Stanley Gibbons Simplified Catalogue

Stamps of the World

2013 Edition

4

Countries **Jersey – New Republic**

Stanley Gibbons Ltd
London and Ringwood

By Appointment to
Her Majesty The Queen
Stanley Gibbons Limited
London
Philatelists

78th Edition
Published in Great Britain by
Stanley Gibbons Ltd
Publications Editorial, Sales Offices and Distribution Centre
7, Parkside, Christchurch Road,
Ringwood, Hampshire BH24 3SH
Telephone +44 (0) 1425 472363

British Library Cataloguing in
Publication Data.
A catalogue record for this book is available
from the British Library.

Volume 4
ISBN 10: 0-85259-857-2
ISBN 13: 978-0-85259-857-3

Boxed Set
ISBN 10: 0-85259-861-0
ISBN 13: 978-0-85259-861-0

Published as Stanley Gibbons Simplified Catalogue from 1934 to 1970, renamed Stamps of the World in 1971, and produced in two (1982-88), three (1989-2001), four (2002-2005) five (2006-2010) and six from 2011 volumes as Stanley Gibbons Simplified Catalogue of Stamps of the World.

Item No. 2881– Set13

Printed and bound in Wales by Stephens & George

Stanley Gibbons
Simplified Catalogue

Stamps of the World

Contents – Volume 4

Est 1856
STANLEY
GIBBONS

About Us

Our History
Edward Stanley Gibbons started trading postage stamps in his father's chemist shop in 1856. Since then we have been at the forefront of stamp collecting for over 150 years. We hold the Royal Warrant, offer unsurpassed expertise and quality and provide collectors with the peace of mind of a certificate of authenticity on all of our stamps. If you think of stamp collecting, you think of Stanley Gibbons and we are proud to uphold that tradition for you.

399 Strand
Our world famous stamp shop is a collector's paradise, with all of our latest catalogues, albums and accessories and, of course, our unrivalled stockholding of postage stamps.
www.stanleygibbons.com   shop@stanleygibbons.com   +44 (0)20 7836 8444

Specialist Stamp Sales
For the collector that appreciates the value of collecting the highest quality examples, Stanley Gibbons is the only choice. Our extensive range is unrivalled in terms of quality and quantity, with specialist stamps available from all over the world.
www.stanleygibbons.com/stamps   shop@stanleygibbons.com   +44 (0)20 7836 8444

Stanley Gibbons Auctions and Valuations
Sell your collection or individual rare items through our prestigious public auctions or our regular postal auctions and benefit from the excellent prices being realised at auction currently. We also provide an unparalleled valuation service.
www.stanleygibbons.com/auctions   auctions@stanleygibbons.com   +44 (0)20 7836 8444

Stanley Gibbons Publications
The world's first stamp catalogue was printed by Stanley Gibbons in 1865 and we haven't looked back since! Our catalogues are trusted worldwide as the industry standard and we print countless titles each year. We also publish consumer and trade magazines, Gibbons Stamp Monthly and Philatelic Exporter to bring you news, views and insights into all things philatelic. Never miss an issue by subscribing today and benefit from exclusive subscriber offers each month.
www.stanleygibbons.com   orders@stanleygibbons.com   +44 (0)1425 472 363

Stanley Gibbons Investments
The Stanley Gibbons Investment Department offers a unique range of investment propositions that have consistently outperformed more traditional forms of investment. You can own your very own piece of history. Whether it is the Penny Black, a Victoria Cross or an official royal document signed by the Queen of England in the 16th century, we have something to amaze you and potentially offer you excellent investment returns.
www.stanleygibbons.com/investment   investment@stanleygibbons.com   +44 (0)1481 708 270

Fraser's Autographs
Autographs, manuscripts and memorabilia from Henry VIII to current day. We have over 60,000 items in stock, including movie stars, musicians, sport stars, historical figures and royalty. Fraser's is the UK's market leading autograph dealer and has been dealing in high quality autographed material since 1978.
www.frasersautographs.com   sales@frasersautographs.com   +44 (0)20 7557 4404

stanleygibbons.com
Our website offers the complete philatelic service. Whether you are looking to buy stamps, invest, read news articles, browse our online stamp catalogue or find new issues, you are just one click away from anything you desire in the world of stamp collecting at stanleygibbons.com. Happy browsing!
www.stanleygibbons.com

Introduction

The ultimate reference work for all stamps issued around the world since the very first Penny Black of 1840, now with an improved layout.

Stamps of the World provides a comprehensive, illustrated, priced guide to postage stamps, and is the standard reference tool for every collector. It will help you to identify those elusive stamps, to value your collection, and to learn more about the background to issues. *Stamps of the World* was first published in 1934 and has been updated every year since 1950.

The helpful article 'Putting on a Good Show' provides expert advice on starting and developing a collection, then making the most of its presentation. Also included is a guide to stamp identification so that you can easily discover which country issued your stamp.

Re-designed to provide more colourful, clearer, and easy-to-navigate listings, these volumes continue to present you with a wealth of information to enhance your enjoyment of stamp collecting.

Features:

▶ Current values for every stamp in the world from the experts

▶ Easy-to-use simplified listings

▶ World-recognised Stanley Gibbons catalogue numbers

▶ A wealth of historical, geographical and currency information

▶ Indexing and cross-referencing throughout the volumes

▶ Worldwide miniature sheets listed and priced

▶ Thousands of new issues since the last edition

For this edition, prices have been thoroughly reviewed for Great Britain up to date, and all Commonwealth countries up to 1970, with further updates for Commonwealth countries which have appeared in our recently-published or forthcoming comprehensive catalogues under the titles *Channel Islands and Isle of Man, Southern and Central Africa, Indian Ocean, Leeward Islands, Cyprus, Gibraltar and Malta, Falkland Islands and Dependencies Australia*. Other countries with complete price updates from the following comprehensive catalogues are: *China, Czech Republic, Slovakia and Poland*. New issues received from all other countries have been listed and priced. The first *Gibbons Stamp Monthly* Catalogue Supplement to this edition is September 2012.

Information for users

Scope of the Catalogue

Stamps of the World contains listings of postage stamps only. Apart from the ordinary definitive, commemorative and air-mail stamps of each country there are sections for the following, where appropriate. Noted below are the Prefixes used for each section (see Guide to Entries for further information):

▶ postage due stamps –	Prefix in listing D
▶ parcel post or postcard stamps –	Prefix P
▶ official stamps –	Prefix O
▶ express and special delivery stamps -	Prefix E
▶ frank stamps –	Prefix F
▶ charity tax stamps –	Prefix J
▶ newspaper and journal stamps –	Prefix N
▶ printed matter stamps –	Prefix
▶ registration stamps -	Prefix R
▶ acknowledgement of receipt stamps –	Prefix AR
▶ late fee and too late stamps –	Prefix L
▶ military post stamps-	Prefix M
▶ recorded message stamps –	Prefix RM
▶ personal delivery stamps –	Prefix P
▶ concessional letter post –	Prefix CL
▶ concessional parcel post –	Prefix CP
▶ pneumatic post stamps –	Prefix PE
▶ publicity envelope stamps –	Prefix B
▶ bulk mail stamps –	Prefix BP
▶ telegraph used for postage –	Prefix PT
▶ telegraph (Commonwealth Countries) –	Prefix T
▶ obligatory tax –	Prefix T
▶ Frama Labels and Royal Mail Postage Labels	No Prefix-

As this is a simplified listing, the following are NOT included:

Fiscal or revenue stamps: stamps used solely in collecting taxes or fees for non-postal purposes. For example, stamps which pay a tax on a receipt, represent the stamp duty on a contract, or frank a customs document. Common inscriptions found include: Documentary, Proprietary, Inter. Revenue and Contract Note.

Local stamps: postage stamps whose validity and use are limited in area to a prescribed district, town or country, or on certain routes where there is no government postal service. They may be issued by private carriers and freight companies, municipal authorities or private individuals.

Local carriage labels and Private local issues: many labels exist ostensibly to cover the cost of ferrying mail from one of Great Britain's offshore islands to the nearest mainland post office. They are not recognised as valid for national or international mail. Examples: Calf of Man, Davaar, Herm, Lundy, Pabay, Stroma.

Telegraph stamps: stamps intended solely for the prepayment of telegraphic communication.

Bogus or "phantom" stamps: labels from mythical places or non-existent administrations. Examples in the classical period were Sedang, Counani, Clipperton Island and in modern times Thomond and Monte Bello Islands. Numerous labels have also appeared since the War from dissident groups as propaganda for their claims and without authority from the home governments. Common examples are the numerous issues for Nagaland.

Railway letter fee stamps: special stamps issued by railway companies for the conveyance of letters by rail. Example: Talyllyn Railway. Similar services are now offered by some bus companies and the labels they issue likewise do not qualify for inclusion in the catalogue.

Perfins ("perforated initials"): stamps perforated with the initials or emblems of firms as a security measure to prevent pilferage by office staff.

Labels: Slips of paper with an adhesive backing. Collectors tend to make a distinction between stamps, which have postal validity and anything else, which has not.

However, Frama Labels and Royal Mail Postage Labels are both classified as postage stamps and are therefore listed in this catalogue.

Cut-outs: Embossed or impressed stamps found on postal stationery, which are cut out if the stationery has been ruined and re-used as adhesives.

Further information on a wealth of terms is in *Philatelic Terms Illustrated*, published by Stanley Gibbons, details are listed under Stanley Gibbons Publications. There is also a priced listing of the postal fiscals of Great Britain in our *Commonwealth & British Empire Stamps 1840-1970* Catalogue and in Volume 1 of the *Great Britain Specialised Catalogue* (5th and later editions). Again, further details are listed under the Stanley Gibbons Publications section (see p.xii).

Organisation of the Catalogue

The catalogue lists countries in alphabetical order with country headers on each page and extra introductory information such as philatelic historical background at the beginning of each section. The Contents list provides a detailed guide to each volume, and the Index has full cross-referencing to locate each country in each volume.

Each country lists postage stamps in order of date of issue, from earliest to most recent, followed by separate sections for

categories such as postage due stamps, express stamps, official stamps, and so on (see above for a complete listing).

"Appendix" Countries

Since 1968 Stanley Gibbons has listed in an appendix stamps which are judged to be in excess of true postal needs. The appendix also contains stamps which have not fulfilled all the normal conditions for full catalogue listing. Full catalogue listing requires a stamp to be:

- ▶ issued by a legitimate postal authority
- ▶ recognised by the government concerned
- ▶ adhesive
- ▶ valid for proper postal use in the class of service for which they are inscribed
- ▶ available to the general public at face value with no artificial restrictions being imposed on their distribution (with the exception of categories as postage dues and officials)

Only stamps issued from component parts of otherwise united territories which represent a genuine political, historical or postal division within the country concerned have a full catalogue listing. Any such issues which do not fulfil this stipulation will be recorded in the Catalogue Appendix only.

Stamps listed in the Appendix are constantly under review in light of newly acquired information about them. If we are satisfied that a stamp qualifies for proper listing in the body of the catalogue it will be moved in the next edition.

"Undesirable Issues"

The rules governing many competitive exhibitions are set by the Federation Internationale de Philatelie and stipulate a downgrading of marks for stamps classed as "undesirable issues".

This catalogue can be taken as a guide to status. All stamps in the main listings are acceptable. Stamps in the Appendix are considered, "undesirable issues" and should not be entered for competition.

Correspondence

We welcome information and suggestions but we must ask correspondents to include the cost of postage for the return of any materials, plus registration where appropriate. Letters and emails should be addressed to Michelle Briggs, 7 Parkside, Christchurch Road, Ringwood, Hampshire BH24 3SH, UK. mrbriggs@stanleygibbons.co.uk. Where information is solicited purely for the benefit of the enquirer we regret we are seldom able to reply.

Identification of Stamps

We regret we do not give opinion on the authenticity of stamps, nor do we identify stamps or number them by our Catalogue.

Thematic Collectors

Stanley Gibbons publishes a range of thematic catalogues (see page xxxix for details) and *Stamps of the World* is ideal to use with these titles, as it supplements those listings with extra information.

Type numbers

Type numbers (in bold) refer to illustrations, and are not the Stanley Gibbons Catalogue numbers.

A brief description of the stamp design subject is given below or beside the illustrations, or close by in the entry, where needed. Where a design is not illustrated, it is usually the same shape and size as a related design, unless otherwise indicated.

Watermarks

Watermarks are not covered in this catalogue. Stamps of the same issue with differing watermarks are not listed separately.

Perforations

Perforations – all stamps are perforated unless otherwise stated. No distinction is made between the various gauges of perforation but early stamp issues which exist both imperforate and perforated are usually listed separately. Where a heading states, "Imperf or perf" or "Perf. or rouletted" this does not necessarily mean that all values of the issue are found in both conditions

Se-tenant Pairs

Se-tenant Pairs – Many modern issues are printed in sheets containing different designs or face values. Such pairs, blocks, strips or sheets are described as being "*se-tenant*" and they are outside the scope of this catalogue, although reference to them may occur in instances where they form a composite design.

Miniature Sheets are now fully listed.

Guide to Entries

Ⓐ Country of Issue

Ⓑ Part Number – shows where to find more detailed listings in the Stanley Gibbons Comprehensive Catalogue. Part 6 refers to France and so on – see p. xli for further information on the breakdown of the Catalogue.

Ⓒ Country Information – Brief geographical and historical details for the issuing country.

Ⓓ Currency – Details of the currency, and dates of earliest use where applicable, on the face value of the stamps. Where a Colony has the same currency as the Mother Country, see the details given in that country.

Ⓔ Year Date – When a set of definitive stamps has been issued over several years the Year Date given is for the earliest issue, commemorative sets are listed in chronological order. As stamps of the same design or issue are usually grouped together a list of King George VI stamps, for example, headed "1938" may include stamps issued from 1938 to the end of the reign.

Ⓕ Stanley Gibbons Catalogue number – This is a unique number for each stamp to help the collector identify stamps in the listing. The Stanley Gibbons numbering system is universally recognized as definitive. The majority of listings are in chronological order, but where a definitive set of stamps has been re-issued with a new watermark, perforation change or imprint date, the cheapest example is given; in such cases catalogue numbers may not be in numerical order.

Where insufficient numbers have been left to provide for additional stamps to a listing, some stamps will have a suffix letter after the catalogue number. If numbers have been left for additions to a set and not used they will be left vacant.

The separate type numbers (in bold) refer to illustrations (see **M**).

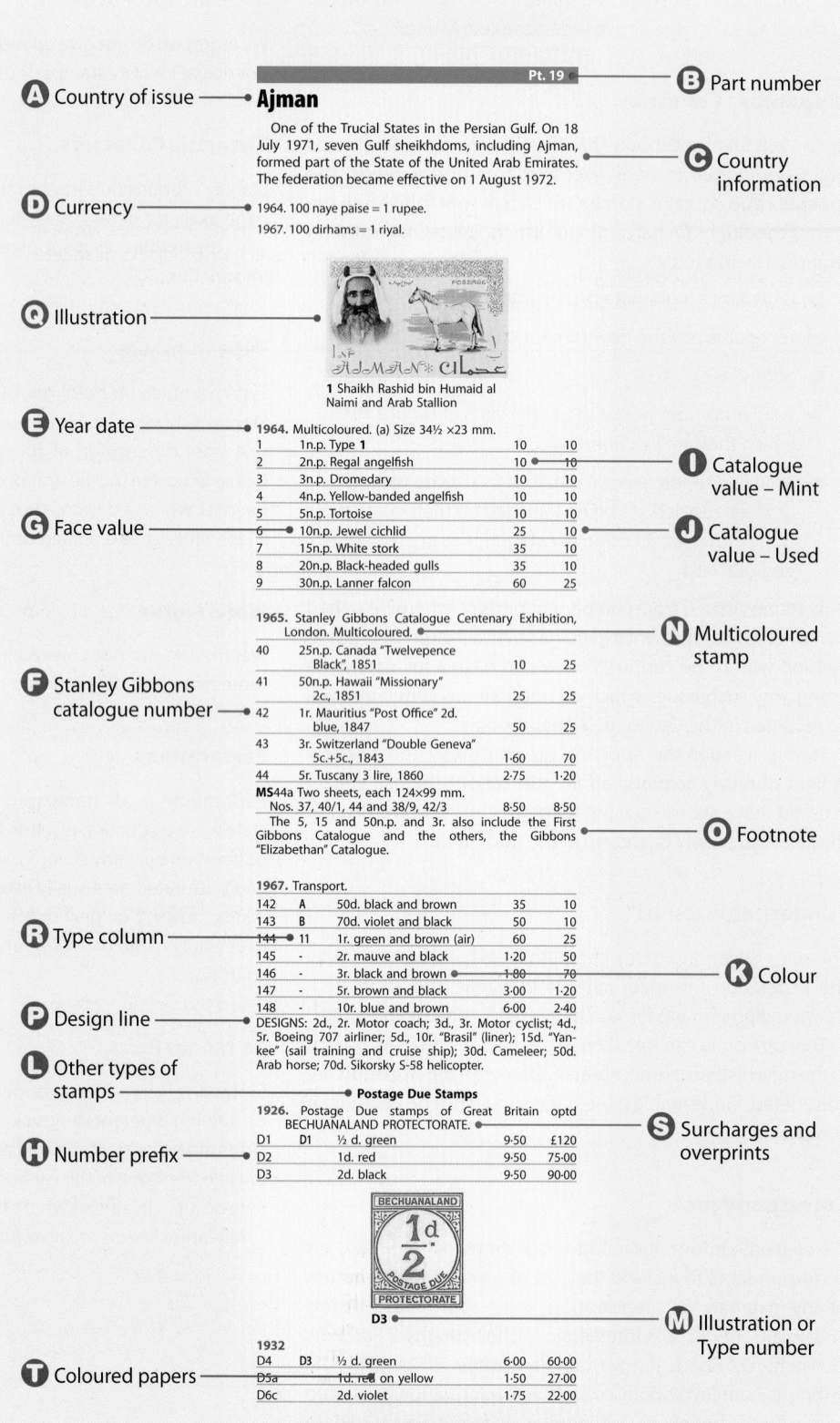

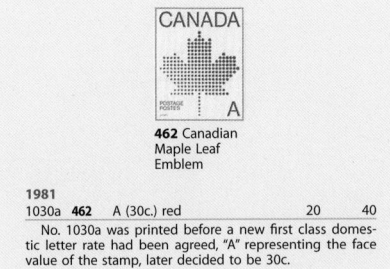

CANADA

462 Canadian
Maple Leaf
Emblem

1981
1030a **462** A (30c.) red 20 40
No. 1030a was printed before a new first class domestic letter rate had been agreed, "A" representing the face
value of the stamp, later decided to be 30c.

Ⓖ Face value – This refers to the value of
each stamp and is the price it was sold
for at the Post Office when issued. Some
modern stamps do not have their values in
figures but instead shown as a letter, see
for example the entry above for Canada
1030a/Illustration 462.

Ⓗ Number Prefix – Stamps other than
definitives and commemoratives have a
prefix letter before the catalogue number.
Such stamps may be found at the end of
the normal listing for each country. (See
Scope of the Catalogue p.viii for a list of
other types of stamps covered, together
with the list of the main abbreviations used
in the Catalogue).

Other prefixes are also used in the
Catalogue. Their use is explained in the
text: some examples are A for airmail, E for
East Germany or Express Delivery stamps.

Ⓘ Catalogue Value – Mint/Unused. Prices
quoted for pre-1945 stamps are for lightly
hinged examples. Prices quoted of unused
King Edward VIII to Queen Elizabeth II
issues are for unmounted mint.

Ⓙ Catalogue Value – Used. Prices generally
refer to fine postally used examples. For
certain issues they are for cancelled-to-
order.

Prices
Prices are given in pence and pounds.
Stamps worth £100 and over are shown in
whole pounds:

Shown in Catalogue as	Explanation
10	10 pence
1.75	£1.75
15.00	£15
£150	£150
£2300	£2300

Prices assume stamps are in 'fine condition';
we may ask more for superb and less
for those of lower quality. The minimum

catalogue price quoted is 10p and is
intended as a guide for catalogue users.
The lowest price for individual stamps
purchased from Stanley Gibbons is £1.

Prices quoted are for the cheapest
variety of that particular stamp. Differences
of watermark, perforation, or other details,
outside the scope of this catalogue, often
increase the value. Prices quoted for mint
issues are for single examples. Those in
se-tenant pairs, strips, blocks or sheets
may be worth more. Where no prices
are listed it is either because the stamps
are not known to exist in that particular
condition, or, more usually, because there
is no reliable information on which to base
their value.

All prices are subject to change without
prior notice and we cannot guarantee
to supply all stamps as priced. Prices
quoted in advertisements are also subject
to change without prior notice. Due to
differing production schedules it is possible
that new editions of Parts 2 to 22 will show
revised prices which are not included in
that year's Stamps of the World.

Ⓚ Colour – Colour of stamp (if fewer
than four colours, otherwise noted as
"multicoloured"– see N below). Colour
descriptions are simple in this catalogue,
and only expanded to aid identification
– see other more comprehensive Stanley
Gibbons catalogues for more detailed
colour descriptions (see p.xxxix).
Where stamps are printed in two or more
colours, the central portion of the design
is the first colour given, unless otherwise
stated.

Ⓛ Other Types of Stamps – See Scope of
the Catalogue p.viii for a list of the types of
stamps included.

Ⓜ Illustration or Type Number – These
numbers are used to help identify stamps,
either in the listing, type column, design line
or footnote, usually the first value in a set.
These type numbers are in a bold type face
– **123**; when bracketed (**123**) an overprint
or a surcharge is indicated. Some type
numbers include a lower-case letter – **123a**,
this indicates they have been added to an
existing set. New cross references are also
normally shown in bold, as in the example
below.

1990. Small Craft of Canada (2nd series). Early Work
Boats. As T **563**. Multicoloured.

Ⓝ Multicoloured – Nearly all modern stamps
are multicoloured; this is indicated in the
heading, with a description of the stamp
given in the listing.

Ⓞ Footnote – further information on
background or key facts on issues

Ⓟ Design line – Further details on design
variations

Ⓠ Illustration – Generally, the first stamp in
the set. Stamp illustrations are reduced to
75%, with overprints and surcharges shown
actual size.

Ⓡ Key Type – indicates a design type (see p.
xii for further details) on which the stamp
is based. These are the bold figures found
below each illustration. The type numbers
are also given in bold in the second column
of figures alongside the stamp description
to indicate the design of each stamp.
Where an issue comprises stamps of similar
design, the corresponding type number
should be taken as indicating the general
design. Where there are blanks in the type
number column it means that the type of
the corresponding stamp is that shown
by the number in the type column of the
same issue. A dash (–) in the type column
means that the stamp is not illustrated.
Where type numbers refer to stamps of
another country, e.g. where stamps of one
country are overprinted for use in another,
this is always made clear in the text.

Ⓢ Surcharges and Overprints – usually
described in the headings. Any actual
wordings are shown in bold type.
Descriptions clarify words and figures used
in the overprint. Stamps with the same
overprints in different colours are not listed
separately. Numbers in brackets after the
descriptions are the catalogue numbers of
the non-overprinted stamps. The words
"inscribed" or "inscription" refer to the
wording incorporated in the design of a
stamp and not surcharges or overprints.

Ⓣ Coloured Papers – stamps printed on
coloured paper are shown – e.g. "brn on
yell" indicates brown printed on yellow
paper. No information on the texture of
paper, e.g. laid or wove, is provided in this
catalogue.

Key-Types

Standard designs frequently occuring on the stamps of the French, German, Portuguese and Spanish colonies are illustrated below together with the descriptive names and letters by which they are referred to in the lists to avoid repetition. Please see the Guide to Entries for further information.

French Group

A "Blanc" **B** "Mouchon" **C** "Merson" **D** "Tablet"

INTERNATIONAL COLONIAL EXHIBITION

E **F** " **G** **H**

I "Faidherbe" **J** "Palms" **K** "Balay" **L** "Natives" **M** "Figure"

German Group

N "Yacht" **O** "Yacht"

Spanish Group

X "Alfonso XII" **Y** "Baby" **Z** "Curly Head"

Portuguese Group

P "Crown" **Q** "Embossed" **R** "Figures" **S** "Carlos" **T** "Manoel" **U** Ceres **V** "Newspaper" **W** "Due"

Selling Your Stamps?

Summary Tip #21: 5 Different Ways to Sell your Stamps: Selling via Auction

Dear Collector,

In Part 3 (Volume 3) of 'Selling your Stamps' we discussed the importance of selecting the right dealers/organisations to approach and ensuring the choice of those with transparent modus operandi.

Here in Part 4 of 'Selling your Stamps' we'll discuss the potential advantages and disadvantages of selling through auction on your own account.

Remember we previously discussed the importance of knowing the strength of your collection. This is never more important than when making the decision to consign your stamps to auction. We have touched upon this in previous 'Stamp Tips of the Trade'. The most important thing to remember – is 'who buys complete stamp collections at auction?'

Collectors want to buy stamps that are missing from their collections: Dealers want to buy complete collections to break out individual stamps/sets to supply to collectors. By breaking collections into individual parts dealers add value/profit. When you consign your collection as one lot to auction – 9 times out of 10 .... it is a dealer that will be buying it. Unless you are a collector that purchases collections, extract the stamps you need, and sell on the rest – you will be looking to buy specific stamps, sets or small 'runs'.

So what is wrong with consigning stamps to auction? Nothing, if it is the right kind of stamps. For example – you need to 'quiz' the auctioneer selected as to what he/she is actually going to do with your stamps. Let's give you an example. A few weeks ago we purchased a 'Birds' thematic collection from public auction. We paid the auctioneer exactly £1011.50= ... but the actual price the stamps were 'knocked down' to us was exactly £800=. The buyer's premium was 26.4375% - and that was before the increase in VAT. If we purchased the same collection today – the buyer's premium would be 27% !

Unless your collection includes valuable stamps/sets that the auctioneer agrees to extract and offer individually ... you are paying an enormous percentage of the value of your stamps for that auction to sell to dealers.

And did the collector realise £800=? NO. Even if the collector was charged just 12% + VAT selling commission – at today's rate the collector would receive £685=. Imagine, this collection has been sold to a dealer for £1011- by an auction who has put no money on the table and yet made a gross profit of £326= on the transaction. The dealer that paid £1,011.50 expects to make a profit. It follows that if you can approach the right dealers in the right way – then you can expect to eliminate much of the money that you pay for that auction to offer your stamps to dealers. Please refer to 'Selling your Stamps?' Tip 19 (Volume 2) for suggestions as to how this may be achieved for more valuable collections.

The 'funniest' thing of all was that the auction does not even pack your purchases .... we had to pay another £35 for a company to collect the stamps, package them and deliver them to us by parcel delivery!

The point is that unless your collection includes valuable stamps/sets that the auctioneer agrees to extract and offer individually ... you are paying an enormous percentage of the value of your stamps for that auction to sell to dealers.

BUT, if your collection is one basically comprised of rarities – then an argument can be made for offering your collection individually lotted. In this way you are going to reach collectors + if yours is a 'named' collection often there is a 'kudos' value/premium that stamps with provenance achieve.

However – so large are the major auctions selling and buyer's premiums today – that even with collections of rarities – leading dealers can often offer to pay in excess of a fair auction estimate immediately – without risk, uncertainty of unsold lots, and immediately. The simple answer is get the auction to underwrite the minimum NET amount that they will guarantee you receive ... and then see by how much the 'trade' will improve upon this. Then you make a fully informed decision.

In Part 5 (Volume 5) of 'Selling your Stamps?' we'll discuss the merits and obstacles of selling your stamps on-line via eBay and other on-line auctions.

Happy collecting from us all,

Andrew

PS. If you find this 'tip' interesting please forward it to a philatelic friend.
Andrew McGavin

Managing Director: Universal Philatelic Auctions, Omniphil & Avon Approvals, Avon Mixtures, UniversalPhilatelic (Ebay)

To read the rest of this series 'SELLING YOUR STAMPS?' see the relevant pages in each volume:

Summary Tip 18 – Volume 1 (opposite Key Types)
Summary Tip 19 – Volume 2 (opposite Key Types)
Summary Tip 20 – Volume 3 (opposite Key Types)
Summary Tip 21 – Volume 4 (opposite Key Types)
Summary Tip 22 – Volume 5 (opposite Key Types)

Please go to Volume 6 (opposite Key Types) to see how UPA can pay you up to 36% more for your collection.

COLECCIONE SELOS DE MACAU
Collect Macao's Stamps

澳門議事亭前地
Largo do Senado, Macau

情牽心意 助拓商貿
Aproximamos Pessoas, Facilitamos Negócios

電話 Tel : (853) 8396 8513, 2857 4491
傳真 Fax : (853) 8396 8603, 2833 6603
電郵 E-mail : philately@macaupost.gov.mo
網址 Website : www.macaupost.gov.mo

Pt. 1

JERSEY

Island in the English Channel off N.W. coast of France. Occupied by German forces from June 1940 to May 1945 with separate stamp issues.

The general issue of 1948 for Channel Islands and the regional issues of 1958 are listed at end of GREAT BRITAIN.

Jersey had its own postal administration from 1969.

1941. 12 pence = 1 shilling; 20 shillings = 1 pound.
1971. 100 (new) pence = 1 pound sterling.

(a) War Occupation Issues

5

1941

| 1 | **5** | ½d. green | 8·00 | 6·00 |
| 2 | **5** | 1d. red | 8·00 | 5·00 |

6 Old Jersey Farm

1943

3	**6**	½d. green	12·00	12·00
4	-	1d. red	3·00	50
5	-	1½d. brown	8·00	5·75
6	-	2d. yellow	7·50	2·00
7a	-	2½d. blue	1·00	1·70
8	-	3d. violet	3·00	2·75

DESIGNS: 1d. Portelet Bay; 1½d. Corbiere Lighthouse; 2d. Elizabeth Castle; 2½d. Mont Orgueil Castle; 3d. Gathering vraic (seaweed).

(b) Independent Postal Administration

14 Elizabeth Castle

1969. Multicoloured.

15	½d. Type **14**	10	60
16	1d. La Hougue Bie (prehistoric tomb)	10	10
17	2d. Portelet Bay	10	10
18	3d. La Corbiere Lighthouse	10	10
19	4d. Mont Orgueil Castle by night	10	10
20	5d. Arms and Royal Mace	10	10
21	6d. Jersey cow	10	10
22	9d. Chart of the English Channel	10	20
23	1s. Mont Orgueil Castle by day	25	25
24	1s.6d. Chart of the English Channel	80	80
25	1s.9d. Queen Elizabeth II (after Cecil Beaton) (vert)	1·00	1·00
26	2s.6d. Jersey Airport	1·60	1·60
27	5s. Legislative Chamber	6·50	6·50
28	10s. The Royal Court	14·00	14·00
29	£1 Queen Elizabeth II (after Cecil Beaton) (vert)	1·90	1·90

28 First Day Cover

1969. Inauguration of Post Office.

30	**28**	4d. multicoloured	10	15
31	**28**	5d. multicoloured	20	10
32	**28**	1s.6d. multicoloured	50	75
33	**28**	1s.9d. multicoloured	80	1·00

29 Lord Coutanche, former Bailiff of Jersey (Sir James Gunn)

1970. 25th Anniv of Liberation. Multicoloured.

34	4d. Type **29**	20	20
35	5d. Sir Winston Churchill (Van Praag)	20	20
36	1s.6d. "Liberation" (Edmund Blampied) (horiz)	90	1·00
37	1s.9d. S.S. Vega (horiz)	90	1·00

33 "A Tribute to Enid Blyton"

1970. "Battle of Flowers" Parade. Multicoloured.

38	4d. Type **33**	20	10
39	5d. "Rags to Riches"	20	20
40	1s.6d. "Gourmet's Delight"	2·50	2·20
41	1s.9d. "We're the Greatest"	2·75	2·20

37 Jersey Airport

1970. Decimal Currency. Nos. 15, etc, but with new colours, new design (6p.) and decimal values, as T **37**.

42	½p. multicoloured (as No. 15)	10	10
43	1p. multicoloured (as No. 18)	10	10
44	1½p. multicoloured (as No. 21)	10	10
45	2p. multicoloured (as No. 19)	10	10
46	2½p. multicoloured (as No. 20)	10	10
47	3p. multicoloured (as No. 16)	10	10
48	3½p. multicoloured (as No. 17)	10	10
49	4p. multicoloured (as No. 22)	10	10
49a	4½p. multicoloured (as No. 20)	75	75
50	5p. multicoloured (as No. 23)	10	10
50a	5½p. multicoloured (as No. 21)	75	75
51	6p. multicoloured (Martello Tower, Archirondel, 23×22 mm)	20	10
52	7½p. multicoloured (as No. 24)	50	50
52a	8p. multicoloured (as No. 19)	75	75
53	9p. multicoloured (as No. 25)	70	70
54	10p. multicoloured (as No. 26)	40	30
55	20p. multicoloured (as No. 27)	90	80
56	50p. multicoloured (as No. 28)	1·50	1·20

38 White Eared-pheasant ("White-eared Pheasant")

1971. Wildlife Preservation Trust (1st series). Multicoloured.

57	2p. Type **38**	20	10
58	2½p. Thick-billed parrot (vert)	20	15
59	7½p. Western black-and-white colobus monkey (vert)	1·75	1·75
60	9p. Ring-tailed lemur	2·50	2·50

See also Nos. 73/6, 217/21, 324/9, 447/51 and 824/9.

43 Poppy Emblem and Field

1971. 50th Anniv of Royal British Legion. Multicoloured.

61	2p. Royal British Legion Badge	20	10
62	2½p. Type **43**	20	10
63	7½p. Jack Counter VC, and Victoria Cross	1·00	1·10
64	9p. Crossed Tricolour and Union Jack	1·00	1·10

46 Tante Elizabeth (E. Blampied)

1971. Paintings. Multicoloured.

65	2p. Type **46**	15	10
66	2½p. English Fleet in the Channel (P. Monamy) (horiz)	20	10
67	7½p. The Boyhood of Raleigh (Millais) (horiz)	95	95
68	9p. The Blind Beggar (W. W. Ouless)	1·10	1·10

See also Nos. 115/118.

50 Jersey Fern

1972. Wild Flowers of Jersey. Multicoloured.

69	3p. Type **50**	20	10
70	5p. Jersey thrift	30	20
71	7½p. Jersey orchid	95	95
72	9p. Jersey viper's bugloss	1·00	1·00

1972. Wildlife Preservation Trust (2nd series). As T **38**. Multicoloured.

73	2½p. Cheetah	30	10
74	3p. Rothschild's mynah (vert)	25	20
75	7½p. Spectacled bear	50	70
76	9p. Tuatara	80	90

58 Artillery Shako

1972. Royal Jersey Militia (1st issue). Multicoloured.

77	2½p. Type **58**	10	10
78	3p. Shako (2nd North Regt.)	10	10
79	7½p. Shako (5th South-West Regt.)	30	20
80	9p. Helmet (3rd Jersey Light Infantry)	50	60

See also Nos. 1253/7.

62 Princess Anne

1972. Royal Silver Wedding. Multicoloured.

81	2½p. Type **62**	10	10
82	3p. Queen Elizabeth and Prince Philip (horiz)	10	10
83	7½p. Prince Charles	35	35
84	20p. The Royal Family (horiz)	35	35

69 Armorican Bronze Coins

1973. Centenary of La Societe Jersiaise. Multicoloured.

85	2½p. Silver cups	10	10
86	3p. Gold torque (vert)	10	10
87	7½p. Royal Seal of Charles II (vert)	25	20
88	9p. Type **69**	30	30

70 Balloon L'Armee de la Loire and Letter, Paris, 1870

1973. Jersey Aviation History. Multicoloured.

89	3p. Type **70**	10	10
90	5p. Astra seaplane, 1912	10	10
91	7½p. Supermarine Sea Eagle amphibian G-EBFK	35	35
92	9p. de Havilland DH.86 Dragon Express G-ACYF "Giffard Bay"	45	45

74 "North Western", 1870

1973. Centenary of Jersey Eastern Railway. Early Locomotives. Multicoloured.

93	2½p. Type **74**	10	10
94	3p. Calvados, 1873	10	10
95	7½p. Carteret at Grouville station, 1893	35	35
96	9p. Caesarea, 1873, and route map	45	45

78 Princess Anne and Capt. Mark Phillips

1973. Royal Wedding.

| 97 | **78** | 3p. multicoloured | 10 | 10 |
| 98 | **78** | 20p. multicoloured | 50 | 50 |

79 Spider Crab

1973. Marine Life. Multicoloured.

99	2½p. Type **79**	10	10
100	3p. Conger eel	10	10
101	7½p. Lobster	30	35
102	20p. Tuberculate ormer	40	45

83 Freesias

1974. Spring Flowers. Multicoloured.

103	3p. Type **83**	10	10
104	5½p. Anemones	15	15
105	8p. Carnations and Gladioli	25	30
106	10p. Daffodils and Iris	30	35

87 First U.K. Pillar box and Contemporary Cover

1974. Centenary of U.P.U. Multicoloured.

107	2½p. Type **87**	10	10
108	3p. Jersey postmen, 1862 and 1969	10	15
109	5½p. Modern pillar-box and cover, 1974	25	20
110	20p. R.M.S. "Aquila" (1874) and B.A.C. One Eleven 200 (1974)	35	40

91 John Wesley

1974. Anniversaries.

111	**91**	3p. black and brown	10	10
112	-	3½p. violet and blue	10	10
113	-	8p. black and lilac	20	20
114	-	20p. black and stone	45	45

PORTRAITS AND EVENTS: 3p. (Bicentenary of Methodism in Jersey); 3½p. Sir William Hillary, founder (150th anniv of R.N.L.I.); 8p. Canon Wace (poet and historian) (800th death anniv; 20p. Sir Winston Churchill (Birth cent).

95 Catherine and Mar" (Royal yachts)

1974. Marine Paintings by Peter Monamy. Multicoloured.

| 115 | 3½p. Type **95** | 10 | 10 |
| 116 | 5½p. French two-decker | 15 | 10 |

| 117 | 8p. Dutch vessel (horiz) | 25 | 20 |
| 118 | 25p. Battle of Cap La Hague, 1692 (55×27 mm) | 55 | 55 |

99 Potato Digger

1975. 19th-century Farming. Multicoloured.

119	3p. Type **99**	10	10
120	3½p. Cider crusher	10	10
121	8p. Six-horse plough	20	20
122	10p. Hay cart	35	40

103 H.M. Queen Elizabeth, the Queen Mother (photograph by Cecil Beaton)

1975. Royal Visit.

| 123 | **103** | 20p. multicoloured | 50 | 45 |

104 Nautilus Shell

1975. Jersey Tourism. Multicoloured.

124	5p. Type **104**	10	10
125	8p. Parasol	10	10
126	10p. Deckchair	30	25
127	12p. Sandcastle with flags of Jersey and the U.K.	40	35
MS128	146×68 mm. Nos. 124/7	90	1·10

108 Common Tern

1975. Sea Birds. Multicoloured.

129	4p. Type **108**	10	10
130	5p. British storm petrel ("Storm-Petrel")	15	10
131	8p. Brent geese	40	25
132	25p. Shag	70	50

112 Armstrong Whitworth Siskin IIIA

1975. 50th Anniv of Royal Air Force Association, Jersey Branch. Multicoloured.

133	4p. Type **112**	10	10
134	5p. Supermarine Southampton I flying boat	15	10
135	10p. Supermarine Spitfire Mk 1	40	25
136	25p. Folland Fo-141 Gnat T1	70	50

116 Map of Jersey Parishes

1976. Multicoloured. (a) Parish Arms and Views.

137	½p. Type **116**	10	10
138	1p. Zoological Park	10	10
139	5p. St. Mary's Church	10	10
140	6p. Seymour Tower	10	10
141	7p. La Corbiere Lighthouse	10	10
142	8p. St. Saviour's Church	15	10
143	9p. Elizabeth Castle	15	10
144	10p. Gorey Harbour	20	10
145	11p. Jersey Airport	25	25

146	12p. Grosnez Castle	25	20
147	13p. Bonne Nuit Harbour	25	20
148	14p. Le Hocq Tower	30	20
149	15p. Morel Farm	30	25

129 Parish Arms and Island Scene

(b) Emblems.

150	20p. Type **129**	45	45
151	30p. Flag and map	55	50
152	40p. Postal H.Q. and badge	80	80
153	50p. Parliament, Royal Court and arms	1·00	1·00
154	£1 Lieutenant-Governor's flag and Government House	3·00	3·00
155	£2 Queen Elizabeth II (vert)	4·00	4·00

135 Sir Walter Raleigh and Map of Virginia

1976. Bicentenary of American Independence. Multicoloured.

160	5p. Type **135**	10	10
161	7p. Sir George Carteret and map of New Jersey	15	10
162	11p. Philippe d'Auvergne and Long Island landing	40	40
163	13p. John Copley and sketch	50	50

139 Dr. Grandin and Map of China

1976. Birth Centenary of Dr. Lilian Grandin (medical missionary).

164	**139**	5p. multicoloured	10	10
165	-	7p. yellow, brown and black	10	10
166	-	11p. multicoloured	35	25
167	-	13p. multicoloured	50	40

DESIGNS: 7p. Sampan on the Yangtze; 11p. Overland trek; 13p. Dr. Grandin at work.

143 Coronation, 1953 (photographed by Cecil Beaton)

1977. Silver Jubilee. Multicoloured.

168	5p. Type **143**	15	10
169	7p. Visit to Jersey, 1957	20	15
170	25p. Queen Elizabeth II (photo by Peter Grugeon)	40	55

146 Coins of 1871 and 1877

1977. Centenary of Currency Reform. Multicoloured.

171	5p. Type **146**	10	10
172	7p. One-twelfth shilling, 1949	15	10
173	11p. Silver crown, 1966	30	30
174	13p. £2 piece, 1972	35	35

150 Sir William Weston and *Santa Anna*, 1530

1977. Centenary of St. John Ambulance. Multicoloured.

| 175 | 5p. Type **150** | 10 | 10 |

176	7p. Sir William Drogo and ambulance, 1877	10	10
177	11p. Duke of Connaught and ambulance, 1917	25	20
178	13p. Duke of Gloucester and stretcher-team, 1977	30	25

154 Arrival of Queen Victoria, 1846

1977. 125th Anniv of Victoria College. Multicoloured.

179	7p. Type **154**	15	10
180	10½p. Victoria College, 1852	20	15
181	11p. Sir Galahad Statue, 1924 (vert)	25	25
182	13p. College Hall (vert)	30	25

158 Harry Vardon Statuette and Map of Royal Jersey Course

1978. Centenary of Royal Jersey Golf Club. Multicoloured.

183	6p. Type **158**	10	10
184	8p. Harry Vardon's grip and swing	15	10
185	11p. Harry Vardon's putt	35	25
186	13p. Golf trophies and book by Harry Vardon	40	35

162 Mont Orgueil Castle

1978. Europa. Castles from Paintings by Thomas Phillips. Multicoloured.

187	6p. Type **162**	10	10
188	8p. St. Aubin's Fort	15	15
189	10½p. Elizabeth Castle	35	25

165 *Gaspé Basin* (P. J. Ouless)

1978. Links with Canada. Multicoloured.

190	6p. Type **165**	10	10
191	8p. Map of Gaspé Peninsula	15	10
192	10½p. *"Century"* (brigantine)	20	15
193	11p. Early map of Jersey	40	25
194	13p. St. Aubin's Bay, town and harbour	45	40

170 Queen Elizabeth and Prince Philip

1978. 25th Anniv of Coronation.

| 195 | **170** | 8p. silver, black and red | 20 | 10 |
| 196 | - | 25p. silver, black and blue | 50 | 45 |

DESIGN: 25p. Hallmarks of 1953 and 1977.

172 Mail Cutter, 1778–1827

1978. Bicentenary of England–Jersey Government Mail Packet Service.

197	**172**	6p. black, brown and yellow	10	10
198	-	8p. black, green and yellow	15	10
199	-	10½p. black, ultram & bl	30	20
200	-	11p. black, purple and lilac	35	30
201	-	13p. black, red and pink	40	40

DESIGNS—SHIPS: 8p. *"Flamer"*, 1831–7; 10½p. *"Diana"*, 1877–90; 11p. *"Ibex"*, 1891–1925; 13p. *"Caesarea"*, 1960–75.

177 Jersey Calf

1979. Ninth Conference of World Jersey Cattle Bureau. Multicoloured.

| 202 | 6p. Type **177** | 10 | 10 |
| 203 | 25p. "Ansom Designette" (calf presented to the Queen, 1978) (46×29 mm) | 50 | 45 |

179 Jersey Pillar Box, c. 1860

1979. Europa. Communications. Multicoloured.

204	8p. Type **179**	15	15
205	8p. Clearing modern post box	15	15
206	10½p. Telephone switchboard, c. 1900	15	15
207	10½p. Modern SPC telephone system	15	15

183 Percival Mew Gull G-AEXF *Golden City*

1979. 25th Anniv International Air Rally. Multicoloured.

208	6p. Type **183**	10	10
209	8p. de Havilland Canada DHC-1 Chipmunk trainer OO-PHS	25	15
210	10½p. Druine D.31 Turbulent	25	20
211	11p. de Havilland DH.82A Tiger Moth	30	25
212	13p. North American AT-6 Harvard F-BRGB	40	35

188 *My First Sermon*

1979. International Year of the Child and 150th Birth Anniversary of Sir John Millais (painter). Paintings. Multicoloured.

213	8p. Type **188**	20	15
214	10½p. Orphans	30	20
215	11p. *The Princes in the Tower*	30	30
216	25p. *Christ in the House of his Parents* (50×32 mm)	50	40

1979. Wildlife Preservation Trust (3rd series). As T **38**. Multicoloured.

217	6p. Pink pigeon (vert)	10	10
218	8p. Orang-utan (vert)	20	15
219	11½p. Waldrapp ("Waldrapp Ibis")	30	30
220	13p. Lowland gorilla (vert)	45	35
221	15p. Rodriguez flying fox (vert)	45	35

197 Plan of Mont Orgueil

1980. Jersey Fortresses. Drawings by Thomas Phillips. Multicoloured.

222	8p. Type **197**	20	15
223	11½p. Plan of La Tour de St. Aubin	30	30
224	13p. Plan of Elizabeth Castle	30	30
225	25p. Map of Jersey showing fortresses (38×27 mm)	50	45

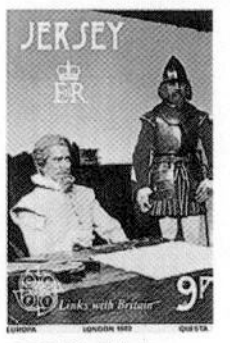

201 Sir Walter Raleigh

1980. Europa. Links with Britain. Multicoloured.

226	9p. Type **201**	15	15
227	9p. Paul Ivy (engineer) discussing Elizabeth Castle	15	15
228	13½p. Sir George Carteret receiving deeds to Smith's Island, Virginia from Charles II	20	20
229	13½p. Lady Carteret, maid and Jean Chevalier	20	20

Nos. 226/7 and 228/9 were issued together, *se-tenant*, forming composite designs.

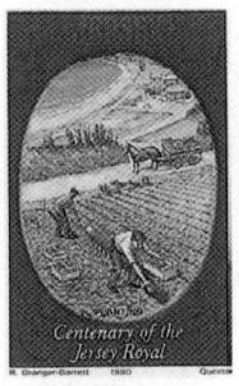

205 Planting

1980. Cent of Jersey Royal Potato. Multicoloured.

230	7p. Type **205**	20	20
231	15p. Digging	30	30
232	17½p. Weighbridge	40	40

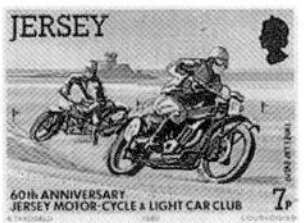

208 Three Lap Event

1980. 60th Anniv of Jersey Motor Cycle and Light Car Club. Multicoloured.

233	7p. Type **208**	15	15
234	9p. Jersey International Road Race	20	15
235	13½p. Scrambling	30	25
236	15p. Sand racing (saloon cars)	30	30
237	17½p. National Hill Climb	35	35

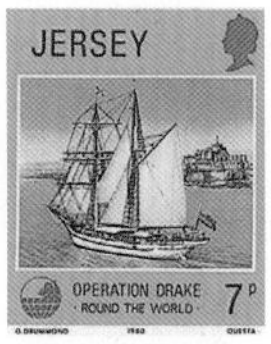

213 *Eye of the Wind*

1980. "Operation Drake" and 150th Anniv of Royal Geographical Society (14p). Multicoloured.

238	7p. Type **213**	15	15
239	9p. Diving from inflatable raft	20	20
240	13½p. Exploration of Papua New Guinea	30	25
241	14p. *"Discovery"*	30	30
242	15p. Aerial walkway, conservation project, Sulawesi	35	35
243	17½p. *"Eye of the Wind"* and Goodyear Aerospace airship *"Europa"*	40	40

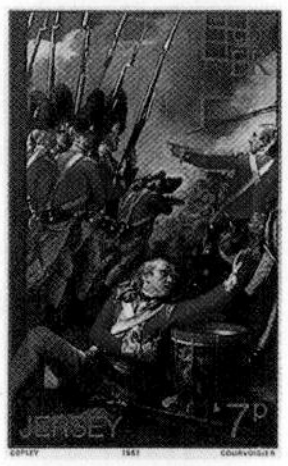

219 Detail of *The Death of Major Peirson*

1981. Bicentenary of Battle of Jersey. Details of J. S. Copley's painting.

244	**219**	7p. multicoloured	15	15
245	-	10p. multicoloured	25	20
246	-	15p. multicoloured	35	30
247	-	17½p. multicoloured	40	35
MS248		144×97 mm. Nos. 244/7	1·40	1·60

Stamps from No. **MS**248 are without white margins.

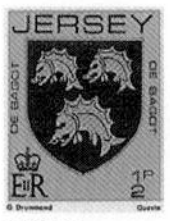

223 De Bagot

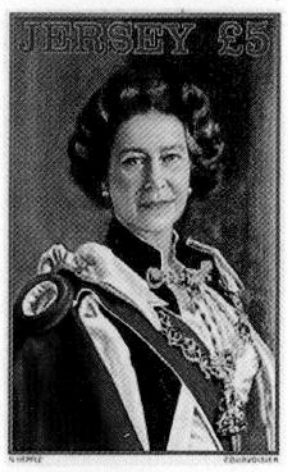

250 "Queen Elizabeth II" (Norman Hepple)

1981. Arms of Jersey Families.

249	**223**	½p. black, silver and green	20	20
250	-	1p. multicoloured	10	10
251	-	2p. multicoloured	10	10
252	-	3p. multicoloured	10	15
253	-	4p. silver, black and mauve	15	15
254	-	5p. multicoloured	15	15
255	-	6p. multicoloured	20	20
256	-	7p. multicoloured	25	25
257	-	8p. multicoloured	30	30
258	-	9p. multicoloured	30	25
259	-	10p. multicoloured	25	25
260	-	11p. multicoloured	30	30
261	-	12p. multicoloured	35	30
262	-	13p. multicoloured	35	35
263	-	14p. multicoloured	40	40
264	-	15p. multicoloured	40	40
265	-	16p. multicoloured	35	35
266	-	17p. multicoloured	45	45
266a	-	18p. multicoloured	50	50
266b	-	19p. multicoloured	60	60
267	-	20p. black, silver and yellow	50	50
268	-	25p. black and blue	45	45
268a	-	26p. black, silver and red	50	50
269	-	30p. multicoloured	50	60
270	-	40p. multicoloured	80	80
271	-	50p. multicoloured	1·00	1·00
272	-	75p. multicoloured	1·50	1·50
273	-	£1 multicoloured	2·00	2·00
274	**250**	£5 multicoloured	8·00	8·00

DESIGNS—As T **223**: 1p. De Carteret; 2p. La Cloche; 3p. Dumaresq; 4p. Payn; 5p. Janvrin; 6p. Poingdestre; 7p. Pipon; 8p. Marett; 9p. Le Breton; 10p. Le Maistre; 11p. Bisson; 12p. Robin; 13p. Herault; 14p. Messervy; 15p. Fiott; 16p. Malet; 17p. Mabon; 18p. De St. Martin; 19p. Hamptonne; 20p. Badier; 25p. L'Arbalestier; 30p. Journeaulx; 40p. Lempriere; 50p. Auvergne; 75p. Remon. 38×22 mm: £1 Jersey crest and map of Channel.

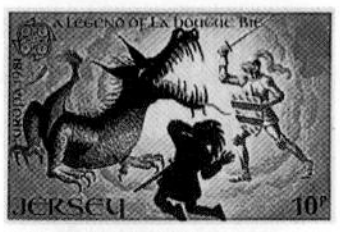

251 Knight of Hambye slaying Dragon

1981. Europa. Folklore. Multicoloured.

275	10p. Type **251**	25	15
276	10p. Servant slaying Knight of Hambye and awaiting execution	25	15
277	18p. St. Brelade celebrating Easter on island	30	20
278	18p. Island revealing itself as a huge fish	30	20

LEGENDS: 10p. (both) Slaying of the Dragon of Lawrence by the Knight of Hambye; 18p. (both) Voyages of St. Brelade.

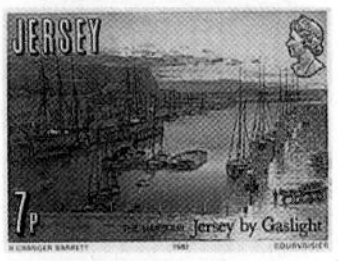

255 The Harbour by Gaslight

1981. 150th Anniv of Gas Lighting in Jersey. Multicoloured.

279	7p. Type **255**	20	15
280	10p. The Quay	25	25
281	18p. Royal Square	40	40
282	22p. Halkett Place	45	45
283	25p. Central Market	55	55

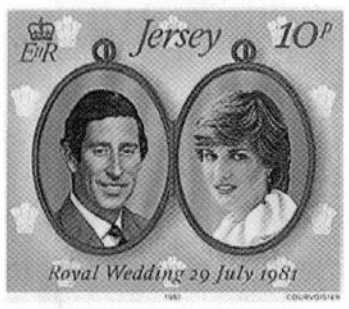

260 Prince Charles and Lady Diana Spencer

1981. Royal Wedding.

284	**260**	10p. multicoloured	20	20
285	**260**	25p. multicoloured	75	90

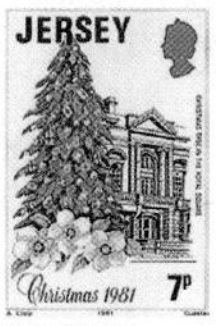

261 Christmas Tree in Royal Square

1981. Christmas. Multicoloured.

286	7p. Type **261**	25	25
287	10p. East window, Parish Church, St. Helier	35	35
288	18p. Boxing Day meet of Jersey Drag Hunt	50	50

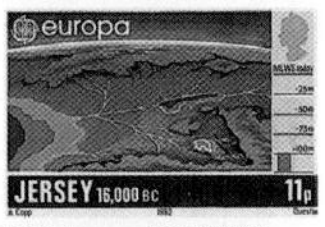

264 Jersey, 16,000 B.C.

1982. Europa. Formation of Jersey. Multicoloured.

289	11p. Type **264**	20	20
290	11p. In 10,000 B.C. (vert)	20	20
291	19½p. In 7,000 B.C. (vert)	45	45
292	19½p. In 4,000 B.C.	45	45

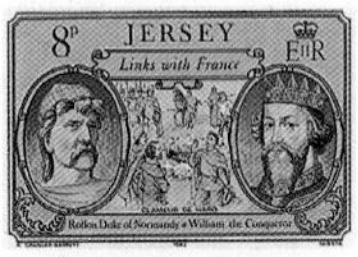

268 Duke Rollo of Normandy, William the Conqueror and "Clameur de Haro" (traditional procedure for obtaining justice)

1982. Links with France. Multicoloured.

293	8p. Type **268**	20	15
294	8p. John of England, Philippe Auguste of France, and Siege of Rouen	20	15
295	11p. Jean Martell (brandy merchant), early still and view of Cognac	30	15
296	11p. Victor Hugo, "Le Rocher des Proscrits" (rock where he used to meditate) and Marine Terrace	30	15
297	19½p. Pierre Teilhard de Chardin (philosopher) and "Maison Saint Louis" (science institute)	45	20
298	19½p. Pere Charles Rey (scientist), anemotachymeter and The Observatory, St. Louis	45	20

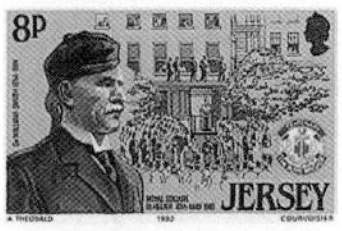

274 Sir William Smith and Proclamation of King George V, Jersey, 1910

1982. Youth Organizations. Multicoloured.

299	8p. Type **274**	20	20
300	11p. Boys' Brigade band, Liberation Parade, 1945 (vert)	20	20
301	24p. Sir William Smith and Lord Baden-Powell at Boys' Brigade Display, 1903	45	50
302	26p. Lord and Lady Baden-Powell, St. Helier, 1924 (vert)	60	60
303	29p. Scouts in summer camp, Jersey	75	70

Nos. 299/301 were issued on the occasion of the 75th anniv of the Boy Scout Movement, the 125th birth anniv of Lord Baden-Powell and centenary of the Boys' Brigade (1983).

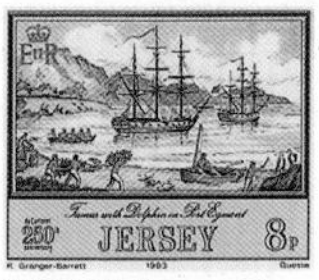

279 H.M.S. *Tamar* and H.M.S. *Dolphin* at Port Egmont

1983. Jersey Adventurers (1st series). 250th Birth anniv of Philippe de Carteret. Multicoloured.

304	8p. Type **279**	20	15
305	11p. H.M.S. *Dolphin* and H.M.S. *Swallow* off Magellan Strait	25	15
306	19½p. Discovering Pitcairn Island	40	35
307	24p. Carteret taking possession of English Cove, New Zealand	45	45
308	26p. H.M.S. *Swallow* sinking a pirate, Macassar Strait	50	50
309	29p. H.M.S. *Endymion* leading convoy from West Indies	65	60

See also Nos. 417/21 and 573/8.

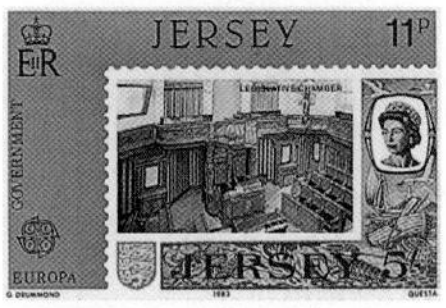

285 1969 5s. Legislative Chamber Definitive

1983. Europa. Multicoloured.

310	11p. Type **285**	25	30
311	11p. Royal Mace (23×32 mm)	25	30
312	19½p. 1969 10s. Royal Court definitive showing green border error	35	35
313	19½p. Bailiff's Seal (23×32 mm)	35	35

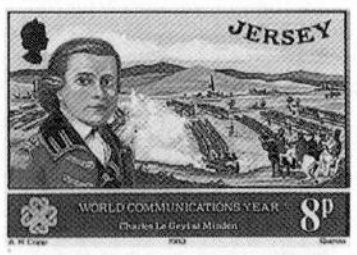

289 Charles Le Geyt and Battle of Minden (1759)

1983. World Communications Year and 250th Birth Anniv of Charles Le Geyt (First Jersey postmaster). Multicoloured.

314	8p. Type **289**	20	20
315	11p. London to Weymouth mail coach	30	30
316	24p. P.O. Mail Packet *"Chesterfield"* attacked by French privateer	55	55
317	26p. Mary Godfray and the Hue Street Post Office	65	65
318	29p. Mail steamer leaving St. Helier harbour	80	80

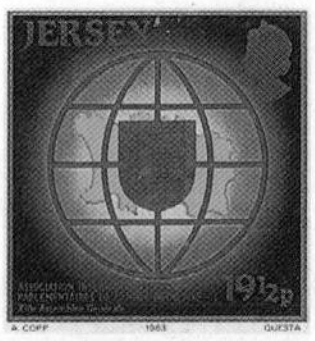

294 Assembly Emblem

1983. 13th General Assembly of the A.I.P.L.F. (Association Internationale des Parlementaires de Langue Francaise) Jersey.

319	**294**	19½p. multicoloured	75	75

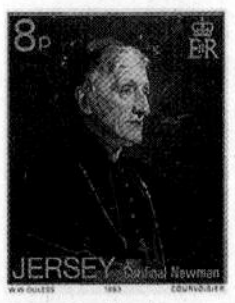

295 *Cardinal Newman*

1983. 50th Death Anniv of Walter Ouless (artist). Multicoloured.

320	8p. Type **295**	30	30
321	11p. "Incident in the French Revolution"	50	50
322	20½p. "Thomas Hardy"	75	75
323	31p. "David with the head of Goliath" (38×32 mm)	1·00	1·00

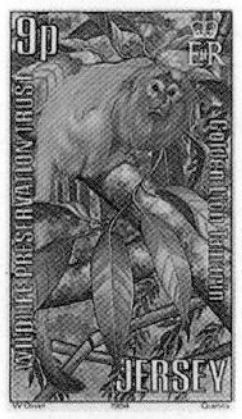

299 Golden Lion Tamarin

1984. Wildlife Preservation Trust (4th series). Multicoloured.

324	9p. Type **299**	25	25
325	12p. Snow leopard	25	25
326	20½p. Jamaican boa	45	45
327	26p. Round island gecko	75	70
328	28p. Coscoroba swan	80	80
329	31p. St. Lucia amazon ("St Lucia Parrot")	1·00	1·00

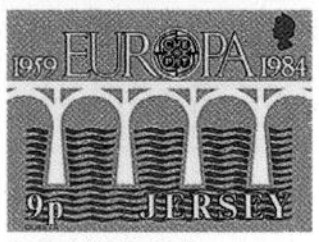

305 C.E.P.T. 25th Anniversary Logo

1984. Europa.

330	**305**	9p. light blue, blue and black	50	50
331	**305**	12p. lt green, green and black	50	50
332	**305**	20½p. lilac, purple and black	90	90

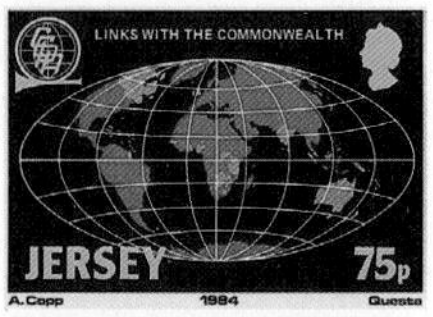

306 Map showing Commonwealth

1984. Links with the Commonwealth. Sheet 108×74 mm.

MS333	**306** 75p. multicoloured	2·00	2·00

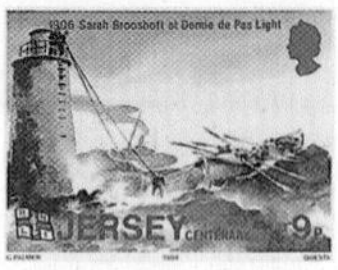

307 *Sarah Bloomshoft* at Demie de Pas Light, 1906

1984. Centenary of Jersey R.N.L.I. Lifeboat Station. Multicoloured.

334	9p. Type **307**	25	15
335	9p. *Hearts of Oak* and *Maurice Georges*, 1949	25	15
336	12p. *Elizabeth Rippon* and *Hanna*, 1949	35	30
337	12p. *Elizabeth Rippon* and *Santa Maria*, 1951	35	30
338	20½p. *Elizabeth Rippon* and *Bacchus*, 1973	60	70
339	20½p. *Thomas James King* and *Cythara*, 1983	60	70

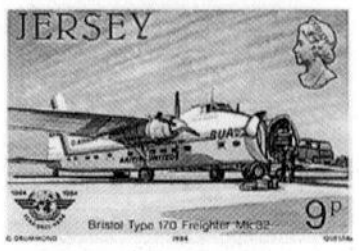

313 Bristol Type 170 Freighter Mk 32 G-ANWM

1984. 40th Anniv of I.C.A.O. Multicoloured.

340	9p. Type **313**	20	15
341	12p. Airspeed A.S.57 Ambassador 2 G-ALZO	35	35
342	26p. de Havilland DH.114 Heron 1B G-AMYU	75	75
343	31p. de Havilland DH.89A Dragon Rapide G-AGPH	1·00	1·00

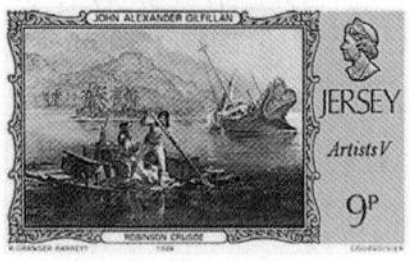

317 *Robinson Crusoe leaves the Wreck*

1984. Links with Australia. Paintings by John Alexander Gilfillan. Multicoloured.

344	9p. Type **317**	25	20
345	12p. *Edinburgh Castle*	30	20
346	20½p. *Maori Village*	60	50
347	26p. *Australian Landscape*	70	60
348	28p. *Waterhouse's Corner, Adelaide*	80	80
349	31p. *Captain Cook at Botany Bay*	80	80

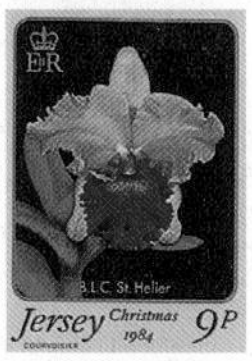

323 "B.L.C. St. Helier"

1984. Christmas. Jersey Orchids (1st series). Multicoloured.

350	9p. Type **323**	50	50
351	12p. "Oda Mt. Bingham"	80	80

See also Nos. 433/7, 613/17, 892/7, 1143/**MS**1149 and 1372/**MS**1378.

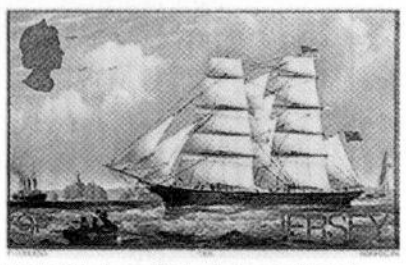

325 *'Hebe off Corbiere, 1874'*

1984. Death Centenary of Philip John Ouless (artist). Multicoloured.

352	9p. Type **325**	25	20
353	12p. *The 'Gaspe' engaging the 'Diomede'*	30	30
354	22p. *The Paddle-steamer 'London' entering Naples, 1856*	65	60
355	31p. *'The Rambler' entering Cape Town, 1840*	1·00	90
356	34p. *St. Aubin's Bay from Mount Bingham, 1871*	1·20	1·00

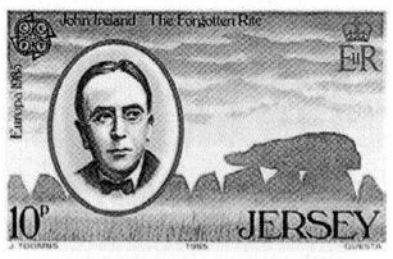

330 John Ireland (composer) and Faldouet Dolmen

1985. Europa. European Music Year. Multicoloured.

357	10p. Type **330**	30	30
358	13p. Ivy St. Helier (actress) and His Majesty's Theatre, London	45	45
359	22p. Claude Debussy (composer) and Elizabeth Castle	80	80

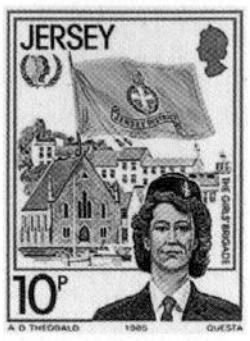

333 Girls' Brigade

1985. International Youth Year. Multicoloured.

360	10p. Type **333**	30	30
361	13p. Girl Guides (75th anniversary)	40	40
362	29p. Prince Charles and Jersey Youth Service Activities Base	70	70
363	31p. Sea Cadet Corps	75	75
364	34p. Air Training Corps	90	90

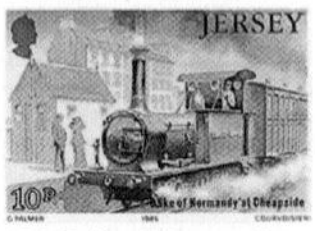

338 *Duke of Normandy* at Cheapside

1985. Jersey Western Railway. Multicoloured.

365	10p. Type **338**	45	45
366	13p. Saddletank at First Tower	50	50
367	22p. *La Moye* at Millbrook	90	90
368	29p. *St. Heliers* at St. Aubin	95	95
369	34p. *St. Aubyns* at Corbiere	1·00	1·00

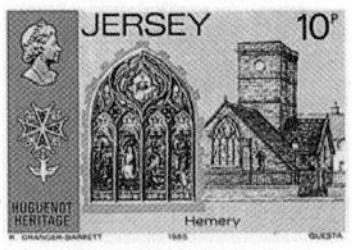

343 Memorial Window to Revd. James Hemery (former Dean) and St. Helier Parish Church

1985. 300th Anniv of Huguenot Immigration. Multicoloured.

370	10p. Type **343**	30	30
371	10p. Judge Francis Jeune, Baron St. Helier, and Houses of Parliament	30	30
372	13p. Silverware by Pierre Amiraux	40	40
373	13p. Francis Voisin (merchant) and Russian port	40	40
374	22p. Robert Brohier, Schweppes carbonation plant and bottles	55	50
375	22p. George Ingouville, V.C., R.N. and attack on Viborg	55	50

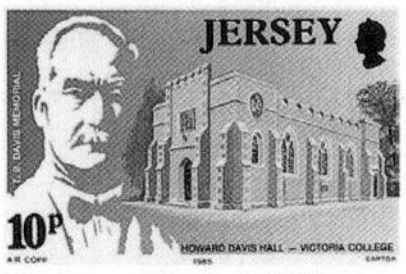

349 Howard Davis Hall, Victoria College

1985. Thomas Davis (philanthropist) Commemoration. Multicoloured.

376	10p. Type **349**	35	35
377	13p. Racing schooner "*Westward*"	50	50
378	31p. Howard Davis Park, St. Helier	70	70
379	34p. Howard Davis Experimental Farm, Trinity	85	85

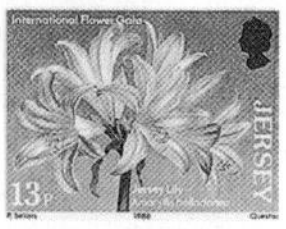

353 *Amaryllis belladonna* (Pandora Sellars)

1986. Jersey Lilies. Multicoloured.

380	13p. Type **353**	45	45
381	34p. "A Jersey Lily" (Lily Langtry) (Sir John Millais) (30×48 mm)	1·00	1·10
MS382	140×96 mm. Nos. 380×4 and 381	2·75	3·00

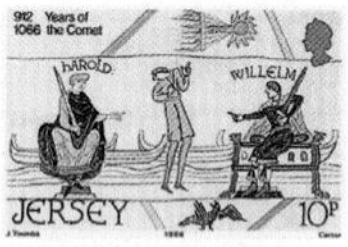

355 King Harold, William of Normandy and Halley's Comet, 1066 (from Bayeux Tapestry)

1986. Appearance of Halley's Comet. Multicoloured.

383	10p. Type **355**	35	35
384	22p. Lady Carteret, Edmond Halley, map and Comet	80	85
385	31p. Aspects of communications in 1910 and 1986 on TV screens	1·00	1·10

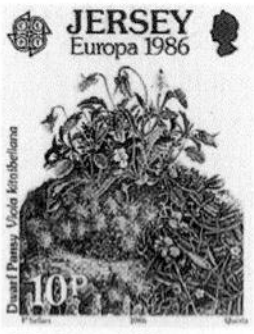

358 Dwarf Pansy

1986. Europa. Environmental Conservation. Multicoloured.

386	10p. Type **358**	35	35
387	14p. Sea stock	45	45
388	22p. Sand crocus	70	70

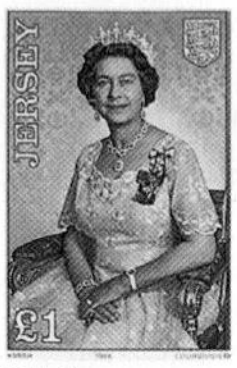

361 Queen Elizabeth II (from photo by Karsh)

1986. 60th Birthday of Queen Elizabeth II.

389	**361**	£1 multicoloured	2·50	2·75

See also No. 491b.

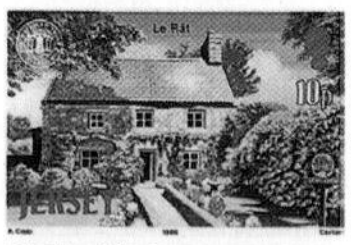

362 Le Rât Cottage

1986. 50th Anniv of National Trust for Jersey. Multicoloured.

390	10p. Type **362**	25	20
391	14p. The Elms (Trust headquarters)	35	30
392	22p. Morel Farm	65	65
393	29p. Quétivel Mill	70	70
394	31p. La Vallette	75	75

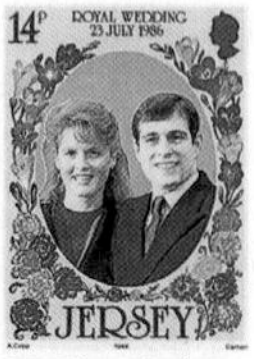

367 Prince Andrew and Miss Sarah Ferguson

1986. Royal Wedding.

395	**367**	14p. multicoloured	35	35
396	**367**	40p. multicoloured	1·20	1·20

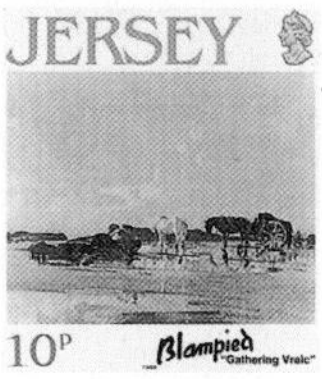

368 *Gathering Vraic*

1986. Birth Centenary of Edmund Blampied (artist).

397	**368**	10p. multicoloured	25	25
398	-	14p. black, blue and grey	40	40
399	-	29p. multicoloured	75	75
400	-	31p. black, orange and grey	90	90
401	-	34p. multicoloured	95	95

DESIGNS: 14p. *Driving Home in the Rain*; 29p. *The Miller*; 31p. *The Joy Ride*; 34p. *Tante Elizabeth*.

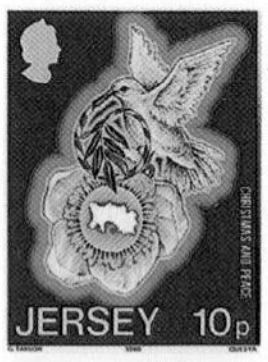

373 Island Map on Jersey Lily, and Dove holding Olive Branch

1986. Christmas. Int Peace Year. Multicoloured.

402	10p. Type **373**	30	30
403	14p. Mistletoe wreath encircling European robin and dove	50	50
404	34p. Christmas cracker releasing dove	1·10	1·10

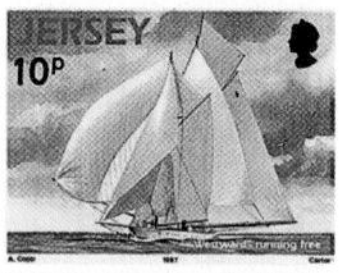

376 *Westward* under Full Sail

1987. Racing Schooner *Westward*. Multicoloured.

405	10p. Type **376**	40	35
406	14p. T. B. Davis at the helm	50	55
407	31p. *Westward* overhauling *Britannia*	95	95
408	34p. *Westward* fitting-out at St. Helier	95	95

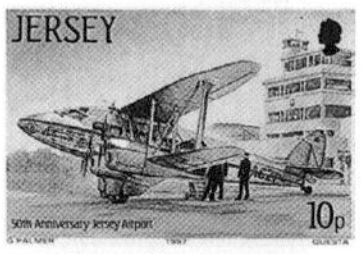

380 de Havilland DH.86 Dragon Express G-ACZP *Belcroute Bay*

1987. 50th Anniv of Jersey Airport. Multicoloured.

409	10p. Type **380**	25	25
410	14p. Boeing 757 and Douglas DC-9-15	40	45
411	22p. Britten-Norman BN-2A Mk III "long nose" Trislander and Islander aircraft	55	50
412	29p. Shorts 330 G-OJUK and Vickers Viscount 800	90	90
413	31p. B.A.C. One Eleven 500 and Handley Page H.P.R.7 Dart Herald	95	95

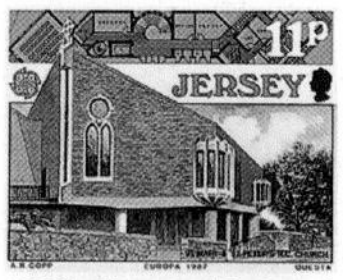

385 St. Mary and St. Peter's Roman Catholic Church

1987. Europa. Modern Architecture. Multicoloured.

414	11p. Type **385**	40	40
415	15p. Villa Devereux, St. Brelade	50	45
416	22p. Fort Regent Leisure Centre, St. Helier (57×29 mm)	75	75

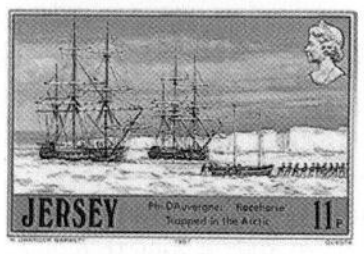

388 H.M.S. *Racehorse* and H.M.S. *Carcass* (bomb ketches) trapped in Arctic

1987. Jersey Adventurers (2nd series). Philippe d'Auvergne. Multicoloured.

417	11p. Type **388**	30	35
418	15p. H.M.S. *Alarm* on fire, Rhode Island	40	45
419	29p. H.M.S. *Arethusa* wrecked off Ushant	70	75
420	31p. H.M.S. *Rattlesnake* stranded on Isle de Trinidad	80	90
421	34p. Mont Orgueil Castle and fishing boats	85	95

See also Nos. 501/6 and 539/44.

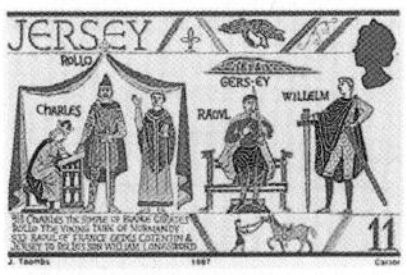

393 Grant of Lands to Normandy, 911 and 933

1987. 900th Death Anniv of William the Conqueror. Multicoloured.

422	11p. Type **393**	30	30
423	15p. Edward the Confessor and Duke Robert I of Normandy landing on Jersey, 1030	35	35
424	22p. King William's Coronation, 1066 and fatal fall, 1087	70	65
425	29p. Death of William Rufus, 1100 and Battle of Tinchebrai, 1106	75	75
426	31p. Civil war between Matilda and Stephen, 1135–41	85	85
427	34p. Henry inherits Normandy, 1151; John asserts Ducal Rights in Jersey, 1213	95	95

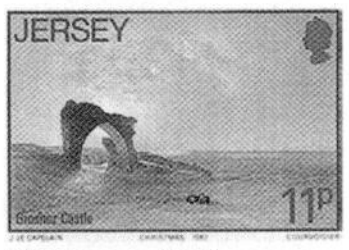

399 *Grosnez Castle*

1987. Christmas. Paintings by John Le Capelain. Multicoloured.

428	11p. Type **399**	35	30
429	15p. *St. Aubin's Bay*	50	50
430	22p. *Mont Orgueil Castle*	65	65
431	31p. *Town Fort and Harbour, St. Helier*	90	80
432	34p. *The Hermitage*	1·00	1·00

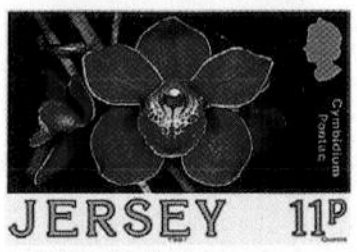

404 *Cymbidium pontac*

1988. Jersey Orchids (2nd series). Multicoloured.

433	11p. Type **404**	40	35
434	15p. *Odontioda* "Eric Young" (vert)	45	45
435	29p. *Lycaste auburn*, "Seaford" and "Ditchling"	70	70
436	31p. *Odontoglossum* "St. Brelade" (vert)	80	80
437	34p. *Cymbidium mavourneen* "Jester"	95	95

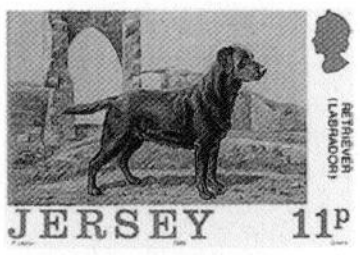

409 Labrador Retriever

1988. Centenary of Jersey Dog Club. Multicoloured.

438	11p. Type **409**	40	40
439	15p. Wire-haired dachshund	60	60
440	22p. Pekingese	80	80
441	31p. Cavalier King Charles spaniel	90	1·00
442	34p. Dalmatian	1·00	1·00

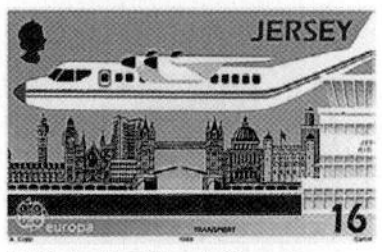

414 de Havilland Canada DHC-7 Dash Seven, London Landmarks and Jersey Control Tower

1988. Europa. Transport and Communications. Multicoloured.

443	16p. Type **414**	40	45
444	16p. Weather radar and Jersey airport landing system (vert)	40	45
445	22p. Hydrofoil, St. Malo and Elizabeth Castle, St. Helier	75	75
446	22p. Port control tower and Jersey Radio maritime communication centre, La Moye (vert)	75	75

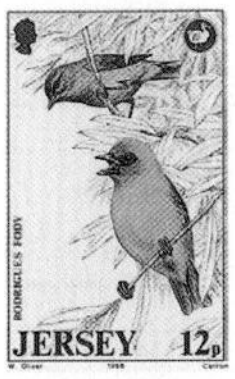

418 Rodriguez Fody ("Rodrigues Fody")

1988. Wildlife Preservation Trust (5th series). Multicoloured.

447	12p. Type **418**	45	45
448	16p. Volcano rabbit (horiz)	55	50
449	29p. White-faced marmoset	90	1·00
450	31p. Ploughshare tortoise (horiz)	1·10	1·10
451	34p. Mauritius kestrel	1·20	1·20

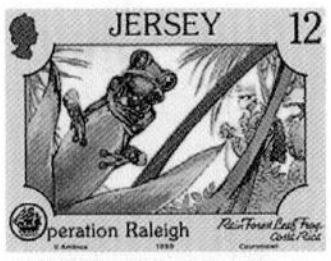

423 Rain Forest Leaf Frog, Costa Rica

1988. Operation Raleigh. Multicoloured.

452	12p. Type **423**	35	25
453	16p. Archaeological survey, Peru	40	40
454	22p. Climbing glacier, Chile	60	60
455	29p. Red Cross Centre, Solomon Islands	70	70
456	31p. Underwater exploration, Australia	80	90
457	34p. *Zebu* (brigantine) returning to St. Helier	90	1·00

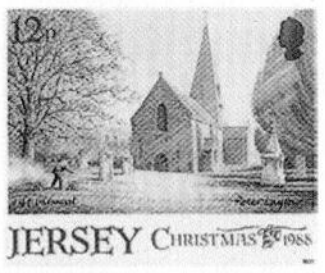

429 St. Clement Parish Church

1988. Christmas. Jersey Parish Churches (1st series). Multicoloured.

458	12p. Type **429**	30	15
459	16p. St. Ouen	45	30
460	31p. St. Brelade	90	90
461	34p. St. Lawrence	85	95

See also Nos. 535/8 and 597/600.

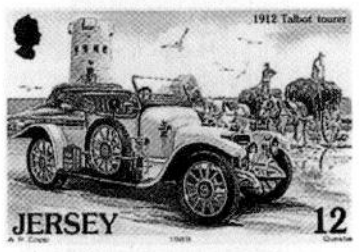

433 Talbot "Type 4 CT Tourer", 1912

1989. Vintage Cars (1st series). Multicoloured.

462	12p. Type **433**	35	30
463	16p. De Dion "Bouton Type 1-D", 1920	50	45
464	23p. Austin 7 "Chummy", 1926	60	55
465	30p. Ford "Model T", 1926	80	80
466	32p. Bentley 8 litre, 1930	1·00	1·00
467	35p. Cadillac "452A–V16 Fleetwood Sports Phaeton", 1931	1·00	1·00

See also Nos. 591/6 and 905/10.

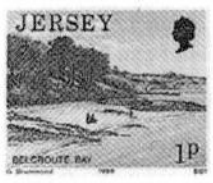

439 Belcroute Bay

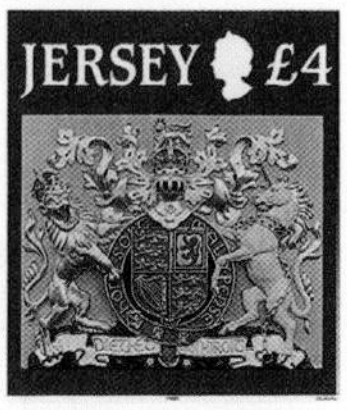

464 Arms of King George VI

1989. Jersey Scenes. Multicoloured.

468	1p. Type **439**	10	10
469	2p. High Street, St. Aubin	10	10
470	4p. Royal Jersey Golf Course	10	10
471	5p. Portelet Bay	10	15
472	10p. Les Charrieres D'Anneport	30	30
473	13p. St. Helier Marina	40	45
474	14p. Sand yacht racing, St. Ouen's Bay	40	45
475	15p. Rozel Harbour	45	50
476	16p. St. Aubin's Harbour	50	55
477	17p. Jersey Airport	50	55
478	18p. Corbiére Lighthouse	55	60
479	19p. Val de la Mare	55	60
480	20p. Elizabeth Castle	45	45
481	21p. Greve de Lecq	50	55
482	22p. Samarés Manor	45	50
483	23p. Bonne Nuit Harbour	75	55
484	24p. Grosnez Castle	60	60
485	25p. Augrés Manor	70	75
486	26p. Central Market	75	80
487	27p. St. Brelade's Bay	80	90
488	30p. St. Ouen's Manor	85	90
489	40p. La Hougue Bie	1·00	1·00
490	50p. Mont Orgueil Castle	1·20	1·40
491	75p. Royal Square, St. Helier	2·00	1·50
491b	£2 Queen Elizabeth II (from photo by Karsh)	4·00	3·25
491c	£4 Type **464**	7·00	6·75

Nos. 469/91 are as Type **439**.

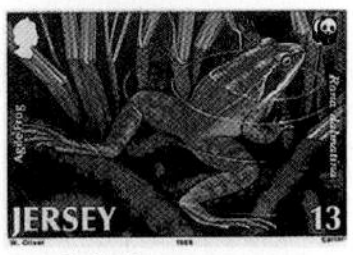

465 Agile Frog

1989. Endangered Jersey Fauna. Multicoloured.

492	13p. Type **465**	80	85
493	13p. *Heteropterus morpheus* (butterfly) (vert)	80	85
494	17p. Barn owl (vert)	80	85
495	17p. Green lizard	80	85

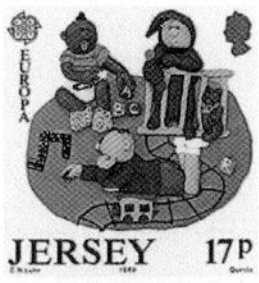

469 Toddlers' Toys

1989. Europa. Children's Toys and Games. Designs showing clay plaques. Multicoloured.

496	17p. Type **469**	60	60
497	17p. Playground games	60	60
498	23p. Party games	1·00	1·00
499	23p. Teenage sports	1·00	1·00

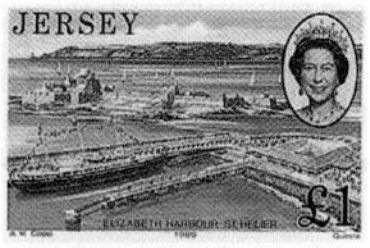

473 Queen Elizabeth II and Royal Yacht *Britannia* in Elizabeth Harbour

1989. Royal Visit.

500	**473** £1 multicoloured	2·75	2·75

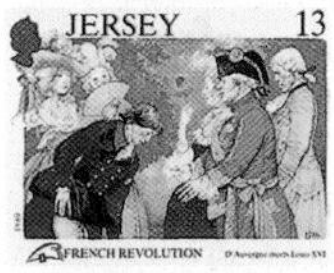

474 Philippe d'Auvergne presented to Louis XVI, 1786

1989. Bicentenary of the French Revolution. Philippe d'Auvergne. Multicoloured.

501	13p. Type **474**	40	30
502	17p. Storming the Bastille, 1789	50	40
503	23p. Marie de Bouillon and revolutionaries, 1790	60	50
504	30p. Auvergne's headquarters at Mont Orgueil, 1795	95	1·00
505	32p. Landing arms for Chouan rebels, 1796	1·00	1·10
506	35p. The last Chouan revolt, 1799	1·20	1·30

See also Nos. 539/44.

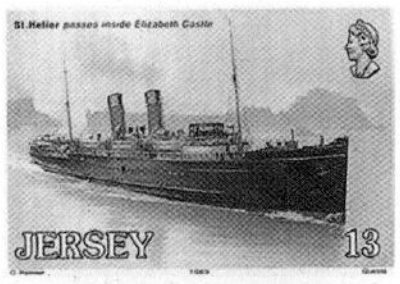

480 *St. Helier* off Elizabeth Castle

1989. Centenary of Great Western Railway Steamer Service to Channel Islands. Multicoloured.

507	13p. Type **480**	30	30
508	17p. *Caesarea II* off Corbière Lighthouse	35	35
509	27p. *Reindeer* in St. Helier harbour	80	80
510	32p. "*bex racing *Frederica* off Portelet	95	95
511	35p. *Lynx* off Noirmont	1·10	1·10

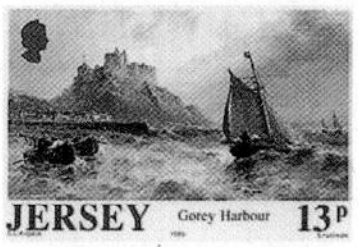

485 *Gorey Harbour*

1989. 150th Birth Anniv of Sarah Louisa Kilpack (artist). Multicoloured.

512	13p. Type **485**	25	25
513	17p. *La Corbière*	30	30
514	23p. *Grève de Lecq*	80	75
515	32p. *Bouley Bay*	85	85
516	35p. *Mont Orgueil*	90	1·00

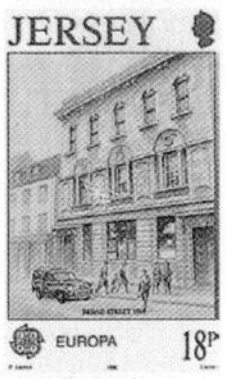

490 Head Post Office, Broad Street, 1969

1990. Europa. Post Office Buildings. Multicoloured.

517	18p. Type **490**	50	40
518	18p. Postal Headquarters, Mont Millais, 1990	50	50
519	24p. Hue Street Post Office, 1815 (horiz)	65	65
520	24p. Head Post Office, Halkett Place, 1890 (horiz)	65	65

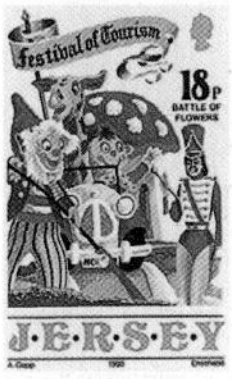

494 "Battle of Flowers" Parade

1990. Festival of Tourism. Multicoloured.

521	18p. Type **494**	55	55
522	24p. Sports	70	70
523	29p. Mont Orgueil Castle and German Underground Hospital Museum	85	85
524	32p. Salon Culinaire	90	90
MS525	151×100 mm. Nos. 521/4	2·75	3·00

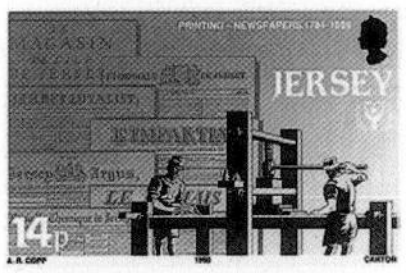

498 Early Printing Press and Jersey Newspaper Mastheads

1990. International Literacy Year. Jersey News Media. Multicoloured.

526	14p. Type **498**	45	45
527	18p. Modern press, and offices of *Jersey Evening Post* in 1890 and 1990	45	45
528	34p. Radio Jersey broadcaster	90	90
529	37p. Channel Television studio cameraman	95	95

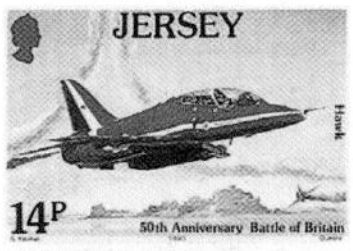

502 British Aerospace Hawk T.1

1990. 50th Anniv of Battle of Britain. Multicoloured.

530	14p. Type **502**	40	45
531	18p. Supermarine Spitfire	55	60
532	24p. Hawker Hurricane Mk I	85	85
533	34p. Vickers-Armstrong Wellington	1·50	1·60
534	37p. Avro Type 683 Lancaster	1·60	1·60

1990. Christmas. Jersey Parish Churches (2nd series). As T **429**. Multicoloured.

535	14p. St. Helier	45	40
536	18p. Grouville	45	40
537	34p. St. Saviour	1·00	1·10
538	37p. St. John	1·20	1·40

1991. 175th Death Anniv of Philippe d'Auvergne. As T **474**. Multicoloured.

539	15p. Prince's Tower, La Hougue Bie	45	40
540	20p. Auvergne's arrest in Paris	55	55
541	26p. Auvergne plotting against Napoleon	70	75
542	31p. Execution of George Cadoudal	90	90
543	37p. H.M.S. *Surly* (cutter) attacking French convoy	1·10	1·10
544	44p. Auvergne's last days in London	1·20	1·20

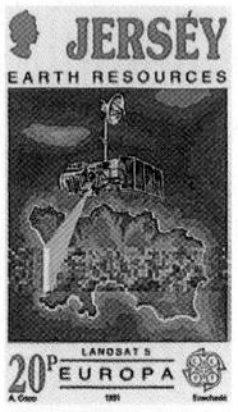

517 "Landsat 5" and Thematic Mapper Image over Jersey

1991. Europa. Europe in Space. Multicoloured.

545	20p. Type **517**	50	50
546	20p. "ERS-1" earth resources remote sensing satellite	50	50
547	26p. "Meteosat" weather satellite	80	85
548	26p. "Olympus" direct broadcasting satellite	80	85

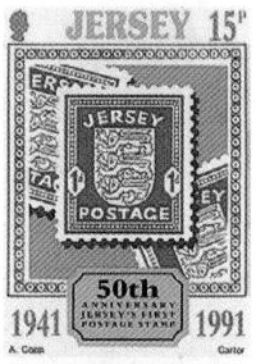

521 1941 1d. Stamp (50th anniv of first Jersey postage stamp)

1991. Anniversaries. Multicoloured.

549	15p. Type **521**	30	30
550	20p. Steam train (centenary of Jersey Eastern Railway extension to Gorey Pier)	50	55
551	26p. Jersey cow and Herd Book (125th anniv of Jersey Herd Book)	60	70
552	31p. Stone-laying ceremony (from painting by P. J. Ouless) (150th anniv of Victoria Harbour)	75	80
553	53p. Marie Bartlett and hospital (250th anniv of Marie Bartlett's hospital bequest)	1·70	1·70

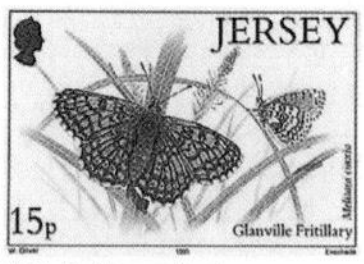

526 *Melitaea cinxia*

1991. Butterflies and Moths. Multicoloured.

554	15p. Type **526**	35	35
555	20p. *Euplagia quadripunctaria*	45	30
556	37p. *Deilephilia porcellus*	1·40	1·50
557	57p. *Inachis io*	1·70	1·90

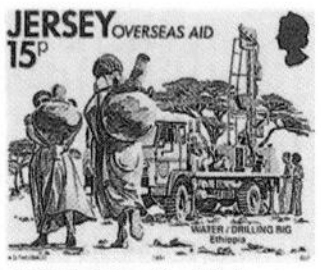

530 Drilling for Water, Ethiopia

1991. Overseas Aid. Multicoloured.

558	15p. Type **530**	45	40
559	20p. Building construction, Rwanda	50	45
560	26p. Village polytechnic, Kenya	70	70
561	31p. Treating leprosy, Tanzania	85	90
562	37p. Ploughing, Zambia	1·10	1·10
563	44p. Immunization clinic, Lesotho	1·20	1·40

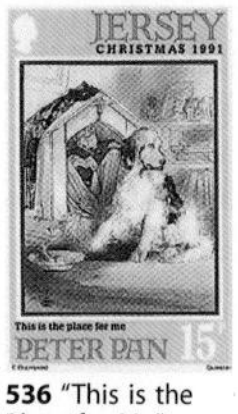

536 "This is the Place for Me"

1991. Christmas. Illustrations by Edmund Blampied for J. M. Barrie's *Peter Pan*. Multicoloured.

564	15p. Type **536**	40	40
565	20p. *The Island Come True*	65	65
566	37p. *The Never Bird*	1·20	1·20
567	53p. *The Great White Father*	1·60	1·60

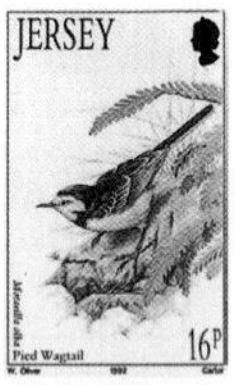

540 Pied Wagtail

1992. Winter Birds. Multicoloured.

568	16p. Type **540**	50	25
569	22p. Firecrest	70	55
570	28p. Common snipe ("Snipe")	80	85
571	39p. Northern lapwing ("Lapwing")	1·20	1·20
572	57p. Fieldfare	1·70	1·70

See also Nos. 635/9.

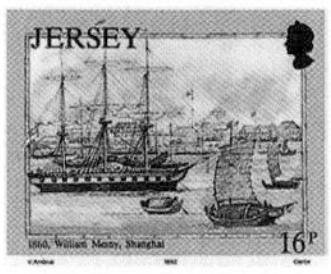

545 Shipping at Shanghai, 1860

1992. Jersey Adventurers (3rd series). 150th Birth Anniv of William Mesny. Multicoloured.

573	16p. Type **545**	40	45
574	16p. Mesny's junk running Taiping blockade, 1862	40	45
575	22p. General Mesny outside river gate, 1874	65	65
576	22p. Mesny in Burma, 1877	65	65
577	33p. Mesny and Governor Chang, 1882	90	95
578	33p. Mesny in mandarin's sedan chair, 1886	90	95

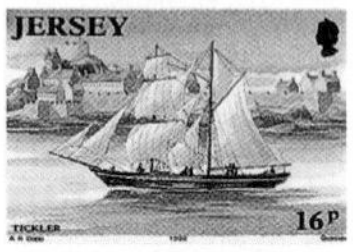

551 *Tickler* (brigantine)

1992. Jersey Shipbuilding. Multicoloured.

579	16p. Type **551**	45	40
580	22p. *Hebe* (brig)	70	75
581	50p. *Gemini* (barque)	1·40	1·50
582	57p. *Percy Douglas* (full-rigged ship)	1·60	1·70
MS583	148×98 mm. Nos. 579/82	4·00	4·25

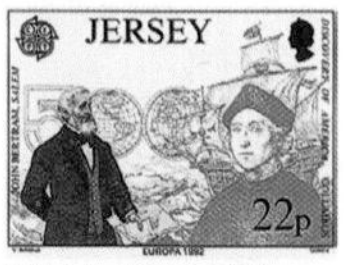

555 John Bertram (ship owner) and Columbus

1992. Europa. 500th Anniv of Discovery of America by Columbus. Multicoloured.

584	22p. Type **555**	65	50
585	28p. Sir George Carteret (founder of New Jersey)	75	80
586	39p. Sir Walter Raleigh (founder of Virginia)	1·10	1·40

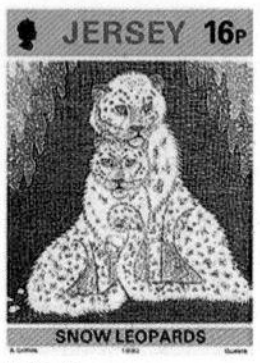

558 "Snow Leopards" (Allison Griffiths)

1992. Batik Designs. Multicoloured.

587	16p. Type **558**	45	40
588	22p. "Three Elements" (Nataly Miorin)	65	45
589	39p. "Three Men in a Tub" (Amanda Crocker)	1·10	1·20
590	57p. "Cockatoos" (Michelle Millard)	1·50	1·70

1992. Vintage Cars (2nd series). As T **433**. Multicoloured.

591	16p. Morris Cowley "Bullnose", 1925	30	30
592	22p. Rolls Royce "20/25", 1932	45	45
593	28p. Chenard and Walcker "T5", 1924	70	75
594	33p. Packard 900 series "Light Eight", 1932	90	95
595	39p. Lanchester "21", 1927	1·00	1·10
596	50p. Buick "30 Roadster", 1913	1·50	1·70

1992. Christmas. Jersey Parish Churches (3rd series). As T **429**. Multicoloured.

597	16p. Trinity	40	30
598	22p. St. Mary	55	50
599	39p. St. Martin	1·10	1·10
600	57p. St. Peter	1·50	1·50

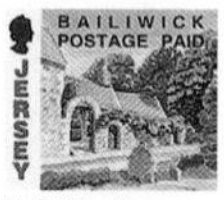

572 Farmhouse

1993. Multicoloured.

601	(–) Type **572**	60	70
602	(–) Trinity Church	60	70
603	(–) Daffodils and cows	60	70
604	(–) Jersey cows	60	70
605	(–) Sunbathing	70	60
606	(–) Windsurfing	70	60
607	(–) Crab (Queen's head at left)	70	60
608	(–) Crab (Queen's head at right)	70	60
609	(–) "Singin' in the Rain" float	85	80
610	(–) "Dragon Dance" float	85	80
611	(–) "Bali, Morning of the World" float	85	80
612	(–) "Zulu Fantasy" float	85	80

The above do not show face values, but are inscribed "BAILIWICK POSTAGE PAID" (Nos. 601/4), "U.K. MINIMUM POSTAGE PAID" (Nos. 605/8) or "EUROPE POSTAGE PAID" (Nos. 609/12). They were initially sold at 17p., 23p. or 28p., but it is intended that these face values will be increased to reflect postage rate changes in the future.

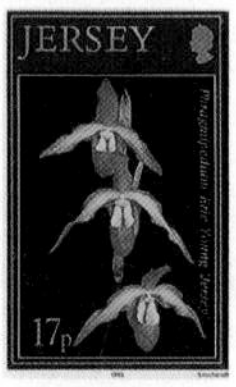

584 *Phragmipedium* Eric Young "Jersey"

1993. Jersey Orchids (3rd series). Multicoloured.

613	17p. Type **584**	45	35
614	23p. *Odontoglossum* Augres "Trinity"	70	65
615	28p. *Miltonia* St. Helier "Colomberie"	80	75
616	39p. *Phragmipedium pearcei*	1·20	1·40
617	57p. *Calanthe* Grouville "Gorey"	1·70	1·90

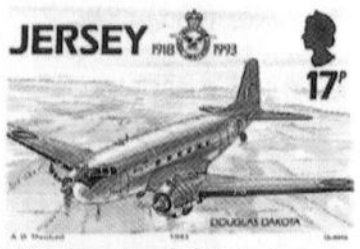

589 Douglas DC-3 Dakota

1993. 75th Anniv of Royal Air Force. Multicoloured.

618	17p. Type **589**	45	30
619	23p. Wight seaplane	60	65
620	28p. Avro Shackleton A.E.W.2	70	70
621	33p. Gloster Meteor Mk III and de Havilland Vampire FB.5	80	85
622	39p. Hawker Siddeley Harrier GR.1A	1·00	1·10
623	57p. Panavia Tornado F.3	1·50	1·60
MS624	147×98 mm. Nos. 619 and 623	4·50	4·75

Nos. 618/24 also commemorate the 50th anniv of the Royal Air Force Association and the 40th anniv of the first air display on Jersey.

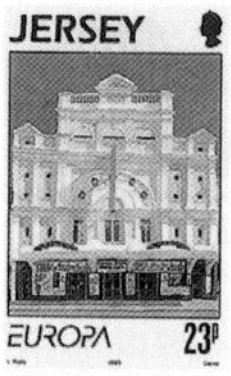

595 *Jersey's Opera House* (Ian Rolls)

1993. Europa. Contemporary Art. Multicoloured.

625	23p. Type **595**	60	60
626	28p. *The Ham and Tomato Bap* (Jonathan Hubbard)	70	70
627	39p. *Vase of Flowers* (Neil MacKenzie)	1·10	1·10

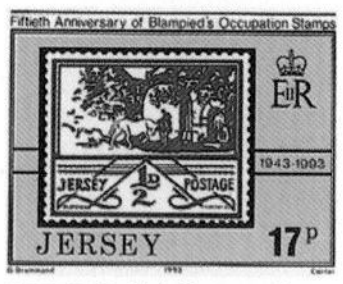

598 1943 ½d. Occupation Stamp

1993. 50th Anniv of Edmund Blampied's Occupation Stamps. Designs showing stamps from the 1943 issue.

628	**598**	17p. green, light green and black	35	35
629	-	23p. red, pink and black	50	50
630	-	28p. brown, cinnamon and black	70	70
631	-	33p. orange, salmon and black	85	85
632	-	39p. blue, cobalt and black	1·20	1·20
633	-	50p. mauve, light mauve and black	1·40	1·40

DESIGNS: 23p. 1d. value; 28p. 1½d. value; 33p. 2d. value; 39p. 2½d. value; 50p. 3d. value.

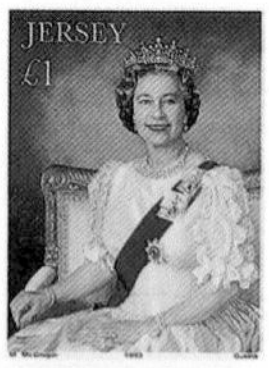

604 Queen Elizabeth II (from painting by Mara McGregor)

1993. 40th Anniv of Coronation.

634	**604**	£1 multicoloured	2·75	2·75

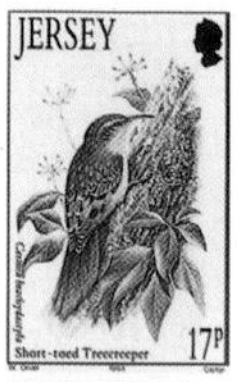

605 Short-toed Treecreeper

1993. Summer Birds. Multicoloured.

635	17p. Type **605**	45	50
636	23p. Dartford warbler	70	75
637	28p. Northern wheatear ("Wheatear")	80	85
638	39p. Cirl bunting	1·20	1·20
639	57p. Jay	1·70	1·70

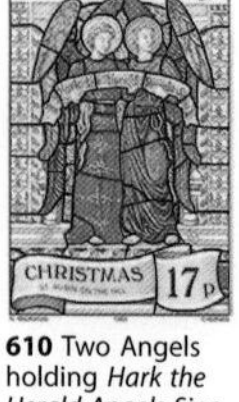

610 Two Angels holding *Hark the Herald Angels Sing* Banner

1993. Christmas. Stained Glass Windows by Henry Bosdet from St. Aubin on the Hill Church. Multicoloured.

640	17p. Type **610**	40	35
641	23p. Two angels playing harps	60	60
642	39p. Two angels playing violins	1·10	1·20
643	57p. Two angels holding *Once in Royal David's City* banner	1·70	1·90

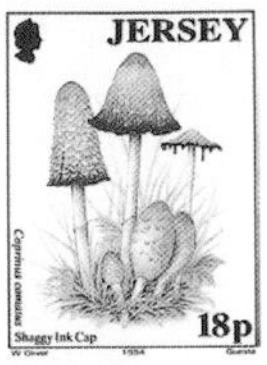

614 *Coprinus comatus*

1994. Fungi. Multicoloured.

644	18p. Type **614**	45	40
645	23p. Amanita muscaria	65	70
646	30p. Cantharellus cibarius	80	85
647	41p. *Macrolepiota procera*	1·20	1·20
648	60p. *Clathrus ruber*	1·60	1·60

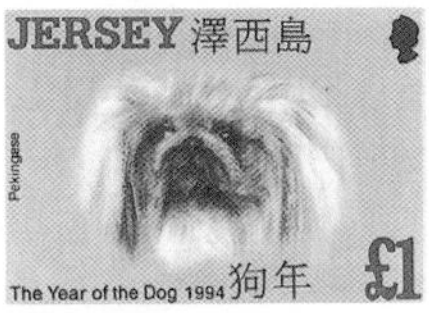

619 Pekingese

1994. "Hong Kong '94" International Stamp Exhibition. "Chinese Year of the Dog". Sheet 110×75 mm.

MS649	**619** £1 multicoloured	2·50	2·75

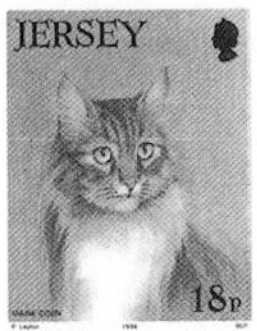

620 Maine Coon

1994. 21st Anniv of Jersey Cat Club. Multicoloured.

650	18p. Type **620**	40	30
651	23p. British shorthair (horiz)	60	50
652	35p. Persian	80	80
653	41p. Siamese (horiz)	1·20	1·20
654	60p. Non-pedigree	1·20	1·50

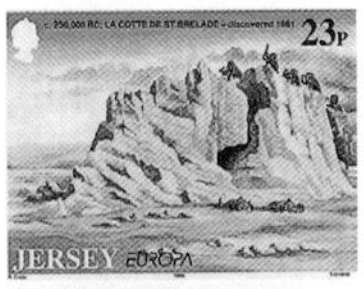

625 Mammoth Hunt, La Cotte de St. Brelade

1994. Europa. Archaeological Discoveries. Multicoloured.

655	23p. Type **625**	50	55
656	23p. Stone Age hunters pulling mammoth into cave	50	55
657	30p. Chambered passage, La Hougue Bie	75	85
658	30p. Transporting stones	75	85

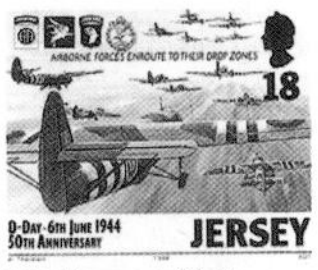

629 Airspeed AS 51 Horsa Gliders and Douglas C-47 Tow Planes approaching France

1994. 50th Anniv of D-Day. Multicoloured.

659	18p. Type **629**	55	50
660	18p. Landing craft approaching beaches	55	50
661	23p. Disembarking from landing craft on Gold Beach	75	70
662	23p. British troops on Sword Beach	75	70
663	30p. Spitfires over beaches	80	75
664	30p. Invasion map	80	75

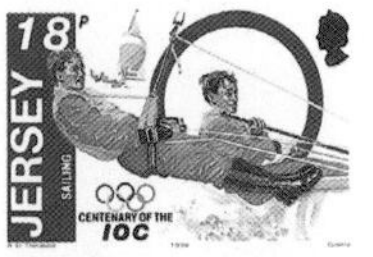

635 Sailing

1994. Centenary of International Olympic Committee. Multicoloured.

665	18p. Type **635**	40	35
666	23p. Rifle-shooting	55	55
667	30p. Hurdling	75	75
668	41p. Swimming	1·10	1·10
669	60p. Hockey	1·50	1·60

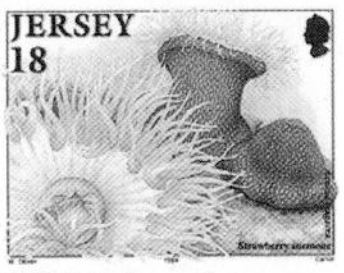

640 Strawberry Anemone

1994. Marine Life. Multicoloured.

670	18p. Type **640**	40	45
671	23p. Hermit crab and parasitic anemone	60	65
672	41p. Velvet swimming crab	1·20	1·40
673	60p. Common jellyfish	1·60	1·60

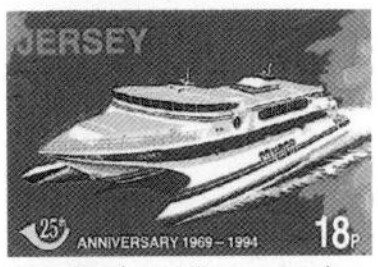

644 *Condor 10* (catamaran)

1994. 25th Anniv of Jersey Postal Administration. Multicoloured.

674	18p. Type **644**	50	45
675	23p. Map of Jersey and pillar box	60	50
676	35p. Vickers Type 953 Vanguard of B.E.A.	85	85
677	41p. Short 360 of Aurigny Air Services	1·10	1·00
678	60p. *Caesarea* (Sealink ferry)	1·60	1·50
MS679	150×100 mm. Nos. 674/8	4·50	4·50

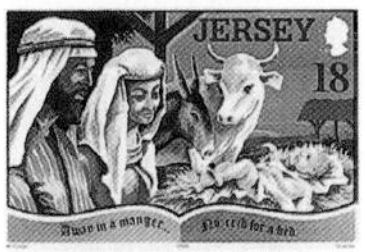

649 "Away in a Manger"

1994. Christmas. Carols. Multicoloured.

680	18p. Type **649**	40	40
681	23p. *Hark! the Herald Angels Sing*	50	50
682	41p. *While Shepherds Watched*	1·20	1·20
683	60p. *We Three Kings of Orient Are*	1·50	1·50

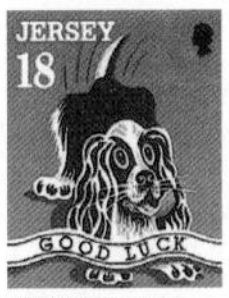

653 Dog and "GOOD LUCK"

1995. Greetings Stamps. Multicoloured.

684	18p. Type **653**	30	20
685	18p. Rose and "WITH LOVE"	30	20
686	18p. Chick and "CONGRATULATIONS"	30	20
687	18p. Bouquet of flowers and "THANK YOU"	30	20
688	23p. Dove with letter and "WITH LOVE"	45	25
689	23p. Cat and "GOOD LUCK"	45	25
690	23p. Carnations and "THANK YOU"	45	25
691	23p. Parrot and "CONGRATULATIONS"	45	25
692	60p. Pig and "HAPPY NEW YEAR" (25×63 mm)	45	25

No. 692 commemorates the Chinese New Year of the Pig.

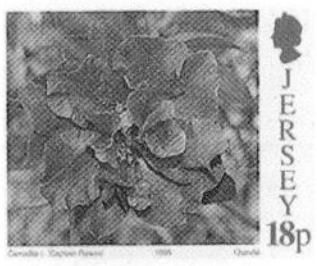

662 Camellia "Captain Rawes"

1994. Camellias. Multicoloured.

693	18p. Type **662**	55	50
694	23p. "Brigadoon"	80	70
695	30p. "Elsie Jury"	90	85
696	35p. "Augusto L'Gouveia Pinto"	1·10	1·20
697	41p. "Bella Romana"	1·20	1·30

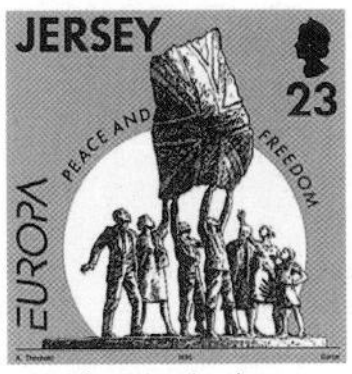

667 *Liberation* (sculpture, Philip Jackson)

1995. Europa. Peace and Freedom.

698	**667**	23p. black and blue	55	55
699	**667**	30p. black and pink	70	95

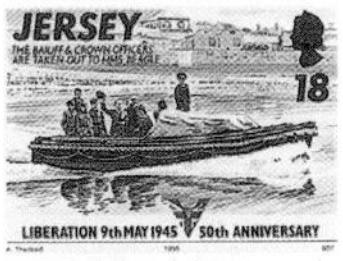

668 Bailiff and Crown Officers in Launch

1995. 50th Anniv of Liberation. Multicoloured.

700	18p. Type **668**	40	40
701	18p. *Vega* (Red Cross supply ship)	40	40
702	23p. H.M.S. *Beagle* (destroyer)	60	60
703	23p. British troops in Ordnance Yard, St. Helier	60	60
704	60p. King George VI and Queen Elizabeth in Jersey	1·50	1·50
705	60p. Unloading supplies from landing craft, St. Aubin's	1·50	1·50
MS706	110×75 mm. £1 Royal Family with Winston Churchill on Buckingham Palace balcony, V.E. Day (80×39 mm)	2·75	2·75

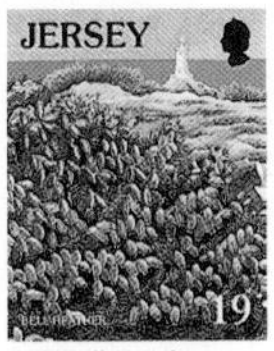

675 Bell Heather

1995. European Nature Conservation Year. Wild Flowers. Multicoloured.

707	19p. Type **675**	40	20
708	19p. Sea campion	40	20
709	19p. Spotted rock-rose	40	20
710	19p. Thrift	40	20
711	19p. Sheep's-bit scabious	40	20
712	23p. Field bind-weed	50	25
713	23p. Common bird's-foot trefoil	50	25
714	23p. Sea-holly	50	25
715	23p. Common centaury	50	25
716	23p. Dwarf pansy	50	25

Nos. 707/11 and 712/16 respectively were printed together, *se-tenant*, forming composite designs.

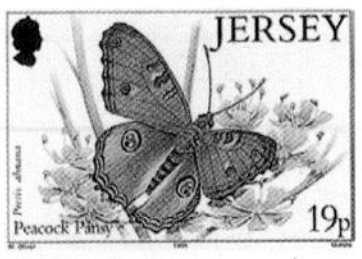

685 *Precis almana*

1995. Butterflies. Multicoloured.

717	19p. Type **685**	50	55
718	23p. *Papilio palinurus*	55	60
719	30p. *Catopsilia scylla*	80	85
720	41p. *Papilio rumanzovia*	1·00	1·10
721	60p. *Troides helena*	1·60	1·70
MS722	150×100 mm. Nos. 720/1	2·40	2·50

No. **MS**722 includes the "Singapore '95" International Stamp Exhibition logo on the sheet margin and shows the two stamp designs without frames.

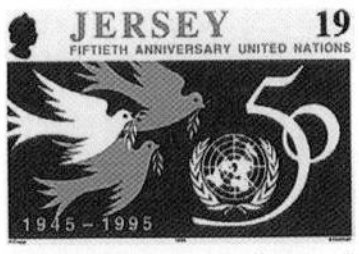

690 Peace Doves and United Nations Anniversary Emblem

1995. 50th Anniv of United Nations.

723	**690**	19p. cobalt and blue	60	50
724	-	23p. turquoise and green	70	70
725	-	41p. green and turquoise	1·20	1·20
726	**690**	60p. blue and cobalt	1·50	1·50

DESIGN: 23p., 41p. Symbolic wheat and anniversary emblem.

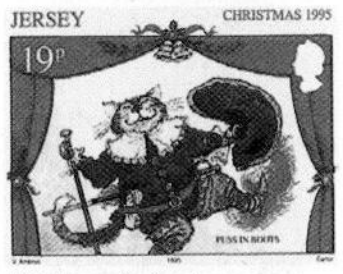

692 *Puss in Boots*

1995. Christmas. Pantomimes. Multicoloured.

727	19p. Type **692**	50	40
728	23p. *Cinderella*	55	45
729	41p. *Sleeping Beauty*	1·00	1·00
730	60p. *Aladdin*	1·60	1·50

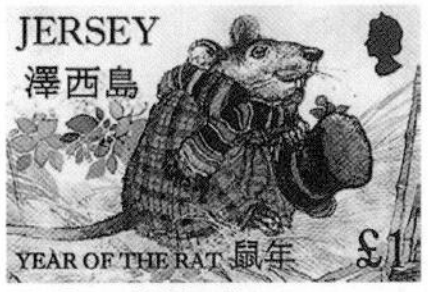

696 Rat with Top Hat

1996. Chinese New Year ("Year of the Rat"). Sheet 110×75 mm.

MS731	**696** £1 multicoloured	2·50	2·50

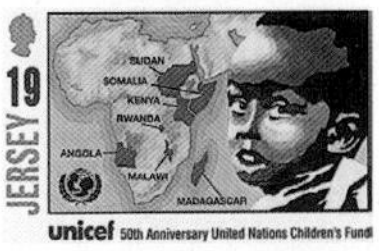

697 African Child and Map

1996. 50th Anniv of UNICEF. Multicoloured.

732	19p. Type **697**	45	40
733	23p. Children and globe	55	45
734	30p. European child and map	70	65
735	35p. South American child and map	90	95
736	41p. Asian child and map	1·00	1·10
737	60p. South Pacific child and map	1·50	1·60

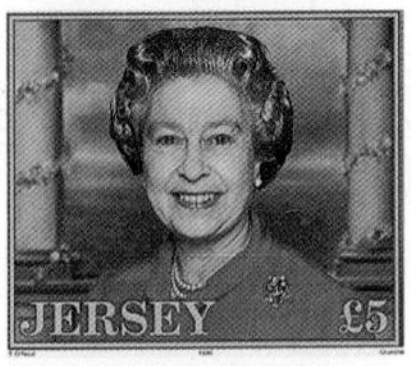

703 Queen Elizabeth II (from photo by T. O'Neill)

1996. 70th Birthday of Queen Elizabeth II.

738	**703**	£5 multicoloured	10·00	10·00

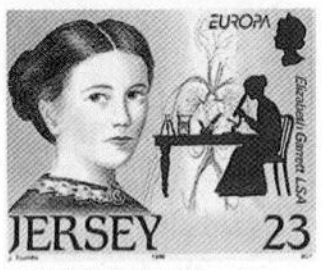

704 Elizabeth Garrett (first British woman doctor)

1996. Europa. Famous Women. Multicoloured.

739	23p. Type **704**	60	60
740	30p. Emmeline Pankhurst (suffragette)	90	90

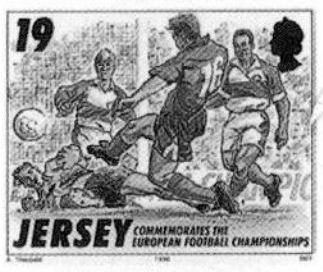

706 Player shooting at Goal

1996. European Football Championship, England. Multicoloured.

741	19p. Type **706**	50	40
742	23p. Two players chasing ball	60	50
743	35p. Player avoiding tackle	95	90
744	41p. Two players competing for ball	1·00	1·00
745	60p. Players heading ball	1·60	1·60

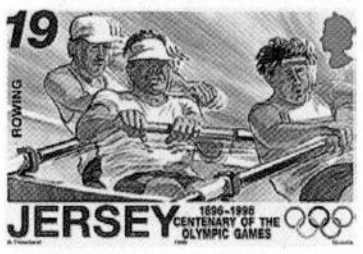

711 Rowing

1996. Sporting Anniversaries. Multicoloured.

746	19p. Type **711**	50	40
747	23p. Judo	60	50
748	35p. Fencing	95	95
749	41p. Boxing	1·00	1·00
750	60p. Basketball	1·60	1·60
MS751	150×100 mm. £1 Olympic torch (50×37 mm)	2·50	2·50

ANNIVERSARIES: Nos. 746/8, 750/1, Centenary of modern Olympic Games; 749, 50th anniv of International Amateur Boxing Association.

No. **MS**751 also includes the "CAPEX '96" International Stamp Exhibition logo.

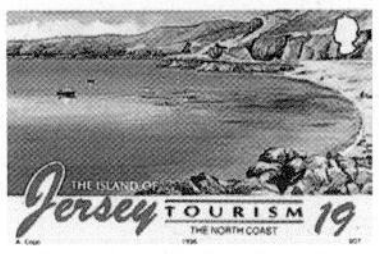

717 Bay on North Coast

1996. Tourism. Beaches. Multicoloured.

752	19p. Type **717**	50	50
753	23p. Portelet Bay	60	60
754	30p. Greve de Lecq Bay	80	80
755	35p. Beauport Beach	95	95
756	41p. Plemont Bay	1·10	1·10
757	60p. St. Brelade's Bay	1·60	1·60

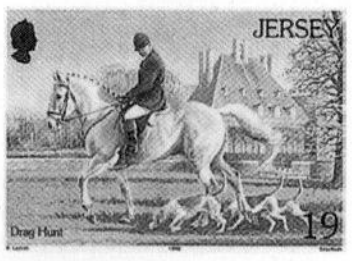

723 Drag Hunt

1996. Horses. Multicoloured.

758	19p. Type **723**	50	50
759	23p. Pony and trap	60	60
760	30p. Training racehorses on beach	80	80
761	35p. Show-jumping	95	95
762	41p. Pony Club event	1·10	1·10
763	60p. Shire mare and foal	1·60	1·60

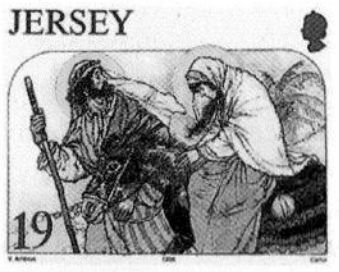

729 The Journey to Bethlehem

1996. Christmas. Multicoloured.

764	19p. Type **729**	50	50
765	23p. The Shepherds	60	70
766	30p. The Nativity	90	95
767	60p. The Three Kings	1·40	1·50

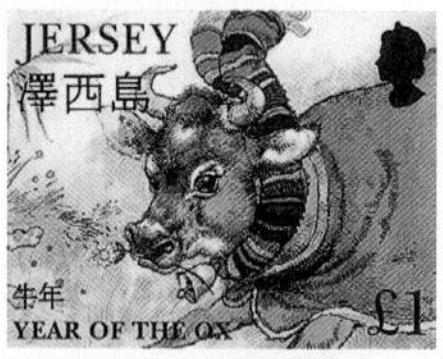

733 Jersey Cow wearing Scarf

1997. Chinese New Year ("Year of the Ox"). Sheet 110×74 mm.

MS768	**733** £1 multicoloured	3·25	3·75

1997. "HONG KONG '97" International Stamp Exhibition. No. **MS**768 optd with exhibition emblem in black and "JERSEY AT HONG KONG '97" in red, both on sheet margin.

MS769	**733** £1 multicoloured	3·75	4·00

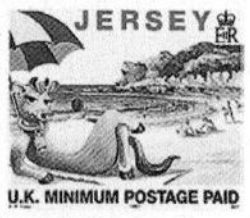

734 Lillie the Cow on the Beach

1997. Tourism. "Lillie the Cow". Multicoloured. Self-adhesive.

770	(23p.) Type **734**	80	85
771	(23p.) Lillie taking photograph	80	85
772	(23p.) Carrying bucket and spade	80	85
773	(23p.) Eating meal at Mont Orgueil	80	85

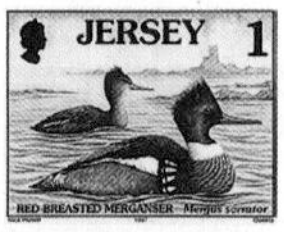

738 Red-breasted Merganser

1997. Seabirds and Waders. Multicoloured.

774	1p. Type **738**	10	10
775	2p. Sanderling	10	10
776	4p. Northern gannet ("Gannet")	10	10
777	5p. Great crested grebe	10	15
778	10p. Common tern	20	25
779	15p. Black-headed gull	30	35
780a	20p. Dunlin	60	45
781	21p. Sandwich tern	40	45
782	22p. Ringed plover	45	50
783	23p. Bar-tailed godwit	45	50
784a	24p. Atlantic puffin ("Puffin")	70	50
785	25p. Brent goose	50	55
786	26p. Grey plover	50	55
787	27p. Black scoter ("Common Scoter")	55	60
788	28p. Lesser black-backed gull	60	65
789	29p. Little egret	60	65
790	30p. Fulmar	60	65
791	31p. Golden plover	60	65
792	32p. Common greenshank ("Greenshank")	65	70
793	33p. Little grebe	65	70
794	34p. Great cormorant ("Common Cormorant")	70	75
795	35p. Western curlew ("Curlew")	70	75
796	37p. Oystercatcher	75	80
797	40p. Ruddy turnstone ("Turnstone")	80	85
798	44p. Herring gull	90	95
799	45p. Rock pipit	90	95
800	50p. Great black-backed gull	1·00	1·10
801	60p. Pied avocet ("Avocet")	1·20	1·40
802	65p. Grey heron	1·20	1·40
803	75p. Common redshank ("Redshank")	2·00	2·10
804	£1 Razorbill	2·50	2·50
805	£2 Shag	5·00	5·25
MS806	Four sheets, each 136×130 mm. (a) Nos. 774, 778/80, 784, 796, 803 and 805. (b) Nos. 775, 777, 781, 785, 790, 797, 801 and 804. (c) Nos. 776, 782, 786, 791/2, 795, 798 and 800. (d) Nos. 783, 787/9, 793/4, 799 and 802 Set of 4 sheets	25·00	25·00

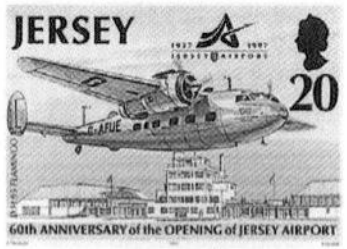

770 de Havilland DH.95 Flamingo

1997. 60th Anniv of Jersey Airport. Multicoloured.

807	20p. Type **770**	45	40
808	24p. Handley Page H.P.R. 5 Marathon	55	40
809	31p. de Havilland DH.114 Heron	65	65
810	37p. Boeing 737-236	95	95
811	43p. Britten-Norman BN-2A Mk III Trislander	1·10	1·10
812	63p. BAe 146-200	1·70	1·70

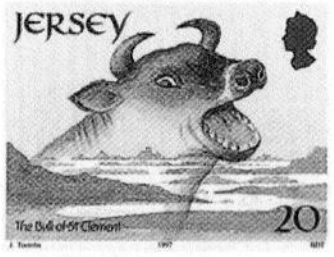

776 The Bull of St. Clement

1997. Europa. Tales and Legends. Multicoloured.

813	20p. Type **776**	65	60
814	24p. The Black Horse of St. Ouen	75	70
815	31p. The Black Dog of Bouley Bay	1·00	1·10
816	63p. Les Fontaines des Mittes	1·25	1·80

Nos. 814/15 include the "EUROPA" emblem.

1997. "Pacific 97" International Stamp Exhibition, San Francisco. No. **MS**806a optd with exhibition emblem on sheet margin.

MS817	136×130 mm. Nos. 774, 778/80, 784, 796, 803 and 805	7·50	8·50

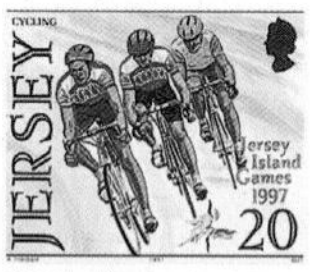

780 Cycling

1997. Seventh Island Games, Jersey. Multicoloured.

818	20p. Type **780**	55	55
819	24p. Archery	65	65
820	31p. Windsurfing	80	80
821	37p. Gymnastics	1·00	1·00
822	43p. Volleyball	1·10	1·10
823	63p. Running	1·70	1·70

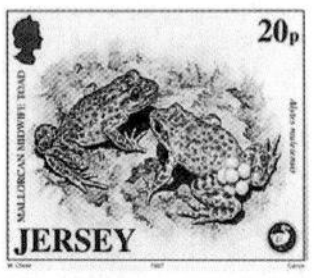

786 Mallorcan Midwife Toad

1997. Wildlife Preservation Trust (6th series). Multicoloured.

824	20p. Type **786**	50	45
825	24p. Aye-aye	60	50
826	31p. Mauritius parakeet ("Echo Parakeet")	90	90
827	37p. Pigmy hog	1·00	1·10
828	43p. St. Lucia whip-tail	1·10	1·20
829	63p. Madagascar teal	1·70	1·80

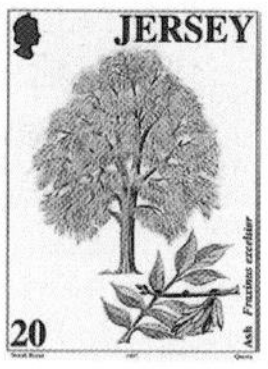

792 Ash

1997. Trees. Multicoloured.

830	20p. Type **792**	50	45
831	24p. Elder	60	50
832	31p. Beech	90	90
833	37p. Sweet chestnut	1·00	1·10
834	43p. Hawthorn	1·10	1·20
835	63p. Common oak	1·70	1·80

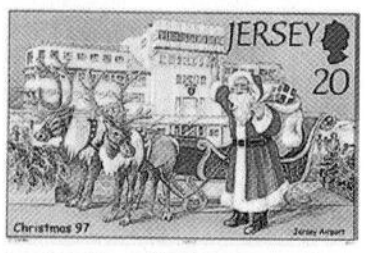

798 Father Christmas and Reindeer outside Jersey Airport

1997. Christmas. Multicoloured.

836	20p. Type **798**	60	60
837	24p. Father Christmas with presents, St. Aubin's Harbour	70	70
838	31p. Father Christmas in sleigh, Mont Orgueil Castle	1·00	1·00
839	63p. Father Christmas with children, Royal Square, St. Helier	1·90	1·90

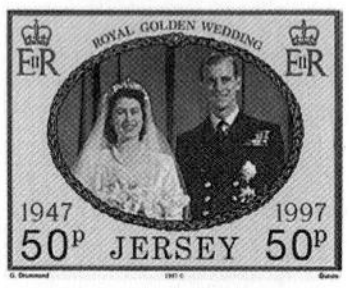

802 Wedding Photograph, 1947

1997. Golden Wedding of Queen Elizabeth and Prince Philip. Multicoloured.

840	50p. Type **802**	1·00	60
841	50p. Queen Elizabeth and Prince Philip, 1997	1·00	60
MS842	150×100 mm. £1.50 Full-length Wedding photograph, 1947 (38×50 mm)	4·50	4·50

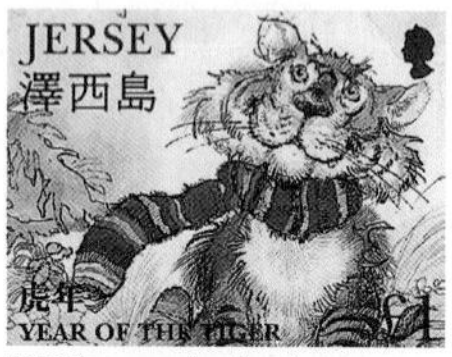

805 Tiger wearing Scarf

1998. Chinese New Year ("Year of the Tiger"). Sheet 110×75 mm.

MS843	**805** £1 multicoloured	2·50	2·75

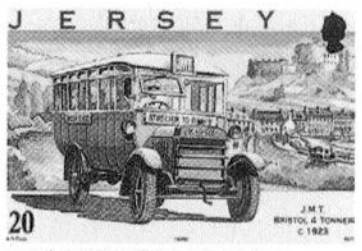

806 J.M.T. Bristol 4 Tonner, 1923

1998. 75th Anniv of Jersey Motor Transport Company. Buses. (1st series). Multicoloured.

844	20p. Type **806**	55	50
845	24p. Safety Coach Service Regent double decker, 1934	65	50
846	31p. Slade's Dennis Lancet, c. 1936	75	70
847	37p. Tantivy Leyland PLSC Lion, 1947	1·00	1·00
848	43p. J.B.S. Morris, c. 1958	1·10	1·10
849	63p. J.M.T. Titan TD4 double decker, c. 1961	1·50	1·60

See also Nos. 1364/**MS**1370.

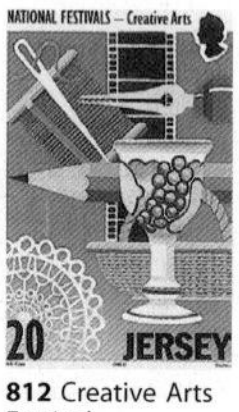

812 Creative Arts Festival

1998. Europa. National Festivals. Multicoloured.

850	20p. Type **812**	65	45
851	24p. Jazz Festival	70	55
852	31p. Good Food Festival	90	1·00
853	63p. Floral Festival	1·70	1·90

Nos. 851/2 include the "EUROPA" emblem.

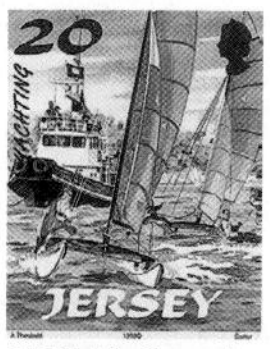

816 Hobie Cat and *Duke of Normandy* (launch)

1998. Opening of Elizabeth Marina, St. Helier (1st issue). Multicoloured.

854	20p. Type **816**	40	20
855	20p. Hobie Cat with white, yellow, red and green sails	40	20
856	20p. Hobie Cats with pink, purple and orange sails	40	20
857	20p. Bow of Hobie Cat with yellow, blue and purple sail	40	20
858	20p. Hobie Cat heeling	40	20
859	24p. Yacht with red, white and blue spinnaker	45	25
860	24p. Yacht with pink spinnaker	45	25
861	24p. Yacht with two white sails	45	25
862	24p. Trimaran	45	25
863	24p. Yacht with blue, white and yellow spinnaker in foreground	45	25

Nos. 854/8 and 859/63 respectively were printed together, *se-tenant*, forming composite designs of yacht races.

See also No. **MS**1319.

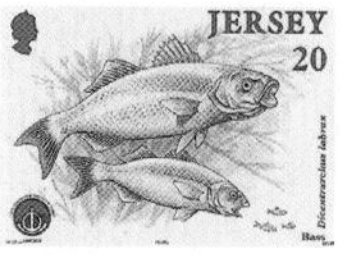

826 Bass

1998. International Year of the Ocean. Fish. Multicoloured.

864	20p. Type **826**	50	50
865	24p. Red gurnard	65	65
866	31p. Skate	80	80
867	37p. Mackerel	1·00	1·00
868	43p. Tope	1·10	1·10
869	63p. Cuckoo wrasse	1·50	1·50

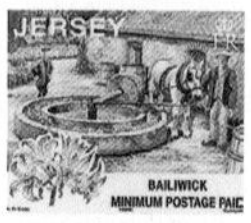

832 Cider-making

1998. Days Gone By. Multicoloured. Self-adhesive.

870	(20p.) Type **832**	90	90
871	(20p.) Potato barrels on cart	90	90
872	(20p.) Collecting seaweed for fertiliser	90	90
873	(20p.) Milking Jersey cows	90	90

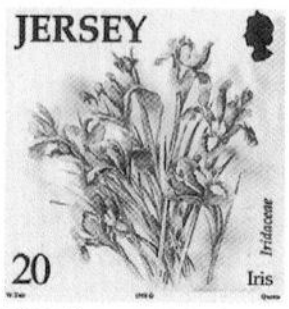

836 Irises

1998. Flowers. Multicoloured.

874	20p. Type **836**	50	40
875	24p. Carnations	60	50
876	31p. Chrysanthemums	75	70
877	37p. Pinks	90	90
878	43p. Roses	1·00	1·10
879	63p. Lilies	1·40	1·50
MS880	150×100 mm. £1.50 *Lilium* "Star Gazer" (50×37 mm)	3·25	3·75

No. **MS**880 includes the "ITALIA '98" stamp exhibition emblem on the margin.

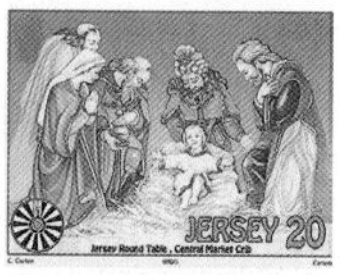

843 Central Market Crib

1998. Christmas. Cribs. Multicoloured.

881	20p. Type **843**	40	40
882	24p. St. Thomas's Church crib	50	55
883	31p. Trinity Parish Church crib	65	65
884	63p. Royal Square crib	1·60	1·60

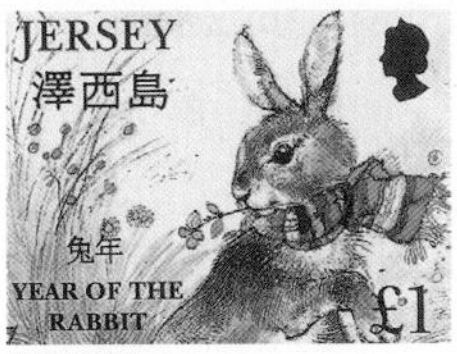

847 Rabbit

1999. Chinese New Year ("Year of the Rabbit"). Sheet 110×75 mm.

MS885	**847** £1 multicoloured	2·50	2·75

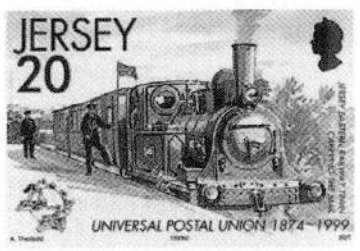

848 Jersey Eastern Railway Mail Train

1999. 125th Anniv of U.P.U. Multicoloured.

886	20p. Type **848**	55	50
887	24p. Brighton (paddle-steamer)	65	60
888	43p. de Havilland DH.86 Dragon Express at Jersey Airport	95	1·10
889	63p. Jersey Postal Service Morris Minor van	1·40	1·70

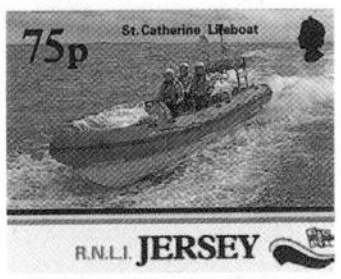

852 *Jessie Eliza*, St. Catherine

1999. 175th Anniv of Royal National Lifeboat Institution. Multicoloured.

890	75p. Type **852**	2·00	80
891	£1 *Alexander Coutanche*, St. Helier	2·50	1·00

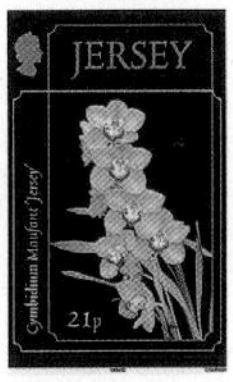

854 *Cymbidium*" Maufant Jersey"

1999. Jersey Orchids (4th series). Multicoloured.

892	21p. Type **854**	55	50
893	25p. *Miltonia Millbrook* "Jersey"	55	50
894	31p. *Paphiopedilum* "Transvaal"	75	70
895	37p. *Paphiopedilum* "Elizabeth Castle"	85	80
896	43p. *Calanthe* "Five Oaks"	90	90
897	63p. *Cymbidium* Icho Tower "Trinity"	2·00	2·00
MS898	150×100 mm. £1.50 *Miltonia* Portelet	4·00	4·50

No. **MS**898 also includes the "Australia '99" World Stamp Exhibition, Melbourne, emblem on the margin at top left.

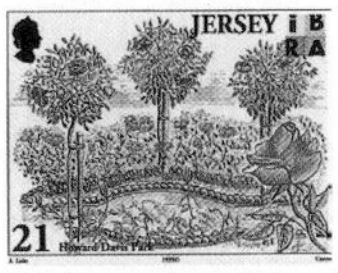

861 Howard Davis Park

1999. Europa. Parks and Gardens. Multicoloured.

899	21p. Type **861**	50	50
900	25p. Sir Winston Churchill Memorial Park	70	70
901	31p. Coronation Park	1·00	1·00
902	63p. La Collette Gardens	2·00	2·00

Nos. 900/1 include the "EUROPA" logo at top left and all four values show the "iBRA '99" International Stamp Exhibition, Nuremberg, emblem at top right.

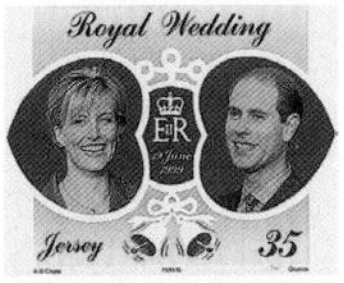

865 Prince Edward and Miss Sophie Rhys-Jones

1999. Royal Wedding.

903	**865**	35p. multicoloured (yellow background)	60	35
904	**865**	35p. multicoloured (blue background)	60	35

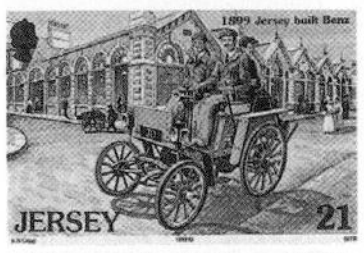

866 Jersey-built Benz, 1899

1999. Vintage Cars (3rd series). Centenary of Motoring in Jersey. Multicoloured.

905	21p. Type **866**	45	45
906	25p. Star Tourer, 1910	55	55
907	31p. Citroen "Traction Avant", 1938	65	65
908	37p. Talbot BG110 Tourer, 1937	1·00	1·00
909	43p. Morris Cowley Six Special Coupe, 1934	1·20	1·20
910	63p. Ford Anglia Saloon, 1946	1·50	1·50

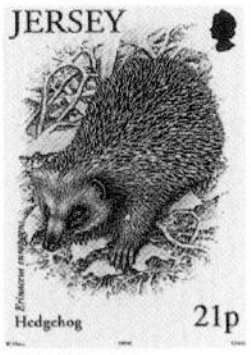

872 West European Hedgehog

1999. Small Mammals. Multicoloured.

911	21p. Type **872**	45	45
912	25p. Eurasian red squirrel	55	55
913	31p. Nathusius pipistrelle	65	65
914	37p. Jersey bank vole	1·00	1·10
915	43p. Lesser white-toothed shrew	1·00	1·10
916	63p. Common mole	2·00	2·20

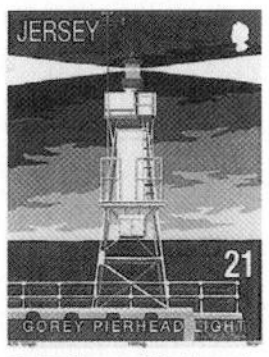

878 Gorey Pierhead Light

1999. 150th Anniv of First Lighthouse on Jersey (1st series). Multicoloured.

917	21p. Type **878**	45	45
918	25p. La Corbiere	55	55
919	34p. Noirmont Point	75	75
920	38p. Demie de Pas	1·00	1·00
921	44p. Greve d'Azette	1·20	1·20
922	64p. Sorel Point	2·00	2·00

See also Nos. 1086/91.

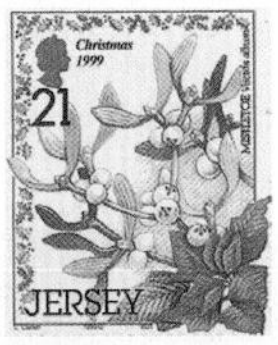

884 Mistletoe

1999. Christmas. Festive Foliage. Multicoloured.

923	21p. Type **884**	45	45
924	25p. Holly	55	55
925	34p. Ivy	1·10	75
926	64p. Christmas Rose	1·60	2·00

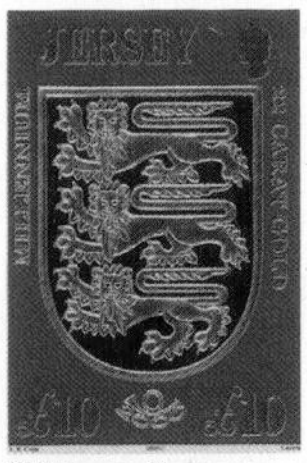

888 Jersey Crest

2000. New Millennium.

927	**888**	£10 gold, red and carmine	20·00	20·00

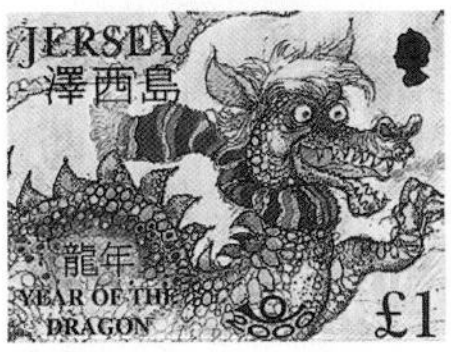

889 Dragon

2000. Chinese New Year ("Year of the Dragon"). Sheet 110×75 mm.

MS928	**889** £1 multicoloured	3·00	3·00

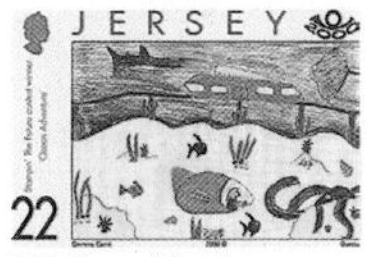

890 *Ocean Adventure* (Gemma Carré)

2000. "Stampin' the Future" (children's stamp design competition) Winners. Multicoloured.

929	22p. Type **890**	65	65
930	22p. *Solar Power* (Chantal Varley-Best)	65	65
931	22p. *Floating City and Space Cars* (Nicola Singleton)	65	65
932	22p. *Conservation* (Carly Logan)	65	65
MS933	150×100 mm. Nos. 929/32	3·00	3·50

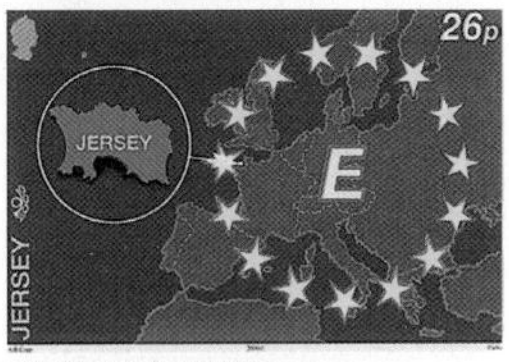

894 "Jersey in Europe"

2000. Europa. Multicoloured.

934	26p. Type **894**	2·00	2·00
935	34p. "Building Europe" (29×39 mm)	3·00	3·50

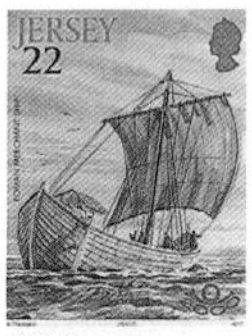

896 Roman Merchant Ship

2000. "The Stamp Show 2000" International Stamp Exhibition, London. Maritime Heritage. Multicoloured.

936	22p. Type **896**	45	25
937	22p. Viking longship	45	25
938	22p. 13th-century warship	45	25
939	22p. 14th–15th-century merchant ship	45	25
940	22p. Tudor warship	45	25
941	26p. 17th-century warship	50	30
942	26p. 18th-century naval cutter	50	30
943	26p. 19th-century barque	50	30
944	26p. 19th-century oyster cutter	50	30
945	26p. 20th-century ketch	50	30
MS946	174×104 mm. Nos. 936/45	6·00	6·00

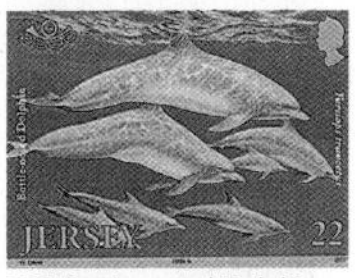

906 Bottle-nosed Dolphins

2000. World Environment Day. Marine Mammals. Multicoloured.

947	22p. Type **906**	50	55
948	26p. Long-finned pilot whales	55	60
949	34p. Common porpoises	80	85
950	38p. Grey seals	1·00	1·10
951	44p. Risso's dolphins	1·10	1·20
952	64p. White-beaked dolphin	1·50	1·70
MS953	150×100 mm. £1.50 Common dolphins (80×29 mm)	4·00	4·50

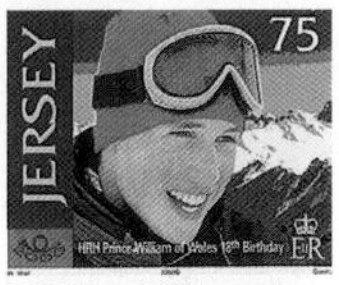

913 Prince William and Alps

2000. 18th Birthday of Prince William. Multicoloured.

954	75p. Type **913**	1·50	1·50
955	75p. Prince William and polo player	1·50	1·50
956	75p. Prince William and Beaumaris Castle	1·50	1·50
957	75p. Prince William and fireworks	1·50	1·50

2000. "World Stamp Expo 2000", Anaheim, U.S.A. As No. **MS**953, but with multicoloured exhibition logo added to top left corner of sheet margin.

MS958	150×100 mm. £1.50 Common dolphins (80×29 mm)	4·00	4·00

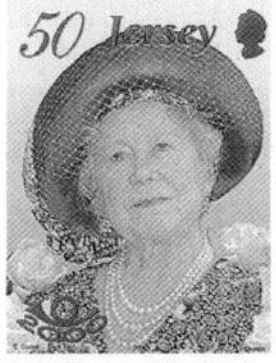

917 Queen Elizabeth the Queen Mother with Roses

2000. Queen Elizabeth the Queen Mother's 100th Birthday. Multicoloured.

959	50p. Type **917**	1·20	1·20
960	50p. Queen Elizabeth the Queen Mother with daisies	1·20	1·20
MS961	150×100 mm. Nos. 959/60	2·50	3·00

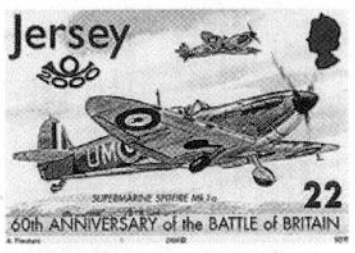

919 Supermarine Spitfire Mk Ia

2000. 60th Anniv of Battle of Britain. Multicoloured.

962	22p. Type **919**	50	55
963	26p. Hawker Hurricane Mk I	60	65
964	36p. Bristol Blenheim Mk IV	80	85
965	40p. Vickers Wellington Mk Ic	90	95
966	45p. Boulton Paul P.82 Defiant Mk I	1·00	1·10
967	65p. Short S.25 Sunderland Mk I	1·50	1·60

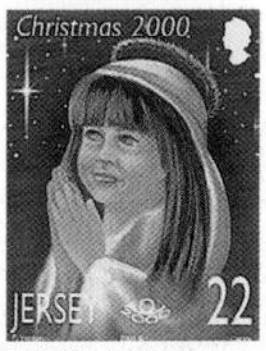

925 Virgin Mary

2000. Christmas. Children's Nativity Play. Multicoloured.

968	22p. Type **925**	55	55
969	26p. Shepherd	65	65
970	36p. Angel	1·00	1·00
971	65p. Magi with gift	1·60	1·60

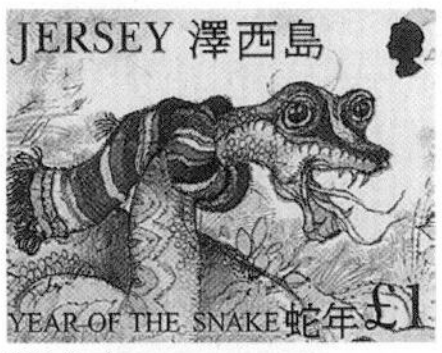

929 Snake

2001. Chinese New Year ("Year of the Snake"). Sheet 110×75 mm.

MS972	**929** £1 multicoloured	2·75	3·00

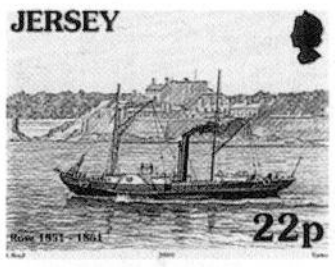

930 *Rose* (1851–61)

2001. Maritime Links with France. Mail Packet Ships. Multicoloured.

973	22p. Type **930**	50	55
974	26p. *Comete* (1856–67)	60	65
975	36p. *Cygne* (1894–1912)	80	85
976	40p. *Victoria* (1896–1918)	90	95
977	45p. *Attala* (1920–25)	1·20	1·30
978	65p. *Brittany* (1933–62)	1·70	1·80

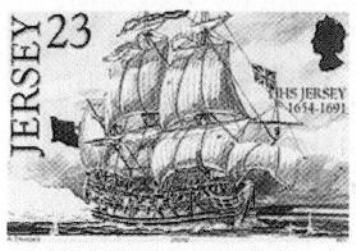

936 H.M.S. *Jersey* (4th Rate), 1654–91

2001. Royal Navy Ships named after Jersey. Multicoloured.

979	23p. Type **936**	50	55
980	26p. H.M.S. *Jersey* (6th Rate), 1694–98	60	65
981	37p. H.M.S. *Jersey* (4th Rate), 1698–1731	80	85
982	41p. H.M.S. *Jersey* (4th Rate), 1736–83	1·00	95
983	46p. H.M.S. *Jersey* (cutter), 1860–73	1·20	1·10

984	66p. H.M.S. *Jersey* (destroyer), 1938–41	1·50	1·60

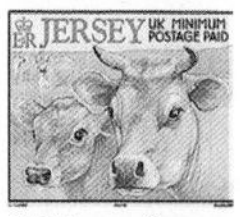

942 Jersey Cows

2001. Jersey Agriculture. Multicoloured. Self-adhesive.

985	(26p.) Type **942**	2·75	2·75
986	(26p.) Potatoes	2·75	2·75
987	(26p.) Tomatoes	2·75	2·75
988	(26p.) Cauliflower and purple-sprouting broccoli	2·75	2·75
989	(26p.) Peppers and courgettes	2·75	2·75

Nos. 985/9, which are inscribed "UK MINIMUM POSTAGE PAID", were initially sold at 26p each.

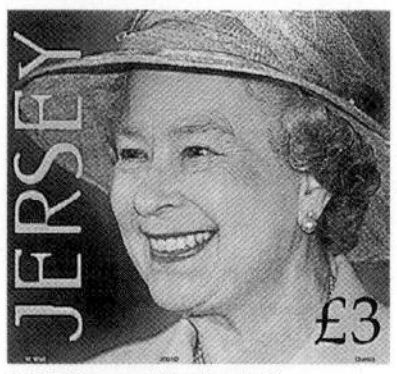

947 Queen Elizabeth II

2001. 75th Birthday of Queen Elizabeth II.

990	**947**	£3 multicoloured	6·00	6·50

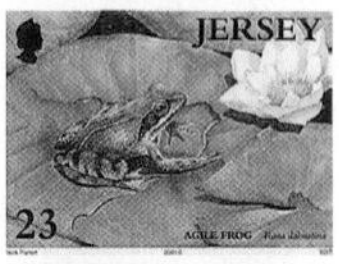

948 Agile Frog

2001. Europa. Pond Life. Multicoloured.

991	23p. Type **948**	60	65
992	26p. Trout	70	75
993	37p. White water-lily	1·00	1·10
994	41p. Common blue damselfly	1·10	1·20
995	46p. Palmate newt	1·20	1·40
996	66p. Tufted duck	2·00	2·20
MS997	150×100 mm. £1.50 Common kingfisher (36×50 mm)	5·00	5·00

The 26 and 37p. values include "EUROPA" emblem.

2001. "Belgica 2001" International Stamp Exhibition, Brussels. No. **MS**997 optd **JERSEY AT BELGICA 2001** on sheet margin.

MS998	150×100 mm. £1.50 Common kingfisher (36×50 mm)	5·00	4·50

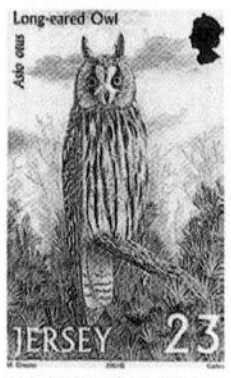

955 Long-eared Owl

2001. Birds of Prey. Multicoloured.

999	23p. Type **955**	50	55
1000	26p. Peregrine falcon	60	65
1001	37p. Short-eared owl	80	85
1002	41p. Western marsh harrier ("Marsh Harrier")	1·00	95
1003	46p. Northern sparrow hawk ("Sparrowhawk")	1·20	1·10
1004	66p. Tawny owl	1·50	1·60
MS1005	110×75 mm. £1.50 Barn owl (30×47 mm)	5·00	5·00

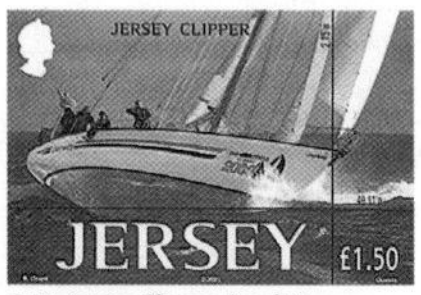

962 *Jersey Clipper* (yacht)

2001. The Times Clipper 2000 Round the World Yacht Race. Sheet 150×100 mm.

MS1006	**962** £1.50 multicoloured	4·00	5·00

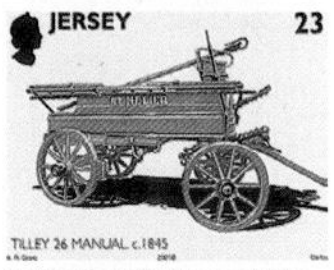

963 Tilley 26 Manual Fire Engine, c. 1845

2001. Centenary of Jersey Fire and Rescue Service. Fire Engines. Multicoloured.

1007	23p. Type **963**	50	55
1008	26p. Albion Merryweather, c. 1935	60	65
1009	37p. Dennis Ace, c. 1940	80	85
1010	41p. Dennis F8 Pump Escape, c. 1952	90	95
1011	46p. Land Rover Merryweather, c. 1968	1·00	1·10
1012	66p. Dennis Carmichael, c. 1989	1·50	1·60

2001. "Hafnia 01" International Stamp Exhibition, Copenhagen. As No. **MS**1005, but with brown-red exhibition logo added to bottom left corner of sheet margin and additionally inscr "Jersey visits Hafnia 01 Denmark".

MS1013	£1.50 Barn owl (30×47 mm)	4·00	4·00

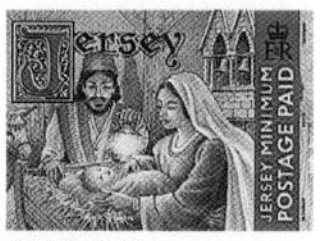

969 Nativity

2001. Christmas. Bells. Multicoloured. Self-adhesive.

1014	(23p.) Type **969**	70	70
1015	(23p.) Street decorations	70	70
1016	(23p.) Carol singers with hand bells	70	70
1017	(23p.) Father Christmas	70	70
1018	(23p.) Christmas tree decorations	70	70
1019	(26p.) Adoration of the shepherds	70	70
1020	(26p.) Carol singers and Father Christmas in sleigh	70	70
1021	(26p.) Paper bell, chains and Christmas tree	70	70
1022	(26p.) Church bells ringing	70	70
1023	(26p.) Christmas cracker	70	70

Nos. 1014/18, which are inscribed "JERSEY MINIMUM POSTAGE PAID", were initially sold for 23p., and Nos. 1019/23, inscribed "U.K. MINIMUM POSTAGE PAID", were sold for 26p.

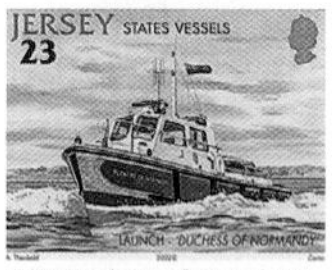

979 *Duchess of Normandy* (launch)

2002. States Vessels. Multicoloured.

1024	23p. Type **979**	50	55
1025	29p. *Duke of Normandy* (tug)	65	70
1026	38p. *Challenger* (customs patrol boat)	80	85
1027	47p. *Le Fret* (pilot boat)	1·20	1·30
1028	68p. *Norman le Brocq* (fisheries protection vessel)	1·70	1·90

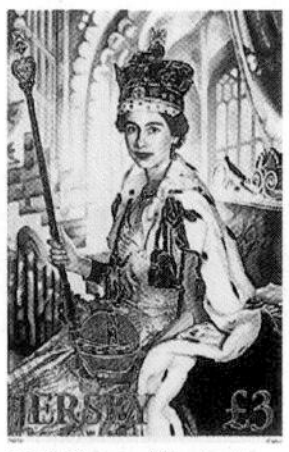

984 Queen Elizabeth in Coronation Robes (after Cecil Beaton)

2002. Golden Jubilee.

1029	**984**	£3 multicoloured	6·25	6·50

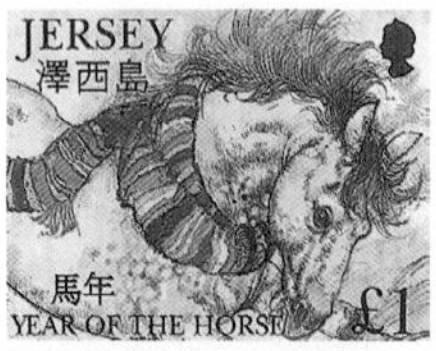

985 Horse

2002. Chinese New Year ("Year of the Horse"). Sheet 110×75 mm.

MS1030	**985** £1 multicoloured	2·20	2·50

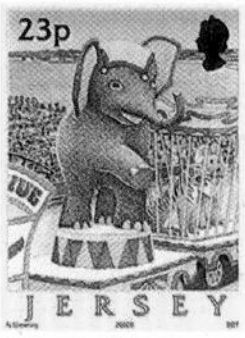

986 Elephant Float, Parish of St. John, 1980

2002. Europa. Circus. Designs showing carnival floats. Multicoloured.

1031	23p. Type **986**	50	55
1032	29p. Clown with red hair, Grouville, 1996	65	70
1033	38p. Clown with white hat, Optimists, 1988	1·00	1·10
1034	68p. Performing seal, Grouville, 1996	1·70	2·00

The 29p. and 38p. values include the "EUROPA" emblem.

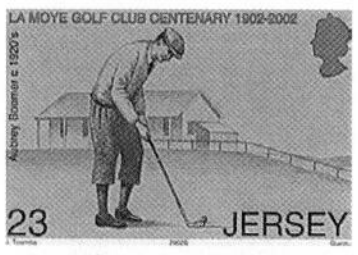

990 Aubrey Boomer

2002. Centenary of La Moye Golf Club. Multicoloured.

1035	23p. Type **990**	50	55
1036	29p. Harry Vardon	65	70
1037	38p. Sir Henry Cotton	80	85
1038	47p. Diagram of golf swing	1·00	1·10
1039	68p. Putting	1·50	1·70

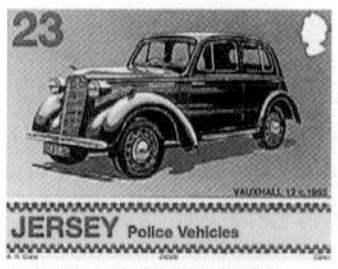

995 Vauxhall 12, 1952

2002. 50th Anniv of States of Jersey Police. Patrol Vehicles. Multicoloured.

1040	23p. Type **995**	50	55
1041	29p. Jaguar 2.4 MkII, 1959–60	65	70
1042	38p. Austin 1800, 1972–73	80	85
1043	40p. Ford Cortina MkIV, 1978	85	90
1044	47p. Honda ST 1100 motorcycle, 1995–2000	1·00	1·10
1045	68p. Vauxhall Vectra, 1998–2000	1·50	1·70

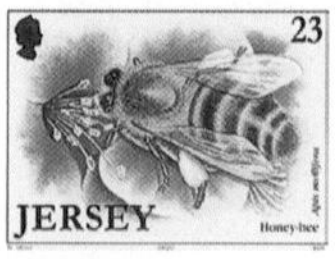

1001 Honey Bee

2002. Insects. Multicoloured.

1046	23p. Type **1001**	50	55
1047	29p. Seven-spot ladybird	65	70
1048	38p. Great green bush-cricket	80	85
1049	40p. Greater horn-tail	85	90
1050	47p. Emperor dragonfly	1·10	1·20
1051	68p. Hawthorn shield bug	1·50	1·70

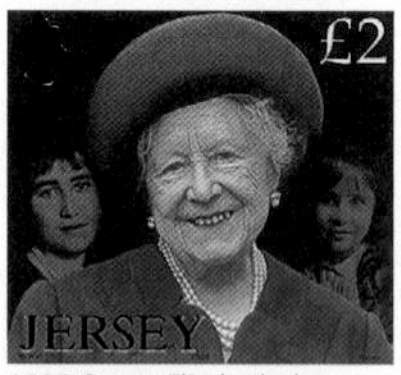

1007 Queen Elizabeth the Queen Mother in 1910, 1923 and 2002

2002. Queen Elizabeth the Queen Mother Commemoration.

1052	**1007**	£2 multicoloured	4·25	4·50

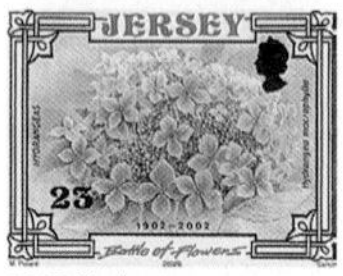

1008 Hydrangeas

2002. Centenary of "Battle of Flowers" Parade. Multicoloured.

1053	23p. Type **1008**	50	55
1054	29p. Chrysanthemums	65	70
1055	38p. Hare's tails and pampas grasses	80	85
1056	40p. Asters	85	90
1057	47p. Carnations	1·00	1·10
1058	68p. Gladioli	1·50	1·70
MS1059	150×100 mm. £2 "Zanzibar" float (winner of Prix d'Honneur, 1999) (75×38 mm)	4·25	4·50

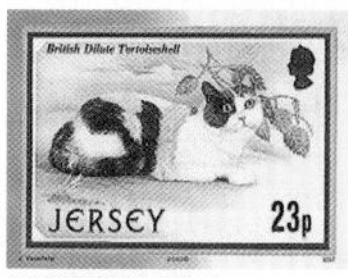

1015 British Dilute Tortoiseshell

2002. 25th Anniv of Caesarea Cat Club. Multicoloured.

1060	23p. Type **1015**	50	55
1061	29p. Cream Persian	65	70
1062	38p. Blue exotic shorthair	80	85
1063	40p. Black smoke Devon rex	85	90
1064	47p. British silver tabby	1·00	1·10
1065	68p. Usual Abyssinian	1·50	1·70
MS1066	110×75 mm. £2 British cream/white bi-colour cross (38×51 mm)	4·25	4·50

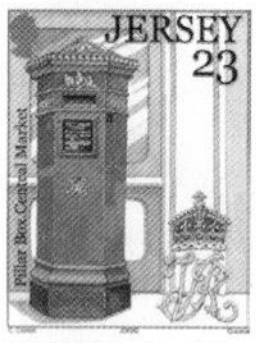

1022 Victorian Pillar Box in Central Market

2002. Jersey Social History (1st series). 150th Anniv of the First Pillar Box. Multicoloured.

1067	23p. Type **1022**	50	55
1068	29p. Edward VII wall box, Colomberie	65	70
1069	38p. George V wall box, St. Clement's Inner Road	80	85
1070	40p. George V "Boite Mobile" ship box	85	90
1071	47p. Elizabeth II pillar box, Parade	1·00	1·10
1072	68p. Modern pillar boxes, La Collette	1·50	1·60
MS1073	150×100 mm. £2 Posting letter in first pillar box, David Place (40×77 mm)	4·25	4·50

See also Nos. 1286/**MS**1072.

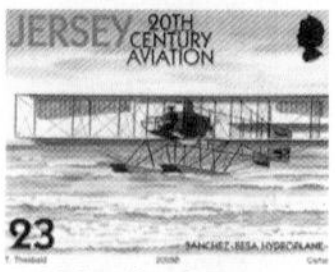

1029 Sanchez-Besa Hydroplane

2003. Centenary of Powered Flight. Multicoloured.

1074	23p. Type **1029**	50	55
1075	29p. Supermarine S.6B seaplane	65	70
1076	38p. de Havilland DH.84 Dragon	80	85
1077	40p. de Havilland DH.89a Rapide	85	90
1078	47p. Vickers 701 Viscount	1·00	1·10
1079	68p. BAC One Eleven	1·50	1·60
MS1080	112×76 mm. £2 Jacob Ellehammer's Biplane, 1906 (60×40 mm)	4·25	4·50

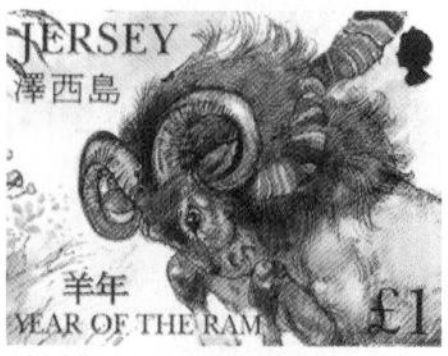

1036 Ram

2003. Chinese New Year ("Year of the Ram"). Sheet 110×75 mm.

MS1081	**1036** £1 multicoloured	2·50	2·75

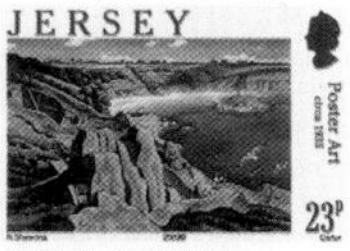

1037 *Portelet* (Adrian Allinson)

2003. Europa. Travel Posters. Multicoloured.

1082	23p. Type **1037**	50	55
1083	29p. "Jersey" (Lander) (vert)	80	80
1084	38p. "Channel Islands Map" (vert)	1·25	1·50
1085	68p. "Jersey, the Sunny Channel Island" (A. Allinson)	1·75	2·00

The 29p. and 38p. values include the **"EUROPA"** emblem.

2003. Jersey Lighthouses (2nd series). T **878**. Multicoloured.

1086	29p. Violet Channel light buoy	50	30
1087	29p. St. Catherine's Breakwater Light	50	30

1088	30p. Frouquie Aubert light buoy	55	35
1089	30p. Mont Ube Lighthouse	55	35
1090	48p. Banc des Ormes light buoy	85	50
1091	48p. Gronez Point Lighthouse	85	50

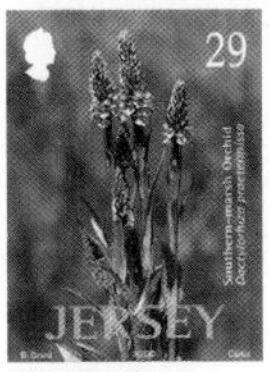

1047 Southern-marsh Orchid

2003. Wild Orchids. Multicoloured.

1092	29p. Type **1047**	60	65
1093	30p. Loose-flowered orchid	60	65
1094	39p. Spotted orchid	80	85
1095	50p. Autumn ladies tresses	1·00	1·10
1096	53p. Green-winged orchid	1·10	1·20
1097	69p. Pyramidal orchid	1·40	1·50
MS1098	110×75 mm. £2 Loose-flowered orchid (different)	4·00	4·25

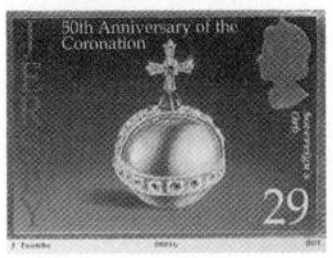

1054 Sovereign's Orb

2003. 50th Anniv of Coronation. Coronation Regalia. Multicoloured.

1099	29p. Type **1054**	60	65
1100	30p. St. Edward's Crown	60	65
1101	39p. Sceptre with Cross	80	85
1102	50p. Ampulla and Spoon	1·00	1·10
1103	53p. Sovereign's Ring	1·00	1·10
1104	69p. Armills	1·40	1·50
MS1105	150×100 mm. Nos. 1099/1104	5·25	5·75

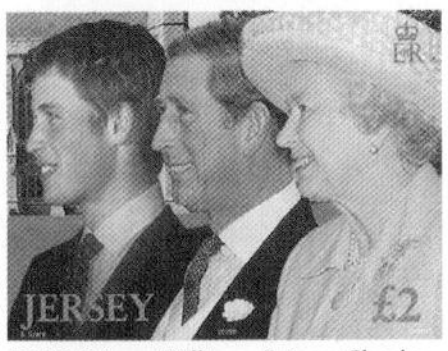

1060 Prince William, Prince Charles and Queen Elizabeth

2003. Royal Links. Sheet 110×75 mm.

MS1106	**1060** £2 multicoloured	4·00	4·25

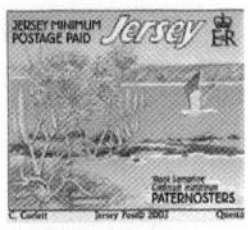

1061 Rock Samphire and Paternosters

2003. Offshore Reefs. Multicoloured. Self-adhesive.

1107	(29p.) Type **1061**	1·10	1·25
1108	(29p.) Bluebells and Les Ecrehous	1·10	1·25
1109	(29p.) Tree-mallow and Les Ecrehous	1·10	1·25
1110	(29p.) Smooth Sow-thistle and Les Minquiers	1·10	1·25
1111	(29p.) Thrift and Les Minquiers	1·10	1·25

Nos. 1107/11 are inscribed "JERSEY MINIMUM POSTAGE PAID" and were initially sold at 29p.

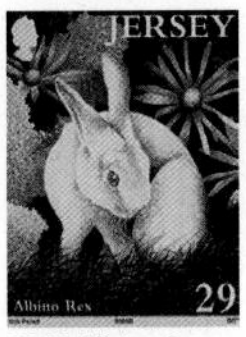

1066 Albino Rex Rabbit

2003. Pets. Multicoloured.

1112	29p. Type **1066**	95	95
1113	30p. Black labrador puppy	95	95
1114	38p. Canary and budgerigar	1·20	1·20
1115	53p. Hamster	1·70	1·70
1116	69p. Guinea pig	2·20	2·20
MS1117	150×100 mm. £2 Border collie (39×51 mm)	5·50	5·50

2003. "Bangkok 2003" International Stamp Exhibition. No. **MS**1098 optd **Jersey at Bangkok 2003** and emblem on sheet margin.

MS1118	110×75 mm. £2 Loose-flowered orchid	5·50	5·50

2003. Winter Flowers. As T **836**. Multicoloured.

1119	29p. Japanese quince	60	65
1120	30p. Winter jasmine	60	65
1121	39p. Snowdrop	80	85
1122	48p. Winter heath	95	1·00
1123	53p. Chinese witch-hazel	1·00	1·10
1124	69p. Winter daphne	1·40	1·50

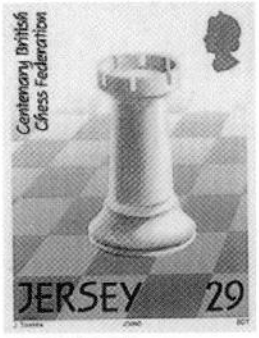

1078 Rook

2004. Jersey Festivals (1st issue). Festival of Chess. Multicoloured.

1125	29p. Type **1078**	95	95
1126	30p. Knight	1·00	1·00
1127	39p. Bishop	1·30	1·30
1128	48p. Pawn	1·60	1·60
1129	53p. Queen	1·70	1·70
1130	69p. King	2·20	2·20

See also Nos. 1204/9 and 1359/63.

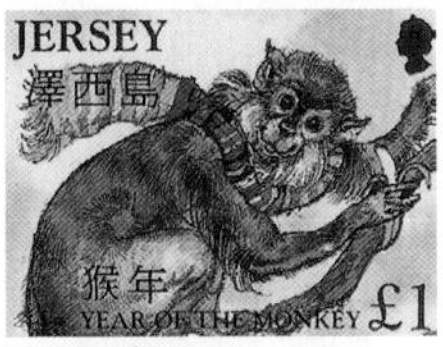

1084 Monkey

2004. Chinese New Year ("Year of the Monkey"). Sheet 110×75 mm.

MS1131	**1084** £1 multicoloured	3·25	3·25

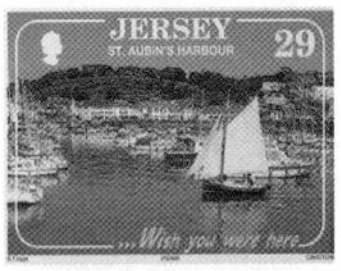

1085 St. Aubin's Harbour

2004. Europa. Holidays. Multicoloured.

1132	29p. Type **1085**	95	95
1133	30p. Mont Orgueil Castle	95	95
1134	39p. Corbiere Lighthouse	1·30	1·30
1135	69p. Rozel Harbour	2·30	2·30

The 30p. and 39p. values include the "EUROPA" emblem.

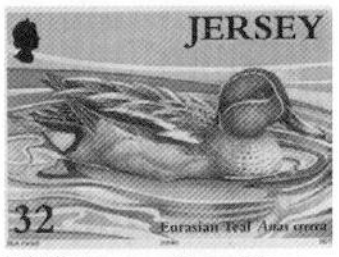

1089 Green-winged Teal ("Eurasian Teal")

2004. Ducks and Swans. Multicoloured.

1136	32p. Type **1089**	1·00	1·00
1137	33p. Mute swan	1·10	1·10
1138	40p. Northern shoveler	1·30	1·30
1139	49p. Common pochard	1·60	1·60
1140	62p. Black swan	2·00	2·00
1141	70p. European Wigeon ("Eurasian Wigeon")	2·30	2·30
MS1142	150×100 mm. £2 Mallard (38×50 mm)	6·50	6·50

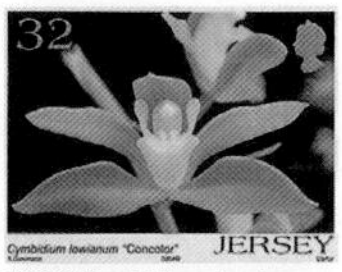

1096 *Cymbidium lowianum* "Concolor"

2004. Jersey Orchids (5th series). Multicoloured.

1143	32p. Type **1096**	1·00	1·00
1144	33p. *Phragmipedium besseae* var. *flavum*	1·10	1·10
1145	40p. *Peristeria elata*	1·30	1·30
1146	54p. *Cymbidium tracyanum*	1·80	1·80
1147	62p. *Paphiopedilum* Victoria Village "Isle of Jersey"	2·00	2·00
1148	70p. *Paphiopedilum hirsutissimum*	2·30	2·30
MS1149	110×75 mm. £2 *Phragmipedium* "Jason Fischer"	6·50	6·50

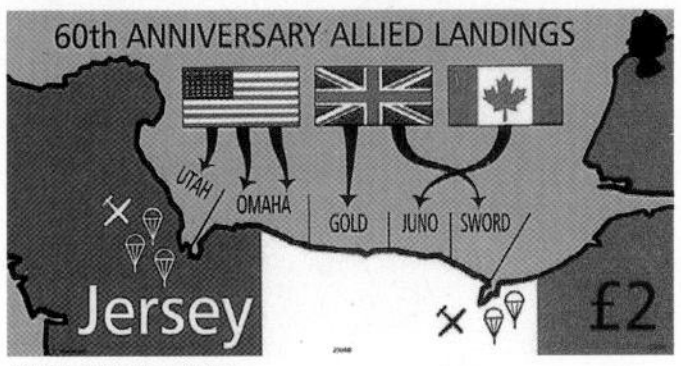

1103 Invasion Map

2004. 60th Anniv of D-Day. Sheet 110×75 mm.

MS1150	**1103** £2 multicoloured	6·50	6·50

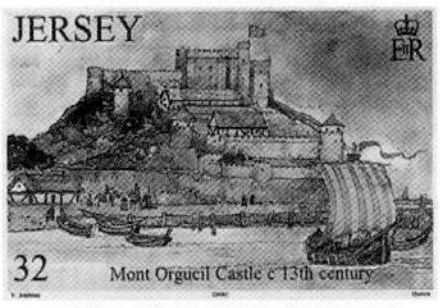

1104 Mont Orgueil Castle in 13th Century

2004. Jersey–"A Peculiar of the Crown". Multicoloured.

1151	32p. Type **1104**	60	35
1152	32p. King John, c. 1204 (23×31 mm)	60	35
1153	33p. Mont Orgueil Castle in 17th century	60	35
1154	33p. King Charles II, c. 1684 (23×31 mm)	60	35
1155	40p. Mont Orgueil Castle, 2004	80	45
1156	40p. Queen Elizabeth II, 2002 (23×31 mm)	80	45

2004. Salon du Timbre Stamp Exhibition, Paris. As No. **MS**1149, but optd **Jersey at Le Salon du Timbre 2004** at top left corner of sheet margin.

MS1157	110×75 mm. £2 *Phragmipedium* (Jason Fischer)	6·50	6·50

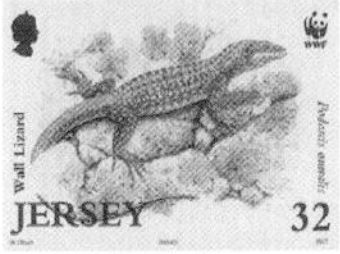

1110 Wall Lizard

2004. Endangered Species. Multicoloured.

1158	32p. Type **1110**	1·00	1·00
1159	33p. Ant lion	1·10	1·10
1160	49p. Field cricket	1·60	1·60
1161	70p. Dartford warbler	2·30	2·30
MS1162	141×174 mm. Nos. 1158/61 each ×2	12·00	12·00

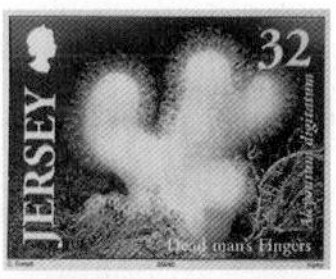

1114 Dead Man's Fingers

2004. Corals. Multicoloured.

1163	32p. Type **1114**	1·00	1·00
1164	33p. Devonshire cup	1·10	1·10
1165	40p. White sea fan	1·30	1·30
1166	54p. Pink sea fan	1·80	1·80
1167	62p. Sunset cup	2·00	2·00
1168	70p. Red fingers	2·30	2·30
MS1169	150×100 mm. Nos. 1166/8	6·00	6·00

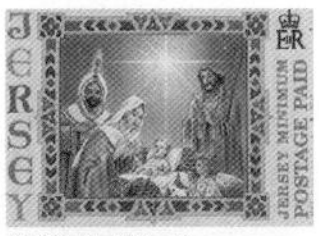

1120 Nativity Scene

2004. Christmas. Illuminations. Multicoloured. Self-adhesive.

1170	(32p.) Type **1120**	1·00	1·00
1171	(32p.) Fairy lights over busy street	1·00	1·00
1172	(32p.) Santa Claus, children and Christmas tree	1·00	1·00
1173	(32p.) Candles in church	1·00	1·00
1174	(32p.) Three candles and holly	1·00	1·00
1175	(33p.) Mary and Jesus	1·10	1·10
1176	(33p.) Stockings and candle on mantelpiece	1·10	1·10
1177	(33p.) Five candles	1·10	1·10
1178	(33p.) Angel and candle	1·10	1·10
1179	(33p.) Candles in window	1·10	1·10

Nos. 1170/4 are inscribed "JERSEY MINIMUM POSTAGE PAID" and were sold for 32p., and Nos. 1175/9 are inscribed "U.K. MINIMUM POSTAGE PAID" and were sold for 33p.

2004. Designs as Nos. 1107/11. Self-adhesive.

1180	(32p.) Type **1061**	1·25	1·50
1181	(32p.) Bluebells and Les Ecrehous	1·25	1·50
1182	(32p.) Tree-mallow and Les Ecrehous	1·25	1·50
1183	(32p.) Smooth Sow-thistle and Les Minquiers	1·25	1·50
1184	(32p.) Thrift and Les Minquiers	1·25	1·50

Nos. 1180/4, which are inscribed "JERSEY MINIMUM POSTAGE PAID" and were initially sold at 32p each. Nos. 1180/4 are inscribed "2004" with copyright symbol after date.

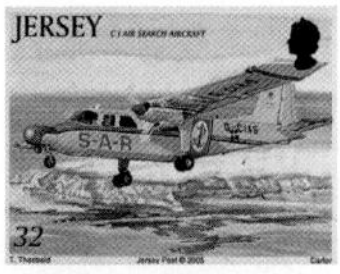

1130 Britten-Norman BN-2 Islander C 1 Air Search Aircraft

2005. Rescue Craft. Multicoloured.

1185	32p. Type **1130**	65	70
1186	33p. Eurocopter AS355 Ecurevil II	65	70
1187	40p. Beach lifeguard service	80	85
1188	49p. Fire rescue inflatable	1·50	1·50
1189	70p. R.A.F. Westland Sea King helicopter	1·75	1·75

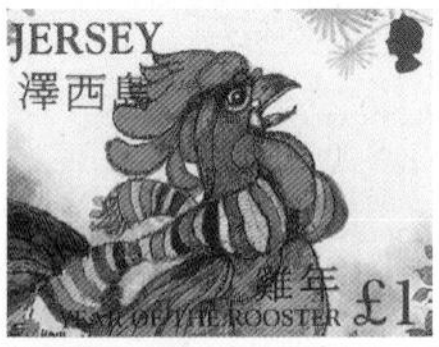

1135 Rooster

2005. Chinese New Year ("Year of the Rooster"). Sheet 110×75 mm.

MS1190	**1135** £1 multicoloured	2·50	2·75

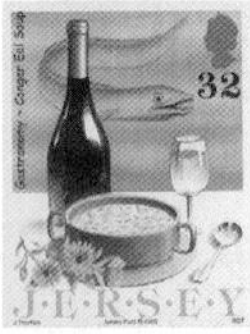

1136 Conger Eel Soup

2005. Europa. Gastronomy. Multicoloured.

1191	32p. Type **1136**	65	70
1192	33p. Oysters	65	70
1193	40p. Bean crock	80	85
1194	70p. Bourdélots with black butter	1·40	1·50

The 33p. and 40p. values include the "EUROPA" emblem.

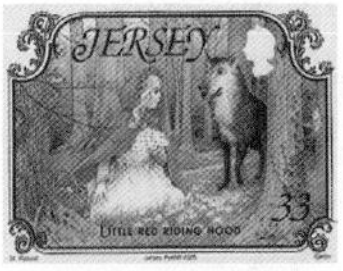

1140 *Little Red Riding Hood*

2005. Fairy Tales. Multicoloured.

1195	33p. Type **1140**	65	70
1196	34p. *The Little Mermaid*	70	75
1197	41p. *Beauty and the Beast*	80	85
1198	50p. *Rumpelstiltskin*	1·50	1·50
1199	73p. *Goose that laid the Golden Egg*	2·00	2·00
MS1200	110×75 mm. £2 *The Ugly Duckling* (50×37 mm)	4·50	4·75

Nos. 1195/**MS**1200 commemorate the birth bicentenary of Hans Christian Andersen.

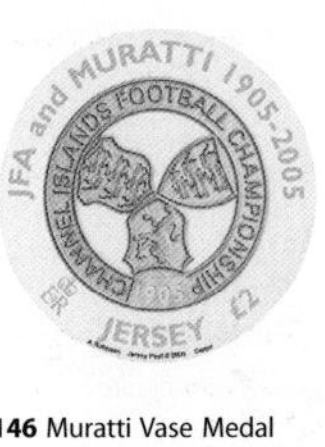

1146 Muratti Vase Medal

2005. Centenary of Jersey Football Association and Muratti Vase. Sheet 110×75 mm.

MS1201	**1146** £2 ochre, black and brown	4·50	4·50

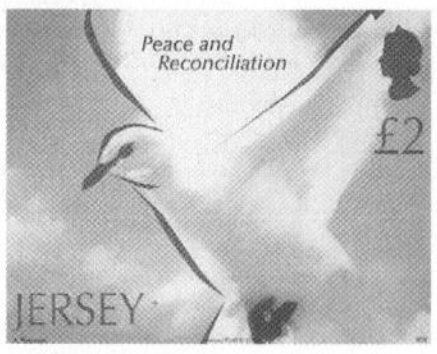

1147 Peace Dove

2005. 60th Anniv of Liberation of Channel Islands. Peace and Reconciliation. Sheet 110×75 mm.

MS1202	**1147** £2 multicoloured	4·50	4·50

2005. "Nordia 2005" Stamp Exhibition, Goteborg, Sweden. No. **MS**1200 optd **Jersey at Nordia 2005** and **Goteborg 26-29 mai SVENSKA FRIMARKET 150 AR.**

MS1203	110×75 mm. £2 *The Ugly Duckling* (50×37 mm)	4·00	4·25

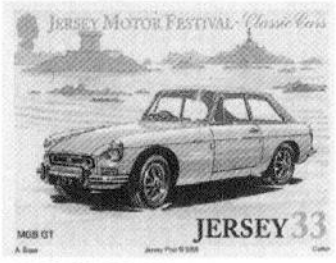

1148 MGB GT

2005. Jersey Festivals (2nd issue). Motor Festival. Classic Cars. Multicoloured.

1204	33p. Type **1148**	65	70
1205	34p. Mini Cooper	70	75
1206	41p. Citroen DS	80	85
1207	50p. Jaguar E Type	1·00	1·10
1208	56p. Volkswagen Beetle	1·10	1·20
1209	73p. Aston Martin DB5	1·50	1·60

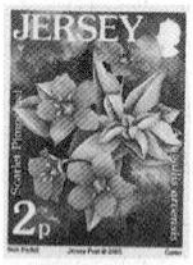

1154 Scarlet Pimpernel

2005. Wild Flowers. Multicoloured.

1210	1p. Yellow bartsia	10	10
1211	2p. Type **1154**	10	10
1212	3p. Wild angelica	10	10
1213	4p. Common knapweed	10	10
1214	5p. Marsh St. Johnswort	10	15
1215	10p. Black bryony	30	30
1216	15p. Bog pimpernel	30	35
1217	20p. Greater stitchwort	40	45
1218	25p. Horseshoe vetch	75	75
1219	30p. Common mallow	60	65
1220	35p. English stone crop	1·00	1·00
1221	40p. White campion	80	85
1222	45p. Tutsan	1·30	1·30
1223	50p. Common dog-violet	1·00	1·10
1224	55p. Oxeye daisy	1·60	1·60
1225	60p. Rook sea spurrey	1·80	1·80
1226	65p. Herb-Robert	1·30	1·40
1227	70p. Ragged robin	1·40	1·50
1228	75p. Brooklime	1·50	1·60
1229	80p. Mouse ear hawkweed	2·30	2·30
1230	85p. Cuckoo flower	1·70	1·80
1231	90p. Yellow iris	1·80	1·90
1232	£1 Three-cornered garlic	2·00	2·10
1233	£1.50 Devil's-bit scabious	4·50	4·50
MS1234	Three sheets, each 150×100 mm. (a) Nos. 1211, 1213, 1217, 1219, 1221, 1223, 1226 and 1232. (b) Nos. 1210, 1212, 1214, 1216, 1227/8 and 1230/1. (c) Nos. 1215, 1218, 1220, 1222, 1224/5, 1229 and 1223 Set of 3 sheets	26·00	27·00

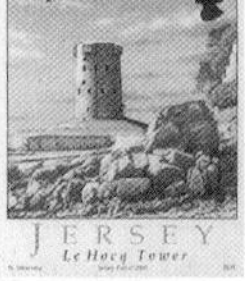

1178 Le Hocq Tower

2005. Coastal Towers. Multicoloured.

1235	33p. Type **1178**	65	70
1236	34p. Seymour Tower	70	75
1237	41p. Archirondel Tower	1·00	85
1238	56p. Kempt Tower	1·50	1·75
1239	73p. Le Rocco Tower	2·00	2·25

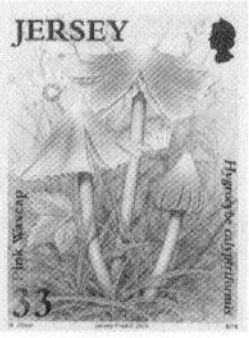

1183 *Hygrocybe calyptriformis*

2005. Fungi. Multicoloured.

1240	33p. Type **1183**	65	70
1241	34p. *Boletus erythropus*	70	75
1242	41p. *Inocybe godeyi*	80	85
1243	50p. *Myriostoma coliforme*	1·00	1·10
1244	56p. *Helvella crispa*	1·10	1·20
1245	73p. *Hygrocybe coccinea*	1·50	1·60
MS1246	150×100 mm. £2 *Marasmius oreades* (50×38 mm)	4·50	4·75

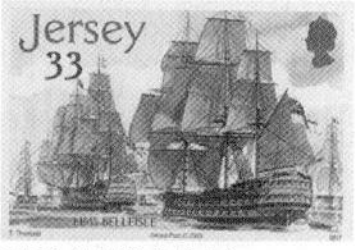

1190 H.M.S. Belleisle

2005. Bicentenary of the Battle of Trafalgar. Multicoloured.

1247	33p. Type **1190**	65	70
1248	34p. H.M.S. *Royal Sovereign*	70	75
1249	41p. H.M.S. *Neptune*	80	95
1250	50p. H.M.S. *Euryalus*	1·50	1·50
1251	73p. H.M.S. *Mars*	2·00	2·00
MS1252	110×75 mm. £2 H.M.S. *Victory* (50×38 mm)	5·00	5·00

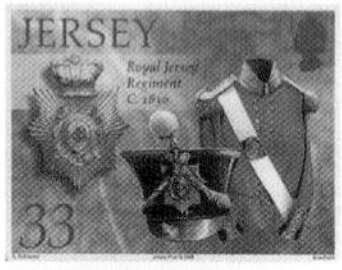

1196 Royal Jersey Regiment, c. 1830

2006. Royal Jersey Militia (2nd series). Uniforms and Badges. Multicoloured.

1253	33p. Type **1196**	65	70
1254	34p. Royal Jersey Regiment, c. 1844	70	75
1255	41p. Royal Jersey Artillery, c. 1881	80	85
1256	50p. Royal Jersey Light Infantry, c. 1890	1·50	1·50
1257	73p. Royal Engineers (modern)	2·00	2·00

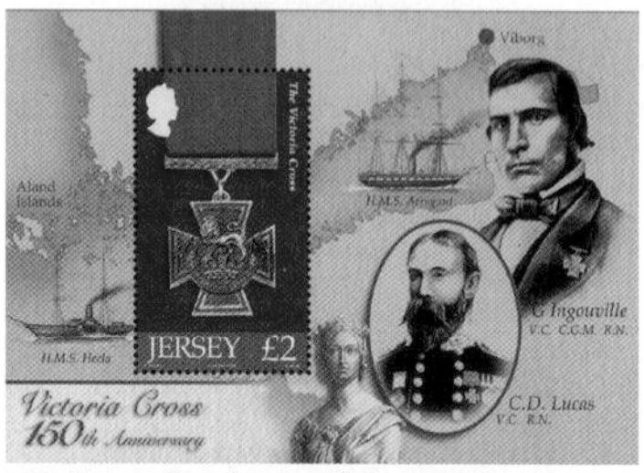

1201 Victoria Cross (image scaled to 44% of original size)

2006. 150th Anniv of the Victoria Cross. Sheet 110×75 mm.

MS1258	**1201** £2 multicoloured	5·00	5·00

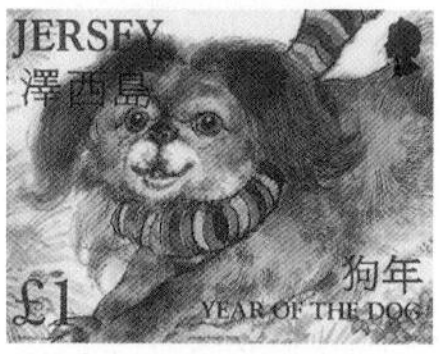

1202 Dog

2005. Chinese New Year ("Year of the Dog"). Sheet 110×75 mm.

MS1259	**1202** £1 multicoloured	3·50	3·75

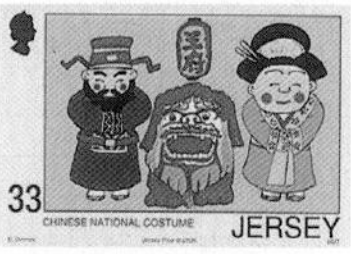

1203 Chinese National Costumes and Mask (Elliott Grimes)

2006. Europa. Winning Entries in Children's Stamp Design Competition. Multicoloured.

1260	33p. Type **1203**	65	70
1261	34p. Portuguese Fado Music Festival (Liam Reynolds)	70	75
1262	41p. Polish Pisanki painted Easter egg design (Kelly Reynolds)	1·75	1·50
1263	73p. Indian national costumes (Olivia Grimes)	2·25	2·25

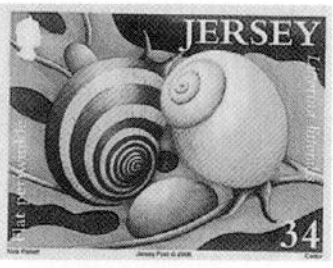

1207 Flat Periwinkle

2006. Sea Shells. Multicoloured.

1264	34p. Type **1207**	70	75
1265	37p. Painted top shell	75	80
1266	42p. Dog cockle	85	90
1267	51p. Variegated scallop	1·00	1·10
1268	57p. Blue rayed limpet	1·10	1·20
1269	74p. European cowrie	1·50	1·60
MS1270	150×100 mm. £2 Ormer shell (oval, 45×30 mm)	4·50	4·50

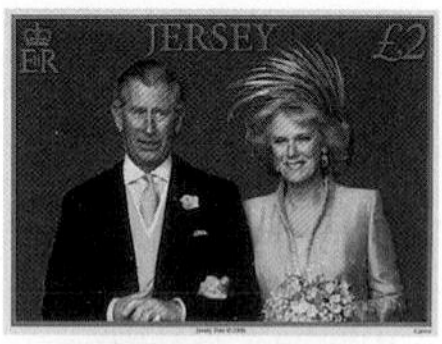

1214 Wedding Photograph

2006. First Wedding Anniversary of Prince Charles and Duchess of Cornwall.

1271	**1214** £2 multicoloured	4·00	4·50

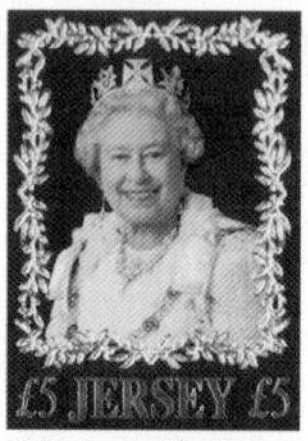

1215 Queen Elizabeth II

2006. 80th Birthday of Queen Elizabeth II. Multicoloured.

1272	£5 Type **1215**	10·00	10·50
MS1273	150×100 mm. £5 Type **1215**; No. 2874 of New Zealand (sold at £7)	15·00	15·00

No. **MS**1273 is identical to **MS**2875 of New Zealand.

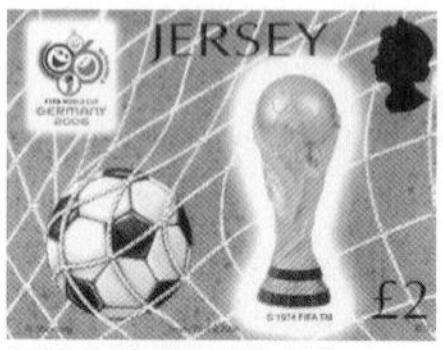

1217 Football and World Cup Trophy

2006. World Cup Football Championship, Germany. Sheet 110×75 mm.

MS1274	**1217** £2 multicoloured	4·75	5·00

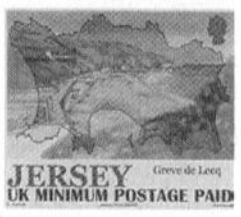

1218 Greve de Lecq

2006. Island Views. Multicoloured. Self-adhesive.

1275	(37p.) Type **1218**	1·50	1·50
1276	(37p.) La Rocque	1·50	1·50
1277	(37p.) Portelet	1·50	1·50
1278	(37p.) St. Brelade's Bay	1·50	1·50

Nos. 1275/8, which are inscribed "UK MINIMUM POSTAGE PAID" and were initially sold at 37p.

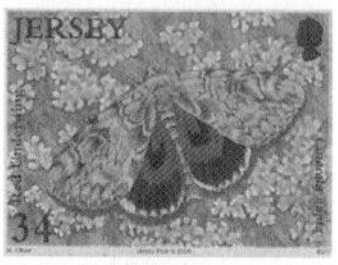

1222 Red Underwing Moth

2006. Butterflies and Moths. Multicoloured.

1279	34p. Type **1222**	70	75
1280	37p. Comma butterfly	75	80
1281	42p. Black arches moth	85	90
1282	51p. Small copper butterfly	1·00	1·10
1283	57p. Holly blue butterfly	1·10	1·20
1284	74p. Orange-tip butterfly	1·50	1·60
MS1285	150×100 mm. Nos. 1282/4	4·50	4·50

Stamps from **MS**1285 have no white borders.

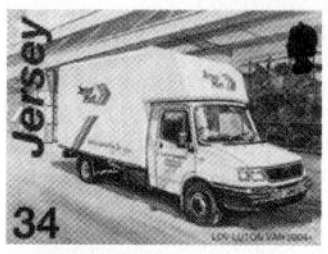

1228 LDV Luton Van, c. 2004

2006. Jersey Postal History (2nd series). Postal Vehicles. Multicoloured.

1286	34p. Type **1228**	70	75
1287	37p. Renault Kangoo, 1999–2004	75	80
1288	42p. LDV Pilot, 1994–2004	85	90
1289	51p. Ford Transit, Luton body, 1988–96	1·00	1·10
1290	57p. Morris Marina, 440/575, c. 1978	1·10	1·20
1291	74p. Morris Minor, c. 1969	1·50	1·60
MS1292	150×100 mm. Nos. 1289/91	4·50	4·75

2006. Belgica '06 International Stamp Exhibition, Brussels. No. **MS**1270 optd **Jersey at and Belgica** emblem on bottom left sheet margin.

MS1293	150×100 mm. £2 Ormer shell (oval, 45×30 mm)	5·00	5·50

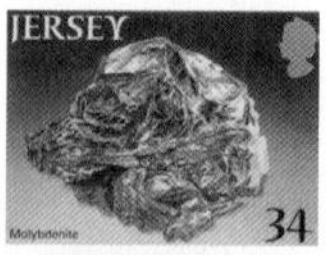

1234 Molybdenite

2007. Mineralogy. Multicoloured.

1294	34p. Type **1234**	1·00	1·00
1295	37p. Muscovite in pegmatite vein, feldspar+quartz	1·10	1·10
1296	42p. Orthoclase and plagioclase	1·20	1·20
1297	51p. Quartz coated with manganese oxide	1·50	1·50
1298	74p. Smoky quartz	2·20	2·20

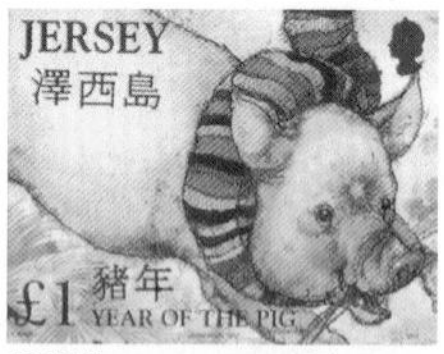

1239 Pig

2007. Chinese New Year ("Year of the Pig"). Sheet 110×75 mm.

MS1299	**1239** £1 multicoloured	3·25	3·50

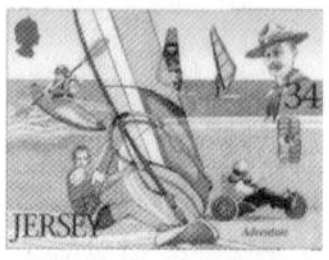

1240 Windsurfing, canoeing and land yachting ("Adventure")

2007. Europa. Centenary of Scouting. Multicoloured.

1300	34p. Type **1240**	1·00	1·00
1301	37p. Scouts playing trumpets and national flags ("International Friendship")	1·10	1·10
1302	42p. Climbing and go-karting ("Developing Young People")	1·20	1·20
1303	74p. Scouts and badges ("Changing the World for Good")	2·20	2·20

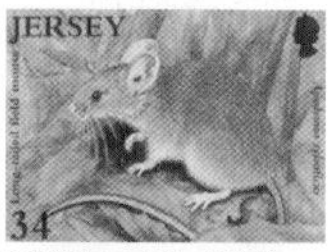

1244 Long-tailed Field Mouse

2007. Countryside Animals. Multicoloured.

1304	34p. Type **1244**	1·00	1·00
1305	37p. Rabbits	1·10	1·10
1306	42p. Polecat	1·30	1·30
1307	51p. Common shrew	1·50	1·50
1308	57p. Stoat	1·70	1·70
1309	74p. Brown rat	2·20	2·20
MS1310	150×100 mm. As Nos. 1307/9	5·50	5·50

Stamps from **MS**1310 have no white borders.

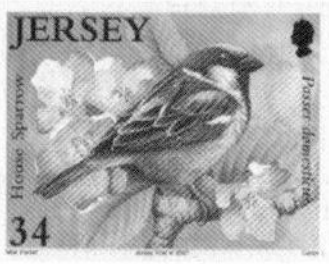

1250 House Sparrow

2007. Jersey Birdlife (1st series). Garden Birds. Multicoloured.

1311	34p. Type **1250**	1·00	1·00
1312	37p. Chaffinch	1·10	1·10
1313	42p. Blue tit	1·30	1·30
1314	51p. Blackbirds (pair)	1·50	1·50
1315	57p. Magpie	1·70	1·70
1316	74p. Great tit	2·20	2·20
MS1317	150×100 mm. Nos. 1314/16	5·25	5·25
MS1318	150×100 mm. Nos. 1311/16	8·75	8·75

Stamps from **MS**1317 have no white borders.

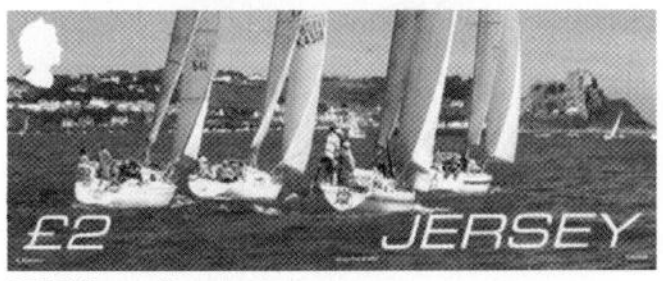

1256 Gorey Regatta

2007. Jersey Yachting (2nd issue). 150th Anniv of Gorey Regatta. Sheet 110×75 mm.

MS1319	**1256** £2 multicoloured	6·00	6·00

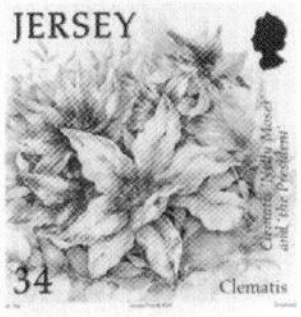

1257 Clematis 'Nelly Moser' and 'The President'

2007. Summer Flowers. Multicoloured.

1320	34p. Type **1257**	1·00	1·00
1321	37p. Rose 'Just Joey'	1·10	1·10
1322	42p. Honeysuckle *Lonicera x Americana*	1·30	1·30
1323	51p. Fuchsia 'Swingtime'	1·50	1·50
1324	57p. Sweet peas	1·70	1·70
1325	74p. Lilac	2·20	2·20

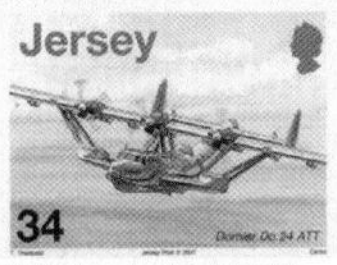

1263 Dornier Do-24 ATT

2007. 60th Anniv of Jersey International Air Display. Multicoloured.

1326	34p. Type **1263**	1·00	1·00
1327	37p. Avro Type 698 Vulcan B.2	1·10	1·10
1328	42p. Junkers Ju 52/3m	1·30	1·30
1329	51p. Sukhoi Su-27 'Flanker'	1·50	1·50
1330	57p. Boeing B-52 Stratofortress	1·70	1·70
1331	74p. Anglo French Concorde	2·20	2·20
MS1332	110×75 mm. £2.50 BAe Hawk T1s of the Red Arrows (60×40 mm)	7·25	7·25

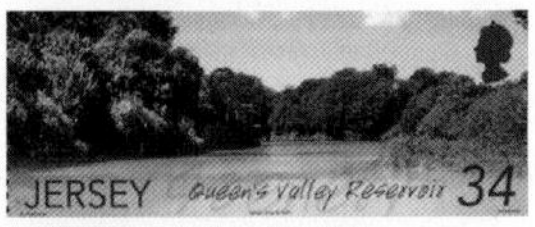

1270 Queen's Valley Reservoir

2007. Jersey Scenery (1st series). Multicoloured.

1333	34p. Type **1270**	1·00	1·00
1334	37p. Mont Orgueil Castle	1·10	1·10
1335	42p. Bonne Nuit Harbour	1·30	1·30
1336	51p. La Hougue Bie	1·50	1·50
1337	57p. Bouley Bay	1·70	1·70
1338	74p. La Corbiere Lighthouse	2·20	2·20

See also Nos. 1364/**MS**1370.

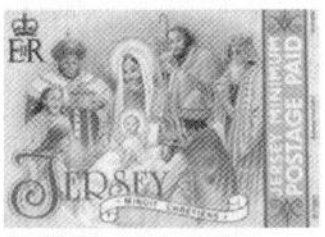

1276 *Minuit Chretiens*

2007. Christmas Carols. Multicoloured. Self-adhesive.

1339	(35p.) Type **1276**	1·00	1·00
1340	(35p.) While Shepherds Watched	1·00	1·00
1341	(35p.) O Come All Ye Faithful	1·00	1·00
1342	(35p.) O Christmas Tree	1·00	1·00
1343	(35p.) Jingle Bells	1·00	1·00
1344	(39p.) Hark the Herald Angels Sing	1·20	1·20
1345	(39p.) We Three Kings	1·20	1·20
1346	(39p.) Ding Dong Merrily on High	1·20	1·20
1347	(39p.) Holly and the Ivy	1·20	1·20
1348	(39p.) Good King Wenceslas	1·20	1·20

Nos. 1339/43 which are inscribed 'JERSEY MINIMUM POSTAGE PAID' were sold for 35p., and Nos. 1344/8 which are inscribed 'U.K. MINIMUM POSTAGE PAID' were sold for 39p.

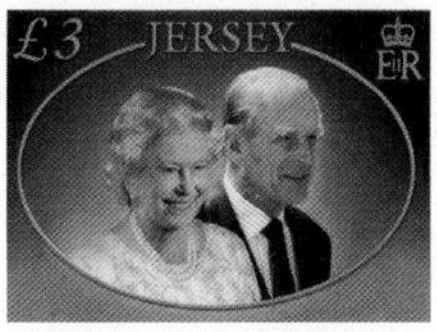

1286 Queen Elizabeth II and Duke of Edinburgh

2007. Diamond Wedding of Queen Elizabeth II and Duke of Edinburgh.

1349	**1286** £3 multicoloured	8·75	8·75

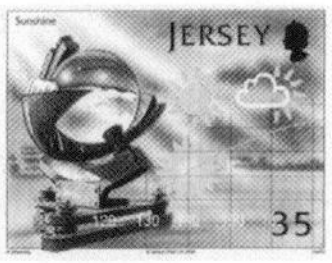

1287 Sunshine

2008. 300th Anniv of Jersey Signal Station. Multicoloured.

1350	35p. Type **1287**	1·00	1·00
1351	39p. Strong wind signals	1·20	1·20
1352	43p. Weather signals	1·30	1·30
1353	58p. Temperature	1·70	1·70
1354	76p. Tides and wave signals	2·30	2·30

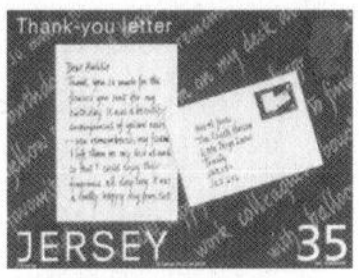

1292 Thank You Letter

2008. Europa. The Letter. Multicoloured.

1355	35p. Type **1292**	1·00	1·00
1356	39p. Love letter	1·20	1·20
1357	43p. Letter to Santa Claus	1·30	1·30
1358	76p. Family letter	2·30	2·30

The 39p. and 43p. values include the "EUROPA" emblem.

1296 Arts and Crafts

2008. Jersey Festivals (3rd issue). Centenary of Jersey Eisteddfod. Multicoloured.

1359	35p. Type **1296**	1·00	1·00
1360	39p. Dance and drama	1·20	1·20
1361	43p. Speech	1·30	1·30
1362	58p. Films and photography	1·70	1·70
1363	76p. Music	2·30	2·30

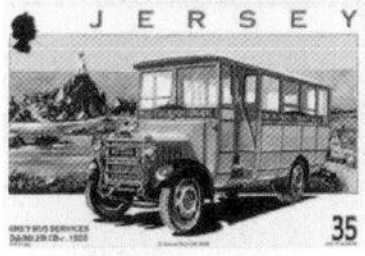

1301 Grey Bus Services Daimler CB, c. 1920

2008. Jersey Transport. Buses (2nd series). Multicoloured.

1364	35p. Type **1301**	85	85
1365	39p. SCS Ex LGOC 'K' single decker, c. 1930	95	95
1366	43p. JMT Town Bus Service, c. 1941	1·00	1·00
1367	52p. JMT Leyland Lion Charcoal Burner, c. 1941	1·30	1·30
1368	58p. JBS Bedford WLB, c. 1956	1·40	1·40
1369	76p. JMT Commer Commando, c. 1963	1·80	1·80
MS1370	110×75 mm. £2.50 JMT Ford Willowbrook, c. 1977 (74×30 mm)	7·25	7·25

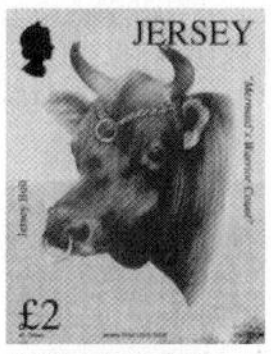

1308 Jersey Bull 'Mermaid's Warrior Count'

2008. 18th World Jersey Cattle Bureau Conference, Jersey. Sheet 110×75 mm.

MS1371	**1308** £2 multicoloured	5·75	5·75

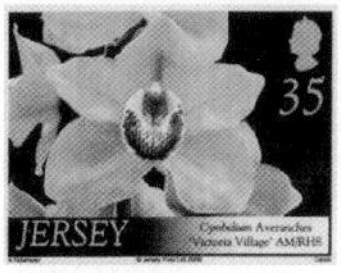

1309 *Cymbidium* Averanches 'Victoria Village'

2008. Jersey Orchids (6th series). Multicoloured.

1372	35p. Type **1309**	1·00	1·00
1373	39p. *Miltonia* 'Tesson Mill'	1·20	1·20
1374	43p. *Anguloa* Victoire 'Trinity'	1·30	1·30
1375	52p. *Phragmipedium* La Hougette	1·50	1·50
1376	58p. *Phragmipedium* Havre des Pas 'Jersey'	1·70	1·70
1377	76p. *Paphiopedilum* Rolfei 'Trinity'	2·30	2·30
MS1378	110×75 mm. £2.50 *Paphiopedilum* Rocco Tower	7·25	7·25

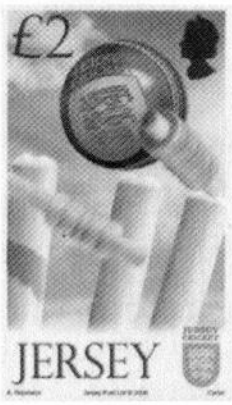

1316 Jersey Cricket Board, Ball hitting Stumps

2008. World Cricket League Division 5 Tournament, Jersey. Sheet 110×75 mm.

MS1379	**1316** £2 multicoloured	5·75	5·75

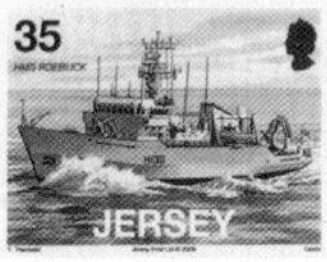

1317 HMS *Roebuck*

2008. Jersey Naval Connections (2nd series). Visiting Naval Vessels. Multicoloured.

1380	35p. Type **1317**	1·00	1·00
1381	39p. HMS *Monmouth*	1·20	1·20
1382	43p. HMS *Edinburgh*	1·30	1·30
1383	52p. HMS *Express*	1·50	1·50
1384	58p. HMS *Severn*	1·70	1·70
1385	76p. HMS *Cottesmore*	2·30	2·30
MS1386	110×75 mm. £2.50 HMY *Britannia* (60×40 mm)	7·25	7·25

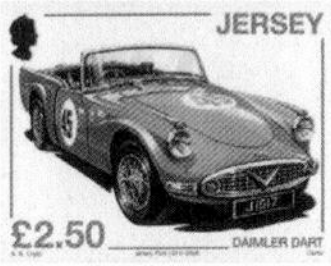

1324 Daimler Dart

2008. Jersey Festival of Speed. Sheet 110×75 mm.

MS1387	**1324** £2.50 multicoloured	7·25	7·25

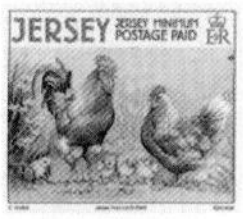

1325 Cockerel, Hen and Chicks

2008. Farm Animals. Multicoloured. Self-adhesive.

1388	(35p.) Type **1325**	1·00	1·00
1389	(35p.) Ewe and lambs	1·00	1·00
1390	(35p.) Sow and piglets	1·00	1·00
1391	(35p.) Geese and goslings	1·00	1·00
1392	(35p.) Jersey cows and calf	1·00	1·00

Nos. 1388/92 are inscribed 'JERSEY MINIMUM POSTAGE PAID' and were sold for 35p. each.

Nos. 1388/92 commemorate the 175th anniversary of the Royal Jersey Agricultural and Horticultural Society.

Nos. 1388/92 were initially released with '2008' imprint dates. They were re-issued on 2nd April 2010 with '2010' imprint dates.

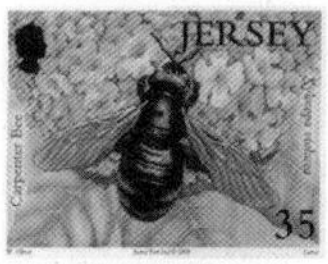

1330 Carpenter Bee

2008. Insects (2nd series). Multicoloured.

1393	35p. Type **1330**	1·00	1·00
1394	39p. Buff-tailed bumblebee	1·20	1·20
1395	43p. Clown-faced bug	1·30	1·30
1396	52p. Large migrant hoverfly	1·50	1·50
1397	58p. Ruby-tailed wasp	1·70	1·70
1398	76p. 22-spot ladybird	2·30	2·30

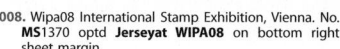

2008. Wipa08 International Stamp Exhibition, Vienna. No. **MS**1370 optd **Jerseyat WIPA08** on bottom right sheet margin.

MS1399	110×75 mm. £2.50 JMT Ford Willowbrook, c. 1977 (74×30 mm)	7·25	7·25

2008. Jersey Birdlife (2nd series). Migrating Birds. As T **1250**. Multicoloured.

1400	35p. Northern wheatear	1·00	1·00
1401	39p. Whinchat	1·20	1·20
1402	43p. Pied flycatcher	1·30	1·30
1403	52p. Yellow wagtail	1·50	1·50
1404	58p. Ring ouzel	1·70	1·70
1405	76p. Common redstart	2·30	2·30
MS1406	150×100 mm. Nos. 1400/5	9·00	9·00
MS1407	150×100 mm. Nos. 1403/5	5·50	5·50

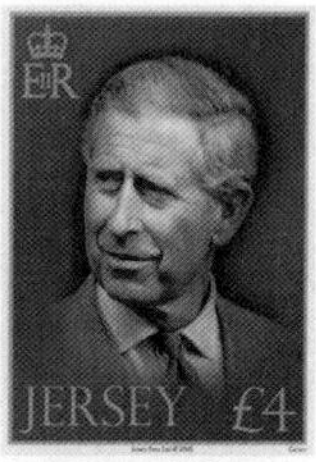

1342 Prince Charles

2008. 60th Birthday of Prince Charles.

1408	**1342** £4 multicoloured	12·00	12·00
MS1409	150×100 mm. No. 1408	12·00	12·00

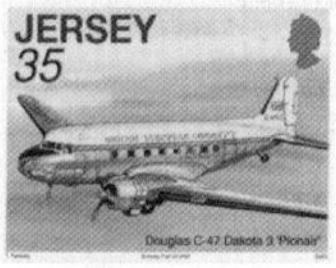

1343 Douglas C-47 Dakota 3 'Pionair'

2009. 75th Anniv of the First Flight from Jersey to Southampton. Multicoloured.

1410	35p. Type **1343**	1·00	1·00
1411	39p. Vickers Viscount 833	1·25	1·25
1412	43p. Handley Page HPR7 Dart-Herald	1·25	1·25
1413	52p. Bristol Superfreighter 32	1·50	1·50
1414	58p. Fokker F-27 Friendship	1·75	1·75
1415	76p. Bombardier Q400 Dash 8	2·25	2·25
MS1416	110×75 mm. £3 de Havilland DH.84 Dragon 2	9·00	9·00

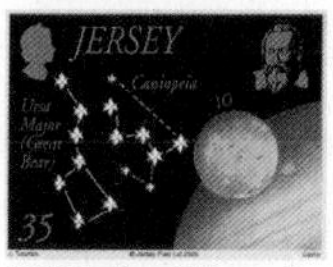

1350 Io, Ursa Major and Cassiopeia

2009. Europa. Astronomy. Satellites of Jupiter and Constellations. Multicoloured.

1417	35p. Type **1350**	1·00	1·00
1418	39p. Europa, Bootes and Corona Borealis	1·25	1·25
1419	43p. Ganymede, Cygnus and Pegasus	1·25	1·25
1420	76p. Callisto, Perseus and Orion	2·25	2·25

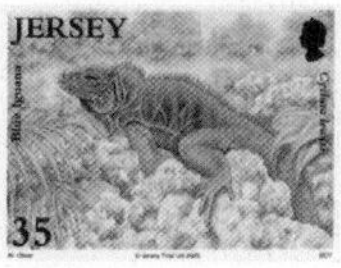

1354 Blue Iguana (*Cyclura lewisi*)

2009. Endangered Species (1st series). 50th Anniv of the Durrell Wildlife Conservation Trust. Multicoloured.

1421	35p. Type **1354**	1·00	1·00
1422	39p. Madagascan giant jumping rat (*Hypogeomys antimena*)	1·25	1·25
1423	43p. Mountain chicken frog (*Leptodactylus fallax*)	1·25	1·25
1424	52p. Livingstone's fruit bat (*Pteropus livingstonii*)	1·50	1·50
1425	58p. Andean bear (*Tremarctos ornatus*)	1·75	1·75
1426	76p. Western lowland gorilla (*Gorilla g. gorilla*)	2·25	2·25

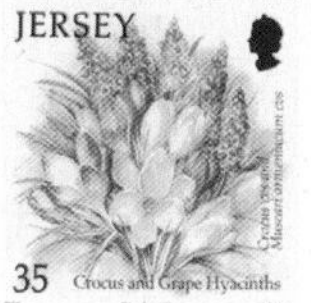

1360 Crocus and Grape Hyacinths

2009. Spring Flowers. Multicoloured.

1427	35p. Type **1360**	1·00	1·00
1428	39p. Daffodils	1·25	1·25
1429	43p. Anemones de Caen	1·25	1·25
1430	52p. Tulips	1·50	1·50
1431	58p. Hyacinths	1·75	1·75
1432	76p. Polyanthus and Primulas	2·25	2·25

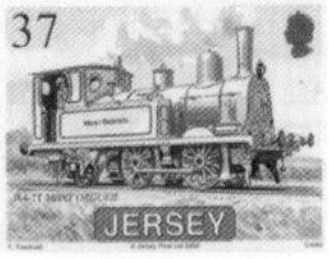

1366 *Mont Orgueil*

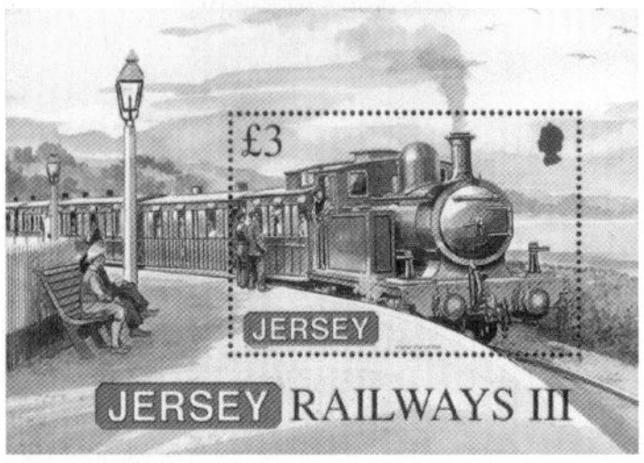

1372 Locomotive No. 5 *La Moye* awaits Departure from St. Aubin (image scaled to 44% of original size)

2009. Jersey Railways (3rd series). Multicoloured.

1433	37p. Type **1366**	1·10	1·10
1434	42p. Corbiere	1·25	1·25
1435	45p. *Carteret*	1·40	1·40
1436	55p. Railcar *Pioneer*	1·60	1·60
1437	61p. *La Moye*	1·75	1·75
1438	80p. *St. Brelades*	2·40	2·40
MS1439	110×75 mm. **1372** £3 multicoloured	9·00	9·00

2009. IBRA International Stamp Exhibition, Essen, Germany. No. **MS**1439 optd **JERSEY AT iBRA** on upper left sheet margin.

MS1440	110×75 mm. **1372** £3 multicoloured	9·00	9·00

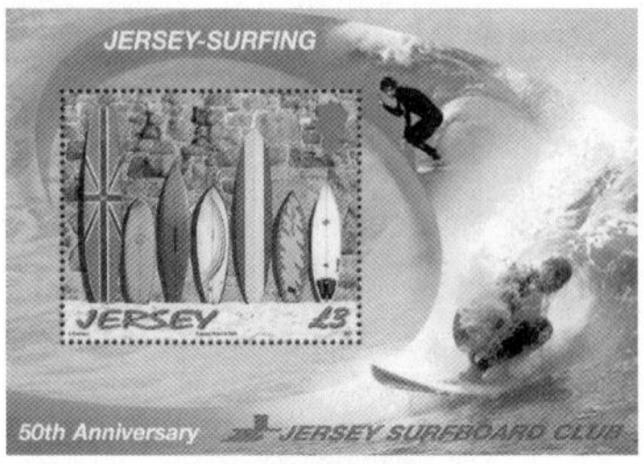

1373 Surfboards (image scaled to 44% of original size)

2009. 50th Anniv of Jersey Surfboard Club. Sheet 110×75 mm.

MS1441	**1373** £3 multicoloured	9·00	9·00

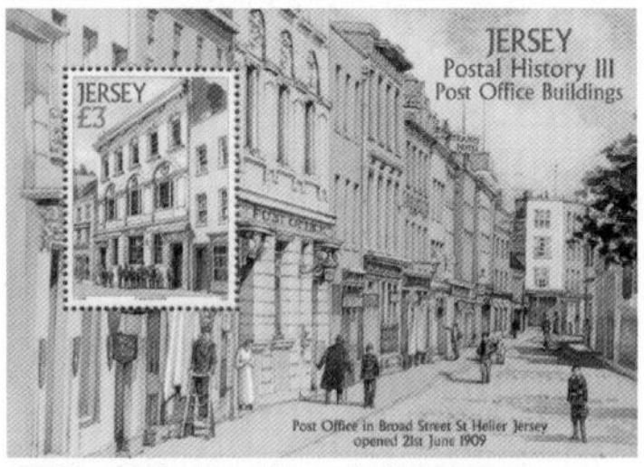

1374 Post Office, Broad Street, St. Helier, 1909 (image scaled to 44% of original size)

2009. Jersey Postal History (3rd series). Post Office Buildings. Sheet 110×75 mm.

MS1442	**1374** £3 multicoloured	9·00	9·00

No. **MS**1442 commemorates the centenary of Jersey's Head Post Office at Broad Street, St. Helier.

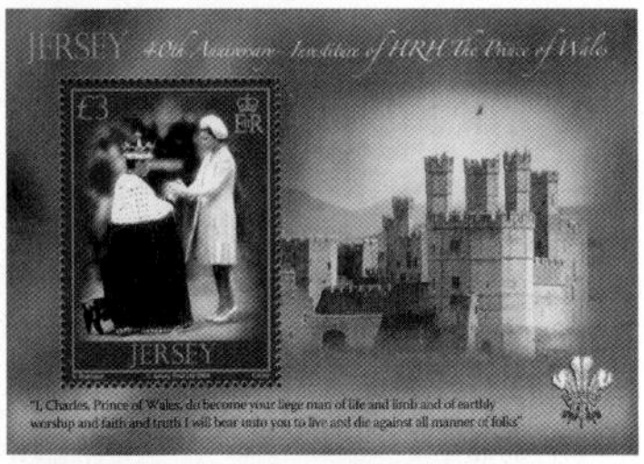

1375 Investiture of the Prince of Wales at Caernarfon Castle, 1969 (image scaled to 44% of original size)

2009. 40th Anniv of the Investiture of Prince Charles as the Prince of Wales. Sheet 110×75 mm.

MS1443	**1375** £3 multicoloured	8·75	8·75

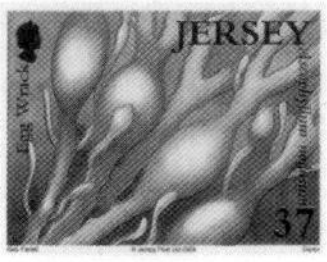

1376 *Ascophyllum nodosum* (egg wrack)

2009. Seaweed. Multicoloured.

1444	37p. Type **1376**	1·00	1·00
1445	42p. *Enteromorpha* sp. (gutweed)	1·25	1·25
1446	45p. *Dilsea carnosa* (red rags)	1·40	1·40
1447	55p. *Ulva lactuca* (sea lettuce)	1·50	1·50
1448	64p. *Laminaria hyperborea*	2·00	2·00
1449	80p. *Codium tomentosum* (velvet horn)	2·40	2·40

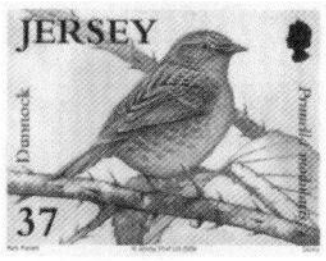

1382 Dunnock

2009. Jersey Birdlife (3rd series). Songbirds. Multicoloured.

1450	37p. Type **1382**	1·00	1·00
1451	42p. Song thrush	1·25	1·25
1452	45p. Wren	1·40	1·40
1453	55p. Blackcap	1·50	1·50
1454	61p. Mistle thrush	2·00	2·00
1455	80p. Robin	2·40	2·40
MS1456	150×100 mm. Nos. 1450/5	9·50	9·50
MS1457	150×100 mm. Nos. 1453/5	5·75	5·75

Stamps from **MS**1457 have no white borders.

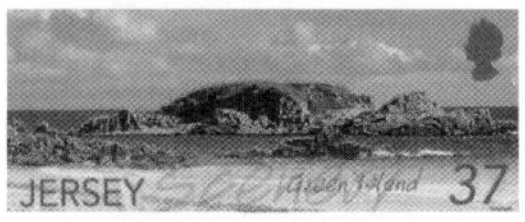

1388 Green Island

2009. Jersey Scenery (2nd series). Multicoloured.

1458	37p. Type **1388**	1·00	1·00
1459	42p. Gorey Castle at night	1·25	1·25
1460	45p. St. Aubin's Harbour	1·40	1·40
1461	55p. St. Peter's Valley	1·50	1·50
1462	61p. La Rocque Harbour	2·00	2·00
1463	80p. Greve de Lecq	2·40	2·40

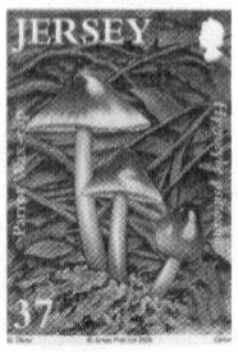

1394 Parrot Wax-cap (*Hygrocybe psittacina*)

2009. Fungi (3rd series). Multicoloured.

1464	**1394**	37p. Type **1394**	1·10	1·10
1465	**1394**	42p. *Russula sardonia*	1·25	1·25
1466	**1394**	45p. Velvet foot (*Flammulina velutipes*)	1·25	1·25
1467	**1394**	55p. Honey fungus (*Armillaria mellea*)	1·60	1·60
1468	**1394**	61p. Orange peel fungus (*Aleuria aurantia*)	1·75	1·75
1469	**1394**	80p. Jewelled deathcap (*Amanita gemmata*)	2·25	2·25

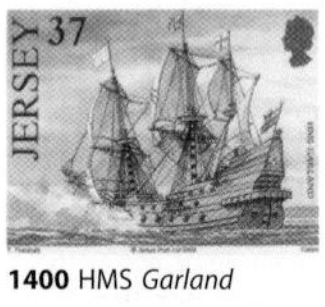

1400 HMS *Garland*

2009. Jersey Naval Connections (3rd series). 400th Birth Anniv of Sir George Carteret. Multicoloured.

1470	37p. Type **1400**	1·10	1·10
1471	42p. HMS *Eighth Lion's Whelp*	1·25	1·25
1472	45p. HMS *Unicorn*	1·25	1·25
1473	55p. HMS *Mary Rose*	1·60	1·60
1474	61p. HMS *Antelope*	1·75	1·75
1475	80p. HMS *Rainbow*	2·25	2·25

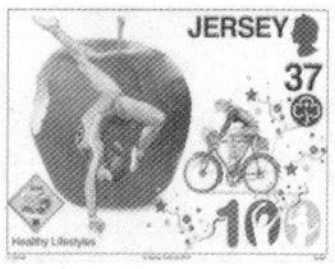

1406 Gymnast and Cyclist ('Healthy Lifestyles')

2010. Centenary of the Girl Guide Association. Multicoloured

1476	37p. Type **1406**	1·00	1·00
1477	42p. Broken globe, tap and young child drinking ('global awareness')	1·25	1·25
1478	45p. Guide salute and hand-shake ('Skills & Relationships')	1·25	1·25
1479	61p. Guides holding hands around globe ('Celebrating Diversity')	1·75	1·75
1480	80p. Guides doing handicrafts and on climbing wall ('Discovery')	2·25	2·25

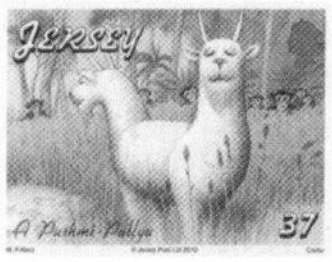

1411 A Pushmi-Pullyu (*The Story of Doctor Dolittle* by Hugh Lofting)

2010. Europa. Children's Books. Multicoloured.

1481	37p. Type **1411**	1·50	1·50
1482	42p. *How the Elephant got his Trunk* (Rudyard Kipling)	1·60	1·60
1483	45p. The Mad Hatter's Tea Party (*Alice's Adventures in Wonderland* by Lewis Carroll)	1·75	1·75
1484	80p. *The Dong with a Luminous Nose* (Edward Lear)d	3·25	3·25

The 42p. and 45p. values are inscr 'EUROPA'.

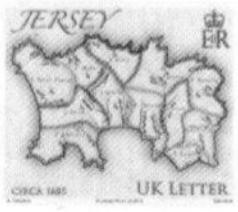

1415 Map, c. 1685

2010. Maps. Multicoloured. Self-adhesive.

1485	(42p.) Type **1415**	1·25	1·25
1486	(42p.) Map, c. 1844	1·25	1·25
1487	(42p.) Map, c. 1980s	1·25	1·25
1488	(42p.) Map, c. 2000	1·25	1·25
1489	(42p.) Satellite view	1·25	1·25

Nos. 1485/9 were inscribed 'UK LETTER' and originally sold for 42p. each.

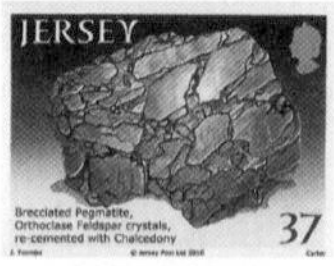

1420 Brecciated Pegmatite, Orthoclase Feldspar Crystals, re-cemented with Chalcedony

2010. Petrology. Multicoloured.

1490	37p. Type **1420**	1·10	1·10
1491	42p. Diorite with Incipient Orbicular Structure	1·25	1·25
1492	45p. Granite	1·25	1·25
1493	61p. Jasper in Andesite	1·75	1·75
1494	80p. Pebbles of Granite, Andesite and Shale in Rozel Conglomerate	2·40	2·40

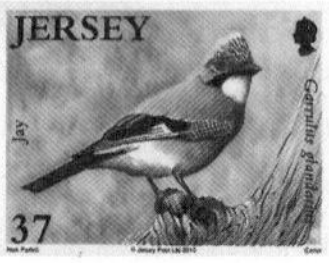

1425 Jay

2010. Jersey Birdlife (4th series). Woodland Birds. Multicoloured.

1495	37p. Type **1425**	1·10	1·10
1496	42p. Great spotted woodpecker	1·25	1·25
1497	45p. Short-toed treecreeper	1·40	1·40
1498	55p. Chiffchaff	1·60	1·60
1499	61p. Long-tailed tit	1·75	1·75
1500	80p. Turtle dove	2·40	2·40
MS1501	150×100 mm. Nos. 1495/500	9·50	9·50
MS1502	150×100 mm. As Nos. 1498/500	5·75	5·75

Stamps from **MS**1502 have no white borders.

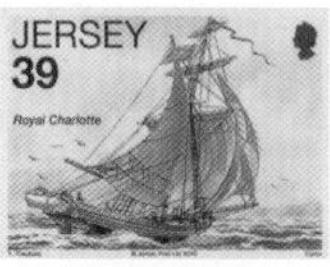

1431 *Royal Charlotte*

2010. Postal History (4th series). Mail Ships. Multicoloured.

1503	39p. Type **1431**	1·10	1·10
1504	45p. *Dispatch*	1·40	1·40
1505	55p. *Diana*	1·60	1·60
1506	60p. *Reindeer*	1·75	1·75
1507	72p. *Caesarea* (II)	2·25	2·25
1508	80p. *St. Patrick* (III)	2·40	2·40
MS1509	150×100 mm. Nos. 1503/8	10·50	10·50
MS1510	110×75 mm. £3 *Watersprite* c. 1827	8·50	8·50

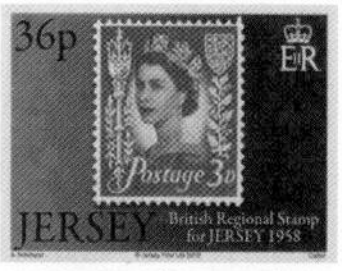

1438 1958 3d. Deep Lilac Stamp

2010. Jersey Postal History (5th series). British Regional Definitive Stamps for Jersey 1958–69. Multicoloured.

1511	36p. Type **1438**	1·10	1·10
1512	39p. 1964 2½d. carmine-red stamp	1·10	1·10
1513	45p. 1966 4d. ultramarine stamp	1·40	1·40
1514	55p. 1968 4d. olive-sepia stamp	1·60	1·60
1515	60p. 1968 5d. royal blue stamp	1·75	1·75
1516	72p. 1969 4d. bright vermilion stamp	2·25	2·25
MS1517	150×100 mm. Nos. 1511/16	9·25	9·25

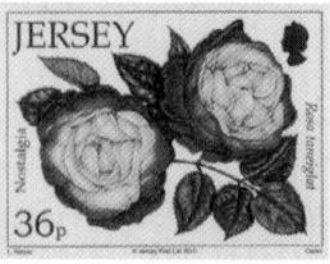

1444 'Nostalgia'

2010. Roses. Multicoloured.

1518	36p. Type **1444**	1·10	1·10
1519	39p. 'Mountbatten'	1·10	1·10
1520	45p. 'Royal William'	1·40	1·40
1521	55p. 'Elina'	1·60	1·60
1522	60p. 'New Dawn'	1·75	1·75
1523	72p. 'Lovers Meeting'	2·25	2·25
MS1524	£3 'Pride of England'	8·50	8·50

2010. Planete Timbres National Stamp Exhibition, Paris. No. **MS**1524 inscr with emblem on top left margin

MS1524a	£3 multicoloured	8·75	8·75

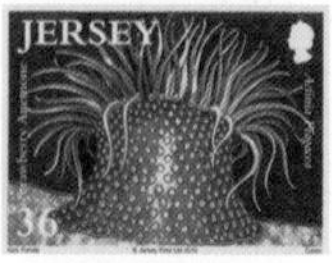

1451 Strawberry Anemone (Actinia fragacea)

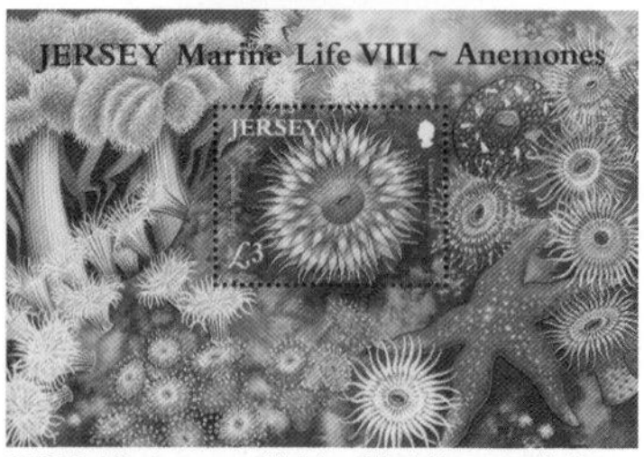

1457 Dahlia Anemone (*Urticina felina*) (image scaled to 44% of original size)

2010. Sea Anemones. Multicoloured.

1525	36p. Type **1451**	1·10	1·10
1526	39p. Snakelocks Anemone (*Anemonia viridis*)	1·10	1·10
1527	45p. Jewel Anemone (*Corynactis viridis*)	1·40	1·40
1528	55p. Parasitic Anemone (*Sagartia parasitica*)	1·60	1·60
1529	60p. Tube Anemone (*Pachycerianthus 'Dorothy'*)	1·75	1·75
1530	72p. Beadlet Anemone (*Actinia equina*)	2·25	2·25
MS1531	**1457** £3 multicoloured	9·00	9·00

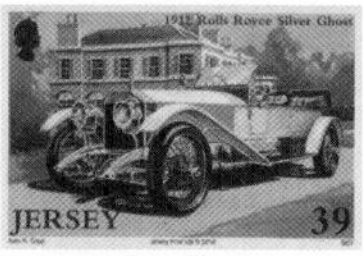

1458 Rolls Royce Silver Ghost, 1912

2010. Vintage Cars (4th series). Multicoloured.

1532	39p. Type **1458**	1·10	1·10
1533	45p. Bugatti Type 37, 1926	1·10	1·10
1534	55p. Austin Seven, 1933	1·40	1·40
1535	60p. Citroën Light 15, 1938	1·60	1·60
1536	72p. Morris 10, 1946	1·75	1·75
1537	80p. Rover 75 Sports Saloon, 1949	2·25	2·25

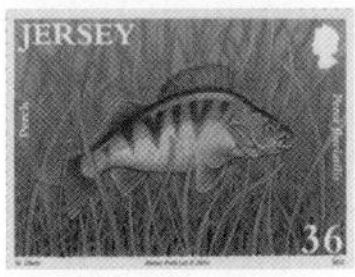

1464 Perch (*Perca fluviatilis*)

2010. Freshwater Fish. Multicoloured.

1538	36p. Type **1464**	1·10	1·10
1539	39p. Tench (*Tinca tinca*)	1·10	1·10
1540	45p. Roach (*Rutilus rutilus*)	1·40	1·40
1541	55p. Rudd (*Scardinius erythrophthalmus*)	1·60	1·60
1542	60p. Mirror Carp (*Cyprinus carpio*)	1·75	1·75
1543	72p. Common Bream (*Abramis brama*)	2·25	2·25
MS1544	110×75 mm. £3 multicoloured	9·00	9·00

Nos. 1538/43 commemorate the 50th anniversary of the Jersey Freshwater Angling Association.

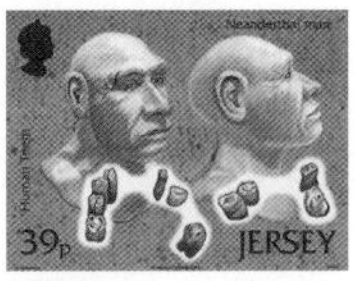

1471 Neanderthal Man and Teeth

2010. Archaeology. La Cotte de St. Brelade. Multicoloured.

1545	39p. Type **1471**	1·10	1·10
1546	45p. Woolly Rhinoceros and Skull	1·40	1·40
1547	55p. Woolly Mammoth, Tusks and Teeth	1·60	1·60
1548	60p. Flint Tools	1·75	1·75
1549	80p. Giant Deer and Antler	2·25	2·25

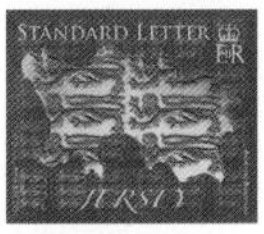

1476 1476

2010. Jersey Map with Lions from Crest of Jersey

1550	(36p.) Type **1476**	1·10	1·10
1551	(39p.) multicoloured	1·10	1·10
1552	(45p.) multicoloured	1·40	1·40

No. 1550 was inscribed 'STANDARD LETTER' and originally sold for 36p. each.

No. 1551 was inscribed 'PRIORITY LETTER' and originally sold for 39p. each.

No. 1552 was inscribed 'UK LETTER' and originally sold for 45p. each.

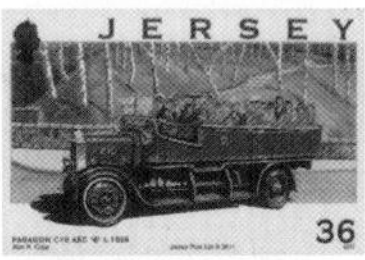

1479 Paragon C10 AEC 'B', c. 1926

2011. Jersey Transport (3rd series). Coaches. Multicoloured.

1553	36p. Type **1479**	1·10	1·10
1554	45p. Rambler Tours Chevrolet, c. 1935	1·40	1·40
1555	55p. JMT Leyland Lioness C14, c. 1938	1·60	1·60
1556	60p. JMT Leyland PLSC1 Lion, c. 1939	1·70	1·70
1557	72p. Mascot Motors Morris CVF 13/5, c. 1948	2·25	2·25
1558	80p. Mascot Motors AEC Regal 4, c. 1961	2·40	2·40

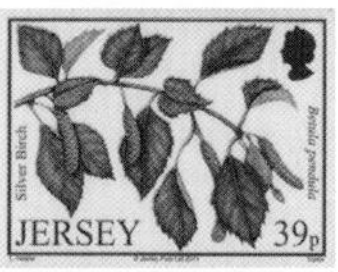

1485 Silver Birch (*Betula pendula*)

2011. Europa. Forests. Multicoloured.

1559	39p. Type **1485**	1·10	1·10
1560	45p. English Oak (*Quercus robur*)	1·40	1·40
1561	55p. Beech (*Fagus sylvatica*)	1·60	1·60
1562	80p. Lime (*Tilia cordata*)	2·40	2·40

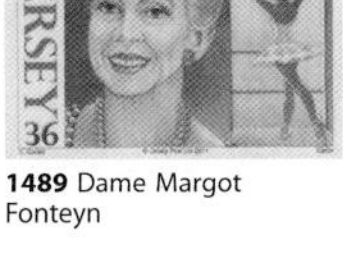

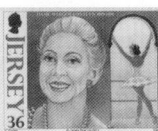

1489 Dame Margot Fonteyn

2011. Women of Achievement. Multicoloured.

1563	36p. Type **1489**	1·10	1·10
1564	45p. Florence Nightingale	1·40	1·40
1565	60p. Marie Curie	1·75	1·75
1566	72p. Mother Teresa	2·25	2·25

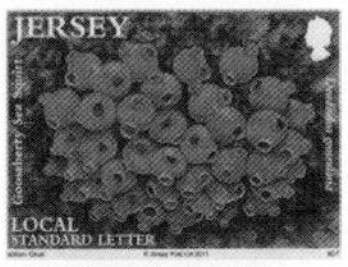

1493 Gooseberry Sea Squirt (*Dendrodoa grossularia*)

2011. Sea Squirts and Sponges. Multicoloured.

1567	(36p.) Type **1493**	1·10	1·10
1568	(39p.) Finger Sponge (*Axinella dissimilis*)	1·10	1·10
1569	(45p.) Purse Sponge (*Scypha ciliata*)	1·40	1·40
1570	60p. Star Squirt (*Botryllus schlosseri*)	1·75	1·75
1571	72p. Light Bulb Sea Squirt (*Clavelina lepadiformis*)	2·25	2·25
1572	80p. Red Sea Squirt (*Polysyncraton lacazei*)	2·40	2·40
MS1573	150×100 mm. As Nos. 1570/2	10·00	10·00

No. 1567 was inscr 'LOCAL STANDARD LETTER' and originally sold for 36p.

No. 1568 was inscr 'LOCAL PRIORITY LETTER' and originally sold for 39p.

No. 1569 was inscr 'UK LETTER' and originally sold for 45p.

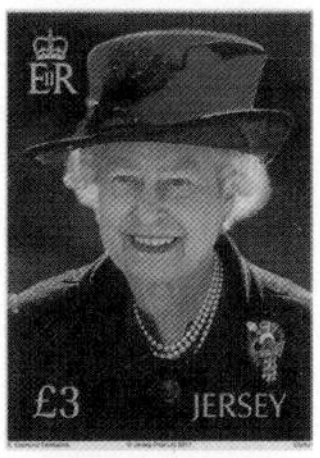

1499 Queen Elizabeth II in Jersey, 2005

2011. 85th Birthday of Queen Elizabeth II

1574	**1499** £3 multicoloured	7·00	7·00
MS1575	150×100 mm. No. 1574	7·00	7·00

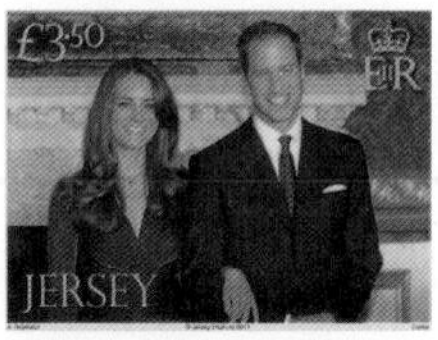

1500 Prince William and Miss Catherine Middleton

2011. Royal Wedding

1576	**1500** £3.50 multicoloured	7·00	7·00

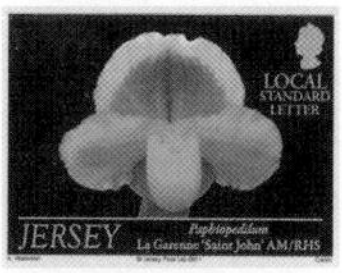

1501 *Paphiopedilum* La Garenne 'St. John'

2011. Jersey Orchids (7th series). Multicoloured.

1577	(36p.) Type **1501**	1·10	1·10
1578	(39p.) *Odontioda* Les Brayes 'Pontac'	1·10	1·10
1579	(45p.) *Phragmipedium* Don Wimber	1·40	1·40
1580	55p. *Kriegerara* Kemp Tower 'Trinity'	1·60	1·60
1581	60p. *Angulocaste* Noirmont 'Isle of Jersey'	1·75	1·75
1582	72p. *Calanthe* Beresford 'Victoria Village'	2·25	2·25
MS1583	110×75 mm. £3 *Miltonia* Point des Pas 'Jersey'	7·00	7·00

No. 1577 was inscr 'LOCAL STANDARD LETTER' and originally sold for 36p.

No. 1578 was inscr 'LOCAL PRIORITY LETTER' and originally sold for 39p.

No. 1579 was inscr 'UK LETTER' and originally sold for 45p.

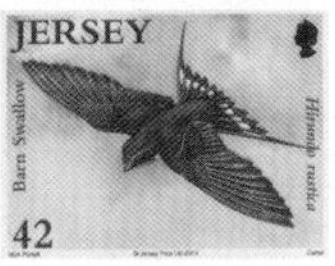

1508 Barn Swallow (*Hirundo rustica*)

2011. Jersey Birdlife (5th series). Summer Visiting Birds. Multicoloured.

1584	42p. Type **1508**	1·25	1·25
1585	50p. Spotted Flycatcher (*Muscicapa striata*)	1·50	1·50
1586	59p. Cuckoo (*Cuculus canorus*)	1·75	1·75
1587	64p. Whitethroat (*Sylvia communis*)	1·90	1·90
1588	79p. Linnet (*Carduelis cannabina*)	2·40	2·40
1589	86p. Swift (*Apus apus*)	2·60	2·60
MS1590	150×100 mm. Nos. 1584/9	11·50	11·50
MS1591	150×100 mm. Nos. 1587/9	7·00	7·00

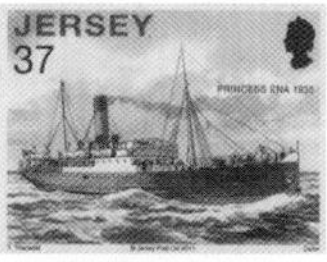

1514 *Princess Ena*, 1935

2011. Shipwrecks. Multicoloured.

1592	37p. Type **1514**	1·10	1·10
1593	49p. *Caledonia*, 1881	1·50	1·50
1594	59p. *Ibex*, 1897	1·75	1·75
1595	64p. *Schokland*, 1943	1·90	1·90
1596	79p. USS PT509, 1944	2·40	2·40
1597	86p. *Superb*, 1850	2·50	2·50
MS1598	110×75 mm. £3 *Roebuck*, 1911	9·00	9·00

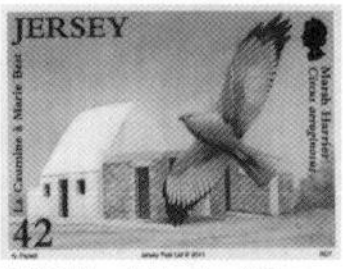

1521 Marsh Harrier (*Circus aeruginosus*) and La Caumine à Marie Best

2011. 75th Anniv of the National Trust for Jersey. Multicoloured.

1599	42p. Type **1521**	1·25	1·25
1600	50p. Swallowtail Butterfly (*Papilio machaon*) and Victoria Tower	1·50	1·50
1601	59p. Dartford Warbler (*Sylvia undata*) and La Cotte Battery	1·75	1·75
1602	64p. Red Squirrel (*Sciurus vulgaris*) and La Moulin de Quétivel	1·90	1·90
1603	75p. Marsh Harrier (*Circus aeruginosus*) and La Caumine à Marie Best painted Green	2·25	2·25
1604	79p. Puffin (*Fratercula arctica*) and North Coast Sea Cliffs	2·40	2·40

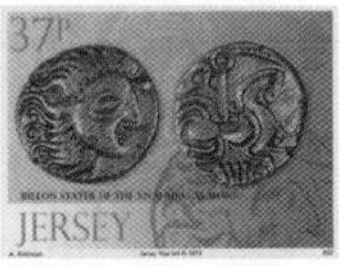

1527 Billion Stater of the XN Series (c. 55-50BC)

2011. Archaeology (2nd series). Buried Treasure. Celtic Coins. Multicoloured.

1605	37p. Type **1527**	1·10	1·10
1606	49p. Durotriges Base Gold Quarter Stater (c. 50-30BC)	1·50	1·50
1607	59p. Baiocasses Gold Stater (c. 50BC)	1·75	1·75
1608	64p. Gold Chute Type Stater (c. 50BC)	1·90	1·90
1609	79p. Southern British Silver Unit (c. 50-30BC)	2·40	2·40
1610	86p. Billion Stater of the Coriosolites Tribe (c. 55-50 BC)	2·50	2·50

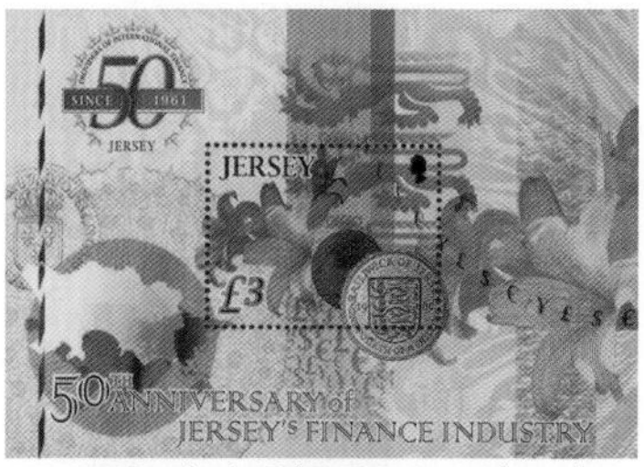

1533 1960 Fourth of a Shilling Coin, Jersey Lilies and Crest (image scaled to 44% of original size)

2011. 50th Anniv of Jersey's Finance Industry. Sheet 110×75 mm

MS1611	**1533** £3 multicoloured	7·00	7·00

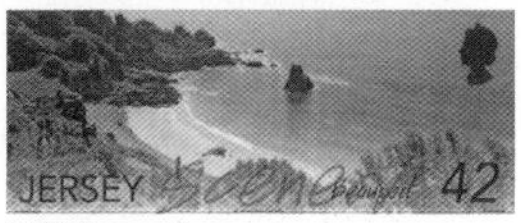

1534 Beauport

2011. Jersey Scenery (3rd series). Multicoloured.

1612	42p. Type **1534**	1·25	1·25
1613	49p. St. Ouen's Bay	1·50	1·50
1614	50p. Ouaisné	1·50	1·50
1615	64p. St. Brelade's Bay	1·90	1·90
1616	79p. Mont Orgueil	2·40	2·40
1617	86p. Portelet	2·50	2·50

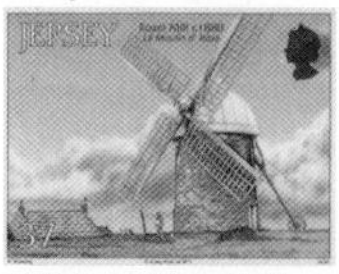

1540 Rozel Mill, c. 1880

2011. Jersey Architecture (1st series). Mills. Multicoloured.

1618	37p. Type **1540**	1·10	1·10
1619	42p. Tesson Mill, c. 1880	1·25	1·25
1620	49p. St. Peter's Mill, c. 1905	1·50	1·50
1621	50p. Ponterrin Mill, 19th century	1·50	1·50
1622	59p. Quétivel Mill, 20th century	1·75	1·75
1623	79p. Gréve De Lecq Mill, 20th century	2·40	2·40

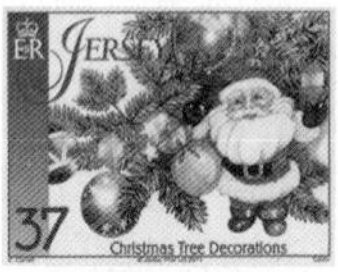

1546 Santa, Baubles and 1970s Light

2011. Christmas. Multicoloured.

1624	37p. Type **1546**	1·10	1·10
1625	42p. Bauble, Bells and Gold Glass Beaded Garland	1·25	1·25
1626	49p. Baubles enclosing Nativity Scenes and Gold Beads	1·50	1·50
1627	50p. Glass Baubles enclosing Santa scenes and 1980s Candle Lights	1·50	1·50
1628	79p. Angel, Bauble and Glass Bead Garland	2·40	2·40
1629	86p. Nativity Bauble and Silver Bead Garland	2·50	2·50

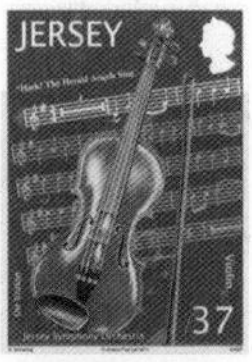

1552 Violin and 'Hark! The Herald Angels Sing' (Mendelssohn)

2011. 25th Anniv of Jersey Symphony Orchestra. Multicoloured.

1630	37p. Type **1552**	1·10	1·10
1631	50p. Trumpets and 'Pomp and Circumstance' (Elgar)	1·50	1·50
1632	59p. Harp and 'Pini di Roma' (Respighi)	1·75	1·75
1633	64p. Timpani and 'La Gazza Ladra' (Rossini)	1·90	1·90
1634	79p. Bassoons and 'Slavonic Dances – Op. 46 No. 1' (Dvorak)	2·40	2·40
1635	86p. French Horn and 'Slavonic Dances – Op. 46 No. 3 (Dvorak)	2·50	2·50

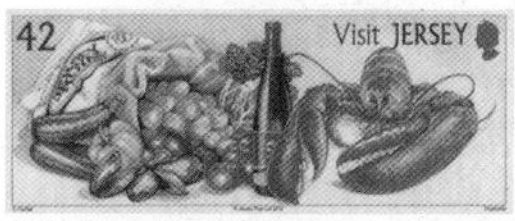

1558 Jersey Produce

2011. Europa. Visit Jersey. Multicoloured.

1636	42p. Type **1558**	1·25	1·25
1637	49p. Surfer, Dinghies and Sand Yachts	1·50	1·50
1638	59p. Cyclist, Family walking and Hikers	1·75	1·75
1639	86p. Re-enactment of 1781 Jersey Militia, Elizabeth Castle and La Hougue Bie	2·50	2·50

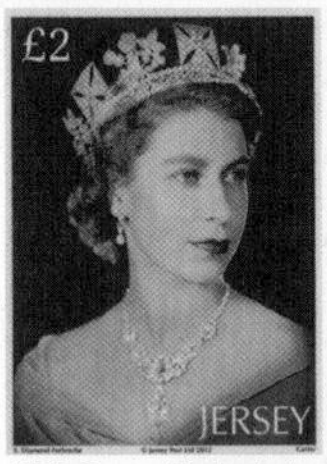

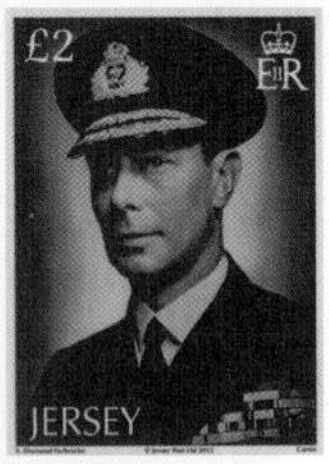

1562 Queen Elizabeth II, 1954 **1563** King George VI

2012. Diamond Jubilee (1st issue)

1640	**1562**	£2 black and new blue	5·00	5·00
1641	**1563**	£2 black and new blue	5·00	5·00
MS1642		126×85 mm. Nos. 1640/1	10·00	10·00

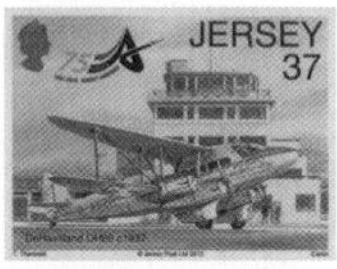

1564 deHavilland DH86, c. 1937

2012. Aviation History (11th series). 75th Anniv of Jersey Airport. Multicoloured.

1643	37p. Type **1564**	1·10	1·10
1644	49p. Bristol 170 Wayfarer, c. 1946	1·50	1·50
1645	50p. Airspeed Ambassador, c. 1953	1·50	1·50
1646	64p. Hawker Siddeley Trident, c. 1966	1·75	1·75
1647	79p. Britten-Norman Trislander, c. 1977	2·25	2·25
1648	86p. Vickers VC10, c. 1987	2·50	2·50
MS1649	110×75 mm. **1570** £3 multicoloured	7·00	7·00

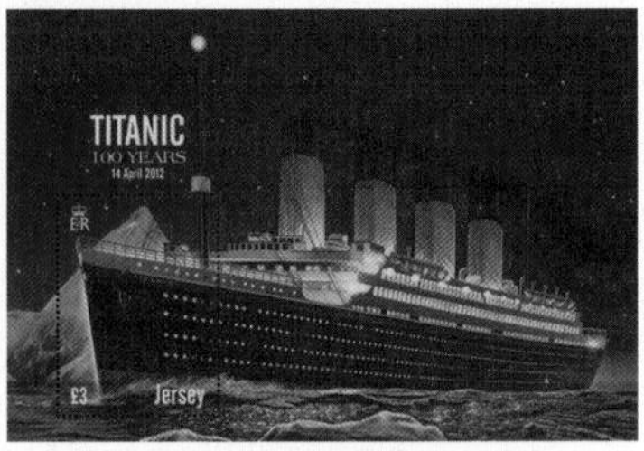

1571 *Titanic (image scaled to 32% of original size)*

2012. Centenary of the Sinking of the *Titanic*. Sheet 150×100 mm

MS1650	**1571** £3 multicoloured	7·00	7·00

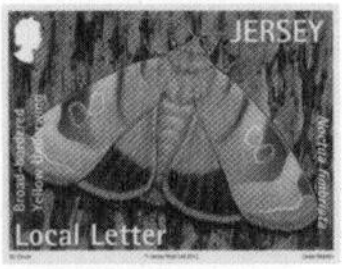

1572 Broad-bordered Yellow Underwing (moth) (*Noctua fimbriata*)

2012. Butterflies and Moths (3rd series). Multicoloured.

1651	(45p.) Type **1572**	1·25	1·25
1652	(55p.) Painted Lady (*Vanessa cardui*)	1·75	1·75
1653	(60p.) Merveille du Jour (moth) (*Dichonia aprilina*)	1·75	1·75
1654	(68p.) Queen of Spain Fritillary (*Issoria lathonia*)	1·90	1·90
1655	(72p.) Large Emerald (moth) (*Geometra papilionaria*)	2·00	2·00
1656	(86p.) Red Admiral (*Vanessa atalanta*)	2·50	2·50
MS1657	150×100 mm. Nos. 1654/6	12·00	12·00

Nos. 1651/6 were inscr 'Local Letter', 'UK Letter', 'Europe', 'Local Large', 'UK Large' and 'International' and were originally sold for 45p., 55p., 60p., 68p., 72p. and 86p. respectively.

POSTAGE DUE STAMPS

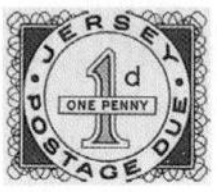

D1

1969

D1	**D1**	1d. violet	65	1·10
D2	**D1**	2d. sepia	90	1·10
D3	**D1**	3d. mauve	1·00	1·10
D4	-	1s. green	5·50	5·00
D5	-	2s.6d. grey	13·00	14·00
D6	-	5s. red	15·00	16·00

DESIGNS: 1s., 2s.6d., 5s. Map.

1971. Decimal Currency. Design as Nos. D4/6, but values in new currency.

D7	½p. black	10	10
D8	1p. blue	10	10
D9	2p. brown	10	10
D10	3p. purple	10	10
D11	4p. red	10	10
D12	5p. green	10	10
D13	6p. orange	10	10
D14	7p. yellow	10	10
D15	8p. blue	15	20
D16	10p. green	15	20
D17	11p. brown	30	35
D18	14p. violet	40	50
D19	25p. green	45	90
D20	50p. purple	1·10	1·70

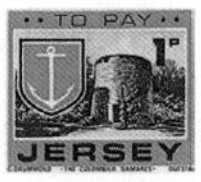

D4 Arms of St. Clement and Dovecote at Samares

1978. Parish Arms and Views.

D21	**D4**	1p. black and green	10	10
D22	-	2p. black and yellow	10	10
D23	-	3p. black and brown	10	10
D24	-	4p. black and red	10	10
D25	-	5p. black and blue	10	10
D26	-	10p. black and olive	10	10
D27	-	12p. black and blue	15	10
D28	-	14p. black and orange	20	15
D29	-	15p. black and mauve	25	30
D30	-	20p. black and green	30	40
D31	-	50p. black and brown	90	80
D32	-	£1 black and blue	1·40	1·40

DESIGNS: 2p. Arms of St. Lawrence and Handois Reservoir; 3p. Arms of St. John and Sorel Point; 4p. Arms of St. Ouen and Pinnacle Rock; 5p. Arms of St. Peter and Quetivel Mill; 10p. Arms of St. Martin and St. Catherine's Breakwater; 12p. Arms of St. Helier and Harbour; 14p. Arms of St. Saviour and Highlands College; 15p. Arms of St. Brelade and Beauport Bay; 20p. Arms of Grouville and La Hougue Bie; 50p. Arms of St. Mary and Perry Farm; £1 Arms of Trinity and Bouley Bay.

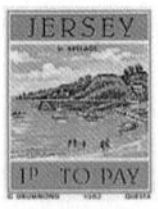

D16 St. Brelade

1982. Jersey Harbours.

D33	**D16**	1p. green	10	10
D34	-	2p. yellow	10	10
D35	-	3p. brown	10	10
D36	-	4p. red	10	10
D37	-	5p. blue	10	10
D38	-	6p. green	10	15
D39	-	7p. mauve	15	20
D40	-	8p. red	15	20
D41	-	9p. green	20	20
D42	-	10p. blue	20	20
D43	-	20p. green	40	40
D44	-	30p. purple	60	60
D45	-	40p. orange	80	80
D46	-	£1 violet	2·00	2·00

DESIGNS: 2p. St. Aubin; 3p. Rozel; 4p. Greve de Lecq; 5p. Bouley Bay; 6p. St. Catherine; 7p. Gorey; 8p. Bonne Nuit; 9p. La Rocque; 10p. St. Helier; 20p. Ronez; 30p. La Collette; 40p. Elizabeth Castle; £1 Upper Harbour Marina.

Pt. 1

JHALAWAR

A state of Rajasthan, India. Now uses Indian stamps.

4 paisa = 1 anna.

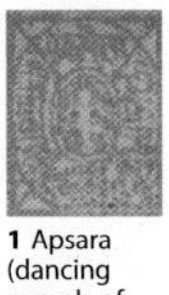

1 Apsara (dancing nymph of Hindu Paradise)

1886. Imperf.

1	**1**	1p. green	5·00	20·00
2	**1**	¼a. green	1·50	2·50

The ¼a. is larger and has a different frame.

Pt. 1

JIND

A "convention" state of the Punjab, India, which now uses Indian stamps.

12 pies = 1 anna; 16 annas = 1 rupee.

J1 (½a.)

1874. Imperf.

J8	**J1**	½a. blue	1·00	5·00
J9	**J1**	1a. purple	3·25	15·00
J3	**J1**	2a. bistre	1·25	6·00
J11	**J1**	4a. green	3·75	20·00
J12	**J1**	8a. purple	8·50	11·00

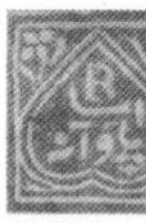

J6 (¼a.)

1882. Various designs and sizes. Imperf or perf.

J16	**J6**	¼a. brown	40	1·50
J19	**J6**	½a. bistre	1·00	60
J20	**J6**	1a. brown	1·75	3·25
J22	**J6**	2a. blue	3·00	1·25
J23	**J6**	4a. green	2·75	1·25
J25	**J6**	8a. red	6·50	4·50

Stamps of India (Queen Victoria) overprinted

1885. Optd **JHIND STATE** vert (curved).

1	**23**	½a. turquoise	9·00	8·00
2	-	1a. purple	55·00	85·00
3	-	2a. blue	27·00	26·00
4	-	4a. green (No. 71)	85·00	£120
5	-	8a. mauve	£550	
6	-	1r. grey (No. 101)	£600	

1885. Optd **JEEND STATE.**

7	**23**	½a. turquoise	£180	
8	-	1a. purple	£180	
9	-	2a. blue	£180	
10	-	4a. green (No. 71)	£275	
11	-	8a. mauve	£250	
12	-	1r. grey (No. 101)	£250	

1886. Optd **JHIND STATE** horiz.

17	**23**	½a. turquoise	1·00	10
18	-	1a. purple	4·25	20
20	-	1a.6p. brown	3·75	5·00
21	-	2a. blue	4·50	40
23	-	3a. orange	6·00	1·25
15		4a. green (No. 71)	80·00	
24	-	4a. green (No. 96)	7·00	3·75
27	-	6a. brown	7·00	22·00
28	-	8a. mauve	15·00	28·00
30	-	12a. purple on red	11·00	32·00
31	-	1r. grey (No. 101)	16·00	75·00
32	**37**	1r. green and red	17·00	80·00
33	**38**	2r. red and orange	£450	£1400
34	**38**	3r. brown and green	£650	£1200
35	**38**	5r. blue and violet	£700	£1000

1900. Optd **JHIND STATE** horiz.

36	**40**	3p. red	1·10	2·75
37	**40**	3p. grey	40	4·50
38	**23**	½a. green	6·50	9·00
40	-	1a. red	2·00	10·00

Stamps of India optd JHIND STATE

1903. King Edward VII.

41	**41**	3p. grey	35	20
43	-	½a. green (No. 122)	3·50	2·25
44	-	1a. red (No. 123)	3·25	2·50
46	-	2a. lilac	4·25	1·25
47	-	2½a. blue	1·75	8·00
48	-	3a. orange	4·50	75
50	-	4a. olive	13·00	14·00
51	-	6a. bistre	11·00	30·00
52	-	8a. mauve	6·00	26·00
54	-	12a. purple on red	5·00	17·00
55	-	1r. green and red	6·50	30·00

1907. King Edward VII (inscr "INDIA POSTAGE and REVENUE").

56	½a. green (No. 149)	1·00	20
57	1a. red (No. 150)	2·50	70

1913. King George V.

58	**55**	3p. grey	10	2·25
59	**56**	½a. green	10	75
60	**57**	1a. red	10	45
61	**59**	2a. purple	15	4·25
62	**62**	3a. orange	1·50	15·00
63	**64**	6a. bistre	11·00	38·00

1914. Stamps of India (King George V) optd **JIND STATE** in two lines.

64	**55**	3p. grey	1·25	60
65	**56**	½a. green	3·50	15
66	**57**	1a. red	1·75	15
80	**57**	1a. brown	6·50	3·75
67	**58**	1½a. brown (A. No. 163)	5·00	7·50
68	**58**	1½a. brown (B. No. 165)	75	1·50
81	**58**	1½a. red (B.)	20	1·75
69	**59**	2a. purple	4·50	1·50
70	**61**	2a.6p. blue	50	5·50
82	**61**	2a.6p. orange	1·75	9·50
71	**62**	3a. orange	50	4·75
83	**62**	3a. blue	3·00	7·00
72	**63**	4a. olive	3·00	9·50
73a	**64**	6a. brown	7·00	20·00
74	**65**	8a. mauve	7·00	24·00
75	**66**	12a. red	6·00	28·00
76	**67**	1r. brown and green	12·00	32·00
77	**67**	2r. red and brown	10·00	£150
78	**67**	5r. blue and violet	55·00	£400

1922. No. 192 of India optd **JIND.**

79	**57**	9p. on 1a. red	1·25	17·00

Stamps of India optd JIND STATE in one line

1927. King George V.

84	**55**	3p. grey	10	10
85	**56**	½a. green	10	35
86	**80**	9p. green	2·25	40
87	**57**	1a. brown	15	10
88	**82**	1a.3p. mauve	25	30
89	**58**	1½a. red	1·00	4·50
90w	**70**	2a. lilac	5·00	40
91w	**61**	2a.6p. orange	1·25	15·00
92	**62**	3a. blue	7·00	23·00
93w	**83**	3a.6p. blue	60	24·00
94w	**71**	4a. green	2·00	4·50
95	**64**	6a. bistre	65	26·00
96	**65**	8a. mauve	9·50	2·25
97w	**66**	12a. red	10·00	26·00
98	**67**	1r. brown and green	8·50	9·50
99	**67**	2r. red and orange	55·00	£180
100	**67**	5r. blue and violet	13·00	50·00
101	**67**	10r. green and red	16·00	18·00
102	**67**	15r. blue and olive	£130	£900
103	**67**	25r. orange and blue	£200	£1200

1934. King George V.

104	**79**	½a. green	30	25
105	**81**	1a. brown	2·00	30
106	**59**	2a. orange	5·50	70
107	**62**	3a. red	3·25	40
108	**63**	4a. olive	3·25	1·75

1937. King George VI.

109	**91**	3p. slate	10·00	3·25
110	**91**	½a. brown	75	6·50
111	**91**	9p. green	75	4·00
112	**91**	1a. red	75	75
113	**92**	2a. red	2·50	24·00
114	-	2a.6p. violet	1·25	30·00
115	-	3a. green	7·00	27·00
116	-	3a.6p. blue	5·00	30·00
117	-	4a. brown	11·00	25·00
118	-	6a. green	8·00	40·00
119	-	8a. violet	8·50	30·00
120	-	12a. red	3·50	40·00
121	**93**	1r. slate and brown	12·00	55·00
122	**93**	2r. purple and brown	15·00	£170
123	**93**	5r. green and blue	32·00	£110
124	**93**	10r. purple and red	55·00	95·00
125	**93**	15r. brown and green	£100	£1000
126	**93**	25r. slate and purple	£800	£1300

1941. Stamps of India (King George VI) optd **JIND.** (a) On issue of 1937.

127	**91**	3p. slate	18·00	26·00
128	**91**	½a. brown	1·25	3·50
129	**91**	9p. green	16·00	23·00
130	**91**	1a. red	1·00	7·50
131	**93**	1r. slate and brown	11·00	35·00
132	**93**	2r. purple and brown	20·00	45·00
133	**93**	5r. green and blue	40·00	£130
134	**93**	10r. purple and red	55·00	£110
135	**93**	15r. brown and green	£170	£225
136	**93**	25r. slate and purple	60·00	£425

(b) On issue of 1940.

137	**100a**	3p. slate	50	2·00
138	**100a**	½a. mauve	50	2·50
139	**100a**	9p. green	75	4·50
140	**100a**	1a. red	2·00	1·50
141	**101**	1a.3p. yellow-brown	1·00	6·50
142	**101**	1½a. violet	10·00	6·00
143	**101**	2a. red	1·75	7·00
144	**101**	3a. violet	25·00	8·00
145	**101**	3½a. blue	9·00	16·00
146	**102**	4a. brown	8·50	8·50
147	**102**	6a. green	9·00	22·00
148	**102**	8a. violet	7·00	20·00
149	**102**	12a. purple	14·00	25·00

OFFICIAL STAMPS
Postage stamps of Jind optd SERVICE

1885. Nos. 1/3 (Queen Victoria).

O1	**O23**	½a. green	3·50	50
O2	-	1a. purple	70	10
O3	-	2a. blue	45·00	50·00

1886. Nos. 17/32 and No. 38 (Queen Victoria).

O12	**23**	½a. turquoise	4·00	10
O22	-	½a. green (No. 38)	4·25	40
O14	-	1a. purple	19·00	1·50
O16	-	2a. blue	3·50	30
O17	-	4a. green (No. 24)	6·50	3·00
O19	-	8a. mauve	9·00	6·00
O21	**37**	1r. green and red	9·00	70·00

1903. Nos. 42/55 (King Edward VII).

O23	**41**	3p. grey	1·50	10
O25	-	½a. green (No. 43)	4·50	10
O26	-	1a. red (No. 44)	4·75	10
O28	-	2a. lilac	2·75	10
O29	-	4a. olive	3·75	45
O31	-	8a. mauve	9·00	1·50
O32	-	1r. green and red	2·75	2·25

1907. Nos. 56/7 (King Edward VII).

O33	½a. green	1·50	10
O34	1a. red	2·75	10

1914. Official stamps of India. Nos. O75/96 (King George V) optd **JIND STATE.**

O35	**55**	3p. grey	10	10
O36	**56**	½a. green	10	10
O37	**57**	1a. red	75	10
O46	**57**	1a. brown	60	10
O39	**59**	2a. purple	25	30
O40	**63**	4a. olive	1·50	20
O41	**64**	6a. bistre	2·75	2·25
O42	**65**	8a. mauve	1·00	1·00
O43	**67**	1r. brown and green	5·00	2·00
O44	**67**	2r. red and brown	18·00	75·00
O45	**67**	5r. blue and violet	32·00	£350

Stamps of India optd JIND STATE SERVICE

1927. King George V.

O47	**55**	3p. grey	10	20
O48	**56**	½a. green	10	1·00
O49	**80**	9p. green	75	15
O50	**57**	1a. brown	10	10
O51	**82**	1a.3p. mauve	40	15
O52	**70**	2a. lilac	25	15
O64	**59**	2a. orange	30	15
O53	**61**	2a.6p. orange	1·50	21·00
O54	**71**	4a. green	35	25
O55w	**64**	6a. bistre	6·50	22·00
O56w	**65**	8a. mauve	75	1·75
O57	**66**	12a. red	2·25	23·00
O58	**67**	1r. brown and green	6·50	7·00
O59	**67**	2r. red and orange	70·00	55·00
O60	**67**	5r. blue and purple	13·00	£350
O61	**67**	10r. green and red	45·00	£180

1934. King George V.

O62	**79**	½a. green	20	15
O63	**81**	1a. brown	20	15
O65	**63**	4a. olive	7·00	30

1937. King George VI.

O66	**91**	½a. brown	80·00	30
O67	**91**	9p. green	4·50	24·00
O68	**91**	1a. red	3·50	30
O69	**93**	1r. slate and brown	55·00	75·00
O70	**93**	2r. purple and brown	60·00	£350
O71	**93**	5r. green and blue	£100	£500
O72	**93**	10r. purple and red	£475	£1400

1939. Official stamps of India optd **JIND**.

O73	**O20**	3p. slate	60	2·00
O74	**O20**	½a. brown	4·00	1·25
O75	**O20**	½a. purple	60	30
O76	**O20**	9p. green	3·00	16·00
O77	**O20**	1a. red	3·75	15
O78	**O20**	1½a. violet	9·00	3·00
O79	**O20**	2a. orange	8·50	30
O80	**O20**	2½a. violet	5·00	13·00
O81	**O20**	4a. brown	8·50	8·50
O82	**O20**	8a. violet	12·00	13·00

1943. Stamps of India (King George VI) optd **JIND SERVICE.**

O83	**93**	1r. slate and brown	18·00	75·00
O84	**93**	2r. purple and brown	42·00	£225
O85	**93**	5r. green and blue	70·00	£550
O86	**93**	10r. purple and red	£170	£750

Pt. 1

JOHORE

A state of the Federation of Malaya, incorporated in Malaysia in 1963.

100 cents = 1 dollar (Straits or Malayan).
1996. 100 sen = 1 ringgit

Queen Victoria stamps of Straits Settlements overprinted

1876. Optd with Crescent and Star.

1	**1**	2c. brown	£21000	£6500

1882. Optd **JOHORE.**

6	2c. pink (with full point)	£200	£200
8	2c. pink (no full point)	£120	£130

1884. Optd **JOHOR.**

10	2c. pink (no full point)	22·00	12·00
14	2c. pink (with full point)	£200	75·00

1891. Surch **JOHOR Two CENTS.**

17	2c. on 24c. green	28·00	40·00

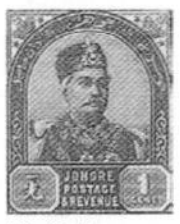

21 Sultan Aboubakar

1891

21	**21**	1c. purple	1·00	50
22	**21**	2c. purple and yellow	60	1·50
23	**21**	3c. purple and red	60	50
24	**21**	4c. purple and black	2·75	20·00
25	**21**	5c. purple and green	7·00	21·00
26	**21**	6c. purple and blue	8·00	21·00
27	**21**	$1 green and red	85·00	£170

1892. Surch **3 cents.**

28	3c. on 4c. purple and black	2·50	50
29	3c. on 5c. purple and green	2·00	3·75
30	3c. on 6c. purple and blue	3·50	6·00
31	3c. on $1 green and red	12·00	75·00

1896. Sultan's Coronation. Optd **KEMAHKOTAAN.**

32	1c. purple	50	1·00
33	2c. purple and yellow	50	1·00
34	3c. purple and red	55	1·00
35	4c. purple and black	80	2·25
36	5c. purple and green	5·50	7·50
37	6c. purple and blue	3·50	6·50
38	$1 green and red	60·00	£130

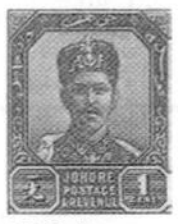

24 Sultan Ibrahim

1896

39	**24**	1c. green	80	2·75
40	**24**	2c. green and blue	50	1·00
41	**24**	3c. green and purple	4·00	4·25
42	**24**	4c. green and red	1·00	3·25
43	**24**	4c. yellow and red	1·50	2·25
44	**24**	5c. green and brown	2·00	4·25
45	**24**	6c. green and yellow	2·00	6·00
46	**24**	10c. green and black	7·00	50·00
47	**24**	25c. green and mauve	9·00	48·00
48	**24**	50c. green and red	16·00	50·00
49	**24**	$1 purple and green	32·00	75·00
50	**24**	$2 purple and red	55·00	80·00
51	**24**	$3 purple and blue	45·00	£120
52	**24**	$4 purple and brown	45·00	85·00
53	**24**	$5 purple and yellow	95·00	£130

1903. Surch in figures and words.

54	3c. on 4c. yellow and red	60	1·10
55	10c. on 4c. green & red (A)	2·50	12·00
58	10c. on 4c. yellow & red (B)	20·00	40·00
59	10c. on 4c. green & red (B)	9·50	70·00
56	50c. on $3 purple and blue	30·00	85·00
60	50c. on $5 purple and yellow	80·00	£170
57	$1 on $2 purple and red	65·00	£120

10c. on 4c. Type A, "cents" in small letters. Type B, "CENTS" in capitals.

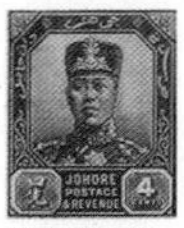

33 Sultan Sir Ibrahim

1904

78	**33**	1c. purple and green	1·25	15
90	**33**	2c. purple and orange	1·00	6·00
63	**33**	3c. purple and black	4·75	60
91	**33**	4c. purple and red	1·75	70
109	**33**	5c. purple and green	50	30
83	**33**	8c. purple and blue	4·00	11·00
84	**33**	10c. purple and black	60·00	3·00
116	**33**	25c. purple and green	4·50	1·00
119	**33**	50c. purple and red	3·75	1·60
120	**33**	$1 green and mauve	3·75	1·25
121	**33**	$2 green and red	10·00	4·00
72	**33**	$3 green and blue	40·00	85·00
73	**33**	$4 green and brown	40·00	£120
124	**33**	$5 green and orange	60·00	50·00
75	**33**	$10 green and black	£110	£200
76	**33**	$50 green and blue	£375	£500
77	**33**	$100 green and red	£550	£900
128	**33**	$500 blue and red	£20000	

1912. Surch **3 CENTS.** and bars.

88	3c. on 8c. purple and blue	10·00	10·00

1918

103	1c. purple and black	30	20
89	2c. purple and green	50	1·50
104	2c. purple and sepia	1·25	4·25
105	2c. green	60	40
106	3c. green	2·00	5·50
107	3c. purple and sepia	1·40	1·50
110	6c. purple and red	50	50
93	10c. purple and blue	2·00	1·40
112	10c. purple and yellow	50	25
113	12c. purple and blue	1·00	1·25
114	12c. blue	55·00	2·25
115	21c. purple and orange	2·00	3·00
117	30c. purple and orange	9·50	12·00
118	40c. purple and brown	9·50	13·00

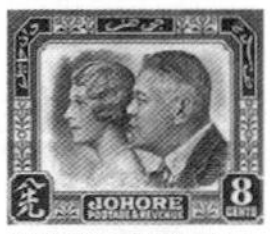

37 Sultan Sir Ibrahim and Sultana

1935

129	**37**	8c. violet and grey	5·00	3·25

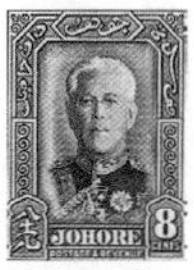

38 Sultan Sir Ibrahim

1940

130	**38**	8c. black and blue	24·00	1·00

1948. Silver Wedding. As T **61/2** of Jamaica.

131	10c. violet	20	75
132	$5 green	26·00	50·00

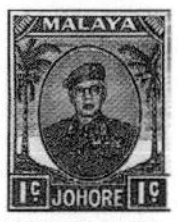

39 Sultan Sir Ibrahim

1949

133	**39**	1c. black	50	10
134	**39**	2c. orange	35	20
135	**39**	3c. green	2·00	1·00
136	**39**	4c. brown	1·75	10
136a	**39**	5c. purple	2·00	30
137	**39**	6c. grey	1·75	20
138	**39**	8c. red	4·50	1·25
138a	**39**	8c. green	8·50	2·25
139	**39**	10c. mauve	1·25	10
139a	**39**	12c. red	10·00	7·50
140	**39**	15c. blue	4·00	10
141	**39**	20c. black and green	2·50	1·00
141a	**39**	20c. blue	2·00	10
142	**39**	25c. purple and orange	3·75	10
142a	**39**	30c. red and purple	2·50	2·75
142b	**39**	35c. red and purple	11·00	1·25
143	**39**	40c. red and purple	7·50	17·00
144	**39**	50c. black and blue	5·00	10
145	**39**	$1 blue and purple	11·00	2·00
146	**39**	$2 green and red	27·00	13·00
147	**39**	$5 green and brown	45·00	17·00

1949. U.P.U. As T **63/6** of Jamaica.

148	10c. purple	30	40
149	15c. blue	2·00	1·25
150	25c. orange	65	3·50
151	50c. black	1·25	3·75

1953. Coronation. As T **71** of Jamaica.

152	10c. black and purple	1·25	10

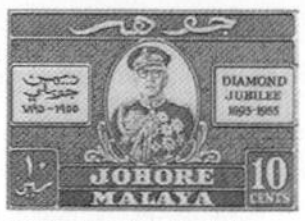

40 Sultan Sir Ibrahim

1955. Diamond Jubilee of Sultan.

153	**40**	10c. red	10	10

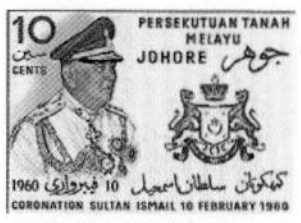

41 Sultan Sir Ismail and Johore Coat of Arms

1960. Coronation of Sultan.

154	**41**	10c. multicoloured	20	20

1960. As Nos. 92/102 of Kedah but with inset portrait of Sultan Sir Ismail.

155	1c. black	10	50
156	2c. red	10	1·25
157	4c. sepia	10	10
158	5c. lake	10	10
159	8c. green	3·00	4·00
160	10c. purple	30	10
161	20c. blue	2·00	1·00
162	50c. black and blue	50	20
163	$1 blue and purple	6·50	7·00
164	$2 green and red	19·00	24·00
165	$5 brown and green	40·00	42·00

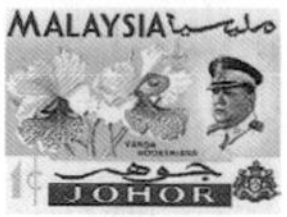

42 *Vanda hookeriana*

1965. Inset portrait of Sultan Ismail. Multicoloured.

166	1c. Type **42**	10	30
167	2c. *Arundina graminifolia*	10	1·00
168	5c. *Paphiopedilum niveum*	10	10
169	6c. *Spathoglottis plicata*	40	30
170	10c. *Arachnis flos-aeris*	40	20
171	15c. *Rhyncostylis retusa*	1·50	10
172	20c. *Phalaenopsis violacea*	1·50	75

The higher values used in Johore were Nos. 20/7 of Malaysia (National Issues).

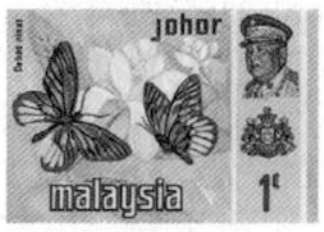

44 *Delias ninus*

1971. Butterflies. Inset portrait of Sultan Ismail. Multicoloured.

175	1c. Type **44**	50	2·00
176	2c. *Danaus melanippus*	1·50	2·75
177	5c. *Parthenos sylvia*	1·50	20
178	6c. *Papilio demoleus*	1·50	2·25
179	10c. *Hebomoia glaucippe*	1·50	20
180	15c. *Precis orithya*	1·75	10
181	20c. *Valeria valeria*	1·75	50

The higher values in use with this issue were Nos. 64/71 of Malaysia (National Issues).

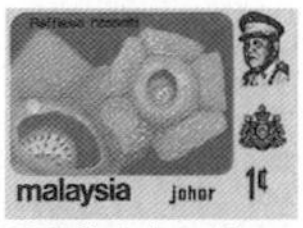

45 *Rafflesia hasseltii* (inset portrait of Sultan Ismail)

1979. Flowers. Multicoloured.

188	1c. Type **45**	10	1·00
189	2c. *Pterocarpus indicus*	10	1·00
190	5c. *Lagerstroemia speciosa*	10	60
191	10c. *Durio zibethinus*	15	10
192	15c. *Hibiscus rosa-sinensis*	15	10
193	20c. *Rhododendron scortechinii*	20	25
194	25c. *Etlingera elatior* (inscr "Phaeomeria speciosa")	40	25

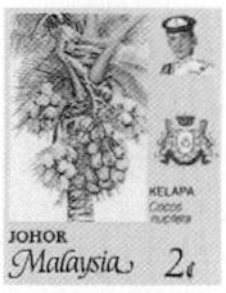

46 Coconuts (inset portrait of Sultan Mahmood)

1986. Agricultural Products of Malaysia. Multicoloured.

202	1c. Coffee	10	20
203	2c. Type **46**	10	40
204	5c. Cocoa	15	10

205	10c. Black pepper	15	10
206	15c. Rubber	25	10
207	20c. Oil palm	25	15
208	30c. Rice	30	15

2003. As T **46** but renominated in 'sen'. Multicoloured.

209	30s. Rice	1·75	10

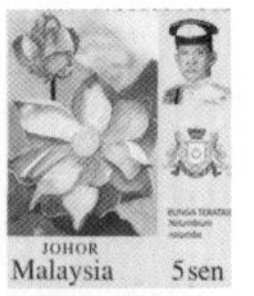

47 *Nelumbium nelumbo* (sacred lotus) (Inset portrait of Sultan Mahmud Iskandar)

2007. Garden Flowers. Multicoloured.

210	5s. Type **47**	10	10
211	10s. *Hydrangea macrophylla*	15	10
212	20s. *Hippeastrum reticulatum*	25	15
213	30s. *Bougainvillea*	40	20
214	40s. *Ipomoea indica*	50	30
215	50s. *Hibiscus rosa-sinensis*	65	35
MS216	100×85 mm. Nos. 210/15	1·40	1·40

POSTAGE DUE STAMPS

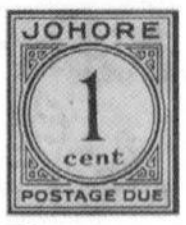

D1

1938

D1	**D1**	1c. red	21·00	50·00
D2	**D1**	4c. green	45·00	40·00
D3	**D1**	8c. orange	50·00	£160
D4	**D1**	10c. brown	50·00	50·00
D5	**D1**	12c. purple	55·00	£140

Pt. 1, Pt. 19

JORDAN

A territory to the E. of Israel, formerly called Transjordan; under British mandate from 1918 to 1946. Independent kingdom since 1946.

1920. 1000 milliemes = 100 piastres = £1 Egyptian.
1927. 1000 milliemes = £1 Palestinian.
1950. 1000 fils = 1 Jordan dinar.
2004. 1 dinar =100 qirsh/piastre=1000 fils.

شرقي الاردن

(1) "East of Jordan"

1920. Stamps of Palestine optd with T **1**.

1	3	1m. brown	2·75	3·75
10	3	2m. green	2·00	3·50
3	3	3m. brown	3·00	3·50
4	3	4m. red	3·25	3·25
5	3	5m. orange	8·00	3·25
14	3	1p. blue	3·00	3·75
15	3	2p. olive	10·00	10·00
16	3	5p. purple	6·00	12·00
17	3	9p. ochre	6·00	45·00
18	3	10p. blue	15·00	45·00
19	3	20p. grey	17·00	70·00

عشر القرش

(2) Tenth of a piastre

القرش

(3) Piastre

1922. Handstamped with T **2** or **3** (piastre values). (a) 1920 issue of Jordan (No. 1 etc).

28	2	1/10p. on 1m. brown	25·00	30·00
29	2	2/10p. on 2m. green	29·00	29·00
22	2	3/10p. on 3m. brown	15·00	15·00
23	2	4/10p. on 4m. red	60·00	65·00
24	2	5/10p. on 5m. orange	£180	£100
31	3	1p. on 1p. blue	£200	60·00
25	3	2p. on 2p. olive	£250	75·00
26	3	5p. on 5p. purple	65·00	80·00
27a	3	9p. on 9p. ochre	£130	£140
33	3	10p. on 10p. blue	£850	£1000
34	3	20p. on 20p. grey	£650	£850

(b) Type **3** of Palestine.

35	10p. on 10p. blue	£1800	£2500
36	20p. on 20p. grey	£2500	£3000

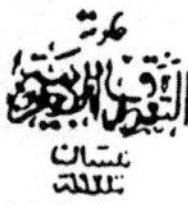

(4) "Arab Government of the East, April, 1921"

1922. Stamps of Jordan handstamped with T **4**.

45	1m. brown	16·00	20·00
46a	2m. green	10·00	10·00
39b	3m. brown	9·00	9·00
40	4m. red	60·00	65·00
41a	5m. orange	19·00	12·00
48a	1p. blue	22·00	11·00
42c	2p. olive	17·00	12·00
43b	5p. purple	65·00	85·00
44b	9p. ochre	70·00	85·00
52a	10p. blue	£1100	£1600
53a	20p. grey	£1100	£1800

حكومة الشرق
العربية
يسان سنة ٩٢١

(5) "Arab Government of the East, April, 1921"

1923. Stamps of Jordan optd with T **5**.

62	1m. brown	19·00	32·00
63	2m. green	18·00	21·00
56	3m. brown	18·00	19·00
57	4m. red	20·00	19·00
64	5m. orange	14·00	14·00
65	1p. blue	14·00	18·00
59	2p. olive	23·00	21·00
60	5p. purple	75·00	£100
66	9p. ochre	90·00	£130
67	10p. blue	85·00	£130
68	20p. grey	85·00	£130

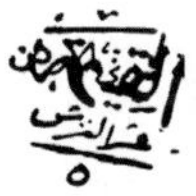

(6)

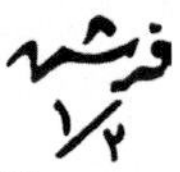

(7)

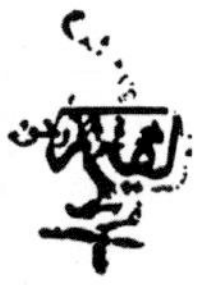

(8)

غرش

(9)

1923. Various stamps surch as T **6/9**. (a) 1920 issue of Jordan (No. 1 etc).

70	-	2½/10thsp. on 5m.	£170	£170
70c	6	5/10p. on 3m.	†	£5000
70d	6	5/10p. on 5m.	£2500	
70e	9	2p. on 20p.		

(b) No. 7 of Palestine.

71	6	5/10p. on 3m.	£3000	

(c) 1922 issue of Jordan (Nos. 22 etc).

72		5/10p. on 3m.	£7000	
73		5/10p. on 5p.	75·00	85·00
73b		5/10p. on 9p.	£1300	
74	7	½p. on 5p.	75·00	85·00
75a	7	½p. on 9p.	£350	£400
77	8	1p. on 5p.	85·00	£110

(d) 1922 issue of Jordan (Nos. 396 etc).

78b	6	5/10p. on 3m.	50·00	60·00
79	6	5/10p. on 5p.	10·00	19·00
79d	6	5/10p. on 9p.		£1200
80c	7	½p. on 2p.	60·00	£110
81a	7	½p. on 5p.	£1000	
83b	8	1p. on 5p.	£2000	£2250

(e) 1923 issue of Jordan (Nos. 56 etc).

84	6	5/10p. on 3m.	29·00	45·00
85	7	½p. on 9p.	95·00	£160
87	9	1p. on 10p.	£2250	£2500
88	9	2p. on 20p.	65·00	85·00

حكومة
الشرق العربية
٩ شعبان ١٣٤١

(10) "Arab Government of the East, 9 Sha'ban, 1341"

1923. Stamps of Saudi Arabia optd with T **10**.

89	11	⅛p. brown	5·00	4·25
96	11	¼ on⅛p. brown (47)	15·00	8·00
90	11	½p. red	5·00	4·25
91	11	1p. blue	4·00	1·25
92	11	1½p. lilac	4·25	2·50
93	11	2p. orange	5·00	8·00
94	11	3p. brown	13·00	19·00
95	11	5p. green	29·00	42·00
97	11	10 on 5p. green (49)	30·00	38·00

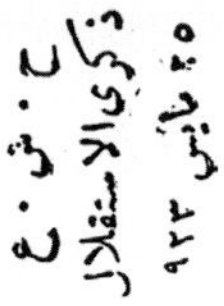

(11) "Arab Government of the East, Commemoration of Independence, 25 May, 1923"

1923. Stamps of Palestine optd with T **11**.

98A	3	1m. brown	23·00	23·00
99A	3	2m. green	42·00	50·00
100A	3	3m. brown	14·00	18·00
101A	3	4m. red	15·00	18·00
102A	3	5m. orange	70·00	80·00
103B	3	1p. blue	70·00	85·00
104A	3	2p. olive	70·00	90·00
105A	3	5p. purple	80·00	90·00
106B	3	9p. ochre	70·00	85·00
107A	3	10p. blue	80·00	£100
108B	3	20p. grey	85·00	£110

1923. No. 107 surch with T **9**.

109	1p. on 10p. blue	£6000	

نصف قرش

(12)

1923. No. 92 surch with T **12**.

110	½p. on 1½p. lilac	12·00	14·00

حكومة
الشرق العربية
٩ شعبان ١٣٤١

(13a) "Arab Government of the East, 9 Sha'ban, 1341"

1923. Stamp of Saudi Arabia handstamped as T **13a**.

112	11	½p. red	15·00	16·00

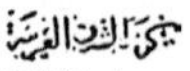

(15) "Arab Government of the East"

1924. Stamps of Saudi Arabia optd with T **15**.

114	½p. red	22·00	16·00
115	1p. blue	£300	£200
116	1½p. violet	£350	

د · ق · ج
ملك العرب
١ ج · ث ٣٤٢

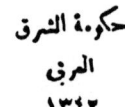

(16) "Commemorating the coming of His Majesty the King of the Arabs" and date

1924. Stamps of Saudi Arabia optd with T **15** and **16**.

117	½p. red	3·25	3·25
118	1p. blue	4·00	3·50
119	1½p. violet	4·25	4·50
120	2p. orange	13·00	13·00

حكومة الشرق
العربي
١٣٤٢

(17) "Government of the Arab East, 1342"

1924. Stamps of Saudi Arabia optd with T **17**.

125	⅛p. brown	1·50	1·25
126	¼p. green	1·50	70
127	½p. red	1·50	70
129	1p. blue	10·00	1·50
130	1½p. lilac	6·50	6·50
131	2p. orange	4·75	3·50
132	3p. red	4·75	4·75
133	5p. green	6·50	6·50
134	10p. purple and mauve	15·00	16·00

حكومة الشرق العربي
سنة ١٣٤٣

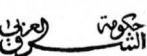

(18) "Government of the Arab East, 1343"

1925. Stamps of Saudi Arabia optd with T **18**.

135	⅛p. brown	1·00	1·50
136	¼p. blue	2·00	3·00
137	½p. red	1·50	60
138	1p. green	1·50	1·50
139	1½p. orange	3·50	4·00
140	2p. blue	4·50	6·00
141	3p. green	5·00	8·00
142	5p. brown	7·50	15·00

شرق
الاردن

(19) "East of the Jordan"

1925. Stamps of Palestine (without Palestine opt) optd with T **19**.

143	3	1m. brown	55	3·00
144	3	2m. yellow	70	60
145	3	3m. blue	2·25	1·50
146	3	4m. red	2·25	3·25
147	3	5m. orange	2·75	50
148	3	6m. green	2·25	2·50
149	3	7m. brown	2·25	2·50
150	3	8m. red	2·25	1·25
151	3	1p. grey	2·25	70
152	3	13m. blue	2·75	3·00
153	3	2p. olive	3·75	4·25
154	3	5p. purple	8·00	9·00
155	3	9p. ochre	11·00	22·00
156	3	10p. blue	24·00	30·00
157	3	20p. violet	40·00	70·00

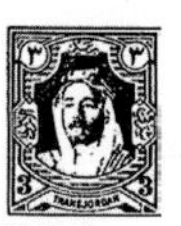

22 Emir Abdullah

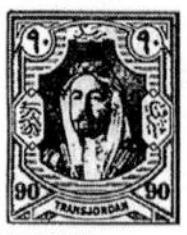

23 Emir Abdullah

1927. Figures at left and right.

159	22	2m. blue	2·25	40
160	22	3m. red	3·50	2·75
161	22	4m. green	4·50	5·00
162	22	5m. orange	2·00	30
163	22	10m. red	3·50	5·00
164	22	15m. blue	3·00	30
165	22	20m. olive	3·00	3·75
166	23	50m. purple	3·00	10·00
167	23	90m. brown	7·00	26·00
168	23	100m. blue	8·00	21·00
169	23	200m. violet	17·00	42·00
170	23	500m. brown	60·00	85·00
171	23	1000m. grey	£100	£140

دستور

(24) "Constitution"

1928. Optd with T **24**.

172	22	2m. blue	5·00	5·00
173	22	3m. red	6·00	8·50
174	22	4m. green	6·00	11·00
175	22	5m. orange	6·00	3·75
176	22	10m. red	6·00	12·00
177	22	15m. blue	6·00	4·25
178	22	20m. olive	12·00	22·00
179	23	50m. purple	17·00	25·00
180	23	90m. brown	23·00	85·00
181	23	100m. blue	23·00	85·00
182	23	200m. violet	80·00	£180

1930. "Locust campaign". Optd **LOCUST CAMPAIGN** in English and Arabic.

183	22	2m. blue	3·25	6·00
184	22	3m. red	2·25	6·50
185	22	4m. green	3·75	15·00
186	22	5m. orange	23·00	14·00
187	22	10m. red	2·25	4·25
188	22	15m. blue	2·25	3·50
189	22	20m. olive	3·50	4·00
190	23	50m. purple	5·00	11·00
191	23	90m. brown	10·00	48·00
192	23	100m. blue	12·00	48·00
193	23	200m. violet	32·00	85·00
194	23	500m. brown	75·00	£200

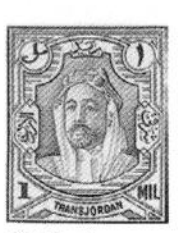

28 Emir

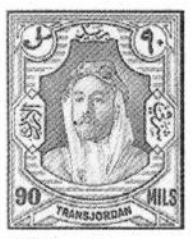

29 Emir

1930

230	28	1m. brown	30	75
195	28	2m. green	75	50
196a	28	3m. green	5·50	85
258	28	3m. pink	35	35
233	28	4m. pink	1·75	2·00
259	28	4m. green	35	35
198	28	5m. orange	2·00	40
199	28	10m. red	3·25	15
260	28	10m. violet	35	35
261	28	12m. red	80	80
200	28	15m. blue	3·25	20
262	28	15m. green	1·00	1·00
201	28	20m. green	3·50	35
263	28	20m. blue	1·10	1·10
202	29	50m. purple	4·25	1·25
203	29	90m. bistre	2·75	4·25
240	29	100m. blue	5·00	1·75
241	29	200m. violet	10·00	14·00
242	29	500m. brown	13·00	12·00
243	29	£P1 grey	24·00	22·00

30 Mushetta

31a The Khasneh at Petra

1933

208	30	1m. black and purple	1·60	1·40
209	-	2m. black and red	4·25	1·25
210	-	3m. green	4·50	1·60
211	-	4m. black and brown	8·50	4·00
212	-	5m. black and orange	5·00	1·25
213	-	10m. red	11·00	4·00
214	31a	15m. blue	6·00	1·25
215	-	20m. black and olive	7·00	5·00
216	-	50m. black and purple	30·00	19·00
217	30	90m. black and yellow	30·00	55·00
218	-	100m. black and blue	30·00	55·00
219	-	200m. black and violet	60·00	£110
220	31a	500m. red and brown	£200	£375
221	-	$P1 black and green	£450	£900

DESIGNS—HORIZ: 2m. Nymphaeum, Jerash; 3, 90m. Kasr Kharana; 4m. Kerak Castle; 5, 100m. Temple of Artemis, Jerash; 10, 200m. Ajlun Castle; 20m. Allenby Bridge over Jordan; 50m. Threshing. VERT: £P1, Emir Abdullah.

Nos. 216 to 221 are larger (33½×24 mm or 24×33½ mm).

35 Map of Jordan

1946. Installation of King Abdullah and National Independence.

249	35	1m. purple	20	20
250	35	2m. orange	20	20
251	35	3m. green	20	20
252	35	4m. violet	20	20
253	35	10m. brown	20	20
254	35	12m. red	20	20
255	35	20m. blue	35	35
256	35	50m. blue	80	80
257	35	200m. green	3·25	3·25

39 Parliament Building

1947. Inauguration of First National Parliament.

276	39	1m. violet	20	20
277	39	3m. red	20	20
278	39	4m. green	20	20
279	39	10m. purple	20	20
280	39	12m. red	20	20
281	39	20m. blue	20	20
282	39	50m. red	35	35
283	39	100m. pink	65	65
284	39	200m. green	1·50	1·50

40 Globe and Forms of Transport

1949. 75th Anniv of U.P.U.

285	40	1m. brown	45	45
286	40	4m. green	80	80
287	40	10m. red	1·00	1·00
288	40	20m. blue	1·70	1·70
289	-	50m. green	2·75	2·75

DESIGN: 50m. King Abdullah.

44 Lockheed Constellation Airliner and Globe

1950. Air.

295	44	5f. purple and yellow	1·10	80
296	44	10f. brown and violet	1·10	80
297	44	15f. red and olive	1·10	80
298	44	20f. black and blue	1·60	1·30
299	44	50f. green and mauve	2·75	1·30
300	44	100f. brown and blue	4·50	3·25
301	44	150f. orange and black	6·75	4·50

1952. Optd **FILS** and bars or **J.D.** (on 1d.).

313	28	1f. on 1m. brown	55	55
314	28	2f. on 2m. green	55	55
315	28	3f. on 3m. green	33·00	
316	28	3f. on 3m. pink	55	55
310	28	4f. on 4m. pink	8·00	4·25
318	28	4f. on 4m. green	55	55
319	28	5f. on 5m. orange	80	80
320	28	10f. on 10m. red	33·00	
321	28	10f. on 10m. violet	1·00	1·00
322	28	12f. on 12m. red	1·00	1·00
312	28	15f. on 15m. blue	36·00	19·00
325	28	15f. on 15m. green	1·30	80
326	28	20f. on 20m. green	35·00	
327	28	20f. on 20m. blue	2·50	1·10
328	29	50f. on 50m. purple	2·50	1·80
329	29	90f. on 90m. bistre	18·00	12·50
330	29	100f. on 100m. blue	11·00	4·00
331	29	200f. on 200m. violet	16·00	5·00
332	29	500f. on 500m. brown	36·00	16·00
333	29	1d. on £P1 grey	85·00	20·00

48 Dome of the Rock and Khazneh at Petra

1952. Unification of Jordan and Palestine.

355	48	1f. green and brown	45	45
356	48	2f. red and green	45	45
357	48	3f. black and red	45	45
358	48	4f. orange and green	45	45
359	48	5f. purple and brown	55	55
360	48	10f. brown and violet	55	55
361	48	20f. black and blue	1·30	80
362	48	100f. sepia and brown	5·00	3·50
363	48	200f. orange and violet	12·50	6·75

49 King Abdullah

1952. (a) Size 18×21½ mm.

364	49	5f. orange	45	45
365	49	10f. lilac	45	45
366	49	12f. red	1·80	1·30
367	49	15f. olive	1·10	45
368	49	20f. blue	1·10	55

(b) Size 20×24½ mm.

369		50f. purple	2·75	1·10
370		90f. brown	7·75	4·00
371		100f. blue	8·25	2·75

1953. Optd with two horiz bars across Arabic commemorative inscription.

378A	48	1f. green and brown	45	45
379A	48	2f. red and green	45	45
380A	48	3f. black and red	45	45
381A	48	4f. orange and green	45	45
382A	48	5f. purple and brown	45	45
383A	48	10f. brown and violet	1·30	80
384A	48	20f. black and blue	1·30	1·00
385A	48	100f. brown and blue	7·75	2·10
386A	48	200f. orange and violet	10·50	6·75

بريد
POSTAGE
(51)

1953. Obligatory Tax stamps optd for postal use as in T **51**. (a) Inscr "MILS".

387	T36	1m. blue	45	45
388	T36	3m. green	45	45
389	T36	5m. purple	£160	£160
390	-	10m. red	60·00	50·00
391	-	15m. black	4·00	2·10
392	-	20m. brown	£130	£100
393	-	50m. violet	1·10	1·00
394	-	100m. red	12·50	10·00

(b) Inscr "MILS" and optd **PALESTINE**.

395	T36	1m. blue	85·00	50·00
396	T36	3m. green	85·00	50·00
397	T36	5m. purple	85·00	50·00
398	-	10m. red	85·00	50·00
399	-	15m. black	85·00	50·00
400	-	20m. brown	85·00	50·00
400a	-	50m. violet		
401	-	100m. red	85·00	50·00

(c) Inscr "MILS", optd **FILS** (T **334**, etc).

402	T36	1f. on 1m. blue	75·00	60·00
403	T36	3f. on 3m. green	75·00	60·00
404	-	10f. on 10m. red	75·00	60·00
405	-	15f. on 15m. black	75·00	60·00
406	-	20f. on 20m. brown	75·00	60·00
407	-	100f. on 100m. red	80·00	80·00

(d) Inscr "FILS".

408	T36	5f. purple	45	20
409	-	10f. red	55	20
410	-	15f. black	1·30	1·10
411	-	20f. brown	2·75	1·80
412	-	100f. orange	6·75	3·50

51a King Hussein

1953. Enthronement of King Hussein.

413	51a	1f. black and green	20	20
414	51a	4f. black and red	35	35
415	51a	15f. black and blue	2·10	45
416	51a	20f. black and lilac	3·50	45
417	51a	50f. black and green	7·75	3·50
418	51a	100f. black and blue	16·00	10·50

52 El-Deir Temple, Petra

54a Temple of Artemis Jerash

1954

445	52	1f. brown & grn (post-age)	20	15
446	-	2f. black and red	20	15
447	52	3f. violet and purple	20	15
448	-	4f. green and brown	20	15
449	52	5f. green and violet	45	20
470	54a	5f. orange and blue (air)	35	20
433	54a	10f. red and brown	80	80
450	-	10f. green and purple	4·00	2·75
451	-	12f. sepia and red	1·70	20
452	-	15f. red and brown	1·00	20
453	-	20f. green and blue	80	20
434	54a	25f. blue and green	1·10	80
435	54a	35f. blue and mauve	1·30	80
436	54a	40f. slate and red	1·70	80
437	54a	50f. orange and blue	2·20	1·10
454	-	50f. red and blue	1·70	20
428	-	100f. blue and green	4·00	1·30
438	54a	100f. brown and blue	2·75	2·00
439	54a	150f. lake and turquoise	4·50	2·75
456	-	200f. blue and lake	10·00	2·75
457	-	500f. purple and brown	36·00	14·50
458	-	1d. lake and olive	60·00	21·00

DESIGNS—VERT: 2f., 4f., 500f., 1d. King Hussein. HORIZ: 10f., 15f., 20f. Dome of the Rock, Jerusalem; 12f., 50f., 100f., 200f. Facade of Mosque of El Aqsa.

1955. Arab Postal Union. As Nos. 502/4 of Egypt but inscr "H. K. JORDAN" at top and "ARAB POSTAL UNION" at foot.

440	15f. green	80	45
441	20f. violet	80	45
442	25f. brown	1·00	80

56 King Hussein and Queen Dina

1955. Royal Wedding.

443	56	15f. blue	2·50	1·00
444	56	100f. lake	9·00	4·00

58 Envelope with Postmarks in English and Arabic

1956. First Arab Postal Congress, Amman.

459	58	1f. brown and black	35	35
460	58	4f. red and black	35	35
461	58	15f. blue and black	35	35
462	58	20f. bistre and black	35	35
463	58	50f. blue and black	80	35
464	58	100f. orange and black	1·20	80

59 "Flame of Freedom"

1958. Tenth Anniv of Declaration of Human Rights.

476	59	5f. red and blue	10	10
477	59	15f. black and brown	35	35
478	59	35f. purple and green	65	65
479	59	45f. black and red	90	90

60 King Hussein

1959. Centres in black.

480	60	1f. green	10	10
481	60	2f. violet	10	10
482	60	3f. red	45	10
483	60	4f. purple	45	10
484	60	7f. green	55	10
485	60	12f. red	80	15
486	60	15f. red	80	15
487	60	21f. green	80	15
488	60	25f. brown	1·10	20
489	60	35f. blue	1·70	20
490	60	40f. green	2·50	20
491	60	50f. red	3·25	20
492	60	100f. green	4·00	80
493	60	200f. purple	10·50	3·25
494	60	500f. blue	28·00	12·50
495	60	1d. purple	50·00	31·00

61 Arab League Centre, Cairo

1960. Inaug of Arab League Centre, Cairo.

496	61	15f. black and green	35	20

62 "Care of Refugees"

1960. World Refugee Year.

497	62	15f. red and blue	35	20
498	62	35f. blue and bistre	65	55

63 Shah of Iran and King Hussein

1960. Visit of Shah of Iran.

499	63	15f. multicoloured	55	55
500	63	35f. multicoloured	80	80
501	63	50f. multicoloured	1·10	1·10

64 Petroleum Refinery, Zarka

1961. Inaug of Jordanian Petroleum Refinery.

502	64	15f. blue and violet	35	20
503	64	35f. brown and violet	55	45

65 Jordanian Families and Graph

1961. First Jordanian Census Commemoration.

504	65	15f. brown	35	20

1961. Dag Hammarskjold Memorial Issue. Optd **IN MEMORIAL OF DAG HAMMARSKJOELD 1904–1961** in English and Arabic and laurel leaves at top and bottom.

505	62	15f. red and blue	6·25	6·25
506	62	35f. blue and bistre	6·25	6·25

67 Campaign Emblem

1962. Malaria Eradication.

507	67	15f. mauve	35	35
508	67	35f. blue	65	45
MS509		75×76 mm. Nos. 507/8	8·25	8·25

68 Telephone Exchange, Amman

1962. Inauguration of Amman's Automatic Telephone Exchange.

510	68	15f. blue and purple	20	35
511	68	35f. purple and green	65	65

69 Aqaba Port and King Hussein

1962. Opening of Aqaba Port.

512	69	15f. black and purple	55	20
513	69	35f. black and blue	1·10	55
MS514		80×93 mm. Nos. 512/13	5·50	5·50

70 Dag Hammarskjold and U.N. Headquarters

1963. 17th Anniv of U.N.

515	70	15f. red, olive and blue	55	20
516	70	35f. blue, red and olive	1·30	65
517	70	50f. olive, blue and red	2·20	1·30
MS518		135×95 mm. Nos. 515/17. Imperf	14·50	14·50

71 Church of Holy Virgin's Tomb, Jerusalem

1963. "Holy Places". Multicoloured.

519	50f. Type **71**	1·70	1·70
520	50f. Basilica of the Agony, Gethsemane	1·70	1·70
521	50f. Holy Sepulchre, Jerusalem	1·70	1·70
522	50f. Nativity Church. Bethlehem	1·70	1·70
523	50f. Haram of Ibrahim, Hebron	1·70	1·70
524	50f. Dome of the Rock, Jerusalem	1·70	1·70
525	50f. Omer-el-Khetab Mosque, Jerusalem	1·70	1·70
526	50f. El-Aqsa Mosque, Jerusalem	1·70	1·70

72 League Centre, Cairo and Emblem

1963. Arab League.

527	72	15f. blue	35	20
528	72	35f. red	1·10	45

73 Wheat and F.A.O. Emblem

1963. Freedom from Hunger.

529	73	15f. green, black and blue	45	20
530	73	35f. green, black and apple	65	45
MS531		98×85 mm. Nos. 529/30	2·20	1·90

74 Canal and Symbols

1963. East Ghor Canal Project.

532	74	1f. black and bistre	20	10
533	74	4f. black and blue	20	10
534	74	5f. black and purple	20	10
535	74	10f. black and green	45	10
536	74	35f. black and orange	2·50	1·80

75 Scales of Justice and Globe

1963. 15th Anniv of Declaration of Human Rights.

537	75	50f. red and blue	1·10	1·10
538	75	50f. blue and red	1·10	1·10

1963. Surch in English and Arabic.

539	60	1f. on 21f. black and green	35	35
540	60	2f. on 21f. black and green	35	35
541	60	4f. on 12f. black and red	20·00	33·00
542	-	4f. on 12f. sepia and red (No. 451)	45	45
543	60	21f. on 21f. black and green	90	65
544	60	25f. on 35f. blue	3·25	1·50

77 King Hussein and Red Crescent

1963. Red Crescent Commemoration.

545	77	1f. purple and red	20	20
546	77	2f. turquoise and red	20	20
547	77	3f. blue and red	20	20
548	77	4f. turquoise and red	20	20
549	77	5f. sepia and red	20	20
550	77	85f. green and red	3·00	2·50
MS551		90×65 mm. 100f. purple and red (larger). Imperf	36·00	36·00

78 Red Cross Emblem

1963. Centenary of Red Cross.

552	78	1f. purple and red	35	35
553	78	2f. turquoise and red	35	35
554	78	3f. blue and red	35	35
555	78	4f. turquoise and red	35	35
556	78	5f. sepia and red	35	35
557	78	85f. green and red	4·75	3·25
MS558		90×65 mm. 100f. purple and red (larger). Imperf	33·00	33·00

79 Kings Hussein of Hejaz and Hussein of Jordan

1963. Arab Renaissance Day.

559	79	15f. multicoloured	90	45
560	79	25f. multicoloured	1·20	65
561	79	35f. multicoloured	2·20	1·50
562	79	50f. multicoloured	4·75	4·00
MS563		112×93 mm. Nos. 559/62	10·00	10·00

80 Al Aqsa Mosque, Pope Paul and King Hussein

1964. Pope Paul's Visit to the Holy Land.

564	80	15f. green and black	45	35
565	-	35f. mauve and black	65	45
566	-	50f. brown and black	1·30	1·00
567	-	80f. blue and black	2·50	1·80
MS567a		138×108 mm. Nos. 564/7. Imperf	29·00	29·00

DESIGNS: 35f. Dome of the Rock (Mosque of Omar), Jerusalem; 50f. Church of the Holy Sepulchre, Jerusalem; 80f. Church of the Nativity, Bethlehem.

81 Prince Abdullah

1964. Second Birthday of Prince Abdullah. Multicoloured.

568	5f. Prince standing by wall	55	20
569	10f. Head of Prince and roses	65	55
570	35f. Type **81**	1·50	1·10

SIZES: 5f. as Type **81** but vert; 10f. diamond (63×63 mm).

NOTE.—A set of ten triangular 20f. stamps showing astronauts and rockets was issued, but very few were put on sale at the Post Office and we are not listing them unless we receive satisfactory evidence as to their status.

82 Basketball

1964. Olympic Games, Tokyo (1st issue).

571	82	1f. red	20	20
572	-	2f. blue	20	20
573	-	3f. green	20	20
574	-	4f. buff	20	20
575	-	5f. violet	20	20
576	-	35f. red	2·50	1·10
577	-	50f. green	4·50	2·20
578	-	100f. brown	6·75	4·00
MS579		88×64 mm. 200f. blue (as 100f. but larger). Imperf	50·00	50·00

DESIGNS—VERT: 2f. Volleyball; 3f. Football; 5f. Running. HORIZ: 4f. Table tennis; 35f. Cycling; 50f. Fencing; 100f. Pole vaulting.

See also Nos. 610/MS618 and 641/MS647.

83 Woman and Child

1964. Fourth Session of Social Studies Seminar, Amman.

580	83	5f. multicoloured	55	55
581	83	10f. multicoloured	55	55
582	83	25f. multicoloured	55	55

84 King Hussein Sports Stadium, Amman

1964. Air. Inaug of "Hussein Sports City".

583	84	1f. multicoloured	35	35
584	84	4f. multicoloured	35	35
585	84	10f. multicoloured	35	35
586	84	35f. multicoloured	65	65
MS587		120×94 mm. Nos. 583/6	3·25	3·25

85 President Kennedy

1964. Pres. Kennedy Memorial Issue.

588	85	1f. violet	45	45
589	85	2f. red	45	45
590	85	3f. blue	45	45
591	85	4f. brown	45	45
592	85	5f. green	45	45
593	85	85f. red	22·00	13·50
MS594		110×77 mm. 85 100f. sepia (larger). Imperf	25·00	25·00

86 Statues at Abu Simbel

1964. Nubian Monuments Preservation.

595	86	4f. black and blue	55	55
596	86	15f. violet and yellow	55	55
597	86	25f. red and green	55	55

87 King Hussein and Map of Palestine in 1920

1964. Arab Summit Conference.

598	87	10f. multicoloured	20	10

599	87	15f. multicoloured	35	15
600	87	25f. multicoloured	45	20
601	87	50f. multicoloured	1·00	35
602	87	80f. multicoloured	1·90	1·60

MS603 110×90 mm. Nos. 598/602.
Imperf. No gum 6·25 6·25

88 Pope Paul VI, King Hussein and Ecumenical Patriarch

1964. Meeting of Pope, King and Patriarch, Jerusalem. Multicoloured, background colour given.

604	88	10f. green	20	20
605	88	15f. purple	35	35
606	88	25f. brown	45	45
607	88	50f. blue	1·00	1·00
608	88	80f. green	1·90	1·90

MS609 130×100 mm. Nos. 604/8.
Imperf. No gum 10·00 10·00

89 Olympic Flame

1964. Olympic Games, Tokyo (2nd issue).

610	89	1f. red	10	10
611	89	2f. violet	15	15
612	89	3f. green	20	20
613	89	4f. brown	30	30
614	89	5f. red	35	35
615	89	35f. blue	1·10	1·10
616	89	50f. olive	1·70	1·70
617	89	100f. blue	4·00	4·00

MS618 108×76 mm. 89 100f. rose
(larger). Imperf 25·00 25·00

90 Scouts crossing River

1964. Jordanian Scouts.

619	90	1f. brown	15	15
620	90	2f. violet	15	15
621	-	3f. ochre	20	20
622	-	4f. lake	20	20
623	-	5f. green	20	20
624	-	35f. blue	6·25	2·50
625	-	50f. green	6·75	3·75

MS626 108×76 mm. 100f. blue (as 50f.
but larger). Imperf 29·00 14·50

DESIGNS: 2f. First aid; 3f. Exercising; 4f. Practising knots; 5f. Cooking meal; 35f. Sailing; 50f. Around camp-fire.

91 Four-coloured Bush Shrike

1964. Air. Birds. Multicoloured.

627		150f. Type 91	33·00	17·00
628		500f. Ornate hawk eagle (vert)	90·00	45·00
629		1000f. Grey-headed kingfisher (vert)	£160	80·00

92 Bykovsky

1965. Russian Astronauts.

630		40f. brown and green (Type 92)	1·60	1·10
631		40f. violet & brown (Gagarin)	1·60	1·10
632		40f. maroon & bl (Nikolaev)	1·60	1·10
633		40f. lilac and bistre (Popovich)	1·60	1·10
634		40f. sepia & blue (Tereshkova)	1·60	1·10

| 635 | | 40f. green and pink (Titov) | 1·60 | 1·10 |

MS636 115×83 mm. 100f. blue and
black (space ship and the six cosmonauts). Imperf 28·00 28·00

MS637 As above opt **VOSKHOD
12/10/64/VLADIMIR KOMATOV/
KONSTANTIN FEOKTISTOV/BORIS
YEGEROV** 28·00 28·00

93 U.N. Headquarters and Emblem

1965. 19th Anniv (1964) of U.N.

| 638 | 93 | 30f. violet, turquoise and brown | 65 | 55 |
| 639 | 93 | 70f. brown, blue and violet | 1·30 | 80 |

MS640 76×102 mm. Nos. 638/9. Imperf 22·00 22·00

94 Olympic Flame

1965. Air. Olympic Games, Tokyo (3rd issue).

641	94	10f. red	45	45
642	94	15f. violet	45	45
643	94	20f. blue	45	45
644	94	30f. green	45	45
645	94	40f. brown	65	65
646	94	60f. mauve	90	90

MS647 102×102 mm. 94 100f. blue
(larger). Imperf 21·00 21·00

95 Dagger on Deir Yassin, Palestine

1965. Deir Yassin Massacre.

| 648 | 95 | 25f. red and olive | 5·00 | 2·75 |

96 Horse-jumping

1965. Army Day.

649	96	5f. green	20	10
650	-	10f. blue	45	20
651	-	35f. brown	1·50	55

DESIGNS: 10f. Tank; 35f. King Hussein making inspection in army car.

97 Volleyball Player and Cup

1965. Arab Volleyball Championships.

652	97	15f. olive	1·20	45
653	97	35f. lake	2·50	1·10
654	97	50f. blue	4·00	2·50

MS655 63×89 mm. 97 100f. brown
(larger). Imperf 31·00 31·00

98 President J. F. Kennedy

1965. First Death Anniv of Pres. Kennedy.

656	98	10f. black and green	55	55
657	98	15f. violet and orange	80	55
658	98	25f. brown and blue	1·20	80
659	98	50f. purple and green	2·50	1·50

MS660 114×90 mm. 98 50f. salmon
and blue. Imperf 22·00 22·00

99 Pope Paul, King Hussein and Dome of the Rock

1965. First Anniv of Pope Paul's Visit to the Holy Land.

661	99	5f. brown and mauve	55	55
662	99	10f. lake and green	1·10	45
663	99	15f. blue and flesh	1·60	55
664	99	50f. grey and pink	4·00	1·90

MS665 102×76 mm. 99 50f. blue and
violet. Imperf 31·00 31·00

100 Cathedral Steps

1965. Air. Jerash Antiquities. Multicoloured.

666		55f. Type 100	1·90	1·90
667		55f. Artemis Temple Gate	1·90	1·90
668		55f. Street of Columns	1·90	1·90
669		55f. Columns of South Theatre	1·90	1·90
670		55f. Forum (horiz)	1·90	1·90
671		55f. South Theatre (horiz)	1·90	1·90
672		55f. Triumphal Arch (horiz)	1·90	1·90
673		55f. Temple of Artemis (horiz)	1·90	1·90

101 Jordan Pavilion at Fair

1965. New York World's Fair.

674	101	15f. multicoloured	20	20
675	101	25f. multicoloured	55	35
676	101	50f. multicoloured	1·20	80

MS677 113×75 mm. 101 100f. multicoloured 4·25 4·25

102 Lamp and Burning Library

1965. Burning of Algiers Library.

| 678 | 102 | 25f. green, red and black | 55 | 35 |

103 I.T.U. Emblem and Symbols

1965. Centenary of I.T.U.

| 679 | 103 | 25f. blue and light blue | 55 | 20 |
| 680 | 103 | 45f. black and green | 90 | 55 |

MS681 40×32 mm. 103 100f. lake and
red (larger). Imperf 3·25 3·25

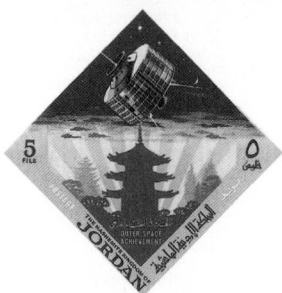

104 "Syncom" Satellite and Pagoda

1965. Space Achievements. Multicoloured.

682		5f. Type 104	45	45
683		10f. North American X-15 rocket airplane	45	45
684		15f. Astronauts	65	55
685		20f. As 10f.	90	65
686		50f. Type 104	2·10	1·60

MS687 101×76 mm. 50f. Syncom Satellite and Earth's sphere. Imperf 21·00 21·00

105 Dead Sea

1985. Dead Sea. Multicoloured.

688		35f. Type 105	1·00	65
689		35f. Boats and palms	1·00	65
690		35f. Qumran Caves	1·00	65
691		35f. Dead Sea Scrolls	1·00	65

1965. Air. Space Flight of McDivitt and White. Nos. 641/6 optd **James McDivitt Edward White 2-6-1965** in English and Arabic and rocket.

692	94	10f. red	1·70	1·70
693	94	15f. violet	2·20	2·20
694	94	20f. blue	3·25	3·25
695	94	30f. green	4·75	4·75
696	94	40f. brown	6·25	6·25
697	94	60f. mauve	9·00	9·00

MS698 102×102 mm. 94 100f. blue
(larger). Imperf 33·00 33·00

107 King Hussein, U.N. Emblem and Headquarters

1965. King Hussein's Visit to France and the U.S.A.

699	107	5f. sepia, blue and pink	45	45
700	-	10f. sepia, green and grey	45	45
701	-	20f. agate, brown and blue	80	80
702	107	50f. lilac, brown and blue	1·90	1·90

MS703 102×102 mm. 107 50f. lilac,
brown and blue. Imperf 13·50 13·50

DESIGNS: 10f. King Hussein, Pres. de Gaulle and Eiffel Tower; 20f. King Hussein, Pres. Johnson and Statue of Liberty.

108 I.C.Y. Emblem

1965. International Co-operation Year.

704	108	5f. red and orange	35	20
705	108	10f. violet and blue	80	35
706	108	45f. purple and green	3·00	2·20

109 A.P.U. Emblem

1965. Tenth Anniv (1964) of Arab Postal Union's Permanent Office at Cairo.

707	**109**	15f. black and blue	20	20
708	**109**	25f. black and green	80	35

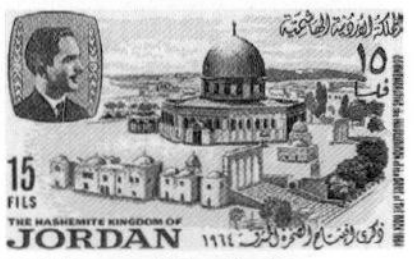

110 Dome of the Rock

1965. Inaug (1964) of "Dome of the Rock".

709	**110**	15f. multicoloured	1·20	45
710	**110**	25f. multicoloured	2·10	1·30

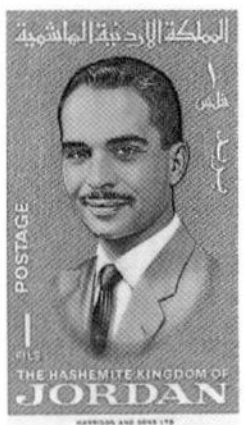

111 King Hussein

1966. (a) Postage. Portraits in blue (1f. to 15f.) or purple (21f. to 150f.); background colours given.

711	**111**	1f. orange	10	10
712	**111**	2f. blue	10	10
713	**111**	3f. violet	10	10
714	**111**	4f. purple	10	10
715	**111**	7f. brown	35	10
716	**111**	12f. mauve	35	10
717	**111**	15f. brown	45	10
718	**111**	21f. green	65	15
719	**111**	25f. blue	80	15
720	**111**	35f. stone	1·00	20
721	**111**	40f. yellow	1·10	35
722	**111**	50f. green	1·20	55
723	**111**	100f. green	2·10	1·20
724	**111**	150f. violet	4·75	1·90

(b) Air. Portraits in brown; background colours given.

725	200f. turquoise	7·25	2·10
726	500f. green	12·50	8·25
727	1d. blue	21·00	13·50

1966. Space Flights of Belyaev and Leonov. Nos. 630/5 optd **Alexei Leonov Pavel Belyaev 18 3-1965** in English and Arabic and spacecraft motif.

728	**92**	40f. brown and green	6·75	6·75
729	-	40f. violet and brown	6·75	6·75
730	-	40f. purple and blue	6·75	6·75
731	-	40f. lilac and bistre	6·75	6·75
732	-	40f. sepia and blue	6·75	6·75
733	-	40f. green and pink	6·75	6·75
MS734		115×83 mm. 100f. blue and black (No. **MS**636)	65·00	65·00
MS735		115×83 mm. 100f. blue and black (No. **MS**637)	65·00	65·00

1966. Pope Paul's Visit to U.N. (1965). Nos. 604/8 optd **PAPA PAULUS VI WORLD PEACE VISIT TO UNITED NATIONS 1965** in English and Arabic.

736	**88**	10f. green	35	10
737	**88**	15f. purple	80	35
738	**88**	25f. brown	80	45
739	**88**	50f. blue	1·50	80
740	**88**	80f. green	2·50	1·20
MS740a		130×100 mm. Nos. 736/40. Imperf. No gum	14·50	14·50

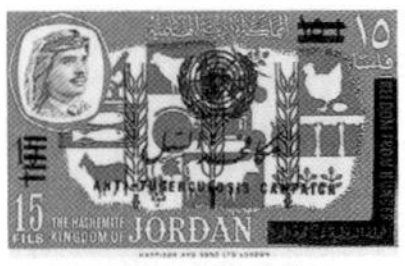

114 Agricultural Symbols

1966. Anti-T.B. Campaign. (a) Unissued "Freedom from Hunger" stamps optd as in T **114**.

741	**114**	15f. multicoloured	55	45
742	**114**	35f. multicoloured	1·50	1·00
743	**114**	50f. multicoloured	2·20	2·10
MS744		108×76 mm. Nos. 741/3. Gold background	17·00	17·00
MS744a		108×76 mm. Nos. 741/2. White background. Imperf	17·00	17·00

(b) As Nos. 741/3 but with additional premium obliterated by bars.

745	15f. multicoloured	55	45
746	35f. multicoloured	1·50	1·00
747	50f. multicoloured	2·20	2·10

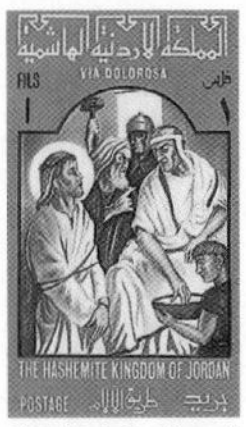

115 First Station of the Cross

1966. Christ's Passion. The Stations of the Cross.

749	**115**	1f. multicoloured	20	10
750	-	2f. multicoloured	20	10
751	-	3f. multicoloured	35	20
752	-	4f. multicoloured	35	20
753	-	5f. multicoloured	55	35
754	-	6f. multicoloured	80	45
755	-	7f. multicoloured	1·10	65
756	-	8f. multicoloured	1·20	75
757	-	9f. multicoloured	1·50	80
758	-	10f. multicoloured	1·60	1·00
759	-	11f. multicoloured	1·90	1·20
760	-	12f. multicoloured	1·90	1·20
761	-	13f. multicoloured	2·00	1·30
762	-	14f. multicoloured	2·10	1·50
MS763		101×76 mm. **115** 100f. multicoloured	39·00	55

DESIGNS: The 14 Stations. The denominations, expressed in Roman numerals, correspond to the numbers of the stations.

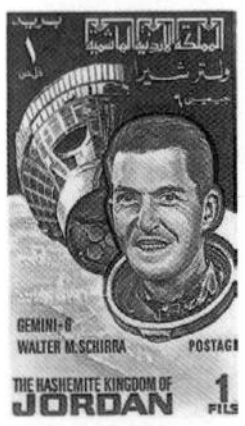

116 Schirra and "Gemini 6"

1966. Space Achievements.

764	**116**	1f. blue, violet and green	20	20
765	-	2f. green, violet and blue	20	20
766	-	3f. violet, blue and green	20	20
767	-	4f. violet, green and ochre	35	20
768	-	30f. turquoise, brn & vio	2·20	1·60
769	-	60f. brown, turq & vio	3·00	2·20
MS770		114×88 mm. 100f. multicoloured (The six astronauts etc). Imperf	27·00	27·00

DESIGNS: 2f. Stafford and "Gemini 6"; 3f. Borman and "Gemini 7"; 4f. Lovell and "Gemini 7"; 30f. Armstrong and "Gemini 8"; 60f. Scott and "Gemini 8".

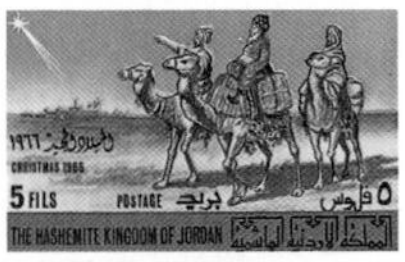

117 The Three Kings

1966. Christmas. Multicoloured.

771	5f. Type **117**	35	10
772	10f. The Magi presenting gifts to the infant Christ	45	20
773	35f. The flight to Egypt (vert)	4·25	1·50
MS774	115×90 mm. 50f. As 10f. Imperf	31·00	31·00

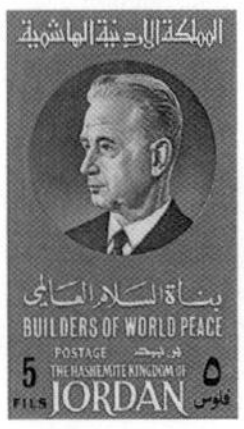

118 Dag Hammarskjold

1967. "Builders of World Peace". Multicoloured. (a) (1st issue).

775	5f. Type **118**	20	20
776	10f. Pandit Nehru	35	20
777	35f. President Kennedy	1·20	65
778	50f. Pope John XXIII	3·00	90
779	100f. King Abdullah (of Jordan)	3·25	2·75
MS780	99×64 mm. 100f. The above five portraits. Imperf	27·00	27·00

(b) (2nd issue).

781	5f. U. Thant	20	20
782	10f. President De Gaulle	35	20
783	35f. President Johnson	1·20	65
784	50f. Pope Paul VI	3·00	90
785	100f. King Hussein	3·25	2·75
MS786	99×64 mm. 100f. The above five portraits	27·00	27·00

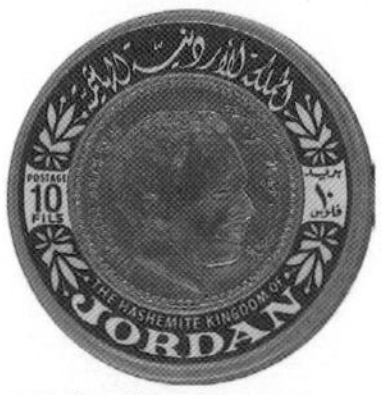

119 King Hussein

1967. "Gold Coins". Circular designs, centre and rim embossed on gold foil. Imperf. (a) As T **119**. (i) Diameter 41 mm.

787	**119**	5f. orange and blue	80	80
788	**119**	10f. orange and violet	80	80

(ii) Diameter 47 mm.

789	50f. lilac and brown	4·25	4·25
790	100f. pink and green	5·25	5·25

(iii) Diameter 54 mm.

791	200f. blue and deep blue	12·50	12·50

(b) Crown Prince Hassan of Jordan. (i) Diameter 41 mm.

792	5f. black and green	80	80
793	10f. black and lilac	80	80

(ii) Diameter 47 mm.

794	50f. black and blue	4·25	4·25
795	100f. black and brown	5·25	5·25

(iii) Diameter 54 mm.

796	200f. black and mauve	12·50	12·50

A similar set was also issued in the same values and sizes but different colours with portrait of John F. Kennedy.

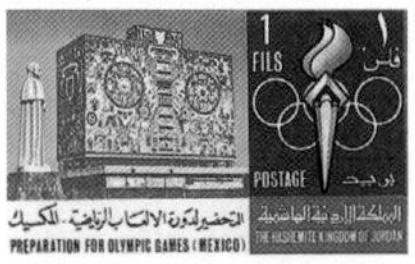

120 University City, Statue and Olympic Torch

1967. Preparation for Olympic Games in Mexico (1968).

797	**120**	1f. red, black and violet	35	35
798	-	2f. black, violet and red	35	35
799	-	3f. violet, red and black	35	35
800	-	4f. blue, brown and green	35	35
801	-	30f. green, blue and brown	80	80
802	-	60f. brown, green and blue	1·60	1·60
MS803		115×90 mm. 100f. brown, green and ultramarine (as 60f.). Imperf	27·00	27·00

DESIGNS (each with Olympic torch): 2f. Fishermen on Lake Patzcuaro; 3f. University City and skyscraper, Mexico City; 4f. Avenida de la Reforma, Mexico City; 30f. Guadalajara Cathedral; 60f. Fine Arts Theatre, Mexico City.

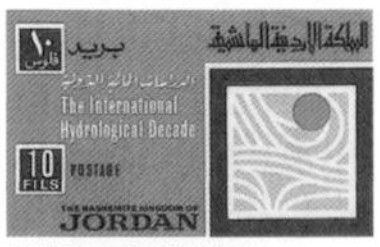

121 Decade Emblem

1967. International Hydrological Decade.

804	**121**	10f. black and red	35	10
805	**121**	15f. black and turquoise	65	35
806	**121**	25f. black and purple	1·20	80

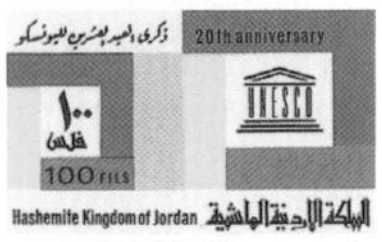

122 UNESCO Emblem

1967. 20th Anniv of UNESCO.

807	**122**	100f. multicoloured	1·70	1·70

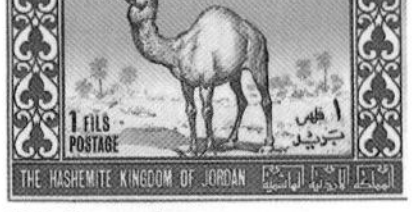

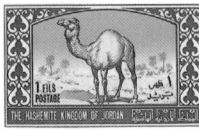

123 Dromedary

1967. Animals. Multicoloured.

808	1f. Type **123** (postage)	2·75	45
809	2f. Karakul sheep	2·75	45
810	3f. Angora goat	2·75	45
811	4f. Striped hyena (air)	2·75	45
812	30f. Arab horses	3·50	90
813	60f. Goitred gazelle	6·25	1·70
MS814	115×89 mm. 100f. (as 30f.) . Imperf	38·00	38·00

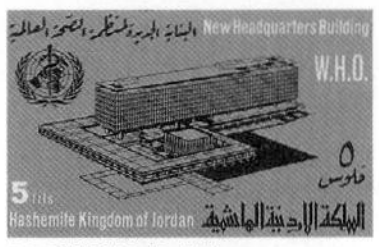

124 W.H.O. Building

1967. Inaug of W.H.O. Headquarters, Geneva.

815	**124**	5f. black and green	20	20
816	**124**	45f. black and orange	90	45

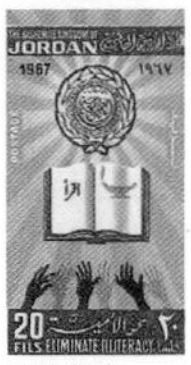

125 Arab League Emblem, Open Book and Reaching Hands

1968. Literacy Campaign.

817	**125**	20f. green and orange	90	35
818	**125**	20f. blue and mauve	65	35

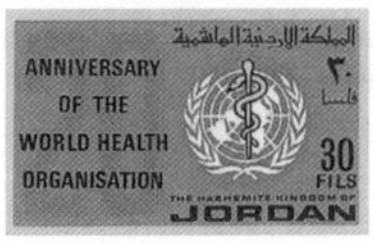

126 W.H.O. Emblem and "20"

1968. 20th Anniv of W.H.O.

819	**126**	30f. multicoloured	90	35
820	**126**	100f. multicoloured	2·75	1·50

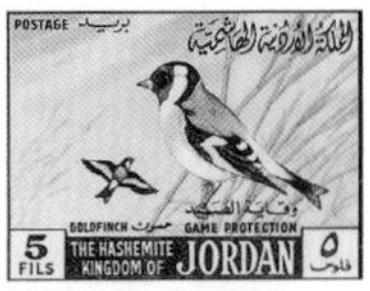

127 Eurasian Goldfinch ("Goldfinch")

1968. Game Protection. Multicoloured.

821	5f. Type **127** (postage)	3·75	1·70
822	10f. Chukar partridge ("Rock Partridge") (vert)	6·75	1·70
823	15f. Ostriches (vert)	9·50	2·10
824	20f. Sand partridge	9·50	2·50
825	30f. Mountain gazelle	6·25	1·90
826	40f. Arabian oryx	8·25	2·10
827	50f. Houbara bustard ("Bustard")	13·50	4·75
828	60f. Ibex (vert) (air)	10·50	5·50
829	100f. Flock of mallard ("Duck")	17·00	10·50

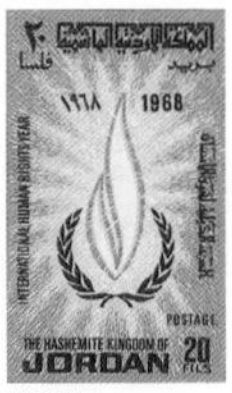

128 Human Rights Emblem

1968. Human Rights Year.

830	**128**	20f. black, buff and brown	35	20
831	**128**	60f. black, blue and green	1·30	1·10

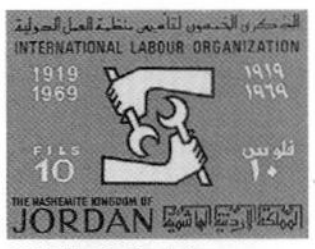

129 I.L.O. Emblem

1969. 50th Anniv of I.L.O.

832	**129**	10f. black and blue	35	10
833	**129**	20f. black and brown	35	20
834	**129**	25f. black and green	45	35
835	**129**	45f. black and mauve	80	55
836	**129**	60f. black and orange	1·10	80

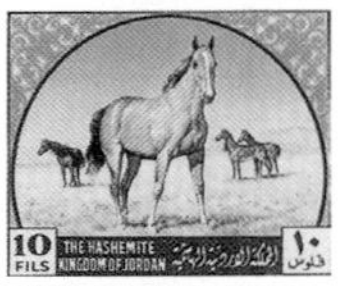

130 Horses in Pasture

1969. Arab Horses. Multicoloured.

837	10f. Type **130**	1·70	35
838	20f. White horse	4·75	1·20
839	45f. Black mare and foal	8·25	3·75

131 Kaaba, Mecca, and Dome of the Rock, Jerusalem

1969. Multicoloured

840	5f. As Type **131**	45	10
841	10f. Dome of the Rock (30×36 mm)	80	55
842	20f. As 10f.	1·50	80
843	45f. As 5f.	3·50	90

132 Oranges

1969. Fruits. Multicoloured.

844	10f. Type **132**	35	10
845	20f. Gooseberry	55	35
846	30f. Lemons	1·20	40
847	40f. Grapes	1·80	45
848	50f. Olives	2·50	1·20
849	100f. Apples	4·00	2·20

133 Prince Hassan and Bride

1969. Wedding of Prince Hassan (1968).

850	– 20f. multicoloured	65	65
851	– 60f. multicoloured	1·60	1·30
852	**133** 100f. multicoloured	2·75	2·75

Nos. 850/1 show a similar design to Type **133**.

134 Wrecked Houses

1969. "Tragedy of the Refugees". Various vert designs as T 134. Multicoloured.

853-882	1f. inclusive	40·00	40·00

135 Bombed Mosque

1969. "Tragedy in the Holy Lands". Various vert designs as T 135. Multicoloured.

883-912	1f. inclusive	40·00	40·00

136 Pomegranate

1970. Flowers. Multicoloured.

913	5f. Type **136**	55	20
914	15f. Wattle	90	20
915	25f. Caper	1·50	20
916	35f. Convolvulus	2·00	35

917	45f. Desert scabious	2·75	1·00
918	75f. Black iris	4·50	3·75

Nos. 913/15 and 917 are wrongly inscribed on the stamps.

137 Football

1970. Sports. Multicoloured.

919	5f. Type **137**	20	10
920	10f. Diving	35	20
921	15f. Boxing	55	20
922	50f. Running	1·70	80
923	100f. Cycling (vert)	4·00	1·50
924	150f. Basketball (vert)	6·25	3·25

138 Arab Children

1970. Children's Day. Multicoloured.

925	5f. Type **138**	35	10
926	10f. Refugee boy with kettle (vert)	35	20
927	15f. Refugee girl in camp (vert)	80	25
928	20f. Refugee child in tent (vert)	1·10	35

139 White-crowned Black Wheatear ("Black Chat")

1970. Birds.

929	**139**	120f. black and orange	16·00	3·25
930	–	180f. brown, black & lilac	19·00	7·25
931	–	200f. multicoloured	25·00	10·00

DESIGNS: 180f. Masked shrike; 200f. Palestine sunbird.

140 Grotto of the Nativity, Bethlehem

1970. Christmas. Church of the Nativity, Bethlehem. Multicoloured.

932	5f. Type **140**	35	20
933	10f. Christmas crib	45	20
934	20f. Crypt Altar	80	35
935	25f. Nave, Church of the Nativity	1·00	35

141 Arab League Flag, Emblem and Map

1971. 25th Anniv (1970) of Arab League.

936	**141** 10f. green, violet and orange	20	20
937	**141** 20f. green, brown and blue	55	25
938	**141** 30f. green, blue and olive	80	35

142 Heads of Four Races and Emblem

1971. Racial Equality Year. Multicoloured.

939	5f. Type **142**	35	35
940	10f. "Plant" and emblem	35	35
941	15f. Doves and emblem (horiz)	45	35

No. 939 is inscribed "KINIGDOM" in error.

143 Shore of the Dead Sea

1971. Tourism. Multicoloured.

942	5f. Type **143**	45	35
943	30f. Ed Deir, Petra	1·60	65
944	45f. Via Dolorosa, Jerusalem (vert)	2·20	90
945	60f. River Jordan	3·75	1·90
946	100f. Christmas Bell, Bethlehem (vert)	5·25	3·75

144 Ibn Sinai (Avicenna)

1971. Famous Arab Scholars. Multicoloured.

947	5f. Type **144**	20	10
948	10f. Ibn Rushd	35	10
949	20f. Ibn Khaldun	55	20
950	25f. Ibn Tufail	1·00	25
951	30f. Ibn El Haytham	1·50	80

145 New U.P.U. H.Q. Building

1971. Inauguration of New U.P.U. Headquarters Building, Berne.

952	**145** 10f. brown, green and yellow	55	35
953	**145** 20f. purple, green and yellow	80	35

146 Young Pupil

1972. International Education Year.

954	**146** 5f. multicoloured	10	10
955	**146** 15f. multicoloured	35	10
956	**146** 20f. multicoloured	55	20
957	**146** 30f. multicoloured	1·20	65

147 Mothers and Children

1972. Mothers Day. Multicoloured.

958	10f. Type **147**	65	35
959	20f. Mother and child (vert)	65	35
960	30f. Bedouin mother and child (vert)	80	35

148 Pope Paul VI leaving Holy Sepulchre, Jerusalem

1972. Easter. Multicoloured.

961	30f. Type **148** (postage)	65	20
962	60f. The Calvary, Church of the Holy Sepulchre (air)	1·30	55
963	100f. "Washing of the Feet", Jerusalem	2·50	1·10

149 Children and UNICEF Emblem

1972. 25th Anniv of UNICEF.

964	**149** 10f. turquoise, blue and brown	55	35

965	– 20f. brown, green and pur	55	35
966	– 30f. brown, mauve and blue	65	35

DESIGNS—VERT: 20f. Child with toy bricks. HORIZ: 30f. Nurse holding baby.

150 Dove of Peace

1972. 25th Anniv (1970) of United Nations.

967	**150** 5f. green, violet and yellow	20	20
968	**150** 10f. green, red and yellow	35	20
969	**150** 15f. blue, black and yellow	80	25
970	**150** 20f. blue, green and yellow	1·00	35
971	**150** 30f. green, brown & yell	1·90	90

151 Al Aqsa Mosque and Pilgrims

1972. Burning of Al Aqsa Mosque (1970). Multicoloured.

972	30f. Type **151**	2·50	35
973	60f. Mosque in flames	6·25	1·70
974	100f. Mosque interior	8·25	3·25

152 Arab with Kestrel

1972. Jordanian Desert Life. Multicoloured.

975	5f. Type **152**	65	35
976	10f. Desert bungalow (horiz)	65	35
977	15f. Camel trooper, Arab Legion (horiz)	65	35
978	20f. Boring operations (horiz)	1·00	40
979	25f. Shepherd (horiz)	1·00	40
980	30f. Dromedaries at water-trough (horiz)	1·80	55
981	35f. Chicken farm (horiz)	1·90	1·00
982	45f. Irrigation scheme (horiz)	3·00	1·80

153 Wasfi el Tell and Dome of the Rock, Jerusalem

1972. Wasfi el Tell (assassinated statesman) Memorial Issue. Multicoloured.

983	5f. Type **153**	35	10
984	10f. Wasfi el Tell, map and flag	45	20
985	20f. Type **153**	1·00	25
986	30f. As 10f.	1·10	90

154 Clay-pigeon shooting

1972. World Clay-pigeon Shooting Championships. Multicoloured.

987	25f. Type **154**	80	35
988	75f. Marksman on range (horiz)	1·60	1·30
989	120f. Marksman taking aim (horiz)	3·00	2·00

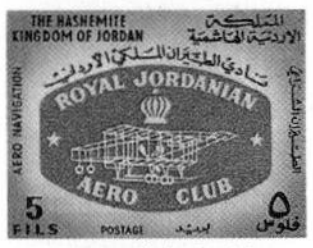

155 Aero Club Emblem

1973. Royal Jordanian Aero Club.

990	**155**	5f. black, blue and yellow (postage)	80	35
991	**155**	10f. black, blue and yellow	80	35
992	-	15f. multicoloured (air)	80	35
993	-	20f. multicoloured	90	40
994	-	40f. multicoloured	1·80	80

DESIGNS: 15f. Piper Cherokee 140 aircraft; 20f. Beech B55 Baron airplane; 40f. Winged horse emblem.

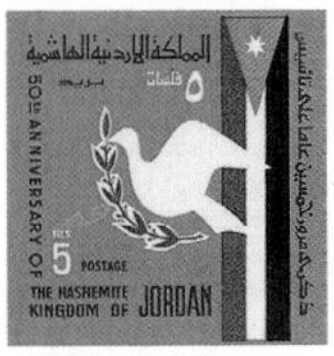

156 Dove and Flag

1973. 50th Anniv of Hashemite Kingdom of Jordan. Multicoloured.

995	5f. Type **156**	10	10
996	10f. Anniversary emblem	35	15
997	15f. King Hussein	80	20
998	30f. Map and emblems	1·70	1·50

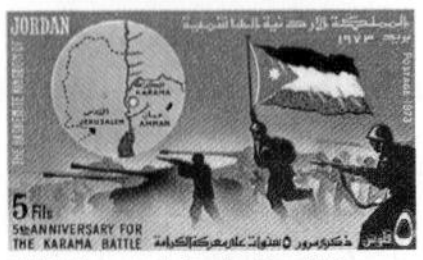

157 Map and Jordanian Advance

1973. Fifth Anniv of Battle of Karama. Multicoloured.

999	5f. Type **157**	35	20
1000	10f. Jordanian attack, and map	65	35
1001	15f. Map, and King Hussein on tank	1·70	1·10

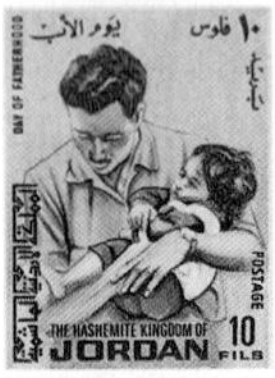

158 Father and Son

1973. Fathers' Day. Multicoloured.

1002	10f. Type **158**	20	20
1003	20f. Father and daughter	80	25
1004	30f. Family group	1·20	55

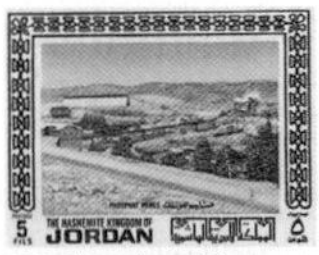

159 Phosphate Mines

1973. Development Projects. Multicoloured.

1005	5f. Type **159**	35	10
1006	10f. Cement factories	45	20
1007	15f. Sharhabil Dam	80	25
1008	20f. Kafrein Dam	1·10	55

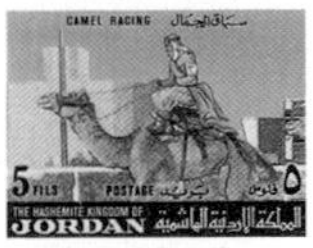

160 Racing Camel

1973. Camel Racing. Multicoloured.

1009	5f. Type **160**	1·00	35
1010	10f. Camels in "paddock"	1·00	35
1011	15f. Start of race	1·00	35
1012	20f. Camel racing	1·00	45

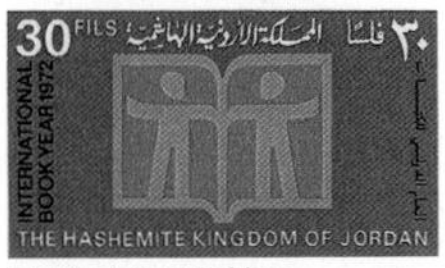

161 Book Year Emblem

1973. International Book Year (1972).

1013	**161**	30f. multicoloured	65	35
1014	**161**	60f. multicoloured	1·60	45

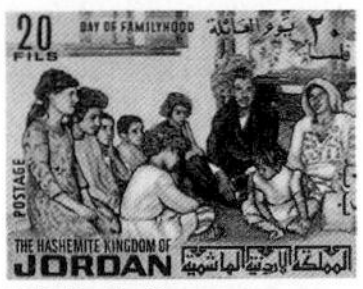

162 Family Group

1973. Family Day.

1015	**162**	20f. multicoloured	65	35
1016	-	30f. multicoloured	65	35
1017	-	60f. multicoloured	1·20	45

DESIGNS: 30, 60f. Different family groups.

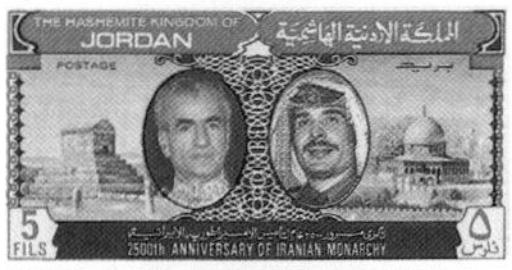

163 Shah of Iran, King Hussein, Cyrus's Tomb and Mosque of Omar

1973. 2500th Anniv of Iranian Monarchy.

1018	**163**	5f. multicoloured	65	20
1019	**163**	10f. multicoloured	90	25
1020	**163**	15f. multicoloured	1·00	35
1021	**163**	30f. multicoloured	2·50	80

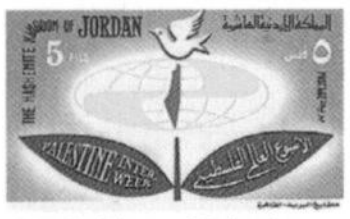

164 Emblem of Palestine Week

1973. Palestine Week. Multicoloured.

1022	5f. Type **164**	55	35
1023	10f. Torch and emblem	80	40
1024	15f. Refugees (26×47 mm)	90	45
1025	30f. Children and map on Globe	2·00	65

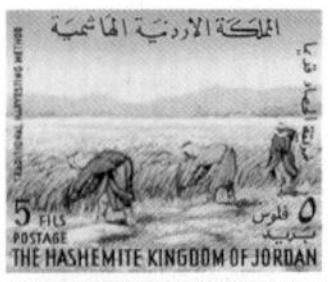

165 Traditional Harvesting

1973. Ancient and Modern Agriculture. Multicoloured.

1026	5f. Type **165** (postage)	20	20
1027	10f. Modern harvesting	35	20
1028	15f. Traditional seeding	65	25
1029	20f. Modern seeding	1·00	25
1030	30f. Traditional ploughing	1·10	35
1031	35f. Modern ploughing	1·30	35
1032	45f. Pest control	1·70	40
1033	60f. Horticulture	3·00	1·50
1034	100f. Agricultural landscape (air)	3·25	1·70

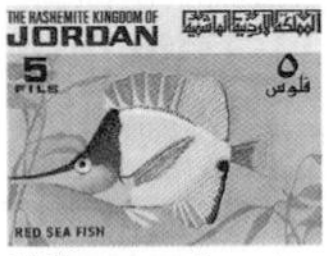

166 Long-nosed Butterflyfish

1974. Red Sea Fishes. Multicoloured.

1035	5f. Type **166**	55	20
1036	10f. Monocle bream	65	20
1037	15f. As No. 1036	1·20	25
1038	20f. Slender-spined mojarra	1·50	35
1039	25f. As No. 1038	2·10	60
1040	30f. Russell's snapper	2·20	65
1041	35f. As No. 1040	3·25	1·10
1042	40f. Blue-barred orange parrotfish	3·25	1·20
1043	45f. As No. 1042	4·25	1·30
1044	50f. Type **166**	4·75	1·50
1045	60f. Yellow-edged lyretail	5·50	1·90

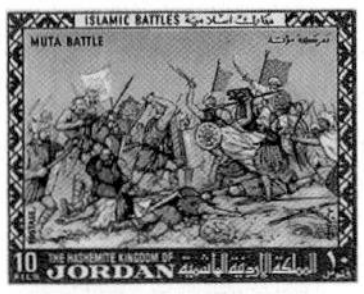

167 Battle of Muta

1974. Islamic Battles against the Crusaders. Multicoloured.

1046	10f. Type **167**	65	25
1047	20f. Battle of Yarmouk	1·70	45
1048	30f. Battle of Hattin	2·75	1·20

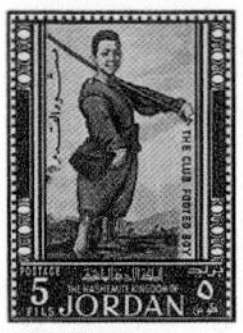

168 *The Club-footed Boy* (Murillo)

1974. Famous Paintings. Multicoloured.

1049	5f. Type **168**	1·50	45
1050	10f. *Praying Hands* (Durer)	1·50	45
1051	15f. *St. George and the Dragon* (Uccello)	1·50	45
1052	20f. *The Mona Lisa* (L. da Vinci)	1·50	45
1053	30f. *Hope* (F. Watts)	1·50	45
1054	40f. *The Angelus* (Jean Millet) (horiz)	1·80	50
1055	50f. *The Artist and her Daughter* (Angelica Kauffmann)	2·20	55
1056	60f. *Whistler's Mother* (J. Whistler) (horiz)	3·25	1·20
1057	100f. *Master Hare* (Sir J. Reynolds)	4·75	2·00

المؤتمر الدولي لتاريخ بلاد الشام
٢٠ – ١٩٧٤/٤/٢٥
الجامعة الاردنية

(169)

1974. International Conference for Damascus History. Nos. 1013/14 optd with T **169**.

1058	**161**	30f. multicoloured	65	45
1059	**161**	60f. multicoloured	1·60	1·00

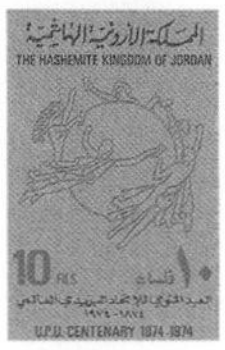

170 U.P.U. Emblem

1974. Centenary of Universal Postal Union.

1060	**170**	10f. multicoloured	45	45
1061	**170**	30f. multicoloured	65	50
1062	**170**	60f. multicoloured	1·20	55

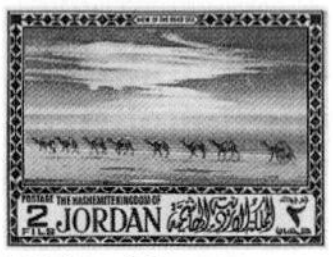

171 Camel Caravan

1974. The Dead Sea. Multicoloured.

1063	2f. Type **171**	20	10
1064	3f. Palm and shore	20	10
1065	4f. Hotel on coast	20	10
1066	5f. Jars from Qumram Caves	1·00	45
1067	6f. Copper scrolls (vert)	1·00	45
1068	10f. Cistern steps, Qumram (vert)	1·00	45
1069	20f. Type **171**	90	20
1070	30f. As 3f.	1·30	35
1071	40f. As 4f.	1·30	65
1072	50f. As 5f.	2·20	55
1073	60f. As 6f.	2·75	65
1074	100f. As 10f.	4·50	1·00

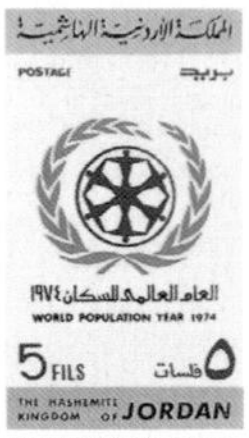

172 W.P.Y. Emblem

1974. World Population Year.

1075	**172**	5f. purple, green & black	20	10
1076	**172**	10f. red, green and black	35	20
1077	**172**	20f. orange, green & blk	80	35

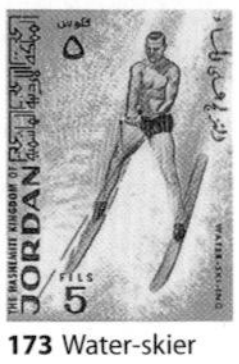

173 Water-skier

1974. Water-skiing. Multicoloured.

1078	5f. Type **173**	45	45
1079	10f. Water-skier (side view) (horiz)	45	45
1080	20f. Skier turning (horiz)	45	45
1081	50f. Type **173**	90	55
1082	100f. As 10f.	1·60	80
1083	200f. As 20f.	3·25	1·60

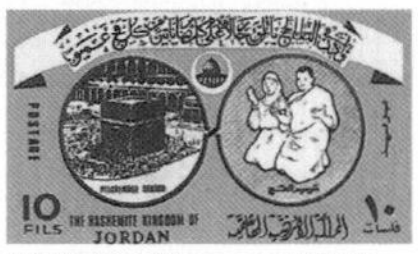

174 Ka'aba, Mecca, and Pilgrims

1974. "Pilgrimage Season".

1084	**174**	10f. multicoloured	35	20
1085	**174**	20f. multicoloured	1·00	65

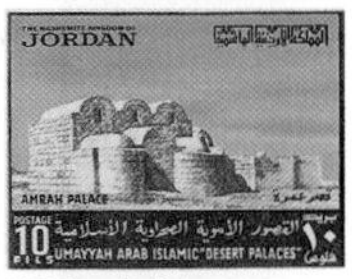

175 Amrah Palace

1974. Desert Ruins. Multicoloured.

1086	10f. Type **175**	35	20
1087	20f. Hisham Palace	80	65
1088	30f. Kharana Castle	2·00	1·00

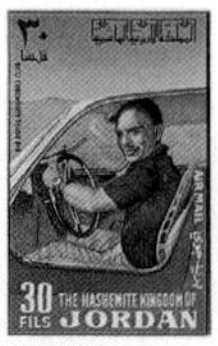

176 King Hussein at Wheel of Car

1975. Air. Royal Jordanian Automobile Club.

1089	**176**	30f. multicoloured	65	20
1090	**176**	60f. multicoloured	2·00	1·10

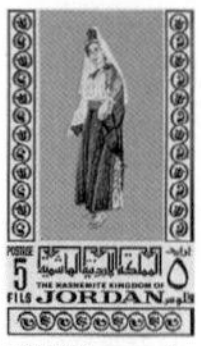

177 Woman in Costume

1975. Jordanian Women's Costumes.

1091	**177**	5f. multicoloured	20	10
1092	-	10f. multicoloured	35	20
1093	-	15f. multicoloured	65	25
1094	-	20f. multicoloured	1·00	35
1095	-	25f. multicoloured	1·30	80

DESIGNS: 10f. to 25f. Various costumes as T **177**.

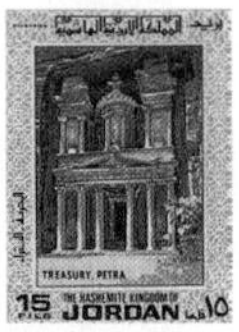

178 Treasury, Petra

1975. Tourism. Multicoloured.

1096	15f. Type **178** (postage)	1·10	45
1097	20f. Ommayyad Palace, Amman (horiz)	1·10	45
1098	30f. Dome of the Rock, Jerusalem (horiz)	1·60	50
1099	40f. Forum columns, Jerash (horiz)	2·10	55
1100	50f. Palms, Aqaba (air)	1·60	55
1101	60f. Obelisk Tomb, Petra (horiz)	2·50	65
1102	80f. Fort of Wadi Rum (horiz)	2·75	75

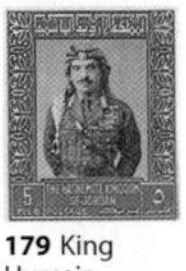

179 King Hussein

1975

1103	**179**	5f. blue and green	35	10
1104	**179**	10f. blue and violet	35	10
1105	**179**	15f. blue and pink	10	10
1106	**179**	20f. blue and brown	65	25

1107	179	25f. blue and ultramarine	65	25
1108	179	30f. blue and brown	20	20
1109	179	35f. blue and violet	35	20
1110	179	40f. blue and red	80	35
1111	179	45f. blue and mauve	45	35
1112	179	50f. blue and green	45	35
1113	179	60f. brown and green	1·50	55
1114	179	100f. brown & lt brown	2·50	65
1115	179	120f. brown and blue	1·20	1·00
1116	179	180f. brown and mauve	2·00	1·50
1117	179	200f. brown and blue	2·50	2·00
1118	179	400f. brown and purple	4·00	3·25
1119	179	500f. brown and red	5·25	5·00

Nos. 1113/19 are larger, 22×27 mm.

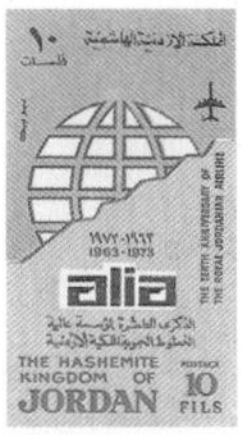

180 Globe and "Desert"

1975. Tenth Anniv of ALIA (Royal Jordanian Airlines). Multicoloured.

1120	10f. Type **180**	35	10
1121	30f. Boeing 707 linking globe and map of Jordan (horiz)	1·10	45
1122	60f. Globe and "ALIA" logo	2·20	1·00

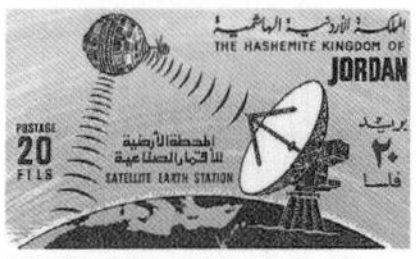

181 Satellite and Earth Station

1975. Satellite Earth Station Opening.

1123	181	20f. multicoloured	90	20
1124	181	30f. multicoloured	1·60	80

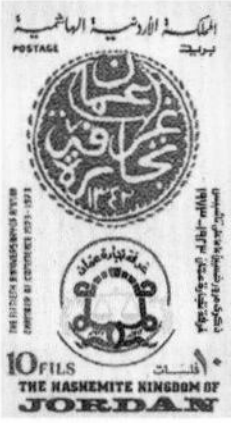

182 Emblem of Chamber of Commerce

1975. 50th Anniv of Amman Chamber of Commerce.

1125	182	10f. multicoloured	20	20
1126	182	15f. multicoloured	45	20
1127	182	20f. multicoloured	65	45

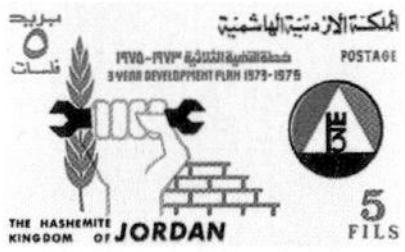

183 Emblem and Hand with Spanner

1975. Completion of Three Year Development Plan.

1128	183	5f. black, red and green	20	20
1129	183	10f. black, red and green	35	35
1130	183	20f. black, red and green	80	45

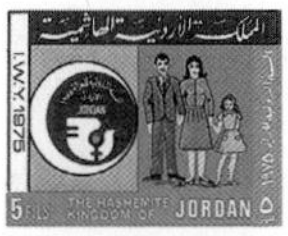

184 Jordanian Family

1976. International Women's Year (1975). Multicoloured.

1131	5f. Type **184**	10	10
1132	25f. Woman scientist	65	35
1133	60f. Woman graduate	1·80	1·00

185 A.L.O. Emblem and Salt Mine

1976. Arab Labour Organization. Multicoloured.

1134	10f. Type **185**	55	45
1135	30f. Welding	55	45
1136	60f. Quayside, Aqaba	1·10	55

1976. Nos. 853-82 surch in English and Arabic.

1137-1146	25f. on 1f. to 10f.
1147-1151	40f. on 11f. to 15f.
1152-1156	50f. on 16f. to 20f.
1157-1161	75f. on 21f. to 25f.
1162-1166	125f. on 26f. to 30f.

1976. Nos. 883-912 surch in English and Arabic.

1167-1176	25f. on 1f. to 10f.
1178-1182	40f. on 11f. to 15f.
1183-1187	50f. on 16f. to 20f.
1188-1192	75f. on 21f. to 25f.
1193-1196	125f. on 26f. to 30f.

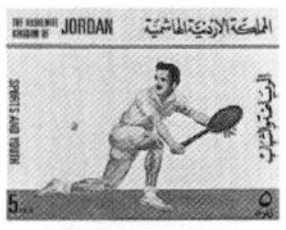

187 Tennis

1976. Sports and Youth. Multicoloured.

1197	5f. Type **187**	20	10
1198	10f. Body-building	35	15
1199	15f. Football	45	20
1200	20f. Show jumping	65	25
1201	30f. Weightlifting	1·10	45
1202	100f. Stadium, Amman	4·50	2·50

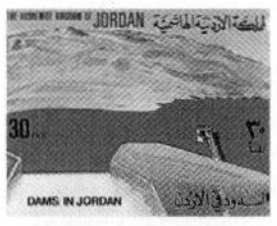

188 Schu'aib Dam

1976. Dams. Multicoloured.

1203	30f. Type **188**	90	45
1204	60f. Al-Kafrein Dam	1·80	55
1205	100f. Ziqlab Dam	3·00	1·00

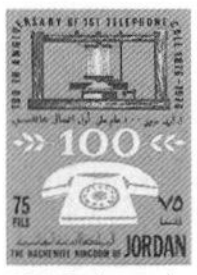

189 Early and Modern Telephones

1977. Telephone Centenary. Multicoloured.

1206	75f. Type **189**	1·70	1·00
1207	125f. Early telephone and modern receiver	2·75	1·70

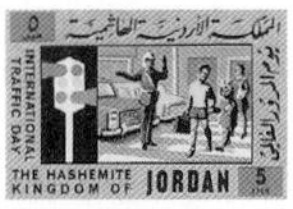

190 Road Crossing and Traffic Lights

1977. International Traffic Day. Multicoloured.

1208	5f. Type **190**	80	35
1209	75f. Roundabout and traffic lights	2·50	1·20
1210	125f. Motorcycle policemen, road signs and traffic lights	3·75	1·70

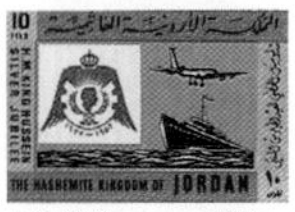

191 Airliner over Ship

1977. Silver Jubilee of King Hussein. Multicoloured.

1211	10f. Type **191**	20	10
1212	25f. Pylons and factories	45	20
1213	40f. Fertilizer plant	65	25
1214	50f. Ground-to-air missile	90	45
1215	75f. Mosque	1·60	80
1216	125f. Ground satellite receiving aerial	2·50	1·60
MS1217	100×70 mm. 100f. Silver Jubilee emblem. Imperf	11·00	11·00

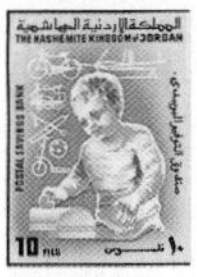

192 Child, Toys and Money-box

1977. Postal Savings Bank. Multicoloured.

1218	10f. Type **192**	10	10
1219	25f. Child with piggy bank	45	20
1220	50f. Savings Bank emblem	1·00	45
1221	75f. Boy and bank teller	2·00	1·00

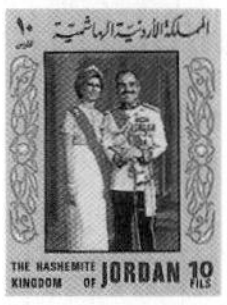

193 King Hussein and Queen Alia

1977

1222	193	10f. multicoloured	20	20
1223	193	25f. multicoloured	45	20
1224	193	40f. multicoloured	80	35
1225	193	50f. multicoloured	1·00	65

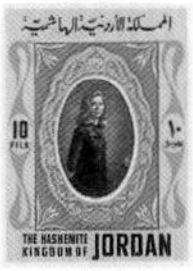

194 Queen Alia

1977. Queen Alia Commemoration.

1226	194	10f. multicoloured	20	20
1227	194	25f. multicoloured	45	20
1228	194	40f. multicoloured	80	35
1229	194	50f. multicoloured	1·00	65

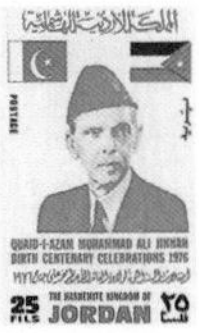

195 Mohammed Ali Jinnah

1977. Birth Centenary of Mohammed Ali Jinnah (First Governor-General of Pakistan).

1230	195	25f. multicoloured	80	35
1231	195	75f. multicoloured	2·20	90

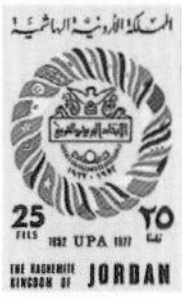

196 A.P.U. Emblem and Flags

1978. 25th Anniv (1977) of Arab Postal Union.

1232	196	25f. multicoloured	90	55
1233	196	40f. multicoloured	1·50	1·00

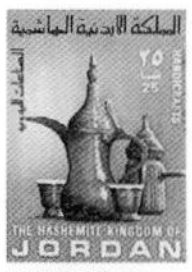

197 Coffee Pots and Cups

1978. Handicrafts. Multicoloured.

1234	25f. Type **197**	45	20
1235	40f. Porcelain plate and ashtray	65	25
1236	75f. Vase, necklace and chains	1·60	65
1237	125f. Containers holding pipes	2·50	1·70

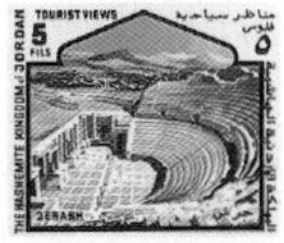

198 Roman Amphitheatre, Jerash

1978. Tourism. Multicoloured.

1238	5f. Type **198**	65	35
1239	20f. Roman columns, Jerash	65	35
1240	40f. Roman mosaic, Madaba	90	45
1241	75f. Rock formations, Rum	2·00	90

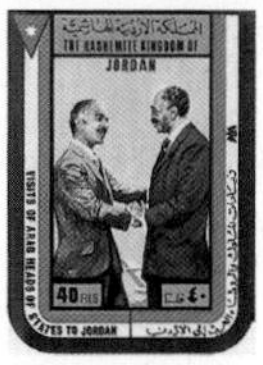

199 King Hussein and Pres. Sadat of Egypt

1978. Visits of Arab Leaders to Jordan. Multicoloured.

1242	40f. Type **199**	65	20
1243	40f. King Hussein and Pres. Assad (horiz)	65	20
1244	40f. King Hussein and King Khalid (horiz)	65	20

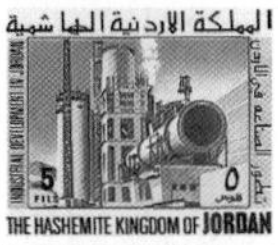

200 Cement Works

1978. Industrial Development. Multicoloured.

1245	5f. Type **200**	10	10
1246	10f. Science laboratory	45	20
1247	25f. Printing press	1·10	35
1248	75f. Fertilizer plant	2·75	1·10

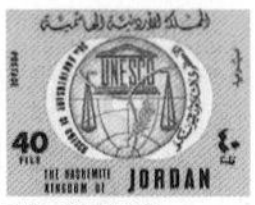

201 UNESCO Emblem

1978. 30th Anniv of UNESCO.

1249	201	40f. multicoloured	90	65
1250	201	75f. multicoloured	2·00	1·50

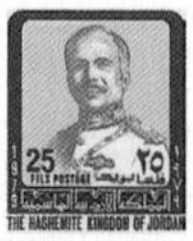

202 King Hussein

1979. Dated "1979".

1251	202	25f. brown, flesh and blue	65	20
1252	202	40f. brown, flesh & pur	1·10	25

See also Nos. 1265/72 for values dated "1980" and Nos. 1309/13 for those dated "1981".

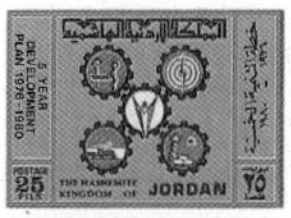

203 Emblems within Cogwheels

1979. Five Year Development Plan.

1253	203	25f. multicoloured	55	20
1254	203	40f. multicoloured	80	25
1255	203	50f. multicoloured	90	55

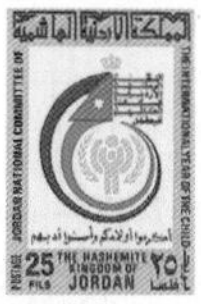

204 I.Y.C. Emblem and Flag of Jordan

1979. International Year of the Child.

1256	204	25f. multicoloured	65	35
1257	204	40f. multicoloured	1·00	40
1258	204	50f. multicoloured	1·60	45

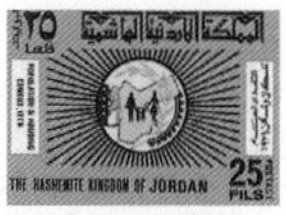

205 Census Emblem

1979. Population and Housing Census.

1259	205	25f. multicoloured	45	20
1260	205	40f. multicoloured	80	25
1261	205	50f. multicoloured	1·10	55

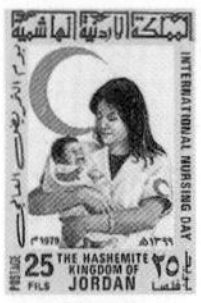

206 Nurse holding Baby

1980. International Nursing Day.

1262	**206**	25f. multicoloured	65	20
1263	**206**	40f. multicoloured	1·10	45
1264	**206**	50f. multicoloured	1·30	80

1980

1265	**202**	5f. brown, pink and green	20	20
1266	**202**	10f. brown, pink & violet	20	20
1267	**202**	20f. brown and pink	20	20
1268	**202**	25f. brown, pink and blue	35	35
1269	**202**	40f. brown and mauve	65	40
1270	**202**	50f. brown, pink & green	80	65
1271	**202**	75f. brown, pink and grey	90	55
1272	**202**	125f. brown, pink and red	2·75	90

Nos. 1265/72 are similar to Nos. 1251/2 but are inscr "1980".

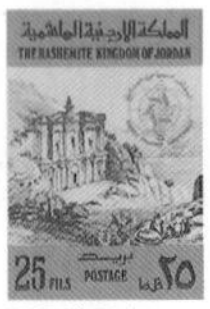

207 El Deir Temple, Petra

1980. World Tourism Conference, Manila.

1273	**207**	25f. black, grey and green	65	35
1274	**207**	40f. black, grey and blue	1·20	45
1275	**207**	50f. black, grey & purple	1·60	55

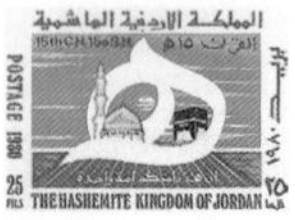

208 Mosque and Kaaba, Mecca

1980. 1400th Anniv of Hegira.

1276	**208**	25f. multicoloured	35	35
1277	**208**	40f. multicoloured	80	45
1278	**208**	50f. multicoloured	1·00	55
1279	**208**	75f. multicoloured	1·80	90
1280	**208**	100f. multicoloured	1·80	1·20
MS1281		127×89 mm. Nos. 1276/80. Imperf	8·25	8·25

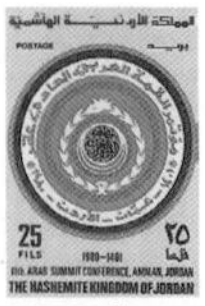

209 Conference Emblem

1980. 11th Arab Summit Conference, Amman.

1282	**209**	25f. multicoloured	35	35
1283	**209**	40f. multicoloured	65	45
1284	**209**	50f. multicoloured	90	55
1285	**209**	75f. multicoloured	1·50	90
1286	**209**	100f. multicoloured	1·80	1·20
MS1287		100×100 mm. Nos. 1282/6. Imperf	8·25	8·25

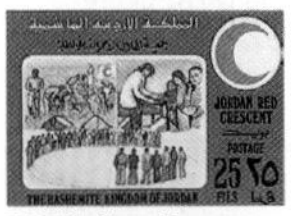

210 Picking Crops, examining Patients and Flag-raising Ceremony

1981. Red Crescent.

1288	**210**	25f. multicoloured	80	35
1289	**210**	40f. multicoloured	1·00	55
1290	**210**	50f. multicoloured	1·10	65

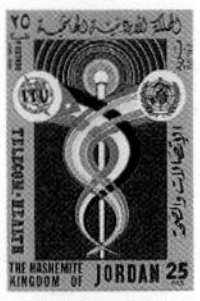

211 I.T.U. and W.H.O. Emblems and Ribbons forming Caduceus

1981. World Telecommunications Day.

1291	**211**	25f. multicoloured	80	35
1292	**211**	40f. multicoloured	1·30	55
1293	**211**	50f. multicoloured	1·80	1·00

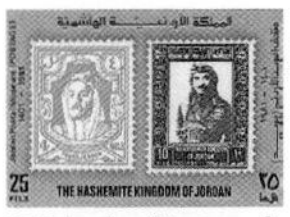

212 Jordan Stamps of 1930 and 1975

1981. Opening of Postal Museum. Multicoloured.

1294	25f. Type **212**	80	20
1295	40f. Jordan stamps of 1933 and 1954 (vert)	1·10	45
1296	50f. Jordan stamps of 1946 and 1952	1·60	80

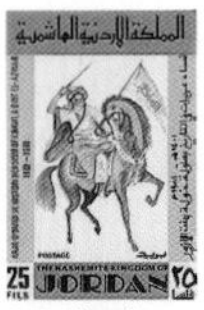

213 Khawla Bint el-Azwar

1981. Arab Women in History. Multicoloured.

1297	25f. Type **213**	1·10	35
1298	40f. El-Khansa (writer)	1·90	55
1299	50f. Rabia el-Adawiyeh (Sufi religious leader)	3·25	1·60

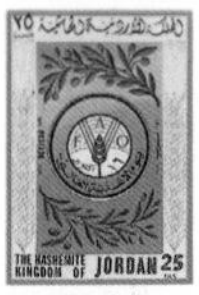

214 F.A.O. Emblem and Olive Branches

1981. World Food Day.

1300	**214**	25f. multicoloured	55	35
1301	**214**	40f. multicoloured	1·00	55
1302	**214**	50f. multicoloured	1·20	55

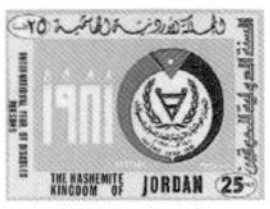

215 I.Y.D.P. Emblem

1981. International Year of Disabled Persons.

1303	**215**	25f. multicoloured	55	35
1304	**215**	40f. multicoloured	1·20	45
1305	**215**	50f. multicoloured	1·60	55

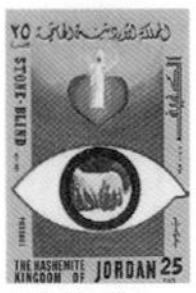

216 Hands reading Braille

1981. The Blind.

1306	**216**	25f. multicoloured	55	35
1307	**216**	40f. multicoloured	1·20	45
1308	**216**	50f. multicoloured	1·60	55

1982

1309	**202**	5f. brown, pink and green	35	20
1310	**202**	10f. brown, pink & violet	35	20
1311	**202**	20f. brown and pink	35	20
1312	**202**	25f. brown, pink and blue	35	20
1313	**202**	40f. brown, pink & pur	55	35

Nos. 1309/13 are similar to Nos. 1251/2, but are inscr "1981".

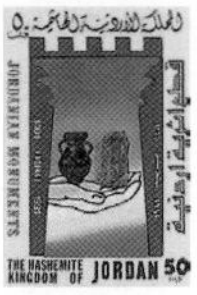

217 Hand holding Jug and Stone Tablets

1982. Jordan Monuments.

1314	**217**	25f. multicoloured	80	25
1315	**217**	40f. multicoloured	1·20	35
1316	**217**	50f. multicoloured	1·60	80

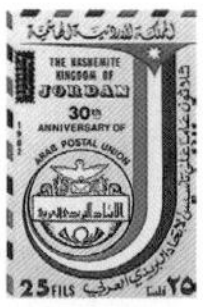

218 A.P.U. Emblem

1982. 30th Anniv of Arab Postal Union.

1317	**218**	10f. multicoloured	65	35
1318	**218**	25f. multicoloured	90	40
1319	**218**	40f. multicoloured	1·20	45
1320	**218**	50f. multicoloured	1·60	55
1321	**218**	100f. multicoloured	3·25	1·10

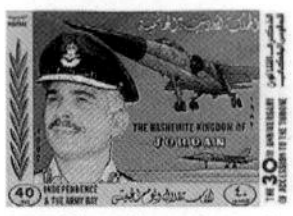

219 King Hussein and Dassault Mirage F1C

1982. Independence, Army Day and 30th Anniv of King's Accession to Throne. Multicoloured.

1322	10f. King Hussein and rockets	35	20
1323	25f. King Hussein and tanks	65	25
1324	40f. Type **219**	1·20	45
1325	50f. King Hussein and tanks (different)	1·60	80
1326	100f. King Hussein and flag being hoisted by armed forces	3·25	2·20

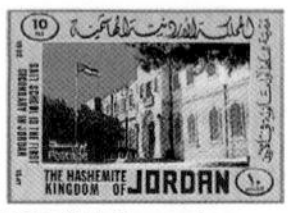

220 Salt Secondary School

1982. Salt Secondary School.

1327	**220**	10f. multicoloured	55	35
1328	**220**	25f. multicoloured	80	40
1329	**220**	40f. multicoloured	1·20	45
1330	**220**	50f. multicoloured	1·30	65
1331	**220**	100f. multicoloured	2·75	1·10

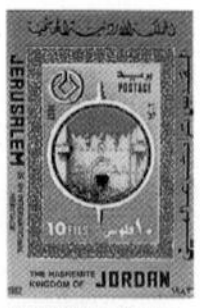

221 City Gate, Jerusalem

1982. Jerusalem. Multicoloured.

1332	10f. Type **221**	35	35
1333	25f. Minaret	1·10	55
1334	40f. Mosque	1·80	1·00
1335	50f. Mosque (different)	2·10	1·10
1336	100f. Dome of the Rock	4·50	2·50

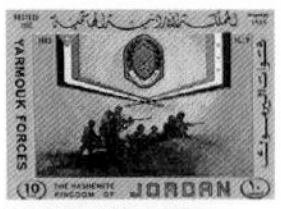

222 Soldiers, Flags and Badge

1982. Yarmouk Forces.

1337	**222**	10f. multicoloured	35	10
1338	**222**	25f. multicoloured	65	20
1339	**222**	40f. multicoloured	1·10	45
1340	**222**	50f. multicoloured	1·30	80
1341	**222**	100f. multicoloured	2·50	1·80
MS1342		71×51 mm. 100f. multicoloured (Forces badge). Imperf	19·00	19·00

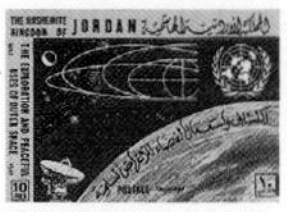

223 Dish Aerial, Earth and U.N. Emblem

1982. Second U.N. Conference on the Exploration and Peaceful Uses of Outer Space, Vienna.

1343	**223**	10f. multicoloured	35	10
1344	**223**	25f. multicoloured	65	20
1345	**223**	40f. multicoloured	1·10	45
1346	**223**	50f. multicoloured	1·30	80
1347	**223**	100f. multicoloured	2·50	2·00

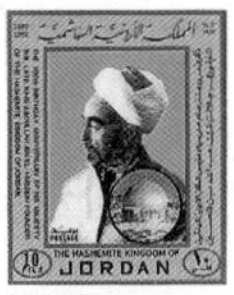

224 King Abdullah and Dome of the Rock

1982. Birth Centenary of King Abdullah.

1348	**224**	10f. multicoloured	35	10
1349	**224**	25f. multicoloured	65	20
1350	**224**	40f. multicoloured	1·10	45
1351	**224**	50f. multicoloured	1·30	80
1352	**224**	100f. multicoloured	2·50	2·00

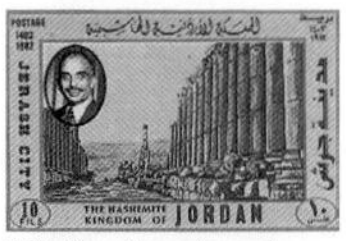

225 King Hussein and Temple Colonnade

1982. Roman Ruins at Jerash. Multicoloured.

1353	10f. Type **225**	90	45
1354	25f. Archway	1·10	45
1355	40f. Temple of Artemis	1·60	55
1356	50f. Amphitheatre	2·00	55
1357	100f. Hippodrome	4·00	1·20

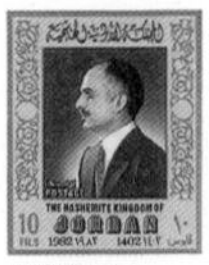

226 King Hussein

1983

1358	**226**	10f. multicoloured	35	35
1359	**226**	25f. multicoloured	35	35
1360	**226**	40f. multicoloured	55	45
1361	**226**	60f. multicoloured	90	55
1362	**226**	100f. multicoloured	1·30	90
1363	**226**	125f. multicoloured	1·80	1·00

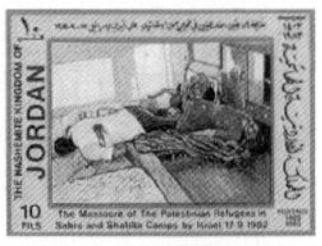

227 Massacre Victims

1983. Massacre of Palestinian Refugees in Sabra and Shatila Camps. Multicoloured.

1364	10f. Type **227**	35	20
1365	25f. Covered bodies	1·00	20
1366	40f. Orphans	1·50	45
1367	50f. Massacre victims in street	2·10	90
1368	100f. Massacre victims (different)	3·25	2·10
MS1369	80×59 mm. 100f. Wounded child in hospital (sold at 1500f.)	22·00	22·00

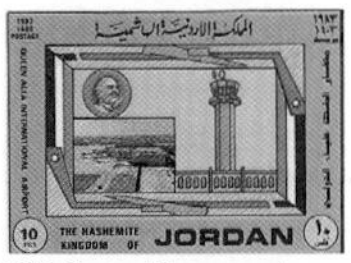

228 Control Tower and Airport Buildings

1983. Opening of Queen Alia International Airport. Multicoloured.

1370	10f. Type **228**	35	10
1371	25f. Tower and terminal building	90	20
1372	40f. Tower and hangar	1·50	45
1373	50f. Tower and aerial view of airport	1·80	90
1374	100f. Tower and embarkation bridge	3·25	2·20

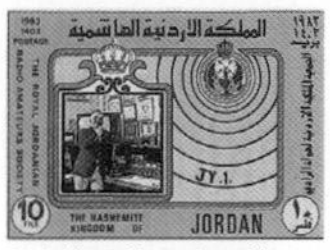

229 King Hussein with Radio Equipment

1983. Royal Jordanian Radio Amateurs Society.

1375	**229**	10f. multicoloured	35	10
1376	**229**	25f. multicoloured	90	20
1377	**229**	40f. multicoloured	1·30	45
1378	**229**	50f. multicoloured	1·50	90
1379	**229**	100f. multicoloured	3·00	2·20

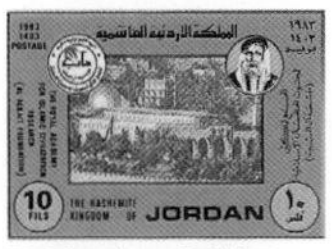

230 Academy Building, Amman

1983. Establishment of Royal Academy for Islamic Civilization Research. Multicoloured.

1380	10f. Type **230**	45	45
1381	25f. Silk rug	90	55
1382	40f. View of Amman	1·30	90
1383	50f. Panorama of Jerusalem	1·60	1·10
1384	100f. Holy sites of Islam	3·50	2·20
MS1385	80×60 mm. 100f. Letter from Mohammed to Heraclius. Imperf	19·00	19·00

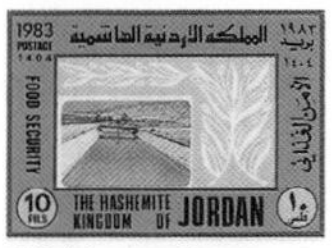

231 Irrigation Canal

1983. Food Security. Multicoloured.

1386	10f. Type **231**	35	20
1387	25f. Growing crops under glass	90	20
1388	40f. Battery hens	1·50	45
1389	50f. Harvesting	1·70	80
1390	100f. Flock of sheep	3·00	2·20

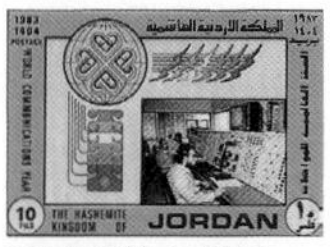

232 Switchboard and Emblem

1983. World Communications Year. Multicoloured.

1391	10f. Type **232**	65	40
1392	25f. Aerial view of satellite receiving station	1·00	45
1393	40f. Microwave antenna and emblems of communication	1·50	50
1394	50f. W.C.Y. emblems	1·90	55
1395	100f. Airmail letter	4·00	1·30

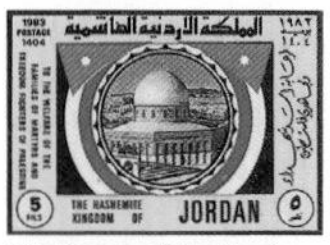

233 Dome of the Rock, Jerusalem

1983. Palestinian Solidarity.

1396	**233**	5f. multicoloured	65	45
1397	**233**	10f. multicoloured	1·30	55

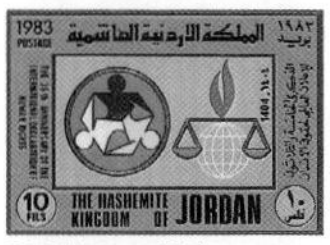

234 Human Rights Emblems

1983. 35th Anniv of Declaration of Human Rights.

1398	**234**	10f. multicoloured	35	10
1399	**234**	25f. multicoloured	90	20
1400	**234**	40f. multicoloured	1·30	45
1401	**234**	50f. multicoloured	1·50	90
1402	**234**	100f. multicoloured	2·75	2·20

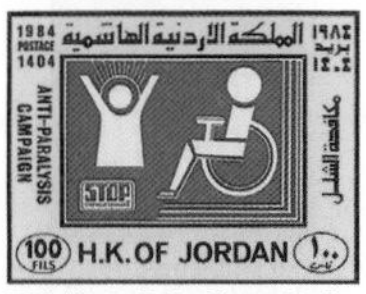

235 "Stop Polio Campaign" Emblem

1984. Anti-poliomyelitis Campaign.

1403	**235**	40f. orange, black & blue	1·20	35
1404	**235**	60f. silver, black and red	2·10	90
1405	**235**	100f. green, black & yell	3·25	1·90

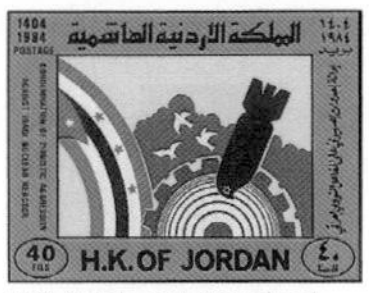

236 Bomb and Cogwheel

1984. Israel's Attack on Iraqi Nuclear Reactor. Multicoloured.

1406	40f. Type **236**	1·70	55
1407	60f. Hand with dagger attacking nuclear symbol	2·20	65
1408	100f. Aircraft bombing nuclear symbol	3·25	1·20

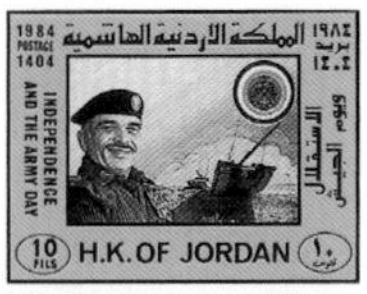

237 King Hussein and Tanks

1984. Independence and Army Day. Multicoloured.

1409	10f. Type **237**	35	20
1410	25f. King Hussein and naval patrol boat	90	30
1411	40f. King Hussein and Camel Corps	1·50	45
1412	60f. King Hussein and soldiers at Independence Monument	2·20	90
1413	100f. Parading soldiers	3·00	2·10

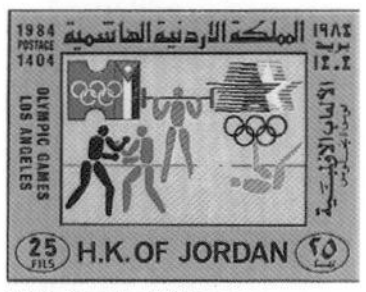

238 Sports Pictogram

1984. Olympic Games. Los Angeles. Multicoloured.

1414	25f. Type **238**	90	45
1415	40f. Swimming	1·50	55
1416	60f. Shooting and archery pictograms	2·20	1·10
1417	100f. Gymnastics (floor exercises)	4·00	1·80
MS1418	90×70 mm. 100f. Pole vaulting. Imperf	17·00	17·00

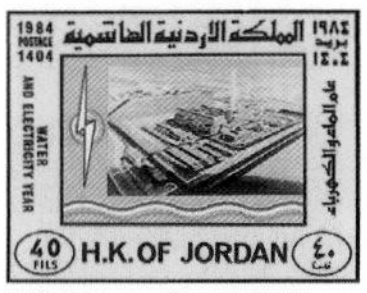

239 Amman Power Station

1984. Water and Electricity Year. Multicoloured.

1419	25f. Power lines and factories	55	20
1420	40f. Type **239**	1·00	35
1421	60f. Reservoirs and water pipe	1·50	90
1422	100f. Telephone lines, street light, water tap and pipeline	2·20	1·50

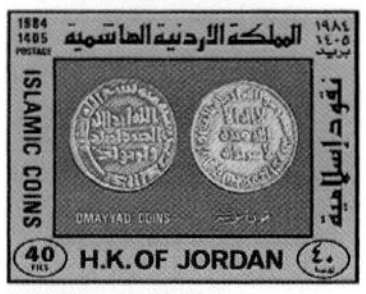

240 Omayyid Coins

1984. Coins. Multicoloured.

1423	40f. Type **240**	1·20	55
1424	60f. Abbasid coins	1·80	80
1425	125f. Hashemite coins	3·75	1·90

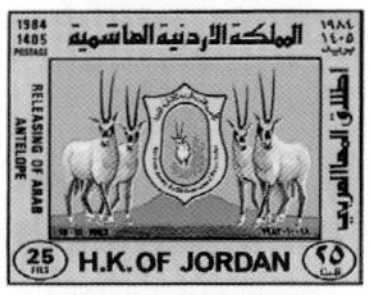

241 Shield and Antelope

1984. Release of Antelope in Jordan. Multicoloured.

1426	25f. Type **241**	80	20
1427	40f. Four antelope	1·30	45
1428	60f. Three antelope	2·10	1·00
1429	100f. Duke of Edinburgh, King Hussein and Queen Alia	3·50	1·60

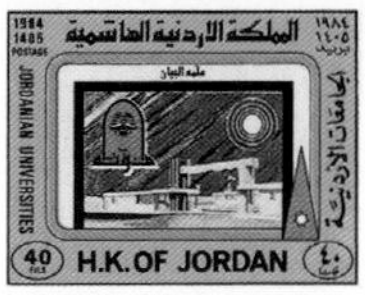

242 Mu'ta Military University, Karak City

1984. Jordanian Universities. Multicoloured.

1430	40f. Type **242**	90	35
1431	60f. Yarmouk University, Irbid City	1·30	65
1432	125f. Jordan University, Amman	2·20	1·50

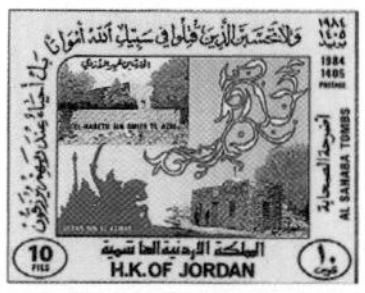

243 Tombs of El-Hareth bin Omier el-Azdi and Derar bin el-Azwar

1984. Al Sahaba Tombs. Multicoloured.

1433	10f. Type **243**	35	10
1434	25f. Tombs of Sharhabil bin Hasna and Abu Obaidah Amer bin el-Jarrah	80	20
1435	40f. Muath bin Jabal's tomb	1·10	35
1436	50f. Tombs of Zaid bin Haretha and Abdullah bin Rawaha	1·20	55
1437	60f. Tomb of Amer bin Abi Waqqas	1·50	90
1438	100f. Jafar bin Abi Taleb's tomb	2·50	1·50

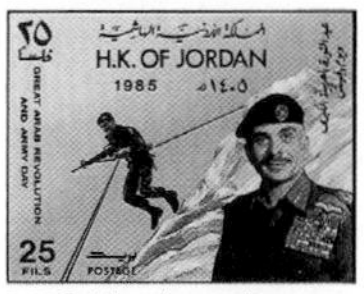

244 Soldier descending Mountain and King Hussein

1985. Independence and Army Day. Multicoloured.

1439	25f. Type **244**	65	20
1440	40f. Flags on map, King Abdullah and King Hussein	1·10	35
1441	60f. Flag, monument and arms	1·70	90
1442	100f. King Hussein, flag, King Abdullah and arms	3·00	2·10

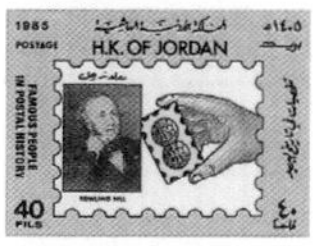

245 Sir Rowland Hill (instigator of first stamps)

1985. Postal Celebrities. Multicoloured.

1443	40f. Type **245**	1·00	35
1444	60f. Heinrich von Stephan (founder of Universal Postal Union)	1·50	90
1445	125f. Yacoub Sukker (first Jordanian stamp designer)	3·00	2·10

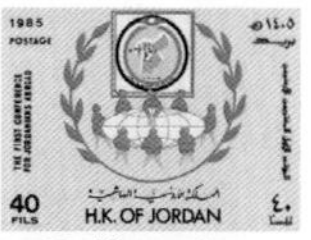

246 Emblem and Delegates round Table

1985. First Jordanians Abroad Conference. Multicoloured.

1446	40f. Type **246**	1·00	35
1447	60f. Conference emblem and globe and hand over torch	1·50	90
1448	125f. Globe encircled by Jordanian flags	3·00	2·10

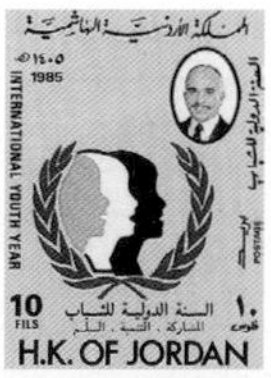

247 I.Y.Y. Emblem

1985. International Youth Year. Multicoloured.

1449	10f. Type **247**	35	20
1450	25f. Arab couple on map, flag and emblem	80	35
1451	40f. Stylized figures flanking globe, flag and emblem	1·10	40
1452	60f. Part of cogwheel, laurel branch and ribbons in jug decorated with emblem	1·70	90
1453	125f. Stylized figures and emblem	3·00	2·10

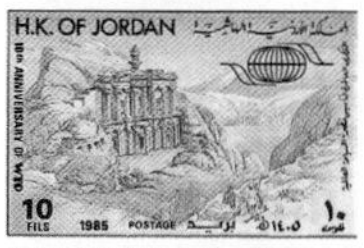

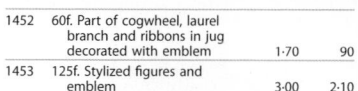

248 El-Deir Temple, Petra

1985. Tenth Anniv of World Tourist Organization. Multicoloured.

1454	10f. Type **248**	35	20
1455	25f. Temple of Artemis (ruins), Jerash	80	35
1456	40f. Amrah Palace	1·10	40
1457	50f. Hill town, Jordan valley	1·30	55
1458	60f. Sailing in Aqaba bay	1·70	1·10
1459	125f. Roman amphitheatre, Amman and city arms	3·00	2·50
MS1460	90×70 mm. 100f. Flower with emblem as vase and flag. Imperf	8·25	8·25

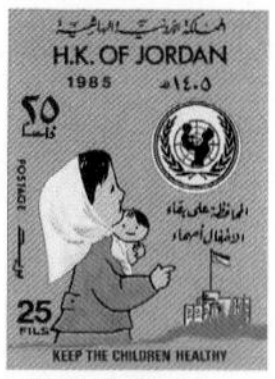

249 Mother and Baby and Hospital

1985. UNICEF Child Survival Campaign. Multicoloured.

1461	25f. Type **249**	80	35
1462	40f. Child being weighed	1·10	45
1463	60f. Childrens' heads as balloons	1·70	1·10
1464	125f. Mother feeding baby	3·00	2·50
MS1465	90×70 mm. 100f. Hands cradling children's heads. Imperf	14·50	14·50

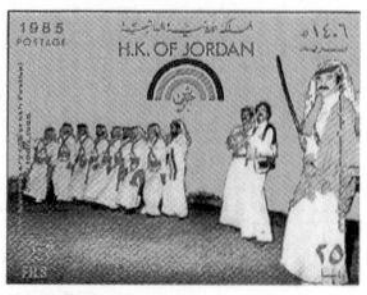

250 Dancers

1985. Fifth Anniv of Jerash Festival. Multicoloured.

1466	10f. Opening ceremony, 1980	35	20
1467	25f. Type **250**	80	35
1468	40f. Dancers (different)	1·10	45
1469	60f. Male choir at Roman theatre	1·70	1·10
1470	100f. King Hussein and his wife	3·00	2·20

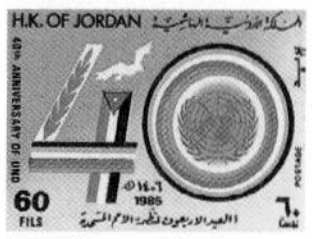

251 Flag and Emblem forming "40"

1985. 40th Anniv of U.N.O.

1471	**251**	60f. multicoloured	1·90	1·20
1472	**251**	125f. multicoloured	3·00	2·20

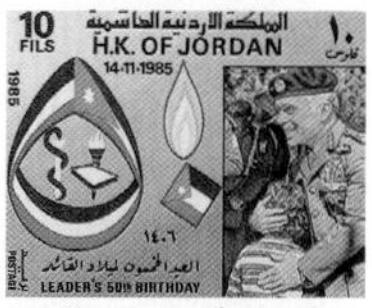

252 Hussein comforting Boy

1985. 50th Birthday of King Hussein. Multicoloured.

1473	10f. Type **252**	35	10
1474	25f. Hussein in Arab robes	80	45
1475	40f. Hussein piloting aircraft	1·10	65
1476	60f. Hussein in army uniform	1·70	1·10
1477	100f. Hussein in Arab headdress	3·00	2·20
MS1478	90×70 mm. 200f. Hussein in uniform, flags and Dome of the Rock, Jerusalem. Imperf	19·00	19·00

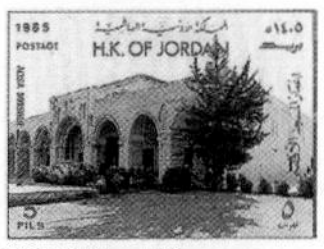

253 El Aqsa Mosque

1985. Compulsory Tax. Restoration of El Aqsa Mosque, Jerusalem.

1479	**253**	5f. multicoloured	1·30	1·30
1480	**253**	10f. multicoloured	3·00	2·10

254 Policeman beside
Car

1985. The Police. Multicoloured.
1481	40f.	Type **254**	1·20	45
1482	60f.	Policeman and crowd of children	1·70	65
1483	125f.	Policeman taking oath	3·75	1·20

255 Satellite over Map of
Arab Countries

1986. First Anniv of Launch of "Arabsat I"
Communications Satellite. Multicoloured.
1484	60f.	Satellite	1·00	45
1485	100f.	Type **255**	1·90	65

256 King presenting
Colours

1986. 30th Anniv of Arabization of Jordanian Army.
Multicoloured.
1486	40f.	Type **256**	90	20
1487	60f.	King Hussein shaking hands with soldier	1·20	45
1488	100f.	King Hussein addressing Army	2·10	1·20
MS1489 90×70 mm. 100f. Text and Hussein addressing Army. Imperf			13·50	13·50

257 King Abdullah decorating
Soldier

1986. 40th Anniv of Independence.
1490	**257**	160f. multicoloured	3·25	1·90

258 King Hussein of
Hejaz and Sons

1986. 70th Anniv of Arab Revolt. Multicoloured.
1491	40f.	Type **258**	90	20
1492	60f.	King Abdullah with armed men	1·60	55
1493	160f.	King leading soldiers on horseback	3·00	2·10
MS1494 90×70 mm. King Abdullah and Independence declaration. Imperf			11·00	11·00

259 Emblem

1986. International Peace Year.
1495	**259**	160f. multicoloured	3·00	1·90
1496	**259**	240f. black, orange & grn	4·00	2·75

260 Cardiac Centre Building

1986. King Hussein Medical City. Multicoloured.
1497	40f.	Type **260**	90	35
1498	60f.	Patient undergoing operation	1·60	80
1499	100f.	View of operating theatre during operation	2·20	1·30

261 Extract of King Hussein's
Speech in Arabic

1986. 40th Anniv of U.N.O. Multicoloured.
1500	40f.	Type **261**	90	20
1501	80f.	Extract of speech in Arabic (different)	1·50	90
1502	100f.	Extract of speech in English	2·10	1·20
MS1503 90×70 mm. 200f. Extracts of speech in Arabic and English and King Hussein making speech. Imperf			10·50	10·50

262 Head Post Office,
Amman

1987. 35th Anniv of Arab Postal Union. Multicoloured.
1504	80f.	Type **262**	1·20	65
1505	160f.	Ministry of Communications, Amman	2·20	1·70

263 Jaber ibn Hayyan
al-Azdi

1987. Arab and Muslim Pharmacists. Multicoloured.
1506	60f.	Type **263**	1·00	45
1507	80f.	Abu-al-Qasem al-Majreeti	1·20	65
1508	240f.	Abu-Bakr al-Razi	3·25	3·00

264 Village

1987. S.O.S. Childrens' Village, Amman. Multicoloured.
1509	80f.	Type **264**	2·00	1·00
1510	240f.	Child and mural	3·50	3·00

265 Soldiers on Wall

1987. 40th Anniv of 4th Army Brigade. Multicoloured.
1511	60f.	Type **265**	1·60	80
1512	80f.	Mortar crew	2·20	1·00
MS1513 70×90 mm. 160f. Soldiers on parade			10·00	10·00

266 Black-headed Bunting

1987. Birds. Multicoloured.
1514	10f.	Hoopoe	1·20	55
1515	40f.	Palestine sunbird	2·10	90
1516	50f.	Type **266**	2·50	1·10
1517	60f.	Spur-winged plover	3·25	1·20
1518	80f.	Western greenfinch ("Greenfinch")	4·00	2·20
1519	100f.	Black-winged stilt	5·00	2·50

267 King
Hussein

1987
1520	**267**	60f. multicoloured	65	55
1521	**267**	80f. multicoloured	1·00	85
1522	**267**	160f. multicoloured	2·20	1·70
1523	**267**	240f. multicoloured	3·25	2·20

268 Horsemen Charging

1987. 800th Anniv of Battle of Hattin. Multicoloured.
1524	60f.	Type **268**	1·50	65
1525	80f.	Horseman and Dome of the Rock	1·90	1·10
1526	100f.	Saladin, horsemen and Dome of the Rock	2·20	1·60
MS1527 90×70 mm. 100f. Saladin (29×44 mm). Perf or imperf			10·00	10·00

269 Arms

1987
1528	**269**	80f. multicoloured	1·20	90
1529	**269**	160f. multicoloured	2·75	1·70

270 Amman Industrial
Estate, Sahab

1987
1530	**270**	80f. multicoloured	1·20	35

271 University Crest

1987. 25th Anniv of Jordan University. Multicoloured.
1531	60f.	Type **271**	1·20	35
1532	80f.	Entrance to campus (47×32 mm)	1·50	65

272 Child's Head in
Droplet

1987. UNICEF Child Survival Campaign. Multicoloured.
1533	60f.	Type **272**	1·00	55
1534	80f.	Hands reaching towards child and flag as "J"	1·90	1·20
1535	160f.	Baby on scales and children reading	2·75	1·90

273 Parliament in Session,
1987

1987. 40th Anniv of Jordanian Parliament.
1536	–	60f. mauve and gold	1·20	90
1537	**273**	80f. multicoloured	2·20	1·90
DESIGN: 60f. 1947 opening ceremony.				

274 Emblem

1987. Extraordinary Arab Summit Conference, Amman.
1538	**274**	60f. multicoloured	1·00	35
1539	**274**	80f. multicoloured	1·30	55
1540	**274**	160f. multicoloured	2·20	1·50
1541	**274**	240f. multicoloured	3·25	2·20
MS1542 90×66 mm. 100f. Emblem, King Hussein and map. Imperf			9·50	9·50

275 King Hussein
receiving Cape

1988. Award of 1987 Dag Hammarskjold Peace Prize to
King Hussein. Multicoloured.
1543	80f.	Type **275**	1·30	55
1544	160f.	King Hussein receiving Prize	2·20	1·50

276 Golden Sword

1988. Jordanian Victory in 1987 Arab Military Basketball
Championship. Multicoloured.
1545	60f.	Type **276**	1·00	35
1546	80f.	King Hussein congratulating winners	1·30	80
1547	160f.	Match scene	2·75	2·20

277 Anniversary
Emblem and National
Flag

1988. 40th Anniv of W.H.O.
1548	**277**	60f. multicoloured	1·20	45
1549	**277**	80f. multicoloured	1·60	80

278 Emblems and
Globe

1988. 75th Anniv of Arab Scout Movement.
1550	**278**	60f. multicoloured	1·20	45
1551	**278**	80f. multicoloured	1·60	80

279 Crested Lark

1988. Birds. Multicoloured.

1552		10f. Type **279**	2·75	45
1553		20f. Stone-curlew	2·75	45
1554		30f. Common redstart ("Red-start")	2·75	45
1555		40f. Blackbird	4·00	55
1556		50f. Feral rock pigeon ("Rock Dove")	4·75	65
1557		160f. White-throated kingfisher ("Smyrna Kingfisher")	14·50	2·20
MS1558	70×90 mm. 310f. Birds as in Nos. 1552/7. Imperf			19·00	19·00

280 City cupped in Hands

1988. Restoration of Sana'a, Yemen Arab Republic.

1559	280	80f. multicoloured	1·10	90
1560	280	160f. multicoloured	2·50	1·80

281 Um al-Rasas

1988. Historic Sites. Multicoloured.

1561		60f. Type **281**	90	65
1562		80f. Umm Qais	1·20	90
1563		160f. Iraq al-Amir	2·50	1·80
MS1564	100×70 mm. Nos. 1561/3. Imperf		6·75	6·75

282 Tennis

1988. Olympic Games, Seoul. Multicoloured.

1565		10f. Type **282**	45	35
1566		60f. Mascot	1·10	65
1567		80f. Running and swimming	1·50	90
1568		120f. Basketball	2·20	1·30
1569		160f. Football	3·25	1·80
MS1570	70×90 mm. 100f. Games emblem. Imperf		19·00	19·00

283 Flame and Figures

1988. 40th Anniv of Declaration of Human Rights.

1571	283	80f. multicoloured	1·20	65
1572	283	160f. multicoloured	1·90	1·10

284 El-Deir Temple, Petra

1988. 25th Anniv of Royal Jordanian Airline. Multicoloured.

1573		60f. Type **284**	1·20	90
1574		80f. Boeing 737 airliner and map of world	1·80	1·00

285 Dome of the Rock, Jerusalem

1989. Palestinian Welfare.

1575	285	5f. multicoloured	35	20
1576	285	10f. multicoloured	35	20

286 Treasury, Petra, Flags and King Hussein

1989. Formation of Arab Co-operation Council (economic grouping of four states). Multicoloured.

1577		10f. Type **286**	10	10
1578		30f. Sana'a, Yemen	45	20
1579		40f. Spiral Tower of Samarra, Iraq	55	35
1580		60f. Pyramids, Egypt	90	45

287 Jordanian Parliament Building

1989. Centenary of Interparliamentary Union.

1581	287	40f. multicoloured	35	20
1582	287	60f. multicoloured	80	45

288 Modern Flats and Emblems

1989. Arab Housing Day and World Refugee Day. Multicoloured.

1583		5f. Type **288**	65	20
1584		40f. Hand supporting refugee family (horiz)	1·20	35
1585		60f. Modern blocks of flats (horiz)	2·20	45

289 King Abdullah, Mosque and King Hussein

1989. Inauguration of King Abdullah Ibn al-Hussein Mosque, Amman.

1586	289	40f. multicoloured	55	20
1587	289	60f. multicoloured	90	35
MS1588	90×70 mm. 289 100f. multi-coloured. Imperf		8·25	8·25

290 Horse's Head

1989. Arabian Horse Festival. Multicoloured.

1589		5f. Horse in paddock and emblem of Royal Stables (horiz)	65	20
1590		40f. Horse rearing and Treasury, Petra (horiz)	1·20	35
1591		60f. Type **290**	2·20	35
MS1592	90×70 mm. 100f. Mare and foal. Imperf		33·00	33·00

291 Trees

1989. 50th Anniv of Ministry of Agriculture. Multicoloured.

1593		5f. Type **291**	1·00	35
1594		40f. Tree and "50"	1·10	40
1595		60f. Orange trees and hives	1·30	45

292 Open Book, Globe and Flags

1989. Jordan Library Association.

1596	292	40f. multicoloured	65	20
1597	292	60f. multicoloured	90	35

293 Man carrying Basket

1989. Mosaics. Multicoloured.

1598		5f. Type **293**	80	35
1599		10f. Philadelphia (modern Amman)	85	40
1600		40f. Deer	1·70	55
1601		60f. Man with stick	2·50	80
1602		80f. Jerusalem (horiz)	3·25	1·10
MS1603	90×70 mm. 100f. As No. 1602. Imperf		19·00	19·00

294 Flags and Map

1990. First Anniv of Arab Co-operation Council.

1604	294	5f. multicoloured	35	35
1605	294	20f. multicoloured	40	40
1606	294	60f. multicoloured	90	55
1607	294	80f. multicoloured	1·10	80

295 Wild Asses at Oasis

1990. Nature Conservation. Multicoloured.

1608		40f. Type **295**	35	35
1609		60f. Rock formation, Rum	55	40
1610		80f. Desert palm trees	80	45

296 Horsemen and Building

1990. 70th Anniv of Arrival of Prince Abdullah in Ma'an.

1611	296	40f. multicoloured	35	35
1612	296	60f. multicoloured	45	40
MS1613	90×73 mm. 200f. multicol-oured. Imperf		7·75	7·75

DESIGN: 200f. King Abdullah, Flags and horseman.

297 Emblem

1990. 40th Anniv of United Nations Development Programme.

1614	297	60f. multicoloured	45	35
1615	297	80f. multicoloured	55	40

298 King Hussein

1990. Multicoloured, frame colour given.

1616	298	5f. yellow	35	35
1617	298	60f. blue	55	35
1620	298	20f. green	35	35
1621	298	40f. red	35	35
1621a	298	80f. mauve	70	25
1623	298	240f. brown	1·70	65
1624	298	320f. purple	2·20	90
1625	298	1d. green	3·25	2·75

299 Nubian Ibex

1991. Endangered Animals. Multicoloured.

1631		5f. Type **299**	20	20
1632		40f. Onager	65	35
1633		80f. Arabian gazelles	1·30	55
1634		160f. Arabian oryx	2·75	1·20

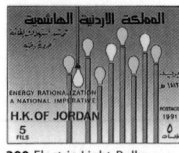

300 Electric Light Bulbs

1991. Energy Rationalization. Multicoloured.

1635		5f. Type **300**	35	35
1636		40f. Solar energy (vert)	40	35
1637		80f. Angle-poise lamp by window (vert)	65	35

301 Grain

1991. Grain Production. Multicoloured.

1638		5f. Type **301**	35	35
1639		40f. Ear of wheat and leaves	40	35
1640		80f. Ear of wheat and field	65	35

302 Drops of Blood on Hand

1991. National Blood Donation Campaign.

1641	302	80f. multicoloured	1·00	55
1642	302	160f. multicoloured	1·80	80

303 Jerusalem and Map

1991. Palestinian "Intifida" Movement.

1643	303	20f. multicoloured	1·30	65

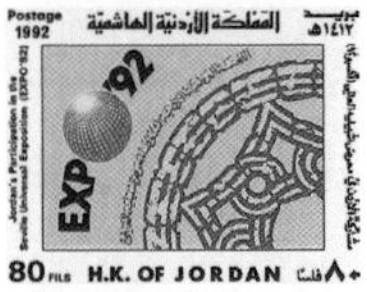

304 Emblem

1992. "Expo '92" World's Fair, Seville.

1644	**304**	80f. multicoloured	55	35
1645	**304**	320f. multicoloured	2·20	1·50

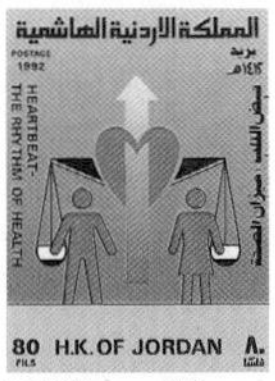

305 Man and Woman balancing Scales

1992. World Health Day. "Heartbeat—the Rhythm of Health".

1646	80f. Type **305**	80	35
1647	125f. Man and heart in balance and cardiograph (horiz)	1·10	55

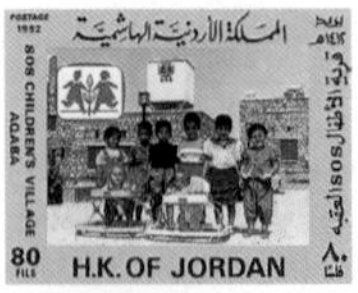

306 Children

1992. S.O.S. Children's Village, Aqaba. Multicoloured.

1648	80f. Type **306**	80	35
1649	125f. Village	1·10	55

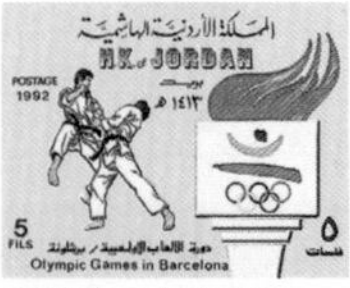

307 Judo and Olympic Flame

1992. Olympic Games, Barcelona. Multicoloured.

1650	5f. Type **307**	35	35
1651	40f. Runners and track (vert)	40	35
1652	80f. Gymnast	65	35
1653	125f. Mascot (vert)	1·20	55
1654	160f. Table tennis	1·50	65
MS1655	70×90 mm. 100f. Motifs as Nos. 1650/4. Imperf	19·00	19·00

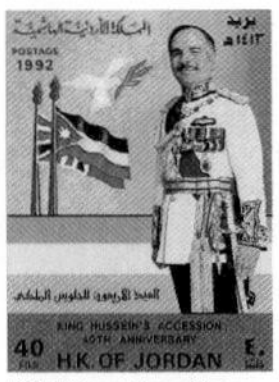

308 King Hussein

1992. 40th Anniv of King Hussein's Accession. Multicoloured.

1656	40f. Type **308**	35	35
1657	80f. National colours, crown and King (horiz)	55	45
1658	125f. King and flags (horiz)	1·00	50
1659	160f. King, crown and anniversary emblem (horiz)	1·20	65
MS1660	90×70 mm. 200f. King Hussein and flame. Imperf	9·00	9·00

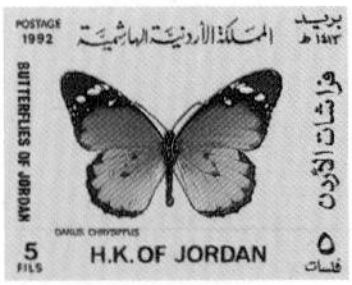

309 African Monarch

1992. Butterflies. Multicoloured.

1661	5f. Type **309**	20	20
1662	40f. Black-veined white	65	35
1663	80f. Swallowtail	1·30	55
1664	160f. *Pseudochazara telephassa*	2·75	1·20
MS1665	90×70 mm. 200f. Butterflies as in Nos. 1661/4. Imperf	18·00	18·00

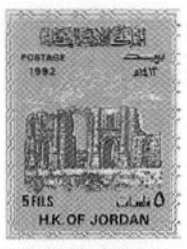

310 Hadrian's Triumphal Arch, Jerash

1993. Variously dated "1992" to "1996".

1666	**310**	5f. brown, blue and black	10	10
1788	**310**	25f. brown, purple & blk	20	20
1718	**310**	40f. brown, green & blk	20	20
1798	**310**	50f. brown, yellow & blk	35	35
1799	**310**	75f. brown, cinn & blk	55	55
1667	**310**	80f. brown, green & blk	45	20
1668	**310**	100f. brown, red & black	55	20
1800	**310**	100f. brown, green & blk	65	65
1801	**310**	120f. brown, green & blk	90	90
1669	**310**	125f. brown, pink & blk	65	20
1721	**310**	125f. brown, blue & blk	80	80
1802	**310**	150f. brown, pink & blk	1·20	1·20
1670	**310**	160f. brown, yell & blk	90	35
1803	**310**	200f. brown, grey & blk	1·50	1·50
1671	**310**	240f. brown, pur & blk	1·20	35
1804	**310**	300f. brown, pink & blk	2·50	2·50
1672	**310**	320f. brown, chest & blk	1·70	45
1805	**310**	400f. brown, blue & blk	3·25	3·25
1793	**310**	500f. brown, ochre & blk	2·75	1·10
1674	**310**	1d. brown, yellow & blk	5·25	1·70

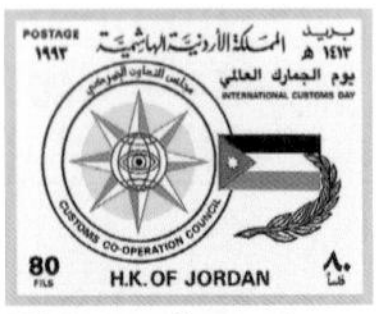

311 Customs Co-operation Council Emblem, Flag and Laurel

1993. International Customs Day.

1680	**311**	80f. multicoloured	80	35
1681	**311**	125f. multicoloured	1·10	55

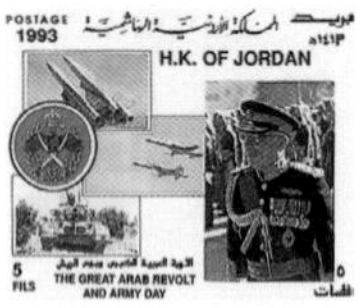

312 King Hussein and Military Equipment

1993. Army Day and 77th Anniv of Arab Revolt. Multicoloured.

1682	5f. Type **312**	20	20
1683	40f. King Hussein, soldier, surgeons and tank	35	25
1684	80f. King Abdullah and Dome of the Rock	65	35
1685	125f. King Hussein of Hejaz, Dome of the Rock and horsemen	1·00	40
MS1686	90×70 mm. 100f. King Hussein, flags of Jordan and Palestine and army emblem. Imperf	7·25	7·25

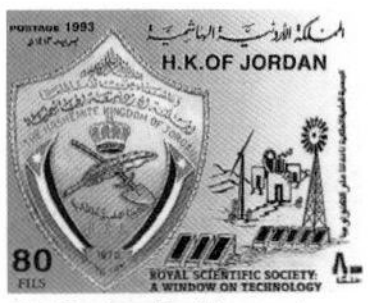

313 Society Emblem and Natural Energy Resources

1993. 23rd Anniv of Royal Scientific Society.

1687	**313**	80f. multicoloured	65	45

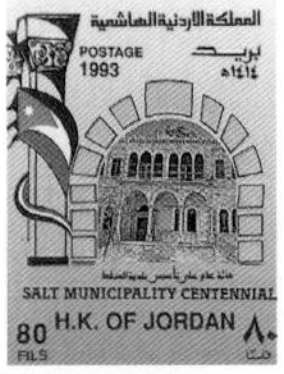

314 Courtyard

1993. Centenary of Salt Municipality.

1688	**314**	80f. multicoloured	80	35
1689	**314**	125f. multicoloured	1·10	55
MS1690		90×71 mm. Nos. 1688/9. Imperf (sold at 200f.)	7·75	7·75

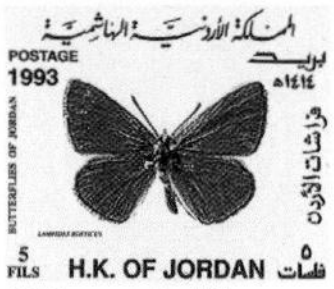

315 Long-tailed Blue

1993. Butterflies. Multicoloured.

1691	5f. Type **315**	45	20
1692	40f. *Melanargria titea*	80	45
1693	80f. *Allancastria deyrollei*	1·10	55
1694	160f. *Gonepteryx cleopatra*	2·75	1·30
MS1695	91×72 mm. 100f. Butterflies as in Nos. 1691/4. Imperf	28·00	28·00

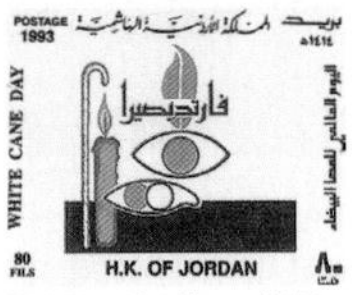

316 Eyes, Candle and White Cane

1993. White Cane Day. Multicoloured.

1696	80f. Type **316**	80	35
1697	125f. Globe, white cane and eye (vert)	1·10	55

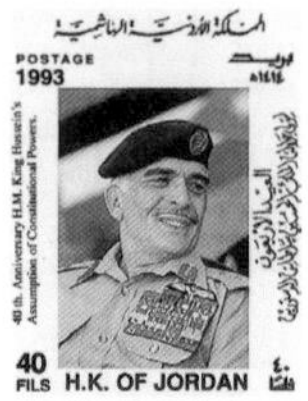

317 King Hussein in Army Uniform

1993. 40th Anniv of King Hussein's Enthronement. Multicoloured.

1698	40f. Type **317**	35	35
1699	80f. King wearing Bedouin costume	65	45
1700	125f. King wearing suit	1·00	50
1701	160f. King with Queen Noor (horiz)	1·30	65
MS1702	90×71 mm. 100f. As No. 1701. Imperf	10·00	10·00

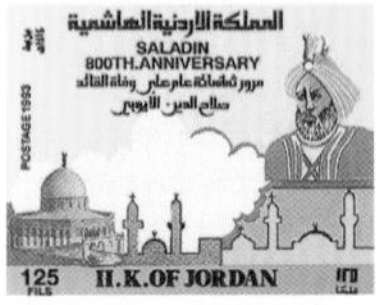

318 Saladin and Dome of the Rock, Jerusalem

1993. 800th Death Anniv of Saladin.

1703	**318**	40f. multicoloured	35	35
1704	**318**	80f. multicoloured	55	35
1705	**318**	125f. multicoloured	1·00	55

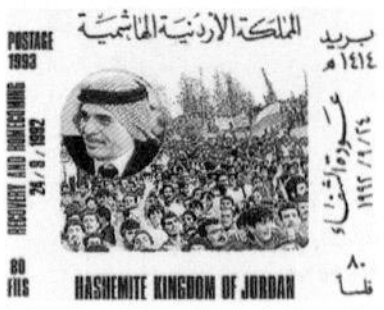

319 King Hussein and Crowd

1993. King Hussein's Return from Surgery in U.S.A. (1992). Multicoloured.

1706	80f. Type **319**	65	35
1707	125f. King waving at crowd	1·00	55
1708	160f. King embracing his mother	1·30	65
MS1709	90×70 mm. 100f. King Hussein at top of steps. Imperf	6·75	6·75

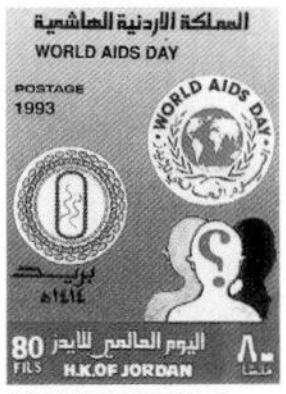

320 Virus, Emblem and Silhouettes

1993. World AIDS Day.

1710	**320**	80f. multicoloured	65	45
1711	**320**	125f. multicoloured	1·00	65
MS1712		91×71 mm. Nos. 1710/11. Imperf (sold at 200f.)	7·75	7·75

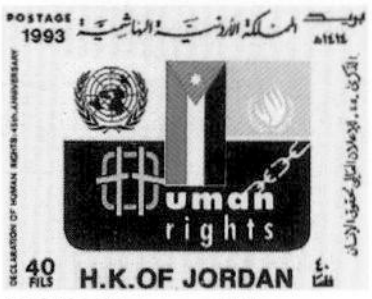

321 Emblems and Flag

1993. 45th Anniv of United Nations Declaration of Human Rights.

1713	**321**	40f. multicoloured	35	35
1714	**321**	160f. multicoloured	1·30	65

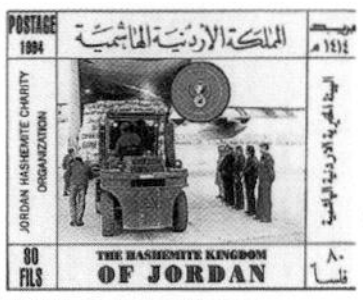

322 Loading Airplane

1994. Jordan Hashemite Charity Organization. Multicoloured.

1715	80f. Type **322**	65	45
1716	125f. Transport plane	1·00	65

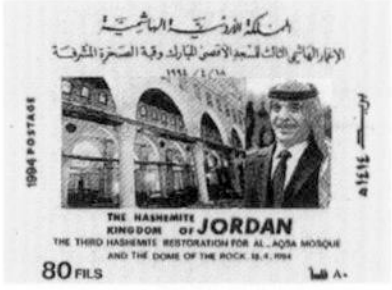

323 Mosque and King Hussein

1994. Refurbishment of El Aqsa Mosque and Dome of the Rock.

1726	80f. Type **323**	65	35
1727	125f. Dome of the Rock and King Hussein	90	55
1728	240f. Dome of the Rock and King Hussein (different)	1·90	90
MS1729	90×70 mm. 100f. King Hussein and interior and exterior view of dome. Imperf	10·00	10·00

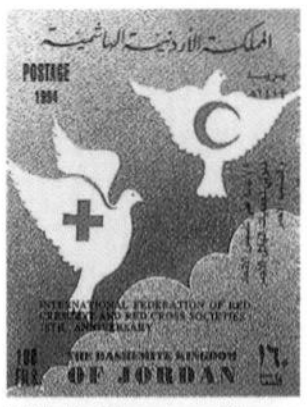

324 Emblems on Doves

1994. 75th Anniv of International Red Cross and Red Crescent Societies. Multicoloured.

1730	80f. Child and emblems (horiz)	65	35
1731	160f. Type **324**	1·20	65
MS1732	70×90 mm. As Nos. 1721/2 but smaller (sold at 200f.)	16·00	16·00

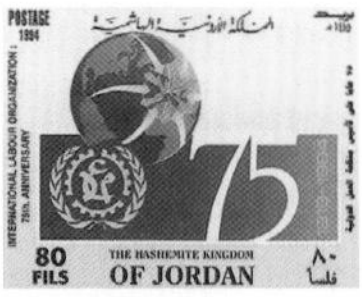

325 Globe, Emblem and "75"

1994. 75th Anniv of I.L.O.

1733	**325**	80f. multicoloured	55	35
1734	**325**	125f. multicoloured	90	45

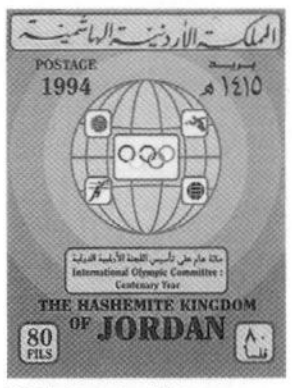

326 Sports Pictograms and Olympic Rings

1994. Centenary of International Olympic Committee. Multicoloured.

1735	80f. Type **326**	55	35
1736	125f. Sports pictograms, flame and "100"	1·00	55
1737	160f. Olympic rings, track and athlete (horiz)	1·20	55
1738	240f. Olympic rings and hand holding torch (horiz)	1·90	1·20
MS1739	90×70 mm. 100f. Olympic rings and Jordanian flag forming "J". Imperf	10·50	10·50

327 King Hussein greeting Soldiers

1994. Jordanian Participation in United Nations Peace-keeping Forces. Multicoloured.

1740		80f. Type **327**	55	35
1741		125f. King Hussein inspecting troops	90	55
1742		160f. U.N. checkpoint	1·00	60

328 Flag, Emblem, Globe, Wheat and Family

1994. International Year of the Family.

1743	**328**	80f. multicoloured	55	35
1744	**328**	125f. multicoloured	1·00	55
1745	**328**	160f. multicoloured	1·20	60

329 Douglas DC-3, Boeing 737 and Emblem

1994. 50th Anniv of I.C.A.O.

1746	**329**	80f. multicoloured	55	55
1747	**329**	125f. multicoloured	80	80
1748	**329**	160f. multicoloured	1·10	1·10

330 Hands around Water Droplet

1994. Water Conservation Campaign. Multicoloured.

1749		80f. Type **330**	80	45
1750		125f. Glass beneath running tap, foodstuffs and industry	1·20	50
1751		160f. Water droplets and boy on lush hillside	1·60	55

331 Crown Prince Hassan

1994. Tenth Anniv of Crown Prince's Award.

1752	**331**	80f. multicoloured	90	45
1753	**331**	125f. multicoloured	1·10	50
1754	**331**	160f. multicoloured	1·60	55

332 University Emblem

1995. Inauguration of Al al-Bayt University.

1755	**332**	80f. gold, blue and black	55	45
1756	**332**	125f. gold, green & black	1·00	50
MS1757		89×70 mm. Nos. 1734/4 (sold at 200f.)	4·75	4·75

333 U.N. Emblem and "50"

1995. 50th Anniv of U.N.O.

1758	**333**	80f. multicoloured	80	45
1759	**333**	125f. multicoloured	1·20	55

334 Labour Emblem and Crowd with Flag

1995. Labour Day. Multicoloured.

1760		80f. Type **334**	55	55
1761		125f. Emblem, world map and miner's head	80	80
1762		160f. Hands holding spanner and torch	1·10	1·10

335 Flags and Globe

1995. Jordan Week in Japan. Multicoloured.

1763		80f. Type **335**	80	55
1764		125f. Hemispheres and flags	1·20	65
1765		160f. Flags, brick wall and globe	1·50	80

336 Artefacts

1995. Petra, "The Rose City". Multicoloured.

1766		50f. Amphitheatre	65	45
1767		75f. Type **336**	90	45
1768		80f. Treasury seen through cleft in rocks	1·00	50
1769		160f. Treasury (vert)	2·10	55
MS1770		90×70 mm. 200f. El-Deir Temple. Imperf	22·00	22·00

337 Emblem

1995. 50th Anniv of Arab League.

1771	**337**	80f. multicoloured	55	55
1772	**337**	125f. multicoloured	80	80
1773	**337**	160f. multicoloured	1·10	1·10

338 Leaves and Emblem

1995. 50th Anniv of F.A.O. Multicoloured.

1774		80f. Type **338**	55	45
1775		125f. Ears of wheat and "50" incorporating F.A.O. emblem	1·00	50
1776		160f. United Nations emblem and "50" incorporating F.A.O. emblem	1·30	55

339 Knotted Ropes, Summit Emblem and National Flags

1995. Middle Eastern and North African Economic Summit, Amman.

1777	**339**	80f. multicoloured	55	45
1778	**339**	125f. multicoloured	1·00	50

340 King Hussein

1995. 60th Birthday of King Hussein. Multicoloured.

1779		25f. Type **340**	45	45
1780		40f. Hussein within shield	45	45
1781		80f. Dove incorporating "60", El-Deir Temple (Petra) and Hussein	55	45
1782		100f. Hussein in military uniform and anniversary emblem	80	50
1783		125f. King Hussein	1·00	55
1784		160f. Hussein, national flag and "60 60 60"	1·30	55
MS1785		90×70 mm. 200f. Dome of the Rock and King Hussein within "60". Imperf	7·75	7·75

341 Hands and Hard of Hearing Emblem

1995. The Deaf. Multicoloured.

1786		80f. Type **341**	55	45
1787		125f. Emblems, sign language and hard of hearing emblem	1·00	50

342 Anniversary Emblem and Map of Jordan

1996. 50th Anniv of Independence. Multicoloured.

1794		100f. Type **342**	80	45
1795		200f. Hussein, map of Jordan and King Abdullah	1·50	80
1796		300f. King Hussein	2·10	1·20
MS1797		85×66 mm. 200f. King Hussein in military uniform. Imperf	8·25	8·25

343 Games Emblem, Olympic Rings and Pictograms

1996. Olympic Games, Atlanta. Multicoloured.

1806		50f. Type **343**	55	45
1807		100f. Games emblem and pictograms	1·00	50
1808		200f. Games emblem forming torch and figure	1·90	65
1809		300f. Games emblem, torch and national flag	2·75	1·00

344 Hand protecting Animals and Plants

1996. Protection of the Ozone Layer.

1810	**344**	100f. multicoloured	1·90	80

345 Anniversary Emblem

1996. 50th Anniv of UNICEF Fund.

1811	**345**	100f. multicoloured	80	55
1812	**345**	200f. multicoloured	1·70	80

346 Playing Polo

1997. 50th Birthday of Crown Prince Hassan. Multicoloured.

1813		50f. Type **346**	55	55
1814		100f. Wearing western dress (vert)	80	60
1815		200f. In military uniform	1·70	80
MS1816		90×69 mm. 200f. Wearing graduation robes. Imperf	9·50	9·50

347 Karak

1997. Centenary of Discovery of Madaba Mosaic Map. Multicoloured.

1817		100f. Type **347**	1·00	55
1818		200f. River Jordan (horiz)	2·10	80
1819		300f. Jerusalem	3·25	1·30
MS1820		90×70 mm. 100f. Remains of map. Imperf	17·00	17·00

348 Von Stephan

1997. Death Centenary of Heinrich von Stephan (founder of U.P.U.).

1821	**348**	100f. multicoloured	1·30	55
1822	**348**	200f. multicoloured	2·75	80

349 Sinai Rosefinch ("Rosefinch")

1997. Sinai Rosefinch ("The Jordanian Rosefinch").

1823	**349**	50f. multicoloured	35	35
1824	**349**	100f. multicoloured	80	80
1825	**349**	150f. multicoloured	1·20	1·20
1826	**349**	200f. multicoloured	1·70	1·70

350 Performers and Hadrian's Triumphal Arch

1997. 15th Anniv of Jerash Festival. Multicoloured.

1827		50f. Type **350**	35	35
1828		100f. Orchestra, Festival emblem and Jerash ruins	80	80
1829		150f. Temple of Artemis and marching band	1·20	1·20
1830		200f. Women dancers and audience at performance	1·70	1·70
MS1831		90×70 mm. 200f. Torch-lighting ceremony. Imperf	10·50	10·50

351 Current and Previous Parliament Buildings

1997. 50th Anniv of First National Parliament. Multicoloured.

1832	100f. Type **351**	80	80
1833	200f. King Hussein addressing, and view of, Chamber of Deputies	1·60	1·60

352 Meeting Emblem

1997. 53rd International Air Transport Assn Annual General Meeting, Amman.

1834	**352**	100f. multicoloured	80	80
1835	**352**	200f. multicoloured	1·60	1·60
1836	**352**	300f. multicoloured	2·50	2·50

353 King Hussein and Queen Noor

1997. 62nd Birthday of King Hussein.

1837	**353**	100f. multicoloured	80	80
1838	**353**	200f. multicoloured	1·60	1·60
1839	**353**	300f. multicoloured	2·50	2·50
MS1840		70×90 mm. 200f. As No. 1838 but 44×61 mm.	9·50	9·50

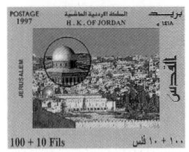

354 Jerusalem and Dome of the Rock

1997. Jerusalem.

1841	**354**	100f.+10f. multicoloured	80	80
1842	**354**	200f.+20f. multicoloured	1·80	1·80
1843	**354**	300f.+30f. multicoloured	2·75	2·75

355 Opening Ceremony

1997. Jordan, Arab Football Champion, 1997. Multicoloured.

1844	50f. Type **355**	45	45
1845	75f. Team saluting national anthem	55	55
1846	100f. Posing for team photograph and police officers patrolling crowd	80	80
MS1847	91×71 mm. 200f. King Hussein and Queen Noor among dignitaries and motorcade. Imperf	13·50	13·50

356 Women

1997. National Women's Forum. Multicoloured.

1848	50f. Type **356**	45	45
1849	100f. National flag, women's profiles and emblems (horiz)	80	80
1850	150f. Forum meeting and emblem (horiz)	1·30	1·30

357 Air Pollution by Factories and Cars

1998. Earth Day. Children's Paintings. Multicoloured.

1851	50f. Polluted air, land and water	45	45
1852	100f. Type **357**	80	80
1853	150f. "Earth" being strangled by pollution (vert)	1·30	1·30

358 King Abdullah and Camel in Desert

1998. 75th Anniv of Recognition of Transjordan as Autonomous State. Multicoloured.

1864	100f. Type **358**	80	80
1865	200f. King Hussein and camel in desert	1·70	1·70
1866	300f. King Abdullah, King Hussein and May 1923 9p. stamp	2·75	2·75
MS1867	89×74 mm. 300f. As No. 1866 but 78×70 mm. Imperf	9·50	9·50

359 Thistle

1998. Flowers. Multicoloured.

1868	50f. Type **359**	45	45
1869	100f. Poppy	80	80
1870	150f. Carnation	1·30	1·30
MS1871	70×90 mm. 200f. Iris. Imperf	9·50	9·50

360 Animals and Trees

1998. Mosaics from Um ar-Rasas. Multicoloured.

1872	100f. Type **360**	80	80
1873	200f. City buildings	1·70	1·70
1874	300f. Mosaic panel	2·75	2·75

361 Honey Bee and Honeycomb

1998. Second Arab Bee-keeping Conference. Multicoloured.

1875	50f. Type **361**	55	50
1876	100f. Bee on flower (vert)	1·00	90
1877	150f. Bee, flower and honeycomb	1·60	1·40
MS1878	90×70 mm. 200f. Bees on flowers. Imperf	9·50	9·50

362 Dove with Stamp

1998. International Stamp Day. Multicoloured.

1879	50f. Type **362**	80	45
1880	100f. World map and U.P.U. emblem	1·30	75
1881	150f. Stamps encircling globe	2·20	1·30

363 King Hussein and Map of Jordan

1998. 63rd Birthday of King Hussein.

1882	**363**	100f. multicoloured	80	75
1883	**363**	200f. multicoloured	1·70	1·60
1884	**363**	300f. multicoloured	2·75	2·50
MS1885		90×70 mm. 300f. King Hussein and map of Jordan (different). Imperf	9·50	9·50

364 King Hussein and Emblem

1998. 25th Anniv of Arab Police and Security Chiefs' Meeting. Multicoloured.

1886	100f. Type **364**	80	80
1887	200f. Flags of member countries of Arab League (vert)	1·70	1·70
1888	300f. Police beret and map of Jordan	2·75	2·75

365 Family and Anniversary Emblem

1998. 50th Anniv of Universal Declaration of Human Rights. Multicoloured.

1889	100f. Type **365**	80	75
1890	200f. Silhouettes of people and United Nations emblem	1·70	1·60

366 Wahbi al Tal

1999. Birth Centenary and 50th Death Anniv of Mustafa Wahbi al Tal (poet).

1891	**366**	100f. multicoloured	1·30	75

367 Mascot and Sports Pictograms

1999. Ninth Arab Sports Tournament. Multicoloured.

1892	50f. Type **367**	55	30
1893	100f. Emblem, mascot and torch	80	55
1894	200f. Sportsmen, emblem and "9" (vert)	1·80	1·10
1895	300f. Jordanian flag, mascot and emblem	2·50	1·60
MS1896	90×70 mm. 200f. Mascot and sports pictograms. Imperf	4·00	4·00

368 Railway Map, Station and Train

1999. Hijazi Railway Museum. Multicoloured.

1897	100f. Type **368**	1·10	1·10
1898	200f. Type **368**	2·20	2·10
1899	300f. Train and station building	3·25	3·25

369 Pachyseris speciosa

1999. Marine Life in the Gulf of Aqaba. Corals. Multicoloured.

1900	50f. Type **369**	45	45
1901	100f. Acropora digitfera	1·00	95
1902	200f. Oxypora lacera	1·80	1·70
1903	300f. Fungia echinata	2·75	2·50
MS1904	70×90 mm. 200f. Gorgonia. Imperf	9·00	9·00

370 "125" and Emblem on Envelope

1999. 125th Anniv of Universal Postal Union. Multicoloured.

1905	100f. Type **370**	80	75
1906	200f. U.P.U. emblem on envelope, target and post emblem	1·80	1·70
MS1907	90×70 mm. 200f. As No. 1906. Imperf	1·80	1·80

371 Children helping Sick Globe

1999. Environmental Protection. Multicoloured.

1908	100f. Type **371**	80	75
1909	200f. Hands holding globe as apple	1·30	1·30

372 Aerial View of Temple

1999. Cradle of Civilizations. Multicoloured. (a) Petra.

1910	100f. Type **372**	80	80
1911	200f. Front view of temple	1·50	1·50
1912	300f. Building in cliffs	2·20	2·20

(b) Jerash.

1913	100f. Path between columns	80	80
1914	200f. Columns	1·50	1·50
1915	300f. Columns and ruined building	2·20	2·20

(c) Amman.

1916	100f. Auditorium	80	80
1917	200f. Columns	1·50	1·50
1918	300f. Statues	2·20	2·20

(d) Aqaba.

1919	100f. Camels, Wadi Rum	80	80
1920	200f. Building with wooden door	1·50	1·50
1921	300f. Fort	2·20	2·20

(e) Baptism Site.

1922	100f. Rushes at water's edge	80	80
1923	200f. Aerial view of site	1·50	1·50
1924	300f. Archaeological site	2·20	2·20

(f) Madaba.

1925	100f. Mosaic of man	80	80
1926	200f. Temple	1·50	1·50
1927	300f. Mosaic of town	2·20	2·20

(g) Pella.

1928	100f. Columns and steps	80	80
1929	200f. Columns and wall	1·50	1·50
1930	300f. Columns and sheep	2·20	2·20

(h) Ajloun.

1931	100f. Castle	80	80
1932	200f. Castle from below	1·50	1·50
1933	300f. Hill top castle	2·20	2·20

(i) Um Quais.

1934	100f. Arches and columns	80	80
1935	200f. Amphitheatre	1·50	1·50
1936	300f. Columns and rubble	2·20	2·20

(j) Desert Palaces.

1937	100f. Mushatta		80	80
1938	200f. Kharaneh		1·50	1·50
1939	300f. Amra		2·20	2·20

373 Jordanian Stamps

1999. 20th Anniv of Jordan Philatelic Club. Multicoloured.

1940	100f. Type **373**		80	80
1941	200f. Jordanian stamps (different)		1·50	1·50

374 Assembly Room

1999. Museum of Political History. Multicoloured.

1942	100f. Type **374**		80	80
1943	200f. Courtyard		1·50	1·50
1944	300f. Entrance		2·20	2·20

375 Jordanian Flag and Emblems

1999. 50th Anniv of S.O.S. Children's Villages. Multicoloured.

1945	100f. Type **375**		80	80
1946	200f. Woman and children		1·50	1·50

376 King Abdullah II

1999. Coronation of King Abdullah II Bin Al-Hussein.

1947	**376**	100f. multicoloured	80	80
1948	**376**	200f. multicoloured	1·50	1·50
1949	**376**	300f. multicoloured	2·20	2·20
MS1950	70×89 mm. 200f. No. 1948 but with gold border		1·50	1·50

377 King Abdullah II and Queen Rania

1999. Coronation of King Abdullah II Bin Al-Hussein and Queen Rania al-Abdullah.

1951	**377**	100f. multicoloured	80	80
1952	**377**	200f. multicoloured	1·50	1·50
1953	**377**	300f. multicoloured	2·20	2·20
MS1954	70×89 mm. 200f. No. 1952 but with gold border		1·50	1·50

378 Crowned Portrait

2000. 38th Birth Anniv of King Abdullah II. Multicoloured.

1955	100f. Type **378**		80	80
1956	200f. King Abdullah II (horiz)		1·50	1·50
1957	300f. King Abdullah II and flag (horiz)		2·20	2·20
MS1958	90×74 mm. 200f. As No. 1956. Imperf		1·50	1·50

379 Red Cross Emblem and Jordanian Flag

2000. 50th Anniv of Geneva Red Cross Conventions. Multicoloured.

1959	**379**	100f. multicoloured	80	80
1960	**379**	200f. multicoloured	1·60	1·60
1961	**379**	300f. multicoloured	2·50	2·50

380 Flag and "2000 A. D."

2000. New Millennium. Multicoloured.

1962	100f. Type **380**		80	80
1963	200f. Palms, sand and fish swimming		1·60	1·60
1964	300f. As No. 1957 but inscription in Arabic		2·50	2·50

381 King Abdullah II, Roofs and Pope John Paul II

2000. 36th Anniv of Pope Paul VI's Visit to Jordan.

1965	**381**	100f. multicoloured	80	80
1966	**381**	200f. multicoloured	1·60	1·60
1967	**381**	300f. multicoloured	2·50	2·50

382 Pope John Paul II, Trees and King Abdullah II

2000. Pope John Paul II's Visit to Jordan.

1968	100f. Type **382**		80	80
1969	200f. Pope John Paul II, river and King Abdullah II		1·60	1·60
1970	300f. Pope John Paul II, flags and King Abdullah II		2·50	2·50
MS1971	70×90 mm. 200f. Pope John Paul II. Imperf		1·60	1·60

383 Globe and Organization Emblem

2000. 50th Anniv of World Meteorological Organization. Multicoloured.

1972	100f. Type **383**		1·00	1·00
1973	200f. Globe and emblem (different)		1·90	1·90

384 Emblem, Flag and "90"

2000. 90th Anniv of Jordan Boy Scouts. Multicoloured.

1974	100f. Type **384**		1·20	1·20
1975	200f. Pyramids		2·50	2·50

1976	300f. "90", flag and pyramids		3·50	3·50
MS1977	90×70 mm. 200f. As No. 1974 but with design enlarged. Imperf		3·50	3·50

385 Clinic Building and Emblem

2000. Al-Amal Cancer Centre. Multicoloured.

1978	200f. Type **385**		1·90	1·90
1979	300f. Emblem and family		3·00	3·00

387 Scales enclosing Palace of Justice

2000. Palace of Justice, Amman. Multicoloured.

1980	100f. Type **387**		1·00	1·00
1981	200f. Building façade		1·90	1·90

388 Dove

2000. Endangered Species. Multicoloured.

1982	50f. Type **388**		45	45
1983	100f. Oryx		1·00	1·00
1984	150f. Caracal		1·60	1·60
1985	200f. Red fox		2·00	2·00
1986	300f. Iris		3·25	3·25
1987	400f. White broom		4·00	4·00

389 Iris

2000. World Conservation Union Conference, Amman.

1988	**389**	200f. multicoloured	2·00	2·00
1989	**389**	300f. multicoloured	3·25	3·25

390 Petra

2000. Tourism. Multicoloured.

1990	50f. Type **390**		35	35
1991	100f. Jerash		80	80
1992	150f. Mount Nebo		1·20	1·20
1993	200f. Dead Sea		1·60	1·60
1994	300f. Aqaba		2·50	2·50
1995	400f. Wadi Rum		3·25	3·25

391 Column Capital

2000. Expo 2000, Hanover. Multicoloured.

1996	200f. Type **391**		2·00	2·00
1997	300f. Statuette		3·25	3·25
MS1998	90×70 mm. 200f. King Abdullah, Queen Rania Al-Abdullah and Expo 2000 buildings		3·75	3·75

392 King Hussein

2000. First Death Anniv of King Hussein. Multicoloured.

1999	50f. Type **392**		45	45
2000	150f. King Hussein enclosed in wreath (horiz)		1·60	1·60
2001	200f. Symbols of industry and King Hussein (horiz)		2·00	2·00
MS2002	90×70 mm. 200f. As No. 2000 but with design enlarged		2·00	2·00

393 Women and Child

2000. 50th Anniv of United Nations High Commissioner for Refugees (2001).

2003	200f. multicoloured		2·00	2·00
2004	300f. green, blue and black		3·25	3·25
DESIGN 300f. UNHCR emblem.

394 Conference Emblem and Jordanian Flag

2001. 13th Arab Summit Conference, Amman. Multicoloured.

2005	50f. Type **394**		45	45
2006	200f. Flags, emblem and map of Arab countries		1·70	1·70
2007	250f. King Abdullah II and emblem		2·20	2·20

395 Mohammed Al Dorra, his Father and Dome

2001. First Death Anniv of Mohammed Al Dorra. Multicoloured.

2008	200f. Type **395**		1·70	1·70
2009	300f. Mohammed Al Dorra and father		2·75	2·75

396 Dome of the Rock with Arms

2001. Al Asqa Intifada. Multicoloured.

2010	200f. Type **396**		1·70	1·70
2011	300f. Dome of the Rock and protesters		2·75	2·75

397 Wheelchair User

2001. Sports for Special Needs. Multicoloured.

2012	200f. Type **397**		1·70	1·70
2013	300f. Woman holding medal		2·75	2·75

398 School Children and No-Smoking Sign

2001. Campaign to stop Smoking amongst Young People. Multicoloured.

2014	200f. Type **398**		1·70	1·70

| 2015 | 300f. Stylized student holding no-smoking sign (vert) | 2·75 | 2·75 |

399 Olive Branches and Map of Jordan

2001. Olive Cultivation. Multicoloured.
| 2016 | 200f. Type **399** | 1·70 | 1·70 |
| 2017 | 300f. Girl holding olives (vert) | 2·75 | 2·75 |

400 Family and World Map

2001. United Nations Year of Dialogue among Civilizations. Multicoloured.
| 2018 | 200f. Type **400** | 1·70 | 1·70 |
| 2019 | 300f. Emblem, clasped hands and olive tree | 2·75 | 2·75 |

401 Sheik Hussein Bridge and Japanese and Jordanian Flags

2001. Japan—Jordan Co-operation. Multicoloured.
| 2020 | 200f. Type **401** | 1·70 | 1·70 |
| 2021 | 300f. King Hussein bridge and clasped hands | 2·75 | 2·75 |

402 Emblem, Star and National Colours

2002. Amman, Arab Cultural Capital, 2002. Multicoloured.
2022	100f. Type **402**	80	80
2023	200f. Flame and pen	1·30	1·30
2024	300f. Emblem and amphi-theatre	2·10	2·10

403 Buildings

2002. Jordanian Artists. Multicoloured.
2025	100f. Type **403**	80	80
2026	150f. Abstract (Mahmoud Taha) (horiz)	1·00	1·00
2027	200f. Woman (Mohanna Durra)	1·30	1·30
2028	300f. Hilltop castle (Wijdan) (horiz)	2·10	2·10

404 Bird carrying Envelope

2002. 25th Anniv of Jordan—China Diplomatic Relations. Multicoloured.
| 2029 | 200f. Type **404** | 1·30 | 1·30 |
| 2030 | 300f. King Abdullah II and Pres. Jiang Zemin | 2·10 | 2·10 |

405 Goldfinch

2002. Birds. Multicoloured.
| 2031 | 100f. Type **405** | 1·00 | 1·00 |

2032	200f. Rufous scrub robin (inscr "rufous bush robin")	1·80	1·80
2033	300f. Stork	2·75	2·75
MS2034	70×90 mm. 200f. Golden oriole, goshawk, bunting and hoopoe	12·50	12·50

406 Symbols of Industry

2002. "Jordan Vision 2002" (campaign for economic development). Multicoloured.
| 2035 | 200f. Type **406** | 1·30 | 1·30 |
| 2036 | 300f. Hand and computer circuit board | 2·10 | 2·10 |

407 Building Facade

2003. Archaeological Museum. Multicoloured.
| 2037 | 150f. Type **407** | 1·00 | 1·00 |
| 2038 | 250f. Building from below | 1·80 | 1·80 |

408 Sherif Hussein bin Ali

2003. Hashemite Dynasty. Sheet 230×90 mm containing T **408** and similar vert designs. Multicoloured.
| MS2039 | 200f.×5 Type **408**; King Abdullah; King Talal bin Abdullah; King Hussein bin Talal; King Abdullah II | 6·75 | 6·75 |

409 Cistanche tubulosa

2003. Flora. Multicoloured.
2040	50f. Type **409**	45	45
2041	100f. Ophioglossum polyphyllum (vert)	1·00	1·00
2042	150f. Narcissus tazetta	1·30	1·30
2043	200f. Gynandriris sisyrinchium (vert)	1·80	1·80

410 Italian Cypress (Cupressus sempervirens)

2003. Trees. Multicoloured.
2044	50f. Type **410**	1·00	1·00
2045	100f. Pistacia atlantica	1·00	1·00
2046	200f. Quercus aegilops	1·30	1·30

411 Short-toed Eagle (Ciraetus gallicus)

2003. Trees. Multicoloured.
2047	100f. Type **411**	1·00	1·00
2048	200f. Peregrine falcon (Falco peregrinus)	1·80	1·80
2049	300f. Northern sparrow hawk (Accipter nisus)	2·75	2·75
MS2050	70×90 mm 200f. Ciraetus gallicus (different). Imperf	9·00	9·00

412 Company Emblem, Colours and Arch

2003. Jordan Post Company. Multicoloured.
| 2051 | 50f. Type **412** | 45 | 45 |
| 2052 | 100f. Columns, stamp outline and emblem | 1·00 | 1·00 |

413 Ferrari F40 (1989)

2003. Royal Car Museum, Amman. Multicoloured.
2053	100f. Type **413**	1·00	1·00
2054	150f. Rolls Royce Phantom V (1968)	1·30	1·30
2055	300f. Mercedes Benz Cabriolet D (1961)	2·75	2·75
MS2056	90×70 mm. 200f. Panther J72 convertible (1972), Mercedes Benz 300sc roadster (1956) and Cadillac 53 (1916). Imperf	6·75	6·75

414 Grey

2004. Arabian Horses. Multicoloured.
2057	5pt. Type **414**	35	35
2058	7pt.50 Light bay, red bridle	55	55
2059	12pt.50 Dark bay	90	90
2060	15pt. Grey, long mane	1·10	1·10
2061	25pt. Chestnut	1·80	1·80
MS2062	90×70 mm. 10pt. Two horses. Imperf	7·75	7·75

415 Camels

2004. Children's Paintings. Multicoloured.
2063	5pt. Type **415**	35	35
2064	7pt.50 Valley	45	45
2065	12pt.50 Sun	80	80
2066	15pt. Sea and buildings	90	90
2067	25pt. Buildings and tree	1·60	1·60
MS2068	90×70 mm. 10pt. Collage of Nos. 2063/7 (detail). Imperf	7·75	7·75

416 Piper and Grapes

2004. Mosaics, Church of the Holy Martyrs, Mount Nebo. Sheet 205×110 mm containing T **416** and similar vert designs. Multicoloured.
| MS2069 | 10pt. Type **416**; 10pt. Man using sickle (68×90 mm); 15pt. House; 25pt. Man carrying basket | 9·00 | 9·00 |

417 Statue

2004. Statues from Ain Ghazal (Neolithic site). Multicoloured.
| 2070 | 5pt. Type **417** | 35 | 35 |
| 2071 | 7pt.50 Female statue | 45 | 45 |

2072	12pt.50 Armless statue	80	80
2073	15pt. Statue with arms	90	90
2074	25pt. Two-headed statue	1·60	1·60
MS2075	70×90 mm. 10pt. Two statues. Imperf	7·75	7·75

418 Nazareth Iris

2004. Nazareth Iris (Iris bismarkiana). Sheet 224×167 mm containing T **418** and similar vert designs. Multicoloured.
| MS2076 | 5pt. Type **418**; 7pt.50 Speckled petals; 10pt. Iris and bud (70×90 mm); 12pt.50 Lined petals; 15pt. Speckled petals below, striped petal above; 25pt. Throat of iris flower | 9·00 | 9·00 |

419 Salt Deposit

2005. EXPO 2005, Aichi, Japan. Sheet 321×111 mm containing T **419** and similar vert designs. Multicoloured.
| MS2077 | 5pt. Type **419**; 7pt.50 Encrusted salt deposit; 12pt.50 Layered salt deposit; 20pt. Cliffs and Dead Sea (70×90 mm) | 5·50 | 5·50 |

420 Twoband Anemonefish

2005. Red Sea Fish. Multicoloured.
2078	5pt. Type **420**	20	20
2079	5pt. Emperor angelfish	55	55
2080	7pt.50 Blue-masked butterflyfish	90	90
2081	12pt.50 Pufferfish	1·60	1·60
MS2082	90×70 mm. 20pt. Ragged-finned firefish	5·50	5·50

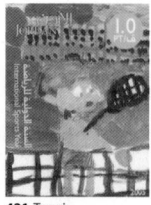

421 Tennis

2005. Children's Drawings. International Year of Sports and Sports Education. Multicoloured.
2083	1pt. Type **421**	20	20
2084	10pt. Medal winner	80	80
2085	15pt. Football (horiz)	1·20	1·20
2086	20pt. Swimmer (horiz)	1·70	1·70
MS2087	70×90 mm. 20pt. Boy. Imperf	5·50	5·50

422 Oryx

2005. Arabian Oryx (Oryx leucoryx). Multicoloured.
2088	1pt.50 Type **422**	35	35
2089	5pt. Mother and calf	90	90
2090	7pt.50 Calf and adults (horiz)	1·20	1·20
2091	12pt.50 Two adults (horiz)	2·00	2·00
MS2092	90×70 mm. 20pt. Head and shoulders	13·50	13·50

423 Mosaic

2005. Islamic Art Revival. Multicoloured.

2093		5pt. Type **423**	55	55
2094		7pt.50 Metalwork	80	80
2095		10pt. Calligraphy	1·00	1·00
2096		15pt. Wood carving	1·50	1·50
MS2097 90×70 mm. 20pt. Circular calligraphy. Imperf			6·75	6·75

424 Adult Hand holding Child's Hand

2005. Child Protection.

2098	**424**	7pt.50 silver and blue	80	80
2099	-	10pt. silver and orange	1·10	1·10
2100	-	12pt.50 silver and carmine	1·50	1·50
MS2101 70×90 mm. 20pt. silver and gold. Imperf			6·75	6·75

DESIGNS: 7pt.50 Type **424**; 10pt.Child enclosed in adult arms; 12pt.50 Adult arms holding toddler; 20pt. Boy with head on hand.

425 Japanese Calligraphy

2005. Jordan—Japan Friendship. Multicoloured.

2102	7pt.50 Type **425**	65	65
2103	12pt.50 Floodlit buildings	1·10	1·10
2104	15pt. Museum by day	1·30	1·30
MS2105 70×90 mm. 20pt. Museum exhibits. Imperf		7·25	7·25

426 Umayyad Coin

2006. Coins. Showing early coins. Multicoloured.

2106	5pt. Type **426**	55	55
2107	7pt.50 Hisham (obverse)	80	80
2108	10pt. Abbasid	1·10	1·10
2109	12pt.50 Ummayyad	1·50	1·50
2110	15pt. Hisham (reverse)	1·70	1·70
MS2111 90×70 mm. 30pt. Umayyad. Imperf		6·75	6·75

427 '2006 FIFA World Cup Germany'

2006. World Cup Football Championship, Germany. Multicoloured.

2112	5pt. Type **427**	55	55
2113	7pt.50 As Type **427**	80	80
2114	10pt. Championship emblem	1·10	1·10
2115	12pt.50 As No. 2114	1·50	1·50
2116	15pt. As No. 2114	1·70	1·70
MS2117 90×70 mm. 30pt. Championship emblem. Imperf		6·75	6·75

428 Waterfront Development

2006. Contemporary Architecture. Multicoloured.

2118	7pt.50 Type **428**	80	80
2119	10pt. Interior (horiz)	1·10	1·10
2120	12pt.50 Garden (horiz)	1·50	1·50
MS2121 90×70 mm. 20pt. Curved facade. Imperf		5·50	5·50

429 Police Vehicle

2006. Public Service Vehicles. Multicoloured.

2122	10pt. Type **429**	80	80
2123	12pt.50 Fire engine	1·10	1·10
2124	17pt.50 Waste disposal truck	1·50	1·50
2125	20pt. Support vans	1·80	1·80
MS2126 90×70 mm. 20pt. Ambulance. Imperf		5·50	5·50

430 Blue Lizard

2006. Desert Reptiles. Multicoloured.

2127	5pt. Type **430**	55	55
2128	7pt.50 Snake	80	80
2129	10pt. Two lizards	1·10	1·10
2130	12pt.50 Lizard	1·50	1·50
2131	15pt. Small lizard (horiz)	1·70	1·70
2132	20pt. Viper	2·20	2·20
MS2133 90×70 mm. 20pt. Monitor lizard. Imperf		6·75	6·75

431 Hearts

2006. Art. Multicoloured.

2134	5pt. Type **431**	55	55
2135	10pt. Dancers	1·10	1·10
2136	15pt. Buildings	1·70	1·70
2137	20pt. Abstract	2·20	2·20
MS2138 90×70 mm. 20pt. Four paintings. Imperf		6·75	6·75

432 King Abdullah II

2006. National Celebration. Multicoloured.

2139	5pt. Type **432**	55	55
2140	7pt.50 King Abdullah II wearing suit	80	80
2141	10pt. Armed forces (horiz)	1·10	1·10
2142	12pt.50 King Abdullah II wearing army uniform	1·50	1·50
2143	15pt. National flag (horiz)	1·70	1·70
2144	20pt. Sharif Hussein bin Ali during a visit to Amman, 1924 (horiz)	2·20	2·20
2145	25pt. Army tanks in parade (horiz)	2·50	2·50
2146	30pt. Rose on flag (horiz)	3·00	3·00

433 Laptop User

2006. ICT in Education. Multicoloured.

2147	7pt.50 Type **433**	80	80
2148	12pt.50 Woman using touch screen	1·50	1·50
2149	15pt. Man using touch screen	1·70	1·70
2150	20pt. Woman using mobile telephone	2·20	2·20
MS2151 70×90 mm. 20pt. Hand and key pad. Imperf		6·75	6·75

434 Orange

2007. Fruit. Multicoloured.

2154	10p. Type **434**	1·10	1·10
2155	15p. Cherries	1·70	1·70
2156	20p. Figs	2·20	2·20
2157	25p. Pomegranate	2·50	2·50
2158	30p. Grapes	2·75	2·75

No. 2153 is vacant.

435 Mafraq

2007. Traditional Women's Clothes. Multicoloured.

2159	10p. Type **435**	1·10	1·10
2160	15p. Ma'an	1·70	1·70
2161	20p. Amman	2·20	2·20
2162	25p. Jerash	2·50	2·50
2163	30p. Salt	2·75	2·75

436 Sculpture

2007. Petra. Multicoloured.

2164	10p. Type **436**	1·10	1·10
2165	15p. Ceramic plate	1·70	1·70
2166	20p. Carved leaves	2·20	2·20
2167	25p. Siq al Barid	2·50	2·50
2168	30p. Rock formation	2·75	2·75
MS2168a 87×105 mm 40p. Treasury		4·50	4·50
MS2168b 71×91 mm. As **MS**2181a. Imperf		4·50	4·50

437 Doorway

2007. Aqaba. Multicoloured.

2169	10p. Type **437**	1·10	1·10
2170	15p. Scuba diver	1·70	1·70
2171	20p. Marina	2·20	2·20
2172	30p. Yacht	2·75	2·75

438 Butterfly

2007. Butterflies. Multicoloured.

2173	10p. Type **438**	1·10	1·10
2174	15p. Brimstone	1·70	1·70
2175	20p. Large white	2·20	2·20
2176	25pt. White admiral (horiz)	2·50	2·50
2177	30pt. Orange tip (horiz)	2·75	2·75
MS2178 90×70 mm. 40pt. Clouded yellow. Imperf		4·50	4·50

439 Metal Jug

2007. Islamic Art. Multicoloured.

2179	10pt. Type **439**	1·10	1·10
2180	20pt. Iron jug with legs and animal head spout	2·20	2·20
2181	30pt. Octagonal incised jug	2·75	2·75
MS2181a 90×70 mm. 25pt. Jug with tall spout. Imperf		4·00	4·00

440 Pile of Books

2007. Culture and Identity. Multicoloured.

2182	10pt. Type **440**	1·10	1·10
2183	20pt. Lute	2·20	2·20
2184	25pt. Desert scene enclosed in bottle	2·50	2·50
2185	30pt. Script	2·75	2·75
MS2186 70×90 mm. 20pt. Details of designs from Nos. 2164/7 and paint brushes. Imperf		3·75	3·75

441 Suspension Bridge

2008. 50th Anniv of Engineers' Association. Multicoloured.

2187	15pt. Type **441**	1·70	1·70
2188	20p. 50	2·20	2·20
2189	25p. Pylons	2·50	2·50

442 Taekwondo

2008. Olympic Games, Beijing. Multicoloured.

2190	20p. Type **442**	2·20	2·20
2191	30p. Equestrian	2·75	2·75
2192	40p. Table Tennis	3·25	3·25
2193	50p. Athletics	3·75	3·75

443 Aoud

2007. Musical Instruments. Multicoloured.

2194	20p. Type **443**	2·20	2·20
2195	40p. Rababah	3·25	3·25
2196	60p. Kanoun	4·00	4·00
2197	80p. Flute	4·25	4·25
2198	100p. Drum	4·75	4·75
MS2199 90×70 mm. 50p. Instruments		5·50	5·50

444 *Silene aegyptiaca* (inscr 'Egyptian Catchfly')

2008. Flowers. Multicoloured.

2200	5pt. Type **444**	60	60
2201	10pt. Inscr 'Lupin'	1·10	1·10
2202	15pt. Judean viper's bugloss (*Echium judaeum*)	1·80	1·80
2203	20pt. Blue pimpernel	2·30	2·30
2204	30pt. Inscr 'Asiatic Crowfoot'	2·75	2·75
2205	40pt. Grape hyacinth	3·25	3·25
2206	50pt. Large flowered sage	3·75	3·75
2207	60pt. Star of Bethlehem	4·00	4·00
2208	80pt. *Orchid pyramidalis*	4·25	4·25
2209	100pt. *Calotropis* (inscr 'calotrpis')	4·75	4·75
MS2210	90×70 mm. 50pt. Cyclamen. Imperf	5·50	5·50

445 Fresco

2008. World Heritage Site. Quseir Amra (early 8th century castle, one of the most important examples of early Islamic art). Designs showing frescoes. Multicoloured.

2211	40pt. Type **445**	3·25	3·25
2212	60pt. Grapes and vine	4·00	4·00
2213	80pt. Games	4·25	4·25
2214	100pt. Face	4·75	4·75
MS2215	90×70 mm. 50pt. Quseir Amra	5·50	5·50

448 Coffee Grinder

2009. Coffee Drinking. Multicoloured.

2228	40pt. Type **448**	3·25	3·25
2229	60pt. Coffee pots and coffee roasting over embers	4·00	4·00
2230	80pt. Coffee pot and cups	4·25	4·25
2231	100pt. Coffee and coffee roasting implements	4·75	4·75
MS2232	70×90 mm. 50pt. Coffee making equipment. Imperf	5·50	5·50

449 Woman wearing Dress with Embroidered Bodice

2009. Traditional Clothes. Multicoloured.

2233	40pt. Type **449**	4·25	4·25
2234	60pt. Woman wearing brown dress and white veil	4·00	4·00
2235	80pt. Woman wearing red headdress and coin jewellery	4·25	4·25
2236	100pt. Couple	4·75	4·75
MS2237	70×90 mm. 50pt. As Type **449** (enlarged detail). Imperf	5·50	5·50

450 Pope Benedict XVI and King Abdullah II

2009. Visit of Pope Benedict XVI. Multicoloured.

2238	20pt. Type **450**	2·30	2·30
2239	30pt. Pope Benedict XVI	2·75	2·75
2240	40pt. Pope Benedict XVI and King Abdullah II (different)	3·25	3·25
MS2241	90×70 mm. 50pt. As No. 2240 (enlarged detail). Imperf	5·50	5·50

451 King Abdullah II

2009. Tenth Anniv of Accession of King Abdullah II.

2242	**451**	10pt. multicoloured	1·10	1·10
2243	**451**	15pt. multicoloured	1·70	1·70
2244	**451**	20pt. multicoloured	2·20	2·20
2245	**451**	25pt. multicoloured	2·50	2·50
2246	**451**	30pt. multicoloured	2·75	2·75
2247	**451**	35pt. multicoloured	3·00	3·00
2248	**451**	40pt. multicoloured	3·25	3·25
2249	**451**	45pt. multicoloured	3·50	3·50
2250	**451**	50pt. multicoloured	3·75	3·75
2251	**451**	1d. multicoloured	4·75	4·75

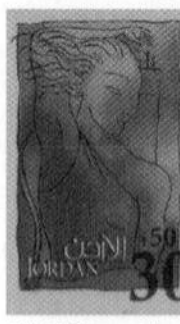

452 Diana, the Huntress (As Type **2342** of USA)

2009. Breast Cancer Awareness Campaign.

2252	**452**	30pt.+50pt. multicoloured	4·25	4·25

453 Horse

2009. Fauna. Multicoloured.

2253	10pt. Type **453**	45	45
2254	20pt. Rabbits	75	75
2255	30pt. Fox	1·30	1·30
2256	40pt. Oryx (inscr 'Maha Gazelle')	1·70	1·70
2257	50pt. Gazelle	2·10	2·10
MS2258	90×70 mm. 60pt. Camel. Imperf	4·25	4·25

No. 2259 is vacant.

454 Cables

2009. e-Government Programme. Multicoloured.

2260	20pt. Type **454**	65	65
2261	30pt. Emblem	1·10	1·10
2262	40pt. 'www.jordan.gov.jo'	1·80	1·80
2263	50pt. Symbols of communication	2·50	2·50

455 Spring-fed Waterfalls

2009. Hammamat Ma'een Hot Springs. Multicoloured.

2264	10pt. Type **455**	45	45
2265	20pt. Resort	75	75
2266	30pt. Waterfall and pool	1·30	1·30
2267	40pt. Waterfalls (different)	1·70	1·70
2268	50pt. Springs and dam	2·10	2·10
MS2269	70×90mm. 60pt. Single waterfall	4·25	4·25

456

457

458

459

460

461

462

463

464

465

2009. Jordanian Universities

2270	**456**	20pt. multicoloured	1·50	1·50
2271	**457**	20pt. multicoloured	1·50	1·50
2272	**458**	20pt. multicoloured	1·50	1·50
2273	**459**	20pt. multicoloured	1·50	1·50
2274	**460**	20pt. multicoloured	1·50	1·50
2275	**461**	20pt. multicoloured	1·50	1·50
2276	**462**	20pt. multicoloured	1·50	1·50
2277	**463**	20pt. multicoloured	1·50	1·50
2278	**464**	20pt. multicoloured	1·50	1·50
2279	**465**	20pt. multicoloured	1·50	1·50

466 Sweetcorn

2009. Vegetables. Multicoloured.

2280	20pt. Type **466**	1·50	1·50
2281	20pt. Garlic and onions	1·50	1·50
2282	20pt. Peas, beans and okra	1·50	1·50
2283	20pt. Cabbages	1·50	1·50
2284	20pt. Aubergines	1·50	1·50
2285	20pt. Sweet peppers	1·50	1·50
2286	20pt. Sweet peppers	1·50	1·50
2287	20pt. Chilli peppers	1·50	1·50
2288	20pt. Turnips, swedes and radishes	1·50	1·50
2289	20pt Tomatoes and courgettes	1·50	1·50

467 Distressed Tree and Litter

2009. Environmental Protection. Multicoloured.

2290	20pt. Type **467**	1·10	1·10
2291	30pt. Litter on fire and children running	1·50	1·50
2292	40pt. Farm animals eating litter	2·40	2·40
2293	50pt. Litter in stream and recycling bins	3·25	3·25

No. 2294 is vacant.

468 Emblem

2009. al-Quds—2009 Arab Capital of Culture

2295	**468**	20pt.+25pts. multicoloured	1·90	1·90
2296		30pts.+25pts. multicoloured	2·30	2·30
2297		40pts+25pts. multicoloured	3·50	3·50
2298		50pts+25pts. multicoloured	5·75	5·75

Nos. 2299/308 are vacant.

470

2009. Nos. 929/31 surch as T **470**

2309	80pt. on 120f. black and salmon (Type **139**)	4·75	4·75
2310	80pt. on 180f. black, deep brown and lilac (930)	4·75	4·75
2311	80pt. on 200f. multicoloured (931)	4·75	4·75

471 Ajlun

2010. Tourism. Multicoloured.

2312	10pt. Type **471**	50	50
2313	20pt. Column and capital, Amman	85	85
2314	30pt. Stone corridor, Karak	1·20	1·20
2315	40pt. Stone staircase, Showbak	1·90	1·90
MS2316	90×70 mm. 50pt. Partial façade, Jerash. Imperf	3·00	3·00

472 *Cortinarius balteatus*

2010. Fungi. Multicoloured.

2317	20pt. Type **472**	1·20	1·20
2318	20pt. *Russula bicolor*	1·20	1·20
2319	20pt. Fly agaric (inscr 'Red Fly Agaric')	1·20	1·20
2320	20pt. Inscr 'Amanita muscaria'	1·20	1·20
2321	20pt. *Boletus edulis*	1·20	1·20
2322	20pt. *Amanita ocreata* (inscr 'Amanita albocreata')	1·20	1·20
2323	20pt. Inscr 'Agaricus Anderwij'	1·20	1·20
2324	20pt. *Agaricus bisporus*	1·20	1·20

473 Jordan University Mosque

2010. Mosques. Multicoloured.

2325	10pt. Type **473**	80	80
2326	20pt. Abu-Darwiesh	1·10	1·10
2327	30pt. Al-Hussainy	1·60	1·60
2328	40pt. King Abdullah Mosque	2·40	2·40
2329	50pt. King Hussain Bin Talal Mosque	2·75	2·75

474 Skydiving

2010. Sports. Multicoloured.

2330	10pt. Type **474**	55	55
2331	20pt. Swimming	85	85
2332	30pt. Air ballooning	1·30	1·30
2333	40pt Yacht racing	1·80	1·80
MS2334	70×90mm. 50pt. Rallying. Imperf	3·00	3·00

OBLIGATORY TAX

T 36 Mosque in Hebron

1947

T264	**T36**	1m. blue	65	45
T265	**T36**	2m. red	80	55
T266	**T36**	3m. green	90	80
T267	**T36**	5m. red	1·10	90
T268	-	10m. red	1·20	1·10
T269	-	15m. grey	1·80	1·30
T270	-	20m. brown	2·75	1·70
T271	-	50m. violet	4·50	3·25
T272	-	100m. red	13·50	9·50
T273	-	200m. blue	39·00	22·00
T274	-	500m. green	80·00	60·00
T275	-	£P1 brown	£160	£130

DESIGNS: Nos. T268/71, Dome of the Rock; Nos. T272/75, Acre.

1950. Optd **Aid** in English and Arabic.

T290	**T28**	5m. orange	21·00	21·00
T291	**T28**	10m. violet	28·00	28·00
T292	**T28**	15m. green	33·00	33·00

T 43 Ruins at Palmyra, Syria

1950. Revenue stamps optd **Aid** in English and Arabic.

T296	**T43**	5m. orange	25·00	19·00
T297	**T43**	10m. violet	25·00	22·00

1951. Values in "FILS".

T302	**T36**	5f. red	80	80
T303	-	10f. red	80	80
T304	-	15f. black	90	90
T305	-	20f. brown	1·10	1·10
T306	-	100f. orange	5·50	5·50

DESIGNS: Nos. T303/305, Dome of the Rock; No. T306, Acre.

1952. Nos. T264/75 optd **J.D.** (T344) or **FILS** (others).

T334	**T36**	1f. on 1m. blue	45	45
T335	**T36**	2f. on 2m. red	£100	
T336	**T36**	3f. on 3m. green	65	45
T337	-	10f. on 10m. red	80	45
T338	-	15f. on 15m. grey	1·60	1·10
T339	-	20f. on 20m. brown	1·80	1·80
T340	-	50f. on 50m. violet	3·25	3·25
T341	-	100f. on 100m. orange	19·00	10·50
T342	-	200f. on 200m. blue	47·00	29·00
T343	-	500f. on 500m. green	£110	80·00
T344	-	1d. on £P1 brown	£180	£160

OFFICIAL STAMPS

(حكومة)
الشرق العربي
١٣٤٢

O16 "Arab Government of the East, 1342"

1924. Type **11** of Saudi Arabia optd with Type **O16**.

O117	½p. red		32·00	£110

POSTAGE DUE STAMPS

حكومة
مستحق
الشرق العربية
٩ شعبان ١٣٤١

مستحق

D12 "Due" (**D13**)

1923. Issue of 1923 (with opt **T 10**) further optd. (a) With Type **D12** (the 3p. also surch as **T 12**).

D112	**11**	½p. on 3p. brown	38·00	40·00
D113	**11**	1p. blue	23·00	25·00
D114	**11**	1½p. lilac	32·00	35·00
D115	**11**	2p. orange	35·00	38·00

(b) With Type **D13** and surch as **T 12**.

D116	½p. on 3p. brown	55·00	60·00

حكومة

الشرق العربية
مستحق
٩ شعبان ١٣٤١

(**D14**)

1923. Stamps of Saudi Arabia handstamped with Type **D14**.

D117	½p. red	3·75	8·00
D118	1p. blue	7·50	7·50
D119	1½p. violet	5·00	8·50
D120	2p. orange	7·50	9·00
D121	3p. brown	18·00	22·00
D122	5p. olive	18·00	32·00

مستحق
شرق الاردن

D20 "Due East of the Jordan"

1925. Stamps of Palestine (without Palestine opt) optd with Type **D20**.

D159	**3**	1m. brown	2·50	12·00
D160	**3**	2m. yellow	4·25	8·00
D161	**3**	4m. red	4·25	17·00
D162	**3**	8m. red	6·00	19·00
D163	**3**	13m. blue	9·50	18·00
D164	**3**	5p. purple	11·00	30·00

مستحق

١ مليم

(**D21**)

1926. Stamps of Palestine as last surch as Type **D21** ("DUE" and new value in Arabic).

D165	1m. on 1m. brown	13·00	23·00
D166	2m. on 1m. brown	12·00	23·00
D167	4m. on 3m. blue	13·00	25·00
D168	8m. on 3m. blue	13·00	25·00
D169	13m. on 13m. blue	18·00	28·00
D170	5p. on 13m. blue	22·00	40·00

The lower line of the surcharge differs for each value.

١ مستحق ١

1 1

(**D25**)

1928. Surch as Type **D25** or optd only.

D183	**22**	1m. on 3m. red	1·75	8·00
D184	**22**	2m. blue	3·00	7·50
D185	**22**	4m. on 15m. blue	3·00	12·00
D186	**22**	10m. red	7·00	9·50
D187	**23**	20m. on 100m. blue	6·00	26·00
D188	**23**	50m. purple	6·00	26·00

D26

1929

D244	**D26**	1m. brown	1·50	5·50
D245	**D26**	2m. yellow	1·75	6·00
D246	**D26**	4m. green	1·75	9·00
D247	**D26**	10m. red	5·50	14·00
D193	**D26**	20m. olive	14·00	22·00
D194	**D26**	50m. blue	18·00	28·00

1952. Optd **FILS FILS** in English and Arabic.

D350	1f. on 1m. brown	1·10	1·50
D351	2f. on 2m. yellow	1·10	1·50
D352	4f. on 4m. green	1·70	2·20
D353	10f. on 10m. red	4·50	5·25
D354	20f. on 20m. olive	9·25	9·25
D346	50f. on 50m. blue	9·50	9·50

D50

1952. Inscr "THE HASHEMITE KINGDOM OF THE JORDAN".

D372	**D50**	1f. brown	65	90
D373	**D50**	2f. yellow	65	90
D374	**D50**	4f. green	65	90
D375	**D50**	10f. red	1·30	1·60
D376	**D50**	20f. brown	1·30	1·80
D377	**D50**	50f. blue	3·75	4·25

1957. As Type **D50**, but inscr "THE HASHEMITE KINGDOM OF JORDAN".

D465	1f. brown	1·10	1·50
D466	2f. yellow	1·10	1·50
D467	4f. green	1·10	2·00
D468	10f. red	1·70	2·00
D469	20f. brown	3·00	4·00

Pt. 19

JORDANIAN OCCUPATION OF PALESTINE

1948. Stamps of Jordan optd **PALESTINE** in English and Arabic.

P1	**28**	1m. brown	80	80
P2	**28**	2m. green	80	80
P3	**28**	3m. green	80	80
P4	**28**	3m. pink	45	45
P5	**28**	4m. green	45	45
P6	**28**	5m. orange	45	45
P7	**28**	10m. violet	1·60	1·60
P8	**28**	12m. red	1·60	90
P9	**28**	15m. green	2·00	2·00
P10	**28**	20m. blue	2·75	1·60
P11	**29**	50m. purple	3·25	3·25
P12	**29**	90m. bistre	17·00	3·25
P13	**29**	100m. blue	19·00	10·00
P14	**29**	200m. violet	7·75	16·00
P15	**29**	500m. brown	65·00	29·00
P16	**29**	£P1 grey	£130	75·00

1949. 75th Anniv of U.P.U. Stamps of Jordan optd **PALESTINE** in English and Arabic.

P30	**40**	1m. brown	80	80
P31	**40**	4m. green	80	80
P32	**40**	10m. red	1·20	1·20
P33	**40**	20m. blue	1·20	1·20
P34	-	50m. green (No. 289)	3·25	3·25

OBLIGATORY TAX

1950. Nos. T264/75 of Jordan optd **PALESTINE** in English and Arabic.

PT35	**T36**	1m. blue	20	80
PT36	**T36**	2m. red	20	80
PT37	**T36**	3m. green	80	90
PT38	**T36**	5m. purple	90	80
PT39	-	10m. red	90	80
PT40	-	15m. black	3·25	90
PT41	-	20m. brown	5·00	1·70
PT42	-	50m. violet	7·25	3·25
PT43	-	100m. red	12·50	5·25
PT44	-	200m. blue	31·00	16·00
PT45	-	500m. green	90·00	47·00
PT46	-	£P1 brown	£170	90·00

POSTAGE DUE STAMPS

1948. Postage Due stamps of Jordan optd **PALESTINE** in English and Arabic.

PD25	**D26**	1m. brown	4·00	5·25
PD26	**D26**	2m. yellow	4·50	6·25
PD18	**D26**	4m. green	4·50	6·25
PD28	**D26**	10m. red	4·50	5·25
PD20	**D26**	20m. olive	4·00	5·00
PD21	**D26**	50m. blue	4·50	6·25

After a time the stamps of Jordan were used in the occupied areas.

Pt. 8

JUBALAND

A district in E. Africa, formerly part of Kenya, ceded by Gt. Britain to Italy in 1925, and incorporated in Italian Somaliland.

100 centesimi = 1 lira.

1925. Stamps of Italy optd **OLTRE GIUBA**.

1	**30**	1c. brown	3·50	16·00
2	**31**	2c. brown	2·50	16·00
3	**37**	5c. green	2·10	10·50
4	**37**	10c. pink	2·10	10·50
5	**37**	15c. grey	2·10	13·00
6	**41**	20c. orange	2·10	13·00
39	**39**	20c. green	9·50	17·00
7	**39**	25c. blue	2·50	13·00
8	**39**	30c. brown	4·25	13·00
40	**39**	30c. grey	9·50	21·00
9	**39**	40c. brown	6·50	10·50
10	**39**	50c. mauve	6·50	10·50
11	**39**	60c. red	6·50	16·00
41	**44**	75c. red and carmine	60·00	65·00
12	**44**	1l. brown and green	13·00	19·00
42	**44**	1l.25 blue and ultramarine	75·00	80·00
13	**44**	2l. green and orange	65·00	45·00
43	**44**	2l.50 green and orange	£100	£160
14	**44**	5l. blue and pink	£130	65·00
15	**44**	10l. green and pink	17·00	75·00

1925. Royal Jubilee stamps of Italy optd **OLTRE GIUBA**.

44B	**82**	60c. red	1·60	10·50
45B	**82**	1l. blue	1·60	21·00
46B	**82**	1l.25 blue	5·25	27·00

1926. St. Francis of Assisi stamps of Italy, as Nos. 191/6, optd **OLTRE GIUBA**.

47	20c. green	3·00	24·00
48	40c. violet	3·00	24·00
49	60c. red	3·00	37·00
50	1l.25 blue	3·00	55·00
51	5l.+2l.50 olive	6·75	80·00

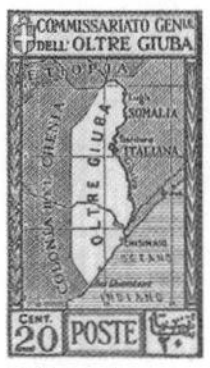

8 Map of Jubaland

1926. First Anniv of Acquisition of Jubaland.

54	**8**	5c. orange	1·40	13·00
55	**8**	20c. green	1·40	13·00
56	**8**	25c. brown	1·40	13·00
57	**8**	40c. red	1·40	13·00
58	**8**	60c. purple	1·40	13·00
59	**8**	1l. blue	1·40	13·00
60	**8**	2l. grey	1·40	13·00

1926. As Colonial Propaganda **T6** of Cyrenaica, but inscr "OLTRE GIUBA".

61	5c.+5c. brown	1·10	7·50
62	10c.+5c. olive	1·10	7·50
63	20c.+5c. green	1·10	7·50
64	40c.+5c. red	1·10	7·50
65	60c.+5c. orange	1·10	7·50
66	1l.+5c. blue	1·10	7·50

EXPRESS LETTER STAMPS

1926. Express Letter stamps of Italy optd **OLTRE GUIBA**.

E52	**E35**	70c. red	26·00	43·00
E53	**E41**	2l.50 blue and pink	38·00	£110

PARCEL POST STAMPS

1925. Parcel Post stamps of Italy optd **OLTRE GIUBA**.

P16	**P53**	5c. brown	9·50	21·00
P17	**P53**	10c. blue	6·50	21·00
P18	**P53**	20c. black	6·50	21·00
P19	**P53**	25c. red	6·50	21·00
P20	**P53**	50c. orange	9·50	21·00
P21	**P53**	1l. violet	7·75	55·00
P22	**P53**	2l. green	12·00	55·00
P23	**P53**	3l. yellow	32·00	75·00
P24	**P53**	4l. grey	13·00	75·00
P25	**P53**	10l. purple	75·00	£110
P26	**P53**	12l. brown	£150	£190
P27	**P53**	15l. olive	£140	£225
P28	**P53**	20l. purple	£140	£225

Unused prices are for complete stamps, used prices for half-stamps.

POSTAGE DUE STAMPS

1925. Postage Due stamps of Italy optd **OLTRE GIUBA**.

D29	**D12**	5c. purple and orange	16·00	13·00
D30	**D12**	10c. purple and orange	16·00	13·00
D31	**D12**	20c. purple and orange	16·00	21·00
D32	**D12**	30c. purple and orange	16·00	21·00
D33	**D12**	40c. purple and orange	21·00	24·00
D34	**D12**	50c. purple and orange	21·00	32·00
D35	**D12**	60c. brown and orange	29·00	43·00
D36	**D12**	1l. purple and blue	29·00	48·00
D37	**D12**	2l. purple and blue	£140	£190
D38	**D12**	5l. purple and blue	£150	£190

Pt. 21

KAMPUCHEA

Following the fall of the Khmer Rouge government which had terminated the Khmer Republic, the People's Republic of Kampuchea was proclaimed on 10 January 1979.

Kampuchea was renamed Cambodia in 1989.

100 cents = 1 riel.

105 Soldiers with Flag and Independence Monument, Phnom Penh

1980. Multicoloured. Without gum.

402	0.1r. Type **105**	4·50	4·50
403	0.2r. Khmer people and flag	7·25	7·25
404	0.5r. Fisherman pulling in nets	11·00	11·00
405	1r. Armed forces and Kam-puchean flag	18·00	18·00

106 Moscow Kremlin and Globe

1982. 60th Anniv of U.S.S.R. Multicoloured.

406	50c. Type **106**	35	20
407	1r. Industrial complex and map of U.S.S.R.	55	25

107 Arms of Kampuchea

1983. Fourth Anniv of People's Republic of Kampuchea. Multicoloured.

408	50c. Type **107**	55	10
409	1r. Open book illustrating national flag and arms (horiz)	90	20
410	3r. Stylized figures and map	2·50	65
MS411	90×109 mm. 6r. Temple, Phnom Penh (28×35 mm)	4·75	90

108 Runner with Olympic Torch

1983. Olympic Games, Los Angeles (1984) (1st issue). Multicoloured.

412	20c. Type **108**	25	10
413	50c. Javelin throwing	35	10
414	80c. Pole vaulting	45	10
415	1r. Discus throwing	55	10
416	1r.50 Relay (horiz)	90	20
417	2r. Swimming (horiz)	1·30	20
418	3r. Basketball	2·00	20
MS419	92×64 mm. 6r. Football (31×39 mm)	4·25	90

See also Nos. 526/**MS**533.

109 Orange Tiger

1983. Butterflies. Multicoloured.

420	20c. Type **109**	20	10
421	50c. *Euploea althaea*	25	10
422	80c. *Byasa polyeuctes* (horiz)	35	10
423	1r. *Stichophthalma howqua* (horiz)	55	10
424	1r.50 Leaf butterfly	1·20	20
425	2r. Blue argus	1·30	20
426	3r. Lemon migrant	2·00	20

110 Srah Srang

1983. Khmer Culture. Multicoloured.

427	20c. Type **110**	20	10
428	50c. Bakong	25	10
429	80c. Ta Som (vert)	35	10

430	1r. North gate, Angkor Thom (vert)	55	20
431	1r.50 Kennora (winged figures) (vert)	1·20	25
432	2r. Apsara (carved figures), Angkor (vert)	1·30	35
433	3r. Banteai Srei (goddess), Tevoda (vert)	2·00	55

111 Dancers with Castanets

1983. Folklore. Multicoloured.

434	50c. Type **111**	25	20
435	1r. Dancers with grass head-dresses	90	25
436	3r. Dancers with scarves	2·00	65
MS437	94×63 mm. 6r. Warrior with blowpipe (31×39 mm)	4·00	90

112 Detail of Fresco

1983. 500th Birth Anniv of Raphael (artist).

438	**112**	20c. multicoloured	20	10
439	-	50c. multicoloured	25	10
440	-	80c. multicoloured	35	10
441	-	1r. multicoloured	80	20
442	-	1r.50 multicoloured	1·30	25
443	-	2r. multicoloured	1·60	50
444	-	3r. multicoloured	2·20	55
MS445	97×75 mm. 6r. multicoloured (39×31 mm)		6·00	1·60

DESIGNS: Nos. 439/44, different details of frescoes by Raphael.

113 Montgolfier Balloon

1983. Bicentenary of Manned Flight. Multicoloured.

446	20c. Type **113**	20	10
447	30c. *La Ville d'Orleans*, 1870	25	10
448	50c. Charles's hydrogen balloon	35	10
449	1r. Blanchard and Jeffries cross-ing Channel, 1785	65	20
450	1r.50 Salomon Andree's balloon flight over Arctic	90	25
451	2r. Auguste Piccard's strato-sphere balloon *F.N.R.S.*	1·30	35
452	3r. Hot-air balloon race	1·80	70
MS453	75×67 mm. 6r. Balloons over European town (vert)	5·75	1·10

114 Cobra

1983. Reptiles. Multicoloured.

454	20c. Crested lizard (horiz)	20	10
455	30c. Type **114**	25	20
456	80c. Trionyx turtle (horiz)	45	20
457	1r. Chameleon	70	25
458	1r.50 Boa constrictor	1·30	45
459	2r. Crocodile (horiz)	1·60	65
460	3r. Turtle (horiz)	2·10	90

115 Rainbow Lory

1983. Birds. Multicoloured.

461	20c. Type **115**	20	10
462	50c. Barn swallow	25	10
463	80c. Golden eagle (horiz)	45	10
464	1r. Griffon vulture (horiz)	90	10
465	1r.50 Javanese collared dove (horiz)	1·60	20
466	2r. Black-billed magpie	2·00	20
467	3r. Great Indian hornbill	3·50	20

116 Sunflower

1983. Flowers. Multicoloured.

468	20c. Type **116**	20	10
469	50c. *Caprifoliaceae*	25	10
470	80c. *Bougainvillea*	35	10
471	1r. *Ranunculaceae*	65	20
472	1r.50 *Nyctagynaeceae*	1·30	20
473	2r. Cockscomb	1·60	25
474	3r. Roses	2·00	45

117 Luge

1983. Winter Olympic Games, Sarajevo (1984) (1st issue). Multicoloured.

475	1r. Type **117**	65	10
476	2r. Biathlon	1·40	20
477	4r. Ski-jumping	2·75	25
478	5r. Two-man bobsleigh	3·25	35
479	7r. Ice hockey	4·75	45
MS480	81×68 mm. 6r. Skiing (35×28 mm)	5·25	90

See also Nos. 496/**MS**503.

118 Cyprinid

1983. Fish. Multicoloured.

481	20c. Type **118**	20	10
482	50c. Loach	25	10
483	80c. Bubblebee catfish	35	10
484	1r. Spiny eel	70	10
485	1r.50 Cyprinid (different)	1·30	20
486	2r. Cyprinid (different)	1·80	20
487	3r. Aberrant fish	2·20	20

119 Factory and Gearwheel

1983. Festival of Rebirth. Multicoloured.

488	50c. Type **119**	25	20
489	1r. Tractor and cow (horiz)	90	20
490	3r. Bulk carrier, diesel locomo-tive, car and bridge	2·00	55
MS491	65×85 mm. 6r. Radio signal (31×39 mm)	5·25	90

120 Red Cross and Sailing Ship

1984. Fifth Anniv of Liberation. Multicoloured.

492	50c. Type **120**	25	20
493	1r. Three soldiers, flags and temple	65	20
494	3r. Crowd surrounding temple	1·80	55
MS495	91×60 mm. 6r. Man carrying containers (31×39 mm)	5·25	1·20

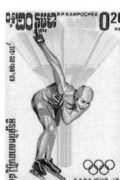
121 Speed Skating

1984. Winter Olympic Games, Sarajevo (2nd issue). Multicoloured.

496	20c. Type **121**	20	10
497	50c. Ice hockey	25	10
498	80c. Skiing	35	10
499	1r. Ski jumping	65	10
500	1r.50 Skiing (different)	1·30	20
501	2r. Cross-country skiing	1·60	25
502	3r. Ice skating (pairs)	2·00	45
MS503	120×80 mm. 6r. Ice skating (individual) (31×29 mm)	5·25	1·10

122 Ilyushin Il-62M Jet over Angkor Vat

1984. Air.

504	**122**	5r. multicoloured	4·00	20
505	**122**	10r. multicoloured	7·50	35
506	**122**	15r. multicoloured	11·00	45
507	**122**	25r. multicoloured	18·00	80

For design as Type **122** but inscribed "R.P. DU KAM-PUCHEA", see Nos. 695/8.

123 Cattle Egret

1984. Birds. Multicoloured.

508	10c. Type **123**	20	10
509	40c. Black-headed shrike	65	10
510	80c. Slaty-headed parakeet	1·20	20
511	1r. Golden-fronted leafbird	1·60	20
512	1r.20 Red-winged crested cuckoo	1·80	25
513	2r. Grey wagtail	3·50	35
514	2r.50 Forest wagtail	3·75	45

124 Doves and Globe

1984. International Peace in South-East Asia Forum, Phnom Penh. Mult, background colour given.

515	**124**	50c. green	25	20
516	**124**	1r. blue	65	20
517	**124**	3r. violet	1·80	55

125 "Luna 2"

1984. Space Research. Multicoloured.
518	10c. "Luna 1"	20	10
519	40c. Type **125**	25	10
520	80c. "Luna 3"	35	10
521	1r. "Soyuz 6" and cosmonauts (vert)	65	10
522	1r.20 "Soyuz 7" and cosmonauts (vert)	90	20
523	2r. "Soyuz 8" and cosmonauts (vert)	1·30	20
524	2r.50 Book, rocket and S. P. Korolev (Russian spaceship designer) (vert)	1·80	20
MS525	81× 80 mm. 6r. "Soyuz"-"Salyut" space complex and Earth (39×31 mm)	5·25	90

126 Throwing the Discus

1984. Olympic Games, Los Angeles (2nd issue). Multicoloured.
526	20c. Type **126**	20	10
527	50c. Long jumping	25	10
528	80c. Hurdling	35	10
529	1r. Relay	90	20
530	1r.50 Pole vaulting	1·20	20
531	2r. Throwing the javelin	1·40	20
532	3r. High jumping	2·00	45
MS533	79×59 mm. 76r. Sprinting	5·25	90

127 Hispano-Suiza "K6", 1933

1984. "Espana 84" International Stamp Exhibition, Madrid. Sheet 71×58 mm.
MS534	**127** 5r. multicoloured	5·25	1·80

128 Coyote

1984. Dog Family. Multicoloured.
535	10c. Type **128**	20	10
536	40c. Dingo	25	10
537	80c. Hunting dog	45	10
538	1r. Golden jackal	90	10
539	1r.20 Red fox	1·10	20
540	2r. Maned wolf (vert)	2·00	20
541	2r.50 Wolf	3·00	20

129 Class BB 1002 Diesel Locomotive, 1966, France

1984. Railway Locomotives. Multicoloured.
542	10c. Type **129**	20	10
543	40c. Class BB 1052 diesel loco-motive, 1966, France	25	10
544	80c. Franco-Belgian-built steam locomotive, 1945, France	35	10
545	1r. Steam locomotive No. 231-505, 1929, France	80	10
546	1r.20 Class 803 diesel railcar, 1968, Germany	1·30	20
547	2r. Class BDE-405 diesel loco-motive, 1957, France	1·60	20
548	2r.50 Class DS-01 diesel railcar, 1925, France	2·75	20

130 Magnolia

1984. Flowers. Multicoloured.
549	10c. Type **130**	20	10
550	40c. Plumeria sp.	15	10
551	80c. Himenoballis sp.	45	10
552	1r. Peltophorum roxburghii	1·10	20
553	1r.20 Couroupita guianensis	1·30	20
554	2r. Lagerstroemia sp.	2·20	20
555	2r.50 Thevetia perubiana	3·50	25

131 Mercedes Benz

1984. Cars. Multicoloured.
556	20c. Type **131**	20	10
557	50c. Bugatti	25	20
558	80c. Alfa Romeo	45	20
559	1r. Franklin	1·00	25
560	1r.50 Hispano-Suiza	1·40	35
561	2r. Rolls Royce	2·00	45
562	3r. Tatra	2·75	70
MS563	68×70 mm. 6r. Mercedes Benz (39×31 mm)	5·75	1·10

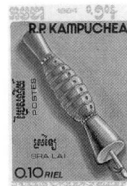

132 Sra Lai (Rattle)

1984. Musical Instruments. Multicoloured.
564	10c. Type **132**	20	10
565	40c. Skor drum (horiz)	25	10
566	80c. Skor drums (different)	35	10
567	1r. Thro khmer (stringed instru-ment) (horiz)	65	20
568	1r.20 Raneat ek (xylophone) (horiz)	1·30	35
569	2r. Raneat kong (bells) (horiz)	1·40	35
570	2r.50 Thro khe (stringed instru-ment) (horiz)	2·20	65

133 Gazelle

1984. Mammals. Multicoloured.
571	10c. Type **133**	20	10
572	40c. Roe deer	25	10
573	80c. Hare (horiz)	35	10
574	1r. Red deer	65	20
575	1r.20 Indian elephant	1·30	20
576	2r. Genet (horiz)	1·40	20
577	2r.50 Kouprey (horiz)	2·20	25

134 Madonna and Child

1984. 450th Death Anniv of Correggio (artist). Multicoloured.
578	20c. Type **134**	20	10
579	50c. Detail showing man strik-ing monk	25	10
580	80c. Madonna and Child (different)	35	10
581	1r. Madonna and Child (dif-ferent)	70	20
582	1r.50 Mystical Marriage of St. Catherine	1·30	20
583	2r. Pieta	1·50	20
584	3r. Detail showing man de-scending ladder	2·00	25
MS585	91×64 mm. 6r. Coronation of the Virgin (39×31 mm)	5·50	95

135 Bullock Cart

1985. National Festival (Sixth Anniv of People's Republic). Multicoloured.
586	50c. Type **135**	45	20
587	1r. Horse-drawn passenger cart	90	25
588	3r. Elephants	2·75	45
MS589	85×64 mm. 6r. Bullock-drawn passenger cart (31×39 mm)	5·75	90

136 Footballers

1985. World Cup Football Championship, Mexico (1986) (1st issue). Designs showing footballers.
590	**136** 20c. multicoloured	20	10
591	- 50c. multicoloured	25	10
592	- 80c. multicoloured	35	10
593	- 1r. multicoloured (horiz)	65	20
594	- 1r.50 mult (horiz)	1·10	20
595	- 2r. multicoloured	1·30	20
596	- 3r. multicoloured	2·00	25
MS597	94×57 mm. 6r. multicoloured (39×31 mm)	5·25	90

See also Nos. 680/**MS**687.

137 Eska-Mofa Motor Cycle, 1939

1985. Centenary of Motor Cycle. Multicoloured.
598	20c. Type **137**	20	10
599	50c. Wanderer, 1939	25	10
600	80c. Premier, 1929	35	20
601	1r. Ardie, 1939	70	25
602	1r.50 Jawa, 1932	1·30	45
603	2r. Simson, 1983	1·50	70
604	3r. "CZ 125", 1984	2·00	90
MS605	100×85 mm. 6r. MBA, 1984 (39×31 mm)	5·75	90

138 Glistening Ink Cap

1985. Fungi. Multicoloured.
606	20c. Gymnophilus spectabilis (horiz)	20	10
607	50c. Type **138**	35	10
608	80c. Panther cap	70	10
609	1r. Fairy cake mushroom	1·00	10
610	1r.50 Fly agaric	2·00	20
611	2r. Shaggy ink cap	2·75	20
612	3r. Caesar's mushroom	3·00	20

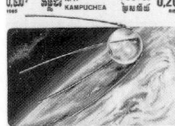

139 "Sputnik 1"

1985. Space Exploration. Multicoloured.
613	20c. Type **139**	20	10
614	50c. "Soyuz" rocket on trans-porter and Yuri Gagarin (first man in space)	25	20
615	80c. "Vostok 6" and Valentina Tereshkova (first woman in space)	35	20
616	1r. Space walker	65	25
617	1r.50 "Salyut"–"Soyuz" link	1·10	35
618	2r. "Lunokhod 1" (lunar vehicle)	1·30	45
619	3r. "Venera" (Venus probe)	2·00	70
MS620	94×59 mm. 6r. "Soyuz" prepar-ing to dock with "Salyut" space station (39×31 mm)	5·25	1·40

140 Absara Dancer

1985. Traditional Dances. Multicoloured.
621	50c. Absara group (horiz)	45	10
622	1r. Tepmonorom dance (horiz)	90	25
623	3r. Type **140**	1·80	70

140a Captured Nazi Standards, Red Square, Moscow

1985. 40th Anniv of End of Second World War. Multicoloured.
623a	50c. Rejoicing soldiers in Berlin	35	10
623b	1r. Type **140a**	80	25
623c	3r. Tank battle	2·40	70

141 Tortoiseshell Cat

1985. Domestic Cats. Multicoloured.
624	20c. Type **141**	20	10
625	50c. Tortoiseshell (different)	25	20
626	80c. Tabby	45	20
627	1r. Long-haired Siamese	1·00	25
628	1t.50 Sealpoint Siamese	1·40	35
629	2r. Grey cat	2·00	45
630	3r. Black cat	2·75	70

142 "Black Dragon" Lily

1985. Flowers. Multicoloured.
631	20c. Type **142**	20	10
632	50c. Iris delavayi	25	10
633	80c. Crocus aureus	35	10
634	1r. Cyclamen persicum	70	20
635	1r.50 Fairy primrose	1·30	25
636	2r. Pansy "Ullswater"	1·80	35
637	3r. Crocus purpureus grandiflorus	2·10	55

143 Per Italiani (Antoine Watteau)

1985. International Music Year. Multicoloured.

638	20c. Type **143**	20	10
639	50c. *St. Cecilia* (Carlos Saraceni)	25	10
640	80c. *Still Life with Violin* (Jean Baptiste Oudry) (horiz)	55	10
641	1r. *Three Musicians* (Fernand Leger)	65	20
642	1r.50 Orchestra	90	25
643	2r. *St. Cecilia* (Bartholomeo Schedoni)	1·30	35
644	3r. *Harlequin with Violin* (Christian Caillard)	1·80	55
MS645	55×89 mm. 6r. *The Fifer* (Edouard Manet) (31×39 mm)	6·50	1·40

144 Lenin and Arms

1985. 115th Birth Anniv of Lenin. Multicoloured.

646	1r. Type **144**	1·10	35
647	3r. Lenin on balcony and map	2·10	70

145 Saffron-cowled Blackbird

1985. "Argentina '85" International Stamp Exhibition, Buenos Aires. Birds. Multicoloured.

648	20c. Type **145**	20	10
649	50c. Saffron finch (vert)	25	10
650	80c. Blue and yellow tanager (vert)	35	10
651	1r. Scarlet-headed blackbird	70	20
652	1r.50 Amazon kingfisher (vert)	1·30	25
653	2r. Toco toucan (vert)	1·80	35
654	3r. Rufous-bellied thrush	2·10	55

146 River Launch, Cambodia, 1942

1985. Water Craft. Multicoloured.

655	10c. Type **146**	20	10
656	40c. River launch, Cambodia, 1948	25	10
657	80c. Tug, Japan, 1913	35	10
658	1r. Dredger, Holland	65	20
659	1r.20 Tug, U.S.A.	90	25
660	2r. River freighter	1·30	35
661	2r.50 River tanker, Panama	1·80	55

147 *The Flood* (Michelangelo)

1985. "Italia '85" International Stamp Exhibition, Rome. Paintings. Multicoloured.

662	20r. Type **147**	20	10
663	50r. *The Virgin of St. Marguerite* (Mazzola)	25	10
664	80r. *The Martyrdom of St. Peter* (Zampieri Domenichino)	35	10
665	1r. *Allegory of Spring* (detail) (Sandro Botticelli)	70	20
666	1r.50 *The Sacrifice of Abraham* (Caliari)	1·30	25
667	2r. *The Meeting of Joachim and Anne* (Giotto)	1·80	35
668	3r. *Bacchus* (Michel Angelo Carraraggio)	2·10	20
MS669	94×64 mm. 6r. Early steam locomotive, Berlin (31×39 mm)	6·50	1·40

148 Son Ngoc Minh

1985. Festival of Rebirth.

670	**148**	50c. multicoloured	35	20
671	**148**	1r. multicoloured	55	25
672	**148**	3r. multicoloured	1·30	45

149 Tiger Barbs

1985. Fish. Multicoloured.

673	20c. Type **149**	20	10
674	50c. Giant snakehead	25	10
675	80c. Veil-tailed goldfish	35	10
676	1r. Pearl gourami	65	20
677	1r.50 Six-banded tiger barbs	1·10	25
678	2r. Siamese fighting fish	1·30	35
679	3r. Siamese tigerfish	2·00	55

150 Footballers

1986. World Cup Football Championship, Mexico (2nd issue).

680	**150**	20c. multicoloured	20	10
681	-	50c. multicoloured	25	10
682	-	80c. multicoloured	35	10
683	-	1r. multicoloured	65	20
684	-	1r.50 multicoloured	90	25
685	-	2r. multicoloured	1·30	35
686	-	3r. multicoloured	1·80	55
MS687	95×92 mm. 6r. multicoloured (31×39 mm)		5·25	90

DESIGNS: 50c. to 6r. Various footballing scenes.

151 Cob

1986. Horses. Multicoloured.

688	20c. Type **151**	20	10
689	50c. Arab	25	10
690	80c. Australian pony	35	10
691	1r. Appaloosa	70	20
692	1r.50 Quarter horse	1·30	20
693	2r. Vladimir heavy draught horse	1·50	20
694	3r. Andalusian	2·00	25

152 "Mir" Space Station and Spacecraft

1986. 27th Russian Communist Party Congress. Multicoloured.

694a	50c. Type **152**	25	10
694b	1r. Lenin	80	35
694c	5r. Statue and launch of space rocket	3·00	65

1986. Air. As Nos. 504/7 but inscr "R.P. DU KAMPUCHEA".

695	**122**	5r. multicoloured	3·50	20
696	**122**	10r. multicoloured	7·25	35
697	**122**	15r. multicoloured	9·00	45
698	**122**	25r. multicoloured	16·00	80

153 Edaphosaurus (⅔-size illustration)

1986. Prehistoric Animals. Multicoloured.

699	20c. Type **153**	35	10
700	50c. Sauroctonus	45	10
701	80c. Mastodonsaurus	90	10
702	1r. Rhamphorhynchus (vert)	1·60	20
703	1r.50 "Brachiosaurus brancai" (vert)	2·50	25
704	2r. "Tarbosaurus bataar" (vert)	3·25	35
705	3r. Indricotherium (vert)	4·50	70

154 "Luna 16"

1986. 25th Anniv of First Man in Space. Multicoloured.

706	10c. Type **154**	20	10
707	40c. "Luna 3"	25	10
708	80c. "Vostok"	35	10
709	1r. Cosmonaut Leonov on space walk	65	20
710	1r.20 "Apollo" and "Soyuz" preparing to dock	1·10	20
711	2r. "Soyuz" docking with "Salyut" space station	1·30	20
712	2r.50 Yuri Gagarin (first man in space) and spacecraft	2·00	25

155 Baksei Chmkrong Temple, 920

1986. Khmer Culture. Multicoloured.

713	20c. Type **155**	20	10
714	50c. Buddha's head	25	10
715	80c. Prea Vihear monastery, Dangrek	35	10
716	1r. Fan with design of man and woman	45	20
717	1r.50 Fan with design of men fighting	65	25
718	2r. Fan with design of dancer	1·10	35
719	3r. Fan with design of dragon-drawn chariot	1·50	70

156 Tricar, 1885

1986. Centenary (1985) of Motor Car. Mercedes Benz Models. Multicoloured.

720	20c. Type **156**	20	10
721	50c. Limousine, 1935	25	10
722	80c. Open tourer, 1907	35	10
723	1r. Light touring car, 1920	65	20
724	1r.50 Cabriolet, 1932	1·10	25
725	2r. "SKK" tourer, 1938	1·30	35
726	3r. "190", 1985	2·00	70

157 Orange Tiger

1986. Butterflies. Multicoloured.

727	20c. Type **157**	20	10
728	50c. Five-bar swallowtail	25	10
729	80c. Chequered swallowtail	35	10
730	1r. Chestnut tiger	70	20
731	1r.50 Idea blanchardi	1·30	25
732	2r. Common mormon	1·50	35
733	3r. Dabasa payeni	2·00	55

158 English Kogge of Richard II's Reign

1986. Medieval Ships.. Multicoloured.

734	20c. Type **158**	20	10
735	50c. Kogge	25	10
736	80c. Knarr	35	10
737	1r. Galley	65	20
738	1r.50 Norman ship	90	25
739	2r. Mediterranean usciere	1·30	45
740	3r. French kogge	1·80	55

159 Solar System, Copernicus, Galileo and Tycho Brahe (astronomers)

1986. Appearance of Halley's Comet. Multicoloured.

741	10c. Type **159**	20	10
742	20c. *Nativity* (Giotto) and comet from Bayeux Tapestry	20	10
743	50c. Comet, 1910, and Mt. Palomar observatory, U.S.A.	25	10
744	80c. Edmond Halley and "Planet A" space probe	45	20
745	1r.20 Diagram of comet's trajectory and "Giotto" space probe	70	25
746	1r.50 "Vega" space probe and camera	90	35
747	2r. Thermal pictures of comet	1·30	55
MS748	87×56 mm. 6r. "Vega" space probe (31×39 mm)	4·25	1·10

160 Ruy Lopez

1986. "Stockholmia 86" International Stamp Exhibition. Chess. Multicoloured.

749	20c. Type **160**	20	10
750	50c. Francois-Andre Philidor	25	10
751	80c. Karl Anderssen and Houses of Parliament, London	35	10
752	1r. Wilhelm Steinitz and Charles Bridge, Prague	70	20
753	1r.50 Emanuel Lasker and medieval knight	1·30	25
754	2r. Jose Raul Capablanca and Morro Castle, Cuba	1·80	35
755	3r. Aleksandr Alekhine	2·10	70
MS756	62×72 mm. 6r. Chess pieces (39×31 mm)	6·50	1·40

No. 751 is wrongly inscribed "Andersen".

161 *Parodia maassii*

1986. Cacti. Multicoloured.

757	20c. Type **161**	20	10
758	50c. *Rebutia marsoneri*	25	10
759	80c. *Melocactus evae*	35	10
760	1r. *Gymnocalycium valnicekianum*	70	20
761	1r.50 *Discocactus silichromus*	1·30	25
762	2r. *Neochilenia simulans*	1·50	35
763	3r. *Weingartia chiquichuquensis*	2·00	55

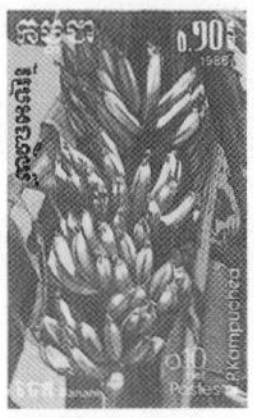

162 Bananas

1986. Fruit. Multicoloured.

764	10c. Type **162**	20	10
765	40c. Papaya	25	20
766	80c. Mangoes	35	20
767	1r. Breadfruit	45	20
768	1r.20 Lychees	65	35
769	2r. Pineapple	1·10	55
770	2r.50 Grapefruit (horiz)	1·50	70

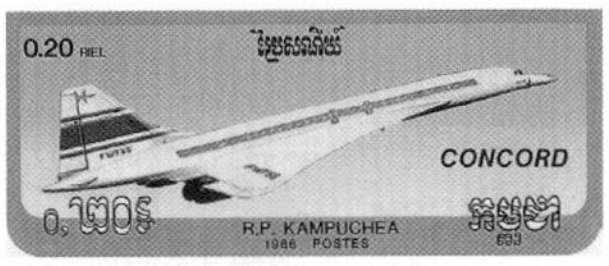

163 Concorde

1986. Aircraft. Multicoloured.

771	20c. Type **163** (wrongly inscr "Concord")	20	10
772	50c. Douglas DC-10	25	10
773	80c. Boeing 747SP	35	10
774	1r. Ilyushin Il-62M	65	20
775	1r.50 Ilyushin Il-86	90	25
776	2r. Antonov An-24 (wrongly inscr "AN-124")	1·30	35
777	3r. Airbus Industrie A300	1·80	70

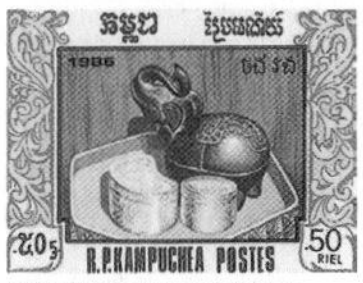

164 Elephant and Silver Containers on Tray

1986. Festival of Rebirth. Silverware. Multicoloured.

778	50c. Type **164**	35	20
779	1r. Tureen	70	25
780	3r. Dish on stand	2·10	45

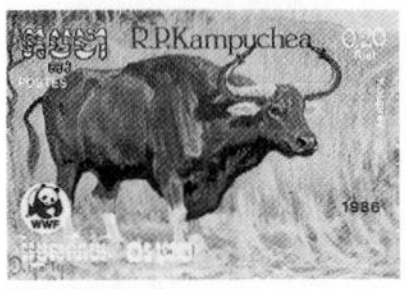

165 Kouprey

1986. Endangered Animals. Cattle. Multicoloured.

781	20c. Type **165**	1·10	20
782	20c. Gaur	1·60	25
783	80c. Bateng cow and calf	4·00	35
784	1r.50 Asiatic water buffalo	6·75	55

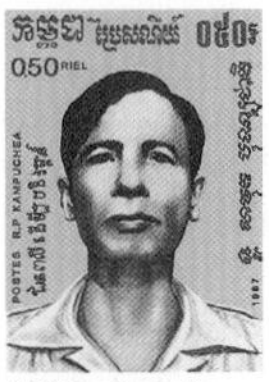

166 Tou Samuth (revolutionary)

1987. National Festival. Eighth Anniv of People's Republic.

785	**166**	50c. multicoloured	25	20
786	**166**	1r. multicoloured	45	25
787	**166**	3r. multicoloured	1·10	45

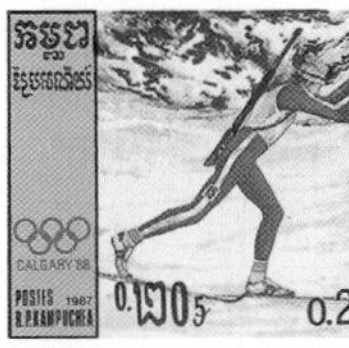

167 Biathlon

1987. Winter Olympic Games, Calgary (1988) (1st issue). Multicoloured.

788	20c. Type **167**	20	10
789	50c. Figure skating	25	10
790	80c. Speed skating	35	10
791	1r. Ice hockey	65	20
792	1r.50 Two-man luge	90	25
793	2r. Two-man bobsleigh	1·30	35
794	3r. Cross-country skiing	1·80	70
MS795	91×65 mm. 6r. Skiing (39×31 mm)	4·25	1·10

See also Nos. 864/**MS**871.

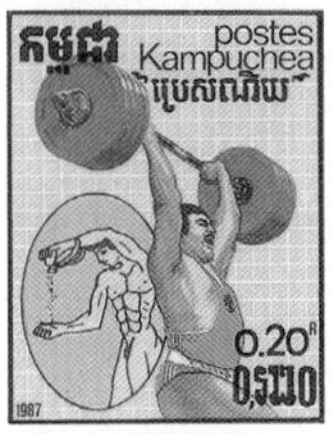

168 Weightlifting

1987. Olympic Games, Seoul (1988) (1st issue). Designs showing ancient Greek and modern athletes. Multicoloured.

796	20c. Type **168**	20	10
797	50c. Archery (horiz)	25	10
798	80c. Fencing (horiz)	35	20
799	1r. Gymnastics	65	20
800	1r.50 Throwing the discus (horiz)	90	20
801	2r. Throwing the javelin	1·30	25
802	3r. Hurdling	1·80	35
MS803	93×63 mm. 6r. Wrestling (39×31 mm)	4·25	1·10

See also Nos. 875/**MS**882.

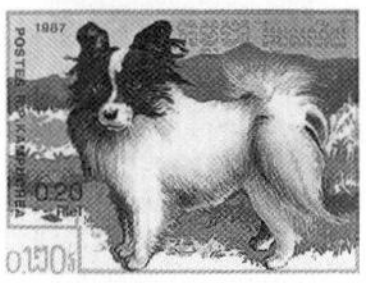

169 Papillon

1987. Dogs. Multicoloured.

804	20c. Type **169**	20	10
805	50c. Greyhound	25	10
806	80c. Great Dane	35	10
807	1r. Dobermann	70	20
808	1r.50 Samoyed	1·30	25
809	2r. Borzoi	1·80	35
810	3r. Rough collie	2·10	55

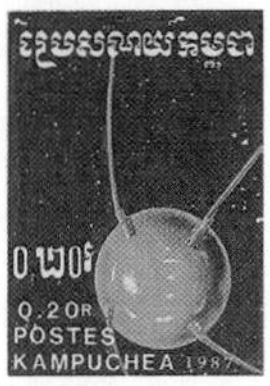

170 "Sputnik 1"

1987. Space Exploration. Multicoloured.

811	20c. Type **170**	20	10
812	50c. "Soyuz 10"	25	10
813	80c. "Proton"	35	10
814	1r. "Vostok 1"	65	20
815	1r.50 "Elektron 2"	90	25
816	2r. "Kosmos"	1·30	35
817	3r. "Luna 2"	1·80	70
MS818	71×48 mm. 6r. "Elektron 4" (39×31 mm)	4·25	1·10

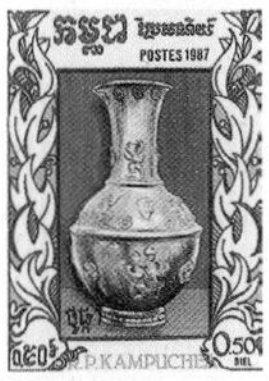

171 Flask

1987. Metalwork. Multicoloured.

819	50c. Type **171**	25	20
820	1r. Repousse box (horiz)	70	25
821	1r.50 Teapot and cups on tray (horiz)	1·10	35
822	3r. Ornamental sword	2·00	55

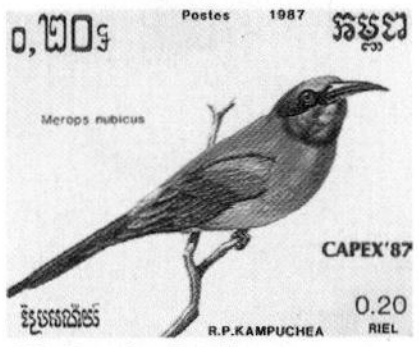

172 Carmine Bee Eater

1987. "Capex'87" International Stamp Exhibition, Toronto. Birds. Multicoloured.

823	20c. Type **172**	20	10
824	50c. Hoopoe (vert)	25	10
825	80c. South African crowned crane (vert)	35	10
826	1r. Barn owl (vert)	65	20
827	1r.50 Grey-headed kingfisher (vert)	1·10	25
828	2r. Red-whiskered bulbul	1·30	35
829	3r. Purple heron (vert)	2·00	55
MS830	70×94 mm. 6r. Asiatic paradise flycatcher (28×39 mm)	6·50	90

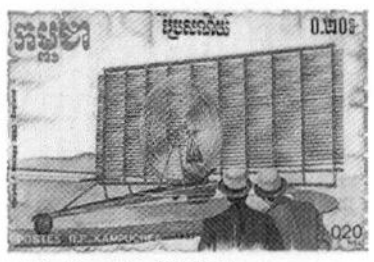

173 Horatio Phillip's "multiplane" Model, 1893

1987. Experimental Aircraft Designs. Multicoloured.

831	20c. Type **173**	20	10
832	50c. John Stringfellow's steam-powered model, 1848	25	10
833	80c. Thomas Moy's model *Aerial Steamer*, 1875	35	10
834	1r. Leonardo da Vinci's "orni-thopter", 1490	65	20
835	1r.50 Sir George Cayley's "convertiplane", 1843	1·10	20
836	2r. Sir Hiram Maxim's *Flying Test Rig*, 1894	1·30	20
837	3r. William Henson's *Aerial Steam Carriage*, 1842	2·00	25
MS838	98×83 mm. 6r. Leonardo da Vinci's drawing of *Flying Man* (31×39 mm)	4·25	90

No. 835 is wrongly dated "1840".

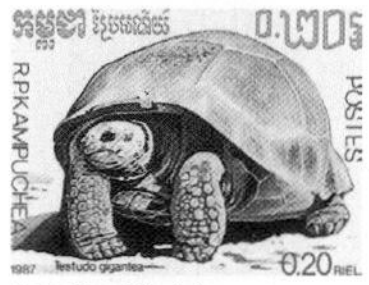

174 Giant Tortoise

1987. Reptiles. Multicoloured.

839	20c. Type **174**	20	10
840	50c. African spiny-tailed lizard	25	10
841	80c. Iguana	35	10
842	1r. Coast horned lizard	65	20
843	1r.50 Northern chuckwalla	90	25
844	2r. Glass lizard	1·30	35
845	3r. Common garter snake	1·80	55

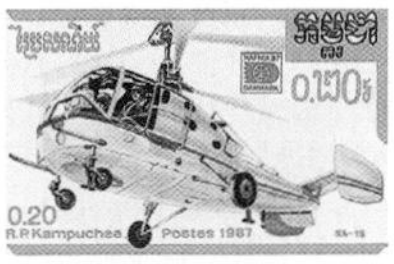

175 Kamov Ka-15

1987. "Hafnia 87" International Stamp Exhibition, Copenhagen. Helicopters. Multicoloured.

846	20c. Type **175**	20	10
847	50c. Kamov Ka-18	25	10
848	80c. Westland WG-13 Lynx	35	10
849	1r. Sud Aviation SA 341 Gazelle	65	20
850	1r.50 Sud Aviation SA 330E Puma	90	20
851	2r. Boeing-Vertol CH-47 Chinook	1·30	20
852	3r. Boeing UTTAS	1·80	25
MS853	65×85 mm. 6r. Fairey rotodyne	4·25	1·10

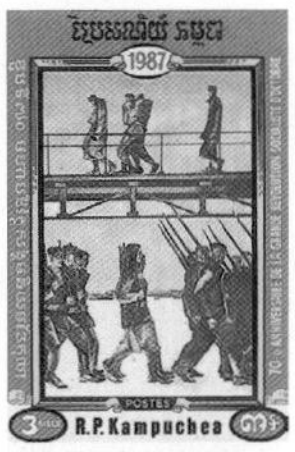

176 Revolutionaries

1987. 70th Anniv of Russian October Revolution. Multicoloured.

853a	2r. Revolutionaries on street corner (horiz)	1·10	20
853b	3r. Type **176**	1·30	45
853c	5r. Lenin receiving ticker-tape message (horiz)	3·00	70

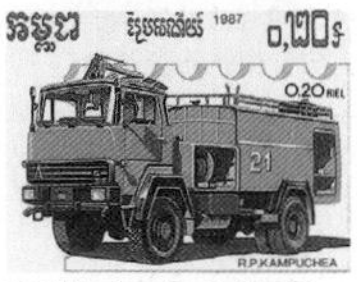

177 Magirus-Deutz No. 21

1987. Fire Engines. Multicoloured.

854	20c. Type **177**	20	10
855	50c. "SIL-131" rescue vehicle	25	10
856	80c. "Cas-25" fire pump	35	10
857	1r. Sirmac Saab "424"	70	20
858	1r.50 Rosenbaum-Falcon	1·30	25
859	2r. Tatra "815-PRZ"	1·80	35
860	3r. Chubbfire "C-44-20"	2·10	55

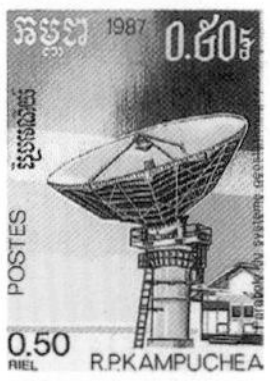

178 Earth Station Dish Aerial

1987. Telecommunications. Multicoloured.

861	50c. Type **178**	35	20
862	1r. Technological building with radio microwave aerial (27×44 mm)	70	25
863	3r. Intersputnik programme earth station (44×27 mm)	1·60	65

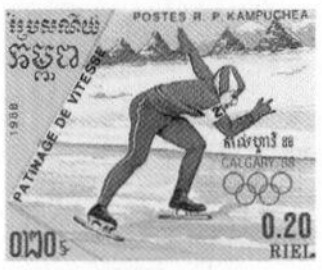

179 Speed Skating

1988. Winter Olympic Games, Calgary (2nd issue). Multicoloured.

864	20c. Type **179**	20	10
865	50c. Ice hockey	25	10
866	80c. Slalom	35	10
867	1r. Ski jumping	65	10
868	1r.50 Biathlon	90	20
869	2r. Ice dancing	1·30	20
870	3r. Cross-country skiing	1·80	20
MS871	66×89 mm. 6r. Four-man bobsleigh (31×39 mm)	4·25	90

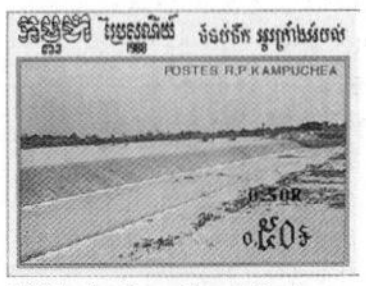

180 Irrigation Canal Bed

1988. Irrigation Projects. Multicoloured.

872	50c. Type **180**	35	20
873	1r. Dam construction	70	25
874	3r. Dam and bridge	1·60	45

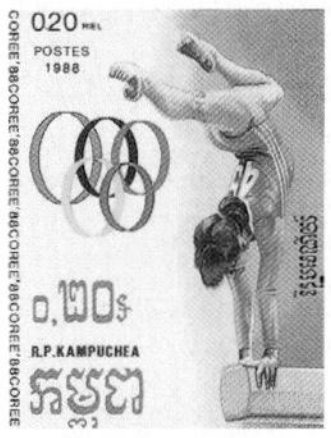

181 Beam Exercise

1988. Olympic Games, Seoul (2nd issue). Women's Gymnastics. Multicoloured.

875	20c. Type **181**	20	10
876	50c. Bar exercise (horiz)	25	10
877	80c. Ribbon exercise	35	10
878	1r. Hoop exercise	55	10
879	1r.50 Baton exercise	70	20
880	2r. Ball exercise (horiz)	1·20	20
881	3r. Floor exercise (horiz)	1·60	20
MS882	84×59 mm. 6r. Ball exercise (different) (28×36 mm)	4·25	90

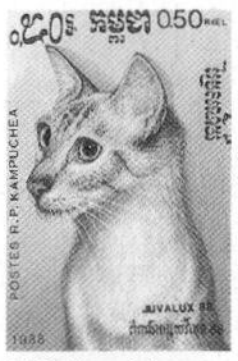

182 Abyssinian

1988. "Juvalux 88" Ninth Youth Philately Exhibition, Luxembourg. Cats. Multicoloured.

883	20c. White long-haired (horiz)	20	10
884	50c. Type **182**	25	10
885	80c. Ginger and white long-haired	35	10
886	1r. Tortoiseshell queen and kitten (horiz)	65	20

887	1r.50 Brown cat	1·10	25
888	2r. Black long-haired cat	1·30	35
889	3r. Grey cat	2·00	55
MS890	61×50 mm. 6r. Kittens (39×31 mm)	7·00	90

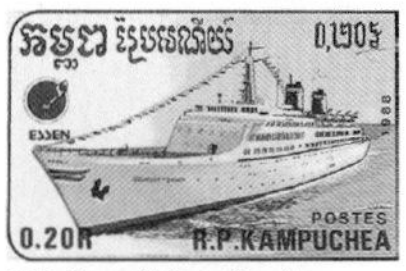

183 *Emerald Seas* (liner)

1988. "Essen 88" International Stamp Fair. Ships. Multicoloured.

891	20c. Type **183**	20	10
892	50c. Car ferry	25	10
893	80c. *Mutsu* (nuclear-powered freighter)	35	10
894	1r. *Kosmonavt Yury Gagarin* (research ship)	65	20
895	1r.50 Tanker	1·10	25
896	2r. Hydrofoil	1·30	35
897	3r. Hovercraft	2·00	55
MS898	95×70 mm. 6r. Hydrofoil (different) (39×31 mm)	4·75	90

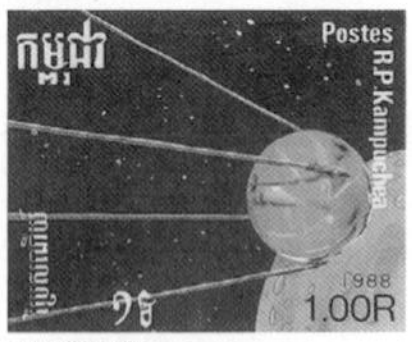

184 Satellite

1988. Space Exploration. Designs showing different satellites.

899	-	20c. multicoloured (vert)	20	10
900	-	50c. multicoloured (vert)	25	10
901	-	80c. multicoloured (vert)	35	10
902	**184**	1r. multicoloured	55	10
903	-	1r.50 multicoloured	80	20
904	-	2r. multicoloured	1·20	20
905	-	3r. multicoloured	1·60	20
MS906		103×63 mm. 6r. multicoloured (39×31 mm)	4·25	90

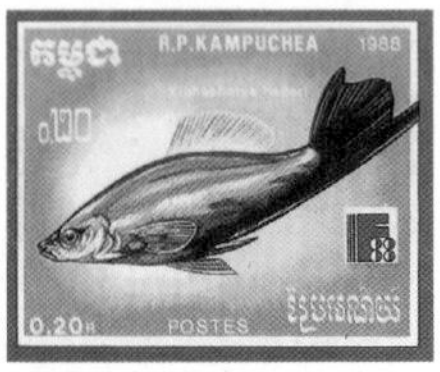

185 Swordtail

1988. "Finlandia 88" International Stamp Exhibition, Helsinki. Tropical Fish. Multicoloured.

907	20c. Type **185**	20	10
908	50c. Head-and-taillight tetra	25	10
909	80c. Paradise fish	35	20
910	1r. Black moor goldfish	65	20
911	1r.50 Cardinal tetra	1·10	20
912	2r. Sword-tailed characin	1·30	25
913	3r. Sail-finned molly	2·00	35
MS914	62×72 mm. 6r. Angel fish (31×39 mm)	5·75	90

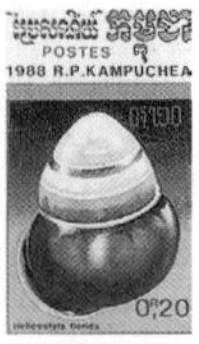

186 Flowery Helicostyla

1988. Sea Shells. Multicoloured.

915	20c. Type **186**	20	10
916	50c. Changing helicostyla	25	10
917	80c. Shining helicostyla	35	10
918	1r. Marinduque helicostyla	65	10
919	1r.50 Siren chlorena	1·10	20
920	2r. Miraculous helicostyla	1·30	20
921	3r. "Helicostyla limansauensis"	2·00	20

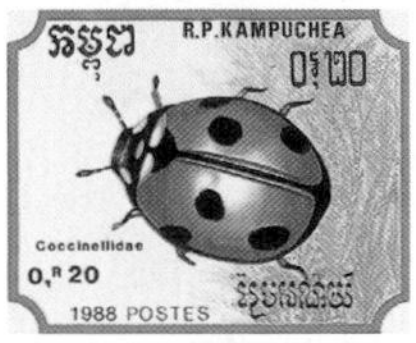

187 Seven-spotted Ladybird

1988. Insects. Multicoloured.

922	20c. Type **187**	20	10
923	50c. *Zonabride geminata* (blister beetle)	25	10
924	80c. *Carabus auronitens* (ground beetle)	35	10
925	1r. Honey bee	65	10
926	1r.50 Praying mantis	1·10	20
927	2r. Dragonfly	1·30	20
928	3r. Soft-winged flower beetle	2·00	20

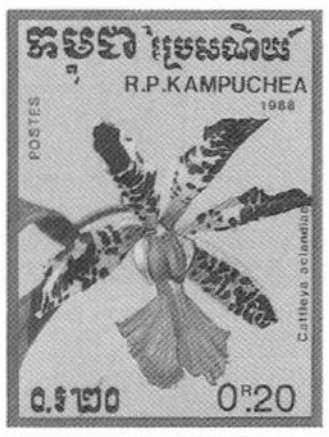

188 *Cattleya aclandiae*

1988. Orchids. Multicoloured.

929	20c. Type **188**	20	10
930	50c. *Odontoglossum* "Royal Sovereign"	25	10
931	80c. *Cattleya labiata*	35	10
932	1r. Bee orchid	65	10
933	1r.50 *Laelia anceps*	90	20
934	2r. *Laelia pumila*	1·30	20
935	3r. *Stanhopea tigrina* (horiz)	1·80	20

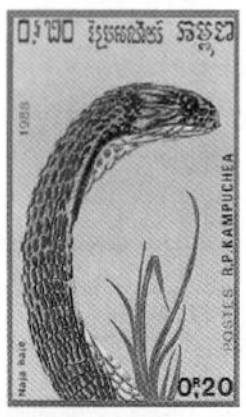

189 Egyptian Banded Cobra

1988. Reptiles. Multicoloured.

936	20c. Type **189**	20	10
937	50c. Common iguana	25	10
938	80c. Long-nosed vine snake (horiz)	35	10
939	1r. Common box turtle (horiz)	65	10
940	1r.50 Iguana (horiz)	1·10	20
941	2r. Viper (horiz)	1·30	20
942	3r. Common cobra	2·00	20

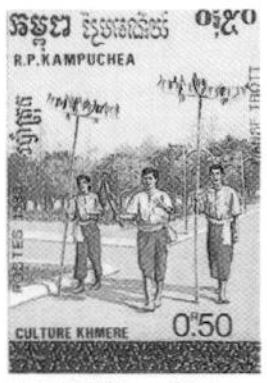

190 Walking Dance

1988. Festival of Rebirth. Khmer Culture. Multicoloured.

943	50c. Type **190**	35	20
944	1r. Peacock dance (horiz)	80	25
945	3r. Kantere dance (horiz)	2·00	65

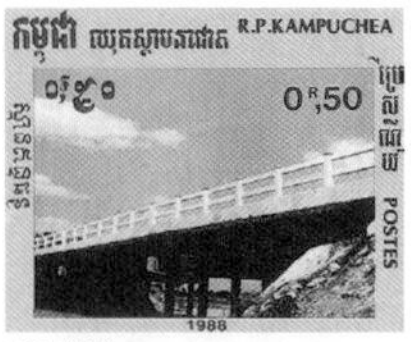

191 Bridge

1989. Multicoloured.. Multicoloured..

946	50c. Type **191**	25	10
947	1r. More distant view of bridge	65	35
948	3r. Closer view of bridge	1·60	90

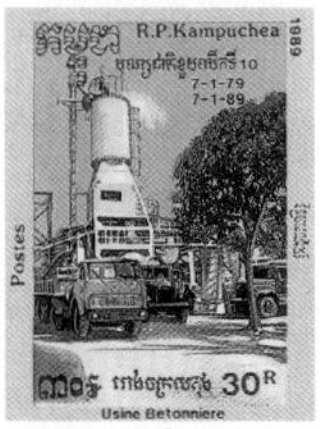

192 Cement Works

1989. National Festival. Tenth Anniv of People's Republic of Kampuchea. Multicoloured.

949	3r. Bayon Earth Station (horiz)	25	10
950	12r. Electricity generating station 4 (horiz)	70	35
951	30r. Type **192**	2·00	90

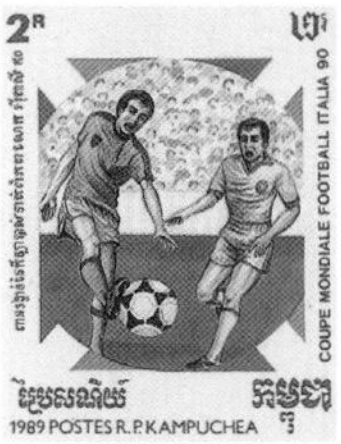

193 Footballers

1989. World Cup Football Championship, Italy (1990).

952	**193**	2r. multicoloured	20	10
953	-	3r. multicoloured	25	10
954	-	5r. multicoloured	35	10
955	-	10r. multicoloured	80	10
956	-	15r. multicoloured	1·20	20
957	-	20r. multicoloured	1·60	20
958	-	35r. multicoloured	2·75	20
MS959		92×54 mm. 45r. multicoloured (goalkeeper) (31×39 mm)	4·25	90

DESIGNS: 3r. to 45r. Various footballing scenes. See also Nos. 1042/**MS**1049.

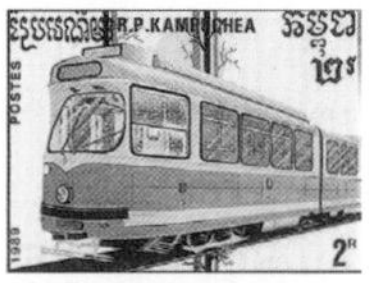

194 Tram

1989. Trams and Trains. Multicoloured.

960	2r. Type **194**	25	10
961	3r. ETR 401 Pendolino express train, 1976, Italy	35	10
962	5r. High speed train, Germany	45	10
963	10r. Theme park monorail train	80	10
964	15r. German Trans Europe Express (TEE) train	1·20	20
965	20r. "Hikari" express train, Sanyo Shinkansenline, Japan	1·60	20
966	35r. TGV express train, France	3·00	20
MS967	85×55 mm. 45r. multicoloured (39×31 mm)	5·25	90

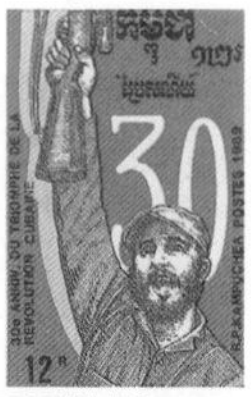

195 Fidel Castro

1989. 30th Anniv of Cuban Revolution.

968	**195**	12r. multicoloured	1·10	55

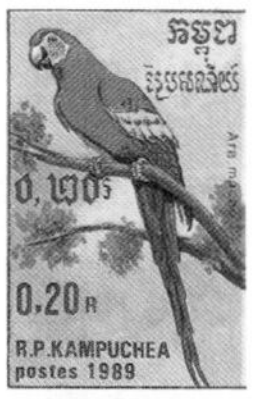

196 Scarlet Macaw

1989. Parrots. Multicoloured.

969	20c. Type **196**	20	10
970	80c. Sulphur-crested cockatoo	25	10
971	3r. Rose-ringed parakeet	35	10
972	6r. Blue and yellow macaw	70	10
973	10r. Brown-necked parrot	90	20
974	15r. Blue-fronted amazon	1·40	20
975	25r. White-capped parrot (horiz)	2·00	20
MS976	65×75 mm. 45r. Red-fronted parakeet (31×39 mm)	6·50	90

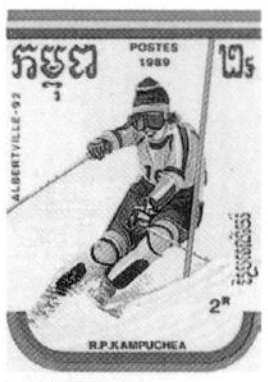

197 Skiing

1989. Winter Olympic Games, Albertville (1992). Multicoloured.

977	2r. Type **197**	20	10
978	3r. Biathlon	25	10
979	5r. Cross-country skiing	35	10
980	10r. Ski jumping	80	10
981	15r. Speed skating	1·10	20
982	20r. Ice hockey	1·30	20
983	35r. Two-man bobsleighing	2·75	20
MS984	75×89 mm. 45r. Figure skating (31×39 mm)	4·25	90

See also Nos. 1069/**MS**1076 and 1152/**MS**1159.

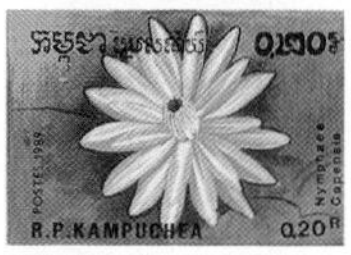

198 *Nymphaea capensis* (pink)

1989. Water Lilies. Multicoloured.

985	20c. Type **198**	20	10
986	80c. *Nymphaea capensis* (mauve)	20	10
987	3r. *Nymphaea lotus dentata*	25	10
988	6r. "Dir. Geo. T. Moore"	45	10
989	10r. "Sunrise"	65	20
990	15r. *Escarbuncle*	1·30	20
991	25r. *Cladstoniana*	2·00	20
MS992	59×79 mm. 45r. "Paul Hariot" (31×39 mm)	4·25	90

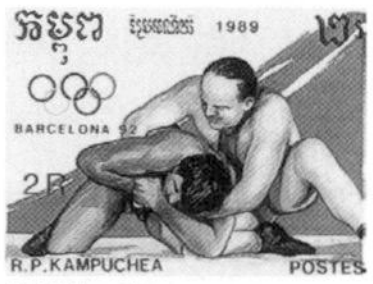

199 Wrestling

1989. Olympic Games, Barcelona (1992). Multicoloured.

993	2r. Type **199**	20	10
994	3r. Gymnastics (vert)	25	10
995	5r. Putting the shot	35	10
996	10r. Running (vert)	70	10
997	15r. Fencing	1·10	20
998	20r. Canoeing (vert)	1·30	20
999	35r. Hurdling (vert)	2·75	20
MS1000	62×87 mm. 45r. Weightlifting (31×39 mm)	4·25	90

See also Nos. 1061/**MS**1068, 1163/**MS**1170, 1208/**MS**1213 and 1241/**MS**1246.

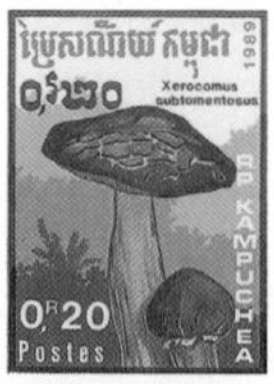

200 Downy Boletus

1989. Fungi. Multicoloured.

1001	20c. Type **200**	20	10
1002	80c. Red-staining inocybe	25	10
1003	3r. Honey fungus	35	10
1004	6r. Field mushroom	70	10
1005	10r. Brown roll-rim	90	20
1006	15r. Shaggy ink cap	1·40	20
1007	25r. Parasol mushroom	2·00	20

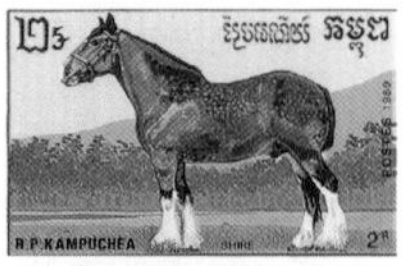

201 Shire Horse

1989. Horses. Multicoloured.

1008	2r. Type **201**	20	10
1009	3r. Brabant	25	10
1010	5r. Bolounais	35	10
1011	10r. Breton	80	10
1012	15r. Vladimir heavy draught horse	1·20	20
1013	20r. Italian heavy draught horse	1·60	20
1014	35r. Freiberger	2·75	20
MS1015	77×56 mm. 45r. Team of four white horses (39×31 mm)	5·25	90

Pt. 10

KARELIA

Northern Karelia, on the border of Finalnd, declared its independence from Russia on 1 October 1921 and issued the following stamps.

100 pennia = 1 markka.

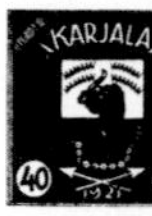

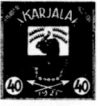

1 Arms of Karelia

1922

1	1	5p. grey	16·00	40·00
2	1	10p. blue	16·00	40·00
3	1	20p. rose	16·00	40·00
4	1	25p. brown	16·00	40·00
5	1	40p. violet	16·00	40·00
6	1	50p. olive	16·00	40·00
7	1	75p. yellow	16·00	40·00
8	1	1m. black and rose	16·00	40·00
9	1	2m. black and green	37·00	90·00
10	1	3m. black and blue	37·00	£110
11	1	5m. black and violet	37·00	£130
12	1	10m. black and brown	37·00	£200
13	1	15m. carmine and green	37·00	£200
14	1	20m. green and mauve	37·00	£200
15	1	25m. blue and yellow	37·00	£200

Stamps inscribed "ITA-KARJALA" (Eastern Karelia) are listed under Finnish Occupation of Eastern Karelia.

Pt. 14

KATANGA

The following stamps were issued by Mr. Tshombe's Government for independent Katanga. In 1963 Katanga was reunited with the Central Government of Congo.

1960. Various stamps of Belgian Congo optd **KATANGA** and bar or surch also. (a) Masks issue of 1948.

1	1f.50 on 1f.25 mauve and blue	80	20
2	3f.50 on 2f.50 green and brown	80	25
3	20f. purple and red	2·75	85
4	50f. black and brown	6·50	3·00
5	100f. black and red	48·00	21·00

(b) Flowers issue of 1952. Flowers in natural colours; colours given are of backgrounds and inscriptions.

6	10c. yellow and purple	20	20
7	15c. green and red	20	20
8	20c. grey and green	35	25
9	25c. orange and green	35	25
10	40c. salmon and green	35	25
11	50c. turquoise and red	45	35
12	60c. purple and green	35	25
13	75c. grey and lake	45	35
14	1f. lemon and red	55	45
15	2f. buff and olive	65	55
16	3f. pink and green	90	65
17	4f. lavender and sepia	1·25	95
18	5f. green and purple	1·25	95
19	6f.50 lilac and red	1·25	85
20	7f. brown and green	1·75	1·25
21	8f. yellow and green	1·75	1·25
22	10f. olive and purple	28·00	17·00

(c) Wild animals issue of 1959.

23	10c. brown, sepia and blue	20	10
24	20c. blue and red	1·60	80
25	40c. brown and blue	20	10
26	50c. multicoloured	20	10
27	1f. black, green and brown	6·75	4·00
28	1f.50 black and yellow	11·00	7·50
29	2f. black, brown and red	50	10
30	3f. black, purple and slate	4·25	3·00
31	5f. brown, green and sepia	75	30
32	6f.50 brown, yellow and blue	95	30
33	8f. bistre, violet and brown	1·40	35
34	10f. multicoloured	2·10	50

(d) Madonna.

35	102	50c. brown, ochre and chestnut	15	15
36	102	1f. brown, violet and blue	15	15
37	102	2f. brown, blue and slate	20	20

(e) African Technical Co-operation Commission. Inscr in French or Flemish.

38	103	3f. salmon and slate	7·00	7·00
39	103	3f.50 on 3f. salmon and slate	2·10	2·10

1960. Independence. Independence issue of Congo optd **11 JUILLET DE L'ETAT DU KATANGA**.

40	106	20c. bistre	10	10
41	106	50c. red	10	10
42	106	1f. green	10	10
43	106	1f.50 brown	10	10
44	106	2f. mauve	10	10
45	106	3f.50 violet	15	10
46	106	5f. blue	15	10
47	106	6f.50 black	15	10
48	106	10f. orange	25	20
49	106	20f. blue	45	30

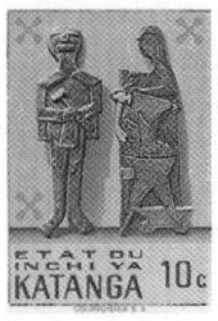

5

1961. Katanga Art.

50	5	10c. green	10	10
51	5	20c. violet	10	10
52	5	50c. blue	10	10
53	5	1f.50 green	10	10
54	5	2f. brown	10	10
55	-	3f.50 blue	10	10
56	-	5f. turquoise	10	10
57	-	6f. brown	10	10
58	-	6f.50 blue	10	10
59	-	8f. purple	15	10
60	-	10f. brown	15	10
61	-	20f. myrtle	25	20
62	-	50f. brown	50	40
63	-	100f. turquoise	85	70

DESIGNS: 3f.50 to 8f. "Preparing food"; 10f. to 100f. "Family circle".

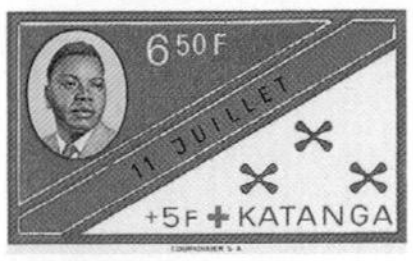

6 Pres. Tshombe

1961. First Anniv of Independence. Portrait in brown.

64	6	6f.50+5f. red, green & gold	1·25	1·00
65	6	8f.+5f. red, green and gold	1·25	1·00
66	6	10f.+5f. red, green and gold	1·25	1·00

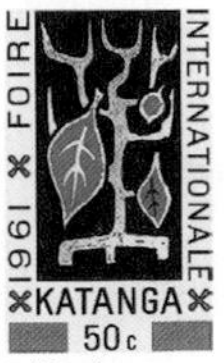

7 "Tree"

1961. Katanga International Fair. Vert symbolic designs as T **7**.

67	7	50c. red, green and black	10	10
68	-	1f. black and blue	10	10
69	-	2f.50 black and yellow	15	15
70	7	3f.50 red, brown and black	15	15
71	-	5f. black and violet	25	25
72	-	6f.50 black and yellow	30	30

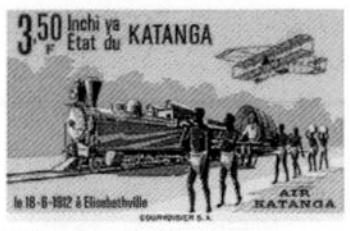

8 Farman H.F.III Biplane, Steam Train and Safari

1961. Air.

73	8	3f.50 multicoloured	3·00	3·25
74	-	6f.50 multicoloured	65	65
75	8	8f. multicoloured	3·00	3·25
76	-	10f. multicoloured	65	65

DESIGNS: 6f.50, 10f. Tail of Boeing 707.

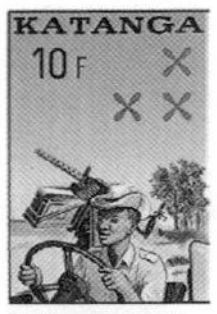

9 Gendarme in armoured Vehicle

1962. Katanga Gendarmerie.

77	9	6f. multicoloured	2·25	2·25
78	9	8f. multicoloured	35	35
79	9	10f. multicoloured	45	45

POSTAGE DUE STAMPS

1960. Postage Due stamps of Belgian Congo handstamped **KATANGA**. (a) On Nos. D270/4.

D50	D 86	10c. olive	80	80
D51	D 86	20c. blue	80	80
D52	D 86	50c. green	1·00	1·00
D53	D 86	1f. brown		
D54	D 86	2f. orange		

(b) On Nos. D330/6.

D55	D 99	10c. brown	3·25	3·25
D56	D 99	20c. purple	3·25	3·25
D57	D 99	50c. green	3·25	3·25
D58	D 99	1f. blue	1·00	1·00
D59	D 99	2f. red	2·00	2·00
D60	D 99	4f. violet	2·75	2·75
D61	D 99	6f. blue	3·25	3·25

Pt. 1

KATHIRI STATE OF SEIYUN

The stamps of Aden were used in Kathiri State of Seiyun from 22 May 1937 until 1942.

1937. 16 annas = 1 rupee.
1951. 100 cents = 1 shilling.
1966. 1000 fils = 1 dinar.

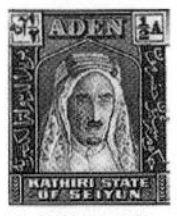

1 Sultan of Seiyun

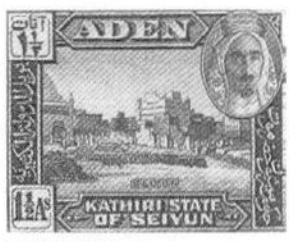

2 Seiyun

1942

1	1	½a. green	20	1·75
2	1	¾a. brown	40	4·00
3	1	1a. blue	70	2·00
4	2	1½a. red	70	2·75
5	-	2a. brown	40	2·50
6	-	2½a. blue	1·25	2·50
7	-	3a. brown and red	1·75	4·00
8	-	8a. red	2·00	70
9	-	1r. green	5·50	4·50
10	-	2r. blue and purple	13·00	23·00
11	-	5r. brown and green	30·00	28·00

DESIGNS—VERT: 2a. Tarim; 2½a. Mosque at Seiyun; 1r. South Gate, Tarim; 5r. Mosque entrance, Tarim. HORIZ: 3a. Fortress at Tarim; 8a. Mosque at Seiyun; 2r. A Kathiri house.

1946. Victory. Optd **VICTORY ISSUE 8TH JUNE 1946**.

12	2	1½a. red	20	65
13	-	2½a. blue (No. 6)	20	35

1949. Royal Silver Wedding. As T **59b/c** of Jamaica.

14	1½a. red	30	3·25
15	5r. green	18·00	12·00

1949. 75th Anniv of U.P.U. As T **59d/g** of Jamaica, surch with new values.

16	2½a. on 20c. blue	15	1·00
17	3a. on 30c. red	1·25	2·50
18	8a. on 50c. orange	25	3·50
19	1r. on 1s. blue	30	1·25

1951. 1942 stamps surch in cents or shillings.

20	1	5c. on 1a. blue	15	1·75
21	-	10c. on 2a. brown	30	1·25
22	-	15c. on 2½a. blue	15	2·00
23	-	20c. on 3a. brown and red	20	2·75
24	-	50c. on 8a. red	20	1·25
25	-	1s. on 1r. green	1·00	3·25
26	-	2s. on 2r. blue and purple	11·00	38·00
27	-	5s. on 5r. brown and green	32·00	55·00

1953. Coronation. As T **61a** of Jamaica.

28	15c. black and green	40	1·75

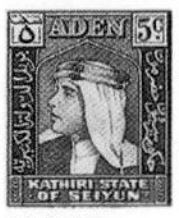

14 Sultan Hussein

1954. As 1942 issue and new designs, but with portrait of Sultan Hussein as in T **14**.

29	14	5c. brown	10	10
30	14	10c. blue	15	10
31	2	15c. green	20	10
32	-	25c. red	20	10
33	-	35c. blue	20	10
34	-	50c. brown and red	20	10
39	-	70c. black	3·00	2·00
35	-	1s. orange	20	10
40	-	1s.25 green	3·00	8·00
41	-	1s.50 violet	3·00	8·00
36	-	2s. green	4·25	2·25
37	-	5s. blue and violet	9·50	8·50
38	-	10s. brown and violet	9·50	8·50

DESIGNS—VERT: 35c. Mosque at Seiyun; 70c. Qarn Adh Dhabi; 2s. South Gate, Tarim; 10s. Mosque entrance, Tarim. HORIZ: 50c. Fortress at Tarim; 1s. Mosque at Seiyun; 1s.25, Seiyun; 1s.50, Gheil Omer; 5s. Kathiri house.

1966. Nos. 29 etc surch **SOUTH ARABIA** in English and Arabic, with value and bar.

42	14	5f. on 5c.	30	20
43	14	5f. on 10c.	30	85
44	2	10f. on 15c.	30	1·50
45	-	15f. on 25c.	30	80
46	-	20f. on 35c.	30	30
47	-	25f. on 50c.	30	75
61	-	35f. on 70c.	2·50	60
49	-	50f. on 1s.	30	20
50	-	65f. on 1s.25	30	20
51	-	75f. on 1s.50	30	30
65	-	100f. on 2s.	4·75	2·50
53	-	250f. on 5s.	1·40	3·75
54	-	500f. on 10s.	1·75	3·75

Each value has two similar surcharges.

1966. Nos. 57, 59, 61/7 variously optd as given below, together with Olympic "rings".

68	10f. on 15c. (**LOS ANGELES 1932**)	35	35
69	20f. on 35c. (**BERLIN 1936**)	45	45
70	35f. on 70c. (**INTERNATIONAL COOPERATION**, etc)	45	45
71	50f. on 1s. (**LONDON 1948**)	50	55
72	65f. on 1s.25 (**HELSINKI 1952**)	50	1·00
73	75f. on 1s.50 (**MELBOURNE 1956**)	60	1·50
74	100f. on 2s. (**ROME 1960**)	70	1·75
75	250f. on 5s. (**TOKYO 1964**)	1·00	3·50
76	500f. on 10s. (**MEXICO CITY 1968**)	1·25	4·00

1966. World Cup Football Championship. Nos. 57, 59, 61/2, 65/7 optd **CHAMPIONS ENGLAND** (10f., 50f. and 250f.) or **FOOTBALL 1966** (others). Both with football symbol.

77	10f. on 15c.	70	50
78	20f. on 35c.	90	60
79	35f. on 70c.	1·25	60
80	50f. on 1s.	1·40	60
81	100f. on 2s.	2·75	2·50
82	250f. on 5s.	6·00	7·00
83	500f. on 10s.	7·50	10·00

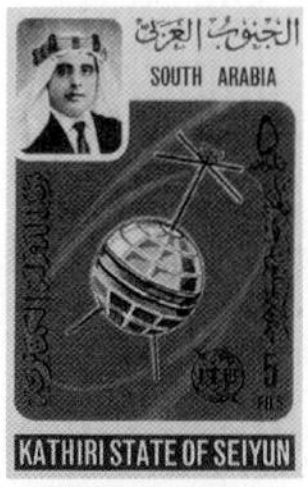

29 "Telstar"

1966. Centenary of I.T.U. (1965).

84	29	5f. green, black and violet	2·00	15
85	-	10f. purple, black and green	2·25	20
86	-	15f. blue, black and orange	2·75	20
87	29	25f. green, black and red	3·25	20
88	-	35f. purple, black and yellow	3·25	20
89	-	50f. blue, black and brown	3·75	25
90	29	65f. green, black and yellow	4·00	30

DESIGNS: 10, 35f. "Relay"; 15, 50f. "Ranger".

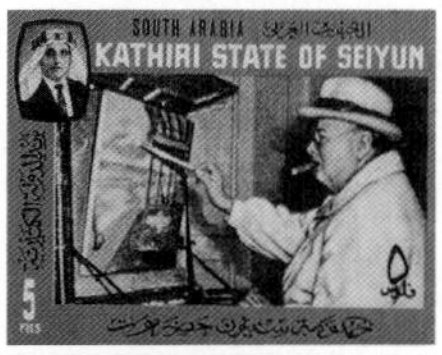

32 Churchill at Easel

1966. Sir Winston Churchill's Paintings. Multicoloured.

91	5f. Type **32**	1·75	15
92	10f. *Antibes*	2·00	15
93	15f. *Flowers* (vert)	2·00	20
94	20f. *Tapestries*	2·00	35
95	25f. *Village, Lake Lugano*	2·00	35
96	35f. *Church, Lake Como* (vert)	2·00	40
97	50f. *Flowers at Chartwell*"(vert)	2·25	65
98	65f. Type **32**	2·75	90

1967. "World Peace". Nos. 57, 59, 61/7 optd **WORLD PEACE** and names as given below.

99	10f. on 15c. (**PANDIT NEHRU**)	4·00	2·00
100	20f. on 35c. (**WINSTON CHURCHILL**)	6·00	2·75
101	35f. on 70c. (**DAG HAMMARSKJOLD**)	50	80
102	50f. on 1s. (**JOHN F. KENNEDY**)	60	90
103	65f. on 1s.25 (**LUDWIG ERHARD**)	70	1·10
104	75f. on 1s.50 (**LYNDON JOHNSON**)	80	1·25
105	100f. on 2s. (**ELEANOR ROOSEVELT**)	1·00	2·25
106	250f. on 5s. (**WINSTON CHURCHILL**)	17·00	12·00
107	500f. on 10s. (**JOHN F. KENNEDY**)	5·00	13·00

40 *Master Crewe as Henry VIII* (Sir Joshua Reynolds)

1967. Paintings. Multicoloured.
108		5f. Type **40**	30	25
109		10f. *The Dancer* (Degas)	35	30
110		15f. *The Fifer* (Manet)	40	35
111		20f. *Stag at Sharkey's* (boxing match, G. Bellows)	45	40
112		25f. *Don Manuel Osorio* (Goya)	50	45
113		35f. *St. Martin distributing his Cloak* (A. van Dyck)	70	65
114		50f. *The Blue Boy* (Gainsborough)	85	75
115		65f. *The White Horse* (Gauguin)	1·10	1·00
116		75f. *Mona Lisa* (Da Vinci) (45×62 mm)	1·40	1·25

1967. American Astronauts. Nos. 57, 59, 61/2 and 65/6 optd as below, all with space capsule.
117		10f. on 15c. (**ALAN SHEPARD JR.**)	55	1·25
118		20f. on 35c. (**VIRGIL GRISSOM**)	70	1·25
119		35f. on 70c. (**JOHN GLENN JR.**)	95	1·50
120		50f. on 1s. (**SCOTT CARPENTER**)	95	1·50
121		100f. on 2s. (**WALTER SCHIRRA JR.**)	1·75	3·50
122		250f. on 5s. (**GORDON COOPER JR.**)	2·50	8·00

50 *Churchill Crown*

1967. Churchill Commemoration.
123	**50**	75f. multicoloured	8·00	7·50

APPENDIX

The following stamps have either been issued in excess of postal needs or have not been made available to the public in reasonable quantities at face value.

1967

Hunting. 20f.
Olympic Games, Grenoble. Postage 10, 25, 35, 50, 75f.; Air 100, 200f.
Scout Jamboree, Idaho. Air 150f.
Paintings—Renoir. Postage 10, 35, 50, 65, 75f.; Air 100, 200, 250f.
Paintings—Toulouse-Lautrec. Postage 10, 35, 50, 65, 75f.; Air 100, 200, 250f.

The National Liberation Front is said to have taken control of Kathiri State of Seiyun on 1 October 1967.

Pt. 10

KAZAKHSTAN

Formerly a constituent republic of the Soviet Union, Kazakhstan declared its independence on 16 December 1991.

1992. 100 kopeks = 1 rouble.
1994. 100 tyin (ty.) = 1 tenge (t.).

1 *"Golden Warrior"*

1992. "Golden Warrior" (from 5th-century B.C. tomb).
1	**1**	50k. multicoloured	35	25

(2)

1992. Nos. 6079/80 of Russia optd as T **2**, in Cyrillic (2, 4) or English (3, 5) capitals.
2		12k. purple	4·25	4·00
3		12k. purple	4·25	4·00
4		13k. violet	4·25	4·00
5		13k. violet	4·25	4·00

(3)

1992. Russian–French Space Flight. Nos. 6072/4 of Russia surch as T **3**.
6		30k. on 2k. brown	2·50	2·00
7		75k. on 3k. green	2·10	2·00
8		1r. on 1k. brown	2·30	2·20

4 *Saiga*

1992
9	**4**	75k. multicoloured	35	20

5 *"Turksib"* (E. K. Kasteev)

1992. Kazakh Art.
10	**5**	1r. multicoloured	40	30

(6)   (7)   (8)

1992. Various stamps of Russia surch as T **6** (11/12), **7** (13/14) or **8** (15/16).
11		1r.50 on 1k. brown (No. 5940)	85	80
12		2r. on 2k. brown (No. 6073)	1·00	95
13		3r. on 6k. blue (No. 4673)	85	80
14		5r. on 6k. blue (No. 4673)	85	80
15		10r. on 1k. brown (No. 5940)	1·00	95
16		24r.50 on 1k. brown (No. 5940)	2·10	2·00

9 *National Flag and Arms*

1992. Republic Day.
17	**9**	5r. multicoloured	2·50	2·40

11 *National Flag*   **10** *Rocket Launch*

1993
18	**10**	1r. green	15	10
19	**10**	3r. red	15	10
20	**10**	10r. bistre	50	50
21	**10**	25r. violet	1·30	1·20
22	**11**	50r. yellow, blue and deep blue	2·50	2·40

See also Nos. 45 etc.

12 *Rocket and Earth*

1993. Space Mail.
23	**12**	100r. multicoloured	2·10	1·40

13 *Cock*

1993. New Year. Year of the Cock.
24	**13**	60r. black, red and yellow	1·30	1·20

14 *Space Station*

1993. Cosmonautics Day.
25	**14**	90r. multicoloured	2·10	1·40

15 *Nazarbaev and Flag on Map*

1993. President Nursultan Nazarbaev (1st series).
26	**15**	50r. multicoloured	85	80

See also No. 28.

16 *Kalkaman-Uly*

1993. 325th Birth Anniv of Bukar Zhyrau Kalkaman-Uly (poet).
27	**16**	15r. multicoloured	40	25

17 *Arms, Flag on Map and Nazarbaev*

1993. President Nursultan Nazarbaev (2nd series).
28	**17**	100r. multicoloured	1·30	1·20

18 *Desert Dormouse*

1993. Mammals. Multicoloured.
29		5r. Type **18**	25	20
30	**10**	10r. Porcupine	35	25
31		15r. Marbled polecat	50	30
32		20r. Asiatic wild ass	65	40
33		25r. Mouflon	85	50
34		30r. Cheetah	90	60

19 *Ice Hockey*

1994. Winter Olympic Games, Lillehammer, Norway (1st issue). Multicoloured.
35		15t. Type **19**	30	20
36		25t. Skiing	45	30
37		90t. Ski jumping	1·40	1·20
38		150t. Speed skating	2·20	2·00

20 *Skiers*

1994. Winter Olympic Games, Lillehammer, Norway (2nd issue). Multicoloured.
39		2t. Type **20**	1·00	85
40		6t.80 Vladimir Smirnov (Kazakh skier)	2·75	2·50

See also No. 42.

21 *Dog*

1994. New Year. Year of the Dog.
41	**21**	30t. black, blue and green	65	50

22 *Smirnov*

1994. Vladimir Smirnov, Winter Olympic Games Medals Winner. As No. 40 but face value changed and with additional inscription in Kazakh.
42	**22**	12t. multicoloured	3·25	3·00

23 *Launch of "Soyuz TM16" at Baikonur*

1994. Cosmonautics Day.
43	**23**	2t. multicoloured	1·30	1·10

24 *Space Shuttle* Buran *on Baikonur Launch Pad and Toktar Aubakrirov*

1994. First Space Flight of Kazakh Cosmonaut. Sheet 107×66 mm.
MS44	**24**	4 ×6t.80 multicoloured	5·00	4·75

1994
45	**10**	15ty. blue	25	15
46	**10**	80ty. purple	1·00	85
76	**10**	20ty. orange	15	10
77	**10**	25ty. yellow	15	10
78	**10**	50ty. grey	15	10
79	**10**	1t. green	25	20
80	**10**	2t. blue	65	50
81	**10**	4t. mauve	90	70
82	**10**	6t. green	1·80	1·60
83	**10**	12t. mauve	2·40	1·80

25 *Mt. Abay*

1994. Fifth "Asia Dauysy" International Music Festival, Almaty. Multicoloured.
47		10t. Type **25**	1·00	85
48		15t. Medeo Ice Stadium, Almaty	1·40	1·30

26 *Horsfield's Tortoises*

1994. Reptiles. Multicoloured.
49		1t. Type **26**	15	10
50		1t.20 Toad-headed agamas	25	20
51		2t. Halys vipers	40	25
52		3t. Turkestan plate-tailed geckos	50	35
53		5t. Steppe agamas	75	60
54		7t. Glass lizards	1·10	95
MS55		93×73 mm. 10t. Transcaspian desert monitor (*Varanus griseus*)	2·30	2·00

27 National Arms

1994. Republic Day.

| 56 | **27** | 2t. multicoloured | 65 | 60 |

28 "Why does the Swallow have a Forked Tail?" (dir. Amen Khaidarov)

1994. Children's Fund. Kazakh Children's Films. Multicoloured.

57	**28**	Type **28**	25	20
58		1t.+30ty. *The Calf and Hare seek a Better Life* (E. Abdra-khmanov)	25	20
59		1t.+30ty. *Asses* (*Lame Kulan* dir. Amen Khaidarov)	25	20

29 Entelodon

1994. Prehistoric Animals. Multicoloured.

60		1t. Type **29**	15	10
61		1t.20 *Saurolophus*	25	20
62		2t. *Plesiosaurus*	40	25
63		3t. "*Sordes pilosus*"	50	35
64		5t. *Mosasaurus*	75	60
65		7t. "*Megaloceros giganteum*"	1·10	95
MS66	92×72 mm. 10t. *Koelodonta antiquitatis*		2·30	2·00

1995. Nos. 45/6 surch.

67	**24**	1t. on 15ty. blue	15	10
68	**24**	2t. on 15ty. blue	20	15
69	**24**	3t. on 80ty. purple	25	20
70	**24**	4t. on 80ty. purple	40	25
71	**24**	6t. on 80ty. purple	65	50
72	**24**	8t. on 80ty. purple	1·30	1·10
73	**24**	12t. on 80ty. purple	1·50	1·30
74	**24**	20t. on 80ty. purple	2·50	1·40

31 Pig

1995. New Year. Year of the Pig.

| 75 | **31** | 10t. blue, black and light blue | 1·30 | 1·10 |

32 Kunanbaev

1995. 150th Birth Anniv of Abai Kunanbaev (writer). Multicoloured.

| 86 | **32** | 4t. Type **32** | 40 | 30 |
| 87 | | 9t. Kunanbaev holding pen and book | 90 | 70 |

33 Flight Path of "Soyuz" Spacecraft

1995. Cosmonautics Day. Multicoloured.

| 88 | **33** | 2t. Type **33** | 3·25 | 3·00 |
| 89 | | 10t. Yuri Malenchenko, Talgat Musabaev and Ulf Merbold (cosmonauts) | 13·00 | 12·00 |

34 Manshuk Mametova and Battle Scene

1995. 50th Anniv of End of Second World War. Multicoloured.

90		1t. Type **34**	75	60
91		3t. Aliya Moldafulova and tank	1·70	1·60
92		5t. Wheat field, dove and eternal flame	3·00	2·75

35 "Spring" (S. Membeev)

1995. Paintings. Multicoloured.

93		4t. Type **35**	65	50
94		9t. *Mountains* (Zh. Shardenov)	1·00	95
95		15t. *Kulash Baiseitova in role of Kyz Zhibek* (G. Ismailova) (vert)	1·70	1·60
96		28t. *Kokpar* (K. Telzhanov)	3·25	3·00

1995. "Asia Dauysy" International Music Festival, Almaty. Nos. 47/8 optd **KAZAKSTAN '95 1995**.

| 97 | | 10t. multicoloured | 1·30 | 1·10 |
| 98 | | 15t. multicoloured | 1·90 | 1·70 |

37 Dauletkerei

1995. 175th Birth Anniv of Dauletkerei (composer and poet).

| 99 | **37** | 2t. multicoloured | 65 | 50 |
| 100 | **37** | 28t. multicoloured | 5·50 | 5·25 |

38 Gandhi, Temple and Spinning Wheel

1995. 125th Birth Anniv (1994) of Mahatma Gandhi.

| 101 | **38** | 9t. red and black | 2·50 | 2·30 |
| 102 | **38** | 22t. red and black | 4·50 | 4·25 |

39 Anniversary Emblem

1995. 50th Anniv of U.N.O.

| 103 | **39** | 10t. gold and blue | 2·50 | 2·40 |
| 104 | **39** | 36t. gold and blue | 5·25 | 5·00 |

40 Cathedral of the Ascension

1995. Buildings in Almaty.

105	**40**	1t. green	25	20
106	-	2t. blue	50	35
107	-	3t. red	75	60
108	-	48t. brown	7·75	7·25

DESIGNS: 2t. Culture Palace; 3t. Opera and Ballet House; 48t. Theatre.
See also Nos. 124/5.

41 White-tailed Sea Eagle

1995. Birds of Prey. Multicoloured.

109		1t. Type **41**	15	10
110		4t. Osprey	25	20
111		5t. Lammergeier	45	30
112		6t. Himalayan griffon	50	35
113		30t. Saker falcon	2·75	2·40
114		50t. Golden eagle	4·50	4·00

42 Rat and Lunar Cycle

1996. Chinese New Year. Year of the Rat.

| 115 | **42** | 25t. red, black and lilac | 3·25 | 3·00 |

43 Baikonur Launch Pad highlighted on Globe

1996. Cosmonautics Day. Multicoloured.

116		6t. Type **43**	1·30	1·20
117		15t. Yuri Gagarin	3·25	3·00
118		20t. Proposed "Alpha" space station	4·50	4·25

44 Carancal (*Felis caracal*)

1996. "Save the Aral Sea". Sheet 128×108 mm containing T **44** and similar horiz designs. Multicoloured.

| **MS**119 | 20t. Type **44**; 20t. Aral trout (*Salmo trutta aralensis*); 20t. Striped hyena (*Hyaena hyaena*); 20t. Kaufmann's shovelnose (*Pseudo-scaphirhynchus kaufmanni*); 20t. Pike asp (*Aspiolucius esocinus*) | | 7·00 | 6·50 |

45 Cycling

1996. Olympic Games, Atlanta. Multicoloured.

120		4t. Type **45**	95	80
121		6t. Wrestling	1·40	1·30
122		30t. Boxing	7·00	6·75
MS123	92×69 mm. 50t. Hurdling (45×27 mm)		5·25	5·00

1996. As T **40** but smaller, size 24×19 mm.

| 124 | | 1t. green | 25 | 25 |
| 125 | | 6t. green | 80 | 65 |

DESIGNS: 1t. Circus; 6t. Academy of Sciences (50th anniv).

46 Zhabaev (after embroidery by G. Atknin)

1996. 150th Birth Anniv of Zhambil Zhabaev (writer).

| 126 | **46** | 12t. multicoloured | 1·30 | 1·10 |

47 Tomb, Dombauyl

1996. Ancient Buildings. Multicoloured.

127		1t. Type **47**	75	60
128		3t. Mausoleum, Aisha Biy	2·30	2·00
129		6t. Mausoleum, Syrly Tam	4·50	4·00
MS130	90×60 mm. 30t. Kozha Ahmet Yasavi Mausoleum, Turkestan		3·75	3·50

48 "Soyuz TM-13" docked with "Mir" Space Station

1996. Fifth Anniv of Toktar Aubakirov's (cosmonaut) Service on "Mir". Multicoloured.

| 131 | | 46t. Type **48** | 4·75 | 4·50 |
| 132 | | 46t. Aubakirov | 4·75 | 4·50 |

Nos. 131/2 were issued together, *se-tenant*, forming a composite design.

49 Map of Kazakhstan and Dove with Letter

1996. World Post Day.

| 133 | **49** | 9t. blue | 1·30 | 1·10 |
| 134 | - | 40t. orange | 5·00 | 4·75 |

DESIGN: 40t. Dove with letter and Universal Postal Union emblem.

1996. Republic Day. No. 56 surch **KAZAKSTAN 1. 1996**.

| 135 | **27** | 21t. on 2t. multicoloured | 1·90 | 1·70 |

51 Saturnia schenki

1996. Butterflies. Multicoloured.

136		4t. Type **51**	40	30
137		6t. *Parnassius patricius*	50	40
138		12t. *Parnasssius ariadne*	75	65
139		46t. *Colias draconis*	2·75	2·50

52 Borzois giving Chase

1996. Hunting Dogs.

| 140 | **52** | 5t. multicoloured | 65 | 60 |
| **MS**141 | 95×70 mm. **52** 100t. multi-coloured | | 5·75 | 5·50 |

53 Bride before Yurte

1996. Traditional Costumes and Dwelling. Multicoloured.

142		10t. Type **53**	90	70
143		16t. Bridegroom before yurte	1·40	1·20
144		45t. Yurte interior	4·00	3·75

Nos. 142/4 were issued together, *se-tenant*, Nos. 142/3 forming a composite design.

54 Writing Materials and Books

1996. Bicentenary of National Archive.

| 145 | **54** | 4t. brown | 30 | 25 |
| 146 | - | 68t. violet | 4·25 | 4·00 |

DESIGN: 68t. Book and documents.

55 Scene from *Angel with Tyubetejka* by Shaken Aimanov

1996. Centenary (1995) of Motion Pictures. Sheet 135×148 mm containing T **55** and similar horiz designs. Multicoloured.
MS147 24t. Type **55**; 24t. *The Zhibek Girl* (S. Kozhykov); 24t. *His Time will Come* (M. Begalin); 24t. *My Name is Kozha* (A. Karsakbaev)   7·00   6·75

56 Head

1997. The Marbled Polecat. Multicoloured.
148	6t. Type **56**	65	50
149	10t. Adult with tail down	90	70
150	32t. Two polecats	2·10	1·90
151	46t. Adult with tail raised	3·00	2·75

57 Ox

1997. New Year. Year of the Ox.
152	**57**	40t. brown, black and green	2·00	1·80

58 Aries

1997. Star Signs. Each violet and purple.
153	1t. Type **58**	15	10
154	2t. Taurus	15	10
155	3t. Gemini	20	15
156	4t. Cancer	20	15
157	5t. Leo	25	20
158	6t. Virgo	30	25
159	7t. Libra	40	30
160	8t. Scorpio	45	35
161	9t. Sagittarius	50	40
162	10t. Capricorn	65	55
163	12t. Aquarius	75	60
164	20t. Pisces	1·00	85
MS165	109×164 mm. Nos. 153/64	6·50	6·25

59 Saturn and Automatic Transfer Vehicle

1997. Cosmonautics Day. Multicoloured.
166	10t. Type **59**	1·00	85
167	10t. Space shuttle and "Mir" space station	1·00	85
168	10t. "Sputnik 1" and Earth	1·00	85

Nos. 166/8 were issued together, *se-tenant*, forming a composite design.

60 Emblem

1997. World Book and Copyright Day.
169	**60**	15t. yellow and green	75	60
170	**60**	60t. yellow and green	3·25	3·00

61 Auezov Museum, Almaty

1997. Birth Centenary of Mukhtar Auezov (philologist). Multicoloured.
171	25t. Type **61**	1·50	1·30
172	40t. Auezov at table (after Shcherkassky)	2·50	2·30

62 Order of Bravery

1997. Orders and Medals. Multicoloured.
173	15t. Type **62**	90	70
174	15t. Medal of Honour	90	70
175	20t. Order of Victory	1·10	95
176	30t. National Order of Merit	1·60	1·40

63 "Tulipa alberti"

1997. Tulips. Multicoloured.
177	15t. *Tulipa regelii*	75	60
178	35t. Type **63**	2·00	1·80
179	35t. *Tulipa greigii*	2·00	1·80

64 "Shepherd" (Sh. Sariev)

1997. Paintings. Multicoloured.
180	25t. Type **64**	1·50	1·30
181	25t. *Fantastic Still Life* (S. Kalmykov)	1·50	1·30
182	25t. *Capturing Horse* (M. Kenbaev) (horiz)	1·50	1·30

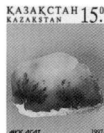

65 Moss Agate

1997. Minerals. Multicoloured.
183	15t. Type **65**	1·00	85
184	15t. Chalcedony	1·00	85
185	20t. Azurite	1·30	1·10
186	20t. Malachite	1·30	1·10
MS187	110×99 mm. Nos. 182/5	4·50	4·25

66 *Gylippus rickmersi*

1997. Arachnidae. Multicoloured.
188	30t. Type **66**	1·80	1·60
189	30t. *Latrodectus pallidus*	1·80	1·60
190	30t. *Oculicosa supermirabilis*	1·80	1·60
191	30t. *Anomalobuthus rickmersi*	1·80	1·60

67 Argali

1997. Karkaraly Nature Park. Sheet 114×148 mm containing T **67** and similar vert designs. Multicoloured.
MS192 30t. Type **67**; 30t. Common juniper; 30t. Cudgel stone   5·00   4·75

68 Horse Race

1997. National Sports. Multicoloured.
193	20t. Type **68**	1·10	95
194	20t. Tearing goatskin ("Koknar")	1·10	95
195	20t. Wrestling	1·10	95
196	20t. Two-horse race	1·10	95

69 Ice Dancing

1998. Winter Sports. Multicoloured.
197	15t. Type **69**	1·00	85
198	30t. Biathlon	2·10	1·90

70 *Little Girl* (A. Ashkiyazara)

1998. Children's Paintings. Multicoloured.
199	15t. Type **70**	1·00	85
200	15t. *My House* (M. Tarakara) (horiz)	1·00	85

71 Tiger and Lunar Cycle

1998. New Year. Year of the Tiger.
201	**71**	30t. brown, black and yellow	1·90	1·70

72 Kurmangazy

1998. 175th Birth Anniv of Kurmangazy (composer).
202	**72**	30t. yellow, brown and black	1·90	1·70

73 Baitursynov

1998. 125th Birth Anniv of Akhmet Baitursynov (writer).
203	**73**	30t. light brown, brown and black	1·90	1·70

74 Winged and Horned Beasts, Issyk Kurgan

1998. Archaeological Finds. Multicoloured.
204	15t. Type **74**	90	70
205	30t. Pendants, Aktasty (vert)	1·80	1·60
206	40t. Gold and jewel-studded open-work ornament depicting animals, Kargaly	2·40	2·20

75 "Apollo 8" Spacecraft and Moon

1998. Cosmonautics Day. Multicoloured.
207	30t. Type **75**	1·40	1·20
208	30t. "Apollo 8", Earth and Moon	1·40	1·20
209	50t. "Vostok 6" orbiting Earth	2·30	2·00

Nos. 207/8 were issued together, *se-tenant*, forming a composite design.

76 Mosque

1998. Astana. New Capital of Kazakhstan.
210	**76**	10t. brown	65	55
211	–	15t. blue (inscr "Akmola")	95	80
212	–	15t. blue (inscr "Astana")	95	80
213	–	20t. blue	1·10	95
214	–	25t. violet	1·30	1·10
MS215	99×73 mm. 100t. multicoloured	5·00	4·75

DESIGNS—VERT: 15t. Petroleum Ministry; 20t. Parliament. HORIZ: 25k. Presidents Palace. 43×25 mm.—100t. Presidents Palace.

77 State Arms

1998
216	**77**	1t. green	15	10
217	**77**	2t. blue	15	10
218	**77**	3t. red	25	20
219	**77**	4t. purple	40	35
220	**77**	5t. yellow	40	35
221	**77**	8t. orange	65	60
225	**77**	20t. orange	90	85
229	**77**	50t. blue	2·10	2·00

78 Climber fixing Tent

1998. Kazakhstan Expedition to Mt. Everest. Sheet 85×67 mm.
MS230 **78** 100t. multicoloured   6·25   6·00

79 Black Stork

1998. Birds. Multicoloured.
231	15t. Type **79**	70	55
232	30t. Greater flamingoes	1·40	1·20
233	50t. Great white crane	2·20	2·00

80 Lynx

1998. Wild Cats. Multicoloured.
234	15t. Type **80**	70	55
235	30t. Sand dune cat	1·40	1·20
236	50t. Snow leopard	2·20	2·00

81 Dove and Emblem

1998. Admission of Kazakhstan to Universal Postal Union (1st issue). Sheet 104×84 mm.
MS237 **81** 50t. multicoloured   3·25   3·00

See also No. **MS278**.

82 Stamp and U.P.U. Emblem

1998. World Post Day.
| 238 | 82 | 30t. bistre | 1·50 | 1·40 |

83 Anniversary Emblem

1998. Fifth Anniv of the Tenge (currency unit).
| 239 | 83 | 40t. orange | 2·10 | 1·90 |

84 Warrior with Sword

1998. Kazakh Horsemen. Multicoloured.
240	20t. Type 84	1·10	95
241	30t. Using bow and arrow	1·70	1·50
242	40t. With spear and shield	2·30	2·00

85 Rock Formation in Lake

1998. Environmental Protection. Buradai National Park. Sheet 110×98 mm containing T **85** and similar vert design. Multicoloured.
| MS243 | 30t. Type 85; 30t. View over lake | 3·25 | 3·00 |

86 Family (census)

1999
244	86	1t. green	25	20
245	-	3t. red	40	30
246	-	9t. green	45	35
247	-	15t. red	50	40
248	-	20t. brown	75	70
249	-	30t. brown	1·30	1·20

DESIGNS—HORIZ: 15t. Kanyish Sambaev (geologist and President of Academy of Sciences, birth centenary) and book; 20t. Sambaev and Academy of Sciences. VERT: 3, 9, 30t. Dish aerial and 'Intelsat' satellite.

87 Rabbit and Lunar Cycle

1999. New Year. Year of the Rabbit.
| 250 | 87 | 40t. green, black and yellow | 1·60 | 1·40 |

88 Steam Locomotive and Railway Route Map

1999. Railway Locomotives. Multicoloured.
251	40t. Type 88	2·30	2·00
252	50t. Electric locomotive	2·75	2·50
253	60t. Diesel railcar	3·25	3·00
254	80t. Electric locomotive (different)	4·25	4·00

89 Satellite

1999. Cosmonautics Day. Multicoloured.
| 255 | 50t. Type 89 | 3·00 | 2·75 |
| 256 | 90t. Astronaut on Moon (30th anniv of first manned Moon landing) (horiz) | 5·00 | 4·75 |

90 *Pseudoeremostachys severzowii*

1999. Flowers. Multicoloured.
257	20t. Type 90	1·10	95
258	30t. *Rhaphidophyton regelii*	1·60	1·40
259	90t. *Niedzwedzkia semiretschenskia*	5·00	4·75

91 Scene from *Turksib* (1929)

1999. 70th Anniv of Kazak Cinema. Multicoloured.
260	15t. Type 91	75	60
261	20t. M. Berkovich (director) and scenes from *Jambul's Youth* (1997) and *Wolf Cub among People* (1998)	1·00	85
262	30t. Scenes from *The Devil Paths* (1935), *Our Dear Doctor* (1957) and *Amangeldy* (1938)	1·80	1·60
263	35t. Scenes from *Zama-ay* (1997), *Biography of a Young Accordionist* (1994) and *Who are you Rider?* (1989)	1·90	1·70
264	50t. Alfred Hitchcock (director) and scene from *The Birds*	2·75	2·50
265	60t. Sergei Eisenstein (director)	3·50	3·00

92 Red Fox

1999. Endangered Species. Foxes. Multicoloured.
266	20t. Type 92	1·30	1·20
267	30t. Dhole	1·90	1·70
268	90t. Corsac fox	5·75	5·25

93 Magnifying Glass and Stamps

1999. 125th Anniv of Universal Postal Union.
| 269 | 93 | 10t. violet | 65 | 60 |

94 Mushroom Cloud

1999. Environmental Protection Sheet 130×108, containing T **94** and similar horiz designs. Multicoloured.
| MS270 | 15t. Type 94 (tenth Anniv of cessation of nuclear testing at Semipalatinsk); 45t. Emblem (International Day for Protection of the Ozone Layer); 60t. Butterflies and landscape | 6·25 | 6·00 |

95 Flower

1999. Endangered Flora (1st series).
| 271 | 95 | 4t. mauve | 25 | 20 |
| 272 | 95 | 30t. green | 1·10 | 95 |

See also Nos. 296/8, 310/11 and 357/63.

96 T. Musabayev

1999. Cosmonauts. Multicoloured.
| 273 | 40t. Type 96 | 1·80 | 1·60 |
| 274 | 50t. T. Aubakirov (first Kazakhstan cosmonaut) (vert) | 2·40 | 2·20 |

97 Ice Hockey Match

1999. Sports. Multicoloured.
275	20t. Type 97	90	70
276	30t. Ice hockey team	1·40	1·20
277	40t. G. Kosanov (athlete)	1·90	1·70

98 Globe and Horse-drawn Carriage

1999. 125th Anniv of U.P.U. (2nd issue). Sheet 120×85 mm.
| MS278 | 98 | 20t. multicoloured | 1·90 | 1·80 |

99 Oil Rig

2000. Centenary of Oil Extraction in Kazakhstan.
| 279 | 99 | 7t. red | 40 | 35 |

100 Yurt, Horse racing and Artifacts

2000. Navruz Bayram Festival. Imperf.
| 280 | 100 | 20t. multicoloured | 1·10 | 95 |

101 Millennium Emblem

2000. New Millennium.
| 281 | 101 | 30t. blue, deep blue and orange | 1·30 | 1·10 |

102 28th Guardsman-Panfilovs Memorial and Eternal Flame, Alma-Ata

2000. 55th Anniv of End of Second World War.
| 282 | 102 | 3t. brown and red | 25 | 20 |

103 "Stride into the Bright Future" (painting, Kostya Balakirev)

2000. International Children's Day. New Millennium. Sheet 127×106 mm.
| MS283 | 103 | 70t. multicoloured | 3·25 | 3·00 |

104 Koumiss (fermented mare's milk) Flask

2000. Joint issue with People's Republic of China. Pots. Multicoloured.
| 284 | 15t. Type 104 | 50 | 40 |
| 285 | 50t. He-pot (Chinese wine vessel) | 1·90 | 1·70 |

105 Mukanov

2000. Birth Centenary of Sabit Mukanov (writer).
| 286 | 105 | 1t. green | 40 | 35 |

106 Dulati

2000. 500th Birth Anniv of Mukhammed Khaidar Dulti (historian) (1999).
| 287 | 106 | 8t. blue | 30 | 25 |

107 Canoeing

2000. Olympics Games, Sydney. Multicoloured.
288	35t. Type 107	1·40	1·20
289	40t. Gymnastics	1·60	1·40
290	40t. Taekwondo	1·60	1·40
291	50t. Triathlon	1·90	1·70

108 "Echo" Telecommunications Satellite

2000
292	108	5t. orange	25	20
293	108	15t. blue	65	50
294	108	20t. blue	75	60

109 Arystan Bab's Mausoleum

2000. 1500th Anniv of Turkestan (town). Sheet 160×140 mm containing T **109** and similar horiz designs. Multicoloured.
| MS295 | 50t. Type 109; 50t. Rabiy Sultan Begim's and Karashash Ana's mausolea; 70t. Kozhah Akhmet Yassauy's mausoleum | 7·00 | 6·50 |

Stamps of a similar design were issued by Turkey.

110 Flower

2000. Endangered Flora (2nd series).

296	**110**	1t. green	15	10
297	**110**	2t. blue	15	10
298	**110**	50t. blue	2·00	1·80

111 Momysh-Uly and Gold Star of Hero of Soviet Union Medal

2000. 90th Birth Anniv of Baurdzhan Momyush-Uly (Soviet military leader).

299	**111**	4t. brown and black	30	25

2001. Nos. 57/9 surch **2001 10.00**.

300		10t. on 1t. +30ty. multicoloured	40	35
301		10t. on 1t. +30ty. multicoloured	40	35
302		10t. on 1t. +30ty. multicoloured	40	35

113 Snail and Lunar Cycle

2001. New Year. Year of the Snail.

303	**113**	40t. black, blue and yellow	1·40	1·20

114 Rocket, Yuri Gagarin and Dogs

2001. Cosmonautics Day (2000). Multicoloured.

304		40t. Type **114** (40th anniv of space flight by Belka and Strelka (dogs))	1·40	1·20
305		70t. Rocket launch (45th anniv of Baikonur cosmodrome) (vert)	2·40	2·20

115 Snake and Lunar Cycle

2001. New Year. Year of the Snake.

306	**115**	40t. black, brown and green	1·40	1·20

116 Dove, Globe and Transport

2001. Tenth Anniv of Ministry of Transportation and Communication. Sheet 100×70 mm.

MS307 **116** 100t. multicoloured		5·00	4·75

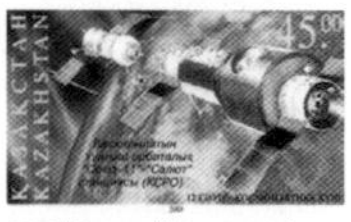

117 "Soyuz-II" Spacecraft and "Salyut" Space Station

2001. Cosmonautics Day. Multicoloured.

308		45t. Type **117**	1·60	1·40
309		70t. Yuri Gagarin and earth (40th anniv of first manned space flight)	2·10	1·90

118 *Aquilegia karatavica*

2001. Endangered Flora (3rd series).

310	**118**	3t. green	15	10
311	**118**	10t. green	40	35

119 Abulkhair-Khan (1693–1748)

2001. Khans (feudal rulers). Multicoloured.

312		50t. Type **119**	1·90	1·70
313		60t. Abylai-Khan (1711–1781)	2·30	2·00

120 Roborovski Hamster (*Phodopus roborovskii*)

2001. Fauna (1st series).

314	**120**	8t. orange	25	20
315	**120**	15t. blue	50	35
316	**120**	20t. blue	75	60
317	**120**	50t. brown	2·00	1·80

See also 351/4 and 386/92.

121 Northern Eagle Owl (*Bubo bubo*)

2001. Owls. Multicoloured.

318		30t. Type **121**	2·10	1·90
319		40t. Long-eared owl (*Asio otis*)	2·75	2·50
320		50t. Hawk owl (*Surnia ulula*)	3·50	3·25

122 Winged Lion and Fibre Optic Cable

2001. National Development Plan. Communications.

321	**122**	40t. multicoloured	1·50	1·30

123 Red Deer (*Cervus elaphus*)

2001. Fauna of Lake Markakol (national park). Sheet 110×98 mm containing T **123** and similar vert designs. Multicoloured.

MS322 Type **123**; 30t. Brown bear (*Ursus arctos*); 30t. Lenok (*Brachymystax lenok*)		4·50	4·25

124 Bobak Marmot (*Marmota bobak*)

2001. Flora and Fauna. Sheet 215×102 mm containing T **124** and similar horiz designs. Multicoloured.

MS323 Type **124**; 12t. Great bustard (*Otis tarda*); 25t. Relict gull (*Larus relictus*); 60t. African wildcat (*Felis silvestris libyca*); 90t. Water lily (*Nymphaea alba*); 100t. Dalmatian pelican (*Pelecanus crispus*)		11·50	11·00

125 Druzhba Station Facade

2001. Anniversaries. Sheet 105×74 mm containing T **125** and similar horiz designs. Multicoloured.

MS324 Type **125** (10th anniv of Kazakhstan–China railway); 20t. Steam locomotive (70th anniv of Turkestan–Siberia railway); 50t. Workmen (opening of Aksu–Delegen railway)		4·50	4·25

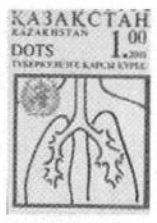

126 Lungs and United Nations Emblem

2001. Health.

325	**126**	1t. green, blue and black	15	10
326	-	5t. red, grey and black	15	10

DESIGNS: Type **126** (tuberculosis prevention campaign); 5t. Ribbon and book (AIDS prevention campaign).

127 River Charyn Cliffs

2001. International Year of Mountains. Multicoloured.

327		35t. Type **127**	1·10	95
328		60t. Mt. Khan Tegri	2·10	1·90

128 Alexej Leonov

2001. Space Anniversaries. Multicoloured.

329		50t. Type **128** (35th anniv of 1st space walk)	2·75	2·50
330		70t. *Soyuz* and *Apollo* space craft (25th anniv of joint USSR–USA space flight) (horiz)	4·00	3·50

129 Children encircling Globe

2001. United Nations Year of Dialogue among Civilizations.

331	**129**	45t. multicoloured	1·60	1·40

130 Wild Ass

2001. Endangered Species. Asiatic Wild Ass (Equus heminus kulan). Multicoloured.

332		9t. Type **130**	40	35
333		12t. Galloping	50	40
334		25t. Fighting	90	70
335		50t. Mare and foal	1·60	1·40

131 School Palace, Alma Ata

2001. Architecture.

336	**131**	7t. mauve	25	20
337	-	30t. green	1·40	1·20

DESIGN: 30t. School Palace, Alma Ata (different).

132 Union Emblem

2001. Tenth Anniv of Union of Independent States.

338	**132**	40t. multicoloured	1·50	1·30

133 Pres. Nursultan Nazarbaev and Pope John Paul II

2001. Visit of Pope John Paul II to Kazakhstan. Multicoloured.

339		20t. Type **133**	75	60
340		50t. Pres. Nazarbaev and Pope John Paul II (different)	1·90	1·70

134 Independence Monument, Almaty

2001. Tenth Anniv of Independence (1st issue). Sheet 110×96 mm containing T **134** and similar vert designs. Multicoloured.

MS341 Type **134**; 25t. Parliament House, Astana; 35t. Pres. Nursultan Nazarbaev		3·00	3·00

See also No. 342.

135 Celebration Emblem and Map

2001. Tenth Anniv of Independence (2nd issue).

342	**135**	40t. yellow, blue and black	1·50	1·30

136 Man's Costume

2001. Traditional Costumes. Multicoloured.

343		25t. Type **136**	90	70
344		35t. Woman's costume	1·30	1·10

Nos. 343/4 were issued together, *se-tenant*, forming a composite design.

137 Women Ice Hockey Players

2002. Winter Olympic Games, Salt Lake City, USA. Multicoloured.

345		50t. Type **137**	2·10	1·90
346		150t. Freestyle ski jump	5·75	5·50

138 Horse and Lunar Cycle

2002. New Year. Year of the Horse.

347	**138**	50t. black, ochre and stone	1·80	1·60

139 Chestnut Horse

2002. Horses. Multicoloured.

348		9t. Type **139**	40	35
349		25t. Dark chestnut, two legs raised	90	70
350		60t. Grey	2·10	1·90

140 Pallid Pygmy Jerboa (*Salpingotus pallidus*)

2002. Fauna (2nd series).

351	**140**	5t. purple	15	10
352	**140**	15t. blue	50	50
353	**140**	40t. brown	1·30	1·10
354	**140**	50t. sepia	1·60	1·40

141 Denis Tito (passenger), Talgat Musabaev and Yury Baturin (crew of Soyuz TM-32)

2002. Cosmonautics Day. Multicoloured.

355	30t. Type **141**	1·00	85
356	70t. Flags of USA, Kazakhstan and Russia	2·40	2·20

142 *Pterygostemon spathulatus*

2002. Endangered Flora (4th series).

357	**142**	1t. green	25	20
358	**142**	2t. blue	25	20
359	**142**	3t. green	25	20
360	**142**	10t. violet	40	35
361	**142**	12t. mauve	50	40
362	**142**	25t. violet	90	80
363	**142**	35t. olive	1·00	90

143 Two Players

2002. World Cup Football Championship, Japan and South Korea. Multicoloured.

364	10t. Type **143**	40	30
365	10t. Player heading ball	40	30

144 Globe

2002. TRANSEURASIA 2002 International Conference.

366	**144**	30t. blue, black and yellow	90	80

145 *Leontopodium fedtschenkoanum* (flower)

2002. Alatau National Park. Sheet 115×110 mm containing T **145** and similar vert designs. Multicoloured.

MS367 30t.×3, Type **145**; Ermine (*Mustela erminea*); Aport Alexander apples 3·50 3·25

146 Trading House

2002. 250th Anniv of Petropavlovsk.

368	**146**	6t. red	25	20
369	-	7t. purple	25	20
370	-	8t. orange (vert)	40	30
371	-	23t. blue (vert)	75	65

DESIGNS: 7t. No. 368; 8t. Karasai and Agyntai (heroes) monument; 23t. No. 371.

147 *Kazakh Composition* (E. Sidorkin)

2002. Art.

372	**147**	8t. brown, bistre and black	40	30
373	-	9t. black and drab	40	30
374	-	60t. sepia, bistre and black	2·10	1·90

DESIGNS: 9t. *Makhambet* (M. Kisametdinov); 60t. *Batyr* (E. Sidorkin).

148 Great Black-headed Gull (Pallas' Gull) (*Larus ichthyaetus Pallas*)

2002. Endangered Species. Birds. Multicoloured.

375	10t. Type **148**	40	30
376	15t. Demoiselle crane (*Anthropoides virgo*)	50	40

Stamps of the same design were issued by Russia.

149 *Huso huso ponticus* (fish)

2002. Endangered Species. Marine Animals. Multicoloured.

377	20t. Type **149**	70	60
378	35t. Caspian seal (*Phoca caspica*)	1·10	95

Stamps of the same design were issued by Ukraine.

150 Mosque

2002. Bimillenary of Taraz. Sheet 115×80 mm.

MS379 **150** 70t. multicoloured 2·75 2·75

151 Altau Mountains

2002. International Year of Mountains. Sheet 90×70 mm.

MS380 **151** 50t. multicoloured 2·00 1·90

152 Gabiden Mustaphin

2002. Birth Centenary of Gabiden Mustaphin (writer).

381	**152**	10t. blue	40	30

153 Gani Muratbaev

2002. Birth Centenary of Gani Muratbaev (politician).

382	**153**	3t. brown	25	20

154 Gabit Musrepov

2002. Birth Centenary of Gabit Musrepov (writer).

383	**154**	20t. multicoloured	65	55

155 Ilyushin IL-86 over Almaty Airport

2002. Aircraft. Multicoloured.

384	20t. Type **155**	65	55
385	40t. Tupelov TU-144 (25th Anniv of flight from Russia to Almaty)	1·30	1·10

156 Desert Dormouse (*Selevinia betpakdalensis*)

2003. Fauna (3rd series).

386	**156**	4t. brown	15	10
387		5t. brown	25	20
388		6t. olive	25	20
389		7t. green	25	20
390		10t. blue	40	25
391		63t. red	2·30	2·00
392		150t. purple	5·00	4·75

157 Argali-Merino Ram

2003. Sheep. Multicoloured.

393	20t. Type **157**	65	55
394	40t. Ram (different)	1·30	1·10
395	50t. Argali ram	1·60	1·40

158 Sheep and Lunar Cycle

2003. New Year ("Year of the Sheep").

396	**158**	50t. black, blue and light blue	1·30	1·10

2003. Fauna. Roborovski Hamster (Phodopus roborovskii) (2nd issue)).

397	**120**	35t. green	1·50	1·30

159 Sputnik "Pioner-10"

2003. Cosmonautics Day. Multicoloured.

398	40t. Type **159**	1·30	1·10
399	70t. "Mir" space station (vert)	2·10	1·90

160 Memorial to Victims of Political Repression

2003. Tenth Anniv of Rehabilitation of Victims of Political Repression Law.

400	**160**	1t. magenta	15	10
401	**160**	8t. brown	25	20

161 IAAS Emblem

2003. Tenth Anniv of the International Association of Academies of Sciences.

402	**161**	50t. multicoloured	1·60	1·40

162 Couple wearing Kazakhstan Costumes

2003. Traditional Costumes. Sheet 115×97 mm containing T **162** and similar vert designs (1st series). Multicoloured.

MS403 35t.×3, Type **162**; Russian; Ukrainian 3·25 3·00

See also No. **MS**453.

163 Dombra

2003. Traditional Instruments. Multicoloured.

404	25t. Type **163**	75	60
405	50t. Kobyz	1·50	1·30

164 "Intelsat" Satellite

2003

406	**164**	3t. red	25	20
407	**164**	9t. blue	40	35
408		84t. orange	2·50	2·30
409		100t. purple	3·00	2·75

165 Aldar Kose and Alasha Khan

2003. Fairy Tale Characters. Multicoloured.

410	30t. Type **165**	90	70
411	40t. Aldar Kose and Karynbaj	1·10	95

166 "Game of a Chess" (A. Richchi)

2003. Museum of Arts Exhibits. Multicoloured.

412	20t. Type **166**	50	35
413	35t. *Portrait of a Shepherd* (sculpture, H. Nauryzbaev)	90	70
414	45t. *Drinking Koumiss* (A. Galimbaeva)	1·10	95

167 Aiteke Bi Baibekuly (1689–1766)

2003. Judges. Multicoloured.

415	60t. Type **167**	1·60	1·40
416	60t. Kazibek Bi Keldibekuly (1667–1763)	1·60	1·40
417	60t. Tole Bi Alibekuly (1663–1756)	1·60	1·40

168 Anniversary Emblem

2003. Tenth Anniv of Halyk Bank.

418	**168**	23t. multicoloured	65	60

169 Conference and UN
Emblems

2003. International Ministerial Transport Co-operation
Conference.
419   **169**   40t. multicoloured   1·10   95

170 Globe and
UPU emblems

2003. World Post Day.
420   **170**   23t. violet and blue   50   55

171 Central
Mosque, Almaty

2003. Religious Buildings. Multicoloured.
421   50t. Type **171**   1·30   1·10
422   50t. Almaty Cathedral   1·30   1·10

172 Anniversary
Emblem

2003. Tenth Anniv of Kazakhstan Currency (tenge).
423   **172**   25t. lemon and blue   70   60

173 Happiness (S.
Aitbaev) (1966)

2003. Paintings. Multicoloured.
424   100t. Type **173**   2·40   2·20
425   100t. Morning Motherhood (R.
Ahmedov) (1962)   2·40   2·20
Stamps of similar designs were issued by Uzbekistan.

174 Populus
diversifolia

2003. Endangered Species. Asiatic Poplar.
426   **174**   100t. multicoloured   2·40   2·20

175 Cow

2003. Tamalgy—UNESCO World Heritage Site.
Petroglyphs (carvings). Multicoloured.
427   25t. Type **175**   65   55
428   30t. Sun and bull (vert)   75   60

2004. No. 45 surch **200t.**
429   200t. on 80t. claret   5·75   5·50

177 Abylhan
Kasteev

2004. Birth Centenary of Abylhan Kasteev (artist).
430   **177**   115t. multicoloured   3·25   3·00

178 Monkey and
Lunar Cycle

2004. New Year. "Year of the Monkey".
431   **178**   35t. blue, ultramarine
and ochre   1·00   85

179 Spacecraft
"Mariner-10"

2004. Cosmonautics Day. Multicoloured.
432   40t. Type **179**   1·00   85
433   50t. "Luna-3" space station
(horiz)   1·40   1·20

180
Kazakhstan
Arms

2004
434   **180**   1t. green   15   10
435   **180**   2t. blue   15   10
436   **180**   4t. purple   20   15
437   **180**   5t. yellow   25   20
438   **180**   10t. olive   40   25
439   **180**   16t. mauve   50   35
440   **180**   20t. mauve   55   40
441   **180**   35t. yellow   1·00   85
442   **180**   50t. emerald   1·40   1·20
443   **180**   72t. orange   2·00   1·80
444   **180**   100t. turquoise   2·75   2·50
445   **180**   200t. vermilion   5·75   5·25

181 National
Flag

2004
451   **181**   25t. blue and lemon   75   60

182 Electric
Locomotive

2004. Centenary of Kazakhstan Railway. Sheet 101×71
mm.
MS452 **182** 150t. multicoloured   4·00   4·00

2004. Traditional Costumes (2nd series). Sheet 110×96
mm containing vert designs as T **162**. Multicoloured.
MS453 65t.×2, Uzbekistan; German   3·75   3·50

183 Player and Emblem

2004. Centenary of FIFA (Federation Internationale de
Football Association). Multicoloured.
454   100t. Type **183**   2·75   2·50
455   100t. Player facing right and
emblem   2·75   2·50

184 Bayan Sulu
(fairy tale)

2004. Children's Drawings. Multicoloured.
456   45t. Type **184** (D. Ishanova)   1·10   95

457   45t. Mountains, yurts and
sheep (A. Sadykov) (horiz)   1·10   95

185 Boxing

2004. Olympic Games, Athens. Sheet 100×90 mm
containing T **185** and similar horiz design.
Multicoloured.
MS458 70t. Type **185**; 115t. Rifle
shooting   5·00   4·75

186 Cinereous Vulture
(Aegypius monachus) (inscr
"Acgypius")

2004. Altyn Yemel National Park. Sheet 80×110 mm
containing T **186** and similar horiz designs.
Multicoloured.
MS459 50t.×3 T **186**; Siberian ibex
(Capra sibirica); Persian gazelle
(Gazella subgutturosa)   4·50   4·25

187 Emblem

2004. Tenth Anniv of Kazakhtelecom Company. Sheet
100×70 mm.
MS460 **187** 70t. multicoloured   2·00   1·90

188 Alkei Margulan

2004. Birth Centenary of Alkei Hakanovich Margulan
(archaeologist).
461   **188**   115t. multicoloured   3·25   3·00

189 Flowers

2004. Greetings Stamp.
462   **189**   25t. multicoloured   65   50

2004. World Post Day.
463   **170**   3t. violet and blue   25   20
464   **170**   30t. lemon and blue   70   55

190 Bauble

2004. "Happy New Year".
465   **190**   65t. multicoloured   1·60   1·40

191 Adyrna

2004. Traditional Musical Instruments. Multicoloured.
466   100t. Type **191**   2·50   2·30
467   100t. Gizhak   2·50   2·30
Stamps of the same design were issued by Tadjikistan.

192 Saken Seifullin

2004. 110th Birth Anniv of Saken Seifullin (writer).
Multicoloured.
468   **192**   35t. multicoloured   90   70

193 Kazakh Woman's
Headdress

2004. Women's Headdress. Multicoloured.
469   72t. Type **193**   2·00   1·80
470   72t. Mongolian woman's
headdress   2·00   1·80
Stamps of the same design were issued by Mongolia.

194
Emblem

2005. Centenary of Research Institute of Veterinary
Science.
471   **194**   7t. vermilion, blue and
ultramarine   25   20

195 Arms
and Book

2005. Tenth Anniv of Constitution.
472   **195**   1t. blue and brown   15   10
473   **195**   2t. mauve and brown   15   10
474   **195**   3t. green and brown   20   15
475   **195**   8t. blue and -brown   25   20
476   **195**   10t. carmine and brown   40   25
477   **195**   A (25t.) purple and
brown   65   50
478   **195**   50t. bistre and brown   1·30   1·10
479   **195**   65t. blue and brown   1·60   1·40

196 Horse and
Bowl of Kumis

2005. Europa. Gastronomy.
480   **196**   90t. multicoloured   3·75   3·50

197 "Rodina-mat"
(statue)

2005. 60th Anniv of End of World War II.
481   **197**   72t. multicoloured   2·00   1·80

198 Soyuz Spacecraft

2005. 50th Anniv of Baikonur Cosmodrome. Sheet
111×71 mm containing T **198** and similar horiz
designs. Multicoloured.
MS482 72t.×3 Type **198**; Buran spacecraft; Parachute and space capsule   5·00   4·75

199 Building Plan of Project

2005. Peace and Harmony Palace Project (designed by
Norman Foster).
483   **199**   65t. multicoloured   1·60   1·40

200 Inscr "Ashirite"

2005. Minerals. Multicoloured.

484	50t. Type **200**	1·30	1·10
485	70t. Tubular agate	2·00	1·80

201 Aldar Kose and Rich Musician

2005. Fairy Tale Characters. Multicoloured.

486	35t. Type **201**	90	70
487	45t. *How Aldar Kose taught the rich man to grow donkeys*	1·30	1·10

202 Anniversary Emblem

2005. Tenth Anniv of Constitution.

488	**202**	72t. multicoloured	2·00	1·80

203 Zhaksylyk Ushkempirov (Graeco-Roman wrestling, Moscow, 1980)

2005. Sport. Olympic Champions. Sheet 139×84 mm containing T **203** and similar horiz designs.

MS489 100t.×4, Type **203**; Vitaly Savin (4×100 metres men's relay, Seoul, 1988); Vasily Zhirov (boxing light heavyweight, Atlanta, 1996); Bekzat Sattarkhanov (boxing featherweight, Sydney, 2000) 8·25 7·75

204

2005. No. 203 optd T **204**.

490	**73**	30t. multicoloured	90	70

205 UPU Emblem

2005. World Post Day.

491	**205**	35t. blue and lilac	1·10	95
492	**205**	40t. violet and claret	1·30	1·10

206 Kazak Tazi (hound)

2005. Hunting Dogs. Multicoloured.

493	138t. Type **206**	4·00	3·50
494	138t. Estonia hound	4·00	3·50

Stamps of similar design were issued by Estonia.

207 "60" and UN Emblem

2005. 60th Anniv of United Nations.

495	**207**	150t. blue, orange and black	4·50	4·00

208 Baiterek Monument, Clock Face and Tree

2005. New Year.

496	**208**	65t. multicoloured	2·00	1·80

209 Evgeny Brusilovsky

2005. Birth Centenary of Evgeny Grigorevich Brusilovsky (composer).

497	**209**	150t. multicoloured	4·50	4·00

210 Flag

2005. State Symbols. Sheet 135×80 mm containing T **210** and similar vert designs. Multicoloured.

MS498 70t. Type **210**; 70t. Words to hymn and statue; 300t. State arms 9·50 9·00

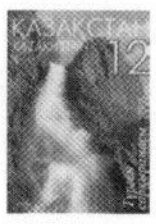
211 Turgen Waterfall

2005. Mountain Landscapes. Multicoloured.

499	12t. Type **211**	45	35
500	100t. Mountain lake (horiz)	3·25	3·00

212 Hans Christian Andersen and Characters from Stories

2005. Birth Bicentenary of Hans Christian Andersen (writer).

501	**212**	200t. multicoloured	6·25	6·00

213 Emblem

2006. Tenth Anniv of Parliament.

502	**213**	50t. multicoloured	1·50	1·30

214 "Ablai Khan" (Aubakir Ismailov)

2006. Art.

503	**214**	94t. multicoloured	3·00	2·75

215 Curling

2006. Winter Olympic Games, Turin.

504	**215**	138t. multicoloured	4·00	3·50

216 "Cosmonauts" (P. M. Popov) (1966)

2006. Cosmonautics Day. Paintings. Multicoloured.

505	100t. Type **216**	3·25	3·00
506	120t. *Cosmonaut* (A. M. Stepanov) (1970)	3·50	3·25

217 Cuff

2006. Jewellery. Multicoloured.

507	110t. Type **217**	3·50	3·00
508	110t. Brooch	3·50	3·00

Stamps of the same design were issued by Latvia.

218 Haloxylon aphyllum

2006

509	**218**	25t. multicoloured	90	70

219 Hands of Many Nations

2006. Europa. Integration.

510	**219**	210t. multicoloured	6·50	6·00

220 "Turksib" (painting) (Abylhan Kasteev)

2006. 75th Anniv of Turkestan—Siberian Railway.

511	**220**	200t. multicoloured	6·25	6·00

221 Football and Emblem

2006. World Cup Football Championship, Germany.

512	**221**	150t. multicoloured	4·50	4·00

222 Emblem

2006. International Year of Deserts and Desertification.

513	**222**	110t. multicoloured	3·50	3·00

223 Astana Mosque

2006

514	**223**	5t. green	25	20
515	**223**	8t. blue	30	25
516	**223**	10t. green	40	30
517	**223**	A (25t.) purple	75	60
517a	**223**	100t. blue	3·25	3·00
518	**223**	110t. brown	3·25	3·00
519	**223**	120t. magenta	3·50	3·00
520	**223**	200t. green	6·25	6·00

224 Akzhan Mashani

2006. Birth Centenary of Akzhan Mashani (geologist).

521	**224**	85t. multicoloured	3·00	2·75

225 Holy Trinity Cathedral Church, Almaty

2006. Places of Worship. Multicoloured.

522	25t. Type **225**	90	70
523	25t. Chabad Lubavich Synagogue, Almaty	90	70

226 Chokan Valikhanov (scientist-historian), 1835–1865

2006. Personalities. Sheet 84×100 mm containing T **226** and similar horiz designs. Multicoloured.

MS524 90t.×4, Type **226**; Saken Sejfullin (writer), 1894–1938; Nazir Tjurjakulov, 1893–1937; Kanysh Satpaev (geologist), 1899–1964 11·50 11·00

227 Flags of Participating Countries and Map

2006. Third Meeting of ECO Postal Authorities.

525	**227**	210t. multicoloured	6·25	6·00

АНКАРА

(228)

2006. Third Meeting of ECO Postal Authorities. No. 525 overprinted with T **228**. Multicoloured.

526	210t. As No. 525	6·25	6·00

229 Ahmet Zhubanov

2006. Birth Centenary of Ahmet Zhubanov (composer).

527	**229**	85t. multicoloured	2·75	2·40

229a Almaty

2006. Town Arms. Multicoloured.

528	17t. Type **229a**	65	50
529	80t. Astana	2·75	2·40

230 Snowman

2006. Happy New Year.

530	**230**	25t. multicoloured	90	70

232 Akzhan Mashani

2006. 75th (2005) Birth Anniv of Manash Kozybaev (historian).

532	**232**	20t. brown	75	60
533	**232**	30t. claret	1·00	85

233 Mukafali Makataev

2006. 75th (2005) Birth Anniv of Mukagali Makataev (writer).

534	**233**	1t. ultramarine	15	10
535	**233**	4t. olive	25	10
536	**233**	7t. claret	50	35
537	**233**	15t. chestnut	65	50

234 18th-century Helmet

2006. Ancient Armour and Weapons.

538	**234**	85t. multicoloured	2·75	2·40

235 "The Silk Girl" (opera)

2006. Theatre Art.

539	**235**	80t. multicoloured	2·50	2·30

236 Nikolai Repinsky

2006. Birth Centenary of Nikolai Repinsky (architect).

540	**236**	2t. ultramarine	15	10
541	**236**	3t. brown	20	10
542	**236**	105t. olive	3·25	2·75
543	**236**	150t. blue	4·50	4·00
544	**236**	500t. purple	8·25	7·50

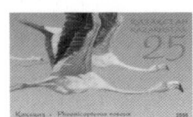

237 *Phoenicopterus roseus*

2006. Kurgalzhinsky Nature Reserve. Sheet 80×110 mm containing T **237** and similar horiz designs. Multicoloured.

MS545	25t. Type **237**; 100t. *Cygnus cygnus*; 120t. *Meles meles*	4·50	4·25

238 Anniversary Emblem

2007. 10th Anniv of KazTransOil.

546	**238**	25t. multicoloured	90	70

239 Konstantin Tsiolkovski (physicist and rocket pioneer) (150th birth anniv)

2007. Cosmonautics Day. Anniversaries. Multicoloured.

547	80t. Type **239**		2·75	2·40
548	110t. Sergei Korolev (rocket engineer and designer) (birth centenary)		3·25	3·00

240 Scout (Danagul Orazymbetova)

2007. Europa. Centenary of Scouting. Children's Drawings. Multicoloured.

549	25t. Type **240**		90	70
550	65t. Scouts wearing packs (Tamara Turta)		2·00	1·80

No. 551 and Type **241** have been left for '60th Anniv of UN ESCAP', issued on 17 May 2007, not yet received.

242 Gali Ormanov

2007. Birth Centenary of Gali Ormanov (writer).

552	**242**	25t. multicoloured	90	70

243 Emblem

2007. 15th Anniv of Conference on Interaction and Confidence Building in Asia (CICA).

553	**243**	80t. multicoloured	2·75	2·40

244 Maulen Balakaev

2007. Birth Centenary of Maulen Balakaev (writer).

554	**244**	1t. brown	15	10
555	**244**	4t. green	25	10
556	**244**	5t. brown	35	10

245 Zebra

2007. 70th Anniv of Almaty Zoo. Multicoloured.

557	25t. Type **245**		90	70
558	110t. Elephant		3·25	3·00

246 Swallow

2007. Swallow (Hirundo rustica).

559	**246**	20t. black and vermilion	75	60
560	**246**	25t. black and vermilion	90	70
561	**246**	50t. black and vermilion	1·70	1·50
562	**246**	100t. black and vermilion	3·00	2·75

247 Kazakhstan Saddle

2007

563	**247**	80t. multicoloured	2·75	2·40

248 *Sputnik I*

2007. 50th Anniv of Space Exploration.

564	**248**	500t. multicoloured	13·00	13·50

2007. Town Arms. As T **229a**. Multicoloured.

565	10t. Pavlodar		40	30
566	10t. Karaganda		40	30

249 Bauble

2007. New Year.

567	**249**	25t. multicoloured	90	70

250 Uigur Couple

2007. Traditional Costumes. Sheet 110×96 mm containing T **250** and similar vert designs. Multicoloured.

MS568	105t.×2, Type **250**; Tatar couple	6·25	6·00

251 Vladimir Smirnov

2007. Olympic Gold Medallists. Sheet 138×83 mm containing T **251** and similar horiz designs. Multicoloured.

MS569	150t.×4, Type **251** (skier) (Lillehammer 1994); Yuri Melinichenko (wrestling) (Atlanta 1996); Olga Shishigina (hurdler) (Sydney 2000); Ermahan Ibraimov (boxer) (Sydney 2000)	15·00	14·50

252 Tulip

2008. Women's Day. Flowers. Sheet 144×144 mm containing T **252** and similar square designs. Multicoloured.

MS570	25t.×6, Type **252**; Tulip, white and yellow flowers; Large yellow and small white chrysanthemums; Part of large orange and several small yellow and white chrysanthemums; Part of large yellow and small white and yellow chrysanthemums; Part of large orange and yellow and white chrysanthemums	5·50	5·00

The stamps, gutter and margins of **MS**570 form a composite design of a bouquet of flowers.

253 Flowers and Couple on Swing

2008. Nauryz (Spring) Festival.

571	**253**	25t. multicoloured	90	70

254 Torch Relay in Alma-Ata

2008. Olympic Games, Beijing.

572	**254**	25t. multicoloured	90	70

255 Main Post Office

2008. 15th Anniv of Kazakhstan Posts.

573	**255**	25t. multicoloured	90	70

256 Space Station *Mir*

2008. Cosmonautics Day. Tenth Anniv of International Space Station. Multicoloured.

574	100t. Type **256**		3·00	2·75
575	150t. Space station		4·50	4·00

257 Dove and Label

2008. Europa. The Letter. Multicoloured.

576	150t. Type **257**		4·50	4·00
577	150t. Label and dove		4·50	4·00

Nos. 576/7 were issued together, *se-tenant*, forming a composite design.

258 Judo

2008. Olympic Games, Beijing. Multicoloured.

578	100t. Type **258**		3·00	2·75
579	100t. Handball		3·00	2·75
580	100t. As Type **258** (grey background)		3·00	2·75
581	100t. As No. 579 (grey background)		3·00	2·75

Nos. 578/9 and 580/1 were issued together, *se-tenant*, each pair forming a composite design.

259 *Cervus elphas*

2008. Fauna. Multicoloured.

582	110t. Type **259**		3·25	3·00
583	110t. *Cervus nippon*		3·25	3·00

Stamps of a similar design were issued by Moldova

260 4th/5th-century Gold Buckle, Kazakhstan

2008. Jewellery. Multicoloured.

584	25t. Type **260**		90	70
585	150t. 17th-century gold medallion, Iran		4·50	4·00

Stamps of a similar design were issued by Iran.

261 Anniversary Emblem

2008. 60th Anniv of Declaration of Human Rights.

586	**261**	25t. multicoloured	90	70

262 Tair Zharokov

2008. Birth Centenary of Tair Zharokov (writer).

587	**262**	25t. multicoloured	90	70

263 Shakarim
Kudaiberdyuly

2008. 150th Birth Anniv of Shakarim Kudaiberdyuly (writer).
588 **263** 25t. multicoloured 90 70

264 Executive
Committee
Meeting Record
(fragment)

2008. 90th (2007) Anniv of Alash (movement for independence).
589 **264** 25t. multicoloured 90 70

265 Zhelbuaz

2008. Musical Instruments. Multicoloured.
590 25t. Type **265** 90 70
591 100t. Dauylpaz 3·00 2·75

266 Portrait of
Kenesary
(Abylkhan Kasteev)

2008. Art. Multicoloured.
592 25t. Type **266** 90 70
593 100t. *Guest has arrived* (Salihit-din Aitbaev) 3·00 2·75

267 Callisthenes
semenovi

2008. Beetles. Multicoloured.
594 25t. Type **267** 90 70
595 100t. Inscr 'Dorcadion ach-arlense' 3·00 2·75

268 Petr Aravin

2008. Birth Centenary of Petr Aravin (musical critic and historian).
596 **268** 10t. multicoloured 40 30

269 Eagle

2008
597 **269** 20t. multicoloured 75 60

270 Atyrau

2008. Arms. Multicoloured.
598 A Type **270** 3·00 2·75
599 A Taraz 3·00 2·75

270a Polar Bear

2009. Preserve Polar Regions and Glaciers.
599a **270a** 230t. multicoloured 4·00 3·75

271 Musician and Dancers

2009. Nauryz (Spring) Festival.
600 **271** 25t. multicoloured 90 70

272 Louis Braille

2009. Birth Bicentenary of Louis Braille (inventor of Braille writing for the blind).
601 **272** 230t. multicoloured 4·00 3·75

273 Constellation, Star
Gazers and Telescope

2009. Europa. Astronomy. Multicoloured.
602 230t. Type **273** 4·00 3·75
603 230t. Galileo Galilei 4·00 3·75

274 5th-6th Century Korean
Earrings

2009. Earrrings. Multicoloured.
604 180t. Type **274** 3·75 3·50
605 180t. 17th-19th century Mongolian 3·75 3·50
606 180t. 1st-2nd century BC Kazakhstan 3·75 3·50

275 Telescope

2009. Astronomy and Space. Multicoloured.
607 180t. Type **275** 3·75 3·50
608 230t. Observatory 4·00 3·75

276 18th Century Shield

2009. Armour.
609 **276** 190t. multicoloured 3·75 3·50

277 Marija Lizogub

2009. Birth Centenary of Marija Lizogub (artist).
610 **277** 180t. multicoloured 3·75 3·50

278 Kenen Azerbaev

2009. 125th Birth Anniv of Kenen Azerbaev (singer and composer).
611 **278** 180t. multicoloured 3·75 3·50

279 Garifolla
Kurmangaliev

2009. Birth Centenary of Garifolla Kurmangaliev (singer).
612 **279** 180t. multicoloured 3·75 3·50

280 Emblem

2009. UNWTO (United Nations world tourist organization) General Assembly, Astana, Kazakhstan 2009
613 **280** 140t new blue, dull ultramarine and magenta 2·75 2·50

281 Giselle

2009. National Ballet. Multicoloured.
MS614 180t. Type **281**; 180t. *Don Quixote*; 180t. *Swan Lake*; 180t. *Tlep and Sarkyzy*; 230t. *Legend about Love*; 230t. *Bahchisarayskiy Fountain* 15·00 15·00

282 Tymak uru

2009. National Sports. Multicoloured.
615 140t. Type **282** 2·75 2·50
616 180t. At omyraulastyru (two horses) 3·25 3·00

283 Abdildy Tazhibaev

2009. Birth Centenary of Abdildy Tazhibaev (poet)
617 **283** 180t. multicoloured 3·25 3·00

284 *Crataegus ambigua*

2009. Flora and Fauna. Multicoloured.
618 180t. Type **284** 3·25 3·00
619 180t. *Mellivora capensis* (honey badger) 3·25 3·00

285 Iskander
Tynyshpaev

2009. Birth Centenary of Iskander Tynyshpaev (actor and cameraman)
620 **285** 25t. multicoloured 90 70

286 Tuleu Basenov

2009. Birth Centenary of Tuleu Basenov (architect)
621 **286** 25t. multicoloured 90 70

287 Birzhan sal
Kozhagululy

2009. 175th Birth Anniv of Birzhan sal Kozhagululy (composer)
622 **287** 25t. multicoloured 90 70

288 Symbols of
Kazakhstan and Map
of Route

2009. Construction of Gas Main through Central Asia
623 **288** 25t. multicoloured 90 70

289 Emblem

2010. Kazakhstan's Chairmanship of OSCE
624 **289** 230t multicoloured 4·00 3·75

290 Symbols of Conflict

2010. 65th Anniv of End of World War II
625 **290** 32st. multicoloured 1·10 1·00

291 Ski Jumper

2010. Winter Olympic Games, Vancouver. Multicoloured.
626 32t. Type **291** 1·10 1·00
627 190t. Alpine skier 3·25 3·00

292 Cat, Wolf and Characters from
Children's Fiction

2010. Europa
628 **292** 240t. multicoloured 4·00 3·75

293 Anniversary Emblem

2010. 50th Anniv of Temirtau
629 **293** 32t. multicoloured 1·10 1·00

294 Khan Shatyr Entertainment Centre, Astana (designed by Norman Foster)

2010. Modern Architecture
630 **294** 32t. multicoloured   1·10   1·00

295 Championship Emblem

2010. World Cup Football Championship, South Africa
631 **295** 240t. multicoloured   4·00   3·75

296 Aktyubinsk

2010. Arms
632 **296** 10t. multicoloured   35   30

297 Chimkent

2010. Arms
633 **297** 5t. multicoloured   15   10

298 Constitution

2010. 15th Anniv of Constitution
634 **298** 32t. mutlcoloured   1·10   1·00

299 Musa Baijanuly

2010. 175th Birth Anniv of Musa Baijanuly (composer)
635 **299** A multicoloured   3·00   2·75

300 Rocket as Dove and Globe

2010. Scientific Research Test Range N.5, Baikonur
636 **300** 190t. multicoloured   3·25   3·00

301 Mukhamedjan Karataev

2010. Birth Centenary of Mukhamedjan Karataev (academician)
637 **301** 20t. multicoloured   70   65

302 Baurjan Momasuhly

2010. Birth Centenary of Baurjan Momasuhly (World War II hero)
MS638 **302** 140t. multicoloured   2·75   2·75

303 Shokan Valikhanov

2010. 175th Birth Anniv of Chokan Chingisovich Valikhanov (scholar, ethnographer and historian)
639 **303** 140t. multicoloured   2·75   2·50

304 Frédéric Chopin

2010. Birth Bicentenary of Fryderyk Franciszek (Frédéric) Chopin (composer)
640 **304** 240t. multicoloured   4·00   3·75

305 Sun over Lake

2010. Tenth Anniv of Kazakhstan–Kyrgyzstan Water Agreement
641 **305** 32t. multicoloured   1·10   1·00

306 Ak Orda Monument

2010. Organization on Safety and Cooperation in Europe Summit, Astana
MS642 32t. Type **306**; 140t. Palace of Independence (right); 190t. Palace of Independence (left) and Palace of World and Consent   7·00   7·00

307 *Phoenicopterus roseus* (greater flamingo)

2010. Ecology of Caspian Sea. Multicoloured.
643   140t. Type **307**   2·75   2·50
644   140t. *Ardeola ralloides* (Squacco heron)   2·75   2·50
Stamps of the same design were issued by Azerbaijan

308 Irbi, Games Mascot

2010. 2011 Asian Winter Games, Astana and Almaty. Multicoloured.
645   190t. Type **308**   3·25   3·00
646   190t. Games emblem   3·25   3·00
647   240t. irbi skating   4·00   3·75
648   240t. Irbi ski jumping   4·00   3·75

309 Mirzhakyp Dulatov

2010. 175th Birth Anniv of Mirzhakyp Dulatov (writer)
649 **309** 50t. multicoloured   1·30   1·20

310 *Tadorna ferruginea* (ruddy shelduck)

2010. Bayanaul Nature Reserve. Fauna. Multicoloured.
MS650 32t. Type **310**; 140t. *Mustela nivalis* (weasel); 190t. *Capreolus pygargus* (Siberian roe deer)   7·00   7·00
The stamps of **MS**650 have a printing error, which shows 'H' instead of 'N' (KAZAKHSTAN) at the end of the country name

311 *Rhinecanthus aculeatus* (Picasso triggerfish)

2010. Astana Oceanarium. Multicoloured.
651   32t. Type **311**   1·10   1·00
652   190t. *Zebrasoma veliferum* (Pacific sailfin tang)   3·25   3·00

290a Horse Race

2010. Navruz Bayram
625a **290a** 32t. multicoloured   1·10   1·00

312 Korean Couple

2010. Traditional Costumes. Multicoloured.
MS653 32t. Type **312**; 190t. Belorussian couple   4·25   4·25

313 Yuri Gagarin

2011. 50th Anniv of First Manned Space Flight
654 **313** 190t. multicoloured   3·25   3·00

314 Forest under Magnifying Glass

2011. Europa. Forests
655 **314** 250t. multicoloured   4·25   4·00

315

2011. Tenth Anniv of Shanghai Organisation of Cooperation
656 **315** 210t. multicoloured   1·00   80

316 AIDS Ribbon

2011. 30th Anniv of AIDS Prevention Campaign
657 **316** 30t. multicoloured   1·00   80

317 Emblem

2011. Tenth Anniv of Eurasian Economic Community (EAEC)
658 **317** 32t. multicoloured   1·00   80

318 Kasym Amanzholov

2011. Birth Centenary of Kasym Amanzholov (poet)
659 **318** 32t multicoloured   1·00   80

319 Coin

320 Coin

321 Coin

322 Coin

2011. Coins. Multicoloured.
660 **319** 32t. multicoloured   1·00   80
661 **320** 32t. multicoloured   1·00   80
662 **321** 32t. multicoloured   1·00   80
663 **322** 32t. multicoloured   1·00   80

2011. Birth Centenary of Orymbek Akhmetbekovich Zhautykov (scientist)
664 **323** 32t. multicoloured   1·00   80

324 Emblem (note different inscription)

2011. Customs Union of EAEC
665 **324** 32t. multicoloured   1·00   80

325 Anniversary Emblem

2011. 20th Anniv of Regional Communication Community (RCC)

666	**325**	150t. multicoloured	1·00	80

326 G. Slanov

2011. Birth Centenary of Gabdol Slanov (writer)

667	**326**	32t. multicoloured	1·00	80

327 Coat of Arms of Kazakhstan

2011. Arms

668	**327**	A (32t.) multicoloured	1·00	80
669	**327**	50t. multicoloured	1·80	1·50
670	**327**	80t. multicoloured	2·10	1·70
671	**327**	100t. multicoloured	2·10	1·70
672	**327**	200t. multicoloured	3·75	3·00
673	**327**	500t. multicoloured	9·50	7·50

328 U. Sultangazin

2011. 75th Birth Anniversary of Umirzak Sultangazin (acientist)

674	**328**	32t. multicoloured	1·00	80

329 Dina Nurpeisova

2011. 150th Birth Anniv of Dina Nurpeisova (composer and musician)

675	**329**	32t. multicoloured	1·00	80

330 Anniversary Emblem

2011. 20th Anniv of Community of Independent States (CIS)

676	**330**	150t. multicoloured	2·75	2·20

Pt. 1

KEDAH

A state of the Federation of Malaya, incorporated in Malaysia in 1963.

100 cents = 1 dollar (Straits or Malayan).

1 Sheaf of Rice

2 Malay ploughing

1912

1	1	1c. black and green	60	25
26	1	1c. brown	1·50	20
52	1	1c. black	1·00	10
27	1	2c. green	1·50	20
2	1	3c. black and red	4·50	30
19	1	3c. purple	65	2·75
53	1	3c. green	2·25	90
3	1	4c. red and grey	10·00	25
20	1	4c. red	7·00	50
54	1	4c. violet	1·00	10
4	1	5c. green and brown	2·25	3·00
55	1	5c. yellow	2·25	10
56	1	6c. red	2·50	65
5	1	8c. black and blue	4·00	3·50
57	1	8c. black	18·00	10
58	2	12c. black and blue	8·00	3·50
6	2	10c. blue and brown	2·25	1·00
31	2	20c. black and green	7·00	2·00
32	2	21c. mauve and purple	2·25	13·00
33	2	25c. blue and purple	2·25	9·00
34	2	30c. black and pink	3·00	11·00
59	2	35c. purple	14·00	42·00
9	2	40c. black and purple	3·50	20·00
36	2	50c. brown and blue	4·00	24·00
37w	-	$1 black and red on yellow	7·00	9·50
38	-	$2 green and brown	13·00	£100
39	-	$3 black and blue on blue	75·00	£100
40	-	$5 black and red	95·00	£160

DESIGN—As Type **2**: $1 to $5, Council Chamber.

1919. Surch in words.

24	50c. on $2 green and brown	70·00	80·00
25	$1 on $3 black and blue on blue	20·00	95·00

1922. Optd **MALAYA-BORNEO EXHIBITION**.

45	1	1c. brown	6·50	28·00
41	1	2c. green	4·25	26·00
46	1	3c. purple	4·75	50·00
47	1	4c. red	4·75	25·00
48	2	10c. blue and sepia	9·50	50·00
42	2	21c. purple	40·00	85·00
43	2	25c. blue and purple	40·00	85·00
44	2	50c. brown and blue	40·00	£100

6 Sultan Abdul Hamid Halimshah

1937

60	6	10c. blue and brown	7·00	2·25
61	6	12c. black and violet	60·00	3·25
62	6	25c. blue and purple	13·00	4·50
63	6	30c. green and red	13·00	10·00
64	6	40c. black and purple	7·00	16·00
65	6	50c. brown and blue	13·00	5·00
66	6	$1 black and green	4·50	10·00
67	6	$2 green and brown	£130	75·00
68	6	$5 black and red	40·00	£170

1948. Silver Wedding. As T **59b/c** of Jamaica.

70	10c. violet	20	40
71	$5 red	28·00	50·00

1949. U.P.U. As T **59d/f** of Jamaica.

72	10c. purple	25	1·25
73	15c. blue	2·00	1·50
74	25c. orange	65	2·50
75	50c. black	1·00	5·75

7 Sheaf of Rice

8 Sultan Badlishah

1950

76	7	1c. black	70	30
77	7	2c. orange	50	15
78	7	3c. green	2·00	1·00
79	7	4c. brown	75	10
79ab	7	5c. purple	4·50	1·00
80	7	6c. grey	70	15
81	7	8c. red	3·00	4·75
81a	7	8c. green	4·25	2·75
82	7	10c. mauve	70	10
82a	7	12c. red	4·25	2·50
83	7	15c. blue	4·00	35
84	7	20c. black and green	3·75	2·50
84a	7	20c. blue	2·50	10
85	8	25c. purple and orange	1·50	30
85a	8	30c. red and purple	5·50	1·25
85b	8	35c. red and purple	5·50	1·50
86	8	40c. red and purple	6·00	9·00
87	8	50c. black and blue	5·00	35
88	8	$1 blue and purple	5·50	7·50
89	8	$2 green and red	26·00	38·00
90	8	$5 green and brown	55·00	75·00

1953. Coronation. As T **71** of Jamaica.

91	10c. black and purple	2·50	60

15 Fishing Craft

1957. Inset portrait of Sultan Badlishah.

92	-	1c. black	10	60
93	-	2c. red	1·00	1·75
94	-	4c. sepia	30	1·00
95	-	5c. lake	30	75
96	-	8c. green	2·00	8·00
97	-	10c. sepia	80	40
98	**15**	20c. blue	2·75	3·25
99	-	50c. black and blue	3·75	4·25
100	-	$1 blue and purple	11·00	19·00
101	-	$2 green and red	38·00	48·00
102	-	$5 brown and green	50·00	48·00

DESIGNS—HORIZ: 1c. Copra; 2c. Pineapples; 4c. Ricefield; 5c. Masjid Alwi Mosque, Kangar; 8c. East Coast Railway "Golden Blowpipe" Express; $1 Govt Offices; $2 Bersilat (form of wrestling); $5 Weaving. VERT: 10c. Tiger; 50c. Aborigines with blowpipe.

20 Sultan Abdul Halim Mu' Adzam Shah

1959. Installation of Sultan.

103	**20**	10c. yellow, brown and blue	80	10

21 Sultan Abdul Halim Shah

1959. As Nos. 92/102 but with inset portrait of Sultan Abdul Halim Shah as in T **21**.

104	1c. black	10	75
105	2c. red	10	2·00
106	4c. sepia	10	75
107	5c. lake	10	10
108	8c. green	3·50	3·50
109	10c. sepia	1·00	10
109a	10c. purple	12·00	1·00
110	20c. blue	1·00	1·00
111a	50c. black and blue	30	60
112	$1 blue and purple	4·50	2·25
113	$2 green and red	13·00	20·00
114	$5 brown and green	16·00	19·00

22 *Vanda hookeriana*

1965. Flowers. Multicoloured.

115	1c. Type **22**	10	1·75
116	2c. *Arundina graminifolia*	10	2·00
117	5c. *Paphiopedilum niveum*	10	40
118	6c. *Spathoglottis plicata*	15	60
119	10c. *Arachnis flos-aeris*	30	20
120	15c. *Rhyncostylis retusa*	1·50	10
121	20c. *Phalaenopsis violacea*	1·75	1·25

The higher values used in Kedah were Nos. 20/7 of Malaysia.

23 *Danaus melanippus*

1971. Butterflies. Multicoloured.

124	1c. *Delias ninus*	30	1·75
125	2c. Type **23**	50	1·75
126	5c. *Parthenos sylvia*	1·25	40
127	6c. *Papilio demoleus*	1·25	2·00
128	10c. *Hebomoia glaucippe*	1·25	10
129	15c. *Precis orithya*	1·25	10
130	20c. *Valeria valeria*	1·50	70

The higher values in use with this issue were Nos. 64/71 of Malaysia.

24 *Pterocarpus indicus*

1979. Flowers. Multicoloured.

135	1c. *Rafflesia hasseltii*	10	90
136	2c. Type **24**	10	90
137	5c. *Lagerstroemia speciosa*	10	60
138	10c. *Durio zibethinus*	15	10
139	15c. *Hibiscus rosa-sinensis*	15	10
140	20c. *Rhododendron scortechinii*	20	10
141	25c. *Etlingera elatior* (inscr "Phaeomeria speciosa")	40	20

25 Sultan Abdul Halim Shah

1983. Silver Jubilee of Sultan's Installation. Multicoloured.

142	20c. Type **25**	70	30
143	40c. Paddy fields (horiz)	1·75	1·75
144	60c. Paddy fields and Mount Jerai (horiz)	2·50	5·25

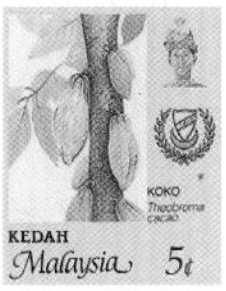

26 Cocoa

1986. Agricultural Products of Malaysia. Multicoloured.

152	1c. Coffee	10	30
153	2c. Coconuts	10	30
154	5c. Type **26**	15	10
155	10c. Black pepper	15	10
156	15c. Rubber	25	10
157	20c. Oil palm	25	15
158	30c. Rice	30	15

2003. As T **26** but redenominated in 'sen'. Multicoloured.

159	30s. Rice	1·40	10

27 *Nelumbium nelumbo* (sacred lotus)

2007. Garden Flowers. As Nos. 210/15 of Johore, but with portrait of Sultan Abdul Halim Shah and Arms of Kedah as in T **27**. Multicoloured.

160	5s. Type **47**	10	10
161	10s. *Hydrangea macrophylla*	15	10
162	20s. *Hippeastrum reticulatum*	25	15
163	30s. *Bougainvillea*	40	20
164	40s. *Ipomoea indica*	50	30
165	50s. *Hibiscus rosa-sinensis*	65	35
MS165	110×85 mm. Nos. 160/5	2·10	2·10

Pt. 1

KELANTAN

A state of the Federation of Malaya, incorporated in Malaysia in 1963.

100 cents = 1 dollar (Straits or Malayan).

1

1911

1a	1	1c. green	6·00	30
15	1	1c. black	1·00	50
16	1	2c. brown	7·50	3·75
16a	1	2c. green	5·50	40
2	1	3c. red	4·25	15
16b	1	3c. brown	5·00	1·00
17	1	4c. black and red	3·50	10
18	1	5c. green and red on yellow	1·75	10
19	1	6c. purple	3·50	1·00
19a	1	6c. red	4·00	3·00
5	1	8c. blue	5·50	1·00
20	1	10c. black and mauve	3·00	10
21	1	30c. purple and red	4·00	5·00
8	1	50c. black and orange	8·50	2·00
9	1	$1 green	48·00	35·00
9a	1	$1 green and brown	75·00	2·00
10	1	$2 green and red	1·50	2·25
11	1	$5 green and blue	4·00	2·50
12	1	$25 green and orange	50·00	£110

1922. Optd **MALAYA BORNEO EXHIBITION**.

37	1c. green	3·50	55·00
30	4c. black and red	6·50	50·00
31	5c. green and red on yellow	6·50	50·00
38	10c. black and mauve	6·50	75·00
32	30c. purple and red	6·50	80·00
33	50c. black and orange	9·50	85·00
34	$1 green and brown	32·00	£110
35	$2 green and red	95·00	£275
36	$5 green and blue	£250	£500

3 Sultan Ismail

1928

40	3	1c. olive and yellow	2·75	55
41	3	2c. green	8·00	20
42	3	4c. red	7·50	1·00
43	3	5c. brown	4·75	10
44	3	6c. lake	20·00	10·00
45	3	8c. olive	4·75	10
46	3	10c. purple	30·00	2·75
47	3	12c. blue	8·00	7·50
48	3	25c. red and purple	9·00	4·25
49	3	30c. violet and red	60·00	25·00
50	3	40c. orange and green	9·50	40·00
51	3	50c. olive and orange	85·00	10·00
39	3	$1 blue	15·00	90·00
52	3	$1 violet and green	55·00	13·00
53	3	$2 brown and red	£300	£200
54	3	$5 red and lake	£600	£800

All except No. 39 are larger than T 3.

1948. Silver Wedding. As T **59b/c** of Jamaica.

55	10c. violet	75	2·75
56	$5 red	29·00	50·00

1949. U.P.U. As T **59d/f** of Jamaica.

57	10c. purple	25	30
58	15c. blue	2·25	2·25
59	25c. orange	40	6·50
60	50c. black	70	3·00

5 Sultan Ibrahim

1951

61	5	1c. black	50	30
62	5	2c. orange	1·25	35
63	5	3c. green	6·00	1·25
64	5	4c. brown	2·00	15
65	5	5c. mauve	1·50	50
66	5	6c. grey	75	20
67	5	8c. red	5·00	4·00
68	5	8c. green	6·00	1·75
69	5	10c. purple	65	10
70	5	12c. red	6·00	3·00
71	5	15c. blue	8·00	60
72	5	20c. black and green	6·00	14·00
73	5	20c. blue	1·75	25
74	5	25c. purple and orange	1·75	55
75	5	30c. red and purple	1·50	6·00
76	5	35c. red and purple	2·25	1·50
77	5	40c. red and purple	16·00	26·00
78	5	50c. black and blue	7·50	40
79	5	$1 blue and purple	9·00	14·00
80	5	$2 green and red	42·00	60·00
81	5	$5 green and brown	65·00	75·00

1953. Coronation. As T **61a** of Jamaica.

82	10c. black and purple	1·25	1·40

1957. As Nos. 92/102 of Kedah but inset portrait of Sultan Ibrahim.

83	1c. black	10	30
84	2c. red	75	1·50
85	4c. sepia	40	10
86	5c. lake	40	10
87	8c. green	3·00	3·25
88	10c. sepia	3·00	10
89	10c. purple	17·00	11·00
90	20c. blue	2·50	30
91	50c. black and blue	50	1·75
92	$1 blue and purple	10·00	1·50
93	$2 green and red	19·00	10·00
94	$5 brown and green	24·00	12·00

6 Sultan Yahya Petra and Arms of Kelantan

1961. Coronation of the Sultan.

95	6	10c. multicoloured	50	1·25

7 Sultan Yahya Petra

1961. As Nos. 83, etc, but with inset portrait of Sultan Yahya Petra as in T **7**.

96	1c. black	20	3·00
97	2c. red	1·25	3·25
98	4c. sepia	2·25	2·25
99	5c. lake	2·25	60
100	8c. green	16·00	17·00
101	10c. purple	1·75	40
102	20c. blue	12·00	3·00

8 *Vanda hookeriana*

1965. As Nos. 115/21 of Kedah but with inset portrait of Sultan Yahya Petra as in T **8**.

103	8	1c. multicoloured	10	1·25
104	-	2c. multicoloured	10	1·75
105	-	5c. multicoloured	15	30
106	-	6c. multicoloured	70	2·50
107	-	10c. multicoloured	30	25
108	-	15c. multicoloured	1·50	25
109	-	20c. multicoloured	1·50	2·00

The higher values used in Kelantan were Nos. 20/7 of Malaysia (National Issues).

9 *Parthenos sylvia*

1971. Butterflies. As Nos. 124/30 of Kedah but with portrait of Sultan Yahya Petra as in T **9**.

112		1c. multicoloured	30	2·25
113		2c. multicoloured	40	2·25
114	9	5c. multicoloured	1·50	60
115	-	6c. multicoloured	1·50	2·50
116	-	10c. multicoloured	1·50	30
117	-	15c. multicoloured	1·50	10
118	-	20c. multicoloured	2·00	1·50

The higher values in use with this series were Nos. 64/71 of Malaysia (National Issues).

10 *Lagerstroemia speciosa*

1979. Flowers. As Nos. 135/41 of Kedah but with portrait of Sultan Yahya Petra as in T **10**.

123	1c. "Rafflesia hasseltii"	10	1·00
124	2c. "Pterocarpus indicus"	10	1·00
125	5c. Type **10**	10	80
126	10c. "Durio zibethinus"	15	10
127	15c. "Hibiscus rosa-sinensis"	15	10
128	20c. "Rhododendron scortechinii"	20	10
129	25c. "Etlingera elatior" (inscr "Phaeomeria speciosa")	40	50

11 Sultan Tengku Ismail Petra

1980. Coronation of Sultan Tengku Ismail Petra.

130	11	10c. multicoloured	40	75
131	11	15c. multicoloured	40	15
132	11	50c. multicoloured	90	2·75

12 Black Pepper

1986. Agricultural Products of Malaysia. Multicoloured.

140	1c. Coffee	10	30
141	2c. Coconuts	10	40
142	5c. Cocoa	50	10
143	10c. Type **12**	20	10
144	15c. Rubber	30	10
145	20c. Oil palm	20	15
146	30c. Rice	40	15

13 *Nelumbium nelumbo* (sacred lotus)

2007. Garden Flowers. As Nos. 210/15 of Johore, but with portrait of Sultan Ismail Petra and Arms of Kelantan as in T **13**. Multicoloured.

147	5s. Type **13**	10	10
148	10s. *Hydrangea macrophylla*	15	10
149	20s. *Hippeastrum reticulatum*	25	15
150	30s. *Bougainvillea*	40	20
151	40s. *Ipomoea indica*	50	30
152	50s. *Hibiscus rosa-sinensis*	65	35
MS153	100×85 mm. Nos. 147/52	1·40	1·40

Pt. 1

KENYA

Formerly part of Kenya, Uganda and Tanganyika (q.v.). Became independent in 1963 and a Republic in 1964.

100 cents = 1 shilling.

1 Cattle Ranching

3 National Assembly

1963. Independence.

1	1	5c. multicoloured	10	55
2	-	10c. brown	10	10
3	-	15c. mauve	1·00	10
4	-	20c. black and green	15	10
5	-	30c. black and yellow	15	10
6	-	40c. brown and blue	15	30
7	-	50c. red, black and green	15	10
8	-	65c. turquoise and yellow	55	65
9	3	1s. multicoloured	20	10
10	-	1s.30 brown, black and green	5·00	30
11	-	2s. multicoloured	1·25	40
12	-	5s. brown, blue and green	1·25	1·00
13	-	10s. brown and blue	8·50	3·00
14	-	20s. black and red	4·00	8·50

DESIGNS—As Type **1**: 10c. Wood-carving; 15c. Heavy industry; 20c. Timber industry; 30c. Jomo Kenyatta facing Mt. Kenya; 40c. Fishing industry; 50c. Kenya flag; 65c. Pyrethrum industry. As Type **3**: 1s.30, Tourism (Treetops hotel); 2s. Coffee industry; 5s. Tea industry; 10s. Mombasa Port; 20s. Royal College, Nairobi.

4 Cockerel

1964. Inauguration of Republic. Multicoloured.

15	15c. Type **4**	15	15
16	30c. Pres. Kenyatta	15	10
17	50c. African lion	15	10
18	1s.30 Hartlaub's turaco	2·00	50
19	2s.50 Nandi flame	20	3·75

5 Thomson's Gazelle

7 Greater Kudu

1966

20	5	5c. orange, black and sepia	20	20
21	-	10c. black and green	10	10
22	-	15c. black and orange	10	10
23	-	20c. ochre, black and blue	10	15
24	-	30c. indigo, blue and black	20	10
25	-	40c. black and brown	60	30
26	-	50c. black and orange	60	10
27	-	65c. black and green	1·25	2·00
28	-	70c. black and purple	5·00	1·75
29	7	1s. brown, black and blue	30	10
30	-	1s.30 blue, green and black	4·00	20
31	-	1s.50 black, brown and green	3·00	2·75
32	-	2s.50 yellow, black and brown	4·25	1·25
33	-	5s. yellow, black and green	75	70
34	-	10s. ochre, black and brown	1·75	3·00
35	-	20s. multicoloured	7·50	13·00

DESIGNS—As Type **5**: 10c. Sable antelope; 15c. Aardvark ("Ant Bear"); 20c. Lesser bushbaby; 30c. Warthog; 40c. Common zebra; 50c. African buffalo; 65c. Black rhinoceros; 70c. Ostrich. As Type **7**: 1s.30, African elephant; 1s.50, Bat-eared fox; 2s.50, Cheetah; 5s. Savanna monkey ("Vervet Monkey"); 10s. Giant ground pangolin; 20s. Lion.

8 Perna Tellin

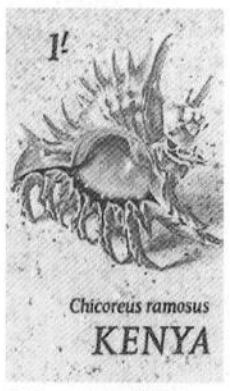

9 Ramose Murex

1971. Sea Shells. Multicoloured.

36	5c. Type **8**	10	30
37	10c. Episcopal mitre	15	10
38	15c. Purplish clanculus	15	20
39	20c. Humpback cowrie	15	20
40	30c. Variable abalone	20	10
41	40c. Flame top shell	20	10
42	50c. Common purple janthina	30	20
43	50c. Common purple janthina	13·00	3·00
44	60c. Bullmouth helmet	30	1·75
45	70c. Chambered or pearly nautilus	45	1·50
46	70c. Chambered or pearly nautilus	11·00	6·00
47a	1s. Type **9**	20	10
48	1s.50 Trumpet triton	1·00	10
49	2s.50 Trapezium horse conch	1·00	10
50a	5s. Great green turban	1·00	10
51	10s. Textile or cloth of gold cone	1·50	15
52a	20s. Scorpion conch	1·50	25

INSCRIPTIONS: No. 42, *Janthina globosa*; 43, *Janthina janthina*; 45, *Nautilus pompileus*; 46, *Nautilus pompilius*.

Nos. 47/52 are larger, as Type **9**.

1975. Nos. 48/9 and 52a surch.

53	2s. on 1s.50 Trumpet triton	6·00	5·50
54	3s. on 2s.50 Trapezium horse conch	9·50	22·00
55	40s. on 20s. Scorpion conch	6·00	14·00

11 Microwave Tower

1976. Telecommunications Development. Multicoloured.

56	50c. Type **11**	10	10
57	1s. Cordless switchboard (horiz)	10	10
58	2s. Telephones	20	30
59	3s. Message switching centre (horiz)	25	45
MS60	120×120 mm. Nos. 56/9. Imperf	1·10	2·50

12 Akii Bua, Ugandan Hurdler

1976. Olympic Games, Montreal. Multicoloured.

61	50c. Type **12**	10	10
62	1s. Filbert Bayi, Tanzanian runner	15	10
63	2s. Steve Muchoki, Kenyan boxer	45	35
64	3s. Olympic flame and East African flags	90	50
MS65	129×154 mm. Nos. 61/4	6·00	7·50

13 Diesel-hydraulic Train, Tanzania–Zambia Railway

1976. Railway Transport. Multicoloured.

66	50c. Type **13**	35	10
67	1s. Nile Bridge, Uganda	60	15
68	2s. Nakuru Station, Kenya	1·50	1·00
69	3s. Uganda Railway Class A steam locomotive, 1896	1·50	1·50
MS70	154×103 mm. Nos. 66/9	8·00	8·00

14 Nile Perch

1977. Game Fish of East Africa. Multicoloured.

71	50c. Type **14**	25	10
72	1s. Nile mouthbrooder ("Tilapia")	30	10
73	3s. Sailfish	60	60
74	5s. Black marlin	80	80
MS75	153×129 mm. Nos. 71/4	7·50	4·00

15 Maasai Manyatta (village), Kenya

1977. Second World Black and African Festival of Arts and Culture, Nigeria. Multicoloured.

76	50c. Type **15**	15	10
77	1s. "Heartbeat of Africa" (Ugandan dancers)	15	10
78	2s. Makonde sculpture, Tanzania	60	1·25
79	3s. "Early man and technology" (skinning hippopotamus)	75	2·00
MS80	132×109 mm. Nos. 76/9	4·00	5·50

16 Rally Car and Villagers

1977. 25th Anniv of Safari Rally. Multicoloured.

81	50c. Type **16**	15	10
82	1s. Pres. Kenyatta starting rally	15	10
83	2s. Car fording river	50	60
84	5s. Car and elephants	1·40	1·50
MS85	126×93 mm. Nos. 81/4	3·75	6·50

17 Canon Kivebulaya

1977. Centenary of Ugandan Church. Multicoloured.

86	50c. Type **17**	10	10
87	1s. Modern Namirembe Cathedral	10	10
88	2s. The first Cathedral	30	55
89	5s. Early congregation, Kigezi	50	1·25
MS90	126×94 mm. Nos. 86/9	1·40	2·50

18 Sagana Royal Lodge, Nyeri, 1952

1977. Silver Jubilee. Multicoloured.

91	2s. Type **18**	15	15
92	5s. Treetops Hotel (vert)	20	35
93	10s. Queen Elizabeth and Pres. Kenyatta	30	60
94	15s. Royal visit, 1972	45	1·00
MS95	Two sheets. (a) 140×60 mm. No. 94. (b) 152×127 mm. 50s. Queen and Prince Philip in Treetops Hotel Set of 2 sheets	2·00	1·40

19 Pancake Tortoise

1977. Endangered Species. Multicoloured.

96	50c. Type **19**	30	10
97	1s. Nile crocodile	40	10
98	2s. Hunter's hartebeest	1·60	40
99	3s. Red colobus monkey	1·75	50
100	5s. Dugong	2·00	75
MS101	127×101 mm. Nos. 97/100	6·00	8·50

20 Kenya-Ethiopia Border Point

1977. Nairobi–Addis Ababa Highway. Multicoloured.

102	50c. Type **20**	15	10
103	1s. Archer's Post	15	10
104	2s. Thika Flyover	30	25
105	5s. Marsabit Game Lodge	50	75
MS106	144×91 mm. Nos. 102/5	2·25	3·50

21 Gypsum **22** Amethyst

1977. Minerals. Multicoloured.

107	10c. Type **21**	1·25	20
108	20c. Trona	2·00	20
109	30c. Kyanite	2·00	20
110	40c. Amazonite	1·40	10
111	50c. Galena	1·40	10
112	70c. Silicified wood	7·50	1·00
113	80c. Fluorite	7·50	60
114	1s. Type **22**	1·40	10
115	1s.50 Agate	1·50	30
116	2s. Tourmaline	1·50	20
117	3s. Aquamarine	1·75	55
118	5s. Rhodolite garnet	1·75	1·10
119	10s. Sapphire	1·75	1·50
120	20s. Ruby	4·50	2·50
121	40s. Green grossular garnet	18·00	20·00

23 Joe Kadenge (Kenya) and Forwards

1978. World Cup Football Championship, Argentina. Multicoloured.

122	50c. Type **23**	10	10
123	1s. Mohamed Chuma (Tanzania) and cup presentation	10	10
124	2s. Omari Kidevu (Zanzibar) and goalmouth scene	30	70
125	3s. Polly Ouma (Uganda) and three forwards	40	95
MS126	136×81 mm. Nos. 122/5	3·75	3·50

24 Boxing

1978. Commonwealth Games, Edmonton. Multicoloured.

127	50c. Type **24**	15	10
128	1s. Welcoming the Olympic Games Team, 1968	15	10
129	3s. Javelin throwing	50	1·00
130	5s. Pres. Kenyatta admiring boxer's trophy	60	1·60

25 "Overloading is Dangerous"

1978. Road Safety. Multicoloured.

131	50c. Type **25**	50	10
132	1s. "Speed does not pay"	70	20
133	1s.50 "Ignoring Traffic Signs may cause death"	85	55
134	2s. "Slow down at School Crossing"	1·25	1·00
135	3s. "Never cross a continuous line"	1·40	2·50
136	5s. "Approach Railway Level Crossing with extreme caution"	2·00	3·50

26 Pres. Kenyatta at Mass Rally, 1963

1978. Kenyatta Day. Multicoloured.

137	50c. "Harambee Water Project"	15	10
138	1s. Handing over of Independence Instruments, 1963	15	10
139	2s. Type **26**	30	35
140	3s. "Harambee, 15 Great Years"	60	1·00
141	5s. "Struggle for Independence, 1952"	80	2·00

27 Freedom Fighters, Namibia

1978. International Anti-Apartheid Year.

142	**27**	50c. multicoloured	15	10
143	-	1s. black and blue	15	10
144	-	2s. multicoloured	30	30
145	-	3s. multicoloured	50	65
146	-	5s. multicoloured	55	1·00

DESIGNS: 1s. International seminar on apartheid; 2s. Steve Biko's tombstone; 3s. Nelson Mandela; 5s. Bishop Lamont.

28 Children Playing

1979. International Year of the Child. Multicoloured.

147	50c. Type **28**	15	10
148	2s. Boy fishing	40	60
149	3s. Children singing and dancing	55	1·10
150	5s. Children with camels	1·00	2·25

29 "The Lion and the Jewel"

1979. Kenya National Theatre. Multicoloured.

151	50c. Type **29**	15	10
152	1s. "Utisi"	15	10
153	2s. Theatre programmes	25	30
154	3s. Kenya National Theatre	35	45
155	5s. "Genesis"	50	75

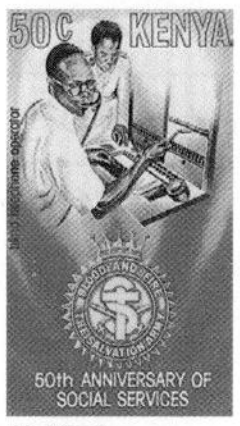

30 Blind Telephone Operator

1979. 50th Anniv of Salvation Army Social Services.

156	50c. Type **30**	30	10
157	1s. Care for the aged	30	10
158	3s. Village polytechnic (horiz)	60	1·50
159	5s. Vocational training (horiz)	1·00	2·50

31 "Father of the Nation" (Kenyatta's funeral procession)

1979. First Death Anniv of President Kenyatta. Multicoloured.

160	50c. Type **31**	10	10
161	1s. "First President of Kenya" (Kenyatta receiving independence)	10	10
162	3s. "Kenyatta the politician" (speaking at rally)	30	50
163	5s. "A true son of Kenya" (Kenyatta as a boy carpenter)	40	95

32 British East Africa Company 1890 1a. Stamp

1979. Death Centenary of Sir Rowland Hill.

164	**32**	50c. multicoloured	15	10
165	-	1s. multicoloured	15	10
166	-	2s. black, red and brown	20	40
167	-	5s. multicoloured	35	1·00

DESIGNS: 1s. Kenya, Uganda and Tanganyika 1935 1s. stamp; 2s. Penny Black; 5s. 1964 2s.50 Inauguration of Republic commemorative.

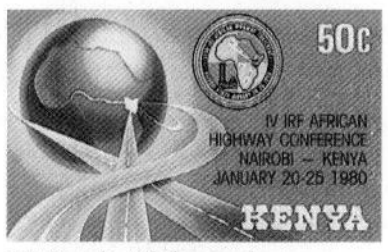

33 Roads, Globe and Conference Emblem

1980. International Road Federation. African Highway Conference, Nairobi. Multicoloured.

168	50c. Type **33**	15	10
169	1s. New weighbridge, Athi River	15	10
170	3s. New Nyali Bridge, Mombasa	40	85
171	5s. Highway to Jomo Kenyatta International Airport	50	2·00

34 Mobile Unit in action in Masailand

1980. Flying Doctor Service. Multicoloured.

172	50c. Type **34**	10	10
173	1s. Donkey transport to Turkana airstrip (vert)	20	10
174	3s. Surgical team in action at outstation (vert)	65	1·00
175	5s. Emergency airlift from North Eastern Province	90	1·60
MS176	146×133 mm. Nos. 172/5	1·60	2·75

35 Statue of Sir Rowland Hill

1980. "London 1980" International Stamp Exhibition.

177	**35** 25s. multicoloured	1·00	2·50
MS178	114×101 mm. No. 177	1·00	2·75

36 Pope John Paul II

1980. Papal Visit. Multicoloured.

179	50c. Type **36**	40	10
180	1s. Pope, arms and cathedral (vert)	40	10
181	5s. Pope, flags and dove (vert)	75	85
182	10s. Pope, President Moi and map of Africa	1·25	1·75

37 Blue-spotted Stingray

1980. Marine Life. Multicoloured.

183	50c. Type **37**	30	10
184	2s. Allard's anemonefish	1·00	80
185	3s. Four-coloured nudibranch	1·25	1·75
186	5s. "Eretmochelys imbricata"	1·75	2·75

38 National Archives

1980. Historic Buildings. Multicoloured.

187	50c. Type **38**	10	10
188	1s. Provincial Commissioner's Office, Nairobi	15	10
189	1s.50 Nairobi House	20	20
190	2s. Norfolk Hotel	25	50
191	3s. McMillan Library	35	95
192	5s. Kipande House	55	1·60

39 "Disabled enjoys Affection"

1981. Int Year for Disabled Persons. Multicoloured.

193	50c. Type **39**	15	10
194	1s. President Moi presenting flag to Disabled Olympic Games team captain	15	10
195	3s. Blind people climbing Mount Kenya, 1975	55	65
196	5s. Disabled artist at work	70	1·00

40 Longonot Complex

1981. Satellite Communications. Multicoloured.

197	50c. Type **40**	15	10
198	2s. "Intelsat V"	40	35
199	3s. "Longonot I"	45	55
200	5s. "Longonot II"	60	85

41 Kenyatta Conference Centre

1981. O.A.U. (Organization of African Unity) Summit Conference, Nairobi.

201	**41**	50c. multicoloured	15	10
202	-	1s. black, yellow and blue	15	10
203	-	3s. multicoloured	40	40
204	-	5s. multicoloured	70	65
205	-	10s. multicoloured	80	1·00
MS206		110×110 mm. No. 205	1·10	1·50

DESIGNS: 1s. "Panaftel" earth stations; 3s. Parliament Building; 5s. Jomo Kenyatta International Airport; 10s. O.A.U. flag.

42 St. Paul's Cathedral

1981. Royal Wedding. Multicoloured.

207	50c. Prince Charles and President Daniel Arap Moi	10	10
208	3s. Type **42**	15	20
209	5s. Royal Yacht Britannia	25	30
210	10s. Prince Charles on safari in Kenya	40	55
MS211	85×102 mm. 25s. Prince Charles and Lady Diana Spencer	75	80

43 Giraffe

1981. Rare Animals. Multicoloured.

212	50c. Type **43**	15	10
213	2s. Bongo	25	25
214	5s. Roan antelope	40	1·00
215	10s. Agile mangabey	60	2·25

44 "Technical Development"

1981. World Food Day. Multicoloured.

216	50c. Type **44**	10	10
217	1s. "Mwea rice projects"	15	10
218	2s. "Irrigation schemes"	30	55
219	5s. "Breeding livestock"	60	1·75

45 Kamba

1981. Ceremonial Costumes (1st series), Multicoloured.

220	50c. Type **45**	40	10
221	1s. Turkana	45	10
222	2s. Giriama	1·25	85
223	3s. Masai	1·60	2·50
224	5s. Luo	1·75	4·25

See also Nos. 329/33, 413/17 and 515/19.

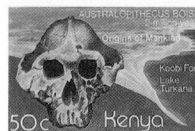

46 Australopithecus boisei

1982. "Origins of Mankind". Skulls. Multicoloured.

225	50c. Type **46**	1·75	30
226	2s. Homo erectus	3·25	1·50
227	3s. Homo habilis	3·25	3·75
228	5s. Proconsul africanus	3·75	5·00

47 Tree-planting

1982. 75th Anniv of Boy Scout Movement (Nos. 229, 231, 233 and 235) and 60th Anniv of Girl Guide Movement (Nos. 230, 232, 234 and 236). Multicoloured.

229	70c. Type **47**	50	80
230	70c. Paying homage	50	80
231	3s.50 "Be Prepared"	1·25	2·00
232	3s.50 "International Friendship"	1·25	2·00
233	5s. Helping disabled	1·50	2·50
234	5s. Community service	1·50	2·50
235	6s.50 Paxtu Cottage (Lord Baden-Powell's home)	1·50	2·75
236	6s.50 Lady Baden-Powell	1·50	2·75
MS237	112×112 mm. Nos. 229, 231, 233 and 235	3·75	3·00

48 Footballer displaying Shooting Skill

1982. World Cup Football Championship, Spain. Footballers silhouetted against Map of World. Multicoloured.

238	70c. Type **48**	1·25	65
239	3s.50 Heading	2·50	2·75
240	3s.50 Goalkeeping	3·50	4·25
241	10s. Dribbling	5·00	8·00
MS242	101×76 mm. 20s. Tackling	5·50	4·00

49 Cattle Judging

1982. 80th Anniv of Agricultural Society of Kenya. Multicoloured.

243	70c. Type **49**	50	10
244	2s.50 Farm machinery	1·25	1·25
245	3s.50 Musical ride	1·50	2·50
246	6s.50 Agricultural Society emblem	2·00	4·25

50 Micro-wave Radio System

1982. I.T.U. Plenipotentiary Conference, Nairobi. Multicoloured.

247	70c. Type **50**	50	10
248	3s.50 Sea-to-shore service link	1·75	1·75
249	5s. Rural telecommunications system	2·25	3·75
250	6s.50 I.T.U. emblem	2·50	4·50

1982. No. 113 surch **70c.**

251	70c. on 80c. Fluorite	1·00	1·25

52 Container Cranes

1983. Fifth Anniv of Kenya Ports Authority. Multicoloured.

252	70c. Type **52**	85	10
253	2s. Port by night	1·75	1·90
254	3s.50 Container cranes (different)	2·50	3·50
255	5s. Map of Mombasa Port	3·25	4·50
MS256	125×85 mm. Nos. 252/5	7·50	9·00

53 Shada Zambarau

54 Waridi Kikuba

1983. Flowers. Multicoloured.

257	10c. Type **53**	40	40
258	20c. Kilua Kingulima	55	40
259	30c. Mwalika Mwiya	55	40
260	40c. Ziyungi Buluu	55	40
261	50c. Kilua Habashia	55	30
262	70c. Chanuo Kato	60	20
262a	80c. As 40c.	4·50	5·00
262b	1s. Waridi Kikuba	4·50	80
263	1s. Type **54**	65	20
264	1s.50 Mshomoro Mtambazi	1·75	60
265	2s. Papatuo Boti	1·75	60
266	2s.50 Tumba Mboni	1·75	60
266a	3s. Mkuku Mrembo	14·00	10·00
267	3s.50 Mtongo Mbeja	1·50	1·50
267b	4s. Mnukia Muuma	4·75	7·00
268	5s. Nyungu Chepuo	1·25	1·50
268a	7s. Mlua Miba	6·50	11·00
269	10s. Muafunili	1·25	1·50
270	20s. Mbake Nyanza	1·25	2·50
271	40s. Njuga Pagwa	2·00	8·00

The 1s.50 to 40s. are in the same format as T **54**.

55 Coffee Plucking

1983. Commonwealth Day. Multicoloured.

272	70c. Type **55**	10	10
273	2s. President Daniel Arap Moi	15	20
274	5s. Satellite view of Earth (horiz)	35	45
275	10s. Masai dance (horiz)	65	1·00

56 Examining Parcels

1983. 30th Anniv of Customs Co-operation Council. Multicoloured.

276	70c. Type **56**	25	10
277	2s.50 Customs Headquarters, Mombasa	65	30
278	3s.50 Customs Council Headquarters, Brussels	75	40
279	10s. Customs patrol boat	2·40	2·50

57 Communications via Satellite

1983. World Communications Year. Multicoloured.

280	70c. Type **57**	60	10
281	2s.50 "Telephone and Postal Services"	1·50	1·75
282	3s.50 Communications by sea and air (horiz)	2·00	3·00
283	5s. Road and rail communications (horiz)	2·50	4·00

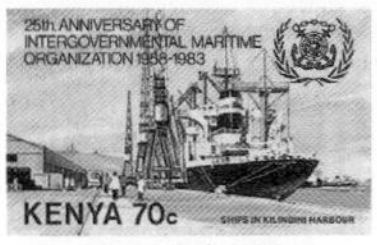

58 "Craftsman" (freighter) in Kilindini Harbour

1983. 25th Anniv of Intergovernmental Maritime Organization. Multicoloured.

284	70c. Type **58**	1·10	10
285	2s.50 Life-saving devices	2·25	1·75
286	3s.50 Mombasa container terminal	2·75	3·00
287	10s. Marine park	3·75	8·50

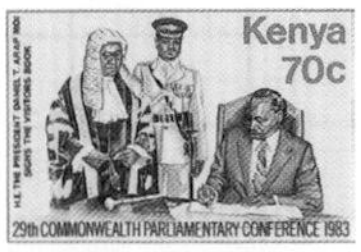

59 President Moi signing Visitors' Book

1983. 29th Commonwealth Parliamentary Conference. Multicoloured.

288	70c. Type **59**	25	10
289	2s.50 Parliament building, Nairobi (vert)	90	1·25
290	5s. State opening of Parliament (vert)	1·60	3·00
MS291	122×141 mm. Nos. 288/90	2·50	6·50

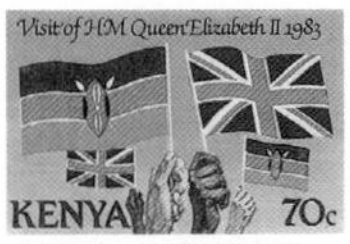

60 Kenyan and British Flags

1983. Royal Visit. Multicoloured.

292	70c. Type **60**	50	10
293	3s.50 Sagana State Lodge	2·00	1·50
294	5s. Treetops Hotel	2·25	2·75
295	10s. Queen Elizabeth II and President Moi	3·50	7·00
MS296	126×100 mm. 25s. Designs as Nos. 292/5, but without face values. Imperf	4·50	7·50

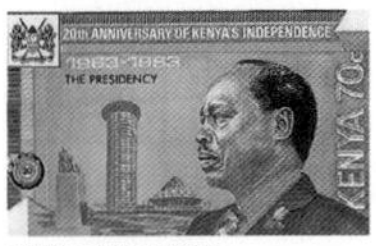

61 President Moi

1983. 20th Anniv of Independence. Multicoloured.

297	70c. Type **61**	10	10
298	2s. President Moi planting tree	15	20
299	3s.50 Kenyan flag and emblem	25	35
300	5s. School milk scheme	40	50
301	10s. People of Kenya	75	1·10
MS302	126×93 mm. 25s. Designs as Nos. 297 and 299/301, but without face values. Imperf	1·50	2·75

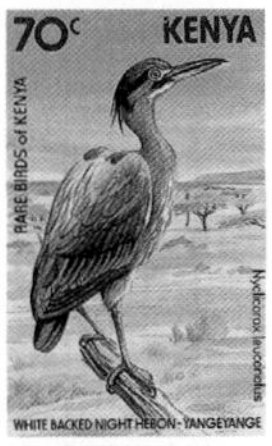

62 White-backed Night Heron

1984. Rare Birds of Kenya. Multicoloured.

303	70c. Type **62**	1·75	30
304	2s.50 Quail plover	3·00	2·50
305	3s.50 Taita olive thrush	3·75	3·75
306	5s. Mufumbiri shrike	4·25	4·25
307	10s. White-winged apalis	5·50	7·00

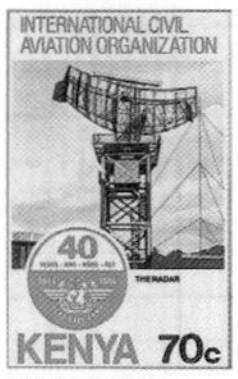

63 Radar Tower

1984. 40th Anniv of International Civil Aviation Organization. Multicoloured.

308	70c. Type **63**	30	10
309	2s.50 Kenya School of Aviation (horiz)	75	70
310	3s.50 Boeing 707 taking off from Moi airport (horiz)	1·10	1·50
311	5s. Air traffic control centre	1·50	2·50

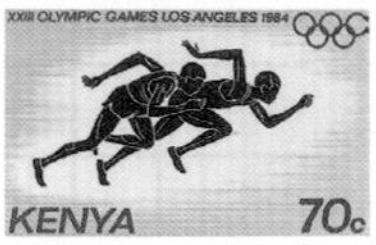

64 Running

1984. Olympic Games, Los Angeles.

312	**64**	70c. black, green and deep green	30	10
313	-	2s.50 black, purple and violet	60	70
314	-	5s. black, blue and deep blue	1·50	2·50
315	-	10s. black, yellow and brown	4·00	6·00
MS316		130×121 mm. 25s. Designs as Nos. 312/15, but without face values. Imperf	3·25	3·25

DESIGNS: 2s.50, Hurdling; 5s. Boxing; 10s. Hockey.

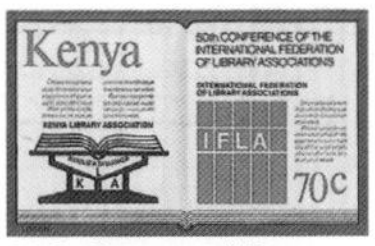

65 Conference and Kenya Library Association Logos

1984. 50th Conference of the International Federation of Library Associations. Multicoloured.

317	70c. Type **65**	10	10
318	3s.50 Mobile library	50	60
319	5s. Adult library	65	1·25
320	10s. Children's library	1·00	3·25

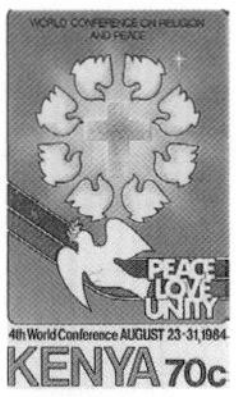

66 Doves and Cross

1984. Fourth World Conference on Religion and Peace. As T **66**, each design showing a different central symbol. Multicoloured.

321	70c. Type **66**	30	10
322	2s.50 Arabic inscription	1·25	1·50
323	3s.50 Peace emblem	1·60	2·50
324	6s.50 Star and Crescent	2·00	4·00

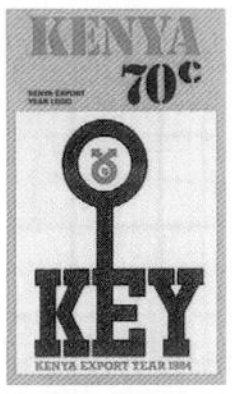

67 Export Year Logo

1984. Kenya Export Year. Multicoloured.

325	70c. Type **67**	30	10
326	3s.50 Forklift truck with air cargo (horiz)	1·75	2·00
327	5s. Loading ship's cargo	2·50	3·00
328	10s. Kenyan products (horiz)	3·75	6·50

1984. Ceremonial Costumes (2nd series). As T **45**. Multicoloured.

329	70c. Luhya	80	15
330	2s. Kikuyu	2·00	1·75
331	3s.50 Pokomo	2·50	2·25
332	5s. Nandi	3·00	3·00
333	10s. Rendile	4·00	6·50

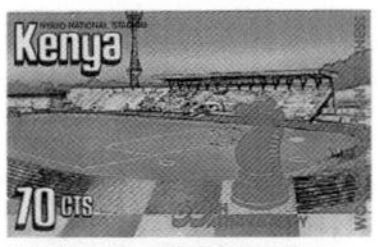

68 Staunton Knight and Nyayo National Stadium

1984. 60th Anniv of International Chess Federation. Multicoloured.

334	70c. Type **68**	2·25	40
335	2s.50 Staunton rook and Fort Jesus	3·25	1·75
336	3s.50 Staunton bishop and National Monument	3·75	2·00
337	5s. Staunton queen and Parliament Building	4·00	3·75
338	10s. Staunton king and Nyayo Fountain	6·00	8·00

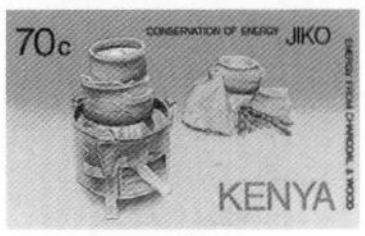

69 Cooking with Wood-burning Stove and Charcoal Fire

1985. Energy Conservation. Multicoloured.

339	70c. Type **69**	20	10
340	2s. Solar energy panel on roof	65	75
341	3s.50 Production of gas from cow dung	75	1·25
342	10s. Ploughing with oxen	2·25	6·00
MS343	110×85 mm. 20s. Designs as Nos. 339/42, but without face values	2·50	2·50

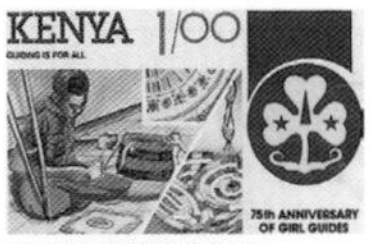

70 Crippled Girl Guide making Table-mat

1985. 75th Anniv of Girl Guide Movement. Multicoloured.

344	1s. Type **70**	75	15
345	3s. Girl Guides doing community service	1·75	1·50
346	5s. Lady Olave Baden-Powell (founder)	2·50	3·00
347	7s. Girl Guides gardening	4·00	6·50

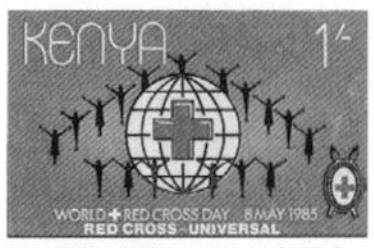

71 Stylized Figures and Globe

1985. World Red Cross Day.

348	**71**	1s. black and red	80	15
349	-	4s. multicoloured	3·00	3·00
350	-	5s. multicoloured	3·25	3·50
351	-	7s. multicoloured	4·50	6·50

DESIGNS: 4s. First Aid Team; 5s. Hearts containing crosses ("Blood Donation"); 7s. Cornucopia ("Famine Relief").

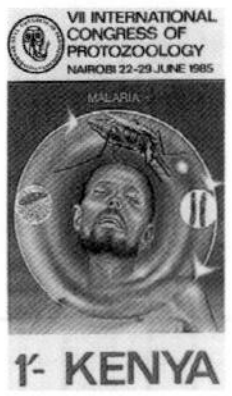

72 Man with Malaria

1985. Seventh International Congress of Protozoology, Nairobi. Multicoloured.

352	1s. Type **72**	2·00	25
353	3s. Child with Leishmaniasis	4·00	2·75
354	5s. Cow with Trypanosomiasis	4·50	4·25
355	7s. Dog with Babesiosis	7·50	8·50

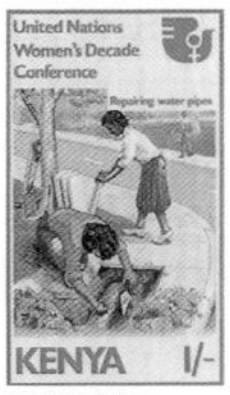

73 Repairing Water Pipes

1985. United Nations Women's Decade Conference. Multicoloured.

356	1s. Type **73**	20	10
357	3s. Traditional food preparation	60	70
358	5s. Basket-weaving	75	1·25
359	7s. Dressmaking	1·00	3·00

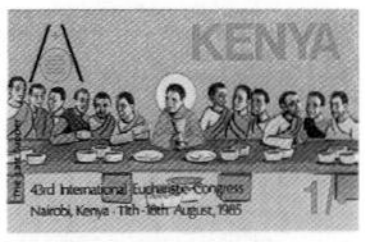

74 The Last Supper

1985. 43rd International Eucharistic Congress, Nairobi. Multicoloured.

360	1s. Type **74**	50	10
361	3s. Village family ("The Eucharist and the Christian Family")	2·25	2·00
362	5s. Congress altar, Uhuru Park	2·50	3·25
363	7s. St. Peter Claver's Church, Nairobi	3·00	5·50
MS364	117×80 mm. 25s. Pope John Paul II	8·50	7·00

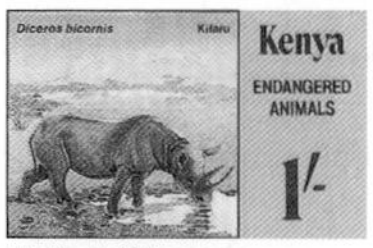

75 Black Rhinoceros

1985. Endangered Animals. Multicoloured.

365	1s. Type **75**	2·75	40
366	3s. Cheetah	3·50	2·75
367	5s. De Brazza's monkey	3·75	4·00
368	10s. Grevy's zebra	7·50	9·00
MS369	129×122 mm. 25s. Endangered species (122×114 mm). Imperf	10·00	7·00

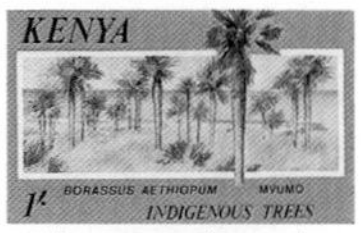

76 "Borassus aethiopum"

1986. Indigenous Trees. Multicoloured.

370	1s. Type **76**	1·25	15
371	3s. *Acacia xanthophloea*	3·50	2·50
372	5s. *Ficus natalensis*	4·50	4·50
373	7s. *Spathodea nilotica*	6·00	9·00
MS374	117×96 mm. 25s. Landscape with trees (109×90 mm). Imperf	3·25	4·00

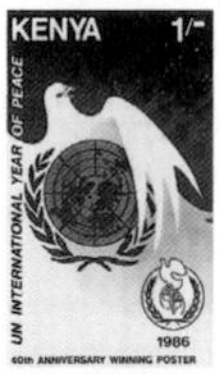

77 Dove and U.N. Logo (from poster)

1986. International Peace Year. Multicoloured.

375	1s. Type **77**	30	10
376	3s. U.N. General Assembly (horiz)	1·00	75
377	7s. Nuclear explosion	2·50	3·50
378	10s. Quotation from Wall of Isaiah, U.N. Building, New York (horiz)	6·50	7·00

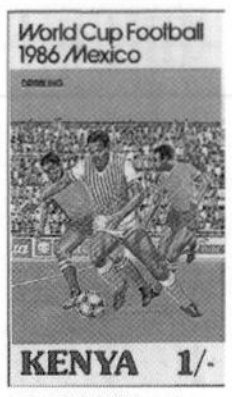

78 Dribbling the Ball

1986. World Cup Football Championship, Mexico. Multicoloured.

379	1s. Type **78**	80	15
380	3s. Scoring from a penalty	2·25	1·25
381	5s. Tackling	3·00	2·00
382	7s. Cup winners	3·75	5·50
383	10s. Heading the ball	4·75	4·25
MS384	110×86 mm. 30s. Harambee Stars football team (102×78 mm). Imperf	3·75	3·75

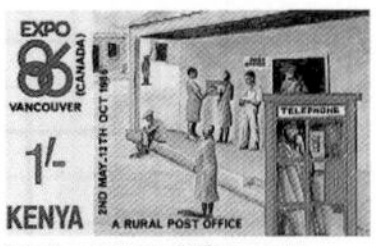

79 Rural Post Office and Telephone

1986. "Expo '86" World Fair, Vancouver. Multicoloured.

385	1s. Type **79**	50	15
386	3s. Container depot, Embakasi	2·50	1·75
387	5s. Piper PA-30B Twin Commanche airplane landing at game park airstrip	4·00	2·75
388	7s. Container ship	4·25	4·50
389	10s. Transporting produce to market	4·50	5·25

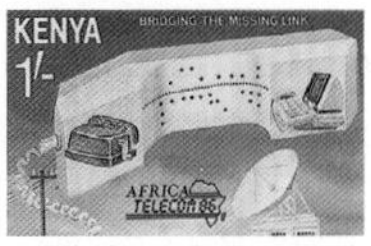

80 Telephone, Computer and Dish Aerial

1986. African Telecommunications. Multicoloured.

390	1s. Type **80**	35	10
391	3s. Telephones of 1876, 1936 and 1986	1·00	85
392	5s. Dish aerial, satellite, telephones and map of Africa	1·25	1·25
393	7s. Kenyan manufacture of telecommunications equipment	1·75	2·25

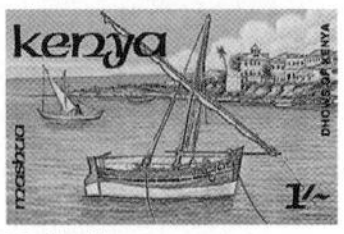

81 Mashua

1986. Dhows of Kenya. Multicoloured.

394	1s. Type **81**	1·25	20
395	3s. Mtepe	2·75	1·50
396	5s. Dau La Mwao	3·25	3·00
397	10s. Jahazi	6·00	7·00
MS398	118×80 mm. 25s. Lamu dhow and map of Indian Ocean	5·00	5·00

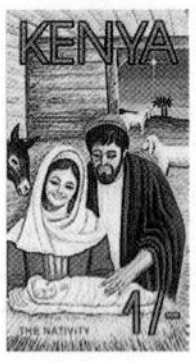

82 Nativity

1986. Christmas. Multicoloured.

399	1s. Type **82**	60	10
400	3s. Shepherd and sheep	1·50	55
401	5s. Angel and slogan "LOVE PEACE UNITY" (horiz)	2·25	1·60
402	7s. The Magi riding camels (horiz)	3·00	3·00

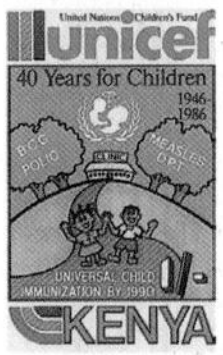

83 Immunization

1987. 40th Anniv of UNICEF. Multicoloured.

403	1s. Type **83**	60	10
404	3s. Food and nutrition	1·25	70
405	4s. Oral rehydration therapy	2·00	1·50
406	5s. Family planning	2·00	1·50
407	10s. Female literacy	2·75	4·00

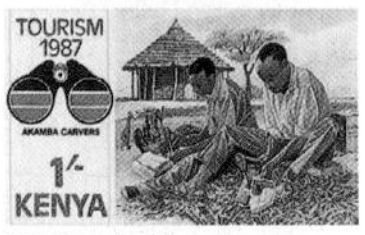

84 Akamba Woodcarvers

1987. Tourism. Multicoloured.

408	1s. Type **84**	55	10
409	3s. Tourism on beach	3·25	1·75
410	5s. Tourist and guide at view point	4·00	4·00
411	7s. Pride of lions	6·00	7·00
MS412	118×81 mm. 30s. Geysers	11·00	11·00

1987. Ceremonial Costumes (3rd series). As T **45**. Multicoloured.

413	1s. Embu	1·00	10
414	3s. Kisii	2·75	70
415	5s. Samburu	3·25	1·75
416	7s. Taita	4·00	4·25
417	10s. Boran	4·25	4·75

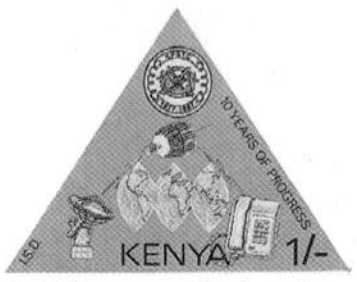

85 Telecommunications by Satellite

1987. Tenth Anniv of Kenya Posts and Telecommunications Corporation. Multicoloured.

418	1s. Type **85**	85	30
419	3s. Rural post office, Kajiado	1·90	2·00
420	4s. Awarding trophy, Welfare Sports	2·00	2·76
421	5s. Village and telephone box	2·50	3·00
422	7s. Speedpost labels and outline map of Kenya	3·50	5·50
MS423	110×80 mm. 25s. Corporation flag	2·50	2·75

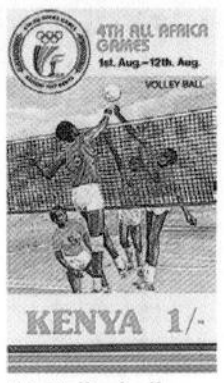

86 Volleyball

1987. Fourth All-Africa Games, Nairobi. Multicoloured.

424	1s. Type **86**	20	10
425	3s. Cycling	85	45
426	4s. Boxing	35	1·25
427	5s. Swimming	40	1·25
428	7s. Steeplechasing	60	2·25
MS429	117×80 mm. 30s. Kasarani Sports Complex (horiz)	2·50	2·75

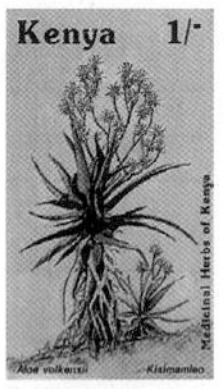

87 *Aloe volkensii*

1987. Medicinal Herbs. Multicoloured.

430	1s. Type **87**	85	10
431	3s. *Cassia didymobotrya*	2·25	1·25
432	5s. *Erythrina abyssinica*	3·00	2·75
433	7s. *Adenium obesum*	3·75	4·75
434	10s. Herbalist's clinic	4·00	5·00

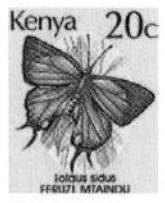

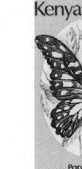

88 "Epamera sidus"

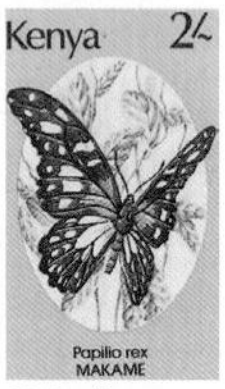

89 *Papilio rex*

1988. Butterflies. Multicoloured.

434a	10c. *Cyrestis camillus*	1·50	2·25
435	20c. Type **88**	35	70
436	40c. *Cynthia cardui*	50	70
437	50c. *Colotis evippe*	50	70
438	70c. *Precis westermanni*	50	70
439	80c. *Colias electo*	50	70
440	1s. *Eronia leda*	50	30
440a	1s.50 *Papilio dardanus*	5·50	30
441	2s. Type **89**	70	40
442	2s.50 *Colotis phisadia*	75	90
443	3s. *Papilio desmondi*	80	90
444	3s.50 *Papilio demodocus*	80	60
445	4s. *Papilio phorcas*	85	1·00
446	5s. *Charaxes druceanus*	90	70
447	7s. *Cymothoe teita*	1·00	2·50
448	10s. *Charaxes zoolina*	1·00	1·75
449	20s. *Papilio dardanus*	1·25	3·50
450	40s. *Charaxes cithaeron*	2·00	8·00

The 10c. to 1s.50 are in the same format as T **88**.

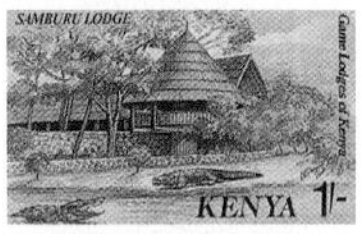

90 Samburu Lodge and Crocodiles

1988. Kenyan Game Lodges. Multicoloured.

451	1s. Type **90**	70	10
452	3s. Naro Moru River Lodge and rock climbing	1·00	60
453	4s. Mara Serena Lodge and zebra with foal	1·25	1·40
454	5s. Voi Safari Lodge and buffalo	1·25	1·40
455	7s. Kilimanjaro Buffalo Lodge and giraffes	2·50	2·75
456	10s. Meru Mulika Lodge and rhinoceroses	2·75	3·25

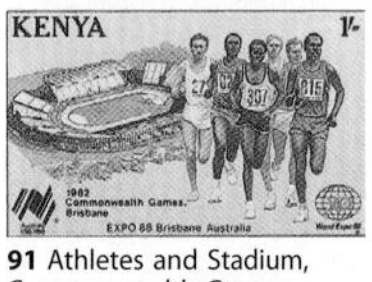

91 Athletes and Stadium, Commonwealth Games, Brisbane, 1982

1988. "Expo '88" World Fair, Brisbane, and Bicent of Australian Settlement. Multicoloured.

457	1s. Type **91**	40	10
458	3s. Flying Doctor Service de Havilland Drover 3 and Piper PA-30B Twin Commanche aircraft	2·75	1·25
459	4s. H.M.S. *Sirius* (frigate), 1788	3·00	2·25
460	5s. Ostrich and emu	3·25	2·50
461	7s. Queen Elizabeth II, Pres. Arap Moi of Kenya and Prime Minister Hawke of Australia	3·00	4·25
MS462	117×80 mm. 30s. Entrance to Kenya Pavilion	1·90	2·00

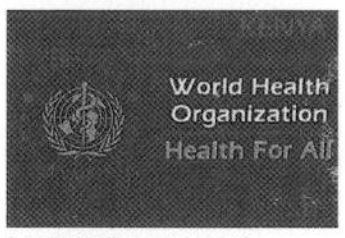

92 W.H.O. Logo and Slogan

1988. 40th Anniv of W.H.O.

463	**92**	1s. blue, gold and deep blue	25	10
464	-	3s. multicoloured	85	70
465	-	5s. multicoloured	1·25	1·50
466	-	7s. multicoloured	1·75	2·50

DESIGNS: 3s. Mother with young son and nutritious food; 5s. Giving oral vaccine to baby; 7s. Village women drawing clean water from pump.

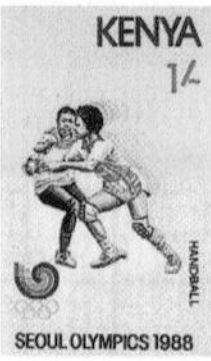

93 Handball

1988. Olympic Games, Seoul. Multicoloured.

467	1s. Type **93**	45	10
468	3s. Judo	75	55
469	5s. Weightlifting	1·00	1·00
470	7s. Javelin	1·25	2·00
471	10s. Relay racing	1·75	3·00
MS472	110×78 mm. 30s. Tennis	2·25	2·50

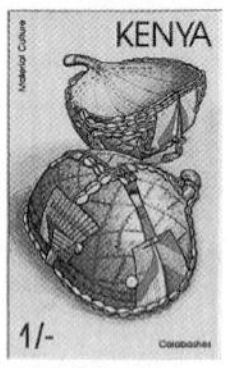

94 Calabashes

1988. Kenyan Material Culture (1st issue). Multicoloured.

473	1s. Type **94**	30	10
474	3s. Milk gourds	75	55
475	5s. Cooking pots (horiz)	85	85
476	7s. Winnowing trays (horiz)	1·25	1·75
477	10s. Reed baskets (horiz)	1·60	2·50
MS478	118×80 mm. 25s. Gourds, calabash and horn (horiz)	1·50	1·60

See also Nos. 646/50.

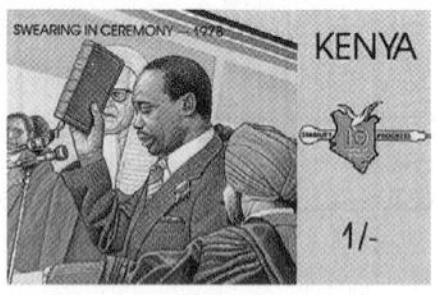

95 Pres. Arap Moi taking Oath, 1978

1988. Tenth Anniv of "Nyayo" Era. Multicoloured.

479	1s. Type **95**	30	10
480	3s. Building soil conservation barrier	1·00	70
481	3s.50 Passengers boarding bus	3·00	1·40
482	4s. Metalwork shop	1·25	1·50
483	5s. Moi University, Eldoret	1·25	1·50
484	7s. Aerial view of hospital	3·00	3·50
485	10s. Pres. Arap Moi and Mrs. Thatcher at Kapsabet Telephone Exchange	8·00	7·00

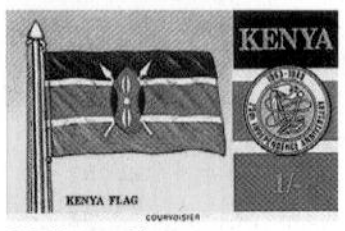

96 Kenya Flag

1988. 25th Anniv of Independence. Multicoloured.

486	1s. Type **96**	75	10
487	3s. Coffee picking	80	50
488	5s. Proposed Kenya Posts and Telecommunications Headquarters building	1·00	1·10
489	7s. Kenya Airways Airbus Industrie A310-300 "Harambee Star"	5·50	3·00
490	10s. New diesel locomotive No. 9401	7·50	5·00

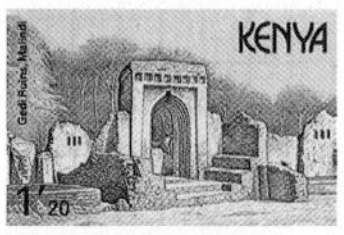

97 Gedi Ruins, Malindi

1989. Historic Monuments. Multicoloured.

491	1s.20 Type **97**	60	10
492	3s.40 Vasco Da Gama Pillar, Malindi (vert)	1·40	1·25
493	4s.40 Ishiakani Monument, Kiunga	1·50	1·75
494	5s.50 Fort Jesus, Mombasa	1·75	2·25
495	7s.70 She Burnan Omwe, Lamu (vert)	2·50	4·00

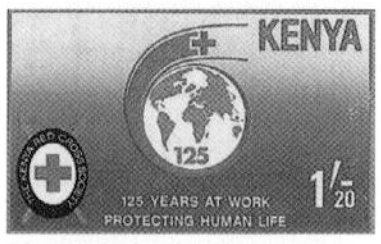

98 125th Anniversary and Kenya Red Cross Logos

1989. 125th Anniv of International Red Cross. Multicoloured.

496	1s.20 Type **98**	50	10
497	3s.40 Red Cross workers with car crash victim	1·25	90
498	4s.40 Disaster relief team distributing blankets	1·40	1·60
499	5s.50 Henri Dunant (founder)	1·50	2·25
500	7s.70 Blood donor	1·75	3·50

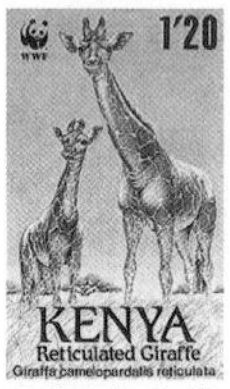

99 Female Giraffe and Calf

1989. Reticulated Giraffe. Multicoloured.

501	1s.20 Type **99**	1·75	30
502	3s.40 Giraffe drinking	3·25	3·00
503	4s.40 Two giraffes	3·75	4·00
504	5s.50 Giraffe feeding	4·50	5·50
MS505	80×110 mm. 30s. Designs as Nos. 501/4, but without face values	5·50	7·00

Designs from No. **MS**505 are without the Worldwide Fund for Nature logo.

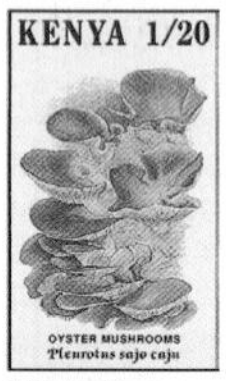

100 *Lentinus sajor-caju*

1989. Mushrooms. Multicoloured.

506	1s.20 Type **100**	1·50	30
507	3s.40 *Agaricus bisporus*	2·50	2·00
508	4s.40 *Agaricus bisporus* (different)	2·75	2·50
509	5s.50 *Termitomyces schimperi*	3·50	3·50
510	7s.70 *Lentinus edodes*	4·25	5·50

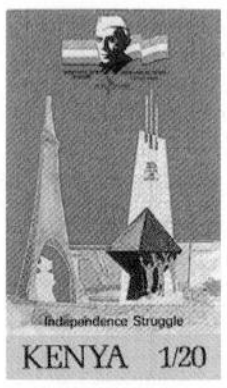

101 Independence Monuments

1989. Birth Centenary of Jawaharlal Nehru (Indian statesman). Multicoloured.

511	1s.20 Type **101**	1·50	30
512	3s.40 Nehru with graduates and open book	3·50	1·75
513	5s.50 Jawaharlal Nehru	4·50	4·00
514	7s.70 Industrial complex and cogwheels	4·76	6·50

1989. Ceremonial Costumes (4th series). As T **45**. Multicoloured.

515	1s.20 Kipsigis	1·50	20
516	3s.40 Rabai	2·50	1·60

517	5s.50 Duruma	3·00	2·75
518	7s.70 Kuria	4·00	4·25
519	10s. Bajuni	4·25	6·00

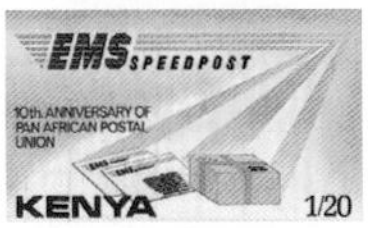

102 EMS Speedpost Letters and Parcel

1990. Tenth Anniv of Pan African Postal Union. Multicoloured.

520	1s.20 Type **102**	15	10
521	3s.40 Mail runner	35	35
522	5s.50 Mandera Post Office	55	70
523	7s.70 EMS Speedpost letters and globe (vert)	80	1·60
524	10s. P.A.P.U. logo (vert)	90	1·60

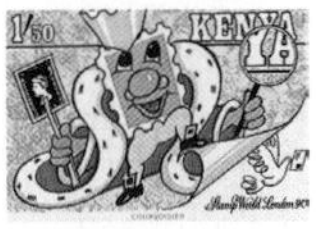
103 "Stamp King" with Tweezers and Magnifying Glass

1990. "Stamp World London '90" International Stamp Exhibition.

525	**103**	1s.50 multicoloured	45	10
526	-	4s.50 multicoloured	1·50	1·25
527	-	6s.50 black, red and blue	1·60	2·00
528	-	9s. multicoloured	2·00	4·00
MS529		113×77 mm. Nos. 525/8	5·00	7·00

DESIGNS: 4s.50, Penny Black and Kenya Stamp Bureau postmark; 6s.50, Early British cancellations; 9s. Ronald Ngala Street Post Office, Nairobi.

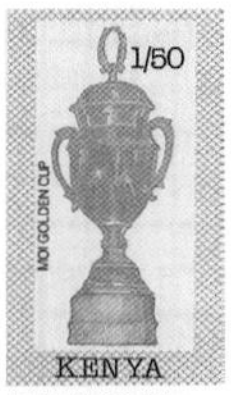
104 Moi Golden Cup

1990. World Cup Football Championship, Italy. Trophies. Multicoloured.

530	1s.50 Type **104**	1·00	10
531	4s.50 East and Central Africa Challenge Cup	2·75	1·75
532	6s.50 East and Central Africa Club Championship Cup	3·75	3·75
533	9s. World Cup	4·00	7·00

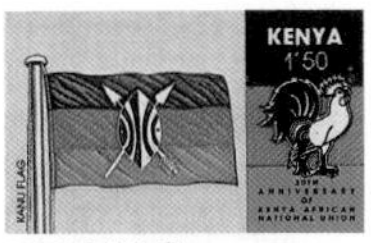
105 K.A.N.U. Flag

1990. 30th Anniv of Kenya African National Union. Multicoloured.

534	1s.50 Type **105**	15	10
535	2s.50 Nyayo Monument	15	15
536	4s.50 Party Headquarters	35	35
537	5s. Jomo Kenyatta (Party founder)	40	40
538	6s.50 President Arap Moi	50	85
539	9s. President Moi addressing rally	80	1·90
540	10s. Queue of voters	80	1·90

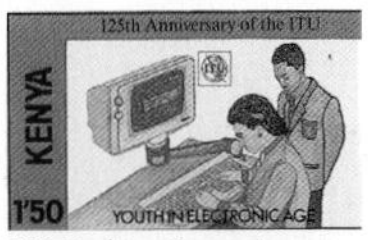
106 Desktop Computer

1990. 125th Anniv of I.T.U. Multicoloured.

541	1s.50 Type **106**	15	10
542	4s.50 Telephone switchboard assembly, Gilgil	35	50
543	6s.50 "125 YEARS"	45	1·00
544	9s. Urban and rural telecommunications	70	2·25

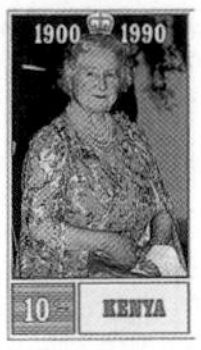
107 Queen Mother at British Museum, 1988

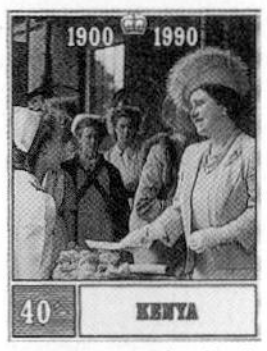
108 Queen Elizabeth at Hospital Garden Party, 1947

1990. 90th Birthday of Queen Elizabeth the Queen Mother.

545	**107**	10s. multicoloured	1·50	1·75
546	**108**	40s. black and green	3·25	5·00

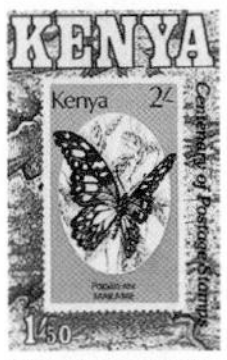
109 Kenya 1988 2s. Definitive

1990. Cent of Postage Stamps in Kenya. Multicoloured.

547	1s.50 Type **109**	1·40	10
548	4s.50 East Africa and Uganda 1903 1a.	2·75	90
549	6s.50 British East Africa Co 1890 ½a. optd on G.B. 1d.	3·25	2·00
550	9s. Kenya and Uganda 1922 20c.	3·75	3·50
551	20s. Kenya, Uganda, Tanzania 1971 2s.50 railway commemorative	6·75	9·50

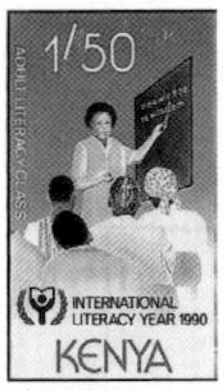
110 Adult Literacy Class

1990. International Literacy Year. Multicoloured.

552	1s.50 Type **110**	30	10
553	4s.50 Teaching by radio	1·00	1·10
554	6s.50 Technical training	1·25	1·75
555	9s. International Literacy Year logo	2·00	3·50

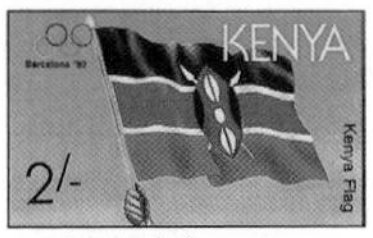
111 National Flag

1991. Olympic Games, Barcelona (1992) (1st issue). Multicoloured.

556	2s. Type **111**	1·10	20
557	6s. Basketball	2·75	1·40
558	7s. Hockey	2·75	2·25
559	8s.50 Table tennis	2·50	3·75
560	11s. Boxing	2·50	4·25

See also Nos. 580/4.

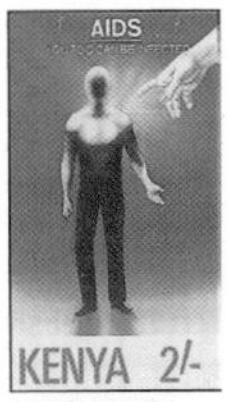
112 Symbolic Man and Pointing Finger

1992. AIDS Day. Multicoloured.

561	2s. Type **112**	1·00	15
562	6s. Victim and drugs	2·50	1·25
563	8s.50 Male and female symbols	3·00	3·50
564	11s. Symbolic figure and hypodermic syringe	4·50	5·00

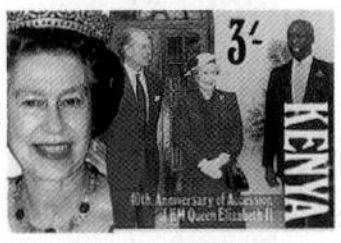
113 Queen and Prince Philip with Pres. Moi

1992. 40th Anniv of Queen Elizabeth II's Accession.

565	3s. Type **113**	50	10
566	8s. Marabou storks in tree	2·00	85
567	11s. Treetops Hotel	1·25	1·00
568	14s. Three portraits of Queen Elizabeth	1·25	1·25
569	40s. Queen Elizabeth II	2·50	4·50

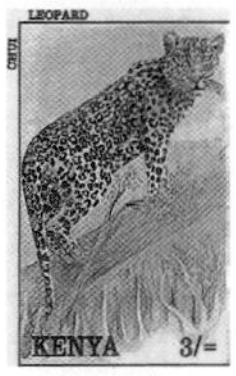
114 Leopard

1992. Kenya Wildlife. Multicoloured.

570	3s. Type **114**	2·00	30
571	8s. Lion	2·75	2·00
572	10s. Elephant	6·50	3·00
573	11s. Buffalo	2·75	3·25
574	14s. Black rhinoceros	8·50	6·00

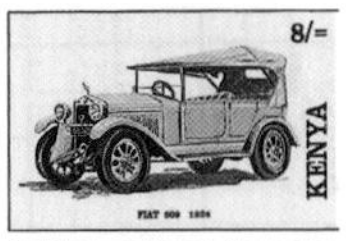
115 International Harvester Safari Truck, 1926

1992. Vintage Cars. Multicoloured.

575	3s. Type **115**	2·25	20
576	8s. Fiat "509", 1924	3·50	2·00
577	10s. Hupmobile, 1923	3·75	3·00
578	11s. Chevrolet "Box Body", 1928	3·75	3·25
579	14s. Bentley/Parkward, 1934	4·25	6·00

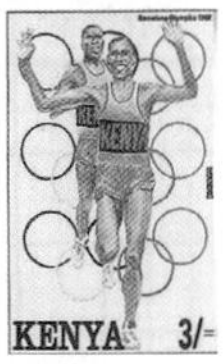
116 Kenyan Athlete winning Race

1992. Olympic Games, Barcelona (2nd issue). Multicoloured.

580	3s. Type **116**	1·00	10
581	8s. Men's judo	2·00	1·25
582	10s. Kenyan women's volleyball players	2·50	2·25
583	11s. Kenyan men's 4×100 m relay runners	2·50	2·50
584	14s. Men's 10,000 m	2·75	5·00

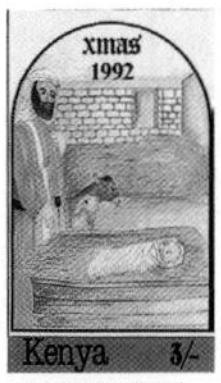
117 Holy Child, Joseph and Animals

1992. Christmas. Multicoloured.

585	3s. Type **117**	30	10
586	8s. Mary with Holy Child	75	50
587	11s. Christmas tree	1·00	80
588	14s. Adoration of the Magi	1·25	2·25

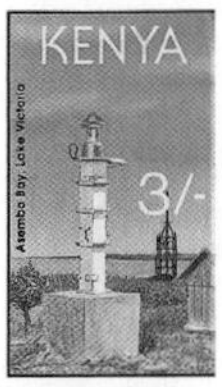
118 Asembo Bay Lighthouse, Lake Victoria

1993. Lighthouses. Multicoloured.

589	3s. Type **118**	2·25	55
590	8s. Old Ras Serani lighthouse, Mombasa	3·50	2·25
591	11s. New Ras Serani lighthouse, Mombasa	3·75	3·50
592	14s. Gingira, Lake Victoria	4·50	6·00

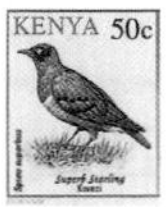
119 Superb Starling

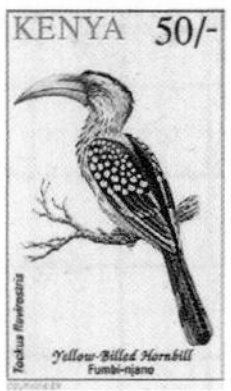
120 Yellow-billed Hornbill

1993. Birds. Multicoloured. (a) As T **119**.

593	50c. Type **119**	15	1·00
594	1s. Red and yellow barbet	25	80
594a	1s.50 Lady Ross's turaco	65	1·00
595	3s. Black-throated honeyguide ("Greater honeyguide")	50	10
595a	5s. African fish eagle	80	60
595b	6s. Vulturine guineafowl	4·50	1·25
596	7s. Malachite kingfisher	70	30
597	8s. Speckled pigeon	70	20
598	10s. Cinnamon-chested bee eater	70	20
599	11s. Scarlet-chested sunbird	70	25
600	14s. Bagalafecht weaver ("Reichenow's weaver")	75	30

(b) As T **120**.

601	50s. Type **120**	1·25	2·00
602	80s. Lesser flamingo	1·60	3·00
603	100s. Hadada ibis	1·90	3·50

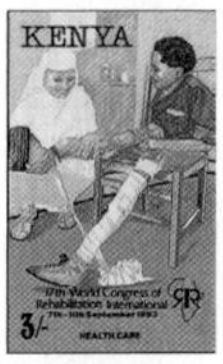
121 Nurse bandaging Boy's Legs

1993. 17th World Congress of Rehabilitation International.

611	**121**	3s. multicoloured	70	10
612	-	8s. multicoloured	1·10	70
613	-	10s. multicoloured	1·25	1·40
614	-	11s. multicoloured	1·25	1·60
615	-	14s. black, blue and orange	1·50	2·50

DESIGNS—HORIZ: 8s. Singing group on crutches; 10s. Vocational training; 11s. Wheelchair race. VERT: 14s. Congress emblem.

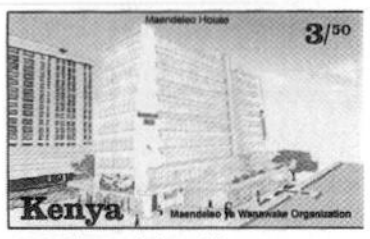
122 Maendeleo House, Nairobi

1994. 40th Anniv of Maendeleo Ya Wanawake Organization. Multicoloured.

616	3s.50 Type **122**	1·00	20
617	9s. Planting saplings	1·40	70
618	11s. Rural family planning clinic (vert)	1·90	1·60
619	12s.50 Women carrying water	1·90	2·75
620	15s.50 Improved wood-burning cooking stove (vert)	2·25	3·50

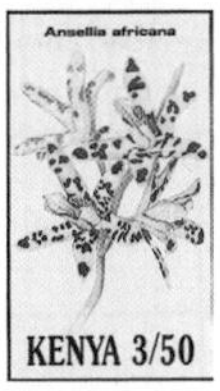
123 *Ansellia africana*

1994. Orchids. Multicoloured.

621	3s.50 Type **123**	2·25	30
622	9s. *Aerangis luteoalba var rhodosticta*	3·00	85
623	12s.50 *Polystachya bella*	3·25	2·50
624	15s.50 *Brachycorythis kalbreyeri*	3·75	3·75
625	20s. *Eulophia guineensis*	4·50	5·50

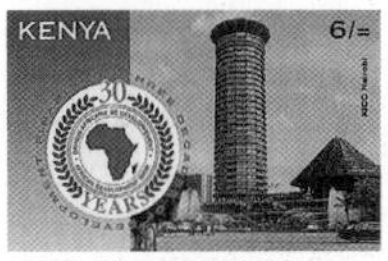
124 Emblem and K.I.C.C. Building, Nairobi

1994. 30th Anniv of African Development Bank. Multicoloured.

626	6s. Type **124**	1·00	25
627	25s. Isinya-Kajiado project	3·50	4·50

125 Kenyan Family

1994. International Year of the Family. Multicoloured.

628	6s. Type **125**	85	10
629	14s.50 Nurse with mother and baby	3·00	1·40
630	20s. Schoolchildren and teacher (horiz)	3·25	3·75
631	25s. Emblem (horiz)	3·25	4·25

126 Paul Harris (founder of Rotary)

1994. 50th Anniv of Rotary Club of Mombasa. Multicoloured.

632	6s. Type **126**	40	10
633	14s.50 Anniversary logo	1·00	70
634	17s.50 Administering polio vaccine	1·40	2·00
635	20s. Women at stand pipe	1·50	2·25
636	25s. Rotary emblem	1·60	2·50

127 Donkey

1995. Kenya Society for Prevention of Cruelty to Animals. Multicoloured.

637	6s. Type **127**	40	10
638	14s.50 Cow	45	45
639	17s.50 Sheep	55	1·00
640	20s. Dog	1·75	2·25
641	25s. Cat	1·75	2·25

128 Male Golfer in Bunker

1995. Golf. Multicoloured.

642	6s. Type **128**	1·25	12
643	17s.50 Female golfer on fairway	2·50	1·75
644	20s. Male golfer teeing-off	2·50	3·00
645	25s. Head of golf club	2·75	3·25

129 Perfume Containers

1995. Kenyan Material Culture (2nd issue). Multicoloured.

646	6s. Type **129**	30	10
647	14s.50 Basketry	75	75
648	17s.50 Preserving pots	85	1·25
649	20s. Gourds	1·10	1·75
650	25s. Wooden containers	1·25	2·00

130 Tsetse Fly

1995. 25th Anniv of I.C.I.P.E. Insect Pests. Multicoloured.

651	14s. Type **130**	50	30
652	26s. Tick	80	80
653	32s. Wild silkmoth	95	1·10
654	33s. Maize borer	1·00	1·75
655	40s. Locust	1·60	2·50

131 Maize

1995. 50th Anniv of F.A.O. Multicoloured.

656	14s. Type **131**	75	30
657	28s. Cattle	1·25	80
658	32s. Chickens	1·75	1·60
659	33s. Fisherman with catch	2·00	2·50
660	40s. Fruit	2·50	3·50

132 Kenyan and United Nations Flags over Headquarters, Nairobi

1995. 50th Anniv of United Nations.

661	**132**	23s. multicoloured	85	70
662	-	26s. multicoloured	95	95
663	-	32s. multicoloured	1·25	1·40
664	-	40s. blue, red and black	1·75	2·50

DESIGNS: 26s. Multi-racial group with emblem; 32s. United Nations helmet; 40s. 50th anniversary emblem.

133 Swimming

1996. Olympic Games, Atlanta (1st issue). Events and Gold Medal Winners. Multicoloured.

665	14s. Type **133**	1·00	1·10
666	20s. Archery	1·00	1·10
667	20s. Weightlifting	1·00	1·10
668	20s. Pole vault (vert)	1·00	1·10
669	20s. Equestrian (vert)	1·00	1·10
670	20s. Diving (vert)	1·00	1·10
671	20s. Sprinting (vert)	1·00	1·10
672	20s. Athlete carrying Olympic Torch (vert)	1·00	1·10
673	20s. Hurdling (vert)	1·00	1·10
674	20s. Kayak (vert)	1·00	1·10
675	20s. Boxing (vert)	1·00	1·10
676	20s. Gymnastics (vert)	1·00	1·10
677	25s. Greg Louganis (U.S.A.) (diving, 1984 and 1988) (vert)	1·25	1·40
678	25s. Cassius Clay (U.S.A.) (boxing, 1960) (vert)	1·25	1·40
679	25s. Nadia Comaneci (Rumania) (gymnastics, 1980) (vert)	1·25	1·40
680	25s. Daley Thompson (Great Britain) (decathlon, 1980 and 1984) (vert)	1·25	1·40
681	25s. Kipchoge Keino (Kenya) (running, 1968) (vert)	1·25	1·40
682	25s. Kornelia Enders (Germany) (swimming, 1976) (vert)	1·25	1·40
683	25s. Jackie Joyner-Kersee (U.S.A.) (long jump, 1988) (vert)	1·25	1·40
684	25s. Michael Jordan (U.S.A.) (basketball, 1984) (vert)	1·25	1·40
685	25s. Shun Fujimoto (Japan) (gymnastics, 1972) (vert)	1·25	1·40
686	32s. Javelin	1·25	1·40
687	40s. Fencing	1·25	1·40
688	50s. Discus	1·50	1·75

MS689 Two sheets, each 79×109 mm. (a) 100s. Athlete with medal (vert). (b) 100s. Athlete carrying Olympic Torch (different) (vert) Set of 2 sheets ..... 6·00 8·00

Nos. 665/7 with 686/8, 668/76 and 677/85 respectively were printed together, *se-tenant*, forming composite designs.

See also Nos. 702/6.

134 Lions

135 Water Buck

1996. Tourism. Multicoloured. (a) Designs as T **134**.

690	6s. Type **134**	30	10
691	14s. Mt. Kenya	35	30
692	20s. Sail boards	55	70
693	25s. Hippopotami	1·25	1·50
694	40s. Couple in traditional dress	1·25	2·50
MS695	100×80 mm. 50s. Female giraffe and calf (vert)	3·00	3·75

(b) Horiz designs as T **135**.

696	20s. Type **135**	1·60	1·90
697	20s. Pair of rhinoceroses	1·60	1·90
698	20s. Cheetah	1·60	1·90
699	20s. Group of oryx	1·60	1·90
700	20s. Pair of giraffes	1·60	1·90
701	20s. Monkey and bongo	1·60	1·90

136 Women's 10,000 Metres

1996. Olympic Games, Atlanta (2nd issue). Multicoloured.

702	6s. Type **136**	35	10
703	14s. Steeple-chasing	55	30
704	20s. Victorious athletes with flag	80	80
705	25s. Boxing	80	1·00
706	40s. Men's 1500 m	1·40	2·50

137 Red Cross Emblem

1996. Kenya Red Cross Society.

707	**137**	6s. red and black	25	10
708	-	14s. multicoloured	45	35
709	-	20s. multicoloured	70	80
710	-	25s. multicoloured	80	95
711	-	40s. multicoloured	1·40	2·00

DESIGNS: 14s. Giving blood; 20s. Immunization; 25s. Refugee child with food; 40s. Cleaning the environment.

138 Impala

1996. East African Wildlife Society. Multicoloured.

712	6s. Type **138**	20	10
713	20s. Colobus monkey	60	70
714	25s. African elephant	1·75	1·50
715	40s. Black rhinoceros	2·50	3·50

139 Kenya Lions Club Logo

1996. Work of Lions Club International in Kenya. Multicoloured.

716	6s. Type **139**	15	10
717	14s. Eye operation	55	45
718	20s. Two disabled children in wheelchair	70	1·25
719	25s. Modern ambulance	1·00	1·50

140 C.O.M.E.S.A. Logo

1997. Inauguration of Common Market for Eastern and Southern Africa. Multicoloured.

720	6s. Type **140**	15	15
721	20s. Kenyan flag and logo	85	1·10

141 *Haplochromis cinctus*

1997. Endangered Species. Lake Victoria Cichlid Fish. Multicoloured.

722	25s. Type **141**	75	1·00
723	25s. *Haplochromis* "Orange Rock Hunter"	75	1·00
724	25s. *Haplochromis chilotes*	75	1·00
725	25s. *Haplochromis nigricans*	75	1·00

142 Class 94 Diesel-electric Locomotive No. 9401, 1981

1997. Kenya Railway Locomotives. Multicoloured.

726	6s. Type **142**	70	15
727	14s. Class 87 diesel-electric No. 8721, 1964	1·10	40
728	20s. Class 59 Garratt steam No. 5905, 1955	1·50	65
729	25s. Class 57 Garratt steam No. 5701, 1939	1·50	1·10
730	30s. Class 23 steam No. 2305, 1923	1·75	2·00
731	40s. Class 10 steam No. 1001, 1914	1·90	2·50

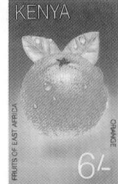

143 Orange

1997. Fruits of East Africa. Multicoloured.

732	6s. Type **143**	65	15
733	14s. Pineapple	1·25	60
734	20s. Mango	2·00	2·00
735	25s. Pawpaw	2·25	3·00

144 Crocodile

1997. Local Tourist Attractions. Multicoloured.

736	10s. Type **144**	1·25	25
737	27s. Lake Bogoria hot springs	2·00	1·50
738	30s. Warthogs	2·00	1·75
739	33s. Windsurfing	2·00	2·25
740	42s. Traditional huts	3·25	3·25

145 Girl Guides
Anniversary Logo

1997. 75th Anniv of Kenyan Girl Guides Anniversary. Multicoloured.

741	10s. Type **145**	55	70
742	10s. Lord Baden-Powell	55	70
743	27s. Girl guides hiking	90	1·10
744	27s. Rangers in camp	90	1·10
745	33s. Girl guides planting seedlings	1·00	1·25
746	33s. Boy scouts giving first aid	1·00	1·25
747	42s. Boy scouts in camp	1·25	1·75
748	42s. Brownies entertaining the elderly	1·25	1·75

146 Portuguese Ships
arriving at Malindi

1998. 500th Anniv of Vasco da Gama's Arrival at Malindi. Multicoloured.

749	10s. Type **146**	65	25
750	24s. Portuguese ships	1·40	80
751	33s. Map of Africa	1·75	2·00
752	42s. Vasco da Gama Pillar and harbour	2·00	2·50

147 Lion

1998. 18th Anniv of Pan African Postal Union. Wildlife. Multicoloured.

753	10s. Type **147**	1·50	25
754	24s. Buffalo	2·00	80
755	33s. Grant's gazelle	2·25	2·50
756	42s. Cheetah	3·25	4·50
MS757	94×76 mm. 50s. Hirola gazelle	2·50	3·25

148 Pres. Arap Moi taking
Oath, 1998

1998. Daniel Arap Moi's Fifth Presidential Term.

758	**148**	14s. multicoloured	1·50	80

149 Leatherback Turtle

2000. Turtles. Multicoloured.

759	17s. Type **149**	1·10	35
760	20s. Green sea turtle	1·40	40
761	30s. Hawksbill turtle	1·75	1·25
762	47s. Olive Ridley turtle	2·50	3·50
763	59s. Loggerhead turtle	3·00	4·50

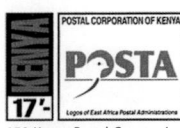

150 Kenya Postal Corporation
Logo

2000. East Africa Postal Administrations' Co-operation. Multicoloured (except 17s.).

764	17s. Type **150** (red, blue and black)	1·00	35
765	35s. Uganda Post Ltd logo	1·75	1·75
766	50s. Tanzania Posts Corporation logo	2·00	3·00
MS767	100×80 mm. 70s. As 50s.	3·50	4·25

151 Cotton   **152** Tea

2001. Crops. Multicoloured. (a) Vert designs as T **151**.

768	2s. Type **151**	10	30
769	4s. Bananas	15	30
770	5s. Avocado	15	30
771	6s. Cassava	15	30
772	8s. Arrowroot	25	30
773	10s. Pawpaw	25	30
774	19s. Orange	50	35
775	20s. Pyrethrum	50	35
776	30s. Groundnuts	80	55
777	35s. Coconut	1·00	60
778	40s. Sisal	1·25	70
779	50s. Cashew nuts	1·40	85

(b) Vert designs as T **152**.

780	60s. Type **152**	1·50	1·00
781	80s. Maize	2·00	1·40
782	100s. Coffee	2·25	1·75
783	200s. Finger millet	4·25	3·75
784	400s. Sorghum	7·50	8·00
785	500s. Sugar cane	9·00	7·50

153 Source of the Nile, Jinja,
Uganda

2002. Historical Sites of East Africa. Multicoloured.

786	19s. Type **153**	1·00	35
787	35s. Kamu Fort, Kenya (35×35 mm)	1·50	1·10
788	40s. Olduvai Gorge, Tanzania	2·75	2·75
789	50s. Thimlich Ohinga (ancient settlement), Kenya (35×35 mm)	2·75	3·25

154 Section of Mombasa Road

2003. 40th Anniv of Kenya—China Diplomatic Relations. Multicoloured.

790	21s. Type **154**	1·50	40
791	66s. Kasarani Stadium	2·75	3·50

155 Lioness and Baby Oryx

2004. Tourism. Multicoloured.

792	21s. Type **155**	1·00	35
793	60s. Leopard and cub	2·00	1·75
794	66s. Zebra and calf	2·00	2·00
795	88s. Bongo and calf	3·25	2·00

156 Risen Christ

2005. Easter. Showing bronze bas-reliefs, each black, brown and yellow.

796	25s. Type **156**	70	45
797	65s. Christ brought before Pilate	1·75	1·60
798	75s. Crucifixion	2·00	2·00
799	95s. Christ praying in Gethsemane	3·00	4·00

157 Polio Vaccination

2005. Centenary of Rotary International. Multicoloured.

800	25s. Type **157**	60	45
801	65s. Donation of Jaipur feet (prosthetics)	1·60	1·60
802	75s. Don Bosco Centre (Nairobi)	1·75	2·00
803	95s. Donation of sewing machine	2·75	3·00

158 Gabbra

2005. Traditional Costumes of East Africa (1st series). Multicoloured.

804	21s. Type **158**	85	35
805	60s. Pokot	2·00	1·75
806	66s. Meru	2·25	2·25
807	88s. Digo	3·25	4·00

See also Nos. 830/3.

159 Elephant Snout Fish

2006. Fish of Lake Victoria. Multicoloured.

808	25s. Type **159**	90	45
809	55s. Sudan catfish	1·75	1·40
810	75s. Nile perch	2·25	2·25
811	95s. Redbreast tilapia	3·25	3·75

160 Emblem

2006. 24th UPU Congress, Nairobi (1st issue).

812	**160**	25s. multicoloured	1·00	1·00

The UPU Congress was moved to Geneva, Switzerland, due to political unrest in Kenya.

161 Owen and Mzee, 2005 (Illustration
reduced. Actual size 60×31 mm)

2006. Owen and Mzee (baby hippopotamus and giant tortoise), Haller Park, Mombasa.

813	**161**	25s. multicoloured	1·25	1·50

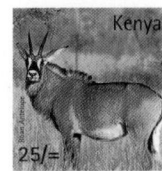

162 Roan Antelope

2006. Tourism. 'Kenya The Land of Opportunity'. Multicoloured.

814	25s. Type **162**	75	75
815	25s. Weaver bird at nest	75	75
816	25s. Monkey	75	75
817	25s. Turkana hut	75	75
818	25s. Athletes in steeplechase	75	75
819	25s. Golf course	75	75
820	25s. Waterfalls, Abadares	75	75
821	25s. Balloon safari	75	75
822	25s. Bullfight	75	75
823	25s. Chimpanzee	75	75
824	25s. Maasai	75	75
825	25s. Kit Makaye (rock formation)	75	75

163 Mt. Kenya

2007. Mountains of East Africa. Multicoloured.

826	25s. Type **163**	75	35
827	75s. Mt. Ruwenzori, Uganda	2·50	2·75
828	95s. Mt. Kilimanjaro, Tanzania	2·75	3·00

164 African Woman

2007. Breast Cancer Research.

829	**164**	25s. multicoloured	1·25	1·25

165 Oglek

2007. Traditional Costumes of East Africa (2nd series). Multicoloured.

830	25s. Type **165**	75	35
831	65s. Sabaot	2·00	1·50
832	75s. Ribe	2·25	2·25
833	95s. Elmolo	3·25	3·75

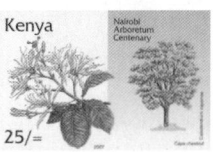

166 *Calodendrum capense* (Cape
chestnut)

2007. Centenary of Nairobi Arboretum. Multicoloured.

834	25s. Type **166**	75	35
835	65s. Tree Centre and *Cupressus torulosa* (Bhutan cypress)	2·00	1·50
836	75s. *Spathodea campanulata* (Nandi flame)	2·25	2·25
837	95s. *Monodora myristica* (calabash nutmeg)	3·25	3·75

167 Sitalunga Gazelle in Saiwa
Swamp

2008. 24th UPU Congress, Nairobi (2nd issue). Multicoloured.

838	25s. Type **167**	75	25
839	65s. Jackson's hartebeest at Ruma Park	2·00	1·50
840	75s. Athlete in steeplechase	2·25	2·25
841	95s. Kenyatta International Conference Centre, Nairobi	3·25	3·75

The UPU Congress was moved to Geneva, Switzerland, due to political unrest in Kenya.

Nos. 842/5, T **168** are left for Olympic Games, Beijing, issued 21 August 2008, not yet received.

169 Oginga Odinga, Pio Gama
Pinto, Tom Mboya and Ronald
Ngala (politicians) (Post
Independence)

2008. Heroes of Kenya. Multicoloured.

846	25s. Type **169**	70	40
847	65s. Bildad Kaggia, Kung'u Karumba, Jomo Kenyatta, Fred Kubai, Paul Ngei and Achieng' Oneko (The Kapenguria Six)	1·75	1·75

848	75s. Dedan Kimathi (Mau Mau rebellion leader), Elijah Masinde (political and religious leader), Mekatilili Wa Menza (anti colonial leader) and Koitalel Samoei (Nandi rebellion leader) (Pre Independence)	2·25	2·25
849	95s. Kenya Army Peacekeeping Force	2·50	3·00

170 Woman loading Donkey with Water Cans

2008. Centenary of Theosophical Order of Service. Provision of Wells and Boreholes.

850	**170**	25s. multicoloured	1·25	1·00

171 Madrasa Programme

2008. Golden Jubilee of the Aga Khan. Multicoloured.

851	25s. Type **171**	70	40
852	65s. Workers in field (Coastal Rural Support Programme)	1·75	1·75
853	75s. Aga Khan Academy, Mombasa (44×29 mm)	2·25	2·25
854	95s. Aga Khan University Hospital, Nairobi (44×29 mm)	2·50	3·00

172 Blind Man

2009. Birth Bicentenary of Louis Braille (inventor of Braille writing for the blind).

855	**172**	25s. multicoloured	1·25	1·00

173 Market Stallholder ('Financial Services')

2009. Tenth Anniv of Postal Corporation of Kenya. Multicoloured.

856	25s. Type **173**	1·10	1·10
857	25s. Parcels ('We Deliver Peace of Mind!')	1·10	1·10
858	25s. Courier and Posta Dispatch vans ('Pick-up Services')	1·10	1·10
859	25s. Boy and stamps ('Say it with Stamps!')	1·10	1·10
860	25s. Brochures in postbox ('Direct Mail Marketing')	1·10	1·10
861	25s. 'Utility Bills Retail Services Salaries' ('Agency Services')	1·10	1·10
862	25s. Woman reading letter ('We Deliver Emotions!')	1·10	1·10
863	25s. Postman and private letter boxes	1·10	1·10
864	25s. 'Financial Services'	1·10	1·10
865	65s. Unloading parcels from airplane ('Expedited Mail Service')	1·90	1·90
866	75s. Narok Post Office	2·40	2·40
867	95s. Water standpipe ('Corporate Social Responsibility')	2·75	2·75

174 Taita African Violet and Amegilla Bee, Taita Hills

2010. Centenary (2009) of the East Africa Natural History Society. Multicoloured.

868	25s. Type **174**	75	75
869	65s. Reed frog, Shimba Hills	2·40	2·40
870	75s. Great blue turaco, Kakamega Forest	2·75	2·75
871	95s. Golden-rumped sengi, Arabuko-Sokoke Forest	3·50	3·50

OFFICIAL STAMPS

Intended for use on official correspondence of the Kenya Government only, but there is no evidence that they were so used.

1964. Stamps of 1963 optd **OFFICIAL**.

O21	**46**	5c. multicoloured	10
O22	-	10c. brown	10
O23	-	15c. mauve	1·25
O24	-	20c. black and green	20
O25	-	30c. black and yellow	30
O26	-	50c. red, black and green	2·75

POSTAGE DUE STAMPS

D3

1967

D13	**D3**	5c. red	15	2·75
D41	**D3**	10c. green	40	1·75
D42	**D3**	20c. blue	40	1·75
D44	**D3**	30c. brown	1·00	2·00
D45	**D3**	40c. purple	1·00	2·00
D46	**D3**	80c. red	1·50	2·25
D49	**D3**	50c. green	10	10
D50	**D3**	1s. orange	10	10
D51	**D3**	2s. violet	10	10
D52	**D3**	3s. blue	10	10
D53	**D3**	5s. red	10	10

Pt. 1

KENYA, UGANDA AND TANGANYIKA (TANZANIA)

From 1903 joint issues were made for British East Africa (later Kenya) and Uganda. In 1933 the postal administrations of Kenya, Uganda and Tanganyika were combined.

On independence of the constituent territories in the 1960s the postal administration became the East African Posts and Telecommunications Corporation. As well as separate issues for each state (q.v.), joint commemorative issues (which however were not valid in Zanzibar) were made until the dissolution of the Corporation in 1977.

1903. 16 annas = 100 cents = 1 rupee.
1922. 100 cents = 1 shilling.

1

2

1903

17	**1**	½a. green	8·50	3·00
2		1a. grey and red	1·75	1·25
19a	**11**	2a. purple	2·75	2·75
21	**11**	2½a. blue	7·50	17·00
22a	**11**	3a. purple and green	4·25	40·00
23	**11**	4a. green and black	7·50	18·00
24	**11**	5a. grey and brown	8·00	15·00
25	**11**	8a. grey and blue	7·00	8·50
9	**2**	1r. green	22·00	60·00
27	**2**	2r. purple	40·00	60·00
28	**2**	3r. green and black	75·00	£110
29	**2**	4r. grey and green	95·00	£160
30	**2**	5r. grey and red	£130	£150
31	**2**	10r. grey and blue	£300	£350
15	**2**	20r. grey and stone	£600	£1500
16	**2**	50r. grey and brown	£1800	£3750

1907

34	**1**	1c. brown	2·50	15
35	**1**	3c. green	18·00	70
36	**1**	6c. red	2·75	10
37	**1**	10c. lilac and olive	9·50	8·50
38	**1**	12c. purple	10·00	2·75
39	**1**	15c. blue	27·00	8·50
40	**1**	25c. green and black	18·00	7·00
41	**1**	50c. green and brown	14·00	14·00
42	**1**	75c. grey and blue	4·50	42·00

1912. As T **1/2** but portraits of King George V.

44	1c. black	30	1·75
45	3c. green	2·00	60
46	6c. red	1·25	40
47	10c. orange	2·00	50
48	12c. grey	2·75	50
49	15c. blue	2·75	80
50	25c. black and red on yellow	50	1·25
51	50c. black and lilac	1·50	1·25
52b	75c. black and green	7·00	7·50
53	1r. black and green	1·75	4·25
54	2r. red and black on blue	20·00	38·00
55	3r. violet and green	24·00	£110
56	4r. red and green on yellow	50·00	£100
57	5r. blue and purple	55·00	£150
58	10r. red and green on green	£190	£300
59	20r. black and purple on red	£400	£400
60	20r. purple and blue on blue	£475	£650
61	50r. red and green	£750	£800
62	100r. purple and black on red	£6500	£3000
63	500r. green and red on green	£27000	

1919. No. 46 surch **4 cents**.

64	4c. on 6c. red	1·25	15

6

7

1922

76	**6**	1c. brown	1·00	3·50
77	**6**	5c. violet	4·50	75
78	**6**	5c. green	2·00	30
79	**6**	10c. green	1·50	30
80	**6**	10c. black	4·00	20
81a	**6**	12c. black	10·00	26·00
82	**6**	15c. red	1·25	10
83	**6**	20c. orange	3·25	10
84	**6**	30c. blue	4·00	50
85	**6**	50c. grey	2·50	10
86	**6**	75c. olive	8·00	9·00
87	**7**	1s. green	4·75	2·50
88	**7**	2s. purple	8·00	16·00
89	**7**	2s.50 brown	19·00	£110
90	**7**	3s. grey	18·00	6·50
91	**7**	4s. grey	30·00	£110
92	**7**	5s. red	23·00	22·00
93	**7**	7s.50 orange	£110	£250
94	**7**	10s. blue	70·00	70·00
95	**7**	£1 black and orange	£200	£300
96	**7**	£2 green and purple	£900	£1600
97	**7**	£3 purple and yellow	£1300	
98	**7**	£4 black and mauve	£2250	
99	**7**	£5 black and blue	£2500	
100	**7**	£10 black and green	£11000	
101	**7**	£20 red and green	£23000	
102	**7**	£25 black and red	£27000	
103	**7**	£50 black and brown	£35000	
104	**7**	£75 purple and grey	£100000	
105	**7**	£100 red and black	£110000	

8 South African Crowned Cranes

9 Dhow on Lake Victoria

1935. King George V.

110	**8**	1c. black and brown	1·00	1·50
111	**9**	5c. black and green	2·75	30
112	-	10c. black and yellow	5·50	60
113	-	15c. black and red	3·00	10
114	**8**	20c. black and orange	3·50	20
115	-	30c. black and blue	3·75	1·00
116	**9**	50c. purple and black	4·50	10
117	-	65c. black and brown	6·00	2·00
118	-	1s. black and green	4·50	1·00
119	-	2s. red and purple	10·00	4·50
120	-	3s. blue and black	14·00	15·00
121	-	5s. black and red	23·00	27·00
122	**8**	10s. purple and blue	90·00	£110
123	-	£1 black and red	£225	£325

DESIGNS—VERT: 10c., £1 Lion; 30c., 5s. Nile Railway Bridge, Ripon Falls. HORIZ: 15c., 2s. Kilimanjaro; 65c. Mt. Kenya; 1s., 3s. Lake Naivasha.

14a Windsor Castle

1935. Silver Jubilee.

124	**14a**	20c. blue and olive	1·75	10
125	**14a**	30c. brown and blue	2·75	3·00
126	**14a**	65c. green and blue	1·75	2·75
127	**14a**	1s. grey and purple	2·25	5·50

14b King George VI and Queen Elizabeth

1937. Coronation.

128	**14b**	5c. green	20	10
129	**14b**	20c. orange	40	30
130	**14b**	30c. blue	60	1·75

15 Dhow on Lake Victoria

1938. As 1935 (except 10c.) but with portrait of King George VI as in T **15**.

131a	**8**	1c. black and brown	30	50
132	**15**	5c. black and green	4·50	50
133	**15**	5c. brown and orange	1·00	5·00
134	-	10c. brown and orange	2·25	10
135	-	10c. black and green	30	2·00
136	-	10c. brown and grey	1·25	55
137a	-	15c. black and red	5·50	3·75
138	-	15c. black and green	3·00	6·00
139b	**8**	20c. black and orange	9·50	10
140	**15**	25c. black and red	1·25	2·25
141b	-	30c. black and blue	2·75	10
142	-	30c. purple and brown	1·50	40
143	**8**	40c. black and blue	1·75	3·25
144e	**15**	50c. purple and black	8·50	55
145a	-	1s. black and brown	15·00	30
146b	-	2s. red and purple	42·00	30
147ac	-	3s. blue and black	48·00	7·50
148b	-	5s. black and red	48·00	1·75
149b	**8**	10s. purple and blue	55·00	6·50
150a	-	£1 black and red	35·00	22·00

DESIGN—HORIZ: 10c. Lake Naivasha.

1941. Stamps of South Africa surch **KENYA TANGANYIKA UGANDA** and value. Alternate stamps inscr in English or Afrikaans.

151	**7**	5c. on 1d. black and red	1·60	15
152	**22a**	10c. on 3d. blue	5·00	30
153	**8**	20c. on 6d. green and red	4·00	20
154	-	70c. on 1s. brown and blue (No. 120)	22·00	45

Prices for Nos. 151/4 are for unused pairs and used singles.

1946. Victory. As T **59a** of Jamaica.

155	20c. orange	30	10
156	30c. blue	30	75

1948. Silver Wedding. As T **59b/c** of Jamaica.

157	20c. orange	15	30
158	£1 red	50·00	70·00

1949. U.P.U. As T **63/3** of Jamaica.

159	20c. orange	15	10
160	30c. blue	1·75	2·25
161	50c. grey	45	60
162	1s. brown	50	40

1952. Visit of Queen Elizabeth II (as Princess) and Duke of Edinburgh. As Nos. 135 and 145ba but inscr "ROYAL VISIT 1952".

163	10c. black and green	30	1·50
164	1s. black and brown	1·40	2·00

1953. Coronation. As T **71** of Jamaica.

165	20c. black and orange	30	10

1954. Royal Visit. As No. 171 but inscr "ROYAL VISIT 1954".

166	**18**	30c. black and blue	65	15

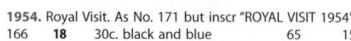

18 Owen Falls Dam

20 Royal Lodge, Sagana

21 Queen Elizabeth II

1954

167		5c. black and brown	1·75	50
168	-	10c. red	1·75	10
169a	-	15c. black and blue	1·00	1·25

170	-	20c. black and orange	2·00	10
171	18	30c. black and blue	1·50	10
172	-	40c. brown	1·25	75
173	-	50c. purple	3·50	10
174	-	65c. green and purple	2·75	1·50
175	-	1s. black and purple	3·75	10
176	-	1s.30 lilac and orange	17·00	10
177	-	2s. black and green	16·00	1·25
178	-	5s. black and orange	30·00	3·50
179	20	10s. black and blue	38·00	5·00
180	21	£1 red and black	19·00	20·00

DESIGNS—VERT (Size as Type **18**): 10, 50c. Giraffe; 20, 40c., 1s. Lion. HORIZ: 15c., 1s.30, 5s. Elephants; 65c., 2s. Mt. Kilimanjaro.

25 Map of E. Africa showing Lakes

1958. Centenary of Discovery of Lakes Tanganyika and Victoria by Burton and Speke.

181	25	40c. blue and green	1·00	40
182	25	1s.30 green and purple	1·00	1·60

26 Sisal

28 Mt. Kenya and Giant Plants

29 Queen Elizabeth II

1960

183	26	5c. blue	10	15
184	-	10c. green	10	10
185	-	15c. purple	30	10
186	-	20c. mauve	20	10
187	-	25c. green	3·25	1·25
188	-	30c. red	15	10
189	-	40c. blue	15	20
190	-	50c. violet	15	10
191	-	65c. olive	30	2·00
192	28	1s. violet and purple	80	10
193	-	1s.30 brown and red	6·50	15
194	-	2s. indigo and blue	8·00	40
195	-	2s.50 olive and turquoise	11·00	2·75
196	-	5s. red and purple	4·50	60
197	-	10s. myrtle and green	13·00	6·50
198	29	20s. blue and lake	25·00	30·00

DESIGNS—As Type **26**: 10c. Cotton; 15c. Coffee; 20c. Blue wildebeest; 25c. Ostrich; 30c. Thomson's gazelle; 40c. Manta; 50c. Common zebra; 65c. Cheetah. As Type **28**: 1s.30, Murchison Falls and hippopotamus; 2s. Mt. Kilimanjaro and giraffe; 2s.50, Candelabra tree and black rhinoceros; 5s. Crater Lake and Mountains of the Moon; 10s. Ngorongoro Crater and African buffalo.

30 Land Tillage

1963. Freedom from Hunger.

199	30	15c. blue and olive	30	10
200	-	30c. brown and yellow	45	10
201	30	50c. blue and orange	60	10
202	-	1s.30 brown and blue	1·10	1·75

DESIGN: 30c., 1s.30, African with corncob.

31 Scholars and Open Book

1963. Founding of East African University.

203	31	30c. multicoloured	10	10
204	31	1s.30 multicoloured	20	30

32 Red Cross Emblem

1963. Centenary of Red Cross.

205	32	30c. red and blue	1·50	30
206	32	50c. red and brown	1·75	1·25

35 East African "Flags"

1964. Olympic Games, Tokyo.

207	-	30c. yellow and purple	15	10
208	-	50c. purple and yellow	20	10
209	35	1s.30 yellow, green and blue	50	10
210	35	2s.50 mauve, violet and blue	60	2·25

DESIGN—VERT: 30, 50c. Chrysanthemum emblem.

36 Rally Badge

1965. 13th East African Safari Rally.

211	36	30c. black, yellow & turq	10	10
212	36	50c. black, yellow and brown	10	10
213	-	1s.30 green, ochre and blue	25	10
214	-	2s.50 green, red and blue	40	1·50

DESIGN: 1s.30, 2s.50, Cars en route.

38 I.T.U. Emblem and Symbols

1965. Centenary of I.T.U. "I.T.U." and symbols in gold.

215	38	30c. brown and mauve	15	10
216	38	50c. brown and grey	15	10
217	38	1s.30 brown and blue	40	10
218	38	2s.50 brown and turquoise	75	2·25

39 I.C.Y. Emblem

1965. International Co-operation Year.

219	39	30c. green and gold	15	10
220	39	50c. black and gold	20	10
221	39	1s.30 blue and gold	40	10
222	39	2s.50 red and gold	90	3·50

40 Game Park Lodge, Tanzania

1966. Tourism. Multicoloured.

223	30c. Type **40**	35	10
224	50c. Murchison Falls, Uganda	65	10
225	1s.30 Lesser flamingoes, Lake Nakuru, Kenya	3·00	30
226	2s.50 Deep sea fishing, Tanzania	2·00	2·25

41 Games Emblem

1966. Eighth British Empire and Commonwealth Games, Jamaica.

227	41	30c. multicoloured	10	10
228	41	50c. multicoloured	15	10
229	41	1s.30 multicoloured	20	10
230	41	2s.50 multicoloured	35	1·50

42 UNESCO Emblem

1966. 20th Anniv of UNESCO.

231	42	30c. black, green and red	65	10
232	42	50c. black, green and brown	75	10
233	42	1s.30 black, green and grey	1·75	20
234	42	2s.50 black, green and yellow	2·50	6·00

43 de Havilland DH.89 Dragon Rapide

1967. 21st Anniv of East African Airways.

235	43	30c. violet, blue and green	30	10
236	-	50c. multicoloured	40	10
237	-	1s.30 multicoloured	85	30
238	-	2s.50 multicoloured	1·25	3·00

DESIGNS: 50c. Vickers Super VC-10; 1s.30, Hawker Siddeley Comet 4B; 2s.50, Fokker F.27 Friendship.

44 Pillar Tomb

1967. Archaeological Relics.

239	44	30c. ochre, black and purple	15	10
240	-	50c. red, black and brown	65	10
241	-	1s.30 black, yellow and green	85	15
242	-	2s.50 black, ochre and red	1·40	2·50

DESIGNS: 50c. Rock painting; 1s.30, Clay head; 2s.50, Proconsul skull.

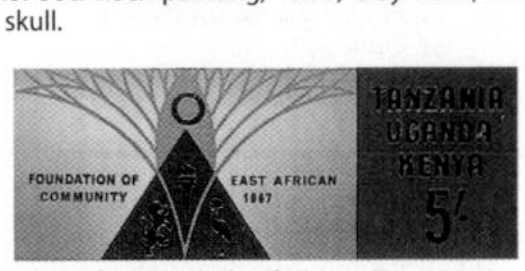

48 Unified Symbols of Kenya, Tanzania and Uganda

1967. Foundation of East African Community.

243	48	5s. gold, black and grey	40	1·50

49 Mountaineering

1968. Mountains of East Africa. Multicoloured.

244	30c. Type **49**	15	10
245	50c. Mt. Kenya	30	10
246	1s.30 Mt. Kilimanjaro	60	10
247	2s.50 Ruwenzori Mountains	90	2·25

50 Family and Rural Hospital

1968. World Health Organization.

248	50	30c. green, lilac and brown	10	10
249	-	50c. slate, lilac and black	15	10
250	-	1s.30 brown, lilac and light brown	20	15
251	-	2s.50 grey, black and lilac	30	1·90

DESIGNS: 50c. Family and nurse; 1s.30, Family and microscope; 2s.50, Family and hypodermic syringe.

51 Olympic Stadium, Mexico City

1968. Olympic Games, Mexico.

252	51	30c. green and black	10	10
253	-	50c. green and black	15	10
254	-	1s.30 red, black and grey	25	15
255	-	2s.50 sepia and brown	35	1·50

DESIGNS—HORIZ: 50c. High-diving boards; 1s.30, Running tracks. VERT: 2s.50, Boxing ring.

52 *Umoja* (railway ferry)

1969. Water Transport.

256	52	30c. blue and grey	30	10
257	-	50c. multicoloured	35	10
258	-	1s.30 green and blue	60	20
259	-	2s.50 orange and blue	1·10	3·25

DESIGNS: 50c. S.S. *Harambee*; 1s.30, M.V. *Victoria*; 2s.50, *St. Michael*.

53 I.L.O. Emblem and Agriculture

1969. 50th Anniv of Int Labour Organization.

260	53	30c. black, green and yellow	10	10
261	-	50c. multicoloured	10	10
262	-	1s.30 black, brown and orange	10	10
263	-	2s.50 black, blue & turq	20	90

DESIGNS—I.L.O. emblem and: 50c. Building-work; 1s.30, Factory-workers; 2s.50, Shipping.

54 Pope Paul VI and Ruwenzori Mountains

1969. Visit of Pope Paul VI to Uganda.

264	54	30c. black, gold and blue	15	10
265	54	70c. black, gold and red	20	10
266	54	1s.50 black, gold and blue	25	20
267	54	2s.50 black, gold and violet	30	1·40

55 Euphorbia Tree shaped as Africa, and Emblem

1969. Fifth Anniv of African Development Bank.

268	55	30c. green and gold	10	10
269	55	70c. green, gold and violet	15	10
270	55	1s.50 green, gold and blue	30	10
271	55	2s.50 green, gold and brown	35	1·00

56 Marimba

1970. Musical Instruments.

272	56	30c. buff and brown	15	10
273	-	70c. green, brown and yellow	25	10
274	-	1s.50 brown and yellow	50	10
275	-	2s.50 orange, yellow and brown	75	2·50

DESIGNS: 70c. Amadinda; 1s.50, Nzomari; 2s.50, Adeudeu.

57 Satellite Earth Station

1970. Inauguration of Satellite Earth Station.

276	**57**	30c. multicoloured	10	10
277	-	70c. multicoloured	15	10
278	-	1s.50 black, violet & orge	30	10
279	-	2s.50 multicoloured	60	2·25

DESIGNS: 70c. Transmitter—daytime; 1s.50, Transmitter—night; 2s. 50, Earth and satellite.

58 Athlete

1970. Ninth Commonwealth Games.

280	**58**	30c. brown and black	10	10
281	**58**	70c. green, brown and black	10	10
282	**58**	1s.50 lilac, brown and black	15	10
283	**58**	2s.50 blue, brown and black	20	1·25

59 "25" and U.N. Emblem

1970. 25th Anniv of United Nations.

284	**59**	30c. multicoloured	10	10
285	**59**	70c. multicoloured	10	10
286	**59**	1s.50 multicoloured	20	10
287	**59**	2s.50 multicoloured	45	2·00

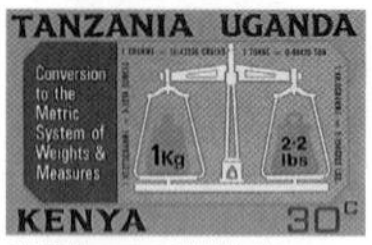

60 Balance and Weight Equivalents

1971. Conversion to Metric System. Multicoloured.

288	30c. Type **60**	10	10
289	70c. Fahrenheit and Centigrade thermometers	10	10
290	1s.50 Petrol pump and liquid capacities	15	10
291	2s.50 Surveyors and land measures	35	2·00

61 Class 11 Tank Locomotive

1971. Railway Transport. Multicoloured.

292	30c. Type **61**	15	10
293	70c. Class 90 diesel-electric locomotive	25	10
294	1s.50 Class 59 steam locomotive	50	20
295	2s.50 Class 30 steam locomotive	90	2·25
MS296	120×88 mm. Nos. 292/5	6·50	10·00

62 Syringe and Cow

1971. O.A.U. Rinderpest Campaign.

297	**62**	30c. black, brown and green	10	10
298	-	70c. black, blue and brown	10	10
299	**62**	1s.50 black, purple & brn	15	10
300	-	2s.50 black, red and brown	25	70

DESIGN: 70c., 2s.50, as Type **62** but with bull facing right.

63 Livingstone meets Stanley

1971. Centenary of Livingstone and Stanley meeting at Ujiji.

301	**63**	5s. multicoloured	30	75

64 Pres. Nyerere and Supporters

1971. Tenth Anniv of Tanzanian Independence. Multicoloured.

302	30c. Type **64**	10	10
303	70c. Ujamaa village	15	10
304	1s.50 Dar-es-Salaam University	30	25
305	2s.50 Kilimanjaro International Airport	1·00	3·25

65 Flags and Trade Fair Emblem

1972. All-Africa Trade Fair.

306	**65**	30c. multicoloured	10	10
307	**65**	70c. multicoloured	10	10
308	**65**	1s.50 multicoloured	10	10
309	**65**	2s.50 multicoloured	25	80

66 Child with Cup

1972. 25th Anniv of UNICEF. Multicoloured.

310	30c. Type **66**	10	10
311	70c. Children with ball	10	10
312	1s.50 Child at blackboard	10	10
313	2s.50 Child and tractor	25	80

67 Hurdling

1972. Olympic Games, Munich. Multicoloured.

314	40c. Type **67**	10	10
315	70c. Running	10	10
316	1s.50 Boxing	20	15
317	2s.50 Hockey	30	1·75
MS318	131×98 mm. Nos. 314/17	4·50	7·00

68 Ugandan Kobs

1972. Tenth Anniv of Ugandan Independence. Multicoloured.

319	40c. Type **68**	30	10
320	70c. Conference Centre	30	10
321	1s.50 Makerere University	65	30
322	2s.50 Coat of arms	1·00	3·50
MS323	132×120 mm. Nos. 319/22	3·50	3·50

69 Community Flag

1972. Fifth Anniv of East African Community.

324	**69**	5s. multicoloured	55	1·90

70 Run-of-the-wind Anemometer

1972. Centenary of IMO/WMO. Multicoloured.

325	40c. Type **70**	10	10
326	70c. Weather balloon (vert)	20	10
327	1s.50 Meteorological rocket	30	15
328	2s.50 Satellite receiving aerial	55	2·25

71 "Learning by Serving"

1973. 24th World Scouting Conference, Nairobi.

329	**71**	40c. multicoloured	15	10
330	-	70c. red, violet and black	20	10
331	-	1s.50 blue, violet and black	45	30
332	-	2s.50 multicoloured	1·00	2·25

DESIGNS: 70c. Baden-Powell's grave, Nyeri; 1s.50, World Scout emblem; 2s.50, Lord Baden-Powell.

72 Kenyatta Conference Centre

1973. I.M.F./World Bank Conference.

333	**72**	40c. green, grey and black	10	10
334	-	70c. brown, grey and black	10	10
335	-	1s.50 multicoloured	25	35
336	-	2s.50 orange, grey and black	35	1·75
MS337		166×141 mm. Nos. 333/6. Imperf	1·40	4·00

DESIGNS: Nos. 334/6 show different arrangements of Bank emblems and the Conference Centre, the 1s.50 being vertical.

73 Police Dog-handler

1973. 50th Anniv of Interpol.

338	**73**	40c. yellow, blue and black	55	15
339	-	70c. green, yellow and black	90	15
340	-	1s.50 violet, yellow and black	1·50	90
341	-	2s.50 green, orange and black	3·75	6·00
342	-	2s.50 green, orange and black	3·75	6·00

DESIGNS: 70c. East African policemen; 1s.50, Interpol emblem; 2s.50 (2), Interpol H.Q.

No. 341 is inscribed "St. Clans" and 342 "St. Cloud".

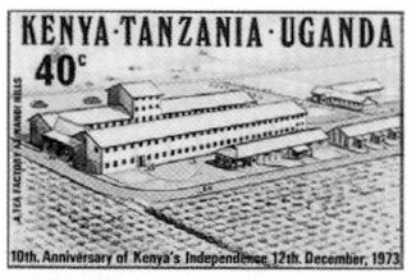

74 Tea Factory

1973. Tenth Anniv of Kenya's Independence. Multicoloured.

343	40c. Type **74**	10	10
344	70c. Kenyatta Hospital	15	10
345	1s.50 Nairobi Airport	50	20
346	2s.50 Kindaruma hydro-electric scheme	65	1·75

75 Party H.Q.

1973. Tenth Anniv of Zanzibar's Revolution. Multicoloured.

347	40c. Type **75**	10	10
348	70c. Housing scheme	15	10
349	1s.50 Colour T.V.	35	30
350	2s.50 Amaan Stadium	70	3·50

76 "Symbol of Union"

1974. Tenth Anniv of Tanganyika–Zanzibar Union. Multicoloured.

351	40c. Type **76**	10	10
352	70c. Handclasp and map	15	10
353	1s.50 "Communications"	35	30
354	2s.50 Flags of Tanu, Tanzania and Afro-Shirazi Party	70	3·00

77 East African Family ("Stability of the Home")

1974. 17th Social Welfare Conference, Nairobi.

355	**77**	40c. yellow, brown and black	10	10
356	-	70c. multicoloured	10	10
357	-	1s.50 yellow, green and black	20	30
358	-	2s.50 red, violet and black	1·00	2·00

DESIGNS: 70c. Dawn and drummer (U.N. Second Development Plan); 1s.50, Agricultural scene (Rural Development Plan); 2s.50, Transport and telephone ("Communications").

78 New Postal H.Q., Kampala

1974. Centenary of U.P.U. Multicoloured.

359	40c. Type **78**	10	10
360	70c. Mail-train and post-van	20	10
361	1s.50 U.P.U. Building, Berne	15	20
362	2s.50 Loading mail into Vickers Super VC-10	55	1·50

79 Family-planning Clinic

1974. World Population Year.

363	**79**	40c. multicoloured	10	10
364	-	70c. mauve and red	10	10
365	-	1s.50 multicoloured	15	20
366	-	2s.50 blue, emerald and green	30	1·90

DESIGNS: 70c. "Tug of War"; 1s.50, "Population scales"; 2s.50, W.P.Y. emblem.

80 Seronera Wildlife Lodge, Tanzania

1975. East African Game Lodges. Multicoloured.

367	40c. Type **80**	15	10
368	70c. Mweya Safari Lodge, Uganda	20	10
369	1s.50 "Ark"—Aberdare Forest Lodge, Kenya	25	30
370	2s.50 Paraa Safari Lodge, Uganda	60	3·00

81 Kitana (wooden comb), Bajun of Kenya

1975. African Arts. Multicoloured.

371	50c. Type **81**	10	10
372	1s. Earring, Chaga of Tanzania	15	10

373	2s. Okoco (armlet), Acholi of Uganda	35	75
374	3s. Kitete, Kamba gourd, Kenya	85	1·75

82 International Airport, Entebbe

1975. O.A.U. Summit Conf, Kampala. Multicoloured.

375	50c. Type **82**	30	10
376	1s. Map of Africa and flag (vert)	30	10
377	2s. Nile Hotel, Kampala	30	85
378	3s. Martyrs' Shrine, Namugongo (vert)	40	1·90

83 Ahmed ("Presidential" Elephant)

1975. Rare Animals. Multicoloured.

379	50c. Type **83**	40	10
380	1s. Albino buffalo	40	10
381	2s. Ahmed in grounds of National Museum	1·25	1·50
382	3s. Abbott's duiker	1·25	3·00

84 Maasai Manyatta (village), Kenya

1975. Second World Black and African Festival of Arts and Culture, Nigeria (1977). Multicoloured.

383	50c. Type **84**	15	10
384	1s. "Heartbeat of Africa" (Ugandan Dancers)	15	10
385	2s. Makonde sculpture, Tanzania	50	85
386	3s. "Early Man and Technology" (skinning animal)	75	1·40

85 Fokker F.27 Friendship at Nairobi Airport

1975. 30th Anniv of East African Airways. Multicoloured.

387	50c. Type **85**	1·00	30
388	1s. Douglas DC-9 at Kilimanjaro Airport	1·10	40
389	2s. Vickers Super VC-10 at Entebbe Airport	3·50	3·50
390	3s. East African Airways crest	3·75	4·25

Further commemorative sets were released during 1976-78 using common designs, but each inscribed for one republic only. See Kenya, Tanzania and Uganda.

Co-operation between the postal services of the three member countries virtually ceased after 30 June 1977. The postal services of Kenya, Uganda and Uganda then operated independently.

OFFICIAL STAMPS

For use on official correspondence of the Tanganyika Government only.

1959. Stamps of 1954 optd **OFFICIAL**.

O1	18	5c. black and brown	10	1·25
O2	-	10c. red	30	1·25
O3	-	15c. black and blue	75	1·25
O4	-	20c. black and orange	20	20
O5	18	30c. black and blue	15	80
O6	-	50c. purple	1·75	20
O7	-	1s. black and red	20	75
O8	-	1s.30 orange and lilac	8·50	2·25
O9	-	2s. black and green	1·25	1·00
O10	-	5s. black and orange	8·50	3·75
O11	20	10s. black and blue	3·25	7·00
O12	21	£1 red and black	6·50	25·00

1960. Stamps of 1960 optd **OFFICIAL**.

O13	26	5c. blue	10	3·00
O14	-	10c. green	10	3·00
O15	-	15c. purple	10	3·00
O16	-	20c. mauve	10	75
O17	-	30c. red	10	10
O18	-	50c. violet	30	1·00
O19	28	1s. violet and purple	30	10
O20	-	5s. red and purple	21·00	65

POSTAGE DUE STAMPS

D1

1923

D1	D 1	5c. violet	2·50	50
D2	D 1	10c. red	2·50	15
D3	D 1	20c. green	3·50	3·25
D4	D 1	30c. brown	22·00	16·00
D5	D 1	40c. blue	6·50	14·00
D6	D 1	1s. green	70·00	£140

D2

1935

D7	D2	5c. violet	2·75	1·75
D8	D2	10c. red	30	50
D9	D2	20c. green	40	50
D10	D2	30c. brown	1·25	50
D11	D2	40c. blue	1·50	3·00
D12	D2	1s. grey	19·00	19·00

Pt. 21

KHMER REPUBLIC

Cambodia was renamed Khmer Republic on 9 October 1970.

Following the fall of the Khmer Republic, the People's Republic of Kampuchea was proclaimed on 10 January 1979.

100 cents = 1 riel.

78 "Attack"

1971. Defence of Khmer Territory.

285	78	1r. multicoloured	15	10
286	78	3r. multicoloured	15	15
287	78	10r. multicoloured	50	25

79 "World Races" and U.N. Emblem

1971. Racial Equality Year.

288	79	3r. multicoloured	25	15
289	79	7r. multicoloured	40	25
290	79	8r. multicoloured	60	40

80 General Post Office, Phnom Penh

1971

291	80	3r. multicoloured	15	10
292	80	9r. multicoloured	50	35
293	80	10r. multicoloured	60	40

81 Global Emblem

1971. World Telecommunications Day.

294	81	3r. multicoloured	25	15
295	81	4r. multicoloured	35	15
296	-	7r. multicoloured	40	25
297	-	8r. red, black and orange	50	25

DESIGN: 7, 8r. I.T.U. emblem.

82 Indian Coral Bean

1971. Wild Flowers. Multicoloured.

298		2r. Type **82**	40	15
299		3r. Orchid tree	50	40
300		6r. Flame-of-the-forest	1·00	40
301		10r. Malayan crape myrtle (vert)	1·20	65

83 Arms of the Republic

84 Monument and Flag

1971. First Anniv of Republic.

302	83	3r. bistre and green	25	10
303	84	3r. multicoloured	25	10
304	84	4r. multicoloured	35	15
305	83	8r. bistre and orange	40	15
306	83	10r. bistre and brown	60	25
307	84	10r. multicoloured	50	35
MS308		Two sheets, each 130×100 mm. (a) Nos. 302 and 305/6 (sold for 25r.); (b) Nos. 303/4 and 307 (sold for 20r.)	4·75	4·00

85 UNICEF Emblem

1971. 25th Anniv of UNICEF.

309	85	3r. purple	25	15
310	85	5r. blue	35	25
311	85	9r. red and violet	65	40

86 Book Year Emblem

1972. International Book Year.

312	86	3r. green, purple and blue	25	15
313	86	8r. blue, green and purple	40	25
314	86	9r. bistre, blue and green	60	40
MS315		160×100 mm. Nos. 312/14 (sold at 25r.)	2·10	1·80

87 Lion of St. Mark's

1972. UNESCO "Save Venice" Campaign.

316	87	3r. brown, buff and purple	35	15
317	-	5r. brown, buff and green	60	25
318	-	10r. brown, blue and green	75	40
MS319		160×100 mm. Nos. 316/18 (sold at 23r.)	3·00	2·50

DESIGNS—HORIZ: 5r. St. Mark's Basilica. VERT: 10r. Bridge of Sighs.

88 U.N. Emblem

1972. 25th Anniv of Economic Commission for Asia and the Far East (C.E.A.E.O.).

320	88	3r. red	25	15
321	88	6r. blue	40	25
322	88	9r. red	60	40
MS323		141×101 mm. Nos. 320/3 (sold at 23r.)	1·90	1·70

89 Dancing Apsaras (relief), Angkor

1972

324	89	1r. brown	25	15
325	89	3r. violet	25	15
326	89	7r. purple	40	25
327	89	8r. brown	40	25
328	89	9r. green	50	25
329	89	10r. blue	65	25
330	89	12r. purple	90	35
331	89	14r. blue	1·20	40

90 "UIT" on T.V. Screen

1972. World Telecommunications Day.

332	90	3r. black, blue and yellow	25	15
333	90	9r. black, blue and mauve	50	25
334	90	14r. black, blue and brown	75	40

91 Conference Emblem

1972. United Nations Environmental Conservation Conference, Stockholm.

335	91	3r. green, brown and violet	25	15
336	91	12r. violet and green	40	25
337	91	15r. green and violet	60	40
MS338		131×100 mm. Nos. 335/7 (sold at 35r.)	2·75	2·30

92 Javan Rhinoceros

1972. Wild Animals.

339	92	3r. black, red and violet	40	15
340	-	4r. violet, bistre and purple	50	15
341	-	6r. brown, green and blue	90	35
342	-	7r. ochre, green and brown	1·30	35
343	-	8r. black, green and blue	1·50	40
344	-	10r. black, blue and green	2·00	60

DESIGNS: 4r. Mainland serow; 6r. Thamin; 7r. Banteng; 8r. Water buffalo; 10r. Gaur.

1972. Olympic Games, Munich. Nos. 164 of Cambodia and 302, 306 and 336/7 of Khmer Republic optd **XXe JEUX OLYMPIQUES MUNICH 1972**, Olympic rings and emblem.

345	83	3r. bistre and green	35	35
346	83	10r. bistre and brown	1·20	65
347	-	12r. green and brown	1·40	85
348	91	12r. violet and green	1·40	85
349	91	15r. green and violet	1·70	1·10

94 Hoisting Flag

1972. Second Anniv of Republic.

350	94	3r. multicoloured	15	10
351	94	5r. multicoloured	25	15
352	94	9r. multicoloured	60	40

1972. Red Cross Aid for War Victims. No. 164 of Cambodia and 302, 306 and 336/7 of Khmer Republic surch **SECOURS AUX VICTIMES DE GUERRE**, red cross and value.

353	83	3r.+2r. bistre and green	25	25
354	83	10r.+6r. bistre and brown	65	65
355	-	12r.+7r. green and brown	75	65
356	91	12r.+7r. violet and green	75	75
357	91	15r.+8r. green and violet	1·30	1·30

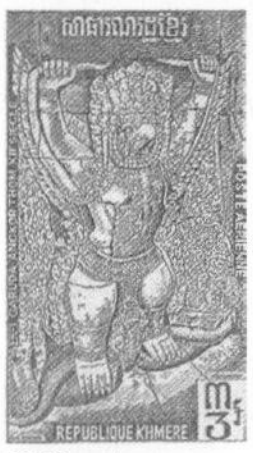

96 Garuda

1973. Air.

358	**96**	3r. red	25	15
359	**96**	30r. blue	1·80	1·00
360	**96**	50r. lilac	3·25	1·80
361	**96**	100r. green	4·50	2·75

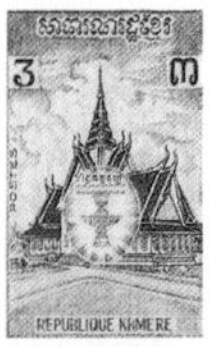

97 Crest and Temple

1973. New Constitution.

362	**97**	3r. multicoloured	15	10
363	**97**	12r. multicoloured	25	15
364	**97**	14r. multicoloured	40	35
MS365 130×100 mm. Nos. 362/4 (sold at 34r.)			1·60	1·40

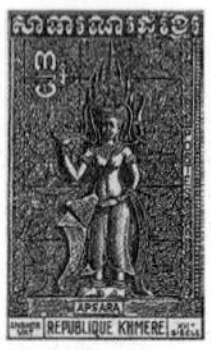

98 Apsara

1973. Angkor Sculptures.

366	**98**	3r. black	25	15
367	-	8r. blue	40	25
368	-	10r. brown	50	40
MS369 130×100 mm. Nos. 366/8 (sold at 25r.)			2·30	2·00

DESIGNS: 8r. Devata (12th century); 10f. Devata (10th century).

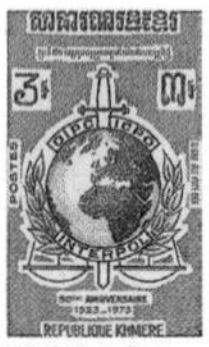

99 Interpol Emblem

1973. 50th Anniv of International Criminal Police Organization (Interpol).

370	**99**	3r. green and turquoise	25	15
371	**99**	7r. green and red	35	25
372	**99**	10r. green and brown	40	40
MS373 130×100 mm. Nos. 370/2 (sold at 30r.)			2·75	2·30

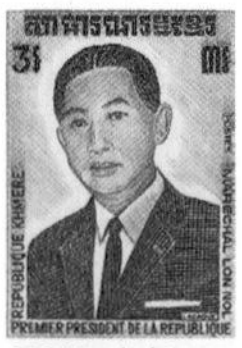

100 Marshal Lon Nol

1973. Honouring Marshal Lon Nol, First President of Republic.

374	**100**	3r. black, brown and green	15	15
375	**100**	8r. black, brown and green	25	25
376	**100**	14r. black, brown and agate	40	25
MS377 130×100 mm. Nos. 374/6 but background colours changed (sold at 50r.)			4·75	4·25

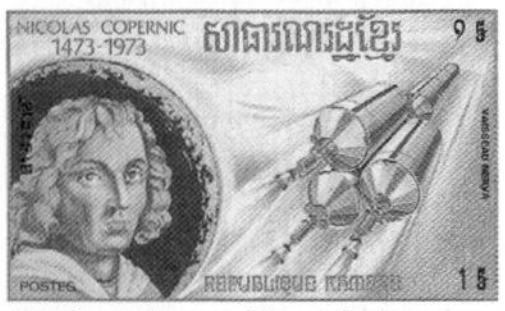

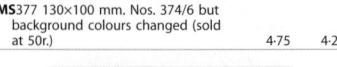

102 Copernicus and Space Rocket

1974. 500th Birth Anniv of Nicolas Copernicus (astronomer). Multicoloured.

382	1r. Type **102** (postage)	20	20
383	5r. Copernicus and "Mariner II"	20	20
384	10r. Copernicus and "Apollo"	50	25
385	25r. Copernicus and "Telstar"	1·10	55
386	50r. Copernicus and space-walker	2·00	1·00
387	100r. Copernicus and spaceship landing on Moon	4·75	2·50
388	150r. Copernicus and Moon-landing craft leaving "Apollo"	7·00	4·00
389	200r. Copernicus and "Skylab III" (air)	8·50	4·00
390	250r. Copernicus and Concorde	14·00	7·50

1974. Fourth Anniv of Republic. Various stamps optd **4E ANNIVERSAIRE DE LA REPUBLIQUE**.

391	**78**	10r. multicoloured	90	85
392	**77**	50r. on 3r. multicoloured	3·00	2·10
393	**94**	100r. on 5r. multicoloured	5·75	5·50

No. 392 is additionally optd **REPUBLIQUE KHMERE** in French and Cambodian.

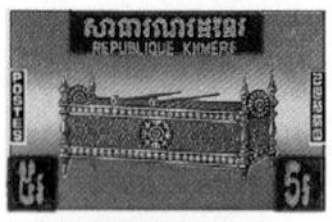

104 Xylophone

1975. Unissued stamps of Cambodia showing musical instruments, surch **REPUBLIQUE KHMERE** in French and Cambodian and new value. Multicoloured.

394	5r. on 8r. Type **104**		
395	20r. on 1r. So (two-stringed violin)		
396	160r. on 7r. Khoung vong (bronze gongs)		
397	180r. on 14r. Two drums		
398	235r. on 12r. Barrel-shaped drum		
399	500r. on 9r. Xylophone (different)		
400	1000r. on 10r. Boat-shaped xylophone		
401	2000r. on 3r. Twenty-stringed guitar on legs		

POSTAGE DUE STAMPS

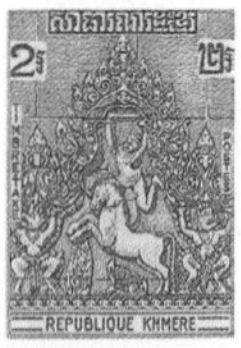

D101 Frieze, Angkor Vat

1974

D378	**D 101**	2r. brown	25	25
D379	**D 101**	6r. green	35	35
D380	**D 101**	8r. red	50	50
D381	**D 101**	10r. blue	65	75

APPENDIX

The following stamps have either been issued in excess of postal needs or have not been available to the public in reasonable quantities at face value. Such stamps may later be given full listing if there is evidence of regular postal use.

1972

Moon Landing of "Apollo 16". Embossed on gold foil. Air 900r.×2.
Visit of Pres. Nixon to China. Embossed on gold foil. Air 900r.×2.
Olympic Games, Munich. Embossed on gold foil. Air 900r.×2.

1973

Gold Medal Winners, Munich Olympics. Embossed on gold foil. Air 900r.×2.
World Cup Football Championship, West Germany (1974). Embossed on gold foil. Air 900r.×4.

1974

Pres. Kennedy and "Apollo 11". Embossed on gold foil. Air 1100r.×2.
500th Birth Anniv of Nicolas Copernicus (astronomer). Embossed on gold foil. Air 1200r.
Centenary of U.P.U. (1st issue). Postage 10, 60r.; Air 700; 1200r. embossed on gold foil.

1975

Olympic Games, Montreal (1976). Postage 5, 10, 15, 25r.; Air 50, 100, 150, 200, 250r.; 1200r. embossed on gold foil.
World Cup Football Championship, West Germany (1974). Postage 1, 5, 10, 25r.; Air 50, 100, 150, 200, 250, 1200r. embossed on gold foil.
Centenary of U.P.U. (2nd issue). Postage 15, 20, 70, 160, 180, 235r.; Air 500, 1000, 2000, 2000r. embossed on gold foil.

Pt. 19

KHOR FAKKAN

From 1965 various issues were produced for this dependency, some being overprinted on, or in the same designs as, issues for Sharjah.

APPENDIX

The following stamps have either been issued in excess of postal needs or have not been available to the public in reasonable quantities at face value. Such stamps may later be given full listing if there is evidence of regular postal use.

1965

Views. Nos. 75/80 of Sharjah optd. Air 10, 20, 30, 40, 75, 100n.p.
Boy and Girl Scouts. Nos. 74 and 89 of Sharjah optd. 2, 2r.
Birds. Nos. 101/6 of Sharjah optd. Air 30, 40, 75, 150n.p., 2, 3r.
Olympic Games, Tokyo 1964. Nos. 95/7 of Sharjah optd. 40, 50n.p., 2r.
New York World's Fair. Nos. 81/3 of Sharjah optd. Air 20, 40n.p., 1r.
Pres. Kennedy Commem. Nos. 98/100 of Sharjah optd. Air 40, 60, 100n.p.
Centenary of I.T.U. Postage 1, 2, 3, 4, 5, 50n.p., 1r., 120n.p.
Pan-Arab Games, Cairo. 50p.x5.

1966

International Co-operation Year. 50n.p.×8.
Churchill Commemoration. 2, 3, 4, 5r.
Roses. 20, 35, 60, 80n.p., 1r., 125n.p.
Fish. 1, 2, 3, 4, 5, 15, 20, 30, 40, 50, 75n.p., 1, 2, 3, 4, 5, 10r.
Int Stamp Exhibition, Washington D.C. (SIPEX). 80, 120n.p., 2r.

New Currency Surcharges in Rials and Piastres.
(a) 1965 I.T.U. Centenary issue. 10p. on 50n.p., 16p. on 120n.p., 1r. on 1r.
(b) Churchill issue. 1r. on 2r., 2r. on 3r., 3r. on 4r., 4r. on 5r.
(c) Roses issue. 1p. on 20n.p., 2p. on 35n.p., 4p. on 60n.p., 6p. on 80n.p., 10p. on 125n.p., 12p. on 1r.

New Currency Surcharges in Dirhams and Riyals.
(a) 1965 Pan-Arab Games issue. 20d. on 50p.x5.
(b) Fish issue. 1d. on 1n.p., 2d. on 2n.p., 3d. on 3n.p., 4d. on 4n.p., 5d. on 5n.p., 15d. on 15n.p., 20d. on 20n.p., 30d. on 30n.p., 40d. on 40n.p., 50d. on 50n.p., 75d. on 75n.p., 1r. on 1r., 2r. on 2r., 3r. on 3r., 4r. on 4r., 5r. on 5r., 10r. on 10r.
3rd Death Anniv of Pres. J. Kennedy. Optd on Int Stamp Exhibition, Washington issue. 80d. on 80n.p., 120d. on 120n.p., 2r. on 2r.
World Football Cup Championship, England. 1/2r.x7.

1967

Fourth Death Anniv of Pres. J. Kennedy. Optd on 1966 Int Stamp Exhibition issue. 80d. on 80n.p., 120d. on 120n.p., 2r. on 2r.

1968

Famous Paintings. Optd on Sharjah. Postage 1, 2, 3, 4, 5, 30, 40, 60, 75d.; Air 1, 2, 3, 4, 5r.
Winter Olympic Games, Grenoble. Optd on Sharjah. Postage 1, 2, 3, 4, 5d.; Air 1, 2, 3r.
Previous Olympic Games. Optd on Sharjah. Air 25, 50, 75d., 1r.50, 3, 4r.
Olympic Games, Mexico. Optd on Sharjah. 10, 20, 30d., 2, 2r.40, 5r.

1969

12th World Jamboree. Optd on 1968 issue of Sharjah. Postage 1, 2, 3, 4, 5, 10d.; Air 30, 50, 60d., 1r.50.
Martyrs of Liberty. Optd on 1968 issue of Sharjah. Air 35d.x4, 60d.x4, 1r.x4
Sportsmen and Women. Optd on 1968 issue of Sharjah. Postage 20, 30, 40, 60d., 1r.50, 2r.50; Air 35, 50d., 1, 2, 3r.25, 4, 4r.

A number of issues on gold or silver foil also exist, but it is understood that these were mainly for presentation purposes, although valid for postage.

In common with the other states of the United Arab Emirates the Khor Fakkan stamp contract was terminated on 1 August 1972, and any further new issues released after that date were unauthorised.

Pt. 17

KIAUTSCHOU (KIAOCHOW)

A port in Shantung, China, leased by Germany from China in 1898. It was occupied by Japan in 1914, but reverted to China in 1922.

1900. 100 pfennige = 1 mark.
1905. 100 cents = 1 dollar (Chinese).

1900. No. 9 of German Post Offices in China surch **5 Pfg.**

3	5pf. on 10pf. red	60·00	70·00

1901. "Yacht" key-types inscr "KIAUTSCHOU".

11	**N**	3pf. brown	2·50	2·30
12	**N**	5pf. green	2·50	2·10
13	**N**	10pf. red	3·25	2·75
14	**N**	20pf. blue	9·50	10·50
15	**N**	25pf. black and red on yellow	18·00	26·00
16	**N**	30pf. black and orange on buff	18·00	22·00
17	**N**	40pf. black and red	20·00	25·00
18	**N**	50pf. black and purple on buff	21·00	30·00
19	**N**	80pf. black and red on pink	40·00	70·00
20	**O**	1m. red	75·00	£130
21	**O**	2m. blue	£110	£140
22	**O**	3m. black	£100	£275
23	**O**	5m. red and black	£300	£850

1905. Chinese currency. "Yacht" key-types inscr "KIAUTSCHOU".

34	**N**	1c. brown	1·60	2·10
35	**N**	2c. green	1·50	1·60
36	**N**	4c. red	1·30	1·60
37	**N**	10c. blue	1·40	4·75
38	**N**	20c. black and red	3·75	21·00
39	**N**	40c. black and red on pink	4·00	70·00
40	**O**	½d. red	12·50	85·00
41	**O**	1d. blue	16·00	90·00
42	**O**	1½d. black	26·00	£275
43	**O**	2½d. red and black	65·00	£650

Pt. 1

KING EDWARD VII LAND

Stamp issued in connection with the Shackleton Antarctic Expedition in 1908. The expedition landed at Cape Royds in Victoria Land, instead of King Edward VII Land, the intended destination.

1908. Stamp of New Zealand optd **KING EDWARD VII LAND.**

A1	**42**	1d. red	£475	40·00

Pt. 9

KIONGA

Part of German E. Africa, occupied by the Portuguese during the 1914/18 war, and now incorporated in Mozambique.

1916. "King Carlos" key-type of Lourenco Marques optd **REPUBLICA** and surch **KIONGA** and new value.

1	**S**	½c. on 100r. blue on blue	17·00	13·50
2	**S**	1c. on 100r. blue on blue	17·00	13·50
3	**S**	2½c. on 100r. blue on blue	17·00	13·50
4	**S**	5c. on 100r. blue on blue	17·00	13·50

Pt. 1

KIRIBATI

This group of islands in the Pacific, formerly known as the Gilbert Islands, achieved independence on 12 July 1979 and was renamed Kiribati.

100 cents = 1 dollar.

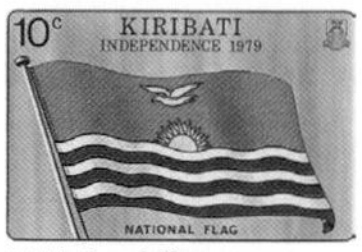

15 National Flag

1979. Independence. Multicoloured.

84	10c. Type **15**	10	35
85	45c. Houses of Parliament and Maneaba ni Maungatabu (House of Assembly)	20	65

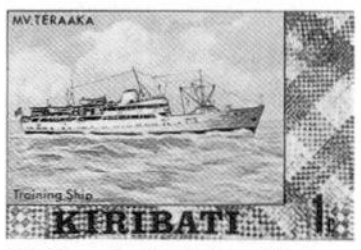

16 *Teraaka* (training ship)

1979. Multicoloured.. Multicoloured..

86	1c. Type **16**	10	90
122	3c. "Tautunu" (inter-island freighter)	15	30
123	5c. Hibiscus	10	15
124	7c. Catholic Cathedral, Tarawa	10	15
125	10c. Maneaba, Bikenibeu	10	15
91	12c. Betio Harbour	15	20
92	15c. Reef heron	35	25
93	20c. Flamboyant tree	20	25
129	25c. Moorish idol (fish)	30	30
95	30c. Frangipani	25	30
96	35c. G.I.P.C. Chapel, Tangintebu	25	30
97	50c. "Hypolimnas bolina" (butterfly)	75	55
133	$1 "Tabakea" (Tarawa Lagoon ferry)	50	75
134	$2 Evening scene	50	75
135	$5 National flag	1·00	2·00

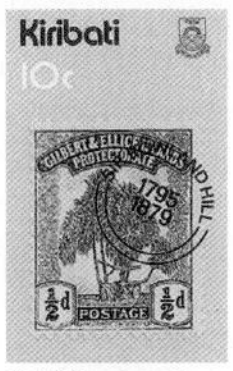

17 Gilbert and Ellice Islands 1911 ½d. Stamp

1979. Death Cent of Sir Rowland Hill. Multicoloured.

100	10c. Type **17**	10	10
101	20c. Gilbert & Ellice Islands 1956 2s.6d. definitive	15	20
102	25c. G.B. Edward VII 2s.6d.	15	20
103	45c. Gilbert and Ellice Islands 1924 10s.	25	35
MS104	113×110 mm. Nos. 100/3	70	1·00

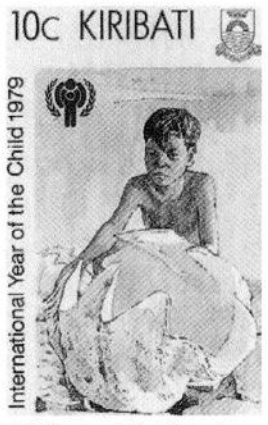

18 Boy with Giant Clam Shell

1979. International Year of the Child. Multicoloured.

105	10c. Type **18**	10	10
106	20c. Child climbing coconut palm (horiz)	10	10
107	45c. Girl reading	15	20
108	$1 Child in traditional costume	30	50

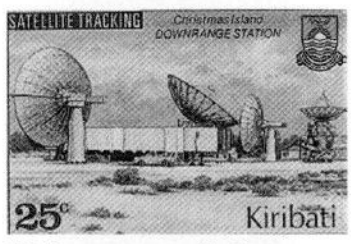

19 Downrange Station, Christmas Island

1980. Satellite Tracking. Multicoloured.

109	25c. Type **19**	10	10
110	45c. Map showing satellite trajectory	15	15
111	$1 Rocket launch, Tanegashima, Japan (vert)	30	35

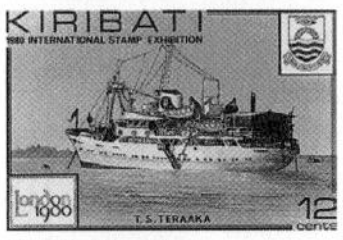

20 T.S. *Teraaka*

1980. "London 1980" Int Stamp Exhibition. Multicoloured.

112	12c. Type **20**	15	10
113	25c. Loading Air Tungaru Britten-Norman BN-2 Islander, Bonriki Airport	15	10
114	30c. Radio operator	15	10
115	$1 Bairiki Post Office	20	35
MS116	139×116 mm. Nos. 112/15	60	85

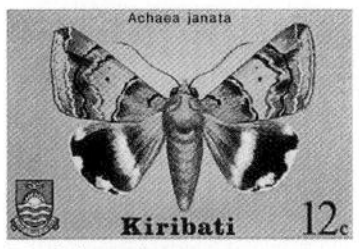

21 *Achaea janata*

1980. Moths. Multicoloured.

117	12c. Type **21**	10	10
118	25c. *Ethmia nigroapicella*	15	15
119	30c. *Utetheisa pulchelloides*	15	15
120	50c. *Anua coronata*	25	25

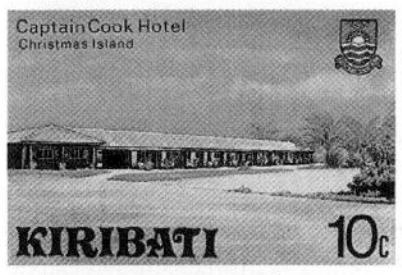

22 Captain Cook Hotel

1980. Development. Multicoloured.

136	10c. Type **22**	10	10
137	20c. Sports stadium	10	10
138	25c. International Airport, Bonriki	15	10
139	35c. National Library and Archives, Bairiki	15	10
140	$1 Otintai Hotel, Bikenibeu	20	40

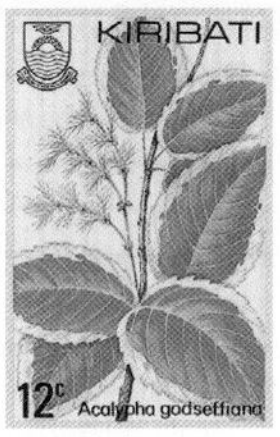

23 *Acalypha godseffiana*

1981. Flowers. Multicoloured.

141	12c. Type **23**	10	10
142	30c. *Hibiscus schizopetalus*	15	15
143	35c. *Calotropis gigantea*	15	15
144	50c. *Euphorbia pulcherrima*	20	20

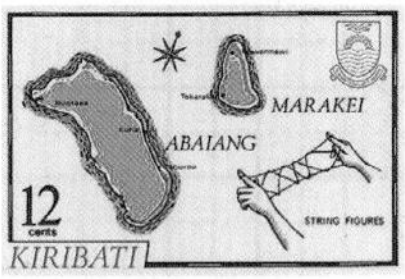

25 Maps of Abaiang and Marakei, and String Figures

1981. Islands (1st series). Multicoloured.

145	12c. Type **25**	15	10
146	30c. Maps of Little Makin and Butaritari, and village house	20	10
147	35c. Map of Maiana and coral road	25	15
148	$1 Map of Christmas Island, and Captain Cook's H.M.S. "Resolution"	70	75

See also Nos. 201/4, 215/18, 237/40, 256/60 and 270/3.

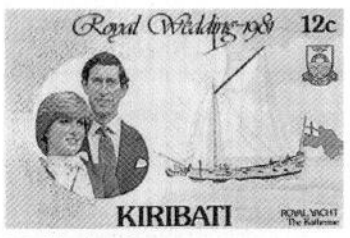

26 *Katherine*

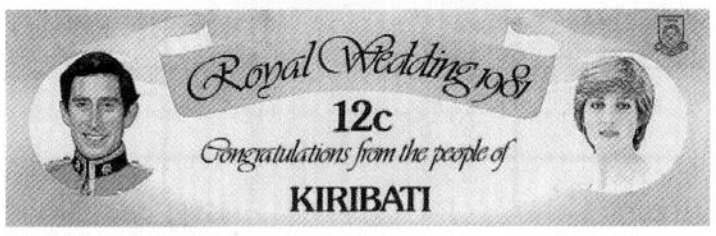

27 Prince Charles and Lady Diana Spencer (image scaled to 59% of original size)

1981. Royal Wedding. Royal Yachts. Multicoloured.

149	12c. Type **26**	10	15
150	12c. Type **27**	20	30
151	50c. *Osborne*	25	40
152	50c. Type **27**	50	75
153	$2 *Britannia*	35	80
154	$2 Type **27**	1·50	2·50
MS155	120×109 mm. $1.20 Type **27**	75	1·00

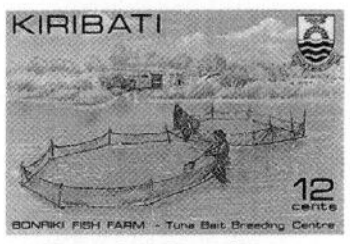

28 Tuna Bait Breeding Centre, Bonriki Fish Farm

1981. Tuna Fishing Industry. Multicoloured.

158	12c. Type **28**	15	10
159	30c. Tuna fishing	20	20
160	35c. Cold storage, Betio	20	25
161	50c. Government Tuna Fishing Vessel *Nei Manganibuka*	30	50
MS162	134×99 mm. Nos. 158/61	1·00	1·40

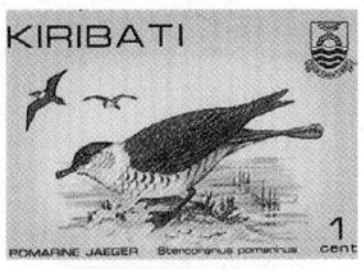

29 Pomarine Skua

1982. Birds. Multicoloured.

163	1c. Type **29**	15	15
164	2c. Mallard	15	15
165	4c. Collared petrel	20	20
166	5c. Blue-faced booby	20	20
167	7c. Friendly quail dove	20	20
168	8c. Common shoveler ("Shoveler")	20	20
169	12c. Polynesian reed warbler	20	20
170	15c. Pacific golden plover ("Pacific Plover")	25	25
171	20c. Reef heron	30	30
171a	25c. Common noddy ("Brown Noddy")	1·75	1·50
172	30c. Brown booby	30	30
173	35c. Audubon's shearwater	60	35
174	40c. White-throated storm petrel (vert)	35	40
175	50c. Bristle-thighed curlew (vert)	40	45
175a	55c. White tern ("Fairy Tern") (vert)	9·00	16·00
176	$1 Kuhl's lory ("Scarlet-breasted Lorikeet") (vert)	1·00	40
177	$2 Long-tailed koel ("Long-tailed Cuckoo") (vert)	1·00	55
178	$5 Great frigate bird (vert)	1·50	1·25

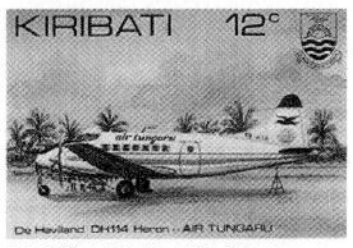

30 Riley Turbo Skyliner

1982. Air. Inaug of Tungaru Airline. Multicoloured.

179	12c. Type **30**	15	10
180	30c. Britten-Norman BN-2A Mk III "short nose" Trislander	20	20
181	35c. Casa-212 Aviocar	20	25
182	50c. Boeing 727-200	30	35

No. 179 is inscr "de Havilland DH114 Heron" in error.

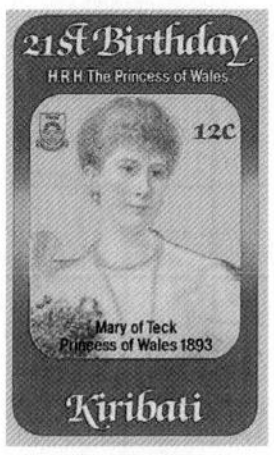

31 Mary of Teck, Princess of Wales, 1893

1982. 21st Birthday of Princess of Wales. Multicoloured.

183	12c. Type **31**	10	10
184	50c. Coat of arms of Mary of Teck	20	35
185	$1 Diana, Princess of Wales	30	70

1982. Birth of Prince William of Wales. Nos. 183/5 optd **ROYAL BABY.**

186	12c. Type **31**	10	15
187	50c. Coat of arms of Mary of Teck	25	50
188	$1 Diana, Princess of Wales	40	70

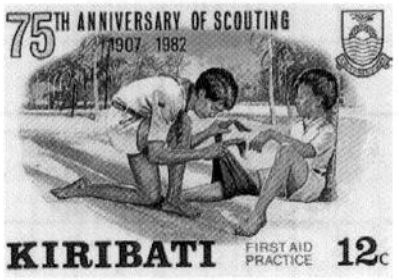

32 First Aid Practice

1982. 75th Anniv of Boy Scout Movement. Multicoloured.

189	12c. Type **32**	20	15
190	25c. Boat repairs	20	30
191	30c. On parade	25	35
192	50c. Gilbert Islands 1977 8c. Scouting stamp and "75"	25	60

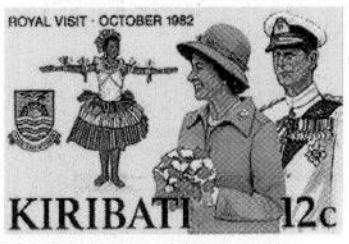

33 Queen and Duke of Edinburgh with Local Dancer

1982. Royal Visit. Multicoloured.

193	12c. Type **33**	15	15
194	25c. Queen, Duke of Edinburgh and outrigger canoe	20	20
195	35c. New Philatelic Bureau building	30	30
MS196	88×76 mm. 50c. Queen Elizabeth II	60	60

On No. **MS**196 the captions on the map for the islands of Teraina and Tabuaeran have been transposed.

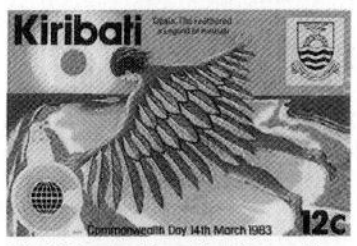

34 "Obaia, The Feathered" (Kiribati legend)

1983. Commonwealth Day. Multicoloured.

197	12c. Type **34**	10	10
198	30c. Robert Louis Stevenson Hotel, Abemama	15	10
199	50c. Container ship off Betio	15	25
200	$1 Map of Kiribati	20	50

1983. Island Maps (2nd series). As T **25**. Multicoloured.

201	12c. Beru, Nikunau and canoe	25	15
202	25c. Abemama, Aranuka, Kuria and fish	25	20
203	35c. Nonouti and reef fishing (vert)	30	35
204	50c. Tarawa and House of Assembly (vert)	30	50

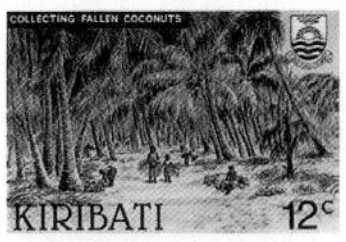

35 Collecting Coconuts

1983. Copra Industry. Multicoloured.

205	12c. Type **35**	20	15
206	25c. Selecting coconuts for copra	35	25
207	30c. Removing husks	35	30
208	35c. Drying copra	35	35
209	50c. Loading copra at Betio	40	45

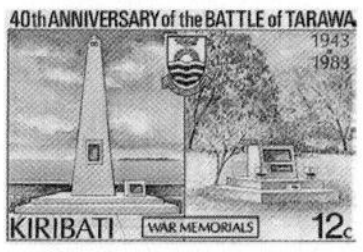

36 War Memorials

1983. 40th Anniv of Battle of Tarawa. Multicoloured.

210	12c. Type **36**	15	15
211	30c. Maps of Tarawa and Pacific Ocean	20	30
212	35c. Gun emplacement	20	35
213	50c. Modern and war-time landscapes	25	55
214	$1 Aircraft carrier U.S.S. *Tarawa*	40	75

1983. Island Maps (3rd series). As T **25**. Multicoloured.

215	12c. Teraina and Captain Fanning's ship "Betsey", 1798	25	15
216	30c. Nikumaroro and hawksbill turtle	30	35
217	35c. Kanton and local postmark	35	40
218	50c. Banaba and flying fish	40	55

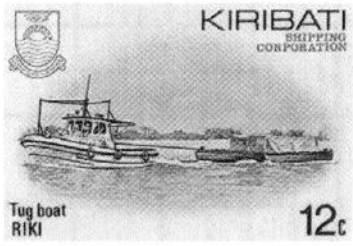

37 Tug *Riki*

1984. Kiribati Shipping Corporation. Multicoloured.

219	12c. Type **37**	40	15
220	35c. Ferry *Nei Nimanoa*	70	35
221	50c. Ferry *Nei Tebaa*	90	60
222	$1 Cargo ship *Nei Momi*	1·25	1·10
MS223	115×98 mm. Nos. 219/22	2·75	5·50

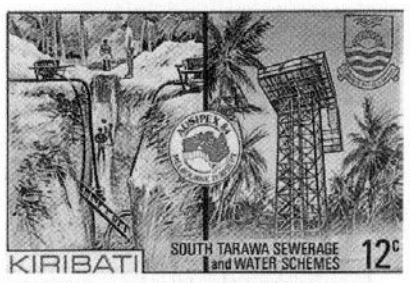

38 Water and Sewage Schemes

1984. "Ausipex" International Stamp Exhibition, Melbourne. Multicoloured.

224	12c. Type **38**	15	15
225	30c. "Nouamake" (game fishing boat)	20	30
226	35c. Overseas training schemes	20	40
227	50c. International communications link	25	55

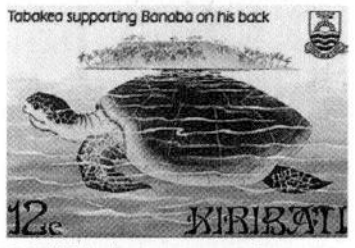

39 "Tabakea supporting Banaba"

1984. Kiribati Legends (1st series). Multicoloured.

228	12c. Type **39**	15	20
229	30c. "Nakaa, Judge of the Dead"	15	35
230	35c. "Naareau and Dragonfly"	15	45
231	50c. "Whistling Ghosts"	20	55

See also Nos. 245/8.

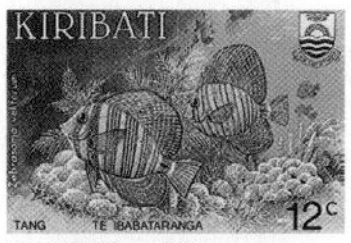

40 Sail-finned Tang

1985. Reef Fish. Multicoloured.

232	12c. Type **40**	60	25

233	25c. Picasso triggerfish	1·00	65
234	35c. Clown surgeonfish	1·25	85
235	80c. Red squirrelfish	2·00	2·50
MS236	140×107 mm. Nos. 232/5	4·75	4·75

1985. Island Maps (4th series). As T **25**. Multicoloured.

237	12c. Tabuaeran and great frigate bird ("Frigate Bird")	1·75	25
238	35c. Rawaki and germinating coconuts	2·25	40
239	50c. Arorae and xanthid crab	2·50	65
240	$1 Tamana and fish hook	3·00	1·50

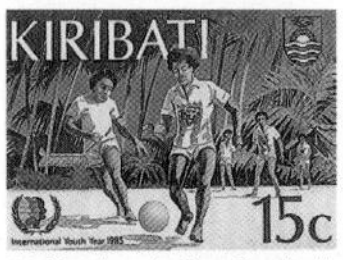

41 Youths playing Football on Beach

1985. International Youth Year. Multicoloured.

241	15c. Type **41**	70	70
242	35c. Logos of I.Y.Y. and Kiribati Youth Year	1·10	1·40
243	40c. Girl preparing food (vert)	1·25	1·60
244	55c. Map illustrating Kiribati's youth exchange links	1·40	2·25

1985. Kiribati Legends (2nd series). As T **39**. Multicoloured.

245	15c. "Nang Kineia and the Tickling Ghosts"	50	35
246	35c. "Auriaria and Tituabine"	85	90
247	40c. "The first coming of Babai at Arorae"	1·00	1·40
248	55c. "Riiki and the Milky Way"	1·25	1·90

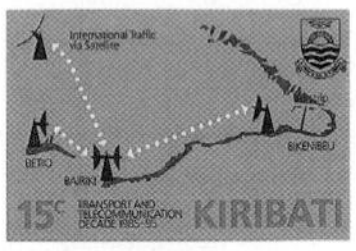

42 Map showing Telecommunications Satellite Link

1985. Transport and Telecommunications Decade (1st issue). Multicoloured.

249	15c. Type **42**	1·50	1·00
250	40c. M. V. "Moanaraoi" (Tarawa–Suva service)	2·75	3·00

See also Nos. 268/9, 293/4 and 314/15.

1986. 60th Birthday of Queen Elizabeth II. As T **230a** of Jamaica. Multicoloured.

251	15c. Princess Elizabeth in Girl Guide uniform, Windsor Castle, 1938	15	15
252	35c. At Trooping the Colour, 1980	20	30
253	40c. With Duke of Edinburgh in Kiribati, 1982	20	35
254	55c. At banquet, Austrian Embassy, London, 1966	25	50
255	$1 At Crown Agents Head Office, London, 1983	45	1·25

1986. Island Maps (5th series). As T **25**. Multicoloured.

256	15c. Manra and coconut crab	2·75	1·50
257	30c. Birnie and McKean Islands and cowrie shells	3·50	2·75
258	35c. Orona and red-footed booby	4·25	2·75
259	40c. Malden Island and whaling ship, 1844	4·25	3·75
260	55c. Vostok, Flint and Caroline Islands and Bellingshausen's "Vostok", 1820	4·25	4·25

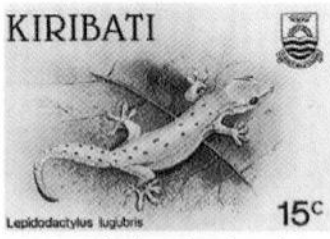

43 *Lepidodactylus lugubris*

1986. Geckos. Multicoloured.

261	15c. Type **43**	1·50	70
262	35c. *Gehyra mutilata*	1·75	1·50
263	40c. *Hemidactylus frenatus*	1·90	1·75
264	55c. *Gehyra oceanica*	2·25	2·50

See also Nos. 274/7.

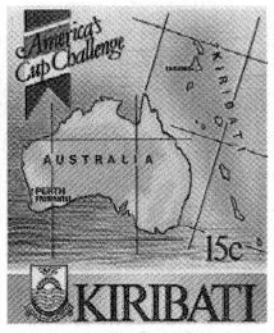

44 Maps of Australia and Kiribati

1986. America's Cup Yachting Championship. Multicoloured.

265	15c. Type **44**	20	65
266	55c. America's Cup and map of course	50	1·25
267	$1.50 *Australia II* (1983 winner)	1·00	1·50

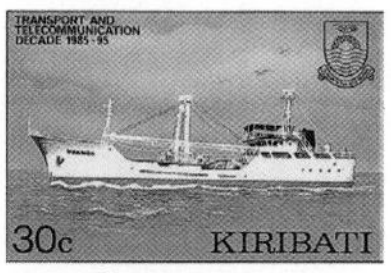

45 Freighter *Moamoa*

1987. Transport and Telecommunications Decade (2nd issue). Multicoloured.

268	30c. Type **45**	2·75	2·50
269	55c. Telephone switchboard and automatic exchange	3·75	3·50

1987. Island Maps (6th series). As T **25**. Multicoloured.

270	15c. Starbuck and red-tailed tropic bird ("Red-tailed Tropicbird"!)	60	80
271	30c. Enderbury and white tern	70	85
272	55c. Tabiteuea and pandanus tree	70	90
273	$1 Onotoa and okai (house)	80	2·50

1987. Skinks. As T **43**. Multicoloured.

274	15c. *Emoia nigra*	30	45
275	35c. *Cryptoblepharus* sp.	30	50
276	40c. *Emoia cyanura*	30	55
277	$1 *Lipinia noctua*	45	1·50
MS278	130×114 mm. Nos. 274/7	1·10	3·25

1987. Royal Ruby Wedding. Nos. 251/5 optd **40TH WEDDING ANNIVERSARY**.

279	15c. Princess Elizabeth in Girl Guide uniform, Windsor Castle, 1938	15	25
280	35c. At Trooping the Colour, 1980	20	30
281	40c. With Duke of Edinburgh in Kiribati, 1982	25	35
282	55c. At banquet, Austrian Embassy, London, 1966	30	45
283	$1 At Crown Agents Head Office, London, 1983	50	1·25

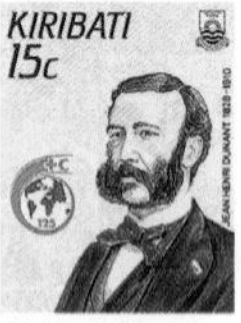

46 Henri Dunant (founder)

1988. 125th Anniv of Int Red Cross. Multicoloured.

284	15c. Type **46**	80	65
285	35c. Red Cross workers in Independence parade, 1979	1·25	1·50
286	40c. Red Cross workers with patient	1·25	1·60
287	55c. Gilbert & Ellice Islands 1970 British Red Cross Centenary 10c. stamp	1·60	1·75

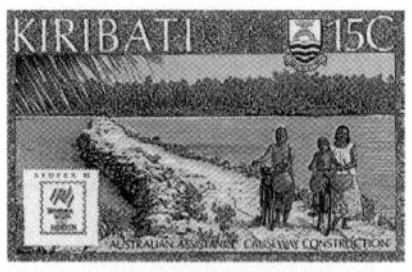

47 Causeway built by Australia

1988. Bicent of Australian Settlement and "Sydpex '88" National Stamp Exn, Sydney. Multicoloured.

288	15c. Type **47**	25	20
289	35c. Capt. Cook and Pacific map	60	60
290	$1 Obverse of Australian $10 Bicentenary banknote	1·00	1·75
291	$1 Reverse of $10 Bicentenary banknote	1·00	1·75
MS292	95×76 mm. $2 "Logistic Ace" (container ship) (37×26 mm)	4·75	5·00

No. **MS**292 also commemorates the 150th anniversary of the first screw-driven steamship.

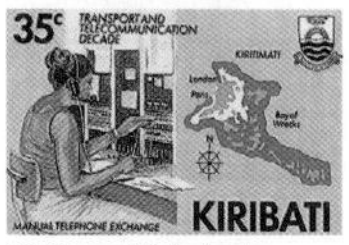

48 Manual Telephone Exchange and Map of Kiritimati

1988. Transport and Telecommunications Decade (3rd issue). Multicoloured.

293	35c. Type **48**	75	75
294	45c. Betio-Bairiki Causeway	1·00	1·00

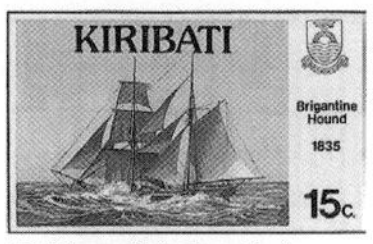

49 "Hound" (brigantine), 1835

1989. Nautical History (1st series). Multicoloured.

295	15c. Type **49**	90	55
296	30c. *Phantom* (brig), 1854	1·50	1·10
297	40c. H.M.S. *Alacrity* (schooner), 1873	1·60	1·60
298	$1 *Charles W. Morgan* (whaling ship), 1851	3·00	3·75

See also Nos. 343/7 and 523/6.

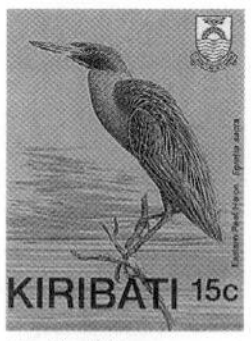

50 Reef Heron ("Eastern Reef Heron")

1989. Birds with Young. Multicoloured.

299	15c. Type **50**	1·25	1·50
300	15c. Reef heron ("Eastern Reef Heron") chicks in nest	1·25	1·50
301	$1 White-tailed tropic bird	2·50	3·25
302	$1 Young white-tailed tropic bird	2·50	3·25

Nos. 299/300 and 301/2 were each printed together, *se-tenant*, each pair forming a composite design.

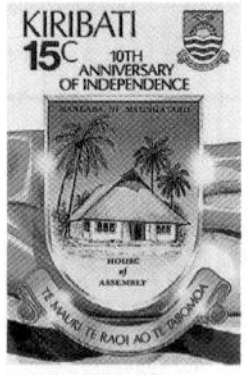

51 House of Assembly

1989. Tenth Anniv of Independence. Multicoloured.

303	15c. Type **51**	25	25
304	$1 Constitution	1·25	1·75

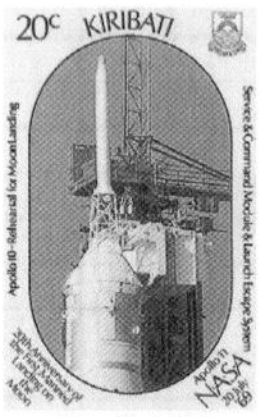

51a "Apollo 10" on Launch Gantry

1989. 20th Anniv of First Manned Landing on Moon. Multicoloured.

305	20c. Type **51a**	30	30
306	50c. Crew of "Apollo 10" (30×30 mm)	70	90
307	60c. "Apollo 10" emblem (30×30 mm)	80	1·00
308	75c. "Apollo 10" splashdown, Hawaii	95	1·25
MS309	82×100 mm. $2.50 "Apollo 11" command module in lunar orbit	6·50	7·50

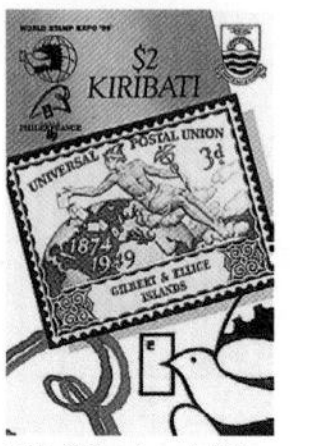

51b Gilbert and Ellice Islands, 1949 75th Anniv of U.P.U. 3d. Stamp

1989. "Philexfrance 89" International Stamp Exhibition, Paris, and "World Stamp Expo '89", Washington (1st issue). Sheet 104×86 mm.

MS310	**51b** $2 multicoloured	3·50	5·00

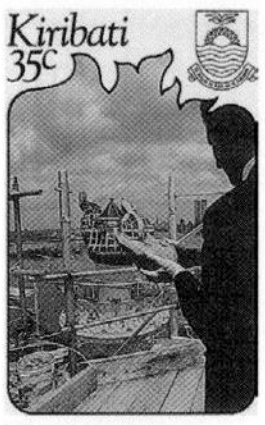

51c Examining Fragment of Statue

1989. "Philexfrance 89" International Stamp Exhibition, Paris, and "World Stamp Expo '89", Washington (2nd issue). Designs showing Statue of Liberty. Multicoloured.

311	35c. Type **51c**	1·10	1·40
312	35c. Workman drilling Statue	1·10	1·40
313	35c. Surveyor with drawing	1·10	1·40

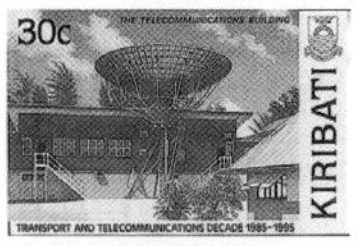

52 Telecommunications Centre

1989. Transport and Telecommunications Decade (4th issue). Multicoloured.

314	30c. Type **52**	1·50	1·25
315	75c. *Mataburo* (inter-island freighter)	4·00	4·25

1989. "Melbourne Stampshow '89". Nos. 301/2 optd with Exhibition emblem showing tram.

316	$1 White-tailed tropic bird	3·00	3·50
317	$1 Young white-tailed tropic bird	3·00	3·50

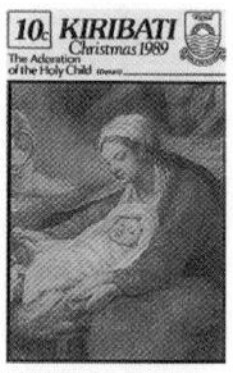

54 Virgin and Child (detail, *The Adoration of the Holy Child* (Denys Calvert))

1989. Christmas. Paintings. Multicoloured.

318	10c. Type **54**	1·00	55
319	15c. *The Adoration of the Holy Child* (Denys Calvert)	1·25	70
320	55c. *The Holy Family and St. Elizabeth* (Rubens)	3·00	1·25
321	$1 *Madonna with Child and Maria Magdalena* (School of Correggio)	4·50	7·00

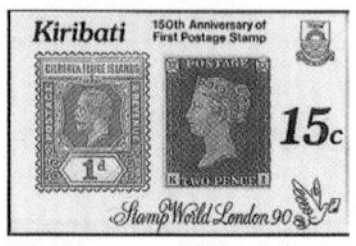

55 Gilbert and Ellice Islands 1912 1d. and G.B. Twopence Blue Stamps

1990. 150th Anniv of the Penny Black and "Stamp World London 90" International Stamp Exhibition. Multicoloured.

322	15c. Type **55**	1·00	1·00
323	50c. Gilbert and Ellice Islands 1911 ½d. and G.B. Penny Black	2·50	2·75
324	60c. Kiribati 1982 1c. bird and G.B. 1870 ½d.	2·50	2·75
325	$1 Gilbert Islands 1976 1c. ship and G.B. 1841 1d. brown	2·75	3·50

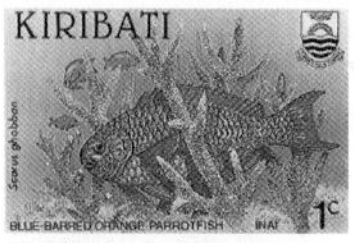

56 Blue-barred Orange Parrotfish

1990. Fish. Multicoloured.

326	1c. Type **56**	30	75
327	5c. Honeycomb grouper	45	75
328	10c. Blue-finned trevally	55	85
329	15c. Hump-backed snapper	70	50
330	20c. Variegated emperor	75	70
356	23c. Bennett's pufferfish	1·00	1·00
331	25c. Rainbow runner	80	65
332	30c. Black-saddled coral grouper	90	65
333	35c. Great barracuda	1·00	75
334	40c. Convict tang	1·00	80
335	50c. Violet squirrelfish	1·25	90

336	60c. Stocky hawkfish	1·75	1·40
337	75c. Pennant coralfish	1·90	1·60
338	$1 Common blue-striped snapper ("Yellow and blue sea perch")	2·25	1·90
339	$2 Sailfish	3·25	4·75
340	$5 White-tipped reef shark	6·50	10·00

1990. 90th Birthday of Queen Elizabeth the Queen Mother. As T **107** (75c.) or **108** ($2) of Kenya.

341	75c. multicoloured	1·25	1·50
342	$2 black and green	2·75	3·50

DESIGNS—21×36 mm: 75c. Queen Elizabeth the Queen Mother. 29×37 mm: $2 King George VI and Queen Elizabeth with air raid victim, London, 1940.

1990. Nautical History (2nd series). As T **49**. Multicoloured.

343	15c. *Herald* (whaling ship), 1851	1·00	70
344	50c. *Belle* (barque), 1849	1·75	1·75
345	60c. *Supply* (schooner), 1851	2·00	2·50
346	75c. *Triton* (whaling ship), 1848	2·00	2·50
MS347	95×75 mm. $2 *Charlotte* (convict transport), 1789	7·50	8·50

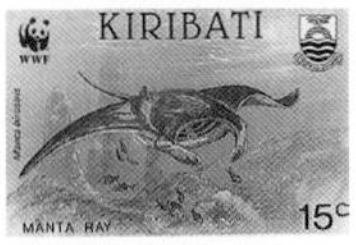

57 Manta

1991. Endangered Species. Fish. Multicoloured.

348	15c. Type **57**	1·10	55
349	20c. Manta (different)	1·25	90
350	30c. Whale shark	1·75	2·00
351	35c. Whale shark (different)	2·00	2·25

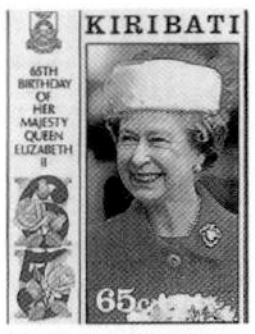

58 Queen Elizabeth II

1991. 65th Birthday of Queen Elizabeth II and 70th Birthday of Prince Philip. Multicoloured.

366	65c. Type **58**	1·25	1·50
367	70c. Prince Philip in R.A.F. uniform	1·25	1·50

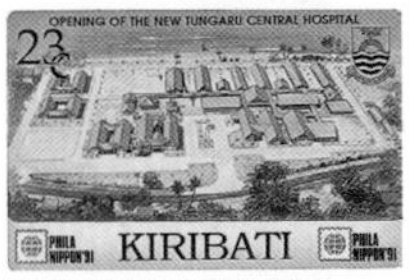

59 Aerial View of Hospital

1991. "Phila Nippon '91" International Stamp Exhibition, Tokyo, and Opening of Tungaru Central Hospital. Multicoloured.

368	23c. Type **59**	40	30
369	50c. Traditional dancers	75	85
370	60c. Hospital entrance	85	1·10
371	75c. Foundation stone and plaques	1·25	1·60
MS372	125×83 mm. $5 Casualty on trolley and ambulance	7·00	8·00

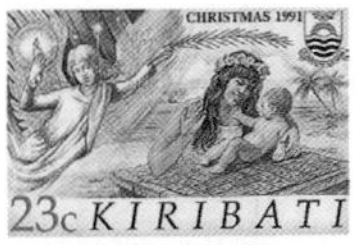

60 Mother and Child

1991. Christmas. Multicoloured.

373	23c. Type **60**	60	40
374	50c. The Holy Family in Pacific setting	1·10	90
375	60c. The Holy Family in traditional setting	1·25	1·50
376	75c. Adoration of the Shepherds	1·50	2·00

1992. 40th Anniv of Queen Elizabeth II's Accession. As T **214** of Lesotho. Multicoloured.

377	23c. Kiribati village	30	30
378	30c. Lagoon at sunset	40	45
379	50c. Tarawa waterfront	60	70
380	60c. Three portraits of Queen Elizabeth	70	90
381	75c. Queen Elizabeth II	90	1·10

1992. "EXPO '92" World's Fair, Seville. Nos. 356, 336/7 and 339 optd **EXPO'92 SEVILLA**.

382	23c. Bennett's pufferfish	55	40
383	60c. Stocky hawkfish	1·25	1·50
384	75c. Pennant coralfish	1·40	1·60
385	$2 Sailfish	3·00	4·00

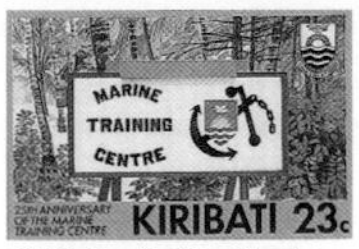

62 Marine Training Centre Sign

1992. 25th Anniv of Marine Training Centre. Multicoloured.

386	23c. Type **62**	45	40
387	50c. Cadets on parade	80	1·00
388	60c. Fire school	80	1·00
389	75c. Lifeboat training	1·10	1·40

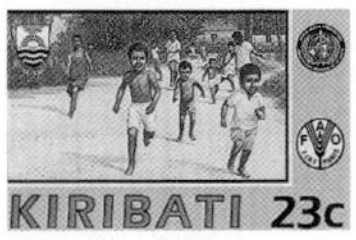

63 Healthy Children

1992. United Nations World Health and Food and Agriculture Organizations. Multicoloured.

390	23c. Type **63**	55	50
391	50c. Fishing at night	1·00	1·00
392	60c. Fruit	1·25	1·50
393	75c. "Papuan Chief" (container ship)	2·50	2·50

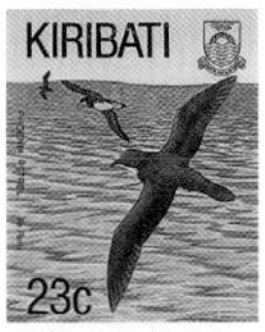

64 Phoenix Petrel

1993. Birds. Multicoloured.

394	23c. Type **64**	40	70
395	23c. Cook's petrel	40	70
396	60c. Pintail ("Northern Pintail")	90	1·25
397	60c. European wigeon ("Eurasian Wigeon")	90	1·25
398	75c. Spectacled tern	1·00	1·25
399	75c. Black-naped tern	1·00	1·25
400	$1 Australian stilt ("Stilt Wader")	1·25	1·40
401	$1 Wandering tattler	1·25	1·40

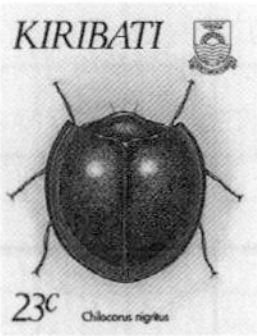

65 *Chilocorus nigritus*

1993. Insects. Multicoloured.

402	23c. Type **65**	1·25	55
403	60c. *Rodolia pumila* (ladybird)	2·25	2·25
404	75c. *Rodolia cardinalis* (ladybird)	2·50	2·75
405	$1 *Cryptolaemus montrouzieri*	2·75	3·25

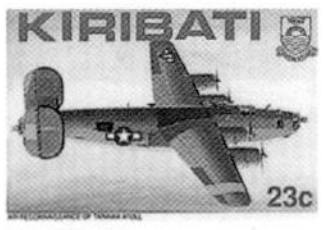

66 U.S. Air Reconnaissance Consolidated B-24 Liberator

1993. 50th Anniv of Battle of Tarawa. Multicoloured.

406	23c. Type **66**	75	75
407	23c. U.S.S. "Nautilus" (submarine)	75	75
408	23c. U.S.S. *Indianapolis* (cruiser)	75	75
409	23c. U.S.S. *Pursuit* (destroyer)	75	75
410	23c. Vought Sikorsky OS2U Kingfisher spotter seaplane	75	75
411	23c. U.S.S. *Ringgold* and *Dashiell* (destroyers)	75	75
412	23c. Sherman tank on seabed	75	75
413	23c. Grumman F6F Hellcat fighter aircraft in lagoon	75	75
414	23c. Naval wreck on seabed	75	75
415	23c. First U.S. aircraft to land on Betio	75	75
416	75c. Landing craft leaving transports	1·25	1·25
417	75c. Marines landing on Betio	1·25	1·25
418	75c. Landing craft approaching beach	1·25	1·25
419	75c. Marines pinned down in surf	1·25	1·25
420	75c. U.S.S. *Maryland* (battleship)	1·25	1·25
421	75c. Aerial view of Betio Island	1·25	1·25
422	75c. U.S. Navy memorial	1·25	1·25
423	75c. Memorial to expatriates	1·25	1·25
424	75c. Japanese memorial	1·25	1·25
425	75c. Plan of Betio Island	1·25	1·25

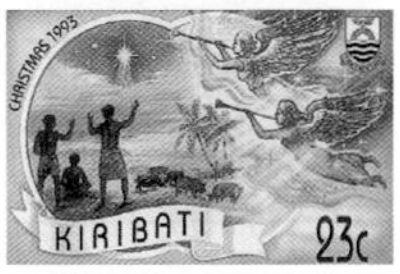

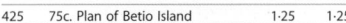

67 Shepherds and Angels

1993. Christmas. Pacific Nativity Scenes. Multicoloured.

426	23c. Type **67**	40	30
427	40c. Three Kings	65	70
428	60c. Holy Family	85	1·25
429	75c. Virgin and Child	1·10	1·50
MS430	100×81 mm. $3 Virgin and Child (different)	3·75	5·50

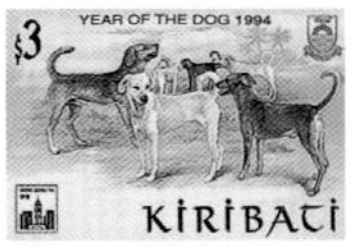

68 Group of Dogs

1994. "Hong Kong '94" International Stamp Exhibition. Chinese New Year ("Year of the Dog"). Sheet 120×90 mm.

MS431	**68** $3 multicoloured	4·00	5·50

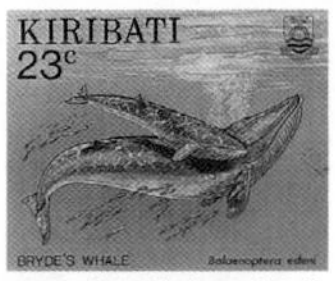

69 Bryde's Whale and Calf

1994. Whales. Multicoloured.

432	23c. Type **69**	1·00	1·25
433	23c. Bryde's whale with two calves	1·00	1·25
434	40c. Blue whale and calf (face value at left)	1·25	1·40
435	40c. Blue whales and calf (face value at right)	1·25	1·40
436	60c. Humpback whale and calf (face value at left)	1·90	2·25
437	60c. Humpback whale and calf (face value at right)	1·90	2·25
438	75c. Killer whale and calf	1·90	2·25
439	75c. Killer whale and two calves	1·90	2·25

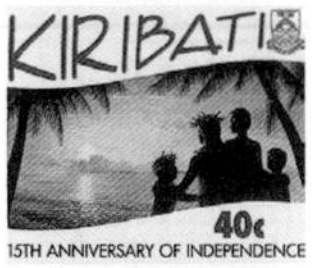

70 Family silhouetted on Beach

1994. 15th Anniv of Independence. Protecting the Environment. Multicoloured.

440	40c. Type **70**	60	60
441	60c. Fish and coral	1·00	1·25
442	75c. Great frigate birds in flight	1·25	1·50

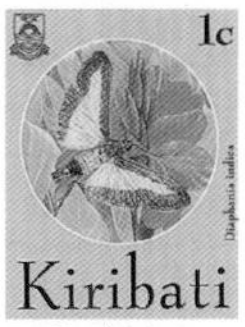

71 *Diaphania indica*

1994. Butterflies and Moths. Multicoloured.

443	1c. Type **71**	10	15
444	5c. *Herpetogramma licarsisalis*	15	20
445	10c. *Parotis suralis*	25	20
446	12c. *Sufetula sunidesalis*	25	20
447	20c. *Aedia sericea*	35	25
448	23c. *Anomis vitiensis*	35	25
449	30c. *Anticarsia irrorata*	45	30
450	35c. *Spodoptera litura*	55	40
451	40c. *Mocis frugalis*	65	50
452	45c. *Agrius convolvuli*	70	50
453	50c. *Cephonodes picus*	75	55
454	55c. *Gnathothlibus erotus*	80	60
455	60c. *Macroglossum hirundo*	80	60
456	75c. *Badamia exclamationis*	1·00	75
457	$1 *Precis villida*	1·40	1·40
458	$2 *Danaus plexippus*	2·25	2·50
459	$3 *Hypolimnas bolina* (male)	2·75	3·25
460	$5 *Hypolimnas bolina* (female)	3·75	4·50

See also No. **MS**527.

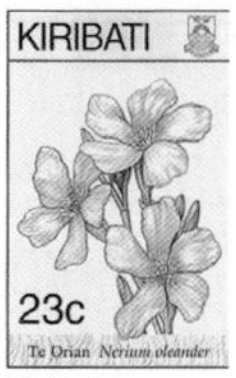

72 *Nerium oleander*

1994. Seasonal Flowers. Multicoloured.

461	23c. Type **72**	30	30
462	60c. *Catharanthus roseus*	80	1·25
463	75c. *Ipomea pes-caprae*	1·00	1·40
464	$1 *Calophyllum inophyllum*	1·40	2·00

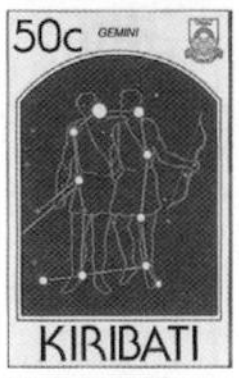

73 Gemini (The Twins)

1995. Night Sky over Kiribati. Multicoloured.

465	50c. Type **73**	75	75
466	60c. Cancer (The Crab)	85	1·00
467	75c. Cassiopeia (The Queen of Ethiopia)	1·00	1·40
468	$1 Southern Cross	1·25	1·75

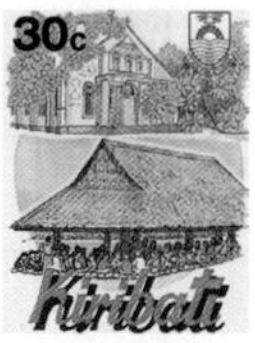

74 Church and Traditional Meeting Hut

1995. Tourism. Multicoloured.

469	30c. Type **74**	85	95
470	30c. Fishermen and outrigger canoes	85	95
471	30c. Gun emplacement and map	85	95
472	30c. Children with marine creatures	85	95
473	30c. Sports	85	95
474	40c. Local girls in traditional costume	85	95
475	40c. Windsurfing	85	95
476	40c. Fishermen and wood carver	85	95
477	40c. Underwater sport	85	95
478	40c. Women weaving	85	95

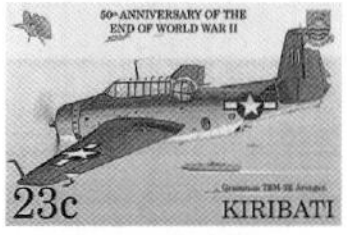

75 Grumman TBF Avenger

1995. 50th Anniv of End of Second World War. American Aircraft. Multicoloured.

489	23c. Type **75**	60	45
490	40c. Curtiss SOC.3-1 Seagull seaplane	80	70
491	50c. Consolidated B-24 Liberator bomber	90	90
492	60c. Grumman G-21 Goose amphibian	1·10	1·10
493	75c. Martin B-26 Marauder bomber	1·40	1·50
494	$1 Northrop P-61 Black Widow bomber	1·60	1·75
MS495	75×85 mm. $2 Reverse of 1939–45 War Medal (vert)	2·50	3·00

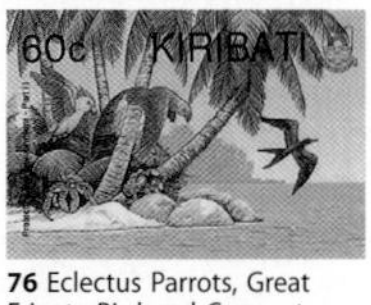

76 Eclectus Parrots, Great Frigate Bird and Coconut Crabs

1995. Protecting the Environment. Multicoloured.

496	60c. Type **76**	85	1·10
497	60c. Red-tailed tropic birds, common dolphin and pantropical spotted dolphin	85	1·10
498	60c. Blue-striped snapper ("Yellow and blue sea perch"), blue-barred orange parrotfish and green turtle	85	1·10

499	60c. Red-breasted wrasse, pennant coralfish and violet squirrelfish	85	1·10

1995. "Jakarta '95" Stamp Exhibition, Indonesia. Nos. 496/9 optd **JAKARTA 95** within emblem.

500	60c. Type **76**	2·00	2·25
501	60c. Red-tailed tropic birds, common dolphin and pan-tropical spotted dolphin	2·00	2·25
502	60c. Blue-striped snapper, blue-barred orange parrotfish and green turtle	2·00	2·25
503	60c. Red-breasted wrasse, pennant coralfish and violet squirrelfish	2·00	2·25

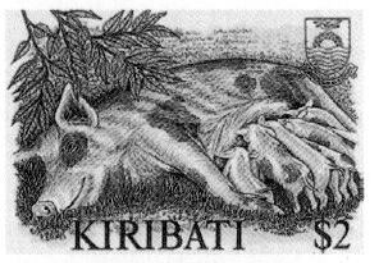

78 Sow feeding Piglets

1995. "Singapore '95" International Stamp Exhibition and Beijing International Coin and Stamp Expo '95. Two sheets, each 113×85 mm, containing T **78**.

MS504	$2 multicoloured ("Singapore '95")	2·50	3·25
MS505	$2 multicoloured ("Beijing '95")	3·00	3·75

Nos. **MS**504/5 show the exhibition logos on the sheet margins.

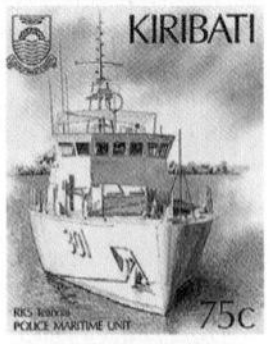

79 *Teanoai* (police patrol boat)

1995. Police Maritime Unit. Multicoloured.

506	75c. Type **79**	1·40	1·75
507	75c. *Teanoai* at sea	1·40	1·75

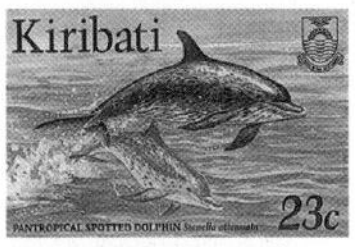

80 Pantropical Spotted Dolphins

1996. Dolphins. Multicoloured.

508	23c. Type **80**	1·00	55
509	60c. Spinner dolphins	1·75	1·25
510	75c. Fraser's dolphins	1·90	1·75
511	$1 Rough-toothed dolphins	2·00	2·25

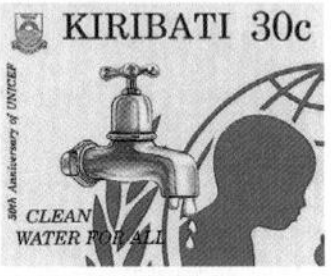

81 Tap and Top Left Segment of UNICEF Emblem

1996. 50th Anniv of UNICEF. Multicoloured.

512	30c. Type **81**	50	70
513	30c. Documents and top right segment	50	70
514	30c. Syringe and bottom left segment	50	70
515	30c. Open book and bottom right segment	50	70

Nos. 512/15 were printed together, *se-tenant*, with each block of 4 showing the complete emblem.

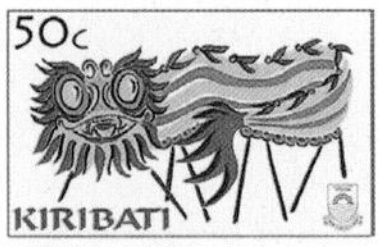

82 Chinese Dragon

1996. "CHINA '96" Ninth Asian International Stamp Exhibition, Peking. Sheet 110×86 mm.

MS516	**82** 50c. multicoloured	1·00	1·50

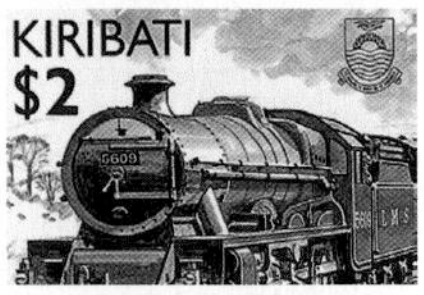

83 L.M.S. No. 5609 *Gilbert and Ellice Islands* Locomotive

1996. "CAPEX '96" International Stamp Exhibition, Toronto. Sheet 111×80 mm.

MS517	**83** $2 multicoloured	2·40	3·00

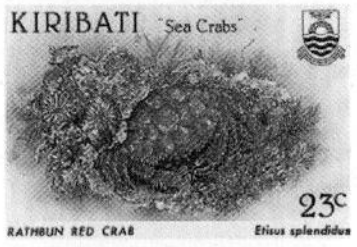

84 Rathbun Red Crab

1996. Sea Crabs. Multicoloured.

518	23c. Type **84**	50	40
519	60c. Red and white painted crab	90	80
520	75c. Red-spotted crab	1·10	1·10
521	$1 Red-spotted white crab	1·60	2·50

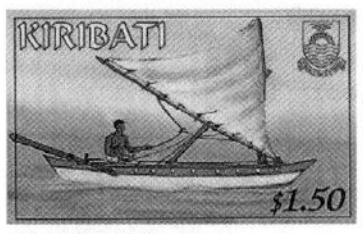

85 Kiribati Canoe

1996. "Taipei '96" International Stamp Exhibition, Taiwan. Sheet 110×86 mm.

MS522	**85** $1.50 multicoloured	3·00	3·50

1996. Nautical History (3rd series). As T **49**. Multicoloured.

523	23c. *Potomac* (whaling ship), 1843	60	40
524	50c. *Southern Cross IV* (missionary ship), 1891	90	90
525	60c. *John Williams III* (missionary sailing ship), 1890	1·10	1·10
526	$1 H.M.S. *Dolphin* (frigate), 1765	1·60	2·00

1997. "HONG KONG '97" International Stamp Exhibition. Sheet 130×90 mm, containing No. 457. Multicoloured.

MS527	$1 *Precis villida*	1·10	1·60

1997. "Pacific '97" International Stamp Exhibition, San Francisco. Nos. 489/94 optd **PACIFIC 97 World Philatelic Exhibition San Francisco, California 29 May - 8 June**.

528	23c. Type **75**	40	35
529	40c. Curtiss SOC.3-1 Seagull seaplane	60	55
530	50c. Consolidated B-24 Liberator bomber	70	70
531	60c. Grumman G-21 Goose amphibian	80	90
532	75c. Martin B-26 Marauder bomber	90	1·10
533	$1 Northrop P-61 Black Widow bomber	1·10	1·40
MS534	75×85 mm. $2 Reverse of 1939–45 War Medal (vert)	2·10	2·75

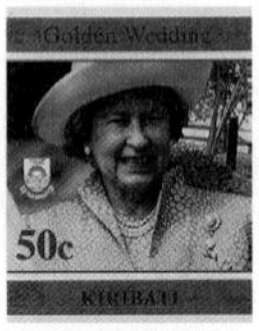

87 Queen Elizabeth II in 1996

1997. Golden Wedding of Queen Elizabeth and Prince Philip. Multicoloured.

535	50c. Type **87**	1·25	1·50
536	50c. Prince Philip carriage-driving at Windsor Horse Show	1·25	1·50
537	60c. Queen in phaeton at Trooping the Colour	1·25	1·50
538	60c. Prince Philip on Montserrat, 1993	1·25	1·50
539	75c. Queen Elizabeth and Prince Philip, 1989	1·25	1·50
540	75c. Prince Edward on horseback	1·25	1·50
MS541	110×70 mm. $2 Queen Elizabeth and Prince Philip in Landau (horiz)	4·00	4·50

Nos. 535/6, 537/8 and 539/40 respectively were printed together, *se-tenant*, with the backgrounds forming composite designs.

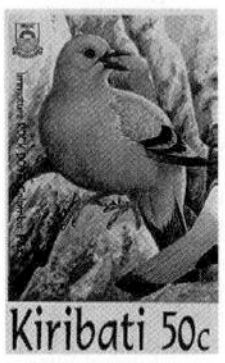

88 Young Rock Dove

1997. Birds. Multicoloured.

542	50c. Type **88**	1·00	1·25
543	50c. Adult rock dove	1·00	1·25
544	60c. Adult Pacific pigeon	1·00	1·25
545	60c. Young Pacific pigeon	1·00	1·25
546	75c. Adult Micronesian pigeon	1·00	1·25
547	75c. Young Micronesian pigeon	1·00	1·25

1997. "ASIA '97" Stamp Exhibition, Bangkok. Nos. 542/3 and 546/7 optd **ASIA '97 KIRIBATI 5 - 14 OCTOBER** and elephant.

548	50c. Type **88**	85	1·25
549	50c. Adult rock dove	85	1·25
550	75c. Adult Micronesian pigeon	1·00	1·40
551	75c. Young Micronesian pigeon	1·00	1·40

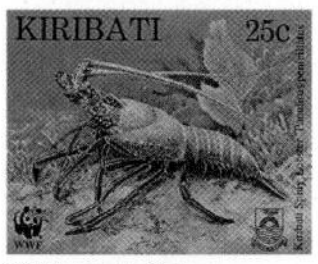

90 Spiny Lobster

1998. Endangered Species. Spiny Lobster. Multicoloured.

552	25c. Type **90**	40	60
553	25c. Facing right	40	60
554	25c. With coral in foreground	40	60
555	25c. On sponge	40	60
MS556	69×49 mm. $1.50 Spiny Lobster	1·90	2·50

No. **MS**556 does not show the W.W.F. panda emblem.

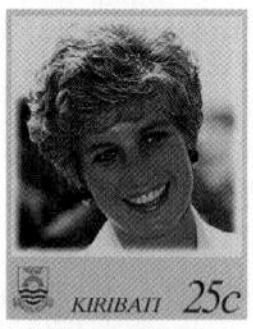

91 Diana, Princess of Wales, 1992

1998. Diana, Princess of Wales Commemoration.

557	**91** 25c. multicoloured	50	60
MS558	145×70 mm. 25c. Type **91**; 50c. Wearing black evening dress, 1981; 60c. With scarf over head, 1992; 75c. Wearing brown jacket, 1993 (sold at $2.10 + 50c. charity premium)	2·00	3·00

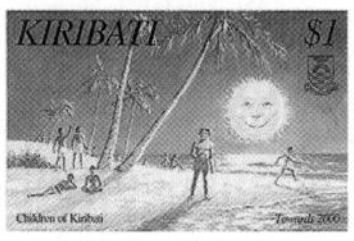

92 Children and Smiling Sun

1998. "Towards the Millennium" (1st issue). Sheet 102×69 mm.

MS559	**92** $1 multicoloured	1·25	2·00

See also Nos. 580/4 and 594/8.

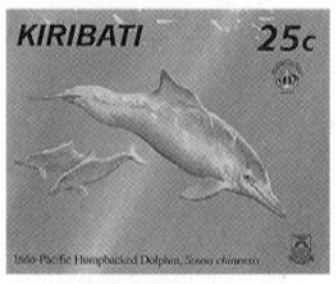

93 Indo-Pacific Humpbacked Dolphin

1998. Whales and Dolphins. Multicoloured.

560	25c. Type **93**	55	65
561	25c. Bottlenose dolphin	55	65
562	60c. Short-snouted spinner dolphin	80	1·00
563	60c. Risso's dolphin	80	1·00
564	75c. Striped dolphin	1·00	1·10
565	75c. Sei whale	1·00	1·10
566	$1 Fin whale	1·25	1·40
567	$1 Minke whale	1·25	1·40

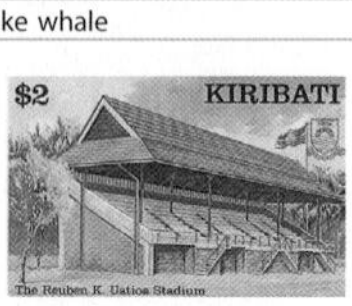

94 Reuben K. Uatioa Stadium, Kiribati

1998. "Italia '98" International Stamp Exhibition, Milan. Sheet 110×85 mm.

MS568	**94** $2 multicoloured	2·00	2·75

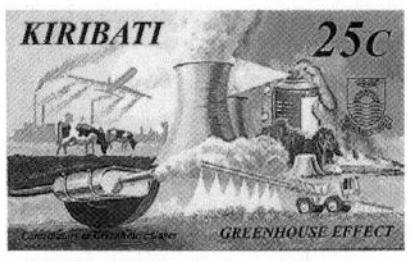

95 Pollutants and Harmful Emissions

1998. The Greenhouse Effect. Multicoloured.

569	25c. Type **95**	30	30
570	50c. Diagram of greenhouse effect	50	50
571	60c. Diagram of rising sea levels on Tarawa	60	65
572	75c. Diagram of rising sea levels on Kiritimati	70	85
MS573	103×69 mm. $1.50 Outrigger canoe	3·50	3·50

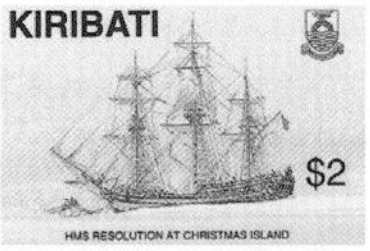

96 H.M.S. *Resolution* (Cook) at Christmas Island, 1777

1999. "Australia '99" World Stamp Exhibition, Melbourne. Sheet 136×56 mm.

MS574	**96** $2 multicoloured	2·25	2·75

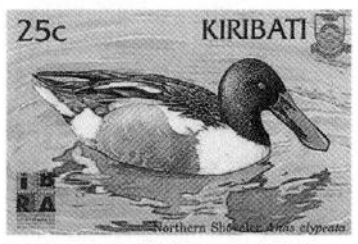

97 Northern Shoveler (male)

1999. "iBRA '99" International Stamp Exhibition, Nuremberg. Ducks. Multicoloured.

575	25c. Type **97**	60	50
576	50c. Northern Shoveler (female) and ducklings	75	65
577	60c. Green-winged teal (male)	80	80
578	75c. Green-winged teal (female) and ducklings	90	1·00
MS579	100×70 mm. $3 Green-winged teal (male) and duckling	3·25	4·25

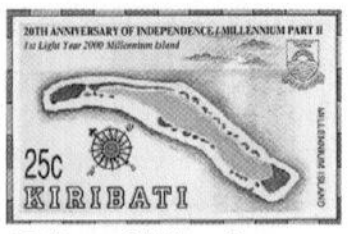

98 Map of Millennium Island

1999. "Towards the Millennium" (2nd issue). 20th Anniv of Independence. Multicoloured.

580	25c. Type **98**	1·00	80
581	60c. Map of Kiribati	1·50	1·25
582	75c. Map of Nikumaroro	1·50	1·25
583	$1 Amelia Earhart (aviator) and Lockheed Model 10 Electra	2·00	2·00
MS584	100×80 mm. Nos. 582/3	2·75	3·50

No. 581 shows Tarawa as "TAROWA" in error.
See also Nos. 594/8.

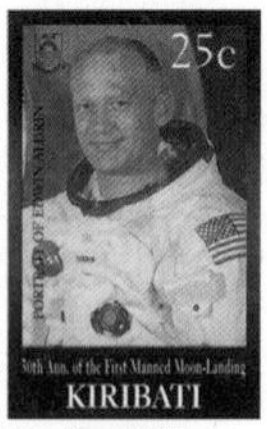

98a Buzz Aldrin (astronaut)

1999. 30th Anniv of First Manned Landing on Moon. Multicoloured.

585	25c. Type **98a**	35	35
586	60c. Service module docking with lunar module	65	75
587	75c. "Apollo 11" on Moon's surface	75	85
588	$1 Command module separating from service section	95	1·10
MS589	90×80 mm. $2 Kiribati as seen from Moon (circular, 40 mm diam)	1·90	2·50

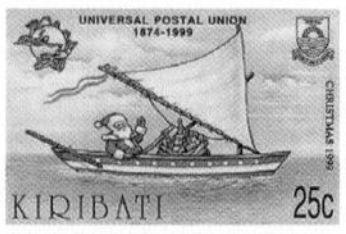

99 Santa Claus in Sailing Canoe

1999. Christmas and 125th Anniv of Universal Postal Union. Multicoloured.

590	25c. Type **99**	35	35
591	60c. Santa and unloading freighter	65	65
592	75c. Santa in sleigh passing aircraft	80	90
593	$1 Santa using computer	1·00	1·50

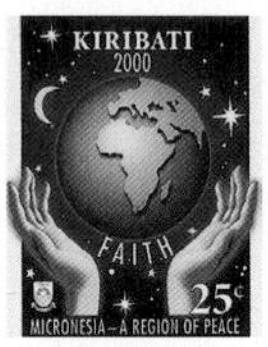

100 Open Hands around Globe ("FAITH")

2000. "Towards the Millennium" (3rd issue). "A Region of Peace". Multicoloured.

594	25c. Type **100**	30	40

595	40c. Solar eclipse ("HARMONY")	45	60
596	60c. Stars and Sun over Earth ("HOPE")	60	80
597	75c. Sun over Earth ("ENLIGHTENMENT")	75	1·00
598	$1 Dove over Earth ("PEACE")	90	1·25

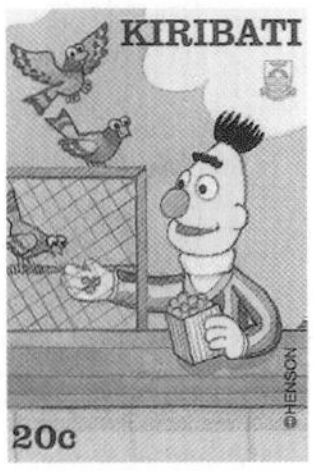

101 Bert feeding Pigeons

2000. *Sesame Street* (children's T.V. programme). Multicoloured.

599	20c. Type **101**	20	30
600	20c. Little Bear flying kite	20	30
601	20c. Grover calling	20	30
602	20c. Elmo and Cookie Monster	20	30
603	20c. Telly leaning out of window	20	30
604	20c. Zoe painting house	20	30
605	20c. Ernie with bird	20	30
606	20c. Big Bird and Rosita reading	20	30
607	20c. Oscar the Grouch and Slimey in dustbin	20	30
MS608	139×86 mm. $1.50 Grover as postman	1·40	1·75

Nos. 599/607 were printed together, *se-tenant*, with the backgrounds forming a composite design.

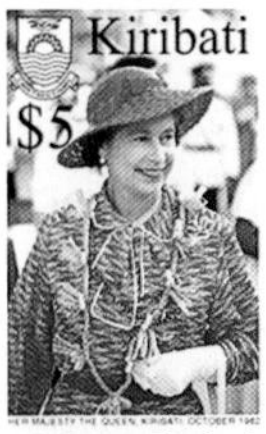

102 Queen Elizabeth II in Kiribati, 1982

2000. "The Stamp Show 2000" International Stamp Exhibition, London. Sheet 80×70 mm.

MS609	**102** $5 multicoloured	4·25	5·50

2000. "EXPO 2000" World's Fair, Hanover. Nos. 444/5, 447, 457 and 459 optd **KIRIBATI AT EXPO 2000 1.06-31.10.2000.**

610	5c. *Herpetogramma licarsisalis*	15	25
611	10c. *Parotis suralis*	15	25
612	20c. *Aedia sericea*	25	30
613	$1 *Precis villida*	1·00	1·25
614	$3 *Hypolimnas bolina* (male)	2·75	3·25

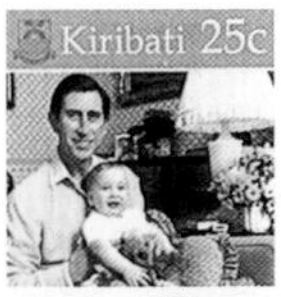

104 Prince William as a Baby with Prince Charles

2000. 18th Birthday of Prince William. Each showing Prince William with Prince Charles. Multicoloured.

615	25c. Type **104**	60	45
616	60c. In Italy, 1985	95	95
617	75c. At Sandringham, Christmas, 1992	1·10	1·10
618	$1 At Balmoral, 1997	1·25	1·75

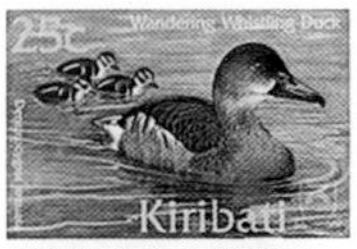

105 Wandering Whistling Duck

2001. Ducks. Multicoloured.

619	25c. Type **105**	80	80
620	25c. Green-winged teal	80	80
621	25c. Mallard	80	80
622	25c. Northern shoveler	80	80
623	25c. Pacific black duck	80	80
624	25c. Mountain duck ("Blue Duck")	80	80
MS625	85×75 mm. $1 Grey teal	3·75	4·00

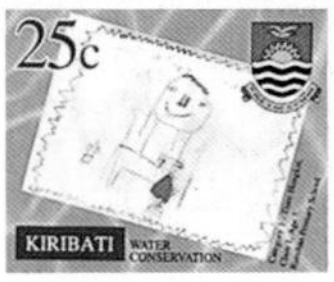

106 Man with Tap (Tiare Hongkai)

2001. Water Conservation. Children's Drawings. Multicoloured.

626	25c. Type **106**	45	40
627	50c. Cooking pot on fire and house in rain (Gilbert Tluanga)	60	50
628	60c. Map in raindrop and cup (Mantokataake Tebaiuea) (vert)	70	55
629	75c. Hand holding drop (Tokaman Karanebo) (vert)	80	70
630	$2 Water management system (Taom Simon)	1·90	3·00

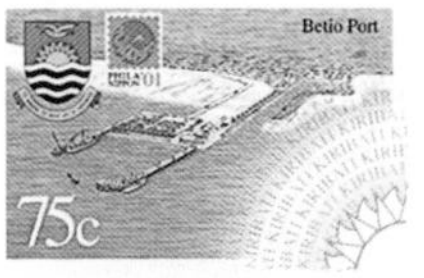

107 Betio Port

2001. "Philanippon '01" International Stamp Exhibition, Tokyo. Development Projects. Multicoloured.

631	75c. Type **107**	1·00	75
632	$2 New Parliament House complex	2·00	2·75

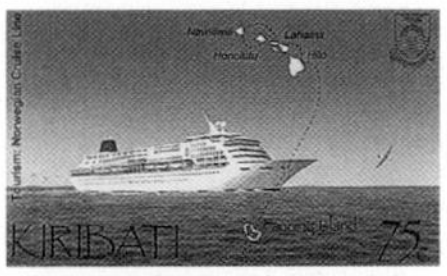

108 Norwegian Cruise Liner and Map of Route

2001. Tourism. Fanning Island. Multicoloured.

633	75c. Type **108**	1·75	1·00
634	$3 *Betsey* (full-rigged sealer) and map of Fanning Island	4·50	5·00

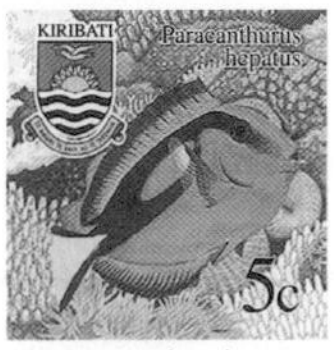

109 *Paracanthrus hepatus*

2002. Tropical Fish. Multicoloured.

635	5c. Type **109**	10	15
636	10c. *Centropyge flavissimus*	15	15
637	15c. *Anthias squamipinnis*	20	20
638	20c. *Centropyge loriculus*	25	20
639	25c. *Acanthurus lineatus*	30	25
640	30c. *Oxycirrhites typus*	35	30
641	40c. *Dascyllus trimaculatus*	45	40
642	50c. *Acanthurus achilles*	50	45
643	60c. *Pomacentrus caeruleus*	60	55
644	75c. *Acanthurus glaucopareius*	75	70
645	80c. *Thalassoma lunare*	80	80
646	90c. *Arothron meleagris*	90	90
647	$1 *Odonus niger*	1·10	1·10
648	$2 *Cephalopholis miniatus*	1·90	2·00
649	$5 *Pomacanthus imperator*	4·50	4·75
650	$10 *Balistoides conspicillum*	9·00	9·50

The 60c. is inscribed "coeruleus" in error.

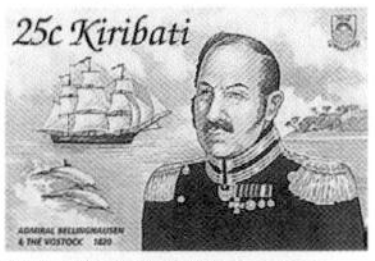

110 Admiral Bellinghausen and *Vostok*, 1820

2002. Pacific Explorers. Multicoloured.

651	25c. Type **110**	75	45
652	40c. Captain Wilkes and the U.S.S. *Vincennes* (sail frigate), 1838–42	85	55
653	60c. Captain Fanning and *Betsey* (full-rigged sealer), 1798	1·00	75
654	75c. Captain Coffin and *Transit* (full-rigged ship), 1823	1·10	80
655	$1 Commodore Byron and H.M.S. *Dolphin* (frigate), 1765	1·40	1·10
656	$3 Captain Broughton and H.M.S. *Providence* (sloop), 1795	3·25	4·00
MS657	92×63 mm. $5 Captain Cook (vert)	7·00	7·50

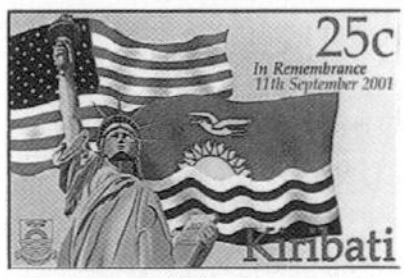

111 Statue of Liberty with U.S. and Kiribati Flags

2002. In Remembrance. Victims of Terrorist Attacks on U.S.A. (11 September 2001).

658	**111**	25c. multicoloured	1·00	1·00
659	**111**	$2 multicoloured	2·25	2·75

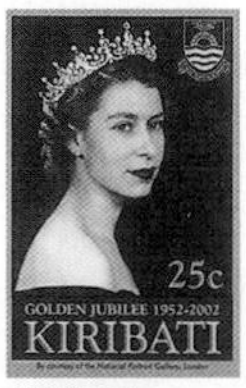

112 Queen Elizabeth in 1953

2002. Golden Jubilee. Featuring photographs by Dorothy Wilding. Multicoloured.

660	25c. Type **112**	1·00	80
MS661	135×110 mm. $2 Queen Elizabeth wearing Garter sash; $2 Queen Elizabeth in evening dress	5·50	6·00

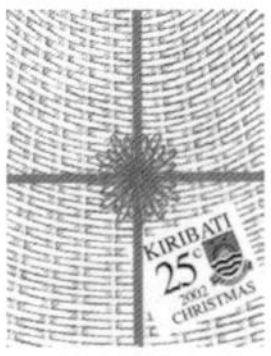

113 Woven "Parcel"

2002. Christmas.

662	**113**	25c. multicoloured	45	25
663	-	60c. multicoloured	65	50
664	-	75c. multicoloured	75	65
665	-	$1 multicoloured	80	85
666	-	$2.50 multicoloured	2·25	3·25

DESIGNS: 60c. to $2.50 show different weave patterns.

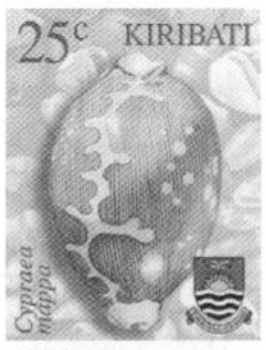

114 *Cypraea mappa*

2003. Cowrie Shells of Kiribati. Multicoloured.

667	25c. Type **114**	35	35
668	50c. *Cypraea eglantine*	50	45
669	60c. *Cypraea mauritiana*	60	55
670	75c. *Cypraea cribraria*	75	75
671	$1 *Cypraea talpa*	80	85
672	$2.50 *Cypraea depressa*	2·25	3·00
MS673	130×95 mm. Nos. 667/72	5·25	6·50

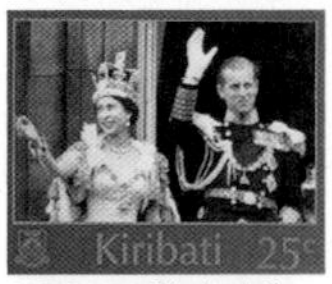

115 Queen Elizabeth II and Duke of Edinburgh waving from Palace Balcony

2003. 50th Anniv of Coronation. Multicoloured.

674	25c. Type **114**	40	25
675	$3 Newly crowned Queen in Coronation ceremony	2·75	3·25
MS676	95×115 mm. $2 As Type **115**; $5 As $3	5·00	6·00

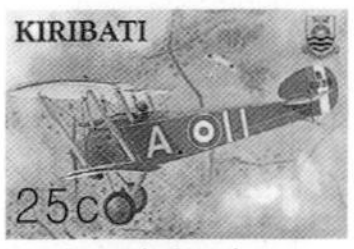

116 Sopwith Camel

2003. Centenary of Powered Flight. Multicoloured.

677	25c. Type **116**	60	45
678	50c. Northrop Alpha	80	60
679	60c. de Havilland DH.106 Comet	90	70
680	75c. Boeing 727	1·00	75
681	$1 English Electric Canberra	1·50	1·10
682	$2.50 Lockheed Martin F22 Raptor	3·25	4·00

MS683	115×65 mm. 40c. Mitsubishi A6M-5 Zero; 60c. Grumman F6F Hellcat	2·25	2·50

No. **MS**680 also commemorates the 60th anniversary of the Battle of Tarawa.

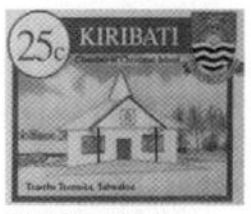

117 Teareba Teomeka, Tabwakea

2003. Christmas. Churches of Christmas Island. Multicoloured.

684	25c. Type **117**	35	25
685	40c. Seventh-Day Adventist Church, London (Port Camp)	45	40
686	50c. St. Teresa Catholic Church, Tabakea Village	50	45
687	60c. Betaera Fou, London	60	55
688	75c. Children standing by church bells, London	80	80
689	$1.50 Emanuira Church, London	1·50	2·00
690	$2.50 Church of Christ (Ana Ekaretia Kristo) (58×22 mm)	2·50	3·50
MS691	144×82 mm. Nos. 681/7	6·00	7·00

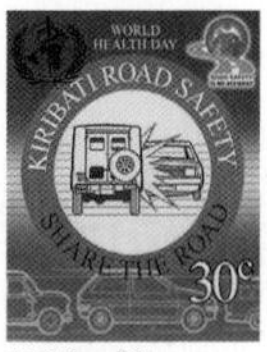

118 Road Sign showing Car Accident

2004. World Health Day. Road Safety. Multicoloured.

692	30c. Type **118**	1·00	1·10
693	40c. Road sign showing speeding car	1·10	1·25
694	50c. Road sign showing cigarette and alcohol	1·25	1·40
695	60c. Road sign showing children	1·40	1·50
MS696	165×58 mm. As Nos. 692/5	4·25	4·75

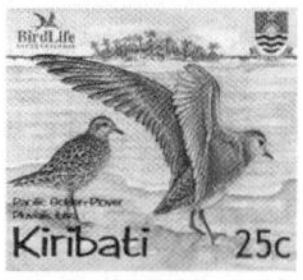

119 Pacific Golden Plover

2004. Bird Life International. Shore Birds. Multicoloured.

697	25c. Type **119**	65	55
698	40c. Whimbrel	85	70
699	50c. Wandering tattler (*Heteroscelus incanus*)	95	75
700	60c. Sanderling	1·10	85
701	75c. Bar-tailed godwit	1·25	90
702	$2.50 Ruddy turnstone	3·50	4·50
MS703	175×80 mm. $1 Head of Bristle-thighed curlew; $1 Front of Bristle-thighed curlew (vert); $1 Back of Bristle-thighed curlew (vert); $1 Two Bristle-thighed curlews; $1 Bristle-thighed curlews and tree	10·00	11·00

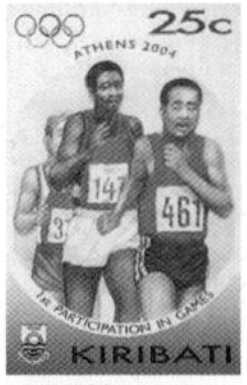

120 Athletes

2004. Olympic Games, Athens. Multicoloured.

704	25c. Type **120**	50	50
705	50c. Taekwondo	75	70
706	60c. Weight-lifting	85	90
707	75c. Sprinting	90	1·25
MS708	98×74 mm. $2.50 Athletes in training; $2.50 Athletes in front of Parliament House	6·00	7·00

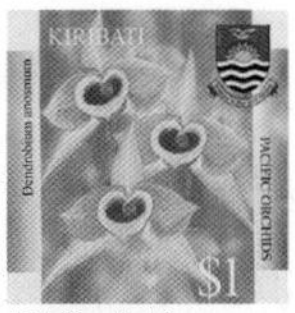

121 *Dendrobium anosmum*

2004. Orchids. Multicoloured.

709	$1 Type **121**	1·40	1·50

710	$1 *Dendrobium chrysotoxum*	1·40	1·50
711	$1 *Dendrobium laevifolium*	1·40	1·50
712	$1 *Dendrobium mohlianum*	1·40	1·50
713	$1 *Dendrobium pseudoglomeratum*	1·40	1·50
714	$1 *Dendrobium purpureum*	1·40	1·50
715	$1 *Grammatophyllum speciosum*	1·40	1·50
716	$1 *Dendrobium williamsianum*	1·40	1·50
717	$1 *Spathoglottis plicata*	1·40	1·50
718	$1 *Vanda hindsii*	1·40	1·50

Nos. 709/18 were printed together, *se-tenant*, with the backgrounds forming composite designs.

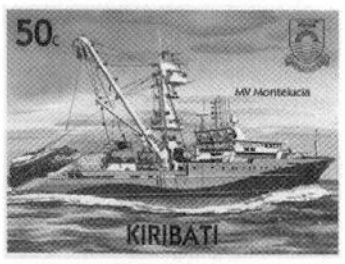

122 MV *Montelucia*

2004. Merchant Ships. Multicoloured.

719	50c. Type **122**	1·25	60
720	75c. MS *Pacific Princess*	1·50	70
721	$2.50 MS *Prinsendam*	3·75	4·00
722	$5 MS *Norwegian Wind*	6·50	7·50

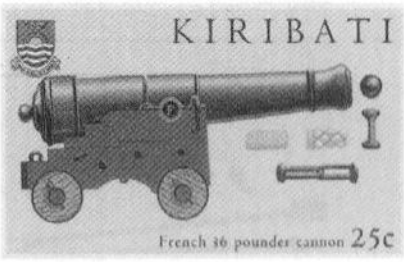

123 French 36 Pounder Cannon

2005. Bicentenary of the Battle of Trafalgar (1st issue). Multicoloured.

723	25c. Type **123**	80	55
724	50c. *San Indefonso* and HMS *Defence* in battle	1·25	70
725	75c. HMS Victory lashed to *Redoubtable*	1·75	1·00
726	$1 Emperor Napoleon Bonaparte (vert)	1·75	1·25
727	$1.50 HMS *Victory*	2·50	2·75
728	$2.50 Vice-Admiral Sir Horatio Nelson (vert)	3·50	4·25
MS729	120×79 mm. $2.50 Admiral Federico Gravina; $2.50 *Santissima Trinidad*	8·00	8·00

No. 727 contains traces of powdered wood from HMS *Victory*.

See also Nos. 743/5.

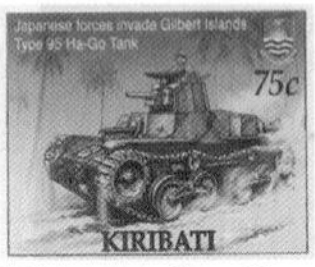

124 Japanese Type 95 Ha-Go Tank

2005. 60th Anniv of the End of World War II. "The Route to Victory". Multicoloured.

730	75c. Type **124**	1·40	1·50
731	75c. Japanese A6M Zero fighter aircraft on Gilbert Islands	1·40	1·50
732	75c. US Marines from USS *Argonaut* and *Nautilus* coming ashore at Butaritari, 6.8.1942 ("Carlson Raid")	1·40	1·50
733	75c. Admiral of Pacific Fleet Chester Nimitz	1·40	1·50
734	75c. USS *Liscome Bay* (sunk by Japanese 24.11.1943)	1·40	1·50
735	75c. US Forces Higgins Landing Craft approaching Tarawa Red Beach, 20.11.1943	1·40	1·50
736	75c. F6F-3 Hellcats providing air cover, Tarawa Red Beach, November 1943	1·40	1·50
737	75c. LVT's reaching shore, Tarawa Red Beach, 20.11.1943	1·40	1·50
738	75c. Sherman tank of C Company, Tarawa Red Beach, 20.11.1943	1·40	1·50
739	75c. US Marines taking cover on Tarawa Red Beach, 20.11.1943	1·40	1·50
MS740	90×60 mm. $5 John Curtin (Australian Prime Minister) and Winston Churchill, London, 1944	10·00	10·00

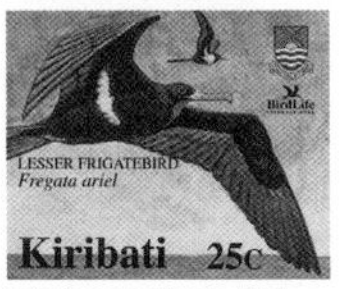

125 Lesser Frigate Bird

2005. Bird Life International (Part II Breeding Birds (**MS**741a) and Part III Seabirds (**MS**741b)). Multicoloured.

MS741	Two sheets, each 170×85 mm. (a) 25c.×6, Type **125**; Red-tailed tropic bird; Blue-grey noddy; Christmas Island shearwater; Sooty tern; Blue-faced ("Masked") booby. (b) $2×6, White-tailed tropic bird; White-capped ("Black") noddy; Red-footed booby; Wedge-tailed shearwater; White tern; Great frigate bird	19·00	22·00

2005. Pope John Paul II Commemoration. As T **126** of Jamaica.

742	$1 multicoloured	2·25	2·25

2005. Bicentenary of the Battle of Trafalgar (2nd issue). Multicoloured As T **339** of Jamaica.

743	25c. HMS *Victory*	1·00	60
744	50c. Ships engaged in battle (horiz)	1·25	70
745	$5 Admiral Lord Nelson	7·50	8·50

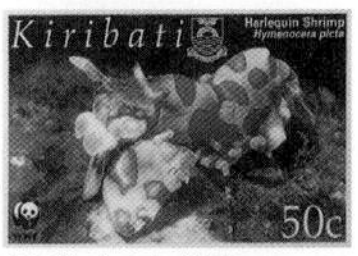

126 Harlequin Shrimp

2005. Endangered Species. Harlequin Shrimp (Hymenocera picta). Multicoloured.

746	50c. Type **126**	85	55
747	60c. Shrimp on yellow rocks	95	65
748	75c. Two shrimp	1·25	80
749	$5 Shrimp on red rocks	7·50	8·50

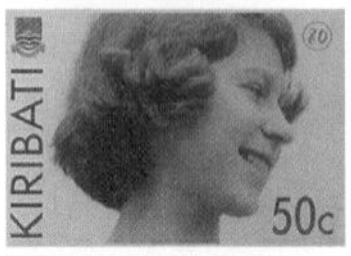

127 Princess Elizabeth

2006. 80th Birthday of Queen Elizabeth II. Multicoloured.

750	50c. Type **127**	1·00	65
751	75c. Queen wearing tiara (looking left)	1·40	85
752	$1 Wearing tiara (facing forward)	1·75	1·40
753	$2 Wearing pink hat and jacket	3·25	4·00
MS754	144×75 mm. $1.50 As No. 752; $2.50 As No. 751	6·50	7·50

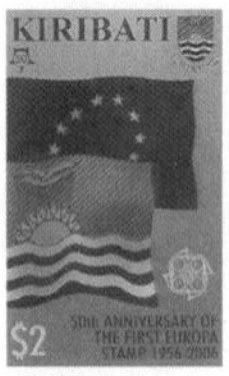

128 Kiribati and EU Flags

2006. 50th Anniv of First Europa Stamps. Multicoloured, background colour given.

755	**128**	$2 grey	2·25	2·50
756	**128**	$2.50 lilac	2·25	2·50
757	**128**	$3 brown and yellow	3·00	3·75
758	**128**	$5 blue	6·00	7·50
MS759		77×122 mm. Nos. 755/8	12·00	15·00

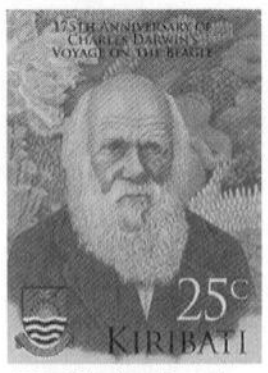

129 Charles Darwin (originator of *Theory of Evolution*) and Corals

2006. Exploration and Innovation. Anniversaries. Multicoloured.

760	25c. Type **129** (175th anniv of voyage on *Beagle*)	90	90
761	25c. Fish and coral reef	90	90
762	50c. Isambard Kingdom Brunel (engineer) (birth bicentenary)	1·40	1·40
763	50c. Foundry	1·40	1·40
764	75c. Christopher Columbus (discoverer of New World) (500th death anniv)	1·75	1·75
765	75c. *Santa Maria*	1·75	1·75
766	$1 Thomas Edison (inventor and physicist) (75th death anniv)	2·00	2·00
767	$1 "Tin foil" phonograph	2·00	2·00
768	$1.25 Wolfgang Amadeus Mozart (composer) (250th birth anniv)	2·75	2·75
769	$1.25 Violin and score	2·75	2·75
770	$1.50 Concorde (30th anniv of inaugural flight)	3·25	3·25
771	$1.50 Concorde on runway and in flight	3·25	3·25

Nos. 760/1, 762/3, 764/5, 766/7, 768/9 and 770/1 were each printed together, *se-tenant*, each pair forming a composite design.

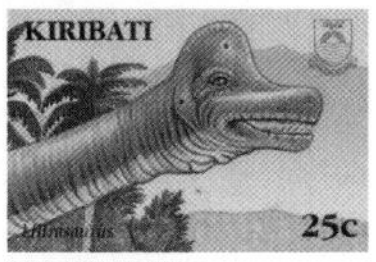

130 Ultrasaurus

2006. Dinosaurs. Multicoloured.

772	25c. Type **130**	75	60
773	50c. Rhamphorhynchus	1·25	1·00
774	60c. Dilophosaurus	1·50	1·50
775	75c. Brachiosaurus	1·60	1·60
776	$1 Minmi paravertebra	1·75	1·75
777	$1 Eoraptor	1·75	1·75
778	$1.25 Stegosaurus	2·00	2·00
779	$1.50 Giganotosaurus	2·25	2·50

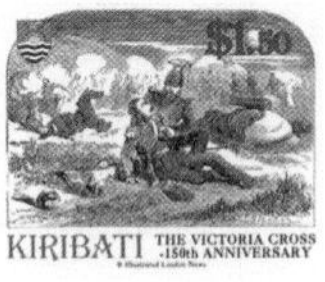

131 Troop Sgt. Major John Berryman refusing to leave Capt. Webb, Balaclava

2006. 150th Anniv of the Victoria Cross. Multicoloured.

780	$1.50 Type **131**	2·75	2·75
781	$1.50 Private W. Norman bringing in single-handed two Russian prisoners	2·75	2·75
782	$1.50 Sgt. Major John Grieve saving officer at Balaclava	2·75	2·75
783	$1.50 Private Thomas Beach rescuing Col. Carpenter, Inkerman	2·75	2·75
784	$1.50 Brevet-Major C. H. Lumley engaged with three Russian gunners in the Redan	2·75	2·75
785	$1.50 Major F. C. Elton working in trenches under heavy fire	2·75	2·75

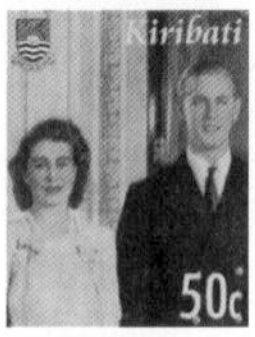

132 Princess Elizabeth and Lt. Philip Mountbatten, 1947

2007. Diamond Wedding of Queen Elizabeth II and Prince Philip. Multicoloured.

786	50c. Type **132**	1·25	1·00
787	75c. Wedding procession down the aisle	1·60	1·60
788	$1 Waving from balcony on wedding day	1·75	1·75
789	$1.50 At Broadlands, Romsey, Hampshire, 1947	2·25	2·25
MS790	125×85 mm. $5 Wedding photograph (42×56 mm)	7·00	7·50

2007. Centenary of Scouting. As T **348** of Jamaica. Multicoloured.

791	25c. Kiribati scouts with their flag	60	35
792	50c. AIDS awareness	1·00	65
793	75c. Scout leaders	1·50	80
794	$2 Scout shelter, Kiribati, 1962	2·50	3·00
MS795	90×65 mm. $1 Kiribati Scouts emblem (vert); $1.50 Lord Baden-Powell (founder) (vert)	4·00	4·00

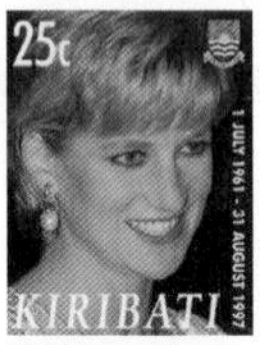

133 Diana, Princess of Wales

2007. Tenth Death Anniv of Diana, Princess of Wales. Multicoloured.

796	25c. Type **133**	65	60
797	25c. In profile	65	60
798	50c. Wearing cream jacket	1·10	65
799	75c. Wearing black and white check dress	1·40	1·25
800	75c. In close up, wearing earrings and emerald choker	1·40	1·25
801	$1 Wearing red dress	1·60	1·50

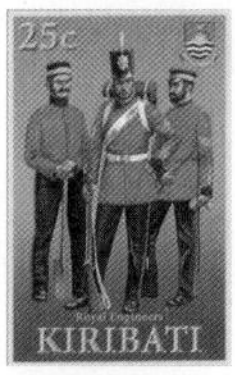

134 Royal Engineers

2007. Military Uniforms. Multicoloured.

802	25c. Type **134**	40	35
803	40c. 95th Rifles	75	55
804	50c. 24th Regiment of Foot	80	60
805	60c. New Zealand soldiers	90	75
806	75c. 93rd Sutherland Highlanders	1·00	80
807	90c. Irish Guards	1·25	1·10
808	$1 Japanese soldiers	1·40	1·25
809	$1.50 United States Marine Corps	1·75	2·25

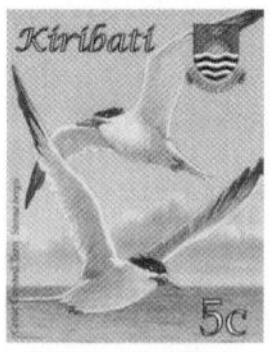

135 Great Crested Terns

2008. Birds. Multicoloured.

810	5c. Type **135**	35	40
811	10c. Eurasian teal	50	50
812	15c. Laughing gulls	70	50
813	20c. Black-tailed godwit	75	50
814	25c. Pectoral sandpipers	75	50
815	50c. Band-rumped storm-petrel	1·25	65
816	60c. Sharp-tailed sandpiper	1·40	80
817	75c. Grey-tailed tattler	1·40	85
818	90c. Red phalarope	1·50	1·25
819	$1 Pink-footed shearwater	1·60	1·25
820	$2 Ring-billed gull	2·50	2·75
821	$5 Bonin petrel	5·50	6·00
MS822	Two sheets, each 120×90 mm. (a) Nos. 810/11, 813/15 and 821. (b) Nos. 812 and 816/20	16·00	16·00

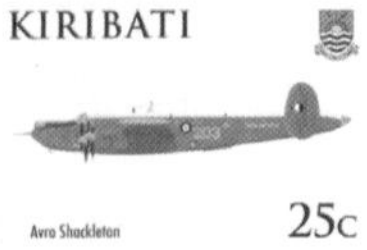

136 Avro Type 696 Shackleton

2008. 90th Anniv of the Royal Air Force. Multicoloured.

822a	25c. Type **136**	60	50
823	50c. Hawker Siddeley (BAe) Harrier	60	50
824	75c. Eurofighter EF-2000 Typhoon	1·00	75
825	$1 Vickers Valiant	1·25	1·10
MS826	110×70 mm. $2.50 Dambusters Raid	3·75	4·00

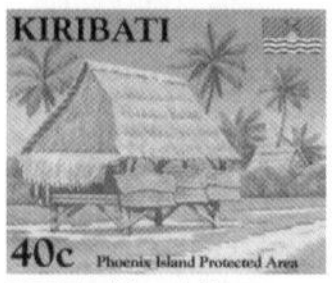

137 Traditional Hut

2008. Phoenix Island Protected Area. Multicoloured.

827	40c. Type **137**	1·00	60
828	75c. Outline map of Kanton Island	1·00	60
829	80c. Map of protected area	1·40	80
830	85c. Phoenix petrel with chick	1·50	1·00
831	$1.25 *Acropora nobilis*(coral)	1·50	1·00
832	$1.75 Blacktip reef shark	2·00	2·00
MS833	170×85 mm. Nos. 827/32	9·00	9·50

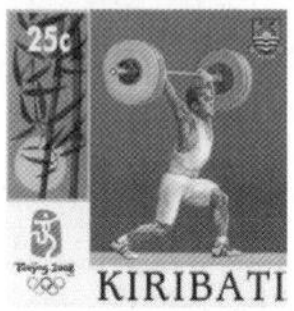

138 Weightlifting

2008. Olympic Games, Beijing. Multicoloured.

834	25c. Type **138**	50	60
835	50c. Running	60	50
836	60c. Cycling	1·00	80

Column 1

837	75c. Javelin-thrower		1·50	1·25

139 Lady Sacred
Heart, Bairiki

2008. Churches of Tarawa, Kiribati. Multicoloured.

838	25c. Type **139**		60	50
839	25c. Kiribati Protestant Church, Bikenibeu		60	50
840	40c. Kaotitaeka RCC, Betio		1·00	60
841	40c. Mormon Church, Iesu Kristo		1·00	60
842	50c. Moaningaina		1·00	80
843	50c. Sacred Heart Cathedral		1·00	80
844	75c. St. Paul's Millennium Church		1·00	80
845	75c. Kainkatikun Kristo, Naninimo, Tarawa		1·50	1·25
MS846	165×92 mm. Nos. 838/45		8·25	8·50

140 Ernest
Shackleton

2009. Seafaring and Exploration. Multicoloured.

847	25c. Type **140**		60	50
848	40c. Robert Falcon Scott		1·00	60
849	50c. Captain James Cook		1·00	80
850	75c. Marco Polo		1·50	1·25
851	$1.50 Matthew Flinders		2·50	2·50
852	$1.75 John Cabot		2·75	3·00

141 Grumman Avenger

2009. Centenary of Naval Aviation. Multicoloured.

853	40c. Type **141**		1·00	60
854	50c. Chance Vought Corsair		1·00	80
855	75c. Westland Whirlwind helicopter		1·50	1·25
856	$1.25 McDonnell Douglas Phantom		2·00	2·00
MS857	110×70 mm. $3 Helicopter on deck of HMS *Ark Royal*		4·50	4·25

142 Mars Science
Laboratory

2009. International Year of Astronomy. 40th Anniv of First
Moon Landing. Multicoloured.

858	40c. Type **142**		1·10	65
859	50c. International Space Station		1·10	85
860	75c. *Endeavour* and Boeing Transporter, 2008		1·75	1·50
861	$1.25 Apollo 12 launch, 1969		2·25	2·00
862	$3 Luna 16, 1970		4·75	4·50
MS863	100×80 mm. $3 *Tradition* (Apollo 11 crew erecting US flag on Moon) (Alan Bean) (39×59 mm). Wmk upright		4·75	4·75

143 Aircraft
Servicing

2010. 70th Anniv of the Battle of Britain. Multicoloured.

864	25c. Type **143**		65	55
865	40c. Pikeman with England standard		1·10	70

Column 2

866	50c. Parachute packing		1·25	90
867	75c. Ground control		1·50	1·00
868	$1 Rescue services		1·60	1·25
869	$1.50 RAF badge		2·10	1·75
MS870	110×70 mm. $3 Sir Douglas Bader		4·75	4·75

Nos. 864/9 show stained glass windows from St.
George's RAF Chapel of Remembrance, Biggin Hill, Kent.

2011. Royal Wedding. Multicoloured.

MS871	$5 Prince William and Miss Catherine Middleton		10·75	10·75

Beatified
1 May 2011
144

2011. Beatification of Pope John Paul II. No. 742 optd
with Type **144**

872	$1 Pope John Paul II		70	60

OFFICIAL STAMPS

1981. Nos. 86/135 optd **O.K.G.S.**

O11	1c. Type **16**		10	50
O12	3c. M.V. "Tautunu" (inter-island freighter)		10	30
O13	5c. Hibiscus		10	20
O14	7c. Catholic Cathedral, Tarawa		10	20
O15	10c. Maneaba, Bikenibeu		10	20
O16	12c. Betio Harbour		30	30
O17	15c. Reef heron		1·75	30
O18	20c. Flamboyant tree		20	30
O19	25c. Moorish idol (fish)		30	30
O20	30c. Frangipani		30	35
O21	35c. G.I.P.C. Chapel, Tangintebu		35	40
O22	50c. "Hypolimnas bolina" (butterfly)		1·00	55
O23	$1 "Tabakea" (Tarawa Lagoon ferry)		65	50
O24	$2 Evening scene		70	70
O25	$5 National flag		1·25	1·75

1983. Nos. 169, 172/3, 175 and 177 optd **O.K.G.S.**

O36	12c. Polynesian reed warbler		40	30
O37	30c. Brown booby		70	50
O38	35c. Audubon's shearwater		80	60
O39	50c. Bristle-thighed curlew		1·00	80
O40	$2 Long-tailed koel		3·00	2·75

POSTAGE DUE STAMPS

D1 Kiribati
Coat of
Arms

1981

D1	**D1**	1c. black and mauve	10	10
D2	**D1**	2c. black and blue	10	10
D3	**D1**	5c. black and green	10	10
D4	**D1**	10c. black and brown	10	15
D5	**D1**	20c. black and blue	15	25
D6	**D1**	30c. black and brown	15	35
D7	**D1**	40c. black and purple	20	45
D8	**D1**	50c. black and green	20	50
D9	**D1**	$1 black and red	30	75

Pt. 1

KISHANGARH

A state of Rajasthan, India. Now uses Indian stamps.

12 pies = 1 anna; 16 annas = 1 rupee.

1

1899. Imperf or perf.

1	**1**	1a. green	22·00	70·00
3	**1**	1a. blue	£475	

2 (¼a.)   **5** (2a.) Maharaja
Sardul Singh

1899. Various arms designs. Perf or imperf.

21	**2**	¼a. green	£375	£650
22a	**2**	¼a. red	25	50
7	**2**	½a. lilac	£200	£425
8	**2**	½a. red	£3750	£1600

Column 3

25	**2**	½a. green	13·00	16·00
26a	**2**	½a. blue	1·25	50
12b	**2**	1a. pink	95·00	£300
27	**2**	1a. grey	6·50	4·50
29	**2**	1a. mauve	75	1·00
15	**5**	2a. orange	6·00	4·50
31	**2**	4a. brown	2·50	7·00
17	**2**	1r. lilac	30·00	42·00
32	**2**	1r. green	11·00	15·00
33	**2**	1r. yellow	£1100	
34	**2**	2r. red	35·00	55·00
35	**2**	5r. mauve	35·00	65·00

11 (½a.)   **12** Maharaja
Sardul Singh

1903. Imperf or perf.

39	**11**	½a. pink	16·00	3·00
40	**12**	2a. orange	3·00	6·00
41	**2**	8a. grey	5·00	8·00

13 Maharaja
Madan Singh

1904

42	**13**	¼a. red	45	75
43a	**13**	½a. brown	1·25	30
44a	**13**	1a. blue	3·25	2·75
45	**13**	2a. orange	15·00	7·00
46a	**13**	4a. brown	15·00	20·00
47	**13**	8a. violet	24·00	38·00
48	**13**	1r. green	30·00	65·00
49	**13**	2r. yellow	38·00	£225
50	**13**	5r. brown	25·00	£250

14 Maharaja
Madan Singh

1912

63	**14**	¼a. blue	20	45
64	**14**	½a. green	30	1·25
65	**14**	1a. red	2·00	2·75
54	**14**	2a. purple	2·50	5·00
67	**14**	4a. blue	6·00	8·00
68	**14**	8a. brown	7·00	50·00
69	**14**	1r. mauve	16·00	£170
70	**14**	2r. green	£140	£450
71	**14**	5r. brown	40·00	£500

15

1913

59	**15**	¼a. blue	30	90
60	**15**	2a. purple	11·00	25·00

16 Maharaja
Yagyanarayan
Singh

1928

72	**16**	¼a. blue	1·50	2·00
73	**16**	½a. green	4·00	2·25
74	**-**	1a. red	1·50	1·50
75	**-**	2a. purple	3·00	8·50
76	**16**	4a. brown	2·00	2·00
77	**16**	8a. violet	6·50	38·00
78	**16**	1r. green	20·00	80·00
79	**16**	2r. yellow	28·00	£325
80	**16**	5r. red	55·00	£375

Nos. 74/5 are larger.

Column 4

OFFICIAL STAMPS

1918. Optd **ON K S D.**

O5	**2**	¼a. green		£160
O6	**2**	¼a. pink	2·25	60
O7	**2**	½a. blue	£550	60·00
O9	**2**	1a. mauve	70·00	2·25
O10	**5**	2a. orange		£180
O11	**2**	4a. brown	90·00	16·00
O16	**2**	8a. grey	£120	24·00
O12	**2**	1r. green	£200	£140
O13	**2**	2r. brown		£1200
O14	**2**	5r. mauve		£3000

1918. Optd **ON K S D.**

O15	**12**	2a. orange	£120	5·00

1918. Optd **ON K S D.**

O17	**13**	¼a. red		£400
O18	**13**	½a. brown	2·00	35
O19	**13**	1a. blue	14·00	4·00
O20	**13**	2a. orange		£1300
O21	**13**	4a. brown	70·00	18·00
O22	**13**	8a. violet	£475	£300
O23	**13**	1r. green	£1200	£1100
O24	**13**	5r. brown		

1918. Optd **ON K S D.**

O28	**14**	¼a. blue	1·50	75
O29	**14**	½a. green	1·75	75
O30a	**14**	1a. red	1·25	1·00
O31	**14**	2a. purple	14·00	6·50
O32	**14**	4a. blue	38·00	18·00
O33	**14**	8a. brown	£160	60·00
O34	**14**	1r. mauve	£425	£375
O35	**14**	2r. green		
O36	**14**	5r. brown	£2500	

1918. Optd **ON K S D.**

O25	**15**	¼a. blue	10·00	
O26	**15**	2a. purple		£130

For later issues see **RAJASTHAN.**

Pt. 18

KOREA

A peninsula to the S. of Manchuria in E. Asia. Formerly an empire under Chinese suzerainty, it was annexed by Japan in 1910 and used Japanese stamps. After the defeat of Japan in 1945, Russian and United States Military administrations were set up in Korea to the north and south of the 38th Parallel respectively; in 1948 South Korea and North Korea became independent republics.

Korean Empire.
1884. 100 mon = 1 tempo.
1895. 5 poon = 1 cheun.
1900. 10 re (or rin) = 1 cheun;
100 cheun = 1 weun.

South Korea.
1946. 100 cheun = 1 weun.
1953. 100 weun = 1 hwan.
1962. 100 chon = 1 won.

North Korea.
100 cheun = 1 won.

KOREAN EMPIRE

1

1894

1	**1**	5m. pink	£110	£6000
2	**-**	10m. blue	29·00	£4250

DESIGN: 10m. Central motif as in Type **1** but different
frame and inscribed "COREAN POST POST".

3 Korean Flag

1895

7	**3**	5p. green	32·00	19·00
8	**3**	10p. blue	70·00	22·00
9	**3**	25p. red	75·00	30·00
10a	**3**	50p. lilac	18·00	11·00

한국

(4)

1897. Optd with T **4**.

12A		5p. green	95·00	35·00
13A		10p. blue	£100	47·00
14A		25p. red	£110	48·00
16A		50p. lilac	95·00	45·00

1899. Surch in Korean characters.

17	**3**	1(p.) on 5p. green (No. 7)	£2250	£900
20	**3**	1(p.) on 5p. green (No. 12)	£950	£250
18	**3**	1(p.) on 25p. red (No. 9)	£500	£160
21	**3**	1(p.) on 25p. red (No. 14)	90·00	55·00

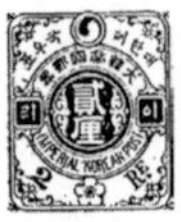

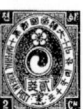

6

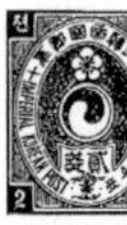

7 National Emblems

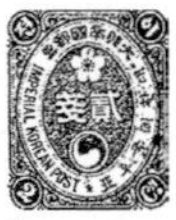

8

1900. T **6**, **7** (2ch.), **8** (2ch.) and similar designs.

22aA	2r. grey	6·00	2·20
23B	1ch. green	11·00	5·25
24A	2ch. blue (T **7**)	55·00	37·00
25B	2ch. blue (T **8**)	8·75	7·50
26B	3ch. orange	13·50	8·00
27B	4ch. red	34·00	15·00
28B	5ch. pink	18·00	11·00
29B	6ch. blue	19·00	12·50
30B	10ch. purple	24·00	18·00
31aB	15ch. purple	37·00	28·00
32B	20ch. red	55·00	41·00
33C	50ch. green and pink	£275	£150
34C	1wn. multicoloured	£800	£225
35C	2wn. green and purple	£1300	£300

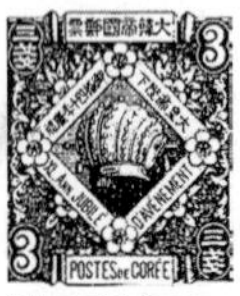

9 Imperial Crown

1902. 40th Anniv of Emperor's Accession as King.

36	**9**	3ch. orange	65·00	33·00

Types **10** to **12** are in two parts, the horizontal strokes (one, two or three) representing the value figures and the bottom part being the character for "cheun".

Some variation can be found in these woodblock overprints.

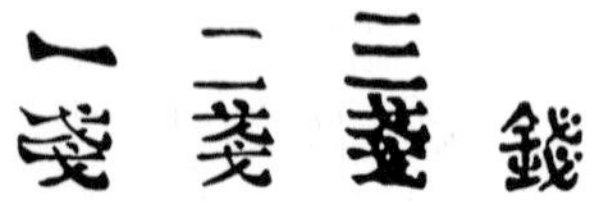

(10) (11) (12) (16)

1902. (a) Surch as Types **10** to **12**.

37B	**3**	1ch. on 25p. red (No. 9)	22·00	7·50
38A	**3**	1ch. on 25p. red (No. 14)	£150	80·00
39B	**3**	2ch. on 25p. red (No. 9)	26·00	8·75
40A	**3**	2ch. on 25p. red (No. 14)	95·00	75·00
42A	**3**	2ch. on 50p. lilac (No 10a)		£475
43B	**3**	3ch. on 25p. red (No. 9)	65·00	£110
44A	**3**	3ch. on 25p. red (No. 14)		
46B	**3**	3ch. on 50p. lilac (No. 10a)	27·00	15·00
47A	**3**	3ch. on 50p. lilac (No. 16)	75·00	55·00

(b) Surch as T **16** (Japanese "sen" character) and strokes.

49	3ch. on 50p. lilac	£1300	£650

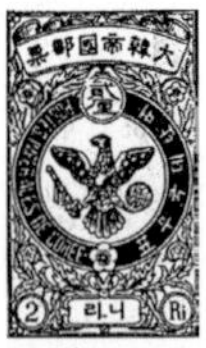

17 Falcon, Sceptre and Orb

1903

50	**17**	2r. grey	12·50	5·00
51	**17**	1ch. purple	13·00	6·50
52	**17**	2ch. green	13·50	6·50
53	**17**	3ch. orange	15·00	6·50
54	**17**	4ch. pink	22·00	7·25
55	**17**	5ch. brown	23·00	8·50
56	**17**	6ch. lilac	27·00	10·00
57	**17**	10ch. blue	31·00	13·50
58	**17**	15ch. red on yellow	50·00	24·00
59	**17**	20ch. purple on yellow	65·00	29·00
60	**17**	50ch. red on green	£190	£100
61	**17**	1wn. lilac on lilac	£350	£225
62	**17**	2wn. purple on orange	£450	£300

SOUTH KOREA

A. UNITED STATES MILITARY GOVERNMENT

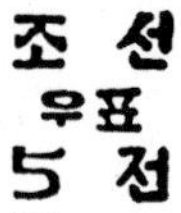

(31)

1946. Stamps of Japan surch as T **31**.

69	5ch. on 5s. purple (No. 396)	13·50	12·00
70	5ch. on 14s. red & brn (No. 324)	2·50	3·00
71	10ch. on 40s. purple (No. 407)	2·50	3·00
72	20ch. on 6s. blue (No. 397)	2·50	3·00
73	30ch. on 27s. red (No. 404)	2·50	3·00
74	5w. on 17s. violet (No. 402)	13·50	12·00

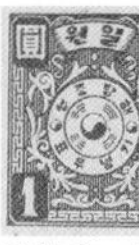

33 National Emblem

1946. Liberation from Japanese Rule.

75	-	3ch. orange	1·50	1·00
76	-	5ch. green	1·50	1·00
77	-	10ch. red	1·50	1·00
78	-	20ch. blue	1·50	1·00
79	**33**	50ch. purple	3·00	1·20
80	**33**	1w. brown	5·25	1·60

DESIGN : 3ch. to 20ch. Family and flag.

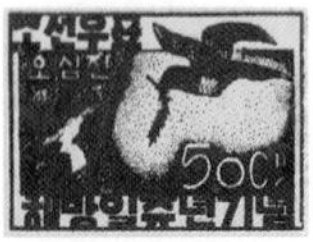

34 Dove of Peace and Map of Korea

1946. First Anniv of Liberation.

81	**34**	50ch. violet	10·00	4·00

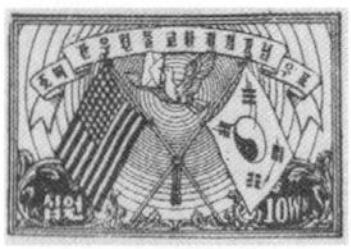

35 U.S. and Korean Flags

1946. Resumption of Postal Service between Korea and U.S.A.

82	**35**	10w. red	8·50	3·25

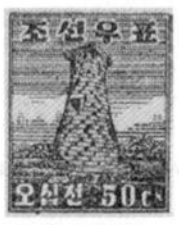

36 Kyongju Observatory

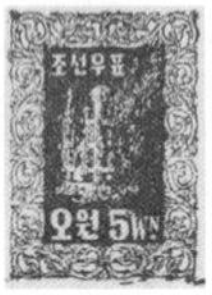

39 Golden Crown of Silla

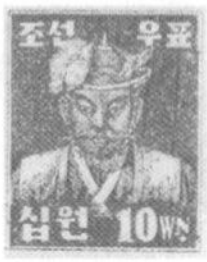

40 Admiral Li Sun Sin

1946

83	**36**	50ch. blue	1·80	1·50
84	-	1w. brown	2·20	1·90
85	-	2w. blue	2·40	1·90
86	**39**	5w. mauve	22·00	11·00
87	**40**	10w. green	24·00	17·00

DESIGNS—As Type **36**: 1w. Hibiscus; 2w. Map of Korea.

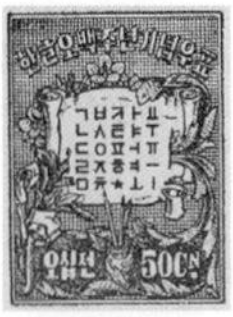

41 Korean Alphabet

1946. 500th Anniv of Creation of Korean Alphabet.

88	**41**	50ch. blue	8·75	4·50

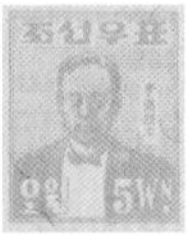

42 Li Jun, patriot

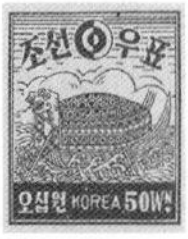

44 16th-century "Turtle" Ship

1947

89	**42**	5w. green	11·00	7·00
90	-	10w. blue	11·00	7·00
91	-	20w. red	7·50	3·75
92	**44**	50w. brown	£130	37·00

DESIGNS: 10w. Admiral Li Sun Sin; 20w. Independence Arch, Seoul.

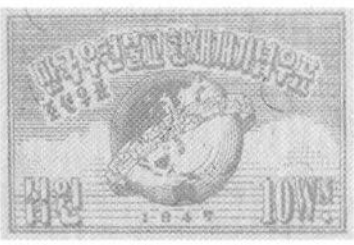

45 Letters Surrounding Globe

1947. Resumption of Int Postal Service.

93	**45**	10w. blue	17·00	7·25

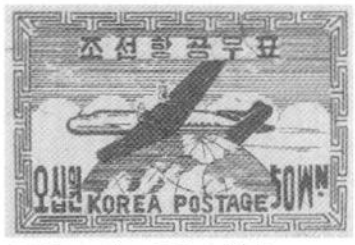

46 Douglas DC-4 Airliner

1947. Air. Inauguration of Air Mail Service.

94	**46**	50w. red	13·50	3·75
126	**46**	150w. blue	3·75	1·50
127	**46**	150w. green	22·00	13·00

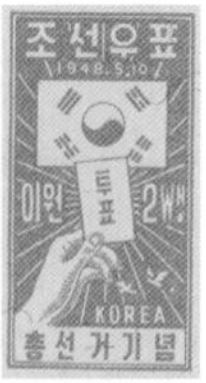

47 Hand and Ballot Slip

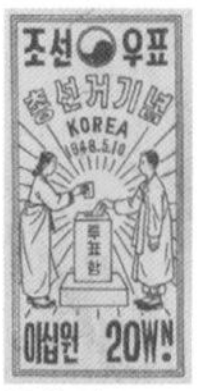

48 Casting Votes

1948. South Korea Election.

95	**47**	2w. orange	20·00	6·50
96	**47**	5w. mauve	33·00	10·00
97	**47**	10w. violet	47·00	16·00
98	**48**	20w. red	65·00	24·00
99	**48**	50w. blue	47·00	21·00

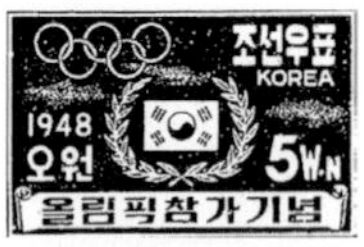

49 Korean Flag and Laurel Wreath

1948. Olympic Games.

100	**49**	5w. green	£150	55·00
101	-	10w. violet	65·00	20·00

DESIGN—VERT: 10w. Runner with torch.

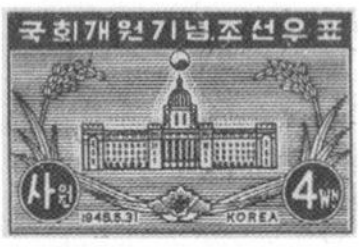

50 Capitol and Ears of Rice

1948. Meeting of First National Assembly.

102	**50**	4w. brown	27·00	10·50

MINIATURE SHEETS. Many of the stamps from 1948 to 1956 exist in miniature sheets from limited printings which were presented to postal and government officials.

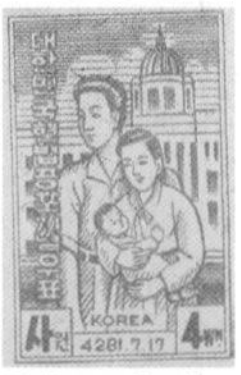

51 Korean Family

1948. Promulgation of Constitution.

103	**51**	4w. green	£120	30·00
104	-	10w. brown	50·00	19·00

DESIGN—HORIZ: 10w. Flag of Korea.

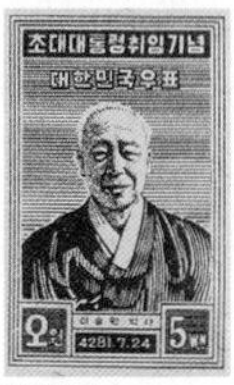

52 Dr. Syngman Rhee (First President)

1948. Election of First President.

105	**52**	5w. blue	£400	£130

B. REPUBLIC OF KOREA

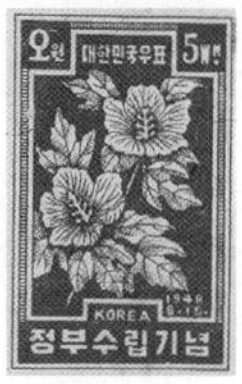

53 Hibiscus

1948. Proclamation of Republic.

106	-	4w. blue	50·00	24·00
107	**53**	5w. mauve	90·00	30·00

DESIGN: 4w. Dove and olive branch.

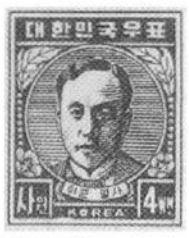

54 Li Jun

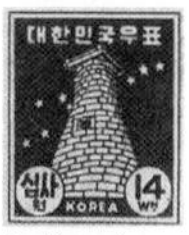

55 Kyongju Observatory

1948

108	**54**	4w. red	1·50	1·10
109	**55**	14w. blue	1·50	1·10

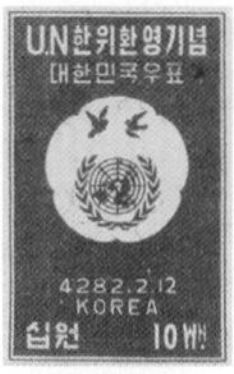

56 Doves and U.N. Emblem

1949. Arrival of U.N. Commission.

110	**56**	10w. blue	60·00	18·00

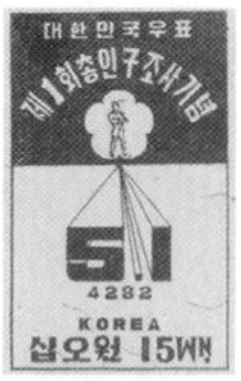

57 Citizen and Date

1949. National Census.

111	**57**	15w. violet	75·00	21·00

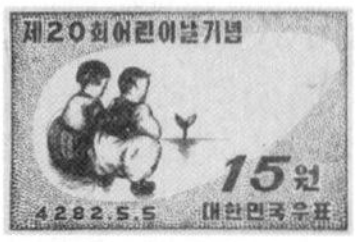

58 Children and Plant

1949. 20th Anniv of Children's Day.

112	**58**	15w. violet	44·00	11·00

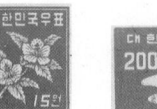

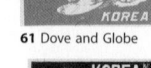

59 Hibiscus

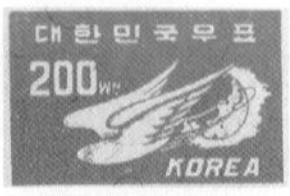

61 Dove and Globe

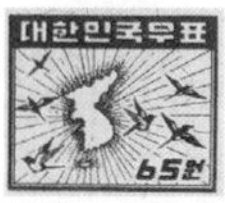

60 Map of Korea and Black-billed Magpies

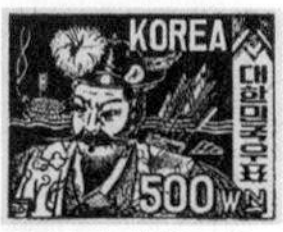

62 Admiral Li Sun Sin

1949

113	-	1w. red	7·75	3·25
114	-	2w. grey	6·75	2·75
115	-	5w. green	27·00	7·50
116	-	10w. green	3·00	1·10
117	**59**	15w. red	1·10	1·00
118	-	20w. brown	1·50	1·00
119	-	30w. green	1·50	1·00
120	-	50w. blue	1·50	1·00
121	**60**	65w. blue	2·50	1·90
122	-	100w. green	1·50	1·00
123	**61**	200w. green	1·10	1·00
124	-	400w. brown	1·10	1·00
125	**62**	500w. blue	1·10	1·00

DESIGNS—As Type **59**: 1w. Postman; 2w. Worker and factory; 5w. Harvesting rice; 10w. Manchurian cranes; 20w. Diamond Mountains; 30w. Ginseng plant; 50w. South Gate, Seoul; 100w. Tabo Pogoda, Kyongju. As Type **61**: 400w. Diamond Mountains.

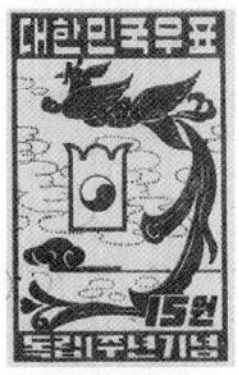

63 Symbol and Phoenix

1949. First Anniv of Independence.

128	**63**	15w. blue	60·00	13·50

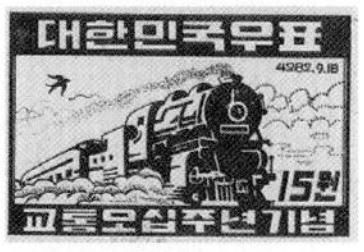

64 Steam Train

1949. 50th Anniv of Korean Railways.

129	**64**	15w. blue	£160	37·00

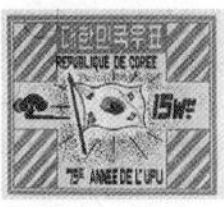

65 Korean Flag

1949. 75th Anniv of U.P.U.

130	**65**	15w. multicoloured	33·00	15·00

66 Post-horse Warrant

1950. 50th Anniv of Membership of U.P.U.

131	**66**	15w. green	50·00	15·00
132	**66**	65w. brown	22·00	7·50

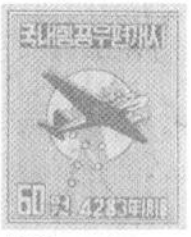

67 Douglas DC-2 Airplane and Globe

1950. Air. Opening of Internal Air Mail Service.

133	**67**	60w. blue	37·00	7·50

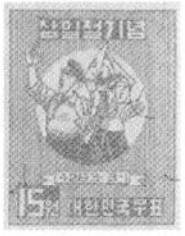

68 Demonstrators

1950. 31st Anniv of Abortive Proclamation of Independence.

134	**68**	15w. green	48·00	15·00
135	**68**	65w. violet	22·00	6·00

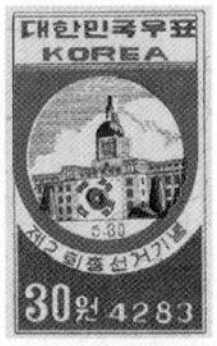

69 Capitol, Seoul

1950. Second South Korean Election.

136	**69**	30w. multicoloured	30·00	6·75

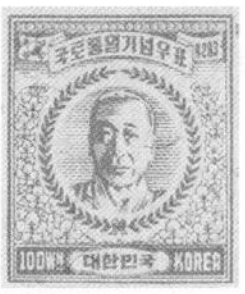

70 Dr. Syngman Rhee

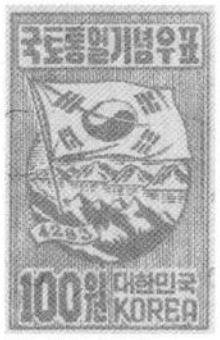

71 Flag and Mountains

1950. Unification of Korea.

137	**70**	100w. blue	7·50	3·00
138	**71**	100w. green	9·50	3·00
139	-	200w. green	6·75	2·20

DESIGN—35×24 mm: 200w. Map of Korea and flags of U.N. and Korea.

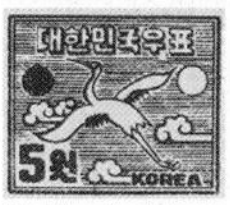

73 Manchurian Crane

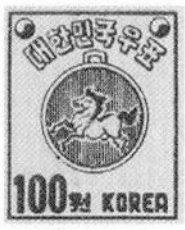

76 Post-horse Warrant

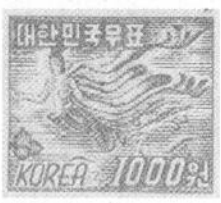

77 Fairy (8th cent painting)

1951. Perf or roul.

140	**73**	5w. brown	3·25	2·20
181	-	20w. violet	3·75	3·00
187	-	50w. green	5·50	2·50
183	**76**	100w. blue	4·50	1·50
193	**77**	1000w. green	11·00	75

DESIGNS—HORIZ: 20w. Astrological Tiger (ancient painting); 50w. Dove and Korean flag.

1951. Surch with new value.

145	**54**	100w. on 4w. red	6·25	3·75
146	**59**	200w. on 15w. red	12·00	5·75
147	**54**	300w. on 4w. red	4·75	3·75
149	**55**	300w. on 14w. blue	9·50	3·75
150	**59**	300w. on 15w. red	4·75	3·75
151	-	300w. on 20w. brown (118)	6·00	4·50
152	-	300w. on 30w. green (119)	4·75	3·75
153	-	300w. on 50w. blue (120)	4·50	3·25
154	**60**	300w. on 65w. blue	5·00	3·75
155	-	300w. on 100w. green (122)	4·75	3·00
156	-	300w. on 10w. green (116)	14·00	5·25

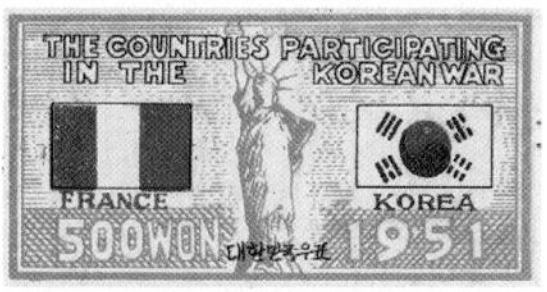

80 Statue of Liberty and Flags

1951. Participation in Korean War. Flags in national colours. A. As Type **80** in green. B. As Type **80** but showing U.N. Emblem and doves in blue.

158A	500w. Australia	12·00	12·00
158B	500w. Australia	10·50	10·50
159A	500w. Belgium	12·00	12·00
159B	500w. Belgium	10·50	10·50
160A	500w. Britain	12·00	12·00
160B	500w. Britain	10·50	10·50
161A	500w. Canada	12·00	12·00
161B	500w. Canada	10·50	10·50
162A	500w. Colombia	12·00	12·00
162B	500w. Colombia	10·50	10·50
163A	500w. Denmark	60·00	60·00
163B	500w. Denmark	37·00	37·00
164A	500w. Ethiopia	12·00	12·00
164B	500w. Ethiopia	10·50	10·50
165A	500w. France	12·00	12·00
165B	500w. France	10·50	10·50
166A	500w. Greece	12·00	12·00
166B	500w. Greece	10·50	10·50
167A	500w. India	50·00	50·00
167B	500w. India	37·00	37·00
168A	500w. Italy (with crown)	60·00	60·00
168B	500w. Italy (with crown)	44·00	44·00
169A	500w. Italy (without crown)	13·50	13·50
169B	500w. Italy (without crown)	22·00	22·00
170A	500w. Luxembourg	50·00	50·00
170B	500w. Luxembourg	37·00	37·00
171A	500w. Netherlands	12·00	12·00
171B	500w. Netherlands	10·50	10·50
172A	500w. New Zealand	12·00	12·00
172B	500w. New Zealand	10·50	10·50
173A	500w. Norway	50·00	50·00
173B	500w. Norway	37·00	37·00
174A	500w. Philippines	12·00	12·00
174B	500w. Philippines	10·50	10·50
175A	500w. Sweden	12·00	12·00
175B	500w. Sweden	10·50	10·50
176A	500w. Thailand	12·00	12·00
176B	500w. Thailand	10·50	10·50
177A	500w. Turkey	12·00	12·00
177B	500w. Turkey	10·50	10·50
178A	500w. Union of South Africa	12·00	12·00
178B	500w. Union of South Africa	10·50	10·50
179A	500w. U.S.A.	10·50	10·50
179B	500w. U.S.A.	8·75	8·75

1951. Air. No. 126 surch **500 WON.**

180	**46**	500w. on 150w. blue	10·50	3·75

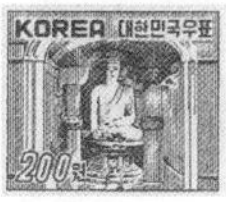

82 Buddha of Sokkuram

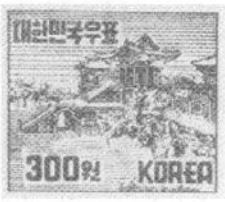

83 Pulguksa Temple, Kyongju

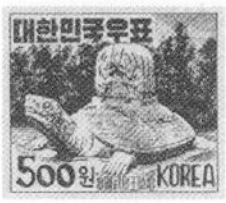

84 Monument to King Muryol, Kyongju

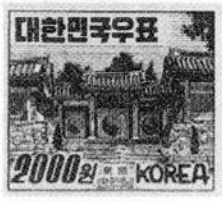

85 Shrine of Admiral Li Sun Sin, Tongyong

1952. Inscr "KOREA".

184	**82**	200w. red	3·75	1·50
185	**83**	300w. green	3·00	75
191	**84**	500w. red	5·25	1·50
192	**84**	500w. blue	44·00	£150
194	**85**	2000w. blue	3·75	75

See also Nos. 200/1 and 205.

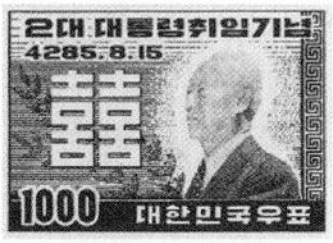

86 President Syngman Rhee

1952. President's Election to Second Term of Office.

195	**86**	1000w. green	13·50	7·50

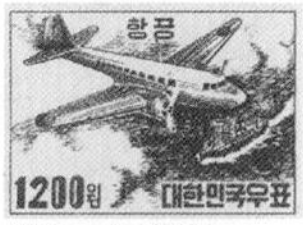

87 Douglas DC-3 over Freighter

1952. Air.

196	**87**	1200w. brown	2·50	75
197	**87**	1800w. blue	2·50	75
198	**87**	4200w. violet	6·50	1·00

For stamps in new currency, see Nos. 210/12.

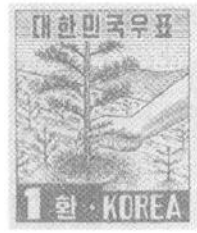

88 Tree-planting

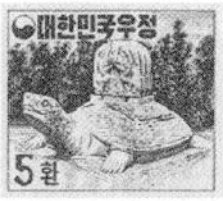

89 Monument to King Muryol, Kyongju

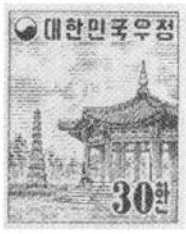

91 Pagoda Park, Seoul

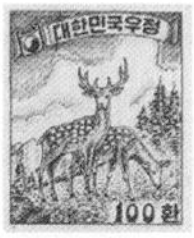

92 Sika Deer

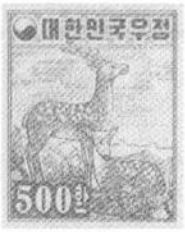

93 Sika Deer

1953. New currency. With character "hwan" after figure of value.

244	**88**	1h. blue	70	45
200	**84**	2h. blue	1·90	40
201	**84**	5h. green	2·30	40
202	**89**	5h. green	2·75	1·20
203	**88**	10h. green	7·00	1·40
204	-	10h. brown	11·00	1·90
205	**85**	20h. brown	8·00	1·50
206	**91**	30h. blue	2·30	1·40
242	**92**	100h. brown	75·00	6·25
243	**91**	200h. violet	15·00	2·30
208	**93**	500h. orange	85·00	5·50
209	**93**	1000h. brown	£200	6·25

DESIGN: No. 204, "Metopta rectifasciata" (moth) and Korean flag.

For designs without character after figure of value, see 1955 issue (No. 273 etc).

1953. Air. Colours changed and new Currency.

210	**87**	12h. blue	3·00	65
211	**87**	18h. violet	3·75	75
212	**87**	42h. green	4·50	1·20

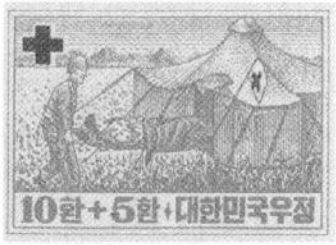

94 Field Hospital

1953. Red Cross Fund. Crosses in red.

213	**94**	10h.+5h. green	17·00	4·75
214	-	10h.+5h. blue	17·00	4·75

DESIGN—VERT: No. 214, Nurses supporting wounded soldier.

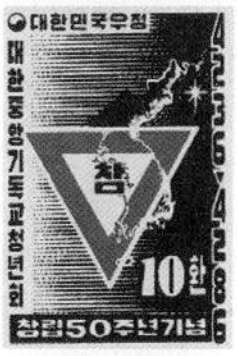

95 Y.M.C.A. Badge and Map

1953. 50th Anniv of Korean Young Men's Christian Association.

215	**95**	10h. red and black	11·00	3·75

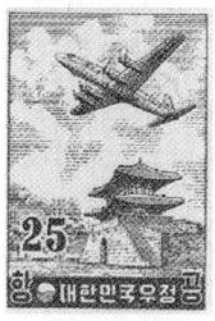

96 Douglas DC-6 over East Gate, Seoul

1954. Air.

216	**96**	25h. brown	6·25	1·40
217	**96**	35h. purple	6·25	1·60
218	**96**	38h. green	6·25	1·80
219	**96**	58h. blue	6·25	2·00
220	**96**	71h. blue	15·00	2·40
258	**96**	70h. green	11·50	3·75
259	**96**	110h. brown	11·50	3·75
260	**96**	205h. mauve	19·00	3·75

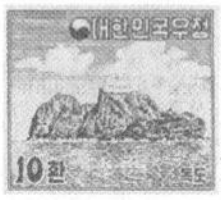

98 Tokto Island

1954

221	-	2h. purple	3·75	2·30
222	-	5h. blue	8·25	2·30
223	**98**	10h. green	12·00	2·30

DESIGN: 2, 5h. Rocks off Tokto Island.

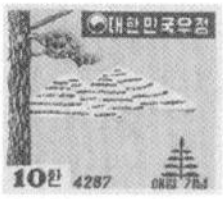

99 Erosion Control

1954. Fourth World Forestry Congress, Dehru Dun.

224	**99**	10h. light green and green	7·00	1·20
225	**99**	19h. light green and green	7·00	1·90

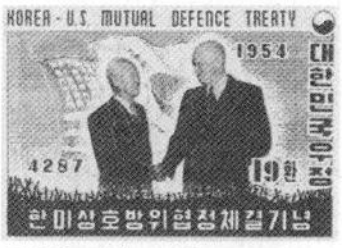

100 Presidents Syngman Rhee and Eisenhower

1954. Korea–United States Mutual Defence Treaty.

226	**100**	10h. blue	5·00	1·50
227	**100**	19h. brown	5·50	1·50
228	**100**	71h. green	9·25	2·30

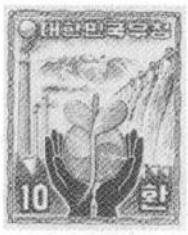

101 "Rebirth of Industry"

1955. Reconstruction.

229A	**101**	10h. brown	5·50	2·75
230B	**101**	15h. violet	5·00	90
231B	**101**	20h. blue	5·00	95
232B	**101**	50h. mauve	9·50	1·30
269	**101**	50h. red	9·25	1·90

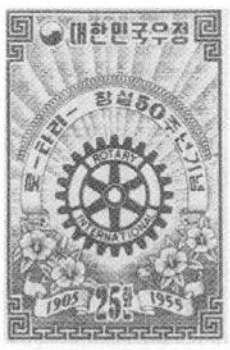

102 Rotary Emblem

1955. 50th Anniv of Rotary International.

236	**102**	20h. violet	9·25	2·75

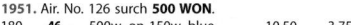

237	102	25h. green	4·75	1·50
238	102	71h. purple	4·75	1·50

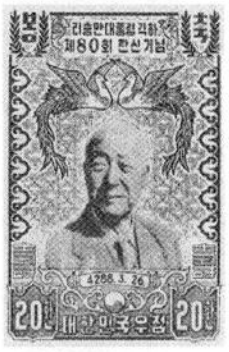

103 Pres. Syngman Rhee

1955. 80th Birthday of President.

239	103	20h. blue	27·00	7·75

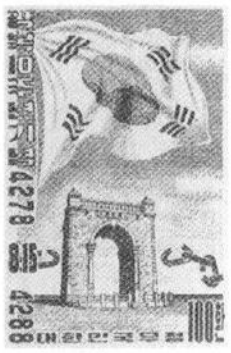

104 Independence Arch, Seoul

1955. Tenth Anniv of Liberation.

240	104	40h. green	11·50	1·90
241	104	100h. brown	11·50	2·75

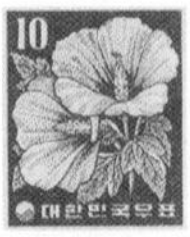
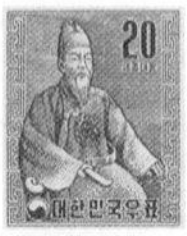
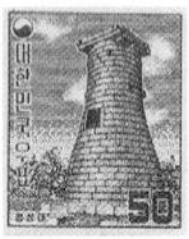

105 Hibiscus **106** King Sejong **107** Kyongju Observatory

1955. Without character after figure of value.

273	88	2h. blue	75	40
309	89	4h. blue	1·20	40
310	89	5h. green	1·20	40
247	105	10h. mauve	1·80	70
277	-	10h. green	1·30	10
248	106	20h. purple	3·50	70
279	105	20h. mauve	1·50	40
280	-	30h. violet	1·50	40
281	106	40h. purple	1·70	30
249	107	50h. violet	4·00	70
315	-	55h. purple	3·25	75
250	92	100h. purple	28·00	4·00
284	107	100h. violet	4·25	45
285	92	200h. purple	5·00	45
286	91	400h. violet	75·00	4·75
251	93	500h. brown	70·00	4·75
288	93	1000h. brown	£150	11·50
MS289 Set of 10 sheets (110×83 mm) each with one of Nos. 273/4, 277, 279/80, 283/6			£1100	

DESIGNS—HORIZ: No. 277, South Gate, Seoul; 280, Tiger. VERT: No. 315, Haegumgang (cliff face).

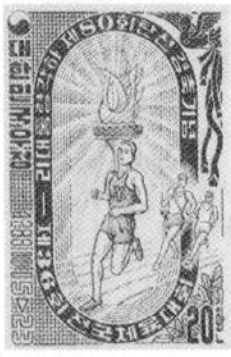

108 Runners and Torch

1955. 36th National Athletic Meeting.

252	108	20h. purple	7·00	1·90
253	108	55h. green	7·00	1·90

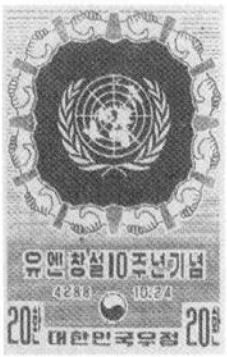

109 U.N. Emblem

1955. Tenth Anniv of U.N.

254	109	20h. green	5·50	1·50
255	109	55h. blue	5·50	1·50

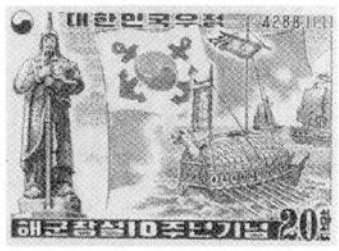

110 Admiral Li Sun Sin and 16th-century "Turtle" Ship

1955. Tenth Anniv of Korean Navy.

256	110	20h. blue	10·50	2·50

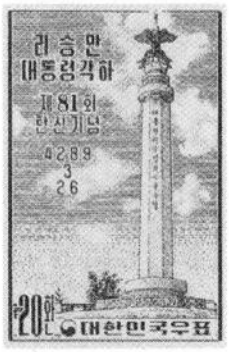

111 Admiration Pagoda

1956. 81st Birthday of President.

257	111	20h. green	7·75	2·20

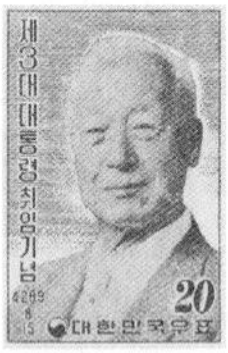

112 Pres. Syngman Rhee

1956. President's Election to Third Term of Office.

261	112	20h. brown	£120	27·00
262	112	55h. blue	55·00	11·50

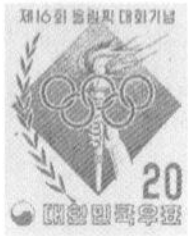

113 Torch and Olympic Rings

1956. Olympic Games.

263	113	20h. brown	6·25	2·30
264	113	55h. green	6·25	2·30

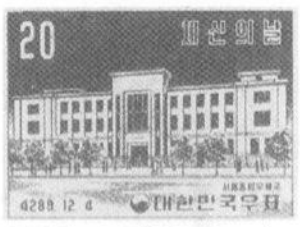

114 Central P.O., Seoul

1956. Stamp Day. Inscr "4289.12.4".

265	114	20h. turquoise	15·00	2·75
266	-	50h. red	23·00	4·75
267	-	55h. green	11·50	1·90

DESIGNS—VERT: 50h. Stamp of 1884. HORIZ: 55h. Man leading post-pony.

MINIATURE SHEETS. Beginning in 1957 miniature sheets were put on sale at post offices. Miniature sheets of earlier issues were intended only for presentation purposes.

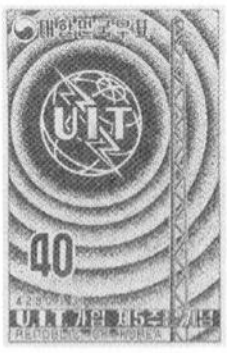

119 I.T.U. Emblem and Radio Mast

1957. Fifth Anniv of Korea's Admission to I.T.U.

290	119	40h. blue	3·00	1·30
291	119	55h. green	3·00	1·30
MS292 110×3 mm. Nos. 290/1. Imperf. No gum.			£950	

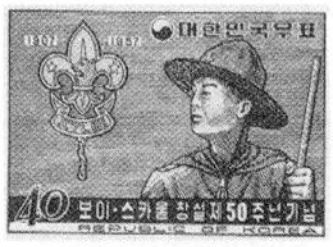

120 Korean Scout and Badge

1957. 50th Anniv of Boy Scout Movement.

293	120	40h. purple	2·75	1·30
294	120	55h. purple	2·75	1·30
MS295 110×83 mm. Nos. 293/4. Imperf			£3250	

1957. Flood Relief Fund. As No. 281 but Korean inscr and premium added and colour changed.

299	121	40h.+10h. green	11·50	2·30
MS300 110×84 mm. No. 299			£250	

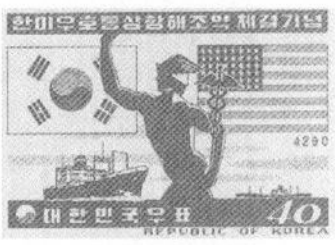

123 Mercury, Flags and Freighters

1957. Korean–American Friendship Treaty.

301	123	40h. orange	2·30	85
302	123	205h. green	4·75	1·70
MS303 110×84 mm. Nos. 301/2. Imperf. No gum			£1700	

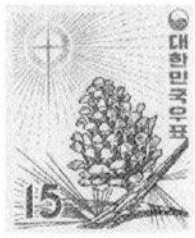

124 Star of Bethlehem and Pine Cone

1957. Christmas and New Year Issue.

304	124	15h. brown, green and orange	11·00	1·90
305	-	25h. green, red and yellow	11·00	1·90
306	-	30h. blue, green and yellow	22·00	2·75
MS307 Three sheets, each 90×60 mm. Nos. 304/6. Imperf			£3750	

DESIGNS: 25h. Christmas tree and tassels; 30h. Christmas tree and dog by window.

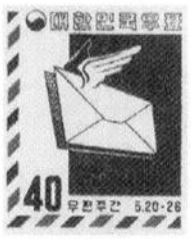

125 Winged Letter

1958. Postal Week.

321	125	40h. blue and red	2·30	75
MS322 90×60 mm. No. 321. Imperf			£2250	

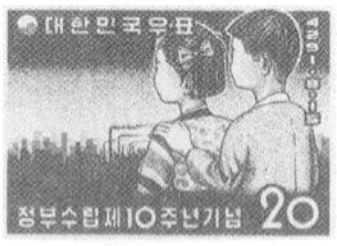

126 Korean Children regarding future

1958. Tenth Anniv of Republic of Korea.

323	126	20h. grey	1·90	60
324	-	40h. red	2·75	85
MS325 110×84 mm. Nos. 323/4. Imperf			£550	£500

DESIGN: 40h. Hibiscus flowers forming figure "10".

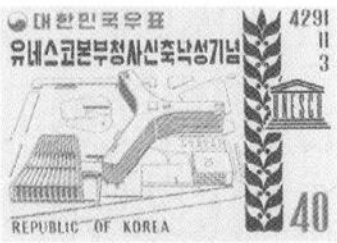

127 UNESCO Headquarters, Paris

1958. Inauguration of UNESCO Building, Paris.

326	127	40h. orange and green	1·50	55
MS327 90×60 mm. No. 326. Imperf			£225	£200

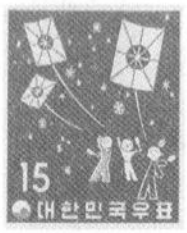

128 Children flying Kites

1958. Christmas and New Year.

330	128	15h. green	2·30	75
331	-	25h. red, yellow and blue	2·30	75
332	-	30h. red, blue and yellow	3·75	1·20
MS333 Three sheets each 90×60 mm. Nos. 330/2. Imperf			£250	£250

DESIGNS—VERT: 25h. Christmas tree, tassels and wicker basket (cooking sieve); 30h. Children in traditional festive costume.

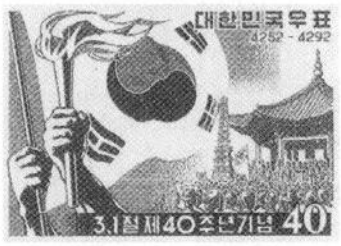

129 Rejoicing Crowds in Pagoda Park, Flag and Torch

1959. 40th Anniv of Abortive Proclamation of Independence.

334	129	40h. purple and brown	1·50	60
MS335 90×60 mm. No. 334			£140	£130

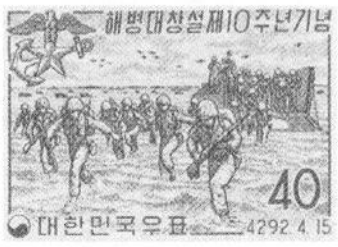

130 Marines going ashore from Landing-craft

1959. Tenth Anniv of Korean Marine Corps.

336	130	40h. bronze green	1·50	60
MS337 90×60 mm. No. 336. Imperf			15·00	12·50

1959. Third Postal Week. Sheet containing Nos. 311/4.

MS338 70×105 mm			11·50	10·50

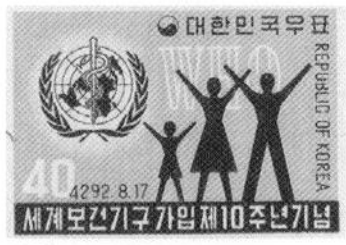

131

1959. Tenth Anniv of Korea's Admission to W.H.O.

339	131	40h. purple and pink	1·50	60
MS340 90×60 mm. No. 339. Imperf			13·00	10·50

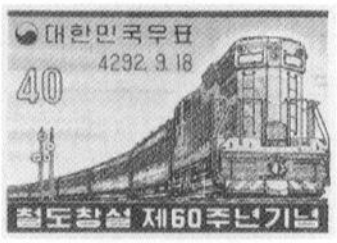

132 Diesel Train

1959. 60th Anniv of Korean Railways.

341	132	40h. sepia and brown	2·50	1·00
MS342 90×60 mm. No. 341. Imperf			31·00	25·00

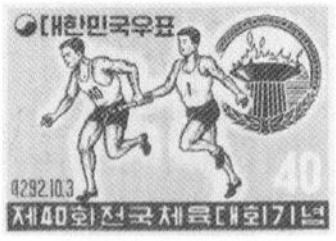

133 Runners in Relay Race

1959. 40th Korean National Games.

343	133	40h. brown and blue	1·70	70
MS344 90×60 mm. No. 343. Imperf			19·00	17·00

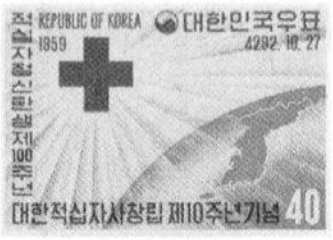

134 Red Cross and Korea

1959. Red Cross. Inscr "1959 4292".

345	134	40h. red and green	1·50	45
346	-	55h. red and mauve	1·50	45
MS347 110×60 mm. Nos. 345/6. Imperf			42·00	38·00

DESIGN: 55h. Red Cross on globe.

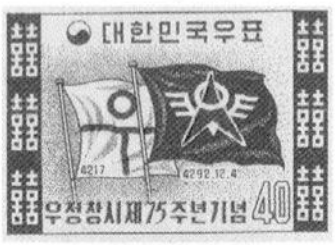

135 Korean Postal Flags Old and New

1959. 75th Anniv of Korean Postal Service.

348	135	40h. red and blue	1·50	55
MS349 90×60 mm. No. 348. Imperf			23·00	21·00

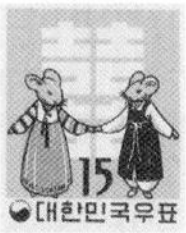

136 Mice in Korean Costume and New Year Emblem

1959. Christmas and New Year.

350	136	15h. pink, blue and grey	1·50	35
351	-	25h. red, green and blue	1·50	40
352	-	30h. red, black and mauve	3·00	50
MS353 Three sheets each 90×60 mm. Nos. 350/2. Imperf			95·00	85·00

DESIGNS: 25h. Carol singers; 30h. Crane.

137 U.P.U. Monument

1960. 60th Anniv of Admission of Korea to U.P.U.
354 **137** 40h. hocolate and blue 1·90 75
MS355 90×60 mm. No. 354. Imperf 39·00 35·00

138
Bee and Clover

1960. Children's Savings Campaign.
356 **138** 10h. yellow, brown and
green 1·50 75
357 - 20h. brown, blue and
pink 1·90 75
DESIGN: 20h. Snail and Korean money-bag.
For these stamps in new currency, see Nos. 452 etc.

139 "Uprooted
Tree"

1960. World Refugee Year.
358 **139** 40h. red, blue and green 1·50 55
MS359 90×60 mm. No. 358. Imperf 60·00 55·00

140 Pres.
Eisenhower

1960. Visit of President Eisenhower of United States.
360 **140** 40h. ultramarine, vermil-
lion and green 4·75 1·90
MS361 90×60 mm. No. 360. Imperf 39·00 38·00

141 Schoolchildren

1960. 75th Anniv of Educational System.
362 **141** 40h. purple, chestnut
and olive 1·50 45
MS363 90×60 mm. No. 362. Imperf 9·25 8·50

142 Assembly

1960. Inauguration of House of Councillors.
364 **143** 40h. grey 1·50 45
MS365 90×60 mm. No. 364. Imperf 9·25 8·50

143 "Liberation"

1960. 15th Anniv of Liberation.
366 **143** 40h. lake, blue and
ochre 1·90 55
MS367 90×60 mm. No. 366. Imperf 9·25 8·50

144 Weightlifting

1960. Olympic Games.
368 **144** 20h. brown, flesh & turq 1·70 75
369 - 40h. brown, blue & turq 1·70 75
MS370 90×60 mm. Nos. 368/9. Imperf 29·00 26·00
DESIGN: 40h. South Gate, Seoul.

145 Barn Swallow
and Insulators

1960. 75th Anniv of Korean Telegraph Service.
371 **145** 40h. violet, grey and
blue 1·70 75
MS372 90×60 mm. No. 371. Imperf 8·50 7·50

146 "Rebirth of Republic"

1960. Establishment of New Government.
373 **146** 40h. green, blue and
orange 1·50 45
MS374 90×60 mm. No. 373. Imperf 7·75 7·00

1960. Postal Week and International Correspondence
Week. Sheet containing Nos. 356/7. Imperf.
MS375 90×60 mm 5·50 5·00

147 "Torch of
Culture"

1960. Cultural Month.
376 **147** 40h. yellow, light blue
and blue 1·50 45
MS377 90×60 mm. No. 376. Imperf 7·75 6·75

148 U.N. Flag

1960. 15th Anniv of U.N.
378 **148** 40h. blue, green and
mauve 1·50 45
MS379 90×60 mm. No. 378. Imperf 7·75 6·75

149 U.N. Emblem
and Gravestones

1960. Establishment of U.N. Memorial Cemetery.
380 **149** 40h. brown and orange 1·50 45
MS381 90×60 mm. No. 380. Imperf 7·75 6·75

150 "National Stocktaking"

1960. Census of Population and Resources.
382 **150** 40h. carmine, drab
and blue 1·50 45
MS383 90×60 mm. No. 382. Imperf 7·75 6·75

151 Festival
Stocking

1960. Christmas and New Year Issue.
384 - 15h. brown, yellow
and grey 2·30 40
385 **151** 25h. red, green and blue 3·00 40
386 - 30h. red, yellow and
blue 3·75 75
MS387 Three sheets, each 90×60 mm.
Nos. 384/6. Imperf 32·00 27·00
DESIGNS: 15h. Ox's head; 30h. Girl bowing in New Year's
greeting.

152 Wind-sock and
Ancient Rain-gauge

1961. World Meteorological Day.
388 **152** 40h. ultramarine and
blue 1·50 45
MS389 90×60 mm. No. 388. Imperf 4·75 4·25

153 Family, Sun and Globe

1961. World Health Day.
390 **153** 40h. brown and orange 1·50 45
MS391 90×60 mm. No. 390. Imperf 4·75 4·25

154 Students'
Demonstration

1961. First Anniv of April Revolution (Overthrow of Pres.
Syngman Rhee).
392 **154** 40h. green, red and blue 1·90 75
MS393 90×60 mm. No. 392. Imperf 11·50 10·50

155 Workers and
Conference Emblem

1961. Int Community Development Conf, Seoul.
394 **155** 40h. green 1·50 55
MS395 90×60 mm. No. 394. Imperf 7·00 6·25

156 Girl Guide, Camp and
Badge

1961. 15th Anniv of Korean Girl Guide Movement.
396 **156** 40h. green 1·90 55
MS397 90×60 mm. No. 396. Imperf 15·00 14·00

157 Soldier's Grave

1961. Memorial Day.
398 **157** 40h. black and drab 3·00 1·30
MS399 90×60 mm. No. 398. Imperf 11·50 10·50

158 Soldier with
Torch

1961. Revolution of 16 May (Seizure of Power by Gen.
Pak Chung Hi).
400 **158** 40h. brown and yellow 3·00 1·30
MS401 90×60 mm. No. 400. Imperf 11·00 9·75

159 "Three
Liberations"

1961. Liberation Day.
402 **159** 40h. multicoloured 3·00 1·30
MS403 90×60 mm. No. 402. Imperf 6·25 5·50

160 Korean Forces, Flag and
Destroyer

1961. Armed Forces Day.
404 **160** 40h. multicoloured 3·00 1·20
MS405 90×60 mm. No. 404. Imperf 5·50 4·75

161 "Korean Art"
(Kyongbok Palace
Art Gallery)

1961. Tenth Korean Art Exhibition.
406 **161** 40h. chocolate and
brown 1·90 55
MS407 90×60 mm. No. 406. Imperf 4·75 4·25

162 Birthday Candle

1961. 15th Anniv of UNESCO.
408 **162** 40h. blue and green 1·90 55
MS409 90×60 mm. No. 408. Imperf 4·75 4·25

163 Mobile X-Ray Unit

1961. Tuberculosis Vaccination Week.
410 **163** 40h. brown, black and
light brown 1·50 55
MS411 90×60 mm. No. 410. Imperf 4·75 4·25

164 Ginseng

165 King Sejong

166 White-bellied
Black Woodpecker

167 Rice
Harvester

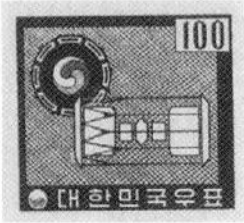

168 Korean Drum

1961

412	**164**	20h. red	2·30	60
413	**165**	30h. purple	6·25	60
414	**166**	40h. blue and red	5·50	60
415	**167**	40h. green	9·25	75
416	**168**	100h. brown	12·50	1·50

See also 1962 issue (No. 537 etc), and for stamps inscribed "REPUBLIC OF KOREA", see Nos. 641 etc and 785/95.

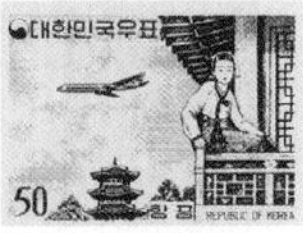

169 Douglas DC-8 Jetliner over Pagoda

1961. Air.

417	**169**	50h. violet and blue	23·00	6·25
418	-	100h. brown and blue	31·00	10·00
419	-	200h. brown and blue	46·00	12·50
420	-	400h. green and blue	55·00	13·00

DESIGNS—Plane over: 100h. West Gate, Suwon; 200h. Gateway and wall of Toksu Palace, Seoul; 400h. Pavilion, Kyongbok Palace, Seoul.

See also Nos. 454 etc.

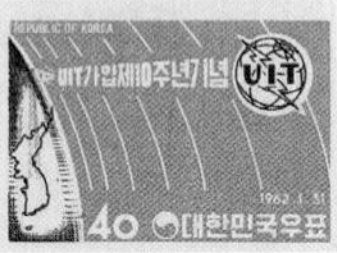

170 I.T.U. Emblem as Satellite

1962. Tenth Anniv of Admission to I.T.U.

421	**170**	40h. red and blue	2·30	1·00
MS422		90×59 mm. No. 421. Imperf	14·00	12·50

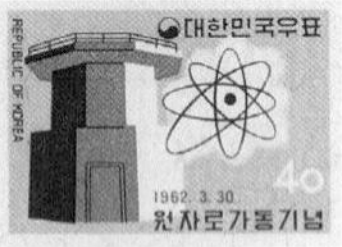

171 Triga Mark II Reactor

1962. First Korean Atomic Reactor.

423	**171**	40h. green, drab and blue	2·30	55

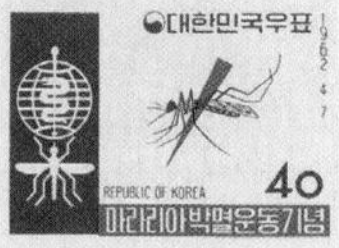

172 Mosquito and Emblem

1962. Malaria Eradication.

424	**172**	40h. red and green	1·50	75
MS425		90×60 mm. No. 424	3·75	3·25

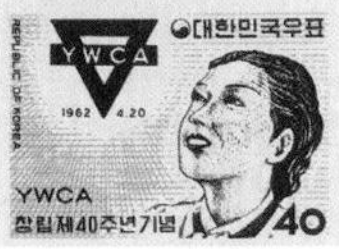

173 Girl and Y.W.C.A. Emblem

1962. 40th Anniv of Korean Young Women's Christian Association.

426	**173**	40h. blue and orange	2·30	55

174 Emblem of Asian Film Producers' Federation

1962. Ninth Asian Film Festival, Seoul.

427	**174**	40h. violet, red and turquoise	3·00	55

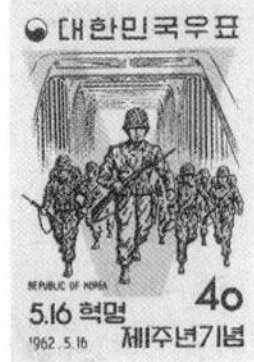

175 Soldiers crossing Han River Bridge

1962. First Anniv of 16th May Revolution.

428	-	30h. green and brown	3·00	1·10
429	**175**	40h. brown, green & turq	3·00	1·10
430	-	200h. yellow, red and blue	34·00	8·50
MS431		Three sheets, each 90×140 mm. Nos. 428/30. Imperf. Inscr in Korean	£120	£110
MS432		As last but sheets inscr in English	£250	£225

DESIGNS—HORIZ: 30h. "Industrial Progress" (men moving cogwheel up slope); 200h. "Egg" containing Korean badge and industrial skyline.

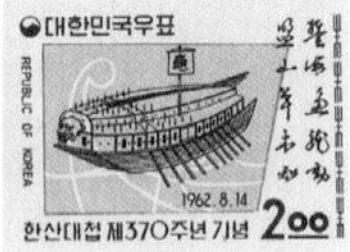

176 20-oared "Turtle" Ship

1962. 370th Anniv of Hansan Naval Victory over Japanese.

433	**176**	2w. blue and light blue	19·00	1·50
434	-	4w. black, violet & turq	24·00	2·30

DESIGN: 4w. 16-oared "turtle" ship.

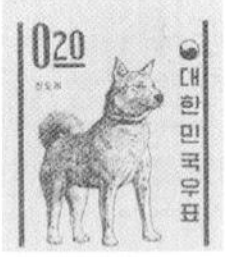

177 Chindo Dog

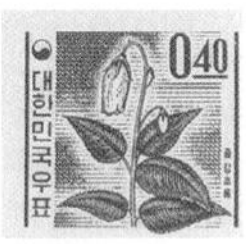

178 *Hanabusaya asiatica*

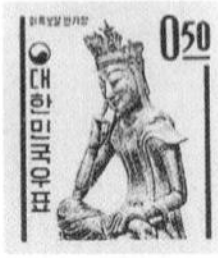

179 Statue of Goddess Mikuk Besal

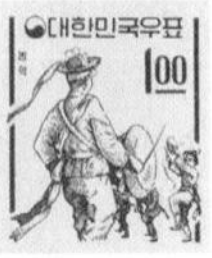

180 Farmers' Dance

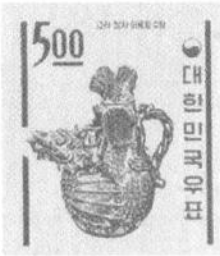

181 12th-century Wine-jug

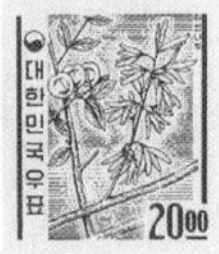

182 Mison

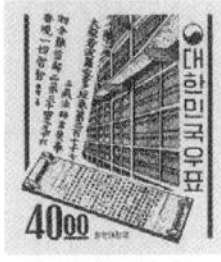

183 13th-century Printing-block and Impression used for *Tripitaka Koreana*

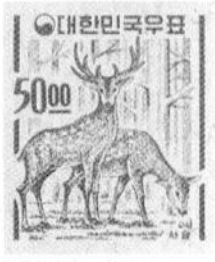

191 Sika Deer

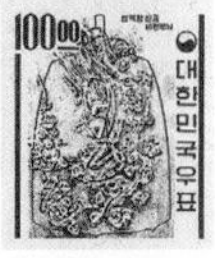

192 Bell of King Kyongdok

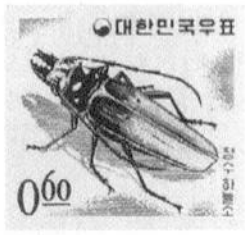

213 Longhorn Beetle

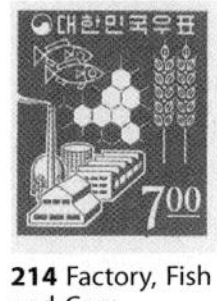

214 Factory, Fish and Corn

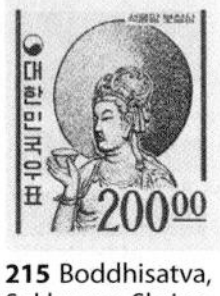

215 Boddhisatva, Sokkuram Shrine

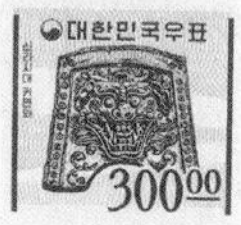

216 Tile, Silla Dynasty

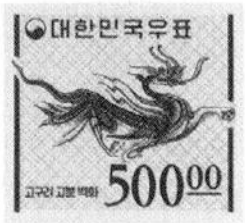

217 *Azure Dragon, Koguryo period*

1962. New Currency.

537	**177**	20ch. brown	75	25
436	**178**	40ch. blue	1·50	40
785	-	40ch. green	1·50	40
539	**179**	50ch. brown	75	25
540	**213**	60ch. brown	95	30
541	**180**	1w. blue	2·30	25
542	**179**	1w.50 grey	75	30
543	**164**	2w. red	3·75	25
472	**165**	3w. purple	14·50	30
545	**167**	4w. green	75	25
442	**181**	5w. blue	6·25	85
547	**214**	7w. mauve	3·00	75
548	**168**	10w. brown	4·75	25
549	**182**	20w. mauve	4·75	40
550	**183**	40w. purple	7·75	1·50
551	**191**	50w. brown	19·00	1·50
552	**192**	100w. green	70·00	2·30
553	**215**	200w. deep green and green	27·00	3·00
554	**216**	300w. green and brown	55·00	3·75
555	**217**	500w. blue and light blue	27·00	3·75

DESIGN—18×72 mm: No. 785, motif as Type **178** but inscriptions differently arranged.

See also Nos. 607, 609 and 641/9.

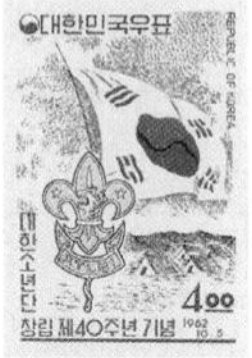

184 Scout Badge and Korean Flag

1962. 40th Anniv of Korean Scout Movement.

446	**184**	4w. brown, red and blue	1·90	75
447	**184**	4w. green, red and blue	1·90	75
MS448		Two sheets, each 90×60 mm. (a) As No. 446; (b) As No. 447	15·00	14·00

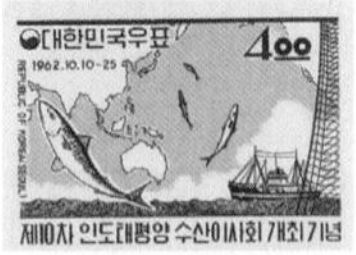

185 Chub Mackerel, Trawler and Nets

1962. Tenth Indo-Pacific Fishery Council Meeting, Seoul.

449	**185**	4w. ultramarine and blue	5·00	75

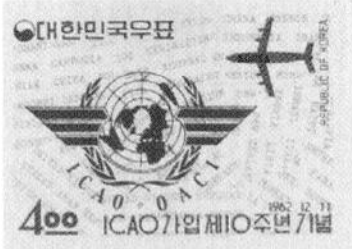

186 I.C.A.O. Emblem

1962. Tenth Anniv of Korea's Entry into I.C.A.O.

450	**186**	4w. blue and brown	2·30	75
MS451		90×60 mm. No. 450. Imperf	10·00	9·00

1962. Children's Savings Campaign. As Nos. 356/7 but new currency.

452		1w. yellow, brown and green	7·00	1·20
453		2w. brown, blue and pink	11·50	1·50

1962. Air. New Currency.

454	**169**	5w. blue and violet	95·00	17·00
512	-	10w. brown and green (As No. 418)	15·00	4·75
513	-	20w. brown and green (As No. 419)	55·00	7·75
563	**169**	39w. drab and blue	11·50	2·30
514	-	40w. green and blue (As No. 420)	29·00	6·25
564	-	64w. green and blue (As No. 418)	10·00	2·75
565	-	78w. blue and green (As No. 419)	27·00	4·75
566	-	112w. green and blue (As No. 420)	13·00	2·75

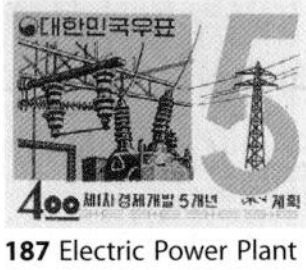

187 Electric Power Plant

1962. Inauguration of First Korean Economic Five Year Plan.

458	**187**	4w. violet and orange	21·00	2·30
459	-	4w. ultramarine and blue	21·00	2·30

DESIGN: No. 459, Irrigation Dam.

See also Nos. 482/3, 528/9, 593/4 and 634/5.

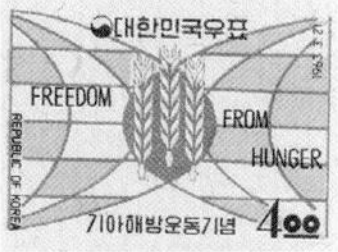

188 Campaign Emblem

1963. Freedom from Hunger.

460	**188**	4w. green, buff and blue	1·50	55
MS461		90×60 mm. No. 460. Imperf	4·75	4·00

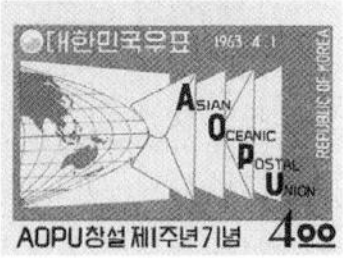

189 Globe and Letters

1963. First Anniv of Asian-Oceanic Postal Union.

462	**189**	4w. purple, green and blue	2·30	55
MS463		90×60 mm. No. 462. Imperf	4·75	4·25

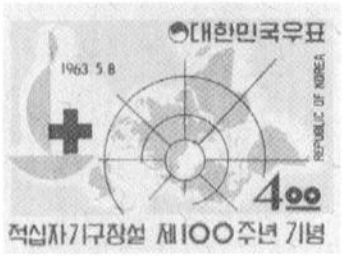

190 Centenary Emblem and Map

1963. Centenary of Red Cross.

464	**190**	4w. red, grey and blue	1·50	55
465	**190**	4w. red, grey and orange	1·50	55
MS466		140×90 mm. Nos. 464/5. Imperf	14·00	12·50

1963. Flood Relief. As No. 545, but new colour and inscr with premium.

479		4w.+1w. blue	9·25	1·20

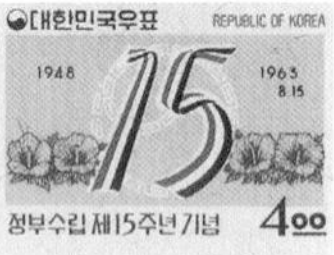

193 "15" and Hibiscus

1963. 15th Anniv of Republic.

480	**193**	4w. red, violet and blue	3·00	1·10

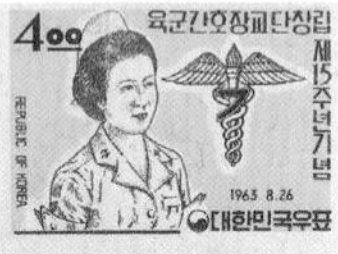

194 Nurse and Emblem

1963. 15th Anniv of Korean Army Nursing Corps.

481	**194**	4w. black, turquoise and green	2·30	95

1963. Five Year Plan. Dated "1963". As T **187**.

482		4w. violet and blue	16·00	1·50
483		4w. chocolate and brown	16·00	1·50

DESIGNS: No. 482, Cement Factory, Mun'gyong, and bag of cement; 483, Miner and coal train, Samch'ok region.

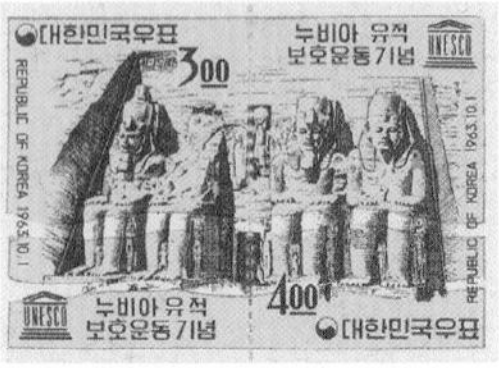

195/6 Rock Temples of Abu Simbel

1963. Nubian Monuments Preservation.

484	**195**	3w. green and drab	5·50	2·20
485	**196**	4w. green and drab	5·50	2·20
MS486		90×60 mm. Nos. 484/5. Imperf	8·50	7·50

Nos. 484/5 were issued together, *se-tenant*, forming the composite design illustrated.

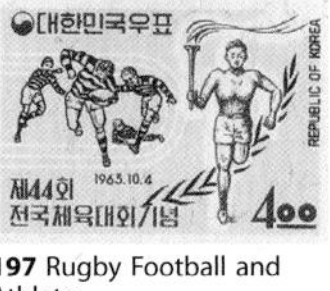

197 Rugby Football and Athlete

1963. 44th National Games.
487 **197** 4w. green, brown and blue 3·75 1·30

198 Nurse and Motor Clinic

1963. Tenth Anniv of Korean Tuberculosis Prevention Society.
488 **198** 4w. blue and red 1·90 75

199 Eleanor Roosevelt

1963. 15th Anniv of Declaration of Human Rights.
489 **199** 3w. brown and blue 1·50 55
490 - 4w. blue, green and buff 1·50 55
MS491 90×60 mm. Nos. 489/90. Imperf 6·25 5·50
DESIGN: 4w. Freedom torch and globe.

200 U.N. Headquarters

1963. 15th Anniv of U.N. Recognition of Korea.
492 **200** 4w. green, blue and black 1·50 45
MS493 90×60 mm. No. 492 5·00 4·50

201 Pres. Pak Chong Hi and Capitol

1963. Inauguration of President Pak Chong Hi.
494 **201** 4w. blue, turquoise and black 60·00 15·00

202 "Tai-Keum" (Bamboo Flute)

1963. Musical Instruments and Players. As T **202**.
495 4w. green, brown and drab 5·25 1·30
496 4w. black, blue and light blue 5·25 1·30
497 4w. green, mauve and pink 5·25 1·30
498 4w. brown, violet and grey 5·25 1·30
499 4w. blue, brown and pink 5·25 1·30
500 4w. turquoise, black and blue 5·25 1·30
501 4w. violet, bistre and yellow 5·25 1·30
502 4w. blue, brown and mauve 5·25 1·30
503 4w. black, blue and purple 5·25 1·30
504 4w. black, brown and pink 5·25 1·30
MUSICAL INSTRUMENTS (and players)—VERT: No. 495, Type **202**; 496, "Wul-keum" (banjo); 497, "Tang-piri" (flageolet); 498, "Na-bal" (trumpet); 499, "Hyang-pipa" (lute); 500, "Pyenkyeng" jade chimes; 501, "Taipyeng-so" (clarinet); 502, "Chang-ko" (double-ended drum). HORIZ: No. 503, "Wa-kong-hu" (harp); 504, "Kaya-ko" (zither).

203 Symbols of Metric System

1964. Introduction of Metric System in Korea.
505 **203** 4w. multicoloured 1·50 45

204 "UNESCO"

1964. Tenth Anniv of Korean UNESCO Committee.
506 **204** 4w. ultramarine, red & blue 1·90 70

205 Symbols of Industry and Census

1964. National Industrial Census (1963).
507 **205** 4w. brown, black and grey 1·90 70

206 Y.M.C.A. Emblem and Profile of Young Man

1964. 50th Anniv of Korean Young Men's Christian Association.
508 **206** 4w. red, blue and green 1·50 45

207 Fair Emblem, Ginseng Root and Freighter

1964. New York World's Fair.
509 **207** 40w. brown, green and yellow 3·75 1·30
510 - 100w. ultramarine, brown and blue 35·00 7·75
MS511 90×60 mm. Nos. 509/10. Imperf 80·00 75·00
DESIGN: 100w. Korean pavilion at Fair.

208 Secret Garden

1964. Background in light blue.
517 **208** 1w. green 1·50 45
518 - 2w. green 1·50 45
519 - 3w. green 1·50 45
520 - 4w. green 3·00 95
521 - 5w. violet 5·50 1·50
522 - 6w. blue 7·00 1·90
523 - 7w. brown 10·00 2·75
524 - 8w. brown 10·50 2·75
525 - 9w. violet 10·50 2·75
526 - 10w. green 15·00 3·00
MS527 Five sheets each 90×60 mm. 1w. and 10w.; 2w. and 9w.; 3w. and 8w.; 4w. and 7w.; 5w. and 6w. Imperf 95·00 85·00
DESIGNS: 2w. Whahong Gate; 3w. Uisang Pavilion; 4w. Mt. Songni; 5w. Paekma River; 6w. Anab Pond; 7w. Choksok Pavilion; 8w. Kwanghan Pavilion; 9w. Whaom Temple; 10w. Chonjeyon Falls.

1964. Five Year Plan. Dated "1964". As T **187**.
528 4w. black and blue 5·50 1·20
529 4w. blue and yellow 5·50 1·20
DESIGNS: No. 528, Trawlers and fish; 529, Oil refinery and barrels.

209 Wheel and Globe

1964. Colombo Plan Day.
530 **209** 4w. light brown, brown and green 1·50 55
MS531 90×60 mm. No. 530. Imperf 5·50 4·75

210 "Helping Hand"

1964. 15th Anniv of Korea's Admission to W.H.O.
532 **210** 4w. black, green and light green 1·50 55
MS533 90×60 mm. No. 532. Imperf 5·50 4·75

211 Running

1964. 45th National Games, Inchon.
534 **211** 4w. pink, green and purple 3·75 1·30

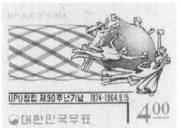

212 U.P.U. Monument, Berne, and Ribbons

1964. 90th Anniv of U.P.U.
535 **212** 4w. brown, blue and pink 1·50 55
MS536 90×60 mm. No. 535. Imperf 5·75 5·00

218 Federation Emblem

1964. Fifth Meeting of Int Federation of Asian and Western Pacific Contractors' Associations.
556 **218** 4w. green, light green and brown 1·50 55

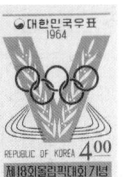

219 Olympic "V" Emblem

1964. Olympic Games, Tokyo.
557 **219** 4w. blue, turquoise and brown 3·00 1·00
558 - 4w. mauve, blue and green 3·00 1·00
559 - 4w. brown, ultramarine and blue 3·00 1·00
560 - 4w. red, brown and blue 3·00 1·00
561 - 4w. brown, purple and blue 3·00 1·00
MS562 Five sheets each 90×60 mm. As Nos. 557/61. Imperf 23·00 21·00
DESIGNS—HORIZ: No. 558, Running; 559, Rowing; 560, Horse-jumping; 561, Gymnastics.

220 Unissued 1884 100m. Stamp

1964. 80th Anniv of Korean Postal Services.
567 **220** 3w. blue, violet and mauve 3·75 95
568 - 4w. black, violet and green 5·50 1·20
DESIGN: 4w. Hong Yong Sik, 1st Korean Postmaster-general.

221 Pine Cone

1965. Korean Plants. Plants multicoloured, background colours given.
571 **221** 4w. green 2·30 75
572 - 4w. brown (Plum blossom) 2·30 75
573 - 4w. blue (Forsythia) 2·30 75
574 - 4w. green (Azalea) 2·30 75
575 - 4w. pink (Lilac) 2·30 75
576 - 4w. grey (Wild rose) 2·30 75
577 - 4w. green (Balsam) 2·30 75
578 - 4w. grey (Hibiscus) 2·30 75
579 - 4w. flesh (Crepe myrtle) 2·30 75
580 - 4w. blue (Ullung chrysanthemum) 2·30 75
581 - 4w. buff (Paulownia, tree) 2·30 75
582 - 4w. blue (Bamboo) 2·30 75
MS583 Twelve sheets each 90×60 mm. Nos. 571/82. Imperf 37·00 30·00

222 Folk Dancing

1965. Pacific Area Travel Assn Conf, Seoul.
584 **222** 4w. violet, brown and green 1·40 45
MS585 90×60 mm. No. 584. Imperf 3·75 3·25

223 Flag and Doves

1965. Military Aid for Vietnam.
586 **223** 4w. brown, blue and yellow 1·40 45
MS587 90×60 mm. No. 586. Imperf 3·75 3·25

224 "Food Production"

1965. Agricultural Seven Year Plan.
588 **224** 4w. brown, green and black 1·40 45

225 "Family Scales"

1965. Family Planning Month.
589 **225** 4w. brown, drab and light green 1·40 45
MS590 90×60 mm. No. 589. Imperf 3·50 3·25

226 I.T.U. Emblem and Symbols

1965. Centenary of I.T.U.
591 **226** 4w. black, red and blue 1·40 45
MS592 90×60 mm. No. 591. Imperf 3·50 3·25

1965. Five Year Plan. Dated "1965". As T **187**.
593 4w. blue and pink 2·30 1·20
594 4w. sepia and brown 2·30 1·20
DESIGNS: No. 593, "Korea" (freighter) at quayside and crates; 594, Fertilizer plant and wheat.

227 Flags of Australia, Belgium, Great Britain, Canada and Colombia

1965. 15th Anniv of Outbreak of Korean War.

595	**227**	4w. multicoloured	1·50	70
596	-	4w. multicoloured	1·50	70
597	-	4w. multicoloured	1·50	70
598	-	4w. multicoloured	1·50	70
599	-	10w. multicoloured	5·50	1·50
MS600 Five sheets each 90×60 mm. Nos. 595/9. Imperf			11·50	10·50

DESIGNS—U.N. Emblem and flags of: No. 596, Denmark, Ethiopia, France, Greece and India; 597, Italy, Luxembourg, Netherlands, New Zealand and Norway; 598, Philippines, Sweden, Thailand, Turkey and South Africa; 599, General MacArthur and flags of Korea, U.N. and U.S.A.

228 Flag and Sky-writing ("20")

1965. 20th Anniv of Liberation.

601	**228**	4w. red, violet and blue	3·00	55
602	-	10w. red, blue and violet	3·75	75

DESIGN: 10w. South Gate and fireworks.

229 Ants and Leaf

1965. Savings Campaign.

603	**229**	4w. brown, ochre and green	1·40	45

230 Hoisting Flag

1965. 15th Anniv of Recapture of Seoul.

604	**230**	3w. green, blue and orange	3·00	1·20

231 Radio Aerial

1965. 80th Anniv of Korean Telecommunications.

605	**231**	3w. green, black and blue	2·30	45
606	-	10w. black, blue and yellow	4·75	75

DESIGN: 10w. Telegraphist of 1885.

1965. Flood Relief. As No. 545 (1962 issue), but colour changed and inscr with premium.

607	4w.+2w. blue	4·75	1·20

232 Pole Vaulting

1965. National Athletic Meeting, Kwangju.

608	**232**	3w. multicoloured	2·30	95

1965. Aid for Children. As No. 545 (1962 issue), but colour changed and inscr with premium.

609	4w.+2w. purple	4·75	1·20

233 I.C.Y. Emblem

1965. International Co-operation Year and 20th Anniv of United Nations.

610	**233**	3w. red, green and deep green	1·20	45
611	-	10w. ultramarine, green and blue	2·30	75
MS612 Two sheets each 90×60 mm. (a) No. 610; (b) No. 611			7·75	7·00

DESIGN—VERT: 10w. U.N. flag and headquarters, New York.

234 Child posting Letter

1965. Tenth Communications Day.

613	**234**	3w. multicoloured	3·00	95
614	-	10w. red, blue and green	6·25	1·70

DESIGN: 10w. Airmail envelope and telephone receiver.

235 Children with Toboggan

1965. Christmas and New Year.

615	**235**	3w. blue, red and green	2·30	55
616	-	4w. blue, red and green	3·75	55
MS617 90×60 mm. Nos. 615/16. Imperf			4·75	4·00

DESIGN: 4w. Boy and girl in traditional costume.

236 Freedom House

1966. Opening of Freedom House, Panmunjom.

618	**236**	7w. black, emerald & grn	2·30	75
619	**236**	39w. black, lilac and green	13·00	3·00
MS620 90×60 mm. Nos. 618/19. Imperf			23·00	19·00

237 Mandarins

1966. Korean Birds. Multicoloured.

621	3w. Type **237**	2·30	1·30
622	5w. Manchurian crane	2·50	1·30
623	7w. Common pheasant	3·75	1·30
MS624 Three sheets each 90×60 mm. Nos. 621/3. Imperf		14·00	12·00

238 Pine Forest

1966. Reafforestation Campaign.

625	**238**	7w. brown, green and light green	1·50	55

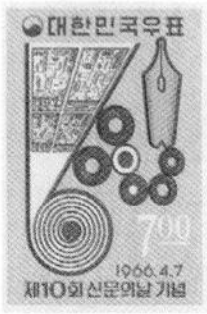

239 Printing Press and Pen

1966. Tenth Newspaper Day.

626	**239**	7w. purple, yellow and green	1·30	55

240 Curfew Bell and Young Koreans

1966. Youth Guidance Month.

627	**240**	7w. orange, green and blue	1·30	55

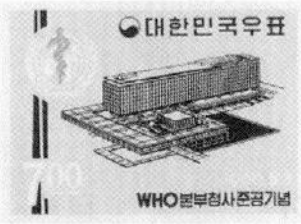

241 W.H.O. Building

1966. Inauguration of W.H.O. Headquarters, Geneva.

628	**241**	7w. black, blue and yellow	1·50	60
629	**241**	39w. red, grey and yellow	11·50	3·50
MS630 90×60 mm. No. 628. Imperf			4·75	3·50

242 Pres. Pak, Handclasp and Flags

1966. Pres. Pak Chung Hi's State Tour of South-East Asia.

631	**242**	7w. multicoloured	7·75	2·50

243 Girl Scout and Flag

1966. 20th Anniv of Korean Girl Scouts.

632	**243**	7w. black, green and yellow	2·30	85

244 Student and Ehwa Women's University

1966. 80th Anniv of Korean Women's Education.

633	**244**	7w. multicoloured	1·30	55

1966. 5-Year Plan. Dated "1966". As T **187**.

634	7w. ultramarine and blue	3·75	1·20
635	7w. black and yellow	3·75	1·20

DESIGNS: No. 634, Map and transport; 635, Radar aerials and telephone.

245 Carrier Pigeons

1966. International Correspondence Week. Unissued sheet (90×60 mm) surch as shown in T **245** and optd **6, 1966.6.13—19** with bars obliterating old inscr.

MS636 7(w.) on 40(h.) deep green, green and red	3·75	3·50

246 Wall-eyed Pollack

1966. Korean Fish. Multicoloured.

637	3w. Type **246**	3·00	85
638	5w. Lenok	3·75	85
639	7w. Manchurian croaker	4·75	1·00
MS640 Three sheets each 90×60 mm. Nos. 637/9. Imperf		11·50	10·00

247 Incense-burner

249 Buddha, Kwanchok Temple

1966. As previous issues (some redrawn) and new designs, all inscr "REPUBLIC OF KOREA".

641	**213**	60ch. green	40	10
642	**180**	1w. green	4·25	40
643	**164**	2w. green	40	10
644	**165**	3w. brown	40	10
645	**181**	5w. blue	5·00	75
646	**214**	7w. blue	5·50	30
789	**168**	10w. blue (22×18 mm)	31·00	70
647	**247**	13w. blue	5·50	75
709	**182**	20w. green and light green	70·00	1·50
710	**183**	40w. green and olive	42·00	1·50
793	**183**	40w. blue and pink (18×22 mm)	46·00	2·30
711	**191**	50w. brown and bistre	8·50	1·50
648	-	60w. green	31·00	1·50
649	**249**	80w. green	11·50	1·50

DESIGN—As Type **247**: 60w. 12th-century porcelain vessel.

250 Children and Hemispheres

1966. 15th Assembly of World Conf of Teaching Profession (WCOTP), Seoul.

650	**250**	7w. violet, brown and blue	1·50	55
MS651 90×60 mm. No. 650. Imperf			3·75	3·50

251 Factory within Pouch

1966. Savings Campaign.

652	**251**	7w. multicoloured	1·30	55

252 People on Map of Korea

1966. National Census.

653	**252**	7w. multicoloured	1·30	55

253 *Lucida lateralis*

1966. Insects. Multicoloured.

654	3w. Type **253**	2·30	85
655	5w. *Hexacentrus japonicus* (grasshopper)	2·30	85
656	7w. *Sericinus montela* (butterfly)	3·00	1·00
MS657 Three sheets each 90×60 mm. (a) No. 654; (b) No. 655; (c) No. 656		11·00	10·00

254 C.I.S.M. Emblem and "Round Table" Meeting

1966. 21st General Assembly of International Military Sports Council (C.I.S.M.), Seoul.

658	**254**	7w. multicoloured	1·30	55
MS659 90×60 mm. No. 658. Imperf			3·75	3·50

255 Soldiers and Flags

1966. First Anniv of Korean Troops in Vietnam.

660	**255**	7w. multicoloured	9·25	2·30

256 Wrestling

1966. 47th Athletic Meeting, Seoul.

661	**256**	7w. multicoloured	2·50	1·20

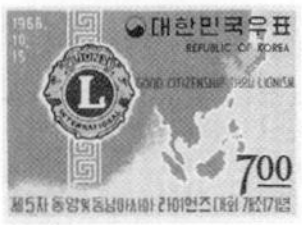

257 Lions Emblem and Map

1966. Fifth Orient and South-East Asian Lions Convention, Seoul.

662	**257**	7w. multicoloured	1·50	55
MS663 90×60 mm. No. 662. Imperf			3·75	3·50

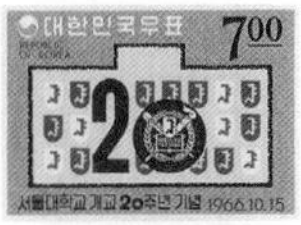

258 University Emblem, "20" and Shields

1966. 20th Anniv of Seoul University.

664	**258**	7w. multicoloured	1·50	55

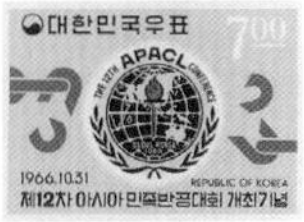

259 A.P.A.C.L. Emblem

1966. 12th Conference of Asian People's Anti-Communist League (A.P.A.C.L.), Seoul.

665	**259**	7w. multicoloured	1·50	55
MS666 90×60 mm. No. 665. Imperf			3·50	3·25

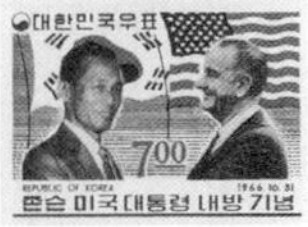

260 Presidents Pak and Johnson

1966. President Johnson's Visit to Korea.

667	**260**	7w. multicoloured	2·30	75
668	**260**	83w. multicoloured	13·00	3·75
MS669 90×60 mm. Nos. 667/8. Imperf			15·00	14·00

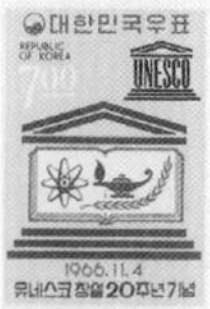

261 UNESCO Symbols and Emblem

1966. 20th Anniv of UNESCO.

670	**261**	7w. multicoloured	1·50	45
MS671 90×60 mm. No. 670. Imperf			3·75	3·50

1966. Hurricane Relief. As No. 646 but colour changed and premium added.

672	**214**	7w.+2w. red	6·25	1·50

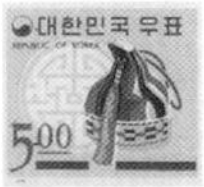

262 "Lucky Bag"

1966. Christmas and New Year. Multicoloured.

673	5w. Type **262**	2·30	40
674	7w. Sheep (vert)	3·75	40
MS675 Two sheets each 90×60 mm. Nos. 673/4. Imperf		7·75	7·00

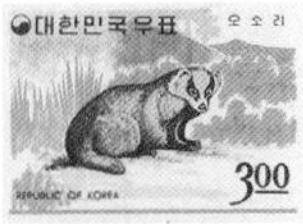

263 Eurasian Badger

1966. Korean Fauna. Multicoloured.

676	3w. Type **263**	3·00	1·10
677	5w. Asiatic black bear	3·00	1·10
678	7w. Tiger	3·75	1·10
MS679 Three sheets each 90×60 mm. Nos. 676/8. Imperf		14·50	13·50

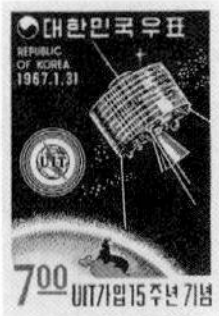

264 "Syncom" Satellite

1967. 15th Anniv of Korea's Admission to I.T.U.

680	**264**	7w. multicoloured	1·50	70
MS681 90×60 mm. No. 680. Imperf			4·25	3·75

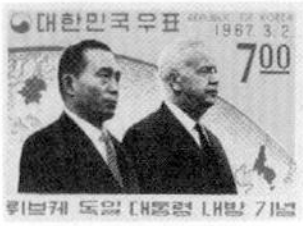

265 Presidents Pak and Lubke

1967. Visit of Pres. Lubke of West Germany to Korea.

682	**265**	7w. multicoloured	2·50	1·20
MS683 90×60 mm. No. 682. Imperf			4·75	4·25

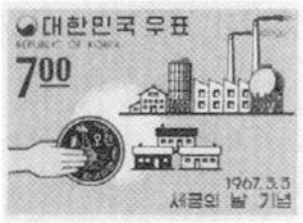

266 Coin, Factories and Houses

1967. First Anniv of Korean Revenue Office.

684	**266**	7w. sepia and green	1·50	55

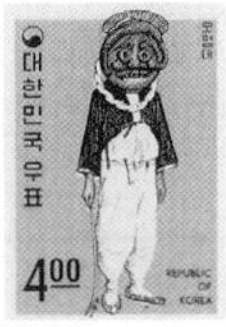

267 Okwangdae Mask

1967. Folklore. Multicoloured.

685	4w. Type **267**	2·30	70
686	5w. Sandi mask (horiz)	2·30	75
687	7w. Mafoe mask	3·00	1·00
MS688 Three sheets each 90×60 mm. Nos. 685/7. Imperf		11·00	9·75

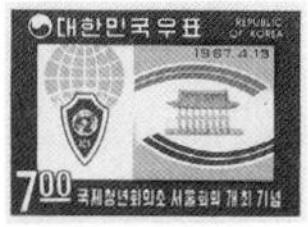

268 J.C.I. Emblem and Pavilion

1967. International Junior Chamber of Commerce Conference, Seoul.

689	**268**	7w. multicoloured	1·40	45
MS690 90×60 mm. No. 689. Imperf			3·75	3·50

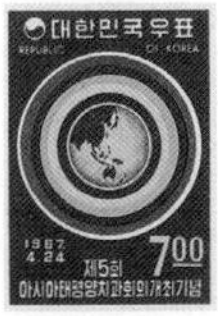

269 Map Emblem

1967. Fifth Asian Pacific Dental Congress, Seoul.

691	**269**	7w. multicoloured	1·40	45
MS692 90×60 mm. No. 691. Imperf			3·75	3·50

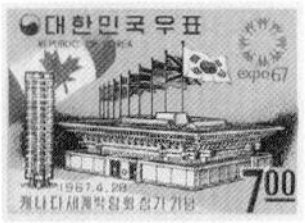

270 Korean Pavilion

1967. World Fair, Montreal.

693	**270**	7w. black, red and yellow	3·75	75
694	**270**	83w. black, red and blue	23·00	5·50
MS695 90×60 mm. Nos. 693/4			19·00	18·00

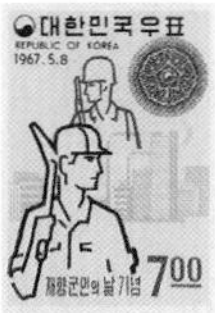

271 Worker and Soldier

1967. Veterans' Day.

696	**271**	7w. multicoloured	1·50	45

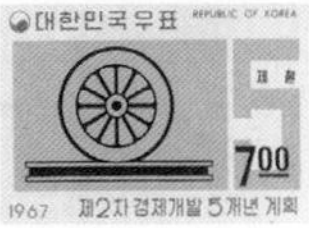

272 Railway Wheel and Rail

1967. Second Five Year Plan. Dated "1967".

697	**272**	7w. black, yellow and brown	7·00	1·20
698	-	7w. orange, brown and black	7·00	1·20

DESIGN: No. 698, Nut and bolt.

See also Nos. 773/4, 833/4, 895/6 and 981/2.

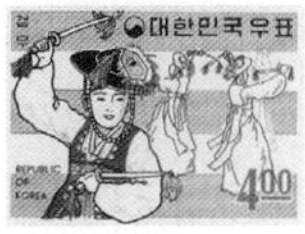

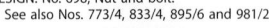

273 Sword Dance

1967. Folklore. Multicoloured.

699	4w. Type **273**	2·30	70
700	5w. Peace dance (vert)	2·30	75
701	7w. Buddhist dance (vert)	3·00	1·00
MS702 Three sheets each 90×60 mm. Nos. 699/701. Imperf		11·00	10·00

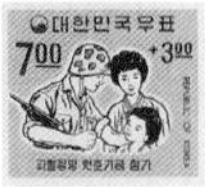

274 Soldier and Family

1967. Fund for Korean Troops Serving in Vietnam.

703	**274**	7w.+3w. black and purple	7·75	1·20

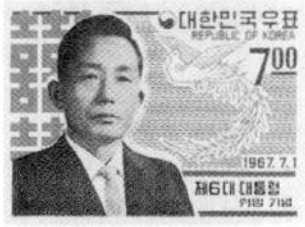

275 President Pak and Phoenix

1967. Inauguration of President Pak for Second Term.

704	**275**	7w. multicoloured	23·00	3·75
MS705 90×60 mm. No. 704. Imperf			65·00	60·00

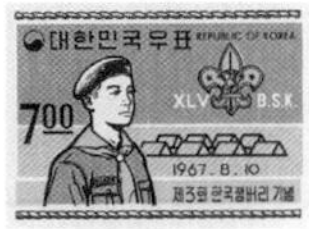

276 Scout, Badge and Camp

1967. Third Korean Scout Jamboree. Multicoloured.

706	7w. Type **276**	1·50	70
707	20w. Scout badge, bridge and tent	5·50	2·20
MS708 Two sheets each 90×60 mm. Nos. 706/7. Imperf		11·00	10·00

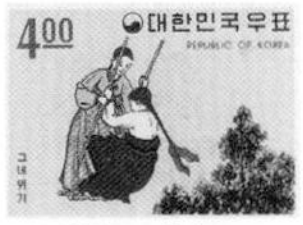

280 Girls on Swing

1967. Folklore. Multicoloured.

712	4w. Type **280**	3·75	75
713	5w. Girls on seesaw (vert)	3·75	95
714	7w. Girls dancing (vert)	6·25	1·10
MS715 Three sheet each 90×60 mm. Nos. 712/14. Imperf		20·00	19·00

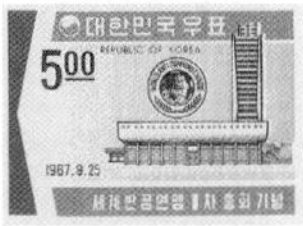

281 Freedom Centre

1967. First World Anti-Communist League Conference, Taipei. Multicoloured.

716	5w. Type **281**	1·50	45
717	7w. Hand grasping chain (vert)	1·50	45
MS718 Two sheets each 90×60 mm. Nos. 716/17. Imperf		11·00	10·00

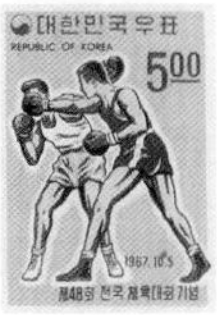

282 Boxing

1967. National Athletic Meeting, Seoul. Multicoloured.

719	5w. Type **282**	2·30	75
720	7w. Basketball	3·00	75

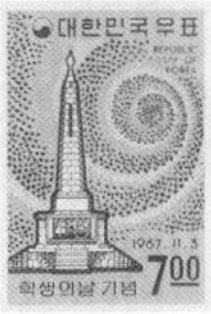

283 Students' Memorial, Kwangjoo

1967. Students' Day.

721	**283**	7w. multicoloured	1·50	45

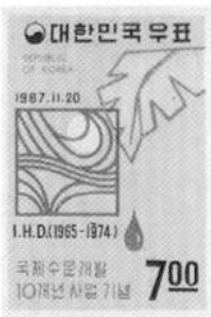

284 Decade Emblem

1967. International Hydrological Decade.

722	**284**	7w. multicoloured	1·50	45

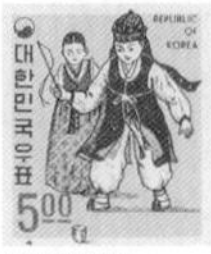

285 Children spinning Top

1967. Christmas and New Year.

723	**285**	5w. blue, red and pink	3·00	40
724	-	7w. brown, blue and bistre	3·75	30
MS725 Two sheets each 90×60 mm. Nos. 723/4. Imperf			7·75	7·00

DESIGN: 7w. Monkey and Signs of the Zodiac.

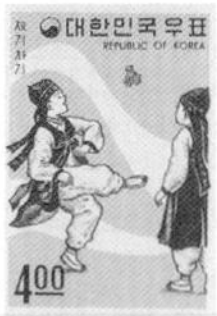

286 Playing Shuttlecock

1967. Folklore. Multicoloured.

726	4w. Type **286**	3·00	1·00
727	5w. "Dalmaji" (horiz)	3·00	1·00
728	7w. Archery	3·00	1·00
MS729 Three sheets each 90×60 mm. Nos. 726/8. Imperf		12·50	11·50

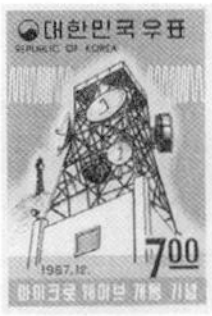

287 Microwave Transmitter

1967. Inauguration of Microwave Telecommunications Service.

730	**287**	7w. black, green and blue	1·50	70
MS731 90×60 mm. No. 730. Imperf			3·75	3·50

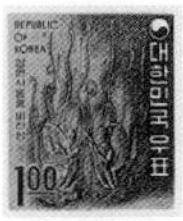

288 Carving, King Songdok's Bell

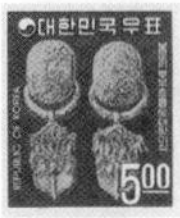

289 5th–6th century Earrings

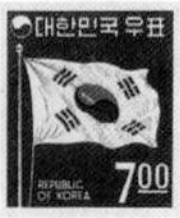

290 Korean Flag

1968

732	**288**	1w. brown and yellow	40	10
733	**289**	5w. yellow and green	3·00	55
734	**290**	7w. red and blue	1·50	25
787	**290**	7w. blue	3·75	40
788	**290**	7w. blue*	1·50	30
790	**290**	10w. blue*	1·50	25

*Nos. 788 and 790 have their face values shown as "7" or "10" only, omitting the noughts shown on Nos. 734 and 787.

For designs similar to Type **290** see Nos. 771, 780 and 827.

291 W.H.O.
Emblem

1968. 20th Anniv of W.H.O.
| 735 | **291** | 7w. multicoloured | 1·50 | 45 |
| MS736 | 90×60 mm. No. 735. Imperf | | 3·75 | 3·50 |

292 E.A.T.A.
Emblem and
Korean Motif

1968. Second East Asia Travel Association Conference, Seoul.
| 737 | **292** | 7w. multicoloured | 1·50 | 45 |
| MS738 | 90×60 mm. No. 737. Imperf | | 4·75 | 4·25 |

293 C.A.C.C.I. Emblem,
Korean Doorknocker
and Factories

1968. Second Conference of Confederation of Asian Chambers of Commerce and Industry (C.A.C.C.I.), Seoul.
| 739 | **293** | 7w. multicoloured | 1·50 | 45 |
| MS740 | 90×60 mm. No. 739. Imperf | | 4·25 | 3·75 |

294 Pres. Pak and
Emperor Haile Selassie

1968. Visit of Emperor of Ethiopia.
| 741 | **294** | 7w. multicoloured | 3·75 | 1·50 |
| MS742 | 90×60 mm. No. 741. Imperf | | 7·75 | 7·00 |

295 Post-bag

1968. Postman's Day. Multicoloured.
| 743 | | 5w. Type **295** | 1·50 | 70 |
| 744 | | 7w. Postman | 1·50 | 70 |

296 Atomic and
Development Symbols

1968. Promotion of Science and Technology.
| 745 | **296** | 7w. blue, green and red | 1·50 | 45 |

297 Kyung Hi University
and Conference Emblem

1968. Second Conf of Int Assn of University Presidents.
| 746 | **297** | 7w. multicoloured | 1·50 | 45 |
| MS747 | 90×60 mm. No. 746. Imperf | | 5·50 | 5·00 |

298 "Liberation"

1968. Liberation of Suppressed Peoples' Campaign.
| 748 | **298** | 7w. multicoloured | 1·50 | 45 |

299 Reservist

1968. Army Reservists' Fund.
| 749 | **299** | 7w.+3w. black & green | 13·00 | 1·50 |

300 Stylized
Peacock

1968. 20th Anniv of Republic.
| 750 | **300** | 7w. multicoloured | 1·50 | 45 |

301 Fair Entrance

1968. First Korean Trade Fair, Seoul.
| 751 | **301** | 7w. multicoloured | 1·50 | 45 |

302 Assembly
Emblem

1968. Third General Assembly of Asian Pharmaceutical Association Federation.
| 752 | **302** | 7w. multicoloured | 1·50 | 45 |

303 Scout Badge

1968. Sixth Far East Scout Conference, Seoul.
| 753 | **303** | 7w. multicoloured | 2·30 | 75 |

304 Soldier and
Battle Scene

1968. 20th Anniv of Korean Armed Forces.
754	**304**	7w. orange and green	7·75	2·30
755	–	7w. blue and light blue	7·75	2·30
756	–	7w. blue and orange	7·75	2·30
757	–	7w. light blue and blue	7·75	2·30
758	–	7w. green and orange	7·75	2·30
DESIGNS: No. 755, Sailor and naval guns; 756, Servicemen and flags; 757, Pilot and Northrop F-5A Freedom Fighters; 758, Marine and landings.

305 Colombo
Plan Emblem and
Globe

1968. 19th Meeting of Colombo Plan Consultative Committee, Seoul.
| 759 | **305** | 7w. multicoloured | 1·50 | 40 |

306 (I) Olympic   **307** (II) Olympic
Emblems   Emblems

1968. Olympic Games, Mexico. Multicoloured.
760		7w. Type **306**	14·50	4·75
761		7w. Type **307**	14·50	4·75
762		7w. Cycling (I)	14·50	4·75
763		7w. Cycling (II)	14·50	4·75
764		7w. Boxing (I)	14·50	4·75
765		7w. Boxing (II)	14·50	4·75
766		7w. Wrestling (I)	14·50	4·75
767		7w. Wrestling (II)	14·50	4·75
MS768 Four sheets each 90×60 mm. Imperf (a) Nos. 760/1; (b) Nos. 762/3; (c) Nos. 764/5; (d) Nos. 766/7 ... 46·00 42·00

The two types of each design may be identified by the position of the country name at the foot of the design—ranged right in types I, and left in types II. On three of the designs (excluding "Cycling") the figures of value are on left and right respectively. Types I and II of each design were issued together horizontally se-tenant within the sheets of 50 stamps.

308 Statue of
Woman

1968. 60th Anniv of Women's Secondary Education.
| 769 | **308** | 7w. multicoloured | 1·50 | 40 |

309 Coin and Symbols

1968. National Wealth Survey.
| 770 | **309** | 7w. multicoloured | 1·50 | 40 |

1968. Disaster Relief Fund. As No. 734, but with additional inscr and premium added.
| 771 | **290** | 7w.+3w. red and blue | 42·00 | 7·75 |
The face value on No. 771 is expressed as "7 00+3 00", see also Nos. 780 and 827.

310 Shin Eui Ju
Memorial

1968. Anniv of Student Uprising, Shin Eui Ju (1945).
| 772 | **310** | 7w. multicoloured | 1·90 | 55 |

1968. Second Five Year Plan. As T **272**. Dated "1968". Multicoloured.
| 773 | | 7w. Express motorway | 13·00 | 1·20 |
| 774 | | 7w. "Clover-leaf" road junction | 7·75 | 1·20 |

311 Demonstrators

1968. Human Rights Year.
| 775 | **311** | 7w. multicoloured | 1·50 | 40 |

312 Christmas
Lanterns

1968. Christmas and New Year. Multicoloured.
| 776 | | 5w. Type **312** | 11·50 | 55 |
| 777 | | 7w. Cockerel | 11·50 | 55 |
MS778 Two sheets each 90×60 mm. Nos. 776/7. Imperf ... 15·00 14·00

314 Korean House and
U.N. Emblems

1968. 20th Anniv of South Korea's Admission to U.N.
| 779 | **314** | 7w. multicoloured | 1·50 | 40 |

1969. Military Helicopter Fund. As No. 734 but colours changed and inscr with premium added.
| 780 | **290** | 7w.+3w. red, blue & grn | 11·50 | 1·30 |

315 Torch and
Monument,
Pagoda Park,
Seoul

1969. 50th Anniv of Samil (Independence) Movement.
| 781 | **315** | 7w. multicoloured | 1·50 | 45 |

316 Hyun Choong Sa
and "Turtle" Ships

1969. Dedication of Rebuilt Hyun Choong Sa (Shrine of Admiral Li Sun Sin).
| 782 | **316** | 7w. multicoloured | 1·50 | 45 |

317 President Pak and
Yang di-Pertuan Agong

1969. Visit of Yang di-Pertuan Agong (Malaysian Head-of-State).
| 783 | **317** | 7w. multicoloured | 3·75 | 1·20 |
| MS784 | 90×60 mm. No. 783. Imperf | | 65·00 | 60·00 |

318 Stone
Temple Lamp

1969
786	**318**	5w. purple	1·10	25
791	–	20w. green	2·30	40
792	–	30w. green	3·75	75
794	–	40w. mauve and blue	2·75	75
795	–	100w. brown and purple	95·00	2·30
DESIGNS—As Type 318. VERT: 20w. Wine jug; 40w. Porcelain Jar, Yi Dynasty; 100w. Seated Buddha (bronze). HORIZ: 30w. "Duck" vase.

323 "Red Cross"
between Faces

1969. 50th Anniv of League of Red Cross Societies.
| 796 | **323** | 7w. multicoloured | 1·90 | 45 |
| MS797 | 90×60 mm. No. 796. Imperf | | 5·50 | 5·00 |

324 "Building the
Nation's Economy"

1969. "Second Economy Drive".
| 798 | **324** | 7w. multicoloured | 1·50 | 45 |

325 Presidents Pak and
Nguyen van Thieu

1969. Visit of President Nguyen van Thieu of South Vietnam.
799 **325** 7w. multicoloured 3·00 1·20
MS800 90×60 mm. No. 799. Imperf 8·50 6·75

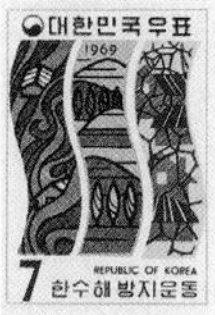

326 Reafforestation and Flooded Fields

1969. Flood and Drought Damage Prevention Campaign. Multicoloured.
801 7w. Type **326** 1·50 40
802 7w. Withered and flourishing plants 1·50 40

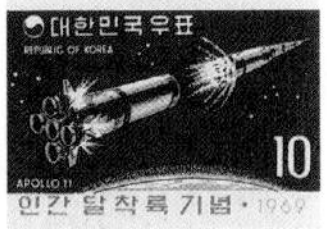

327 Ignition of Second-stage Rocket

1969. First Man on the Moon.
803 **327** 10w. blue, black and red 3·75 1·10
804 - 10w. blue, black and red 3·75 1·10
805 - 20w. multicoloured 3·75 1·10
806 - 20w. multicoloured 3·75 1·10
807 - 40w. blue, red and black 3·75 1·10
MS808 160×110 mm. Nos. 803/7. Imperf 35·00 31·00
DESIGNS: No. 804, Separation of modules from rocket; 805, Diagram of lunar orbit; 806, Astronauts on Moon; 807, Splashdown of "Apollo 11".

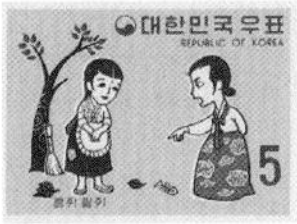

328 Stepmother admonishing Kongji

1969. Korean Fairy Tales (1st series). *Kongji and Patji*. Multicoloured.
809 5w. Type **328** 3·75 95
810 7w. Kongji and sparrows 3·75 95
811 10w. Kongji and ox 6·25 1·30
812 20w. Kongji in sedan-chair 6·25 1·30
MS813 Four sheets each 90×60 mm. Imperf. (a) No. 809; (b) No. 810; (c) No. 811; (d) No. 812 25·00 22·00
See also Nos. 828/**MS**832, 839/**MS**843, 844/**MS**848 and 853/**MS**857.

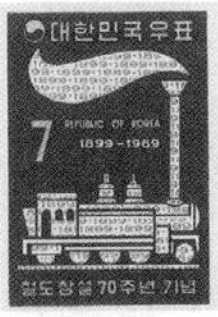

332 Steam Locomotive of 1899

1969. 70th Anniv of Korean Railways. Multicoloured.
814 7w. Type **332** 1·90 70
815 7w. Early steam and modern diesel locomotives 1·90 70

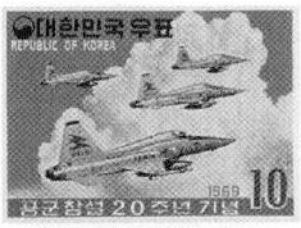

333 Northrop F-5A Freedom Jet Fighters

1969. 20th Anniv of Korean Air Force. Multicoloured.
816 10w. Type **333** 5·50 75
817 10w. McDonnell-Douglas F-4D Phantom II jet fighter 7·00 75

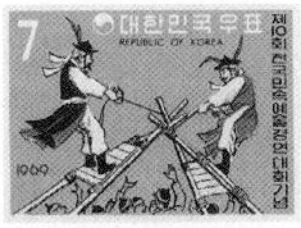

334 Game of Cha-jun

1969. Tenth Korean Traditional Arts Contest, Taegu.
818 **334** 7w. multicoloured 1·20 40

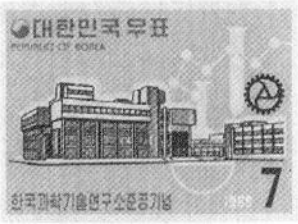

335 Molecule and Institute Building

1969. Completion of Korean Institute of Science and Technology.
819 **335** 7w. multicoloured 1·20 40

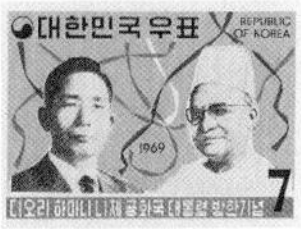

336 Presidents Pak and Hamani

1969. Visit of President Hamani of Niger Republic.
820 **336** 7w. multicoloured 2·30 1·00
MS821 90×60 mm. No. 820. Imperf 14·00 12·50

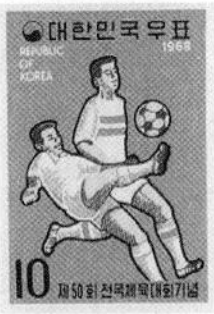

337 Football

1969. 50th Anniv of National Athletic Meeting. Multicoloured.
822 10w. Type **337** 3·00 75
823 10w. Volleyball 3·00 75
824 10w. Korean wrestling (horiz) 3·00 75
825 10w. Fencing (horiz) 3·00 75
826 10w. Taekwondo (karate) (horiz) 3·00 75

1969. Searchlight Fund. As T **290** but with additional inscr and premium. Face value expressed as "7+3".
827 7w.+3w. red and blue 39·00 1·70

1969. Korean Fairy Tales (2nd series). *The Hare's Liver*. As T **328**. Multicoloured.
828 5w. Princess and Doctors 2·30 70
829 7w. Hare arriving at Palace 2·30 70
830 10w. Preparing to remove the Hare's liver 2·30 95
831 20w. Escape of the Hare 3·75 95
MS832 Four sheets each 90×60 mm. Imperf. (a) No. 828; (b) No. 829; (c) No. 830; (d) No. 831 22·00 20·00

1969. Second Five-year Plan. As T **272**. Dated "1969". Multicoloured.
833 7w. "Agriculture and Fisheries" 1·50 45
834 7w. Industrial emblems 1·50 45

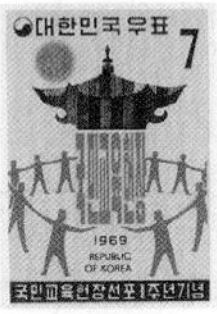

342 Students ringing "Education"

1969. First Anniv of National Education Charter.
835 **342** 7w. multicoloured 1·20 3·75

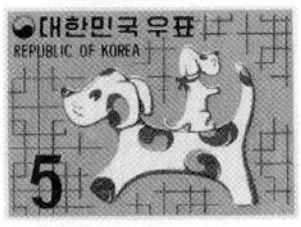

343 Toy Dogs

1969. Lunar New Year ("Year of the Dog"). Multicoloured.
836 5w. Type **343** 1·50 45
837 7w. Candle and lattice doorway 1·50 45

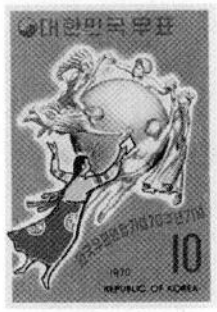

344 Woman with Letter and U.P.U. Monument, Berne

1970. 70th Anniv of Korea's Admission to U.P.U.
838 **344** 10w. multicoloured 11·50 3·75

1970. Korean Fairy Tales (3rd series). *The Sun and the Moon*. As T **328**. Multicoloured.
839 5w. Mother meets the tiger 2·30 70
840 7w. Tiger in disguise 2·30 70
841 10w. Children chased up a tree 2·30 95
842 20w. Children escape to Heaven 3·75 1·20
MS843 Four sheets each 90×60 mm. Imperf. (a) No. 839; (b) No. 840; (c) No. 841; (d) No. 842 22·00 20·00

1970. Korean Fairy Tales (4th series). *The Woodcutter and the Fairy*. As T **328**. Multicoloured.
844 10w. Woodcutter hiding Fairy's dress 2·75 1·00
845 10w. Fairy as Woodcutter's Wife 2·75 1·00
846 10w. Fairy and children fly to Heaven 2·75 1·00
847 10w. Happy reunion 2·75 1·00
MS848 Four sheets each 90×60 mm. Imperf. (a) No. 844; (b) No. 845; (c) No. 846; (d) No. 847 22·00 20·00

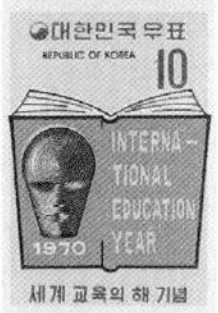

353 I.E.Y. Emblem on Open Book

1970. International Education Year.
849 **353** 10w. multicoloured 6·25 2·30

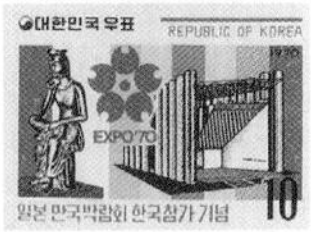

354 Seated Buddha and Korean Pavilion

1970. "EXPO 70" World Fair, Osaka, Japan.
850 **354** 10w. multicoloured 6·25 1·60

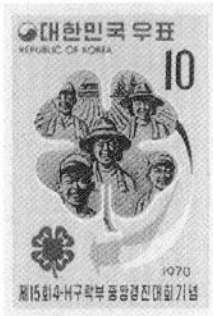

355 "4-11" Club Emblem

1970. 15th "4-11" Club (young farmers' organization) Central Contest, Suwon.
851 **355** 10w. multicoloured 1·90 75

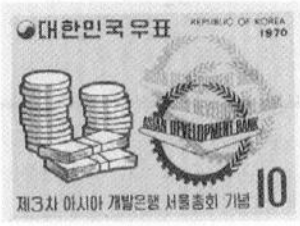

356 Bank Emblem and Cash

1970. Third General Meeting of Asian Development Bank, Seoul.
852 **356** 10w. multicoloured 1·90 75

1970. Korean Fairy Tales (5th series). *Heungbu and Nolbu*. As T **328**. Multicoloured.
853 10w. Heungbu tending swallow 6·25 1·20
854 10w. Heungbu finds treasure in pumpkin 6·25 1·20
855 10w. Nolbu with pumpkin 6·25 1·20
856 10w. Nolbu chased by devil 6·25 1·20
MS857 Four sheets each 90×60 mm. Imperf. (a) No. 853; (b) No. 854; (c) No. 855; (d) No. 856 60·00 55·00

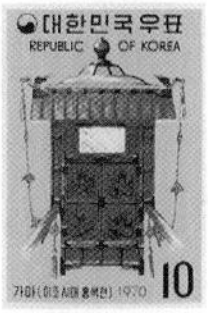

361 Royal Palanquin (Yi dynasty)

1970. Early Korean Transport.
858 **361** 10w. multicoloured 2·75 95
859 - 10w. multicoloured 2·75 95
860 - 10w. multicoloured 2·75 95
861 - 10w. black, stone and blue 2·75 95
DESIGNS—HORIZ: No. 859, Tramcar, 1899; 860, Emperor Sunjong's cadillac, 1903; 861, Nieuport 28 biplane, 1922.

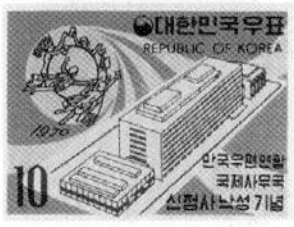

362 New Headquarters Building

1970. Opening of New U.P.U. Headquarters Building, Berne.
862 **362** 10w. multicoloured 1·50 40

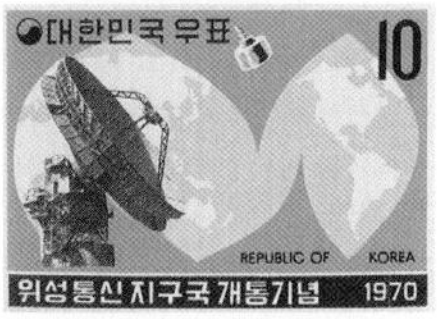

363 Dish Aerial and Hemispheres

1970. Inauguration of Satellite Communications Station, Kum San.
863 **363** 10w. multicoloured 1·90 75

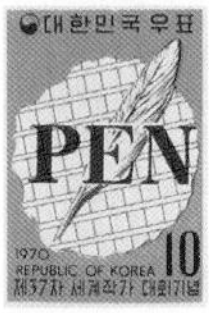

364 "PEN" and Quill Pen

1970. 37th International P.E.N. (literary organization) Congress, Seoul.
864 **364** 10w. multicoloured 1·50 40

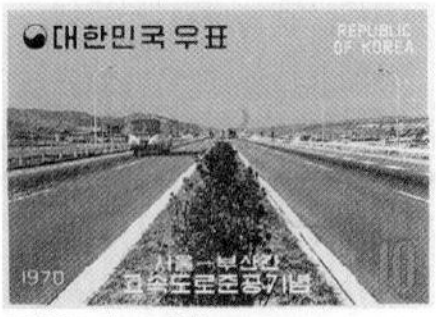

365 Section of Motorway

1970. Opening of Seoul–Pusan Motorway.
865 **365** 10w. multicoloured 1·90 75

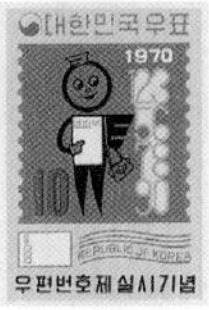

366 Postal Code Symbol

1970. Introduction of Postal Codes.
866 **366** 10w. multicoloured 1·50 40

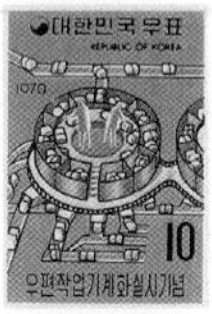

367 Parcel Sorting Area

1970. Inauguration of Postal Mechanization.
867 **367** 10w. multicoloured 1·50 40
MS868 130×90 mm. Nos. 866/7×2 £100 90·00

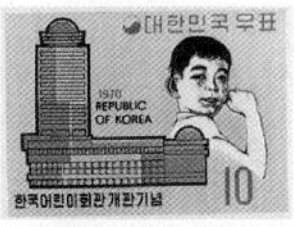

368 Children's Hall and Boy

1970. Opening of Children's Hall, Seoul.
869 **368** 10w. multicoloured 1·50 40

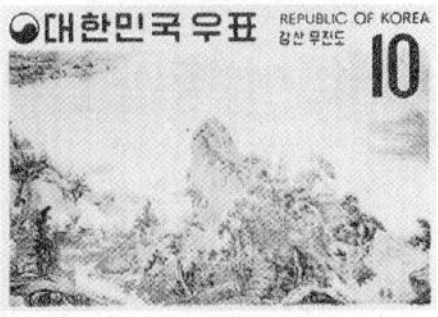

369 *Mountain and River* (Yi In Moon)

1970. Korean Paintings of Yi Dynasty (1st series). Multicoloured.
870 10w. Type **369** 2·75 75
871 10w. *Jongyangsa Temple* (Chong Son) 2·75 75
872 10w. *Mountain and River by Moonlight* (Kim Doo Ryang) (vert) 2·75 75
MS873 Three sheets each 130×90 mm. Nos. 870/2×2 14·00 12·50
See also Nos. 887/**MS**890, 897/**MS**900, 947/**MS**953, 956/**MS**953, 956/**MS**959 and 961/**MS**966.

370 P.T.T.I. Emblem

1970. Councillors' Meeting, Asian Chapter of Postal, Telegraph and Telephone International (Post Office Trade Union Federation).
874   **370**   10w. multicoloured   1·50   45

371 WAC and Corps Badge

1970. 20th Anniv of Korean Women's Army Corps.
875   **371**   10w. multicoloured   1·50   45

372 Pres. Pak and Flag

1970
876   **372**   10w. multicoloured   9·25   3·75
877   –   10w. black, green and blue   14·00   3·75
DESIGN—VERT: No. 877, Pres. Pak and industrial complex.

373 Presidents Pak and Sanchez Hernandez

1970. Visit of Pres. Sanchez Hernandez of El Salvador.
878   **373**   10w. multicoloured   3·00   1·50
MS879 90×60 mm. No. 878. Imperf (inscr "SOLVADOL")   39·00   38·00

374 "People and Houses"

1970. National Census.
880   **374**   10w. multicoloured   1·50   40

375 Diving

1970. 51st National Athletic Games, Seoul.
881   10w. Type **375**   4·75   1·20
882   10w. Hockey   4·75   1·20
883   10w. Baseball   4·75   1·20
MS884 Three sheets each 91×87 mm. Nos. 881/3×2. Imperf   30·00   29·00

376 Police Badge and Activities

1970. National Police Day.
885   **376**   10w. multicoloured   1·50   55

377 Bell and Globe

1970. 25th Anniv of United Nations.
886   **377**   10w. multicoloured   1·50   45

1970. Korean Paintings of the Yi Dynasty (2nd series). Vert designs as T **369**, showing animals. Multicoloured.
887   30w. *Fierce Tiger* (Shim Sa Yung)   12·50   1·90
888   30w. *Cats and Sparrows* (Pyun Sang Byuk)   12·50   1·90
889   30w. *Dog with Puppies* (Yi Am)   12·50   1·90
MS890 Three sheets each 130×90 mm. Nos. 887/9×2.   £170   £160

378 Kite and Reel

1970. Lunar New Year ("Year of the Pig"). Multicoloured.
891   10w. Type **378**   1·50   40
892   10w. Toy pig   1·50   40
MS893 Two sheets each 90×60 mm. Nos. 891/2×3   15·00   14·00

379 Quotation and Emblems on Globe

1970. 15th Communications Day.
894   **379**   10w. multicoloured   1·50   55

1970. Second Five Year Plan. As T **272**. Dated "1970". Multicoloured.
895   10w. "Port Development"   1·50   40
896   10w. "House Construction"   1·50   40

1970. Korean Paintings of the Yi Dynasty (3rd series). Vert designs as T **369**. Multicoloured.
897   10w. *Chokpyokdo* (river cliff) (Kim Hong Do)   2·75   75
898   10w. *Hen and Chicks* (Pyn Sang Byuk)   2·75   75
899   10w. *The Flute-player* (Shin Yun Bok)   2·75   75
MS900 Three sheets each 90×60 mm. Nos. 897/9×2. Perf or imperf   28·00   25·00

380 Fields ("Food Production")

1971. Economic Development (1st series). Multicoloured.
901   10w. Type **380**   1·90   55
902   10w. Dam ("Electric Power") (horiz)   1·90   55
903   10w. Map on crate ("Exports") (horiz)   1·90   55
MS904 Three sheets each 90×60 mm. Nos. 901/3. Imperf   21·00   19·00
See also Nos. 905/7 and 910/12.

381 Coal-mining

1971. Economic Development (2nd series). Multicoloured.
905   10w. Type **381**   1·50   40
906   10w. Cement works (vert)   1·50   40
907   10w. Fertilizer plant   1·50   40
MS908 Three sheets each 90×60 mm. Nos. 905/7×2. Imperf   21·00   19·00

382 Globe, Torch and Spider

1971. Anti-espionage Month.
909   **382**   10w. multicoloured   1·50   45

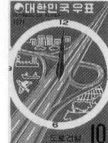

383 Motorway Junction

1971. Economic Development (3rd series). Multicoloured.
910   10w. Type **383**   1·50   40
911   10w. Scales ("Gross National Income") (horiz)   1·50   40
912   10w. Bee and coins ("Increased Savings") (horiz)   1·50   40
MS913 Three sheets each 90×60 mm. Nos. 910/12×2. Imperf   16·00   14·50

384 Reservist and Badge

1971. Third Home Reserve Forces Day.
914   **384**   10w. multicoloured   1·50   45

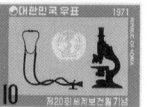

385 W.H.O. Emblem, Stethoscope and Microscope

1971. 20th World Health Day.
915   **385**   10w. multicoloured   1·40   55

386 Underground Train

1971. Construction of Seoul Underground Railway System.
916   **386**   10w. multicoloured   1·40   40

387 Footballer

1971. First Asian Soccer Games, Seoul.
917   **387**   10w. multicoloured   1·90   75

388 Veteran and Association Flag

1971. 20th Korean Veterans' Day.
918   **388**   10w. multicoloured   1·40   45

389 Girl Scouts

1971. 25th Anniv of Korean Girl Scouts Federation.
919   **389**   10w. multicoloured   1·40   30

390 Torch and Economic Symbols

1971. Tenth Anniv of May 16th Revolution.
920   **390**   10w. multicoloured   1·40   40

391 "Tele-communications"

1971. Third World Telecommunications Day.
921   **391**   10w. multicoloured   1·40   45

392 F.A.O. Emblem

1971. "The Work of the United Nations Organization".
922   –   10w. mauve, black and green   3·75   1·20
923   **392**   10w. blue, black and mauve   3·75   1·20
924   –   10w. multicoloured   3·75   1·20
925   –   10w. blue, black and mauve   3·75   1·20
926   –   10w. mauve, black and green   3·75   1·20
927   –   10w. blue, black and mauve   3·75   1·20
928   –   10w. mauve, black and blue   3·75   1·20
929   –   10w. black, green and mauve   3·75   1·20
930   –   10w. mauve, black and blue   3·75   1·20
931   –   10w. blue, black and mauve   3·75   1·20
932   –   10w. mauve, black and blue   3·75   1·20
933   –   10w. black, mauve and green   3·75   1·20
934   –   10w. mauve, blue and black   3·75   1·20
935   –   10w. black, mauve and green   3·75   1·20
936   –   10w. mauve, black and blue   3·75   1·20
937   –   10w. blue, black and mauve   3·75   1·20
938   –   10w. mauve, black and blue   3·75   1·20
939   –   10w. black, mauve and green   3·75   1·20
940   –   10w. mauve, black and blue   3·75   1·20
941   –   10w. blue, black and mauve   3·75   1·20
942   –   10w. mauve, black and green   3·75   1·20
943   –   10w. black, blue and mauve   3·75   1·20
944   –   10w. multicoloured   3·75   1·20
945   –   10w. blue, black and mauve   3·75   1·20
946   –   10w. black, mauve and green   3·75   1·20

EMBLEMS: No. 992, I.L.O.; 924, General Assembly and New York Headquarters; 925, UNESCO; 926, W.H.O.; 927, World Bank; 928, International Development Association; 929, Security Council; 930, International Finance Corporation; 931, International Monetary Fund; 932, International Civil Aviation Organization; 933, Economic and Social Council; 934, South Korean flag; 935, Trusteeship Council; 936, U.P.U.; 937, I.T.U.; 938, World Meteorological Organization; 939, Int Court of Justice; 940, I.M.C.O.; 941, UNICEF; 942, International Atomic Energy Agency; 943, United Nations Industrial Development Organization; 944, United Nations Commission for the Unification and Rehabilitation of Korea; 945, United Nations Development Programme; 946, United Nations Conference on Trade and Development.

393 Boating (Shin Yun Bok)

1971. Korean Paintings of the Yi Dynasty (4th series). Multicoloured.
947   10w. Type **393**   6·25   1·90
948   10w. *Greeting Travellers*   6·25   1·90
949   10w. *Tea Ceremony*   6·25   1·90
950   10w. *Lady and Servants on Country Road*   6·25   1·90
951   10w. *Couple Walking*   6·25   1·90
952   10w. *Fairy and Boy beneath Pine Tree* (Li Chae Kwan) (vert)   6·25   1·90
MS953 Six sheets each 130×90 mm. Nos. 947/52×2   75·00   65·00
Nos. 947/51 show "Folk Customs" paintings by Shin Yun Bok.

394 Pres. Pak, Emblem and Motorway

1971. Re-election of Pres. Pak for Third Term.
954 **394** 10w. multicoloured 23·00 2·30
MS955 90×60 mm. No. 954×2 75·00 70·00

1971. Korean Paintings of the Yi Dynasty (5th series). As T **393**. Multicoloured.
956 10w. *Chasing the Cat* (Kim Deuk Shin) 3·00 1·30
957 10w. *Valley Family* (Li Chae Kwan) (vert) 3·00 1·30
958 10w. *Man Reading* (Li Chae Kwan) (vert) 3·00 1·30
MS959 Three sheets each 130×90 mm. Nos. 956/8×2 25·00 23·00

395 Campfire and Badge

1971. 13th World Scout Jamboree, Asagiri, Japan.
960 **395** 10w. multicoloured 1·40 40

1971. Korean Paintings of the Yi Dynasty (6th series). As T **393** but vert. Multicoloured.
961 10w. *Classroom* 5·50 2·75
962 10w. *Wrestling Match* 5·50 2·75
963 10w. *Dancer with Musicians* 5·50 2·75
964 10w. *Weavers* 5·50 2·75
965 10w. *Drawing Water at the Well* 5·50 2·75
MS966 Five sheets each 130×90 mm. Nos. 961/5×2 60·00 55·00
Nos. 961/5 depict genre paintings by Kim Hong Do.

396 Cogwheel and Asian Map

1971. Third Asian Labour Minister's Conference, Seoul.
967 **396** 10w. multicoloured 1·40 45
MS968 90×60 mm. No. 967×2 50·00 45·00

397 Judo

1971. 52nd National Athletic Meeting, Seoul. Multicoloured.
969 10w. Type **397** 2·30 75
970 10w. Archery 2·30 75
MS971 Two sheets each 91×87 mm. Nos. 969/70×3 70·00 65·00

398 Korean Symbol on Palette

1971. 20th National Fine Art Exhibition.
972 **398** 10w. multicoloured 1·40 30

399 Doctor and Globe

1971. Seventh Congress of Medical Associations from Asia and Oceania.
973 **399** 10w. multicoloured 1·40 30

400 Emblems and "Vocational Skills"

1971. Second National Vocational Skill Contest for High School Students.
974 **400** 10w. multicoloured 1·40 30
MS975 90×60 mm. No. 974×2 42·00 38·00

401 Callipers and "K" Emblem

1971. Tenth Anniv of Industrial Standardisation.
976 **401** 10w. multicoloured 1·40 30

402 Fairy Tale Rats

1971. Lunar New Year ("Year of the Rat"). Multicoloured.
977 10w. Type **402** 1·90 40
978 10w. Flying crane 1·90 40
MS979 Two sheets each 90×60 mm. Nos. 977/8×3 55·00 49·00

403 Emblem and Hangul Alphabet

1971. 50th Anniv of Hangul Hakhoe (Korean Language Research Society).
980 **403** 10w. multicoloured 1·40 30

1971. Second Five Year Plan. As T **272**. Dated "1971". Multicoloured.
981 10w. Atomic power plant 1·50 40
982 10w. Hydro-electric power project 1·50 40

404 Korean Red Cross Building on Map

1971. South–North Korean Red Cross Conference, Panmunjom.
983 **404** 10w. multicoloured 1·50 60
MS984 125×90 mm. No. 983×2 12·50 11·00

405 Globe and Open Book

1971. International Book Year.
985 **405** 10w. multicoloured 1·20 30
MS986 90×60 mm. No. 985×2 11·50 10·50

406 "Intelsat 4" and Korean Earth Station

1971. 20th Anniv of Korea's Membership of I.T.U.
987 **406** 10w. multicoloured 1·20 40

407 Speed Skating

1972. Winter Olympic Games, Sapporo, Japan. Multicoloured.
988 10w. Type **407** 1·50 60
989 10w. Figure-skating 1·50 60
MS990 90×60 mm. Nos. 988/9 11·50 10·50

408 Forestry Map

1972. "Trees for Unity" Campaign.
991 **408** 10w. multicoloured 1·20 40

409 Scarab Beetles and Emblem

1972. 20th Anniv of Korean Junior Chamber of Commerce.
992 **409** 10w. multicoloured 1·20 40

410 E.C.A.F.E. Emblem and Industrial Symbols

1972. 25th Anniv of U.N. Economic Commission for Asia and the Far East.
993 **410** 10w. multicoloured 1·20 40

411 Flags of Member Countries

1972. Tenth Anniv of Asian and Oceanic Postal Union.
994 **411** 10w. multicoloured 1·20 40

412 Reserve Forces' Flag

1972. Home Reserve Forces Day.
995 **412** 10w. multicoloured 1·50 45

413 Emblem and "Terias harina"

1972. 50th Anniv of Korean Young Women's Christian Association.
996 **413** 10w. multicoloured 1·70 45

414 Rural Activities

1972. "New Community" (rural development) Movement.
997 **414** 10w. multicoloured 1·20 40

415 "Anti-Espionage" and Korean Flag

1972. Anti-Espionage Month.
998 **415** 10w. multicoloured 1·20 40

416 Children with Balloons

1972. 50th Children's Day.
999 **416** 10w. multicoloured 1·20 40

417 Leaf Ornament from Gold Crown

1972. Treasures from King Munyong's Tomb. Multicoloured.
1000 10w. Type **417** 1·20 40
1001 10w. Gold earrings (horiz) 1·20 40

418 Lake Paengnokdam, Mt. Halla Park
419 Kalkot, Koje Island, Hanryo Straits Park

1972. National Parks (1st series).
1002 **418** 10w. multicoloured 3·00 45
1003 **419** 10w. multicoloured 3·00 45
See also Nos. 1018/19 and 1026/7.

420 Marguerite and Conference Emblem

1972. U.N. Environmental Conservation Conference, Stockholm.
1004 **420** 10w. multicoloured 1·20 40
MS1005 90×60 mm. No. 1004×2 7·75 7·00

421 Gwanghwa Gate and National Flags

1972. Seventh Asian and Pacific Council (ASPAC) Ministerial Meeting, Seoul.
1006 **421** 10w. multicoloured 1·20 40

422 Pasture ("Development of Rural Economy")

1972. Third Five Year Plan. Dated "1972". Multicoloured.
1007 10w. Type **422** 1·90 55
1008 10w. Foundry ladle ("Heavy Industries") 1·90 55
1009 10w. Crate and Globe ("Increased Exports") 1·90 55

423 "Love Pin"

1972. Disaster Relief Fund.
1010 **423** 10w.+5w. red and blue   1·90   75

424 Judo

1972. Olympic Games, Munich. Multicoloured.
1011   20w. Type **424**   1·20   55
1012   20w. Weightlifting   1·20   55
1013   20w. Wrestling   1·20   55
1014   20w. Boxing   1·20   55
MS1015 Two sheets each 90×60 mm.
(a) Nos. 1011/12; (b) Nos. 1013/14   12·50   11·00

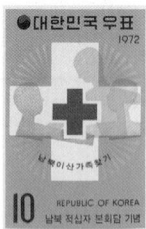

425 Family Reunion
through Red Cross

1972. First Plenary Meeting of South–North Korean Red
Cross Conference, Pyongyang.
1016 **425** 10w. multicoloured   1·90   75
MS1017 125×90 mm. No. 1016×2   27·00   26·00

426 Bulkuk Temple,   **427** Statue and Bopju
Kyongju Park   Temple, Mt. Sokri Park

1972. National Parks (2nd series).
1018 **426** 10w. multicoloured   1·40   45
1019 **427** 10w. multicoloured   1·40   45

428 Conference
Emblem within
"5"

1972. Fifth Asian Judicial Conference, Seoul.
1020 **428** 10w. multicoloured   1·20   40

429 Lions Badge
between Korean
Emblems

1972. 11th Orient and South-East Asian Lions
Convention, Seoul.
1021 **429** 10w. multicoloured   1·20   40

430 Scout taking Oath

1972. 50th Anniv of Korean Boy Scouts Movement.
1022 **430** 10w. multicoloured   1·50   45

431 Dolls and
Ox's Head

1972. Lunar New Year ("Year of the Ox"). Multicoloured.
1023   10w. Type **431**   1·20   40
1024   10w. Revellers in balloon   1·20   40
MS1025 Two sheets each 90×60 mm.
Nos. 1023/4×2   9·25   8·50

432 Temple, Mt.   **433** Madeungryong
Naejang Park   Pass, Mt. Sorak Park

1972. National Parks (3rd series).
1026 **432** 10w. multicoloured   1·20   40
1027 **433** 10w. multicoloured   1·20   40

434 President Pak, Flag and
"Development"

1972. Re-election of President Pak.
1028 **434** 10w. multicoloured   7·75   1·50
MS1029 130×90 mm. Nos. 1028×2   65·00   60·00

435 National Central   **436** Temple, Mt. Sorak
Museum, Kyongbok
Palace

1973. Korean Tourist Attractions (1st series).
1030 **435** 10w. multicoloured   1·20   40
1031 **436** 10w. multicoloured   1·20   40
See also Nos. 1042/3, 1048/9, 1057/8 and 1075/6.

437 Korean
Family

1973. Korean Unification Campaign.
1032 **437** 10w. multicoloured   1·20   30

438 "V" Sign and
Flags

1973. Return of Korean Forces from South Vietnam.
1033 **438** 10w. multicoloured   1·20   30

439 Construction
Workers and
Cogwheel

1973. Tenth Workers' Day.
1034 **439** 10w. multicoloured   85   30

440 W.M.O.
Emblem and
Satellite

1973. Centenary of World Meteorological Organization.
1035 **440** 10w. multicoloured   85   30
MS1036 90×60 mm. No. 1035×2   4·75   4·25

442 Wonsam Costume
(woman's ceremonial)

1973. Korean Court Costumes of the Yi Dynasty (1st
series). Multicoloured. Background colours given.
1037   10w. orange   3·75   70
1038 **442** 10w. orange   3·75   70
MS1039 Two sheets each 125×90 mm.
Nos. 1037/8×2   16·00   15·00
DESIGN: No. 1037, Kujangbok (king's ceremonial cos-
tume).
See also Nos. 1045/**MS**1047, 1053/**MS**1055, 1060/
MS1062 and 1078/**MS**1080.

443 Nurse with Lamp

1973. 50th Anniv of Korean Nurses' Association.
1040 **443** 10w. multicoloured   95   25

444 Reservists
and Flag

1973. Home Reserve Forces Day.
1041 **444** 10w. multicoloured   1·20   40

445 Palmi Island   **446** Sain-am
Rock, Mt. Dokjol

1973. Korean Tourist Attractions (2nd series).
1042 **445** 10w. multicoloured   1·20   30
1043 **446** 10w. multicoloured   1·20   30

447 Table Tennis Player

1973. Victory of South Korean Women's Team in World
Table Tennis Championships, Sarajevo.
1044 **447** 10w. multicoloured   1·90   70

1973. Korean Court Costumes of the Yi Dynasty (2nd
series). As T **442**. Mult. Background colours given.
1045   10w. purple   3·50   60
1046   10w. green   3·50   60
MS1047 Two sheets each 125×90 mm.
Nos. 1045/6×2   14·00   13·00
DESIGNS: No. 1045, Konryongpo (king's costume); 1046,
Jokui (queen's ceremonial costume).

450 Admiral Li   **451** Limestone
Sun Sin's Shrine,   Cavern, Kusan-ni
Asan

1973. Korean Tourist Attractions (3rd series).
1048 **450** 10w. multicoloured   1·50   40
1049 **451** 10w. multicoloured   1·50   40

452 Children's Choir

1973. 20th Anniv of World Vision Int.
1050 **452** 10w. multicoloured   1·20   30

453 Love Pin
and "Disasters"

1973. Disaster Relief Fund.
1051 **453** 10w.+5w. mult   1·20   45

454 Steel
Converter

1973. Inauguration of Pohang Steel Works.
1052 **454** 10w. multicoloured   95   30

1973. Korean Court Costumes of the Yi Dynasty (3rd
series). As T **442**. Mult. Background colours given.
1053   10w. blue   3·00   60
1054   10w. pink   3·00   60
MS1055 Two sheets each 125×90 mm.
Nos. 1053/4×2   10·50   8·50
DESIGNS: No. 1053, Kangsapo (crown prince's) costume;
1054, Tangui (princess's) costume.

457 Table
Tennis Bat
and Ball

1973. Table Tennis Gymnasium Construction Fund.
1056   **457**   10w.+5w. mauve and
green   1·20   30

458 Namhae   **459** Hongdo Island
Suspension Bridge

1973. Korean Tourist Attractions (4th series).
1057 **458** 10w. multicoloured   1·20   30
1058 **459** 10w. multicoloured   1·20   30

460 Interpol and
Korean Police Emblems

1973. 50th Anniv of International Criminal Police
Organization (Interpol).
1059 **460** 10w. multicoloured   85   20

1973. Korean Court Costumes of the Yi Dynasty (4th
series). As T **442**. Mult. Background colours given.
1060   10w. yellow   1·50   55
1061   10w. blue   1·50   55
MS1062 Two sheets each 125×90 mm.
Nos. 1060/1×2   8·50   8·00
DESIGNS: No. 1060, Kumkwanchobok (court official's) costume; 1061, Hwalot (queen's wedding) costume.

465   **466** Sommal   **467**
Manchurian   Lily   Motorway and
Cranes   Farm

1973
1063   –   1w. brown   45   15
1063a   –   3w. black and blue   75   25
1064   –   5w. brown   40   15
1064a   –   6w. turquoise and green   45   15
1065   **465**   10w. ultramarine & blue   1·20   25
1066   **466**   10w. red, black & green   1·50   40

1067 **467** 10w. green and red 75 15
1068 - 30w. brown and yellow 85 15
1068a - 50w. green and brown 75 25
1068b - 60w. brown and yellow 75 25
1068c - 80w. black and brown 1·50 30
1069 - 100w. yellow and brown 39·00 2·30
1069a - 100w. red 1·90 25
1069b - 200w. brown and pink 1·90 30
1069c - 300w. red and lilac 2·75 70
1069d - 500w. multicoloured 23·00 1·50
1069e - 500w. purple and brown 11·50 1·20
1069f - 1000w. green 10·00 1·50

DESIGNS—VERT: 1w. Mask of old man; 5w. Siberian chipmunk; 6w. Lily; 30w. Honey bee; 50w. Pot with lid; 60w. Jar; 100w. (No. 1069) Gold Crown, Silla dynasty; 100w. (No. 1069a) Admiral Yi Soon Shin; 300w. Pobjusa Temple; 500w. (No. 1069d) Gold Crown; 500w. (No. 1069e) Carved dragon (tile Backje Dynasty). LARGER 24×33 mm: 100w. Flying deities (relief from bronze bell, Sangweon Temple). HORIZ: 3w. Black-billed magpie; 80w. Ceramic horseman; 200w. Muryangsujeon Hall, Busok Temple.

For designs similar to Type **465** but with frame, see Type **703**.

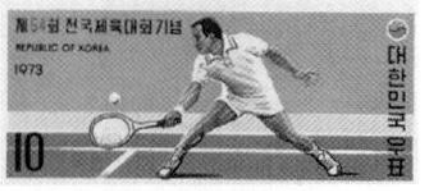

470 Tennis

1973. 54th National Athletic Meeting, Pusan. Multicoloured.
1070 10w. Type **470** 95 30
1071 10w. Hurdling 95 30

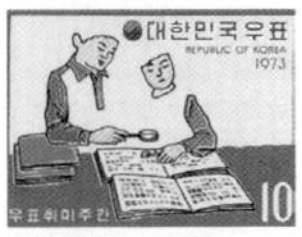

471 Children with Stamp Albums

1973. Philatelic Week.
1072 **471** 10w. multicoloured 75 30
MS1073 90×60 mm. No. 1072×2 15·00 14·00

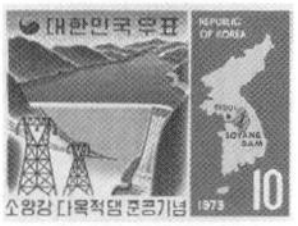

472 Soyang River Dam

1973. Inauguration of Soyang River Dam.
1074 **472** 10w. multicoloured 55 15

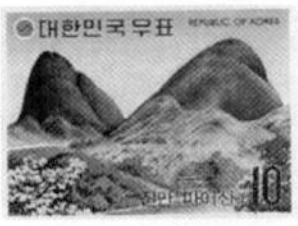

473 Mt. Mai, Chinan

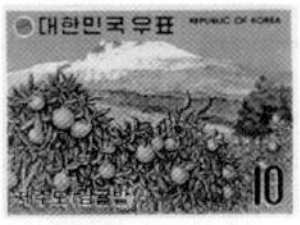

474 Tangerine Grove, Cheju Island

1973. Korean Tourist Attractions (5th series).
1075 **473** 10w. multicoloured 75 25
1076 **474** 10w. multicoloured 75 25

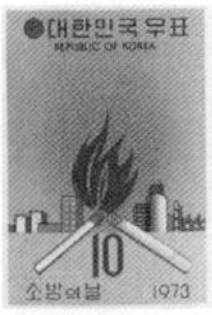

475 Match, Cigarette and Flames

1973. Tenth Fire Prevention Day.
1077 **475** 10w. multicoloured 55 15

1973. Korean Court Costumes of the Yi Dynasty (5th series). As T **442**. Mult. Background colours given.
1078 10w. orange 1·50 45
1079 10w. pink 1·50 45
MS1080 Two sheets each 125×90 mm. Nos. 1078/9×2 8·50 8·00

DESIGNS: No. 1078, Pyongsangbok (official's wife) costume; 1079, Kokunbok (military officer's) costume.

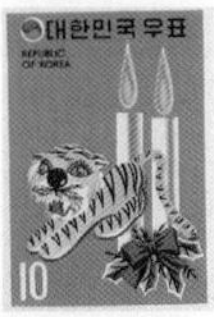

478 Tiger and Candles

1973. Lunar New Year ("Year of the Tiger"). Multicoloured.
1081 10w. Type **478** 75 30
1082 10w. Decorated top 75 30

MS1083 Two sheets each 90×60 mm. Nos. 1081/2×2 9·25 7·75

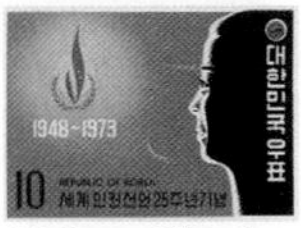

479 Korean Girl and Flame Emblem

1973. 25th Anniv of Declaration of Human Rights.
1084 **479** 10w. multicoloured 60 15

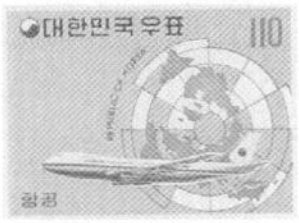

480 Boeing 747-200 Jetliner and Polar Zone

1973. Air.
1085 **480** 110w. blue and pink 10·00 3·75
1086 - 135w. red and green 11·00 3·75
1087 - 145w. red and blue 14·00 4·75
1088 - 180w. yellow and lilac 35·00 7·00

DESIGNS—Boeing 747-200 jetliner and postal zones on map: 135w. South-east Asia; 145w. India, Australasia and North America; 180w. Europe, Africa and South America.

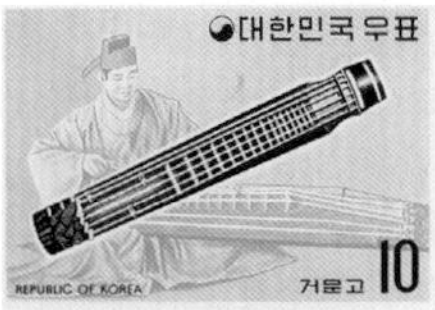

481 "Komunko" (zither)

1974. Traditional Musical Instruments (1st series). Multicoloured. Background colours given.
1089 **481** 10w. blue 1·20 30
1090 - 30w. orange 3·00 60
MS1091 Two sheets each 125×90 mm. (a) No. 1089×2; (b) No. 1090×2 13·00 12·00

DESIGN: 30w. "Nagak" (trumpet triton).

See also Nos. 1098/**MS**1100, 1108/**MS**1110, 1117/**MS**1119 and 1132/**MS**1134.

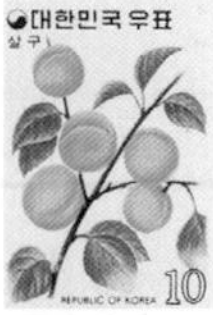

483 Apricots

1974. Fruits (1st series). Multicoloured.
1092 10w. Type **483** 75 30
1093 30w. Strawberries 2·30 45
MS1094 Two sheets each 90×60 mm. (a) No. 1092×2; (b) No. 1093×2 11·00 10·00

See also Nos. 1104/**MS**1106, 1111/**MS**1113, 1120/**MS**1122 and 1143/**MS**1145.

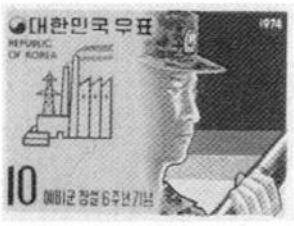

485 Reservist and Factory

1974. Home Reserve Forces Day.
1095 **485** 10w. multicoloured 55 15

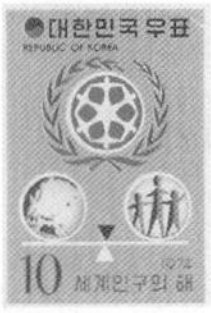

486 W.P.Y. Emblem

1974. World Population Year.
1096 **486** 10w. multicoloured 45 15
MS1097 90×60 mm. No. 1096×2 4·75 4·25

1974. Traditional Musical Instruments (2nd series). As T **481**. Multicoloured. Background colours given.
1098 10w. blue 1·00 25
1099 30w. green 2·30 55
MS1100 Two sheets each 125×90 mm. (a) No. 1098×2; (b) No. 1099×2 9·25 8·50

DESIGNS: 10w. "Tchouk"; 30w. "Eu".

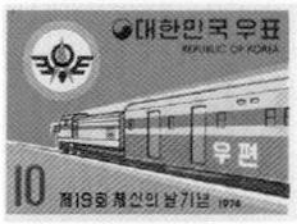

489 Diesel Mail Train and Communications Emblem

1974. Communications Day.
1101 **489** 10w. multicoloured 95 25

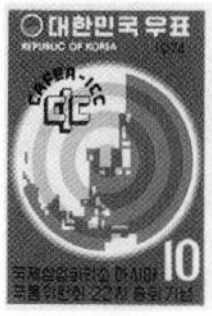

490 C.A.F.E.A.-I.C.C. Emblem on Globe

1974. 22nd Session of International Chamber of Commerce's Commission on Asian and Far Eastern Affairs, Seoul.
1102 **490** 10w. multicoloured 45 10

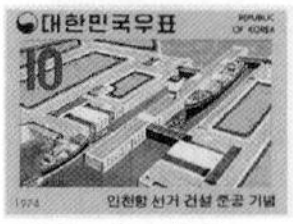

491 Port Installations

1974. Inaug of New Port Facilities, Inchon.
1103 **491** 10w. multicoloured 55 10

1974. Fruits (2nd series). As T **483**. Multicoloured.
1104 10w. Peaches 75 30
1105 30w. Grapes 2·30 45
MS1106 Two sheets each 90×60 mm. No. 1104/5×2 10·50 9·50

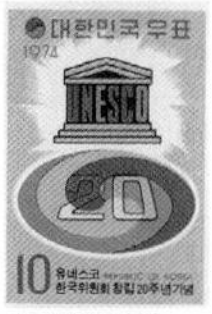

494 UNESCO Emblem and Extended Fan

1974. 20th Anniv of South Korean UNESCO Commission.
1107 **494** 10w. multicoloured 45 10

1974. Traditional Musical Instruments (3rd series). As T **481**. Multicoloured. Background colours given.
1108 10w. orange 95 15
1109 30w. pink 1·90 40
MS1110 Two sheets each 125×90 mm. Nos. 1108/9×2 8·50 7·75

DESIGNS: 10w. "A-chaing" (stringed instrument); 30w. "Kyobang-ko" (drum).

1974. Fruits (3rd series). As T **483**. Multicoloured.
1111 10w. Pears 60 15
1112 30w. Apples 2·30 45
MS1113 Two sheets each 91×61 mm. Nos. 1111/12×2 11·00 9·75

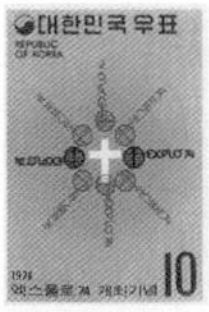

499 Cross and Emblems

1974. "Explo 74" Second International Training Congress on Evangelism. Multicoloured.
1114 10w. Type **499** 40 10
1115 10w. Emblem and Korean map on Globe 40 10

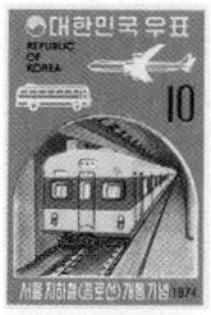

501 Underground Train

1974. Opening of Seoul Underground Railway.
1116 **501** 10w. multicoloured 1·00 25

1974. Traditional Musical Instruments (4th series). As T **481**. Multicoloured. Background colours given.
1117 10w. blue 95 30
1118 30w. pink 1·90 45
MS1119 Two sheets each 125×90 mm. Nos. 1117/18×2 7·75 7·00

DESIGNS: No. 1117, So ("Pan pipes"); 1118, Haikem (Two-stringed fiddle).

1974. Fruits (4th series). As T **483**. Multicoloured.
1120 10w. Cherries 70 25
1121 30w. Persimmons 1·50 45
MS1122 Two sheets each 91×61 mm. Nos. 1120/1×2 5·50 5·00

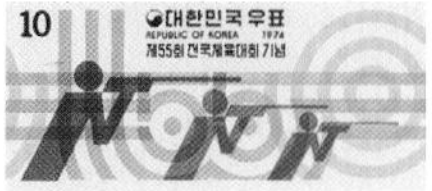

506 Rifle Shooting

1974. 55th National Athletic Meeting, Seoul. Multicoloured.
1123 10w. Type **506** 45 15
1124 30w. Rowing 1·30 40

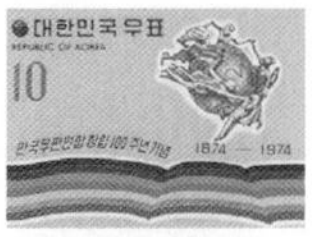

508 U.P.U. Emblem

1974. Centenary of U.P.U.
1125 **508** 10w. multicoloured (postage) 45 15
1126 **508** 110w. multicoloured (air) 2·30 1·00
MS1127 Two sheets each 90×60 mm. Nos. 1125/6×2 20·00 18·00

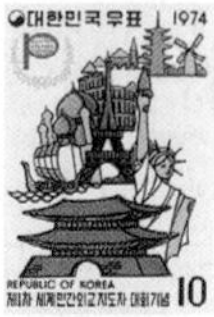

509 Symbols of Member Countries

1974. First World Conference of People-to-People International.
1128 **509** 10w. multicoloured 45 10

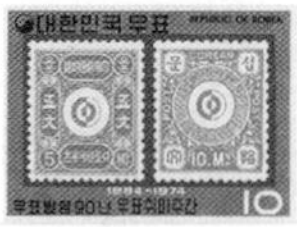

510 Korean Stamps of 1884

1974. Philatelic Week and 90th Anniv of First Korean Stamps.
1129 **510** 10w. multicoloured 55 10
MS1130 91×61 mm. No. 1129×2 8·50 7·75

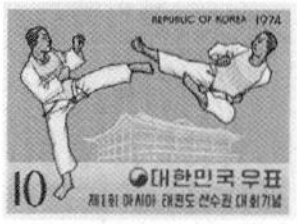

511 Taekwondo Contestants

1974. First Asian Taekwondo Championships, Seoul.
1131 **511** 10w. multicoloured 55 10

1974. Traditional Musical Instruments (5th series). As T **481**. Multicoloured. Background colours given.
1132 10w. pink 95 25
1133 30w. ochre 1·90 45
MS1134 Two sheets each 125×90 mm. Nos. 1132/3×2 7·75 7·00

DESIGNS: 10w. Pak (clappers); 30w. Pyenchong (chimes).

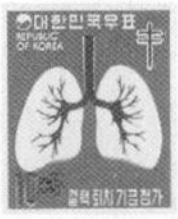

514 Lungs

1974. Tuberculosis Control Fund.
1135 **514** 10w.+5w. red & green 95 25

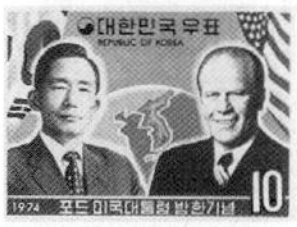

515 Presidents Pak and Ford

1974. State Visit of President Ford of United States.
1136 **515** 10w. multicoloured 85 30
MS1137 89×59 mm. No. 1136×2 7·75 7·00

516 Yook Young Soo (wife of Pres. Pak)

1974. Yook Young Soo Memorial Issue.

1138	516	10w. green	85	30
1139	516	10w. orange	85	30
1140	516	10w. violet	85	30
1141	516	10w. blue	85	30
MS1142	91×125 mm. No. 1138/41		35·00	31·00

1974. Fruits (5th series). As T **483**. Multicoloured.

1143	10w. Tangerines	55	15
1144	30w. Chestnuts	1·30	40
MS1145	Two sheets each 91×61 mm. Nos. 1143/4×2	5·75	5·25

519 "Good Luck" Purse

1974. Lunar New Year ("Year of the Rabbit"). Multicoloured.

1146	10w. Type **519**	60	20
1147	10w. Toy rabbits	60	20
MS1148	Two sheets each 91×61 mm. Nos. 1146/7×2	7·75	7·00

521 U.P.U. Emblem and "75"

1975. 75th Anniv of Korea's Membership of U.P.U. Multicoloured.

1149	10w. Type **521**	45	10
1150	10w. U.P.U. emblem and paper dart	45	10

523 Dove with "Good Luck" Card

1975. Inauguration of National Welfare Insurance System.

1151	523	10w. multicoloured	40	10

524 Dr. Schweitzer, Map and Syringe

1975. Birth Centenary of Dr. Albert Schweitzer.

1152	524	10w. bistre	95	40
1153	524	10w. mauve	95	40
1154	524	10w. orange	95	40
1155	524	10w. green	95	40

525 Salpuli Dancer

1975. Korean Folk Dances (1st series). Multicoloured. Background colour given.

1156	525	10w. green	70	25
1157	525	10w. blue	70	25
MS1158	Two sheets each 90×60 mm. Nos. 1156/7×2		3·75	3·50

DESIGN: No. 1157, Exorcism in dance.
See also Nos. 1168/**MS**1170, 1175/**MS**1177, 1193/**MS**1195 and 1208/**MS**1210.

527 Globe and Rotary Emblem

1975. 70th Anniv of Rotary International.

1159	527	10w. multicoloured	40	10

528 Women and I.W.Y. Emblem

1975. International Women's Year.

1160	528	10w. multicoloured	40	10

529 Violets

1975. Flowers (1st series). Multicoloured.

1161	10w. Type **529**	75	25
1162	10w. Anemones	75	25

See also Nos. 1171/2, 1184/5, 1199/1200 and 1213/4.

531 Saemaeul Township

1975. National Afforestation Campaign. Multicoloured.

1163	10w. Type **531**	75	30
1164	10w. Lake and trees	75	30
1165	10w. "Green" forest	75	30
1166	10w. Felling timber	75	30

Nos. 1163/6 were issued together, *se-tenant*, forming a composite design.

535 H.R.F. Emblem on Map of Korea

1975. Homeland Reserve Forces Day.

1167	535	10w. multicoloured	60	10

536 Butterfly Dance

1975. Folk Dances (2nd series). Multicoloured. Background colour given.

1168	536	10w. green	75	25
1169		10w. yellow	75	25
MS1170	Two sheets each 90×60 mm. Nos. 1168/9×2		3·50	3·00

DESIGN: No. 1169, Victory dance.

538 Rhododendron

1975. Flowers (2nd series). Multicoloured.

1171	10w. Type **538**	75	25
1172	10w. Clematis	75	25

540 Metric Symbols

1975. Centenary of Metric Convention.

1173	540	10w. multicoloured	40	10

541 Soldier and Incense Pot

1975. 20th Memorial Day.

1174	541	10w. multicoloured	40	10

542 Mokjoong Dance

1975. Folk Dances (3rd series). Multicoloured.

1175	542	10w. blue	75	25
1176	-	10w. pink	75	25
MS1177	Two sheets each 90×60 mm. Nos. 1175/6×2		3·50	3·00

DESIGN: No. 1176, Malttungi dancer.

544 Flags of South Korea, U.N. and U.S.

1975. 25th Anniv of Korean War. Multicoloured.

1178	10w. Type **544**	75	30
1179	10w. Flags of Ethiopia, France, Greece, Canada and South Africa	75	30
1180	10w. Flags of Luxembourg, Australia, U.K., Colombia and Turkey	75	30
1181	10w. Flags of Netherlands, Belgium, Philippines, New Zealand and Thailand	75	30

548 Presidents Pak and Bongo

1975. State Visit of President Bongo of Gabon.

1182	548	10w. multicoloured	55	10
MS1183	90×60 mm. No. 1182×2		2·75	2·40

549 Iris

1975. Flowers (3rd series). Multicoloured.

1184	10w. Type **549**	75	25
1185	10w. Thistle	75	25

551 Scout Scarf

1975. "Nordjamb 75" World Scout Jamboree, Norway. Multicoloured.

1186	10w. Type **551**	75	30
1187	10w. Scout oath	75	30
1188	10w. Scout camp	75	30
1189	10w. Axe and rope	75	30
1190	10w. Camp fire	75	30

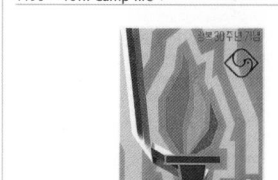

552 Freedom Flame

1975. 30th Anniv of Liberation. Multicoloured.

1191	20w. Type **552**	70	25
1192	20w. Balloon emblems	70	25

554 Drum Dance

1975. Folk Dances (4th series). Multicoloured. Background colour given.

1193	554	20w. yellow	1·00	45
1194	-	20w. orange	1·00	45
MS1195	Two sheets each 90×60 mm. Nos. 1193/4×2		5·50	5·00

DESIGN: No. 1194, Bara dance.

556 Taekwondo Contestant

1975. Second World Taekwondo Championships, Seoul.

1196	556	20w. multicoloured	45	10

557 Assembly Hall

1975. Completion of National Assembly Hall.

1197	557	20w. multicoloured	45	10

558 Dumper Truck and Emblem

1975. Contractors' Association Convention, Seoul.

1198	558	20w. multicoloured	45	10

559 Broad-bell Flower

1975. Flowers (4th series). Multicoloured.

1199	20w. Type **559**	1·20	30
1200	20w. Bush clover	1·20	30

561 Morse Key and Dish Aerial

1975. 90th Anniv of Korean Telecommunications.

1201	561	20w. black, orange & pur	45	10

562 Yeongweol Caves

1975. International Tourism Day. Multicoloured.
1202	20w.	Type 562	45	10
1203	20w.	Mount Sorak	45	10

564 Flag and Missiles

1975. Korean Armed Forces Day.
1204	**564**	20w. multicoloured	40	10

565 "Gymnastics"

1975. 56th National Athletic Meeting. Multicoloured.
1205	20w.	Type 565	40	10
1206	20w.	"Handball"	40	10

567 "Kangaroo" Collector

1975. Philatelic Week.
1207	**567**	20w. multicoloured	40	10

568 Sogo Dance

1975. Folk Dances (5th series). Multicoloured. Background colour given.
1208	**568**	20w. blue	1·10	45
1209	–	20w. yellow	1·10	45
MS1210 Two sheets each 90×60 mm.				
		Nos. 1208/9×2	4·75	4·25

DESIGN: No. 1209, Bupo Nori dance.

570 U.N. Emblem and Handclasps

1975. 30th Anniv of United Nations.
1211	**570**	20w. multicoloured	40	10

571 Red Cross and Emblems

1975. 70th Anniv of Korean Red Cross.
1212	**571**	20w. multicoloured	45	10

572 Camellia

1975. Flowers (5th series). Multicoloured.
1213	20w.	Type 572	1·70	55
1214	20w.	Gentian	1·70	55

574 Union Emblem

1975. Tenth Anniv of Asian Parliamentary Union.
1215	**574**	20w. multicoloured	40	10

575 Children Playing

1975. Lunar New Year. Multicoloured.
1216	20w.	Type 575	55	15
1217	20w.	Dragon ("Year of the Dragon")	55	15
MS1218 Two sheets each 90×60 mm.				
		Nos. 1216/17×2	3·75	3·50

577 Electric Train

1975. Opening of Cross-country Electric Railway.
1219	**577**	20w. multicoloured	75	15

578 *Dilipa fenestra*

1976. Butterflies (1st series). Multicoloured, background colour given.
1220	**578**	20w. red	1·50	30
1221	–	20w. blue	1·50	30

DESIGN: No. 1221, *Luehdorfia puziloi*.
See also Nos. 1226/7, 1246/7, 1254/5 and 1264/5.

580 Institute Emblem and Science Emblems

1976. Tenth Anniv of Korean Institute of Science and Technology.
1222	**580**	20w. multicoloured	40	10

581 Japanese White-naped Crane

1976. Birds (1st series). Multicoloured.
1223	20w.	Type 581	1·50	40
1224	20w.	Great bustard	1·50	40
		See also Nos. 1243/4, 1251/2, 1257/8 and 1266/7.		

583 Globe and Telephones

1976. Telephone Centenary.
1225	**583**	20w. multicoloured	40	10

584 *Papilio xuthus*

1976. Butterflies (2nd series). Multicoloured, background colour given.
1226	**584**	20w. yellow	1·50	30
1227	–	20w. green	1·50	30

DESIGN: No. 1227, *Parnassius bremeri*.

586 "National Development"

1976. Homeland Reserve Forces Day.
1228	**586**	20w. multicoloured	40	10

587 Eye and People

1976. World Health Day. Prevention of Blindness.
1229	**587**	20w. multicoloured	40	10

588 Pres. Pak and Flag

1976. Sixth Anniv of Saemaul Movement (community self-help programme). Multicoloured.
1230	20w.	Type 588	1·50	45
1231	20w.	People ("Intellectual edification")	1·50	45
1232	20w.	Village ("Welfare")	1·50	45
1233	20w.	Produce and fields ("Production")	1·50	45
1234	20w.	Produce and factory ("Increase of Income")	1·50	45

589 Ruins of Moenjodaro

1976. Moenjodaro (Pakistan) Preservation Campaign.
1235	**589**	20w. multicoloured	45	10

590 U.S. Flags of 1776 and 1976

1976. Bicentenary of American Revolution. Each black, blue and red.
1236	100w.	Type 590	3·00	1·20
1237	100w.	Statue of Liberty	3·00	1·20
1238	100w.	Map of United States	3·00	1·20
1239	100w.	Liberty Bell	3·00	1·20
1240	100w.	American astronaut	3·00	1·20
MS1241 91×61 mm. No. 1236			6·25	5·50

591 Camp Scene on Emblem

1976. 30th Anniv of Korean Girl Scouts Federation.
1242	**591**	20w. multicoloured	95	15

592 Blue-winged Pitta

1976. Birds (2nd series). Multicoloured.
1243	20w.	Type 592	1·50	40
1244	20w.	White-bellied black woodpecker	1·50	40

594 Buddha and Temple

1976. UNESCO Campaign for Preservation of Borobudur Temple (in Indonesia).
1245	**594**	20w. multicoloured	40	10

595 Eastern Pale Clouded Yellow

1976. Butterflies (3rd series). Multicoloured, background colour given.
1246	**595**	20w. olive	1·50	30
1247	–	20w. violet	1·50	30

DESIGN: No. 1247, Chinese windmill.

597 Protected Family

1976. National Life Insurance.
1248	**597**	20w. multicoloured	40	10

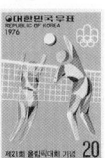

598 Volleyball

1976. Olympic Games, Montreal. Multicoloured.
1249	20w.	Type 598	45	10
1250	20w.	Boxing	45	10

600 Black Wood Pigeon

1976. Birds (3rd series). Multicoloured.
1251	20w.	Type 600	1·50	40
1252	20w.	Oystercatcher	1·50	40

602 Children and Books

1976. Books for Children.
1253	**602**	20w. multicoloured	40	10

603 *Hestina assimilis*

1976. Butterflies (4th series). Multicoloured, background colour given.
1254	**603**	20w. brown	2·20	85
1255	–	20w. drab	2·20	85

DESIGN: No. 1255, Blue triangle.

604a Corps Members and Flag

1976. First Anniv of Korean Civil Defence Corps.
1256 **604a** 20w. multicoloured   40   10

605 Black-faced Spoonbill

1976. Birds (4th series). Multicoloured.
1257   20w. Type **605**   1·50   40
1258   20w. Black stork   1·50   40

607 Chamsungdan, Mani Mountain

1976. International Tourism Day. Multicoloured.
1259   20w. Type **607**   75   25
1260   20w. Ilchumun Gate, Tongdosa   75   25

609 Cadet and Parade

1976. 30th Anniv of Korean Military Academy.
1261 **609** 20w. multicoloured   45   15

610 "Musa basjoo" (flower arrangement, Cheong Jo the Great)

1976. Philatelic Week.
1262 **610** 20w. black, red and drab   45   10
MS1263 91×61 mm. No. 1262×2   3·75   3·50

611 Yellow-legged Tortoiseshell

1976. Butterflies (5th series). Multicoloured, background colour given.
1264 **611** 20w. light green   2·30   95
1265 –   20w. purple   2·30   95
DESIGN: No. 1265, *Fabriciana nerippe*.

613 Cinereous Vulture

1976. Birds (5th series). Multicoloured.
1266   20w. Type **613**   3·75   1·40
1267   20w. Tundra swan   3·75   1·40

615 Snake (bas-relief, Kim Yu Shin's tomb)

1976. Lunar New Year (Year of the Snake). Multicoloured.
1268   20w. Type **615**   55   25
1269   20w. Door knocker with Manchurian cranes   55   25
MS1270 Two sheets each 90×60 mm. Nos. 1268/9×2   3·75   3·50

617 "Training Technicians"

1977. Fourth Five Year Economic Development Plan. Multicoloured.
1271   20w. Type **617**   60   15
1272   20w. Tanker ("Heavy Industries")   60   15

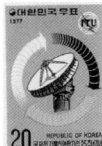
619 Dish Aerial

1977. 25th Anniv of Korea's I.T.U. Membership.
1273 **619** 20w. multicoloured   45   15

620 Korean Broadcasting Centre

1977. 50th Anniv of Broadcasting in Korea.
1274 **620** 20w. multicoloured   45   15

621 Jar with Grape Design

1977. Korean Ceramics (1st series). Multicoloured, background colours given.
1275   20w. Type **621** (brown)   1·90   30
1276   20w. Celadon vase (grey)   1·90   30
See also Nos. 1285/6, 1287/8, 1290/1 and 1300/1.

623 "Two-children" Family

1977. Family Planning.
1277 **623** 20w. green, turq & orge   1·90   25

624 Reserve Soldier

1977. Ninth Homeland Reserve Forces Day.
1278 **624** 20w. multicoloured   40   10

625 Diagram of Brain

1977. Tenth Anniv of Science Day.
1279 **625** 20w. multicoloured   40   10

626 Medical Book and Equipment

1977. 35th International Military Medicine Meeting.
1280 **626** 20w. multicoloured   55   10

627 Child with Flowers

1977. 20th Anniv of Children's Charter.
1281 **627** 20w. multicoloured   40   10

628 Veterans' Flag and Emblem

1977. 25th Anniv of Korean Veterans' Day.
1282 **628** 20w. multicoloured   55   10

629 Statue of Buddha, Sokkulam Grotto

1977. 2600th Birth Anniv of Buddha.
1283 **629** 20w. green and brown   55   10
MS1284 90×60 mm. No. 1283×2   4·75   4·25

630 Celadon Jar

1977. Korean Ceramics (2nd series). Multicoloured, background colours given.
1285   20w. Type **630** (pink)   75   30
1286   20w. Porcelain vase (blue) (vert)   75   30

632 "Buddha" Celadon Wine Jar

1977. Korean Ceramics (3rd series). Multicoloured, background colours given.
1287   20w. Type **632** (mauve)   75   25
1288   20w. Celadon vase (pale blue)   75   25

수해구제
+10
(**634**)

1977. Flood Relief. No. 791 surch with T **634**.
1289   20w.+10w. green   7·75   6·75

635 Celadon Vase, Black Koryo Ware

1977. Korean Ceramics (4th series). Multicoloured, background colours given.
1290   20w. Type **635** (stone)   75   25
1291   20w. White porcelain bowl (green) (horiz)   75   25

637 Ulleung-do Island

1977. World Tourism Day. Multicoloured.
1292   20w. Type **637**   45   10
1293   20w. Haeundae Beach   45   10

639 Servicemen

1977. Armed Forces Day.
1294 **639** 20w. multicoloured   40   10

640/1 *Mount Inwang Clearing-up after the Rain* (detail from drawing by Chung Seon)

1977. Philatelic Week.
1295 **640** 20w. multicoloured   95   25
1296 **641** 20w. multicoloured   95   25
MS1297 90×60 mm. Nos. 1285/6   7·00   6·25
Nos. 1295/6 were issued together, *se-tenant*, forming the composite design illustrated.

642 Rotary Emblem and Koryo Dynasty Bronze Bell

1977. 50th Anniv of Korean Rotary Club.
1298 **642** 20w. multicoloured   70   15

643 South Korean Flag over Everest

1977. South Korean Conquest of Mount Everest.
1299 **643** 20w. multicoloured   70   15

644 Punch'ong Bottle

1977. Korean Ceramics (5th series). Multicoloured, background colours given.
1300   20w. Type **644** (brown)   75   25
1301   20w. Celadon cylindrical bottle (pale brown)   75   25

646 Hands preserving Nature

1977. Nature Conservation.
1302 **646** 20w. blue, green and brown   75   15

647 Children with Kites

1977. Lunar New Year ("Year of the Horse"). Multicoloured.
1303   20w. Type **647**   45   15
1304   20w. Horse (bas-relief, Kim Yu Shin's tomb)   45   15
MS1305 Two sheets each 90×60 mm.
(a) No. 1303×2; (b) No. 1304×2   4·25   4·00

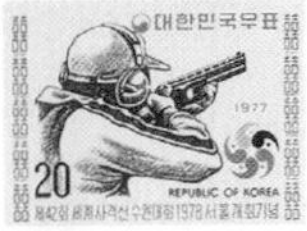
649 Clay Pigeon Shooting

1977. 42nd World Shooting Championships, Seoul. Multicoloured.
1306 20w. Type **649** 55 10
1307 20w. Air pistol shooting 55 10
1308 20w. Air rifle shooting 55 10
MS1309 Three sheets each 90×60 mm. (a) No. 1306×2; (b) No. 1307×2; (c) No. 1308×2 11·50 10·50

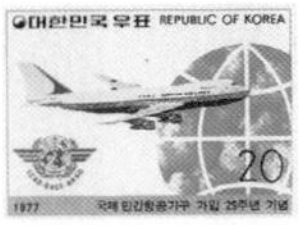
652 Korean Airlines Boeing 747-200

1977. 25th Anniv of Korean Membership of I.C.A.O.
1310 **652** 20w. multicoloured 60 15

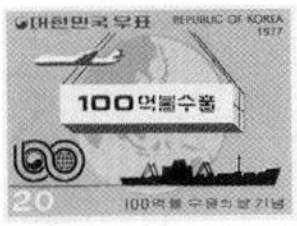
653 "Exports"

1977. Korean Exports.
1311 **653** 20w. multicoloured 45 10

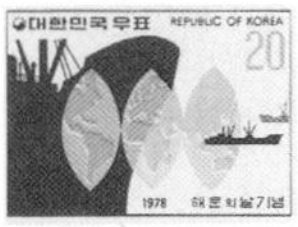
654 Ships and World Map

1978. National Maritime Day.
1312 **654** 20w. multicoloured 40 10

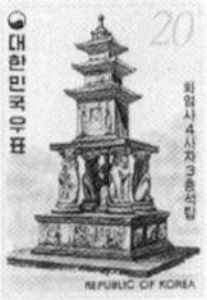
655 Three-storey Pagoda, Hwaom Temple

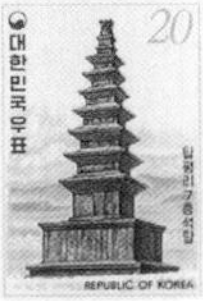
656 Seven-storey Pagoda, T'app'yong-ri

1978. Stone Pagodas (1st series).
1313 **655** 20w. multicoloured 1·20 30
1314 **656** 20w. multicoloured 1·20 30
See also Nos. 1319/20, 1322/5 and 1340/1.

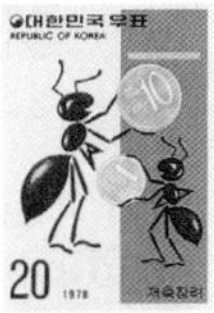
657 Ants with Coins

1978. Savings Encouragement.
1315 **657** 20w. multicoloured 55 10

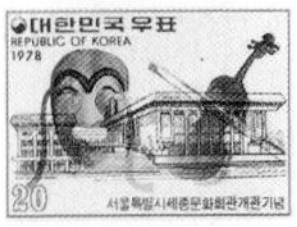
658 Seoul Sejong Cultural Centre, Hahoe Mask and Violin

1978. Opening of Seoul Sejong Cultural Centre.
1316 **658** 20w. multicoloured 70 15

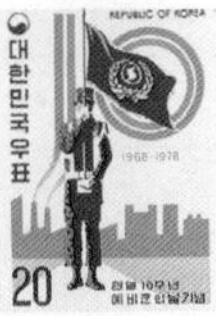
659 Standard Bearer

1978. Tenth Homeland Reserve Forces Day.
1317 **659** 20w. multicoloured 40 10

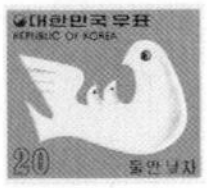
660 Pigeon and Young

1978. Family Planning.
1318 **660** 20w. black and green 1·00 30

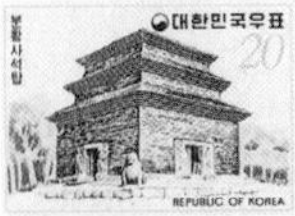
661 Pagoda, Punhwang Temple

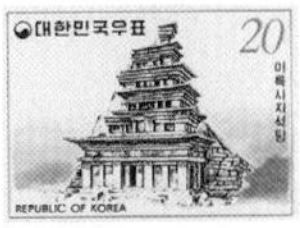
662 Pagoda, Miruk Temple

1978. Stone Pagodas (2nd series).
1319 **661** 20w. multicoloured 1·20 30
1320 **662** 20w. multicoloured 1·20 30

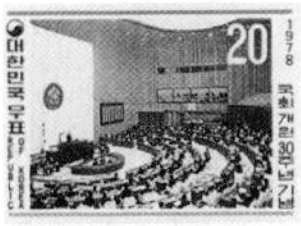
663 National Assembly

1978. 30th Anniv of National Assembly.
1321 **663** 20w. multicoloured 40 10

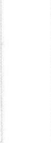

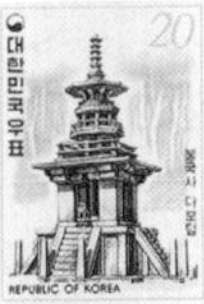
664 Tabo Pagoda, Pulguk Temple

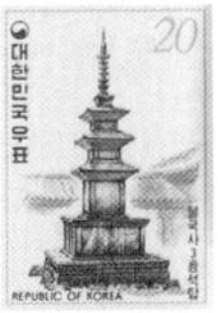
665 Three-storey Pagoda, Pulguk Temple

1978. Stone Pagodas (3rd series).
1322 **664** 20w. multicoloured 75 25
1323 **665** 20w. multicoloured 75 25

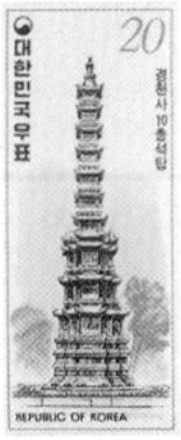
666 Ten-storey Pagoda, Kyongch'on Temple

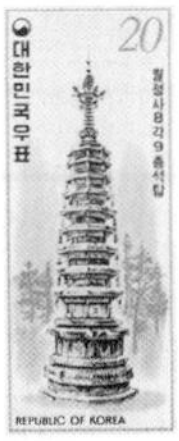
667 Nine-storey Octagonal Pagoda, Wolchong Temple

1978. Stone Pagodas (4th series).
1324 **666** 20w. multicoloured 1·20 30
1325 **667** 20w. multicoloured 1·20 30

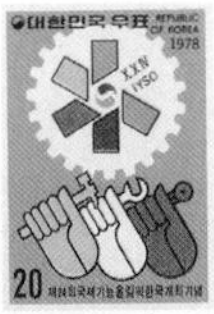
668 Emblem and Hands with Tools

1978. 24th International Youth Skill Olympics, Pusan.
1326 **668** 20w. multicoloured 40 10
MS1327 90×60 mm. No. 1326×1 3·00 2·75

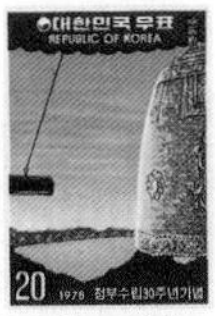
669 Crater Lake, Mt. Baeguda and Bell of Joy

1978. 30th Anniv of Republic of Korea.
1328 **669** 20w. multicoloured 40 10

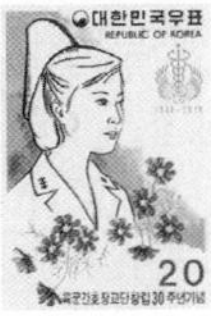
670 Army Nursing Officer

1978. 30th Anniv of Army Nursing Corps.
1329 **670** 20w. multicoloured 40 10

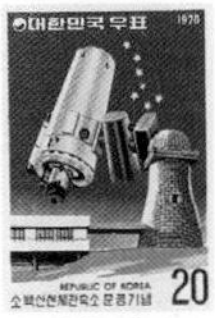
671 Sobaeksan Observatory and Telescope

1978. Opening of Sobaeksan Observatory.
1330 **671** 20w. multicoloured 45 10

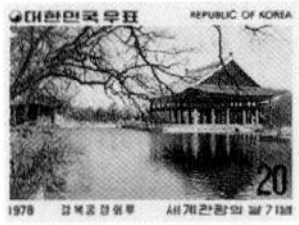
672 Kyonghoeru Pavilion, Kyonbok Palace

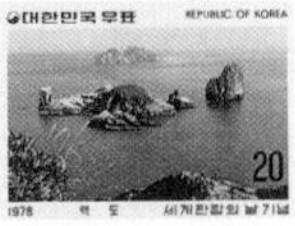
673 Baeg-do Island

1978. World Tourism Day.
1331 **672** 20w. multicoloured 40 10
1332 **673** 20w. multicoloured 40 10

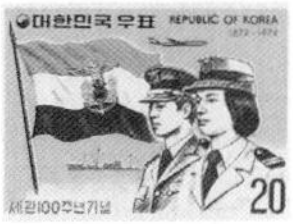
674 Customs Officers and Flag

1978. Centenary of Custom House.
1333 **674** 20w. multicoloured 40 10

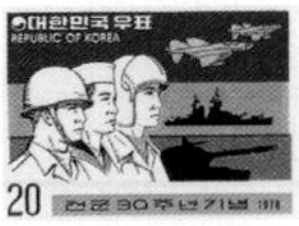
675 Armed Forces

1978. 30th Anniv of Korean Armed Forces.
1334 **675** 20w. multicoloured 40 10

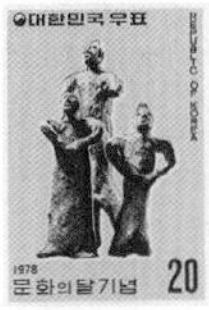
676 Earthenware Figures, Silla Dynasty

1978. Culture Month.
1335 **676** 20w. black and green 40 10

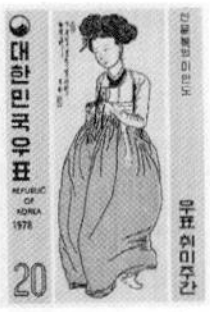
677 *Painting of a Lady* (Shin Yoon-bok)

1978. Philatelic Week.
1336 **677** 20w. multicoloured 45 10
MS1337 91×60 mm. No. 1336×2 3·75 3·50

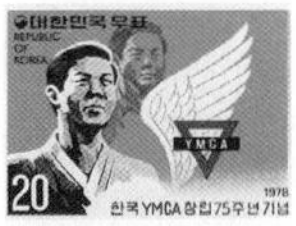
678 Young Men and Y.M.C.A. Emblem

1978. 75th Anniv of Korean Y.M.C.A.
1338 **678** 20w. multicoloured 40 10

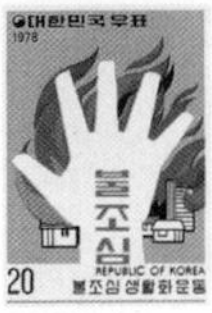
679 Hand smothering Fire

1978. Fire Prevention Campaign.
1339 **679** 20w. multicoloured 30 10

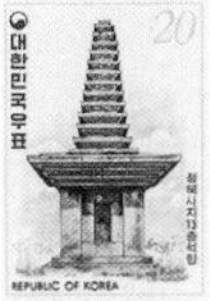
680 Thirteen-storey Pagoda, Jeonghye Temple

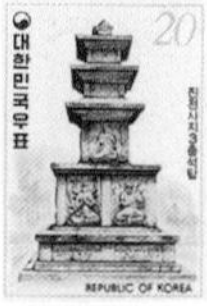
681 Three-storey Pagoda, Jinjeon Temple

1978. Stone Pagodas (5th series).
1340 **680** 20w. multicoloured 55 10
1341 **681** 20w. multicoloured 55 10

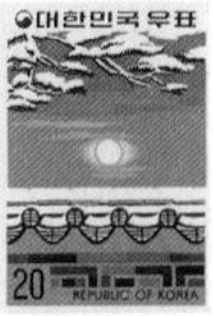
682 Snow Scene

1978. Lunar New Year ("Year of the Sheep"). Multicoloured.
1342 20w. Type **682** 45 10
1343 20w. Sheep (bas-relief, Kim Yu Shin's tomb) 45 10
MS1344 Two sheets each 90×60 mm. Nos. 1342/3×2 3·50 3·00

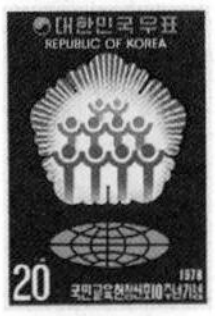
684 People within Hibiscus

1978. Tenth Anniv of National Education Charter.
1345 **684** 20w. multicoloured 40 10

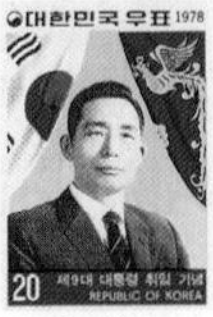
685 President Pak

1978. Re-election of President Pak.
1346 **685** 20w. multicoloured 85 30
MS1347 90×60 mm. No. 1346×2 12·50 11·00

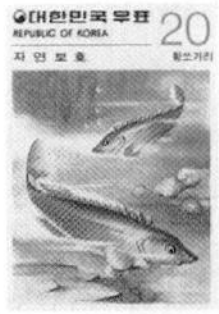
686 Golden Mandarinfish

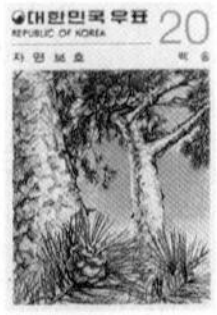
687 Lace Bark Pine

1979. Nature Conservation.
1348 **686** 20w. multicoloured 1·50 15
1349 **687** 20w. multicoloured 1·50 15

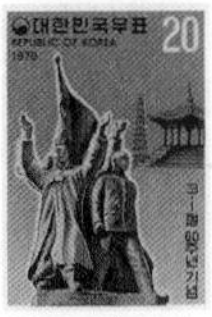
688 Samil Monument

1979. 60th Anniv of Samil Independence Movement.
1350 **688** 20w. multicoloured 40 10

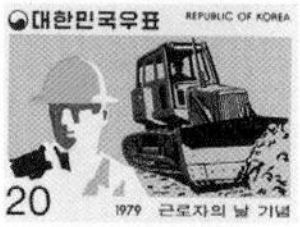
689 Worker and Bulldozer

1979. Labour Day.

1351	**689**	20w. multicoloured	40	10

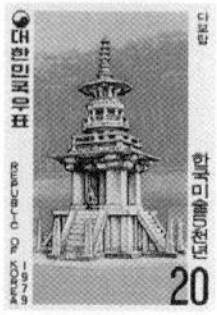
690 Tabo Pagoda, Pulgak Temple

1979. Korean Art. Multicoloured.

1352	20w. Type **690**	45	15
1353	20w. Gilt-bronze Maitreya	45	15
1354	20w. Gold crown of Silla	45	15
1355	20w. Celadon vase	45	15
1356	60w. "Tano Day Activities" (silk screen) (50×33 mm)	85	30
MS1357	90×126 mm. No. 1356×2	3·25	3·00

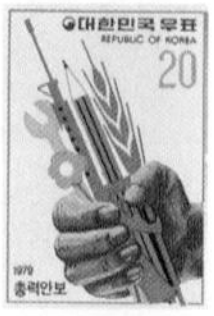
695 Hand holding Symbols of Security

1979. Strengthening National Security.

1358	**695**	20w. multicoloured	40	10

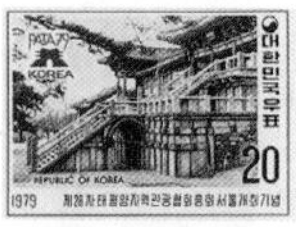
696 Pulguk Temple and P.A.T.A. Emblem

1979. 28th Pacific Area Travel Association Conference, Seoul.

1359	**696**	20w. multicoloured	40	10

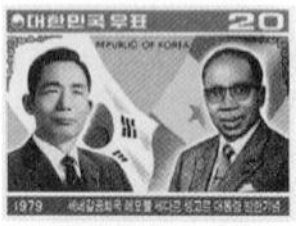
697 Presidents Pak and Senghor

1979. Visit of President Senghor of Senegal.

1360	**697**	20w. multicoloured	40	10
MS1361		90×60 mm. No. 1360×2	1·50	1·40

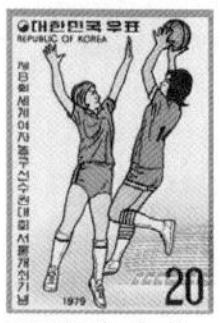
698 Basketball

1979. Eighth World Women's Basketball Championships, Seoul.

1362	**698**	20w. multicoloured	55	10

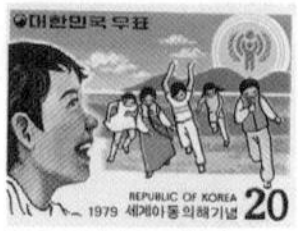
699 Children playing

1979. International Year of the Child.

1363	**699**	20w. multicoloured	40	10
MS1363a		90×60 mm. No. 1363×2	1·50	1·40

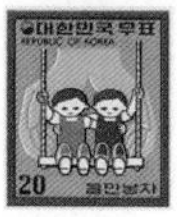
700 Children on Swing

1979. Family Planning.

1364	**700**	20w. multicoloured	75	30

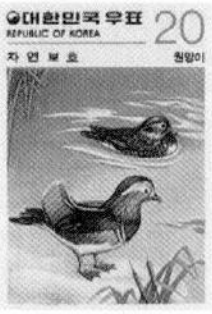
701 Mandarins

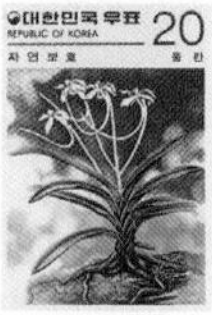
702 *Neofinettia falcata* (orchid)

1979. Nature Conservation.

1365	**701**	20w. multicoloured	1·50	25
1366	**702**	20w. multicoloured	1·50	25

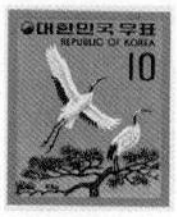
703 Manchurian Cranes

1979

1367	**703**	10w. black and green	70	25
1368	-	15w. deep green and green	40	10
1369	-	20w. bistre, black & blue	40	10
1370	-	30w. multicoloured	45	10
1371	-	40w. multicoloured	55	10
1372	-	50w. brown, red & orge	40	10
1373	-	60w. grey, purple & mve	45	10
1374	-	70w. multicoloured	75	15
1375	-	80w. yellow, black & red	85	25
1376	-	90w. buff, green and orange	1·10	25
1377	-	100w. purple and mauve	95	25
1377a	-	100w. black	2·75	25
1378	-	150w. black, bistre and blue	1·00	25
1379	-	200w. brown and green	1·50	30
1380	-	300w. blue	2·30	30
1381	-	400w. green, brown and deep green	5·00	40
1381a	-	400w. blue, ochre, brown and grey	3·50	40
1382	-	450w. brown	2·75	40
1383	-	500w. dp green & green	2·75	40
1383a	-	550w. black	3·00	40
1384	-	600w. multicoloured	3·00	75
1385	-	700w. multicoloured	4·25	75
1386	-	800w. multicoloured	3·75	1·20
1387	-	1000w. lt brown & brn	4·25	45
1388	-	1000w. lt brown & brn	4·25	45
1389	-	5000w. multicoloured	27·00	5·50

DESIGNS—As T **703**: HORIZ: 15w. Mt. Sorak; 50w. Earthenware model of wagon; 90w. Paikryung Island; 1000w. Duck earthenware vessels (1387 facing right; 1388 facing left). VERT: 20w. Tolharubang (stone grandfather); 30w. National flag; 40w. "Hibiscus syriacus"; 60w. Porcelain jar, Yi Dynasty; 70w. Kyongju Observatory; 80w. Mounted warrior (pottery vessel); 100w. (1377) Ryu Kwan Soon; 100w. (1377a) Chung Yak Yong (writer); 150w. Porcelain jar, Chosun Dynasty; 200w. Ahn Joong Geun; 300w. Ahn Chang Ho; 400w. Koryo celadon incense burner; 450, 550w. Kim Ku (organizer of Korean Independence Party); 500w. Brick with mountain landscape; 600w. Hong Yung Sik (postal reformer); 700w. Duck (lid of incense burner). 29×41 mm: 800w. Dragon's head flagpole finial; 5000w. Tiger.

See also No. 1065.

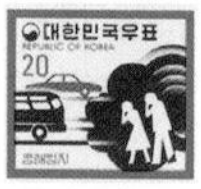
725 People suffering from Traffic Pollution

1979. Environmental Protection.

1390	**725**	20w. brown and green	75	25

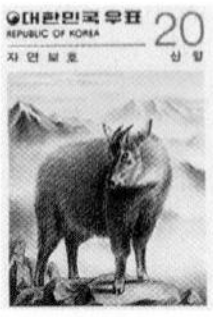
726 Common Goral

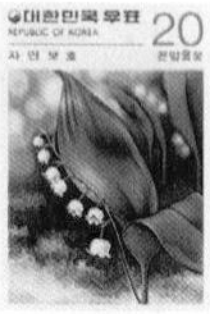
727 *Convallaria leiskei* Miquel

1979. Nature Conservation.

1391	**726**	20w. multicoloured	1·50	15
1392	**727**	20w. multicoloured	1·50	15

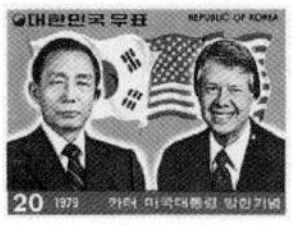
728 Presidents Pak and Carter

1979. Visit of President Carter of United States.

1393	**728**	20w. multicoloured	40	10
MS1394		90×60 mm. No. 1393×2	1·50	1·40

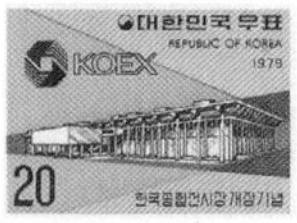
729 Exhibition Building and Emblem

1979. Opening of Korea Exhibition Centre.

1395	**729**	20w. multicoloured	30	10

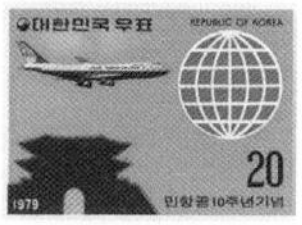
730 Boeing 747-200 Jetliner and Globe

1979. Tenth Anniv of Korean Air Lines.

1396	**730**	20w. multicoloured	40	10

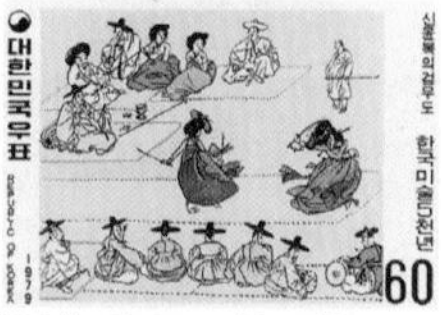
731 *The Courtesans' Sword Dance* (Shin Yun-bok)

1979. United States "5000 Years of Korean Art" Exhibition (1st issue).

1397	**731**	60w. multicoloured	85	30
MS1398		89×125 mm. No. 1397×2	4·25	3·75

See also Nos. 1402/3, 1406/7, 1420/**MS**1422, 1426/7, 1433/4, 1441/2 and 1457/8.

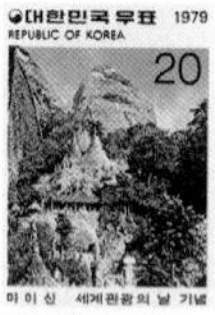
732 Mount Mai, North Cholla Province

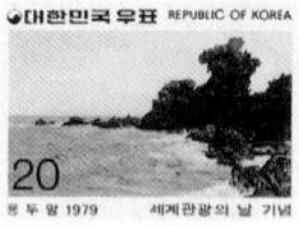
733 Dragon's Head Rock, Cheju Island

1979. World Tourism Day.

1399	**732**	20w. multicoloured	40	10
1400	**733**	20w. multicoloured	40	10

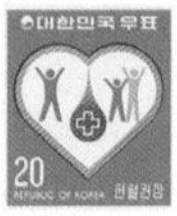
734 Heart, Donors and Blood Drop

1979. Blood Donors.

1401	**734**	20w. red and green	75	15

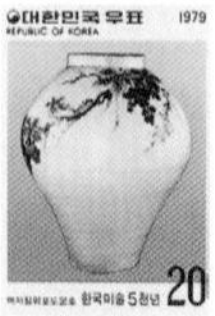
735 White Porcelain Jar with Grape Design

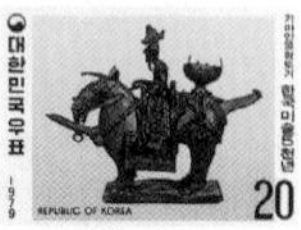
736 Mounted Warrior (pottery vessel)

1979. "5000 Years of Korean Art" Exhibition (2nd issue).

1402	**735**	20w. multicoloured	60	15
1403	**736**	20w. multicoloured	60	15

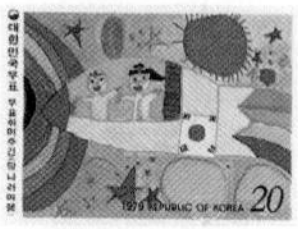
737 "Moon Travel" (Park Chung Jae)

1979. Philatelic Week.

1404	**737**	20w. multicoloured	30	10
MS1405		90×66 mm. No. 1404×2	1·40	1·30

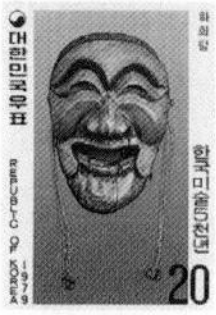
738 Hahoe Mask

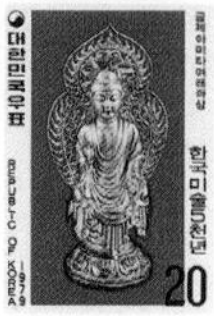
739 Golden Amitabha with Halo

1979. "5000 Years of Korean Art" Exhibition (3rd issue).

1406	**738**	20w. multicoloured	55	15
1407	**739**	20w. multicoloured	55	15

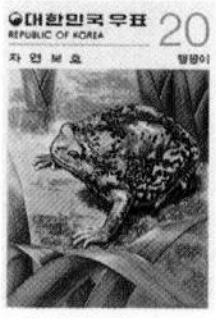
740 Rain Frog

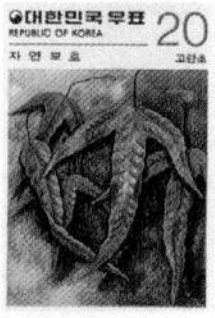
741 Asian Polypody

1979. Nature Conservation.

1408	**740**	20w. multicoloured	1·60	15
1409	**741**	20w. multicoloured	1·60	15

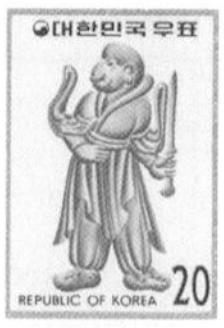
742 Monkey (bas-relief, Kim Yun Shin's tomb)

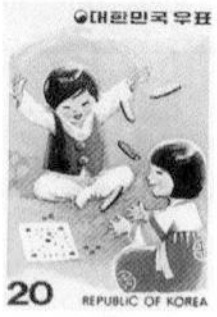
743 Children playing Yut

1979. Lunar New Year ("Year of the Monkey").

1410	**742**	20w. multicoloured	40	10
1411	**743**	20w. multicoloured	40	10
MS1412		Two sheets each 90×60 mm. (a) No. 1410×2; (b) No. 1411×2	1·40	1·20

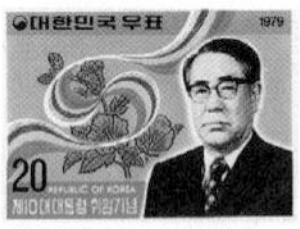
744 President Choi Kyu Hah

1979. Presidential Inauguration.

1413	**744**	20w. multicoloured	50	10
MS1414		91×61 mm. No. 1413×2	5·75	5·50

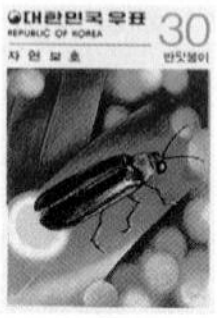
745 Firefly

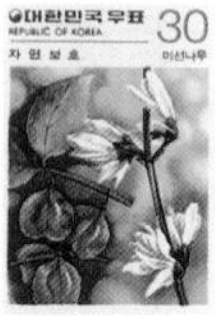
746 Meesun Tree

1980. Nature Conservation (5th series).

1415	**745**	30w. multicoloured	1·60	15
1416	**746**	30w. multicoloured	1·60	15

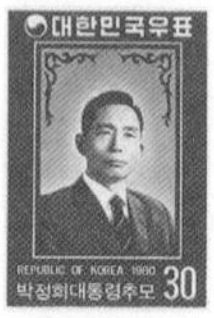
747 President Pak

1980. President Pak Commemoration.

1417	**747**	30w. red	50	15
1418	**747**	30w. purple	50	15
MS1419		90×60 mm. Nos. 1417/18	4·50	4·25

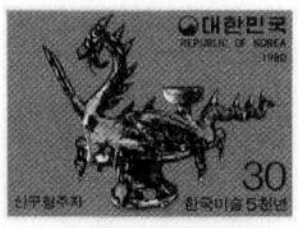
748 Earthenware Kettle

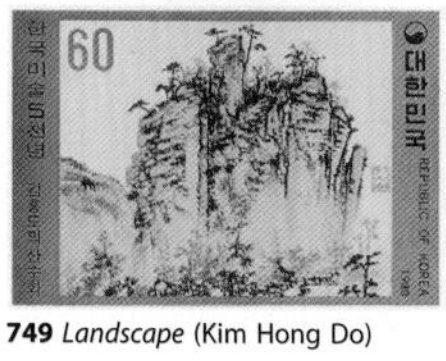
749 *Landscape* (Kim Hong Do)

1980. "5000 Years of Korean Art" Exhibition (4th issue).
1420 **748** 30w. multicoloured 65 15
1421 **749** 60w. multicoloured 1·00 30
MS1422 90×128 mm. No. 1421×2 3·50 3·50

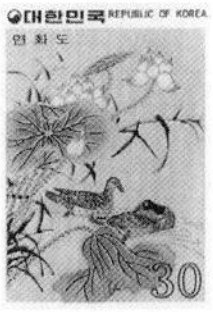
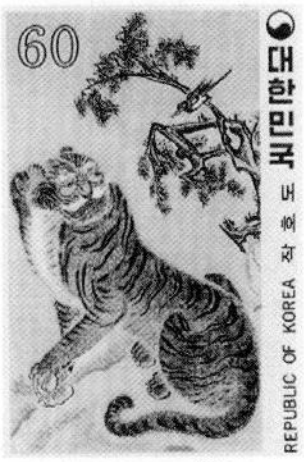

750 "Lotus" **751** *Magpie and Tiger*

1980. Folk Paintings (1st series).
1423 **750** 30w. multicoloured 65 15
1424 **751** 60w. multicoloured 1·60 55
See also Nos. 1429/31, 1437/40 and 1453/6.

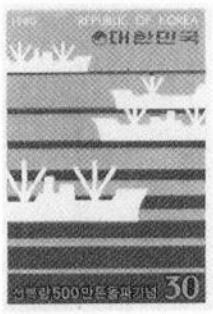

752 Merchant Ships

1980. Korean Merchant Navy.
1425 **752** 30w. multicoloured 40 10

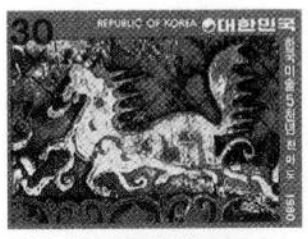
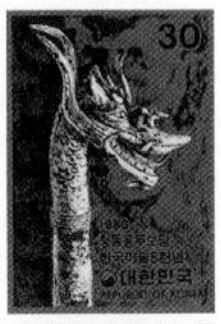

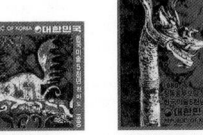

753 *Heavenly Horse* (tomb painting) **754** Banner Staff with Dragonhead Finial

1980. "5000 Years of Korean Art" Exhibition (5th series).
1426 **753** 30w. multicoloured 65 15
1427 **754** 30w. multicoloured 65 15

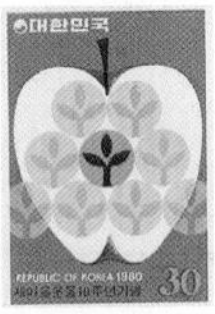

755 "Fruition"

1980. Tenth Anniv of Saemaul Movement (community self-help programme).
1428 **755** 30w. multicoloured 40 10

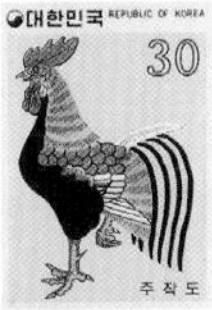

756 "Red Phoenix"

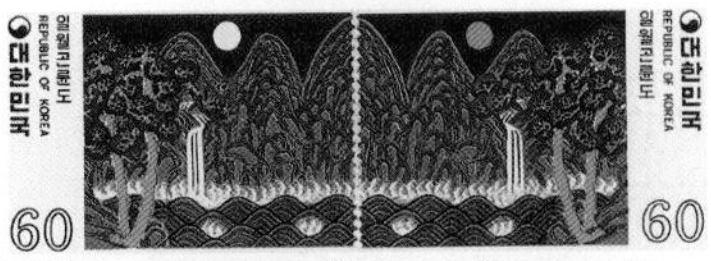

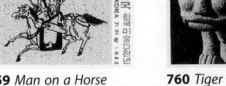

757/8 *Sun and Moon over Mt. Konryun (image scaled to 47% of original size)*

1980. Folk Paintings (2nd series).
1429 **756** 30w. multicoloured 55 15
1430 **757** 60w. multicoloured 1·60 45
1431 **758** 60w. multicoloured 1·60 45
MS1432 127×91 mm. Nos. 1430/1 5·75 5·50
Nos. 1430/1 were issued together, *se-tenant*, forming a composite design.

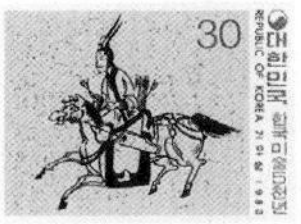
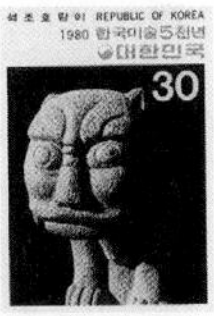

759 *Man on a Horse* (mural, Koguryo period) **760** *Tiger* (granite sculpture)

1980. "5000 Years of Korean Art" Exhibition (6th issue).
1433 **759** 30w. multicoloured 65 15
1434 **760** 30w. multicoloured 65 15

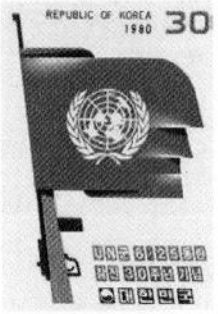

761 U.N. Flag and Rifle

1980. 30th Anniv of Intervention of U.N. Forces in Korean War.
1435 **761** 30w. multicoloured 40 10

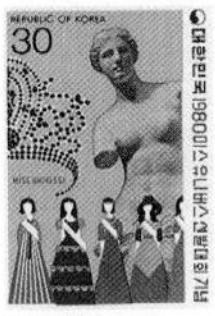

762 *Venus de Milo* and Contestants

1980. "Miss Universe" Beauty Contest, Seoul.
1436 **762** 30w. multicoloured 40 10

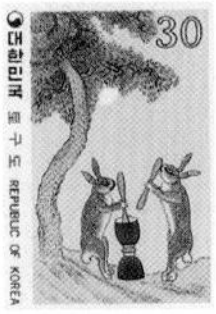
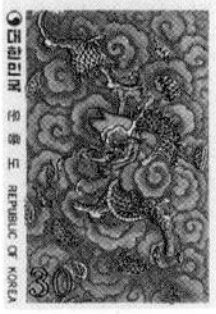

763 *Rabbits pounding Grain in a Mortar* **764** *Dragon in Cloud*

1980. Folk Paintings (3rd series).
1437 **763** 30w. multicoloured 65 25
1438 **764** 30w. multicoloured 65 25

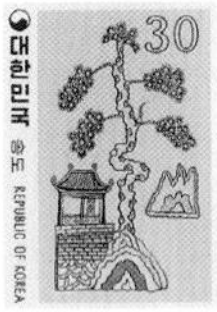
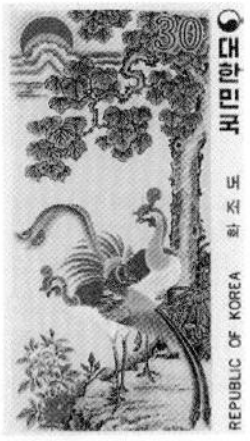

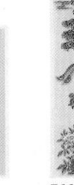

765 *Pine Tree* **766** *Flowers and Manchurian Cranes* (detail, folding screen)

1980. Folk Paintings (4th series).
1439 **765** 30w. multicoloured 65 25
1440 **766** 30w. multicoloured 1·20 30

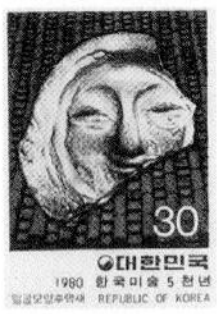
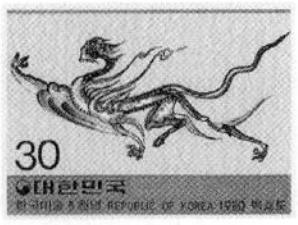

767 Human faced Roof Tile **768** *White Tiger* (mural)

1980. "5000 Years of Korean Art" Exhibition (7th issue).
1441 **767** 30w. multicoloured 55 15
1442 **768** 30w. multicoloured 55 15

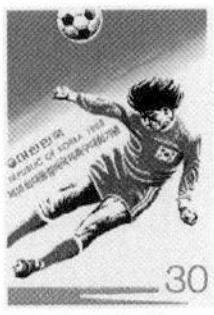

769 Football

1980. Tenth President's Cup Football Tournament.
1443 **769** 30w. multicoloured 40 10

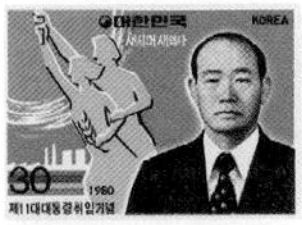

770 President Chun Doo Hwan

1980. Presidential Inauguration.
1444 **770** 30w. multicoloured 50 15
MS1445 90×60 mm. No. 1444×2 3·25 2·75

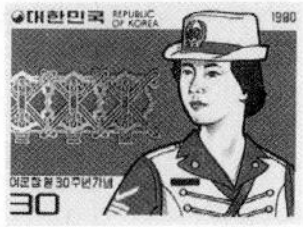

771 Woman Soldier and Emblem

1980. 30th Anniv of Women's Army Corps.
1446 **771** 30w. multicoloured 40 10

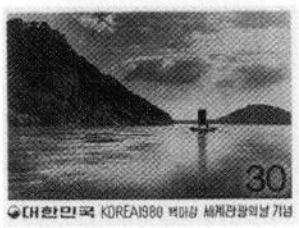
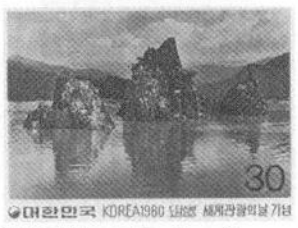

772 River Baegma **773** Three Peaks of Dodam

1980. World Tourism Day.
1447 **772** 30w. pink and purple 40 10
1448 **773** 30w. yellow, green and blue 40 10

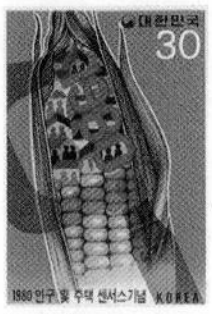

774 Corn-cob and Micrometer

1980. Population and Housing Census.
1449 **774** 30w. multicoloured 40 10

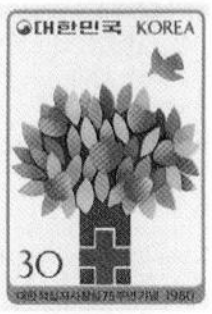

775 Tree

1980. 75th Anniv of Korean Red Cross.
1450 **775** 30w. multicoloured 50 10

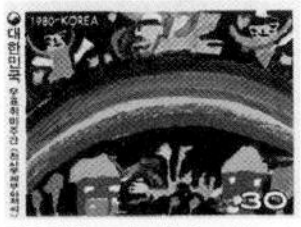

776 "Angels delivering Mail" (Kim Ki Chul)

1980. Philatelic Week.
1451 **776** 30w. multicoloured 40 10
MS1452 91×60 mm. No. 1451×2 1·50 1·30

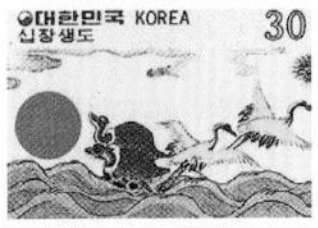

777 *Ten Long-life Symbols*

1980. Folk Paintings (5th series). Multicoloured.
1453 30w. Type **777** 1·50 25
1454 30w. "Herb of eternal youth" and deer 1·50 25
1455 30w. Pine and deer eating herb 1·50 25
1456 30w. Pine, water and rock 1·50 25
Nos. 1453/6 were issued together, *se-tenant*, forming a composite design.

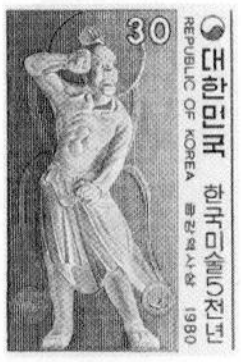

781 Deva King (sculpture)

1980. "5000 Years of Korean Art" Exhibition (8th series).
1457 **781** 30w. black 65 15
1458 **781** 30w. red 65 15

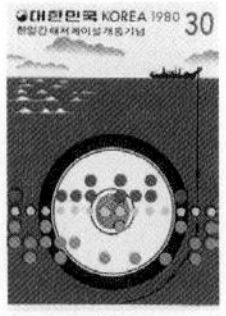

782 *Cable Enterprise* (cable ship) and Cross-section of Cable

1980. Inauguration of Korea–Japan Submarine Cable.
1459 **782** 30w. multicoloured 50 10

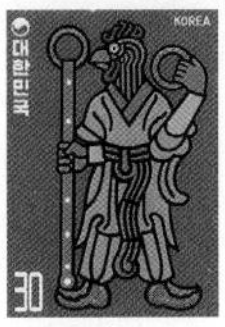
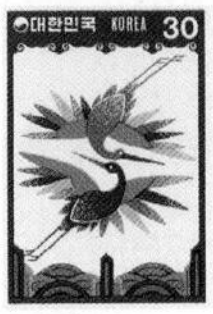

783 Cock (bas-relief, Kim Yu Shin's tomb) **784** Cranes

1980. Lunar New Year ("Year of the Cock").
1460 **783** 30w. multicoloured 50 10
1461 **784** 30w. multicoloured 50 10
MS1462 Two sheets each 90×60 mm. (a) No. 1460×2; (b) No. 1461×2 3·00 2·75

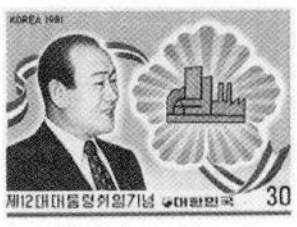

785 President Chun Doo Hwan and Factory within "Hibiscus syriacus"

1981. Presidential Inauguration.
1463 **785** 30w. multicoloured 40 10
MS1464 90×60 mm. No. 1463×2 1·40 1·30

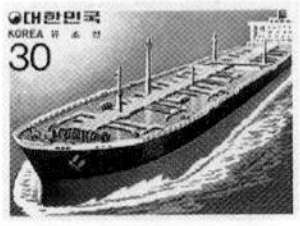
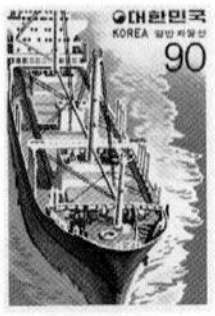

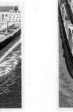

786 *Korea Sun* (tanker) **787** *Asia Yukho* (freighter)

1981. Ships (1st series).
1465 **786** 30w. multicoloured 60 10
1466 **787** 90w. multicoloured 90 25
See also Nos. 1470/1, 1482/5 and 1501/2.

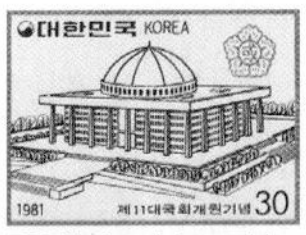

788 National Assembly Building

1981. Inaugural Session of 11th National Assembly.
1467 **788** 30w. brown and gold 40 10

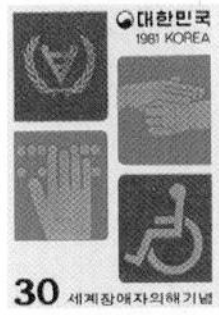
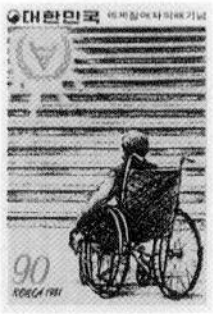

789 Symbols of Disability and I.Y.D.P. Emblem **790** Disabled Person in Wheelchair at Foot of Steps

1981. International Year of Disabled Persons.
1468 **789** 30w. multicoloured 40 10
1469 **790** 90w. multicoloured 85 40

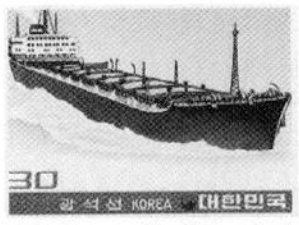
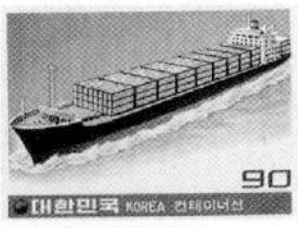

791 *Saturn* (bulk-carrier) **792** *Hanjin Seoul* (container ship)

1981. Ships (2nd series).
1470 **791** 30w. deep purple, purple and blue 60 10
1471 **792** 90w. grey, blue and red 1·00 30

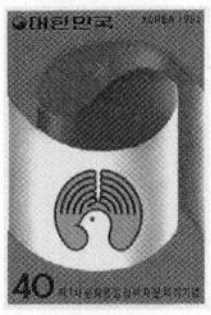

793 Council Emblem on Ribbon

1981. Advisory Council on Peaceful Unification Policy.
1472 **793** 40w. multicoloured 40 10

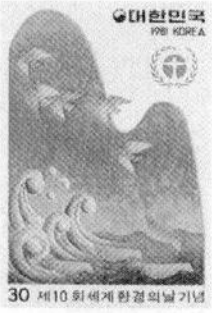

794 "Clean Rivers and Air"

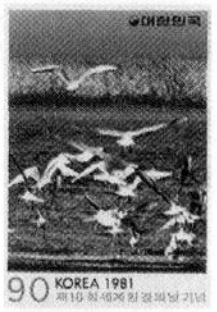

795 White Storks visiting Breeding Grounds

1981. World Environment Day.

1473	**794**	30w. multicoloured	40	10
1474	**795**	90w. multicoloured	90	25

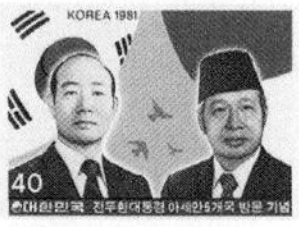

796 Presidents Chun and Suharto of Indonesia

1981. Presidential Visit to A.S.E.A.N. Countries. Multicoloured.

1475	40w. Type **796**	65	10
1476	40w. Pres. Chun and Sultan of Malaysia	65	10
1477	40w. Handshake and flags of South Korea and Singapore	65	10
1478	40w. Pres. Chun and King of Thailand	65	10
1479	40w. Presidents Chun and Marcos of Philippines	65	10
1480	40w. Pres. Chun and flags of Korea, Singapore, Malaysia and Philippines (39×43 mm)	65	10
MS1481	Two sheets each 126×90 mm. (a) Nos. 1475/9; (b) No. 1480×2	5·50	5·00

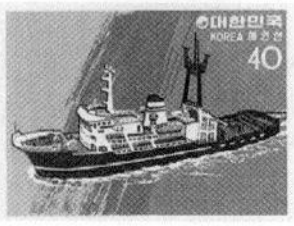

802 *Chung Ryong No. 3* (tug)

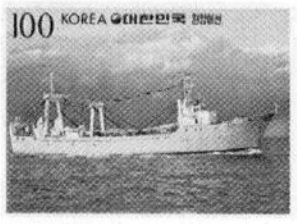

803 *Soo Gong No. 71* (trawler)

1981. Ships (3rd series).

1482	**802**	40w. multicoloured	75	15
1483	**803**	100w. multicoloured	1·30	40

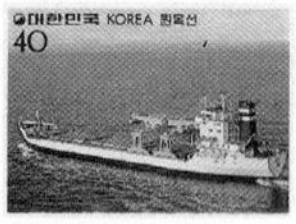

804 *Aldebaran* (log carrier)

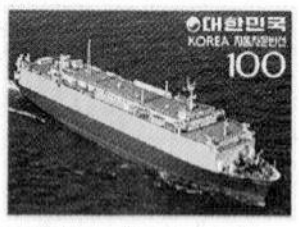

805 *Hyundai No. 1* (car carrier)

1981. Ships (4th series).

1484	**804**	40w. multicoloured	75	15
1485	**805**	100w. multicoloured	1·30	30

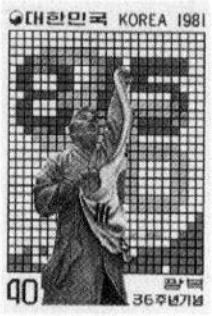

806 Korean with Flag and Dates on Graph

1981. 36th Anniv of Liberation.

1486	**806**	40w. multicoloured	40	10

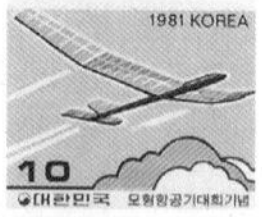

807 Glider

1981. Third Model Aeronautic Competition. Multicoloured.

1487	10w. Type **807**	60	10
1488	20w. Elastic-powered airplane	60	10
1489	40w. Line-controlled airplane	60	20
1490	50w. Radio-controlled airplane	75	30
1491	80w. Radio-controlled helicopter	1·00	40

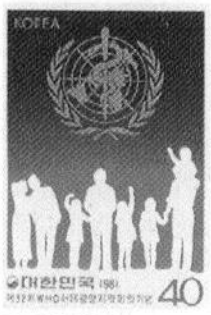

812 W.H.O. Emblem and Citizens

1981. 32nd Session of W.H.O. Regional Committee for the Western Pacific, Seoul.

1492	**812**	40w. multicoloured	40	10

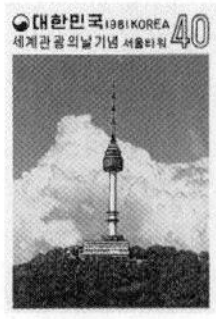

813 Seoul Communications Tower

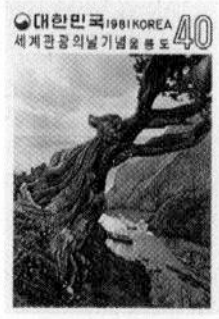

814 Ulreung Island

1981. World Tourism Day.

1493	**813**	40w. multicoloured	40	10
1494	**814**	40w. multicoloured	40	10

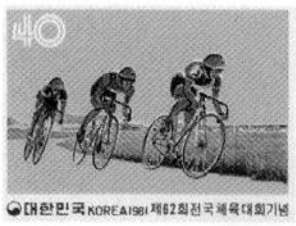

815 Cycling

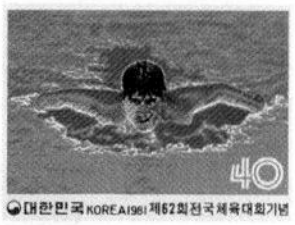

816 Swimming

1981. 62nd National Sports Meeting, Seoul.

1495	**815**	40w. multicoloured	50	10
1496	**816**	40w. multicoloured	50	10

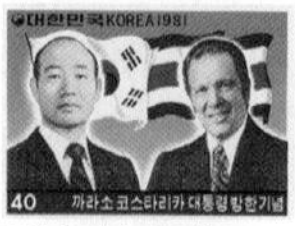

817 Presidents Chun and Carazo Odio

1981. Visit of President Carazo Odio of Costa Rica.

1497	**817**	40w. multicoloured	45	10

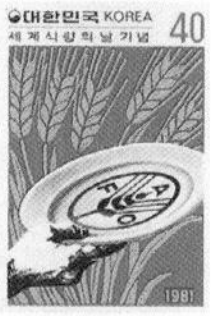

818 Hand holding Plate with F.A.O. Emblem

1981. World Food Day.

1498	**818**	40w. multicoloured	45	10

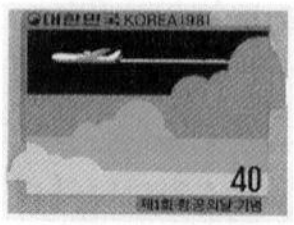

819 Airliner and Clouds

1981. National Aviation Day.

1499	**819**	40w. orange, brown and silver	50	10

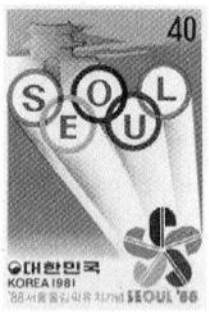

820 South Gate of Seoul and Olympic Rings

1981. Choice of Seoul as 1988 Olympic Host City.

1500	**820**	40w. multicoloured	65	15

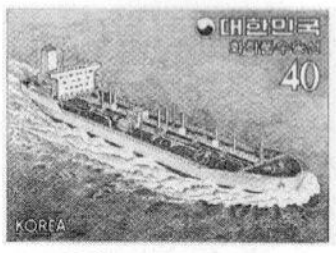

821 *Stolt Hawk* (chemical carrier)

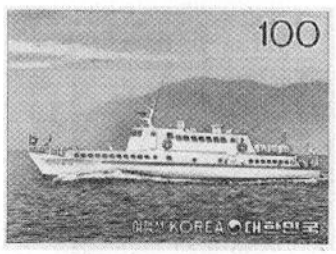

822 Passenger Ferry

1981. Ships (5th series).

1501	**821**	40w. black	65	15
1502	**822**	100w. blue	1·20	30

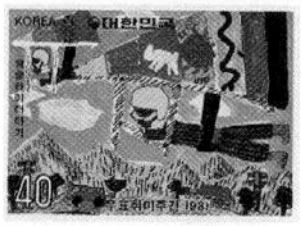

823 "Hang-gliding" (Kim Kyung Jun)

1981. Philatelic Week.

1503	**823**	40w. multicoloured	40	10
MS1504		90×60 mm. No. 1503×2	1·80	1·70

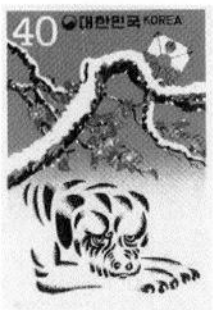

824 Camellia and Dog

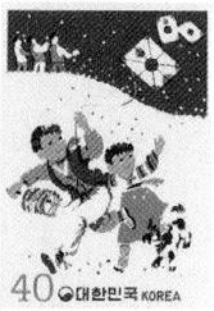

825 Children flying Kite

1981. Lunar New Year ("Year of the Dog").

1505	**824**	40w. multicoloured	40	10
1506	**825**	40w. multicoloured	40	10
MS1507		Two sheets each 90×60 mm. (a) No. 1505×2; (b) No. 1506×2	3·75	3·50

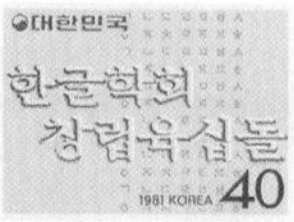

826 "Hangul Hakhoe"

1981. 60th Anniv of Hangul Hakhoe (Korean Language Society).

1508	**826**	40w. multicoloured	50	10

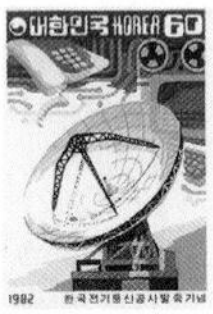

827 Telephone and Dish Aerial

1982. Inauguration of Korea Telecommunication Authority.

1509	**827**	60w. multicoloured	60	10

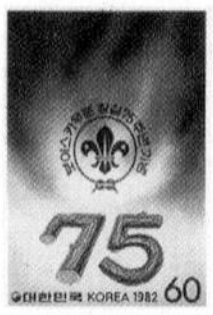

828 Scout Emblem and Logs forming "75"

1982. 75th Anniv of Boy Scout Movement.

1510	**828**	60w. multicoloured	65	15

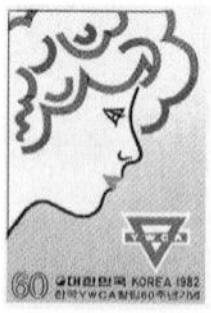

829 Young Woman

1982. 60th Anniv of Korean Young Women's Christian Association.

1511	**829**	60w. multicoloured	50	10

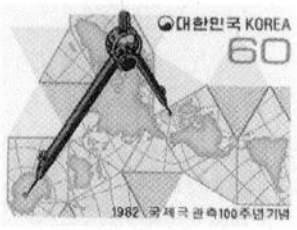

830 Dividers and World Map

1982. Centenary of International Polar Year.

1512	**830**	60w. multicoloured	65	15

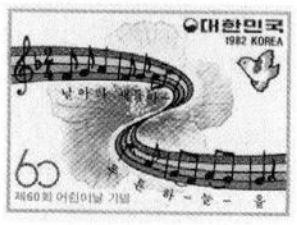

831 Music and *Hibiscus syriacus*

1982. Children's Day.

1513	**831**	60w. multicoloured	50	10

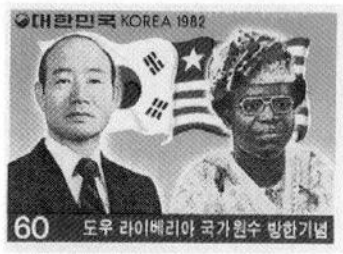

832 President Chun and Samuel Doe

1982. Visit of Samuel Doe (Liberian Head of State).

1514	**832**	60w. multicoloured	60	15
MS1515		100×60 mm. No. 1514×2	1·80	1·70

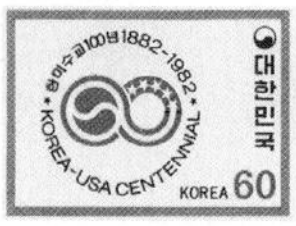

833 Centenary Emblem

1982. Centenary of Korea–United States Friendship Treaty.

1516	**833**	60w. multicoloured	50	15
1517	-	60w. multicoloured	50	15
MS1518		90×60 mm. Nos. 1516/17	3·75	3·50

DESIGN: No. 1517, Statue of Liberty and Seoul South Gate.

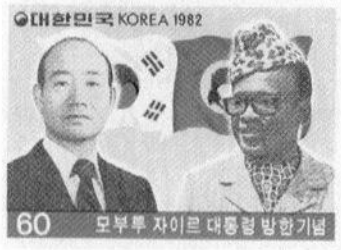

835 Presidents Chun and Mobutu

1982. Visit of President Mobutu of Zaire.

1519	**835**	60w. multicoloured	50	15
MS1520		100×60 mm. No. 1519×2. Imperf	1·80	1·70

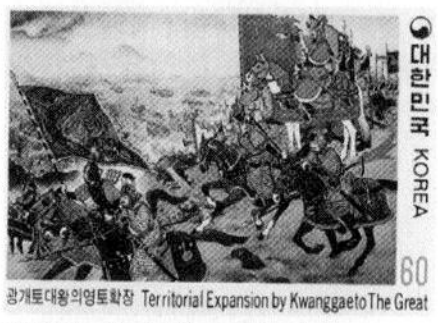

836 *Territorial Expansion by Kwanggaeto the Great* (Lee Chong Sang)

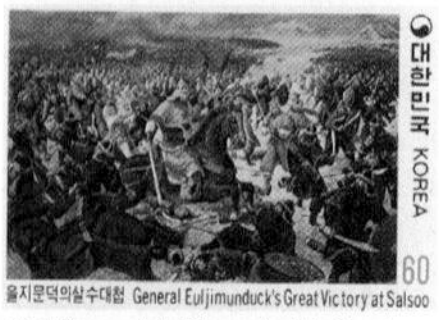

837 *General Euljimunduck's Great Victory at Salsoo* (Park Kak Soon)

1982. Documentary Paintings (1st series).

1521	**836**	60w. multicoloured	85	40
1522	**837**	60w. multicoloured	1·30	45

See also Nos. 1523/4, 1537/8 and 1548/9.

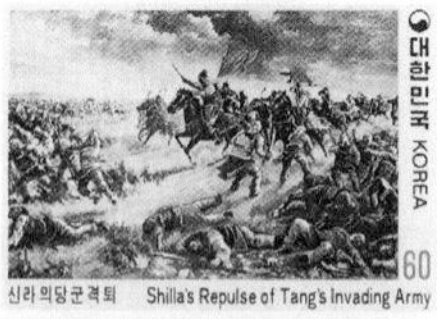

838 *Shilla's Repulse of Invading Tang Army* (Oh Seung Woo)

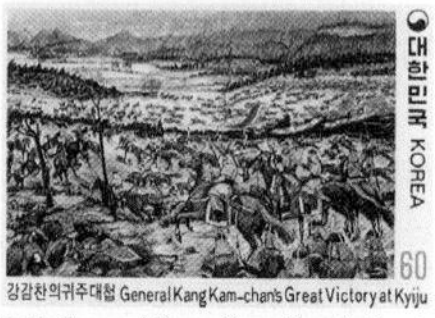

839 *General Kang Kam Chan's Great Victory at Kyiju* (Lee Yong Hwan)

1982. Documentary Paintings (2nd series).

1523	**838**	60w. multicoloured	75	30
1524	**839**	60w. multicoloured	75	30

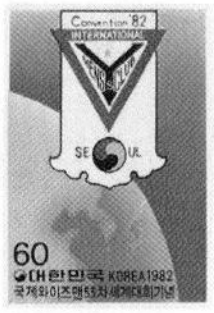

840 Convention Emblem and Globe

1982. 55th International Y's Men's Club Convention, Seoul.

1525	**840**	60w. multicoloured	40	10

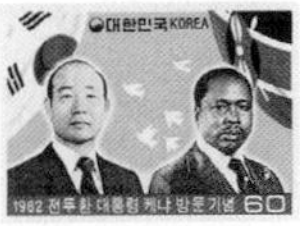

841 Presidents Chun and Moi of Kenya

1982. Presidential Visits to Africa and Canada. Multicoloured.

1526	60w. Type **841**	50	10
1527	60w. Presidents Chun and Shagari of Nigeria	50	10
1528	60w. Presidents Chun and Bongo of Gabon	50	10
1529	60w. Presidents Chun and Diouf of Senegal	50	10
1530	60w. Flags of South Korea and Canada	50	10
MS1531	Five sheets each 90×60 mm. (a) No. 1526×2; (b) No. 1527×2; (c) No. 1528×2; (d) No. 1529×2; (e) No. 1530×2	12·50	11·50

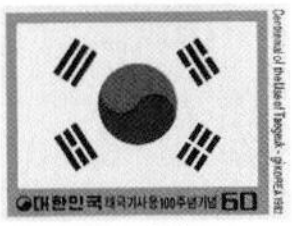

846 National Flag

1982. Centenary of National Flag.

1532	**846**	60w. multicoloured	50	10
MS1533		90×60 mm. No. 1532×2	2·50	2·30

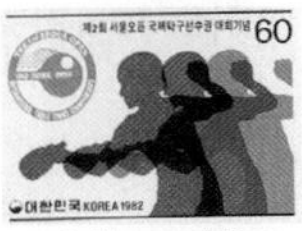

847 Emblem and Player

1982. Second Seoul Table Tennis Championships.

1534	**847**	60w. multicoloured	60	10

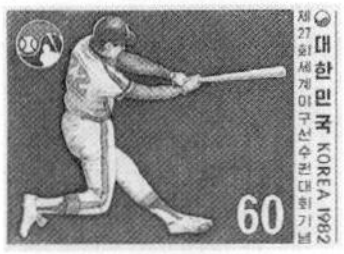

848 Baseball Player

1982. 27th World Baseball Championship Series, Seoul.

1535	**848**	60w. brown	60	15

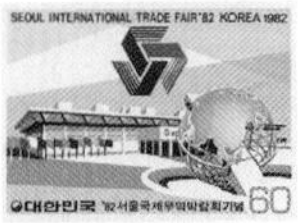

849 Exhibition Centre

1982. Seoul International Trade Fair.

1536	**849**	60w. multicoloured	40	10

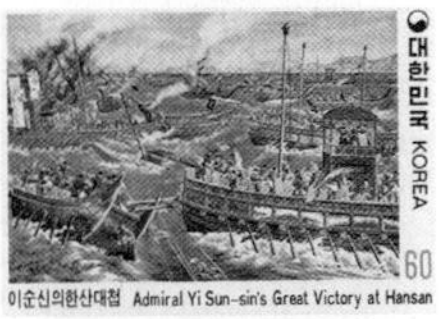

850 *Admiral Yi Sun Sin's Great Victory at Hansan* (Kim Hyung Ku)

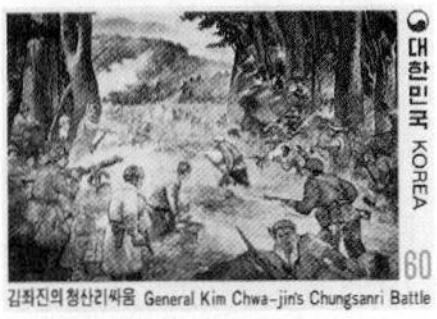

851 *General Kim Chwa Jin's Chungsanri Battle* (Sohn Soo Kwang)

1982. Documentary Paintings (3rd series).

1537	**850**	60w. multicoloured	1·10	40
1538	**851**	60w. multicoloured	1·10	40

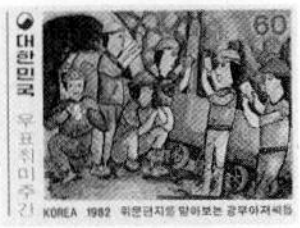

852 "Miners reading Consolatory Letters" (Um Soon Keun)

1982. Philatelic Week.

1539	**852**	60w. multicoloured	40	10
MS1540		90×60 mm. No. 1539×2	1·70	1·50

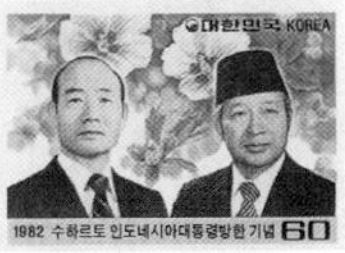

853 Presidents Chun and Suharto

1982. Visit of President Suharto of Indonesia.

1541	**853**	60w. multicoloured	40	10
MS1542		100×60 mm. No. 1541. Imperf×2	1·50	1·40

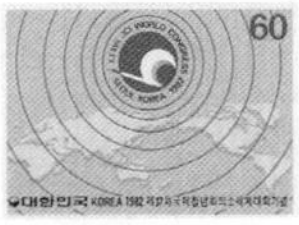

854 J.C.I. Emblem over World Map

1982. 37th Junior Chamber International World Congress, Seoul.

1543	**854**	60w. multicoloured	40	10

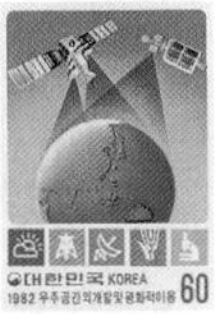

855 "Intelsat 5" and "4-A" orbiting Globe

1982. Second U.N. Conference on the Exploration and Peaceful Uses of Outer Space, Vienna.

1544	**855**	60w. multicoloured	50	10

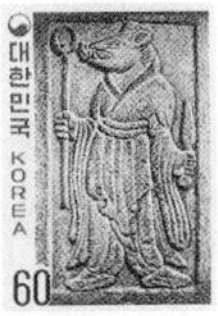

856 Pig (bas-relief, Kim Yu Shin's tomb)

1982. Lunar New Year ("Year of the Pig").

1545	60w. Type **856**	50	10
1546	60w. Black-billed magpies and Korean moneybag	50	10
MS1547	Two sheets each 90×60 mm. (a) No. 1545×2; (b) No. 1546×2	4·25	3·75

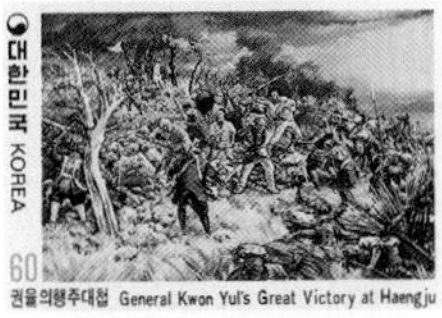

858 *General Kwon Yul's Great Victory at Haengju* (Oh Seung Woo)

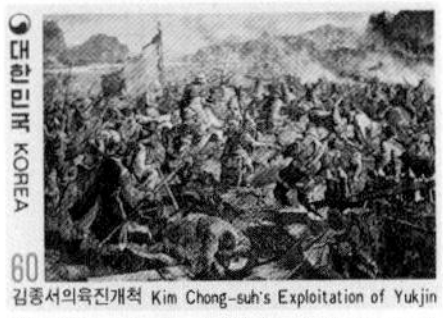

859 *Kim Chong Suh's Exploitation of Yukin* (Kim Tae)

1982. Documentary Paintings (4th series).

1548	**858**	60w. multicoloured	1·30	40
1549	**859**	60w. multicoloured	1·30	40

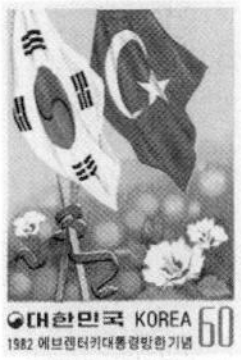

860 Flags of South Korea and Turkey

1982. Visit of President Evran of Turkey.

1550	**860**	60w. multicoloured	50	10
MS1551		100×60 mm. No. 1550×2. Imperf	1·70	1·50

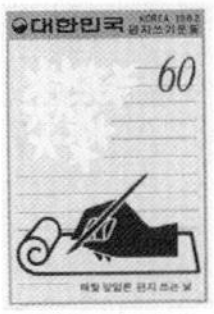

861 Hand writing Letter

1982. Letter Writing Campaign.

1552	**861**	60w. multicoloured	40	10

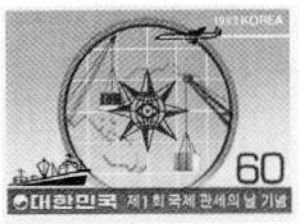

862 Emblem, Airliner, Container Ship and Cranes

1983. International Customs Day.

1553	**862**	60w. multicoloured	60	10

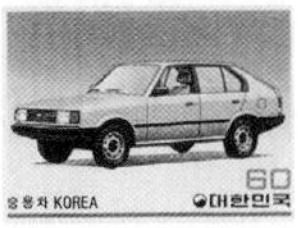

863 Hyundai "Pony 2"

1983. Korean-made Vehicles (1st series). Multicoloured.

1554	60w. Type **863**	85	25
1555	60w. Keohwa Jeep	85	25

See also Nos. 1558/9, 1564/5, 1572/3 and 1576/7.

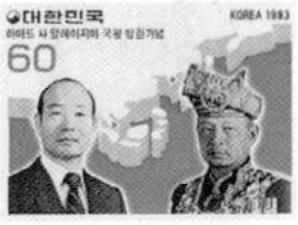

865 President Chun and Sultan of Malaysia

1983. Visit of King of Malaysia.

1556	**865**	60w. multicoloured	40	10
MS1557		90×60 mm. No. 1556×2	1·40	1·30

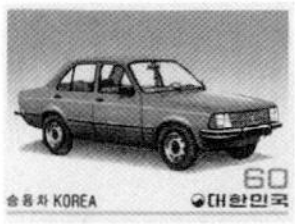

866 Daewoo "Maepsy"

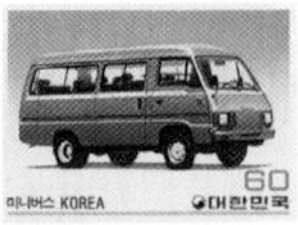

867 Kia "Bongo" Minibus

1983. Korean-made Vehicles (2nd series).

1558	**866**	60w. multicoloured	85	25
1559	**867**	60w. multicoloured	85	25

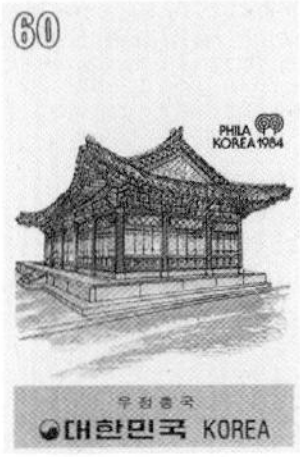

868 Former General Bureau of Postal Administration

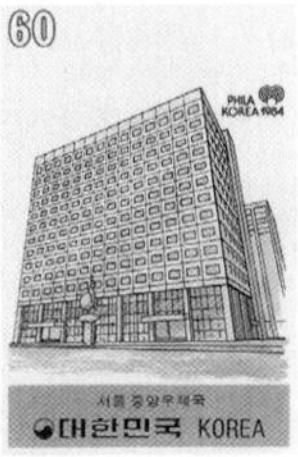

869 Central Post Office, Seoul

1983. "Philakorea 84" International Stamp Exhibition, Seoul. Centenary of Korean Postal Service (1st series).

1560	**868**	60w. multicoloured	65	15
1561	**869**	60w. multicoloured	65	15

See also Nos. 1566/7, 1574/5 and 1603/6.

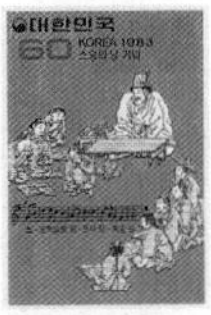

870 Old Village Schoolroom

1983. Teachers' Day.

1562	**870**	60w. multicoloured	50	10
MS1563		90×60 mm. No. 1562×2	2·10	1·90

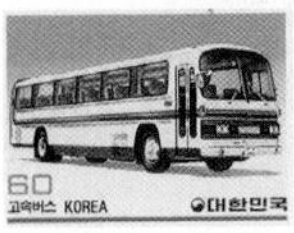

871 Asia Motor Co. Bus

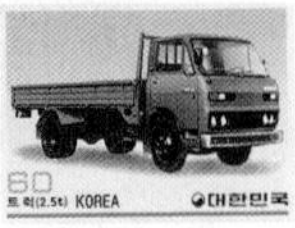

872 Kia "Super Titan" Truck

1983. Korean-made Vehicles (3rd series).

1564	**871**	60w. multicoloured	85	25
1565	**872**	60w. multicoloured	85	25

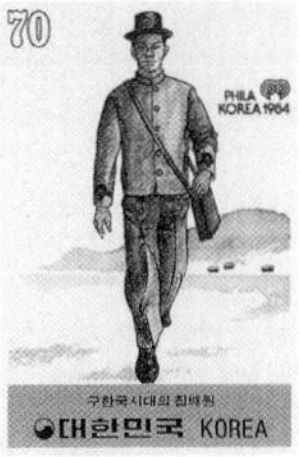

873 Early Postman

1983. "Philakorea 84" International Stamp Exhibition, Seoul. Centenary of Korean Postal Service (2nd series).

1566	**873**	70w. multicoloured	85	25
1567	-	70w. multicoloured	85	25

DESIGN: No. 1567, Modern postman on motor-cycle.

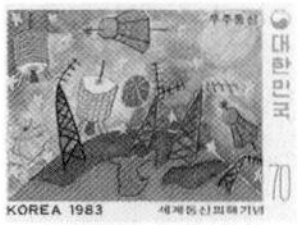

875 "Communications in Outer Space" (Chun Ja Eun)

1983. World Communications Year.

1568	**875**	70w. multicoloured	40	10
MS1569		90×60 mm. No. 1568×2	1·50	1·40

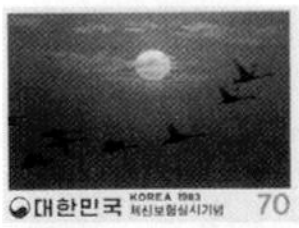

876 Whooper Swans at Sunrise

1983. Inauguration of Communications Insurance.

1570	**876**	70w. multicoloured	85	15

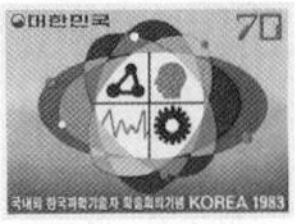

877 Emblems of Science and Engineering

1983. Korean Symposium on Science and Technology, Seoul.

1571	**877**	70w. multicoloured	60	15

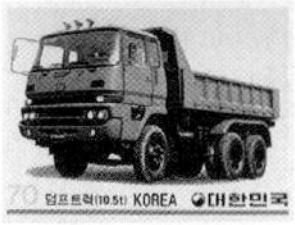

878 Daewoo Dump Truck

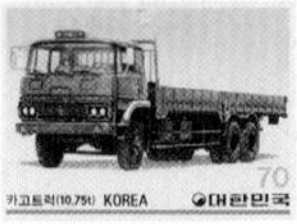

879 Hyundai Cargo Lorry

1983. Korean-made Vehicles (4th series).

1572	**878**	70w. multicoloured	95	25
1573	**879**	70w. multicoloured	95	25

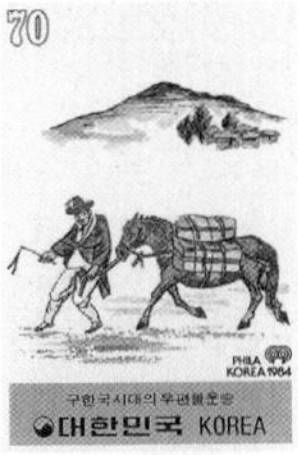

880 Mail carried by Horse

1983. "Philakorea 84" International Stamp Exhibition, Seoul. Centenary of Korean Postal Service (3rd series). Multicoloured.

1574	70w. Type **880**	1·00	25
1575	70w. Mail truck and Douglas DC-8-60 Super Sixty jetliner	1·00	25

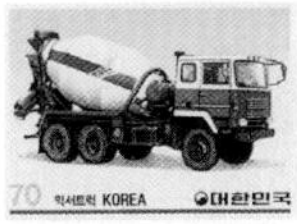

882 Dong-A Concrete Mixer Truck

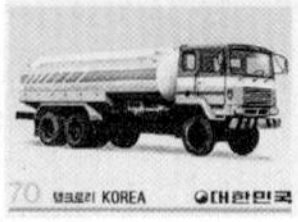

883 Dong-A Tanker

1983. Korean-made Vehicles (5th series).

1576	**882**	70w. multicoloured	95	25
1577	**883**	70w. multicoloured	95	25

884 President Chun and King Hussein

1983. Visit of King Hussein of Jordan.
1578	**884**	70w. multicoloured	50	10

MS1579 100×60 mm. No. 1578×2.
Imperf   1·60   1·40

885 Woman with Fan

1983. 53rd American Society of Travel Agents World Congress, Seoul.
1580	**885**	70w. multicoloured	50	10

886 I.P.U. Emblem and Flags

1983. 70th Inter-Parliamentary Union Conference, Seoul.
1581	**886**	70w. multicoloured	50	10

MS1582 90×60 mm. No. 1581×2.   1·60   1·40

887 Gymnastics   **888** Football

1983. 64th National Sports Meeting, Inchon.
1583	**887**	70w. multicoloured	70	15
1584	**888**	70w. multicoloured	70	15

889 Presidents Chun and U San Yu of Burma

1983. Presidential Visits. Multicoloured.
1585		70w. Type **889**	1·60	75
1586		70w. Presidents Chun and Giani Zail Singh of India	1·60	75
1587		70w. Presidents Chun and Jayewardene of Sri Lanka	1·60	75
1588		70w. Flags of South Korea and Australia	1·60	75
1589		70w. Flags of South Korea and New Zealand	1·60	75

MS1590 Five sheets each 90×60 mm.
(a) No. 1585×2; (b) No. 1586×2; (c) No. 1587×2; (d) No. 1588×2; (e) No. 1589×2   28·00   25·00

894 Rain Drops containing Symbols of Industry, Light and Food

1983. Development of Water Resources and Tenth Anniv of Soyang-gang Dam.
1591	**894**	70w. multicoloured	50	10

895 Centenary Dates

1983. Centenary of First Korean Newspaper "Hansong Sunbo".
1592	**895**	70w. multicoloured	50	10

896 Tree with Lungs and Cross of Lorraine

1983. 30th Anniv of Korean National Tuberculosis Association.
1593	**896**	70w. multicoloured	50	10

897 Presidents Chun and Reagan

1983. Visit of President Reagan of United States of America.
1594	**897**	70w. multicoloured	50	10

MS1595 90×60 mm. No. 1594×2.   2·50   2·30

898 Child collecting Stamps

1983. Philatelic Week.
1596	**898**	70w. multicoloured	50	10

MS1597 90×60 mm. No. 1596×2.   2·50   2·30

899 Rat
(bas-relief, Kim Yu Shin's tomb)

1983. Lunar New Year ("Year of the Rat"). Multicoloured.
1598		70w. Type **899**	50	10
1599		70w. Manchurian cranes and pine	50	10

MS1600 Two sheets each 90×60 mm.
(a) No. 1598×2; (b) No. 1599×2   5·25   4·75

901 Bicentenary Emblem

1984. Bicentenary of Catholic Church in Korea.
1601	**901**	70w. red, violet and silver	50	10

MS1602 90×60 mm. No. 1601×2.   3·25   3·00

902 5m. and 10m. Stamps, 1884

1984. "Philakorea 84" International Stamp Exhibition, Seoul. Centenary of Korean Postal Service (4th series). Multicoloured.
1603		70w. Type **902**	70	15
1604		70w. 5000w. stamp of 1983	70	15

904 Old Postal Emblem and Post Box

1984. "Philakorea 84" International Stamp Exhibition, Seoul. Centenary of Korean Postal Service (5th series). Multicoloured.
1605		70w. Type **904**	70	15
1606		70w. Modern postal emblem and post box	70	15

906 President Chun and Sultan

1984. Visit of Sultan of Brunei.
1607	**906**	70w. multicoloured	50	10

MS1608 100×60 mm. No. 1607×2.   1·70   1·50

907 President Chun and Sheikh Khalifa

1984. Visit of Sheikh Khalifa of Qatar.
1609	**907**	70w. multicoloured	50	10

MS1610 100×60 mm. No. 1609×2.   1·70   1·50

908 Child posting Letter

1984. Centenary of Korean Postal Administration. Multicoloured.
1611		70w. Type **908**	50	10
1612		70w. Postman in city	50	10

MS1613 Two sheets each 90×60 mm.
(a) No. 1611×2; (b) No. 1612×2   3·25   2·75

910 Pope John Paul II

1984. Visit of Pope John Paul II.
1614	**910**	70w. black	60	10
1615	**910**	70w. multicoloured	60	10

MS1616 100×60 mm. Nos. 1614/15.   2·50   2·30

911 Cogwheel, Worker's Tools and Flowers

1984. Labour Festival.
1617	**911**	70w. multicoloured	45	10

912 Globe, Jetliner, Container Ship and Emblem

1984. 63rd/64th Sessions of Customs Co-operation Council, Seoul.
1618	**912**	70w. multicoloured	70	10

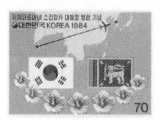

913 Map and Flags of S. Korea and Sri Lanka

1984. Visit of President Jayewardene of Sri Lanka.
1619	**913**	70w. multicoloured	50	10

MS1620 90×60 mm. No. 1619×2.   1·60   1·40

914 Symbols and Punctuation Marks

1984. 14th Asian Advertising Congress, Seoul.
1621	**914**	70w. multicoloured	50	10

915 Expressway

1984. Opening of 88 Olympic Expressway.
1622	**915**	70w. multicoloured	70	15

916 Laurel, "Victory" and Olympic Rings

1984. 90th Anniv of International Olympic Committee.
1623	**916**	70w. multicoloured	50	15

917 A.B.U. Emblem and Microphone

1984. 20th Anniv of Asia-Pacific Broadcasting Union.
1624	**917**	70w. multicoloured	50	10

918 Flags of S. Korea and Senegal

1984. Visit of President Abdou Diouf of Senegal.
1625	**918**	70w. multicoloured	50	15

MS1626 100×60 mm. No. 1625×2.
Imperf   2·30   2·00

919 Archery

1984. Olympic Games, Los Angeles. Multicoloured.
1627		70w. Type **919**	80	30
1628		440w. Fencing	3·00	75

921
Crucifixion

1984. Centenary of Korean Protestant Church. Multicoloured.

1629	70w. Type **921**	80	30
1630	70w. Cross, vine and dove	80	30
MS1631	80×100 mm. Nos. 1629/30	6·00	5·50

923 Man carrying Silk-covered Lantern

1984. Folk Customs (1st series). "Wedding" (Kim Kyo Man). Multicoloured.

1632	70w. Type **923**	80	30
1633	70w. Bridegroom on horse	80	30
1634	70w. Man playing clarinet	80	30
1635	70w. Bride in sedan chair (51×35 mm)	80	30
MS1636	90×61 mm. No. 1635	2·50	2·30

See also Nos. 1657/8, 1683/4, 1734/8, 1808/11, 1840/3, 1858/61 and 1915/18.

927 Pres. Chun and Mt. Fuji

1984. Pres. Chun's Visit to Japan.

1637	**927**	70w. multicoloured	60	15
MS1638	100×60 mm. No. 1637×2. Imperf		2·20	1·90

928 Flags of S. Korea and Gambia

1984. Visit of President Sir Dawada Kairaba Jawara of Gambia.

1639	**928**	70w. multicoloured	60	15
MS1640	100×60 mm. No. 1639×2. Imperf		2·20	1·90

929 Symbols of International Trade

1984. "Sitra '84" International Trade Fair, Seoul.

1641	**929**	70w. multicoloured	50	10

930 Namsan Tower and National Flags

1984. Visit of President El Hadj Omar Bongo of Gabon.

1642	**930**	70w. multicoloured	60	10
MS1643	100×60 mm. No. 1642×2. Imperf		1·90	1·70

931 Badminton

1984. 65th National Sports Meeting, Taegu. Multicoloured.

1644	70w. Type **931**	50	10
1645	70w. Wrestling	50	10

932 Magnifying Glass and Exhibition Emblem

1984. "Philakorea 1984" International Stamp Exhibition, Seoul. Multicoloured.

1646	70w. Type **932**	50	10
1647	70w. South Gate, Seoul, and stamps (horiz)	50	10
MS1648	Two sheets each 124×90 mm. (a) Nos. 1646×2; (b) No. 1647×4	7·75	7·00
MS1649	124×90 mm. 5000w. No. 1389	37·00	32·00

934 Presidents Chun and Gayoom

1984. Visit of President Maumoon Abdul Gayoom of the Maldives.

1650	**934**	70w. multicoloured	50	10
MS1651	100×60 mm. No. 1650×2. Imperf		2·20	1·90

935 "100" and Industrial Symbols

1984. Centenary of Korean Chamber of Commerce and Industry.

1652	**935**	70w. multicoloured	50	10

936 Children playing Jaegi-chagi

937 Ox (bas-relief, Kim Yu Shin's tomb)

1984. Lunar New Year ("Year of the Ox").

1653	**936**	70w. multicoloured	60	15
1654	**937**	70w. multicoloured	60	15
MS1655	Two sheets each 90×60 mm. (a) No. 1653×2; (b) No. 1654×2		3·75	3·50

938 I.Y.Y. Emblem

1985. International Youth Year.

1656	**938**	70w. multicoloured	50	10

939 Pounding Rice for New Year Rice Cake

940 Welcoming Year's First Full Moon

1985. Folk Customs (2nd series).

1657	**939**	70w. multicoloured	80	25
1658	**940**	70w. multicoloured	80	25

941 Seoul Olympic Emblem

1985. Olympic Games, Seoul (1988) (1st issue). Multicoloured.

1659	70w.+30w. Type **941**	80	30
1660	70w.+30w. Hodori (mascot)	80	30
MS1661	90×60 mm. Nos. 1659/60	2·20	1·90

See also Nos. 1673/4, 1678/8, 1694/5, 1703/10, 1747/50, 1752/5, 1784/7, 1814/17, 1826/7, 1835/6 and 1844/7.

943 Still Life with Doll (Lee Chong Woo)

944 Rocky Mountain in Early Spring Morning (Ahn Jung Shik)

1985. Modern Art (1st series).

1662	**943**	70w. multicoloured	80	30
1663	**944**	70w. multicoloured	80	30

See also Nos. 1680/1, 1757/60, 1791/4 and 1875/8.

945 Flags, Statue of Liberty and President Chun

1985. Presidential Visit to United States.

1664	**945**	70w. multicoloured	50	10
MS1665	100×60 mm. No. 1664×2		2·20	1·90

946 Flags, Seoul South Gate and National Flower

1985. Visit of President Mohammed Zia-ul-Haq of Pakistan.

1666	**946**	70w. multicoloured	60	15
MS1667	90×60 mm. No. 1666×2		2·30	2·00

947 Underwood Hall

1985. Centenary of Yonsei University.

1668	**947**	70w. black, buff and green	50	10

948 Flags and Map

1985. Visit of President Luis Alberto Monge of Costa Rica.

1669	**948**	70w. multicoloured	60	15
MS1670	90×60 mm. No. 1669×2		2·10	1·90

949 Rasbora   **950** Sailfish

1985. Fish (1st series).

1671	**949**	70w. multicoloured	80	25
1672	**950**	70w. multicoloured	80	25

See also Nos. 1730/3, 1797/1800, 1881/4, 1903/6 and 1951/4.

951 Rowing

1985. Olympic Games, Seoul (1988) (2nd issue). Multicoloured.

1673	70w.+30w. Type **951**	80	30
1674	70w.+30w. Hurdling	80	30
MS1675	90×60 mm. Nos. 1673/4	2·20	1·90

For designs similar to Type **951** see Nos. 1687/**MS**1689 and 1694/**MS**1696.

952 National Flags

1985. Visit of President Hussain Muhammed Ershad of Bangladesh.

1676	**952**	70w. multicoloured	60	15
MS1677	90×60 mm. No. 1676×2. Imperf		1·70	1·50

953 National Flags

1985. Visit of President Joao Bernardo Vieira of Guinea-Bissau.

1678	**953**	70w. multicoloured	70	15
MS1679	90×60 mm. No. 1678×2. Imperf		1·70	1·50

954 Spring Day on the Farm (Huh Paik Ryun)

955 The Exorcist (Kim Chung Hyun)

1985. Modern Art (2nd issue).

1680	**954**	70w. multicoloured	80	30
1681	**955**	70w. multicoloured	80	30

956 Heavenly Lake, Paekdu and National Flower

1985. 40th Anniv. of Liberation.

1682	**956**	70w. multicoloured	60	15

957 Wrestling   **958** Janggi

1985. Folk Customs (3rd series).

1683	**957**	70w. multicoloured	80	25
1684	**958**	70w. multicoloured	80	25

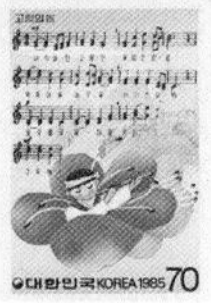

959 *The Spring of My Home* (Lee Won Su and Hong Nan Pa)

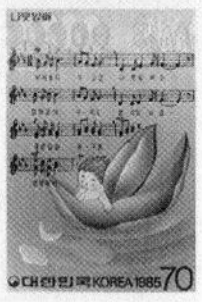

960 *A Leaf Boat* (Park Hong Keun and Yun Yong Ha)

1985. Korean Music (1st series).

1685	**959**	70w. multicoloured	80	25
1686	**960**	70w. multicoloured	80	25

See also Nos. 1728/9, 1776/7, 1854/5, 1862/3, 1893/4, 1935/6, 1996/7 and 2064/5.

1985. Olympic Games, Seoul (1988) (3rd issue). As T **951**. Multicoloured.

1687	70w.+30w. Basketball	80	30
1688	70w.+30w. Boxing	80	30
MS1689	90×60 mm. Nos. 1687/8	2·20	1·90

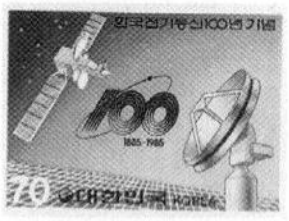

961 Satellite, "100" and Dish Aerial

1985. Centenary of First Korean Telegraph Service.

1690	**961**	70w. multicoloured	60	15

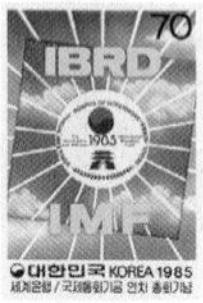

962 Meetings Emblem

1985. World Bank and International Monetary Fund Meetings, Seoul.

1691	**962**	70w. multicoloured	60	15

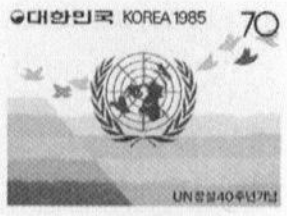

963 U.N. Emblem and Doves

1985. 40th Anniv of U.N.O.

1692	**963**	70w. multicoloured	60	15

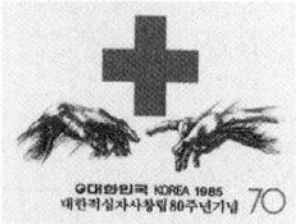

964 Red Cross and Hands (detail "Creation of Adam", Michelangelo)

1985. 80th Anniv of Korea Red Cross.

1693	**964**	70w. black, red and blue	70	25

1985. Olympic Games, Seoul (1988) (4th issue). As T **951**. Multicoloured.

1694	70w.+30w. Cycling	80	30
1695	70w.+30w. Canoeing	80	30
MS1696	90×60 mm. Nos. 1694/5	2·20	1·90

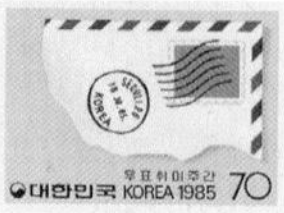

965 Cancelled Stamp on Envelope

1985. Philatelic Week.

1697	**965**	70w. multicoloured	60	15

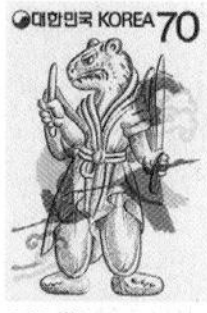

966 Tiger (bas-relief, Kim Yu Shin's tomb)

1985. Lunar New Year ("Year of the Tiger").

1698	**966**	70w. multicoloured	70	30

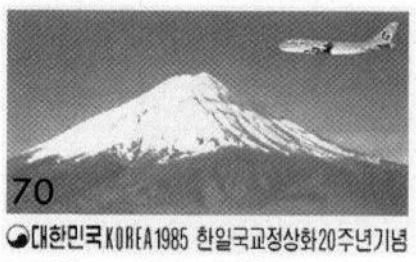

967 Mount Fuji and Boeing 747 Jetliner

1985. 20th Anniv of Korea–Japan Treaty on Basic Relations.

1699	**967**	70w. mult (postage)	80	30
1700	**967**	370w. multicoloured (air)	3·00	95

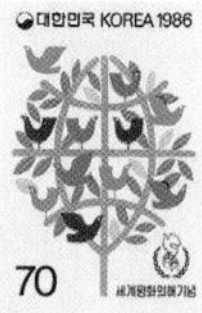

968 Doves and Globe

1986. International Peace Year.

1701	**968**	70w. multicoloured	60	15
1702	**968**	400w. multicoloured	4·25	1·50

1986. Olympic Games, Seoul (1988) (5th series). As T **951**. Multicoloured.

1703	70w.+30w. Show jumping (postage)	85	40
1704	70w.+30w. Fencing	85	40
1705	70w.+30w. Football	85	40
1706	70w.+30w. Gymnastics	85	40
1707	370w.+100w. As No. 1703 (air)	2·50	1·20
1708	400w.+100w. As No. 1704	3·00	1·40
1709	440w.+100w. As No. 1705	3·50	1·50
1710	470w.+100w. As No. 1706	4·00	1·70

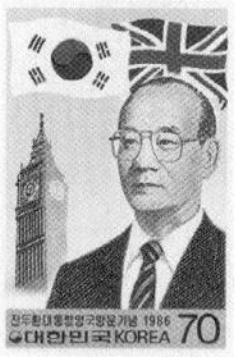

970 Pres. Chun, Big Ben and Korean and British Flags

1986. Presidential Visit to Europe. Multicoloured.

1711	70w. Type **970**	85	30
1712	70w. Pres. Chun, Eiffel Tower and Korean and French flags	85	30
1713	70w. Pres. Chun, Belgian Parliament and Korean and Belgian flags	85	30
1714	70w. Pres. Chun, Cologne Cathedral and Korean and West German flags	85	30
MS1715	4 sheets each 100×60 mm. (a) No. 1711×2; (b) No. 1712×2; (c) No. 1713×2; (d) No. 1714×2	14·00	12·50

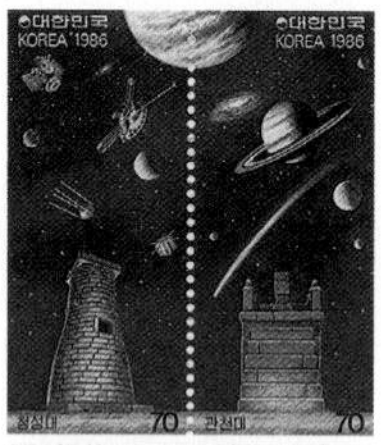

974/5 Kyongju and Kwanchon Observatories

1986. Science (1st series). Appearance of Halley's Comet.

1716	**974**	70w. multicoloured	2·50	85
1717	**975**	70w. multicoloured	2·50	85

See also Nos. 1781/2, 1833/4, 1864/5 and 1898/9.

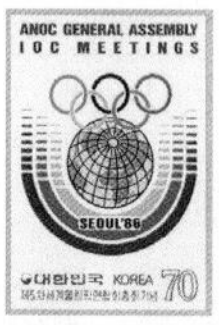

976 General Assembly Emblem

1986. Fifth Association of National Olympic Committees General Assembly, Seoul.

1718	**976**	70w. multicoloured	70	15

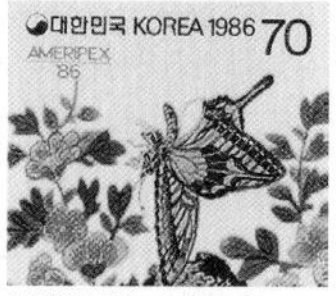

977 Swallowtail and Flowers

1986. "Ameripex '86" International Stamp Exhibition, Chicago. Multicoloured.

1719	70w. Type **977**	3·50	1·50
1720	370w. "Papilio bianor"	3·50	1·50
1721	400w. Swallowtails	3·50	1·50
1722	440w. Swallowtail and frog	3·50	1·50
1723	450w. Swallowtail	3·50	1·50
1724	470w. "Papilio bianor"	3·50	1·50

Nos. 1719/24 were printed together, *se-tenant*, forming a composite design.

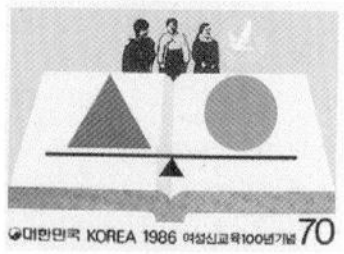

983 Male and Female Symbols in Balance

1986. Centenary of Korean Women's Education.

1725	**983**	70w. multicoloured	60	10

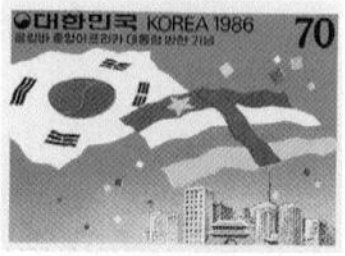

984 National Flags

1986. Visit of President Andre Kolingba of Central African Republic.

1726	**984**	70w. multicoloured	60	10
MS1727		100×60 mm. No. 1726×2. Imperf	1·60	1·40

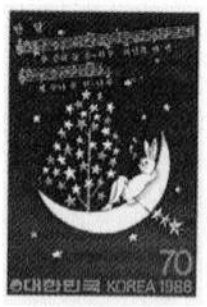

985 *Half Moon* (Yun Keuk Young)

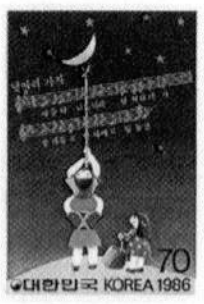

986 *Let's Go and Pick the Moon* (Yun Seok Jung and Park Tae Hyun)

1986. Korean Music (2nd series).

1728	**985**	70w. multicoloured	1·00	30
1729	**986**	70w. multicoloured	1·60	55

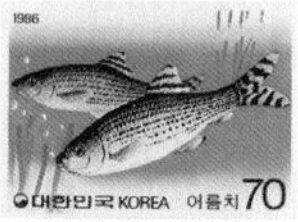

987 Cyprinid Fish

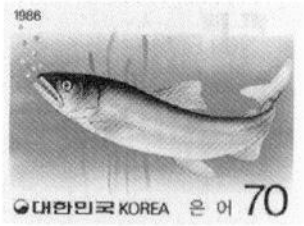

988 Ayu

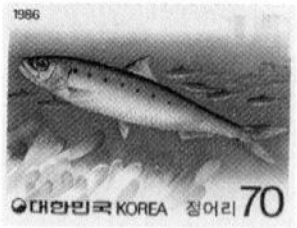

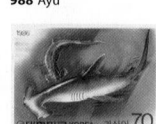

989 Black-spotted Sardine

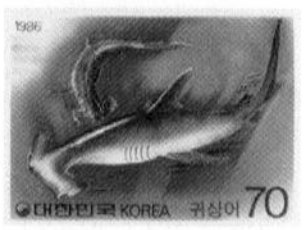

990 Hammerheads

1986. Fish (2nd series).

1730	**987**	70w. multicoloured	1·70	55
1731	**988**	70w. multicoloured	1·70	55
1732	**989**	70w. multicoloured	1·70	55
1733	**990**	70w. multicoloured	1·70	55

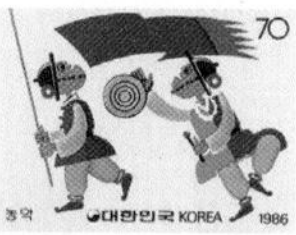

991 Flag Carrier and Gong Player

1986. Folk Customs (4th series). Farm Music. Multicoloured.

1734	70w. Type **991**	1·30	30
1735	70w. Drummer and piper	1·30	30
1736	70w. Drummer and gong player	1·30	30
1737	70w. Men with ribbons	1·30	30
1738	70w. Man and woman with child	1·30	30

Nos. 1734/8 were printed together, *se-tenant*, forming a composite design.

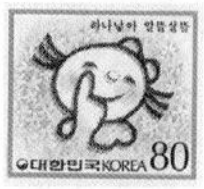

996 Child

1986. Family Planning.

1739	**996**	80w. multicoloured	1·00	25

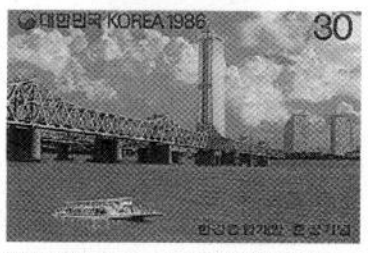

997 Bridge and "63" Building, Seoul

1986. Completion of Han River Development. Multicoloured.

1740	30w. Type **997**	1·30	30
1741	60w. Buildings and excursion boat	1·30	30
1742	80w. Rowing boat and Seoul Tower	1·30	30

Nos. 1740/2 were printed together, *se-tenant*, forming a composite design.

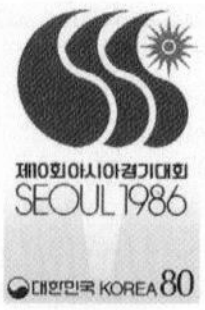

1000 Emblem

1986. Tenth Asian Games, Seoul. (1st issue). Multicoloured.

1743	80w. Type **1000**	80	30
1744	80w. Firework display	80	30
MS1745	Two sheets each 90×60 mm. (a) No. 1743×2; (b) No. 1744×2	14·00	12·50

See also No. **MS**1751.

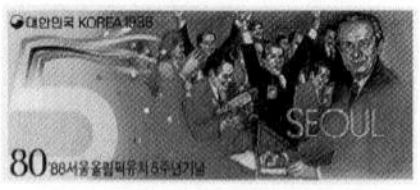

1002 "5", Delegates and Juan Antonio Samaranch (President of International Olympic Committee)

1986. Fifth Anniv of Choice of Seoul as 1988 Olympic Games Host City.

1746	**1002**	80w. multicoloured	1·00	40

1986. Olympic Games, Seoul (1988) (6th issue). As T **951**. Multicoloured.

1747	80w.+50w. Weightlifting (postage)	1·70	85
1748	80w.+50w. Handball	1·70	85
1749	370w.+100w. As No. 1747 (air)	3·00	1·40
1750	400w.+100w. As No. 1748	3·00	1·40

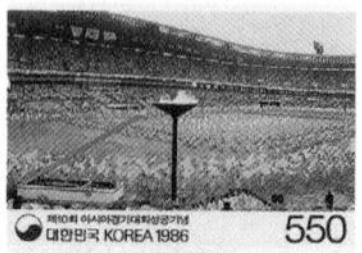

1003 Main Stadium

1986. Tenth Asian Games, Seoul (2nd issue). Sheet 130×90 mm.

MS1751	**1003**	550w. multicoloured	24·00	22·00

1986. Olympic Games, Seoul (1988) (7th issue). As T **951**. Multicoloured.

1752	80w.+50w. Judo (postage)	1·70	85
1753	80w.+50w. Hockey	1·70	85
1754	440w.+100w. As No. 1752 (air)	3·50	1·50
1755	470w.+100w. As No. 1753	4·00	1·70

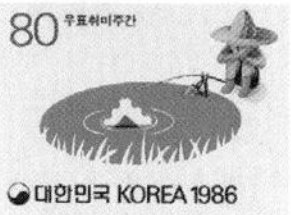

1004 Boy fishing for Stamp

1986. Philatelic Week.

1756	**1004**	80w. multicoloured	70	25

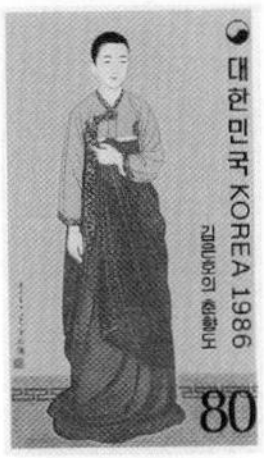

1005 *Chunhyang-do* (Kim Un Ho)

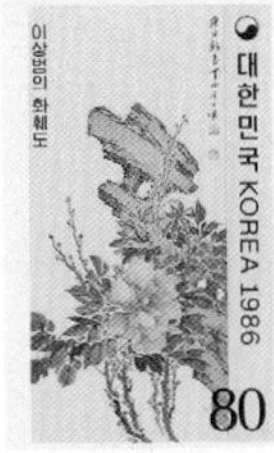

1006 *Flowers* (Lee Sang Bum)

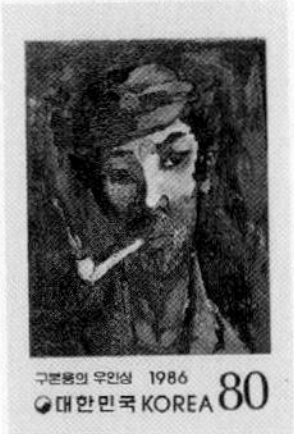

1007 *Portrait of a Friend* (Ku Bon Wung)

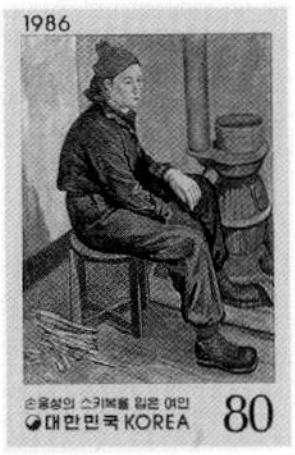

1008 *Woman in a Ski Suit* (Son Ung Seng)

1986. Modern Art (3rd series).

1757	**1005**	80w. multicoloured	1·30	40
1758	**1006**	80w. multicoloured	1·30	40
1759	**1007**	80w. multicoloured	1·30	40
1760	**1008**	80w. multicoloured	1·30	40

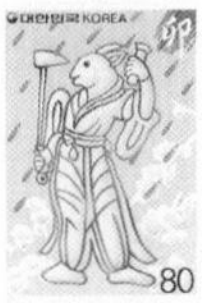

1009 Rabbit

1986. Lunar New Year ("Year of the Rabbit").

1761	**1009**	80w. multicoloured	85	30

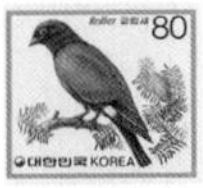

1010 Eastern Broad-billed Roller ("Roller")

1986. Birds. Multicoloured.

1762A	80w. Type **1010**	1·30	40
1763A	80w. Japanese waxwing ("Waxwing")	1·30	40
1764A	80w. Black-naped oriole ("Oriole")	1·30	40
1765A	80w. Black-capped kingfisher ("Kingfisher")	1·30	40
1766A	80w. Hoopoe	1·30	40

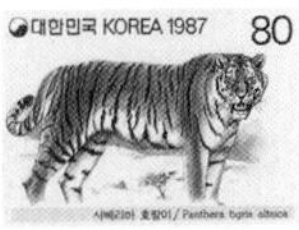

1011 Siberian Tiger

1987. Endangered Animals. Multicoloured.

1767	80w. Type **1011**	2·20	70
1768	80w. Leopard cat	2·20	70
1769	80w. Red fox	2·20	70
1770	80w. Wild boar	2·20	70

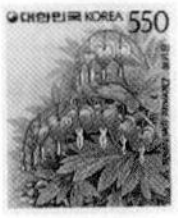

1012 Bleeding Heart (*Dicentra spectabilis*)

1987. Flowers. Multicoloured.

1771A	550w. Type **1012**	2·50	60
1772A	550w. Diamond bluebell ("Hanabusaya asiatica")	2·50	60
1773A	550w. "Erythronium japonicum"	2·50	60
1774A	550w. Pinks ("Dianthus chinensis")	2·50	60
1775A	550w. "Chrysanthemum zawadskii"	2·50	60

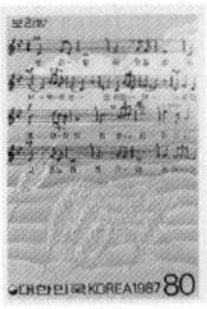

1013 *Barley Field* (Park Wha Mok and Yun Yong Ha)

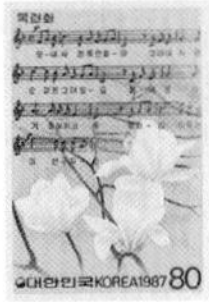

1014 *Magnolia* (Cho Young Shik and Kim Dong Jin)

1987. Korean Music (3rd series).

1776	**1013**	80w. multicoloured	3·00	1·00
1777	**1014**	80w. multicoloured	3·00	1·00

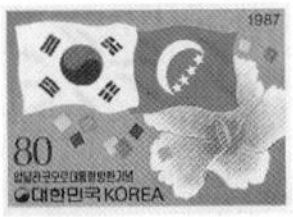

1015 National Flags and Korean National Flower

1987. Visit of President Ahmed Abdallah Abderemane of Comoros.

1778	**1015**	80w. multicoloured	60	10
MS1779		90×60 mm. No. 1778×2	2·20	1·90

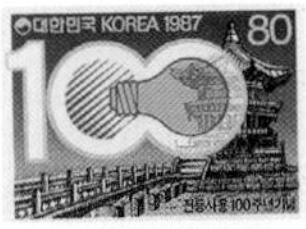

1016 "100", Light Bulb and Hyang Woen Jeong

1987. Centenary of Electric Light in Korea.

1780	**1016**	80w. multicoloured	60	10

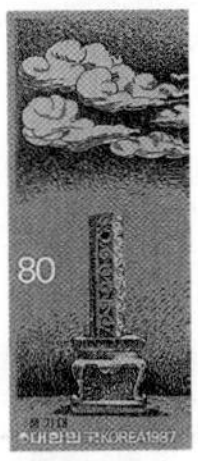

1017 Punggi Wind Observatory

1987. Science (2nd series).

1781	**1017**	80w. dp brown & brown	3·00	1·00
1782	-	80w. brown & dp brown	3·00	1·00

DESIGN: No. 1782, Rain gauge.

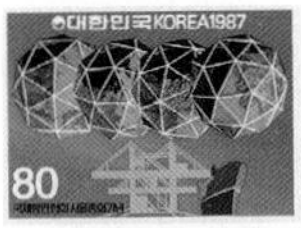

1019 Globes, Crane and Ship

1987. 15th International Association of Ports and Harbours General Session, Seoul.

1783	**1019**	80w. multicoloured	60	10

1987. Olympic Games, Seoul (1988) (8th issue). As T **951**. Multicoloured.

1784	80w.+50w. Wrestling	1·20	40
1785	80w.+50w. Tennis	1·20	40
1786	80w.+50w. Diving	1·20	40
1787	80w.+50w. Show jumping	1·20	40
MS1788	Four sheets each 90×60 mm. (a) No. 1784×2; (b) No. 1785×2; (c) No. 1786×2; (d) No. 1787×2	11·00	10·00

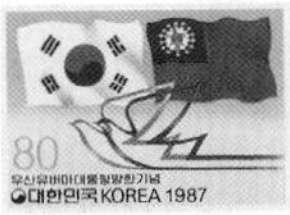

1020 Flags and Doves

1987. Visit of President U San Yu of Burma.

1789	**1020**	80w. multicoloured	60	10
MS1790		90×60 mm. No. 1789×2	1·90	1·70

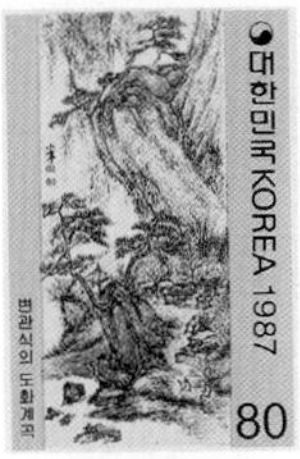

1021 *Valley of Peach Blossoms* (Pyen Kwan Sik)

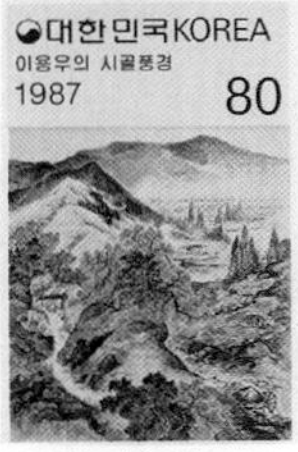

1022 *Rural Landscape* (Lee Yong Wu)

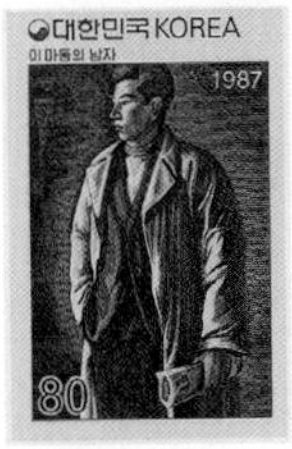

1023 *Man* (Lee Ma Dong)

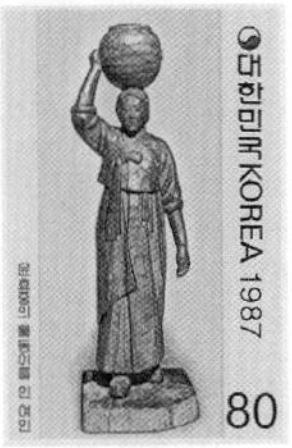

1024 *Woman with Water Jar on Head* (sculpture, Yun Hyo Chung)

1987. Modern Art (4th series).

1791	**1021**	80w. multicoloured	2·50	95
1792	**1022**	80w. multicoloured	2·50	95
1793	**1023**	80w. multicoloured	2·50	95
1794	**1024**	80w. multicoloured	2·50	95

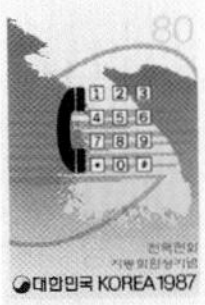

1025 Map and Digital Key Pad

1987. Completion of Automatic Telephone Network (1795) and Communications for Information Year (1796).

1795	80w. Type **1025**	70	25
1796	80w. Emblem	70	25

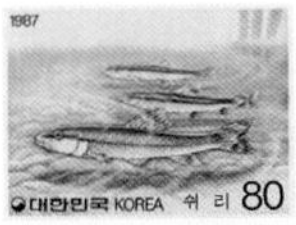

1027 Cyprinid Fishes

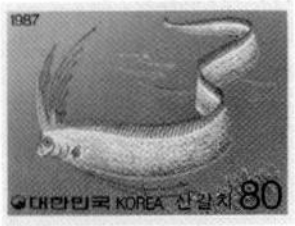

1028 Russell's Oarfish

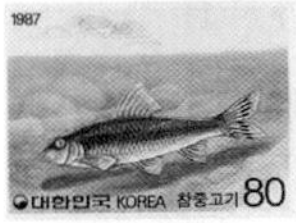

1029 Cyprinid Fish

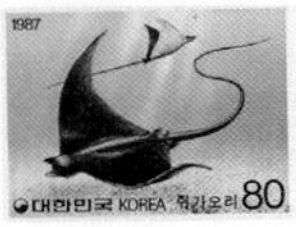

1030 Spine-tailed Mobula

1987. Fish (3rd series).

1797	**1027**	80w. multicoloured	2·50	95
1798	**1028**	80w. multicoloured	2·50	95
1799	**1029**	80w. multicoloured	2·50	95
1800	**1030**	80w. multicoloured	2·50	95

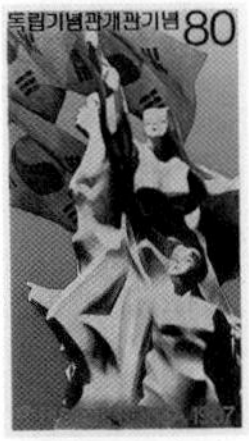

1031 Statue of Indomitable Koreans (detail) and Flags

1987. Opening of Independence Hall. Multicoloured.

1801	80w. Type **1031**	1·10	30
1802	80w. Monument of the Nation and aerial view of Hall	1·10	30
MS1803	Two sheets each 125×90 mm. (a) No. 1801×2; (b) No. 1802×2	24·00	22·00

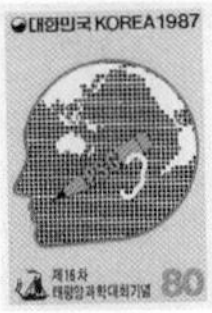

1033 Map and Pen within Profile

1987. 16th Pacific Science Congress, Seoul.

1804	**1033**	80w. multicoloured	70	15
MS1805		90×60 mm. No. 1804×2	3·00	2·75

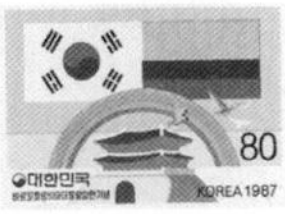

1034 Flags and Seoul South Gate

1987. Visit of President Virgilio Barco of Colombia.

1806	**1034**	80w. multicoloured	70	15
MS1807		90×60 mm. No. 1806×2	2·20	1·90

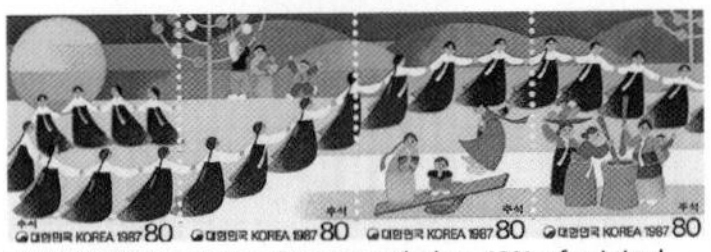

1035/1038 Festivities (image scaled to 42% of original size)

1987. Folk Customs (5th series). Harvest Moon Day.

1808	**1035**	80w. multicoloured	3·50	1·00
1809	**1036**	80w. multicoloured	3·50	1·00
1810	**1037**	80w. multicoloured	3·50	1·00
1811	**1038**	80w. multicoloured	3·50	1·00

Nos. 1808/11 were issued together, *se-tenant*, forming a composite design.

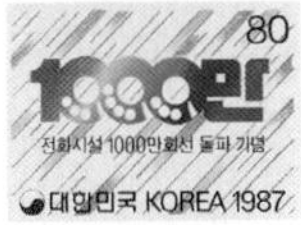

1039 Telephone Dials forming Number

1987. Installation of over 10,000,000 Telephone Lines.

1812	**1039**	80w. multicoloured	70	25

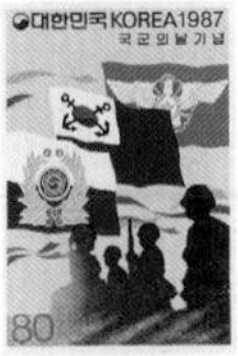

1040 Service Flags and Servicemen

1987. Armed Forces Day.

1813	**1040**	80w. multicoloured	70	25

1987. Olympic Games, Seoul (1988) (9th issue). As T **951**. Multicoloured.

1814	80w.+50w. Table tennis	1·20	40
1815	80w.+50w. Shooting	1·20	40
1816	80w.+50w. Archery	1·20	40
1817	80w.+50w. Volleyball	1·20	40
MS1818	4 sheets each 90×60 mm. (a) No. 1814×2; (b) No. 1815×2; (c) No. 1816×2; (d) No. 1817×2	11·00	10·00

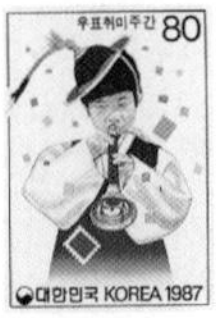

1041 Stamps around Child playing Trumpet

1987. Philatelic Week.

1819	**1041**	80w. multicoloured	70	25

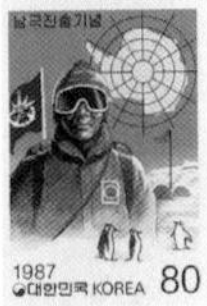

1042 Korean Scientist and Map

1987. First Anniv of South Korea's Signing of Antarctic Treaty.

1820	**1042**	80w. multicoloured	1·30	40

1043 Dragon

1987. Lunar New Year ("Year of the Dragon").
1821	**1043**	80w. multicoloured	1·00	30

1044 Scattered Sections
of Apple

1988. Compulsory Pension Programme.
1822	**1044**	80w. multicoloured	70	25

1045 Base and
Gentoo Penguins

1988. Completion of Antarctic Base.
1823	**1045**	80w. multicoloured	1·00	30

1046 Flag, Olympic
Stadium and President
Roh Tae Woo

1988. Presidential Inauguration.
1824	**1046**	80w. multicoloured	1·30	40
MS1825		90×60 mm. No. 1824×2	19·00	17·00

1047 Dinghy
Racing

1988. Olympic Games, Seoul (1988) (10th issue).
Multicoloured.
1826		80w.+20w. Type **1047**	85	40
1827		80w.+20w. Taekwondo	85	40
MS1828		Two sheets each 90×60 mm.		
		(a) No. 1826×2; (b) No. 1827×2	8·75	7·75

1049 Crane

1988. Japanese White-naped Crane. Multicoloured.
1829		80w. Type **1049**	1·60	70
1830		80w. Crane taking off	1·60	70
1831		80w. Crane with wings spread	1·60	70
1832		80w. Two cranes in flight	1·60	70

1053 Water
Clock

1988. Science (3rd series). Multicoloured.
1833		80w. Type **1053**	85	30
1834		80w. Sundial	85	30

Nos. 1833/4 were issued together, *se-tenant*, forming a
composite design.

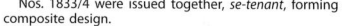

1055 Torch Carrier

1988. Olympic Games, Seoul (1988) (11th issue).
Multicoloured.
1835		80w.+20w. Type **1055**	85	40
1836		80w.+20w. Stadium	85	40
MS1837		Two sheets each 90×60 mm.		
		(a) No. 1835×2; (b) No. 1836×2	6·00	5·50

1057 Globe and
Red Cross as
Candle

1988. 125th Anniv of International Red Cross.
1838	**1057**	80w. multicoloured	70	25

1058 Computer
Terminal

1988. First Anniv of National Use of Telepress.
1839	**1058**	80w. multicoloured	70	25

1059 Woman
sitting by Pool
and Woman on
Swing

1988. Folk Customs (6th series). Tano Day. Multicoloured.
1840	80w. Type **1059**	1·30	40
1841	80w. Women dressing their hair	1·30	40
1842	80w. Woman on swing and boy smelling flowers	1·30	40
1843	80w. Boys wrestling	1·30	40

Nos. 1840/3 were issued together, *se-tenant*, forming a
composite design.

1063 Olympic Flag and
Pierre de Coubertin
(founder of modern
Games)

1988. Olympic Games, Seoul (1988) (12th issue).
Multicoloured.
1844	80w. Type **1063**	85	30
1845	80w. Olympic monument	85	30
1846	80w. View of Seoul (vert)	85	30
1847	80w. Women in Korean cos- tume (vert)	85	30
MS1848	Four sheets each 90×60 mm.		
	(a) No. 1844×2; (b) No. 1845×2; (c)		
	No. 1846×2; (d) No. 1847×2	8·75	7·75

1067 Stamps
forming Torch
Flame

1988. "Olymphilex '88" Olympic Stamps Exhibition, Seoul.
1849	**1067**	80w. multicoloured	70	25
MS1850		90×60 mm. No. 1849×2	2·20	1·90

1068 Pouring Molten
Metal from Crucible

1988. 22nd International Iron and Steel Institute
Conference, Seoul.
1851	**1068**	80w. multicoloured	70	25

1069 Gomdoori
(mascot)

1988. Paralympic Games, Seoul.
1852		80w. Type **1069**	1·10	60
1853		80w. Archery	80	30

1071 *Homesick*
(Lee Eun Sang
and Kim Dong
Jin)

1072 *The Pioneer*
(Yoon Hae
Young and Cho
Doo Nam)

1988. Korean Music (4th series).
1854	**1071**	80w. multicoloured	80	30
1855	**1072**	80w. multicoloured	80	30

1073 Girls on
See-saw

1988. Lunar New Year ("Year of the Snake").
1856	**1073**	80w. multicoloured	70	25

1074 Flags at Opening
Ceremony

1988. Olympic Games, Seoul (13th issue). Sheet 130×90
mm.
MS1857	**1074**	550w. multicoloured	16·00	14·00

1075 Dancers

1989. Folk Customs (7th series). Mask Dance.
Multicoloured.
1858	80w. Type **1075**	1·30	40
1859	80w. Dancer with fans	1·30	40
1860	80w. Dancer holding branch	1·30	40
1861	80w. Dancer with "Lion"	1·30	40

Nos. 1858/61 were issued together, *se-tenant*, forming a
composite design.

1079 *Arirang*

1080
Doraji-taryong

1989. Korean Music (5th series).
1862	**1079**	80w. multicoloured	70	25
1863	**1080**	80w. multicoloured	70	25

1081/2 Wooden and metal
Type Printing

1989. Science (4th series).
1864	**1081**	80w. brown, bis & stone	1·70	40
1865	**1082**	80w. brown, bis & stone	1·70	40

Nos. 1864/5 were issued together, *se-tenant*, forming a
composite design.

1083 Teeth,
Globe, Pencil
and Book

1989. 14th Asian–Pacific Dental Congress.
1866	**1083**	80w. multicoloured	60	15

1084 Hand
with Stick in
Heart

1989. Respect for the Elderly.
1867	**1084**	80w. multicoloured	2·40	30

1085 Emblem

1989. Rotary Int Convention, Seoul.
1868	**1085**	80w. multicoloured	60	15

1086 Profiles
within Heart

1989. 19th International Council of Nurses Congress,
Seoul.
1869	**1086**	80w. multicoloured	60	15

1087 "Communication"

1989. National Information Technology Month.
1870	**1087**	80w. multicoloured	60	15

1088 "Longevity"

1989. World Environment Day.
1871	**1088**	80w. multicoloured	60	15

1089 Satellite,
Globe and Dish
Aerial

1989. Tenth Anniv of Asia–Pacific Telecommunity.
1872 **1089** 80w. multicoloured 60 15

1090 "Liberty guiding
the People" (detail,
Eugene Delacroix)

1989. Bicentenary of French Revolution.
1873 **1090** 80w. multicoloured 60 15

1091 Apple and Flask

1989. Fifth Asian and Oceanic Biochemists Federation
Congress, Seoul.
1874 **1091** 80w. multicoloured 60 15

1092 White Ox (Lee Joong Sub)

1093 Street Stall (Park **1094** Little Girl (Lee
Lae Hyun) Bong Sang)

1095 Autumn Scene (Oh Ji Ho)

1989. Modern Art (5th series).
1875 **1092** 80w. multicoloured 80 30
1876 **1093** 80w. multicoloured 80 30
1877 **1094** 80w. multicoloured 80 30
1878 **1095** 80w. multicoloured 80 30

1096 Hunting Scene

1989. Seoul Olympics Commemorative Festival and
World Sports Festival for Ethnic Koreans.
1879 **1096** 80w. multicoloured 60 15

1097 Goddess of Law
and Ancient Law Code

1989. First Anniv of Constitutional Court.
1880 **1097** 80w. multicoloured 60 15

1098 Banded Knifejaw **1099** Banded Loach

1100 Torrent Catfish **1101** Japanese
Pinecone Fish

1989. Fish (4th series).
1881 **1098** 80w. multicoloured 85 30
1882 **1099** 80w. multicoloured 85 30
1883 **1100** 80w. multicoloured 85 30
1884 **1101** 80w. multicoloured 85 30

1102 Emblem

1989. 44th International Eucharistic Congress, Seoul.
1885 **1102** 80w. multicoloured 60 15

1103 Control Tower and
Boeing 747 Jetliner

1989. 29th International Civil Airports Association World
Congress, Seoul.
1886 **1103** 80w. multicoloured 60 15

1104 Scissors
cutting
Burning
Banner

1989. Fire Precautions Month.
1887 **1104** 80w. multicoloured 2·40 30

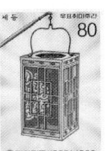

1105 Lantern

1989. Philatelic Week.
1888 **1105** 80w. multicoloured 70 25
MS1889 90×60 mm. No. 1888×2 2·20 1·90

1106 Cranes **1107** New Year Custom

1989. Lunar New Year ("Year of the Horse").
1890 **1106** 80w. multicoloured 60 15
1891 **1107** 80w. multicoloured 60 15
MS1892 Two sheets each 90×60 mm.
(a) No. 1890×2; (b) No. 1891×2 3·50 3·00

1108 Pakyon Fall **1109** Chonan
Samgori

1990. Korean Music (6th series).
1893 **1108** 80w. multicoloured 70 25
1894 **1109** 80w. multicoloured 70 25

1110 Clouds, Umbrella
and Satellite

1990. World Meteorological Day.
1895 **1110** 80w. multicoloured 60 15

1111 Child with
Rose

1990. 40th Anniv of UNICEF's Work in Korea.
1896 **1111** 80w. multicoloured 60 15

1112 Cable, Fish and
Route Map

1990. Completion of Cheju Island–Kohung Optical
Submarine Cable.
1897 **1112** 80w. multicoloured 60 15

1113/4 Gilt-bronze Maitreya,
Spear and Dagger Moulds

1990. Science (5th series). Metallurgy.
1898 **1113** 100w. multicoloured 70 25
1899 **1114** 100w. multicoloured 70 25
 Nos. 1898/9 were issued together, se-tenant, forming
the composite design illustrated.

1115 Housing and "20"

1990. 20th Anniv of Saemaul Movement (community
self-help programme).
1900 **1115** 100w. multicoloured 60 15

1116 Youths

1990. Youth Month.
1901 **1116** 100w. multicoloured 60 15

1117 Butterfly
Net catching
Pollution

1990. World Environmental Day.
1902 **1117** 100w. multicoloured 4·75 30

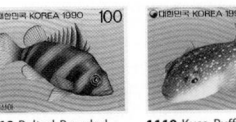 

1118 Belted Bearded **1119** Kusa Pufferfish
Grunt

1120 Cherry Salmon **1121** Rosy Bitterling

1990. Fish (5th series).
1903 **1118** 100w. multicoloured 85 30
1904 **1119** 100w. multicoloured 85 30
1905 **1120** 100w. multicoloured 85 30
1906 **1121** 100w. multicoloured 85 30

1122 Automatic Sorting
Machines

1990. Opening of Seoul Mail Centre.
1907 **1122** 100w. multicoloured 60 15
MS1908 90×60 mm. No. 1907×2 2·20 1·90

1123
Bandaged
Teddy Bear in
Hospital Bed

1990. Road Safety Campaign.
1909 **1123** 100w. multicoloured 1·60 30

1124 Campfire

1990. Eighth Korean Boy Scouts Jamboree, Kosong.
1910 **1124** 100w. multicoloured 60 15

1125 Lily

1990. Wild Flowers (1st series). Multicoloured.
1911 **1125** 370w. Type **1125** 2·10 85
1912 400w. Asters 2·40 95
1913 440w. Pheasant's eye 2·50 1·00
1914 470w. Scabious 2·75 1·10
 See also Nos. 1956/9, 1992/5, 2082/5, 2133/6, 2162/5,
2191/4 and 2244/7.

1129 Washing Wool

1990. Folk Customs (8th series). Hand Weaving.
1915 **1129** 100w. red, yellow & blk 85 30
1916 - 100w. multicoloured 85 30
1917 - 100w. multicoloured 85 30
1918 - 100w. multicoloured 85 30
DESIGNS: No. 1916, Spinning; 1917, Dyeing spun yarn;
1918, Weaving.

1133 Church

1990. Centenary of Anglican Church in Korea.
1919 **1133** 100w. multicoloured 60 15

1134 Top of
Tower

1990. Tenth Anniv of Seoul Communications Tower.
1920 **1134** 100w. black, blue
and red 60 15

1135 Peas in Pod

1990. Census.
1921 **1135** 100w. multicoloured 60 15

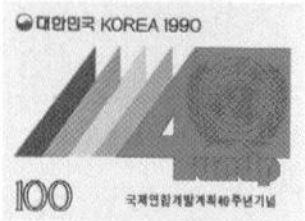
1136 "40" and U.N. Emblem

1990. 40th Anniv of U.N. Development Programme.
1922 **1136** 100w. multicoloured 60 15

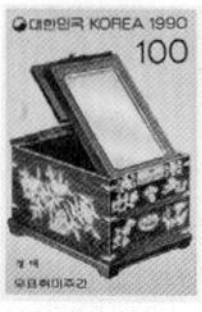
1137 Inlaid Case with Mirror

1990. Philatelic Week.
1923 **1137** 100w. multicoloured 70 15
MS1924 90×60 mm. No. 1923×2 4·00 3·50

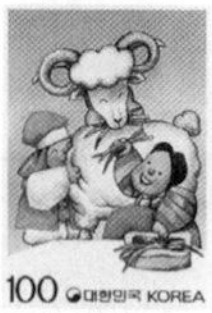
1138 Children feeding Ram

1990. Lunar New Year ("Year of the Sheep"). Multicoloured.
1925 100w. Type **1138** 60 15
1926 100w. Crane flying above mountains 60 15
MS1927 90×60 mm. Nos. 1925/6 4·75 4·25

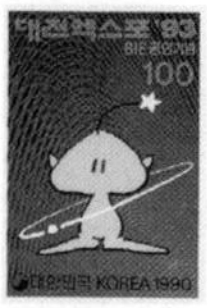
1140 Mascot

1990. "Expo '93" World's Fair, Taejon (1st issue). Multicoloured.
1928 100w. Type **1140** 85 30
1929 440w. Yin and Yang (exhibition emblem) 2·20 95
MS1930 Two sheets each 90×60 mm. (a) No. 1928×2; (b) No. 1929×2 7·00 6·00
See also Nos. 1932/**MS**1934, 2001/**MS**2002 and 2058/**MS**2062.

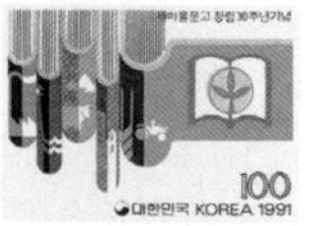
1142 Books and Emblem

1991. 30th Anniv of Saemaul Minilibrary.
1931 **1142** 100w. multicoloured 60 15

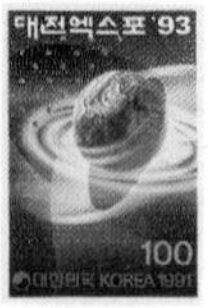
1143 Earth

1991. "Expo '93" World's Fair, Taejon (2nd issue). Multicoloured.
1932 100w. Type **1143** 85 30
1933 100w. Expo Tower 85 30
MS1934 Two sheets each 90×60 mm. (a) No. 1932×2; (b) No. 1933×2 4·25 3·75

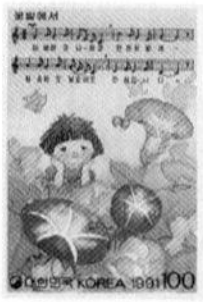
1145 *In a Flower Garden* (Uh Hyo Sun and Kwon Kil Sang)

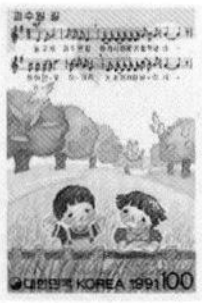
1146 *Way to the Orchard* (Park Hwa Mok and Kim Kong Sun)

1991. Korean Music (7th series).
1935 **1145** 100w. multicoloured 80 30
1936 **1146** 100w. multicoloured 80 30

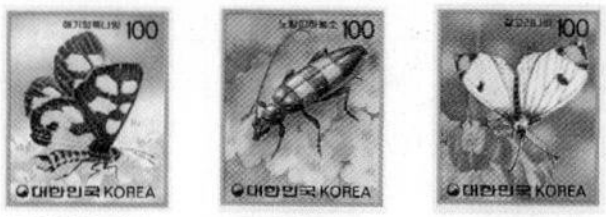
1147 Moth
1148 Beetle
1149 Butterfly

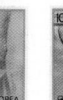

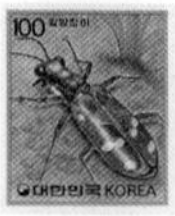
1150 Beetle

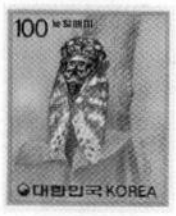
1151 Cicada

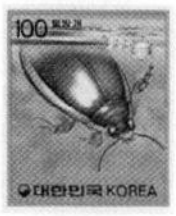
1152 Water Beetle

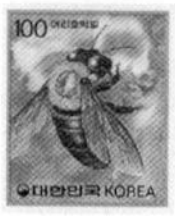
1153 Hornet

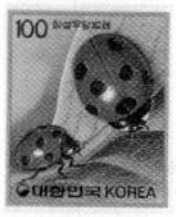
1154 Ladybirds

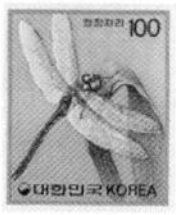
1155 Dragonfly

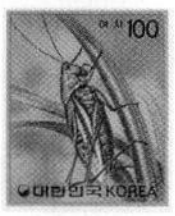
1156 Grasshopper

1991. Insects.
1937 **1147** 100w. multicoloured 1·00 25
1938 **1148** 100w. multicoloured 1·00 25
1939 **1149** 100w. multicoloured 1·00 25
1940 **1150** 100w. multicoloured 1·00 25
1941 **1151** 100w. multicoloured 1·00 25
1942 **1152** 100w. multicoloured 1·00 25
1943 **1153** 100w. multicoloured 1·00 25
1944 **1154** 100w. multicoloured 1·00 25
1945 **1155** 100w. multicoloured 1·00 25
1946 **1156** 100w. multicoloured 1·00 25

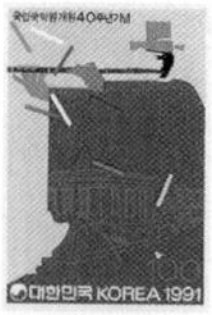
1157 Flautist and Centre

1991. 40th Anniv of Korean Traditional Performing Arts Centre.
1947 **1157** 100w. multicoloured 60 20

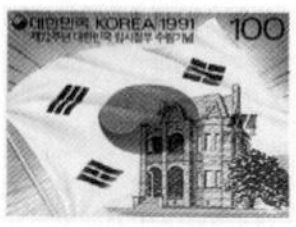
1158 Flag and Provisional Government Building

1991. 72nd Anniv of Establishment of Korean Provisional Government in Shanghai.
1948 **1158** 100w. multicoloured 60 20

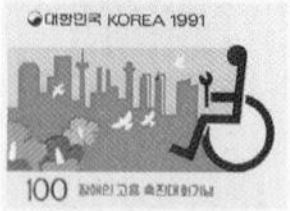
1159 Urban Landscape and Emblem

1991. Employment for Disabled People.
1949 **1159** 100w. multicoloured 60 20

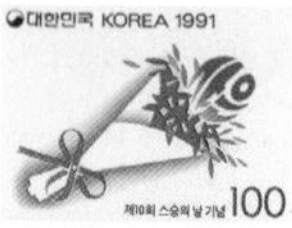
1160 Bouquet

1991. Teachers' Day.
1950 **1160** 100w. multicoloured 60 20

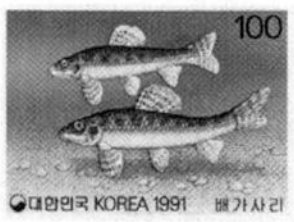
1161 Asian Minnow

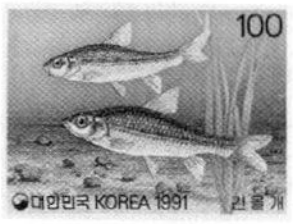
1162 Majime Minnows

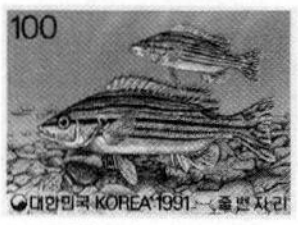
1163 Blotched Grunter

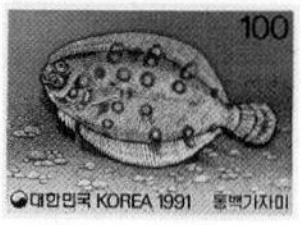
1164 Ijima's Left-eyed Flounder

1991. Fish (6th series).
1951 **1161** 100w. multicoloured 80 25
1952 **1162** 100w. multicoloured 80 25
1953 **1163** 100w. multicoloured 80 25
1954 **1164** 100w. multicoloured 80 25

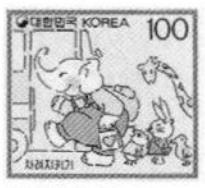
1165 Animals waiting to Board Bus

1991. "Waiting One's Turn" Campaign.
1955 **1165** 100w. multicoloured 1·60 30

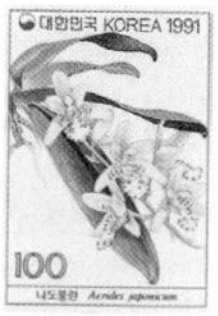
1166 *Aerides japonicum*

1991. Wild Flowers (2nd series). Multicoloured.
1956 100w. Type **1166** 70 25
1957 100w. *Heloniopsis orientalis* 70 25
1958 370w. *Aquilegia buergeriana* 1·80 70
1959 440w. *Gentiana zollingeri* 2·20 80

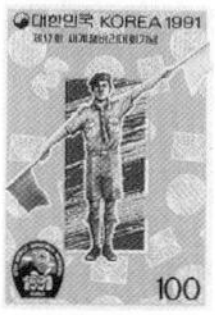
1167 Scout with Semaphore Flags

1991. 17th World Scout Jamboree.
1960 **1167** 100w. multicoloured 65 15
MS1961 90×60 mm. No. 1960×2 1·40 1·20

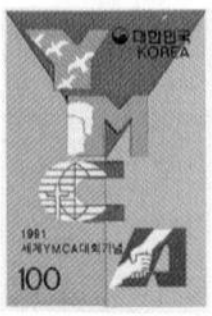
1168 "Y.M.C.A."

1991. Young Men's Christian Association World Assembly, Seoul.
1962 **1168** 100w. multicoloured 65 15

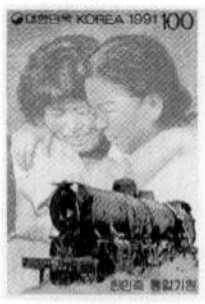
1169 Derelict Steam Locomotive and Family Members Reunited

1991. "North–South Reunification".
1963 **1169** 100w. multicoloured 80 20

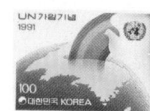

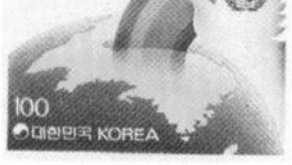
1170 Globe, Rainbow, Dove and U.N. Emblem

1991. Admission of South Korea to United Nations Organization.
1964 **1170** 100w. multicoloured 65 15

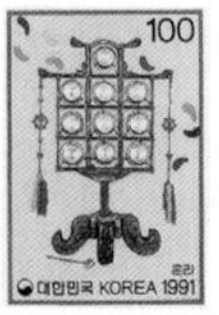
1171 Unra

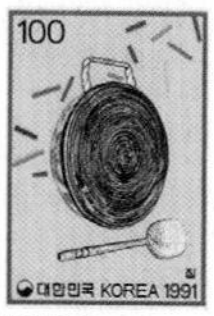
1172 Jing

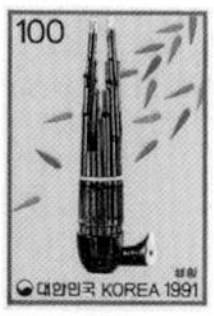
1173 Galgo

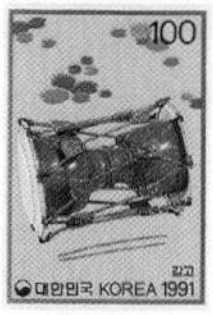
1174 Saeng-hwang

1991. Traditional Musical Instruments (1st series).
1965 **1171** 100w. multicoloured 70 30
1966 **1172** 100w. multicoloured 70 30
1967 **1173** 100w. multicoloured 70 30
1968 **1174** 100w. multicoloured 70 30
See also Nos. 1981/4.

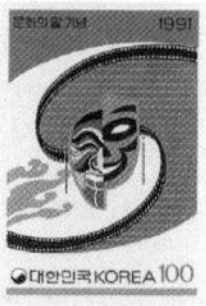
1175 Film and Theatrical Masks

1991. Culture Month.
1969 **1175** 100w. multicoloured 65 15

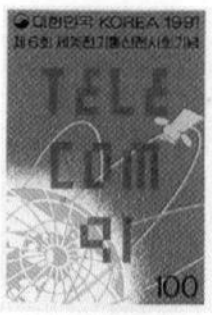
1176 Globe and Satellite

1991. "Telecom 91" Int Telecommunications Exhibition, Geneva.
1970 **1176** 100w. multicoloured 65 15

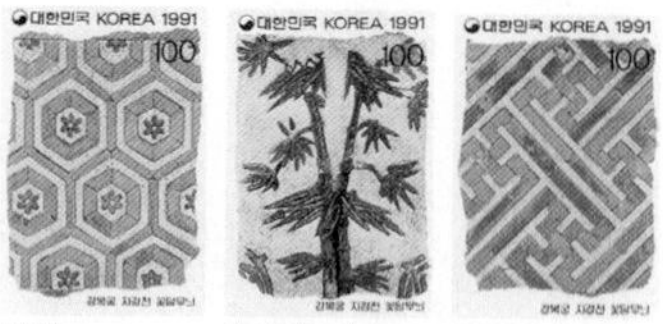
1177 Hexagonals
1178 Bamboo
1179 Geometric

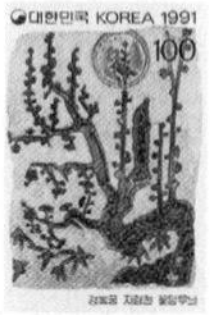
1180 Tree

1991. Korean Beauty (1st series). Kottams (patterns on walls) from Jakyung Hall, Kyungbok Palace.
1971 **1177** 100w. multicoloured 1·00 30
1972 **1178** 100w. multicoloured 1·00 30
1973 **1179** 100w. multicoloured 1·00 30
1974 **1180** 100w. multicoloured 1·00 30
See also Nos. 2006/9, 2068/71, 2103/6, 2157/60, 2219/22, 2257/60, 2308/15, 2350/6 and 2437/40.

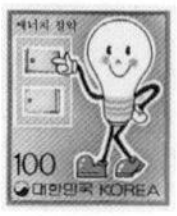
1181 Light Bulb turning off Switch

1991. Energy Saving Campaign.
1975 **1181** 100w. multicoloured 1·60 30

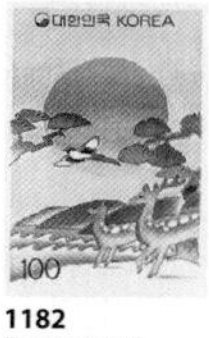
1182 "Longevity"

1991. Lunar New Year ("Year of the Monkey"). Multicoloured.
1976 100w. Type **1182** 65 15
1977 100w. Flying kites 65 15
MS1978 Two sheets each 90×60 mm. (a) No. 1976×2; (b) No. 1977×2 3·50 3·25

1184 Stamps

1991. Philatelic Week.
1979 **1184** 100w. multicoloured 65 15
MS1980 90×60 mm. No. 1979×2 1·60 1·50

1185 Yonggo **1186** Chwago **1187** Kkwaenggwari

1188 T'ukchong

1992. Traditional Musical Instruments (2nd series).
1981 **1185** 100w. multicoloured 70 30
1982 **1186** 100w. multicoloured 70 30
1983 **1187** 100w. multicoloured 70 30
1984 **1188** 100w. multicoloured 70 30

1189 White Hibiscus

1992. *Hibiscus syriacus* (national flower). Multicoloured.
1985 100w. Type **1189** 1·10 40
1986 100w. Pink hibiscus 1·10 40

1191 Satellite

1992. Science Day.
1987 **1191** 100w. multicoloured 55 15

1192 Yoon Pong Gil

1992. 60th Death Anniv of Yoon Pong Gil (independence fighter).
1988 **1192** 100w. multicoloured 55 15

1193 Children and Heart

1992. Child Protection.
1989 **1193** 100w. multicoloured 1·60 25

1194 Japanese Warship attacking Korean Settlement

1992. 400th Anniv of Start of Im-Jin War.
1990 **1194** 100w. multicoloured 55 15

1195 Farmer

1992. 60th International Fertilizer Industry Association Conference, Seoul.
1991 **1195** 100w. multicoloured 55 15

1992. Wild Flowers (3rd series). As T **1166**. Multicoloured.
1992 100w. "Lychnis wilfordii" 65 30
1993 100w. *Lycoris radiata* 65 30
1994 370w. *Commelina communis* 1·70 65
1995 440w. *Calanthe striata* 2·00 70

1196 *Longing for Mt. Keumkang* (Han Sang Ok and Choi Young Shurp) **1197** *The Swing* (Kim Mal Bong and Geum Su Hyeon)

1992. Korean Music (8th series).
1996 **1196** 100w. multicoloured 70 25
1997 **1197** 100w. multicoloured 70 25

1198 Gymnastics

1992. Olympic Games, Barcelona. Multicoloured.
1998 100w. Type **1198** 65 15
1999 100w. Pole vaulting 65 15

1199 Stylized View of Exhibition

1992. "Expo '93" World's Fair, Taejon (3rd issue). Multicoloured.
2000 100w. Type **1199** 55 15
2001 100w. "Expo 93" 55 15
MS2002 Two sheets each 90×60 mm.
(a) No. 2000×2; (b) No. 2001×2 3·50 3·00

1201 Korea Exhibition Centre and South Gate, Seoul

1992. 21st Universal Postal Union Congress, Seoul (1st issue). Multicoloured.
2003 **1201** 100w. multicoloured 55 15
2004 100w. Tolharubang (stone grandfather), Cheju 55 15
MS2005 Two sheets each 90×60 mm.
(a) No. 2003×2; (b) No. 2004×2 3·25 3·00
See also Nos. 2075/2077, 2088/**MS**2089 and 2112/**MS**2117.

1203 Woven Pattern **1204** Fruit and Flower Decorations **1205** Carved Decorations

1206 Coral, Butterfly and Pine Resin Decorations

1992. Korean Beauty (2nd series). Maedeups (tassels).
2006 **1203** 100w. multicoloured 80 30
2007 **1204** 100w. multicoloured 80 30
2008 **1205** 100w. multicoloured 80 30
2009 **1206** 100w. multicoloured 80 30

1207 Lee Pong Chang

1992. 60th Death Anniv of Lee Pong Chang (independence fighter).
2010 **1207** 100w. brown and orange 55 15

1208 Hwang Young Jo (Barcelona, 1992)

1992. Korean Winners of Olympic Marathon. Multicoloured.
2011 100w. Type **1208** 70 30
2012 100w. Shon Kee Chung (Berlin, 1936) 70 30
MS2013 90×60 mm. Nos. 2011/12 4·50 4·00

1209 Sails on Map of Americas

1992. 500th Anniv of Discovery of America by Columbus.
2014 **1209** 100w. multicoloured 55 15

1210 Heads and Speech Balloon

1992. Campaign for Purification of Language.
2015 **1210** 100w. multicoloured 1·60 30

1211 Flowers and Stamps

1992. Philatelic Week.
2016 **1211** 100w. multicoloured 55 15
MS2017 60×90 mm. No. 2016×2 1·80 1·60

1212 Cockerels in Snow-covered Yard

1992. Lunar New Year ("Year of the Cock"). Multicoloured.
2018 100w. Type **1212** 60 15
2019 100w. Flying kites 60 15
MS2020 Two sheets each 90×60 mm.
(a) No. 2018×2; (b) No. 2019×2 3·00 2·50

1214 Emblem, Globe and Woman holding Bowl

1992. International Nutrition Conference, Rome.
2021 **1214** 100w. multicoloured 55 15

1215 View of Centre and Logo

1993. Inauguration of Seoul Arts Centre's Opera House.
2022 **1215** 110w. multicoloured 65 25

1216 Pres. Kim Young Sam, Flag and Mt. Paekdu Lake

1993. Inauguration of 14th President.
2023 **1216** 110w. multicoloured 90 30
MS2024 90×60 mm. No. 2023×2 7·25 6·50

1217 National Flag

1993. No. 2036a orange, black and pink, others multicoloured.
2025 10w. Type **1217** 35 15
2026 20w. White stork 25 15
2026a 20w. Black-crowned night heron 25 10
2027 30w. White magnolia 35 15
2027a 30w. *Vitis amurensis* 65 40
2028 40w. Korean white pine 45 15
2028a 40w. *Purpuricenus lituralus* (beetle) 35 30
2028b 50w. Water cock 35 15
2029 60w. Squirrel 55 15
2030 70w. Chinese lanterns (plant) 55 15
2030a 80w. Japanese white eye on japonica branch 35 15
2031 90w. Oriental scops owl 70 25
2031a 100w. Dishcloth gourd 55 15
2032 110w. *Hibiscus syriacus* (plant) 1·00 15
2033 120w. As 110w. 90 15
2034 130w. Narcissi 90 25
2034c 140w. As 130w. 1·00 15
2035 150w. Painted porcelain jar 1·40 80
2036 160w. Pine tree (horiz) 1·50 25
2036a 170w. Crayfish 1·30 30
2036c 170w. Far eastern curlew 55 25
2037 180w. Little tern (horiz) 1·40 25
2037a 190w. As 110w. 1·20 30
2038 200w. Turtle (horiz) 1·40 30
2038a 200w. Snow crab (horiz) 90 40
2038b 210w. As 180w. 1·40 25
2038c 260w. As 180w. 1·80 40
2039 300w. Eurasian skylark (horiz) 1·30 40
2040 370w. Drum and drum dance (horiz) 2·75 50
2041 400w. Celadon cockerel water dropper (horiz) 1·50 40
2042 420w. As 370w. 3·00 50
2043 440w. Haho'i mask and Ssirum wrestlers (horiz) 3·50 55
2044 480w. As 440w. 3·00 55
2045 500w. Celadon pomegranate water dropper 2·00 65
2045a 600w. Hong Yong-sik (first Postmaster General) 2·30 80
2046 700w. Gilt-bronze Bongnae-san incense burner (23×34 mm) 4·00 80
2046a 700w. Cloud and crane jade ornament, Koryo Dynasty 2·20 80
2046b 710w. King Sejong and alphabet 5·00 70
2046c 800w. Cheju ponies 2·75 65
2047 900w. Gilt-bronze buddha triad (23×34 mm) 6·00 95
2048 910w. As 710w. 6·00 90
2049 930w. Celadon pitcher (blue background) (23×31 mm) 2·75 50
2049a 930w. As No. 2049 (brown background) 3·25 2·40
2049b 1000w. Stone guardian animal (from tomb of King Mury-ong) (32×21 mm) 4·50 1·30
2050 1050w. As 930w. 5·50 95
2050a 1170w. Bronze incense burner 5·00 2·10
2050b 1190w. As 930w. 5·00 2·30
2050c 2000w. Crown from tomb of Shinch'on-ni 6·00 1·60

1243 Student and Computer

1993. Korean Student Inventions Exhibition.

2051	**1243**	110w. mauve and silver	60	15

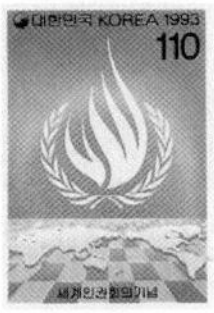
1244 Emblem and Map

1993. International Human Rights Conference, Vienna, Austria.

2052	**1244**	110w. multicoloured	60	15

1245 Hand scooping Globe from Water

1993. "Water is Life".

2053	**1245**	110w. multicoloured	1·20	25

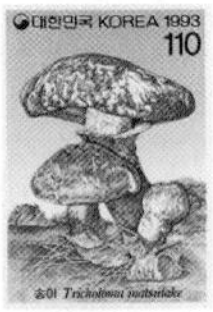
1246 Matsu-take Mushroom (*Tricholoma matsutake*)

1993. Fungi (1st series). Multicoloured.

2054	110w. Type **1246**	70	25
2055	110w. *Ganoderma lucidum*	70	25
2056	110w. *Lentinula edodes*	70	25
2057	110w. Oyster fungus (*Pleurotus ostreatus*)	70	25

See also Nos. 2095/8, 2146/9, 2207/10, 2249/52 and 2293/6.

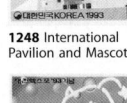

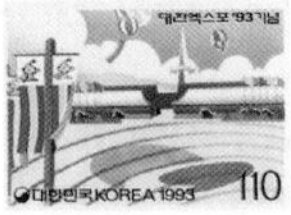
1247 Government Pavilion

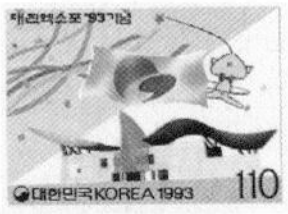
1248 International Pavilion and Mascot

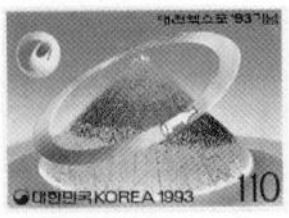
1249 Recycling Art Pavilion

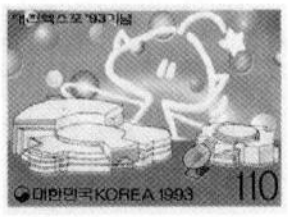
1250 Telecom Pavilion

1993. "Expo '93" World's Fair, Taejon (4th issue).

2058	**1247**	110w. multicoloured	60	25
2059	**1248**	110w. multicoloured	60	25
2060	**1249**	110w. multicoloured	60	25
2061	**1250**	110w. multicoloured	60	25
MS2062		Four sheets each 90×60 mm. (a) No. 2058×2; (b) No. 2059×2; (c) No. 2060×2; (d) No. 2061×2	6·50	6·00

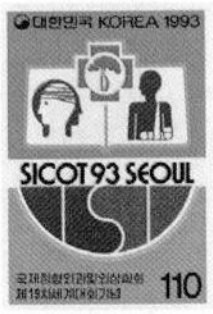
1251 Emblems

1993. 19th Congress of International Society of Orthopaedic and Trauma Surgery.

2063	**1251**	110w. multicoloured	60	15

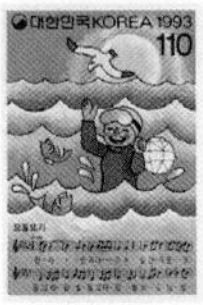
1252 *O Dol Ddo Gi* (Cheju Island folk song)

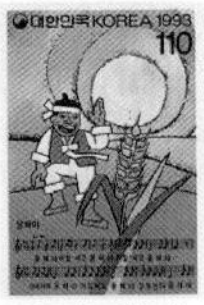
1253 *Ong He Ya* (barley threshing song)

1993. Korean Music (9th series).

2064	**1252**	110w. multicoloured	70	25
2065	**1253**	110w. multicoloured	70	25

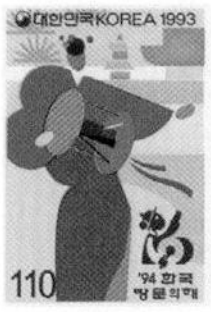
1254 Janggu Drum Dance

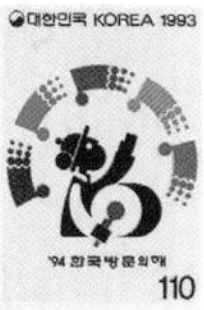
1255 Emblem

1993. "Visit Korea" Year (1994) (1st issue).

2066	**1254**	110w. multicoloured	60	15
2067	**1255**	110w. multicoloured	60	15

See also Nos. 2086/7.

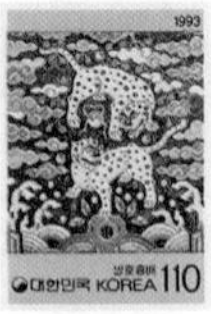
1256 *Twin Tigers* (military officials, 1st to 3rd rank)

1993. Korean Beauty (3rd series). Hyoongbae (embroidered insignia of the Chosun dynasty). Multicoloured.

2068	110w. Type **1256**	70	25
2069	110w. "Single Crane" (civil officials, 4th to 9th rank)	70	25
2070	110w. "Twin Cranes" (civil officials, 1st to 3rd rank)	70	25
2071	110w. "Dragon" (King)	70	25

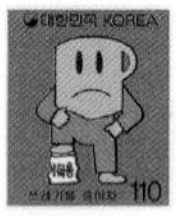
1260 Campaign Emblem

1993. Anti-litter Campaign.

2072	**1260**	110w. multicoloured	1·30	25

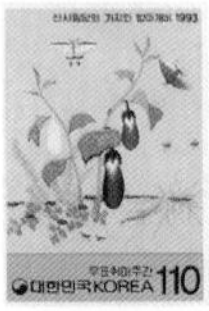
1261 *Eggplant and Oriental Long-nosed Locust* (Shin Saim Dang)

1993. Philatelic Week.

2073	**1261**	110w. multicoloured	60	25
MS2074		90×60 mm. No. 2073×2	1·60	1·40

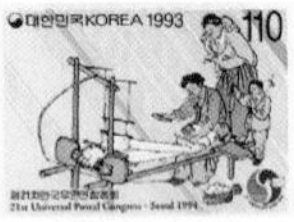
1262 *Weaving*

1993. 21st U.P.U. Congress, Seoul (2nd issue). Paintings by Kim Hong Do. Multicoloured.

2075	110w. Type **1262**	60	25
2076	110w. *Musicians and a Dancer* (vert)	60	25
MS2077	Two sheets each 90×60 mm. (a) No. 2075×2; (b) No. 2076×2	3·00	2·75

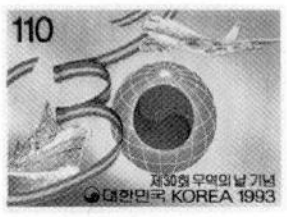
1263 Ribbon and Globe as "30", Freighter and Ilyushin Il-86 Airliner

1993. 30th Trade Day.

2078	**1263**	110w. multicoloured	60	25

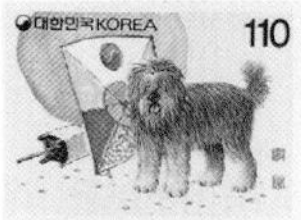
1264 Sapsaree and Kite

1993. Lunar New Year ("Year of the Dog"). Multicoloured.

2079	110w. Type **1264**	60	25
2080	110w. Puppy with New Year's Greetings bow	60	25
MS2081	Two sheets each 90×60 mm. (a) No. 2079×2; (b) No. 2080×2	3·00	2·75

1993. Wild Flowers (4th series). As T **1166**.

2082	110w. "Weigela hortensis"	70	25
2083	110w. *Iris ruthenica*	70	25
2084	110w. *Aceriphyllum rosii*	70	25
2085	110w. Marsh marigold "*Caltha palustris*)	70	25

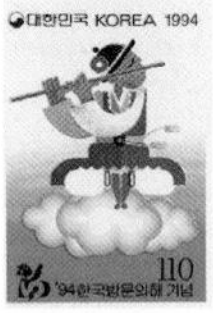
1266 Flautist on Cloud

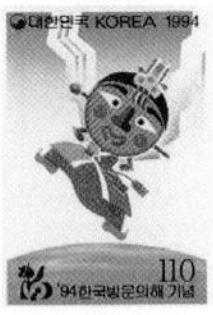
1267 T'alch'um Mask Dance

1994. "Visit Korea" Year (2nd issue).

2086	**1266**	110w. multicoloured	60	15
2087	**1267**	110w. multicoloured	60	25

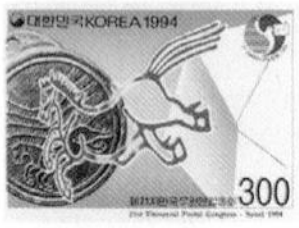
1268 Map'ae, Horse, Envelope and Emblem

1994. 21st U.P.U. Congress, Seoul (3rd issue).

2088	**1268**	300w. multicoloured	1·40	55
MS2089		90×60 mm. No. 2088×2	3·50	3·00

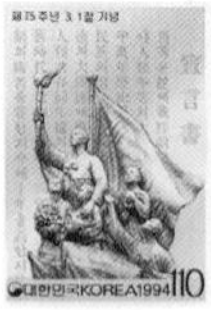
1269 Monument

1994. 75th Anniv of Samil (Independence) Movement.

2090	**1269**	110w. multicoloured	60	15

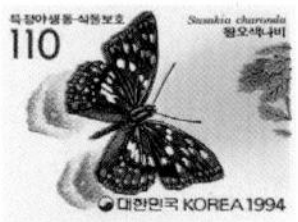
1270 Great Purple (*Sasakia charonda*)

1994. Protection of Wildlife and Plants (1st series). Multicoloured.

2091	110w. Type **1270** (butterfly)	70	30
2092	110w. *Allomyrina dichotoma* (beetle)	70	30
MS2093	Two sheets each 90×60 mm. (a) No. 2091×2; (b) No. 2092×2	3·50	3·00

See also Nos. 2143/**MS**2145 and 2186/**MS**2188, 2241/**MS**2243, 2277/**MS**2279, 2326/**MS**2330, 2383/**MS**2387 and 2481/**MS**2485.

See also Nos. 2143/4, 2186/7, 2241/2, 2275/8, 2326/9, 2383/6 and 2481/4.

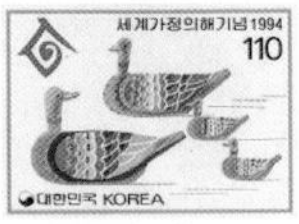
1271 Family of Mandarins

1994. International Year of the Family.

2094	**1271**	110w. multicoloured	60	15

1994. Fungi (2nd series). As T **1246**. Multicoloured.

2095	110w. Common morel (*Morchella esculenta*)	70	25
2096	110w. *Gomphus floccosus*	70	25
2097	110w. *Cortinarius purpurascens*	70	25
2098	110w. *Oudemansiella platyphylla*	70	25
MS2099	Four sheets each 90×60 mm. (a) No. 2095×2; (b) No. 2096×2; (c) No. 2097×2; (d) No. 2098×2	6·50	6·00

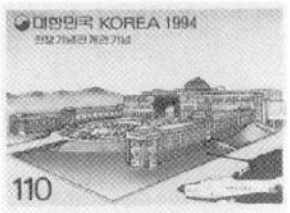
1272 Museum

1994. Inauguration of War Memorial Museum, Yongsan (Seoul).

2100	**1272**	110w. multicoloured	60	15

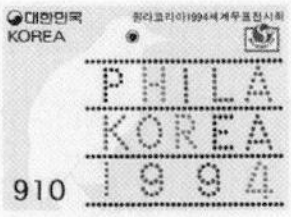
1273 Text and Dove

1994. "Philakorea 1994" International Stamp Exhibition, Seoul (1st issue).

2101	**1273**	910w. multicoloured	4·00	1·60
MS2102		90×60 mm. No. 2101	4·75	4·25

See also Nos. 2107/**MS**2111.
See also Nos. 2107/9.

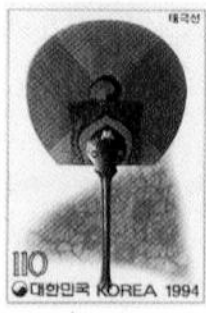
1274 Taeguk (Yin-Yang) Fan

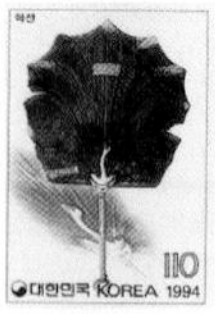
1275 Crane Fan

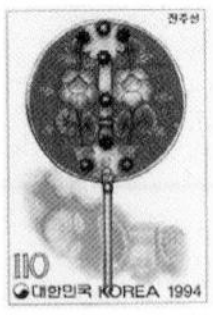
1276 Pearl Fan

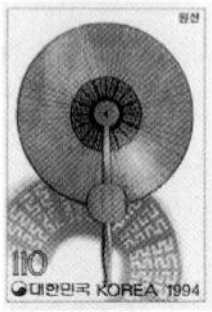
1277 Wheel Fan

1994. Korean Beauty (4th series). Fans.

2103	**1274**	110w. multicoloured	70	25
2104	**1275**	110w. multicoloured	70	25
2105	**1276**	110w. multicoloured	70	25
2106	**1277**	110w. multicoloured	70	25

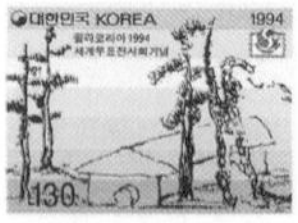
1278 "Wintry Days" (Kim Chong Hui)

1994. "Philakorea 1994" International Stamp Exhibition, Seoul (2nd issue). Multicoloured.

2107	130w. Type **1278**	60	15
2108	130w. *Grape* (Choe Sok Hwan)	60	15
2109	130w. *Riverside Scene* (Kim Duk Sin)	60	15
MS2110	Three sheets each 90×60 mm. (a) No. 2107×2; (b) No. 2108×2; (c) No. 2109×2	4·00	3·50
MS2111	130w. Manchurian crane and mountains; 300w. Manchurian crane and sun; 370w. Manchurian cranes in treetops; 400w. Deer (vert); 440w. Turtle in stream (vert); 470w. Tree and stream (vert); 930w. Trees (vert)	10·50	9·75

See also Nos. 2196/**MS**2198, 2234/**MS**2236, 2280/**MS**2282, 2322/**MS**2325; 2498/**MS**2501, 2594/**MS**2596 and 2697/**MS**2699.

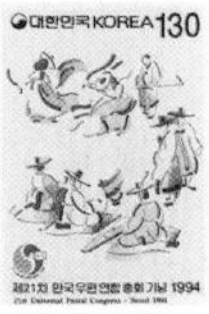
1282 *Sword Dance* (Sin Yun Bok)

1994. 21st U.P.U. Congress, Seoul (4th issue). Multicoloured.

2112	130w. Type **1282**	60	15
2113	130w. *Book Shelves* (detail of folk painting showing stamps)	60	15
2114	130w. Congress emblem	60	15
2115	130w. Hong Yung Sik (postal reformer) and Heinrich von Stephan (founder of U.P.U.) (horiz)	60	15
MS2116	Four sheets each 90×60 mm. (a) No. 2112×2; (b) No. 2113×2; (c) No. 2114×2; (d) No. 2115×2	7·25	6·75
MS2117	125×86 mm. Nos. 2112/15	4·00	3·50

1283 Old Map

1994. 600th Anniv of Adoption of Seoul as Capital of Korea (1st issue).
2118 **1283** 130w. multicoloured 60 15
See also No. 2139.

1284 Mail Van

1994. Transport. Multicoloured.
2121 300w. Type **1284** 2·10 30
2122 330w. Boeing 747 2·10 40
2122a 340w. Boeing 747 facing left 2·10 50
2122b 380w. As 340w. 2·30 55
2123 390w. Boeing 747 (different) 3·00 50
2124 400w. As 330w. 2·10 40
2126 540w. Streamlined diesel train 3·50 55
2127 560w. As 330w. 3·50 65
2130 1190w. River cruiser 7·75 75
2131 1300w. As 330w. 6·75 1·20
2132 1340w. As 340w. 5·75 1·80
2132a 1380w. As 340w. 6·25 2·00

1994. Wild Flowers (5th series). As T **1166**. Multicoloured.
2133 130w. *Gentiana jamesii* 60 25
2134 130w. *Geranium eriostemon* var. *megalanthum* 60 25
2135 130w. *Leontopodium japonicum* 60 25
2136 130w. *Lycoris aurea* 60 25

1285 *Water Melon and Field Mice* (detail of folding screen, Shin Saimdang)

1994. Philatelic Week.
2137 **1285** 130w. multicoloured 60 25
MS2138 90×60 mm. No. 2137×2 1·50 1·30

1286 "600"

1994. 600th Anniv of Seoul as Capital (2nd issue).
2139 **1286** 130w. multicoloured 60 10

1287 Pigs travelling in Snow

1994. Lunar New Year ("Year of the Pig"). Multicoloured.
2140 130w. Type **1287** 60 10
2141 130w. Family in forest 60 10
MS2142 Two sheets each 90×60 mm.
(a) No. 2140×2; (b) No. 2141×2 3·00 2·75

1995. Protection of Wildlife and Plants (2nd series). As T **1270**. Multicoloured.
2143 130w. Plancy's green pond frog (*Rana plancyi*) 60 25
2144 130w. Common toad (*Bufo bufo*) 60 25
MS2145 Two sheets each 125×86 mm.
(a) No. 2143×2; (b) No. 2144×2 3·25 3·00

1995. Fungi (3rd series). As T **1246**. Multicoloured.
2146 130w. Shaggy ink caps (*Coprinus comatus*) 70 25
2147 130w. Chicken mushroom (*Laetiporus sulphureus*) 70 25
2148 130w. *Lentinus lepideus* 70 25
2149 130w. Cracked green russula (*Russula virescens*) 70 25
MS2150 Four sheets each 90×60 mm.
(a) No. 2146×2; (b) No. 2147×2; (c) No. 2148×2; (d) No. 2149×2 6·50 6·00

1290 Spheres around Reactor

1995. Completion of Hanaro Research Reactor.
2151 **1290** 130w. multicoloured 70 15

1291 Scales of Justice

1995. Centenary of Judicial System.
2152 **1291** 130w. multicoloured 70 15

1292 Tiger

1995. Centenary of Law Education.
2153 **1292** 130w. multicoloured 70 15

1293 Dooly the Little Dinosaur (Kim Soo Jeung) **1294** Kochuboo (Kim Yong Hwan)

1995. Cartoons (1st series). Multicoloured.
2154 **1293** 130w. multicoloured 70 25
2155 **1294** 440w. multicoloured 1·60 65
MS2156 Two sheets each 90×60 mm.
(a) No. 2154; (b) No. 2155 4·75 4·50
See also Nos. 2196/MS2198, 2234/MS2236, 2280/MS2282, 2322/MS2325, 2402/MS2404, 2498/MS2500, 2594/MS2596, 2697/MS2699 and 2754/MS2756.

1295 Gate of Eternal Youth, Changdokkung Palace **1296** Fish Water Gate, Chuhamru Pavilion, Changdokkung Palace **1297** Pomosa Temple Gate, Pusan City

1298 Yangban Residence Gate, Hahoe Village

1995. Korean Beauty (5th series). Gates.
2157 **1295** 130w. multicoloured 75 25
2158 **1296** 130w. multicoloured 75 25
2159 **1297** 130w. multicoloured 75 25
2160 **1298** 130w. multicoloured 75 25

1299 Lion and Emblem

1995. 78th Convention of Lions Clubs International.
2161 **1299** 130w. multicoloured 65 15

1995. Wild Flowers (6th series). As T **1166**. Multicoloured.
2162 130w. *Halenia corniculata* 60 25
2163 130w. *Erythronium japonicum* 60 25
2164 130w. *Iris odaesanensis* 60 25
2165 130w. *Leontice microrrhyncha* 60 25

1300 National Flag

1995. 50th Anniv of Liberation. Multicoloured.
2166 130w. Type **1300** 60 25
2167 440w. Anniversary emblem (96×19 mm) 1·90 55
MS2168 Two sheets each 125×85 mm.
(a) No. 2166×2; (b) No. 2167 4·75 4·25

1301 Telescope

1995. Inauguration of Mt. Bohyun Optical Astronomy Observatory.
2169 **1301** 130w. multicoloured 65 15

1302 Turtle's Back Song **1303** Song from *Standards of Musical Science*

1995. Literature (1st series).
2170 **1302** 130w. multicoloured 60 15
2171 **1303** 130w. multicoloured 60 15
MS2172 Two sheets each 90×60 mm.
(a) No. 2170×2; (b) No. 2171×2 3·00 2·75
See also Nos. 2212/MS2214, 2269/MS2271, 2301/MS2303 and 2344/MS2348.

1304 "50 Th" incorporating Man with Wheat

1995. 50th Anniv of F.A.O.
2173 **1304** 150w. black and violet 75 25

1305 Open Bible

1995. Centenary of Korean Bible Society.
2174 **1305** 150w. multicoloured 75 25

1306 Families in Houses

1995. Population and Housing Census.
2175 **1306** 100w. multicoloured 75 25

1307 Dove of Flags

1995. 50th Anniv of United Nations Organization.
2176 **1307** 100w. multicoloured 75 25

1308 Rontgen

1995. Centenary of Discovery of X-Rays by Wilhelm Rontgen.
2177 **1308** 150w. multicoloured 75 25

1309 "Water Pepper and Mantis" (detail of folding screen, Shin Saim Dang)

1995. Philatelic Week.
2178 **1309** 150w. multicoloured 75 25
MS2179 90×60 mm. No. 2178×2 1·70 1·50

1310 Rat and Snowman

1995. Lunar New Year ("Year of the Rat"). Multicoloured.
2180 150w. Type **1310** 75 25
2181 150w. Cranes and pine trees (horiz) 75 25
MS2182 Two sheets each 90×60 mm.
(a) No. 2180×2; (b) No. 2181×2 3·25 3·00

1312 Miroku Bosatsu, Koryu Temple, Kyoto

1995. 30th Anniv of Resumption of Korea–Japan Diplomatic Relations.
2183 **1312** 420w. multicoloured 2·10 70

1313 Cable Route

1996. Inauguration of Korea–China Submarine Cable.
2184 **1313** 420w. multicoloured 2·10 70

1314 "30" and Molecule

1996. 30th Anniv of Korea Institute of Science and Technology.
2185 **1314** 150w. multicoloured 75 25

1996. Protection of Wildlife and Plants (3rd series). As T **1270**. Multicoloured.
2186 150w. Black pond turtle (*Geoclemys reevesii*) 75 25
2187 150w. Ground skink (*Scincella laterale*) 75 25
MS2188 Two sheets each 125×86 mm.
(a) No. 2186×2; (b) No. 2187×2 3·25 3·00

1315 Satellite and Launching Pad

1996. Launch of "Mugunghwa 2" Telecommunications Satellite.
2189 **1315** 150w. multicoloured 75 25

1316 So Chae P'il (founder) and Leader from First Issue

1996. Centenary of "Tongnip Shinmun" (first independent newspaper).
2190 **1316** 150w. multicoloured 75 25

1996. Wild Flowers (7th series). As T **1166**. Multicoloured.
2191 150w. *Cypripedium macranthum* 75 25
2192 150w. *Trilium tschonoskii* 75 25

2193	150w. *Viola variegata*	75	25
2194	150w. *Hypericum ascyron*	75	25

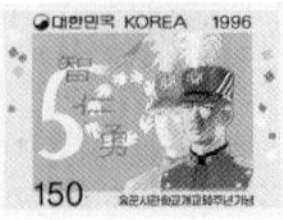

1317 Anniversary Emblem and Cadets

1996. 50th Anniv of Korean Military Academy.

2195	**1317**	150w. multicoloured	75	25

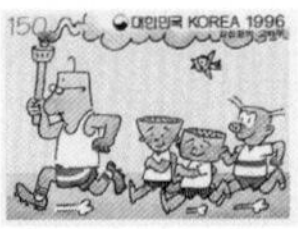

1318 Gobau (Kim Song Hwan)

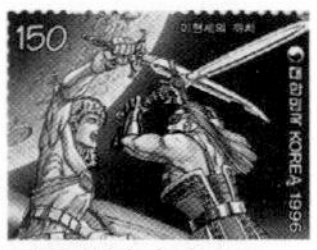

1319 Battle between Kkach'i and Caesarius (Lee Hyun Se) (from film "Armageddon")

1996. Cartoons (2nd series).

2196	**1318**	150w. multicoloured	75	25
2197	**1319**	150w. multicoloured	75	25

MS2198 Two sheets each 90×60 mm. (a) No. 2196×2; (b) No. 2197 3·00 2·75

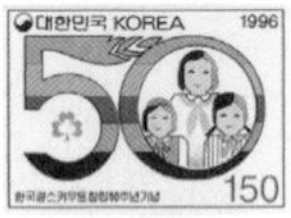

1320 Anniversary Emblem

1996. 50th Anniv of Korean Girl Scouts.

2199	**1320**	150w. multicoloured	75	25

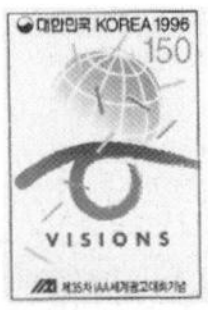

1321 Globe and Congress Emblem

1996. 35th World Congress of International Advertising Association, Seoul.

2200	**1321**	150w. multicoloured	75	25

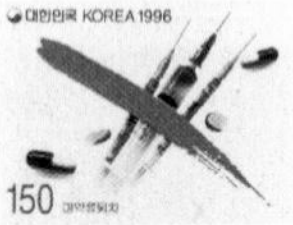

1322 Syringes and Drugs

1996. International Anti-drug Day.

2201	**1322**	150w. multicoloured	75	25

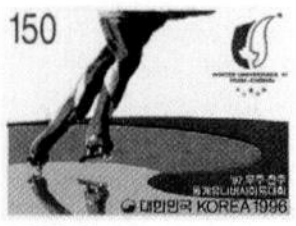

1323 Skater

1996. World University Students' Games, Muju and Chonju (1st issue). Multicoloured.

2202	150w. Type **1323**	75	25
2203	150w. Games emblem (vert)	75	25

See also Nos. 2228/9.

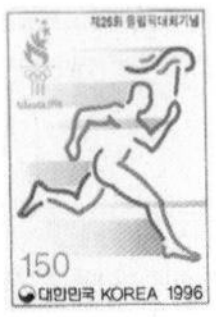

1324 Torch Bearer

1996. Olympic Games, Atlanta. Multicoloured.

2204	150w. Type **1324**	75	25
2205	150w. Games emblem	75	25

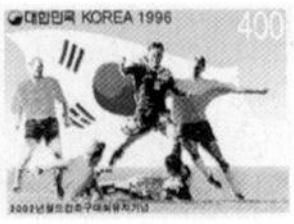

1325 Match Scene

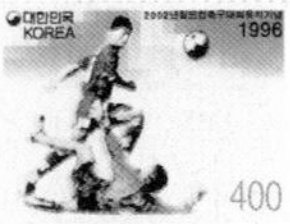

1326 South Korean Team scoring Goal

1996. World Cup Football Championship (2002), South Korea and Japan. Two sheets each 134×78 mm. Multicoloured.

MS2206 Two sheets. (a) 400w.×4, Type **1325**; (b) 400w.×4, Type **1326** 21·00 18·00

1996. Fungi (4th series). As T **1246**. Multicoloured.

2207	150w. *Amanita inaurata*	75	25
2208	150w. *Paxillus atrotomentosus*	75	25
2209	150w. *Rhodophyllus crassipes*	75	25
2210	150w. *Sarcodon imbricatum*	75	25

MS2211 Four sheets each 90×60 mm. (a) No. 2207×2; (b) No. 2208×2; (c) No. 2209×2; (d) No. 2210×2 6·75 6·25

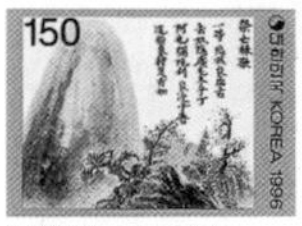

1327 *Requiem for a Deceased Sister*

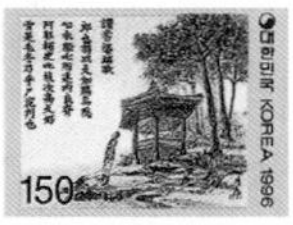

1328 *Ode to Knight Kip'a*

1996. Literature (2nd series).

2212	**1327**	150w. multicoloured	75	25
2213	**1328**	150w. multicoloured	75	25

MS2214 Two sheets, each 90×61 mm. (a) No. 2212×2; (b) No. 2213×2 3·25 3·00

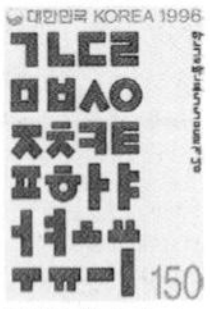

1329 Alphabet

1996. 550th Anniv of Han-Gul (Korean alphabet created by King Sejong).

2215	**1329**	150w. black and grey	75	25

MS2216 90×60 mm. No. 2215×2 1·70 1·50

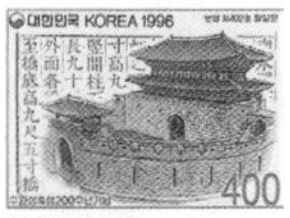

1330 Castle

1996. Bicentenary of Suwon Castle.

2217	**1330**	400w. multicoloured	2·10	80

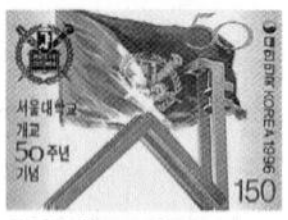

1331 Front Gate, University Flag and Emblem

1996. 50th Anniv of Seoul National University.

2218	**1331**	150w. multicoloured	75	25

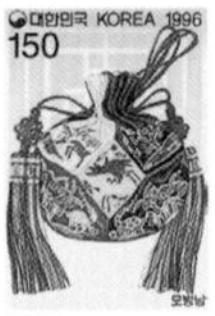

1332 Five-direction Pouch

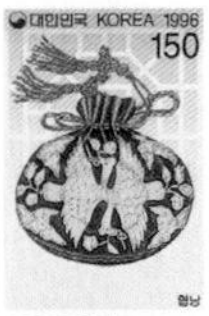

1333 Chinese Phoenix Pouch (Queen's Court Pouch)

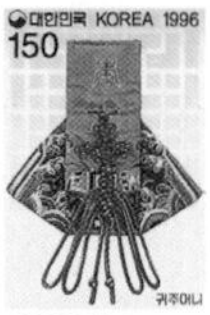

1334 Princess Pokon's Wedding Pouch

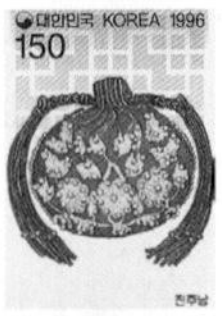

1335 Queen Yunbi's Pearl Pouch

1996. Korean Beauty (6th series). Pouches.

2219	**1332**	150w. multicoloured	75	25
2220	**1333**	150w. multicoloured	75	25
2221	**1334**	150w. multicoloured	75	25
2222	**1335**	150w. multicoloured	75	25

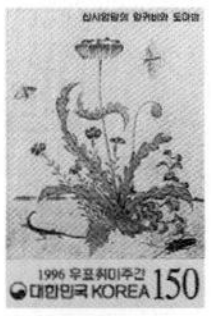

1336 *Poppy and Lizard* (detail of folding screen, Shin Saimdang)

1996. Philatelic Week.

2223	**1336**	150w. multicoloured	75	25

MS2224 90×60 mm. No. 2223×2 1·70 1·50

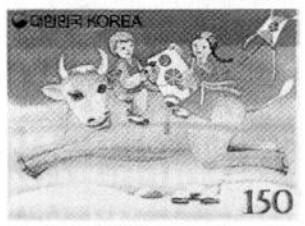

1337 Children riding Ox

1996. Lunar New Year ("Year of the Ox"). Multicoloured.

2225	150w. Type **1337**	75	25
2226	150w. Boy piper and resting ox	75	25

MS2227 Two sheets, each 90×60 mm. (a) No. 2225×2; (b) No. 2226×2 3·25 3·00

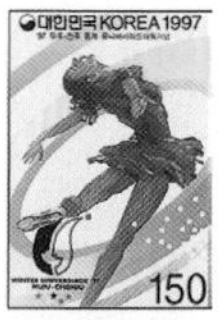

1339 Figure Skating

1997. World University Students' Games, Muju and Chonju (2nd issue). Multicoloured.

2228	150w. Type **1339**	65	25
2229	150w. Skiing	65	25

MS2230 Two sheets, each 60×90 mm. (a) No. 2228×2; (b) No. 2229×2 2·75 2·40

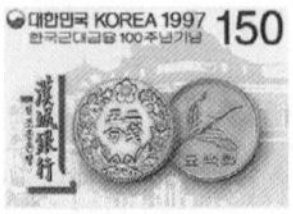

1340 Coins forming "100"

1997. Centenary of Foundation of Hansong Bank (first commercial bank in Korea).

2231	**1340**	150w. multicoloured	65	25

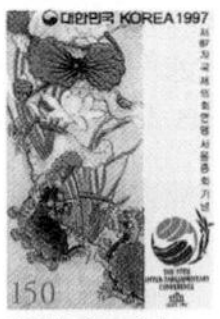

1341 *Auspicious Turtles*(painting)

1997. Interparliamentary Union Conference, Seoul.

2232	**1341**	150w. multicoloured	70	25

1342 Globe, Pen and open Book (Jeon Chong Kwan)

1997. World Book and Copyright Day.

2233	**1342**	150w. multicoloured	1·20	25

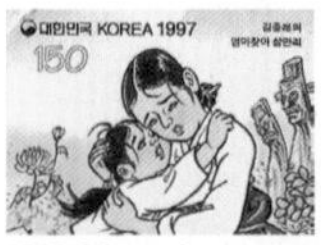

1343 A Long, Long Journey in Search of Mummy (Kim Chong Nae)

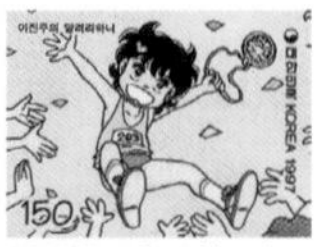

1344 Run, Run, Hannie (Lee Chin Ju)

1997. Cartoons (3rd series).

2234	**1343**	150w. multicoloured	70	25
2235	**1344**	150w. multicoloured	70	25

MS2236 Two sheets, each 90×60 mm. (a) No. 2234; (b) 2235 2·30 2·00

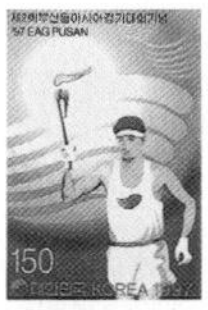

1345 Torch Bearer

1997. Second East Asian Games, Pusan.

2237	**1345**	150w. multicoloured	70	25

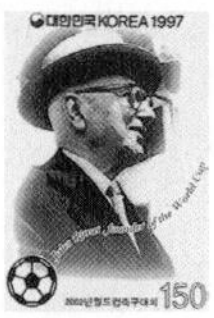

1346 Jules Rimet (founder)

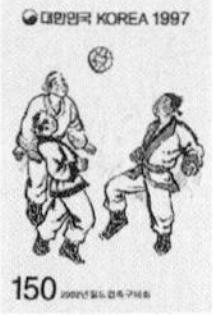

1347 "Chukkuk" (Lee Chul Joo)

1997. World Cup Football Championship (2002), South Korea and Japan (1st issue).

2238	**1346**	150w. multicoloured	70	25
2239	**1347**	150w. multicoloured	70	25

MS2240 Two sheets, each 134×78 mm. (a) 2238×2; (b) 2242×2 5·25 4·75

See also Nos. 2284/**MS**2288.

1997. Protection of Wildlife and Plants (4th series). As T **1270**. Multicoloured.

2241	150w. Chinese nine-spined sticklebacks (*Pungitius sinensis*)	70	25
2242	150w. Spot-eared brook perch (*Coreoperca kawamebari*)	70	25

MS2243 Two sheets, each 125×86 mm. (a) 2241×2; (b) No. 2242×2 2·75 2·40

1997. Wild Flowers (8th series). As T **1166**. Multicoloured.

2244	150w. *Belamcanda chinensis*	70	25
2245	150w. *Belamcanda chinensis*	70	25
2246	150w. *Campanula takesimana*	70	25
2247	150w. *Magnolia sieboldii*	70	25

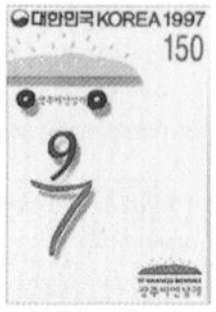

1348 Emblem and "97" forming Face

1997. Second Art Biennale, Kwangju.

2248	**1348**	150w. multicoloured	70	25

1997. Fungi (5th series). As T **1246**. Multicoloured.

2249	150w. *Inocybe fastigiata*	70	25
2250	150w.	70	25
2251	150w. *Ramaria flava*	70	25
2252	150w. Fly agaric (*Amanita muscaria*)	70	25

MS2253 Four sheets, each 90×60 mm. (a) No. 2249×2; (b) No. 2250×2; (c) No. 2251×2; (d) No. 2252×2 5·50 5·00

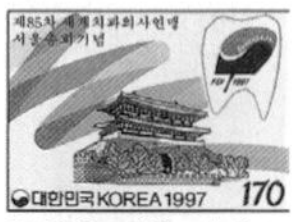

1349 Seoul South Gate and Emblem

1997. 85th World Dental Congress, Seoul.

2254	**1349**	170w. multicoloured	70	25

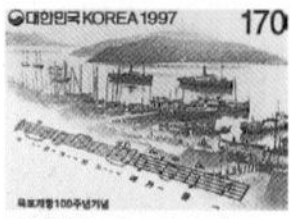

1350 Harbour and Score

1997. Centenary of Mokpo Port.

2255	**1350**	170w. multicoloured	70	25

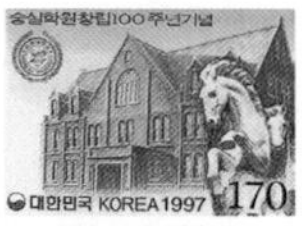

1351 Main Building, Pyongyang

1997. Centenary of Founding of Soongsil Academy in Pyongyang (now situated in Seoul).

2256	**1351**	170w. multicoloured	70	25

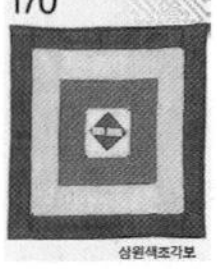

1352 Concentric Squares

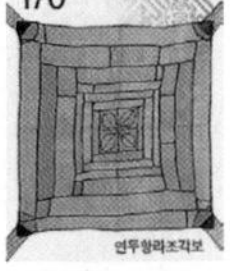

1353 Green Silk

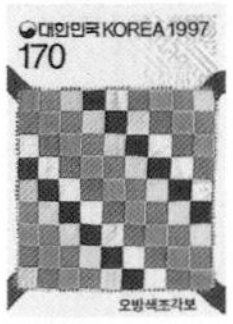

1354 Pattern of Squares

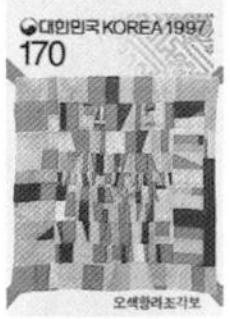

1355 Pattern of Squares and Triangles

1997. Korean Beauty (7th series). Patchwork Pojagi (wrapping cloths).

2257	**1352**	170w. multicoloured	70	25
2258	**1353**	170w. multicoloured	70	25
2259	**1354**	170w. multicoloured	70	25
2260	**1355**	170w. multicoloured	70	25

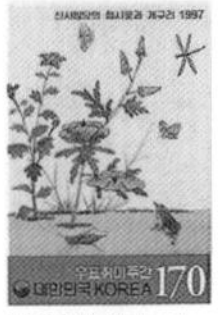

1356 *Hollyhock and Frog* (detail of folding screen, Shin Saimdang)

1997. Philatelic Week.

2261	**1356**	170w. multicoloured	70	25
MS2262		90×60 mm. No. 2261×2	1·40	1·10

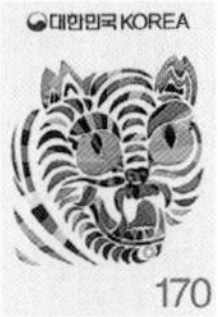

1357 Tiger's Head

1997. Lunar New Year ("Year of the Tiger"). Multicoloured.

2263	170w. Type **1357**	70	25
2264	170w. *Magpie and Tiger* (folk painting)	70	25
MS2265	Two sheets, each 90×60 mm. (a) No. 2263×2; (b) No. 2264×2	2·75	2·40

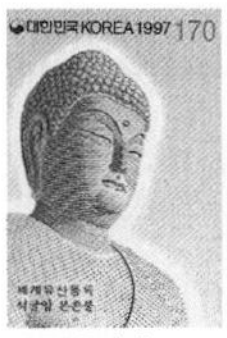

1359 Buddha, Sokkuram Shrine

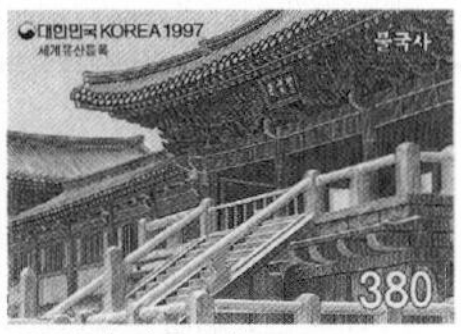

1360 Pulguk Temple

1997. World Heritage Sites (1st series).

2266	**1359**	170w. multicoloured	1·30	90
2267	**1360**	380w. multicoloured	5·25	3·50
MS2268		144×88 mm. Nos. 2266/7	6·50	6·00

See also Nos. 2317/**MS**2319, 2365/**MS**2367, 2457/**MS**2459 and 2533/**MS**2535.

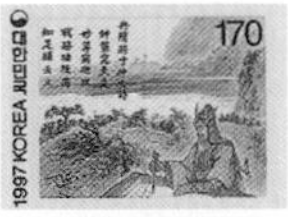

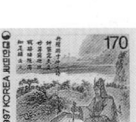

1361 *Poem to Sui General Yu Zhong Wen* (Ulchi Mundok)

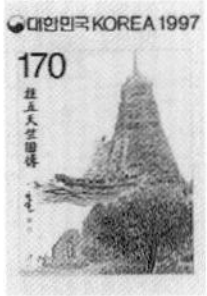

1362 *Record of Travel to Five Indian Kingdoms* (Hye Ch'o)

1997. Literature (3rd series).

2269	**1361**	170w. multicoloured	65	25
2270	**1362**	170w. multicoloured	65	25
MS2271		Two sheets, each 90×60 mm. (a) No. 2269×2; (b) No. 2270×2	2·75	2·40

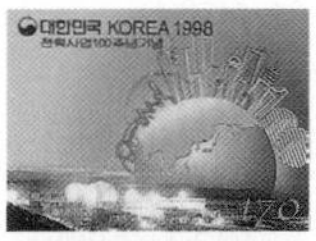

1363 Neon Lights on Globe and Nuclear Power Plant

1998. Centenary of Introduction of Electricity to Korea.

2272	**1363**	170w. multicoloured	65	15

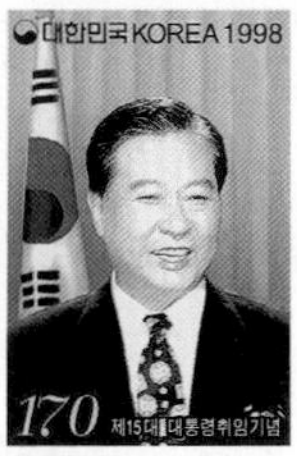

1364 Pres. Kim Dae Jung and Flag

1998. Inauguration of 15th President of South Korea.

2273	**1364**	170w. multicoloured	1·10	40
MS2274		120×110 mm. No. 2273	6·00	5·75

1998. Protection of Wildlife and Plants (5th series). Vert designs as T **1270**. Multicoloured.

2275	340w. Korean leopard (*Panthera pardus orientalis*)	2·00	30
2276	340w. Asiatic black bears (*Selenarctos thibetanus*)	2·00	30
2277	340w. European otters (*Lutra lutra*)	2·00	30
2278	340w. Siberian musk deers (*Moschus moschiferus*)	2·00	30
MS2279	129×123 mm. Nos. 2275/8	8·25	7·00

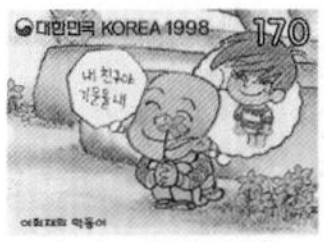

1365 Aktong-i (Lee Hi Jae)

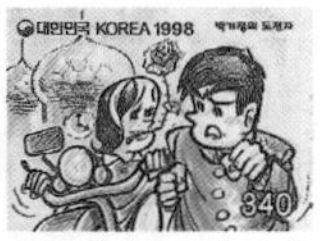

1366 Challenger (Park Ki Jong)

1998. Cartoons (4th series).

2280	**1365**	170w. multicoloured	80	25
2281	**1366**	340w. multicoloured	1·70	1·20
MS2282		Two sheets, each 90×60 mm. (a) No. 2280; (b) No. 2281	3·25	2·75

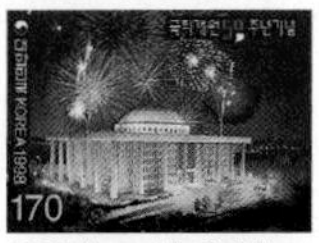

1367 Assembly Building and Firework Display

1998. 50th Anniv of National Assembly.

2283	**1367**	170w. multicoloured	65	15

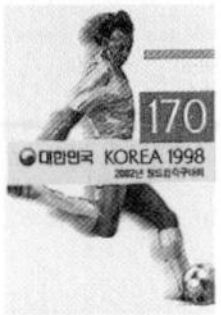

1368 Player with Ball

1998. World Cup Football Championship (2002), Korea and Japan (2nd issue). Multicoloured.

2284	170w. Type **1368**	90	25
2285	170w. Two players chasing ball	90	25
2286	170w. Players heading ball	90	25
2287	170w. Player kicking ball over head	90	25
MS2288	134×78 mm. No. 2284/7	4·00	3·25

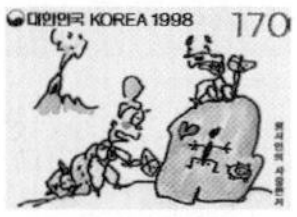

1369 Writing on Stone Tablets

1998. Information Technology. Multicoloured.

2289	170w. Type **1369**	80	25
2290	170w. Pony Express	80	25
2291	170w. Man using telephone and post box	80	25
2292	170w. Old and modern forms of communication (68×22 mm)	1·60	50

1998. Fungi (6th series). As T **1246**. Multicoloured.

2293	170w. *Pseudocolus schellenbergiae*	90	40
2294	170w. *Cyptotrama asprata*	90	40
2295	170w. *Laccaria vinaceoavellanea*	90	40
2296	170w. *Phallus rugulosus*	90	40
MS2297	114×144 mm. Nos. 2293/6	5·00	4·50

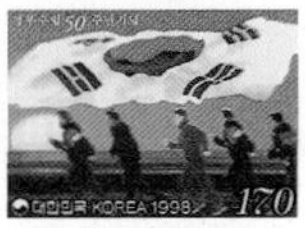

1373 Flag and Runners

1998. 50th Anniv of Proclamation of Republic.

2298	**1373**	170w. multicoloured	65	25

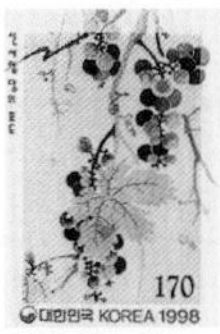

1374 *Grapes* (Lady Shin Saimdang)

1998. Philatelic Week.

2299	**1374**	170w. multicoloured	65	25
MS2300		90×60 mm. No. 2299×2	1·70	1·40

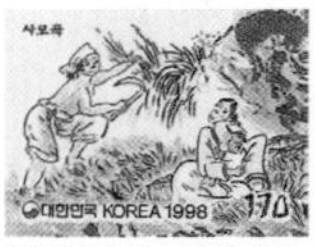

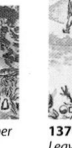

1375 *Thinking of Mother*

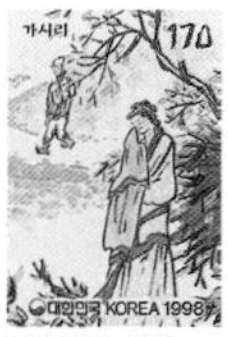

1376 *Would You Leave Me Now?*

1998. Literature (4th series). Sogyo Songs.

2301	**1375**	170w. multicoloured	65	25
2302	**1376**	170w. multicoloured	65	25
MS2303		Two sheets 90×20 mm. (a) No. 2301; (b) No. 2302	2·20	1·80

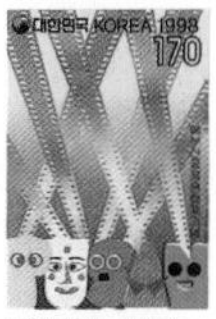

1377 Film Strips and Masks

1998. Third Pusan International Film Festival.

2304	**1377**	170w. multicoloured	65	25

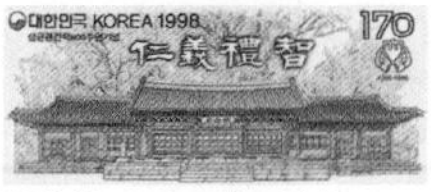

1378 Myungnyundang Hall

1998. 600th Anniv of Sungkyunkwan University.

2305	**1378**	170w. multicoloured	65	25

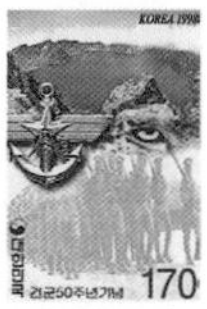

1379 National Constabulary, Badge and Lake Ch'onji

1998. 50th Anniv of Korean Armed Forces.

2306	**1379**	170w. multicoloured	65	25

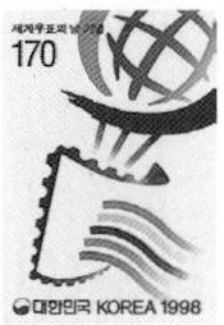

1380 Hot-air Balloon

1998. World Stamp Day.

2307	**1380**	170w. multicoloured	65	25

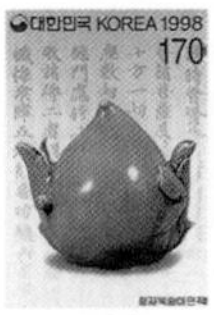

1381 Peach

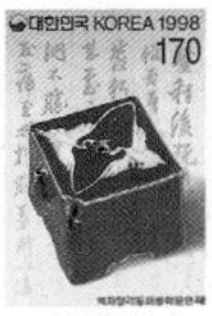

1382 Double Crane

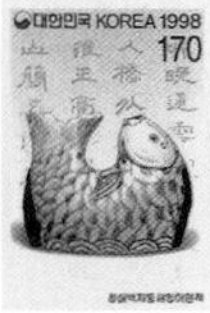

1383 Carp

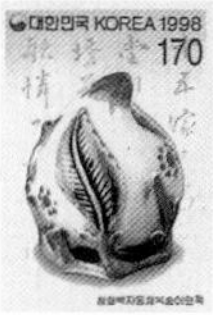

1384 Peach

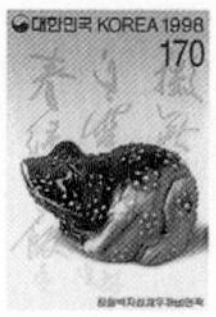

1385 Toad

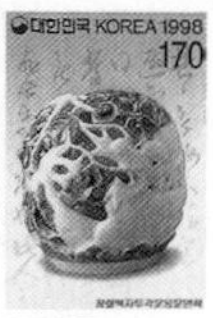

1386 Dragon and Cloud

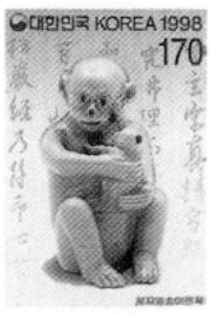

1387 Monkey

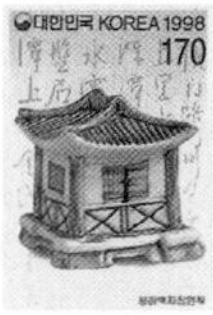

1388 House

1998. Korean Beauty (8th series). Porcelain Water Droppers.

2308	**1381**	170w. multicoloured	1·10	40
2309	**1382**	170w. multicoloured	1·10	40
2310	**1383**	170w. multicoloured	1·10	40
2311	**1384**	170w. multicoloured	1·10	40
2312	**1385**	170w. multicoloured	1·10	40
2313	**1386**	170w. multicoloured	1·10	40
2314	**1387**	170w. multicoloured	1·10	40
2315	**1388**	170w. multicoloured	1·10	40

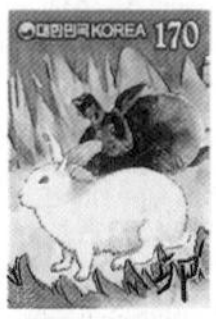

1389 Rabbits

1998. Lunar New Year ("Year of the Rabbit").

2316	**1389**	170w. multicoloured	65	25

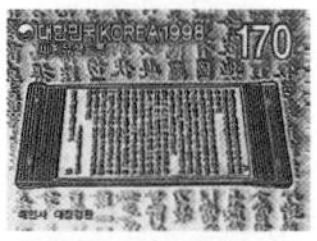

1390 Tripitaka Koreana (scriptures engraved on wooden blocks)

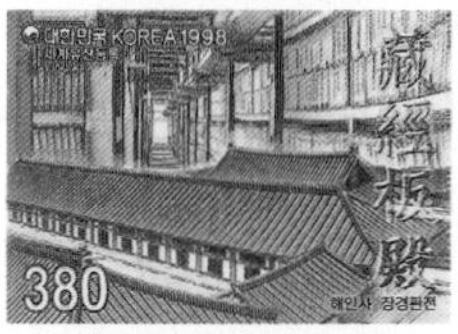

1391 Changgyong P'anjon (woodblock repository)

1998. World Heritage Sites (2nd series). Haein Temple.

2317	**1390**	170w. multicoloured	1·10	55
2318	**1391**	380w. multicoloured	3·25	1·60
MS2319		144×88 mm. Nos. 2317/18	21·00	11·00

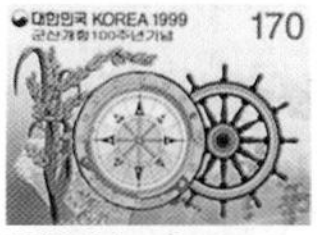

1392 Maize, Compass and Ship's Wheel

1999. Centenary of Kunsan Port.

2320	**1392**	170w. multicoloured	65	30

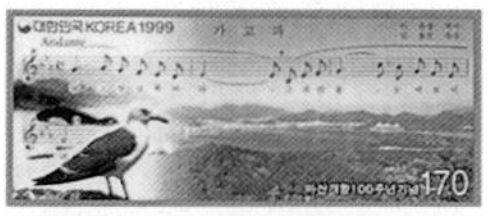

1393 Masan and Score of *I Want to Go* by Lee Eun Sang

1999. Centenary of Masan Port.

2321	**1393**	170w. multicoloured	65	30

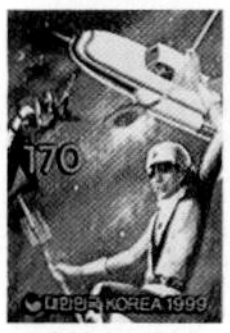

1394 Rai-Fi (Kim San Ho)

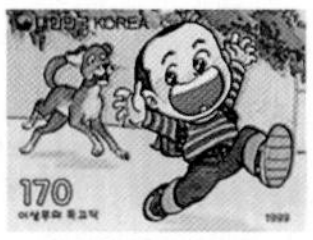

1395 Tokgo T'ak (Lee Sang Mu)

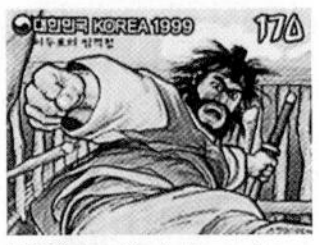

1396 Im Kkuk Jung (Lee Du Ho)

1999. Cartoons (5th series).

2322	**1394**	170w. multicoloured	65	30
2323	**1395**	170w. multicoloured	65	30
2324	**1396**	170w. multicoloured	65	30
MS2325		Three sheets, each 88×58 mm. multicoloured. (a) 340w. Type **1394**; (b) 340w. No. 2323; (c) 340w. No. 2324	6·00	5·75

1999. Protection of Wildlife and Plants (6th series). Vert designs as T **1270**.

2326	170w. Peregrine falcon (*Falco peregrinus*)	1·30	30
2327	170w. Grey frog hawk (*Accipiter soloensis*)	1·30	30
2328	340w. Steller's sea eagle (*Haliaeetus pelagicus*)	2·75	65
2329	340w. Northern eagle owl (*Bubo bubo*)	2·75	65
MS2330	136×133 mm. Nos. 2326/9	8·25	7·75

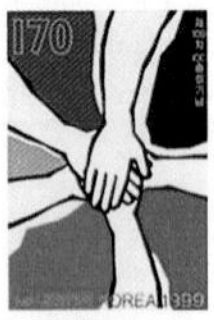

1397 Five clasped Hands

1999. 109th International Olympic Committee Congress, Seoul.

2331	**1397**	170w. multicoloured	65	30

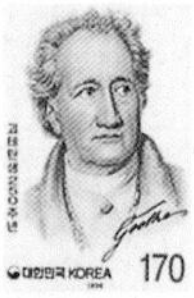

1398 Goethe (after Joseph Stieler)

1999. 250th Birth Anniv of Johann Wolfgang von Goethe (poet and playwright).

2332	**1398**	170w. multicoloured	80	30
MS2333		110×94 mm. **1398** 480w. multicoloured	2·75	2·40

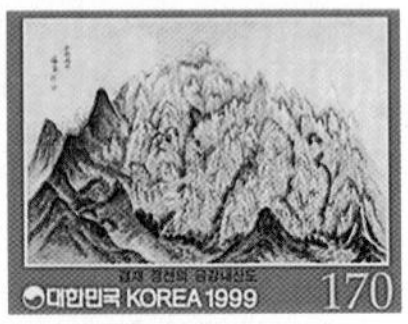

1399 *Kumgang Mountain* (Kyomjae Chong Son)

1999. Philatelic Week.

2334	**1399**	170w. multicoloured	65	30
MS2335		120×90 mm. **1399** 340w. multicoloured	1·70	1·60

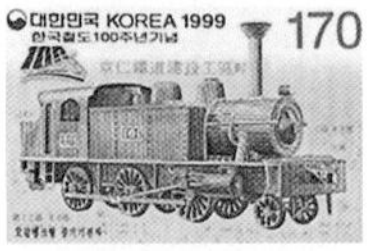

1400 Mogul Tank Locomotive No. 101 (first locomotive in Korea)

1999. Centenary of Railway in Korea.

2336	**1400**	170w. multicoloured	1·00	30

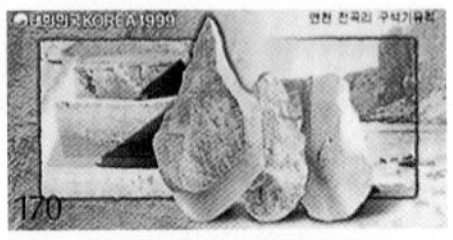

1401 Flint Tools and Paleolithic Ruins, Chungok-ri, Yonch'on

1999. New Millennium (1st series). Multicoloured.

2337	170w. Type **1401**	90	30
2338	170w. Comb-patterned pottery, burnt-out and reconstructed Neolithic dwellings, Amsa-dong, Seoul	90	30
2339	170w. Shell bracelets, bone spear heads and Neolithic shell mounds, Tongsam-dong, Pusan	90	30
2340	170w. Dolmen, Pukon-ri, Kanghwa-do Island	90	30
2341	170w. Bronze and stone daggers and Bronze-age earthenware, Son-gguk-ri, Puyo	90	30
2342	170w. Rock carvings, Pan'gudae	90	30

See also Nos. 2357/62, 2374/8, 2388/92, 2397/2401, 2406/10, 2420/5, 2431/6, 2460/5, 2487/91 and 2511/15.

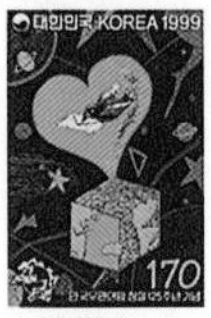

1402 Bird carrying Letter

1999. 125th Anniv of Universal Postal Union.

2343	**1402**	170w. multicoloured	65	30

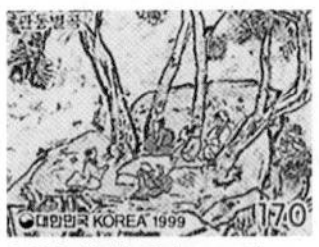

1403 *Little Odes on the Kwandong Area* (Chong Ch'ol)

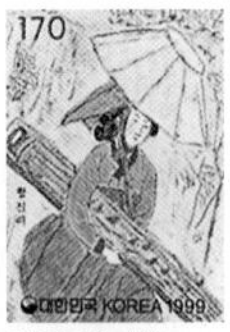

1404 *Alas! How foolish I am!* (Hwang Jin-i)

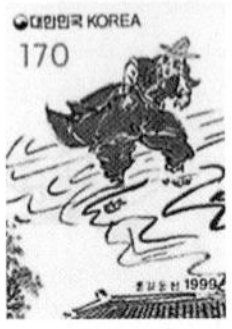

1405 *Story of Hong Kil-dong* (Ho Kyun)

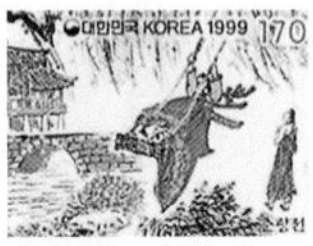

1406 *Story of Ch'unhyang*

1999. Literature (5th series).

2344	**1403**	170w. multicoloured	65	30
2345	**1404**	170w. multicoloured	65	30
2346	**1405**	170w. multicoloured	65	30
2347	**1406**	170w. multicoloured	65	30
MS2348		Four sheets, each 90×60 mm. (a) No. 2344; (b) 90×60 mm. No. 2345; (c) 60×90 mm. No. 2346; (d) 60×90 mm. No. 2347	5·50	5·00

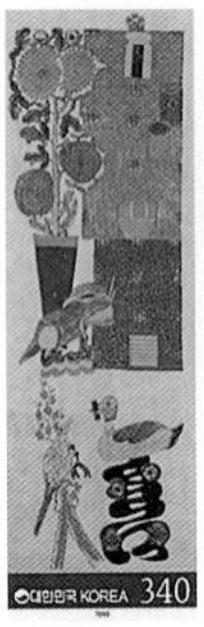

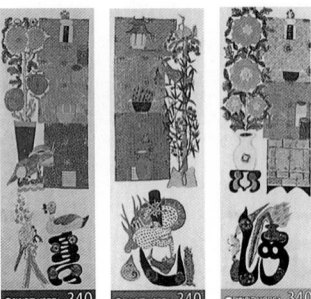

1407 Chrysanthemum, Bird and Duck

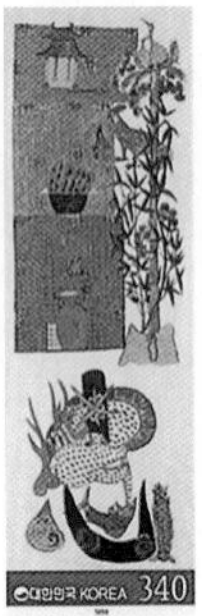

1408 Birds in Tree and Snake on Korean Character

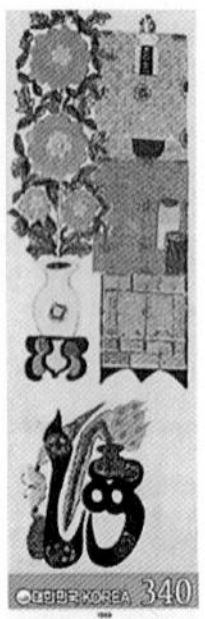

1409 Pot Plant with Butterfly on Korean Character

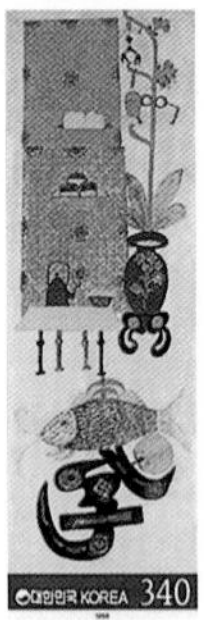

1410 Fish on Korean Character

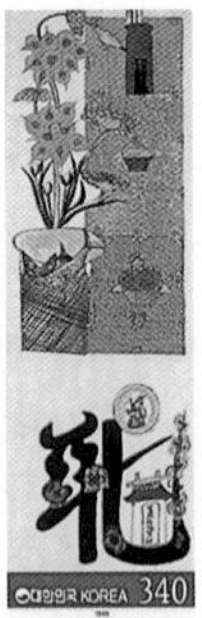

1411 Plant behind Tub of Fishes

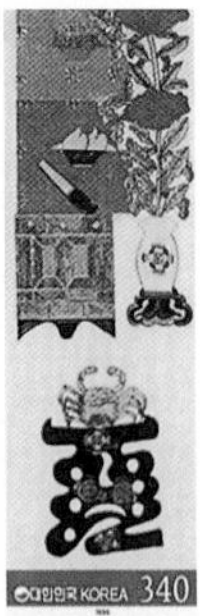

1412 Crab on Korean Character

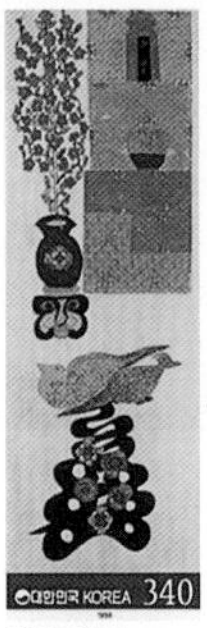

1413 Bird on Korean Character

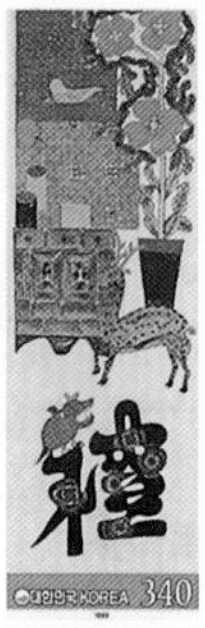

1414 Chest and Plant behind Deer

1999. Korean Beauty (9th series).

2349	**1407**	340w. multicoloured	1·50	65
2350	**1408**	340w. multicoloured	1·50	65
2351	**1409**	340w. multicoloured	1·50	65
2352	**1410**	340w. multicoloured	1·50	65
2353	**1411**	340w. multicoloured	1·50	65
2354	**1412**	340w. multicoloured	1·50	65
2355	**1413**	340w. multicoloured	1·50	65
2356	**1414**	340w. multicoloured	1·50	65

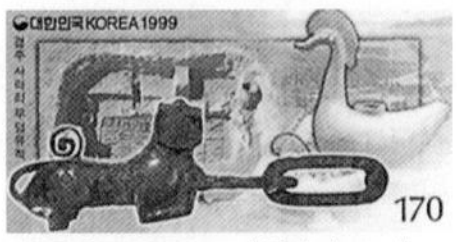

1415 Ornament and Bird-shaped Vase

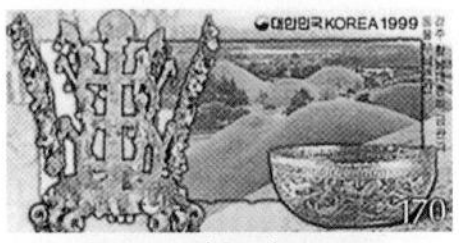

1416 Crown and Bowl

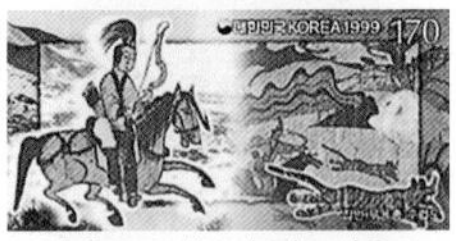

1417 Man on Horseback and Cave Paintings

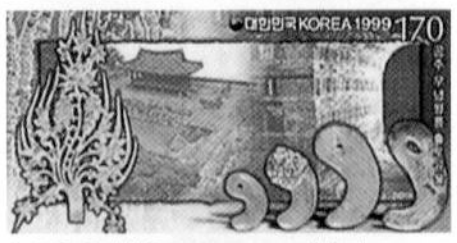

1418 Gold Ornament and Jade Jewellery

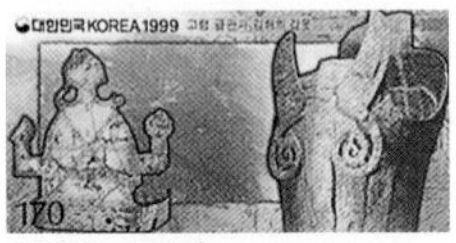

1419 Stone Crafts

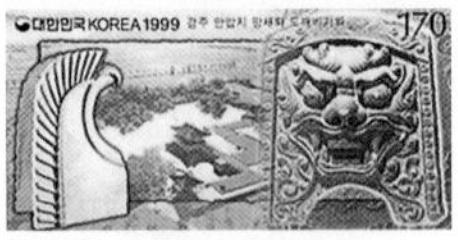

1420 Carved Stone Face

1999. New Millennium (2nd series).

2357	**1415**	170w. multicoloured	80	30
2358	**1416**	170w. multicoloured	80	30
2359	**1417**	170w. multicoloured	80	30
2360	**1418**	170w. multicoloured	80	30
2361	**1419**	170w. multicoloured	80	30
2362	**1420**	170w. multicoloured	80	30

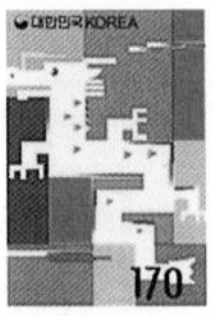

1421 Dragon

1999. Lunar New Year "Year of the Dragon".

2363	**1421**	170w. multicoloured	60	30
MS2364		90×61 mm. No. 2363×2	1·50	1·20

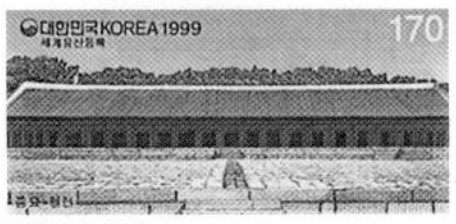

1422 Building

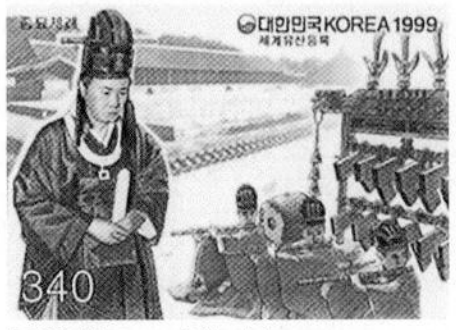

1423 Man and Musicians

1999. World Heritage Sites (3rd series).

2365	**1422**	170w. multicoloured	80	35
2366	**1423**	340w. multicoloured	2·00	70
MS2367		144×96 mm. Nos. 2365/6	11·50	4·50

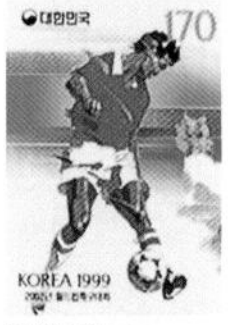

1424 Player

1999. World Cup Football Championship, Japan and Korea (2002). Multicoloured.

2368	170w. Type **1424**	70	35
2369	170w. Players tackling	70	35
2370	170w. Player receiving ball	70	35
2371	170w. Goalkeeper catching ball	70	35
MS2372	134×78 mm. Nos. 2368/71	3·50	3·25

Nos. 2368/71 were issued together, *se-tenant*, forming a composite design.

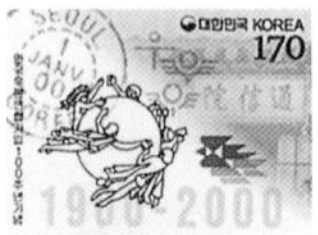

1425 Emblem

2000. Centenary of South Korea's Membership of Universal Postal Union.

2373	**1425**	170w. multicoloured	60	30

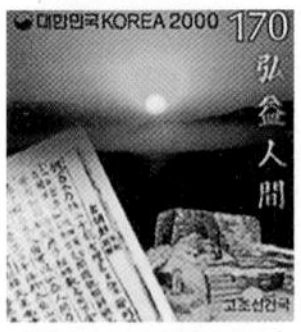

1426 Sunset, Altar and Tablet

2000. New Millennium (3rd series). Multicoloured.

2374	170w. Type **1426**	80	35
2375	170w. Cave painting of wrestlers	80	35
2376	170w. Inscribed bronze disc and warrior	80	35
2377	170w. Silhouettes of archers and inscribed standing stone	80	35
2378	170w. Junk and warrior	80	35

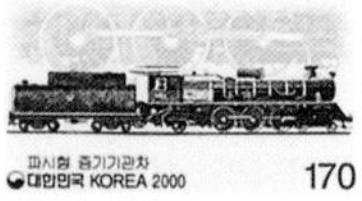

1427 Pashi Steam Locomotive

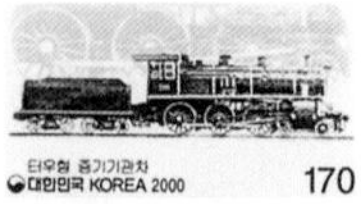

1428 Teho Steam Locomotive

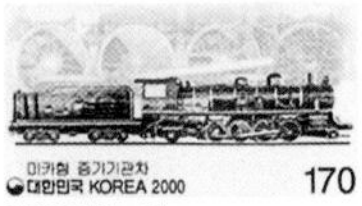

1429 Mika Steam Locomotive

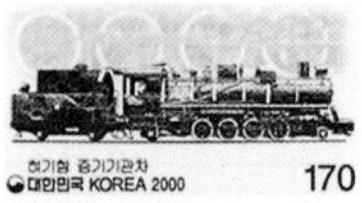

1430 Hyouki Steam Locomotive

2000. Railways (1st series).

2379	**1427**	170w. black, violet and mauve	80	30
2380	**1428**	170w. black, violet and mauve	80	30
2381	**1429**	170w. black, violet and grey	80	30
2382	**1430**	170w. black, violet and bistre	80	30

See also Nos. 2477/80, 2585/8; 2682/5 and 2741/4.

2000. Protection of Wildlife and Plants (7th series). As T **1270**. Multicoloured.

2383 170w. *Lilium cernum* 1·00 30
2384 170w. *Sedirea japonica* 1·00 30
2385 170w. *Hibiscus hamabo* 1·00 30
2386 170w. *Cypripedium japonicum* 1·00 30
MS2387 136×133 mm. Nos. 2383/6 4·25 4·00

Nos. 2383/**MS**2387 are impregnated with scent of flowers.

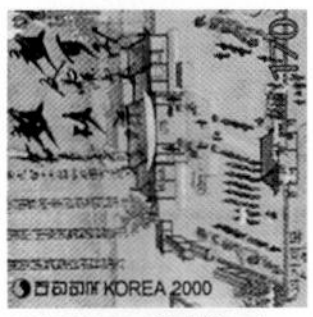

1431 State Civil Service Examination and Text

2000. New Millennium (4th series). Multicoloured.

2388 170w. Type **1431** 80 40
2389 170w. Man carving wood blocks 80 40
2390 170w. Pieces of metal type 80 40
2391 170w. An-Hyang (scholar) and Korean script 80 40
2392 170w. Mun Ik-jom (scholar), spinning wheel and cotton plant 80 40

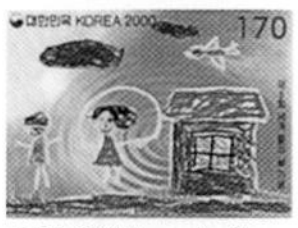

1432 Children playing and House (Kim Chin Sook)

2000. World Water Day. Winning Design in Children's Painting Competition.

2393 **1432** 170w. multicoloured 60 40

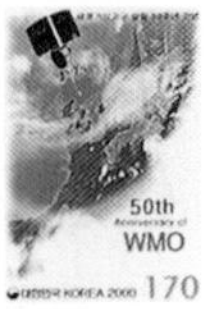

1433 Globe and Satellite

2000. 50th Anniv of World Meteorological Organization.

2394 **1433** 170w. multicoloured 60 40

1434 Hand holding Rose

2000. "Share Love" (good neighbour campaign).

2395 **1434** 170w. multicoloured 1·20 40

No. 2395 is impregnated with the scent of roses.

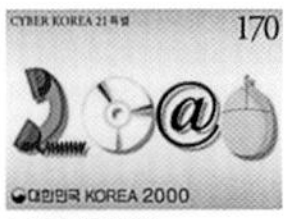

1435 "2000"

2000. "CYBER KOREA 21".

2396 **1435** 170w. multicoloured 60 40

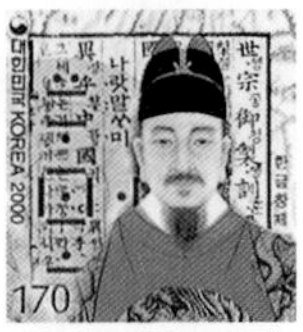

1436 King Sejong and Korean Script

2000. New Millennium (5th series). Multicoloured.

2397 170w. Type **1436** 80 50
2398 170w. Lady Shin Saimdang (calligrapher poet and painter) and detail of *Ch'ochung-do* (painting) 80 50
2399 170w. Yi Hwang and Yi I (founders of Confucian Academy) 80 50
2400 170w. Admiral Yi Sun-shin and model of "turtle" ship 80 50
2401 170w. Sandae-nori (mask-dance drama) 80 50

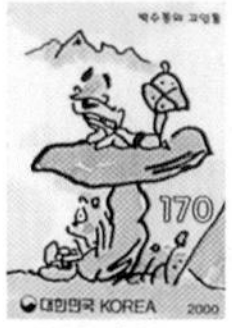

1437 Park Soo Dong

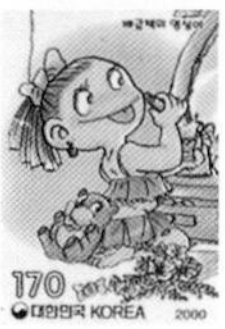

1438 Bae Gum Taek

2000. Cartoons (6th series).

2402 **1437** 170w. multicoloured 60 50
2403 **1438** 170w. multicoloured 60 50
MS2404 Two sheets, each 90×60 mm. (a) No. 2402; (b) No. 2403 1·80 1·60

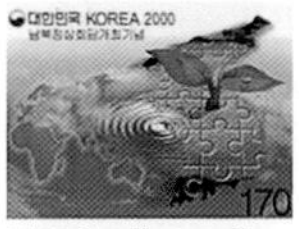

1439 Seedling on Map of Korean Peninsula

2000. Pyongyang, Korean Summit.

2405 **1439** 170w. multicoloured 80 65

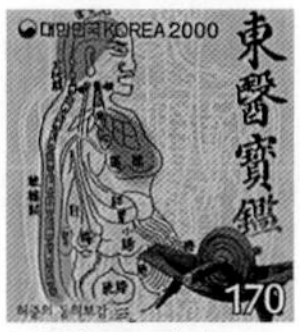

1440 Anatomical Diagram from *Tonui Pogam* (medical treatise by Huh Joan)

2000. Millennium (6th series). Multicoloured.

2406 170w. Type **1440** 80 40
2407 170w. *Dancer with Musicians* (illustration by Kim Hong Do) 80 40
2408 170w. *Plum Blossoms and Bird* (painting, Chong Yak Yong) and house in Kangjin where he served his exile 80 40
2409 170w. Map of Korea by Kim Chong Ho and wheel chart 80 40
2410 170w. Chon Bong Joan (revolutionary) and Tonghak Peasant Uprising monument 80 40

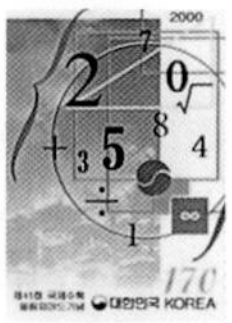

1441 Numbers and Mathematical Symbols

2000. International Mathematical Olympiad (high school mathematics competition).

2411 **1441** 170w. multicoloured 60 40

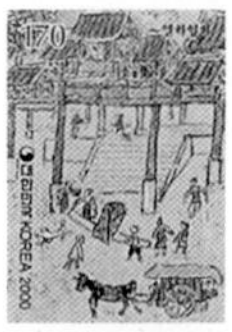

1442 *Yolha Diary* (Park Ji Won)

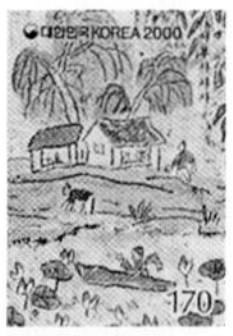

1443 *Fisherman's Calender*

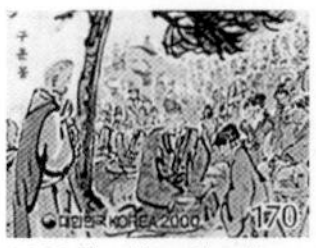

1444 *The Nine-Cloud Dream*

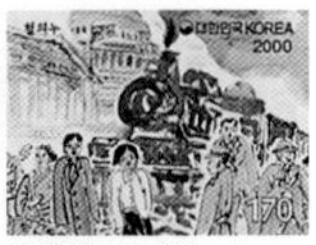

1445 *Tears of Blood*

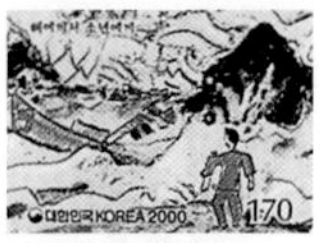

1446 *From the Sea to a Child*

2000. Literature (6th series).

2412 **1442** 170w. multicoloured 70 40
2413 **1443** 170w. multicoloured 70 40
2414 **1444** 170w. multicoloured 70 40
2415 **1445** 170w. multicoloured 70 40
2416 **1446** 170w. multicoloured 70 40
MS2417 Five sheets. (a) 60×90 m. No. 2414; (b) 60×90 mm. No. 2413; (c) 90×60 mm. No. 2414; (d) 90×60 mm. No. 2415; (e) 90×60 mm. No. 2416 5·00 4·50

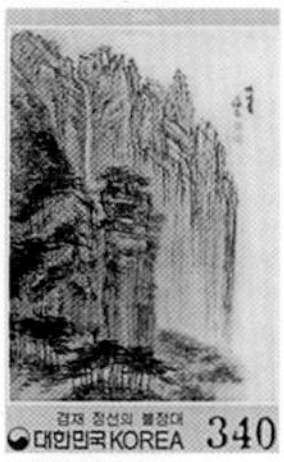

1447 Mountain

2000. Philately Week.

2418 **1447** 340w. multicoloured 1·30 70
MS2419 120×90 mm. No. 2418 1·70 1·50

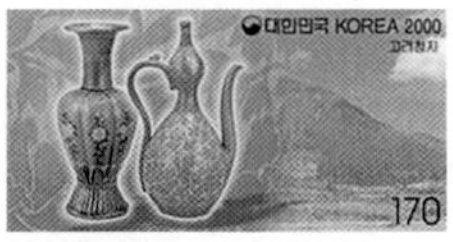

1448 Porcelain

2000. Millennium (7th series). Multicoloured.

2420 170w. Type **1448** 80 40
2421 170w. *Bongjongsa* Temple (Paradise Pavilion) 80 40
2422 170w. Hahoe Tal masks 80 40
2423 170w. Royal Palace 80 40
2424 170w. Landscape painting 80 40
2425 170w. Water clock 80 40

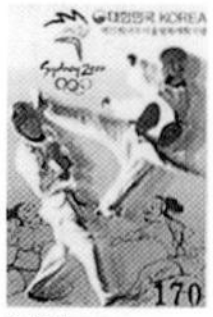

1454 Taekwondo

2000. Olympic Games, Sydney.

2426 **1454** 170w. multicoloured 75 50

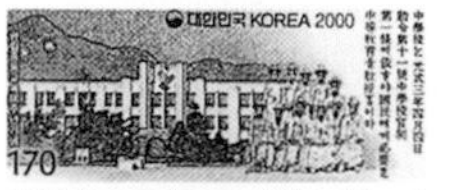

1455 Former Kyunngi High School Building, Hwadong

2000. Centenary of Public Secondary Schools.

2427 **1455** 170w. multicoloured 75 50

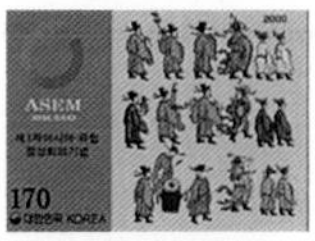

1456 *Returning to the Retirement House* (illustration from *Album of the Gathering of Old Statesmen*)

2000. Third Asia-Europe Meeting, Seoul.

2428 **1456** 170w. multicoloured 75 50

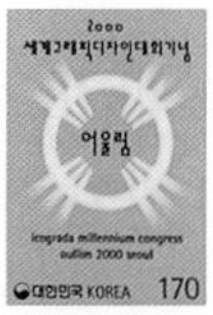

1457 Emblem

2000. Icograde Millennium Congress, Seoul.

2429 **1457** 170w. black and yellow 75 50

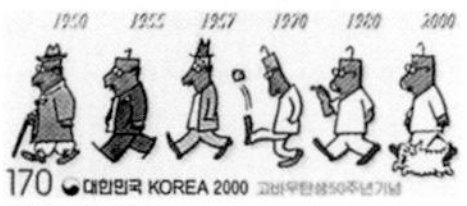

1458 Mr. Gobau

2000. 50th Anniv of Mr. Gobau (cartoon character).

2430 **1458** 170w. multicoloured 75 50

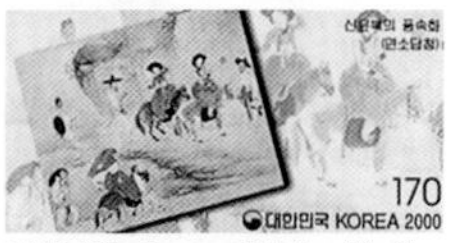

1459 18th-Century Painting (Sin Yun Bok)

2000. Millennium (8th series). Multicoloured.

2431 170w. Type **1459** 80 40
2432 170w. Calligraphy by Kim Jeong Hui 80 40
2433 170w. Bongdon-Chiseong Hwaseong Fortress, Suwon 80 40
2434 170w. Myeongdong Cathedral 80 40
2435 170w. Wongaska theatre actors 80 40
2436 170w. The KITSat-satellite 80 40

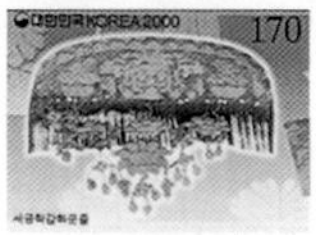

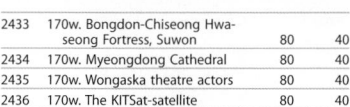

1460 Decorated Comb

2000. Korean Beauty (10th series). Multicoloured.

2437 170w. Type **1460** 75 40
2438 170w. Woman's ceremonial headdress 75 40
2439 170w. Butterfly-shaped hairpin 75 40
2440 170w. Hairpin with dragon decoration and jade hairpin with Chinese phoenix decoration 75 40

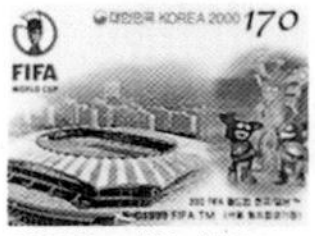

1461 Seoul World Cup Stadium

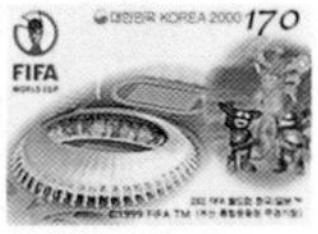

1462 Busan Sports Complex Main Stadium

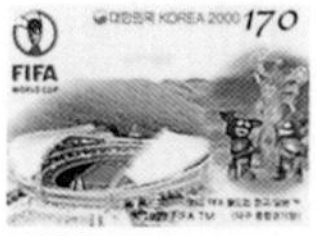

1463 Daegu Sports Complex Stadium

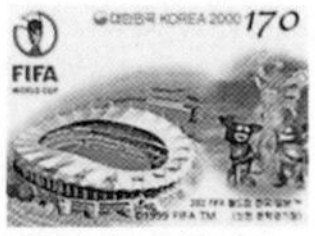

1464 Incheon Munhak Stadium

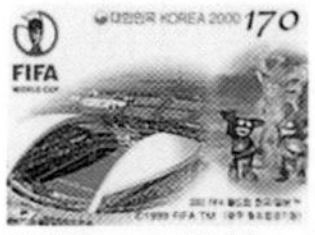

1465 Gwangu World Cup Stadium

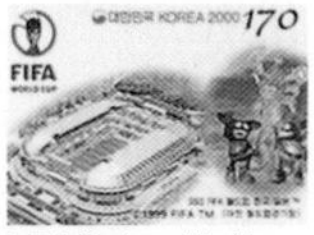

1466 Daejeon World Cup Stadium

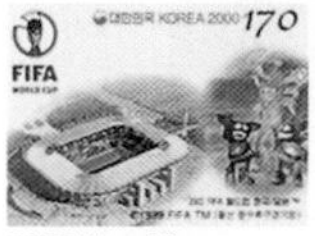

1467 Ulsan Munsu Football Stadium

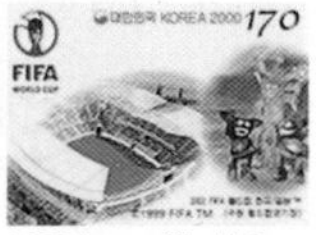

1468 Suwon World Cup Stadium

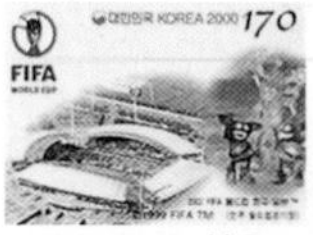

1469 Jeonju World Cup Stadium

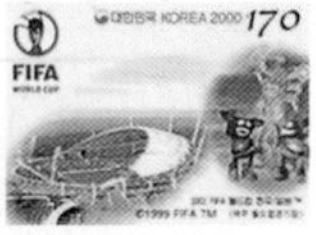

1470 Jeju World Cup Stadium

2000. World Cup Football Championship (2002), South Korea and Japan.

2441 **1461** 170w. multicoloured 1·20 40
2442 **1462** 170w. multicoloured 1·20 40
2443 **1463** 170w. multicoloured 1·20 40
2444 **1464** 170w. multicoloured 1·20 40
2445 **1465** 170w. multicoloured 1·20 40
2446 **1466** 170w. multicoloured 1·20 40
2447 **1467** 170w. multicoloured 1·20 40
2448 **1468** 170w. multicoloured 1·20 40
2449 **1469** 170w. multicoloured 1·20 40
2450 **1470** 170w. multicoloured 1·20 40
MS2451 Five sheets each, 60×90 mm. (a) 170w. No. 2442; (b) 170w. Nos. 2443/4; (c) 170w. Nos. 2445/6; (d) 170w. Nos. 2447/8; (e) 170w. Nos. 2449/50 15·00 14·50

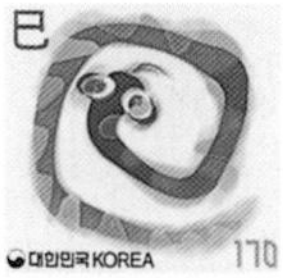

1471 Snake

2000. Lunar New Year "Year of the Snake". Ordinary or self-adhesive gum. (No. 2452).

2452 **1471** 170w. multicoloured 80 40
MS2453 170w. 107×69 mm. No. 2452×3 1·50 1·30

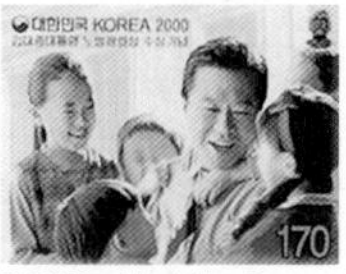

1472 President Kim Dae Jung and Children

2000. Award of Nobel Peace Prize to President Kim Dae Jung.

| 2455 | **1472** | 170w. multicoloured | 80 | 40 |
| MS2456 | 118×70 mm. No. 2455×2 | | 2·50 | 2·20 |

1473 Repository, Jeongjok Mountain and Taejo Sillok (script)

2000. World Heritage Sites (4th series). Multicoloured.

2457	340w. Type **1473**	2·00	1·20
2458	340w. King Sejong and script	2·00	1·20
MS2459	143×89 mm. Nos. 2457/8	5·00	3·00

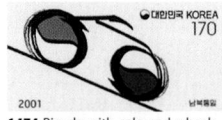

1474 Bicycle with coloured wheels (reunification of Korea)

2001. Millennium (9th series). Multicoloured.

2460	170w. Type **1474**	80	45
2461	170w. Rainbow (environmental protection)	80	45
2462	170w. Human D.N.A. and figure (eradication of incurable diseases)	80	45
2463	170w. Satellite and mobile telephone (communications technology)	80	45
2464	170w. Space (space travel)	80	45
2465	170w. Solar panels, solar-powered car and windmills (alternative energy sources)	80	45

1475 Oksunn Peaks (Kim Hong Do)

2001. Visit Korea Year 2001.

| 2466 | **1475** | 170w. multicoloured | 70 | 40 |

1476 Plough

2001. Agricultural Implements. Multicoloured.

2467	170w. Type **1476**	1·50	40
2468	170w. Harrow	1·50	40
2469	170w. Sowing basket and namtae	1·50	40
2470	170w. Short-handled hoes	1·50	40
2471	170w. Manure barrel and fertilizer ash container	1·50	40
2472	170w. Water dipper	1·50	40
2473	170w. Winnower and thresher	1·50	40
2474	170w. Square straw drying mat and wicker tray	1·50	40
2475	170w. Pestle, mortar and grinding stones	1·50	40
2476	170w. Rice basket and carrier	1·50	40

1486 2000 Series Diesel-electric Locomotive

1487 7000 Series Diesel-electric Locomotive

1488 Diesel Urban Commuter Train

1489 Diesel Saemaul Train

2001. Railways (2nd series).

2477	**1486**	170w. multicoloured	70	45
2478	**1487**	170w. multicoloured	70	45
2479	**1488**	170w. multicoloured	70	45
2480	**1489**	170w. multicoloured	70	45

2001. Protection of Wildlife and Plants (8th series). Vert designs as T **1270**. Multicoloured.

2481	170w. *Jeffersonia dubia*	90	55
2482	170w. *Diapensia lapponica*	90	55
2483	170w. *Rhododendron aureum*	90	55
2484	170w. *Sedum orbiculatum*	90	55
MS2485	170w. 125×108 mm. Nos. 2481/4	3·75	3·50

Nos. 2481/4 are impregnated with the scent of the Ume tree.

1490 Incheon Airport and Emblem

2001. Inauguration of Incheon Airport.

| 2486 | **1490** | 170w. multicoloured | 70 | 40 |

1491 Kim Ku (leader of Independence Movement)

2001. Millennium (10th series). Multicoloured.

2487	170w. Type **1491**	80	40
2488	170w. Statue commemorating the March 1st Independence Movement	80	40
2489	170w. Interim Korean Government Headquarters, Shanghai and Members	80	40
2490	170w. Ahn Ik Tae (composer) and music score	80	40
2491	170w. Yun Dong Ju (poet) and *Seosi* (poem)	80	40

1492 Emblem

2001. International Olympic Fair, Seoul.

| 2492 | **1492** | 170w. multicoloured | 70 | 40 |
| MS2493 | 105×70 mm. No. 2492×2 | | 2·00 | 1·80 |

1493 Bears hugging

2001. Greetings Stamps. Multicoloured.

2494	170w. Type **1493**	2·00	80
2495	170w. Flower	2·00	80
2496	170w. Trumpets (Congratulations)	2·00	80
2497	170w. Cake	2·00	80

1494 Iljimae (Ko Woo Young)   **1495** Kkeobeongi (Kil Chang Duk)

2001. Cartoons (7th series).

2498	**1494**	170w. multicoloured	70	40
2499	**1495**	170w. multicoloured	70	40
MS2500	Two sheets, each 90×60 mm. (a) No. 2498. (b) No. 2499 Price for 2 sheets		2·00	1·80

1496 Players and Mountains (Switzerland, 1954)

2001. World Cup Football Championship, Japan and South Korea. Multicoloured.

2501	170w. Type **1496**	90	40
2502	170w. Players and Ancient settlement (Mexico, 1986)	90	40
2503	170w. Players and Coliseum (Italy, 1990)	90	40
2504	170w. Players and buildings (United States of America, 1994)	90	40
2505	170w. Players and Eiffel Tower (France, 1998)	90	40
MS2506	Five sheets, each 60×90 mm. (a) No. 2501×2. (b) No. 2502×2. (c) No. 2503×2. (d) No. 2504×2. (e) No. 2505×2 Set for 5 sheets		10·00	9·75

1497 Baechu Kimchi (Chinese Cabbage)   **1498** Bossam Kimchi

1499 Dongchimi   **1500** Klakdugi

2001. Korean Foods (1st series).

2507	**1497**	170w. multicoloured	80	40
2508	**1498**	170w. multicoloured	80	40
2509	**1499**	170w. multicoloured	80	40
2510	**1500**	170w. multicoloured	80	40

See also Nos. 2599/2602, 2705/8, 2758/61 and 2810/13.

1501 Raising Flag (Liberation, 1945)

2001. Millennium (11th series). Multicoloured.

2511	170w. Type **1501**	80	40
2512	170w. Soldiers embracing (statue) (Korean War)	80	40
2513	170w. Seoul–Busan Expressway	80	40
2514	170w. Working in fields (Saemaul Undong movement)	80	40
2515	170w. Athletes forming emblem (Olympic Games, Seoul, 1988)	80	40

1502 Red Queen

1503 Pink Lady

2001. "Philakorea 2002" International Stamp Exhibition, Seoul. (1st issue). Roses.

2516	**1502**	170w. multicoloured	70	40
2517	**1503**	170w. multicoloured	70	40
MS2518	Two sheets, each 115×73 mm. (a) No. 2516×2. (b) No. 2517×2 Set for 2 sheets		4·00	3·75

See also Nos. 2604/MS2606 and 2639/MS2640.

1504 Roses in Heart

2001. Philately Week.

| 2519 | **1504** | 170w. multicoloured | 70 | 40 |
| MS2520 | 108×69 mm. No. 2519×2 | | 1·80 | 1·60 |

1505 Goryeo Dynasty Porcelain Vase and Exhibition Emblem

2001. World Ceramics Expo, Icheon, Yeoju, and Gwangju.

| 2521 | **1505** | 170w. multicoloured | 70 | 40 |

1506 Conference Emblem

2001. International Statistical Institute (ISI) Conference, Seoul.

| 2522 | **1506** | 170w. multicoloured | 70 | 40 |

1507 Joseon Coin and Stamping Machine

2001. 50th Anniv of Korea Minting and Security Printing Corporation (KOMSEP).

| 2523 | **1507** | 170w. multicoloured | 70 | 40 |

1508 Multicoloured Ball (Oullim Globe)

2001. International Council of Societies of Industrial Design (ICSID) Conference, Seoul.

| 2524 | **1508** | 170w. multicoloured | 70 | 40 |

1509 Children encircling Globe

2001. United Nations Year of Dialogue among Civilizations.

| 2525 | **1509** | 170w. multicoloured | 70 | 40 |

1510 Conference Emblem

2001. International Organization of Supreme Audit Institutions (INTOSAI) Conference, Seoul.

| 2526 | **1510** | 170w. ultramarine and vermilion | 70 | 40 |

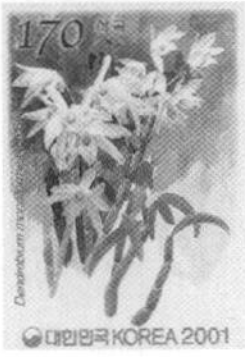

1511 *Dendrobium moniliforme*

2001. Orchids (1st series). Multicoloured.

2527	170w. Type **1511**	80	40
2528	170w. *Gymnadenia camtschatica*	80	40
2529	170w. *Habenaria radiate*	80	40
2530	170w. *Orchis cyclochila*	80	40

Nos. 2527/30 are impregnated with the scent of orchid.
See also Nos. 2670/3; 2727/30 and 2789/92.

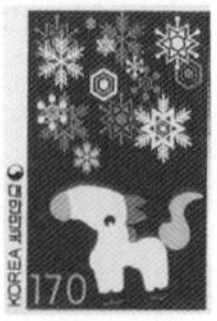

1512 Snowflakes and Horse

2001. New Year. Year of the Horse.

2531	**1512** 170w. multicoloured	70	40
MS2532	90×60 mm. No. 2531×2	1·80	1·60

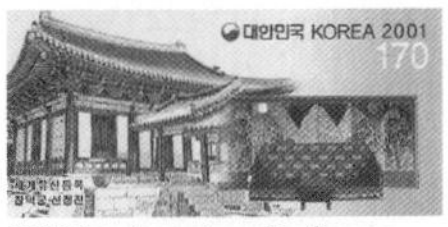

1513 Seonjeongjeon Conference Hall, Changdeok Palace

2001. World Heritage Sites (5th series). Multicoloured.

2533	170w. Type **1513**	1·00	40
2534	340w. Injeongjeon coronation hall, Changdeok Palace (52×36 mm)	2·00	80
MS2535	144×96 mm. Nos. 2533/4	3·75	1·50

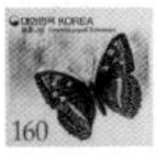

1514 *Limenitis populi*

2002. Fauna.

2536	60w. *Eophona migratoria*	80	40
2546	160w. Type **1514**	80	40
2547	210w. *Falco tinnunculus*	1·10	40
2548	280w. *Ficedula zanthopygia*	1·50	50

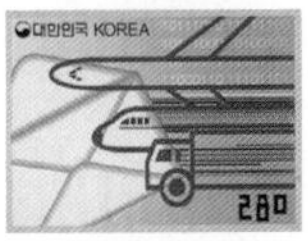

1515 Airplane, Locomotive and Lorry

2002. Transport.

2550	**1515** 280w. multicoloured	1·50	50
2551	**1515** 310w. multicoloured	1·60	55
2551a	**1515** 420w. multicoloured	1·40	95
2552	**1515** 1380w. multicoloured	4·50	2·50
2553	**1515** 1410w. multicoloured	4·75	2·75
2554	**1515** 1580w. multicoloured	5·00	4·00
2555	**1515** 1610w. multicoloured	5·00	4·00

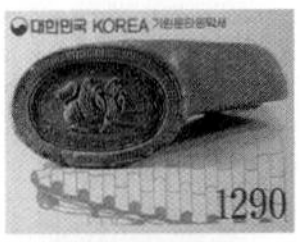

1516 Kylin Roof Tile

2002. Roof Tiles. Multicoloured.

2565	1290w. Type **1516**	4·00	2·50
2566	1310w. Ridge-end tile	4·50	2·75
2567	1490w. As No. 2566 background colour altered	4·50	3·50
2568	1510w. As No. 2565 background colour altered	4·50	3·50

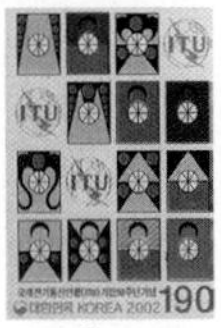

1518 Chungmu (signalling) Kites

2002. 50th Anniv of Membership of International Telecommunications Union.

2584	**1518** 190w. multicoloured	80	40

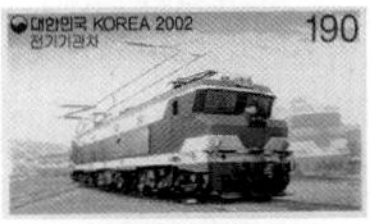

1519 EL8000 Electric Locomotive

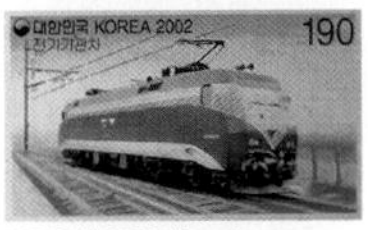

1520 EL8100 Electric Locomotive

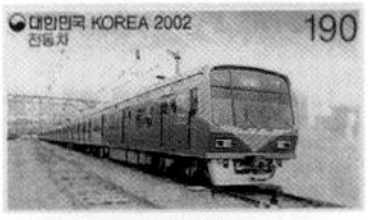

1521 Express Rail Car

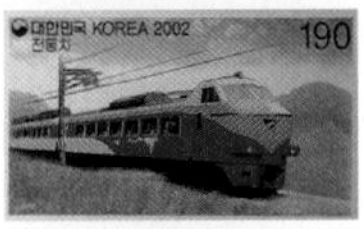

1522 Express Electric Rail Car

2002. Railways (3rd series).

2585	**1519** 190w. multicoloured	80	40
2586	**1520** 190w. multicoloured	80	40
2587	**1521** 190w. multicoloured	80	40
2588	**1522** 190w. multicoloured	80	40

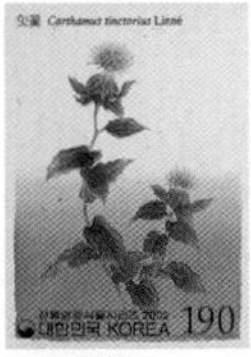

1523 Safflower (*Carthamus tinctorius*)

2002. Traditional Dye Plants (1st series). Multicoloured.

2589	190w. Type **1523**	80	40
2590	190w. *Lithospermum erythrorhizon*	80	40
2591	190w. Ash tree (*Fraxinus rhynchophylla*)	80	40
2592	190w. Indigo plant (*Persicaria tinctoria*)	80	40

See also Nos. 2689/9, 2745/8 and 2801/4.

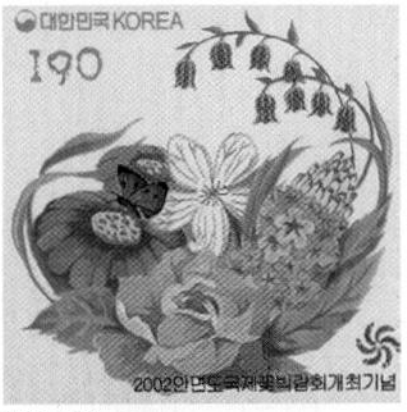

1524 Flowers

2002. International Flower Exhibition, Anmyeondo.

2593	**1524** 190w. multicoloured	50	40

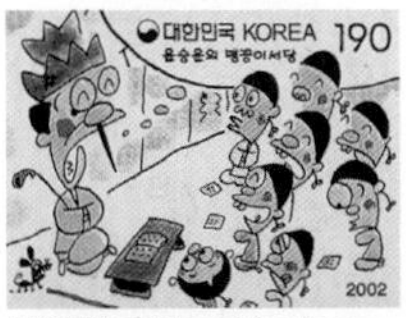

1525 "Mengkkong-i-Seodang Village School" (Yoon Seung-woon)

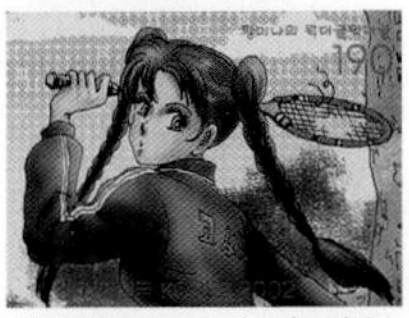

1526 "Wogdoggle Dugdoggle" (Hwang Mi-na)

2002. Cartoons (8th series).

2594	**1525** 190w. multicoloured	80	40
2595	**1526** 190w. multicoloured	80	40
MS2596	Two sheets, each 90×60 mm. (a) No. 2594; (b) No. 2595. Set of 2 sheets	2·40	2·10

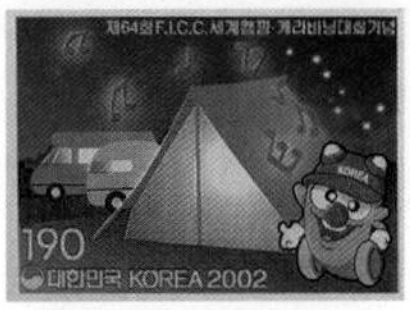

1527 Campervan, Caravan and Tent

2002. 64th International Camping and Caravanning Rally.

2597	**1527** 190w. multicoloured	80	40

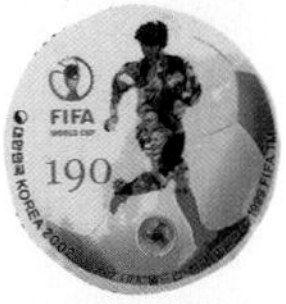

1528 Footballer (Europe)

2002. World Cup Football Championship, Japan and South Korea. Six sheets, each 60×90 mm containing T **1528** and similar circular designs. Multicoloured.

MS2598 (a) 190w.×2, Type **1528**×2; (b) 190w.×2, Central & North America×2; (c) 190w.×2, Asia×2; (d) 190w.×2, South America×2; (e) 190w.×2, Africa×2; (f) 170×240 mm. As Nos. **MS**2598a/e 20·00 20·00

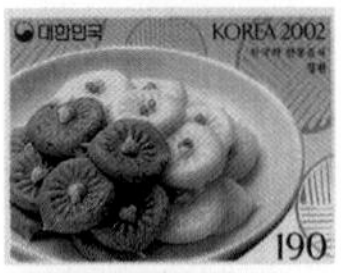

1529 Jeolpyeon

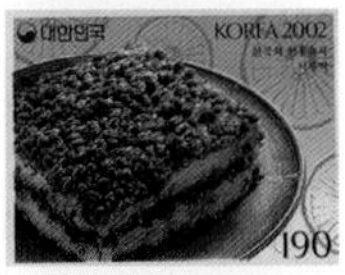

1530 Sirutteok

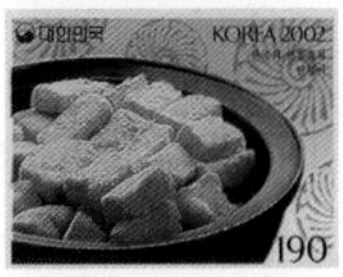

1531 Injeolmi

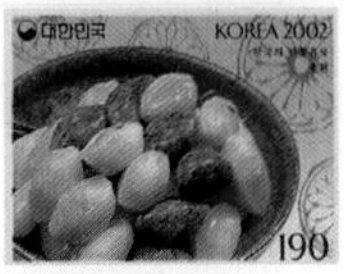

1532 Songpyeon

2002. Korean Foods (2nd series).

2599	**1529** 190w. multicoloured	80	40
2600	**1530** 190w. multicoloured	80	40
2601	**1531** 190w. multicoloured	80	40
2602	**1532** 190w. multicoloured	80	40

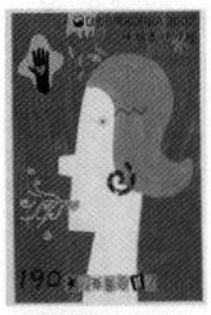

1533 Woman's Face

2002. Women's Week.

2603	**1533** 190w. multicoloured	80	40

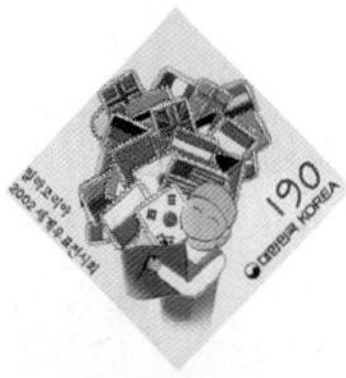

1534 Child holding Flags

2002. Philakorea 2002 International Stamp Exhibition, Seoul (2nd issue). Multicoloured.

2604	190w. Type **1534**	80	40
2605	190w. Children and globe	80	40
MS2606	Two sheets, each 115×73 mm. (a) No. 2604×2; (b) No. 2605. Set of 2 sheets	4·00	3·75

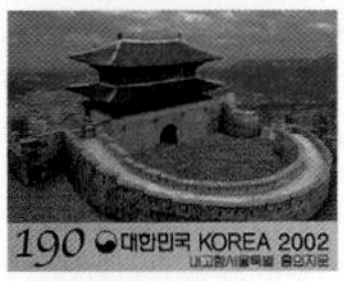

1535 Heung-injimun Fortress, Seoul

2002. Hometowns. Multicoloured.

2607	190w. Type **1535**	90	40
2608	190w. Two masked dancers, Seou	90	40
2609	190w. Basalt cliffs, Incheon	90	40
2610	190w. Dancers wearing white, Chamseongdan altar, Incheon	90	40
2611	190w. Freedom House, Paju, Gyeonggi	90	40
2612	190w. Yangjubyeol Sandaenori dancers one with raised arm, Gyeonggi	90	40
2613	190w. Ulsanbawi rock, Mt. Seoraksan, Gangwon	90	40
2614	190w. Two dancers one holding fan, Gangwon	90	40
2615	190w. Sail boat, Chungnam	90	40
2616	190w. Weaver, Chungnam	90	40
2617	190w. Tower, Expo Science Park, Daejeon	90	40
2618	190w. Scientist, Daedeok Science Town, Daejeon	90	40
2619	190w. Mt. Mai peaks, Jeonbuk	90	40
2620	190w. Iri folk band drummers, Jeonbuk	90	40
2621	190w. Odong island, Jeonnam	90	40
2622	190w. Ganggang Sullae circle dance, Jeonnam	90	40
2623	190w. May 18th monument, Gwangju	90	40
2624	190w. Gossaum Nori tug of war, Gwangju	90	40
2625	190w. Beopju temple, Mt. Songni, Chungbuk	90	40
2626	190w. Taekgyeon martial art, Chungbuk	90	40
2627	190w. Gwangbong Seokjoyeorae statue, Daegu	90	40
2628	190w. Dalseong forest, Daegu	90	40
2629	190w. Taejeondae cliffs, Busan	90	40
2630	190w. Three Dongnaeyaryu festival dancers, Busan	90	40
2631	190w. Dokdo islands, Gyeongbuk	90	40
2632	190w. Andongchajeon Nori log tying game, Gyeongbuk	90	40
2633	190w. Haegeumgang island, Gyeongnam	90	40
2634	190w. Goseong Ogwangdae clown dance, Gyeongnam	90	40
2635	190w. Cheonjeonnigakseok rock wall, Ulsan	90	40
2636	190w. Three Cheoyongmu masked dancers, Ulsan	90	40
2637	190w. Mt. Halla and Baeknokdam crater, Jeju	90	40
2638	190w. House, Jeju	90	40

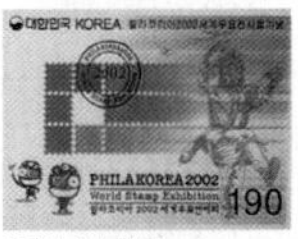

1536 Exhibition Emblem and Talchum Masked Dancer

2002. Philakorea 2002 International Stamp Exhibition, Seoul (3rd issue).

2639	**1536** 190w. multicoloured	80	40
MS2640	90×60 mm. No. 2639×2. Imperf	2·00	1·50

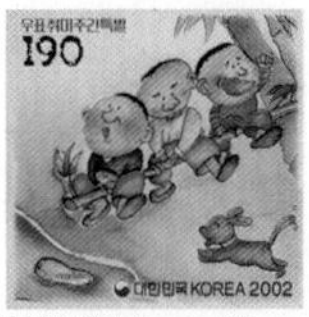

1537 Children and Dog

2002. Philately Week.

2641	**1537** 190w. multicoloured	80	40
MS2642	108×69 mm. Nos. 2641×2	2·00	1·60

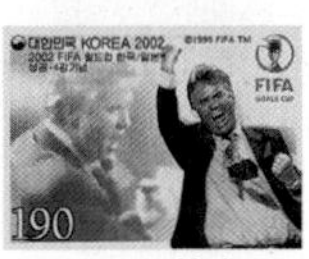

1538 Guus Hiddink (coach)

2002. South Korea—Semi-Finalists, World Cup Football Championship, Japan and South Korea. Showing team members. Multicoloured.

2643	190w. Type **1538**	90	40
2644	190w. No. 1 player	90	40
2645	190w. No. 2	90	40
2646	190w. No. 3	90	40
2647	190w. No. 4	90	40
2648	190w. No. 5	90	40
2649	190w. No. 6	90	40
2650	190w. No. 7	90	40
2651	190w. No. 8	90	40
2652	190w. No. 9	90	40
2653	190w. No. 10	90	40
2654	190w. No. 11	90	40
2655	190w. Goalkeeper	90	40
2656	190w. No. 13	90	40
2657	190w. No. 14	90	40
2658	190w. No. 15	90	40
2659	190w. No. 16	90	40
2660	190w. No. 17	90	40
2661	190w. No. 18	90	40
2662	190w. No. 19	90	40
2663	190w. No. 20	90	40
2664	190w. No. 21	90	40
2665	190w. No. 22	90	40
2666	190w. Goalkeeper (different)	90	40

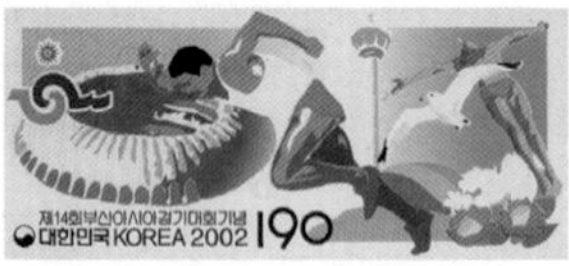

1539 Stadium, Runner, Tower, Seagull and Diver

2002. 14th Asian Games, Busan.

2667	**1539** 190w. multicoloured	80	40
MS2668	120×70 mm. No. 2667×2	2·00	1·80

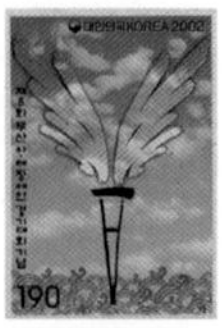

1540 Stylized Torch

2002. Eighth Far East and South Pacific Games for the Disabled (FESPIC), Busan.

2669	**1540** 190w. multicoloured	80	40

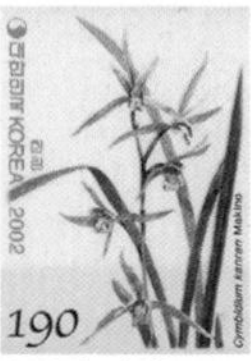

1541 *Cymbidium kanran*

2002. Orchids (2nd series). Multicoloured.

2670	190w. Type **1541**	80	40
2671	190w. *Gastrodia elata*	80	40
2672	190w. *Pogonia japonica*	80	40
2673	190w. *Cephalanthera falcate*	80	40

Each stamp impregnated with the scent of orchid.

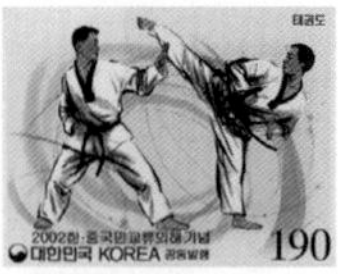

1542 Taekwondo

2002. Tenth Anniv of South Korea—China Diplomatic Relations. Martial Arts. Multicoloured.

2674	190w. Type **1542**	80	40
2675	190w. Wushu	80	40

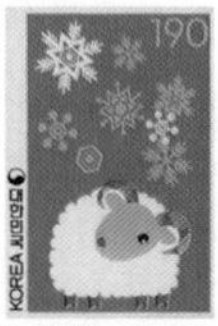

1543 Sheep

2002. New Year. "Year of the Sheep".

2676	**1543** 190w. multicoloured	80	40
MS2677	90×60 mm. No. 2676×2	1·80	1·60

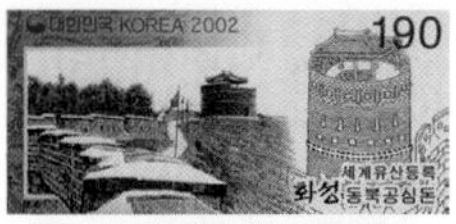

1544 Gongsimdon Observatory Tower

2002. Hwaseong Fortress—UNESCO World Heritage Site. Sheet 145×232 mm containing T **1544** and similar horiz design. Multicoloured.

MS2678	190w.×5 Type **1544**; 280w. Banghwasuryu Pavilion (52×36 mm)	10·00	9·75

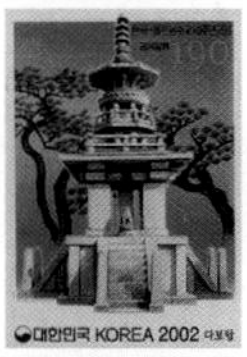

1545 Dabo Pagoda, Bulguk Temple, Gyeongju

2002. Tenth Anniv of South Korea—Vietnam Diplomatic Relations. Multicoloured.

2679	190w. Type **1545**	80	40
2680	190w. One Pillar Pagoda, Hanoi	80	40

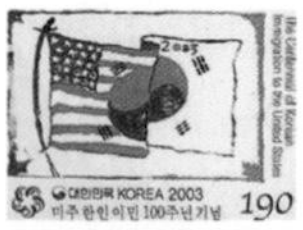

1546 American and Korean Flags Combined

2003. Centenary of Korean Emigration to United States of America.

2681	**1546** 190w. multicoloured	80	40

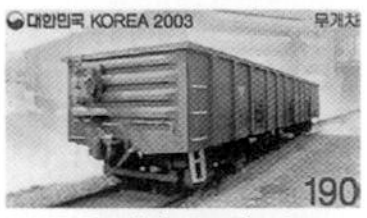

1547 Gondola Freight Car

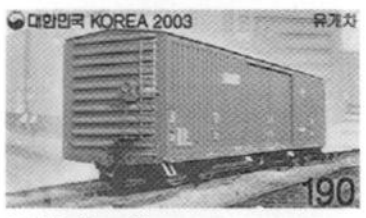

1548 Box Car

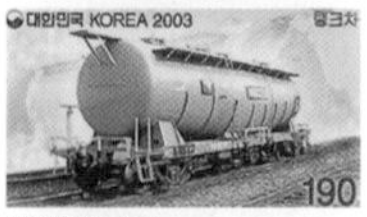

1549 Tanker

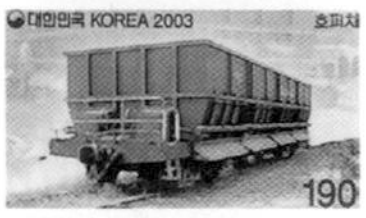

1550 Hopper

2003. Railways (4th series).

2682	**1547** 190w. multicoloured	80	40
2683	**1548** 190w. multicoloured	80	40
2684	**1549** 190w. multicoloured	80	40
2685	**1550** 190w. multicoloured	80	40

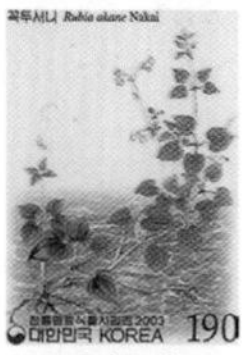

1551 *Rubia akane*

2003. Traditional Dye Plants (2nd series). Multicoloured.

2686	190w. Type **1551**	80	40
2687	190w. *Rhus javanica*	80	40
2688	190w. *Sophora japonica*	80	40
2689	190w. *Isatis tinctoria*	80	40

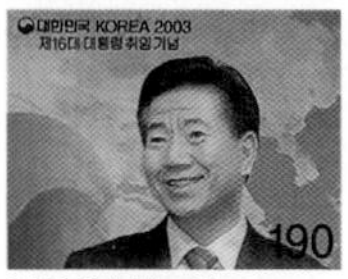

1552 Roh Moo Hyun

2003. Inauguration of President Roh Moo Hyun. Sheet 115×70 mm.

2689a	**1522** 190w. multicoloured	80	40
MS2690	190w. multicoloured	2·00	1·80

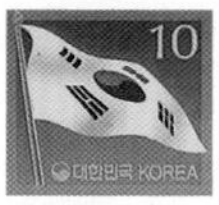

1553 Flag

2003

2691	**1553** 10w. multicoloured	20	10

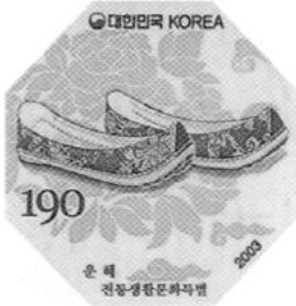

1554 Unhye (embroidered shoes)

2003. Traditional Culture (1st issue). Each chocolate, brown and indigo.

2692	190w. Type **1554**	80	40
2693	190w. Mokhwa (ankle boots)	80	40
2694	190w. Jipsin (straw shoes)	80	40
2695	190w. Namaksin (wooden clogs)	80	40

See also Nos. 2700/3, 2712/15; 2720/3; 2762/5 and 2771/4.

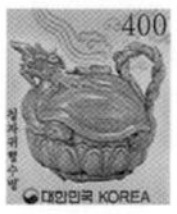

1555 Tortoise-shaped Celadon Jug

2003

2696	**1555** 400w. multicoloured	1·20	95

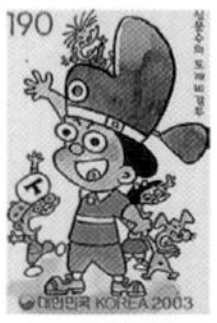

1556 "Goblin's Cap" (Shin Moon Soo)

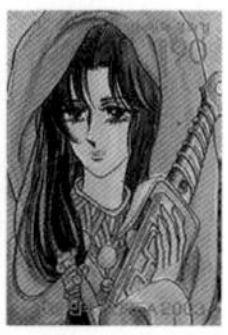

1557 "Sword of Fire" (Kim Hye Rin)

2003. Cartoons (9th series).

2697	**1556** 190w. multicoloured	80	40
2698	**1557** 190w. multicoloured	80	40
MS2699	Two sheets, each 90×60 mm. (a) No. 2697; (b) No. 2698 Set of 2 sheets	3·00	2·75

2003. Traditional Culture (2nd issue). As T **1554**. Each black and brown.

2700	190w. Eoyeon (royal sedan chair)	80	40
2701	190w. Choheon (single-wheeled sedan chair)	80	40
2702	190w. Saingyo (wedding sedan chair)	80	40
2703	190w. Namyeo (small open sedan chair)	80	40

Nos. 2700/3 were issued in horizontal *se-tenant* strips of four stamps within the sheet.

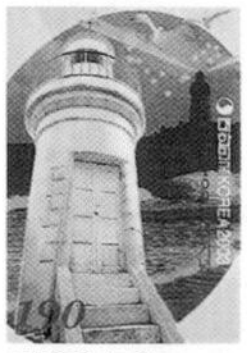

1558 Palmido Lighthouse

2003. Centenary of Lighthouse Building.

2704	**1558** 190w. multicoloured	80	40

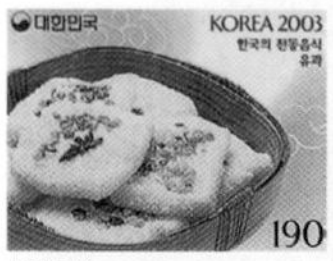

1559 Yugwa

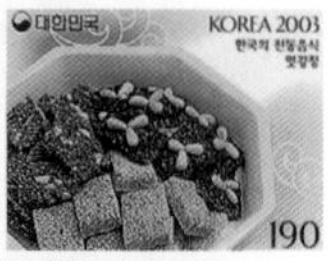

1560 Yeot Gangjeong

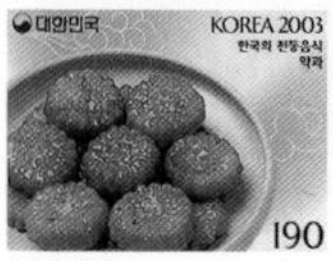

1561 Yakgwa

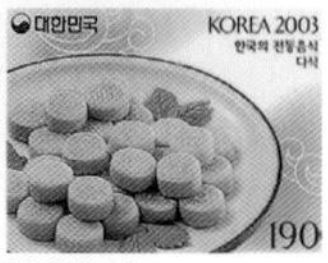

1562 Dasik

2003. Korean Foods (3rd series).

2705	**1559** 190w. multicoloured	80	40
2706	**1560** 190w. multicoloured	80	40
2707	**1561** 190w. multicoloured	80	40
2708	**1562** 190w. multicoloured	80	40

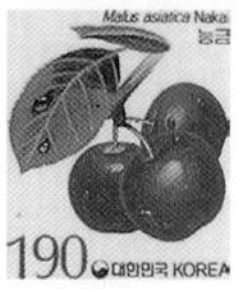

1563 *Malus asiatica*

2003. Fruit and Flower. Multicoloured. Self-adhesive.

2709	190w. Type **1563**	1·00	40
2710	190w. *Aquilegia flabellate* (horiz)	1·00	40

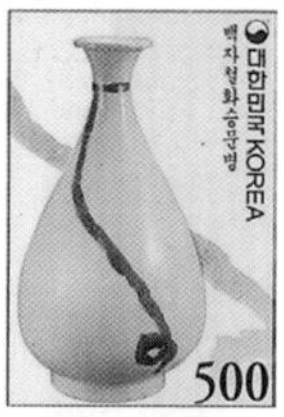

1564 Porcelain Vase

2003

2711	**1564** 500w. multicoloured	1·60	1·10

2003. Traditional Culture (3rd issue). As T **1554**. Each agate and chocolate.

2712	190w. Jojokdeung lantern	80	40
2713	190w. Deungjan (lamp-oil container)	80	40
2714	190w. Juchilmokje yukgakje-deung (hexagonal portable lantern)	80	40
2715	190w. Chot-dae (brass candlestick)	80	40

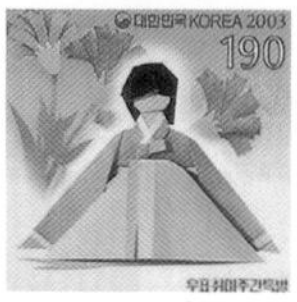

1565 Origami figure ("Expression of Gratitude")

2003. Philately Week.

2716	**1565** 190w. multicoloured	80	40
MS2717	109×69 mm. Nos. 2716×2 Imperf	2·00	1·80

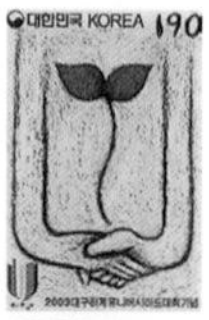

1566 Leaves and Clasped Hands

2003. Summer Universiade (games), Daegu.

2718	**1566** 190w. multicoloured	80	40
MS2719	91×60 mm. Nos. 2718×2	1·80	1·60

2003. Traditional Culture (4th issue). As T **1554**. Each indigo and claret.

2720	190w. Gujok-ban (table with decorated top)	80	40
2721	190w. Punghyeol-ban (tray table)	80	40
2722	190w. Ilju-ban (single stemmed table)	80	40
2723	190w. Haeju-ban (straight-sided table)	80	40

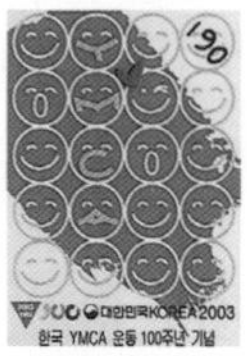

1567 Faces

2003. Centenary of Korean YMCA (Young Men's Christian Association) Movement.

2724	**1567** 190w. multicoloured	80	40

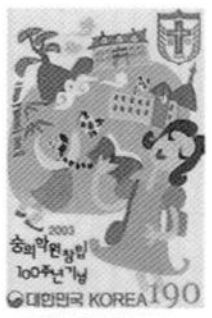

1568 Stylised Teacher and Pupil

2003. Centenary of Soong Eui Girl's School.

| 2725 | 1568 | 190w. multicoloured | 80 | 40 |

1569 Hearts as TB Symbol

2003. 50th Anniv of National Tuberculosis Association.

| 2726 | 1569 | 190w. vermilion, ultramarine and grey | 80 | 40 |

1570 Cremastra appendiculata

2003. Orchids (3rd series). Multicoloured.

2727		190w. Type 1570	80	40
2728		190w. Cymbidium lancifolium	80	40
2729		190w. Orchis graminifolia	80	40
2730		190w. Bulbophyllum drymoglossum	80	40

Each stamp is impregnated with the scent of orchid.

1571 Monkey

2003. New Year. "Year of the Monkey".

| 2731 | 1571 | 190w. multicoloured | 80 | 40 |
| MS2732 | 90×60 mm. No. 2731×2 | | 1·80 | 1·60 |

1572 Dolmen, Ganghwa

2002. Ganghwa, Hwasoon and Gochang—UNESCO World Heritage Sites. Sheet 145×232 mm containing T **1572** and similar horiz design. Multicoloured.

MS2733 190w.×5 Type **1572**; 280w.
Dolmen (52×36 mm) .... 10·00 ... 9·75

1573 Cheomseongdae, Gyeongju

2003. 30th Anniv of South Korea—India Diplomatic Relations. Observatories. Multicoloured.

| 2734 | | 190w. Type 1573 | 80 | 40 |
| 2735 | | 190w. Jantar Mantar, Jaipur | 80 | 40 |

1574 Calystegia soldanella

2004. Dokdo Island. Multicoloured.

2736		190w. Type 1574	60	40
2737		190w. Aster spathulifolius	60	40
2738		190w. Calonectris leucomelas (inscr "laucomelas")	60	40
2739		190w. Larus crassirostris	60	40

Nos. 2736/9 were issued together, se-tenant, forming a composite design.

1575 Emblems

2004. 50th Anniv of National UNESCO Commission.

| 2740 | 1575 | 190w. multicoloured | 60 | 40 |

1576 Multiple Tie Tamper

1577 Ballast Regulator

1578 Track Inspection Car

1579 Ballast Cleaner

2004. Railways (5th series).

2741	1576	190w. multicoloured	60	40
2742	1577	190w. multicoloured	60	40
2743	1578	190w. multicoloured	60	40
2744	1579	190w. multicoloured	60	40

1580 Juglans regia

2004. Traditional Dye Plants (3rd series). Multicoloured.

2745		190w. Type 1580	60	40
2746		190w. Acer ginnala	60	40
2747		190w. Pinus densiflora	60	40
2748		190w. Punica granatum	60	40

1581 Heart enclosing Water Droplet

2004. International Water Day.

| 2749 | 1581 | 190w. multicoloured | 60 | 40 |

1582 Satellite, Dish and Weather Symbols

2004. Centenary of Meteorological Service.

| 2750 | 1582 | 190w. multicoloured | 60 | 40 |

1583 Locomotive

2004. Inauguration of High Speed Trains.

| 2751 | 1583 | 190w. multicoloured | 60 | 40 |

1584 Space Exploration (Radhika Kakrania)

2004. Science Day. Winning Entries in International Stamp Design Competition. Multicoloured.

| 2752 | | 190w. Type 1584 | 60 | 40 |

2753 | | 190w. Mysteries of Life (Kim dong-min) (vert) | 60 | 40 |

1585 "Wicked Boy Simsultong" (Lee Jeong-moon)

1586 "Nation of Winds" (Kim Jin)

2004. Cartoons (10th series).

| 2754 | 1585 | 190w. multicoloured | 60 | 40 |
| 2755 | 1586 | 190w. multicoloured | 60 | 40 |

MS2756 Two sheets, each 90×60 mm.
(a) No. 2754; (b) No. 2755 .... 1·20 ... 1·10

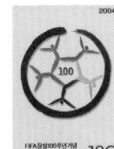

1587 Emblem

2004. Centenary of FIFA (Federation Internationale de Football).

| 2757 | 1587 | 190w. multicoloured | 60 | 40 |

1588 Gujeolpan

1589 Hwayangjeok

1590 Bibimbap

1591 Sinsello

2004. Korean Foods (4th series).

2758	1588	190w. multicoloured	60	40
2759	1589	190w. multicoloured	60	40
2760	1590	190w. multicoloured	60	40
2761	1591	190w. multicoloured	60	40

2004. Traditional Culture (5th issue). As T **1554**. Each purple and green.

2762		190w. Work box	60	40
2763		190w. Thimble	60	40
2764		190w. Bobbin	60	40
2765		190w. Needle case	60	40

1592 Symbols of Science

1593 Symbols of Art

2004. 50th Anniv of National Academies of Science and Art.

| 2766 | 1592 | 190w. multicoloured | 60 | 40 |
| 2767 | 1593 | 190w. multicoloured | 60 | 40 |

Nos. 2766/7 were issued together, se-tenant, forming a composite design.

1594 Animals Celebrating

2004. Philately Week.

| 2768 | 1594 | 190w. multicoloured | 60 | 40 |
| MS2769 | 109×69 mm. Nos. 2768×2 | | 1·00 | 95 |

1595 Acropolis

2004. Olympic Games, Athens.

| 2770 | 1595 | 190w. multicoloured | 60 | 40 |

2004. Traditional Culture (6th issue). As T **1554**. Each maroon and blue.

2771		190w. Golden crown	60	40
2772		190w. Bamboo hat	60	40
2773		190w. Gauze hat	60	40
2774		190w. Horsehair hat	60	40

1596 Geumcheongyo Bridge

1596a Jeongotgyo

1596b Jincheon Nongdari

1596c Seungseongyo

2004. Bridges (1st series).

2775	1596	190w. multicoloured	60	40
2776	1596a	190w. multicoloured	60	40
2777	1596b	190w. multicoloured	60	40
2778	1596c	190w. multicoloured	60	40

See also Nos. 2826/9.

1597 Emblem

2004. International Council of Museums (ICOM) Conference, Seoul.

| 2779 | 1597 | 190w. multicoloured | 60 | 40 |

1598 Obaegnahan Mountain

1598a Seonjakjiwat

1598b Baengnokdam

1598c Oreum

2004. Mountains (1st series).

2780	**1598**	190w. multicoloured	60	40
2781	**1598a**	190w. multicoloured	60	40
2782	**1598b**	190w. multicoloured	60	40
2783	**1598c**	190w. multicoloured	60	40

See also Nos. 2830/3.

1599 White Hibiscus

2004. *Hibiscus syriacus.*

2784	190w. Type **1599**	50	40
2785	220w. Three white blooms and two buds	60	50
2786	240w. Red hibiscus	65	50
2787	310w. Five red blooms	80	65

1600 White Porcelain with Iron-painted Plum and Bamboo Design

2004

2788	**1600**	1520w. multicoloured	5·50	4·50

1601 *Goodyera maximowicziana*

2004. Orchids (4th series). Multicoloured.

2789	190w. Type **1601**	60	50
2790	190w. *Sarcanthus scolpendrifolius*	60	50
2791	190w. *Calanthe sieboldii*	60	50
2792	190w. *Bletilla striata*	60	50

Nos. 2789/92 are impregnated with the scent of orchid.

1602 Hen and Chicks

2004. New Year. "Year of the Rooster". Multicoloured.
MS2793 90×60 mm. 220w.×2, Type

1602×2	1·20	1·00

1603 Daeneungwon Tumuli Park

2004. Gyenongju—UNESCO World Heritage Site. Sheet 145×232 mm containing T **1603** and similar horiz design. Multicoloured.
MS2794 310w.×10 Type **1603**×5;

Anapji×5 (each, 52×36 mm)	8·00	7·25

1604 *Girella punctata*

2005. Marado Island. Multicoloured.

2795	190w. Type **1604**	60	50
2796	190w. *Epinephelus septemfasciatus*	60	50
2797	190w. *Chromis notata*	60	50
2798	190w. *Sebastiscus marmoratus*	60	50

Nos. 2795/6 were issued together, *se-tenant*, forming composite design.

1605 Cells and Wheelchair User

2005. Stem Cell Research.

2799	**1605**	220w. multicoloured	70	50

1606 Emblem, Heart and Flying Figure

2005. Centenary of Rotary International.

2800	**1606**	220w. multicoloured	70	50

1607 *Clerodendron trichotomum*

2005. Traditional Dye Plants (4th series). Multicoloured.

2801	220w. Type **1607**	70	50
2802	220w. *Gardenia jasminoides*	70	50
2803	220w. *Taxus cuspidate*	70	50
2804	220w. *Smilax china*	70	50

1608 Vase, Mask and Dove

2005. Tourism. Visit Gyeonggi.

2805	**1608**	220w. multicoloured	70	50

1609 Children

2005. 50th Anniv of Information and Communication Day. Multicoloured.

2806	220w. Type **1609**	70	50
2807	220w. Boy, computer screen and sheep (vert)	70	50

1610 Inchon Memorial Hall

2005. Centenary of Korea University.

2808	**1610**	220w. agate, silver and magenta	70	50

1611 *Eschrichtius robustus*

2005. International Whaling Commission Meeting, Ulsan.

2809	**1611**	220w. multicolourd	70	50

1612 Hwajeon (pan-fried rice with flower petals) / **1613** Bindaetteok (pan-fried ground mung beans)

1614 Jeongol (casserole) / **1615** Neobani (boiled beef)

2005. Korean Foods (5th series).

2810	**1612**	220w. multicoloured	70	50
2811	**1613**	220w. multicoloured	70	50
2812	**1614**	220w. multicoloured	70	50
2813	**1615**	220w. multicoloured	70	50

1616 Ancient Sword and Armoured Mounted Soldier

2005. Goguryeo (1st issue). Multicoloured.

2814	310w. Type **1616**	80	65
2815	310w. Oneyo fortress	80	65

See also Nos. 2869/70.

1617 Girl icing Birthday Cake

2005. Philately Week.

2817	**1617**	220w. multicoloured	70	50

1618 Buncheong Jar

2005

2818	**1618**	1720w. multicoloured	6·00	5·75

1619 Provisional Government Building and Charter

2005. 60th Anniv of Liberation. Multicoloured.

2819	480w. Type **1619**	1·00	80
2820	520w. Declaration of Independence	1·20	95
2821	580w. Freedom fighters taking oath of allegiance	1·40	1·10
2822	600w. Anniversary emblem	1·50	1·20

1620 Colours and Hand holding Cutlery

2005. Fusion Culture.

2824	**1620**	220w. multicoloured	70	50

1621 *Strix aluco*

2005

2825	**1621**	50w. multicoloured	50	40

1622 Hangang Bridge

1623 Expogyo Bridge

1624 Tongyeong Bridge

1625 Banghwa Bridge

2005. Bridges (2nd series).

2826	**1622**	220w. multicoloured	80	65
2827	**1623**	220w. multicoloured	80	65
2828	**1624**	220w. multicoloured	80	65
2829	**1625**	220w. multicoloured	80	65

1626 Cheonwangbong Peak / **1627** Baraebong Peak

1628 Ikki Falls

1629 Piagol Valley

2005. Mountains (2nd series). Mount Jirisan.

2830	**1626**	220w. multicoloured	80	65
2831	**1627**	220w. multicoloured	80	65
2832	**1628**	220w. multicoloured	80	65
2833	**1629**	220w. multicoloured	80	65

1630 Emblem

2005. Centenary of Korean Red Cross.

2834	**1630**	220w. multicoloured	80	65

1631 Buddha

2005. Relocation and Reopening of National Museum.

2835	**1631**	220w. multicoloured	80	65

1632 *Epipactis thunbergii*

2005. Orchids (5th series). Multicoloured.

2836	220w. Type **1632**	80	65
2837	220w. *Cymbidium goeringii*	80	65
2838	220w. *Cephalanthera erecta*	80	65
2839	220w. *Spiranthes sinensis*	80	65

1633 Nurimaru APEC House, Dongbaek Island

2005. APEC Economic Leaders' Meeting, Busan. Multicoloured.

2840	220w. Type **1633**	80	65
2841	220w. *The Sun, the Moon and Five Peaks* (traditional painting)	80	65

1634 Puppy

2005. New Year. Year of the Dog.

2842	**1634**	220w. multicoloured	80	65

1635 *Jikjisimcheyojeol* (oldest book created using moveable type)

2005. Registration of Korean Cultural Treasures as UNESCO World Heritage. Sheet 145×232 mm containing T **1635** and similar horiz design. Multicoloured.

MS2843 310w.×10, Type **1635**×5; *Seungjeongwon Ilgi* (Diaries of the Royal Secretariat)×5 (52×36 mm) ... 8·00 7·75

1636 Plans and Design Layout

2005. Construction of Multifunctional Administrative City, Chungcheong.

2844	**1636**	220w. multicoloured	80	65

1637 *Phoca vitulina largha*

2006. Baengnyeongdo Island. Multicoloured.

2845	220w. Type **1637**	80	65
2846	220w. *Phalacrocorax pelagicus*	80	65
2847	220w. *Orithyia sinica*	80	65
2848	220w. *Ammodytes personatus*	80	65

Nos. 2845/8 were issued in sheets with enlarged illustrated margins, the whole forming a composite design of the island.

1638 Fruit, Horses, Flowers and Stone Grandfather

2006. First Anniv of Jeju as Designated Island of World Peace.

2849	**1638**	220w. multicoloured	80	65

1639 *Crinum asiaticum*

2006.

2850	**1639**	100w. multicoloured	80	65

1640 Car (automobile industries)

2006. Korean Industries. Multicoloured.

2851	220w. Type **1640**	80	65
2852	220w. Computer chips (semiconductors)	80	65
2853	220w. Chemical symbols (petrochemical)	80	65
2854	220w. TV screen and mobile telephone (electronics)	80	65
2855	220w. Robotic arms (engineering)	80	65
2856	220w. Ships (ship building)	80	65
2857	220w. Rolls of steel (steel industry)	80	65
2858	220w. Fabric (textile industry)	80	65

1641 Rainbow, Children and Computer (Lee Annr Rulloda)

2006. "Ubiquitous World" (pervasive computing). Winning Designs in Children's Painting Competition. Multicoloured.

2859	220w. Type **1641**	80	65
2860	220w. "Green IT" (Kim Jeonghee) (horiz)	80	65

1642 Iguanodon

2006. Gyeongnam Goseong Dinosaurs World Expo. Multicoloured. Self-adhesive.

2861	220w. Type **1642**	80	65
2862	220w. Megaraptor	80	65

1643 Myeongjingwan Building

2006. Centenary of Dongguk University.

2863	**1643**	220w. multicoloured	80	65

1644 Second Foundation Campus

2006. Centenary of Sookmyung Women's University.

2864	**1644**	220w. multicoloured	80	65

No. 2865 and Type **1645** are now vacant.

1646 *Parus major*

2006.

2866	**1646**	90w. multicoloured	80	65

1647 Football, Emblem and Mascot

2006. World Cup Football Championship, Germany. Multicoloured.

2867	220w. Type **1647**	80	65
2868	220w. Players	80	65

2006. Goguryeo (2nd issue). As T **1616**. Multicoloured.

2869	480w. Janggunchong	1·50	1·20
2870	480w. Gods	1·50	1·20

1648 Fingerprints as Heart

2006. Philately Week. Marriage. Multicoloured.

2871	220w. Type **1648**	80	65
2872	220w. As No. 2871 but with country inscription and face value at top	80	65

1649 Tail Stole

2006. Extreme Sports (1st issue). Skateboarding. Sheet 75×106 mm containing T **1649** and similar vert designs. Multicoloured. Self-adhesive.

MS2873 220w.×4 Type **1649**; Drop in; Backside spin; Backside grab ... 3·50 3·25

The stamps of MS2873 form a composite background design.

1650 Ginseng Root

2006. World Ginseng Expo, Geumsan.

2874	**1650**	220w. multicoloured	80	65

1651 Olympic Bridge

1652 Seohae Bridge

1653 Jindo Bridge

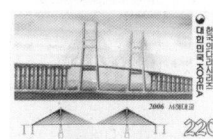

1654 Changseon-Samcheonpo Bridge

2006. Bridges (3rd series).

2875	**1651**	220w. multicoloured	80	65
2876	**1652**	220w. multicoloured	80	65
2877	**1653**	220w. multicoloured	80	65
2878	**1654**	220w. multicoloured	80	65

1655 Script

2006. 560th Anniv of Hangeul (Korean script) Day.

2879	**1655**	220w. multicoloured	80	65

1656 Building Facade

2006. Centenary of Sahmyook University.

2880	**1656**	220w. multicoloured	80	65

1657 Flower

2006. My Own Stamp.

2881	**1657**	250w. multicoloured	1·00	80

1658 *Ninox scutulata*

2006.

2882	**1658**	250w. multicoloured	1·00	80

1659 Swans

2006.

2883	**1659**	340w. multicoloured	1·30	1·00

1660 Buncheong Ware Vase

2006.

2884	**1660**	1750w. multicoloured	7·00	6·50

1661 'Lineage'

2006. Online Computer Games. Self adhesive.

2885	250w. Type **1661**	1·00	80
2886	250w. 'Maple Story'	1·00	80
2887	250w. 'Ragnarok'	1·00	80
2888	250w. 'Gersang'	1·00	80
2889	250w. 'Legend of Mir III'	1·00	80
2890	250w. 'Kartrider'	1·00	80
2891	250w. 'Mu'	1·00	80
2892	250w. 'Pangya'	1·00	80
2893	250w. 'Fortress2 Blue'	1·00	80
2894	250w. 'Mabinogi'	1·00	80

1662 Daecheongbong Peak

1663 Sibiseonnyeotang Valley

1664 Janggunbong Peak

1665 Ulsanbawi Rock

2006. Mountains (3rd series). Mount Seoraksan.

2895	**1662**	250w. multicoloured	1·00	80
2896	**1663**	250w. multicoloured	1·00	80
2897	**1664**	250w. multicoloured	1·00	80
2898	**1665**	250w. multicoloured	1·00	80

1666 Pig

2006. New Year.Year of the Pig.

2899	**1666**	250w. multicoloured	1·00	80

1667 Script, Singer and Drummer

2006. UNESCO Masterpiece of Oral and Intangible Heritage of Humanity. Pansori Songs and Singers. Multicoloured.

2900	**1667**	480w. multicoloured	2·00	1·60
2901		480w. Singer, musician and audience (51×35 mm)	2·00	1·60

1668 Faces and Hands holding Flowers (Kim Han-yun)

2006. Caring Neighbourhood and Donation Culture. Multicoloured.

2902	**1668**	250w. Type **1668**	1·00	80
2903		250w. Man watering tree seedling	1·00	80

1669 Spring

1670 Summer

1671 Autumn

1672 Winter

2007. Rivers (1st issue). Nakdong River.

2904	**1669**	250w. multicoloured	1·10	90
2905	**1670**	250w. multicoloured	1·10	90
2906	**1671**	250w. multicoloured	1·10	90
2907	**1672**	250w. multicoloured	1·10	90

1673 *Megatron/Matrix*

2007. First Death Anniv of Nam June Paik (artist). Multicoloured.

2908	**1673**	250w. Type **1673**	1·10	90
2909		250w. *TV Buddha*	1·10	90
2910		250w. *The More the Better*	1·10	90
2911		250w. *Oh-Mah* (Mother)	1·10	90

1674 Ring with National Flag

2007. Centenary of National Debt Repayment Movement.

2912	**1674**	205w. multicoloured	75	60

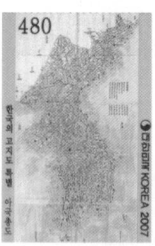
1675 Aguk Chong-do (map of Korea)

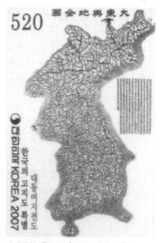
1676 Daedong Yeoji Jeon-do (territorial map of Great East (Korea))

1677 Paldo Chong-do (map of Eight-Provinces (Korea))

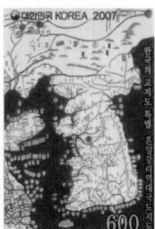
1678 Honilgangni Yeokdae Gukdo-jido (early world map showing enlarged Korea)

2007. Ancient Maps. Multicoloured.

2913	**1675**	480w. multicoloured	2·00	1·60
2914	**1676**	520w. multicoloured	2·20	1·80
2915	**1677**	580w. multicoloured	2·30	1·90
2916	**1678**	600w. multicoloured	2·40	1·90

1679 Clock Tower

2007. Centenary of Daehan Hospital.

2917	**1679**	250w. multicoloured	1·10	90

1680 *Cypripedium agnicapitatum*

2007. Ninth Asia–Pacific Orchid Conference.

2918	**1680**	250w. multicoloured	1·10	90

1681 Chromosome

2007. Year of Biology.

2919	**1681**	250w. multicoloured	1·10	90

1682 Golden Piglet

2007. Personal Stamps (My Own Stamp). Multicoloured.

2920	**1682**	250w. Type **1682**	1·10	90
2921		250w. Four-leaf clover	1·10	90
2922		250w. Sunflower	1·10	90

1683 Chinese Wedding Costume

2007. Wedding Costumes. Designs showing couples in wedding costumes. Multicoloured.

2923	**1683**	250w. Type **1683**	1·10	90
2924		250w. Indian	1·10	90
2925		250w. Malay	1·10	90
2926		250w. Eurasian	1·10	90
2927		480w. Korean (sun, moon and five mountains backdrop)	2·00	1·60
2928		520w. Korean (peonies backdrop)	2·20	1·80
2929		580w. Korean (ducks and water-lily backdrop (bridegroom wearing dark blue robe))	2·30	1·90
2930		600w. Korean (mandarin ducks backdrop (bridegroom wear-ing pale blue robe))	2·40	1·90

1684 Sukjeonnmun Gate

2007. Opening of Fortress Wall, Mount Bugaksan, Seoul.

2931	**1684**	250w. multicoloured	1·10	90

1685 *The Internet Culture that Unites the World into One* (Choi Mi-Yeon) (Korea)

2007. Internet Culture. Ethics. Multicoloured.

2932	**1685**	250w. Type **1685**	1·10	90
2933		250w. *The Internet Culture that Brightens Up the Future* (Daren Kaye C. Aquino) (Philippines)	1·10	90

1686 Child

2007. 50th Anniv of National Children's Charter. Self-adhesive.

2934	**1686**	250w. multicoloured	1·10	90

1687 Lee Sang-sol, Lee Chun and Lee Wi-Jong

2007. Centenary of Special Envoys to Second Peace Conference, the Hague.

2935	**1687**	250w. multicoloured	1·10	90

2007. Goguryeo (3rd issue). As T **1616**. Multicoloured.

2936		480w. Kitchen (mural, Anak Tomb No. 3, South Hwang-hae Province, North Korea)	2·00	1·60
2937		480w. Host welcoming guest (mural, Muyong Tomb, Jian , China)	2·00	1·60

1688 *Arctous ruber*

2007

2938	**1688**	70w. multicoloured	55	45

1689 1884 5m. Stamp (As Type **1**)

2007. Philately Week. Multicoloured.

2939	**1689**	250w. Type **1689**	1·10	90
2940		250w. 1884 10m. Stamp (As No. 2)	1·10	90
MS2941		140×70 mm. 250w.×2, Nos. 2917/18	2·20	2·20

2007. Extreme Sports (2nd issue). Skateboarding. As T **1649**. Multicoloured. Self-adhesive.

2942		250w. Drop in	1·10	90
2943		250w. Flip	1·10	90
2944		250w. Spin	1·10	90
2945		250w. Grind	1·10	90

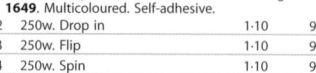
1690 Outline of Figure cradling Bird

2007. Centenary of Bar Association

2946	**1690**	250w. multicoloured	1·10	90

1691 Seongsan Bridge

1692 Yeongjong Bridge

1693 Gwangan Bridge

1694 Seongsu Bridge

2007. Bridges (4th issue).

2947	**1691**	250w. multicoloured	1·10	90
2948	**1692**	250w. multicoloured	1·10	90
2949	**1693**	250w. multicoloured	1·10	90
2950	**1694**	250w. multicoloured	1·10	90

1695 Dove

2007. Inter-Korean Summit, Pyongyang.

| 2951 | **1695** | 250w. multicoloured | 1·10 | 90 |

1696 Hyeongje Falls

1697 Rimyeongsu Falls

1698 Lake Samjiyeon

1699 Lake Chonji

2007. Mountains (4th issue). Mount Baekdusan.

2952	**1696**	250w. multicoloured	1·10	90
2953	**1697**	250w. multicoloured	1·10	90
2954	**1698**	250w. multicoloured	1·10	90
2955	**1699**	250w. multicoloured	1·10	90

1700 Arirang

1701 Looking for Love

1702 Ownerless Ferryboat

1703 Chunyangjeon

2007. Korean Cinema (1st issue).

2956	**1700**	250w. multicoloured	1·10	90
2957	**1701**	250w. multicoloured	1·10	90
2958	**1702**	250w. multicoloured	1·10	90
2959	**1703**	250w. multicoloured	1·10	90

1704 Love for Eternity (Roh Hye-rim (Korea))

2007. United Nations Convention on the Rights of the Child. Winning Designs in International Stamp Design Competition. Multicoloured.

| 2960 | 250w. Type **1704** | 1·10 | 90 |
| 2961 | 250w. Fathers Hands (Robert Brun (Slovakia)) (horiz) | 1·10 | 90 |

1705 Early and Modern Buildings

2007. Opening of New Central Post Office, Seoul. Multicoloured.

| 2962 | 250w. Type **1705** | 1·10 | 90 |
| 2963 | 250w. New building (Post tower) | 1·10 | 90 |

1706 Rat

2007. Chinese New Year. Year of the Rat.

| 2964 | **1706** | 250w. multicoloured | 1·10 | 90 |

1707 Procession

2007. UNESCO Masterpiece of Oral and Intangible Heritage of Humanity. Gangneung Danoje Festival. Multicoloured.

| 2965 | 480w. Type **1707** | 2·00 | 1·60 |
| 2966 | 480w. Masked players (51×35 mm) | 2·00 | 1·60 |

1708 Spring

1709 Summer

1710 Autumn

1711 Winter

2008. Rivers (2nd issue). Seomjin River.

2967	**1708**	250w. multicoloured	1·10	90
2968	**1709**	250w. multicoloured	1·10	90
2969	**1710**	250w. multicoloured	1·10	90
2970	**1711**	250w. multicoloured	1·10	90

Nos. 2971/2 and Type **1712** are left for King Sejong Station, issued on 15 February 2008, not yet received.

1713 Pres. Lee Myung Bak

2008. Inauguration of President Lee Myung Bak.

| 2973 | **1713** | 250w. multicoloured | 1·10 | 90 |
| MS2974 | 115×80 mm. 250w. As Type **1713** | 1·10 | 1·10 |

1714 Mask

2008. African Savannah. Sheet 155×170 mm containing T **1714** and similar fan-shaped designs. Multicoloured. Self-adhesive.

| MS2975 | 250w.×4, Type **1714**; Leopard; Elephant; Zebra | 4·25 | 4·25 |

The stamps of **MS**2975 form a circular design enclosing a central circle showing a map of Africa.

1715 Buchaechum   **1716** Salpurichum

1717 Seungmu   **1718** Taepyeongmu

2008. PHILAKOREA 2009–Asian International Stamp Exhibition. Dance.

2976	**1715**	250w. multicoloured	1·10	90
2977	**1716**	250w. multicoloured	1·10	90
2978	**1717**	250w. multicoloured	1·10	90
2979	**1718**	250w. multicoloured	1·10	90
MS2979a	165×75 mm. Nos. 2976/9 plus label	4·25	4·25

1719 World in a Post Box (Hamzah D. Marbella (Philippines))

2008. Mailbox of the Future–Winning designs in Children's Painting Competition. Multicoloured.

| 2980 | 250w. Type **1719** | 1·10 | 90 |
| 2981 | 250w. Spacecraft collecting and delivering post (Lau Tsun Yin (Hong Kong)) | 1·10 | 90 |

1720 Mothers with Children/ Mothers without Children (Jazayeri Shirin (Iran))

2008. Nurturing Children–Winning Designs in International Stamp Design Competition. Multicoloured.

| 2982 | 250w. Type **1720** | 1·10 | 90 |
| 2983 | 250w. Mother and child (Isaiah Otieno Nondoh (Kenya)) | 1·10 | 90 |

1721 World Map and @

2008. OECD Ministerial Meeting on the Future of Internet Economy, Seoul.

| 2984 | **1721** | 250w. multicoloured | 1·10 | 90 |

1722 Yun Bong-Gil

2008. Birth Centenary of Yun Bong-Gil (patriot).

| 2985 | **1722** | 250w. multicoloured | 1·10 | 90 |

1723 Euryale ferox

2008. Self-adhesive.

| 2986 | **1723** | 250w. multicoloured | 1·10 | 90 |

1724 Hwanung descending onto Siddansu on Taebaek Mountain

2008. Dangun Wanggeom (legend of founding of Korea). Multicoloured.

2987	250w. Type **1724**	1·10	90
2988	250w. Bear and tiger who desire to become human	1·10	90
2989	250w. Birth of Dangun Wanggeom	1·10	90
2990	250w. Dangun Wanggeom (founder of capital city)	1·10	90

1725 Plugs as Flowers (unplugging electronic equipment)

2008. Energy Conservation. Multicoloured.

2991	250w. Type **1725**	1·10	90
2992	250w. Thermometers (regulating temperature in the home)	1·10	90
2993	250w. Energy efficient products	1·10	90
2994	250w. Passenger straps growing leaves (using public transport)	1·10	90

1726 1902 3ch. Stamp (As Type 9)

2008. Philately Week. Multicoloured.

2995	250w. Type **1726**	1·10	90
2996	250w. 1951 300w. on 14w. Stamp (As No. 149)	1·30	1·00
MS2997	140×70 mm. 250w.×2, Nos. 2995/6	2·40	1·90

1727 Gymnast

2008. Olympic Games, Beijing.

| 2998 | **1727** | 250w. multicoloured | 1·10 | 90 |

1728 '60'

2008. 60th Anniv of Republic of Korea.
2999 **1728** 250w. multicoloured   1·10   90

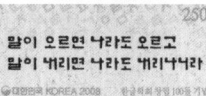

1729 *Hannara Mal* (Sigyeong Ju)

2008. Centenary of Korean Language Society.
3000 **1729** 250w. multicoloured   1·10   90

1730 Tap filling
Glass

2008. Centenary of Seoul Waterworks.
3001 **1730** 250w. multicoloured   1·10   90

1731 Runner and
Radio Waves

2008. 14th Amateur Radio Direction Finding (ARDF)
Championships.
3002 **1731** 250w. multicoloured   1·10   90

2008. Extreme Sports (3rd issue). Snowboarding. As T
1649. Multicoloured. Self-adhesive.
3003   250w. Carving turn   1·10   90
3004   250w. Indy grab   1·10   90
3005   250w. Nose grab   1·10   90
3006   250w. Air   1·10   90

1732 Charity Pot

2008. Centenary of Salvation Army in Korea.
3007 **1732** 250w. multicoloured   1·10   90

1733 '60th' Tag on
Dove-shaped Chain

2008. 60th Anniv of Armed Forces.
3008 **1733** 250w. multicoloured   1·10   90

1734 Grand Palace (Thailand)

2008. 50th Anniv of Korea–Thailand Diplomatic Relations.
Multicoloured.
3009   250w. Type **1734**   1·10   90
3010   250w. Changdeokgung Palace
         (Korea)   1·10   90

1735 Panorama

1736 Sangpaldam's Pools

1737 Manmulsang

1738 Gwimyeonam Rock

2008. Mountains (5th issue). Mount Geumgangsan.
3011 **1735** 250w. multicoloured   1·10   90
3012 **1736** 250w. multicoloured   1·10   90
3013 **1737** 250w. multicoloured   1·10   90
3014 **1738** 250w. multicoloured   1·10   90

1739 *A Coachman*

1739a *The Seashore Village*

1740 *Mother and a Guest*

1740a *The Wedding Day*

2008. Korean Cinema (2nd issue).
3015 **1739** 250w. multicoloured   1·10   90
3016 **1739a** 250w. multicoloured   1·10   90
3017 **1740** 250w. multicoloured   1·10   90
3018 **1740a** 250w. multicoloured   1·10   90

1741 Wetlands

2008. Tenth Meeting of Conference of the Contracting
Parties to the Ramsar Convention on Wetlands
3019 **1741** 250w. multicoloured   1·10   90

1742 Big Head
Buddha (Chinese
Lion Dance)

2008. Masks. Multicoloured.
3020   250w. Type **1742**   1·10   90
3021   250w.   1·10   90

Stamps of a similar design were issued by Hong Kong.

1743 Ox

2008. Chinese New Year. Year of the Ox.
3022 **1743** 250w. multicoloured   1·10   90

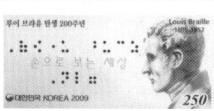

1744 Braille Script, Korean Script
and Louis Braille

2009. Birth Bicentenary of Louis Braille (inventor of
Braille writing for the blind).
3023 **1744** 250w. multicoloured   1·10   90

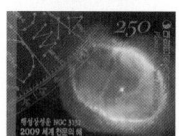

1745 Nebula NGC 3132

2009. International Year of Astronomy. Multicoloured.
3024   250w. Type **1745**   1·10   90
3025   250w. Whirlpool Galaxy M51   1·10   90

1746 Spring

1747 Summer

1748 Autumn

1749 Winter

2009. Rivers (3rd issue). Geum River.
3026 **1746** 250w. multicoloured   1·10   90
3027 **1747** 250w. multicoloured   1·10   90
3028 **1748** 250w. multicoloured   1·10   90
3029 **1749** 250w. multicoloured   1·10   90

1750 Hangawi Sonori (cow
play), Korea

2009. 60th Anniv of Philippines–South Korea Diplomatic
Relations. Multicoloured.
3030   250w. Type **1750**   1·10   90
3031   250w. Panagbenga Flower
         Festival, Philippines   1·10   90

1751 Conifer,
Cheonhwangsa
Temple (Natural
Monument No. 495)

1752 Zelkova Tree, Danjeon-ri
(No. 478)

1753 Tree (called
Seoksongnyeong),
Cheonhyang (No. 294)

1754 Ginko
Tree,
Yongmunsa
(No. 30)

2009. Ancient and Historic Trees of Korea.
3032 **1751** 250w. multicoloured   1·10   90
3033 **1752** 250w. multicoloured   1·10   90
3034 **1753** 250w. multicoloured   1·10   90
3035 **1754** 250w. multicoloured   1·10   90

1755 Tank, Ship and
Helicopters

2009. 60th Anniv of Marine Corps.
3036 **1755** 250w. multicoloured   1·10   90

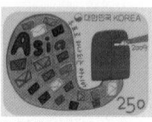

1756 Envelopes and
Post Box (Jaesong Yun)

2009. Asia becoming One Through Stamps. Winning
Designs in Children's Design a Stamp Competition.
Multicoloured.
3037   250w. Type **1756**   1·10   90
3038   250w. Envelope, flags in heart
         shape and children of many
         nations (Yu Hoi Dick Cherie)
         (vert)   1·10   90

1757 Tree on Globe (Seo
Hye Min)

2009. Love for the Earth. Winning Designs in Design a
Stamp Competition. Multicoloured.
3039   250w. Type **1757**   1·10   90
3040   250w. Smiling globe (Cho Zaw
         Aung) (vert)   1·10   90

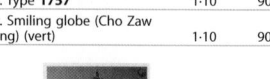

1757a Geumdongdaetap
(gilt-bronze pagoda)

2009. Cultural Heritage
3041 **1757a** 2000w. multicoloured   8·00   7·50

1758 *Mr. Gobau, Run Hany,
Little Dino Dooly,
Mengkkongi Village School
and Robot Zzibba*

2009. Centenary of Korean Cartoons.
3042 **1758** 250w. multicoloured   1·10   90

1759 17th–19th century
Mongolian

2009. Earrings. Multicoloured.
3043   250w. Type **1759**   1·10   90
3044   250w. 1st–2nd century BC
         Kazakhstan   1·10   90

3045	250w. 5th–6th Century Korean Earrings	1·10	90
MS3045a	87×137 mm. 250w.×3, Nos. 3043/5	3·25	3·25

1760 Yongcheondonggul Lava Tube

2009. World Heritage Site. Jeju Volcanic Island. Multicoloured.

3046	250w. Type 1760	1·10	90
3047	250w. Dangcheomuldonggul (52×36 mm)	1·10	90

1761 1900 3ch. Stamp (As No. 23A)

2009. Philately Week. Multicoloured.

3048	250w. Type 1761	1·10	90
3049	250w. 1969 7w. Stamp (As No. 787)	1·10	90
MS3050	140×70 mm. 250w.×2, Nos. 3048/9	4·25	4·25

1762 Cock Pheasant

2009. PHILAKOREA 2009–Asian International Stamp Exhibition, South Korea. Designs showing Yeongmohwa paintings. Multicoloured.

3051	250w. Type 1762	1·10	90
3052	250w. Eagle leaning forward	1·10	90
3053	250w. Female duck	1·10	90
3054	250w. Crane with raised head	1·10	90
3055	250w. Hen pheasant	1·10	90
3056	250w. Eagle facing left	1·10	90
3057	250w. Male duck with head on back	1·10	90
3058	250w. Crane (different)	1·10	90

Nos. 3051 and 3055, 3052 and 3056, 3053 and 3057, 3054 and 3058, respectively, were printed together, se-tenant, forming composite designs.

1763 The God's Command moving Country's Capital

2009. Geumwawang of Buyeo Kingdom (from Samgukyusa (by Venerable Ilyeon)). Multicoloured.

3059	250w. Type 1763	1·10	90
3060	250w. Horse riders (establishment of East Buyeo)	1·10	90
3061	250w. Birth of King Geumwawang	1·10	90
3062	250w. King Geumwawang's enthronement	1·10	90

Nos. 3059/60 and 3061/2 were printed, se-tenant, forming a composite design.

1764 House with Solar Thermal Roof Panels

2009. Green Energy. Multicoloured.

3063	250w. Type 1764	1·10	90
3064	250w. Car with photo voltaic panels	1·10	90
3065	250w. Wind turbines	1·10	90
3066	250w. Tidal power generator	1·10	90

Nos. 3067/73 and Types 1765/6 are vacant.

1767 World Map and Graph

2009. OECD World Forum, Busan, Korea

3074	1767	250w. multicoloured	1·20	90

1768 A Road to Sampo

1769 Never Never Forget Me

1770 Yalkae, A Joker In High School

1771 Chilsu and Mansu

2009. Korean Cinema (3rd issue)

3075	1768	250w. multicoloured	1·20	90
3076	1769	250w. multicoloured	1·20	90
3077	1770	250w. multicoloured	1·20	90
3078	1771	250w. multicoloured	1·20	90

1772 ncheon Bridge, South Korea

1773 Octávio Frias de Oliveira bridge, Brazil

2009. Brazil–South Korea Diplomatic Relations.

3079	1772	250w. multicoloured	1·20	90
3080	1773	250w. multicoloured	1·20	90

Stamps of a similar design were issued by Brazil.

1774 Tiger

2009. Chinese New Year. Year of the Tiger

3081	1774	250w. multicoloured	1·20	90

1775 Taegeukmaji (Jaekuk Jung)

1776 Saekdongeolgul (Yongsoon Na)

2010. Visit Korea

3082	1775	250w. multicoloured	1·20	90
3083	1776	250w. multicoloured	1·20	90

1777 Figure Skating

2010. Winter Olympic Games, Vancouver. Multicoloured.

3084	250w. Type 1777	1·20	90
3085	250w. Speed skating	1·20	90

1778 Malayan Tiger (Panthera tigris jacksoni)

2010. 50th Anniv of Korea–Malaysia Diplomatic Relations. Multicoloured.

3086	250w. Type 1778	1·20	90
3087	250w. Korean tiger (Panthera tigris altaica)	1·20	90

1779 Ahn Jung-geun, Script written on Stylized Taegeukgi (national flag)

2010. Death Centenary of Ahn Jung-geun (independence activist, nationalist, and pan-Asianist). Multicoloured.

3088	250w. Type 1779	1·20	90
3089	250w. Ahn Jung-geun's hand print with script inscribed on missing ring-finger	1·20	90

1780 National University of Technology, Seoul

2010. Centenary of National University of Technology, Seoul and Jinju National University

3090	250w. Type 1780	1·20	90
3091	250w. Jinju National University (vert)	1·20	90

1781 Old Buddha's Plum Tree at Baegyangsa Temple, Jangseong (Natural Monuments No. 486)

1782 Conifer, Samsong-ri, Goesan (No. 290)

1783 Two Chinese Junipers at Songgwangsa Temple (No. 88)

1784 Thunbergii camphor, Samsan-ri, Jangheung (No. 481)

2010. Ancient and Historic Trees of Korea

3092	1781	250w. multicoloured	1·20	90
3093	1782	250w. multicoloured	1·20	90
3094	1783	250w. multicoloured	1·20	90
3095	1784	250w. multicoloured	1·20	90

1785 Mo Tae Bum (speed skater)

2010. Korea's Skating Victories at Winter Olympic Games, Vancouver

3096	250w. Type 1785	1·20	90
3097	250w. Lee Sang Hwa (speed skater) (rose)	1·20	90
3098	250w. Lee Seung Hoon (speed skater) (dull yellow green)	1·20	90
3099	250w. Kim Yu Na (world champion figure skater) (deep mauve)	1·20	90
3100	250w. Kwak Yoon Gy (short track) (pale orange)	1·20	90
3101	250w. Kim Seoung Il (short track) (pale blue-green)	1·20	90
3102	250w. Park Seung Hi (short track) (pale slate-lilac)	1·20	90
3103	250w. Sung Si Bak (short track) (lavender)	1·20	90
3104	250w. Lee Eun Byul (short track) (bright lilac)	1·20	90
3105	250w. Lee Jung Su (short track) (violet-blue)	1·20	90
3106	250w. Lee Ho Suk (short track) (dark flesh)	1·20	90

1786 Autumn

1787 Winter

1788 Spring

1789 Summer

2010. Rivers (4th issue)

3107	1786	250w. multicoloured	1·20	90
3108	1787	250w. multicoloured	1·20	90
3109	1788	250w. multicoloured	1·20	90
3110	1789	250w. multicoloured	1·20	90

1790 Players and Championship Emblem

2010. World Cup Football Championship, South Africa

3111	1790	250w. multicoloured	1·20	90

1791 Children and Women making 'Hands of Protection' (UNHCR emblem)

2010. Tenth Anniv of World Refugee Day

3112	1791	250w. multicoloured	1·20	90

1792 Chimney of Mt. Amisan in Gyeongbokgung Palace, Korea

1793 Traditional Air-conditioning Tower, UAE

2010. 30th Anniv of Korea–United Arab Emirates Diplomatic Relations

3113	**1792**	250w. multicoloured	1·20	90
3114	**1793**	250w. multicoloured	1·20	90

1794 Barbed Wire and Butterfly

2010. 60th Anniv of Start of Korean War

3115	**1794**	250w. multicoloured	1·20	90

1795 1980 30w. Stamp (As Type **781**)

2010. Philately Week

3116	250w. black and vermilion	1·20	90
3117	250w. black, vermilion and new blue	1·20	90
MS3118	140×70 mm. 250w.×2, Nos. 3116/17	2·40	2·40

DESIGNS: No. 3116, Type **1795**; No. 3117, 1980 30w. Stamp (As No. 1458)

1796 Herrerasaurus

2010. The Age of Dinosaurs (1st issue). Multicoloured.

3119	250w. Type **1796**	1·20	90
3120	250w. Coelophysis	1·20	90
3121	250w. Plateosaurus	1·60	1·10
3122	250w. Riojasaurus	1·60	1·10

1797 Stylized Trees and Symbols of Life

2010. IUFRO–Global Network for Forest Science Co-operation Congress, Seoul

3123	**1797**	340w. multicoloured	1·60	1·10

C. NORTH KOREAN OCCUPATION

1 "Democratic People's Republic of Korea"

1950. Nos. 116 and 118/19 optd with Type **1**.

1	10w. green	65·00
2	20w. brown	25·00
3	30w. green	31·00

NORTH KOREA.

A. RUSSIAN OCCUPATION

GUM. All stamps of North Korea up to No. N1506 are without gum, except where otherwise stated.

1 Hibiscus

2 Diamond Mountains

1946. Perf, roul or imperf.

N1	**1**	20ch. red	75·00	50·00
N2	**2**	50ch. green	50·00	40·00
N4b	**2**	50ch. red	13·50	13·50
N5b	**2**	50ch. violet	12·50	14·50

4 Gen. Kim Il Sung and Flag

1946. First Anniv of Liberation from Japan.

N6	**4**	50ch. brown	£250	£190

5 Peasants

1947. Perf, roul or imperf.

N7	**5**	1wn. green	6·75	5·75
N8	**5**	1wn. violet	21·00	21·00
N9	**5**	1wn. blue on buff	8·50	6·75
N10	**5**	1wn. blue	4·25	3·25

6

1948. Second Anniv of Labour Law.

N11	**6**	50ch. blue	£300	£300

7

1948. Third Anniv of Liberation from Japan.

N12	**7**	50ch. red	£180	£600

8

1948. Promulgation of Constitution.

N13	**8**	50ch. blue and red	£225	£110

B. KOREAN PEOPLE'S DEMOCRATIC REPUBLIC

9 North Korean Flag

1948. Establishment of People's Republic. Roul.

N16	**9**	25ch. violet	4·50	4·50
N17	**9**	50ch. blue	8·00	7·75

10

1949. Roul or perf.

N18	**10**	6wn. red and blue	3·00	3·50

11 Kim Il Sung University, Pyongyang

11a Kim Il Sung University, Pyongyang

1949. Roul.

N19	**11**	1wn. violet	£110	60·00
N20	**11a**	1wn. blue	£150	41·00

12 North Korean Flags

1949. Fourth Anniv of Liberation from Japan. Roul or perf.

N22	**12**	1wn. red, green and blue	£140	50·00

13 Order of the National Flag

1950. Perf, roul or imperf. Various sizes.

N24	**13**	1wn. green (A)	5·50	1·40
N25	**13**	1wn. orange (A)	70·00	55·00
N26	**13**	1wn. orange (B)	22·00	18·00
N27	**13**	1wn. green (C)	5·50	2·00
N28	**13**	1wn. olive (D)	9·25	5·75

SIZES: (A) 23¼×37½ mm. (B) 20×32½ mm. (C) 22×35½ mm. (D) 22½×36½ mm.

14 Liberation Monument, Pyongyang

15 Soldier and Flags

16 Peasant and Worker

17 Tractor

1950. Fifth Anniv of Liberation from Japan. Roul, perf or imperf. Various sizes.

N29	**14**	1wn. red, indigo and blue	1·60	1·10
N30	**14**	1wn. orange	9·25	8·75
N31	**15**	2wn. black, blue and red	1·60	1·20
N32	**16**	6wn. green (A)	2·20	1·60
N36	**16**	6wn. red (B)	17·00	13·50
N33	**17**	10wn. brown (C)	3·25	2·40
N37	**17**	10wn. brown (D)	25·00	16·00

SIZES: (A) 20×30 mm. (B) 22×33 mm. (C) 20×28 mm. (D) 22×30 mm.

18 Capitol, Seoul

1950. Capture of Seoul by North Korean Forces. Roul.

N38	**18**	1wn. red, blue and green	50·00	44·00

19

1951. Order of Admiral Li Sun Sin. Imperf or perf.

N39	**19**	6wn. orange	8·50	7·00

20 Kim Gi Ok and Aeroplane

1951. Air Force Hero Kim Gi Ok. Imperf.

N40	**20**	1wn. blue	10·50	6·75

21 Russian and North Korean Flags

22 Kim Ki U (hero)

23 N. Korean and Chinese Soldiers

1951. Sixth Anniv of Liberation from Japan. Roul or perf.

N41A	**21**	1wn. blue	4·50	3·25
N42A	**21**	1wn. red	4·50	3·25
N43A	**22**	1wn. blue	4·50	3·25
N44A	**22**	1wn. red	5·00	3·25
N45A	**23**	2wn. blue	9·25	6·50
N46A	**23**	2wn. red	13·50	11·50

All values exist on buff and on white paper.

24 Order of Soldier's Honour

1951. Imperf or perf.

N47	**24**	40wn. red	12·50	5·75

25

1951. Co-operation of Chinese People's Volunteers. Imperf or perf.

N49	**25**	10wn. blue	7·25	6·50

26 Woman Partisan, Li Su Dok

1952. Partisan Heroes. Imperf or perf.

N50	**26**	70wn. brown	5·50	1·60

27

1952. Peace Propaganda. Imperf or perf.

N51	**27**	20wn. blue, green and red	8·00	2·75

28 Gen. P'eng Teh-huai

1952. Honouring Commander of Chinese People's Volunteers. Imperf.

N52	**28**	10wn. purple	16·00	6·50

29 Munition Worker

1952. Labour Day. Imperf or perf.

N53	**29**	10wn. red	42·00	40·00

30

1952. Sixth Anniv of Labour Law. Imperf or perf.

N54a	**30**	10wn. blue	21·00	16·00

31

1952. Anti-U.S. Imperialism Day. Imperf or perf.

N55	**31**	10wn. red	31·00	30·00

32

1952. North Korean and Chinese Friendship. Imperf or perf.

N56a	**32**	20wn. deep blue	14·00	13·50

33 **34**

1952. Seventh Anniv of Liberation from Japan. Imperf or perf.

N57	**33**	10wn. red	31·00	30·00
N58	**34**	10wn. red	24·00	23·00

35

1952. Int Youth Day. With gum. Imperf or perf.

N59	**35**	10wn. green	17·00	17·00

36 **37**

1953. Fifth Anniv of People's Army. Imperf or perf.

N60	**36**	10wn. red	32·00	31·00
N61	**37**	40wn. purple	21·00	20·00

38 **39**

1953. Int Women's Day. With gum. Imperf or perf.

N62	**38**	10wn. red	22·00	19·00
N63	**39**	40wn. green	24·00	21·00

40 **41**

1953. Labour Day. Imperf or perf.

N64	**40**	10wn. green	16·00	15·00
N65	**41**	40wn. orange	16·00	15·00

42 **43**

1953. Anti-U.S. Imperialism Day. With gum. Imperf or perf.

N66	**42**	10wn. turquoise	31·00	30·00
N67	**43**	40wn. red	31·00	30·00

44 **45**

1953. Fourth World Youth Festival, Bucharest. With gum. Imperf or perf.

N68	**44**	10wn. blue and green	18·00	17·00
N69	**45**	20wn. green and pink	15·00	8·75

46

1953. Armistice and Victory Issue. With gum. Imperf or perf.

N70a	**46**	10wn. brown and yellow	90·00	85·00

47

1953. Eighth Anniv of Liberation from Japan. Imperf.

N71	**47**	10wn. red	£400	£375

48

1953. Fifth Anniv of People's Republic. Imperf or perf.

N72	**48**	10wn. blue and red	20·00	19·00

49 Liberation Monument, Pyongyang

1953. With gum. Imperf or perf.

N73	**49**	10wn. slate	19·00	9·75

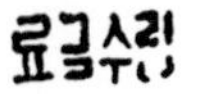

(50)

1954. No. N18 optd **"Fee Collected"** in Korean characters, T **50**.

N74	**10**	6wn. red and blue	£250	£250

(51)

1954. Nos. N18 and N39 surch with T **51**.

N75	**10**	5wn. on 6wn. red and blue	29·00	19·00
N76	**19**	5wn. on 6wn. orange	75·00	55·00

52

1954. Post-war Economic Reconstruction. With gum. Imperf or perf.

N77	**52**	10wn. blue	31·00	18·00

53

1954. Sixth Anniv of People's Army. With gum. Imperf or perf.

N78	**53**	10wn. red	£110	£110

54

1954. Int Women's Day. With gum. Imperf or perf.

N79	**54**	10wn. red	25·00	24·00

55

1954. Labour Day. With gum. Imperf or perf.

N80	**55**	10wn. red	20·00	19·00

56

1954. Anti-U.S. Imperialism Day. With gum. Imperf or perf.

N81	**56**	10wn. red	37·00	33·00

57 Taedong Gate, Pyongyang

1954. Imperf or perf.

N82	**57**	5wn. lake	4·25	1·50
N83	**57**	5wn. brown	4·25	1·50

58

1954. National Young Activists' Conference With gum. Imperf or perf.

N84	**58**	10wn. red, blue and slate	5·25	5·00

59 Soldier

1954. Ninth Anniv of Liberation from Japan. With gum. Imperf or perf.

N85	**59**	10wn. red	12·00	11·50

60 North Korean Flag

1954. Sixth Anniv of People's Republic. With gum. Imperf or perf.

N86	**60**	10wn. blue and red	9·75	9·25

61 Hwanghae Iron Works **62** Hwanghae Iron Works and Workers

1954. Economic Reconstruction. Imperf or perf.

N87	**61**	10wn. blue	8·75	1·20
N88	**62**	10wn. brown	8·75	1·20

63

1955. Seventh Anniv of People's Army. With gum. Imperf or perf.

N89	**63**	10wn. red	11·50	9·75

64

1955. Int Women's Day. With gum. Imperf or perf.

N90	**64**	10wn. deep blue	11·50	9·75

65 **66**

1955. Labour Day. With gum. Imperf or perf.

N91	**65**	10wn. green	8·25	7·75
N92	**66**	10wn. red	8·25	7·75

67 Admiral Li Sun Sin

1955. Imperf or perf.

N93	**67**	1wn. blue on green	4·75	60
N94	**67**	2wn. red on buff	5·25	60
N95	**67**	2wn. red	10·00	1·10

68

1955. Ninth Anniv of Labour Law. With gum. Imperf or perf.

N96	**68**	10wn. red	12·50	11·50

69 Liberation Monument and Flags

1955. Tenth Anniv of Liberation from Japan. Imperf or perf.

N97	**69**	10wn. green	4·25	3·75
N98	**69**	10wn. red, blue and brown (29½×42½ mm)	3·75	3·25

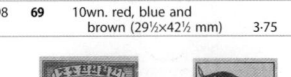

70 **71**

1955. Soviet Union Friendship Month. Imperf or perf.
N99	70	10wn. red	2·75	1·50
N100	70	10wn. red and blue	3·50	2·20
N101	71	20wn. red and slate	4·75	3·25
N102	71	20wn. red and blue	2·75	1·70

SIZES: No. N99, 22×32½ mm; N100, 29½×43 mm; N101, 18½×32 mm; N102, 25×43 mm.

72 Son Rock

1956. Haegumgang Maritime Park. Imperf or perf.
| N103 | 72 | 10wn. blue on blue | 6·00 | 3·25 |

73

1956. Eighth Anniv of People's Army. Imperf or perf.
| N104 | 73 | 10wn. red on green | 14·00 | 12·50 |

74

1956. Labour Day. Imperf or perf.
| N105 | 74 | 10wn. blue | 11·50 | 8·00 |

75 Machinist   76 Taedong Gate, Pyongyang

77 Woman Harvester   78 Moranbong Theatre, Pyongyang

1956. Imperf or perf.
N106	75	1wn. brown	2·00	95
N107	76	2wn. blue	8·50	1·90
N108	77	10wn. red	1·60	1·10
N109	78	40wn. green	11·00	5·50

79 Miner

1956. Tenth Anniv of Labour Law. Imperf or perf.
| N110 | 79 | 10wn. brown | 3·25 | 1·40 |

80 Boy Bugler and Girl Drummer

1956. Tenth Anniv of Children's Union. Imperf or perf.
| N111 | 80 | 10wn. brown | 5·50 | 3·50 |

81 Workers

1956. Tenth Anniv of Sex Equality Law. Imperf or perf.
| N112 | 81 | 10wn. brown | 3·25 | 2·10 |

82 Industrial Plant

1956. Tenth Anniv of Nationalization of Industry. Imperf or perf.
| N113 | 82 | 10wn. brown | 50·00 | 33·00 |

83 Liberation Tower

1956. 11th Anniv of Liberation from Japan. Imperf or perf.
| N114 | 83 | 10wn. red | 4·25 | 1·80 |

84 Kim Il Sung University

1956. Tenth Anniv of Kim Il Sung University. Imperf or perf.
| N115 | 84 | 10wn. brown | 3·50 | 3·25 |

85 Boy and Girl

1956. Fourth Democratic Youth League Congress. Imperf or perf.
| N116 | 85 | 10wn. brown | 3·50 | 2·00 |

86 Pak Ji Won

1957. 220th Birth Anniv of Pak Ji Won "Yonam", (statesman). Imperf or perf.
| N117 | 86 | 10wn. blue | 2·00 | 1·00 |

87 Tabo Pagoda, Pulguksa   88 Ulmil Pavilion, Pyongyang

1957. Imperf, perf or roul.
| N118 | 87 | 5wn. blue | 1·80 | 1·20 |
| N119 | 88 | 40wn. green | 2·75 | 1·80 |

89 Furnaceman

1957. Production and Economy Campaign. With or without gum. Imperf or perf.
| N121 | 89 | 10wn. blue | 4·25 | 2·75 |

90 Furnaceman   91 Voters and Polling Booth

1957. Second General Election. Imperf or perf.
N122	90	1wn. orange	1·10	45
N123	90	2wn. brown	1·10	45
N124	91	10wn. red	6·50	1·80

92 Ryongwangjong, Pyongyang

1957. 1530th Anniv of Pyongyang. Imperf or perf.
| N125 | 92 | 10wn. green | 1·30 | 35 |

93 Lenin and Flags   94 Kim Il Sung at Pochonbo   95 Lenin

96 Pouring Steel

1957. 40th Anniv of Russian Revolution. Imperf or perf.
N126	93	10wn. green	1·00	55
N127	94	10wn. red	1·00	55
N128	95	10wn. blue	1·00	55
N129	96	10wn. orange	2·50	55

No. N126 exists with gum.

97 Congress Emblem

1957. Fourth World Trade Unions Federation Congress. Leipzig. Imperf (with or without gum) or perf.
| N130 | 97 | 10wn. blue and green | 1·60 | 65 |

98 Liberation Monument, Spassky Tower and Flags

1957. Russian Friendship Month. Imperf or perf.
| N131 | 98 | 10wn. green | 2·20 | 60 |

99 Weighing a Baby   100 Bandaging a Hand

1957. Red Cross. Imperf, perf or roul.
N132	99	1wn. red	7·50	1·20
N133	99	2wn. red	7·50	1·20
N134	100	10wn. red	20·00	3·50

No. N133 exists with and without gum.

101 Koryo Celadon Jug (12th century)   102 Koryo Incense-burner (12th century)

1958. Korean Antiquities. Imperf (with or without gum) or perf.
| N135 | 101 | 10wn. blue | 6·25 | 95 |
| N136 | 102 | 10wn. green | 6·25 | 95 |

103 Woljong Temple Pagoda

1958. With gum (5wn.), without gum (10wn.). Imperf or perf.
| N137 | 103 | 5wn. green | 1·50 | 80 |
| N138 | 103 | 10wn. blue | 2·50 | 1·40 |

104 Soldier

1958. Tenth Anniv of People's Army. No gum (No. N139) with or without gum (No. N140). Imperf or perf.
| N139 | 104 | 10wn. blue | 3·25 | 60 |
| N140 | 104 | 10wn. red | 6·00 | 80 |

DESIGN—HORIZ (37½×26 mm): No. N140, Soldier, flag and Hwanghae Iron Works.

106 Lisunov Li-2 Airliner over Pyongyang

1958. Air. Imperf or perf.
| N141 | 106 | 20wn. blue | 7·00 | 1·20 |

107 Sputniks   108 Sputnik encircling Globe

1958. I.G.Y. Inscr "1957–1958". Imperf or perf.
N142	107	10wn. slate	5·25	3·25
N143	108	20wn. slate	5·25	3·25
N144	107	40wn. slate	5·25	3·25
N145	107	70wn. slate	11·50	9·75

DESIGN—HORIZ: 40wn. Sputnik over Pyongyang Observatory.

Nos. N142/4 exist with or without gum.

109 Furnaceman

1958. Young Socialist Constructors' Congress, Pyongyang. Imperf or perf.
| N146 | 109 | 10wn. blue | 3·75 | 70 |

110 Hwanghae Iron Works

1958. Opening of Hwanghae Iron Works. Imperf or perf.
| N147 | 110 | 10wn. blue | 5·50 | 80 |

111 Commemorative Badge

1958. Farewell to Chinese People's Volunteers (1st issue). Imperf or perf.
| N148 | 111 | 10wn. purple and blue | 2·75 | 70 |

See also No. N158.

112 Federation Emblem

1958. Fourth International Women's Federation Democratic Congress. Imperf or perf.
| N149 | 112 | 10wn. blue | 1·30 | 50 |

113 Conference Emblem

1958. First World Young Workers' Trade Union Federation Conference, Prague. Imperf or perf.

N150	**113**	10wn. brown and green	2·30	95

114 Flats, East Ward, Pyongyang

115 Workers' Flats, Pyongyang

1958. Rehousing Progress. Imperf or perf.

N151	**114**	10wn. blue	2·75	70
N152	**115**	10wn. green	2·75	70

117 Pyongyang Railway Station

119 Textile Worker

1958. Tenth Anniv of Korean People's Republic. Imperf or perf.

N153	-	10wn. green	3·50	65
N154	**117**	10wn. green	12·50	2·00
N155	-	10wn. brown and buff	2·20	65
N156	**119**	10wn. brown	10·00	2·30
N157	-	10wn. brown	12·00	4·50

DESIGNS—HORIZ: No. N153, Hungnam Fertiliser Plant; N157, Yongp'ung Dam, Pyongyang. VERT: No. N155, Arms of People's Republic.

121 Volunteer and Steam Troop Train

1958. Farewell to Chinese People's Volunteers (2nd issue). Imperf or perf.

N158	**121**	10wn. sepia	30·00	9·75

122 Transplanting Rice

1958. Imperf or perf.

N159	**122**	10wn. sepia	1·10	30

123 Winged Horse of Chollima

1958. National Production Executives' Meeting, Pyongyang. With or without gum. Imperf or perf.

N160	**123**	10wn. red	1·90	30

124 N. Korean and Chinese Flags

1958. North Korean–Chinese Friendship Month. With or without gum. Imperf or perf.

N161	**124**	10wn. red, blue green	1·60	40

125 Farm Workers

1959. National Co-operative Farming Congress, Pyongyang. With or without gum. Imperf or perf.

N162	**125**	10wn. blue	1·40	35

126 Gen. Ulji Mun Dok

1959. With gum. Imperf or perf.

N163	**126**	10wn. red and yellow	2·75	65

See also Nos. N165/7 and N216/19.

127 Women with Banner

1959. National Conference of Women Socialist Constructors, Pyongyang. With or without gum.

N164	**127**	10ch. brown and red	2·75	70

1959. Revalued currency. Portraits as T **126**. Imperf (with or without gum) or perf (with gum).

N165	-	2ch. blue on green	1·20	20
N166	-	5ch. purple on buff	1·40	25
N167	**126**	10ch. red on cream	2·40	30

PORTRAITS: 2ch. General Kang Gam Chan; 5ch. General Chon Bong Jun.

128 Rocket and Moon

1959. Launch of Soviet Moon Rocket. With or without gum. Imperf or perf.

N168	**128**	2ch. purple on buff	8·50	3·00
N169	**128**	10ch. blue on green	16·00	4·00

129 "Irrigation"

1959. Land Irrigation Project. Imperf or perf.

N170	**129**	10ch. multicoloured	5·75	1·30

130 Inscribed Tree at Partisan H.Q., Chongbong

131 Kim Il Sung Statue

132 Mt. Paekdu

1959. Partisan Successes against Japanese, 1937–39. With gum (No. N172) or no gum (others). Perf (N172) or imperf or perf (others).

N171	**130**	5ch. multicoloured	3·75	70
N172	**131**	10ch. blue and turquoise	1·90	45
N173	**132**	10ch. violet	3·25	90

133 "Flying Horse" Tractor

1959. "Great Perspectives" (1st issue: Development of Industrial Mechanization). With or without gum. Perf, roul or imperf.

N174	**133**	1ch. red, olive and green	1·70	25
N175	-	2ch. multicoloured	8·50	2·00
N176	-	2ch. red, pink and violet	1·60	30
N177	-	5ch. orange, brown and ochre	1·60	60
N178	-	10ch. blue, green & brn	2·00	50
N179	-	10ch. grn, lt grn & brn	3·75	65

DESIGNS: No. N175, Electric mine locomotive; N176, "Red Star 58" bulldozer; N177, "Flying Horse" excavator; N178, "SU-50" universal lathe; N179, "Victory 58" lorry.

See also Nos. N189a/200 and N275/79.

134 Armistice Building, Panmunjom

135 Protest Meeting

136 "Hoisting link between N. and S. Korea"

1959. Campaign for Withdrawal of U.S. Forces from S. Korea. With gum. Perf (20ch.) or imperf or perf (others).

N180	**134**	10ch. blue & ultramarine	1·20	30
N181	**135**	20ch. deep blue and blue	1·50	50
N182	**136**	70ch. brown, cream and purple	20·00	8·00

137 Emigration "Pickets"

1959. Campaign Against Emigration of South Koreans. With gum.

N183	**137**	20ch. brown and sepia	4·50	1·30

138 Korean Type of "1234"

139 Books breaking Chains

140 Emblems of Peace, Labour and Letters

141 Korean Alphabet of 1443

1959. International Book Exhibition, Leipzig. With gum (No. N184, N186) or no gum (others).

N184	**138**	5ch. sepia	20·00	6·50
N185	**139**	5ch. red and green	6·25	1·90
N186	**140**	10ch. blue	6·25	1·90
N187	**141**	10ch. violet and blue	9·25	3·25
MSN187a		152×122 mm. Nos. N184/7	85·00	44·00

142 Pig Farm

1959. Animal Husbandry. With gum (5ch.) or no gum (2ch.).

N188	-	2ch. brown, green & buff	3·00	65
N189	**142**	5ch. cream, blue & brn	3·75	95

DESIGN—HORIZ: 2ch. Cow-girl with Cattle.

143 Rotary Cement Kiln

1959. "Great Perspectives" (2nd issue: Production Targets). With gum (Nos. N190 and N192) or no gum (others). Perf (N197/8 and N200), perf or imperf (others).

N189a	**143**	1ch. cinnamon, brn & bl	40	25
N190	-	2ch. multicoloured	75	30
N191	-	5ch. multicoloured	70	35
N192	-	10ch. multicoloured	1·30	50
N193	-	10ch. purple, yell & bl	1·30	50
N194	-	10ch. yellow, grn & red	1·30	50
N195	-	10ch. multicoloured	1·30	50
N196	-	10ch. blue, light blue and green	1·30	50
N197	-	10ch. multicoloured	1·30	50
N198	-	10ch. green, buff and brown	1·30	50
N199	-	10ch. brown and orange	1·30	50
N200	-	10ch. multicoloured	1·30	50

DESIGNS—VERT: No. N190, Electric power lines and dam; N191, Loading fertilizers into goods wagon. HORIZ: No. N192, Factory, electric power lines and dam; N163, Harvesting; N194, Sugar-beet, factory and pieces of sugar; N195, Steel furnace; N196, Trawlers; N197, Pig-iron workers; N198, Coal miners; N199, Girl picking apples; N200, Textile worker.

144 Sika Deer

1959. Game Preservation. No gum (5ch.), with gum (10ch.).

N201		5ch. multicoloured	5·00	60
N202		5ch. yellow, brown & bl	5·00	60
N203		5ch. sepia, green & brn	5·00	60
N204		5ch. brown, black & blue	5·00	60
N205	**144**	10ch. multicoloured	5·00	65
N206	-	10ch. red, brown and green on cream	13·50	1·80

DESIGNS—HORIZ: No. N201, Chinese water deer; N202, Siberian weasel; N203, Steppe polecat; N204, European otter; N206, Common pheasant.

145 Congress Emblem

1960. Third Korean Trade Unions Federation Congress. With gum.

N207	**145**	5ch. multicoloured	70	25

146 *Chungnyon-ho* (freighter)

1959. Transport. With gum.

N208	-	5ch. purple	18·00	2·00
N209	**146**	10ch. green	4·50	1·30

DESIGN: 5ch. Electric train.

147 Soldier, Tractor and Plough

1960. 12th Anniv of Korean People's Army. With gum.

N210	**147**	5ch. violet and blue	70·00	55·00

148 Knife Dance

1960. Korean National Dances. Multicoloured.

N211	5ch. Type **148**	4·25	25
N212	5ch. Drum dance	4·25	25
N213	10ch. Farmers' dance	4·25	30

149 Women of Three
Races

1960. 50th Anniv of Int Women's Day. With gum.
| N214 | 149 | 5ch. mauve and blue | 1·20 | 15 |
| N215 | - | 10ch. green and orange | 1·20 | 30 |

DESIGN—VERT: 10ch. Woman operating lathe.

150 Kim Jong Ho
(geographer)

1960. Korean Celebrities. With gum.
N216	150	1ch. grey and green	1·30	10
N217	-	2ch. blue and yellow	1·60	10
N218	-	5ch. blue and yellow	5·75	25
N219	-	10ch. brown and ochre	1·60	15

PORTRAITS: 2ch. Kim Hong Do (painter); 5ch. Pak Yon (musician); 10ch. Chong Da San (scholar).

151 Grapes

1960. Wild Fruits. Fruits in natural colours. With or without gum (N221/2), with gum (others).
N220	5ch. olive and turquoise	2·75	65
N221	5ch. drab and blue	2·75	65
N222	5ch. olive and blue	2·75	65
N223	10ch. olive and orange	3·25	90
N224	10ch. green and pink	3·25	90

FRUITS: No. N220, T **151**; N221, Fruit of "Actinidia arguta planch"; N222, Pine-cone; N223, Hawthorn berries; N224, Horse-chestnut.

152 Lenin

1960. 90th Birth Anniv of Lenin. With gum.
| N225 | 152 | 10ch. purple | 90 | 20 |

153 Koreans
and American
Soldier
(caricature)

1960. Campaign Day for Withdrawal of U.S. Forces from South Korea. With gum.
| N226 | 153 | 10ch. blue | 4·50 | 50 |

154 Arch of Triumph
Square, Pyongyang

1960. Views of Pyongyang.
N227	154	10ch. green	75	15
N228	-	20ch. slate	1·50	25
N229	-	40ch. green	2·50	55
N230	-	70ch. green	4·50	1·20
N231	-	1wn. blue	5·75	2·10

VIEWS OF PYONGYANG: 20ch. River Taedong promenade; 40ch. Youth Street; 70ch. People's Army Street; 1wn. Sungri Street.

155 Russian
Flag on Moon
(14.9.59)

1960. Russian Cosmic Rocket Flights. With gum (5ch.) or no gum (10ch.).
| N232 | | 5ch. turquoise | 7·50 | 7·25 |
| N233 | 155 | 10ch. multicoloured | 11·00 | 3·50 |

DESIGN: 5ch. "Lunik 3" approaching Moon (4.10.59).

156 "Mirror Rock"

1960. Diamond Mountains Scenery (1st issue). Multicoloured.
N234	5ch. Type **156**	1·30	20
N235	5ch. Devil-faced Rock	1·30	20
N236	10ch. Dancing Dragon Bridge (horiz)	4·75	30
N237	10ch. Nine Dragon Falls	4·25	30
N238	10ch. Mt. Diamond on the Sea (horiz)	1·70	15

See also Nos. N569/72, N599/601 and N1180/4.

157 Lily

1960. Flowers. Multicoloured. With gum (N242), with or without gum (others).
N239	5ch. Type **157**	1·50	25
N240	5ch. Rhododendron	1·50	25
N241	10ch. Hibiscus	2·50	40
N242	10ch. Blue campanula	2·50	40
N243	10ch. Mauve campanula	2·50	40

158 Guerrillas in the Snow

1960. Revolutionary Leadership of Kim Il Sung.
N244	158	5ch. red	65	15
N245	-	10ch. blue	1·20	15
N246	-	10ch. red	1·20	15
N247	-	10ch. blue	1·20	15
N248	-	10ch. red	1·20	15

DESIGNS: No. N245, Kim Il Sung talks to guerrillas; N246, Kim Il Sung at Pochonbo; N247, Kim Il Sung on bank of Amnok River; N248, Kim Il Sung returns to Pyongyang.

159 Korean and
Soviet Flags

1960. 15th Anniv of Liberation from Japan.
| N249 | 159 | 10ch. red, blue & brown | 1·00 | 20 |

160 "North
Korean–Soviet
Friendship"

1960. North Korean–Soviet Friendship Month.
| N250 | 160 | 10ch. lake on cream | 60 | 20 |

161 Okryu Bridge,
Pyongyang

1960. Pyongyang Buildings.
N251	161	10ch. blue	3·25	30
N252	-	10ch. violet	2·75	15
N253	-	10ch. green	1·00	15

DESIGNS: No. N252, Grand Theatre, Pyongyang; N253, Okryu Restaurant.

162 Tokro River Dam

1960. Inauguration of Tokro River Hydro-electric Power Station. With gum.
| N254 | 162 | 5ch. blue | 1·20 | 20 |

163

1960. 15th Anniv of World Federation of Trade Unions.
| N255 | 163 | 10ch. lt blue, ultram & bl | 65 | 20 |

164 Quayside
Welcome

1960. Repatriation of Korean Nationals from Japan.
| N256 | 164 | 10ch. purple | 3·25 | 25 |

165 Lenin and
Workers

1960. Korea–Soviet Friendship. With gum.
| N257 | 165 | 10ch. brown and flesh | 70 | 20 |

166 Football

1960. Liberation Day Sports Meeting, Pyongyang. Multicoloured.
N258	5ch. Running (vert)	85	15
N259	5ch. Weightlifting (vert)	85	15
N260	5ch. Cycling (vert)	2·50	20
N261	5ch. Gymnastics (vert)	85	15
N262	5ch. Type **166**	1·30	20
N263	10ch. Swimming	1·00	50
N264	10ch. Moranbong Stadium, Pyongyang	85	50

167 Friendship
Monument,
Pyongyang

1960. Tenth Anniv of Entry of Chinese Volunteers into Korean War. With gum.
| N265 | | 5ch. mauve | 60 | 15 |
| N266 | 167 | 10ch. blue | 60 | 15 |

DESIGN—HORIZ: 5ch. Chinese and Korean soldiers celebrating.

168 Federation
Emblem

1960. 15th Anniv of World Democratic Youth Federation.
| N267 | 168 | 10ch. multicoloured | 55 | 20 |

169
White-backed
Woodpecker

1960. Birds.
N268	169	2ch. multicoloured	7·50	80
N268a	-	5ch. multicoloured	11·00	65
N269	-	5ch. brown, yellow & bl	13·50	1·80
N270	-	10ch. yellow, brn & grn	9·25	80

DESIGNS—HORIZ: 5ch. (N268a), Mandarins; 10ch. Black-naped oriole. VERT: 5ch. (N269), Oriental scops owl.

170 Korean Wrestling

1960. Sports and Games. Multicoloured.
N271	170	5ch. Type **170**	80	15
N272		5ch. Riding on swing (vert)	80	15
N273		5ch. Archery	3·25	40
N274		10ch. Jumping on see-saw (vert)	80	15

171 Cogwheel and
Textiles

1961. "Great Perspectives" (3rd issue: Targets of Seven-Year Plan, 1961–67. Inscr "1961"). Multicoloured.
N275	5ch. Type **171**	1·10	15
N276	5ch. Cogwheel and Corn ("Mechanization of Rural Economy")	2·10	15
N277	10ch. Hammer, sickle and torch on flag (vert)	55	15
N278	10ch. Cogwheels around power station	1·10	15
N279	10ch. Cogwheel and molten steel	80	15

172 Wild
Ginseng
(perennial
herb)

1961. Multicoloured.. Multicoloured..
| N280 | 5ch. Type **172** | 3·50 | 25 |
| N281 | 10ch. Cultivated ginseng | 3·50 | 25 |

173 Aldehyde Shop

1961. Construction of Vinalon Factory. With gum.
N282	173	5ch. red and yellow	1·00	15
N283	-	10ch. green and yellow	2·30	25
N284	-	10ch. blue and yellow	2·30	25
N285	-	20ch. purple and yellow	3·00	50

DESIGNS: No. N283, Glacial acetic acid shop; N284, Polymerization and saponification shop; N285, Spinning shop.

See also Nos. N338/41.

174 Construction
Work

1961. Construction of Children's Palace, Pyongyang. With gum.
| N286 | 174 | 2ch. red on yellow | 60 | 20 |

175 Museum Building

1961. Completion of Museum of Revolution, Pyongyang. With gum.

N287	**175**	10ch. red	50	20

176 Cosmic Rocket

1961. Launching of Soviet Venus Rocket.

N288	**176**	10ch. red, yellow & blue	6·25	25

177 Wheat Harvester

1961. Agricultural Mechanization. With gum.

N289	-	5ch. violet	70	15
N290	-	5ch. green	70	15
N291	**177**	5ch. green	70	15
N292	-	10ch. blue	1·00	15
N293	-	10ch. purple	1·00	15

DESIGNS: No. N289, Tractor-plough; N290, Disc-harrow; N292, Maize-harvester; N293, Tractors.

178

1961. Opening of Training Institute.

N294	**178**	10ch. brown on buff	90	20

179 Agriculture

1961. 15th Anniv of Land Reform Law. With gum.

N295	**179**	10ch. green on yellow	85	20

180

1961. 15th Anniv of National Programme. With gum.

N296	**180**	10ch. purple and yellow	50	20

181 Chub Mackerel

1961. Marine Life.

N297	**181**	5ch. multicoloured	2·75	25
N298	-	5ch. black and blue	6·50	80
N299	-	10ch. blue, black & lt bl	7·50	35
N300	-	10ch. multicoloured	2·75	25
N301	-	10ch. brown, yell & grn	2·75	25

DESIGNS: No. N298, Common dolphin; N299, Whale sp; N300, Yellow-finned tuna; N301, Pacific cod.

182 Tractor-crane

1961. With gum.

N302	**182**	1ch. brown	1·30	15
N303	-	2ch. brown	1·30	15
N304	-	5ch. green	1·90	15
N305	-	10ch. violet	1·80	25

DESIGNS—HORIZ: 2ch. Heavy-duty lorry; 5ch. Eight-metres turning lathe. VERT: 10ch. 3000-ton press.

See also Nos. N378/9c.

183 Tree-planting

1961. Re-afforestation Campaign. With gum.

N306	**183**	10ch. green	1·60	30

184 "Peaceful Unification" Banner

1961. Propaganda for Peaceful Reunification of Korea.

N307	**184**	10ch. multicoloured	20·00	2·00

185 Pioneers visiting Battlefield

1961. 15th Anniv of Children's Union. Mult.

N308	5ch. Pioneers bathing	1·30	25
N309	10ch. Pioneer bugler	3·25	50
N310	10ch. Type **185**	1·30	25

186 "Labour Law"

1961. 15th Anniv of Labour Law. With gum.

N311	**186**	10ch. blue on yellow	85	25

187 Apples

1961. Fruit. Multicoloured.

N312	5ch. Peaches	1·10	15
N313	5ch. Plums	1·10	15
N314	5ch. Type **187**	1·10	15
N315	10ch. Persimmons	1·10	15
N316	10ch. Pears	1·10	15

188 Yuri Gagarin and "Vostok 1"

1961. World's First Manned Space Flight.

N317	**188**	10ch. ultramarine & blue	1·90	55
N318	**188**	10ch. violet and blue	1·90	55

189 Power Station

1961. 15th Anniv of Nationalization of Industries Law. With gum.

N319	**189**	10ch. brown	15·00	80

190 Women at Work

1961. 15th Anniv of Sex Equality Law. With gum.

N320	**190**	10ch. red	60	20

191 Children planting Tree

1961. Children. Multicoloured.

N321	5ch. Type **191**	1·30	15
N322	5ch. Reading book	65	15
N323	10ch. Playing with ball	65	20
N324	10ch. Building a house	65	20
N325	10ch. Waving flag	65	20

192 Poultry and Stock-breeding

1961. Improvement in Living Standards. Mult.

N326	5ch. Type **192**	1·00	15
N327	10ch. Fabrics and textile factory	1·60	25
N328	10ch. Trawler and fish (horiz)	1·50	25
N329	10ch. Grain-harvesting (horiz)	85	15

193 Soldiers on March (statue)

1961. 25th Anniv of Fatherland Restoration Association. With gum.

N330	-	10ch. violet	65	30
N331	-	10ch. violet	65	30
N332	**193**	10ch. blue and buff	95	30

DESIGNS—Marshal Kim Il Sung: No. N330, Seated under tree; N331, Working at desk.

194 Party Emblem and Members

1961. Fourth Korean Workers' Party Congress, Pyongyang. With gum.

N333	**194**	10ch. green	55	30
N334	-	10ch. purple	55	30
N335	-	10ch. red	55	30

DESIGNS—VERT: No. N334, "Chollima" statue, Pyongyang. HORIZ: No. N335, Marshal Kim Il Sung.

195 Miner

1961. Miners' Day. With gum.

N336	**195**	10ch. brown	11·00	80

196 Pak in Ro

1961. 400th Birth Anniv of Pak in Ro (poet).

N337	**196**	10ch. indigo on blue	95	20

197 Aldehyde Shop

1961. Completion of Vinalon Factory. With gum.

N338	**197**	5ch. red and yellow	1·00	15
N339	-	10ch. brown and yellow	1·60	15
N340	-	10ch. blue and yellow	1·60	15
N341	-	20ch. purple and yellow	2·50	30

DESIGNS: No. N339, Glacial-acetic shop; N340, Polymerization and saponification shop; N341, Spinning shop.

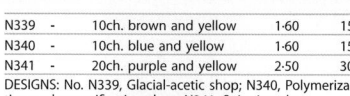

198 Korean and Chinese Flags

1961. North Korean Friendship Treaties with China and the U.S.S.R.

N342		10ch. multicoloured	80	30
N343	**198**	10ch. red, blue & yellow	80	30

DESIGN: No. N342, Korean and Soviet flags.

199 Basketball

1961. Physical Culture Day. With gum.

N344	-	2ch. grey	1·00	15
N345	-	5ch. blue	1·70	15
N346	**199**	10ch. blue	1·70	25
N347	-	10ch. blue	1·70	25
N348	-	10ch. purple	1·70	25
N349	-	20ch. purple	1·30	40

DESIGNS: 2ch. Table tennis; 5ch. Flying model glider; 10ch. (N347) Rowing; 10ch. (N348) High jumping; 20ch. Sports emblem.

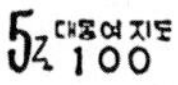

(200)

1961. Centenary of Publication of Map "Taidong Yu Jido" by Kim Jung Ho. No. N216 surch with T **200**.

N350	**150**	5ch. on 1ch. grey and green	65·00	50·00

201 General Rock

1961. Mt. Chilbo Scenery. With gum.

N351	**201**	5ch. blue	90	15
N352	-	5ch. brown	90	15
N353	-	10ch. violet	1·70	25
N354	-	10ch. blue	1·70	25
N355	-	10ch. blue	1·70	25

DESIGNS—HORIZ: No. N352, Chonbul Peak; N354, Tiled House Rock; N355, Rainbow Rock. VERT: No. N353, Mansa Peak.

202 "Agriculture and Industry"

1961. With gum.

N356	**202**	10ch. green	65	20

203 Winged Horse and Congress Emblem

1961. Fifth World Federation of Trade Unions Congress, Moscow. With gum.

N357	**203**	10ch. blue, purple and violet	40	20

204 Class "Red Banner"
Electric Locomotive

1961. Railway Electrification. With gum.
N358 **204** 10ch. violet and yellow   18·00   2·10

205 Ice Hockey

1961. Winter Sports. With gum.
N359 -   10ch. brown and green   1·30   25
N360 -   10ch. brown and green   1·30   25
N361 **205** 10ch. brown and blue   1·30   25
N362 -   10ch. brown and green   1·30   25
DESIGNS—No. N359, Figure skating; N360, Speed skating;
N362, Skiing.

206 Grain Harvest

1962. "Six Heights" of Production Targets (1st series).
Inscr "1962". With gum.
N363 5ch. red, violet and grey   1·00   25
N364 5ch. brown and grey   6·75   65
N365 **206** 10ch. yellow, black & bl   1·00   25
N366 -   10ch. red, yellow & blue   3·25   25
N367 -   10ch. black and blue   3·00   30
N368 -   10ch. yellow, brown & bl   1·00   25
DESIGNS—No. N363, Ladle and molten steel; N364, Elec-
tric mine train; N366, Fabrics and mill; N367, Trawler and
catch; N368, Construction of flats.
See also Nos. N440/5.

207 Tiger

1962. Animals.
N369 **207** 2ch. multicoloured   3·75   25
N370 -   2ch. brown and green   2·75   15
N371 -   5ch. yellow and green   1·70   15
N372 -   10ch. brown and green   3·00   30
ANIMALS—HORIZ: 2ch. (N370), Racoon-dog; 5ch. Chinese
ferret-badger; 10ch. Asiatic black bear.

208 Kayagum
Player

1962. Musical Instruments and Players (1st series).
Multicoloured.
N373 10ch. Type **208**   2·75   30
N374 10ch. Man playing haegum
(two-stringed bowed instru-
ment)   2·75   30
N375 10ch. Woman playing wolgum
(banjo)   2·75   30
N376 10ch. Man playing chotdae
(flute)   2·75   30
N377 10ch. Woman playing wagon-
ghu (harp)   2·75   30
See also Nos. N473/7.

1962. As T **182**. Inscr "1962". With gum (Nos. N379 and
379b), no gum (others).
N378   5ch. green   1·20   15
N379   10ch. blue   2·10   20
N379a 10ch. brown   12·50
N379b 5wn. brown   18·00   4·00
N379c 10wn. purple   23·00   8·00
DESIGNS—VERT: 5ch. Hydraulic press; 10ch. (2), Three-
ton hammer; 10wn. Tunnel drill. HORIZ: 5wn. Hobbing
machine.
See also Nos. N415/22, N513/15 and N573.

209 "Leuhdorfia
puziloi"

1962. Butterflies. Multicoloured.
N380 5ch. Type **209**   4·25   20
N381 10ch. *Sericinus telamon* (purple
background)   4·25   20
N382 10ch. Keeled apollo (lilac
background)   4·25   20
N383 10ch. Peacock (green back-
ground)   4·25   20

210 G. S. Titov and "Vostok 2"

1962. Second Soviet Manned Space Flight.
N384 **210** 10ch. multicoloured   3·00   30

211 Marshal Kim Il Sung and
(inset) addressing Workers

1962. Marshal Kim Il Sung's 50th Birthday. With gum.
N385 **211** 10ch. red   65   25
N386 -   10ch. green   65   25
N387 -   10ch. blue   65   25
DESIGN: No. 387, Kim Il Sung in fur hat and (inset) in-
specting battle-front.

212 Kim Chaek

1962. Korean Revolutionaries (1st series). With gum.
N388 **212** 10ch. sepia   85   15
N389 -   10ch. blue   85   15
N390 -   10ch. red   85   15
N391 -   10ch. purple   85   15
N392 -   10ch. green   85   15
N393 -   10ch. blue   85   15
N394 -   10ch. brown   85   15
PORTRAITS: No. N389, Kang Gon; N390, An Gil; N391, Ryu
Gyong Su; N392/3, Kim Jong Suk; N394, Choe Chun Guk.
See also Nos. N478/82 and N733/5.

213 Mother with Children

1962. National Mothers' Meeting, Pyongyang.
N395 **213** 10ch. multicoloured   65   20

214 Black-faced
Spoonbill

1962. Birds. Inscr "1962". Multicoloured.
N396 5ch. Type **214**   2·30   30
N397 5ch. Brown hawk owl   8·00   40
N398 10ch. Eastern broad-billed roller   4·75   50
N399 10ch. Black paradise flycatcher   4·75   50
N400 20ch. Tundra swan   5·75   80

215 Victory
Flame

1962. 25th Anniv of Battle of Pochonbo.
N401 **215** 10ch. multicoloured   90   20

216 Japanese Croaker

1962. Fish. Multicoloured.
N402 5ch. Type **216**   2·10   15
N403 5ch. Hairtail   2·10   15
N404 10ch. Dotted gizzard shad
(head pointing to right)   3·00   25
N405 10ch. Japanese spotted seabass
(blue background)   3·00   25
N406 10ch. Japanese croaker (green
background)   3·00   25

217 Waterdropper

1962. Antiques. With gum.
N407 -   4ch. black and blue   1·30   15
N408 **217** 5ch. black and ochre   1·30   15
N409 **A** 10ch. black and green   1·70   20
N410 **B** 10ch. black and orange   1·70   20
N411 **C** 10ch. black and purple   1·70   20
N412 **D** 10ch. black and brown   1·70   20
N413 **E** 10ch. black and yellow   1·70   20
N414 -   40ch. black and grey   5·00   50
DESIGNS—VERT: 4ch. Brush pot; 40ch. Porcelain decanter.
HORIZ: A, Inkstand; B, Brushstand; C, Turtle paperweight;
D, Inkstone; E, Document case.

218 Radial
Drill

1962. Double frame-line. With gum.
N415 2ch. green   45   10
N415a 2ch. brown   6·25
N416 4ch. blue   3·00   10
N417 **218** 5ch. blue   85   10
N418 -   5ch. purple   95   10
N419 -   10ch. purple   1·30   10
N420 -   40ch. blue   6·50   25
N421 -   90ch. blue   2·75   40
N422 -   1wn. brown   8·25   65
DESIGNS—VERT: 2ch. Vertical milling machine; 5ch.
(N418), Hydraulic hammer; 1wn. Spindle drill. HORIZ: 4ch.
"Victory April 15" motor-car; 10ch. All-purpose excavator;
40ch. Trolley-bus; 90ch. Planing machine.
See also Nos. N513/15 and N573.

219 Chong Da
San

1962. Birth Bicentenary of Chong Da San (philosopher).
N423 **219** 10ch. purple   55   20

220 Voter

1962. Election of Deputies to National Assembly.
Multicoloured.
N424 10ch. Type **220**   1·30   25
N425 10ch. Family going to poll   1·30   25

221 Pyongyang

1962. 1535th Anniv of Pyongyang. With gum.
N426 **221** 10ch. black and blue   85   20

222 Globe and
"Vostok 3" and "4"

1962. First "Team" Manned Space Flight.
N427 **222** 10ch. indigo, blue & red   3·00   65

223 Spiraea

1962. Korean Plants. Plants in natural colours; frame and
inscr colours given.
N428 **223** 5ch. light green & green   1·50   15
N429 -   10ch. green and red   1·50   15
N430 -   10ch. blue and purple   1·50   15
N431 -   10ch. green and olive   1·50   15
PLANTS: No. N429, Ginseng; N430, Campanula; N431,
Rheumcoreanum makai (Polyonaceae).

224 "Uibang
Ryuchui"

1962. 485th Anniv of Publication of "Uibang Ryuchui"
(medical encyclopaedia).
N432 **224** 10ch. multicoloured   5·00   40

225 Science Academy

1962. Tenth Anniv of Korean Science Academy.
N433 **225** 10ch. blue and turquoise   1·30   20

226
Fisherwomen

1962
N434 **226** 10ch. blue   1·30   20

227 European Mink

1962. Animals.
N435 **227** 4ch. brown and green   2·10   35
N436 -   5ch. blue, drab and
green   2·10   35
N437 -   10ch. blue and yellow   2·50   35
N438 -   10ch. sepia and
turquoise   2·50   35
N439 -   20ch. brown and blue   5·00   60
ANIMALS—HORIZ: No. N436, Chinese hare. VERT: No.
N437, Eurasian red squirrel; N438, Common goral; N439,
Siberian chipmunk.

228 Harvesting

1963. "Six Heights" of Production Targets (2nd issue).
Inscr "1963". Multicoloured.
N440 5ch. Miner   1·00   25
N441 10ch. Type **228**   75   15
N442 10ch. Furnaceman   75   15
N443 10ch. Construction worker   75   15
N444 10ch. Textiles loom operator   1·00   15
N445 40ch. Fisherman and trawler   2·50   55

229 Soldier

1963. 15th Anniv of Korean People's Army. With gum.

N446	-	5ch. brown	50	10
N447	**229**	10ch. red	85	15
N448	-	10ch. blue	1·30	15

DESIGNS: 5ch. Airman; 10ch. Sailor.

230 Peony

1963. Korean Flowers. Multicoloured.

N449	5ch. Type **230**	85	15
N450	10ch. Rugosa rose	1·30	15
N451	10ch. Azalea	1·30	15
N452	20ch. Campion	1·30	15
N453	40ch. Orchid	3·75	50

231 *Sadang-ch'um* (Korean folk dance)

1963. International Music and Dancing Contest, Pyongyang. Multicoloured.

N454	10ch. Type **231**	3·25	25
N455	10ch. Dancer with fan	3·25	25

232 Revolutionaries

1963. Third Anniv of South Korean Rising of April, 1960.

N456	**232**	10ch. multicoloured	60	20

233 Karl Marx

1963. 145th Birth Anniv of Karl Marx. With gum.

N457	**233**	10ch. blue	55	20

234 Children in Chemistry Class

1963. Child Care and Amenities. Multicoloured.

N458	2ch. Type **234**	1·10	25
N459	5ch. Children running	90	15
N460	10ch. Boy conducting choir	2·50	25
N461	10ch. Girl chasing butterfly	5·00	30

235 Armed Koreans and American Soldier (caricature)

1963. Campaign Month for Withdrawal of U.S. Forces from South Korea.

N462	**235**	10ch. multicoloured	85	20

236 *Cyrtoclytus capra*

1963. Korean Beetles. Multicoloured designs. Colours of beetles given.

N463	5ch. Type **236**	1·70	25
N464	10ch. multicoloured	2·50	25
N465	10ch. red and blue	2·50	25
N466	10ch. indigo, blue and purple	2·50	25

BEETLES: No. N464, *Cicindela chinensis* (tiger beetle); N465, *Purpuricenus lituratus*; N466, *Agapanthia pilicornis*.

237 Soldier with Flag

1963. Tenth Anniv of Victory in Korean War.

N467	**237**	10ch. multicoloured	90	20

238 North Korean Flag

1963. 15th Anniv of People's Republic. Multicoloured.

N468	10ch. Type **238**	50	25
N469	10ch. North Korean Badge	50	25

239 Namdae Gate, Kaesong

1963. Ancient Korean Buildings (1st series). With gum.

N470	**239**	5ch. black	40	15
N471	-	10ch. blue	70	20
N472	-	10ch. brown	70	20

BUILDINGS: No. N471, Taedong Gate, Pyongyang; N472, Potong Gate, Pyongyang.

See also Nos. N537/8.

240 Ajaeng (bowed zither)

1963. Musical Instruments and Players (2nd series). Multicoloured. Nos. N473 and N476 with gum.

N473	3ch. Type **240**	1·70	15
N474	5ch. Pyongyon (jade chimes)	1·70	15
N475	10ch. Saenap (brass bowl)	2·10	20
N476	10ch. Rogo (drums in frame)	2·10	20
N477	10ch. Piri ("wooden pipe")	2·10	20

1963. Korean Revolutionaries (2nd issue). As T **212**. With gum.

N478	5ch. brown	35	10
N479	5ch. purple	35	10
N480	10ch. rose	40	15
N481	10ch. slate	40	15
N482	10ch. dull purple	40	15

PORTRAITS: No. N478, Kwon Yong Byok; N479, Ma Dong Hui; N480, Li Je Sun; N481, Pak Dal; N482, Kim Yong Bom.

241 Nurse with Children

1963. Child Welfare. Multicoloured.

N483	10ch. Type **241**	50	20
N484	10ch. Children in playground	50	20

242 Hwajang Hall

1963. Mount Myohyang Resort. Multicoloured.

N485	5ch. Type **242**	65	15
N486	10c. Mountain stream and chalet	1·30	15
N487	10ch. Kwanum Pavilion and stone pagoda (horiz)	1·30	15
N488	10ch. Rope bridge across river (horiz)	3·25	15

243 Furnaceman

1963. Seven Year Plan. With gum.

N489	**243**	5ch. red	40	15
N490	-	10ch. grey	3·00	40
N491	-	10ch. red	3·00	40
N492	-	10ch. lilac	1·80	15

DESIGNS—VERT: No. N490, Construction workers. HORIZ: No. N491, Power technicians; N492, Miners.

244 Children hoeing

1963. *Hung Bo* (fairytale). Multicoloured.

N493	5ch. Type **244**	45	25
N494	10ch. Tying up broken leg of swallow	1·40	25
N495	10ch. Barn swallow dropping gourd seed	1·40	25
N496	10ch. Sawing through giant gourd	75	25
N497	10ch. Treasure inside gourd	75	25

245 Marksman

1963. Marksmanship. Multicoloured.

N498	5ch. Type **245**	50	15
N499	10ch. Marksman with small-bore rifle	75	15
N500	10ch. Marksman with standard rifle	75	15

246 Sinuiju Chemical Fibre Factory

1964. Chemical Fibres Factories. With gum.

N501	**246**	10ch. slate	1·00	15
N502	-	10ch. purple	1·00	15

DESIGN: No. N502, Chongjin Chemical Fibre Factory.

247 Strikers

1964. 35th Anniv of Wonsan General Strike. With gum.

N503	**247**	10ch. brown	85	20

248 Korean Alphabet

1964. 520th Anniv of Korean Alphabet.

N504	**248**	10ch. green, buff & brn	85	25

249 Lenin

1964. 40th Death Anniv of Lenin. With gum.

N505	**249**	10ch. red	55	20

250 Whale-catcher

1964. Fishing Industry. Multicoloured.

N506	5ch. Type **250**	85	15
N507	5ch. Trawler No. 051	85	15
N508	10ch. Trawler No. 397	1·70	40
N509	10ch. Trawler No. 738	1·70	40

251 Insurgents

1964. 45th Anniv of Rising of 1st March. With gum.

N510	**251**	10ch. purple	45	20

252 Warring Peasants

1964. 70th Anniv of Kabo Peasants' War. With gum.

N511	**252**	10ch. purple	45	20

253 Students' Palace, Pyongyang

1964. With gum.

N512	**253**	10ch. green	45	20

254 "Changbaek" Excavator

1964. Single frame-line. Dated "1964" or "1965" (No. N573). With gum.

N513	-	5ch. violet	1·10	15
N514	**254**	10ch. green	1·70	15
N515	-	10ch. blue	1·70	15
N573	-	10ch. violet	1·50	25

DESIGNS—VERT: 5ch. 200 metre drill; 10ch. (N573) "Horning 500" machine. HORIZ: 10ch. (N515) 400 h.p. Diesel engine.

255 "On the March"

1964. Fifth Korean Democratic Youth League Congress, Pyongyang.

N516	**255**	10ch. multicoloured	45	20

256 Electric Train

1964. Inauguration of Pyongyang–Sinuiju Electric Railway.

N517	**256**	10ch. multicoloured	10·00	30

257 Rejoicing in Chongsan-ri Village

1964. Popular Movement at Chongsan-ri. With gum.
N517a **257** 5ch. brown   £250

258 Drum Dance

1964. Korean Dances.
N518 **258** 2ch. mauve, buff & black   2·10   40
N519   – 5ch. red, black & yellow   2·50   40
N520   – 10ch. multicoloured   3·00   40
DESIGNS: 5ch. "Ecstasy" (solo); 10ch. Tabor.

259 "For the Sake of the Fatherland"

1964. Li Su Bok Commemorative. With gum.
N521 **259** 5ch. red   65   15

260 Nampo Smelting Works

1964. With gum.
N522 **260** 5ch. green   3·75   15
N523   – 10ch. slate   4·00   25
DESIGN: 10ch. Hwanghae iron works.

261 Torch, Chollima Statue and Cogwheel

1964. Asian Economic Seminar, Pyongyang. Multicoloured.
N524 5ch. Type **261**   40   15
N525 10ch. Flags, statue and cogwheel   55   20

262 Korean People and Statue of Kang Ho Yong (war hero)

1964. Struggle for Reunification of Korea.
N526 **262** 10ch. multicoloured   70   15

263 Hawk Fowl

1964. Domestic Poultry. Multicoloured.
N527 2ch. Type **263**   85   15
N528 4ch. White fowl   85   15
N529 5ch. Ryongyon fowl   1·30   15
N530 5ch. Black fowl   1·30   15
N531 40ch. Helmet guineafowl   4·25   1·30

264 Skiing

1964. Winter Olympic Games, Innsbruck.
N532 **264** 5ch. red, blue and buff   65   10
N533   – 10ch. blue, green & buff   1·10   15
N534   – 10ch. blue, red and buff   1·10   15
DESIGNS: No. N533, Ice skating; N534, Skiing (slalom).

265 *Tobolsk* (passenger ship) and Flags

1964. Fifth Anniv of Agreement for Repatriation of Koreans in Japan.
N535 **265** 10ch. red, blue & lt blue   1·60   25
N536   – 30ch. multicoloured   1·60   15
DESIGN: 30ch. Return of repatriates.

266 Tonggun Pavilion Uiju

1964. Ancient Korean Buildings (2nd series). With gum.
N537 **266** 5ch. purple   35   15
N538   – 10ch. green   40   15
DESIGN: 10ch. Inpang Pavilion, Kanggye City.

267 Cycling

1964. Olympic Games, Tokyo.
N539 2ch. brown and blue   35   15
N540 **267** 5ch. brown and green   1·00   15
N541   – 10ch. orange and blue   40   15
N542   – 10ch. orange and green   40   15
N543   – 40ch. brown and blue   85   50
DESIGNS—HORIZ: 2ch. Rifle-shooting; 10ch. blue, Running. VERT: 10ch. green, Wrestling; 40ch. Volleyball.

268 Burning of the *General Sherman*

1964. The *General Sherman* Incident, 1866. With gum.
N544 **268** 30ch. brown   3·00   40

269 Organizing Guerrillas

1964. Guerrilla Operations in the 1930s against the Japanese. With gum.
N545 **269** 2ch. violet   40   15
N546   – 5ch. blue   55   15
N547   – 10ch. black   65   15
DESIGNS: 5ch. Kim Il Sung addressing guerillas; 10ch. Battle scene at Xiaowangqing.

270 Students attacking

1964. Kwangju Students Rising, 1929. With gum.
N548 **270** 10ch. violet   2·20   15

271 Weightlifting

1964. "GANEFO" Athletic Games, Djakarta, Indonesia (1963). Multicoloured.
N549 2ch. Type **271**   40   15
N550 5ch. Athlete breasting tape   40   15
N551 5ch. Boxing (horiz)   40   15
N552 10ch. Football (horiz)   75   15
N553 10ch. Globe emblem (horiz)   65   15

272 Lynx

1964. Animals. With gum.
N554 2ch. sepia (Type **272**)   1·50   25
N555 5ch. sepia (Leopard cat)   3·75   25
N556 10ch. brown (Leopard)   4·50   25
N557 10ch. sepia (Yellow-throated marten)   4·50   25

273 Vietnamese Attack

1964. Support for People of Vietnam.
N558 **273** 10ch. multicoloured   55   15

274 Prof. Kim Bong Han and Emblems

1964. Kyongrak Biological Systems.
N559 **274** 2ch. purple and olive   90   15
N560   – 5ch. green, orange & bl   1·30   15
N561   – 10ch. red, yellow & blue   1·70   15
DESIGNS—33×23½ mm: 5ch. "Bonghan" duct; 10ch. "Bonghan" corpuscle. Each include emblems as in Type **274**.

275 Farmers, Tractor and Lorry

1964. Agrarian Programme. Multicoloured.
N562 5ch. Type **275**   25   10
N563 10ch. Peasants with scroll and book   40   15
N564 10ch. Peasants, one writing in book   40   15

276 Chung Jin gets a Pistol

1964. The Struggle to capture Japanese Arms. With gum.
N565 **276** 4ch. brown   60   15

277 Girl with Korean Products

1964. Economic 7 Year Plan. Multicoloured. With gum (5ch.) or no gum (others).
N566 5ch. Type **277**   75   10
N567 10ch. Farm girl   75   15
N568 10ch. Couple on winged horse (23½×23½ mm)   50   15

278 Three Fairies Rock

1964. Diamond Mountains Scenery (2nd issue). Inscr "1964". Multicoloured. Without gum (2, 4ch.) or with gum (others).
N569 2ch. Type **278**   1·00   15
N570 4ch. Ryonju Falls   3·50   20
N571 10ch. The Ten Thousand Rocks, Manmulsang   1·00   15
N572 10ch. Chinju Falls   3·50   20

280 Soldiers Advancing, Fusong

1965. Guerrilla Operations against the Japanese, 1934–40. With gum.
N574 **280** 10ch. violet   45   15
N575   – 10ch. violet   45   15
N576   – 10ch. green   45   15
DESIGNS: No. N575, Soldiers descending hill, Hongqihe; N576, Soldiers attacking hill post, Luozigou.

281 Tuman River

1965. Korean Rivers. Multicoloured.
N577 2ch. Type **281**   60   10
N578 5ch. Taedong (vert)   2·10   15
N579 10ch. Amnok   85   15

282 Union Badge

1965. First Congress of Landworkers' Union, Pyongyang. With gum.
N580 **282** 10ch. multicoloured   70   15

283 Furnacemen and Workers

1965. 10 Major Tasks of 7 Year Plan. With gum.
N581 **283** 10ch. multicoloured   55   15

284 Miners' Strike, Sinhung Colliery

1965. 35th Anniv of Strikes and Peasants' Revolt. With gum.
N582 **284** 10ch. olive   1·70   15
N583   – 10ch. brown   2·10   15
N584   – 40ch. purple   1·40   25
DESIGNS: 10ch. Strikers at Pyongyang Rubber Factory; 40ch. Revolt of Tanchon peasants.

285 Embankment Construction

1965. Sunhwa River Works. With gum.
N585 **285** 10ch. multicoloured   40   15

286 Hand holding Torch

1965. Fifth Anniv of South Korean Rising of April 19th. Multicoloured. With gum.
N586 10ch. Type **286**   35   15
N587 40ch. Student-hero, Kim Chio   70   15

287 Power Station
under Construction

1965. Construction of Thermal Power Station, Pyongyang. With gum.

| N588 | **287** | 5ch. brown and blue | 75 | 15 |

288 African and Asian

1965. Tenth Anniv of First Afro-Asian Conference, Bandung. With gum.

| N589 | **288** | 10ch. multicoloured | 50 | 15 |

289 Rejoicing of Koreans

1965. Tenth Anniv of General Association of Koreans in Japan. With gum.

| N590 | **289** | 10ch. blue and red | 45 | 15 |
| N591 | - | 40ch. indigo, blue & red | 70 | 25 |

DESIGN: 40ch. Patriot and flag.

290 Workers in Battle

1965. Second Afro-Asian Conference, Algiers. With gum.

| N592 | **290** | 10ch. black, yellow red | 1·10 | 15 |
| N593 | - | 40ch. black, yellow red | 1·80 | 40 |

DESIGN: 40ch. Korean and African soldiers.
The Algiers Conference did not take place.

291 "Victory 64"
10-ton Lorry

1965. With gum.

| N594 | **291** | 10ch. green | 1·70 | 25 |

292 Kim Chang Gol

1965. War Heroes (1st series). With gum.

N595	**292**	10ch. green	40	15
N596	-	10ch. brown	40	15
N597	-	40ch. purple	1·30	50

PORTRAITS: No. N596, Cho Gun Sil and machine-gun; N597, An Hak Ryong and machine-gun.
See also Nos. N781/3 and N842/3.

293 Marx and Lenin

1965. Postal Ministers' Congress, Peking. With gum.

| N598 | **293** | 10ch. black, yellow red | 2·00 | 30 |

294 Lake Samil

1965. Diamond Mountains Scenery (3rd issue). Multicoloured. With gum.

N599	2ch. Type **294**	85	15
N600	5ch. Chipson Peak	1·40	15
N601	10ch. Kwanum Falls	3·75	30

295 Amnok River,
Kusimuldong

1965. Scenes of Japanese War. With gum.

| N602 | **295** | 5ch. green and blue | 50 | 15 |
| N603 | - | 10ch. turquoise and blue | 85 | 15 |

DESIGN: 10ch. Lake Samji.

296 Footballer
and Games'
Emblem

1965. "GANEFO" Football Games, Pyongyang. Multicoloured. With gum.

| N604 | 10ch. Type **296** | 1·30 | 20 |
| N605 | 10ch. Games emblem and Moranbong Stadium | 1·30 | 20 |

297 Workers and
Map

1965. 20th Anniv of Liberation from Japan. With gum.

| N606 | **297** | 10ch. multicoloured | 40 | 15 |

298 Engels

1965. 145th Birth Anniv of Engels. With gum.

| N607 | **298** | 10ch. brown | 40 | 15 |

299 Pole Vaulting

1965. Sports. Multicoloured. With gum.

N608	2ch. Type **299**	50	10
N609	4ch. Throwing the javelin	2·10	25
N610	10ch. Throwing the discus	60	15
N611	10ch. High jumping (horiz)	60	15
N612	10ch. Putting the shot (horiz)	60	15

301 Korean Fighters

1965. 20th Anniv of Korean Workers' Party. Each black, yellow and red. With gum.

N613	10ch. Type **301**	1·10	40
N614	10ch. Party emblem	1·10	40
N615	10ch. Lenin and Marx	1·10	40
N616	10ch. Workers marching	1·10	40
N617	10ch. Fighters	1·10	40
N618	40ch. Workers	1·10	40
MSN619	191×99 mm. Nos. N613/18	40·00	23·00

Nos. N613/8 each have a red banner in the background and were issued together in blocks of 6 (3×2), forming a composite design, within the sheet.

302 Kim Chaek Iron Works

1965. With gum.

| N620 | **302** | 10ch. purple | 5·00 | 15 |
| N621 | - | 10ch. brown | 5·00 | 15 |

DESIGN: No. 621, Chongjin Steel Works.

303 Grass Carp

1965. Freshwater Fish. Multicoloured. With gum.

N622	2ch. Rainbow trout	1·00	15
N623	4ch. Dolly Varden charr	1·10	15
N624	10ch. Brown trout (surfacing water)	2·10	15
N625	10ch. Common carp diving (date at left)	2·10	15
N626	10ch. Type **303**	2·10	15
N627	40ch. Crucian carp	3·25	40

304 Building
House

1965. Kim Hong Do's Drawings. With gum.

N628	2ch. green (Type **304**)	60	15
N629	4ch. purple (Weaving)	1·30	15
N630	10ch. brown (Wrestling)	1·10	15
N631	10ch. blue (School class)	1·10	15
N632	10ch. red (Dancing)	1·70	15
N633	10ch. violet (Blacksmiths)	1·50	15

305 Children in
Workshop

1965. Life at Pyongyang Children's and Students' Palace. Multicoloured. With gum.

N634	2ch. Type **305**	25	10
N635	4ch. Boxing	25	10
N636	10ch. Chemistry	1·00	20
N637	10ch. Playing violin and accordion	1·00	20

306 Whale-catcher

1965. Korean Fishing Boats. With gum.

| N638 | **306** | 10ch. blue | 1·70 | 35 |
| N639 | - | 10ch. green | 1·70 | 35 |

DESIGN: No. N639, Fishing fleet service vessel.

307 Great Tit

1965. Korean Birds. Inscr "1965". Multicoloured. With gum.

N640	4ch. Black-capped kingfisher (vert)	2·40	35
N641	10ch. Type **307**	3·25	55
N642	10ch. Pied wagtail (facing left)	3·25	55
N643	10ch. Azure-winged magpie (facing right)	3·25	55
N644	40ch. Black-tailed hawfinch	8·50	1·10

308 Silkworm
Moth ("Bombyx
mori") and
Cocoon

1965. Korean Sericulture. With gum.

N645	**308**	2ch. green	42·00	1·50
N646	-	10ch. brown	42·00	1·50
N647	-	10ch. purple	42·00	1·50

MOTHS AND COCOONS: No. N646, Ailathus silk moth ("Samia cynthia"); N647, Chinese oak silk moth ("Antheraea pernyi").

309 Hooded
Crane

1965. Wading Birds. With gum.

N648	**309**	2ch. brown	4·50	40
N649	-	10ch. blue	5·00	65
N650	-	10ch. purple	5·00	65
N651	-	40ch. green	9·25	1·40

BIRDS: No. N649, Japanese white-naped crane; N650, Manchurian crane; N651, Grey heron.

310 Japanese Common
Squid

1965. Korean Molluscs. Multicoloured. With gum.

| N652 | 5ch. Type **310** | 2·10 | 30 |
| N653 | 10ch. Giant Pacific octopus | 3·00 | 45 |

311 Spotbill Duck

1965. Korean Ducks. Multicoloured. With gum.

N654	2ch. Type **311**	3·25	40
N655	4ch. Ruddy shelduck	3·25	45
N656	10ch. Mallard	5·00	90
N657	40ch. Baikal teal	7·25	1·60

312 Circus Theatre,
Pyongyang

1965. Korean Circus. With gum except No. N661.

N658	**312**	2ch. blue, black & brown	65	20
N659	-	10ch. blue, red and black	1·70	30
N660	-	10ch. red, black & green	1·70	30
N661	-	10ch. orange, sepia and green	1·70	30
N662	-	10ch. red, yellow & turq	1·70	30

DESIGNS—VERT: No. N659, Trapeze artistes; N660, Performer with hoops on seesaw; N661, Tightrope dancers; N662, Performer with revolving cap on stick.

313 "Marvel of
Peru" (*Mirabilis
jalapa*)

1965. Korean Flowers. Multicoloured. With gum except No. N663.

N663	4ch. Type **313**	2·20	25
N664	10ch. Peony	3·50	40
N665	10ch. Moss rose	3·50	40
N666	10ch. Magnolia	3·50	40

314 "Finn" Class Dinghy

1965. Yachts. Multicoloured. With gum.

N667	2ch. Type **314**	75	25
N668	10ch. "5.5m" class yacht	1·20	40
N669	10ch. "Dragon" class yacht	1·20	40
N670	40ch. "Star" class yacht	2·50	85

315 Cuban, Korean and African

1966. African-Asian and Latin American Friendship Conference, Havana. With gum.

N671	**315**	10ch. multicoloured	40	15

316 Hosta

1966. Wild Flowers. Mult. With gum. (a) 1st series.

N672	2ch. Type **316**	1·10	25
N673	4ch. Dandelion	1·10	25
N674	10ch. Pink convolvulus	1·60	25
N675	10ch. Lily-of-the-valley	1·60	25
N676	40ch. Catalpa blossom	4·75	65

(b) 2nd series.

N677	2ch. Polyanthus	1·10	25
N678	4ch. Lychnis	1·10	25
N679	10ch. Adonis	1·60	25
N680	10ch. Orange lily	1·60	25
N681	90ch. Rhododendron	7·50	80

Nos. N672/6 exist imperf and without gum.

317 Farmer and Wife

1966. 20th Anniv of Land Reform Law. With gum.

N682	**317**	10ch. multicoloured	40	15

318 Troops advancing, Dashahe

1966. Paintings of Guerrilla Battles, 1937–39. With gum, except No. N684.

N683	**318**	10ch. red	50	15
N684	-	10ch. turquoise	50	15
N685	-	10ch. purple	50	15

DESIGNS AND BATTLES: No. N684, Troops firing from trees, Taehongdan; N685, Troops on hillside, Jiansanfeng.

319 Silla Bowl

1966. Art Treasures of Silla Dynasty. With gum.

N686	**319**	2ch. ochre	1·70	30
N687	-	5ch. black	1·70	30
N688	-	10ch. violet	1·70	30

DESIGNS: 5ch. Earthenware jug. 10ch. Censer.

320 Hands holding Torch, Rifle and Hammer

1966. 80th Anniv of Labour Day. With gum.

N689	**320**	10ch. multicoloured	45	15

321 Torch and Patriots

1966. 30th Anniv of Association for Restoration of Fatherland.

N690	**321**	10ch. red and yellow	50	15

322 Harvester

1966. Aid for Agriculture. Multicoloured.

N691	5ch. Type **322**	35	15
N692	10ch. Labourer	45	15

323 Young Pioneers

1966. 20th Anniv of Korean Children's Union. Without gum.

N693	**323**	10ch. multicoloured	45	15

324 Kangson Steel Works

1966. Korean Industries. With gum.

N694	**324**	10ch. grey	5·00	20
N695	-	10ch. red (Pongung Chemical Works)	5·00	20

325 Pacific Saury

1966. Korean Fish. With gum, except Nos. N699/700.

N696	**325**	2ch. blue, green and purple	1·20	25
N697	-	5ch. purple, green & brn	1·50	25
N698	-	10ch. blue, buff & green	2·75	50
N699	-	10ch. purple and green	2·75	50
N700	-	40ch. green, buff & blue	6·25	85

FISH: 5ch. Pacific cod; 10ch. (N698), Chum salmon, (N699), Yellowfish; 40ch. Pink salmon.

326 Professor Kim Bong Han

1966. Kyungrak Biological System. With gum.

N701	**326**	2ch. blue, green and yellow	85	25
N702	-	4ch. multicoloured	85	25
N703	-	5ch. multicoloured	85	25
N704	-	10ch. multicoloured	85	25
N705	-	10ch. multicoloured	85	25
N706	-	10ch. multicoloured	85	25
N707	-	15ch. multicoloured	85	25
N708	-	40ch. multicoloured	85	25
MSN709		117×141 mm. Nos. N701/8	24·00	23·00

DESIGNS: No. N704, Kyongrak Institute; N708, Figure of Man; N702/3, 705/7, Diagram of system.

Nos. N701/8 were issued together, *se-tenant*, forming a composite design.

327 Leonov in Space ("Voskhod 2")

1966. Cosmonauts Day. Multicoloured.

N710	5ch. Type **327**	25	15
N711	10ch. "Luna 9"	85	40
N712	40ch. "Luna 10"	1·60	65

328 Footballers

1966. World Cup Football Championship. Multicoloured.

N713	10ch. Type **328**	1·70	40
N714	10ch. Jules Rimet Cup, football and boots	1·70	40
N715	10ch. Goalkeeper saving goal (vert)	1·70	40

329 Defence of Seoul

1966. Korean War of 1950–53. With gum.

N716	**329**	10ch. green	65	15
N717	-	10ch. purple	65	15
N718	-	10ch. purple	65	15

DESIGNS: No. N717, Battle on Mt. Napal; N718, Battle for Height 1211.

330 Women in Industry

1966. 20th Anniv of Sex Equality Law.

N719	**330**	10ch. multicoloured	45	15

331 Industrial Workers

1966. 20th Anniv of Industrial Nationalization.

N720	**331**	10ch. multicoloured	1·30	20

332 Water-jar Dance

1966. Korean Dances. Multicoloured. 5, 40ch. with or without gum; others without.

N721	5ch. Type **332**	1·30	20
N722	10ch. Bell dance	2·10	35
N723	10ch. "Dancer in a Mural Painting"	2·10	35
N724	15ch. Sword dance	2·10	40
N725	40ch. Gold Cymbal dance	3·75	70

333 Korean attacking U.S. Soldier

1966. Korean Reunification Campaign. With gum.

N726	**333**	10ch. green	85	20
N727	-	10ch. purple	85	20
N728	-	10ch. lilac	5·00	1·10

DESIGNS: No. N727, Korean with young child; N728, Korean with shovel, industrial scene and electric train.

334 Yakovlev Yak-12M Crop-spraying

1966. Industrial Uses of Aircraft. With gum except 2 and 5ch.

N729	**334**	2ch. green and purple	50	10
N730	-	5ch. brown and green	7·25	80
N731	-	10ch. brown and blue	1·70	30
N732	-	40ch. brown and blue	1·70	30

DESIGNS: 5ch. Yakovlev Yak-18U (forest-fire observation); 10ch. Lisunov Li-2 (geological survey); 40ch. Lisunov Li-2 (detection of fish shoals).

1966. Korean Revolutionaries (3rd issue). As T **212**. With gum.

N733	10ch. violet (O Jung Hub)	
N734	10ch. green (Kim Gyong Sok)	
N735	10ch. blue (Li Dong Gol)	

335 Kim Il Sung University

1966. 20th Anniv of Kim Il Sung University. With gum.

N736	**335**	10ch. violet	65	15

336 Judo

1966. Ganefo Games, Phnom Penh.

N737	**336**	5ch. black, green and blue	60	20
N738	-	10ch. blk, grn & dp grn	60	20
N739	-	10ch. black and red	60	20

DESIGNS: No. N738, Basketball; N739, Table tennis.

337 Hoopoe

1966. Korean Birds. Multicoloured. Inscr "1966".

N740	2ch. Common rosefinch (horiz)	1·80	30
N741	5ch. Type **337**	2·10	35
N742	10ch. Black-breasted thrush (blue background) (horiz)	2·50	55
N743	10ch. Crested lark (green background) (horiz)	2·50	55
N744	40ch. White-bellied black woodpecker	5·75	1·10

338 Building Construction

1966. "Increased Production with Economy". Multicoloured. Without gum (40ch.) or with gum (others).

N745	5ch. Type **338**	35	10
N746	10ch. Furnaceman and graph	60	15
N747	10ch. Machine-tool production	60	15
N748	40ch. Miners and pit-head	1·80	50

339 Parachuting

1966. National Defence Sports. With gum.

N749	**339**	2ch. brown	1·00	20
N750	-	5ch. red	65	15
N751	-	10ch. blue	3·50	60
N752	-	40ch. green	2·10	40

DESIGNS: 5ch. Show jumping; 10ch. Motor cycle racing; 40ch. Radio receiving and transmitting competition.

340 *Samil Wolgan* (Association Magazine)

1966. 30th Anniv of *Samil Wolgan* Magazine.
N753 **340** 10ch. multicoloured 1·20 20

341 Red Deer

1966. Korean Deer. Multicoloured.
N754 2ch. Type **341** 85 25
N755 5ch. Sika deer 1·30 25
N756 10ch. Indian muntjac (erect) 2·10 25
N757 10ch. Reindeer (grazing) 2·10 25
N758 70ch. Fallow deer 6·25 80

342 Blueberries

1966. Wild Fruit. Multicoloured.
N759 2ch. Type **342** 50 15
N760 5ch. Wild pears 75 20
N761 10ch. Wild raspberries 1·00 20
N762 10ch. Schizandra 1·00 20
N763 10ch. Wild plums 1·00 20
N764 40ch. Jujube 2·75 45

343 Onpo Rest Home

1966. Korean Rest Homes. With gum.
N765 **343** 2ch. violet 40 15
N766 - 5ch. turquoise 40 15
N767 - 10ch. green 65 20
N768 - 40ch. black 1·30 30
REST HOMES: 5ch. Mt. Myohyang; 10ch. Songdowon; 40ch. Hongwon.

344 Soldier

1967. 19th Anniv of Army Day. Without gum.
N769 **344** 10ch. green, yellow and red 40 15

345 Sow

1967. Domestic Animals. Multicoloured. Without gum. 40ch. also with gum.
N770 5ch. Type **345** 1·30 40
N771 10ch. Goat 1·70 40
N772 40ch. Ox 4·25 1·00

346 Battle Scene

1967. 30th Anniv of Battle of Pochonbo. With gum.
N773 **346** 10ch. orange, red and green 65 20

347 Students

1967. Compulsory Technical Education for Nine Years.
N774 **347** 10ch. multicoloured 40 15

348 Table Tennis Player

1967. 29th Int Table Tennis Championships, Pyongyang. Designs showing players in action. 5ch. with or without gum.
N775 **348** 5ch. multicoloured 60 15
N776 - 10ch. multicoloured 1·00 20
N777 - 40ch. multicoloured 1·50 35

349 Anti-aircraft Defences

1967. Paintings of Guerrilla War against the Japanese. With gum.
N778 **349** 10ch. blue 40 15
N779 - 10ch. purple 3·75 40
N780 - 10ch. violet 40 15
PAINTINGS: No. N779, Blowing-up railway bridge; N780, People helping guerrillas in Wangyugou.

1967. War Heroes (2nd series). As T **292**. Designs showing portraits and combat scenes. With gum.
N781 10ch. slate 50 15
N782 10ch. violet 50 15
N783 10ch. blue 1·30 20
PORTRAITS: No. N781, Li Dae Hun and grenade-throwing; N782, Choe Jong Un and soldiers charging; N783, Kim Hwa Ryong and Lavochkin La-11.

350 Workers

1967. Labour Day.
N784 **350** 10ch. multicoloured 40 15

351 Card Game

1967. Korean Children. Multicoloured.
N785 5ch. Type **351** 1·10 20
N786 10ch. Children modelling tractor 60 15
N787 40ch. Children playing with ball 1·20 30

352 Victory Monument

1967. Unveiling of Battle of Ponchonbo Monument.
N788 **352** 10ch. multicoloured 50 15

353 Attacking Tank

1967. Monuments to War of 1950–53. 2ch. with or without gum.
N789 **353** 2ch. green and turquoise 25 10
N790 - 5ch. sepia and green 65 10
N791 - 10ch. brown and buff 50 15
N792 - 40ch. brown and blue 1·30 50
MONUMENTS: 5ch. Soldier-musicians; 10ch. Soldier; 40ch. Soldier with children.

354 *Polygonatum japonicum*

1967. Medicinal Plants. Multicoloured; background colour of 10ch. values given to aid identification. Nos. 793/5 and 797 with or without gum.
N793 2ch. Type **354** 1·20 20
N794 5ch. *Hibiscus manihot* 1·20 20
N795 10ch. *Scutellaria baicalensis* (turquoise) 1·40 25
N796 10ch. *Pulsatilla koreana* (blue) 1·40 25
N797 10ch. *Rehmannian glutinosa* (yellow) 1·40 25
N798 40ch. *Tanacetum boreale* 3·75 85

355 Servicemen

1967. People's Army. Multicoloured. 5ch. with or without gum.
N799 5ch. Type **355** 25 10
N800 10ch. Soldier and farmer 35 15
N801 10ch. Officer decorating soldier 35 15

356 Freighter *Chollima*

1967. With gum.
N802 **356** 10ch. green 1·50 30

357 Reclamation of Tideland

1967. *Heroic Struggle of the Chollima Riders*. Paintings. Without gum (5ch.) or with gum (others).
N803 - 5ch. brown 50 15
N804 **357** 10ch. grey 65 20
N805 - 10ch. green 1·10 20
DESIGNS—VERT: 5ch. *Drilling Rock Precipice*; 10ch. (N805), *Felling Trees*.

358 "Erimaculus isenbeckii"

1967. Crabs. Multicoloured.
N806 2ch. Type **358** 1·00 20
N807 5ch. *Neptunus trituberculatus* 1·30 20
N808 10ch. *Paralithodes camtschatica* 1·80 35
N809 40ch. *Chionoecetes opilio* 3·25 65

359 Electric Train and Hand switching Points

1967. Propaganda for Reunification of Korea.
N810 **359** 10ch. multicoloured 3·25 75

360 Tongrim Waterfall

1967. Korean Waterfalls. 2ch. with or without gum. Multicoloured.
N811 2ch. Type **360** 3·50 55
N812 10ch. Sanju waterfall, Mt. Myohyang 4·25 75
N813 40ch. Sambang waterfall, Mt. Chonak 6·75 1·40

361 Chollima Flying Horse and Banners

1967. "The Revolutionary Surge Upwards". Various designs incorporating the Chollima Flying Horse.
N814 - 5ch. blue 4·25 35
N815 - 10ch. red 75 15
N816 - 10ch. green 75 15
N817 - 10ch. lilac 75 15
N818 **361** 10ch. red 65 15
DESIGNS—HORIZ: 5ch. Ship, electric train and lorry (Transport); N815, Bulldozers (Building construction); N816, Tractors (Rural development); N817, Heavy presses (Machine-building industry).

362 Lenin

1967. 50th Anniv of Russian October Revolution.
N819 **362** 10ch. brown, yell & red 50 15

363 Voters and Banner

1967. Korean Elections. Multicoloured.
N820 10ch. Type **363** 45 15
N821 10ch. Woman casting vote (vert) 45 15

364 Cinereous Black Vulture

1967. Birds of Prey. Multicoloured. With gum.
N822 2ch. Type **364** 3·00 60
N823 10ch. Booted eagle (horiz) 5·75 1·10
N824 40ch. White-bellied sea eagle 7·50 1·50

365 Chongjin

1967. North Korean Cities. With gum.
N825 **365** 5ch. multicoloured 90 20
N826 - 10ch. lilac 90 20
N827 - 10ch. violet 90 20
DESIGNS: No. N826, Humhung; N827, Sinuiju.

366 Soldier brandishing Red Book

1967. "Let us carry out the Decisions of the Workers' Party Conference!". Multicoloured.
N828 10ch. Type **366** 40 15
N829 10ch. Militiaman holding bayonet 40 15
N830 10ch. Foundryman and bayonet 40 15

367 Whaler firing
Harpoon

1967. With gum.
N831 **367** 10ch. blue   1·10   40

368 Airman,
Soldier and Sailor

1968. 20th Anniv of People's Army. Mult. With gum.

N832	10ch. Type **368**	40	20
N833	10ch. Soldier below attack in snow	40	20
N834	10ch. Soldier below massed ranks	40	20
N835	10ch. Soldier holding flag	40	20
N836	10ch. Soldier holding book	40	20
N837	10ch. Soldiers and armed workers with flag	40	20
N838	10ch. Furnaceman and soldier	40	20
N839	10ch. Soldier saluting	40	20
N840	10ch. Charging soldiers	40	20
N841	10ch. Soldier, sailor and airman below flag	40	20

1968. War Heroes (3rd series). As T 292. With gum.

N842	10ch. violet	40	15
N843	10ch. purple	40	15

PORTRAITS: No. N842, Han Gye Ryol firing Bren gun; N843, Li Su Bok charging up hill.

369 Dredger *September 2*   **370** Ten-storey Flats, East Pyongyang

371 Palace of Students and Children, Kaesong

1968. With gum.

N844	**369**	5ch. green	1·00	20
N845	**370**	10ch. blue	45	15
N846	**371**	10ch. blue	45	15

372 Marshal Kim Il Sung

1968. Marshal Kim Il Sung's 56th Birthday. With gum.

N847	**372**	40ch. multicoloured	85	50

373 Kim Il Sung with Mother

1968. Childhood of Kim Il Sung. Multicoloured.

N848	10ch. Type **373**	50	15
N849	10ch. Kim Il Sung with his father	50	15
N850	10ch. Setting out from home, aged 13	50	15
N851	10ch. Birthplace at Mangyongdae	50	15
N852	10ch. Mangyong Hill	50	15

374 Matsu-take
Mushroom

1968. Mushrooms. With gum.

N853	**374**	5ch. brown and green	25·00	1·40
N854		10ch. ochre, brn & grn	42·00	1·50
N855		10ch. brown and green	42·00	1·50

DESIGNS: No. N854, Black mushroom; N855, Cultivated mushroom.

375 Leaping Horseman

1968. 20th Anniv of Korean People's Democratic Republic. Multicoloured. With gum.

N856	10ch. Type **375**	1·40	30
N857	10ch. Four servicemen	1·40	30
N858	10ch. Soldier with bayonet	1·40	30
N859	10ch. Advancing with banners	1·40	30
N860	10ch. Statue	1·40	30
N861	10ch. Korean flag	1·40	30
N862	10ch. Soldier and peasant with flag	1·40	30
N863	10ch. Machine-gunner with flag	1·40	30

376 Domestic Products

1968. Development of Light Industries. Multicoloured. With gum.

N864	2ch. Type **376**	35	15
N865	5ch. Textiles	1·40	15
N866	10ch. Tinned produce	50	15

377 Proclaiming the Ten Points

1968. Kim Il Sung's Ten Point Political Programme. Multicoloured.

N867	2ch. Type **377**	20	10
N868	5ch. Soldier and artisan (horiz)	30	10

378 Livestock

1968. Development of Agriculture. Multicoloured. With gum.

N869	5ch. Type **378**	35	10
N870	10ch. Fruit-growing	35	15
N871	10ch. Wheat-harvesting	35	15

379 Yesso Scallop

1968. Shellfish. Multicoloured. With gum.

N872	5ch. Type **379**	1·70	20
N873	5ch. Meretrix chione (venus clam)	1·70	20
N874	10ch. "Modiolus hanleyi" (mussel)	3·00	35

380 Kim Il Sung at Head of Columns

1968. Battle of Pochonbo Monument. Detail of Monument. Multicoloured.

N875	10ch. Type **380**	35	20
N876	10ch. Head of right-hand column	35	20
N877	10ch. Tail of right-hand column	35	20
N878	10ch. Head of left-hand column	35	20
N879	10ch. Tail of left-hand column	35	20
N880	10ch. Centre of right-hand column	35	20
N881	10ch. Centre of left-hand column	35	20

SIZES—HORIZ: Nos. N876/8, 43×28 mm. 880/1, 56×28 mm.

The centrepiece of the Monument is flanked by two columns of soldiers, headed by Kim Il Sung.

381 Museum of the Revolution, Pochonbo

382 Grand Theatre, Pyongyang

1968

N883	**381**	2ch. green	30	10
N884	**382**	10ch. brown	90	20

383 Irrigation

1969. Rural Development. Multicoloured.

N885	3ch. Type **383**	25	10
N886	5ch. Agricultural mechanization	25	10
N887	10ch. Electrification	50	15
N888	40ch. Applying fertilizers and spraying trees	85	20

384 Grey Rabbits

1969. Rabbits. Multicoloured. With or without gum.

N889	2ch. Type **384**	1·50	25
N890	10ch. Black rabbits	1·70	25
N891	10ch. Brown rabbits	1·70	25
N892	10ch. White rabbits	1·70	25
N893	40ch. Doe and young	4·50	50

385 "Age and Youth"

1969. Public Health Service.

N894	2ch. brown and blue	50	10
N895	10ch. blue and red	1·00	20
N896	40ch. green and yellow	2·10	40

DESIGNS: 10ch. Nurse with syringe; 40ch. Auscultation by woman doctor.

386 Sowing Rice Seed

1969. Agricultural Mechanization.

N897	**386**	10ch. green	75	20
N898	-	10ch. orange	75	20
N899	-	10ch. black	75	20
N900	-	10ch. brown	75	20

DESIGNS: No. N898, Rice harvester; N899, Weed-spraying machine; N900, Threshing machine.

387 Ponghwa

1969. Revolutionary Historical Sites. Multicoloured.

N901	10ch. Type **387**	55	15
N902	10ch. Mangyongdae, birthplace of Kim Il Sung	55	15

388 Kim crosses into Manchuria, 1926, aged 13

1969. Kim Il Sung in Manchuria. Multicoloured. No. N907 with gum.

N903	10ch. Type **388**	50	20
N904	10ch. Leading strike of Yuwen Middle School boys, 1927	50	20
N905	10ch. Leading anti-Japanese demonstration in Kirin, 1928	50	20
N906	10ch. Presiding at meeting of Young Communist League, 1930	50	20
N907	10ch. Meeting of young revolutionaries	50	20

389 Birthplace at Chilgol

1969. Commemoration of Mrs. Kang Ban Sok, mother of Kim Il Sung. Multicoloured.

N908	10ch. Type **389**	40	15
N909	10ch. With members of Women's Association	40	15
N910	10ch. Resisting Japanese police	3·50	75

390 Pegaebong Bivouac

1969. Bivouac Sites in the Guerrilla War against the Japanese. Multicoloured.

N911	5ch. Type **390**	25	10
N912	10ch. Mupo site (horiz)	40	15
N913	10ch. Chongbong site	40	15
N914	40ch. Konchang site (horiz)	1·40	55

391 Chollima Statue   **392** Museum of the Revolution, Pyongyang

1969

N915	**391**	10ch. blue	40	15
N916	**392**	10ch. green	40	15

393 Mangyong Chickens

1969. Korean Poultry.

N917	**393**	10ch. blue	1·30	25
N918	-	10ch. violet	3·75	45

DESIGN: No. N918, Kwangpo ducks.

394 Marshal Kim Il Sung and Children

1969. Kim Il Sung's Educational System. Multicoloured.

N919	2ch. Type **394**	10	10
N920	10ch. Worker with books	25	15
N921	40ch. Students with books	1·00	55

395 Statue of Marshal Kim Il Sung

1969. Memorials on Pochonbo Battlefield. Inscr "1937.6.4". Multicoloured.

N922	5ch. Machine-gun post	35	15
N923	10ch. Type **395**	35	15
N924	10ch. "Aspen-tree" monument	35	15
N925	10ch. Glade Konjang Hill	35	15

396 Teaching at Myongsin School

1969. Commemoration of Kim Hyong Jik, father of Kim Il Sung. Multicoloured.

N926	10ch. Type **396**	45	15
N927	10ch. Secret meeting with Korean National Association members	45	15

397 Relay Runner

1969. 20th Anniv of Sports Day.

N928	**397**	10ch. multicoloured	55	15

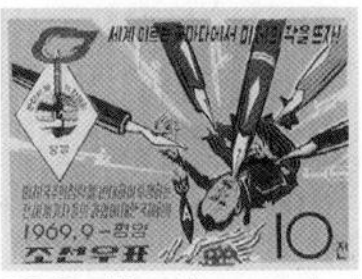

398 President Nixon attacked by Pens

1969. Anti-U.S. Imperialism Journalists' Conference, Pyongyang.

N929	**398**	10ch. multicoloured	1·20	15

399 Fighters and Battle

1969. Implementation of Ten-Point Programme of Kim Il Sung. Multicoloured.

N930	5ch. Type **399** (Reunification of Korea)	40	15
N931	10ch. Workers upholding slogan (vert)	40	15

400 Bayonet Attack over U.S. Flag

1969. Anti-American Campaign.

N932	**400**	10ch. multicoloured	50	15

401 Armed Workers

1969. Struggle for the Reunification of Korea. Multicoloured.

N933	10ch. Workers stabbing U.S. soldier (vert)	25	15
N934	10ch. Kim Il Sung and crowd with flags (vert)	25	15
N935	50ch. Type **401**	70	25

402 Buri

1969. Korean Fishes. Multicoloured.

N936	5ch. Type **402**	85	15
N937	10ch. Eastern dace	1·30	20
N938	40ch. Flat-headed grey mullet	3·00	45

403 Freighter *Taesungsan*

1969

N939	**403**	10ch. purple	1·00	20

405 Dahwangwai (1935)

1970. Guerrilla Conference Places.

N940	**405**	2ch. blue and green	35	10
N941	-	5ch. brown and green	35	10
N942	-	10ch. lt green & green	35	10

DESIGNS: 5ch. Yaoyinggou (barn) (1935); 10ch. Xiaohaerbaling (tent) (1940).

406 Lake Chon

1970. Mt. Paekdu, Home of Revolution (1st issue). Inscr "1970".

N943	**406**	10ch. black, brown & grn	50	20
N944	-	10ch. black, green & yell	50	20
N945	-	10ch. purple, blue & yell	50	20
N946	-	10ch. black, blue and pink	50	20

DESIGNS: No. N944, Piryu Peak; N945, Pyongsa (Soldier) Peak; N946, Changgun (General) Peak.

See also Nos. N979/81.

407 Vietnamese Soldier and Furnaceman

1970. Help for the Vietnamese People.

N947	**407**	10ch. green, brown & red	40	15

408 Receiving his Father's Revolvers from his Mother

1970. Revolutionary Career of Kim Il Sung. Multicoloured.

N948	10ch. Type **408**	90	25
N949	10ch. Receiving smuggled weapons from his mother	90	25
N950	10ch. Talking to farm workers	90	25
N951	10ch. At Kalun meeting, 1930	90	25

409 Lenin

1970. Birth Centenary of Lenin.

N952	**409**	10ch. brown & cinnamon	45	15
N953	-	10ch. brown and green	45	15

DESIGN: No. N953, Lenin making a speech.

410 March of Koreans

1970. 15th Anniv of Association of Koreans in Japan.

N954	**410**	10ch. red	30	15
N955	**410**	10ch. purple	30	15

411 Uniformed Factory Worker

1970. Workers' Militia.

N956	**411**	10ch. green, brn & mve	30	10
N957	-	10ch. green, brown & bl	30	10

DESIGN—HORIZ: No. N957, Militiaman saluting.

412 Students and Newspapers

1970. Peasant Education. Multicoloured.

N958	2ch. Type **412**	50	10
N959	5ch. Peasant with book	25	10
N960	10ch. Students in class	25	10

413 "Electricity Flows"

1970. Commemoration of Army Electrical Engineers.

N961	**413**	10ch. brown	50	15

414 Soldier with Rifle

1970. Campaign Month for Withdrawal of U.S. Troops from South Korea.

N962	**414**	5ch. violet	15	10
N963	-	10ch. purple	40	10

DESIGN: 10ch. Soldier and partisan.

415 Rebel wielding Weapons

1970. Struggle in South Korea against U.S. Imperialism.

N964	**415**	10ch. violet	30	15

416 Labourer ("Fertilizers")

1970. Encouragement of Increased Productivity.

N965	**416**	10ch. green, pink & brn	50	15
N966	-	10ch. green, red & brn	1·00	20
N967	-	10ch. blue, green & brn	50	15
N968	-	10ch. bistre, brn & grn	50	15
N969	-	10ch. violet, green & brn	65	15

DESIGNS: No. N966, Furnaceman ("Steel"); N967, Operative ("Machines"); N968, Labourer ("Building Construction"); N969, Miner ("Mining").

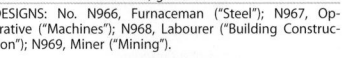

417 Railway Guard

1970. "Speed the Transport System".

N970	**417**	10ch. blue, orange & grn	1·70	35

418 Agriculture

1970. Executive Decisions of the Workers' Party Congress. Designs embodying book.

N971	**418**	5ch. red	35	10
N972	-	10ch. green	1·50	25
N973	-	40ch. green	1·50	25

DESIGNS: 10ch. Industry; 40ch. The Armed Forces.

419 Chollima Statue and Workers' Party Banner

1970. 25th Anniv of Korean Workers' Party.

N974	**419**	10ch. red, brown & buff	35	15

420 Kim Il Sung and the People

1970. Fifth Congress of Workers' Party. Miniature sheet (153×92 mm) comprising ten stamps as T **420** (10ch. values with symbols and inscr in panel at right).

MSN975	Multicoloured, comprising 40ch. T **420** and nine 10ch. stamps showing Family and new housing; Advance with Kim Il Sung's programme; People's army; Furnaceman and industry; Anti-U.S. Imperialism; Peasants and agriculture; Students with books; Schoolgirl with book; Collaboration with Freedom Fighters	18·00	8·00

421 Emblem of League

1971. 25th Anniv of League of Socialist Working Youth.

N976	**421**	10ch. red, brown & blue	30	15

422 Log Cabin, Nanhutou

1971. 35th Anniv of Nanhutou Guerrilla Conference.

N977	**422**	10ch. multicoloured	30	15

423 Tractor Driver

1971. 25th Anniv of Land Reform Law.

N978	**423**	2ch. red, green and black	30	15

1971. Mt. Paekdu, Home of Revolution (2nd issue). As T **406** but inscr "1971".

N979	2ch. black, olive and green	50	15
N980	5ch. pink, black and slate	3·00	60
N981	10ch. black, red and grey	85	20

DESIGNS—HORIZ: 2ch. General view; 10ch. Western peak. VERT: 5ch. Waterfall.

424 Popyong Museum

1971. Museum of the Revolution.

N982	**424**	10ch. brown and yellow	25	15
N983	-	10ch. blue and orange	25	15
N984	-	10ch. green and orange	25	15

DESIGNS: No. N983, Mangyongdae Museum; N984, Chunggang Museum.

425 Miner

1971. Six Year Plan for Coal Industry.

N985	**425**	10ch. multicoloured	65	25

426 Kim Il Sung

1971. Founding of Anti-Japanese Guerrilla Army. Multicoloured.

N986	10ch. Type **426**	50	20
N987	10ch. Kim Il Sung founding Anti-Japanese Guerrilla Army (horiz)	50	20
N988	10ch. Kim Il Sung addressing the people (horiz)	50	20
N989	10ch. Kim Il Sung and members of Children's Corps (horiz)	50	20

428 Hands holding Hammer and Rifle

1971. 85th Anniv of Labour Day.

N990	**428**	1wn. red, brown and buff	3·00	55

429 Soldiers and Map

1971. 35th Anniv of Association for Restoration of Fatherland.

N991	**429**	10ch. red, buff and black	50	20

430 Monument

1971. Battlefields in Musan Area, May 1939. Multicoloured.

N992	5ch. Type **430**	15	10
N993	10ch. Machine guns in perspex cases (horiz)	35	15
N994	40ch. Huts among birch trees (horiz)	90	55

431 Koreans Marching

1971. Solidarity of Koreans in Japan.

N995	**431**	10ch. brown	30	15

432 Flame Emblem

1971. 25th Anniv of Korean Childrens' Union.

N996	**432**	10ch. red, yellow and blue	30	15

433 Marchers and Banners

1971. Sixth Congress of League of Socialist Working Youth.

N997	**433**	5ch. red, buff and black	25	10
N998	-	10ch. red, green & black	35	15

DESIGN: 10c. Marchers and banner under globe.

434 Foundryman

1971. 25th Anniv of Labour Law.

N999	**434**	5ch. black, purple & buff	30	15

435 Young Women

1971. 25th Anniv of Sex Equality Law.

N1000	**435**	5ch. multicoloured	30	15

436 Schoolchildren

1971. 15th Anniv of Compulsory Primary Education.

N1001	**436**	10ch. multicoloured	55	15

437 Choe Yong Do and Combat Scene

1971. Heroes of the Revolutionary Struggle in South Korea.

N1002	**437**	5ch. black and green	35	10
N1003	-	10ch. red and brown	35	10
N1004	-	10ch. black and red	35	10

DESIGNS: No. N1003, Revolutionary with book; N1004, Kim Jong Tae and scene of triumph.

438 Two Foundrymen

1971. 25th Anniv of Nationalization of Industry Law.

N1005	**438**	5ch. black, green & brn	2·10	35

439 Struggle in Korea

1971. The Anti-Imperialist and Anti-U.S. Imperialist Struggles.

N1006	**439**	10ch. red, black and brown	35	15
N1007	-	10ch. brown, black and blue	50	15
N1008	-	10ch. red, black and pink	65	15
N1009	-	10ch. black, olive and green	35	15
N1010	-	10ch. orange, black and red	65	15
N1011	-	40ch. green, black and pink	65	20

DESIGNS: No. N1007, Struggle in Vietnam; N1008, Soldier with rifle and airplane marked "EC"; N1009, Struggle in Africa; N1010, Cuban soldier and Central America; N1011, Bayoneting U.S. soldier.

440 Kim Il Sung University

1971. 25th Anniv of Kim Il Sung University.

N1012	**440**	10ch. grey, red & yellow	30	10

441 Iron-ore Ladle (Mining)

1971. Tasks of Six Year Plan. Multicoloured.

N1013	10ch. Type **441**	2·10	35
N1014	10ch. Workers and text	40	15
N1015	10ch. Electric train and track (Transport)	2·10	35
N1016	10ch. Hand and wrench (Industry)	85	25
N1017	10ch. Mechanical scoop (Construction)	2·10	35
N1018	10ch. Manufactured goods (Trade)	40	15
N1019	10ch. Crate on hoists (Exports)	35	10
N1020	10ch. Lathe (Heavy Industries)	2·10	35
N1021	10ch. Freighter (Shipping)	85	25
N1022	10ch. Household equipment (Light Industries)	40	15
N1023	10ch. Corncob and wheat (Agriculture)	50	15

442 Technicians

1971. Cultural Revolution. Multicoloured.

N1024	2ch. Type **442**	25	10
N1025	5ch. Mechanic	35	10
N1026	10ch. Schoolchildren	40	10
N1027	10ch. Chemist	65	10
N1028	10ch. Composer at piano	1·10	10

443 Workers with Red Books

1971. Ideological Revolution. Multicoloured.

N1029	10ch. Type **443**	25	10
N1030	10ch. Workers reading book	25	10
N1031	10ch. Workers' lecture	25	10
N1032	10ch. Worker and pneumatic drill	25	10

444 Korean Family

1971. Improvement in Living Standards.

N1033	**444**	10ch. multicoloured	25	10

445 Furnaceman

1971. Implementation of Decisions of Fifth Workers' Party Conference.

N1034	**445**	10ch. multicoloured	1·40	25

446

1971. Solidarity with South Korean Revolutionaries.

N1036	**446**	10ch. brown, bl & blk	40	15
N1037	-	10ch. brn, flesh & red	40	15
N1038	-	10ch. multicoloured	40	15
N1039	-	10ch. multicoloured	40	15

DESIGNS—VERT: No. N1037, U.S. soldier attacked by poster boards; N1038, Hands holding rifles aloft. HORIZ: No. N1039, Men advancing with rifles.

447 6000-ton Press

1971

N1040	**447**	2ch. brown	90	15
N1041	-	5ch. blue	1·30	25
N1042	-	10ch. green	1·50	25
N1043	-	10ch. green	1·50	25

DESIGNS: No. N1041, Refrigerated freighter "Ponghwasan"; N1042, 300 h.p. bulldozer; N1043, "Sungrisan" lorry.

448 Title-page and Militants

1971. 35th Anniv of "Samil Wolgan" Magazine.

N1044	**448**	10ch. red, green & black	60	15

452 Poultry Chicks

1972. Poultry Breeding.

N1051	**452**	5ch. yellow, black and brown	35	10
N1052	-	10ch. orange, bistre and brown	50	10
N1053	-	40ch. blue, orange and deep blue	85	50

DESIGNS: 10ch. Chickens and battery egg house; 40ch. Eggs and fowls suspended from hooks.

453 Scene from *Village Shrine*

1972. Films of Guerrilla War.

N1054	**453**	10ch. grey and green	1·00	20

N1055	-	10ch. blue, pur & orge	1·00	20
N1056	-	10ch. purple, blue & yell	1·00	20

DESIGNS: No. N1055, Patriot with pistol (*A Sea of Blood*); N1056, Guerrilla using bayonet (*The Lot of a Self-Defence Corps Member*).

454 Kim Il Sung acknowledging Greetings

1972. Kim Il Sung's 60th Birthday. Scenes in the life of Kim Il Sung, dated "1912–1972". Mult.

N1057	5ch. Type **454**	25	10
N1058	5ch. In campaign H.Q.	25	10
N1059	5ch. Military conference (horiz)	25	10
N1060	10ch. In wheatfield (horiz)	40	10
N1061	10ch. Directing construction (horiz)	2·75	50
N1062	10ch. Talking to foundry workers (horiz)	25	10
N1063	10ch. Aboard whaler (horiz)	75	10
N1064	10ch. Visiting a hospital (horiz)	1·00	10
N1065	10ch. Viewing orchard (horiz)	25	10
N1066	10ch. With survey party on Haeju–Hasong railway line (horiz)	2·75	50
N1067	10ch. Meeting female workers at silk factory (horiz)	1·40	15
N1068	10ch. Village conference (horiz)	25	10
N1069	10ch. Touring chicken factory (horiz)	50	10
N1070	40ch. Relaxing with children	60	25
N1071	1wn. Giant portrait and marchers	90	50
MSN1072	100×79 mm. 3wn. Kim Il Sung by Lake Chon (horiz). Imperf	8·50	6·00

455 Bugler sounding "Charge"

1972. 40th Anniv of Guerrilla Army.

N1073	**455**	10ch. multicoloured	60	15

456 Pavilion of Ryongpo

1972. Historic Sites of the 1950–53 War. Multicoloured.

N1074	2ch. Type **456**	20	10
N1075	5ch. Houses at Onjong	20	10
N1076	10ch. Headquarters, Kosanjin	20	10
N1077	40ch. Victory Museum, Chonsung-dong	40	15

457 Volleyball

1972. Olympic Games, Munich. Multicoloured.

N1078	2ch. Type **457**	35	10
N1079	5ch. Boxing (horiz)	40	10
N1080	10ch. Judo	50	15
N1081	10ch. Wrestling (horiz)	50	15
N1082	40ch. Rifle-shooting	1·30	55

458 Chollima Street, Pyongyang

1971. Chollima Street, Pyongyang.

N1083	-	5ch. orange and black	2·20	55

N1084	**458**	10ch. yellow and black	85	20
N1085	-	10ch. green and black	85	20

DESIGNS: No. N1083, Bridge and skyscraper blocks; N1085, Another view looking up street.

459 Dredger

1972. Development of Natural Resources. Multicoloured.

N1086	5ch. Type **459**	50	10
N1087	10ch. Forestry	65	10
N1088	40ch. Reclaiming land from the sea	85	20

460 Ferrous Industry

1972. Tasks of the Six-Year Plan. The Metallurgical Industry. Inscr "1971–1976". Multicoloured.

N1089	10ch. Type **460**	2·10	15
N1090	10ch. Non-ferrous Industry	60	15

461 Iron Ore Industry

1972. Tasks of the Six-Year Plan. The Mining Industry. Inscr "1971–1976". Multicoloured.

N1091	10ch. Type **461**	85	15
N1092	10ch. Coal mining industry	3·25	45

462 Electronic and Automation Industry

1972. Tasks of the Six-Year Plan. The Engineering Industry. Inscr "1971–1976". Multicoloured.

N1093	10ch. Type **462**	85	15
N1094	10ch. Single-purpose machines	60	15
N1095	10ch. Machine tools	60	15

463 Clearing Virgin Soil

1972. Tasks of the Six-Year Plan. Rural Economy. Multicoloured.

N1096	10ch. Type **463**	65	15
N1097	10ch. Irrigation	65	15
N1098	10ch. Harvesting	65	15

464 Automation

1972. Tasks of the Six-Year Plan. Inscr "1971–1976". Multicoloured.

N1099	10ch. Type **464**	1·00	25
N1100	10ch. Agricultural mechanization	65	15
N1101	10ch. Lightening of household chores	65	15

465 Chemical Fibres and Materials

1972. Tasks of the Six-Year Plan. The Chemical Industry. Inscr "1971–1976". Multicoloured.

N1102	10ch. Type **465**	85	15
N1103	10ch. Fertilizers, insecticides and weed killers	85	15

466 Textiles

1972. Tasks of the Six-Year Plan. Consumer Goods. Inscr "1971–1976". Multicoloured.

N1104	10ch. Type **466**	90	20
N1105	10ch. Kitchen ware and overalls	65	15
N1106	10ch. Household goods	65	15

467 Fish, Fruit and Vegetables

1972. Tasks of the Six-Year Plan. The Food Industry. Multicoloured.

N1107	10ch. Type **467**	90	20
N1108	10ch. Tinned foods	90	20
N1109	10ch. Food packaging	90	20

468 Electrifying Railway Lines

1972. Tasks of the Six-Year Plan. Transport. Inscr "1971–1976". Multicoloured.

N1110	10ch. Type **468**	65	15
N1111	10ch. Laying new railway track	65	15
N1112	10ch. Freighters	60	15

469 Soldier with Shell

1972. North Korean Armed Forces. Multicoloured.

N1113	10ch. Type **469**	50	15
N1114	10ch. Marine	50	15
N1115	10ch. Air Force pilot	50	15

470 "Revolution of 19 April 1960"

1972. The Struggle for Reunification of Korea. Multicoloured.

N1116	10ch. Type **470**	25	15
N1117	10ch. Marchers with banner	25	15
N1118	10ch. Insurgents with red banner	25	15
N1119	10ch. Attacking U.S. and South Korean soldiers	25	15
N1120	10ch. Workers with posters	25	15
N1121	10ch. Workers acclaiming revolution	5·00	90
N1122	10ch. Workers and manifesto	25	15

471 Single-spindle Automatic Lathe

1972. Machine Tools.

N1123	**471**	5ch. green and purple	35	15
N1124	-	10ch. blue and green	50	15
N1125	-	40ch. green and brown	1·20	20

DESIGNS—HORIZ: 10ch. "Kusong-3" lathe; VERT: 40ch. 2,000 ton crank press.

472 Casting Vote

1972. National Elections. Multicoloured.

N1126	10ch. Type **472**	40	15
N1127	10ch. Election campaigner	40	15

475 Soldier

1973. 25th Anniv of Founding of Korean People's Army. Multicoloured.

N1130	10ch. Type **475**	25	10
N1131	10ch. Sailor	40	10
N1132	40ch. Airman	1·00	65

476 Wrestling Site

1973. Scenes of Kim Il Sung's Childhood, Mangyongdae. Multicoloured.

N1133	2ch. Type **476**	15	15
N1134	5ch. Warship rock	15	15
N1135	10ch. Swinging site (vert)	25	15
N1136	10ch. Sliding rock	25	15
N1137	40ch. Fishing site	85	25

477 Monument to Socialist Revolution and Construction, Mansu Hill

1973. Museum of the Korean Revolution.

N1138	**477**	10ch. multicoloured	35	10
N1139	-	10ch. multicoloured	35	10
N1140	-	40ch. multicoloured	75	15
N1141	-	3wn. green and yellow	3·75	80

DESIGNS—As Type **477**: 10ch. (N1139) Similar monument but men in military clothes; 40ch. Statue of Kim Il Sung. HORIZ—60×29 mm: 3wn. Museum building.

478 Karajibong Camp

1973. Secret Camps by Tuman-Gang in Guerrilla War, 1932. Multicoloured.

N1142	10ch. Type **478**	20	10
N1143	10ch. Soksaegol Camp	20	15

479

1973. Menace of Japanese Influence in South Korea.

N1144	**479**	10ch. multicoloured	30	10

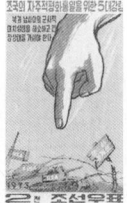

480 Wrecked U.S. Tanks

1973. Five-point Programme for Reunification of Korea. Multicoloured.

N1145	2ch.	Type **480**	60	10
N1146	5ch.	Electric train and crane lifting tractor	3·75	50
N1147	10ch.	Leaflets falling on crowd	25	10
N1148	10ch.	Hand holding leaflet and map of Korea	60	10
N1149	40ch.	Banner and globe	90	25

481 Lorries

1973. Lorries and Tractors. Multicoloured.

N1150	10ch.	Type **481**	50	15
N1151	10ch.	Tractors and earth-moving machine	50	15

482 Volleyball

1973. Socialist Countries' Junior Women's Volleyball Games, Pyongyang.

N1152	**482**	10ch. multicoloured	55	15

483 Battlefield

1973. 20th Anniv of Victory in Korean War.

N1153	**483**	10ch. green, pur & blk	35	15
N1154	-	10ch. brown, bl & blk	35	15

DESIGN: 10ch. Urban fighting.

484 *The Snow Falls*

1973. Mansudae Art Troupe. Dances. Multicoloured.

N1155	10ch.	Type **484**	75	15
N1156	25ch.	*A Bumper Harvest of Apples*	1·70	40
N1157	40ch.	*Azalea of the Fatherland*	2·10	45

485 Schoolchildren

1973. Ten Years Compulsory Secondary Education.

N1158	**485**	10ch. multicoloured	40	15

486 *Fervour in the Revolution*

1973. The Works of Kim Il Sung (1st series).

N1159	**486**	10ch. brown, red and yellow	20	15
N1160	-	10ch. brown, green and yellow	20	15
N1161	-	10ch. lake, brown and yellow	20	15

DESIGNS: No. N1160, Selected works; N1161, *Strengthen the Socialist System*.
See also Nos. N1217/18.

487 Celebrating Republic

1973. 25th Anniv of People's Republic. Multicoloured.

N1162	5ch.	Type **487**	20	10
N1163	10ch.	Fighting in Korean War	20	10
N1164	40ch.	Peace and reconstruction	2·20	60

488 Pobwang Peak

1973. Mt. Myohyang. Multicoloured.

N1165	2ch.	Type **488**	30	10
N1166	5ch.	Inhodae Pavilion	35	15
N1167	10ch.	Taeha Falls (vert)	1·60	40
N1168	40ch.	Rongyon Falls (vert)	4·50	70

489 Party Memorial Building

1973. Party Memorial Building.

N1169	**489**	1wn. brn, grey & buff	1·80	45

490 Football and Handball

1973. National People's Sports Meeting. Multicoloured.

N1170	2ch.	Type **490**	75	15
N1171	5ch.	High jumper and woman sprinter	35	10
N1172	10ch.	Skaters and skiers	60	15
N1173	10ch.	Wrestling and swinging	40	10
N1174	40ch.	Parachutist and motor cyclists	4·25	70

491 Weightlifting

1973. Junior Weightlifting Championships of Socialist Countries.

N1175	**491**	10ch. blue, brn & grn	50	15

492 Chongryu Cliff

1973. Scenery of Moran Hill, Pyongyang. Multicoloured.

N1176	2ch.	Type **492**	1·00	20
N1177	5ch.	Moran Waterfall	4·25	80
N1178	10ch.	Pubyok Pavilion	1·10	20
N1179	40ch.	Ulmil Pavilion	1·30	25

493 Rainbow Bridge

1973. Diamond Mountains Scenery (4th issue). Multicoloured.

N1180	2ch.	Type **493**	2·00	35
N1181	5ch.	Suspension footbridge, Okryudong (horiz)	2·00	35
N1182	10ch.	Chonnyo Peak	1·00	20
N1183	10ch.	Chilchung Rock and Sonji Peak (horiz)	1·00	20
N1184	40ch.	Sujong and Pari Peaks (horiz)	1·20	25

494 Magnolia Flower

1973

N1185	**494**	10ch. multicoloured	1·80	40

495 S. Korean Revolutionaries

1973. South Korean Revolution. Multicoloured.

N1186	10ch.	Type **495**	20	15
N1187	10ch.	Marching revolutionaries	20	15

496 Cock sees Butterflies

1973. Scenes from *Cock Chasing Butterflies*. Fairy Tale. Multicoloured.

N1188	2ch.	Type **496**	2·10	35
N1189	5ch.	Butterflies discuss how to repel cock	2·10	35
N1190	10ch.	Cock chasing butterflies with basket	3·00	40
N1191	10ch.	Cock chasing butterfly up cliff	3·00	45
N1192	40ch.	Cock chasing butterflies over cliff	3·25	55
N1193	90ch.	Cock falls into sea and butterflies escape	5·00	60

497 Yonpung

1973. Historical Sites of War and Revolution (40ch.). Multicoloured.

N1196	2ch.	Type **497**	15	10
N1197	5ch.	Hyangha	15	10
N1198	10ch.	Changgol	15	15
N1199	40ch.	Paeksong	85	20

498 Science Library, Kim Il Sung University

1973. New Buildings in Pyongyang.

N1200	**498**	2ch. violet	75	15
N1201	-	5ch. green	25	15
N1202	-	10ch. brown	35	15
N1203	-	40ch. brown and buff	85	20
N1204	-	90ch. buff	1·40	40

DESIGNS—HORIZ: 10ch. Victory Museum; 40ch. People's Palace of Culture; 90ch. Indoor stadium. VERT: 5ch. Building No. 2, Kim Il Sung University.

499 Red Book

1973. Socialist Constitution of North Korea. Multicoloured.

N1205	10ch.	Type **499**	35	15
N1206	10ch.	Marchers with red book and banners	35	15
N1207	10ch.	Marchers with red book and emblem	35	15

500 Oriental Great Reed Warbler

1973. Korean Songbirds. Multicoloured.

N1208	5ch.	Type **500**	2·50	45
N1209	10ch.	Grey starling (facing right)	3·75	70
N1210	10ch.	Daurian starling (facing left)	3·75	70

503 Chollima Statue

1974. The Works of Kim Il Sung (2nd series). Multicoloured.

N1217	10ch.	Type **503**	90	20
N1218	10ch.	Bayonets threatening U.S. soldier	15	15

504 Train in Station

1974. Opening of Pyongyang Metro. Multicoloured.

N1219	10ch.	Type **504**	90	15
N1220	10ch.	Escalators	90	15
N1221	10ch.	Station hall	90	15

505 Capital Construction Front

1974. Five Fronts of Socialist Construction. Multicoloured.

N1222	10ch.	Type **505**	20	15
N1223	10ch.	Agricultural front	35	15
N1224	10ch.	Transport front	1·80	35
N1225	10ch.	Fisheries front	1·10	20
N1226	10ch.	Industrial front (vert)	35	15

506 Marchers with Banners

1974. Tenth Anniv of Publication of *Theses on the Socialist Rural Question in Our Country*. Multicoloured.

N1227	10ch.	Type **506**	25	10
N1228	10ch.	Book and rejoicing crowd	25	10
N1229	10ch.	Tractor and banners	25	10

Nos. N1227/9 were issued together, *se-tenant*, forming a composite design.

507 Manure Spreader

1974. Farm Machinery.

N1230	**507**	2ch. green, black & red	60	15
N1231	-	5ch. red, black and blue	60	15
N1232	-	10ch. red, black and green	60	15

DESIGNS: 5ch. "Progress" tractor; 10ch. "Mount Taedoksan" tractor.

508 Archery (Grenoble)

1974. North Korean Victories at International Sports Meetings. Multicoloured.

N1233	2ch. Type **508**	1·30	25
N1234	5ch. Gymnastics (Varna)	25	15
N1235	10ch. Boxing (Bucharest)	35	15
N1236	20ch. Volleyball (Pyongyang)	25	15
N1237	30ch. Rifle shooting (Sofia)	65	20
N1238	40ch. Judo (Tbilisi)	1·00	25
N1239	60ch. Model aircraft flying (Vienna) (horiz)	1·70	35
N1240	1wn. 50 Table tennis (Peking) (horiz)	3·00	65

509 Book and Rejoicing Crowd

1974. The First Country with No Taxes.

N1241	**509** 10ch. multicoloured	40	10

510 Drawing up Programme in Woods

1974. Kim Il Sung during the Anti-Japanese Struggle. Multicoloured.

N1242	10ch. Type **510**	35	15
N1243	10ch. Giving directions to Pak Dal	35	15
N1244	10ch. Presiding over Nanhutou Conference	35	15
N1245	10ch. Supervising creation of strongpoint	35	15

511 Sun Hui loses her Sight

1974. Scenes from *The Flower Girl* (revolutionary opera). Multicoloured.

N1246	2ch. Type **511**	1·00	20
N1247	5ch. Death of Ggot Bun's mother	1·00	20
N1248	10ch. Ggot Bun throws boiling water at landlord	2·10	35
N1249	40ch. Ggot Bun joins revolutionaries	2·75	45
MSN1250	111×62 mm. 50ch. Ggot Bun amid flowers of revolution. Imperf	3·75	1·50

512 Leopard Cat

1974. 15th Anniv of Pyongyang Zoo. Multicoloured.

N1251	2ch. Type **512**	75	15
N1252	5ch. Lynx	75	15
N1253	10ch. Red fox	75	15
N1254	10ch. Wild boar	75	15
N1255	20ch. Dhole	75	15
N1256	40ch. Brown bear	85	40
N1257	60ch. Leopard	1·50	40
N1258	70ch. Tiger	2·10	45
N1259	90ch. Lion	2·75	55
MSN1260	140×100 mm. Diamond-shaped designs: 10ch. Wildcat; 30ch. Lynx; 50ch. Leopard; 60ch. Tiger. Imperf	29·00	8·00

513 *Rosa acucularis lindly*

1974. Roses. Multicoloured.

N1261	2ch. Type **513**	75	15
N1262	5ch. Yellow sweet briar	85	20
N1263	10ch. Pink aromatic rose	1·00	20
N1264	10ch. Aronia sweet briar (yellow centres)	1·00	20
N1265	40ch. Multi-petal sweet briar	2·50	35

514 Kim Il Sung greeted by Children

1974. 30th Anniv of Korean Children's Union. Sheet 126×95 mm.

MSN1266	**514** 1w.20 multicoloured	4·50	3·25

515 Weigela

1974. Flowering Plants of Mt. Paekdu. Multicoloured.

N1267	2ch. Type **515**	60	15
N1268	5ch. Amaryllis	60	15
N1269	10ch. Red lily	60	15
N1270	20ch. Orange lily	85	20
N1271	40ch. Azalea	1·10	20
N1272	60ch. Yellow lily	1·80	35

516 Postwoman and Construction Site

1974. Centenary of U.P.U. and Admission of North Korea to Union. Multicoloured.

N1273	10ch. Type **516**	1·80	30
N1274	25ch. Chollima monument	20	20
N1275	40ch. Globe and Antonov An-12 transport planes	1·30	30

517 Common Pond Frog

1974. Amphibians. Multicoloured.

N1276	2ch. Type **517**	3·00	30
N1277	5ch. Oriental fire-bellied toad	3·25	30
N1278	10ch. Bullfrog	3·75	45
N1279	40ch. Common toad	5·50	65

518 Women of Namgang Village

1974. Korean Paintings. Multicoloured.

N1281	2ch. Type **518**	75	15

N1282	5ch. *An Old Man on the Rakdong River* (60×49 mm)	85	20
N1283	10ch. *Morning in the Naekumgang* (bridge)	1·80	35
N1284	20ch. *Mt. Kumgang* (60×49 mm)	1·70	30
MSN1285	116×115 mm. 1wn.50 *Evening Glow in Kangson.* Imperf	6·25	4·50

519 "Elektron 1" and "Elektron 2", 1964

1974. Cosmonauts Day. Multicoloured.

N1286	10ch. Type **519**	15	10
N1287	20ch. "Proton 1", 1965	25	15
N1288	30ch. "Venera 3", 1966	50	15
N1289	10ch. "Venera 5" and "Venera 6", 1969	60	20
MSN1290	80×120 mm. 1wn. Dogs Belka and Strelka. Imperf	29·00	2·75

520 Satellite

1974. Fourth Anniv of Launching of First Chinese Satellite. Sheet 80×120 mm. Imperf.

MSN1291	**520** 50ch. multicoloured	3·75	1·40

521 Antonov An-2 Biplane

1974. Civil Aviation. Multicoloured.

N1292	2ch. Type **521**	85	15
N1293	5ch. Lisunov Li-2	85	15
N1294	10ch. Ilyushin Il-14P	1·10	20
N1295	40ch. Antonov An-24	1·50	45
N1296	60ch. Ilyushin Il-18	2·75	70
MSN1297	96×68 mm. 90ch. Airliner. Imperf	6·25	4·75

522 *Rhododendron redowskianum*

1974. Plants of Mt. Paekdu. Multicoloured.

N1298	2ch. Type **522**	50	10
N1299	5ch. *Dryas octopetala*	50	15
N1300	10ch. *Potentilla fruticosa*	60	15
N1301	20ch. *Papaver somniferum*	75	15
N1302	40ch. *Phyllodoce caerulea*	1·00	30
N1303	60ch. *Oxytropis anertii*	2·20	55

523 *Sobaek River in the Morning*

1974. Modern Korean Paintings (1st series). Multicoloured.

N1304	10ch. Type **523**	1·30	20
N1305	20ch. *Combatants of Mt. Laohei* (60×40 mm)	1·50	25
N1306	30ch. *Spring in the Fields*	1·80	25
MSN1307	40ch. *Tideland Night*	5·75	85
N1308	60ch. *Daughter* (60×54 mm)	2·10	60

See also Nos. N1361/5, N1386/96 and N1485/9.

524

1974. Bologna Exhibition for 50th Anniv of L'Unita (organ of the Italian communist party). Sheet 148×98 mm. Imperf.

MSN1309	1wn.50 multicoloured	6·25	2·10

525 Log Cabin, Unha Village

1974. Historic Sites of the Revolution. Multicoloured.

N1310	5ch. Munmyong	20	10
N1311	10ch. Type **525**	20	10

526 Sesame

1974. Oil-producing Plants. Multicoloured.

N1312	2ch. Type **526**	90	20
N1313	5ch. *Perilla frutescens*	1·00	20
N1314	10ch. Sunflower	1·20	25
N1315	40ch. Castor bean	1·70	55

527 Kim Il Sung as Guerrilla Leader

1974. Kim Il Sung. Multicoloured.

N1316	10ch. Type **527**	35	15
N1317	10ch. Commander of the People's Army (52×35 mm)	35	15
N1318	10ch. "The commander is also a son of the people" (52×35 mm)	35	15
N1319	10ch. Negotiating with the Chinese anti-Japanese unit (52×35 mm)	35	15

528

1974. Grand Monument on Mansu Hill. Multicoloured.

N1320	10ch. Type **528**	25	15
N1321	10ch. As T **528** but men in civilian clothes	25	15
N1322	10ch. As T **528** but men facing left	25	15
N1323	10ch. As No. N1322 but men in civilian clothes	25	15

529 Factory Ship *Chilbosan*

1974. Deep-sea Fishing. Multicoloured.

N1324	2ch. Type **529**	1·20	30
N1325	5ch. Trawler support ship *Paekdusan*	1·20	30
N1326	10ch. Freighter *Moranbong*	1·20	30
N1327	20ch. Whale-catcher	1·20	30
N1328	30ch. Trawler	1·20	30
N1329	40ch. Stern trawler	1·20	30

539 Kim Il Sung crossing River Agrok

1975. 50th Anniv of Kim Il Sung's crossing of River Agrok.

N1349	**539**	10ch. multicoloured	40	15

540 Pak Yong Sun "World Table Tennis Queen"

1975. Pak Yong Sun, Winner of 33rd World Table Tennis Championships, Calcutta.

N1350	**540**	10ch. multicoloured	1·50	15
MS	N1351	80×119 mm. 80ch. "Table Tennis Crown". Imperf	2·75	80

541 Zebra

1975. Pyongyang Zoo. Multicoloured.

N1352	10ch. Type **541**	85	15
N1353	10ch. African buffalo	85	15
N1354	20ch. Giant panda (horiz)	2·10	25
N1355	25ch. Bactrian camel	1·70	40
N1356	30ch. Indian elephant	3·25	45

542 Blue Dragon

1975. 7th-century Mural Paintings from Koguryo Tombs, Kangso.

N1357	10ch. Type **542**	90	15
N1358	15ch. "White Tiger"	1·30	25
N1359	25ch. "Red Phoenix" (vert)	1·50	30
N1360	40ch. "Snake-turtle"	2·10	40

543 Spring in the Guerrilla Base (1968)

1975. Modern Korean Paintings (2nd series). Anti-Japanese struggle. Multicoloured.

N1361	10ch. Type **543**	50	15
N1362	10ch. *Revolutionary Army landing at Unggi* (1969)	50	15
N1363	15ch. *Sewing Team Members* (1961)	85	20
N1364	20ch. *Girl Watering Horse* (1969)	1·50	25
N1365	30ch. *Kim Jong Suk giving Guidance to Children's Corps* (1970)	1·20	25

544 Cosmonaut

1975. Cosmonauts' Day. Multicoloured.

N1366	10ch. Type **544**	15	10
N1367	30ch. "Lunokhod" moon vehicle (horiz)	65	15
N1368	40ch. "Soyuz" spacecraft and "Salyut" space laboratory (horiz)	90	25

545 Victory Monument

1975. Commemoration of Battle of Pochonbo. Sheet 140×98 mm. Imperf.

MS	N1369 **545** 1wn. multicoloured	5·75	3·00

546 The Beacon lit at Pochonbo, 1937

1975. Kim Il Sung during the Guerrilla War against the Japanese. Multicoloured.

N1370	10ch. Type **546**	35	15
N1371	10ch. "A Bowl of Parched-rice Powder", 1938	35	15
N1372	10ch. Guiding the Nanpaizi meeting, November, 1938	35	15
N1373	10ch. Welcoming helper	35	15
N1374	10ch. Lecturing the guerrillas	35	15
N1375	15ch. Advancing into the homeland, May 1939	40	15
N1376	25ch. By Lake Samji, May 1939	60	25
N1377	30ch. At Sinsadong, May 1939	75	30
N1378	40ch. Xiaoaerbaling meeting, 1940	1·10	40

547 Vase of Flowers and Kim Il Sung's Birthplace

1975. Kim Il Sung's 63rd Birthday. Multicoloured.

N1379	10ch. Type **547**	20	10
N1379a	40ch. Kim Il Sung's birthplace, Mangyongdae	65	15

548 South Korean Insurgent

1975. 15th Anniv of April 19th Rising.

N1380	**548** 10ch. multicoloured	30	10

549 Kingfisher at a Lotus Pond

1975. Paintings of Li Dynasty. Multicoloured.

N1381	5ch. Type **549**	2·10	30
N1382	10ch. *Crabs*	1·30	25
N1383	15ch. *Rose of Sharon*	2·10	35
N1384	25ch. *Lotus and Water Cock*	3·00	50
N1385	30ch. *Tree Peony and Red Junglefowl*	4·25	75

1975. Modern Korean Paintings (3rd series). Fatherland Liberation War. Dated designs as T **543**. Multicoloured.

N1386	5ch. *On the Advance Southward* (1966) (vert)	25	15
N1387	10ch. *The Assigned Post* (girl sentry) (1968) (vert)	35	15
N1388	15ch. *The Heroism of Li Su Bok* (1965)	40	15
N1389	25ch. *Retaliation* (woman machine-gunner) (1970)	75	25
N1390	30ch. *The awaited Troops* (1970)	90	25

1975. Modern Korean Paintings (4th series). Socialist Construction. As T **543**. Multicoloured.

N1391	10ch. *Pine Tree* (1966) (vert)	1·00	20
N1392	10ch. *The Blue Signal Lamp* (1960) (vert)	3·75	55
N1393	15ch. *A Night of Snowfall* (1963)	1·10	20
N1394	20ch. *Smelters* (1968)	1·30	25
N1395	25ch. *Tideland Reclamation* (1961)	1·30	25
N1396	30ch. *Mount Paekgum* (1966)	1·30	25

550 Flag and Building

1975. 20th Anniv of "Chongryon" Association of Koreans in Japan.

N1397	**550** 10ch. multicoloured	40	10
N1398	**550** 3wn. multicoloured	9·50	85

551 Marathon Runners

1975. Marathon Race of Socialist Countries. Sheet 105×74 mm. Imperf.

MS	N1399 1wn. multicoloured	4·25	1·40

552 "Feet first" entry (man)

1975. Diving. Multicoloured.

N1400	10ch. Type **552**	15	10
N1401	25ch. Piked somersault (man)	65	30
N1402	40ch. "Head first" entry (woman)	1·30	40

553

1975. Campaign against U.S. Imperialism.

N1403	**553** 10ch. multicoloured	40	15

554 Silver Carp

1975. Fresh-water Fish. Multicoloured.

N1404	10ch. Type **554**	85	15
N1405	10ch. Elongate ilisha (swimming to right)	85	15
N1406	15ch. Banded minnow	1·30	20
N1407	25ch. Bare-headed bagrid	1·80	30
N1408	30ch. Amur catfish (swimming to right)	2·50	40
N1409	30ch. Chevron snakehead (swimming to left)	2·50	40

555

1975. Tenth Socialist Countries' Football Tournament, Pyongyang.

N1410	**555** 5ch. multicoloured	50	10
N1411	- 10ch. multicoloured	50	15
N1412	- 15ch. multicoloured	60	15
N1413	- 20ch. multicoloured	75	25
N1414	- 50ch. multicoloured	1·40	50
MS	N1415 112×80 mm. 1wn. multicoloured. Imperf	6·25	4·00

DESIGNS: 10ch. to 1wn. Various footballers.

556 Blue and Yellow Macaw

1975. Birds. Multicoloured.

N1416	10ch. Type **556**	1·70	35
N1417	15ch. Sulphur-crested cockatoo	2·00	40
N1418	20ch. Blyth's parakeet	2·75	50
N1419	25ch. Rainbow lory	3·00	65
N1420	30ch. Budgerigar	3·25	70

557 Flats

1975. New Buildings in Pyongyang. Multicoloured.

N1421	90ch. Saesallim (formerly Sarguson) Street	5·00	90
N1422	1wn. Type **557**	5·00	95
N1423	2wn. Potonggang Hotel	10·00	2·00

558 White Peach Blossom

1975. Blossoms of Flowering Trees. Multicoloured.

N1424	10ch. Type **558**	60	15

N1425	15ch. Red peach blossom	60	15
N1426	20ch. Red plum blossom	1·00	25
N1427	25ch. Apricot blossom	1·20	25
N1428	30ch. Cherry blossom	1·70	40

559 Sejongbong

1975. Landscapes in the Diamond Mountains. Multicoloured.

N1429	5ch. Type **559**	50	10
N1430	10ch. Chonsondae	75	15
N1431	15ch. Pisamun	1·00	25
N1432	25ch. Manmulsang	1·30	30
N1433	30ch. Chaehabong	1·50	35

560 Azalea

1975. Flowers of the Azalea Family. Multicoloured.

N1434	5ch. Type **560**	65	15
N1435	10ch. White azalea	65	25
N1436	15ch. Wild rhododendron	1·00	25
N1437	20ch. White rhododendron	1·00	25
N1438	25ch. Rhododendron	1·30	30
N1439	30ch. Yellow rhododendron	1·70	40

561 Gliders

1975. Training for National Defence. Multicoloured.

N1440	5ch. Type **561**	60	10
N1441	5ch. Radio-controlled model airplane	60	10
N1442	10ch. "Free fall parachutist" (vert)	75	20
N1443	10ch. Parachutist landing on target (vert)	75	20
N1444	20ch. Parachutist with bouquet of flowers (vert)	1·30	30
MSN1445 90×68 mm. 50ch. Three parachutists in circle. Imperf		2·75	75

562 Wild Apple

1975. Fruit Tree Blossom. Multicoloured.

N1446	10ch. Type **562**	65	25
N1447	15ch. Wild pear	65	25
N1448	20ch. Hawthorn	1·00	30
N1449	25ch. Chinese quince	1·30	40
N1450	30ch. Flowering quince	1·40	50

563 Torch of Juche

1975. 30th Anniv of Korean Workers' Party. Multicoloured.

N1451	2ch. "Victory" and American graves	15	10
N1452	2ch. Sunrise over Mt. Paekdusan	15	10
N1453	5ch. Type **563**	15	10
N1454	5ch. Chollima Statue and sunset over Pyongyang	15	10
N1455	10ch. Korean with Red Book	15	10
N1456	10ch. Chollima Statue	15	10
N1457	25ch. Crowds and burning building	50	25
N1458	70ch. Flowers and map of Korea	1·60	80
MSN1459 Two sheets (a) 85×120 mm. 90ch. Kim Il Sung delivering speech; (b) 120×85 mm. 1wn. Kim Il Sung leading crowd		6·25	4·75

564 Welcoming Crowd

1975. 30th Anniv of Kim Il Sung's Return to Pyongyang.

| N1460 | **564** 20ch. multicoloured | 35 | 15 |

565 Workers holding "Juche" Torch

1975. 30th Anniv of *Rodong Simmun* (Journal of the Central Committee of the Worker's Party).

| N1461 | 10ch. multicoloured | 60 | 15 |
| **MS**N1462 95×68 mm. **565** 1wn. multicoloured. Imperf | | 3·00 | 2·10 |

566 Hyonmu Gate

1975. Ancient Wall-Gates of Pyongyang. Multicoloured.

N1463	10ch. Type **566**	15	10
N1464	10ch. Taedong Gate	15	10
N1465	15ch. Potong Gate	25	15
N1466	20ch. Chongum Gate	40	25
N1467	30ch. Chilsong Gate (vert)	60	40

567

1975. Views of Mt. Chilbo.

N1468	**567** 10ch. multicoloured	50	15
N1469	– 10ch. multicoloured	50	20
N1470	– 15ch. multicoloured	75	25
N1471	– 20ch. multicoloured	90	30
N1472	– 30ch. multicoloured	1·00	35

DESIGNS: Nos. N1468/72, Various views.

568 Right-hand Section of Monument

1975. Historic Site of Revolution in Wangjaesan. Multicoloured.

N1473	10ch. Type **568**	15	10
N1474	15ch. Left-hand section of monument	25	10
N1475	25ch. Centre section of monument (38×60 mm)	40	15
N1476	30ch. Centre section, close up (60×38 mm)	50	25

569 Marchers with Flags

1976. 30th Anniv of Korean League of Socialist Working Youth. Multicoloured.

| N1477 | 2ch. Flags and Emblem | 20 | 15 |
| N1478 | 70ch. Type **569** | 1·30 | 65 |

570 Geese

1976. Ducks and Geese. Multicoloured.

N1479	10ch. Type **570**	85	15
N1480	20ch. "Perennial" duck	1·80	25
N1481	40ch. Kwangpo duck	3·25	45

571 Oath

1976. Korean Peoples Army (sculptural works). Multicoloured.

N1482	5ch. Type **571**	25	10
N1483	10ch. *Union of Officers with Men* (horiz)	35	10
N1484	10ch. *This Flag to the Height*	35	10

572 *Rural Road at Evening*

1976. Modern Korean Paintings (5th series). Social Welfare. Multicoloured.

N1485	10ch. Type **572**	60	15
N1486	15ch. *Passing on Technique* (1970)	65	20
N1487	25ch. *Mother (and Child)* (1965)	90	20
N1488	30ch. *Medical Examination at School* (1970) (horiz)	1·70	35
N1489	40ch. *Lady Doctor of Village* (1970) (horiz)	2·00	45

573 Worker holding Text of Law

1976. 30th Anniv of Agrarian Reform Law.

| N1490 | **573** 10ch. multicoloured | 30 | 15 |

574 Telephones and Satellite

1976. Centenary of First Telephone Call. Multicoloured. With or without gum.

N1491	2ch. Type **574**	60	10
N1492	5ch. Satellite and antenna	60	10
N1493	10ch. Satellite and telecommunications systems	65	15
N1494	15ch. Telephone and linesman	1·40	35
N1495	25ch. Satellite and map of receiving stations	2·10	45
N1496	40ch. Satellite and cable-laying barge	3·25	60
MSN1497 94×70 mm. 50ch. Old telephone and satellite. Without gum		2·50	60

575 Cosmos

1976. Flowers. Multicoloured.

N1498	5ch. Type **575**	40	15
N1499	10ch. Dahlia	40	15
N1500	20ch. Zinnia	60	20
N1501	40ch. China aster	1·00	40

576 Fruit and Products

1976. Pukchong Meeting of Korean Workers' Party Presidium. Multicoloured.

| N1502 | 5ch. Type **576** | 85 | 20 |
| N1503 | 10ch. Fruit and orchard scene | 85 | 20 |

577 "Pulgungi" Electric Locomotive

1976. Railway Locomotives. Multicoloured.

N1504	5ch. Type **577**	50	15
N1505	10ch. "Chaju" underground train	1·00	20
N1506	15ch. "Saebyol" diesel locomotive	1·20	30

578 Satellite

1976. Space Flight. With or without gum.

N1507	**578** 2ch. multicoloured	15	10
N1508	– 5ch. multicoloured	15	10
N1509	– 10ch. multicoloured	25	15
N1510	– 15ch. multicoloured	40	15
N1511	– 25ch. multicoloured	60	25
N1512	– 40ch. multicoloured	1·00	30
MSN1513 77×98 mm. 50ch. Moon vehicle		1·30	55

DESIGNS: 5ch. to 50ch. Various satellite and space craft.

579 Kim Il Sung beside Car

1976. Kim Il Sung's 64th Birthday.

| N1514 | **579** 10ch. multicoloured | 50 | 20 |
| **MS**N1515 120×80 mm. 40ch. Kim Il Sung and rejoicing crowd | | 4·50 | 1·30 |

580 Bat and Ribbon

1976. Third Asian Table Tennis Championships. Multicoloured. Without gum.

| N1516 | 5ch. Type **580** | 35 | 10 |
| N1517 | 10ch. Three women players with flowers | 35 | 15 |

N1518	20ch. Player defending	60	30
N1519	25ch. Player making attacking shot	1·00	40
MSN1520	74×99 mm. 50ch. Player making backhand shot. Imperf	2·50	80

581 Kim Il Sung announcing Establishment of Association

1976. 40th Anniv of Association for the Restoration of the Fatherland. Without gum.
N1521	**581**	10ch. multicoloured	25	15

582 Golden Pheasant

1976. Pheasants. Multicoloured. With or without gum.
N1522	2ch. Type **582**	1·00	25
N1523	5ch. Lady Amherst's pheasant	1·10	25
N1524	10ch. Silver pheasant	1·30	30
N1525	15ch. Reeves's pheasant	1·50	40
N1526	25ch. Temminck's tragopan	2·00	60
N1527	40ch. Common pheasant (albino)	2·30	80
MSN1528	77×58 mm. 50ch. Ring-necked pheasant	5·00	2·10

583 Monument and Map of River

1976. Potong River Monument. Without gum.
N1529	**583**	10ch. brown and green	25	15

584 Running

1976. Olympic Games, Montreal. Multicoloured.
N1530	2ch. Type **584**	15	15
N1531	5ch. Diving	35	15
N1532	10ch. Judo	75	15
N1533	15ch. Gymnastics	1·30	35
N1534	25ch. Gymnastics	1·70	35
N1535	40ch. Fencing	3·50	85
MSN1536	109×85 mm. 50ch. Runner with torch and Olympic Stadium	4·25	2·10

585 Bronze Medal (Hockey, Pakistan)

1976. Olympic Medal Winners (1st issue). Multicoloured.
N1537	2ch. Type **585**	1·10	15
N1538	5ch. Bronze medal (shooting, Rudolf Dollinger)	35	10
N1539	10ch. Silver medal (boxing, Li Byong Uk)	35	15
N1540	15ch. Silver medal (cycling, Daniel Morelon)	3·00	45
N1541	25ch. Gold medal (marathon, Waldemar Cierpinski)	1·30	30
N1542	40ch. Gold medal (boxing, Ku Yong Jo)	1·70	35
MSN1543	109×84 mm. 50ch. Three medals	2·10	2·10

586 Boxing (Ku Yong Jo)

1976. Olympic Medal Winners (2nd issue). Multicoloured.
N1544	2ch. Type **586**	35	10
N1545	5ch. Gymnastics (Nadia Comaneci)	35	10
N1546	10ch. Pole vaulting (Tadeusz Slusarki)	35	15
N1547	15ch. Hurdling (Guy Drut)	40	15
N1548	25ch. Cycling (Bernt Johansson)	3·75	55
N1549	40ch. Football (East Germany)	2·20	40
MSN1550	104×84 mm. 50ch. Ku Yong Jo (boxing champion)	2·50	55

587 U.P.U. Headquarters, Berne

1976. International Festivities. Multicoloured.
N1551	2ch. Type **587**	60	10
N1552	5ch. Footballers (World Cup)	60	10
N1553	10ch. Olympic Stadium	65	15
N1554	15ch. Olympic Village	1·40	25
N1555	25ch. Junk and satellite	1·20	35
N1556	40ch. Satellites	1·20	60
MSN1557	85×105 mm. 50ch. World map	2·10	1·40

588 Azure-winged Magpies

1976. Embroidery. Multicoloured. With or without gum.
N1558	2ch. Type **588**	2·00	40
N1559	5ch. White magpie	1·40	30
N1560	10ch. Roe deer	50	15
N1561	15ch. Black-naped oriole and magnolias	2·10	40
N1562	25ch. Fairy with flute (horiz)	1·20	25
N1563	40ch. Tiger	2·50	65
MSN1564	94×105 mm. 50ch. Tiger (52×82 mm)	10·00	90

589 Roman "5" and Flame

1976. Fifth Non-aligned States' Summit Conference, Colombo. Without gum.
N1565	**589**	10ch. multicoloured	25	15

590 Trophy and Certificate

1976. World Model Plane Championships (1975). Multicoloured. Without gum.
N1566	5ch. Type **590**	25	10
N1567	10ch. Trophy and medals	40	10
N1568	20ch. Model airplane and emblem	60	20
N1569	40ch. Model glider and medals	1·00	50

591 "Pulgungi" Diesel Shunting Locomotive

1976. Locomotives. Multicoloured.
N1570	2ch. Type **591**	60	15
N1571	5ch. "Saebyol" diesel locomotive	85	20
N1572	10ch. "Saebyol" diesel shunting locomotive	90	20
N1573	15ch. Electric locomotive	1·10	25
N1574	25ch. "Kumsong" diesel locomotive	1·50	30
N1575	40ch. "Pulgungi" electric locomotive	1·80	35
MSN1576	100×68 mm. 50ch. "Kumsong" type diesel locomotive. Imperf	7·50	3·75

592 House of Culture

1976. House of Culture. Without gum.
N1577	**592**	10ch. brown and black	20	15

593 Kim Il Sung visiting Tosongrang

1976. Revolutionary Activities of Kim Il Sung. Multicoloured.
N1578	2ch. Type **593**	25	10
N1579	5ch. Kim Il Sung visits pheasants	25	10
N1580	10ch. Kim Il Sung on hilltop	35	10
N1581	15ch. Kim Il Sung giving house to farmhand	40	15
N1582	25ch. Kim Il Sung near front line	1·00	20
N1583	40ch. Kim Il Sung walking in rain	1·00	35
MSN1584	105×85 mm. 50ch. Kim Il Sung with child at roadside	1·80	1·40

594 Kim Il Sung with Union Members

1976. 50th Anniv of Down-with-Imperialism Union. Without gum.
N1585	**594**	20ch. multicoloured	50	20

604 Searchlights and Kim Il Sung's Birthplace

1977. New Year. Without gum.
N1589	**604**	10ch. multicoloured	25	15

605 Spring Costume

1977. National Costumes of Li Dynasty. Multicoloured.
N1590	10ch. Type **605** (postage)	65	15
N1591	15ch. Summer costume	90	20

N1592	20ch. Autumn costume	1·00	25
N1593	40ch. Winter costume (air)	1·70	40

606 Two Deva Kings (Koguryo Dynasty)

1977. Korean Cultural Relics. Multicoloured.
N1594	2ch. Type **606** (postage)	60	15
N1595	5ch. Gold-copper decoration, Koguryo Dynasty	60	15
N1596	10ch. Copper Buddha, Koryo Dynasty	85	20
N1597	15ch. Gold-copper Buddha, Paekje Dynasty	1·00	20
N1598	25ch. Gold crown, Koguryo Dynasty	1·20	30
N1599	40ch. Gold-copper sun decoration, Koguryo Dynasty (horiz)	1·40	35
N1600	50ch. Gold crown, Silla Dynasty (air)	1·50	50

607 Worker with Five-point Programme

1977. Five-point Programme for Remaking Nature. Without gum.
N1601	**607**	10ch. multicoloured	30	15

608 Pine Branch and Map of Korea

1977. 60th Anniv of Korean National Association. Without gum.
N1602	**608**	10ch. multicoloured	55	20

609 Championship Emblem and Trophy

1977. 34th World Table Tennis Championships. Multicoloured. Without gum.
N1603	10ch. Type **609** (postage)	25	10
N1604	15ch. Pak Yong Sun	40	15
N1605	20ch. Pak Yong Sun with trophy	65	20
N1606	40ch. Pak Yong Ok and Yang Ying (air)	1·30	40

610 Kim Il Sung founds Guerrilla Army at Mingyuegou

1977. Kim Il Sung's 65th Birthday. Multicoloured.
N1607	2ch. Type **610**	15	10
N1608	5ch. In command of army	15	10
N1609	10ch. Visiting steel workers in Kangson	35	10
N1610	15ch. Before battle	25	10
N1611	25ch. In schoolroom	35	15
N1612	40ch. Viewing bumper harvest	50	15
MSN1613	85×94 mm. 50ch. "Kim Il Sung among the Artists"	1·30	90

611 "Chollima 72" Trolleybus

1977. Trolleybuses. Without gum.
| N1614 | **611** | 5ch. blue, lilac and black | 1·50 | 30 |
| N1615 | - | 10ch. red, green & black | 1·50 | 30 |

DESIGN: 10ch. "Chollima 74" trolleybus.

612 Red Flag and
Hand holding Rifle

1977. 45th Anniv of Korean People's Revolutionary Army.
Without gum.
| N1616 | **612** | 40ch. red, yellow & blk | 85 | 25 |

613 Proclamation and
Watchtower

1977. 40th Anniv of Pochonbo Battle. Without gum.
| N1617 | **613** | 10ch. multicoloured | 25 | 15 |

614 Koryo White Ware
Teapot

1977. Korean Porcelain. Multicoloured.
N1618		10ch. Type **614** (postage)	75	15
N1619		15ch. White vase, Li Dynasty	1·00	20
N1620		20ch. Celadon vase, Koryo Dynasty	1·30	30
N1621		40ch. Celadon vase with lotus decoration, Koryo Dynasty (air)	1·80	40

615 Postal Transport

1977. Postal Services. Multicoloured. Without gum.
N1623		2ch. Type **615**	1·50	30
N1624		10ch. Postwoman delivering letter	60	15
N1625		30ch. Mil Mi-8 helicopter	1·50	40
N1626		40ch. Ilyushin Il-18 airliner and world map	1·70	45

616 Rapala arata

1977. Butterflies and Dragonflies. Multicoloured.
N1627		2ch. Type **616** (postage)	65	10
N1628		5ch. *Colias aurora*	1·00	15
N1629		10ch. Poplar admiral	1·30	20
N1630		15ch. *Anax partherope* (dragonfly)	1·70	35
N1631		25ch. *Sympetrum pedemontanum* (dragonfly)	2·20	45
N1632		50ch. *Papilio maackii* (air)	2·75	60

617 Grey Cat

1977. Cats. Multicoloured.
| N1634 | | 2ch. Type **617** | 1·70 | 30 |

| N1635 | | 10ch. Black and white cat | 2·20 | 40 |
| N1636 | | 25ch. Ginger cat | 3·75 | 55 |

618

1977. Dogs. Multicoloured.
N1638		5ch. Type **618** (postage)	1·30	25
N1639		15ch. Chow	1·50	25
N1640		50ch. Pungsang dog (air)	2·30	45

619 Kim Il Sung and
President Tito

1977. Visit of President Tito.
N1642	**619**	10ch. multicoloured	15	10
N1643	**619**	15ch. multicoloured	15	10
N1644	**619**	20ch. multicoloured	25	15
N1645	**619**	40vh. multicoloured	40	25

620 Girl and Symbols of
Education

1977. Fifth Anniv of 11-year Compulsory Education.
Without gum.
| N1646 | **620** | 10ch. multicoloured | 25 | 15 |

621 Chinese Mactra
and Cobia

1977. Shellfish and Fish. Multicoloured.
N1647		2ch. Type **621** (postage)	50	10
N1648		5ch. Bladder moon	65	20
N1649		10ch. *Arca inflata* and pomfret	1·00	20
N1650		25ch. Thomas's rapa whelk and grouper	1·40	35
N1651		50ch. Thomas's rapa whelk and globefish (air)	2·30	65

622 Students and
"Theses"

1977. Kim Il Sung's "Theses on Socialist Education".
Multicoloured. Without gum.
| N1653 | | 10ch. Type **622** | 25 | 10 |
| N1654 | | 20ch. Students, crowd and text | 30 | 15 |

623 "Juche" Torch

1977. Seminar on the Juche Idea. Multicoloured. Without
gum.
N1655		2ch. Type **623**	25	10
N1656		5ch. Crowd and red book	25	10
N1657		10ch. Chollima Statue and flags	25	10
N1658		15ch. Handclasp and red flag on world map	25	10
N1659		25ch. Map of Korea and anti-U.S. slogans	35	15
N1660		40ch. Crowd and Mt. Paekdu-san	40	15
MSN1661	117×78 mm. 50ch. Emblem of Juche seminar		1·30	55

624 Jubilant Crowd

1977. Election of Deputies to Supreme People's
Assembly. Without gum.
| N1662 | **624** | 10ch. multicoloured | 25 | 15 |

625 Footballers

1977. World Cup Football Championship, Argentina.
Without gum.
N1663	**625**	10ch. multicoloured	1·10	25
N1664	-	15ch. multicoloured	1·50	35
N1665	-	40ch. multicoloured	2·50	50
MSN1666	132×82 mm. 50ch. Footballers		2·20	55

DESIGNS: 15ch. to 50ch. Different football scenes.

626 Kim Il Sung with Rejoicing Crowds

1977. Re-election of Kim Il Sung. Without gum.
| N1667 | **626** | 10ch. multicoloured | 30 | 15 |

627 Chollima Statue
and Symbols of
Communication

1977. 20th Anniv of Socialist Countries' Communication
Organization. Without gum.
| N1668 | **627** | 10ch. multicoloured | 30 | 15 |

638 Chollima Statue and City
Skyline

1978. New Year. Without gum.
| N1687 | **638** | 10ch. multicoloured | 30 | 15 |

639 Skater in
19th-century Costume

1978. Winter Olympic Games, Sapporo and Innsbruck.
Multicoloured.
N1688		2ch. Type **639** (postage)	60	15
N1689		5ch. Skier	60	15
N1690		10ch. Woman skater	60	15
N1691		15ch. Hunter on skis	65	20
N1692		20ch. Woman (in 19th-century costume) on skis	65	20
N1693		25ch. Viking with longbow	3·25	50
N1694		40ch. Skier (air)	1·80	35
MSN1695	Two sheets. (a) 78×97 mm. 50ch. Innsbruck skyline; (b) 97×78 mm. 60ch. Skater		3·00	1·30

640 Post-rider and
"Horse-ticket"

1978. Postal Progress. Multicoloured.
N1696		2ch. Type **640** (postage)	35	10
N1697		5ch. Postman on motor cycle	2·10	45
N1698		10ch. Electric train and post-van	2·10	45
N1699		15ch. Mail steamer and Mil Mi-8 helicopter	1·20	25
N1700		25ch. Tupolev Tu-154 jetliner and satellite	1·10	25
N1701		40ch. Dove and U.P.U. headquarters (air)	65	20
MSN1702	Two sheets each 97×79 mm. (a) 50ch. Dove and UPU symbol; (b) 60ch. Dove and UPU headquarters		6·25	3·25

641 Self-portrait

1978. 400th Birth Anniv of Rubens.
N1703	**641**	2ch. multicoloured	35	15
N1704	**641**	5ch. multicoloured	35	15
N1705	**641**	40ch. multicoloured	2·10	45
MSN1706	96×79 mm. 50ch. multicoloured		2·50	1·70

642 "Chungsong" Tractor

1978. Farm Machines. Without gum.
| N1707 | **642** | 10ch. red and black | 65 | 20 |
| N1708 | - | 10ch. brown and black | 65 | 20 |

DESIGN: No. N1708, Sprayer.

643 Show Jumping

1978. Olympic Games, Moscow (1980) (1st issue). Equestrian Events. Multicoloured.

N1709	2ch. Type **643**	35	10
N1710	5ch. Jumping bar	35	10
N1711	10ch. Cross-country	65	15
N1712	15ch. Dressage	65	25
N1713	25ch. Water splash	1·00	40
N1714	40ch. Dressage (different)	1·70	75
MSN1715	75×111 mm. 50ch. Jumping triple bar	2·50	55

See also Nos. N1861/**MS**N1866, N1873/**MS**N1880 and N1887/**MS**N1893.

644 Soldier

1978. Korean People's Army Day. Multicoloured. Without gum.

N1716	5ch. Type **644**	25	10
N1717	10ch. Servicemen saluting	25	10

645 Mangyongbong (Freighter)

1978. Korean Ships. Multicoloured.

N1718	2ch. Type **645** (postage)	2·10	50
N1719	5ch. *Hyoksin* (freighter)	35	15
N1720	10ch. *Chongchongang* (gas carrier)	65	15
N1721	30ch. *Sonbong* (tanker)	1·30	40
N1722	50ch. *Taedonggang* (freighter) (air)	1·50	85

646 Uruguayan Footballer

1978. World Cup Football Championship Winners. Multicoloured.

N1724	5ch. Type **646** (postage)	60	10
N1725	10ch. Italian player	60	10
N1726	15ch. West German player	60	15
N1727	25ch. Brazilian player	60	15
N1728	40ch. English player	1·00	35
N1729	50ch. Hands holding World Cup (vert) (air)	1·70	50
MSN1730	110×74 mm. 50ch. Italian and North Korean players (air)	3·75	1·00

647 Footballers (1930 Winners, Uruguay)

1978. History of World Cup Football Championship. Multicoloured.

N1731	20ch. Type **647** (postage)	1·00	35
N1732	20ch. Italy, 1934	1·00	35
N1733	20ch. France, 1938	1·00	35

N1734	20ch. Brazil, 1950	1·00	35
N1735	20ch. Switzerland, 1954	1·00	35
N1736	20ch. Sweden, 1958	1·00	35
N1737	20ch. Chile, 1962	1·00	35
N1738	20ch. England, 1966	1·00	35
N1739	20ch. Mexico, 1970	1·00	35
N1740	20ch. West Germany, 1974	1·00	35
N1741	20ch. Argentina, 1978	1·00	35
N1742	50ch. Footballers and emblem (air)	2·50	1·00
MSN1743	73×98 mm. 50ch. World Cup and championship emblem	2·10	60

648 Sea of Blood (opera)

1978. Art from the Period of Anti-Japanese Struggle. Multicoloured.

N1744	10ch. Type **648**	35	15
N1745	15ch. Floral kerchief embroidered with map of Korea	50	15
N1746	20ch. *Tansimjul* (maypole dance)	65	25
MSN1747	100×69 mm. 40ch. Notation of *Song of Korea*	1·60	60

649 Red Flag and "7", Electricity and Coal

1978. Second 7 Year Plan. Multicoloured. Without gum.

N1748	5ch. Type **649**	35	10
N1749	10ch. Steel and non-ferrous metal	35	10
N1750	15ch. Engineering and chemical fertilizer	50	15
N1751	30ch. Cement and fishing	75	25
N1752	50ch. Grain and tideland reclamation	1·00	50

650 Gymnastics (Alfred Flatow)

1978. Olympic Games History and Medal-winners. Multicoloured.

N1753	20ch. Type **650**	90	35
N1754	20ch. Runners (Michel Theato)	90	35
N1755	20ch. Runners (Wyndham Halswelle)	90	35
N1756	20ch. Rowing (William Kinnear)	90	35
N1757	20ch. Fencing (Paul Anspach)	1·70	50
N1758	20ch. Runners (Ugo Frigerio)	90	35
N1759	20ch. Runners (Ahmed El Quafi)	90	35
N1760	20ch. Cycling (Robert Charpentier)	2·10	50
N1761	20ch. Gymnastics (Josep Stalder)	90	35
N1762	20ch. Boxing (Lazio Papp)	1·20	40
N1763	20ch. Runners (Ronald Delany)	90	35
N1764	20ch. High jump (Jolanda Balas)	90	35
N1765	20ch. High jump (Valery Brumel)	90	35
N1766	20ch. Gymnastics (Vera Caslavska)	90	35
N1767	20ch. Rifle shooting (Li Ho Jun)	90	35
MSN1768	105×95 mm. 50ch. Boxing (Ku Yong Jo)	1·70	85

651 Douglas DC-8-63 and Comte AC-4 Gentleman

1978. Airplanes. Multicoloured.

N1769	2ch. Type **651**	75	15
N1770	10ch. Ilyushin Il-62M and Avia BH-25	1·00	15
N1771	15ch. Douglas DC-8-63 and Savoia Marchetti S-71	1·10	25
N1772	20ch. Tupolev Tu-144 and Kalinin K-5	1·30	25

N1773	25ch. Tupolev Tu-154 and Antonov An-2 biplane	1·30	25
N1774	30ch. Ilyushin Il-18	1·30	25
N1775	40ch. Concorde and Wibault 283 trimotor	3·00	75
MSN1776	102×75 mm. 50ch. Airbus Industries A300B2 jetliner and Focke Wulf A-17 Mowe	2·75	60

652 White-bellied Black Woodpecker and Map

1978. White-bellied Black Woodpecker Preservation. Multicoloured.

N1777	5ch. Type **652**	1·10	40
N1778	10ch. Woodpecker and eggs	1·30	50
N1779	15ch. Woodpecker feeding young	1·70	65
N1780	25ch. Woodpecker feeding young (different)	2·10	85
N1781	50ch. Adult woodpecker on tree trunk	3·25	1·20

653 Demonstrators and Korean Map

1978. 30th Anniv of Democratic People's Republic of Korea. Multicoloured. Without gum.

N1783	10ch. Type **653**	25	15
N1784	10ch. Flag and soldiers	25	15
N1785	10ch. Flag and "Juche"	25	15
N1786	10ch. Red Flag	25	15
N1787	10ch. Chollima Statue and city skyline	25	15
N1788	10ch. "Juche" torch and men of three races	25	15

654 Cat and Pup

1978. Animal Paintings by Li Am. Multicoloured.

N1789	10ch. Type **654**	3·00	65
N1790	15ch. *Cat up a tree*	3·00	65
N1791	40ch. *Wild geese*	3·00	65

655 Footballers

1978. Argentina's Victory in World Cup Football Championship. Without gum.

N1792	**655** 10ch. multicoloured	90	20
N1793	- 15ch. multicoloured	1·10	25
N1794	- 25ch. multicoloured	1·30	40
MSN1795	94×69 mm. 50ch. multicoloured	2·10	1·70

DESIGNS: 15ch. to 50ch. Different football scenes.

668 Red Flag and Pine Branch

1979. New Year. Without gum.

N1812	**668** 10ch. multicoloured	30	15

669 Kim Il Sung with Children's Corps Members, Maanshan

1979. International Year of the Child (1st issue). Multicoloured. (a) Paintings of Kim Il Sung and children.

N1813	5ch. Type **669**	10	10
N1814	10ch. Kim Il Sung and Children's Corps members in classroom	25	10
N1815	15ch. New Year gathering	40	25
N1816	20ch. Kim Il Sung and children in snow	60	35
N1817	30ch. Kim Il Sung examines children's schoolbooks (vert)	85	40

(b) Designs showing children.

N1818	10ch. Tug-of-war	25	10
N1819	15ch. Dance *Growing up Fast*	40	15
N1820	20ch. Children of many races and globe	50	25
N1821	25ch. Children singing	85	40
N1822	30ch. Children in toy spaceships	85	40
MSN1823	Two sheets (a) 90×72 mm. 50ch. Kim Il Sung visits a kindergarten (vert); (b) 124×85 mm. 50ch. As No. N1820	5·00	4·25

See also Nos. N1907/**MS**N1918.

670 Rose

1979. Roses. Multicoloured.

N1824	1wn. Red rose		
N1825	3wn. White rose		
N1826	5wn. Type **670**		
N1827	10wn. Deep pink rose		

See also Nos. N1837/42.

671 Warriors on Horseback

1979. *The Story of Two Generals*. Multicoloured. Without gum.

N1828	5ch. Type **671**	25	10
N1829	10ch. Farm labourer blowing feather	40	15
N1830	10ch. Generals fighting on foot	40	15
N1831	10ch. Generals on horseback	40	15

672 Red Guard and Industrial Skyline

1979. 20th Anniv of Worker-Peasant Red Guards. Without gum.

N1832	**672** 10ch. multicoloured	30	15

673 Clement-Bayard Airship *Fleurus*

1979. Airships. Multicoloured. Without gum.
N1833	10ch. Type **673**	1·30	30
N1834	20ch. N.1 *Norge*	1·30	30
MSN1835 80×79 mm. 50ch. *Graf Zeppelin*		2·20	60

674 Crowd of Demonstrators

1979. 60th Anniv of First March Popular Uprising. Without gum.
N1836	**674** 10ch. blue and red	30	15

1979. Roses. As Nos. N1824/7. Multicoloured.
N1837	5ch. As Type **670** (postage)	25	10
N1838	10ch. As No. N1827	35	10
N1839	15ch. As No. N1824	35	10
N1840	20ch. Yellow rose	60	15
N1841	30ch. As No. 1825	75	25
N1842	50ch. Deep pink rose (different) (air)	1·10	50

675 Table Tennis Trophy

1979. 35th World Table Tennis Championship, Pyongyang. Multicoloured. With or without gum.
N1843	5ch. Type **675**	25	10
N1844	10ch. Women's doubles	25	10
N1845	15ch. Women's singles	40	15
N1846	20ch. Men's doubles	65	15
N1847	30ch. Men's singles	1·00	35
MSN1848 84×108 mm. 50ch. Chollima Statue and championship emblem		2·50	1·70

676 Marchers with Red Flag

1979. Socialist Construction under Banner of Juche Idea. Multicoloured. Without gum.
N1849	5ch. Type **676**	30	15
N1850	10ch. Map of Korea	30	15
N1851	10ch. Juche torch	30	15

677 Badge

1979. Order of Honour of the Three Revolutions. Without gum.
N1852	**677** 10ch. blue	25	10

678 Emblem, Satellite orbiting Globe and Aerials

1979. World Telecommunications Day. Without gum.
N1853	**678** 10ch. multicoloured	40	15

679 Advancing Soldiers and Monument

1979. 40th Anniv of Battle in Musan Area. Without gum.
N1854	**679** 10ch. mauve, light blue and blue	30	15

680 Exhibition Entrance

1979. Int Friendship Exhibition. Without gum.
N1855	**680** 10ch. multicoloured	25	15

681 Peonies

1979. 450th Death Anniv (1978) of Albrecht Durer (artist) (1st issue). Multicoloured.
N1856	15ch. Type **681**	85	25
N1857	20ch. *Columbines*	1·40	35
N1858	25ch. *A Great Tuft of Grass*	1·40	35
N1859	30ch. *Wing of a Bird*	2·10	55
MSN1860 92×67 mm. 50ch. As No. 1859		3·25	85

See also Nos. N2012/**MS**N2013.

682 Fencing

1979. Olympic Games, Moscow (2nd issue). Multicoloured. With gum (10, 40ch. only).
N1861	5ch. Type **682**	1·50	35
N1862	10ch. Gymnastics	60	15
N1863	20ch. Yachting	85	35
N1864	30ch. Athletics	1·00	40
N1865	40ch. Weightlifting	1·30	60
MSN1866 106×77 mm. 50ch. Equestrian event		3·25	1·70

683 Hunting

1979. Horse-riding (people of Koguryo Dynasty). Multicoloured.
N1867	5ch. Type **683**	85	35
N1868	10ch. Archery contest	85	35
N1869	15ch. Man beating drum on horseback	35	10
N1870	20ch. Man blowing horn	35	10
N1871	30ch. Man and horse, armoured with chainmail	40	15
N1872	50ch. Hawking (air)	2·75	55

684 Judo

1979. Olympic Games, Moscow (3rd issue). Multicoloured. With gum (5, 15, 20, 30ch. only).
N1873	5ch. Type **684**	40	10
N1874	10ch. Volleyball	40	10
N1875	15ch. Cycling	1·70	40
N1876	20ch. Basketball	65	25
N1877	25ch. Canoeing	65	25
N1878	30ch. Boxing	1·00	35
N1879	40ch. Shooting	90	35
MSN1880 79×108 mm. 50ch. Gymnastics		1·30	50

685 Warrior's Costume

1979. Warrior Costumes of Li Dynasty.
N1881	**685** 5ch. multicoloured	25	15
N1882	- 10ch. multicoloured	25	15
N1883	- 15ch. multicoloured	40	15
N1884	- 20ch. multicoloured	60	20
N1885	- 30ch. multicoloured	1·00	30
N1886	- 50ch. multicoloured (air)	1·30	50

DESIGNS: 10ch. to 50ch. Different costumes.

686 Wrestling

1979. Olympic Games, Moscow (4th issue). Multicoloured.
N1887	10ch. Type **686**	40	15
N1888	15ch. Handball	40	15
N1889	20ch. Archery	2·10	50
N1890	25ch. Hockey	2·10	60
N1891	30ch. Rowing	1·00	35
N1892	40ch. Football	2·00	50
MSN1893 77×106 mm. 50ch. Equestrian events		3·25	1·40

687 Monument

1979. Chongbong Monument. Without gum.
N1894	**687** 10ch. multicoloured	30	15

688 Bottle-feeding Fawn

1979. Sika Deer. Multicoloured.
N1895	5ch. Type **688** (postage)	25	15
N1896	10ch. Doe and fawn	25	15
N1897	15ch. Stag drinking from stream	25	15
N1898	20ch. Stag	35	15
N1899	30ch. Stag and doe	40	35
N1900	50ch. Antlers and deer (air)	65	50

689 Moscovy Ducks

1979. Central Zoo, Pyongyang. Multicoloured.
N1901	5ch. Type **689** (postage)	35	15
N1902	10ch. Ostrich	65	25
N1903	15ch. Common turkey	90	35
N1904	20ch. Dalmatian pelican	1·10	40
N1905	30ch. Vulturine guineafowl	1·30	50
N1906	50ch. Mandarins (air)	2·00	85

690 Girl with Model Viking Ship

1979. International Year of the Child (2nd issue). Multicoloured.
N1907	20ch. Type **690**	1·50	40
N1908	20ch. Boys with model steam railway locomotive	3·25	40
N1909	20ch. Boy with model biplane	1·70	40
N1910	20ch. Boy with model spaceman	1·30	40
N1911	30ch. Boy with model speedboat	2·50	60
N1912	30ch. Boy sitting astride toy electric train	3·25	60
N1913	30ch. Boy and model airplane	2·50	60
N1914	30ch. Boy and flying spaceman	1·90	60
MSN1915 Four sheets, each 77×104 mm. (a) 80ch. Boy and Concorde; (b) 80ch. Girl and satellite; (c) Boy and model liner; (d) 80ch. Children with model train		29·00	6·75

691 Footballers

1979. International Year of the Child (3rd issue). Multicoloured.
N1916	20ch. Type **691**	1·30	50
N1917	30ch. Footballers (different)	2·10	75
MSN1918 104×78 mm. 80ch. Footballers (different)		6·75	2·10

692 Japanese Stonefish

1979. Marine Life. Multicoloured.
N1919	20ch. Type **692**	1·10	40
N1920	30ch. Schlegel's redfish	1·30	50
N1921	50ch. Northern sealion	2·20	85

693 Cross-country Skiing (Sergei Saveliev)

1979. Winter Olympic Games, Lake Placid. Multiloured.
N1922	10ch. Figure skating (Irina Rodnina and Aleksandr Zaitsev) (horiz)	60	20
N1923	20ch. Ice hockey (Russian team) (horiz)	1·00	30
N1924	30ch. Women's 5 km relay (horiz)	1·40	55
N1925	40ch. Type **693**	2·00	85
N1926	50ch. Women's speed skating (Tatiana Averina)	3·00	1·10
MSN1927 81×68 mm. 60ch. Ice dancing (Ludmila Pakhomova and Aleksandr Gorshkov)		6·25	4·75

694 The Honey Bee collecting Nectar

1979. The Honey Bee. Multicoloured.

N1928	20ch. Type **694**	1·70	35
N1929	30ch. Bee and flowers	2·00	40
N1930	50ch. Bee hovering over flower	2·20	50

695 Kim Jong Suk's Birthplace, Heoryong

1979. Historic Revolutionary Sites.

N1931	**695** 10ch. multicoloured	35	15
N1932	- 10ch. brown, blue & blk	35	15

DESIGN: No. N1932, Sinpa Revolutionary Museum.

696 Mt. Paekdu

1980. New Year.

N1933	**696** 10ch. multicoloured	75	15

697 Student and Books

1980. Studying.

N1934	**697** 10ch. multicoloured	35	15

698 Conveyor Belt

1980. Unryul Mine Conveyor Belt.

N1935	**698** 10ch. multicoloured	75	15

699 Children of Three Races

1980. International Day of the Child. Multicoloured.

N1936	10ch. Type **699**	40	15
N1937	10ch. Girl dancing to accordion	65	15
N1938	10ch. Children in fairground airplane	60	15
N1939	10ch. Children as astronauts	40	15
N1940	10ch. Children on tricycles	1·70	40
N1941	10ch. Children with toy diesel train	2·50	60
N1942	10ch. "His loving care for the children, future of the fatherland" (59½×38 mm)	40	15
MSN1943	69×89 mm. 50ch. "Father Marshal visiting Kindergarten" (52×44 mm)	3·00	1·40

700 Monument

1980. Chongsan-ri Historic Site. Multicoloured.

N1944	5ch. Type **700**	15	15
N1945	10ch. Meeting place of the General Membership	25	15

701 Monument

1980. Monument marking Kim Jong Suk's Return.

N1946	**701** 10ch. multicoloured	25	15

702 Vasco Nunez de Balboa

1980. Conquerors of the Earth. Multicoloured.

N1947	10ch. Type **702**	65	25
N1948	20ch. Francisco de Orellana	1·00	35
N1949	30ch. Haroun Tazieff	1·40	50
N1950	40ch. Edmund Hillary and Sherpa Tenzing	2·10	85
MSN1951	75×105 mm. 70ch. Ibn Battuta	3·50	1·70

703 Museum

1980. Ryongpo Revolutionary Museum.

N1952	**703** 10ch. blue and black	25	10

704 Rowland Hill and Stamps

1980. Death Centenary (1979) of Sir Rowland Hill. Multicoloured.

N1953	30ch. Type **704**	3·75	1·10
N1954	50ch. Rowland Hill and stamps (different)	5·50	1·40

705 North Korean Red Cross Flag

1980. World Red Cross Day. Multicoloured.

N1955	10ch. Type **705**	1·00	35
N1956	10ch. Henri Dunant (founder)	1·00	35
N1957	10ch. Nurse and child	1·00	35
N1958	10ch. Polikarpov Po-2 biplane and ship	1·30	50
N1959	10ch. Mil Mi-4 helicopter	1·50	50
N1960	10ch. Children playing at nurses	1·00	35
N1961	10ch. Red Cross map over Korea and forms of transport	3·50	1·30
MSN1962	83×93 mm. 50ch. Nurse with syringe	5·00	2·50

706 Fernando Magellan

1980. Conquerors of the Sea. Multicoloured.

N1963	10ch. Type **706**	2·10	75
N1964	20ch. Fridtjof Nansen	2·10	75
N1965	30ch. Auguste and Jacques Piccard	3·00	1·00
N1966	40ch. Jacques-Yves Cousteau	3·50	1·30
MSN1967	75×105 mm. 70ch. James Cook	6·75	1·80

707 Korean Stamps and Penny Black

1980. "London 1980" International Stamp Exhibition. Multicoloured.

N1968	10ch. Type **707** (postage)	3·00	1·00
N1969	20ch. Korean cover and British Guiana 1c. black and red	3·00	1·00
N1970	30ch. Early Korean stamp and modern cover	2·10	75
N1971	30ch. Korean stamps	2·20	85
N1972	40ch. Korean stamp and miniature sheet (air)	3·50	1·30
MSN1973	110×138 mm. 20ch. Type **707**; 30ch. As No. N1969; 50ch. As No. N1970	9·25	3·25

708 Wright Brothers

1980. Conquerors of Sky and Space. Multicoloured.

N1974	10ch. Type **708**	85	30
N1975	20ch. Louis Bleriot	1·30	50
N1976	30ch. Anthony Fokker	1·70	65
N1977	40ch. Secondo Campini and Sir Frank Whittle	2·50	85
MSN1978	76×106 mm. 70ch. Count Ferdinand Zeppelin	3·25	1·00

709 Space Station on Planet

1980. Conquerors of the Universe. Multicoloured.

N1979	10ch. Orbiting space station	35	15
N1980	20ch. Type **709**	50	25
N1981	30ch. Prehistoric animals and spaceships	1·30	50
N1982	40ch. Prehistoric animals and birds and spaceship	1·70	60
MSN1983	77×105 mm. 70ch. Planetary scene	3·25	1·70

710 Flag and Banners

1980. 25th Anniv of General Association of Korean Residents in Japan (Chongryon).

N1984	**710** 10ch. multicoloured	25	15

711 Hospital

1980. Pyongyang Maternity Hospital.

N1985	**711** 10ch. blue, purple & blk	60	20

712 Health Centre

1980. Changgangwon Health Centre, Pyongyang.

N1986	**712** 2ch. black and blue	35	15

713 Hand holding Rifle

1980. 50th Anniv of Revolutionary Army.

N1987	**713** 10ch. multicoloured	35	15

714 Workers' Hostel, Samjiyon

1980

N1988	**714** 10ch. brown, blue & blk	40	15
N1989	- 10ch. black and green	65	25
N1990	- 10ch. black and red	65	25
N1991	- 10ch. black and yellow	65	25
N1992	- 10ch. multicoloured	40	15
N1993	- 10ch. multicoloured	40	15
N1994	- 10ch. multicoloured	1·70	50
N1995	- 10ch. green and black	1·30	40
N1996	- 10ch. grey, blue & black	5·00	85
N1997	- 10ch. multicoloured	5·75	85

DESIGNS: No. N1989, "Taedonggang" rice transplanter; N1990, "Chongsan-ri" rice harvester; N1991, Maize harvester; N1992, Revolutionary building, Songmun-ri; N1993, Revolutionary building, Samhwa; N1994, Sundial of 1438; N1995, 16th-century "turtle" ship; N1996, Pungsan dog; N1997, Japanese quail.

715 Party Emblem

1980. Sixth Korean Workers' Party Congress. Multicoloured.

N1998	10ch. Type **715**	25	15
N1999	10ch. Students and Laurel leaf on globe	25	15
N2000	10ch. Group with accordion	65	15
N2001	10ch. Group with banner, microscope, book and trophy	40	25
N2002	10ch. Worker with book and flag	1·30	40
N2003	10ch. Worker with spanner and flag	1·30	40
N2004	10ch. Marchers with torch and flags	25	15
N2005	10ch. Emblem, marchers and map	35	20
MSN2006	Two sheets each 94×77 mm. (a) 50ch. "The great Leader inspires and encourages Colliers on the Spot" (41×50 mm); (b) 50ch. "Leading the Van in the arduous March" (38×60 mm)	2·50	1·70

716 Dribbling Ball

1980. World Cup Football Championship, 1978–82. Multicoloured.

N2007	20ch. Type **716**	3·50	1·30
N2008	30ch. Tackle	4·25	1·70
MSN2009	147×118 mm. 40ch. Tackling (different); 60ch. Moving in to tackle	7·25	2·75

717 Irina Rodnina and Aleksandr Zaitsev

1980. Winter Olympic Gold Winners. Multicoloured.

N2010	20ch. Type **717**	6·75	2·30
MSN2011	67×94 mm. 1wn. Natalia Linitshchnuk and Gennadi Karponosov	7·25	2·50

718 *Soldier with Horse*

1980. 450th Death Anniv (1978) of Albrecht Durer (artist) (2nd issue). Multicoloured.

N2012 20ch. Type **718**	7·25	2·75
MSN2013 81×106 mm. 1wn. *Horse and Rider*	11·00	3·75

719 *Kepler, Astrolabe and Satellites*

1980. 350th Death Anniv of Johannes Kepler (astronomer). Multicoloured.

N2014 20ch. Type **719**	3·75	1·70
MSN2015 93×75 mm. 1wn. Kepler astrolabe and satellites (different)	6·75	2·10

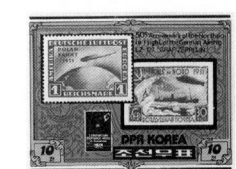

720 *German 1m. and Russian 30k. Zeppelin Stamps*

1980. Third International Stamp Fair, Essen. Multicoloured.

N2016 10ch. Type **720**	1·20	40
N2017 20ch. German 2m. and Russian 35k. Zeppelin stamps	2·50	90
N2018 30ch. German 4m. and Russian 1r. Zeppelin stamps	3·50	1·30
MSN2019 137×82 mm. 50ch. Russian 2r. Polar Flight stamp and Korean 50ch. IYC stamp	8·50	3·50

721 *Shooting (Aleksandr Melentev)*

1980. Olympic Medal Winners. Multicoloured.

N2020 10ch. Type **721**	40	15
N2021 20ch. Cycling (Robert Dill-Bundi)	4·50	1·60
N2022 25ch. Gymnastics (Stoyan Deltchev)	65	35
N2023 30ch. Wrestling (Chang Se Hong and Li Ho Pyong)	65	35
N2024 35ch. Weightlifting (Ho Bong Chol)	65	35
N2025 40ch. Running (Marita Koch)	70	40
N2026 50ch. Modern Pentathlon (Anatoli Starostin)	1·00	50
MSN2027 Two sheets. (a) 100×76 mm. 70ch. Boxing (Teofilo Stevenson); (b) 107×163 mm. 70ch. Ancient Greek rider on horse	5·75	3·75

722 *Tito*

1980. President Tito of Yugoslavia Commemoration.

N2028 **722** 20ch. multicoloured	50	15

723 *Convair CV 340 Airliner*

1980. 25th Anniv of First Post-war Flight of Lufthansa. Multicoloured.

N2029 20ch. Type **723**	6·25	2·50
MSN2030 90×75 mm. 1wn. Airbus A 300	8·50	3·25

724 *The Rocket*

1980. 150th Anniv of Liverpool—Manchester Railway. Multicoloured.

N2031 20ch. Type **724**	7·25	2·75
MSN2032 105×60 mm. 1wn. Locomotive drawing carriage and horsebox	8·50	3·25

725 *Steam and Electric Locomotives*

1980. Centenary of First Electric Train. Multicoloured.

N2033 20ch. Type **725**	7·25	2·50
MSN2084 106×86 mm. 1wn. Opening Ceremony of first electric railway	14·50	5·00

726 *Hammarskjold*

1980. 75th Birth Anniv of Dag Hammarskjold (former Secretary General of United Nations). Multicoloured.

N2035 20ch. Type **726**	4·25	3·00
MSN2036 87×68 mm. 1wn. Hammarskjold (different)	5·50	3·25

727 *Bobby Fischer and Boris Spassky*

1980. World Chess Championship, Merano. Multicoloured.

N2037 20ch. Type **727**	8·00	2·50
MSN2038 84×84 mm. 1wn. Viktor Korchnoi and Anatoly Karpov	10·00	2·50

728 *Stolz*

1980. Birth Centenary of Robert Stolz (composer). Multicoloured.

N2039 20ch. Type **728**	3·75	1·30
MSN2040 94×76 mm. 1wn. Stolz examining stamp with magnifying glass	6·25	1·80

729 *Chollima Statue*

1981. New Year. Without gum.

N2041 **729** 10ch. multicoloured	40	15

730 *Russian Fairy Tale*

1981. International Year of the Child (1979) (4th issue). Fairy Tales. Multicoloured.

N2042 10ch. Type **730**	1·80	60
N2043 10ch. Icelandic tale	1·80	60
N2044 10ch. Swedish tale	1·80	60
N2045 10ch. Irish tale	1·80	60
N2046 10ch. Italian tale	1·80	60
N2047 10ch. Japanese tale	1·80	60
N2048 10ch. German tale	1·80	60
MSN2049 95×117 mm. 70ch. Korean tale	4·75	3·50

731 *Changgwang Street*

1981. Changgwang Street, Pyongyang.

N2050 **731** 10ch. multicoloured	40	15

732 *Footballers*

1981. World Cup Football Championship, Spain (1982) (1st issue). Multicoloured.

N2051 10ch. Type **732**	3·50	1·00
N2052 20ch. Hitting ball past defender	3·50	1·00
N2053 30ch. Disputing possession of ball	3·50	1·00
MSN2054 95×103 mm. 70ch. Three players	8·50	3·50

See also Nos. N2055/**MS**N2060 and N2201/**MS**N2207.

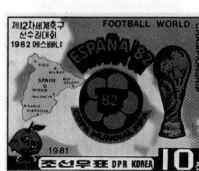

733 *Map, Emblem and World Cup*

1981. World Cup Football Championship, Spain (1982) (2nd issue). Multicoloured.

N2055 10ch. Type **733**	2·20	85
N2056 15ch. Footballers	2·20	85
N2057 20ch. Heading ball	2·20	85
N2058 25ch. Footballers (different)	2·20	85
N2059 30ch. Footballers (different)	2·20	85
MSN2060 96×92 mm. 70ch. Footballers (different)	8·50	3·50

734 *Workers with Book and Marchers with Banner*

1981. Implementation of Decision of the Sixth Koreans' Party Congress. Multicoloured.

N2061 2ch. Type **734**	15	10
N2062 10ch. Worker with book	20	10
N2063 10ch. Workers and industrial plant	35	15
N2064 10ch. Electricity and coal (horiz)	1·60	35
N2065 10ch. Steel and non-ferrous metals (horiz)	35	15
N2066 10ch. Cement and fertilizers (horiz)	35	15
N2067 30ch. Fishing and fabrics (horiz)	50	15
N2068 40ch. Grain and harbour (horiz)	65	25
N2069 70ch. Clasped hands	1·20	50
N2070 1wn. Hand holding torch	1·70	75

735 *Footballers*

1981. Gold Cup Football Championship, Uruguay. Multicoloured.

N2071 20ch. Type **735**	3·75	1·50
MSN2072 99×84 mm. 1wn. Goalkeeper diving for ball	6·25	3·25

736 *Dornier Do-X Flying Boat*

1981. "Naposta '81" International Stamp Exhibition, Stuttgart. Multicoloured.

N2073 10ch. Type **736**	3·50	65
N2074 20ch. Airship LZ-120 *Bodensee*	3·50	65
N2075 30ch. *Gotz von Berlichingen*	2·10	60
MSN2076 135×80 mm. 70ch. Mercedes-Benz "W 196" car	6·25	3·00

737 *Telecommunications Equipment*

1981. World Telecommunications Day.

N2077 **737** 10ch. multicoloured	2·50	40

738 *"Iris pseudacorus"*

1981. Flowers. Multicoloured.

N2078 10ch. Type **738**	1·10	15
N2079 20ch. *Iris pallasii*	1·40	25
N2080 30ch. *Gladiolus gandavensis*	2·00	40

739 *Austrian "WIPA 1981" and Rudolf Kirchschlager Stamps*

1981. "WIPA 1981" International Stamp Exhibition, Vienna. Multicoloured.

N2081	20ch. Type **739**	2·50	75
N2082	30ch. Austrian Maria Theresa and Franz Joseph stamps	3·25	1·20
MSN2083	133×87 mm. 50ch. Kim Il Sung and choir (38×60 mm)	6·25	3·00

740 Rings Exercise

1981. Centenary of International Gymnastic Federation. Multicoloured.

N2084	10ch. Type **740**	50	25
N2085	15ch. Horse exercise	60	25
N2086	20ch. Backwards somersault	1·00	25
N2087	25ch. Floor exercise	1·10	35
N2088	30ch. Exercise with hoop	1·30	40
MSN2089	104×77 mm. 70ch. Exercise with wand (horiz)	2·50	1·10

741 Armed Workers

1981. 50th Anniv of Mingyuehgou Meeting.

N2090	**741**	10ch. multicoloured	30	15

742 Farm Building, Sukchon

1981. 20th Anniv of Agricultural Guidance System and Taean Work System.

N2091	**742**	10ch. green, black and gold	30	15
N2092	–	10ch. blue, black and gold	30	15

DESIGN: No. N2092, Taean Revolutionary Museum.

743 Woman and Banner

1981. 55th Anniv of Formation of Women's Anti-Japanese Association.

N2093	**743**	5wn. multicoloured	5·25	1·10

743a Scene from Opera

1981. Tenth Anniv of *Sea of Blood* (opera).

N2094	**743a**	10wn. multicoloured	14·50	6·25

744 Joan of Arc

1981. 550th Death Anniv of Joan of Arc. Multicoloured.

N2095	10ch. Type **744**	3·25	85

N2096	10ch. Archangel Michael	3·50	85
N2097	70ch. Joan of Arc in armour	3·50	85
MSN2098	96×124 mm. No. N2097	6·25	2·10

745 Torch, Mountains and Flag

1981. 55th Anniv of Down with Imperialism Union.

N2099	**745**	1wn.50 multicoloured	1·60	75

746 *Young Girl by the Window*

1981. 375th Birth Anniv of Rembrandt (artist). Multicoloured.

N2100	10ch. Type **746**	75	35
N2101	20ch. *Rembrandt's Mother*	1·70	60
N2102	30ch. *Saskia van Uylenburgh*	1·70	1·00
N2103	40ch. *Pallas Athene*	3·00	1·30
MSN2104	91×105 mm. 70ch. *Self-portrait*	6·25	3·25

747 Emblem and Banners over Pyongyang

1981. Symposium of Non-Aligned Countries on Food Self-Sufficiency, Pyongyang. Multicoloured.

N2105	10ch. Type **747**	25	15
N2106	50ch. Harvesting	65	35
N2107	90ch. Factories, tractors and marchers with banner	1·30	65

748 St. Paul's Cathedral

1981. Wedding of Prince of Wales (1st issue). Multicoloured.

N2108	10ch. Type **748**	2·50	85
N2109	20ch. Great Britain Prince of Wales Investiture stamp	2·50	85
N2110	30ch. Lady Diana Spencer	2·50	85
N2111	40ch. Prince Charles in military uniform	2·50	85
MSN2112	93×96 mm. 70ch. Engagement day portrait of couple	10·50	6·25

See also Nos. N2120/**MS**2124.

749 *Four Philosophers* (detail)

1981. Paintings by Rubens. Multicoloured.

N2113	10ch. Type **749**	85	40
N2114	15ch. *Portrait of Helena Fourment*	1·30	60
N2115	20ch. *Portrait of Isabella Brandt*	1·70	65

N2116	25ch. *Education of Maria de Medici*	2·10	85
N2117	30ch. *"Helena Fourment and her Child"*	2·50	90
N2118	40ch. *Helena Fourment in her Wedding Dress*	3·00	1·30
MSN2119	92×110 mm. 70ch. *Portrait of Nikolaas Rubens*	6·25	3·00

750 Royal Couple

1981. Wedding of Prince of Wales (2nd issue). Multicoloured.

N2120	10ch. Type **750**	3·75	1·30
N2121	20ch. Couple on balcony after wedding	3·75	1·30
N2122	30ch. Couple outside St. Paul's Cathedral	3·75	1·30
N2123	70ch. Full-length wedding portrait of couple	3·75	1·30
MSN2124	85×106 mm. 70ch. Royal couple and Queen Elizabeth on balcony	13·00	7·25

751 Rowland Hill and Stamps

1981. "Philatokyo '81" International Stamp Exhibition. Multicoloured.

N2125	10ch. Korean 2ch. Seminar on Juche Idea stamp (41×29 mm)	1·30	35
N2126	10ch. Korean and 70ch. stamps (41×29 mm)	3·00	1·20
N2127	10ch. Type **751**	3·00	1·20
N2128	20ch. Korean Fairy Tale stamps	2·50	60
N2129	30ch. Japanese stamps	4·25	1·30
MSN2130	93×105 mm. 70ch. Medals, building and pigeon carrying letter	8·00	2·20

752 League Members and Flag

1981. Seventh League of Socialist Working Youth Congress, Pyongyang.

N2131	**752**	10ch. multicoloured	25	10
N2132	**752**	80ch. multicoloured	85	40

753 Government Palace, Sofia, Bulgarian Arms and Khan Asparuch

1981. 1300th Anniv of Bulgarian State.

N2133	**753**	10ch. multicoloured	35	10

754 Dimitrov

1981. Birth Centenary of Georgi Dimitrov (Bulgarian statesman).

N2134	**754**	10ch. multicoloured	35	10

755 Emblem, Boeing 747-200, City Hall and Mercedes "500"

1981. "Philatelia '81" International Stamp Fair, Frankfurt-am-Main.

N2135	**755**	20ch. multicoloured	3·25	50

756 Concorde, Airship *Graf Zeppelin* and Count Ferdinand von Zeppelin

1981. "Philexfrance 82" International Stamp Exhibition, Paris. Multicoloured. (a) As T **756**.

N2136	10ch. Type **756**	3·75	60
N2137	20ch. Concorde, Breguet Provence airliner and Santos-Dumont's biplane *14 bis*	4·50	1·10
N2138	30ch. *Mona Lisa* (Leonardo da Vinci) and stamps	2·50	40
MSN2139	99×105 mm. 60ch. French Rembrandt and Picasso stamps	8·00	2·50

(b) Size 32×53 mm.

N2140	10ch. Hotel des Invalides, Paris	1·40	60
N2141	20ch. President Mitterrand of France	1·40	60
N2142	30ch. International Friendship Exhibition building	1·40	60
N2143	70ch. Kim Il Sung	1·40	60

757 Rising Sun

1982. New Year.

N2144	**757**	10ch. multicoloured	40	10

758 Emblem and Flags

1982. "Prospering Korea". Multicoloured.

N2145	2ch. Type **758**	15	10
N2146	10ch. Industry	35	15
N2147	10ch. Agriculture	35	15
N2148	10ch. Mining	60	15
N2149	10ch. Arts	35	15
N2150	10ch. Al Islet lighthouse, Uam-ri	3·50	60
N2151	40ch. Buildings	65	25

759 The Hair-do

1982. Birth Centenary of Pablo Picasso (artist). Multicoloured.

N2152	10ch. Type **759**	1·10	25
N2153	10ch. *Paulo on a donkey*	2·50	50
N2154	20ch. *Woman leaning on Arm*	1·30	35
N2155	20ch. *Harlequin*	2·50	50
N2156	25ch. *Child with Pigeon*	2·75	65

N2157	25ch. *Reading a Letter*	2·50	50
N2158	35ch. *Portrait of Gertrude Stein*	2·10	40
N2159	35ch. *Harlequin (different)*	2·50	50
N2160	80ch. *Minotaur*	2·50	50
N2161	90ch. *Mother with Child*	2·50	50

MSN2162 Two sheets each 78×96 mm.
(a) No. N2160; (b) No. 2161   7·50   4·25

760 Fireworks over
Pyongyang

1982. Kim Il Sung's 70th Birthday. Multicoloured.

N2163	10ch. Kim Il Sung's birthplace, Mangyongdae	25	10
N2164	10ch. Type **760**	25	10
N2165	10ch. "The Day will dawn on downtrodden Korea" (horiz)	25	10
N2166	10ch. Signalling start of Pochonbo Battle (horiz)	25	10
N2167	10ch. Kim Il Sung starting Potong River project (horiz)	25	10
N2168	10ch. Embracing bereaved children (horiz)	25	10
N2169	10ch. Kim Il Sung as Supreme Commander (horiz)	25	10
N2170	10ch. "On the Road of Advance" (horiz)	25	10
N2171	10ch. Kim Il Sung kindling flame of Chollima Movement, Kangsong Steel Plant (horiz)	25	10
N2172	10ch. Kim Il Sung talking to peasants (horiz)	25	10
N2173	10ch. Kim Il Sung fixing site of reservoir (horiz)	25	10
N2174	20ch. Kim Il Sung visiting Komdok Valley (horiz)	25	10
N2175	20ch. Kim Il Sung visiting Red Flag Company (horiz)	25	10
N2176	20ch. Kim Il Sung teaching Juche farming methods (horiz)	25	10
N2177	20ch. Kim Il Sung visiting iron works (horiz)	25	10
N2178	20ch. Kim Il Sung talking with smelters (horiz)	25	10
N2179	20ch. Kim Il Sung at chemical plant (horiz)	25	10
N2180	20ch. Kim Il Sung with fishermen (horiz)	25	10

MSN2181 Two sheets. (a) 93×82 mm.
60ch. Kim Il Sung as a boy (35×47
mm); (b) 60ch. "Long live Comrade
Kim Il Sung" (35×46 mm)   4·25   2·10

761 Soldier saluting

1982. 50th Anniv of People's Army.

N2182	**761** 10ch. multicoloured	35	10

762 *The Bagpiper*
(Durer)

1982. Fourth Essen International Stamp Fair.

N2183	**762** 30ch. multicoloured	5·50	65

763 Surveyors

1982. Implementation of Four Nature-remaking Tasks.

N2184	**763** 10ch. multicoloured	60	10

764 Princess as Baby

1982. 21st Birthday of Princess of Wales.

N2185	**764** 10ch. multicoloured	65	25
N2186	- 20ch. multicoloured	1·50	40
N2187	- 30ch. multicoloured	1·80	60
N2188	- 50ch. multicoloured	1·90	1·00
N2189	- 60ch. multicoloured	1·90	1·00
N2190	- 70ch. multicoloured	1·90	1·00
N2191	- 80ch. multicoloured	1·90	1·00

MSN2192 Two sheets each 88×100
mm. (a) 40ch. Princess with her
brother; (b) No. N2191   11·00   5·00

DESIGNS: 20 to 80ch. Princess at various ages.

765 Tower of the
Juche Idea,
Pyongyang

1982

N2193	**765** 2wn. multicoloured	2·75	85
N2194	- 3wn. orange and black	3·25	90

DESIGN (26×38 mm): 3wn. Arch of Triumph.

766 Tiger

1982. Tigers.

N2195	**766** 20ch. multicoloured	2·20	65
N2196	- 30ch. multicoloured	3·00	65
N2197	- 30ch. mult (horiz)	3·75	1·10
N2198	- 40ch. mult (horiz)	3·75	1·10
N2199	- 80ch. mult (horiz)	3·75	1·10

MSN2200 105×54 mm. 80ch. multicoloured (horiz)   7·75   2·50

DESIGNS: 30 to 80ch. Tigers.

767 Group 1 Countries

1982. World Cup Football Championship, Spain (3rd
issue). Multicoloured.

N2201	**767** 10ch. Type **767**	75	25
N2202	20ch. Group 2 countries	1·50	60
N2203	30ch. Group 3 countries	2·20	90
N2204	40ch. Group 4 countries	2·50	1·10
N2205	50ch. Group 5 countries	3·00	1·30
N2206	60ch. Group 6 countries	3·75	1·40

MSN2207 133×92 mm. 1wn. World
Cup, footballers and emblem   10·00   5·00

768 Rocket Launch

1982. The Universe. Multicoloured.

N2208	10ch. Type **768**	2·10	85
N2209	20ch. Spaceship over globe	2·10	85
N2210	80ch. Spaceship between globe and moon	2·50	85

MSN2211 71×103 mm. 80ch. Spaceship
over crags   4·25   1·70

769 Charlotte von
Stein

1982. 150th Death Anniv of Johann von Goethe (writer).
Multicoloured.

N2212	10ch. Type **769**	65	35
N2213	10ch. Goethe's mother	2·10	60
N2214	20ch. Goethe's sister	1·00	40
N2215	20ch. Angelika Kauffmann	2·10	60
N2216	25ch. Charlotte Buff	1·30	50
N2217	25ch. Anna Amalia	2·10	60
N2218	35ch. Lili Schonemann	1·70	55
N2219	35ch. Charlotte von Lengefeld	2·10	60
N2220	80ch. Goethe	2·10	60

MSN2221 126×84 mm. 80ch. Goethe
(different)   5·00   2·10

770 Player holding aloft World
Cup

1982. World Cup Football Championship Results.
Multicoloured.

N2222	20ch. Type **770**	1·70	40
N2223	30ch. Group of players with World Cup	2·50	65
N2224	30ch. Type **770**	3·50	90
N2225	40ch. As No. N2203	3·50	90
N2226	80ch. King Juan Carlos of Spain and two players with World Cup	3·50	90

MSN2227 105×78 mm. No. N2226   5·75   2·75

771 Princess and Prince
William of Wales

1982. First Wedding Anniv of Prince and Princess of
Wales. Multicoloured.

N2228	30ch. Type **771**	6·50	3·25

MSN2229 135×102 mm. 80ch. Prince
and Princess of Wales with Prince
William   11·00   4·25

772 Royal Couple with
Prince William

1982. Birth of Prince William of Wales. Multicoloured.

N2230	10ch. Couple with Prince William (different)	90	65
N2231	10ch. Princess of Wales holding bouquet	2·75	1·00
N2232	20ch. Couple with Prince William (different)	1·80	85
N2233	20ch. Prince Charles carrying baby, and Princess of Wales	2·75	1·00
N2234	30ch. Type **772**	3·00	1·30
N2235	30ch. Prince Charles carrying baby, and Princess of Wales (different)	2·75	1·00
N2236	40ch. Princess with baby	3·75	1·90
N2237	40ch. Prince and Princess of Wales (horiz)	3·25	1·50
N2238	50ch. Princess with baby (different)	4·75	2·10
N2239	50ch. Prince and Princess of Wales in evening dress (horiz)	3·25	1·50
N2240	80ch. Couple with Prince William (different)	2·75	1·00
N2241	80ch. Prince Charles holding baby, and Princess of Wales (horiz)	3·25	1·50

MSN2242 Two sheets each 115×90
mm. (a) 80ch. Princess of Wales
holding Prince William and
royal family; (b) 80ch. Princess of
Wales holding Prince William and
godparents   27·00   10·00

773 Airship *Nulli Secundus II*,
1908

1982. Bicentenary of Manned Flight (1st issue).
Multicoloured.

N2243	10ch. Type **773**	1·50	50
N2244	10ch. Pauley and Durs Egg's dirigible balloon *The Dolphin*, 1818	2·75	85
N2245	20ch. Tissandier Brothers' airship, 1883	1·80	60
N2246	20ch. Guyton de Morveau's balloon with oars, 1784	2·75	85
N2247	30ch. Parseval airship PL-VII, 1912	2·50	65
N2248	30ch. Sir George Cayley's airship design, 1837	2·75	85
N2249	40ch. Count de Lennox's balloon *Eagle*, 1834	2·75	65
N2250	40ch. Camille Vert's balloon *Poisson Volant*, 1859	2·75	85
N2251	80ch. Dupuy de Lome's airship, 1872	2·75	85

MSN2252 71×100 mm. 80ch. Masse
oar-powered balloon, 1784 (vert)   5·00   2·50

774 *Utopic Balloon Post*
(Balthasar Antoine
Dunker)

1982. Bicentenary of Manned Flight (2nd issue).
Multicoloured.

N2253	10ch. Type **774**	1·30	50
N2254	10ch. Montgolfier balloon at Versailles, 1783	4·25	1·00
N2255	20ch. ... and they fly in heaven and have no wings ...	2·50	1·00
N2256	20ch. Montgolfier Brothers' balloon, 1783	4·25	1·00
N2257	30ch. Pierre Testu-Brissy's balloon ascent on horseback, 1798	3·75	1·70
N2258	30ch. Charles's hydrogen balloon landing at Nesle, 1783	4·25	1·00
N2259	40ch. Gaston Tissandier's test flight of *Zenith*, 1875	5·00	2·10
N2260	40ch. Blanchard and Jeffries' balloon flight over English Channel, 1785	4·25	1·00
N2261	80ch. Henri Giffard's balloon *Le Grand Ballon Captif* at World Fair, 1878	4·25	1·00

MSN2262 130×96 mm. 80ch. Night
flight of balloon   5·00   2·50

775 Turtle with Scroll

1982. *Tale of the Hare*. Multicoloured.

N2263	10ch. Type **775**	1·10	25
N2264	20ch. Hare riding on turtle	1·50	35
N2265	30ch. Hare and turtle before Dragon King	1·80	50
N2266	40ch. Hare back on land	2·75	60

776 Flag, Red Book and City

1982. Tenth Anniv of Socialist Constitution.
N2267 **776** 10ch. multicoloured 40 15

777 Tower of Juche Idea

1983. New Year.
N2268 **777** 10ch. multicoloured 30 15

778 Children reading *Saenal*

1983. 55th Anniv of *Saenal* Newspaper.
N2269 **778** 10ch. multicoloured 75 25

779 *Man in Oriental Costume*

1983. Paintings by Rembrandt. Multicoloured.
N2270 10ch. Type **779** 90 35
N2271 10ch. *Child with dead Peacocks* (detail) 2·50 85
N2272 20ch. *The Noble Slave* 1·80 50
N2273 20ch. *Old Man in Fur Hat* 2·50 85
N2274 30ch. *Dr. Tulp's Anatomy Lesson* (detail) 3·25 90
N2275 30ch. *Portrait of a fashionable Couple* 2·50 85
N2276 40ch. *Two Scholars disputing* 2·75 60
N2277 40ch. *Woman with Child* 2·50 85
N2278 80ch. *Woman holding an Ostrich Feather Fan* 2·50 85
MSN2279 102×69 mm. 80ch. *Self-portrait* 4·25 2·10

780 Airships *Gross Basenach II* and *Graf Zepplin* over Cologne

1983. "Luposta" International Air Mail Exhibition, Cologne. Multicoloured.
N2280 30ch. Type **780** 4·25 1·30
N2281 40ch. Parsevel airship PL-II over Cologne 4·25 1·30
MSN2282 86×95 mm. 80ch. *Virgin and Child* (Stephan Lochner) (vert) 4·25 2·10

781 Banner and Monument

1983. 50th Anniv of Wangjaesan Meeting.
N2283 **781** 10ch. multicoloured 30 15

782 Karl Marx

1983. Death Centenary of Karl Marx.
N2284 **782** 10ch. multicoloured 1·10 40

783 Scholar, Marchers and Map of Journey

1983. 60th Anniv of Thousand-ri Journey for Learning.
N2285 **783** 10ch. multicoloured 1·40 15

784 *Madonna of the Goldfinch*

1983. 500th Birth Anniv of Raphael. Multicoloured.
N2286 10ch. Type **784** 1·80 50
N2287 20ch. *The School of Athens* (detail) 2·10 65
N2288 30ch. *Madonna of the Grand Duke* 3·00 75
N2289 50ch. *Madonna of the Chair* 3·50 85
N2290 50ch. *Madonna of the Lamb* 2·10 65
N2291 80ch. *The Beautiful Gardener* 2·10 65
MSN2292 80×106 mm. 80ch. *Sistine Madonna* 5·00 2·10

785 Department Store No. 1

1983. Pyongyang Buildings. Multicoloured.
N2293 2ch. Chongryu Restaurant 25 10
N2294 10ch. Part of Munsu Street 40 10
N2295 10ch. Ice Rink 50 15
N2296 40ch. Type **785** 95 55
N2297 70ch. Grand People's Study House 1·70 75

786 Emblem and Crowd

1983. Fifth Anniv of International Institute of Juche Idea.
N2298 **786** 10ch. multicoloured 30 15

787 Judo

1983. Olympic Games, Los Angeles (1st issue). Multicoloured.
N2299 20ch. Type **787** 1·30 60
N2300 20ch. Wrestling 2·50 60
N2301 30ch. Judo (different) (value in gold) 1·30 60

N2302 30ch. Judo (different) (value in black) 2·50 60
N2303 40ch. Boxing 1·30 60
N2304 40ch. Li Ho Jun (1972 shooting gold medalist) 2·50 60
N2305 50ch. Weightlifting 1·30 60
N2306 50ch. Wrestling (different) 2·50 60
N2307 80ch. Boxing (different) 2·50 60
MSN2308 95×74 mm. 80ch. Judo (different) 5·00 1·80
See also Nos. N2359/**MS**N2365.

788 Satellite, Masts and Dish Aerial

1983. World Communications Year (1st issue).
N2309 **788** 10ch. multicoloured 2·10 40
See also Nos. N2349/**MS**N2354.

789 Emblem, Giant Panda and Stamp

1983. "Tembal 83" International Thematic Stamp Exhibition, Basel. Multicoloured.
N2310 20ch. Type **789** 2·50 85
N2311 30ch. Emblem, flag and Basel Town Post stamp 2·75 90

790 *Colourful Cow* (kogge), 1402

1983. Old Ships. Multicoloured.
N2312 20ch. Type **790** 1·60 65
N2313 20ch. *Kwi-Sun* ("turtle" ship), 1592 3·75 1·10
N2314 35ch. *Great Harry* (warship), 1555 2·10 75
N2315 35ch. Admiral Li Sun Sin and "turtle" ship 3·75 1·10
N2316 50ch. *Eagle of Lubeck* (galleon), 1567 3·00 1·00
N2317 50ch. *Merkur* (full-rigged sailing ship), 1847 3·75 1·10
N2318 80ch. *Herzogin Elisabeth* (cadet ship) 3·75 1·10
MSN2319 104×82 mm. 80ch. *Cristoforo Colombo* (cadet ship) 7·25 5·00

791 *Locomotion*, 1825, Great Britain

1983. Railway Locomotives. Multicoloured.
N2320 20ch. Type **791** 1·70 65
N2321 20ch. *Drache*, 1848, Germany 6·25 1·70
N2322 35ch. *Adler*, 1835, Germany 3·25 1·50
N2323 35ch. Korean steam locomotive 6·25 1·70
N2324 50ch. *Austria*, 1837, Austria 4·25 2·10
N2325 50ch. Bristol and Exeter Railway steam locomotive, 1853 6·25 1·70
N2326 80ch. Caledonian Railway locomotive, 1859 6·25 1·70
MSN2327 106×64 mm. 80ch. *Ilmarinen*, 1860 50·00 4·25

792 Map, Hand and Weapons

1983. Tenth Anniv of Publication of Five-point Policy for Korea's Reunification.
N2328 **792** 10ch. multicoloured 60 15

793 Emblem, Tower of Juche Idea and Fireworks

1983. World Conference on Journalists against Imperialism and for Friendship and Peace, Pyongyang. Multicoloured.
N2329 10ch. Type **793** 35 10
N2330 40ch. Emblem and rainbow and clasped hands 60 25
N2331 70ch. Emblem, map and hand with raised forefinger 90 40

794 Worker and Banners

1983. "Let's Create the Speed of the 80s".
N2332 **794** 10ch. multicoloured 40 15

795 Soldier and Rejoicing Crowd

1983. 30th Anniv of Victory in Liberation War.
N2333 **795** 10ch. multicoloured 35 10

796 *Gorch Fock* (cadet barque) and Korean 1978 2ch. Stamp

1983. "Bangkok 1983" International Stamp Exhibition. Multicoloured.
N2334 40ch. Type **796** 4·25 1·70
MSN2335 195×71 mm. 80ch. Bangkok, Penny Black and Korean IYC stamp 6·75 3·25

797 Skiing

1983. Winter Olympic Games, Sarajevo (1984). Multicoloured.
N2336 10ch. Type **797** 90 40
N2337 20ch. Figure skating (vert) 3·25 85
N2338 30ch. Skating (pair) 2·50 1·30
N2339 50ch. Ski jumping 3·00 1·40
N2340 50ch. Ice hockey (vert) 3·25 85
N2341 80ch. Speed skating (vert) 3·25 85
MSN2342 74×87 mm. 80ch. Shooting (biathlon) (vert) 5·00 2·10

798 Workers and Soldier with Books

1983. 35th Anniv of Korean People's Democratic Republic.
N2343 **798** 10ch. multicoloured 55 15

799 Archery

1983. Folk Games. Multicoloured.

N2344	10ch. Type **799**	3·75	60
N2345	10ch. Flying kites	90	35
N2346	40ch. See-sawing	90	35
N2347	40ch. Swinging	90	35

800 Girls holding Hands

1983. Korean–Chinese Friendship.

N2348	**800**	10ch. multicoloured	65	20

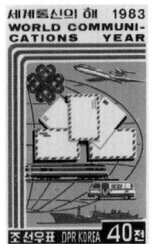

801 Envelopes and Forms of Transport

1983. World Communications Year (2nd issue). Multicoloured.

N2349	30ch. Mail van, motorcyclist and hand holding magazines	6·25	1·40
N2350	30ch. Satellite, globe and dish aerial	1·70	60
N2351	40ch. Type **801**	6·25	1·40
N2352	40ch. Television cameraman	1·70	60
N2353	80ch. Telephone and aerial	1·70	60
MSN2354	96×75 mm. 80ch. WCY emblem and satellite	4·50	2·10

802 Portrait

1983. Paintings by Rubens. Multicoloured.

N2355	40ch. Type **802**	1·80	75
N2356	40ch. Portrait (different) (horiz)	2·30	1·00
N2357	80ch. *The Sentencing of Midas* (horiz)	2·30	1·00
MSN2358	129×95 mm. 80ch. *The Bear Hunt*	3·25	1·20

803 Sprinting

1983. Olympic Games, Los Angeles (2nd issue). Multicoloured.

N2359	10ch. Type **803**	90	25
N2360	20ch. Show jumping	2·50	85
N2361	30ch. Cycling	3·75	85
N2362	50ch. Handball	2·50	85
N2363	50ch. Fencing	2·50	85
N2364	80ch. Gymnastics	2·50	85
MSN2365	109×75 mm. 80ch. Judo	4·25	1·80

804 *St. Catherine*

1983. 450th Death Anniv (1984) of Antonio Correggio (artist). Multicoloured.

N2366	20ch. Type **804**	2·10	65
N2367	20ch. *Morning* (detail)	2·50	85
N2368	35ch. *Madonna*	2·10	65
N2369	35ch. *Morning* (different)	2·50	85
N2370	50ch. *Madonna with St. John*	2·10	65
N2371	50ch. *St. Catherine* (different)	2·50	85
N2372	80ch. *Madonna and Child*	2·50	85
MSN2373	58×73 mm. 80ch. *Madonna and Child with Music-making Angels*	5·50	2·10

804a Cat

1983. Cats. Multicoloured, frame colour given.

N2373a	**804a**	10ch. green	1·40	20
N2373b	-	10ch. gold	1·40	20
N2373c	-	10ch. blue	1·40	20
N2373d	-	10ch. red	1·40	20
N2373e	-	10ch. silver	1·40	20

DESIGNS: Different cats' heads.

805 Kimilsungflower

1983. New Year.

N2374	**805**	10ch. multicoloured	85	15

806 Worker and Workers' Party Flag

1984. "Under the Leadership of the Workers' Party". Multicoloured.

N2375	10ch. Type **806**	35	10
N2376	10ch. Ore-dressing plant No. 3, Komdok General Mining Enterprise, and Party Flag	50	10

807 Farm Worker, Rice and Maize

1984. 20th Anniv of Publication of "Theses of the Socialist Rural Question in Our Country".

N2377	**807**	10ch. multicoloured	30	10

808 Changdok School, Chilgol

1984. Kim Il Sung's 72nd Birthday.

N2378	**808**	5ch. green, black & blue	40	15
N2379	-	10ch. multicoloured	40	15

DESIGN: 10ch. Birthplace, Mangyongdae, and rejoicing crowd.

809 *Spanish Riding School* (Julius von Blaas)

1984. "Espana 84" International Stamp Exhibition, Madrid. Multicoloured.

N2380	10ch. Type **809**	2·20	65
N2381	20ch. *Ferdinand of Austria* (Rubens)	2·20	65
MSN2382	73×96 mm. 80ch. *Spanish Riding School* (Julius von Blaas) (different)	5·75	2·50

810 *La Donna Velata*

1984. 500th Birth Anniv (1983) of Raphael (artist). Multicoloured.

N2383	10ch. *Portrait of Agnolo Doni*	1·90	75
N2384	20ch. Type **810**	1·90	75
N2385	30ch. *Portrait of Jeanne d'Aragon*	1·90	75
MSN2386	79×105 mm. 80ch. *St. Sebastian*	5·25	2·50

811 Map and Second Stage Pumping Station

1984. 25th Anniv of Kiyang Irrigation System.

N2387	**811**	10ch. multicoloured	65	20

812 Construction Site

1984. Construction on Five District Fronts.

N2388	**812**	10ch. red, black & yell	65	25

813 Bobsleighing (East Germany)

1984. Winter Olympic Games Medal Winners. Multicoloured.

N2389	10ch. Ski jumping (Matti Nykaenen)	3·00	65
N2390	20ch. Speed skating (Karin Enke)	2·10	60
N2391	20ch. Slalom (Max Julen)	3·00	65
N2392	30ch. Type **813**	2·10	60
N2393	30ch. Downhill skiing (Maria Walliser)	2·30	65
N2394	40ch. Cross-country skiing (Thomas Wassberg)	3·75	75
N2395	80ch. Cross-country skiing (Marja-Liisa Hamalainen)	3·75	75
MSN2396	106×86 mm. 80ch. Biathlon (Peter Angerer) (vert)	4·50	2·10

814 Steam Locomotive, 1919

1984. Essen International Stamp Fair. Multicoloured.

N2397	20ch. Streamlined steam locomotive, 1939	5·50	1·20
N2398	30ch. Type **814**	5·50	1·20
MSN2399	94×86 mm. 80ch. Type "D" locomotive	9·25	2·20

815 *Mlle. Fiocre in the Ballet `La Source'*

1984. 150th Birth Anniv of Edgar Degas (artist). Multicoloured.

N2400	10ch. Type **815**	2·00	50
N2401	20ch. *The Dance Foyer at the Rue le Peletier Opera*	3·00	55
N2402	30ch. *Race Meeting*	5·00	90
MSN2403	108×89 mm. 80ch. *Dancers at the Barre*	4·50	2·10

816 Map of Pyongnam Irrigation System and Reservoir

1984. Irrigation Experts Meeting, Pyongyang.

N2404	**816**	2ch. multicoloured	55	15

817 Korean Stamp and Building

1984. U.P.U. Congress Stamp Exn, Hamburg.

N2405	**817**	20ch. multicoloured	3·75	65
MSN2406	106×76 mm. 80ch. *Gorch Fock* (cadet barque) and Koren "turtle" stamp	6·25	3·25

818 Crowd and Banners

1984. Proposal for Tripartite Talks.

N2407	**818**	10ch. multicoloured	55	15

819 Nobel experimenting

1984. 150th Birth Anniv (1983) of Alfred Bernhard Nobel (inventor). Multicoloured.

N2408	20ch. Type **819**	3·75	65
N2409	30ch. Portrait of Nobel	4·25	65
MSN2410	109×99 mm. 80ch. Portrait of Nobel (different)	6·25	3·25

820 Drinks, Tinned Food, Clothes and Flats

1984. Improvements of Living Standards.

N2411	**820**	10ch. multicoloured	65	15

821 Sunhwa School, Mangyongdae

1984. School of Kim Hyong Jik (Kim Il Sung's Father).
N2412 **821** 10ch. multicoloured   60   15

822 Armed Crowd with Banners

1984. 65th Anniv of Kuandian Conference.
N2413 **822** 10ch. multicoloured   65   15

823 *Thunia bracteata*

1984. Flowers. Multicoloured.
N2414 10ch. *Cattleya loddigesii*   90   10
N2415 20ch. Type **823**   1·40   35
N2416 30ch. *Phalaenopsis amabilis*   1·80   50
MSN2417 67×94 mm. Kimilsung flower   4·50   1·70

824 Swordfish and Trawler

1984. Fishing Industry. Multicoloured.
N2418 5ch. Type **824**   90   25
N2419 10ch. Blue marlin and trawler   1·30   40
N2420 40ch. Sailfish and game fishing launch   3·50   1·20

825 Revolutionary Museum, Chilgol

1984
N2421 **825** 10ch. multicoloured   55   15

826 Kim Hyok, Cha Gwang Su and Youth

1984. "Let's All become the Kim Hyoks and Cha Gwang Sus of the '80s".
N2422 **826** 10ch. multicoloured   55   15

827 Inauguration of a French Railway Line, 1860

1984. Centenary (1983) of *Orient Express*. Multicoloured.
N2423 10ch. Type **827**   1·60   35
N2424 20ch. Opening of a British railway line, "1821"   3·00   65
N2425 30ch. Inauguration of Paris–Rouen line, 1843   4·25   1·10
MSN2426 11×81 mm. Interiors of Wagons-lits Car, 1905   7·50   3·00

828 Clock Face

1984. Centenary of Greenwich Meridian. Multicoloured.
N2427 10ch. Type **828**   3·25   1·30
MSN2428 112×81 mm. 80ch. Cholliuma statue, buildings and clock   5·00   2·10

829 Grand Theatre, Hamburg

1984
N2429 **829** 10ch. blue   55   15

830 Turning on Machinery

1984. Automation of Industry.
N2430 **830** 40ch. multicoloured   75   40

831 Dragon Angler

1984. Paintings. Multicoloured.
N2431 10ch. Type **831**   1·10   20
N2432 20ch. *Ox Driver* (Kim Du Ryang) (47×35 mm)   1·40   40
N2433 30ch. *Bamboo* (Kim Jin U) (47×35 mm)   2·10   60
MSN2434 85×43 mm. 80ch. *Autumn Night*   5·50   5·50

832 Tsiolkovsky

1984. K. E. Tsiolkovsky (space scientist). Multicoloured.
N2435 20ch. Type **832**   1·10   35
N2436 30ch. "Sputnik" orbiting Earth   1·60   60
MSN2437 100×70 mm. 80ch. Rocket launch   5·00   1·30

833 Pongdaesan

1984. Container Ships. Multicoloured.
N2438 10ch. Type **833**   1·30   25
N2439 20ch. *Ryongnamsan*   1·40   50
N2440 30ch. *Rungrado*   1·80   75
MSN2441 97×107 mm. 80ch. *Kumgangsan*   6·25   1·90

834 Caracal

1984. Animals. Multicoloured.
N2442 10ch. Spotted hyenas   75   15
N2443 20ch. Type **834**   1·10   35
N2444 30ch. Black-backed jackals   1·60   60
N2445 40ch. Foxes   2·10   85
MSN2446 80×104 mm. 80ch. Lanner falcon (vert)   7·50   2·50

835 Marie Curie

1984. 50th Death Anniv of Marie Curie (physicist). Multicoloured.
N2447 10ch. Type **835**   2·50   35
MSN2448 78×103 mm. 80ch. Portrait of Marie Curie   5·00   2·10

836 Chestnut-eared Aracari ("Toucan")

1984. Birds. Multicoloured.
N2449 10ch. Hoopoe   1·40   25
N2450 20ch. South African crowned cranes ("Crowned Crane")   1·80   50
N2451 30ch. Saddle-bill stork ("Stork")   2·52   65
N2452 40ch. Type **836**   3·50   90
MSN2453 104×74 mm 80ch. Black kite   9·25   2·50

837 Cosmonaut

1984. Space Exploration. Multicoloured.
N2454 10ch. Type **837**   65   15
N2455 20ch. Cosmonaut on space-walk   1·00   35
N2456 30ch. Cosmonaut (different)   1·40   50
MSN2457 77×90 mm. 80ch. Moon vehicle   4·50   1·70

838 *Arktika*

1984. Russian Ice-breakers. Multicoloured.
N2458 20ch. Type **838**   1·60   50
N2459 30ch. *Ermak*   2·20   65
MSN2460 97×67 mm. 80c. *Lenin*   6·25   2·10

839 Mendeleev

1984. 150th Birth Anniv of Dmitiri Mendeleev (chemist). Multicoloured.
N2461 10ch. Type **839**   1·20   25

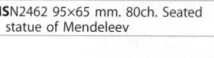

MSN2462 95×65 mm. 80ch. Seated statue of Mendeleev   5·00   2·10

840 Kim Il Sung in U.S.S.R.

1984. Kim Il Sung's Visits to Eastern Europe. Multicoloured.
N2463 10ch. Type **840**   85   20
N2464 10ch. In Poland   85   20
N2465 10ch. In German Democratic Republic   85   20
N2466 10ch. In Czechoslovakia   85   20
N2467 10ch. In Hungary   85   20
N2468 10ch. In Bulgaria   85   20
N2469 10ch. In Rumania   85   20
MSN2470 80×105 mm. 10ch. In China   1·70   1·70

841 Freesia

1985. New Year.
N2471 **841** 10ch. multicoloured   90   25

842 Journey Route, Steam Locomotive and Memorials

1985. 60th Anniv of 1000 ri Journey by Kim Il Sung. Multicoloured.
N2472 5ch. Type **842**   1·60   25
N2473 10ch. Boy trumpeter and schoolchildren following route   60   10
Nos. N2472/3 were issued together, *se-tenant*, forming a composite design.

843 Cugnot's Steam Car, 1769

1985. History of the Motor Car (1st series). Multicoloured.
N2474 10ch. Type **843**   1·60   20
N2475 15ch. Goldsworthy Gurney steam omnibus, 1825   1·60   25
N2476 20ch. Gottlieb Daimler diesel car, 1885   1·60   35
N2477 25ch. Benz three-wheeled diesel car, 1886   1·70   50
N2478 30ch. Peugeot diesel car, 1891   2·20   60
MSN2479 92×75 mm. 80c. black and gold (Wind car)   5·00   2·20
See also Nos. N2562/**MS**N2567.

844 Camp, Mt. Paekdu

1985. Korean Revolution Headquarters.
N2480 **844** 10ch. multicoloured   55   30

845 Taechodo Lighthouse

1985. Lighthouses. Multicoloured.

N2481	10ch. Type **845**	2·20	20
N2482	20ch. Sodo	2·50	40
N2483	30ch. Pido	3·00	65
N2484	40ch. Suundo	3·50	1·00

846 Hedgehog challenges Tiger

1985. *The Hedgehog defeats the Tiger* (fable). Multicoloured.

N2485	10ch. Type **846**	75	15
N2486	20ch. Tiger goes to stamp on rolled-up hedgehog	1·10	35
N2487	30ch. Hedgehog clings to tiger's nose	1·60	60
N2488	35ch. Tiger flees	1·70	65
N2489	40ch. Tiger crawls before hedgehog	2·00	85

847 *Pleurotus cornucopiae*

1985. Fungi. Multicoloured.

N2490	10ch. Type **847**	1·40	20
N2491	20ch. Oyster fungus	1·70	40
N2492	30ch. *Catathelasma ventricosum*	2·50	65

848 West Germany v. Hungary, 1954

1985. World Cup Football Championship Finals.

N2493	**848** 10ch. black, buff & brn	75	20
N2494	- 10ch. multicoloured	75	20
N2495	- 20ch. black, buff & brn	1·10	35
N2496	- 20ch. multicoloured	1·10	35
N2497	- 30ch. black, buff & brn	1·60	60
N2498	- 30ch. multicoloured	1·60	60
N2499	- 40ch. black, buff & brn	2·00	85
N2500	- 40ch. multicoloured	2·00	85

MSN2501 Two sheets, (a) 105×75 mm. 80ch. black, cinnamon and gold; (b) 94×95 mm. 80ch.multicoloured ... 10·00 ... 4·25

DESIGNS—VERT: No. N2493, Type **848**; N2496, West Germany v. Netherlands, 1974; N2499, England v. West Germany,**MS**N2501 (b), Azieca Stadium, Mexico (venue of 1966 final). HORIZ: N2494, Brazil v. Italy, 1970; N2495, Brazil v. Sweden, 1958; N2497, Brazil v. Czechoslovakia, 1963; N2498 Argentina v Netherlands, 1968. **MS**N2500, Italy v West Germany, 1982; **MS**N2501 (a) North Korea's quarter-final place, 1966.

849 Date and Kim Il Sung's Birthplace

1985. 73rd Birthday of Kim Il Sung.

N2502	**849** 10ch. multicoloured	55	15

850 Horn Player

1985. 4th-century Musical Instruments. Multicoloured.

N2503	10ch. Type **850**	1·70	20
N2504	20ch. So (pipes) player	1·70	35

851 Chongryon Hall, Tokyo

1985. 30th Anniv of Chongryon (General Association of Korean Residents in Japan).

N2505	**851** 10ch. brown	55	15

852 Common Marmoset

1985. Mammals. Multicoloured.

N2506	5ch. Type **852**	1·10	20
N2507	10ch. Ring-tailed lemur	1·10	20

853 National Emblem

1985. Sheet 51×70 mm.

MSN2508 **853** 80ch. multicoloured ... 1·90 ... 65

854 Buenos Aires and Argentina 1982 Stamp

1985. "Argentina '85" International Stamp Exhibition, Buenos Aires. Multicoloured.

N2509	10ch. Type **854**	90	20
N2510	20ch. Iguacu Falls and Argentina 1984 and North Korea 1978 stamps (horiz)	3·00	35

MSN2511 73×100 mm. 80ch. Gaucho ... 6·25 ... 5·00

855 Dancer and Gymnast

1985. 12th World Youth and Students' Festival, Moscow. Multicoloured.

N2512	10ch. Type **855**	75	15
N2513	20ch. Spassky Tower, Moscow, and Festival emblem	1·10	35
N2514	40ch. Youths of different races	2·00	85

856 Peace Pavilion, Youth Park

1985. Pyongyang Buildings.

N2515	**856** 2ch. black and green	25	10
N2516	- 40ch. brown & lt brn	60	25

DESIGN: 40ch. Multi-storey flats, Chollima Street.

857 Liberation Celebrations

1985. 40th Anniv of Liberation.

N2517	5ch. red, black and blue	20	10
N2518	10ch. multicoloured	50	15
N2519	10ch. brown, blk & grn	50	15
N2520	10ch. multicoloured	50	15
N2521	**857** 10ch. yellow, blk & red	50	15
N2522	- 10ch. red, orange & blk	50	15
N2523	- 40ch. multicoloured	1·20	75

MSN2524 68×50 mm. 90ch. multicoloured ... 2·75 ... 1·90

DESIGNS—HORIZ: No. N2517, Soldiers with rifles and flag; N2518, Crowd with banners and Flame of Juche; N2519, Korean and Soviet soldiers raising arms; N2520, Japanese soldiers laying down weapons; N2523, Students bearing banners. VERT: No. N2522, Liberation Tower, Moran Hill, Pyongyang; **MS**N2524, Monument.

858 Halley and Comet

1985. Appearance of Halley's Comet. Multicoloured.

N2525	10ch. Type **858**	90	15
N2526	20ch. Diagram of comet's flight and space probe	1·40	35

MSN2527 144×128 mm. 80ch. ultramarine and gold (Comet's trajectory) ... 5·00 ... 2·20

859 *Camellia japonica*

1985. Flowers. Multicoloured.

N2528	10ch. *Hippeastrum hybridum*	90	35
N2529	20ch. Type **859**	1·40	40
N2530	30ch. *Cyclamen persicum*	1·80	60

860 "Hunting"

1985. Koguryo Culture.

N2531	10ch. "Hero" (vert)	75	15
N2532	15ch. "Heroine" (vert)	90	35
N2533	20ch. "Flying Fairy"	1·10	35
N2534	25ch. Type **860**	1·40	50

MSN2535 90×80 mm. 80ch. "Pine Tree" (28×48 mm) ... 4·25 ... 1·30

861 Party Founding Museum

1985. 40th Anniv of Korean Workers' Party. Multicoloured.

N2536	5ch. Type **861**	20	10
N2537	10ch. Soldier with gun and workers	50	15
N2538	10ch. Soldiers and flag	50	15
N2539	40ch. Statue of worker, peasant and intellectual holding aloft party emblem	1·20	75

MSN2540 60×75 mm. 90ch. People with flowers ... 2·20 ... 90

862 Arch of Triumph, Pyongyang

1985. 40th Anniv of Kim Il Sung's Return.

N2541	**862** 10ch. brown and green	55	15

863 Colosseum, Rome, and N. Korea 1975 10ch. Stamp

1985. "Italia '85" International Stamp Exhibition, Rome. Multicoloured.

N2542	10ch. Type **863**	75	25
N2543	20ch. *The Holy Family* (Raphael) (vert)	1·10	40
N2544	30ch. Head of *David* (statue, Michelangelo) (vert)	1·60	60

MSN2545 67×47 mm. 80ch. Pantheon, Rome ... 5·00 ... 2·20

864 Mercedes Benz Type "300"

1985. South-West German Stamp Fair, Sindelfingen. Multicoloured.

N2546	10ch. Type **864**	1·10	15
N2547	15ch. Mercedes Benz Type "770"	1·70	25
N2548	20ch. Mercedes Benz "W 150"	1·80	35
N2549	30ch. Mercedes Type "600"	2·50	60

MSN2550 84×57 mm. 80ch. Mercedes Benz "W31" ... 5·50 ... 1·50

865 Tackle

1985. World Cup Football Championship, Mexico (1st issue). Multicoloured.

N2551	20ch. Type **865**	1·50	40
N2552	30ch. Three players	1·70	60

MSN2553 106×76 mm. 80ch. Goalkeeper and Mexican monuments ... 5·00 ... 1·90

See also Nos. N2558/**MS**N2560 and 2577/**MS**N2583.

866 Dancers

1985. International Youth Year. Multicoloured.

N2554	10ch. Type **866**	75	20
N2555	20ch. Sports activities	1·10	35
N2556	30ch. Technology	1·60	60

MSN2557 75×60 mm. 80ch. Young people ... 5·75 ... 2·10

867 Players

1985. World Cup Football Championship, Mexico (2nd issue). Multicoloured.

N2558	20ch. Type **867**	1·50	40
N2559	30ch. Goalkeeper and players	1·70	60
MSN2560	102×80 mm. 80ch. Goal-keeper and bullfighter	5·00	2·10

868 Juche Torch

1986. New Year.

N2561	**868**	10ch. multicoloured	55	15

869 Amedee Bollee and Limousine, 1901

1986. History of the Motor Car (2nd series). Multicoloured.

N2562	10ch. Type **869**	90	15
N2563	20ch. Stewart Rolls, Henry Royce and *Silver Ghost*, 1906	1·60	35
N2564	25ch. Giovanni Agnelli and Fiat car, 1912	1·70	50
N2565	30ch. Ettore Bugatti and *Royal* coupe, 1928	2·00	60
N2566	40ch. Louis Renault and fiacre, 1906	3·00	85
MSN2567	75×80 mm. 80ch. Gottiebo Daimler, Karl Benz and Mercedes "S", 1927	5·75	1·50

870 Gary Kasparov

1986. World Chess Championship, Moscow.

N2568	**870**	20ch. multicoloured	3·00	35
MSN2569	60×82 mm. 80ch. Anatoly Karpov and Kasparov	5·75	2·50

871 Cemetery Gate

1986. Revolutionary Martyrs' Cemetery, Pyongyang. Multicoloured.

N2570	5ch. Type **871**	25	10
N2571	10ch. Bronze sculpture (detail)	65	15

872 Tongdu Rock, Songgan

1986. 37th Anniv of Pres. Kim Il Sung's Visit to Songgan Revolutionary Site.

N2572	**872**	10ch. multicoloured	55	15

873 Buddhist Scriptures Museum

1986. Mt. Myohyang Buildings.

N2573	**873**	10ch. brown and green	50	15
N2574	–	20ch. violet and red	60	15

DESIGN: 20ch. Taeung Hall.

874 Tomato Anemonefish

1986. Fish. Multicoloured.

N2575	10ch. Pennant coralfish	1·20	15
N2576	20ch. Type **874**	1·70	40

875 Footballers and Flags of Italy, Bulgaria and Argentina

1986. World Cup Football Championship, Mexico (3rd issue). Designs showing footballers and flags of participating countries. Multicoloured.

N2577	10ch. Type **875**	75	15
N2578	20ch. Mexico, Belgium, Paraguay and Iraq	1·10	35
N2579	25ch. France, Canada, U.S.S.R. and Hungary	1·40	50
N2580	30ch. Brazil, Spain, Algeria and Northern Ireland	1·60	60
N2581	35ch. West Germany, Uruguay, Scotland and Denmark	1·70	65
N2582	40ch. Poland, Portugal, Morocco and England	2·00	85
MSN2583	100×70 80ch. Ball, boots, footballers and trophy	5·00	2·30

876 Singer, Pianist and Emblem

1986. Fourth Spring Friendship Art Festival, Pyongyang.

N2584	**876**	1wn. multicoloured	1·70	1·10

877 Daimler "Motorwagen", 1886

1986. 60th Anniv of Mercedes-Benz (car manufacturers). Multicoloured.

N2585	10ch. Type **877**	65	15
N2586	10ch. Benz "velo", 1894	65	15
N2587	20ch. Mercedes car, 1901	1·00	35
N2588	20ch. Benz limousine, 1909	1·00	35
N2589	30ch. Mercedes "tourenwagen", 1914	1·40	50
N2590	30ch. Mercedes-Benz "170" 6-cylinder, 1931	1·40	50
N2591	40ch. Mercedes-Benz "380", 1933	1·80	90
N2592	40ch. Mercedes-Benz "540 K", 1936	1·80	90
MSN2593	75×60 mm. 80ch. Mercedes-Simplex "phaeton", 1904	5·75	2·30

878 Mangyong Hill

1986. 74th Birthday of Kim Il Sung.

N2594	**878**	10ch. multicoloured	50	10

879 Crowd

1968. 50th Anniv of Association for the Restoration of the Fatherland.

N2595	**879**	10ch. multicoloured	40	10

880 Dove carrying Letter

1986. International Peace Year. Multicoloured.

N2596	10ch. Type **880**	50	35
N2597	20ch. U.N. Headquarters, New York	1·00	65

N2598	30ch. Dove, globe and broken missiles	1·50	1·00
MSN2599	72×90 mm. 80ch. Sculpture	3·75	1·30

881 *Mona Lisa* (Leonardo da Vinci)

1986

N2600	**881**	20ch. multicoloured	1·20	40

882 Pink Iris

1986. Irises. Multicoloured.

N2601	20ch. Type **882**	1·50	40
N2602	30ch. Violet iris	1·70	60
MSN2603	84×64 80ch. Magenta iris	5·00	2·10

883 Kim Un Suk

1986. Tennis Players. Multicoloured.

N2604	10ch. Type **883** (postage)	2·20	50
N2605	20ch. Ivan Lendl	2·20	50
N2606	30ch. Steffi Graf	2·20	50
N2607	50ch. Boris Becker (air)	2·20	50

884 Sulphur-crested Cockatoo ("Cockatoo")

1986. "Stampex '86" Stamp Exhibition. Adelaide, Australia. Multicoloured.

N2608	10ch. Type **884**	1·80	35
MSN2609	75×60 mm. 80ch. Kangaroo	5·00	2·10

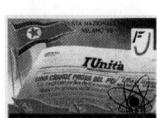

885 First Issue of "L'Unita"

1986. National "L'Unita" (Italian Communist Party newspaper) Festival, Milan. Multicoloured.

N2610	10ch. Type **885**	70	40
N2611	20ch. Milan Cathedral	1·30	85
N2612	30ch. "Pieta" (Michelangelo) (vert)	1·80	1·30
MSN2613	85×65 mm. 80ch. Enrico Berlingoer (former General Secretary of Italian Communist Part) (vert)	2·50	1·00

886 *Express II* (icebreaker) and Sweden 1872 20 ore Stamp

1986. "Stockholmia 86" International Stamp Exhibition, Stockholm.

N2614	10ch. multicoloured	2·50	25
MSN2615	86×60 mm. 80ch. UPU emblem, mail coach and Swedish stamps (horiz)	4·50	1·80

887 Reprint of First Stamp

1986. 40th Anniv of First North Korean Stamps (1st issue). Multicoloured.

N2616	10ch. Type **887** (postage)	50	40
N2617	15ch. Imperforate reprint of first stamp	75	60
N2618	50ch. 1946 50ch. violet stamp (air)	2·50	1·70

See also Nos. N2619/21.

888 Postal Emblems and 1962 and 1985 Stamps

1986. 40th Anniv of First North Korean Stamps (2nd issue). Multicoloured.

N2619	10ch. Type **888** (postage)	2·20	40
N2620	15ch. General Post Office and 1976 and 1978 stamps	1·20	25
N2621	50ch. Kim Il Sung, first stamp and reprint (vert) (air)	1·80	65

1986. World Cup Football Championship Results. Nos. N2577/82 optd **1st: ARG 2nd: FRG 3rd: FRA 4th: BEL**.

N2622	10ch. multicoloured	1·20	15
N2623	20ch. multicoloured	1·40	40
N2624	25ch. multicoloured	1·70	50
N2625	30ch. multicoloured	1·80	60
N2626	35ch. multicoloured	2·10	75
N2627	40ch. multicoloured	2·50	85
MSN2628	100×70 mm. 80ch. multicoloured	5·75	1·70

890 Flag and Man with raised Fist

1986. 60th Anniv of Down-with-Imperialism Union.

N2629	**890**	10ch. multicoloured	40	25

891 Gift Animals House

1986. First Anniv of Gift Animals House, Central Zoo, Pyongyang.

N2630	**891**	2wn. multicoloured	4·25	1·40

892 Schoolchildren

1986. 40th Anniv of UNESCO. Multicoloured.

N2631	10ch. Type **892**	50	35
N2632	50ch. Anniversary emblem, Grand People's Study House and telecommunications (horiz)	2·50	1·70

893 Communications Satellite

1986. 15th Anniv of Intersputnik.

N2633	**893**	5wn. multicoloured	9·25	4·25

894 Oil tanker leaving Lock

1986. West Sea Barrage.

N2634	**894**	10ch. multicoloured	65	15
N2635	-	40ch. grn, blk & gold	1·70	35
N2636	-	1wn. 20 multicoloured	3·50	85

DESIGNS: 20ch. Aerial view of dam; 1wn.20, Aerial view of lock.

895 Common Morel

1986. Minerals and Fungi. Multicoloured.

N2637		10ch. Lengenbachite (postage)	2·10	40
N2638		10ch. Common funnel cap	2·10	40
N2639		15ch. Rhodochrosite	2·10	40
N2640		15ch. Type **895**	2·10	40
N2641		50ch. Annabergite (air)	2·10	40
N2642		50ch. Blue russula	2·10	40

896 Machu Picchu, Peru, and N. Korea Taedong Gate Stamp

1986. North Korean Three-dimensional Photographs and Stamp Exhibition, Lima, Peru. Multicoloured.

N2643		10ch. Type **896**	1·70	35
MSN2644		110×75 mm. 80ch. Korean and Peruvian children	5·00	1·80

897 Pine Tree

1987. New Year. Multicoloured.

N2645		10ch. Type **897**	90	20
N2646		40ch. Hare	1·20	40

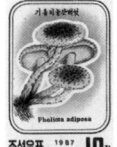

898 Pholiota adiposa

1987. Fungi. Multicoloured.

N2647		10ch. Type **898**	1·80	40
N2648		20ch. Chanterelle	1·90	40
N2649		30ch. Boletus impolitus	2·30	45
MSN2650		50×70 mm. 80ch. Gomphidius rutilus	5·75	2·30

899 Kim Ok Song (composer)

1987. Musicians' Death Anniversaries. Multicoloured.

N2651		10ch. Maurice Ravel (composer, 50th anniv)	1·70	30

N2652		10ch. Type **899** (22nd anniv)	1·70	30
N2653		20ch. Giovanni Lully (composer, 300th anniv)	1·70	30
N2654		30ch. Franz Liszt (composer, centenary (1986))	1·70	30
N2655		40ch. Violins (250th anniv of Antonio Stradivari (violin maker))	1·70	30
N2656		40ch. Christoph Gluck (composer, bicent)	1·70	30

900 King Jong II

1997. Kim Jong Il's Birthday. Sheet 85×105 mm.

MSN2657		80ch. multicoloured	1·80	65

901 East Pyongyang Grand Theatre

1987. Buildings.

N2658	**901**	5ch. green	40	10
N2659	-	10ch. brown	50	15
N2660	-	3wn. blue	4·50	1·60

DESIGNS—VERT: 10ch. Pyongyang Koryo Hotel. HORIZ: 3wn. Rungnado Stadium.

902 Gorch Fock (German cadet barque)

1987. Sailing Ships. Multicoloured.

N2661		20ch. Type **902** (postage)	85	30
N2662		30ch. Tovarishch (Russian cadet barque) (vert)	1·20	40
N2663		50ch. Belle Poule (cadet schooner) (vert) (air)	1·70	65
N2664		50ch. Sagres II (Portuguese cadet barque) (vert)	1·70	65
N2665		1wn. Koryo period merchantman	3·75	1·30
N2666		1wn. Dar Mlodziezy (Polish cadet full-rigged ship) (vert)	3·75	1·30

903 Road Signs

1987. Road Safety.

N2667	**903**	10ch. blue, red and black (postage)	1·30	10
N2668	-	10ch. red and black	1·30	10
N2669	-	20ch. blue, red & black	1·70	30
N2670	-	50ch. red and black (air)	1·80	75

DESIGNS: Nos. N2668/70, Different road signs.

904 Fire Engine

1987. Fire Engines.

N2671	**904**	10ch. mult (postage)	2·20	40
N2672	-	20ch. multicoloured	2·50	45
N2673	-	30ch. multicoloured	3·25	55
N2674	-	50ch. multicoloured (air)	4·25	75

DESIGNS: N2672/4, 20ch. to 50ch. Different machines.

905 Apatura ilia and Spiraea

1987. Butterflies and Flowers. Multicoloured.

N2675		10ch. Type **905**	90	25
N2676		10ch. Ypthima argus and fuchsia	90	25
N2677		10ch. Neptis philyra and aquilegia	1·30	30
N2678		20ch. Papilio protenor and chrysanthemum	1·30	30
N2679		40ch. Parantica sita and celosia	2·10	65
N2680		40ch. Vanessa indica and hibiscus	2·10	65

906 Association Monument, Pyongyang

1987. 70th Anniv of Korean National Association (independence movement).

N2681	**906**	10ch. red, silver & black	40	20

907 Doves, Emblem and Tree

1987. Fifth Spring Friendship Art Festival, Pyongyang.

N2682	**907**	10ch. multicoloured	40	20

908 Mangyong Hill

1987. 75th Birthday of Kim Il Sung. Multicoloured.

N2683		10ch. Type **908**	35	10
N2684		10ch. Kim Il Sung's birthplace, Mangyongdae (horiz)	35	10
N2685		10ch. "A Bumper Crop of Pumpkins" (62×41 mm)	35	10
N2686		10ch. "Profound Affection for the Working Class"	35	10

909 Bay

1987. Horses. Multicoloured.

N2687		10ch. Type **909**	40	20
N2688		10ch. Bay (different)	40	20
N2689		40ch. Grey rearing	1·70	1·20
N2690		40ch. Grey on beach	1·70	1·20

910 "Sputnik 1" (first artificial satellite)

1987. Transport. Multicoloured.

N2691		10ch. "Juche" high speed train (horiz)	50	10
N2692		10ch. Electric locomotive "Mangyongdae" (horiz)	50	10
N2693		10ch. Type **910** (30th anniv of flight)	50	10

N2694		20ch. Laika (30th anniv of first animal in space)	90	30
N2695		20ch. Tupolev Tu-144 super-sonic airliner (horiz)	90	30
N2696		20ch. Concorde (11th anniv of first commercial flight) (horiz)	90	30
N2697		30ch. Count Ferdinand von Zeppelin (70th death anniv) and airship LZ-4 (horiz)	1·30	40
N2698		80ch. Zeppelin and diagrams and drawings of airships (horiz)	3·75	1·50

911 Musk Ox

1987. "Capex '87" International Stamp Exhibition, Toronto. Multicoloured.

N2699		10ch. Type **911**	85	15
N2700		40ch. Jacques Cartier, his ship Grande Hermine and Ierry Fox (ice-breaker) (horiz)	2·20	55
N2701		60ch. Ice hockey (Winter Olympics, Calgary, 1988) (horiz)	2·20	85

912 Trapeze Artistes

1987. International Circus Festival, Monaco. Multicoloured.

N2702		10ch. Type **912**	50	15
N2703		10ch. "Brave Sailors" (North Korean acrobatic act) (vert)	50	15
N2704		20ch. Clown and elephant (vert)	90	30
N2705		20ch. North Korean artiste receiving "Golden Clown" award	90	30
N2706		40ch. Performing horses and cat act	2·75	45
N2707		50ch. Prince Rainier and his children applauding	1·80	65

913 Attack on Watch Tower

1987. 50th Anniv of Battle of Pochonbo.

N2708	**913**	10ch. brown, black and ochre	40	20

914 Sports

1987. Angol Sports Village.

N2709	**914**	5ch. brown and gold	15	10
N2710	-	10ch. blue and gold	25	10
N2711	-	40ch. brown and gold	85	30
N2712	-	70ch. blue and gold	1·40	45
N2713	-	1wn. red and gold	2·20	75
N2714	-	1wn.20 violet	2·75	1·10

DESIGNS: Exteriors of—10ch. Indoor swimming pool; 40ch. Weightlifting gymnasium; 70ch. Table tennis gymnasium; 1wn. Football stadium; 1wn.20, Handball gymnasium.

915 Mandarins

1987. Mandarins. Multicoloured.

N2715		20ch. Type **915**	1·70	45
N2716		20ch. Mandarins on shore	1·70	45
N2717		20ch. Mandarins on branch	1·70	45
N2718		40ch. Mandarins in water	2·50	65

916 Exhibition Site and
1987 3wn. Stamp

1987. "Olymphilex '87" Olympic Stamps Exhibition, Rome.
Multicoloured.
N2719 10ch. Type **916**   1·30   20
MSN2720 95×80 mm. 80ch. Exhibition
emblem and 5ch. and 1wn. Angol
Sports Village stamps   4·25   1·60

917 Underground Station and
Guard

1987. Railway Uniforms. Multicoloured.
N2721 10ch. Type **917**   50   10
N2722 10ch. Underground train and
station supervisor   50   10
N2723 20ch. Guard and electric train   75   15
N2724 30ch. Guard with flag and
electric train   1·10   30
N2725 40ch. "Orient Express" guard
and steam locomotive   1·40   40
N2726 40ch. German ticket controller
and diesel train   1·40   40

918 White Stork

1987. "Hafnia 87" International Stamp Exhibition,
Copenhagen. Multicoloured.
N2727 40ch. Type **918**   2·20   55
N2728 60ch. *Danmark* (cadet full-
rigged ship) and "Little
Mermaid", Copenhagen   2·50   65

919 Ice Skating

1987. Winter Olympic Games, Calgary (1988).
Multicoloured.
N2729 40ch. Type **919**   1·20   40
N2730 40ch. Ski jumping   1·20   40
N2731 40ch. Skiing (value on left)
(horiz)   1·20   40
N2732 40ch. Skiing (value on right)
(horiz)   1·20   40
MSN2733 73×100 mm. 80ch. Skiing   3·75   1·40

920 Victory Column

1987. 750th Anniv of Berlin and "Philatelia '87"
International Stamp Exhibition, Cologne.
Multicoloured.
N2734 10ch. Type **920**   50   10
N2735 20ch. Reichstag (horiz)   85   30
N2736 30ch. Pfaueninsel Castle   1·30   40
N2737 40ch. Charlottenburg Castle
(horiz)   1·40   55
MSN2738 77×94 mm. 80ch. Olympic
stadium (horiz)   3·75   1·40

921 Garros and Bleriot XI

1987. Birth Centenary of Roland Garros (aviator) and
Tennis as an Olympic Sport. Multicoloured.
N2739 20ch. Type **921**   1·80   30
N2740 20ch. Ivan Lendl (tennis player)   3·00   40
N2741 40ch. Steffi Graf (tennis player)   3·75   55
MSN2742 80×102 mm. 80ch. Steffi Graf
(different)   5·00   1·40

922 Kim Jong Suk

1987. 70th Birth Anniv of Kim Jong Suk (revolutionary).
Sheet 80×100 mm.
MSN2743 **922** 80ch. multicoloured   1·60   75

923 Pyongyang Buildings

1988. New Year. Multicoloured.
N2744 10ch. Type **923**   25   10
N2745 40ch. Dragon   85   30

924 Banner and
Newspaper

1988. 60th Anniv of "Saenal" Newspaper.
N2746 **924**   10ch. multicoloured   60   20

925 Birthplace, Mt.
Paekdu

1988. King Jongs Il's Birthday. Multicoloured.
N2747 109×85 mm. 10ch. Type **925**   35   10
MSN2748 109×85 mm. Kim Jong Il
(41×63 mm.)   1·80   65

926 Henry Dunant (founder)

1988. 125th Anniv of International Red Cross.
Multicoloured.
N2749 10ch. Type **926**   75   10
N2750 20ch. North Korean Red Cross
emblem and map   1·20   30
N2751 20ch. International Committee
headquarters, Geneva   1·20   30

N2752 40ch. Pyongyang Maternity
Hospital, doctor and baby   1·20   40
MSN2753 70×100 mm. 80ch. Red
Cross and Red Crescent flags and
anniversary emblem   2·50   95

927 Santa Maria

1988. 500th Anniv (1992) of Discovery of America by
Christopher Columbus. Multicoloured.
N2754 10ch. Type **927**   1·70   20
N2755 20ch. *Pinta*   1·70   30
N2756 30ch. *Nina*   1·70   45
MSN2757 80×102 mm. 80ch. *Columbus
on the deck of his Flagship* (detail,
Karl von Piloty)   3·50   95
Nos. N2754/6 were issued together, se-tenant, forming
a composite design of Columbus's ships leaving Palos.

928 Montgolfier
Balloon and Modern
Hot-air Balloons

1988. "Juvalux '88" International Youth Stamp Exhibition,
Luxembourg. Multicoloured.
N2758 40ch. Type **928**   1·10   40
N2759 60ch. Steam locomotive and
railway map of Luxembourg,
1900   2·10   55

929 Dancers

1988. Sixth Spring Friendship Art Festival, Pyongyang.
Multicoloured.
N2760 10ch. Singer (poster)   25   10
N2761 1wn.20 Type **929**   3·25   1·30

930 Inaugural
Congress Emblem

1988. Tenth Anniv of International Institute of the Juche
Idea.
N2762 **930**   10ch. multicoloured   40   10

931 Birthplace,
Mangyongdae

1988. 76th Birthday of Kim Il Sung. Multicoloured.
N2763 10c. Type **931**   40   10
MSN2764 135×95 mm. 80ch. Kim Il
Sung and schoolchildren (40×62
mm.)   1·40   65

932 Urho (ice-breaker)

1988. "Finlandia 88" International Stamp Exhibition,
Helsinki. Multicoloured.
N2765 40ch. Type **932**   1·80   40
N2766 60ch. Matti Nykaenen (Olympic
Games ski-jumping medallist)   1·70   55

933 Postcard for 1934
Championship

1988. World Cup Football Championship, Italy (1st issue).
Multicoloured.
N2767 10ch. Football match   65   15
N2768 20ch. Type **933**   1·10   30
N2769 30ch. Player tackling (horiz)   1·70   40
MSN2770 100×75 mm. 80ch. Winning
Italian team, 1982 (horiz)   2·50   95
See also Nos. N2924/7.

934 Emblem

1988. 13th World Youth and Students' Festival,
Pyongyang (1st issue). Multicoloured.
N2771 5ch. Type **934**   10   10
N2772 10ch. Dancer   50   10
N2773 10ch. Gymnast and gymnasium,
Angol Sports Village   25   10
N2774 10ch. Map of Korea, globe
and doves   35   10
N2775 10ch. Finger pointing at shat-
tered nuclear rockets   90   20
N2776 1wn.20 Three differently col-
oured hands and dove   2·75   1·00
See also Nos. N2860/3 and N2879/80.

935 Fairy

1988. *Eight Fairies of Mt. Kumgang* (tale). Multicoloured.
N2777 10ch. Type **935**   25   10
N2778 15ch. Fairy at pool and fairies
on rainbow   40   10
N2779 20ch. Fairy and woodman
husband   60   20
N2780 25ch. Couple with baby   75   20
N2781 30ch. Couple with son and
daughter   85   30
N2782 35ch. Family on rainbow   1·00   35

936 Mallards

1988. "Praga '88" International Stamp Exhibition, Prague.
Multicoloured.
N2783 20ch. Type **936**   1·50   30
N2784 40ch. Vladimir Remek (Czecho-
slovak cosmonaut)   1·10   40

937 Red Crossbill

1988. Birds. Multicoloured.

N2785	10ch. Type **937**	75	20
N2786	15ch. Common stonechat	1·00	30
N2787	20ch. Eurasian nuthatch	1·50	40
N2788	25ch. Great spotted wood-pecker	1·70	45
N2789	30ch. River kingfisher	2·00	55
N2790	35ch. Bohemian waxwing	2·10	65

938 Fair Emblem

1988. 40th International Stamp Fair, Riccione. Multicoloured.

N2791	20ch. Type **938**	50	40
MSN2792	101×75 mm. 80ch. Drum dancer (vert)	2·10	75

939 Emu

1988. Bicentenary of Australian Settlement. Multicoloured.

N2793	10ch. Type **939**	85	20
N2794	15ch. Satin bowerbirds	1·10	30
N2795	30ch. Laughing kookaburra (vert)	1·80	45
MSN2796	101×73 mm. 80ch. HMS "Resolution" (Cook's ship)	3·00	1·00

940 Floating Crane *5-28*

1988. Ships. Multicoloured.

N2797	10ch. Type **940**	50	20
N2798	20ch. Freighter *Hwanggumsan*	85	30
N2799	30ch. Freighter *Changjasan Chongnyon-ho*	1·00	40
N2800	40ch. Liner *Samjiyon*	1·30	45

941 *Hansa*

1988. 150th Birth Anniv of Count Ferdinand von Zeppelin (airship pioneer). Multicoloured.

N2801	10ch. Type **941**	35	10
N2802	20ch. *Schwaben*	65	30
N2803	30ch. *Viktoria Luise*	90	40
N2804	40ch. LZ-3	1·30	45
MSN2805	102×80 mm. 1wn. Portrait of Zeppelin (vert)	3·25	1·40

942 Kim Il Sung and Jambyn Batmunkh

1988. Kim Il Sung's Visit to Mongolia.

N2806	**942** 10ch. multicoloured	25	10

943 Hero and Labour Hero of the D.P.R.K. Medals

1988. National Heroes Congress.

N2807	**943** 10ch. multicoloured	25	10

944 Tower of Juche Idea

1988. 40th Anniv of Democratic Republic. Multicoloured.

N2808	5ch. Type **944**	15	10
N2809	10ch. Smelter and industrial buildings	25	10
N2810	10ch. Soldier and Mt. Paekdu	25	10
N2811	10ch. Map of Korea and globe	25	10
N2812	10ch. Hand holding banner, globe and doves	25	10
MSN2813	118×105 mm. 1wn.20 Kim Il Sung designing national flag and emblem (41×63 mm)	3·00	1·10

945 *Sunflowers* (Vincent van Gogh)

1988. "Filacept 88" Stamp Exhibition, The Hague. Multicoloured.

N2814	40ch. Type **945**	2·20	1·70
N2815	60ch. *The Chess Game* (Lucas van Leyden) (horiz)	3·25	2·40

946 Emblem

1988. 16th Session of Socialist Countries' Post and Telecommunications Conference, Pyongyang.

N2816	**946** 10ch. multicoloured		10

947 Chaju "82" 10-ton Truck

1988. Tipper Trucks. Multicoloured.

N2817	20ch. Type **947**	50	40
N2818	40ch. Kumsusan-ho 40-ton truck	1·00	75

948 Owl

1988. Paintings by O Un Byol. Multicoloured.

N2819	10ch. Type **948**	2·20	30
N2820	15ch. *Dawn* (red junglefowl)	1·10	30
N2821	20ch. *Beautiful Rose received by Kim Il Sung*	85	25
N2822	25ch. *Sun and Bamboo*	1·00	25
N2823	30ch. *Autumn* (fruit tree)	1·20	30

949 Chunggi Steam Locomotive No. 35

1988. Railway Locomotives. Multicoloured.

N2824	10ch. Type **949**	65	15
N2825	20ch. *Chunggi* steam locomotive No. 22	90	20
N2826	30ch. *Chongiha* electric locomotive No. 3	1·10	30
N2827	40ch. *Chunggi* steam locomotive No. 307	1·30	40

950 Pirmen Zurbriggen (downhill skiing)

1988. Winter Olympic Games, Calgary, Medal Winners. Multicoloured.

N2828	10ch. Type **950**	25	10
N2829	20ch. Yvonne van Gennip (speed skating)	50	40
N2830	30ch. Marjo Matikainen (cross-country skiing)	75	55
N2831	40ch. U.S.S.R. (ice hockey) (horiz)	1·00	75
MSN2832	Two sheets, each 105×95 mm. (a) 80ch. Katarina Witt (figure skating); (b) 80ch. As sheet (a) but with names of winners printed in margin	4·25	1·60

951 Yuri Gagarin

1988. First Man and Woman in Space. Multicoloured.

N2833	20ch. Type **951**	40	30
N2834	40ch. Valentina Tereshkova	90	65

952 Nehru

1988. Birth Centenary of Jawaharlal Nehru (Indian statesman) and "India 89" International Stamp Exhibition, New Delhi.

N2835	**952** 20ch. purple, black and gold	85	20
MSN2836	90×74 mm. 60ch. multicoloured (Dancer)	1·70	55

953 Chollima Statue

1989. New Year. Multicoloured.

N2837	10ch. Type **953**	25	10
N2838	20ch. *The Dragon Angler* (17th-century painting)	85	20
N2839	40ch. *Tortoise and Serpent* (Kangso tomb painting) (horiz)	1·20	40

954 Archery

1989. National Defence Training. Multicoloured.

N2840	10ch. Type **954**	1·20	30
N2841	15ch. Rifle shooting	40	10
N2842	20ch. Pistol shooting	50	20
N2843	25ch. Parachuting	65	25
N2844	30ch. Launching model glider	75	30

955 Dobermann Pinscher

1989. Animals presented to Kim Il Sung. Multicoloured.

N2845	10ch. Type **955**	65	20
N2846	20ch. Labrador	90	25
N2847	25ch. German shepherd	1·20	30
N2848	30ch. Rough collies (horiz)	1·30	35
N2849	35ch. Serval (horiz)	1·70	40
MSN2850	95×75 mm. 80ch. "Felis libica" (horiz)	3·75	95

956 Begonia *Kimjongil*

1989. Kim Jong Il Birthday. Sheet 78×100 mm.

MSN2851	**956** 80ch. multicoloured	1·80	65

957 Agriculture

1989. 25th Anniv of Publication of "Theses on the Socialist Rural Question in our Country" by Kim Il Sung.

N2852	**957** 10ch. multicoloured	50	15

958 The Gypsy and Grapes

1989. Fungi and Fruits. Multicoloured.

N2853	10ch. Type **958**	65	15
N2854	20ch. Caesar's mushroom and magnolia vine	1·10	30
N2855	25ch. *Lactarius hygrophoides* and *Eleagnus crispa*	1·50	35
N2856	30ch. *Agaricus placomyces* and Chinese gooseberries	1·70	40
N2857	35ch. Horse mushroom and *Lycium chinense*	2·10	40
N2858	40ch. Elegant boletus and *Juglans cordiformis*	2·20	45
MSN2859	100×78 mm. 1wn. *Gomphidius roseus* and Diospyros lotus" (48×30 mm)	4·50	1·40

959 Korean Girl

1989. 13th World Youth and Students' Festival, Pyongyang (2nd issue). Multicoloured.

N2860	10ch. Type **959**	25	10
N2861	20ch. Children of different races	45	30

| N2862 | 30ch. Fairy and rainbow | 65 | 45 |
| N2863 | 40ch. Young peoples and Tower of Juche Idea | 90 | 65 |

960 *Parnassius eversmanni*

1969. Insects. Multicoloured.
N2864	10ch. Type **960**	1·00	30
N2865	15ch. *Colias heos*	1·00	30
N2866	20ch. *Dilipa fenestra*	1·00	30
N2867	25ch. *Buthus martensis*	1·00	30
N2868	30ch. *Trichogramma ostriniae*	1·00	30
N2869	40ch. *Damaster constricticollis*	1·00	30
MSN2870	82×65 mm. 80ch. *Parnassius nomion*	3·25	1·10

961 Dancers
(poster)

1989. Spring Friendship Art Festival, Pyongyang.
| N2871 | **961** | 10ch. multicoloured | 60 | 15 |

962 Birthplace, Mangyongdae

1989. 77th Birthday of Kim Il Sung.
| N2872 | **962** | 10ch. multicoloured | 35 | 10 |

963 Battle Plan and Monument to the Victory

1989. 50th Anniv of Battle of the Musan Area.
| N2873 | **963** | 10ch. blue, flesh and red | 85 | 20 |

964 Modern Dance

1989. Chamo System of Dance Notation. Multicoloured.
N2874	10ch. Type **964**	60	20
N2875	20ch. Ballet	75	30
N2876	25ch. Modern dance (different)	1·00	35
N2877	30ch. Traditional dance	1·10	40
MSN2878	85×105 mm. 80ch. Dancers	3·00	75

965 Hands supporting Torch

1989. 13th World Youth and Students' Festival, Pyongyang (3rd issue).
| N2879 | **965** | 5ch. blue | 15 | 10 |
| N2880 | - | 10ch. brown | 25 | 10 |
DESIGN: 10ch. Youth making speech.

966 Victorious Badger

1989. "Badger measures the Height" (cartoon film). Multicoloured.
N2881	10ch. Cat, bear and badger race to flag pole	1·10	20
N2882	40ch. Cat and bear climb pole while badger measures shadow	1·70	40
N2883	50ch. Type **966**	2·00	45

967 Kyongju Observatory and Star Chart

1989. Astronomy.
| N2884 | 20ch. multicoloured | 1·30 | 25 |
| MSN2885 | 102×85 mm. 80ch. Planet Saturn (horiz) | 5·50 | 75 |

968 "Liberty guiding the People" (Eugene Delacroiz)

1989. "Philexfrance 89" International Stamp Exhibition, Paris. Sheet 107×88 mm.
| MSN2886 | **968** | 70ch. multicoloured | 1·80 | 95 |

969 Pele (footballer) and 1978 25ch. Stamp

1989. "Brasiliana 89" International Stamp Exhibition, Rio de Janeiro.
| N2887 | **969** | 40ch. multicoloured | 1·30 | 45 |

970 Nurse and Ambulance

1989. Emergency Services. Multicoloured.
N2888	10ch. Type **970**	25	10
N2889	20ch. Surgeon and ambulance	40	20
N2890	30ch. Fireman and fire engine	3·00	30
N2891	40ch. Fireman and engine (different)	3·00	40

971 Kaffir Lily

1989. Plants presented to Kim Il Sung. Multicoloured.
| N2892 | 10ch. Type **971** | 40 | 10 |
| N2893 | 15ch. Tulips | 50 | 15 |

N2894	20ch. Flamingo lily	75	20
N2895	25ch. *Rhododendron obtusum*	90	25
N2896	30ch. Daffodils	1·10	30
MSN2897	84×104 mm. 80ch. *Gerbera hybrida*	3·00	75

972 Air Mail Letter and Postal Transport

1989. 150th Anniv of the Penny Black and "Stamp World London 90" International Stamp Exhibition (1st issue). Multicoloured.
N2898	5ch. Type **972**	40	10
N2899	10ch. Post box and letters	60	15
N2900	20ch. Stamps, tweezers and magnifying glass	65	20
N2901	30ch. First North Korean stamps	85	30
N2902	40ch. Universal Postal Union emblem and headquarters, Berne	1·10	40
N2903	50ch. Sir Rowland Hill and Penny Black	1·50	55
See also No. N2956/MSN2957.

973 *Bistorta incana*

1989. Alpine Flowers. Multicoloured.
N2904	10ch. *Iris setosa*	50	15
N2905	15ch. *Aquilegia japonica*	65	20
N2906	20ch. Type **973**	85	25
N2907	25ch. *Rodiola elongata*	90	30
N2908	30ch. *Sanguisorba sitchensis*	1·00	35
MSN2909	62×49 mm. 80ch. *Trollius japonicus*	2·75	85

974 Tree, Mt. Paekdu

1989. Slogan-bearing Trees (1st series). Multicoloured.
N2910	10ch. Type **974**	25	10
N2911	3wn. Tree, Oun-dong, Pyongyang	8·50	6·50
N2912	5wn. Tree, Mt. Kanbaek	14·50	10·50
See also No. N2931.

975 Skipping

1989. Children's Games. Multicoloured.
N2913	10ch. Type **975**	25	10
N2914	20ch. Windmill	1·70	30
N2915	30ch. Kite	75	35
N2916	40ch. Whip and top	1·00	40

976 Marchers

1989. International March for Peace and Reunification of Korea. Sheet 100×77 mm.
| MSN2917 | **976** | 80ch. multicoloured | 2·10 | 1·40 |

977 Diesel Train and Sinpa Youth Station

1989. Railway Locomotives. Multicoloured.
| N2918 | 10ch. Type **977** | 50 | 10 |

N2919	20ch. *Pulgungi* electric locomotive	75	20
N2920	25ch. Diesel goods train	85	30
N2921	30ch. Diesel train	1·00	35
N2922	40ch. Steam locomotive	1·30	40
N2923	50ch. Steam locomotive (different)	1·30	45

978 Players and Map of Italy

1989. World Cup Football Championship, Italy (2nd issue). Multicoloured.
N2924	10ch. Type **978**	90	20
N2925	20ch. Free kick	50	20
N2926	30ch. Goal mouth scrimmage	75	30
N2927	40ch. Goalkeeper diving for ball	1·00	35

979 Magellan (navigator) and his Ship *Vitoria*

1989. "Descobrex '89" International Stamp Exhibition, Portugal.
| N2928 | **979** | 30ch. multicoloured | 1·50 | 30 |

980 Mangyong Hill and Pine Branches

1990. New Year. Multicoloured.
| N2929 | 10ch. Type **980** | 25 | 10 |
| N2930 | 20ch. Koguryo mounted archers | 1·10 | 20 |

1990. Slogan-bearing Trees (2nd series). As T **974**. Multicoloured.
| N2931 | 5ch. Tree, Mt. Paekdu | 35 | 10 |

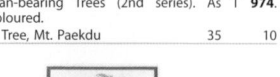

981 Ryukwoli

1990. Dogs. Multicoloured.
N2932	20ch. Type **981**	1·30	30
N2933	30ch. Palryuki	1·30	30
N2934	40ch. Komdungi	1·30	30
N2935	50ch. Oulruki	1·30	30

982 Birthplace, Mt. Paekdu

1990. Birthday of Kim Jong Il.
| N2936 | **982** | 10ch. brown | 35 | 10 |

983 Stone Instruments and Primitive Man

1990. Evolution of Man. Multicoloured.
| N2937 | 10ch. Type **983** | 2·50 | 20 |
| N2938 | 40ch. Palaeolithic and Neolithic man | 3·25 | 30 |

984 Rungna Bridge, Pyongyang

1990. Bridges. Multicoloured.
| N2939 | 10ch. Type **984** | 50 | 10 |

N2940 20ch. Potong bridge, Pyongyang | 75 | 20
N2941 30ch. Sinuiji-Ryucho Island Bridge | 1·00 | 30
N2942 40ch. Chungsongui Bridge, Pyongyang | 1·30 | 40

985 Infantryman

1990. Warriors' Costumes. Multicoloured.
N2943 20ch. Type **985** | 40 | 30
N2944 30ch. Archer | 65 | 55
N2945 50ch. Military commander in armour | 1·20 | 95
N2946 70ch. Officer's costume, 10th–14th centuries | 1·60 | 1·20

Nos. N2943/5 depict costumes from the 3rd century B.C. to the 7th century A.D.

986 *Atergatis subdentatus* (poster)

1990. Crabs. Multicoloured.
N2947 20ch. Type **986** | 50 | 20
N2948 30ch. *Platylambrus validus* | 75 | 30
N2949 50ch. *Uca arcuata* | 1·30 | 45

987 Dancers

1990. Spring Friendship Art Festival, Pyongyang.
N2950 **987** 10ch. multicoloured | 35 | 10

988 Monument at Road Folk, Mangyongdae

1990. 78th Birthday of Kim Il Sung.
N2951 **988** 10ch. green and gold | 35 | 10
MSN2952 85×105 mm. 80ch. multicoloured (Kim Il Sung) (38×60 mm) | 2·10 | 75

989 *Gymnocalycium* sp.

1990. Cacti. Multicoloured.
N2953 10ch. Type **989** | 50 | 10
N2954 30ch. *Pyllocactus hybridus* | 90 | 30
N2955 50ch. *Epiphyllum truncatum* | 1·50 | 45

990 Exhibition Emblem

1990. "Stamp World London 90" International Stamp Exhibition (2nd issue).
N2956 **990** 20ch. red and black | 60 | 20
MSN2957 49×66 mm. 70ch. grey, black and gold | 2·00 | 1·90

DESIGN: 70ch. Sir Rowland Hill.

991 Congo Peafowl

1990. Peafowl. Multicoloured.
N2958 10ch. Type **991** | 1·00 | 20
N2959 20ch. Common peafowl | 1·80 | 45
MSN2960 96×82 mm. 70ch. Common peafowl displaying tail | 3·25 | 95

992 Dolphin and Submarine

1990. Bio-engineering. Multicoloured.
N2961 10ch. Type **992** | 1·40 | 45
N2962 20ch. Bat and dish aerial | 1·40 | 45
N2963 30ch. Owl and Tupolev Tu-154 jetliner | 1·40 | 45
N2964 40ch. Squid, "Soyuz" rocket and Concorde supersonic jetliner | 1·40 | 45

993 *Self-portrait* (Rembrandt)

1990. "Belgica 90" International Stamp Exhibition, Brussels. Multicoloured.
N2965 10ch. Type **993** | 35 | 10
N2966 20ch. *Self-portrait* (Raphael) | 60 | 20
N2967 30ch. *Self-portrait* (Rubens) | 75 | 30

994 K. H. Rummenigge (footballer)

1990. "Dusseldorf '90" International Youth Stamp Exhibition. Multicoloured.
N2968 20ch. Steffi Graf (tennis player) | 85 | 20
N2969 30ch. Exhibition emblem | 75 | 30
N2970 70ch. Type **994** | 1·70 | 65

995 Workers' Stadium, Peking, and Games Mascot

1990. 11th Asian Games, Peking (Nos. N2971/2) and 3rd Asian Winter Games, Samjiyon (N2973). Multicoloured.
N2971 10ch. Type **995** | 25 | 10
N2972 30ch. Chollima Statue and sportsmen | 75 | 40
N2973 40ch. Sportsmen and Games emblem | 1·10 | 45

996 Ball

1990. West Germany, Winners of World Cup Football Championship. Multicoloured.
N2974 15ch. Emblem of F.I.F.A. (International Federation of Football Associations) | 40 | 10
N2975 20ch. Jules Rimet | 60 | 20
N2976 25ch. Type **996** | 65 | 30
N2977 30ch. Olympic Stadium, Rome (venue of final) | 75 | 35
N2978 35ch. Goalkeeper | 90 | 40
N2979 40ch. Emblem of West German Football Association | 1·10 | 45
MSN2980 106×92 mm. 80ch. German Football Association emblem and trophy (horiz) | 2·10 | 1·40

997 Kakapo and Map of New Zealand

1990. "New Zealand 1990" International Stamp Exhibition, Auckland.
N2981 **997** 30ch. multicoloured | 1·50 | 55

998 "Summer at Chipson Peak"

1990. "Europa 90" International Stamp Fair, Riccione. Sheet 90×70 mm.
MSN2982 **998** 80cn. multicoloured | 2·10 | 75

999 Head of Procession

1990. Koguryo Wedding Procession. Multicoloured.
N2983 10ch. Type **999** | 1·30 | 40
N2984 30ch. Bridegroom | 1·30 | 40
N2985 50ch. Bride in carriage | 1·30 | 40
N2986 1wn. Drummer on horse | 1·30 | 40

Nos. N2983/6 were issued together, *se-tenant*, forming a composite design.

1000 Marchers descending Mt. Paekdu

1990. Rally for Peace and Reunification of Korea. Multicoloured.
N2987 10ch. Type **1000** | 25 | 10
MSN2988 106×70 mm. 1wn. Crowd watching dancers | 2·20 | 85

1001 Praying Mantis

1990. Insects. Multicoloured.
N2989 20ch. Type **1001** | 50 | 20
N2990 30ch. Ladybird | 75 | 30
N2991 40ch. *Pheropsophus jessoensis* | 1·10 | 35
N2992 70ch. *Phyllium siccifolium* | 1·70 | 55

1002 Footballers

1990. North–South Reunification Football Match, Pyongyang. Multicoloured.
N2993 10ch. Type **1002** | 75 | 10
N2994 20ch. Footballers (different) | 75 | 20
MSN2995 105×80 mm. 1wn. Teams parading | 2·20 | 85

1003 Concert Emblem

1990. National Reunification Concert.
N2996 **1003** 10ch. multicoloured | 35 | 10

1004 Ox

1990. Farm Animals.
N2997 **1004** 10ch. brown and green | 25 | 10
N2998 - 20ch. lilac and yellow | 45 | 20
N2999 - 30ch. grey and red | 60 | 30
N3000 - 40ch. green and yellow | 85 | 35
N3001 - 50ch. brown and blue | 1·10 | 40

DESIGNS: 20ch. Pig; 30ch. Goat; 40ch. Sheep; 50ch. Horse.

1005 Chinese and North Korean Soldiers

1990. 40th Anniv of Participation of Chinese Volunteers in Korean War. Multicoloured.
N3002 10ch. Type **1005** | 25 | 10
N3003 20ch. Populace welcoming volunteers (horiz) | 45 | 20
N3004 30ch. Rejoicing soldiers and battle scene (horiz) | 60 | 25
N3005 40ch. Post-war reconstruction (horiz) | 85 | 30
MSN3006 95×75 mm. 80ch. Friendship Tower, Moran Hill, Pyongyang | 1·70 | 70

1006 Anniversary Emblem

1990. 40th Anniv of United Nations Development Programme.
N3007 **1006** 1wn. blue, silver & blk | 3·00 | 2·10

1007 Mikado Sturgeon

1990. Fish.
N3008 **1007** 10ch. brown and green | 25 | 10
N3009 - 20ch. green and blue | 60 | 20
N3010 - 30ch. blue and purple | 80 | 30
N3011 - 40ch. brown and blue | 1·10 | 40
N3012 - 50ch. violet and green | 1·40 | 50

DESIGNS: 20ch. Large-headed sea bream; 30ch. Agoo flyingfish; 40ch. Fat greenling; 50ch. Tobiji-ei eagle ray.

1008 Sheep

1990. New Year.
N3013　**1008**　40ch. multicoloured　　85　30

1009 Moorhen

1990. Birds.
N3014	**1009**	10ch. blue, green & blk	50	10
N3015	–	20ch. brown, bistre and black	85	30
N3016	–	30ch. green, grey and black	1·10	50
N3017	–	40ch. brown, orange and black	1·60	60
N3018	–	50ch. ochre, brown and black	2·20	80

DESIGNS: 20ch. Jay; 30ch. Three-toed woodpecker; 40ch. Whimbrel; 50ch. Water rail.

1010 Giant Panda

1991. "Phila Nippon '91" International Stamp Exhibition, Tokyo. Multicoloured.
N3019	10ch. Type **1010**	25	10
N3020	20ch. Two giant pandas feeding	45	20
N3021	30ch. Giant panda clambering onto branch	60	25
N3022	40ch. Giant panda on rock	95	30
N3023	50ch. Two giant pandas	1·10	40
N3024	60ch. Giant panda in tree fork	1·30	50
MSN3025	115×85 mm. Giant panda	6·00	1·50

1011 Changsan

1991. Revolutionary Sites.. Multicoloured.
| N3026 | 5ch. Type **1011** | 15 | 10 |
| N3027 | 10ch. Oun | 25 | 20 |

1012 Black-faced Spoonbills

1991. Endangered Birds. Multicoloured.
N3028	10ch. Type **1012**	25	10
N3029	20ch. Grey herons	60	20
N3030	30ch. Great egrets	85	30
N3031	40ch. Manchurian cranes	1·20	40
N3032	50ch. Japanese white-naped cranes	1·60	50
N3033	70ch. White storks	2·20	70

1013 *Clossiana angarensis*

1991. Alpine Butterflies. Multicoloured.
N3034　10ch. Type **1013**　　15　10

N3035	20ch. "Erebia embla"	35	30
N3036	30ch. Camberwell beauty	50	40
N3037	40ch. Comma	70	50
N3038	50ch. Eastern pale clouded yellow	95	70
N3039	60ch. *Theela betulae*	1·20	80

1014 Hedgehog Fungus

1991. Fungi. Multicoloured.
N3040	10ch. Type **1014**	15	10
N3041	20ch. *Phylloporus rhodoxanthus*	45	20
N3042	30ch. *Calvatia craniiformis*	60	30
N3043	40ch. Cauliflower clavaria	80	40
N3044	50ch. *Russula integra*	1·00	50

1015 Kumchon

1991. Revolutionary Sites. Multicoloured.
| N3045 | 10ch. Type **1015** | 15 | 10 |
| N3046 | 40ch. Samdung | 70 | 50 |

1016 Dr. Kye Ung Sang (researcher)

1991. Silkworm Research. Multicoloured.
N3047	10ch. Type **1016**	15	10
N3048	20ch. Chinese oak silk moth	35	30
N3049	30ch. *Attacus ricini*	50	40
N3050	40ch. *Antheraea yamamai*	70	50
N3051	50ch. Silkworm moth	95	70
N3052	60ch. *Aetias artemis*	1·10	80

1017 Emblem and Venue

1991. Ninth Spring Friendship Art Festival, Pyongyang.
N3053　**1017**　10ch. multicoloured　　20　10

1018 Emperor Penguins

1991. Antarctic Exploration. Multicoloured.
N3054	10ch. Type **1018**	45	20
N3055	20ch. Research station	45	20
N3056	30ch. Elephant seals	50	30
N3057	40ch. Research ship	95	40
N3058	50ch. Southern black-backed gulls	1·60	60
MSN3059	75×105 mm. 80ch. National flag and map of Antarctica	1·60	90

1019 People's Palace of Culture (venue)

1991. 85th Interparliamentary Union Conference, Pyongyang.
| N3060 | **1019** | 10ch. dp green, grn & sil | 25 | 10 |
| N3061 | – | 1wn.50 multicoloured | 2·75 | 2·10 |

DESIGN: 1wn.50, Conference emblem and azalea.

1020 Map and Kim Jong Ho

1991. 130th Anniv of Publication of Kim Jong Ho's Map *Taidong Yu Jido*.
N3062　**1020**　90ch. black, brn & sil　　1·90　1·30

1021 Cynognathus

1991. Dinosaurs. Multicoloured.
N3063	10ch. Type **1021**	35	10
N3064	20ch. Brontosaurus	70	40
N3065	30ch. Stegosaurus and allosaurus	1·00	50
N3066	40ch. Pterosauria	1·40	80
N3067	50ch. Ichthyosaurus	1·70	90

1022 Sprinting

1991. Olympic Games, Barcelona (1992) (1st issue). Multicoloured.
N3068	10ch. Type **1022**	15	10
N3069	10ch. Hurdling	15	10
N3070	20ch. Long jumping	45	20
N3071	20ch. Throwing the discus	45	20
N3072	30ch. Putting the shot	60	30
N3073	30ch. Pole vaulting	60	30
N3074	40ch. High jumping	95	50
N3075	40ch. Throwing the javelin	95	50
MSN3076	Two sheets, each 105×85 mm. (a) 80ch. Breasting the tape; (b) 80ch. Running	3·50	1·90

See also Nos. N3142/**MS**3148.

1023 Cats and Eurasian Tree Sparrows

1991. Cats. Multicoloured.
N3077	10ch. Type **1023**	50	40
N3078	20ch. Cat and rat	1·00	60
N3079	30ch. Cat and butterfly	1·60	80
N3080	40ch. Cats with ball	2·10	1·10
N3081	50ch. Cat and frog	2·75	1·30

1024 "Wisteria Flowers and Pups" (detail)

1991. "Riccione '91" Stamp Fair and Exhibition, Italy. Sheet 116×80 mm. International.
MSN3082　**1024**　80ch. multicoloured　　3·50　95

1025 Wild Horse

1991. Horses. Multicoloured.
N3083	10ch. Type **1025**	15	10
N3084	20ch. Hybrid of wild ass and wild horse	50	20
N3085	30ch. Przewalski's horse	70	30
N3086	40ch. Wild ass	95	50
N3087	50ch. Wild horse (different)	1·20	60

1026 Pennant Coralfish

1991. Fish. Multicoloured.
N3088	10ch. Type **1026** (postage)	15	10
N3089	20ch. Clown triggerfish	45	20
N3090	30ch. Tomato anemonefish	60	30
N3091	40ch. Palette surgeonfish	95	50
N3092	50ch. Freshwater angelfish (air)	1·30	70
MSN3093	88×60 mm. 80ch. Tetras ("Hyhessobrycon innesi") (51×31 mm)	3·00	95

1027 Rhododendrons

1991. Flowers. Multicoloured.
N3094	10ch. Begonia	25	10
N3095	20ch. Gerbera	35	30
N3096	30ch. Type **1027**	50	40
N3097	40ch. Phalaenopsis	70	50
N3098	50ch. *Impatiens sultanii*	95	70
N3099	60ch. Streptocarpus	1·10	80

Nos. N3097/9 commemorate "CANADA '92" international youth stamp exhibition, Montreal.

1028 Panmunjom

1991
N3100　**1028**　10ch. multicoloured　　20　10

1029 Magnolia

1991. National Flower.
N3101　**1029**　10ch. multicoloured　　20　10

1030 Players

1991. Women's World Football Championship, China. Multicoloured.
N3102	10ch. Type **1030**	25	10
N3103	20ch. Dribbling the ball	35	30
N3104	30ch. Heading the ball	50	40
N3105	40ch. Overhead kick	70	50
N3106	50ch. Tackling	95	70
N3107	60ch. Goalkeeper	1·10	80

1031 Squirrel Monkeys

1992. Monkeys. Multicoloured.
N3108 10ch. Type **1031** 45 20
N3109 20ch. Pygmy marmosets 80 40
N3110 30ch. Red-handed tamarins 1·40 50
MSN3111 65×91 mm. 80ch. Monkey leaping (33×51 mm) 2·30 1·70

1032 Eagle Owl

1992. Birds of Prey. Multicoloured.
N3112 10ch. Type **1032** 35 10
N3113 20ch. Common buzzard 80 40
N3114 30ch. African fish eagle 1·10 50
N3115 40ch. Steller's sea eagle 1·50 80
N3116 50ch. Golden eagle 1·90 90
MSN3117 78×59 mm. 80ch. Common kestrel (41×31 mm) 2·20 95

1033 Birthplace, Mt. Paekdu

1992. Birthday of Kim Jong Il. Mt. Paekdu. Multicoloured.
N3118 10ch. Type **1033** 15 10
N3119 20ch. Mountain summit 35 30
N3120 30ch. Lake Chon (crater lake) 50 40
N3121 40ch. Lake Sarryi 70 50
MSN3122 162×87 mm. 80ch. "Snow-storm on Mt. Paekdu" (41×63 mm) 1·70 95

1034 Service Bus

1992. Transport.
N3123 **1034** 10ch. multicoloured 15 10
N3124 - 20ch. multicoloured 35 30
N3125 - 30ch. multicoloured 50 40
N3126 - 40ch. multicoloured 70 50
N3127 - 50ch. multicoloured 95 70
N3128 - 60ch. multicoloured 1·10 80
DESIGNS: 20ch. to 60ch. Different buses and electric trams.

1035 Dancers and Emblem

1992. Spring Friendship Art Festival, Pyongyang.
N3129 **1035** 10ch. multicoloured 20 10

1036 Birthplace, Mangyongdae

1992. 80th Birthday of Kim Il Sung. Revolutionary Sites. Multicoloured.
N3130 10ch. Type **1036** (postage) 15 10
N3131 10ch. Party emblem and Turubong monument 15 10
N3132 10ch. Map and Ssuksom 15 10
N3133 10ch. Statue of soldier and Tongchang 15 10
N3134 40ch. Cogwheels and Taean 70 50
N3135 50ch. Chollima Statue and Kangson 70 50
N3136 1wn.20 Monument and West Sea Barrage (air) 2·40 1·90

1037 Kang Ban Sok

MSN3137 160×160 mm. 80ch. "April spring Friendship Art Festival" (41×63 mm) 1·70 95

1992. Birth Centenary of Kang Ban Sok (mother of Kim Il Sung). Sheet 80×103 mm.
MSN3138 **1037** 80ch. multicoloured 1·70 95

1038 Soldiers on Parade

1992. 60th Anniv of People's Army. Multicoloured.
N3139 10ch. Type **1038** 15 10
N3140 10ch. Couple greeting soldier 15 10
N3141 10ch. Army, air force and navy personnel 15 10

1039 Hurdling

1992. Olympic Games, Barcelona (2nd issue). Multicoloured.
N3142 10ch. Type **1039** 15 10
N3143 20ch. High jumping 35 30
N3144 30ch. Putting the shot 50 40
N3145 40ch. Sprinting 70 50
N3146 50ch. Long jumping 95 70
N3147 60ch. Throwing the javelin 1·10 80
MSN3148 105×85 mm. 80ch. Running 1·70 95

1040 Planting Crops

1992. Evolution of Man. Designs showing life in the New Stone Age (10, 20ch.) and the Bronze Age (others). Multicoloured.
N3149 10ch. Type **1040** (postage) 45 10
N3150 20ch. Family around cook-ing pot 70 30
N3151 30ch. Ploughing fields 1·10 40
N3152 40ch. Performing domestic chores 1·40 50
N3153 50ch. Building a dolmen (air) 2·40 70

1041 White-bellied Black Woodpecker

1992. Birds. Multicoloured.
N3154 10ch. Type **1041** 15 10
N3155 20ch. Common pheasant 45 30
N3156 30ch. White stork 50 40
N3157 40ch. Blue-winged pitta 80 50
N3158 50ch. Pallas's sandgrouse 1·00 45
N3159 60ch. Black grouse 1·40 80
MSN3160 98×63 mm. 80ch. Daurian starling 1·70 1·50

1042 Map and Hands holding Text

1992. 20th Anniv of Publication of North–South Korea Joint Agreement.
N3161 **1042** 1wn.50 multicoloured 2·75 2·10
MSN3162 112×76 mm. No. 3161×2 6·00 4·50

1043 Bougainvillea spectabilis

1992. Flowers. Multicoloured.
N3163 10ch. Type **1043** 15 10
N3164 20ch. Ixora chinensis 35 30
N3165 30ch. Dendrobium taysuwie 50 40
N3166 40ch. Columnea gloriosa 70 50
N3167 50ch. Crinum 95 70
N3168 60ch. Ranunculus asiaticus 1·10 80

1044 Venus, Earth, Mars and Satellite

1992. The Solar System. Multicoloured.
N3169 50ch. Type **1044** 95 70
N3170 50ch. Jupiter 95 70
N3171 50ch. Saturn 95 70
N3172 50ch. Uranus 95 70
N3173 50ch. Neptune and Pluto 95 70
MSN3174 90×71 mm. 80ch. Planet Earth 1·70 1·40
Nos. N3169/73 were issued together, *se-tenant*, forming a composite design.

1045 "470" Dinghy

1992. "Riccione '92" Stamp Fair. Multicoloured.
N3175 10ch. Type **1045** 15 10
N3176 20ch. Sailboard 35 30
N3177 30ch. Sailing dinghy 50 40
N3178 40ch. "Finn" dinghy 70 50
N3179 50ch. "420" dinghy 95 70
N3180 60ch. Fair emblem 1·10 80

1046 Moreno Mannini (defender)

1992. Sampdoria, Italian Football Champion, 1991. Multicoloured.
N3181 20ch. Type **1046** 35 30
N3182 30ch. Gianluca Vialli (forward) 50 40
N3183 40ch. Pietro Vierchowod (defender) 70 50
N3184 50ch. Fausto Pari (defender) 95 70
N3185 60ch. Roberto Mancini (forward) 1·20 80
N3186 1wn. Paolo Mantovani (club president) 1·90 1·50
MSN3187 92×66 mm. 1wn. Vialli and Riccardo Garrone (president of club sponsor) (51×33 mm) 1·90 1·50

1047 Black-belts warming up

1992. Eighth World Taekwondo Championship, Pyongyang. Multicoloured.
N3188 10ch. Type **1047** (postage) 15 10
N3189 30ch. "Roundhouse" kick 50 40
N3190 50ch. High kick 95 70
N3191 70ch. Flying kick 1·30 95
N3192 90ch. Black-belt breaking tiles with fist 1·70 1·30
MSN3193 93×75 mm. 1wn.20 Flight scene (33×51 mm) (air) 2·30 1·70

1048 Common Toad (Bufo bufo)

1992. Frogs and Toads. Multicoloured.
N3194 40ch. Type **1048** (postage) 70 50
N3195 40ch. Moor frog (Rana arvalis) 70 50
N3196 40ch. Rana chosenica 70 50
N3197 70ch. Common pond frog (Rana nigromaculata) 1·40 95
N3198 70ch. Japanese tree toad (Hyla japonica) 1·40 95
N3199 70ch. Rana coreana (air) 1·40 95

1049 Rhododendron mucronulatum

1992. World Environment Day. Multicoloured.
N3200 10ch. Type **1049** (postage) 25 10
N3201 30ch. Barn swallow 50 40
N3202 40ch. Stewartia koreana (flower) 70 50
N3203 50ch. Dictyoptera aurora (beetle) 95 70
N3204 70ch. Metasequoia glypto-stroboides (tree) 1·30 95
N3205 90ch. Chinese salamander 1·70 1·30
N3206 1wn. 20 Ginkgo biloba (tree) (air) 2·30 1·70
N3207 1wn. 40 Alpine bullhead 2·75 1·90

1050 Fin Whale (Balaenoptera physalus)

1992. Whales and Dolphins. Multicoloured.
N3208 50ch. Type **1050** 1·30 70
N3209 50ch. Common dolphin (Delphinus delphis) 1·30 70
N3210 50ch. Killer Whale (Orcinus orca) 1·30 70
N3211 50ch. Hump-backed whale (Megaptera nodosa) 1·30 70
N3212 50ch. Bottle-nosed whale (Berardius bairdii) 1·30 70
N3213 50ch. Sperm whale (Physeter catadon) (air) 1·30 70

1051 Mother and Chicks

1992. New Year. Roosters in various costumes. Multicoloured.
N3214 10ch. Type **1051** 15 10
N3215 20ch. Lady 35 30
N3216 30ch. Warrior 50 40
N3217 40ch. Courtier 70 50
N3218 50ch. Queen 95 70
N3219 60ch. King 1·10 80
MSN3220 112×80 mm. 1wn.20 Sultan 2·50 1·50

1052 Choe Chol Su (boxing)

1992. Gold Medal Winners at Barcelona Olympics. Multicoloured.
N3221 10ch. Type **1052** 15 10
N3222 20ch. Pae Kil Su (gymnastics) 35 30
N3223 50ch. Ri Hak Son (freestyle wrestling) 95 70
N3224 60ch. Kim Il (freestyle wrestling) 1·10 80

MSN3225 28×120 mm. Nos. N3221/4;
30ch. Flags of Spain and North
Korea, flame, gold medal and archer;
40ch. Church of the Holy Family
(Barcelona), games mascot and
emblem   4·00   3·00

1053 Golden
Mushroom

1993. Fungi. Multicoloured.
N3227	10ch. Type **1053**	15	10
N3228	20ch. Shaggy caps	35	30
N3229	30ch. *Ganoderma lucidum*	50	40
N3230	40ch. Brown mushroom	70	50
N3231	50ch. *Volvaria bombycina*	95	70
N3232	60ch. *Sarcodon aspratus*	1·10	80

MSN3233 59×60 mm. 1wn. Scarlet
caterpillar fungus   2·20   1·50

1054 *Keumkangsania
asiatica*

1993. Plants. Multicoloured.
N3234	10ch. Type **1054**	15	10
N3235	20ch. *Echinosophora koreensis*	35	30
N3236	30ch. *Abies koreana*	50	40
N3237	40ch. *Benzoin angustifolium*	70	50
N3238	50ch. *Abeliophyllum distichum*	95	70
N3239	60ch. *Abelia mosanensis*	1·10	80

MSN3240 73×93 mm. 1wn. *Pentactina
rupicola* (27×38 mm)   1·90   1·50

1055 League
Members and Flag

1993. Eighth League of Socialist Working Youth Congress.
Multicoloured.
N3241	10ch. Type **1055**	15	10
N3242	40ch. Flame, League emblem and text	70	50

1056 Phophyong
Revolutionary Site
Tower and March
Corps Emblem

1993. 70th Anniv of 1000-ri Journey for Learning.
N3243 **1056** 10ch. multicoloured   20   10

1057 Tower of
Juche Idea and
Grand Monument,
Mt. Wangjae

1993. 60th Anniv of Wangjaesan Meeting.
N3244 **1057** 5ch. multicoloured   10   10

1058 *Kimjomgil*
(begonia)

1993. 51st Birthday if Kim Jong Li. Multicoloured.
N3245 10ch. Type **1058**   20   10

MSN3246 170×95 mm. 1wn. Kim Il
Sung writing paean to Kim Jong Il
on his 59th birthday (50×41 mm)   1·90   1·20

1059 Pilot Fish

1993. Fish. Multicoloured.
N3247	10ch. Type **1059**	15	10
N3248	20ch. Japanese stingray	35	30
N3249	30ch. Opah	50	40
N3250	40ch. Coelacanth	70	50
N3251	50ch. Moara grouper	1·00	70

MSN3252 96×70 mm. 1wn.20 Mako
shark   2·75   1·50

1060/1064 *Spring on the Hill* (image scaled to 42% of
original size)

1993. 18th-century Korean Painting.
N3253	**1060**	40ch. multicoloured	70	50
N3254	**1061**	40ch. multicoloured	70	50
N3255	**1062**	40ch. multicoloured	70	50
N3256	**1063**	40ch. multicoloured	70	50
N3257	**1064**	40ch. multicoloured	70	50

Nos. N3253/7 were issued together, *se-tenant*, forming
the composite design illustrated.

1065 Violinist, Dancers and
Emblem

1993. Spring Friendship Art Festival, Pyongyang.
N3258 **1065** 10ch. multicoloured   20   10

1066 Books

1993. 81st Birthday of Kim Li Sung and Publication of his
Reminiscences *With the Country*. Multicoloured.
N3259 10ch. Type **1066**   20   10

MSN3260 140×105 mm. 1wn. Kim Il
Sung writing (62×412 mm)   2·00   1·30

1067 Kwangbok Street

1993. Pyongyang. Multicoloured.
N3261	10ch. Type **1067**	15	10
N3262	20ch. Chollima Street	35	30
N3263	30ch. Munsu Street	50	40
N3264	40ch. Moranbong Street	70	50
N3265	50ch. Thongil Street	1·00	70

MSN3266 115×74 mm. 1wn. Chang-
gwang street   1·90   1·50

1068 *Trichogramma
dendrolimi* (fly)

1993. Insects. Multicoloured.
N3267	10ch. Type **1068**	15	10
N3268	20ch. *Brachymeria obscurata* (fly)	35	30
N3269	30ch. *Metrioptera brachyptera* (cricket)	50	40
N3270	50ch. European field cricket	95	70
N3271	70ch. *Geocoris pallidipennis* (beetle)	1·40	95
N3272	90ch. *Cyphonony x dorsalis* (wasp) fighting spider	1·70	1·30

1069 Ri In Mo

1993. Return from Imprisonment of Ri in Mo (war
correspondent). Multicoloured.
N3273 10ch. Type **1069**   20   10

MSN3274 110×80 mm. 1wn.20 Ri in
Mo and flowers (47×35 mm)   2·50   1·50

1070 Footballers

1993. World Cup Football Championship, U.S.A.
N3275	**1070**	10ch. multicoloured	15	10
N3276	-	20ch. multicoloured	35	30
N3277	-	30ch. multicoloured	50	40
N3278	-	50ch. multicoloured	1·00	70
N3279	-	70ch. multicoloured	1·40	95
N3280	-	90ch. multicoloured	1·70	1·30

DESIGNS: 20ch. to 90ch. Various footballing scenes.

1071 Grey-headed
Woodpecker

1993. Birds. Multicoloured.
N3281	10ch. Type **1071**	15	10
N3282	20ch. King bird of paradise	35	30
N3283	30ch. Lesser bird of paradise	50	40
N3284	40ch. Paradise whydah	70	50
N3285	50ch. Magnificent bird of paradise	1·00	70
N3286	60ch. Greater bird of paradise	1·10	80

Nos. N3283/4 also commemorate "Indopex '93" international stamp exhibition, Surabaya.

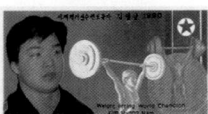

1072 Korean Peninsula and Flag (image scaled to 58% of
original size)

1993. Self-adhesive. Roul.
N3287 **1072** 1wn.50 multicoloured   2·50   1·90

No. N3287 is for any one of the six stamps which together make up the design illustrated. They are peeled
from a card backing.

1073 Kim Myong Nam
(weightlifting, 1990)

1993. World Champions. Multicoloured.
N3293	10ch. Type **1073**	15	10
N3294	20ch. Kim Kwang Suk (gymnas-tics, 1991)	35	30
N3295	30ch. Pak Yong Sun (table ten-nis, 1975, 1977)	50	40
N3296	50ch. Kim Yong Ok (radio direction-finding, 1990)	1·00	70
N3297	70ch. Han Yun Ok (taekwondo, 1987, 1988, 1990)	1·40	95
N3298	90ch. Kim Yong Sik (free-style wrestling, 1986, 1989)	1·70	1·20

1074 Cabbage and
Chilli Peppers

1993. Fruits and Vegetables. Multicoloured.
N3299	10ch. Type **1074**	15	10
N3300	20ch. Squirrels and horse chestnuts	35	30
N3301	30ch. Grapes and peach	50	40
N3302	40ch. Birds and persimmon	70	50
N3303	50ch. Tomatoes, aubergine and cherries	1·00	70
N3304	60ch. Radish, onion and garlic	1·10	80

1075 State
Arms

1993
N3305 **1075** 10ch. red   20   10

1076 Soldiers and Civilians

1993. 40th Anniv of Victory in Liberation War.
Multicoloured.
N3306	10ch. Type **1076**	20	10
N3307	10ch. Officer and soldier	20	10
N3308	10ch. Guided missiles on low-loaders on parade	20	10
N3309	10ch. Anti-aircraft missiles on lorries on parade	20	10
N3310	10ch. Self-propelled missile launchers (tracked vehicles) on parade	20	10
N3311	10ch. Machine gun emplace-ment (30×48 mm)	20	10
N3312	10ch. Soldier holding flag (bronze statue) (30×48 mm)	20	10
N3313	40ch. Soldiers and flags ("Let us become Kim Jims and Ri Su Boks of the 90s") (30×48 mm)	80	50
N3314	10ch. Kim Il Sung at strategic policy meeting	20	10
N3315	10ch. Kim Il Sung directing battle for Height 1211	20	10
N3316	10ch. Kim Il Sung at munitions factory	20	10
N3317	10ch. Kim Il Sung with tank commanders	20	10
N3318	10ch. Kim Il Sung with trium-phant soldiers	20	10
N3319	20ch. Kim Il Sung with artil-lery unit	40	30
N3320	20ch. Kim Il Sung encouraging machine gun crew	40	30
N3321	20ch. Kim Il Sung studying map of Second Front	40	30
N3322	20ch. Kim Il Sung with airmen	40	30
N3323	20ch. Musicians ("Alive is art of Korea")	40	30

MSN3324 Four sheets, (a) 150×90
mm; 80ch. Kim Il Sung beside tank
(39×50 mm); (b) 131×75 mm. 80ch.
Kim Il Sung and victory celebrations
(33×51 mm); (c) 1wn. Kim Il sung
making speech (47×35 mm); (d)
190×93 mm. 1wn. king Il Sung tak-
ing salute (38×49 mm)   7·75   4·25

1077 Choe Yong Do

1993. National Reunification Prize Winners. Multicoloured.

N3325	10ch. Type **1077**	20	10
N3326	20ch. Kim Ku	40	30
N3327	30ch. Hong Myong Hui	60	40
N3328	40ch. Ryo Un Hyong	80	50
N3329	50ch. Kim Jong Thae	1·10	75
N3330	60ch. Kim Chaek	1·30	85

1078 *Robinia* sp.

1993. "Taipei '93" International Stamp Exhibition, Taipeh. Multicoloured.

N3331	20ch. Type **1078**	40	30
N3332	30ch. "Hippeastrum"	60	40
MSN3333	75×105 mm. 1wn. Deer (33×51 mm)	2·10	1·60

1079 Newton

1993. 350th Birth Anniv (1992) of Sir Isaac Newton (mathematician and scientist). Multicoloured.

N3334	10ch. Type **1079**	20	10
N3335	20ch. Apple tree and formula of law of gravitation	40	30
N3336	30ch. Satellite, reflecting telescope, dish aerial, globe and rocket	70	40
N3337	50ch. Formula of binomial theorem	1·10	75
N3338	70ch. Newton's works and statue	1·60	1·00

1080 King Tongmyong shooting Bow

1993. Restoration of King Tongmyong of Koguryo's Tomb. Multicoloured.

N3339	10ch. Type **1080**	20	10
N3340	20ch. King Tongmyong saluting crowd	40	30
N3341	30ch. Restoration monument	70	40
N3342	40ch. Temple of the Tomb of King Tongmyong (horiz)	90	60
N3343	50ch. Tomb (horiz)	1·10	75
MSN3344	95×105 mm. 80ch. Kim Il Sung visiting tomb (41×63 mm)	1·90	1·60

1081 First North Korea and Thailand Stamps

1993. "Bangkok 1993" International stamp Exhibition, Thailand. Sheet 76×81 mm.

MSN3345	**1081** 1wn. 20 multicoloured	2·50	2·10

1082 *Cyrtopodium andresoni*

1993. Orchids. Multicoloured.

N3346	10ch. Type **1082**	20	10
N3347	20ch. *Cattleya*	40	30
N3348	30ch. *Cattleya intermedia Oculata*	70	40
N3349	40ch. *Potinaria Maysedo godensia*	90	60
N3350	50ch. Kim Il Sung flower	1·10	75

모택동탄생100돐
毛泽东诞生100周年
1893-1993

(1083)

1993. Birth Centenary of Mao Tse-tung (1st issue). No. MSN3006 optd with T **1083**.

MSN3351	95×75 mm. 80ch. multicoloured	1·90	1·60

See also Nos. N3352/**MS**N3357.

1084 Mao Tse-tung at Yanan, 1944

1993. Birth Centenary of Mao Tse-tung. Multicoloured.

N3352	10ch. Type **1084**	20	10
N3353	20ch. Seated portrait (Peking, 1960)	40	30
N3354	30ch. Casting a vote, 1953	70	40
N3355	40ch. With pupils at Shaoshan Secondary School, 1959	90	60
MSN3356	110×70 mm. 1wn. Mao Tse-tung and Pres. Kim Il Sung of North Korea (47×35 mm)	2·10	1·60
MSN3357	169×130 mm. Nos. N3352/ **MS**N3356 25ch. Mao Tse-tung proclaiming foundation of Chinese People's Republic, 1949 (47×35 mm); 25ch. Mao Tse-tung with son Mao An-ying (47×35 mm)	5·25	4·25

1085 Phungsan

1994. New Year. Dogs. Multicoloured.

N3358	10ch. Type **1085**	20	10
N3359	20ch. Yorkshire terriers	40	30
N3360	30ch. Gordon setter	70	40
N3361	40ch. Pomeranian	80	60
N3362	50ch. Spaniel with pups	1·20	85
MSN3363	80×66 mm. 1wn. Pointer	2·10	1·60

1086 Purple Hyosong Flower

1994. 52nd Birthday of Kim Jong Il. Multicoloured.

N3364	10ch. Type **1086**	20	10
N3365	40ch. Yellow hyosong flower	90	60
MSN3366	156×82 mm. 1wn. Kim Il Sung and Kim Jong surrounded by flowers (44×53 mm)	2·10	1·60

1087 Red and Black Dragon-eyed

1994. Goldfishes. Multicoloured.

N3367	10ch. Type **1087**	20	10
N3368	30ch. Red and white bubble-eyed	70	40
N3369	50ch. Red and white veil-tailed wenyu	1·10	75
N3370	70ch. Red and white fringe-tailed	1·60	1·00

1088 Crowd with Banners

1994. 20th Anniv of Publication of *Programme for Modelling the Whole Society on the Juche Idea* **by Kim Jong Il. Multicoloured.**

N3371	20ch. Type **1088**	25	10
MSN3372	145×95 mm. 1wn.20 Kim Jong Il making speech (41×63 mm)	2·50	1·60

1089 Wheat, Banner and Woman writing

1994. 30th Anniv of Publication of *Theses on the Socialist Rural Question in Our Country* **by Kim Il Sung. Multicoloured.**

N3373	10ch. Type **1089**	20	10
N3374	10ch. Electricity generating systems and pylon	20	10
N3375	10ch. Lush fields, grain and tractor	20	10
N3376	40ch. Modern housing, books, food crops and laboratory technician	90	60
N3377	40ch. Revellers	90	60
MSN3378	Two sheets, each 134×111 mm. (a) 1wn. KimIl Sung in field (38×59 mm); (b) 1wn. Peasants with Kim Il Jong (41×63 mm)	4·50	3·00

1090 *Mangyongbong-92* (ferry)

1994. Ships. Multicoloured.

N3379	20ch. Type **1090**	40	30
N3380	30ch. *Osandok* (freighter)	80	40
N3381	40ch. *Ryongaksan* (stern trawler)	90	60
N3382	50ch. Stern trawler	1·10	75
MSN3383	131×112 mm. Nos. 3379/82; 80ch.×2 *Maekjon-1* (passenger ship)	6·25	5·25

1091 National Flag

1994

N3384	**1091** 10ch. red and blue	25	10

1092 Birthplace and Magnolia (national flower)

1994. 82nd Birthday of Kim Il Sung. Multicoloured.

N3385	10ch. Type **1092**	20	10

N3386	40ch. Birthplace, Manyongdae, and Kim Il Sung flower	90	60
MSN3387	162×103 mm. 40ch.×5 Composite design of Lake Chon (crater lake of Mt. Paekdu) and score of *Song of General Kim Il Sung*	4·50	3·00

1093 *Chrysosplenium sphaerospermum*

1994. Alpine Plants on Mt. Paekdu. Multicoloured.

N3388	10ch. Type **1093**	20	10
N3389	20ch. *Campanula cephalotes*	40	30
N3390	40ch. *Trollius macropetalus*	90	60
N3391	40ch. *Gentiana algida*	90	60
N3392	50ch. *Sedum kamtschaticum*	1·10	75
MSN3393	78×64 mm. 1wn. *Dianthus repens*	2·10	1·60

1094 National Olympic Committee Emblem

1994. Centenary of International Olympic Committee. Multicoloured.

N3394	10ch. Type **1094**	20	10
N3395	20ch. Pierre de Coubertin (founder)	40	30
N3396	30ch. Olympic flag and flame	70	40
N3397	50ch. Emblem of Centennial Olympic Congress, Paris	1·10	75
MSN3398	Two sheets, each 75×105 mm. (a) 1wn. Torch carrier; (b) 1wn. Juan Antonio Samaranch (IOC President) and entrance headquarters	4·50	3·75

1095 Red Cross Launch ("Relief on the Sea")

1994. 75th Anniv of International Red Cross and Red Crescent Federation. Multicoloured.

N3399	10ch. Electric tram, pedestrians on footbridge and traffic lights ("Prevention of Traffic Accident")	20	10
N3400	20ch. Type **1095**	40	30
N3401	30ch. Planting tree ("Protection of Environment")	70	40
N3402	40ch. Dam ("Prevention of Drought Damage")	90	60

1994. No. N3287 surch 160 in circle.

N3403	**1072** 1wn.60 on 1wn.50 multicoloured	4·50	3·75

1097 Northern Fur Seal

1994. Marine Mammals. Multicoloured.

N3404	10ch. Type **1097**	20	10
N3405	40ch. Southern elephant seal	90	60
N3406	60ch. Southern sealion	1·40	95
MSN3407	Two sheets, (a) 80×130 mm. 20ch. Californian sealion; 30ch. Ringed seal; 50ch. Walrus. (b) 80×88nn. 1wn. Harp seal	4·75	4·25

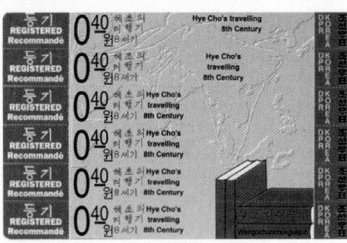

1098 Map of Asia and Books (image scaled to 57% of original size)

1994. 8th-century Travels of Hye Cho. Self-adhesive. Roul.
N3408 **1098** 40ch. multicoloured   70   50
No. N3408 is for any one of the six stamps which together make up the design illustrated. They are peeled from a card backing.

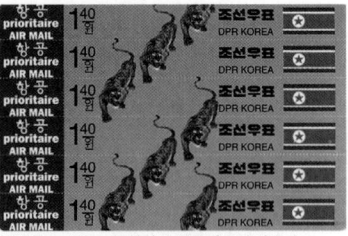

1099 Tigers (image scaled to 57% of original size)

1994. Self-adhesive. Roul.
N3409 **1099** 1wn.40 multicoloured   2·50   2·10
No. N3409 is for any one of the six stamps which together make up the design illustrated. They are peeled from a card backing.

1100 Kim Jong Il on Mt. Paekdu

1994. 30th Anniv of Kim Jong Il's Leadership of Korean Workers' Party. Two Sheets containing multicoloured designs as T 1100 showing various scenes featuring Kim Jong Il.
MSN3410 Two sheets. (a) 148×182 mm. 40ch. Type **1100**; 40ch With engineers surveying bay; 40ch. Visiting the set of *Star of Korea* (film); 40ch. Visiting Chongryu Restaurant; 40ch. Reviewing tank corps; 40k. Shaking hands with international figures. (b) 145×95 mm. 1wn. At desk (41×63 mm)   7·50   6·25

1101 "Turtle" Ships (image scaled to 57% of original size)

1994. Self-adhesive. Roul.
N3411 **1101** 1wn.80 multicoloured   3·00   2·50
No. N3411 is for any one of the six stamps which together make up the design illustrated. They are peeled from a card backing.

1102 Striped Bonnet

1994. Molluscs. Multicoloured.
N3412 30ch. Type **1102**   70   40
N3413 40ch. Equilateral venus   95   60
MSN3414 103×75 mm. 1wn.20 Bladder moon   2·75   2·10
MSN3415 Two sheets, each 127×73 mm. (a) Nos. N3413/MSN3414; 10ch. "Cardium muticum" (cockle). (b) Nos. N3412 and MSN3412 and MSN3414; 20ch. "Buccinum bayani" (whelk)   7·25   6·25

1103 Trapeze

1994. Circus Acrobatics. Multicoloured.
N3416 10ch. Type **1103**   20   10
N3417 20ch. Reino (Swedish acrobat) performing rope dance   40   30
N3418 30ch. Seesaw performer   70   40
N3419 40ch. Unicycle juggler   90   60

1104 Korean Script and "100"

1994. Birth Centenary of Kim Hyong Jik (father of Kim Il Sung). Multicoloured.
N3420 10c. Type **1104**   80   10
MSN3421 61×85 mm. 1wn. Kim Hyong Jik (30×48 mm)   2·10   1·60

1105 Jon Pong Jun and Battle Scene

1994. Centenary of Kabo Peasant War.
N3422 **1105** 10ch. multicoloured   25   10

1106 Inoue Shuhachi

1994. Award of First International Kim Il Sung Prize to Inoue Shuhachi (Director Genaral to Juche Idea International Institute). Sheet 103×78 mm.
MSN3423 **1106** 1wn.20 multicoloured   2·50   1·60
See also Nos. N3458/MSN3464.

1107 Workers and Banner

1994. Revolutionary Economic Strategy.
N3424 **1107** 10ch. multicoloured   25   10

1108 Onsong Fish

1994. Fossils. Multicoloured.
N3425 40ch. Type **1108**   90   60
N3426 40ch. Metasequoia   90   60
N3427 40ch. Mammoth teeth   90   60
N3428 80ch. Archaeopteryx   1·80   1·20

1109 "Acorus calamus"

1994. Medicinal Plants. Multicoloured.
N3429 20ch. Type **1109**   40   30
N3430 30ch. Arctium lappa   70   40
MSN3431 Two sheet. (a) 133×86 mm. 80ch. *Lilium lancifolium*; 80ch. *Codonopsis lanceolata*. (b) 56×83 mm. 1wn. Ginseng (vert)   5·50   4·25

1110 Ribbon Exercise

1994. Callisthenics. Multicoloured.
N3432 10ch. Type **1110**   20   10
N3433 20ch. Ball exercise   40   30
N3434 30ch. Hoop exercise   70   40
N3435 40ch. Ribbon exercise (different)   90   60
N3436 50ch. Club exercise   1·10   75

1111 Chou En-lai at Tianjun, 1919

1994. 96th Birth Anniv of Chou En-lai (Chinese statesman). Multicoloured.
N3437 10ch. Type **1111**   20   10
N3438 20ch. Arrival in Northern Shanxi from Long March   40   30
N3439 30ch. At Conference of Asian and African Countries, Bandung, Indonesia, 1955   70   40
N3440 40ch. Surrounded by children in Wulumuqi, Xinjiang Province   90   60
MSN3441 106×70 mm. 80ch. green, silver and black (Kim Il Sung proposing to Chou En-li during Korean visit, 1970) (46½×35 mm)   1·90   1·60
MSN3442 Two sheets, each 144×110 mm. (a) Nos. N3440/MSN3441; 20ch. Leading Nanchang Uprising, 1927 (46½×35 mm). (b) N3438/9 and MS3441; 20ch. At airport on return from foreign visit (46½×35 mm)   6·75   5·25

1113 Kim Il Sung as Youth, 1927

1994. Kim Il Sung Commemoration (1st issue). (a) As T **1113**. Each red, gold and black.
N3444 40ch. Type **1113**   90   60
N3445 40ch. Kim Il Sung and Kim Jong Suk   90   60
N3446 40ch. Kim Il Sung as young man   90   60

(b) Horiz designs as T **1115**. Each purple, gold and black.
N3447 40ch. Kim Il Sung making speech, Pyongyang, 1945   90   60
N3448 40ch. Kim Il Sung sitting at desk   90   60
N3449 40ch. Kim Il Sung at microphone   90   60

(c) Miniature sheet.
MSN3450 78×106 mm. 1wn. Kim Il Sung smiling (35×46 mm)   2·10   1·60
See also Nos. N3459/63.

1114 Player No. 4

1994. World Cup Football Championship, U.S.A. Multicoloured.
N3451 10ch. Type **1114**   20   10
N3452 20ch. Player No. 5   40   30
N3453 30ch. Player No. 6   70   40
N3454 40ch. Player No. 7   90   60
N3455 1wn. Player No. 8   2·10   1·60
N3456 1wn.50 Player No. 9   3·50   2·30

MSN3457 Two sheets. (a) 79×112 mm. 2wn.50 Stadium, players and trophy (41×48 mm); (b) 200×223 mm. 1wn.×6, each depicting player, trophy and different view   18·00   11·50

1115 Kim Il Sung making Radio Broadcast, 1950

1994. Kim Il Sung Commemoration (2nd issue). (a) Each green, gold and black.
N3458 40ch. Type **1115**   90   60
N3459 40ch. Kim Il Sung with four soldiers, 1951   90   60
N3460 40ch. Kim Il Sung and crowd of soldiers, 1953   90   60

(b) Multicoloured (N3463) or lilac, gold and black (others).
N3461 40ch. Kim Il Sung with workers at Chongjin Steel Plant, 1959   90   60
N3462 40ch. Kim Il Sung on Onchon Plain   90   60
N3463 40ch. Kim Il Sung at desk using telephone   90   60

(c) Miniature sheet.
MSN3464 78×106 mm. 1wn. Kim Il Sung and Kim Jong Il (35×47 mm)   2·10   1·60

1116 National Flags and Flowers

1994. Korean—Chinese Friendship. Multicoloured.
N3465 10ch. Type **1116**   90   60
MSN3466 79×100 mm. 1wn.20 black, grey and gold (Mao Tse-tung and Kim Il Sung) (53×44 mm)   2·50   2·10

1117 Ri Myon Sang and Score of *Snow Falls*

1994. Composers. Multicoloured.
N3467 50ch. Type **1117**   1·10   75
N3468 50ch. Pak Han Kyu and score of *Nobody Knows*   1·10   75
N3469 50ch. Ludwig van Beethoven and score of piano sonata No. 14   1·10   75
N3470 50ch. Wolfgang Amadeus Mozart and score of symphony No. 39   1·10   75

1118 National Emblem

1994
N3471 **1118** 1wn. green   2·40   1·60
N3472 **1118** 3wn. brown   6·25   4·75

1119 P. Wiberg (Alpine combined skiing)

1994. Winter Olympic Games, Lillehammer, Gold Medal Winners. Multicoloured.
N3473 10ch. Type **1119**   20   10
N3474 20ch. D. Compagnoni (slalom)   40   30
N3475 30ch. O. Baiul (figure skating)   70   40
N3476 40ch. D. Jansen (speed skating)   90   60
N3477 1wn. L. Yegorova (cross-country skiing)   2·10   1·60
N3478 1wn.50 B. Blair (speed skating)   3·25   2·30

MSN3479 Seven sheets, each 102×75 mm (a/f) or 131×895 mm (g). (a) 1wn. Norwegian skiing team and B. Daehile (Alpine combine); (b) 1wn. Gordeyeva and Grinkov (pairs figure skating); (c) 1wn. G. Hackl (luge); (e) 1wn. J. Weissflog (ski jumping); (f) 1wn. Kono, Ogiwara and Abe (cross-country skiing); (g.) 2wn.50 T. Moe (downhill) (50×35 mm)   18·00   11·50

1120 Pig Couple

1995. New Year. Year of the Pig. Multicoloured.

N3480	20ch. Type **1120**	40	30
N3481	40ch. Pigs carrying bucket and spade	90	60

MSN3482 40ch. Two sheets, each 72×70 mm. (a) 1wn. Adult pig greeting young pigs; (b) 1wn. Pig couple carrying pumpkin   4·75   4·25

See also No. **MS3533**.

1121 Pison Waterfalls, Mt. Myohyang

1995. 20th Anniv of World Tourism Organization. Multicoloured.

N3483	30ch. Tower of Juche Idea, Pyongyang	70	40
N3484	30ch. Type **1121**	70	40
N3485	30ch. Myogilsang (cliff-face carving of Buddha), Mt. Kumgang	70	40

1122 Mangyongdae, Badaogou and Badge

1995. 70th Anniv of 1000-ri (250 mile) Journey by Kim Il Sung to Restore Fatherland.

N3486	**1122** 40ch. multicoloured	90	60

1123 Monument bearing 50th Birthday Ode, Mt. Paekdu

1995. 53rd Birthday of Kim Jung Il. Multicoloured.

N3487	10ch. Type **1123**	20	10

MSN3488 Three sheets. (a) 75×90 mm. 20ch. Kim Il Sung and Kim Jong Il (horiz); 80ch, Kim Jong Il on balcony overlooking West Sea Barrage (horiz); (b) 90×75 mm. 40ch. Kim Jong Il in public park; 50ch. Kim Jong before memorial in Taesongsan Revolutionary Martyrs' Cemetery; (c) 96×75 mm. 1wn. Kim Jong Il on visit to Tyongsong Machine Complex, 1984 (31×50 mm)   6·25   5·25

1124 Reconstruction Monument

1995. Completion of Reconstruction of King Tangun's Tomb. Multicoloured.

N3489	10ch. Type **1124**	20	10
N3490	30ch. Bronze dagger on plinth	70	45
N3491	50ch. Monument inscribed with exploits of King Tangun	1·10	75
N3492	70ch. Gateway (horiz)	1·60	1·10

MSN3493 103×60 mm. 1wn.40 King Tangun   3·75   2·50

1125 Jamaedo Lighthouse

1995. Lighthouses. Multicoloured.

N3494	20ch. Type **1125**	40	20
N3495	1wn. Phido Lighthouse, West Sea Barrage	2·50	1·20

1126 Cracked Green Russula

1995. Fungi. Multicoloured.

N3496	20ch. Type **1126**	40	20
N3497	30ch. *Russula atropurpurea*	70	25

MSN3498 68×90 mm. 1wn. Kim Il Sung and children (29×41 mm)   2·10   1·50

1127 Couple planting Tree

1995. Tree Planting Day.

N3499	**1127** 10ch. multicoloured	20	10

1128 Birthplace, Mangyongdae

1995. 20th Anniv of Kim Il Sung's Visit to China.

N3500	1129 10ch. multicoloured	20	10
N3501	40ch. multicoloured	90	60

MSN3502 84×80 mm. 50ch. purple, gold and black   2·20   1·50

DESIGNS: As T **1129** but vert—20ch. Deng Xiaoping of China sitting in armchair. 60×38 mm—50ch. Kim Il Sung and Deng Xiaoping.

1129 Deng Xiaoping waving

1995. 20th Anniv of Kim Il Sung's Visit to China. Multicoloured.

N3503	10ch. Type **1129**	20	10
N3504	20ch. Deng Xiaoping of China sitting in armchair (vert)	40	20

MSN3505 84×80 mm. 50ch. Kim Il Sung and Deng Xiaoping (60×38 mm)   1·10   65

1130 Venue

1995. 40th Anniv of Asian–African Conference, Bandung.

N3506	**1130** 10ch. black, buff and red	20	10
N3507	– 50ch. brown, gold and black	1·10	45

MSN3508 88×85 mm. 1wn. brown and black   2·10   1·50

DESIGN: 50ch. Kim Il Sung receiving honorary Doctorate at Indonesia University.

1131 Emblem

1995. International Sports and Cultural Festival for Peace, Pyongyang. Multicoloured.

N3509	20ch. Type **1131**	40	20
N3510	40ch. Dancer	90	40
N3511	40ch. Inoki Kanji (leader of Sports Peace Party of Japan)	90	40

MSN3512 87×70 mm. 1wn. Rikidozan (wrestler)   2·10   1·50

1132 Amethyst

1995. Minerals.

N3513	**1132** 20ch. multicoloured	40	20

1133 Eurasian Tree Sparrow

1995. White Animals. Multicoloured.

N3514	40ch. Type **1133**	90	40
N3515	40ch. *Stichopus japonicus* (sea slug)	90	40

1134 Ostrea

1995. Fossils. Multicoloured.

N3516	50ch. Type **1134**	1·10	45
N3517	1wn. Cladophlebis (fern)	2·10	1·00

1135 Chess

1995. Traditional Games. Multicoloured.

N3518	30ch. Type **1135**	70	25
N3519	60ch. Taekwondo	1·30	60
N3520	70ch. Yut	1·60	65

1136 National Flag and Korean Hall, Tokyo

1995. 40th Anniv of Association of Koreans in Japan.

N3521	**1136** 1wn. multicoloured	2·10	1·00

1137 Weightlifting

1995. Olympic Games, Atlanta (1996). Multicoloured.

N3522	50ch. Type **1137**	1·10	45
N3523	50ch. Boxing	1·10	45

MSN3524 62×78 mm. 1wn. Clay-pigeon shooting   2·10   1·50

DESIGNS: 50ch. Kim Il Sung receiving honorary Doctorate at Indonesia University. 1wn. Kim Il Sung and Kim Jong Il at conference tenth anniversary ceremony, Djakarta.

1138 *Russula citrina*

1995. Fungi. Multicoloured.

N3525	40ch. Type **1138**	90	40
N3526	60ch. Black trumpets	1·30	60
N3527	80ch. Shaggy caps	1·80	80

1139 Kim Il Sung greeting Pres. Mugabe of Zimbabwe

1995. First Death Anniv of Kim Il Sung. Four sheets containing designs as T **1139** inscriptions in black, frames in gold, centre colour listed.

MSN3528 Four sheets (a) 109×85 mm. 10ch. blue; 70ch. sepia. (b) 130×66 mm. 20ch. blue; 50ch. chocolate. (c) 129×66 mm. 30ch. blue; 40ch. purple. (d) 80×107 mm. 1wn. plum   7·00   4·75

DESIGNS—VERT: 70ch. With King Norodom Sihanouk of Cambodia. HORIZ: Kim Il Sung being awarded title of Honorary Doctor of Algeria University, 1975; 30ch. With Pres. Ho Chi Minh of Vietnam; 40ch. Greeting Che Cuevara; 50ch. With Pres. Fidel Castro of Cuba; 1wn. Giving speech.

1140 Mt. Paekdu and Revolutionaries

1995. 50th Anniv of Liberation. Multicoloured.

N3529	10ch. Type **1140**	20	10
N3530	30ch. Map of Korea and family	70	25
N3531	60ch. Medal	1·30	60

MSN3532 Two sheets, each 120×110 mm. (a) 2×20ch. Revolutionary and crowd with banners; (b) No. N3530×2; 2×40ch. Revolutionaries   6·00   4·25

1995. "Singapore '95" International Stamp Exibition. Sheet 139×90 mm. Multicoloured.

MSN3533 Nos. N3480/1, each×2   2·40   1·70

1141 Markswoman

1995. First Military World Games, Rome.

N3534	**1141** 40ch. multicoloured	90	40

1142 Kim Il Sung With Prime Minister Chou En-lai of China, 1970

1995. Korean—Chinese Friendship. Three sheets containing designs as T **1142** inscriptions in black, frames in gold, centre colour listed below.

MSN3535 Three sheets. (a) 50ch. purple (Type **1142**); 50ch. green (With Deng Ying-chao of China, 1979). (b) 85×100 mm. 80ch. green (Greeting Mao Tse-tung of China, 1958) (vert). (c) 85×100 mm. 80ch. purple (In Hamburg with Prime Minister Chou En-lai of China) (vert)   5·75   4·00

1143 Emblem and Banner

1995. 50th Anniv of Korean Workers' Party. Multicoloured.

N3536	10ch. Type **1143**	20	10
N3537	20ch. Statue of worker, peasant and intellectual	40	20
N3538	30ch. Party monument	70	25
MSN3539	108×75 mm. 1wn. Kim Il Sung (founder) (38×50 mm)	2·10	1·50

1144 Arch of Triumph, Pyongyang

1995. 50th Anniv of Kim Il Sung's Return to Homeland.

N3540	**1144** 10ch. multicoloured	20	10

1145 Tuna

1995. Designs as T **1145**. Each brown and black. (a) Fishes.

N3541	40ch. Type **1145**	95	40
N3542	50ch. Pennant coralfish (with two bands)	1·20	45
N3543	50ch. Needlefish	1·20	45
N3544	60ch. Seascorpion	1·40	60
N3545	5wn. Emperor angelfish	11·50	5·00

(b) Buildings on Kwangbok Street, Pyongyang.

N3546	60ch. Circus	1·40	65
N3547	70ch. Flats	1·60	65
N3548	80ch. Ryanggang Hotel	1·80	80
N3549	90ch. Tower apartment block (vert)	1·90	85
N3550	1wn. Sosan Hotel (vert)	2·10	1·00

(c) Machines.

N3551	10ch. Kamsusan tipper truck	30	10
N3552	20ch. Bulldozer	60	20
N3553	30ch. Excavator	80	25
N3554	40ch. Earth mover (vert)	1·30	40
N3555	10wn. "Chollima 80" tractor (vert)	21·00	10·00

(d) Animals.

N3556	30ch. Giraffe	70	25
N3557	40ch. Ostrich (vert)	90	40
N3558	60ch. Bluebuck (vert)	1·30	60
N3559	70ch. Bactrian camel	1·60	65
N3560	3wn. Indian rhinoceros	6·25	3·00

(e) Sculptures of Children.

N3561	30ch. Boy holding bird (vert)	70	25
N3562	40ch. Boy with goose (vert)	90	40
N3563	60ch. Girl with geese (vert)	1·30	60
N3564	70ch. Boy and girl with football (vert)	1·60	75
N3565	2wn. Boy and girl arguing over football (vert)	4·50	2·00

1146 Kim Hyong Gwon

1995. 90th Birth Anniv of Hyong Gwon (uncle of Kim Il Sung). Sheet 90×70 mm.

MSN3566	**1146** 1wn. black and gold	2·10	1·50

1147 Guinea Pig

1996. Rodents. Multicoloured.

N3567	20ch. Type **1147**	40	20
N3568	20ch. Squirrel	40	20
N3569	30ch. White mouse	70	25

1148 Emblem, Badge and Flag

1996. 50th Anniv of League of Socialist Working Youth.

N3570	**1148** 10ch. multicoloured	20	10

1149 Restoration Mounument

1996. Reconstruction of Tomb of King Wanggon. Multicoloured.

N3571	30ch. Type **1149**	70	25
N3572	40ch. Entrance gate	90	40
N3573	50ch. Tomb	1·10	45

1150 Teng Li-Chuang (singer)

1996. Sheet 130×86 mm.

MSN3574	**1150** 49ch. multicoloured	1·20	60

1151 Kim Song Sung

1996. Third Asian Games, Harbin, China. Speed Skaters. Sheet 130×81 containing T **1151** and similar vert design. Multicoloured.

MSN3575	30ch. Type **1551**; 30ch. Ye Qiaobo	1·50	1·00

1152 Jong Il Peak and Kim Jong Il Flower

1996. 54th Birthday of Kim Jong Il. Multicoloured.

N3576	10ch. Type **1152**	20	10
MSN3577	96×78 mm. 80ch. Kim Jong Il and servicemen in snow (35×78 mm)	1·80	1·20

1153 Pairs Skating

1996. Fifth Paektusan Prize Figure Skating Championships. Multicoloured.

N3578	10ch. Type **1153**	20	10
N3579	20ch. Pairs skating (different)	40	20
N3580	30ch. Pairs skating (different)	70	25
N3581	50ch. Women's individual skating	1·10	45
MSN3582	100×116 mm. No. 3575/82.	2·40	1·70

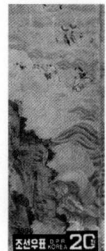
1154 Left-hand detail

1996. *Folk Tail* (screen painting) by Ryu Suk. Sheet 206×84 mm containing T **1154** and similar vert designs. Multicoloured.

MSN3583	8×20ch. Composite design of the painting	3·50	2·40

1155 Farm Worker

1996. 50th Anniv of Agrarian Reform Law.

N3584	**1155** 10ch. multicoloured	20	10

1156 1946 20ch. Stamp and Tower of Juche Idea

1996. 50th Anniv of First North Korean Stamps.

N3585	**1156** 1wn. multicoloured	2·10	1·00

1157 Yangzhou, China

1996. Centenary of founding of Chinese Imperial Post. Two sheets each 108×90 mm containing Type **1157** or similar horiz designs. Multicoloured.

MSN3586	Two sheets (a) 50ch. Type **1157**; (b) 50ch. Taihu Lake, Jiangsu	4·50	3·00

1158 Birthplace, Mangyongdae

1996. 83rd Birthday of Kim Il Sung. Multicoloured.

N3587	10ch. Type **1158**	20	10
MSN3588	105×115 mm. 1wn. *Eternal Image* (portrait of Kim Il Sung) (41×62 mm)	2·10	1·50

1159 Gateway

1996. "China '96" Asian International Stamp Exhibition, Peking. Landmarks in Zhejiang. Multicoloured.

N3589	10ch. Type **1159**	20	10
N3590	10ch. Haiyin Pool	20	10
MSN3591	105×80 mm. Pantuo Stone (60×38 mm)	1·30	85

1160 Hopscotch

1996. Children's Games. Multicoloured.

N3592	20ch. Type **1160**	40	20
N3593	40ch. Shuttlecock	90	40
N3594	50ch. Sledging	1·10	45

1161 Association Pamphlets

1996. 60th Anniv of Association for Restoration of the Fatherland.

N3595	**1161** 10ch. multicoloured	20	10

1162 Ri Po lk

1996. 120th Birth Anniv of Ri Po lk (grandmother of Kim Il Sung). Sheet 80×90 mm.

MSN3596	**1162** 1wn. grey, black and gold	2·10	1·50

1163 Arctic Fox

1996. Polar Animals. Multicoloured.

N3597	50ch. Type **1163**	1·20	50
N3598	50ch. Polar bear	1·20	50
N3599	50ch. Emperor penguins	1·20	50
N3600	50ch. Leopard seals	1·20	50

1164 Boy Saluting

1996. 50th Anniv of Korean Children's Union. Multicoloured.

N3601	10ch. Type **1164**	20	10
MSN3602	83×98 mm. 1wn. *There's Nothing to envy in the World* (painting of Kim Il Sung with Union members) (33×51 mm)	2·10	1·50

1165 Steam Locomotive

1996. Railway Locomotives. Multicoloured.

N3603	50ch. Type **1165**	1·20	50
N3604	50ch. Electric locomotive (green livery)	1·20	50
N3605	50ch. Steam locomotive (facing right)	1·20	50
N3606	50ch. Diesel locomotive (red and yellow livery)	1·20	50

1166 Kim Chol Ju

1996. 80th Birth Anniv of Kim Chol Ju (brother of Kim Il Sung). Sheet 58×77 mm.

MSN3607	**1166** 1wn.50 brown, gold black	3·75	2·50

1167 Open Book and Characters

1996. 760th Anniv of Publication of *Complete Collection of Buddhist Scriptures printed from 80,000 Wooden Blocks.*

N3608 **1167** 40ch. multicoloured   95   45

1168 Worker using Microphone

1996. 50th Anniv of Labour Law.

N3609 **1168** 50ch. multicoloured   30   15

1169 Eastern Broad-billed Roller

1996. Birds. (1st series). 110×92 mm containing T **1169** and similar horiz designs. Multicoloured.

MSN3610 Type **1169**; 40ch. Yellow-rumped flycatcher; 50ch. European cuckoo   3·25   2·30

1170 Ye Qiaobo

1996. Third Asian Winter Games, Harbin, China (2nd issue). As No. **MS**N3575 but with right hand-stamp changed.

MSN3611 30ch. Type **1151**; 30ch. Type **1170**   1·50   1·10

1171 Kumsusan Memorial Palace

1996. Second Death Anniv of Kim Il Sung. Multicoloured.

N3612 10ch. Type **1171**   20   10

MSN3613 Three sheets. (a) 116×71 mm. 1wn. Statue of Kim Il Sung, Kumsusan Memorial Palace (29×41 mm). (b) 80×106 mm. 1wn. Bars of *The Leader will always be with Us* (44×53 mm). (c) 115×105 mm. 1wn. Crowd visiting statue of Kim Il Sung, Manus Hill (34×51 mm) Set of 3 sheets   7·00   5·00

1172 Kim Il Sung meeting Jiang Zemin of China, 1991

1996. 35th Anniv of Korean–Chinese Treaty for Friendship, Co-operation and Mutual Assistance.

N3614 **1172** 10ch. brown, gold and black   20   10
N3615 – 10ch. green, gold and black   20   10
MSN3616 70×80 mm. 80ch. ultramarine, gold and black   1·90   1·40

DESIGNS—VERT: 10ch. Kim Il Sung meeting Pres. Mao Zedong of China, 1954. HORIZ: 80ch. Kim Il Sung meeting Deng Xiaoping of China, 1982.

1173 Football and Ancient Greek Athletes

1996. Centenary of Modern Olympic Games and Olympic Games, Atlanta. Multicoloured.

N3617 50ch. Type **1173**   1·30   55

N3618 50ch. Tennis, Olympic Anthem and 1896 5l. Greek stamp   1·30   55
N3619 50ch. Throwing the hammer and advertisement poster for first modern olympics   1·30   55
N3620 50ch. Baseball and Olympic stadium, Atlanta   1·30   55

1174 Couple

1996. 50th Anniv of Sex Equality Laws.

N3621 **1174** 10ch. multicoloured   35   15

1996. Birds (2nd series). Sheet 110×92 mm containing horiz design as T **1169**. Multicoloured.

MSN3622 10ch. crested shelduck; 40ch. Demoiselle crane; 50c. Mute Swan   3·25   2·30

1175 State Arms and Symbols of Industry and Communications

1996. 50th Anniv of Nationalization of Industries.

N3623 **1175** 10ch. bistre and brown   30   15

1176 Boy with Ball

1996. 50th Anniv of UNICEF. Multicoloured.

N3624 10ch. Type **1176**   25   10
N3625 20ch. Boy with building blocks   45   25
N3626 50ch. Boy eating melon   1·30   55
N3627 60ch. Girl playing accordion   1·50   70

1177 Pae Kil Su (men's pommel) (N. Korea)

1996. First Asian Gymnastics Championships, Changsha, China. Sheet 167×127 mm containing T **1177** and similar vert designs. Multicoloured.

MSN3628 15ch. Type **1177**; 15ch. Li Jing (China); 15ch. Chen Cui Ting on rings (China); 15ch. Kim Kwang Suk (asymmetrical bars) (N. Korea)   1·60   1·10

1178 University Buildings, Pyongyang

1996. 50th Anniv of Kim Il Sung University.

N3629 **1178** 10ch. multicoloured   25   10

1179 Tiger

1996. World Conservation Union Congress, Montreal, Canada. Multicoloured.

N3630 50ch. Type **1179**   1·40   55
N3631 50ch. Royal spoonbill   1·40   55
MSN3632 80×66 mm. 80ch. Dove-hand protecting sapling growing from globe (horiz)   2·30   1·60

1180 Red Flag and Tower of Juche Idea

1996. 70th Anniv of Down-with-Imperialism Union.

N3633 **1180** 10ch. multicoloured   35   15

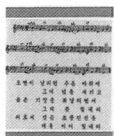

1181 Score of Theme Song from "Red Mountain Ridge" (film)

1996. 44th Death Anniv of Huang Ji Guang (Chinese volunteer in Korean War).

MSN3634 142×80 mm. 10ch. multicoloured (Type **1181**); 30ch. brown, silver and black (Huang Ji Guang); 30ch. multicoloured Huang Ji Guang) blocking gun muzzle with body)   1·80   1·30

1182 Archeozoic Era

1996. History of the Earth. Sheet 160×70 mm containing T **1182** and similar vert designs. Multicoloured.

MSN3635 50ch. Type **1182**; 50ch. Proterozoic era; 50ch. Palaeozoic era; 50ch. Mesozoic era; 50ch. Cainozoic era   6·25   4·50

1183 Japanese Eel

1996. Freshwater Fish. Multicoloured.

N3636 20ch. Type **1183**   65   25
N3637 20ch. Menada grey mullet (*Liza haematocheila*)   65   25
MSN3638 74×53 mm. 80ch. Silver carp   2·30   1·50

1184 Soldiers and Supreme Commander's Flag

1996. Fifth Anniv of Appointment of Kim Jong Il as Supreme Commander of the People's Army.

N3639 **1184** 20ch. multicoloured   50   25

1185 Ox Driver (Kim Tu Ryang)

1997. New Year. Year of the Ox. Multicoloured.

N3640 70ch. Type **1185**   2·00   85
N3641 70ch. Bronze ritual plate of two bulls and a tiger   2·00   85
N3642 70ch. Boy with bull (ceramic)   2·00   85
N3643 70ch. Boy flautist sitting on bull (sculpture)   2·00   85
MSN3644 83×82 mm. 80ch. *People's support of the Front* (drawing, Jong Jong Yo) (60×38 mm)   2·20   1·60

1186 Left-hand Detail

1997. *Flowers and Butterflies* by Nam Kye U. Multicoloured.

N3645 50ch. Type **1186**   1·40   60
N3646 50ch. Centre detail   1·40   60
N3647 50ch. Right-hand detail   1·40   60

Nos. N3645/7 were issued together, *se-tenant*, forming a composite design of the painting.

1187 Kitten with Dogs in Basket

1997. Paintings of Cats and Dogs. Multicoloured.

N3648 50ch. Type **1187**   1·40   60
N3649 50ch. Pup in vine-wreathed basket, kitten and pumpkin   1·40   60
MSN3650 Two sheets, each 96×114 mm. (a) 50ch.×2, Kitten in basket of vegetables, pup, fruit and flowers; 50ch. Kitten in basket of flowers, pup and ball of wool; No. N3648. (b) 50c.×2, Kittens, pup and vegetables (as in sheet a); No. 3649 Set of 2 sheets   6·75   4·00

1188 Bank of China

1997. Return of Hong Kong to China. Sheet 145×100 mm containing T **1188** and similar vert designs. Multicoloured.

MSN3651 20ch. Type **1188**; 20ch. Building with spire; 20ch. High-rise buildings   3·75   3·00

1189 Birthplace, Mt. Paekdu

1997. 55th Birthday of Kim Jong Il. Multicoloured.

N3652 10ch. Type **1189**   35   15

MSN3653 Two sheets, each 64×86 mm. (a) 1wn.Kim Jong Il inspecting farm equipment (47×53 mm); (b) 1wn. Kim Jong Il receiving flowers from soldier (47×35 mm) Set of 2 sheets   5·50   3·75

1190 Pair

1997. Sixth Paektusan Prize International Figure Skating Championships, Pyongyang. Multicoloured.

N3654 50ch. Type **1190**   1·40   60
N3655 50ch. Pair (mauve)   1·40   60
N3656 50ch. Pair (green)   1·40   60

1191 Kye Sun Hui

1997. North Korean Gold Medal in Women's Judo at Olympic Games, Atlanta. Sheet 90×100 mm.
MSN3657 **1191** 80ch. multicoloured   2·20   1·60

1192 Choe Un A

1997. Choe Un A (competitor in World Go championships at seven years). Sheet 90×110 mm.
MSN3658 **1192** 80ch. multicoloured   2·20   1·60

1193 "Prunus ansu"

1997. Apricots. Multicoloured.
N3659 50ch. Type **1193**   1·50   65
N3660 50ch. *Prunus mandshurica*   1·50   65
N3661 50ch. Hoeryong white apricot (*Prunus armeniaca*)   1·50   65
N3662 50ch. Puksan apricot (*Prunus sibirica*)   1·50   65

1194 Foundation Monument

1997. 80th Anniv of Foundation of Korean National Association.
N3663 **1194** 10ch. brown and green   35   10

1195 Sapling

1997. 50th Anniv of Reforestation Day. Multicoloured.
N3664 10ch. Type **1195**   35   15
MSN3665 90×100 mm. 1wn. Kim Il Sung planting sapling on Munsa Hill   2·20   1·50

1196 Birthplace, Mangyongdae

1997. 85th Birth Anniv of Kim Il Sung. Multicoloured.
N3666 10ch. Type **1196**   25   10
N3667 20ch. Sliding Rock (horiz)   50   25
N3668 40ch. Warship Rock (horiz)   1·10   50
MSN3669 Two sheets. (a) 110×90 mm. 1wn. Kim Il Sung in crowd (50×41 mm). (b) 100×120 mm. 1wn. Kim Il Sung on flowered hill-top (33×51 mm) Set of 2 sheets   5·50   3·75

1197 Cap Badge and Modern Weapons

1997. 65th Anniv of People's Army. Multicoloured.
N3670 10ch. Type **1197**   25   10
MSN3671 75×90 mm. 1wn. Soldier applauding Kin Il Sung and Kim Jong Il (35×49 mm)   2·75   1·90

1198 Map of Korea

1997. 25th Anniv of Publication of North—South Korea joint Agreement.
N3672 10ch. Type **1198**   25   10
MSN3673 105×70 mm. 1wn. Kim Il Sung's Autograph Monument, Phammunjom (60×38 mm)   2·75   1·90

1199 Tower of Juche Idea, People and Flag

1997. Posters reflecting Joint New Year Newspaper Editorials. Multicoloured.
N3674 10ch. Type **1199**   25   10
N3675 10ch. Man with flag   25   10
N3676 10ch. Soldier, miner, farmer, intellectual and bugler   25   10

1200 Exhibition Centre

1997. International Friendship Exhibition, Myohyang Mountains. Four sheetd containing designs as T **1200**. Multicoloured.
MSN3677 Four sheets, each 105×120 mm. (a) 70ch. Type **1200**. (b) 70ch. Statue of Kim Il Sung in entrance hall; (c) 70ch. *Native Home in Mangyongdae* (ivory sculpture from China) (horiz); (d) 70ch. Stuffed crocodile holding cups on salver and wooden ash tray (from Nicaragua) Set of 4 sheets   7·50   5·25

1201 Memorial Post and Blazing Fortress

1997. 60th Anniv of Battle of Pochonbo.
N3678 **1201** 40ch. multicoloured   1·10   50

1202 Kim Il Sung transplanting Rice

1997. 50th Anniv of Kim Il Sung's Visit to Mirin Plain Paddy-fields. Two sheets, each 75×105 mm, containing designs as T **1202**.
MSN3679 Two sheets. (a) 1wn. black and gold (Type **1202**); (b) 1wn. multicoloured (Kim Il Sung inspecting rice-transplanting machine) Set of 2 sheets   6·25   4·25

1203 Signing Nanjing Treaty, 1842

1997. Return og Hong Kong to China. Two sheets containing multicoloured designs as T **1203**.
MSN3680 Two sheets. (a) 124×117 mm. 20ch. Type **1203**; 20ch. Signing China—Britain Joint Statement, Peking, 1984; 20ch. Deng Xiaoping and Margaret Thatcher; 20ch. Jiang Zemin and Tong Jiahua (Mayor of Hong Kong), 1996. (b) 124×95 mm. 97 mm. Deng Xiaoping (circular, diameter 42 mm) (pair sold at 1wn.80) Set of 2 sheets   5·00   3·50

1204 *Redlichia chinensis*

1997. Fossils. Multicoloured.
N3681 50ch. Type **1204**   1·40   60
N3682 1wn. "Ptychoparia coreanica"   2·75   1·30

1205 Kim Il Sung at Kim Chaek Ironworks, June 1985

1997. Third Death Anniv of Kim Il Sung. Multicoloured.
N3683 50ch. Kim Il Sung at microphones (party conference, October 1985)   1·40   60
N3684 50ch. Type **1205**   1·40   60
N3685 50ch. Kim Il Sung and farmers holding wheat (Songsin Co-operative Farm, Sadong District, 1993)   1·40   60
N3686 50ch. Performing artists applauding Kim Il Sung, 1986   1·40   60
N3687 50ch. Kim Il Sung at Jonchon Factory, Jagang Province, 1991   1·40   60
N3688 50ch. Kim Il Sung receiving flowers at People's Army Conference, 1989   1·40   60

1206 Blindman's Buff

1997. Children's Games. Multicoloured.
N3689 30ch. Type **1206**   85   35
N3690 60ch. Five stones   1·60   80
N3691 70ch. Arm wrestling   2·00   85

1207 Spring

1997. Women's National Costumes. Multicoloured.
N3692 10ch. Type **1207**   25   10
N3693 40ch. Summer   1·10   50
N3694 50ch. Autumn   1·40   60
N3695 60ch. Winter   1·60   80

1208 Aerial View

1997. Chongryu Bridge, Pyongyang. Multicoloured.
N3696 50ch. Type **1208**   1·40   60
N3697 50ch. Chongryu Bridge and birds   1·40   60

1209 Sun, Magnolias and Balloons

1997. 85th Anniv of Juche Era and Sun Day. Multicoloured.
N3698 10ch. Type **1209**   25   10
MSN3699 85×115 mm. 1wn. Kim Il Sung (circular, diameter 45 mm)   2·75   2·00

1210 Korean Text and Kim Il Sung University

1997. 20th Anniv of Publication of Theses on Socialist Education.
N3700 **1210** 10ch. multicoloured   25   10

1211 Tupolev Tu-134

1997. 20th Anniv of Korean Membership of International Civil Aviation Oraganization. Three sheets, each 165×58 mm. containing designs as T **1211**. Multicoloured.
MSN3701 Three sheets. (a) 2×20ch. Type **1211**; (b) 2×30ch. Tupolev Tu-154; (c) 2×50ch. Illyushin IL-62   5·75   4·00

1212 Chonbul Peak

1997. Tenth Anniv of Korean Membership of World Tourism Organization. Mt Chilbo. Multicoloured.
N3702 50ch. Type **1212**   1·40   60
N3703 50ch. Sea-Chilbo (coast)   1·40   60
N3704 50ch. Rojok Peak   1·40   60

1213 Podok Hermitage

1997. Kumgang Mountains. Multicoloured.
N3705 50ch. Type **1213**   1·40   60
N3706 50ch. Kumgang Gate   1·40   60

1214 School, Pupil and Mt. Paekdu

1997. 50th Anniv of Mangyongdae Revolutionary School.
N3707 **1214** 40ch. multicoloured   1·10   50

1215 Lion

1997. Animals presented as Gifts to Kim Il Sung. Multicoloured.

N3708	20ch. Type **1215** (Ethiopia, 1987)	50	25
N3709	30ch. Jaguar (Japan, 1992)	85	35
N3710	50ch. Barbary sheep (Czechoslovakia, 1992)	1·40	60
N3711	80ch. Scarlet macaw (Austria, 1979)	2·20	1·00

1216 Bust

1997. 27th Anniv of Participation in Korean War by Chinese People's Volunteers. Qu Shao Yun. Sheet 145×80 mm containing T **1216** and similar vert designs. Multicoloured.

MSN3712	10ch. Statue; 30ch. Type **1216**; 30ch. Qu Shao Yun on fire	2·00	1·40

1217 Ten-pin Bowling

1997. Sports. Multicoloured.

N3713	50ch. Type **1217**	1·40	60
N3714	50ch. Golf	1·40	60
N3715	50ch. Fencing	1·40	60

1218 Snails

1997. Snails. Multicoloured.

N3716	50ch. Type **1218**	1·50	60
N3717	50ch. Two snails on leaf	1·50	60
N3718	50ch. Snail laying eggs	1·50	60

1219 Shanghai

1997. International Stamp and Coin Exhibition, Shanghai. Sheet 145×199 mm containing T **1219** and similar vert design.

MSN3719	30ch. Type **1219**; 50ch. Shanghai (different)	2·20	1·60

1220 "Juche 87" and Temple

1997. New Year. Year of the Tiger. Multicoloured.

N3720	10ch. Type **1220**	25	10
N3721	50ch. Tiger in rocket (24×34 mm)	60	35
N3722	50ch. Tiger steering ship (24×34 mm)	60	35
MSN3723	(a) 112×75 mm. 80ch. Tiger driving train (24×34 mm). (b) 82×115 mm. Nos. 3721/2; 80ch. As No. **MS**3723a	4·50	3·25

1221 Birthplace, Hoeryong

1997. 80th Birth Anniv of Kim Jong Sok (revolutionary). Multicoloured.

N3724	10ch. Type **1221**	25	10
MSN3725	85×115 mm. 1wn. Kim Jong Suk (41×50 mm)	2·75	1·90

1222 Skiing

1998. Winter Olympic Ganes, Nagano, Japan. Multicoloured.

N3726	20ch. Type **1222**	25	10
N3727	40ch. Speed skating	60	25

1223 Birthdate and Celebration Ribbon

1998. 50th Birth Anniv of Kim Jong Il. Multicoloured.

N3728	10ch. Type **1223**	25	10
MSN3729	3wn. Log cabin (birthplace, Mt. Paekdu)	4·25	3·00

1224 Korean Tigers

1998. Wildlife Paintings. Multicoloured.

N3730	50ch. Type **1224**	75	35
N3731	50ch. Manchurian cranes	75	35
MSN3732	102×157 mm. 50ch. Nos. N3730/1; 50ch. Bears; 50ch. Racoon dogs	3·00	2·10

1225 Route Map, Birthplace at Mangyongdae and Trail Followers

1998. 75th Anniv of 1000-ri (250 mile) Journey by Kim Il Sung.

N3733	**1225** 10ch. multicoloured	25	10

1226 Soldiers and Balloons

1998. Fifth Anniv of Appointment of Kim Jong Il as Chairman of National Defence Commission.

N3734	**1226** 10ch. multicoloured	25	10

1227 Flags and Birthplace, Mangyongdae

1228 Kim Il Sung as Child

1998. 86th Birth Anniv of Kim Il Sung. Multicoloured.

N3735	**1227** 10ch. multicoloured	25	10
MSN3736	Eight sheets, each 84×155 mm. (a) 80ch. Type **1228**; (b) 80ch. As student (wearing cap with rectangular badge); (c) 80ch. Commander of revolutionary army (wearing cap with star badge); (d) 80ch. In jacket and tie (three-quarter face) 80ch. In army uniform; (f) 80ch. In Mao jacket; (g) 80ch. In jacket and tie (full-face); (h) 80ch. Wearing glasses Set of 8 sheets	9·00	6·25

1229 United Front Tower and Moranbong Theatre

1998. 50th Anniv of North–South Conference, Pyongyang.

N3737	**1229** 10ch. brown, blue and black	25	10

1230 Players and Championship Emblem

1998. World Cup Football Championship, France. Multicoloured.

N3738	30ch. Type **1230**	35	15
N3739	50ch. Player winning ball and emblem	75	35
MSN3740	62×87 mm. 80ch. Tackling and emblem	1·10	80

1231 Cabbages

1998. Vegetables. Multicoloured.

N3741	10ch. Type **1231**	25	10
N3742	40ch. Radishes	50	25
N3743	50ch. Spring onions	60	35
N3744	60ch. Cucumbers	85	40
N3745	70ch. Pumpkins	1·00	45
N3746	80ch. Carrots	1·10	50
N3747	90ch. Garlic	1·20	60
N3748	1wn. Peppers	1·40	70

1232 Countryside in May (Jong Jong Yo)

1998. Paintings. Multicoloured.

N3749	60ch. Type **1232**	1·00	35
N3750	1wn.40 Dance (Kim Yong Jun)	2·20	85
MSN3751	80×80 mm. 3wn. Heart to Heart talk with a Peasant (Yu Yong Gwan) (59×58 mm.)	4·25	3·00

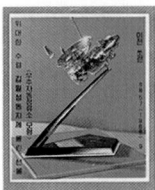

1233 Model of Automatic Space Station (from U.S.S.R.)

1998. International Friendship Exhibition, Myohyang Mountains (2nd series). Multicoloured.

N3752	1wn. Type **1233**	1·40	60
N3753	1wn. Ceramic flower vase (from Egypt)	1·40	60
N3754	1wn. "Crane" (statuette, from Billy Graham (evangelist))	1·40	60
MSN3755	86×100 mm. 1wn. claret and black (Kim Il Sung) (35×56 mm)	1·40	95

1234 Research Ship, Buoy and Dolphins in Globe and Hydro- meteorological Headquarters

1998. International Year of the Ocean. Multicoloured.

N3756	10ch. Type **1234**	35	15

N3757	80ch. Sailing dinghies and mother with child	1·10	70
MSN3758	128×105 mm. 5wn. Vasco da Gama (vert)	6·75	4·75

1235 Stone Age Implement

1998. Korean Central History Museum, Pyongyang. Multicoloured.

N3759	10ch. Type **1235**	25	10
N3760	2wn.50 Fossil skull of monkey	3·50	1·70
MSN3761	80×75 mm. 4wn. claret, grey and black (Kim Il Sung visiting museum) (60×38 mm)	5·75	4·00

1236 Commander of Hedgehog Unit and Squirrel

1998. "Squirrels and Hedgehogs" (cartoon film). Multicoloured.

N3762	20ch. Type **1236**	25	10
N3763	30ch. Commander of hedgehog unit receiving invitation to banquet	35	15
N3764	60ch. Weasel ordering mouse to poison bear	85	45
N3765	1wn.20 Squirrel with poisoned bear	1·90	85
N3766	2wn. Weasel and mice invade Flower Village	2·75	1·30
N3767	2wn.50 Hedgehog scout rescues squirrel	3·50	1·70

1237 Ri Sung Gi and Molecular Model

1998. Second Death Anniv of Ri Sung Gi (inventor of vinalon material). Multicoloured.

N3768	40ch. Type **1237**	60	25
MSN3769	80×65 mm. 80ch. Ri Sung Gi working in laboratory	1·10	80

1238 Tiger Cub

1998. Young Mammals. Multicoloured.

N3770	10ch. Type **1238**	25	10
N3771	50ch. Donkey foal	75	50
N3772	1wn.60 Elephant	2·40	1·70
N3773	2wn. Two lion cubs	2·75	2·00

1239 "Victory" (Liberation War Monument, Pyongyang) and Medal

1998. 45th Anniv of Victory in Liberation War.

N3774	**1239** 10ch. brown and pink	25	15
MSN3775	Two sheets, each 62×87 mm. multicoloured. (a) 2w. "Gaz-67" jeep and route map of Kim Il Sung's wartime inspections (30×48 mm). (b) 2wn. "Kim Il Sung inspecting Frontline" (painting) (48×30 mm) Set of 2 sheets	5·50	3·75

1240 *White Herons in Forest*

1998. Embroidery. Multicoloured.

N3776	10ch. Type **1240**	25	15
N3777	40ch. *Carp*	1·90	1·30
N3778	1wn.20 *Hollyhock*	1·90	1·30
N3779	1wn.50 *Cockscomb*	2·20	1·60
MSN3780	80×65 mm. 4wn. *Pine and Cranes*	5·75	4·00

1241 *Pouch*

1998. Traditional Costume Adornments. Multicoloured.

N3781	10ch. Type **1241**	25	10
N3782	50ch. *Tassels*	75	50
N3783	1wn.50 *Hairpin*	2·10	1·50
N3784	1wn.90 *Silver knife*	2·75	1·90

1242 *Rocket and State Flag*

1998. Launch of first Korean Artificial satellite "Kwangmyongsong 1".

N3785	40ch. Type **1242**	60	45
MSN3786	81×115 mm. 1wn.50 Rocket and satellite orbit (41×63 mm)	2·40	1·70

1243 *Kim Jong Il Flower*

1998. Re-election of Kim Jung Il as Chairman of National dfence Commission. Multicoloured.

N3787	10ch. Type **1243**	25	15
MSN3788	69×94 mm. 1wn. Kim Jonh II (circular, diameter 42 mm)	1·40	95

1244 *Tower of Juche Idea, State Arms and Flag*

1998. 50th Anniv of Democratic Republic (1st issue). Multicoloured.

N3789	10ch. Type **1244**	25	15
N3790	1wn. Painting *The Founding of the Democratic People's Republic of Korea, Our Glorious Fatherland* (Kim Il Sung waving from balcony) (48×30 mm)	1·40	95
N3791	1wn. Painting *Square of Victory* (Kim Il Sung and crowd with banners) (48×30 mm)	1·40	95
N3792	1wn. Poster *The Sacred Marks of the Great Leader Kim Il Sung will shine on this Land of Socialism* (Kim Il Sung with produce against panoramic background of Korea) (48×30 mm)	1·40	95

1245 *"Let Us Push Ahead with the Forced March for Final Victory"*

1998.

N3793	**1245**	10ch. multicoloured	25	15

1246 *State Flag and Arms forming "50"*

1998. 50th Anniv of Democratic Republic (2nd issue). Two sheets containing T **1246** or similar multicoloured design.

MSN3794	Two sheets. (a) 108×84 mm. 40ch. Type **1246**; (b) 108×125 mm. 1wn. Celebration Parade (31×38 mm) Set of 2 sheets	2·20	1·60

1247 *Cycling*

1998. Olympic Games, Sydney, Australia (2000). Multicoloured.

N3795	20ch. Type **1247**	25	15
N3796	50ch. Football	75	50
N3797	80ch. Show jumping	1·10	80
N3798	1wn.50 Throwing the javelin	2·20	1·60
MSN3799	57×80 mm. 2wn.50 Basketball	3·75	2·50

1248 *Cyclamen persicum*

1998. Plants presented as Gifts to Kim Jong Il. Multicoloured.

N3800	20ch. Type **1248** (France, 1994)	35	25
N3801	2wn. *Dianthus chinensis* var. *laciniatus* (Japan, 1994)	2·75	1·90

1249 *Oral Vaccination*

1998. National Vaccination Day.

N3802	**1249**	40ch. multicoloured	60	45

1250 *Leopard*

1998. The Leopard. Multicoloured.

N3803	1wn. Type **1250**	1·50	1·00
N3804	1wn. Leopard in snow	1·50	1·00
N3805	1wn. Leopard looking to left	1·50	1·00
N3806	1wn. Leopard's face	1·50	1·00

1251 *Canal*

1998. Land and Environment Conservation Day. Multicoloured.

N3807	10ch. Type **1251**	25	10
N3808	40ch. Motorway, tower blocks and lorry	65	45

MSN3809	85×71 mm. 1wn. Kim Il Sung shovelling earth to signal start of Pothong River improvement	1·50	1·00

1252 *Emblem and Milan Cathedral*

1998. "Italia98" International Stamp Exhibition, Milan, Italy. Sheet 108×90 mm.

MSN3810	2wn. multicoloured	3·00	2·10

1253 *Peng Dehuai and Kim Il Sung*

1998. Birth Centenary of Peng Dehuai (commander of Chinese People's Volunteers in Korea Liberation War). Sheet 131×112 mm containing T **1253** and similar multicoloured designs.

MSN3811	20ch. Type **1253**; 20ch. Mao Tse-tung (Chinese communist leader), Chou Enlai (Chinese states-man) and Peng Dehuai; 30ch. Peng Dehuai in marshal's uniform (27×38 mm); 30ch. "On the Front" (painting), He Kong De) (27×38 mm)	1·60	1·10

1254 *Liu Shaoqi*

1998. Birth Centenary of Liu Shaoqi (Chairman of Chinese People's Republic, 1959–68). Multicoloured.

N3812	10ch. Type **1254**	25	10
N3813	20ch. Liu Shaoqi and Mao Tse-tung	40	20
N3814	30ch. Liu Shaoqi and his daughter, Xiao Xiao	55	40
N3815	40ch. Liu Shaoqi and his wife, Wang Guangmei	65	45
MSN3816	100×70 mm. 1wn. Liu Shaoqi and Kim Il Sung (46½×35 mm.)	1·50	1·00

1255 *Victory in Yonsong Monument, Yonan Fortress and Banners*

1998. 400th Anniv of Victory in Korean–Japanese War. Multicoloured.

N3817	10ch. Type **1255**	25	10
N3818	30ch. Naval Victory in Myon-gryang Monument, General Ri Sun Sin and "turtle" ship	40	30
N3819	1wn.60 Monument to Hyujong in Kwangwon province, Hyujong (Buddhist priest), sword and helmet	2·40	1·70
MSN3820	12×68 mm. 10wn. "Sea Battle off Hansan Islet in 1592" (painting)	15·00	12·00

1256 *Dish Aerial, Artificial Satellite, Globe and Relay Tower*

1998. 15th Anniv of North Korean Membership of Intersputnik.

N3821	**1256**	1wn. dp grn & grn	1·60	1·10

1257 *Goat*

1998

N3822	**1257**	10ch. black and green	30	20
N3823	**1257**	1wn. black and red	1·70	1·20

1258 *"A Floral Carriage of Happiness"* (sculpture) and Palace

1998. Mangyongdae School-children' palace. Multicoloured.

N3824	40ch. Type **1258**	70	50
MSN3825	85×4? mm. 1wn. Quotation of Kim Il Sung "Children are the treasure of our country. Korea of the future is theirs"	1·70	1·20

1259 *Emblem*

1998. 50th Anniv of Universal Declaration of Human Rights.

N3826	**1259**	20ch. multicoloured	30	20

1260 *Reeves's Turtle*

1998. Reptiles and Amphibians. Multicoloured.

N3827	10ch. Type **1260**	30	20
N3828	40ch. Skink	70	50
N3829	60ch. Loggerhead turtle	1·00	70
N3830	1wn.20 Leatherback turtle	2·00	1·40

Nos. N3827/30 were issued together, *se-tenant*, forming a composite design.

1261 *Thajong Rock*

1998. Mt. Chilbo. Multicoloured.

N3831	30ch. Type **1261**	40	30
N3832	50ch. Peasant Rock	85	60
N3833	1wn.70 Couple Rock	2·75	1·90

1262 *Ri Mong Ryong marrying Song Chun Hyang*

1998. Tale of Chun Hyang. Multicoloured.

N3834	40ch. Type **1262**	70	50
N3835	1wn.60 Pyon Hak Do watching Chun Hyang	2·50	1·90
N3836	2wn.50 Ri Mong Ryong and Chun Hyang	4·00	3·00
MSN3837	110×95 mm. Nos. N3834/6; 2wn. Chun Hyang in wedding veil	10·50	8·75

1263 *Chollima Statue*

1998. Pyongyang Monuments.

N3838 ·	**1263**	10ch. red	20	15
N3839	A	10ch. red	20	15
N3840	B	10ch. red	20	15

N3841	**A**	20ch. orange	30	20
N3842	**1263**	30ch. orange	55	40
N3843	**A**	40ch. yellow	70	50
N3844	**B**	40ch. yellow	70	50
N3845	**1263**	70ch. green	1·10	85
N3846	**B**	70ch. green	1·10	85
N3847	**B**	1wn.20 green	2·00	1·50
N3848	**1263**	1wn.50 green	2·50	1·90
N3849	**A**	2wn. blue	3·50	2·50
N3850	**B**	3wn. blue	5·00	3·75
N3851	**1263**	5wn. blue	8·50	6·25
N3852	**A**	10wn. violet	17·00	12·50

DESIGNS: A, Arch of Triumph; B, Tower of Juche Idea.

1264 Rabbit meeting Lion

1999. New Year. Year of the Rabbit. Multicoloured.

N3853	10ch. Type **1264**	30	20
N3854	1wn. Rabbit with mirror and lion	1·70	1·30
N3855	1wn.50 Lion in trap	2·50	1·90
N3856	2wn.50 Rabbit	4·00	3·00
MSN3857	160×70 mm. 10ch. Type **1264**; 1wn. No. N3854; 1wn.50 No. N3855; 2wn.50 No. N3856	8·50	6·50

1265 Automatic Rifle and Star

1999. 40th Anniv of Worker-Peasant Red Guards.

N3858	**1265**	10ch. multicoloured	30	20

1266 Log Cabin (birthplace, Mt. Paekdu)

1999. 57th Birth Anniv of Kim Jong Il.

N3859	**1266**	40ch. multicoloured	70	55

1267 Cranes, Rice Sheaf and "35"

1999. 35th Anniv of Publication of Theses on the Socialist Rural Question in Our Country by Kim Il Sung.

N3860	**1267**	10ch. multicoloured	30	20

1268 Korean Script and Crowd

1999. 80th Anniv of 1 March Uprising.

N3861	**1268**	10ch. black and brown	30	20

1269 16th-century "Turtle" Ship

1999. "Australia '99" International Stamp Exhibition, Melbourne.

N3862	**1269**	2wn. multicoloured	2·40	1·80
MSN3863		100×75 mm. **1269** 2wn. multicoloured	2·75	2·00

1270 Birthplace, Mangyondae

1999. 87th Birth Anniv of Kim Il Sung.

N3864	**1270**	10ch. brown, flesh and grey	30	20
MSN3865		68×95 mm. 2wn. multicoloured (Kim Il Sung 94×62 mm)	2·75	2·00

1271 Player

1999. 45th Table Tennis Championship, Belgrade, Yugoslavia.

N3866	**1271**	1wn.50 multicoloured	2·00	1·50

1272 Korean Sports Stamps and Emblem

1999. "iBRA'99" International Stamp Exhibition, Nuremberg, Germany.

N3867	**1272**	1wn. multicoloured	1·30	95

1273 *Benzoin obtus*

1999. 40th Anniv of Central Botanical Garden, Mt. Taesong, Pyongyang. Multicoloured.

N3868	10ch. Type **1273**	30	20
N3869	30ch. *Styrax obassia*	40	30
N3870	70ch. *Petunia hybrida*	1·00	75
N3871	90ch. *Impatiens hybrida*	1·30	95
MSN3872	65×75 mm. 2wn. Kimilsung-flower and Kimjongil (begonia)	2·75	2·00

1274 Chimpanzee and Rhinoceros

1999. 40th Anniv of Central Zoo, Mt. Taesong, Pyongyang. Multicoloured.

N3873	50ch. Type **1274**	70	55
N3874	60ch. Manchurian crane and deer	85	65
N3875	70ch. Common zebra and kangaroo	1·00	75
MSN3876	95×75 mm. 2wn. Tiger	2·75	2·00

1275 Light Industry Hall

1999. Three Revolutions Museum, Ryonmotdong, Pyongyang. Multicoloured.

N3877	60ch. Type **1275**	85	65
N3878	80ch. Heavy Industry Hall	1·10	85

1276 Methods of Communication, Satellite and Globe

1999. 20th Anniv of Asia–Pacific Telecommunications Union.

N3879	**1276**	1wn. multicoloured	1·40	1·10

1277 Monument

1999. 60th Anniv of Victory in Battle of Musan.

N3880	**1277**	10ch. multicoloured	30	20

1278 Seagulls

1999. 190th Birth Anniv of Charles Darwin (naturalist). Multicoloured.

N3881	30ch. Type **1278**	40	30
N3882	50ch. Bats	70	55
N3883	1wn. Dolphins	1·40	1·10
N3884	1wn.20 Man on horseback	1·70	1·30
N3885	1wn.50 Dancer	2·10	1·60
MSN3886	76×67 mm. 2wn. Charles Darwin (26×39 mm)	3·50	2·75

1279 *Princess Margarita in a White Dress*

1999. 400th Birth Anniv of Diego Velazquez (artist). Multicoloured.

N3887	50ch. Type **1279**	70	55
N3888	50ch. *Men drawing Water from a Well*	70	55
N3889	3wn.50 *Self-portrait*	4·50	3·50
MSN3890	68×118 mm. No. N3889	4·75	3·75

1280 Rimyongsu Power Station

1999. Hydro-electric Power Stations. Multicoloured.

N3891	50ch. Type **1280**	70	55
N3892	1wn. Jangjasan Power Station	1·40	1·10

1281 Players tackling

1999. Third Women's World Football Championship, U.S.A. Multicoloured.

N3893	1wn. Type **1281**	1·40	1·10
N3894	1wn.50 Player No. 3 and player wearing blue and white strip tackling	2·10	1·60
N3895	1wn.50 Player and goalkeeper	2·10	1·60
N3896	2wn. Player No. 7 and player wearing blue strip	2·75	2·10

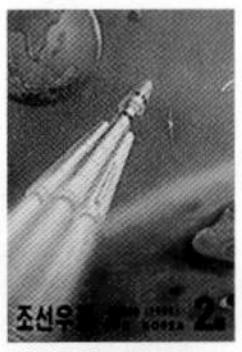
1282 The Earth, Space Rocket and Mars

1999. Exploration of Planet Mars. Sheet 110×75 mm. containing T **1282** and similar vert designs. Multicoloured.

MSN3897	2wn. Type **1282**; 2wn. Satellite orbiting Mars; 2wn. Probe landing on Mars	8·50	6·50

1283 Man with Candlesticks

1999. *The Nation and Destiny* (Korean film). Scenes from the film. Multicoloured.

N3898	1wn. Type **1283**	1·30	95
N3899	1wn. Woman holding gun and man in white suit	1·30	95
N3900	1wn. Man behind bars	1·30	95
N3901	1wn. Man with protective goggles on head	1·30	95

1284 Samil Lagoon

1999. Mt. Kumgang. Multicoloured.

N3902	20ch. Type **1284**	30	20
N3903	40ch. Samson Rocks (vert)	55	45
N3904	60ch. Rock, Kumgang Sea	85	65
N3905	80ch. Kuryong Waterfall (vert)	1·00	75
N3906	1wn. Kwimyon Rock (vert)	1·30	95

1285 Emblem, Girl and Dove

1999. 125th Anniv of Universal Postal Union. Sheet 87×67 mm.

MSN3907	**1285**	2wn. multicoloured	3·00	2·40

1286 France 1870 20c. Stamp and North Korea 20ch. 1946 Stamp

1999. "Philexfrance99" International Stamp Exhibition, Paris. Sheet 102×77 mm.

MSN3908	**1286**	2wn.50 multicoloured	3·50	2·50

1287 Mercedes Motor Car

1999. Fifth Death Anniv of Kim Il Sung. Multicoloured.

N3909	1wn. Type **1287**	1·70	1·30
N3910	1wn. Railway carriage	1·70	1·30

1288 Chinese Characters and Mangyong Hill

1999. 105th Birth Anniv of Kim Hyong Jik (revolutionary).

N3911	**1288**	10ch. multicoloured	30	20

1289 Patterned Vessel

1999. Ceramics. Multicoloured.

N3912	70ch. Type **1289**	1·00	75
N3913	80ch. Wit and Beauty jar	1·10	85

N3914	1wn. Patterned vase	1·30	95
N3915	1wn.50 Celadon kettle	2·00	1·50
N3916	2wn.50 White china vase	3·25	2·50

1290 Silver Carp

1999. Fish Breeding. Multicoloured.

N3917	50ch. Type **1290**		70	55
N3918	1wn. Common carp	1·40	1·10
N3919	1wn.50 Spotted silver carp	2·10	1·60

1291 Map and Crowd

1999. Year of National Independence and Solidarity.

| N3920 | **1291** 40ch. multicoloured | 55 | 45 |

1292 Samjiyon with Maps of Japan and Korea

1999. 40th Anniv of Repatriation of Korean Nationals in Japan.

| N3921 | **1292** 1wn.50 multicoloured | 2·50 | 1·90 |

1293 Symbols of Prosperity

1999

| N3922 | **1293** 40ch. multicoloured | 55 | 45 |

1294 100 m Race

1999. World Athletics Championships, Seville, Spain. Multicoloured.

N3923	30ch. Type **1294**	45	35
N3924	40ch. Hurdles	60	45
N3925	80ch. Discus	1·20	80

1295 Acalypha hispida

1999. Plants presented to Kim Il Sung. Multicoloured.

N3926	40ch. Type **1295**	75	55
N3927	40ch. Allamanda neriifolia	75	55
N3928	40ch. Begonia x hiemalis	75	55
N3929	40ch. Fatsia japonica	75	55
N3930	40ch. Streptocarpus hybrida	75	55
N3931	40ch. Streptocarpus rexii	75	55

Nos. N3926/31 were issued together, *se-tenant*, forming a composite design.

1296 Play a Flute to call the Phoenix

1999. "CHINA 1999" International Stamp Exhibition and 22nd UPU Congress, Beijing. T **1296** and similar vert designs. Multicoloured.

MSN3932 40ch. Type **1296**; 40ch. "Relics kept in Bamboo Field"; 40ch. "Six Friends in a Pine Forest"; 40ch. "Lady's Morning Dressing"   3·00   2·20

1297 Grifola frondosa

1999. Mushrooms. Multicoloured.

N3933	40ch. Type **1297**	75	55
N3934	60ch. Lactarius volemus	1·00	80
N3935	1wn. Coriolus versicolor	1·80	1·30

1298 Aporocactus flagelliformis

1999. Cacti. Multicoloured.

N3936	40ch. Type **1298**	75	55
N3937	50ch. Astrophytum ornatum	90	65
N3938	60ch. Gymnocalycium michano vichii	1·00	80

1299 Rat

1999. Animals of Eastern Zodiac. Two sheets, each 110×160 mm containing T **1299** and similar circular multicoloured designs.

MSN3942 Two sheets (a) 10ch. Type **1299**; 10ch. Ox; 10ch. Tiger; 10ch Rabbit; 10ch. Dragon; 10ch. Snake. (b) 10ch. Horse; 10ch. Sheep; 10ch. Monkey; 10ch. Cockerel; 10ch. Dog; Sow and piglets (each sold at 1wn.)   3·50   2·75

1300 Shrimp

1999. Crustacea. Multicoloured.

N3943	50ch. Type **1300**	90	65
N3944	70ch. Shrimp	1·20	90
N3945	80ch. Lobster	1·50	1·10

1301 Jong Song Ok (marathon runner)

1999. Victory of Jong Song Ok at World Athletic Championship, Seville.

| N3946 | 40ch. Type **1301** | 75 | 55 |

MSN3947 90×70 mm. 2wn. Jong Song Ok (vert)   3·50   2·75

1302 Mt. Kumgang, North Korea

1999. 50th Anniv of North Korean–China Diplomatic Relations. Multicoloured.

| N3948 | 40ch. Type **1302** | 75 | 55 |
| N3949 | 60ch. Mt. Lushan, China | 1·00 | 80 |

MSN3950 142×93 mm. Nos. N3948/9   2·10   1·70

1303 Deng Xiaoping

1999. Return of Macao to China. Four sheets containing T **1303** and similar multicoloured designs.

MSN3951 Four sheets. (a) 155×100m. 20ch. Type **1303** (green frame); 20ch. Jiang Zemin (President of People's Republic of China) and He Houba (mayor of Macao Special Administrative Region) (green frame); 80ch. Mao Tse-tung (green frame); (b) 155×100 mm. As No. MSN3951a but gold frames; (c) 90×122 mm. 1wn. Jiang Zemin (green frame) (circular design); (d) As MSN3951c but with gold frame   8·25   6·75

1304 Steel Worker holding Torch

2000. New Year. 40th Anniv of 19 April Rising.

| N3952 | **1304** 10ch. multicoloured | 30 | 20 |

1305 Yellow Dragon

2000. Koguryo Era Tomb Murals, Jian. Multicoloured.

| N3953 | 70ch. Type **1305** | 1·20 | 90 |

MSN3954 90×60 mm. 1wn.60 Blue dragon (51×33 mm)   3·00   2·20

1306 Weeding

2000. *Rural Life* (anon). Showing details from the painting. Multicoloured.

N3955	40ch. Type **1306**	75	55
N3956	40ch. Hemp cloth weaving	75	55
N3957	40ch. Threshing	75	55
N3958	40ch. Riverside market	75	55

1307 Views across Lake Chou

2000. Mt. Paektu. Multicoloured.

N3959	20ch. Type **1307**	45	35
N3960	20ch. Eagle-shaped rock formation	45	35
N3961	20ch. Owl-shaped rock formation	45	35

1308 Chuibari Mask Dance

2000. Pongsan Mask Dance. Depicting masks and characters from component dances. Multicoloured.

N3962	50ch. Type **1308**	90	65
N3963	80ch. Ryangban Mask Dance	1·50	1·10
N3964	1wn. Malttugi Mask Dance	2·10	1·60

1309 Cat

2000. Cats. Multicoloured.

N3965	50ch. Type **1309**	1·00	80
N3966	50ch. Three kittens	1·00	80
N3967	50ch. Mother and kittens	1·00	80

1310 Singapura Cat

2000. Fauna. Multicoloured.

N3968	2wn. Type **1310**	3·75	2·75
N3969	2wn. Blue Abyssinian cat	3·75	2·75
N3970	2wn. Oriental cat	3·75	2·75
N3971	2wn. Scottish fold tabby cat	3·75	2·75
N3972	2wn. Shiba inu	3·75	2·75
N3973	2wn. Yorkshire terrier	3·75	2·75
N3974	2wn. Japanese chin	3·75	2·75
N3975	2wn. Afghan hound	3·75	2·75
N3976	2wn. Przewalski's horse	3·75	2·75
N3977	2wn. Grey cob	3·75	2·75
N3978	2wn. White horse rearing	3·75	2·75
N3979	2wn. Donkeys	3·75	2·75
N3980	2wn. Panda in tree	3·75	2·75
N3981	2wn. Panda eating	3·75	2·75
N3982	2wn. Panda scratching against tree	3·75	2·75
N3983	2wn. Mother and cub	3·75	2·75
N3984	2wn. Two polar bears (Ursus maritimus)	3·75	2·75
N3985	2wn. Mother and cub	3·75	2·75
N3986	2wn. Standing bear	3·75	2·75
N3987	2wn. Bear lying down	3·75	2·75
N3988	2wn. Mexican lance-headed rattlesnake (Crotalus polystictus)	3·75	2·75
N3989	2wn. Scarlet king snake (Lampropeltis triangulum elapsoides)	3·75	2·75
N3990	2wn. Green tree python (Chondropython viridis)	3·75	2·75
N3991	2wn. Blood python (Python curtus)	3·75	2·75
N3992	2wn. Corythosaurus	3·75	2·75
N3993	2wn. Psittacosaurus	3·75	2·75
N3994	2wn. Megalosaurus	3·75	2·75
N3995	2wn. Muttaburrasaurus	3·75	2·75
N3996	2wn. Burmeister's porpoise (Phocoena spinipinnis)	3·75	2·75
N3997	2wn. Finless porpoise (Neophocaena phocaenoides)	3·75	2·75
N3998	2wn. Bottle-nosed dolphin (Tursiops truncatus)	3·75	2·75
N3999	2wn. Curvier's beaked whale (Ziphius cavirostris)	3·75	2·75
N4000	2wn. Port Jackson shark (Heterodontus portusjacksoni)	3·75	2·75
N4001	2wn. Great hammerhead shark (Sphyrna mokarran) (inscr "mokkarran")	3·75	2·75
N4002	2wn. Zebra shark (Stegostoma fasciatum)	3·75	2·75
N4003	2wn. Ornate wobbegong (Orectolobus ornatus)	3·75	2·75
N4004	2wn. Ruddy shelduck (Tadorna ferruginea)	3·75	2·75
N4005	2wn. European widgeon (Anas penelope)	3·75	2·75
N4006	2wn. Mandarin drake (Aix galericulata)	3·75	2·75
N4007	2wn. Hottentot teal (Anas hottentota)	3·75	2·75
N4008	2wn. Little owl (Athene noctua)	3·75	2·75
N4009	2wn. Ural owl (Strix uralensis)	3·75	2·75
N4010	2wn. Great horned owl (Bubo virginianus)	3·75	2·75
N4011	2wn. Snowy owl (Nyctea scandiaca)	3·75	2·75
N4012	2wn. Slaty-headed parakeet (Psittacula himalayana)	3·75	2·75
N4013	2wn. Male eclectus parrot (Eclectus roratus)	3·75	2·75
N4014	2wn. Major Mitchell's cockatoo (Cacatua leadbeateri)	3·75	2·75
N4015	2wn. Female eclectus parrot (Eclectus roratus)	3·75	2·75
N4016	2wn. Indian leaf butterfly (Kallima paralekta)	3·75	2·75
N4017	2wn. Spanish festoon (Zerynthia rumina)	3·75	2·75

N4018	2wn. Male and female emerald swallowtails (*Papilio palinurus*)	3·75	2·75
N4019	2wn. *Bhutanitis lidderdalii*	3·75	2·75
N4020	2wn. Bumble bee	3·75	2·75
N4021	2wn. Bumble bee on flower	3·75	2·75
N4022	2wn. Honey bee (*Apis mellifera*)	3·75	2·75
N4023	2wn. Honey bee attacking spider	3·75	2·75
N4024	2wn. *Micrommata virescens* (spider)	3·75	2·75
N4025	2wn. *Araneus quadratus* (spider)	3·75	2·75
N4026	2wn. *Dolomedes fimbriatus* (spider)	3·75	2·75
N4027	2wn. *Aculepeira ceropegia* (spider)	3·75	2·75

Nos. N3980/3 are wrongly inscr "Aculepeira ceropegia".

1311 Log Cabin (birthplace, Mt. Paekdu)

2000. 58th Birth Anniv of Kim Jong Il.
N4028	**1311**	40ch. multicoloured	75	55

1312 Styracosaurus

2000. Dinosaurs. Sheet 120×80 mm, containing T **1312** and similar multicoloured designs.
MSN4029	1wn. Type **1312**; 1wn. Saltasaurus (29×41 mm); 1wn. Tyrannosaurus	6·25	5·00

1313 Peacock (*Inachis io*)

2000. Butterflies. Multicoloured.
N4030	40ch. Type **1313**	90	65
N4031	60ch. Swallowtail (*Papilio machaon*)	1·20	90
N4032	80ch. Mimic (*Hypolimnas misippus*)	1·50	1·10
N4033	1wn.20 *Papilio bianor Cramer*	2·40	1·80

1314 Patas Monkey (*Erythrocebus patas*)

2000. Primates. Multicoloured.
N4035	10ch. Type **1314**	1·00	80
N4036	50ch. Western tarsier (*Tarsius spectrm*)	1·00	80
MSN4037	Sheet 75×65 mm. 2wn. Mona monkey (*Cercopithecus mona*)	4·25	3·00

1315 Red Flag, Top of Chollima Statue and Emblem

2000. 55th Anniv of Korean Worker's Party (1st issue).
N4038	**1315**	10ch. multicoloured	30	20

See also Nos. N4083/MSN4084.

1316 Demonstrators

2000. 40th Anniv of 19 April Uprising, South Korea.
N4039	**1316**	10ch. multicoloured	30	20

1317 Kim Il Sun Flower

2000. 88th Birth Anniv of Kim Il Sung.
N4040	**1317**	40ch. multicoloured	90	65

1318 Mun Ik Hwan

2000. Sixth Death Anniv of Mun Ik Hwan (National Reunification Prize winner).
N4041	**1318**	50ch. multicoloured	1·00	80

1319 Symbols of Technology, Globe, Flag and Chollima Statue

2000. New Millennium. 55th Anniv of Korean Worker's Party. Multicoloured.
N4042	40ch. Type **1319**	90	65
N4043	1wn.20 Dove with envelope, globe and satellites	2·40	1·80

1320 Cattleya intermedia

2000. Orchids. Multicoloured.
N4044	20ch. Type **1320**	45	35
N4045	50ch. *Dendrobium moschatum*	1·00	80
N4046	70ch. *Brassolaeliocattleya*	1·50	1·10
MSN4047	85×60 mm. 2wn. *Laeliocattleya*	4·25	3·00

1321 Okryu Bridge (River Taedong)

2000. Bridges.
N4048	20ch. Type **1321**	60	45
N4049	30ch. Ansan Bridge (River Pothong)	90	65
N4050	1wn. Rungna Bridge (River Taedong)	2·75	2·00

1322 Okryugum and Jaengggang Dancers

2000. Air. "WIPA 2000" International Stamp Exhibition, Vienna. Traditional Instruments and Folk Dances. Sheet 150×84 mm, containing T **1322** and similar vert designs. Multicoloured.
MSN4051	1wn. Type **1322**; 1wn.50 Oungum and Full Moon Viewing; 1wn.50 Janggo (drum) and Trio	8·00	6·75

The 1wn. stamp does not carry an airmail inscription.

1323 Half Moon (Yun Kuk Yong)

2000. Children's Songs. Multicoloured.
N4052	40ch. Type **1323**	90	65
N4053	60ch. *Kangnam Nostalgia* (Kim Sok Song and An Ki Yong)	1·20	90
MSN4054	95×80 mm. 1.50wn. *Spring in Home Village* (Ri Won Su and Hong Ran Pha)	3·00	2·20

1324 Pearly Nautilus (*Nautilus pompilius*)

2000. Cephalopods. Multicoloured.
N4055	40ch. Type **1324**	90	65
N4056	60ch. Common octopus (*Octopus vulgaris*)	1·20	90
N4057	1w.50 Squid (*Ommastrephes sloanei pacificus*)	3·00	2·20
MSN4058	60×70 mm. 1wn.50 No. N4057×	3·00	2·20

1325 Drake and Duck

2000. Mandarin Ducks. Multicoloured.
N4059	50ch. Type **1325**	1·10	80
N4060	50ch. Drake with duck and couple on bridge	1·10	80
MSN4061	92×75 mm. 1wn. Duck, drake and ducklings	2·10	1·60

1326 Table Tennis

2000. "World Expo 2000" International Stamp Exhibition, Anaheim, California. Sport. Multicoloured.
N4062	80ch. Type **1326**	1·70	1·30
N4063	1wn. Basketball	2·00	1·50
N4064	1wn.20 Baseball	2·40	1·90

1327 Sungri-61 NA

2000. Trucks. Multicoloured.
N4065	40ch. Type **1327**	90	70
N4066	70ch. Tipper truck	1·70	1·30
N4067	1wn.50 Konsol 25 ton dump truck	3·00	2·30

1328 Ri Tae Hun (artillery company commander) and 76 mm Field Gun

2000. Weaponry. Multicoloured.
N4068	60ch. Type **1328**	1·40	1·10

N4069	80ch. Ko Hyon Bin (tank commander) and T-34 tank	1·80	1·40
N4070	1wn. Squadron leader Paek Ki Rak and Yakovlev Yak-9P pursuit plane	2·10	1·60

1329 Fluorite

2000. Minerals. Multicoloured.
N4071	30ch. Type **1329**	60	45
N4072	60ch. Graphite	1·40	1·10
N4073	1w.60 Magnesite	3·50	2·75
MSN4074	74×74 mm. 1w.60 No. N4073	3·75	3·00

2000. "Indonesia 2000" International Stamp Exhibition, Jakarta. Nos. N4059/MSN4061 optd **WORLD PHILATELIC EXHIBITION JAKARTA 15-21 AUGUST 2000** and emblem, No. MSN4061 optd in the margin.
N4075	40ch. multicoloured	1·10	90
N4076	50ch. multicoloured	1·10	90
MSN4077	1wn. multicoloured	2·30	1·90

1331 Swimming

2000. Olympic Games, Sydney. Triathlon. Sheet 78×110 mm, containing T **1331** and similar horiz designs. Multicoloured.
MSN4078	80ch. Type **1331**; 1w.20 Cycling; 2w. Running	9·00	7·75

1332 Sanju Falls

2000. Myohyang Mountain. Multicoloured.
N4079	40ch. Type **1332**	90	70
N4080	40ch. Inho rock	90	70
N4081	1w.20 Sangwon valley	2·75	2·10

2000. "Espana 2000" International Stamp Exhibition, Madrid. No. MSN4029 optd **Exposioion Mundial de Filatolia 2000. 0.6 - 14.** in the margin.
MSN4082	120×80 mm. 1w. Type **1312**; 1w. Saltasaurus; 1w. Tyrannosaurus	6·25	5·00

1334 Anniversary Emblem and Party Museum

2000. 55th Anniv of Korean Worker's Party (2nd issue). Multicoloured.
N4083	10ch. Type **1334**	30	25
MSN4084	120×85 mm. 50ch. Kim Il Sung (35×56 mm); 50ch. Kim Jong Il (35×56 mm); 50ch. Kim Jong Suk (35×56 mm)	3·50	2·75

1335 Flag, Bulldozer and Fields

2000. Land Re-organization.
N4085	**1335**	10ch. multicoloured	30	25

1336 Potatoes, Pigs, Fields and Scientist

2000. Taehongdan (potato production centre). Multicoloured.
N4086	40ch. Type **1336**	90	70
MSN4087	110×92 mm. 2w. Kim Il Sung with farmers in potato field (42×34 mm)	4·50	3·50

1337 Kim Jong Il and Pres. Jiang Zemin

2000. Visit of Kim Jong Il to People's Republic of China. Sheet 110×80 mm.

MSN4088 **1337** 1w.20 multicoloured ... 2·75 ... 2·20

1338 Kim Jong Il and Pres. Kim Dae Jung

2000. North Korea–South Korea Summit Meeting, Pyongyang. Sheet 85×110 mm.

MSN4089 **1338** 2w. multicoloured ... 4·50 ... 3·50

1339 Kim Jong Il and Pres. Putin

2000. Visit of Pres. Vladimir Putin of Russian Federation. Sheet 94×108 mm.

MSN4090 **1339** 1w.50 multicoloured ... 3·50 ... 2·75

1340 Soldiers crossing River Amnok

2000. 50th Anniv of Chinese People's Volunteers Participation in Korean War (1st issue). Sheet 139×164 mm, containing T **1340** and similar horiz designs. Multicoloured.

MSN4091 10ch. Type **1340**; 10ch. Battle; 50ch. Chinese and Korean soldiers; 50ch. Mao Tse-tung and Chinese leaders; 80ch. Soldiers and gun emplacement ... 4·50 ... 3·50

1341 Chinese and Korean Soldiers

2000. 50th Anniv of Chinese People's Volunteers Participation in Korean War (2nd issue).

N4092 **1341** 30ch. multicoloured ... 75 ... 60

1342 *Aquilegia oxysepala*

2000. Alpine Flowers. Multicoloured.

N4093 30ch. Type **1342** ... 75 ... 60
N4094 50ch. Brilliant campion (*Lychnis fulgens*) ... 1·20 ... 95
N4095 70ch. Self-heal (*Prunela vulgaris*) ... 1·70 ... 1·30

1343 Women presenting Prisoners with Flowers

2000. Repatriation of Long-term Prisoners of War. Sheets containing horiz designs as T **1343**. Multicoloured.

MSN4096 Two sheets. (a) 139×87 mm. 80ch. Type **1343**. (b) 165×120 mm. 1w.20 Prisoners and crowd. Price for 2 sheets ... 4·50 ... 3·75

1344 Flag, Factories and Trees

2001. New Year (1st issue).

N4097 **1344** 10ch. multicoloured ... 30 ... 25

1345 White Snake meeting Xu Xian

2001. New Year (2nd issue). Tale of the White Snake. Multicoloured.

N4098 10ch. Type **1345** ... 30 ... 25
N4099 40ch. Stealing the Immortal Grass ... 90 ... 75
N4100 50ch. White and Green snakes and Xu Xian ... 1·10 ... 90
N4101 80ch. Flooding of Jinshan Hill ... 1·70 ... 1·40
MSN4102 105×80 mm. 1wn.20 White snake and Green snake (32×52 mm) ... 2·75 ... 2·30

1346 E. Lasker and J-R. Capablanca

2001. World Chess Champions. 165th Birth Anniv of Wilhelm Steinitz (19th-century champion) (MSN4109). Multicoloured.

N4103 10ch. Type **1346** ... 35 ... 30
N4104 20ch. A. Alekhine and M. Euwe ... 65 ... 55
N4105 30ch. M. Botvinnik and V. Smylov ... 80 ... 70
N4106 40ch. T. Petrosian and M. Tal ... 1·00 ... 85
N4107 50ch. B. Spassky and R. Fisher ... 1·20 ... 95
N4108 1wn. A. Karpov and G. Kasparov ... 2·30 ... 1·90
MSN4109 105×80 mm. 2wn.50 Wilhelm Steinitz (32×52 mm) ... 6·25 ... 5·25

1347 White Suit and Black Hat

2001. Ri-Dynasty Men's Costumes. Multicoloured.

N4110 10ch. Type **1347** ... 35 ... 30
N4111 40ch. White suit with blue waistcoat ... 1·00 ... 85
N4112 50ch. White trousers, brown jacket and pagoda-shaped hat ... 1·20 ... 95
N4113 70ch. Knee-length pale blue coat, black hat and stick ... 1·60 ... 1·40
MSN4114 110×80 mm. 1wn.50 Blue knee-length coat with ornamental cummerbund and black boots ... 3·50 ... 3·00

1348 Small Appliance (fire)

2001. Fire Engines. Designs showing engines and fire hazards. Multicoloured.

N4115 20ch. Type **1348** ... 50 ... 40
N4116 30ch. Large engine with hydraulic ladder (oil can) ... 65 ... 55
N4117 40ch. Small engine with two-door cab and closed back (match) ... 1·00 ... 85
N4118 60ch. Small engine with ladder, spotlight and external hose reel (gas canister) ... 1·50 ... 1·20
N4119 2wn. Older-style engine (cigarette) ... 5·00 ... 4·25
MSN4120 95×90 mm. 2wn. As No. N4119 (32×52 mm) ... 5·25 ... 4·50

1349 Black-naped Oriole (*Oriolus chinensis*)

2001. "HONG KONG 2001" International Stamp Exhibition. Sheet 72×80 mm.

MSN4121 **1349** 1wn.40 multicoloured ... 3·25 ... 2·75

1350 Jjong Il Peak and Flower

2001. 59th Birth Anniv of Kim Jong Il.

N4122 **1350** 10ch. multicoloured ... 35 ... 30

1351 Flag and Symbols of Industry and Agriculture

2001. New Millennium. Rodong Sinmun, Josoninmingun and Chongnyonjonwi Newspapers Joint Editorial.

N4123 **1351** 10ch. multicoloured ... 35 ... 30

1352 Log Cabin (revolutionary headquarters, Mt. Paekdu)

2001
N4124 **1352** 40ch. multicoloured ... 1·00 ... 85

1353 Family Home, Mangyongdae

2001. 89th Birth Anniv of Kim Il Sung. Multicoloured.

N4125 10ch. Type **1353** ... 50 ... 30
MSN4126 170×103 mm. 80ch.×8, Eight different portraits of Kim Il Sung (vert) ... 16·00 ... 14·00

1354 Kim Jong Il

2001. Army as Priority. Sheet 140×75 mm.

MSN4127 **1354** 1w. multicoloured ... 2·50 ... 2·10

1355 Pyongyang—Kaesong Motorway

2001. Roads. Multicoloured.

N4128 40ch. Type **1355** ... 1·00 ... 85
N4129 70ch. Pyongyang—Hyanngsan expressway ... 1·60 ... 1·40
N4130 1w. 20 Pyongyang—Nampo motorway ... 3·00 ... 2·50
N4131 1w. 50 Pyongyang—Wonsan expressway ... 3·50 ... 3·00

1356 Ryongwang Pavilion, Pyongyang

2001. Cultural Heritage. Pavilions. Multicoloured.

N4132 40ch. Type **1356** ... 1·00 ... 85
N4133 80ch. Inphung, Kanggye ... 2·00 ... 1·70
N4134 1w. 50 Paeksang, Anju ... 3·50 ... 3·00
N4135 2w. Thonggun, Uiju ... 5·00 ... 4·25

1357 Man with raised Arm

2001
N4136 **1357** 10ch. Multicoloured ... 35 ... 30

1358 Blue-throat (*Luscinia svecica*)

2001. Birds. Multicoloured.

N4137 10ch. Type **1358** ... 35 ... 30
N4138 40ch. Grey lag goose (*Anser anser*) ... 1·00 ... 85
N4139 80ch. Short-tailed albatross (*Diomedea albatrus*) ... 2·00 ... 1·70
N4140 1w. Little ring plover (*Charadrius dubius*) ... 2·50 ... 2·10
N4141 1w. 20 Common guillemot (*Uria aalge*) ... 3·00 ... 2·50
N4142 1w. 50 House martin (*Delichon urbica*) ... 3·50 ... 3·00

1359 Mao Zedong

2001. 80th Anniv of Chinese Communist Party. Three sheets, each 152×67 mm containing T **1359** and similar horiz designs. Multicoloured.

MSN4143 (a) 80ch. Type **1359**; (b) 80ch. Deng Xiaping; (c) 80ch. Jiang Zemin ... 6·00 ... 5·00

1360 Woljong Temple, Mt. Kuwol

2001. Kumol Mountain. Multicoloured.

N4144 10ch. Type **1360** ... 35 ... 30
N4145 40ch. Revolutionary building ... 1·00 ... 85
N4146 70ch. Potnamu Pavilion ... 1·60 ... 1·40
N4147 1w. 30 Tak Peak ... 3·25 ... 2·75
N4148 1w. 50 Ryongyon Falls ... 3·50 ... 3·00

1361 *Rheum coreanum*

2001. Endangered Species. Plants. Multicoloured.
N4149	10ch. Type **1361**	35	30
N4150	40ch. *Forsythia densiflora*	1·00	85
N4151	1w. *Rhododendron yedoense*	2·50	2·10
N4152	2w. *Iris setosa*	5·00	4·25

1362 *Eria pannea*

2001. Orchids. Multicoloured.
N4153	10ch. Type **1362**	35	30
N4154	40ch. *Cymbidium*	1·00	85
N4155	90ch. *Sophrolaeliocattleya*	2·10	1·80
N4156	1w. 60 *Cattleya trianae*	4·00	3·25
N4157	2w. *Cypripedium macranthum*	5·00	4·25
MSN4158	142×96 mm. No. N4157	5·25	4·50

1363 *Pibaldo Lighthouse*

2001. Lighthouses. Multicoloured.
N4159	40ch. Type **1363**	1·00	85
N4160	70ch. Soho, Hamhung	1·60	1·40
N4161	90ch. Komalsan, Chongjin	2·10	1·80
N4162	1w. 50 Alsom, Rason	3·50	3·00
MSN4163	81×95 mm. No. N4162	3·75	3·25

1364 *Kim Po Hyon*

2001. 130th Birth Anniv of Kim Po Hyon. Sheet 80×90 mm.
MSN4164	**1364** 1w. black and bronze	2·50	2·10

1365 *Black Stork (Ciconia nigra)*

2001. Endangered Species. Fauna. Multicoloured.
N4165	10ch. Type **1365**	35	30
N4166	40ch. Cinereous vulture (*Aegypius monchus*)	1·00	85
N4167	70ch. Chinese water deer (*Hydropotes inermis*)	1·60	1·40
N4168	90ch. Goral (*Nemorhaedus goral*)	2·10	1·80
N4169	1w. 30 Northern eagle owl (*Bubo bubo*)	3·25	2·75
MSN4170	106×81 mm. No. N4169	3·50	3·00

1366 *Deng Ya Ping receiving Gold Medal for Table Tennis from Juan Antonio Samaranch (Olympic president)*

2001. Olympic Games 2008, Beijing. Sheet 152×115 mm containing T **1366** and similar circular designs. Multicoloured.
MSN4171	56ch.×5, Type **1366**; Jiang Zemin (pres. People's Republic of China); Wang Jun Xia (athletics); Li Ning (gymnast); Fu Ming Xia (diver)	7·50	6·25

1367 *Cycle Football*

2001. Cycling. Sheet 90×145 mm containing T **1367** and similar vert designs. Multicoloured.
MSN4172	10ch. Type **1367**; 40ch. Road racing; 1w. Cyclo-cross; 2w. Indoor racing	9·75	8·25

1368 *Yuri Gagarin*

2001. Space Exploration. Multicoloured.
N4173	10ch. Type **1368** (cosmonaut)	35	30
N4174	40ch. Apollo 11 space ship	1·00	85
N4175	1w. 50 Kwangmyongsong satellite	3·50	3·00
N4176	2w. Edmund Halley (astronomer). Halley's comet and Giotto satellite	5·00	4·25
MSN4177	140×197 mm. Nos. N4173/6	9·75	8·25

1369 *Presidents Vladimir Putin and Kim Jong II*

2001. Visit of Kim Jong II to Russia. Sheet 92×105 mm.
MSN4178	**1369** 1w.50 mulicoloured	3·50	3·00

1370 *Presidents Kim Jong II and Jiang Zemin*

2001. Meeting between Pres. Kim Jong II and Jiang Zemin (pres. People's Republic of China). Sheet 72×104 mm.
MSN4179	**1370** 1w.50 multicoloured	3·50	3·00

1371 *Kim Jong Suk protecting Kim II Sung during Battle*

2001. 84th Birth Anniv of Kim Jong Suk (revolutionary fighter). Sheet 168×100 mm.
MSN4180	**1371** 1w.60 multicoloured	4·00	3·25

1372 *Kim Jong II inspecting Troops*

2001. Tenth Anniv of Kim Jong II's election as Supreme Commander of Korean People's Army. Sheet 90×110 mm.
MSN4181	1w. multicoloured	2·50	2·10

1373 *Chollima Statue*

2002
N4182	**1373** 10ch. multicoloured	35	30

1374 *Grey Horse*

2002. New Year ("Year of the Horse"). *Ten Horses* (paintings by Wang Zhi Cheng) (Nos. N4183/6). Multicoloured.
N4183	10ch. Type **1374**	35	30
N4184	40ch. Bay	1·00	85
N4185	60ch. Skewbald	1·50	1·20
N4186	1w.30 Piebald	3·25	2·75
MSN4187	(a) 106×80 mm. 1w.60. *Jiu Fang Gao* (painting by Xu Bei Hong) (36×57 mm). (b) 168×104 mm. Nos. N4183/6 and **MS**4187a	14·00	11·50

1375 *Flower Basket*

2002. 60th Birth Anniv of Kim Jong II. Multicoloured.
N4188	10ch. Type **1375**	35	30
MSN4189	(a) 124×94 mm. 1w.20×3, Kim II Sung (father) (32×52 mm); Kim Jong II as child (32×52 mm); Kim Jong Suk (mother) (32×52 mm). (b) 105×85 mm. 1w.50 Kim Jong II with soldiers (45×34 mm). (c) 77×117 mm. 2w. Kim Jong II as young man (42×64 mm)	18·00	16·00

1376 *Zeppelin LZ1*

2002. Centenary of First Zeppelin Airship Flight. Multicoloured.
N4190	40ch. Type **1376**	80	70
N4191	80ch. LZ	1·60	1·40
N4192	1w. 20 Zeppelin NT	2·50	2·10
MSN4193	(a) 110×80 mm. 2w.40 Zeppelin NT (different). (b) 132×110 mm. Nos. N4190/**MSN**4193a	15·00	13·00

2002. Rodong Sinmun, Josoninmingun and Chongnyonjonwi Newspapers Joint Editorial.
N4194	**1377** 10ch. multicoloured	35	30

1378 *Collybia confluens*

2002. Fungi. Multicoloured.
N4195	10ch. Type **1378**	35	30
N4196	40ch. *Sparassis laminose*	80	70
N4197	80ch. Grisette (*Amanita vaginata*) (inscr "Amanjta")	1·60	1·40
N4198	1w. 20 *Russla integra*	2·50	2·10
N4199	1w. 50 Scaly pholita (*Pholita squarrosa*)	3·00	2·50

1379 *Family Home, Mangyongdae*

2002. 90th Birth Anniv of Kim II Sung. Multicoloured.
N4200	10ch. Type **1379**	35	30
MSN4201	(a) 105×85 mm. 1w.50 Kim II Sung as young man (45×54 mm). (b) 105×85 mm. 1w.50 With Kim Jong Suk (wife) (45×54 mm). (c) 105×85 mm. 1w.50 With Kim Chaeck (revolutionary) (45×54 mm). (d) 76×117 mm. 2w. Wearing black jacket (42×64 mm)	13·50	12·00

1380 *Kang Pan Sok*

2002. 110th Birth Anniv of Kang Pan Sok (mother of Kim II Sung). Sheet 70×100 mm.
MSN4202	**1380** 1w. multicoloured	2·00	1·70

1381 *Emblem, Doves, Dancers and Music*

2002. 20th April Spring Friendship Art Festival.
N4203	**1381** 10ch. multicoloured	35	30

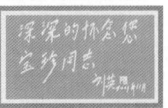

1382 *Electric Locomotive*

2002. 20th-century Locomotives. Multicoloured.
N4204	10ch. Type **1382**	35	30
N4205	40ch. Electric locomotive (different)	80	70
N4206	1w. 50 Steam locomotive	2·75	2·30
N4207	2w. Steam locomotive (different)	3·50	3·00
MSN4208	65×55 mm. 2w. Diesel locomotive	3·50	3·00

1383 *Inscription*

2002. Birth Centenary of He Baozhen (first wife of Liu Shaoqi (Chinese politician)). Sheet 150×110 mm containing T **1383** and similar multicoloured designs.

MSN4209	10ch. Type **1383**; 20ch. Arch; 30ch. Building; 40ch. Family (33×45 mm); 1w. He Baozhen and Liu Shaoqi (33×45 mm)	4·00	3·50

1384 *Cristaria plicata*

2002. Shellfish. Multicoloured.

N4210	10ch. Type **1384**	35	30
N4211	40ch. *Lanceolaria cospidata*	65	55
N4212	1w. *Schistodesmus lampreyanus*	1·60	1·40
N4213	1w. 50 *Lamprotula coreana*	2·50	2·10

1385 Soldiers

2002. 70th Anniv of Korean People's Army. Multicoloured.

N4214	10ch. Type **1385**	35	30
MSN4215	60×85 mm. 1w.60 Kim Il Sung and Kim Jong Il (39×51 mm). Perf or imperf	3·25	2·75

1386 Actors

2002. Arirang Festival. Multicoloured.

N4216	10ch. Type **1386**	35	30
N4217	20ch. Animation and cartoon characters	50	40
N4218	30ch. Dancer holding fan	65	55
N4219	40ch. Dancers	80	70
MSN4220	120×93 mm. 1w. Woman holding tambourine (54×45 mm)	2·00	1·70

1387 Ri Rang and Song Bu

2002. Arirang Legend. Sheet 176×88 mm containing T **1387** and similar vert designs. Multicoloured.

MSN4221	10ch. Type **1387**; 40ch. As young adults; 50ch. Ri Rang killing landlord; 1w.50 Song Bu	4·25	3·50

1388 Symbols of Modern Industry

2002. Science and Technology.

N4222	10ch. multicoloured	35	30

1389 Squid-shaped Stalactite

2002. Ryongmun Cavern. Sheet 160×105 mm containing T **1389** and similar vert designs. Multicoloured.

MSN4223	10ch. Type **1389**; 20ch. Chandelier-shaped stalactite; 30ch. Hill-shaped stalagmite; 40ch. Stalagmite with rough surface	2·00	1·70

1390 Monument

2002. 30th Anniv of Charter of Three Principles for Re-unification.

N4224	**1390**	10ch. multicoloured	35	30

1391 *Stauropus fagi*

2002. Butterflies and Moths. Multicoloured.

N4225	10ch. Type **1391**	35	30
N4226	40ch. *Agrias claudina*	65	55
N4227	1w. 50 *Catocala nupta*	2·50	2·10
N4228	2w. Blue morpho (*Morpho rhetenor*)	3·25	2·75

(1392)

2002. 16th Chinese Communist Party Conference, Beijing. Nos. **MS**N4143a/c optd in the margin with T **1392**.

MSN4229	(a) 80ch. Type **1359**. (b) 80ch. Deng Xiaping. (c) 80ch. Jiang Zemin	6·00	5·00

1393 Child and Old Man

2002. 50th Anniv of Free Medical Care.

N4230	**1393**	10ch. multicoloured	35	30

1394 Kim Jong Suk as Child

2002. 85th Birth Anniv of Kim Jong Suk (wife of Kim Il Sung). Sheet containing T **1394** and similar vert designs. Multicoloured.

MSN4231	10ch. Type **1394**; 40ch. As young woman; 1w. Wearing uniform; 1w.50 In middle age	5·00	4·25

1395 Workers, Soldiers and Symbols of Industry

2002. 30th Anniv of Constitution.

N4232	**1395**	10ch. multicoloured	35	30

1396 Returnees

2002. Red Cross and Red Crescent (humanitarian organizations) Day. Multicoloured.

N4233	3w. Type **1396**	35	30
N4234	12w. Red Cross workers	80	70
N4235	80w. Family (AIDS awareness)	1·60	1·40
N4236	150w. Humanitarian aid to flood victims	3·00	2·50
MSN4237	(a) 150×115 mm. Nos. N4233/4 and N4326, each×2. (b) 85×113 mm. No. N4325	1·80	1·50

1397 Hong Chang Su

2002. Hong Chang Su—2000 World Super-Flyweight Champion. Sheet 110×75 mm.

MSN4238	**1397**	75w. multicoloured	1·60	1·40

1398 Kim Jong Il and President Vladimir Putin

2002. Kim Jong Il's Visit to Russia. Two sheets containing T **1398** and similar multicoloured design.

MSN4239	(a) 85×70 mm. 70w. Type **1398**; (b) 120×100 mm. 120w. President Putin and Kim Jong Il shaking hands (vert)	4·00	3·50

1399 Seal-point Shorthair Cat

2002. Cats and Dogs. Multicoloured.

N4240	3w. Type **1399**	25	20
N4241	12w. Pungsan dog	35	30
N4242	100w. White shorthair cat	2·50	2·10
N4243	150w. Black and white shorthair cat	3·50	3·00
MSN4244	57×70 mm. 150w. Cavalier King Charles spaniel	3·75	3·25

1400 Iron Pyrite

2002. Minerals. Multicoloured.

N4245	3w. Type **1400**	25	20
N4246	12w. Magnetite	35	30
N4247	130w. Calcite	3·00	2·50
N4248	150w. Galena	3·50	3·00

1401 Prime Minister Koizumi Junichiro and Kim Jong Il signing Declaration

2002. Japan—Korea Bilateral Declaration. Two sheets containing T **1401** and similar horiz design. Multicoloured.

MSN4249	(a) 90×80 mm. 120w. Type **1401**; (b) 75×65 mm. 150w. Prime Minister Junichiro and Kim Jong Il shaking hands	5·75	5·25

1402 Family Home, Mangyongdae

2002. National Symbols.

N4250	**1402**	1w. brown	15	15
N4251	-	3w. green (vert)	15	15
N4252	-	5w. agate	25	20
N4253	-	10w. crimson (vert)	25	20
N4254	-	12w. claret (17×26 mm)	10 10	
N4255	-	20w. scarlet and ultramarine (17×26 mm)	50	40
N4256	-	30w. red (vert)	65	55
N4257	-	40w. blue (vert)	1·00	85
N4258	-	50w. brown (17×26 mm)	1·20	95
N4259	-	70w. sepia (17×26 mm)	1·60	1·40
N4260	-	100w. brown (17×26 mm)	2·50	2·10
N4261	-	200w. crimson (17×26 mm)	5·00	4·25

DESIGNS: Type **1402**; 3w. Mount Paeku; 5w. Hoeryong; 10w. Kimilsungia; 12w. Torch (Tower of Juche Idea); 20w. Flag; 30w. Kimjongilia; 40w. Magnolia blossom; 50w. National emblem; 70w. Chollima statue; 100w. Victorious Fatherland monument; 200w. Workers Party monument.

1403 Workers and Soldiers

2003. New Year.

N4262	**1403**	3w. multicoloured	25	20

1404 Bald Eagle steals Young Antelope

2003. Antelope defeats Bald Eagle (fairy tale). Multicoloured.

N4263	3w. Type **1404**	25	20
N4264	50w. Antelopes unite to defeat eagle	1·30	1·10
N4265	70w. Eagle eating fish poisoned by antelopes	1·70	1·40
N4266	100w. Mother antelope and rescued baby	2·50	2·10
MSN4267	110×80 mm. 150w. Antelopes carrying fruit (54×45 mm)	3·25	2·75

1405 Greeting Full Moon (January 15th festival)

2003. Folk Festivals. Multicoloured.

N4268	3w. Type **1405**	25	20
N4269	12w. Dance greeting full moon (January 15th)	35	30
N4270	40w. Swinging (Surinal festival)	1·00	85
N4271	70w. Woman and child (Hangawi festival)	1·70	1·40
N4272	140w. Peasant dance (Hangawi)	3·25	2·75
MSN4273	110×90 mm. 112w. Wrestling (Surinal)	2·75	2·40

1406 Soldier

2003. Rodong Sinmun, Josoninmingun and Chongnyonjonwi Newspapers Joint Editorial.

N4274	**1406**	12w. multicoloured	50	40

1407 Weapons

2003. Withdrawal from NPT.

N4275	**1407**	30w. multicoloured	85	70

1408 Ode Monument

2003. 61st Birth Anniv of Kim Jong II. Multicoloured.

N4276	3w. Type **1408**	25	20
MSN4277	90×60 mm. 75w. Mt. Paektu (64×42 mm)	1·80	1·60

1409 *Paekmagang* (cargo ship)

2003. Ships. Multicoloured.

N4278	15w. Type **1409**	40	35
N4279	50w. *Konsol* (dredger)	1·20	1·00
N4280	70w. *Undok No. 2* (passenger ship)	1·70	1·40
N4281	112w. *Piryugang* (cargo ship)	2·75	2·40
MSN4282	78×52 mm. 150w. *Pyongyang No. 1* (pleasure cruiser)	3·25	2·75

1410 Zis

2003. Kim Il Sung's Presidential Cars. Multicoloured.

N4283	3w. Type **1410**	25	20
N4284	14w. Gaz	40	35
N4285	70w. Pobeda	1·70	1·40
N4286	90w. Mercedes Benz	2·20	1·80
MSN4287	100×80 mm. 150w. *Delaying His Urgent Journey* (painting by Kim Sam Gon) (64×42 mm)	3·25	2·75

1411 Book Cover

2003. 30th Anniv of Publication of *On the Art of the Cinema* by Kim Jong II. Sheet 95×75 mm.

MSN4288	**1411** 120w. mult	3·00	2·50

1412 Trumpeter and Symbols of Journey

2003. 80th Anniv of Kim Il Sung's 250 Mile Journey for Learning.

N4289	**1412** 15w. multicoloured	50	40

1413 Soldier and Workers

2003. Korean People's Army.

N4290	**1413** 3w. multicoloured	25	20

1414 Flags and Emblem

2003. Tenth Anniv of Election of Kim Jong II as Chairman of National Defence Commission. Multicoloured.

N4291	3w. Type **1414**	25	20
MSN4292	175×75 mm. 12w. Kim Jong II with computers (51×49 mm); 70w. With soldiers (51×49 mm); 112w. With raised hand (51×49 mm)	5·75	5·00

1415 Birthplace, Mangyongdae and Kimilsungia

2003. 91st Birth Anniv of Kim Il Sung.

N4293	**1415** 3w. multicoloured	25	20

1416 Order of Suhbaatar (Mongolia)

2003. Kim Il Sung's Medals and Orders. Multicoloured.

N4294	12w. Type **1416**	35	30
N4295	35w. Order of Grand Cross (Madagascar)	1·00	85
N4296	70w. Order of Lenin (USSR)	2·20	1·80
N4297	140w. Order of Playa Giron (Cuba)	4·25	3·50
MSN4298	108×91 mm. 120w. Fidel Castro (president of Cuba) and Kim Il Sung (horiz)	3·25	2·75

1417 *Pantala flavescens*

2003. Insects. Multicoloured.

N4299	15w. Type **1417**	50	40
N4300	70w. *Tibicen japonicus*	1·70	1·40
N4301	220w. *Xylotrupes dichotomus*	5·75	5·00
N4302	300w. *Lycaena dispar*	8·50	7·00
MSN4303	150×85 mm. Nos. N4299/302	17·00	16·00

1418 Glutinous Rice Cakes

2003. Traditional Food. Multicoloured.

N4304	3w. Type **1418**	25	20
N4305	30w. Tongkimchi	85	70
N4306	70w. Sinsollo	2·00	1·70
MSN4307	100×83 mm. 120w. Pyongyang raengmyon	3·25	2·75

1419 Victory Monument, Taechongdan Hill

2003. Sheet 98×71 mm.

MSN4308	**1419** 90w. multicoloured	2·75	2·30

1420 Manse Pavilion

2003. Ryangchon Temple, Kowon, South Hamgyong Province. Multicoloured.

N4309	3w. Type **1420**	25	20
N4310	12w. Three statues	35	30
N4311	40w. Buddha and two saints (painting)	1·20	1·00
N4312	50w. Buddha and four saints (painting)	1·50	1·30
MSN4313	100×80 mm. 120w. Taeung Hall	3·00	2·50

1421 Music Score

2003. *We are One* (song). Sheet 70×100 mm.

MSN4314	**1421** 60w. multicoloured	1·50	1·30

1422 Tigers

2003. Animals. Sheet 157×72 mm containing T **1422** and similar vert designs. Multicoloured.

MSN4315	3w. Type **1422**; 70w. Bears; 150w. Wild boar; 230w. Deer	12·50	11·50

1423 Public Bonds

2003. Public Bond Purchase Campaign.

N4316	**1423** 140w. multicoloured	3·75	3·00

1424 Distinguished Service Medal

2003. 50th Anniv of Liberation. Multicoloured.

N4317	3w. Type **1424**	25	20
MSN4318	Three sheets, all 146×106 mm. (a) 12w. Kim Il Sung and radio microphone (38×31 mm); 35w. Kim Il Sung with soldiers (38×31 mm); 70w. Kim Il Sung signing document (38×31 mm); 140w. Kim Il Sung (43×43 mm) (circular). (b) 12w. Kim Il Sung with soldiers (38×31 mm); 35w. Kim Il Sung inspecting soldier's weapons (38×31 mm); 70w. Kim Il Sung and Kim Jong II (38×31 mm); 140w. Kim Il Sung (43×43 mm) (circular). (c) 12w. Kim Jong II receiving bouquet (38×31 mm); 35w. Kim Jong II with soldiers (38×31 mm); 70w. Kim Jong II with unit commander (38×31 mm); 140w. Kim Jong II (43×43 mm) (circular)	20·00	18·00
MSN4319	65×90 mm. 120w. President Kim Il Sung	3·00	2·50

1425 *Minicattleya*

2003. Orchids. Multicoloured.

N4320	75w. Type **1425**	2·00	1·70
N4321	100w. *Phalaenopsis Aphrodite* (inscr "Phalanopsis")	2·50	2·10
N4322	150w. *Calanthe discolour*	3·75	3·25
N4323	200w. *Dendrobium snowflake* (inscr "Den.")	5·00	4·25

Nos. N4320/23 were issued together, *se-tenant*, forming a composite design.

1426 Japanese White-necked Crane (*Grus vipio*)

2003. Birds. Multicoloured.

N4324	12w. Type **1426**	35	30
N4325	70w. Black-crowned night heron (*Nycticorax nycticorax*)	2·10	1·80
N4326	100w. Domestic pigeon (*Columba livia domestica*)	3·00	2·50
N4327	120w. Cockatiel (*Nymphicus hollandicus*)	3·50	3·00
N4328	150w. Tawny owl (*Strix aluco*)	4·25	3·75
MSN4329	70×90 mm. 225w. Inscr "Pseudogyps africanus" (39×51 mm)	6·75	6·00

1427 Adelie Penguin (*Pygoscelis adeliae*)

2003. Arctic and Antarctic Fauna. Sheet 160×114 mm containing T **1427** and similar horiz designs. Multicoloured.

MSN4330	15w. Type **1427**; 70w. Walrus (*Odobenus rosmarus*); 140w. Polar bear (*Thalarctos maritimus*); 150w. Bowhead whale (*Balaena mysticetus*) (inscr "mysticegus"); 220w. Spotted seal (*Phoca largha*)	16·00	14·50

The stamps and margins of MSN4330 form a composite design.

1428 *Pholiota flammans*

2003. Fungi. Multicoloured.

N4331	3w. Type **1428**	25	20
N4332	12w. *Geastrum fimbriatum*	35	30
N4333	70w. *Coprinus atramentarius*	1·90	1·60
N4334	130w. *Pleurotus cornucopiae*	3·50	3·00
MSN4335	80×65 mm. 250w. *Elfvingia applanata*	6·75	6·00

1429 Exhibition Hall

2003. National Stamp Exhibition. Multicoloured.

N4336	3w. Type **1429**	25	20
N4337	60w. Stamps and display stands (horiz)	1·70	1·50

1430 Emblem and Flag

2003. 55th Anniv of Democratic Peoples' Republic of Korea. Multicoloured.

N4338	3w. Type **1430**	25 20

MSN4339 Four sheets, each 65×120 mm. (a) 60w. "The Birth of New Korea"; 60w. "On the Road supporting Kim Il Sung"; (b) 60w. "Braving Rain of Bullets"; 60w. "Giving command for Counter Offensive"; (c) 60w. "We Trust and Follow You"; 60w. "Kim Il Sung at Power Plant"; (d) 60w. "Victory Assured"; 60w. "Keeping up Shongun Politics"   13·50   12·50

MSN4340 75×105 mm. 120w. Kim Il Sung (43×43 mm) (circular)   3·50   3·00

1431

2003. Bangkok 2003 International Stamp Exhibition, Thailand. No. **MS**N4244 optd in the margin with T **1431**.

MSN4341 57×70 mm. 150w. Cavalier King Charles spaniel   3·75   3·25

1432 Mao Zedong

2003. 110th Birth Anniv of Mao Zedong (Chinese leader 1945—1976). Multicoloured. Imperf (140w.) or perf (others).

N4342	20w. Type **1432**	70 60
N4343	20w. During the "Long March"	70 60
N4344	30w. With female companion	85 75
N4345	30w. Seated in room of men	85 75
N4346	30w. Addressing partisans	85 75
N4347	30w. With partisans wearing long coat	85 75
N4348	30w. Addressing crowd in Beijing	85 75
N4349	30w. With people from many nations	85 75

1433 Workers and Soldiers

2004. New Year.

N4351	**1433** 3w. multicoloured	25 25

1434 *Cebus paella*

2004. Monkeys. Multicoloured.

N4352	3w. Type **1434**	25 25
N4353	60w. *Papio doguera*	1·70 1·50
N4354	70w. *Cercopithecus aethiops*	2·10 1·80
N4355	100w. *Saguinus Oedipus*	3·00 2·50

MSN4356 71×85 mm. 155w. *Macaca mulatta*   4·25   3·75

1435 Children

2004. Lunar New Year.

N4357	**1435** 3w. multicoloured	25 25

1436 Yong Liwei

2004. Yong Liwei—First Chinese Astronaut. Multicoloured.

N4358	91w. Type **1436**	2·50 2·30
N4359	98w. Returned space capsule (54×45 mm)	2·75 2·40

MSN4360 142×100 mm. Nos. N4358/9   5·50   4·75

1437

2004. Hong Kong 2004 International Stamp Exhibition. Nos. N4352/**MS**N4356 optd with T **1437**.

N4361	3w. multicoloured	25 25
N4362	60w. multicoloured	1·70 1·50
N4363	70w. multicoloured	2·10 1·80
N4364	100w. multicoloured	3·00 2·50

MSN4365 71×85 mm. 155w. multicoloured   4·25   3·75

1438 Book, Weapons and Slogan

2004. Rodong Sinmun, Josoninmingun and Chongnyonjonwi Newspapers Joint Editorial.

N4366	**1438** 3w. multicoloured	25 25

1440 Kim Jong Il

2004. 30th Anniv of Publication of Juche Idea Programme. Sheet 151×80 mm.

MSN4372 **1440** 120w. multicoloured   3·50   3·00

1441 Fields and Goat Herd

2004. 40th Anniv of Publication of *Thesis on Rural Socialist Question* by Kim Il Sung. Multicoloured.

N4373	3w. Type **1441**	25 25

MSN4374 117×86 mm. 120w. Kim Il Sung and farmer (49×51 mm)   3·25   2·75

1442 Sokgundo Lighthouse

2004. Lighthouses. Multicoloured.

N4375	3w. Type **1442**	25 25
N4376	12w. Yubundo	50 45
N4377	100w. Jangdokdo	2·50 2·30
N4378	195w. Amryongdan	5·25 4·50

MSN4379 131×121 mm. Nos. N4375/8   8·75   7·50

1443 Korean Chess

2004. Board Games. Multicoloured.

N4380	3w. Type **1443**	25 25
N4381	12w. Go	50 45
N4382	90w. Yut	2·40 2·10
N4383	120w. Koni	3·25 2·75

MSN4384 110×114 mm. Nos. N4380/3   6·75   6·00

MSN4385 97×81 mm. 98w. Men and child playing chess (54×45 mm)   2·50   2·30

1444 Birthplace, Mangyongdae

2004. 92nd Birth Anniv of Kim Il Sung. Multicoloured.

N4386	3w. Type **1444**	25 25

MSN4387 94×76 mm. 120w. Kim Il Sung (39×51 mm)   3·25   2·75

1445 18th-century Map of Korea

2004. Tok Islet. Multicoloured.

N4388	3w. Type **1445**	25 25
N4389	12w. Western islet	50 45
N4390	106w. Eastern islet	3·00 2·50
N4391	116w. Both islets (circular) (45×45 mm)	3·25 2·75

MSN4392 101×121 mm. Nos. N4388/90   3·75   3·25

MSN4393 160×81 mm. 116w. No. N4391   3·50   3·00

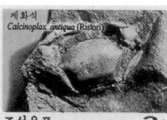

1446 *Calcinoplax antique*

2004. Fossils. Multicoloured.

N4394	3w. Type **1446**	25 25
N4395	12w. *Podozamites lanceolatus*	50 45
N4396	70w. *Comptonia naumannii*	1·90 1·70
N4397	120w. *Tingia carbonica*	3·25 2·75
N4398	140w. *Clinocardium asagaiense*	3·75 3·25

MSN4399 135×86 mm. Nos. N4394/6 and N4398   6·75   5·75

MSN4400 102×76 mm. 120w. No. N4397   3·50   3·00

1447 *Notocactus leninghausii*

2004. Cacti. Multicoloured.

N4401	70w. Type **1447**	1·70 1·50
N4402	90w. *Echinocactus grusonii*	2·30 2·00
N4403	100w. *Gymnocalycium baldianum*	2·50 2·30
N4404	140w. *Mammillaria insularis*	3·75 3·25

MSN4405 148×93 mm. Nos. N4401/4   10·50   9·50

1448 Kim Jong Il and Hu Jintao

2004. Kim Jong Il's visit to China. Multicoloured

N4406	3w. Type **1448**	25 25
N4407	3w. With Wen Jiabao	25 25
N4408	12w. With Jiang Zemin	35 30
N4409	12w. With Jia Qinglin	35 30
N4410	40w. With Wu Bangguo	1·00 90
N4411	40w. Seated with Zeng Qinghong	1·00 90
N4412	60w. With Huang Guo and others	1·60 1·40
N4413	60w. Inspecting Tianjin (new city)	1·60 1·40
N4414	74w. With Hu Jintao (41×60 mm)	2·10 1·80

MSN4415 Two sheets, each 160×130 mm. (a) Nos. N4406, N4408, N4410 and N4412 (b) Nos. N4407, N4409, N4411 and N4413   6·50   5·50

MSN4416 90×120 mm. N4414 (41×60 mm)   2·30   2·00

1449 Flag

2004. 40th Anniv of Kim Il Jong at WPK. Multicoloured.

N4417	3w. Type **1449**	25 25

MSN4418 Three sheets, each 150×75 mm. (a) Size 54×45 mm. 12w. Kim Il Jong at desk; 100w. With paintings. (b) Size 54×45 mm. 12w. Inspecting power station; 100w. With soldiers. (c) Size 54×45 mm. 12w. Wearing safety hat and glasses; 100w. Kim Il Jong   9·00   7·75

MSN4419 84×100 mm. Size 42×60 mm. 130w. Kim Il Sung and Kim Il Jong   2·10   1·80

1450 Monument and Kimilsungia

2004. Kim Il Sung Commemoration. Multicoloured.

N4420	3w. Type **1450**	25 25

MSN4421 Four sheets, each 116×120 mm. (a) Size 51×39 mm. 12w. Kim Il Sung with workers; 116w. With farmers. (b) Size 51×39 mm. 12w. With soldiers; 116w. With children. (c) Size 51×39 mm. 12w. With Kim Il Jong at Academy; 116w. With Kim Il Jong on Mt. Paektu. (d) Size 51×39 mm. 12w. With Mun Ik Hwan; 116w. Holding telephone   12·50   11·00

MSN4422 70×90 mm. Size 39×51 mm. 112w. Kim Il Sung   2·75   2·40

1451 Kim Hyong Jik and Kim Il Sung as a Child (statue)

2004. 110th Birth Anniv of Kim Yong Jik (father of Kim Il Sung). Sheet 150×96 mm.

MSN4423 **1451** 112w. mult   2·75   2·40

1452 Deng Xiaoping
as Young Man

2004. Birth Centenary of Deng Xiaoping (Chinese leader). Multicoloured.

N4424	3w. Type **1452**	25	25
N4425	12w. Wearing shorts	35	30
N4426	35w. Wearing uniform	85	75
N4427	50w. Giving speech	1·20	1·10
MSN4428	175×115 mm. Nos. N4424/7; 70w. Visiting shopping centre (51×39 mm)	5·25	4·50
MSN4429	100×70 mm. 80w. Deng Xiaoping (51×39 mm)	2·10	1·80

1453 Boxing

2004. Olympic Games, Athens. Multicoloured.

N4430	3w. Type **1453**	25	25
N4431	12w. Football	35	30
N4432	85w. High jump	2·30	2·00
N4433	140w. Gymnastics	3·50	3·00

1454 Carassius auratus

2004. Fish. Sheet 110×140 mm containing T **1454** and similar horiz designs. Multicoloured.

MSN4434	3w. Type **1454**; 12w. *Tilapia nilotica*; 140w. *Ophiocephalus argus*; 165w. *Clarias gariepinus*	8·50	7·50

1455 Mercedes Benz Fire Appliance

2004. Fire Engines. Multicoloured.

N4435	3w. Type **1455**	30	25
N4436	12w. Fire truck	35	30
N4437	40w. Jelcz fire appliance	1·00	90
N4438	105w. Mercedes Benz without ladders, facing right	2·50	2·30
MSN4439	115×88 mm. Nos. N4435/8	4·25	3·50
MSN4440	85×75 mm. 97w. Mercedes Benz with ladders, facing left	2·40	2·10

1456 Airbus A340–600

2004. Aircraft. Multicoloured.

N4441	3w. Type **1456**	30	25
N4442	97w. Concorde	2·50	2·30
N4443	104w. *Graff Zeppelin II*	2·75	2·40
N4444	116w. Junkers	3·00	2·50
MSN4445	126×1058 mm. Nos. N4432/5	8·75	7·50

Nos. N4441/2 and N4443/4, respectively each form a composite design. The two pairs combine with the margin in MSN4445 to form a composite design of an airfield.

1457 Kim Il Sung and
Prime Minister Koizumi

2004. Kim Il Jong's Meeting with Japanese Prime Minister Junichiro Koizumi. Sheet 150×75 mm.

MSN4446	**1457** 220w. multicoloured	5·25	4·50

1458 An Jung Gun

2004. 125th Birth Anniv of An Jung Gun (revolutionary). Sheet 68×90 mm.

MSN4447	**1458** 112w. multicoloured	2·50	2·30

1459 Kim Jong Suk's Pistol

2004. Kim Jong Suk (Kim Il Sung's wife and revolutionary fighter) Commemoration. Multicoloured.

N4448	3w. Type **1459**	25	25
MSN4449	103×85 mm. 97w. Kim Jong Suk (85×42 mm)	2·50	2·30

1460 Anser cygnoides

2004. Swan Goose (*Anser cygnoides*). Multicoloured.

N4450	3w. Type **1460**	30	25
N4451	97w. Facing left	2·75	2·30
N4452	104w. Two geese	2·75	2·50
N4453	120w. Two geese swimming	3·00	2·75

1461 Temple Building

2004. Simwon Temple. Multicoloured.

N4454	3w. Type **1461**	30	25
MSN4455	120×80 mm. 97w. Buddha (56×42 mm)	3·00	2·50

1462 Diesel Locomotive

2004. Railways. Multicoloured.

N4456	15w. Type **1462**	55	45
N4457	40w. Yellow locomotive	1·10	95
N4458	75w. Electric locomotive	2·10	1·90
N4459	120w. Older electric locomotive	3·50	3·00
N4460	150w. Red locomotive	4·25	3·75
MSN4461	165×91 mm. Nos. N4456/8 and N4460	11·50	10·50
MSN4462	95×58 mm. 120w. No. N4459	3·75	3·25

1463 Kim Il Sung and
Children

2004. 45th Anniv of Repatriation. Sheet 85×77 mm.

MSN4464	**1463** 80w. multicoloured	1·30	1·30

No. 4463 is vacant.

MARIO CESAR KINDELAND MESA
(CUBA)

(1464)

2004. Olympic Games, Athens. Nos. N4430/3 optd as T **1464** with medal winners' names and country. Multicoloured.

N4465	3w. Boxing (Mario Cesar Kinde-lan Mesa) (Cuba)	30	25
N4466	12w. Football (Argentina)	35	30
N4467	85w. High jump (Yelena Slesarenko) (Russia)	2·30	2·00
N4468	140w. Gymnastics (Teng Haibin) (China)	3·50	3·00

1465 Soldier

2005. New Year.

N4469	**1465** 3w. multicoloured	30	25

1466 Chick

2005. New Year. Year of the Rooster. Designs showing carved wooden fowl (N4470/MS4476). Multicoloured.

N4470	3w. Type **1466**	30	25
N4471	12w. Hen	35	30
N4472	30w. Hen sitting on eggs	90	75
N4473	70w. Hen pecking	2·00	1·70
N4474	100w. Rooster	2·50	2·20
N4475	140w. Basket of eggs	3·50	3·00
MSN4476	84×112 mm. Nos. N4470, N4473/5	8·50	7·50
MSN4477	80×130 mm. 97w. Hen and chicks (painting) (50×60 mm)	2·50	2·20

1467 Kim Il Sung

2005. 80th Anniv (2003) of Kim Il Sung's 250 Mile Journey for Learning. Sheet 125×90 mm.

MSN4478	**1467** 120w. multicoloured	3·00	2·50

1468 Statue

2005. 45th Anniv of Chongsanri Method. Sheet 136×95 mm.

MSN4479	**1468** 120w. multicoloured	3·00	2·50

The stamps and margins of MSN4479 form a composite design.

1469 Sunset

2005. Landscapes. Sheet 136×95 mm containing T **1469** and similar horiz designs. Multicoloured.

MSN4480	3w. Type **1469**; 12w. Snow covered weapons; 40w. Flowering trees and mountain; 50w. Waterside town; 60w. Waterfall in autumn; 70w. Tractors working in fields; 80w. Flower fields; 100w. Paddy fields	9·50	8·50

1470 Flowers and
Mount Paektu

2005. 63rd Birth Anniv of Kim Jong Il. Multicoloured.

N4481	3w. Type **1470**	30	25
MSN4482	Two sheets, each 192×60 mm. (a) 50w.×3, Snow covered peaks, left; Snow covered main peak at sunrise; Snow covered peaks, right. (b) 50w.×3, Peaks and clouds, left; Peaks and lake; Peaks and lake, right	30	7·75

The stamps of MSN4482a/b, each form a composite design of a mountain range.

1471 Monuments

2005. Rodong Sinmun, Josoninmingun and Chongnyonjonwi Newspapers Joint Editorial.

N4483	**1471** 3w. multicoloured	30	25

1472 Orchid

2005. 40th Anniv of Orchid Festival. Multicoloured.

N4484	3w. Type **1472**	30	25
MSN4485	107×80 mm. 120w. Kim Il Sung and President Sukarno of Indonesia (54×45 mm)	3·00	2·50

1473 Kimilsungii
and Birthplace,
Mangyongdae

2005. 93rd Birth Anniv of Kim Il Sung. Multicoloured.

N4486	3w. Type **1473**	30	25
MSN4487	105×78 mm. 112w. Kim Il Sung (39×51 mm)	2·75	2·30

1474 Pack Yong Sun

2005. World Table Tennis Championship, Shanghai. Multicoloured.

N4488	3w. Type **1474**	30	25
N4489	5w. Mao Zedong	30	25
N4490	12w. Wang Liqin	35	30
N4491	20w. Jan-Ove Waldner	70	60
N4492	30w. Zhang Yining	90	75
N4493	102w. Werner Schlager	2·50	2·20
MSN4494	155×187 mm. Nos. N4488/93	5·25	4·75

1475 Panda

2005. Giant Panda (*Ailuropoda melanoleuca*). Multicoloured.

N4495	15w. Type **1475**	55	45
N4496	45w. Walking	1·20	1·00
N4497	70w. Two pandas	2·00	1·70
N4498	120w. Mother and cub	3·00	2·50
N4499	140w. Eating bamboo	3·50	3·00
MSN4500	150×105 mm. Nos. N4495/9	10·50	9·25
MSN4501	80×130 mm. 120w. Mother and cub	3·25	2·75

1477 Family

2005. 50th Anniv of Korean Residents in Japan Association (Chongryon). Multicoloured.

N4507	3w. Type **1477**	30	25
MSN4508	85×102 mm. 130w. Kim Il Sung and Chongryon leader (45×54 mm)	3·25	2·75

1478 *Panthera tigris altaika*

2005. Far Eastern Animals. Multicoloured.

N4509	40w. Type **1478**	1·10	95
N4510	40w. *Martes zibellina*	1·10	95

Stamps of a similar design were issued by Russia.

1479 General's Tomb, Koguryo

2005. Relics and Remains of Koguryo Dynasty (277BC–668AD). Multicoloured.

N4511	3w. Type **1479**	30	25
N4512	70w. Hunting (tomb mural)	2·00	1·70
N4513	97w. King Kwanggaetho's mausoleum (37×56 mm)	2·40	2·10
N4514	100w. Fortress, Mt. Songsan	2·50	2·20
N4515	130w. Gilded arrow heads	3·25	2·75
MSN4516	135×120 mm. Nos. N4511/12 and N4514/15	8·00	7·00
MSN4517	130×90 mm. 97w. No. N4513	2·50	2·20

1480 Kim Chol Ju

2005. Kim Chol Ju (revolutionary) Commemoration. Sheet 75×100 mm.

MSN4518	**1480** 170w. multicoloured	4·50	3·75

1481 Kim Jong Il and Kim Dae-jung (President South Korea 1998–2003)

2005. Fifth Anniv of North–South Joint Declaration. Two sheets containing T **1481** and similar multicoloured designs showing Kim Il Jong and Kim Dae-jung.

MSN4519	120×125 mm. 112w.×4, Type **1481**; Kim Jong Il and Kim Dae-jung (different); At banquet (horiz); At conference table (horiz)	13·50	12·50
MSN4520	90×110 mm. 167w. Shaking hands (54×45 mm)	4·50	3·75

1482 White Tiger

2005. White Tiger (*Panthera tigris altaika*). Multicoloured.

N4521	3w. Type **1482**	30	25
N4522	12w. Snarling head	35	30
N4523	130w. Head and shoulders	3·25	2·75
N4524	200w. Snarling facing right	5·25	4·75
MSN4525	160×100 mm. Nos. N4521/4	9·50	8·50
MSN4526	131×105 mm. 150w. Mother and cubs (42×64 mm)	4·00	3·50

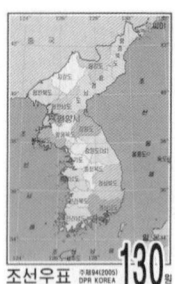

1483 Map of Korea

2005. Sheet 113×89 mm.

MSN4527	**1483** 130w. multicoloured	3·25	2·75

1484 Soldier

2005. Period of Struggle.

N4528	**1484** 3w. multicoloured	30	25

1485 Monument

2005. 60th Anniv of National Liberation. Designs showing Kim Il Sung. Multicoloured.

N4529	3w. Type **1485**	30	25
MSN4530	Two sheets, each 111×145 mm (a) 60w.×4, Kim Il Sung at home (horiz); On horseback (horiz); With fighters in woodland (horiz); Planning strategy (horiz); 102w. In uniform (44×44 mm. circular). (b) 60w.×4, On board ship (horiz); With workers (horiz); Giving speech (horiz); With family (horiz); 102w. At microphone (44×44 mm. circular)	20·00	19·00
MSN4531	98×126 mm. 128w. Kim Il Sung (44×44 mm. circular)	3·25	2·75

(1486)

2005. Taipei 2005 International Stamp Exhibition. Nos. N4490/2, N4494 and MSN4496 overprinted as T **1486**.

N4532	15w. As Type **1475**	55	45
N4533	45w. Walking (As N4491)	1·20	1·00
N4534	70w. Two pandas (As N4492)	2·10	1·90
N4535	140w. Eating bamboo (As N4494)	3·50	3·00
MSN4536	80×80 mm. 120w. Mother and cub (As MSN4496)	3·00	2·50

1487 Red Robes

2005. National Costume. Multicoloured.

N4537	3w. Type **1487**	30	25
N4538	80w. Blue and yellow robe	2·20	1·90
N4539	100w. Green and cream robe with cranes	2·50	2·20
N4540	120w. Brocade coat	3·00	2·50
MSN4541	140×80 mm. Nos. N45237/40	8·25	7·25
MSN4542	70×94 mm. 140w. Children (39×51 mm)	3·50	3·00

1488 Marchers

2005. Joint Slogans.

N4543	**1488** 3w. multicoloured	30	25

1489 Monument

2005. 60th Anniv of Korean Workers Party. Multicoloured.

N4544	3w. Type **1489**	30	25
MSN4545	Two sheets, each 153×125 mm. Horiz, size 51×39 mm. (a) 12w Kim Il Sung; 30w. Kim Il Sung and Kim Jong Il; 60w. Kim Il Sung with military leaders; 90w. Kim Jong Il. (b) 12w. Early discussions; 30w. Joining together; 60w. Planning; 90w. Giving speech	10·50	9·75
MSN4546	Two sheets, each 81×100 mm. Circular, size 46×46 mm. (a) 120w. Kim Jong Il. (b) 120w. Kim Il Sung	6·00	5·50

1490 Queen emerging

2005. Bees (*Apis mellifera*). Multicoloured.

N4547	3w. Type **1490**	30	25
N4548	12w. Two bees and grubs	35	30
N4549	128w. Bee and honey	3·25	2·75
N4550	200w. Bee in flight	5·25	4·75
MSN4551	140×80 mm. Nos. N4547/50	9·75	9·00

1491 "60" and Emblem

2005. 60th Anniv of United Nations.

N4552	**1491** 15w. multicoloured	30	25

1492 Pagoda

2005. Relics of Kaesong (1st issue). Two sheets, each 180×125 mm containing T **1492** and similar multicoloured designs.

MSN4553	(a) 35w.×3, Type **1492**; Monument; Pagoda (different); 75c. Buildings (64×42 mm). (b) 35w.×3, Small building; Steps; Tablet (32×32 mm circular); 75w. Gateway (64×42 mm)	5·75	5·00

See also Nos. MSN4556.

1493 Kim Hyong Gwon

2005. Birth Centenary of Kim Hyong Gwon (revolutionary). Sheet 75×110 mm.

MSN4554	**1493** 120w. multicoloured	3·00	2·50

1494 Manuscript and "X"

2005. Centenary of False Five Point Treaty.

N4555	**1494** 12w. multicoloured	35	30

2005. Relics of Kaesong (2nd issue). Three sheets, each 180×125 mm containing multicoloured designs as T **1492**.

MSN4556	(a) 35w.×2, Bridge; Statue; 75w. Waterfall (42×64 mm). (b) 35w.×2, Yeongjo of Joseon (32×32 mm circular); Gateway (45×33 mm); 75w. Burial mound (64×42 mm). (c) 35w.×6, Raised building and tunnel; Two burial mounds; Stone bridge; Steps and gateway; Buddha; Pillars and mound	14·00	13·00

The larger stamps in MSN4550a/b merge with the margins to form composite background designs.

1495 President Hu Jintao and Kim Il Jong

2005. Visit of President Hu Jintao to Korea. Sheet 149×118 mm containing T **1495** and similar multicoloured designs.

MSN4557	35w.×3, Type **1495**; With business men; Seated at flower strewn table; 102w. Shaking hands (36×57 mm)	5·50	4·75

1496 Flowers and Mountain

2006. New Year.

N4558	**1496** 3w. multicoloured	30	25

1497 Dog

2006. New Year. Year of the Dog (1st issue). Multicoloured.

N4559	3w. Type **1497**	30	25
N4560	15w. Hound	55	45
N4561	70w. White and brown Spitz type	2·00	1·70
N4562	100w. Black and white Spitz type	2·50	2·20
N4563	130w. Spaniel	3·25	2·75
MSN4564	150×104 mm. Nos. N4559/63 plus stamp size label	9·00	8·00
MSN4565	80×80 mm. 130w. No. N4563	3·50	3·00

See also Nos. 4568/**MS**4569.

1498 Kim Jong Il

2006. 60th Anniv of Kim Jong Il's Socialist Youth League. Two sheets containing T **1498** and similar vert designs. Multicoloured.

MSN4566	115×80 mm. 3w. Type **1498**; 111w. Kim Jong Il and young people; 150w. Passing torch	7·00	6·50
MSN4567	130×115 mm. 128w. With young socialists (42×64 mm)	3·25	2·75

The stamp and margins of **MS**N4567 form a composite design.

1499 Dog

2006. New Year. Year of the Dog (2nd issue). Multicoloured.

N4568	12w. Type **1499**	35	30
MSN4569	80×130 mm. 70w. Mastiff (painting) (50×60 mm)	2·00	1·80

1500 Revolutionary Tools

2006. Rodong Sinmun, Josoninmingun and Chongnyonjonwi Newspapers Joint Editorial.

N4570	**1500** 3w. multicoloured	30	25

1501 Ice Dance

2006. Winter Olympic Games, Turin. Multicoloured.

N4571	15w. Type **1501**	55	45
N4572	85w. Ice hockey	2·30	2·00
N4573	110w. Ski jump	2·75	2·30
N4574	135w. Speed skating	3·50	3·00
MSN4575	140×112 mm. Nos. N4571/4	9·25	8·50

1502 Mount Paektu and Flowers

2006. 64th Birth Anniv of Kim Jong Il. Multicoloured.

N4576	3w. Type **1502**	30	25
MSN4577	140×76 mm. 12w. *Polemorium racemosum*; 45w. *Lilium concolor*; 100w. *Taraxacum platycarpum*; 140w. *Parnassia palustris*	9·00	8·00

1503 Crop Research Institute

2006. Kim Jong Il's Visit to China. Two sheets containing T **1503** and similar multicoloured designs showing Kim Jong Il.

MSN4578	170×120 mm. 3w. Type **1503**; 12w. Fibre optic production; 35w. Outside at Three Gorges Dam; 70w. Inside at Guangzhou International Conference and Exhibition Centre; 100w. Inside at Gree Air-Conditioner Production Company; 120w. Outside at Yandian Port	10·00	9·00
MSN4579	160×120 mm. 102w. With President Hu Jintao (42×64 mm)	2·50	2·20

1504 Irrigation

2006. 60th Anniv of Agrarian Reform Law. Multicoloured.

N4580	12w. Type **1504**	35	30
MSN4581	96×72 mm. 150w. Kim Il Sung and farmer (51×39 mm)	4·00	3·50

1505 As No. 4b

2006. 60th Anniv of First Postage Stamps. Sheet 100×80 mm.

MSN4582	**1505** 158w. multicoloured	4·25	3·75

1506 Pibong Falls

2006. Mount Kumgang. Multicoloured designs.

N4583	3w. Type **1506**	30	25
N4584	12w. Podok Hermitage	35	30
N4585	35w. Sokka Peak	1·00	85
N4586	50w. Jipson Peak	1·30	1·20
N4587	70w. Chongsok rocks (horiz)	2·00	1·70
N4588	100w. Sejon Peak (horiz)	2·50	2·20
N4589	120w. Chonhwa rock (horiz)	3·00	2·50
N4590	140w. Piro Peak (horiz)	3·50	3·00

1507 Jules Verne (writer)

2006. Belgica 2006 International Stamp Exhibition. Multicoloured.

N4591	140w. Type **1507**	3·50	3·00
N4592	140w. *Tursiops truncates*	3·50	3·00
N4593	140w. Alaskan malamute dog and Birman cat	3·50	3·00
N4594	140w. *Australopithecus afarensis* heads	3·50	3·00
N4595	140w. *Sunflowers* (Vincent Van Gogh)	3·50	3·00
N4596	140w. *Nymphalidae* and *Disa grandiflora*	3·50	3·00

N4597	140w. Football, chess piece, table tennis bat and ball	3·50	3·00
N4598	140w. *Tyto alba*	3·50	3·00
N4599	140w. Ernst Grube Type S 4000-1 fire appliance (1962) (horiz)	3·50	3·00
N4600	140w. Maglev train (horiz)	3·50	3·00

1508 Kimilsungia

2006. 94th Birth Anniv of Kim Il Sung.

N4601	**1508** 3w. multicoloured	30	25

1509 Site of Donggang Meeting and Inaugural Declaration

2006. 70th Anniv of Foundation for the Restoration of the Fatherland.

N4602	**1509** 3w. multicoloured	30	25

1510 Pothong River Improvement Monument

2006. 60th Anniv of Pothong River Improvement Project.

N4603	**1510** 12w. multicoloured	35	30

1511 Necktie and Badge

2006. 60th Anniv of Children's Union.

N4604	**1511** 3w. multicoloured	30	25

1512 Chasing Ball

2006. World Cup Football Championship, Germany. Showing two players. Multicoloured.

N4605	3w. Type **1512**	30	25
N4606	130w. Tackling	3·25	2·75
N4607	160w. Kicking ball into goal	4·25	3·75
N4608	210w. Heading ball	5·75	5·00

1513 Kim Chol Ju and Zhang Weihua

2006. 90th Birth Anniv of Kim Chol Ju (revolutionary). Sheet 65×83 mm.

MSN4609	**1513** 170w. multicoloured	4·50	3·75

1514 Ri Su Bok

2006. Ri Su Bok (poet and soldier) Commemoration. Sheet 145×85 mm.

MSN4610	**1514** 120w. multicoloured	3·00	2·50

The stamp and margin of **MS**N4610 form a composite design.

1515 Trapeze Artistes

2006. Circus. Sheet 125×150 mm containing T nnnnnnn and similar multicoloured designs.

MSN4611	3w. Type **1515**; 12w. Four trapeze artistes; 130w. Acrobat; 200w. Blindfolded juggler (42×64 mm)	10·00	9·25

The stamps and margin of **MS**N4611 form a composite design.

1516 Kimchi

2006. Traditional Food. Multicoloured.

N4612	3w. Type **1516**	30	25
N4613	12w. Umegi	35	30
N4614	130w. Rice cake dumplings	3·25	2·75
N4615	200w. Sweet rice	5·25	4·75

1517 *Megaptera nodosa*

2006. Sea Mammals. Multicoloured.

N4616	3w. Type **1517**	30	25
N4617	70w. *Balaenoptera musculus*	2·00	1·70
N4618	160w. *Physter catodon*	4·25	3·75
N4619	240w. *Inia geoffrensis*	6·00	5·25

1518 Early Motor Cycle

2006. Motor Cycles. Multicoloured.

N4620	3w. Type **1518**	30	25
N4621	102w. Blue motor cycle with full faring	2·50	2·20
N4622	150w. Early motor cycle	4·00	3·50
N4623	240w. Red motor cycle with partial faring	6·50	5·50
MSN4624	175×100 mm. Nos. N4620/3, each×2	27·00	25·00

1519 *General Sherman* in Flames

2006. 140th Anniv of Sinking of *General Sherman*.

N4625	**1519** 130w. multicoloured	3·25	2·75

1520 *Tyto alba*

2006. Owls. Multicoloured.

N4626	12w. Type **1520**	35	30
N4627	111w. *Strix uralensis*	2·75	2·30
N4628	130w. *Strix aluco*	3·25	2·75
N4629	160w. *Nyctea scandiaca*	4·25	3·75

1521 Kim Il Sung (statue)

2006. 60th Anniv of Kim Il Sung University. Sheet 90×115 mm.

MSN4630 **1521** 70w. multicoloured   2·00   1·70

1522 Ulji Mundok

2006. Personalities. Multicoloured.

N4631	3w. Type **1522**	30	25
N4632	12w. So Hui	35	30
N4633	35w. Kim Ung So	1·00	85
N4634	70w. Kang Kam Chan	2·00	1·70
N4635	102w. Yongae Somun	2·50	2·20
N4636	130w. Ri Kyu Bo	3·25	2·75
N4637	160w. Mun Ik Jom	4·25	3·75

1523 Flag

2006. 80th Anniv of Anti-Imperialism Union. Multicoloured.

N4638 **1523** 3w. Type **1523**   30   25

MSN4639 160×100 mm. 70w. Founder members in the countryside (51×40 mm); 102w. Kim Il Sung as young man (46×46 mm) (circular); 120w. Kim Il Sung and members on rail track   9·00   7·75

1524 Flag and Red Cross Vehicles

2006. 60th Anniv of Red Cross Society.

N4640 **1524** 30wn. multicoloured   90   75

1525 Students (image scaled to 38% of original size)

2006. 60th Anniv of Secondary Education Fund for Koreans in Japan. Sheet 150×95 mm.

MSN4641 **1525** 110w. multicoloured   2·75   2·30

1526 Ruler

2006. 60th Anniv of UNESCO. Tomb Murals, Anak. Sheet 165×112 mm containing T **1526** and similar multicoloured designs.

MSN4642 3w. Type **1526**; 70w. Consort; 130w. Subak (martial art) (horiz); 135w. Procession (horiz); 160w. Kitchen (horiz)   13·50   12·00

1527 University Buildings

2006. 50th Anniv of Joson University. Sheet 150×95 mm.

MSN4643 **1527** 110w. multicoloured   2·75   2·30

(1528)

2006. Belgica 2006 International Stamp Exhibition. Owls. Nos. N4625/8 overprinted as T **1528**. Multicoloured.

N4644	12w. As Type **1520**	35	30
N4645	111w. As No. N4627	2·75	2·30
N4646	130w. As No. N4628	3·25	2·75
N4647	160w. As No. N4629	4·25	3·75

1529 Carving

2006. Army's Gift to Kim Jong Il. Sheet 90×130 mm.

MSN4648 **1529** 130w. multicoloured   3·25   2·75

The stamp and margin of MSN4648 form a composite design.

1530 Bell and Snow-covered Pagoda

2007. New Year.

N4649 **1530** 3w. multicoloured   30   25

1531 Pig

2007. New Year. Year of the Pig. Multicoloured.

N4650	3w. Type **1531**	30	25
N4651	45w. Pot-bellied pig	1·20	1·00
N4652	70w. Saddle back	2·00	1·70
N4653	130w. Large white	3·25	2·75
MSN4654	115×86 mm. Nos. N4650/3	7·00	6·50
MSN4655	80×57 mm. 70w. No. N4653	2·00	1·80

1532 Begonia 'Kimjongilhwa'

2007. 65th Birth Anniv of Kim Jong Il. Multicoloured.

N4656 3w. Type **1532**   30   25

MSN4657 170×100 mm. Size 36×57 mm. 12w. Score, mountains and lake (left); 70w. Score, mountains (two peaks) and lake (centre); 100w. Score, mountains and lake (larger); 140w. Score, mountains and lake (right)   8·50   7·50

The stamps and margins of MSN4657 form a composite design of a lake ringed by mountains.

1533 Symbols of Industry and Agriculture

2007. Rodong Sinmun

N4658 **1533** 3w. multicoloured   30   35

1534 *Callicore selima*

2007. Butterflies. Multicoloured.

N4659	15w. Type **1534**	40	35
N4660	85w. *Morpho rhetenor*	2·20	1·90
N4661	110w. *Atrophaneura alcinous*	2·75	2·50
N4662	160w. *Parnassius bremeri*	4·25	3·75

1535 Horses in Stable

2007. World Heritage Sites. Tomb Murals, Anak. Multicoloured.

N4663	3w. Type **1535**	30	25
N4664	70w. Well	2·00	1·70
N4665	130w. Women milling (30×42 mm)	3·25	3·75
N4666	160w. Horn (30×42 mm)	4·25	3·75

MSN4667 135×110 mm. 3w. As Type **1535**; 70w. As N4664; 130w. As N4665 (vert); 160w. As N4666 (vert)   13·50   12·00

1536 Building

2007. 90th Anniv of Korean National Association.

N4668 **1536** 12w. multicoloured   35   30

1537 Beethoven and Score

2007. 180th Death Anniv of Ludwig van Beethoven (composer).

N4669 **1537** 80w. multicoloured   2·10   1·80

1538 Mangyongdae (birthplace)

2007. 94th Birth Anniv of Kim Il Sung. Multicoloured.

N4670 3w. Type **1538**   30   25

MSN4671 92×112 mm. 130w. Kim Il Sung and family (64×42 mm)   3·25   2·75

1539 *Sciurius vulgaris*

2007. Rodents. Sheet 145×85 mm containing T **1539** and similar triangular designs. Multicoloured.

MSN4673 3w. Type **1539**; 12w. *Muscardinus avellanarius*; 20w. *Hypogeomys antimena*; 30w. *Lemniscomys striatus*; 40w. *Pedetes capensis*; 50w. *Rattus norvegicus*; 80w. *Eliomys quercinus*; 102w. *Micromys minutes*   13·50   12·00

1540 Soldiers

2007. 75th Anniv of National Army. Multicoloured.

N4674 12w. Type **1540**   35   30

MSN4675 124×76 mm. Size 51×39 mm. 80w. Kim Il Sung inspecting troops; 100w. Kim Jong Il and soldiers   4·50   4·00

MSN4676 132×90 mm. Size 64×42 mm. 120w. Kim Il Sung and Kim Jong Il on podium   3·00   2·40

1541 Spraying

2007. Avian Flu Prevention Campaign.

N4677 **1541** 85w. multicoloured   2·20   1·90

1542 Banknote (1947)

2007. 60th Anniv of National Currency. Sheet 118×160 mm containing T **1542** and similar horiz designs. Multicoloured.

MSN4678 3w. Type **1542**; 35w. Banknote (1947) (different); 35w. Banknote (1959); 50w. Banknote (1959) (different); 70w. Banknote (1978); 110w. Banknote (1978) (different); 130w. Banknote (1992); 160w. Banknote (1992) (different)   7·00   6·25

1543 Kim Il Sung

2007. 70th Anniv of Pochonbo Battle. Sheet 140×102 mm.

MSN4679 **1543** 120w. multicoloured   3·50   3·00

1544 *Naso lituratus*

2007. Fish. Multicoloured.

N4680	15w. Type **1544**	15	10
N4681	50w. *Carassius auratus*	1·30	1·10
N4682	110w. Inscr 'A. citrinellus'	2·75	2·30
N4683	200w. *Symphysodon discus*	5·25	4·75

1545 Ri Jun

2007. Death Centenary of Ri Jun (cultural activist).
N4684 **1545** 110w. chocolate and
green 2·75 2·30

1546 Tetracorallia

2007. Fossils. Multicoloured.
N4685 15w. Type **1546** 15 10
N4686 70w. Neuropteridium 2·00 1·70
N4687 130w. Yoldia 3·25 2·75
N4688 200w. Rhinoceros 5·25 4·75

1547 *Oncidium wyattianum*

2007. Orchids. Multicoloured.
N4689 3w. Type **1547** 30 25
N4690 70w. *Cymbidium* Red Beauty
'Carmen' 2·00 1·70
N4691 127w. *Dendrobium thyrsiflorum* 3·00 2·50
N4692 140w. *Dendrobium* Candy Stripe
'Kodama' 3·50 3·00
MSN4692a 192×91 mm. Nos. N4689/
N4692

1548 Players

2007. Women's Football. Two sheets containing T **1548**
and similar circular designs. Multicoloured.
MSN4693 152×110 mm. 12w. Type
1548; 40w. Reverse kick; 70w. Heading the ball; 110w. Preparing to kick;
140w. Tackle 9·75 9·00
MSN4694 96×65 mm. 130w. Two players running for ball 3·25 2·75

1549 Gladiolus gandavensis

2007. Flowers. Multicoloured.
N4695 30w. Type **1549** 30 25
N4696 30w. *Iris ensata* Thumb 30 25
N4697 30w. *Rosa hybrida* 30 25
N4698 30w. *Nelumbo nucifera* 30 25
MSN4699 130×84 mm. N4695/N4698
Nos. N4695/8 were issued together, *se-tenant*, form-
ing a composite design. The stamps and margins of
MSN4699 form a composite design.
Stamps of a similar design were issued by Russia.

1550 Beibei

2007. Olympic Games, Beijing. Two sheets containing T
1550 and similar circular designs. Multicoloured.
MSN4700 152×110 mm. 3w. Type
1550; 12w. Jingjing; 30w. Huanhuan;
70w. Yingying; 140w. Nini 7·00 6·50
MSN4701 150×120mm. Size 44x44mm
(circular). 3w. Beibei; 12w. Jungjing;
30w. Huazhuan; 70w. Yingying;
140w. Niri

No. MSN4701 has been left for sheet not yet received.

1551 Box

2007. Traditional Furniture. Multicoloured.
N4702 3w. Type **1551** 30 25
N4703 12w. Ornamental chest of
drawers 35 30
N4704 40w. Collapsible dressing tables 1·00 80
N4705 70w. Wardrobe with perforated
front 2·00 1·70
N4706 110w. Triple chest of drawers
inlaid with mother of pearl 2·75 2·30
N4707 130w. Red lacquered triple
chest of drawers 3·25 2·75

1552 Glutinous Potato Cake

2007. Traditional Food. Multicoloured.
N4708 12w. Type **1552** 35 30
N4709 50w. Yongchae kimchi 1·30 1·10
N4710 70w. Fermented flatfish 2·00 1·70
N4711 110w. Frozen potato cake 2·75 3·00

1553 Roo Moo Hyun
(president of South Korea)
and Kim Jong II (leader of
North Korea)

2007. North–South Summit Meeting. Sheet 110×80 mm.
MSN4712 **1553** 170w. multicoloured 4·50 3·75

1554 Parade (image scaled to 29% of original size)

2007. Arirang Festival. Two sheets each 195×155 mm
containing T **1554** and similar circular designs.
Multicoloured.
MSN4713 (a) 12w. Type **1554**; 50w.
Floodlit parade (93×35 mm); (b)
120w. Two performers and massed
performance; 155w. Massed performance (93×35 mm) 7·75 6·50

1555 Ploughing

2007. Paintings by Kim Hong Do. Multicoloured.
N4714 13w. Type **1555** 35 30
N4715 50w. Weaving 1·30 1·10
N4716 70w. Threshing 2·00 1·70
N4717 110w. Archery 2·75 3·00

1555a Nong Duc Manh and Kim Jong
II

2007. Visit of Nong Duc Manh (General Secretary of the
Communist Party of Vietnam) to Pyongyang. Sheet
98×76 mm.
MSN4718 **1555a** 120w. multicoloured 3·00 2·50

1556 Kim Jong Suk's Home

2007. 90th Birth Anniv of Kim Jong Suk (Kim Il Sung's
wife and revolutionary fighter). Multicoloured.
N4719 3w. Type **1556** 30 25
MSN4720 30w. Kim Jong Suk and Kim
Il Sung (53×44 mm); 70w. Kim Jong
Suk (circular (45×45 mm)); 110w.
With soldiers (53×44 mm) 5·00 4·25

1557 Flag and Skyline

2008. New Year.
N4721 **1557** 3w. multicoloured 30 25

1558 Frontpage and Couple

2008. 80th Anniv of Publication of Saenal Sinmum
Newspaper.
N4722 **1558** 85w. multicoloured 2·20 1·90

1559 Emblem

2008. Rodong Sinmun, Josoninmingun and
Chongnyonjonwi Newspapers Joint Editorial.
Multicoloured.
N4723 3w. Type **1559** 30 25
N4724 3w. Soldier leading crowd 30 25
N4725 12w. Soldier with arm raised 35 30
N4726 12w. Construction workers and
soldiers (horiz) 35 30
N4727 30w. Woman and food (horiz) 1·00 85
N4728 120w. Musicians 3·00 2·50
N4729 135w. Demonstrators from 6.15
Unification Alliance 3·25 2·75

1560 *Melopsittacus
undulatus* (budgerigar)

2008. Cage Birds. Multicoloured.
N4730 15w. Type **1560** 15 10
N4731 85w. *Agapornis personata*
(lovebird) 2·20 1·90
N4732 155w. *Agapornis personata*
(horiz) 4·00 3·50
N4733 170w. *Melopsittacus undulatus*
(horiz) 4·50 3·75

1561 Kim Il Sung and Kim Jong II amongst Flowers

2008. 20th Anniv of Dedication of Kimjongilia. Sheet
155×100 mm.
MSN4734 **1561** 85w. multicoloured 2·20 2·20

1562 *Pyrethrum
hybridum*

2008. 66th Birth Anniv of Kim Jong II. T **1562** and similar
multicoloured designs.
N4735 3w. Type **1562** 30 25
MSN4736 100×105 mm. 12w. *Tulipa
gesneriana*; 70w. *Adonis amurensis*;
120w. *Mathiola incana*; 155w. *Begon-
iax tuberhybrida Voss* 'Kimjongilhwa'
(43×43 mm (circular)) 9·25 9·25

No. N4737 and Type **1563** have been left for 'Mangyongdae', issued on 15 March 2008, not yet received.

1564 Guitarist

2008. 35th Anniv of Publication of On the Art of Cinema.
Sheet 105×167 mm containing T **1564** and similar
horiz designs. Multicoloured.
MSN4738 3w. Type **1564**; 85w. Fur-clad
fighter; 135w. Martial arts; 170w.
Family and young woman 10·00 10·00

1565 Map of Route

2008. 85th Anniv of Kim Il Sung's 250 Mile Journey for
Learning.
N4739 **1565** 15w. multicoloured 20 15

1566 Football

2008. Olympic Games, Beijing. Multicoloured.
N4740 3w. Type **1566** 10 10
N4741 12w. Basketball 25 2·00
N4742 30w. Tennis 35 30
N4743 70w. Table tennis 1·00 85

1567 Choe Yong

2008. Personalities. Each brown.
N4744 85w. Type **1567** 1·20 1·00
N4745 160w. Ho Jun 2·30 2·00

1568 Flowers and Flags

2008. 15th Anniv of Kim Il Jong's Chairmanship of National Defence Commission. Multicoloured.
N4746 12w. Type **1568**   25   20
MSN4747 90×118 mm. 120w. Kim Il
  Jong (42×64 mm)   1·70   1·50

1569 Jug

2008. International Friendship Exhibition, Mt. Myohyang. Multicoloured.
N4748 3w. Type **1569**   10   10
N4749 85w. Cockerel (painting)   1·20   1·00
N4750 155w. Throne   2·00   1·90
MSN4751 101×80 mm. 135w. Vase   2·00   2·00

1570 Mornabong Theatre (conference venue)

2008. 60th Anniv of Joint North—South Conference.
N4752 **1570** 12w. olive   25   20

1571 Amanita muscaria

2008. Fungi. Multicoloured.
N4753 12w. Type**1571**   25   20
N4754 50w. Armillariella mellea   75   65
N4755 135w. Macrolepiota procera   2·00   1·70
N4756 155w. Tricholoma terreum   2·20   1·90

1572 Building and Mountain

2008. Tourism. Mount Ryongak, Pyongyang. Multicoloured.
N4757 35w. Type **1572**   40   35
N4758 155w. Building and mountain
  (different)   2·20   1·90

1573 Hyangbipha

2008. Musical Instruments. Multicoloured.
N4759 15w. Type**1573**   20   15
N4760 50w. Phiri   75   65
N4761 120w. Jangsaenap   1·70   1·50
N4762 160w. Kayagum (horiz)   2·30   2·00

1574 Woman and Score (Sea of Blood)

2008. Five Revolutionary Operas. Designs showing images from the operas and scores. Multicoloured.
N4763 3w. Type **1574**   10   10
N4764 12w. Girl with basket of flowers
  (Flower Girl)   25   20
N4765 85w. Woman in uniform (True
  Daughter of the Party)   1·20   1·00
N4766 120w. Man in snow covered
  landscape (Tell Oh Forest)   1·70   1·50
N4767 155w. Women (The Song of Mt.
  Kumgang)   2·20   1·90

1575 1946 20ch. Stamp (As Type 1)

2008. EFIRO 2008–International Stamp Exhibition, Romania.
N4768 **1575**   85w. multicoloured   1·30   1·10

1576 USS Pueblo (AGER-2) (US ship held in Pyongyang)

2008. Conflict.
N4769 **1576** 12w. multicoloured   30   25
  No. N4770 and Type **1577** are left for Olympic Torch Relay, issued on 26 June 2008, not yet received.

1578 Serpentine (Magnesium Iron Silicate Hydroxide)

2008. Minerals. Multicoloured.
N4771 12w. Type **1578**   30   25
N4772 75w. Copper pyrites   1·10   90
N4773 135w. Zinc blende (sphalerite)   2·10   1·80
N4774 155w. Molybdenite (molybde-
  num disulfide)   2·30   2·00

1579 Kim Il Sung commanding Crossing of Han River

2008. 55th Anniv of End of Korean War. Three sheets containing T **1579** and similar multicoloured designs.
MSN4775 90×130 mm. 3w. Type **1579**;
  120w. Kim Il Sung, soldiers and villagers in snow   1·80   1·80

MSN4776 90×130 mm. 35w. Kim Il
  Sung picnicking with soldiers; 155w.
  Kim Il Sung and cheering crowd   2·75   2·50
MSN4777 144×95 mm. 85w. Kim Il
  Sung and commanders (56×70 mm)   1·30   1·10

1580 Jong Il Peak

2008. 20th Anniv of Naming of Jong Il Peak. Sheet 160×90 mm.
MSN4778 **1580** 120w. multicoloured   1·80   1·80

1581 Rice-Wormwood Cake

2008. Traditional Foods. Multicoloured.
N4779 3w. Type **1581**   50   45
N4780 70w. Nochi (rice cakes)   1·30   1·10
N4781 135w. Green gram pancake   2·10   1·80
N4782 155w. Young garlic preserved
  in soy   2·30   2·00

1582 Kim Jong Il

2008. Songun Revolutionary Leadership. Multicoloured.
N4782a12w. Soldiers   30   25
MSN4783 154×105 mm. 3w. Type
  1582; 12w. With factory workers;
  120w. In laboratory; 170w. With
  cooks in kitchen   10·50 10·50
MSN4784 154×120 mm. 135w. With
  soldiers in persimmon orchard
  (54×90 mm)   2·00   2·00

1583 Mask Dance

2008. World Heritage Sites. King Kogukwon's Tomb Murals, Anak. Sheet 135×112 containing T **1583** and similar multicoloured designs.
MSN4785 3w. Type **1583**: 90w. Jang-
  hadock (aide to the King) (30×42
  mm); 120w. Butchery; 155w. Stable   5·25   5·25
  :

1584 Flag

2008. National Flag.
N4786 **1584**   3w. bright rosine and
  ultramarine   30   25
N4787 **1584** 155w. bright rosine,
  ultramarine and new
  blue   2·20   1·90

1585 Chollima Statue and Flag

2008. 60th Anniv of the Republic. Multicoloured.
N4788 3w. Type **1585**   20   15
N4789 12w. Workers and soldier   30   25
N4790 70w. Soldiers   90   80
N4791 120w. Workers and soldiers on
  flying horses   1·70   1·50
N4792 160w. Hands   2·30   2·00
MSN4793 135×98 mm. 155w. When
  National Flag and Emblem were Born
  (68×54 mm)   2·30   2·30

1586 Husky Sled Team

2008. Modes of Transport. Multicoloured.
N4794 680w. Type **1586**   5·00   5·00
N4795 680w. Cycling   5·00   5·00
N4796 680w. Ferrari Enzo   5·00   5·00
N4797 680w. Mercedes Benz LF 16 fire
  appliance   5·00   5·00
N4798 680w. Steam locomotive (inscr
  'Paravoz Y-127 1910 Russia')   5·00   5·00
N4799 680w. LZ 129 Hindenburg   5·00   5·00
N4800 680w. Concorde   5·00   5·00
N4801 680w. Sputnik 2 spacecraft and
  Laika (1st animal in space)   5·00   5·00
N4802 680w. Eurostar locomotive   5·00   5·00
N4803 680w. Nina (Columbus' ship)   5·00   5·00

1587 Salvelinus malma m. chonjiensis

2008. Endangered Species. Sheet 100×70 mm.
MSN4804 **1587** 135w. multicoloured   2·10   1·80

1588 Choesung Pavilion

2008. Moran Hill. Sheet 188×128 mm containing T **1588** and similar horiz designs. Multicoloured.
MSN4805 3w. Type **1588**: 45w. Pagoda
  and stone pathway; 100w. Shrubs
  and Pyongyang; 135w. Pagoda, steps
  and gateway   4·25   4·25

1589 Children using Computers

2008. 50th Anniv of Universal Compulsory Secondary Education.
N4806 **1589** 12w. multicoloured   30   35

1590 Soldier

2008. Posters. Multicoloured.
N4807 12w. Type **1590**   30   35

N4808 85w. Woman holding bean halms   1·30   1·10

1591 Haeju Table

2008. Traditional Furniture. Multicoloured.
N4809   50w. Type **1591**   75   65
N4810   70w. Inkstone table with drawer and mother-of-pearl inlay   1·10   90
N4811   120w. Red lacquer collapsible dressing table   1·00   85
N4812   170w. Decorated cow horn trunk   2·30   2·00

1592 Pavilion

2008. Ulmil Pavilion, Pyongyang. Sheet 130×85 mm.
MSN4813 **1592** 85w. multicoloured   1·30   1·20

1593 Snow Scene

2009. New Year.
N4814 **1593**   3w. multicoloured   30   35

1594 Red Guards

2009. 50th Anniv of Worker–Peasant Red Guards. Multicoloured.
N4815   12w. Type **1594**   30   25
MSN4816 64×78 mm. 160w. Kim Il Sung and Red Guards (51×39 mm)   1·20   2·10

1595 Tug of War

2009. Traditional Games. Multicoloured.
N4817   3w. Type **1595**   40   35
N4818   120w. Knee fighting   1·50   1·40

1596 *Crinum bracteatum*

2009. 67th Birth Anniv of Kim Jong Il. Multicoloured.
N4819   3w. Type **1596**   20   15
N4820   12w. *Begonia* Irene Nuss   35   30
N4821   120w. *Callistemon phoeniceus*   1·60   1·50
N4822   160w. *Plumeria rubra*   2·20   2·00

1597 Kim Jong Il

2009. 35th Anniv of Publication of Juche Idea Programme. Sheet 120×85 mm.
MSN4823 **1597** 170w. multicoloured   2·40   2·20

1598 Torch and Chollima Statue

2009. Rodong Sinmun, Josoninmingun and Chongnyonjonwi Newspapers Joint Editorial. Four sheets, each 110×85 mm containing T **1598** and similar horiz designs. Multicoloured.
MSN4824 3w. Type **1598**; 170w. Symbols of industry   20   15
MSN4825 12w. Wheat sheaf and other produce; 150w. Musical instruments   2·20   2·20
MSN4826 30w. Hand holding weapon; 120w. Soldiers and flag   2·20   2·20
MSN4827 80w. Emblem; 100w. Hands on weapons   2·40   2·40

1599 Peonies and Butterflies

2009. China 2009 International Stamp Exhibition, Luoyang. Multicoloured.
N4827a 3w. Type **1599**   20   15
N4827b 12w. Tang horse and building   30   35
N4827c 90w. Temple and statue   1·20   1·00
N4827d 100w. Pink peonies   1·50   2·30
MSN4828 155×90 mm. 3w. As Type **1599**; 100w. As No. N4827d   1·50   1·50
MSN4829 155×90 mm. 12w. As No. N4827b; 90w. As No. N4827c   1·50   1·50

1600 Protestors

2009. 90th Anniv of 1 March Uprising.
N4830 **1600**   90w. multicoloured   1·20   1·00

1601 Mother and Child

2009. Centenary of Women's Day.
N4831 **1601**   35w. multicoloured   45   40

1602 Horses (painting)

2009. 96th Birth Anniv of Kim Il Sung. Gifts. Multicoloured.
N4832   3w. Type **1602**   20   15
N4833   12w. Fossil   45   40
N4834   140w. Rifle   2·00   1·70
N4835   150w. Bear skin   2·10   2·00

1603 *Anthropoides paradisea* (blue crane)

2009. 50th Anniv of Central Zoo. Multicoloured.
N4836   12w. Type **1603**   45   40
N4837   70w. *Accipiter gentilis* (goshawk)   75   70
N4838   120w. *Larus argentatus* (herring gull)   1·70   1·50
N4839   140w. *Balearica pavonina* (black crowned crane)   1·90   1·70

1604 *Catalpa ovata* (Chinese catalpa)

2009. 50th Anniv of Central Botanical Garden. Multicoloured.
N4840   3w. Type **1604**   20   15
N4841   50w. *Betula platyphylla* (Asian white birch)   75   60
N4842   120w. *Juglans cordiformis* (Japanese walnut)   1·70   1·60
N4843   160w. *Metasequoia glyptostroboides* (dawn redwood)   2·10   2·00

1605 Baseball

2009. Sports. Multicoloured.
N4844   12w. Type **1605**   20   15
N4845   90w. Tenpin bowling   1·20   1·10
N4846   160w. Fencing   2·20   2·00
N4847   200w. Golf   3·00   2·75

(1606)

2009. IBRA '09 International Stamp Exhibition. No. MSN4193b surch and overprinted in gold as T **1606**. Multicoloured.
MSN4848 20w. on 40ch. Zeppelin LZ1; 40w. on 80ch. LZ 120; 109w. on 1w.20 Zeppelin NT; 168w. on 2w.40 Zeppelin NT (different)   5·00   5·00

1607 Mountaineering

2009. Children's Union Camp. Multicoloured.
N4849   3w. Type **1607**   20   15
N4850   80w. Children with butterfly net   1·00   90
N4851   120w. Cooking over camp fire   1·60   1·50
N4852   170w. At the seaside   2·30   2·10

2009. 23rd Asian International Exhibition, Hong Kong. Sheet 130×42 mm containing horiz designs as T **1607**. Multicoloured.
MSN4853 3w. As Type **1607**; 80w. As N4850; 120w. N4851; 170w. N4852   5·25   5·25

1608 Kim Il Sung

2009. 70th Anniv of Musan Battle. Sheet 130×45 mm.
MSN4854 **1608** 120w. multicoloured   1·80   1·70

1609 UPU Emblem

2009. 135th Anniv of Universal Postal Union.
N4855 **1609**   50w. multicoloured   80   70

1610 *Vespa mandarinia*

2009. Insects. Multicoloured.
N4856   50w. Type **1610**   70   65
N4857   90w. *Cicindela japaonica*   1·30   1·40
N4858   120w. *Locusta migratoria*   1·80   1·70
N4859   140w. *Aphaenogaster famelica*   2·00   1·90

1611 Kim Chaek University of Technology Library

2009. Prominent Buildings in Pyongyang. Multicoloured.
N4860   12w. Grand Theatre   35   30
MSN4861 145×97 mm. 3w. Type **1611**; 70w. Taedongmun Cinema; 90w. Okyryu Restaurant (70×28 mm); 150w. Chongryu Restaurant (70×28 mm)   4·75   4·50

1612 *Kim Il Sung drawing Party Emblem*

2009. Juche Idea. Sheet 190×84 mm containing T **1612** and similar horiz designs showing paintings. Multicoloured.
MSN4862 12w. Type **1612**; 50w. *First Military Flags*; 70w. *Birth*; 140w. *Every Field with a Bumper Harvest*   4·00   4·00

1613 Nurse and Child

2009. Public Health. Multicoloured.
N4863   12w. Type **1613**   45   40
N4864   150w. Symbols of health care   2·20   2·00

1614 Unha-2 Rocket

2009. Launch of Satellite—Kwangmyongsong 2. Sheet 127×100mm.
MSN4865 **1614** 120w. multicoloured   1·80   1·80

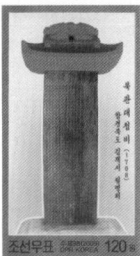

1615 Monument

2009. Re-erection of Victory Monument. Sheet 160×70mm.
MSN4866 **1615** 120w. multicoloured   1·80   1·80

1616 Saenap

2009. Traditional Musical Instruments. Multicoloured.
N4867 12w. Type **1616**   30   35
N4868 80w. Drum   1·30   1·20
N4869 140w. Songonghu   2·10   1·00
N4870 170w. Flute   2·40   2·30

1617 Worker

2009. 150–Day Campaign for Innovation.
N4871 **1617** 12w. multicoloured   45   40

1617a Dogs and Total Solar Eclipse

2009. International Year of Astronomy. Multicoloured.
N4871a 95w. Type **1617a**   1·20   1·10
N4871b 95w. Cholima statue   1·20   1·10
N4871c 95w. Hares and partial solar
          eclipse   1·20   1·10
N4871d 95w. Satellite, Galilean tel-
          escope and Galileo Galilei   1·20   1·10
N4871e 95w. Galaxy and planets   1·20   1·10
N4871f 95w. Chomsongdae–7th
          century observatory   1·20   1·10
MSN4871g 135×86 mm. 95w. As Type
          1617a   2·40   2·40
MSN4871h 140×95 mm. 95w.×2, Nos.
          N4871b and N4771d   2·40   2·40
MSN4871i 140×95 mm. 95w.×2, Nos.
          N4871c and N4871e   2·40   2·40
MSN4871j 140×95 mm. 95w.×2, As
          Type **1617a** and N4871f   2·40   2·40

1618 *Theragra chalcogramma*

2009. Fish. Multicoloured.
N4872 15w. Type **1618**   50   40
N4873 60w. *Cyprinus carpio*   80   75
N4874 140w. *Euthynnus pelamis*   1·90   1·70
N4875 160w. *Mugil cephalus*   2·20   2·00

1619 DPRK—China Friendship Stamps (image scaled to 34% of original size)

1620 DPRK—China Friendship Stamps (image scaled to 34% of original size)

2009. DPRK—China Friendship. Two sheets, each 140×110mm, containing T **1619** and similar horiz designs. Multicoloured.
MSN4876 60w.×2, Type **1619**   1·40   1·40
MSN4877 60w.×2, Type **1620**   1·40   1·40

1621 *Coturnicops exquistus* (Swinhoe's rail)

2009. Bird Pex. Multicoloured.
N4878 12w. Type **1621**   45   40
N4879 90w. *Porzana pusilla* (Baillon's
          crake)   1·40   1·20
N4880 170w. *Porzana fusca* (ruddy-
          breasted crake)   2·40   2·20
MSN4880a 166×121 mm. 12w.×2 As
          Type **1621**×2 (*Coturnicops exquistus*
          (Swinhoe's rail)): 90w. ×2, No.
          N4879×2, (*Porzana pusilla* (Baillon's
          crake)); 170w. No. N4880 (*Porzana
          fusca* (ruddy-breasted crake))   6·25   6·25

1621a Henry Dunant

2009. Year of Red Cross and Red Crescent. 150th Anniv of Battle of Solferino (witnessed by Henry Dunant who instigated campaign resulting in establishment of Geneva Conventions and Red Cross). Sheet 120×84 mm containing T **1621a** and similar vert designs. Multicoloured.
MSN4880b 75w. Type **1621a**; 95w.
Trees and water (disaster risk reduction); Red Cross workers and patient
(first aid)   4·50   4·50

1622 Kim Jong Suk

2009. 60th Death Anniv of Kim Jong Suk (Kim Il Sung's first wife and Kim Jong Il's mother). Sheet 93×106 mm containing T **1622** and similar multicoloured design.
MSN4881 90w. Type **1622**; 100w. With
soldiers (57×36 mm)   5·00   5·00

1622a Hu Jintao and *In Praise of Harmony*

2009. 60th Anniv of People's Republic of China. Sheet 160×133 mm containing T **1622a** and similar horiz designs. Multicoloured.
MS4881a 10w. Type **1622a**; 67w.
Chinese cosmonauts; 67w. National
Stadium, China; 84w. National Grand
Theatre, China   3·00   3·00

1622b Spoonbill

2009. Endangered Species. Spoonbill (*Platalea minor*). Multicoloured.
N4881b 3w. Type **1622b**   20   15
N4881c 12w. Holding fish   45   40
N4881d 99w. In flight   1·40   1·20
N4881e 266w. With wings raised   4·00   4·00

1623 *Chamaeleo jacksonii* (Jackson's chameleon)

2009. Reptiles. Multicoloured.
N4882 15w. Type **1623**   55   50
N4883 50w. (*Naja naja* (cobra)   80   75
N4884 110w. *Caretta caretta* (logger-
          head sea turtle) (horiz)   1·70   1·50
N4885 160w. *Crocodylus niloticus* (Nile
          crocodile) (horiz)   2·40   2·20

1624 Stamp of 2006 (As No. N4608)

2009. Italia 2009–International Stamp Exhibition. Sheet 164×83 mm.
MSN4886 **1624** 210w. multicoloured   3·25   3·25
Nos. N4887/91 and Type **1625** are left for Lighthouses issued on 24 October 2009, not yet received.

1626 Kim Il Sung and Returnees

2009. Repatriation
MSN4892 **1626** 160w. multicoloured   2·20   1·90

1627 Rocket and Satellite (space)

2009. Year of Realizing Ideals. Multicoloured.
MSN4893 159×125 mm. 10w. Type
1627; 20w. Computer controlled
machines (CNC); 20w. Power plant,
girders and transport; 30w. Building
site; 50w. Refinery; 50w. Cityscape;
57w. Sturgeon, ostriches and farm
animals; 70w. Arable land; 80w.
Footballers and singer   3·50   3·50
MSN4894 162×113 mm. 100w. Kim
Jong Il and workmen (72×57 mm)   1·00   1·00

1628 Party Founding Monument, Mansu Hill

2010. New Year
N4895 **1628** 10w. multicoloured   30   25

1629 Tiger (painting by He Xiangning)

2010. Chinese New Year. Year of the Tiger
N4896 30w. Type **1629**   40   35
N4897 67w. Tiger (embroidery by Ri
          Won In)   90   85

1630 *Ailuropoda melanoleuca* (panda)

2010. Fauna. Multicoloured.
N4899 35w. Type **1630**   40   35
N4900 60w. *Aix galericulata* (Mandarin
          duck)   80   75·00
N4901 80w. *Lagenorhynchus obliq-
          uidens* (Pacific white-sided
          dolphin)   95   90
N4902 110w. *Panthera pardus* (leopard)   1·20   1·10

1631 Ice Hockey

2010. Winter Olympic Games, Vancouver. Multicoloured.
N4903 10w. Type **1631**   35   30
N4904 40w. Figure skating   45   40
N4905 50w. Speed skating   60   55
N4906 70w. Skiing   90   85

1632 *Impatiens sultani*

2010. 68th Birth Anniv of Kim Jong Il. Multicoloured.
N4907 10w. Type **1632**   30   25
N4908 50w. *Gazania hybrida*   60   55
N4909 70w. *Paeonia suffruticosa*   90   85
N4910 110w. *Bougainvillea glabra*   1·20   1·10

1633 Workers, Soldier and Party Founding Monument

2010. *Rodong Sinmun, Josoninmingun* and *Chongnyonjonwi* Newspapers Joint Editorial. Multicoloured.
MSN4911 10w. Type **1633**; 20w.
Woman factory worker and goods;
30w. Woman carrying sheaf of corn;
57w. Worker holding walkie-talkie,
molten metal and symbols of development; 67w. Two soldiers; 95w. Two
men and one woman with left arms
raised; 125w. Doves and globe   3·50   3·50

1634 Korean Soldiers

2010. Posters
N4912 76w. Type **1634** | 90 | 85
N4913 95w. Japanese soldier and bayonet | 1·10 | 1·00

1635 Kitten and Chicks

2010. Domestic Cats. Multicoloured.
N4914 10w. Type **1635** | 30 | 25
N4915 70w. Two ginger and white cats | 90 | 85
N4916 133w. Tabby and white cat and mouse | 1·10 | 1·00
N4917 170w. Cat and kittens | 1·20 | 1·10

1636 Brachyramphus perdix

2010. BIRDPEX 2010 and ANTVERPIA 2010 International Stamp Exhibitions. Multicoloured.
MSN4918 30w. Type **1636**; 125w. *Gallinago solitaria*; 133w. *Porzana paykullii* | 2·75 | 2·75

1637 Ceramic Eagle

2010. 98th Birth Anniv of Kim Il Sung
N4922 Type **1637** | 30 | 25
N4923 30w. Ceramic white crane | 40 | 35
N4924 95w. Embroidered tiger | 1·10 | 1·00
N4925 152w. Stuffed turtle (horiz) | 1·20 | 1·10

1638 1638 *Sophronitis brevipedunculata* (inscr 'Sophronitella brevipendunculata')

2010. Orchids. Multicoloured.
N4926 30w. Type **1638** | 40 | 35
N4927 80w. *Epidendrum radiatum* | 95 | 90
N4928 120w. *Cymbidium* | 1·10 | 1·00
N4929 152w. *Dendrobium* | 1·20 | 1·00

1639 Cholima Statue, Pyongyang

2010. Expo 2010, Shanghai (1st issue). Multicoloured.
MSN4930 10w. Type **1639**; 80w. Wind turbines, dolphins, children watering plant, skyline and animals | 1·10 | 1·00

1640 Forehand

Table Tennis. Multicoloured.
N4931 10w. Type **1640** | 10 | 10
N4932 30w. Serve | 25 | 25
N4933 95w. Backhand | 80 | 80
N4934 152w. Pushing ball | 1·40 | 1·40
MSN4935 150×107 mm. Nos. N4931/4 | 2·50 | 2·50

1641 Worker with Megaphone and Soldiers

2010. 65th Anniv of Workers' Party
N4936 **1641** 10w. multicoloured | 30 | 25
No. N4937 is left for Winter Olympic Games Winners issued on 25 May 2010, not yet received.

1642 Two Players

2010. World Cup Football Championships, South Africa. Multicoloured.
N4938 20w. Type **1642** | 10 | 10
N4939 57w. Players, No. 9 (yellow strip) and No. 4 (blue strip) | 60 | 55
N4940 114w. No. 5 (blue and yellow strip) player being tackled | 1·20 | 1·10
N4941 190w. No. 7 (red strip) and No. 9 player tackling | 1·70 | 1·60
MSN4942 160×95 mm 20w. As Type **1642**; 57w. As No. N4939; 190w. As No. N4941 | 1·90 | 1·90
MSN4943 85×61 mm. 114w. As No. N4940 | 1·20 | 1·10

1643 Children in Carriage

2010. 60th Anniv of Children's Day
MSN4944 **1643** 95w. multicoloured | 1·10 | 1·10

1644 Symbols of Peace

2010. Tenth Anniv of Publication of June 15 Joint Declaration
N4945 **1644** 190w. multicoloured | 1·70 | 1·70

1645 Brontosaurus

2010. Dinosaurs. Multicoloured.
N4947 10w. Type **1645** | 30 | 25
N4948 125w. Allosaurus | 1·10 | 1·00
N4949 152w. Pterodactylus | 1·20 | 1·10

1645a Visiting Dalian Bingshan Group

MSN4950 180×114 mm. 10w. As Type **1645**; 125w. As No. N4948; 152w. As No. N4949 | 3·50 | 3·50

2010. Unofficial Visit of Kim Jong Il to China (1st issue)
MSN4950a 150×126 mm. 20w. Type **1645a**; 35w. Visiting Dalian Locomotive Company; 80w. Visiting Liaoning Fishery Group | 1·40 | 1·40
MSN4950b 150×126 mm. 20w. Visiting Dalian Xuelong Group; 40w. Visiting Tianjin Port; 67w. Visiting Beiling Park | 1·20 | 1·20
MSN4950c 170×129 mm. 30w. Visiting Boao Biological Co.; 40w. With President Hu Jintao; 70w. Shaking hands with Pres. Jintao in farewell | 1·30 | 1·30
MSN4950d 157×110 mm. 60w. Pres. Jintao greeting Kim Jong Il (42×64 mm) | 55 | 55

1646 Butterfly and Cockerel

2010. Children's Animated Films. Multicoloured.
MSN4951 10w. Type **1646**; 30w. *Clever Racoon Dog*; 95w. *Hedgehog defeats Tiger*; 133w. *Rabbit's Regret* | 3·50 | 3·50

1647 *Rhododendron mucronulatum*

2010. Snow Azalea
MSN4952 **1647** 80w.multicoloured | 1·10 | 1·00

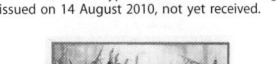

1648 Score

2010. National Anthem, written by Pak Se Yong and composed by Kim Wyon Gyun
MSN4953 **1648** 50w. multicoloured | 65 | 50
Nos. N4954/9 and Type **1649** are left for Relics issued on 30 July 2010, not yet received.
Nos. N4960/1 and Type **1650** are left for Singapore 2010 issued on 14 August 2010, not yet received.

1651 Kim Il Sung with Soldiers

2010. 65th Anniv of End of Anti-Japanese War
MSN4962 155×102 mm. 10w. Type **1651**; 15w. Soldiers in snow; 20w. Kim Il Sung and soldiers among azaleas; 40w. Kim Il Sung wearing civilian dress with civilians and soldiers; 100w. Kim Il Sung and Kim Jong Il as child seated with soldiers and peasants | 2·50 | 2·50
MSN4963 138×98 mm. 60w. Kim Il Sung, family and soldiers in snow (60×42 mm) | 2·00 | 2·00

1652 Workers and Soldier

2010. 50th Anniv of Songun Revolutionary Leadership. Multicoloured.
N4964 10w. Type **1652** | 15 | 10
MSN4965 167×112 mm. 15w. Kim Jong Il and soldiers in snow (64×42 mm); 30w. With soldiers and flags (51×39 mm); 55w. Looking over valley (51×39 mm); 80w. On roadway with jubilant soldiers (51×39 mm) | 2·00 | 2·00
MSN4966 130×95 mm. 70w. Kim Jong Il on snowy mountain top (78×51 mm) | 90 | 90

1653 Pres. Fidel Castro of Cuba and Kim Il Sung

2010. 50th Anniv of North Korea–Cuba Diplomatic Relations
N4967 **1653** 85w. multicoloured | 1·00 | 1·00

1654 *Pine Tree and Hawk* (Sin Yun Bok)

2010. Korean Paintings. Multicoloured.
N4968 15w. Type **1654** | 10 | 10
N4969 35w. *Waves of Ongchon* (Jong Son) | 40 | 35
N4970 70w. *Reeds and Wild Geese* (Jo Sok Jin) | 65 | 60
N4971 100w. *After picking Medicinal Herbs* (Kim Hong Do) | 95 | 90

1655 Founding Guerrilla Army

2010. Sun of the Nation (1st issue). Birth Centenary of Kim Il Sung (2012)
MSN4972 104×112 mm. 10w. Type **1655**; 20w. With crowd celebrating formation of revolutionary government; 35w. With soldiers and flags during anti-Japanese war; 90w. Addressing soldiers at founding of Association for the Restoration of Fatherland | 1·10 | 1·10
MSN4973 166×100 mm.10w. In snow during 250 mile Journey for Learning; 30w. With workers in demonstration against railway; 40w. Addressing meeting; 55w. Receiving pistols from Kang Pan Sok, women's leader | 1·10 | 1·10
MSN4974 140×87 mm. 20w. Firing pistol into air; 30w. Burning documents; 40w. With children and soldiers in snow; 45w. With soldiers, holding binoculars | 95 | 95
MSN4975 150×68 mm. 20w. As child with father; 55w. As child writing, whilst mother sews | 80 | 80
MSN4976 150×116 mm. 25w. Kim Jong Suk defending Kim Il Sung (64×42 mm); 30w. With Kim Jong Suk at Mt. Paektu camp; 45w. With family and soldiers on horseback | 1·00 | 1·00
MSN4977 158×101 mm. 50w. Addressing crowd (39×51 mm) | 60 | 60
MSN4978 147×83 mm. 60w. With soldiers in snow, holding binoculars (39×51 mm) | 65 | 65

1656 Emblem of DPRK Pavilion, Expo 2010

2010. Expo 2010, Shanghai (2nd issue)
N4979 **1656**　25w. multicoloured　　15　10

1657 Chinese Soldier and Korean Woman

2010. 60th Anniv of Chinese People's Volunteers' Entry into Korean War
N4980　25w. Type **1657**　　15　10

MSN4981 135×105 mm. 10w. Chinese committee deciding to send volunteer force (60×42 mm); 15w. Two soldiers (30×42 mm); 20w. *For Peace* (bronze statue) (60×42 mm); 27w. Children holding doves (30×42 mm)　75　75

(1657a)

2010. Europhila 2010 International Youth Stamp Collector's Exhibition, Stockholm. Multicoloured.
MSN4982 10w. As Type **1645**; 125w. As No. N4948; 152w. As No.N4949　2·75　2·75

1658 Workers' Party Flag

2010. 65th Anniv of Workers' Party (2nd issue)
N4983　10w. Type **1658**　　10　10

MSN4984 165×106 mm. 10w. As Type **1658**; 20w. Kim Il Sung on military vessel; 25w. Kim Il Sung and railway workers; 50w. Kim Il Sung and farmers; 50w. Kim Il Sung with scientists and equipment; 60w. Kim Il Sung in fabric shop　1·20　1·20

MSN4985 145×97 mm. 70w. Kim Il Sung examining party flag (45×54 mm)　80　80

1659 Kim Jong Il and Pres. Hu Jintao of China

2010. Unofficial Visit of Kim Jong Il to China
N4986　70w. Type **1659**　　65　60

MSN4987 140×130 mm. 30w. Signing register at Jilin Yuwen Middle School (42×35 mm); 42w. Examining railway carriage (42×35 mm); 70w. Examining bottles at Harbin Huijiang Foodstuff Company (42×35 mm)　1·20　1·20

1660 WPK Flag and Kimjongilia

2010. Workers' Party of Korea Conference
N4988　**1660**　30w. multicoloured　25　25

1662 Two Rabbits

2011. Chinese New Year. Year of the Rabbit
N4990　70w. Type **1662**　　60　60

N4991　140w. Large white and small brown rabbits　1·10　1·10

MSN4992 115×85 mm. Nos. N4990/1　1·70　1·70

1663 DPRK National Flag and Air Koryo Airliner

2011. INDIPEX 2011 International Philatelic Exhibition, New Delhi. Sheet 100×72 mm
MSN4993 **1663**　70w. multicoloured　60　60

1664 Capra Hircus

2011. 68th Birth Anniv of Kim Jong Il. Animal Gifts from Kuwait
N4994　30w. Type **1664**　　25　25

N4995　42w. *Ceropithecus aethiops* (green monkey)　30　30

N4996　112w. *Cebuella pygmaea* (pygmy marmoset)　1·00　1·00

N4997　125w. *Hystrix indica* (porcupine) (horiz)　1·10　1·10

1666 Celebrating Workers and Soldiers

2011. *Rodong Sinmun, Josoninmingun* and *Chongnyonjonwi* Newspapers Joint Editorial
N4999　10w. Type **1666**　　10　10

N5000　10w. News vendor and symbols of productivity　10　10

N5001　30w. Farmer carrying sheaf of corn and symbols of agriculture　25　25

N5002　70w. Flags and service personnel　60　60

N5003　112w. Map, three figures and broken missile (vert)　1·00　1·00

1667 *Paradisaea raggiana* (bird-of-paradise)

2011. Birds. Multicoloured.
N5004　30w. Type **1667**　　25　25

N5005　42w. *Cygnus olor* (mute swan)　35　35

N5006　75w. *Pulsatrix perspicillata* (spectacled owl)　65　65

N5007　133w. *Goura victoria* (Victoria crowned pigeon)　1·20　1·20

1668 Flag, Flowers and 1946 50ch. Stamp (As Type **2**)

2011. 65th Anniv of First Postage Stamp
N5008　**1668**　30w. multicoloured　25　25

1669 Mao Zedong (painting)

2011. 50th Anniv of Treaty of Friendship, Cooperation and Mutual Assistance with China
MSN5009 10w.×6, Type **1669**; Mao Zedong and Kim Il Sung (54×45 mm); Mao Zedong addressing rally (painting) (56×39 mm); Mao Zedong wearing blue; Mao Zedong wearing black (28×39 mm); Mao Zedong and Deng Xiaoping (56×39 mm)　55　55

MSN5010 10w.×6, Mao Zedong and Peng Dehuai (45×33 mm); Kim Il Sung and Mao Zedong (36×45 mm); Mao Zedong and Chen Yi (45×33 mm); Mao Zedong and Liu Shaoqi wearing overcoats (56×39 mm); Mao Zedong and Zhou Enlai (28×39 mm); Zhu De and Mao Zedong applauding (56×39 mm)　55　55

1670 Young Couple (Disaster Risk Reduction)

2011. International Year of Volunteers. Multicoloured.
MSN5011 30w. Type **1670**; 42w. Red Cross worker (Promotion Activities); Rescue workers (Emergency Relief Activities)　65　65

1671 Apples

2011. 50th Anniv. of Pukchong Meeting of Presidium of WPK Central Committee
N5012　30w. Type **1671**　　65　65

MSN5013 114×79 mm. 70w. Kim Il Sung (39×51 mm)　25　25

1672 Kimilsungia

2011. 99th Birth Anniv of Kim Il Sung. Floral Gifts. Multicoloured.
N5014　30w. Type **1672**　　1·00　1·00

N5015　42w. *Callistephus chinensis*　25　25

N5016　70w. *Iris ensata*　35　35

N5017　98w. *Rosa hybrida*　60　60

N5018　112w. *Lilium*　80　80

MSN5019 165×97 mm. Nos. N5014/18　3·00　3·00

1673 Pyongyang Metro

2011. Tourism. Pyongyang. Multicoloured.
N5020　30w. Type **1673**　　25　25

N5021　42w. Mangyongdae Children's Palace　35　35

N5022　56w. May Day Stadium　45　45

N5023　70w. People's Palace of Culture　60　60

N5024　84w. Arch of Triumph　75　75

N5025　98w. State Theatre　80　80

N5026　112w. Party Museum　1·00　1·00

N5027　140w. Kim Il Sung's Birthplace, Mangyongdae　1·10　1·10

1674 Kimilsungia

2011. International Horticultural Exposition in Xi'an, China
N5028　10w. Type **1674**　　95　95

N5029　30w. *Magnolia sieboldi*　10　10

N5030　30w. *Kimjongilia* (30×36 mm)　25　25

N5031　42w. *Paeonia suffruticosa*　25　25

MSN5032 117×130 mm. 10w. As Type **1674**; 30w. As No. N5030; 42w. As No. N5031　35　35

1675 Aerial Acrobat

2011. Circus. Multicoloured.
MSN5033 42w. Type **1675**; 70w. Aerial juggler; Highwire unicycle juggler; Skipping　95　95

1676 Cholima Statue

2011. Chollima Statue. Sheet 140×80mm
MSN5034 **1676**　98w. multicoloured　80　80

1677 Apples

2011. Taedonggang Combined Fruit Farm. Sheet 120×70 mm
MSN5035 **1677**　70w. multicoloured　60　60

1678 Vanda hybrida

2011. Orchids. Multicoloured.
N5036　10w. Type **1678**　　10　10

N5037　30w. *Laeliocattlea*　35　25

N5038　70w. *Laelia gouldiana*　60　60

N5039　142w. *Phalaennnopsis*　1·10　1·10

1679 With Workers at Kangson Steel Works

2011. Sun of the Nation (2nd issue). Birth Centenary of Kim Il Sung (2012)
N5040　10w. Type **1679**　　10　10

N5041　10w. With his grandparents　10　10

N5042　10w. At Pyongyang Railway Works　10　10

N5043　30w. Digging at Pothong River Improvement Project　25　25

N5044　30w. Land redistribution　25　25

N5045　30w. On Ssuk Island　25　25

N5046　30w. With bereaved children　25　25

N5047　30w. Machine gun demonstration with Kim Jong Suk　25　25

N5048　30w. Tank training　25　25

N5049　30w. With airmen　25　25

N5050　30w. Operational instruction to armed services　25　25

N5051　30w. With tanks and soldiers　25　25

N5052　30w. Outlining frontline strategy　35　35

N5053　42w. With soldiers and musicians　35　35

N5054　42w. With female soldier at frontline　35　35

N5055　42w. With plough women　35　35

N5056　42w. Party meeting at Rakwon Machine Plant　35　35

N5057　42w. In soldiers' canteen　35　35

N5058　42w. With railway engineers　35　35

N5059　42w. With soldiers, tank and motorcycle　35　35

N5060　42w. With returning soldiers　35　35

N5061　42w. Directing Han River crossing　35　35

N5062　42w. With soldiers and map　35　35

MSN5063 150×116 mm. 25w. Holding papers in garden (64×42 mm); 30w. Drawing party emblem; 45w. Giving speech   90   90

MSN5064 159×86 mm. 40w. Addressing crowd from balcony (36×45 mm)   35   35

MSN5065 159×86 mm. 50w. With soldiers in snow (39×51 mm)   40   40

MSN5066 130×88 mm. 60w. Seated with soldiers (39×51 mm)   55   55

1680 With Management Personnel

2011. Unofficial Visit of Kim Jong Il to China (3rd issue). Multicoloured.
MSN5067 90w. Type **1680**   80   80
MSN5068 90w. With Pres. Jintao   80   80
MSN5069 90w. Examining 3D display (horiz)   80   80

1681 Kim Jong Il and EU Delegation

2011. Tenth Anniv of European Union–DPRK Diplomatic Relations. Sheet 122×92 mm
MSN5070 **1681** 140w. multicoloured   1·10   1·10

1682 *Gymnocalycium schuetzianum*

2011. Cacti. Multicoloured.
N5071   30w. Type **1682**   2·75   2·75
N5072   70w. *Rebutia euanthema*   25   25
N5073   98w. *Rebutia xanthocapa*   60   60
N5074   112w. *Notocactus herteri*   80   80
MSN5075 95×105 mm. Nos. N5071/4   1·00   1·00

1683 *Megalosaurus bucklandi*

2011. Dinosaurs. Multicoloured.
N5076   42w. Type **1683**   35   35
N5077   98w. *Staurikosaurus pricei*   80   80
N5078   140w. *Chamosaurus belli*   1·10   1·10

1684 ZIL Fire Appliance

2011. Fire Appliances. Multicoloured.
N5079   30w. Type **1684**   25   25
N5080   70w. Mercedes-Benz   60   60
N5081   98w. ZIL with ladders   80   80
N5082   140w. Mercedes-Benz with ladders   1·10   1·10
MSN5083 102×90 mm. Nos. N5079 and N5082   1·10   1·10
MSN5084 102×90 mm. Nos. N5080/1   1·40   1·40

APPENDIX

The following stamps have either been issued in excess of postal needs or have not been available to the public in reasonable quantities at face value. Such stamps may later be given full listing if there is evidence of regular postal use.

1976

Olympic Games, Montreal. Three-dimensional stamps showing Olympic events. 5, 10, 15, 20, 25, 40ch.

1977

Olympic Games, Montreal. Three-dimensional stamps showing medals. 5, 10, 15, 20, 25, 40ch.
Olympic Games, Montreal. 1976 Olympic Games issue optd with winners' names. 5, 10, 15, 20, 25, 40ch.

1979

XIII Winter Olympic Games, 1980. Nos. N1688/94 optd. 2, 5, 10, 15, 20, 25, 40ch.

1981

Nobel Prizes for Medicine. Nos. N1955/61 optd. 7×10ch.
World Cup Football Championship, Spain (1982). Nos. N1731/41 optd. 12×20ch.
World Cup Football Championship, Spain (1982). Three-dimensional stamps. Air 20, 30ch.

1982

21st Birthday of Princess of Wales. Nos. N2108/11 and N2120/3 optd. 10, 20, 30, 40ch.; 10, 20, 30, 70ch.
Birth of Prince William of Wales. Nos. N2185/91 optd. 10, 20, 30, 50, 60, 70, 80ch.
World Cup Football Championship, Spain, Results. Nos. N2201/6 optd. 10, 20, 30, 40, 50, 60ch.
Birth of Prince William of Wales. Three-dimensional stamps. 3×30ch.

1983

XXIII Olympic Games, Los Angeles, 1984. Nos. N2084/8 optd. 10, 15, 20, 25, 30ch.

1984

European Royal History. 81×10ch.

Pt. 3

KOSOVO REPUBLIC

The Republic of Kosovo declared independence on the 17th February 2008.

100 cents = 1 euro.

41 William Walker (head of OSCE cease-fire verification mission)

2009. Tenth Anniv of Racak Massacre. Multicoloured.
118   50c. Type **41**   2·30   2·30
119   70c. Broken stone inscribed RECAK   2·50   2·50

44 Monastery Building

2010. UNESCO World Heritage Site
123   €1 Type **44**   5·50   5·50
124   €2 Early building   15·00   15·00
MS125 80×104 mm. Vert. €1 Window; €2 Head of Christ (fresco)   21·00   21·00

45 EU Stars, Man, Child and Telescope and Map

2009. Europa. Multicoloured.
126   €1 Type **45**   5·50   5·50
127   €2 Boy and rocket boosters   15·00   15·00
MS128 180×69 mm. €2 As No. 127   21·00   21·00
The stamp of **MS128** has the design to the edge of the stamp and, with the margins, forms a composite design

46 Children

2009. Children's Day. Multicoloured.
129   20c. Type **46**   1·90   1·90
130   50c. Children holding balloon and kite   2·75   2·75
131   70c. Child's hand in adult's hand   3·25   3·25
132   €1 Child's silhouette   6·00   6·00

47 Flags of Kosovo and USA as Hands touching

2009. Kosovo–USA Friendship
133   **47**   €2 multicoloured   10·50   50

48 Lorenc Antoni and Piano

2009. Birth Centenary of Lorenc Antoni (composer)
134   **48**   €1 multicoloured   5·50   5·50

49 Flags of Germany and Kosovo intertwined as Waves

2009. German Weeks
1335   **49**   €1 multicoloured   5·50   5·50

50 Parchment and Script

2009. 320th Death Anniv of Pjeter Bogdani (author of *Cuneus Prophetarum* (The Band of the Prophets), first prose work written in Albanian)
136   **50**   €1 multicoloured   5·50   5·50

51 Head (Teuta Beqiri)

2009. Visual Arts. Multicoloured.
137   30c. Type **51**   2·20   2·20
138   50c. White horses (I. Kodra)   2·75   2·75
139   70c. Abstract (G. J. G. Jokaj)   3·00   3·00
140   €1 Back view of figure carrying rucksac (M. Mulliqi)   5·00   5·00

52 Faruk Begolli (actor)

2010. Kosovo Cinema. Multicoloured.
141   30c. Type **52**   2·20   2·20
142   70c. Melihate Qena (actress)   3·25   3·25
143   €1 Abdurrahman Shala (producer and director)   5·50   5·50
MS144 81×105mm. 30c. Hadi Shehu (actor); 70c. Muharrem Qena (actor)   5·50   5·50

53 TMK (Protection Corps), SHPK (Police Force) and FSK (Security Force (replaced TMK)) Badges

2010. Independence Day. Multicoloured.
145   30c. Type **53**   2·20   2·20
146   50c. SHPK personnel   2·75   2·75
147   70c. FSK soldiers   3·25   3·25

54 Reading beneath Tree of Books

2010. Multicoloured
148   €1 Type **54**   5·50   5·50
149   €2 Figure emerging from book pages carrying letter 'A'   10·50   10·50
MS150 80×69mm. €2 Boy reading   11·00   11·00

55 National Team Emblem and Map of Africa as Football Pitch

2010. World Cup Football Championships, South Africa. Multicoloured.
151   €1 Type **55**   5·50   5·50
152   €2 National team emblem, globe and stream of colours   10·50   10·50
MS153 104×80mm. 50c.×2, Kosovo colours looped to football; Kosovo flag as football   5·50   5·50

56 Azem Galica, Shote Galica and Albanian Flag

2010. Azem Galica (Azem Bejta) and his wife, Shote Galica (Qerime Radisheva) (nationalists) Commemoration
154   **56**   €2 multicoloured   11·00   11·00

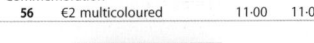

57 Waterfall, Mirusha Park

2010. National Parks. Multicoloured.
155   20c. Type **57**   1·90   1·90
156   50c. Lake and conifers, Rugova   2·50   2·50
157   70c. Lake and rocky hillside, Gjeravica   3·50   3·50
158   €1 Tree covered hillside and mountains, Sharri   5·50   5·50

58 Mother Teresa

2010. Birth Centenary of Agnes Gonxha Bojaxhiu (Mother Teresa) (founder of Missionaries of Charity)
159   **58**   €1 multicoloured   5·50   5·50

59 Streaming towards EU Stars as '8'

2010. European Integration. Multicoloured.
160   70c. Type **59**   3·50   3·50
MS161 70×53mm. €1 Stars, streamers and '8' on map of Europe   5·50   5·50

60 Barn Swallows

2010. Birds. Multicoloured.

162	30c. Type **60**	2·20	2·20
163	50c. Tree swallow	2·75	2·75
164	70c. Redwing	3·50	3·50
165	€1 Red-rumped swallow	5·50	5·50
MS166	80×105 mm. 30c. Bluethroat; 30c. Dark barn swallow facing right; 70c. Barn swallow in flight; 70c. Barn swallow facing left	11·00	11·00

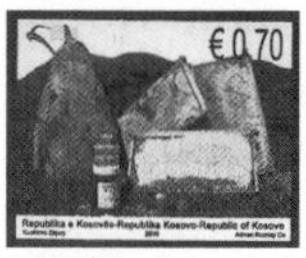

61 Beehive, Honeycomb and Honey Jars.

2010. Local Foods. Multicoloured.

167	70c. Type **61**	2·75	2·75
168	€1 Table with local dishes displayed	5·50	5·50

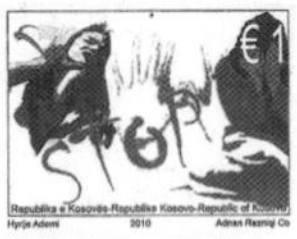

62 Symbols of Violence against Women

2010. Campaign to End Violence against Women

169	**62**	€1 multicoloured	5·50	5·50

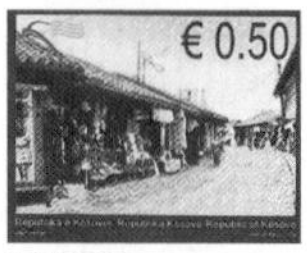

63 Shops

2010. Cultural Heritage. Multicoloured.

170	50c. Type **63**	2·20	2·20
171	70c. Village street	2·75	2·75
172	€1 Market place	5·50	5·50

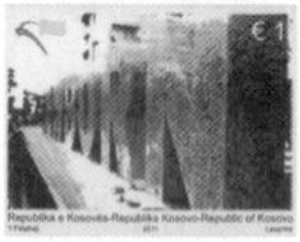

64 Letters

2011. Third Anniv of Independence. Multicoloured.

173	€1 Type **64**	5·50	5·50
174	€2 Fireworks over city	10·00	10·00

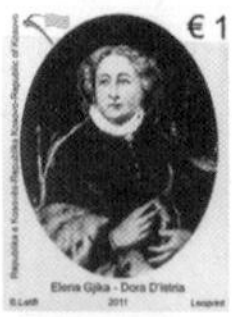

65 Elena Gjika

2011. Elena Gjika (author) Commemoration

175	**65**	€1 multicoloured	5·50	5·50

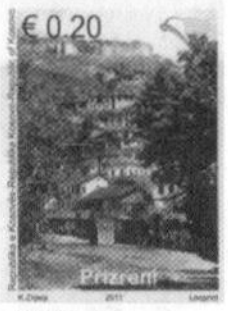

66 Houses

2011. Cities of Kosovo: Prizreni. Multicoloured.

176	20c. Type **66**	1·00	1·00
177	50c. Houses	2·20	2·20
178	70c. View over city	2·75	2·75

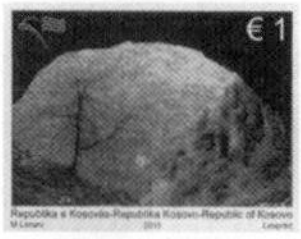

67 Forest

2011. Europa. Forests. Multicoloured.

179	€1 Type **67**	5·50	5·50
180	€2 Forest and mountains	10·00	10·00
MS181	69x53mm. €2 Forest clearing	10·00	10·00

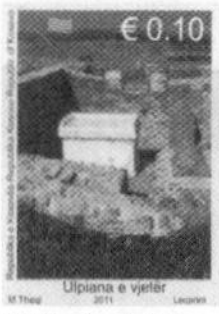

68 Ancient Ruins

2011. Archaeology. Multicoloured.

182	10c. Type **68**	50	50
183	15c. Ancient ruins	75	75
184	€1 Relief	5·50	5·50

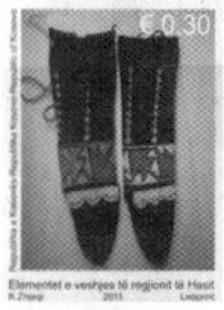

69 Decorated Socks

2011. National Costumes. Multicoloured.

185	30c. Type **69**	1·50	1·50
186	50c. National dress	2·20	2·20
187	70c. Decorated bag	2·75	2·75
188	€1 Decorated dress	5·50	5·50
MS189	80x104mm €2 Headdress	10·00	10·00

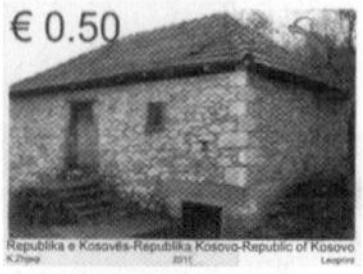

70 Mill

2011. Old Mills. Multicoloured.

190	50c. Type **70**	2·20	2·20
191	70c. Brick mill	2·75	2·75
192	€1 Wooden water mill	5·50	5·50
MS193	61x85mm. €2 Mill	10·00	10·00

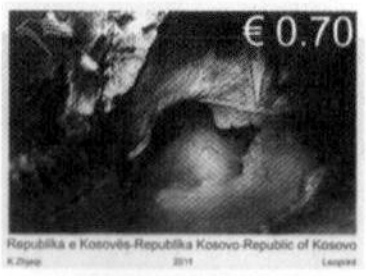

71 Interior, Cave of the Grand Canyon, Peja

2011. The Cave of the Grand Canyon, Peja. Multicoloured.

194	70c. Type **71**	2·75	2·75
195	€1 Cave interior	5·50	5·50

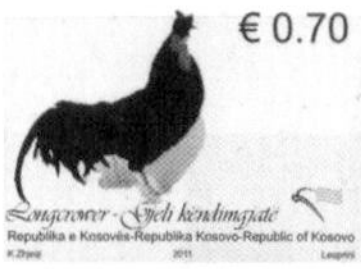

72 Rooster

2011. Roosters. Multicoloured.

196	70c. Type **72**	2·75	2·75
197	€1 Rooster	5·50	5·50

Pt. 17

KOUANG TCHEOU (KWANGCHOW)

An area and port of S. China, leased by France from China in April 1898. It was returned to China in February 1943.

1906. 100 centimes = 1 franc.
1919. 100 cents = 1 piastre.

Unless otherwise stated the following are optd or surch on stamps of Indo-China.

1906. Surch **Kouang Tcheou-Wan** and value in Chinese.

1	**8**	1c. green	7·00	10·00
2	**8**	2c. red on yellow	6·00	5·50
3	**8**	4c. mauve on blue	5·00	8·25
4	**8**	5c. green	9·25	11·50
5	**8**	10c. red	10·50	8·75
6	**8**	15c. brown on blue	13·00	24·00
7	**8**	20c. red on green	8·00	12·00
8	**8**	25c. blue	6·50	9·25
9	**8**	30c. brown on cream	9·00	16·00
10	**8**	35c. black on yellow	15·00	21·00
11	**8**	40c. black on grey	9·25	14·50
12	**8**	50c. brown on cream	32·00	60·00
13	**D**	75c. brown on orange	60·00	65·00
14	**8**	1f. green	50·00	65·00
15	**8**	2f. brown on yellow	55·00	65·00
16	**D**	5f. mauve on lilac	£200	£200
17	**8**	10f. red on green	£250	£250

1908. Native types surch **KOUANG-TCHEOU** and value in Chinese.

18	**10**	1c. black and brown	1·00	1·00
19	**10**	2c. black and brown	1·00	1·50
20	**10**	4c. black and blue	1·20	1·80
21	**10**	5c. black and green	1·50	1·40
22	**10**	10c. black and red	2·30	2·50
23	**10**	15c. black and violet	4·00	6·50
24	**11**	20c. black and violet	6·75	11·00
25	**11**	25c. black and blue	8·50	12·00
26	**11**	30c. black and brown	10·50	26·00
27	**11**	35c. black and green	24·00	36·00
28	**11**	40c. black and brown	22·00	36·00
29	**11**	50c. black and red	25·00	42·00
30	**12**	75c. black and orange	18·00	42·00
31	-	1f. black and red	25·00	48·00
32	-	2f. black and green	55·00	70·00
33	-	5f. black and blue	85·00	£110
34	-	10f. black and violet	£130	£130

1919. Nos. 18/34 surch in figures and words.

35	**10**	⅖c. on 1c. black and brown	75	6·25
36	**10**	⅘c. on 2c. black and brown	75	5·75
37	**10**	1⅗c. on 4c. black and blue	1·00	5·75
38	**10**	2c. on 5c. black and green	6·00	8·00
39	**10**	4c. on 10c. black and red	4·75	4·00
40	**10**	6c. on 15c. black and violet	5·00	4·75
41	**11**	8c. on 20c. black and violet	11·00	11·50
42	**11**	10c. on 25c. black and blue	25·00	32·00
43	**11**	12c. on 30c. black & brown	7·75	9·25
44	**11**	14c. on 35c. black and green	5·50	9·00
45	**11**	16c. on 40c. black & brown	5·00	8·00
46	**11**	20c. on 50c. black and red	5·75	7·75
47	**12**	30c. on 75c. black & orange	11·00	21·00
48	-	40c. on 1f. black and red	18·00	18·00
49	-	80c. on 2f. black and green	13·00	26·00
50	-	2p. on 5f. black and blue	£150	£160
51	-	4p. on 10f. black and violet	34·00	60·00

1923. Native types optd **KOUANG-TCHEOU** only. (Value in cents and piastres).

52	**10**	⅒c. red and grey	40	7·25
53	**10**	⅕c. black and blue	40	7·25
54	**10**	⅖c. black and brown	45	6·25
55	**10**	⅘c. black and red	55	7·50
56	**10**	1c. black and brown	55	6·50
57	**10**	2c. black and green	1·00	8·00
58	**10**	3c. black and violet	65	8·25
59	**10**	4c. black and orange	1·20	6·75
60	**10**	5c. black and red	1·20	4·25
61	**11**	6c. black and red	80	8·75
62	**11**	7c. black and green	60	7·25
63	**11**	8c. black on lilac	2·00	8·50
64	**11**	9c. black and yellow on green	3·00	8·50
65	**11**	10c. black and blue	2·30	8·25
66	**11**	11c. black and violet	2·50	8·25
67	**11**	12c. black and brown	3·50	6·50
68	**11**	15c. black and orange	4·00	10·00
69	**11**	20c. black and blue on buff	4·75	9·25
70	**11**	40c. black and red	4·50	12·00
71	**11**	1p. black and green on green	10·00	32·00
72	**11**	2p. black and purple on pink	15·00	50·00

1927. Pictorial types optd **KOUANG-TCHEOU**.

73	**22**	⅒c. green	35	6·25
74	**22**	⅕c. yellow	35	6·50
75	**22**	⅖c. blue	40	7·25
76	**22**	⅘c. brown	55	4·75
77	**22**	1c. orange	1·00	7·25
78	**22**	2c. green	1·00	6·75
79	**22**	3c. blue	1·40	7·50
80	**22**	4c. pink	80	7·75
81	**22**	5c. violet	1·20	6·75
82	**23**	6c. red	1·40	5·00
83	**23**	7c. brown	1·50	8·00
84	**23**	8c. green	1·60	8·00
85	**23**	9c. purple	1·60	7·25
86	**23**	10c. blue	2·30	7·75
87	**23**	11c. orange	3·00	8·75
88	**23**	12c. grey	2·00	8·00
89	**24**	15c. brown and red	5·00	9·25
90	**24**	20c. grey and violet	3·75	10·00
91	-	25c. mauve and brown	3·50	10·00
92	-	30c. olive and blue	3·25	8·75
93	-	40c. blue and red	3·50	8·50
94	-	50c. grey and green	3·25	9·00
95	-	1p. black, yellow and blue	5·50	15·00
96	-	2p. blue, orange and red	8·50	16·00

1937. International Exhibition, Paris. As No. **MS**246a of Indo-China (Diane de Poitiers) but colour changed and optd **KOUANG-TCHEOU** in black.

MS97	30c. green	20·00	27·00

1937. 1931 issue optd **KOUANG-TCHEOU**.

98	**33**	⅒c. blue	30	6·75
99	**33**	⅕c. lake	30	7·25
100	**33**	⅖c. red	60	7·50
101	**33**	½c. brown	30	7·25
102	**33**	⅘c. violet	35	7·00
103	**33**	1c. brown	30	7·25
104	**33**	2c. green	30	6·75
105	-	3c. green	2·75	7·75
126	-	3c. brown	30	7·50
106	-	4c. blue	3·75	8·25
127	-	4c. green	60	7·00
128	-	4c. yellow	11·00	14·50
107	-	5c. purple	4·00	7·75
129	-	5c. green	80	7·50
108	-	6c. red	1·00	7·75
130	-	7c. black	80	7·75
131	-	8c. lake	80	7·75
132	-	9c. black on yellow	2·75	9·00
109	-	10c. blue	4·00	8·00
133	-	10c. blue on pink	1·40	8·25
110	-	15c. blue	1·10	7·75
134	-	18c. blue	1·20	7·75
111	-	20c. red	80	7·75
112	-	21c. green	60	7·75
135	-	22c. green	3·25	8·50
113	-	25c. purple	6·50	12·00
136	-	25c. blue	1·50	7·75
114	-	30c. brown	1·40	7·75
115	**36**	50c. brown	85	8·50
116	**36**	60c. purple	65	8·50
137	**36**	70c. blue	2·50	7·50
117	**36**	1p. green	1·80	9·50
118	**36**	2p. red	2·50	9·75

1939. New York World's Fair. As T **28** of Mauritania.

119	13c. red	1·20	8·25
120	23c. deep blue and blue	1·60	8·25

1939. 150th Anniv of French Revolution. As T **29** of Mauritania.

121	6c.+2c. green	7·00	18·00
122	7c.+3c. brown	7·00	18·00
123	9c.+4c. orange	7·00	18·00
124	13c.+10c. red	7·00	18·00
125	23c.+20c. blue	7·00	18·00

Pt. 1, Pt. 19

KUWAIT

An independent Arab Shaikhdom on the N.W. coast of the Persian Gulf with Indian and later British postal administration. On 1 February 1959 the Kuwait Government assumed responsibility for running its own postal service. In special treaty relations with Great Britain until 19 June 1961 when Kuwait became completely independent.

1923. 12 pies = 1 anna; 16 annas = 1 rupee.
1957. 100 naye paise = 1 rupee.
1961. 1000 fils = 1 dinar.

1923. King George V.

16	**56**	½a. green	6·50	1·75
16b	**79**	½a. green	6·00	1·40
2	**57**	1a. brown	6·00	4·50
17b	**81**	1a. brown	11·00	1·25
3	**58**	1½a. brown (No. 163)	4·75	8·50
4	**59**	2a. lilac	4·25	7·00
18	**70**	2a. lilac	6·00	1·25
19	**70**	2a. orange	20·00	90·00
19c	**59**	2a. orange	5·00	2·50
5	**61**	2a.6p. blue	2·75	8·00
6	**62**	3a. orange	4·25	22·00
20	**62**	3a. blue	2·75	2·50
21	**62**	3a. red	5·50	4·25
22	**71**	4a. green	25·00	£100
22a	**63**	4a. green	11·00	14·00
9	**64**	6a. bistre	8·50	13·00
23	**65**	8a. mauve	35·00	13·00
11	**66**	12a. red	14·00	50·00
12	**67**	1r. brown and green	38·00	50·00
26	**67**	2r. red and orange	21·00	65·00
27	**67**	5r. blue and violet	£120	£300
28	**67**	10r. green and red	£250	£500
29	**67**	15r. blue and olive	£850	£1000

1933. Air.

31	**72**	2a. green	22·00	27·00
32	**72**	3a. blue	4·50	2·50
33	**72**	4a. olive	£150	£225
34	**72**	6a. bistre	6·50	4·50

1939. King George VI.

36	**91**	½a. brown	7·00	2·50
38	**91**	1a. red	7·00	2·75
39	**92**	2a. orange	7·50	3·50
41	-	3a. green	9·00	2·50
43	-	4a. brown	40·00	26·00
44	-	6a. turquoise	25·00	17·00
45	-	8a. violet	28·00	32·00
46	-	12a. lake	20·00	85·00
47	**93**	1r. slate and brown	25·00	7·00
48	**93**	2r. purple and brown	7·50	24·00
49	**93**	5r. green and blue	19·00	28·00
50	**93**	10r. purple and red	80·00	95·00
51	**93**	15r. brown and green	£325	£350

1942. King George VI stamps of 1940.

52	**100a**	3p. slate	4·00	8·50
53	**100a**	½a. purple	2·75	4·75
54	**100a**	9p. green	3·75	16·00
55	**100a**	1a. red	3·50	2·25
56	**101**	1½a. violet	4·25	9·50
57	**101**	2a. red	5·00	7·50
58	**101**	3a. violet	5·50	13·00
59	**101**	3½a. blue	5·00	15·00
60	**102**	4a. brown	6·50	3·75
60a	**102**	6a. turquoise	14·00	19·00
61	**102**	8a. violet	7·00	13·00
62	**102**	12a. lake	8·50	8·00
63	-	14a. purple (No. 277)	15·00	22·00

Stamps of Great Britain surch KUWAIT and new values in Indian currency

From 1948 onwards, for stamps with similar surcharges, but without name of country, see British Postal Agencies in Eastern Agencies

1948. King George VI.

64	**128**	½a. on ½d. green	3·25	3·50
84	**128**	½a. on ½d. orange	2·75	1·50
65	**128**	1a. on 1d. red	3·25	1·75
85	**128**	1a. on 1d. blue	2·75	1·60
66	**128**	1½a. on 1½d. brown	3·50	1·75
86	**128**	1½a. on 1½d. green	2·75	2·25
67	**128**	2a. on 2d. orange	3·25	1·75
87	**128**	2a. on 2d. brown	2·75	1·50
68	**128**	2½a. on 2½d. blue	3·50	1·00
88	**128**	2½a. on 2½d. red	2·75	2·75
69	**128**	3a. on 3d. violet	3·25	80
89	**129**	4a. on 4d. blue	2·75	1·50
70	**129**	6a. on 6d. purple	3·25	75
71	**130**	1r. on 1s. brown	7·00	2·00
72	**131**	2r. on 2s.6d. green	8·00	8·50
73	**131**	5r. on 5s. red	10·00	8·50
73a	-	10r. on 10s. blue (No. 478a)	55·00	11·00

From 1948 onwards, for stamps with similar surcharges, but without name of country, see British Postal Agencies in Eastern Arabia.

1948. Silver Wedding.

74	**137**	2½a. on 2½d. blue	2·25	2·50
75	**138**	15r. on £1 blue	38·00	48·00

1948. Olympic Games.

76	**139**	2½a. on 2½d. blue	1·25	4·50
77	**140**	3a. on 3d. violet	1·25	4·50
78	-	6a. on 5d. purple	1·50	4·25
79	-	1r. on 1s. brown	1·50	4·25

1949. U.P.U.

80	**143**	2½a. on 2½d. blue	1·25	3·25
81	**144**	3a. on 3d. violet	1·25	3·75
82	-	6a. on 6d. purple	1·25	3·75
83	-	1r. on 1s. brown	1·25	1·75

1951. Pictorial high values.

90	**147**	2r. on 2s.6d. green	24·00	8·00
91	-	5r. on 5s. red (No. 510)	30·00	10·00
92	-	10r. on 10s. blue (No. 511)	50·00	15·00

1952. Queen Elizabeth II.

93	**154**	½a. on ½d. orange	20	2·00
94	**154**	1a. on 1d. blue	20	10
95	**154**	1½a. on 1½d. green	15	1·75
96	**154**	2a. on 2d. brown	35	10
97	**155**	2½a. on 2½d. red	15	1·75
98	**155**	3a. on 3d. lilac	40	10
99	**155**	4a. on 4d. blue	1·25	1·00
100	**157**	6a. on 6d. purple	2·00	10
101	**160**	12a. on 1s.3d. green	5·50	2·50
102	**160**	1r. on 1s.6d. blue	4·50	10

1953. Coronation.

103	**161**	2½a. on 2½d. red	3·50	3·50
104	-	4a. on 4d. blue	3·50	3·50
105	**163**	12a. on 1s.3d. green	5·00	5·50
106	-	1r. on 1s.6d. blue	4·00	1·25

1955. Pictorials.

107	**166**	2r. on 2s.6d. brown	10·00	3·25
108	-	5r. on 5s. red	10·00	7·50
109	-	10r. on 10s. blue	10·00	5·00

1957. Queen Elizabeth II.

120	**157**	1n.p. on 5d. brown	10	70
121	**154**	3n.p. on ½d. orange	60	3·75
122	**154**	6n.p. on 1d. blue	60	1·25
123	**154**	9n.p. on 1½d. green	60	3·00
124	**154**	12n.p. on 2d. brown	60	4·00
125	**155**	15n.p. on 2½d. red	60	5·00
126	**155**	20n.p. on 3d. lilac	60	30
127	**155**	25n.p. on 4d. blue	2·75	3·25
128	**157**	40n.p. on 6d. purple	1·00	30
129	**158**	50n.p. on 9d. olive	5·50	4·00
130	**160**	75n.p. on 1s.3d. green	6·00	5·00

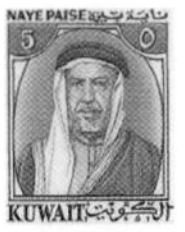

20 Shaikh Abdullah

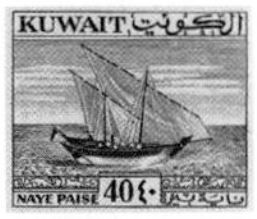

21 Dhow

1958

131	**20**	5n.p. green	75	10
132	**20**	10n.p. red	55	10
133	**20**	15n.p. brown	30	20
134	**20**	20n.p. violet	30	20
135	**20**	25n.p. orange	55	20
136	**20**	40n.p. purple	4·00	1·00
137	**21**	40n.p. blue	65	20
138	-	50n.p. red	55	20
139	-	75n.p. green	65	45
140	-	1r. purple	75	55
141	-	2r. blue and brown	3·75	95
142	-	5r. green	6·00	2·75
143	-	10r. lilac	19·00	6·50

DESIGNS—HORIZ: As Type **21**: 50n.p. Oil pipe-lines; 75n.p. Shuwaikh Power Station. 36×20 mm: 1r. Oil rig; 2r. Single-masted dhow; 5r. Kuwait Mosque; 10r. Main Square, Kuwait Town.

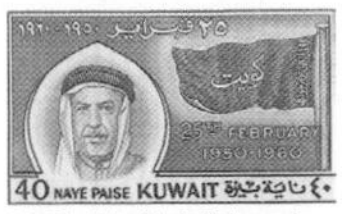

22 Shaikh Abdullah and Flag

1960. Tenth Anniv of Shaikh's Accession.

144	**22**	40n.p. red and green	65	20
145	**22**	60n.p. red and blue	95	30

1961. As 1958 issue but currency changed and new designs.

146	**20**	1f. green	10	10
147	**20**	2f. red	10	10
148	**20**	4f. brown	10	10
149	**20**	5f. violet	10	10
150	**20**	8f. red	10	10
151	**20**	15f. purple	20	10
152	-	20f. green (as No. 142)	30	15
153	-	25f. blue	55	30
154	-	30f. blue and brown (as No. 141)	65	30
155	-	35f. black and red	75	30
156	**21**	40f. blue (32×22 mm)	85	30
157	-	45f. brown	95	30
158	-	75f. brown & grn (as No. 141)	1·40	75
159	-	90f. brown and blue	1·30	65
160	-	100f. red	1·60	30
161	**21**	250f. green (32×22 mm)	10·50	1·60
162	-	1d. orange	19·00	5·25
163	-	3d. red (as No. 142)	43·00	32·00

NEW DESIGNS—37×20 mm: 25, 100f. Vickers Viscount 700 airliner over South Pier, Mina al Ahmadi; 35, 90f. Shuwaikh Secondary School; 45f., 1d. Wara Hill.

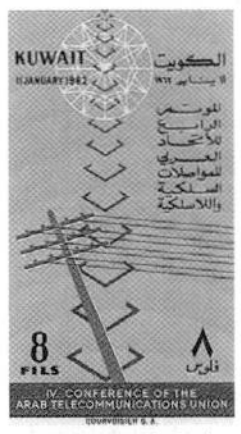

23 Telegraph Pole

1962. Fourth Arab Telecommunications Union Conference.

164	**23**	8f. blue and black	45	10
165	**23**	20f. red and black	95	55

1962. Arab League Week. As T **76** of Libya.

166	20f. purple	30	20
167	45f. brown	75	65

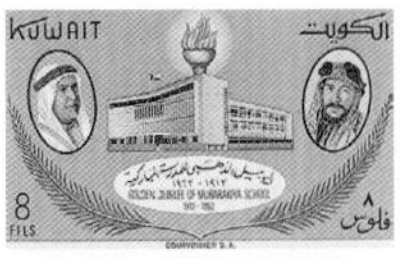

25 Mubarakiya School, Shaikh Abdullah and Shaikh Mubarak

1962. Golden Jubilee of Mubarakiya School.

168	**25**	8f. multicoloured	45	10
169	**25**	20f. multicoloured	85	45

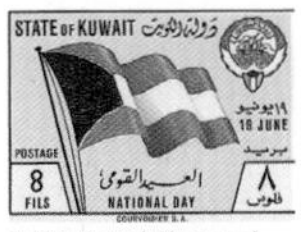

26 National Flag and Crest

1962. National Day.

170	**26**	8f. multicoloured	20	20
171	**26**	20f. multicoloured	55	30
172	**26**	45f. multicoloured	1·20	45
173	**26**	90f. multicoloured	1·80	1·20

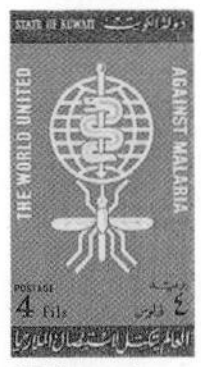

27 Campaign Emblem

1962. Malaria Eradication.

174	**27**	4f. green and turquoise	20	10
175	**27**	25f. grey and green	85	75

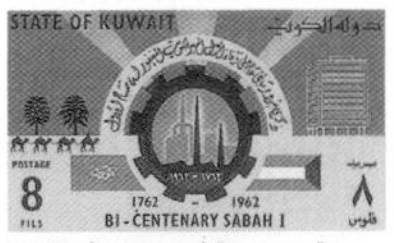

28 "Industry and Progress"

1962. Bicentenary of Sabah Dynasty.

176	**28**	8f. multicoloured	20	10
177	**28**	20f. multicoloured	65	30
178	**28**	45f. multicoloured	1·30	65
179	**28**	75f. multicoloured	2·10	1·10

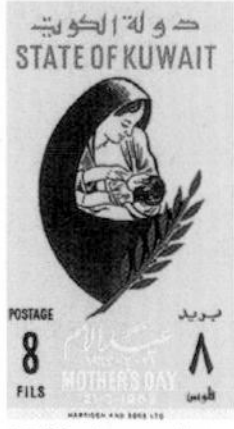

29 Mother and Child

1963. Mothers' Day. Centres black and green; value black; country name red.

180	**29**	8f. yellow	20	10
181	**29**	20f. blue	55	45
182	**29**	45f. olive	1·10	65
183	**29**	75f. grey	1·90	75

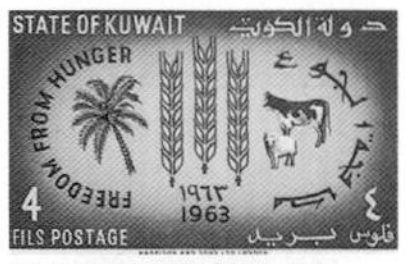

30 Campaign Emblem, Palm and Domestic Animals

1963. Freedom from Hunger. Design in brown and green. Background colours given.

184	**30**	4f. blue	30	20
185	**30**	8f. yellow	65	45
186	**30**	20f. lilac	1·20	75
187	**30**	45f. pink	2·75	1·80

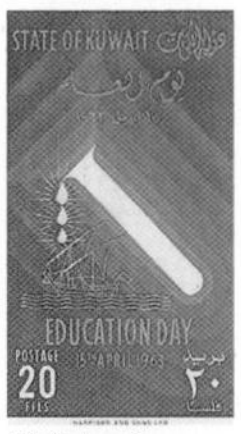

31 "Education from Oil"

1963. Education Day.

188	**31**	4f. brown, blue and yellow	20	10
189	**31**	20f. green, blue and yellow	75	30
190	**31**	45f. purple, blue and yellow	1·40	65

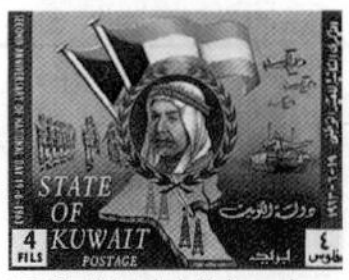

32 Shaikh Abdullah and Flags

1963. Second Anniv of National Day. Flags in green, black and red; values in black.

191	**32**	4f. blue	85	65
192	**32**	5f. ochre	1·30	1·10
193	**32**	20f. violet	6·50	4·75
194	**32**	50f. brown	13·00	8·00

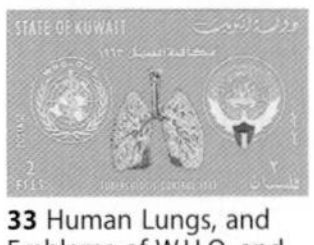

33 Human Lungs, and Emblems of W.H.O. and Kuwait

1963. W.H.O. "Tuberculosis Control" Campaign. Emblem yellow; arms black, green and red.

195	**33**	2f. black and stone	20	10
196	**33**	4f. black and green	20	10
197	**33**	8f. black and blue	55	20
198	**33**	20f. black and red	1·80	75

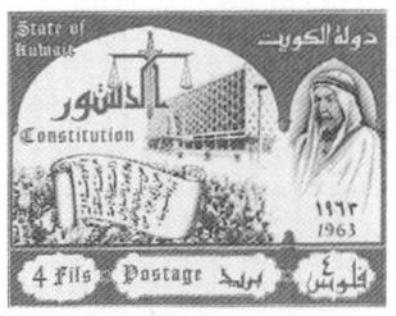

34 Municipal Hall and Scroll

1963. New Constitution. Centres dull purple; Amir red.

199	**34**	4f. red	20	10
200	**34**	8f. green	30	15
201	**34**	20f. purple	65	30
202	**34**	45f. brown	1·10	65
203	**34**	75f. violet	1·80	1·30
204	**34**	90f. blue	2·40	1·60

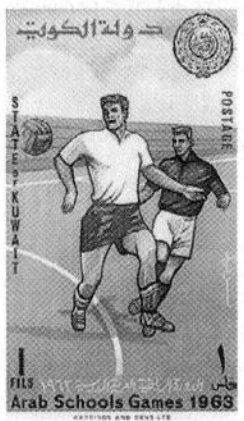
35 Football

1963. Arab Schools Games. Multicoloured.

205	1f. Type **35**	20	10
206	4f. Basketball	20	10
207	5f. Swimming (horiz)	20	10
208	8f. Running	30	15
209	15f. Throwing the javelin (horiz)	75	30
210	20f. Pole vaulting (horiz)	1·10	30
211	35f. Gymnastics (horiz)	2·10	75
212	45f. Gymnastics	3·25	1·60

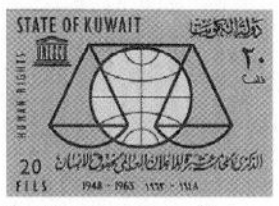
36 Scales of Justice and Globe

1963. 15th Anniv of Declaration of Human Rights.

213	**36**	8f. black, green and violet	20	10
214	**36**	20f. black, yellow and grey	95	55
215	**36**	25f. black, brown and blue	1·50	85

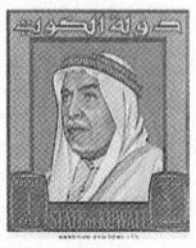
37 Shaikh Abdullah

1964. Multicoloured, frame colours given.

216	**37**	1f. grey	20	10
217	**37**	2f. blue	20	10
218	**37**	4f. brown	20	10
219	**37**	5f. brown	20	10
220	**37**	8f. brown	30	10
221	**37**	10f. green	45	10
222	**37**	15f. green	55	10
223	**37**	20f. blue	60	10
224	**37**	25f. green	65	30
225	**37**	30f. green	75	30
226	**37**	40f. violet	1·20	45
227	**37**	45f. violet	1·30	55
228	**37**	50f. yellow	1·40	55
229	**37**	70f. purple	1·60	65
230	**37**	75f. red	2·10	75
231	**37**	90f. blue	3·25	75
232	**37**	100f. lilac	3·75	65
233	**37**	250f. brown (25×30 mm)	9·00	2·75
234	**37**	1d. purple (25×30 mm)	32·00	10·50

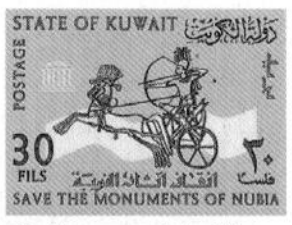
38 Rameses II in War Chariot

1964. Nubian Monuments Preservation.

235	**38**	8f. purple, blue and buff	45	10
236	**38**	20f. violet, blue and light blue	95	55
237	**38**	30f. violet, blue and turquoise	1·30	65

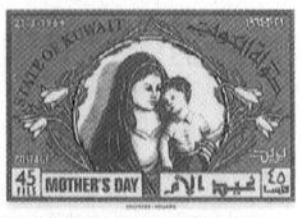
39 Mother and Child

1964. Mother's Day.

238	**39**	8f. blue, green and grey	20	10
239	**39**	20f. blue, green and red	65	20
240	**39**	30f. blue, green and bistre	85	45
241	**39**	45f. indigo, green and blue	1·10	65

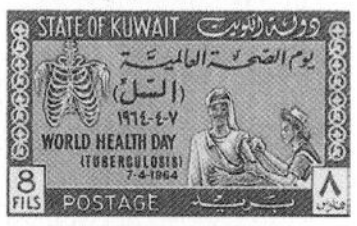
40 Nurse giving B.C.G. Vaccine to Patient, and Bones of Chest

1964. World Health Day.

242	**40**	8f. green and brown	65	10
243	**40**	20f. red and green	1·50	55

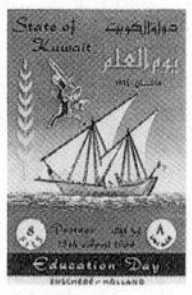
41 Dhow and Microscope

1964. Education Day.

244	**41**	8f. multicoloured	20	10
245	**41**	15f. multicoloured	30	20
246	**41**	20f. multicoloured	55	30
247	**41**	30f. multicoloured	75	65

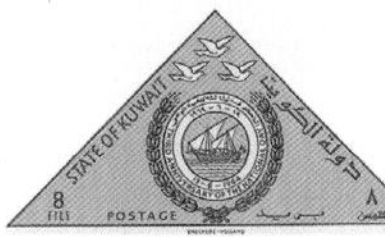
42 Dhow and Doves

1964. Third Anniv of National Day. Badge in blue, brown, black, red and green.

248	**42**	8f. black and brown	30	20
249	**42**	20f. black and green	55	30
250	**42**	30f. black and grey	85	55
251	**42**	45f. black and blue	1·20	75

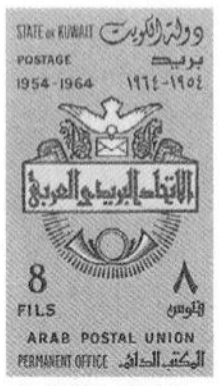
43 A.P.U. Emblem

1964. Tenth Anniv of Arab Postal Union's Permanent Office, Cairo.

252	**43**	8f. brown and blue	55	10
253	**43**	20f. blue and yellow	75	30
254	**43**	45f. brown and green	1·40	85

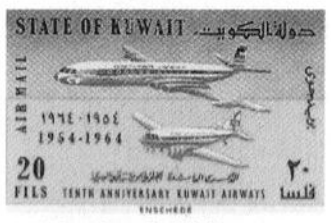
44 Hawker Siddeley Comet 4C and Douglas DC-3 Airliners

1964. Air. Tenth Anniv of Kuwait Airways. Sky in blue; aircraft blue, red and black.

255	**44**	20f. black and bistre	75	30
256	**44**	25f. black and brown	95	30
257	**44**	30f. black and green	1·10	55
258	**44**	45f. black and brown	1·50	75

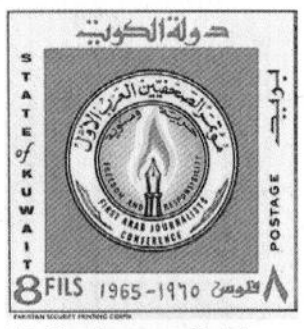
45 Conference Emblem

1965. First Arab Journalists' Conference, Kuwait.

259	**45**	8f. multicoloured	45	10
260	**45**	20f. multicoloured	75	30

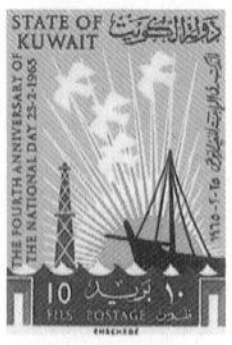
46 Dhow, Doves and Oil-drilling Rig

1965. Fourth Anniv of National Day.

261	**46**	10f. multicoloured	30	10
262	**46**	15f. multicoloured	75	20
263	**46**	20f. multicoloured	1·10	45

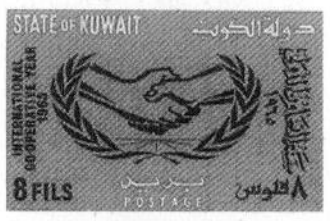
47 I.C.Y. Emblem

1965. International Co-operation Year.

264	**47**	8f. black and red	45	20
265	**47**	20f. black and blue	75	30
266	**47**	30f. black and green	1·50	55

The stamps are inscribed "CO-OPERATIVE".

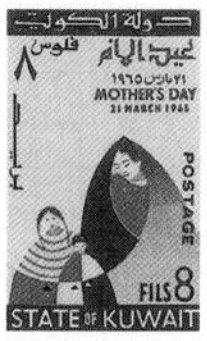
48 Mother and Children

1965. Mothers' Day.

267	**48**	8f. multicoloured	45	10
268	**48**	15f. multicoloured	65	45
269	**48**	20f. multicoloured	1·10	65

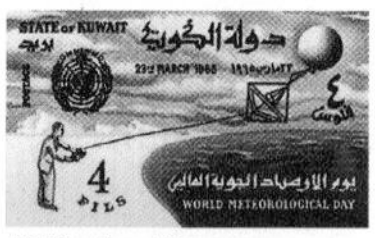
49 Weather Kite

1965. World Meteorological Day.

270	**49**	4f. blue and yellow	55	10
271	**49**	5f. blue and orange	55	20
272	**49**	20f. blue and green	2·10	1·10

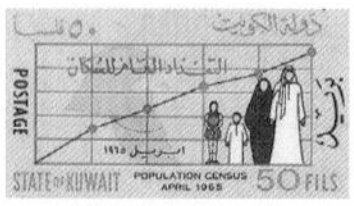
50 Census Graph

1965. Population Census.

273	**50**	8f. black, brown and blue	30	10
274	**50**	20f. black, pink and green	85	30
275	**50**	50f. black, green and red	2·00	85

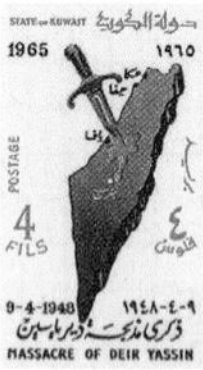
50a Dagger on Deir Yassin, Palestine

1965. Deir Yassin Massacre.

276	**50a**	4f. red and blue	45	30
277	**50a**	45f. red and green	2·75	1·30

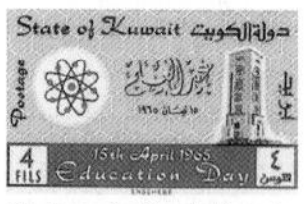
51 Atomic Symbol and Tower of Shuwaikh Secondary School

1965. Education Day.

278	**51**	4f. multicoloured	30	10
279	**51**	20f. multicoloured	75	45
280	**51**	45f. multicoloured	1·60	1·10

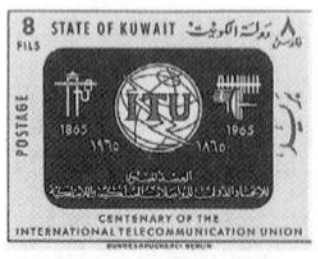
52 I.T.U. Emblem and Symbols

1965. I.T.U. Centenary.

281	**52**	8f. red and blue	30	20
282	**52**	20f. red and green	1·30	30
283	**52**	45f. blue and red	3·25	1·30

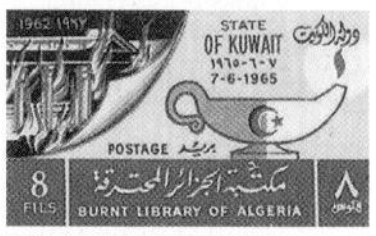
52a Lamp and Burning Library

1965. Reconstitution of Burnt Algiers Library.

284	**52a**	8f. green, red and black	65	20
285	**52a**	15f. red, green and black	1·70	45

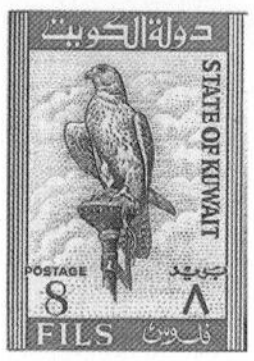
53 Saker Falcon

1965. Centre in brown.

286	**53**	8f. purple	2·75	30
287	**53**	15f. green	2·10	30
288	**53**	20f. blue	3·75	55
289	**53**	25f. red	4·00	75
290	**53**	30f. green	4·75	85
291	**53**	45f. blue	9·00	1·30
292	**53**	50f. purple	10·50	1·40
293	**53**	90f. red	17·00	2·75

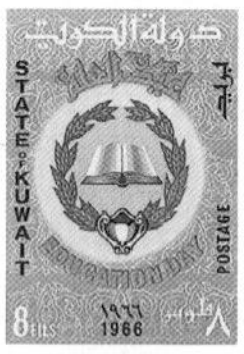
54 Open Book

1966. Education Day.

294	**54**	8f. multicoloured	30	10
295	**54**	20f. multicoloured	95	45
296	**54**	30f. multicoloured	1·40	65

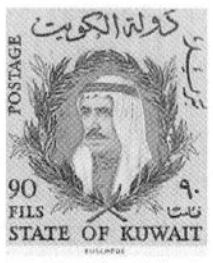
55 Shaikh Sabah

1966

297	**55**	4f. multicoloured	10	10
298	**55**	5f. multicoloured	20	10
299	**55**	20f. multicoloured	55	15
300	**55**	30f. multicoloured	75	20
301	**55**	40f. multicoloured	95	30
302	**55**	45f. multicoloured	1·20	45
303	**55**	70f. multicoloured	2·75	1·10
304	**55**	90f. multicoloured	3·25	1·60

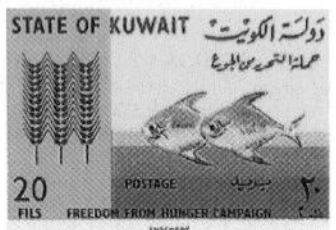
56 Pomfrets and Ears of Wheat

1966. Freedom from Hunger.

305	**56**	20f. multicoloured	2·75	75
306	**56**	45f. multicoloured	3·75	1·40

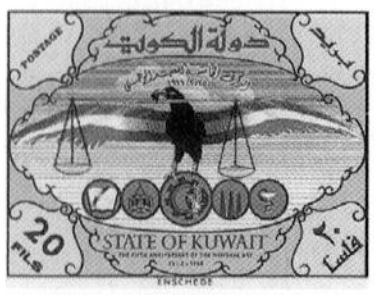
57 Eagle and Scales of Justice

1966. Fifth Anniv of National Day.

307	**57**	20f. multicoloured	1·60	30
308	**57**	25f. multicoloured	1·60	55
309	**57**	45f. multicoloured	3·50	1·30

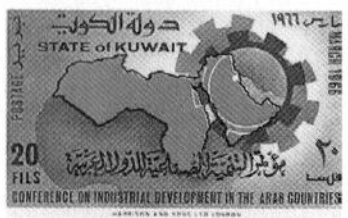
58 Cogwheel and Map of Arab States

1966. Arab Countries Industrial Development Conference, Kuwait.

310	**58**	20f. green black and blue	85	30
311	**58**	50f. green, black and brown	1·50	75

59 Mother and Children

1966. Mothers' Day.
312	**59**	20f. multicoloured	75	30
313	**59**	45f. multicoloured	1·60	75

60 Red Crescent and Emblem of Medicine

1966. Fifth Arab Medical Conference, Kuwait.
314	**60**	15f. red and blue	55	85
315	**60**	30f. red, blue and pink	1·20	85

61 "Man and his Cities"

1966. World Health Day.
316	**61**	8f. multicoloured	75	20
317	**61**	10f. multicoloured	1·10	20

62 W.H.O. Building

1966. Inaug of W.H.O. Headquarters, Geneva.
318	**62**	5f. green, blue and red	75	20
319	**62**	10f. green, blue and turquoise	1·40	20

62a Traffic Signals

1966. Traffic Day.
320	**62a**	10f. red, emerald and green	75	20
321	**62a**	20f. emerald, red and green	1·10	45

63 Symbol of Blood Donation

1966. Blood Bank Day.
322	**63**	4f. multicoloured	65	20
323	**63**	8f. multicoloured	1·50	55

64 Shaikh Ahmad and *British Fusilier* (tanker)

1966. 20th Anniv of 1st Crude Oil Shipment.
324	**64**	20f. multicoloured	1·10	55
325	**64**	45f. multicoloured	2·40	1·10

65 Ministry Building

1966. Inauguration of Ministry of Guidance and Information Building.
326	**65**	4f. red and brown	20	10
327	**65**	5f. brown and green	20	10
328	**65**	8f. green and violet	45	15
329	**65**	20f. orange and blue	95	30

66 Dhow, Lobster, Fish and Crab

1966. F.A.O. Near East Countries Fisheries Conference, Kuwait.
330	**66**	4f. multicoloured	75	20
331	**66**	20f. multicoloured	2·10	95

67 U.N. Flag

1966. U.N. Day.
332	**67**	20f. multicoloured	1·30	30
333	**67**	45f. multicoloured	2·75	1·30

68 UNESCO Emblem

1966. 20th Anniv of UNESCO.
334	**68**	20f. multicoloured	1·10	20
335	**68**	45f. multicoloured	2·75	1·10

69 Ruler and University Shield

1966. Opening of Kuwait University.
336	**69**	8f. multicoloured	45	10
337	**69**	10f. multicoloured	45	10
338	**69**	20f. multicoloured	1·10	30
339	**69**	45f. multicoloured	2·10	1·30

70 Ruler and Heir-Apparent

1966. Appointment of Heir-Apparent.
340	**70**	8f. multicoloured	45	10
341	**70**	20f. multicoloured	95	30
342	**70**	45f. multicoloured	2·10	1·20

71 Scout Badge

1966. 30th Anniv of Kuwait Scouts.
343	**71**	4f. brown and green	1·50	45
344	**71**	20f. green and brown	3·75	1·50

72 Symbols of Learning

1967. Education Day.
345	**72**	10f. multicoloured	45	20
346	**72**	45f. multicoloured	1·20	55

73 Fertiliser Plant

1967. Inauguration of Chemical Fertiliser Plant.
347	**73**	8f. multicoloured	55	10
348	**73**	20f. multicoloured	1·40	45

74 Ruler, Dove and Olive-branch

1967. Sixth Anniv of National Day.
349	**74**	8f. multicoloured	45	10
350	**74**	20f. multicoloured	1·10	45

75 Map and Municipality Building

1967. First Arab Cities Organization Conf, Kuwait.
351	**75**	20f. multicoloured	1·60	55
352	**75**	30f. multicoloured	2·75	1·40

76 Arab Family

1967. Family's Day.
353	**76**	20f. multicoloured	1·60	55
354	**76**	45f. multicoloured	2·75	1·40

77 Arab League Emblem

1967. Arab Cause Week.
355	**77**	8f. blue and grey	45	10
356	**77**	10f. green and yellow	85	20

78 Sabah Hospital

1967. World Health Day.
357	**78**	8f. multicoloured	85	10
358	**78**	20f. multicoloured	2·40	55

79 Nubian Statues

1967. Arab Week for Nubian Monuments Preservation.
359	**79**	15f. green, brown and yellow	95	20
360	**79**	20f. green, purple and blue	1·70	55

80 Traffic Policeman

1967. Traffic Day.
361	**80**	8f. multicoloured	1·10	30
362	**80**	20f. multicoloured	2·75	75

81 I.T.Y. Emblem

1967. International Tourist Year.
363	**81**	20f. black, blue & turquoise	1·10	20
364	**81**	45f. black, blue and mauve	2·10	1·10

82 "Reaching for Knowledge"

1967. "Eliminate Illiteracy" Campaign.
365	**82**	8f. multicoloured	1·40	10
366	**82**	20f. multicoloured	2·40	65

83 Map of Palestine

1967. U.N. Day.
367	**83**	20f. red and blue	75	20
368	**83**	45f. red and orange	1·60	75

84 Factory and Cogwheels

1967. Third Arab Labour Ministers' Conference.
369	**84**	20f. yellow and red	1·10	20
370	**84**	45f. yellow and grey	2·40	1·40

85 Open Book and Kuwaiti Flag

1968. Education Day.
371	**85**	20f. multicoloured	65	10
372	**85**	45f. multicoloured	2·00	1·20

86 Oil Rig and Map

1968. 30th Anniv of Oil Discovery in Greater Burgan Field.
373	**86**	10f. multicoloured	1·10	20
374	**86**	20f. multicoloured	2·10	1·10

87 Ruler and Sun's Rays

1968. Seventh Anniv of National Day.
375	**87**	8f. multicoloured	45	10
376	**87**	10f. multicoloured	45	20
377	**87**	15f. multicoloured	55	20
378	**87**	20f. multicoloured	75	20

88 Book, Eagle and Sun

1968. Teachers' Day.
379	**88**	8f. multicoloured	45	10

380	**88**	20f. multicoloured	95	20
381	**88**	45f. multicoloured	1·80	1·10

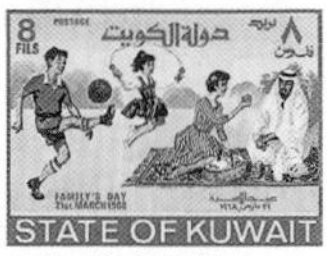

89 Family Picnicking

1968. Family Day.

382	**89**	8f. multicoloured	30	10
383	**89**	10f. multicoloured	45	10
384	**89**	15f. multicoloured	55	15
385	**89**	20f. multicoloured	75	20

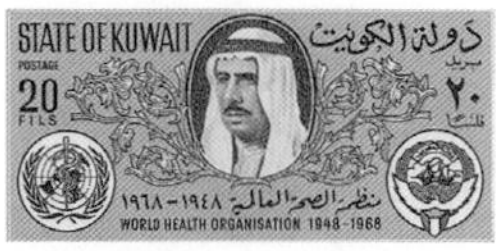

90 Ruler, W.H.O. and State Emblems

1968. World Health Day and 20th Anniv of W.H.O.

386	**90**	20f. multicoloured	1·10	55
387	**90**	45f. multicoloured	2·10	1·30

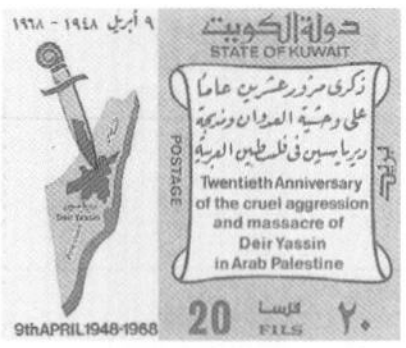

91 Dagger on Deir Yassin, and Scroll

1968. 20th Anniv of Deir Yassin Massacre.

388	**91**	20f. red and blue	1·30	55
389	**91**	45f. red and violet	4·00	1·10

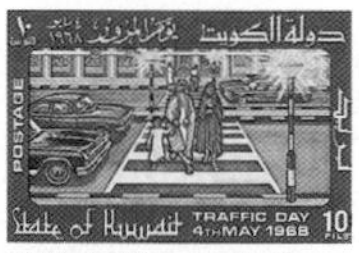

92 Pedestrians on Road Crossing

1968. Traffic Day.

390	**92**	10f. multicoloured	1·10	30
391	**92**	15f. multicoloured	1·60	55
392	**92**	20f. multicoloured	3·25	75

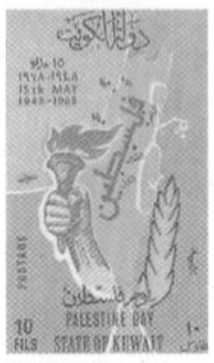
93 Torch and Map

1968. Palestine Day.

393	**93**	10f. multicoloured	1·40	45
394	**93**	20f. multicoloured	2·10	55
395	**93**	45f. multicoloured	4·50	1·80

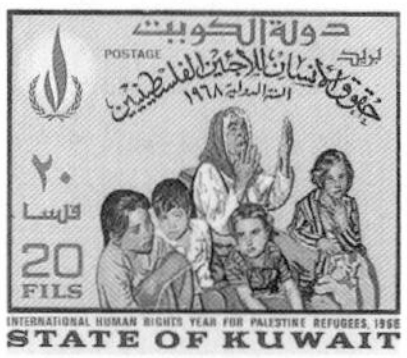

94 Palestine Refugees

1968. Human Rights Year.

396	**94**	20f. multicoloured	30	20
397	**94**	30f. multicoloured	55	45
398	**94**	45f. multicoloured	1·10	55
399	**94**	90f. multicoloured	2·10	1·80

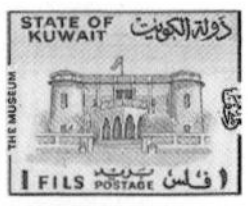

95 National Museum

1968

400	**95**	1f. green and brown	10	10
401	**95**	2f. green and purple	10	10
402	**95**	5f. red and black	20	10
403	**95**	8f. green and brown	30	10
404	**95**	10f. purple and blue	45	15
405	**95**	20f. blue and brown	65	20
406	**95**	25f. orange and blue	75	25
407	**95**	30f. green and blue	1·10	30
408	**95**	45f. deep purple and purple	1·70	65
409	**95**	50f. red and green	2·10	1·10

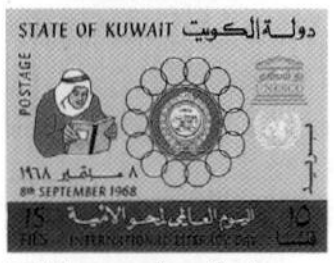

96 Man reading Book

1968. International Literacy Day.

410	**96**	15f. multicoloured	45	10
411	**96**	20f. multicoloured	1·10	30

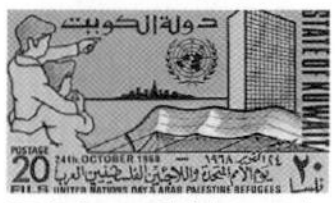

97 Refugee Children and U.N. Headquarters

1968. United Nations Day.

412	**97**	20f. multicoloured	45	10
413	**97**	30f. multicoloured	65	45
414	**97**	45f. multicoloured	1·10	55

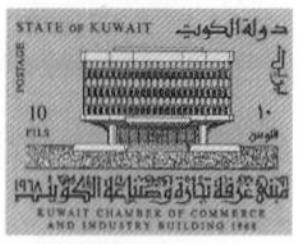

98 Chamber of Commerce Building

1968. Inauguration of Kuwait Chamber of Commerce and Industry Building.

415	**98**	10f. purple and orange	45	10
416	**98**	15f. blue and mauve	45	20
417	**98**	20f. green and brown	65	45

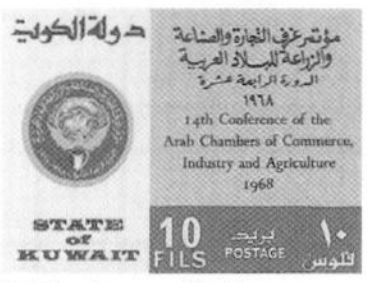

99 Conference Emblem

1968. 14th Arab Chambers of Commerce, Industry and Agriculture Conference.

418	**99**	10f. multicoloured	45	10
419	**99**	15f. multicoloured	45	10
420	**99**	20f. multicoloured	65	45
421	**99**	30f. multicoloured	85	55

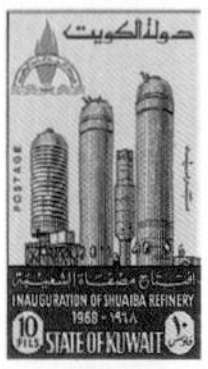

100 Refinery Plant

1968. Inauguration of Shuaiba Refinery.

422	**100**	10f. multicoloured	55	10
423	**100**	20f. multicoloured	95	20
424	**100**	30f. multicoloured	1·20	55
425	**100**	45f. multicoloured	2·10	1·10

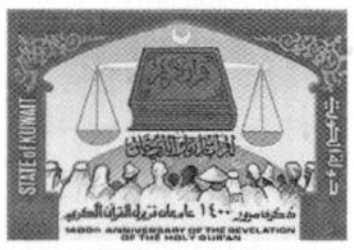
101 Holy Koran, Scales and People

1968. 1,400th Anniv of the Holy Koran.

426	**101**	8f. multicoloured	55	10
427	**101**	20f. multicoloured	1·10	20
428	**101**	30f. multicoloured	1·60	55
429	**101**	45f. multicoloured	2·10	95

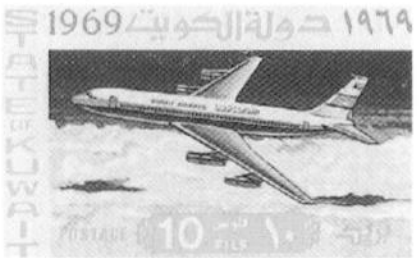

102 Boeing 707 Airliner

1969. Inauguration of Boeing 707 Aircraft by Kuwait Airways.

430	**102**	10f. multicoloured	55	20
431	**102**	20f. multicoloured	1·10	45
432	**102**	25f. multicoloured	1·60	75
433	**102**	45f. multicoloured	2·75	95

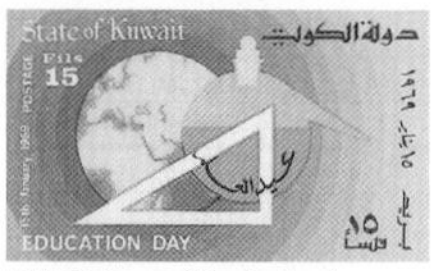

103 Globe and Symbols of Engineering and Science

1969. Education Day.

434	**103**	15f. multicoloured	65	20
435	**103**	20f. multicoloured	85	65

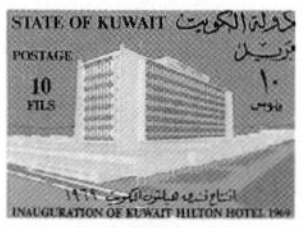

104 Hilton Hotel

1969. Inauguration of Kuwait Hilton Hotel.

436	**104**	10f. multicoloured	45	20
437	**104**	20f. multicoloured	95	30

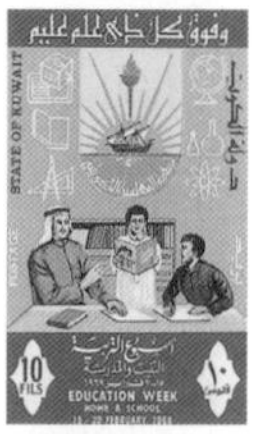

105 Family and Teachers' Society Emblem

1969. Education Week.

438	**105**	10f. multicoloured	45	20
439	**105**	20f. multicoloured	95	30

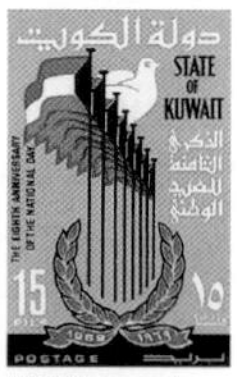

106 Flags and Laurel

1969. Seventh Anniv of National Day.

440	**106**	15f. multicoloured	45	20
441	**106**	20f. multicoloured	65	30
442	**106**	30f. multicoloured	85	55

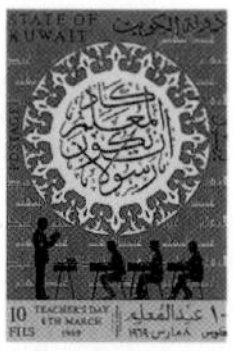
107 Emblem, Teacher and Class

1969. Teachers' Day.

443	**107**	10f. multicoloured	45	20
444	**107**	20f. multicoloured	75	55

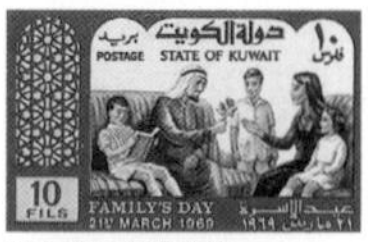

108 Kuwaiti Family

1969. Family Day.

445	**108**	10f. multicoloured	55	20
446	**108**	20f. multicoloured	1·10	30

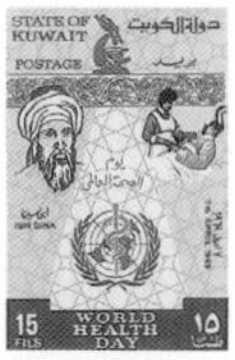

109 Ibn Sina, Nurse with Patient and W.H.O. Emblem

1969. World Health Day.

447	**109**	15f. multicoloured	1·10	20
448	**109**	20f. multicoloured	1·30	30

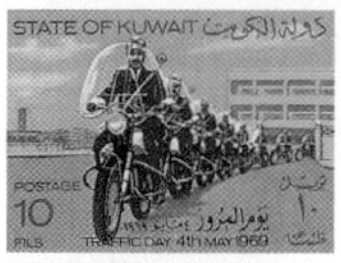

110 Motor-cycle Police

1969. Traffic Day.

449	**110**	10f. multicoloured	1·60	20
450	**110**	20f. multicoloured	3·25	55

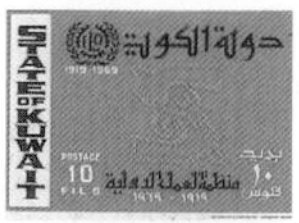

111 I.L.O. Emblem

1969. 50th Anniv of I.L.O.

451	**111**	10f. gold, black and red	45	20
452	**111**	20f. gold, black and green	85	30

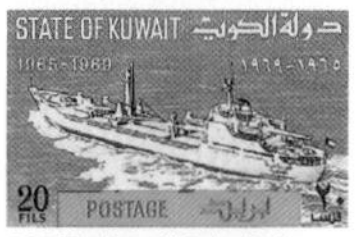

112 Tanker *Al Sabahiah*

1969. Fourth Anniv of Kuwait Shipping Company.

453	**112**	20f. multicoloured	1·30	55
454	**112**	45f. multicoloured	3·00	1·50

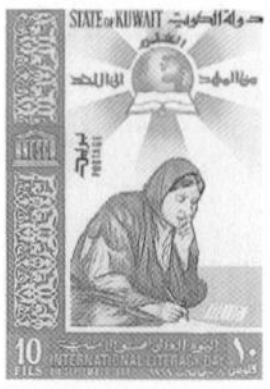
113 Woman writing Letter

1969. International Literacy Day.

455	**113**	10f. multicoloured	45	10
456	**113**	20f. multicoloured	85	45

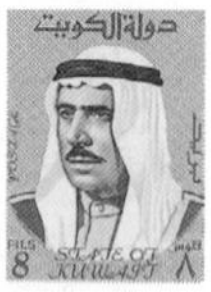
114 Amir Shaikh Sabah

1969. Portraits mult; background colours given.

457	**114**	8f. blue	45	10
458	**114**	10f. pink	45	10
459	**114**	15f. grey	55	20
460	**114**	20f. yellow	55	20
461	**114**	25f. lilac	75	30
462	**114**	30f. orange	1·10	45
463	**114**	45f. grey	1·50	55
464	**114**	50f. green	1·70	65
465	**114**	70f. blue	1·80	75
466	**114**	75f. blue	2·75	85
467	**114**	90f. brown	2·75	1·10
468	**114**	250f. purple	8·50	2·75
469	**114**	500f. green	16·00	10·00
470	**114**	1d. purple	28·00	17·00

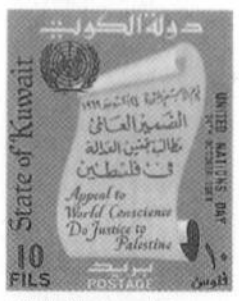

115 "Appeal to World Conscience"

1969. United Nations Day.

471	**115**	10f. blue, black and green	55	10
472	**115**	20f. blue, black and stone	1·20	20
473	**115**	45f. blue, black and red	2·50	95

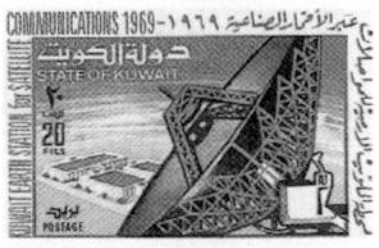

116 Earth Station

1969. Inauguration of Kuwait Satellite Communications Station. Multicoloured.

474		20 Type **116**	1·70	20
475		45f. Dish aerial on Globe (vert)	2·75	1·10

117 Refugee Family

1969. Palestinian Refugee Week.
476 **117** 20f. multicoloured 2·10 55
477 **117** 45f. multicoloured 4·75 1·90

118 Globe, Symbols and I.E.Y. Emblem

1970. International Education Year.
478 **118** 20f. multicoloured 65 20
479 **118** 45f. multicoloured 1·50 95

119 Shoue

1970. Kuwait Sailing Dhows. Multicoloured.
480 8f. Type **119** 65 20
481 10f. Sambuk 75 30
482 15f. Baggala 1·20 45
483 20f. Battela 1·50 65
484 25f. Bum 1·80 75
485 45f. Baggala 3·25 1·40
486 50f. Dhow-building 3·75 1·60

120 Kuwaiti Flag

1970. Ninth Anniv of National Day.
487 **120** 15f. multicoloured 95 30
488 **120** 20f. multicoloured 1·20 30

121 Young Commando and Dome of the Rock, Jerusalem

1970. Support for Palestinian Commandos. Multicoloured.
489 10f. Type **121** 1·50 85
490 20f. Commando in battle-dress 2·75 1·70
491 45f. Woman commando 6·50 3·75

122 Parents with "Children"

1970. Family Day.
492 **122** 20f. multicoloured 55 20
493 **122** 30f. multicoloured 95 30

123 Arab League Flag, Emblem and Map

1970. 25th Anniv of Arab League.
494 **123** 20f. brown, green and blue 75 20
495 **123** 45f. violet, green and orange 1·10 55

124 Census Emblem and Graph

1970. Population Census.
496 **124** 15f. multicoloured 45 10
497 **124** 20f. multicoloured 65 75
498 **124** 30f. multicoloured 85 55

125 Cancer the Crab in "Pincers"

1970. World Health Day.
499 **125** 20f. multicoloured 1·10 55
500 **125** 30f. multicoloured 1·70 75

126 Traffic Lights and Road Signs

1970. Traffic Day.
501 **126** 20f. multicoloured 1·60 65
502 **126** 30f. multicoloured 2·10 1·10

127 Red Crescent

1970. International Red Cross and Crescent Day.
503 **127** 10f. multicoloured 65 15
504 **127** 15f. multicoloured 95 45
505 **127** 30f. multicoloured 2·75 75

128 New Headquarters Building

1970. Opening of New U.P.U. Headquarters Building, Berne.
506 **128** 20f. multicoloured 95 30
507 **128** 30f. multicoloured 1·40 75

129 Amir Shaikh Sabah

1970
508 **129** 20f. multicoloured 95 20
509 **129** 45f. multicoloured 2·50 1·10
MS510 127×101 mm. Nos. 508/9.
Imperf 6·00 6·00

130 U.N. Symbols

1970. 25th Anniv of United Nations.
511 **130** 20f. multicoloured 55 20
512 **130** 45f. multicoloured 1·10 55

131 Medora (tanker) at Sea Island Jetty

1970. Oil Shipment Facilities, Kuwait.
513 **131** 20f. multicoloured 1·60 30
514 **131** 45f. multicoloured 2·75 1·10

132 Kuwaiti and U.N. Emblems and Hand writing

1970. International Literacy Day.
515 **132** 10f. multicoloured 1·10 20
516 **132** 15f. multicoloured 1·30 55

133 Guards and Badge

1970. First Graduation of National Guards.
517 **133** 10f. multicoloured 75 20
518 **133** 20f. multicoloured 1·60 55

134 Symbols and Flag

1971. Tenth Anniv of National Day.
519 **134** 20f. multicoloured 1·10 45
520 **134** 30f. multicoloured 1·60 55

135 Dr. C. Best and Sir F. Banting (discoverers of insulin) and Syringe

1971. World Health Day, and 50th Anniv of Discovery of Insulin.
521 **135** 20f. multicoloured 1·60 45
522 **135** 45f. multicoloured 3·25 75

136 Map of Palestine on Globe

1971. Palestine Day.
523 **136** 20f. multicoloured 1·60 20
524 **136** 45f. multicoloured 3·25 1·10

137 I.T.U. Emblem

1971. World Telecommunications Day.
525 **137** 20f. black, brown and silver 1·10 30
526 **137** 45f. black, brown and gold 2·40 75

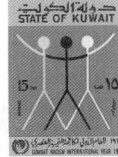

138 "Three Races"

1971. Racial Equality Year.
527 **138** 15f. multicoloured 65 20
528 **138** 30f. multicoloured 1·20 65

139 A.P.U. Emblem

1971. 25th Anniv of Founding of Arab Postal Union at Sofar Conference.
529 **139** 20f. multicoloured 95 30
530 **139** 45f. multicoloured 1·80 75

140 Book, Pupils, Globes and Pen

1971. International Literacy Day.
531 **140** 25f. multicoloured 85 20
532 **140** 60f. multicoloured 2·10 1·10

141 Footballers

1971. Regional Sports Tournament, Kuwait. Multicoloured.
533 20f. Type **141** 1·50 55
534 30f. Footballer blocking attack 2·10 95

142 Emblems of UNICEF and Kuwait

1971. 25th Anniv of UNICEF.
535 **142** 25f. multicoloured 55 30
536 **142** 60f. multicoloured 1·40 75

143 Book Year Emblem

1972. International Book Year.
537 **143** 20f. black and brown 75 45
538 **143** 45f. black and green 1·70 95

144 Crest and Laurel

1972. 11th Anniv of National Day.
539 **144** 20f. multicoloured 1·10 15
540 **144** 45f. multicoloured 2·10 95

145 Telecommunications Centre

1972. Inauguration of Telecommunications Centre, Kuwait.
541 **145** 20f. multicoloured 1·60 30
542 **145** 45f. multicoloured 4·25 1·30

146 Human Heart

1972. World Health Day and World Heart Month.
543	146	20f. multicoloured	1·60	55
544	146	45f. multicoloured	4·25	1·30

147 Nurse and Child

1972. International Red Cross and Crescent Day.
545	147	8f. multicoloured	75	30
546	147	40f. multicoloured	4·00	1·30

148 Football

1972. Olympic Games, Munich. Multicoloured.
547	2f. Type **148**		10	10
548	4f. Running		20	10
549	5f. Swimming		20	10
550	8f. Gymnastics		45	10
551	10f. Throwing the discus		50	15
552	15f. Show jumping		75	20
553	20f. Basketball		95	25
554	25f. Volleyball		1·20	55

149 Produce and Fishing Boat

1972. 11th F.A.O. Near East Regional Conference, Kuwait.
555	149	5f. multicoloured	45	45
556	149	10f. multicoloured	1·50	1·10
557	149	20f. multicoloured	3·00	2·10

150 Bank Emblem

1972. 20th Anniv of National Bank of Kuwait.
558	150	10f. multicoloured	45	10
559	150	35f. multicoloured	1·70	85

151 Ancient Capitals

1972. Archaeological Excavations on Failaka Island. Multicoloured.
560	2f. Type **151**		20	20
561	5f. View of excavations		45	20
562	10f. "Leaf" capital		65	25
563	15f. Excavated building		1·40	30

152 Floral Emblem

1973. 12th Anniv of National Day.
564	152	10f. multicoloured	45	10
565	152	20f. multicoloured	85	30
566	152	30f. multicoloured	1·40	65

153 Interpol Emblem

1973. 50th Anniv of International Criminal Police Organization (Interpol).
567	153	10f. multicoloured	85	20
568	153	15f. multicoloured	1·60	45
569	153	20f. multicoloured	1·80	95

154 C.I.S.M. Badge and Flags

1973. 25th Anniv of International Military Sports Council (C.I.S.M.).
570	154	30f. multicoloured	1·10	55
571	154	40f. multicoloured	1·60	75

155 Airways Building

1973. Opening of Kuwait Airways H.Q. Building.
572	155	10f. multicoloured	55	10
573	155	15f. multicoloured	75	20
574	155	20f. multicoloured	95	45

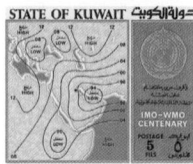

156 Weather Map of Middle East

1973. Centenary of World Meteorological Organization.
575	156	5f. multicoloured	55	20
576	156	10f. multicoloured	85	30
577	156	15f. multicoloured	1·30	65

157 Shaikhs Ahmed and Sabah

1973. 50th Anniv of 1st Kuwait Stamp Issue (overprints on India of 1923).
578	157	10f. multicoloured	65	10
579	157	20f. multicoloured	1·20	20
580	157	70f. multicoloured	3·75	1·50

158 Mourning Dove

1973. Birds and Hunting Equipment. Multicoloured. (a) Size 32×32 mm.
581	5f. Type **158**		75	20
582	5f. Hoopoe (Upupa epops)		75	20
583	5f. Feral rock pigeon (Columba livia)		75	20
584	5f. Stone-curlew (Burhinus oedicnemus)		75	20
585	8f. Great grey shrike (Lanius excubitor)		1·10	25
586	8f. Red-backed shrike (Lanius collurio)		1·10	25
587	8f. Black-headed shrike (Lanius schach)		1·10	25
588	8f. Golden oriole (Oriolus chinensis)		1·10	25
589	10f. Willow warbler (Phylloscopus trochilus)		1·20	30
590	10f. Great reed warbler (Acrocephalus arundinaceus)		1·20	30
591	10f. Blackcap (Sylvia atricapilla)		1·20	30
592	10f. Barn swallow (Hirundo rustica)		1·20	30
593	15f. Rock thrush (Monticola solitarius)		1·70	45
594	15f. Common redstart (Phoenicurus phoenicurus)		1·70	45
595	15f. Northern wheatear (Oenanthe oenanthe)		1·70	45
596	15f. Bluethroat (Luscinia svecica)		1·70	45
597	20f. Houbara bustard (Chlamydotis undulata)		2·40	55
598	20f. Pin-tailed sandgrouse (Pterocles alchata)		2·40	55
599	20f. Greater wood rail (Aramides ypecaha)		2·40	55
600	20f. Spotted crake (Porzana porzana)		2·40	55

(b) Size 38×38 mm.
601	25f. American kestrel (Falco sparverius)		3·25	65
602	25f. Great black-backed gull (Larus marinus)		3·25	65
603	25f. Purple heron (Ardea purpurea)		3·25	65
604	25f. Wryneck (Jynx torquilla)		3·25	65
605	30f. European bee eater (Merops apiaster)		3·50	75
606	30f. Saker falcon (Accipiter)		3·50	75
607	30f. Grey wagtail (Motacilla cinerea)		3·50	75
608	30f. Pied wagtail (Motacilla alba)		3·50	75
609	45f. Bird traps		5·00	1·60
610	45f. Driving great grey shrikes into net		5·00	1·60
611	45f. Stalking Feral rock pigeon with hand net		5·00	1·60
612	45f. Great grey shrike and disguised lure		5·00	1·60

159 Flame Emblem

1973. 25th Anniv of Declaration of Human Rights.
613	159	10f. multicoloured	55	10
614	159	40f. multicoloured	1·60	55
615	159	75f. multicoloured	2·75	1·50

160 Congress Emblem

1974. Fourth Congress of Arab Veterinary Union, Kuwait.
616	160	30f. multicoloured	95	45
617	160	40f. multicoloured	1·40	95

161 Flag and Wheat Ear Symbol

1974. 13th Anniv of National Day.
618	161	20f. multicoloured	55	20
619	161	30f. multicoloured	85	30
620	161	70f. multicoloured	1·80	1·60

162 A.M.U. Emblem

163 Tournament Emblem

1974. 12th Conference of Arab Medical Union and 1st Conference of Kuwait Medical Society.
621	162	30f. multicoloured	1·80	55
622	162	40f. multicoloured	3·00	1·10

1974. Third Arabian Gulf Trophy Football Tournament, Kuwait.
623	163	25f. multicoloured	1·50	45
624	163	45f. multicoloured	2·50	1·10

164 Institute Buildings

1974. Inauguration of Kuwait Institute for Scientific Research.
625	164	15f. multicoloured	1·50	45
626	164	20f. multicoloured	1·90	65

165 Emblems of Kuwait, Arab Postal Union and U.P.U.

1974. Centenary of U.P.U.
627	165	20f. multicoloured	45	20
628	165	30f. multicoloured	50	45
629	165	60f. multicoloured	75	75

166 Symbolic Telephone Dial

1974. World Telecommunications Day.
630	166	20f. multicoloured	45	20
631	166	30f. multicoloured	1·20	55
632	166	40f. multicoloured	1·70	65

167 Council Emblem and Flags of Member States

1974. 17th Anniv of Signing Arab Economic Unity Agreement.
633	167	20f. green, black and red	95	45
634	167	30f. red, black and green	1·10	65

168 "Population Growth"

1974. World Population Year.
635	168	30f. multicoloured	1·10	20
636	168	70f. multicoloured	2·75	1·50

169 Fund Building

1974. Kuwait Fund for Arab Economic Development.
637	169	10f. multicoloured	75	20
638	169	20f. multicoloured	1·20	45

170 Shuaiba Emblem

1974. Tenth Anniv of Shuaiba Industrial Area.

639	170	10f. multicoloured	65	20
640	170	20f. multicoloured	1·50	45
641	170	30f. multicoloured	2·10	95

171 Arms of Kuwait and "14"

1975. 14th Anniv of National Day.

642	171	20f. multicoloured	65	15
643	171	70f. multicoloured	1·70	1·20
644	171	75f. multicoloured	2·50	1·50

172 Census Symbols

1975. Population Census.

645	172	8f. multicoloured	10	10
646	172	20f. multicoloured	45	20
647	172	30f. multicoloured	65	45
648	172	70f. multicoloured	1·80	1·10
649	172	100f. multicoloured	3·00	1·30

173 I.W.Y. and Kuwait Women's Union Emblems

1975. International Women's Year.

650	173	15f. multicoloured	85	20
651	173	20f. multicoloured	90	30
652	173	30f. multicoloured	1·60	65

174 Classroom within Open Book

1975. International Literacy Day.

653	174	20f. multicoloured	75	20
654	174	30f. multicoloured	1·40	65

175 I.S.O. Emblem

1975. World Standards Day.

655	175	10f. multicoloured	45	20
656	175	20f. multicoloured	85	45

176 U.N. Flag, Rifle and Olive-branch

1975. 30th Anniv of U.N.O.

657	176	20f. multicoloured	75	20
658	176	45f. multicoloured	1·70	75

177 Shaikh Sabah

1975

659	177	8f. multicoloured	30	10
660	177	20f. multicoloured	85	20
661	177	30f. multicoloured	1·40	45
662	177	50f. multicoloured	2·10	65
663	177	90f. multicoloured	3·75	1·20
664	177	100f. multicoloured	4·25	1·30

178 Kuwait "Skyline"

1976. 15th Anniv of National Day.

665	178	10f. multicoloured	75	20
666	178	20f. multicoloured	1·40	30

178a Emblem, Microscope and Operation

1976. Second Annual Conference of Kuwait Medical Association.

667	178a	5f. multicoloured	65	20
668	178a	10f. multicoloured	1·30	45
669	178a	30f. multicoloured	3·50	1·50

179 Early and Modern Telephones

1976. Telephone Centenary.

670	179	5f. black and orange	45	20
671	179	15f. black and blue	95	30

180 Eye

1976. World Health Day.

672	180	10f. multicoloured	65	20
673	180	20f. multicoloured	1·10	30
674	180	30f. multicoloured	2·00	85

181 Red Crescent Emblem

1976. Tenth Anniv of Kuwait Red Crescent Society.

675	181	20f. multicoloured	65	20
676	181	30f. multicoloured	1·10	55
677	181	45f. multicoloured	2·00	85
678	181	75f. multicoloured	3·25	2·10

182 Suburb of Manama

1976. U.N. Human Settlements Conference.

679	182	10f. multicoloured	55	20
680	182	20f. multicoloured	1·20	30

183 Basketball

1976. Olympic Games, Montreal. Multicoloured.

681	4f. Type **183**		10	10
682	8f. Running		20	10
683	10f. Judo		30	15
684	15f. Handball		45	20
685	20f. Figure-skating		55	30
686	30f. Volleyball		75	55
687	45f. Football		1·20	75
688	70f. Swimming		1·80	1·10

184 Ethnic Heads and Map of Sri Lanka

1976. Non-Aligned Countries' Congress, Colombo.

689	184	20f. multicoloured	65	20
690	184	30f. multicoloured	85	55
691	184	45f. multicoloured	1·30	75

185 Torch, UNESCO. Emblem and Kuwaiti Arms

1976. 30th Anniv of UNESCO.

692	185	20f. multicoloured	65	20
693	185	45f. multicoloured	1·50	55

186 Pot-throwing

1977. Popular Games. Multicoloured.

694	5f. Type **186**		30	10
695	5f. Kite-flying		30	10
696	5f. Balancing sticks		30	10
697	5f. Spinning tops		30	10
698	10f. Blind-man's-buff (horiz)		65	30
699	10f. Rowing (horiz)		65	30
700	10f. Rolling hoops (horiz)		65	30
701	10f. Rope game (horiz)		65	30
702	15f. Skipping		95	55
703	15f. Marbles		95	55
704	15f. Carting		95	55
705	15f. Teetotum (tops)		95	55
706	20f. Halma (horiz)		1·30	65
707	20f. Model boating (horiz)		1·30	65
708	20f. Pot and candle (horiz)		1·30	65
709	20f. Hide-and-seek (horiz)		1·30	65
710	30f. Knucklebones		1·90	95
711	30f. Hiding the stone		1·90	95
712	30f. Hopscotch		1·90	95
713	30f. Catch-as-catch-can		1·90	95
714	40f. Bowls (horiz)		2·50	1·30
715	40f. Hockey (horiz)		2·50	1·30
716	40f. Guessing which hand (horiz)		2·50	1·30
717	40f. Jacks (horiz)		2·50	1·30
718	60f. Hiding the cake (horiz)		3·75	2·00
719	60f. Chess (horiz)		3·75	2·00
720	60f. Story-telling (horiz)		3·75	2·00
721	60f. Treasure hunt (horiz)		3·75	2·00
722	70f. Hobby horses (horiz)		4·50	2·10
723	70f. Hide-and-seek (horiz)		4·50	2·10
724	70f. Catch shadow (horiz)		4·50	2·10
725	70f. Throwing game (horiz)		4·50	2·10

187 Diseased Knee

1977. World Rheumatism Year.

726	187	20f. multicoloured	65	20
727	187	30f. multicoloured	85	30
728	187	45f. multicoloured	1·40	55
729	187	75f. multicoloured	1·60	1·10

188 Shaikh Sabah

1977. 16th National Day.

730	188	10f. multicoloured	20	10
731	188	15f. multicoloured	45	20
732	188	30f. multicoloured	95	30
733	188	80f. multicoloured	2·10	85

189 Kuwait Tower

1977. Inauguration of Kuwait Tower.

734	189	30f. multicoloured	85	20
735	189	80f. multicoloured	2·40	1·10

190 A.P.U. Emblem and Flags

1977. 25th Anniv of Arab Postal Union.

736	190	5f. multicoloured	20	10
737	190	15f. multicoloured	30	20
738	190	30f. multicoloured	75	30
739	190	80f. multicoloured	2·10	1·10

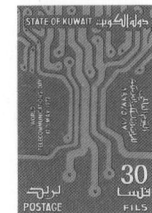

191 Printed Circuit

1977. World Telecommunications Day.

740	191	30f. orange and brown	1·20	20
741	191	80f. orange and green	3·00	1·50

192 Shaikh Sabah

1977

742	192	15f. brown, black and blue	1·40	30
743	192	25f. brown, black and yellow	2·10	45
744	192	30f. brown, black and red	2·40	55
745	192	80f. brown, black and lilac	5·25	1·50
746	192	100f. brown, black and orange	7·00	1·80
747	192	150f. brown, black and blue	10·50	2·75
748	192	200f. brown, black and green	14·00	3·50

192a Aerogramme stamp

1977. Aerogramme stamp. Imperf.

748a	**192a**	55f. red and blue		

No. 748a was applied before sale to aerogrammes to uprate the imprinted 25f. stamp. It was not available separately.

193 Championship Emblem

1977. Fourth Asian Youth Basketball Championships.

749	**193**	30f. multicoloured	1·10	20
750	**193**	80f. multicoloured	2·10	1·10

194 *Popular Dancing* (O. Al-Nakeeb)

1977. Children's Paintings. Multicoloured.

751	15f. Type **194**	30	10
752	15f. *Al Deirah* (A. M. al-Onizi)	30	10
753	30f. *Fishing* (M. al-Jasem)	75	20
754	30f. *Dugg al-Harees* (B. al-Sa'adooni) (vert)	75	20
755	80f. *Fraisa Dancing* (M. al-Mojaibel) (vert)	2·10	1·10
756	80f. *Kuwaiti Girl* (K. Ghazi) (vert)	2·10	1·10

195 Dome of the Rock and Palestinian Freedom Fighters

1978. Palestinian Freedom Fighters.

757	**195**	30f. multicoloured	2·10	1·10
758	**195**	80f. multicoloured	5·25	2·10

196 Dentist treating Patient

1978. Tenth Arab Dental Union Congress.

759	**196**	30f. multicoloured	1·10	20
760	**196**	80f. multicoloured	2·40	1·40

197 Carrying Water from Dhows

1978. Water Resources. Multicoloured.

761	5f. Type **197**	20	10
762	5f. Camel	20	10
763	5f. Water carrier	20	10
764	5f. Pushing water in cart	20	10
765	10f. Irrigation with donkey	45	15
766	10f. Water troughs in desert	45	15
767	10f. Pool by a town	45	15
768	10f. Watering crops	45	15
769	15f. Bedouin watering sheep	65	20
770	15f. Bedouin women by pool	65	20
771	15f. Camels watered by pipeline	65	20
772	15f. Water skins in Bedouin tent	65	20
773	20f. Oasis with wells	85	30
774	20f. Washing and drinking at home	85	30
775	20f. Water urn	85	30
776	20f. Filling vessels from taps	85	30
777	25f. Desalination plant	1·10	40
778	25f. Water tanker	1·10	40
779	25f. Filling water tankers	1·10	40
780	25f. Modern water tanks	1·10	40
781	30f. Catching water during storm (vert)	1·30	45
782	30f. Water tank (vert)	1·30	45
783	30f. Sheet to catch rain (vert)	1·30	45
784	30f. Trees by water tanks (vert)	1·30	45
785	80f. Carrying water on donkey (vert)	3·50	1·20
786	80f. Woman carrying water-can (vert)	3·50	1·20
787	80f. Woman with water-skins (vert)	3·50	1·20
788	80f. Tanker delivering water to house (vert)	3·50	1·20
789	100f. Tanker delivering to courtyard tank (vert)	4·25	1·40
790	100f. Household cistern (vert)	4·25	1·40
791	100f. Filling cistern (vert)	4·25	1·40
792	100f. Drawing water from well (vert)	4·25	1·40

198 Symbols of Development

1978. 17th National Day.

793	**198**	30f. multicoloured	55	20
794	**198**	80f. multicoloured	1·60	75

199 Face of Smallpox Victim

1978. Global Eradication of Smallpox.

795	**199**	30f. multicoloured	65	20
796	**199**	80f. multicoloured	1·70	95

200 Microwave Antenna

1978. Tenth World Telecommunications Day.

797	**200**	30f. multicoloured	55	20
798	**200**	80f. multicoloured	1·60	85

201 Shaikh Jabir

1978. Portrait in brown; background colour given.

799	**201**	15f. green	55	30
800	**201**	30f. orange	1·20	55
801	**201**	80f. purple	2·75	1·30
802	**201**	100f. green	3·00	1·50
803	**201**	130f. brown	4·75	2·10
804	**201**	180f. violet	7·00	2·75
805	**201**	1d. red (24×29 mm)	21·00	13·00
806	**201**	4d. blue (24×29 mm)	75·00	32·00

202 Mount Arafat, Pilgrims and Kaaba

1978. Pilgrimage to Mecca.

807	**202**	30f. multicoloured	85	20
808	**202**	80f. multicoloured	2·40	1·10

203 U.N. and Anti-Apartheid Emblems

1978. International Anti-Apartheid Year.

809	**203**	30f. multicoloured	65	30
810	**203**	80f. multicoloured	1·50	1·10
811	**203**	180f. multicoloured	3·25	2·10

204 Refugees

1978. 30th Anniv of Declaration of Human Rights.

812	**204**	30f. multicoloured	75	30
813	**204**	80f. multicoloured	2·00	75
814	**204**	100f. multicoloured	2·50	1·60

205 Information Centre

1978. Kuwait Information Centre.

815	**205**	5f. multicoloured	10	10
816	**205**	15f. multicoloured	30	20
817	**205**	30f. multicoloured	75	30
818	**205**	80f. multicoloured	2·00	95

206 Kindergarten

1979. International Year of the Child.

819	**206**	30f. multicoloured	75	20
820	**206**	80f. multicoloured	1·90	1·10

207 Kuwaiti Flag and Doves

1979. 18th National Day.

821	**207**	30f. multicoloured	55	45
822	**207**	80f. multicoloured	1·40	1·10

208 Crops and Greenhouse

1979. Fouth Arab Agriculture Ministers' Congress.

823	**208**	30f. multicoloured	55	20
824	**208**	80f. multicoloured	1·60	1·10

209 World Map, Koran and Symbols of Arab Achievements

1979. The Arabs.

825	**209**	30f. multicoloured	65	20
826	**209**	80f. multicoloured	1·70	1·10

210 Children flying Kites

1979. Children's Paintings. Multicoloured.

827	30f. Type **210**	1·10	55
828	30f. Girl and doves	1·10	55
829	30f. Crowd and balloons	1·10	55
830	80f. Boys smiling (horiz)	2·50	1·30
831	80f. Children in landscape (horiz)	2·50	1·30
832	80f. Tug-of-war (horiz)	2·50	1·30

211 Wave Pattern and Television Screen

1979. World Telecommunications Day.

833	**211**	30f. multicoloured	55	20
834	**211**	80f. multicoloured	1·60	95

212 International Military Sports Council Emblem

1979. 29th International Military Football Championship.

835	**212**	30f. multicoloured	65	30
836	**212**	80f. multicoloured	1·80	1·30

213 Child and Industrial Landscape

1979. World Environment Day.

837	**213**	30f. multicoloured	1·20	55
838	**213**	80f. multicoloured	3·25	1·60

214 Children supporting Globe

1979. 50th Anniv of Int Bureau of Education.

839	**214**	30f. multicoloured	55	20
840	**214**	80f. multicoloured	1·60	95
841	**214**	130f. multicoloured	2·10	1·50

215 Children with Television

1979. 25th Anniv of Kuwaiti Kindergartens. Children's Drawings. Multicoloured.

842	30f. Type **215**	65	20
843	80f. Children with flags	1·70	95

216 The Kaaba, Mecca

1979. Pilgrimage to Mecca.

844	**216**	30f. multicoloured	85	20
845	**216**	80f. multicoloured	2·40	95

217 Figure, with Dove and Torch, clothed in Palestinian Flag

1979. Int Day of Solidarity with Palestinians.

846	**217**	30f. multicoloured	2·10	75
847	**217**	80f. multicoloured	5·25	1·90

218 Boeing 747 and Douglas DC-3 Airliners

1979. 25th Anniv of Kuwait Airways.

848	**218**	30f. multicoloured	1·10	55
849	**218**	80f. multicoloured	2·75	1·60

219 *Pinctada* Shell bearing Map of Kuwait

1980. 19th National Day.

850	**219**	30f. multicoloured	65	20
851	**219**	80f. multicoloured	1·70	95

220 Graph with Human Figures

1980. Population Census.

852	**220**	30f. black, silver and blue	75	30
853	**220**	80f. black, gold and orange	1·80	95

221 Campaign Emblem

1980. World Health Day. Anti-smoking Campaign.

854	**221**	30f. multicoloured	1·10	20
855	**221**	80f. multicoloured	2·40	1·20

222 Municipality Building

1980. 50th Anniv of Kuwait Municipality.

856	**222**	15f. multicoloured	45	10
857	**222**	30f. multicoloured	75	30
858	**222**	80f. multicoloured	2·00	1·20

223 "The Future"

1980. Children's Imagination of Future Kuwait. Multicoloured.

859	30f. Type **223**	85	45
860	80f. Motorways	2·40	1·20

224 Hand blotting out Factory

1980. World Environment Day.

861	**224**	30f. multicoloured	85	45
862	**224**	80f. multicoloured	2·10	85

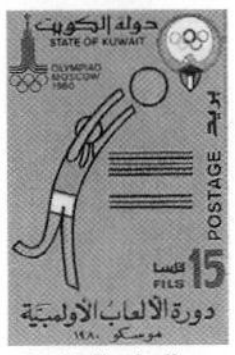

225 Volleyball

1980. Olympic Games, Moscow. Multicoloured.

863	15f. Type **225**	45	20
864	15f. Tennis	45	20
865	30f. Swimming	55	30
866	30f. Weightlifting	55	30
867	30f. Basketball	55	30
868	30f. Judo	55	30
869	80f. Gymnastics	1·40	1·10
870	80f. Badminton	1·40	1·10
871	80f. Fencing	1·40	1·10
872	80f. Football	1·40	1·10

226 O.P.E.C. Emblem and Globe

1980. 20th Anniv of Organization of Petroleum Exporting Countries.

873	**226**	30f. multicoloured	95	30
874	**226**	80f. multicoloured	2·00	1·20

227 Mosque and Kaaba, Mecca

1980. 1400th Anniv of Hegira.

875	**227**	15f. multicoloured	45	20
876	**227**	30f. multicoloured	95	45
877	**227**	80f. multicoloured	2·40	1·30

228 Dome of the Rock

1980. International Day of Solidarity with Palestinian People.

878	**228**	30f. multicoloured	2·10	85
879	**228**	80f. multicoloured	5·25	2·40

229 Ibn Sina (Avicenna)

1980. Birth Millenary of Ibn Sina (philosopher and physician).

880	**229**	30f. multicoloured	75	20
881	**229**	80f. multicoloured	2·10	1·20

230 Islamic Symbols

1981. First Islamic Medicine Conference, Kuwait.

882	**230**	30f. multicoloured	85	20
883	**230**	80f. multicoloured	1·90	1·50

231 Person in Wheelchair playing Snooker

1981. International Year of Disabled Persons. Multicoloured.

884	30f. Type **231**	85	30
885	80f. Girl in wheelchair	2·40	1·30

232 Symbols of Development and Progress

1981. 20th National Day.

886	**232**	30f. multicoloured	85	30
887	**232**	80f. multicoloured	2·10	1·30

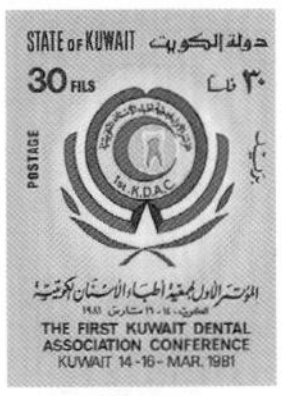

233 Emblem of Kuwait Dental Association

1981. First Kuwait Dental Association Conference.

888	**233**	30f. multicoloured	2·00	75
889	**233**	80f. multicoloured	5·00	1·90

234 "Lamp"

1981. World Red Cross and Red Crescent Day.

890	**234**	30f. multicoloured	1·50	65
891	**234**	80f. multicoloured	3·75	1·70

235 Emblems of I.T.U. and W.H.O. and Ribbons forming Caduceus

1981. World Telecommunications Day.

892	**235**	30f. multicoloured	1·30	20
893	**235**	80f. multicoloured	3·00	1·70

236 Tanker polluting Sea and Car polluting Atmosphere

1981. World Environment Day.

894	**236**	30f. multicoloured	1·40	45
895	**236**	80f. multicoloured	3·50	1·70

237 Sief Palace

1981

896	**237**	5f. multicoloured	10	10
897	**237**	10f. multicoloured	10	10
898	**237**	15f. multicoloured	20	10
899	**237**	25f. multicoloured	30	10
900	**237**	30f. multicoloured	45	10
901	**237**	40f. multicoloured	55	20
902	**237**	60f. multicoloured	75	30
903	**237**	80f. multicoloured	1·10	30
904	**237**	100f. multicoloured	1·30	45
905	**237**	115f. multicoloured	1·50	55
906	**237**	130f. multicoloured	1·70	65
907	**237**	150f. multicoloured	1·90	75
908	**237**	180f. multicoloured	2·40	85
909	**237**	250f. multicoloured	3·25	1·20
910	**237**	500f. multicoloured	6·50	2·40
911	**237**	1d. multicoloured	13·00	4·75
912	**237**	2d. multicoloured	26·00	9·00
913	**237**	3d. multicoloured	39·00	14·00
914	**237**	4d. multicoloured	50·00	18·00

Nos. 911/14 are larger, 33×28 mm and have a different border.

238 Pilgrims

1981. Pilgrimage to Mecca.

915	**238**	30f. multicoloured	1·30	45
916	**238**	80f. multicoloured	3·25	1·30

239 Palm Trees, Sheep, Camel, Goat and F.A.O. Emblem

1981. World Food Day.

917	**239**	30f. multicoloured	1·30	45
918	**239**	80f. multicoloured	3·25	1·30

240 Television Emblem

1981. 20th Anniv of Kuwait Television.

919	**240**	30f. multicoloured	1·30	45
920	**240**	80f. multicoloured	3·25	1·30

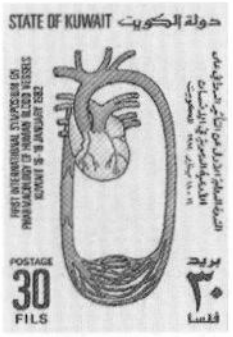

241 Blood Circulation Diagram

1982. First International Symposium on Pharmacology of Human Blood Vessels.

921	**241**	30f. multicoloured	1·50	1·20
922	**241**	80f. multicoloured	3·50	1·70

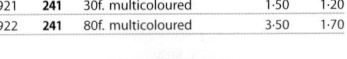

242 Symbols of Development, Progress and Peace

1982. 21st National Day.

923	**242**	30f. multicoloured	85	45
924	**242**	80f. multicoloured	2·10	1·20

243 Emblem of Kuwait Boy Scouts Association on Globe

1982. 75th Anniv of Boy Scout Movement.

925	**243**	30f. multicoloured	1·20	65
926	**243**	80f. multicoloured	3·25	1·50

244 Emblem of Arab Pharmacists Union

1982. Arab Pharmacists Day.

927	**244**	30f. multicoloured	1·60	45
928	**244**	80f. multicoloured	3·75	1·50

245 Red Crescent, Arab and W.H.O. Emblem

1982. World Health Day.

929	**245**	30f. multicoloured	1·50	95
930	**245**	80f. multicoloured	4·50	2·75

246 A.P.U. Emblem

1982. 30th Anniv of Arab Postal Union.

931	**246**	30f. black, orange and green	1·60	45
932	**246**	80f. black, green and orange	3·75	1·50

247 Lungs and Microscope

1982. Centenary of Discovery of Tubercle Bacillus.

933	**247**	30f. multicoloured	2·10	85
934	**247**	80f. multicoloured	6·50	2·40

248 Crest and Emblems of Kuwait Football Association and Olympic Committee

1982. World Cup Football Championship, Spain.

935	**248**	30f. multicoloured	1·40	45
936	**248**	80f. multicoloured	3·50	1·50

249 Museum Exhibits

1982. Tenth Anniv of Science and Natural History Museum.

937	**249**	30f. multicoloured	3·25	55
938	**249**	80f. multicoloured	6·50	2·40

250 *Al-Wattyah* (container ship)

1982. Sixth Anniv of United Arab Shipping Company. Multicoloured.

939		30f. Type **250**	1·20	45
940		80f. *Al-Salimiah* (freighter)	3·25	1·30

251 Palm Trees

1982. Arab Palm Tree Day.

941	**251**	30f. multicoloured	85	45
942	**251**	80f. multicoloured	1·90	1·30

252 Pilgrims

1982. Pilgrimage to Mecca.

943	**252**	15f. multicoloured	65	10
944	**252**	30f. multicoloured	1·30	45
945	**252**	80f. multicoloured	3·50	1·30

253 Desert Flower

1983. Desert Plants. As T **253**. Multicoloured; background colours given. (a) Vert designs.

946	10f. green	10	10
947	10f. violet	10	10
948	10f. salmon	10	10
949	10f. pink (blue flowers)	10	10
950	10f. bistre	10	10
951	10f. green	10	10
952	10f. light orange	10	10
953	10f. red (poppy)	10	10
954	10f. brown	10	10
955	10f. blue	10	10
956	15f. green	20	20
957	15f. purple	20	20
958	15f. blue	20	20
959	15f. blue (iris)	20	20
960	15f. olive	20	20
961	15f. red	20	20
962	15f. brown	20	20
963	15f. blue (bellflowers)	20	20
964	15f. mauve	20	20
965	15f. pink	20	20
966	30f. brown	55	45
967	30f. mauve	55	45
968	30f. blue	55	45
969	30f. green	55	45
970	30f. pink	55	45
971	30f. blue	55	45
972	30f. green	55	45
973	30f. mauve	55	45
974	30f. bistre	55	45
975	30f. yellow	55	45

(b) Horiz designs.

976	40f. red (fungi)	75	55
977	40f. green (fungi)	75	55
978	40f. violet	75	55
979	40f. blue	75	55
980	40f. grey	75	55
981	40f. green	75	55
982	40f. mauve	75	55
983	40f. brown	75	55
984	40f. blue	75	55
985	40f. green (daisies)	75	55
986	80f. violet	1·60	85
987	80f. green	1·60	85
988	80f. yellow (yellow flowers)	1·60	85
989	80f. brown (green leaves)	1·60	85
990	80f. blue	1·60	85
991	80f. yellow	1·60	85
992	80f. green	1·60	85
993	80f. violet (red berries)	1·60	85
994	80f. brown (yellow flowers)	1·60	85
995	80f. yellow (red and blue flowers)	1·60	85

DESIGNS: Various plants.

254 Peace Dove on Map of Kuwait

1983. 22nd National Day.

996	**254**	30f. multicoloured	85	30
997	**254**	80f. multicoloured	2·40	1·30

255 I.M.O. Emblem

1983. 25th Anniv of International Maritime Organization.

998	**255**	30f. multicoloured	55	30
999	**255**	80f. multicoloured	1·60	85

256 Virus and Map of Africa

1983. Third International Conference on Impact of Viral Diseases on Development of Middle East and African Countries.

1000	**256**	15f. multicoloured	45	20
1001	**256**	30f. multicoloured	85	45
1002	**256**	80f. multicoloured	2·10	1·50

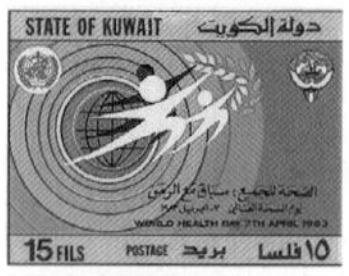

257 Stylized Figures exercising

1983. World Health Day.

1003	**257**	15f. multicoloured	65	30
1004	**257**	30f. multicoloured	1·30	65
1005	**257**	80f. multicoloured	3·25	1·90

258 U.P.U., W.C.Y. and I.T.U. Emblems

1983. World Communications Year.

1006	**258**	15f. multicoloured	55	30
1007	**258**	30f. multicoloured	1·10	65
1008	**258**	80f. multicoloured	2·75	1·90

259 Map of Kuwait and Dhow

1983. World Environment Day.

1009	**259**	15f. multicoloured	65	30
1010	**259**	30f. multicoloured	1·30	65
1011	**259**	80f. multicoloured	3·50	1·90

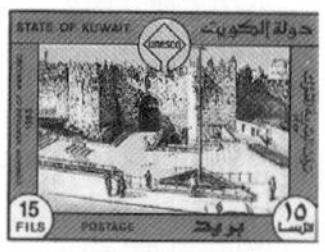

260 Walls of Jerusalem

1983. World Heritage Convention.

1012	**260**	15f. multicoloured	55	20
1013	**260**	30f. multicoloured	95	45
1014	**260**	80f. multicoloured	2·50	1·50

261 Pilgrims in Mozdalipha

1983. Pilgrimage to Mecca.

1015	**261**	15f. multicoloured	55	20
1016	**261**	30f. multicoloured	1·10	45
1017	**261**	80f. multicoloured	3·00	1·50

262 Arab within Dove

1983. International Day of Solidarity with Palestinian People.

1018	**262**	15f. multicoloured	65	30
1019	**262**	30f. multicoloured	1·30	65
1020	**262**	80f. multicoloured	3·50	1·70

263 Kuwait Medical Association and Congress Emblems

1984. 21st Pan-Arab Medical Congress.

1021	**263**	15f. multicoloured	65	30
1022	**263**	30f. multicoloured	1·20	65
1023	**263**	80f. multicoloured	3·00	1·80

264 State Arms within Key

1984. Inauguration of New Health Establishments.

1024	**264**	15f. multicoloured	55	20
1025	**264**	30f. multicoloured	95	45
1026	**264**	80f. multicoloured	2·50	1·50

265 Dove and Globe

1984. 23rd National Day.

1027	**265**	15f. multicoloured	55	20
1028	**265**	30f. multicoloured	1·20	45
1029	**265**	80f. multicoloured	3·00	1·50

266 Symbols of Medicine within Head

1984. Second International Medical Science Conference.

1030	**266**	15f. multicoloured	65	30
1031	**266**	30f. multicoloured	1·30	65
1032	**266**	80f. multicoloured	3·50	1·70

267 Douglas DC-3 Airliner

1984. 30th Anniv of Kuwait Airways Corporation.

1033	**267**	30f. blue, dp blue & yell	1·20	85
1034	**267**	80f. blue, dp blue & mve	3·25	1·70

268 Magazine Covers

1984. 25th Anniv of *Al-Arabi* (magazine).

1035	**268**	15f. multicoloured	55	20
1036	**268**	30f. multicoloured	1·10	45
1037	**268**	80f. multicoloured	2·75	1·50

269 Family and Emblems

1984. World Health Day.

1038	**269**	15f. multicoloured	55	20

| 1039 | 269 | 30f. multicoloured | 1·10 | 45 |
| 1040 | 269 | 80f. multicoloured | 3·00 | 1·50 |

270 Sudanese Orphan
and Village

1984. Hanan Kuwaiti Village, Sudan.

1041	270	15f. multicoloured	55	20
1042	270	30f. multicoloured	1·20	45
1043	270	80f. multicoloured	3·00	1·50

271 I.C.A.O., Kuwait
Airport and Kuwait
Airways Emblems

1984. 40th Anniv of I.C.A.O.

1044	271	15f. multicoloured	65	30
1045	271	30f. multicoloured	1·20	65
1046	271	80f. multicoloured	3·25	1·80

272 Map of Arab
Countries and
Youths

1984. Arab Youth Day.

| 1047 | 272 | 30f. multicoloured | 1·30 | 65 |
| 1048 | 272 | 80f. multicoloured | 3·25 | 1·70 |

273 Swimming

1984. Olympic Games, Los Angeles. Multicoloured.

1049		30f. Type **273**	55	55
1050		30f. Hurdling	55	55
1051		80f. Judo	1·60	1·60
1052		80f. Equestrian	1·60	1·60

274 Anniversary Emblem,
Camera, Airplane, Al-Aujairy
Observatory and Wind
Tower

1984. Tenth Anniv of Science Club.

1053	274	15f. multicoloured	65	30
1054	274	30f. multicoloured	1·30	65
1055	274	80f. multicoloured	3·50	1·80

275 Stoning the Devil

1984. Pilgrimage to Mecca.

| 1056 | 275 | 30f. multicoloured | 1·30 | 75 |
| 1057 | 275 | 80f. multicoloured | 3·00 | 2·00 |

276 Anniversary Emblem

1984. 20th Anniv of International Tele-communications
Satellite Consortium (Intelsat).

| 1058 | 276 | 30f. multicoloured | 1·30 | 75 |
| 1059 | 276 | 80f. multicoloured | 3·00 | 2·00 |

277 Council Emblem

1984. Fifth Supreme Council Session of Gulf Co-operation
Council.

| 1060 | 277 | 30f. multicoloured | 1·30 | 85 |
| 1061 | 277 | 80f. multicoloured | 3·00 | 2·10 |

278 Hands
breaking Star

1984. International Day of Solidarity with Palestinian
People.

| 1062 | 278 | 30f. multicoloured | 1·30 | 75 |
| 1063 | 278 | 80f. multicoloured | 3·00 | 2·00 |

279 Company Emblem
as Satellite

1984. 50th Anniv of Kuwait Oil Company.

| 1064 | 279 | 30f. multicoloured | 1·30 | 75 |
| 1065 | 279 | 80f. multicoloured | 3·00 | 2·00 |

280 I.Y.Y. Emblem

1985. International Youth Year.

| 1066 | 280 | 30f. multicoloured | 75 | 30 |
| 1067 | 280 | 80f. multicoloured | 1·90 | 1·20 |

281 "24", Hand
holding Flame and
Dove

1985. 24th National Day.

| 1068 | 281 | 30f. multicoloured | 1·10 | 45 |
| 1069 | 281 | 80f. multicoloured | 3·00 | 1·20 |

282 Programme
Emblem

1985. International Programme for Communications
Development.

| 1070 | 282 | 30f. multicoloured | 1·10 | 45 |
| 1071 | 282 | 80f. multicoloured | 2·75 | 1·50 |

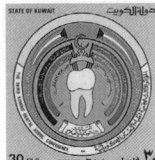

283 Emblem

1985. First Arab Gulf Social Work Week.

| 1072 | 283 | 30f. multicoloured | 1·10 | 45 |
| 1073 | 283 | 80f. multicoloured | 2·75 | 1·50 |

284 Molar

1985. Third Kuwait Dental Association Conference.

| 1074 | 284 | 30f. multicoloured | 1·10 | 75 |
| 1075 | 284 | 80f. multicoloured | 2·40 | 2·00 |

285 Emblem

1985. Population Census.

| 1076 | 285 | 30f. multicoloured | 1·20 | 45 |
| 1077 | 285 | 80f. multicoloured | 3·25 | 1·50 |

286 Globe and
Figures

1985. World Health Day.

| 1078 | 286 | 30f. multicoloured | 1·30 | 55 |
| 1079 | 286 | 80f. multicoloured | 2·50 | 1·60 |

287 Arabic Script

No. 1080
No. 1081
No. 1082
No. 1083
No. 1084
No. 1085
No. 1086
No. 1087

1985. 50th Anniv of Central Library. Designs showing
titles of books and names of authors in Arabic script
(first line of text illustrated above).

1080		30f. gold	1·40	75
1081		30f. gold	1·40	75
1082		30f. gold	1·40	75
1083		30f. gold	1·40	75
1084		80f. black and gold	3·50	1·40
1085		80f. black and gold	3·50	1·40
1086		80f. black and gold	3·50	1·40
1087		80f. black and gold	3·50	1·40

288 Seascape

1985. World Environment Day.

| 1088 | 288 | 30f. multicoloured | 1·50 | 75 |
| 1089 | 288 | 80f. multicoloured | 3·75 | 2·00 |

289 Anniversary Emblem

1985. 25th Anniv of Organization of Petroleum Exporting
Countries.

| 1090 | 289 | 30f. ultramarine, bl & mve | 1·20 | 55 |
| 1091 | 289 | 80f. ultramarine, bl & brn | 3·25 | 1·60 |

290 Emblem and Heads

1985. Introduction of Civilian Identity Cards.

| 1092 | 290 | 30f. multicoloured | 1·20 | 45 |
| 1093 | 290 | 80f. multicoloured | 3·25 | 1·50 |

291 Flag on Globe
within Symbolic Design

1985. International Day of Solidarity with Palestinian
People.

1094	291	15f. multicoloured	75	45
1095	291	30f. multicoloured	1·60	85
1096	291	80f. multicoloured	4·25	2·40

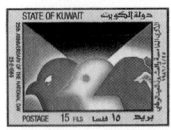

292 Birds

1986. 25th National Day.

1097	292	15f. multicoloured	65	30
1098	292	30f. multicoloured	1·30	65
1099	292	80f. multicoloured	3·50	1·80

293 Emblem

1986. 20th Anniv of Kuwait Red Crescent.

1100	293	10f. multicoloured	1·10	30
1101	293	25f. multicoloured	1·30	55
1102	293	70f. multicoloured	3·75	1·80

294 W.H.O.
Emblem as Flower

1986. World Health Day.

1103	294	20f. multicoloured	1·10	65
1104	294	25f. multicoloured	1·40	75
1105	294	70f. multicoloured	4·00	2·40

295 I.P.Y. Emblem

1986. International Peace Year.

1106	295	20f. green, blue and black	1·10	30
1107	295	25f. blue, yellow and black	1·30	55
1108	295	70f. blue, mauve and black	3·75	1·80

296 Al Mirqab

1986. Tenth Anniv of United Arab Shipping Company.
Container Ships. Multicoloured.

| 1109 | | 20f. Type **296** | 1·10 | 55 |
| 1110 | | 70f. Al Mubarakiah | 4·25 | 1·80 |

297 Bank Emblem on Map

1986. 25th Anniv of Gulf Bank.
1111	**297**	20f. multicoloured	1·10	55
1112	**297**	25f. multicoloured	1·30	65
1113	**297**	70f. multicoloured	3·75	1·70

298 Zig-zags and Diamonds

1986. Sadu Art. Multicoloured.
1114	20f. Type **298**		75	30
1115	70f. Triangles and symbols		2·50	1·30
1116	200f. Stripes and triangles		7·50	3·75

299 Dove on Manacled Hand pointing to Map

1986. International Day of Solidarity with Palestinian People.
1117	**299**	20f. multicoloured	1·50	60
1118	**299**	25f. multicoloured	1·90	80
1119	**299**	70f. multicoloured	5·25	2·10

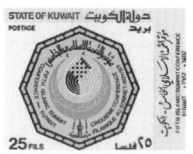

300 Conference Emblem

1987. Fifth Islamic Summit Conference.
1120	**300**	25f. multicoloured	95	35
1121	**300**	50f. multicoloured	1·90	80
1122	**300**	150f. multicoloured	6·00	2·30

301 Map in National Colours and Symbols of Development

1987. 26th National Day.
1123	**301**	50f. multicoloured	1·60	60
1124	**301**	150f. multicoloured	4·75	2·00

302 Health Science Centre

1987. Third Kuwait International Medical Sciences Conference: Infectious Diseases in Developing Countries.
1125	**302**	25f. multicoloured	75	35
1126	**302**	150f. multicoloured	4·75	2·00

303 Campaign Emblem

1987. World Health Day. Child Immunization Campaign.
1127	**303**	25f. multicoloured	85	35
1128	**303**	50f. multicoloured	1·70	70
1129	**303**	150f. multicoloured	5·00	2·00

304 Jerusalem

1987. "Jerusalem is an Arab City".
1130	**304**	25f. multicoloured	85	35
1131	**304**	50f. multicoloured	1·70	80
1132	**304**	150f. multicoloured	5·00	2·50

305 Pilgrims in Miqat Wadi Mihrim

1987. Pilgrimage to Mecca.
1133	**305**	25f. multicoloured	85	35
1134	**305**	50f. multicoloured	1·70	80
1135	**305**	150f. multicoloured	5·00	2·50

306 Emblem

1987. Arab Telecommunications Day.
1136	**306**	25f. multicoloured	75	35
1137	**306**	50f. multicoloured	1·40	80
1138	**306**	150f. multicoloured	4·25	2·50

307 Buoy and Container Ship

1987. World Maritime Day.
1139	**307**	25f. multicoloured	95	35
1140	**307**	50f. multicoloured	1·90	70
1141	**307**	150f. multicoloured	6·00	2·00

308 Project Monument and Site Plan

1987. Al-Qurain Housing Project.
1142	**308**	25f. multicoloured	75	25
1143	**308**	50f. multicoloured	1·50	60
1144	**308**	150f. multicoloured	4·75	1·50

309 Unloading Container Ship

1987. Tenth Anniv of Ports Public Authority.
1145	**309**	25f. multicoloured	95	35
1146	**309**	50f. multicoloured	1·40	80
1147	**309**	150f. multicoloured	6·00	2·50

310 Symbolic Design

1987. International Day of Solidarity with Palestinian People.
1148	**310**	25f. multicoloured	75	35
1149	**310**	50f. multicoloured	1·40	70
1150	**310**	150f. multicoloured	4·25	2·00

311 Emblem

1988. 25th Anniv of Women's Cultural and Social Society.
1151	**311**	25f. multicoloured	65	25
1152	**311**	50f. multicoloured	1·20	60
1153	**311**	150f. multicoloured	3·75	1·50

312 Emblem

1988. 27th National Day.
1154	**312**	25f. multicoloured	65	25
1155	**312**	50f. multicoloured	1·20	60
1156	**312**	150f. multicoloured	3·75	1·50

313 Hands holding W.H.O. Emblem

1988. World Health Day. 40th Anniv of W.H.O.
1157	**313**	25f. multicoloured	75	35
1158	**313**	50f. multicoloured	1·50	70
1159	**313**	150f. multicoloured	4·75	2·00

314 Regional Maritime Protection Organization Symbol

1988. Tenth Anniv of Kuwait Regional Convention for Protection of Marine Environment.
1160	**314**	35f. ultram, blue & brn	1·10	35
1161	**314**	50f. ultram, blue & grn	1·60	80
1162	**314**	150f. ultram, blue & pur	4·75	2·50

315 Society Emblem

1988. 25th Anniv of Kuwait Teachers' Society.
1163	**315**	25f. multicoloured	75	25
1164	**315**	50f. multicoloured	1·40	60
1165	**315**	150f. multicoloured	4·25	1·70

316 Pilgrims at al-Sail al-Kabir Miqat

1988. Pilgrimage to Mecca.
1166	**316**	25f. multicoloured	85	25
1167	**316**	50f. multicoloured	1·70	60
1168	**316**	150f. multicoloured	5·00	1·70

317 Gang of Youths lying in wait for Soldiers

1988. Palestinian "Intifda" Movement.
1169	**317**	50f. multicoloured	2·75	60
1170	**317**	150f. multicoloured	7·00	1·70

318 Ring of Dwellings around Key

1988. Arab Housing Day.
1171	**318**	50f. multicoloured	1·30	60
1172	**318**	100f. multicoloured	2·75	1·20
1173	**318**	150f. multicoloured	4·00	1·70

319 Map of Palestine highlighted on Globe

1988. International Day of Solidarity with Palestinian People.
1174	**319**	50f. multicoloured	1·30	60
1175	**319**	100f. multicoloured	2·75	1·20
1176	**319**	150f. multicoloured	4·00	1·70

320 Volunteers embracing Globe

1988. International Volunteer Day.
1177	**320**	50f. multicoloured	1·30	60
1178	**320**	100f. multicoloured	2·50	1·20
1179	**320**	150f. multicoloured	3·75	1·70

321 Conference, Kuwait Society of Engineers and Arab Engineers Union Emblems

1989. 18th Arab Engineering Conference.
1180	**321**	50f. multicoloured	1·20	60
1181	**321**	100f. multicoloured	2·40	1·20
1182	**321**	150f. multicoloured	3·50	1·70

322 Flags as Figures supporting Map

1989. 28th National Day.
1183	**322**	50f. multicoloured	1·20	60
1184	**322**	100f. multicoloured	2·50	1·20
1185	**322**	150f. multicoloured	3·50	1·80

323 Conference Emblem

1989. Fifth Kuwait Dental Association Conference.

1186	**323**	50f. multicoloured	1·10	60
1187	**323**	150f. multicoloured	3·25	1·20
1188	**323**	250f. multicoloured	5·50	3·00

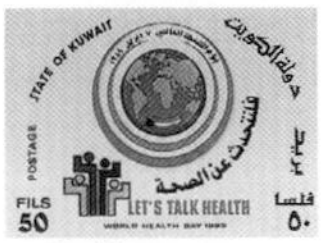

324 Emblems

1989. World Health Day.

1189	**324**	50f. multicoloured	90	50
1190	**324**	150f. multicoloured	2·75	1·40
1191	**324**	250f. multicoloured	4·75	2·40

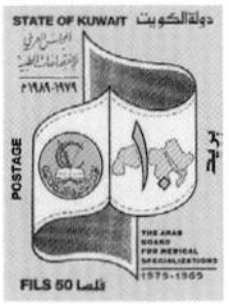

325 Anniversary Emblem

1989. Tenth Anniv of Arab Board for Medical Specializations.

1192	**325**	50f. multicoloured	90	50
1193	**325**	150f. multicoloured	2·75	1·40
1194	**325**	250f. multicoloured	4·75	2·40

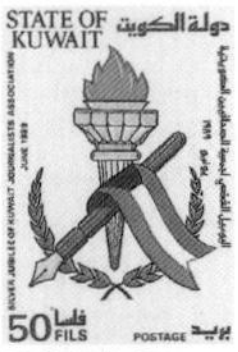

326 Torch, Pen and Flag

1989. 25th Anniv of Kuwait Journalists' Association.

1195	**326**	50f. multicoloured	1·00	60
1196	**326**	200f. multicoloured	4·00	2·40
1197	**326**	250f. multicoloured	5·00	3·00

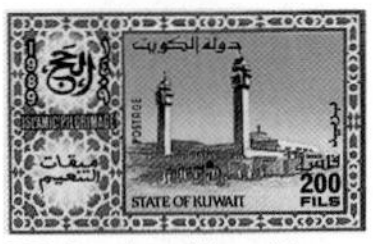

327 Attan'eem Miqat, Mecca

1989. Pilgrimage to Mecca.

1198	**327**	50f. multicoloured	1·10	60
1199	**327**	150f. multicoloured	3·25	1·80
1200	**327**	200f. multicoloured	4·50	2·40

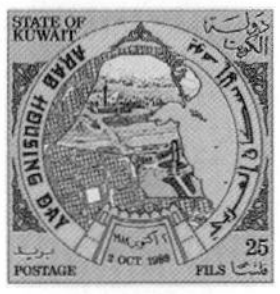

328 Al-Qurain Housing Project

1989. Arab Housing Day.

1201	**328**	25f. multicoloured	90	25
1202	**328**	50f. multicoloured	1·90	60
1203	**328**	150f. multicoloured	5·50	1·80

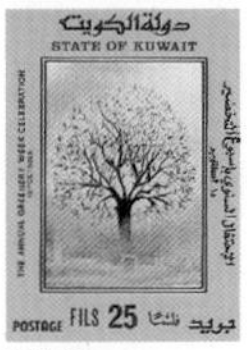

329 Tree

1989. Greenery Week.

1204	**329**	25f. multicoloured	90	25
1205	**329**	50f. multicoloured	1·90	60
1206	**329**	150f. multicoloured	5·50	1·80

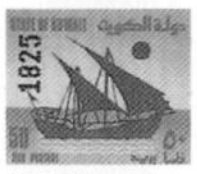

330 Dhow

1989. Coil Stamps.

1207	**330**	50f. gold and green	2·10	2·10
1208	**330**	100f. gold and blue	4·00	4·00
1209	**330**	200f. gold and red	8·25	8·25

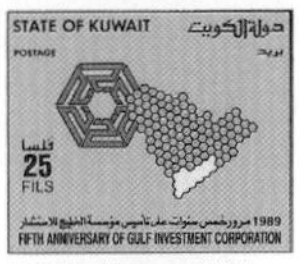

331 Emblem and Map

1989. Fifth Anniv of Gulf Investment Corporation.

1210	**331**	25f. multicoloured	90	25
1211	**331**	50f. multicoloured	1·90	60
1212	**331**	150f. multicoloured	5·50	1·80

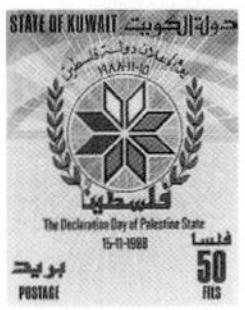

332 Emblem

1989. First Anniv of "Declaration of Palestine State".

1213	**332**	50f. multicoloured	1·10	60
1214	**332**	150f. multicoloured	3·25	1·80
1215	**332**	200f. multicoloured	4·50	2·40

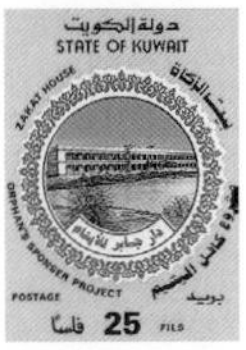

333 Zakat House

1989. Orphanage Sponsorship Project.

1216	**333**	25f. multicoloured	65	35
1217	**333**	50f. multicoloured	1·20	85
1218	**333**	150f. multicoloured	3·75	2·40

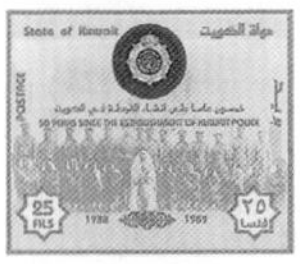

334 Shaikh Sabah al-Salem as-Sabah (former Chief) and Officers

1989. 50th Anniv (1988) of Kuwait Police.

1219	**334**	25f. multicoloured	65	35
1220	**334**	50f. multicoloured	1·20	85
1221	**334**	150f. multicoloured	3·75	2·40

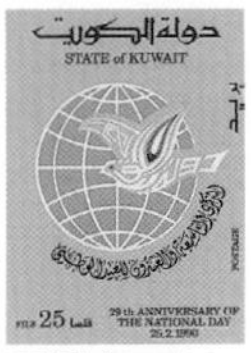

335 Globe and Dove

1990. 29th National Day.

1222	**335**	25f. multicoloured	65	35
1223	**335**	50f. multicoloured	1·20	85
1224	**335**	150f. multicoloured	3·75	2·40

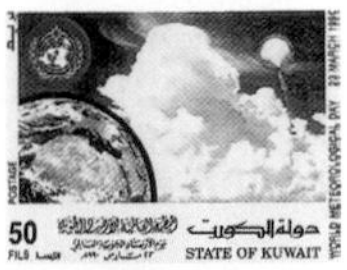

336 Earth, Clouds and Weather Balloon

1990. World Meteorological Day.

1225	**336**	50f. multicoloured	1·20	70
1226	**336**	100f. multicoloured	2·50	1·40
1227	**336**	150f. multicoloured	3·50	2·20

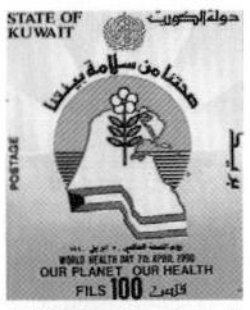

337 Map bordered by National Flag

1990. World Health Day.

1228	**337**	50f. multicoloured	1·20	70
1229	**337**	100f. multicoloured	2·50	1·40
1230	**337**	150f. multicoloured	3·50	2·20

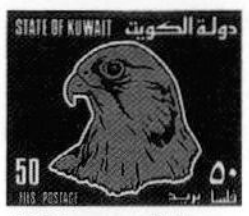

338 Lanner Falcon

1990

1231	**338**	50f. gold and blue	9·00	9·00
1232	**338**	100f. gold and red	9·00	9·00
1233	**338**	150f. gold and green	9·00	9·00

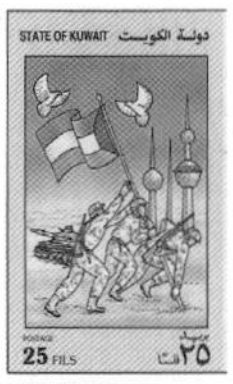

339 Soldiers carrying Kuwait Flag

1991. Liberation (1st issue).

1234	**339**	25f. multicoloured	65	50
1235	**339**	50f. multicoloured	1·50	95
1236	**339**	150f. multicoloured	4·00	3·00

See also Nos. 1243/**MS**1285.

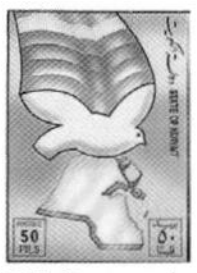

340 Dove and Map

1991. Peace.

1237	**340**	50f. multicoloured	1·50	85
1238	**340**	100f. multicoloured	3·00	1·90
1239	**340**	150f. multicoloured	4·00	2·75

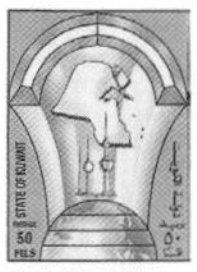

341 Flag, Map, Kuwait Towers and Globe

1991. Reconstruction.

1240	**341**	50f. multicoloured	1·30	95
1241	**341**	150f. multicoloured	4·00	2·75
1242	**341**	200f. multicoloured	5·25	3·50

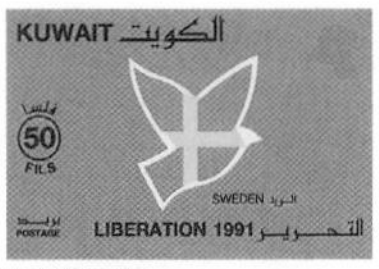

342 Sweden

1991. Liberation (2nd issue). Each showing a dove coloured with the flag of one of the assisting nations. Multicoloured.

1243	50f. Type **342**	1·30	1·20
1244	50f. Soviet Union	1·30	1·20
1245	50f. United States of America	1·30	1·20
1246	50f. Kuwait	1·30	1·20
1247	50f. Saudi Arabia	1·30	1·20
1248	50f. United Nations	1·30	1·20
1249	50f. Singapore	1·30	1·20
1250	50f. France	1·30	1·20
1251	50f. Italy	1·30	1·20
1252	50f. Egypt	1·30	1·20
1253	50f. Morocco	1·30	1·20
1254	50f. United Kingdom	1·30	1·20
1255	50f. Philippines	1·30	1·20
1256	50f. United Arab Emirates	1·30	1·20
1257	50f. Syria	1·30	1·20
1258	50f. Poland	1·30	1·20
1259	50f. Australia	1·30	1·20
1260	50f. Japan	1·30	1·20
1261	50f. Hungary	1·30	1·20
1262	50f. Netherlands	1·30	1·20
1263	50f. Denmark	1·30	1·20
1264	50f. New Zealand	1·30	1·20
1265	50f. Czechoslovakia	1·30	1·20
1266	50f. Bahrain	1·30	1·20
1267	50f. Honduras	1·30	1·20
1268	50f. Turkey	1·30	1·20
1269	50f. Greece	1·30	1·20
1270	50f. Oman	1·30	1·20
1271	50f. Qatar	1·30	1·20
1272	50f. Belgium	1·30	1·20
1273	50f. Sierra Leone	1·30	1·20
1274	50f. Argentina	1·30	1·20
1275	50f. Norway	1·30	1·20
1276	50f. Canada	1·30	1·20
1277	50f. Germany	1·30	1·20
1278	50f. South Korea	1·30	1·20
1279	50f. Bangladesh	1·30	1·20
1280	50f. Bulgaria	1·30	1·20
1281	50f. Senegal	1·30	1·20
1282	50f. Spain	1·30	1·20
1283	50f. Niger	1·30	1·20
1284	50f. Pakistan	1·30	1·20
MS1285	87×134 mm. 1d. Flag and dove. Imperf	22·00	22·00

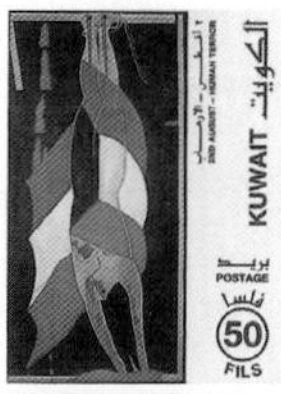

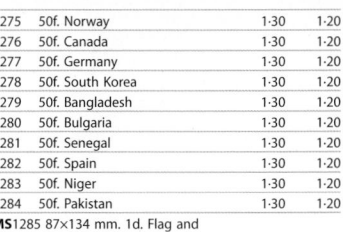

343 "Human Terror"

1991. First Anniv of Iraqi Invasion. Multicoloured.

1286	50f. Type **343**	1·50	95
1287	100f. "Invasion of Kuwait"	2·75	1·80
1288	150f. "Environmental Terrorism" (horiz)	4·25	2·75
MS1289	90×65 mm. 250f. "Desert Storm" (liberation campaign). Imperf	7·75	7·75

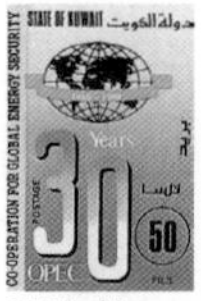

344 Emblem

1991. 30th Anniv (1990) of Organization of Petroleum Exporting Countries.

1290	**344**	25f. multicoloured	65	50
1291	**344**	50f. multicoloured	1·50	95
1292	**344**	150f. multicoloured	4·00	3·00

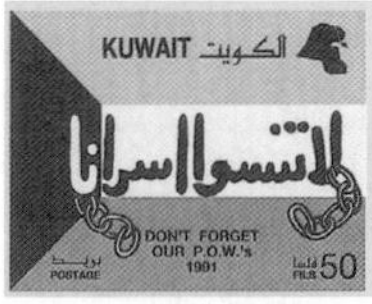

345 National Flag, Arabic Script and Broken Chains

1991. Campaign to Free Kuwaiti Prisoners of War. Each black and yellow.

1293	50f. Type **345**	1·30	60
1294	150f. Prison bars, "Don't Forget Our P.O.W.'s" and broken chains	4·00	2·10
MS1295	121×101 mm. No. 1293×2; No. 1294×2	11·00	11·00

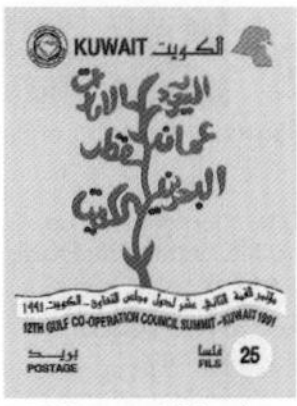

346 Names of Member Countries forming Tree

1991. 12th Gulf Co-operation Council Summit Conference, Kuwait. Multicoloured.

1296	25f. Type **346**	55	50
1297	150f. National flags as leaves of plant	3·50	2·40
MS1298	Two sheets, each 100×120 mm. (a) No. 1296×2, No. 1297×2; (b) No. 1297×2; 2×25f. Similar to No. 1296 but with tree multicoloured	18·00	18·00

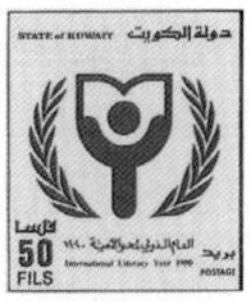

347 I.L.Y. Emblem

1992. International Literacy Year (1990).

1299	**347**	50f. blue and brown	1·20	85
1300	**347**	100f. blue and yellow	2·50	1·70
1301	**347**	150f. blue and mauve	3·50	2·40

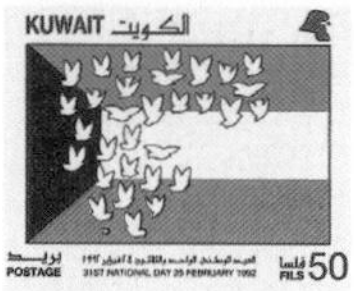

348 Doves and National Flag

1992. 31st National Day (1302) and 1st Anniv of Liberation (1303).

1302	**348**	50f. black, green and red	65	50
1303	-	150f. multicoloured	2·20	1·60
MS1304 120×99 mm. No. 1302×2; No. 1303×2			6·25	6·25

DESIGN: 150f. Assisting nations' flags.

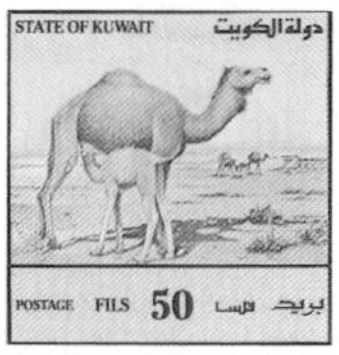

349 Dromedaries

1992

1305	**349**	25f. multicoloured	45	45
1306	**349**	50f. multicoloured	90	90
1307	**349**	150f. multicoloured	2·75	2·75
1308	**349**	200f. multicoloured	3·25	3·25
1309	**349**	350f. multicoloured	6·25	6·25

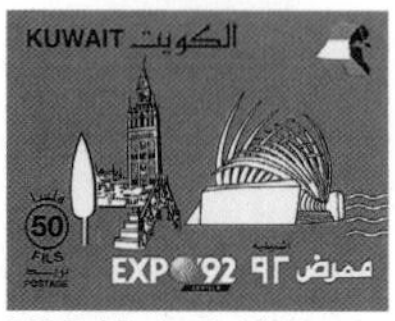

350 Paddle, La Giralda Tower and Kuwaiti Pavilion

1992. "Expo '92" World's Fair, Seville. Multicoloured.

1310	50f. Type **350**	65	65
1311	50f. Dhows	65	65
1312	50f. Dhow	65	65
1313	50f. Kuwaiti Pavilion and dhow	65	65
1314	150f. Kuwaiti Pavilion on Spanish flag	1·90	1·90
1315	150f. Paddle and La Giralda Tower on hoist of Kuwaiti flag	1·90	1·90
1316	150f. Paddle, La Giralda Tower and dhow on Spanish flag	1·90	1·90
1317	150f. Kuwaiti Pavilion and dhow on fly of Kuwaiti flag	1·90	1·90
MS1318 120×169 mm. Nos. 1310/17		10·50	10·50

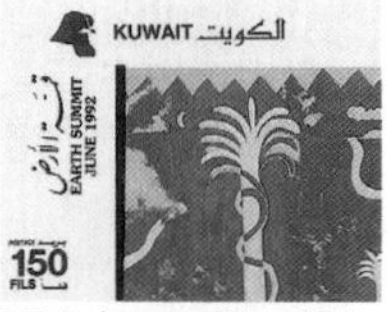

351 Snake around Top of Palm Tree

1992. Second U.N. Conference on Environment and Development, Rio de Janeiro, Brazil. Mult.

1319	150f. Type **351**	2·20	1·60
1320	150f. Snakes, Kuwait colours on map and palm tree	2·20	1·60
1321	150f. Skull, snake around tree trunk and dead fish	2·20	1·60
1322	150f. Snake around camel's neck and bird	2·20	1·60
MS1323 121×101 mm. Nos. 1319/22		9·50	9·50

Nos. 1319/22 were issued together, *se-tenant*, forming a composite design of the painting *Environmental Terrorism*.

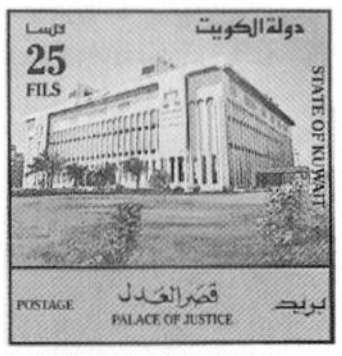

352 Palace of Justice

1992

1324	**352**	25f. multicoloured	35	25
1325	**352**	50f. multicoloured	80	50
1326	**352**	100f. multicoloured	1·50	95
1327	**352**	150f. multicoloured	2·20	1·40
1328	**352**	250f. multicoloured	3·50	2·40

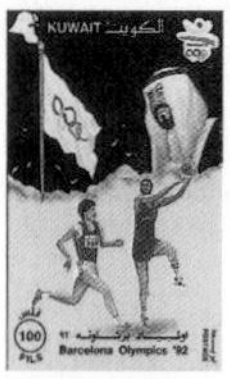

353 Running and Handball

1992. Olympic Games, Barcelona. Multicoloured.

1329	50f. Swimming and football	1·10	70
1330	100f. Type **353**	2·20	1·40
1331	150f. Judo and show jumping	3·25	2·20

Each value also portrays the Olympic flag and Prince Fahed al-Ahmad al-Sabah, President of several sports organizations, who was killed in the Iraqi invasion.

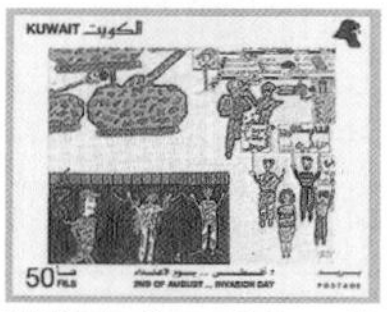

354 Tanks, Demonstrators with Placards and Executed Civilians

1992. Second Anniv of Iraqi Invasion. Children's Drawings. Multicoloured.

1332	50f. Type **354**	65	65
1333	50f. Soldiers rounding up civilians	65	65
1334	50f. Military vehicles and Kuwait Towers	65	65
1335	50f. Battle scene	65	65
1336	150f. Tanks, bleeding eye and soldiers	1·90	1·90
1337	150f. Battle scene around fortifications	1·90	1·90
1338	150f. Liberation	1·90	1·90
1339	150f. Soldiers and military vehicles	1·90	1·90
MS1340 121×171 mm. Nos. 1332/9		10·00	10·00

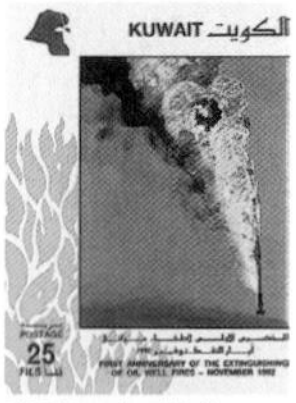

355 Burning Well

1992. First Anniv of Extinguishing of Oil Well Fires. Multicoloured.

1341	25f. Type **355**	35	35
1342	50f. Spraying dampener on fire	70	70
1343	150f. Close-up of spraying	2·00	2·00
1344	250f. Extinguished well (horiz)	3·50	3·50

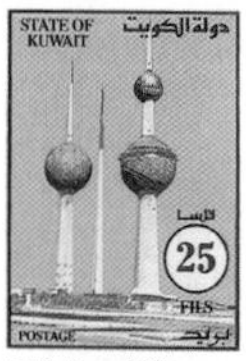

356 Kuwait Towers

1993

1345	**356**	25f. multicoloured	35	35
1346	**356**	100f. multicoloured	1·30	1·30
1347	**356**	150f. multicoloured	2·00	2·00

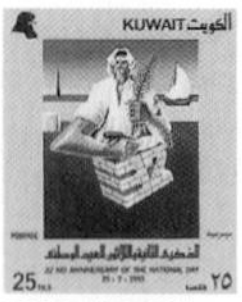

357 Laying Bricks to form "32"

1993. 32nd National Day.

1348	**357**	25f. multicoloured	35	35
1349	**357**	50f. multicoloured	70	70
1350	**357**	150f. multicoloured	2·00	2·00

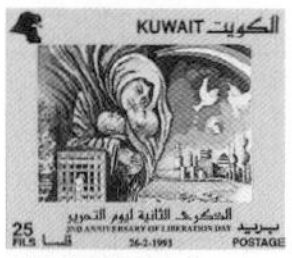

358 Symbols of Oppression and Freedom

1993. Second Anniv of Liberation.

1351	**358**	25f. multicoloured	35	35
1352	**358**	50f. multicoloured	70	70
1353	**358**	150f. multicoloured	2·00	2·00

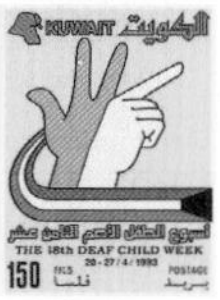

359 Hands Signing

1993. Deaf Child Week.

1354	**359**	25f. multicoloured	35	35
1355	**359**	50f. multicoloured	70	70
1356	**359**	150f. multicoloured	2·00	2·00
1357	**359**	350f. multicoloured	4·75	4·75

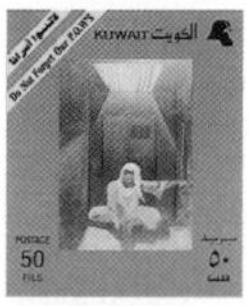

360 Chained Prisoner

1993. Campaign to Free Kuwaiti Prisoners of War. Multicoloured.

1358	50f. Type **360**	70	70
1359	150f. Chained hand, hoopoe and barred window (horiz)	2·00	2·00
1360	200f. Screaming face on wall of empty cell	2·50	2·50

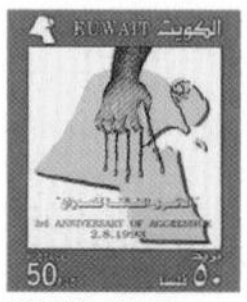

361 Hand scratching Map

1993. Third Anniv of Iraqi Invasion.

1361	**361**	50f. multicoloured	60	60
1362	**361**	150f. multicoloured	2·00	2·00

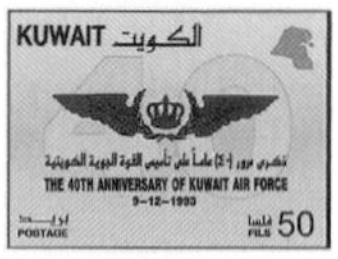

362 Emblem

1993. 40th Anniv of Kuwait Air Force.

1363	**362**	50f. multicoloured	60	60
1364	**362**	150f. multicoloured	2·00	2·00

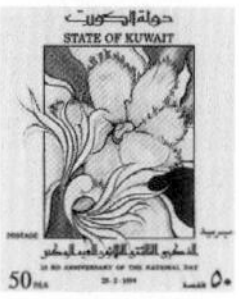

363 Flower and Dove

1994. 33rd National Day.

1365	**363**	25f. multicoloured	40	40
1366	**363**	50f. multicoloured	75	75
1367	**363**	150f. multicoloured	2·10	2·10

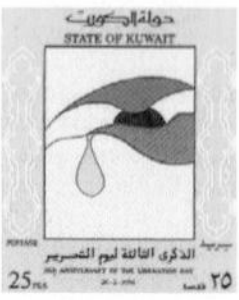

364 Anniversary Emblem

1994. Third Anniv of Liberation.

1368	**364**	25f. multicoloured	40	40
1369	**364**	50f. multicoloured	75	75
1370	**364**	150f. multicoloured	2·10	2·10

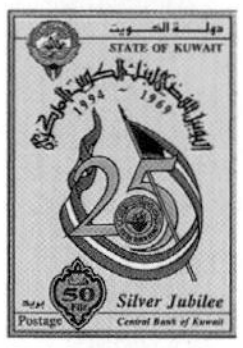

365 Anniversary Emblem

1994. 25th Anniv of Central Bank of Kuwait.

1371	**365**	25f. multicoloured	40	40
1372	**365**	50f. multicoloured	75	75
1373	**365**	150f. multicoloured	2·40	2·40

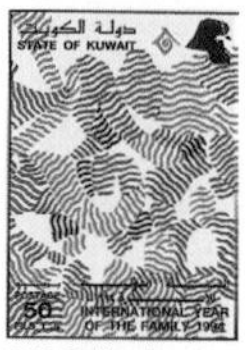

366 Stylized Emblems

1994. Int Year of the Family. Multicoloured.

1374	50f. Type **366**	75	75
1375	150f. Three I.Y.F. emblems	2·40	2·40
1376	200f. Globe, emblem and spheres (horiz)	3·25	3·25

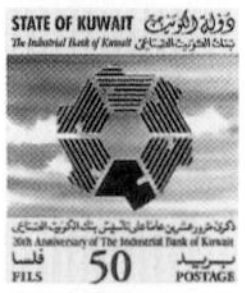

367 Emblem on Sky

1994. 20th Anniv of Industrial Bank of Kuwait.

1377	**367**	50f. multicoloured	75	75
1378	**367**	100f. gold, blue and black	1·50	1·50
1379	**367**	150f. multicoloured	2·30	2·30

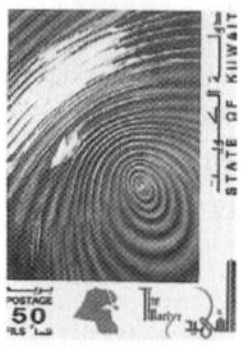

368 Fingerprint in Water

1994. Martyrs' Day. Multicoloured.

1380	50f. Type **368**	75	75
1381	100f. Fingerprint in sand	1·50	1·50
1382	150f. Fingerprint in national colours	2·30	2·30
1383	250f. Fingerprint in clouds over Kuwait Towers	3·75	3·75
MS1384 91×111 mm. Nos. 1380/3		8·25	8·25

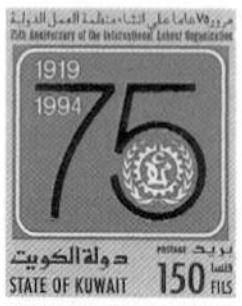

369 Anniversary Emblem

1994. 75th Anniv of I.L.O.

1385	**369**	50f. multicoloured	75	75
1386	**369**	150f. multicoloured	2·30	2·30
1387	**369**	350f. gold, blue and black	5·25	5·25

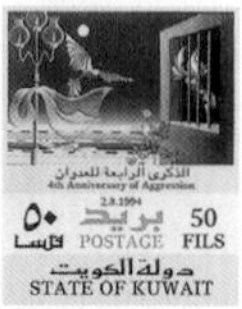

370 Free and Imprisoned Doves

1994. Fourth Anniv of Iraqi Invasion.

1388	**370**	50f. multicoloured	75	75
1389	**370**	150f. multicoloured	2·30	2·30
1390	**370**	350f. multicoloured	5·25	5·25

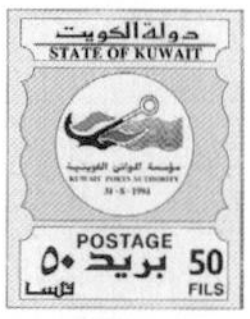

371 Emblem

1994. Kuwait Ports Authority.

1391	**371**	50f. multicoloured	75	75
1392	**371**	150f. multicoloured	2·30	2·30
1393	**371**	350f. multicoloured	5·25	5·25

372 Anniversary Emblem

1994. 20th Anniv of Kuwait Science Club.
1394	372	50f. multicoloured	75	75
1395	372	100f. multicoloured	1·50	1·50
1396	372	150f. multicoloured	2·30	2·30

373 Map and Building

1994. Inauguration of Arab Towns Organization Permanent Headquarters. Multicoloured.
1397		50f. Type 373	75	75
1398		100f. Close-up of arched facade	1·50	1·50
1399		150f. Door	4·00	4·00

374 I.C.A.O. and Kuwait International Airport Emblems

1994. 50th Anniv of I.C.A.O. Multicoloured.
1400		100f. Type 374	1·60	1·60
1401		150f. Emblems and control tower	2·40	2·40
1402		350f. Airplane and "50 years"	5·50	5·50

375 Anniversary Emblem

1994. 40th Anniv of Kuwait Airways.
1403	375	50f. multicoloured	75	75
1404	375	100f. multicoloured	1·50	1·50
1405	375	150f. multicoloured	2·30	2·30

376 Family

1995. Population Census.
1406	376	50f. multicoloured	75	75
1407	376	100f. multicoloured	1·50	1·50
1408	376	150f. multicoloured	2·30	2·30

377 Children waving Flags

1995. 34th National Day.
1409	377	25f. multicoloured	40	40
1410	377	50f. multicoloured	75	75
1411	377	150f. multicoloured	2·40	2·40

378 Falcon dragging Kuwaiti Flag from Snake's Grip

1995. Fourth Anniv of Liberation.
1412	378	25f. multicoloured	40	40
1413	378	50f. multicoloured	75	75
1414	378	150f. multicoloured	2·40	2·40

379 Conference Venue

1995. International Medical Conference. Multicoloured.
1415		50f. Type 379	75	75
1416		100f. Lecture	1·50	1·50
1417		150f. Emblem on map of Kuwait in national colours	2·30	2·30

380 Anniversary Emblem and Flags

1995. 50th Anniv of Arab League. Multicoloured.
1418		50f. Type 380	75	75
1419		100f. Kuwaiti and League flags and League emblem (horiz)	1·50	1·50
1420		150f. Handshake and League emblem	2·30	2·30

381 Emblem

1995. World Health Day. "A World without Polio".
1421	381	50f. multicoloured	75	75
1422	381	150f. multicoloured	2·40	2·40
1423	381	200f. multicoloured	3·25	3·25

382 "100"

1995. Centenary of Volleyball.
1424	382	50f. multicoloured	75	75
1425	382	100f. multicoloured	1·60	1·60
1426	382	150f. multicoloured	2·40	2·40

383 Olive Branch falling from Wounded Dove's Beak

1995. Fifth Anniv of Iraqi Invasion.
1427	383	50f. multicoloured	75	75
1428	383	100f. multicoloured	1·60	1·60
1429	383	150f. multicoloured	2·40	2·40

384 Doves and Anniversary Emblem

1995. 50th Anniv of U.N.O.
1430	384	25f. multicoloured	75	75
1431	384	100f. multicoloured	1·60	1·60
1432	384	150f. multicoloured	2·40	2·40

385 Farmer with Animals

1995. 50th Anniv of F.A.O. Multicoloured.
1433		50f. Type 385	75	75
1434		100f. Fish market	1·60	1·60
1435		150f. Agriculture	2·40	2·40
MS1436		120×70 mm. Nos. 1433/5	4·75	4·75

386 Emblems within Ruler

1995. World Standards Day. Multicoloured.
1437		50f. Type 386	75	75
1438		100f. Emblems and aspects of industry (48×27 mm)	1·60	1·60
1439		150f. As No. 1438	2·40	2·40

387 Onobrychis ptolemaica

1995. Flowers. Multicoloured.
1440		5f. Type 387	15	15
1441		15f. Convolvulus oxyphyllus	40	40
1442		25f. Corn poppy	75	75
1443		50f. Moltkiopsis ciliata	1·30	1·30
1444		150f. Senecio desfontainei	3·75	3·75

388 Coins forming Map of Kuwait

1996. Money Show.
1445	388	25f. multicoloured	45	45
1446	388	100f. multicoloured	1·70	1·70
1447	388	150f. multicoloured	2·40	2·40

389 Boy Scout in Watchtower

1996. 60th Anniv of Scout Movement in Kuwait. Multicoloured.
1448		50f. Type 389	1·10	1·10
1449		100f. Scout drawing water from well	2·40	2·40
1450		150f. Scouts planting sapling	3·50	3·50

390 Hands supporting Ear of Wheat

1996
1451	390	50f. multicoloured	85	85
1452	390	100f. multicoloured	1·70	1·70
1453	390	150f. multicoloured	2·50	2·50

391 Saker Falcon trailing National Colours, Falcon and City

1996. 35th National Day.
1454	391	25f. multicoloured	45	45
1455	391	50f. multicoloured	85	85
1456	391	150f. multicoloured	2·40	2·40

392 Horses

1996. Fifth Anniv of Liberation.
1457	392	25f. multicoloured	45	45
1458	392	50f. multicoloured	85	85
1459	392	150f. multicoloured	2·40	2·40

393 View through Gateway

1996. Arab City Day.
1460	393	50f. multicoloured	85	85
1461	393	100f. multicoloured	1·70	1·70
1462	393	150f. multicoloured	2·50	2·50

394 Emblem

1996. Seventh Kuwait Dental Association Conference.
1463	394	25f. multicoloured	45	45
1464	394	50f. multicoloured	85	85
1465	394	150f. multicoloured	2·40	2·40

395 Figures holding Open Book within Bird

1996. 50th Anniv of UNESCO.
1466	395	25f. multicoloured	45	45
1467	395	100f. multicoloured	1·70	1·70
1468	395	150f. multicoloured	2·40	2·40

396 Flags, Anniversary Emblem and Tanker

1996. 50th Anniv of First Oil Shipment from Kuwait.
1469	396	25f. multicoloured	45	45
1470	396	100f. multicoloured	1·70	1·70
1471	396	150f. multicoloured	2·40	2·40

397 Shaikh Mubarak al-Sabah

1996. Centenary of Accession as Emir of Shaikh Mubarak al-Sabah. Multicoloured.
1472		25f. Type 397	45	45
1473		50f. Shaikh Mubarak al-Sabah and ribbons	85	85
1474		150f. Type 397	2·40	2·40

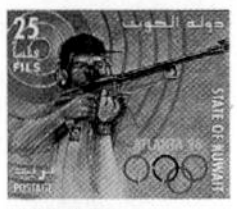
398 Rifle Shooting

1996. Olympic Games, Atlanta. Multicoloured.

1475	25f. Type **398**	45	45
1476	50f. Running	85	85
1477	100f. Weightlifting	1·70	1·70
1478	150f. Fencing	2·75	2·75

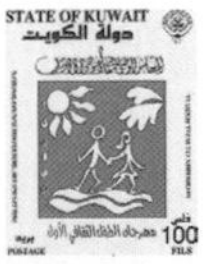

399 Festival Emblem

1996. National Council for Culture, Art and Letters. First Children's Cultural Festival.

1479	**399**	25f. multicoloured	45	45
1480	**399**	100f. multicoloured	1·70	1·70
1481	**399**	150f. multicoloured	2·40	2·40

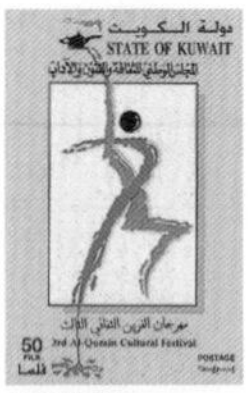

400 Emblem

1996. Third Al-Qurain Cultural Festival.

1482	**400**	50f. multicoloured	85	85
1483	**400**	100f. multicoloured	1·70	1·70
1484	**400**	150f. multicoloured	2·50	2·50

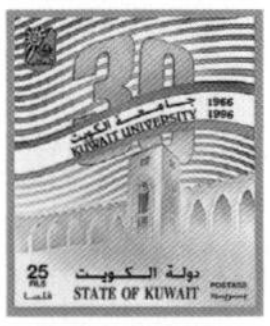

401 University

1996. 30th Anniv of Kuwait University.

1485	**401**	25f. multicoloured	45	45
1486	**401**	100f. multicoloured	1·70	1·70
1487	**401**	150f. multicoloured	2·40	2·40

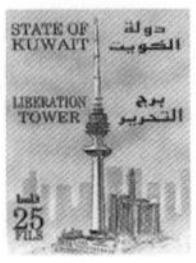

402 Liberation Tower

1996

1488	**402**	5f. multicoloured	15	15
1489	**402**	10f. multicoloured	30	30
1490	**402**	15f. multicoloured	45	45
1491	**402**	25f. multicoloured	55	55
1492	**402**	50f. multicoloured	1·30	1·30
1493	**402**	100f. multicoloured	2·40	2·40
1494	**402**	150f. multicoloured	3·75	3·75
1495	**402**	200f. multicoloured	5·00	5·00
1496	**402**	250f. multicoloured	6·25	6·25
1497	**402**	350f. multicoloured	8·50	8·50

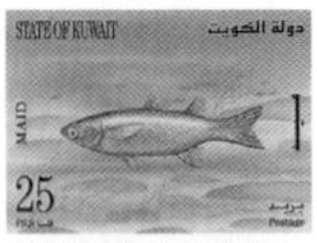

403 Sehel's Grey Mullet

1997. Marine Life. Multicoloured. (a) Fish.

1498	25f. Type **403**	45	45
1499	50f. Yellow-finned seabream	85	85
1500	100f. Greasy grouper	1·70	1·70
1501	150f. Silver-backed seabream	2·50	2·50
1502	200f. Silver grunt	3·50	3·50
1503	350f. Silver pomfret	6·00	6·00

(b) Shrimps.

1504	25f. Tail and body segments of shrimps	45	45
1505	25f. Head and body segments of shrimps	45	45
1506	25f. Underside of fish and body and legs of shrimp	45	45
1507	25f. Head of shrimp, fish and body and legs of shrimp	45	45
1508	50f. Tail and body segments of two shrimps	85	85
1509	50f. Legs and body segments of shrimp	85	85
1510	50f. Body segments of shrimp and fish	85	85
1511	50f. Head of shrimp, seaweed and body and legs of shrimp	85	85
1512	100f. Tail and body segments of two shrimps	1·70	1·70
1513	100f. Head, legs and body segments of shrimps	1·70	1·70
1514	100f. Body of shrimp	1·70	1·70
1515	100f. Part of head, legs, tail and body of three shrimps	1·70	1·70
1516	150f. Body segments of two shrimps and upper half of fish	2·75	2·75
1517	150f. Front part of bodies of two shrimps and tail of fish	2·75	2·75
1518	150f. Heads of two shrimps, complete shrimp and fish	2·75	2·75
1519	150f. Body segments of two shrimps and front part of shrimps head	2·75	2·75

Nos. 1504/19 were issued together, *se-tenant*, forming a composite design of shrimps in a marine environment.

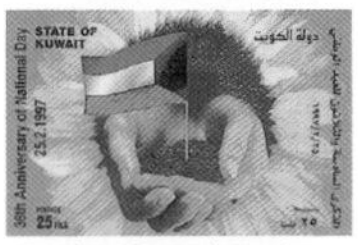

404 Flag, Cupped Hands and Sunflower

1997. 36th National Day.

1520	**404**	25f. multicoloured	45	45
1521	**404**	50f. multicoloured	85	85
1522	**404**	150f. multicoloured	2·40	2·40

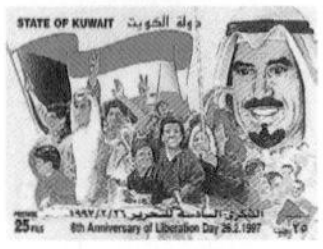

405 Flag, rejoicing Crowd and Shaikh Jabir

1997. Sixth Anniv of Liberation.

1523	**405**	25f. multicoloured	45	45
1524	**405**	50f. multicoloured	85	85
1525	**405**	150f. multicoloured	2·40	2·40

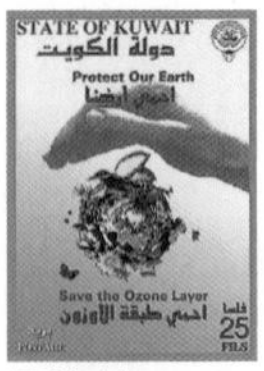

406 Emblem

1997. Tenth Anniv of Montreal Protocol (on reduction of use of chlorofluorocarbons).

1526	**406**	25f. multicoloured	45	45
1527	**406**	50f. multicoloured	85	85
1528	**406**	150f. multicoloured	2·75	2·75

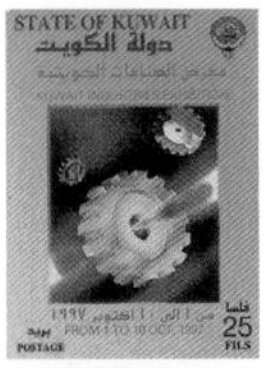

407 Emblem

1997. Kuwait Industries Exhibition.

1529	**407**	25f. multicoloured	45	45
1530	**407**	50f. multicoloured	85	85
1531	**407**	150f. multicoloured	2·75	2·75

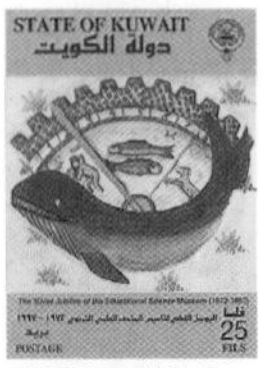

408 Signs of Zodiac and Whale

1997. 25th Anniv of Educational Science Museum.

1532	25f. Type **408**	45	45
1533	50f. Space shuttle orbiting Earth, whale, astronaut and dinosaur (horiz)	85	85
1534	150f. Symbols of past, present and future around whale	2·75	2·75
MS1535	100×75 mm. 150f. Coelacanth (horiz)	17·00	17·00

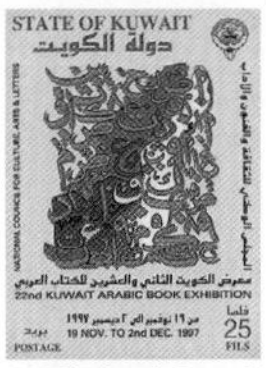

409 National Council for Culture, Arts and Letters Emblem

1997. 22nd Kuwait Arabic Book Exhbition.

1536	**409**	25f. multicoloured	45	45
1537	**409**	50f. multicoloured	85	85
1538	**409**	150f. multicoloured	2·75	2·75

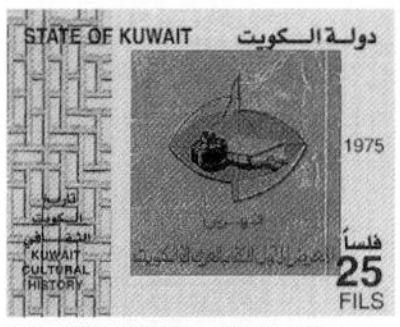

410 Ink-well and Book (first book fair, 1975)

1997. Kuwait Cultural History.

1539	25f. Type **410**	45	45
1540	25f. Front page of *Kuwait Magazine* (1928)	45	45
1541	25f. Front page *A'lam al-Fikr* (periodical) (1970)	45	45
1542	25f. Pyramids and dhow (*Al'Bitha* magazine, 1946)	45	45
1543	25f. Rising sun over open book and quill (*Al'am al Ma'rifa* (periodical), 1978)	45	45
1544	25f. Book with dhow on front cover (*Dalil Almohtar Fi Alaam Al-Bihar*, 1923)	45	45
1545	25f. Arabic script and "brick" design (*Al-Arabi* magazine, 1958)	45	45
1546	25f. Open book (inauguration of first public library, 1923)	45	45
1547	25f. Two covers showing Arabic script in boxes and cosmic explosion (*Al Thaqafa Al-Alamiya* (periodical), 1981)	45	45
1548	25f. Actors and curtain (*The World Theatre* (periodical), 1969)	45	45
1549	50f. Entrance to Qibliya Girls' School (1937)	45	45
1550	50f. Scissors cutting ribbon (first Fine Arts Exhibition, 1959)	1·00	1·00
1551	50f. Mubarakiya School (1912)	1·00	1·00
1552	50f. Family entering Kuwait National Museum (1958)	1·00	1·00
1553	50f. Shuwaikh Secondary School (1953)	1·00	1·00
1554	50f. Door and three windows (Al-Marsam Al-Hor, 1959)	1·00	1·00
1555	50f. Decorated screen (Alma'had Aldini, 1947)	1·00	1·00
1556	50f. Courtyard of Folklore Centre (1956)	1·00	1·00
1557	50f. Three columns of Arabic script (Al Ma'arif printing press, 1947)	1·00	1·00
1558	50f. Class photograph (Literary Club, 1924)	1·00	1·00
1559	150f. Heads and curtains (Folk Theatre Group, 1956)	2·75	2·75
1560	150f. Musical instruments and notes (Academy of Music, 1972)	2·75	2·75
1561	150f. Film frames, audience and camera (opening of Al-Sharqiya cinema, 1955)	2·75	2·75
1562	150f. Curtains around couple at oasis (Theatrical Academy, 1967)	2·75	2·75
1563	150f. Marine views in film frame (*Bas Ya Bahar* (first Kuwaiti feature film), 1970)	2·75	2·75

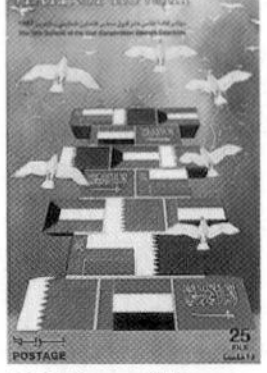

411 Doves flying over Members' Flags

1997. 18th Gulf Co-operation Council Summit, Kuwait. Multicoloured.

1564	25f. Type **411**	55	55
1565	50f. Members' flags forming doves wheeling over map (horiz)	1·10	1·10
1566	150f. Doves perched atop wall of members' flags	3·50	3·50

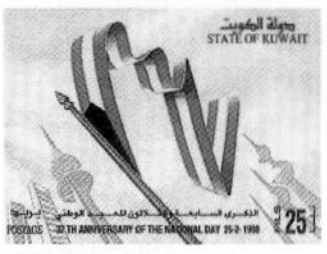

412 State Flag

1998. 37th National Day.

1567	**412**	25f. multicoloured	55	55
1568	**412**	50f. multicoloured	1·10	1·10
1569	**412**	150f. multicoloured	3·50	3·50

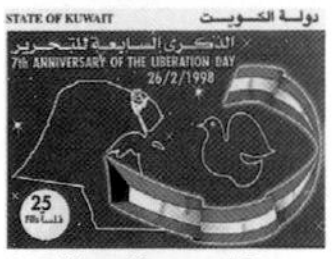

413 Flag, Map and Dove

1998. Seventh Anniv of Liberation.

1570	**413**	25f. multicoloured	55	55
1571	**413**	50f. multicoloured	1·10	1·10
1572	**413**	150f. multicoloured	3·50	3·50

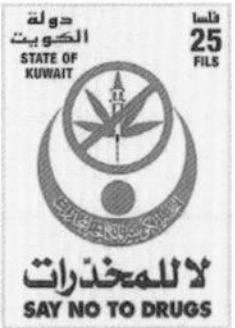

414 Emblem

1998. Anti-drugs Campaign.

1573	**414**	25f. multicoloured	55	55
1574	**414**	50f. multicoloured	1·10	1·10
1575	**414**	150f. multicoloured	3·50	3·50

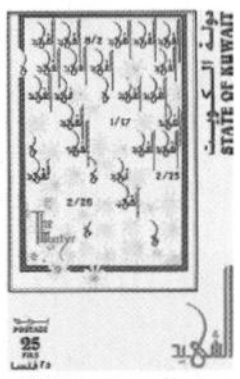

415 Text on Open Page with Flowers

1998. Martyrs' Day. Multicoloured.

1576	25f. Type **415**	55	55
1577	50f. Tree	1·10	1·10
1578	150f. Calligraphy	3·50	3·50
MS1579	60×54 mm. 500f. Shaikh Jabir; 500f. People of Kuwait	23·00	23·00

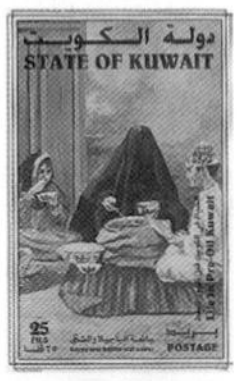

416 Woman selling Cooked Vegetables

1998. Life in Pre-Oil Kuwait (1st series). Multicoloured.

1580	25f. Type **416**	55	55
1581	50f. Ship-building	1·10	1·10
1582	100f. Sailor strapping his box	2·30	2·30
1583	150f. Pearl divers wading out to boat	3·50	3·50
1584	250f. Delivering fresh water	6·00	6·00
1585	350f. Pigeon trainer	7·75	7·75

See also Nos. 1599/604.

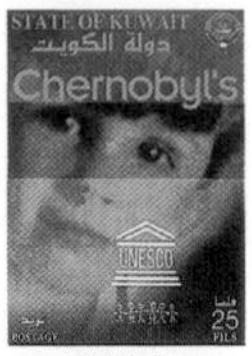

417 Child's Face

1998. 12th Anniv of Chernobyl Nuclear Disaster.

1586	**417**	25f. multicoloured	55	55
1587	**417**	50f. multicoloured	1·10	1·10
1588	**417**	150f. multicoloured	3·50	3·50

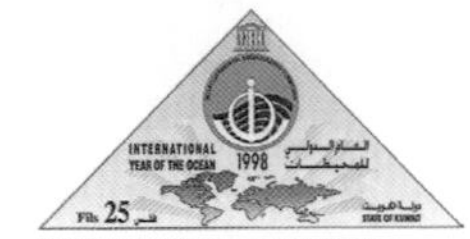

418 World Map and Emblem

1998. International Year of the Ocean. Multicoloured.

1589	25f. Type **418**	55	55
1590	50f. Motifs as in Type **418** but differently arranged in rectangle (27×37 mm)	1·10	1·10
1591	150f. Type **418**	3·50	3·50

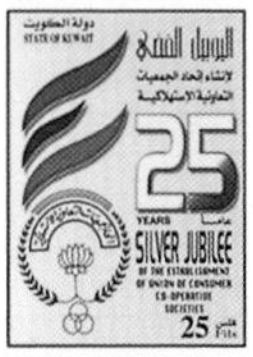

419 Emblem

1998. 25th Anniv of Union of Consumer Co-operative Societies. Multicoloured.

1592	**419**	25f. multicoloured	55	55
1593	**419**	50f. multicoloured	1·10	1·10
1594	**419**	150f. multicoloured	3·50	3·50

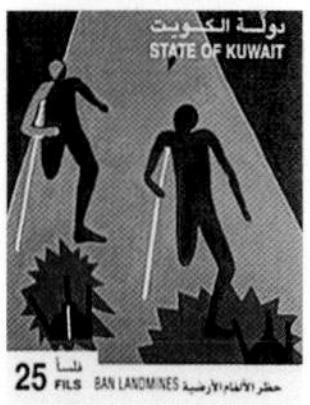

420 Men on Crutches

1998. Anti-landmine Campaign. Details from painting by Jafar Islah. Multicoloured.

1595	25f. Type **420**	55	55
1596	50f. Man on crutch	1·10	1·10
1597	150f. Man on crutches and woman helping child	3·50	3·50
MS1598	96×89 mm. 500f. Motifs of Nos. 1596/7	11·50	11·50

1998. Life in Pre-Oil Kuwait (2nd series). As T **416**. Multicoloured.

1599	25f. Hairdresser	65	65
1600	50f. Hand-grinding	1·10	1·10
1601	100f. Tailor	2·30	2·30
1602	150f. Artist	3·25	3·25
1603	250f. Potter	5·75	5·75
1604	350f. Hand-spinning	8·00	8·00

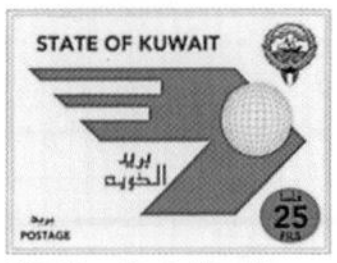

421 New Postal Emblem

1998

1605	**421**	25f. multicoloured	50	50
1606	**421**	50f. multicoloured	1·10	1·10
1607	**421**	100f. multicoloured	2·10	2·10
1608	**421**	150f. multicoloured	3·25	3·25
1609	**421**	250f. multicoloured	5·25	5·25

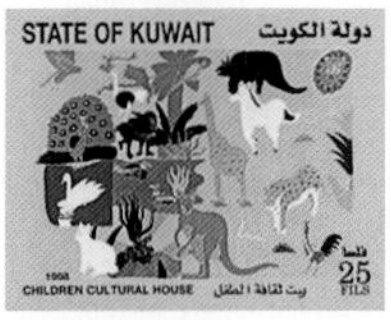

422 Child's Painting

1998. Children's Cultural House.

1610	**422**	25f. multicoloured	50	50
1611	**422**	50f. multicoloured	1·10	1·10
1612	**422**	150f. multicoloured	3·25	3·25

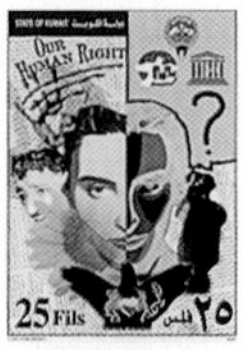

423 Collage

1998. 50th Anniv of Universal Declaration of Human Rights.

1613	**423**	25f. multicoloured	50	50
1614	**423**	50f. multicoloured	1·10	1·10
1615	**423**	150f. multicoloured	3·25	3·25

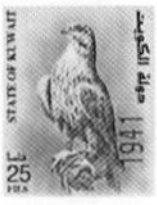

424 Falcon

1998

1616	25f. Type **424**	95	95
1617	50f. Young camels	1·90	1·90
1618	150f. Dhow	5·25	5·25

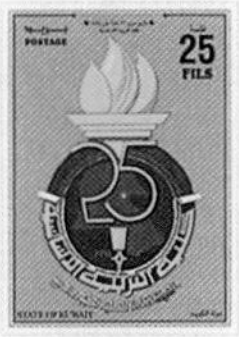

425 Emblem

1998. 25th Anniv of Public Authority for Applied Education and Training.

1619	**425**	25f. multicoloured	50	50
1620	**425**	50f. multicoloured	1·00	1·00
1621	**425**	150f. multicoloured	3·00	3·00

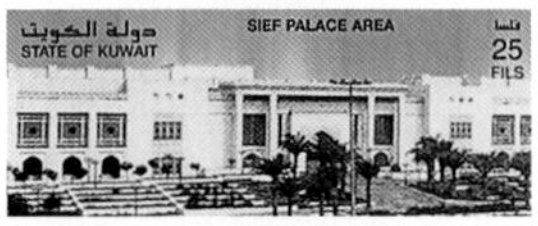

426 Entrance and Palm Trees

1999. Seif Palace. Different views of the Palace. Multicoloured.

1622	25f. Type **426**	35	35
1623	50f. Palace buildings	85	85
1624	100f. Tower	1·70	1·70
1625	150f. Type **426**	2·75	2·75
1626	250f. As No. 1623	4·50	4·50
1627	350f. As No. 1624	6·00	6·00

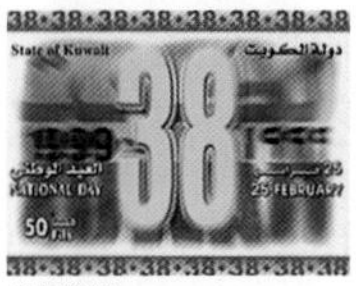

427 "38"

1999. 38th National Day.

1628	**427**	50f. multicoloured	85	85
1629	**427**	150f. multicoloured	2·50	2·50

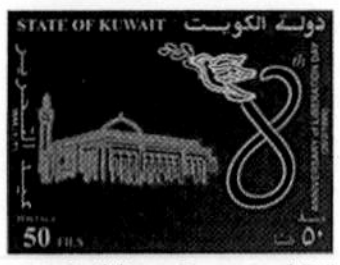

428 Building, Dove and "8"

1999. Eighth Anniv of Liberation.

1630	**428**	50f. multicoloured	85	85
1631	**428**	150f. multicoloured	2·50	2·50

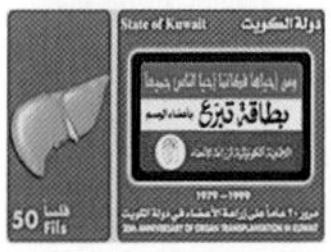

429 Liver and Kuwait Flag

1999. 20th Anniv of Organ Transplantation in Kuwait. Multicoloured.

1632	50f. Type **429**	85	85
1633	150f. Heart and Kuwait flag	2·50	2·50

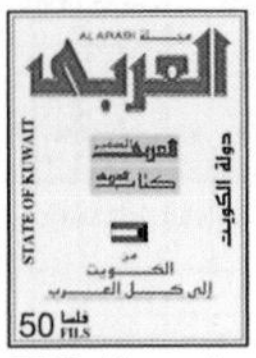

430 Emblem and Kuwait Flag

1999. 40th Anniv of Al-Arabi (magazine).

1634	**430**	50f. multicoloured	85	85
1635	**430**	150f. multicoloured	2·50	2·50

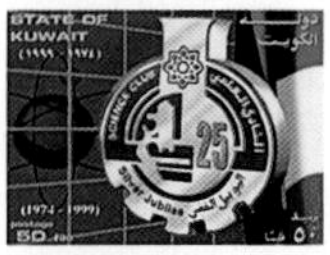

431 Emblem

2000. 25th Anniv (1999) of Kuwait Science Club.

1636	**431**	50f. multicoloured	1·00	1·00
1637	**431**	150f. multicoloured	3·25	3·25
1638	**431**	350f. multicoloured	5·00	5·00

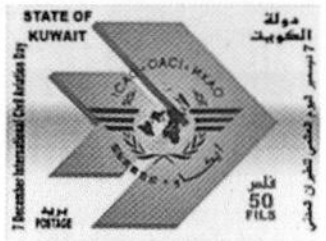

432 Emblem

2000. International Civil Aviation Day.

1639	**432**	50f. multicoloured	1·00	1·00
1640	**432**	150f. multicoloured	3·25	3·25
1641	**432**	250f. multicoloured	5·00	5·00

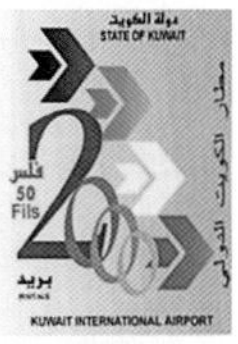

433 "2000" and Emblem

2000. Kuwait International Airport.

1642	**433**	50f. multicoloured	50	50
1643	**433**	150f. multicoloured	1·20	1·20
1644	**433**	250f. multicoloured	3·50	3·50

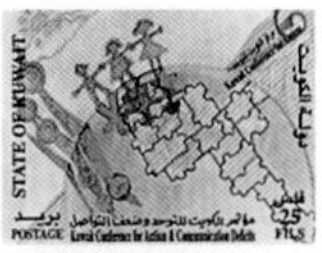

434 Children, Globe and Jigsaw Pieces

2000. International Conference on Autism and Communication Deficiencies, Kuwait. Children's paintings. Multicoloured.

1645	25f. Type **434**	50	50
1646	50f. Globe and children	1·20	1·20
1647	150f. Children holding hands	3·50	3·50

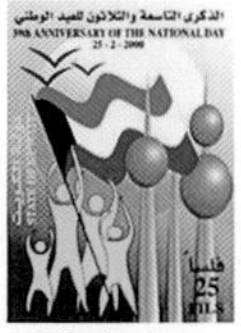

435 Stylized Figures and Flag

2000. 39th National Day.

1648	**435**	25f. multicoloured	50	50
1649	**435**	50f. multicoloured	1·20	1·20
1650	**435**	150f. multicoloured	3·50	3·50

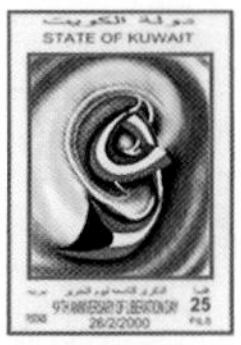

436 State Flag

2000. Ninth Anniv of Liberation.

1651	**436**	25f. multicoloured	1·00	1·00
1652	**436**	50f. multicoloured	3·25	3·25
1653	**436**	150f. multicoloured	7·75	7·75

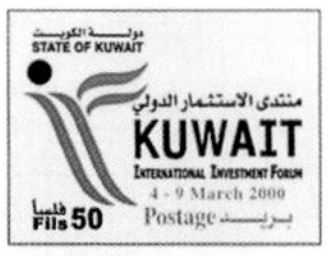

437 Emblem

2000. International Investment Forum, Kuwait.

1654	**437**	25f. multicoloured	50	50
1655	**437**	50f. multicoloured	1·20	1·20
1656	**437**	150f. multicoloured	3·50	3·50

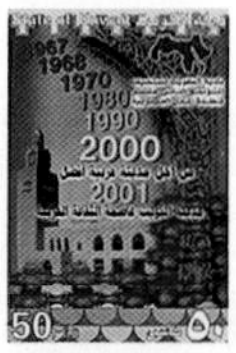

438 View over City

2000. Kuwait City.

1657	**438**	50f. multicoloured	85	85
1658	**438**	150f. multicoloured	2·40	2·40
1659	**438**	350f. multicoloured	5·50	5·50

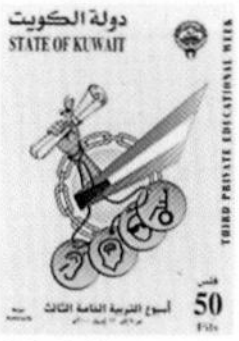

439 Emblem and Hand holding Scroll

2000. Third Private Education Week.

1660	**439**	50f. multicoloured	85	85
1661	**439**	150f. multicoloured	2·40	2·40
1662	**439**	350f. multicoloured	5·50	5·50

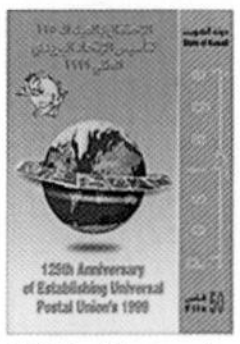

440 Emblem and Stamps Encircling Globe

2000. 125th Anniv of Universal Postal Union.

1663	**440**	50f. multicoloured	85	85
1664	**440**	150f. multicoloured	2·40	2·40
1665	**440**	350f. multicoloured	5·50	5·50
MS1666		100×75 mm. 1d. Stamps encircling globes	15·00	15·00

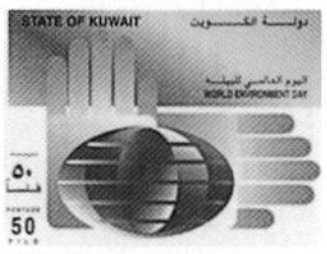

441 Hands and Emblem

2000. World Environment Day.

1667	**441**	50f. multicoloured	85	85
1668	**441**	150f. multicoloured	2·40	2·40
1669	**441**	350f. multicoloured	5·50	5·50

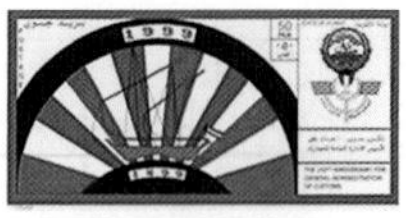

442 Galleon and Emblem

2000. Cent of General Customs' Administration.

1670	**442**	50f. multicoloured	85	85
1671	**442**	150f. multicoloured	2·40	2·40
1672	**442**	350f. multicoloured	5·50	5·50
MS1673		100×5 mm. **442** 1d. multicoloured	15·00	15·00

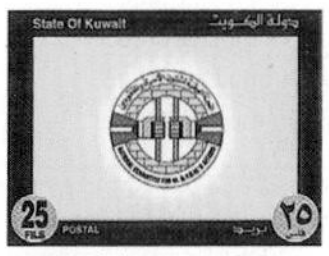

443 Emblem

2000. Tenth Anniv of Committee for Missing and Prisoners of War Affairs. Multicoloured.

1674	25f. Type **443**	35	35
1675	50f. Emblem and chains	85	85
1676	150f. Emblem forming "10"	2·20	2·20

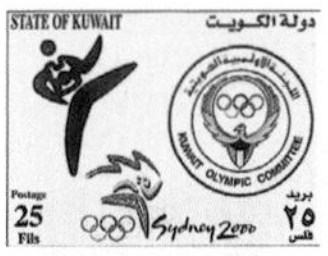

444 Kick-boxing and Emblem

2000. Olympic Games, Sydney. Multicoloured.

1677	25f. Type **444**	35	35
1678	50f. Shooting	85	85
1679	150f. Swimming	2·40	2·40
1680	200f. Weight-lifting	3·25	3·25
1681	250f. Running	4·00	4·00
1682	350f. Football	5·50	5·50

A 1d. imperforate miniature sheet, the design consisting of the emblem and pictograms as depicted on the stamps, exists in a cover inscribed "With the Compliments of Ministry of Communications - Post Sector".

445 Emblem and
Outline of Tooth

2000. 25th Anniv of Kuwait Dental Association.
1683	445	50f. multicoloured	85	85
1684	445	50f. multicoloured	2·40	2·40
1685	445	350f. multicoloured	5·50	5·50

446 Emblem

2000. Sixth Gulf Cooperation Council (G.C.C.) Joint Stamp
Exhibition, Kuwait.
1686	446	25f. multicoloured	50	50
1687	446	50f. multicoloured	1·20	1·20
1688	446	150f. multicoloured	3·50	3·50

MS1689 146×111 mm. 1d. Emblems
of current and previous exhibitions.
Imperf   17·00   17·00

447 Building and "15" in
Laurel Wreath

2000. 15th Anniv of Gulf Investment Corporation
and Inauguration of New Headquarters Building.
Multicoloured.
| 1690 | 447 | 25f. Type **447** | 50 | 50 |
| 1691 | | 50f. Building in centre with
"15" at left | 1·20 | 1·20 |
| 1692 | | 150f. Building at right with "15"
in centre | 3·50 | 3·50 |

448 Letters and
Book

2000. National Council for Culture, Arts and Letters.
1693	448	25f. multicoloured	50	50
1694	448	50f. multicoloured	1·20	1·20
1695	448	150f. multicoloured	3·50	3·50

MS1695a **448** 500f. multicoloured
(85×95 mm)   10·00   10·00

449 Map and Emblems

2001. Arab Cultural Capital.
1696	449	25f. multicoloured	50	50
1697	449	50f. multicoloured	1·20	1·20
1698	449	150f. multicoloured	3·50	3·50

450 Emblem

2001. "Long Live February".
1699	450	25f. multicoloured	50	50
1700	450	50f. multicoloured	1·20	1·20
1701	450	150f. multicoloured	3·50	3·50

451 Anniversary
Emblem

2001. 40th Anniv of National Day.
1702	451	25f. multicoloured	50	50
1703	451	50f. multicoloured	1·20	1·20
1704	451	150f. multicoloured	3·50	3·50

452 Doves

2001. 10th Anniv of Liberation Day.
1705	452	25f. multicoloured	50	50
1706	452	50f. multicoloured	1·20	1·20
1707	452	150f. multicoloured	3·50	3·50

453 Buildings

2001. 40th Anniv of Kuwait Fund For Arab Economic
Development.
| 1708 | 453 | 25f. multicoloured | 50 | 50 |
| 1709 | 453 | 50f. multicoloured | 1·20 | 1·20 |

454 Anniversary Emblem

2001. 50th Anniv of United Nations Commissioner for
Refugees. Multicoloured.
| 1710 | 454 | 25f. Type **454** | 50 | 50 |
| 1711 | | 50f. Anniversary emblem (verti-
cal blue band) | 1·20 | 1·20 |
| 1712 | | 150f. Anniversary emblem
(different) | 3·50 | 3·50 |

455 Pierced Flag

2001. Prisoners.
1713	455	25f. multicoloured	50	50
1714	455	50f. multicoloured	1·20	1·20
1715	455	150f. multicoloured	3·50	3·50

456 Anniversary Emblem

2001. 50th Anniv of Radio Kuwait.
1716	456	25f. multicoloured	50	50
1717	456	50f. multicoloured (vert)	1·20	1·20
1718	456	150f. multicoloured (vert)	3·50	3·50

457 Mosque and Colours

2001. Al Aqsa Uprising. Multicoloured.
| 1719 | 457 | 25f. Type **457** | 50 | 50 |
| 1720 | | 50f. Mosque dome and uprising | 1·20 | 1·20 |
| 1721 | | 150f. Mosque dome and upris-
ing (different) | 3·50 | 3·50 |

458 Children
encircling Globe

2001. United Nations Year of Dialogue among
Civilizations.
1722	458	25f. multicoloured	50	50
1723	458	50f. multicoloured	1·20	1·20
1724	458	150f. multicoloured	3·50	3·50

459 Script

2001. Heritage Management Foundation. Multicoloured.
1725		25f. Type **459**	50	50
1726		50f. Sheikh Abdulla	1·20	1·20
1727		150f. Sheikh Jabir	3·50	3·50

460 Stylised Tree
with Nine Leaves

2001. 25th Anniv of Tourism Enterprise. Multicoloured.
| 1728 | | 25f. Type **460** | 50 | 50 |
| 1729 | | 50f. Twig with six long leaves | 1·20 | 1·20 |
| 1730 | | 100f. Many-branched tree with
falling leaves | 2·50 | 2·50 |
| 1731 | | 150f. Tree with two branches | 3·50 | 3·50 |

MS1732 60×80 mm. 250f. As Nos.
1728/31. Imperf   6·00   6·00

461 Face covered
by Hands

2001. Human Rights. Multicoloured.
| 1733 | | 25f. Type **461** | 50 | 50 |
| 1734 | | 50f. Faces and barbed wire
(horiz) | 1·20 | 1·20 |
| 1735 | | 150f. Chains, globe and child's
face (horiz) | 3·50 | 3·50 |

462 Metal Artefact

2001. Tenth Anniv of Scientific Diving Team.
Multicoloured.
1736		25f. Type **462**	50	50
1737		50f. Divers	1·20	1·20
1738		150f. Turtle (vert)	3·50	3·50

463 Original Building
Facade

2002. 50th Anniv of National Bank. Multicoloured.
| 1739 | | 50f. Type **463** | 50 | 50 |
| 1740 | | 100f. Modern building | 1·20 | 1·20 |
| 1741 | | 150f. Anniversary emblem and
camels | 3·50 | 3·50 |

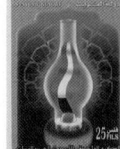

464 Flag enclosed
Lamp

2002. First Anniv of National Day. Multicoloured.
1742	464	25f. multicoloured	50	50
1743	464	50f. multicoloured	1·20	1·20
1744	464	150f. multicoloured	3·50	3·50

465 Monument,
Doves, Flag and
Map

2002. 11th Anniv of Liberation Day. Multicoloured.
1745	465	25f. multicoloured	50	50
1746	465	50f. multicoloured	1·20	1·20
1747	465	150f. multicoloured	3·50	3·50

466 Camel Caravan

2002. Arab Nomads. Multicoloured.
1748	466	25f. multicoloured	50	50
1749	466	50f. multicoloured	1·20	1·20
1750	466	150f. multicoloured	3·50	3·50

467 Emblem and
Gas Tower

2002. Rehabilitation of Al-Qurain Landfill Site.
Multicoloured.
1751	467	25f. multicoloured	50	50
1752	467	50f. multicoloured	1·20	1·20
1753	467	150f. multicoloured	3·50	3·50

468 Northern
Lapwing

2002. Kuwait Scientific Centre. Multicoloured.
1754	468	25f. Type **468**	1·70	1·70
1755		25f. Spur-winged plover	1·70	1·70
1756		25f. Otter	1·70	1·70
1757		25f. Crocodile	1·70	1·70
1758		25f. Fennec fox	1·70	1·70
1759		25f. Caracal	1·70	1·70
1760		25f. Protoreaster	1·70	1·70
1761		25f. Sepia	1·70	1·70
1762		25f. Nurse shark	1·70	1·70
1763		25f. Lionfish	1·70	1·70
1764		25f. Kestrel	1·70	1·70
1765		25f. Fruit bat	1·70	1·70
1766		50f. Centre building (45×27
mm)	3·50	3·50

MS1767 80×60 mm. 250f. Dock and
building. Imperf   12·50   12·50

469 Adult and
Child's Hands

2002. Tenth Anniv of Social Development Office. Multicoloured.

| 1768 | 469 | 25f. multicoloured | 50 | 50 |
| 1769 | 469 | 50f. multicoloured | 1·20 | 1·20 |

470 Engineering Symbols

2002. 40th Anniv of Society of Engineers. Multicoloured.

1770	470	25f. multicoloured	50	50
1771	470	50f. multicoloured	1·20	1·20
1772	470	150f. multicoloured	3·50	3·50

471 Anniversary Emblems

2002. 25th Anniv of Science Foundation. Multicoloured.

1773	471	25f. Type **471**	50	50
1774	471	50f. Building	1·20	1·20
1775	471	150f. Map of Kuwait (vert)	3·50	3·50

472 Organization Emblem

2002. International Year of Volunteers. KNPVC (welfare organization).

1776	472	25f. multicoloured	50	50
1777	472	50f. multicoloured	1·20	1·20
1778	472	150f. multicoloured	3·50	3·50

473 Engineering Workers

2002. 20th Anniv of Professional Education Programme. Multicoloured.

1779	473	25f. Type **473**	50	50
1780	473	50f. Theatre nurse	1·20	1·20
1781	473	100f. Man checking dials	2·20	2·20
1782	473	150f. Flag and "20"	3·50	3·50
1783	473	250f. Emblem	5·50	5·50

474 Traditional Boat

2003

| 1784 | 474 | 100f. multicoloured | 2·00 | 2·00 |

475 Greek Ruins, Failaka Island

2003. 42nd Anniv of National Day. Multicoloured.

1785	475	25f. multicoloured	70	70
1786	475	50f. multicoloured	1·40	1·40
1787	475	150f. multicoloured	4·00	4·00

476 Bureau Emblem and Boat

2003. The Martyrs' Bureau. Multicoloured.

| 1788 | 476 | 25f. Type **476** | 70 | 70 |

1789		50f. National flag on Qarow Island	1·20	1·20
1790		150f. Fingerprint on stone	3·50	3·50
1791		350f. "746" and map	8·50	8·50

477 Leafless Tree and Dunes

2003. International Day to Combat Desertification. Multicoloured.

1792		25f. Type **477**	70	70
1793		50f. Log in valley	1·20	1·20
1794		150f. Oasis	3·50	3·50

478 Statuette

2003. Kuwait Design. Multicoloured.

1795		25f. Type **478**	70	70
1796		100f. Statuette (different)	2·40	2·40
1797		150f. Group of statuettes	3·50	3·50

479 "43" and Star

2003. 43rd Anniv of Commercial Bank. Multicoloured.

1798		25f. Type **479**	70	70
1799		50f. "43" and original building	1·30	1·30
1800		150f. "43" and modern building	3·50	3·50

480 Stylised Family

2004. Tenth Anniv of Awqaf Public Foundation. Multicoloured.

1801		50f. Type **480**	1·10	1·10
1802		100f. Hand	2·10	2·10
1803		150f. Scholar and minaret	3·00	3·00

481 Palm Tree as Flag

2004. 43rd Anniv of National Day. Multicoloured.

1804		25f. Type **481**	70	70
1805		50f. Pearl shell as flag and "43" as pearl	1·20	1·20
1806		150f. Flags flying above gateway	3·50	3·50
1807		350f. Boat and towers	7·75	7·75

482 Ground Crew and Boeing 727

2004. 50th Anniv of Kuwait Airways. Multicoloured.

1808		25f. Type **482**	45	45
1809		50f. Aircraft and maintenance crew	75	75
1810		75f. Airbus A340 in flight	1·20	1·20
1811		100f. Airbus A340 on runway	1·50	1·50

| 1812 | | 125f. Boeing 747 and support trucks | 2·00 | 2·00 |
| 1813 | | 150f. Passengers embarking | 2·30 | 2·30 |

483 Building, Trees and Water

2005. 25th Anniv of Petroleum Corporation. Multicoloured.

1814		50f. Type **483**	80	80
1815		75f. At sunset	1·30	1·30
1816		125f. At night	2·10	2·10

484 Flag and Sheiks

2005. 14th Anniv of Liberation. Multicoloured.

| 1817 | | 50f. Type **484** | 1·30 | 1·30 |
| 1818 | | 150f. Flags and sheiks (different) | 2·10 | 2·10 |

485 Emblem and Sheiks

2005. 44th Anniv of National Day. Multicoloured.

| 1819 | | 75f. Type **485** | 80 | 80 |
| 1820 | | 125f. Sheiks (different) | 2·40 | 2·40 |

486 Emblem

2005. 50th Anniv of Technical Education.

1821	486	25f. multicoloured	50	50
1822	486	50f. multicoloured	80	80
1823	486	75f. multicoloured	1·30	1·30
1824	486	125f. multicoloured	2·10	2·10

487 Support Workers and Vehicles

2005. Civil Defence. Multicoloured.

1825		50f. Type **487**	90	90
1826		75f. Support workers and children	1·20	1·20
1827		125f. Support workers carrying stretcher	2·10	2·10

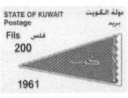

488 Flag

2005. Flags and Emblems. Multicoloured. (a) Ordinary gum. (i) 30×20 mm.

| 1828 | | 200f. Type **488** (ships and harbour flag) | 2·40 | 2·40 |
| 1829 | | 250f. 1940 (official flag) | 3·25 | 3·25 |

(ii) 40×30 mm.

| 1830 | | 350f. 1903 (state emblems) | 4·00 | 4·00 |
| 1831 | | 500f. 1941–50 (ruling family flag) | 6·50 | 6·50 |

(iii) 60×30 mm.

| 1832 | | 1d. Two flags (Shaikh Mubarak Al-Sabah (1914)) | 11·50 | 11·50 |
| 1833 | | 1d. 1956–62 and 1921–40 (state emblems) | 11·50 | 11·50 |

(b) Self-adhesive. (i) 39×34 mm.

| 1834 | | 100f. 1956–62 (official emblem) | 2·10 | 2·10 |
| 1835 | | 100f. 1921–40 (official emblem) | 2·10 | 2·10 |

1836		175f. Shaikh Mubarak Al-Sabah flag (1914)	3·75	3·75
1837		175f. Shaikh Mubarak Al-Sabah (1914) (different)	3·75	3·75
1838		175f. Shaikh Mubarak Al-Sabah flag (1914) (different)	3·75	3·75
1839		350f. 1866 (special event flag)	5·75	5·75
1840		350f. 1903 (special event flag)	5·75	5·75
1841		350f. 1921 (special event flag)	5·75	5·75
1842		500f. 1921–40 (ruling family flag)	9·75	9·75
1843		500f. 1921–40 (different)	9·75	9·75
1844		500f. 1941–50 (different)	9·75	9·75

(ii) 29×20 mm.

1845		200f. 1921 (ships and harbour flag) (pennant)	4·00	4·00
1846		200f. 1921 (rectangular)	4·00	4·00
1847		200f. 1961 (ships and harbour flag) (pennant)	4·00	4·00
1848		200f. 1961 (rectangular)	4·00	4·00
1849		250f. 1914–1961 (official flag)	5·75	5·75
1850		250f. 1971–1914 (official flag)	5·75	5·75
1851		250f. 1746–1871 (official flag)	5·75	5·75
1852		250f. 1940 (official flag)	5·75	5·75
1853		250f. 1921–61 (official flag)	5·75	5·75

489 Children riding Pegasus

2006. 20th Anniv of "Al-Arabi Al Saghir" Children's Magazine. Multicoloured, background colour given.

1854	489	100f. blue	1·50	1·50
1855	489	200f. yellow	3·75	3·75
1856	489	350f. red	6·75	6·75

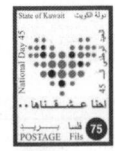

490 Heart Shape

2006. 45th Anniv of National Day. Multicoloured, background colour given.

| 1857 | 490 | 75f. ultramarine | 95 | 95 |
| 1858 | 490 | 200f. green | 3·00 | 3·00 |

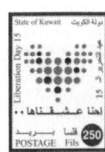

491 Heart Shape

2006. 15th Anniv of Liberation. Multicoloured, background colour given.

| 1859 | 491 | 250f. black | 4·25 | 4·25 |
| 1860 | 491 | 350f. red | 5·50 | 5·50 |

No. 1861 and Type **492** have been left for single stamp not yet received.

2006. 25th Anniv of Gulf Co-operation Council. As T 166. Multicoloured.

MS1862 165×105 mm. 500f. Flags of member states. Imperf ... 10·00 10·00

Stamps of similar designs were issued by Bahrain, Oman, Qatar, Saudi Arabia and United Arab Emirates.

493 'Annual Meeting of the IDB Group'

494 Coin

495 Coin

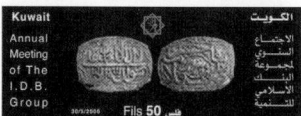
496 Coin

497 Coin

498 Coin

499 Coin

500 Coin

501 Coin

502 Coin

503 Coin

504 Coin

505 Coin

506 Coin

507 Coin

508 Coin

509 Coin

510 Coin

511 Coin

512 Coin

513 Coin

514 Coin

515 'Annual Meeting of the IDB Group'

516 Coin

517 Coin

518 Coin

519 Coin

520 Coin

521 Coin

522 Coin

523 Coin

524 Coin

525 Coin

526 Coin

527 Coin

528 Coin

529 Coin

530 Coin

531 Coin

2006. Islamic Development Meeting.

1863	493	50f. multicoloured	60	60
1864	494	50f. multicoloured	60	60
1865	495	50f. multicoloured	60	60
1866	496	50f. multicoloured	60	60
1867	497	50f. multicoloured	60	60
1868	498	50f. multicoloured	60	60
1869	499	50f. multicoloured	60	60
1870	500	50f. multicoloured	60	60
1871	501	50f. multicoloured	60	60
1872	502	50f. multicoloured	60	60
1873	503	50f. multicoloured	60	60
1874	504	50f. multicoloured	60	60
1875	505	50f. multicoloured	60	60
1876	506	50f. multicoloured	60	60
1877	507	50f. multicoloured	60	60
1878	508	50f. multicoloured	60	60
1879	509	50f. multicoloured	60	60
1880	510	50f. multicoloured	60	60
1881	511	50f. multicoloured	60	60
1882	512	50f. multicoloured	60	60
1883	513	50f. multicoloured	60	60
1884	514	50f. multicoloured	60	60
1885	515	150f. multicoloured	1·80	1·80
1886	516	150f. multicoloured	1·80	1·80
1887	517	150f. multicoloured	1·80	1·80
1888	518	150f. multicoloured	1·80	1·80
1889	519	150f. multicoloured	1·80	1·80
1890	520	150f. multicoloured	1·80	1·80
1891	521	150f. multicoloured	1·80	1·80
1892	522	150f. multicoloured	1·80	1·80
1893	523	150f. multicoloured	1·80	1·80
1894	524	150f. multicoloured	1·80	1·80
1895	525	150f. multicoloured	1·80	1·80
1896	526	150f. multicoloured	1·80	1·80
1897	527	150f. multicoloured	1·80	1·80
1898	528	150f. multicoloured	1·80	1·80
1899	529	150f. multicoloured	1·80	1·80
1900	530	150f. multicoloured	1·80	1·80
1901	531	150f. multicoloured	1·80	1·80
1902	532	150f. multicoloured	1·80	1·80
1903	533	150f. multicoloured	1·80	1·80
1904	534	150f. multicoloured	1·80	1·80
1905	535	150f. multicoloured	1·80	1·80
1906	536	150f. multicoloured	1·80	1·80

537 Emblem

2006. 40th Anniv of Kuwait University. Multicoloured, background colour given.

1907	537	25f. lavender	55	55
1908	537	50f. yellow	90	90
1909	537	150f. green	2·75	2·75
1910	537	350f. rose	6·25	6·25

538 Tennis

2006. DOHA 2006–15th Asian Games. Multicoloured.

1911		25f. Type 538	50	50
1912		50f. Ten pin bowling	80	80
1913		150f. Shooting	2·40	2·40
1914		250f. Equestrian	4·00	4·00
1915		350f. Fencing	5·75	5·75

539 Emblem

2007. Campaign to Fight Hypertension. Multicoloured, background colour given.

1916	539	50f. green	85	85
1917	539	150f. vermilion	2·50	2·50
1918	539	350f. brown	6·00	6·00

540 Ship

2007. 46th Anniv of National Day.

1919	540	25f. multicoloured	55	55
1920	540	50f. multicoloured	90	90
1921	540	150f. multicoloured	2·75	2·75

541 Flag and Doves

2007. 16th Anniv of Liberation Day.

1922	541	25f. multicoloured	55	55
1923	541	50f. multicoloured	90	90
1924	541	150f. multicoloured	2·75	2·75

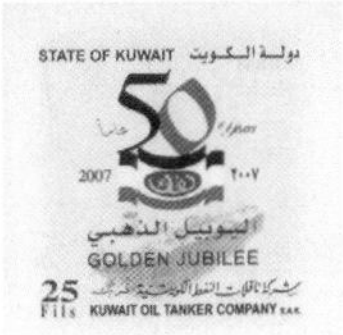

542 Anniversary Emblem

2007. 50th Anniv of Kuwait Oil Tanker Company.

1925	**542**	25f. multicoloured	90	90
1926	**542**	50f. multicoloured	1·30	1·30
1927	**542**	150f. multicoloured	3·25	3·25

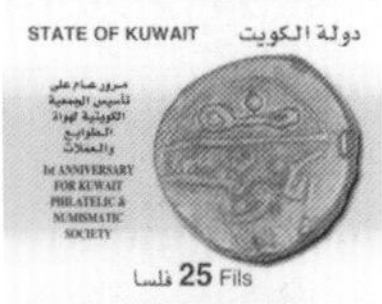

543 Early Coin

2007. 1st Anniv of Philatelic and Numismatic Society. Multicoloured.

1928	25f. Type **543**	70	70
1929	50f. 1959 40n. stamp (As Type **21**)	1·10	1·10
1930	150f. Early coin and stamp (60×35 mm)	3·00	3·00

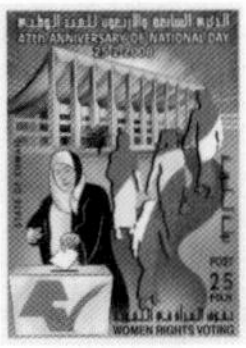

544 Women voting

2008. 47th National Day. Multicoloured.

1931	25f. Type **544**	70	70
1932	150f. Symbols of Kuwait (horiz)	2·75	2·75

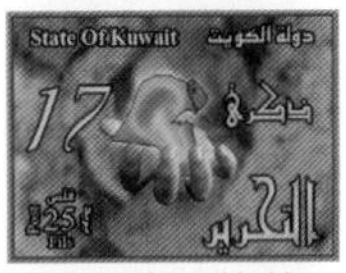

545 '17' and Hand holding Map of Kuwait

2008. 17th Anniv of Liberation Day.

1933	**545**	25f. multicoloured	70	70
1934	**545**	50f. multicoloured	1·10	1·10

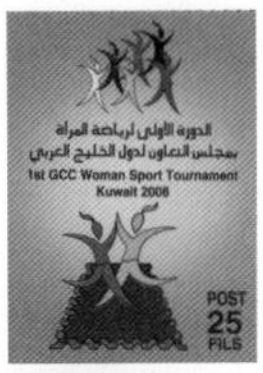

546 Stylized Gymnasts and Games Emblem

2008. First GCC Women's Sports Tournament, Kuwait. Designs showing stylized women athletes. Multicoloured.

1935	25f. Type **546**	80	80
1936	25f. Runners	80	80
1937	25f. Rifle shooting	80	80
1938	25f. Basketball	80	80
1939	25f. Table tennis	80	80
1940	150f. Games emblem and stylized athletes, orange background (horiz)	3·00	3·00
1941	150f. As No. 1940, red background (horiz)	3·00	3·00
1942	150f. As No. 1940, violet background (horiz)	3·00	3·00
1943	150f. As No. 1940, green background (horiz)	3·00	3·00
1944	150f. As No. 1940, mauve background (horiz)	3·00	3·00

Nos. 1945/6 and Type **547** are left for 45th Anniv of Kuwait–Romania Diplomatic Relations, issued on 21 June 2008, not yet received.

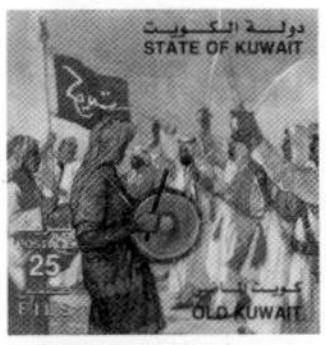

548 Drummer and Procession

2008. Old Kuwait. Designs showing paintings. Multicoloured.

1947	25f. Type **548**	80	80
1948	50f. Two drummers and men caulking boat	1·20	1·20
1949	100f. Covered street	2·20	2·20
1950	150f. Funfair	3·00	3·00
1951	200f. Minarets and male figure	3·50	3·50
1952	250f. Donkey riders and wooden gateway	3·75	3·75
1953	350f. Shoreline and boats disembarking	4·25	4·25
1954	500f. Stone gateway and male figures	5·50	5·50

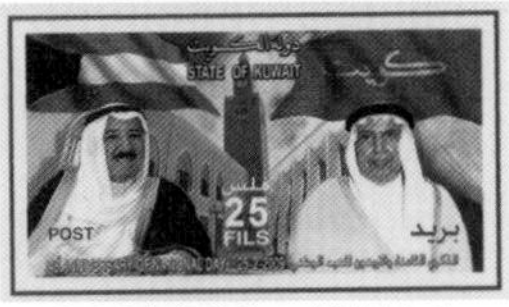

549 Emir Sabah Al Ahmad Al Jabir Al Sabah and Flags

2009. 48th National Day.

1955	**549**	25f. multicoloured	80	80
1956	**549**	50f. multicoloured	1·20	1·20
1957	**549**	150f. multicoloured	3·00	3·00
MS1958		100×66 mm. 250f. As Type **549**. Imperf	3·75	3·75

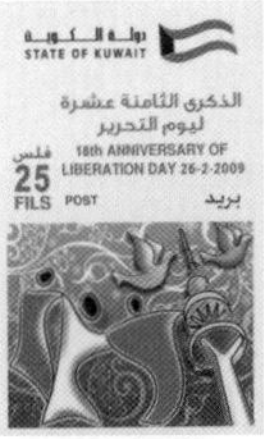

550 Symbols of Liberation

2009. 18th Anniv of Liberation Day.

1959	**550**	25f. multicoloured	80·00	80·00
1960	**550**	50f. multicoloured	1·20	1·20
1961	**550**	150f. multicoloured	3·00	3·00

OFFICIAL STAMPS

1923. Stamps of India (King George V) optd **KUWAIT SERVICE**.

O1	**56**	½a. green	5·50	42·00
O2	**57**	1a. brown	4·75	23·00
O3	**58**	1½a. brown (No. 163)	4·00	60·00
O4	**59**	2a. lilac	9·00	42·00
O17	**70**	2a. lilac	70·00	£250
O5	**61**	2a.6p. blue	4·50	75·00
O6	**62**	3a. orange	4·00	70·00
O19	**62**	3a. blue	4·50	50·00
O8	**63**	4a. green	4·00	70·00
O20	**71**	4a. green	4·25	85·00
O9	**65**	8a. mauve	6·00	£110
O22	**66**	12a. red	40·00	£200
O10	**67**	1r. brown and green	30·00	£190
O11	**67**	2r. red and orange	30·00	£275
O12	**67**	5r. blue and violet	£110	£450
O13	**67**	10r. green and red	£200	£400
O14	**67**	15r. blue	£350	£600

POSTAGE DUE STAMPS

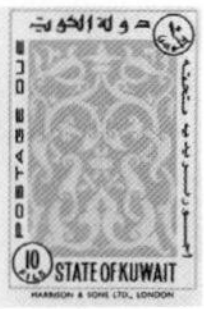

D34

1963

D199	**D34**	1f. brown and black	10	30
D200	**D34**	2f. lilac and black	30	45
D201	**D34**	5f. blue and black	45	30
D202	**D34**	8f. green and black	85	55
D203	**D34**	10f. yellow and black	1·10	1·10
D204	**D34**	25f. red and black	2·50	3·25

The above stamps were not sold to the public unused until 1 July 1964.

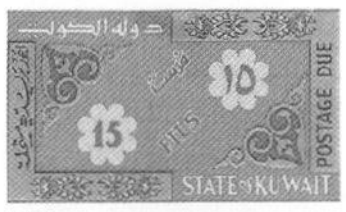

D51

1965

D276	**D51**	4f. pink and yellow	20	30
D277	**D51**	15f. red and blue	75	55
D278	**D51**	40f. blue and green	1·60	1·20
D279	**D51**	50f. green and mauve	2·10	1·70
D280	**D51**	100f. blue and yellow	3·75	3·25

Pt. 10

KYRGYZSTAN

Formerly Kirghizia, a constituent republic of the Soviet Union, Kyrgyzstan became independent in 1991. Its capital Frunze reverted to its previous name of Bishkek.

1992. 100 kopeks = 1 rouble.
1993. 100 tyin = 1 som.

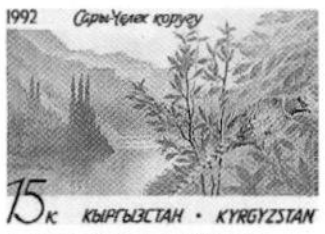

1 Sary-C'helek Nature Reserve

1992

1	**1**	15k. multicoloured	50	40

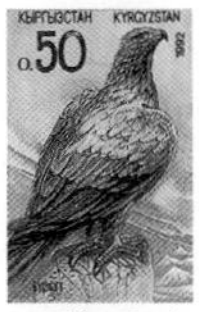

2 Golden Eagle

1992

2	**2**	50k. multicoloured	60	50

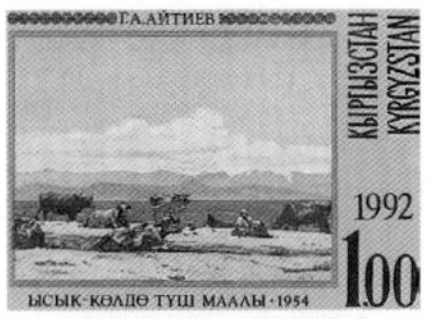

3 *Cattle at Issyk-Kule* (G. A. Aitiev)

1992

3	**3**	1r. multicoloured	60	50

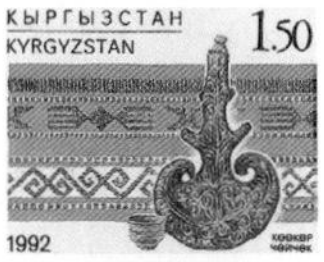

4 Carpet and Samovar

1992

4	**4**	1r.50 multicoloured	60	50

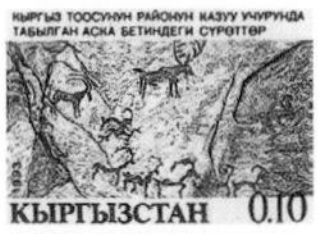

5 Cave Paintings

1993. National Monuments. Multicoloured.

5	10k. Type **5**	15	10
6	50k. 11th-century tower, Burana (vert)	15	10
7	1r.+25k. Mausoleum of Manas, Talas (vert)	15	10
8	2r.+50k. Mausoleum, Uzgen	25	15
9	3r. Yurt	25	15
10	5r.+50k. Statue of Manas, Bishkek	45	35
11	9r. Cultural complex, Bishkek	70	60
MS12	61×91 mm. 10r. Cockle jewellery	1·70	1·70

The premium on Nos. 7/8 and 10 were used for the financing of a Manas museum.

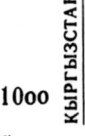

КЫРГЫЗСТАН
10оо

(6)

1993. Nos. 5940, 6073 and 4671 of Russia surch as T **6**.

13	10k. on 1k. brown	35	25
14	20k. on 2k. brown	60	50
15	30k. on 3k. red	85	75

КЫРГЫЗСТАН
20 т.

(7)

1993. Nos. 4672/3 of Russia surch as T **7**.

16	20t. on 4k. red	70	60
17	30t. on 6k. blue	95	85

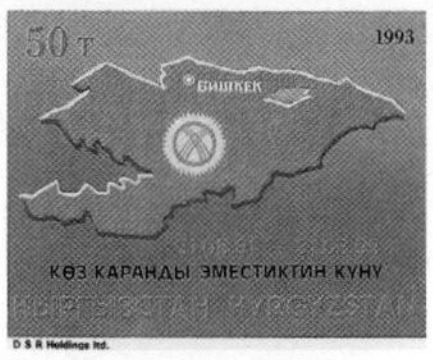

8 Map

1993. Second Anniv of Independence (18) and First Anniv of Admission to United Nations (19). Multicoloured.

18	50t. Type **8**	95	85
19	60t. U.N. emblem, national flag and Government Palace, Bishkek (vert)	1·00	90

See also No. **MS**35.

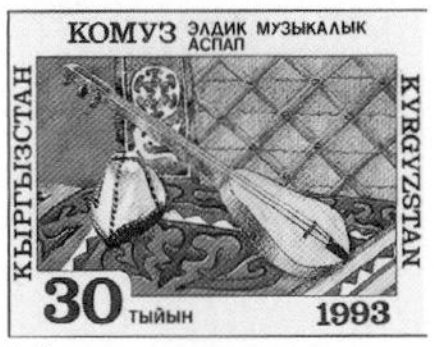

9 Komuz

1993. Music.

20	**9**	30t. multicoloured	85	75
MS21		84×67 mm. 140t. Similar design to Type **9** but with motifs reversed (51×39 mm)	13·00	12·50

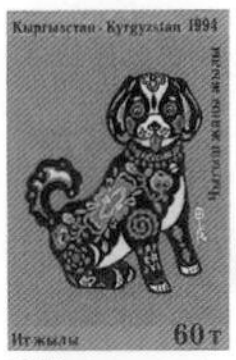

10 Dog

1994. New Year. Year of the Dog.

22	**10**	60t. multicoloured	95	85

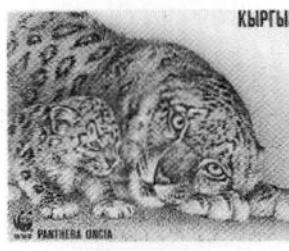

11 Adult and Cub

1994. The Snow Leopard. Multicoloured.

23	10t. Type **11**	35	25
24	20t. Lying curled-up	50	40
25	30t. Sitting	70	60
26	40t. Head	95	85

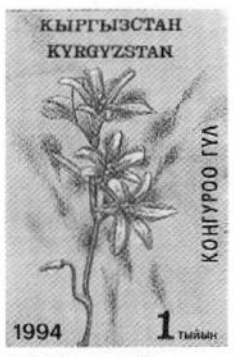

12 Mauve Flowers

1994. Flowers. Multicoloured.

27	1t. Type **12**	10	10
28	3t. Daisies (horiz)	15	10
29	10t. Tulip	40	35
30	16t. Narcissi	45	40
31	20t. Deep pink flower	50	45
32	30t. White flower	60	50
33	40t. Yellow flower	75	65
MS34	70×90 mm. 50t. *Trollius altaicum*	1·00	90

1994. Third Anniv of Independence and Second Anniv of Admission to United Nations. Sheet containing stamps as Nos. 18/19 but with face values changed. Multicoloured.

MS35	110×80 mm. 120t. Type **8**; 130t. As No. 19	8·75	8·50

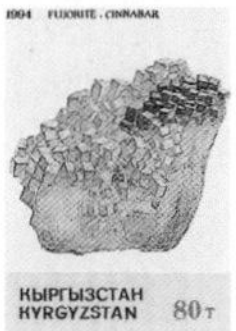

13 Fluorite

1994. Minerals. Multicoloured.

36	80t. Type **13**	50	40
37	90t. Calcite	60	50
38	100t. Getchellite	70	60
39	110t. Barite	75	65
40	120t. Auripigment	80	65

41	140t. Antimonite	95	85
MS42	135×95 mm. 200t. Cinnabar	1·60	1·50

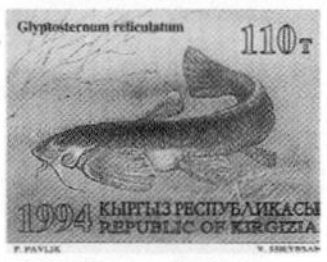

14 Turkestan Catfish

1994. Fish. Multicoloured.

43	110t. Type **14**	70	60
44	120t. Schmidt's dace	80	65
45	130t. Scaleless osman	85	75
46	140t. Spotted stone loach	95	85
MS47	82×57 mm. 200t. Common carp (*Cyprinus carpio*)	1·90	1·80

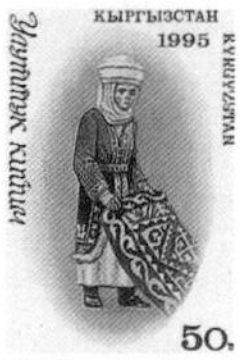

15 Woman with Rug

1995. Traditional Costumes. Multicoloured.

48	50t. Type **15**	45	35
49	50t. Musician	45	35
50	100t. Falconer	70	60
51	100t. Woman with long plaits	70	60

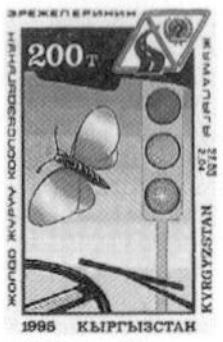

16 Butterfly, Traffic Lights and Emblem

1995. Road Safety Week.

52	**16** 200t. multicoloured	1·30	1·10

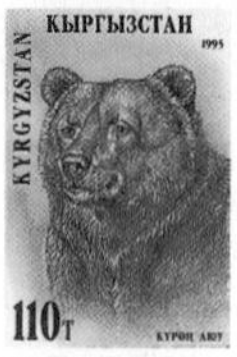

17 Brown Bear

1995. Animals. Multicoloured.

53	110t. Type **17**	40	30
54	120t. Snow leopard (horiz)	50	40
55	130t. Golden eagle	65	50
56	140t. Menzbier's marmot (horiz)	80	65
57	150t. Short-toed eagle (horiz)	90	75
58	160t. Golden eagle (different)	1·00	90
59	190t. Red fox (horiz)	1·20	1·00
MS60	90×70 mm. 130t. Golden eagle (*different*); 170t. Argali	2·00	1·90

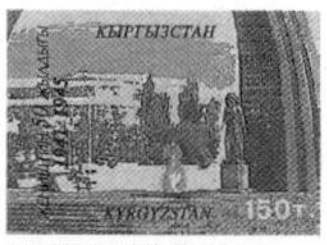

18 Memorial Flame, Bishkek

1995. 50th Anniv of End of Second World War. Sheet 90×70 mm.

MS61	**18** 150t. multicoloured	1·20	1·10

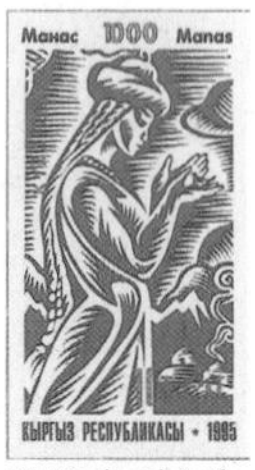

19 Aitschurek (wife of Manas)

1995. Millenary of *Manas* (epic poem). Each blue and gold.

62	10t.+5t. Type **19**	40	30
63	20t.+10t. Hoopoe on youth's wrist	50	40
64	30t.+10t. Birth of Semetey, son of Manas	65	50
65	30t.+10t. Woman carrying spear and leading horse	65	50
66	40t.+15t. Warrior astride dead dragon	80	65
67	50t.+15t. Jakyp, father of Manas	90	75
68	50t.+15t. Manas on horseback	90	75
69	50t.+15t. Seytek, grandson of Manas	90	75
MS70	Two sheets. (a) 166×107 mm. 2s.+50t. Saryakbai (Manas singer) cradling injured warrier (37×51 mm). (b) 148×131 mm. 2s.+50t. Sagymbai (Manas singer) (37×51 mm)	6·75	6·50

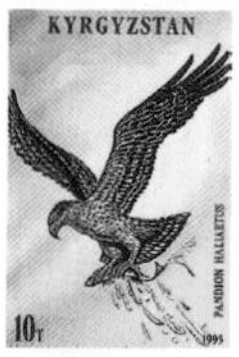

20 Osprey

1995. Birds. Multicoloured.

71	10t. Type **20**	15	15
72	50t. Tawny eagle	25	20
73	100t. Lammergeier	50	40
74	140t. Saker falcon	80	65
75	150t. Short-toed eagle	90	75
76	200t. Lammergeier	1·00	90
77	300t. Golden eagle	1·60	1·40
MS78	90×70 mm. 600t. White-tailed sea eagle (*Haliaeetus albicilla*) (29×40 mm)	3·00	2·75

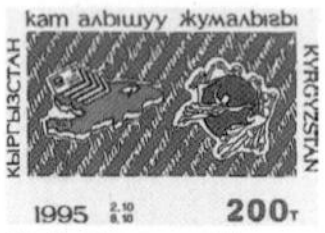

21 Envelopes on Map and U.P.U. Emblem

1995. Postage Stamp Week.

79	**21** 200t. multicoloured	1·00	90

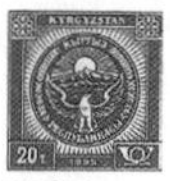

22 State Arms

1995

80	**22** 20t. violet	15	15
81	**22** 50t. blue	25	20
82	**22** 100t. brown	50	40
83	**22** 500t. green	2·20	2·00

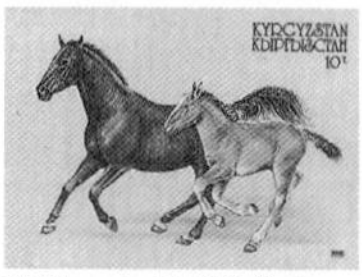

23 Mare and Foal Galloping

1995. Horses. Multicoloured.

89	10t. Type **23**	15	15
90	50t. Palamino mare and foal (vert)	25	20
91	100t. Brown mare and foal (vert)	50	40
92	140t. Chestnut mare and foal (vert)	80	65
93	150t. Chestnut mare and foal	90	75
94	200t. Grey mare and foal	1·20	1·00
95	300t. Pair of foals	1·40	1·30
MS96	91×71 mm. 600t. brown and cream (Mongolian wild horses) (*Equus caballus*) (vert)	3·25	3·25

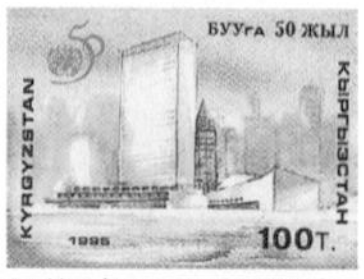

24 Headquarters, New York

1995. 50th Anniv of United Nations Organization. Sheet 71×91 mm containing T **24** and similar horiz design. Multicoloured.

MS97	100t. Type **24**; 100t. Rainbow and mountains	1·20	1·10

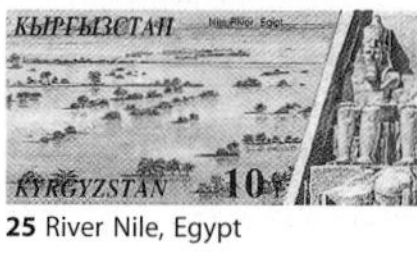

25 River Nile, Egypt

1995. Natural Wonders of the World. Multicoloured.

98	10t. Type **25**	15	15
99	50t. Mt. Kilimanjaro, Tanzania	25	20
100	100t. Sahara Desert, Algeria	50	40
101	140t. Amazon River, Brazil (vert)	80	65
102	150t. Grand Canyon, U.S.A. (vert)	90	75
103	200t. Victoria Falls, Zimbabwe (vert)	1·30	1·10
104	350t. Mt. Everest, Nepal	1·60	1·40
105	400t. Niagara Falls, Canada	1·80	1·60
MS106	Two sheets, each 90×70 mm. (a) Gull over Issyk-Kule lake, Kyrgyzstan; (b) Eagle over Issyk-Kule lake	5·75	5·75

No. 98 is wrongly inscribed "Egipt".

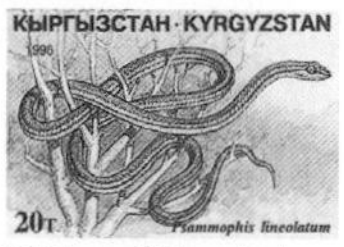

26 Steppe Ribbon Snake

1996. Reptiles. Multicoloured.

107	20t. Type **26**	15	15
108	50t. Fat-tailed panther gecko	25	20
109	50t. Tessellated water snake	25	20
110	100t. Central Asian viper	50	40
111	150t. Arguta	1·00	90
112	200t. Dione snake	1·30	1·10
113	250t. *Asyblepharus* sp. (wrongly inscr "Asymblepharus")	1·60	1·40
MS114	91×71 mm. 500t. Sand lizard (*Lacerta agilis*)	3·25	3·25

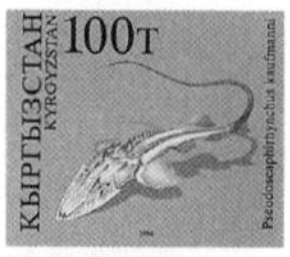

27 Kaufmann's Shovelnose (*Pseudoscphirhyncus kafmanni*)

1996. "Save the Aral Sea". Sheet 128×108 mm containing T **27** and similar horiz designs. Multicoloured.

MS115	100t. Caracal (*Felis caracal*); 100t. Aral trout (*Salmo trutta aralensis*); 100t. Striped hyena (*Hyaena hyaena*); 100t. Type **27**; 100t. Pike asp (*Aspiolucius esocinus*)	6·50	6·25

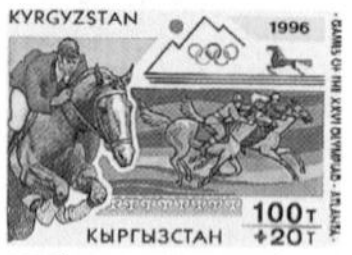

28 Show Jumping and Traditional Horse Race

1996. Olympic Games, Atlanta, U.S.A. Multicoloured.

116	100t.+20t. Type **28**	50	40
117	140t.+30t. Boxing and traditional wrestling match	80	65
118	150t.+30t. Archer and mounted archer shooting at eagle	90	75
119	300t.+50t. Judo competitor, ballooning, yachting and water-skiing	1·80	1·60

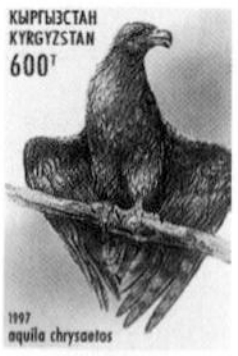

29 Golden Eagle

1997. Animals. Multicoloured.

120	600t. Type **29**	1·70	1·50
121	600t. Markhor (*Capra falconeri*)	1·70	1·50
122	600t. Argali (*Ovis ammon*)	1·70	1·50
123	600t. Himalayan griffon (*Gyps himalayensis*)	1·70	1·50
124	600t. Asiatic wild ass (*Equus hemionus*)	1·70	1·50
125	600t. Wolf (*Canis lupus*)	1·70	1·50
126	600t. Brown bear (*Ursus arctos*) (wrongly inscr "arctor")	1·70	1·50
127	600t. Saiga (*Saiga tatarica*)	1·70	1·50

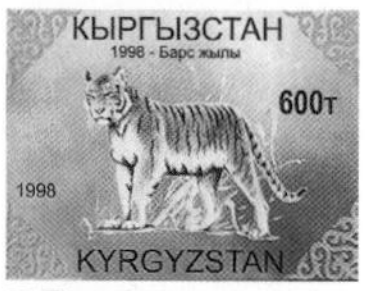

30 Tiger

1998. New Year. Year of the Tiger.

128	**30** 600t. multicoloured	1·30	1·10

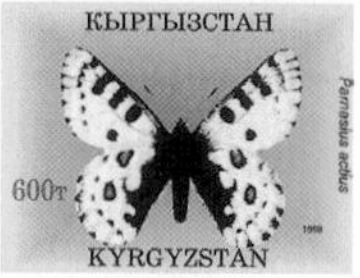

31 "Parnassius actius"

1998. Butterflies. Multicoloured.

129	600t. Type **31** (wrongly inscr "Parnasius")	1·30	1·10
130	600t. *Colias christophi*	1·30	1·10
131	600t. Swallowtail (*Papilio machaon*)	1·30	1·10
132	600t. *Colias thisoa*	1·30	1·10
133	600t. *Parnassius delphius*	1·30	1·10
134	600t. *Parnassius tianschanicus*	1·30	1·10

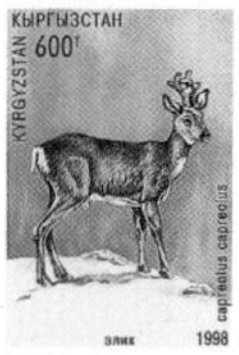

32 Roe Deer

1998. Animals. Multicoloured.

135	600t. Type **32**	1·60	1·40
136	600t. Osprey ("Pandion haliaetus")	1·60	1·40
137	600t. Hoopoe ("Upupa epops")	1·60	1·40
138	600t. White stork ("Ciconia ciconia")	1·60	1·40
139	1000t. Golden oriole ("Oriolus oriolus")	2·50	2·40
140	1000t. Snow leopard	2·50	2·40
141	1000t. River kingfisher ("Alcedo althis")	2·50	2·40
142	1000t. Common kestrel ("Falco tinnunculus")	2·50	2·40

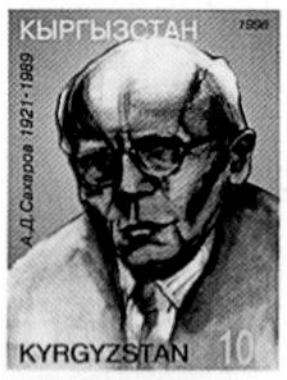

33 Andrei Dimitriyevich Sakharov (physicist)

1998. 50th Anniv of Universal Declaration of Human Rights. Multicoloured.

143	10s. Type **33**	1·20	1·00
144	10s. Crowd cheering	1·20	1·00
145	10s. Martin Luther King (civil rights leader)	1·20	1·00
146	10s. Mahatma Ghandi (Indian leader)	1·20	1·00
147	10s. Eleanor Roosevelt (humanitarian)	1·20	1·00

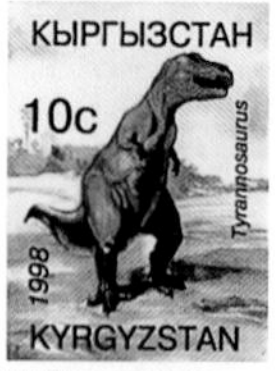

34 Tyrannosaurus

1998. Prehistoric Animals. Multicoloured.

148	10s. Type **34**	1·60	1·40
149	10s. Saurolophus	1·60	1·40
150	10s. Gallimimus (horiz)	1·60	1·40
151	10s. Euoplocephalus (horiz)	1·60	1·40
152	10s. Protoceratops (horiz)	1·60	1·40
153	10s. Velociraptor (horiz)	1·60	1·40

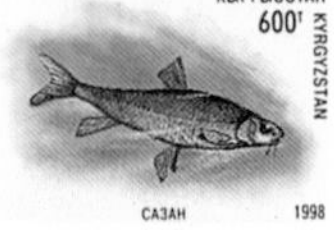

35 Fish

1998. Fauna. Multicoloured.

154	600t. Type **35**	1·00	90
155	600t. Fish (with orange tail and fins)	1·00	90
156	1000t. Bar-headed goose	1·70	1·50
157	1000t. Chukar partridge	1·70	1·50
158	1000t. Goosander by water	1·70	1·50
159	1000t. Common shelduck swimming	1·70	1·50
160	1000t. Rodent	1·70	1·50

161 1000t. Himalayan snowcock standing on one leg 1·70 1·50

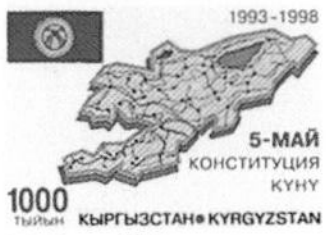

36 Map of Kyrgyzstan

1998. Fifth Anniv of Constitution.
162 **36** 1000t. multicoloured 2·00 1·80

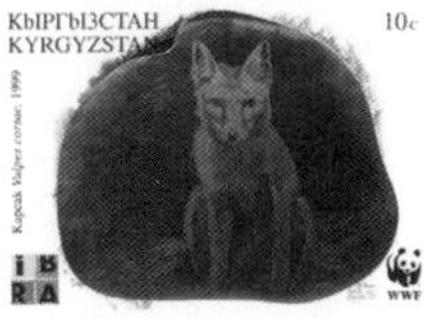

37 Fox

1999. "iBRA" International Stamp Exhibition, Nuremberg, Germany. The Corsac Fox (*Vulpes corsac*). Multicoloured.
163 10s. Type **37** 80 65
164 10s. Fox sleeping 80 65
165 30s. Two foxes standing 2·30 2·10
166 50s. Mother and cubs 4·00 3·75

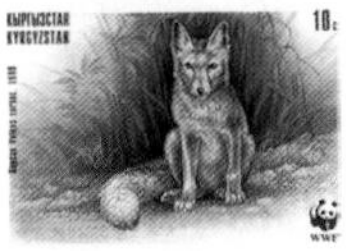

38 Fox

1999. The Corsac Fox (*Vulpes corsac*). Multicoloured.
167 10s. Type **38** 80 65
168 10s. Fox sleeping 80 65
169 30s. Two foxes standing 2·30 2·10
170 50s. Mother and cubs 4·00 3·75

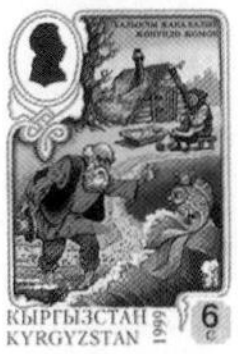

39 *The Fisherman and the Golden Fish* (poem)

1999. Birth Bicentenary of Alexander Sergeevich Pushkin. Multicoloured.
171 36t. *Ruslan and Lyudmila* (poem) 15 10
172 6s. Type **39** 90 75
173 10s. *Tsar Saltan* (poem) 1·60 1·40
174 10s. *The Golden Cockerel* (fairy tale) 1·60 1·40
MS175 74×99 mm. 20s. Pushkin 4·00 3·75

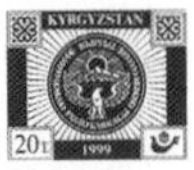

40 State Arms

1999
176 **40** 20t. blue 15 10

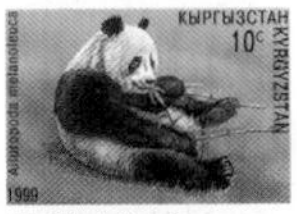

41 Giant Panda (*Ailuropoda melanoleuca*)

1999. "China '99" International Stamp Exhibition, Beijing, China. Sheet 90×90 mm containing T **41** and similar horiz design. Multicoloured.
MS180 10s. Type **41**; 15s. Brown wood owl (*Strix leptogrammica*) 3·50 3·25

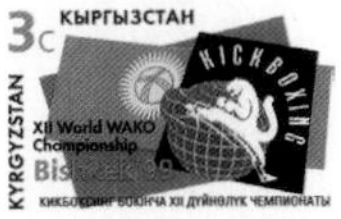

42 State Flag and Emblem

1999. World Kick Boxing Championships, Bishkek. Multicoloured.
181 3s. Type **42** 65 50
182 3s. Emblem on blue background with Cyrillic championship title in red 65 50
183 3s. "WORLD" in green across globe and emblem 65 50
MS184 121×62 mm. 6s. "WORLD" in blue across globe and emblem (different); 6s. "KICKBOXING" and emblem on yellow rectangle 2·50 2·50

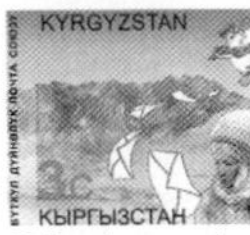

43 Envelopes and Emblem

1999. 125th Anniv of Universal Postal Union. Multicoloured.
185 3s. Type **43** 65 50
186 6s. Airplane, envelopes, horseman and emblem 1·20 1·00

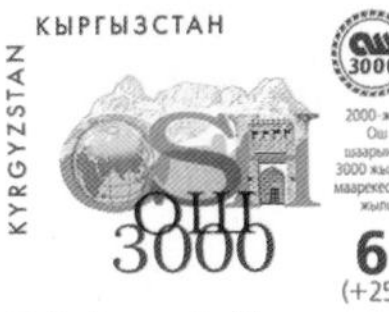

44 Anniversary Emblem

2000. 3000th Anniv of Osh. Sheet 139×109 mm containing Multicoloured.
MS187 6s.+25t. Type **44**; 6s.+25t. Ravat Abdullakhan Mosque; 6s.+25t. Tahti Suleiman Mosque; 6s.+25t. Asaf ibn Burhia tower 4·50 4·50

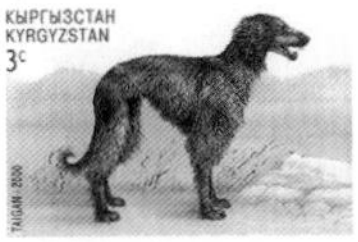

45 Taigan

2000. Asian Dogs. Multicoloured.
188 3s. Type **45** 40 25
189 6s. Tasy 80 65
190 6s. Afghan hound 80 65
191 10s. Saluki 1·20 1·00
192 15s. Mid-Asian shepherd 1·80 1·50
193 15s. Akbash 1·80 1·50
194 20s. Chow Chow 2·20 2·00
195 25s. Akita-inu 2·75 2·50

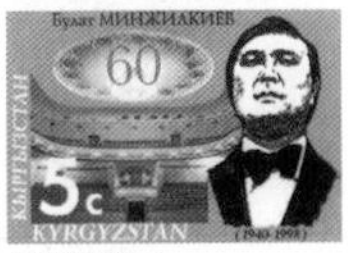

46 Minjilkiev

2000. 60th Birth Anniv of Bulat Minzhilkiev (opera singer).
196 **46** 5s. multicoloured 80 65
No. 196 is wrongly inscribed "1940–1998" instead of "1940–1997".

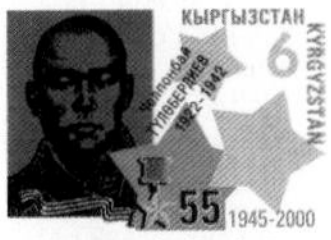

47 Private Cholponbai Tuleberdiev and Medal

2000. 55th Anniv of End of Second World War. Showing recipients of Gold Star of Hero of Soviet Union Medal. Multicoloured.
197 6s. Type **47** 90 75
198 6s. Major-General Ivan Vasilievich Panfilov (vert) 90 75
199 6s. Private Duishenkul Shopokov 90 75

2000. No. 27 surch **36t.**
200 36t. on 1t. multicoloured 25 20

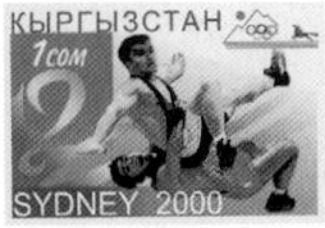

49 Wrestling

2000. Olympic Games, Sydney. Multicoloured.
201 1s. Type **49** 25 20
202 3s. Hurdling (vert) 50 40
203 6s. Boxing 80 65
204 10s. Weightlifting (vert) 1·00 90

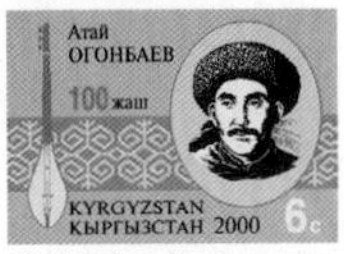

50 Atai Ogonbaev

2000. Birth Centenary of Atai Ogonbaev (musician).
205 **50** 6s. multicoloured 1·30 1·10

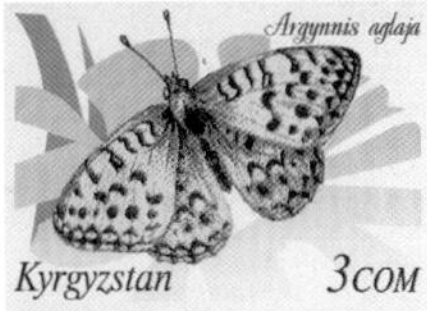

51 Dark Green Fritillary (*Argynnis aglaja*)

2000. Butterflies. Multicoloured.
206 3s. Type **51** 65 50
207 3s. Swallowtail (*Papilo machaon*) 65 50
208 3s. Peacock (*Inachis io*) 65 50
209 3s. Apollo (*Parnassius Apollo*) 65 50
210 3s. Small tortoiseshell (*Aglais urticae*) 65 50
211 3s. *Colias thisoa* 65 50

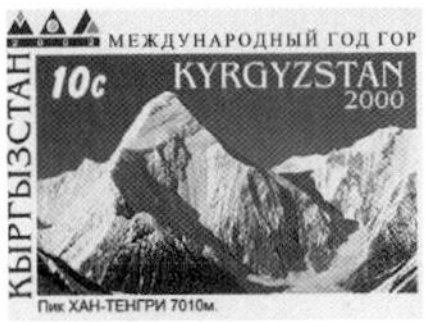

52 Khan-Tegri

2000. International Year of Mountains (1st series). Multicoloured.
212 10s. Type **52** 1·30 1·10
213 10s. Lenin Peak 1·30 1·10
214 10s. Victory Peak 1·30 1·10
See also Nos. 228/**MS**231.

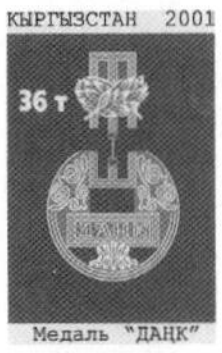

53 Dank Medal (bravery)

2001. Orders and Medals. Multicoloured.
215 36t. Type **53** 15 10
216 48t. Baatyrene (women's medal) 15 10
217 1s. Manas 3rd class order 15 10
218 2s. Manas 2nd class order 25 20
219 3s. Manas 1st class order 40 25
220 6s. Danaker order (bravery) 65 50
221 10s. Ak Shumkar (Hero of Kyrgyz Republic) 1·00 90

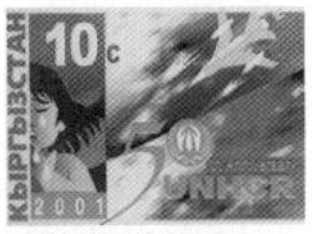

54 Crying Child and Military Aircraft

2001. 50th Anniv of United Nations High Commissioner for Refugees.
222 **54** 10s. multicoloured 1·00 90

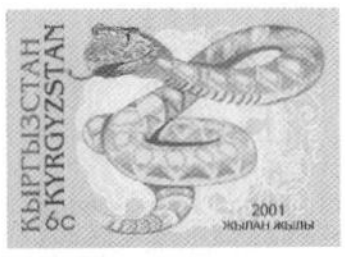

55 Snake

2001. New Year. Year of the Snake.
223 **55** 6s. multicoloured 90 75

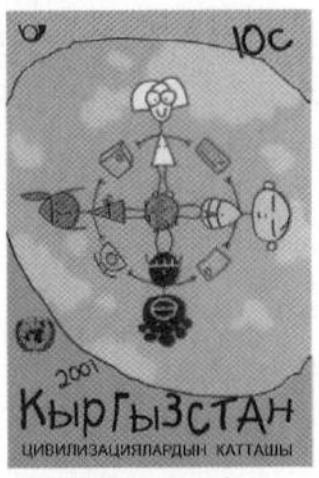

56 Children encircling Globe

2001. United Nations Year of Dialogue among Civilizations.
224 **56** 10s. multicoloured 1·00 90

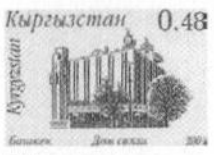

57 Communication House

2001. Bishkek.
225 **57** 48t. green 15 10
226 - 1s. green 25 20
227 - 3s. brown 50 40
DESIGNS: 1s. Government House; 3s. National Opera House.

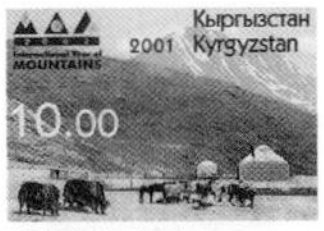

58 Yaks in Pasture

2001. International Year of Mountains (2nd series). Multicoloured.
228 10s. Type **58** 1·30 1·10
229 10s. Horses crossing river 1·30 1·10
230 10s. Forested slopes 1·30 1·10
MS231 10×83 mm. Designs as Nos. 228/30 4·00 3·75

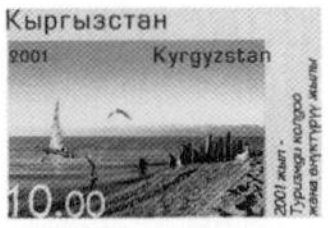

59 Yacht on Lake Issyk-Kul

2001. International Year of Eco-tourism. Multicoloured.
232 10s. Type **59** 1·20 1·00
233 10s. Lake Sary-Chelek 1·20 1·00
234 10s. Suusamyr Valley 1·20 1·00
MS235 119×89 mm. 10s. Mosque, Naryn (vert) 2·75 2·75

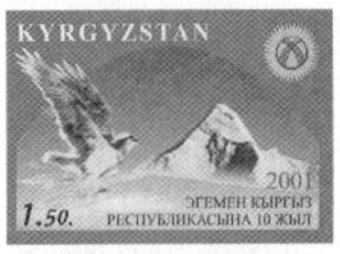

60 Ak-Shumkar (legendary bird) and Khan-Tengri Mountain

2001. Tenth Anniv of Independence. Multicoloured.
236 1s.50 Type **60** 25 20
237 7s. Pres. Askar Akaev and national flag 1·30 1·10
MS238 126×90 mm. 11s.50 Government House, Bishkek 2·00 1·90

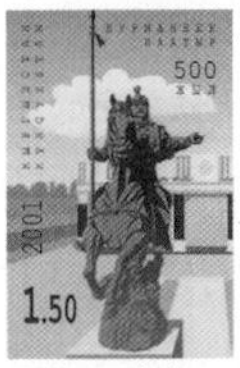

61 Kurmanbek (statue), Djalal-Abad

2001. 500th Birth Anniv of Kurmanbek Khan (military leader).
239 **61** 1s.50 multicoloured 90 75

2001. 40th Anniv of Worldwide Fund for Nature. Nos. 163/6 overprinted **40th Anniversary 1961–2001** or surcharged.
240 25s. on 10s. Fox 1·80 1·60
241 25s. on 10s. Fox sleeping 1·80 1·60
242 30s. Two foxes standing 2·20 2·00
243 50s. Mother and cubs 3·75 3·50
Nos. 240/1 with both change of face value and celebratory inscription, and Nos. 242/3 with only celebratory inscription.

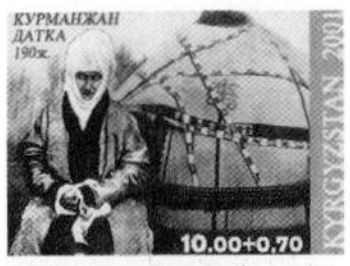

63 Kurmandjan Datka

2001. 190th Birth Anniv of Kurmandjan Dakta (aka Alai Queen, female tribal leader).
244 **63** 10s.+70t. black 1·30 1·10

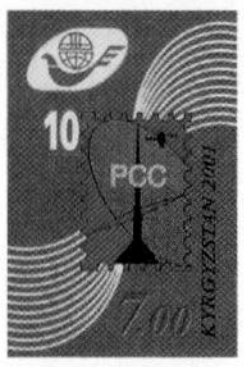

64 RCC and Kyrgyzstan Post

2001. Tenth Anniv of Regional Communications Community.

245	**64**	7s. multicoloured	90	75

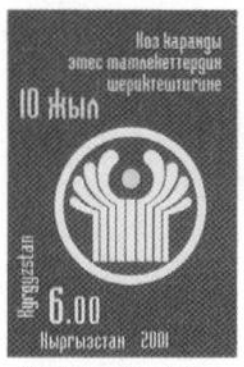

65 Union Emblem Office Emblems

2001. Tenth Anniv of Union of Independent States.

246	**65**	6s. blue and yellow	80	65

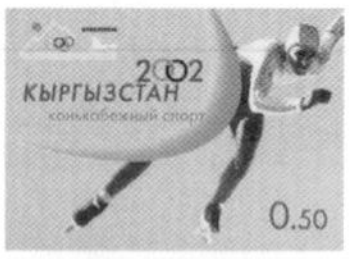

66 Skating

2002. Olympic Games, Salt Lake City, USA. Multicoloured.

247	50t. Type **66**	15	10
248	1s.50 Biathlon	25	20
249	7s. Hockey	80	65
250	10s. Ski jumping	1·00	90
MS251	88×89 mm. 50s. Alpine skiing	5·75	5·75

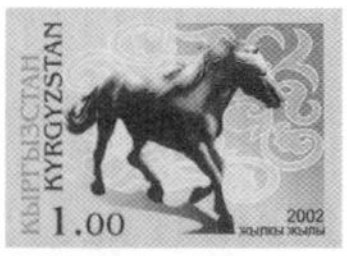

67 Horse

2002. Chinese New Year ("Year of the Horse").

252	**67**	1s. multicoloured	40	25

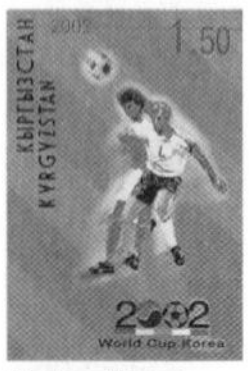

68 Two Players

2002. World Cup Football Championships, Japan and South Korea. Sheet 136×118 mm containing T **68** and similar vert designs. Multicoloured.

MS253 1s.50 Type **68**; 3s. Players tackling for ball; 7s.20 Player dribbling ball; 12s. Player defending; 24s. Players jumping for ball; 60s. Player chasing another — 16·00 15·00

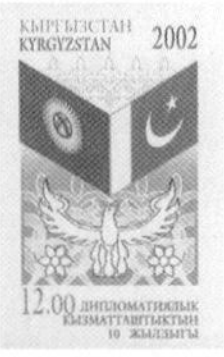

69 Kyrgyzstan and Pakistan Flags and Dove

2002. Tenth Anniv of Kyrgyzstan—Pakistan Diplomatic Relations.

254	**69**	12s. multicoloured	1·30	1·10

2002. No. **MS**253 surch **Final BRAZIL 2 : 0 GREMANY Third Place TURKEY : KOREA** in either gold or silver.

MS255 (a) As No. **MS**253 (gold ovpt)
(b) As No. **MS**253 (silver ovpt) — 23·00 23·00

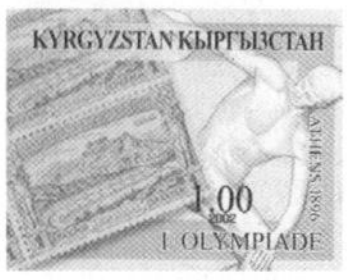

71 Greek Stamp and Discus Thrower (Athens, 1896)

2002. History of Summer Olympic Games. Four sheets, each 140×110 mm containing T **71** and similar horiz designs. Multicoloured.

MS256 (a) 1s. Type **71**; 2s. Boxer and French stamp (Paris 1900); 3s. Diver and American stamp (St. Louis 1904); 5s. Weightlifting and English stamp (London 1908); 7s. Rower and Swedish stamp (Stockholm 1912). 7s. Athlete and Belgian stamp (Antwerp 1920). (b) 1s. Gymnast and French stamp (Paris 1924); 2s. Diver and Dutch stamp (Amsterdam 1928); 3s. Table tennis and American stamp (Los Angeles 1932); 5s. Runner and German stamp (Berlin 1936); 7s. Fencing and English stamp (London 1948); 7s. Gymnast and Finnish stamp (Helsinki 1952). (c) 1s.50 Volleyball and Australian stamp (Melbourne 1956); 3s. Tennis and Italian stamp (Rome 1960); 5s. Swimmer and Japan stamp (Tokyo 1964); 5s. Wrestlers and Mexican stamp (Mexico 1968); 7s.20 Kayaker and German stamp (Munich 1972); 12s. Yacht and Canadian stamp (Montreal 1976). (d) 1s. Gymnast and USSR stamp (Moscow 1980); 3s. Synchronised swimmer and USA stamp (Los Angeles 1984); 5s. Cyclist and Korean stamp (Seoul 1988); 5s. High jumper and Spanish stamp (Barcelona 1992); 7s.20 Wind surfer and USA stamp (Atlanta 1996); 12s. Gymnast and Australian stamp (Sydney 2000) — 21·00 20·00

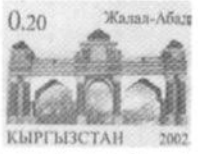

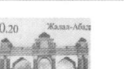

72 Zhalal-Abad

2002. Regional Cities.

257	**72**	20t. purple	15	10
258	-	50t. purple	15	10
259	-	60t. purple	15	10
260	-	1s. blue	20	15
261	-	1s.50 blue	25	20
262	-	2s. slate	35	25
263	-	3s. slate	50	40
264	-	7s. slate	1·00	80
265	-	10s. blue	1·30	1·10

DESIGNS: 20t. Zhalal-Abad; 50t. Talas; 60t. Osh; 1s. Zhalal-Abad; 1s.50 Talas; 2s. Osh; 3s. Zhalal-Abad; 7s. Talas; 10s. Osh.

2002. No. 27 surch **2000 1.50**.

266	1s.50 on 1t. multicoloured	25	20

2002. No. 28 surch **3.60**.

267	3s.60 on 3t. multicoloured	50	40

2002. No. 29 surch **7.00 2002**.

268	7s. on 10t. multicoloured	90	75

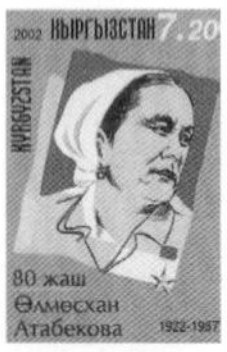

76 Olmoskhan Atabekova

2003. 80th (2002) Birth Anniversary of Olmoskhan Atabekova (war heroine).

269	**76**	7s.20 multicoloured	1·00	90

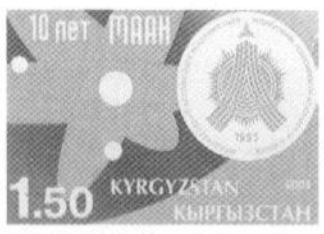

77 Atomic Symbol and Association Emblem

2003. Tenth Anniversary of the International Association of Academies of Sciences. Multicoloured.

270	1s.50 Type **77**	25	20
271	7s.20 Emblem	1·00	90

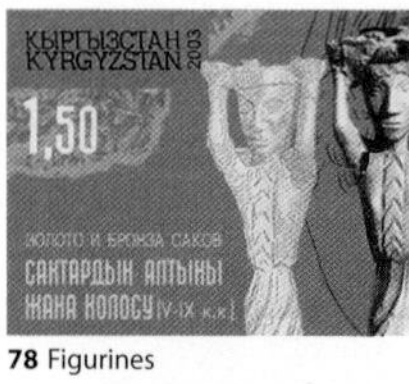

78 Figurines

2003. 2200th Anniv of Nationhood (1st issue). Saki Tribal Gold and Bronze Artefacts. Two sheets containing T **78** and similar horiz designs. Multicoloured. Imperf (MS272a) or imperf (MS272).

MS272 (a) 119×140 mm. 1s.50 Type **78**; 3s. Shield; 3s.60 Lion; 5s. Horned head; 7s. Bird; 10s. Two goat heads with joined horns; 20s.Coin; 42s. Animal headed staff.(b) 125×89 mm. 42s. Mask — 22·00 21·00

See also No. **MS**277.

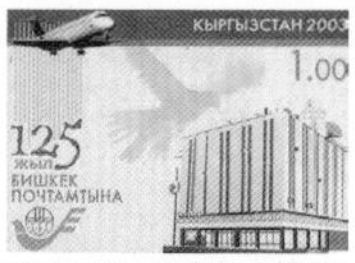

79 Airplane and Post Office Building, Bishkek

2003. 125th Anniv of Bishkek Post Office. Multicoloured.

273	1s. Type **79**	25	20
274	3s. Wagon, jeep and building	45	30
275	7s. Building, dove and wagon	85	70
MS276	119×88 mm. 50s. Dove and building (different). Imperf	5·75	5·75

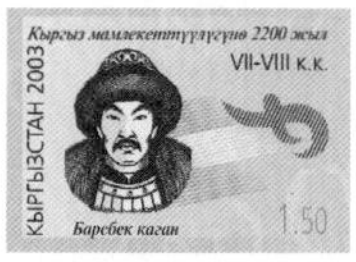

80 Barsbek

2003. 2200th Anniv of Nationhood (2nd issue). Rulers. Sheet 99×160 mm containing T **80** and similar horiz designs. Multicoloured.

MS277 1s.50 Type **80** (7th-century leader); 3s. Alp Sol; 3s.60 Mukhammed; 5s. Manap; 7s.20 Zharban; 10s. Kubatbek; 18s. Azhy; 20s. Ormon; 25s. Alymbek; 30s. Shabdan — 16·00 15·00

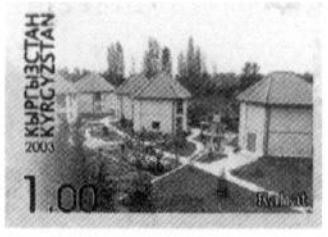

81 Rabat

2003. Tourism. Issyk Kul Resorts. Sheet 167×148 mm containing T **81** and similar horiz designs showing resorts. Multicoloured.

MS278 1s. Type **81**; 1s.50 Raduga; 2s. Teltoru; 3s. Kyrgyzskoe Vzmorije; 3s.60 Tamga; 5s. Solnyshko; 7s. Vityaz; 8s. AkBermet; 12s. Royal Beach; 20s. Inscr "Luchezarnoe poberejie" — 8·50 8·25

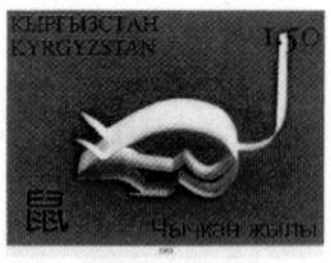

82 Rat

2003. Chinese Lunar Calendar. Sheet 210×171 mm containing T **82** and similar horiz designs showing Chinese lunar animals. Multicoloured.

MS279 1.50 "Year of the Rat"; 3s. "Year of the Ox"; 5s. "Year of the Tiger"; 7s. "Year of the Rabbit"; 12s. "Year of the Dragon"; 12s. "Year of the Snake"; 15s. "Year of the Horse"; 15s. "Year of the Sheep"; 20s. "Year of the Monkey"; 20s. "Year of the Cock"; 25s. "Year of the Dog"; 25s. "Year of the Pig" — 16·00 15·00

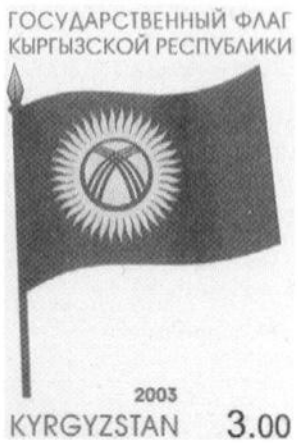

83 Flag

2003. National Symbols.

280	**83**	3s. vermilion, yellow and black	50	40
281	-	3s. black	50	40
282	-	5s. multicoloured	65	50

MS283 (a) 136×81 mm. Nos. 280/2 (b) 103×74 mm. 12s. multicoloured (52×37 mm) — 3·00 2·75

DESIGNS: Type **83**; 3s. Anthem; 5s. National arms; 12s. "Notes" (written by Syma Tsjan (Chinese historian).

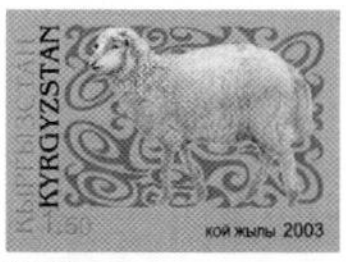

84 Sheep

2003. New Year. "Year of the Sheep".

284	**84**	1s.50 multicoloured	80	75

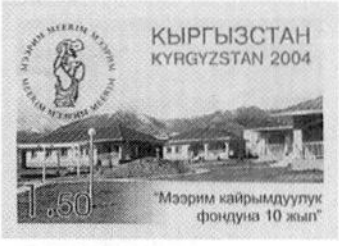

85 Buildings

2004. Tenth Anniv of Meerim Welfare Fund. Multicoloured.

285	1s.50 Type **85**	25	20
286	7s. Buildings (different)	90	75
MS287	74×103 mm. 20s. Emblem (37×52 mm)	2·20	2·00

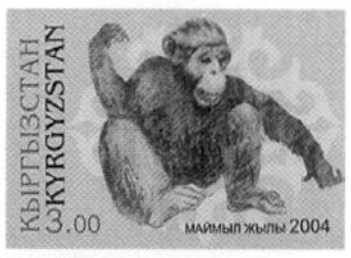

86 Monkey

2004. New Year. Year of the Monkey.

288	**86**	3s. multicoloured	50	40

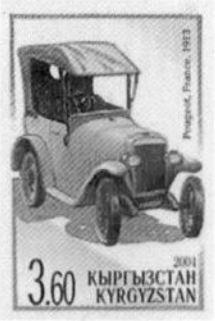

87 Peugeot (1913)

2004. Cars. Sheet 123×108 mm containing T **87** and similar vert designs. Multicoloured.

MS289 3s.60 Type **87**; 3s.60 Mercedes Benz (1999); 10s. Volvo S40 (1996); 10s. Ford (1908); 15s. Alfa Romeo (1932); 15s. VAZ 2101 (1972); 25s. Nissan (1998); 25s. ZIS 110 (1950) — 9·00 8·75

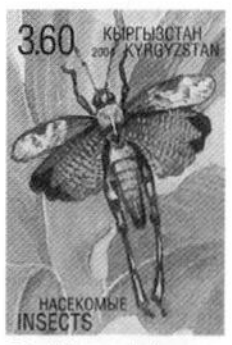

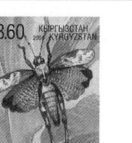

88 Winged Insect

2004. Singapore International Stamp Exhibition. Insects. Sheet 123×108 mm containing T **88** and similar vert designs. Multicoloured.

MS290 3s.60 Type **88**; 3s.60 Grasshopper; 10s. Cicada; 10s. Ladybirds; 15s. Dragonfly; 15s. Praying mantis; 25s. Moth; 25s. Bee — 9·00 8·75

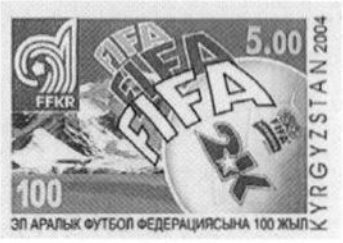

89 "FIFA" and Football

2004. Centenary of FIFA (Federation Internationale de Football Association). Multicoloured.

291	5s. Type **89**	50	40
292	6s. Anniversary emblem	60	45
293	7s. Player	65	50
294	10s. Player heading ball	90	75

2004

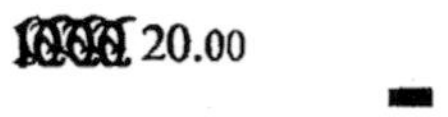

(90)

2004. Second International Festival of Arts. Peace and Respect. No. **MS**12 surch as T **90**.

MS295	20t. on 10r. multicoloured	2·50	2·50

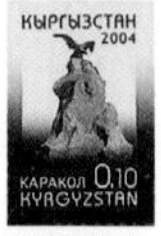

91 Karakol Region

2004. Regions.

296	**91**	10t. blue	15	10
297	-	20t. green	15	10
298	-	50t. sepia	15	10
299	-	60t. ultramarine	15	10
300	-	1s. blue	15	10
301	-	2s. brown	25	20
302	-	3s. violet	40	25

303	-	5s. emerald	50	40
304	-	7s. brown	80	65

DESIGNS: 20t. Monument, Naryn; 50t. Castle, Tokmok; 60t. Tower, Karakol; 1s. As No. 297; 2s. As No. 298; 3s. As No. 296; 5s. As No. 297; 7s. As No. 298.

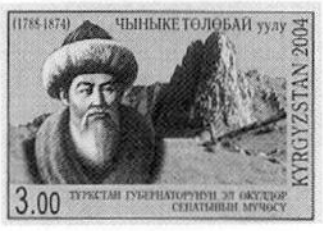

92 Chynykei Biy

2004. Chynykei Biy Commemoration.

305	**92**	3s. chocolate and black	50	40

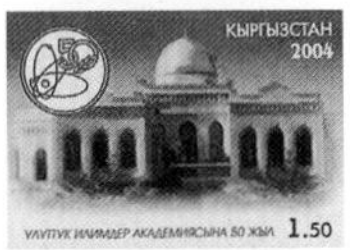

93 Original Academy Building

2004. 50th Anniv of National Academy of Sciences. Multicoloured.

306	1s.50 Type **93**	25	20
307	3s.60 Modern Academy building	60	45

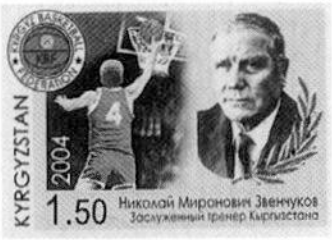

94 Nikolay Zvenchukov

2004. Basketball. Multicoloured.

308	1s.50 Type **94**	25	20
309	3s.60 Kubat Karabekov	60	45

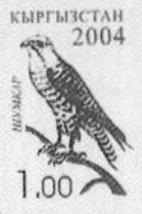

95 Falcon

2004

309a		50t. blue	15	10
309b		60t. violet	15	10
310	**95**	10t. green	15	10
311	**95**	50t. blue	15	10
311a	**95**	50t. blue	15	10
312	**95**	60t. violet	15	10
320	**95**	1s. brown	25	20
321	**95**	1s. claret	25	20
323	**95**	3s. brown	75	50

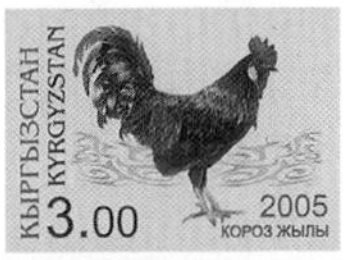

96 Rooster

2005. New Year. Year of the Rooster.

330	**96**	3s. multicoloured	80	65

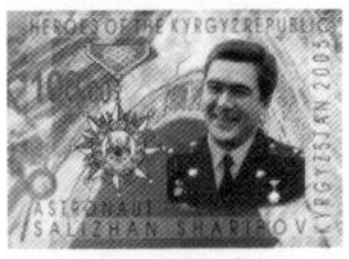

97 Salizhan Sharipov

2005. Salizhan Sharipov (cosmonaut). Sheet 100×70 mm.

MS331 **97**	100s. multicoloured	10·50	10·00

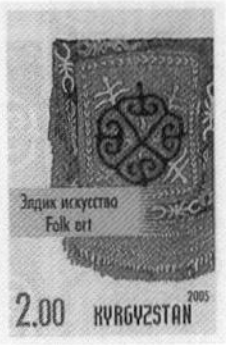

98 Carpet

2005. National Museum of Graphic Arts. Multicoloured.

332	2s. Type **98**	15	10
333	3s.60 Carpet with border	20	15
334	7s. Cloth with orange border and red central design	50	40
335	12s. Black and white cloth	90	75
336	15s. Saddle	1·20	1·00
337	20s. Pots	1·40	1·30
MS338	70×100 mm. 40s. multicoloured cloth (detail)	4·00	3·75

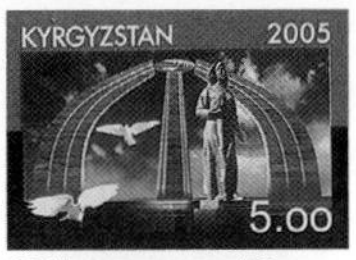

99 Monuments and Doves

2005. 60th Anniv of End of World War II.

339	**99**	5s. multicoloured	40	30

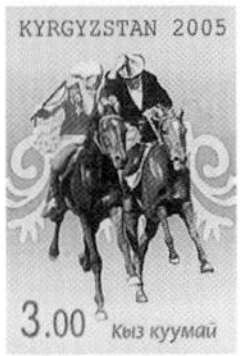

100 Horse Riders

2005. National Games (Kyz Kuumai).

340	**100**	3s. multicoloured	35	25

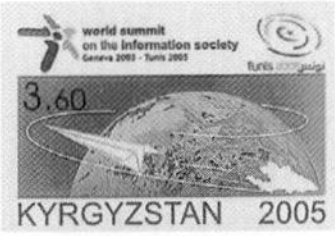

101 Paper Aeroplane, Globe and Kyrgyzstan Map

2005. World Information Society Summit, Tunis.

341	**101**	3s.60 multicoloured	40	30

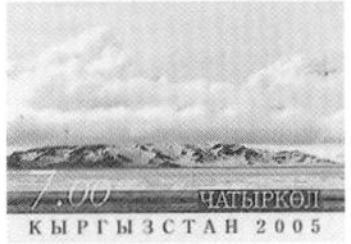

102 Chatyrul Lake

2005. Lakes. Sheet 109×83 mm containing T **102** and similar horiz designs. Multicoloured.

MS342	7s. Type **102**; 20s. Sonkul; 25s. Sarychelek; 30s. Issykkul	7·50	7·25

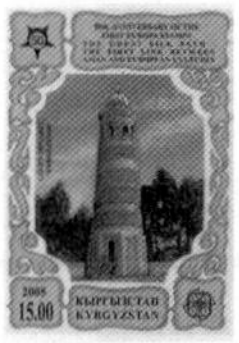

103 Minaret, Uzgen

2005. 50th Anniv of Europa Stamps. Multicoloured.

343	15s. Type **103**	1·00	90
344	20s. Acropolis, Athens	1·40	1·30
345	25s. Buran tower	2·10	1·90
346	60s. Tash Rabat	3·50	3·50
347	85s. St. Mark's Basilica, Italy	6·50	6·25
MS348	134×130 mm. Nos. 343/7. Perf or imperf	17·00	16·00

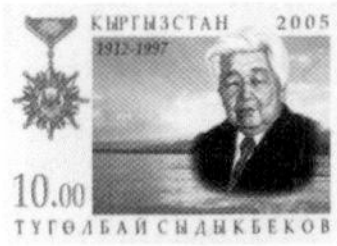

104 Tugolbai Sydykbekov

2006. Tugolbai Sydykbekov (writer) Commemoration.

349	**104**	10s. multicoloured	80	65

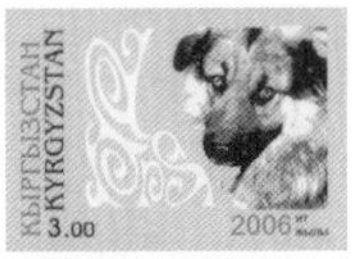

105 Dog

2006. New Year. Year of the Dog.

350	**105**	3s. multicoloured	40	30

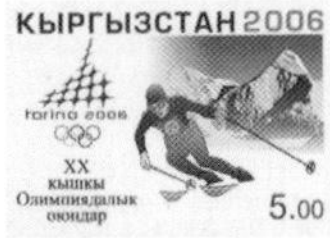

106 Skier

2006. Winter Olympic Games, Turin.

351	**106**	5s. multicoloured	40	20

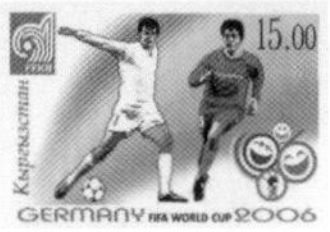

107 Players

2006. World Cup Football Championship, Germany.

352	**107**	15s. multicoloured	1·80	80

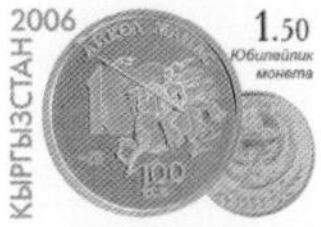

108 100s. Gold Coin (Manas millenary) (2000)

2006. Commemorative Coins. Multicoloured.

353	1s.50 Type **108**	10	10
354	3s. 10s. silver coin (showing horseman (Manas millenary) (1995)	20	10
355	16s. 100s. coin showing Sule-iman-Toho and the Davan Horses petroglyphs (3000th anniv of Osh) (2001)	1·00	80
356	20s. 10s. coin showing mountains (10th anniv of Independence and International Year of Mountains)	1·40	1·20
357	24s. 10s. coin showing edelweiss (International Year of Mountains) (2002)	2·00	1·80
358	28s. 10s. coin showing mountain arkhar (sheep) (International Year of Mountains) (2002)	2·30	2·10
359	30s. 10s. coin showing coins (10th anniv of national currency) (2003)	2·40	2·20
360	40s. 10s. coin showing head of a tiger, Turgesh coin and tower of Burana (statehood) (2003)	2·75	2·50
361	45s. 10s. coin showing woman, yurt and Victory Memorial (60th anniv of end of World War II) (2005)	2·75	2·50
362	50s. 10s. coin showing Tashrabat (Great Silk road) (2005)	3·00	2·75

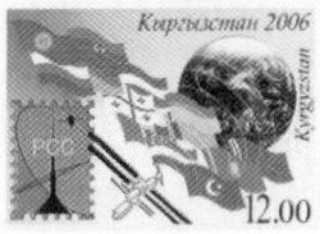

109 Symbols of Communications

2006. 15th Anniv of RCC (Regional Commonwealth of Communications).

363	**109**	12s. multicoloured	90	70

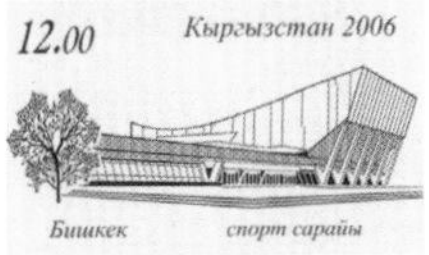

110 Palace of Sport

2006. Architecture of Bishkek. Sheet 125×80 mm containing T **110** and similar horiz design. Each black on stone.

MS364	12s.×4, Type **110**; Theatre; Philharmonic Society building; Museum	3·00	2·75

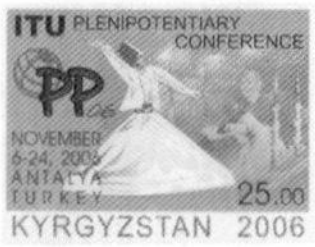

111 Dancer

2006. International Telecommunication Union (ITU) Plenipotentiary Conference, Antalya, Turkey.

365	**111**	25s. multicoloured	2·00	1·80

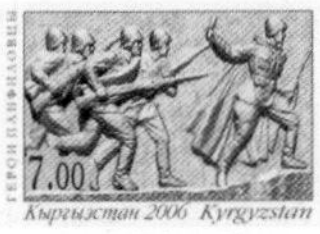

112 Heroes of Panfilovtsy (bas relief)

2006. 65th Anniv of Defence of Moscow.

366	**112**	7s. multicoloured	50	30

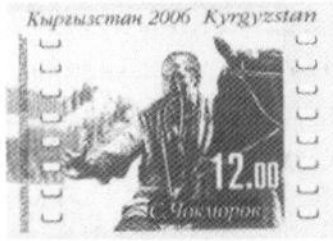

113 Suimenkul Chokmorov

2006. 65th Anniv of National Cinema. T **113** and similar horiz designs showing actors. Each brown and flesh.

MS367	12s.×4, Type **113**; Bolot Bejshenaliev; Tattybyubyu Tursunbaeva; Baken Kydykeeva	3·00	2·75

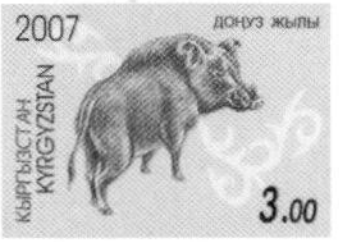

114 Pig

2007. New Year. Year of the Pig.

368	**114**	3s. multicoloured	20	10

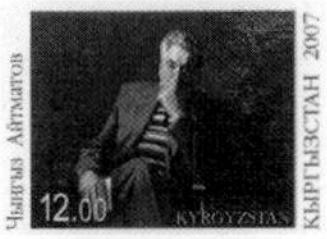

115 *Chingiz Aitmatov*

2007. Art. Sheet 130×70 mm containing Showing portraits. Multicoloured.

MS369	12s.×5, Type **115**; *Syimenkul Chokmorov; Kurmangazy Azykbaev; Omor Sultanov; Zhylkychy Zhakypov*	4·50	4·50

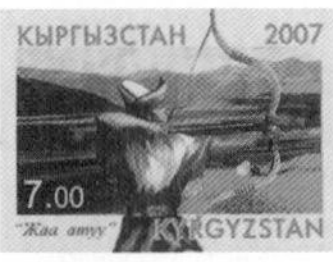

116 Archer

2007. National Sports (1st series).

370	**116**	7s. multicoloured	50	30

See also No. 387.

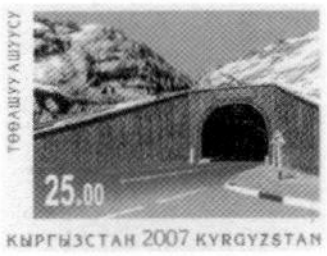

117 Tunnel

2007. 50th Anniv of Bishkek-Osh Highway. Sheet 97×126 mm containing T **117** and similar horiz designs. Multicoloured.

MS371	25s.×4, Type **117**; Highway and lake; Highway and snow-capped mountains; Highway with hills on either side	9·00	9·00

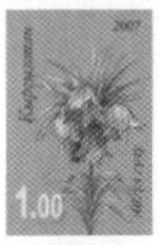

118 Flowers

2007. Aigul (*Pentelium eduardi*).

372	1s. Type **118**	10	10
MS373	67×87 mm. 100s. As No. 372 (30×40 mm)	5·75	5·75

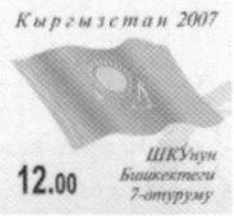

119 Kazakhstan

2007. Shanghai Cooperation Organization Conference. Sheet 95×82 mm containing T **119** and similar horiz designs showing flags of member countries. Multicoloured.

MS374	12s.×6, Type **119**; Kyrgyzstan; China; Russia; Tajikistan; Uzbekistan	5·50	5·50

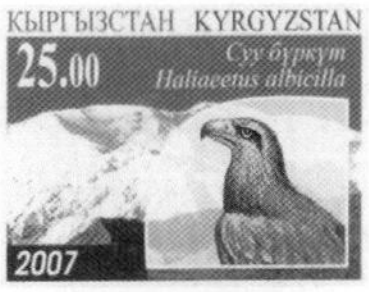

120 *Haliaeetus albicilla* (white-tailed eagle)

2007. Birds of Prey. Sheet 145×85 mm containing T **120** and similar horiz designs. Multicoloured.

MS375	25s.×6, Type **120**; *Falco rusticolus* (gyrfalcon); *Aquila chrysaetus* (golden eagle); *Accipiter gentilis* (goshawk); *Milvus migrans* (black kite); *Falco peregrinus* (peregrine falcon)	13·00	13·00

121 Santa Claus,
Blue Birds and
Letters

2007. Letters to Santa Claus.
376 **121** 3s. multicoloured 20 10

122 Rat

2008. New Year. Year of the Rat.
377 **122** 7s. multicoloured 50 30

123 *Ailuropoda
melanoleuca*
(giant panda)

2008. Fauna. Multicoloured.
378 7s. Type **123** 50 30
379 7s. *Uncia uncia* (snow leopard) 50 30
380 12s. *Ailurus fulgens* (red panda) 90 75
381 12s. *Panthera tigris* (tiger) 90 75
382 16s. *Pygathrix roxellana* (golden
   snub-nosed monkey) 1·00 80
383 16s. *Hystrix cristata* (porcupine) 1·00 80
384 25s. *Ovis ammon* (argali) 2·00 1·80
385 25s. *Felis manul* (Pallas' cat) 2·00 1·80
MS386 128×93 mm. Nos. 378/85 7·75 7·75

It is reported that Nos. 378/MS386 were also issued
imperforate.

124 Horse
Wrestlers

2008. National Sport (2nd series).
387 **124** 5s. multicoloured 40 20

125 Javelin

2008. Olympic Games, Beijing. Multicoloured.
388 20s. Type **124** 1·40 1·20
389 20s. Football 1·40 1·20
390 20s. Wrestling 1·40 1·20
391 20s. Basketball 1·40 1·20

126 Khan Tengri Peak,
Kyrgyzstan

2008. Mountains. Sheet 110×56 mm containing T **126**
and similar vert design. Multicoloured.
MS392 16s.×2, Type **126**; Sabalan
   peak, Iran 2·00 2·00

127 Stamp
Outline,
Mountains and
Postal Emblem

2008. National Postal Service.
393 **127** 1s. multicoloured 10 10
394 **127** 3s. multicoloured 20 10

128 Sabira Kumushalieva

2008. Sabira Kumushalieva (actress) Commemoration.
395 **128** 10s. brown and black 1·20 1·00

129 Absamat Masaliev

2008. Absamat Masaliyevich Masaliyev (politician)
Commemoration.
396 **129** 15s. sepia and black 1·20 1·00

2008. Postal Service. As T **130**.
397 **130** 50t. multicoloured 20 15
398 **130** 7s. multicoloured 70 55

131 Yakovlev Yak-12

2008. Aviation (1st issue). Multicoloured.
MS399 20s.×8, Type **131**; Mil Mi-2;
Antonov An-2; Tupolev Tu-154;
Ilyushin Il-14; Ilyushin Il-18; Antonov
An-24; Mil Mi-4 13·00 13·00

132 Hat

2008. Traditional Hats. Multicoloured.
400 **130** 6s. Type **132** 70 45
401 **130** 7s. With black embroidery and tassel 75 50
402 **130** 12s. With brown embroidery and blue tassel 1·10 90
403 **130** 50s. Quartered hat with
   black highlights 4·25 4·00

133 Yak

2008. Yaks. Multicoloured.
404 25s. Type **133** 1·70 1·50
405 25s. Black horned yak against
   mountains 1·70 1·50
406 25s. Brown horned yak against
   green valley 1·70 1·50
407 25s. Grey yak against mountains 1·70 1·50

134 Isa Akhunbaev

2008. Birth Centenary of Isa Akhunbaev (surgeon).
408 **134** 12s. multicoloured 2·20 1·90

2008. Civil Aviation (2nd issue). Sheet 130×115 mm
containing horiz designs as T **131**. Multicoloured.
MS409 20s.×7, Antonov An-28; Yakov-
lev Yak-40; Antonov An-26;Tupolev
Tu-134; Ilyushin Il-76; Airbus A320;
Mil Mi-8 helicopter 2·50 2·50

2008. Aviation (3rd issue). Multicoloured.
MS410 20s.×7, Antonov An-28;Yakovlev
Yak-40; Antonov An-26;Tupolev
Tu-134; Ilyushin Il-76; Airbus A320;
Mil Mi-8 12·00 12·00

Nos. 411/16 are vacant.

К. Бегалиев жана Р. Түмөнбаев–
XXIX Олимпиаданын жеңүүчүлөрү

(135)

2008
417 **134** 20s. Javelin (388) 1·40 1·20
418 **134** 20s. Football (389) 1·40 1·20

419 **134** 20s. Wrestling (390) 1·40 1·20
420 **134** 20s. Basketball (391) 1·40 1·20

136 Poppy Heads,
Syringe and
Powder

2008. Drug Abuse Awareness Campaign.
421 **136** 12s. multicoloured 90 70

137 Ox

2008. Chinese New Year. Year of the Ox.
422 **137** 25s. multicoloured 2·10 2·00

138 Ishembay
Abdraimov and
Honored Pilot
Medal

2009. Ishembay Abdraimov (test pilot) Commemoration.
423 **138** 10s. multicoloured 75 60

139 Horses and Riders

2009. National Sport (Kok-Boru).
424 **139** 25s. multicoloured 2·00 1·00

140 Bright Bay

2009. The Kyrgyz Horse. Sheet 130×101 mm containing
T **140** and similar horiz designs showing horses.
Multicoloured.
425 16s. Type **140** 1·50 1·30
426 42s. Yellow dun 2·00 1·80
427 50s. Grey 2·20 2·00
428 60s. Bay with four white socks 2·40 2·10
MS429 130×101 mm. Nos. 425/8 8·00 8·00

141 Saker Falcon

2009. Endangered Species. Saker Falcon (*Falco cherrug*).
Designs showing falcons. Multicoloured.
430 10s. Type **141** 75 65
431 15s. On nest 1·00 85
432 25s. In flight 1·60 1·40
433 50s. Adult and chicks 3·00 2·75

142 Woman (*Zhamiyla*)

2009. Chyngyz Aitmatov (writer) Commemoration. Sheet
131×116 mm containing T **142** and similar horiz
designs showing scenes from his writing. Each slate-
grey and scarlet-vermilion.
MS434 7s. Type **142**; 12s. Man and
horse (*Gulsarat*); 16s. Woman and
lorry (*Delbirim*); 21s. Woman and
locomotive (*Samanchynyn Jolu*); 28s.
Man carrying boy (*Birinchi Mughale*);
30s. Boy with binoculars and
stag(*Ak-Keme*); 45s. Horseman and
cranes (*Zrte Zhazdagy Turnalar*); 60s.
Canoe in stormy weather 16·00 16·00

143 Barpy
Alykulov

2009. 125th Birth Anniv of Barpy Alykulov (poet).
435 **143** 16s. multicoloured 1·00 80

144 Building Facade

2009. 75th Anniv of National Library.
436 **144** 12s. multicoloured 95 80

145 Ak-Sai Glacier

2009. Glaciers of Kyrgyzstan. Sheet 130×82 mm
containing T **145** and similar horiz designs showing
glaciers. Multicoloured.
MS437 12s. Type **145**; 16s. Kotur; 21s.
Semenovsky; 28s. Zvezdochka; 45s.
North Inylchek; 60s. South Inylchek 11·00 11·00

146 Railway Station

2009. Railways. Multicoloured.
438 16s. Type **146** 1·50 1·30
439 42s. Diesel train on bridge
   over river 2·00 1·80
440 50s. Locomotive emerging from
   covered way 2·20 2·00
441 60s. Diesel train on bridge over
   roadway 2·40 2·20

147 Children

2010. 50th Anniv of United Nations Declaration of Rights
of the Child
442 **147** 21s. multicoloured 2·10 2·00

148 Tiger

2010. Chinese New Year. Year of the Tiger
443 **148** 25s. multicoloured 2·10 2·00

149 Nordic Skiing

2010. Winter Olympic Games, Vancouver. Multicoloured.
444 21s. Type **149** 1·80 1·60
445 28s. Biathlon 2·00 2·00
446 45s. Skiing 3·75 3·50
447 60s. Snowboarding 2·75 2·50

150 Peonies

2010. Peonies. Multicoloured.

448	25s. Type **150**	2·10	2·00
449	30s. Single flower	2·50	2·20
MS450	144×115 mm. As No. 449	2·50	2·50

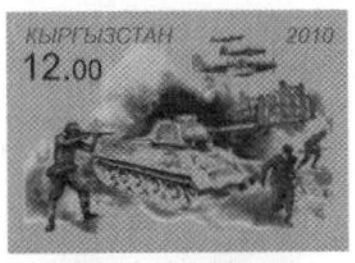

151 Tank and Soldiers

2010. 65th Anniv of End of World War II

451	**151**	12s. multicoloured	95	80

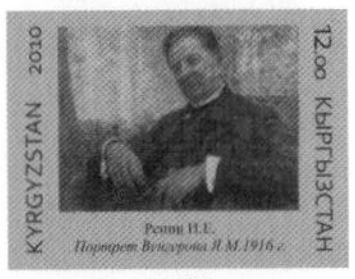

152 Portrait of Vengerov , 1916 (I. E. Repin)

2010. 75th Anniv of National Museum of Art. Multicoloured.

MS452 12s. Type **152**; 16s. *Field of Cabbage* , 1910 (R. R. Falk); 21s. *Still-life on Red Cloth* , 1916 (P. P. Konchalovsky); 24s. *Sea in Crimea* , 1866 (I. K. Aivazovsky); 28s. *Autumn in Jailoo* (autumn in summer pastures), 1945 (S. A. Chuikov); 30s. *Evening in South Kirgizia*, 1967 (G. A. Aitiev); 42s. *Autumn Garden*, 1989 (A. Ignatev); 45s. *By night* , 1971 (D. N. Deimant) 7·00 7·00

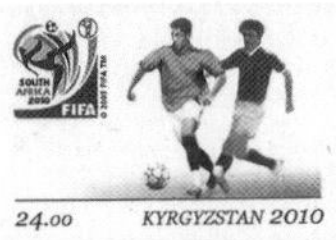

153 Games Emblem and Players

2010. World Cup Football Championships, South Africa. Multicoloured.

453	24s. Type **153**	1·90	1·70
454	30s. World Cup trophy and two players	1·70	1·50
455	42s. Games emblem and two players	2·00	1·80
456	60s. Trophy and goalkeeper	2·40	2·10

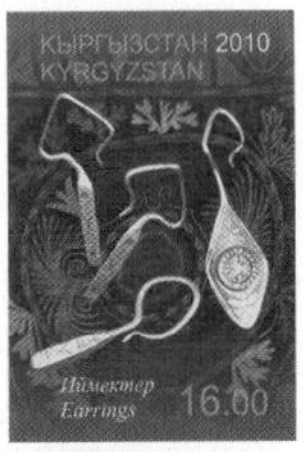

154 Earrings

2010. Jewellery. Multicoloured.

457	16s. Type **154**	1·50	1·30
458	24s. Six buttons	2·30	2·10
459	58s. Bangles	2·40	2·20
460	66s. Hair ornaments	2·50	2·30

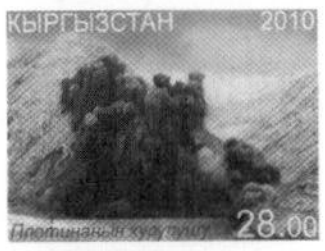

155 Explosion

2010. Hydroelectric Power Station. Multicoloured.

MS461 28s. Type **155**; 42s. Power station in valley; 60s. Building work 4·50 4·50

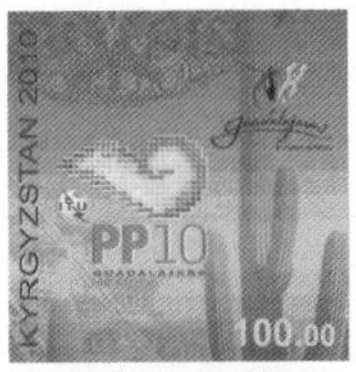

156 Conference Emblem

2010. Plenipotentiary Conference in Mexico

MS462 **156** 100s. multicoloured 7·00 7·00

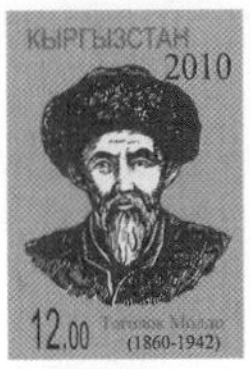

157 Togolok Moldo

2010. 150th Birth Anniversaries. Multicoloured.

463	12s. Type **157**	90	70
464	16s. Murataly Kurenkeev	1·50	1·30
465	21s. Zhenizhok Coco uulu	2·10	1·90

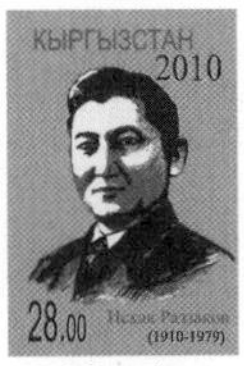

158 I. Razzakov

2010. Birth Centenary of Iskhak Razzakovich Razzakov (politician)

466	**158**	28s. multicoloured	2·20	2·00

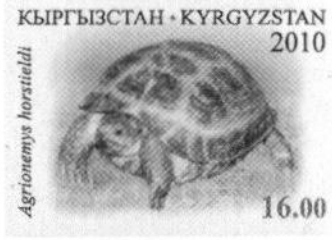

159 *Agrionemys horsfieldi* (inscr 'Agrionemys horstieldi')

2010. Turtles and Tortoises. Multicoloured.

467	16s. Type **159**	1·00	80
468	24s. *Pseudemys scripta*	1·60	1·40
469	48s. *Geochelone elegans*	2·20	2·00
470	72s. *Testudo kleimanni*	3·75	3·50

Pt. 9

LA AGUERA

An administrative district of Spanish Sahara, whose stamps it later used.

1920. Rio de Oro stamps optd **LA AGUERA**.

1	**15**	1c. green	2·75	2·75
2	**15**	2c. brown	2·75	2·75
3	**15**	5c. green	2·75	2·75
4	**15**	10c. red	2·75	2·75
5	**15**	15c. yellow	2·75	2·75
6	**15**	20c. violet	2·75	2·75
7	**15**	25c. blue	2·75	2·75
8	**15**	30c. brown	2·75	2·75
9	**15**	40c. pink	2·75	2·75
10	**15**	50c. blue	9·00	9·00
11	**15**	1p. red	18·00	18·00
12	**15**	4p. purple	50·00	50·00
13	**15**	10p. orange	£110	£110

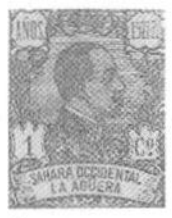

2

1923

14	**2**	1c. blue	1·70	1·10
15	**2**	2c. green	1·70	1·10
16	**2**	5c. green	1·70	1·10
17	**2**	10c. red	1·70	1·10
18	**2**	15c. brown	1·70	1·10
19	**2**	20c. yellow	1·70	1·10
20	**2**	25c. blue	1·70	1·10
21	**2**	30c. brown	1·70	1·10
22	**2**	40c. red	2·40	1·60
23	**2**	50c. purple	6·75	5·00
24	**2**	1p. mauve	14·00	10·50
25	**2**	4p. violet	41·00	30·00
26	**2**	10p. orange	65·00	46·00

Pt. 1

LABUAN

An Island off the N. coast of Borneo, ceded to Great Britain in 1846, and a Crown Colony from 1902. Incorporated with Straits Settlements in 1906, it used Straits stamps till it became part of N. Borneo in 1946.

100 cents = 1 dollar.

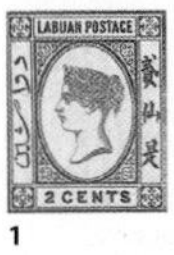

1

1879

17	**1**	2c. green	26·00	42·00
39	**1**	2c. red	6·50	3·50
6	**1**	6c. orange	£130	£140
40	**1**	6c. green	11·00	4·50
7	**1**	8c. red	£130	£130
41	**1**	8c. violet	9·50	16·00
43	**1**	10c. brown	24·00	8·00
9	**1**	12c. red	£300	£375
45	**1**	12c. blue	12·00	6·50
10	**1**	16c. blue	£100	£110
46	**1**	16c. grey	12·00	16·00
47	**1**	40c. orange	23·00	45·00

1880. (a) Surch **8**.

11	8 on 12c. red	£1800	£850

(b) Surch **6 6** or **8 8**.

12	6 on 16c. blue	£3500	£1100
13	8 on 12c. red	£2250	£1200

1881. Surch **EIGHT CENTS**.

14x	8c. on 12c. red	£400	£450

1881. Surch **Eight Cents**.

15	8c. on 12c. red	£140	£150

1883. Manuscript surch **one Dollar A.S.H.**

22	$1 on 16c. blue	£4250	

1885. Surch **2 CENTS** horiz.

23	2c. on 8c. red	£225	£500
24	2c. on 16c. blue	£950	£900

1885. Surch **2 Cents** horiz.

25	2c. on 16c. blue	£110	£160

1885. Surch with large **2 Cents** diag.

26	2c. on 8c. red	75·00	£130

1891. Surch **6 Cents**.

35	6c. on 8c. violet	15·00	13·00
37	6c. on 16c. blue	£2750	£2000
38	6c. on 40c. orange	£12000	£5000

1892. Surch as **Two CENTS** or **Six CENTS**.

49	2c. on 40c. orange	£170	90·00
50	6c. on 16c. grey	£375	£150

Where there are three price columns, prices in the second column are for postally used stamps and those in the third column are for stamps cancelled with black bars.

1894. Types of North Borneo (different colours) optd **LABUAN**.

62	**24**	1c. black and mauve	1·50	12·00
63	**25**	2c. black and blue	2·50	12·00
64a	**26**	3c. black and yellow	15·00	9·00
65a	**27**	5c. black and green	45·00	21·00
67	**28**	6c. black and red	2·50	21·00
69	**29**	8c. black and pink	9·00	29·00
70	**30**	12c. black and orange	23·00	50·00
71	**31**	18c. black and brown	24·00	55·00
74a	**32**	24c. blue and mauve	16·00	50·00
80	-	25c. green (as No. 81)	35·00	42·00
81	-	50c. purple (as No. 82)	35·00	42·00
82	-	$1 blue (as No. 83)	80·00	75·00

1895. No. 83 of North Borneo surch **LABUAN** and value in cents.

75	4c. on $1 red	2·25	3·75
76	10c. on $1 red	8·50	1·40
77	20c. on $1 red	42·00	14·00
78	30c. on $1 red	45·00	60·00
79	40c. on $1 red	45·00	50·00

1896. Jubilee of Cession of Labuan to Gt. Britain. Nos. 62/8 optd **1846 JUBILEE 1896**.

83	**24**	1c. black and mauve	23·00	24·00
84d	**25**	2c. black and blue	50·00	22·00
85	**26**	3c. black and yellow	50·00	22·00
86	**27**	5c. black and green	70·00	16·00
87	**28**	6c. black and red	40·00	27·00
88b	**29**	8c. black and pink	55·00	15·00

1897. Stamps of North Borneo, Nos. 92 to 106 (different colours), optd **LABUAN**. Opt at top of stamp.

89	1c. black and purple	5·50	4·75
90	2c. black and blue	23·00	5·50
91b	3c. black and yellow	9·00	7·00
92a	5c. black and green	55·00	60·00
93b	6c. black and red	12·00	21·00
94a	8c. black and pink	22·00	12·00
95a	12c. black and orange	32·00	50·00

Overprint at foot of stamp.

98a	12c. black and orange (as No. 106)	48·00	50·00

Opt at foot. Inscr "POSTAL REVENUE".

96a	18c. black and bistre (as No. 108)	12·00	45·00

Opt at foot. Inscr "POSTAGE AND REVENUE".

99a	18c. black and bistre (as No. 110)	85·00	60·00

Opt at top. Inscr "POSTAGE AND REVENUE".

101b	18c. black and bistre (as No. 110)	50·00	55·00

Opt at top. "POSTAGE AND REVENUE" omitted.

97a	24c. blue and lilac (as No. 109)	12·00	50·00

Opt at top. Inscr "POSTAGE AND REVENUE".

100	24c. blue and mauve (No. 111)	42·00	60·00

1899. Stamps of Labuan surch **4 CENTS**.

102	4c. on 5c. black & grn (92a)	50·00	26·00
103	4c. on 6c. black & red (93b)	27·00	19·00
104a	4c. on 8c. black and pink (94a)	48·00	32·00
105	4c. on 12c. black and orange (98a)	55·00	35·00
106	4c. on 18c. black and olive (101b)	32·00	18·00
107a	4c. on 24c. blue and mauve (100)	26·00	25·00
108	4c. on 25c. green (80)	6·00	7·50
109	4c. on 50c. purple (81)	8·00	7·50
110	4c. on $1 blue (82)	8·00	7·50

1900. Stamps of North Borneo, as Nos. 95 to 107, optd **LABUAN**.

111	2c. black and green	3·75	2·50
112	4c. black and brown	8·50	60·00
113a	4c. black and red	5·00	14·00
114	5c. black and blue	20·00	20·00
115	10c. brown and grey	55·00	£100
116	16c. green and brown	50·00	£140

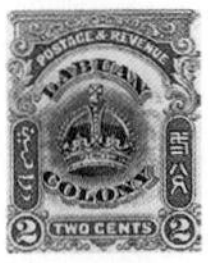

18

1902

117	**18**	1c. black and purple	6·00	7·00
118	**18**	2c. black and green	4·50	6·50
119	**18**	3c. black and brown	3·25	19·00
120	**18**	4c. black and red	3·25	3·50
121	**18**	8c. black and orange	14·00	9·00
122	**18**	10c. brown and blue	3·25	19·00
123	**18**	12c. black and yellow	12·00	21·00
124	**18**	16c. green and brown	4·75	30·00
125	**18**	18c. black and brown	3·25	30·00
126	**18**	25c. green and blue	7·50	24·00
127	**18**	50c. purple and lilac	11·00	50·00
128	**18**	$1 red and orange	8·50	50·00

1904. Surch **4 cents**.

129	4c. on 5c. black and green (92a)	55·00	45·00
130	4c. on 6c. black and red (93b)	12·00	42·00
131	4c. on 8c. black and pink (94a)	25·00	55·00
132	4c. on 12c. black and orange (98a)	30·00	48·00
133	4c. on 18c. black and olive (101b)	23·00	50·00
134a	4c. on 24c. blue and mauve (100)	38·00	40·00
135	4c. on 25c. green (80)	8·50	29·00
136	4c. on 50c. purple (81)	8·50	29·00
137	4c. on $1 blue (82)	10·00	29·00

1904. Nos. 81, 83 and 84/6 of North Borneo optd **LABUAN**.

138	25c. indigo	£1100	†
139	$1 blue	†	†
140	$2 green	£3250	£3250
141	$5 purple	£6000	†
142	$10 brown	£48000	†

Dangerous forgeries exist.

POSTAGE DUE STAMPS

1901. Optd **POSTAGE DUE**.

D1	2c. black and green (111)	23·00	40·00
D2	3c. black and yellow (91)	29·00	£120
D3b	4c. black and red (113)	50·00	£110
D4	5c. black and blue (114)	50·00	£150
D5	6c. black and red (93b)	45·00	£120
D6	8c. black and pink (94a)	95·00	£120
D7b	12c. black and orange (98a)	£120	£170
D8	18c. black and olive (101b)	32·00	£140
D9c	24c. blue and mauve (100)	65·00	£130

Pt. 1

LAGOS

A British colony on the southern coast of Nigeria. United with Southern Nigeria in 1906 to form the Colony and Protectorate of Southern Nigeria.

12 pence = 1 shilling;
20 shillings = 1 pound.

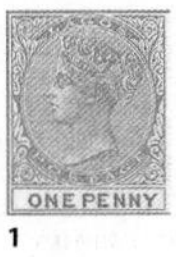

1

1874

21	1	½d. green	2·00	80
17	1	1d. mauve	28·00	21·00
22	1	1d. red	2·00	80
11	1	2d. blue	70·00	13·00
23	1	2d. grey	90·00	8·50
19	1	3d. brown	26·00	7·00
5	1	4d. red	£130	45·00
24	1	4d. violet	£150	8·50
25	1	6d. green	8·00	55·00
26	1	1s. orange	14·00	20·00
27	1	2s.6d. black	£350	£275
28	1	5s. blue	£700	£475
29	1	10s. brown	£1600	£1000

1887

30	2d. mauve and blue	7·00	2·00
31	2½d. blue	7·00	1·75
32	3d. mauve and brown	2·50	3·25
33	4d. mauve and black	2·25	1·75
34	5d. mauve and green	2·00	11·00
35	6d. mauve	4·75	3·00
36	7½d. mauve and red	3·25	30·00
37	10d. mauve and yellow	3·75	13·00
38	1s. green and black	5·50	24·00
39	2s.6d. green and red	23·00	80·00
40	5s. green and blue	45·00	£150
41	10s. green and brown	£110	£250

1893. Surch **HALF PENNY** and bars.

42	½d. on 4d. mauve and black	8·00	2·50

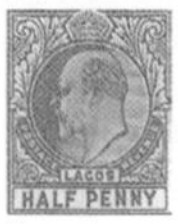

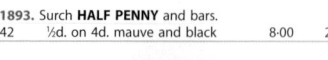

3

1904

44	3	½d. green	2·00	5·50
45	3	1d. purple and black on red	1·00	15
56	3	2d. purple and blue	3·25	2·75
47	3	2½d. purple and blue on blue	1·00	1·50
48	3	3d. purple and brown	2·25	1·75
59a	3	6d. purple and mauve	4·25	1·50
60a	3	1s. green and black	24·00	2·25
61	3	2s.6d. green and red	24·00	70·00
62	3	5s. green and blue	25·00	£100
63a	3	10s. green and brown	90·00	£225

Pt. 21

LAOS

Previously part of French Indo-China, the Kingdom of Laos was proclaimed in 1947. In 1949 it became an Associated State within the French Union and in 1953 it became fully independent within the Union.

Laos left the French Union in 1956. In 1976 it became a Republic.

1951. 100 cents = 1 piastre.
1955. 100 cents = 1 kip.

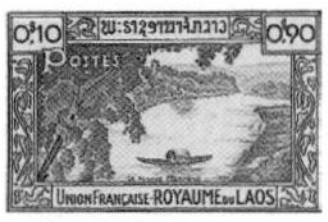

1 River Mekong

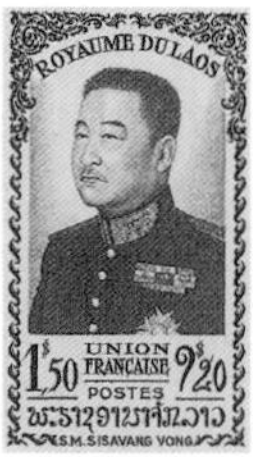

2 King Sisavang Vong

1951

1	1	10c. green and turquoise	35	35
2	1	20c. red and purple	35	35
3	1	30c. blue and indigo	1·50	1·10
4	-	50c. brown and deep brown	35	35
5	-	60c. orange and red	35	35
6	-	70c. turquoise and blue	35	35
7	-	1p. violet and deep violet	75	75
8	2	1p.50 purple and brown	1·10	1·10
9	-	2p. green and turquoise	15·00	5·50
10	-	3p. red and purple	1·10	90
11	-	5p. blue and indigo	1·50	1·10
12	-	10p. purple and brown	2·20	1·50

DESIGNS—As Type **1**: 50c. to 70c. Luang Prabang; 1p. and 2p. to 10p. Vientiane.

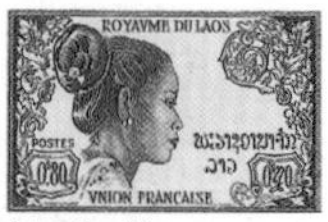

3 Laotian Woman

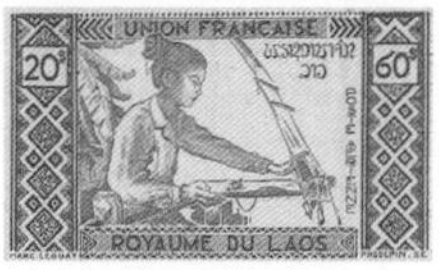

4 Laotian Woman Weaving

1952

13	3	30c. violet and blue (postage)	75	35
14	3	80c. turquoise and green	75	35
15	3	1p.10 red and crimson	75	75
16	3	1p.90 blue and indigo	1·10	1·10
17	3	3p. deep brown and brown	1·10	1·10
18	-	3p.30 violet and deep violet (air)	1·10	75
19	4	10p. green and blue	1·80	1·10
20	4	20p. red and crimson	3·75	2·50
21	4	30p. brown and black	5·50	5·50

DESIGN—As Type **4**: 3p.30, Vat Pra Keo shrine.

1952. Anniv of First Issue of Laos Stamps. Souvenir booklet containing 26 sheets inscr "ROYAUME DU LASO" in French and Laotian. Nos. 1/2, 13/17, 19/21 and D22/7.

MS21b 26 sheets each 130×90 mm £325

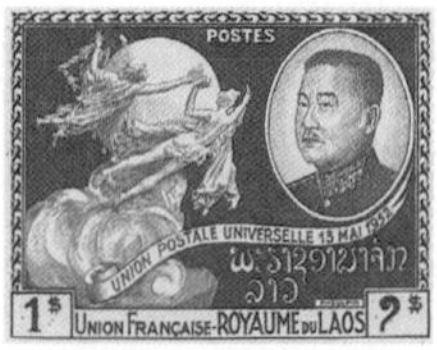

5 King Sisavang Vong and U.P.U. Monument

1952. First Anniv of Admission to U.P.U.

22	5	80c. violet, blue and indigo (postage)	1·10	1·10
23	5	1p. brown, red and lake	1·10	1·10
24	5	1p.20 blue and violet	1·10	1·10
25	5	1p.50 brown, emerald and green	1·10	1·10
26	5	1p.90 turquoise and sepia	1·10	1·10
27	5	25p. indigo and blue (air)	4·50	4·50
28	5	50p. sepia, purple and brown	4·50	4·50

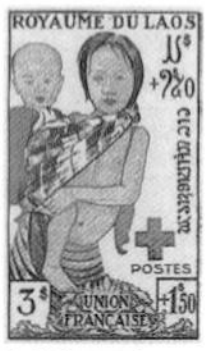

6 Girl carrying her Brother

1953. Red Cross Fund. Cross in red.

29	6	1p.50+1p. purple and blue	2·50	2·50
30	6	3p.+1p.50 red and green	2·50	2·50
31	6	3p.90+2p.50 purple and brn	3·00	3·00

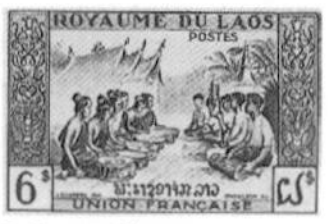

7 Court of Love

1953

32	7	4p.50 turquoise and blue	95	75
33	7	6p. brown and slate	95	75

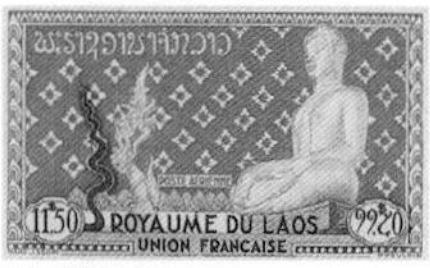

8 Buddha

1953. Air. Statues of Buddha.

34	-	4p. green	95	75
35	-	6p.50 green	1·30	95
36	-	9p. green	1·90	1·30
37	8	11p.50 orange, brown and red	3·00	2·50
38	-	40p. purple	7·00	2·50
39	-	100p. green	13·50	9·50

DESIGNS—HORIZ: 4p. Reclining. VERT: 6p.50, Seated; 9p. Standing (full-face); 40p. Standing (facing right); 100p. Buddha and temple dancer.

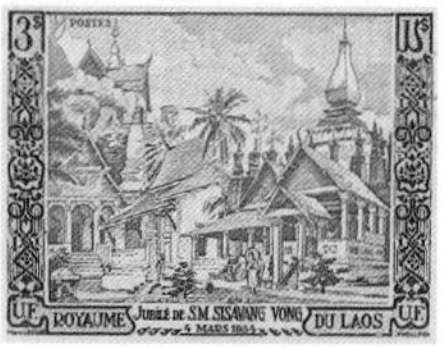

9 Vientiane

1954. Golden Jubilee of King Sisavang Vong.

40	9	2p. violet and blue (postage)	48·00	31·00
41	9	3p. red and brown	48·00	34·00
42	9	50p. turquoise and blue (air)	£150	£150

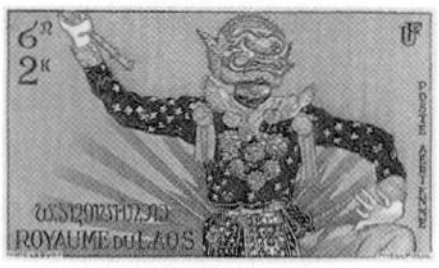

10 Ravana

1955. Air. *Ramayana* (dramatic poem).

43	10	2k. blue, emerald and green	95	75
44	-	4k. red and brown	1·30	1·10
45	-	5k. green, brown and red	2·50	1·50
46	-	10k. black, orange and brown	4·50	3·00
47	-	20k. olive, green and violet	5·50	3·75
48	-	30k. black, brown and blue	7·50	5·25

DESIGNS—HORIZ: 4k. Hanuman, the white monkey; 5k. Ninh Laphath, the black monkey. VERT: 10k. Sita and Rama; 20k. Luci and Ravana's friend; 30k. Rama.

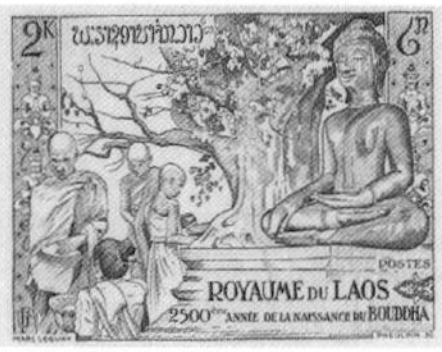

11 Buddha and Worshippers

1956. 2500th Anniv of Buddhist Era.

49	11	2k. brown (postage)	3·00	2·50
50	11	3k. black	3·75	2·50
51	11	5k. sepia	5·50	3·00
52	11	20k. carmine and red (air)	34·00	27·00
53	11	30k. green and bistre	35·00	32·00

Nos. 49/53 were wrongly inscribed as commemorating the birth anniversary of Buddha.

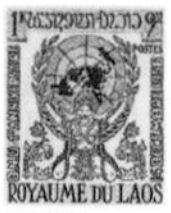

12 U.N. Emblem

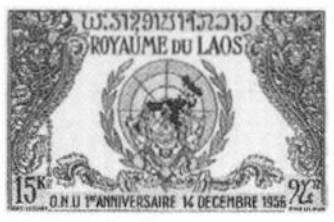

13 U.N. Emblem

1956. First Anniv of Admission to U.N.

54	12	1k. black (postage)	75	60
55	12	2k. blue	95	90
56	12	4k. red	1·30	95
57	12	6k. violet	1·60	1·30
58	13	15k. blue (air)	6·25	6·25
59	13	30k. red	8·75	8·75

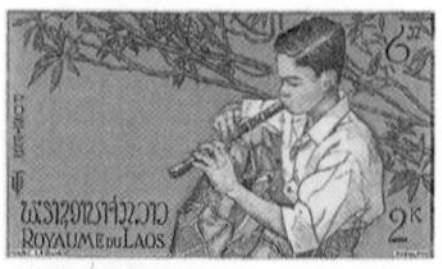

14 Flute Player

1957. Native Musicians.

60	14	2k. multicoloured (postage)	1·80	1·30
61	-	4k. multicoloured	1·80	1·30
62	-	8k. blue, brown and orange	3·25	1·50
63	-	12k. multicoloured (air)	2·50	2·50
64	-	14k. multicoloured	3·00	3·00
65	-	20k. multicoloured	3·75	3·75

DESIGNS—VERT: 4k. Piper; 14k. Violinist; 20k. Drummer. HORIZ: 8k. Xylophonist; 12k. Bells player.

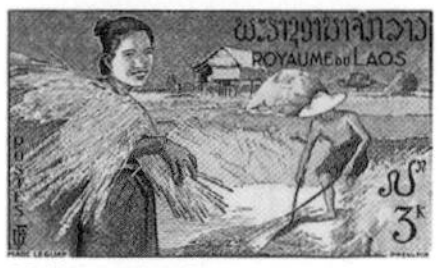

15 Harvesting Rice

1957. Rice Cultivation.

66	15	3k. multicoloured	1·10	60
67	-	5k. brown, red and green	1·10	75
68	-	16k. violet, olive and blue	2·20	1·30
69	-	26k. chocolate, brown and green	3·00	2·20

DESIGNS—VERT: 5k. Drying rice; 16k. Winnowing rice. HORIZ: 26k. Polishing rice.

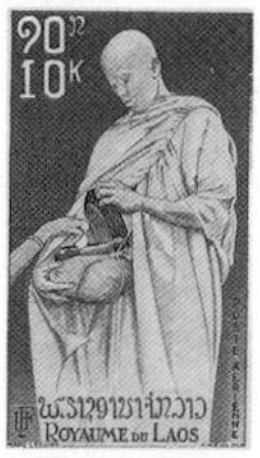

16 "The Offertory"

1957. Air. Buddhism.

70	16	10k. multicoloured	90	90
71	-	15k. brown, yellow & choc	1·30	1·30
72	-	18k. yellow and green	1·60	1·60
73	-	24k. red, black and yellow	3·75	3·75

DESIGNS—As T **16**: HORIZ: 15k. "Meditation" (children on river craft). 48×36½ mm: 24k. "The Great Renunciation" (dancers with horse). VERT: 18k. "Serenity" (head of Buddhist).

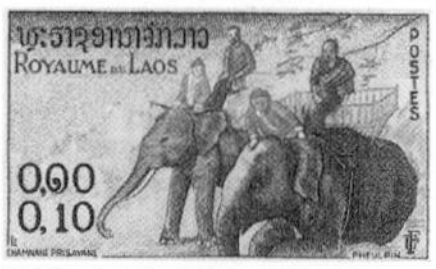

17 Carrier Elephants

1958. Laotian Elephants. Multicoloured.

74	10c. Type **17**	50	35
75	20c. Elephant's head with head-dress	50	35
76	30c. Elephant with howdah (vert)	50	35
77	2k. Elephant hauling log	1·00	35
78	5k. Elephant walking with calf (vert)	2·40	1·10
79	10k. Caparisoned elephant (vert)	3·00	1·10
80	13k. Elephant bearing throne (vert)	4·00	2·20

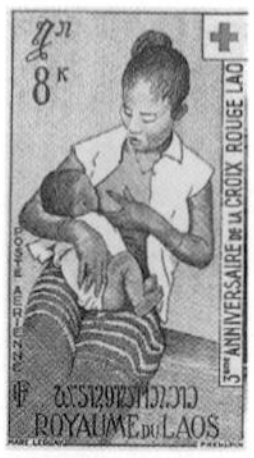

18 Mother and Child

1958. Air. Third Anniv of Laotian Red Cross. Cross in red.

81	18	8k. black and grey	1·10	1·10
82	18	12k. olive and brown	1·10	1·10
83	18	15k. turquoise and green	1·30	1·30
84	18	20k. violet and bistre	1·50	1·50

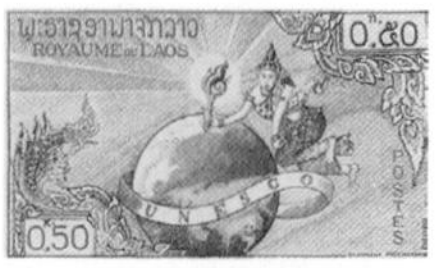

19

1958. Inauguration of UNESCO Headquarters Building, Paris.

85	19	50c. blue, orange and red	35	20
86	-	60c. violet, brown and green	35	20
87	-	70c. blue, brown and red	35	20
88	-	1k. red, blue and bistre	75	45

DESIGNS—VERT: 60c. Woman, children and part of exterior of UNESCO building; 70c. Woman and children hailing UNESCO building superimposed on globe. HORIZ: 1k. General view of UNESCO building and Eiffel Tower.

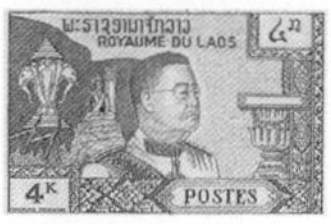

20 King Sisavang Vong

1959

89	20	4k. lake	50	50

90	20	6k.50 red	50	50
91	20	9k. mauve	50	50
92	20	13k. green	75	75

21 Stage Performance

1959. Education and Fine Arts.

93	21	1k. multicoloured	35	20
94	-	2k. lake, violet and black	35	20
95	-	3k. black, green and purple	75	20
96	-	5k. green, yellow and violet	75	45

DESIGNS—VERT: 2k. Student and "Lamp of Learning"; 5k. Stage performers and Buddhist temple. HORIZ: 3k. Teacher and children with "Key to Education".

22 Portal of Vat Phou Temple, Pakse

1959. Laotian Monuments. Multicoloured.

97	-	50c. Type 22	20	15
98	-	1k.50 That Ing Hang, Savannakhet (horiz)	35	20
99	-	2k.50 Vat Phou Temple, Pakse (horiz)	45	35
100	-	7k. That Luang, Vientiane	75	45
101	-	11k. As 7k., but different view (horiz)	80	65
102	-	12k.50 Phou-Si Temple, Luang Prabang	1·10	80

1960. World Refugee Year. Nos. 89 and 79 surch ANNEE MONDIALE DU REFUGIE 1959–1960 and premium.

103	-	4k.+1k. red	3·75	3·75
104	-	10k.+1k. multicoloured	5·50	5·50

24 Plain of Jars, Xieng Khouang

1960. Air. Tourism.

105	24	9k.50 red, bistre and blue	75	75
106	-	12k. brown, violet and green	95	95
107	-	15k. red, green and brown	1·20	1·20
108	-	19k. brown, orange and green	1·40	1·40

DESIGNS—HORIZ: 12k. Phapheng Falls, Champassak; 15k. Pair of bullocks with cart. VERT: 19k. Buddhist monk and village.

25 Funeral Urn

1961. Funeral of King Sisavang Vong.

109	25	4k. bistre, black and red	1·10	1·10
110	-	6k.50 brown and black	1·10	1·10
111	-	9k. brown and black	1·10	1·10
112	-	25k. black	3·00	3·00

DESIGNS: 6k.50. Urn under canopy; 9k. Catafalque on dragon carriage; 25k. King Sisavang Vong.

26 Temples and Statues ("Pou Gneu Nha Gneu")

1962. Air. Festival of Makha Bousa.

113	26	11k. brown, red and green	75	75
114	-	14k. blue and orange	90	90
115	-	20k. green, yellow and mauve	1·30	1·30
116	-	25k. red, blue and green	1·60	1·60

DESIGNS—As T 26: 14k. Bird ("Garuda"); 20k. Flying deities ("Hanuman"). 36×48 mm: 25k. Warriors ("Nang Teng One").

27 King Savang Vatthana

1962

117	27	1k. brown, red and blue	20	20
118	27	2k. brown, red and mauve	45	20
119	27	5k. brown, red and blue	45	35
120	27	10k. brown, red and bistre	80	45

28 Laotian Boy

1962. Malaria Eradication.

121	28	4k. olive, black and green	35	15
122	-	9k. brown, black & turq	45	35
123	-	10k. red, yellow and green	80	45

MS123a 130×100 mm. Nos. 121/2. Imperf £225

DESIGN: 9k. Laotian girl; 10k. Campaign emblem.

29 Royal Courier

1962. Philatelic Exhibition, Vientiane, and Stamp Day.

124	-	50c. multicoloured	50	50
125	-	70c. multicoloured	50	50
126	-	1k. black, green and red	1·10	1·10
127	29	1k.50 multicoloured	90	90

MS127a Two sheets (each 129×100 mm) containing Nos. 124/5 and 126/7 75·00

MS127b As above but imperf 75·00

DESIGNS—HORIZ: 50c. Modern mail transport; 70c. Dancer and globe. VERT: 1k. Royal courtier on elephant.

30 Fisherman

1963. Freedom from Hunger.

128	30	1k. bistre, violet and green	35	20

129	-	4k. blue, brown and green	50	35
130	-	5k. blue, bistre and green	50	45
131	-	9k. blue, green and brown	90	50

MS131a 220×100 mm. Nos. 128/31. Imperf 3·75 3·75

DESIGNS—VERT: 4k. Threshing rice; 9k. Harvesting rice. HORIZ: 5k. Ploughing paddy field.

31 Queen of Laos

1963. Red Cross Centenary.

132	31	4k. red, blue and brown	50	50
133	31	6k. multicoloured	60	60
134	31	10k. red, blue and brown	95	95

MS134a 140×100 mm. Nos. 132/4 4·50 4·50

32 Laotian supporting U.N. Emblem

1963. 15th Anniv of Declaration of Human Rights.

135	32	4k. purple, blue and red	1·30	90

33 Temple, Map and Rameses II

1964. Nubian Monuments Preservation.

136	33	4k. multicoloured	35	35
137	33	6k. multicoloured	50	50
138	33	10k. multicoloured	75	75

MS138a 185×100 mm. Nos. 136/8 (sold at 25k.) 2·75 2·75

34 Offertory Vase and Horn

1964. "Constitutional Monarchy". Multicoloured.

139	-	10k. Type 34	45	20
140	-	15k. Seated Buddha of Vat Pra Keo	50	30
141	-	20k. Laotians walking across map	60	45
142	-	40k. Royal Palace, Luang Prabang	1·10	60

MS142a 140×140 mm. Nos. 139/42 3·75 3·75

35 Phra Vet and Wife

1964. Folklore. Phra Vet Legend. Multicoloured.

143	35	10k. Type 35	45	45
144	-	32k. "Benediction"	65	65
145	-	45k. Phame and wife	95	95
146	-	55k. Arrest of Phame	1·30	1·30

MS146a 140×80 mm. Nos. 143/6. Imperf 6·25 6·25

36 Meo Warrior

1964. "People of Laos".

147	-	25k. black, brown and green (postage)	75	75
148	36	5k. multicoloured (air)	30	15
149	-	10k. pink, grey and green	45	20
150	-	50k. brown, drab and lilac	1·60	90

MS150a 150×115 mm. Nos. 147/50 4·50 5·50

DESIGNS: 10k. Kha hunter; 25k. Girls of three races; 50k. Thai woman.

37 Red Lacewing

1965. Butterflies and Moths.

151	37	10k. chestnut, brown and green (postage)	95	50
152	-	25k. blue, black and yellow	1·90	75
153	-	40k. yellow, brown & green	4·00	1·50
154	-	20k. red and yellow (air)	2·20	1·10

BUTTERFLIES—As Type 37: 25k. Yellow pansy. 48×27 mm: 20k. Atlas moth; 40k. *Dysphania militaris* (moth).

38 Wattay Airport ("French Aid")

1965. Foreign Aid.

155	38	25k. mauve, brown & turq	35	20
156	-	45k. brown and green	50	45
157	-	55k. brown and blue	75	60
158	-	75k. multicoloured	1·10	80

DESIGNS—VERT: 45k. Mother bathing child (water resources: "Japanese Aid"); 75k. School and plants (education and cultivation: "American Aid"). HORIZ: 55k. Studio of radio station ("British Aid").

39 Hophabang

1965

159	39	10k. multicoloured	30	20

40 Teleprinter Operator, Globe and Map

1965. I.T.U. Centenary.

160	40	5k. brown, violet and purple	35	20
161	-	30k. brown, blue and green	50	45
162	-	50k. multicoloured	95	80

MS162a 150×100 mm. Nos. 160/2 2·75 2·75

DESIGNS: 30k. Globe, map, telephonist and radio operator; 50k. Globe, radio receiver and mast.

1965. Nos. 89/90 surch.

163	20	1k. on 4k. lake	15	10
164	20	5k. on 6k.50 brown	20	15

220 Laos

42 Mother and Baby

1965. 6th Anniv of U.N. "Protection of Mother and Child".
MS165a 130×100 mm. No. 165   3·75   3·75

43 Leopard Cat

1965. Air. Laotian Fauna.
166	**43**	25k. yellow, brown & green	45	35
167	-	55k. brown, sepia and blue	75	65
168	-	75k. brown and green	90	80
169	-	100k. brown, black & yell	1·60	1·10
170	-	200k. black and red	3·75	2·50

DESIGNS: 55k. Phayre's flying squirrel; 75k. Javan mongoose; 100k. Chinese porcupine; 200k. Binturong.

44 U.N. Emblem on Map

1965. 20th Anniv of U.N.
171	**44**	5k. blue, grey and green	20	20
172	**44**	25k. blue, grey and mauve	45	35
173	**44**	40k. blue, grey and turquoise	65	65

45 Bulls in Combat

1965. Laotian Pastimes.
174	**45**	10k. brown, black and orange	35	20
175	-	20k. blue, red and green	35	30
176	-	25k. red, blue and green	50	35
177	-	50k. multicoloured	75	60

DESIGNS: 20k. Tikhy (form of hockey); 25k. Pirogue race; 50k. Rocket festival.

46 Slaty-headed Parakeet

1966. Birds.
178	**46**	5k. green, brown and red	50	45
179	-	15k. brown, black & turq	75	50
180	-	20k. sepia, ochre and blue	1·30	90
181	-	45k. blue, sepia and violet	3·00	2·20

BIRDS: 15k. White-crested laughing thrush; 20k. Osprey; 45k. Indian roller (or "blue jay").

47 W.H.O. Building

1966. Inaug of W.H.O. Headquarters, Geneva.
182	**47**	10k. blue and turquoise	35	20
183	**47**	25k. green and red	35	30
184	**47**	50k. black and blue	75	60

MS185 150×100 mm. Nos. 182/4 (sold at 150k.)   16·00   16·00

48 Ordination of Priests

1966. Laotian Ceremonies. Multicoloured.
186		10k. Type **48**	35	20
187		25k. Sand-hills ceremony	45	35
188		30k. "Wax pagoda" procession (vert)	65	45
189		40k. "Sou-Khouan" ceremony (vert)	80	50

49 UNESCO Emblem

1966. 20th Anniv of UNESCO.
190	**49**	20k. orange and black	20	20
191	**49**	30k. blue and black	45	35
192	**49**	40k. green and black	50	45
193	**49**	60k. red and black	75	65

MS194 140×140 mm. Nos. 190/3 (sold at 250k.)   2·75   2·75

50 Letter, Carrier Pigeon and Emblem

1966. International Correspondence Week.
195	**50**	5k. blue, brown and red	20	15
196	**50**	20k. purple, black and green	45	30
197	**50**	40k. brown, red and blue	50	35
198	**50**	45k. black, green and purple	75	60

MS199 130×100 mm. Nos. 195/8 (sold at 240k.)   3·00   3·00

51 Flooded Village

1967. Mekong Delta Flood Relief. Multicoloured.
200		20k.+5k. Type **51**	50	50
201		40k.+10k. Flooded market-place	80	80
202		60k.+15k. Flooded airport	1·30	1·30

MS203 150×100 mm. Nos. 200/2 (sold at 250k.)   4·50   4·50

52 Carving, Siprapouthbat Pagoda

1967. Buddhist Art.
204	**52**	5k. green and brown	20	20
205	-	20k. blue and sepia	45	20
206	-	50k. purple and sepia	95	60
207	-	70k. grey and brown	1·30	90

DESIGNS (carvings in temple pagodas, Luang Prabang): 30k. Visoun; 50k. Xiengthong; 70k. Visoun (different).

53 General Post Office

1967. Opening of New G.P.O. Building, Vientiane.
208	**53**	25k. brown, green and purple	30	15
209	**53**	50k. blue, green and slate	45	35
210	**53**	70k. red, green and brown	75	60

54 Giant Snakehead

1967. Fishes.
211	**54**	20k. black, bistre and blue	50	35
212	-	35k. slate, bistre and blue	60	45
213	-	45k. sepia, ochre and green	1·10	65
214	-	60k. black, bistre and green	1·50	75

DESIGNS: 35k. Giant catfish; 45k. Tire-track spiny eel; 60k. Bronze knifefish.

55 "Cassia fistula"

1967. Flowers.
215	**55**	30k. yellow, green and mauve	50	35
216	-	55k. red, green and orange	75	45
217	-	75k. red, green and blue	1·10	80
218	-	80k. yellow, mauve and green	1·50	90

DESIGNS: 55k. *Cucuma singulario*; 75k. *Poinciana regia*; 80k. *Plumeria acutifolia*.

56 Harvesting

1967. Tenth Anniv of Laotian Red Cross.
219	**56**	20k.+5k. multicoloured	35	35
220	**56**	50k.+10k. multicoloured	75	75
221	**56**	60k.+15k. multicoloured	1·20	1·20

MS222 185×99 mm. Nos. 219/21 (sold at 250k.+30k.)   2·50   2·50

57 Banded Krait

1967. Reptiles.
223	**57**	5k. blue, yellow and green	35	35
224	-	40k. brown, bistre and green	75	60
225	-	100k. chocolate, brown and green	2·75	1·60
226	-	200k. black, brown and green	5·25	3·00

DESIGNS: 40k. Marsh crocodile; 100k. Pit viper; 200k. Water monitor.

58 Human Rights Emblem

1968. Human Rights Year. Emblem in red and green.
227	**58**	20k. green	35	20
228	**58**	30k. brown	35	20
229	**58**	50k. blue	75	50

MS230 190×100 mm. Nos. 227/9 (sold at 250k.)   2·75   2·75

59 Military Parade

1968. Army Day. Multicoloured.
231	**59**	15k. Type **59** (postage)	35	20
232		20k. Soldiers and tank in battle	35	30
233		60k. Soldiers and Laotian flag	65	50

234		200k. Parade of colours before National Assembly building (air)	1·30	90
235		300k. As No. 234	2·10	1·30

MS236 80×110 mm. Nos. 231/5 (sold at 600k.)   5·25   5·25

60 W.H.O. Emblem

1968. 20th Anniv of W.H.O.
237	**60**	15k. brown, red and purple	20	20
238	**60**	30k. brown, green and blue	35	30
239	**60**	70k. brown, purple and red	60	35
240	**60**	110k. light brown, purple and brown	95	75
241	**60**	250k. brown, blue and green	2·20	1·60

MS242 130×115 mm. Nos. 237/41 (sold at 500k.)   5·25   5·25

61 "Chrysochroa mnizechi"

1968. Beetles.
243	**61**	30k. blue, yellow and green (postage)	60	35
244	-	50k. black, orange & purple	95	45
245	-	90k. blue, orange and ochre	1·60	80
246	-	120k. black and orange (air)	1·30	50
247	-	160k. multicoloured	1·90	80

INSECTS—VERT: 50k. *Aristobia approximator*; 90k. *Eutaenia corbetti*. HORIZ: 120k. "*Dorysthenes walkeri*; 160k. *Megaloxantha bicolor*.

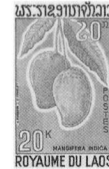

62 "Mangifera indica"

1968. Laotian Fruits.
248	**62**	20k. green, blue and black	35	20
249	-	50k. green, red and blue	50	30
250	-	180k. green, brown and orange	1·80	1·10
251	-	250k. green, brown and yellowl	2·50	1·60

DESIGNS—VERT: 50k. *Tamarindus indica*. HORIZ: 180k. *Artocarpus integrifolia*; 250k. *Citrullus vulgaris*.

63 Hurdling

1968. Olympic Games, Mexico.
252	**63**	15k. green, blue and brown	20	20
253	-	80k. brown, turquoise and blue	60	45
254	-	100k. blue, brown and green	75	50
255	-	110k. brown, red and blue	80	60

DESIGNS: 80k. Tennis; 100k. Football; 110k. High jumping.

64 Oriental Door, Wat Ongtu (detail)

1969. Wat Ongtu Temple.

256	**64**	150k. gold, black and red	1·80	1·10
257	-	200k. gold, black and red	2·40	1·60

DESIGN: 200k. Central door, Wat Ongtu.

65 "Pharak praying to the Gods"

1969. Laotian *Ballet Royal*. Designs showing dance characters. Multicoloured.

258	10k. Type **65** (postage)		35	20
259	15k. "Soukhib ordered to attack"		50	35
260	20k. "Thotsakan reviewing troops"		60	50
261	30k. "Nang Sida awaiting punishment"		95	60
262	40k. "Pharam inspecting his troops"		1·30	75
263	60k. "Hanuman about to rescue Nang Sida"		1·90	1·30
264	110k. "Soudagnou battling with Thotsakan" (air)		2·75	2·20
265	300k. "Pharam dancing with Thotsakkan"		6·25	4·00

MS266 Two sheets, each 106×106 mm. (a) Nos. 258/60, 265 (sold at 650k.); (b) Nos. 261/4 (sold at 480k.). Imperf | 8·75 | 8·75

66 Handicrafts Workshop, Vientiane

1969. Tenth Anniv of I.L.O.

267	**66**	30k. violet and purple (postage)	35	35
268	**66**	60k. brown and green	75	65
269	-	300k. black and brown (air)	4·00	2·75

DESIGN: 300k. Elephants moving logs.

67 Chinese Pangolin

1969. Wild Animals (1st series). Multicoloured.

270	15k. Type **67** (postage)		35	15
271	30k. Type **67**		75	35
272	70k. Sun bear (air)		95	60
273	120k. Common gibbon (vert)		1·80	1·10
274	150k. Tiger		2·40	1·30

See also Nos. 300/3 and 331/5.

68 Royal Mausoleum, Luang Prabang

1969. Tenth Death Anniv of King Sisavang Vong.

275	**68**	50k. ochre, blue and green	75	50
276	-	70k. ochre and lake	75	50

DESIGN: 70k. King Sisavang Vong (medallion).

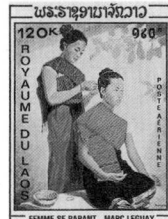

69 Lao Woman being Groomed (Leguay)

1969. Air. Paintings by Marc Leguay (1st series). Multicoloured.

277	10k. Type **69**		1·50	75
278	150k. *Village Market* (horiz)		2·20	1·10

See also Nos. 285, 307/9 and 357/61.

70 Carved Capital, Wat Xiengthong

1970. Laotian Pagodas. Multicoloured.

279	70k. Type **70** (postage)		1·10	75
280	100k. Library, Wat Sisaket (air)		90	35
281	120k. Wat Xiengthong (horiz)		1·30	75

71 "Noon" Drum

1970. Laotian Drums.

282	**71**	30k. mult (postage)	75	60
283	-	55k. black, green and brown	1·10	90
284	-	125k. brown, yellow and flesh (air)	2·20	1·50

DESIGNS—HORIZ: 55k. Bronze drum. VERT: 125k. Wooden drum.

1970. Air. Paintings by Marc Leguay (2nd series). As T **69**. Multicoloured.

285	150k. *Banks of the Mekong* (horiz)		1·80	1·30

72 Franklin D. Roosevelt

1970. Air. 25th Death Anniv of Franklin D. Roosevelt (American statesman).

286	**72**	120k. slate and green	1·80	1·10

73 Lenin explaining Electrification Plan (L. Shmatko)

1970. Birth Centenary of Lenin.

287	**73**	30k. multicoloured	1·30	45
288	**73**	70k. multicoloured	80	60

1970. "Support for War Victims". Nos. 258/65 (*Ballet Royal*) surch **Soutien aux Victimes de la Guerre** and premium.

289	10k.+5k. mult (postage)		45	45
290	15k.+5k. multicoloured		45	45
291	20k.+5k. multicoloured		45	45
292	30k.+5k. multicoloured		45	45
293	40k.+5k. multicoloured		90	90
294	60k.+5k. multicoloured		1·00	1·00
295	110k.+5k. mult (air)		2·20	2·20
296	300k.+5k. multicoloured		3·25	3·25

75 Weaving Silk

1970. "EXPO 70" World Fair, Osaka, Japan. Laotian Silk Industry.

297	**75**	30k. bl, brn & red (postage)	45	30
298	-	70k. multicoloured	90	60
299	-	125k. multicoloured (air)	1·30	90

DESIGNS: 70k. Silk-spinning; 125k. Winding skeins.

76 Wild Boar

1970. Wild Animals (2nd series).

300	**76**	20k. brown and green (postage)	45	20
301	-	60k. brown and olive	90	45
302	-	210k. brown, red and yellow (air)	2·20	1·60
303	-	500k. green, brown and orange	4·50	3·00

ANIMALS: 210k. Leopard; 500k. Gaur.

77 Buddha, U.N. Emblem and New York H.Q.

1970. 25th Anniv of U.N.O.

304	**77**	30k. brown, mauve and blue (postage)	60	35
305	**77**	70k. brown, blue and green	90	50
306	-	125k. multicoloured (air)	1·90	1·10

DESIGN—26×36 mm: 125k. Nang Thorani ("Goddess of the Earth") and New York Headquarters.

1970. Air. Paintings by Marc Leguay (3rd series). As T **69**. Multicoloured.

307	100k. *Village Track*		1·10	50
308	120k. *Paddy-field in the Rainy Season* (horiz)		1·50	60
309	150k. *Village Elder*		1·60	80

78 "Nakhanet"

1971. Laotian Mythology (1st series). Frescoes from Triumphal Arch, Vientiane. Multicoloured.

310	**78**	70k. orange, brown and red (postage)	60	45
311	-	85k. green, yellow and blue	75	50
312	-	125k. multicoloured (air)	1·50	80

DESIGNS: As T **78**: 85k. "Rahu". 49×36 mm: 125k. "Underwater duel between Nang Matsa and Hanuman". See also Nos. 352/4 and 385/7.

79 Silversmiths

1971. Laotian Traditional Crafts. Multicoloured.

313	30k. Type **79**		20	20
314	50k. Potters		35	20
315	70k. Pirogue-builder (49×36 mm)		65	35

80 Laotian and African Children

1971. Racial Equality Year.

316	**80**	30k. blue, red and green	30	20
317	-	60k. violet, red and yellow	50	30

DESIGN: 60k. Laotian dancers and musicians.

81 Buddhist Monk at That Luang

1971. 50th Anniv of Vientiane Rotary Club.

318	**81**	30k. violet, brown and blue	35	20
319	-	70k. grey, red and blue	1·10	50

DESIGN—VERT: 70k. Laotian girl on "Dragon" staircase.

82 "Dendrobium agregatum"

1971. Laotian Orchids. Multicoloured.

320	30k. Type **82** (postage)		75	35
321	40k. *Rynchostylis giganterum*		75	50
322	50k. *Ascocentrum miniatur* (horiz)		1·10	45
323	60k. *Paphiopedilum exul*		1·30	75
324	70k. *Trichoglottis fasciata* (horiz)		1·50	80
325	80k. Cattleya (horiz)		1·60	80
326	125k. Brazilian cattleya (horiz) (air)		3·25	1·10
327	150k. *Vanda teres* (horiz)		3·75	1·30

Nos. 321, 323 and 325 are smaller, 22×36 or 36×22 mm. Nos. 326/7 are larger, 48×27 mm.

83 Dancers from France and Laos

1971. Air. "Twin Cities" of St. Astier (France) and Keng-Kok (Laos).

328	**83**	30k. brown and light brown	20	15
329	**83**	70k. purple and plum	35	15
330	**83**	100k. green and deep green	50	20

84 Common Palm Civet

1971. Wild Animals (3rd series).

331	**84**	25k. black, violet and blue (postage)	50	30
332	**84**	40k. black, green and olive	75	45
333	-	50k. orange and green	1·10	60
334	-	85k. brown, green and emerald	1·80	95
335	-	300k. brown and green (air)	4·00	2·40

DESIGNS: 50k. Lesser Malay chevrotain; 85k. Sambar; 300k. Javan rhinoceros.

85 Laotian Woman (design from 1952 issue)

1971. 20th Anniv of Laotian Stamps.

336	**85**	30k. chocolate, brown and violet (postage)	20	15
337	-	40k. multicoloured	45	20
338	-	50k. black, flesh and blue	60	35
339	-	125k. violet, brn & grn (air)	1·40	90

MS340 180×110 mm. **85** 30k. chocolate, brown and violet; 60k. red and brown; 85k. deep green, green and blue   3·00   3·00

DESIGNS: 36×48 mm—40k. Violinist (1957 issue); 50k. Rama (1965 issue); 125k. "The Offertory" 1957 issue.

86 Sunset on the Mekong

1971. Air. Paintings by Chamnane Prisayane. Multicoloured.

341		125k. Type **86**	1·20	90
342		150k. Quiet Morning at Ban Tane Pieo	1·60	1·10

87 Children reading Book

1972. International Book Year.

343	**87**	30k. green (postage)	20	15
344	-	70k. brown	50	35
345	-	125k. violet (air)	1·10	80

DESIGNS—36×22 mm: 70k. Laotian illustrating manuscript. 48×27 mm: 125k. Father showing manuscripts to children.

88 Nam Ngum Dam and Obelisk

1972. 25th Anniv of U.N. Economic Commission for Asia and the Far East (E.C.A.F.E.). Multicoloured.

346	**88**	40k. Type **88** (postage)	30	20
347	**88**	80k. Type **88**	60	35
348		145k. Lake and spill-way, Nam Ngum Dam (air)	1·10	75

89 The Water-carrier

1972. 25th Anniv of UNICEF Drawings by Lao Schoolchildren. Multicoloured.

349	**89**	50k. Type **89** (postage)	60	35
350		80k. Teaching Bamboo-weaving	75	45
351		120k. Riding a Water-buffalo (air)	1·10	80

90 "Nakharath"

1972. Air. Laotian Mythology (2nd series).

352	**90**	100k. turquoise	75	60
353	-	120k. lilac	95	75
354	-	150k. brown	1·30	90

DESIGNS: 120k. "Nang Kinnali"; 150k. "Norasing".

91 Festival Offerings

1972. Air. That Luang Religious Festival.

355	**91**	110k. brown	75	50
356	-	125k. purple	1·10	75

DESIGN: 125k. Festival procession.

1972. Air. Paintings by Marc Leguay (4th series). As T **69**. Multicoloured.

357		50k. In the Paddy Field (detail)	45	35
358		50k. In the Paddy Field (different detail)	45	35
359		70k. Village in the Rainy Season (detail)	65	45
360		70k. Village in the Rainy Season (different detail)	65	45
361		120k. Laotian Mother	1·50	90

Nos. 357/8 and 359/60 when placed together form the complete painting in each case.

92 Attopeu Religious Costume

1973. Regional Costumes.

362	**92**	40k. yellow, mauve & brown (postage)	45	20
363	-	90k. black, red and brown	95	45
364	-	120k. brown, sepia and mauve (air)	90	60
365	-	150k. ochre, red and brown	1·10	80

DESIGNS: 90k. Phongsaly festival costume; 120k. Luang Prabang wedding costume; 150k. Vientiane evening dress.

93 "Lion" Guardian, That Luang

1973. 55th Anniv of Lions International.

366	**93**	40k. red, purple and bluel (postage)	45	20
367	**93**	80k. red, yellow and blue	75	45
368	-	150k. multicoloured (air)	1·20	90

DESIGN—48×27 mm: 150k. Lions emblems and statue of King Saysetthathirath, Vientiane.

94 Satellite passing Rahu

1973. Traditional and Modern Aspects of Space. Multicoloured.

369		80k. Type **94**	50	35
370		150k. Landing module and Laotian festival rocket	95	50

95 Dr. Gerhard Hansen and Map of Laos

1973. Centenary of Identification of Leprosy Bacillus by Hansen.

371	**95**	40k. purple, deep purple and orange	50	35
372	**95**	80k. purple, brown and yellow& yell	95	45

96 "Benediction"

1973. 25th Anniv of Laotian Boy Scouts Association.

373	**96**	70k. yellow and brown (postage)	65	35
374	-	110k. violet and orange (air)	65	35
375	-	150k. blue, drab and brown	90	50

DESIGNS—48×27 mm: 110k. Campfire entertainment; 150k. Scouts helping flood victims, Vientiane, 1966.

97 "Nang Mekhala". (Goddess of the Sea)

1973. Air. Centenary of World Meteorological Organization.

376	**97**	90k. lilac, red and brown	65	35
377	-	150k. brown, red & lt brn	1·20	50

DESIGN—HORIZ: 150k. "Chariot of the Sun".

99 Interpol H.Q., Paris

1973. 50th Anniv of Int Criminal Police Organization (Interpol).

382	**99**	40k. blue (postage)	30	20
383	**99**	80k. brown and light brown	45	30
384	-	150k. violet, red and green (air)	90	50

DESIGN—48×27 mm: 150k. Woman in opium poppy field.

100 "Phra Sratsvady"

1974. Air. Laotian Mythology (3rd series).

385	**100**	100k. red, brown and lilac	75	45
386	-	110k. brown, lilac and red	95	50
387	-	150k. violet, brown and light brown	1·50	80

DESIGNS: 110k. "Phra Indra"; 150k. "Phra Phrom".

101 Boy and Postbox

1974. Centenary of U.P.U.

388	**101**	70k. brown, green and blue (postage)	50	35
389	**101**	80k. brown, blue and green	60	50
390	-	200k. brown and red (air)	2·20	1·50

DESIGN—48×36 mm: 200k. Laotian girls with letters, and U.P.U. Monument, Berne (Type **105**).

102 Eranthemum nervosum

1974. Laotian Flora.

391	**102**	30k. violet & grn (postage)	50	35
392	-	50k. multicoloured	75	45
393	-	80k. red, green and brown	1·10	75
394	-	500k. green & brown (air)	4·00	2·50

DESIGNS—As T **102**: HORIZ: 50k. Water lily; 80k. Red silk-cotton. 36×36 mm: 500k. Pitcher plant.

103 Mekong Ferry carrying Bus

1974. Laotian Transport.

395	**103**	25k. brown & orge	35	20
396	-	90k. brown and bistre	1·80	90
397	-	250k. brown & green (air)	1·90	1·10

DESIGNS—VERT: 90k. Bicycle rickshaw. HORIZ: 250k. Mekong house boat.

104 Marconi, and Laotians with Transistor Radio

1974. Birth Centenary of Guglielmo Marconi (radio pioneer).

398	**104**	60k. grey, green and brown (postage)	35	20
399	**104**	90k. grey, brown and green	1·80	90
400	-	200k. blue and brown (air)	1·90	1·10

DESIGN: 200k. Communications methods.

105 U.P.U. Monument and Laotian Girls

1974. Air Centenary of U.P.U.

401	**105**	500k. lilac and red	4·50	2·75

MS402 135×105 mm. No. 401   4·50   4·50

For 200k. as T **105** see No. 390.

106 Diastocera wallichi

1974. Beetles.

403	**106**	50k. brown, black and green (postage)	75	45
404	-	90k. black, turquoise and green	1·10	60
405	-	100k. black, orange and brown	1·50	90
406	-	110k. violet, red and green (air)	1·30	50

DESIGNS: 90k. Macrochenus isabellunus; 100k. Purpuricenus malaccensis; 110k. Sternocera multipunctata.

107 Pagoda and Sapphire

1974. "Mineral Riches".

407	**107**	100k. brown, green and blue	75	50
408	-	110k. brown, blue and yellow	90	50

DESIGN: 110k. Gold-panning and necklace.

108 King Savang Vatthana, Prince Souvanna Phouma and Prince Souvanouvong

1975. First Anniv (1974) of Laotian Peace Treaty.

409	**108**	80k. brown, ochre and green	75	35
410	**108**	300k. brown, ochre and purple	1·30	1·10
411	**108**	420k. brown, ochre and turquoise	1·50	1·10

109 Fortune-teller's Chart

1975. Chinese New Year ("Year of the Rabbit").

413	**109**	40k. brown and green	50	20
414	-	200k. black, brown and green	1·30	50
415	-	350k. brown, green and blue	2·40	1·30

DESIGNS—HORIZ: 200k. Fortune-teller. VERT: 350k. Woman riding hare.

110 U.N. Emblem and Frieze

1975. International Women's Year.

416	**110**	100k. blue and turquoise	35	30
417	-	200k. orange and green	75	35
MS418	130×100 mm. Nos. 416/17		4·75	4·75

DESIGN: 200k. IWY emblem.

111 King Savang Vatthana, Prince Souvanna Phouma and Prince Souvanouvong

1975. First Laotian Peace Treaty (2nd issue). Sheet 90×70 mm.

MS419	**111** 2000k. gold, red and green		8·75	8·75

112

1975. "Pravet Sandone" Religious Festival.

420	**112**	80k. multicoloured	50	30
421	-	110k. multicoloured	50	35
422	-	120k. multicoloured	65	45
423	-	130k. multicoloured	1·10	60

DESIGNS: 110k. to 130k. Various legends.

113 Buddha and Stupas

1975. UNESCO Campaign for Preservation of Borobudur Temple (in Indonesia).

424	**113**	100k. green, blue and brown	65	35
425	-	200k. ochre, green and brown	1·30	80
MS426	130×100 mm. Nos. 424/5		1·50	1·50

DESIGN: 200k. Temple sculptures.

114 Laotian Arms

1976. Multicoloured, background colour given.

427	**114**	1k. blue	15	15
428	**114**	2k. mauve	15	15
429	**114**	5k. green	20	15
430	**114**	10k. violet	45	35
431	**114**	200k. orange	3·00	2·20
MS432	165×70 mm. Nos. 427/31		11·00	11·00

115 Thathiang, Vien-Tran

1976. Pagodas. Multicoloured.

433		1k. Type **115**	15	15
434		2k. Phonsi, Luang Prabang	20	15
435		30k. Type **115**	75	50
436		80k. As 2k.	1·50	1·10
437		100k. As 2k.	2·20	1·50
438		300k. Type **115**	3·75	2·75
MS439	Two sheets, each 113×75 mm. (a) Nos. 433, 435 and 438; (b) Nos. 434 and 436/7		8·00	8·00

116 Silversmith

1977. Laotian Crafts. Multicoloured.

440		1k. Type **116**	10	10
441		2k. Weaver	15	10
442		20k. Potter	75	20
443		50k. Basket-weaver (vert)	1·30	45
MS444	Four sheets, 90×81 mm (d) or 81×90 mm (others). (a) No. 440×2; (b) No. 441×2; (c) No. 442×2; (d) No. 443×2		11·00	11·00

117 Gubarev, Grechko and "Salyut" Space Station

1977. 60th Anniv of Russian Revolution. Multicoloured.

445		5k. Type **117**	10	10
446		20k. Lenin	20	15
447		50k. As 20k.	50	30
448		60k. Type **117**	60	45
449		100k. Government Palace, Vientiane, and Kremlin, Moscow (horiz)	1·00	75
450		250k. As 100k.	2·40	1·90
MS451	Two sheets, each 141×81 mm. (a) Nos. 445, 447 and 450; (b) Nos. 446 and 448/9		8·75	8·75

118 Laotian Arms

1978

452	**118**	5k. yellow and black	15	15
453	**118**	10k. sepia and black	15	15
454	**118**	50k. purple and black	50	15
455	**118**	100k. green and black	95	50
456	**118**	250k. violet and black	1·90	1·10

119 Soldiers with Flag

1978. Army Day. Multicoloured.

457		20k. Type **119**	15	15
458		40k. Soldiers attacking village (horiz)	20	15
459		300k. Anti-aircraft guns	1·80	1·10

120 Marchers with Banner

1978. National Day. Multicoloured.

460		20k. Type **120**	35	15
461		50k. Women with flag	35	15
462		400k. Dancer	2·20	1·50
MS463	Two sheets, each 160×105 mm, each containing Nos. 460/2, arranged from left (a) 20, 50, 400k.; (b) 400, 50, 20k. Imperf		8·75	8·75

121 Printed Circuit and Map of Laos

1979. World Telecommunications Day.

464	**121**	30k. orange, brown and silver	15	10
465	-	250k. multicoloured	1·50	80

DESIGN: 250k. Printed circuit, map of Laos and transmitter tower.

122 Woman posting Letter

1979. 15th Anniv of Asian-Oceanic Postal Union. Multicoloured.

466		5k. Type **122**	10	10
467		10k. Post Office counter	10	10
468		80k. As 10k.	80	35
469		100k. Type **122**	95	50

123 Children playing Ball

1979. International Year of the Child (1st issue). Multicoloured. Without gum.

470		20k. Type **123**	20	15
471		50k. Children at school (horiz)	45	15
472		200k. Mother feeding child	2·20	80
473		500k. Nurse immunising child	6·25	1·80
MS474	215×110 mm. Nos. 470/3. Imperf		15·00	15·00

See also Nos. 479/MS482.

124 Elephant, Buffalo and Pirogues

1979. Transport. Multicoloured.

475		5k. Type **124**	15	15
476		10k. Buffalo carts	15	15
477		70k. As No. 476	75	20
478		500k. Type **124**	2·75	1·50

125 Dancing Child

1979. International Year of the Child (2nd issue). Multicoloured. Without gum.

479		100k. Children playing musical instruments (horiz)	50	35

480		200k. Child releasing dove	95	75
481		600k. Type **125**	3·25	1·80
MS482	189×109 mm. Nos. 479/81. Imperf		12·50	12·50

126 Forest and Paddy Field

1980. Fifth Anniv of Republic (1st issue) and 25th Anniv of People's Front. Multicoloured. Without gum.

483		30c. Type **126**	15	15
484		50c. Classroom and doctor examining baby (horiz)	35	15
485		1k. Three women	50	35
486		2k. Dam and electricity pylons (horiz)	1·30	1·10
MS487	170×99 mm. Nos. 483/6. Imperf		8·75	7·50

127 Lenin Reading

1980. 110th Birth Anniv of Lenin. Multicoloured.

488		1k. Type **127**	20	15
489		2k. Lenin writing	45	20
490		3k. Lenin and Red Flag (vert)	60	35
491		4k. Lenin making speech (vert)	1·10	50
MS492	136×95 mm. Nos. 488/91. Imperf		4·50	4·50

128 Workers in Field

1980. Fifth Anniv of Republic (2nd issue). Multicoloured. Without gum.

493		50c. Type **128**	15	10
494		1k.60 Loading logs on lorry and elephant hauling logs	35	15
495		4k.60 Veterinary workers tending animals	75	30
496		5k.40 Workers in paddy field	1·10	45
MS497	207×165 mm. Nos. 193/6. Imperf		8·75	7·50

129 Emblems of Industry, Technology, Transport, Sport and Art

1981. 26th P.C.U.S. (Communist Party) Congress. Multicoloured.

498		60c. Type **129**	15	10
499		4k.60 Communist star breaking manacles and globe	1·50	45
500		5k. Laurel branch and broken bomb	2·10	50
MS501	140×106 mm. Nos. 498/500 (sold at 15k.)		6·25	4·00

130 Giant Pandas

1981. "Philatokyo 81" International Stamp Exhibition, Tokyo. Sheet 90×60 mm.

MS502	**130** 10k. multicoloured		5·50	2·20

131 Player heading Ball

1981. World Cup Football Championship, Spain (1982) (1st issue). Multicoloured.

503	1k. Type **131**		15	10
504	2k. Receiving ball		35	15
505	3k. Passing ball		50	15
506	4k. Goalkeeper diving for ball (horiz)		80	15
507	5k. Dribbling		1·10	35
508	6k. Kicking ball		1·60	45

See also Nos. 545/50.

132 Disabled Person on Telephone

1981. International Year of Disabled Persons. Multicoloured.

509	3k. Type **132**		1·10	35
510	5k. Disabled teacher		1·30	75
511	12k. Person in wheelchair mending net		3·25	1·10

133 Wild Cat

1981. Wild Cats. Multicoloured.

512	10c. Type **133**		15	15
513	20c. Fishing cat		15	15
514	30c. Caracal		15	15
515	40c. Clouded leopard		15	15
516	50c. Flat-headed cat		15	15
517	9k. Jungle cat		3·25	65

134 Dish Aerial and Flag

1981. Sixth National Day Festival. Multicoloured.

518	3k. Type **134**		45	30
519	4k. Soldier and flag		65	35
520	5k. Girls presenting flowers to soldier, flag and map of Laos		95	45

135 Indian Elephant

1982. Indian Elephant. Multicoloured.

521	1k. Type **135**		20	15
522	2k. Elephant carrying log		50	15
523	3k. Elephant with passengers		65	20
524	4k. Elephant in trap		90	30
525	5k. Elephant and young		1·20	35
526	5k.50 Herd of elephants		1·50	50

136 Laotian Wrestling

1982. Wrestling.

527	**136**	50c. multicoloured	15	15
528	-	1k.20 multicoloured	15	15
529	-	2k. multicoloured	35	15
530	-	2k.50 multicoloured	60	20
531	-	4k. multicoloured	95	35
532	-	5k. multicoloured	1·50	50

DESIGNS: 1k.20 to 5k. Various wrestling scenes.

137 *Nymphaea zanzibariensis*

1982. Water Lilies. Multicoloured.

533	30c. Type **137**		15	15
534	40c. *Nelumbo nucifera* "Gaertn Rose"		15	15
535	60c. *Nymphaea rosea*		15	15
536	3k. *Nymphaea nouchali*		65	35
537	4k. *Nymphaea* White		95	35
538	7k. *Nelumbo nucifera* "Gaertn White"		1·90	45

138 Barn Swallow

1982. Birds. Multicoloured.

539	50c. Type **138**		15	15
540	1k. Hoopoe		15	15
541	2k. River kingfisher		50	15
542	3k. Black-naped blue monarch		75	20
543	4k. Grey wagtail (horiz)		1·00	20
544	10k. Long-tailed tailor bird (horiz)		2·50	75

139 Football

1982. World Cup Football Championship, Spain (2nd issue).

545	**139**	1k. multicoloured	20	15
546	-	2k. multicoloured	35	15
547	-	3k. multicoloured	50	15
548	-	4k. multicoloured	75	20
549	**139**	5k. multicoloured	95	30
550	-	6k. multicoloured	1·30	45

MS551 81×63 mm. 15k. multicoloured (footballer and flag) (36×28 mm) 3·50 1·30

DESIGNS: 2, 3, 4, 6, 15k. Various football scenes.

140 "Herona marathus"

1982. Butterflies. Multicoloured.

552	1k. Type **140**		20	15
553	2k. *Neptis paraka*		45	15
554	3k. *Euripus halitherses*		65	20
555	4k. *Lebadea martha*		95	20
556	5k. *Iton semamora* (42×26 mm)		1·50	35
557	6k. Common palm fly (59×41 mm)		1·80	45

141 Buddhist Temple, Vientiane

1982. "Philexfrance 82" International Stamp Exhibition, Paris. Sheet 86×64 mm.

MS558 **141** 10k. multicoloured 2·75 1·30

142 River Raft

1982. River Craft. Multicoloured.

559	50c. Type **142**		15	15
560	60c. River sampan		15	15
561	1k. River house boat		20	15
562	2k. River passenger steamer		50	15
563	3k. River ferry		65	20
564	8k. Self-propelled barge		1·60	50

143 Vat Chanh

1982. Pagodas. Multicoloured.

565	50c. Type **143**		15	15
566	60c. Vat Inpeng		15	15
567	1k. Vat Dong Mieng		20	15
568	2k. Ho Tay		50	15
569	3k. Vat Ho Pha Keo		65	20
570	8k. Vat Sisaket		1·60	50

1982. Various stamps optd **1982**.

571	**114**	1k. multicoloured		
572	**116**	1k. multicoloured		
573	-	2k. multicoloured (441)		
574	**117**	5k. multicoloured		
575	**118**	5k. yellow and black		
576	**122**	5k. multicoloured		
577	**124**	5k. multicoloured		
578	-	10k. multicoloured (467)		
579	-	10k. multicoloured (476)		
580	-	20k. multicoloured (446)		
581	**119**	20k. multicoloured		
582	**121**	30k. orange, brown & sil		
583	-	40k. multicoloured (458)		
584	-	50k. multicoloured (443)		
585	-	70k. multicoloured (477)		
586	-	80k. multicoloured (468)		
587	**122**	100k. multicoloured		
588	**114**	200k. multicoloured		
589	**121**	250k. multicoloured		

145 Poodle

1982. Dogs. Multicoloured.

591	50c. Type **145**		15	15
592	60c. Samoyed		15	15
593	1k. Boston terrier		20	15
594	2k. Cairn terrier		65	15
595	3k. Chihuahua		90	35
596	8k. Bulldog		2·40	60

146 Woman watering Crops

1982. World Food Day. Multicoloured.

597	7k. Type **146**		1·30	45
598	8k. Woman transplanting rice		1·50	50

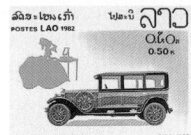

147 Fiat, 1925

1982. Cars. Multicoloured.

599	50c. Type **147**		15	15
600	60c. Peugeot, 1925		15	15
601	1k. Berliet, 1925		30	15
602	2k. Ballot, 1925		60	15
603	3k. Renault, 1926		90	35
604	8k. Ford, 1925		1·80	60

148 President Souphanouvong

1982. Seventh Anniv of Republic. Multicoloured.

605	50c. Type **148**		15	15
606	1k. Tractors (horiz)		20	15
607	2k. Cow (horiz)		30	15
608	3k. Lorry passing dish aerial (horiz)		50	20
609	4k. Nurse examining child		75	35
610	5k. Classroom (horiz)		1·00	35
611	6k. Dancer		1·50	45

149 Dimitrov, Flag and Arms of Bulgaria

1982. Birth Centenary of Georgi Dimitrov (Bulgarian statesman).

612 **149** 10k. multicoloured 1·60 90

150 Kremlin and Arms of U.S.S.R.

1982. 60th Anniv of U.S.S.R. Multicoloured.

613	3k. Type **150**		50	35
614	4k. Doves and maps of U.S.S.R. and Laos		95	50

MS615 96×92 mm. Nos. 613/14 3·25 1·30

151 Hurdling

1983. Olympic Games, Los Angeles (1984) (1st issue). Multicoloured.

616	50c. Type **151**		15	15
617	1k. Javelin		20	15
618	2k. Basketball		30	15
619	3k. Diving		50	15
620	4k. Gymnastics		75	35
621	10k. Weightlifting		2·20	75

MS622 91×62 mm. 15k. Football (31×39 mm) 3·25 1·30

See also Nos. 708/**MS**715.

152 Bucking Horse

1983. Horses. Multicoloured.

623	50c. Type **152**		15	15
624	1k. Rearing black horse		20	15
625	2k. Trotting brown horse		35	15

626	3k. Dappled grey horse	65	20
627	4k. Wild horse crossing snow	80	30
628	10k. Horse in paddock	2·50	75

153 St. Catherine of Alexandria

1983. 500th Birth Anniv of Raphael (artist). Multicoloured.

629	50c. Type 153	15	15
630	1k. Adoration of the Kings	20	15
631	2k. Madonna of the Grand Duke	35	15
632	3k. St. George and the Dragon	65	20
633	4k. The Vision of Ezekiel	80	30
634	10k. Adoration of the Kings (different)	2·50	75
MS635	74×123 mm. 10k. Coronation of the Virgin (39×31 mm)	3·00	90

154 A. Gubarev (Soviet) and V. Remek (Czechoslovak)

1983. Cosmonauts. Multicoloured.

636	50c. Type 154	15	15
637	50c. P. Klimuk (Soviet) and Miroslaw Hermaszewski (Polish)	15	15
638	1k. V. Bykovsky (Soviet) and Sigmund Jahn (East German)	20	15
639	1k. Nikolai Rukavishnikov (Soviet) and Georgi Ivanov (Bulgarian)	20	15
640	2k. V. Kubasov (Soviet) and Bertalan Farkas (Hungarian)	35	15
641	3k. V. Dzhanibekov (Soviet) and Gurragchaa (Mongolian)	60	20
642	4k. L. Popov (Soviet) and D. Prunariu (Rumanian)	75	20
643	6k. Soviet cosmonaut and Arnaldo Tamayo (Cuban)	1·10	35
644	10k. Soviet and French cosmonauts	2·20	75
MS645	92×90 mm. 10k. V. Gorbatko (Soviet) and Pham Tuan (Vietnamese) (28×35 mm)	2·50	90

155 Jacques Charles's Hydrogen Balloon, 1783

1983. Bicentenary of Manned Flight. Multicoloured.

646	50c. Type 155	15	15
647	1k. Blanchard and Jeffries' balloon, 1785	20	15
648	2k. Vincenzo Lunardi's balloon (London–Ware flight), 1784	35	15
649	3k. Modern hot-air balloon over city	75	20
650	4k. Massed balloon ascent, 1890	90	35
651	10k. Auguste Piccard's stratosphere balloon F.N.R.S., 1931	2·50	75
MS652	100×83 mm. 10k. Balloon Double Eagle II (312×39 mm)	2·50	95

156 German Maybach Car

1983. "Tembal 83" Stamp Exhibition, Basle. Sheet 95×72 mm.

MS653	156 10k. multicoloured	3·00	95

157 Dendrobium sp.

1983. Flowers. Multicoloured.

654	1k. Type 157	20	15
655	2k. Aerides odoratum	35	15
656	3k. Dendrobium aggregatum	60	20
657	4k. Dendrobium	75	20
658	5k. Moschatum	1·00	30
659	6k. Dendrobium sp. (different)	1·50	45

158 Downhill Skiing

1983. Winter Olympic Games, Sarajevo (1984) (1st issue). Multicoloured.

660	50c. Type 158	15	15
661	1k. Slalom	20	15
662	2k. Ice hockey	35	15
663	3k. Speed skating	65	20
664	4k. Ski jumping	80	30
665	10k. Luge	2·20	75
MS666	91×57 mm. 15k. Bobsleigh (39×31 mm)	3·25	1·10

See also Nos. 696/MS703.

183 Motor Cycle

1983. "Bangkok 1983" International Stamp Exhibition. Sheet 93×72 mm.

MS667	159 10k. multicoloured	2·50	90

160 Clown Knifefish

1983. Fish of Mekong River. Multicoloured.

668	1k. Type 160	20	15
669	2k. Common carp	35	15
670	3k. Lesser Mekong catfish	65	20
671	4k. Giant barb	75	20
672	5k. Black shark	1·20	30
673	6k. Nile mouthbrooder	1·60	45

161 Magellan and Vitoria

1983. Explorers and their Ships. Multicoloured.

674	1k. Type 161	20	15
675	2k. Jacques Cartier and Grande Hermine	35	15
676	3k. Columbus and Santa Maria	75	20
677	4k. Pedro Alvares Cabral and El Ray	90	20
678	5k. Cook and H.M.S. Resolution	1·10	30
679	6k. Charcot and Pourquoi-pas?	1·60	45

No. 679 is wrongly inscribed "Cabot".

162 Tabby Cat

1983. Domestic Cats. Multicoloured.

680	1k. Type 162	20	15
681	2k. Long-haired Persian	75	15
682	3k. Siamese	65	20
683	4k. Burmese	80	20
684	5k. Persian	1·20	30
685	6k. Tortoiseshell	1·60	45

1983. Nos. 430 and 466 optd **1983**.

685a	122 5k. multicoloured		
685b	114 10k. multicoloured		

163 Marx, Book, Sun and Signature

1983. Death Centenary of Karl Marx. Multicoloured.

686	1k. Marx, dove, globe and flags	30	15
687	4k. Type 163	1·00	15
688	6k. Marx and flags	1·80	50

164 Elephant dragging Log

1983. Eighth Anniv of Republic. Multicoloured.

689	1k. Type 164	30	15
690	4k. Cattle and pig (horiz)	1·00	15
691	6k. Crops	1·80	50

165 Carrier Pigeon and Telex Machine

1983. World Communications Year. Multicoloured.

692	50c. Type 165	15	15
693	1k. Early telephone, handset and receiver	20	15
694	4k. Television tube and aerial	90	30
695	6k. Satellite and dish aerial	1·50	50

166 Ice Skating

1984. Winter Olympic Games, Sarajevo (2nd issue). Multicoloured.

696	50c. Type 166	15	15
697	1k. Speed skating	20	15
698	2k. Biathlon	35	15
699	3k. Luge (horiz)	90	30
700	4k. Downhill skiing (horiz)	95	30
701	5k. Ski jumping	1·30	45
702	6k. Slalom	1·60	50
MS703	89×55 mm. 10k. Ice hockey (31×39 mm)	2·50	90

167 Tiger

1984. Endangered Animals. The Tiger. Multicoloured.

704	25c. Type 167	35	15
705	25c. Tigers (horiz)	35	15
706	3k. Tiger and cubs (horiz)	4·00	50
707	4k. Tiger cubs	6·25	1·00

168 Diving

1984. Olympic Games, Los Angeles (2nd issue). Multicoloured.

708	50c. Type 168	15	15
709	1k. Volleyball	30	15
710	2k. Running	60	15
711	4k. Basketball	1·20	15
712	5k. Judo	1·30	30
713	6k. Football	1·80	35
714	7k. Gymnastics	2·10	45
MS715	98×81 mm. 10k. Wrestling (31×39 mm)	2·50	90

169 Tuned Drums

1984. Musical Instruments. Multicoloured.

716	1k. Type 169	20	15
717	2k. Xylophone	45	15
718	3k. Pair of drums	80	20
719	4k. Hand drum	1·00	30
720	5k. Barrel drum	1·30	30
721	6k. Pipes and string instrument	2·10	45

170 National Flag

1984. National Day. Multicoloured.

722	60c. Type 170	20	15
723	1k. National arms	45	15
724	2k. As No. 723	60	20

171 Chess Game

1984. 60th Anniv of World Chess Federation. Multicoloured.

725	50c. Type 171	15	15
726	1k. Renaissance game from The Three Ages of Man (miniature attr. to Estienne Porchier)	20	15
727	2k. Woman teaching girls	50	15
728	2k. Margrave Otto IV of Brandenburg playing chess with his wife	50	15
729	3k. Four men at chessboard	90	30
730	4k. Two women playing	1·30	30
731	8k. Two men playing	2·75	45
MS732	87×70 mm. 10k. Human chess game (31×39 mm)	2·50	90

Nos. 725, 727 and 729/31 show illustrations from King Alfonso X's Book of Chess, Dice and Tablings.

172 Cardinal Nino de Guevara (El Greco)

1984. "Espana 84" International Stamp Exhibition, Madrid. Multicoloured.

733	50c. Type 172	15	15
734	1k. Gaspar de Guzman, Duke of Olivares, on Horseback (Velazquez)	30	15
735	2k. The Annunciation (Murillo)	45	15
736	2k. Portrait of a Lady (Zurbaran)	45	15
737	3k. The Family of Charles IV (Goya)	65	30
738	4k. Two Harlequins (Picasso)	95	30

173 Adonis aestivalis

| 739 | 8k. Abstract (Miro) | 1·90 | 45 |

MS740 63×80 mm. 10k. Burial of the Count of Orgaz (El Gerco) — 2·50 90

1984. Woodland Flowers. Multicoloured.

741	50c. Type 173	15	15
742	1k. Alpinia speciosa	20	15
743	2k. Cassia lechenaultiana	45	15
744	2k. Aeschynanthus speciosus	45	15
745	3k. Datura meteloides	75	30
746	4k. Quamoclit pennata	95	30
747	8k. Commelina benghalensis	1·90	45

174 Nazzaro

1984. 19th Universal Postal Union Congress Philatelic Salon, Hamburg. Cars. Multicoloured.

748	50c. Type 174	15	15
749	1k. Daimler	20	15
750	2k. Delage	45	15
751	2k. Fiat "S 57/14B"	45	15
752	3k. Bugatti	90	30
753	4k. Itala	1·30	30
754	8k. Blitzen Benz	2·40	45

MS755 79×52 mm. 10k. Winton "Bullet" — 2·50 95

175 Madonna and Child

1984. 450th Death Anniv of Correggio (artist). Multicoloured.

756	50c. Type 175	15	15
757	1k. Detail showing horsemen resting	30	15
758	2k. Madonna and Child (different)	50	15
759	2k. Mystical Marriage of St. Catherine	50	15
760	3k. Four Saints	75	30
761	4k. Noli me Tangere	1·10	30
762	8k. Christ bids Farewell to the Virgin Mary	2·20	45

MS763 80×107 mm. 10k. Madonna and Child (different) (31×39 mm) — 3·25 95

176 "Luna 1"

1984. Space Exploration. Multicoloured.

764	50c. Type 176	15	15
765	1k. "Luna 2"	20	15
766	2k. "Luna 3"	45	15
767	2k. Kepler and "Sputnik 2"	45	15
768	3k. Newton and Lunokhod 2	95	20
769	4k. Jules Verne and "Luna 13"	1·30	35
770	8k. Copernicus and space station	2·40	60

177 Malaclemys Terrapin

1984. Reptiles. Multicoloured.

771	50c. Type 177	15	15
772	1k. Banded krait	20	15
773	2k. Indian python (vert)	45	15
774	2k. Reticulated python	45	15
775	3k. Tokay gecko	95	20
776	4k. Natrix subminiata (snake)	1·30	35
777	8k. Dappled ground gecko	2·50	60

178 Greater Glider

1984. "Ausipex 84" International Stamp Exhibition, Melbourne. Marsupials. Multicoloured.

778	50c. Type 178	15	15
779	1k. Platypus	30	15
780	2k. Southern hairy-nosed wombat (Lasiorhinus latifrons)	45	15
781	2k. Tasmanian devil (Sarcophilus harrisii)	45	15
782	3k. Thylacine	95	20
783	4k. Tiger cat	1·20	35
784	8k. Wallaby	2·10	60

MS785 95×58 mm. 10k. Red kangaroo (31×39 mm) — 2·50 90

179 Nurse with Mother and Child

1984. Anti-poliomyelitis Campaign. Multicoloured.

| 786 | 5k. Type 179 | 1·10 | 50 |
| 787 | 6k. Doctor inoculating child | 1·30 | 50 |

180 Dragon Stair-rail

1984. Laotian Art. Multicoloured.

788	50c. Type 180	15	15
789	1k. Capital of column	20	15
790	2k. Decorative panel depicting god	35	15
791	2k. Decorative panel depicting leaves	35	15
792	3k. Stylized leaves (horiz)	75	20
793	4k. Triangular flower decoration (horiz)	1·30	35
794	8k. Circular lotus flower decoration	2·40	60

181 River House Boats

1984. Ninth Anniv of Republic. Multicoloured.

795	1k. Type 181	45	15
796	2k. Passengers boarding Fokker Friendship airliner	65	20
797	4k. Building a bridge	1·30	60
798	10k. Building a road	2·75	1·20

182 Players with Ball

1985. World Cup Football Championship, Mexico (1986) (1st issue). Multicoloured.

799	50c. Type 182	15	15
800	1k. Heading the ball	20	15
801	2k. Defending the ball	60	15
802	3k. Running with ball	90	15
803	4k. Taking possession of ball	1·30	30
804	5k. Heading the ball (different)	1·60	35
805	6k. Saving a goal	1·90	60

MS806 56×72 mm. 10k. Flag, player and ball (31×39 mm) — 2·75 90

See also Nos. 868/MS875.

183 Motor Cycle

1985. Centenary of Motor Cycle. Multicoloured.

807	50c. Type 183	15	15
808	1k. Gnome Rhone, 1920	20	15
809	2k. F.N. "M67C", 1928	50	15
810	3k. Indian "Chief", 1930	75	15
811	4k. Rudge Multi, 1914	1·10	30
812	5k. Honda "Benly J", 1953	1·30	35
813	6k. CZ, 1938	1·60	60

1985. Various stamps optd 1985.

813a	-	40k. multicoloured (458)		
813b	-	50k. multicoloured (443)		
813c	-	50k. multicoloured (447)		
813d	-	70k. multicoloured (477)		
813e	-	80k. multicoloured (468)		
813f	-	100k. multicoloured (449)		
813g	122	100k. multicoloured		
813h	114	200k. multicoloured		
813i	-	250k. multicoloured (450)		
813j	118	250k. violet and black		
813k	121	250k. multicoloured		
813m	-	300k. multicoloured (459)		

184 Fly Agaric

1985. Fungi. Multicoloured.

814	50c. Type 184	15	15
815	1k. Cep	20	15
816	2k. Shaggy ink cap (Coprinus comatus)	50	15
817	2k. The blusher (Amanita rubescens)	50	15
818	3k. Downy boletus	1·00	30
819	4k. Parasol mushroom	1·60	35
820	8k. Brown roll-rim	2·75	65

184a Battle Plan, Kursk, and Tanks

1985. 40th Anniv of End of Second World War. Multicoloured.

820a	1k. Type 184a	35	15
820b	2k. Monument and military parade, Red Square, Moscow	65	15
820c	4k. Street battle and battle plan, Stalingrad	1·30	35
820d	5k. Battle plan and Reichstag, Berlin	1·60	45
820e	6k. Soviet Memorial, Berlin-Treptow, and military parade at Brandenburg Gate	1·90	50

185 Lenin reading "Pravda"

1985. 115th Birth Anniv of Lenin. Multicoloured.

821	1k. Type 185	35	15
822	2k. Lenin (vert)	60	15
823	10k. Lenin addressing meeting (vert)	2·50	75

186 Cattleya percivaliana

1985. "Argentina '85" International Stamp Exhibition, Buenos Aires. Orchids. Multicoloured.

824	50c. Type 186	15	15
825	1k. Odontoglossum luteo-purpureum	20	15
826	2k. Cattleya lueddemanniana	45	15
827	2k. Maxillaria sanderiana	45	15
828	3k. "Miltonia vexillaria	75	20
829	4k. Oncidium varicosum	1·00	30
830	8k. Cattleya dowiana	2·20	60

MS831 82×63 mm. 10k. Catasetum fimbriatum (31×39 mm) — 3·00 95

187 Rhesus Macaque

1985. Mammals. Multicoloured.

832	2k. Type 187	30	15
833	3k. Kouprey	60	15
834	4k. Porcupine (horiz)	90	30
835	5k. Asiatic black bear (horiz)	1·10	30
836	10k. Chinese pangolin	2·40	60

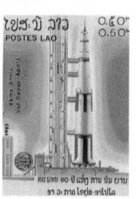
188 "Saturn" Rocket on Launch Pad

1985. Tenth Anniv of "Apollo"–"Soyuz" Space Link. Multicoloured.

837	50c. Type 188	15	15
838	1k. Soviet rocket on launch pad	30	15
839	2k. "Apollo" approaching "Soyuz 19" (horiz)	45	15
840	2k. "Soyuz 19" approaching "Apollo" (horiz)	45	15
841	3k. "Apollo" and crew T. Stafford, V. Brand and D. Stayton (horiz)	75	20
842	4k. "Soyuz 19" and crew A. Leonov and V. Kubasov (horiz)	1·00	30
843	8k. "Apollo" and "Soyuz 19" docked (horiz)	2·10	60

189 Fiat Biplane

1985. "Italia '85" International Stamp Exhibition, Rome. Multicoloured. (a) Aircraft. As T 189.

844	50c. Type 189	15	15
845	1k. Cant Z.501 Gabbiano flying boat	20	15
846	2k. Marina Fiat MF.5 flying boat	45	15
847	3k. Macchi Castoldi MC-100 flying boat	65	20
848	4k. Anzani biplane	90	30
849	5k. Ambrosini biplane	95	30
850	6k. Piaggio P-148	1·30	45

MS851 86×54 mm. 10k. Marina Fiat MF.4 flying boat (39×31 mm) — 2·50 1·00

(b) Columbus and his Ships. Size 40×29 mm.

852	1k. Pinta	20	15
853	2k. Nina	45	15
854	3k. Santa Maria	65	20
855	4k. Christopher Columbus	90	30
856	5k. Map of Columbus's first voyage	1·10	35

190 U.N. and National Flags on Globe

1985. 40th Anniv of U.N.O. Multicoloured.

857	2k. Type 190	65	20
858	3k. U.N. emblem and Laotian arms on globe	95	30
859	10k. Map on globe	2·75	95

191 Woman feeding Child

1985. Lao Health Services. Multicoloured.

860	1k. Type **191**		20	15
861	3k. Red Cross nurse injecting child (horiz)		80	15
862	4k. Red Cross nurse tending patient (horiz)		1·00	30
863	10k. Mother breast-feeding baby		2·20	75

192 Soldier, Workers and Symbols of Industry and Agriculture

1985. Tenth Anniv of Republic. Multicoloured.

864	3k. Type **192**	65	20
865	10k. Soldier, workers and symbols of transport and communications	2·50	90

193 Soldier with Flag and Workers

1985. 30th Anniv of Lao People's Revolutionary Party. Multicoloured.

866	2k. Type **193**	90	15
867	8k. Soldier with flag and work-ers (different)	2·75	60

194 Footballers

1986. World Cup Football Championship, Mexico (2nd issue).

868	**194**	50c. multicoloured	15	15
869	-	1k. multicoloured	20	15
870	-	2k. multicoloured	45	15
871	-	3k. multicoloured	65	20
872	-	4k. multicoloured	75	20
873	-	5k. multicoloured	95	30
874	-	6k. multicoloured	1·30	35
MS875	92×92 mm. 10k. multicoloured (39×31 mm)		3·75	90

DESIGNS: 1k. to 10k. Various football scenes.

194a Cosmonaut, "Mir" Space Complex and Earth

1986. 17th Soviet Communist Party Congress. Multicoloured.

875a	4k. Type **194a**	1·00	30
875b	20k. Lenin and Red Flag	4·00	95

195 "Pelargonium grandiflorum"

1986. Flowers. Multicoloured.

876	50c. Type **195**		15	15
877	1k. Columbine		20	15
878	2k. Fuchsia globosa		45	15
879	3k. Crocus aureus		65	20
880	4k. Hollyhock		75	20
881	5k. Gladiolus purpureo		95	30
882	6k. Hyacinthus orientalis		1·30	35

196 Aporia hippia

1986. Butterflies. Multicoloured.

883	50c. Type **196**		15	15
884	1k. Euthalia irrubescens		20	15
885	2k. Japonica lutea		45	15
886	3k. Pratapa ctesia		65	20
887	4k. Leaf butterfly		75	20
888	5k. Yellow orange-tip		95	30
889	6k. Chestnut tiger		1·30	35

197 Rocket launch at Baikanur Space Centre

1986. 25th Anniv of First Man in Space. Multicoloured.

890	50c. Type **197**		15	15
891	1k. "Molniya" communications satellite		30	15
892	2k. "Salyut" space station (horiz)		45	15
893	3k. Yuri Gagarin, "Sputnik 1" and rocket debris (horiz)		80	15
894	4k. "Luna 3" and Moon		1·10	20
895	5k. Vladimir Komarov on first space walk		1·60	35
896	6k. "Luna 16" lifting off from Moon		1·80	45
MS897	88×66 mm. 10k. "Soyuz" preparing to dock with "Salyut" (39×31 mm)		2·50	90

198 Giraffe

1986. Animals. Multicoloured.

898	50c. Type **198**		15	15
899	1k. Lion		20	15
900	2k. African elephant		45	15
901	3k. Red kangaroo		65	20
902	4k. Koala		90	20
903	5k. Greater flamingo		1·00	30
904	6k. Giant panda		1·80	50
MS905	80×60 mm. 10k. American bison (31×39 mm)		2·50	1·00

199 Boeing 747-100

1986. Air. Aircraft. Multicoloured.

906	20k. Type **199**	3·75	30

907	50k. Ilyushin Il-86	8·75	80

200 Great Argus Pheasant

1986. Pheasants. Multicoloured.

908	50c. Type **200**	15	15
909	1k. Silver pheasant	20	15
910	2k. Common pheasant	45	15
911	3k. Lady Amherst's pheasant	65	20
912	4k. Reeves's pheasant	75	20
913	5k. Golden pheasant	95	30
914	6k. Copper pheasant	1·30	35

201 Scarlet King Snake

1986. Snakes. Multicoloured.

915	50c. Corn snake	15	15
916	1k. Type **201**	20	15
917	1k. Richard's blind snake (vert)	45	15
918	2k. Western ring-necked snake	65	20
919	4k. Mangrove snake	75	20
920	5k. Indian python	95	30
921	6k. Common cobra (vert)	1·30	35

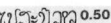

202 Bayeux Tapestry (detail) and Comet Head

1986. Appearance of Halley's Comet. Multicoloured.

922	50c. Comet over Athens (65×21 mm)	15	15
923	1k. Type **202**	20	15
924	2k. Edmond Halley (astrono-mer) and comet tail (20×21 mm)	45	15
925	3k. "Vega" space probe and comet head	65	20
926	4k. Galileo and comet tail (20×21 mm)	75	20
927	5k. Comet head (20×21 mm)	95	30
928	6k. "Giotto" space probe and comet tail	1·30	35
MS929	100×45 mm. 10k. Surface of Earth and comet head (39×31 mm)	2·50	90

Nos. 923/4, 925/6 and 927/8 reseptcnively were issued together, *se-tenant*, each pair forming a composite design.

203 Keeshond

1986. "Stockholmia 86" International Stamp Exhibition. Dogs. Multicoloured.

930	50c. Type **203**	15	15
931	1k. Elkhound (horiz)	20	15
932	2k. Bernese (horiz)	50	15
933	3k. Pointing griffon (horiz)	80	20
934	4k. Collie (horiz)	80	20
935	5k. Irish water spaniel (horiz)	1·00	30
936	6k. Briard (horiz)	1·60	50
MS937	78×60 mm. 10k. Brittany spaniels chasing grey partridge (39×31 mm)	2·50	1·00

204 "Mammillaria matudae"

1986. Cacti. Multicoloured.

938	50c. Type **204**	15	15
939	1k. Mammillaria theresae	20	15
940	2k. Ariocarpus trigonus	45	15
941	3k. Notocactus crassigibbus	65	20
942	4k. Astrophytum asterias hybrid	75	20
943	5k. Melocactus manzanus	95	30
944	6k. Astrophytum ornatum hybrid	1·30	35

205 Arms and Dove on Globe

1986. International Peace Year.

945	**205** 3k. multicoloured	80	20
946	- 5k. black, blue and red	1·30	35
947	- 10k. multicoloured	2·50	90

DESIGNS: 5k. Dove on smashed bomb; 10k. People sup-porting I.P.Y. emblem.

206 Vat Phu Champasak

1987. 40th Anniv of UNESCO. Multicoloured.

948	3k. Type **206**	65	20
949	4k. Dish aerial and map of Laos on globe	90	30
950	9k. People reading books (horiz)	1·80	60

207 Speed Skating

1987. Winter Olympic Games, Calgary (1988) (1st issue). Multicoloured.

951	50c. Type **207**	15	15
952	1k. Biathlon	20	15
953	2k. Figure skating (pairs)	45	15
954	3k. Luge (horiz)	65	20
955	4k. Four-man bobsleigh (horiz)	75	20
956	5k. Ice hockey (horiz)	95	30
957	6k. Ski jumping (horiz)	1·30	35
MS958	78×58 mm. 10k. Skiing (31×39 mm)	2·50	1·00

See also Nos. 1046/**MS**1052.

208 Gymnast and Urn

1987. Olympic Games, Seoul (1988) (1st issue). Sports and Greek Pottery. Multicoloured.

959	50c. Type **208**	15	15
960	1k. Throwing the discus and vase (horiz)	20	15
961	2k. Running and urn	45	15
962	3k. Show jumping and bowl (horiz)	65	20
963	4k. Throwing the javelin and plate	75	20
964	5k. High jumping and bowl with handles (horiz)	95	30
965	6k. Wrestling and urn	1·30	35
MS966	82×55 mm. 10k. Runner leaving blocks (39×31 mm)	2·20	90

See also Nos. 1053/**MS**1060.

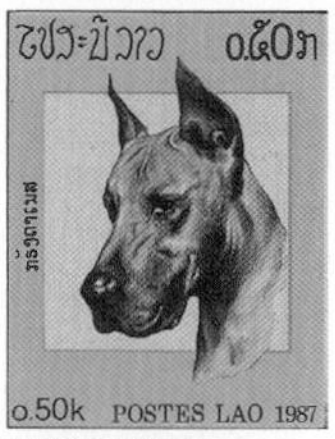

209 Great Dane

1987. Dogs. Multicoloured.

967	50c. Type **209**	15	15
968	1k. Black labrador	20	15
969	2k. St. Bernard	45	15
970	3k. Tervuren shepherd dog	75	20
971	4k. German shepherd	80	20
972	5k. Beagle	1·30	30
973	6k. Golden retriever	1·50	50

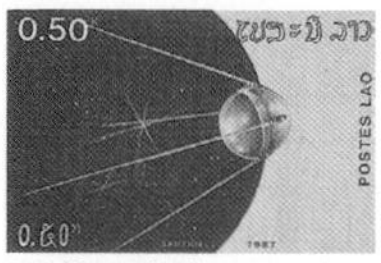

210 "Sputnik 1"

1987. 30th Anniv of Launch of First Artificial Satellite. Multicoloured.

974	50c. Type **210**	15	15
975	1k. "Sputnik 2"	20	15
976	2k. "Cosmos 97"	45	15
977	3k. "Cosmos"	65	20
978	4k. "Mars"	75	20
979	5k. "Luna 1"	95	30
980	9k. "Luna 3" (vert)	1·50	45

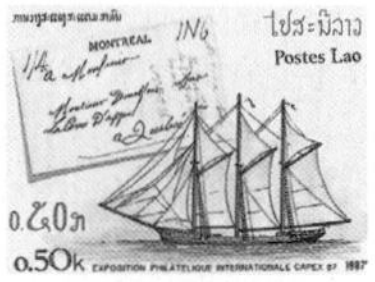

211 "MONTREAL" Handstamp on Letter to Quebec and Schooner

1987. "Capex 87" International Stamp Exhibition, Toronto. Ships and Covers. Multicoloured.

981	50c. Type **211**	15	15
982	1k. "PAID MONTREAL" on letter and schooner	20	15
983	2k. Letter from Montreal to London and *William D. Lawrence* (full-rigged ship)	45	15
984	3k. 1840 letter to Williamsburgh and *Neptune* (steamer)	65	20
985	4k. 1844 letter to London and *Athabasca* (screw-steamer)	75	20
986	5k. 1848 letter and *Chicora* (paddle-steamer)	95	30
987	6k. 1861 letter and *Passport* (river paddle-steamer)	1·30	35
MS988	80×60 mm. 10k. 1949 4c. Canadian stamp (39×31 mm)	2·20	90

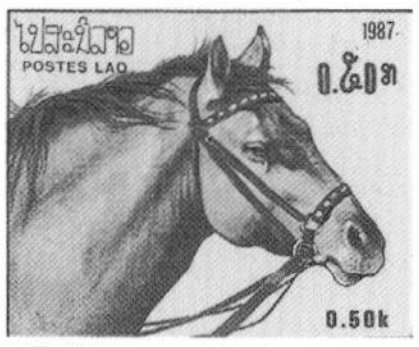

212 Horse

1987. Horses. Multicoloured.

989	50c. Type **212**	15	15
990	1k. Chestnut (vert)	20	15
991	2k. Black horse with sheepskin noseband (vert)	45	15
992	3k. Dark chestnut (vert)	65	20
993	4k. Black horse (vert)	75	20
994	5k. Chestnut with plaited mane (vert)	95	30
995	6k. Grey (vert)	1·30	35

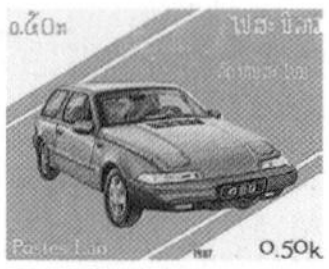

213 Volvo "480"

1987. Motor Cars. Multicoloured.

996	50c. Type **213**	15	15
997	1k. Alfa Romeo "33"	20	15
998	2k. Ford "Fiesta"	45	15
999	3k. Ford "Fiesta" (different)	75	20
1000	4k. Ford "Granada"	80	20
1001	5k. Citroen "AX"	1·30	30
1002	6k. Renault "21"	1·50	50
MS1003	65×52 mm. 10k. Skoda "Estelle" (39×31 mm)	2·75	95

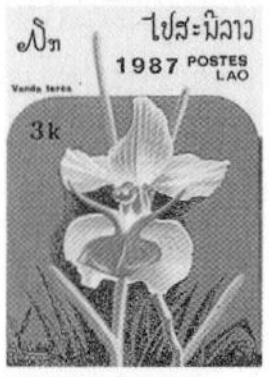

214 *Vanda teres*

1987. Orchids. Multicoloured.

1004	3k. Type **214**	15	15
1005	7k. *Laeliocattleya* sp.	15	15
1006	10k. *Paphiopedilum* hybrid	20	15
1007	39k. *Sobralia* sp.	80	20
1008	44k. *Paphiopedilum* hybrid (different)	90	30
1009	47k. *Paphiopedilum* hybrid (different)	1·00	35
1010	50k. *Cattleya trianaei*	1·20	35
MS1011	52×75 mm. 95k. *Vanda tricolour* (31×39 mm)	2·50	90

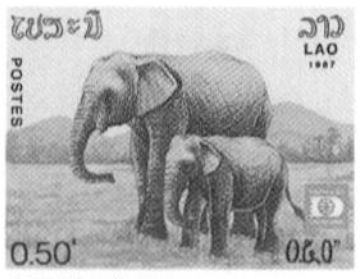

215 Elephants

1987. "Hafnia 87" International Stamp Exhibition, Copenhagen. Elephants. Multicoloured.

1012	50c. Type **215**	15	15
1013	1k. Three elephants	20	15
1014	2k. Elephant feeding	45	15
1015	3k. Elephant grazing on grass	65	20
1016	4k. Adult with calf	75	20
1017	5k. Elephant walking	95	30
1018	6k. Elephant (vert)	1·30	35
MS1019	64×44 mm. 10k. Adults and calf (39×31 mm)	2·20	90

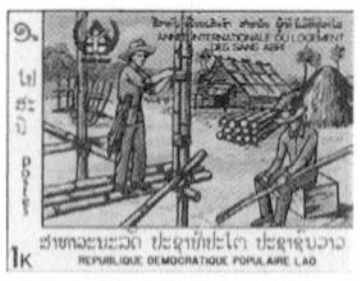

216 Building Bamboo House

1987. International Year of Shelter for the Homeless. Multicoloured.

1020	1k. Type **216**	15	15
1021	27k. Building wooden house	60	20
1022	46k. House on stilts	1·20	30
1023	70k. Street of houses on stilts	1·80	60

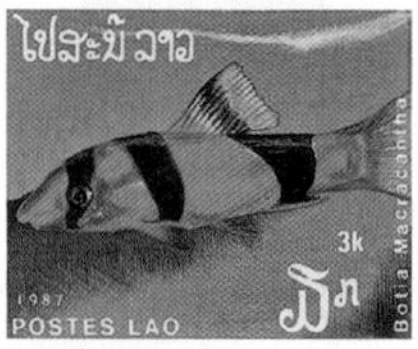

217 Clown Loach

1987. Fishes. Multicoloured.

1024	3k. Type **217**	15	15
1025	7k. Harlequin filefish	15	15
1026	10k. Silver-spotted squirrelfish	20	15
1027	39k. Mandarin fish	80	20
1028	44k. Coral hind	90	30
1029	47k. Zebra lionfish	1·00	35
1030	50k. Semicircle angelfish	1·20	35

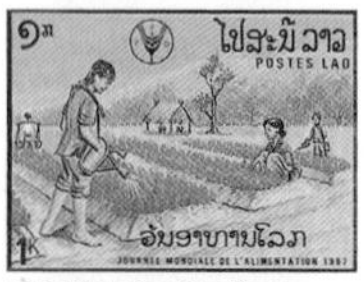

218 Watering Seedlings

1987. World Food Day. Multicoloured.

1031	1k. Type **218**	15	15
1032	3k. Harvesting maize (vert)	15	15
1033	5k. Harvesting rice	15	15
1034	63k. Children with fish (vert)	1·30	45
1035	142k. Tending pigs and poultry	3·00	90

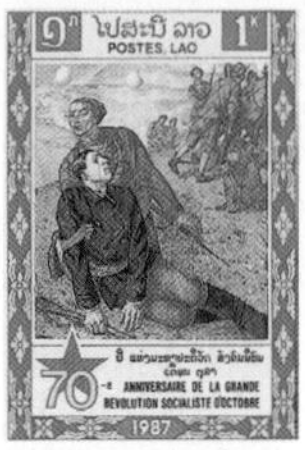

219 Wounded Soldiers on Battlefield

1987. 70th Anniv of Russian Revolution. Multicoloured.

1036	1k. Type **219**	20	15
1037	2k. Mother and baby	45	20
1038	4k. Storming the Winter Palace	80	20
1039	8k. Lenin amongst soldiers and sailors	1·60	45
1040	10k. Lenin labouring in Red Square	2·20	60

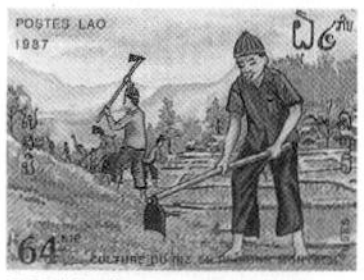

220 Hoeing

1987. Rice Culture in Mountain Regions. Mult.

1041	64k. Type **220**	1·40	30
1042	100k. Working in paddy fields	2·40	75

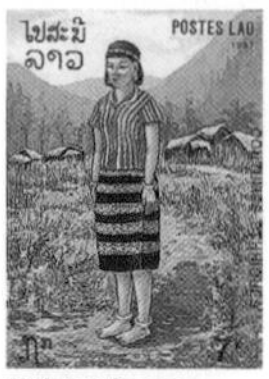

221 Laotheung Costume

1987. Ethnic Costumes. Multicoloured.

1043	7k. Type **221**	15	15
1044	38k. Laoloum costume	80	20
1045	144k. Laosoun costume	3·00	1·00

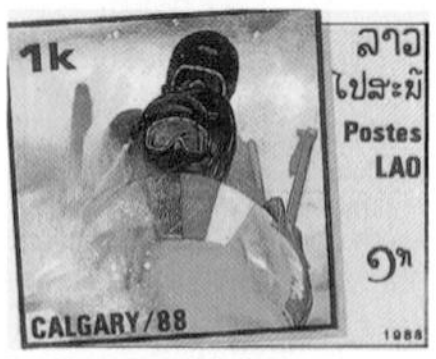

222 Two-man Bobsleigh

1988. Winter Olympic Games, Calgary (2nd issue). Multicoloured.

1046	1k. Type **222**	15	15
1047	4k. Biathlon (shooting)	15	15
1048	20k. Cross-country skiing	45	15
1049	42k. Ice hockey	90	30
1050	63k. Speed skating	1·30	45
1051	70k. Slalom	1·50	50
MS1052	74×45 mm. 95k. Skiing (39×31 mm)	2·20	90

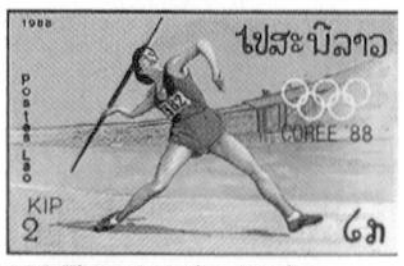

223 Throwing the Javelin

1988. Olympic Games, Seoul (2nd issue). Multicoloured.

1053	2k. Type **223**	15	15
1054	5k. Triple jumping	15	15
1055	10k. Men's gymnastics	20	15
1056	12k. Pirogue racing	35	15
1057	38k. Women's gymnastics	1·00	20
1058	46k. Fencing	1·30	30
1059	100k. Wrestling	2·75	65
MS1060	100×67 mm. 95k. Men's gymnastics (36×38 mm)	2·20	90

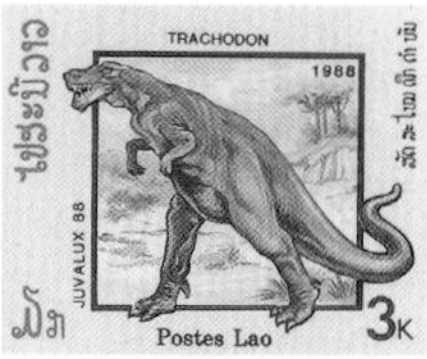

224 Tyrannosaurus

1988. "Juvalux 88" Youth Philately Exhibition, Luxembourg. Prehistoric Animals. Multicoloured.

1061	3k. Type **224** (wrongly inscr "Trachodon")	15	15
1062	7k. "Ceratosaurus nasicornis" (vert)	20	15
1063	39k. "Iguanodon bernissartensis" (vert)	1·10	20
1064	44k. Scolosaurus (vert)	1·10	35
1065	47k. "Phororhacus" sp. (vert)	1·10	35
1066	50k. Anatosaurus (wrongly inscr "Tyrannosaurus")	1·50	35
MS1067	73×94 mm. 95k. Pteranodon (39×31 mm)	2·40	90

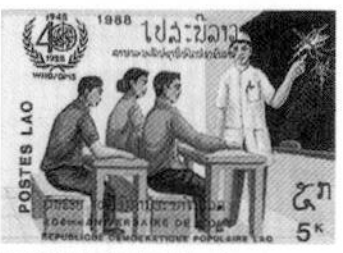

225 Adults in Hygiene Class

1988. 40th Anniv of W.H.O. Multicoloured.

1068	5k. Type **225**	15	15
1069	27k. Fumigating houses	50	15
1070	164k. Woman pumping fresh water (vert)	3·50	1·20

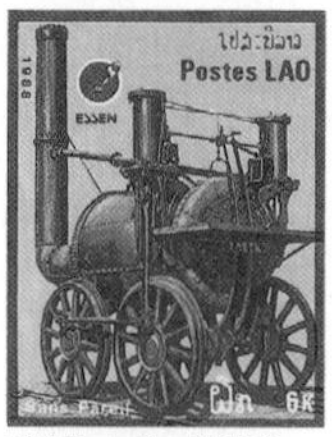

226 "Sans Pareil", 1829

1988. "Essen 88" International Stamp Fair. Early Railway Locomotives. Multicoloured.

1071	6k. Type **226**	15	15
1072	15k. *Rocket*, 1829	35	15
1073	20k. *Royal George*, 1827 (horiz)	45	15
1074	25k. Trevithick's locomotive, 1803 (horiz)	60	20
1075	30k. *Novelty*, 1829 (horiz)	90	20
1076	100k. *Tom Thumb*, 1829 (horiz)	2·40	75
MS1077	82×70 mm. 95k. Stephenson's *Locomotio*", 1825 (34×28 mm)	2·75	95

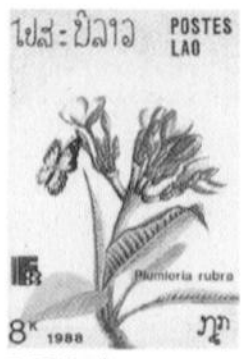

227 Red Frangipani

1988. "Finlandia 88" International Stamp Exhibition, Helsinki. Flowers. Multicoloured.

1078	8k. Type **227**	15	15
1079	9k. Hollyhock	20	15
1080	15k. Flame-of-the forest	30	15
1081	33k. Golden shower	65	20
1082	64k. *Dahlia coccinea* (red)	1·30	45
1083	69k. *Dahlia coccinea* (yellow)	1·50	50
MS1084	76×58 mm. 95k. Hollyhock, frangipani and flame-of-the-forest (31×39 mm)	2·75	1·00

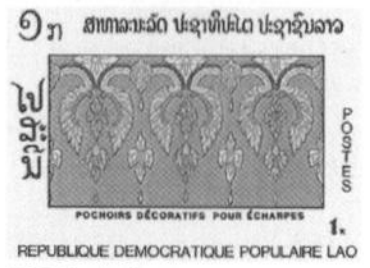

228 Sash Pattern

1988. Decorative Stencil Patterns.

1085	**228**	1k. multicoloured	15	15
1086	-	2k. yellow, red and black	15	15
1087	-	3k. multicoloured	20	15
1088	-	25k. multicoloured	65	20
1089	-	163k. multicoloured	3·25	1·40

DESIGNS (stencils for)—VERT: 2k. Pagoda doors; 3k. Pagoda walls. HORIZ: 25k. Pagoda pillars; 163k. Skirts.

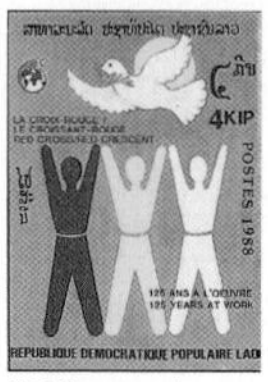

229 Dove and Figures

1988. 125th Anniv of Red Cross Movement. Multicoloured.

1090	4k. Type **229**	15	15
1091	52k. Red Cross workers with handicapped people	1·20	50
1092	144k. Red Cross worker vaccinating baby (horiz)	4·00	1·60

230 Stork-billed Kingfisher

1988. Birds. Multicoloured.

1093	6k. Type **230**	15	15
1094	10k. Japanese quail	20	15
1095	13k. Blossom-headed parakeet	30	15
1096	44k. Orange-breasted green pigeon	65	20
1097	63k. Black-crested bulbul	1·30	45
1098	64k. Mountain imperial pigeon	1·50	50

231 Red Cross Workers loading Supplies into Pirogue

1988. Completion of 1st Five Year Plan. Multicoloured.

1099	20k. Type **231**	50	20
1100	40k. Library	90	35
1101	50k. Irrigating fields	1·30	50
1102	100k. Improvement in communications	2·20	1·00

232 Ruy Lopez Segura

1988. Chess Masters. Multicoloured.

1103	1k. Type **232**	15	15
1104	2k. Karl Anderssen	15	15
1105	3k. Paul Morphy (wrongly inscr "Murphy")	15	15
1106	6k. Wilhelm Steinitz	20	15
1107	7k. Emanuel Lasker	30	15
1108	12k. Jose Raul Capablanca	45	20
1109	172k. Aleksandr Alekhine	4·00	1·00

233 Tortoiseshell and White

1989. "India 89" International Stamp Exhibition, New Delhi. Cats. Multicoloured.

1110	5k. Type **233**	15	15
1111	6k. Brown tabby	15	15
1112	10k. Black and white	35	15
1113	20k. Red tabby	60	15
1114	50k. Black	1·20	35
1115	172k. Silver tabby and white	4·00	90
MS1116 70×94 mm. 95k. Brown tabby and white (31×39 mm)		2·75	1·10

234 Gunboat, Tank, Soldiers and Flags

1989. 40th Anniv of People's Army. Multicoloured.

1117	1k. Type **234**	15	15
1118	2k. Soldier teaching mathematics (vert)	15	15
1119	3k. Army medics vaccinating civilians	15	15
1120	250k. Peasant, revolutionary, worker and soldiers	6·75	95

235 Footballers

1989. World Cup Football Championship, Italy (1990) (1st issue). Multicoloured.

1121	10k. Type **235**	20	15
1122	15k. Footballer looking to pass ball	30	15
1123	20k. Ball hitting player on chest	45	15
1124	25k. Tackle	60	20
1125	45k. Dribbling ball	90	30
1126	105k. Kicking ball	2·40	75
MS1127 52×65 mm. 95k. Players and goalkeeper (38×29 mm)		2·20	1·10

See also Nos. 1168/**MS**1174.

236 Couple planting Sapling

1989. Preserve Forests Campaign. Multicoloured.

1128	4k. Type **236**	15	15
1129	10k. Burning and fallen trees	20	15
1130	12k. Man felling tree (vert)	20	20
1131	200k. Trees on map (vert)	4·50	90

237 Camilo Cienfuegos, Fidel Castro and Flag

1989. 30th Anniv of Cuban Revolution. Multicoloured.

| 1132 | 45k. Type **237** | 1·10 | 35 |
| 1133 | 50d. Cuban and Laotian flags | 1·10 | 35 |

238 Skaters

1989. Winter Olympic Games, Albertville (1992) (1st issue). Figure Skating. Multicoloured.

1134	9k. Type **238**	20	15
1135	10k. Pair (horiz)	30	15
1136	15k. Ice dancing	45	15
1137	24k. Female skater	50	20
1138	29k. Pair	65	20
1139	114k. Male skater	2·75	90
MS1140 49×78 mm. 95k. Pair (different) (31×39 mm)		2·20	1·10

See also. Nos. 1195/**MS**1202, 1237/**MS**1242 and 1276/**MS**1281.

239 High Jumping

1989. Olympic Games, Barcelona (1992) (1st issue). Multicoloured.

1141	5k. Type **239**	15	15
1142	15k. Gymnastics	30	15
1143	20k. Cycling (horiz)	45	20
1144	70k. Boxing (horiz)	50	30
1145	70k. Archery	1·30	50
1146	120k. Swimming	2·75	60
MS1147 65×91 mm. 95k. Baseball (31×39 mm)		2·20	1·10

See also Nos. 1179/**MS**1185, 1231/**MS**1236 and 1282/**MS**1287.

240 Poor on Seashore

1989. "Philexfrance '89" International Stamp Exhibition, Paris. Paintings by Picasso. Multicoloured.

1148	5k. Type **240**	15	15
1149	7k. "Motherhood"	20	15
1150	8k. *Portrait of Jaime S. le Bock*	20	15
1151	9k. *Harlequins*	45	20
1152	105k. *Boy with Dog*	2·75	60
1153	114k. *Girl on Ball*	2·75	75
MS1154 65×75 mm. 95k. *Woman in Hat* (31×39 mm)		2·75	1·10

241 Sapodillas

1989. Fruits. Multicoloured.

1155	5k. Type **241**	15	15
1156	20k. Sugar-apples	50	20
1157	20k. Guavas	50	20
1158	30k. Durians	75	30
1159	50k. Pomegranates	1·30	45
1160	172k. *Moridica charautia*	4·50	90

242 Sikhotabong Temple, Khammouane

1989. Temples. Multicoloured.

1161	5k. Type **242**	15	15
1162	15k. Dam Temple, Vientiane	30	20
1163	61k. Ing Hang Temple, Savannakhet	1·20	50
1164	161k. Ho Vay Phra Luang Temple, Vientiane	3·75	1·00

243 Nehru and Woman

1989. Birth Centenary of Jawaharlal Nehru (Indian statesman). Multicoloured.

1165	1k. Type **243**	15	15
1166	60k. Nehru and group of children (horiz)	1·30	45
1167	200k. Boy garlanding Nehru	4·50	1·00

244 Footballer

1990. World Cup Football Championship, Italy (2nd issue).

1168	**244**	10k. multicoloured	20	15
1169	–	15k. multicoloured	30	15
1170	–	20k. multicoloured	45	15
1171	–	25k. multicoloured	50	20
1172	–	45k. multicoloured	95	30
1173	–	105k. multicoloured	2·40	75
MS1174 90×67 mm. 95k. multicoloured (31×39 mm)			2·20	1·10

DESIGNS: 15 to 95k. Different football scenes.

245 Teacher and Adult Class

1990. International Literacy Year. Multicoloured.

1175	10k. Type **245**	20	15
1176	50k. Woman teaching child (vert)	1·20	65
1177	60k. Monk teaching adults	1·30	45
1178	150k. Group reading and writing under tree	3·25	1·00

246 Basketball

1990. Olympic Games, Barcelona (1992) (2nd issue). Multicoloured.

1179	10k. Type **246**	20	15
1180	30k. Hurdling	60	15
1181	45k. High jumping	95	20
1182	50k. Cycling	1·20	30
1183	60k. Throwing the javelin	1·30	45
1184	90k. Tennis	2·20	75
MS1185 86×102 mm. 95k. Gymnastics (31×39 mm)		2·20	1·10

247 Great Britain 1840 Penny Black and Mail Coach

1990. "Stamp World London 90" International Stamp Exhibition. Multicoloured.

1186	15k. Type **247**	30	15
1187	20k. U.S 1847 5c. stamp and early steam locomotive	45	20
1188	40k. France 1849 20c. stamp and mail balloons, Paris, 1870	90	20
1189	50k. Sardinia 1851 5c. stamp and post rider	1·00	30
1190	60k. Indo-China 1892 1c. stamp and elephant	1·30	45
1191	100k. Spain 1850 6c. stamp and Spanish galleon	1·90	65
MS1192 54×54 mm. 95k. Laos 1976 1k. stamp and Douglas DC-8 airliner (36×28 mm)		2·20	1·10

248 Ho Chi Minh addressing Crowd

1990. Birth Centenary of Ho Chi Minh. Multicoloured.

1193	40k. Type **248**	1·00	45
1194	60k. Ho Chi Minh and Laotian President	1·60	60
1195	160k. Ho Chi Minh and Vietnamese flag (vert)	4·50	1·60

249 Speed Skating

1990. Winter Olympic Games, Albertville (1992) (2nd issue). Multicoloured.

1196	10k. Type **249**	20	15
1197	25k. Cross-country skiing (vert)	50	15
1198	30k. Downhill skiing	60	20
1199	35k. Tobogganing	90	20
1200	80k. Figure skating (pairs) (vert)	1·60	50
1201	90k. Biathlon	2·10	60
MS1202 97×83 mm. 95k. Ice hockey (31×39 mm)		2·20	1·10

250 That Luang, 1990

1990. 430th Anniv of That Luang. Multicoloured.

1203	60k. That Luang, 1867 (horiz)	1·60	45
1204	70k. That Luang, 1930 (horiz)	2·20	60
1205	130k. Type **250**	3·75	1·00

251 Parson Bird

1990. "New Zealand 1990" International Stamp Exhibition, Auckland. Multicoloured.

1206	10k. Type **251**	20	15
1207	15k. Eurasian sky lark	30	15
1208	20k. Oystercatcher	45	20
1209	50k. Variable cormorant	1·30	30
1210	60k. Great Reef heron	1·50	45
1211	100k. Brown kiwi	2·75	75
MS1212	56×82 mm. 95k. Rough-faced cormorant (30×37 mm)	2·75	1·10

252 Brown-antlered Deer

1990. Mammals. Multicoloured.

1213	10k. Type **252**	20	15
1214	20k. Gaur	45	15
1215	40k. Wild water buffalo	95	20
1216	45k. Kouprey	1·10	30
1217	120k. Javan rhinoceros	2·75	90

253 Surgeons Operating

1990. 40th Anniv of United Nations Development Programme. Multicoloured.

1218	30k. Type **253**	90	30
1219	45k. Fishermen inspecting catch	1·50	30
1220	80k. Air-traffic controller (vert)	2·20	90
1221	90k. Electricity plant workers	2·50	1·20

254 Rice Ceremony

1990. New Year. Multicoloured.

1222	5k. Type **254**	20	15
1223	10k. Elephant in carnival parade	30	15
1224	50k. Making offerings at temple	1·10	30
1225	150k. Family ceremony	3·25	1·10

255 Memorial, Wreath and Eternal Flame

1990. 15th National Day Festival. Multicoloured.

1226	15k. Type **255**	45	20
1227	20k. Celebration parade	65	45
1228	80k. Hospital visit	2·20	90
1229	120k. Girls parading with banner	3·25	1·20

256 West German World Cup Football Champion

1991. West Germany, World Cup Football Champion. Sheet 86×58 mm.

MS1230	**256** 95k. multicoloured	2·20	1·10

257 Two-man Kayak

1991. Olympic Games, Barcelona (1992) (3rd issue). Multicoloured.

1231	22k. Type **257**	15	15
1232	32k. Canoeing	15	15
1233	285k. Diving (vert)	90	20
1234	330k. Racing dinghies (vert)	1·10	30
1235	1000k. Swimming	2·75	90
MS1236	83×55 mm. 700k. Two-man canoeing (39×31 mm)	2·75	1·10

258 Bobsleighing

1991. Winter Olympic Games, Albertville (1992) (3rd issue). Multicoloured.

1237	32k. Type **258**	15	15
1238	135k. Cross-country skiing (horiz)	45	15
1239	250k. Ski jumping (horiz)	75	20
1240	275k. Biathlon (horiz)	90	30
1241	900k. Speed skating (horiz)	2·75	90
MS1242	80×63 mm. 700k. Skiing (31×39 mm)	2·75	1·10

259 Pha Pheng Falls, Champassak

1991. Tourism. Multicoloured.

1243	155k. Type **259**	50	20
1244	220k. Pha Tang mountains, Vangvieng	75	30
1245	235k. Tat Set waterfall, Saravane (vert)	90	50
1246	1000k. Plain of Jars, Xieng Khouang (vert)	3·50	1·10

260 Match Scene

1991. World Cup Football Championship, U.S.A. (1994) (1st issue). Multicoloured.

1247	32k. Type **260**	15	15
1248	330k. Goalkeeper catching ball	95	20
1249	340k. Player controlling ball (vert)	1·20	20
1250	400k. Player dribbling ball	1·50	30
1251	500k. Tackle	1·80	75
MS1252	75×57 mm. 700k. Player shooting at goal (31×39 mm)	2·75	1·10

See also Nos. 1292/**MS**1297, 1370/**MS**1375 and 1386/**MS**1391.

261 Planting Saplings

1991. National Tree Planting Day. Multicoloured.

1253	350k. Type **261**	75	30
1254	700k. Planting saplings (different)	2·20	75
1255	800k. Removing saplings from store	2·50	1·10

262 *Mallard*, 1938, Great Britain

1991. "Espamer '91" Spain–Latin America Stamp Exhibition, Buenos Aires. Railway Locomotives. Multicoloured.

1256	25k. Type **262**	15	15
1257	32k. Class 4500 steam locomotive, France (inscr "Pacific 231")	20	15
1258	285k. Streamlined steam locomotive, U.S.A.	95	30
1259	650k. Canadian Pacific Class T1b steam locomotive, 1938	1·90	65
1260	750k. East African Railways Class 59 steam locomotive, 1955	2·75	95
MS1261	80×64 mm. 700k. Class VT601 diesel-hydraulic intercity express (39×31 mm)	2·75	1·10

263 Spindle Festival

1991. Traditional Music. Multicoloured.

1262	20k. Type **263**	15	15
1263	220k. Mong player (vert)	65	20
1264	275k. Siphandone singer (vert)	75	30
1265	545k. Khap ngum singer	1·80	65
1266	690k. Phouthaydam dance	2·20	90

264 Great Purple

1991. "Phila Nippon '91" International Stamp Exhibition, Tokyo. Butterflies. Multicoloured.

1267	55k. Type **264**	20	15
1268	90k. *Luehdorfia puziloi* (wrongly inscr "Luendorfia")	30	15
1269	255k. *Papilio bianor*	90	20
1270	285k. Swallowtail	1·00	30
1271	900k. Mikado swallowtail	3·00	90
MS1272	60×77 mm. 700k. Common map butterfly (39×31 mm)	2·75	1·10

265 Emblem and Pattern

1991. International Decade for Cultural Development (1988–97). Multicoloured.

1273	285k. Type **265**	75	30
1274	330k. Emblem and drum	90	30
1275	1000k. Emblem and pipes	2·75	1·10

266 Bobsleighing

1992. Winter Olympic Games, Albertville (4th issue). Multicoloured.

1276	200k. Type **266**	50	15
1277	220k. Slalom skiing	65	20
1278	250k. Downhill skiing (horiz)	75	20
1279	500k. One-man luge	1·60	30
1280	600k. Figure skating	1·80	75
MS1281	77×61 mm. 700k. Speed skating (31×39 mm)	2·75	90

267 Running

1992. Olympic Games, Barcelona (4th issue). Multicoloured.

1282	32k. Type **267**	15	15
1283	245k. Baseball	65	20
1284	275k. Tennis	90	20
1285	285k. Basketball	90	30
1286	900k. Boxing (horiz)	3·00	75
MS1287	71×59 mm. 700k. Diving (39×31 mm)	2·75	90

268 Pest Control

1992. World Health Day. Multicoloured.

1288	200k. Type **268**	60	20
1289	255k. Anti-smoking campaign	65	30
1290	330k. Donating blood	95	60
1291	1000k. Vaccinating child (vert)	3·00	1·20

269 Argentinian and Italian Players and Flags

1992. World Cup Football Championship, U.S.A. (1994) (2nd issue). Multicoloured.

1292	260k. Type **269**	60	15
1293	305k. German and English players and flags	80	20
1294	310k. United States flag, ball and trophy	90	30
1295	350k. Italian and English players and flags	1·30	45
1296	800k. German and Argentinian players and flags	2·75	90
MS1297	60×88 mm. 700k. Goalkeeper catching ball (31×39 mm)	3·00	90

270 Common Cobra

1992. Snakes. Multicoloured.

1298	280k. Type **270**	80	20
1299	295k. Common cobra	80	20
1300	420k. Wagler's pit viper	1·30	30
1301	700k. King cobra (vert)	2·75	90

271 Doorway and Ruins

1992. Restoration of Wat Phou. Multicoloured.

1302	185k. Type **271**	60	35
1303	220k. Doorway (different)	65	35
1304	1200k. Doorway with collapsed porch (horiz)	4·00	1·60

272 *Pinta* and Juan Martinez's Map

1992. "Genova '92" International Thematic Stamp Exhibition. Multicoloured.

1305	100k. Type **272**	20	15
1306	300k. Piri Reis's map and caravelle (vert)	90	20
1307	350k. Magellan's ship and Paolo del Pozo Toscanelli's world map	1·20	20
1308	400k. Gabriel de Vallesca's map and Vasco da Gama's flagship *Sao Gabriel*	1·30	45
1309	455k. Juan Martinez's map and Portuguese four-masted caravel	1·60	65
MS1310 94×63 mm. 700k. *Santa Maria* (39×31 mm)		3·00	90

273 Woman in Traditional Costume

1992. Traditional Costumes of Laotian Mountain Villages.

1311	**273**	25k. multicoloured	15	15
1312	-	55k. multicoloured	20	15
1313	-	400k. multicoloured	1·30	45
1314	-	1200k. multicoloured	4·00	1·20

DESIGNS: 55 to 1200k. Different costumes.

274 Boy Drumming

1992. International Children's Day. Children at Play. Multicoloured.

1315	220k. Type **274**	60	20
1316	285k. Girls skipping (horiz)	80	20
1317	330k. Boys racing on stilts	1·20	30
1318	400k. Girls playing "escape" game (horiz)	1·50	60

275 Praying before Buddha

1992. National Customs. Multicoloured.

1319	100k. Type **275**	30	15
1320	140k. Wedding (horiz)	45	20
1321	160k. Religious procession (horiz)	75	20
1322	1500k. Monks receiving alms (horiz)	4·75	2·20

276 Crested Gibbon

1992. Climbing Mammals. Multicoloured.

1323	10k. Type **276**	20	15
1324	100k. Variegated langur	30	20
1325	250k. Pileated gibbon	80	30
1326	430k. Francois's monkey	1·50	45
1327	800k. Lesser slow loris	3·00	80

277 New York

1993. 130th Anniv of Underground Railway Systems. Multicoloured.

1328	15k. Type **277**	15	15

1329	50k. West Berlin	20	15
1330	100k. Paris	30	20
1331	200k. London	80	30
1332	900k. Moscow	3·00	1·20
MS1333 85×55 mm. 700k. Royal Mail underground system, London (31×39 mm)		3·00	90

278 Malayan Bullfrog

1993. Amphibians. Multicoloured.

1334	55k. Type **278**	20	15
1335	90k. Muller's clawed frog	30	15
1336	100k. Glass frog (vert)	45	20
1337	185k. Giant toad	65	30
1338	1200k. Common tree frog (vert)	4·00	1·20

279 Common Tree-shrew

1993. Mammals. Multicoloured.

1339	45k. Type **279**	20	15
1340	60k. Philippine flying lemur	20	15
1341	120k. Loris	45	20
1342	500k. Eastern tarsier	1·60	65
1343	600k. Giant gibbon	1·90	1·20

280 Noble Scallop

1993. Molluscs. Multicoloured.

1344	20k. Type **280**	15	15
1345	30k. Precious wentletrap	15	15
1346	70k. Spider conch	30	20
1347	500k. Aulicus cone	1·60	65
1348	1000k. Milleped spider conch	3·00	1·20

281 Drugs and Skull smoking

1993. Anti-drugs Campaign. Multicoloured.

1349	200k. Type **281**	65	30
1350	430k. Burning seized drugs	1·40	60
1351	900k. Instructing on dangers of drugs	3·00	1·20

282 House

1993. Traditional Houses. Multicoloured.

1352	32k. Type **282**	15	15
1353	200k. Thatched house with gable end (horiz)	75	20
1354	650k. Thatched house (horiz)	1·90	60
1355	750k. House with tiled roof (horiz)	2·40	1·20

283 Greater Spotted Eagle

1993. Birds of Prey. Multicoloured.

1356	10k. Type **283**	15	15
1357	100k. Spotted little owl	45	20
1358	330k. Pied harrier (horiz)	1·60	45
1359	1000k. Short-toed eagle	4·00	1·30

284 Fighting Forest Fire

1993. Environmental Protection. Multicoloured.

1360	32k. Type **284**	15	15
1361	40k. Wildlife on banks of River Mekong	15	15
1362	260k. Paddy fields	90	30
1363	1100k. Oxen in river	4·00	1·20

285 *Narathura atosia*

1993. "Bangkok 1993" International Stamp Exhibition. Butterflies. Multicoloured.

1364	35k. Type **285**	15	15
1365	80k. *Parides philoxenus*	20	15
1366	150k. *Euploea harrisi*	45	20
1367	220k. Yellow orange-tip	65	30
1368	500k. Female common palm fly	1·90	80
MS1369 85×69 mm. 700k. *Stichophtlalma Louisa* (39×31 mm)		3·00	90

286 Footballer

1993. World Cup Football Championship, U.S.A. (3rd issue). Multicoloured.

1370	10k. Type **286**	15	15
1371	20k. Brazil player	15	15
1372	285k. Uruguay player	80	20
1373	400k. Germany player	1·40	45
1374	800k. Forward challenging goalkeeper	2·75	1·20
MS1375 99×72 mm. 700k. Ball on pitch (31×39 mm)		3·00	90

287 Hesperornis

1994. Prehistoric Birds. Multicoloured.

1376	10k. Type **287**	15	15
1377	20k. Mauritius dodo	15	15
1378	150k. Archaeopteryx	60	20
1379	600k. Phororhachos	1·80	45
1380	700k. Giant moa	2·50	90
MS1381 80×65 mm. 700k. *Teratornis mirabilis* (Teratornis) (39×31 mm)		3·00	90

288 Olympic Flag and Flame

1994. Centenary of International Olympic Committee. Multicoloured.

1382	100k. Type **288**	30	15
1383	250k. Ancient Greek athletes (horiz)	80	20
1384	1000k. Pierre de Coubertin (founder) and modern athlete	3·50	1·40

289 Bridge and National Flags

1994. Opening of Friendship Bridge between Laos and Thailand.

1385	**289**	500k. multicoloured	1·90	1·20

290 World Map and Players

1994. World Cup Football Championship, U.S.A. (4th issue).

1386	**290**	40k. multicoloured	15	15
1387	-	50k. multicoloured	20	15
1388	-	60k. multicoloured	20	15
1389	-	320k. multicoloured	1·20	45
1390	-	900k. multicoloured	3·50	1·20
MS1391 82×59 mm. 700k. multicoloured (31×39 mm)			2·50	90

DESIGNS: 50 to 900k. Different players on world map.

291 Pagoda

1994. Pagodas.

1392	**291**	30k. multicoloured	15	15
1393	-	150k. multicoloured	45	20
1394	-	380k. multicoloured	1·20	30
1395	-	1100k. multicoloured	3·50	1·20

DESIGNS: 150 to 1100k. Different gabled roofs.

292 Bear eating

1994. The Malay Bear. Multicoloured.

1396	50k. Type **292**	35	15
1397	90k. Bear's head	80	20
1398	200k. Adult and cub	1·80	30
1399	220k. Bear	1·90	45

293 Grass Snake

1994. Amphibians and Reptiles. Multicoloured.

1400	70k. Type **293**	20	15
1401	80k. Tessellated snake	20	15
1402	90k. Fire salamander	30	15
1403	600k. Alpine newt	1·90	60
1404	800k. Green lizard (vert)	2·50	1·20
MS1405 79×50 mm. 700k. Great crested newt (39×31 mm)		2·50	90

294 Phra
Xayavoraman 7

1994. Buddhas. Multicoloured.

1406	15k. Type **294**	15	15
1407	280k. Phra Thong Souk	90	30
1408	390k. Phra Manolom	1·30	45
1409	800k. Phra Ongtu	2·50	1·20

295 Family
supporting Healthy
Globe

1994. International Year of the Family. Multicoloured.

1410	200k. Type **295**	65	30
1411	500k. Mother taking child to school (horiz)	1·60	80
1412	700k. Mother and children	2·40	1·20
MS1413	50×70 mm. 700k. Family and flag	2·50	90

296 Kong Hang

1994. Traditional Laotian Drums. Multicoloured.

1414	370k. Type **296**	1·30	35
1415	440k. Kong Leng (portable drum)	1·50	45
1416	450k. Kong Toum (drum on stand)	1·50	45
1417	600k. Kong Phene (hanging drum)	2·10	65

297 Elephant in Procession

1994. Ceremonial Elephants. Multicoloured.

1418	140k. Type **297**	45	20
1419	400k. Elephant in pavilion	1·30	80
1420	890k. Elephant in street procession (vert)	2·75	1·30

298 Theropodes

1994. Prehistoric Animals. Multicoloured.

1421	50k. Type **298**	20	15
1422	380k. Iguanodontides	1·80	60
1423	420k. Sauropodes	2·10	65

299 Playing Musical
Instruments

1995. 20th Anniv of World Tourism Organization. Multicoloured.

1424	60k. Type **299**	20	15
1425	250k. Women dancing	80	20
1426	400k. Giving alms to monks	1·30	45
1427	650k. Waterfall (vert)	1·80	80
MS1428	40×83 mm. 700k. Close-up view of waterfall in No. 1427 (31×39 mm)	2·40	80

300 Trachodon

1995. Prehistoric Animals. Multicoloured.

1429	50k. Type **300**	15	15
1430	70k. Protoceratops	15	15
1431	300k. Brontosaurus	80	30
1432	400k. Stegosaurus	1·10	45
1433	600k. Tyrannosaurus	1·80	65

301 Indian Jungle Mynah

1995. Birds. Multicoloured.

1434	50k. Type **301**	15	15
1435	150k. Jerdon's starling	45	15
1436	300k. Common mynah	90	35
1437	700k. Southern grackle	1·90	80

302 Children and
Emblem

1995. 25th Anniv of Francophonie. Multicoloured.

1438	50k. Type **302**	15	15
1439	380k. Golden roof decorations	1·20	60
1440	420k. Map	1·30	65

303 Pole Vaulting

1995. Olympic Games, Atlanta, U.S.A. (1st issue). Multicoloured.

1441	60k. Type **303**	15	15
1442	80k. Throwing the javelin	20	15
1443	200k. Throwing the hammer	60	20
1444	350k. Long jumping	1·00	35
1445	700k. High jumping	2·10	80
MS1446	90×60 mm. 700k. Baseball (39×31 mm)	2·40	80

See also Nos. 1484/**MS**1489.

304 Chalice

1995. Antique Vessels. Multicoloured.

1447	70k. Type **304**	15	15
1448	200k. Resin and silver bowl (horiz)	50	20
1449	450k. Geometrically decorated bowl (horiz)	1·30	50
1450	600k. Religious chalice (horiz)	1·80	65

305 Procession

1995. Rocket Festival. Multicoloured.

1451	80k. Launching rocket (vert)	20	15
1452	160k. Type **305**	45	15
1453	500k. Musicians in procession	1·40	50
1454	700k. Crowds and rockets	2·10	80

306 Red Tabby Longhair

1995. Cats. Multicoloured.

1455	40k. Type **306**	15	15
1456	50k. Siamese sealpoint	20	15
1457	250k. Red tabby longhair (different)	80	20
1458	400k. Tortoiseshell shorthair	1·30	30
1459	650k. Head of tortoiseshell shorthair (vert)	1·60	65
MS1460	49×70 mm. 700k. Tortoiseshell shorthair (different) (39×31 mm)	2·40	80

307 Nepenthes villosa

1995. Insectivorous Plants. Multicoloured.

1461	90k. Type **307**	20	15
1462	100k. Dionaea muscipula	30	15
1463	350k. Sarracenia flava	1·00	30
1464	450k. Sarracenia purpurea	1·30	30
1465	500k. Nepenthes ampullaria	1·50	60
MS1466	59×77 mm. 1000k. Nepenthes gracillis (31×39 mm)	3·00	90

308 Stag Beetle

1995. Insects. Multicoloured.

1467	40k. Type **308**	15	15
1468	50k. May beetle	20	15
1469	500k. Blue carpenter beetle	1·40	45
1470	800k. Great green grasshopper	2·40	80

309 Cattle grazing

1995. 50th Anniv of F.A.O. Multicoloured.

1471	80k. Type **309**	20	15
1472	300k. Working paddy-field	90	45
1473	1000k. Agriculture	3·00	1·20

310 At Meeting

1995. 50th Anniv of U.N.O. Peoples of Different Races. Multicoloured.

1474	290k. Type **310**	80	35
1475	310k. Playing draughts	90	45
1476	440k. Children playing	1·40	65

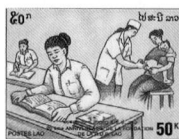

311 Students and Nurse
vaccinating Child

1995. 20th Anniv of Republic. Multicoloured.

1477	50k. Type **311**	15	15
1478	280k. Agricultural land	80	45
1479	600k. Bridge	1·80	90

312 Mong

1996. Traditional New Year Customs. Multicoloured.

1480	50k. Type **312**	15	15
1481	280k. Phouthai	90	30
1482	380k. Ten Xe	1·20	45
1483	420k. Lao Loum	1·30	45

313 Cycling

1996. Olympic Games, Atlanta, U.S.A. (2nd issue). Multicoloured.

1484	30k. Type **313**	15	15
1485	150k. Football	30	15
1486	200k. Basketball (vert)	45	20
1487	300k. Running (vert)	65	30
1488	500k. Shooting	1·20	60
MS1489	80×60 mm. 1000k. High jumping (38×30 mm)	2·20	2·20

314 Sun Bear

1996. Animals. Multicoloured.

1490	40k. Type **314**	15	15
1491	60k. Grey pelican	15	15
1492	200k. Leopard	45	20
1493	250k. Swallowtail	60	30
1494	700k. Indian python	1·50	80

315 Weaving

1996. International Women's Year. Multicoloured.

1495	20k. Type **315**	15	15
1496	290k. Physical training instructress	65	30
1497	1000k. Woman feeding child (vert)	2·20	1·10

316 Rat

1996. New Year. Year of the Rat.

1498	**316**	50k. multicoloured	15	15
1499	–	340k. multicoloured	1·20	60
1500	–	350k. multicoloured	1·30	60
1501	–	370k. multicoloured	1·30	65

DESIGNS: 340k. to 370k. Different rats.

317 Players

1996. World Cup Football Championship, France (1998) (1st issue).

1502	**317**	20k. multicoloured	15	15
1503	–	50k. multicoloured	15	15
1504	–	300k. multicoloured	65	30
1505	–	400k. multicoloured	90	45
1506	–	500k. multicoloured	1·10	50
MS1507	63×92 mm. 1000k. multicoloured (30×37 mm)		2·20	2·20

DESIGNS: 50k. to 1000k. Different football scenes.
See also Nos. 1589/**MS**1595.

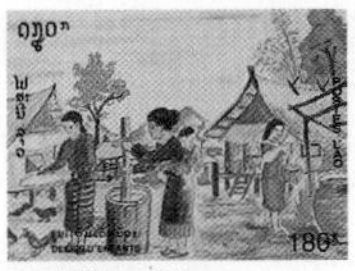

318 Village Women grinding Rice

1996. Children's Drawings. Multicoloured.

1508	180k. Type **318**	65	30
1509	230k. Women picking fruit	80	35
1510	310k. Village women preparing food	1·10	50
1511	370k. Women tending vegetable crops	1·30	65

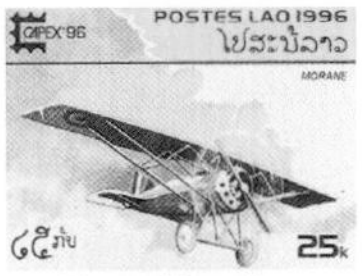

319 Morane Monoplane

1996. "Capex'96" International Stamp Exhibition, Toronto, Canada. Aircraft. Multicoloured.

1512	25k. Type **319**	15	15
1513	60k. Sopwith Camel biplane	15	15
1514	150k. de Havilland D.H.4 biplane	30	15
1515	250k. Albatros biplane	50	30
1516	800k. Caudron biplane	1·80	90

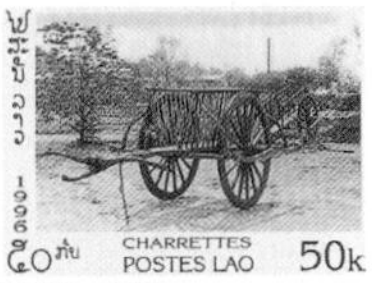

320 Front View

1996. Ox-carts. Multicoloured.

1517	50k. Type **320**	15	10
1518	100k. Side view	20	15
1519	440k. Oxen pulling cart	1·00	50

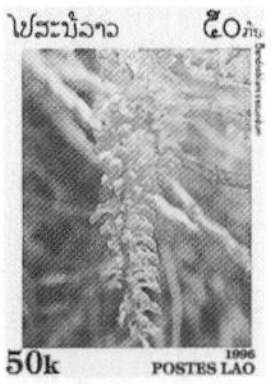

321 *Dendrobium secundum*

1996. Orchids (1st series). Multicoloured.

1520	50k. Type **321**	15	15
1521	200k. *Ascocentrum miniatum*	45	20
1522	500k. *Aerides multiflorum*	1·10	60
1523	520k. *Dendrobium aggregatum*	1·30	60

See also Nos. 1563/**MS**1569, 1626/9, 1685/**MS**1689 and 1836/46.

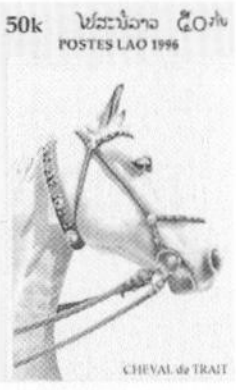

322 White Horse

1996. Saddle Horses. Multicoloured.

1524	50k. Type **322**	15	15
1525	80k. Horse with red and black bridle	15	15
1526	200k. Bay horse with white bridle and reins	45	20
1527	400k. Horse with red and yellow cords braided into mane	90	45
1528	600k. Chestnut horse with white blaze	1·30	65
MS1529	89×69 mm. 1000k. Horse with ornate yellow and red bridle (28×36 mm)	2·20	2·20

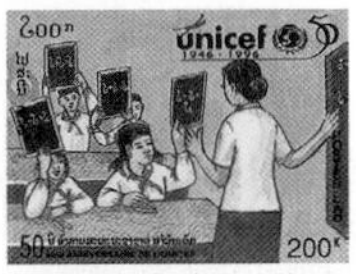

323 Pupils displaying Slates to Teacher

1996. 50th Anniv of UNICEF. Multicoloured.

1530	200k. Type **323**	65	30
1531	500k. Mother breastfeeding (vert)	1·80	80
1532	600k. Woman drawing water at public well	2·10	1·10

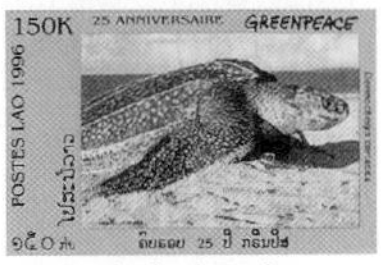

324 Leatherback Turtle

1996. 25th Anniv of Greenpeace (environmental organization). Turtles. Multicoloured.

1533	150k. Type **324**	50	20
1534	250k. Leatherback turtle at water's edge	90	45
1535	400k. Hawksbill turtle	1·50	75
1536	450k. *Chelonia agassizi*	1·60	80

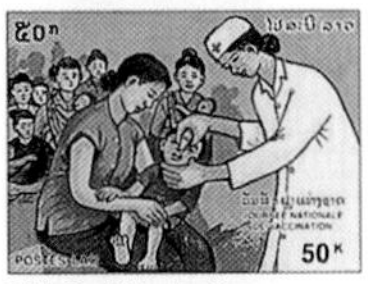

325 Oral Vaccination

1997. National Vaccination Day. Multicoloured.

1537	50k. Type **325**	15	15
1538	340k. Nurse injecting child's leg	1·20	60
1539	370k. Nurse pushing child in wheelchair	1·30	65

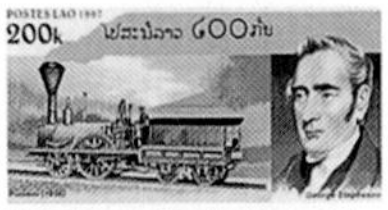

326 George Stephenson and *Pioneer*, 1836

1997. Steam Railway Locomotives. Multicoloured.

1540	100k. "Kinnaird", 1846 (44×27 mm)	20	15
1541	200k. Type **326**	45	20
1542	300k. Robert Stephenson and long-boiler express locomotive, 1848	65	30
1543	400k. Stephenson locomotive *Adler*, 1835, Germany	90	45
1544	500k. *Lord of the Isles*, 1851–84	1·20	60
1545	600k. *The Columbine*, 1845	1·40	65
MS1546	69×93 mm. 2000k. South Carolina Railroad locomotive *Best Friend of Charleston*, 1830 (39×31 mm)	4·50	4·50

The 200 and 300k. are wrongly inscr "Stepheson".

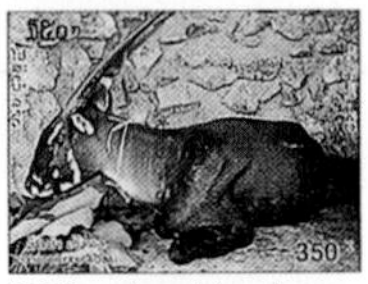

327 Pseudoryx lying down

1997. Pseudoryx (Saola). Multicoloured.

1547	350k. Type **327**	1·30	1·30
1548	380k. Grazing (vert)	1·40	1·40
1549	420k. Scratching with hind leg	1·50	1·50

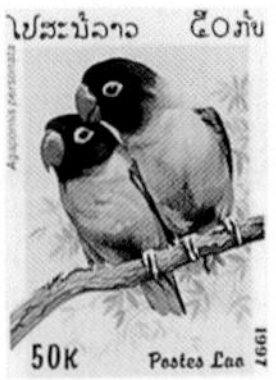

328 Masked Lovebirds (*Agapornis personata*)

1997. Lovebirds. Multicoloured.

1550	50k. Type **328**	15	15
1551	150k. Grey-headed lovebird (*Agapornis cana*)	30	15
1552	200k. Nyasa lovebirds (*Agapornis lilianae*)	45	20
1553	400k. Fischer's lovebirds (*Agapornis fischeri*)	90	45
1554	500k. Black-cheeked lovebirds (*Agapornis nigrigenis*)	1·10	60
1555	800k. Peach-faced lovebird (*Agapornis roseicollis*)	1·90	90
MS1556	91×74 mm. 2000k. Black-winged lovebirds (31×38 mm)	4·50	4·50

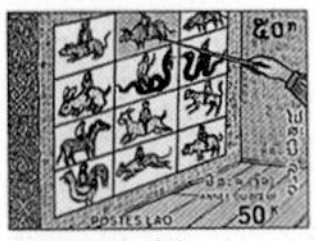

329 Signs of the Chinese Zodiac

1997. New Year. Year of the Ox. Multicoloured.

1557	50k. Type **329**	15	15
1558	300k. Woman riding ox (vert)	1·20	1·20
1559	440k. Ox on float in procession	1·60	1·60

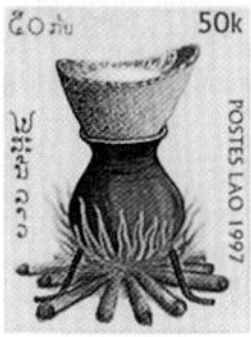

330 Steaming Rice

1997. Food Preparation. Multicoloured.

1560	50k. Type **330**	15	15
1561	340k. Water containers (horiz)	75	35
1562	370k. Table laid with meal (horiz)	80	35

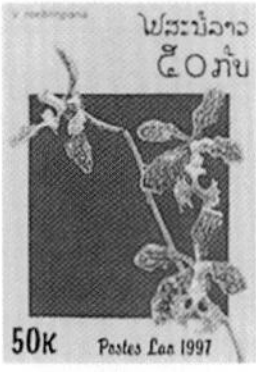

331 *Vanda roeblingiana*

1997. Orchids (2nd series). Multicoloured.

1563	50k. Type **331**	15	15
1564	100k. *Dendrobium findleyanum*	20	15
1565	150k. *Dendrobium crepidatum*	30	15
1566	250k. *Sarcanthus birmanicus*	50	30
1567	400k. *Cymbidium lowianum*	90	45
1568	1000k. *Dendrobium gratiosissimum*	2·40	1·10
MS1569	95×70 mm. 2000k. *Paphiopedilum chamberlainanum* (31×37 mm)	4·50	4·50

See also Nos. 1626/9, 1685/**MS**1689 and 1836/46.

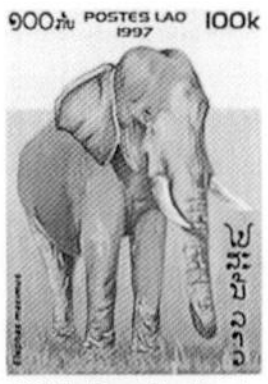

332 Indian Elephant (*Elephas maximus*)

1997. Elephants. Multicoloured.

1570	100k. Type **332**	20	15
1571	250k. Indian elephant carrying log (horiz)	50	30
1572	300k. Indian elephant with young (horiz)	65	30
1573	350k. African elephant ("Loxodonta africana") (horiz)	80	35
1574	450k. African elephant in water (horiz)	1·00	50
1575	550k. African elephant with ears flapping	1·30	60
MS1576	117×74 mm. 2000k. Forequarter of African elephant (31×39 mm)	4·50	4·50

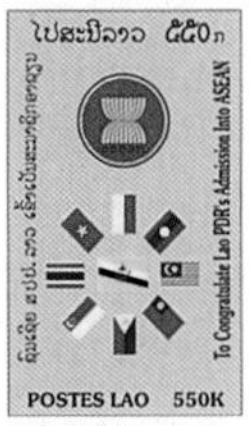

333 Emblem and Brunei Flag

1997. Admission of Laos into Association of South East Asian Nations. Members' flags, centre flag given.

1577	550k. Type **333**	80	80
1578	550k. Indonesia (red and white bands)	80	80
1579	550k. Laos (red, blue with white circle, red bands)	80	80
1580	550k. Malaysia (crescent and star on blue quarter, red and white stripes)	80	80
1581	550k. Myanmar (flower and stars on blue quarter, red)	80	80
1582	550k. Philippines (sun and stars on white triangle, blue and red bands)	80	80
1583	550k. Singapore (crescent and five stars on red band, white band)	80	80
1584	550k. Thailand (red, white, blue, red bands)	80	80
1585	550k. Vietnam (yellow star on red)	80	80
MS1586	Nine sheets, each 138×110 mm. (a) No. 1577; (b) No. 1578; (c) No. 1582; (d) No. 1580; (e) No. 1581; (f) No. 1582; (g) No. 1583; (h) No. 1584; (i) No. 1585	7·25	7·25

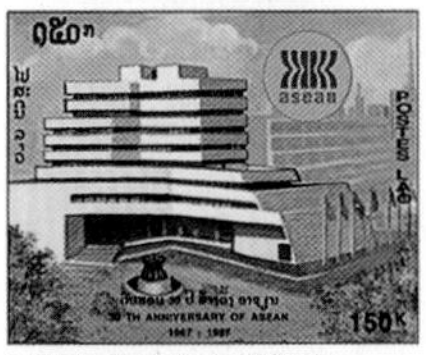

335 Headquarters, Djakarta, Indonesia

1997. 30th Anniv of Association of South East Asian Nations. Multicoloured.

1587	150k. Type **335**	60	60
1588	600k. Map of Laos and state flag	2·50	2·50

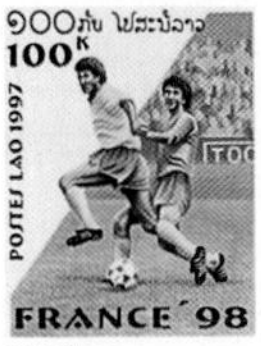

336 Players

1997. World Cup Football Championship, France (1998) (2nd issue).

1589	**336**	100k. multicoloured	20	15
1590	-	200k. multicoloured	45	20
1591	-	250k. multicoloured	50	30
1592	-	300k. multicoloured	65	30
1593	-	350k. multicoloured	80	35
1594	-	700k. multicoloured	1·50	75
MS1595		111×84 mm. 2000k. multicoloured	4·50	4·50

DESIGNS: 200k. to 2000k. Various football scenes.

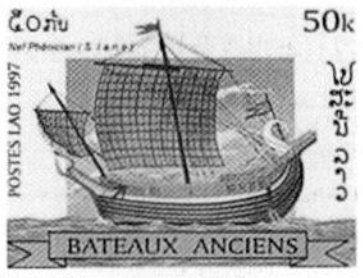

337 Phoenician Nef

1997. Sailing Ships. Multicoloured.

1596	50k. Type **337**	15	15
1597	100k. 13th-century nef	20	15
1598	150k. 15th-century nef	30	15
1599	200k. 16th-century Portuguese caravel	45	20
1600	400k. 17th-century Dutch ship	90	45
1601	900k. H.M.S. *Victory* (Nelson's flagship)	2·10	1·00
MS1602	80×60 mm. 2000k. *Great Harry* (sail warship), 1514	4·50	4·50

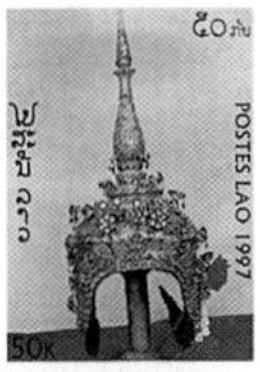

338 Headdress

1997. Headdresses and Masks. Multicoloured.

1603	50k. Type **338**	15	15
1604	100k. Headdress with flower at left	20	15
1605	150k. Mask with curved tusks (horiz)	30	15
1606	200k. Mask tipped with headdress decorated with two faces	50	20
1607	350k. Mask with green face	75	35

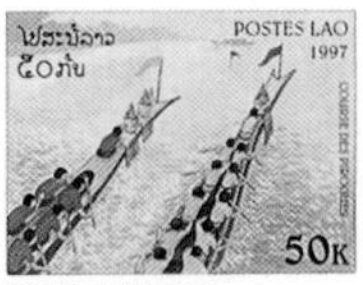

339 Two Pirogues

1997. Pirogue Race. Multicoloured.

1608	50k. Type **339**	15	15
1609	100k. Crowd cheering competitors from land	20	15
1610	300k. Side view of two competing pirogues	65	30
1611	500k. People cheering on spectator boat	1·10	50

340 Sunken Net

1998. Traditional Fishing Methods. Multicoloured.

1612	50k. Type **340**		15	15
1613	100k. Fisherman throwing net (horiz)		30	30
1614	450k. Funnel net (horiz)		1·40	1·40
1615	650k. Lobster pots (horiz)		1·90	1·90

341 Man riding Tiger

1998. New Year. Year of the Tiger.

1616	**341**	150k. multicoloured	60	60
1617	**341**	350k. multicoloured	1·40	1·40
1618	**341**	400k. multicoloured	1·80	1·80

342 Wat Sisaket Shrine

1998. Temples. Multicoloured.

1619	10000k. Type **342**		7·50	7·50
1620	25000k. Wat Phou temple, Pakse (horiz)		15·00	15·00
1621	45000k. That Luang (royal mausoleum) (horiz)		22·00	22·00

343 Boat and Pole

1998. Water Transport. Multicoloured.

1622	1100k. Type **343**		1·10	1·10
1623	1200k. Covered canoe		1·20	1·20
1624	2500k. Motorized canoe		2·50	2·50

344 Buddha, Luang Phabang Temple

1998

1625	**344**	3000k. multicoloured	2·10	2·10

345 *Paphiopedilum callosum*

1998. Orchids (3rd series). Multicoloured.

1626	900k. Type **345**		1·40	1·40
1627	950k. *Paphiopedilum concolor*		1·50	1·50
1628	1000k. *Dendrobium thyrsiflorum* (vert)		1·60	1·60
1629	1050k. *Dendrobium lindleyi*		1·60	1·60

See also Nos. 1685/**MS**1689 and 1836/46.

346 Children in Classroom

1998. 50th Anniv of Universal Declaration of Human Rights. Multicoloured.

1630	300k. Type **346**		35	35
1631	1700k. Woman posting vote into ballot box		2·20	2·20

347 Gaeng

1998. Wind Instruments. Multicoloured.

1632	900k. Type **347**		1·30	1·30
1633	1200k. Khuoy (flute)		1·80	1·80
1634	1500k. Khaen (bamboo pipes of various lengths)		2·20	2·20

348 Military Personnel and Flag

1999. 50th Anniv of People's Army. Multicoloured.

1635	1300k. Type **348**		1·10	1·10
1636	1500k. Soldier with upraised arm and jungle fighters (vert)		1·30	1·30

349 Inscribed Monument (world heritage)

1999. UNESCO World Heritage Site. Luang Prabang. Multicoloured.

1637	400k. Type **349**		35	35
1638	1150k. House with veranda and dovecote (horiz)		95	95
1639	1250k. Wat Xiengthong (horiz)		1·00	1·00

350 Yao Children celebrating New Year, Muong Sing

1999. Tourism Year (1st issue). Multicoloured.

1640	200k. Type **350**		15	15
1641	500k. Phadeang, Vangvieng district		35	35
1642	1050k. Wat That Makmo, Luang Prabang		80	80
1643	1300k. Patuxay (victory monument), Vientiane (vert)		1·00	1·00

See also No. **MS**1653 and 1714/17.

351 Rabbit and Chinese Zodiac Animals

1999. New Year. Year of the Rabbit. Multicoloured.

1644	1500k. Type **351**		75	75
1645	1600k. White rabbit (horiz)		1·60	1·60

352 Iron Plough

1999. Traditional Farming Implements. Multicoloured.

1646	1500k. Type **352**		1·10	1·10
1647	2000k. Harrow		1·50	1·50
1648	3200k. Wooden plough		2·40	2·40

353 Collared Owlet (*Glaucidium brodiei*)

1999. Owls and Bat. Multicoloured.

1649	900k. Type **353**		75	75
1650	1600k. Collared scops owl (*Otus lempiji*)		1·50	1·50
1651	2100k. Barn owl (*Tyto alba*)		2·20	2·20
1652	2800k. Black capped fruit bat (*Chironax melanocephalus*)		3·00	3·00

354 Patuxay (victory monument), Vientiane

1999. Tourism (2nd issue). Sheet 135×100 mm containing T 354 and similar horiz designs.

MS1653	2500k. Type **354**; 4000k. Ho Phra Keo, Vientiane; 5500k. Wat Xieng Thong, Luang Prabang; 8000k. Pha That Luang, Vientiane		10·50	10·50

355 Envelope and Globe

1999. 125th Anniv of Universal Postal Union. Multicoloured.

1654	2600k. Type **355**		1·80	1·80
1655	3400k. Postman delivering letter		2·50	2·50

356 Carved Tree Stump

1999. International Horticultural Exposition, Kunming, China. Exposition buildings. Multicoloured.

1656	300k. Type **356**		20	20
1657	900k. China Hall		45	45
1658	2300k. Science and Technology Hall		1·20	1·20
1659	2500k. Traditional Laotian house		1·40	1·40

357 Javan Rhino (*Rhinoceros sondaicus*)

1999. Animals. Multicoloured.

1660	700k. Type **357**		50	50
1661	900k. Water buffalo (*Bubalus bubalis*) (vert)		65	65
1662	1700k. Spotted linsang (*Prionodon pardicolor*)		1·30	1·30
1663	1800k. Sambar deer (*Cervus unicolor*)		1·30	1·30
1664	1900k. Lion (*Panthera leo*) (vert)		1·40	1·40

358 Airport and Hospital

2000. Millennium (1st issue). Multicoloured.

1665	2000k. Type **358**		75	75
1666	2000k. Temple		75	75
1667	2000k. Building with portico		75	75
1668	2000k. River and traditional buildings		75	75
MS1669	124×181 mm. Nos. 1665/8		3·00	3·00

Nos. 1665/8 were issued together, *se-tenant*, forming a composite design.
See also Nos. 1718/19.

359 Kor Loma

2000. Women's Regional Costumes (1st series). Multicoloured.

1670	100k. Type **359**		10	10
1671	200k. Kor Pchor		10	10
1672	500k. Nhuan Krom		15	15
1673	900k. Taidam		30	30
1674	2300k. Yao		65	65
1675	2500k. Meuy		75	75
1676	2600k. Sila		80	80
1677	2700k. Hmong		80	80
1678	2800k. Yao (different)		80	80
1679	3100k. Kor Nukkuy		90	90
1680	3200k. Kor Pouxang		95	95
1681	3300k. Yao Lanten		1·00	1·00
1682	3400k. Khir		1·10	1·10
1683	3500k. Kor		1·00	1·00
1684	3900k. Hmong (different)		1·20	1·20

See also Nos. 1777/87.

360 *Dendrobium draconis*

2000. Orchids (4th series). Bangkok 2000 International Stamp Exhibition (MS1689) Multicoloured.

1685	500k. Type **360**		15	15
1686	900k. *Paphiopedilum hirsutissimum*		30	30
1687	3000k. *Dendrobium sulcatum*		95	95
1688	3400k. *Rhynchostylis gigantean*		1·10	1·10
MS1689	111×145 mm. Nos. 1686/90		3·00	3·00

See also Nos. 1836/46.

361 Dragon and Chinese Zodiac

2000. Year of the Dragon. Multicoloured.

1690	1800k. Type **361**		50	50
1691	2300k. Dragon swimming		75	75

362 River, Deer and Trees

2000. Children's Paintings. Multicoloured.

1692	300k. Type **362**		15	15
1693	400k. Animals running from fire		15	15
1694	2300k. Animals and birds		95	95
1695	3200k. Animals and birds (vert)		1·30	1·30

363 Peacock

2000. The Peacock. Multicoloured.

1696	700k. Type **363**	20	20
1697	1000k. With tail displayed	35	35
1698	1800k. Peahen (horiz)	60	60
1699	3500k. Pair (horiz)	1·20	1·20
MS1700 146×110 mm. 10000k. Front showing tail displayed		3·50	3·50

364 Bridge

2000. Pakse Bridge over Mekong River. Multicoloured.

1701	900k. Type **364**	30	30
1702	2700k. Overview of bridge	95	95
1703	3200k. Bridge from right	1·10	1·10
MS1704 180×122 mm. 4000k. No. 1701; 7500k. No. 1702; 8500k. No. 1703r		6·75	6·75

365 Cycling

2000. Olympic Games, Sydney. Multicoloured.

1705	500k. Type **365**	15	15
1706	900k. Boxing	30	30
1707	2600k. Kick boxing	90	90
1708	3600k. Canoeing	1·30	1·30
MS1709 124×180 mm. Nos. 1705/8		3·25	3·25

366 Lao Theung

2000. Regional Wedding Costumes. Multicoloured.

1710	800k. Type **366**	30	30
1711	2300k. Lao Lum	75	75
1712	3400k. Lao Sung	1·20	1·20

367 Phousy Stupa, Luang Prabang

2000. Tourism (3rd issue). Multicoloured.

1713	300k. Type **367**	15	15
1714	600k. Tham Chang cave	20	20
1715	2800k. Inhang Stupa	1·20	1·20
1716	3300k. Buddha, Phiawal temple, Xiengkhuang	1·40	1·40

368 Building Facade

2000. 25th Anniv of Republic of Laos.

1717	**368** 4000k. multicoloured	1·30	1·30

369 Satellites and Child writing

2001. Millennium (2nd issue). Multicoloured.

1718	3200k. Type **369**	1·00	1·00
1719	4000k. Electricity pylons and dam	1·30	1·30

370 Roadway

2001. Route 13 Highway Improvement Project. Sheet 120×190 mm containing T **370** and similar horiz designs. Multicoloured.

MS1720 4000k. Type **370**; 4000k. Bridge and mountains; 4000k. Bridge (different)		4·00	4·00

371 Yao mane Huaphanh

2001. Men's Regional Costumes. Multicoloured.

1721	100k. Type **371**	10	10
1722	200k. Gnaheun Champasak	10	10
1723	500k. Katou Sarvane	15	15
1724	2300k. Hmong Dam Oudomxay	80	80
1725	2500k. Harlak Xekong	90	90
1726	2600k. Kui Luangnamtha	90	90
1727	2700k. Krieng Xekong	95	95
1728	3100k. Khmu Nhuan Luang-namtha	1·10	1·10
1729	3200k. Ta Oy Saravane	1·10	1·10
1730	3300k. TaiTheng Bolihamxay	1·20	1·20
1731	3400k. Hmong Khao Huaphanh	1·20	1·20
1732	3500k. Gnor Khammouane	1·30	1·30
1733	3600k. Phouthai Na Gnom ZVK	1·30	1·30
1734	4000k. Yao Ventiane	1·40	1·40
1735	5000k. Hmong LPQ	1·80	1·80

372 Cocks

2001. Fighting Cocks. Multicoloured.

1736	500k. Type **372**	20	20
1737	900k. Pair with wings out-stretched	35	35
1738	3200k. Pair, one in flight	1·30	1·30
1739	3500k. Pair resting	1·40	1·40
MS1740 140×111 mm. 10000k. Cock crowing (36×51 mm)		4·00	4·00

373 Pou Nyer and Nya Nyer

2001. Luang Prabang New Year Celebrations. Multicoloured.

1741	300k. Type **373**	10	10
1742	600k. Hae Nang Sangkhan	20	20
1743	1000k. Sand Stupa (horiz)	35	35
1744	2300k. Hae Prabang	80	80
1745	4000k. Takbat	1·50	1·50

374 Snake

2001. Year of the Snake. Multicoloured.

1746	900k. Type **374**	30	30
1747	3500k. Snake and Chinese zodiac symbols	1·20	1·20

375 The Gate of Heavenly Peace (Tian An Men)

2001. 40th Anniv of Laos–China Diplomatic Relations.

1748	**375** 1000k. multicoloured	35	35

376 Nurse, Mother and Children

2001. Polio Eradication Campaign. Sheet 135×101 mm containing T **376** and similar horiz design.

MS1749 900k. Type **376**; 2500k. Family and map		1·10	1·10

377 Mekong River

2001. Mekong River at Twilight. Multicoloured.

1750	900k. Type **377**	30	30
1751	2700k. River with boats in foreground	90	90
1752	3400k. River (different)	1·10	1·10

378 Poppy Field

2001. Anti-Drug Campaign. Multicoloured.

1753	100k. Type **378**	35	35
1754	4000k. Burning seized drugs	1·10	1·10

379 Intermediate Egret (*Egretta intermedia*)

2001. Birds. Philanippon '01 International Stamp Exhibition. Multicoloured.

1755	700k. Type **379**	20	20
1756	800k. Bulbucus ibis (33×49 mm)	20	20
1757	3100k. Grey heron (*Ardea cinera*) (33×49 mm)	95	95
1758	3400k. Great egret (*Egretta alba*)	1·00	1·00
MS1759 200×146 mm. Nos. 1755/8		3·00	3·00

380 Temple Door

2001. Buddhist Temple Doors.

1760	**380** 600k. multicoloured	20	20
1761	– 2300k. multicoloured	80	80
1762	– 2500k. multicoloured	90	90
1763	– 2600k. multicoloured	90	90

DESIGNS: 2300k. to 2600k. Different temple doors.

381 White Frangipani

2001. The Frangipani. Multicoloured.

1764	1000k. Type **381**	35	35
1765	2500k. Pink frangipani (vert)	90	90
1766	3500k. Red frangipani	1·20	1·20
MS1767 145×111 mm. Nos. 1764/6		2·40	2·40

382 Women using Pestles and Mortar

2001. Traditional Mortars. Multicoloured.

1768	900k. Type **382**	30	30
1769	2600k. Wheel driven pestle and mortar (horiz)	80	80
1770	3500k. Fulcrum and lever pestle and mortar	1·10	1·10

383 Himavanta

2001. *Vessantara* (Buddhist story illustrating charity). Multicoloured.

1771	200k. Type **383**	10	10
1772	900k. Vanapavesa	35	35
1773	3200k. Kumarakanda	1·30	1·30
1774	3600k. Sakkapabba	1·50	1·50
MS1775 120×151 mm. Nos. 1772/4		3·25	3·25

384 People and Emblem

2001. International Year of Volunteers.

1776	**384** 1000k. multicoloured	35	35

2002. Women's Regional Costumes (2nd series). As T **359**. Multicoloured.

1777	200k. Meuy	10	10
1778	300k. Leu	10	10
1779	500k. Tai Kouane	15	15
1780	700k. Tai Dam	25	25
1781	1000k. Tai Man	30	30
1782	1500k. Lanten	45	45
1783	2500k. Hmong	80	80
1784	3000k. Phouxang	95	95
1785	3500k. Taitheng	1·10	1·10
1786	4000k. Tai O	1·20	1·20
1787	5000k. Tai Dam (different)	1·50	1·50

385 Phou Phamane

2002. International Year of Mountains. Multicoloured.

1788	1500k. Type **385**	55	55
1789	1500k. Pha Tang	55	55

386 Horse

2002. Chinese New Year ("Year of the Horse"). Multicoloured.

1790	1500k. Type **386**	55	55
1791	3500k. Galloping horse	1·10	1·10

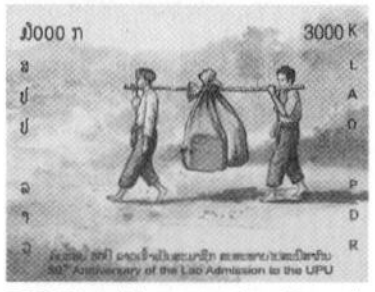

387 Two Men carrying Parcels on Pole

2002. 50th Anniv of Laos Admission to Universal Postal Union.

1792 **387**	3000k. black	85	85

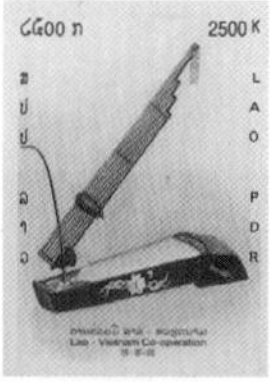

388 Laotian and Vietnamese Musical Instruments

2002. 40th Anniv of Laos—Vietnam Diplomatic Relations. 25th Anniv of Friendship Treaty.

1793 **388**	2500k. multicoloured	70	70
1794 -	3500k. black and orange (horiz)	1·00	1·00

DESIGNS: 2500k. Type **388**; 3500k. Prince Souvanna Vong and Ho Chi Minh (Vietnamese leader).

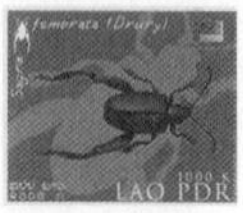

389 *Sagra femorata*

2002. Beetles. PhilaKorea 2002. Multicoloured.

1795	1000k. Type **389**	25	25
1796	1000k. *Cerambycidae*	25	25
1797	1000k. *Chrysoxhroa mniszechii*	25	25
1798	1000k. *Anoplophora*	25	25
1799	1000k. *Chrysochroa saundersi*	25	25
1800	1000k. *Mouhotia batesi*	25	25
1801	1000k. *Megaloxantha assamensis*	25	25
1802	1000k. *Eupatorus gracillicornis*	25	25
MS1803	150×210 mm. 1000k. ×8, *Sagra femorata* (different); *Cerambycidae* (different); *Chrysoxhroa mniszechii* (different); *Anoplophora* (different);*Chrysochroa saundersi* (different); *Mouhotia batesi* (different); *Megaloxantha assamensis* (different); *Eupatorus gracillicornis* (different)	2·00	2·00

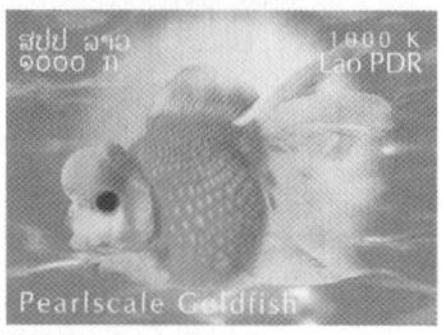

390 Pearlscale Oranda

2002. Goldfish. Multicoloured.

1804	1000k. Type **390**	35	35
1805	1000k. Moor	35	35
1806	1000k. Bubble eye	35	35
1807	1000k. Red-capped oranda	35	35
1808	1000k. Lionhead	35	35
1809	1000k. Pom pom	35	35
1810	1000k. Ranchu	35	35
1811	1000k. Fantail	35	35
1812	1000k. Celestial	35	35
1813	1000k. Ryukin	35	35
1814	1000k. Brown oranda	35	35
1815	1000k. Veiltail (inscr "Veitail")	35	35

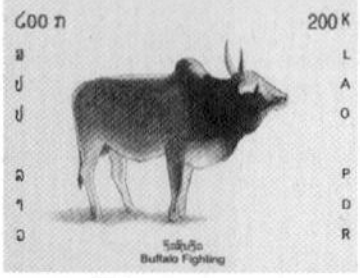

391 Buffalo

2002. Buffalo Fighting. Multicoloured.

1816	200k. Type **391**	15	15
1817	300k. Two buffalos with raised heads	15	15
1818	3000k. Two with locked horns	85	85
1819	4000k. Two chasing one another	1·10	1·10

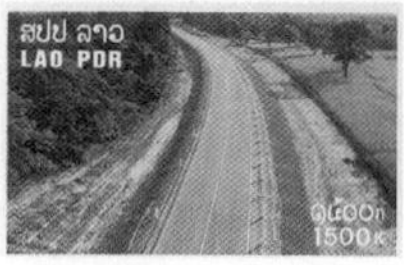

392 Roadway

2002. Route 9 Highway Improvement Project. Sheet 190×116 mm containing T **392** and similar horiz designs. Multicoloured.

MS1820	1500k. ×3, Type **392**; Road junction; Open road	1·40	1·40

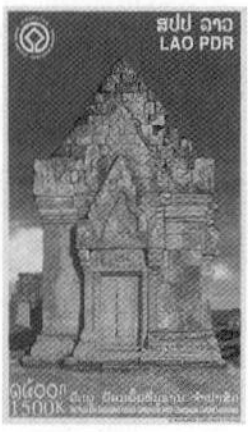

393 Arched Doorway

2003. World Heritage Site. Wat Phou Temple, Champasak. Multicoloured.

1821	1500k. Type **393**	30	30
1822	3000k. Wat Phou (horiz)	70	70
1823	4000k. Internal doorway and Buddha	1·20	1·20
MS1824	145×150 mm. 10000k. Carving showing three-headed elephant (96×30 mm)	2·60	2·60

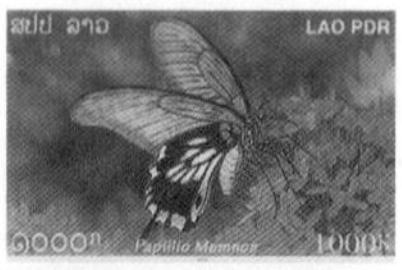

394 Great Mormon (*Papillio memnon*)

2003. Butterflies. Multicoloured.

1825	1000k. Type **394**	30	30
1826	1000k. *Pachliopta aristolochiae*	30	30
1827	1000k. Inscr "Dalias pasithoe"	30	30
1828	1000k. *Castalius rosimon*	30	30
1829	1000k. *Polyura Schreiber*	30	30
1830	1000k. Blue triangle (*Graphium sarpedon*)	30	30
1831	1000k. *Spindasis lohita*	30	30
1832	1000k. *Hasora schoenherr*	30	30
MS1833	156×129 mm. 1000k. *Danaus genutia*	2·60	2·60

No. **MS**1833 was cut round in the shape of a butterfly.

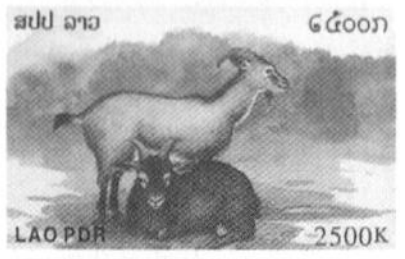

395 Two Goats

2003. New Year ("Year of the Goat"). Multicoloured.

1834	2500k. Type **395**	70	70
1835	5000k. Goat wearing bell and saddle cloth	1·40	1·40

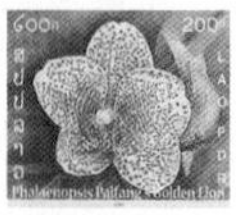

396 *Phalaenopsis paifang*

2003. Orchids (5th series). Multicoloured.

1836	200k. Type **396**	10	10
1837	300k. *Coelogyne lentiginosa*	15	15
1838	500k. *Phalaenopsis sumatrana*	25	25
1839	1000k. *Phalaenopsis bellina*	30	30
1840	1500k. *Paphiopedilum appletonianum*	30	30
1841	2000k. *Vanda bensonii*	50	50
1842	2500k. *Dendrobium harveyanum*	60	60
1843	3000k. *Paphiopedilum glaucophyllum*	75	75
1844	3500k. *Paphiopedilum gratrixianum*	90	90
1845	4000k. *Vanda roeblingiana*	1·00	1·00
1846	5000k. *Phalaenopsis Lady Sakara*	1·30	1·30

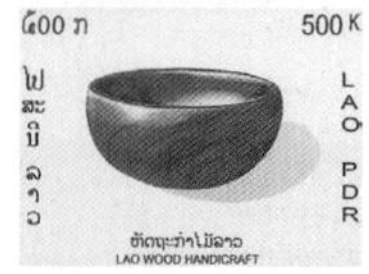

397 Bowl

2003. Wooden Crafts. Multicoloured.

1847	500k. Type **397**	15	10
1848	1500k. Drinks set	40	40
1849	2500k. Flower-shaped bowl	65	65
1850	3500k. Vase (vert)	95	95

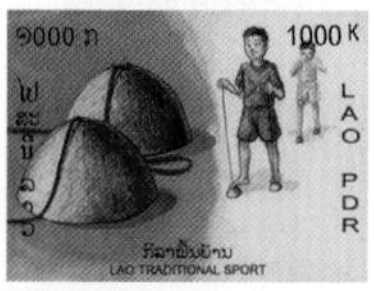

398 Children using Coconut Feet Lifters

2003. Traditional Sports and Games. Multicoloured.

1851	1000k. Type **398**	30	30
1852	3000k. Spinning tops	80	80
1853	4000k. Tee knee (hockey)	1·00	1·00

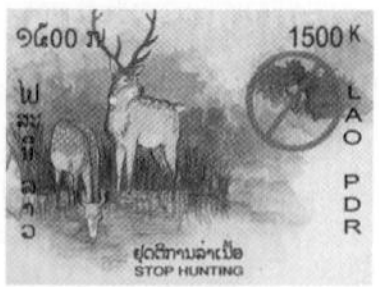

399 Deer and "Stop" Sign

2003. "Stop Hunting" Campaign. Multicoloured.

1854	1500k. Type **399**	40	40
1855	2000k. Rifle and bow	50	50
1856	4500k. Prey animals	1·20	1·20

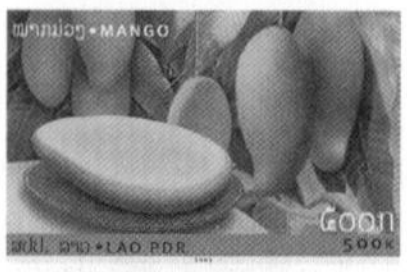

400 Mango

2003. Fruit. Multicoloured.

1857	500k. Type **400**	15	15
1858	1500k. Water melon	40	40
1859	2500k. Custard apple	65	65
1860	4000k. Pineapple	1·00	1·00

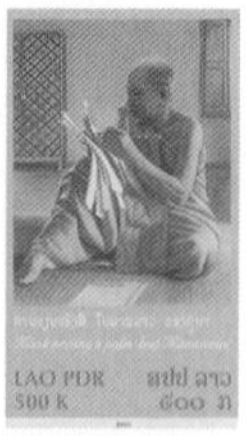

401 Monk writing on Palm Leaf

2003. Palm Leaf Manuscripts. Multicoloured.

1861	500k. Type **401**	15	15
1862	1500k. Manuscript book	30	30
1863	2500k. Manuscript casket	55	55
1864	3000k. Ho Tai temple archive	65	65

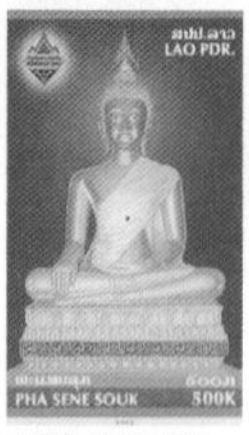

402 Buddha (Pha Sene Souk)

2003. Luang Prabang Statues. Statues of Buddha. Multicoloured.

1865	500k. Type **402**	15	15
1866	1500k. Pha Gnai	30	30
1867	3000k. Pha Ong Luang	55	55
1868	3500k. Pha Ong Sene	65	65
MS1869	110×144 mm. 1000k. Pha Attharatsa (30×96 mm)	2·50	2·50

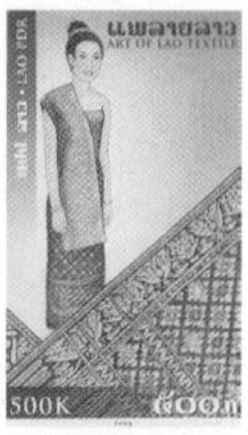

403 Traditional Cloth and Woman wearing Sin Mai (skirt) and Bieng Phae (scarf)

2003. Laotian Textiles. Showing cloth and woman. Multicoloured.

1870	500k. Type **403**	15	15
1871	1000k. Woman at right and brown patterned cloth	25	25
1872	3000k. Woman at left and green patterned cloth	65	65
1873	4000k. Woman at right and block patterned cloth	80	80

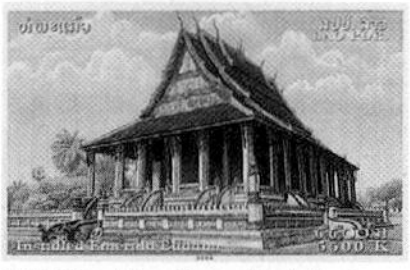

404 Haw Pha Keaw (Installed Emerald Buddha), Vientiane

2004

1874 **404**	5500k. multicoloured	1·20	1·20

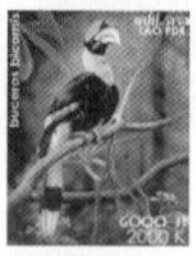

405 *Buceros bicornis*

2004. Birds. Multicoloured.

1875	2000k. Type **405**	55	55
1876	2500k. *Pycnonotus jocosus*	65	65
1877	3000k. *Ploceus hypoxanthus*	80	80
1878	3500k. *Alcedo atthis*	80	80
1879	4000k. *Megalaima* (inscr "Magalaima") *incognita*	90	90
1880	4500k. *Serilophus lunatus*	1·10	1·10
1881	5000k. *Eurylaimus ochromalus*	1·20	1·20
1882	5500k. *Lacedo pulchella*	1·40	1·40

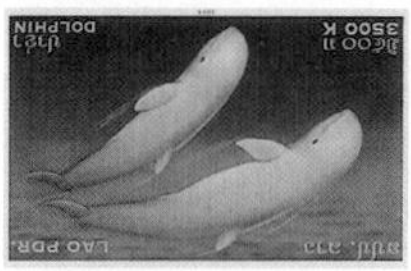

406 Two Dolphins

2004. Endangered Species. Irrawaddy Dolphins. Multicoloured.

1883	1500k. Type **406**	30	30
1884	2500k. Leaping	55	55
1885	3500k. With heads raised	65	65

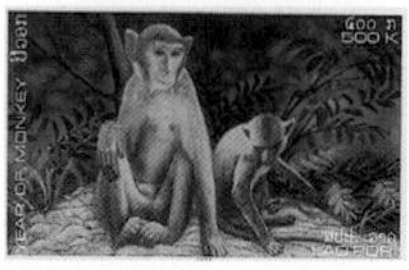

407 Two Monkeys

2004. New Year "Year of the Monkey". Multicoloured.

1886	500k. Type **407**	15	15
1887	4500k. Monkey king	1·10	1·10

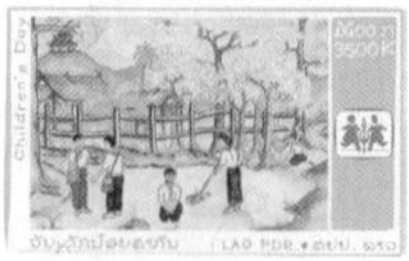

409 Children

2004. Children's Day Multicoloured.

1890	3500k. Type **409**	95	95
1891	4500k. Children (different)	1·30	1·30

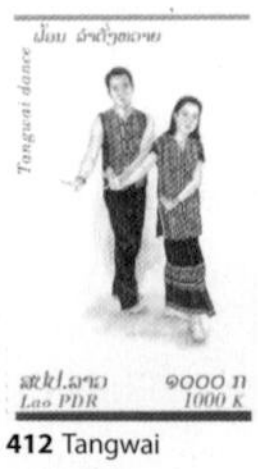

412 Tangwai

2004. Dances. Multicoloured.

1897	1000k. Type **412**	25	25
1898	1500k. Khabthoume Luangprabang	40	40
1899	2000k. Lao Lamvong	40	40
1900	2500k. Salavan	60	60

413 Marigold

2004. Marigold. Multicoloured.
1901	3500k. Type **413**	80	80
1902	5000k. Marigold (different)	1·10	1·10
1903	5500k. Hats and marigold garlands	1·20	1·20

414 Demons

2004. Ramakian. Multicoloured.
1904	3500k. Type **414**	80	80
1905	4500k. Hanuman, Rama and Lakshman	90	90
1906	5500k. Hanuman, Rama and Lakshman (different)	1·10	1·10
1907	6500k. Demon, Hanuman, Rama and Lakshman	1·20	1·20

415 Gods and Naga

2004. Naga Fire. Multicoloured.
1908	2000k. Type **415**	50	50
1909	3000k. Naga in kingdom beneath the water (horiz)	75	75
1910	3500k. Naga in river (horiz)	80	80
1911	4000k. Naga rearing out of water	85	85

416 Betel Nuts and Equipment

2004. Betel Tray. Multicoloured.
1912	2000k. Type **416**	50	50
1913	4000k. Leaf tray and wrappings	85	85
1914	6000k. Decorated tray and equipment	1·40	1·40

417 Elephant, Wat, Building and Reindeer

2004. 40th Anniv of Laos—Sweden Diplomatic Relations.
| 1915 | **417** | 8500k. multicoloured | 1·80 | 1·80 |

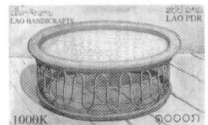
418 Woven Table

2005. Handicrafts. Multicoloured.
1916	1000k. Type **418**	30	30
1917	2000k. Paddle	50	50
1918	2500k. Basket (vert)	70	70
1919	5500k. Hanging lidded basket (vert)	1·50	1·50

419 Rooster, Hen and Chicks

2005. New Year. Year of the Rooster. Multicoloured.
| 1920 | 2000k. Type **419** | 50 | 50 |
| 1921 | 7500k. Rooster | 1·80 | 1·80 |

420 Sunday's Buddha

2005. Days of the Week. Designs showing Buddha. Multicoloured.
1922	500k. Type **420**	20	20
1923	1000k. Monday	35	35
1924	1500k. Tuesday (horiz)	35	35
1925	2000k. Wednesday	50	50
1926	2500k. Thursday	65	65
1927	3000k. Friday	80	80
1928	3500k. Saturday	95	95

421 Growing Rice

2005. Rice. Multicoloured.
1929	1500k. Type **421**	40	40
1930	3000k. Cooked rice on woven tray (horiz)	80	80
1931	6500k. Rice straw (horiz)	1·70	1·70

422 Catfish

2005. Mekong River Giant Catfish (*Pangasianodon giga*). Multicoloured.
| 1932 | 3500k. Type **422** | 95 | 95 |
| 1933 | 6500k. Catfish (different) | 1·70 | 1·70 |

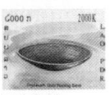
423 Gold Panning Sieve

2005. Tools. Multicoloured.
| 1934 | 2000k. Type **423** | 55 | 55 |
| 1935 | 7500k. Woman using sieve (vert) | 1·80 | 1·80 |

424 Musician and Singer

2005. Folk Music. Multicoloured.
1936	1000k. Type **424**	30	30
1937	3500k. Seated singer and musician	75	75
1938	5500k. Singer and three musicians (horiz)	1·20	1·20

425 Harvesting

2005. 50th Anniv of Laos—United Nations Co-operation. Multicoloured.
1939	3000k. Type **425**	75	75
1940	3000k. Child immunization	75	75
1941	3000k. Education	75	75

426 Stonehenge, UK and Field of Jars, Laos

2005. 50th Anniv of Europa Stamps. Multicoloured.
1943	6000k. Type **426**	75	75
1944	7000k. Knossos, Greece and Patuxay, Laos	80	80
1945	7000k. Coliseum, Rome and Wat Phu, Laos	80	80

1946	7500k. Lom Church, Norway and Wat Xieng Thong, Laos	85	85
1947	7500k. Notre Dame Cathedral, Paris and That Lauang, Laos	85	85
1948	8000k. Trier Cathedral, Germany	1·00	1·00
MS1949	142×90 mm. Nos. 1943/8	4·75	4·75

427 Flag and Government Building

2005. 30th Anniv of Laos People's Democratic Republic. Multicoloured.
1950	500k. Type **427**	20	20
1951	1000k. Flag, map and figures	35	35
1952	2000k. State arms and flag	70	70
1953	5000k. "30" enclosing state arms	1·40	1·40

428 Cement Works

2005. 30th Anniv of Laos People's Democratic Republic (2nd issue). Multicoloured.
| 1954 | 15500k. Type **428** | 2·40 | 2·40 |
| **MS**1955 | 170×130 mm. 2000k. As No. 1954 | 45 | 45 |

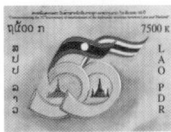
429 Flags and "55"

2005. 55th Anniv of Laos—Thailand Diplomatic Relations.
| 1956 | **429** | 7500k. multicoloured | 90 | 90 |

430 Cherry Blossom and Frangipani

2005. 50th Anniv of Laos—Japan Diplomatic Relations.
| 1957 | **430** | 7000k. multicoloured | 85 | 85 |

431 King Phangum Lenglathorany

2006. King Phangum Lenglathorany.
| 1958 | **431** | 8500k. multicoloured | 1·30 | 1·30 |

No. 1958 was issued both in sheets and premium miniature sheets, 110×145 mm, which were on sale for 20000k.

No. 1959 is vacant.

432 Dog

2006. New Year. Year of the Dog. Multicoloured.
| 1960 | 2000k. Type **432** | 35 | 35 |
| 1961 | 6500k. Dog surrounded by astrological animals | 1·10 | 1·10 |

433 Laotian and Russian Women

2006. Vientiane—Moscow Friendship. Multicoloured.
1962	7500k. Type **433**	90	90
1963	87500k. Laotian and Russian statues and buildings	9·25	9·25
MS1964	130×170 mm. Nos. 1962/3	10·00	10·00

434 Vehicles

2006. 15th Anniv of Insurance Provision in Laos. Multicoloured.
1965	8000k. Type **434**	1·00	1·00
1966	8500k. Map showing provinces	2·30	2·30
1967	9500k. Family	2·50	2·50

435 Images of China and Laos

2006. 45th Anniv of Laos—China Diplomatic Relations.
| 1968 | **435** | 8500k. multicoloured | 1·30 | 1·30 |

436 Garden

2006. Wat Xieng Khouang (garden of Buddhas). Multicoloured.
1969	1000k. Type **436**	15	15
1970	2500k. Demon	40	40
1971	3000k. Centre of garden	50	50
1972	5000k. Reclining Buddha	80	80

437 Shrimps

2006. Shrimps. Multicoloured.
1973	1000k. Type **437**	15	15
1974	2000k. Facing left	35	35
1975	4000k. Facing right	65	65
1976	6000k. Amongst weeds	95	95
MS1977	170×130 mm. Nos. 1973/6		

438 Leopold Senghor

2006. Birth Centenary of Leopold Senghor (poet and president of Senegal 1960–1980).
| 1978 | **438** | 8500k. multicoloured | 1·30 | 1·30 |

439 Drum

2006. Drums. Multicoloured.
1978a	2000k. Type **439**	35	35
1978b	3500k. Drum with two handles	45	45
1978c	7500k. Waisted drum	95	95
MS1979	130×170 mm. 2000k. As Type **439**; 3500k. As No. 1978b; 7500k. As 1978c	1·90	1·90

2006. Drums. Sheet 130×170 mm containing T 439 and similar horiz designs. Multicoloured.

MS1979 2000k. Type **439**; 3500k. Drum with two handles; 7500k. Waisted drum   2·20   2·20

440 Green Bananas

2006. Bananas. Multicoloured.

1980	1000k. Type **440**	15	15
1981	2000k. Double bunch	35	35
1982	4000k. Long bunch	65	65
1983	8000k. Long bunch with stalk	1·30	1·30

441 Bridge Over Mekong River and Japanese, Thai and Laotian Flags

2006. Friendship Bridge. Multicoloured.

| 1984 | 7500k. Type **441** | 1·20 | 1·20 |
| 1985 | 7500k. Bridge at night | 1·20 | 1·20 |

442 Pig and Signs of Chinese Zodiac

2007. New Year. Year of the Pig. Mutlicoloured.

| 1986 | 7500k. Type **442** | 1·20 | 1·20 |
| 1987 | 7500k. Pig and piglets | 1·20 | 1·20 |

443 Earrings

2007. Jewellery. Multicoloured.

1988	2000k. Type **443**	35	35
1989	5000k. Bracelet	80	80
1990	7000k. Circular earrings	1·10	1·10
1991	7500k. Pendant	1·20	1·20
MS1992 127×170 mm. Nos. 1988/91		3·50	3·50

444 Crab

2007. Crabs. Multicoloured.

1993	1000k. Type **444**	15	15
1994	2000k. Purple crab facing right	35	35
1995	7000k. Facing left	1·10	1·10
1996	7500k. With one enlarged pincer	1·20	1·20
MS1997 128×170 mm. Nos. 1993/6		2·75	2·75

444a Traditional House, Laos

2007. 40th Anniv of ASEAN. Multicoloured.

1998	700k. Type **444a**	20	20
1999	700k. Secretariat Building, Bandar Seri Bagwan, Brunei	20	20
2000	700k. National Museum of Cambodia	20	20
2001	700k. Fatahillah Museum, Jakarta, Indonesia	20	20

2002	700k. Railway Headquarters Building, Kuala Lumpur, Malaysia	20	20
2003	700k. Post Office, Yangon, Myanmar	20	20
2004	700k. Malcanang Palace, Philippines	20	20
2005	700k. National Museum of Singapore	20	20
2006	700k. Vimanmek Mansion, Bangkok, thailand	20	20
2007	700k. Presidential Palace, Hanoi, Vietnam	20	20
2008	7000k. As Type **444a** with additional Laotian script	95	95

432a Elephant and Rider

2008. Elephant Festival. Multicoloured.

2008a	1000k. Type **432a**	15	15
2008b	2000k. Two elephants and riders	35	35
2008c	3000k. Crowd, parasol and presentation	50	50
2008d	5000k. Elephant with rider wearing hat	80	80
2008e	7500k. Woman dressing elephant	95	95
2008f	8500k. Elephants moving logs	1·30	1·30

MS2008g 146×110 mm. 20000k. Two elephants with riders wearing red. Imperf   3·50   3·50

445 Monks and Women

2008. Tak Bat Dok Mai Floral Festival (giving alms to monks including Dok Khao Phansa flowers that only come into bloom during the Buddhist Lent). Multicoloured.

2009	2000k. Type **445**	35	35
2010	5000k. Monks receiving alms	80	80
2011	7500k. Women preparing alms	1·20	1·20

446 Aircraft

2008. Transport. Multicoloured.

2012	2000k. Type **446**	35	35
2013	5000k. Ferry	80	80
2014	7500k. Lorry convoy	1·20	1·20

447 Monks and Festival Goers

2008. That Luang Festival. Multicoloured.

2015	2000k. Type **447**	35	35
2016	5000k. Procession	80	80
2017	8000k. Illuminated temple	1·30	1·30

448 Sticky Rice cooked in Bamboo Tube

2008. Traditional Foods. Multicoloured.

2018	2000k. Type **448**	35	35
2019	5500k. Green papaya salad	90	90
2020	7500k. Grilled chicken	1·20	1·20

449 Gibbon

2008. Endangered Species. Lar Gibbon (white-handed gibbon) (*Hylobates lar*). Multicoloured.

2021	6000k. Type **449**	1·00	1·00
2022	7000k. Mother and baby	1·10	1·10
2023	8000k. Gibbon howling	1·40	1·40
2024	9000k. Two gibbons	1·50	1·50

450 Coffee Cup and Beans

2008. Coffee. Multicoloured.

2025	3000k. Type **450**	45	45
2026	5000k. Coffee berries	80	80
2027	6000k. Coffee beans	1·10	1·10

A miniature sheet 110×141 mm, containing one example each of Nos. 2025/7, was on sale for 18000k., 4000k. above face value.

451 Woman separating Seeds from Fibres

2008. Cotton. Multicoloured.

2028	1000k. Type **451**	15	15
2029	5000k. Cotton flower	80	80
2030	5500k. Cotton bolls	90	90

452 Judo

2008. Olympic Games, Beijing. Multicoloured.

2031	5000k. Type **452**	80	80
2032	5000k. Cycling	80	80
2033	5000k. Football	80	80
2034	5000k. High jump	80	80

453 Bees on Honeycomb

2008. Bees. Multicoloured.

2035	1000k. Type **453**	15	15
2036	4000k. Bees on flower	70	70
2037	6000k. Swarm	1·00	1·00
2038	8500k. Bee in flight	1·40	1·40

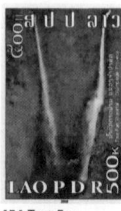

454 Taat Fan, Champasak

2008. Waterfalls. Multicoloured.

2039	500k. Type **454**	10	10
2040	2000k. Tad Sae, Luangprabang (horiz)	35	35
2041	5000k. Kuang Si, Luangprabang	80	80
2042	6500k. Khonphapheng, Champasak (horiz)	1·00	1·00

455 White Aubergines

456 Humong Woman

2008. Aubergines. Multicoloured.

2043	2043 Type **455**	15	15·00
2044	2000k. Circular green	35	35
2045	4000k. Circular green striped	70	70
2046	5500k. Long thin purple	90	90

2008. Humong New Year. Multicoloured.

2047	1000k. Type **456**	15	15
2048	5500k. Fighting bulls (horiz)	90	90
2049	6000k. Musician dancing	1·00	1·00
2050	7500k. Two actors wearing traditional dress (horiz)	1·20	1·20
MS2051 151×123 mm. Nos. 2047/50		3·25	3·25

457 Haw Phra Kaew

2009. Antiquities. Multicoloured.

2052	1000k. Type **457**	15	15
2053	2000k. Plain of jars	35	35
2054	4000k. Phat That Luang	70	70
2055	7500k. Temple	1·20	1·20
MS2056 137×170 mm. Nos. 2052/5		2·50	2·50

458 Early Soldiers

2009. 60th Anniv of Lao People's Army. Multicoloured.

2057	2000k. Type **458**	35	35
2058	2000k. Soldiers on parade, marching right	35	35
2059	2000k. Soldiers, heads, facing left	35	35
2060	2000k. Soldiers wearing helmets, facing left	35	35

459 Locomotive and Train

2009. Opening of Laos–Thailand Rail Link. Multicoloured.

2061	3000k. Type **459**	45	45
2062	3000k. Train in station	45	45
2063	3000k. Rail link bridge	45	45

460 Kalachuchi

2009. China 2009–World Stamp Exhibition, Luoyang. Multicoloured.

| 2064 | 7500k. Type **460** | 1·20 | 1·20 |
| 2065 | 7500k. Peony | 1·20 | 1·20 |

461 Inscr 'Mari Flower'

2009. Flowers. Multicoloured.

2066	500k. Type **461**	10	10
2067	2000k. Ixora	35	35
2068	4000k. White crown flowers (inscr 'Vuddhish Flowers')	70	70
2069	7500k. Mauve crown flowers (inscr 'Vuddhish Flowers')	1·20	1·20

462 Pot with Straws

2009. Rice Alcohol. Multicoloured.

2070	1000k. Type **462**	15	15
2071	2000k. Drinking horn	35	35
2072	5500k. Drinking through straw from large pot	90	9·00

463 R. P. Vientiane

2009. Post Day. Each royal blue and black.

2073	2000k. Type **463**	35	35
2074	2000k. Centre de Tri	35	35
2075	2000k. Phongsaly	35	35
2076	2000k. Luangnamtha	35	35
2077	2000k. Oudomxay	35	35
2078	2000k. Bokeo	35	35
2079	2000k. Luangpabang	35	35
2080	2000k. Huaphan	35	35
2081	2000k. Sayaboury	35	35
2082	2000k. Xiengkhouang	35	35
2083	2000k. Vientiane	35	35
2084	2000k. Bolikhamxay	35	35
2085	2000k. Khammouane	35	35
2086	2000k. Savannakhet	35	35
2087	2000k. Saravan	35	35
2088	2000k. Sekong	35	35
2089	2000k. Champasack	35	35
2090	2000k. Attapeu	35	35

464 Champa and Champi, Games Mascots

2009. 25th Southeast Asian Games, Vientiane. Multicoloured.

2091	5000k. Type **464**	80	8·00
2092	7000k. Champa, Champi and Laotian flag	1·10	1·10

465 Female Statue

2009. Wat Si Muang (Wat Simuong). Multicoloured.

2093	4000k. Type **465**	70	70
2094	5000k. Stone ruin	80	80
2095	6000k. Temple	1·00	1·00

Nos. 2096/8 and Type **466** are left for Village Life, issued on 15 February 2010, not yet received.

Nos. 2099/101 and Type **467** are left for Architecture, issued on 15 March 2010, not yet received.

Nos. 2102/5 and Type **468** are left for Landscapes, issued on 1April 2010, not yet received.

469 *Litsea cubeba*

2010. Flora. Multicoloured.

2106	1000k. Type **469**	60	60
2107	3000k. *Orthosiphon stamineus* (vert)	2·00	2·00
2108	4000k. *Strychnos nux vomica* (vert)	2·40	2·40
2109	5000k. *Zingiber*	2·50	2·50
2110	8000k. *Styrax tonkinensis* (vert)	3·75	3·75
2111	9000k. *Aquilaria crassna* (vert)	5·00	5·00

POSTAGE DUE STAMPS

D5 Vat Sisaket Shrine

D6 Sampans

1952

D22	**D5**	10c. brown	15	15
D23	**D5**	20c. violet	15	15
D24	**D5**	50c. red	15	15
D25	**D5**	1p. green	20	20
D26	**D5**	2p. blue	20	20
D27	**D5**	5p. purple	75	75
D28	**D6**	10p. blue	1·10	1·10

D98 Serpent

1973

D378	**D98**	10k. black, brn & yell	15	15
D379	**D98**	15k. black, yell & grn	15	15
D380	**D98**	20k. black, green & bl	15	15
D381	**D98**	50k. black, blue & red	35	35

APPENDIX

The following stamps have either been issued in excess of postal needs or have not been available to the public in reasonable quantities at face value. Such stamps may later be given full listing if there is evidence of regular postal use.

1975

Centenary of U.P.U. Postage 10, 15, 30, 40k.; Air 1000, 1500k. On gold foil 2500, 3000k.

"Apollo–Soyuz" Space Link. Postage 125, 150, 200, 300k.; Air 450, 700k.

Bicentenary of American Revolution. Postage 10, 15, 40, 50, 100, 125, 150, 200k.; Air 1000, 1500k.

Pt. 1

LAS BELA

A state of Baluchistan. Now part of Pakistan.

12 pies = 1 anna; 16 annas = 1 rupee.

1

1897

1	1	½a. black on white	42·00	22·00
3	1	½a. black on grey	28·00	14·00
11	1	½a. black on blue	25·00	12·00
12	1	½a. black on green	26·00	12·00
8	-	1a. black on orange	42·00	45·00

The 1a. has the English inscription in a circle with the native inscription across the centre.

Pt. 6, Pt. 19

LATAKIA

The former state of the Alaouites which changed its name to Latakia. in 1930. Latakia was merged with Syria in 1936.

100 centimes = 1 piastre.

The former state of the Alaouites which changed its name to Latakia in 1930.

Latakia was merged with Syria in 1936.

1931. As 1930 stamps of Syria (T 26/7) optd **LATTAQUIE** in French and Arabic.

65	0p.10 mauve	2·00	4·25
66	0p.20 blue	30	2·50
67	0p.20 red	1·80	6·50
68	0p.25 green	1·30	4·00
69	0p.25 violet	3·25	6·25
70	0p.50 violet	2·10	5·75
71	0p.75 red	3·50	8·00
72	1p. green	2·50	2·30
73	1p.50 brown	5·00	9·00
74	1p.50 green	10·00	10·00
75	2p. violet	4·00	2·75
76	3p. green	9·00	7·75
77	4p. orange	5·00	2·30
78	4p.50 red	7·75	13·00
79	6p. green	8·00	13·00
80	7p.50 blue	7·00	5·00
81	10p. brown	8·50	16·00
82	15p. green	12·00	26·00
83	25p. purple	30·00	50·00
84	50p. brown	36·00	50·00
85	100p. red	65·00	£110

1931. Air. As 1931 air stamps of Syria optd **LATTAQUIE** in French and Arabic.

86	0p.50 yellow	1·60	3·75
87	0p.50 brown	2·75	6·00
88	1p. brown	2·40	3·25
89	2p. blue	5·00	7·25
90	3p. green	4·50	7·75
91	5p. purple	7·75	18·00
92	10p. blue	10·00	14·50
93	15p. red	11·00	24·00
94	25p. orange	30·00	55·00
95	50p. black	32·00	60·00
96	100p. mauve	38·00	55·00

POSTAGE DUE STAMPS

1931. Nos. D197/8 of Syria optd **LATTAQUIE** in French and Arabic.

D86	8p. black on blue	29·00	55·00
D87	15p. black on pink	16·00	28·00

Pt. 10

LATVIA

A country on the Baltic Sea. Previously part of the Russian Empire. Latvia was independent from 1918 to 1940 when it became part of the U.S.S.R.

Following the dissolution of the U.S.S.R. in 1991, Latvia once againbecame an independent republic.

4

1919. Liberation of Riga. Imperf.

24	**4**	5k. red	25	25
25	**4**	15k. green	25	25
26	**4**	35k. brown	35	65

For stamps of Types **1** and **4** optd with a cross, with or without Russian letters "Z A", see under North-West Russia Nos. 21/42.

5 Rising Sun

1919. Imperf or perf.

27	**5**	10k. blue	85	35

6

1919. First Anniv of Independence. (a) Size 33×45 mm.

32	**6**	10k. red and brown	70	2·20

1

1918. Printed on back of German war maps. Imperf or perf.

15	**1**	3k. lilac	25	25
16	**1**	5k. red	25	25
17	**1**	10k. blue	25	25
18	**1**	15k. green	25	25
41	**1**	20k. orange	25	10
20	**1**	25k. grey	25	25
21	**1**	35k. brown	25	25
42	**1**	40k. purple	25	10
22	**1**	50k. violet	25	25
44	**1**	75k. green	60	10
29	**1**	3r. red and blue	85	90
30	**1**	5r. red and brown	85	75

(b) Size 28×38 mm.

33	10k. red and brown	25	30
34	35k. green and blue	25	30
35	1r. red and green	35	35

7

1919. Liberation of Courland.

36	**7**	10k. red and brown	25	15
37	**7**	25k. green and blue	25	25
38	**7**	35k. blue and black	25	40
39	**7**	1r. brown and green	25	80

8

1920. Red Cross stamps. (a) On backs of blue Bolshevist notes. Perf.

46	**8**	20-30k. red and brown	1·30	1·00
47	**8**	40-55k. red and blue	1·30	1·00
48	**8**	50-70k. red and green	1·00	1·80
49	**8**	1r.-1r.30 red and grey	1·50	1·80

(b) On backs of green Western Army notes. Perf.

50	20-30k. red and brown	1·30	1·30
51	40-55k. red and blue	1·30	1·30
52	50-70k. red and green	1·00	1·80
53	1r.-1r.30 red and grey	1·90	1·80

(c) On backs of red, green and brown Bolshevist notes. Imperf.

54	20-30k. red and brown	1·70	2·75
55	40-55k. red and blue	1·70	2·75
56	50-70k. red and green	1·70	2·75
57	1r.-1r.30 red and grey	3·50	4·50

CHARITY PREMIUMS. In the above and later issues where two values are expressed, the lower value represents the franking value and the higher the price charged, the difference being the charity premium.

9

1920. Liberation of Latgale.

58	**9**	50k. pink and green	40	45
59	**9**	1r. brown and green	40	45

10

1920. First Constituent Assembly.

60A	**10**	50k. red	85	25
61A	**10**	1r. blue	85	25
62A	**10**	3r. green and brown	85	85
63A	**10**	5r. purple and grey	2·10	90

1920. Surch in white figures on black oval.

64	**6**	10r. on 1r. red and green	1·70	1·70
65	**6**	20r. on 1r. red and green	4·25	3·50
66	**6**	30r. on 1r. red and green	6·00	4·50

1920. Surch **2 DIWI RUBLI**. Perf.

67	**1**	2r. on 10k. blue	3·00	8·00
68	**4**	2r. on 35k. brown	85	5·00

1920. (a) Surch **WEENS** or **DIVI**, value and **RUBLI**.

69	**7**	1 (WEENS) r. on 35k. blue and black	50	40
70	**7**	2 (DIVI) r. on 10k. red and brown	1·00	90
71	**7**	2 (DIVI) r. on 25k. green and blue	60	50

(b) Surch **DIWI RUBLI 2**.

72	**6**	2r. on 35k. green and blue	60	50

(c) Surch **DIVI 2 RUB. 2**.

73	**10**	2r. on 50k. red	85	70

(d) Surch **Desmit rubli**.

74	**6**	10r. on 10r. on 1r. red and green (No. 64)	2·10	90

1921. Red Cross. Nos. 51/3 surch **RUB 2 RUB**.

75	**8**	2r. on 20-30k. red and brown	3·00	4·50

76	8	2r. on 40-55k. red and blue	3·00	4·50
77	8	2r. on 50-70k. red and green	3·00	4·50
78	8	2r. on 1r.-1r.30k. red and grey	3·00	4·50

1921. Surch in figures and words over thick bar of crossed lines.

79	9	10r. on 50k. pink and green	2·10	90
80	9	20r. on 50k. pink and green	6·25	4·50
81	9	30r. on 50k. pink and green	8·50	4·50
82	9	50r. on 50k. pink and green	12·50	6·00
83	9	100r. on 50k. pink and green	30·00	18·00

19 Bleriot XI

1921. Air. Value in "RUBLU". Imperf or perf.

84	19	10r. green	5·00	3·00
85	19	20r. blue	5·00	1·50

See also Nos. 155/7.

21 Latvian Coat of Arms

22 Great Seal of Latvia

1921. Value in "Kopeks" or "Roubles".

86	21	50k. violet	50	10
87b	21	1r. yellow	25	25
88	21	2r. green	15	10
89	21	3r. green	70	45
90	21	5r. red	1·40	25
91	21	6r. red	2·10	90
92	21	9r. orange	1·30	60
93	21	10r. blue	1·30	15
94	21	15r. blue	4·00	80
95c	21	20r. lilac	16·00	1·50
96	22	50r. brown	30·00	3·50
97	22	100r. blue	34·00	3·50

1923. Value in "Santimi" or "Lats".

127	21	1s. mauve	15	15
129	21	2s. yellow	25	10
130	21	3s. red	15	10
100	21	4s. green	1·00	25
132	21	5s. green	85	15
133	21	6s. green and yellow	15	10
134	21	7s. green	85	15
103	21	10s. red	2·50	25
136d	21	10s. green and yellow	8·00	15
104	21	12s. mauve	40	35
105c	21	15s. purple and orange	4·00	15
107	21	20s. blue	2·50	15
139	21	20s. pink	2·10	10
108	21	25s. blue	85	15
109	21	30s. pink	8·50	25
140	21	30s. blue	3·75	15
141	21	35s. blue	2·50	15
110	21	40s. purple	3·50	25
143	21	50s. grey	4·25	35
144	22	1l. brown and bistre	13·50	30
116	22	2l. blue and light blue	34·00	1·50
117	22	5l. green and light green	£100	4·50
118	22	10l. red and light red	4·75	10·00

1923. Charity. War Invalids. Surch **KARA INVALIDIEM S.10S.** and cross.

112	21	1s.+10s. mauve	60	90
113	21	2s.+10s. yellow	60	95
114	21	4s.+10s. green	60	1·00

24 Town Hall

1925. 300th Anniv of City of Libau.

119	-	6-12s. blue and red	4·25	6·25
120	24	15-25s. brown and blue	2·50	4·50
121	-	25-35s. green and violet	4·25	4·25
122	-	30-40s. lake and blue	7·50	13·00
123	-	50-60s. violet and green	11·00	17·00

DESIGNS—HORIZ: 6-12s. Harbour and lighthouse; 25-35s. Spa health pavilion. VERT: 30-40s. St. Anna's Church; 50-60s. Arms of Libau.

1927. Surch.

124	1	15s. on 40k. purple	85	45
125	1	15s. on 50k. violet	2·50	1·80
126	10	1l. on 3r. green and brown	21·00	8·75

28 Pres. J. Cakste

1928. Death of President Cakste and Memorial Fund.

150	28	2-12s. orange	4·25	3·50
151	28	6-16s. green	4·25	3·50
152	28	15-25s. lake	4·25	3·50
153	28	25-35s. blue	4·25	3·50
154	28	30-40s. red	4·25	3·50

1928. Air. Value in "SANTIMU" or "SANTIMI".

156	19	15s. red	3·50	1·70
157	19	25s. blue	6·25	1·90
193A	19	10s. green	1·70	85

29 Ruins at Rezekne

1928. Tenth Anniv of Independence. Views.

158	29	6s. purple and green	1·70	35
159	-	15s. green and brown	1·70	35
160	-	20s. green and red	1·70	40
161	-	30s. brown and blue	2·50	35
162	-	50s. pink and grey	2·50	90
163	-	1l. sepia and brown	6·25	1·80

DESIGNS: 15s. Jelgava (Mitau); 20s. Cesis (Wenden); 30s. Liepaja (Libau); 50s. Riga; 1l. National Theatre, Riga.

30 Venta

1928. Liberty Memorial Fund. Imperf or perf.

164B	30	6-16s. green	3·00	3·00
165B	-	10-20s. red	3·00	3·00
166B	-	15-25s. brown	3·00	3·00
167B	-	30-40s. blue	3·00	3·00
168B	-	50-60s. black	3·00	3·00
169B	-	1l.-1l.10s. purple	3·00	3·00

DESIGNS: 10-20s. "Latvia" (Woman); 15-25s. Mitau; 30-40s. National Theatre, Riga; 50-60s. Wenden; 1l.-1l.10s. Trenches, Riga Bridge.

32 Z. A. Meierovics

1929. Third Death Anniv of Meierovics (Foreign Minister). Imperf or perf.

170B	32	2-4s. yellow	4·75	4·75
171B	32	6-12s. green	4·75	4·75
172B	32	15-25s. purple	4·75	4·75
173B	32	25-35s. blue	4·75	4·75
174B	32	30-40s. blue	4·75	4·75

33 J. Rainis

1930. Memorial Fund for J. Rainis (writer and politician). Imperf or perf.

175A	33	1-2s. purple	1·30	1·30
176A	33	2-4s. orange	1·30	1·30
177A	33	4-8s. green	1·30	1·30
178A	33	6-12s. brown and green	1·30	1·30
179A	33	10-20s. red	35·00	35·00
180A	33	15-30s. green and brown	35·00	35·00

34 Klemm Kl-20 over Durbe Castle

1930. Air. J. Rainis Memorial Fund. Imperf or perf.

181A	34	10-20s. green and red	11·00	16·00
182A	34	15-30s. red and green	11·00	16·00

35

36

1930. Anti-T.B. Fund.

183	-	1-2s. red and purple	85	45
184	-	2-4s. red and orange	85	45
185	35	4-8s. red and green	85	90
186	-	5-10s. brown and green	1·70	1·30
187	-	6-12s. yellow and green	1·70	90
188	-	10-20s. black and red	2·50	1·80
189	-	15-30s. green and brown	2·50	1·80
190	-	20-40s. blue and red	2·50	2·20
191	-	25-50s. lilac, blue and red	3·50	2·20
192	36	30-60s. lilac, green and blue	4·25	4·50

DESIGNS—VERT: As Type **35**: 1-2s., 2-4s. The Crusaders' Cross; 5-10s. G. Zemgalis; 6-12s. Tower; 10-20s. J. Cakste; 15-30s. Floral design; 20-40s. A. Kviesis. HORIZ: As Type **36**: 25-50s. Sanatorium.

1931. Nos. 183/92 surch.

196		9 on 6-12s. yellow and green	1·70	2·20
197		16 on 1-2s. red and purple	21·00	26·00
198		17s. on 2-4s. red and orange	2·10	2·20
199		19 on 4-8s. red and green	6·25	9·75
200		20 on 5-10s. brown and green	4·25	9·75
201		23 on 15-30s. green and brown	1·70	1·60
202		25 on 10-20s. black and red	4·25	5·25
203		35 on 20-40s. blue and red	6·25	8·00
204		45 on 25-50s. lilac, blue and red	17·00	23·00
205		55 on 30-60s. lilac, green & bl	21·00	37·00

1931. Air. Charity. Nos. 155/7 surch **LATVIJAS AIZSARGI** and value. Imperf or perf.

206A	19	50 on 10s. green	14·50	17·00
207A	19	1l. on 15s. red	14·50	17·00
208A	19	1l.50 on 2s. blue	14·50	17·00

38 Foreign Invasion

1932. Militia Maintenance Fund. Imperf or perf.

209A	-	1-11s. blue and purple	3·50	3·75
210A	38	2-17s. orange and olive	3·50	3·75
211A	-	3-23s. red and brown	3·50	3·75
212A	-	4-34s. green	3·50	3·75
213A	-	5-45s. green	3·50	3·75

DESIGNS: 1-11s. The Holy Oak and Kriva telling stories; 3-23s. Lacplesis, the deliverer; 4-34s. The Black Knight (enemy) slaughtered; 5-45s. Laimdota, the spirit of Latvia, freed.

39 Infantry Manoeuvres

1932. Militia Maintenance Fund. Imperf or perf.

214B	-	6-25s. purple and brown	6·75	6·25
215B	39	7-35s. blue and green	6·75	6·25
216B	-	10-45s. sepia and green	6·75	6·25
217B	-	12-55s. green and red	6·75	6·25
218B	-	15-75s. violet and red	6·75	6·25

DESIGNS—HORIZ: 6-25s. Troops on march. VERT: 10-45s. First aid to soldier; 12-55s. Army kitchen; 15-75s. Gen. J. Balodis.

41

1932. Air. Charity. Imperf or perf.

219A	41	10-20s. black and green	19·00	31·00
220A	41	15-30s. red and grey	19·00	31·00
221A	41	25-50s. blue and grey	19·00	31·00

1932. Riga Exn of Lettish Products. Optd **Latvijas razojumu izstade Riga. 1932.g.10.-18.IX.**

222	21	3s. red	85	35
223	21	10s. green on yellow	85	45
224	21	20s. pink	1·70	85
225	21	35s. blue	4·25	85

43 Leonardo da Vinci

1932. Air. Charity. Pioneers of Aviation. Imperf or perf.

226A	-	5-25s. green and brown	21·00	22·00
227A	43	10-50s. green and brown	21·00	22·00
228A	-	15-75s. green and red	21·00	22·00
229A	-	20-100s. mauve and green	21·00	22·00
230A	-	25-125s. blue and brown	21·00	22·00

DESIGNS—VERT: 5s. Icarus; 15s. Jacques Charles's hydrogen balloon, 1783 (inscr "Charliers"). HORIZ: 20s. Wright Type A biplane; 25s. Bleriot XI monoplane.

44 "Mourning Mother" Memorial, Riga

1933. Air. Wounded Latvian Airmen Fund. Imperf or perf.

231A	-	2-52s. brown and black	14·50	22·00
232A	44	3-53s. red and black	14·50	22·00
233A	-	10-60s. green and black	14·50	22·00
234A	-	20-70s. red and black	14·50	22·00

DESIGNS: 2s. Fall of Icarus; 10s., 20s. Proposed tombs for airmen.

1933. Air. Charity. Riga–Bathurst Flight. Nos. 155/7 optd **LATVIJA-AFRIKA 1933** or surch also.

235		10s. green	65·00	90·00
236		15s. red	65·00	90·00
237		25s. blue	65·00	90·00
238		50s. on 15s. red	£300	£550
239		100s. on 25s. blue	£300	£550

In the event the aircraft crashed at Neustettin, Germany, and the mail was forwarded by ordinary post.

46 Biplane under Fire at Riga

1933. Air. Charity. Wounded Latvian Airmen Fund. Imperf or perf.

240A	-	3-53s. blue and orange	38·00	44·00
241A	46	7-57s. brown and blue	38·00	44·00
242A	-	35-135s. black and blue	38·00	44·00

DESIGNS: 3s. Monoplane taking off; 35s. Map and aircraft.

47 Glanville Brothers' Gee Bee Super Sportster

1933. Air. Charity. Wounded Latvian Airmen Fund. Imperf or perf.

243A	47	8-68s. grey and brown	50·00	80·00
244A	-	12-112s. green and purple	50·00	80·00
245A	-	30-130s. grey and blue	50·00	80·00
246A	-	40-190s. blue and purple	50·00	80·00

DESIGNS: 12s. Supermarine S6B seaplane; 30s. Airship *Graf Zeppelin* over Riga; 40s. Dornier Do-X flying boat.

48 President's Palace

1934. 15th Anniv of New Constitution.

247	48	3s. red	25	20
248	-	5s. green	25	15
249	-	10s. green	1·70	10
250	-	20s. red	1·70	10
251	-	35s. blue	60	20
252	48	40s. brown	60	20

DESIGNS: 5, 10s. Arms and shield; 20s. Allegory of Latvia; 35s. Government Building.

50 A. Kronvalds

1936. Lettish Intellectuals.

253	**50**	3s. red	2·50	5·00
254	-	10s. green	2·50	5·00
255	-	20s. mauve	2·50	5·75
256	-	35s. blue	2·50	5·75

PORTRAITS: 10s. A. Pumpurs; 20s. J. Maters; 35s. Auseklis.

51

1936. White Cross Fund. Designs incorporating Cross and Stars device as in T **51**.

257	**51**	3s. red	2·50	4·50
258	-	10s. green	2·50	4·50
259	-	20s. mauve	2·50	5·25
260	-	35s. blue	2·50	5·25

DESIGNS: 10s. Oak leaves; 20s. Doctors and patient; 35s. Woman holding shield.

53 Independence Monument, Rauna (Ronneburg)

1937. Monuments.

261	**53**	3s. red	40	90
262	-	5s. green	40	90
263	-	10s. green	40	45
264	-	20s. red	1·30	90
265	-	30s. blue	1·70	1·80
266	-	35s. blue	1·70	1·80
267	-	40s. brown	3·00	2·75

DESIGNS—VERT: 10s. Independence Monument, Jelgava (Mitau); 20s. War Memorial, Valka (Walk); 30s. Independence Monument, Iecava (Eckau); 35s. Independence Monument, Riga; 40s. Col. Kalpak's Grave, Visagalas Cemetery. HORIZ: 5s. Cemetery Gate, Riga.

54 President Ulmanis

1937. President Ulmanis's 60th Birthday.

268	**54**	3s. red and orange	15	10
269	**54**	5s. light green and green	15	20
270	**54**	10s. deep green and green	40	45
271	**54**	20s. purple and red	85	45
272	**54**	25s. grey and blue	1·40	70
273	**54**	30s. deep blue and blue	1·40	90
274	**54**	35s. indigo and blue	1·30	60
275	**54**	40s. light brown and brown	1·30	90
276	**54**	50s. green and black	1·40	85

55 Palace of Justice

1938. National Building Fund. Sheet 140×100 mm comprising 35 (s.) blue (T **55**) and 40 (s.) brown (Power Station, Kegums).

MS277	Sold at 2l.	19·00	75·00

56 Gaizinkalns, Livonia **57** General J. Balodis

1938. 20th Anniv of Independence.

278	**56**	3s. red	15	15
279	-	5s. green	15	15
280	**57**	10s. green	25	15
281	-	20s. mauve	15	15
282	-	30s. blue	1·00	20
283	-	35s. slate	1·00	15
284	-	40s. mauve	85	25

DESIGNS: As Type **56**: 5s. Latgale landscape; 30s. City of Riga; 35s. Rumba waterfall, Courland; 40s. Zemgale landscape. As Type **57**: 20s. President Ulmanis.

58 Elementary School, Riga

1939. Fifth Anniv of Authoritarian Government.

285	**58**	3s. brown	40	75
286	-	5s. green	85	75
287	-	10s. green	1·30	85
288	-	20s. red	2·50	1·40
289	-	30s. blue	1·70	90
290	-	35s. blue	2·50	1·80
291	-	40s. purple	3·50	90
292	-	50s. black	3·50	90

DESIGNS: 5s. Jelgava Castle; 10s. Riga Castle; 20s. Independence Memorial; 30s. Eagle and National Flag; 35s. Town Hall, Daugavpils; 40s. War Museum and Powder-magazine, Riga; 50s. Pres. Ulmanis.

1939. Fifth Year of Office of Pres. Ulmanis. Sheet as **MS**277 optd **1934 1939 14/V**.

MS293	Sold at 2l.	30·00	£110

59 Reaping

1939. Harvest Festival. Dated "8 X 1939".

294	**59**	10s. green	85	90
295	-	20s. red (Apples)	85	75

60 Arms of Courland, Livonia and Latgale

1940

296	**60**	1s. violet	40	45
297	**60**	2s. yellow	60	45
298	**60**	3s. red	10	20
299	**60**	5s. brown	10	20
300	**60**	7s. green	40	45
301	**60**	10s. green	1·30	25
302	**60**	20s. red	1·30	25
303	**60**	30s. brown	1·70	45
304	**60**	35s. blue	10	90
305	**60**	50s. green	2·50	90
306	**60**	1l. olive	5·00	2·75

61 Arms of Latvian Soviet Socialist Republic

1940. Incorporation of Latvia in U.S.S.R.

307	**61**	1s. violet	15	15
308	**61**	2s. yellow	15	15
309	**61**	3s. red	10	15
310	**61**	5s. olive	10	15
311	**61**	7s. green	10	90
312	**61**	10s. green	2·10	40
313	**61**	20s. red	1·30	15
314	**61**	30s. blue	2·50	45
315	**61**	35s. blue	10	50
316	**61**	40s. brown	2·10	1·20
317	**61**	50s. grey	2·50	1·20
318	**61**	1l. brown	3·50	1·70
319	**61**	5l. green	25·00	15·00

64 Latvian Arms **65** Latvian Arms

1991

320	**64**	5k. silver, brown & lt brn	3·00	3·00
321	**64**	10k. silver, brown & drab	25	25
322	**64**	15k. silver, sepia & brown	35	30
323	**64**	20k. silver, blue & lt blue	50	50
324	**64**	40k. silver, green and light green	1·00	80
325	**64**	50k. silver, brown and lilac	1·50	1·20
326	**65**	100k. multicoloured	2·50	3·25
327	**65**	200k. multicoloured	4·75	4·75

1991. Nos. 6073 and 6077a of Russia surch **LATVIJA** and new value.

332	100k. on 7k. blue	85	85
333	300k. on 2k. brown	1·30	1·10
334	500k. on 2k. brown	2·10	1·90
335	1000k. on 2k. brown	4·25	4·25

67 Main Statue, Liberty Monument, Riga

1991

336	**67**	10k. multicoloured	15	15
337	**67**	15k. multicoloured	85	1·40
338	**67**	20k. multicoloured	60	40
339	**67**	30k. multicoloured	60	40
340	**67**	50k. multicoloured	60	50
341	**67**	100k. multicoloured	60	75

68 Olympic Committee Symbol

1992. Recognition of Latvian Olympic Committee.

342	**68**	50k.+25k. red, silver and drab	85	75
343	-	50k.+25k. red, silver and grey	1·70	1·30
344	**68**	100k.+50k. red, gold and bistre	1·30	1·00

DESIGN: No. 343, as T **68** but symbols smaller and inscribed "BERLIN 18.09.91." at left.

69 Vaidelotis

1992. Statues from the base of the Liberty Monument, Riga.

345	-	10k. black and brown	10	50
346	**69**	20k. brown and grey	15	20
347	-	30k. deep lilac and lilac	35	30
348	**69**	30k. deep brown and brown	35	30
349	-	40k. blue and grey	40	45
350	**69**	50k. green and grey	40	45
351	-	50k. black and grey	40	45
352	-	100k. purple and mauve	70	90
353	-	200k. deep blue and blue	1·40	1·30

DESIGNS: Nos. 345, 347, 353, Kurzeme (warrior with shield); 349, 351/2, Lachplesis (two figures).

1992. Nos. 4672, 6073 and 6077a of Russia surch **LATVIJA** and new value.

354a	1r. on 7k. blue	70	45
355	3r. on 2k. brown	40	40
356	5r. on 2k. brown	85	75
357	10r. on 2k. brown	1·30	1·10
358	25r. on 4k. red	3·00	2·75

1992. Birds of the Baltic. As Nos. 506/9 of Lithuania.

359	5r. black and red	70	65
360	5r. brown, black and red	70	65
361	5r. sepia, brown and red	70	65
362	5r. brown, black and red	70	65

DESIGNS: Nos 359, Osprey (*Pandion haliaetus*); 360, Black-tailed godwit (*Limosa limosa*); 361, Goosander (*Mergus merganser*); 362, Common shelducks (*Tadorna tadorna*).

72 Children in Fancy Dress around Christmas Tree

1992. Christmas. Multicoloured.

363	2r. Type **72**	85	85
364	3r. Angel choir	40	45
365	10r. Type **72**	1·30	1·10
366	15r. Adoration of the Kings	1·70	1·80

1993. Nos. 4855, 5296 and 5295 of Russia surch **LATVIJA** and new value.

367	50r. on 6k. multicoloured	70	80
368	100r. on 6k. multicoloured	1·50	1·40
369	300r. on 6k. multicoloured	3·50	3·50

74 Kuldiga Couple

1993. Traditional Costumes. Multicoloured.

370	5s. Type **74**	15	10
371	10s. Alsunga	35	35
372	20s. Lielvarde	40	40
373	50s. Rucava	1·30	1·40
374	100s. Zemgale	2·50	2·50
375	500s. Ziemellatgale	12·50	12·50
MS376	103×88 mm. Nos. 370/5	27·00	24·00

See also Nos. 428/**MS**429, 442/**MS**443, 467/**MS**468 and 491/**MS**492.

75 Emblem

1993. National Song Festival.

377	**75**	3s. black, gold and brown	15	20
378	**75**	5s. black, gold and lilac	25	25
379	-	15s. multicoloured	40	60

DESIGN: 15s. Abstract.

76 Pope John Paul II

1993. Papal Visit.

380	**76**	15s. multicoloured	85	80

77 Flags

1993. 75th Anniv of First Republic.

381	**77**	5s. multicoloured	25	25
382	**77**	15s. multicoloured	60	65

78 Valters

1994. 100th Birthday of Evalds Valters (actor).

383	**78**	15s. brown, light brown and gold	60	60

79 Biathlon

1994. Winter Olympic Games, Lillehammer, Norway. Multicoloured.

384	5s. Type **79**	40	40
385	10s. Two-man bobsleigh	40	40
386	15s. One-man luge	40	50
387	100s. Figure skating	3·00	3·25
MS388	55×80 mm. 200s. As No. 385	6·75	8·25

80 Reed Hut

1994. 70th Anniv of Latvian Ethnological Open-air Museum, Bergi.

389	**80**	5s. multicoloured	25	25

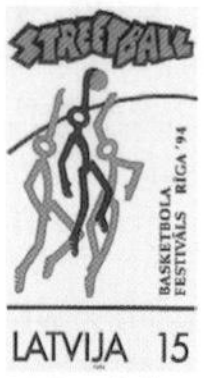

81 Streetball

1994. Basketball Festival, Riga.

390	**81**	15s. black, grey and orange	50	55

82 Kurzeme

1994. Arms (1st series). (a) Size 18×21 mm.

391	**82**	1s. red, black and silver	10	15
392	-	2s. multicoloured	10	10
393	-	3s. silver, black and blue	40	35
394	-	5s. silver, black and red	25	35
395	-	8s. silver, black and blue	35	30
396	-	10s. silver, black and blue	40	45
396a	-	10s. multicoloured	40	35
397	-	13s. black, gold and silver	50	50
397a	-	16s. multicoloured	70	55
398	-	20s. silver, black and grey	85	75
398a	-	20s. multicoloured	85	75
399	-	24s. green, black and silver	95	80
399a	-	28s. multicoloured	75	90
400	-	30s. multicoloured	1·30	1·20
401	-	36s. silver, black and red	1·10	1·10
402	-	50s. multicoloured	2·10	1·90

(b) Size 29×23½ mm.

403	100s. multicoloured	4·25	3·25
404	200s. multicoloured	9·25	8·50

DESIGNS: 2s. Auce; 3s. Zemgale; 5s. Vidzeme; 8s. Livani; 10s. (396) Latgale; 10s. (396a) Valmiera; 13s. Preila; 16s. Ainazi; 20s. (398) Grobina; 20s. (398a) Rezekne; 24s. Tukums; 28s. Madona; 30, 100s. Riga; 36s. Priekule; 50, 200s. State arms.

See also Nos. 501/6.

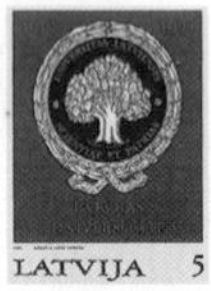

83 Emblem

1994. 75th Anniv of Latvia University.

405	**83**	5s. gold, blue and green	25	25

84 Coins in Scales

1994. Europa. Multicoloured.

406	10s. Type **84**	85	60
407	50s. Money chest and notes in scales	2·10	2·00

85 Eating Cherries

1994. The Fat Dormouse. Multicoloured.

408	5s. Type **85**	25	25
409	10s. Eating strawberries	50	45
410	10s. On leafy branch	50	45
411	15s. On branch of apple tree	85	65

86 Angel

1994. Christmas. Multicoloured.

412	3s. Type **86**	15	15
413	8s. Angels playing violin and flute	40	35
414	13s. Angels singing	40	40
415	100s. Wreath of candles	3·25	2·50

87 Gnome with Candle

1994. 80th Birthday of Margarita Staraste (children's writer and illustrator). Multicoloured.

416	5s. Type **87**	35	30
417	10s. Bear	35	40
418	10s. Child on sledge	35	40

88 Emblem

1994. Road Safety Year.

419	**88**	10s. multicoloured	40	35

89 Emblem

1995. 50th Anniv of U.N.O.

420	**89**	15s. blue, red and silver	50	55

90 Bauska Castle (Latvia)

1995. Via Baltica Motorway Project. Multicoloured.

421	8s. Type **90**	40	40
MS422	100×110 mm. 18s. Beach Hotel, Parnu (Estonia); 18s. Type **90**; 18s. Kaunas (Lithuania)	2·10	2·20

91 White-backed Woodpecker

1995. European Nature Conservation Year. Birds. Multicoloured.

423	8s. Type **91**	85	55
424	20s. Corncrake	1·30	95
425	24s. White-winged black tern	1·30	1·10

92 Vaivods

1995. Birth Centenary of Cardinal Julijans Vaivods.

426	**92**	8s. multicoloured	40	40

93 Sun and Open Book

1995. 60th Anniv of Karlis Ulmaris Schools Appeal.

427	**93**	8s. multicoloured	40	40

1995. Traditional Costumes. As T **74**. Multicoloured.

428	8s. Nica	40	40
MS429	100s. As No. 428	3·50	3·50

94 National Opera House

1995. 800th Anniv of Riga (1st issue). Multicoloured.

430	8s. Type **94**	35	30
431	16s. National Theatre	50	55
432	24s. Art School (44×26 mm)	70	85
433	36s. Art Museum (44×26 mm)	1·00	1·30

See also Nos. 456/9, 479/82, 493/6, 522/5, 540/3 and 560/3.

95 Lacplesis, the Bear Slayer

1995. European Peace and Freedom. Multicoloured.

434	16s. Type **95**	85	75
435	50s. Spidola	2·10	2·00

96 Christmas Tree at Night

1995. Christmas. Multicoloured.

436	6s. Type **96**	35	30
437	6s. Elf flying with candle	35	30
438	15s. Cottage at night	50	55
439	24s. Elf with dog and cat	1·00	1·00

97 Stradins

1996. Birth Centenary of Pauls Stradins (surgeon).

440	**97**	8s. multicoloured	25	25

98 Zenta Maurina (writer)

1996. Europa. Famous Women.

441	**98**	36s. multicoloured	1·70	1·50

1996. Traditional Costumes. As T **74**. Multicoloured.

442	8s. Barta	40	35
MS443	100×70 mm. 100s. As No. 422	3·00	3·25

99 Children with Toys

1996. Sheet 96×97 mm.

MS444	**99** 48s. multicoloured	2·10	3·00

100 Cycling

1996. Olympic Games, Atlanta. Multicoloured.

445	8s. Type **100**	25	25
446	16s. Basketball	50	50
447	24s. Walking	70	90
448	36s. Canoeing (horiz)	1·10	1·20
MS449	85×60 mm. 100s. Throwing the javelin (horiz)	3·50	3·50

101 Swallowtail

1996. Butterflies. Multicoloured.

450	8s. Type **101**	35	30
451	24s. *Clifden's nonpareil*	85	85
452	80s. Large tiger moth	2·10	2·30

102 1912 Russo-Balt Fire Engine

1996. Latvian Car Production. Multicoloured.

453	8s. Type **102**	25	25
454	24s. 1899 Leutner-Russia carriage	85	90
455	36s. 1939 Ford-Vairogs motor car	1·00	1·10

103 Apartment Block (E. Laube)

1996. 800th Anniv of Riga (2nd issue). Multicoloured.

456	8s. Type **103**	35	30
457	16s. Stained glass window (F. Sefels) (30×26 mm)	60	55
458	24s. Turreted buildings (E. Laube) (38×26 mm)	85	75
459	30s. Couple welcoming charioteer (mural, J. Rozentals) (38×26 mm)	1·20	1·10

104 Elves and Presents

1996. Christmas. Multicoloured.

460	6s. Type **104**	15	10
461	14s. Children with dog and Father Christmas on skis	70	60
462	20s. Child at tree and Father Christmas in armchair	70	65

105 European Nightjar

1997. 75th Anniv of Birdlife International (conservation organization). Multicoloured.

463	10s. Type **105**	40	40
464	20s. Greater spotted eagle	85	80
465	30s. Aquatic warbler	1·30	1·20

106 Symbols of Independence

1997. Sixth Anniv of Independence.

466	**106**	10s. multicoloured	40	35

1997. Traditional Costumes. As T **74**. Multicoloured.

467	10s. Rietumvidzeme	60	50
MS468	100×70 mm. 100s. As No. 467	3·50	3·50

107 Turaidas Roze

1997. Europa. Tales and Legends.

469	**107**	32s. multicoloured	1·30	1·30

108 *Wappen der Herzogin von Kurland* (galleon)

1997. Baltic Sailing Ships. Multicoloured.

470	10s. Type **108**	60	50
MS471	110×70 mm. 20s. As No. 470 but with different frame; 20s. Kurshes ship (Lithuania); 20s. Maasilinn ship (Estonia)	2·50	2·30

109 Hermes and Neptune

1997. Centenary of Ventspils International Commercial Port.

472	**109**	20s. blue, silver and yellow	70	70

110 Stamp Collecting

1997. Children's Leisure Pursuits. Multicoloured.

473	10s. Type **110**	35	30
474	12s. Motor cycle trials (vert)	40	40
475	20s. Ice hockey and skiing (vert)	70	60
476	30s. Tennis, football and basketball	1·10	90

111 Moricsala

1997. Nature Reserves. Multicoloured.

477	10s. Type **111**	40	35
478	30s. Slitere	1·30	1·00

112 Woman, Wooden Building and Jewellery (12th century)

1997. 800th Anniv of Riga (3rd issue). 12th–16th Centuries. Multicoloured.

479	10s. Type **112**	35	30
480	20s. 13th-century Cathedral cloister, statue (K. Bernevics) and seal of Bishop Albert, rosary beads and writing implement	70	60
481	30s. Livonian Order's castle, statue of V. von Plettenberg (Order Master) and weapons	95	85
482	32s. *Three Brothers* terrace, statue of St. John and seal (27×27 mm)	1·00	95

113 Man and Bear

1997. Christmas. Mummers. Multicoloured.

483	8s. Type **113**	35	30
484	18s. Witches	70	60
485	28s. Horse	1·00	80

114 Flames

1998. Winter Olympic Games, Nagano, Japan.

486	**114**	20s. multicoloured	70	60

115 Sculpture of Character

1998. Spridisi Memorial (to Anna Brigadere (writer)) Museum, Tervete.

487	**115**	10s. multicoloured	40	35

116 Song Festival

1998. Europa. National Festivals.

488	**116**	30s. multicoloured	1·30	1·30

117 Grini

1998. Nature Reserves. Multicoloured.

489	10s. Type **117**	35	30
490	30s. Teici	95	85

1998. Traditional Costumes. As T **74**. Multicoloured.

491	10s. Krustpils	60	50
MS492	100×69 mm. 100s. As No. 491 but man with Midsummer Festival headdress	3·75	3·75

118 Dannenstern House, Wooden Sculpture and Polish and Swedish Coins

1998. 800th Anniv of Riga (4th issue). 16th–20th Centuries. Multicoloured.

493	10s. Type **118**	35	35
494	20s. Library, medallion and monument to G. Herder (poet and philosopher)	60	60
495	30s. Arsenal, Victory column, octant and compass	85	85
496	40s. Entrance gate to Warrior's Cemetery, "Mother Latvia" (statue) and 5l. coin	1·20	1·20

1988. Arms (2nd series). As T **82**.

496a	1s. multicoloured	10	10
496b	2s. multicoloured	10	10
496c	3s. multicoloured	10	10
497	5s. multicoloured	10	10
497a	5s. multicoloured	35	25
497b	5s. multicoloured	35	25
497c	5s. multicoloured	40	40
499	10s. multicoloured	35	25
499a	10s. multicoloured	40	40
499b	10s. black, red and silver	35	25
499c	10s. multicoloured	60	60
500	15s. multicoloured	35	35
501	15s. black, blue and silver	35	40
502	15s. multicoloured	35	15
503	15s. multicoloured	35	40
504	15s. black, silver and red	35	40
504a	15s. multicoloured	35	50
504b	15s. silver and black	35	40
504c	15s. multicoloured	35	50
504d	15s. multicoloured	35	15
504e	15s. multicoloured	35	15
505	20s. multicoloured	35	15
505a	20s. blue, silver and black	85	50
505b	22s. multicoloured	1·30	1·30
506	30s. multicoloured	70	50
506a	33s. scarlet, bronze and black	75	55
506b	35s. emerald, bronze and black	80	60
508	40s. multicoloured	1·30	75
509	40s. multicoloured	1·00	1·30
509a	60s. bronxe, emerald and black	1·40	1·00

DESIGNS: 496a, Kurzeme; 496b, Auce; 496c, Zemgale; 497, Smiltene; 497a, Ludza; 497b, Valka; 499, Valmiera; 499a, Dobeje; 499b, Balvi; 497c, Staicele Sabile; 500, Bauska; 501, Ogre; 502, Daugavpils; 503, Jurmala; 504, Kuldiga; 504a, Sigulda; 504b, Gulbene; 504c, Ventspils; 504d, Cesis; 504e, Talis; 505, Aluksne; 505a, Dagda; 505b, Vecummeki; 506, Liepaja; 506a, Saldus; 506b, Balozi; 508, Jelgava; 509, Jekabpils; 509a, Stende.

119 1918 5k. Stamp

1998. 70th Anniv of First Latvian Stamp.

510	**119**	30s. red, cream and grey	1·00	90

120 Dome Church, Riga

1998. Churches.

511	**120**	10s. multicoloured	40	35

121 Janis Cakste (1922–27)

1998. Presidents.

512	**121**	10s. multicoloured	40	35

122 State Flag

1998. 80th Anniv of Declaration of Independence. Multicoloured.

513	10s. Type **122**	25	25
514	30s. State arms and flags	85	80

123 Elves building Snowman

1998. Christmas. Multicoloured.

515	10s. Type **123**	35	30
516	20s. Elves decorating tree	60	55
517	30s. Elves sledging	85	80

124 Krustkalnu Nature Reserve

1999. Europa. Parks and Gardens.

518	30s. Type **124**	1·30	1·10
519	60s. Gauja National Nature Park	2·50	2·10

125 Playing Cards and Edgars (from novel *Purva Bridejs*)

1999. Latvian Literature. Rudolfs Blaumanis.

520	**125**	110s. multicoloured	3·00	2·75

126 Council Emblem

1999. 50th Anniv of Council of Europe.

521	**126**	30s. multicoloured	1·30	1·10

127 *Widwud* (schooner)

1999. 800th Anniv of Riga (5th issue). Transport. Multicoloured.

522	10s. Electric tramcar No. 258 (30×26½ mm)	25	25
523	30s. Type **127**	85	80
524	40s. Biplane	1·10	1·00
525	70s. Steam locomotive No. Tk-236	2·00	2·00

128 Aglona Basilica

1999. Churches.

526	**128**	15s. multicoloured	50	45

129 Family and State Flag

1999. Tenth Anniv of Baltic Chain (human chain uniting capitals of Latvia, Lithuania and Estonia).

527	**129**	15s. multicoloured	60	40
MS528		110×72 mm. 30s. Type **129**; 30s. Family and Lithuanian flag; 30s. Family and Estonian flag	2·20	2·20

130 Rundale Palace

1999. Palaces.

529	**130**	20s. multicoloured	70	60

131 *Perse*

1999. 90th Death Anniv of Julijs Feders (painter).

530	**131**	15s. multicoloured	60	50

132 Gustavs Zemgals (1927–30)

1999. Presidents.
531 **132** 15s. multicoloured 60 50

133 Harbour, Letters and Emblem

1999. 125th Anniv of Universal Postal Union.
532 **133** 40s. multicoloured 1·70 1·30

134 Father Christmas and Candle

1999. Christmas. Multicoloured.
533 12s. Type **134** 60 50
534 15s. Children watching television 70 55
535 40s. Father Christmas placing toys under tree 1·70 1·30

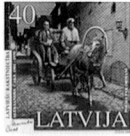
135 Artist's Model (J. Rosentals)

2000
536 **135** 40s. multicoloured 1·70 1·30

136 Scene from The Wagon Driver (poem)

2000. 50th Death Anniv of Aleksandrs Caks (poet).
537 **136** 40s. multicoloured 1·50 1·30

137 "Building Europe"

2000. Europa.
538 **137** 60s. multicoloured 3·00 2·20

138 Ice Hockey Players

2000. Ice Hockey.
539 **138** 70s. multicoloured 2·20 2·20

140 Central Market

2000. 800th Anniv of Riga (6th issue). Tourist Sights. Multicoloured.
540 20s. Type **140** 85 65
541 40s. Dome Church organ (25×30 mm) 1·50 1·10
542 40s. Zoo (44×26 mm) 1·50 1·10
543 70s. The Powder Tower (25×30 mm) 2·50 2·00

141 Jelgava Palace

2000. Palaces.
544 **141** 40s. multicoloured 1·70 1·70

142 Globe and Olympic Rings

2000. Olympic Games, Sydney.
545 **142** 40s. multicoloured 1·70 1·70
546 **142** 70s. multicoloured 2·10 2·10

143 Main Statue, Liberty Monument, Riga (Karlis Zale)

2000. New Millennium. Multicoloured.
547 15s. Type **143** 70 70
548 50s. Brotherhood of Blackheads meeting house, Riga 2·10 2·10

144 Alberts Kviesis (1930–36)

2000. Presidents.
549 **144** 15s. multicoloured 70 70

145 Orthodox Church, Riga

2000. Churches.
550 **145** 40s. multicoloured 1·70 1·70

146 Nurses tending to Elderly Lady

2000. Latvian Red Cross.
551 **146** 15s. multicoloured 70 70

147 Elf and Sleigh

2000. Christmas. Multicoloured.
552 12s. Type **147** 50 50
553 15s. Cherubs 60 60
554 15s. Mary and baby Jesus 60 60

148 People around Bonfire

2001. Sovereignty.
555 **148** 40s. multicoloured 1·50 1·30

149 When Silava's Forest Wakes (V. Purvitis)

2001
556 **149** 40s. multicoloured 1·70 1·30

150 Karlis Ulmanis (1936–40)

2001. Presidents.
557 **150** 15s. multicoloured 60 50

151 ML Series Steam Locomotive

2001. Narrow-gauge Railway.
558 **151** 40s. multicoloured 1·70 1·30

152 Ventas Rumba (waterfall), Kuldiga

2001. Europa. Water Resources.
559 **152** 60s. multicoloured 2·10 1·80

153 Modern View of Riga

2001. 800th Anniv of Riga (7th issue). Multicoloured.
560 15s. Type **153** 70 55
561 15s. Modern View of Riga with three spires 3·00 3·00
562 60s. 16th-century view of Riga 3·50 2·40
563 70s. 17th-century view of Riga 1·70 1·70

Nos. 560/1 are 29×32 mm and 562/3 are 52×29 mm. Nos. 560/1 were issued together, *se-tenant*, forming a composite design.

154 Cat with Pipe ("Pussy's Water Mill" (fairytale))

2001. Literature. Karlis Skalbe (writer) Commemoration.
564 **154** 40s. multicoloured 1·70 1·30

155 Tals

2001. Tenth Death Anniv of Mikhail Nekhemevich Tal (World Chess Champion, 1960–1961). Sheet 98×68 mm.
MS565 **155** 100s. multicoloured 4·25 4·25

156 Beach, Vidzeme, Latvia

2001. Baltic Sea Coast. Multicoloured.
566 15s. Type **156** 70 55

MS567 125×60 mm. 30s. As Type **156**; 30s. Sand dunes, Palanga, Lithuania; 30s. Rocky coastline, Lahemaa, Estonia 3·75 3·25

Stamps in similar designs were issued by Estonia and Lithuania.

157 Cesvaines Palace

2001. Palaces.
568 **157** 40s. multicoloured 1·70 1·30

158 Synagogue, Riga

2001
569 **158** 70s. multicoloured 3·00 2·40

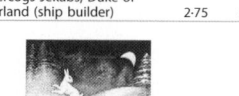
159 Krisjanis Valdemars (image scaled to 56% of original size)

2001. Ship Building, Trade and Discovery. Multicoloured.
570 15s. Type **159** (founder of Naval College and ship builder) 70 60
571 70s. Hercogs Jekabs, Duke of Courland (ship builder) 2·75 2·40

160 White Rabbits

2001. Christmas. Multicoloured.
572 12s. Type **160** 60 50
573 15s. Dog and rabbit 60 55
574 15s. Sheep 60 55

161 Cross-country Skiers

2002. Winter Olympic Games, Salt Lake City.
575 **161** 40s. multicoloured 1·40 1·20

162 Downhill Skier

2002. Winter Paralympic Games, Salt Lake City.
576 **162** 15s. multicoloured 60 55

163 Refugees (Jekabs Kazaks)

2002. Art.
577 **163** 40s. multicoloured 1·50 1·30

164 Clowns

2002. Europa. Circus.
578   **164**   60s. multicoloured   2·50   2·30

165 Lady's Slipper Orchid (*Cypripedium calceolus*)

2002. Plants. Multicoloured.
579   15s. Type **165**   50   50
580   40s. Water chestnut (*Trapa natans*)   1·40   1·20

166 Soldier and Flag

2002. Armed Forces.
581   **166**   40s. multicoloured   1·40   1·20

167 Jancis standing in Brook (*The White Book*)

2002. Literature. 40th Death Anniv of Janis Jaunsudrabins (writer).
582   **167**   40s. multicoloured   1·40   1·20

168 Kristians Johan Dals

2002. Kristians Johan Dals (sailor and founder of maritime school) Commemoration.
584   **168**   70s. multicoloured   2·40   2·10

169 Atlantic Cod (*Gadus morhua*)

2002. Fish. Multicoloured.
585   15s. Type **169**   50   50
586   40s. Wels (*Silurus glanis*)   1·40   1·20

170 Bridge over River Venta

2002. Sheet 100×70 mm.
MS587   **170**   100s. multicoloured   3·50   3·50

171 Jaunmoku Palace

2002. Palaces.
588   **171**   40s. multicoloured   1·40   1·20

172 Grebenschikov Old Believers Praying House, Riga

2002. Churches.
589   **172**   70s. multicoloured   2·40   2·10

173 Mittens and Couple wearing Traditional Winter Clothes

2002. Mittens (1st series).
590   **173**   15s. multicoloured   60   50
  See also Nos. 606, 628 and 650.

174 Christmas Tree and Elf Musician

2002. Christmas. Multicoloured.
591   12s. Type **174**   40   40
592   15s. Elf musicians on present   50   50
593   15s. Angel   50   50

175 *Man enters Room* (Niklavs Srtunke)

2003. Art.
594   **175**   40s. multicoloured   1·30   1·10

176 Fly Orphide (*Ophrys insectifera*)

2003. Plants. Multicoloured.
595   15s. Type **176**   60   55
596   40s. Yew (*Taxus baccata*)   1·10   1·00

177 *Scene from Straumei* (poem)

2003. Literature. 40th Death Anniv of Edvarts Virza (writer).
597   **177**   40s. multicoloured   1·50   1·30

178 *Riga's Towers* (Valda Batraks)

2003. Europa. Poster Art.
598   **178**   60s. multicoloured   2·50   2·50

179 Kolka Lighthouse

2003
599   **179**   60s. multicoloured   2·00   1·80

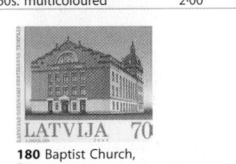

180 Baptist Church, Riga

2003. Churces.
600   **180**   70s. multicoloured   2·40   2·10

181 Bridge over River Gauja, Sigulda.

2003. Sheet 100×70 mm.
MS601   **181**   100s. multicoloured   3·00   3·00

182 *Thymallus thymallus*

2003. Fish. Multicoloured.
602   15s. Type **182**   60   60
603   30s. *Salmo salar*   1·10   1·10

183 Pied Wagtail (*Motacilla alba*)

2003
604   **183**   15s. multicoloured   60   60

184 Birinu Palace

2003. Palaces.
605   **184**   40s. multicoloured   1·50   1·50

185 Mittens and Couple, Liv

2003. Mittens (2nd series).
606   **185**   15s. multicoloured   60   60
  See also No. 628.

186 Motorcycle and Sidecar

2003. Motor Sports.
607   **186**   70s. multicoloured   2·50   2·50

187 Mary and Jesus visited by Angels

2003. Christmas. Multicoloured.
608   12s. Type **187**   60   60
609   15s. Holy Family   60   60
610   15s. Annunciation of Mary   60   60

188 *Still Life with Triangular Ruler* (Romans Suta)

2004. Art.
611   **188**   40s. multicoloured   2·40   2·40

189 Scene from *Times of Land Surveyors*

2004. Literature. Reinis and Matiss Kaudzites (writers) Commemoration.
612   **189**   40s. multicoloured   2·50   2·50

190 Gentian (*Gentiana cruciata*)

2004. Plants. Multicoloured.
613   15s. Type **190**   90   90
614   30s. *Onobrychis arenaria*   1·80   1·80

191 Crowd of Fans

2004. International Ice Hockey Federation Championship, Riga (2006).
615   **191**   30s. multicoloured   80   80

192 Stars

2004. Enlargement of European Union. Multicoloured.
616   30s. Type **192**   80   80
617   30s. Flags of new members   80   80

193 Family in Rowing Boat

2004. Europa. Holidays.
618   **193**   60s. multicoloured   1·70   1·70

194 Footballers

2004. Euro 2004 Football Championship, Portugal.
619   **194**   30s. multicoloured   85   85

195 *Oncrhynchus mykiss*

2004. Fish. Multicoloured.
620   15s. Type **195**   75   75
621   30s. *Psetta maxima*   1·50   1·50

196 Statues of Liberty, New York and Riga

2004. Tenth Anniv of Visit of Bill Clinton (president of USA, 1993–2001).
622   **196**   40s. multicoloured   2·50   2·50

197 Bridge over River Daugava, Riga.

2004. Sheet 100×70 mm.
MS623 100s. multicoloured   6·00   6·00

198 Wrestlers

2004. Olympic Games, Athens.
624   **198**   30s. multicoloured   1·80   1·80

199 St. Jacob's Cathedral, Riga

2004. Churches.
625   **199**   40s. multicoloured   2·50   2·50

200 Mikelbaka Lighthouse

2004
626   **200**   60s. multicoloured   3·75   3·75

201 Jaunpils Palace

2004. Palaces.
627   **201**   40s. multicoloured   2·50   2·50

202 Mittens and Couple, Piebalga

2004. Mittens (3rd series).
628   **202**   15s. multicoloured   1·00   1·00

203 Heart, Rabbit, Bluebird and Children

2004. Christmas.
629   12s. Type **203**   70   70
630   15s. Snowman   90   90
631   15s. Angel   90   90

204 Revolution Monument, Riga

2005. Centenary of Russian Revolution.
632   **204**   12s. multicoloured   1·00   1·00

205 Gentian (*Pulsatilla patens*)

2005. Plants. Multicoloured.
633   15s. Type **205**   75   75
634   30s. *Allium ursinum*   1·50   1·50

206 St. Jacob's Cathedral, Riga

2005. Churches.
635   **206**   40s. multicoloured   2·20   2·20

207 Baron Minhauzen

2005. Adventures of Baron Minhauzen (Munchausen).
636   **207**   30s. multicoloured   1·60   1·60

208 Pig's Head, Sausages and Beer

2005. Europa. Gastronomy.
637   **208**   60s. multicoloured   3·25   3·25

209 Mother and Child (Janis Rozentals)

2005
638   **209**   40s. multicoloured   2·10   2·20

210 Baumanu Karlis and Music Score

2005. 170th Birth Anniv of Karlis Baumanis (Baumanu Karlis) (composer of national anthem).
639   **210**   20s. multicoloured   1·20   1·20

211 Kaive Oak

2005. Nature Protection. Oldest Oak Tree in Latvia. Self-adhesive.
640   **211**   15s. multicoloured   80   80

212 *Lampetra fluviatilis*

2005. Fish. Multicoloured.
641   15s. Type **212**   80   80
642   40s. *Salmo salar*   2·20   2·20

213 Pope John Paul II

2005. Pope John Paul II Commemoration.
643   **213**   15s. multicoloured   80   80

214 Library Building

2005. National Library (Castle of Light) designed by Gunnar Birkerts. Sheet 100×70 mm.
MS644 **214** 100s. multicoloured   5·50   5·50

215 "Uguns un Nakts"

2005. Literature. Janis Rainis (writer) Commem.
645   **215**   40s. multicoloured   2·20   2·20

216 Viaduct, Riga.

2005. Bridges. Sheet 100×70 mm.
MS646 **216** 100s. multicoloured   5·50   5·50

217 Daugavgrivas Lighthouse

2005
647   **217**   40s. multicoloured   2·20   2·20

218 Monument and Gunars Astra

2005. Gunars Astra (human rights activist) Commemoration.
648   **218**   15s. multicoloured   80   80

219 Durbe Palace

2005. Palaces.
649   **219**   40s. multicoloured   2·20   2·20

220 Mittens and Couple, Southern Latgale

2005. Mittens (4th series).
650   **220**   15s. multicoloured   80   80

221 Goat riding Wolf

2005. Christmas. Multicoloured. Self-adhesive.
651   12s. Type **221**   65   65
652   15s. Woman, tree and dog (vert)   80   80
653   15s. Cat and woman carrying cockerel in basket (vert)   80   80

222 1996 36s. Stamp (Type 98)

2006. 50th Anniv of Europa Stamps. Multicoloured.
654   10s. Type **222**   55   55
655   15s. 1997 32s. stamp (Type 108)   75   75
656   15s. 1998 30s. stamp (Type 117)   75   75
657   20s. 1999 30s. and 60s. stamps (As Nos. 518/19)   1·10   1·10
MS658 110×75 mm. Nos. 654/7   3·25   3·25

223 Snowboarder

2006. Winter Olympic Games, Turin.
659   **223**   45s. multicoloured   2·20   2·20

224 Stamerienas Palace

2006. Palaces.
660   **224**   95s. multicoloured   4·50   4·50

225 Zvartes Rock

2006. Nature Protection. Self-adhesive.
661   **225**   22s. multicoloured   1·10   1·10

226 Railway Bridge, Ruanu

2006. Bridges. Sheet 100×70 mm.
MS662 **226** 100s. multicoloured   5·75   5·75

227 Player

2006. World Ice Hockey Championships, Riga.
663   **227**   55s. multicoloured   3·25   3·25

228 Victory Monument

2006. 800th Anniv of Cesis. Multicoloured.
664   **228**   22s. Type **228**   1·10   1·10
665   31s. St. John's Church   1·60   1·60

666	45s. Castle Manor (horiz)		2·30	2·30
667	55s. New Castle (horiz)		7·50	7·50

229 Brooch

2006. Jewellery. Multicoloured.

668	22s. Type **229**		1·10	1·10
669	22s. Cuff		1·10	1·10

Stamps of a similar design were issued by Kazakhstan.

230 Figures, Trees and Horses

2006. Europa. Integration.

670	**230**	85s. multicoloured	4·25	4·25

231 *The Young Gypsy* (Karlis Huns)

2006. Art.

671	**231**	40s. multicoloured	2·20	2·20

232 Painting inscribed "Jekabs Beckers"

2006. Personal Stamps. Multicoloured.

672	31s. Type **232**		1·60	1·60
673	31s. Postal emblem (horiz)		1·60	1·60

233 Lielais Kristaps (statue)

2006. Lielais Kristaps (Big Christopher) (protector of Riga).

674	**233**	36s. multicoloured	2·10	2·10

234 Hills, Sheep and House (Paula Anna Koskina)

2006. Winning Design in Children's Painting Competition. Self-adesive.

675	**234**	22s. multicoloured	1·30	1·30

235 Uniformed Volunteers

2006. Emergency Volunteer Corps.

676	**235**	22s. multicoloured	1·30	1·30

236 Cliffs, Staburags

2006. Natural Heritage.

677	**236**	58s. multicoloured	3·25	3·25

237 *Lynx lynx*

2006. Fauna. Multicoloured.

678	45s. Type **237**		2·30	2·30
679	55s. *Cervus elaphus*		3·00	3·00
680	45s. As Type **237** (30×48 mm)		2·30	2·30
681	45s. As Type **237** (30×48 mm)		2·30	2·30

238 *Pansija Pili*

2006. Literature. A. Eglitis (writer) Commemoration.

682	**238**	67s. multicoloured	3·75	3·75

239 Mersraga Lighthouse

2006

683	**239**	40s. multicoloured	2·20	2·20
684	**239**	45s. As Type **239** (30×47 mm)	2·30	2·30
685	**239**	45s. As Type **239** (30×47 mm)	2·30	2·30

240 City Skyline

2006. NATO Summit, Riga.

686	**240**	55s. multicoloured	3·25	3·25

241 Tree-shaped Cookie

2006. Christmas. Cookies. Multicoloured. Self-adhesive.

687	18s. Type **241**		1·10	1·10
688	22s. Star and trail		1·40	1·40
689	31s. Bell		1·90	1·90
690	45s. Moon		2·40	2·40

242 Oskar Kalpaks

2007. 125th Birth Anniv of Oskar Kalpaks (first commander in chief national armed forces).

691	**242**	22s. multicoloured	1·30	1·30

243 Air Balloon

2007. 15th Anniv of Mobile Telephony.

692	**243**	22s. multicoloured	1·30	1·30

244 *Tornkalna Bridge* (Ludolfs Libert)

2007. Art.

693	**244**	58s. multicoloured	3·25	3·25

245 Museum Artefacts

2007. 50th Anniv of Pauls Stradins History of Medicine Museum.

694	**245**	22s. multicoloured	1·30	1·30

246 Baltic Coast

2007. Natural Heritage. Self-adhesive.

695	**246**	22s. multicoloured	1·30	1·30

247 Papes Lighthouse

2007

696	**247**	67s. multicoloured	4·00	4·00

248 Emblem, Compass and Scouts

2007. Europa. Centenary of Scouting.

697	**248**	85s. multicoloured	5·00	5·00

249 Sigulda Castle

2007. 800th Anniv of Sigulda. Multicoloured. Self-adhesive.

698	22s. Type **249**		1·30	1·30
699	31s. Bobsleigh track		2·00	2·00
700	40s. New castle ruins		2·50	2·50

250 Krutspils Castle

2007

701	**250**	22s. multicoloured	1·30	1·30

251 House of Blackheads, Riga

2007. World Heritage Sites, Riga and Vismar. Multicoloured.

702	36s. Type **251**		2·00	2·00
703	45s. City Hall, Schtralsund and St George's Church, Vismar		2·75	2·75

Stamps of a similar design were issued by Germany.

252 *Vaccinium vitis*

2007. Berries and Fungi. Multicoloured.

704	22s. Type **252**		1·30	1·30
705	58s. *Cantharellus cibarius*		3·25	3·25

253 Ball containing Player

2007. Centenary of National Football.

706	**253**	45s. multicoloured	2·50	2·50

254 Railway Bridge

2007. Bridges. Sheet 100×70 mm.

MS707	**254**	100s. multicoloured	5·75	5·75

255 Early Postal Delivery

2007. 375th Anniv of Latvian Post. Multicoloured. Self-adhesive.

708	22s. Type **255**		1·30	1·30
709	31s. Modern postal delivery		1·70	1·70

256 Decorated Metal Work

2007. Archaeology.

710	**256**	60s. multicoloured	3·50	3·50

257 *Vulpes vulpes* (fox)

2007. Fauna. Multicoloured.

711	45s. Type **257**		2·50	2·50
711a	55s. *Alces alces* (elk)		3·25	3·25

258 Child Musicians

2007. Christmas. Designs showing children. Multicoloured. Self-adhesive.

712	22s. Type **258**		1·40	1·40
713	31s. Baking		1·90	1·90
714	45s. Sledding		2·50	2·50

259 Salaspils

2008. Arms. Multicoloured.

715		22s. Type **259**	1·40	1·40
716		28s. Plavinas	2·10	2·10
717		45s. Saulkrasti	2·50	2·50

260 Egg in Nest

2008. Easter.

718	**260**	22s. multicoloured	1·10	1·10

261 *Still Life* (Leo Svemps)

2008. Art.

719	**261**	63s. multicoloured	2·70	2·70

262 Order of
Three Stars
(Latvia)

2008. Baltic State's Orders. Multicoloured.

720		31s. Type **262**	1·40	1·40

MS721 116×51 mm. 31s.×3, As Type
262; Order of Vytautas the Great
with Golden Chain (Lithuania); Order
of National Coat of Arms (Estonia)   4·25   4·25

Stamps of similar design were issued by Estonia and
Lithuania.

263 *Barbastella
barbastellus*

2008. Bats. Multicoloured.

722		22s. Type **263**	1·10	1·10
723		31s. *Myotis dasycneme*	1·40	1·40
724		45s. *Barbastella barbastellus* (vert)	1·90	1·90
725		55s. *Myotis dasycneme* (vert)	2·40	2·40

264 Envelopes

2008. Europa. The Letter. Multicoloured.

726		45s. Type **264**	1·90	1·90
727		85s. Writing letter	4·25	4·25

265 Akmenraga
Baka

2008. Lighthouses.

728	**265**	63s. multicoloured	2·70	2·70

266 Athlete and
Controls

2008. European Orienteering Championship.

729	**266**	45s. multicoloured	2·75	2·75

267 Rock

2008. Natural Heritage. Self-adhesive.

730	**267**	22s. multicoloured	5·00	5·00

268 Exhibits

2008. Museum Foundations.

731	**268**	22s. multicoloured	5·00	5·00

269 Basketball

2008. Olympic Games, Beijing.

732	**269**	63s. multicoloured	14·00	14·00

270 Horse Dancer

2008. Fairytales.

733	**270**	22s. multicoloured	1·50	1·50

271 *Vaccinium
myrtillus* (bilberry)

2008. Berry and Fungi. Multicoloured.

734		22s. Type **271**	1·60	1·60
735		58s. *Leccinum aurantiacum* (orange cap boletus)	3·50	3·50

272 Bridge over Abava
River, Kandavas

2008. Bridges. Sheet 100×70 mm.

MS736	**272**	100s. multicoloured	6·50	6·50

273 Masthead

2008. 20th Anniv of Latvijas Tautas Frontei (Latvian
People's Front) and *Atmoda* (Awakening) (first
independent opposition newspaper).

737	**273**	22s. multicoloured	1·50	1·50

274 *Martes martes*
(European pine
marten)

2008. Fauna. Multicoloured.

738		45s. Type **274**	2·75	2·75
739		55s. *Castor fiber* (beaver)	3·75	3·75

275 Maris Strombergs

2008. Maris Strombergs–BMX Olympic Gold Medallist.

740	**275**	22s. multicoloured	1·50	1·50

276 Brooches and
Woollen Shawl

2008. Cultural Heritage. Decoration.

741	**276**	28s. multicoloured	2·00	2·00

277 Map as Flag and Arms

2008. 90th Anniv of Republic.

742	**277**	31s. multicoloured	2·00	2·00

278 Mezotnes Palace,
Bauska

2008. Palaces.

743	**278**	63s. multicoloured	2·00	2·00

279 Decorated
Trees

2008. Christmas.

744	**279**	25s. multicoloured	1·50	1·50

280 Metalwork

2009. Cultural Heritage. Decoration.

745	**280**	98s. multicoloured	5·25	5·25

281 Dancing Boy and
Animals

2009. Fairy Tales.

746	**281**	40s. multicoloured	1·70	1·70

282 Polar Bear

2009. Preserve Polar Regions and Glaciers. Sheet 120×75
mm containing T **282** and similar vert design.
Multicoloured.

MS747		35s. Type **282**; 55s. Penguin and chick	5·50	5·50

283 Janis Ikaunieks
and Schmidt
Telescope, Baldone
Observatory

2009. Europa. Astronomy. Multicoloured.

748		50s. Type **283**	2·75	2·75
749		55s. Astronomers and images of space	3·50	3·50

284 Museum Building
and Exhibits

2009. National History Museum of Latvia.

750	**284**	35s. multicoloured	2·10	2·10

285 Latvija Player
(European Champions,
1935)

2009. Basketball–National Sport. Multicoloured.

751		35s. Type **285**	2·40	2·40
752		40s. TTT Riga player (women's club)	2·75	2·75
753		60s. ASK Riga player (men's club)	3·00	3·00
MS754		100×70 mm. 120s. Young players	8·25	8·25

286 Bauska Castle

2009. 400th Anniv of Bauska.

755	**286**	38s. multicoloured	2·40	2·40

287 Steam Locomotive

2009. Latvian Railways.

756	**287**	35s. multicoloured	3·25	3·25

288 Dienvidu Bridge, Riga

2009. Bridges. Sheet 100×70 mm.

MS757	**288**	100s. multicoloured	21·00	21·00

289 *Fragaria vesca*
(strawberry)

2009. Berry and Fungi. Multicoloured.

758		55s. Type **289**	3·25	3·25
759		60s. *Russula paludosa*	3·75	3·75

290 *Canes lupus* (wolf)

2009. Fauna. Multicoloured.

760		35s. Type **290**	3·00	3·00
761		98s. *Lepus europaeus* (hare)	5·25	5·25

Pt. 6, Pt. 19

LEBANON

A territory north of the Holy Land, formerly part of the Turkish Empire, Greater Lebanon was given a separate status under French Mandate in 1920. Until September 1923, the French occupation stamps of Syria were used and these were followed by the joint issue of 1923, Nos. 97 etc., of Syria. Independence was proclaimed in 1941, but the country was not evacuated by French troops until 1946.

100 centimes = 1 piastre;
100 piastres = 1 Lebanese pound.

1924. Stamps of France surch **GRAND LIBAN** and value. (a) Definitive stamps.

1	**11**	10c. on 2c. purple	1·00	2·50
2	**18**	25c. on 5c. orange	1·70	1·50
3	**18**	50c. on 10c. green	2·00	1·10
4	**15**	75c. on 15c. green	3·25	5·75
5	**18**	1p. on 20c. brown	3·00	1·60
6	**18**	1.25p. on 25c. blue	5·00	3·75
7	**18**	1.50p. on 30c. orange	4·00	8·25
8	**18**	1.50p. on 30c. red	3·75	8·50
10	**13**	2p. on 40c. red and blue	2·30	1·10
9	**15**	2.50p. on 50c. blue	2·50	1·30
11	**13**	3p. on 60c. violet and blue	8·25	11·00
12	**13**	5p. on 1f. red and yellow	9·25	8·75
13	**13**	10p. on 2f. orange and green	18·00	20·00
14	**13**	25p. on 5f. blue and buff	35·00	60·00

(b) Pasteur issue.

15	**30**	50c. on 10c. green	1·70	4·00
16	**30**	1,50p. on 30c. red	3·25	9·75
17	**30**	2,50p. on 50c. blue	1·30	4·25

(c) Olympic Games issue.

18	**31**	50c. on 10c. green and light green	28·00	85·00
19	-	1,25p. on 25c. deep red and red	11·00	85·00
20	-	1,50p. on 30c. red and black	17·00	70·00
21	-	2,50p. on 50c. blue	12·00	65·00

1924. Air. Stamps of France surch **Poste par Avion GRAND LIBAN** and value.

22	**13**	2p. on 40c. red and blue	13·00	38·00
23	**13**	3p. on 60c. violet and blue	13·00	38·00
24	**13**	5p. on 1f. red and yellow	13·00	16·00
25	**13**	10p. on 2f. orange and green	13·00	35·00

1924. Stamps of France surch Grand Liban (T **13**) or **Gd Liban** (others) and value in French and Arabic. (a) Definitive stamps.

26	**11**	0p.10 on 2c. purple	30	1·10
27	**18**	0p.25 on 5c. orange	1·30	1·20
28	**18**	0p.50 on 10c. green	3·25	3·50
29	**15**	0p.75 on 15c. green	90	4·25
30	**18**	1p. on 20c. brown	1·10	25
31	**18**	1p.25 on 25c. blue	3·25	5·00
32	**18**	1p.50 on 30c. red	2·30	2·50
33	**18**	1p.50 on 30c. orange	75·00	80·00
34	**18**	2p. on 35c. violet	2·75	8·50
35	**13**	2p. on 40c. red and blue	4·25	55
36	**13**	2p. on 45c. green and blue	25·00	40·00
37	**13**	3p. on 60c. violet and blue	3·00	2·00
38	**15**	3p. on 60c. violet	3·75	10·00
39	**15**	4p. on 85c. red	1·00	3·50
40	**13**	5p. on 1f. red and yellow	3·00	3·00
41	**13**	10p. on 2f. orange and green	8·25	18·00
42	**13**	25p. on 5f. blue and buff	11·00	34·00

(b) Pasteur issue.

43	**30**	0p.50 on 10c. green	85	30
44	**30**	0p.75 on 15c. green	3·25	8·75
45	**30**	1p.50 on 30c. red	3·00	55
46	**30**	2p. on 45c. red	4·00	8·75
47	**30**	2p.50 on 50c. blue	90	45
48	**30**	4p. on 75c. blue	2·30	3·00

(c) Olympic Games issue.

49	**31**	0p.50 on 10c. green and light green	16·00	60·00
50	-	1p.25 on 25c. deep red and red	18·00	75·00
51	-	1p.50 on 30c. red and black	16·00	60·00
52	-	2p.50 on 50c. ultramarine and blue	23·00	46·00

(d) Ronsard issue.

53	**35**	4p. on 75c. blue on bluish	90	10·50

1924. Air. Stamps of France surch **Gd Liban Avion** and value in French and Arabic.

54	**13**	2p. on 40c. red and blue	6·25	35·00
55	**13**	3p. on 60c. violet and blue	6·25	35·00
56	**13**	5p. on 1f. red and yellow	6·25	35·00
57	**13**	10p. on 2f. orange and green	8·75	38·00

5 Cedar of Lebanon

6 Beirut

1925. Views.

58	**5**	0p.10c. violet	50	1·60
59	**6**	0p.25c. black	1·00	2·30
60	-	0p.50c. green (Tripoli)	1·60	1·40
61	-	0p.75c. red (Beit ed-Din)	2·00	4·00
62	-	1p. purple (Baalbek ruins)	2·75	35
63	-	1p.25 green (Mouktara)	3·50	4·00
64	-	1p.50 pink (Tyre)	1·90	50
65	-	2p. brown (Zahle)	2·40	65
66	-	2p.50 blue (Baalbek)	2·30	1·00
67	-	3p. brown (Deir el-Kamar)	1·20	75
68	-	5p. violet (Sidon)	7·00	7·25
69	**7**	10p. purple	9·00	6·50
70	-	25p. blue (Beirut)	11·00	28·00

7 Tripoli

1925. Air. Nos. 65 and 67/9 optd **AVION** in French and Arabic.

71		2p. brown	4·75	12·00
72		3p. brown	5·00	12·00
73		5p. violet	5·00	12·00
74	**7**	10p. purple	4·75	10·00

1926. Air. Nos. 65 and 67/9 optd with *Bleriot XI* airplane.

75	-	2p. brown	5·00	14·50
76	-	3p. brown	4·50	14·50
77	-	5p. violet	5·00	14·50
78	**7**	10p. purple	4·50	14·50

1926. War Refugee Charity. Various stamps surch **Secours aux Refugies Afft** and premium in French and Arabic. (a) Postage. Stamps of 1925.

79	**6**	0p.25+0p.25 black	2·20	7·00
80	-	0p.50+0p.25 green	3·00	14·00
81	-	0p.75+0p.25 red	1·80	11·00
82	-	1p.+0p.50 purple	2·50	13·50
83	-	1p.25+0p.50 green	2·30	17·00
84	-	1p.50+0p.50 pink	4·25	14·00
85	-	2p.+0p.75 brown	5·50	13·00
86	-	2p.50+0p.75 blue	3·00	20·00
87	-	3p.+1p. brown	3·50	19·00
88	-	5p.+1p. violet	7·00	22·00
89	**7**	10p.+2p. purple	7·00	28·00
90	-	25p.+5p. blue	7·25	34·00

(b) Air. Nos. 75/78 surch.

91		2p.+1p. brown	5·00	20·00
92		3p.+2p. brown	5·00	17·00
93		5p.+3p. violet	5·00	17·00
94	**7**	10p.+5p. purple	5·00	24·00

1926. Stamps of 1925 surch in English and Arabic.

95	-	3p.50 on 0p.75 red	3·25	3·75
97b	**6**	4p. on 0p.25 black	4·00	85
98	-	4p.50 on 0p.75 red	4·50	3·75
99	-	6p. on 2p.50 blue	4·00	4·00
100	-	7p.50 on 2p.50 blue	3·75	90
101	-	12p. on 1p.25 green	3·00	4·25
102	-	15p. on 25p. blue	5·00	2·00
103	-	20p. on 1p.25 green	10·00	19·00

1927. Stamps of 1925 and provisional stamps of Lebanon optd **Republique Libanaise**.

104	**5**	0p.10 violet	55	1·80
105	-	0p.50 green	1·20	65
106	-	1p. purple	55	35
107	-	1p.50 pink	2·00	1·70
108	-	2p. brown	3·75	2·00
109	-	3p. brown	1·60	55
110	**6**	4p. on 0p.25 black (No. 96)	1·80	35
111	-	4p.50 on 0p.75 red (No. 98)	1·30	70
112	-	5p. violet	3·75	4·25
113	-	7p.50 on 2p.50 bl (No. 100)	2·30	65
114	**7**	10p. purple	4·50	4·50
115	-	15p. on 25p. blue (No. 102)	11·00	6·00
117	-	25p. blue	12·00	42·00

1927. Air. Nos. 75/78 optd **Republique Libanaise**.

118		2p. brown	5·50	14·50
119		3p. brown	5·50	14·50
120		5p. violet	5·50	14·50
121	**7**	10p. purple	5·50	14·50

1928. Nos. 104/117 optd with T **10** or surch also.

145	**5**	05 on 0p.10 violet	10	1·20
124	**5**	0p.10 violet	55	50
125	-	0p.50 green	2·75	1·80
146	-	0p.50 on 0p.75 red	1·00	70
126	-	1p. purple	1·60	35
127	-	1p.50 pink	3·25	3·25
128	-	2p. brown	5·75	11·00
147	-	2p. on 1p.25 green	1·40	45
129	-	3p. brown	3·25	80
148	**6**	4p. on 0p.25 black	3·50	20
131	-	4p.50 on 0p.75 red	2·75	2·75
132a	-	5p. violet	3·25	9·00
149	-	7p.50 on 2p.50 blue	2·40	20
134	**7**	10p. purple	11·00	10·50
123	-	15p. on 25p. blue	13·00	38·00
136	-	25p. blue	12·50	19·00

الجمهورية اللبنانية

(10)

1928. Air. Optd or surch with airplane, **Republique Libanaise** and line of Arabic as T **10**.

151	-	0p.50 green	1·10	5·00
152	-	0p.50 on 0p.75 red (No. 146)	1·70	2·75
153	-	1p. purple	2·50	3·75
141		2p. brown	4·25	8·00
154	-	2p. on 1p.25 grn (No. 147)	2·50	3·25
142		3p. brown	2·75	4·50
143		5p. violet	4·50	5·75
144	**7**	10p. purple	4·50	3·75
155	-	15p. on 25p. blue (No. 123)	£200	£225
156	-	25p. blue	£130	£130

14 Silkworm Larva, Cocoon and Moth

1930. Silk Congress.

157	**14**	4p. sepia	13·00	23·00
158	**14**	4½p. red	13·00	23·00
159	**14**	7½p. blue	13·00	30·00
160	**14**	10p. violet	14·00	25·00
161	**14**	15p. green	14·00	23·00
162	**14**	25p. purple	14·00	23·00

15 Cedars of Lebanon

16a Baalbek

1930. Views.

163b	-	0p.10 orange (Beirut)	2·30	1·60
164	**15**	0p.20 brown	1·20	2·30
165	-	0p.25 blue (Baalbek)	60	2·10
166	-	0p.50 brown (Bickfaya)	1·10	65
166b	-	0p.75 brown (Baalbek)	3·75	3·00
167	-	1p. green (Saida)	5·50	50
167a	-	1p. purple (Saida)	8·25	65
168	-	1p.50 purple (Beit ed-Din)	4·50	1·80
168a	-	1p.50 green (Beit ed-Din)	10·50	45
169	-	2p. blue (Tripoli)	6·50	65
170	-	3p. sepia (Baalbek)	7·75	65
171	-	4p. brown (Nahr-el-Kalb)	7·75	45
172	-	4p.50 red (Beaufort)	6·50	70
173	-	5p. green (Beit ed-Din)	3·25	50
251	-	5p. blue (Nahr el-Kalb)	3·25	90
174	-	6p. purple (Tyre)	9·25	85
175	**16a**	7p.50 blue	6·75	55
176	-	10p. green (Hasbaya)	10·00	85
177	-	15p. purple (Afka Falls)	11·00	85
178	-	25p. green (Beirut)	11·00	1·10
179	-	50p. green (Deir el-Kamar)	50·00	18·00
180	-	100p. black (Baalbek)	46·00	24·00

17 Jebeil (Byblos)

1930. Air. Potez 29-4 biplane and views as T **17**.

181		0p.50 purple (Rachaya)	1·80	2·00
182		1p. green (Broumana)	70	1·60
183		2p. orange (Baalbek)	1·10	1·70
184		3p. red (Hasroun)	2·20	2·00
185		5p. green (Byblos)	2·00	1·80
186		10p. red (Kadisha)	2·75	1·70
187		15p. brown (Beirut)	2·50	1·70
188		25p. violet (Tripoli)	3·00	2·75
189		50p. lake (Kabelais)	7·00	5·50
190		100p. brown (Zahle)	10·50	10·00

18 Skiing

1936. Air. Tourist Propaganda.

191	**18**	0p.50 green	3·25	3·00
192	-	1p. orange	4·25	4·25
193	**18**	2p. violet	2·20	3·00
194	-	3p. green	3·00	3·00
195	**18**	5p. red	6·00	5·50
196	-	10p. brown	6·50	7·25
197	-	15p. red	41·00	38·00
198	**18**	25p. green	£130	£140

DESIGN: 1, 3, 10, 15p. Jounieh Bay.

20 Cedar of Lebanon

21 President Edde

22 Lebanese Landscape

1937

199	**20**	0p.10 red	10	10
200	**20**	0p.20 blue	1·00	5·50
201	**20**	0p.25 lilac	65	5·25
202	**20**	0p.50 mauve	55	10
203	**20**	0p.75 brown	30	1·70
207	**21**	3p. violet	4·25	1·90
208	**21**	4p. brown	2·75	35
209	**21**	4p.50 red	2·75	35
211	**22**	10p. red	3·75	35
212	**22**	12½p. blue	1·80	35
213	**22**	15p. green	4·25	35
214	**22**	20p. brown	4·00	75
215	**22**	25p. red	7·50	55
216	**22**	50p. violet	12·50	3·25
217	**22**	100p. sepia	17·00	5·50

23 Exhibition Pavilion, Paris

1937. Air. Paris International Exhibition.

218	**23**	0p.50 black	1·80	2·30
219	**23**	1p. green	1·80	3·25
220	**23**	2p. brown	1·80	3·25
221	**23**	3p. green	1·80	3·25
222	**23**	5p. green	1·80	3·25
223	**23**	10p. red	11·00	23·00
224	**23**	15p. purple	7·75	27·00
225	**23**	25p. brown	14·50	42·00

25 Ruins of Baalbek

1937. Air.

226	-	0p.50 blue	15	35
227	-	1p. red	2·00	2·30
228	-	2p. sepia	2·40	2·75
229	-	3p. red	6·00	5·00
230	-	5p. green	2·75	2·30
231	**25**	10p. violet	2·30	10
232	-	15p. blue	2·30	3·50
233	-	25p. violet	6·00	3·50
234	-	50p. green	11·00	2·50
235	-	100p. brown	6·00	6·75

DESIGN: 0p.50 to 5p. Beit ed-Din.

1938. Nos. 207/8 surch in English and Arabic figures.

236	**21**	2p. on 3p. violet	2·00	20
237	**21**	2½p. on 4p. brown	3·00	20

27 Medical College, Beirut

1938. Air. Medical Congress.

238	**27**	2p. green	3·25	7·00
239	**27**	3p. orange	4·25	5·00
240	**27**	5p. violet	5·00	11·00
241	**27**	10p. red	11·00	23·00

28 Maurice Nogues and Liore et Olivier LeO H.24-3 Flying Boat over Beirut

1938. Air. Tenth Anniv of 1st Air Service between France and Lebanon.

242	**28**	10p. purple	7·50	14·50
MS242a		161×120 mm. No. 242 in block of four	70·00	75·00

16a Baalbek

1938. Surch.

243	**16a**	6p. on 7p.50 blue	3·25	1·30
244	-	7p.50 on 50p. grn (No. 179)	3·50	3·50
245	-	7p.50 on 100p. blk (No. 180)	2·75	3·25
246	**22**	12p.50 on 7p.50 blue	6·50	1·60
247	**22**	12½p. on 7p.50 blue	3·25	35

1939. As T **16a**, but with differing figures and Arabic inscriptions in side panels, and imprint at foot "IMP. CATHOLIQUE-BEYROUTH-LIBAN" instead of "HELIO VAUGIRARD".

248		1p. green	1·00	80
249		1p.50 purple	1·60	1·10
250		7p.50 red	2·30	35

DESIGN: 1p. to 7p.50, Beit ed-Din.

32 Emir Bechir Chehab

1942. First Anniv of Proclamation of Independence.

252	**32**	0p.50 green (postage)	3·50	3·50
253	**32**	1p.50 purple	3·50	3·50
254	**32**	6p. red	3·50	3·50
255	**32**	15p. blue	3·50	3·50
256	-	10p. purple (air)	6·00	6·00
257	-	50p. green	6·50	6·50

DESIGN: 10, 50p. Airplane over mountains.

1943. Surch in English and Arabic and with old values cancelled with ornaments.

258	**21**	2p. on 4p. brown	7·00	6·50
259	-	6p. on 7p.50 red (No. 250)	2·50	1·50
260	**22**	10p. on 12½p. blue	2·40	1·20
261	-	2p. on 5p. blue (No. 251)	1·40	85
262	-	3p. on 5p. blue (No. 251)	1·40	85
263	**22**	6p. on 12½p. blue	2·00	1·50
264	**22**	7½p. on 12½p. blue	2·40	2·00

37 Parliament House

38 Bechamoun

1944. Second Anniv of Proclamation of Independence.

265	**37**	25p. red (postage)	10·50	10·50
266	-	50p. blue	10·50	10·50
267	**37**	150p. blue	10·50	10·50
268	-	200p. purple	10·50	10·50

DESIGN: 50p., 200p. Government House.

269	**38**	25p. green (air)	4·25	2·75
270	**38**	50p. orange	4·25	2·75
271	-	100p. brown	4·25	3·75
272	-	200p. violet	5·25	3·75
273	-	300p. green	18·00	18·00
274	-	500p. brown	49·00	34·00

DESIGNS: 100p., 200p. Rachaya Citadel; 300p., 500p. Beirut.

38a Beirut Isolation Hospital

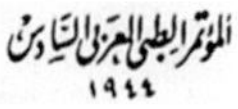

(39)

1944. Sixth Medical Congress. Optd with T **39**.

275	**38a**	10p. red (postage)	7·00	7·00
276	**38a**	20p. blue	8·00	8·00
277	-	20p. orange (air)	3·50	3·50
278	-	50p. blue	4·50	4·50
279	-	100p. purple	6·00	6·00

DESIGN: Nos. 277/9, Bhannes Sanatorium.

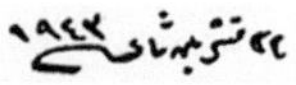

40 Trans "Nov. 23, 1943"

1944. First Anniv of President's Return to Office. Nos. 265/74 optd with T **40**.

280	**37**	25p. red (postage)	18·00	18·00
281	-	50p. blue	18·00	18·00
282	**37**	150p. blue	18·00	18·00
283	-	200p. purple	18·00	18·00
284	**38**	25p. green (air)	9·00	9·00
285	-	50p. orange	15·00	15·00
286	-	100p. brown	19·00	19·00
287	-	200p. violet	30·00	30·00
288	-	300p. green	41·00	41·00
289	-	500p. brown	70·00	70·00

41 Crusader Castle, Byblos

42 Falls of R. Litani

1945

397	**41**	7p.50 red (postage)	3·25	20
398	**41**	10p. purple	4·75	30
399	**41**	12p.50 blue	12·00	30
290	**41**	15p. brown	5·25	5·25
291	**41**	20p. green	6·50	5·25
292	-	25p. blue	6·50	5·25
400	**41**	25p. violet	24·00	75
293	-	50p. red	7·50	5·25
401	**41**	50p. green	55·00	6·00
294	**42**	25p. brown (air)	3·50	2·40
295	**42**	50p. purple	6·00	4·00
296	-	200p. violet	17·00	6·50
297	-	300p. black	30·00	13·00

DESIGNS—HORIZ: Nos. 292/3, Crusader Castle, Tripoli; 296/7, Cedar of Lebanon and skier.

43 V(ictory) and National Flag

1946. Victory. "V" in design. (a) Postage.

298	**43**	7p.50 brown, red and pink	85	10
299	**43**	10p. purple, pink and red	1·30	10
300	**43**	12p.50 purple, blue and red	1·90	15
301	**43**	15p. green, emerald and red	3·25	20
302	**43**	20p. myrtle, green and red	2·75	20
303	**43**	25p. blue, light blue and red	4·25	45
304	**43**	50p. blue, violet and red	7·00	2·40
305	**43**	100p. black, blue and red	12·00	4·50

44 V(ictory) and Lebanese Soldiers at Bir-Hakeim

(b) Air.

306	**44**	15p. blue, yellow and red	75	20
307	**44**	20p. red and blue	85	55
308	**44**	25p. blue, yellow and red	85	55
309	**44**	50p. black, violet and red	1·90	55
310	**44**	100p. violet and red	4·75	1·60
311	**44**	150p. brown and red	6·00	2·75
MS311a		142×230 mm. Nos. 298/311. Colours changed. Text in brown (with gum) or blue (without gum)	£130	£130

1946. As T **43** but without "V" sign.

312		7p.50 lake, red and mauve	1·30	20
313		10p. violet, mauve and red	1·90	20
314		12p.50 brown, green and red	2·75	25
315		15p. brown, pink and red	3·75	30
316		20p. blue, orange and red	3·25	30
317		25p. myrtle, green and red	6·00	45
318		50p. blue, light blue and red	10·50	1·90
319		100p. black, blue and red	18·00	4·75

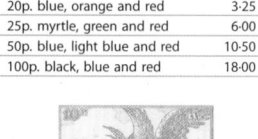

45 Grey Herons

1946

320	**45**	12p.50 red (postage)	34·00	3·75
321	**45**	10p. orange (air)	8·50	1·30
322	**45**	25p. blue	10·50	65
323	**45**	50p. green	24·00	1·80
324	**45**	100p. purple	43·00	8·00

46 Cedar of Lebanon

1946

325	**46**	0p.50 brown	55	20
326	**46**	1p. purple	1·10	20
327	**46**	2p.50 violet	3·75	20
328	**46**	5p. red	3·75	20
329	**46**	6p. grey	3·75	20

47

1946. Air. Arab Postal Congress.

330	**47**	25p. blue	1·30	75
331	**47**	50p. green	1·70	1·20
332	**47**	75p. red	3·00	1·90
333	**47**	150p. violet	7·00	3·50

48 Cedar of Lebanon

1947

333a	**48**	0p.50 brown	1·70	20
333b	**48**	2p.50 green	2·40	20
333c	**48**	5p. red	4·25	45

49 President, Bridge and Tablet

1947. Air. Evacuation of Foreign Troops from Lebanon.

334	**49**	25p. blue	1·30	55
335	**49**	50p. red	1·80	1·10
336	**49**	75p. black	3·75	1·60
337	**49**	150p. green	6·50	3·25

50 Crusader Castle, Tripoli

51 Jounieh Bay

1947

338	**50**	12p.50 red (postage)	10·50	55
339	**50**	25p. blue	13·00	55
340	**50**	50p. green	43·00	1·20
341	**50**	100p. violet	55·00	8·50
342	**51**	5p. green (air)	55	20
343	**51**	10p. mauve	55	20
344	**51**	15p. red	95	20
403	**51**	15p. green	10·50	1·60
345	**51**	20p. orange	1·80	20
345a	**51**	20p. red	1·90	45
346	**51**	25p. blue	2·40	20
347	**51**	50p. red	5·25	55
348	**51**	100p. purple	10·50	85
349	-	150p. purple	21·00	1·80
350	-	200p. slate	32·00	85
351	-	300p. black	50·00	19·00

DESIGN: 150p. to 300p. Grand Serail Palace.

54 Phoenician Galley

1947. Air. 12th Congress of U.P.U., Paris.

352	-	10p. blue	1·20	55
353	-	15p. red	1·70	75
354	-	25p. blue	2·40	1·30
355	**54**	50p. green	5·25	1·50
356	-	75p. violet	7·00	2·10
357	-	100p. brown	9·75	4·75

DESIGN—VERT: 10p. to 25p. Posthorn.

55 Faraya Bridge and Statue

1947. Air. Red Cross Fund. Cross in red.

358	**55**	12p.50+25p. green	9·75	7·50
359	**55**	25p.+50p. blue	10·50	8·50
360	-	50p.+100p. brown	14·00	10·50
361	-	75p.+150p. violet	28·00	21·00
362	-	100p.+200p. grey	55·00	38·00

DESIGN: 50p. to 100p. Djounie Bay and statue.

56 Cedar of Lebanon

58 Lebanese Landscape

1948

363	**56**	0p.50 blue (postage)	20	10
364	**56**	1p. brown	55	10
395	**56**	1p. orange	1·30	10
365	**56**	2p.50 mauve	85	10
366	**56**	3p. green	2·10	15
367	**56**	5p. red	2·75	20
368	-	7p.50 red	7·50	30
369	-	10p. purple	4·75	30
370	-	12p.50 blue	12·00	45
371	-	25p. blue	17·00	95
372	-	50p. green	39·00	7·50
373	**58**	5p. red (air)	75	20
374	**58**	10p. mauve	1·30	20
375	**58**	15p. brown	3·75	20
376	**58**	20p. slate	6·00	25
377	**58**	25p. blue	10·50	1·50
378	**58**	50p. black	20·00	2·10

DESIGN—As T **58**: Nos. 368/72, Zebaide Aqueduct.

59 Europa on Bull

1948. Third Meeting of UNESCO, Beirut.

379	**59**	10p. orange and red (postage)	2·75	1·90
380	**59**	12p.50 mauve and violet	3·75	2·75
381	**59**	25p. green and light green	4·50	2·75
382	-	30p. buff and brown	6·00	3·50
383	-	40p. green and turquoise	8·50	3·50

DESIGN—VERT: 30, 40p. Avicenna (philosopher and scientist).

61 Apollo on Sun Chariot

384	**61**	7p.50 blue & lt blue (air)	2·40	1·90
385	**61**	15p. black and grey	2·75	1·90
386	**61**	20p. brown and pink	4·75	2·75
387	-	35p. red	8·00	3·75
388	-	75p. green	16·00	8·50
MS388a 142×205 mm. Nos. 379/88. Imperf. No gum			£350	£350

DESIGN—HORIZ: 35, 75p. Symbolic figure.

63 Camel

64 Sikorsky S-51 Helicopter

1949. 75th Anniv of U.P.U.

389	**63**	5p. violet (postage)	1·80	1·20
390	**63**	7p.50 red	2·50	2·00
391	**63**	12p.50 blue	4·25	2·50
392	**64**	25p. blue (air)	9·00	4·00
393	**64**	50p. green	14·00	6·50
MS393a 135×190 mm. Nos. 389/93. Imperf (sold at 150p.)			90·00	90·00

65 Cedar of Lebanon

66 Nahr el-Kalb Bridge

1950

407	**65**	0p.50 red	30	20
408	**65**	1p. red	95	20
409	**65**	2p.50 violet	1·50	20
410	**65**	5p. purple	2·75	20
411	**66**	7p.50 red	3·50	20
412	**66**	10p. lilac	4·25	20
413	**66**	12p.50 blue	7·00	30
414	**66**	25p. blue	13·00	1·40
415	**66**	50p. green	38·00	7·50

67 Congressional Flags

1950. Lebanese Emigrants' Congress. Inscr "MOIS DES EMIGRES-ETE 1950".

416	**67**	7p.50 green (postage)	95	30
417	**67**	12p. mauve	95	30
418	-	5p. blue (air)	2·75	75
419	-	15p. violet	3·75	1·10
420	-	25p. brown	1·90	1·10
421	-	35p. green	3·75	1·90
MS421a 134×184 mm. Nos. 416/21. Imperf. No gum			85·00	85·00

DESIGNS: 5, 15p. House martins; 25, 35p. Pres. Bishara al-Khoury and building.

70 Crusader Castle, Sidon

1950. Air.

422	**70**	10p. brown	75	20
423	**70**	15p. green	1·20	20
424	**70**	20p. red	3·75	55
425	**70**	25p. blue	6·50	1·30
426	**70**	50p. grey	12·00	3·25

1950. Surch with figures and bars.

427	**56**	1p. on 3p. green	75	30
428	**46**	2p.50 on 6p. grey	1·10	30

73 Cedar of Lebanon

74 Nahr el-Kalb Bridge

75 Crusader Castle, Sidon

1951

429	**73**	0p.50 red (postage)	30	10
430	**73**	1p. brown	75	10
431	**73**	2p.50 grey	3·75	10
432	**73**	5p. purple	4·25	10
433	**74**	7p.50 red	4·50	45
434	**74**	10p. purple	6·00	30
435	**74**	12p.50 turquoise	10·50	55
436	**74**	25p. blue	17·00	1·90
437	**74**	50p. green	39·00	10·00
438	**75**	10p. turquoise (air)	1·20	20
439	**75**	15p. brown	2·75	20
440	**75**	20p. red	2·75	30
441	**75**	25p. blue	2·75	30
442	**75**	35p. mauve	7·50	3·75
443	**75**	50p. blue	14·00	2·75

Type **74** is similar to Type **66** but left value tablets differ.

For design as Type **74** but inscr "LIBAN", see Nos. 561/3.

76 Cedar of Lebanon

77 Baalbek

1952

444	**76**	0p.50 green (postage)	85	10
445	**76**	1p. brown	85	10
446	**76**	2p.50 blue	1·40	30
447	**76**	5p. red	2·40	30
448	**77**	7p.50 red	3·25	65
449	**77**	10p. violet	7·00	75
450	**77**	12p.50 blue	7·00	75
451	**77**	25p. blue	8·50	1·90
452	-	50p. green	26·00	3·50
453	-	100p. brown	55·00	10·50
454	-	5p. red (air)	45	10
455	-	10p. grey	65	20
456	-	15p. mauve	1·20	20
457	-	20p. orange	1·90	45
458	-	25p. blue	1·90	55
459	-	35p. blue	3·25	65
460	-	50p. green	10·50	75
461	-	100p. blue	75·00	3·25
462	-	200p. green	43·00	6·00
463	-	300p. sepia	60·00	13·00

DESIGNS—As Type **77**: Nos. 452/3, Beaufort Castle; 454/9, Beirut Airport; 460/3, Amphitheatre, Byblos.

78 Cedar of Lebanon

79 General Post Office

80 Douglas DC-4

1953

559	**78**	0p.50 blue (postage)	30	15
465	**78**	1p. red	1·10	10
466	**78**	2p.50 violet	1·40	30
560	**78**	2p.50 purple	85	15
467	**78**	5p. green	2·40	30
468	**79**	7p.50 red	3·75	55
469	**79**	10p. green	4·50	75
470	**79**	12p.50 turquoise	6·50	85
471	**79**	25p. blue	9·75	1·70
472	**79**	50p. brown	17·00	3·75
473	**80**	5p. green (air)	45	10
474	**80**	10p. red	85	10
475	**80**	15p. red	1·20	10
476	**80**	20p. turquoise	1·90	10
477	**80**	25p. blue	4·75	20
478	**80**	35p. brown	7·00	30
479	**80**	50p. blue	9·75	65
480	**80**	100p. sepia	18·00	6·50

For 20p. green as Type **79** see No. 636.

81 Cedar of Lebanon

82 Beit ed-Din Palace

83 Baalbek

1954

481	**81**	0p.50 blue (postage)	30	20
482	**81**	1p. orange	55	20
483	**81**	2p.50 violet	85	30
484	**81**	5p. green	1·70	30
485	**82**	7p.50 red	2·75	65
486	**82**	10p. green	4·25	65
487	**82**	12p.50 blue	7·00	85
488	**82**	25p. deep blue	9·75	3·50
489	**82**	50p. turquoise	17·00	6·00
490	**82**	100p. sepia	43·00	12·00
491	**83**	5p. green (air)	55	10
492	**83**	10p. lilac	1·10	10
493	**83**	15p. red	1·20	10
494	**83**	20p. brown	1·70	10
495	**83**	25p. blue	1·90	30
496	**83**	35p. sepia	2·75	30
497	-	50p. green	8·50	55
498	-	100p. red	14·00	85
499	-	200p. sepia	28·00	2·75
500	-	300p. blue	48·00	6·00

DESIGN—As T **83**: 50p. to 300p. Litani Irrigation Canal.

For other values as Nos. 497/500, see Nos. 564/7.

84 Khalde Airport, Beirut

1954. Air. Opening of Beirut International Airport.

501	**84**	10p. red and pink	75	30
502	**84**	25p. blue and ultramarine	1·90	55
503	**84**	35p. brown and sepia	2·75	95
504	**84**	65p. green and turquoise	6·50	3·75

84a

1955. Arab Postal Union.

505	**84a**	12p.50 green (postage)	75	55
506	**84a**	25p. violet	1·10	55
507	**84a**	2p.50 brown (air)	55	45

85 Rotary Emblem

1955. Air. 50th Anniv of Rotary International.

508	**85**	35p. green	1·40	1·10
509	**85**	65p. blue	2·40	1·60

86 Cedar of Lebanon

87 Jeita Grotto

88 Skiers

1955

510	**86**	0p.50 blue (postage)	30	20
511	**86**	1p. red	40	20
512	**86**	2p.50 violet	65	20
552	**86**	2p.50 blue	9·00	20
513	**86**	5p. green	1·10	20
514	**87**	7p.50 orange	1·40	20
515	**87**	10p. green	2·40	20
516	**87**	12p.50 blue	2·50	20
517	**87**	25p. blue	6·00	45
518	**87**	50p. green	9·75	1·10
519	**88**	5p. turquoise (air)	75	55
520	**88**	15p. red	1·30	30
521	**88**	20p. violet	2·10	30
522	**88**	25p. blue	4·25	45
523	**88**	35p. brown	6·50	75
524	**88**	50p. brown	12·00	1·10
525	**88**	65p. blue	21·00	3·50

The face value on No. 510 reads "0.50 PIASTRE"; on No. 512 the "2" and "50" are different sizes and the 1 and 5p. have no dash under "P".

For other colours and new values as Type **88** see Nos. 568/70 and for redrawn Type **86** see Nos. 582/5, 686 and 695/7.

89 Visitor from Abroad

1955. Air. Tourist Propaganda.

526	**89**	2p.50 slate and purple	20	10
527	**89**	12p.50 blue & ultramarine	55	30
528	**89**	25p. blue and indigo	1·20	55
529	**89**	35p. blue and green	1·60	75
MS529a 159×110 mm. Nos. 526/9. Imperf			28·00	28·00

90 Cedar of Lebanon

91 Globe and Columns

92 Oranges

1955

530	**90**	0.50p. blue (postage)	10	10
531	**90**	1p. orange	20	10
532	**90**	2p.50 violet	45	10
533	**90**	5p. green	75	10
534	**91**	7p.50 red and orange	1·10	10
535	**91**	10p. green and brown	1·20	15
536	**91**	12p.50 blue and green	1·30	15
537	**91**	25p. blue and mauve	2·75	25
538	**91**	50p. green and blue	3·75	55
539	**91**	100p. brown and orange	6·00	1·30
540	**92**	5p. yellow and green (air)	55	15
541	**92**	10p. orange and green	1·10	15
542	**92**	15p. orange and green	1·30	15
543	**92**	20p. orange and brown	1·60	15
544	-	25p. violet and blue	2·40	20
545	-	35p. purple and green	3·75	30
546	-	50p. yellow and black	4·25	40
547	-	65p. yellow and green	8·00	45
548	-	100p. orange and green	10·50	1·20
549	-	200p. red and green	21·00	6·00

DESIGNS—VERT: 25p. to 50p. Grapes. HORIZ: 4p. to 200p. Quinces.

93 U.N. Emblem

1956. Air. Tenth Anniv of U.N.

550	**93**	35p. blue	6·00	4·75
551	**93**	65p. green	8·00	6·00
MS551a 90×70 mm. Nos. 550/1. Imperf			£110	£110

94 Masks, Columns and Gargoyle

1956. Air. Baalbek International Drama Festival. Inscr "FESTIVAL INTERNATIONAL DE BAALBECK".

553	**94**	2p.50 sepia	55	20
554	**94**	10p. green	75	30
555	-	12p.50 blue	85	55
556	-	25p. violet	1·30	65
557	-	35p. purple	2·75	1·10
558	-	65p. slate	4·50	2·40

DESIGNS—HORIZ: 12p.50, 25p. Temple ruins at Baalbek. VERT: 35p., 65p. Double bass, masks and columns.

1957. As earlier designs but redrawn. (a) Postage. As T **74** but inscr "LIBAN".

561		7p.50 red	1·70	15
562		10p. brown	2·40	15
563		12p.50 blue	2·75	15

(b) Air. Arabic inscription changed. New values and colours.

564	-	10p. violet	45	15
565	-	15p. orange	55	15
566	-	20p. green	65	20
567	As	25p. blue	1·10	20
568	88	35p. green	3·25	30
569	88	65p. purple	6·00	85
570	88	100p. brown	9·00	1·80

DESIGN: 10p. to 25p. As Nos. 497/500.

95 Pres. Chamoun and King Faisal II of Iraq

1957. Air. Arab Leaders' Conference, Beirut.

571	95	15p. orange	95	55
572	-	15p. blue	95	55
573	-	15p. maroon	95	55
574	-	15p. purple	95	55
575	-	15p. green	95	55
576	-	25p. turquoise	1·10	60
577	-	100p. brown	6·50	3·50
MS577a		106×151 mm. Nos. 571/6.		
		Imperf	85·00	85·00

DESIGNS—As T **95**: 15p. values show Pres. Chamoun and: King Hussein of Jordan (No. 572), Abdallah Khalil of Sudan (No. 573), Pres. Shukri Bey al-Quwatli of Syria (No. 574) and King Saud of Saudi Arabia (No. 575); 25p. Map and Pres. Chamoun. 44×44 mm (Diamond shape): 100p. The six Arab Leaders.

97 Runners

1957. Second Pan-Arabian Games, Beirut.

578	97	2p.50 sepia (postage)	95	55
579	-	12p.50 blue	1·40	75
580	-	35p. purple (air)	3·75	1·50
581	-	50p. green	4·50	2·10
MS581a		132×185 mm. Nos. 576/81.		
		Imperf. No gum	£130	£130

DESIGNS—VERT: 12p.50, Footballers. HORIZ: 35p. Fencers; 50p. Stadium.

98 Miners

1957

582	86	0p.50 blue (16½×20½ mm) (postage)	20	15
582a	86	0p.50 violet (17×21½ mm)	30	15
583	86	1p. brown (16½×20½ mm)	30	15
583a	86	1p. purple (17×21½ mm)	30	15
584	86	2p.50 violet (16½×20½ mm)	55	15
584a	86	2p.50 violet (17×21¼ mm)	55	15
585	86	5p. green (16½×20½ mm)	75	15
586	98	7½p. pink	1·20	15
587	98	10p. brown	1·50	20
588	98	12½p. blue	2·10	20
589	-	25p. blue	2·40	25
590	-	50p. green	3·75	45
591	-	100p. brown	6·50	1·30
592	-	5p. green (air)	30	10
593	-	10p. orange	30	10
594	-	15p. brown	40	10
595	-	20p. purple	55	15
596	-	25p. blue	75	20
597	-	35p. purple	1·20	45
598	-	50p. green	2·10	65
599	-	65p. brown	3·75	70
600	-	100p. grey	4·75	1·30

DESIGNS: POSTAGE—As Type **86**: 50c. inscr "0 P.50", 2p.50, Figures in uniform size; 1p., 5p. Short dash under "P". As Type **98**: 25p. to 100p. Potter. AIR—As Type **98**: HORIZ: 5p. to 25p. Cedar of Lebanon with signs of the Zodiac, bird and ship; 35 to 100p. Chamoun Electric Power Station.

99 Cedar of Lebanon

100 Soldier and Flag

101 Douglas DC-6B at Khalde Airport

1959

601	99	0p.50 blue (postage)	20	15
602	99	1p. orange	30	15
603	99	2p.50 violet	55	15
604	99	5p. green	75	15
605	100	12p.50 blue	1·50	20
606	100	25p. blue	1·70	20
607	100	50p. brown	2·75	30
608	100	100p. sepia	5·25	65
609	101	5p. green (air)	85	10
610	101	10p. purple	90	10
611	101	15p. violet	1·20	15
612	101	20p. red	1·70	15
613	101	25p. violet	2·10	40
614	-	35p. myrtle	1·70	30
615	-	50p. turquoise	2·10	40
616	-	65p. sepia	4·25	65
617	-	100p. blue	4·75	1·10

DESIGN—HORIZ: Nos. 614/17, Factory, cogwheel and telegraph pylons.

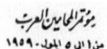

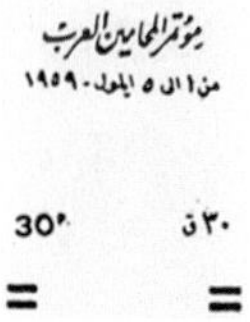

(102)

1959. Lawyers' Conference. Nos. 538 and 546 surch as T **102**.

618		30p. on 50p. myrtle and blue (postage)	1·70	85
619		40p. on 50p. yellow & blk (air)	1·80	95

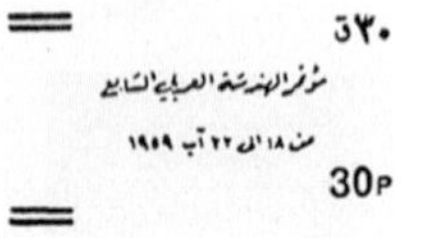

(103)

1959. Air. Engineers' Conference. Nos. 614 and 616 surch as T **103**.

620		30p. on 35p. myrtle	1·10	75
621		40p. on 65p. sepia	1·80	1·10

(104)

1959. Emigrants' Conference. No. 590 surch as T **104**.

622		30p. on 50p. green	1·10	30
623		40p. on 50p. green	1·60	65

105 Discus Thrower

1959. Air. Third Mediterranean Games, Beirut.

624	105	15p. green	75	30
625	-	30p. brown	1·10	55
626	-	40p. blue	2·50	95
MS626a		106×130 mm. Nos. 624/6.		
		Imperf (sold at 100p.)	£275	£275
MS626b		As last but with sheet values in margins	80·00	80·00

DESIGNS—VERT: 30p. Weightlifting. HORIZ: 40p. Games emblem.

106 Soldiers with Standard

1959. Air. 16th Anniv of Independence.

627	106	40p. red and black	1·40	70
628	106	60p. red and green	1·80	90

1959. Surch.

629	100	7p.50 on 12p.50 blue	55	10
630	100	10p. on 12p.50 blue	65	10
631	100	15p. on 25p. blue	75	15
632	-	40p. on 50p. green (No. 590)	1·70	55
633	88	40p. on 65p. purple (No. 569) (air)	3·75	65

108 Planting Tree

1960. Air. 25th Anniv of Friends of the Tree Society.

634	108	20p. purple and green	1·10	75
635	108	40p. sepia and green	1·70	1·10

1960. Air. As T **79** but colours of name and value tablets reversed.

636		20p. green	1·10	65

109 Pres. Chehab

1960. Air.

637	109	5p. green	15	10
638	109	10p. blue	15	10
639	109	15p. brown	20	15
640	109	20p. sepia	20	15
641	109	30p. olive	45	20
642	109	40p. red	50	30
643	109	50p. blue	85	40
644	109	70p. purple	1·60	45
645	109	100p. green	3·50	85

110 Arab League Centre

1960. Inaug of Arab League Centre, Cairo.

646	110	15p. turquoise	75	55

111 "Uprooted Tree"

1960. Air. World Refugee Year. (a) Size 20½×36½ mm.

647	111	25p. brown	1·10	75
648	111	40p. green	1·70	1·10
MS648a		90×110 mm. Nos. 647/8.		
		Imperf (sold at 150p.)	55·00	55·00

(b) Size 19½×35½ mm.

648b		25p. brown	1·50	1·10
648c		40p. green	1·80	1·50

112 Martyrs' Monument

1960. Air. Martyrs' Commemoration.

649	112	20p. purple and green	75	45

650	112	40p. blue and green	1·10	75
651	-	70p. olive and black	2·50	1·10

DESIGN—VERT: 70p. Detail of statues on monument.

113 Pres. Chehab and King Mohammed V

1960. Air. Visit of King Mohammed V of Morocco.

652	113	30p. chocolate and brown	1·20	55
653	113	70p. brown and black	2·40	85

114 Pres. Chehab

1960

654	114	50c. green	15	15
655	114	2p.50 olive	15	15
656	114	5p. green	20	15
657	114	7p.50 red	45	20
658	114	15p. blue	75	30
659	114	50p. purple	1·80	45
660	114	100p. brown	3·75	75

115 Child

1960. Air. Mother and Child Days.

661	115	20p. red and yellow	55	20
662	115	20p.+10p. red and yellow	75	30
663	-	60p. blue and light blue	1·80	1·30
664	-	60p.+15p. blue & lt bl	2·75	1·40

DESIGN: Nos. 663/4, Mother and child.

116 Dove, Map and Flags

1960. Air. World Lebanese Union Meeting, Beirut. Multicoloured.

665		20p. Type **116**	30	30
666		40p. Cedar of Lebanon and homing pigeons	1·10	55
667		70p. Globes and Cedar of Lebanon (horiz)	1·30	75
MS667a		110×139 mm. Nos. 665/7.		
		Imperf (sold at 150p.)	27·00	27·00

(117)

1960. Arabian Oil Congress, Beirut. Optd with T **117**.

668	86	5p. green (No. 585)	45	10
669	110	15p. turquoise	95	55

1960. Air. World Refugee Year. Nos. 648b/c surch in English and Arabic.

669a	111	20p.+10p. on 40p. grn	10·50	10·50
669b	111	30p.+15p. on 25p. brn	15·00	15·00

119 Boxing

1961. Olympic Games.

670	**119**	2p.50+2p.50 brown and blue (postage)	20	20
671	-	5p.+5p. brown & orge	45	30
672	-	7p.50+7p.50 brn & vio	65	55
673	-	15p.+15p. brown & red (air)	3·50	3·25
674	-	25p.+25p. brown & grn	3·50	3·25
675	-	35p.+35p. brown & bl	3·75	3·25

MS675a 137×118 mm. Nos. 673/5. Imperf (sold at 150p.) 39·00 39·00

DESIGNS: 5p. Wrestling; 7p.50, Putting the shot; 15p. Fencing; 25p. Cycling; 35p. Swimming.

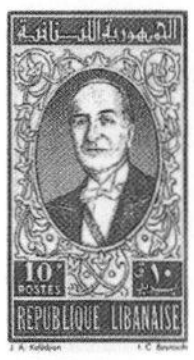

120 Pres. Chehab

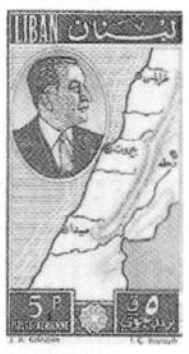

121 Pres. Chehab and Map of Lebanon

1961

676	**120**	2p.50 ultramarine and blue (postage)	15	10
677	**120**	7p.50 violet and mauve	20	10
678	**120**	10p. brown and yellow	55	15
679	**121**	5p. green & lt green (air)	20	20
680	**121**	10p. brown and ochre	55	20
681	**121**	70p. violet and mauve	2·75	65
682	-	200p. blue and bistre	6·50	2·75

DESIGN—HORIZ: 200p. Casino, Maameltein.

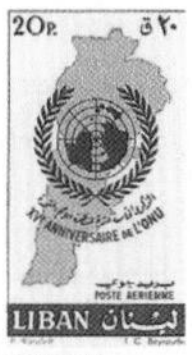

122 U.N. Emblem and Map

1961. Air. 15th Anniv of U.N.O.

683	**122**	20p. purple and blue	65	30
684	-	30p. green and brown	1·10	55
685	-	50p. blue and ultramarine	1·80	85

MS685a 100×132 mm. Nos. 683/5. Imperf (sold at 125p.) 10·50 10·50

DESIGNS—VERT: 30p. U.N. emblem and Baalbek ruins. HORIZ: 50p. View of U.N. Headquarters and Manhattan.

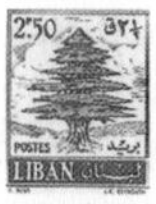

123 Cedar of Lebanon

1961. Redrawn version of T **86** (different arrangement at foot). Shaded background.

686	**123**	2p.50 myrtle	65	10

See also Nos. 695/7.

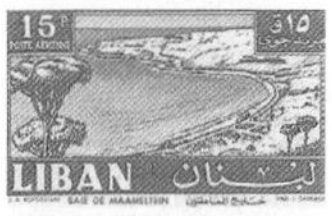

124 Bay of Maameltein

1961. Air.

687	**124**	15p. lake	55	20
688	**124**	30p. blue	85	45
689	**124**	40p. sepia	1·30	65

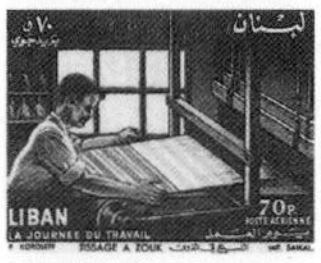

125 Weaving

1961. Air. Labour Day.

690	-	30p. red	1·80	85
691	**125**	70p. blue	3·50	1·80

DESIGN: 30p. Pottery.

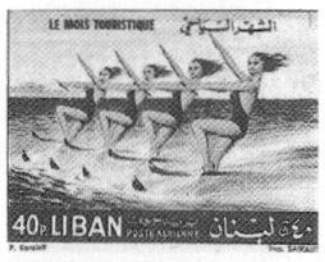

126 Water-skiers

1961. Air. Tourist Month.

692	-	15p. violet and blue	85	45
693	**126**	40p. blue and flesh	1·80	65
694	-	70p. olive and flesh	2·75	1·40

DESIGNS—VERT: 15p. Firework display. HORIZ: 70p. Tourists in punt.

1961. As T **123** but plain background.

695		2p.50 yellow	55	15
696		5p. lake	60	15
697		10p. black	75	20

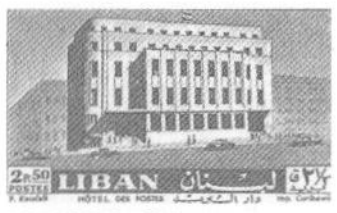

127 G.P.O., Beirut

1961

698	**127**	2p.50 mauve (postage)	55	15
699	**127**	5p. green	75	20
700	**127**	15p. blue	85	30
701	-	35p. green (air)	75	45
702	-	50p. brown	1·30	55
703	-	100p. black	1·80	85

DESIGN: 35p. to 100p. Motor highway, Dora.

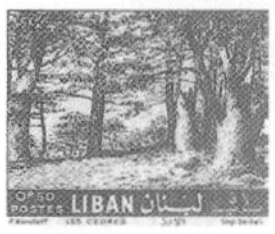

128 Cedars of Lebanon

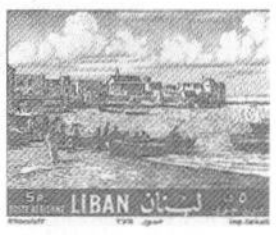

129 Tyre Waterfront

1961

704	**128**	0p.50 green (postage)	15	15
705	**128**	1p. brown	15	15
706	**128**	2p.50 blue	20	15
707	**128**	5p. red	45	20
708	**128**	7p.50 violet	65	20
709	-	10p. purple	1·40	25
710	-	15p. blue	1·90	45
711	-	50p. green	2·10	1·30
712	-	100p. black	5·25	1·90
713	**129**	5p. red (air)	30	15
714	**129**	10p. violet	45	15
715	**129**	15p. blue	75	15
716	**129**	20p. orange	80	20
717	**129**	30p. green	85	25
718	-	40p. purple	1·30	45
719	-	50p. blue	1·60	65
720	-	70p. green	2·10	1·10
721	-	100p. sepia	3·75	1·70

DESIGNS—HORIZ: Nos. 709/12, Zahle. VERT: Nos. 718/21, Afka Falls.

See also Nos. 729/34.

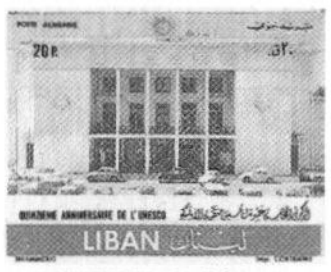

130 UNESCO Building, Beirut

1961. Air. 15th Anniv of UNESCO. Multicoloured.

722		20p. Type **130**	65	25
723		30p. UNESCO emblem and cedar (vert)	85	55
724		50p. UNESCO Building, Paris	1·70	80

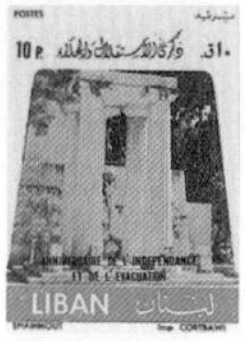

131 Tomb of Unknown Soldier

1961. Independence and Evacuation of Foreign Troops Commemoration. Multicoloured.

725		10p. Type **131** (postage)	55	10
726		15p. Soldier and flag	65	20
727		25p. Cedar emblem (horiz) (air)	55	55
728		50p. Emirs Bashir and Fakhreddine (horiz)	75	65

1962. As Nos. 704/21 but with larger figures of value.

729	**128**	50c. green (postage)	30	15
730	**128**	1p. brown	45	15
731	**128**	2p.50 blue	55	20
732	-	15p. blue	3·75	30
733	**129**	5p. red (air)	20	10
734	-	40p. purple	8·50	1·10

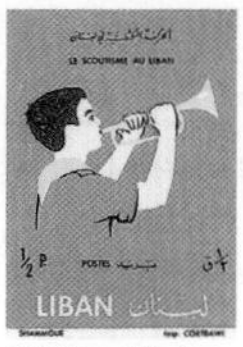

132 Scout Bugler

1962. Lebanese Scout Movement Commemorative.

735		½p. black, yell & grn (postage)	10	10
736		1p. multicoloured	10	10
737		2½p. green, black and red	20	10
738		6p. multicoloured	55	10
739		10p. yellow, black and blue	85	15
740		15p. multicoloured (air)	1·10	20
741		20p. yellow, black and violet	1·20	30
742		25p. multicoloured	1·70	1·10

DESIGNS—VERT: ½p. Type **132**; 6p. Lord Baden-Powell; 20p. Saluting hand. HORIZ: 1p. Scout with flag, cedar and badge; 2½p. Stretcher party, badge and laurel; 10p. Scouts at campfire; 15p. Cedar and Guide badge; 25p. Cedar and Scout badge.

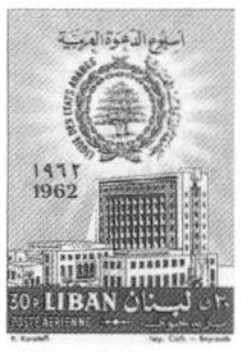

133 Arab League Centre, Cairo, and Emblem

1962. Air. Arab League Week.

743	**133**	20p. ultramarine and blue	55	30
744	**133**	30p. lake and pink	65	55
745	**133**	50p. green and turquoise	1·20	85

See also Nos. 792/5.

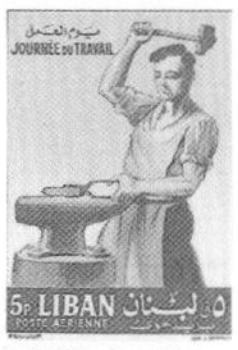

134 Blacksmith

1962. Air. Labour Day.

746	**134**	5p. green and blue	20	10
747	**134**	10p. blue and pink	30	15
748	-	25p. violet and pink	75	30
749	-	35p. mauve and blue	1·10	55

DESIGN—HORIZ: 25, 35p. Tractor.

1962. European Shooting Championships. Nos. 670/5 optd **CHAMPIONNAT D'EUROPE DE TIR 2 JUIN 1962** in French and Arabic.

750	**119**	2p.50+2p.50 (postage)	30	30
751	-	5p.+5p.	75	75
752	-	7p.50+7p.50	85	85
753	-	15p.+15p. (air)	1·30	1·30
754	-	25p.+25p.	3·00	3·00
755	-	35p.+35p.	3·50	3·50

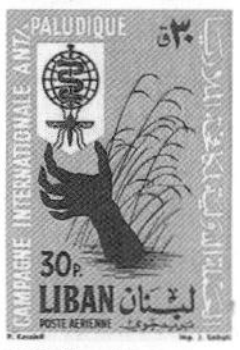

136 Hand grasping Emblem

1962. Air. Malaria Eradication.

756	**136**	30p. brown & light brown	1·10	65
757	-	70p. violet and lilac	1·80	1·20

DESIGN: 70p. Campaign emblem.

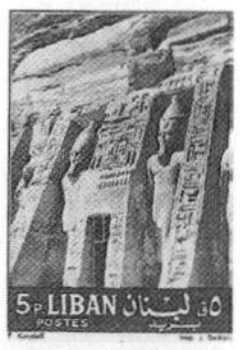

137 Rock Temples of Abu Simbel

1962. Nubian Monuments.

758	**137**	5p. bl & ultram (postage)	65	20
759	**137**	15p. lake and brown	85	30
760	-	30p. yellow and green (air)	2·10	75
761	-	50p. olive and grey	3·75	1·60

DESIGNS: 30, 50p. Bas-relief.

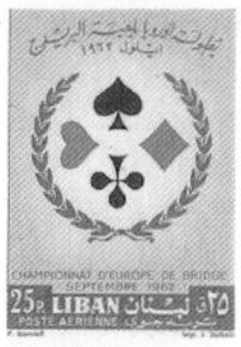

138 Playing-card Symbols

1962. Air. European Bridge Championships.

762	**138**	25p. multicoloured	5·00	3·00
763	**138**	40p. multicoloured	5·25	3·00

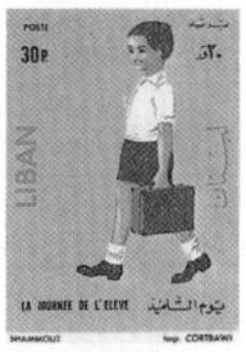

139 Schoolboy

1962. Schoolchildren's Day.

764	**139**	30p. mult (postage)	75	30
765	-	45p. multicoloured (air)	1·10	65

DESIGN: 45p. Teacher.

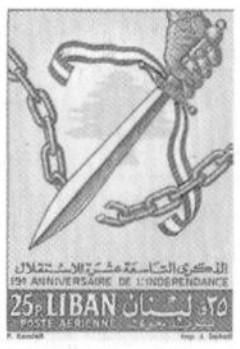

140

1962. Air. 19th Anniv of Independence.

766	**140**	25p. green, red & turq	1·20	65
767	**140**	25p. violet, red & turq	1·20	65
768	**140**	25p. blue, red & turquoise	1·20	65

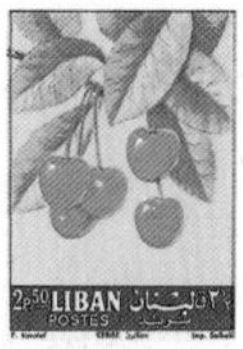

141 Cherries

1962. Fruits. Multicoloured.

769		0p.50 Type **141** (postage)	30	10
770		1p. Figs	55	10
771		2p.50 Type **141**	65	10
772		5p. Figs	75	10
773		7p.50 Type **141**	30	10
774		10p. Grapes	55	15
775		17p.50 Grapes	1·10	20
776		30p. Grapes	1·90	30
777		50p. Oranges	3·50	75
778		100p. Pomegranates	7·00	1·90
779		5p. Apricots (air)	20	10
780		10p. Plums	45	15
781		20p. Apples	75	20
782		30p. Plums	1·10	45
783		40p. Apples	1·20	50
784		50p. Pears	1·40	55
785		70p. Medlars	2·10	65
786		100p. Lemons	3·75	1·30

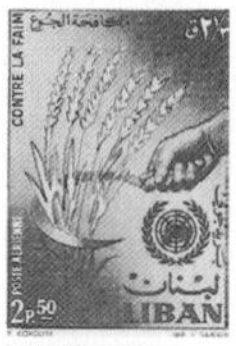

142 Reaping

1963. Air. Freedom from Hunger.

787	**142**	2p.50 yellow and blue	10	10
788	**142**	5p. yellow and green	10	10
789	**142**	7p.50 yellow and purple	30	15
790	-	15p. green and red	75	20
791	-	20p. green and red	1·10	55

DESIGN—HORIZ: 15, 20p. Three ears of wheat within hand.

1963. Air. Arab League Week. As T **133** but inscr "1963".

792		5p. violet and blue	10	10
793		10p. green and blue	30	30
794		15p. brown and blue	55	45
795		20p. grey and blue	85	75

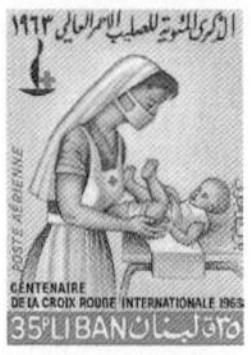

143 Nurse tending Baby

1963. Air. Red Cross Centenary.

796	-	5p. green and red	10	10
797	-	20p. blue and red	45	20
798	**143**	35p. red and black	75	45
799	**143**	40p. violet and red	1·30	65

DESIGN—HORIZ: 5, 20p. Blood transfusion.

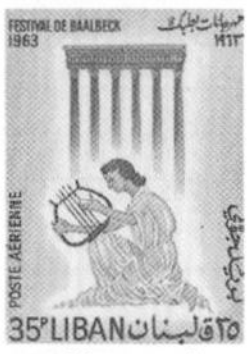

144 Allegory of Music

1963. Air. Baalbek Festival.

800	**144**	35p. orange and blue	1·30	65

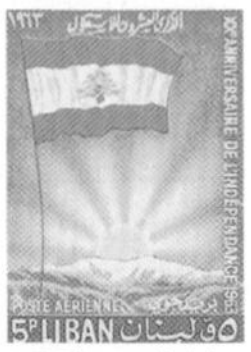

145 Flag and rising Sun

1963. Air. 20th Anniv of Independence. Flag and sun in red and yellow.

801	**145**	5p. turquoise	20	15
802	**145**	10p. green	55	45
803	**145**	25p. blue	75	65
804	**145**	40p. drab	1·20	1·10

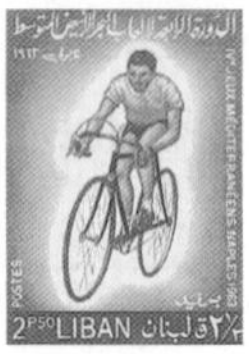

146 Cycling

1964. Fourth Mediterranean Games, Naples (1963).

805	**146**	2p.50 brown and purple (postage)	20	10
806	-	5p. orange and blue	30	10
807	-	10p. brown and violet	55	20
808	-	15p. orange and green (air)	60	30
809	-	17p.50 brown and blue	65	45
810	-	30p. brown and turquoise	1·10	65

MS810a 152×112 mm. Nos. 808/10. Imperf (sold at 100p.) 16·00 16·00

DESIGNS—VERT: 5p. Basketball; 10p. Running; 15p. Tennis. HORIZ: 17p.50, Swimming; 30p. Skiing.

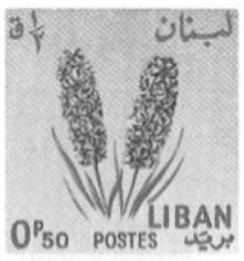

147 Hyacinth

1964. Flowers. Multicoloured.

811	0p.50 Type **147** (postage)	10	10
812	1p. Type **147**	10	10
813	2p.50 Type **147**	10	10
814	5p. Cyclamen	15	10
815	7p.50 Cyclamen	20	10
816	10p. Poinsettia (vert)	45	15
817	17p.50 Anemone (vert)	85	25
818	30p. Iris (vert)	1·80	65
819	50p. Poppy (vert)	4·25	1·10
820	5p. Lily (vert) (air)	45	30
821	10p. Ranunculus (vert)	75	30
822	20p. Anemone (vert)	95	40
823	40p. Tuberose (vert)	1·70	65
824	45p. Rhododendron (vert)	1·80	65
825	50p. Jasmine (vert)	2·10	75
826	70p. Yellow broom (vert)	3·25	1·10

Nos. 816/26 are size 26½×37 mm.

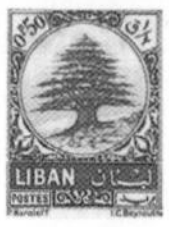

148 Cedar of Lebanon

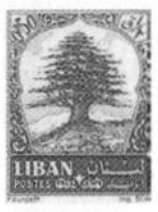

149 Cedar of Lebanon

1964

827	**148**	0p.50 green	55	20
828	**149**	0p.50 green	30	20
829	**149**	2p.50 blue	30	20
830	**149**	5p. mauve	45	20
831	**149**	7p.50 orange	85	20
832	**149**	17p.50 purple	1·60	25

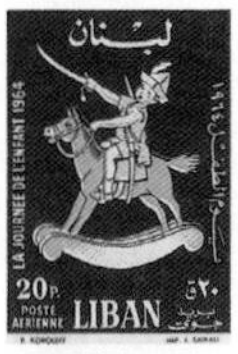

150 Child on Rocking-horse

1964. Air. Children's Day.

833	-	5p. red, orange and green	20	10
834	-	10p. red, orange and brown	30	20
835	**150**	20p. orange, blue and ultramarine	65	55
836	**150**	40p. yellow, blue and purple	1·30	85

DESIGN—HORIZ: 5, 10p. Girls skipping.

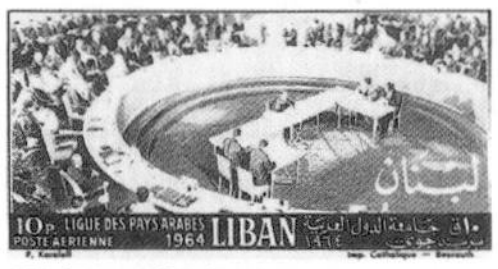

151 League Session

1964. Air. Arab League Meeting.

837	**151**	5p. buff, brown and black	55	30
838	**151**	10p. black	65	40
839	**151**	15p. turquoise	95	45
840	**151**	20p. mauve, brn & sepia	1·50	65

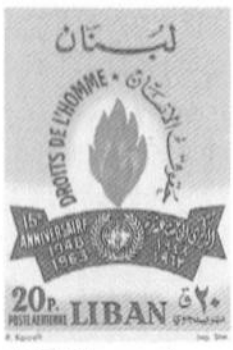

152 "Flame of Freedom"

1964. Air. 15th Anniv of Declaration of Human Rights.

841	**152**	20p. red, pink and brown	30	20
842	-	40p. orange, blue and light blue	65	30

DESIGN: 40p. Flame on pedestal bearing U.N. emblem.

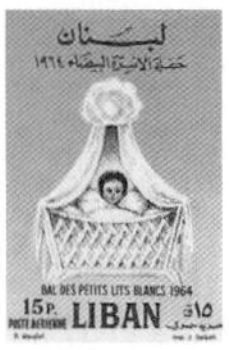

153 Sick Child

1964. Air. "Bal des Petits Lits Blancs" (Ball for children's charity).

843	**153**	2p.50 multicoloured	10	10
844	**153**	5p. multicoloured	15	10
845	**153**	15p. multicoloured	25	15
846	-	17p.50 multicoloured	65	30
847	-	20p. multicoloured	75	40
848	-	40p. multicoloured	1·30	45

DESIGN—55×25½ mm: 17p.50 to 40p. Children in front of palace (venue of ball).

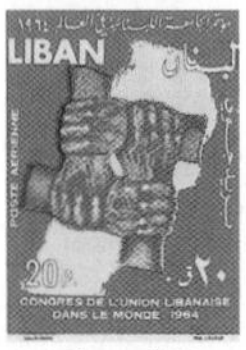

154 Clasped Wrists

1964. Air. World Lebanese Union Congress, Beirut.

849	**154**	20p. black, yellow & green	75	30
850	**154**	40p. black, yellow & pur	1·40	75

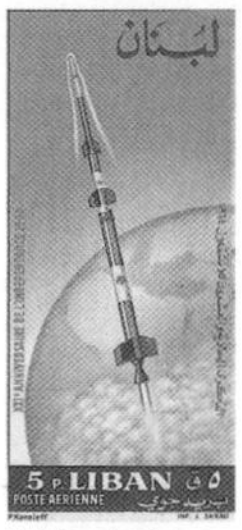

155 Rocket in Flight

1964. Air. 21st Anniv of Independence.

851	**155**	5p. multicoloured	30	20
852	**155**	10p. multicoloured	30	20
853	-	40p. blue and black	1·20	75
854	-	70p. purple and black	2·10	1·60

DESIGNS—HORIZ: 40p. to 70p. "Struggle for Independence" (battle scene).

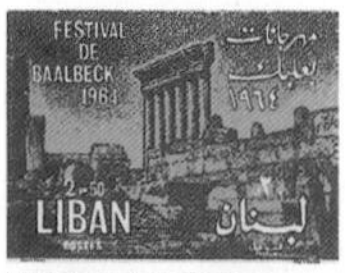

156 Temple Columns

1965. Baalbek Festival.

855	**156**	2p.50 black and orange (postage)	20	20
856	-	7p.50 black and blue	55	30
857	-	10p. multicoloured (air)	20	10
858	-	15p. multicoloured	45	15
859	-	25p. multicoloured	75	55
860	-	40p. multicoloured	1·50	65

DESIGNS—28×55 mm: 10, 15p. Man in costume; 25, 40p. Woman in costume.

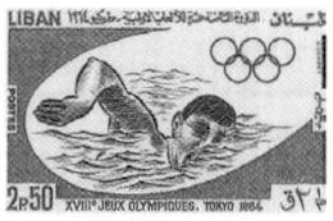

157 Swimming

1965. Olympic Games, Tokyo.

861	**157**	2p.50 black, blue and mauve (postage)	20	10
862	-	7p.50 purple, green & brn	1·10	75
863	-	10p. grey, brown & green	1·40	85
864	-	15p. black and green (air)	30	10
865	-	25p. green and purple	75	30
866	-	40p. brown and blue	1·20	55

MS866a 140×100 mm. Nos. 864/6. Imperf (sold at 100p.) 21·00 21·00

DESIGNS—HORIZ: 7p.50, Fencing; 15p. Horse-jumping; 40p. Gymnastics. VERT: 10p. Basketball; 25p. Rifle-shooting.

1965. (a) Postage. Birds.

867	5p. multicoloured	1·60	20
868	10p. multicoloured	2·40	20
869	15p. chocolate, orange & brn	4·25	30
870	17p.50 purple, red and blue	6·50	45
871	20p. black, yellow and green	7·50	55
872	32p.50 yellow, brown & grn	18·00	1·20

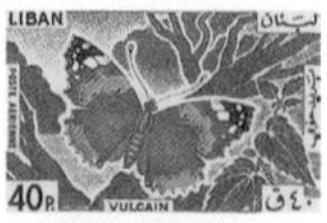

158 Red Admiral

(b) Air. Butterflies.

873	-	30p. yellow, brown and red	1·80	20
874	-	35p. blue, red and bistre	2·75	45
875	**158**	40p. brown, red and green	3·50	55
876	-	45p. brown, yellow & blue	4·25	65
877	-	70p. multicoloured	6·50	95
878	-	85p. black, orange & green	7·50	1·20
879	-	100p. blue and plum	10·50	1·30
880	-	200p. brown, blue & pur	19·00	1·50
881	-	300p. sepia, yellow & green	28·00	4·50
882	-	500p. brown, blue and light blue	55·00	9·00

DESIGNS—As T **158**. BIRDS: 5p. Northern bullfinch; 10p. Eurasian goldfinch; 15p. Hoopoe; 17p.50, Red-legged partridge; 20p. Golden oriole; 32p.50, European bee eater. BUTTERFLIES: 30p. Large tiger moth; 35p. Small postman; 45p. Common grayling; 70p. Swallowtail; 85p. Orange-tip; 100p. Blue morpho; 200p. *Erasmia sanguiflua*; 300p. *Papilio crassus*. 35½×25 mm: 500p. Amelia's charakes.

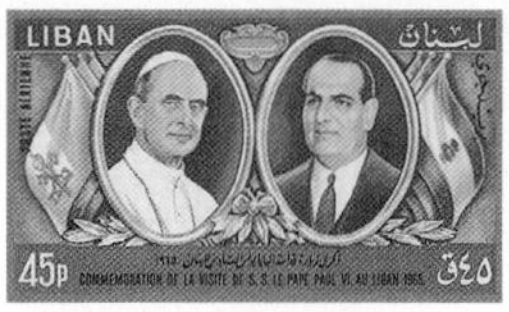

159 Pope Paul and Pres. Helou

1965. Air. Pope Paul's Visit to Lebanon.

883	**159**	45p. violet and gold	6·50	2·75

MS883a 100×81 mm. No. 883. Imperf (sold at 100p.) 65·00 65·00

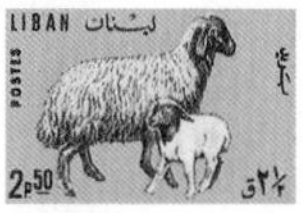

160 Sheep

1965

884	-	50c. multicoloured	2·00	20
885	-	1p. grey, black and mauve	2·10	20
886	**160**	2p.50 yellow, sepia & grn	2·30	20

DESIGNS: 50c. Cow and calf; 1p. Rabbit.

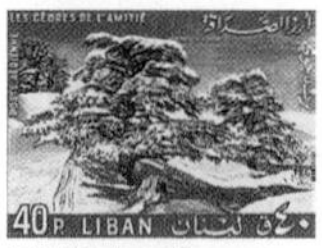

161 "Cedars of Friendship"

1965. Air.

887	**161**	40p. multicoloured	1·80	30

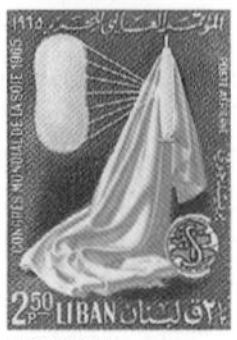

162 "Silk Manufacture"

1965. Air. World Silk Congress, Beirut. Multicoloured.

888	2p.50 Type **162**	75	20
889	5p. Type **162**	80	20
890	7p.50 Type **162**	95	20
891	15p. Weaver and loom	1·10	25
892	30p. As 15p.	2·75	45
893	40p. As 15p.	4·00	65
894	50p. As 15p.	5·25	95

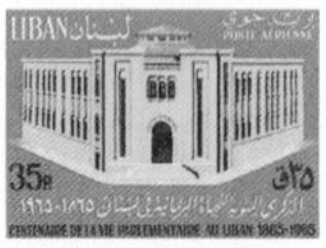

163 Parliament Building

1965. Air. Centenary of Lebanese Parliament.

895	**163**	35p. brown, ochre and red	75	45
896	**163**	40p. brown, ochre & green	1·10	65

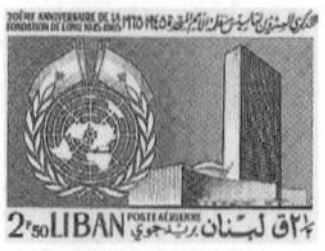

164 U.N. Emblem and Headquarters

1965. Air. 20th Anniv of U.N.O.

897	**164**	2p.50 blue	10	10
898	**164**	10p. red	15	10
899	**164**	17p.50 violet	25	15
900	**164**	30p. green	55	30
901	**164**	40p. brown	65	65

MS901a 101×80 mm. No. 901 in violet. Imperf (sold at 50p.) 18·00 18·00

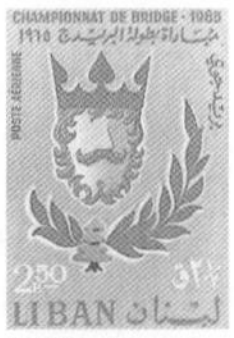

165 Playing-card "King"

1965. Air. World Bridge Championships, Beirut.

902	**165**	2p.50 multicoloured	20	10
903	**165**	15p. multicoloured	95	20
904	**165**	17p.50 multicoloured	1·50	30

905 165 40p. multicoloured 3·00 1·30
MS905a 105×85 mm. Nos. 903 and 905. Imperf or perf (sold at 75p.) 28·00 28·00

166 Dagger on Deir Yassin, Palestine

1965. Air. Deir Yassin Massacre.
906 166 50p. multicoloured 5·25 1·40

167 I.T.U. Emblem and Symbols

1966. Air. Centenary (1965) of I.T.U.
907 167 2p.50 multicoloured 10 10
908 167 15p. multicoloured 45 15
909 167 17p.50 multicoloured 65 20
910 167 25p. multicoloured 1·40 30
911 167 40p. multicoloured 1·90 55

168 Stage Performance

1966. Air. Baalbek Festival. Multicoloured.
912 2p.50 Type 168 20 15
913 5p. Type 168 20 15
914 7p.50 Ballet performance (vert) 45 20
915 15p. Ballet performance (vert) 45 20
916 30p. Concert 95 45
917 40p. Concert 1·40 55

169 Tabarja

1966. Tourism. Multicoloured.
918 50c. Hippodrome, Beirut (postage) 15 10
919 1p. Pigeon Grotto, Beirut 15 10
920 2p.50 Type 169 15 10
921 5p. Ruins, Beit-Mery 15 10
922 7p.50 Ruins, Anjar 15 10
923 10p. Djezzine Falls (air) 20 10
924 15p. Sidon Castle 25 10
925 20p. Amphitheatre, Byblos 40 10
926 30p. Sun Temple, Baalbek 55 15
927 50p. Palace, Beit ed-Din 1·40 20
928 60p. Nahr-el Kalb 1·60 40
929 70p. Tripoli 2·40 55

170 W.H.O. Building

1966. Air. Inauguration of W.H.O. Headquarters, Geneva.
930 170 7p.50 green 30 10
931 170 17p.50 red 55 40
932 170 25p. blue 95 55

171 Skiing

1966. Air. International Cedars Festival.
933 171 2p.50 brown, red and green 20 15
934 - 5p. multicoloured 20 15
935 - 17p.50 multicoloured 45 30
936 - 25p. red, brown and green 1·30 55
DESIGNS: 5p. Tobogganing; 17p.50, Cedar in snow; 25p. Ski-lift.

172 Inscribed Sarcophagus

1966. Air. Phoenician Invention of the Alphabet.
937 172 10p. brown, black and green 10 10
938 - 15p. brown, ochre and mauve 45 15
939 - 20p. sepia, blue and ochre 55 30
940 - 30p. brown, orange and yellow 1·10 55
DESIGNS: 15p. Phoenician sailing ship; 20p. Mediterranean route map showing spread of Phoenician alphabet; 30p. Kadmus with alphabet tablet.

173 Child in Bath

1966. Air. Int Children's Day. Multicoloured.
941 2p. Type 173 10 10
942 5p. Boy and doll in rowing boat 10 10
943 7p.50 Girl skiing 30 10
944 15p. Girl giving food to bird 75 20
945 20p. Boy doing homework 1·10 55
MS946 100×69½ mm. 50p. Children of various races (horiz). Imperf 9·00 9·00

174 Decade Emblem

1966. Air. International Hydrological Decade.
947 174 5p. ultramarine, bl & orge 10 10
948 174 10p. red, blue and orange 20 10
949 - 15p. sepia, green & orange 30 15
950 - 20p. blue, green & orange 75 30
DESIGN: 15p., 20p. Similar "wave" pattern.

175 Rev. Daniel Bliss (founder)

1966. Air. Centenary of American University, Beirut.
951 175 20p. brown, yellow & grn 55 25
952 - 30p. green, brown and blue 65 40
MS953 125×85 mm. 50p. brown, orange and green. Imperf 2·75 2·75
DESIGNS—VERT: 30p. University Chapel. Horiz (59×37 mm)—50p. Rev. Daniel Bliss, University and emblem.

176 I.T.Y. Emblem

1967. International Tourist Year (1st issue). (a) Postage.
954 176 50c. multicoloured 10 10
955 176 1p. multicoloured 10 10
956 176 2p.50 multicoloured 10 10
957 176 5p. multicoloured 10 10
958 176 7p.50 multicoloured 15 10

177 Beit ed-Din Palace

(b) Air. Multicoloured.
959 10p. Tabarja 20 10
960 15p. Pigeon Rock, Beirut 30 10
961 17p.50 Type 177 40 10
962 20p. Sidon 45 10
963 25p. Tripoli 50 15
964 30p. Byblos 55 20
965 35p. Ruins, Tyre 75 20
966 40p. Temple, Baalbek 1·20 20
See also Nos. 977/MS980a.

178 Signing Pact, and Flags

1967. Air. 22nd Anniv of Arab League Pact.
967 178 5p. multicoloured 10 10
968 178 10p. multicoloured 15 10
969 178 15p. multicoloured 40 30
970 178 20p. multicoloured 75 45

179 Veterans War Memorial Building, San Francisco

1967. Air. San Francisco Pact of 1945. Multicoloured.
971 2p.50 Type 179 75 25
972 5p. Type 179 75 25
973 7p.50 Type 179 75 25
974 10p. Scroll and flags of U.N. and Lebanon 30 25
975 20p. As 10p. 45 25
976 30p. As 10p. 65 25

180 Temple Ruins, Baalbek

1967. Air. International Tourist Year (2nd issue). Multicoloured.
977 5p. Type 180 10 10
978 10p. Ruins, Anjar 15 10
979 15p. Ancient bridge, Nahr-Ibrahim 30 15
980 20p. Grotto, Jeita 55 20
MS980a 112×90 mm. 50p. Beirut (plus flag and map of Lebanon). Imperf 27·00 27·00

181

1967. Air. India Day.
981 181 2p.50 red 15 15
982 181 5p. purple 15 15
983 181 7p.50 brown 15 15
984 181 10p. blue 20 15
985 181 15p. green 55 20

182

1967. Air. 22nd Anniv of Lebanon's Admission to U.N.O.
986 182 2p.50 red 10 10
987 182 5p. blue 10 10
988 182 7p.50 green 10 10
989 - 10p. red 10 15
990 - 20p. blue 30 15
991 - 30p. green 55 20
MS991a 109×85 mm. 100p. red (T 182). Imperf 7·50 7·50
DESIGN: 10, 20, 30p. U.N. Emblem.

183 Goat and Kid

1967. Animals and Fishes. Multicoloured.
992 50c. Type 183 (postage) 45 15
993 1p. Cattle 45 15
994 2p.50 Sheep 45 15
995 5p. Dromedaries 45 15
996 10p. Donkey 1·10 20
997 20p. Horses 2·10 20
998 20p. Basking shark (air) 2·10 20
999 30p. Garfish 2·10 20
1000 40p. Pollack 3·50 25
1001 50p. Cuckoo wrasse 3·75 30
1002 70p. Striped red mullet 9·75 45
1003 100p. Rainbow trout 12·00 55

184 Ski Jumping

1968. Air. International Ski Congress, Beirut.
1004 184 2p.50 multicoloured 15 10
1005 - 5p. multicoloured 25 10
1006 - 7p.50 multicoloured 30 15
1007 - 10p. multicoloured 40 20
1008 - 25p. multicoloured 1·10 30
MS1008a 121×91 mm. 50p. multicoloured. Imperf 8·50 8·50
DESIGNS: 5p. to 10p. Skiing (all different); 25p. Congress emblem of Cedar and skis.

185 Princess Khaskiah

1968. Air. Emir Fakhreddine II Commem. Multicoloured.
1009 185 2p.50 Type 185 10 15
1010 5p. Emir Fakhreddine II 10 15
1011 10p. Sidon Citadel (horiz) 20 15
1012 15p. Chekif Citadel (horiz) 30 15
1013 17p.50 Beirut Citadel (horiz) 55 20
MS1013a 120×86 mm. 50p. Battle of Anjar. Imperf 14·00 14·00

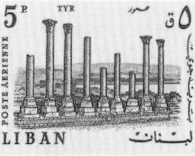

186 Colonnade

1968. Air. Tyre Antiquities.
1014 - 2p.50 brn, cream & pink 10 10
1015 186 5p. brown, blue & yellow 20 10
1016 - 7p.50 brown, buff & grn 30 15
1017 - 10p. brown, blue & orange 55 30
MS1018 120×80 mm. 10p. brown and blue. Perf or imperf (sold at 50p.) 27·00 27·00
DESIGNS—VERT: 2p.50, Roman bust; 10p. Bas-relief. HORIZ: 7p.50, Arch.

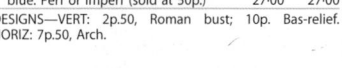

187 Justinian and Mediterranean Map

1968. Air. First Anniv of Faculty of Law, Beirut.
1019 5p. Justinian (vert) 10 10
1020 10p. Justinian (vert) 10 10
1021 15p. Type 187 20 10
1022 20p. Type 187 30 20

188 Arab League
Emblem

1968. Air. Arab Appeal Week.
1023	188	5p. multicoloured	10	10
1024	188	10p. multicoloured	20	10
1025	188	15p. multicoloured	30	15
1026	188	20p. multicoloured	55	20

189 Cedar on Globe

1968. Air. Third World Lebanese Union Congress, Beirut.
1027	189	2p.50 multicoloured	10	10
1028	189	5p. multicoloured	15	10
1029	189	7p.50 multicoloured	25	10
1030	189	10p. multicoloured	30	25

190 Jupiter's Temple Ruins,
Baalbek

1968. Air. Baalbek Festival. Multicoloured.
1031		5p. Type **190**	10	10
1032		10p. Bacchus's Temple	20	15
1033		15p. Corniche, Jupiter's Temple	30	20
1034		20p. Portal, Bacchus's Temple	55	30
1035		25p. Columns, Bacchus's Temple	75	55

191 Long Jumping and Atlantes

1968. Air. Olympic Games, Mexico.
1036	191	5p. black, yellow and blue	10	10
1037	-	10p. black, blue & purple	15	10
1038	-	15p. multicoloured	30	15
1039	-	20p. multicoloured	55	30
1040	-	25p. brown	75	55

DESIGNS (each incorporating Aztec relic): 10p. High jumping; 15p. Fencing; 20p. Weightlifting; 25p. "Sailing boat" with oars.

192 Lebanese
driving Tractor
("Work protection")

1968. Air. Human Rights Year. Multicoloured.
1041		10p. Type **192**	10	10
1042		15p. Citizens ("Social Security")	20	15
1043		25p. Young men of three races ("Unity")	45	25

193 Minshiya Stairs

1968. Air. Centenary of First Municipal Council (Deir el-Kamar). Multicoloured.
1044		10p. Type **193**	10	10
1045		15p. Serai kiosk	20	15
1046		25p. Ancient highway	45	40

194 Nurse and Child

1969. Air. UNICEF. Multicoloured.
1047	194	5p. black, brown and blue	10	10
1048	-	10p. black, green & yell	10	10
1049	-	15p. black, red and purple	20	10
1050	-	20p. black, blue & yellow	30	15
1051	-	25p. black, ochre & mve	45	20

DESIGNS: 10p. Produce; 15p. Mother and child; 20p. Child with book; 25p. Children with flowers.

195 Ancient Coin

1969. Air. 20th Anniv of International Museums Council (I.C.O.M.). Exhibits in National Museum, Beirut. Multicoloured.
1052		2p.50 Type **195**	10	10
1053		5p. Gold dagger, Byblos	20	10
1054		7p.50 Detail of Ahiram's Sarcophagus	30	15
1055		30p. Jewelled pectoral	65	30
1056		40p. Khalde "bird" vase	95	85

196 Water-skiing

1969. Air. Water Sports. Multicoloured.
1057		2p.50 Type **196**	10	10
1058		5p. Water-skiing (group)	15	10
1059		7p.50 Paraskiing (vert)	25	15
1060		30p. Racing dinghies (vert)	75	45
1061		40p. Racing dinghies	95	85

197 Frontier Guard

1969. Air. 25th Anniv of Independence. The Lebanese Army.
1062		2p. Type **197**	10	10
1063		5p. Unknown Soldier's Tomb	10	10
1064		7p.50 Army Foresters	20	10
1065		15p. Road-making	30	15
1066		30p. Military ambulance and Sud Aviation Alouette III helicopter	75	45
1067		40p. Skiing patrol	1·10	55

198 Concentric Red
Crosses

1971. Air. 25th Anniv of Lebanese Red Cross.
| 1068 | 198 | 15p. red and black | 55 | 20 |
| 1069 | - | 85p. red and black | 2·00 | 1·30 |

DESIGN: 85p. Red Cross in shape of cedar of Lebanon.

199 Foil and Flags of Arab
States

1971. Air. Tenth International Fencing Championships. Multicoloured.
1070		10p. Type **199**	10	10
1071		15p. Foil and flags of foreign nations	20	15
1072		35p. Contest with foils	75	55
1073		40p. Epee contest	85	65
1074		50p. Contest with sabres	1·30	75

200 "Farmers at Work"
(12th-century Arab painting)

1971. Air. 50th Anniv (1969) of I.L.O.
| 1075 | 200 | 10p. multicoloured | 20 | 10 |
| 1076 | 200 | 40p. multicoloured | 95 | 55 |

201 U.P.U. Monument and
New H.Q. Building, Berne

1971. Air. New U.P.U. Headquarters Building, Berne.
| 1077 | 201 | 15p. red, black and yellow | 20 | 10 |
| 1078 | 201 | 35p. yellow, black and orange | 95 | 55 |

202 "Ravens setting
fire to Owls"
(14th-century
painting)

1971. Air. Children's Day. Multicoloured.
| 1079 | | 15p. Type **202** | 65 | 20 |
| 1080 | | 85p. *The Lion and the Jackal* (13th-century painting) (39×29 mm) | 3·00 | 1·30 |

203 Arab League Flag and
Map

1971. Air. 25th Anniv of Arab League.
| 1081 | 203 | 30p. multicoloured | 65 | 30 |
| 1082 | 203 | 70p. multicoloured | 1·50 | 95 |

204 Jamhour Electricity
Sub-station

1971. Air. Multicoloured.
1083		5p. Type **204**	30	15
1084		10p. Maameltein Bridge	30	15
1085		15p. Hoteliers' School	30	15
1086		20p. Litani Dam	30	15
1087		25p. Interior of T.V. set	45	20
1088		35p. Bziza Temple	85	30
1089		40p. Jounieh Harbour	95	40
1090		45p. Radar scanner, Beirut Airport	1·20	45
1091		50p. Hibiscus	1·60	50
1092		70p. School of Sciences Building	2·40	55
1093		85p. Oranges	2·75	65
1094		100p. Satellite Communications Station, Arbanieh	3·75	1·40

205 Insignia of Imam al
Ouzai (theologian)

1971. Air. Lebanese Celebrities.
| 1095 | 205 | 25p. brown, gold & green | 45 | 25 |

1096	-	25p. brown, gold & yell	45	25
1097	-	25p. brown, gold & yell	45	25
1098	-	25p. brown, gold & green	45	25

PORTRAITS: No. 1096, Bechara el Khoury (poet and writer); 1097, Hassan Kamel el Sabbah (scientist); 1098, Gibran Khalil Gibran (writer).

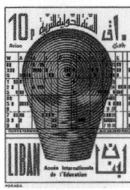

206 I.E.Y. Emblem
and Computer Card

1971. Air. International Education Year.
| 1099 | 206 | 10p. black, blue and violet | 20 | 10 |
| 1100 | 206 | 40p. black, yellow and red | 95 | 55 |

207 Dahr-el-Basheq
Sanatorium

1971. Air. Tuberculosis Relief Campaign.
| 1101 | 207 | 50p. multicoloured | 1·50 | 65 |
| 1102 | - | 100p. multicoloured | 2·10 | 1·10 |

DESIGN: 100p. Different view of Sanatorium.

208 "Solar Wheel"
Emblem

1971. Air. 16th Baalbek Festival.
| 1103 | 208 | 15p. orange and blue | 20 | 10 |
| 1104 | - | 85p. black, blue and orange | 1·50 | 95 |

DESIGN: 85p. Corinthian capital.

209 Field-gun

1971. Air. Army Day. Multicoloured.
1105		15p. Type **209**	45	20
1106		25p. Dassault Mirage IIICJ jet fighters	75	30
1107		40p. Army Command H.Q.	1·20	55
1108		70p. *Tarablous* (naval patrol boat)	2·40	1·10

210 Interior
Decoration

1971. Air. Second Anniv of Burning of Al-Aqsa Mosque, Jerusalem.
| 1109 | 210 | 15p. brown and deep brown | 75 | 20 |
| 1110 | 210 | 35p. brown and deep brown | 1·70 | 75 |

211 Lenin

1971. Air. Birth Centenary of Lenin. Multicoloured.
| 1111 | | 30p. Type **211** | 75 | 45 |
| 1112 | | 70p. Lenin in profile | 1·70 | 1·10 |

212 U.N. Emblem

1971. Air. 25th Anniv of United Nations.
| 1113 | 212 | 15p. multicoloured | 20 | 10 |
| 1114 | 212 | 85p. multicoloured | 1·70 | 95 |

213 Europa Mosaic, Byblos

1971. Air. World Lebanese Union.
| 1115 | 213 | 10p. multicoloured | 20 | 10 |
| 1116 | 213 | 40p. multicoloured | 1·70 | 55 |

1972. Various stamps surch.
1117		5p. on 7p.50 (No. 922) (postage)	55	30
1118		5p. on 7p.50 (No. 958)	55	30
1119		25p. on 32p.50 (No. 872)	3·25	2·10
1120		5p. on 7p.50 (No. 1016) (air)	55	30
1121		100p. on 300p. (No. 881)	7·50	3·50
1122		100p. on 500p. (No. 882)	7·50	3·50
1123		200p. on 300p. (No. 881)	12·00	7·50

217 Morning Glory

1973. Air. Multicoloured.
1124	217	2p.50 Type 217	20	10
1125		5p. Roses	30	15
1126		15p. Tulips	55	30
1127		25p. Lilies	75	40
1128		40p. Carnations	1·10	45
1129		50p. Iris	1·60	45
1130		70p. Apples	2·50	50
1131		75p. Grapes	2·75	65
1132		100p. Peaches	3·75	1·30
1133		200p. Pears	6·50	1·10
1134		300p. Cherries	8·50	1·90
1135		500p. Oranges	13·00	3·25

218 Ornate Arches

1973. Air. Lebanese Domestic Architecture.
1136	-	35p. multicoloured	95	30
1137	218	50p. multicoloured	1·40	65
1138	-	85p. multicoloured	2·40	85
1139	-	100p. multicoloured	2·50	1·20

DESIGNS: Nos. 1136 and 1138/39, Various Lebanese dwellings.

219 Girl with Lute

1973. Air. Ancient Costumes. Multicoloured.
1140		5p. Woman with rose	45	20
1141		10p. Shepherd	55	30
1142		20p. Horseman	65	45
1143		25p. Type 219	75	55

220 Swimming

1973. Air. Fifth Pan-Arab Schools' Games, Beirut. Multicoloured.
1144		5p. Type 220	15	10
1145		10p. Running	20	10
1146		15p. Gymnastics	30	10
1147		20p. Volleyball	50	15
1148		25p. Basketball	55	20
1149		50p. Table-tennis	1·20	45
1150		75p. Handball	1·80	55

| 1151 | | 100p. Football | 2·75 | 1·60 |
| MS1152 | 121×71 mm. No. 1151. Imperf | | 4·50 | 4·50 |

221 Brasilia

1973. Air. 150th Anniv of Brazil's Independence. Multicoloured.
1153		5p. Type 221	20	15
1154		20p. Salvador (Bahia) in 1823	30	15
1155		25p. Map and Phoenician galley	55	20
1156		50p. Emperor Pedro I and Emir Fakhreddine II	1·30	55

222 Marquetry

1973. Air. Lebanese Handicrafts. Multicoloured.
1157		10p. Type 222	45	15
1158		20p. Weaving	75	20
1159		35p. Glass-blowing	1·60	25
1160		40p. Pottery	2·00	45
1161		50p. Metal-working	2·40	55
1162		70p. Cutlery-making	3·75	65
1163		85p. Lace-making	5·25	95
1164		100p. Handicrafts Museum	5·25	1·70

223 Cedar of Lebanon

1974
| 1165 | 223 | 50c. green, brown and orange | 30 | 15 |

224 Camp Site and Emblems

1974. Air. 11th Arab Scout Jamboree, Smar-Jubeil, Lebanon. Multicoloured.
1166		2p.50 Type 224	20	15
1167		5p. Scout badge and map	20	15
1168		7p.50 Map of Arab countries	45	20
1169		10p. Lord Baden-Powell and Baalbek	45	20
1170		15p. Guide and camp	45	20
1171		20p. Lebanese Guide and Scout badge	65	20
1172		25p. Scouts around campfire	95	25
1173		30p. Globe and Scout badge	1·10	45
1174		35p. Flags of participating countries	1·50	50
1175		50p. Scout chopping wood for old man	2·10	75

225 Mail Train

1974. Centenary of U.P.U. Multicoloured.
1176		5p.50 Type 225	1·10	65
1177		20p. Container ship	75	15
1178		25p. Congress building, Lausanne, and U.P.U. H.Q., Berne	80	20
1179		50p. Mail plane	1·30	75

226 Congress Building, Sofar

1974. Air. 25th Anniv of Arab Postal Union. Multicoloured.
1180		5p. Type 226	20	15
1181		20p. View of Sofar	45	20
1182		25p. A.P.U. H.Q., Cairo	55	20

| 1183 | | 50p. Ministry of Posts, Beirut | 2·40 | 1·30 |

227 Mountain Road (O. Onsi)

1974. Air. Lebanese Paintings. Multicoloured.
1184		50p. Type 227	1·40	75
1185		50p. Clouds (M. Farroukh)	1·40	75
1186		50p. Woman (G. K. Gebran)	1·40	75
1187		50p. Embrace (C. Gemayel)	1·40	75
1188		50p. Self-portrait (H. Serour)	1·40	75
1189		50p. Portrait (D. Corm)	1·40	75

228 Hunter killing Lion

1974. Air. Hermel Excavations. Multicoloured.
1190		5p. Type 228	30	15
1191		10p. Astarte	55	20
1192		25p. Dogs hunting boar	2·10	65
1193		35p. Greco-Roman tomb	4·75	2·40

229 Book Year Emblem

1974. Air. International Book Year (1972).
1194	229	5p. multicoloured	20	15
1195	229	10p. multicoloured	55	20
1196	229	25p. multicoloured	2·10	65
1197	229	35p. multicoloured	3·00	2·40

230 Magnifying Glass

1974. Air. Stamp Day. Multicoloured.
1198		5p. Type 230	20	15
1199		10p. Linked posthorns	20	15
1200		15p. Stamp-printing	45	20
1201		20p. "Stamp" in mount	75	45

231 Georgina Rizk in Lebanese Costume

1974. Air. Miss Universe 1971 (Georgina Rizk). Multicoloured.
1202		5p. Type 231	10	10
1203		20p. Head-and-shoulders portrait	75	30
1204		25p. Type 231	95	45
1205		50p. As 20p.	2·00	1·40
MS1206	156×112 mm. Nos. 1202/5. Imperf		9·75	9·75

232 Winds

1974. Air. U.N. Conference on Human Environment, Stockholm, 1972. Multicoloured.
1207		5p. Type 232	10	10
1208		25p. Mountains and plain	70	15
1209		30p. Trees and flowers	75	30
1210		40p. Sea	95	45
MS1211	153×113 mm. Nos. 1207/1210. Imperf		8·50	8·50

233 UNICEF Emblem and Sikorsky S-55 Helicopter

1974. Air. 25th Anniv of UNICEF. Multicoloured.
1212		20p. Type 233	85	20
1213		25p. Emblem and child welfare clinic	45	15
1214		35p. Emblem and kindergarten class	85	30
1215		70p. Emblem and schoolgirls in laboratory	1·60	45
MS1216	158×112 mm. Nos. 1212/1215. Imperf		7·00	7·00

234 Discus-throwing

1974. Air. Olympic Games, Munich (1972). Multicoloured.
1217		5p. Type 234	20	15
1218		10p. Putting the shot	20	15
1219		15p. Weight-lifting	20	15
1220		35p. Running	85	45
1221		50p. Wrestling	1·10	50
1222		85p. Javelin-throwing	2·10	65
MS1223	175×130 mm. Nos. 1217/22. Imperf		9·75	9·75

235 Symbols of Archaeology

1975. Air. Beirut—"University City". Multicoloured.
1224		20p. Type 235	70	20
1225		25p. Science and medicine	75	30
1226		35p. Justice and commerce	1·30	85
1227		70p. Industry and commerce	2·50	1·20

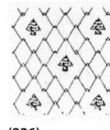
(236)

1978. Air. Various stamps optd with different patterns as T 236. (a) Tourist Views. Nos. 1090, 1092/3.
1228		45p. Radar scanner, Beirut Airport	2·00	75
1229		70p. School of Sciences Building	4·25	95
1230		85p. Oranges	4·50	1·50

(b) Flowers and Fruits. Nos. 1124/35.
1231		2p.50 Type 217	55	55
1232		5p. Roses	55	55
1233		15p. Tulips	1·10	55
1234		25p. Lilies	2·00	55
1235		40p. Carnations	2·00	75
1236		50p. Iris	3·00	75
1237		70p. Apples	4·25	95
1238		75p. Grapes	5·25	95
1239		100p. Peaches	5·25	1·90
1240		200p. Pears	12·00	6·00
1241		300p. Cherries	17·00	9·75
1242		500p. Oranges	26·00	15·00

(c) Lebanese Domestic Architecture. Nos. 1136/9.
1243	-	35p. multicoloured	2·40	55
1244	218	50p. multicoloured	3·00	75
1245	-	85p. multicoloured	4·50	1·50
1246	-	100p. multicoloured	5·25	1·90

(d) Ancient Costumes. Nos. 1140/3.
1247		5p. Woman with rose	55	55
1248		10p. Shepherd	65	55
1249		20p. Horseman	1·20	55
1250		25p. Type 219	2·00	55

(e) Lebanese Handicrafts. Nos. 1157/8, 1160/4.

1251	10p. Type **222**		65	55
1252	20p. Weaving		1·20	55
1253	40p. Pottery		2·00	75
1254	50p. Metal-working		3·50	75
1255	70p. Cutlery-making		4·25	95
1256	85p. Lace-making		4·50	1·50
1257	100p. Handicraft Museum		5·25	1·90

237 Mikhail Naimy (poet) and View of al-Chakroub Baskinta

1978. Air. Mikhail Naimy Festival Week. Multicoloured.

1258	25p. Mikhail Naimy and San- nine mountains		45	10
1259	50p. Type **237**		85	45
1260	75p. Mikhail Naimy (vert)		1·40	75

238 Heart and Arrow

1978. Air. World Health Day. "Down with Blood Pressure".

1261	**238**	50p. blue, red and black	1·30	65

239 Army Badge

1980. Army Day. Multicoloured.

1262	25p. Type **239** (postage)		75	30
1263	50p. Statue of Emir Fakhr el Dine on horseback (air)		1·30	55
1264	75p. Soldiers with flag (horiz)		1·90	55

240 13th-century European King

1980. Air. 50th Anniv (1974) of International Chess Federation. Multicoloured.

1265	50p. Rook, knight and Jubilee emblem (horiz)		1·60	1·10
1266	75p. Type **240**		2·75	2·10
1267	100p. Rook and Lebanon Chess Federation emblem		4·25	3·25
1268	150p. 18th-century French rook, king and knight		6·00	4·25
1269	200p. Painted faience rook, queen and bishop		7·50	5·25

241 Congress, U.P.U. and Lebanon Post Emblems

1981. Air. 18th U.P.U. Congress, Rio de Janeiro (1979).

1270	**241**	25p. blue, brown and black	1·60	75
1271	**241**	50p. pink, brown & black	2·75	1·40
1272	**241**	75p. green, brown and black	4·25	2·10

242 Children on Raft

1981. Air. International Year of the Child (1979).

1273	**242**	100p. multicoloured	5·25	3·25

243 President Sarkis

1981. 5th Anniv of Election of President Sarkis.

1274	**243**	125p. multicoloured	1·60	85
1275	**243**	300p. multicoloured	4·75	1·90
1276	**243**	500p. multicoloured	8·00	2·75

244 Society Emblem and Children

1981. Air. Centenary (1978) of Al-Makassed Islamic Welfare Society. Multicoloured.

1277	50p. Type **244**		85	20
1278	75p. Institute building		1·30	30
1279	100p. Al-Makassed (founder)		1·60	55

245 Stork carrying Food

1982. World Food Day (1981). Multicoloured.

1280	50p. Type **245**		1·30	45
1281	75p. Ear of wheat and globe		1·90	55
1282	100p. Fruit, fish and grain		2·75	95

246 W.C.Y. Emblem

1983. World Communications Year.

1283	**246**	300p. multicoloured	6·50	3·00

247 Phoenician Galley flying Scout Flag

1983. 75th Anniv of Boy Scout Movement. Multicoloured.

1284	200p. Type **247**		3·25	1·60
1285	300p. Scouts lowering flag and signalling by semaphore		4·25	2·10
1286	500p. Camp		8·00	3·25

248 The Soul is Back

1983. Birth Centenary of Gibran (poet and painter). Multicoloured.

1287	200p. Type **248**		3·25	1·60
1288	300p. *The Family*		4·25	2·10
1289	500p. *Gibran*		8·00	3·25
1290	1000p. *The Prophet*		15·00	8·00

MS1291 130×151 mm. Nos. 1287/90.
Imperf (sold at L£25)   45·00   45·00

249 Cedar of Lebanon

1984

1292	**249**	5p. multicoloured	75	20

250 Iris

1984. Flowers. Multicoloured.

1293	10p. Type **250**		45	20
1294	25p. Periwinkle		75	45
1295	50p. Barberry		1·60	65

251 Dove with Laurel over Buildings

1984. Lebanese Army. Multicoloured.

1296	75p. Type **251**		1·90	75
1297	150p. Cedar and soldier hold- ing rifle		3·75	1·70
1298	300p. Broken chain, hand hold- ing laurel wreath and cedar		9·00	3·75

252 Temple Ruins, Fakra

1984. Multicoloured.

1299	100p. Type **252**		1·60	65
1300	200p. Temple ruins, Bziza		3·25	1·50
1301	500p. Roman arches and relief, Tyre		8·00	3·25

253 President taking Oath

1988. Installation of President Amin Gemayel.

1302	**253**	L£25 multicoloured	1·30	90

254 Map of South America and Cedar of Lebanon

1988. First World Festival of Lebanese Youth in Uruguay.

1303	**254**	L£5 multicoloured	65	25

255 Satellite, Flags and Earth

1988. "Arabsat" Telecommunications Satellite.

1304	**255**	L£10 multicoloured	75	50

256 Children

1988. UNICEF Child Survival Campaign.

1305	**256**	L£15 multicoloured	1·30	75

257 Arabic "75" and Scout Emblems

1988. 75th Anniv (1987) of Arab Scouts Movement.

1306	**257**	L£20 multicoloured	1·50	90

258 President, Map and Dove

1988. International Peace Year (1986).

1307	**258**	L£50 multicoloured	2·50	1·30

259 Red Cross and Figures

1988. Red Cross.

1308	**259**	L£10+L£1 red, silver and black	1·00	65
1309	-	L£20+L£2 multicoloured	1·60	1·10
1310	-	L£30+L£3 silver, green and red	2·50	1·50

DESIGNS: L£20, Helmeted heads; L£30, Globe, flame, and dove holding map of Lebanon.

260 Cedar of Lebanon

1989

1311	**260**	L£50 green and mauve	75	25
1312	**260**	L£70 green and brown	1·00	50
1313	**260**	L£100 green and yellow	1·60	75
1314	**260**	L£200 green and blue	3·25	1·50
1315	**260**	L£500 deep green and green	8·75	3·75

261 Dining in the Open at Zahle, 1883

1993. 50th Anniv of Independence. Multicoloured.

1316	L£200 Type **261**		1·30	1·00
1317	L£300 Castle ruins, Saida (vert)		2·50	1·80
1318	L£500 Presidential Palace, Baabda		3·75	2·50
1319	L£1000 Sword ceremony (vert)		6·25	3·75
1320	L£3000 Model for the rebuild- ing of central Beirut		12·50	7·50
1321	L£5000 President Elias Hrawi and state flag (vert)		25·00	15·00

MS1322 130×149 mm. L£10000 As Nos.
1319/24 but smaller and without
face values. Imperf   75·00   75·00

262 Protection of Plants

1994. Environmental Protection. Multicoloured.

1323	L£100 Type **262**	90	40
1324	L£200 Protection against forest fires	1·30	65
1325	L£500 Reforesting with cedars	3·00	1·50
1326	L£1000 Creation of urban green zones	5·50	3·25
1327	L£2000 Trees	9·50	5·00
1328	L£5000 Green tree in town	30·00	15·00

263 Martyrs' Monument, Beirut

1995. Martyrs' Day.

1329	**263**	L£1500 multicoloured	7·50	7·50

264 Arabic Script under Magnifying Glass and Headquarters

1996. Anniversaries and Events. Multicoloured.

1330	L£100 Type **264** (inauguration of Postal Museum, Arab League Headquarters, Cairo)	90	65
1331	L£500 Anniversary emblem (50th anniv of UNICEF) (horiz)	4·00	3·25
1332	L£500 Ears of wheat and anniversary emblem (50th anniv (1995) of F.A.O.)	4·00	3·25
1333	L£1000 U.N. Building (New York) and anniversary emblem (50th anniv (1995) of U.N.O.)	8·25	6·25
1334	L£1000 Emblem (International Year of the Family (1994)) (horiz)	8·25	6·25
1335	L£2000 Anniversary emblem (75th anniv (1994) of I.L.O.) (horiz)	16·00	12·50
1336	L£2000 Emblem (50th anniv of Arab League)	16·00	12·50
1337	L£3000 Emblem (75th anniv (1994) of Lebanese Law Society)	24·00	19·00
1338	L£3000 Rene Moawad (former President, 70th birth anniv (1995))	24·00	19·00

265 Commemorative Medallion

1997. First Anniv of Shelling of Cana Refugee Camp.

1339	**265**	L£1100 multicoloured	12·50	12·50

266 Pope John Paul II and President Hrawi

1998. Papal Visit.

1340	**266**	L£10000 multicoloured	£140	£140

1999. Various stamps optd with a Fleuon values unchanged. Original numbers given.

1341	L£100 multicoloured (No. 1330)	3·25	3·25
1342	L£200 multicoloured (No. 1316)	7·50	7·50
1343	L£500 multicoloured (No. 1318)	19·00	19·00
1344	L£500 multicoloured (No. 1319)	19·00	19·00
1346	L£500 multicoloured (No. 1331)	19·00	19·00
1347	L£500 multicoloured (No. 1332)	38·00	38·00
1348	L£1000 multicoloured (No. 1326)	38·00	38·00
1349	L£1000 multicoloured (No. 1333)	38·00	38·00
1350	L£1100 multicoloured (No. 1339)	44·00	44·00
1351	L£1500 multicoloured (No. 1329)	55·00	55·00
1352	L£2000 multicoloured (No. 1335)	65·00	65·00
1353	L£3000 multicoloured (No. 1337)	£110	£110
1354	L£5000 multicoloured (No. 1328)	£190	£190
1355	L£10000 multicoloured (No. 1340)	£375	£375

268 Cedar of Lebanon

1999

1356	**268**	L£100 red	40	40
1357	**268**	L£500 grey	1·00	1·00
1358	**268**	L£1000 blue	3·25	3·25
1359	**268**	L£300 turquoise	1·60	1·60
1360	**268**	L£1100 brown	3·50	3·50
1361	**268**	L£1500 violet	4·75	4·75

100L.L.

(269)

1100 L L

(270)

1999. Nos. 1295/6 surch as T 269. No. 1092 surch as T **270**.

1368	L£100 on L£50 multicoloured	75	75
1369	L£300 on L£75 multicoloured	1·80	1·80
1370	L£1100 on L£70 multicoloured	6·25	6·25

271 Emir Chehab's Palace, Hasbaya

1999. Buildings. Multicoloured.

1371	L£100 Type **271**	65	65
1372	L£300 UN Economic and Social Commission for Western Asia, Beirut	1·30	1·30
1373	L£500 Emir Fakhreddine's Palace, Deir-el-Kamar (horiz)	2·50	2·50
1374	L£1100 Grand Serail, Beirut (horiz)	5·75	5·75

1999. Nos. 1335 and 1338 optd with a Fleuron, values unchanged.

1375	L£2000 multicoloured	15·00	15·00
1376	L£3000 multicoloured	21·00	21·00

272 Flag and Soldiers

2001. Return of South Lebanon (1st series).

1377	**272**	L£1100 multicoloured	4·50	4·50

See also No. **MS**1991.

273 Ibrahim Abd el Al

2001. 93rd Birth Anniv of Ibrahim Abd el Al (engineer).

1378	**273**	L£1000 multicoloured	5·00	5·00

274 Hand and Bars

2001. Prisoners.

1379	**274**	L£500 multicoloured	2·00	2·00

275 Emblem

2001. SOS Children's Villages.

1380	**275**	L£300 multicoloured	1·30	1·30

276 Hand holding "50"

2001. 50th Anniversaries.

1381	**276**	L£500 olive (Geneva Convention)	2·00	2·00
1382	-	L£1100 lilac (Geneva Convention)	4·00	4·00
1383	-	L£1500 multicoloured (Red Cross and Red Crescent)	5·75	5·75

DESIGNS: L£500 Type **276**; L£1100 Fist around bars and "50"; L£1500 Hand holding stylized people.

277 Ahas Abu Chabke

2001. 97th Birth Anniv of Ahas Abu Chabke (writer).

1384	**277**	L£1500 multicoloured	5·50	5·50

278 Father Monnot and Emblem

2001. 125th Anniv of Saint Joseph University, Beirut.

1385	**278**	L£5000 multicoloured	19·00	19·00

279 Abdallah Zakher

2001. 319th Birth Anniv of Abdallah Zakher (first Arab printer).

1386	**279**	L£1000 multicoloured	4·00	4·00

280 UN Emblem

2001. 25th. Anniv of UN Economic and Social Commission for Western Asia.

1387	**280**	L£10000 ultramarine, blue and mauve	39·00	39·00

281 Arabic Script

2002. Day of the Arab Woman.

1388	**281**	L£1000 multicoloured	4·00	4·00

282 Emblem

2002. Arab Summit Conference, Beirut. Multicoloured.

1389	L£2000 Type **282**	7·75	7·75
1390	L£3000 Cedar tree and Pres. Emile Lahoud	11·50	11·50

283 Pres. Emile Lahoud

2002. Return of Southern Lebanon (2nd series). Sheet 160×108 mm containing T **283** and similar vert designs. Multicoloured.

MS1391	L£1100×4 Type **283**; Pres. Lahoud with raised arm; Pres. Lahoud and map; Sword ceremony	19·00	19·00

284 Judges, Scales and Cedar Tree

2002. Martyrs. Sheet 120×90 mm.

MS1392	**284**	L£3000 multicoloured	11·50	11·50

285 UPU Emblem and Cedar Tree

2002. 125th Anniv of Universal Postal Union.

1393	**285**	L£2000 multicoloured	6·25	6·25

286 Men seated at Table, Zouk Mikael

2002. Souks. Multicoloured.

1394	L£100 Type **286**	30	30
1395	L£300 Vendor with wheeled stall, Saida Souk	1·10	1·10
1396	L£500 Byblos (UNESCO world heritage site)	1·90	1·90
1397	L£1000 Carpet mender, Tripoli	3·75	3·75

287 Emblem and National Colours

2002. Ninth Francophile States Summit, Beirut. Multicoloured.

1398	L£1500 Type **287**	4·75	4·75
1399	L£1500 Pres. Lahoud	4·75	4·75

288 Emblem

2002. Beirut, Arab Culture Capital, 2002.

1400	**288**	L£2000 multicoloured	6·25	6·25

289 Roman
Temple, Bziza

2002. Ruins. Multicoloured.
1401	L£1100 Type **289**	3·75	3·75
1402	L£1500 Arqa	5·25	5·25
1403	L£2000 Niha	7·50	7·50
1404	L£3000 Castle, Mousailaha	13·50	13·50

290 Lebanese Amber

2002. Fossils. Multicoloured.
| 1405 | L£5000 Type **290** | 22·00 | 22·00 |
| 1406 | L£10000 *Nematonotus longispinus* | 44·00 | 44·00 |

291 Tree, Signatures, Lebanese
and French Leaders

2003. 60th Anniv of Independence. Multicoloured.
1407	L£1250 Type **291**	2·30	2·30
1408	L£1250 Tree, signatures and parade	2·30	2·30
1409	L£1750 Tree, signatures and dignitaries	3·25	3·25
1410	L£1750 Tree and signatures	3·25	3·25
MS1411	160×110 mm. L£6000 Nos. 1407/10. Imperf	11·00	11·00

292 Postal
Building before
Restoration, Riad El
Solh–Beirut

2004. Restoration of Posts and Telecommunications
Buildings. Multicoloured.
| 1412 | L£100 Type **292** | 30 | 30 |
| 1413 | L£300 Restored building | 45 | 45 |

293 Snow Scene, Faqra

2004. Tourism.
| 1414 | **293** | L£500 multicoloured | 95 | 95 |

294 Musical Score and
Emblem

2004. Al Bustan Music Festival, Riad El Solh–Beirut.
| 1415 | **294** | L£1000 multicoloured | 1·90 | 1·90 |

295 Kamouaa

2004. Tourism. Ski Resorts. Multicoloured.
1416	L£100 Type **295**	30	30
1417	L£100 Aayoun Siman	30	30
1418	L£250 Laklouk (vert)	65	65
1419	L£300 Zaarour	70	70
1420	L£300 Kanat Bakish	70	70
1421	L£1000 Cedres	1·10	1·10

296 Anniversary
Emblem and
Hospital (½-size
illustration)

2004. 125th Anniv of St. Georges Hospital, Beirut.
| 1422 | **296** | L£3000 multicoloured | 5·50 | 5·50 |

297 Baalbeck
International Festival

2004. Festivals. Multicoloured.
1423	L£500 Type **297**	1·10	1·10
1424	L£1250 Tyre (vert)	2·75	2·75
1425	L£1400 Beiteddine (vert)	3·25	3·25
1426	L£1750 Byblos (vert)	3·75	3·75

298 Rafic Hariri
International Airport

2005. Buildings. Multicoloured.
1427	L£100 Type **298**	30	30
1428	L£250 Parliament	80	80
1429	L£300 Camille Chamoun Sports Centre	95	95
1430	L£500 National Museum	1·60	1·60
1431	L£1000 Government Palace	3·25	3·25
1432	L£1250 National Bank	4·00	4·00
1433	L£1400 St. Paul Cathedral	4·50	4·50
1434	L£1750 Bahaeddine Hariri Mosque	5·50	5·50
1435	L£2000 Presidential Palace	6·25	6·25

299 Centenary
Emblem

2005. Centenary of Rotary International.
| 1436 | **299** | L£3000 multicoloured | 5·50 | 5·50 |

300 Rafic Hariri, Towers and
Statue

2006. Rafic Hariri (prime minister 1992–8 and 2000–4)
Commemoration. Multicoloured.
1437	L£1250 Type **300**	4·00	4·00
1438	L£1250 Rafic Hariri and flag	4·00	4·00
1439	L£1750 Mosque	5·50	5·50
1440	L£1750 Child kissing portrait1	5·50	5·50
MS1441	160×110 mm. Nos. 1437/40. Imperf	19·00	19·00

301 Pile of Books

2007. 50th Anniv of Book Fair.
| 1442 | **301** | L£1000 multicoloured | 3·25 | 3·25 |

302 Basil Fuleihan

2007. Basil Fuleihan (Minister of Economy and Finance
2000–2003 (assassinated in 2005)) Commemoration.
Multicoloured.
1443	L£500 Type **302**	1·60	1·60
1444	L£1500 Seated at desk, signing agreement and national and EU flags	4·75	4·75
1445	L£2000 Head in hand and national flag	6·25	6·25

303 President Chehab

2007. President Fouad Chehab Commemoration.
| 1446 | **303** | L£1400 multicoloured | 4·50 | 4·50 |

304 Globe and Emblem

2007. World Information Society Summit, Tunis.
| 1447 | **304** | L£100 multicoloured | 30 | 30 |

305 '125' (Arabic) enclosing
Emblem

2007. 125th Anniv of Makassed Islamic Welfare
Organization in Beirut (2003) (1448/50 and 1453)
and Saida (2004) (1451/2). Multicoloured.
1448	L£250 Type **305**	80	80
1449	L£500 Saeb Salam (prime minister 1952, 1953, 1960–1961, 1970–1973) (Makassed chairman 1957–1982)	1·60	1·60
1450	L£1400 Rafic Hariri (prime minister 1992–1998, 2000–2004 (assassinated 2005))	4·50	4·50
1451	L£1400 Rafic Hariri (different)	4·50	4·50
1452	L£1750 Riad El Solh (first prime minister)	5·50	5·50
1453	L£1750 Omar El Daouk	5·50	5·50

306 Leopold Senghor

2007. Birth Centenary of Leopold Sedar Senghor
(poet and president of Senegal 1960–1980). La
Francophonie (organization of French speaking
countries).
| 1454 | **306** | L£300 multicoloured | 95 | 95 |

307 Athlete (sculpture)

2007. International Year of Sports and Sports Education
(2005).
| 1455 | **307** | L£500 multicoloured | 1·60 | 1·60 |

308 Names of Artistes

2007. 50th Anniv of Baalbek International Festival.
Multicoloured.
| 1456 | L£1000 Type **308** | 3·25 | 3·25 |
| 1457 | L£5000 Female artistes | 8·50 | 8·50 |

309 '30'

2007. 30th Anniv of OPEC Development Fund.
| 1458 | **309** | L£1400 multicoloured | 4·50 | 4·50 |

310 Maxime Chaya and Flag on
Summit

2007. Maxime Chaya (1st Lebanese climber to reach top
of Mount Everest). Sheet 160×110 mm.
| **MS**1459 | 310L£3000 multicoloured | 7·75 | 7·75 |

311 *Hills* (detail) (painting by Nizar
Daher)

2007. Sheet 160×110 mm.
| **MS**1460 | **311** L£5000 multicoloured | 11·00 | 11·00 |

312 Dove and Broken Bars (image scaled to 30% of
original size)

2007. Return of Prisoners. Sheet 160×110 mm. Imperf.
| **MS**1461 | **312** L£5000 multicoloured | 11·00 | 11·00 |

313 Mother and Child

2008. 125th Birth Anniv of Gibran Khalil Gibran (writer
and artist). Multicoloured.
1462	L£100 Type **313**	30	30
1463	L£500 Sultana	1·60	1·60
1464	L£1400 Gibran Museum	4·50	4·50
1465	L£2000 Khalil Gibran	6·25	6·25
MS1466	160×110 mm. L£4000 As Nos. 1462/5. Imperf	9·50	9·50

314 Flags as Rowers

2008. Rotary International Conference, Beirut.
1467 **314** L£2000 multicoloured 6·25 6·25

315 Pigeon

2008. Arab Post Day. Sheet 170×60 mm containing T 315 and similar horiz design. Multicoloured.
MS1468 L£5000 Type 315; L£5 000 Camels 11·00 11·00

316 Soldier, Flag and Moon

2008. Army Day. Multicoloured.
1469 L£500 Type **316** 1·60 1·60
1470 L£1000 Script and tree 3·25 3·25
1471 L£1250 Hand holding grain 4·00 4·00
1472 L£1750 Eye enclosing emblem 5·50 5·50
MS1473 160× 110 mm. L£4500 As Nos. 1469/72. Imperf 10·00 10·00

317 Aircraft and Envelope

2008. Tenth Anniv of LIBANPOST. Multicoloured.
1474 L£1250 Type **317** 4·00 4·00
1475 L£1750 10th ANNIVERSARY 5·50 5·50
MS1476 160× 110 mm. L£3000 As Nos. 1474/5. Imperf 6·25 6·25

318 Oak, Map of Mediterranean and Cedar Tree

2008. Lebanon—France Relations.
1477 **318** L£1750 multicoloured 5·50 5·50
A stamp of a similar design was issued by France.

319 Francois El Hajj

2008. First Death Anniv of General Francois El Hajj.
1478 **319** L£1750 multicoloured 5·50 5·50

320 Charles Malik (member of Commission)

2008. 60th Anniv of Universal Declaration of Human Rights.
1479 **320** L£2000 multicoloured 6·25 6·25

321 Emblem

2009. al-Quds—2009 Capital of Arab Culture.
1480 **321** L£1000 multicoloured 3·25 3·25

322 Pierre Deschamps (founder)

2009. Centenary of Mission Laique Francaise (network of French schools abroad).
1481 **322** L£500 multicoloured 1·80 1·80

323 Emblem

2009. Beirut—Book Capital of the World.
1482 **323** L£750 multicoloured 2·10 2·10

324 Emblem

2009. Sixth Francophone Games.
1483 **324** L£1000 multicoloured 3·25 3·25

325 Civil Defence Workers

2010. Civil Defence. Multicoloured.
1484 L£100 Type **325** 35 35
1485 L£250 Firefighters 80 80

326 Plants

2010. Lebanon Nature Reserves
1486 **326** L£300 multicoloured 1·10 1·10

327 Building with Colonnade

2010. Traditional Buildings. Multicoloured.
1487 L£500 Type **327** 1·60 1·60
1488 L£1000 Two storied building with white glazed door and blue shutters 3·25 3·25
1489 L£1250 Two storied building with blue door and shutters 4·00 4·00

328 Soaps

2010. Trsditional Industries. Soap
1490 **328** L£1400 multicoloured 4·50 4·50

329 Soldier carrying Map of Lebanon as Bag

2010. Lebanese Army
1491 L£1750 multicoloured 5·50 5·50

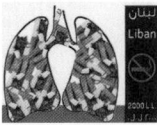

330 Lungs full of Cigarette Butts

2010. Anti Drugs and Tobacco Awareness Campaign
1492 L£2000 multicoloured 6·25 6·25
1493 L£5000 black and scarlet-vermilion (vert) 10·00 10·00
Designs: L£2000 Type 330; L£5000 Needle and emblem.

331 Al Imam Al Ouzai (inscr 'Al Imam Al Ouzaai')

2010. Al Imam Al Ouzai Commemoration
1490 **331** L£1000 multicoloured 3·25 3·25

332 President-Elect Bachir Gemayel

2010. Martyrs. Multicoloured.
1495 L£1400 Type **332** 4·50 4·50
1496 L£1400 Kamal Jumblatt (politician) (inscr 'Kamal Joumblat') (vert) 4·50 4·50
1497 L£1400 Prime Minister Rashid Karame (vert) 4·50 4·50
1498 L£1400 Mufti Hassan Khaled 4·50 4·50
1499 L£1400 President Rene Mouawad (vert) 4·50 4·50
1500 L£1400 Músá al-Ṣadr (vert) 4·50 4·50

333 Woman and Globe

2010. World Tourism Day. 'An Open Door for Women'
1501 **333** L£2000 multicoloured 6·25 6·25

334 Dove and Flowers

2010. Peace
1502 **334** L£3000 multicoloured 9·00 9·00

335 Early Writing

2011. Cradle of the Alphabet
1503 **335** L£250 multicoloured 80 80

336

2011. Arab Permanent Postal Commission
1504 **336** L£500 multicoloured 1·60 1·60

337 Sabah

2011. Sabah (Jeanette Gergi Feghali) (singer and actress)
1505 **337** L£1750 multicoloured 5·50 5·50

338 Nabih Abou El-Hossn

2011. Nabih Abou El-Hossn (actor)
1506 **338** L£2250 multicoloured 6·50 6·50

339 Hassan Alaa Eddine

2011. Hassan Alaa Eddine ('Chouchou') (comedian)
1507 **339** L£2750 multicoloured 7·00 7·00

340 Caracalla

2011. Caracalla (dance troup)
1508 **340** L£3000 multicoloured 8·00 8·00

341 Michel, Alfred, and Youssef Basbous

2011. Basbous Brothers (sculptors)
1509 **341** L£5000 multicoloured 10·00 10·00

342 Said Akl

2011. Said Akl (poet)
1510 **342** L£10000 multicoloured 6·25 6·25

343 Ehden Reserve

2011. Ehden Reserve
1511 **343** L£750 multicoloured 2·75 2·75

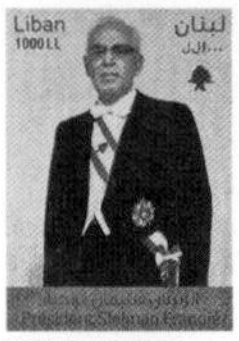

344 President Frangiè

2011. President Sleiman Frangiè (Suleiman Kabalan Frangieh) Commemoration

1512	**344**	L£1000 multicoloured	3·25	3·25

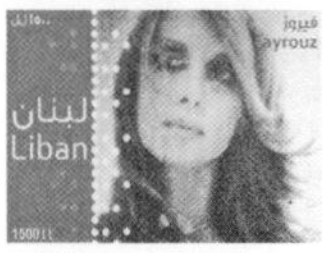

345 Fayrouz (Fairuz)

2011. Fayrouz (Nouhad Wadi Haddad) (singer)

1513	**345**	L£1500 multicoloured	4·75	4·75

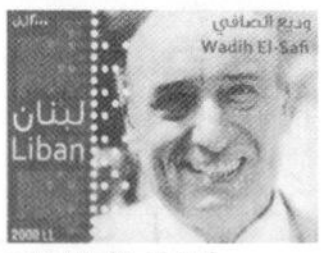

346 Wadih El Safi

2011. Wadih El Safi (Wadi' Francis) (singer, songwriter and actor)

1514	**346**	L£2000 multicoloured	6·25	6·25

POSTAGE DUE STAMPS

1924. Postage Due stamps of France surch **GRAND LIBAN** and value in "CENTIEMES" or "PIASTRES".

D26	**D11**	50c. on 10c. brown	3·50	5·00
D27	**D11**	1p. on 20c. green	4·25	11·00
D28	**D11**	2p. on 30c. red	3·50	8·25
D29	**D11**	3p. on 50c. purple	3·75	7·75
D30	**D11**	5p. on 1f. purple on yellow	3·50	7·00

1924. Postage Due stamps of France surch **Gd Liban** and value in French and Arabic.

D58		0p.50 on 10c. brown	2·75	7·25
D59		1p. on 20c. green	3·50	7·00
D60		2p. on 30c. red	4·75	7·00
D61		3p. on 50c. purple	6·25	9·25
D62		5p. on 1f. purple on yell	4·50	9·75

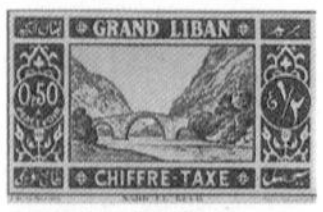

D7 Nahr el-Kalb

1925

D75	**D7**	0p.50 brown on yellow	1·30	3·50
D76	-	1p. red on pink	1·10	5·50
D77	-	2p. black on blue	2·40	4·00
D78	-	3p. brown on orange	2·50	11·50
D79	-	5p. black on green	2·00	10·50

DESIGNS—HORIZ: 1p. Pine Forest, Beirut; 2p. Pigeon Grotto, Beirut; 3p. Beaufort Castle; 5p. Baalbeck.

1927. Optd **Republique Libanaise**.

D122	**D7**	0p.50 brown on yellow	1·20	4·25
D123	-	1p. red on pink	£140	7·25
D124	-	2p. black on blue	2·75	9·00
D125	-	3p. brown on orange	3·00	6·25
D126	-	5p. black on green	4·50	16·00

1928. Nos. D122/6 optd with T **10**.

D145	**D7**	0p.50 brown on yellow	2·75	7·00
D146	-	1p. red on pink	2·50	8·25
D147	-	2p. black on blue	2·20	8·25
D148	-	3p. brown on orange	3·00	14·00
D149	-	5p. black on green	3·75	21·00

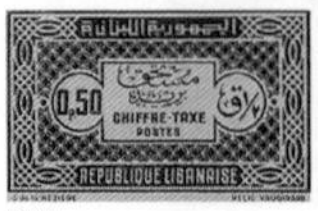

D18

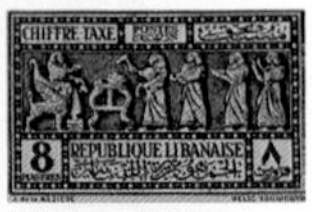

D19 Bas-relief from Sarcophagus of King Ahiram at Byblos

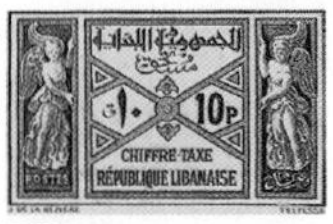

D32

1931

D191	**D18**	0p.50 black on pink	1·00	2·50
D192	-	1p. black on blue	1·90	2·30
D193	-	2p. black on yellow	2·50	2·00
D194	-	3p. black on green	3·73	2·75
D195	**D32**	5p. black on orange	12·00	12·00
D196	**D19**	8p. black on pink	6·75	11·50
D252	**D32**	10p. green	14·50	18·00
D197	-	15p. black	4·50	6·50

DESIGNS: 1p. Bas-relief of Phoenician galley; 2p. Arabesque; 3p. Garland; 15p. Statuettes.

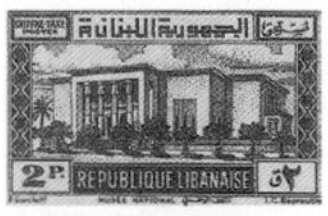

D43 National Museum

1945

D298	**D43**	2p. black on lemon	5·25	5·25
D299	**D43**	5p. blue on pink	6·50	6·50
D300	**D43**	25p. blue on green	8·50	8·50
D301	**D43**	50p. purple on blue	9·75	9·75

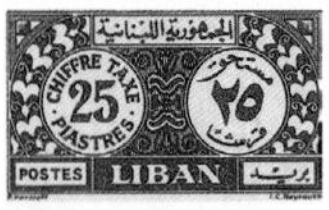

D53

1947

D352	**D53**	5p. black on green	7·00	1·80
D353	**D53**	25p. black on yellow	70·00	4·75
D354	**D53**	50p. black on blue	36·00	12·00

D59 Monument at Hermel

1948

D379	**D59**	2p. black on yellow	4·50	1·20
D380	**D59**	3p. black on pink	9·75	4·25
D381	**D59**	10p. black on blue	26·00	8·00

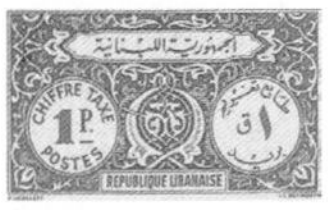

D67

1950

D416	**D67**	1p. red	1·10	20
D417	**D67**	5p. blue	5·25	1·10
D418	**D67**	10p. green	7·50	2·10

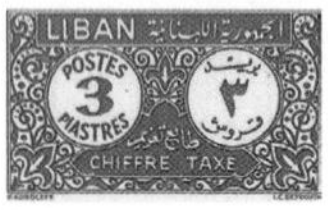

D78

1952

D464	**D78**	1p. mauve	30	10
D465	**D78**	2p. violet	55	30
D466	**D78**	3p. green	65	30
D467	**D78**	5p. blue	95	45
D468	**D78**	10p. brown	1·80	75
D469	**D78**	25p. black	14·00	1·80

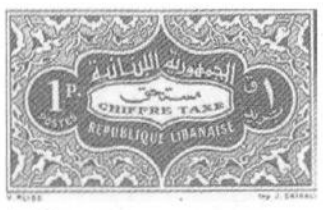

D81

1953

D481	**D81**	1p. red	20	10
D482	**D81**	2p. green	20	20
D483	**D81**	3p. orange	20	20
D484	**D81**	5p. purple	30	30
D485	**D81**	10p. brown	95	45
D486	**D81**	15p. blue	1·80	95

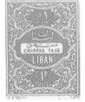

D93

1955

D550	**D93**	1p. brown	20	20
D551	**D93**	2p. green	20	20
D552	**D93**	3p. turquoise	20	20
D553	**D93**	5p. purple	20	20
D554	**D93**	10p. green	65	30
D555	**D93**	15p. blue	70	40
D556	**D93**	25p. purple	1·60	1·10

D178

1967

D967	**D178**	1p. green	20	25
D968	**D178**	5p. mauve	20	30
D969	**D178**	15p. blue	55	75

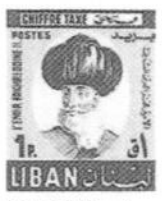

D184 Emir Fakhreddine II

1968

D1004	**D184**	1p. slate and grey	10	10
D1005	**D184**	2p. turquoise & green	10	10
D1006	**D184**	3p. orange & yellow	10	15
D1007	**D184**	5p. purple and red	10	15
D1008	**D184**	10p. olive and yellow	20	25
D1009	**D184**	15p. blue and violet	45	55
D1010	**D184**	25p. blue & lt blue	75	85

POSTAL TAX STAMPS

These were issued between 1945 and 1962 for compulsory use on inland mail (and sometimes on mail to Arab countries) to provide funds for various purposes.

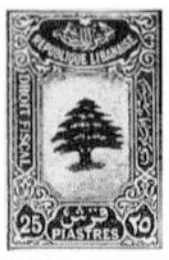

T41

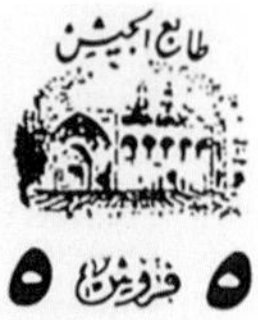

(T42)

1945. Lebanese Army. Fiscal stamp as Type T **41** surch with Type T **42**.

T289	**T41**	5p. on 30c. brown	£650	3·75

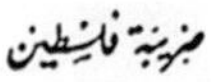

(T50)

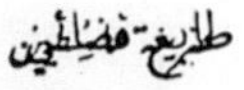

(T51)

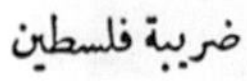

(T 52)

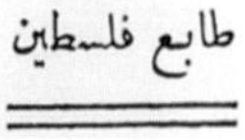

T56 "Palestine stamp"

1947. Aid to War in Palestine. Surch as Type T **42**. (a) With top line Type T **50**.

T338	5p. on 25c. green	30·00	2·75
T339	5p. on 30c. brown	39·00	5·25
T340	5p. on 60c. blue	65·00	3·75
T341	5p. on 3p. pink	30·00	4·75
T342	5p. on 15p. blue	30·00	1·90

(b) With top line Type T 51.

T343	5p. on 10p. red	£130	8·50

(c) With top line Type T 52.

T344	5p. on 3p. pink	27·00	2·75

(d) As No. T344 but with figure "5" at left instead of "0" and without inscr between figures.

T345	5p. on 3p. pink	£475	34·00

1948. Palestine Aid. No. T289 optd with Type T **56**.

T363	5p. on 30c. brown	27·00	3·50

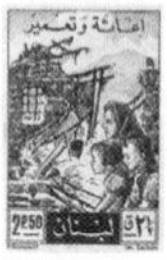

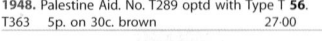

T95 Family and Ruined House

1956. Earthquake Victims.

T559	**T95**	2p.50 brown	4·75	30

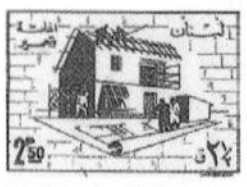

T99 Rebuilding

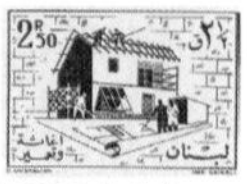

T100 Rebuilding

1957. Earthquake Victims.

T601	**T99**	2p.50 brown	4·75	30
T602	**T99**	2p.50 green	2·75	30
T603	**T100**	2p.50 brown	3·25	20

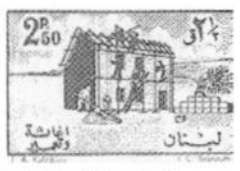

T132 Rebuilding

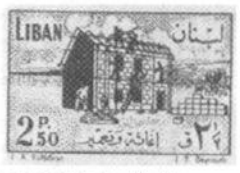

T133 Rebuilding

1961. Earthquake Victims.

T729	**T132**	2p.50 brown	2·75	20
T730	**T133**	2p.50 blue	2·75	20

Pt. 1

LEEWARD ISLANDS

A group of islands in the Br. W. Indies, including Antigua, Barbuda, British Virgin Islands, Dominica (till end of 1939), Montserrat, Nevis and St. Christopher (St. Kitts). Stamps of Leeward Islands were used concurrent with the issues for the respective islands until they were withdrawn on the 1 July 1956.

1890. 12 pence = 1 shilling; 20 shillings = 1 pound.
1951. 100 cents = 1 West Indian dollar.

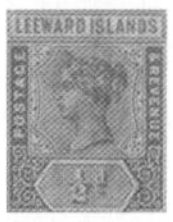

1

1890

1	**1**	½d. mauve and green	3·50	1·25
2	**1**	1d. mauve and red	7·50	20
3	**1**	2½d. mauve and blue	8·50	30
4	**1**	4d. mauve and orange	10·00	9·00
5	**1**	6d. mauve and brown	12·00	13·00
6	**1**	7d. mauve and grey	10·00	17·00
7	**1**	1s. green and red	23·00	55·00
8	**1**	5s. green and blue	£140	£300

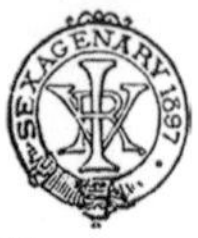

(3)

1897. Diamond Jubilee. Optd with T **3**.

9	½d. mauve and green	7·00	22·00
10	1d. mauve and red	8·00	22·00
11	2½d. mauve and blue	8·50	22·00
12	4d. mauve and orange	55·00	80·00
13	6d. mauve and brown	60·00	£130
14	7d. mauve and grey	60·00	£130
15	1s. green and red	£130	£275
16	5s. green and blue	£450	£800

1902. Surch One Penny.

17	1d. on 4d. mauve and orange	6·00	9·00
18	1d. on 6d. mauve and brown	8·00	15·00
19	1d. on 7d. mauve and grey	6·50	12·00

1902. As T **1**, but portrait of King Edward VII.

29	½d. purple and green	3·75	2·00
21	1d. purple and red	8·00	20
22	2d. purple and brown	2·75	4·25
23	2½d. purple and blue	6·00	2·25
24	3d. purple and black	8·00	7·50
25	6d. purple and brown	2·50	8·00
26	1s. green and red	7·50	25·00
27	2s.6d. green and black	28·00	75·00
28	5s. green and blue	65·00	90·00

1907. As last, but colours changed.

36	¼d. brown	2·75	1·75
37	½d. green	4·00	1·25
38	1d. red	11·00	80
39	2d. grey	4·50	9·00
40	2½d. blue	8·00	4·25
41	3d. purple and yellow	3·50	7·50
42	6d. purple	9·00	7·50
43	1s. black on green	7·00	21·00
44	2s.6d. black and red on blue	42·00	55·00
45	5s. green and red on yellow	48·00	65·00

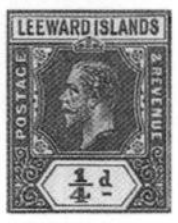

10 King George V

1912

46	**10**	¼d. brown	1·75	1·00
59	**10**	½d. green	1·25	75
60	**10**	1d. red	2·25	55
61	**10**	1d. violet	2·25	1·00
63	**10**	1½d. red	5·00	2·00
64	**10**	1½d. brown	1·25	10
65	**10**	2d. grey	2·50	80
66	**10**	2½d. yellow	10·00	60·00
67	**10**	2½d. blue	3·50	1·25
68	**10**	3d. blue	12·00	29·00
69	**10**	3d. purple on yellow	5·00	6·50
70	**10**	4d. black and red on yellow	3·25	21·00
71	**10**	5d. purple and green	2·50	4·25

53	10	6d. purple	3·50	8·50
54	10	1s. black on green	3·00	8·00
74a	10	2s. purple and blue on blue	8·50	48·00
75	10	2s.6d. black and red on blue	8·50	23·00
76	10	3s. green and violet	12·00	35·00
77	10	4s. black and red	18·00	42·00
57b	10	5s. green and red on yellow	45·00	85·00

Larger type, as T **15** of Malta.

79	13	10s. green and red on green	80·00	£130
80	13	£1 purple and black on red	£225	£275

1935. Silver Jubilee. As T **14a** of Kenya, Uganda and Tanganyika.

88	1d. blue and red	1·90	3·00
89	1½d. blue and grey	2·75	1·25
90	2½d. brown and blue	4·25	4·50
91	1s. grey and purple	25·00	35·00

1937. Coronation. As T **14b** of Kenya, Uganda and Tanganyika.

92	1d. red	80	1·00
93	1½d. brown	80	1·50
94	2½d. blue	90	1·50

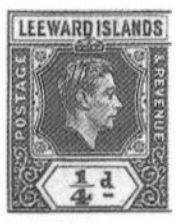

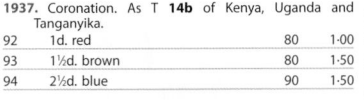

14 King George VI

1938

95a	14	¼d. brown	30	1·75
96	14	½d. green	1·00	70
97	14	½d. grey	2·00	1·50
99	14	1d. red	2·25	1·75
100	14	1d. green	55	15
101	14	1½d. brown	1·00	50
102	14	1½d. orange and black	1·50	40
103	14	2d. grey	3·25	2·25
104	14	2d. red	1·40	1·25
105a	14	2½d. blue	80	1·25
106	14	2½d. black and purple	80	15
107a	14	3d. orange	50	85
108	14	3d. blue	80	15
109a	14	6d. purple	10·00	3·50
110b	14	1s. black on green	4·25	1·00
111a	14	2s. purple and blue on blue	12·00	2·00
112b	14	5s. green and red on yellow	35·00	15·00
113c	-	10s. green and red on green	£120	£100
114b	-	£1 purple and black on red	45·00	28·00

The 10s. and £1 are as Type **15** of Bermuda but with portrait of King George VI.

1946. Victory. As T **60** of Jamaica.

115	1½d. brown	15	75
116	3d. orange	15	75

1949. Silver Wedding. As T **61/2** of Jamaica.

117	2½d. blue	10	10
118	5s. green	7·00	7·00

1949. U.P.U. As T **63/66** of Jamaica.

119	2½d. black	15	2·50
120	3d. blue	2·00	2·50
121	6d. mauve	15	2·50
122	1s. turquoise	15	2·50

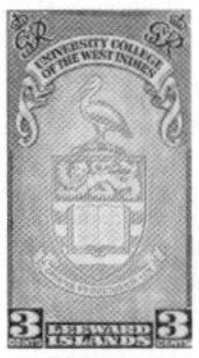

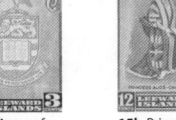

15a Arms of University

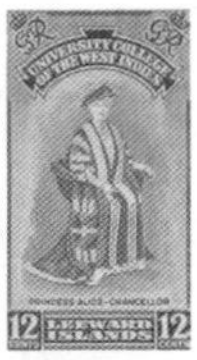

15b Princess Alice

1951. Inauguration of B.W.I. University College.

123	15a	3c. orange and black	30	2·00
124	15b	12c. red and violet	70	2·00

1953. Coronation. As T **71** of Jamaica.

125	3c. black and green	1·00	2·25

1954. As T **14** but portrait of Queen Elizabeth II facing left.

126	½c. brown	10	60
127	1c. grey	1·25	1·25
128	2c. green	1·75	10
129	3c. yellow and black	2·50	1·00
130	4c. red	1·75	10
131	5c. black and purple	2·25	1·00
132	6c. yellow	2·25	60
133	8c. blue	2·50	10
134	12c. purple	2·00	10
135	24c. black and green	2·00	20
136	48c. purple and blue	8·00	2·75
137	60c. brown and green	6·00	2·25
138	$1.20 green and red	7·00	3·50

Larger type as T 15 of Malta, but portrait of Queen Elizabeth II facing left.

139	$2.40 green and red	11·00	6·00
140	$4.80 purple and black	15·00	11·00

Pt. 1

LESOTHO

Formerly Basutoland, attained independence on 4 October 1966 and changed its name to Lesotho.

1966. 100 cents = 1 rand.
1979. 100 lisente = 1 (ma)loti.

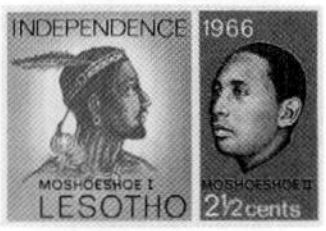

33 Moshoeshoe I and Moshoeshoe II

1966. Independence.

106	33	2½c. brown, black and red	10	10
107	33	5c. brown, black and blue	10	10
108	33	10c. brown, black and green	15	10
109	33	20c. brown, black and purple	20	15

1966. Nos. 69 etc. of Basutoland optd **LESOTHO**.

110A	8	½c. black and sepia	10	10
111A	-	1c. black and green	10	10
112A	-	2c. blue and orange	60	10
113B	26	2½c. sage and red	50	10
114A	-	3½c. indigo and blue	30	10
115A	-	5c. brown and green	10	10
116A	-	10c. bronze and purple	10	10
117B	-	12½c. brown and turquoise	30	20
118A	-	25c. blue and red	30	20
119B	-	50c. black and red	70	50
120B	9	1r. black and purple	65	75

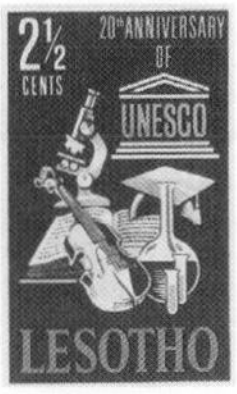

35 "Education, Culture and Science"

1966. 20th Anniv of UNESCO.

121	35	2½c. yellow and green	10	10
122	35	5c. green and olive	15	10
123	35	12½c. blue and red	35	15
124	35	25c. orange and blue	60	75

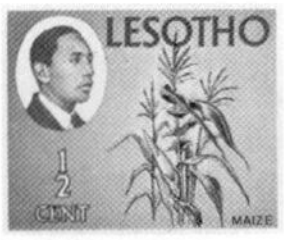

36 Maize

1967

125	36	½c. green and violet	10	10
126	-	1c. sepia and red	10	10
149	-	2c. yellow and green	10	10
128	-	2½c. black and ochre	10	10
151	-	3c. chocolate, green and brown	15	15
152	-	3½c. blue and yellow	15	10
130	-	5c. bistre and blue	20	10
131	-	10c. brown and grey	10	10
132	-	12½c. black and orange	20	10
133	-	25c. black and blue	55	20
134	-	50c. black, blue & turquoise	4·50	1·90
135	-	1r. multicoloured	65	75
136	-	2r. black, gold and purple	1·00	1·75

DESIGNS—HORIZ: 1c. Cattle; 2c. Aloes; 2½c. Basotho hat; 3c. Sorghum; 3½c. Merino sheep ("Wool"); 5c. Basotho pony; 10c. Wheat; 12½c. Angora goat ("Mohair"); 25c. Maletsunyane Falls; 50c. Diamonds; 1r. Arms of Lesotho. VERT: 2r. Moshoeshoe II.

See also Nos. 191/203.

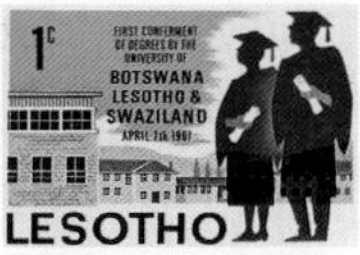

46 Students and University

1967. First Conferment of University Degrees.

137	46	1c. sepia, blue and orange	10	10
138	46	2½c. sepia, ultramarine & bl	10	10
139	46	12½c. sepia, blue and red	10	10
140	46	25c. sepia, blue and violet	15	15

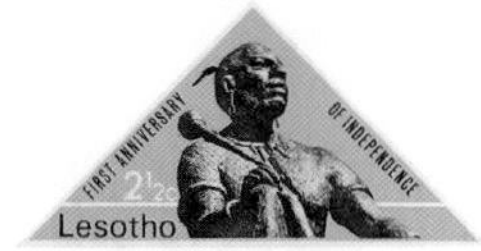

47 Statue of Moshoeshoe I

1967. First Anniv of Independence.

141	47	2½c. black and green	10	10
142	-	12½c. multicoloured	25	15
143	-	25c. black, green and ochre	35	25

DESIGNS: 12½c. National flag; 25c. Crocodile (national emblem).

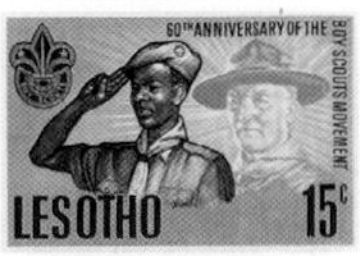

50 Lord Baden-Powell and Scout Saluting

1967. 60th Anniv of Scout Movement.

144	50	15c. multicoloured	20	10

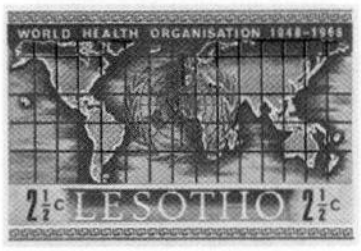

51 W.H.O. Emblem and World Map

1968. 20th Anniv of World Health Organization.

145	51	2½c. blue, gold and red	15	10
146	-	25c. multicoloured	45	60

DESIGN: 25c. Nurse and child.

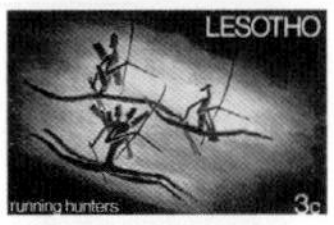

55 Running Hunters

1968. Rock Paintings.

160	55	3c. brown, turquoise and green	20	10
161	-	3½c. yellow, olive and sepia	25	10
162	-	5c. red, ochre and brown	25	10
163	-	10c. yellow, red and purple	35	10
164	-	15c. buff, yellow and brown	50	30
165	-	20c. green, yellow and brown	60	55
166	-	25c. yellow, brown and black	65	75

DESIGNS—HORIZ: 3½c. Baboons; 10c. Archers; 20c. Eland; 25c. Hunting scene. VERT: 5c. Javelin thrower; 15c. Blue cranes.

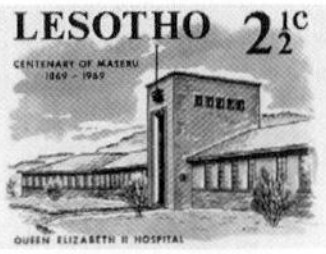

62 Queen Elizabeth II Hospital

1969. Centenary of Maseru (capital). Multicoloured.

167	2½c. Type **62**	10	10
168	10c. Lesotho Radio Station	10	10
169	12½c. Leabua Jonathan Airport	35	10
170	25c. Royal Palace	25	15

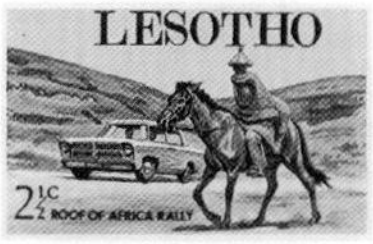

66 Rally Car passing Basuto Tribesman

1969. "Roof of Africa" Car Rally.

171	66	2½c. yellow, mauve and plum	15	10
172	-	12½c. blue, yellow and grey	20	10
173	-	15c. blue, black and mauve	20	10
174	-	20c. black, red and yellow	20	10

DESIGNS: 12½c. Rally car on mountain road; 15c. Chequered flags and "Roof of Africa" Plateau; 20c. Map of rally route and Independence Trophy.

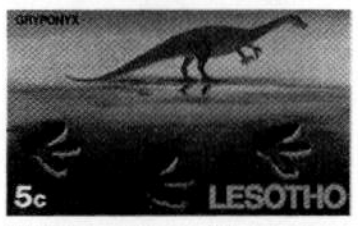

71 Gryponyx and Footprints

1970. Prehistoric Footprints (1st series).

175		3c. brown and sepia	90	70
176	71	5c. purple, pink and sepia	1·10	30
177	-	10c. yellow, black and sepia	1·40	35
178	-	15c. yellow, black and sepia	2·00	2·25
179	-	25c. blue and black	2·75	2·25

DESIGNS: 3c. Dinosaur footprints at Moyeni; 10c. Plateosauravus and footprints; 15c. Tritylodon and footprints; 25c. Massospondylus and footprints.

No. 175 is larger, 60×23 mm.

See also Nos. 596/8.

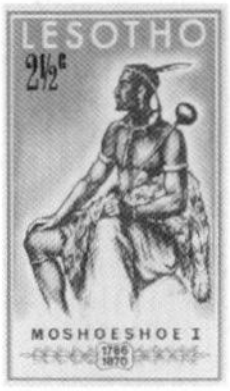

75 Moshoeshoe I as a Young Man

1970. Death Centenary of Chief Moshoeshoe I.

180	75	2½c. green and mauve	10	10
181	-	25c. blue and brown	20	20

DESIGN: 25c. Moshoeshoe I as an old man.

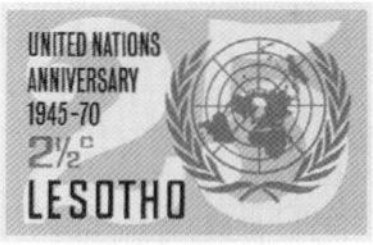

77 U.N. Emblem and "25"

1970. 25th Anniv of United Nations.

182	77	2½c. pink, blue and purple	10	10
183	-	10c. multicoloured	10	10
184	-	12½c. red, blue and drab	10	25
185	-	25c. multicoloured	15	65

DESIGNS: 10c. U.N. Building; 12½c. "People of the World"; 25c. Symbolic dove.

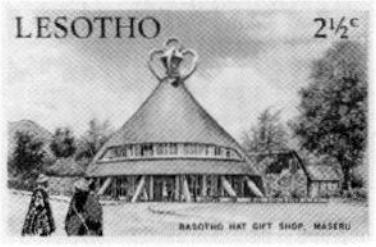

78 Gift Shop, Maseru

1970. Tourism. Multicoloured.

186	2½c. Type **78**	10	10
187	5c. Trout fishing	20	10
188	10c. Pony trekking	25	10
189	12½c. Skiing, Maluti Mountains	50	10
190	20c. Holiday Inn, Maseru	40	50

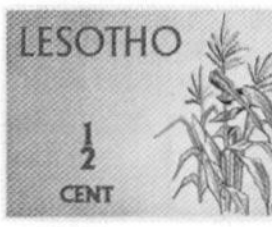

79 Maize

1971. As Nos. 147/58 but in new format omitting portrait, as in T **79**. New designs for 4c., 2r.

191	79	½c. green and violet	10	10
192	-	1c. brown and red	10	10
193	-	2c. yellow and green	10	10
194	-	2½c. black, green and yellow	10	10
195	-	3c. brown, green and yellow	10	10
196	-	3½c. blue and yellow	10	10
196a	-	4c. multicoloured	20	10
197	-	5c. brown and blue	15	10
198	-	10c. brown and grey	15	10
199	-	12½c. brown and orange	25	30
200	-	25c. slate and blue	60	40

201	-	50c. black, blue and green	6·00	4·50
202	-	1r. multicoloured	1·25	1·75
401	-	2r. brown and blue	70	2·25

DESIGNS—HORIZ: 4c. National flag. VERT: 2r. Statue of Moshoeshoe I.

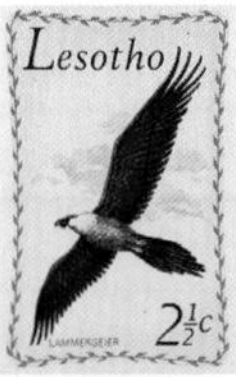

80 Lammergeier

1971. Birds. Multicoloured.

204	2½c. Type **80**	2·50	20
205	5c. Bald ibis	3·50	2·50
206	10c. Orange-breasted rock-jumper	3·50	2·00
207	12½c. Blue bustard ("Blue korhaan")	3·75	3·50
208	15c. Painted-snipe	4·25	4·50
209	20c. Golden-breasted bunting	4·25	4·50
210	25c. Ground woodpecker	4·75	4·50

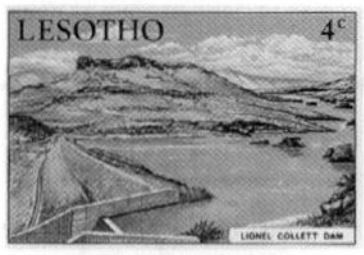

81 Lionel Collett Dam

1971. Soil Conservation. Multicoloured.

211	4c. Type **81**	10	10
212	10c. Contour ridges	10	10
213	15c. Earth dams	25	10
214	25c. Beaver dams	35	35

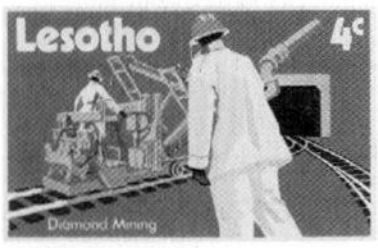

82 Diamond Mining

1971. Development. Multicoloured.

215	4c. Type **82**	75	40
216	10c. Pottery	30	10
217	15c. Weaving	45	60
218	20c. Construction	55	1·50

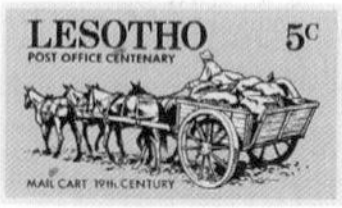

83 Mail Cart

1972. Centenary of Post Office.

219	**83**	5c. brown and pink	15	20
220	-	10c. multicoloured	15	10
221	-	15c. blue, black and brown	20	15
222	-	20c. multicoloured	30	90

DESIGNS—HORIZ: 10c. Postal bus; 20c. Maseru Post Office. VERT: 15c. 4d. Cape of Good Hope stamp of 1876.

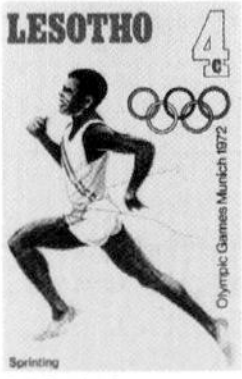

84 Sprinting

1972. Olympic Games, Munich. Multicoloured.

223	4c. Type **84**	15	10
224	10c. Shot putting	20	10
225	15c. Hurdling	30	10
226	25c. Long-jumping	35	55

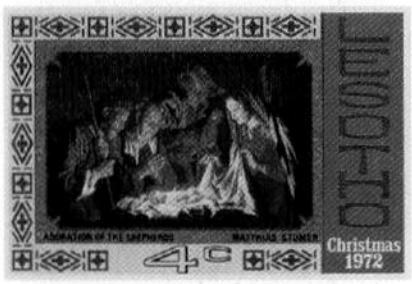

85 "Adoration of the Shepherds" (Matthias Stomer)

1972. Christmas.

227	**85**	4c. multicoloured	10	10
228	**85**	10c. multicoloured	10	10
229	**85**	25c. multicoloured	15	20

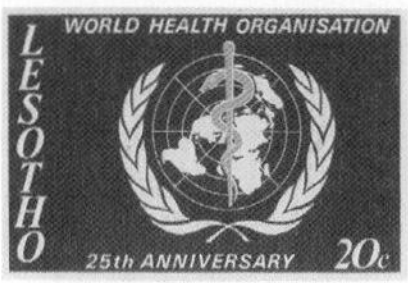

86 W.H.O. Emblem

1973. 25th Anniv of W.H.O.

230	**86**	20c. yellow and blue	30	30

1973. O.A.U. 10th Anniv. Nos. 194 and 196a/8 optd **O.A.U. 10th Anniversary Freedom in Unity**.

231	2½c. black, green and brown	10	10
232	4c. multicoloured	10	10
233	5c. brown and blue	10	10
234	10c. brown and blue	15	15

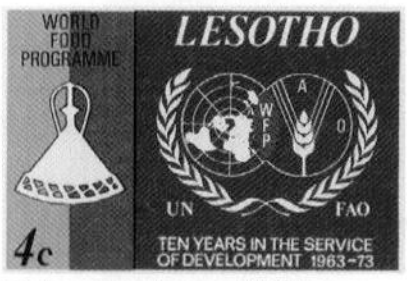

88 Basotho Hat and W.F.P. Emblem

1973. Tenth Anniv of World Food Programme. Multicoloured.

235	4c. Type **88**	10	10
236	15c. School feeding	20	15
237	20c. Infant feeding	20	20
238	25c. "Food for work"	25	25

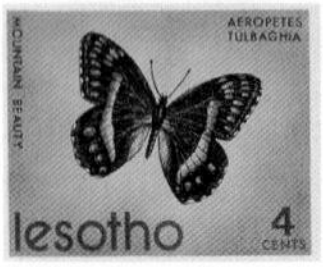

89 "Aeropetes tulbaghia"

1973. Butterflies. Multicoloured.

239	4c. Type **89**	85	10
240	5c. *Papilio demodocus*	95	50
241	10c. *Cynthia cardui*	1·50	50
242	15c. *Precis hierta*	2·75	1·75
243	20c. *Precis oenone*	2·75	1·75
244	25c. *Danaus chrysippus*	3·00	2·75
245	30c. *Colotis evenina*	3·00	3·75

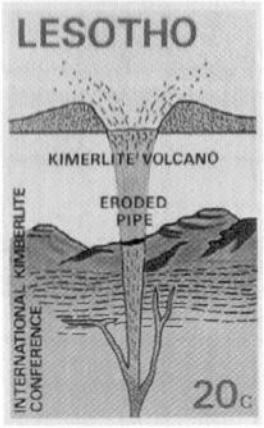

90 Kimberlite Volcano

1973. International Kimberlite Conference. Multicoloured.

246	10c. Map of diamond mines (horiz)	2·00	50
247	15c. Kimberlite-diamond rock (horiz)	2·25	2·25
248	20c. Type **90**	2·25	2·50
249	30c. Diamond prospecting	3·75	7·00

1974. Youth and Development. Multicoloured.

250	4c. Type **91**	10	10
251	10c. "Education"	15	10
252	20c. "Agriculture"	20	10
253	25c. "Industry"	30	20
254	30c. "Service"	30	25

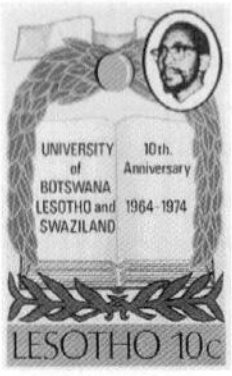

92 Open Book and Wreath

1974. Tenth Anniv of U.B.L.S. Multicoloured.

255	10c. Type **92**	15	10
256	15c. Flags, mortar-board and scroll	20	20
257	20c. Map of Africa	25	25
258	25c. King Moshoeshoe II capping a graduate	25	65

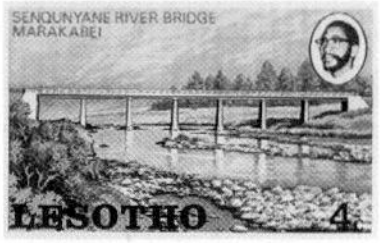

93 Senqunyane River Bridge, Marakabei

1974. Rivers and Bridges. Multicoloured.

259	4c. Type **93**	10	10
260	5c. Tsoelike River and bridge	10	10
261	10c. Makhaleng River Bridge	20	10
262	15c. Seaka Bridge, Orange/Senqu River	35	35
263	20c. Masianokeng Bridge, Phuthiatsana River	40	40
264	25c. Mahobong Bridge, Hlotse River	45	45

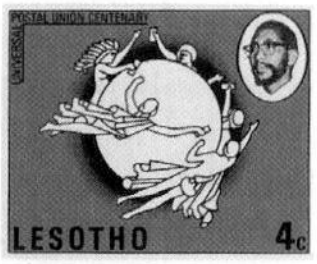

94 U.P.U. Emblem

1974. Centenary of U.P.U.

265	**94**	4c. green and black	10	10
266	-	10c. orange, yellow & black	15	10
267	-	15c. multicoloured	20	60
268	-	20c. multicoloured	45	85

DESIGNS: 10c. Map of airmail routes; 15c. Post Office H.Q., Maseru; 20c. Horseman taking rural mail.

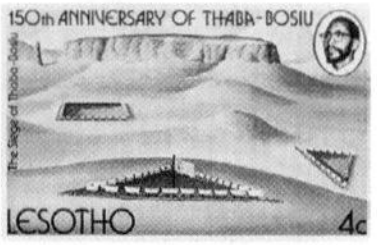

95 Siege of Thaba-Bosiu

1974. 150th Anniv of Siege of Thaba-Bosiu. Multicoloured.

269	4c. Type **95**	10	10
270	5c. The wreath-laying	10	10
271	10c. Moshoeshoe I (vert)	25	10
272	20c. Makoanyane, the warrior (vert)	90	55

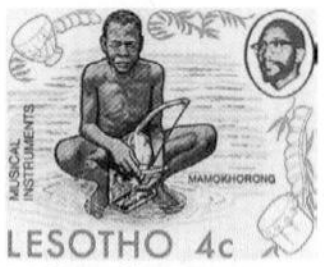

96 Mamokhorong

1974. Basotho Musical Instruments. Multicoloured.

273	4c. Type **96**	10	10
274	10c. Lesiba	10	10
275	15c. Setolotolo	15	20
276	20c. Meropa	15	20
MS277	108×92 mm. Nos. 273/6	1·00	2·00

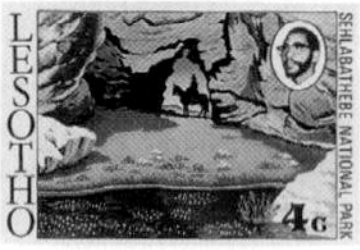

97 Horseman in Rock Archway

1975. Sehlabathebe National Park. Multicoloured.

278	4c. Type **97**	30	10
279	5c. Mountain view through arch	30	10
280	15c. Antelope by stream	50	45
281	20c. Mountains and lake	50	50
282	25c. Tourists by frozen waterfall	65	75

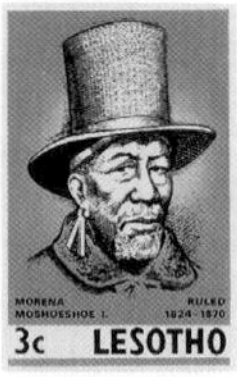

98 Morena Moshoeshoe I

1975. Leaders of Lesotho.

283	**98**	3c. black and blue	10	10
284	-	4c. black and mauve	10	10
285	-	5c. black and pink	10	10
286	-	6c. black and brown	10	10
287	-	10c. black and red	10	10
288	-	15c. black and red	20	20
289	-	20c. black and green	25	30
290	-	25c. black and blue	25	40

DESIGNS: 4c. King Moshoeshoe II; 5c. Morena Letsie I; 6c. Morena Lerotholi; 10c. Morena Letsie II; 15c. Morena Griffith; 20c. Morena Seeiso Griffith Lerotholi; 25c. Mofumahali Mantsebo Seeiso, O.B.E.

The 25c. also commemorates International Women's Year.

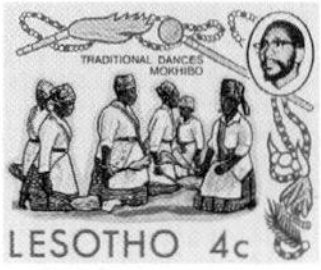

99 Mokhibo Dance

1975. Traditional Dances. Multicoloured.

291	4c. Type **99**	15	10
292	10c. Ndlamo	20	10
293	15c. Baleseli	35	75
294	20c. Mohobelo	40	1·25
MS295	111×100 mm. Nos. 291/4	3·75	3·50

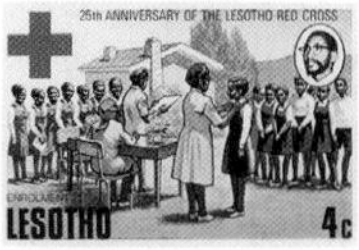

100 Enrolment

1976. 25th Anniv of Lesotho Red Cross. Multicoloured.

296	4c. Type **100**	50	10
297	10c. Medical aid	70	10
298	15c. Rural service	1·00	1·25
299	25c. Relief supplies	1·40	2·50

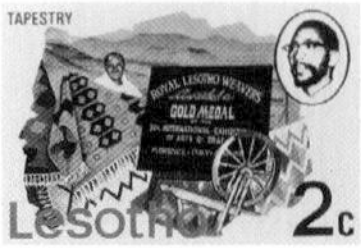

101 Tapestry

1976. Multicoloured.

300	2c. Type **101**	10	35
301	3c. Mosotho horseman	20	30
302	4c. Map of Lesotho	1·50	10
303	5c. Lesotho Brown diamond	75	1·00
304	10c. Lesotho Bank	30	10
305	15c. Lesotho and O.A.U. flags	2·00	1·00
306	25c. Sehlabathebe National Park	60	35
307	40c. Pottery	60	1·00
308	50c. Prehistoric rock art	2·75	2·00
309	1r. King Moshoeshoe II (vert)	60	1·75

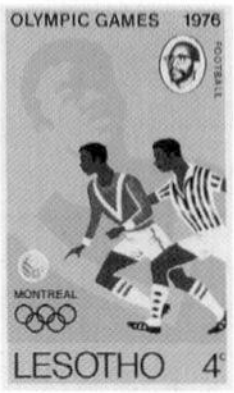

102 Football

1976. Olympic Games, Montreal. Multicoloured.

310	4c. Type **102**	15	10
311	10c. Weightlifting	15	10
312	15c. Boxing	35	35
313	25c. Throwing the discus	50	80

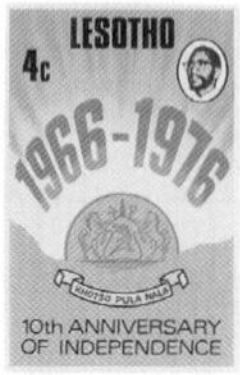

103 "Rising Sun"

1976. Tenth Anniv of Independence. Multicoloured.

314	4c. Type **103**	10	10
315	10c. Open gates	10	10
316	15c. Broken chains	40	20
317	25c. Britten Norman Islander aircraft over hotel	50	35

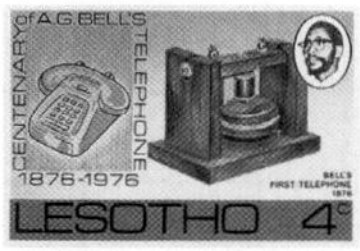

104 Telephones, 1876 and 1976

1976. Centenary of Telephone. Multicoloured.

318	4c. Type **104**	10	10

319	10c.	Early handset and telephone-user, 1976	15	10
320	15c.	Wall telephone and telephone exchange	25	20
321	25c.	Stick telephone and Alexander Graham Bell	45	50

105 "Aloe striatula"

1977. Aloes and Succulents. Multicoloured.

322	3c. Type 105	25	10
323	4c. *Aloe aristata*	25	10
324	5c. *Kniphofia caulescens*	25	10
325	10c. *Euphorbia pulvinata*	35	10
326	15c. *Aloe saponaria*	1·00	30
327	20c. *Caralluma lutea*	1·00	50
328	25c. *Aloe polyphylla*	1·25	70

See also Nos. 347/54.

106 Large-toothed Rock Hyrax

1977. Animals. Multicoloured.

329	4c. Type 106	3·50	30
330	5c. Cape porcupine	3·50	75
331	10c. Zorilla (polecat)	3·50	30
332	15c. Klipspringer	11·00	2·50
333	25c. Chacma baboon	12·00	3·75

107 "Rheumatic Man"

1977. World Rheumatism Year.

334	107	4c. yellow and red	10	10
335	-	10c. blue and deep blue	15	10
336	-	15c. yellow and blue	30	10
337	-	25c. red and black	40	45

DESIGNS—Each show the "Rheumatic Man" as Type 107: 10c. Surrounded by "pain"; 15c. Surrounded by "chain"; 25c. Supporting globe.

108 Small-mouthed Yellowfish

1977. Fish. Multicoloured.

338	4c. Type 108	30	10
339	10c. Mudfish	45	10
340	15c. Rainbow trout	70	35
341	25c. Barnard's mudfish	80	60

1977. No. 198 surch 3.

| 342 | 3c. on 10c. brown and blue | 1·00 | 1·00 |

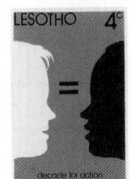

110 Black and White Heads

1977. Decade for Action to Combat Racism.

343	110	4c. black and mauve	10	10
344	-	10c. black and blue	10	10
345	-	15c. black and orange	15	15
346	-	25c. black and green	25	25

DESIGNS: 10c. Jigsaw pieces; 15c. Cogwheels; 25c. Handshake.

1978. Flowers. As T 105. Multicoloured.

| 347 | 2c. *Papaver aculeatum* | 10 | 50 |
| 348 | 3c. *Diascia integerrima* | 10 | 50 |

349	4c. *Helichrysum trilineatum*	10	10
350	5c. *Zaluzianskya maritima*	10	10
351	10c. *Gladiolus natalensis*	15	10
352	15c. *Chironia krebsii*	20	40
353	25c. *Wahlenbergia undulata*	35	1·00
354	40c. *Brunsvigia radulosa*	65	2·00

111 Edward Jenner vaccinating Child

1978. Global Eradication of Smallpox. Multicoloured.

| 355 | 5c. Type 111 | 25 | 35 |
| 356 | 25c. Head of child and W.H.O. emblem | 75 | 90 |

112 Tsoloane Falls

1978. Waterfalls. Multicoloured.

357	4c. Type 112	15	10
358	10c. Qiloane Falls	25	10
359	15c. Tsoelikana Falls	35	60
360	25c. Maletsunyane Falls	55	1·75

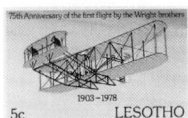

113 Wright Flyer III, 1903

1978. 75th Anniv of First Powered Flight. Multicoloured.

| 361 | 5c. Type 113 | 15 | 30 |
| 362 | 25c. Wilbur and Orville Wright | 40 | 60 |

114 "Orthetrum farinosum"

1978. Insects. Multicoloured.

363	4c. Type 114	10	10
364	10c. *Phymateus viridipes*	20	10
365	15c. *Belonogaster lateritis*	30	55
366	25c. *Sphodromantis gastrica*	50	90

115 Oudehout Branch in Flower

1979. Trees. Multicoloured.

367	4c. Type 115	10	10
368	10c. Wild olive	15	10
369	15c. Blinkblaar	30	80
370	25c. Cape holly	55	1·50

116 Mampharoane

1979. Reptiles. Multicoloured.

371A	4s. Type 116	10	10
372A	10s. Qoaane	20	10
373A	15s. Leupa	30	80
374A	25s. Masumu	60	1·50

117 Basutoland 1933 1d. Stamp

1979. Death Centenary of Sir Rowland Hill.

375	117	4s. multicoloured	10	10
376	-	15s. multicoloured	30	20
377	-	25s. black, orange & bistre	40	30
MS378	118×95 mm. 50s. multicoloured		60	80

DESIGNS: 15s. Basutoland 1962 ½c. new currency definitive; 25s. Penny Black; 50s. 1972 15c. Post Office Centenary commemorative.

118 Detail of painting "Children's Games" by Brueghel

1979. International Year of the Child.

379	118	4s. multicoloured	10	10
380	-	10s. multicoloured	10	10
381	-	15s. multicoloured	15	15
MS382	113×88 mm. 25s. multicoloured (horiz)		55	45

DESIGNS: 10, 15s, 25s. Different details taken from Brueghel's *Children's Games.*

119 Beer Strainer, Broom and Mat

1980. Grasswork. Multicoloured.

383	4s. Type 119	10	10
384	10s. Winnowing basket	10	10
385	15s. Basotho hat	20	40
386	25s. Grain storage	35	65

120 Praise Poet

1980. Centenary of Gun War. Multicoloured.

387	4s. Type 120	15	10
388	5s. Lerotholi, Commander of Basotho Army	15	10
389	10s. Ambush at Qalabane	20	10
390	15s. Snider and Martini-Henry rifles	60	55
391	25s. Map showing main areas of action	70	1·25

121 Olympic Flame, Flags and Kremlin

1980. Olympic Games, Moscow. Multicoloured.

392	25s. Type 121	25	25
393	25s. Doves, flame and flags	25	25
394	25s. Football	25	25
395	25s. Running	25	25
396	25s. Opening ceremony	25	25
MS397	110×85 mm. 1m.40 Ancient and modern athletes carrying Olympic torch		1·10	1·25

101 Tapestry

1980. Nos. 203 and 300/9 surch s or new value.

| 402A | 2s. on 2c. Type 101 | 10 | 30 |

403A	3s. on 3c. Mosotho horseman	20	30
404B	6s. on 4c. Map of Lesotho	1·00	30
406A	40s. on 40c. Pottery	45	50
409A	1m. on 1r. King Moshoeshoe II	80	1·25
410A	5s. on 5c. Lesotho Brown diamond	1·50	10
411B	10s. on 10c. Lesotho Bank	10	10
412A	25s. on 25c. Sehlabathebe National Park	25	30
414A	50s. on 50c. Prehistoric rock art	2·00	55
415B	75s. on 15c. Lesotho and O.A.U. flags	1·50	1·25
417A	2m. on 2r. Statue of King Moshoeshoe I	80	1·60

123 Beer Mug

1980. Pottery. Multicoloured.

418	4s. Type 123	10	10
419	10s. Beer brewing pot	10	10
420	15s. Water pot	15	15
421	25s. Pot shapes	25	30
MS422	150×110 mm. 40s. × 4 Wedgwood plaques of Prince Philip; Queen Elizabeth II; Prince Charles; Princess Anne (each 22×35 mm).		50	90

No. MS422 was issued to commemorate the 250th birth anniversary of Josiah Wedgwood.

124 Queen Elizabeth the Queen Mother with Prince Charles

1980. 80th Birthday of The Queen Mother. Multicoloured.

423	5s. Type 124	25	25
424	10s. The Queen Mother	25	25
425	1m. 1947 Basutoland Royal Visit 2d. stamp (54×43 mm)	90	90

125 Lesotho Evangelical Church, Morija

1980. Christmas. Multicoloured.

426	4s. Type 125	10	10
427	15s. St. Agnes' Anglican Church, Teyateyaneng	10	10
428	25s. Cathedral of Our Lady of Victories, Maseru	15	10
429	75s. University Chapel, Roma	45	50
MS430	110×85 mm. 1m.50 Nativity scene (43×29 mm)		50	80

126 "Voyager" Satellite and Jupiter

1981. Space Exploration. Multicoloured.

431	25c. Type 126	30	25
432	25c. "Voyager" and Saturn	30	25
433	25c. "Voyager" passing Saturn	30	25
434	25c. "Space Shuttle" releasing satellite	30	25
435	25c. "Space Shuttle" launching into space	30	25
MS436	111×85 mm. 1m.40 Saturn		1·40	1·00

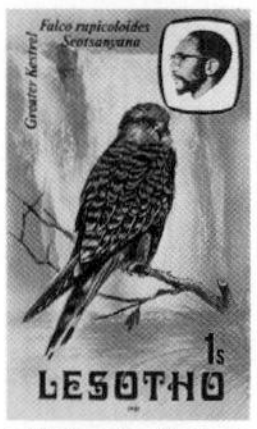

127 Greater Kestrel

1981. Birds. Multicoloured.

437	1s. Type **127**	15	40
438	2s. Speckled pigeon ("Rock Pigeon") (horiz)	15	40
439	3s. South African crowned crane ("Crowned Crane")	20	40
440	5s. Bokmakierie shrike ("Bokmakierie")	20	40
448	1m. Red bishop (horiz)	1·50	75
449	2m. Egyptian goose (horiz)	1·00	1·50
450	5m. Lilac-breasted roller (horiz)	1·25	4·00
504	6s. Cape robin chat ("Cape Robin")	30	10
505	7s. Yellow canary	30	10
506	10s. Red-billed pintail ("Red-billed Teal") (horiz)	30	10
507	25s. Malachite kingfisher	80	30
508	40s. Yellow-tufted malachite sunbird ("Malachite Sunbird") (horiz)	1·00	45
509	60s. Cape longclaw ("Orange-throated Longclaw") (horiz)	1·25	90
510	75s. Hoopoe ("African Hoppoe") (horiz)	1·50	90

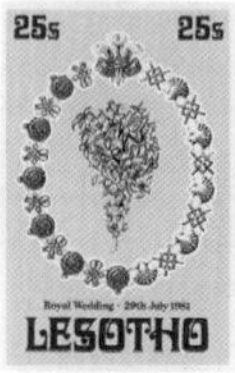

128 Wedding Bouquet from Lesotho

1981. Royal Wedding (1st issue). Multicoloured.

451	25s. Type **128**	10	10
452	50s. Prince Charles riding	20	25
453	75s. Prince Charles and Lady Diana Spencer	30	50

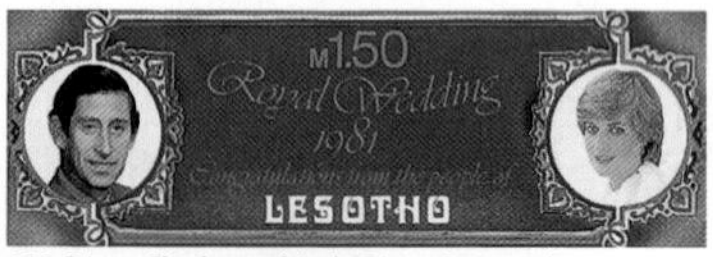

129 Prince Charles and Lady Diana Spencer (image scaled to 57% of original size)

1981. Royal Wedding (2nd issue). Sheet 115×90 mm.

MS454	**129** 1m.50 multicoloured	1·00	1·25

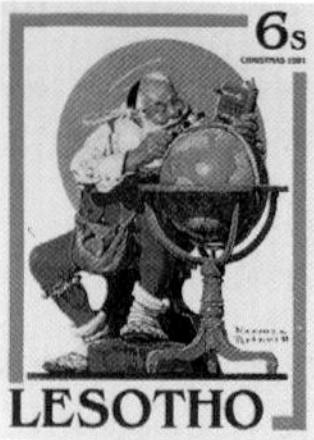

130 "Santa planning his Annual Visit"

1981. Christmas. Paintings by Norman Rockwell. Multicoloured.

455	6s. Type **130**	15	10
456	10s. *Santa reading his Mail*	20	10
457	15s. *The Little Spooners*	25	20
458	20s. *Raleigh Rockwell Travels*	25	25
459	25s. *Ride 'em Cowboy*	25	30
460	60s. *The Discovery*	30	1·00
MS461	111×85 mm. 1m.25 *Mystic Nativity* (48×31 mm)	1·10	1·10

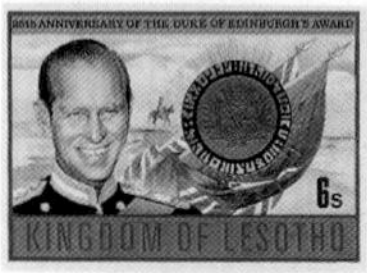

131 Duke of Edinburgh, Award Scheme Emblem and Flags

1981. 25th Anniv of Duke of Edinburgh Award Scheme. Multicoloured.

462	6s. Type **131**	10	10
463	7s. Tree planting	10	10
464	25s. Gardening	25	20
465	40s. Mountain climbing	40	40
466	75s. Award Scheme emblem	70	75
MS467	111×85 mm. 1m.40 Duke of Edinburgh (45×30 mm)	1·25	1·25

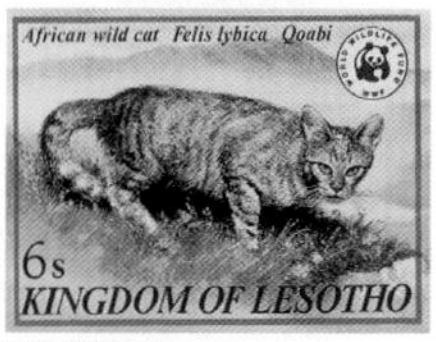

132 Wild Cat

1981. Wildlife. Multicoloured.

468	6s. Type **132**	1·25	30
469	20s. Chacma baboon (44×31 mm)	2·00	70
470	25s. Cape eland	2·50	75
471	40s. Porcupine	3·25	1·75
472	50s. Oribi (44×31 mm)	3·25	1·75
MS473	111×85 mm. 1m.50 Black-backed Jackal (47×31 mm)	2·75	1·90

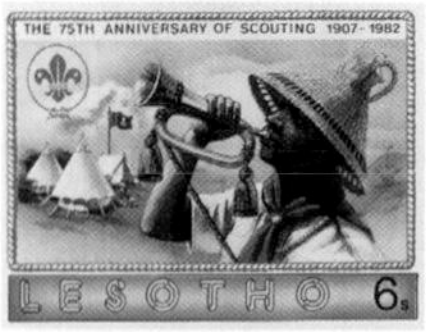

133 Scout Bugler

1982. 75th Anniv of Boy Scout Movement. Multicoloured.

474	6s. Type **133**	30	25
475	30s. Scouts hiking	35	50
476	40s. Scout sketching	40	60
477	50s. Scout with flag	40	65
478	75s. Scouts saluting	45	80
MS479	117×92 mm. 1m.50 Lord Baden-Powell	1·00	2·00

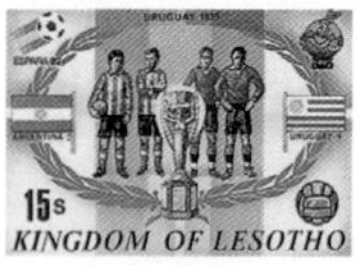

134 Jules Rimet Trophy with Footballers and Flags of 1930 Finalists (Argentina and Uruguay)

1982. World Cup Football Championship, Spain. Each showing Trophy with Players and Flags from Past Finals. Multicoloured.

480	15s. Type **134**	25	25
481	15s. Czechoslovakia and Italy, 1934	25	25
482	15s. Hungary and Italy, 1938	25	25
483	15s. Brazil and Uruguay, 1950	25	25
484	15s. Hungary and W. Germany, 1954	25	25
485	15s. Sweden and Brazil, 1958	25	25
486	15s. Czechoslovakia and Brazil, 1962	25	25
487	15s. W. Germany and England, 1966	25	25
488	15s. Italy and Brazil, 1970	25	25
489	15s. Holland and W. Germany, 1974	25	25
490	15s. Holland and Argentina, 1978	25	25
491	15s. Map of World on footballs	25	25
MS492	118×93 mm. 1m.25 Bernabeu Stadium, Madrid (47×35 mm)	1·10	1·25

Nos. 480/8 show the Jules Rimet Trophy and Nos. 489/91 the World Cup Trophy.

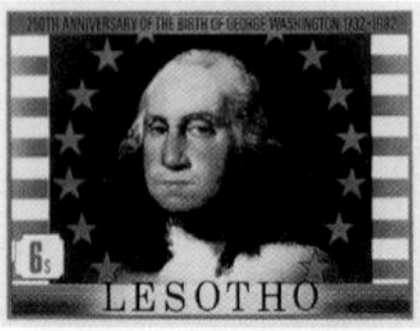

135 Portrait of George Washington

1982. 250th Birth Anniv of George Washington. Multicoloured.

493	6s. Type **135**	10	10
494	7s. Washington with step-children and dog	10	10
495	10s. Washington with Indian chief	15	10
496	25s. Washington with troops	25	30
497	40s. Washington arriving in New York	30	40
498	1m. Washington on parade	75	1·10
MS499	117×92 mm. 1m.25 Washington crossing the Delaware	1·00	1·00

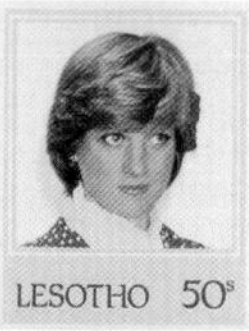

136 Lady Diana Spencer in Tetbury, May 1981

1982. 21st Birthday of Princess of Wales. Multicoloured.

514a	30s. Lesotho coat of arms	40	50
515	50s. Type **136**	50	50
516	75s. Wedding picture at Buckingham Palace	60	80
517	1m. Formal portrait	80	1·25

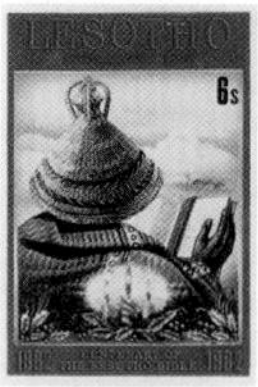

137 Mosotho reading Sesotho Bible

1982. Centenary of Sesotho Bible. Multicoloured.

518	6s. Type **137**	15	20
519	15s. Sesotho bible and Virgin Mary holding infant Jesus	20	25
520	1m. Sesotho bible and Cathedral (62×42 mm)	50	75

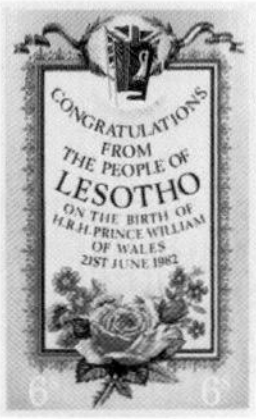

138 Birthday Greetings

1982. Birth of Prince William of Wales. Multicoloured.

521	6s. Type **138**	3·00	4·00
522	60s. Princess Diana and Prince William	60	1·00

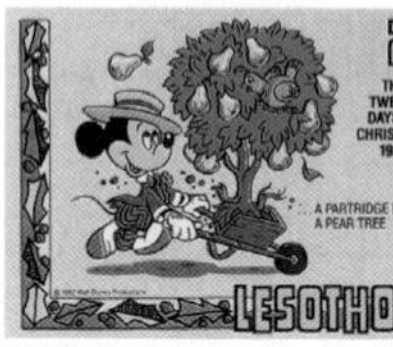

139 "A Partridge in a Pear Tree"

1982. Christmas. "The Twelve Days of Christmas". Walt Disney cartoon characters. Multicoloured.

523	2s. Type **139**	10	10
524	2s. "Two turtle doves"	10	10
525	3s. "Three French hens"	10	10
526	3s. "Four calling birds"	10	10
527	4s. "Five golden rings"	10	10
528	4s. "Six geese a-laying"	10	10
529	75s. "Seven swans a-swimming"	1·40	1·75
530	75s. "Eight maids a-milking"	1·40	1·75
MS531	126×101 mm. 1m.50, "Nine ladies dancing, ten lords a-leaping, eleven pipers piping, twelve drummers drumming"	2·40	2·75

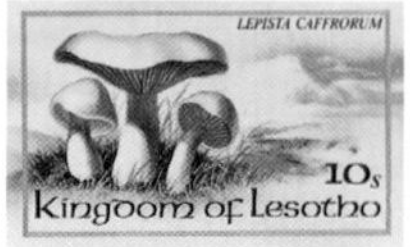

140 "Lepista caffrorum"

1983. Fungi. Multicoloured.

532	10s. Type **140**	15	10
533	30s. *Broomeia congregata*	30	40
534	50s. *Afroboletus luteolus*	60	90
535	75s. *Lentinus tuber-regium*	90	1·40

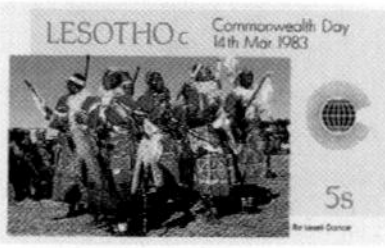

141 Ba-Leseli Dance

1983. Commonwealth Day. Multicoloured.

536	5s. Type **141**	10	10
537	30s. Tapestry weaving	15	30
538	60s. Queen Elizabeth II (vert)	25	65
539	75s. King Moshoeshoe II (vert)	30	80

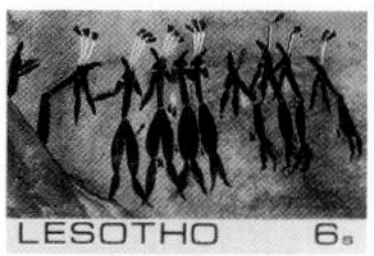

142 "Dancers in a Trance" (rock painting from Ntloana Tsoana)

1983. Rock Paintings. Multicoloured.

540	6s. Type **142**	20	10
541	25s. "Baboons", Sehonghong	45	35
542	60s. "Hunters attacking Mountain Reedbuck", Makhetha	50	1·10
543	75s. "Eland", Lehaha la Likhomo	50	1·60
MS544	166×84 mm. Nos. 540/3 and 10s. "Cattle herding", Sehonghong (52×52 mm)	1·25	3·50

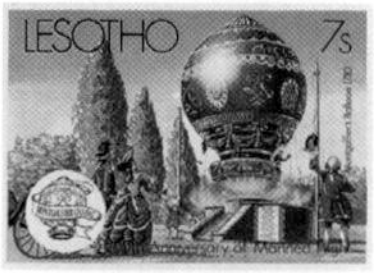

143 Montgolfier Balloon, 1783

1983. Bicentenary of Manned Flight. Multicoloured.

545	7s. Type **143**	15	10
546	30s. Wright brothers and Flyer I	30	40
547	60s. First airmail flight	50	1·25
548	1m. Concorde	2·25	2·50
MS549	180×92 mm. Nos. 545/8 and 6s. Dornier Do-28D Skyservant of Lesotho Airways (60×60 mm)	2·75	2·75

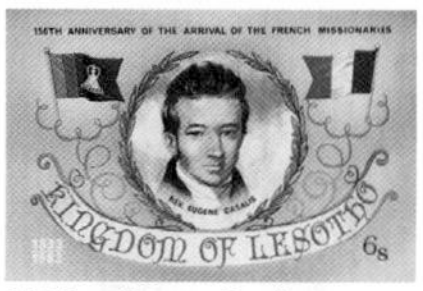

144 Rev. Eugene Casalis

1983. 150th Anniv of Arrival of the French Missionaries. Multicoloured.

550	6s. Type **144**	10	10
551	25s. The founding of Morija	10	10
552	40s. Baptism of Libe	10	15
553	75s. Map of Lesotho	20	25

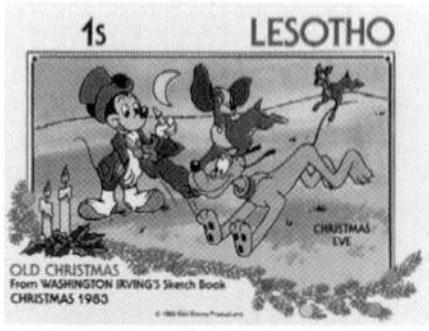

145 Mickey Mouse and Pluto greeted by Friends

1983. Christmas. Walt Disney Characters in scenes from "Old Christmas" (Washington Irving's sketchbook). Multicoloured.

554	1s. Type **145**	10	10
555	2s. Donald Duck and Pluto	10	10
556	3s. Donald Duck with Huey, Dewey and Louie	10	10
557	4s. Goofy, Donald Duck and Mickey Mouse	10	10
558	5s. Goofy holding turkey, Donald Duck and Mickey Mouse	10	10
559	6s. Goofy and Mickey Mouse	10	10
560	75s. Donald and Daisy Duck	2·00	2·40
561	1m. Goofy and Clarabell	2·50	2·75
MS562	132×113 mm. 1m.75 Scrooge McDuck, Pluto and Donald Duck	3·25	4·50

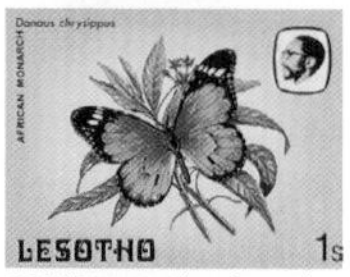

146 "Danaus chrysippus"

1984. Butterflies. Multicoloured.

563	1s. Type **146**	30	60
564	2s. *Aeropetes tulbaghia*	30	60
565	3s. *Colotis evenina*	35	60
566	4s. *Precis oenone*	35	60
567	5s. *Precis hierta*	35	60
568	6s. *Catopsilia florella*	35	10
569	7s. *Phalanta phalantha*	35	10
570	10s. *Acraea stenobea*	40	10
571	15s. *Cynthia cardui*	75	10
572	20s. *Colotis subfasciatus*	75	10

573	30s. *Charaxes jasius*	75	30
574	50s. *Terias brigitta*	75	40
575	60s. *Pontia helice*	75	50
576	75s. *Colotis regina*	75	50
577	1m. *Hypolimnas misippus*	75	1·50
578	5m. *Papilio demodocus*	1·50	7·50

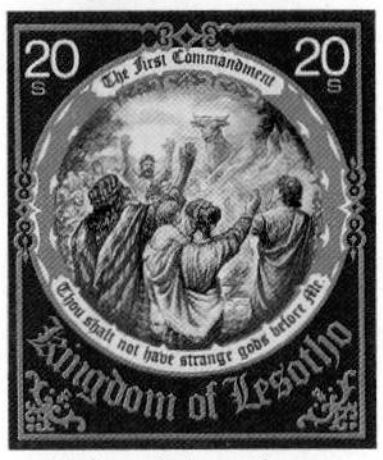

147 "Thou shalt not have Strange Gods before Me"

1984. Easter. The Ten Commandments. Multicoloured.

579	20s. Type **147**	25	30
580	20s. "Thou shalt not take the name of the Lord thy God in vain"	25	30
581	20s. "Remember thou keep holy the Lord's Day"	25	30
582	20s. "Honour thy father and mother"	25	30
583	20s. "Thou shalt not kill"	25	30
584	20s. "Thou shalt not commit adultery"	25	30
585	20s. "Thou shalt not steal"	25	30
586	20s. "Thou shalt not bear false witness against thy neighbour"	25	30
587	20s. "Thou shalt not covet thy neighbour's wife"	25	30
588	20s. "Thou shalt not covet thy neighbour's goods"	25	30
MS589	102×73 mm. 1m.50 Moses with Tablets (45×28 mm)	1·00	2·50

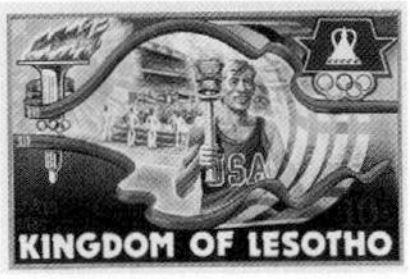

148 Torch Bearer

1984. Olympic Games, Los Angeles. Multicoloured.

590	10s. Type **148**	10	10
591	30s. Horse-riding	10	10
592	50s. Swimming	15	20
593	75s. Basketball	20	25
594	1m. Running	25	30
MS595	101×72 mm. 1m.50 Olympic Flame and flags	1·25	2·75

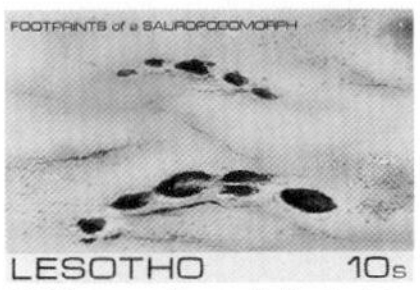

149 Sauropodomorph Footprints

1984. Prehistoric Footprints (2nd series). Multicoloured.

596	10s. Type **149**	30	30
597	30s. Lesothosaurus footprints	40	1·00
598	50s. Footprint of carnivorous dinosaur	50	1·50

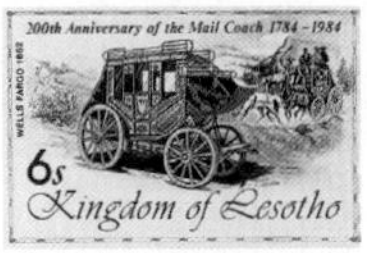

150 Wells Fargo Coach, 1852

1984. "Ausipex" Int Stamp Exhibition, Melbourne. Bicent of First Mail Coach Run. Multicoloured.

599	6s. Type **150**	10	10
600	7s. Basotho mail cart, circa 1900	10	10
601	10s. Bath mail coach, 1784	10	10
602	30s. Cobb coach, 1853	15	15
603	50s. Exhibition logo and Royal Exhibition Buildings, Melbourne (82×25 mm)	50	80
MS604	147×98 mm. 1m.75 G.B. Penny Black, Basutoland 1934 "OFFICIAL" optd 6d. and Western Australia 1854 4d. with frame inverted (82×25 mm)	2·25	3·75

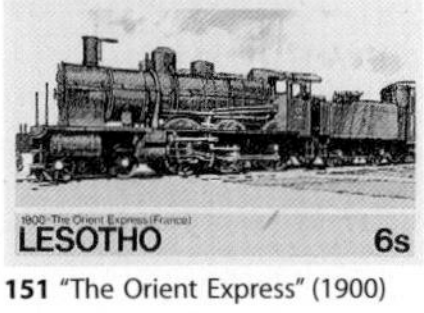

151 "The Orient Express" (1900)

1984. Railways of the World. Multicoloured.

605	6s. Type **151**	30	15
606	15s. Class 05 streamlined steam locomotive No. 001, Germany (1935)	30	30
607	30s. Caledonian Railway steam locomotive *Cardean* (1906)	35	60
608	60s. Atchison, Topeka & Santa Fe *Super Chief* express (1940)	40	1·75
609	1m. L.N.E.R. *Flying Scotsman* (1934)	40	2·00
MS610	108×82 mm. 2m. South African Railways *The Blue Train* (1972)	1·00	2·50

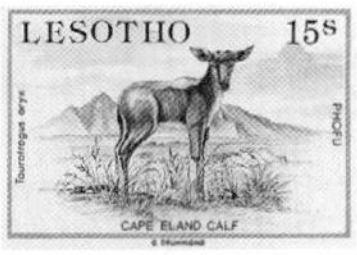

152 Eland Calf

1984. Baby Animals. Multicoloured.

611	15s. Type **152**	35	20
612	20s. Young chacma baboons	35	25
613	30s. Oribi calf	35	40
614	75s. Young Natal red hares	50	1·60
615	1m. Black-backed jackal pups (46×27 mm)	50	2·00

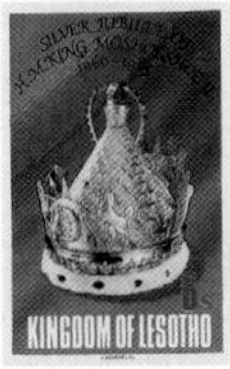

153 Crown of Lesotho

1985. Silver Jubilee of King Moshoeshoe II. Multicoloured.

616	6s. Type **153**	10	10
617	30s. King Moshoeshoe in 1960	20	30
618	75s. King Moshoeshoe in traditional dress, 1985	50	85
619	1m. King Moshoeshoe in uniform, 1985	70	1·25

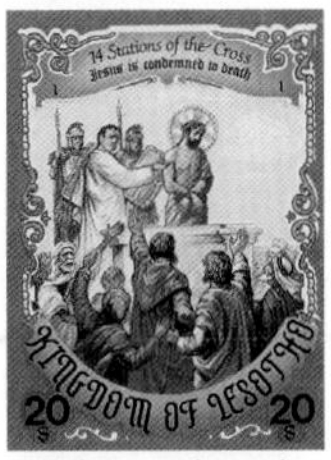

154 Christ condemned to Death

1985. Easter. The Stations of the Cross. Multicoloured.

620	20s. Type **154**	25	35
621	20s. Christ carrying the Cross	25	35
622	20s. Falling for the first time	25	35
623	20s. Christ meets Mary	25	35
624	20s. Simon of Cyrene helping to carry the Cross	25	35
625	20s. Veronica wiping the face of Christ	25	35
626	20s. Christ falling a second time	25	35
627	20s. Consoling the women of Jerusalem	25	35
628	20s. Falling for the third time	25	35
629	20s. Christ being stripped	25	35
630	20s. Christ nailed to the Cross	25	35
631	20s. Dying on the Cross	25	35
632	20s. Christ taken down from the Cross	25	35
633	20s. Christ being laid in the sepulchre	25	35
MS634	138×98 mm. 2m. "The Crucifixion" (Mathias Grunewald)	1·50	3·50

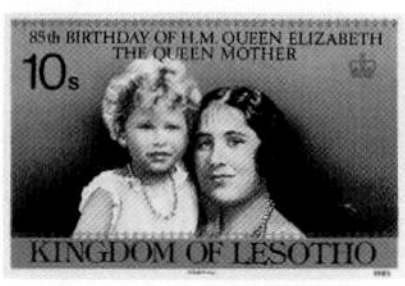

155 Duchess of York with Princess Elizabeth, 1931

1985. Life and Times of Queen Elizabeth the Queen Mother. Multicoloured.

635	10s. Type **155**	25	10
636	30s. The Queen Mother in 1975	70	50
637	60s. Queen Mother with Queen Elizabeth and Princess Margaret, 1980	80	90
638	2m. Four generations of Royal Family at Prince Harry's christening, 1984	1·25	2·50
MS639	139×98 mm. 2m. Queen Elizabeth with the Princess of Wales and her children at Prince Harry's christening (37×50 mm)	2·25	2·75

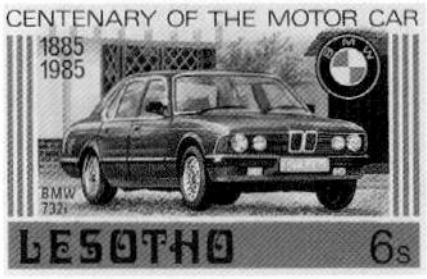

156 B.M.W. "732i"

1985. Century of Motoring. Multicoloured.

640	6s. Type **156**	25	15
641	10s. Ford "Crown Victoria"	35	15
642	30s. Mercedes-Benz "500SE"	75	50
643	90s. Cadillac "Eldorado Biarritz"	1·50	2·50
644	2m. Rolls-Royce "Silver Spirit"	2·00	4·00
MS645	139×98 mm. 2m. Rolls-Royce "Silver Ghost Tourer", 1907 (37×50 mm)	4·00	6·00

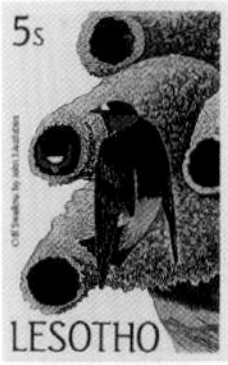

157 American Cliff Swallow

1985. Birth Bicentenary of John J. Audubon (ornithologist). Designs showing original paintings. Multicoloured.

646	5s. Type **157**	40	30
647	6s. Great crested grebe (horiz)	40	30
648	10s. Vesper sparrow ("Vester Sparrow") (horiz)	55	30
649	30s. Common greenshank ("Greenshank") (horiz)	1·25	75
650	60s. Stilt sandpiper (horiz)	1·75	2·75
651	2m. Glossy ibis (horiz)	2·50	6·00

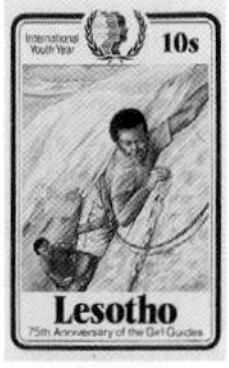

158 Two Youths Rock-climbing

1985. International Youth Year and 75th Anniv of Girl Guide Movement. Multicoloured.

652	10s. Type **158**	20	10
653	30s. Young technician in hospital laboratory	50	40
654	75s. Three guides on parade	1·00	1·25
655	2m. Guide saluting	1·75	3·00
MS656	138×98 mm. 2m. *Olave, Lady Baden-Powell* (Grace Wheatley) (37×50 mm)	2·40	2·75

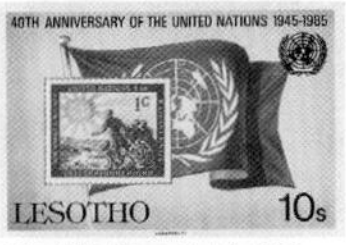

159 U.N. (New York) 1951 1c. Definitive and U.N. Flag

1985. 40th Anniversary of U.N.O.

657	**159**	10s. multicoloured	25	10
658	-	30s. multicoloured	60	35
659	-	50s. multicoloured	95	85
660	-	2m. black and green	5·00	6·50

DESIGNS—VERT: 30s. Ha Sofonia Earth Satellite Station; 2m. Maimonides (physician, philosopher and scholar). HORIZ: 50s. Lesotho Airways Fokker F.27 Friendship at Maseru Airport.

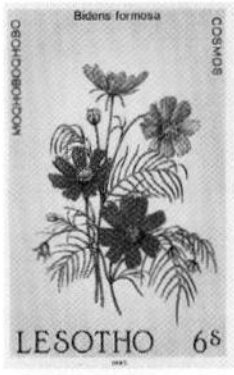

160 Cosmos

1985. Wild Flowers. Multicoloured.

661	6s. Type **160**	40	15
662	10s. Small agapanthus	55	15
663	30s. Pink witchweed	1·10	70
664	60s. Small iris	1·50	2·00
665	90s. Wild geranium or cranesbill	1·75	3·00
666	1m. Large spotted orchid	3·00	5·00

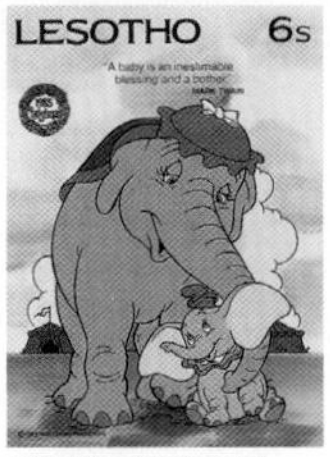

160a Mrs Jumbo and Baby Dumbo

1985. 150th Birth Anniv of Mark Twain. Walt Disney cartoon characters illustrating various Mark Twain quotations. Multicoloured.

667	6s. Type **160a**	50	15
668	50s. Uncle Scrooge and Goofy reading newspaper	1·50	1·00
669	90s. Winnie the Pooh, Tigger, Piglet and Owl	2·00	2·00
670	1m.50 Goofy at ship's wheel	3·00	3·00
MS671	127×102 mm. 1m.25 Mickey Mouse as astronaut	4·75	3·75

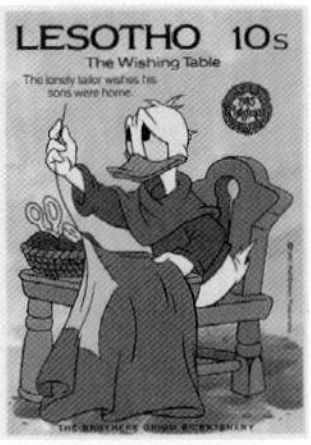

160b Donald Duck as the Tailor

1985. Birth Bicentenaries of Grimm Brothers (folklorists). Walt Disney cartoon characters in scenes from *The Wishing Table*. Multicoloured.

672	10s. Type **160b**	50	20
673	60s. The second son (Dewey) with magic donkey and gold coins	1·50	1·50
674	75s. The eldest son (Huey) with wishing table laden with food	1·75	1·75
675	1m. The innkeeper stealing the third son's (Louie) magic cudgel	2·00	2·75
MS676	127×102 mm. 1m.50 The tailor and eldest son with wishing table	4·75	5·50

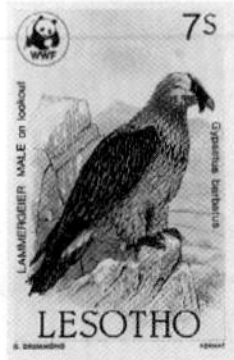

161 Male Lammergeier on Watch

1986. Flora and Fauna of Lesotho. Multicoloured.

677	7s. Type **161**	1·75	65
678	9s. Prickly pear	70	20
679	12s. Stapelia	70	20
680	15s. Pair of lammergeiers	2·50	60
681	35s. Pig's ears	1·10	60
682	50s. Male lammergeier in flight	3·75	2·75
683	1m. Adult and juvenile lammergeiers	3·75	4·75
684	2m. Columnar cereus	3·75	6·50
MS685	125×106 mm. 2m. Verreaux's eagle ("Black Eagle")	8·50	12·00

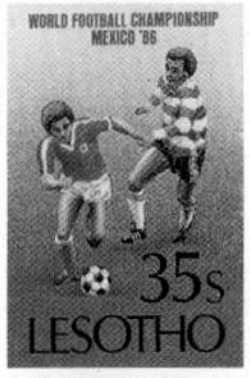

162 Two Players chasing Ball

1986. World Cup Football Championship, Mexico. Multicoloured.

686	35s. Type **162**	1·25	50
687	50s. Goalkeeper saving goal	1·75	1·25
688	1m. Three players chasing ball	3·00	2·75
689	2m. Two players competing for ball	5·00	5·00
MS690	104×74 mm. 3m. Player heading ball	9·00	8·50

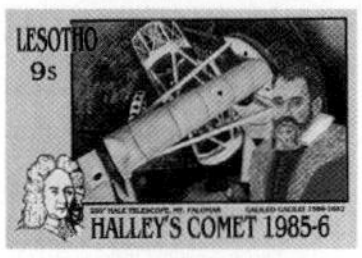

162a Galileo and 200 inch Hale Telescope at Mount Palomar Observatory, California

1986. Appearance of Halley's Comet. Multicoloured.

691	9s. Type **162a**	75	15
692	15s. Halley's Comet and "Pioneer Venus 2" spacecraft	90	20
693	70s. Halley's Comet of 684 A.D. (from *Nuremberg Chronicle*, 1493)	1·60	1·40
694	3m. Comet and landing of William the Conqueror, 1066	4·25	5·50
MS695	101×70 mm. 4m. Halley's Comet over Lesotho	6·50	7·00

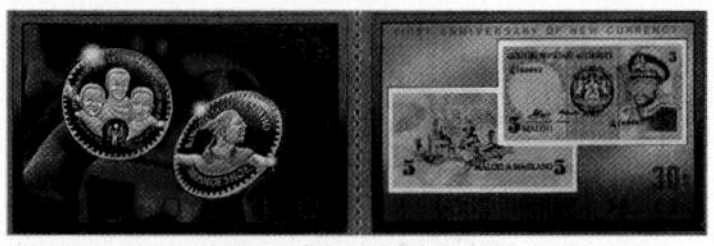

163 International Year of the Child Gold Coin (image scaled to 52% of original size)

1986. First Anniv of New Currency (1980). Multicoloured.

696	30s. Type **163**	4·00	6·50
697	30s. Five maloti banknote	4·00	6·50
698	30s. Fifty lisente coin	4·00	6·50
699	30s. Ten maloti banknote	4·00	6·50
700	30s. One sente coin	4·00	6·50

These stamps were prepared in 1980, but were not issued at that time.

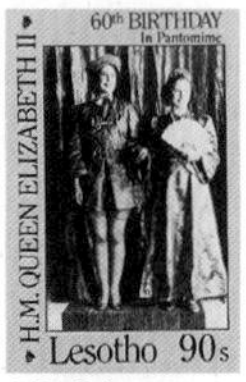

163a Princess Elizabeth in Pantomime

1986. 60th Birthday of Queen Elizabeth II.

701	**163a**	90s. black and yellow	50	60
702	-	1m. multicoloured	55	65
703	-	2m. multicoloured	90	1·40
MS704		119×85 mm. 4m. black and grey-brown	1·75	3·25

DESIGNS: 1m. Queen at Windsor Horse Show, 1971; 2m. At Royal Festival Hall, 1971; 4m. Princess Elizabeth in 1934.

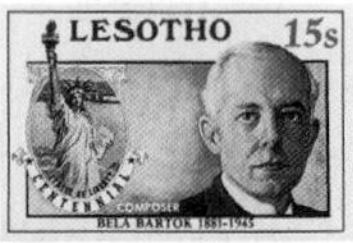

163b Statue of Liberty and Bela Bartok (composer)

1986. Centenary of Statue of Liberty. Immigrants to the U.S.A. Multicoloured.

705	15s. Type **163b**	85	30
706	35s. Felix Adler (philosopher)	85	30
707	1m. Victor Herbert (composer)	3·50	2·00
708	3m. David Niven (actor)	4·50	4·25
MS709	103×74 mm. 3m. Statue of Liberty (vert)	3·50	5·00

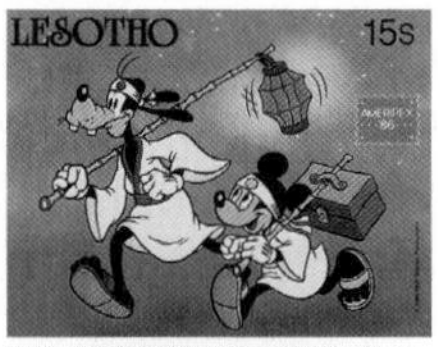

163c Mickey Mouse and Goofy as Japanese Mail Runners

1986. "Ameripex" International Stamp Exhibition, Chicago. Walt Disney cartoon characters delivering mail. Multicoloured.

710	15s. Type **163c**	80	20
711	35s. Mickey Mouse and Pluto with mail sledge	1·25	30
712	1m. Goofy as postman riding Harley-Davidson motorcycle	2·50	2·75
713	2m. Donald Duck operating railway mailbag apparatus	2·75	4·00
MS714	127×101 mm. 4m. Goofy driving mail to aircraft	6·50	7·00

1986. Various stamps surch. (a) On Nos. 437 etc. (Birds).

729	9s. on 5s. Bokmakierie shrike	75	20
715	9s. on 10s. Red-billed pintail (horiz)	4·00	1·25
716	15s. on 1s. Type **127**	8·00	3·00
717	15s. on 2s. Speckled pigeon (horiz)	4·00	4·50
718	15s. on 5s. Bokmakierie shrike	3·00	35
719	15s. on 60s. Cape longclaw (horiz)	20	10
730	16s. on 25s. Malachite kingfisher	3·50	1·00
731	35s. on 25s. Malachite kingfisher	2·25	60
721	35s. on 75s. Hoopoe	22·00	16·00

(b) On Nos. 563 etc (Butterflies).

722	9s. on 30s. *Charaxes jasius*	15	10
723	9s. on 60s. *Pontia helice*	3·25	4·00
724	15s. on 1s. Type **146**	2·00	2·25
725	15s. on 2s. *Aeropetes tulbaghia*	20	20
726	15s. on 3s. *Colotis evenina*	20	20
727	15s. on 5s. *Precis hierta*	20	20
732	20s. on 4s. *Precis oenone*	20	10
728	35s. on 75s. *Colotis regina*	35	35
733	40s. on 7s. *Phalanta phalantha*	20	20

(c) No. 722 further surch.

734	3s. on 9s. on 30s. *Charaxes jasius*	1·50	1·50
735	7s. on 9s. on 30s. *Charaxes jasius*	1·75	1·50

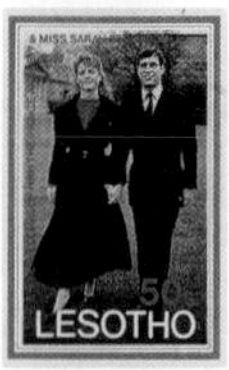

170a Prince Andrew and Miss Sarah Ferguson

1986. Royal Wedding. Multicoloured.

736	50s. Type **170a**	40	40
737	1m. Prince Andrew	70	80
738	3m. Prince Andrew piloting helicopter	2·75	2·25
MS739	88×88 mm. 4m. Prince Andrew and Miss Sarah Ferguson (different)	3·50	4·50

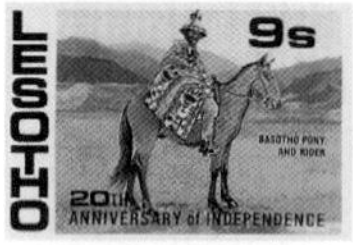

171 Basotho Pony and Rider

1986. 20th Anniv of Independence. Multicoloured.

740	9s. Type **171**	40	10
741	15s. Basotho woman spinning mohair	40	15
742	35s. Crossing river by rowing boat	50	30
743	3m. Thaba Tseka Post Office	1·00	3·00
MS744	109×78 mm. 4m. King Moshoeshoe I	4·75	8·00

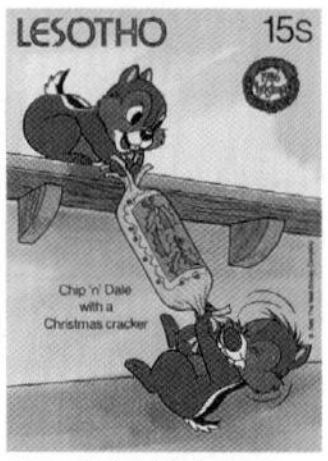

171a Chip'n' Dale pulling Christmas Cracker

1986. Christmas. Walt Disney cartoon characters. Multicoloured.

745	15s. Type **171a**	80	20
746	35s. Mickey and Minnie Mouse	1·10	30
747	1m. Pluto pulling Christmas taffy	1·90	2·75
748	2m. Aunt Matilda baking	2·25	4·00
MS749	126×102 mm. 5m. Huey and Dewey with gingerbread house	5·50	7·00

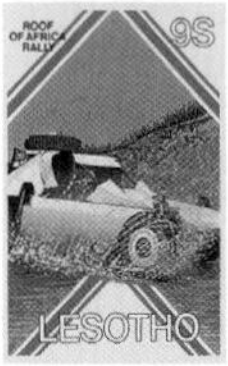

172 Rally Car

1987. Roof of Africa Motor Rally. Multicoloured.

750	9s. Type **172**	30	10
751	15s. Motorcyclist	35	15
752	35s. Motorcyclist (different)	55	35
753	4m. Rally car (different)	3·00	5·00

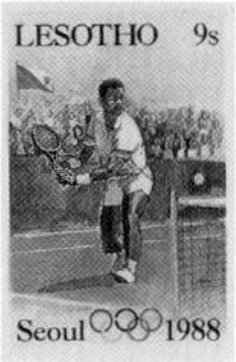

173 Lawn Tennis

1987. Olympic Games, Seoul (1988) (1st issue). Multicoloured.

754	9s. Type **173**	70	10
755	15s. Judo	70	15
756	20s. Athletics	75	20
757	35s. Boxing	85	30
758	1m. Diving	1·10	1·75
759	3m. Ten-pin bowling	2·75	5·50
MS760	Two sheets, each 75×105 mm. (a) 2m. Lawn tennis (different). (b) 4m. Football. Set of 2 sheets	6·00	5·00

See also Nos. 838/41.

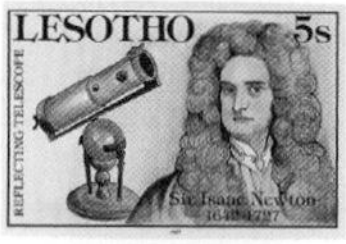

174 Isaac Newton and Reflecting Telescope

1987. Great Scientific Discoveries. Multicoloured.

761	5s. Type **174**	30	10
762	9s. Alexander Graham Bell and first telephone	30	15
763	75s. Robert Goddard and liquid fuel rocket	80	75
764	4m. Chuck Yeager and Bell XS-1 rocket plane	2·75	4·50
MS765	98×68 mm. 4m. "Mariner 10" spacecraft	2·75	3·00

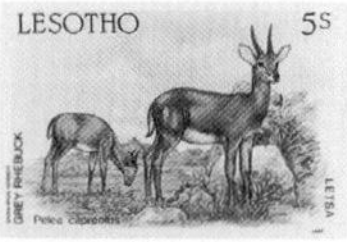

175 Grey Rhebuck

1987. Flora and Fauna. Multicoloured.

766	5s. Type **175**	40	15
767	9s. Cape clawless otter	40	15
768	15s. Cape grey mongoose	55	20
769	20s. Free State daisy (vert)	60	20
770	35s. River bells (vert)	75	30
771	1m. Turkey flower (vert)	1·75	2·50
772	2m. Sweet briar (vert)	2·25	3·75
773	3m. Mountain reedbuck	2·75	5·00
MS774	Two sheets, each 114×98 mm. (a) 2m. Pig-Lily (vert). (b) 4m. Cape Wildebeest	6·00	10·00

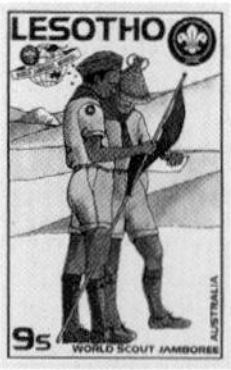

176 Scouts hiking

1987. World Scout Jamboree, Australia. Multicoloured.

775	9s. Type **176**	60	20
776	15s. Scouts playing football	65	20
777	35s. Kangaroos	80	50
778	75s. Scout saluting	1·75	1·25
779	4m. Australian scout windsurfing	3·75	6·50
MS780	96×66 mm. 4m. Outline map and flag of Australia	3·25	4·00

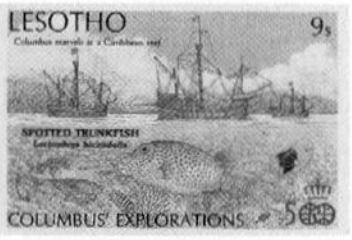

177 Spotted Trunkfish and Columbus's Fleet

1987. 500th Anniv (1992) of Discovery of America by Columbus. Multicoloured.

781	9s. Type **177**	65	20
782	15s. Green turtle and ships	80	20
783	35s. Columbus watching common dolphins from ship	1·00	40
784	5m. White-tailed tropic bird and fleet at sea	6·50	8·00
MS785	105×76 mm. 4m. *Santa Maria* and Cuban Amazon in flight	5·50	4·00

No. 782 is inscribed "Carribbean" in error.

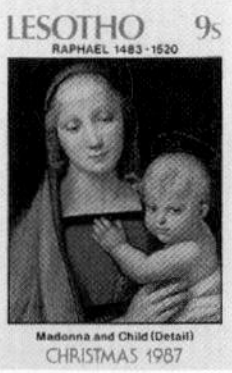

178 "Madonna and Child" (detail)

1987. Christmas. Paintings by Raphael. Multicoloured.

786	9s. Type **178**	30	10
787	15s. *Marriage of the Virgin*	45	15
788	35s. *Coronation of the Virgin* (detail)	90	40
789	90s. *Madonna of the Chair*	2·00	3·50
MS790	75×100 mm. 3m. *Madonna and Child enthroned with Five Saints* (detail)	3·00	3·00

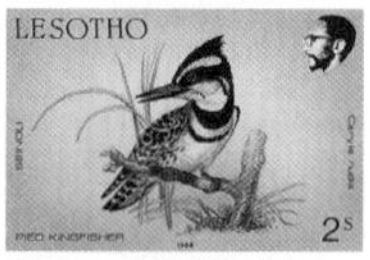

179 Lesser Pied Kingfisher

1988. Birds. Multicoloured.

791	2s. Type **179**	20	30
792	3s. Three-banded plover	20	30
793	5s. Spur-winged goose	20	30
794	10s. Clapper lark	20	20
795	12s. Red-eyed bulbul	30	10
796	16s. Cape weaver	30	10
797	20s. Paradise sparrow ("Red-headed Finch")	30	10
798	30s. Mountain wheater ("Mountain Chat")	35	20
799	40s. Common stonechat ("Stone Chate")	40	20
800	55s. Pied barbet	50	25
801	60s. Red-shouldered glossy starling	55	50
802	75s. Cape sparrow	60	60
803	1m. Cattle egret	60	80
804	3m. Giant kingfisher	90	2·50
805	10m. Helmeted guineafowl	1·90	7·00

1988. Royal Ruby Wedding. Nos. 701/3 optd **40TH WEDDING ANNIVERSARY H.M. QUEEN ELIZABETH II H.R.H. THE DUKE OF EDINBURGH**.

806	90s. black and yellow	90	65
807	1m. multicoloured	1·00	80
808	2m. multicoloured	1·75	1·40
MS809	119×85 mm. 4m. black and grey-brown	3·25	2·75

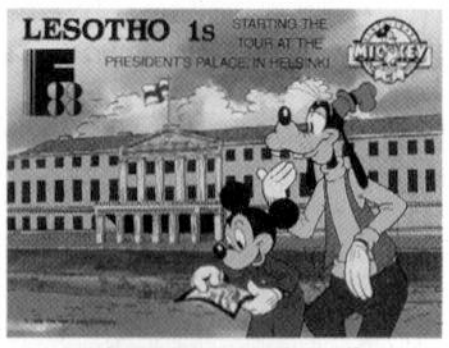

181 Mickey Mouse and Goofy outside Presidential Palace, Helsinki

1988. "Finlandia '88" International Stamp Exhibition, Helsinki. Designs showing Walt Disney cartoon characters in Finland. Multicoloured.

810	1s. Type **181**	10	10
811	2s. Goofy and Mickey Mouse in sauna	10	10
812	3s. Goofy and Mickey Mouse fishing in lake	10	10
813	4s. Mickey and Minnie Mouse and Finlandia Hall, Helsinki	10	10
814	5s. Mickey Mouse photographing Goofy at Sibelius Monument, Helsinki	10	10
815	10s. Mickey Mouse and Goofy pony trekking	10	10
816	3m. Goofy, Mickey and Minnie Mouse at Helsinki Olympic Stadium	4·50	3·00
817	5m. Mickey Mouse and Goofy meeting Santa at Arctic Circle	5·50	4·00
MS818	Two sheets, each 127×102 mm. (a) 4m. Mickey Mouse and nephew as Lapps. (b) 4m. Daisy Duck, Goofy, Mickey and Minnie Mouse by fountain, Helsinki. Set of 2 sheets	5·50	7·00

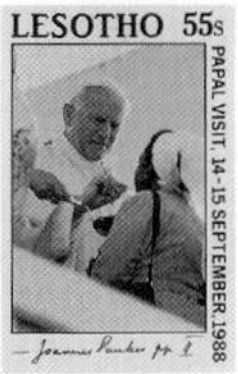

182 Pope John Paul II giving Communion

1988. Visit of Pope John Paul II. Multicoloured.

819	55s. Type **182**	40	25
820	2m. Pope leading procession	1·25	1·50
821	3m. Pope at airport	1·75	2·00
822	4m. Pope John Paul II	2·25	2·75
MS823	98×79 mm. 5m. Archbishop Morapeli (horiz)	5·00	4·50

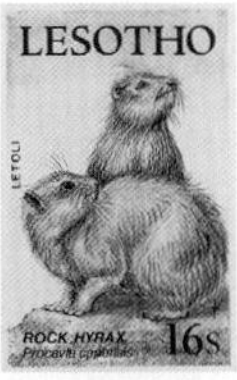

183 Large-toothed Rock Hyrax

1988. Small Mammals of Lesotho. Multicoloured.

824	16s. Type **183**	55	15
825	40s. Ratel and black-throated honey guide (bird)	2·00	55
826	75s. Small-spotted genet	1·50	85
827	3m. Yellow mongoose	3·25	5·50
MS828	110×78 mm. 4m. Meerkat	3·75	4·00

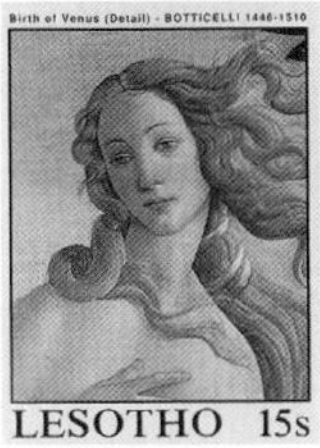

184 "Birth of Venus" (detail) (Botticelli)

1988. Famous Paintings. Multicoloured.

829	15s. Type **184**	30	15
830	25s. *View of Toledo* (El Greco)	35	20
831	40s. *Maids of Honour* (detail) (Velasquez)	45	25
832	50s. *The Fifer* (Manet)	55	30
833	55s. *Starry Night* (detail) (Van Gogh)	55	30
834	75s. *Prima Ballerina* (Degas)	70	70
835	2m. *Bridge over Water Lilies* (Monet)	1·75	2·25
836	3m. *Guernica* (detail) (Picasso)	1·75	2·75
MS837	Two sheets, each 110×95 mm. (a) 4m. *The Presentation of the Virgin in the Temple* (Titian). (b) 4m. *The Miracle of the Newborn Infant* (Titian)	4·00	4·50

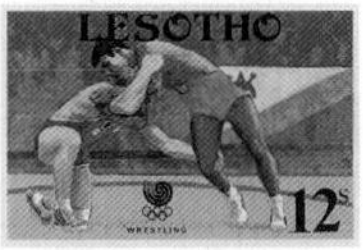

185 Wrestling

1988. Olympic Games, Seoul (2nd series). Multicoloured.

838	12s. Type **185**	10	10
839	16s. Show jumping (vert)	10	10
840	55s. Shooting	20	30
841	3m.50 As 16s. (vert)	1·40	2·00
MS842	108×77 mm. 4m. Olympic flame (vert)	2·75	3·50

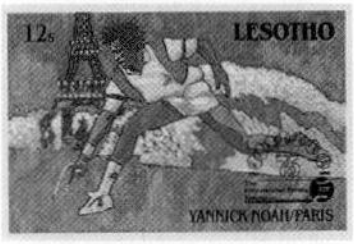

186 Yannick Noah and Eiffel Tower, Paris

1988. 75th Anniv of Int Tennis Federation. Multicoloured.

843	12s. Type **186**	60	25
844	20s. Rod Laver and Sydney Harbour Bridge and Opera House	1·75	30
845	30s. Ivan Lendl and Prague	65	25
846	65s. Jimmy Connors and Tokyo (vert)	80	40
847	1m. Arthur Ashe and Barcelona (vert)	1·25	60
848	1m.55 Althea Gibson and New York (vert)	1·25	90
849	2m. Chris Evert and Vienna (vert)	1·50	1·25
850	2m.40 Boris Becker and Houses of Parliament, London (vert)	1·75	1·75
851	3m. Martina Navratilova and Golden Gate Bridge, San Francisco	2·00	2·00
MS852	98×72 mm. 4m. Steffi Graf and Berlin	3·00	3·75

No. 844 is inscribed "SIDNEY" in error.

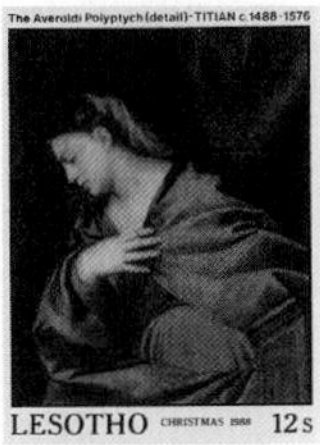

186a "The Averoldi Polyptych" (detail)

1988. Christmas. 500th Birth Anniv of Titian (artist). Multicoloured.

853	12s. Type **186a**	20	10
854	20s. *Christ and the Adulteress* (detail)	20	10
855	35s. *Christ and the Adulteress* (different detail)	30	20
856	45s. *Angel of the Annunciation*	40	30
857	65s. *Saint Dominic*	55	50
858	1m. *The Vendramin Family* (detail)	75	80
859	2m. *Mary Magdalen*	1·25	1·75
860	3m. *The Tribute Money*	1·75	2·50
MS861	(a) 94×110 mm. 5m. *Mater Dolorosa*. (b) 110×94 mm. 5m.*Christ and the Woman taken in Adultery* (horiz)	6·00	8·00

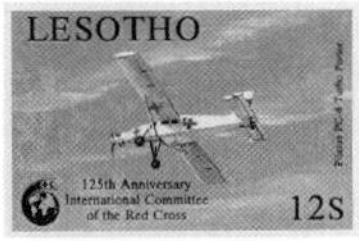

187 Pilatus PC-6 Turbo Porter

1989. 125th Anniv of International Red Cross. Aircraft. Multicoloured.

862	12s. Type **187**	70	20
863	20s. Unloading medical supplies from Cessna Caravan I	1·00	25
864	55s. de Havilland D.H.C.6 Twin Otter 200/300	1·40	50
865	3m. Douglas DC-3	3·00	3·75
MS866	109×80 mm. 4m. Red Cross logo and Douglas DC-3 (vert)	7·00	4·00

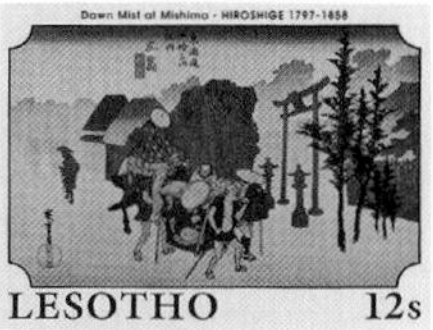

187a "Dawn Mist at Mishima"

1989. Japanese Art. Paintings by Hiroshige. Multicoloured.

867	12s. Type **187a**	30	10
868	16s. *Night Snow at Kambara*	35	10
869	20s. *Wayside Inn at Mariko Station*	35	10
870	35s. *Shower at Shono*	55	10
871	55s. *Snowfall on the Kisokaido near Oi*	65	40
872	1m. *Autumn Moon at Seba*	85	85
873	3m.20 *Evening Moon at Ryogoku Bridge*	2·00	3·00
874	5m. *Cherry Blossoms at Arashiyama*	2·25	3·75
MS875	Two sheets, each 102×76 mm. (a) 4m. *Listening to the Singing Insects at Dokanyama*. (b) 4m. *Moonlight, Nagakubo*	6·00	7·50

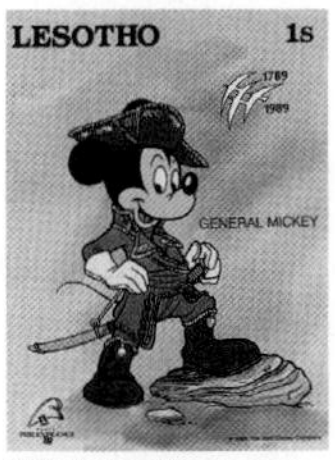

188 Mickey Mouse as General

1989. "Philexfrance 89" International Stamp Exhibition, Paris. Designs showing Walt Disney cartoon characters in French military uniforms of the Revolutionary period. Multicoloured.

876	1s. Type **188**	10	10
877	2s. Ludwig von Drake as infantryman	10	10
878	3s. Goofy as grenadier	10	10
879	4s. Horace Horsecollar as cavalryman	10	10
880	5s. Pete as hussar	10	10
881	10s. Donald Duck as marine	10	10
882	3m. Gyro Gearloose as National Guard	3·25	3·25
883	5m. Scrooge McDuck as admiral	4·00	4·25
MS884	Two sheets, each 127×102 mm. (a) 4m. Mickey and Minnie Mouse as King Louis XVI and Marie Antoinette with Goofy as a National Guard (horiz). (b) 4m. Mickey Mouse as drummer. Set of 2 sheets	7·50	9·00

No. 879 is inscribed "CALVARYMAN" in error.

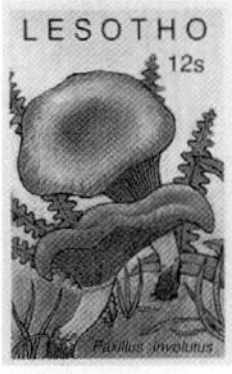

189 "Paxillus involutus"

1989. Fungi. Multicoloured.

900	12s. Type **189**	20	10
901	16s. *Ganoderma applanatum*	20	15
902	55s. *Suillus granulatus*	45	35
903	5m. *Stereum hirsutum*	3·25	4·50
MS904	96×69 mm. 4m. *Scleroderma cepa* ("flavidum")	5·00	5·50

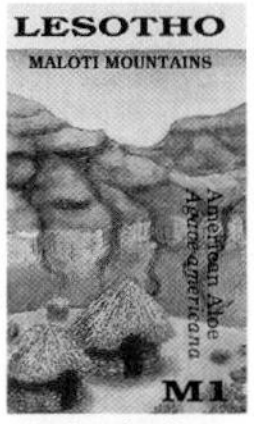

190 Sesotho Huts

1989. Maloti Mountains. Multicoloured.

905	1m. Type **190**	70	1·00
906	1m. American aloe and mountains	70	1·00
907	1m. River valley with waterfall	70	1·00
908	1m. Sesotho tribesman on ledge	70	1·00
MS909	86×117 mm. 4m. Spiral Aloe	3·00	4·00

Nos. 905/8 were printed together, se-tenant, forming a composite design.

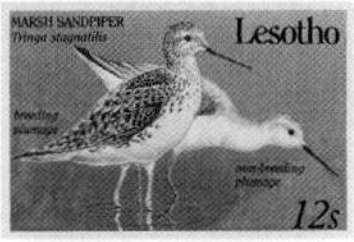

191 Marsh Sandpiper

1989. Migrant Birds. Multicoloured.

910	12s. Type **191**	80	30
911	65s. Little stint	1·50	70
912	1m. Ringed plover	2·00	1·50
913	4m. Curlew sandpiper	3·50	5·50
MS914	97×69 mm. 5m. Ruff (vert)	9·00	9·50

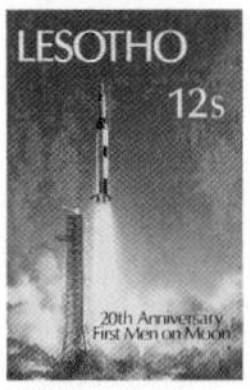

192 Launch of "Apollo 11"

1989. 20th Anniv of First Manned Landing on Moon. Multicoloured.

915	12s. Type **192**	25	10
916	16s. Lunar module "Eagle" landing on Moon (horiz)	25	15
917	40s. Neil Armstrong leaving "Eagle"	45	25
918	55s. Edwin Aldrin on Moon (horiz)	50	30
919	1m. Aldrin performing scientific experiment (horiz)	85	85
920	2m. "Eagle" leaving Moon (horiz)	1·50	1·75
921	3m. Command module "Columbia" in Moon orbit (horiz)	2·00	2·25
922	4m. Command module on parachutes	2·50	2·75
MS923	81×111 mm. 5m. Astronaut on Moon	5·50	6·00

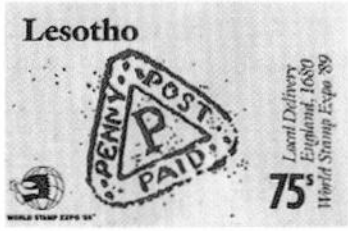

193 English Penny Post Paid Mark, 1680

1989. "World Stamp Expo '89" International Stamp Exhibition, Washington (1st issue). Stamps and Postmarks.

924	**193**	75s. red, black and stone	80	80
925	-	75s. black, grey and red	80	80
926	-	75s. violet, black & brown	80	80
927	-	75s. brown, black and light brown	80	80
928	-	75s. black and yellow	80	80
929	-	75s. multicoloured	80	80
930	-	75s. black and lilac	80	80
931	-	75s. black, red and brown	80	80
932	-	75s. red, black and yellow	80	80

DESIGNS: No. 925, German postal seal and feather, 1807; 926, British Post Office in Crete 1898 20pa. stamp; 927, Bermuda 1848 Perot 1d. provisional; 928, U.S.A. Pony Express cancellation, 1860; 929, Finland 1856 5k. stamp; 930, Fiji 1870 "Fiji Times" 1d. stamp, 1870; 931, Sweden newspaper wrapper handstamp, 1823; 932, Bhor 1879 ½a. stamp.

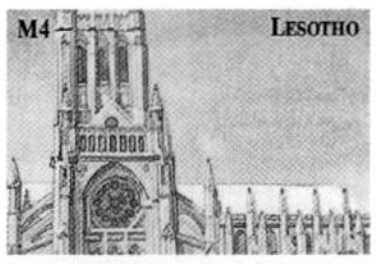

193a Cathedral Church of St. Peter and St. Paul, Washington

1989. "World Stamp Expo '89" International Stamp Exhibition, Washington (2nd issue). Sheet 78×61 mm.

MS933	**193a** 4m. multicoloured	2·50	3·00

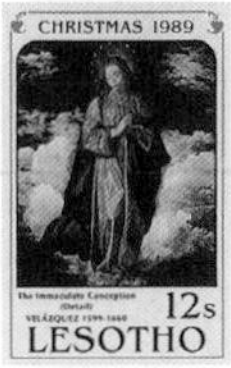

193b "The Immaculate Conception"

1989. Christmas. Paintings by Velazquez. Multicoloured.

934	12s. Type **193b**	10	10
935	20s. *St. Anthony Abbot and St. Paul the Hermit*	15	10
936	35s. *St. Thomas the Apostle*	25	25
937	55s. *Christ in the House of Martha and Mary*	35	35
938	1m. *St. John writing The Apocalypse on Patmos*	60	75
939	3m. *The Virgin presenting the Chasuble to St. Ildephonsus*	1·60	2·25
940	4m. *The Adoration of the Magi*	2·00	2·75
MS941	71×96 mm. 5m. *The Coronation of the Virgin*	7·00	8·00

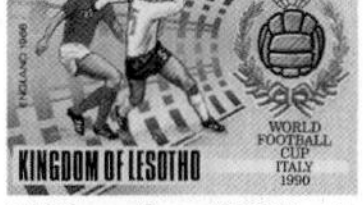

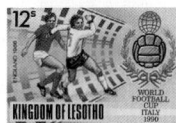

194 Scene from 1966 World Cup Final, England

1989. World Cup Football Championship, Italy. Scenes from past finals. Multicoloured.

942	12s. Type **194**	50	10
943	16s. 1970 final, Mexico	50	15
944	55s. 1974 final, West Germany	1·00	40
945	5m. 1982 final, Spain	3·75	5·50
MS946	106×85 mm. 4m. Player's legs and symbolic football	6·00	7·00

1990. No. 889 and 798/9 surch **16 s.**

948	16s. on 12s. Red-eyed bulbul	2·25	20
948e	16s. on 30s. Common wheater	1·00	15
948f	16s. on 40s. Common stonechat	1·00	15

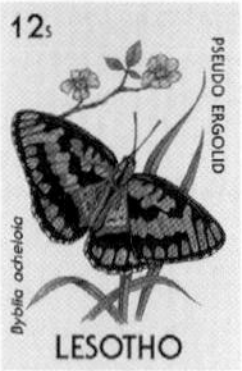

197 "Byblia anvatara"

1990. Butterflies. Multicoloured.

949	12s. Type **197**	80	15
950	16s. *Cynthia cardui*	90	15
951	55s. *Precis oenone*	1·40	40
952	65s. *Pseudacraea boisduvali*	1·40	65
953	1m. *Precis orithya*	2·25	1·25
954	2m. *Precis sophia*	3·25	2·50
955	3m. *Danaus chrysippus*	4·25	4·25
956	4m. *Druryia antimachus*	5·00	6·50
MS957	105×70 mm. 5m. *Papilio demodocus*	8·50	10·00

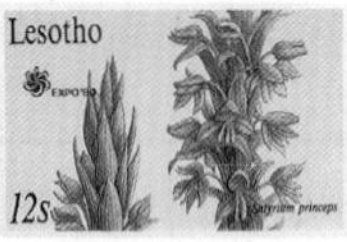

198 "Satyrium princeps"

1990. "EXPO 90" International Garden and Greenery Exhibition, Osaka. Local Orchids. Multicoloured.

958	12s. Type **198**	55	15
959	16s. *Huttonaea pulchra*	60	15
960	55s. *Herschelia graminifolia*	1·25	30
961	1m. *Ansellia gigantea*	1·75	75
962	1m.55 *Polystachya pubescens*	2·00	1·75
963	2m.40 *Penthea filicornis*	2·00	2·25
964	3m. *Disperis capensis*	2·25	3·25
965	4m. *Disa uniflora*	3·00	4·00
MS966	95×68 mm. 5m. *Stenoglottis longifolia*	7·50	9·00

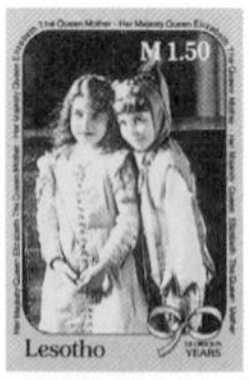

198a Lady Elizabeth Bowes-Lyon and Brother in Fancy Dress

1990. 90th Birthday of Queen Elizabeth the Queen Mother.

967	**198a**	1m.50 black and mauve	1·25	1·25
968	-	1m.50 black and mauve	1·25	1·25
969	-	1m.50 black and mauve	1·25	1·25
MS970		90×75 mm. 5m. brown, black and mauve	4·25	4·25

DESIGNS: 12s. No. 968, Lady Elizabeth Bowes-Lyon in evening dress; 969, Lady Elizabeth Bowes-Lyon wearing hat; **MS**970, Lady Elizabeth Bowes-Lyon as a child.

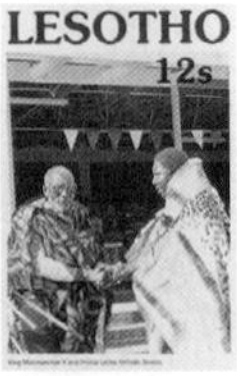

199 King Moshoeshoe II and Prince Mohato wearing Seana-Marena Blankets

1990. Traditional Blankets. Multicoloured.

971	12s. Type **199**	10	10
972	16s. Prince Mohato wearing Seana-Marena blanket	10	10
973	1m. Pope John Paul II wearing Seana-Marena blanket	1·75	1·10
974	3m. Basotho horsemen wearing Matlama blankets	2·00	3·00
MS975	85×104 mm. 5m. Pope John Paul II wearing hat and Seana-Marena blanket (horiz)	4·50	4·75

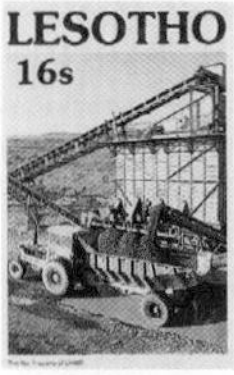

200 Filling Truck at No. 1 Quarry

1990. Lesotho Highlands Water Project. Multicoloured.

976	16s. Type **200**	1·00	10
977	20s. Tanker lorry on Pitseng–Malibamatso road	1·00	20
978	55s. Piers for Malibamatso Bridge	1·00	30
979	2m. Excavating Mphosong section of Pitseng–Malibamatso road	3·00	3·75
MS980	104×85 mm. 5m. Sinking blasting borcholes on Pitseng–Malibamatso road	7·00	8·00

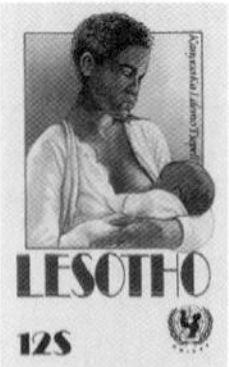

201 Mother breastfeeding Baby

1990. UNICEF Child Survival Campaign. Multicoloured.

981	12s. Type **201**	75	10
982	55s. Baby receiving oral rehydration therapy	1·25	45
983	1m. Weight monitoring	1·75	3·25

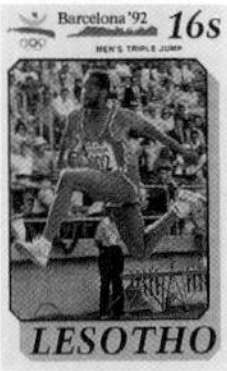

202 Men's Triple Jump

1990. Olympic Games, Barcelona (1992). Multicoloured.

984	16s. Type **202**	70	10
985	55s. Men's 200 m race	95	25
986	1m. Men's 5000 m race	1·60	1·25
987	4m. Show jumping	4·25	6·00
MS988	100×70 mm. 5m. Olympic flame (horiz)	7·00	8·00

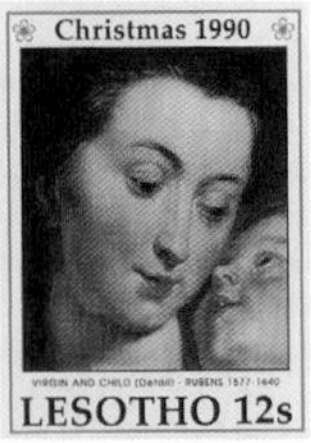

203 "Virgin and Child" (detail, Rubens)

1990. Christmas. Paintings by Rubens. Multicoloured.

989	12s. Type **203**	20	10
990	16s. *Adoration of the Magi* (detail)	20	10
991	55s. *Head of One of the Three Kings*	45	25
992	80s. *Adoration of the Magi* (different detail)	60	60
993	1m. *Virgin and Child* (different detail)	70	70
994	2m. *Adoration of the Magi* (different detail)	1·25	1·75
995	3m. *Virgin and Child* (different detail)	2·00	2·50
996	4m. *Adoration of the Magi* (different detail)	2·25	3·25
MS997	71×100 mm. 5m. *Assumption of the Virgin* (detail)	4·25	6·00

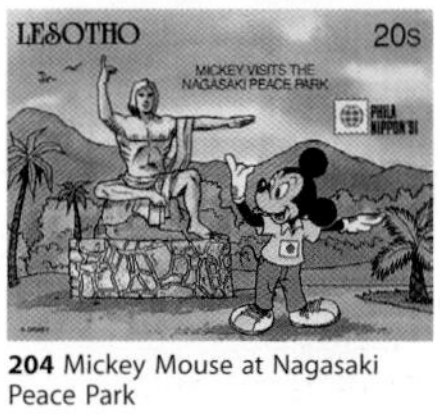

204 Mickey Mouse at Nagasaki Peace Park

1991. "Phila Nippon '91" International Stamp Exhibition, Tokyo. Walt Disney cartoon characters in Japan. Multicoloured.

998	20s. Type **204**	80	15
999	30s. Mickey Mouse on Kamakura Beach	85	20
1000	40s. Mickey and Donald Duck with Bunraku puppet	95	25
1001	50s. Mickey and Donald eating soba	1·00	35
1002	75s. Mickey and Minnie Mouse at tea house	1·40	70
1003	1m. Mickey running after "Hikari" express train	1·40	1·00
1004	3m. Mickey Mouse with deer at Todaiji Temple, Nara	3·25	3·50
1005	4m. Mickey and Minnie outside Imperial Palace	3·25	4·00
MS1006	Two sheets, each 127×112 mm. (a) 5m. Mickey Mouse skiing. (b) 5m. Mickey and Minnie having a picnic. Set of 2 sheets	8·00	8·50

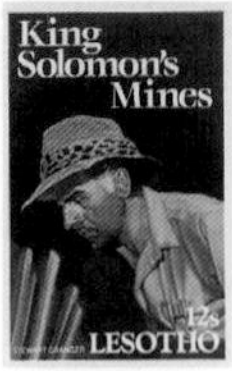

205 Stewart Granger ("King Solomon's Mines")

1991. Famous Films with African Themes. Multicoloured.

1007	12s. Type **205**	35	20
1008	16s. Johnny Weissmuller (*Tarzan the Ape Man*)	35	20
1009	30s. Clark Gable and Grace Kelly (*Mogambo*)	50	35
1010	55s. Sigourney Weaver and gorilla (*Gorillas in the Mist*)	75	55
1011	70s. Humphrey Bogart and Katharine Hepburn (*The African Queen*)	90	80
1012	1m. John Wayne and capture of rhinoceros (*Hatari!*)	1·25	1·00
1013	2m. Meryl Streep and de Havilland Gipsy Moth light aircraft (*Out of Africa*)	2·00	2·25
1014	4m. Arsenio Hall and Eddie Murphy (*Coming to America*)	2·75	3·50
MS1015	108×77 mm. 5m. Elsa the Lioness (*Born Free*)	3·75	4·50

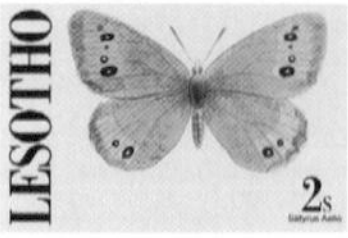

206 "Satyrus aello"

1991. Butterflies. Multicoloured.

1016B	2s. Type **206**	40	65
1017B	3s. *Erebia medusa*	40	65
1018A	5s. *Melanargia galathea*	30	50
1019B	10s. *Erebia aethiops*	40	50
1020A	20s. *Coenonympha pamphilus*	20	10
1021B	25s. *Pyrameis atalanta*	45	20
1022B	30s. *Charaxes jasius*	50	10
1023B	40s. *Colias palaeno*	55	10
1024B	50s. *Colias cliopatra*	55	10
1025B	60s. *Colias philodice*	60	30
1026B	70s. *Rhumni gonepterix*	65	10
1027B	1m. *Colias caesonia*	1·00	50
1028B	2m. *Pyrameis cardui*	2·00	1·25
1029cA	3m. *Danaus chrysippus*	1·40	2·00
1030B	10m. *Apatura iris*	6·50	7·50

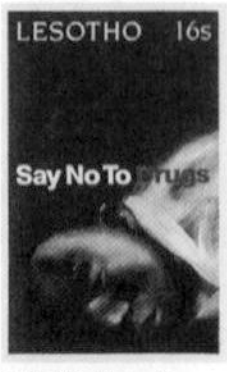

207 Victim of Drug Abuse

1991. "Say No To Drugs" Campaign.

1031	**207**	16s. multicoloured	2·00	60

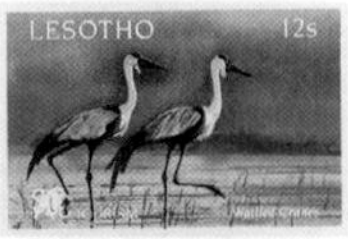

208 Wattled Cranes

1991. Southern Africa Development Co-ordination Conference Tourism Promotion. Multicoloured.

1032	12s. Type **208**	2·00	1·00
1033	16s. Butterfly on flowers	2·00	1·00
1034	25s. Zebra and tourist bus at Mukorob (rock formation), Namibia	2·50	1·50
MS1035	75×117 mm. 3m. Basotho women in ceremonial dress	4·00	5·00

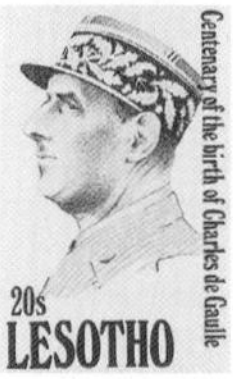

209 De Gaulle in 1939

1991. Birth Centenary of Charles de Gaulle (French statesman).

1036	**209**	20s. black and brown	80	15
1037	-	40s. black and purple	1·00	1·25
1038	-	50s. black and green	1·00	40
1039	-	60s. black and blue	1·00	70
1040	-	4m. black and red	3·50	4·50

DESIGNS: 40s. General De Gaulle as Free French leader; 50s. De Gaulle as provisional President of France, 1944–46; 60s. Charles de Gaulle in 1958; 4m. Pres. De Gaulle.

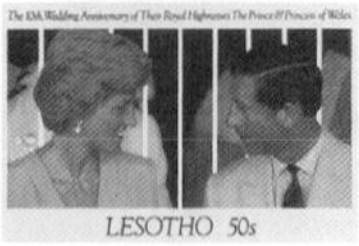

210 Prince and Princess of Wales

1991. Tenth Wedding Anniv of Prince and Princess of Wales. Multicoloured.

1041	50s. Type **210**	1·50	25
1042	70s. Prince Charles at polo and Princess Diana holding Prince Harry	1·50	45
1043	1m. Prince Charles with Prince Harry and Princess Diana in evening dress	1·60	70
1044	3m. Prince William and Prince Harry in school uniform	2·25	3·00
MS1045	68×91 mm. 4m. Portraits of Prince with Princess and sons	5·50	4·25

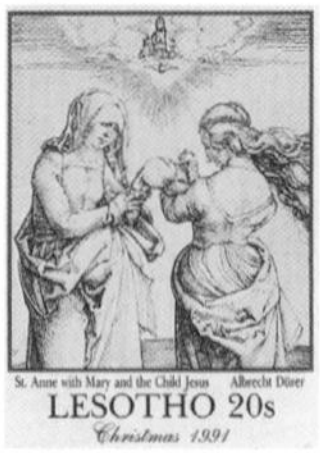

211 "St. Anne with Mary and the Child Jesus"

1991. Christmas. Drawings by Albrecht Durer.

1046	**211**	20s. black and mauve	60	10
1047	-	30s. black and blue	75	20
1048	-	50s. black and green	90	25
1049	-	60s. black and red	95	30
1050	-	70s. black and yellow	1·00	60
1051	-	1m. black and orange	1·25	1·10
1052	-	2m. black and purple	2·50	2·75
1053	-	4m. black and blue	3·50	6·00
MS1054		Two sheets, each 102×127 mm. (a) 5m. black and red. (b) 5m. black and blue	6·00	7·50

DESIGNS: 30s. *Mary on Grass Bench*; 50s. *Mary with Crown of Stars*; 60s. *Mary with Child beside Tree*; 70s. *Mary with Child beside Wall*; 1m. *Mary in Halo on Crescent Moon*; 2m. *Mary breastfeeding Child*; 4m. *Mary with Infant in Swaddling Clothes*

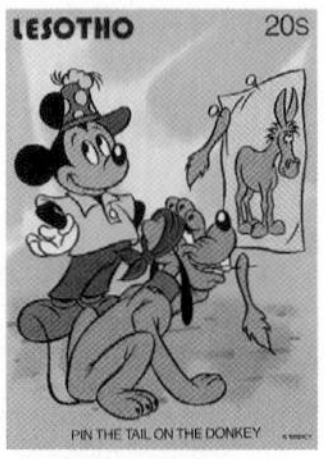

212 Mickey Mouse and Pluto pinning the Tail on the Donkey

1991. Children's Games. Walt Disney cartoon characters. Multicoloured.

1055	20s. Type **212**	65	15
1056	30s. Mickey playing mancala	70	20
1057	40s. Mickey rolling hoop	80	20
1058	50s. Minnie Mouse hula-hooping	90	25
1059	70s. Mickey and Pluto throwing a frisbee	1·25	75

1060	1m. Donald Duck with a diabolo	1·60	1·40
1061	2m. Donald's nephews playing marbles	2·50	3·00
1062	3m. Donald with Rubik's cube	3·00	4·00

MS1063 Two sheets, each 127×112 mm. (a) 5m. Donald's and Mickey's nephews playing tug-of-war. (b) 5m. Mickey and Donald mock fighting. Set of 2 sheets 8·50 9·00

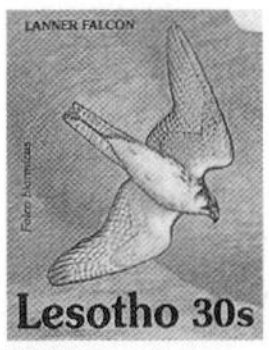

213 Lanner Falcon

1992. Birds. Multicoloured.

1064	30s. Type **213**	75	60
1065	30s. Bateleur	75	60
1066	30s. Paradise sparrow (inscr "Red-headed Finch")	75	60
1067	30s. Lesser striped swallow	75	60
1068	30s. Alpine swift	75	60
1069	30s. Didric cuckoo ("Diederik Cuckoo")	75	60
1070	30s. Yellow-tufted malachite sunbird ("Malachite Sunbird")	75	60
1071	30s. Burchell's gonolek ("Crimson-breasted Shrike")	75	60
1072	30s. Pin-tailed whydah	75	60
1073	30s. Lilac-breasted roller	75	60
1074	30s. Black bustard ("Korhaan")	75	60
1075	30s. Black-collared barbet	75	60
1076	30s. Secretary bird	75	60
1077	30s. Red-billed quelea	75	60
1078	30s. Red bishop	75	60
1079	30s. Ring-necked dove	75	60
1080	30s. Yellow canary	75	60
1081	30s. Cape longclaw ("Orange-throated Longclaw")	75	60
1082	30s. Cordon-bleu (inscr "Blue Waxbill")	75	60
1083	30s. Golden bishop	75	60

Nos. 1064/83 were printed together, *se-tenant*, forming a composite design.

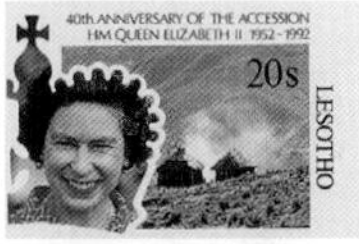

214 Queen Elizabeth and Cooking at a Mountain Homestead

1992. 40th Anniv of Queen Elizabeth II's Accession. Multicoloured.

1084	20s. Type **214**	40	15
1085	30s. View from mountains	40	20
1086	1m. Cacti and mountain	1·25	65
1087	4m. Thaba-Bosiu	3·00	3·50

MS1088 75×97 mm. 5m. Mountains at sunset 4·50 4·50

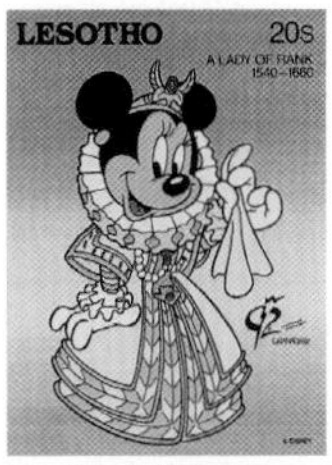

215 Minnie Mouse as Spanish Lady, 1540–1660

1992. International Stamp Exhibitions. Walt Disney cartoon characters. Multicoloured. (a) "Granada '92", Spain. Traditional Spanish Costumes.

1089	20s. Type **215**	1·00	20
1090	50s. Mickey Mouse as Don Juan at Lepanto, 1571	1·25	40
1091	70s. Donald in Galician costume, 1880	1·50	70
1092	2m. Daisy Duck in Aragonese costume, 1880	3·00	3·75

MS1093 127×112 mm. 5m. Goofy the bullfighter 4·50 5·50

(b) "World Columbian Stamp Expo '92". Red Indian Life.

1094	30s. Donald Duck making arrowheads	90	30
1095	40s. Goofy playing lacrosse	95	40
1096	1m. Mickey Mouse and Donald Duck planting corn	1·50	1·10
1097	3m. Minnie Mouse doing bead work	3·00	3·50

MS1098 127×112 mm. 5m. Mickey paddling canoe 4·50 5·50

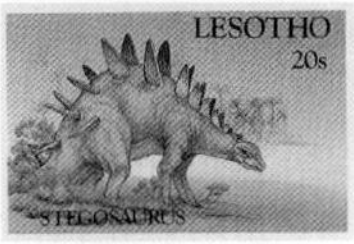

216 Stegosaurus

1992. Prehistoric Animals. Multicoloured.

1099	20s. Type **216**	1·00	30
1100	30s. Ceratosaurus	1·10	35
1101	40s. Procompsognathus	1·40	45
1102	50s. Lesothosaurus	1·60	55
1103	70s. Plateosaurus	1·60	70
1104	1m. Gasosaurus	2·00	1·25
1105	2m. Massospondylus	2·50	3·25
1106	3m. Archaeopteryx	2·50	4·00

MS1107 Two sheets, each 105×77 mm. (a) 5m. As 50s. (b) 5m. As 3m. Set of 2 sheets 11·00 10·00

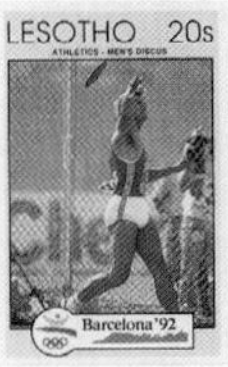

217 Men's Discus

1992. Olympic Games, Albertville and Barcelona. Multicoloured.

1108	20s. Type **217**	20	15
1109	30s. Men's long jump	25	15
1110	40s. Women's 4×100 m relay	30	25
1111	70s. Women's 100 m	50	50
1112	1m. Men's parallel bars	70	70
1113	2m. Men's double luge (horiz)	1·40	1·75
1114	3m. Women's 30k cross-country skiing (horiz)	1·75	2·50
1115	4m. Men's biathlon	2·00	2·75

MS1116 Two sheets, each 100×70 mm. (a) 5m. Women's figure skating. (b) 5m. Ice hockey (horiz). Set of 2 sheets 6·75 7·50

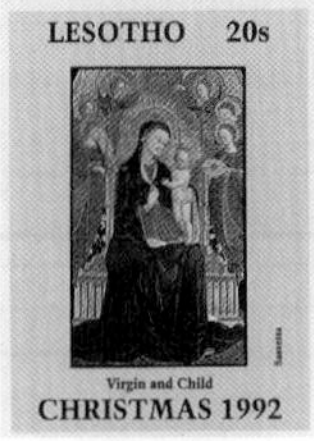

218 "Virgin and Child" (Sassetta)

1992. Christmas. Religious Paintings. Multicoloured.

1117	20s. Type **218**	55	15
1118	30s. *Coronation of the Virgin* (Master of Bonastre)	65	20
1119	40s. *Virgin and Child* (Master of SS. Cosmas and Damian)	75	25
1120	70s. *The Virgin of Great Panagia* (detail) (12th-century Russian school)	1·25	55
1121	1m. *Madonna and Child* (Vincenzo Foppa)	1·75	1·10
1122	2m. *Madonna and Child* (School of Lippo Memmi)	2·50	2·75
1123	3m. *Virgin and Child* (Barnaba da Modena)	3·00	3·75
1124	4m. *Virgin and Child with Saints* (triptych) (Simone dei Crocifissi)	3·25	4·00

MS1125 Two sheets, each 76×102 mm. (a) 5m. *Virgin and Child with Saints* (different detail) (Simone dei Crocifissi). (b) 5m. *Virgin and Child enthroned and surrounded by Angels* (Cimabue) 10·00 12·00

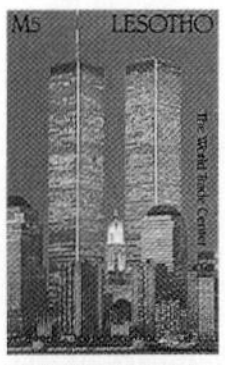

219 World Trade Centre, New York

1992. Postage Stamp Mega Event, New York. Sheet 100×70 mm.

MS1126 5m. **219** multicoloured 6·00 7·00

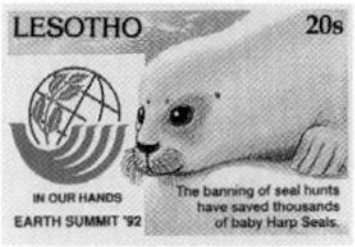

220 Baby Harp Seal (Earth Summit '92, Rio)

1993. Anniversaries and Events. Multicoloured.

1127	20s. Type **220**	1·25	50
1128	30s. Giant panda (Earth Summit '92, Rio)	1·75	50
1129	40s. Airship "Graf Zeppelin" over globe (75th death anniv of Count Ferdinand von Zeppelin)	1·60	50
1130	70s. Woman grinding maize (International Conference on Nutrition, Rome)	60	55
1131	4m. Lt. Robinson's Royal Aircraft Factory B.E.2C shooting down Schutte Lanz SL-11 airship (75th death anniv of Count Ferdinand von Zeppelin)	3·75	4·75
1132	5m. Valentina Tereshkova and "Vostok 6" (30th anniv of first woman in space)	3·75	4·75

MS1133 Two sheets, each 100×70 mm. (a) 5m. Dr. Ronald McNair ("Challenger" astronaut) (International Space Year). (b) 5m. South African crowned crane (Earth Summit '92, Rio) 10·00 10·00

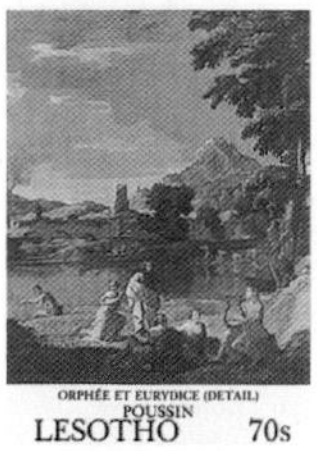

221 "Orpheus and Eurydice" (detail)

1993. Bicentenary of the Louvre, Paris. Paintings by Poussin. Multicoloured.

1134	70s. Type **221**	80	80
1135	70s. *Rape of the Sabine Women* (left detail)	80	80
1136	70s. *Rape of the Sabine Women* (right detail)	80	80
1137	70s. *The Death of Sapphira* (left detail)	80	80
1138	70s. *The Death of Sapphira* (right detail)	80	80
1139	70s. *Echo and Narcissus* (left detail)	80	80
1140	70s. *Echo and Narcissus* (right detail)	80	80
1141	70s. *Self-portrait*	80	80

MS1142 70×100 mm. 5m. *The Money Lender and his Wife* (57×89 mm) (Metsys) 4·75 5·00

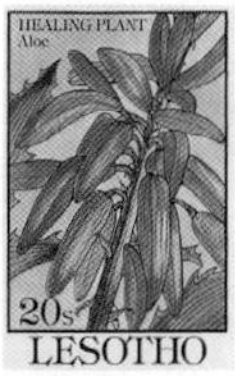

222 Aloe

1993. Flowers. Multicoloured.

1143	20s. Type **222**	40	10
1144	30s. Calla lily	45	15
1145	40s. Bird of paradise plant	45	15
1146	70s. Amaryllis	75	40
1147	1m. Agapanthus	90	60
1148	2m. Crinum	3·75	2·25
1149	4m. Watsonia	2·50	3·25
1150	5m. Gazania	2·50	3·50

MS1151 Two sheets, each 98×67 mm. (a) 7m. Plumbago. (b) 7m. Desert Rose 8·00 8·50

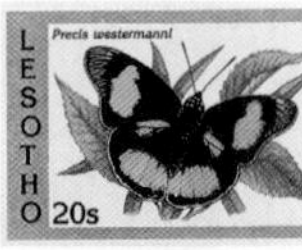

223 "Precis westermanni"

1993. Butterflies. Multicoloured.

1152	20s. Type **223**	40	15
1153	40s. *Precis sophia*	50	20
1154	70s. *Precis terea*	65	45
1155	1m. *Byblia acheloia*	75	75
1156	2m. *Papilio antimachus*	1·25	1·50
1157	5m. *Pseudacraea boisduvali*	1·75	3·00

MS1158 Two sheets, each 96×62 mm. (a) 7m. *Precis oenone*. (b) 7m. *Precis octavia* 7·00 7·00

No. 1157 is inscribed "Pesudacraea boisduvali" in error.

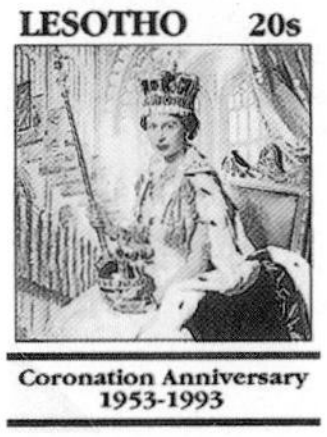

224 Queen Elizabeth II at Coronation (photograph by Cecil Beaton)

1993. 40th Anniv of Coronation.

1159	**224**	20s. multicoloured	90	90
1160	-	40s. multicoloured	1·25	1·25
1161	-	1m. black and green	1·60	1·60
1162	-	5m. multicoloured	3·50	3·50

MS1163 70×100 mm. 7m. multicoloured (42½×28½ mm) 6·50 6·50

DESIGNS—VERT: 40s. St. Edward's Crown and Sceptre; 1m. Queen Elizabeth the Queen Mother; 5m. Queen Elizabeth II and family. HORIZ: 7m. *Conversation Piece at Royal Lodge, Windsor* (detail) (Sir James Gunn).

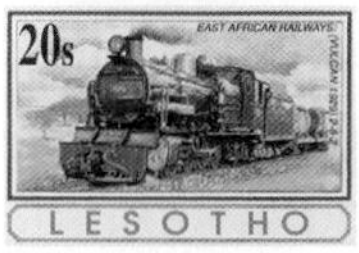

225 East African Railways Vulcan Steam Locomotive, 1929

1993. African Railways. Multicoloured.

1164	20s. Type **225**	85	25
1165	30s. Beyer-Garratt Class 15A steam locomotive, Zimbabwe Railways, 1952	95	30
1166	40s. Class 25 steam locomotive, South African Railways, 1953	1·00	30
1167	70s. Class A 58 steam locomotive, East African Railways	1·50	60
1168	1m. Class 9E electric locomotives, South African Railways	1·60	85
1169	2m. Class 87 diesel-electric locomotive, East African Railways, 1971	2·00	1·75
1170	3m. Class 92 diesel locomotive, East African Railways, 1971	2·25	2·50
1171	5m. Class 26 steam locomotive No. 3450, South African Railways, 1982	2·75	3·75

MS1172 Two sheets, each 104×82 mm. (a) 7m. Class 6E electric locomotive, South African Railways, 1969. (b) 7m. Class 231-132BT steam locomotive, Algerian Railways, 1937 11·00 11·00

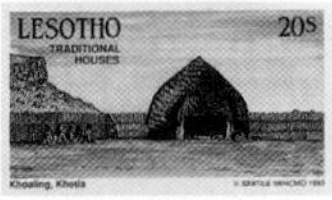

226 Court-house

1993. Traditional Houses. Multicoloured.

1173	20s. Type **226**	50	10
1174	30s. House with reed fence	55	15
1175	70s. Unmarried girls' house	1·00	40
1176	4m. Hut made from branches	3·50	5·00

MS1177 81×69 mm. 4m. Decorated houses 4·00 4·50

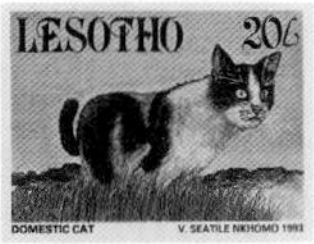

227 Black and White Shorthair

1993. Domestic Cats. Multicoloured.

1178	20s. Type **227**	75	25
1179	30s. Shorthair tabby lying down	75	25
1180	70s. Head of shorthair tabby	1·00	40
1181	5m. Black and white shorthair with shorthair tabby	3·00	4·00

MS1182 113×89 mm. 5m. Shorthair Tabby with rat (vert) 4·25 4·50

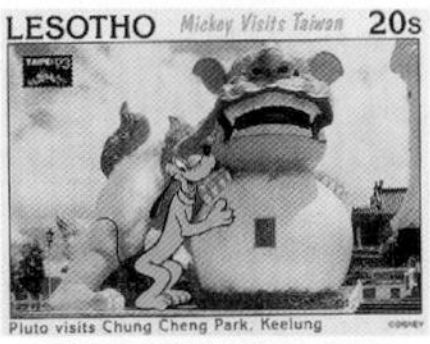

228 Pluto in Chung Cheng Park, Keelung

1993. "Taipei '93" Asian International Stamp Exhibition, Taiwan. Walt Disney cartoon characters in Taiwan. Multicoloured.

1183	20s. Type **228**	65	10
1184	30s. Donald Duck at Chiao-Tienkung Temple Festival	75	15
1185	40s. Goofy with lantern figures	85	20
1186	70s. Minnie Mouse shopping at temple festival	1·25	40
1187	1m. Daisy Duck at Queen's Head Rock, Yehliu (vert)	1·50	70
1188	1m.20 Mickey and Minnie at National Concert Hall (vert)	1·60	1·60
1189	2m. Donald at Chiang Kai-shek Memorial Hall (vert)	1·75	2·00
1190	2m.50 Donald and Daisy at the Grand Hotel, Taipei	2·00	2·75
MS1191	Two sheets, each 128×102 mm. (a) 5m. Goofy over National Palace Museum, Taipei. (b) 6m. Mickey and Minnie at Presidential Palace Museum, Taipei (vert)	8·50	8·50

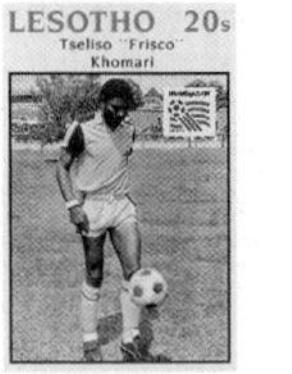

229 Tseliso "Frisco" Khomari (Lesotho)

1994. World Cup Football Championship, U.S.A. Multicoloured.

1192	20s. Type **229**	50	10
1193	30s. Thato "American Spoon" Mohale (Lesotho)	55	15
1194	40s. Jozic Davor (Yugoslavia) and Freddy Rincorn (Colombia)	65	20
1195	50s. Lefika "Mzee" Lekhotla (Lesotho)	70	25
1196	70s. Litsiso "House-on-fire" Khali (Lesotho)	85	55
1197	1m. Roger Milla (Cameroun)	1·00	85
1198	1m.20 David Platt (England)	1·50	2·00
1199	2m. Karl Heinz Rummenigge (Germany) and Soren Lerby (Denmark)	1·75	2·50
MS1200	Two sheets, each 100×70 mm. (a) 6m. Klaus Lindenberger (Czechoslovakia). (b) 6m. Franco Baresi (Italy) and Ivan Hasek (Czechoslovakia) (horiz)	9·00	9·00

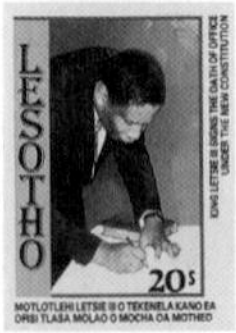

230 King Letsie III signing Oath of Office

1994. First Anniv of Restoration of Democracy. Multicoloured.

1201	20s. Type **230**	20	20
1202	30s. Parliament building (horiz)	25	20
1203	50s. Swearing-in of Dr. Ntsu Mokhehle as Prime Minister (horiz)	40	25
1204	70s. Maj-Gen P. Ramaema handing Instruments of Government to Dr. Ntsu Mokhehle (horiz)	70	45

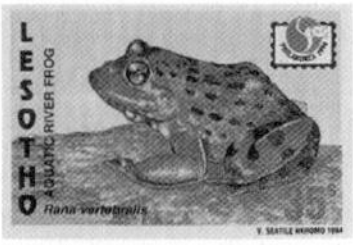

231 Aquatic River Frog

1994. "Philakorea '94" International Stamp Exhibition, Seoul. Frogs and Toads. Multicoloured.

1205	35s. Type **231**	25	10
1206	50s. Bubbling kassina	35	15
1207	1m. Guttural toad	60	60
1208	1m.50 Common river frog	80	1·25
MS1209	Two sheets, each 102×72 mm. (a) 5m. Jade frog (sculpture). (b) 5m. Black Spotted frog and oriental white-eye (bird) (vert)	9·00	9·00

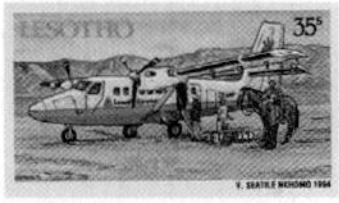

232 De Havilland D.H.C.6 Twin Otter and Emblem

1994. 50th Anniv of I.C.A.O. Multicoloured.

1210	35s. Type **232**	60	15
1211	50s. Fokker F.27 Friendship on runway	75	20
1212	1m. Fokker F.27 Friendship over Moshoeshoe I International Airport	1·25	80
1213	1m.50 Cessna light aircraft over mountains	1·60	2·00

1995. No. 1022 surch **20s.**

1214a	20s. on 30s. "Charaxes jasius"	1·50	65

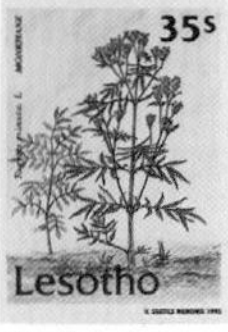

234 "Tagetes minuta"

1995. Medicinal Plants. Multicoloured.

1215	35s. Type **234**	35	10
1216	50s. *Plantago lanceolata*	40	15
1217	1m. *Amaranthus spinosus*	65	60
1218	1m.50 *Taraxacum officinale*	1·10	2·00
MS1219	120×91 mm. 5m. *Dativa stramonium*	2·50	3·25

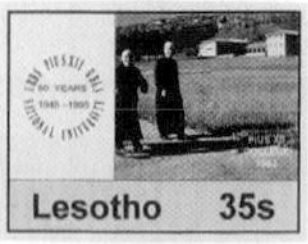

235 Pius XII College, 1962

1995. 50th Anniv of University Studies in Lesotho. Multicoloured.

1220	35s. Type **235**	20	10
1221	50s. Campus, University of Basutoland, Bechuanaland and Swaziland, 1966	25	15
1222	70s. Campus, University of Botswana, Lesotho and Swaziland, 1970	35	15
1223	1m. Administration Block, University of Botswana, Lesotho and Swaziland, 1975	55	40
1224	1m.50 Administration Block, National University of Lesotho, 1988	75	1·10
1225	2m. Procession of Vice-Chancellors, National University of Lesotho, 1995	1·00	1·75

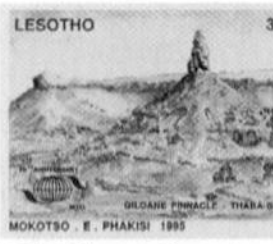

236 Qiloane Pinnacle, Thaba-Bosiu

1995. 20th Anniv of World Tourism Organization. Multicoloured.

1226	35s. Type **236**	25	10
1227	50s. Ha Mohalenyane rock formation	30	15
1228	1m. Botsoela Falls (vert)	55	45
1229	1m.50 Backpackers in Makhaleng River Gorge	80	1·50
MS1230	143×88 mm. 4m. Red Hot Pokers (38×57 mm)	2·25	3·00

No. **MS**1230 is inscribed "RED HOT PORKERS" in error.

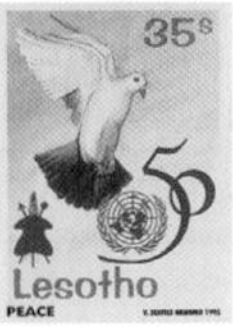

237 "Peace"

1995. 50th Anniv of United Nations. Multicoloured.

1231	35s. Type **237**	30	10
1232	50s. "Justice" (scales)	40	20
1233	1m.50 "Reconciliation" (clasped hands) (horiz)	1·00	1·90

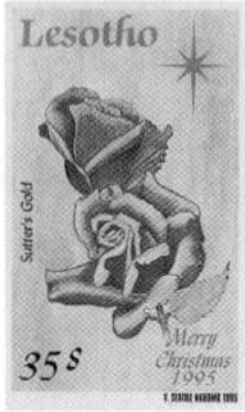

238 "Sutter's Gold Rose"

1995. Christmas. Roses. Multicoloured.

1234	5s. Type **238**	30	10
1235	50s. "Michele Meilland"	35	10
1236	1m. "J. Otto Thilow"	60	50
1237	2m. "Papa Meilland"	95	1·60

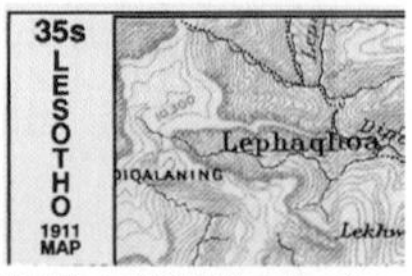

239 Part of 1911 Map showing Lephaqhoa

1996. Completion of New Standard Map of Lesotho (1994). Map Sections of Malibamatso Valley. Multicoloured. (a) 1911 Map.

1238	35s. Type **239**	40	40
1239	35s. Boritsa Tsuene	40	40
1240	35s. Molapo	40	40
1241	35s. Nkeu	40	40
1242	35s. Three rivers flowing east	40	40
1243	35s. Tibedi and Rafanyane	40	40
1244	35s. Two rivers flowing east	40	40
1245	35s. Madibatmatso River	40	40
1246	35s. Bokung River	40	40
1247	35s. Semena River	40	40

(b) 1978 Map.

1248	35s. Mountains and river valley	40	40
1249	35s. Pelaneng and Lepaqoa	40	40
1250	35s. Mamohau	40	40
1251	35s. Ha Lejone	40	40
1252	35s. Ha Thoora	40	40
1253	35s. Ha Mikia	40	40
1254	35s. Ha Kosetabole	40	40
1255	35s. Ha Seshote	40	40
1256	35s. Ha Rapooane	40	40
1257	35s. Bokong Ha Kennan	40	40

(c) 1994 Map.

1258	35s. Mafika-Lisiu Pass	40	40
1259	35s. Ha Lesaoana	40	40
1260	35s. Ha Masaballa	40	40
1261	35s. Ha Nkisi	40	40
1262	35s. Ha Rafanyane	40	40
1263	35s. Laitsoka Pass	40	40
1264	35s. "Katse Reservoir"	40	40
1265	35s. Seshote	40	40
1266	35s. Sephareng	40	40
1267	35s. Katse Dam	40	40

Nos. 1238/47, 1248/57 and 1258/67 respectively were printed together, *se-tenant*, forming composite designs.

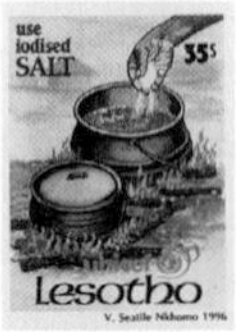

240 Adding Iodized Salt to Cooking Pot

1996. 50th Anniv of UNICEF. Multicoloured.

1268	35s. Type **240**	25	10
1269	50s. Herdboys with livestock (horiz)	35	20
1270	70s. Children in class (horiz)	45	20
1271	1m.50 Boys performing traditional dance (horiz)	90	1·50

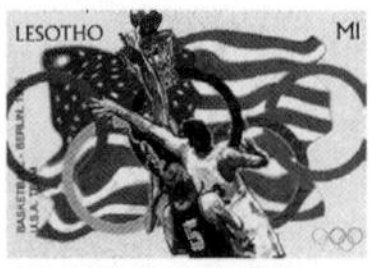

241 U.S.A. Basketball Team, 1936

1996. Olympic Games, Atlanta. Previous Gold Medal Winners. Multicoloured.

1272	1m. Type **241**	50	20
1273	1m.50 Brandenburg Gate and stadium, Berlin, 1936	50	30
1274	1m.50 Glen Morris (U.S.A.) (decathlon, 1936) (vert)	50	50
1275	1m.50 Saidi Aouita (Morocco) (5000 m running, 1984) (vert)	50	50
1276	1m.50 Arnie Robinson (U.S.A.) (long jump, 1976) (vert)	50	50
1277	1m.50 Hans Woellke (Germany) (shot put, 1936) (vert)	50	50
1278	1m.50 Renate Stecher (Germany) (100 m running, 1972) (vert)	50	50
1279	1m.50 Evelyn Ashford (U.S.A.) (100 m running, 1984) (vert)	50	50
1280	1m.50 Willie Davenport (U.S.A.) (110 m hurdles, 1968) (vert)	50	50
1281	1m.50 Bob Beamon (U.S.A.) (long jump, 1968) (vert)	50	50
1282	1m.50 Heidi Rosendhal (Germany) (long jump, 1972) (vert)	50	50
1283	2m. Jesse Owens (U.S.A.) (track and field, 1936) (vert)	65	70
1284	3m. Speed boat racing	85	1·00
MS1285	Two sheets, each 110×80 mm. (a) 8m. Michael Gross (Germany) (swimming, 1984) (vert). (b) 8m. Kornelia Ender (Germany) (swimming, 1976) (vert)	7·50	7·50

No. 1273 is inscribed "BRANDEBOURG GATE" in error. No. 1274 incorrectly identifies Glen Morris as the gold medal winner in the 1936 long jump.

Nos. 1274/82 were printed together, *se-tenant*, with the backgrounds forming a composite design.

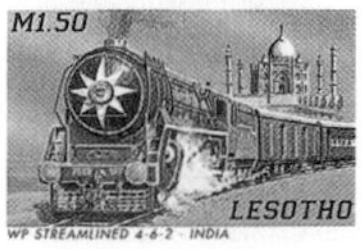

242 Class WP Steam Locomotive (India)

1996. Trains of the World. Multicoloured.

1286	1m.50 Type **242**	85	85
1287	1m.50 Canadian Pacific steam locomotive No. 2471 (Canada)	85	85
1288	1m.50 The *Caledonian* (Great Britain)	85	85
1289	1m.50 Steam locomotive *William Mason* (U.S.A.)	85	85
1290	1m.50 *Trans-Siberian Express* (Russia)	85	85
1291	1m.50 Steam train (Switzerland)	85	85
1292	1m.50 ETR 450 high speed train (Italy)	85	85
1293	1m.50 TGV express train (France)	85	85
1294	1m.50 XPT high speed train (Australia)	85	85
1295	1m.50 *The Blue Train* (South Africa)	85	85
1296	1m.50 Intercity 225 express train (Great Britain)	85	85
1297	1m.50 *Hikari* express train (Japan)	85	85
MS1298	Two sheets, each 98×68 mm. (a) 8m. Class 52 steam locomotive (Germany) (57×43 mm). (b) 8m. ICE high speed train (Germany) (57×43 mm)	7·50	8·50

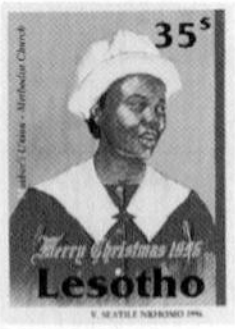

243 Mothers' Union Member, Methodist Church

1996. Christmas. Mothers' Unions. Multicoloured.

1299	35s. Type **243**	30	10
1300	50s. Roman Catholic Church	35	10
1301	1m. Lesotho Evangelical Church	65	40
1302	1m.50 Anglican Church	1·00	1·50

No. 1302 is inscribed "Anglian" in error.

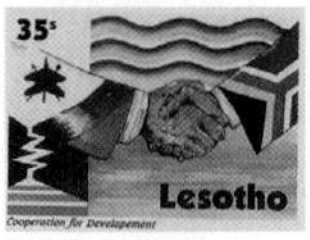

244 Hand Clasp (Co-operation for Development)

1997. Tenth Anniv of Lesotho Highland Water Project (1996). Multicoloured.

1303	35s. Type **244**	25	10
1304	50s. Lammergeier and rock painting (Nature and Heritage)	1·40	45
1305	1m. Malibamatso Bridge (Engineering)	70	55
1306	1m.50 Katse Valley in 1986 and 1996 (75×28 mm)	1·00	1·75

No. 1305 is inscribed "Developement" in error.

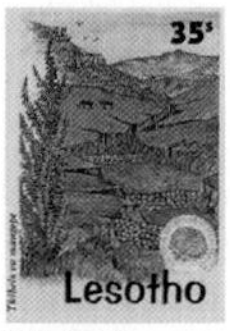

245 Land Reclamation

1997. Environment Protection. Multicoloured.

1307	35s. Type **245**	30	10
1308	50s. Throwing rubbish into bin	35	15

1309	1m. Hands holding globe and tree	65	40
1310	1m.20 Recycling symbol and rubbish	75	1·00
1311	1m.50 Collecting rain water	85	1·10

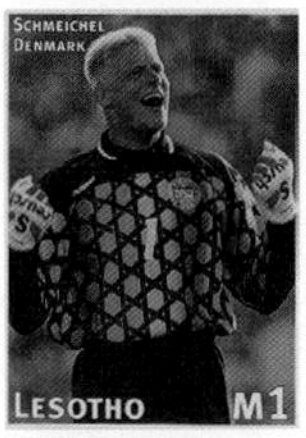

246 Schmeichel, Denmark

1997. World Cup Football Championship, France (1998). Multicoloured.

1312	1m. Type **246**	40	20
1313	1m.50 Bergkamp, Netherlands	55	55
1314	1m.50 Argentine players celebrating	55	55
1315	1m.50 Argentine and Dutch players competing for ball	55	55
1316	1m.50 Players heading ball	55	55
1317	1m.50 Goalkeeper deflecting ball	55	55
1318	1m.50 Goal-mouth melee	55	55
1319	1m.50 Argentine player kicking ball	55	55
1320	2m. Southgate, England	70	70
1321	2m.50 Asprilla, Colombia	80	85
1322	3m. Gascoigne, England	90	95
1323	4m. Giggs, Wales	1·10	1·25
MS1324	Two sheets, each 127×102 mm. (a) 8m. Littbarski, West Germany (horiz). (b) 8m. Shearer, England	6·50	7·00

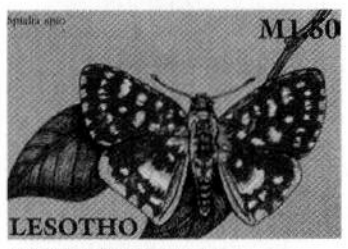

247 "Spialia spio"

1997. Butterflies. Multicoloured.

1325	1m.50 Type **247**	60	60
1326	1m.50 *Leptotes pirithous*	60	60
1327	1m.50 *Acratea satis*	60	60
1328	1m.50 *Belenois aurota aurota*	60	60
1329	1m.50 *Spindasis natalensis*	60	60
1330	1m.50 *Torynesis orangica*	60	60
1331	1m.50 *Lepidochysops variabilis*	60	60
1332	1m.50 *Pinacopteryx eriphia*	60	60
1333	1m.50 *Anthene butleri livida*	60	60
MS1334	Two sheets, each 106×76 mm. (a) 8m. *Bematistes aganice.* (b) 8m. *Papilio demodocus*	8·00	8·00

Nos. 1325/33 were printed together, *se-tenant*, with the backgrounds forming a composite design.

No. 1326 is inscribed "Cyclyrius pirithous", No. 1332 "Pinacopteryx eriphea" and No. **MS**1334(b) "Papalio demodocus", all in error.

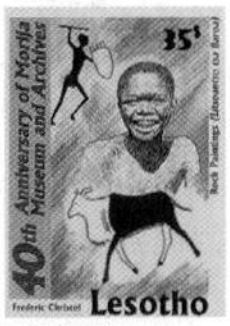

248 Rock Paintings and Boy

1998. 40th Anniv of Morija Museum and Archives. Multicoloured.

1335	35s. Type **248**	25	10
1336	45s. Hippopotamus and lower jaw bone (horiz)	40	20
1337	50s. Woman and cowhide skirt	30	20
1338	1m. Drum and "thomo" (musical bow)	40	40
1339	1m.50 Warrior with "khau" (gorget awarded for valour)	60	1·00
1340	2m. Herders with ox (horiz)	75	1·25

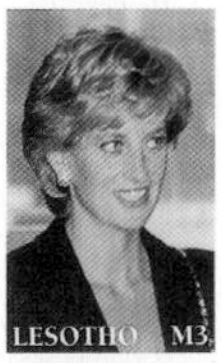

249 Diana, Princess of Wales

1998. Diana, Princess of Wales Commemoration. Multicoloured.

1341	3m. Type **249**	1·10	1·25
1342	3m. Wearing grey jacket	1·10	1·25
1343	3m. Wearing white polo-necked jumper	1·10	1·25
1344	3m. Wearing pearl necklace	1·10	1·25
1345	3m. Wearing white evening dress	1·10	1·25
1346	3m. Wearing pale blue jacket	1·10	1·25
MS1347	70×100 mm. 9m. Accepting bouquet	6·50	6·50

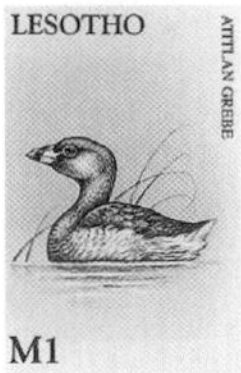

250 Atitlan Grebe

1998. Fauna of the World. Multicoloured. (a) Vert designs as T **250**.

1348	1m. Type **250**	40	40
1349	1m. Cabot's tragopan	40	40
1350	1m. Spider monkey	40	40
1351	1m. Dibatag	40	40
1352	1m. Right whale	40	40
1353	1m. Imperial amazon ("Imperial Parrot")	40	40
1354	1m. Cheetah	40	40
1355	1m. Brown-eared pheasant	40	40
1356	1m. Leatherback turtle	40	40
1357	1m. Imperial woodpecker	40	40
1358	1m. Andean condor	40	40
1359	1m. Barbary deer	40	40
1360	1m. Grey gentle lemur	40	40
1361	1m. Cuban amazon ("Cuban Parrot")	40	40
1362	1m. Numbat	40	40
1363	1m. Short-tailed albatross	40	40
1364	1m. Green turtle	40	40
1365	1m. White rhinoceros	40	40
1366	1m. Diademed sifaka	40	40
1367	1m. Galapagos penguin	40	40

(b) Horiz designs, each 48×31 mm.

1368	1m.50 Impala	55	55
1369	1m.50 Black bear	55	55
1370	1m.50 American buffalo	55	55
1371	1m.50 African elephant	55	55
1372	1m.50 Kangaroo	55	55
1373	1m.50 Lion	55	55
1374	1m.50 Giant panda	55	55
1375	1m.50 Tiger	55	55
1376	1m.50 Zebra	55	55
MS1377	Four sheets, each 98×68 mm. (a) 8m. White-bellied sunbird. (b) 8m. Golden-shouldered parrot. (c) 8m. Snail darter. (d) 8m. Monkey (47×31 mm)	10·00	10·00

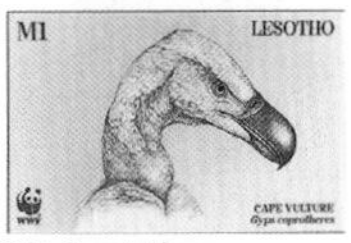

251 Cape Vulture

1998. Endangered Species. Cape Vulture. Multicoloured.

1378	1m. Type **251**	50	65
1379	1m. Looking towards ground	50	65
1380	1m. Looking over shoulder	50	65
1381	1m. Facing right	50	65

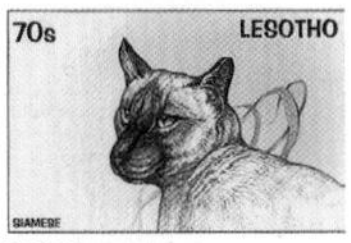

252 Siamese

1998. Cats of the World. Multicoloured.

1382	70s. Type **252**	30	20
1383	1m. Chartreux	40	25
1384	2m. Korat	65	65
1385	2m. Japanese bobtail	65	65
1386	2m. British white	65	65
1387	2m. Bengal	65	65
1388	2m. Abyssinian	65	65
1389	2m. Snowshoe	65	65
1390	2m. Scottish fold	65	65
1391	2m. Maine coon	65	65
1392	2m. Balinese	65	65
1393	2m. Persian	65	65
1394	2m. Javanese	65	65
1395	2m. Turkish angora	65	65
1396	2m. Tiffany	65	65
1397	3m. Egyptian mau	85	85
1398	4m. Bombay	95	1·10
1399	5m. Burmese	1·10	1·25
MS1400	Two sheets, each 98×69 mm. (a) 8m. Tonkinese. (b) 8m. Singapura	6·50	7·00

Nos. 1385/90 and 1391/6 respectively were printed together, *se-tenant*, with the backgrounds forming composite designs.

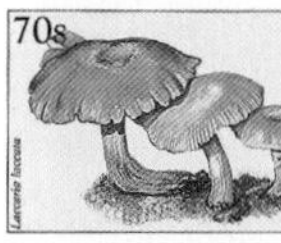

253 "Laccaria laccata"

1998. Fungi of the World. Multicoloured.

1401	70s. Type **253**	30	20
1402	1m. *Mutinus caninus*	40	40
1403	1m. *Hygrophorus psittacinus*	40	40
1404	1m. *Cortinarius obtusus*	40	40
1405	1m. *Volvariella bombycina*	40	40
1406	1m. *Cortinarius caeryelescens*	40	40
1407	1m. *Laccaria amethystina*	40	40
1408	1m. *Tricholoma aurantium*	40	40
1409	1m. *Amanita excelsa* (spissa)	40	40
1410	1m. *Clavaria helvola*	40	40
1411	1m. Unidentified species (inscr "Cortinarius caerylescens")	40	40
1412	1m. *Russula queletii*	40	40
1413	1m. *Amanita phalloides*	40	40
1414	1m. *Lactarius deliciosus*	40	40
1415	1m.50 *Tricholoma lascivum*	55	55
1416	2m. *Clitocybe geotropa*	65	65
1417	3m. *Amanita excelsa*	85	90
1418	4m. Red-capped bolete	95	1·10
MS1419	Two sheets, each 98×68 mm. (a) 8m. *Amanita pantherina.* (b) 8m. *Boletus satanas*	5·50	6·50

Nos. 1406, 1407, 1414, 1416 and **MS**1419b are inscribed "Continarius caerylescens", "Laccaria amethystea", "Lactarius delicious", "Clitocybe geotrapa" and "Boletys satanus", all in error.

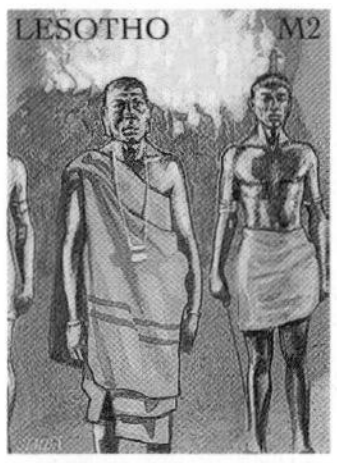

254 "Simba"

1998. World Cinema. Multicoloured. (a) Films about Africa.

1420	2m. Type **254**	60	60
1421	2m. *Call to Freedom*	60	60
1422	2m. *Cry the Beloved Country*	60	60
1423	2m. *King Solomon's Mines*	60	60
1424	2m. *Flame and the Fire*	60	60
1425	2m. *Cry Freedom*	60	60
1426	2m. *Bopha!*	60	60
1427	2m. *Zulu*	60	60

(b) Japanese Film Stars.

1428	2m. Takamine Hideko	60	60
1429	2m. James Shigeta	60	60
1430	2m. Miyoshi Umeki	60	60
1431	2m. May Ishimara	60	60
1432	2m. Sessue Hayakawa	60	60
1433	2m. Miiko Taka	60	60
1434	2m. Mori Masayuki	60	60
1435	2m. Hara Setsuko	60	60
1436	2m. Kyo Machiko	60	60
MS1437	Two sheets. (a) 68×98 mm. 10m. Lion cubs from "Born Free" (horiz). (b) 70×100 mm. 10m. Toshiro Mifune	6·50	7·00

Nos. 1420/7 and 1428/36 respectively were printed together, *se-tenant*, with the backgrounds forming composite designs.

No. 1423 is inscribed "KING SOLOMAN'S MINES" in error.

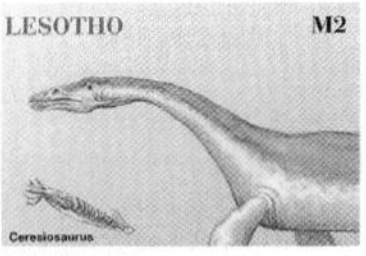

255 Ceresiosaurus

1998. Prehistoric Animals. Multicoloured.

1438	2m. Type **255**	60	60
1439	2m. Rhomaleosaurus	60	60
1440	2m. Anomalocaris	60	60
1441	2m. Mixosaurus	60	60
1442	2m. Stethacanthus	60	60
1443	2m. Dunklosteus	60	60
1444	2m. Tommotia	60	60
1445	2m. Sanctacaris	60	60
1446	2m. Ammonites	60	60
1447	2m. Rhamphorhynchus	60	60
1448	2m. Brachiosaurus	60	60
1449	2m. Mamenchisaurus hochuanensis	60	60
1450	2m. Ceratosaurus nasicornis	60	60
1451	2m. Archaeopteryx	60	60
1452	2m. Leaellynasaura amicagraphica	60	60
1453	2m. Chasmosaurus belli	60	60
1454	2m. Deinonychus and Pachyrhinosaurus	60	60
1455	2m. Deinonychus	60	60
1456	2m. Nyctosaurus	60	60
1457	2m. Volcanoes	60	60
1458	2m. Eudimorphodon	60	60
1459	2m. Apatosaurus	60	60
1460	2m. Peteinosaurus	60	60
1461	2m. Tropeognathus	60	60
1462	2m. Pteranodon ingens	60	60
1463	2m. Ornithodesmus	60	60
1464	2m. Wuerhosaurus	60	60
MS1465	Three sheets, each 100×70 mm. (a) 10m. Coelophysis (vert). (b) 10m. Tyrannosaurus (vert). (c) 10m. Woolly Rhinoceros	8·50	10·00

Nos. 1438/46, 1447/55 and 1456/64 respectively were printed together, *se-tenant*, with the back-grounds forming composite designs.

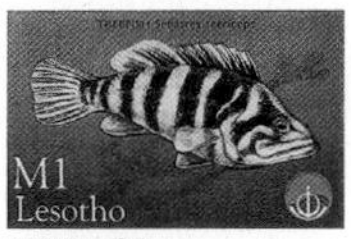

256 Treefish

1998. Year of the Ocean. Fish. Multicoloured.

1466	1m. Type **256**	30	30
1467	1m. Tigerbarb	30	30
1468	1m. Bandtail puffer	30	30
1469	1m. Cod	30	30
1470	1m.50 Clown loach	45	45
1471	1m.50 Christy's lyretail	45	45
1472	1m.50 Filefish	45	45
1473	1m.50 Sicklefin killie	45	45
1474	2m. Brook trout	55	55
1475	2m. Emerald betta	55	55
1476	2m. Pacific electric ray	55	55
1477	2m. Bighead searobin	55	55
1478	2m. Weakfish	55	55
1479	2m. Red drum	55	55
1480	2m. Blue marlin	55	55
1481	2m. Yellowfin tuna	55	55
1482	2m. Barracuda	55	55
1483	2m. Striped bass	55	55
1484	2m. White shark	55	55
1485	2m. Permit	55	55
1486	2m. Purple firefish	55	55
1487	2m. Harlequin sweetlips	55	55
1488	2m. Clown wrasse	55	55
1489	2m. Bicolour angelfish	55	55
1490	2m. False cleanerfish	55	55
1491	2m. Mandarinfish	55	55
1492	2m. Regal tang	55	55
1493	2m. Clownfish	55	55
1494	2m. Bluegill	55	55
1495	2m. Grayling	55	55
1496	2m. Walleye	55	55
1497	2m. Brown trout	55	55
1498	2m. Atlantic salmon	55	55
1499	2m. Northern pike	55	55
1500	2m. Large-mouth bass	55	55
1501	2m. Rainbow trout	55	55
1502	2m. Platy variatus	55	55
1503	2m. Archerfish	55	55
1504	2m. Clown knifefish	55	55
1505	2m. Angelicus	55	55
1506	2m. Black arowana	55	55
1507	2m. Spotted scat	55	55
1508	2m. Kribensis	55	55
1509	2m. Golden pheasant	55	55
1510	3m. Harlequin tuskfish	80	80
1511	4m. Half-moon angelfish	90	90
1512	5m. Spotted trunkfish	1·10	1·10
1513	6m. Wolf eel	1·40	1·50
1514	7m. Cherubfish	1·50	1·60
MS1515	Four sheets, each 98×73 mm. (a) 12m. Common Carp. (b) 12m. Sockeye Salmon. (c) 12m. Winter Flounder. (d) 12m. Horn Shark	10·00	11·00

Nos. 1470/3 show the face value as "M1.5".

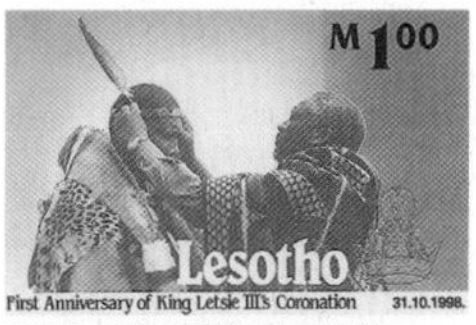

257 Crowning of King Letsie III

1998. First Anniv of Coronation of King Letsie III. Multicoloured.

1516	1m. Type **257**	65	65
1517	1m. King saluting Basotho nation	65	65
1518	1m. King Letsie in profile	65	65

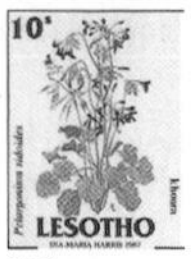

258 "Pelargonium sidoides"

1998. Flowers. Multicoloured.

1519	10s. Type **258**	10	50
1520	15s. *Aponogeton ranunculiflorus*	10	50
1521	20s. *Sebaea leiostyla*	10	50
1522	40s. *Sebaea grandis*	15	30
1523	50s. *Satyrium neglectum*	15	20
1524	60s. *Massonia jasminiflora*	20	20
1525	70s. *Ajuga ophrydis*	20	20
1526	80s. *Nemesia fruticans*	20	20
1527	1m. *Aloe broomii*	30	20
1528	2m. *Wahlenbergia androsacea*	45	30
1529	2m.50 *Phygelius capensis*	55	40
1530	3m. *Dianthus basuticus*	65	50
1531	4m.50 *Rhodohypoxis baurii*	90	90
1532	5m. *Turbina oblongata*	1·00	1·25
1533	6m. *Hibiscus microcarpus*	1·25	1·50
1534	10m. *Lobelia erinus* ("Moraea stricta")	2·00	2·50

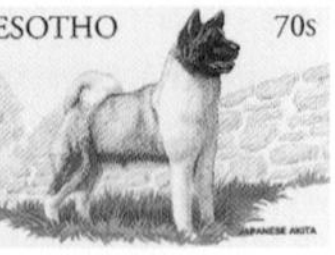

259 Japanese Akita

1999. Dogs. Multicoloured.

1535	70s. Type **259**	40	20
1536	1m. Canaan dog	45	20
1537	2m. Husky ("ESKIMO DOG")	60	60
1538	2m. Cirneco dell'Etna	60	60
1539	2m. Afghan hound	60	60
1540	2m. Finnish spitz	60	60
1541	2m. Dalmatian	60	60
1542	2m. Basset hound	60	60
1543	2m. Shar-pei	60	60
1544	2m. Boxer	60	60
1545	2m. Catalan sheepdog	60	60
1546	2m. English toy spaniel	60	60
1547	2m. Greyhound	60	60
1548	2m. Keeshond	60	60
1549	2m. Bearded collie	60	60
1550	4m.50 Norwegian elkhound	1·50	1·60

MS1551 Two sheets, each 98×69 mm. (a) 8m. Rough Collie. (b) 8m. Borzoi 6·50 6·50

Nos. 1538/43 and 1544/9 were printed together, *se-tenant*, with the backgrounds forming composite designs.

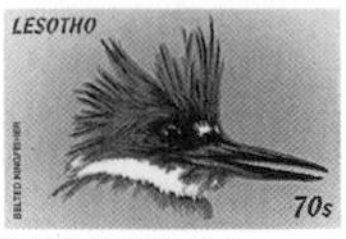

260 Belted Kingfisher

1999. Birds. Multicoloured.

1552	70s. Type **260**	60	20
1553	1m.50 Palm cockatoo (vert)	85	45
1554	2m. Red-tailed hawk	85	70
1555	2m. Evening grosbeak	85	85
1556	2m. Blue-winged pitta ("Lesser Blue-winged Pitta")	85	85
1557	2m. Lichtenstein's oriole ("Atlamira Oriole")	85	85
1558	2m. Rose-breasted grosbeak	85	85
1559	2m. Yellow warbler	85	85
1560	2m. Akiapolaau	85	85
1561	2m. American goldfinch	85	85
1562	2m. Common flicker ("Northern Flicker")	85	85
1563	2m. Western tanager	85	85
1564	2m. Blue jay (vert)	85	85
1565	2m. Common cardinal ("Northern Cardinal") (vert)	85	85
1566	2m. Yellow-headed blackbird (vert)	85	85
1567	2m. Red crossbill (vert)	85	85
1568	2m. Cedar waxwing (vert)	85	85
1569	2m. Vermilion flycatcher (vert)	85	85
1570	2m. Pileated woodpecker (vert)	85	85
1571	2m. Western meadowlark (vert)	85	85
1572	2m. Belted kingfisher ("Kingfisher") (vert)	85	85
1573	3m. Tufted puffin	1·00	1·25
1574	4m. Reddish egret	1·25	1·50
1575	5m. Hoatzin (vert)	1·25	1·75

MS1576 Two sheets. (a) 76×106 mm. 8m. Great egret. (b) 106×76 mm. 8m. Chestnut-flanked white-eye "Zosterops erythropleura" 7·50 8·00

No. 1553 shows the face value as "M1.5".

Nos. 1555/63 and 1564/72 were printed together, *se-tenant*, with the backgrounds forming composite designs.

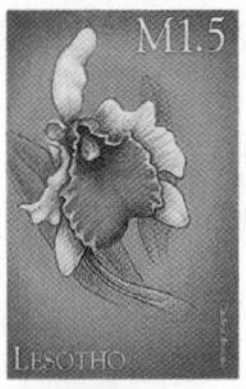

261 "Cattleya dowiana"

1999. Orchids of the World. Multicoloured.

1577	1m.50 Type **261**	75	30
1578	2m. *Cochleanthes discolor*	75	75
1579	2m. *Cischweinfia dasyandra*	75	75
1580	2m. *Ceratostylis retisquama*	75	75
1581	2m. *Comparettia speciosa*	75	75
1582	2m. *Cryptostylis subulata*	75	75
1583	2m. *Cycnoches ventricosum*	75	75
1584	2m. *Dactylorhiza maculata*	75	75
1585	2m. *Cypripedium calceolus*	75	75
1586	2m. *Cymbidium finlaysonianum*	75	75
1587	2m. *Apasia epidendroides*	75	75
1588	2m. *Barkaria lindleyana*	75	75
1589	2m. *Bifrenaria tetragona*	75	75
1590	2m. *Bulbophyllum graveolens*	75	75
1591	2m. *Brassavola flagellaris*	75	75
1592	2m. *Bollea lawrenceana*	75	75
1593	2m. *Caladenia carnea*	75	75
1594	2m. *Catasetum macrocarpum*	75	75
1595	2m. *Cattleya aurantiaca*	75	75
1596	2m. *Dendrobium bellatulum*	75	75
1597	2m. *Dendrobium trigonopus*	75	75
1598	2m. *Dimerandra emarginata*	75	75
1599	2m. *Dressleria eburnea*	75	75
1600	2m. *Dracula tubeana*	75	75
1601	2m. *Disa kirstenbosch*	75	75
1602	2m. *Encyclia alata*	75	75
1603	2m. *Epidendrum pseudepidendrum*	75	75
1604	2m. *Eriopsis biloba*	75	75
1605	3m. *Diurus behrii*	1·00	1·00
1606	4m. *Ancistrochilus rothchildianus*	1·25	1·25
1607	5m. *Aerangis curnowiana*	1·40	1·40
1608	7m. *Arachnis flos-aeris*	1·75	2·00
1609	8m. *Aspasia principissa*	1·75	2·25

MS1610 Four sheets, each 110×82 mm. (a) 10m. *Paphiopedilum tonsum*. (b) 10m. *Ansellia africana*. (c) 10m. *Laelia rubescens*. (d) 10m. *Ophrys apifera* 14·00 15·00

No. 1583 was inscribed "Cycnoches ventricsum" in error.

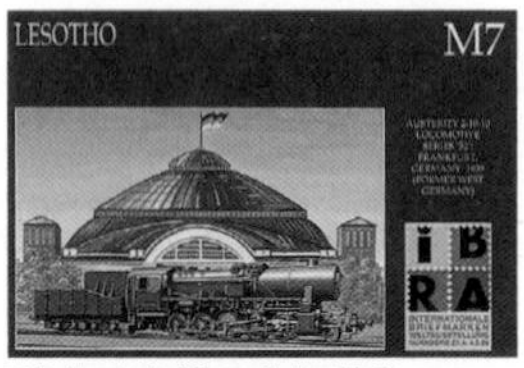

262 "Austerity" Type Series 52 Steam Locomotive, Frankfurt, 1939

1999. "iBRA '99" International Stamp Exhibition, Nuremburg. Railway Locomotives. Multicoloured.

1611	7m. Type **262**	2·00	2·00
1612	8m. "Adler" and Brandenburg Gate, Berlin, 1835	2·00	2·00

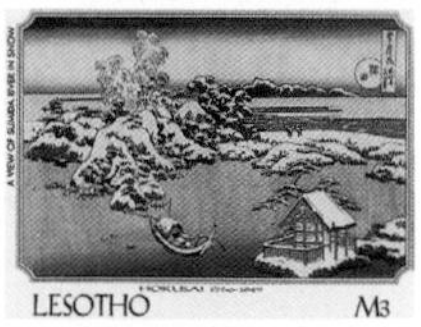

263 "View of Sumida River in Snow"

1999. 150th Death Anniv of Katsushika Hokusai (Japanese artist). Multicoloured.

1613	3m. Type **263**	75	75
1614	3m. *Two Carp*	75	75
1615	3m. *The Blind* (woman with eyes closed)	75	75
1616	3m. *The Blind* (woman with one eye open)	75	75
1617	3m. *Fishing by Torchlight*	75	75
1618	3m. *Whaling off the Goto Islands*	75	75
1619	3m. *Makamaro watching the Moon from a Hill*	75	75
1620	3m. *Peonies and Butterfly*	75	75
1621	3m. *The Blind* (old man with open eyes)	75	75
1622	3m. *The Blind* (old man with one eye open)	75	75
1623	3m. *People crossing an Arched Bridge* (four people on bridge)	75	75
1624	3m. *People crossing an Arched Bridge* (two people on bridge)	75	75

MS1625 Two sheets, each 102×72 mm. (a) 10m. *Bell-flower and Dragonfly* (vert). (b) 10m. *Moon above Yodo River and Osaka Castle* (vert). Set of 2 sheets 5·50 6·00

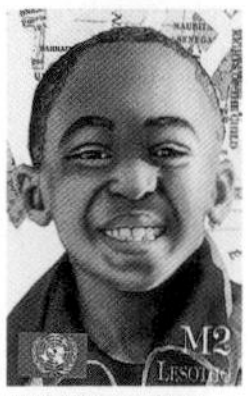

264 African Boy

1999. 10th Anniv of United Nations Rights of the Child Convention. Multicoloured.

1626	2m. Type **264**	85	90
1627	2m. Asian girl	85	90
1628	2m. European boy	85	90

Nos. 1626/8 were printed together, *se-tenant*, the backgrounds forming a composite design.

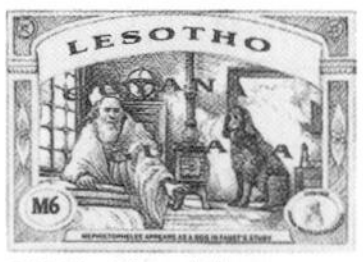

265 Mephistopheles appearing as Dog in Faust's Study

1999. 250th Birth Anniv of Johann von Goethe (German writer).

1629	**265**	6m. multicoloured	1·40	1·75
1630	-	6m. blue, lilac and black	1·40	1·75
1631	-	6m. multicoloured	1·40	1·75

MS1632 76×106 mm. 12m. red, violet and black 2·75 3·25

DESIGNS—HORIZ: No. 1630, Goethe and Schiller; 1631, Mephistopheles disguised as a dog scorching the Earth. VERT: No. **MS**1632, Mephistopheles.

No. 1629, in addition to the normal country name, shows "GUYANA" twice in violet across the centre of the design.

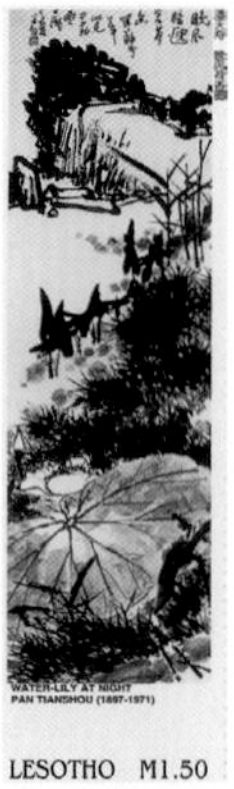

266 "Water Lily at Night" (Pan Tianshou)

1999. "China '99" International Stamp Exhibition, Beijing. Paintings of Pan Tianshou (Chinese artist). Multicoloured.

1633	1m.50 Type **266**	40	50
1634	1m.50 *Hen and Chicks*	40	50
1635	1m.50 *Plum Blossom and Orchid*	40	50
1636	1m.50 *Plum Blossom and Banana Tree*	40	50
1637	1m.50 *Crane and Pine*	40	50
1638	1m.50 *Swallows*	40	50
1639	1m.50 *Eagle on the Pine* (bird looking up)	40	50
1640	1m.50 *Palm Tree*	40	50
1641	1m.50 *Eagle on the Pine* (bird looking down)	40	50
1642	1m.50 *Orchids*	40	50

MS1643 138×105 mm. 6m. *Sponge Gourd* (51×39 mm); 6m. *Dragonfly* (51×39 mm) 4·25 4·75

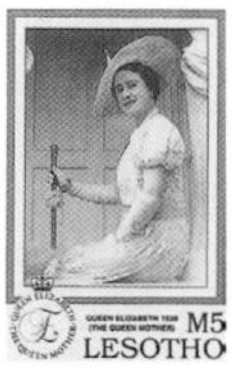

267 Queen Elizabeth, 1938

1999. "Queen Elizabeth the Queen Mother's Century".

1644	**267**	5m. black and gold	1·50	1·50
1645	-	5m. multicoloured	1·50	1·50
1646	-	5m. black and gold	1·50	1·50
1647	-	5m. multicoloured	1·50	1·50

MS1648 153×152 mm. 15m. multicoloured 3·75 4·00

DESIGNS: No. 1645, King George VI and Queen Elizabeth, 1948; 1646, Queen Mother wearing tiara, 1963; 1647, Queen Mother wearing blue hat, Canada, 1989. 37×50 mm.—No. **MS**1648, Queen Mother outside Clarence House.

No. **MS**1648 also shows the Royal Arms embossed in gold.

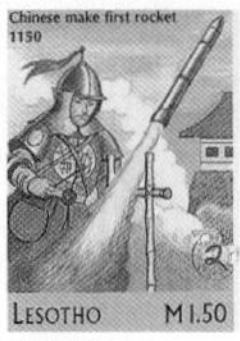

268 Chinese Soldier firing Rocket, 1150

1999. New Millennium. People and Events of Twelfth Century (1150–99). Multicoloured.

1649	1m.50 Type **268**	60	60
1650	1m.50 Burmese temple guardian, 1150	60	60
1651	1m.50 Troubadour serenading Lady, 1150	60	60
1652	1m.50 Abbot Suger (advisor to French Kings), 1150	60	60
1653	1m.50 Pope Adrian IV, 1154	60	60
1654	1m.50 Henry II of England, 1154	60	60
1655	1m.50 Bust of Frederick Barbarossa, King of Germany, and Holy Roman Emperor, 1155	60	60
1656	1m.50 Shogun Yoritomo of Japan, 1156	60	60
1657	1m.50 Count and Countess of Vaudemont (Crusader monument), 1165	60	60
1658	1m.50 Ibn Rushd (Arab translator), 1169	60	60
1659	1m.50 Archbishop Thomas a Becket, 1170	60	60
1660	1m.50 Leaning Tower of Pisa, 1174	60	60
1661	1m.50 Pivot windmill, 1180	60	60
1662	1m.50 Saladin (Saracen general), 1187	60	60
1663	1m.50 King Richard the Lionheart of England, 1189	60	60
1664	1m.50 Moai (statues), Easter Island, 1150 (59×39 mm)	60	60
1665	1m.50 Crusader, 1189	60	60

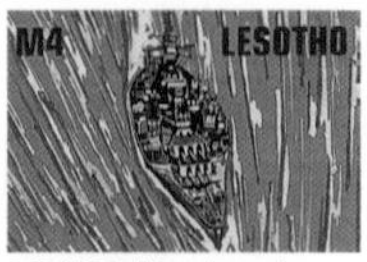

269 U.S.S. "New Jersey" (battleship)

1999. Maritime Developments 1700–2000. Multicoloured.

1666	4m. Type **269**	1·00	1·00
1667	4m. "Aquila" (Italian aircraft carrier)	1·00	1·00
1668	4m. "De Zeven Provincien" (Dutch cruiser)	1·00	1·00
1669	4m. H.M.S. "Formidable" (aircraft carrier)	1·00	1·00
1670	4m. "Vittorio Veneto" (Italian cruiser)	1·00	1·00
1671	4m. H.M.S. "Hampshire" (destroyer)	1·00	1·00
1672	4m. "France" (French liner)	1·00	1·00
1673	4m. "Queen Elizabeth 2" (liner)	1·00	1·00
1674	4m. "United States" (American liner)	1·00	1·00
1675	4m. "Queen Elizabeth" (liner)	1·00	1·00
1676	4m. "Michelangelo" (Italian liner)	1·00	1·00
1677	4m. "Mauretania" (British liner)	1·00	1·00
1678	4m. "Shearwater" (British hydrofoil ferry)	1·00	1·00
1679	4m. British Class M submarine	1·00	1·00
1680	4m. SRN 130 hovercraft	1·00	1·00
1681	4m. Italian Second World War submarine	1·00	1·00
1682	4m. SRN 3 hovercraft	1·00	1·00
1683	4m. "Soucoupe Plongeante" (oceanographic submersible)	1·00	1·00
1684	4m. "James Watt" (early steamship)	1·00	1·00
1685	4m. "Savannah" (steam/sail ship), 1819	1·00	1·00
1686	4m. "Amistad" (slave schooner)	1·00	1·00
1687	4m. American Navy brig	1·00	1·00
1688	4m. "Great Britain" (liner)	1·00	1·00
1689	4m. "Sirius" (paddle steamer)	1·00	1·00

MS1690 Four sheets, each 106×76 mm. (a) 15m. U.S.S. "Enterprise" (aircraft carrier) (vert). (b) 15m. "Titanic" (liner). (c) 15m. German U-boat. (d) 15m. "E. W. Morrison" (Great Lakes schooner) (vert). Set of 4 sheets 15·00 16·00

Nos. 1686 and 1687 both have their names wrongly inscribed as "ARMISTAD" and "BRICK" on the sheet margin.

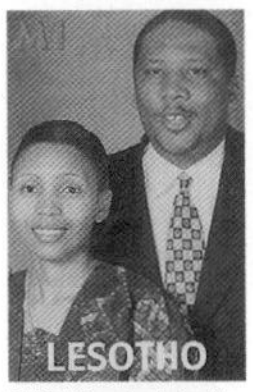

270 King Letsie III and Miss Karabo Anne Motsoeneng

2000. Wedding of King Letsie III. Multicoloured.

1691	1m. Type **270**	75	75
1692	1m. Miss Karabo Anne Motsoeneng	75	75
1693	1m. King Letsie III	75	75
1694	1m. King Letsie III and Miss Karabo Motsoeneng in traditional dress	75	75

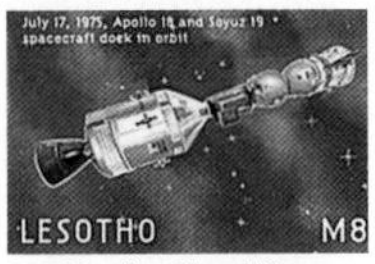

271 "Apollo 18" and "Soyuz 19" docked in Orbit

2000. 25th Anniv of "Apollo–Soyuz" Joint Project. Multicoloured.

1695	8m. Type **271**	2·00	2·00
1696	8m. "Apollo 18" and docking module	2·00	2·00
1697	8m. "Soyuz 19"	2·00	2·00
MS1698	106×76 mm. 15m. Docking module and "Soyuz 19"	4·00	4·50

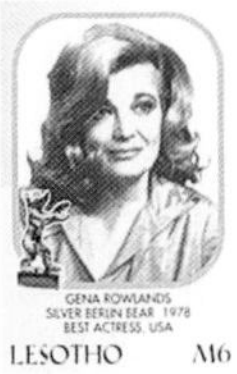

272 Gena Rowlands (actress), 1978

2000. 50th Anniv of Berlin Film Festival. Showing actors, directors and film scenes with awards. Multicoloured.

1699	6m. Type **272**	1·25	1·40
1700	6m. Vlastimil Brodsky (actor), 1975	1·25	1·40
1701	6m. Carlos Saura (director), 1966	1·25	1·40
1702	6m. Scene from *La Collectionneuse*, 1967	1·25	1·40
1703	6m. Scene from *Le Depart*, 1967	1·25	1·40
1704	6m. Scene from *Le Diable Probablement*, 1977	1·25	1·40
MS1705	97×103 mm. 15m. Scene from *Stammeheim*, 1986	4·25	4·50

No. 1704 is inscribed "LE DIIABLE PROBABLEMENT" in error.

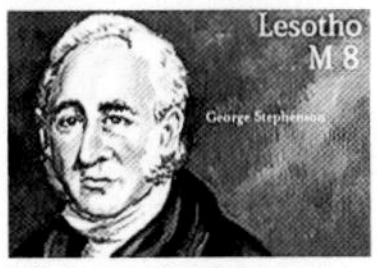

273 George Stephenson

2000. 175th Anniv of Stockton and Darlington Line (first public railway). Multicoloured.

1706	8m. Type **273**	2·25	2·25
1707	8m. Stephenson's Patent locomotive	2·25	2·25
1708	8m. Robert Stephenson's Britannia Tubular Bridge, Menai Straits	2·25	2·25

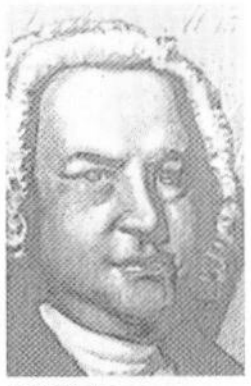

274 Johann Sebastian Bach

2000. 250th Death Anniv of Johann Sebastian Bach (German composer). Sheet 105×101 mm.

MS1709 **274** 15m. multicoloured 4·50 4·50

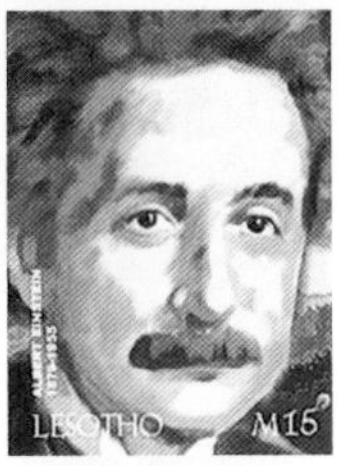

275 Albert Einstein

2000. Election of Albert Einstein (mathematical physicist) as Time Magazine "Man of the Century". Sheet 117×91 mm.

MS1710 **275** 15m. multicoloured 3·75 4·00

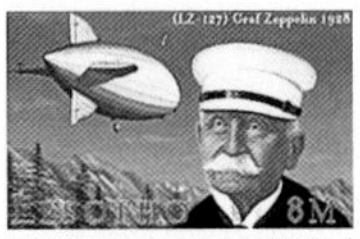

276 Ferdinand Zeppelin and LZ-127 *Graf Zeppelin*, 1928

2000. Centenary of First Zeppelin Flight. Mult.

1711	8m. Type **276**	2·00	2·00
1712	8m. LZ-130 *Graf Zeppelin II*, 1938	2·00	2·00
1713	8m. LZ-10 *Schwaben*, 1911	2·00	2·00
MS1714	83×119 mm. 15m. LZ-130 *Graf Zeppelin II*, 1938 (50×37 mm)	3·75	4·25

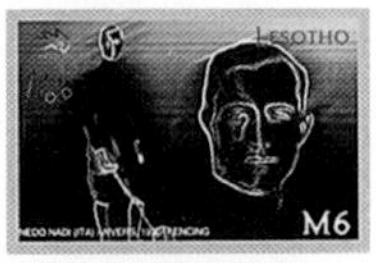

277 Nedo Nadi (Italian fencer), 1920

2000. Olympic Games, Sydney. Multicoloured.

1715	6m. Type **277**	1·75	2·00
1716	6m. Swimming (butterfly stroke)	1·75	2·00
1717	6m. Aztec Stadium, Mexico City, 1968	1·75	2·00
1718	6m. Ancient Greek boxing	1·75	2·00

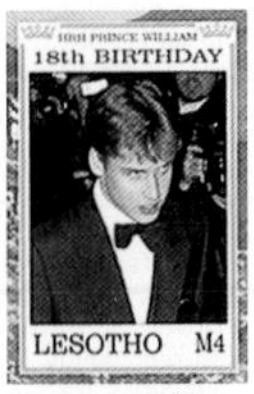

278 Prince William in Evening Dress

2000. 18th Birthday of Prince William. Multicoloured.

1719	4m. Type **278**	1·40	1·40
1720	4m. Wearing coat and scarf	1·40	1·40
1721	4m. Wearing striped shirt and tie	1·40	1·40
1722	4m. Getting out of car	1·40	1·40
MS1723	100×80 mm. 15m. Prince William (37×50 mm)	4·50	4·50

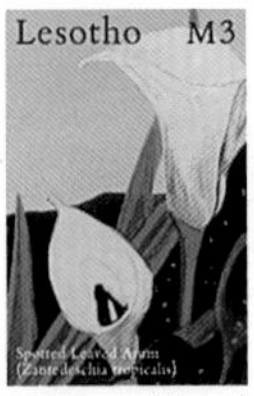

279 Spotted-leaved Arum

2000. African Flowers. Multicoloured.

1724	3m. Type **279**	85	85
1725	3m. Christmas bells	85	85
1726	3m. Lady Monson	85	85
1727	3m. Wild pomegranate	85	85
1728	3m. Blushing bride	85	85
1729	3m. Bot River protea	85	85
1730	3m. Drooping agapanthus	85	85
1731	3m. Yellow marsh Afrikander	85	85
1732	3m. Weak-stemmed painted lady	85	85
1733	3m. Impala lily	85	85
1734	3m. Beatrice Watsonia	85	85
1735	3m. Pink arum	85	85
1736	3m. Starry gardenia	85	85
1737	3m. Pink hibiscus	85	85
1738	3m. Dwarf poker	85	85
1739	3m. Coast kaffirboom	85	85
1740	3m. Rose cockade	85	85
1741	3m. Pride of Table Mountain	85	85
1742	4m. Moore's crinum	1·50	1·50
1743	5m. Flame lily	1·50	1·50
1744	6m. Cape clivia	1·60	1·60
1745	8m. True sugarbush	1·75	2·00
MS1746	Two sheets, each 107×77 mm. (a) 15m. Red Hairy Erika (horiz). (b) 15m. Green Arum. Set of 2 sheets	9·00	11·00

Nos. 1724/9, 1730/5 and 1736/41 were each printed together, se-tenant, with the backgrounds forming composite designs.

No. 1733 is inscribed "Llly", No. 1736 "Gardenia thunbengii" and No. 1741 "Disa unoflora", all in error.

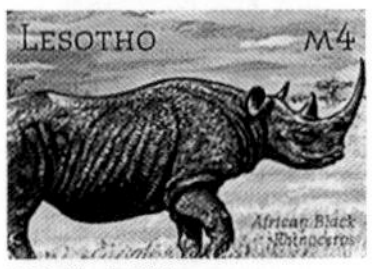

280 Black Rhinoceros

2000. "The Stamp Show 2000", International Stamp Exhibition, London. Endangered Wildlife. Multicoloured.

1747	4m. Type **280**	1·25	1·25
1748	4m. Leopard	1·25	1·25
1749	4m. Roseate tern	1·25	1·25
1750	4m. Mountain gorilla	1·25	1·25
1751	4m. Mountain zebra	1·25	1·25
1752	4m. Zanzibar red colobus monkey	1·25	1·25
1753	4m. Cholo alethe	1·25	1·25
1754	4m. Temminck's pangolin	1·25	1·25
1755	4m. Cheetah	1·25	1·25
1756	4m. African elephant	1·25	1·25
1757	4m. Chimpanzee	1·25	1·25
1758	4m. Northern white rhinoceros	1·25	1·25
1759	5m. Blue wildebeest	1·25	1·25
1760	5m. Tree hyrax	1·40	1·40
1761	5m. Red lechwe	1·40	1·40
1762	5m. Eland	1·40	1·40
MS1763	Two sheets, each 65×118 mm. (a) 15m. Dugong (vert). (b) 15m. West African Manatee (vert). Set of 2 sheets	9·00	11·00

Nos. 1747/52, 1753/8 and 1759/62 were each printed together, *se-tenant*, with the backgrounds forming composite designs.

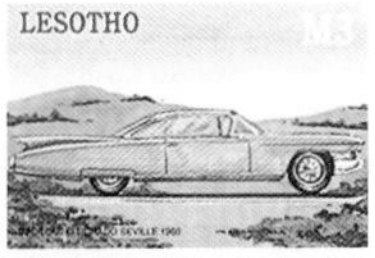

281 Cadillac Eldorado Seville (1960)

2000. Classic Cars. Multicoloured.

1764	3m. Type **281**	90	90
1765	3m. Citroen DS (1955–75)	90	90
1766	3m. Ford Zephyr Zodiac MK II (1961)	90	90
1767	3m. MG TF (1945–55)	90	90
1768	3m. Porsche 356 (1949–65)	90	90
1769	3m. Ford Thunderbird (1955)	90	90
1770	3m. Cisitalia 202 Coupe (1948–52)	90	90
1771	3m. Dodge Viper (1990s)	90	90
1772	3m. TVR Vixen SI (1968–69)	90	90
1773	3m. Lotus 7 (1957–70)	90	90
1774	3m. Ferrari 275 GTB/4 (1964–68)	90	90
1775	3m. Pegasus - Touring Spider (1951–58)	90	90
1776	4m. Fiat Type O (1913)	90	90
1777	4m. Stutz Bearcat (1914)	90	90
1778	4m. French Leyat (1924)	90	90
1779	4m. Benz gasoline-driven Motorwagon (1886)	90	90
1780	4m. Isotta Fraschini Type 8A (1925)	90	90
1781	4m. Markus Motor Carriage (1887)	90	90
1782	4m. Morris Minor (1951)	90	90
1783	4m. Hispano-Suiza Type 68 (1935)	90	90
1784	4m. MG TC (1949)	90	90
1785	4m. Morgan 4/4 (1955)	90	90
1786	4m. Jaguar XK120 (1950)	90	90
1787	4m. Triumph 1800/2000 Roadster (1946–49)	90	90
MS1788	Four sheets. (a) 110×85 mm. 15m. AC ACE (1953–63). (b) 110×85 mm. 15m. Morris Minor 1000 (1948–71). (c) 85×110 mm. 15m. Ferrari F 40 (vert). (d) 110×85 mm. 15m. Bersey Electric Cab (1896). Set of 4 sheets	15·00	16·00

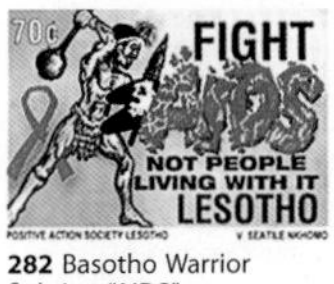

282 Basotho Warrior fighting "AIDS"

2001. Fight Against Aids. Multicoloured.

1789	70c. Type **282**	55	20
1790	1m. "Speed Kills So Does Aids"	80	30
1791	1m.50 "People with Aids need friends not rejection"	1·25	1·25
1792	2m.10 "Even when you're off duty protect the nation"	1·50	1·75

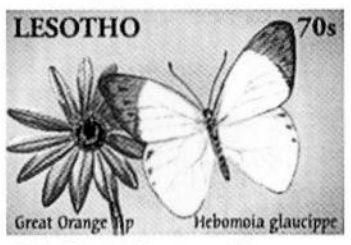

283 Great Orange Tip

2001. Butterflies. Multicoloured.

1793	70s. Type **283**	50	20
1794	1m. Red-banded pereute	60	20
1795	1m.50 Sword grass brown	80	45
1796	2m. Striped blue crow	80	65
1797	2m. Orange-banded sulphur	65	80
1798	2m. Large wood nymph	65	80
1799	2m. The postman	65	80
1800	2m. Palmfly	65	80
1801	2m. Gulf fritillary	65	80
1802	2m. Cairns birdwing	65	80
1803	2m. Common morpho	65	80
1804	2m. Common dotted border	65	80
1805	2m. African migrant	65	80
1806	2m. Large oak blue	65	80
1807	2m. The wanderer	65	80
1808	2m. Tiger swallowtail	65	80
1809	2m. Union jack	65	80
1810	2m. Saturn	65	80
1811	2m. Broad-bordered grass yellow	65	80
1812	2m. Hewitson's uraneis	65	80
1813	3m. Bertoni's antwren bird	85	85
1814	3m. Clorinde	85	85
1815	3m. Iolas blue	85	85
1816	3m. Mocker swallowtail	85	85
1817	3m. Common Indian crow	85	85
1818	3m. Grecian shoemaker	85	85
1819	3m. Small flambeau	85	85
1820	3m. Orchid swallowtail	85	85
1821	3m. Alfalfa butterfly	85	85
1822	4m. Doris butterfly	95	1·25
MS1823	Two sheets, each 70×100 mm. (a) 15m. Forest Queen. (b) 15m. Crimson Tip. Set of 2 sheets	12·00	13·00

Nos. 1797/1804, 1805/12 and 1813/20 were each printed together, *se-tenant*, with the backgrounds forming composite designs.

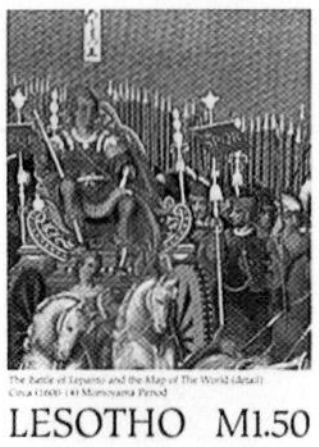

284 Roman General and Soldiers from "Battle of Lepanto and Map of the World" (anon)

2001. "Philanippon 01" International Stamp Exhibition, Tokyo. Paintings from Momoyama Era. Multicoloured.

1824	1m.50 Type **284**	60	30
1825	2m. Pikemen and musketeers from "Battle of Lepanto and Map of the World"	90	40
1826	3m. Manchurian crane from "Birds and Flowers of the Four Seasons" (Kano Eitoku)	1·00	65
1827	4m. Travellers in the mountains from "Birds and Flowers of the Four Seasons"	1·00	1·00
1828	5m. "Portrait of a Lady" (24½×81½ mm)	1·00	1·00
1829	5m. "Honda Tadakatsu" (24½×81½ mm)	1·00	1·00
1830	5m. "Wife of Goto Tokujo" (24½×81½ mm)	1·00	1·00
1831	5m. "Emperor Go-Yozei" (Kano Takanobu) (24½×81½ mm)	1·00	1·00
1832	5m. "Tenzuiin Hideyoshi's Mother, Hoshuku Sochin" (24½×81½ mm)	1·00	1·00
1833	6m. "Hosokawa Yusai" (Ishin Suden) (24½×81½ mm)	1·25	1·25
1834	6m. "Sen No Rikyu" (attr Hasegawa Tohaku) (24½×81½ mm)	1·25	1·25
1835	6m. "Oichi No Kata" (24½×81½ mm)	1·25	1·25
1836	6m. "Inaba Ittetsu" (attr Hasegawa Tohaku) (24½×81½ mm)	1·25	1·25
1837	6m. "Oda Nobunaga" (Kokei Sochin) (24½×81½ mm)	1·25	1·25
1838	7m. "Viewing the Maples at Mount Takao"	1·50	2·00
1839	8m. "The Four Accomplishments" (Kaiho Yusho)	1·50	2·25

MS1840 Two sheets. (a) 98×131 mm. 15m. "Tokugawa Ieyasu". (b) 114×134 mm. 15m. "Toyotomi Hideyoshi". Set of 2 sheets 9·50 11·00

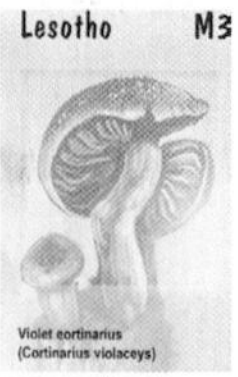

285 *Cortinarius violaceus*

2001. "Belgica 2001" International Stamp Exhibition, Brussels. African Fungi. Multicoloured.

1841 3m. Type **285** 1·10 1·10
1842 3m. *Pleurocybella porrigens* 1·10 1·10
1843 3m. *Collybia velutibes* 1·10 1·10
1844 3m. *Lentinellus cochleatus* 1·10 1·10
1845 3m. *Anthurua aseroiformis* 1·10 1·10
1846 3m. Caesar's mushroom 1·10 1·10
1847 4m. *Cortinarius traganus* 1·10 1·10
1848 4m. *Peziza sarcosphaera* 1·10 1·10
1849 4m. *Russula emetica* 1·10 1·10
1850 4m. *Stropharia ambigua* 1·10 1·10
1851 4m. *Phlogiotis helvelloides* 1·10 1·10
1852 4m. *Clitocybe odora* 1·10 1·10
1853 5m. Golden false pholiota 1·25 1·25
1854 5m. *Coprinus micaceus* 1·25 1·25
1855 5m. *Hygrophorus camarophyllus* 1·25 1·25
1856 5m. *Panaeolus campanulatus* 1·25 1·25
MS1857 Two sheets, each 75×55 mm. (a) 15m. *Boletus parasiticus* (horiz). (b) 15m. *Hygrophorus hygrocybe conicus* (horiz). Set of 2 sheets 14·00 14·00

No. 1841 is inscribed "violaceys", 1842 "Pleyrocybella", 1844 "Cochleathus", 1852 "Clitoeybe" and 1856 "Panaelus companulatus", all in error.

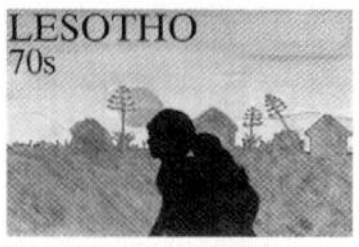

286 "Woman with Baby in Sunset" (Leila Hall)

2001. Winners of United Nations Children's Art Competition. Multicoloured.

1858 70s. Type **286** 50 15
1859 1m. "Herdboy with Lamb" (Chambeli Ramathe) 65 30
1860 1m.50 "Girl with A.I.D.S. Ribbon" (Chambeli Ramathe) (vert) 1·00 1·00
1861 2m.10 "Satellite Dish and Map seen through Keyhole" (Mika Sejake) (vert) 1·25 1·50

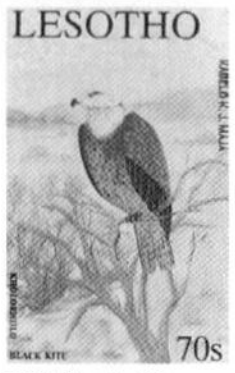

287 Black Kite

2001. Birds of Prey. Multicoloured.

1862 70s. Type **287** 55 30
1863 1m. Martial eagle 70 35
1864 1m.50 Bateleur 90 80
1865 2m.10 African goshawk 1·25 1·25
1866 2m.50 Lammergeier ("Bearded Vulture") 1·25 1·50
1867 3m. Jackal buzzard 1·40 1·75

No. 1865 is inscribed "GASHAWK" in error.

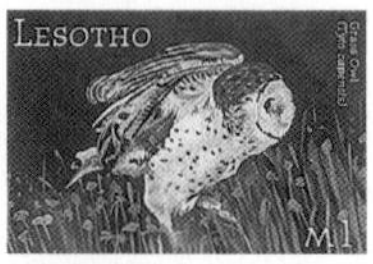

288 Grass Owl

2001. Wildlife of Southern Africa. Multicoloured.

1868 1m. Type **288** 1·00 60
1869 2m.10 Klipspringer 1·00 70
1870 3m. Saddle-backed jackal 1·25 80
1871 4m. Aardvark 1·25 1·25
1872 4m. Common kestrel ("Rock Kestrel") 1·25 1·25
1873 4m. Black-footed cat 1·25 1·25
1874 4m. Springhare 1·25 1·25
1875 4m. Aardwolf 1·25 1·25
1876 4m. Rock hyrax 1·25 1·25
1877 4m. Damara zebra 1·25 1·25
1878 4m. Bontebok 1·25 1·25
1879 4m. Eland 1·25 1·25
1880 4m. Lion 1·25 1·25
1881 4m. Saddle-backed jackal 1·25 1·25
1882 4m. Black kite ("Yellow-billed Kite") 1·25 1·25
1883 5m. Black wildebeest 1·25 1·50
MS1884 Two sheets, each 90×64 mm. (a) 15m. Black-shouldered kite. (b) 15m. Caracal (vert). Set of 2 sheets 10·00 11·00

Nos. 1871/6 and 1877/82 were each printed together, *se-tenant*, with the backgrounds forming composite designs.

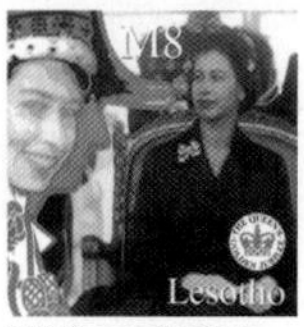

289 Queen Elizabeth wearing Purple Coat

2002. Golden Jubilee. Multicoloured.

1885 8m. Type **289** 2·50 2·50
1886 8m. Queen Elizabeth with Duke of Edinburgh on launch 2·50 2·50
1887 8m. Queen Elizabeth with mayor 2·50 2·50
1888 8m. Duke of Edinburgh wearing sunglasses 2·50 2·50
MS1889 76×108 mm. 20m. Queen Elizabeth inspecting R.A.F. guard of honour 6·50 7·00

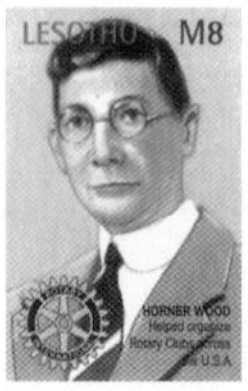

290 Homer Wood (Rotary pioneer)

2002. 25th Anniv of Rotary International in Lesotho. Multicoloured.

1890 8m. Type **290** 2·00 2·00
1891 10m. Paul Harris (founder of Rotary International) 2·25 2·25
MS1892 Two sheets. (a) 60×75 mm. 25m. Coloured globe and Rotary logo. (b) 75×60 mm. 25m. Golden Gate Bridge, San Francisco, and Rotary logo (horiz) 12·00 14·00

No. 1890 is inscribed "HORNER" in error.

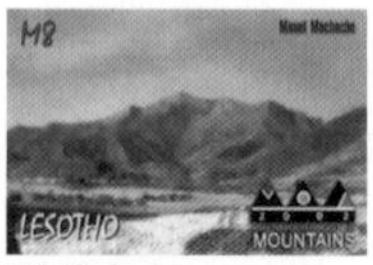

291 Machache

2002. International Year of Mountains. Showing Lesotho mountains (except No. MS1897). Multicoloured.

1893 8m. Type **291** 2·00 2·00
1894 8m. Thabana-li-Mele 2·00 2·00
1895 8m. Qiloane 2·00 2·00
1896 8m. Thaba-Bosiu 2·00 2·00
MS1897 64×83 mm. 25m. The Matterhorn, Switzerland (vert) 7·50 8·50

No. **MS**1897 is inscribed "Mount Rainer" in error.

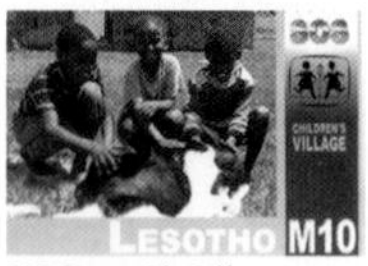

292 Boys with Calf, Lithabaneng

2002. S.O.S. Children's Villages (Kinderdorf International).

1898 **292** 10m. multicoloured 2·75 3·00

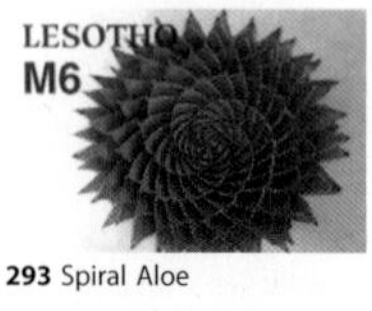

293 Spiral Aloe

2002. U.N. Year of Eco Tourism. Multicoloured.

1899 6m. Type **293** 1·60 1·75
1900 6m. Athrixia gerradii (flower) 1·60 1·75
1901 6m. Horseman and packhorse 1·60 1·75
1902 6m. Lion 1·60 1·75
1903 6m. Frog 1·60 1·75
1904 6m. Thatched building 1·60 1·75
MS1905 77×83 mm. 20m. European bee eater (vert) 7·00 8·00

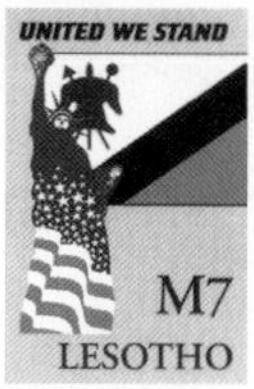

294 U.S. Flag as Statue of Liberty with Lesotho Flag

2002. "United We Stand". Support for Victims of 11 September 2001 Terrorist Attacks.

1906 **294** 7m. multicoloured 1·60 2·00

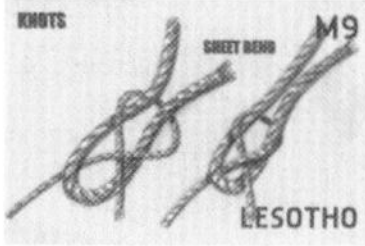

295 Sheet Bend Knot

2002. 20th World Scout Jamboree, Thailand. Multicoloured.

1907 9m. Type **295** 2·00 2·25
1908 9m. Pup and forester tents 2·00 2·25
1909 9m. Scouts in canoe 2·00 2·25
1910 9m. Life-saving 2·00 2·25
MS1911 75×59 mm. 25m. Scouts asleep in tent 7·00 8·00

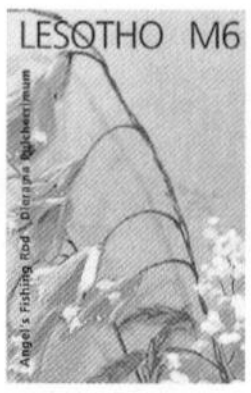

296 Angel's Fishing Rod (*Dierama pulcherrimum*)

2002. Flowers, Orchids and Insects. Multicoloured.

MS1912 100×180 mm. 6m. Type **296**; 6m. Marigold (*Calendula officinalis*); 6m. Dianthus "Joan's Blood"; 6m. Mule pink (*Dianthus plumarius*); 6m. Tiger lily (*Lilium lancifolium*); 6m. Clematis viticella "Comtesse de Bouchaud" 8·50 9·00
MS1913 180×100 mm. 6m. Leaf grasshopper (*Brochopeplu exalatus*); 6m. Golden-ringed dragonfly (*Cordulegaster boltoni*); 6m. Weevil-hunting wasp (*Cerceris arenaria*); 6m. European grasshopper (*Oedipoda miniata*); 6m. Thread-waisted Wasp (Ammophilia alberti); 6m. Mantid (*Mantis acontista*) (all horiz) 8·50 9·00
MS1914 95×103 mm. 6m. *Phragmipedium besseae*; 6m. *Cypripedium calceolus*; 6m. Cattleya "Louise Georgiana"; 6m. *Brassocattleya binosa*; 6m. *Laelia gouldiana*; 6m. *Paphiopedilum maudiae* "Alba" 8·50 9·00
MS1915 Three sheets. (a) 63×75 mm. 20m. Bleeding heart (*Dicentra spectabilis*. (b) 75×63 mm. 20m. Orb web spider (*Argiope bruennichi*). (c) 75×63 mm. 20m. *Brassavola tuberculata* Set of 3 16·00 18·00

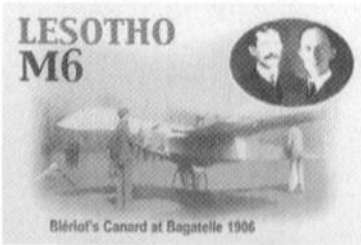

297 Bleriot's Canard at Bagatelle, 1906

2004. Centenary of Powered Flight. Multicoloured.

MS1916 177×97 mm. 6m. Type **297**; 6m. Bleriot's Double-winged Libellule, 1907; 6m. Bleriot's No. VIII in Toury–Artenay cross-country flight, 1908; 6m. Bleriot's X12 Test Flight, 1909 5·00 5·50
MS1917 66×97 mm. 15m. Louis Bleriot's No. XI 4·00 4·25

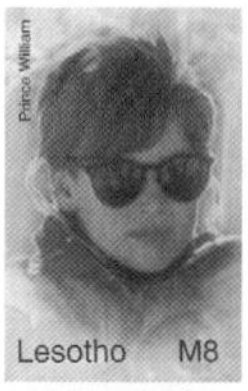

298 Prince William

2004. 21st Birthday of Prince William. Multicoloured.

MS1918 77×148 mm. 8m. Type **298**; 8m. Wearing grey suit and tie; 8m. Wearing yellow polo shirt 6·50 7·00
MS1919 98×68 mm. 15m. Young Prince William 4·25 4·50

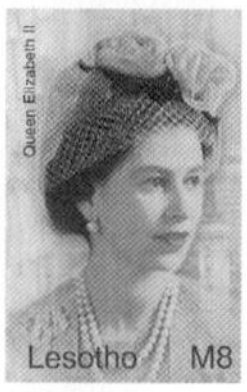

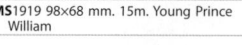

299 Queen Elizabeth II

2004. 50th Anniv (2003) of Coronation. Multicoloured.

MS1920 148×85 mm. 8m. Type **299**; 8m. Wearing ivory suit and hat; 8m. Wearing royal uniform 6·50 7·00
MS1921 68×97 mm. 15m. Queen Elizabeth II 4·25 4·50

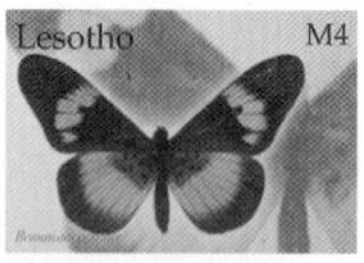

300 *Bematistes aganice*

2004. Butterflies. Multicoloured.

1922 1m.50 *Acraea rabbaiae* 80 40
1923 2m.10 *Alaena margaritacea* 1·00 55
1924 4m Type **300** 1·75 2·00
1925 6m. *Acraea quirina* 2·50 3·00
MS1926 117×116 mm. 6m. *Bematistes excise* (male); 6m. *Bematistes excise* (female); 6m. *Bematistes epiprotea*; 6m. *Bematistes poggei* 8·50 9·00
MS1927 67×98 mm. 15m. *Acraea satis* 5·00 5·50

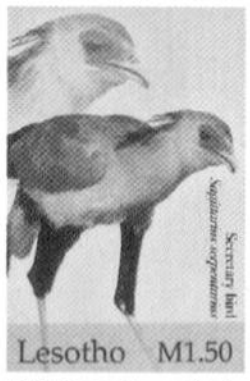

301 Secretary Bird

2004. Birds. Multicoloured.

1928 1m.50 Type **301** 80 50
1929 2m.10 South African crowned crane ("Gray-crowned Crane") 1·00 70
1930 3m. Pied avocet 1·50 1·50
1931 5m. Common kestrel 2·00 2·50
MS1932 108×136 mm. 6m. European roller; 6m. European cuckoo ("Common Cuckoo"); 6m. Great spotted cuckoo; 6m. Pel's fishing owl 9·50 11·00
MS1933 68×97 mm. 15m. Kori bustard 5·00 5·50

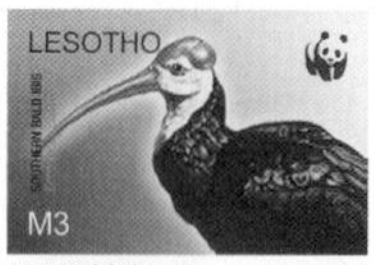

302 Bald Ibis

2004. Endangered Species. Bald Ibis. Multicoloured.

1934 3m. Type **302** 1·50 1·50
1935 3m. Bald Ibis at rest 1·50 1·50
1936 3m. Bald Ibis on nest 1·50 1·50
1937 3m. Bald Ibis in flight (facing right) 1·50 1·50
MS1938 207×132 mm. Designs as Nos. 1934/6 and 1937 (Bald Ibis facing left), each ×2 10·00 11·00

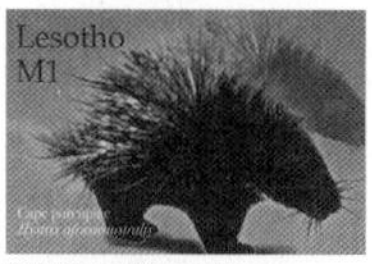

303 Cape Porcupine

2004. Animals. Multicoloured.

1939 1m. Type **303** 50 20
1940 1m.50 Brown rat 70 45
1941 2m.10 Springhare (vert) 90 70
1942 5m. South African galago (vert) 1·75 2·25
MS1943 117×136 mm. 5m. Striped grass mouse; 5m. Greater galago; 5m. Ground pangolin; 5m. Banded mongoose 7·50 8·50
MS1944 68×98 mm. 15m. Egyption rousette (vert) 4·50 5·00

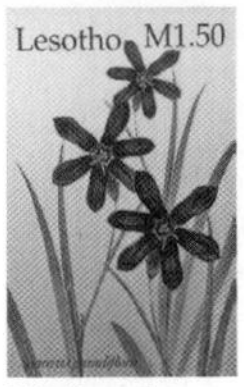

304 *Sparaxis grandiflora*

2004. Flowers. Multicoloured.

1945	1m.50 Type **304**	70	30
1946	2m.10 *Agapanthus africanus*	90	65
1947	3m. *Protea linearis*	1·25	1·25
1948	5m *Nerine cultivars*	1·75	2·25
MS1949	104×117 mm. 5m. *Kniphofia uvaria*; 5m. *Amaryllis belladonna*; 5m. *Gazania splendens*; 5m. *Erica coronata*	7·50	8·50
MS1950	68×98 mm. 15m. *Saintpaulia cultivars*	4·50	5·00

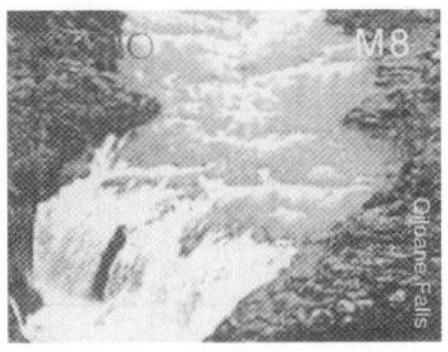

305 Qiloane Falls

2004. International Year of Freshwater. T **305** and similar horiz designs. Multicoloured.

MS1951	85×167 mm. 8m. Type **305**; 8m. Halfway down Qiloane Falls; 8m. Base of Qiloane Falls	8·50	9·50
MS1952	118×84 mm. 15m. Orange River	4·50	5·00

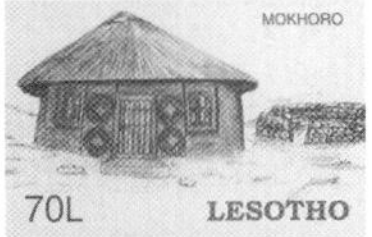

306 Mokhoro (Round House and Cooking Hut)

2005. Basotho Houses. Multicoloured.

1953	70s. Type **306**	40	15
1954	1m. Heisi (Rectangular house) Type **306**	65	35
1955	1m.50 Typical homestead	90	70
1956	2m.10 Mathule (Round house with porch)	1·25	1·75

No. 1953 is inscribed "70L" and No. 1956 "Mohlongoafat'se", both in error.

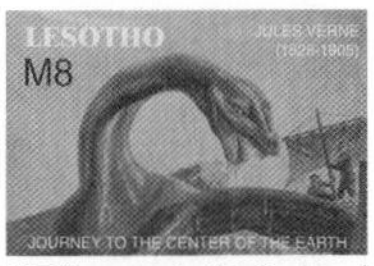

307 "Journey to the Centre of the Earth"

2005. Death Centenary of Jules Verne (writer). Multicoloured.

1957	8m. Type **307**	2·25	2·25
1958	8m. Jules Verne and "100 YEARS"	2·25	2·25
1959	8m. "20,000 Leagues under the Sea"	2·25	2·25
MS1960	107×83 mm. 15m. Jules Verne (vert)	4·00	4·50

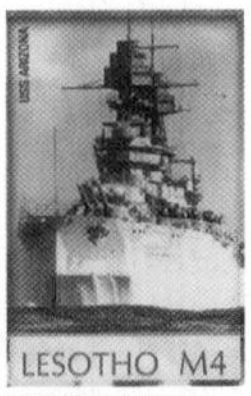

308 USS *Arizona* (battleship)

2005. 60th Anniv of Victory in Japan. Multicoloured.

1961	4m. Type **308**	1·60	1·60
1962	4m. Bunker at Chula Beach, Tinian Island	1·60	1·60
1963	4m. Flight crew of Bockscar (B-29 aircraft)	1·60	1·60
1964	4m. Men showing newspaper headline	1·60	1·60
1965	4m. Marker of second atomic bomb loading pit, Tinian Island	1·60	1·60

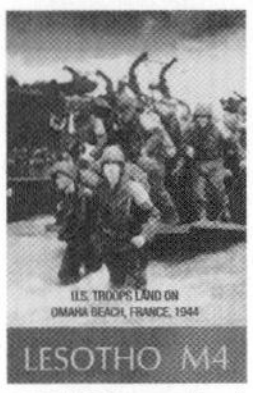

309 US Troops land on Omaha Beach

2005. 60th Anniv of Victory in Europe. Multicoloured.

1966	4m. Type **309**	1·60	1·60
1967	4m. General George C. Marshall	1·60	1·60
1968	4m. Field Marshall Wilhelm Keitel	1·60	1·60
1969	4m. General Dwight D. Eisenhower and Lt. General George S. Patton	1·60	1·60
1970	4m. Soldiers searching through rubble	1·60	1·60

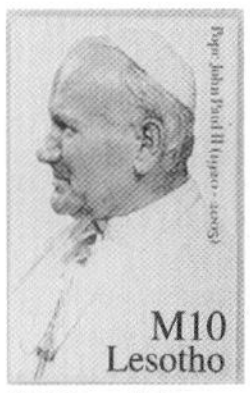

310 Pope John Paul II

2005. Pope John Paul II Commemoration.

1971	**310**	10m. multicoloured	4·00	4·00

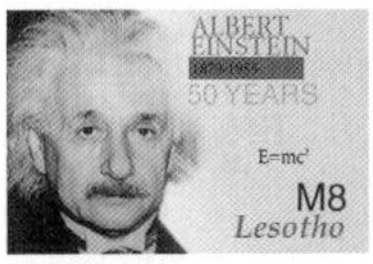

311 Albert Einstein

2005. 50th Death Anniv of Albert Einstein (physicist). Multicoloured.

1972	8m. Wearing glasses	2·25	2·25
1973	8m. With Nikola Tesla (inscr "Testa") and Charles Steinmetz	2·25	2·25
1974	8m. Type **311**	2·25	2·25
MS1975	100×70 mm. 15m. On the cover of *Time magazine* (vert)	4·00	4·50

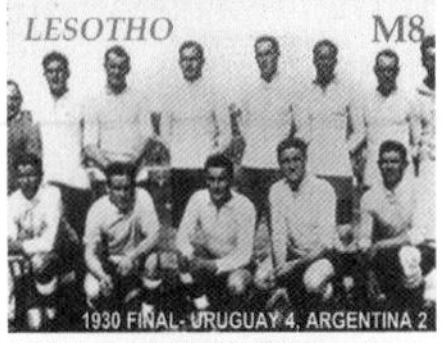

312 Uruguay Football Team, 1930

2005. 75th Anniv of First World Cup Football Championship, Uruguay. Multicoloured.

1976	8m. Type **312**	2·25	2·25
1977	8m. Opposing players and referee	2·25	2·25
1978	8m. German team	2·25	2·25
MS1979	105×70 mm. 15m. Bodo Illgner (Germany) (vert)	4·00	4·50

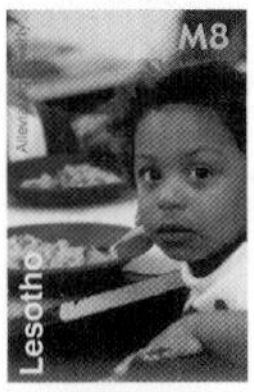

313 Child eating

2005. Centenary of Rotary International. Multicoloured.

1980	8m. Type **313**	2·25	2·25
1981	8m. Classroom scene	2·25	2·25
1982	8m. Children	2·25	2·25

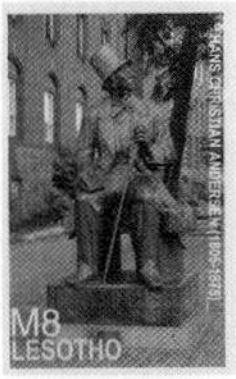

314 Hans Christian Andersen (statue)

2005. Birth Bicentenary of Hans Christian Andersen (writer). Multicoloured.

1983	8m. Type **314**	2·25	2·25
1984	8m. Former home of Hans Christian Andersen, Odense	2·25	2·25
1985	8m. "The Steadfast Tin Soldier"	2·25	2·25
MS1986	75×82 mm. 15m. "The Little Mermaid"	4·00	4·50

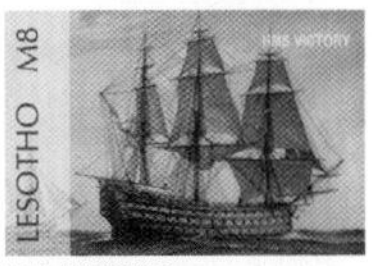

315 HMS *Victory*

2005. Bicentenary of the Battle of Trafalgar. Multicoloured.

1987	8m. Type **315**	3·50	3·00
1988	8m. Admiral Lord Horatio Nelson	3·50	3·00
1989	8m. Admiral Nelson fatally wounded	3·50	3·00
1990	8m. Ships engaged in battle	3·50	3·00
MS1991	70×100 mm. 25m. Admiral Lord Horatio Nelson and crew (50×38 mm)	13·00	13·00

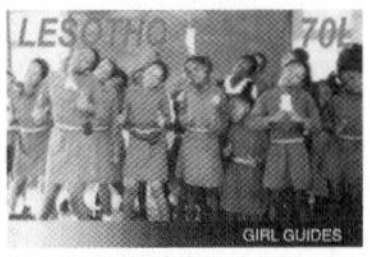

316 Brownies

2005. 80th Anniv of Lesotho Girl Guides Association. Multicoloured.

1992	70l. Type **316**	40	15
1993	1m. Procession of rangers and guides	60	30
1994	1m.50 Rangers recycling tin cans (vert)	90	80
1995	2m.10 Ranger and guides at Lesotho Girl Guides Headquarters	1·25	1·50
MS1996	66×98 mm. 10m. Queen 'Mamohato Seeiso (patron 1966—2003)	3·50	4·00

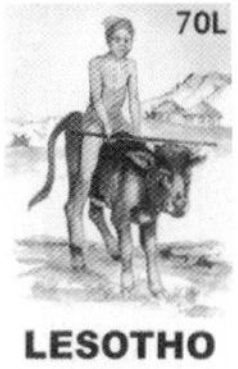

317 Herdboy riding Calf

2006. Herdboys. Multicoloured.

1997	70l. Type **317**	30	10
1998	1m. Feeding cattle	50	25
1999	1m.50 Three herdboys playing morabaraba and grazing cattle	70	65
2000	2m. Carrying newborn lamb on shoulders	90	1·25
MS2001	95×65 mm. 10m. Herdboys dancing ndlamo and practicing stick fighting	3·50	4·00

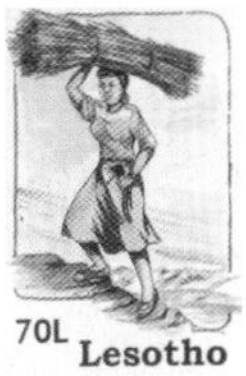

318 Woman carrying Thatch Grass

2006. Head Carrying by Mosotho Women. Multicoloured.

2002	70l. Type **318**	30	10
2003	1m. Carrying iron cooking pot on head	50	25
2004	1m.50 Carrying clay water pot on head	70	65
2005	2m.10 Carrying basket of pumpkins and maize on head and baby on back	90	1·25
MS2006	96×67 mm. 10m. Girl carrying basket of maize flour on head	3·50	4·00

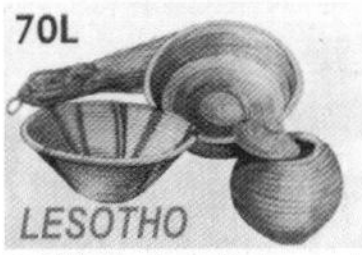

319 Woven Grass Baskets and Broom

2006. Handicrafts. Multicoloured.

2007	70l. Type **319** 21	30	10
2008	1m. Artist and tapestry (vert)	50	25
2009	1m.50 Calabash, clay pots and pipe	70	65
2010	2m.10 Horn, carved fish and bird	90	1·25
MS2011	96×65 mm. 10m. Young girl wearing traditional headband and necklace of clay beads (vert)	3·50	4·00

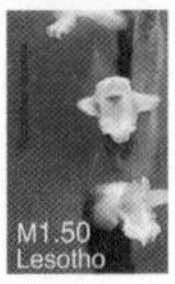

320 *Spiranthes laciniata*

2007. Orchids of the World. Multicoloured.

2012	1m.50 Type **320**	70	50
2013	2m.10 *Triphora craigheadii*	90	70
2014	3m. *Arethusa bulbosa*	1·25	1·00
2015	6m. *Encyclia tampensis*	2·50	2·50
2016	6m. *Prosthechea cochleata*	2·50	2·50
2017	6m. *Vanilla pompona*	2·50	2·50
2018	6m. *Cypripedium acaule*	2·50	2·50
2019	10m. *Calypso bulbosa*	3·75	4·50
MS2020	Two sheets, each 98×68 mm. (a) 15m. *Epidendrum radicans* (horiz). (b) 15m. *Vanilla barbellata*	11·00	12·00

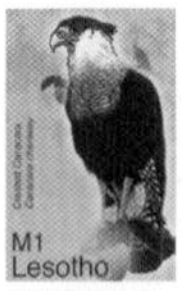

321 Crested Caracara

2007. Birds of the World. Multicoloured.

2021	1m. Type **321**	55	30
2022	1m.50 Wood stork	70	50
2023	2m.10 Tawny-shouldered blackbird	90	70
2024	6m. Great blue heron	2·50	2·50
2025	6m. Anna's hummingbird	2·50	2·50
2026	6m. Grey Silky-flycatcher	2·50	2·50
2027	6m. Limpkin	2·50	2·50
2028	15m. Jabiru	5·50	6·25
MS2029	Two sheets, each 68×97 mm. (a) 15m. Monk parakeet. (b) 15m. Western reef-heron	11·00	12·00

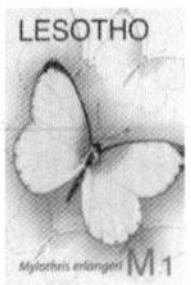

322 *Mylothris erlangeri*

2007. Butterflies of Africa. Multicoloured.

2030	1m. Type **322**	55	30
2031	1m.50 *Papilio nireus*	70	50
2032	2m.10 *Acraea terpiscore*	90	70
2033	10m. *Salamis temora*	3·75	4·50
MS2034	133×110 mm. 6m.×4 *Danaus chrysippus*; *Myrina silenus*; *Chrysiridiamadagascariensis*; *Hypolimnas dexithea*	9·00	10·00
MS2035	Two sheets, each 103×72 mm. (a) 15m. *Amphicallia tigris*. (b) 15m. *Papiliodemodocus*	11·00	12·00

The stamps and margins of No. **MS**2034 form a composite background design showing flowers.

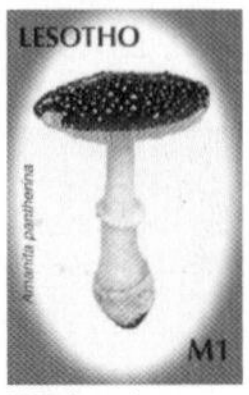

323 *Amanita pantherina*

2007. African Mushrooms. Multicoloured.

2036	1m. Type **323**	55	30
2037	1m.50 *Agaricus xanthodermus*	70	50
2038	2m.10 *Amanita rubescens*	90	70
2039	6m. *Amanita phalloides*	2·50	2·50
2040	6m. *Amanita pantherina*	2·50	2·50
2041	6m. *Panaeolus papilionaceus*	2·50	2·50
2042	6m. *Amanita rubescens* (different)	2·50	2·50
2043	15m. *Amanita phalloides* (different)	5·50	6·25
MS2044	Two sheets, each 103×73 mm. (a) 15m. *AmanitaPanther*. (b) 15m. *Podaxispistillaris*	11·00	12·00

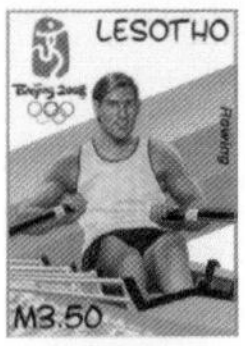

324 Rowing

2008. Olympic Games, Beijing. Multicoloured.

2045	3m.50 Type **324**	1·10	1·25
2046	3m.50 Softball	1·10	1·25
2047	3m.50 Wrestling	1·10	1·25
2048	3m.50 Volleyball	1·10	1·25

2010. Third Joint Issue of Southern Africa Postal Operators Association Members. World Cup Football Championship, South Africa. Multicoloured.

MS2049	5m.×9 Namibia; South Africa; Zimbabwe; Malawi; Swaziland; Botswana; Mauritius; Lesotho; Zambia	11·00	12·00

Similar designs were issued by Botswana, Malawi, Mauritius, Namibia, South Africa, Swaziland, Zambia and Zimbabwe.

POSTAGE DUE STAMPS

1966. Nos. D9/10 of Basutoland optd **LESOTHO**.

D11	**D2**	1c. red	30	75
D12	**D2**	5c. violet	30	90

D3

1967

D13	**D3**	1c. blue	15	3·00
D14	**D3**	2c. red	15	3·50
D15	**D3**	5c. green	20	3·50

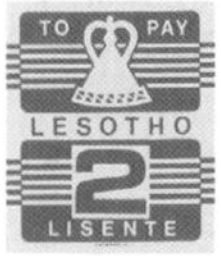

D4

1986

D19	**D4**	2s. green	20	1·25
D20	**D4**	5s. blue	20	1·25
D21	**D4**	25s. violet	70	1·50

APPENDIX

The following stamps have either been issued in excess of postal needs, or have not been available to the public in reasonable quantities at face value.

1981

15th Anniv of Independence. Classic Stamps of the World. 10m.×40, each embossed on gold foil.

Pt. 13

LIBERIA

A republic on the W. coast of Africa, founded as a home for freed slaves.

100 cents = 1 dollar.

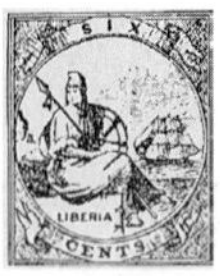

1

1860

7	1	6c. red	23·00	32·00
8	1	12c. blue	20·00	32·00
9	1	24c. green	23·00	32·00

1880

13	1c. blue	3·25	4·75
14	2c. red	2·25	3·25
15	6c. mauve	4·25	5·50
16	12c. yellow	4·25	6·00
17	24c. red	5·00	6·75

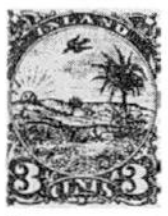

2

1881

18	**2**	3c. black	4·25	4·00

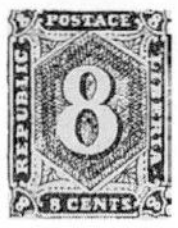

3

1882

47	**3**	8c. blue	3·25	3·25
20	**3**	16c. red	4·25	3·25

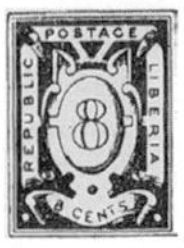

4

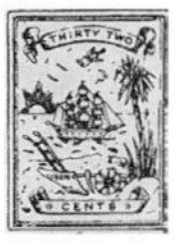

5 "Alligator" (first settlers' ship)

1886

49	**3**	1c. red	95	95
50	**3**	2c. green	95	1·00
23		3c. mauve	1·00	1·00
52	**3**	4c. brown	1·10	1·00
27		6c. grey	1·50	1·50
54	**4**	8c. grey	2·75	2·75
55	**4**	16c. yellow	4·25	4·25
29	**5**	32c. blue	17·00	17·00

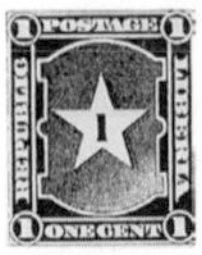

7 Liberian Star

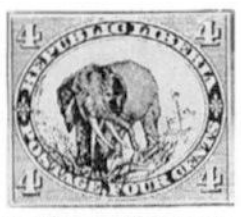

8 African Elephant

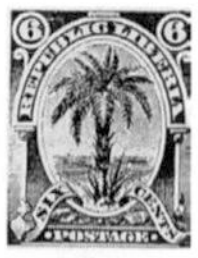

9 Oil Palm

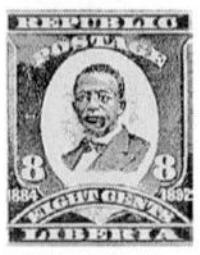

10 Pres. H. R. W. Johnson

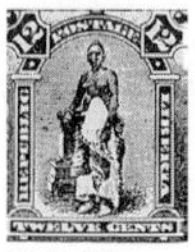

11 Vai Woman

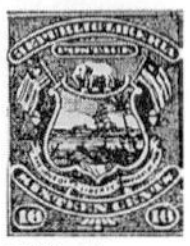

12 Seal

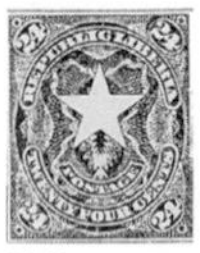

13 Star

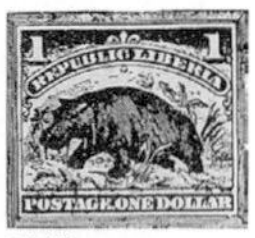

15 Hippopotamus

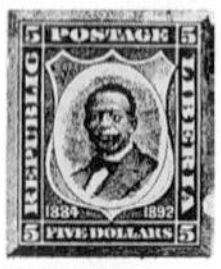

17 President Johnson

1892

75	**7**	1c. red	30	30
76	**7**	2c. blue	30	30
77	**8**	4c. black and green	2·10	1·60
78	**9**	6c. green	85	75
79	**10**	8c. black and brown	60	75
80	**11**	12c. red	60	85
81	**12**	16c. lilac	2·10	1·60
82	**13**	24c. green on yellow	1·50	1·25
83	**12**	32c. blue	3·00	2·50
84	**15**	$1 black and blue	10·00	5·75
85	**13**	$2 brown on buff	4·25	3·75
86	**17**	$5 black and red	5·50	5·50

1893. Surch **5 5 Five Cents.**

103	**9**	5c. on 6c. green	1·50	1·50

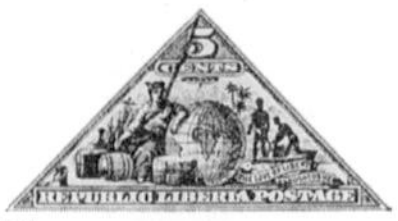

24

1894. Imperf or roul.

117	**24**	5c. black and red	6·25	6·25

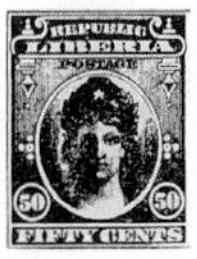

35

1897

144	**9**	1c. purple	70	35
145	**9**	1c. green	85	50
146	**15**	2c. black and bistre	1·50	1·10
147	**15**	2c. black and red	1·60	1·40
148	**8**	5c. black and lake	1·60	1·10
149	**8**	5c. black and blue	3·00	2·00
150	**10**	10c. blue and yellow	60	50
151	**11**	15c. black	60	65
152	**12**	20c. red	1·90	1·25
153	**13**	25c. green	1·25	85
154	**12**	30c. blue	4·25	3·00
155	**35**	50c. black and brown	2·10	2·75

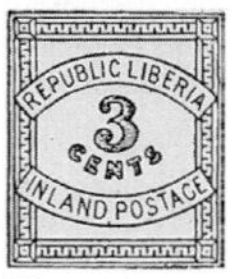

36

1897

156	**36**	3c. red and green	25	40

1901. Official stamps of 1892–98 optd ORDINARY.

175	**9**	1c. purple (No. O157)	50·00	35·00
176	**9**	1c. green (O158)	28·00	32·00
177	**7**	2c. blue (O120)	75·00	80·00
178	**15**	2c. black and brown (O159)	£100	45·00
179	**15**	2c. black and red (O160)	28·00	32·00
180	**24**	5c. green and lilac (O130)	£225	£225
181	**8**	5c. black and red (O161)	£150	£150
182	**8**	5c. black and blue (O162)	22·00	28·00
183	**10**	8c. black and brown (O122)	75·00	
184	**10**	10c. blue and yellow (O163)	28·00	32·00
169	**11**	12c. red (O92)	£100	£100
185	**11**	15c. black (O164)	28·00	32·00
170	**12**	16c. lilac (O93)		
186	**12**	16c. lilac (O124)	£325	£325
187	**12**	20c. red (O165)	32·00	38·00
171	**13**	24c. green and yellow (O94)	£300	£300
188	**13**	24c. green on yellow (O125)	32·00	38·00
189	**13**	25c. green (O166)	32·00	38·00
190	**12**	30c. blue (O167)	28·00	32·00
191	**13**	32c. blue (O126)	£150	£150
192	**35**	50c. black & brown (O168)	38·00	42·00
172	**15**	$1 black and blue (O96)	£1300	£1300
193	**15**	$1 black and blue (O127)	£225	£250
194	**13**	$2 brown on buff (O128)	£1300	£1300
174	**17**	$5 black and red (O98)	£3000	£3000
196	**17**	$5 black and red (O129)	£1400	£1400

1902. Surch **75c.** and bar.

206	**15**	75c. on $1 black and blue	8·25	7·75

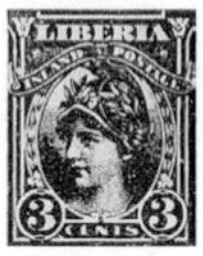

40 Liberty

1903

209	**40**	3c. black	25	15

1903. Surch in words.

216	**12**	10c. on 16c. lilac	2·50	4·50
217	**13**	15c. on 24c. green on yell	3·00	5·00
218	**12**	20c. on 32c. blue	4·25	5·25

1904. Surch.

219	**9**	1c. on 5c. on 6c. green (No. 103)	60	80
220	**8**	2c. on 4c. black and green (No. O89)	2·50	3·25
221	**12**	2c. on 30c. blue (No. 154)	6·25	9·25

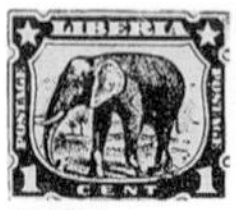

50 African Elephant

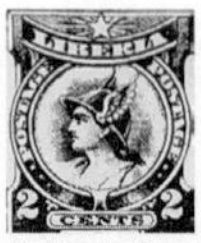

51 Head of Mercury

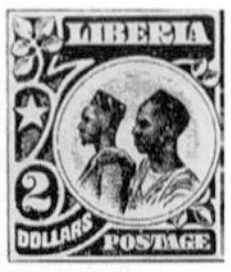

52 Mandingo Tribesmen

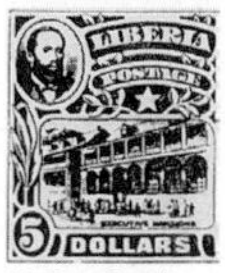

53 Pres. Barclay and Executive Mansion

1906

224	**50**	1c. black and green	1·00	50
225	**51**	2c. black and red	15	15
226	-	5c. black and blue	2·00	75
227	-	10c. black and red	3·00	90
228	-	15c. green and violet	7·00	2·75
229	-	20c. black and orange	7·25	2·50
230	-	25c. grey and blue	75	20
231	-	30c. violet	70	15
232	-	50c. black and green	75	20
233	-	75c. black and brown	7·00	2·10
234	-	$1 black and pink	1·90	25
235	**52**	$2 black and green	3·00	35
236	**53**	$5 grey and red	5·75	50

DESIGNS—As Type **50**: 5c. Chimpanzee; 15c. Agama lizard; 75c. Pygmy hippopotamus. As Type **51**: 10c. Great blue turaco; 20c. Great egret; 25c. Head of Liberty on coin; 30c. Figures "30"; 50c. Liberian flag. As Type **53**: $1 Head of Liberty.

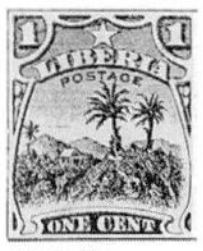

55 Coffee Plantation

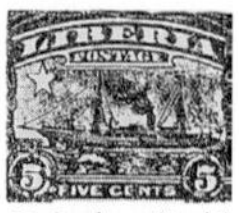

56 Gunboat "Lark"

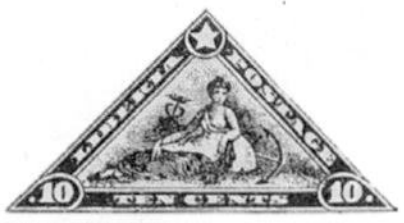

57 Commerce

1909. The 10c. is perf or roul.

250	**55**	1c. black and green	25	15
251	-	2c. black and red	25	15
252	**56**	5c. black and blue	1·75	35
254	**57**	10c. black and purple	25	20
255	-	15c. black and blue	1·25	35
256	-	20c. green and red	2·50	50
257	-	25c. black and brown	1·75	35
258	-	30c. brown	1·75	35
259	-	50c. black and green	2·75	60
260	-	75c. black and brown	2·25	45

DESIGNS—As Type **55**: 2c. Pres. Barclay; 15c. Vai woman spinning cotton; 20c. Pepper plant; 25c. Village hut; 30c. Pres. Barclay (in picture frame). As Type **56**: 50c. Canoeing; 75c. Village (design shaped like a book).

1909. No. 227 surch Inland **3 Cents**.

261	3c. on 10c. black and red	4·75	5·25

1910. Surcharged **3 CENTS INLAND POSTAGE**. Perf or rouletted.

274	**57**	3c. on 10c. black and purple	35	25

1913. Various types surch with new value and bars or ornaments.

322	-	1c. on 2c. black and red (No. 251)	2·25	3·00
290	**57**	+ 2c. on 3c. on 10c. black and purple	60	2·00
323	**56**	2c. on 5c. black and blue	2·25	3·00
292	-	2c. on 15c. black and blue (No. 255)	1·25	1·25
279	-	2c. on 25c. grey & blue (A) (No. 230)	7·50	3·75
281	-	2c. on 25c. black and brown (A) (No. 257)	7·50	3·75
295	-	2c. on 25c. black and brown (B) (No. 257)	6·25	6·25
296	-	5c. on 20c. green and red (No. 256)	85	4·50
280	-	5c. on 30c. violet (C) (No. 231)	7·50	3·75
282	-	5c. on 30c. brown (C) (No. 258)	7·50	3·75
297	-	5c. on 30c. brown (D) (No. 258)	3·75	3·75
278	**36**	8c. on 3c. red and green	60	30
283	-	10c. on 50c. black and green (E) (No. 259)	9·25	5·75
299	-	10c. on 50c. black and green (F) (No. 259)	6·75	6·75
303	-	20c. on 75c. black and brown (No. 260)	3·25	6·25
304	**53**	25c. on $1 black and pink	32·00	32·00
305	-	50c. on $2 black and green (No. 235)	9·25	9·25
308	-	$1 on $5 grey and red (No. 236)	42·00	42·00

Descriptions of surcharges. (A) **1914 2 CENTS.** (B) **2** over ornaments. (C) **1914 5 CENTS.** (D) **5** over ornaments. (E) **1914 10 CENTS.** (F) **10** and ornaments.

64 House on Providence Is

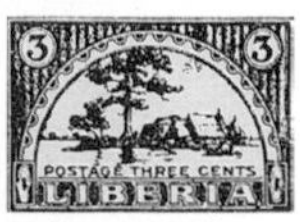

65 Monrovia Harbour, Providence Is

1915

288	**64**	2c. red	20	10
289	**65**	3c. violet	20	10

1916. Liberian Frontier Force. Surch **LFF 1 C**.

332	**9**	1c. on 1c. green	£120	£120
333	**50**	1c. on 1c. black and green	£375	£375
334	**55**	1c. on 1c. black and green	2·75	4·25
335	-	1c. on 2c. black and red (No. 251)	2·75	4·25

1916. Surch **1916** over new value.

339	**1**	3c. on 6c. mauve	32·00	32·00
340	**1**	5c. on 12c. yellow	4·00	4·00
341	**1**	10c. on 24c. red	3·25	3·75

1917. Surch **1917** and value in words.

342	**13**	4c. on 25c. green	8·25	9·25
343	**52**	5c. on 30c. violet (No. 231)	60·00	65·00

1918. Surch **3 CENTS**.

345	**57**	3c. on 10c. black & purple	2·40	3·75

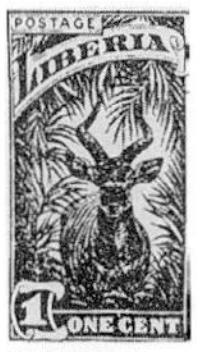

91 Bongo

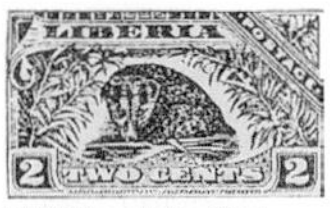

92 African Palm Civet

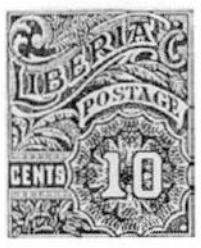

93

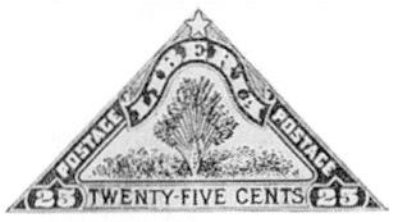

94 Traveller's Tree

1918

349	**91**	1c. black and green	65	25
350	**92**	2c. black and red	65	25
351	-	5c. black and blue	15	10
352	**93**	10c. green	20	10
353	-	15c. green and black	2·50	20
354	-	20c. black and red	50	15
355	**94**	25c. green	3·25	25
356	-	30c. black and mauve	11·00	95
357	-	50c. black and blue	13·00	1·10
358	-	75c. black and olive	1·00	25
359	-	$1 blue and brown	4·25	25
360	-	$2 black and violet	6·00	30
361	-	$5 brown	6·00	40

DESIGNS—As Type **91**: 5c. Coat of Arms; 15c. Oil palm; 20c. Statue of Mercury; 75c. Heads of Mandingos; $5 "Liberia" seated. As Type **92**: 50c. West African mudskipper; $1 Coast view; $2 Liberia College. As Type **93**: 30c. Palm-nut Vulture.

1918. Geneva Red Cross Fund. Surch **TWO CENTS** and red cross.

375	**91**	1c.+2c. black and green	75	75
376	**92**	2c.+2c. black and red	75	75
377	-	5c.+2c. black and blue	25	1·00
378	**93**	10c.+2c. green	50	1·00
379	-	15c.+2c. green and black	2·40	1·75
380	-	20c.+2c. black and red	1·50	3·00
381	**94**	25c.+2c. green	3·25	3·25
382	-	30c.+2c. black and mauve	10·50	5·75
383	-	50c.+2c. black and blue	7·00	5·75
384	-	75c.+2c. black and olive	2·10	5·25
385	-	$1+2c. blue and brown	4·25	7·00
386	-	$2+2c. black and violet	5·75	11·50
387	-	$5+2c. brown	14·00	23·00

1920. Surch **1920** and value and two bars.

393	**91**	3c. on 1c. black & green	1·50	2·75
394	**92**	4c. on 2c. black and red	1·50	3·00
395	**R 42**	5c. on 10c. black & blue	3·75	4·25
396	**R 42**	5c. on 10c. black and red	3·75	4·25
397	**R 42**	5c. on 10c. black & grn	3·75	4·25
398	**R 42**	5c. on 10c. black & vio	3·75	4·25
399	**R 42**	5c. on 10c. black and red	3·75	4·25

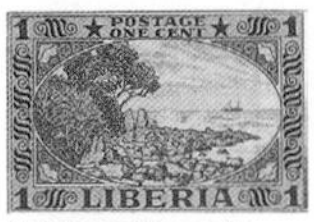

100 Cape Mesurado

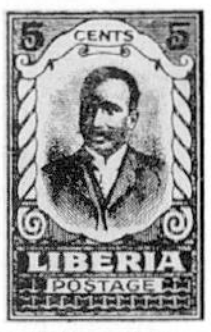

101 Pres. D. E. Howard

1921

402	**100**	1c. green	20	10
403	**101**	5c. black and blue	25	10
404	-	10c. blue and red	80	10
405	-	15c. green and purple	3·00	50
406	-	20c. green and red	1·50	25
407	-	25c. black and yellow	2·75	50
408	-	30c. purple and green	1·00	15
409	-	50c. blue and yellow	1·00	25
410	-	75c. sepia and red	1·00	40
411	-	$1 black and red	17·00	1·00
412	-	$2 violet and yellow	24·00	1·40
413	-	$5 red and purple	22·00	1·50

DESIGNS—VERT: 10c. Arms. HORIZ: 15c. Crocodile; 20c. Pepper plant; 25c. Leopard; 30c. Village; 50c. "Kru" boatman; 75c. St. Paul's River; $1 Bongo (antelope); $2 Great Indian hornbill; $5 African elephant.

1921. Optd **1921**.

414	**100**	1c. green	9·25	50
415	**64**	2c. red	9·25	50
416	**65**	3c. violet	12·50	50
417	**101**	5c. black and blue	2·75	50
418	-	10c. blue and red	20·00	50
419	-	15c. green and purple	11·50	1·00
420	-	20c. green and red	5·25	60
421	-	25c. black and yellow	11·50	1·00
422	-	30c. purple and green	3·00	50
423	-	50c. blue and yellow	3·00	70
424	-	75c. sepia and red	3·75	50
425	-	$1 black and red	30·00	1·50
426	-	$2 violet and yellow	28·00	1·60
427	-	$5 red and purple	32·00	5·25

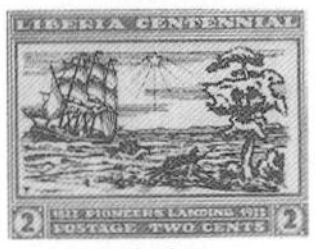

107 Arrival of First Settlers in "Alligator"

1923. Centennial issue.

466	**107**	1c. black and blue	14·00	70
467	**107**	2c. brown and red	17·00	70
468	**107**	5c. blue and olive	17·00	70
469	**107**	10c. mauve and green	4·75	70
470	**107**	$1 brown and red	7·00	70

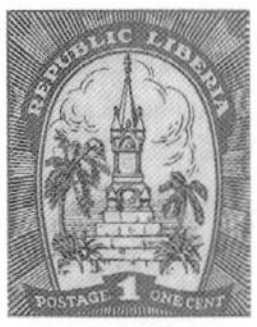

108 J. J. Roberts Memorial

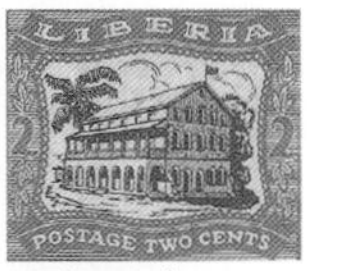

109 House of Representatives, Monrovia

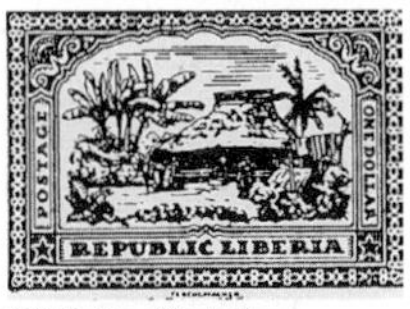

110 Rubber Plantation

1923

471	**108**	1c. green	3·75	10
472	**109**	2c. brown and red	3·75	10
473	-	3c. black and lilac	25	10
474	-	5c. black and blue	42·00	15
475	-	10c. brown and grey	25	10
476	-	15c. blue and bistre	18·00	50
477	-	20c. mauve and green	2·00	50
478	-	25c. brown and red	65·00	50
479	-	30c. mauve and brown	50	20
480	-	50c. orange and purple	1·00	40
481	-	75c. blue and grey	1·50	65
482	**110**	$1 violet and red	3·75	1·00
483	-	$2 blue and orange	4·00	65
484	-	$5 brown and green	10·00	65

DESIGNS—As Type **108**: 3c. Star; 5, 10c. Pres. King; 50c. Pineapple. As Type **109**: 15c. Hippopotamus; 20c. Kob (antelope); 25c. African buffalo; 30c. Natives making palm oil; 75c. Carrying elephant tusk. As Type **110**: $2 Stockton lagoon; $5 Styles of huts.

1926. Surch **Two Cents** and thick bar or wavy lines or ornamental scroll.

504	**91**	2c. on 1c. black and green	3·00	3·25

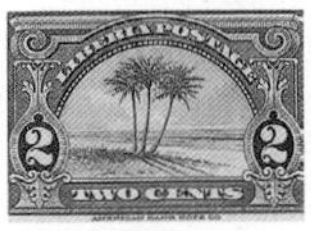

116 Palm Trees

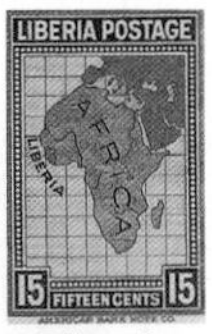

117 Map of Africa

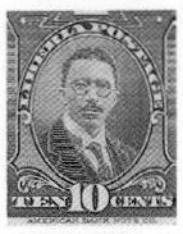

118 President King

1928

511	**116**	1c. green	40	15
512	**116**	2c. violet	20	20
513	**116**	3c. brown	35	20
514	**117**	5c. blue	55	35
515	**118**	10c. grey	70	35
516	**117**	15c. purple	3·75	1·40
517	**117**	$1 brown	42·00	15·00

1936. Nos. O518 and 512/13 surch **AIR MAIL SIX CENTS**.

525	**116**	6c. on 1c. green	£170	90·00
526	**116**	6c. on 2c. violet	£170	90·00
527	**116**	6c. on 3c. brown	£170	90·00

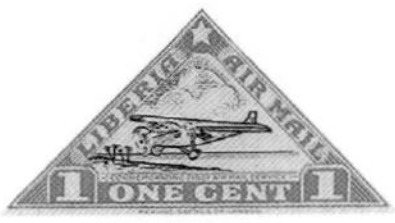

122 Ford "Tin Goose"

1936. Air. Firstt Air Mail Service of 28th February.

530	**122**	1c. black and green	25	10
531	**122**	2c. black and red	25	10
532	**122**	3c. black and violet	40	10
533	**122**	4c. black and orange	40	15
534	**122**	5c. black and blue	45	15
535	**122**	6c. black and green	45	20

1936. Nos. 350/61 surch 1936 and new values in figures.

536		1c. on 2c. black and red	30	50
537		3c. on 5c. black and blue	30	45
538		4c. on 10c. green	25	40
539		6c. on 15c. green and black	30	55
540		8c. on 20c. black and red	20	60
541		12c. on 30c. black and mauve	1·25	1·40
542		14c. on 50c. black and blue	1·50	1·75
543		16c. on 75c. black and olive	50	60
544		18c. on $1 blue and brown	60	80
545		22c. on $2 black and violet	60	95
546		24c. on $5 brown	75	1·25

1936. Nos. O363/74 optd with star and **1936** or surch also in figures and words.

547		1c. on 2c. black and red	30	50
548		3c. on 5c. black and blue	25	50
549		4c. on 10c. green	20	45
550		6c. on 15c. green and brown	25	60
551		8c. on 20c. black and lilac	30	60
552		12c. on 30c. black and violet	95	1·25
553		14c. on 50c. black and brown	1·00	1·50
554		16c. on 75c. black and brown	45	60
555		18c. on $1 blue and olive	50	65
556		22c. on $2 black and olive	60	90
557		24c. on $5 green	75	95
558		25c. green and brown	75	1·25

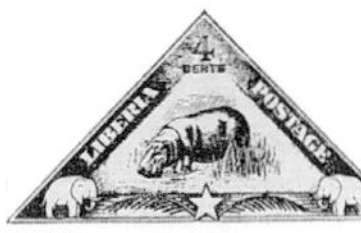

126 Hippopotamus

1937

559	-	1c. black and green	1·25	60
560	-	2c. black and red	1·00	30
561	-	3c. black and purple	1·00	35
562	**126**	4c. black and orange	1·50	60
563	-	5c. black and blue	1·75	85
564	-	6c. black and green	45	20

DESIGNS: 1c. Black and white casqued hornbill; 2c. Bushbuck; 3c. African buffalo; 5c. Western reef heron; 6c. Pres. Barclay.

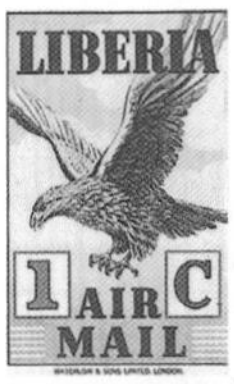

127 Tawny Eagle in Flight

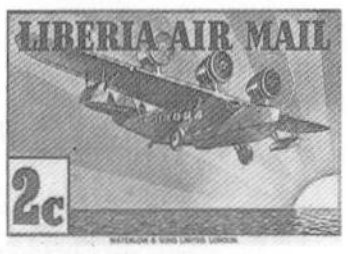

128 Three-engine Flying Boat

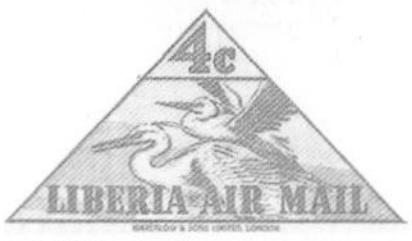

129 Little Egrets

1938. Air.

565	**127**	1c. green	25	20
566	**128**	2c. red	15	10
567	-	3c. olive	35	20
568	**129**	4c. orange	50	10
569	-	5c. green	65	20
570	**128**	10c. violet	25	10
571	-	20c. mauve	30	15
572	-	30c. grey	1·25	20
573	**127**	50c. brown	1·75	20
574	-	$1 blue	1·40	25

DESIGNS—VERT: 20c., $1 Sikorsky S-43 amphibian. HORIZ: 3, 30c. Lesser black-backed gull in flight.

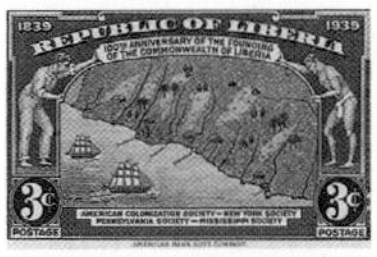

130 Immigrant Ships nearing Liberian Coast

1940. Centenary of Founding of Liberian Commonwealth.

575	**130**	3c. blue	50	15
576	-	5c. brown	20	10
577	-	10c. green	25	15

DESIGNS: 5c. Seal of Liberia and Flags of original Settlements; 10c. Thos. Buchanan's house and portrait.

1941. Centenary of First Postage Stamps. Nos. 575/7 optd **POSTAGE STAMP CENTENNIAL 1840–1940** and portrait of Rowland Hill.

578	**130**	3c. blue (postage)	1·75	1·75
579	-	5c. brown	1·75	1·75
580	-	10c. green	1·75	1·75
581	**130**	3c. blue (air)	1·40	1·40
582	-	5c. brown	1·40	1·40
583	-	10c. green	1·40	1·40

Nos. 581/3 are additionally optd with airplane and **AIR MAIL**.

1941. Red Cross Fund. Nos. 575/7 surch **RED CROSS** plus Red Cross and **TWO CENTS**.

584	**130**	+ 2c. on 3c. bl (postage)	1·40	1·40
585	-	+ 2c. on 5c. brown	1·40	1·40
586	-	+ 2c. on 10c. green	1·40	1·40
587	**130**	+ 2c. on 3c. blue (air)	1·40	1·40
588	-	+ 2c. on 5c. brown	1·40	1·40
589	-	+ 2c. on 10c. green	1·40	1·40

Nos. 587/9 are additionally optd with airplane and **AIR MAIL**.

1941. Air. First Flight to U.S.A. Nos. 565/74 surch **First Flight LIBERIA - U.S. 1941 50c** and bar.

594	**127**	50c. on 1c.	£2500	£225
595	**128**	50c. on 2c.	£150	75·00
596	-	50c. on 3c.	£180	90·00
597	**129**	50c. on 4c.	60·00	38·00
598	**129**	50c. on 5c.	60·00	38·00
599	**128**	50c. on 10c.	45·00	38·00
600	-	50c. on 20c.	£1500	£150
601	-	50c. on 30c.	60·00	24·00
602	**127**	50c. brown	60·00	24·00
603	-	$1 blue	45·00	30·00

The first flight was cancelled and covers were sent by ordinary mail. The flight took place in 1942 and the stamps were reissued but with the date obliterated.

1942. As Nos. 594/601 but with date "1941" obliterated by two bars.

604	**127**	50c. on 1c. green	7·00	7·00
605	**128**	50c. on 2c. red	6·00	6·75
606	-	50c. on 3c. green	5·50	4·75
607	**129**	50c. on 4c. orange	4·00	6·25
608	**129**	50c. on 5c. green	2·40	2·40
609	**128**	50c. on 10c. violet	5·25	6·25
610	-	50c. on 20c. mauve	5·25	6·25
611	-	50c. on 30c. grey	4·00	4·00
612	**127**	50c. brown	4·00	4·00
613	-	$1 blue	6·25	7·50

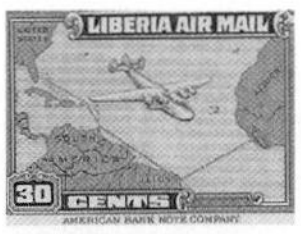

138 Miami–Monrovia Air Route

1942. Air.

614	**138**	10c. red	20	10
615	-	12c. blue	30	10
616	-	24c. green	35	10
617	**138**	30c. green	35	10
618	**138**	35c. lilac	40	15
619	**138**	50c. purple	50	15
620	**138**	70c. olive	55	30
621	**138**	$1.40 red	75	50

DESIGN: 12, 24c. Boeing 247 airliner over Liberian Agricultural and Industrial Fair.

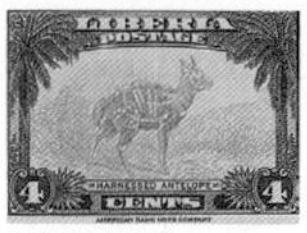

139 Bushbuck

1942

622	-	1c. brown and violet	80	20
623	-	2c. brown and blue	80	20
624	-	3c. brown and green	1·25	45
625	139	4c. red and black	2·00	70
626	-	5c. brown and olive	1·75	70
627	-	10c. black and red	3·75	1·10

DESIGNS—HORIZ: 1c. Royal antelope; 2c. Water chevrotain; 3c. Jentink's duiker; 5c. Banded duiker. VERT: 10c. Diana monkey.

1944. Stamps of 1928 and 1937 surch.

628	116	1c. on 2c. violet	7·50	7·50
634	126	1c. on 4c. black & orange	48·00	40·00
629	118	1c. on 10c. grey	10·00	6·25
635	-	2c. on 3c. black and purple (No. 561)	50·00	40·00
630	117	2c. on 5c. blue	3·25	3·25
632	116	3c. on 2c. violet	27·00	30·00
636	-	4c. on 5c. black and blue (No. 563)	18·00	18·00
633	118	4c. on 10c. grey	3·25	3·25
637	-	5c. on 1c. black and green (No. 559)	85·00	45·00
638	-	6c. on 2c. black and red (No. 560)	12·50	12·50
639	-	10c. on 6c. black and green (No. 564)	14·00	12·50

1944. Air stamps of 1936 and 1938 surch.

643	128	10c. on 2c. red	27·00	30·00
644	129	10c. on 5c. green	9·50	9·50
640	122	30c. on 1c. black & green	80·00	50·00
645	122	30c. on 3c. olive (No. 567)	£120	55·00
646	129	30c. on 4c. orange	9·50	9·50
641	122	50c. on 3c. black & violet	20·00	23·00
642	122	70c. on 2c. black and red	50·00	50·00
647	-	$1 on 3c. olive (No. 567)	25·00	25·00
648	127	$1 on 50c. brown	35·00	25·00

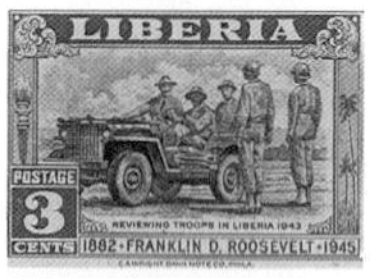

150 Pres. Roosevelt reviewing Troops

1945. Pres. Roosevelt Memorial.

650	150	3c. black & pur (postage)	15	15
651	150	5c. black and blue	30	25
652	150	70c. black and brown (air)	1·00	1·00

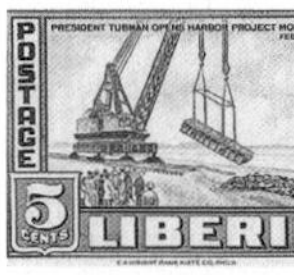

151 Opening Monrovia Harbour Project

1946. Opening of Monrovia Harbour Project by Pres. Tubman.

653	151	5c. blue (postage)	25	15
654	151	24c. green (air)	1·90	2·10

1947. As T **151**, but without inscr at top.

655	5c. violet (postage)	15	15
656	25c. red (air)	1·00	1·10

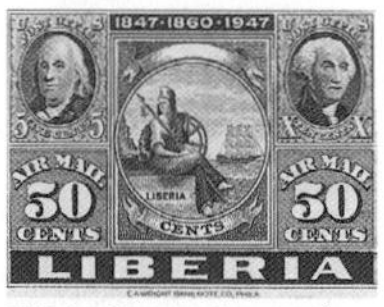

152 1st Postage Stamps of United States and Liberia

1947. U.S. Postage Stamps Centenary and 87th Anniv of Liberian Postal Issues.

657	152	5c. red (postage)	30	15
658	152	12c. green (air)	40	15
659	152	22c. violet	50	20
660	152	50c. blue	60	25
MS661		89×193 mm. Nos. 657/60. Imperf	2·00	2·00

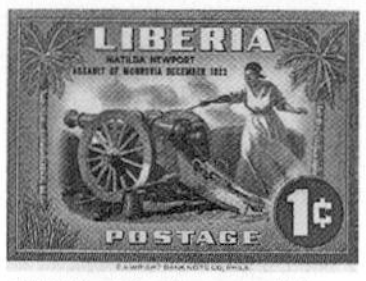

153 Matilda Newport Firing Canon

1947. 125th Anniv of Defence of Monrovia.

662	153	1c. black & green (postage)	15	10
663	153	3c. black and violet	20	10
664	153	5c. black and blue	20	15
665	153	10c. black and yellow	1·50	45
666	153	25c. black and red (air)	1·40	35

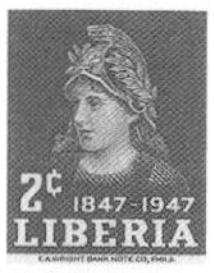

154 Liberty

1947. Centenary of National Independence.

667	-	1c. green (postage)	20	10
668	154	2c. purple	20	10
669	-	3c. purple	30	15
670	-	5c. blue	40	15
671	-	12c. orange (air)	60	20
672	-	25c. red	75	35
673	-	50c. brown	90	70

DESIGNS—VERT: 1c. Liberian star; 3c. Arms of Liberia; 4c. Map of Liberia; 12c. J. J. Roberts Monument; 25c. Liberian Flag; 50c. (26½×33 mm) Centenary Monument.

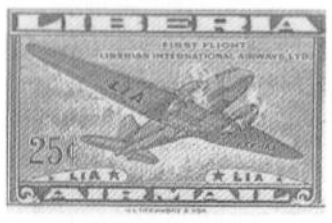

156 Douglas DC-3

1948. Air. First Liberian International Airways Flight (Monrovia–Dakar).

674	156	25c. red	1·50	1·00
675	156	50c. blue	2·40	1·50

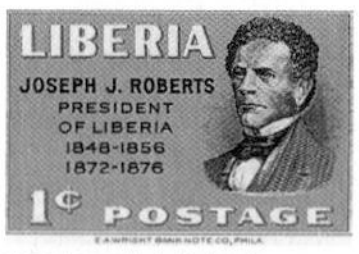

157 Joseph J. Roberts

1949. Liberian Presidents. Portrait and name in black. (a) Postage.

676	-	1c. green (Roberts)	1·60	3·25
677	157	1c. green	15	10
678	-	1c. pink (Roberts)	25	15
679	-	2c. pink (Benson)	35	35
680	-	2c. yellow (Benson)	35	15
681	-	3c. mauve (Warner)	35	35
682	-	4c. olive (Payne)	35	55
683	-	5c. blue (Mansion)	45	55
684	-	6c. orange (Roye)	55	95
685	-	7c. green (Gardner and Russell)	70	1·25
686	-	8c. red (Johnson)	70	1·40
687	-	9c. purple (Cheeseman)	1·10	1·10
688	-	10c. yellow (Coleman)	75	35
689	-	10c. grey (Coleman)	40	20
690	-	15c. orange (Gibson)	85	40
691	-	15c. blue (Gibson)	25	15
692	-	20c. grey (A. Barclay)	1·25	70
693	-	20c. red (A. Barclay)	50	45
694	-	25c. red (Howard)	1·60	1·10
695	-	25c. blue (Howard)	50	45
696	-	50c. turquoise (King)	3·25	95
697	-	50c. purple (King)	70	60
698	-	$1 mauve (E. Barclay)	5·75	70
699	-	$1 brown (E. Barclay)	4·00	55

(b) Air.

700	25c. blue (Tubman)	1·00	55
701	25c. green (Tubman)	75	35

Nos. 676 and 678 have a different portrait of Roberts wearing a moustache.

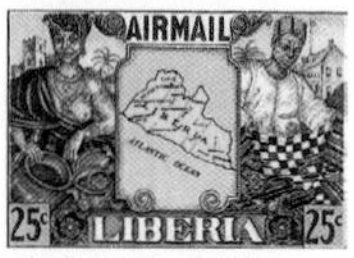

158 Colonists and Map

1949. Multicoloured.. Multicoloured..

702	1c. Settlers approaching village (postage)	50	75
703	2c. Rubber tapping and planting	50	75
704	3c. Landing of first colonists in 1822	1·00	1·50
705	5c. Jehudi Ashmun and Matilda Newport defending stockade	50	75
706	25c. Type **158** (air)	1·25	1·50
707	50c. Africans and coat of arms	2·75	3·25

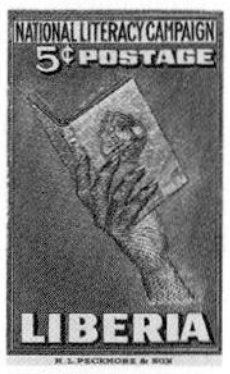

159 Hand holding Book

1950. National Literacy Campaign.

708	159	5c. blue (postage)	20	15
709	-	25c. red (air)	70	70
MS710		140×82 mm. Nos. 708/9. Imperf	1·10	1·10

DESIGN—VERT: 25c. Open book and rising sun.

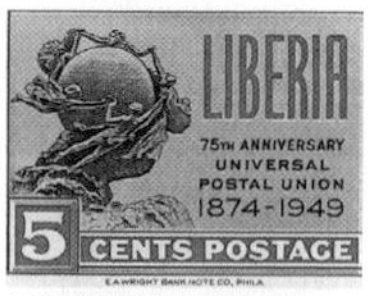

160 U.P.U. Monument, Berne

1950. 75th Anniv of U.P.U.

711	160	5c. black and green (post)	20	15
712	-	10c. black and mauve	30	30
713	-	25c. purple & orange (air)	3·25	3·25
MS714		215×251 mm. Nos. 711/13. Imperf	3·75	3·75

DESIGNS—HORIZ: 10c. Standehaus, Berne. VERT: 25c. U.P.U. Monument, Berne.

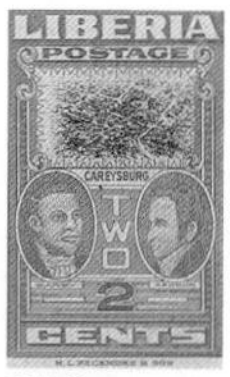

161 Carey, Ashmun and Careysburg

1952. Designs all show portrait of Ashmun.

715		1c. green (postage)	10	10
716	161	2c. blue and red	10	10
717	-	3c. green and purple	10	10
718	-	4c. green and brown	15	10
719	-	5c. red and blue	20	15
720	-	10c. blue and red	25	20
721	-	25c. black and purple (air)	35	35
722	-	50c. red and blue	1·00	45
MS723		215×252 mm. Nos. 715/22. Imperf	2·40	2·40

DESIGNS—VERT: 1c. Seal of Liberia; 3c. Harper and Harper City; 5c. Buchanan and Upper Buchanan. HORIZ: 4c. Marshall and Marshall City; 10c. Roberts and Robertsport; 25c. Monroe and Monrovia; 50c. Tubman and map.

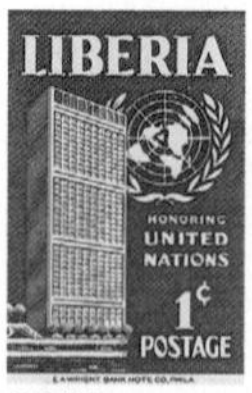

162 U.N. Headquarters

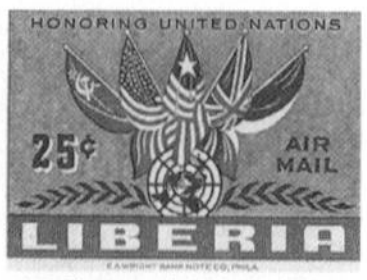

163 Flags and U.N. Emblem

1952. U.N. Commemoration.

724	162	1c. blue (postage)	10	10
725	-	4c. blue and pink	15	10
726	-	10c. brown and yellow	25	20
727	163	25c. red and blue (air)	55	45

DESIGNS—HORIZ: 4c. Liberian and U.N. flags and scroll; 10c. Liberian and U.N. emblems.

1952. World Health Conference, Monrovia. Two sheets each 153×85 mm. Nos. 724/7. Perf or imperf.

MS728	Two sheets	2·25	2·25

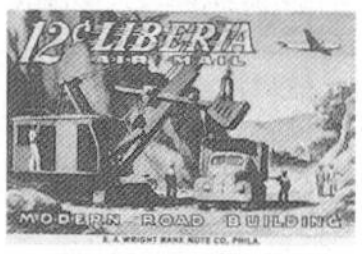

164 Modern Road-building

1953. Air. Transport.

729	164	12c. brown	15	15
730	-	25c. purple	75	30
731	-	35c. violet	1·60	30
732	-	50c. orange	65	25
733	-	70c. green	1·25	40
734	-	$1 blue	1·40	55

DESIGNS: 25c. "African Glen" (freighter) in Monrovia Harbour; 35c. Diesel locomotive; 50c. Free Port of Monrovia; 70c. Roberts Field Airport; $1 Tubman Bridge.

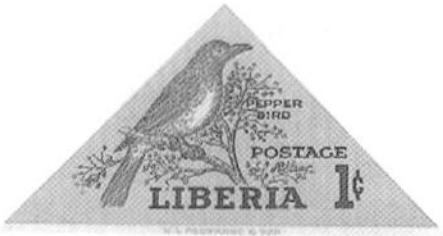

165 Garden Bulbul ("Pepper Bird")

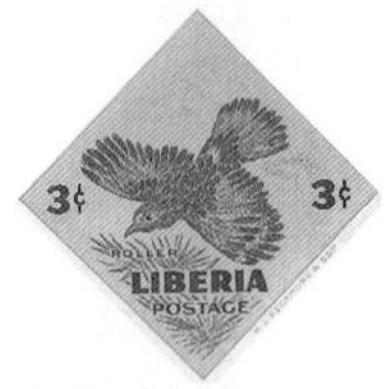

166 Blue-throated Roller ("Roller")

1953. Imperf or perf.

735	165	1c. red and blue	1·00	20
736	166	3c. blue and salmon	1·00	25
737	-	4c. brown and yellow	1·50	30
738	-	5c. turquoise and mauve	1·75	35
739	-	10c. mauve and green	1·75	35
740	-	12c. orange and brown	2·75	50

BIRDS: As Type **165**: 4c. Yellow-casqued hornbill ("Hornbill"); 5c. Giant kingfisher ("Kingfisher"). As Type **166**: 10c. African jacana ("Jacana"); 12c. Broad-tailed paradise whydah ("Weaver").

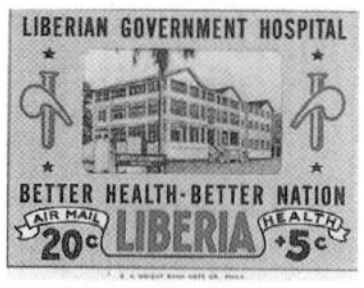

167 Hospital

1954. Liberian Govt. Hospital Fund.

741		5c.+5c. black and purple (postage)	20	15
742		10c.+5c. black and red (air)	15	20
743	167	20c.+5c. black & green	25	25
744	-	25c.+5c. black, red and blue	30	20

DESIGNS—As Type **167**: 5c. Medical research workers; 10c. Nurses. 46×35 mm: 25c. Doctor examining patient.

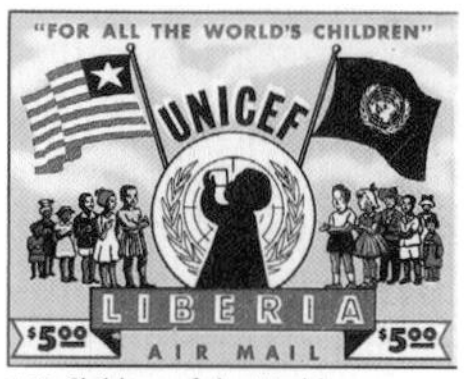

168 Children of the World

1954. Air. UNICEF.

745	168	$5 ultramarine, red and blue	27·00	23·00

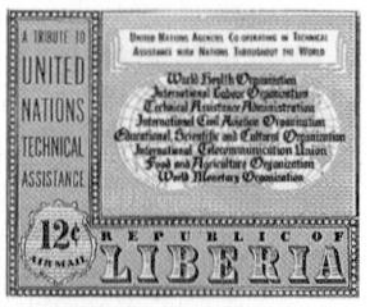

169 U.N. Organizations

1954. Air. U.N. Technical Assistance.

746	169	12c. black and blue	25	15
747	-	15c. brown and yellow	25	15
748	-	20c. black and green	30	20
749	-	25c. blue and red	35	25

DESIGNS: 15c. Printers; 20c. Mechanic; 25c. Teacher and students.

1954. Air. Visit of President Tubman to U.S.A. As Nos. 729/34 but colours changed and inscr "COMMEMORATING PRESIDENTIAL VISIT U.S.A.—1954".

750	12c. orange	20	20
751	25c. blue	80	25
752	35c. red	4·00	1·50
753	50c. mauve	80	30
754	70c. brown	1·10	50
755	$1 green	1·60	3·25

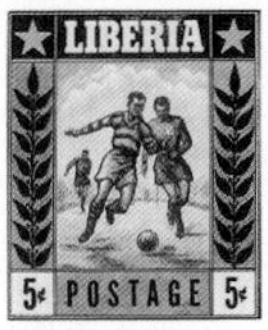

170 Football

1955. Sports.

756	-	3c. red and green (postage)	15	10
757	**170**	5c. black and orange	15	10
758	-	25c. violet and yellow	25	20
759	-	10c. blue and mauve (air)	20	15
760	-	12c. brown and blue	15	15
761	-	25c. red and green	20	20
MS762 90×140 mm. Nos. 758 and 761 Perf or imperf			90	90

DESIGNS—VERT: 3c. Tennis; 25c. Boxing (No. 758). HORIZ: 10c. Baseball; 12c. Swimming; 25c. Running (No. 761).

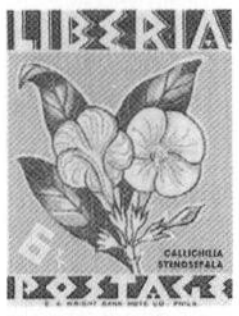

171 "Callichilia stenosepala"

1955. Flowers.

763	**171**	6c. yellow, salmon and green (postage)	15	10
764	-	7c. red, yellow and green	15	10
765	-	8c. buff, blue and green	20	10
766	-	9c. green and orange	25	15
767	-	20c. yellow, green and violet (air)	15	15
768	-	25c. yellow, green and red	20	20

FLOWERS—VERT: 7c. "Gomphia subcordata"; 8c. "Listrostachys chudata"; 9c. "Mussaenda isertiana". HORIZ: 20s. "Costus"; 25c. "Barteria nigritiana".

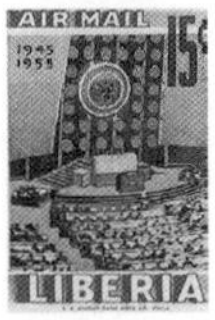

172 U.N. General Assembly

1955. Air. Tenth Anniv of U.N.

769		10c. blue and red	20	10
770	**172**	15c. black and violet	25	15
771	-	25c. brown and green	35	15
772	-	50c. green and red	1·00	20

DESIGNS—VERT: 10c. U.N. emblem; 25c. Liberian Secretary of State signing U.N. Charter. HORIZ: 50c. Page from U.N. Charter.

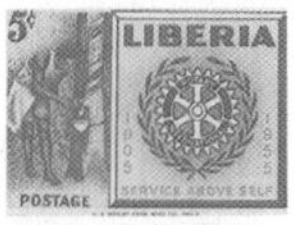

173 Tapping Rubber and Rotary Emblem

1955. 50th Anniv of Rotary International.

773	**173**	5c. green & yell (postage)	25	15
774	-	10c. blue and red (air)	15	50
775	-	15c. brown, yellow and red	20	65
MS776 128×77 mm. 50c. blue and scarlet (as 10c. but without leaves)			80	80

DESIGNS: 10c. Rotary International H.Q., Evanston; 15c. View of Monrovia.

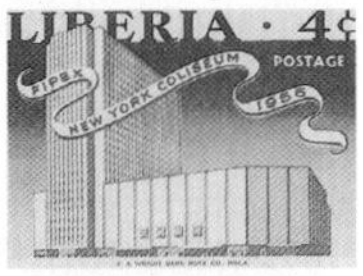

174 Coliseum, New York

1956. Fifth Int Philatelic Exhibition, New York.

777		3c. brown and green (postage)	15	10
778	**174**	4c. brown and green	10	25
779	-	6c. purple and black	20	10
780	**174**	10c. blue and red (air)	25	15
781	-	12c. violet and orange	20	15
782	-	15c. purple and turquoise	25	20
MS783 78×129 mm. 50c. brown and emerald (as No. 782)			85	85

DESIGNS—VERT: 3c., 15c. Statue of Liberty. HORIZ: 6c., 12c. The Globe.

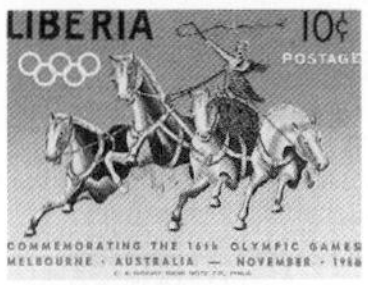

175 Chariot Race

1956. Olympic Games.

784		4c. brown & olive (postage)	10	10
785		6c. black and green	15	10
786		8c. brown and blue	20	10
787	**175**	10c. black and red	25	10
788	-	12c. purple and green (air)	20	15
789	-	20c. multicoloured	30	20
MS790 128×76 mm. 40c. multicoloured (as No. 789)			70	70

DESIGNS—HORIZ: 4c. Olympic rings, eastern grey kangaroo and emu; 8c. Goddess of Victory; 12c., 20c. Olympic torch superimposed on map of Austrialia. VERT: 6c. Discus thrower.

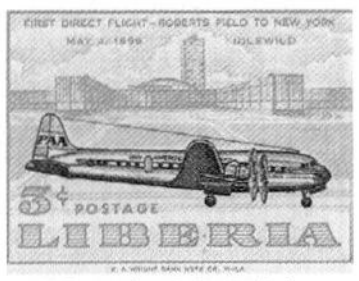

176 Douglas DC-6B "John Alden" at Idlewild Airport

1957. First Anniv of Inauguration of Liberia–U.S. Direct Air Service.

791	**176**	3c. blue & orange (postage)	15	15
792	-	5c. black and mauve	20	20
793	**176**	12c. blue and green (air)	30	25
794	-	15c. black and brown	30	25
795	**176**	25c. blue and red	45	25
796	-	50c. black and blue	85	30

DESIGN: 5, 15, 50c. President Tubman and "John Alden" at Roberts Field, Liberia.

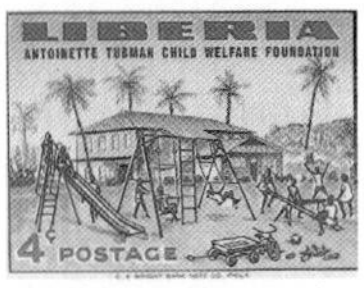

177 Children's Playground

1957. Inauguration of Antoinette Tubman Child Welfare Foundation. Inscr as in T **177**.

797	**177**	4c. green and red (postage)	10	10
798	-	5c. brown and turquoise	15	10
799	-	6c. violet and bistre	15	10
800	-	10c. blue and red	20	15
801	-	15c. brown and blue (air)	20	15
802	-	35c. purple and grey	35	25
MS803 127×77 mm. 70c. lilac, red and blue (as No. 800)			85	85

DESIGNS: 5c. Teacher with pupil; 6c. National anthem with choristers; 10c. Children viewing welfare home; 15c. Nurse inoculating youth; 35c. Kamara triplets.

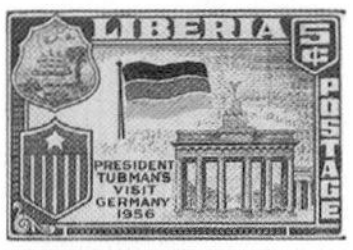

178 German Flag and Brandenburg Gate

1958. Pres. Tubman's European Tour. Flags in national colours.

804	**178**	5c. blue (postage)	15	10
805	-	5c. brown	15	10
806	-	5c. red	15	10
807	-	10c. black (air)	25	15
808	-	15c. green	25	20
809	-	15c. blue	25	20
810	-	15c. violet	25	20

DESIGNS: Flags of: Netherlands and windmill (No. 805); Sweden and Royal Palace, Stockholm (No. 806); Italy and Colosseum (No. 807); France and Arc de Triomphe (No. 808); Switzerland and Alpine chalet (No. 809); Vatican City and St. Peter's Basilica (No. 810).

179 Map of the World

1958. Tenth Anniv of Declaration of Human Rights.

811	**179**	3c. blue and black	25	15
812	-	5c. brown and blue	20	20
813	-	10c. orange and black	30	75
814	-	12c. black and red	40	35

DESIGNS: 5c. U.N. Emblem and H.Q. building; 10c. U.N. Emblem; 12c. U.N. Emblem and initials of U.N. agencies.

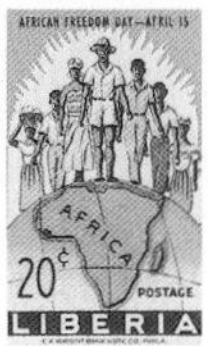

180 Africans and Map

1959. Africa Freedom Day.

816	**180**	20c. orge & brn (postage)	30	30
817	-	25c. brown and blue (air)	35	20

DESIGN: 25c. Two Africans looking at Pres. Tubman's declaration of Africa Freedom Day.

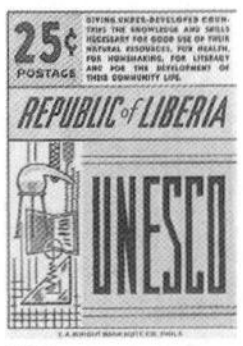

181

1959. Inaug of UNESCO Building, Paris.

818	**181**	25c. purple & grn (postage)	35	40
819	-	25c. red and blue (air)	35	30

DESIGN—HORIZ: No. 819 UNESCO Headquarters, Paris.

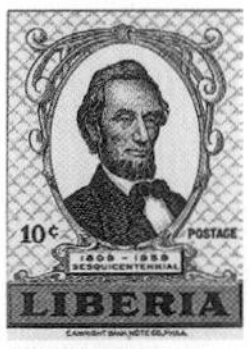

182 Abraham Lincoln

1959. 150th Birth Anniv of Abraham Lincoln.

821	**182**	10c. black & blue (postage)	25	30
822	**182**	15c. black and orange	30	30
823	**182**	25c. black and green (air)	55	50
MS824 140×85 mm. Nos. 821/3. Imperf			1·10	1·10

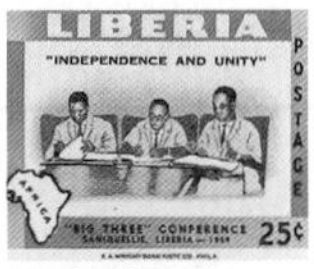

183 Presidents Toure, Tubman and Nkrumah at Conference Table

1960. "Big Three" Conf, Saniquellie, Liberia.

825	**183**	25c. black & red (postage)	35	25
826	-	25c. black, bl & buff (air)	35	25

DESIGN: No. 826, Medallion portraits of Presidents Toure (Guinea), Tubman (Liberia) and Nkrumah (Ghana).

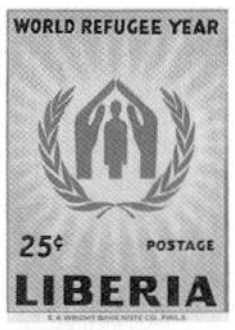

184 "Care of Refugees"

1960. World Refugee Year.

827	**184**	25c. green & blk (postage)	35	30
828	**184**	25c. blue and black (air)	55	40
MS829 134×83 mm. Nos. 827/8			1·00	1·00

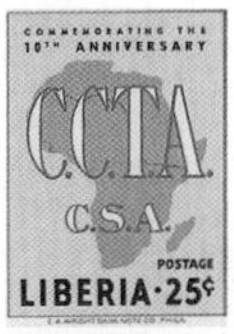

185

1960. Tenth Anniv of African Technical Co-operation Commission (C.C.T.A.).

830	**185**	25c. green & blk (postage)	35	50
831	-	25c. brown and blue (air)	45	35

DESIGN: No. 831, Map of Africa with symbols showing fields of assistance.

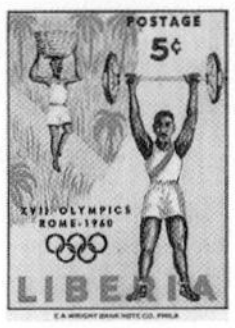

186 Weightlifting

1960. Olympic Games, Rome.

832	**186**	5c. brown & grn (postage)	20	15
833	-	10c. brown and purple	40	75
834	-	15c. brown and orange	35	30
835	-	25c. brown and blue (air)	70	80
MS836 130×80 mm. 50c. brown and violet (Athlete and Olympic Stadium). Imperf			1·50	1·50

DESIGNS—HORIZ: 10c. Rowing; 25c. Javelin-throwing. VERT: 15c. Walking.

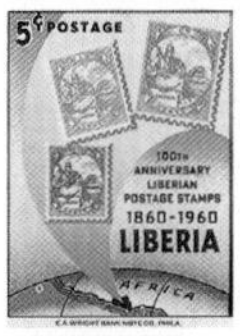

187 Stamps of 1860 and Map

1960. Liberian Stamp Centenary. Stamps, etc., in green, red and blue. Colours of map and inscriptions given.

837	**187**	5c. black (postage)	25	15
838	**187**	20c. brown	40	40
839	**187**	25c. blue (air)	50	40
MS840 130×79 mm. 50c. multicoloured			1·10	1·10

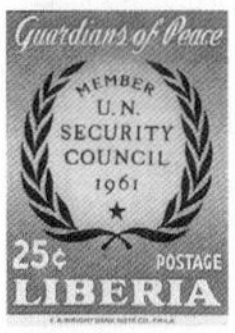

188 "Guardians of Peace"

1961. Membership of U.N. Security Council.

841	**188**	25c. blue and red (postage)	45	35
842	-	25c. blue and red (air)	45	25
MS843 128×77 mm. 50c. green and brown (Globe and Dove). Imperf			1·10	1·10
MS844 134×88 mm. Nos. 841/2 and 50c. (as in No. **MS**843). Imperf			2·75	2·75

DESIGN—HORIZ: No. 842, Dove of Peace, Globe and U.N. Emblem.

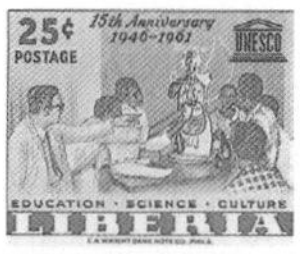

189 Anatomy Class, University of Liberia

1961. 15th Anniv of UNESCO.

845	**189**	25c. brown & grn (postage)	35	35
846	-	25c. brown and violet (air)	35	25
MS847 127×76 mm. 50c. brown and blue			85	85

DESIGNS: Nos. 846 and **MS**847, Science class (different), University of Liberia.

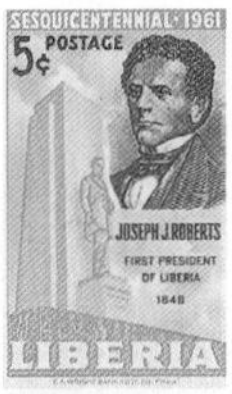

190 President Roberts

1961. 150th Birth Anniv of Joseph J. Roberts (first President of Liberia).

848	**190**	5c. sepia & orge (postage)	20	15
849	-	10c. sepia and blue	35	15
850	-	25c. sepia and green (air)	45	35
MS851 140×83 mm. Nos. 848/50. Imperf			1·10	1·10

DESIGNS—HORIZ: 10c. Pres. Roberts and old and new presidential mansions; 25c. Pres. Roberts and Providence Is.

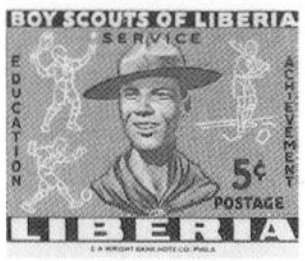

191 Scout and Sports

1961. Liberian Boy Scout Movement.

852	**191**	5c. sepia & violet (postage)	25	20
853	-	10c. ochre and blue	30	20
854	-	25c. sepia and green (air)	40	30
MS855		126×76 mm. 35c. brown and blue (as No. 852)	75	75

DESIGNS—HORIZ: 10c. Scout badge and scouts in camp. VERT: 25c. Scout and badge.

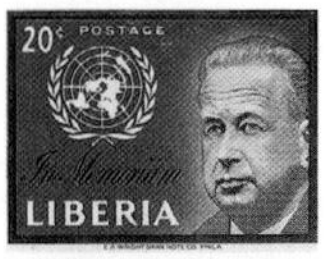

192 Hammarskjold and U.N. Emblem

1962. Dag Hammarskjold Commem.

856	**192**	20c. black & blue (postage)	30	20
857	**192**	25c. black and purple (air)	35	25
MS858		127×76 mm. 50c. black and blue. Imperf	85	85

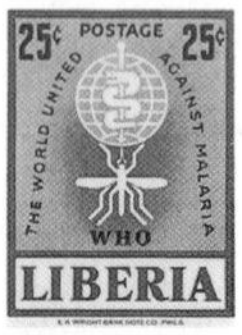

193 Campaign Emblem

1962. Malaria Eradication.

859	**193**	25c. green & red (postage)	35	25
860	-	25c. orange and violet (air)	35	25
MS861		127×71 mm. 50c. red and blue (as No. 860). Imperf	85	85

DESIGN—HORIZ: No. 860, Campaign emblem and slogan.

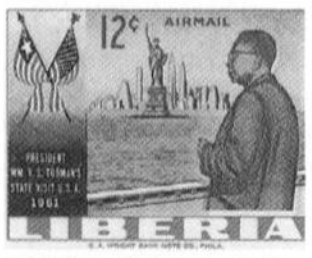

194 Pres. Tubman and New York Skyline

1962. Air. President's Visit to U.S.A.

862	**194**	12c. multicoloured	25	15
863	**194**	25c. multicoloured	35	30
864	**194**	50c. multicoloured	70	55

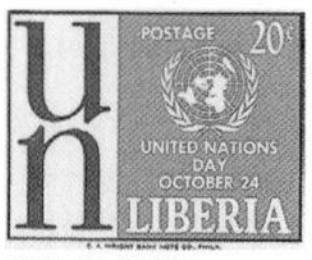

195 U.N. Emblem

1962. U.N. Day.

865	**195**	20c. bistre & grn (postage)	35	30
866	-	25c. blue & deep blue (air)	45	30
MS867		127×71 mm. 50c. black and green (UN Emblem). Imperf	1·00	1·00

DESIGN: 25c. U.N. emblem and flags.

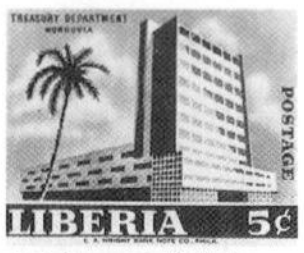

196 Treasury Building

1962. Liberian Government Buildings.

868		1c. orange & blue (postage)	10	15
869	**196**	5c. violet and blue	15	10
870	-	10c. brown and buff	25	15
871	-	15c. blue and salmon	25	20
872	-	80c. yellow and brown	1·60	1·00
873	-	12c. red and green (air)	25	15
874	-	50c. blue and orange	1·00	90
875	-	70c. blue and mauve	1·40	1·00
876	**196**	$1 black and orange	2·00	1·10

BUILDINGS: 1, 80c. Executive; 10, 50c. Information; 12, 15, 70c. Capitol.

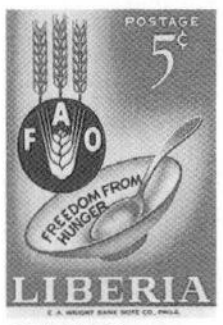

197 F.A.O. Emblem, Bowl and Spoon

1963. Freedom from Hunger.

877	**197**	5c. purple & turq (postage)	15	10
878	-	25c. yellow and green (air)	35	20
MS879		128×77 mm. 50c. blue and green (as 5c.)	80	80

DESIGN: 25c. FAO emblem and globe.

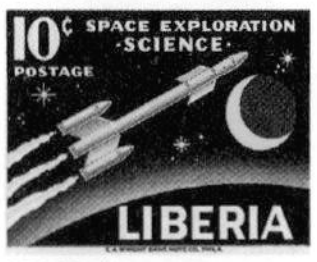

198 Rocket

1963. Space Exploration.

880	**198**	10c. yellow & bl (postage)	20	15
881	-	15c. brown and blue	35	40
882	-	25c. green and orange (air)	45	30
MS883		127×76 mm. 50c. yellow and blue	1·00	1·00

DESIGNS—HORIZ: 15c. Space capsule. VERT: 25c. "Telstar" TV satellite; 50c. "Telstar" and rocket.

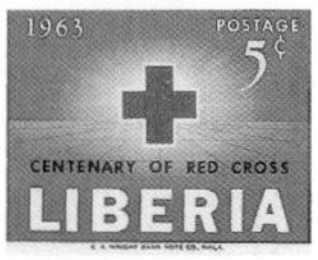

199 Red Cross

1963. Red Cross Centenary.

884	**199**	5c. green and red (postage)	15	15
885	-	10c. grey and red	20	20
886	-	25c. violet and red (air)	35	30
887	-	50c. blue and red	1·00	85

DESIGNS—VERT: 10c. Emblem and torch. HORIZ: 25c. Red Cross and Globe; 50c. Emblem and Globe.

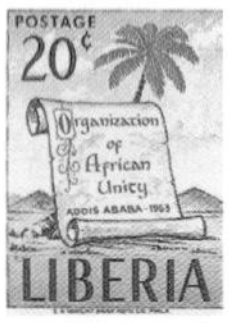

200 "Unity" Scroll

1963. Conference of African Heads of State, Addis Ababa.

888	**200**	20c. brn & grn (postage)	40	35
889	-	25c. red and green (air)	45	30

DESIGN: 25c. Map of Africa (inscr "AFRICAN SUMMIT CONFERENCE").

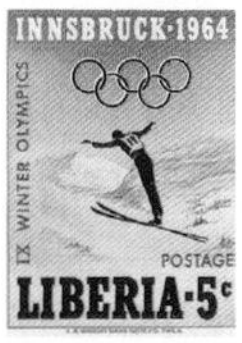

201 Ski-jumping

1963. Winter Olympic Games, Innsbruck. (1964).

890	**201**	5c. blue and red (postage)	20	20
891	-	10c. red and blue (air)	25	25
892	-	25c. orange and green	35	35
MS893		128×77 mm. 50c. red and black	85	85

DESIGNS—VERT: 10c. Olympic flame. HORIZ: 25c. Olympic rings; 50c. Torch and mountains. All have mountain scenery as backgrounds.

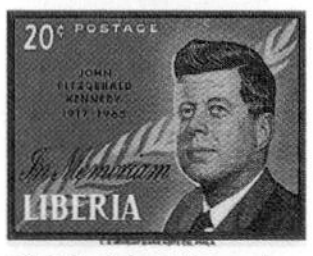

202 President Kennedy

1964. President Kennedy Memorial Issue.

894	**202**	20c. black & blue (postage)	35	20
895	-	25c. black and purple (air)	45	25
MS896		127×78 mm. 50c. black and purple (as 20c.)	1·10	1·10

DESIGN—VERT: 25c. President Kenny, full face portrait.

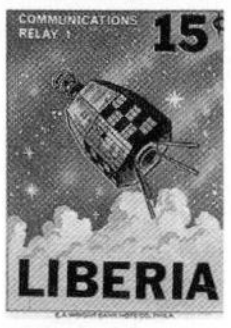

203 "Relay I" Satellite

1964. Space Communications.

897		10c. orange and green	20	15
898	**203**	15c. blue and mauve	25	20
899	-	25c. yellow, black and blue	45	25
MS900		127×77 mm. 50c. red and blue	1·10	1·10

SATELLITES: 10c. "Syncom"; 25c. Mariner II" 50c. Rocket in space.

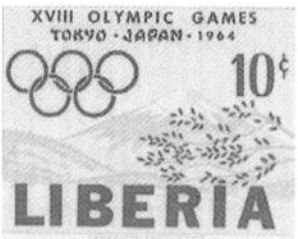

204 Mt. Fuji

1964. Olympic Games, Tokyo.

901	**204**	10c. green and yellow	15	10
902	-	15c. purple and red	20	15
903	-	25c. red and buff	45	20
MS904		128×77 mm. 50c. blue and red	1·10	1·10

DESIGNS:15c. Japanese arch and Olympic flame; 25c. Cherry blossom and stadium; 50c. Runner and Olympic "rings".

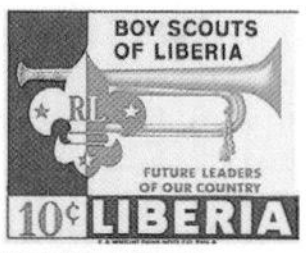

205 Scout Bugle

1965. Liberian Boy Scouts.

905		5c. brown and blue (postage)	25	15
906	**205**	10c. ochre and green	40	25
907	-	25c. blue and red (air)	50	35
MS908		128×77 mm. 50c. lemon and purple (Scout badge and Globe)	1·10	1·10

DESIGNS—VERT: 5c. Scout badge and saluting hand; 25c. Liberian flag within scout badge.

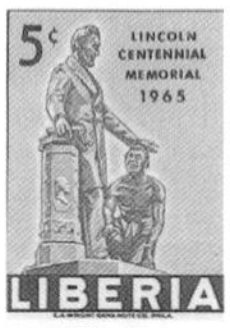

206 "The Great Emancipator" (statue)

1965. Death Centenary of Abraham Lincoln.

909	**206**	5c. brown and sepia	20	25
910	-	20c. green and light brown	35	30
911	-	25c. blue and purple	40	40
MS912		128×77 mm. 50c. purple and drab (as 20c.)	85	85

DESIGNS—HORIZ: 20c. Bust of Lincoln, and Pres. Kennedy. VERT: 25c. Lincoln statue, Chicago (after St. Gaudens).

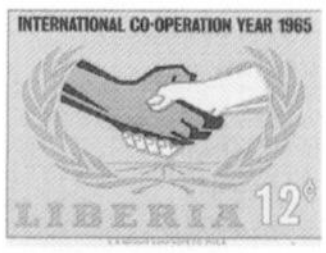

207 I.C.Y. Emblem

1965. International Co-operation Year.

913	**207**	12c. brown and orange	70	25
914	**207**	25c. brown and blue	40	25
915	**207**	50c. brown and green	80	70
MS916		128 ×77 mm. 50c. brown and rosine	85	85

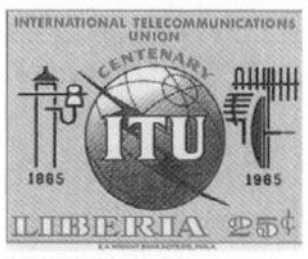

208 I.T.U. Emblem and Symbols

1965. Centenary of I.T.U.

917	**208**	25c. brn & grn (postage)	40	50
918	**208**	35c. mauve and black	60	50
919	**208**	50c. blue and red (air)	80	45
MS920		128×77 mm. Nos. 917/19. Imper	1·75	1·75

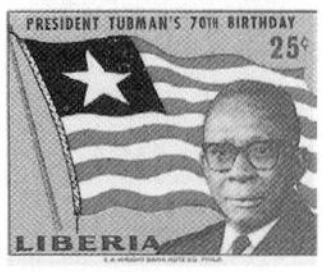

209 Pres. Tubman and Flag

1965. Pres. Tubman's 70th Birthday. Multicoloured.

921	25c. Type **209** (postage)	35	30
922	25c. President and Liberian arms (air)	35	25
MS923	128×77 mm. Nos. 921/2. Imperf	75	75

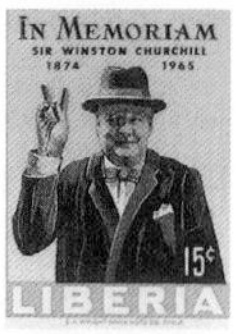

210 Sir Winston Churchill

1966. Churchill Commemoration.

924	**210**	15c. black & orge (postage)	30	30
925	-	20c. black and green	35	25
926	-	25c. black and blue (air)	40	30
MS927		126×77 mm. 50c. black and purple	85	85

DESIGNS—HORIZ: 20c. Churchill in uniform of Trinity House Elder Brother; 25c. Churchill and Houses of Parliament; 50c. Portrait after Karsh.

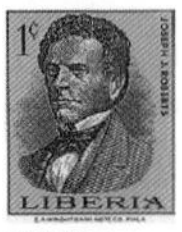

211 Pres. Roberts

1966. Liberian Presidents.

928	**211**	1c. black & pink (postage)	10	10
929	-	2c. black and yellow	10	10
930	-	3c. black and violet	10	10
931	-	4c. black and yellow	75	50
932	-	5c. black and orange	10	10
933	-	10c. black and green	15	10
934	-	25c. black and blue	35	20
935	-	50c. black and mauve	70	65
936	-	80c. black and red	1·25	95
937	-	$1 black and brown	1·40	15
938	-	$2 black and purple	3·25	2·75
939	-	25c. black and green (air)	35	25

PRESIDENTS: 2c. Benson; 3c. Warner; 4c. Payne; 5c. Roye; 10c. Coleman; 25c. (postage) Howard; 25c. (air) Tubman; 50c. King; 80c. Johnson; $1 Barclay; $2 Cheesman.

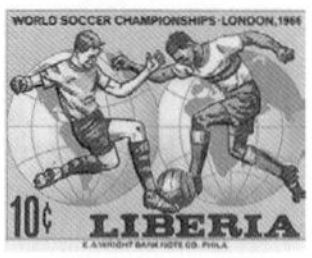

212 Footballers and Hemispheres

1966. World Cup Football Championships.

940	**212**	10c. brown and turquoise (postage)	15	15
941	-	25c. brown and mauve	35	30
942	-	35c. brown and orange	50	45
MS943		127×77 mm. 50c. brown and blue (air)	1·50	1·10

DESIGNS—VERT: 25c. Presentation cup, football and boots; 35c. Footballer. HORIZ: 50c. World Cup match.

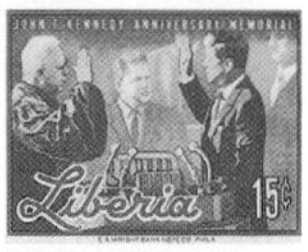

213 Pres. Kennedy taking Oath

1966. Third Death Anniv of Pres. Kennedy.

944	**213**	15c. black & red (postage)	25	15
945	-	20c. purple and blue	35	20
946	-	25c. blue, black and ochre (air)	45	30
947	-	35c. blue and pink	85	45
MS948		77×127 mm. 40c. multicoloured	1·00	1·00

DESIGNS: 20c. Kennedy stamps of 1964; 35c. Pres. Kennedy and rocket on launch pad. Cape Kennedy; 40c. Flame of Remembrance.

214 Children on See-saw

1966. 20th Anniv of UNICEF.
949	**214**	5c. blue and red	20	20
950	-	80c. brown and green	1·50	1·50

DESIGN: 80c. Child playing "Doctors".

215 Giraffe

1966. Wild Animals. Multicoloured.
951	2c. Type **215**	10	10
952	3c. Lion	20	15
953	5c. Crocodile (horiz)	15	10
954	10c. Chimpanzees	40	20
955	15c. Leopard (horiz)	50	25
956	20c. Black rhinoceros (horiz)	60	40
957	25c. African elephant	70	50

216 Scout Emblem and Various Sports

1967. World Scout Jamboree, Idaho.
958	-	10c. purple and green (postage)	20	15
959	**216**	25c. red and blue	35	50
960	-	40c. brown and green	85	60

MS961 127×77 mm. 50c. violet and red (air) 75 75

DESIGNS——VERT: Jamboree emblem. HORIZ: 40, 50c. Scout by campfire and Moon landing.

217 Pre-Hispanic Sculpture

1967. Publicity for Olympic Games, Mexico (1968).
962	**217**	10c. violet and orange	75	85
963	-	25c. orange, black and blue	35	40
964	-	40c. red and green	60	65

DESIGNS—VERT: 25c. Aztec calendar. HORIZ: 40c. Mexican sombrero, guitar and ceramics.

218 W.H.O. Building, Brazzaville

1967. Inauguration of W.H.O.'s Regional Office, Brazzaville.
966	**218**	5c. yellow and mauve	20	20
967	-	80c. green and yellow	1·25	1·25

DESIGN—VERT: 80c. As Type **218** but in vertical format.

219 Boy with Rattle

1967. Musicians and Instruments. Multicoloured.
968	2c. Type **219**	15	15
969	3c. Tomtom and soko violin (horiz)	20	20
970	5c. Mang harp (horiz)	25	25
971	10c. Alimilim	30	30
972	15c. Xylophone drums	35	35
973	25c. Tomtoms	50	40

974	35c. Oral harp	75	60

220 Ice-hockey

1967. Publicity for Winter Olympic Games, Grenoble (1968).
975	**220**	10c. blue and green (postage)	15	20
976	-	25c. violet and blue	35	30
977	-	40c. brown and orange	85	50

MS978 127×76½ mm. 50c. black and vermillion (air) 1·00 1·00

DESIGNS: 25c. Ski-jumping, 40c. Tobogganing; 50c. Ice skating.

221 Pres. Tubman

1967. Re-election of Pres. Tubman for 6th Term.
979	**221**	25c. brown and blue	35	25

MS980 78×78 mm. 50c. brown and blue. Imperf 75 75

222 Human Rights Emblem

1968. Human Rights Year.
981	**222**	3c. blue and red (postage)	10	10
982	**222**	80c. green and brown	1·60	1·60

MS983 128×78 mm. 80c. vermillion and blue (air) 1·60 1·60

223 Dr. King and Hearse

1968. Martin Luther King Commemoration.
984	**223**	15c. brown and blue (postage)	25	20
985	-	25c. brown and blue	40	30
986	-	35c. black and olive	60	65

MS987 127×76 mm. 55c. black and brown (air) 1·00 1·00

DESIGNS—VERT: 25c. Dr. Martin Luther King. HORIZ: 35c. Dr. King and Lincoln Monument; 55c. President Kennedy congratulating Dr. King upon award of Nobel Peace Prize.

224 Throwing the Javelin and Statue of Diana

1968. Olympic Games, Mexico.
988	**224**	15c. violet and brown (postage)	25	15
989	-	25c. blue and red	35	15
990	-	35c. brown and green	50	30

MS991 128×77 mm. 50c. brown and blue (air) 75 75

DESIGNS: Throwing the discus and Quetzalcoatl and sculpture; 35c. High-diving and Xochilcalco bas-relief; 50c. Horse-jumping and Aztec god.

225 President Tubman

1968. 25th Anniv of Pres. Tubman's Administration.
992	**225**	25c. black, brown & silver	1·10	50

MS993 78×78 mm. 80c. red, blue and silver. Imperf 2·50 2·50

DESIGN: 80c. Unification Monument, Voinjama.

226 I.L.O. Symbol

1969. 50th Anniv of I.L.O.
994	**226**	25c. blue & gold (postage)	35	35
995	-	80c. green and gold (air)	1·50	1·40

DESIGN: 80c. As Type **226** but vert.

227 "Prince Balthasar Carlos" (Velasquez)

1969. Paintings (1st series). Multicoloured.
996	3c. Type **227**	10	10
997	5c. "Red Roofs" (Pissarro) (horiz)	20	10
998	10c. "David and Goliath" (Caravaggio) (horiz)	30	15
999	12c. "Still Life" (Chardin) (horiz)	30	15
1000	15c. "The Last Supper" (Leonardo da Vinci) (horiz)	35	15
1001	20c. "Regatta at Argenteuil" (Monet) (horiz)	50	20
1002	25c. "Judgement of Solomon" (Giorgione)	45	25
1003	35c. "The Sistine Madonna" (Raphael)	85	30

See also Nos. 1010/1017.

228 Bank Emblem on "Tree"

1969. 5th Anniv of African Development Bank.
1004	**228**	25c. brown and blue	45	40
1005	**228**	80c. red and green	1·50	1·10

229 Memorial Plaque

1969. 1st Man on the Moon.
1006	**229**	15c. blue and ochre (postage)	25	15
1007	-	25c. blue and orange	70	20
1008	-	35c. red and slate	1·00	25

MS1009 127×76 mm. 65c. blue and vemillion 95 95

DESIGNS——VERT: 25c. Moon landing and Liberian "Kennedy" 35c. stamp of 1966; 35c. Module lifting off from Moon. HORIZ: 65c. "Apollo 1" astronauts.

1969. Paintings (2nd series). As T **227**. Multicoloured.
1010	3c. "The Gleaners" (Millet) (horiz)	15	10
1011	5c. "View of Toledo" (El Greco)	20	15

1012	10c. "Heads of Negroes" (Rubens) (horiz)	30	15
1013	12c. "The Last Supper" (El Greco) (horiz)	30	20
1014	15c. "Peasants Dancing" (Brueghel) (horiz)	35	20
1015	20c. "Hunters in the Snow" (Brueghel) (horiz)	40	25
1016	25c. "Descent from the Cross" (detail, Weyden)	45	30
1017	35c. "The Conception" (Murillo)	60	40

230 Peace Dove and Emblems

1970. 25th Anniv of United Nations.
1018	**230**	5c. green & sil (postage)	15	25
1019	-	$1 blue and silver (air)	1·25	1·00

DESIGN: $1, U.N. emblem and olive branch.

231 World Cup "Football" Emblem

1970. World Cup Football Championship, Mexico.
1020	**231**	5c. brown and blue	20	15
1021	-	10c. brown and green	25	20
1022	-	25c. gold and purple	45	30
1023	-	35c. red and blue	60	45

MS1024 127×76 mm. 55c. blue, yellow and green 90 90

DESIGNS——VERT: 10c. Tlaloc Mexican Rain God; 25c. Jules Rimet Cup. HORIZ: 35c. Football in sombrero; 55c. Players in Aztec Stadium.

232 Japanese Singer and Festival Plaza

1970. Expo 70. Multicoloured.
1025	2c. Type **232**	10	10
1026	3c. Japanese singer and Expo hall	15	10
1027	5c. Aerial view of "EXPO 70"	30	10
1028	7c. "Tanabata" Festival	30	10
1029	8c. "Awa" Dance Festival	30	15
1030	25c. "Sado-Okesa" Dance Festival	1·10	25

MS1031 80×115 mm. Ricoh Pavilion (vert) 2·00 2·00

233 New H.Q. Building

1970. Inauguration of New U.P.U. Headquarters Building, Berne.
1032	**233**	25c. brown and blue	35	35
1033	-	80c. brown and chestnut	1·50	1·50

DESIGN—VERT: 80c. Similar to Type **233** but with larger U.P.U. monument.

234 "The First Consul" (Vien)

1970. Birth Bicentenary of Napoleon Bonaparte. Multicoloured.
1034	3c. Type **234**	20	10
1035	5c. "Napoleon visiting school" (unknown artist)	30	15
1036	10c. "Napoleon Bonaparte" (detail, Isabey)	35	15

1037	12c. "The French Campaign" (Meissonier)	40	20
1038	20c. "The Abdication" (Bouchot)	80	30
1039	25c. "Meeting of Napoleon and Pope Pius VII" (Demarne)	1·50	35
MS1040	77×102 mm. 50c. "The Coronation" (David). Imperf	2·75	2·75

Design of 10c. is incorrectly attributed to Gerard on the stamp.

235 Pres. Tubman

1970. Pres. Tubman's 75th Birthday.

| 1041 | **235** 25c. multicoloured | 75 | 25 |
| MS1042 | 86×112 mm. 50c. multicoloured | 1·40 | 1·40 |

236 "Adoration of the Magi" (Van der Weyden)

1970. Christmas. "The Adoration of the Magi" by artists as below. Multicoloured.

1043	3c. Type **236**	10	10
1044	5c. H. Memling	15	10
1045	10c. S. Lochner	25	15
1046	12c. A. Altdorfer (vert)	30	15
1047	20c. H. van der Goes	35	15
1048	25c. H. Bosch (vert)	40	30
MS1049	99×70 mm. 50c. Triptych by Andrea Mantegna. Imperf	85	85

The design in MS1049 is larger 58×40 mm.

237 Bapende Mask

1971. African Ceremonial Masks. Masks from different tribes. Multicoloured.

1050	2c. Type **237**	10	10
1051	3c. Dogon	15	10
1052	5c. Baoule	15	15
1053	6c. Dedougou	20	15
1054	9c. Dan	25	15
1055	15c. Bamileke	30	20
1056	20c. Bapende (different)	40	30
1057	25c. Bamileke costume	60	30

238 Astronauts on Moon

1971. "Apollo 14" Moon Mission. Multicoloured.

1058	3c. Type **238**	15	10
1059	5c. Astronaut and Moon vehicle	15	10
1060	10c. Erecting U.S. flag on Moon	20	10
1061	12c. Splashdown	40	15
1062	20c. Astronauts leaving capsule	45	15
1063	25c. "Apollo 14" crew	60	20
MS1064	127×85 mm. 50c. Earth, Moon and "star"	1·25	1·25

239 Pres. Tubman and Women at Ballot Box

1971. 25th Anniv of Liberian Women's Suffrage.

| 1065 | **239** 3c. blue and brown | 15 | 30 |
| 1066 | - 80c. brown and green | 1·50 | 1·50 |

DESIGN—HORIZ: 80c. Pres. Tubman, women and map.

240 Hall of Honour, Munich

1971. Olympic Games, Munich (1972) (1st issue). Views of Munich. Multicoloured.

1067	3c. Type **240**	15	10
1068	5c. View of central Munich	15	10
1069	10c. National Museum	20	10
1070	12c. Max Joseph's Square	25	10
1071	20c. Propylaen, King's Square	40	15
1072	25c. Liesel-Karlstadt Fountain	60	20
MS1073	115×84 mm. 25c. Olympic Village, Kiel; 30c. Yachts at Kiel	1·25	1·25

See also Nos. 1106/MS1112.

241 American Scout

1971. World Scout Jamboree, Asagiri, Japan. Scouts in national uniforms. Multicoloured.

1074	3c. Type **241**(postage)	15	10
1075	5c. West Germany	15	10
1076	10c. Australia	20	15
1077	12c. Great Britain	25	15
1078	20c. Japan	40	20
1079	25c. Liberia	60	30
MS1080	102×76 mm. 50c. Scouts around camp fire (horiz) (air)	1·25	1·25

242 Pres. William Tubman

1971. Pres. Tubman Memorial Issue.

| 1081 | **242** 3c. brown, blue and black | 10 | 10 |
| 1082 | **242** 25c. brown, purple & blk | 35 | 35 |

243 Common Zebra and Foal

1971. 25th Anniv of UNICEF. Animals with young. Multicoloured.

1083	5c. Type **243**	20	10
1084	7c. Koalas	30	15
1085	8c. Guanaco	35	15
1086	10c. Red fox and cubs	45	15
1087	20c. Savanna monkeys	65	25
1088	25c. Brown bears	90	35
MS1089	102×77 mm. 50c. Bengal tiger	1·75	1·75

244 Cross-country Skiing and Sika Deer

1971. Winter Olympic Games, Sapporo, Japan. Sports and Hokkaido Animals. Multicoloured.

1090	2c. Type **244** (postage)	10	10
1091	3c. Tobogganing and black woodpecker	70	20
1092	5c. Ski-jumping and brown bear	15	10
1093	10c. Bobsleighing and common guillemots	1·00	20
1094	15c. Figure-skating and northern pika	30	20
1095	25c. Slalom skiing and Manchurian cranes	2·00	50
MS1096	102×77 mm. 50c. Japanese Imperial Family (air)	3·75	3·75

245 A.P.U. Emblem, Dove and Letter

1971. Tenth Anniv of African Postal Union.

| 1097 | **245** 25c. orange and blue | 35 | 50 |
| 1098 | **245** 80c. brown and grey | 1·10 | 1·00 |

246 "Elizabeth" (emigrant ship) at Providence Island

1972. 150th Anniv of Liberia.

1099	**246** 3c. green and blue (postage)	70	50
1100	- 20c. blue and orange	35	20
1101	**246** 25c. purple and orange	2·00	55
1102	- 35c. purple and green	1·10	75
MS1103	127×78 mm. 50c. red and blue (air)	3·75	3·75

DESIGNS—VERT: Arms and Founding Fathers Monument, Monrovia. HORIZ: 50c. "Elizabeth" crossing the Atlantic.

247 Pres. Tolbert and Map

1972. Inaug of Pres. Wm. R. Tolbert Jnr.

| 1104 | **247** 25c. brown and green | 35 | 25 |
| 1105 | - 80c. brown and blue | 1·60 | 80 |

DESIGN—VERT: 80c. Pres. Tolbert standing by desk.

248 Football

1972. Olympic Games, Munich (2nd issue). Multicoloured.

1106	3c. Type **248** (postage)	10	10
1107	5c. Swimming	15	10
1108	10c. Show-jumping	25	10
1109	12c. Cycling	30	15
1110	20c. Long-jumping	45	20
1111	25c. Running	60	25
MS1112	102×70 mm. 55c. Olympic Stadium (air)	1·25	1·25

249 Globe and Emblem

1972. 50th Anniv of Int Y's Men's Clubs.

| 1113 | **249** 15c. violet and gold | 40 | 15 |
| 1114 | - 90c. green and blue | 1·75 | 1·75 |

DESIGN: 90c. Club emblem on World Map.

250 Astronaut and Moon Rover

1972. Moon Mission of "Apollo 16". Multicoloured.

1115	3c. Type **250** (postage)	10	10
1116	5c. Reflection on visor	10	10
1117	10c. Astronauts with cameras	15	10
1118	12c. Setting up equipment	50	15
1119	20c. "Apollo 16" emblem	65	20
1120	25c. Astronauts in Moon Rover	90	50
MS1121	97×71 mm. 55c. "Apollo 16" crew (air)	1·75	1·75

251 Emperor Haile Selassie

1972. Emperor Haile Selassie of Ethiopia's 80th Birthday.

1122	**251** 20c. green and yellow	40	30
1123	**251** 25c. purple and yellow	45	40
1124	**251** 35c. brown and yellow	85	85

252 H.M.S. "Ajax" (ship of the line), 1809

1972. Famous Ships of the British Royal Navy. Multicoloured.

1125	3c. Type **252** (postage)	35	25
1126	5c. HMS "Hogue" (screw ship of the line), 1848	65	25
1127	7c. HMS "Ariadne" (frigate), 1816	85	30
1128	15c. HMS "Royal Adelaide" (ship of the line), 1828	1·00	55
1129	20c. HMS "Rinaldo" (screw sloop), 1860	1·40	70
1130	25c. HMS "Nymphe" (screw sloop), 1888	1·90	1·00
MS1131	102×76 mm. 50c. HMS "Victory" (battleship), 1765 (air)	3·50	3·50

253 Pres. Tolbert taking Oath

1972. First Year of President Tolbert Presidency.

1132	**253** 15c. multicoloured (postage)	65	55
1133	**253** 25c. multicoloured	95	95
MS1134	96×72 mm. 55c. multicoloured (air)	1·90	1·90

254 Klaus Dibiasi and Italian Flag

1973. Olympic Games, Munich. Gold-medal Winners. Multicoloured.

1135	5c. Type **254**	10	10
1136	8c. Borzov and Soviet flag	15	10
1137	10c. Yanagida and Japanese flag	15	10
1138	12c. Spitz and U.S. flag	20	15
1139	15c. Keino and Kenyan flag	25	15
1140	25c. Meade and Union Jack	35	25
MS1141	95×70 mm. 55c. Hans Winkler and West German flag	85	85

255 Astronaut on Moon

1973. Moon Flight of "Apollo 17". Multicoloured.

1142	2c. Type **255** (postage)	10	10
1143	3c. Testing lunar rover at Cape Kennedy	10	10
1144	10c. Collecting Moon rocks	15	10
1145	15c. Lunar rover on Moon	20	15
1146	20c. "Apollo 17" crew at Cape Kennedy	30	20
1147	25c. Astronauts on Moon	35	25
MS1148	102×77 mm. 55c. "Apollo 17" emblem (air)	85	85

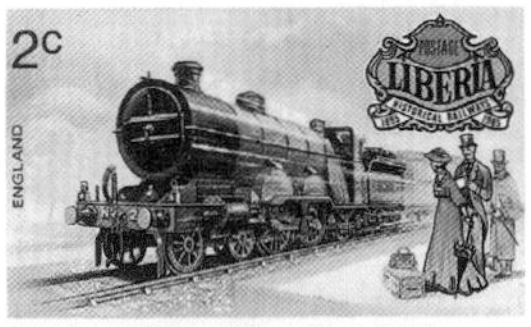

256 Steam Locomotive, Great Britain

1973. Historical Railways. Steam locomotives of 1895–1905. Multicoloured.

1149	2c. Type **256** (postage)	25	10
1150	3c. Netherlands	35	10
1151	10c. France	65	15
1152	15c. No. 1800, U.S.A.	95	20
1153	20c. Class 150 No. 1, Japan	2·00	25
1154	25c. Germany	3·00	30
MS1155	102×77 mm. 55c. Switzerland (air)	4·50	4·50

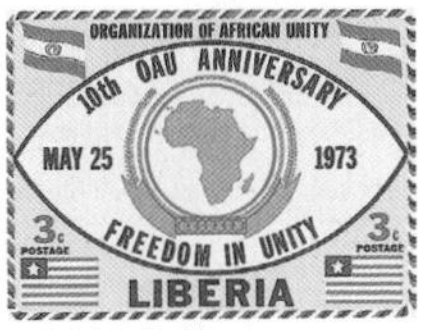

257 O.A.U. Emblem

1973. 10th Anniv of Organization of African Unity.

1156	**257**	3c. multicoloured	10	10
1157	**257**	5c. multicoloured	10	10
1158	**257**	10c. multicoloured	15	10
1159	**257**	15c. multicoloured	20	15
1160	**257**	25c. multicoloured	35	25
1161	**257**	50c. multicoloured	1·00	1·00

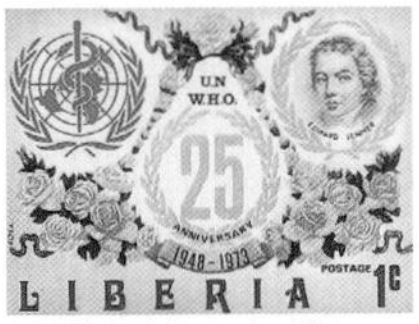

258 Edward Jenner and Roses

1973. 25th Anniv of W.H.O. Multicoloured.

1162	1c. Type **258** (postage)	15	10
1163	4c. Sigmund Freud and violets	15	10
1164	10c. Jonas Salk and chrysanthemums	25	10
1165	15c. Louis Pasteur and scabious	40	15
1166	20c. Emil von Behring and mallow	45	20
1167	25c. Sir Alexander Fleming and rhododendrons	85	25
MS1168	102×77 mm. 55c. Paul Ehrlich and anemones (air)	1·50	1·50

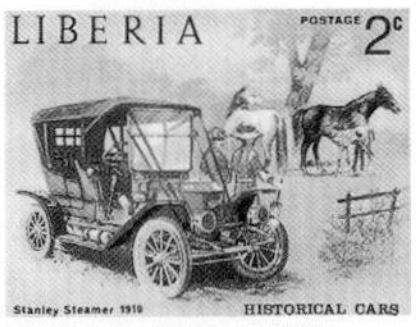

259 Stanley Steamer, 1910

1973. Vintage Cars. Multicoloured.

1169	2c. Type **259** (postage)	10	10
1170	3c. Cadillac Model A, 1903	10	10
1171	10c. Clement-Baynard, 1904	15	10
1172	15c. Rolls-Royce Silver Ghost tourer, 1907	25	15
1173	20c. Maxwell gentleman's speedster, 1905	35	20
1174	25c. Chadwick, 1907	50	25
MS1175	103×77 mm. 55c. Franklin 10 hp Crossed-engine, 1904 and 1905 (air)	1·00	1·00

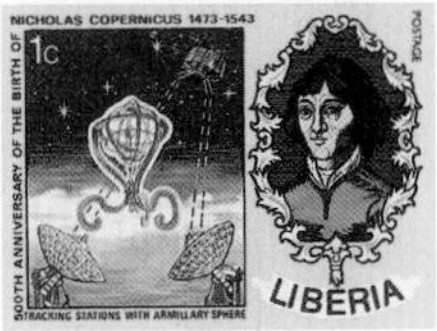

260 Copernicus, Armillary Sphere and Satellite Communications System

1973. 500th Birth Anniv of Copernicus. Multicoloured.

1176	1c. Type **260** (postage)	10	10
1177	4c. Eudoxus solar system	10	10
1178	10c. Aristotle, Ptolemy and Copernicus	15	10
1179	15c. "Saturn" and "Apollo" spacecraft	25	15
1180	20c. Astronomical observatory satellite	35	20
1181	25c. Satellite tracking-station	50	25
MS1182	114×77 mm. 55c. Satellite in Mars orbit (air)	1·00	1·00

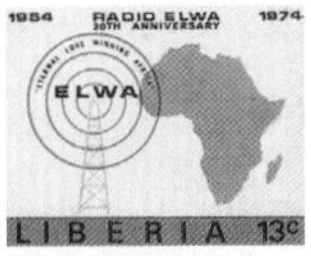

261 Radio Mast and Map of Africa

1974. 20th Anniv of "Eternal Love Winning Africa". Radio Station. Multicoloured.

1183	13c. Type **261**	25	25
1184	15c. Radio mast and map of Liberia	35	25
1185	17c. Type **261**	35	50
1186	25c. As 15c.	50	40

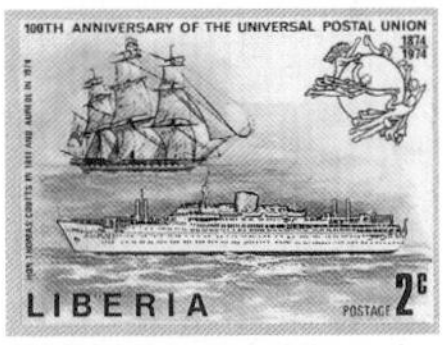

262 "Thomas Coutts" (full-rigged sailing ship) and "Aureol" (liner)

1974. Cent of U.P.U. Multicoloured.

1187	2c. Type **262** (postage)	20	10
1188	3c. Boeing 707 airliner and "Brasil" (liner), satellite and Monrovia Post Office	30	10
1189	10c. U.S. and Soviet Telecommunications satellites	15	10
1190	15c. Postal runner and Boeing 707 airliner	25	20
1191	20c. British Advanced Passenger Train (APT) and Liberian mail-van	1·50	25
1192	25c. American Pony Express rider	50	35
MS1193	115×77 mm. 55c. English mail-coach, 1784 (air)	1·00	1·00

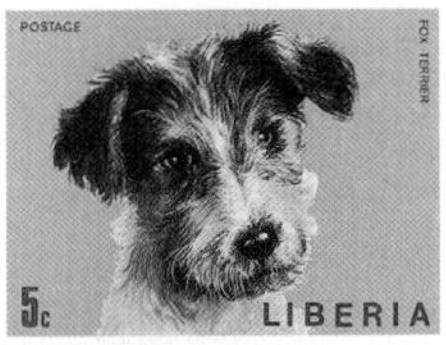

263 Fox Terrier

1974. Dogs. Multicoloured.

1194	5c. Type **263**	15	10
1195	10c. Boxer	20	10
1196	16c. Chihuahua	30	15
1197	19c. Beagle	35	20
1198	25c. Golden retriever	40	25
1199	50c. Collie	1·10	50
MS1200	115×77 mm. 75c. Kuvasz (Hungarian sheepdog)	1·60	1·60

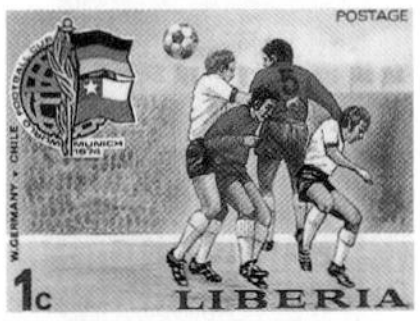

264 West Germany v. Chile Match

1974. World Cup Football Championship, West Germany. Scenes from semi-final matches. Multicoloured.

1201	1c. Type **264** (postage)	10	10
1202	2c. Australia v. East Germany	10	10
1203	5c. Brazil v. Yugoslavia	15	10
1204	10c. Zaire v. Scotland	20	10
1205	12c. Netherlands v. Uruguay	25	15
1206	15c. Sweden v. Bulgaria	30	15
1207	20c. Italy v. Haiti	40	20
1208	25c. Poland v. Argentina	60	25
MS1209	102×77 mm. 60c. World Cup and Stadium (air)	1·60	1·60

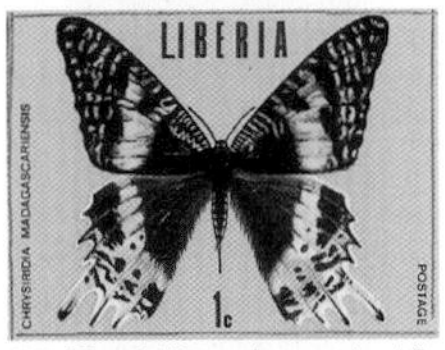

265 "Chrysiridia madagascariensis"

1974. Tropical Butterflies. Multicoloured.

1210	1c. Type **265** (postage)	10	10
1211	2c. "Catagramma sorana"	10	10
1212	5c. "Erasmia pulchella"	20	10
1213	17c. "Morpho cypris"	50	25
1214	25c. "Agrias amydon"	70	35
1215	40c. "Vanessa cardui"	1·40	45
MS1216	114×77 mm. 60c. "Pierella merels" (air)	2·00	2·00

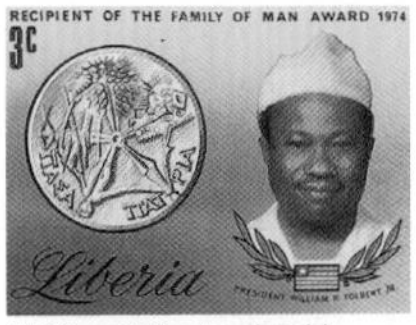

266 Pres. Tolbert and Gold Medallion

1974. "Family of Man" Award to President Tolbert. Multicoloured.

1217	3c. Type **266**	10	25
1218	$1 Pres. Tolbert, medallion and flag	1·40	1·40

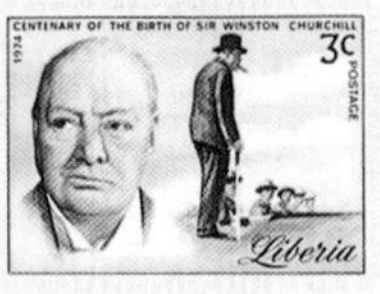

267 Churchill with Troops

1975. Birth Centenary of Sir Winston Churchill. Multicoloured.

1219	3c. Type **267** (postage)	10	10
1220	10c. Churchill and aerial combat	30	10
1221	15c. Churchill aboard "Liberty" ship in Channel	55	15
1222	17c. Churchill reviewing troops in desert	30	15
1223	20c. Churchill crossing Rhine	40	20
1224	25c. Churchill with Roosevelt	50	25
MS1225	113×77 mm. 60c.Chruchill paint (air)	1·60	1·60

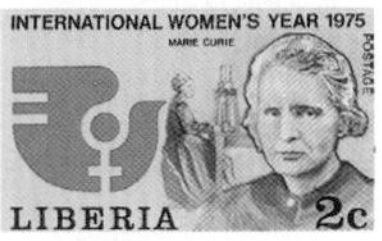

268 Marie Curie

1975. International Women's Year. Multicoloured.

1226	2c. Type **268** (postage)	10	10
1227	3c. Mahalia Jackson	10	10
1228	5c. Joan of Arc	10	10
1229	10c. Eleanor Roosevelt	15	10
1230	25c. Matilda Newport	50	25
1231	50c. Valentina Tereshkova	70	55
MS1232	106×80 mm. 75c. Vijaya Lakshmi Pandit (air)	1·25	1·25

269 Old State House, Boston, and U.S. 2c. "Liberty Bell" Stamp of 1926

1975. Bicentenary of American Independence.

1233	5c. Type **269**	15	10
1234	10c. George Washington and 1928 "Valley Forge" stamp	30	10
1235	15c. Philadelphia and 1937 "Constitution" stamp	45	15
1236	20c. Benjamin Franklin and 1938 "Ratification" stamp	50	15
1237	25c. Paul Revere's Ride and 1925 "Lexington-Concord" stamp	70	20
1238	50c. "Santa Maria" and 1893 "Columbus' Landing" stamp	2·25	55
MS1239	78×100 mm. 75c. "Mayflower" and US Pilgrim Fathers stamp of 1920	2·75	2·75

See also Nos. 1297/**MS**1299.

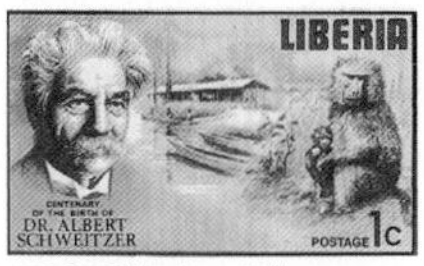

270 Dr. Schweitzer, Yellow Baboon and Lambarene Hospital

1975. Birth Centenary of Dr Albert Schweitzer. Multicoloured.

1240	1c. Type **270** (postage)	10	10
1241	3c. Schweitzer, African elephant and canoe	15	10
1242	5c. Schweitzer, African buffalo and canoe	25	20
1243	6c. Schweitzer, kob and dancer	30	10
1244	25c. Schweitzer, lioness and village woman	75	25
1245	50c. Schweitzer, common zebras and clinic scene	1·40	65
MS1246	76×97 mm. 60c. Schweitzer and staff in operating theatre (air)	2·10	2·10

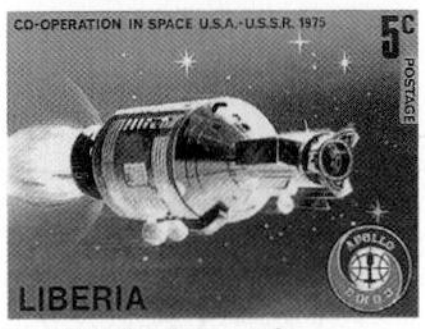

271 "Apollo" Spacecraft

1975. "Apollo–Soyuz" Space Link. Multicoloured.

1247	5c. Type **271**	10	10
1248	10c. "Soyuz" spacecraft	15	10
1249	15c. American–Russian handclasp	20	15
1250	20c. Flags and maps of America and Russia	25	15
1251	25c. Leonov and Kubasov	35	20
1252	50c. Slayton, Brand and Stafford	95	50
MS1253	155×78 mm. 75c. "Apollo" and "Soyuz" spacecraft docked together	1·25	1·25

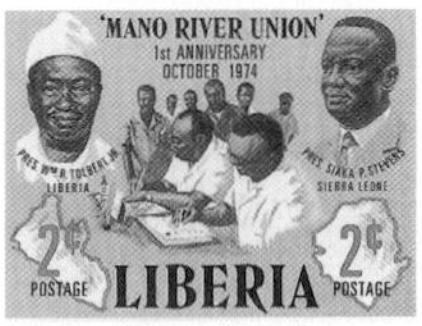

272 Presidents Tolbert and Stevens, and Signing Ceremony

1975. Liberia–Sierra Leone Mano River Union Agreement.

1254	**272**	2c. multicoloured	10	10
1255	**272**	3c. multicoloured	10	10
1256	**272**	5c. multicoloured	10	10
1257	**272**	10c. multicoloured	15	10
1258	**272**	25c. multicoloured	35	25
1259	**272**	50c. multicoloured	70	70

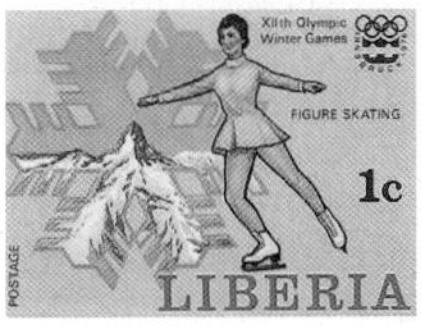

273 Figure Skating

1976. Winter Olympic Games, Innsbruck. Multicoloured.

1260	1c. Type **273** (postage)	10	10
1261	4c. Ski jumping	20	20
1262	10c. Skiing (slalom)	30	20
1263	25c. Ice hockey	60	30
1264	35c. Speed skating	90	40
1265	50c. Two-man bobsledding	1·25	65
MS1266	117×78 mm. 75c. Downhill skiing (air)	1·75	1·75

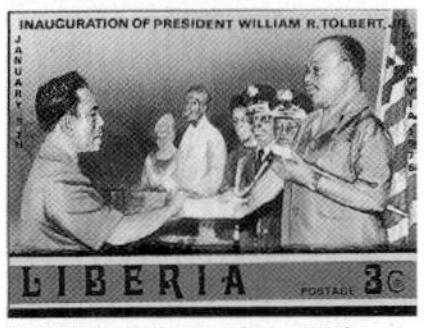

274 Pres. Tolbert taking Oath

1976. Inauguration of President William R. Tolbert, Jr. Multicoloured.

1267	3c. Type **274**	10	10
1268	25c. Pres. Tolbert in Presidential Chair (vert)	35	25
1269	$1 Liberian crest, flag and commemorative gold coin	1·90	1·40

275 Weightlifting

1976. Olympic Games, Montreal. Multicoloured.

1270	2c. Type **275** (postage)	10	10
1271	3c. Pole-vaulting	10	10
1272	10c. Hammer and shot-put	30	15
1273	25c. "Tempest" dinghies	65	35
1274	35c. Gymnastics	90	60
1275	50c. Hurdling	1·25	65
MS1276 115×77 mm. 75c. Dressage and show jumping (air)		1·75	1·75

276 Bell's Telephone and Receiver

1976. Telephone Centenary. Multicoloured.

1277	1c. Type **276** (postage)	10	10
1278	4c. Mail-coach	10	10
1279	5c. "Intelsat 4" satellite	15	10
1280	25c. Cable-ship "Dominia", 1926	1·25	30
1281	40c. British Advanced Passenger Train (APT)	1·60	50
1282	50c. Wright Flyer I, airship "Graf Zeppelin" and Concorde	1·75	60
MS1283 116×78 mm. 75c. Bell making telephone call (air)		3·00	3·00

277 Gold Nugget Pendant

1976. Liberian Products (1st series). Multicoloured.

1284	1c. Mano River Bridge	10	10
1285	3c. Type **277**	10	10
1286	5c. "V" ring	10	10
1286a	7c. As No. 1286	15	25
1287	10c. Rubber tree and tyre	15	10
1287a	15c. Combine harvester	20	10
1287b	17c. As No. 1289	45	10
1288	20c. Hydro-electric plant	60	45
1288	25c. Mesurado shrimp	75	25
1288a	27c. Dress and woman tie-dying cloth	80	60
1289	55c. Great barracuda	1·40	35
1289a	$1 Train carrying iron ore	4·50	60

For designs as T **277** but in a smaller size, see Nos. 1505/8.

278 Black Rhinoceros

1976. Animals. Multicoloured.

1290	2c. Type **278** (postage)	10	10
1291	3c. Bongo	10	10
1292	5c. Chimpanzee (vert)	15	10
1293	15c. Pygmy hippopotamus	40	15
1294	25c. Leopard	80	40
1295	$1 Gorilla	3·00	90
MS1296 103×78 mm. 50c. Elephant (air)		1·60	1·60

279 Statue of Liberty and Unification Monument on Maps of U.S.A. and Liberia

1976. Bicentenary of American Revolution. Multicoloured.

1297	25c. Type **279** (postage)	35	25
1298	$1 Presidents Washington and Ford (U.S.A.), Roberts and Tolbert (Liberia)	1·75	65
MS1299 78×104m. 75c. As $1 (air)		1·75	1·75

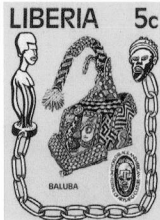

280 Baluba Masks

1977. Second World Black and African Festival of Arts and Culture, Lagos (Nigeria). Tribal Masks. Multicoloured.

1300	5c. Type **280** (postage)	10	10
1301	10c. Bateke	15	10
1302	15c. Basshilele	20	15
1303	20c. Igungun	30	15
1304	25c. Maisi	60	20
1305	50c. Kifwebe	1·10	45
MS1306 102×77 mm. 75c. Lbo mask		11·60	1·60

281 Latham's Francolin

1977. Liberian Wild Birds. Multicoloured.

1307	5c. Type **281**	50	10
1308	10c. Narina's trogon ("Narina Trogon")	80	15
1309	15c. Rufous-crowned roller	80	20
1310	20c. Brown-cheeked hornbill	85	25
1311	25c. Garden bulbul ("Pepper Bird")	1·00	35
1312	50c. African fish eagle ("Fish Eagle")	1·10	85
MS1313 104×77 mm. 80c. Gold Coast touraco		2·00	2·00

282 Alwin Schockemohle (individual jumping)

1977. Olympic Games, Montreal. Equestrian Gold-medal Winners. Multicoloured.

1314	5c. Edmund Coffin (military dressage) (postage)	15	10
1315	15c. Type **282**	40	20
1316	20c. Christine Stuckelberger (dressage)	50	30
1317	25c. "Nations Prize" (French team)	70	35
1318	55c. Military dressage (U.S.A. team) (air)	1·25	70
MS1319 78×104 mm. 80c. West German team (tean dressagr)		1·75	1·75

283 Queen Elizabeth II

1977. Silver Jubilee of Queen Elizabeth II. Multicoloured.

1320	15c. Type **283** (postage)	35	15
1321	25c. Queen Elizabeth and Prince Philip with President and Mrs. Tubman of Liberia	55	25
1322	80c. Queen Elizabeth, Prince Philip and Royal Arms	2·40	70
MS1323 116×78 mm. 75c. Full-faced portrait of Queen Elizabeth (air)		2·25	2·25

284 "Blessing the Children"

1977. Christmas. Multicoloured.

1324	20c. Type **284**	50	25
1325	25c. "The Good Shepherd"	70	35
1326	$1 "Jesus and the Woman of Samaria at the Well"	2·00	1·00

285 Dornier Do-X Flying Boat

1978. "Progress in Aviation". Multicoloured.

1327	2c. Type **285**	10	10
1328	3c. Space shuttle "Enterprise" on Boeing 747	10	10
1329	5c. Edward Rickenbacker and Douglas DC-3	10	10
1330	25c. Charles Lindbergh and "Spirit of St. Louis"	45	20
1331	35c. Louis Bleriot and Bleriot XI monoplane	65	35
1332	50c. Wright Brothers and Flyer I	90	55
MS1333 119×80 mm. 80c. Concorde		1·40	1·40

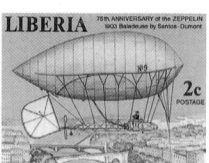

286 Santos-Dumont's Airship "Ballon No. 9 La Badaleuse", 1903

1978. 75th Anniv of First Zeppelin Flight. Multicoloured.

1334	2c. Type **286** (postage)	10	10
1335	3c. Thomas Baldwin's airship "U.S. Military No. 1", 1908	10	10
1336	5c. Tissandier brothers' airship, 1883	10	10
1337	25c. Parseval airship PL-VII, 1912	40	20
1338	40c. Airship "Nulli Secundus II", 1908	75	35
1339	50c. Beardmore airship R-34, 1919	85	55
MS1340 108×81 mm. 75c. Goodyear airship (air)		1·40	1·40

287 Tackling

1978. World Cup Football Championship, Argentina.

1341	**287**	2c. multicoloured (postage)	10	10
1342	-	3c. multicoloured (horiz)	10	10
1343	-	10c. multicoloured (horiz)	15	10
1344	-	25c. multicoloured (horiz)	60	20
1345	-	35c. multicoloured (horiz)	80	25
1346	-	50c. multicoloured (horiz)	1·25	50
MS1347 102×78 mm. 75c. multicoloured (air)			1·60	1·60

DESIGNS: 1341/**MS**1347 Different match scenes.

288 Coronation Chair

1978. 25th Anniv of Coronation. Multicoloured.

1348	5c. Type **288** (postage)	10	25
1349	25c. Imperial State Crown	35	25
1350	$1 Buckingham Palace (horiz)	1·75	1·00
MS1351 103×78 mm. 75c. Coronation coach (horiz) (air)		1·10	1·10

289 Mohammed Ali Jinnah and Flags

1978. Birth Centenary of Mohammed Ali Jinnah (first Governor-General of Pakistan).

1352	**289**	30c. multicoloured	1·50	1·50

290 Carter and Tolbert Families

1978. Visit of President Carter of U.S.A. Multicoloured.

1353	5c. Type **290**	10	10
1354	25c. Presidents Carter and Tolbert with Mrs. Carter at microphones	50	45
1355	$1 Presidents Carter and Tolbert in open car	2·00	2·00

291 Italy v. France

1978. Argentina's Victory in World Cup Football Championship. Multicoloured.

1356	1c. Brazil v. Spain (horiz) (postage)	10	10
1357	2c. Type **291**	10	10
1358	10c. Poland v. West Germany (horiz)	15	10
1359	27c. Peru v. Scotland	65	25
1360	35c. Austria v. West Germany	80	55
1361	50c. Argentinian players with Cup	1·25	80
MS1362 128×103 mm. 75c. Argentinian team (horiz) (air)		1·60	1·60

292 Timber Truck

1978. Eighth World Forestry Congress, Djakarta. Multicoloured.

1363	5c. Chopping up log (horiz)	10	10
1364	10c. Type **292**	15	10
1365	25c. Felling trees (horiz)	60	20
1366	50c. Loggers (horiz)	1·10	70

293 Presidents Gardner and Tolbert with Monrovia Post Office

1979. Centenary of U.P.U. Membership. Multicoloured.

1367	5c. Type **293**	10	10
1368	35c. Presidents Gardner and Tolbert with U.P.U. emblem	90	90

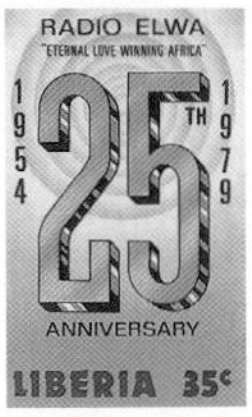

294 "25" and Radio Waves

1979. 25th Anniv of Radio ELWA. Multicoloured.

1369	35c. Type **294**	75	75
1370	$1 Radio tower	2·10	2·10

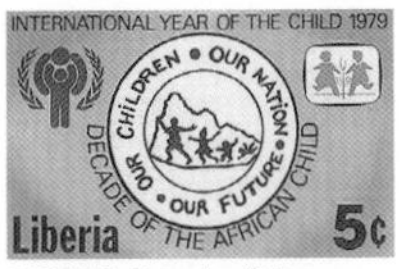

295 I.Y.C., Decade of the African Child and S.O.S. Villages Emblems

1979. International Year of the Child. Multicoloured.

1371	5c. Type **295**	10	10
1372	25c. As Type **295** but with UNICEF instead of S.O.S. Villages emblem	25	20
1373	35c. Type **295**	50	25
1374	$1 As No. 1372	1·40	1·40

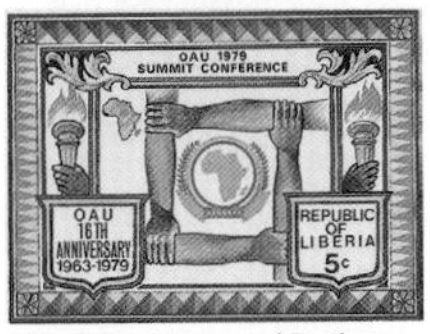

296 Clasped Arms and Torches

1979. Organization for African Unity Summit Conference, Monrovia. Multicoloured.

1375	5c. Type **296**	10	10
1376	27c. Masks	40	25
1377	35c. African animals	50	50
1378	50c. Thatched huts and garden bulbuls	1·50	65

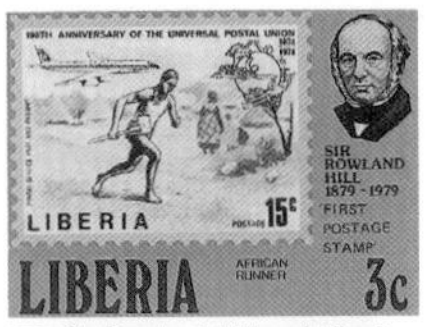

297 Sir Rowland Hill and Liberian 15c. Stamp, 1974

1979. Death Centenary of Sir Rowland Hill. Multicoloured.

1379	3c. Type **297**	10	10
1380	10c. Pony Express rider	15	10
1381	15c. British mail coach	20	35
1382	25c. "John Penn" (paddle-steamer)	75	55
1383	27c. Class "Coronation" stream-lined steam locomotive No. 6235, Great Britain	1·10	25
1384	50c. Concorde	1·50	90
MS1385	102×77 mm. $1 Curtiss "Jenny", 1916	3·00	3·00

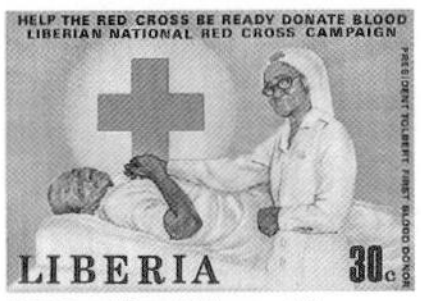

298 President Tolbert giving Blood

1979. National Red Cross Blood Donation Campaign. Multicoloured.

1386	30c. Type **298**	45	25
1387	50c. President Tolbert and Red Cross	1·00	1·00

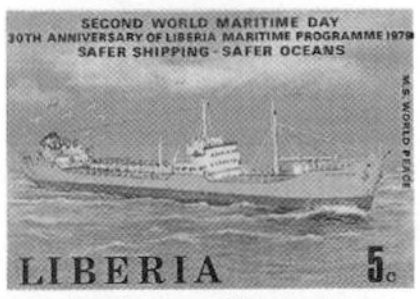

299 "World Peace" (tanker)

1979. Second World Maritime Day and 30th Anniv of Liberia Maritime Programme. Multicoloured.

1388	5c. Type **299**	30	15
1389	$1 "World Peace" (different)	2·25	2·00

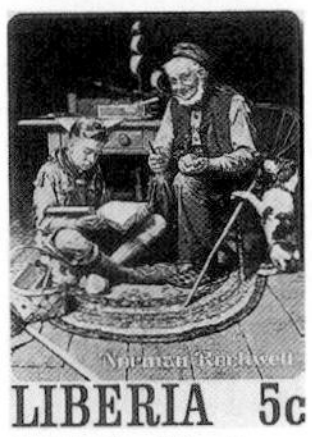

300 "A Good Turn"

1979. Scout Paintings by Norman Rockwell. Multicoloured.

1390	5c. Scout giving first aid to pup ("A Good Scout")	20	15
1391	5c. Type **300**	20	15
1392	5c. "Good Friends"	20	15
1393	5c. "Spirit of America"	20	15
1394	5c. "Scout Memories"	20	15
1395	5c. "The Adventure Trail"	20	15
1396	5c. "On My Honour"	20	15
1397	5c. "A Scout is Reverent"	20	15
1398	5c. "The Right Way"	20	15
1399	5c. "The Scoutmaster"	20	15
1400	10c. "A Scout is Loyal"	40	25
1401	10c. "An Army of Friendship"	35	20
1402	10c. "Carry on"	35	20
1403	10c. "A Good Scout"	35	20
1404	10c. "The Campfire Story"	35	20
1405	10c. "High Adventure"	35	20
1406	10c. "Mighty Proud"	35	20
1407	10c. "Tomorrow's Leader"	35	20
1408	10c. "Ever Onward"	35	20
1409	10c. "Homecoming"	35	20
1410	15c. "Scouts of Many Trails"	40	25
1411	15c. "America builds for Tomorrow"	40	25
1412	15c. "The Scouting Trail"	40	25
1413	15c. "A Scout is Reverent"	40	25
1414	15c. "A Scout is Helpful"	40	25
1415	15c. "Pointing the Way"	40	25
1416	15c. "A Good Sign All Over the World"	40	25
1417	15c. "To Keep Myself Physically Strong"	40	25
1418	15c. "A Great Moment"	40	25
1419	15c. "Growth of a Leader"	40	25
1420	25c. "A Scout is Loyal"	60	35
1421	25c. "A Scout is Friendly"	60	35
1422	25c. "We Too, Have a Job to Do"	60	35
1423	25c. "I Will do my Best"	60	35
1424	25c. "A Guiding Hand"	60	35
1425	25c. "Breakthrough for Freedom"	1·25	40
1426	25c. "Scouting is Outing"	60	35
1427	25c. "Beyond the Easel"	60	35
1428	25c. "Come and Get It"	60	35
1429	25c. "America's Manpower begins with Boypower"	60	35
1430	35c. "All Together"	80	45
1431	35c. "Men of Tomorrow"	80	45
1432	35c. "Friend in Need"	80	45
1433	35c. "Our Heritage"	80	45
1434	35c. "Forward America"	80	45
1435	35c. "Can't Wait"	80	45
1436	35c. "From Concord to Tranquility"	80	45
1437	35c. "We Thank Thee"	80	45
1438	35c. "So Much Concern"	80	45
1439	35c. "Spirit of '76"	80	45

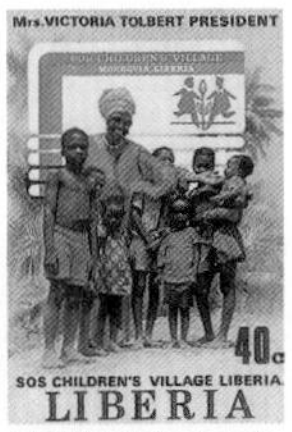

301 Mrs. Tolbert and Children

1979. S.O.S. Children's Village, Monrovia. Multicoloured.

1440	25c. Mrs. Tolbert and children (different) (horiz)	35	50
1441	40c. Type **301**	90	90

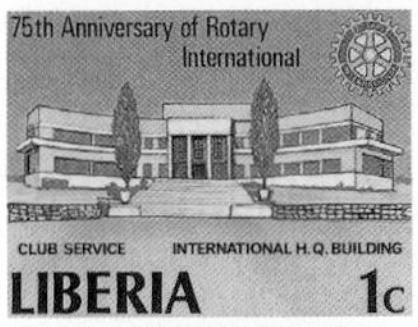

302 International Headquarters, Evanston, Illinois

1979. 75th Anniv of Rotary International. Multicoloured.

1442	1c. Type **302**	10	10
1443	5c. Vocational services	10	10
1444	17c. Wheelchair patient and nurse (community service) (vert)	20	35
1445	27c. Flags (international service)	40	50
1446	35c. Different races holding hands around globe (health, hunger and humanity)	50	50
1447	50c. President Tolbert and map of Africa (17th anniv of Monrovia Rotary Club) (vert)	1·00	1·00
MS1448	102×84 mm. $1 Heart (gift of life)	2·00	2·00

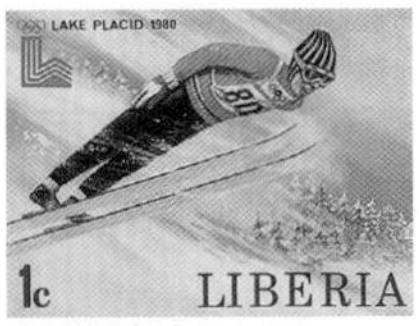

303 Ski Jumping

1980. Winter Olympic Games, Lake Placid. Multicoloured.

1449	1c. Type **303**	10	10
1450	5c. Pairs figure skating	10	10
1451	17c. Bobsleigh	20	35
1452	27c. Cross-country skiing	75	75
1453	35c. Speed skating	75	75
1454	50c. Ice hockey	1·00	1·00
MS1455	105×80 mm. $1 Downhill skiing	2·00	2·00

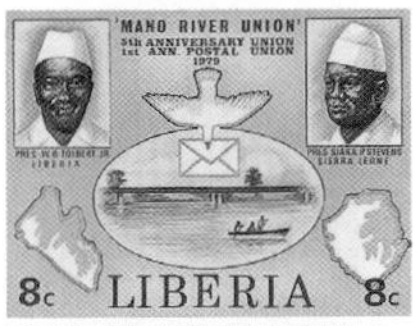

304 Presidents Tolbert of Liberia and Stevens of Sierra Leone and View of Mano River

1980. Fifth Anniv of Mano River Union and 1st Anniv (1979) of Postal Union.

1456	**304**	8c. multicoloured	15	10
1457	**304**	27c. multicoloured	45	50
1458	**304**	35c. multicoloured	80	75
1459	**304**	80c. multicoloured	1·75	1·75

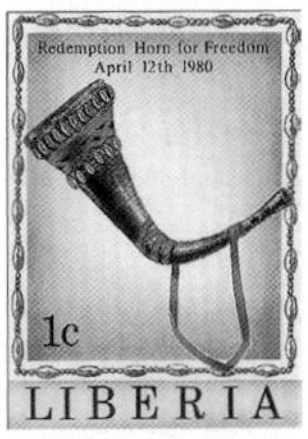

305 Redemption Horn

1981. People's Redemption Council (1st series). Multicoloured.

1460	1c. Type **305**	10	10
1461	10c. M/Sgt. Doe and allegory of redemption (horiz)	10	10
1462	14c. Map, soldier and citizens (horiz)	15	15
1463	$2 M/Sgt. Samuel Doe (chairman of Council)	3·75	3·75

See also Nos. 1475/8.

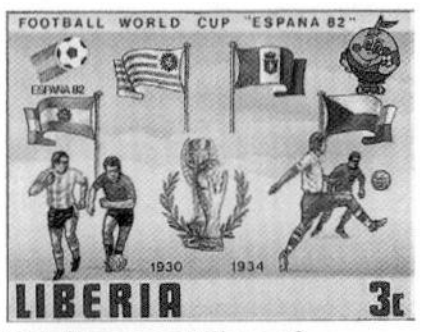

306 Players and Flags of Argentine, Uruguay, Italy and Czechoslovakia

1981. World Cup Football Championship, Spain (1982). Multicoloured.

1464	3c. Type **306**	10	10
1465	5c. Players and flags of Hungary, Italy, Germany, Brazil and Sweden	10	10
1466	20c. Players and flags of Italy, Germany, Brazil and Sweden	20	20
1467	27c. Players and flags of Czechoslovakia, Brazil, Great Britain and Germany	25	25
1468	40c. Players and flags of Italy, Brazil, Germany and Netherlands	60	60
1469	55c. Players and flags of Netherlands and Uruguay	1·10	1·10
MS1470	192×78 mm. $1 Spanish team	1·75	1·75

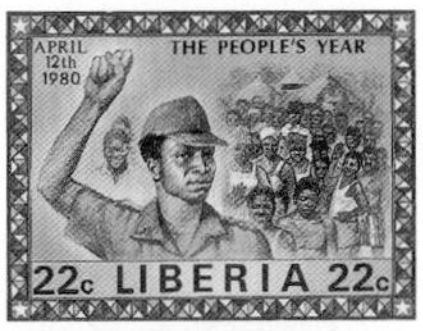

307 M/Sgt. Doe and Crowd

1981. First Anniv of People's Redemption Council. Multicoloured.

1471	22c. Type **307**	20	20
1472	27c. M/Sgt. Doe and national flag	25	25
1473	30c. Hands clasping arms, sunrise and map	45	45
1474	$1 M/Sgt. Doe, "Justice" and soldiers	1·75	1·75

1981. People's Redemption Council (2nd series).

1475	6c. Type **305**	10	10
1476	23c. As No. 1461	20	20
1477	31c. As No. 1462	45	45
1478	41c. As No. 1463	60	60

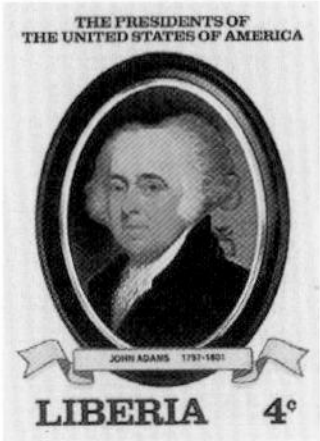

308 John Adams

1981. Presidents of the United States (1st series). Multicoloured.

1479	4c. Type **308**	10	10
1480	5c. William Henry Harrison	10	10
1481	10c. Martin Van Buren	15	15
1482	17c. James Monroe	20	20
1483	20c. John Quincy Adams	25	25
1484	22c. James Madison	25	25
1485	27c. Thomas Jefferson	35	30
1486	30c. Andrew Jackson	55	50
1487	40c. John Tyler	80	70
1488	80c. George Washington	1·50	1·50
MS1489	102×83 mm. $1 Washington crossing the Delaware	1·75	1·75

See also Nos. 1494/**MS**1504, 1519/**MS**1528 and 1533/**MS**1543.

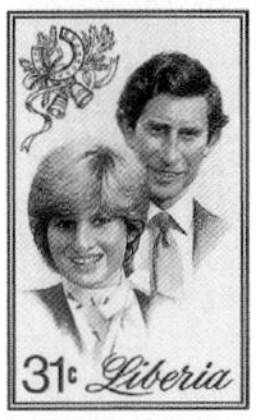

309 Prince Charles and Lady Diana Spencer

1981. British Royal Wedding. Multicoloured.

1490	31c. Type **309**	30	30
1491	41c. Intertwined initials	40	40
1492	62c. St. Paul's Cathedral	1·10	1·10
MS1493	106×80 mm. $1 Prince Charles and Lady Dianna Spencer (horiz 58×44 mm)	1·40	1·40

1981. Presidents of the United States (2nd series). As T **308**. Multicoloured.

1494	6c. Rutherford B. Hayes	10	10
1495	12c. Ulysses S. Grant	15	15
1496	14c. Millard Fillmore	20	15
1497	15c. Zachary Taylor	20	15
1498	20c. Abraham Lincoln	25	20
1499	27c. Andrew Johnson	30	25
1500	31c. James Buchanan	50	45
1501	41c. James A. Garfield	70	60
1502	50c. James K. Polk	80	70
1503	55c. Franklin Pierce	1·00	85
MS1504	101×82 mm. $1 Washington crossing the Delaware (horiz)	1·75	1·75

1981. Liberian Products (2nd series). As T **277**, but smaller, 33×20 mm. Multicoloured.

1504a	1c. Mano River Bridge	10	10
1505	3c. Type **277**	10	10

1506	6c. Rubber tree and tyre	10	10
1506a	15c. Combine harvester	20	15
1507	25c. Mesurado shrimp	35	35
1508	31c. Hydro-electric plant	70	70
1509	41c. Dress and woman tie-dying cloth	60	55
1509a	80c. Great barracuda	2·50	1·50
1510	$1 Diesel train carrying iron ore	5·75	1·60

310 Disabled Children

1982. International Year of Disabled People (1981). Multicoloured.

1515	23c. Type **310**	35	35
1516	62c. Child leading blind woman	1·25	95

311 Examination Room

1982. 30th Anniv of West African Examination Council.

1517	**311**	6c. multicoloured	10	10
1518	**311**	31c. multicoloured	45	45

1982. Presidents of the United States (3rd series). As T **308**. Multicoloured.

1519	4c. William Taft	10	25
1520	5c. Calvin Coolidge	10	10
1521	6c. Benjamin Harrison	15	15
1522	10c. Warren Harding	20	25
1523	22c. Grover Cleveland	45	45
1524	27c. Chester Arthur	50	70
1525	31c. Woodrow Wilson	60	60
1526	41c. William McKinley	70	80
1527	80c. Theodore Roosevelt	1·50	1·60
MS1528	101×83 mm. $1 Signing the Constitution (horiz)	1·75	1·75

312 Lady Diana Spencer

1982. Princess of Wales. 21st Birthday. Multicoloured.

1529	31c. Type **312**	70	70
1530	41c. Lady Diana Spencer (different)	85	85
1531	62c. Lady Diana accepting flower	1·25	1·25
MS1532	103×78 mm. $1 Prince and Princess of Wales (wedding photograph)	1·75	1·75

1982. Presidents of the United States (4th series). As T **308**. Multicoloured.

1533	4c. Jimmy Carter	10	10
1534	6c. Gerald Ford	15	15
1535	14c. Harry Truman	25	25
1536	17c. Franklin D. Roosevelt	30	30
1537	23c. Lyndon B. Johnson	40	40
1538	27c. Richard Nixon	45	50
1539	31c. John F. Kennedy	50	60
1540	35c. Ronald Reagan	60	80
1541	50c. Herbert Hoover	80	90
1542	55c. Dwight D. Eisenhower	1·00	1·00
MS1543	102×83 mm. $1 "Battle of Yorktown" (horiz)	1·75	1·75

1982. Birth of Prince William of Wales. Nos. 1529/31 optd **ROYAL BABY 21-6-82 PRINCE WILLIAM.**

1544	31c. Type **312**	45	45
1545	41c. Lady Diana Spencer (different)	60	60
1546	62c. Lady Diana accepting flower	95	95
MS1547	103×78 mm. $1 Prince and Princess of Wales (wedding photograph)	1·60	1·60

314 Lt. Col. Fallah nGaida Varney

1983. Third Anniv of National Redemption Day. Multicoloured.

1548	3c. Type **314**	10	10
1549	6c. Commander-in-Chief Samuel Doe	10	10
1550	10c. Major-General Jlatoh Nicholas Podier	15	15
1551	15c. Brigadier-General Jeffery Sei Gbatu	20	15
1552	31c. Brigadier-General Thomas Gunkama Quiwonkpa	50	45
1553	41c. Colonel Abraham Doward Kollie	60	80
MS1554	103×78 mm. $1 As No. 1549	1·50	1·50

315 National Archives Centre

1983. Opening of National Archives Centre. Multicoloured.

1555	6c. Type **315**	10	10
1556	31c. National Archives Centre	50	45

316 "Circumcision of Christ"

1983. Christmas. 500th Birth Anniv of Raphael. Multicoloured.

1557	6c. Type **316**	10	10
1558	15c. "Adoration of the Magi" (detail)	20	15
1559	25c. "The Annunciation" (detail)	40	35
1560	31c. "Madonna of the Baldachino"	50	45
1561	41c. "Holy Family" (detail)	60	55
1562	62c. "Madonna and Child with Five Saints" (detail)	90	85
MS1563	102×77 mm. $1.25 "Foligno Madonna" (horiz)	1·90	1·90

317 Graduates of M.U.R. Training Programmes

1984. Tenth Anniv (1983) of Mano River Union. Multicoloured.

1564	6c. Type **317**	10	10
1565	25c. Map of Africa	40	35
1566	31c. Presidents and map of member states	50	45
1567	41c. President of Guinea signing Accession Agreement	70	85
MS1568	102×77 mm. 75c. Guinea's accession	1·25	1·25

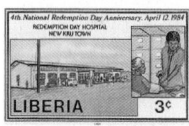

318 Redemption Day Hospital, New Kru Town

1984. Fourth Anniv of National Redemption Day. Multicoloured.

1569	3c. Type **318**	10	10
1570	10c. Ganta–Harpa Highway project	15	15

1571	20c. Opening of Constitution Assembly	35	30
1572	31c. Commander-in-Chief Doe launching Ganta–Harper Highway project	50	45
1573	41c. Presentation of Draft Constitution	70	85

319 "Adoration of the Magi"

1984. Rubens Paintings (1st series). Multicoloured.

1574	6c. Type **319**	10	10
1575	15c. "Coronation of Catherine"	25	20
1576	25c. "Adoration of the Magi"	70	70
1577	31c. "Madonna and Child with Halo"	85	85
1578	41c. "Adoration of the Shepherds"	1·10	1·10
1579	62c. "Madonna and Child with Saints"	1·75	1·75
MS1580	102×77 mm. $1.25 "Adoration of the Saints"	3·25	3·25

See also Nos. 1612/MS1618.

320 Jesse Owens

1984. Olympic Games, Los Angeles. Multicoloured.

1581	3c. Type **320**	10	10
1582	4c. Rafer Johnson	10	10
1583	25c. Miruts Yifter	65	65
1584	41c. Kipchoge Keino	1·10	1·10
1585	62c. Muhammad Ali	1·75	1·75
MS1586	103×77 mm. $1.25 Wilma Rudolph (horiz)	3·25	3·25

321 Liberian Ducks and Water Birds

1984. Louisiana World Exposition. Multicoloured.

1587	6c. Type **321**	20	20
1588	31c. Bulk carrier loading ore at Buchanan Harbour	1·60	75
1589	41c. Peters' mormyrid, electric catfish, Nile perch, krib and jewel cichlid	1·50	1·10
1590	62c. Diesel train carrying iron ore	1·75	90

322 Mother and Calf

1984. Pygmy Hippopotami. Multicoloured.

1591	6c. Type **322**	20	10
1592	10c. Pair of hippopotami	80	80
1593	20c. Close-up of hippopotamus	1·40	1·40
1594	31c. Hippopotamus and map	2·10	2·10

323 Mrs. Doe and Children

1984. Indigent Children's Home, Bensonville. Multicoloured.

1595	6c. Type **323**	10	10
1596	31c. Mrs. Doe and children (different)	50	50

324 New Soldiers' Barracks

1985. Fifth Anniv of National Redemption Day. Multicoloured.

1597	6c. Type **324**	10	10
1598	31c. Pan-African Plaza	50	50

325 Bohemian Waxwing

1985. Birth Bicentenary of John J. Audubon (ornithologist). Multicoloured.

1599	1c. Type **325**	15	10
1600	3c. Bay-breasted warbler	30	10
1601	6c. White-winged crossbill	35	15
1602	31c. Grey phalarope ("Red Phalarope")	2·00	1·00
1603	41c. Eastern bluebird	2·50	1·50
1604	62c. Common cardinal ("Northern Cardinal")	3·50	2·40

326 Germany v. Morocco, 1970

1985. World Cup Football Championship, Mexico (1986). Multicoloured.

1605	6c. Type **326**	10	10
1606	15c. Zaire v. Brazil, 1974	20	15
1607	25c. Tunisia v. Germany, 1978	60	60
1608	31c. Cameroun v. Peru, 1982 (vert)	75	75
1609	41c. Algeria v. Germany, 1982	95	95
1610	62c. Senegal team	1·40	1·40
MS1611	102×77 mm. $1.25 Liberia v Nigeria	2·75	2·75

327 "Mirror of Venus"

1985. Rubens Paintings (2nd series). Multicoloured.

1612	6c. Type **327**	10	10
1613	15c. "Adam and Eve in Paradise" (detail)	20	15
1614	25c. "Andromeda" (detail)	60	60
1615	31c. "The Three Graces" (detail)	75	75
1616	41c. "Venus and Adonis" (detail)	95	95
1617	62c. "The Daughters of Leucippus" (detail)	1·40	1·40
MS1618	102×77 mm. $1.25 "The Judgement of Paris" (horiz)	2·75	2·75

328 Women transplanting Rice

1985. World Food Day.

1619	**328**	25c. multicoloured	1·25	85
1620	**328**	31c. multicoloured	1·50	1·10

329 Queen
Mother in Garter
Robes

1985. 85th Birthday of Queen Elizabeth the Queen
Mother. Multicoloured.

1621	31c. Type **329**	35	30
1622	41c. At the races	80	55
1623	62c. Waving to the crowds	1·10	1·10
MS1624	79×104 mm. $1.25 Wearing tiara	2·00	2·00

330 Alamo, San
Antonio, Texas

1986. "Ameripex '86" International Stamp Exhibition,
Chicago. Multicoloured.

1625	25c. Type **330**	60	60
1626	31c. Liberty Bell, Philadelphia	75	75
1627	80c. Magnifying glass, emblem and Liberian stamps	3·00	2·25

331 Unveiling
Ceremony, 1886
(after E. Moran)

1986. Centenary of Statue of Liberty. Multicoloured.

1628	20c. Type **331**	30	50
1629	31c. Frederic-Auguste Bartholdi (sculptor) and statue	75	75
1630	$1 Head of statue	2·40	2·40

332 Max Julen (Men's Giant
Slalom)

1987. Winter Olympic Games, Calgary (1988). 1984
Games Gold Medallists. Multicoloured.

1631	3c. Type **332**	10	10
1632	6c. Debbi Armstrong (women's giant slalom)	10	10
1633	31c. Peter Angerer (biathlon)	35	55
1634	60c. Bill Johnson (men's downhill)	1·10	1·10
1635	80c. East German team (four-man bobsleigh)	1·40	1·40
MS1636	104×77 mm. $1.25 H.Strangassinger and F. Wembacher (double luge)	2·00	2·00

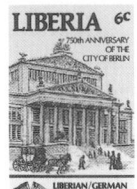

333 Royal Theatre.
Gendarmenmarkt

1987. Liberian–German Friendship. 750th Anniv of Berlin.

1637	6c. multicoloured	10	10
1638	31c. multicoloured	35	35
1639	60c. multicoloured	1·10	1·10
1640	80c. multicoloured	1·40	1·40
MS1641	100×100 mm. $1.50 buff and brown	2·50	2·50

DESIGNS: 31c. Kaiser Frederik Museum, River spree; 60c. Charlottenburg Palace; 80c. Kaiser Wilhelm Memorial Church; $1.50 "Mirak" rocket and scientists, Spaceship Society airfield, Reinckendorf.

No. **MS**1641 has a diagram on the reverse identifying the people portrayed.

334 Othello and Desdemona
("Othello")

1987. William Shakespeare. Multicoloured.

1642	3c. Type **334**	10	10
1643	6c. Romeo and Juliet ("Romeo and Juliet")	10	10
1644	10c. Falstaff ("The Merry Wives of Windsor")	15	10
1645	15c. Falstaff, Doll Tearsheet and Prince Hal ("Henry IV", Part 2)	20	15
1646	31c. Hamlet holding Yorick's skull ("Hamlet")	60	50
1647	60c. Macbeth and the three witches ("Macbeth")	1·25	1·25
1648	80c. Lear and companions in the storm ("King Lear")	1·75	1·75
1649	$2 William Shakespeare and Globe Theatre, Southwark	4·00	4·00

335 Emblem

1987. Amateur Radio Week. 25th Anniv of Liberia Radio
Amateur Association. Multicoloured.

1650	10c. Type **335**	15	10
1651	10c. Amateur radio enthusiasts	15	10
1652	35c. Certificate awarded to participants in anniversary "On the Air" activity	80	70
1653	35c. Globe, flags and banner	80	70

336 Illuminated Torch Flame

1987. Centenary of Statue of Liberty. Multicoloured.

1654	6c. Type **336**	10	10
1655	6c. Scaffolding around statue's head	10	10
1656	6c. Men working on head	10	10
1657	6c. Men working on crown	10	10
1658	6c. Statue's toes	10	10
1659	15c. Statue behind "Sir Winston Churchill" (cadet schooner)	45	20
1660	15c. "Bay Queen" (harbour ferry)	45	20
1661	15c. Posters on buildings and crowd	20	15
1662	15c. Tug and schooner in bay	45	20
1663	15c. Decorated statues around building	20	15
1664	31c. Fireworks display around statue	60	50
1665	31c. Statue floodlit	60	50
1666	31c. Statue's head	60	50
1667	31c. Fireworks display around statue (different)	60	50
1668	31c. Statue (half-length)	60	50
1669	60c. Wall poster on building (vert)	1·10	1·00
1670	60c. Yachts and cabin cruisers on river (vert)	1·50	1·00
1671	60c. Measuring statue's nose (vert)	1·10	1·00
1672	60c. Plastering nose (vert)	1·10	1·00
1673	60c. Finishing off repaired nose (vert)	1·10	1·00

337 Dr. Doe
(President), Dr. Moniba
(Vice-President), Flags
and Hands

1988. Second Anniv of Second Republic.

1674	337	10c. multicoloured	15	10
1675	337	35c. multicoloured	65	55

338 Breast-feeding

1988. UNICEF Child Survival and Development
Campaign. Multicoloured.

1676	3c. Type **338**	10	10
1677	6c. Oral rehydration therapy (vert)	10	10
1678	31c. Immunization	60	50
1679	$1 Growth monitoring (vert)	2·00	2·00

339 Chief Justice
Emmanuel N. Gbalazeh
swearing-in Dr. Samuel
Kanyon Doe

1988. Inauguration of Second Republic.

1680	339	6c. multicoloured	10	10

340 Footballer and
Stadium

1988. 2nd Anniv of Opening of Samuel Kanyon Doe
Sports Complex.

1681	340	31c. multicoloured	60	50

341 Child and Volunteer
reading

1988. 25th Anniv of U.S. Peace Corps in Liberia.

1682	341	10c. multicoloured	10	10
1683	341	35c. multicoloured	70	60

342 Pres. Doe, Farm
Workers and Produce

1988. Green Revolution.

1684	342	10c. multicoloured	25	10
1685	342	35c. multicoloured	85	35

343 Olympic Rings

1988. Olympic Games, Seoul and Stamp Exhibition.

MS1686	343	$3 multicoloured	5·50	5·50

344 Emblem

1988. 25th Anniv of Organization of African Unity.

1687	344	10c. multicoloured	10	10
1688	344	35c. multicoloured	70	60
1689	344	$1 multicoloured	2·00	2·00

345 Type GP10 Diesel
Locomotive, Nimba

1988. Locomotives. Multicoloured.

1690	10c. Type **345**	25	15
1691	35c. Triple-headed diesel iron ore train	85	50

MS1692	Four sheets, each 110×80m. (a) $2 "Ince Castle" pulling the "Bristolian". (b) $2 "75 XX" class locomotive No. 3697. (c) $2 "King Edward II". (d) $2 Locomotive No. 1408 on Lostwithel–Fowey line Set of 4 sheets	14·00	14·00

346 Helping Boy to
Walk

1988. 25th Anniv of St. Joseph's Catholic Hospital.
Multicoloured.

1693	10c. Type **346**	10	10
1694	10c. Medical staff and hospital	10	10
1695	35c. Monk, child, candle and hospital	65	65
1696	$1 Map behind doctor with nurse holding baby	1·90	1·90

347 Baseball

1988. Olympic Games, Seoul. Multicoloured.

1697	10c. Type **347**	10	10
1698	35c. Hurdling	65	65
1699	45c. Fencing	80	80
1700	80c. Synchronized swimming	1·40	1·40
1701	$1 Yachting	1·75	1·75
MS1702	107×89 mm. $1.50 Lawn tennis	2·40	2·40

348 Monkey
Bridge

1988. Multicoloured

1703	10c. Type **348**	10	10
1704	35c. Sasa players (horiz)	40	60
1705	45c. Snake dancers	70	75

349 Tending
Crops

1988. Tenth Anniv of International Fund for Agricultural
Development. Multicoloured.

1706	10c. Type **349**	10	10
1707	35c. Farmers tending livestock and spraying crops	70	60

350 Destruction
of Royal
Exchange, 1838

1988. 300th Anniv of Lloyd's of London. Multicoloured.

1708	10c. Type **350**	10	10
1709	35c. Britten Norman Islander airplane (horiz)	60	60
1710	45c. "Chevron Antwerp" (tanker) (horiz)	70	75
1711	$1 "Lakonia" (liner) ablaze, 1963	2·00	2·00

351 Honouring Head of
Operational Smile Team

1989. Third Anniv of Second Republic.

1712	**351**	10c. black and blue	10	10
1713	**351**	35c. black and red	80	85
1714	-	50c. black and mauve	1·25	1·25

DESIGN: 50c. Pres. Samuel Doe at John F. Kennedy Memorial Hospital.

1989. Presidents of United States (5th series). As T 308. Multicoloured.

1715	$1 George Bush	2·50	2·50

352 "Harmony"

1989. Liberia–Japan Friendship. 50th Anniv of Rissho Kosei-Kai (lay Buddhist association). Multicoloured.

1716	10c. Type **352**	10	10
1717	10c. Nikkyo Niwano (founder and president of association)	10	10
1718	10c. Rissho Kosei-Kai headquarters, Tokyo	10	10
1719	50c. Eternal Buddha, Great Sacred Hall	1·40	1·40
MS1720	109×75 mm. 75c. Liberian silver $10 Hirohito coin; 75c. Liberian gold $250 Hirohito coin (each 40×22 mm)	3·35	3·25

No. **MS**1720 commemorates the death of Emperor Hirohito of Japan.

353 Union Glass Factory, Gardersville, Monrovia

1989. 15th Anniv of Mano River Union. Multicoloured.

1721	10c. Type **353**	15	10
1722	35c. Presidents of Guinea, Sierra Leone and Liberia	70	60
1723	45c. Monrovia–Freetown highway	85	80
1724	50c. Flags, map and mail van	85	85
1725	$1 Presidents at 1988 Summit	2·00	1·90

354 Symbols of International Co-operation

1989. World Telecommunications Day.

1726	**354**	50c. multicoloured	85	85

355 "March of the Women on Versailles" (detail)

1989. Bicentenary of French Revolution and Philexfrance 89 International Stamp Exhibition, Paris. Sheet 115×100 mm.

MS1727 **355**	$1.50 grey, black and red	2·40	2·40

357 Helicopter Carrier U.S.S. "Okinawa"

1989. 20th Anniv of First Manned Landing on Moon. Multicoloured.

1728	10c. Type **357**	60	15
1729	35c. Edwin Aldrin, Neil Armstrong and Michael Collins (crew) (28×28 mm)	70	60
1730	45c. "Apollo 11" flight emblem (28×28 mm)	1·00	1·00
1731	$1 Aldrin descending to Moon's surface	2·00	2·00
MS1732	100×83 mm. $2 Astronaut and capsule on Moon's surface	3·75	3·75

358 Renovation of Statue of Liberty

1989. "Philexfrance '89" International Stamp Exhibition, Paris, and "World Stamp Expo '89" International Stamp Exhibition, Washington D.C. Multicoloured.

1733	25c. Type **358**	55	45
1734	25c. French contingent at statue centenary celebrations	55	45
1735	25c. Statue, officials and commemorative plaque	55	45

359 Exhibition Emblem

1989. World Stamp Expo 89 International Stamp Exhibition, Washington DC (2nd issue). Sheet 110×130 mm.

MS1736 **359**	$2 black	3·75	3·75

360 Nehru and Flag

1989. Birth Centenary of Jawaharlal Nehru (Indian statesman). Multicoloured.

1737	45c. Type **360**	85	70
1738	50c. Nehru	95	80

361 Close View of Station

1990. New Standard A Earth Satellite Station. Multicoloured.

1739	10c. Type **361**	15	10
1740	35c. Distant view of station	85	85

362 Emblem

1990. 25th Anniv of United States Educational and Cultural Foundation in Liberia. Multicoloured.

1741	10c. Type **362**	15	10
1742	45c. Similar to Type **362** but differently arranged	85	70

363 Flags, Arms, Map and Union Emblem

1990. Tenth Anniv of Pan-African Postal Union.

1743	**363**	35c. multicoloured	70	55

364 Bomi County

1990. County Flags. Multicoloured.

1744	10c. Type **364**	10	10
1745	10c. Bong	10	10
1746	10c. Grand Bassa	10	10
1747	10c. Grand Cape Mount	10	10
1748	10c. Grand Gedeh	10	10
1749	10c. Grand Kru	10	10
1750	10c. Lofa	10	10
1751	10c. Margibi	10	10
1752	10c. Maryland	10	10
1753	10c. Montserrado	10	10
1754	10c. Nimba	10	10
1755	10c. Rivercress	10	10
1756	10c. Sinoe	10	10
1757	35c. Type **364**	65	55
1758	35c. Bong	65	55
1759	35c. Grand Bassa	65	55
1760	35c. Grand Cape Mount	65	55
1761	35c. Grand Gedeh	65	55
1762	35c. Grand Kru	65	55
1763	35c. Lofa	65	55
1764	35c. Margibi	65	55
1765	35c. Maryland	65	55
1766	35c. Montserrado	65	55
1767	35c. Nimba	65	55
1768	35c. Rivercress	65	55
1769	35c. Sinoe	65	55
1770	45c. Type **364**	85	70
1771	45c. Bong	85	70
1772	45c. Grand Bassa	85	70
1773	45c. Grand Cape Mount	85	70
1774	45c. Grand Gedeh	85	70
1775	45c. Grand Kru	85	70
1776	45c. Lofa	85	70
1777	45c. Margibi	85	70
1778	45c. Maryland	85	70
1779	45c. Montserrado	85	70
1780	45c. Nimba	85	70
1781	45c. Rivercress	85	70
1782	45c. Sinoe	85	70
1783	50c. Type **364**	1·10	1·10
1784	50c. Bong	1·10	1·10
1785	50c. Grand Bassa	1·10	1·10
1786	50c. Grand Cape Mount	1·10	1·10
1787	50c. Grand Gedeh	1·10	1·10
1788	50c. Grand Kru	1·10	1·10
1789	50c. Lofa	1·10	1·10
1790	50c. Margibi	1·10	1·10
1791	50c. Maryland	1·10	1·10
1792	50c. Montserrado	1·10	1·10
1793	50c. Nimba	1·10	1·10
1794	50c. Rivercress	1·10	1·10
1795	50c. Sinoe	1·10	1·10
1796	$1 Type **364**	2·00	2·00
1797	$1 Bong	2·00	2·00
1798	$1 Grand Bassa	2·00	2·00
1799	$1 Grand Cape Mount	2·00	2·00
1800	$1 Grand Gedeh	2·00	2·00
1801	$1 Grand Kru	2·00	2·00
1802	$1 Lofa	2·00	2·00
1803	$1 Margibi	2·00	2·00
1804	$1 Maryland	2·00	2·00
1805	$1 Montserrado	2·00	2·00
1806	$1 Nimba	2·00	2·00
1807	$1 Rivercress	2·00	2·00
1808	$1 Sinoe	2·00	2·00

365 Lady Elizabeth Bowes-Lyon as Girl

1991. 90th Birthday (1990) of Queen Elizabeth the Queen Mother. Multicoloured.

1809	10c. Type **365**	15	10
1810	$2 As Duchess of York (29×36½ mm)	4·00	4·00

367 Clasped Hands and Map

1991. National Unity. Multicoloured.

1812	35c. Type **367**	65	50
1813	45c. National flag and map of Africa (ECOMOG (West African States Economic Community peace-keeping forces))	85	65
1814	50c. Brewer, Konneh and Michael Francis (co-chairmen) and national flag (All-Liberia Conference)	95	75

368 Boxing

1992. Olympic Games, Barcelona. Multicoloured.

1815	45c. Type **368**	85	65
1816	50c. Football	95	75
1817	$1 Weightlifting	1·90	1·75
1818	$2 Water polo	3·75	3·50
MS1819	120×75 mm. $1.50 Running	2·75	2·75

369 "Disarm Today"

1993. Peace and Redevelopment. Multicoloured.

1820	50c. Type **369**	95	70
1821	$1 "Join your Parents and build Liberia"	1·90	1·40
1822	$2 "Peace must prevail in Liberia"	3·75	2·75

OFFICIAL STAMPS

1892. Stamps of 1892 optd **OFFICIAL**.

O87	**7**	1c. red	30	40
O88	**7**	2c. blue	30	50
O89	**8**	4c. black and green	50	50
O104	**9**	5c. on 6c. green (No. 89)	80	80
O90	**9**	6c. green	60	50
O91	**10**	8c. black and brown	45	45
O92	**11**	12c. red	1·10	1·10
O93	**12**	16c. lilac	1·10	1·10
O94	**13**	24c. green on yellow	1·10	1·10
O95	**12**	32c. blue	1·10	1·10
O96	**15**	$1 black and blue	22·00	8·75
O97	**13**	$2 brown on buff	9·00	6·25
O98	**17**	$5 black and red	13·50	5·75

1894. Stamps of 1892 optd **O S**.

O119	**7**	1c. red	30	20
O120	**7**	2c. blue	60	25
O121	**8**	4c. black and green	95	35
O122	**10**	8c. black and brown	80	35
O123	**11**	12c. red	1·10	40
O124	**12**	16c. lilac	1·10	40
O125	**13**	24c. green on yellow	1·10	45
O126	**12**	32c. blue	1·60	55
O127	**12**	$1 black and blue	13·50	13·50
O128	**12**	$2 brown on buff	13·50	13·50
O129	**12**	$5 black and red	80·00	55·00

1894. Stamp of 1894 in different colours optd **O S**. Imperf or roul.

O130	**24**	5c. green and lilac	1·75	2·00

1898. Stamps of 1897 optd **O S**.

O157	**9**	1c. purple	35	35
O158	**9**	1c. green	35	35
O159	**15**	2c. black and bistre	1·00	30
O160	**15**	2c. black and red	1·50	70
O161	**8**	5c. black and lake	1·50	70
O162	**8**	5c. black and blue	1·90	70
O163	**10**	10c. blue and yellow	85	80
O164	**11**	15c. black	85	80
O165	**12**	20c. red	1·40	95
O166	**13**	25c. green	85	80
O167	**12**	30c. blue	2·40	1·40
O168	**35**	50c. black and brown	2·10	1·40

1903. Stamp of 1903, but different colour, optd **O S**.

O210	**40**	3c. green	20	15

1904. Nos. O104 and 167 surch ONE **O.S.** and bars or **OS 2** and bars.

O222	**9**	1c. on 5c. on 6c. green	1·10	1·10
O223	**12**	2c. on 30c. blue	7·75	7·50

1906. Stamps of 1906, but different colours, optd **OS**.

O237	**50**	1c. black and green	50	50
O238	**51**	2c. black and red	15	15
O239	-	5c. black and blue	55	35
O240	-	10c. black and violet	2·50	60
O241	-	15c. black and brown	2·00	40
O242	-	20c. black and green	2·50	50
O243	-	25c. grey and purple	30	15
O244	-	30c. brown	50	15
O245	-	50c. green and brown	50	20
O246	-	75c. black and blue	1·10	75
O247	-	$1 black and green	55	25
O248	**52**	$2 black and purple	1·50	25
O249	**53**	$5 black and orange	3·75	30

1909. Stamps of 1909, but different colours, optd **OS. 10c.** perf or roul.

O262	**55**	1c. black and green	15	10
O263	-	2c. brown and red	15	10
O264	**56**	5c. black and blue	1·00	15
O266	**57**	10c. blue and black	50	25
O267	-	15c. black and purple	50	25
O268	-	20c. green and bistre	75	45
O269	-	25c. green and blue	70	50
O270	-	30c. blue	60	40
O271	-	50c. green and brown	2·25	40
O272	-	75c. black and violet	1·10	40

1910. No. O266 surch **3 CENTS INLAND POSTAGE**. Perf or roul.

O276	**57**	3c. on 10c. blue and black	55	45

1914. Official stamps surch: (A) **1914 2 CENTS**. (B) +2c. (C) 5. (D) **CENTS 20 OFFICIAL**.

O291	**57**	+2c. on 3c. on 10c. blue and black (B) (No. O275)	60	1·60
O284	-	2c. on 25c. grey and purple (A) (No. O243)	15·00	6·25
O285	-	5c. on 30c. blue (C) (No. O270)	5·25	3·00
O286	-	20c. on 75c. black and violet (D) (No. O272)	7·00	3·00

1914. No. 233 surch **CENTS 20 OFFICIAL**.

O287	20c. on 75c. black and brown	5·25	3·00

1915. Official stamps of 1906 and 1909 surch in different ways.

O325	-	1c. on 2c. brown and red (No. O263)	2·25	2·50
O326	**56**	2c. on 5c. black and blue (No. O264)	2·50	3·00
O310	-	2c. on 15c. black and purple (No. O267)	65	45
O311	-	2c. on 25c. green and blue (No. O269)	3·75	3·75
O312	-	5c. on 20c. green and bistre (No. O268)	65	50
O313	-	5c. on 30c. green and brown (No. O270)	5·75	5·75
O314	-	10c. on 50c. green and brown (No. O271)	6·50	7·50
O316	-	20c. on 75c. black and violet (No. O272)	2·00	2·00
O317	-	25c. on $1 black and green (No. O247)	13·50	13·50
O318	**52**	50c. on $2 black and purple (No. O248)	15·00	15·00
O320	**53**	$1 on $5 black and orange (No. O249)	15·00	15·00

1915. No. O168 surch **10 10** and ornaments and bars.

O321	**35**	10c. on 50c. black & brn	9·75	9·75

1915. Military Field Post. Official stamps surch **L E F 1 c**.

O336	**50**	1c. on 1c. black and green (No. O237)	£325	£325
O337	**55**	1c. on 1c. black and green (No. O262)	3·00	3·50
O338	-	1c. on 2c. brown and red (No. O263)	2·40	2·50

1917. No. O244 surch **FIVE CENTS 1917** and bars.

O344	5c. on 30c. brown	15·00	15·00

1918. No. O266 surch **3 CENTS**.

O348	**57**	3c. on 10c. blue and black	1·40	1·50

1918. Stamps of 1918, but in different colours, optd **O S**.

O362	**91**	1c. brown and green	50	15
O363	**92**	2c. black and red	50	15
O364	-	5c. black and blue	75	10
O365	**93**	10c. blue	35	10
O366	-	15c. green and brown	1·75	40
O367	-	20c. black and lilac	55	10
O368	**94**	25c. green and brown	3·25	45
O369	-	30c. black and violet	4·75	50
O370	-	50c. black and brown	5·00	50
O371	-	75c. black and brown	2·00	15
O372	-	$1 blue and olive	3·75	30
O373	-	$2 black and olive	6·25	20
O374	-	$5 green	8·25	20

1920. Nos. O362/3 surch **1920** and value and two bars.

O400	**91**	3c. on 1c. brown & green	95	50
O401	**92**	4c. on 2c. black and red	60	50

1921. Stamps of 1915 and 1921, in different colours, optd **O S** or **OFFICIAL**.

O428	**100**	1c. green	70	10
O429	**64**	2c. red	4·50	10
O430	**65**	3c. brown	70	10
O431	**101**	5c. brown and blue	70	10
O432	-	10c. black and purple	35	15
O433	-	15c. green and black	2·75	50
O434	-	20c. blue and brown	1·10	25
O435	-	25c. green and orange	3·75	50
O436	-	30c. red and brown	75	15
O437	-	50c. green and black	75	25
O438	-	75c. purple and blue	1·90	25
O439	-	$1 black and blue	12·50	55
O440	-	$2 green and orange	16·00	1·00
O441	-	$5 blue and green	17·00	1·75

1921. Nos. O400/41 optd **1921**.

O442	**100**	1c. green	4·00	20
O443	**64**	2c. red	4·00	20
O444	**65**	3c. brown	4·00	25
O445	**101**	5c. brown and blue	2·40	25
O446	-	10c. black and purple	4·00	25
O447	-	15c. green and black	4·25	15
O448	-	20c. blue and brown	4·25	35
O449	-	25c. green and orange	5·00	40
O450	-	30c. red and brown	4·00	30
O451	-	50c. green and black	4·75	15
O452	-	75c. purple and blue	2·75	15
O453	-	$1 black and blue	8·75	1·10
O454	-	$2 green and orange	15·00	1·75
O455	-	$5 blue and green	16·00	3·00

1923. Stamps of 1923, but different colours, optd **O S**.

O485	**108**	1c. black and green	5·25	10
O486	**109**	2c. brown and red	5·25	10
O487	-	3c. black and blue	5·25	10
O488	-	5c. green and orange	5·25	10
O489	-	10c. purple and olive	5·25	10
O490	-	15c. blue and green	75	40
O491	-	20c. blue and lilac	75	40
O492	-	25c. brown	16·00	40
O493	-	30c. brown and blue	70	20
O494	-	50c. brown and bistre	70	30
O495	-	75c. green and grey	70	25
O496	**110**	$1 green and red	1·50	40
O497	-	$2 red and purple	2·00	50
O498	-	$5 brown and blue	3·75	50

1926. No. O362 surch **Two Cents** and either thick bar, wavy lines, ornamental scroll or two bars.

O506	**91**	2c. on 1c. brown & green	90	80

1928. Stamps of 1928 optd **OFFICIAL SERVICE**.

O518	**116**	1c. green	70	35
O519	**116**	2c. violet	1·40	50
O520	**116**	3c. brown	1·40	15
O521	**117**	5c. blue	80	15
O522	**118**	10c. grey	2·40	1·00
O523	**117**	15c. lilac	1·40	60
O524	**117**	$1 brown	40·00	16·00

1944. No. O522 surch.

O649	**118**	4c. on 10c. grey	8·00	8·00

POSTAGE DUE STAMPS

1892. Stamps of 1886 surch **POSTAGE DUE** and value in frame.

D99	**4**	3c. on 3c. mauve	1·25	1·25
D100	**4**	6c. on 6c. grey	6·25	6·25

D23

1894

D110	**D23**	2c. black and orange on yellow	95	55
D111	**D23**	4c. black & red on rose	95	55
D112	**D23**	6c. black & brn on buff	95	75
D113	**D23**	8c. black & blue on bl	1·00	75
D114	**D23**	10c. black and green on mauve	1·25	95
D115	**D23**	20c. black and violet on grey	1·25	95
D116	**D23**	40c. black and brown on green	2·50	1·75

REGISTRATION STAMPS

R22

1893

R105	**R22**	(10c.) black (Buchanan)	£275	£350
R106	**R22**	(10c.) blk ("Grenville")	£1000	£1250
R107	**R22**	(10c.) black (Harper)	£1000	£1250
R108	**R22**	(10c.) black (Monrovia)	40·00	£175
R109	**R22**	(10c.) blk (Robertsport)	£500	£575

1894. Surch **10 CENTS 10** twice.

R140	10c. blue on pink (Buchanan)	3·75	3·75
R141	10c. green on buff (Harper)	3·75	3·75
R142	10c. red on yellow (Monrovia)	3·75	3·75
R143	10c. red on blue (Robertsport)	3·75	3·75

R42 Pres. Gibson

1904

R211	**R42**	10c. black and blue (Buchanan)	1·50	25
R212	**R42**	10c. black and red ("Grenville")	1·50	25
R213	**R42**	10c. black and green (Harper)	1·50	25
R214	**R42**	10c. black and violet (Monrovia)	1·50	25
R215	**R42**	10c. black and purple (Robertsport)	1·50	25

R96 Patrol Boat "Quail"

1919. Roul or perf.

R388	**R96**	10c. blue and black (Buchanan)	90	5·75
R389	**R96**	10c. black and brown ("Grenville")	90	7·50
R390	**R96**	10c. black and green (Harper)	90	5·25
R391	**R96**	10c. blue and violet (Monrovia)	90	5·75
R392	**R96**	10c. black and red (Robertsport)	90	7·50

R106 Gabon Viper

1921

R456	**R106**	10c. black and red (Buchanan)	23·00	2·50
R457	**R106**	10c. black and red (Greenville)	14·00	2·50
R458	**R106**	10c. black and blue (Harper)	18·00	2·50
R459	**R106**	10c. black and orange (Monrovia)	14·00	2·50
R460	**R106**	10c. black and green (Robertsport)	14·00	2·50

1921. Optd 1921.

R461	10c. black and lake	20·00	4·25
R462	10c. black and red	20·00	4·25
R463	10c. black and blue	20·00	4·25
R464	10c. black and orange	20·00	4·25
R465	10c. black and green	20·00	4·25

R111 Sailing Skiff (Buchanan)

1923. Various sea views.

R499	**R111**	10c. red and black	8·50	55
R500	-	10c. green and black	8·50	55
R501	-	10c. orange and black	8·50	55
R502	-	10c. blue and black	8·50	55
R503	-	10c. violet and black	8·50	55

DESIGNS: No. R500, Lighter (Greenville); R501, Full-rigged sailing ship (Harper); R502, "George Washington" (liner) (Monrovia); R503, Canoe (Robertsport).

1941. No. 576 surch **REGISTERED 10 CENTS 10**.

R592	10c. on 5c. brown (postage)	1·40	1·40
R593	10c. on 5c. brown (air)	1·40	1·40

No. R593 is additionally optd with airplane and **AIR MAIL**.

SPECIAL DELIVERY STAMPS

1941. No. 576 surch with postman and **SPECIAL DELIVERY 10 CENTS 10**.

S590	10c. on 5c. brown (postage)	1·40	1·40
S591	10c. on 5c. brown (air)	1·40	1·40

No. S591 is additionally optd with airplane and **AIR MAIL**.

APPENDIX

The following stamps have either been issued in excess of postal needs, or have not been available to the public in reasonable quantities at face value.

1993

Flora. 70c.×6; 70c.×6.
Wildlife. 90c.×6; 90c.×6.

1994

African Children. 20c.+10c.; 70c.+20c.; 75c.+15c.; 80c.+20c.
Birds. $1×6; $1×6.
HONG KONG '94. Queen Elizabeth, the Queen Mother. 10c.; $2.
50th Anniv of Roberts Airfield, Monrovia. 35c.×8.
National Red Cross Society. 70c.; $1×2; $2.

1995

SOS Children's Village. Tenth Anniv of National Association for the Blind. 25c.+10c.; 80c.+20c.×2; $1.50+50c.×2.
African Animals. 70c.×2; 90c.; $1; $2.
SINGAPORE '95. Orchids. 70c.×8.
George Weah—Golden Ball Winner, 1989 and 1994. 50c.+20c.; 75c.+25c.; 80c.+20c.;$1.50+50c.
50th Anniv of United Nations Organization. 25; 50c.; $1; $2.
20th Anniv of ECOWAS. 25; 50c.; $1.

1996

Centenary of Modern Olympics. 20; 35; 50c.; $1.
Butterflies. 70c.×9.
Fish. 90c.×12.
Birds. 25c.×18; 35c.; 90c.; $1.
Butterflies. 20c.×12; 25c.×12.
Olympic Games, Atlanta. 20c.×2; 35c.×2; 35c.×18; 50c.×2; $1×2.
70th Birth Anniv of Marilyn Munroe. 20c.
Rock Performers. 35c.×8.
50th Anniv of UNICEF. 30; 70c.; $1.
Birds. 75c.×5.
20th Death Anniv of Mao Zedong . $1×2.
Freedom Camp. $1; $2×2.

1997

Animals. 50c.×12.
Return of Hong Kong to China. Deng Xiaoping Commemoration. 50c.; 70c.×2; $1; $1.20.
50th Wedding Anniv of Queen Elizabeth II. 50c.×6.
World Heritage Sites. 50c.×16; 70c.×4.
Tenth Anniv of Chernobyl Tragedy. $1.
"Rapunzel" story by Grimm Brothers. $1×4.
Winter Olympic, Nagano. 50c.; 70c.; 41; $2.
African Fauna. 50c.×8.
Flowers. 50c.×10.
Owls. 50c.×6.
Birds. 1; 2; 3; 4; 5; 10; 15; 20; 25; 50; 70; 75; 90c.; $1; $2; $3.
First Death Anniv of Marcello Mastroianni. 75c.×4.
World Cup Football Championship, France. 50c.; 50c.×8; 70c.; $1; $1.50; $2.×2.

1998

Noah's Ark. 15c.×25.
Endangered Species. Liberian Mongoose. 32c.×4.
Fungi. 10; 15; 20; 30; 40c.×18; 50; 75c.
Monarchs. 50c.×6; 50c.×6; 50c.×6.
Birds. 32c.×8; 30c.×12.
Mahatma Gandhi Commemoration 50c.
Pablo Picasso Commemoration. 50; 70c.; $1.
80th Anniv of Royal Air Force. 70c.×4.
World Scout Jamboree, Chile. $1×3.
Birth Centenary of Enzo Ferrari. $1×3.
Birth Centenary of Chou Enlai. 50c.×6.
American Presidents. 75c.×4; 75c.×4; 75c.×4; 75c.×4.
Classic Cars. 32c.×4; 59c.×12.

1999

Raptors. 50c.; 50c.×12; 70c.; $1; $1.50.
Birds. 50c.×2; 50c.×12; 70c.×2; $1; $1.50.
New Year. Year of the Rabbit. Paintings by Liu Jiyou. 50c.×2
Pre-historic Animals (1st issue). 40c.×16; 50c.×2; 70c.×2; $1; $2.
Flora and Fauna. 20c.×12. Flora. 50c.; 50c.×12; 70c.; $1; $2.
Orchids. 30c.×8; 50c.×2; 70c.×2; $1; $1.50.
Queen Elizabeth, the Queen Mother. $1×4.
CHINA '99, Macao. $20; $25×2.
Trains. 32c.; 40c.; 40c.×18; 50c.; 70c.
Dogs (1st issue). 50c.; 50c.×6; 70c.
Cats. 50c.×6; $1; $1.50.
Three Stooges. 40c.×9.
Christmas. Fauna. $5; $10; $20; $25; $30.
Cats. $5; $10; $25×6.
20th-century Ships and Aircraft. $5; $10; $15; $20; $25; $25×18; $30.
Pre-historic Animals (2nd issue). $10×48.
History of Aviation. $15×18.
Horses. $25×6.
Wild Dogs. $20×12.
Wild Cats. $20×12.
Dogs (2nd issue). $25; $25×6; $30.
30th Anniv of First Moon Landing. 50c.×6.
Marine Life. $10; $15×10; $20; $25; $30.

Pt. 8, Pt. 13

LIBYA

A former Italian colony in N. Africa, comprising the governorates of Cyrenaica and Tripolitania. From the end of 1951 an independent kingdom including the Fezzan also. Following a revolution in 1969 the country became the Libyan Arab Republic.

1912. 100 centesimi = 1 lira.
1952. 1000 milliemes = 1 Libyan pound.
1972. 1000 dirhams = 1 dinar.

A. ITALIAN COLONY

1912. Stamps of Italy optd LIBYA (No. 5) or Libia (others).

1	**30**	1c. brown	2·00	1·90
2	**31**	2c. brown	2·00	1·90
3	**37**	5c. green	2·00	2·00
4	**37**	10c. red	6·00	1·30
5	**41**	15c. grey	£225	3·75
6	**37**	15c. grey	5·00	1·30
7	**33**	20c. orange	5·00	1·30
8	**41**	20c. orange	5·25	7·50
9	**39**	25c. blue	5·00	1·30
10	**39**	40c. brown	13·00	2·10
11	**33**	45c. green	36·00	37·00
12	**39**	50c. violet	32·00	3·25
13	**39**	60c. red	19·00	27·00
14	**34**	1l. brown and green	85·00	3·75
15	**34**	5l. blue and red	£475	£375
16	**34**	10l. green and pink	£200	£180

1915. Red Cross stamps of Italy optd LIBIA.

17	**53**	10c.+5c. red	4·25	16·00
18	**54**	15c.+5c. grey	17·00	32·00
19	**54**	20c. on 15c.+5c. grey	17·00	37·00
20	**54**	20c.+5c. orange	4·25	37·00

1916. No. 100 of Italy optd LIBIA.

21	**41**	20c. on 15c. grey	45·00	16·00

4 Roman Legionary

5 Goddess of Plenty

6 Roman Galley leaving Tripoli

7 Victory

1921

22A	**4**	1c. brown and black	2·10	6·50
23A	**4**	2c. brown and black	2·10	6·50
24A	**4**	5c. green and black	3·25	1·10
50	**4**	7½c. brown and black	80·00	8·50
51	**5**	10c. pink and black	2·10	65·00
52	**5**	15c. orange and brown	6·50	4·25
27A	**5**	25c. blue and deep blue	3·25	60
54	**6**	30c. brown and black	2·10	1·10
55	**6**	50c. green and black	2·10	65
30A	**6**	55c. violet and black	10·50	25·00
57	**7**	75c. red and purple	4·00	55
58	**7**	1l. brown	9·50	65
59	**6**	1l.25 blue and indigo	45	55
32A	**7**	5l. blue and black	26·00	32·00
33A	**7**	10l. green and blue	£225	£170

1922. Victory stamps of Italy optd LIBIA.

34	**62**	5c. green	2·10	8·50
35	**62**	10c. red	2·10	8·50
36	**62**	15c. grey	2·10	13·00
37	**62**	25c. blue	2·10	13·00

1922. Nos. 9 and 12 of Libya surch.

38	**39**	40c. on 50c. mauve	4·25	4·25
39	**39**	80c. on 25c. blue	4·25	10·50

9 "Libyan Sibyl" by Michelangelo

1924

41	**9**	20c. green	1·30	55
42	**9**	40c. brown	2·50	1·60
43	**9**	60c. blue	1·30	55
44	**9**	1l.75 orange	45	10
45	**9**	2l. red	4·75	2·75
46	**9**	2l.55 violet	7·50	16·00

1928. Air. Air stamps of Italy optd Libia.

63	**88**	50c. pink	13·00	16·00
64	**88**	80c. brown and purple	34·00	70·00

1928. Types of Italy optd LIBIA (No. 67) or Libia (others).

65	**92**	7½c. brown	6·00	43·00
66	**34**	1l.25 blue	60·00	17·00
67	**91**	1l.75 brown	65·00	4·25

10 Bedouin Woman

1936. Tenth Tripoli Trade Fair.

68	**10**	50c. violet	3·75	2·75
69	**10**	1l.25 blue	3·25	8·00

1936. Air. Nos. 96 and 99 of Cyrenaica optd LIBIA.

70	-	50c. violet	90	60
71	**17**	1l. black	2·40	1·30

1937. Air. Stamps of Tripolitania optd LIBIA.

72	**18**	50c. red	65	60
73	**18**	60c. red	1·10	
74	**18**	75c. blue	1·40	37·00
75	**18**	80c. purple	1·80	60·00
76	**19**	1l. blue	3·25	1·30
77	**19**	1l.20 brown	2·75	60·00
78	**19**	1l.50 orange	2·75	58·00
79	**19**	5l. green	2·75	£110

11 Triumphal Arch

12 Roman Theatre, Sabrata

1937. Inauguration of Coastal Highway.

80	**11**	50c. red (postage)	3·25	8·50
81	**11**	1l.25 blue	3·25	15·00
82	**12**	50c. purple (air)	3·25	8·50
83	**12**	1l. black	3·25	15·00

1937. 11th Tripoli Trade Fair. Optd XI FIERA DI TRIPOLI.

84	**11**	50c. red (postage)	16·00	27·00
85	**11**	1l.25 blue	16·00	27·00
86	**12**	50c. purple (air)	21·00	27·00
87	**12**	1l. black	21·00	27·00

14 Benghazi Waterfront

1938. 12th Tripoli Trade Fair.

88	**14**	5c. brown (postage)	45	2·10
89	-	10c. brown	45	2·10
90	**14**	25c. green	85	1·10
91	-	50c. violet	85	1·10
92	**14**	75c. red	2·10	3·25
93	-	1l.25 blue	2·10	5·25

DESIGN: 10c., 50c., 1l.25, Fair Buildings.

94	50c. brown (air)	45	3·25
95	1l. blue	2·10	5·25

DESIGN—VERT: View of Tripoli.

16 Statue of Augustus

17 Eagle and Serpent

1938. Birth Bimillenary of Augustus the Great.

96	**16**	5c. green (postage)	45	1·10
97	-	10c. red	45	1·10
98	**16**	25c. green	1·30	85
99	-	50c. mauve	1·30	65
100	**16**	75c. red	3·75	1·80
101	-	1l.25 blue	3·75	2·40
102	**17**	50c. brown (air)	85	1·50
103	**17**	1l. mauve	1·30	3·75

DESIGN: 10, 50c., 1l.25, Statue of Goddess of Plenty.

18 Agricultural Landscape

1939. 13th Tripoli Trade Fair. Inscr "XIII FIERA CAMPIONARIA DE TRIPOLI" etc.

104	**18**	5c. green (postage)	65	85
105	-	20c. red	1·30	95
106	**18**	50c. mauve	1·40	95
107	-	75c. red	1·40	1·80
108	**18**	1l.25 blue	1·40	2·95

DESIGN: 20, 75c. View of Ghadames.

109	25c. green (air)	65	1·50
110	50c. green	85	1·60
111	1l. mauve	1·10	2·10

DESIGNS—Fiat G18V airplane over: 25c., 1l. Arab and camel in desert; 50c. Fair entrance.

19 Buildings

1940. Naples Exhibition.

112	**19**	5c. brown (postage)	55	1·10
113	-	10c. orange	55	1·10
114	-	25c. green	1·10	1·70
115	**19**	50c. violet	1·40	1·70
116	-	75c. red	1·40	4·25
117	-	1l.25 blue	2·10	7·50
118	-	2l.+75c. red	2·10	24·00

DESIGNS—HORIZ: 10, 75c., 2l. Oxen and plough. VERT: 25c., 1l.25, Mosque.

119	50c. black (air)	1·10	2·75
120	1l. brown	1·10	2·75
121	2l.+75c. blue	1·60	9·50
122	5l.+2l.50 brown	1·60	13·00

DESIGNS—HORIZ: 50c., 2l. Savoia Marchetti S.M.75 airplane over city; 1, 5l. Savoia Marchetti S-73 airplane over oasis.

19a Hitler and Mussolini

1941. Rome–Berlin Axis Commemoration.

123	**19a**	5c. orange (postage)	1·50	6·50
124	**19a**	10c. brown	1·50	6·50
125	**19a**	20c. purple	2·40	6·50
126	**19a**	25c. green	2·40	6·50
127	**19a**	50c. violet	2·40	6·50
128	**19a**	75c. red	2·40	21·00
129	**19a**	1l.25 blue	2·40	21·00
130	**19a**	50c. green (air)	4·25	32·00

B. INDEPENDENT

ليبيا

LIBYA

(20)

1951. Stamps of Cyrenaica optd. (a) For use in Cyrenaica, optd as T **20**.

131	**24**	1m. brown	15	15
132	**24**	2m. red	20	20
133	**24**	3m. yellow	25	25
134	**24**	4m. green	28·00	19·00
135	**24**	5m. brown	35	35
136	**24**	8m. orange	40	40
137	**24**	10m. violet	60	60
138	**24**	12m. red	1·10	1·10
139	**24**	20m. blue	1·50	1·50
140	**25**	50m. blue and brown	8·75	8·75
141	**25**	100m. red and black	14·50	14·50
142	**25**	200m. violet and blue	45·00	40·00
143	**25**	500m. yellow and green	£150	£130

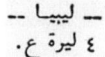

-- ليبيا --
٤ ليرة ع.

4 MAL.
LIBYA

(21)

(b) For use in Tripolitania. Surch as T **21** in Military Authority lire.

151	**24**	1mal. on 2m. red	25	25
152	**24**	2mal. on 4m. green	25	25
153	**24**	4mal. on 8m. orange	25	25
154	**24**	5mal. on 10m. violet	35	35
155	**24**	6mal. on 12m. red	35	35
156	**24**	10mal. on 20m. blue	65	65
157	**25**	24 mal. on 50m. blue and brown	3·00	3·00
158	**25**	48mal. on 100m. red	11·00	11·00
159	**25**	96mal. on 200m. violet and blue	27·00	27·00
160	**25**	240mal. on 500m. yellow and green	70·00	70·00

-- ليبيا --
٨ فرنك

8 FRANCS
LIBYA

(22)

(c) For use in Fezzan. Surch as T **22**.

166	**24**	2f. on 2m. red	20	20
167	**24**	4f. on 4m. green	30	30
168	**24**	8f. on 8m. orange	35	40
169	**24**	10f. on 10m. violet	50	50
170	**24**	12f. on 12m. red	75	70
171	**24**	20f. on 20m. blue	2·00	2·00
172	**25**	48f. on 50m. blue & brown	38·00	35·00
173	**25**	96f. on 100m. red and black	40·00	35·00
174	**25**	192f. on 200m. violet and blue	£110	80·00
175	**25**	480f. on 500m. yellow and green	£190	£190

23 King Idris

1952

176	**23**	2m. brown	10	10
177	**23**	4m. grey	10	10
178	**23**	5m. green	12·50	35
179	**23**	8m. red	40	25
180	**23**	10m. violet	12·50	15
181	**23**	12m. red	75	15
182	**23**	20m. blue	13·50	45
183	**23**	25m. brown	13·50	45
184	-	50m. blue and brown	1·75	65
185	-	100m. red and black	3·75	1·90
186	-	200m. violet and blue	6·00	3·50
187	-	500m. orange and green	25·00	17·00

Nos. 184/7 are larger.

1955. Arab Postal Union. As T **84a** of Lebanon but inscr "LIBYE" at top.

200	5m. brown	£126	60
201	10m. green	1·90	50
202	30m. violet	4·25	2·00

مؤتمر البريد العربي
القاهرة
١٥ مارس ١٩٥٥

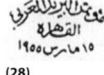

(28)

1955. Second Arab Postal Congress, Cairo. Nos. 200/2 optd with T **28**.

203	5m. brown	40	30
204	10m. green	90	50
205	30m. violet	2·25	1·25

1955. No. 177 surch.

206	**23**	5m. on 4m. grey	1·25	45

30

1955

207	**30**	1m. black on yellow	10	10
208	**30**	2m. bistre	1·40	50
209	**30**	2m. brown	10	10
210	**30**	3m. blue	10	50
211	**30**	4m. black	1·50	15
212	**30**	4m. lake	20	20
213	**30**	5m. green	40	20
214	**30**	10m. lilac	65	25
215	**30**	18m. red	15	10
216	**30**	20m. orange	25	15
217	**30**	30m. blue	50	20
218	**30**	35m. brown	65	25
219	**30**	40m. lake	1·10	40
220	**30**	50m. olive	85	25
221	-	100m. purple and slate	1·75	50
222	-	200m. lake and blue	9·25	1·40
223	-	500m. orange and green	15·00	7·25
224	-	£L1 green, brown and sepia on yellow	21·00	11·50

Nos. 221/4 are larger, 27×32 mm.
See also Nos. 242/57.

33 Immam's Tomb at Djaghboub

1956. Death Centenary of Imam Essayed Mohamed Aly el Senussi.
225	33	5m. green	20	20
226	33	10m. lilac	35	20
227	33	15m. red	95	75
228	33	30m. blue	1·60	1·25

34 Map of Libya

1956. First Anniv of Admission to U.N.
229	34	15m. buff and blue	30	15
230	34	35m. buff, purple and blue	1·00	30

35

1957. Arab Postal Congress, Tripoli.
231	35	15m. blue	1·75	90
232	35	500m. brown	12·50	6·50

36

1958. Tenth Anniv of Declaration of Human Rights.
233	36	10m. violet	20	15
234	36	15m. green	25	20
235	36	30m. blue	95	15

37 F.A.O. Emblem and Date Palms

1959. First Int Dates Conference, Tripoli.
236	37	10m. black and violet	20	15
237	37	15m. black and green	50	20
238	37	45m. black and red	1·00	50

1960. Inauguration of Arab League Centre, Cairo. As T **110** of Lebanon, but with Arms of Libya and inscr "LIBYA".
239	10m. black and green	50	20

39

1960. World Refugee Year.
240	39	10m. black and violet	25	15
241	39	45m. black and blue	1·25	75

1960. As Nos. 207 etc. On coloured paper.
242	30	1m. black on grey	10	10
243	30	2m. brown on buff	10	10
244	30	3m. indigo on blue	10	10
245	30	4m. lake on red	10	10
246	30	5m. green on green	10	10
247	30	10m. lilac on violet	10	10
248	30	15m. sepia on buff	10	10
249	30	20m. orange on orange	20	10
250	30	30m. red on pink	20	15
251	30	40m. lake on red	30	20
252	30	45m. blue on blue	35	20

253	30	50m. olive on bistre	35	20
254	-	100m. purple & slate on blue	1·25	35
255	-	200m. lake and blue on blue	3·25	1·40
256	-	500m. orange and green on green	23·00	5·50
257	-	£1 green, brown and sepia	23·00	11·00

40 Palm Tree and Radio Mast

1960. Third Arab Telecommunications Conference, Tripoli.
258	40	10m. violet	15	10
259	40	15m. turquoise	20	10
260	40	45m. lake	1·40	65

41 Military Watchtower (medallion)

1961. Army Day.
261	41	5m. brown and green	20	10
262	41	15m. brown and blue	60	15

42 Zelten Field and Marsa Brega Port

1961. Inauguration of First Libyan Petrol Pipeline.
263	42	15m. green and buff	25	10
264	42	50m. brown and lavender	75	40
265	42	100m. blue and light blue	2·25	90

43 Broken Chain and Agricultural Scenes

1961. Tenth Anniv of Independence.
266	43	15m. sepia, turquoise and green	15	10
267	-	50m. sepia, brown and buff	45	25
268	-	100m. sepia, blue & salmon	2·10	80

DESIGNS—(embodying broken chain): 50m. Modern highway and buildings; 100m. Industrial machinery.

44 Tuareg Camel Riders

1962. International Fair, Tripoli.
269	44	10m. chestnut and brown	60	10
270	-	15m. green and purple	75	25
271	-	50m. blue and green	2·00	1·60
MS272	148×105 mm. Nos. 269/71. Imperf		15·00	6·00

DESIGNS: 15m. Well; 50m. Oil derrick.

45 Campaign Emblem

1962. Malaria Eradication.
273	45	15m. multicoloured	25	20
274	45	50m. multicoloured	1·10	90

MS275	Two sheets each 68×103 mm. Nos. 273/4 (sold at 20m. and 70m. respectively)	8·50	5·00

46 Ahmed Rafik

1962. First Death Anniv of Ahmed Rafik el Mehdawi (poet).
276	46	15m. green	15	10
277	46	20m. brown	55	20

47 Scout Badge and Handclasp

1962. Third Boy Scouts' Meeting, Tripoli.
278	47	5m. sepia, red and yellow	10	10
279	-	10m. sepia, yellow and blue	20	10
280	-	15m. sepia, yellow and grey	25	20
MS281	130×95 mm. 20, 30 and 50m. in colours and designs of Nos. 278/80. Imperf		2·00	1·50

DESIGNS: 10m. Scouts and badge; 15m. Badge and camp.

48 City within Oildrop

1962. Inauguration of Essider Terminal, Sidrah Oil Pipeline.
282	48	15m. purple and green	45	15
283	48	50m. olive and brown	1·10	45

49 Red Crescent encircling Globe

1963. International Red Cross Centenary.
284	49	10m. multicoloured	20	15
285	49	15m. multicoloured	25	20
286	49	20m. multicoloured	90	60

50 Rainbow over Map of Tripoli

1963. International Trade Fair, Tripoli.
287	50	15m. multicoloured	25	20
288	50	30m. multicoloured	70	20
289	50	50m. multicoloured	1·40	60

51 Palm and Well

1963. Freedom from Hunger.
290	51	10m. green, brown and blue	20	10
291	-	15m. ochre, purple & green	25	20
292	-	45m. sepia, blue and salmon	1·10	75

DESIGNS: 15m. Camel and sheep; 45m. Farmer sowing and tractor.

52 "Emancipation"

1963. 15th Anniv of Declaration of Human Rights.
293	52	5m. brown and blue	10	10
294	52	15m. purple and blue	20	10
295	52	50m. green and blue	45	30

54 Map and Fair Entrance

1964. International Fair, Tripoli.
300	54	10m. green, brown and red	75	15
301	54	15m. green, brown & purple	1·00	50
302	54	30m. green, brown and blue	1·40	75

55 Child playing in Sun

1964. Children's Day. Sun Gold.
303	55	5m. violet, red and pink	10	10
304	-	15m. brown, bistre and buff	20	15
305	55	45m. violet, blue & lt blue	1·25	65
MS306	80×130 mm. Nos. 303/5 (sold at 100m.)		2·00	2·00

DESIGN: 15m. Child in bird's nest.

56 Lungs and Stethoscope

1964. Anti-tuberculosis Campaign.
307	56	20m. violet	90	25

57 Crown and Map

1964. First Anniv of Libyan Union.
308	57	5m. orange and green	15	10
309	57	50m. yellow and blue	1·00	50

58 Libyan Woman, Silk Moth and Cocoon

1964. Emancipation of Libyan Women.
310	58	10m. blue and green	15	10
311	58	20m. blue and yellow	55	35
312	58	35m. blue and pink	85	80
MS313	125×107 mm. Nos. 310/12 (sold at 100m.)		1·80	1·80

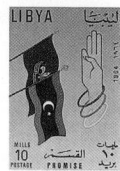

59 Flags and Scout Salute

1964. Libyan Scouts. Multicoloured.
314		10m. Type **59**	65	20
315		20m. Scout badge and saluting hands	1·25	60
MS316		120×85 mm. Nos. 314/15 (sold at 50m.)	1·80	1·80

60 Bayonet

1964. Foundation of the Senussi Army.
317	**60**	10m. brown and green	15	10
318	**60**	20m. black and orange	65	40

61 Ahmed Bahloul (poet)

1964. Ahmed Bahloul El-Sharef Commem.
319	**61**	15m. purple	20	10
320	**61**	20m. blue	65	20

62 Football

1964. Olympic Games, Tokyo. Rings in Gold.
321		5m. black and blue (Type **62**)	25	20
322		10m. black & purple (Cycling)	25	20
323		20m. black and red (Boxing)	50	20
324		30m. black and buff (Runner)	65	50
325		35m. black and olive (High-diving)	65	50
326		50m. black & green (Hurdling)	65	50
MS327		160×110 mm. Six stamps each 15m. in colours and designs of Nos. 321/6 (sold at 100m.)	9·00	9·00

Nos. 321/6 were arranged together se-tenant in the sheets, each block of six being superimposed with the Olympic "rings" symbol.

63 A.P.U. Emblem

1964. Tenth Anniv of Arab Postal Union.
328	**63**	10m. blue and yellow	10	10
329	**63**	15m. brown and lilac	20	10
330	**63**	30m. brown and green	95	65

64 I.C.Y. Emblem

1965. International Co-operation Year.
331	**64**	5m. gold and blue (postage)	25	10
332	**64**	15m. gold and red	90	25
333	**64**	50m. gold and violet (air)	1·50	35
MS334		102×76 mm. No. 333. Imperf	3·25	3·25

65 European Bee Eater

1965. Birds. Multicoloured.
335	5m. Long-legged buzzard (vert)	1·10	30
336	10m. Type **65**	1·50	30
337	15m. Black-bellied sandgrouse	2·25	30
338	20m. Houbara bustard	2·75	55
339	30m. Spotted sandgrouse	3·50	90
340	40m. Barbary partridge (vert)	4·25	1·25

66 Fair Emblem

1965. International Trade Fair, Tripoli.
341	**66**	50m. multicoloured	75	50

67 Compass, Rocket and Balloons

1965. World Meteorological Day.
342	**67**	10m. multicoloured	10	10
343	**67**	15m. multicoloured	20	15
344	**67**	50m. multicoloured	1·00	70

68 I.T.U. Emblem and Symbols

1965. Centenary of I.T.U.
345	**68**	10m. brown	10	10
346	**68**	20m. purple	15	10
347	**68**	50m. mauve	90	65

69 Lamp and Burning Library

1965. Reconstitution of Burnt Algiers Library.
348	**69**	15m. multicoloured	20	10
349	**69**	50m. multicoloured	90	25
MS350		Two sheets each 97×73 mm. Nos. 348/9 in blocks of four	4·50	4·50

70 Rose

1965. Flowers. Multicoloured.
351	1m. Type **70**	10	10
352	2m. Iris	10	10
353	3m. Cactus flower	10	10
354	4m. Sunflower	50	10

71 Sud Aviation Super Caravelle over Globe

1965. Inauguration of Kingdom of Libya Airlines.
355	**71**	5m. multicoloured	10	10
356	**71**	10m. multicoloured	20	10
357	**71**	15m. multicoloured	70	10

72 Forum, Cyrene

1965
358	**72**	50m. olive and blue	70	25
359	-	100m. brown and blue	1·25	45
360	-	200m. blue and purple	3·00	95

361	-	500m. green and red	6·50	2·75
362	-	£1 brown and green	14·00	6·50

DESIGNS–VERT: 100m. Trajan's Arch, Leptis Magna; 200m. Apollo's Temple, Cyrene. HORIZ: 500m. Antonine Temple, Sabratha; £1 Theatre, Sabratha.

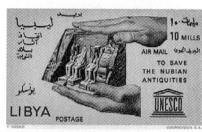

73 "Helping Hands"

1966. Air. Nubian Monuments Preservation.
363	**73**	10m. brown and bistre	20	10
364	**73**	15m. brown and green	25	10
365	**73**	40m. brown and chestnut	1·10	50
MS366		Three sheets each 125×87 mm. Nos. 363/5 in blocks of four	6·00	6·00

74 Germa Mausoleum

1966
367	**74**	70m. violet and brown	1·40	75

See also No. E368.

75 Globe and Satellites

1966. International Trade Fair, Tripoli.
369	**75**	15m. black, gold and green	20	10
370	**75**	45m. black, gold and blue	70	20
371	**75**	55m. black, gold and purple	95	60

76 League Centre, Cairo, and Emblem

1966. Arab League Week.
372	**76**	20m. red, green and black	10	10
373	**76**	55m. blue, red and black	65	50

77 W.H.O. Building

1966. Air. Inauguration of W.H.O. Headquarters, Geneva.
374	**77**	20m. black, yellow and blue (air)	20	10
375	**77**	50m. black, green and red	65	25
376	**77**	65m. black, salmon and lake	95	70
MS377		80×69 mm. 50m. black, blue and gold (air). Imperf	2·50	2·50

DESIGN: 50m. WHO Building as T 77 on UN flag.

78 Tuareg with Camel

79 Three Tuaregs on Camels (image scaled to 30% of original size)

1966. Tuaregs.
378	**78**	10m. red	95	65
379	-	20m. blue	2·25	1·25
380	-	50m. multicoloured	4·50	3·25
MS381		160×110 mm. **79** 100m. multicoloured. Imperf	8·50	8·50

DESIGNS–VERT: 20m. As Type **78** but positions of Tuareg and camel reversed. 62×39 mm: 50m. Tuareg with camel (different).

80 Leaping Deer

1966. First Arab Girl Scouts Camp (5m.) and Seventh Arab Boy Scouts Camp (25 and 65m.). Multicoloured.
382	5m. Type **80**	10	10
383	25m. Boy scouts Camp emblem (vert)	20	10
384	65m. As 25m.	1·00	50

81 Airline Emblem

1966. Air. First Anniv of Kingdom of Libya Airlines.
385	**81**	25m. multicoloured	20	15
386	**81**	60m. multicoloured	1·00	75
387	**81**	85m. multicoloured	1·40	1·00

82 UNESCO Emblem

1967. 20th Anniv of UNESCO.
388	**82**	15m. multicoloured	20	10
389	**82**	25m. multicoloured	90	20

83 Castle of Columns, Tolemaide

1967. Tourism.
390	**83**	25m. black, brown & violet	20	10
391	-	55m. brown, violet & black	90	50

DESIGN—HORIZ: 55m. Sebba Fort.

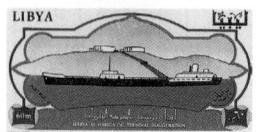

84 "British Confidence" (tanker) at Oil Terminal

1967. Inauguration of Marsa al Hariga Oil Terminal.
392	**84**	60m. multicoloured	1·75	65

85 Fair Emblem

1967. International Fair, Tripoli.
393	**85**	15m. multicoloured	50	10
394	**85**	55m. multicoloured	75	50

86 I.T.Y. Emblem

1967. International Tourist Year.

395	86	5m. black and blue	10	10
396	86	10m. blue and black	10	10
397	86	45m. black, blue and pink	60	15

87 Running

1967. Mediterranean Games, Tunisia. Designs showing action "close-ups".

398	87	5m. black, orange and blue	10	10
399	–	10m. black, brown and blue	10	10
400	–	15m. black, violet and blue	10	10
401	–	45m. black, red and blue	30	25
402	–	75m. black, green and blue	75	30

DESIGNS: 10m. Throwing the javelin; 15m. Cycling; 45m. Football; 75m. Boxing.

88 Open Book and Arab League Emblem

1967. Literacy Campaign.

403	88	5m. orange and violet	10	10
404	88	10m. green and violet	10	10
405	88	15m. purple and violet	15	10
406	88	25m. blue and violet	20	15

89 Human Rights Emblem

1968. Human Rights Year.

407	89	15m. red and green	15	10
408	89	60m. blue and orange	65	25

90 Cameleers, Fokker Friendship, Oil Rig and Map

1968. International Fair, Tripoli.

409	90	55m. multicoloured	95	30

91 Arab League Emblem

1968. Arab League Week.

410	91	10m. red and blue	10	10
411	91	45m. green and orange	65	50

92 Children "Wrestling" (statue)

1968. Children's Day. Multicoloured.

412	92	25m. Type 92	45	15
413		55m. Libyan mother and children	80	55

93 W.H.O. Emblem and Reaching Hands

1968. 20th Anniv of W.H.O.

414	93	25m. blue and purple	25	15
415	93	55m. brown and blue	40	25

94 Oil Pipeline Map

1968. Inauguration of Zueitina Oil Terminal.

416	94	10m. multicoloured	20	10
417	94	60m. multicoloured	1·10	65

95 "Teaching the People"

1968. "Eliminate Illiteracy".

418	95	5m. mauve	10	10
419	95	10m. orange	10	10
420	95	15m. blue	10	10
421	95	20m. green	20	20

96 Conference Emblem

1968. Fourth Session of Arab Labour Ministries Conference, Tripoli.

422	96	10m. multicoloured	10	10
423	96	15m. multicoloured	20	10

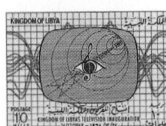

97 Treble Clef, Eye and T.V. Screen

1968. Inauguration of Libyan Television Service.

424	97	10m. multicoloured	10	10
425	97	30m. multicoloured	65	20

98 Bridge, Callipers and Road Sign

1968. Opening of Wadi El Kuf Bridge.

426	98	25m. multicoloured	15	15
427	98	60m. multicoloured	70	25

99 Melons

1969. Fruits. Multicoloured.

428	99	5m. Type 99	10	10
429		10m. Dates	10	10
430		15m. Lemons	10	10
431		20m. Oranges	15	10
432		25m. Peaches	50	15
433		35m. Pears	90	50

100 Fair Emblem

1969. Eighth International Trade Fair, Tripoli.

434	100	25m. multicoloured	15	10
435	100	35m. multicoloured	25	15
436	100	40m. multicoloured	60	20

101 Hoisting Weather Balloon

1969. World Meteorological Day.

437	101	60m. multicoloured	1·10	65

102 Family on Staircase within Cogwheel

1969. Tenth Anniv of Libyan Social Insurance.

438	102	15m. multicoloured	15	10
439	102	55m. multicoloured	30	25

103 I.L.O. Emblem

1969. 50th Anniv of I.L.O.

440	103	10m. green, black & turq	10	10
441	103	60m. green, black and red	70	50

104 Emblem and Desert Scene

1969. African Tourist Year.

442	104	15m. multicoloured	15	10
443	104	30m. multicoloured	65	50

105 Members of the Armed Forces and Olive Branch

1969. Revolution of 1st September.

444	105	5m. multicoloured	25	10
445	105	10m. multicoloured	35	20
446	105	15m. multicoloured	55	25
447	105	25m. multicoloured	85	40
448	105	45m. multicoloured	1·00	60
449	105	60m. multicoloured	2·10	1·00

On Nos. 444/9 the value is in white and the designer's name appears at the foot of design.

106 Dish Aerial and Flags

1970. Fifth Anniv of Arab Satellite Communications Co-operation Agreement.

450	106	15m. multicoloured	50	15
451	106	20m. multicoloured	75	20
452	106	25m. multicoloured	1·00	25
453	106	40m. multicoloured	1·50	75

107 Arab League Flag, Arms and Map

1970. Silver Jubilee of Arab League.

454	107	10m. sepia, green and blue	10	10
455	107	15m. brown, green & orge	15	15
456	107	20m. purple, green & olive	50	25

1970. Revolution of 1 September. Designs as T **105**, but without imprint "M. A. Siala" at foot, and figures of value differently inscr.

457	87	5m. multicoloured	25	10
458	87	10m. multicoloured	35	20
459	87	15m. multicoloured	55	25
460	87	25m. multicoloured	85	40
461	87	45m. multicoloured	1·00	60
462	87	60m. multicoloured	2·10	1·00

108 New Headquarters Building

1970. New U.P.U. Headquarters Building, Berne.

463	108	10m. multicoloured	15	10
464	108	25m. multicoloured	20	20
465	108	60m. multicoloured	95	60

1970. Nos. 358 and 360/2 with "KINGDOM OF LIBYA" inscriptions obliterated.

465a	72	50m. olive and blue
466	–	200m. blue and purple
467	–	500m. green and pink
468	–	£L1 brown and green

These stamps were sold only for use on parcel post items. Other values may exist so overprinted, but were unauthorized.

See also Nos. 518/23.

109 Arms and Soldiers

1970. Evacuation of Foreign Military Bases in Libya.

469	109	15m. black and red	15	15
470	109	25m. yellow, blue and red	45	20
471	109	45m. yellow, red and green	1·25	30

110 Soldiers and Libyan Flag

1970. First Anniv of Libyan Arab Republic.

472	110	20m. multicoloured	55	15
473	110	25m. multicoloured	70	15
474	110	30m. multicoloured	1·25	75

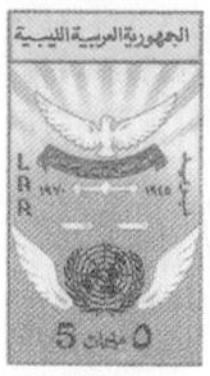

111 U.N. Emblem, Dove and Scales

1970. 25th Anniv of United Nations.

475	**111**	5m. brown, red and green	25	10
476	**111**	10m. green, red & emerald	65	15
477	**111**	60m. green, red and blue	1·75	75

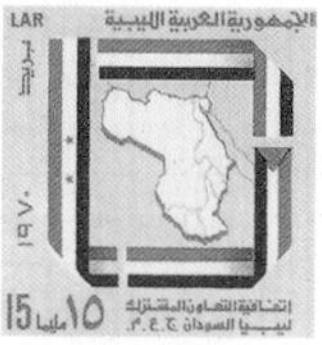

112 Map and Flags

1970. Signing of Tripoli Charter of Co-operation.

478	**112**	15m. green, black and red	5·00	1·50

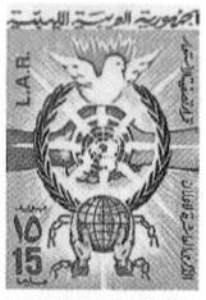

113 Dove, U.N. Emblem and Globe

1971. Tenth Anniv of U.N. De-colonisation Declaration.

479	**113**	15m. multicoloured	50	15
480	**113**	20m. multicoloured	75	20
481	**113**	60m. multicoloured	1·90	75

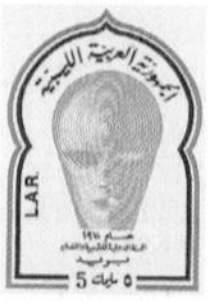

114 Education Year Emblem

1971. International Education Year.

482	**114**	5m. brown, red and black	15	10
483	**114**	10m. green, red and black	50	10
484	**114**	20m. blue, red and black	1·10	15

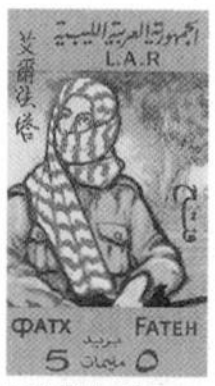

115 Palestinian Guerrilla

1971. "Al-Fatah" Movement for the Liberation of Palestine.

485	**115**	5m. multicoloured	15	10
486	**115**	10m. multicoloured	50	15
487	**115**	100m. multicoloured	1·75	1·00

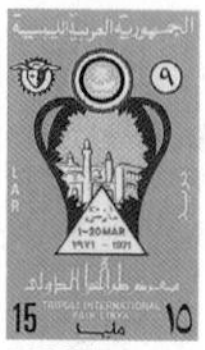

116 Fair Emblem

1971. Ninth International Trade Fair, Tripoli.

488	**116**	15m. multicoloured	15	10
489	**116**	30m. multicoloured	65	20

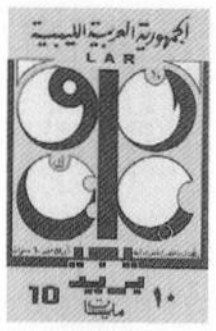

117 O.P.E.C. Emblem

1971. Organization of Petroleum Exporting Countries (O.P.E.C.).

490	**117**	10m. brown and yellow	15	10
491	**117**	70m. violet and pink	1·25	65

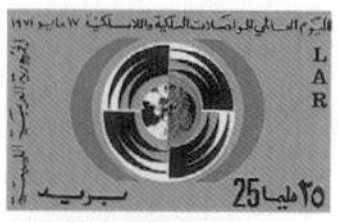

118 Global Symbol

1971. World Telecommunications Day (Nos. 494/5) and Pan-African Telecommunications Network.

492	-	5m. multicoloured	10	10
493	-	15m. multicoloured	10	10
494	**118**	25m. multicoloured	20	15
495	**118**	35m. multicoloured	50	25

DESIGN: 5m., 15m. Telecommunications map of Africa.

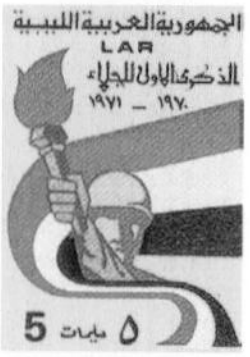

119 Soldier, Torch and Flag

1971. First Anniv of Evacuation of Foreign Troops.

496	**119**	5m. multicoloured	10	10
497	**119**	10m. multicoloured	15	10
498	**119**	15m. multicoloured	20	15

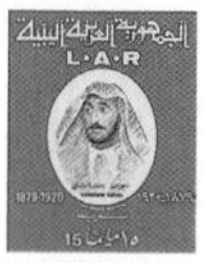

120 Ramadan Suehli

1971. Ramadan Suehli (patriot). Commem.

499	**120**	15m. multicoloured	15	10
500	**120**	55m. multicoloured	75	35

For similar portraits see Nos. 503/4, 507/8, 526/7 and 553/4.

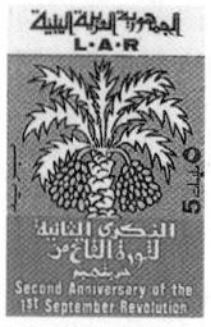

121 Palm and Dates

1971. Second Anniv of 1 September Revolution.

501	**121**	5m. multicoloured	20	10
502	**121**	15m. multicoloured	1·00	15

1971. 40th Death Anniv of Omar el Mukhtar (patriot). As T **120**.

503		5m. multicoloured	10	10
504		100m. multicoloured	1·75	90

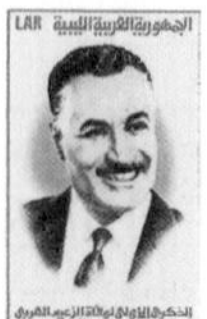

122 Pres. Gamal Nasser

1971. First Death Anniv of Pres. Nasser of Egypt.

505	**122**	5m. black, green & purple	10	10
506	**122**	15m. black, purple & green	95	10

1971. 21st Death Anniv of Ibrahim Usta Omar (poet). As T 120.

507		25m. multicoloured	25	15
508		30m. multicoloured	80	20

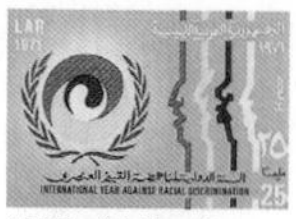

123 Racial Equality Year Emblem

1971. Racial Equality Year.

509	**123**	25m. multicoloured	25	15
510	**123**	35m. multicoloured	70	15

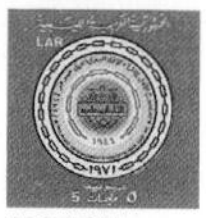

124 A.P.U. Emblem

1971. 25th Anniv of Founding of Arab Postal Union at Sofar Conference.

511	**124**	5m. multicoloured	10	10
512	**124**	10m. multicoloured	20	10
513	**124**	15m. multicoloured	15	10

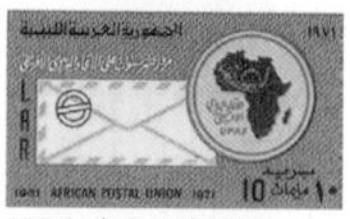

125 Arab Postal Union Emblem and Envelopes

1971. Tenth Anniv of African Postal Union. Multicoloured.

514	10m. Type **125**	10	10
515	15m. Type **125**	15	10
516	25m. A.P.U. Emblem and dove with letter	25	15
517	55m. As 25m.	95	35

1971. Nos. 423/33 with "KINGDOM OF LIBYA" inscriptions obliterated.

518	5m. Type **99**
519	10m. Dates
520	15m. Lemons
521	20m. Oranges
522	25m. Peaches
523	35m. Pears

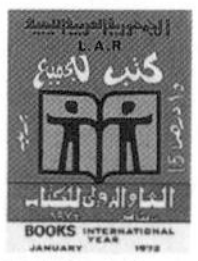

126 Book Year Emblem

1972. International Book Year.

524	**126**	15m. multicoloured	15	10
525	**126**	20m. multicoloured	25	20

1972. Ahmed Gnaba (poet) Commem. As T **120**.

526	20m. multicoloured	25	10
527	35m. multicoloured	65	20

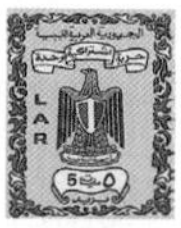

127 Libyan Arms

1972. Values in Milliemes.

528	**127**	5m. multicoloured	10	10
529	**127**	10m. multicoloured	10	10
530	**127**	25m. multicoloured	15	10
531	**127**	30m. multicoloured	20	10
532	**127**	35m. multicoloured	25	10
533	**127**	40m. multicoloured	50	15
534	**127**	45m. multicoloured	60	15
535	**127**	55m. multicoloured	85	20
536	**127**	60m. multicoloured	1·00	35
537	**127**	90m. multicoloured	1·60	90

For values in dirhams and dinars see Nos. 555/62.

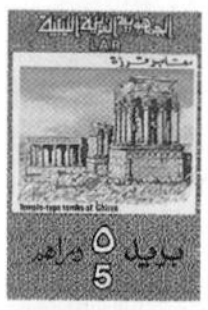

128 Tombs, Ghirza

1972. Libyan Antiquities. Multicoloured.

538	5m. Type **128**	10	10
539	10m. Cufic inscription, Ajdabiya	10	10
540	15m. Marcus Aurelius' Arch, Tripoli (horiz)	15	10
541	25m. Exchanging Weapons (cave painting, Wadi Zigza)	65	15
542	55m. Garamantian chariot (wall drawing, Wadi Zigza)	1·40	65
543	70m. "Libya crowning Cyrene" (Roman relief, Cyrene)	2·50	90

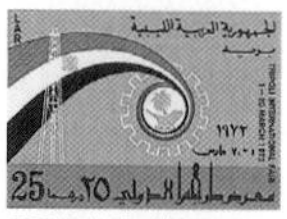

129 Fair Emblem

1972. Tenth International Trade Fair, Tripoli.

544	**129**	25m. multicoloured	20	15
545	**129**	35m. multicoloured	25	20
546	**129**	50m. multicoloured	95	25
547	**129**	70m. multicoloured	1·40	35

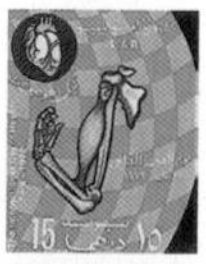

130 Heart and Skeletal Arm

1972. World Health Day.

548	**130**	15m. multicoloured	1·10	25
549	**130**	25m. multicoloured	2·25	75

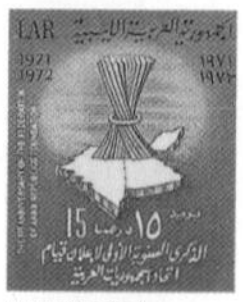

131 "Unity" Symbol on Map

1972. First Anniv of Libyan–Egyptian Federation Agreement.

550	**131**	15m. yellow, blue and black	10	10
551	**131**	20m. yellow, green & emer	20	10
552	**131**	25m. yellow, red and black	80	20

1972. Birth Centenary (1970) of Suleiman el Baruni (writer). As T **120**.

553	10m. multicoloured	95	15
554	70m. multicoloured	1·25	75

1972. New Currency (Dirhams and Dinars). As T **127**. (a) Size 19×24 mm.

555	**127**	15dh. multicoloured	10	10
556	**127**	65dh. multicoloured	75	50
557	**127**	70dh. multicoloured	90	65
558	**127**	80dh. multicoloured	1·25	65

(b) Size 27×32 mm.

559	100dh. multicoloured	1·75	2·00
560	200dh. multicoloured	3·25	1·60
561	500dh. multicoloured	7·50	5·00
562	1D. multicoloured	13·50	10·00

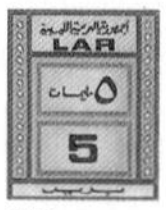

132

1972

563	**132**	5m. multicoloured	1·90	50
564	**132**	20m. multicoloured	7·50	1·40
565	**132**	50m. multicoloured	18·00	3·75

Nos. 563/5 were also issued with the Arabic face values expressed in the new currency.

See also Nos. 657/9.

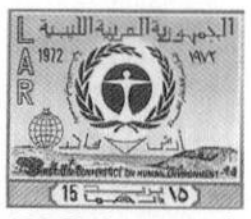

133 Environmental Emblem

1972. U.N. Environmental Conservation Conference, Stockholm.

566	**133**	15dh. multicoloured	50	10
567	**133**	55dh. multicoloured	1·10	35

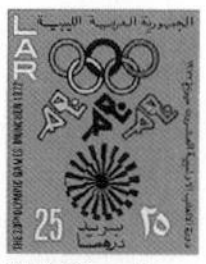

134 Olympic Emblems

1972. Olympic Games, Munich.

568	**134**	25dh. multicoloured	1·50	35
569	**134**	35dh. multicoloured	2·25	90

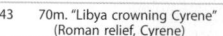

135 Symbolic Tree and "Fruit"

1972. Third Anniv of 1 September Revolution.
| 570 | 135 | 15dh. multicoloured | 15 | 10 |
| 571 | 135 | 25dh. multicoloured | 70 | 15 |

136 Dome of the Rock

1973. Dome of the Rock, Jerusalem.
| 572 | 136 | 10dh. multicoloured | 10 | 10 |
| 573 | 136 | 25dh. multicoloured | 50 | 15 |

137 Nicolas Copernicus

1973. 500th Birth Anniv of Copernicus. Mult.
| 574 | | 15dh. Type 137 | 15 | 10 |
| 575 | | 25dh. "Copernicus in his Observatory" (horiz) | 50 | 15 |

138 Libyan Eagle and Fair

1973. 11th International Trade Fair, Tripoli.
576	138	5dh. multicoloured	15	10
577	138	10dh. multicoloured	50	10
578	138	15dh. multicoloured	90	15

139 Blind Persons and Occupations

1973. Role of the Blind in Society.
| 579 | 139 | 20dh. multicoloured | 5·50 | 1·25 |
| 580 | 139 | 25dh. multicoloured | 10·00 | 2·50 |

140 Map and Laurel

1973. Tenth Anniv of Organization of African Unity.
| 584 | 140 | 15dh. multicoloured | 20 | 10 |
| 585 | 140 | 25dh. multicoloured | 65 | 45 |

141 Interpol H.Q., Paris

1973. 50th Anniv of International Criminal Police Organization (Interpol).
586	141	10dh. multicoloured	10	10
587	141	15dh. multicoloured	15	10
588	141	25dh. multicoloured	60	20

142 Map and Emblems

1973. Census.
589	142	10dh. blue, black and red	3·00	65
590	142	25dh. green, black and blue	4·25	1·25
591	142	35dh. orange, black and grn	8·00	2·50

143 W.M.O. Emblem

1973. W.M.O. Centenary.
| 592 | 143 | 5dh. blue, black and red | 10 | 10 |
| 593 | 143 | 10dh. blue, black and green | 15 | 10 |

144 Footballers

1973. Second Palestine Cup Football Championship.
| 594 | 144 | 5dh. brown and green | 45 | 20 |
| 595 | 144 | 25dh. brown and red | 80 | 15 |

145 Revolutionary Torch

1973. Fourth Anniv of 1 September Revolution.
| 596 | 145 | 15dh. multicoloured | 20 | 10 |
| 597 | 145 | 25dh. multicoloured | 85 | 10 |

146 "Writing Ability"

1973. Literacy Campaign.
| 598 | 146 | 25dh. multicoloured | 50 | 15 |

147 Doorway of Old City Hall

1973. Centenary of Tripoli Municipality. Mult.
599		10dh. Type 147	20	10
600		25dh. Khondok fountain	50	10
601		35dh. Clock tower	75	40

148 Militiamen and Flag

1973. Libyan Militia.
| 602 | 148 | 15dh. multicoloured | 15 | 10 |
| 603 | 148 | 25dh. multicoloured | 55 | 10 |

149 Arabic Quotation from Speech of 15 April 1973

1973. Declaration of Cultural Revolution by Col. Gaddafi. Multicoloured.
| 604 | | 25dh. Type 149 | 20 | 10 |
| 605 | | 70dh. As Type 149 but text in English | 60 | 30 |

150 Ploughing with Camel

1973. Tenth Anniv of World Food Programme.
606	150	10dh. multicoloured	10	10
607	150	25dh. multicoloured	20	10
608	150	35dh. multicoloured	55	15

151 Human Rights Emblem

1973. 25th Anniv of Declaration of Human Rights.
| 609 | 151 | 25dh. red, purple and blue | 20 | 10 |
| 610 | 151 | 70dh. red, green and blue | 1·10 | 30 |

152 Flat-headed Grey Mullet

1973. Fish. Multicoloured.
611		5dh. Type 152	15	10
612		10dh. Zebra seabream	70	10
613		15dh. Grouper	1·00	15
614		20dh. Painted comber	1·50	20
615		25dh. Yellow-finned tunny	2·75	30

153 Lookout Post and Scout Salute

1974. 20th Anniv of Scouting in Libya.
616	153	5dh. multicoloured	95	10
617	153	20dh. multicoloured	2·50	50
618	153	25dh. multicoloured	4·00	1·25

154 Emblem formed with National Flags

1974. 12th International Trade Fair, Tripoli.
619	154	10dh. multicoloured	50	10
620	154	25dh. multicoloured	75	15
621	154	35dh. multicoloured	1·25	35

155 Family within Protective Hands

1974. World Health Day.
| 622 | 155 | 5dh. multicoloured | 15 | 10 |
| 623 | 155 | 25dh. multicoloured | 50 | 20 |

156 Minaret within Star

1974. Inauguration of Benghazi University.
624	156	10dh. multicoloured	20	10
625	156	25dh. multicoloured	75	15
626	156	35dh. multicoloured	1·10	25

157 U.P.U. Emblem within Star

1974. Centenary of U.P.U.
| 627 | 157 | 25dh. multicoloured | 5·50 | 75 |
| 628 | 157 | 70dh. multicoloured | 10·00 | 1·50 |

158 Traffic Lights and Signs

1974. Motoring and Touring Club of Libya.
629	158	5dh. multicoloured	10	10
630	158	10dh. multicoloured	15	10
631	158	25dh. multicoloured	15	10

159 Tank, Refinery and Pipeline

1974. Fifth Anniv of 1 September Revolution.
632	159	5dh. multicoloured	10	10
633	159	20dh. multicoloured	15	10
634	159	25dh. multicoloured	15	10
635	159	35dh. multicoloured	20	15
MS636		121×81 mm. 55dh. lake, yellow and black	2·25	1·60

DESIGN: 26×39 mm.—55dh. Figure "5" and symbols.

160 W.P.Y. Emblem and People

1974. World Population Year.
| 637 | 160 | 25dh. multicoloured | 20 | 10 |
| 638 | 160 | 35dh. multicoloured | 50 | 20 |

161

1975. 13th International Trade Fair, Tripoli. Libyan Costumes.
639	161	5dh. multicoloured	10	10
640	-	10dh. multicoloured	10	10
641	-	15dh. multicoloured	10	10
642	-	20dh. multicoloured	20	10
643	-	25dh. multicoloured	75	10
644	-	50dh. multicoloured	1·10	20

DESIGNS: 10dh. to 50dh. Various costumes.

162 Congress Emblem

1975. Arab Workers' Congress.
645	**162**	10dh. multicoloured	10	10
646	**162**	25dh. multicoloured	15	15
647	**162**	35dh. multicoloured	50	15

163 Teacher at Blackboard

1975. Teachers' Day.
648	**163**	10dh. multicoloured	10	10
649	**163**	25dh. multicoloured	20	10

164 Human Figures, Text and Globe

1975. World Health Day.
650	**164**	20dh. multicoloured	15	10
651	**164**	25dh. multicoloured	20	10

165 Readers and Bookshelves

1975. Arab Book Exhibition.
652	**165**	10dh. multicoloured	10	10
653	**165**	25dh. multicoloured	20	10
654	**165**	35dh. multicoloured	50	15

166 Festival Emblem

1975. Second Arab Youth Festival.
655	**166**	20dh. multicoloured	15	10
656	**166**	20dh. multicoloured	20	15

1975. As Nos. 563/5 but without "L.A.R.".
657	**132**	5dh. black, orange & blue	35	10
658	**132**	20dh. black, yellow & blue	75	10
659	**132**	50dh. black, green and blue	1·40	15

167 Games Emblem

1975. Seventh Mediterranean Games, Algiers.
660	**167**	10dh. multicoloured	10	10
661	**167**	25dh. multicoloured	45	10
662	**167**	50dh. multicoloured	85	20

168 Dove of Peace

1975. Sixth Anniv of 1 September Revolution. Multicoloured.
663	**168**	25dh. Type **168**	20	10
664		70dh. Peace dove with different background	95	25
MS665	120×81 mm. 100dh. Colonel Gaddafi and desert scene. Imperf		1·25	1·25

169 Khalil Basha Mosque

1975. Mosques. Multicoloured.
666	**169**	5dh. Type **169**	10	10
667		10dh. Sidi Abdulla El Shaab	10	10
668		15dh. Sidi Ali El Fergani	10	10
669		20dh. Al Kharruba (vert)	15	10
670		25dh. Katiktha (vert)	20	10
671		30dh. Murad Agha (vert)	45	15
672		35dh. Maulai Mohamed (vert)	55	15

170 Arms and Crowds

1976. National People's Congress.
673	**170**	35dh. multicoloured	20	10
674	**170**	40dh. multicoloured	25	10

171 Dialogue Emblem

1976. Islamic–Christian Dialogue Seminar.
675	**171**	40dh. multicoloured	50	15
676	**171**	115dh. multicoloured	1·40	60

172 Woman blowing Bugle

1976. International Trade Fair, Tripoli. Multicoloured
677		10dh. Type **172**	10	10
678		20dh. Lancer	15	10
679		30dh. Drummer	65	10
680		40dh. Bagpiper	75	20
681		100dh. Woman with jug on head	1·90	35

173 Early and Modern Telephones

1976. Telephone Centenary. Multicoloured.
682		40dh. Type **173**	1·60	15
683		70dh. Alexander Graham Bell	2·75	50
MS684	Two sheets, each 120×100 mm. (a) No. 682×4; (b) No. 683×4		14·00	4·00

174 Mother and Child

1976. International Children's Day.
685	**174**	85dh. multicoloured	75	30
686	**174**	110dh. multicoloured	1·10	40

175 Hands supporting Eye

1976. World Health Day.
687	**175**	30dh. multicoloured	20	10
688	**175**	35dh. multicoloured	20	10
689	**175**	40dh. multicoloured	50	15

176 Great Grey Shrike

1976. Libyan Birds. Multicoloured.
690		5dh. Little bittern	75	25
691		10dh. Type **176**	1·40	40
692		15dh. Fulvous babbler	2·00	50
693		20dh. European bee eater (vert)	2·75	70
694		25dh. Hoopoe	3·00	95

177 Barabekh Plant

1976. Natural History Museum. Multicoloured.
695		10dh. Type **177**	10	10
696		15dh. Fin whale (horiz)	15	10
697		30dh. Lizard (horiz)	20	10
698		40dh. Elephant's skull (horiz)	70	15
699		70dh. Bonnelli's eagle	4·50	55
700		115dh. Barbary sheep	2·00	40

178 Cycling

1976. Olympic Games, Montreal. Multicoloured.
701	**178**	10dh. Type **178**	10	10
702		25dh. Boxing	20	10
703		70dh. Football	95	20
MS704	120×78 mm. 150dh. Symbolic motif depicting Olympic sports		1·25	1·25

179 Global "Tree"

1976. Non-Aligned Countries' Colombo Conference.
705	**179**	115dh. multicoloured	95	35

180 Agricultural and Industrial Symbols

1976. Seventh Anniv of Revolution.
706	**180**	30dh. multicoloured	15	10
707	**180**	40dh. multicoloured	45	15
708	**180**	100dh. multicoloured	90	55
MS709	120×80 mm. 200dh. Musicians and oil pipeline (24×41 mm)		2·00	2·00

181 Various Sports

1976. Fifth Arab Games, Damascus.
710	**181**	15dh. multicoloured	10	10
711	**181**	30dh. multicoloured	15	10
712	**181**	100dh. multicoloured	1·00	55
MS713	120×80 mm. 145dh. Wrestlers and sporting emblems		2·10	2·10

182 Chessboard and Pieces

1976. Arab Chess Olympiad, Tripoli.
714	**182**	15dh. multicoloured	95	15
715	**182**	30dh. multicoloured	1·60	60
716	**182**	100dh. multicoloured	5·00	95

183 Ratima

1976. Libyan Flora. Multicoloured.
717		15dh. Type **183**	15	10
718		20dh. "Sword of Crow"	15	10
719		35dh. "Lasef"	50	10
720		40dh. "Yadid"	80	15
721		70dh. Esparto grass	1·90	25

184 Emblem and Text

1976. International Archives Council.
722	**184**	15dh. multicoloured	10	10
723	**184**	35dh. multicoloured	15	10
724	**184**	70dh. multicoloured	55	20

186 Kaaba, Mecca

1976. Pilgrimage to Mecca.
729	**186**	15dh. multicoloured	10	10
730	**186**	30dh. multicoloured	15	10
731	**186**	70dh. multicoloured	30	20
732	**186**	100dh. multicoloured	75	30

187

1977. Coil Stamps.

733	**187**	5dh. multicoloured	10	10
734	**187**	20dh. multicoloured	10	10
735	**187**	50dh. multicoloured	55	40

188 Basket

1977. 15th International Trade Fair, Tripoli. Mult.

736	**188**	10dh. Type **188**	10	10
737		20dh. Leather bag	10	10
738		30dh. Vase	15	10
739		40dh. Slippers	45	15
740		60dh. Saddle	60	15
MS741		139×100 mm. 100dh. Horse wearing saddle and harness (49×53 mm). Imperf	65	65

189 Girl with Flowers

1977. Children's Day. Multicoloured.

742		10dh. Type **189**	10	10
743		30dh. Clothes shop	15	10
744		40dh. Orchard	20	15

190 Fighters and Machine-gun

1977. Ninth Anniv of Battle of Al-Karamah.

745	**190**	15dh. multicoloured	10	10
746	**190**	25dh. multicoloured	15	10
747	**190**	70dh. multicoloured	80	25

191 Protected Child

1977. World Health Day.

748	**191**	15dh. multicoloured	10	10
749	**191**	30dh. multicoloured	15	10

192 A.P.U. Emblem

1977. 25th Anniv of Arab Postal Union.

750	**192**	15dh. multicoloured	10	10
751	**192**	20dh. multicoloured	15	10
752	**192**	40dh. multicoloured	20	15

193 Maps of Libya and Africa

1977. Organization of African Unity Conference, Tripoli.

753	**193**	40dh. multicoloured	1·00	20
754	**193**	70dh. multicoloured	1·50	30

194 Heart on Map of Libya

1977. Red Crescent Commemoration.

755	**194**	5dh. multicoloured	10	10
756	**194**	10dh. multicoloured	15	10
757	**194**	30dh. multicoloured	65	15

195 Messenger and Jet Fighter

1977. Communications Progress. Multicoloured.

758		20dh. Type **195**	15	10
759		25dh. Arab rider and Concorde	30	15
760		60dh. Satellite and aerial	55	20
761		115dh. Television relay via satellite	1·10	65
762		150dh. Camel rider and Boeing 727 airliner loading	1·75	90
763		200dh. "Apollo–Soyuz" link	2·25	1·10
MS764		Two sheets each 118×89 mm. (a) 300dh. Zeppelin (51×35 mm); (b) 300dh. Planetary system (51×35 mm)	4·50	4·50

196 Mosque

1977. Libyan Mosques.

765	**196**	40dh. multicoloured	20	15
766	-	50dh. multicoloured (vert)	50	15
767	-	70dh. multicoloured	70	20
768	-	90dh. multicoloured	85	30
769	-	100dh. multicoloured (vert)	1·00	35
770	-	115dh. multicoloured	1·25	75

DESIGNS: 50dh. to 115dh. Various mosques.

197 Archbishop Capucci

1977. Third Anniv of Archbishop Capucci's Imprisonment.

771	**197**	30dh. multicoloured	15	10
772	**197**	40dh. multicoloured	20	15
773	**197**	115dh. multicoloured	1·25	60

198 Clasped Hands and Emblems

1977. Eighth Anniv of Revolution.

774	**198**	15dh. multicoloured	10	10
775	**198**	30dh. multicoloured	15	10
776	**198**	85dh. multicoloured	80	25
MS777		120×80 mm. 100dh. Star emblem	1·80	1·80

199 Swimming

1977. Arab School Sports. Multicoloured.

778		5dh. Type **199**	10	10
779		10dh. Handball (horiz)	10	10
780		15dh. Football	15	10
781		25dh. Table tennis (horiz)	50	20
782		40dh. Basketball	1·10	65

200 Championship Emblem

1977. First International Turf Championships, Tripoli. Multicoloured.

783		5dh. Horse jumping fence (facing left)	10	10
784		10dh. Arab horseman	10	10
785		15dh. Type **200**	15	10
786		45dh. Horse jumping fence (facing right)	55	15
787		115dh. Arab horseman racing	1·40	80
MS788		124×83 mm. 100dh. 115dh. Arab horsemen racing	75	75

201 Dome of the Rock

1977. Palestine Welfare.

789	**201**	5dh. multicoloured	10	10
790	**201**	10dh. multicoloured	10	10

202 Fort, and Hands writing Arabic Script in Book

1977. "The Green Book". Multicoloured.

791		35dh. Type **202**	15	10
792		40dh. Type **202** (text in English)	20	15
793		115dh. Dove with "Green Book" and map	1·25	70

203 Emblem

1977. World Standards Day.

794	**203**	5dh. multicoloured	10	10
795	**203**	15dh. multicoloured	10	10
796	**203**	30dh. multicoloured	15	10

204 Giraffe

1978. Rock Drawings from Wadi Mathendous. Multicoloured.

797		10dh. Crocodiles (horiz)	10	10
798		15dh. Elephant hunt (horiz)	10	10
799		20dh. Type **204**	15	10
800		30dh. Antelope (horiz)	45	15
801		40dh. Elephant (horiz)	65	20

205 Silver Pendant

1978. 16th Tripoli International Fair.

802	**205**	5dh. silver, black and red	10	10
803	-	10dh. silver, black & violet	10	10
804	-	20dh. silver, black & green	10	10
805	-	25dh. silver, black and blue	15	10
806	-	115dh. silver, black & blue	1·10	70

DESIGNS: 10dh. Silver ornamental plate; 20dh. Necklace with three pendants; 25dh. Crescent-shaped silver brooch; 115dh. Silver armband.

206 Compass and Lightning Flash

1978. Arab Cultural Education Organization.

807	**206**	30dh. multicoloured	20	15
808	**206**	115dh. multicoloured	1·40	65

207 Dancing a Round

1978. Children's Day. Children's Paintings. Multicoloured.

809		40dh. Type **207**	20	15
810		40dh. Children with placards	20	15
811		40dh. Shopping street	20	15
812		40dh. Playground	20	15
813		40dh. Wedding ceremony	20	15

208 Brickwork Clenched Fist

1978. The Arabs.

814	**208**	30dh. multicoloured	20	15
815	**208**	115dh. multicoloured	1·10	35

209 Blood Pressure Meter

1978. World Hypertension Month.

816	**209**	30dh. multicoloured	15	15
817	**209**	115dh. multicoloured	1·25	35

210 Microwave Antenna

1978. World Telecommunications Day.

818	**210**	30dh. multicoloured	15	15
819	**210**	115dh. multicoloured	1·00	35

211 Games Emblem

1978. Third African Games, Algiers.

820	**211**	15dh. copper, violet & blk	10	10
821	**211**	30dh. silver, lilac and black	15	10
822	**211**	115dh. gold, purple & blk	1·10	35

212 Aerial View of Airport

1978. Inauguration of Tripoli International Airport. Multicoloured.

823	40dh. Type **212**	30	10
824	115dh. Terminal building	1·25	65

213 Ankara

1978. Turkish–Libyan Friendship.

825	**213**	30dh. multicoloured	15	10
826	**213**	35dh. multicoloured	15	10
827	**213**	115dh. multicoloured	1·10	35

214 "Armed Forces"

1978. Ninth Anniv of 1 September Revolution. Multicoloured.

828	30dh. Type **214**	60	15
829	35dh. Tower, Green Book and symbols of progress	15	10
830	115dh. "Industry"	95	70
MS831	116×90 mm. 100dh. "Green Book" and buildings (50×40 mm)	95	70

215 Crater

1978. Second Symposium on Geology of Libya. Multicoloured.

832	30dh. Type **215**	15	10
833	40dh. Oasis	20	15
834	115dh. Crater (different)	1·10	60

216 "Green Book" and Different Races

1978. International Anti-Apartheid Year.

835	**216**	30dh. multicoloured	15	10
836	**216**	40dh. multicoloured	20	15
837	**216**	115dh. multicoloured	85	35

217 Pilgrims, Minarets and Kaaba

1978. Pilgrimage to Mecca.

838	**217**	5dh. multicoloured	10	10
839	**217**	10dh. multicoloured	10	10
840	**217**	15dh. multicoloured	10	10
841	**217**	20dh. multicoloured	15	10

218 Clasped Hands and Globe

1978. U.N. Conference for Technical Co-operation between Developing Countries.

842	**218**	30dh. multicoloured	15	10
843	**218**	40dh. multicoloured	20	15
844	**218**	115dh. multicoloured	85	35

219 Workers, Rifles, Torch and Flag

1978. Arab Countries Summit Conference. Multicoloured.

845	30dh. Type **219**	15	10
846	40dh. Map of Middle East, eagle and crowd (horiz)	20	15
847	115dh. As 40dh.	85	35
848	145dh. Type **219**	1·00	45

220 Human Figure and Scales

1978. 30th Anniv of Declaration of Human Rights.

849	**220**	15dh. multicoloured	10	10
850	**220**	30dh. multicoloured	20	15
851	**220**	115dh. multicoloured	50	35

221 Horse Racing and Fort

1978. Libyan Study Centre.

852	**221**	20dh. multicoloured	15	10
853	**221**	40dh. multicoloured	20	15
854	**221**	115dh. multicoloured	95	60

222 Lilienthal's Biplane Glider

1978. 75th Anniv of First Powered Flight. Multicoloured

855	20dh. Type **222**	10	10
856	25dh. Lindbergh's "Spirit of St. Louis"	10	10
857	30dh. Admiral Richard Byrd's Trimotor "Floyd Bennett"	80	25
858	50dh. Bleriot 5190 Santos Dumont flying boat and airship "Graf Zeppelin"	95	35
859	115dh. Wright brothers and Wright Type A	1·10	75
MS860	Two sheets each 96×103 mm. (a) 100dh. Daedalus and Icarus: (b) 100dh. Eagle and Boeing "727"	2·10	2·10

223 Libyans, Torch and Laurel Wreath

1979

861	**223**	5dh. multicoloured	10	10
862	**223**	10dh. multicoloured	10	10
863	**223**	15dh. multicoloured	10	10
864	**223**	30dh. multicoloured	20	10
865	**223**	50dh. multicoloured	20	10
866	**223**	60dh. multicoloured	25	15
867	**223**	70dh. multicoloured	30	15
868	**223**	100dh. multicoloured	75	25
869	**223**	115dh. multicoloured	85	30
870	**223**	200dh. multicoloured	1·10	45
870a	**223**	250dh. multicoloured	1·90	65
871	**223**	500dh. multicoloured	3·50	65
872	**223**	1000dh. multicoloured	6·75	3·50
872a	**223**	1500dh. multicoloured	12·50	4·25
872b	**223**	2500dh. multicoloured	23·00	7·50

Nos. 861/9 measure 18×23 mm and Nos. 870/2b 26×32 mm.

224 Mounted Dorcas Gazelle Head

1979. Coil Stamps.

873	**224**	5dh. multicoloured	15	10
874	**224**	20dh. multicoloured	25	10
875	**224**	50dh. multicoloured	80	25

225 Tortoise

1979. Libyan Animals. Multicoloured.

876	5dh. Type **225**	10	10
877	10dh. Addax (vert)	10	10
878	15dh. Algerian hedgehog	20	10
879	20dh. North African crested porcupine	20	10
880	30dh. Dromedaries	30	15
881	35dh. Wild cat (vert)	40	15
882	45dh. Dorcas gazelle (vert)	95	25
883	115dh. Cheetah	1·90	75

226 Carpet

1979. 17th Tripoli International Trade Fair.

884	**226**	10dh. multicoloured	10	10
885	-	15dh. multicoloured	10	10
886	-	30dh. multicoloured	15	10
887	-	45dh. multicoloured	15	10
888	-	115dh. multicoloured	85	35

DESIGNS: 15dh. to 115dh. Different carpets.

227 Aircraft and People

1979. International Year of the Child. Children's Paintings (1st series). Multicoloured.

889	20dh. Type **227**	10	10
890	20dh. Shepherd with flock	10	10
891	20dh. Open air cafe	10	10
892	20dh. Boat in storm	10	10
893	20dh. Policeman on traffic duty	10	10

See also Nos. 975/9.

228 World Map, Koran and Symbols of Arab Achievements

1979. The Arabs.

894	**228**	45dh. multicoloured	20	15
895	**228**	70dh. multicoloured	55	20

229 Radar Tower and Map

1979. World Meteorological Day.

896	**229**	15dh. multicoloured	10	10
897	**229**	30dh. multicoloured	15	10
898	**229**	50dh. multicoloured	20	15

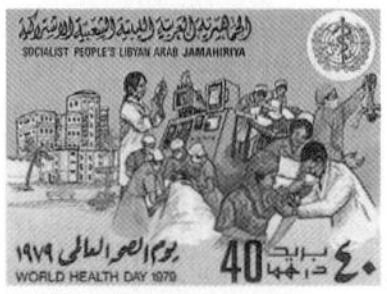
230 Medical Care

1979. World Health Day.

899	**230**	40dh. multicoloured	20	15

231 "Carpobrotus acinaciformis"

1979. Libyan Flowers. Multicoloured.

900	10dh. Type **231**	10	10
901	15dh. "Caralluma europaea"	10	10
902	20dh. "Arum cirenaicum"	10	10
903	35dh. "Lavatera arborea"	50	15
904	40dh. "Capparis spinosa"	50	15
905	50dh. "Ranunculus asiaticus"	60	15

232 Farmer and Sheep

1979. Tenth Anniv of Revolution. Multicoloured

906	15dh. Type **232**	10	10
907	15dh. Crowd with Green Book	10	10
908	15dh. Oil field	10	10
909	15dh. Refinery	10	10
910	30dh. Dish aerial	15	10
911	30dh. Hospital	15	10
912	30dh. Doctor examining patient	15	10
913	30dh. Surgeon	15	10
914	40dh. Street, Tripoli	20	15
915	40dh. Steel mill	20	15
916	40dh. Tanks	20	15
917	40dh. Tuareg horsemen	20	15
918	70dh. Revolutionaries and Green Book	70	20
919	70dh. Crowd within map of Libya	70	20
920	70dh. Mullah	70	20
921	70dh. Student	70	20
MS922	Two sheets each 97×102 mm. (a) 50dh. Revolutionary symbols (82×28 mm); (b) 50dh. Monument (83×35 mm). Imperf	1·10	1·10

233 Volleyball

1979. "Universiada '79" World University Games, Mexico City. Multicoloured.

923	45dh. Type **233**	20	15
924	115dh. Football	1·10	30

234 Emblem

1979. Third World Telecommunications Exhibition, Geneva.

925	**234**	45dh. multicoloured	20	15
926	**234**	115dh. multicoloured	1·25	30

235 Seminar Emblem and Crowd

1979. International Seminar on the "Green Book". Multicoloured.

927	10dh. Type **235**	10	10
928	35dh. Seminar in progress (horiz) (70×43 mm)	45	15
929	100dh. Colonel Gaddafi with "Green Book"	1·00	30
MS930	89×114 mm. 100dh. Colonel Gaddafi holding "Green Book". Imperf	1·25	1·25

236 Horsemen in Town

1979. Evacuation of Foreign Forces. Multicoloured.

931	30dh. Type **236**	15	10
932	40dh. Tuareg horsemen	20	15
MS933	99×100 mm. 100dh. Symbols of industry, education and agriculture (86×30 mm). Imperf	55	55

237 Football Match

1979. Mediterranean Games, Split.

934	**237**	15dh. multicoloured	10	10
935	**237**	30dh. multicoloured	50	10
936	**237**	70dh. multicoloured	1·25	20

238 Cyclist and Emblem

1979. Junior Cycling Championships, Tripoli. Multicoloured.

937	15dh. Type **238**	10	10
938	30dh. Cyclists and emblem	15	10

239 Horse-jumping

1979. Pre-Olympics. Multicoloured.

939	45dh. Type **239**	20	15
940	60dh. Javelin	55	15
941	115dh. Hurdles	1·10	55
942	160dh. Football	1·40	65
MS943	Two sheets each 103×81 mm. (a) 150dh. As No. 941; (b) 150dh. As No. 942	2·60	2·60

Nos. 939/42 exist from sheets on which an overall Moscow Olympics emblem in silver was superimposed on the stamps.

240 Figure clothed in Palestinian Flag

1979. Solidarity with Palestinian People.

944	**240**	30dh. multicoloured	15	10
945	**240**	115dh. multicoloured	1·10	30

241 Ploughing

1980. World Olive Oil Year.

946	**241**	15dh. multicoloured	10	10
947	**241**	30dh. multicoloured	15	10
948	**241**	45dh. multicoloured	20	15

242 Hockey (left)

1980. National Sports. Multicoloured.

949	10dh. Type **242**	10	10
950	10dh. Hockey (right)	10	10
951	10dh. Leap-frog (left)	10	10
952	10dh. Leap-frog (right)	10	10
953	15dh. Long jump (left)	10	10
954	15dh. Long jump (right)	10	10
955	15dh. Ball catching (left)	10	10
956	15dh. Ball catching (right)	10	10
957	20dh. Wrestling (left)	10	10
958	20dh. Wrestling (right)	10	10
959	20dh. Stone throwing (left)	10	10
960	20dh. Stone throwing (right)	10	10
961	30dh. Tug-of-war (left)	15	10
962	30dh. Tug-of-war (right)	15	10
963	30dh. Jumping (left)	15	10
964	30dh. Jumping (right)	15	10
965	45dh. Horsemen (left)	45	15
966	45dh. Horsemen (right)	45	15
967	45dh. Horsemen with whips (left)	45	15
968	45dh. Horsemen with whips (right)	45	15

Nos. 949/68 were issued together, divided into se-tenant blocks of four within the sheet, each horizontal pair forming a composite design.

243 Pipes

1980. 18th Tripoli International Fair. Multicoloured.

969	5dh. Drum (horiz)	10	10
970	10dh. Drum (different) (horiz)	10	10
971	15dh. Type **243**	10	10
972	20dh. Bagpipes (horiz)	10	10
973	25dh. Stringed instrument and bow (horiz)	15	10
MS974	68×87 mm. 100dh. Musicians	55	55

1980. International Year of the Child (1979) (2nd issue). As T **227**. Multicoloured.

975	20dh. "Horse Riding"	10	10
976	20dh. "Beach scene"	10	10
977	20dh. "Fish"	10	10
978	20dh. "Birthday party"	10	10
979	20dh. "Sheep Festival"	10	10

244 Mosque and Kaaba

1980. 400th Anniv of Hejira.

980	**244**	50dh. multicoloured	25	15
981	**244**	115dh. multicoloured	1·10	55

245 Surgical Operation and Hospital

1980. World Health Day.

982	**245**	20dh. multicoloured	10	10
983	**245**	50dh. multicoloured	50	15

246 Battle of Shoghab "Shahat", 1913

1980. Battles (1st series). Multicoloured.

984	20dh. Gardabia, 1915	20	15
985	35dh. Gardabia	10	10
986	20dh. Type **246**	10	10
987	35dh. Shoghab "Shahat"	20	15
988	20dh. Fundugh al-Shibani "Garian"	10	10
989	35dh. Fundagh al-Shibani "Garian"	20	15
990	20dh. Yefren	10	10
991	35dh. Yefren	20	15
992	20dh. Ghira "Brak"	20	15
993	35dh. Ghira "Brak"	20	15
994	20dh. El Hani (Shiat)	35	15
995	35dh. El Hani (Shiat)	60	25
996	20dh. Sebah	20	15
997	35dh. Sebah	20	15
998	20dh. Sirt	10	10
999	35dh. Sirt	10	10

The two values commemorating each battle were issued in se-tenant pairs, each pair forming a composite design.

See also Nos. 1027/50, 1140/63 and 1257/80.

247 Flame

1980. Sheikh Zarruq Festival.

1000	**247**	40dh. multicoloured	20	15
1001	**247**	115dh. multicoloured	1·00	65
MS1002		93×75 mm. 100dh. multicoloured	1·40	1·40

DESIGN: 93×75 mm. 100dh. Domes and minaret of mosque.

248 Ghadames

1980. Arabian Towns Organization. Mult.

1003	15dh. Type **248**	10	10
1004	30dh. Derna	15	10
1005	50dh. Ahmad Pasha Mosque, Tripoli	50	15

249 Guides on Hike

1980. 14th Pan-Arab Scout Jamboree. Multicoloured.

1006	15dh. Type **249**	10	10
1007	30dh. Guides cooking	15	10
1008	50dh. Cub Scouts cooking	25	15
1009	115dh. Scouts map-reading	1·10	60
MS1010	Two sheets each 67×95 mm. (a) 100dh. Type **249**; (b) 100dh. As No. 1008	1·50	1·50

250 Oil Refinery

1980. 11th Anniv of Revolution. Multicoloured.

1011	5dh. Type **250**	10	10
1012	10dh. Recreation and youth	10	10
1013	15dh. Agriculture	10	10
1014	25dh. Boeing 727-200 airplane and liner	60	15
1015	40dh. Education	20	15
1016	115dh. Housing	95	30
MS1017	70×79 mm. 100dh. Students and workers (29×49 mm)	80	80

251 Camels, Map of Libya and Conference Emblem

1980. World Tourism Conference, Manila. Mult.

1018	45dh. Type **251**	20	15
1019	115dh. Emblem, map and camel riders	95	30

252 Figures supporting O.P.E.C. Emblem

1980. 20th Anniv of Organization of Petroleum Exporting Countries. Multicoloured.

1020	45dh. O.P.E.C. emblem and globe	20	15
1021	115dh. Type **252**	95	30

253 Death of Omar el Mukhtar

1980. 49th Death Anniv of Omar el Mukhtar (patriot).

1022	**253**	20dh. multicoloured	10	10
1023	**253**	35dh. multicoloured	20	15
MS1024		104×85 mm. 253 100dh. multicoloured	55	55

253a Map of Libya and Science Symbols

1980. Birth Millenary of Avicenna (philosopher) and School Scientific Exhibition. Multicoloured.

1025	45dh. Type **253a**	20	15
1026	115d. Avicenna and Exhibition Emblem	1·10	30

1981. Battles (2nd series). As T 246. Mult.

1027	20dh. Zuara	10	10
1028	35dh. Zuara	15	15
1029	20dh. Tawargha	10	10
1030	35dh. Tawargha	15	15
1031	20dh. Dernah	10	10
1032	35dh. Dernah	15	15
1033	20dh. Bir Tagreft	10	10
1034	35dh. Bir Tagreft	15	15
1035	20dh. Funduk El Jamel "Misurata"	10	10
1036	35dh. Funduk El Jamel "Misurata"	15	15
1037	20dh. Sidi El Khemri "Gusbat"	10	10
1038	35dh. Sidi El Khemri "Gusbat"	15	15
1039	20dh. El Khoms	10	10
1040	35dh. El Khoms	15	15
1041	20dh. Roghdalin "Menshia"	10	10
1042	35dh. Roghdalin "Menshia"	15	15
1043	20dh. Ain Zara "Tripoli"	10	10
1044	35dh. Ain Zara "Tripoli"	15	15
1045	20dh. Rughbat el Naga "Benina"	10	10
1046	35dh. Rughbat el Naga "Benina"	15	15
1047	20dh. Tobruk	10	10
1048	35dh. Tobruk	15	15
1049	20dh. Ikshadia "Werfella"	10	10
1050	35dh. Ikshadia "Werfella"	15	15

The two values commemorating each battle were issued in se-tenant pairs, each pair forming a composite design.

254 Tent, Trees and Sun

1981. Children's Day. Children's Paintings. Multicoloured.

1051	20dh. Type **254**		10	10
1052	20dh. Women		10	10
1053	20dh. Picnic		10	10
1054	20dh. Aeroplane and playing children		10	10
1055	20dh. Mosque and man with camel		10	10

255 Central Bank

1981. 25th Anniv of Central Bank of Libya.

1056	**255**	45dh. multicoloured	15	15
1057	**255**	115dh. multicoloured	95	35
MS1058 87×61 mm. 255 50dh. multicoloured			20	20

256 Pots

1981. Tripoli International Fair. Multicoloured.

1059	5dh. Type **256**	10	10
1060	10dh. Silver coffee pot (vert)	10	10
1061	15dh. Long-necked vase (vert)	10	10
1062	45dh. Round-bellied vase	45	15
1063	115dh. Jug	1·10	35

257 Crowd and "Green Book" Stamp of 1977

1981. People's Authority Declaration.

1064	**257**	50dh. multicoloured	15	15
1065	**257**	115dh. multicoloured	95	35

258 Tajoura Hospital, Medical Complex, Patients receiving Treatment and W.H.O. Emblem

1981. World Health Day.

1066	**258**	45dh. multicoloured	15	15
1067	**258**	115dh. multicoloured	95	35

259 Eye and Man on Crutches

1981. International Year of Disabled People.

1068	**259**	20dh. green, blue & black	10	10
1069	-	45dh. green, black & blue	15	15
1070	-	115dh. blue and green	1·00	35

DESIGNS: 45dh. Globe and I.Y.D.P. emblem; 115dh. Hands holding shield with I.Y.D.P. emblem, eye and man on crutch.

260 Horse

1981. Libyan Mosaics. Multicoloured.

1071	10dh. Type **260**	10	10
1072	20dh. Ship	10	10
1073	30dh. Birds, fish and flowers	10	10
1074	40dh. Leopard	40	15
1075	50dh. Man playing musical instrument	50	15
1076	115dh. Fishes	1·10	35

261 Racial Discrimination Emblem

1981. Int Year Against Racial Discrimination.

1077	**261**	45dh. multicoloured	25	25
1078	**261**	50dh. multicoloured	55	30

262 Jet Fighters and Sud Aviation Alouette III Helicopter (left-hand stamp)

1981. 12th Anniv of Revolution.

1079	**262**	5dh. blue and light blue	15	10
1080	-	5dh. blue and light blue	15	10
1081	-	5dh. blue and light blue	10	10
1082	-	5dh. blue and light blue	10	10
1083	-	10dh. black and blue	10	10
1084	-	10dh. black and blue	10	10
1085	-	10dh. black and blue	10	10
1086	-	10dh. black and blue	10	10
1087	-	15dh. brown & lt brown	10	10
1088	-	15dh. brown & lt brown	10	10
1089	-	15dh. brown & lt brown	10	10
1090	-	15dh. brown & lt brown	10	10
1091	-	20dh. blue and green	15	15
1092	-	20dh. blue and green	15	15
1093	-	20dh. blue and green	15	15
1094	-	20dh. blue and green	15	15
1095	-	25dh. brown and yellow	15	15
1096	-	25dh. brown and yellow	15	15
1097	-	25dh. brown and yellow	15	15
1098	-	25dh. brown and yellow	15	15
MS1099 127×102 mm. 50dh. multi-coloured			30	30

DESIGNS—VERT: No. 1080, Jet fighter (right-hand stamp); 1081/2, Parachutists; 1083/4, Tank parade; 1085/6, Marching frogmen; 1087/8, Anti-aircraft rocket trucks; 1089/90, Missile trucks. HORIZ: 1091/2, Marching sailors; 1093/4, Jeeps and anti-aircraft rocket trucks; 1095/6, Armoured vehicles and landrovers; 1097/8, Tank parade 50dh.Marching sailors (59×34 mm).

Each pair forms a horizontal composite design, the first number being the left-hand stamp in each instance.

263 Wheat and Plough

1981. World Food Day.

1100	**263**	45dh. multicoloured	25	25
1101	**263**	200dh. multicoloured	1·75	95

264 "Pseudotergumia fidia"

1981. Butterflies. Multicoloured.

1102	5dh. Type **264**	15	10
1103	5dh. "Chazara prieuri" (sun in background)	15	10
1104	5dh. "Polygonia c-album" (trees in background)	15	10
1105	5dh. "Colias crocea" (mosque in background)	15	10
1106	10dh. "Anthocharis bellia" (face value bottom right)	15	10
1107	10dh. "Pandoriana pandora" (face value bottom left)	15	10
1108	10dh. "Melanargia ines" (face value top right)	15	10
1109	10dh. "Charaxes jasius" (face value top left)	15	10
1110	15dh. "Nymphales antiopa" (face value bottom right)	30	30
1111	15dh. "Eurodryas desfontainii" (face value bottom left)	30	30
1112	15dh. "Iphiclides podalirius" (face value top right)	30	30
1113	15dh. "Glaucopsyche melanops" (face value top left)	30	30
1114	25dh. "Spialia sertorius" (face value bottom right)	50	45
1115	25dh. "Pieris brassicae" (face value bottom left)	50	45
1116	25dh. "Lysandra albicans" (face value top right)	50	45
1117	25dh. "Celastrina argiolus" (face value top left)	50	45
MS1118 213×144 mm. Nos. 1102/17		4·25	4·25

The four designs of each value were issued together in small sheets of four, showing composite background designs.

265 Grapes

1981. Fruit. Multicoloured.

1119	5dh. Type **265**	10	10
1120	10dh. Dates	10	10
1121	15dh. Lemons	10	10
1122	20dh. Oranges	15	15
1123	35dh. Barbary figs	20	20
1124	55dh. Pomegranate	65	30

266 I.Y.D.P. Emblem and Globe

1981. International Year of Disabled Persons.

1125	**266**	45dh. multicoloured	25	25
1126	**266**	115dh. multicoloured	90	55

267 Animals (looking right)

1982. Libyan Mosaics. Multicoloured.

1127	45dh. Type **267**	50	25
1128	45dh. Orpheus	50	25
1129	45dh. Animals (looking left)	50	25
1130	45dh. Fishes	50	25
1131	45dh. Fishermen	50	25
1132	45dh. Fishes and ducks	50	25
1133	45dh. Farm	50	25
1134	45dh. Birds and fruit	50	25
1135	45dh. Milking	50	25

268 Koran Texts leading to Ka'aba

1982. Third Koran Reading Contest. Multicoloured.

1136	10dh. Type **268**	10	10
1137	35dh. Koran and formation of the World	20	20
1138	115dh. Reading the Koran	95	55
MS1139 111×80 mm. 100dh. As No. 1138		80	80

1982. Battles (3rd series). As T **246**. Multicoloured.

1140	20dh. Hun "Gioffra"	15	15
1141	35dh. Hun "Gioffra"	20	20
1142	20dh. Gedabia	15	15
1143	35dh. Gedabia	20	20
1144	20dh. El Asaba "Gianduba"	15	15
1145	35dh. El Asaba "Gianduba"	20	20
1146	20dh. El Habela	15	15
1147	35dh. El Habela	20	20
1148	20dh. Suk El Ahad "Tarhuna"	15	15
1149	35dh. Suk El Ahad "Tarhuna"	20	20
1150	20dh. El Tangi	15	15
1151	35dh. El Tangi	20	20
1152	20dh. Sokna	15	15
1153	35dh. Sokna	20	20
1154	20dh. Wadi Smalus "Jabel El Akdar"	15	15
1155	35dh. Wadi Smalus "Jabel El Akdar"	20	20
1156	20dh. Sidi Abuagela "Agelat"	15	15
1157	35dh. Sidi Abuagela "Agelat"	20	20
1158	20dh. Sidi Surur "Zeliten"	15	15
1159	35dh. Sidi Surur "Zeliten"	20	20
1160	20dh. Kuefia	15	15
1161	35dh. Kuefia	20	20
1162	20dh. Abunjeim	15	15
1163	35dh. Abunjeim	20	20

The two values commemorating each battle were issued in se-tenant pairs, each pair forming a composite design.

269 Grinding Flour

1982. Tripoli International Fair. Multicoloured.

1164	5dh. Type **269**	10	10
1165	10dh. Ploughing	10	10
1166	25dh. Stacking hay	15	15
1167	35dh. Weaving	20	20
1168	45dh. Cooking	50	25
1169	100dh. Harvesting	95	50

270 "ALFATAH" forming Farm Vehicle

1982. People's Authority Declaration. Multicoloured.

1170	100dh. Type **270**	75	50
1171	200dh. Colonel Gaddafi, old man, "Green Book" and guns	1·75	95
1172	300dh. Rejoicing crowd	2·50	1·40

271 Scout flying Model Airship

1982. 75th Anniv of Boy Scout Movement. Multicoloured

1173	100dh. Type **271**	75	50

1174	200dh. Scouts helping injured dog	1·75	95
1175	300dh. Scout reading to old man	1·75	1·40
1176	400dh. Scout with model rocket	3·75	2·25
MS1177	Two sheets each 77×73 mm. (a) 500dh. Colonel Gaddafi and scouts (38×41 mm); (b) 500dh. "Green Book" (38×41 mm)	4·75	4·75

272 Map of Africa and A.F.C. Emblem

1982. African Football Cup Competition.

1178	**272**	100dh. multicoloured	95	50
1179	**272**	200dh. multicoloured	1·90	95

273 Footballer

1982. World Cup Football Championship, Spain. Multicoloured.

1180	45dh. Type **273**	25	25
1181	100dh. Footballer (different)	75	50
1182	200dh. As No. 1173	1·60	95
1183	300dh. Footballer and goal-keeper	2·25	1·40
MS1184	135×112 mm. 500dh. Type **273**	3·50	3·50

274 Palestinian Children

1982. Palestinian Children's Day. Multicoloured.

1185	20dh. Type **274**	15	15
1186	20dh. Girl with dish	15	15
1187	20dh. Child with turban	15	15
1188	20dh. Young child	15	15
1189	20dh. Young boy	15	15

275 Lanner Falcon

1982. Birds. Multicoloured.

1190	15dh. Type **275**	35	25
1191	15dh. Eurasian swift	35	25
1192	15dh. Peregrine falcon	35	25
1193	15dh. Greater flamingo	35	25
1194	25dh. Whitethroat	60	35
1195	25dh. Turtle dove	60	35
1196	25dh. Black-bellied sandgrouse	60	35
1197	25dh. Egyptian vulture	60	35
1198	45dh. Golden oriole	1·00	60
1199	45dh. European bee eater	1·00	60
1200	45dh. River kingfisher	1·00	60
1201	45dh. European roller	1·00	60
1202	95dh. Barbary partridge	2·00	1·25
1203	95dh. Barn owl	2·00	1·25
1204	95dh. Cream-coloured courser	2·00	1·25
1205	95dh. Hoopoe	2·00	1·25
MS1206	142×214 mm. Nos. 1190/1205	14·00	14·00

The four designs of each value were printed together in *se-tenant* blocks of four, forming a composite design.

276 Nurses' Class, Operating Theatre and Doctor examining Child

1982. Teaching Hospitals.

1207	**276**	95dh. multicoloured	85	50
1208	**276**	100dh. multicoloured	85	50
1209	**276**	205dh. multicoloured	2·00	1·10

277 Map of Libya and A.P.U. Emblem

1982. 30th Anniv of Arab Postal Union.

1210	**277**	100dh. multicoloured	95	50
1211	**277**	200dh. multicoloured	1·90	95

278 19th-century Chinese King and Diagram of Fischer v Spassky, 1972

1982. World Chess Championship, Moscow. Multicoloured

1212	100dh. Type **278**	1·25	50
1213	100dh. African king and diagram of Karpov v Korchnoi, 1978	1·25	50
1214	100dh. Modern bishop and diagram of Smyslov v Karpov, 1971	1·25	50
1215	100dh. 19th-century European rook and diagram of Tal v Vadasz, 1977	1·25	50
MS1216	87×68 mm. 500dh. Chess-piece on board	4·75	4·75

Nos. 1212/15 were printed together, *se-tenant*, forming a composite design.

279 Hexagonal Pattern

1982. World Telecommunications Day.

1217	**279**	100dh. multicoloured	75	50
1218	**279**	200dh. multicoloured	1·50	95

280 Map of Libya and "Green Book"

1982. 51st Anniv of International Philatelic Federation (F.I.P.).

1219	**280**	200dh. multicoloured	1·75	95
MS1220		70×80 mm. 280 300dh. multicoloured	2·25	2·25

281 Family and Flag

1982. Organization of African Unity Summit. Multicoloured.

1221	50dh. Type **281**	30	30
1222	100dh. Map, dove and symbols of industry and agriculture	75	50
1223	200dh. Pres. Gaddafi and crowd with "Green Book" (65×36 mm.)	1·90	95

282 Pres. Gaddafi and Jet Aircraft

1982. 13th Anniv of Revolution. Multicoloured.

1225	15dh. Type **282**	15	10
1226	20dh. Gaddafi, soldiers and rockets	15	10
1227	30dh. Gaddafi, sailors and naval vessels	50	25
1228	45dh. Gaddafi, soldiers and tanks	25	25
1229	70dh. Gaddafi, and armed forces	60	35
1230	100dh. Gaddafi and women soldiers	90	50
MS1231	114×100 mm. 200dh. Gaddafi, crowd and armed forces. Imperf	1·90	95

283 Palm Tree and Red Crescent

1982. 25th Anniv of Libyan Red Crescent. Multicoloured.

1232	100dh. Type **283**	95	50
1233	200dh. "25" within crescents	1·90	95

284 Globe, Dove and Rifle

1982. Solidarity with Palestinian People.

1234	**284**	100dh. black, mauve and green	95	40
1235	**284**	200dh. black, blue and green	1·90	80

285 Gaddafi, Crowd, "Green Book" and Emblems

1982. Al Fateh University Symposium on the "Green Book". Multicoloured.

1236	100dh. Type **285**	95	45
1237	200dh. Gaddafi, "Green Book", map and emblems	1·90	95

286 Philadelphus

1983. Flowers. Multicoloured.

1238	25dh. Type **286**	15	10
1239	25dh. Hypericum	15	10
1240	25dh. Antirrhinum	15	10
1241	25dh. Lily	15	10
1242	25dh. Capparis	15	10
1243	25dh. Tropaeolum	15	10
1244	25dh. Roses	15	10
1245	25dh. Chrysanthemum	15	10
1246	25dh. "Nigella damascena"	15	10
1247	25dh. "Guilladia lanceolata"	15	10
1248	25dh. Dahlia	15	10
1249	25dh. "Dianthus caryophyllus"	15	10
1250	25dh. "Notobasis syriaca"	15	10
1251	25dh. "Nerium oleander"	15	10
1252	25dh. "Iris histroides"	15	10
1253	25dh. "Scolymus hispanicus"	15	10

287 Customs Council Building, Brussels, and Warrior on Horseback

1983. 30th Anniv of Customs Co-operation Council. Multicoloured.

1254	25dh. Type **287**	15	10
1255	50dh. Customs building	25	20
1256	100dh. Customs building and warrior with sword	50	45

1983. Battles (4th series). As T **246**. (a) Battle of Ghaser Ahmed.

1257	50dh. multicoloured	25	20
1258	50dh. multicoloured	25	20

(b) Battle of Sidi Abuarghub.

1259	50dh. multicoloured	25	20
1260	50dh. multicoloured	25	20

(c) Battle of Ghar Yunes.

1261	50dh. multicoloured	25	20
1262	50dh. multicoloured	25	20

(d) Battle of Bir Otman.

1263	50dh. multicoloured	25	20
1264	50dh. multicoloured	25	20

(e) Battle of Sidi Sajeh.

1265	50dh. multicoloured	25	20
1266	50dh. multicoloured	25	20

(f) Battle of Ras el-Hamam.

1267	50dh. multicoloured	25	20
1268	50dh. multicoloured	25	20

(g) Battle of Zawiet Ishghefa.

1269	50dh. multicoloured	25	20
1270	50dh. multicoloured	25	20

(h) Battle of Wadi Essania.

1271	50dh. multicoloured	25	20
1272	50dh. multicoloured	25	20

(i) Battle of El-Meshiashta.

1273	50dh. multicoloured	25	20
1274	50dh. multicoloured	25	20

(j) Battle of Gharara.

1275	50dh. multicoloured	25	20
1276	50dh. multicoloured	25	20

(k) Battle of Abughelan.

1277	50dh. multicoloured	20	20
1278	50dh. multicoloured	20	20

(l) Battle of Mahruka.

1279	50dh. multicoloured	20	20
1280	50dh. multicoloured	20	20

The two values for each battle were printed together in *se-tenant* pairs, forming composite designs.

288 Camel

1983. Farm Animals. Multicoloured.

1281	25dh. Type **288**	15	10
1282	25dh. Cow	15	10
1283	25dh. Horse	15	10
1284	25dh. Bull	15	10
1285	25dh. Goat	15	10
1286	25dh. Sheep dog	15	10
1287	25dh. Ewe	15	10
1288	25dh. Ram	15	10
1289	25dh. Greylag goose	35	25
1290	25dh. Helmeted guineafowl	35	25
1291	25dh. Rabbit	15	10
1292	25dh. Wood pigeon	35	25
1293	25dh. Common turkey	35	25
1294	25dh. Cockerel	15	10
1295	25dh. Hen	15	10
1296	25dh. Goose	15	10

289 Musician with Twin-horned Pipe

1983. Tripoli International Fair. Multicoloured.

1297	40dh. Type **289**	20	15
1298	45dh. Bagpipes (horiz)	25	20
1299	50dh. Horn	25	20
1300	55dh. Flute (horiz)	30	25
1301	75dh. Pipe	65	35
1302	100dh. Man and woman at well	90	45

290 Phoenician Galley

1983. 25th Anniv of International Maritime Organization. Multicoloured.

1303	100dh. Type **290**		1·25	55
1304	100dh. Ancient Greek galley		1·25	55
1305	100dh. Ancient Egyptian ship		1·25	55
1306	100dh. Roman sailing ship		1·25	55
1307	100dh. Viking longship		1·25	55
1308	100dh. Libyan xebec		1·25	55

291 Motorist

1983. Children's Day. Multicoloured.

1309	20dh. Type **291**		10	10
1310	20dh. Tractor and trailer		10	10
1311	20dh. Child with dove and globe		10	10
1312	20dh. Scout camp		10	10
1313	20dh. Dinosaur		10	10

292 Pres. Gaddafi with Children

1983. World Health Day. Multicoloured.

1314	25dh. Type **292**		15	10
1315	50dh. Gaddafi and old man in wheelchair		25	20
1316	100dh. Gaddafi visiting sick girl (horiz)		80	45

293 Gaddafi, Map and "Green Book"

1983. First World "Green Book" Symposium. Mult.

1317	50dh. Type **293**		25	20
1318	70dh. Syposium in session and emblem (56×37 mm)		60	30
1319	80dh. Gaddafi, "Green Book", emblem and "Jamahiriya"		65	35
MS1320 148×80 mm. 100dh. Gaddafi and "Green Books" (horiz 53×44 mm)			80	80

294 Economic Emblems on Map of Africa

1983. 25th Anniv of African Economic Committee.

1321	**294**	50dh. multicoloured	25	20
1322	**294**	100dh. multicoloured	90	45
1323	**294**	250dh. multicoloured	1·90	1·10

295 Ali Siala

1983. Libyan Scientists. Sheet 127×101 mm containing T **295** and similar vert design. Multicoloured.

MS1324	100dh. Type **295**; 100dh. Ali el-Najar		1·75	1·75

296 Cuckoo Wrasse ("Labrus bimaculatus")

1983. Fish. Multicoloured.

1325	25dh. Type **296**		30	15
1326	25dh. Streaked gurnard ("Trigoporus lastoviza")		30	15
1327	25dh. Peacock wrasse ("Thalassoma pavo")		30	15
1328	25dh. Mediterranean cardinalfish ("Apogon imberbis")		30	15
1329	25dh. Atlantic mackerel ("Scomber scombrus")		30	15
1330	25dh. Black seabream ("Spondyliosoma cantharus")		30	15
1331	25dh. Greater weaver ("Trachinus draco")		30	15
1332	25dh. Peacock blenny ("Blennius pavo")		30	15
1333	25dh. Lesser red scorpionfish ("Scorpaena notata")		30	15
1334	25dh. Painted comber ("Serranus scriba")		30	15
1335	25dh. Angler ("Lophius piscatorius")		30	15
1336	25dh. Stargazer ("Uranoscopus scaber")		30	15
1337	25dh. Frigate mackerel ("Auxis thazard")		30	15
1338	25dh. John dory ("Zeus faber")		30	15
1339	25dh. Flying gurnard ("Dactylopterus volitans")		30	15
1340	25dh. Corb ("Umbrina cirrosa")		30	15

297 "Still-life" (Gauguin)

1983. Paintings. Multicoloured.

1341	50dh. Type **297**		25	20
1342	50dh. Abstract		25	20
1343	50dh. "The Conquest of Tunis by Charles V" (Rubens)		25	20
1344	50dh. "Arab Band in Horse-drawn Carriage"		25	20
1345	50dh. "Apotheosis of Gaddafi" (vert)		25	20
1346	50dh. Horses (detail of Raphael's "The Triumph of David over the Assyrians") (vert)		25	20
1347	50dh. "Workers" (vert)		25	20
1348	50dh. "Sunflowers" (Van Gogh) (vert)		25	20

298 Basketball

1983. Olympic Games, Los Angeles. Mult.

1349	10dh. Type **298**		10	10
1350	15dh. High jumping		10	10
1351	25dh. Running		15	10
1352	50dh. Gymnastics		25	20
1353	100dh. Windsurfing		80	45
1354	200dh. Shot-putting		1·50	95

299 I.T.U. Building, Antenna and W.C.Y. Emblem

1983. World Communications Year.

1356	**299**	10dh. multicoloured	10	10
1357	**299**	50dh. multicoloured	25	20
1358	**299**	100dh. multicoloured	75	45

300 "The House is to be served by its Residents"

1983. Extracts from the Green Book. Multicoloured.

1359	10dh. Type **300**		10	10
1360	15dh. "Power, wealth and arms are in the hands of the people"		10	10
1361	20dh. "Masters in their own castles" (vert)		10	10
1362	35dh. "No democracy without popular congresses"		20	15
1363	100dh. "The authority of the people" (vert)		50	45
1364	140dh. "The Green Book is the guide of humanity for final release"		1·10	70
MS1365 119×78 mm. 200dh. Pres. Gaddafi (vert 32×47 mm)			80	80

301 Handball

1983. Second African Youth Festival. Multicoloured.

1366	100dh. Type **301**		85	45
1367	100dh. Basketball		85	45
1368	100dh. High jumping		85	45
1369	100dh. Running		85	45
1370	100dh. Football		85	45

302 Marching Soldiers

1983. 14th Anniv of September Revolution. Multicoloured

1371	65dh. Type **302**		35	30
1372	75dh. Weapons and communications training		40	35
1373	90dh. Women with machine-guns and bazookas		70	40
1374	100dh. Machine-gun training		75	45
1375	150dh. Bazooka training		1·10	70
1376	250dh. Rifle training		2·00	1·10
MS1377 129×100 mm. 200dh. Pres. Gaddafi and aides at graduation parade (58×35 mm)			1·60	1·60

303 Saluting Scouts

1983. Scout Jamborees. Multicoloured.

1378	50dh. Type **303**		25	20
1379	100dh. Scouts around camp fire		90	45
MS1380 148×92 mm. 100dh.×2 Nos. 1323/4			1·75	1·75

EVENTS: 50dh. Second Islamic Scout Jamboree; 100dh. 15th Pan Arab Scout Jamboree.

304 Traffic Cadets

1983. Traffic Day. Multicoloured.

1381	30dh. Type **304**		40	15
1382	70dh. Traffic policeman		70	30
1383	200dh. Police motorcyclists		1·90	1·25

305 Saadun

1983. 90th Birth Anniv of Saadun (patriot soldier).

1384	**305**	100dh. multicoloured	90	45

306 Walter Wellman's airship "America", 1910

1983. Bicentenary of Manned Flight. Multicoloured

1385	100dh. Type **306**		1·00	55
1386	100dh. Airship "Nulli Secundus", 1907		1·00	55
1387	100dh. Jean-Baptiste Meusnier's balloon design, 1784		1·00	55
1388	100dh. Blanchard and Jeffries' Channel crossing, 1785 (vert)		1·00	55
1389	100dh. Pilatre de Rozier's hydrogen/hot-air balloon flight, 1784 (vert)		1·00	55
1390	100dh. First Montgolfier balloon, 1783 (vert)		1·00	55

307 Globe and Dove

1983. Solidarity with Palestinian People.

1393	**307**	200dh. green, blue & blk	1·60	95

308 Gladiators fighting

1983. Mosaics. Multicoloured.

1394	50dh. Type **308**		50	20
1395	50dh. Gladiators fighting (different)		50	20
1396	50dh. Gladiators and slave		50	20
1397	50dh. Two musicians		50	20
1398	50dh. Three musicians		50	20
1399	50dh. Two gladiators		50	20
1400	50dh. Two Romans and bound victim		50	20
1401	50dh. Leopard and man hunting deer		50	20
1402	50dh. Deer and man with boar		50	20

309 Traditional Architecture

1983. Achievements of the Revolution. Multicoloured.

1403	10dh. Type **309**		10	10
1404	15dh. Camels drinking and mechanization of farming		10	10
1405	20dh. Computer operator and industrial scene		10	10
1406	35dh. Modern architecture		15	10
1407	100dh. Surgeons and nurses treating patients and hospital		90	40
1408	140dh. Airport and airplane		1·25	75
MS1409 118×78 mm. 200dh. Pres. Gaddafi (35×50 mm)			1·75	1·75

THE GREAT MAN-RIVER BUILDER

310 Flooding a River Bed

1983. Colonel Gaddafi—River Builder. Multicoloured.
1410	50dh. Type **310**	20	15
1411	50dh. Irrigation pipe and agricultural produce	20	15
1412	100dh. Colonel Gaddafi, irrigation pipe and farmland (62×44 mm)	1·00	40
1413	100dh. Colonel Gaddafi and map (68×32 mm)	1·00	40
1414	150dh. Colonel Gaddafi explaining irrigation project (35×32 mm)	1·40	65
MS1415	108×66 mm. 300dh. As No. 1413 (70×35 mm) (1984)	2·75	2·75

Nos. 1410/12 were printed together in se-tenant strips of three forming a composite design.

311 Mahmud Burkis

1984. Personalities. Multicoloured.
1416	100dh. Type **311**	1·00	40
1417	100dh. Ahmed el-Bakbak	1·00	40
1418	100dh. Mohamed el-Misurati	1·00	40
1419	100dh. Mahmud Ben Musa	1·00	40
1420	100dh. Abdulhamid el-Sherif	1·00	40
1421	100dh. Mehdi el-Sherif	1·00	40
1422	100dh. Mahmud Mustafa Dreza	1·00	40
1423	100dh. Hosni Fauzi el-Amir	1·00	40
1424	100dh. Ali Haidar el-Saati	1·00	40
1425	200dh. Ahmed el-Feghi Hasan	1·50	80
1426	200dh. Bashir el-Jawab	1·50	80
1427	200dh. Ali el-Gariani	1·50	80
1428	200dh. Muktar Shakshuki	1·50	80
1429	200dh. Abdurrahman el-Busayri	1·50	80
1430	200dh. Ibbrahim Bakir	1·50	80
1431	200dh. Mahmud el-Janzuri	1·50	80

312 Windsurfing

1984. Water Sports. Multicoloured.
1432	25dh. Type **312**	30	10
1433	25dh. Dinghy sailing (orange and red sails)	30	10
1434	25dh. Dinghy sailing (mauve sails)	30	10
1435	25dh. Hang-gliding on water skis	20	10
1436	25dh. Water-skiing	20	10
1437	25dh. Angling from boat	30	10
1438	25dh. Men in speed boat	30	10
1439	25dh. Water-skiing (different)	20	10
1440	25dh. Fishing	30	10
1441	25dh. Canoeing	20	10
1442	25dh. Surfing	20	10
1443	25dh. Water-skiing (different)	20	10
1444	25dh. Scuba diving	30	10
1445	25dh. Diving	30	10
1446	25dh. Swimming in snorkel and flippers	30	10
1447	25dh. Scuba diving for fish	30	10

AFRICAN CHILDREN DAY

313 Col. Gaddafi with Schoolchildren

1984. African Children's Day. Multicoloured.
1448	50dh. Type **313**	50	15
1449	50dh. Colonel Gaddafi and children in national dress	50	15
1450	100dh. Colonel Gaddafi on map and children at various activities (62×43 mm)	1·90	60

314 Women in National, Casual and Military Dress

1984. Libyan Women's Emancipation. Multicoloured.
1451	55dh. Type **314**	50	20
1452	70dh. Women in traditional, casual and military dress (vert)	75	25
1453	100dh. Colonel Gaddafi and women in military dress	95	40

315 Theatre, Sabratha

1984. Roman Ruins of Cyrenaica. Multicoloured.
1454	50dh. Type **315**	20	15
1455	60dh. Temple, Cyrene	50	20
1456	70dh. Monument, Sabratha (vert)	60	25
1457	100dh. Amphitheatre, Leptis Magna	90	40
1458	150dh. Temple, Cyrene (different)	1·40	65
1459	200dh. Basilica, Leptis Magna	1·90	80

316 Silver Dirham, 115h.

1984. Arabic Islamic Coins (1st series).
1460	**316**	200dh. silver, yellow and black	1·90	85
1461	-	200dh. silver, mauve and black	1·90	85
1462	-	200dh. silver, green and black	1·90	85
1463	-	200dh. silver, orange and black	1·90	85
1464	-	200dh. silver, blue and black	1·90	85

DESIGNS: No. 1461, Silver dirham, 93h; 1462, Silver dirham, 121h; 1463, Silver dirham, 49h; 1464, Silver dirham, 135h.
See also Nos. 1643/5.

317 Men at Tea Ceremony

1984. International Trade Fair, Tripoli. Multicoloured
1465	25dh. Type **317**	15	10
1466	35dh. Woman making tea	15	15
1467	45dh. Men taking tea	20	15
1468	55dh. Family taking tea	50	20
1469	75dh. Veiled women pouring tea	70	30
1470	100dh. Robed men taking tea	1·00	40

318 Muktar Shiaker Murabet

1984. Musicians. Multicoloured.
1471	100dh. Type **318**	1·25	65
1472	100dh. El-Aref el-Jamal	1·25	65
1473	100dh. Ali Shiaalia	1·25	65
1474	100dh. Bashir Fehmi	1·25	65

319 Playing among Trees

1984. Children's Day. Designs showing children's paintings. Multicoloured.
1475	20dh. Type **319**	10	10
1476	20dh. A rainy day	10	10
1477	20dh. Weapons of war	10	10
1478	20dh. Playing on the swing	10	10
1479	20dh. Playing in the park	10	10

320 Crest and "39"

1984. 39th Anniv of Arab League.
1480	**320**	30dh. multicoloured	15	15
1481	**320**	40dh. multicoloured	20	15
1482	**320**	50dh. multicoloured	55	20

321 Red Four-seater Car

1984. Motor Cars and Steam Locomotives. Multicoloured
1483	100dh. Type **321**	1·25	65
1484	100dh. Red three-seater car	1·25	65
1485	100dh. Yellow two-seater car with three lamps	1·25	65
1486	100dh. Covered red four-seater car	1·25	65
1487	100dh. Yellow two-seater car with two lamps	1·25	65
1488	100dh. Cream car with spare wheel at side	1·25	65
1489	100dh. Green car with spare wheel at side	1·25	65
1490	100dh. Cream four-seater car with spare wheel at back	1·25	65
1491	100dh. Locomotive pulling wagon and coach	1·40	45
1492	100dh. Purple and blue locomotive	1·40	45
1493	100dh. Cream locomotive	1·40	45
1494	100dh. Lilac and brown locomotive	1·40	45
1495	100dh. Lilac and black locomotive with red wheels	1·40	45
1496	100dh. Cream and red locomotive	1·40	45
1497	100dh. Purple and black locomotive with red wheels	1·40	45
1498	100dh. Green and orange locomotive	1·40	45

322 Stylized People and Campaign Emblem

1984. World Health Day. Anti-Polio Campaign. Multicoloured.
1499	20dh. Type **322**	10	10
1500	30dh. Stylized people and 1981 20dh. stamp	15	15
1501	40dh. Stylized people and Arabic emblem	50	15

323 Man making Slippers

1984. Handicrafts. Multicoloured.
1502	150dh. Type **323**	1·60	65
1503	150dh. Man making decorative harness	1·60	65
1504	150dh. Women forming cotton into skeins	1·60	65
1505	150dh. Woman spinning by hand	1·60	65
1506	150dh. Man weaving	1·60	65
1507	150dh. Women weaving	1·60	65

324 Telephones, Dial and Mail

1984. Postal and Telecommunications Union Congress. Multicoloured.
1508	50dh. Type **324**	50	20
1509	50dh. Woman working at computer console, dial and man working on computer	50	20
1510	100dh. Satellite, map, laurel branches and telephone handset	1·00	40

325 Armed Soldiers and Civilians

1984. Abrogation of 17 May Treaty. Multicoloured.
1511	50dh. Type **325**	65	20
1512	50dh. Map, dove and burning banner	65	20
1513	50dh. Soldiers shaking hands and crowd with banners (30×40 mm)	65	20
1514	100dh. Hands tearing treaty, Gaddafi and crowd (62×40 mm)	1·25	40
1515	100dh. Gaddafi addressing crowd	1·25	40

Nos. 1512/14 were printed together in se-tenant strips of three, forming a composite design.

326 Children behind Barbed Wire

1984. Child Victims of Invasion Day. Multicoloured.
1516	70dh. Torn flags on barbed wire	70	25
1517	100dh. Type **326**	1·00	40

THE PARTY SYSTEM ABORTS DEMOCRACY

327 "The Party System Aborts Democracy"

1984. Quotations from "The Green Book". Multicoloured.
1518	100dh. Type **327**	95	40
1519	100dh. Colonel Gaddafi	95	40
1520	100dh. "Partners not wage-workers"	95	40
1521	100dh. "No representation in lieu of the people. Representation is falsification"	95	40
1522	100dh. The Green Book	95	40
1523	100dh. "Committees everywhere"	95	40
1524	100dh. "Forming parties splits societies"	95	40
1525	100dh. Skyscraper and earthmover	95	40
1526	100dh. "No democracy without popular congresses"	95	40

328 Man in Brown Robes

1984. Costumes. Multicoloured.

1527	100dh. Type **328**	1·25	65
1528	100dh. Woman in green dress and red shawl	1·25	65
1529	100dh. Man in ornate costume and turban	1·25	65
1530	100dh. Man in short trousers and plain shirt	1·25	65
1531	100dh. Woman in shift and trousers with white shawl	1·25	65
1532	100dh. Man in long white robe and red shawl	1·25	65

329 Footballer tackling

1984. World Cup Football Championship. Multicoloured

1533	70dh. Type **329**	70	25
1534	70dh. Footballers in magenta and green shirts	70	25
1535	70dh. Footballers in orange and lemon shirts	70	25
1536	70dh. Goalkeeper failing to save ball	70	25
1537	70dh. Footballers in yellow and brown shirts	70	25
1538	70dh. Top of Trophy and footballer in green striped shirt	70	25
1539	70dh. Top of Trophy and footballers in blue and pink shirts	70	25
1540	70dh. Footballers in black and white striped and green and red striped shirts	70	25
1541	70dh. Footballers in green and red striped shirts	70	25
1542	70dh. Foot of trophy and footballers in orange striped and blue shirts	70	25
1543	70dh. Foot of trophy and goalkeeper	70	25
1544	70dh. Goalkeeper saving headed ball	70	25
1545	70dh. Referee and footballers	70	25
1546	70dh. Footballers in white with red striped sleeves and orange shirts	70	25
1547	70dh. Footballers in white and green striped and orange shirts	70	25
1548	70dh. Footballer in pink shirt	70	25

Nos. 1533/48 were printed in sheetlets of 16 stamps, the backgrounds to the stamps forming an overall design of a stadium.

330 Football

1984. Olympic Games, Los Angeles. Multicoloured

1549	100dh. Type **330**	1·25	65
1550	100dh. Swimming	1·25	65
1551	100dh. Throwing the discus	1·25	65
1552	100dh. Windsurfing	1·25	65
1553	100dh. Basketball	1·25	65
1554	100dh. Running	1·25	65
MS1555	Two sheets each 85×66 mm. (a) 250dh. Show jumping; (b) 250dh. Rider on rearing horse	3·25	3·25

331 Palm Trees

1984. Ninth World Forestry Congress. Multicoloured

1556	100dh. Four types of forest	1·10	40
1557	200dh. Type **331**	2·10	1·10

332 Modern Building

1984. 15th Anniv of Revolution. Multicoloured.

1558	25dh. Type **332**	15	10
1559	25dh. Front of building	15	10
1560	25dh. Building by pool	15	10
1561	25dh. Col. Gaddafi (three-quarter portrait)	15	10
1562	25dh. High-rise block	15	10
1563	25dh. Crane and mosque	15	10
1564	25dh. Motorway interchange	15	10
1565	25dh. House and garden	15	10
1566	25dh. Shepherd and flock	15	10
1567	25dh. Combine harvester	15	10
1568	25dh. Tractors	15	10
1569	25dh. Scientific equipment	15	10
1570	25dh. Col. Gaddafi (full face)	15	10
1571	25dh. Water pipeline	15	10
1572	25dh. Lighthouse	15	10
1573	25dh. Liner at quay	45	10

333 Armed Man

1984. Evacuation of Foreign Forces. Multicoloured (a) As T **333**.

1574	50dh. Type **333**	50	20
1575	50dh. Armed man (different)	50	20
1576	100dh. Men on horseback charging (62×40 mm)	1·00	40

334 Soldier flogging Civilian

(b) As T **334**.

1577	100dh. Type **334**	1·00	40
1578	100dh. Girl on horse charging soldiers	1·00	40
1579	100dh. Mounted soldiers and wounded being tended by women	1·00	40

335 Woman riding Skewbald Showjumper

1984. Equestrian Events. Multicoloured.

1580	25dh. Type **335**	15	10
1581	25dh. Man riding black showjumper (stands in background)	15	10
1582	25dh. Jockey riding chestnut horse (stands in background)	15	10
1583	25dh. Man on chestnut horse jumping in cross-country event	15	10
1584	25dh. Man riding bay horse in showjumping competition	15	10
1585	25dh. Woman on black horse in dressage competition	15	10
1586	25dh. Man on black horse in dressage competition	15	10
1587	25dh. Woman riding chestnut horse in cross-country event	15	10
1588	25dh. Jockey riding bay horse	15	10
1589	25dh. Woman on bay horse in dressage competition	15	10
1590	25dh. Man on grey horse in dressage competition	15	10
1591	25dh. Jockey riding grey steeplechaser	15	10
1592	25dh. Woman riding grey showjumper	15	10
1593	25dh. Woman riding through water in cross-country competition	15	10
1594	25dh. Woman on chestnut horse in cross-country competition	15	10
1595	25dh. Man riding dun showjumper	15	10

Nos. 1580/95 were printed together in sheetlets of 16 stamps, the backgrounds of the stamps forming an overall design of an equestrian ring.

336 Man cleaning Corn

1984. Traditional Agriculture. Multicoloured.

1596	100dh. Type **336**	1·25	65
1597	100dh. Man using oxen to draw water from well	1·25	65
1598	100dh. Man making straw goods	1·25	65
1599	100dh. Shepherd with sheep	1·25	65
1600	100dh. Man treating animal skin	1·25	65
1601	100dh. Man climbing coconut tree	1·25	65

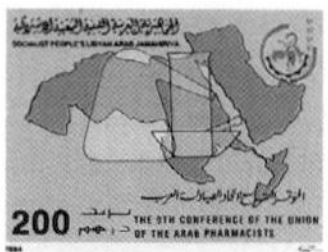

337 Map and Pharmaceutical Equipment

1984. 9th Conference of Arab Pharmacists Union.

1602	**337**	100dh. multicoloured	1·25	40
1603	**337**	200dh. multicoloured	2·50	1·10

338 Crowd with Banner showing Map of North Africa

1984. Arab–African Unity. Multicoloured.

1604	100dh. Type **338**	1·25	65
1605	100dh. Crowd and men holding flags	1·25	65

339 1982 and 1983 Solidarity Stamps and Map of Palestine

1984. Solidarity with Palestinian People.

1606	**339**	100dh. multicoloured	1·25	40
1607	**339**	150dh. multicoloured	1·90	1·00

340 Boeing 747SP, 1975

1984. 40th Anniv of International Civil Aviation Organization. Multicoloured.

1608	70dh. Type **340**	95	30
1609	70dh. Concorde, 1969	95	30
1610	70dh. Lockheed TriStar 500, 1978	95	30
1611	70dh. Airbus Industrie A310, 1982	95	30
1612	70dh. Tupolev Tu-134A, 1962	95	30
1613	70dh. Shorts 360, 1981	95	30
1614	70dh. Boeing 727-100, 1963	95	30
1615	70dh. Sud Aviation Caravelle 10R, 1965	95	30
1616	70dh. Fokker Friendship, 1955	95	30
1617	70dh. Lockheed Constellation, 1946	95	30
1618	70dh. Martin M-130 flying boat, 1955	95	30
1619	70dh. Douglas DC-3, 1936	95	50
1620	70dh. Junkers Ju-52/3m, 1932	95	30
1621	70dh. Lindbergh's "Spirit of St. Louis", 1927	95	30
1622	70dh. De Havilland Moth, 1925	95	30
1623	70dh. Wright Flyer I, 1903	95	30

Nos. 1608/23 were printed together in sheetlets of 16 stamps, the backgrounds of the stamps forming an overall design of a runway.

341 Coin

1984. 20th Anniv of African Development Bank. Multicoloured.

1624	50dh. Type **341**	55	20
1625	70dh. Map of Africa and "20"	1·00	25
1626	100dh. "20" and symbols of industry and agriculture	1·25	65

342 Mother and Son

1985. UNICEF Child Survival Campaign. Multicoloured.

1627	70dh. Type **342**	1·00	50
1628	70dh. Couple and children	1·00	50
1629	70dh. Col. Gaddafi and children	1·00	50
1630	70dh. Boys in uniform	1·00	50

343 Mohamed Hamdi

1985. Musicians and Instruments. Multicoloured.

1631	100dh. Kamel el-Ghadi	1·25	65
1632	100dh. Fiddle rebab	1·25	65
1633	100dh. Ahmed el-Khogia	1·25	65
1634	100dh. Violin	1·25	65
1635	100dh. Mustafa el-Fallah	1·25	65
1636	100dh. Zither	1·25	65
1637	100dh. Type **343**	1·25	65
1638	100dh. Mask	1·25	65

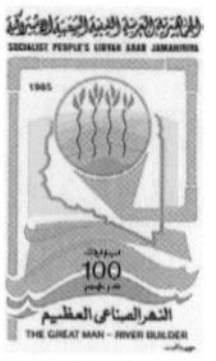

344 Pipeline, River, Plants and Map

1985. Col. Gaddafi—River Builder. Multicoloured.

1639	100dh. Type **344**	1·25	65
1640	100dh. Water droplet, river and flowers	1·25	65
1641	100dh. Dead tree with branch thriving in water droplet	1·25	65
MS1642	117×80 mm. 200dh. Map and droplet (39×39 mm)	2·25	2·25

345 Gold Dinar, 105h.

1985. Arabic Islamic Coins (2nd series). Multicoloured

1643	200dh. Type **345**	2·50	1·25
1644	200dh. Gold dinar, 91h.	2·50	1·25
1645	200dh. Gold dinar, 77h.	2·50	1·25
MS1646	110×80 mm. 300dh. Gold dinar minted in Zuela	3·50	3·50

346 Fish

1985. Fossils. Multicoloured.

1647	150dh. Type **346**	3·00	90
1648	150dh. Frog	1·90	55
1649	150dh. Mammal	1·90	55

347 Gaddafi in Robes and Hat

1985. People's Authority Declaration. Multicoloured

1650	100dh. Type **347**	1·25	65
1651	100dh. Gaddafi in black robe holding book	1·25	65
1652	100dh. Gaddafi in dress uniform without cap	1·25	65
1653	100dh. Gaddafi in black dress uniform with cap	1·25	65
1654	100dh. Gaddafi in white dress uniform	1·25	65

348 Cymbal Player

1985. International Trade Fair, Tripoli. Multicoloured.

1655	100dh. Type **348**	1·25	65
1656	100dh. Piper and drummer	1·25	65
1657	100dh. Drummer and bagpipes player	1·25	65
1658	100dh. Drummer	1·25	65
1659	100dh. Tambour player	1·25	65

349 Goalkeeper catching Ball

1985. Children's Day. Multicoloured.

1660	20dh. Type **349**	10	10
1661	20dh. Child on touchline with ball	10	10
1662	20dh. Letters of alphabet as players	10	10
1663	20dh. Goalkeeper saving ball	10	10
1664	20dh. Player heading ball	10	10

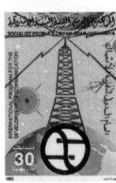

350 Emblem, Radio Transmitter and Satellite

1985. International Communications Development Programme.

1665	**350**	30dh. multicoloured	15	10
1666	**350**	70dh. multicoloured	75	25
1667	**350**	100dh. multicoloured	1·10	65

351 Nurses and Man in Wheelchair

1985. World Health Day. Multicoloured.

1668	40dh. Type **351**	50	10
1669	60dh. Nurses and doctors	75	15
1670	100dh. Nurse and child	1·25	65

352 "Mytilidae"

1985. Sea Shells. Multicoloured.

1671	25dh. Type **352**	40	15
1672	25dh. Purple dye murex ("Muricidae")	40	15
1673	25dh. Tuberculate cockle ("Cardiidae")	40	15
1674	25dh. "Corallophilidae"	40	15
1675	25dh. Trunculus murex ("Muricidae")	40	15
1676	25dh. "Muricacea"	40	15
1677	25dh. "Turridae"	40	15
1678	25dh. Nodose paper nautilus ("Argonautidae")	40	15
1679	25dh. Giant tun ("Tonnidae")	40	15
1680	25dh. Common pelican's-foot ("Aporrhaidae")	40	15
1681	25dh. "Trochidae"	40	15
1682	25dh. "Cancellariidae"	40	15
1683	25dh. "Epitoniidae"	40	15
1684	25dh. "Turbinidae"	40	15
1685	25dh. Zoned mitre ("Mitridae")	40	15
1686	25dh. Cat's-paw scallop ("Pectinidae")	40	15

Nos. 1671/86 were printed se-tenant, the backgrounds forming an overall design of the sea bed.

353 Books and Emblem

1985. International Book Fair, Tripoli.

| 1687 | **353** | 100dh. multicoloured | 1·25 | 60 |
| 1688 | **353** | 200dh. multicoloured | 2·25 | 1·25 |

354 Girls Skipping

1985. International Youth Year. Multicoloured.

1689	20dh. Type **354**	10	10
1690	20dh. Boys playing with stones	10	10
1691	20dh. Girls playing hopscotch	10	10
1692	20dh. Boys playing with sticks	10	10
1693	20dh. Boys playing with spinning top	10	10
MS1694 133×90 mm. 100dh. Footballer; 100dh. Basketball players		95	95

355 Abdussalam Lasmar Mosque

1985. Minarets. Multicoloured.

1695	50dh. Type **355**	50	15
1696	50dh. Zaoviat Kadria Mosque	50	15
1697	50dh. Zaoviat Amura Mosque	50	15
1698	50dh. Gurgi Mosque	50	15
1699	50dh. Mizran Mosque	50	15
1700	50dh. Salem Mosque	50	15
1701	50dh. Ghat Mosque	50	15
1702	50dh. Ahmed Karamanli Mosque	50	15
1703	50dh. Atya Mosque	50	15
1704	50dh. El Kettani Mosque	50	15
1705	50dh. Benghazi Mosque	50	15
1706	50dh. Derna Mosque	50	15
1707	50dh. El Derug Mosque	50	15
1708	50dh. Ben Moussa Mosque	50	15
1709	50dh. Ghadames Mosque	50	15
1710	50dh. Abdulwahab Mosque	50	15

356 Jamila Zemerli

1985. Teachers' Day. Multicoloured.

| 1711 | 100dh. Type **356** | 1·25 | 65 |
| 1712 | 100dh. Hamida El-Anezi | 1·25 | 65 |

357 "Philadelphia" exploding

1985. Battle of the "Philadelphia". Multicoloured.

1713	50dh. Type **357**	60	20
1714	50dh. Men with swords	60	20
1715	100dh. Men fighting and ship's rigging (59×45 mm)	1·25	45

Nos. 1713/15 were printed together, se-tenant, forming a composite design.

358 Gaddafi and Followers

1986. Colonel Gaddafi's Islamic Pilgrimage. Multicoloured.

1716	200dh. Gaddafi writing	2·50	1·25
1717	200dh. Gaddafi praying	2·50	1·25
1718	200dh. Gaddafi, crowds and Kaaba	2·50	1·25
1719	200dh. Gaddafi and mirror	2·50	1·25
1720	200dh. Type **358**	2·50	1·25
MS1721 116×83 mm. 300dh. Koran on stand		3·50	3·50

359 "Leucopaxillus lepistoides"

1985. Mushrooms. Multicoloured.

1722	50dh. Type **359**	1·10	25
1723	50dh. "Amanita caesarea"	1·10	25
1724	50dh. "Coriolus hirsutus"	1·10	25
1725	50dh. "Cortinarius subfulgens"	1·10	25
1726	50dh. "Dermocybe pratensis"	1·10	25
1727	50dh. "Macrolepiota excoriata"	1·10	25
1728	50dh. "Amanita curtipes"	1·10	25
1729	50dh. "Trametes ljubarskyi"	1·10	25
1730	50dh. "Pholiota aurivella"	1·10	25
1731	50dh. "Boletus edulis"	1·10	25
1732	50dh. "Geastrum sessile"	1·10	25
1733	50dh. "Russula sanguinea"	1·10	25
1734	50dh. "Cortinarius herculeus"	1·10	25
1735	50dh. "Pholiota lenta"	1·10	25
1736	50dh. "Amanita rubescens"	1·10	25
1737	50dh. "Seleroderma polyrhizum"	1·10	25

Nos. 1722/37 were printed together, se-tenant, the backgrounds of the stamps forming an overall design of map of Mediterranean.

360 Woman in Purple Striped Dress

1985. Traditional Women's Costumes. Multicoloured.

1738	100dh. Type **360**	1·25	65
1739	100dh. Woman in robes covering her face	1·25	65
1740	100dh. Woman in colourful robes with heavy jewellery	1·25	65
1741	100dh. Woman in long blue striped dress	1·25	65
1742	100dh. Woman in red dress and trousers	1·25	65

361 "In Need Freedom is Latent"

1985. Quotations from "The Green Book".

1743	**361**	100dh. lt green, grn & blk	45	35
1744	-	100dh. multicoloured	45	35
1745	-	100dh. lt green, grn & blk	45	35
1746	-	100dh. lt green, grn & blk	45	35
1747	-	100dh. multicoloured	45	35
1748	-	100dh. lt green, grn & blk	45	35
1749	-	100dh. lt green, grn & blk	45	35
1750	-	100dh. multicoloured	45	35
1751	-	100dh. lt green, grn & blk	45	35

DESIGNS: No. 1744, Gaddafi in uniform reading; 1745, "To make a party you split society"; 1746, "Public sport is for all the masses"; 1747, "Green Books" and doves; 1748, "Wage-workers are a type of slave, however improved their wages may be"; 1749, "People are only harmonious with their own arts and heritages"; 1750, Gaddafi addressing crowd; 1751, "Democracy means popular rule not popular expression".

362 Tree and Citrus Fruits

1985. 16th Anniv of Revolution. Multicoloured.

1752	100dh. Type **362**	1·25	65
1753	100dh. Oil pipeline and tanks	1·25	65
1754	100dh. Capital and olive branch	1·25	65
1755	100dh. Mosque and modern buildings	1·25	65
1756	100dh. Flag and mountains	1·25	65
1757	100dh. Telecommunications	1·25	65
MS1758 100×80 mm. 200dh. Gaddafi		2·40	2·40

363 Zauiet Amoura, Janzour

1985. Mosque Gateways. Multicoloured.

1759	100dh. Type **363**	1·25	65
1760	100dh. Shiaieb El-Ain, Tripoli	1·25	65
1761	100dh. Zauiet Abdussalam El-Asmar, Zliten	1·25	65
1762	100dh. Karamanli, Tripoli	1·25	65
1763	100dh. Gurgi, Tripoli	1·25	65

364 Players in Red
No. 5 and Green
Shirts

1985. Basketball. Multicoloured.
1764	25dh. Type **364**	15	10
1765	25dh. Players in green number 7 and red shirts	15	10
1766	25dh. Players in green number 8 and red shirts	15	10
1767	25dh. Players in red number 6 and green shirts	15	10
1768	25dh. Players in red number 4 and green number 7 shirts	15	10
1769	25dh. Players in green numbers 6 and 5 and red number 9 shirts	15	10
1770	25dh. Basket and one player in red and two in green shirts	15	10
1771	25dh. Players in red number 8 and green number 7 shirts	15	10
1772	25dh. Two players in green shirts and two in red shirts, one number 4	15	10
1773	25dh. Players in red numbers 4 and 7 and green shirts	15	10
1774	25dh. Players in red numbers 4 and 9 and green numbers 7 and 4 shirts	15	10
1775	25dh. Players in red number 6 and green shirts	15	10
1776	25dh. Players in red number 9 and green number 8 shirts	15	10
1777	25dh. Players in red number 8 and green number 5 shirts	15	10
1778	25dh. Players in red number 4 and green shirts	15	10
1779	25dh. Players in red number 5 and green number 10 shirts	15	10

Nos. 1764/79 were printed together *se-tenant*, the backgrounds of the stamps forming an overall design of basketball court and basket.

365 People in Light Ray

1985. Evacuation of Foreign Forces. Multicoloured.
1780	100dh. Man on crutches in web and light shining on tree	1·25	65
1781	100dh. Hands pulling web away from man	1·25	65
1782	100dh. Type **365**	1·25	65

366 Stockbook, Magnifying Glass and Stamps

1985. Stamp Day. "Italia '85" International Stamp Exhibition, Rome. Multicoloured.
1783	50dh. Man and desk on flying stamp above globe	65	15
1784	50dh. Type **366**	65	15
1785	50dh. Stamps escaping from wallet	65	15

367 Players

1985. World Cup Football Championship, Mexico (1st issue). Multicoloured.
1786	100dh. Type **367**	1·25	65
1787	100dh. Players in red and white number 10 and yellow shirts	1·25	65
1788	100dh. Goalkeeper and player defending goal against attack	1·25	65
1789	100dh. Goalkeeper diving to make save	1·25	65
1790	100dh. Goalkeeper jumping to make save	1·25	65
1791	100dh. Player in red and white shirt tackling player in lime shirt	1·25	65
MS1792	70×81 mm. 200dh. Players	2·25	2·25

See also Nos. 1824/MS1830.

368 Hands releasing Dove

1985. Solidarity with Palestinian People.
1793	**368**	100dh. multicoloured	95	35
1794	**368**	150dh. multicoloured	1·60	75

370 Headquarters and Dish Aerial

1986. First Anniv of General Posts and Telecommunications Corporation.
1807	**370**	100dh. multicoloured	1·00	30
1808	**370**	150dh. multicoloured	1·50	75

371 Paper and Quill in Hand

1986. Peoples' Authority Declaration. Multicoloured.
1809	50dh. Type **371**	65	40
1810	50dh. Paper and globe in hand	65	40
1811	100dh. "Green Books" and dove (53×37 mm)	1·25	65

372 Flute

1986. International Trade Fair, Tripoli. Multicoloured.
1812	100dh. Type **372**	1·25	65
1813	100dh. Drums	1·25	65
1814	100dh. Double pipes	1·25	65
1815	100dh. Tambourines	1·25	65
1816	100dh. Drum hung from shoulder	1·25	65

373 Boy Scout with Fish on Hook

1986. Children's Day. Multicoloured.
1817	50dh. Type **373**	1·10	25
1818	50dh. Boy on camel	65	15
1819	50dh. Boy catching butterflies	65	15
1820	50dh. Boy playing drum	65	15
1821	50dh. Boy and giant goalkeeper on football pitch	65	15

374 Emblem, Man and Skull in Blood Droplet

1986. World Health Day. Multicoloured, background colours given.
1822	**374**	250dh. silver	2·50	1·25
1823	**374**	250dh. gold	2·50	1·25

375 Footballers

1986. World Cup Football Championship, Mexico (2nd issue). Multicoloured.
1824	50dh. Type **375**	65	15
1825	50dh. Player jumping over player on ground	65	15
1826	50dh. Referee and players	65	15
1827	50dh. Goalkeeper trying to save ball	65	15
1828	50dh. Player about to tackle	65	15
1829	50dh. Player jumping over ball	65	15
MS1830	Two sheets each 90×90 mm. (a) 200dh. Match scene; (b) 200dh. First Libyan team, 1931	2·25	2·25

376 Peas

1986. Vegetables. Multicoloured.
1831	50dh. Type **376**	45	15
1832	50dh. Marrow	45	15
1833	50dh. Beans	45	15
1834	50dh. Aubergine	45	15
1835	50dh. Corn on the cob	45	15
1836	50dh. Tomato	45	15
1837	50dh. Red pepper	45	15
1838	50dh. Zucchini	45	15
1839	50dh. Garlic	45	15
1840	50dh. Cabbage	45	15
1841	50dh. Cauliflower	45	15
1842	50dh. Celery	45	15
1843	50dh. Onions	45	15
1844	50dh. Carrots	45	15
1845	50dh. Potato	45	15
1846	50dh. Radishes	45	15

Nos. 1831/46 were printed together in sheetlets of 16 stamps, the backgrounds of the stamps forming an overall design of a garden.

377 Health Programmes

1986. Jamahiriya Thought. Multicoloured.
1847	50dh. Type **377**	50	15
1848	50dh. Education programmes	50	15
1849	100dh. "Green Book", agricultural and agriculture scenes and produce (agriculture programmes) (62×41 mm)	1·75	45

378 Gaddafi studying Plan

1986. Colonel Gaddafi, "Great man-made River Builder". Multicoloured.
1850	100dh. Type **378**	95	30
1851	100dh. Gaddafi showing planned route on map	95	30
1852	100dh. Gaddafi and old well	95	30
1853	100dh. Gaddafi in desert	95	30
1854	100dh. Gaddafi and pipe	95	30
1855	100dh. Gaddafi at pumping station	95	30
1856	100dh. Gaddafi and storage tank	95	30
1857	100dh. Workers' hut	95	30
1858	100dh. Water in cupped hands and irrigation equipment	95	30
1859	100dh. Gaddafi turning wheel at opening ceremony	95	30
1860	100dh. Laying pipes	95	30
1861	100dh. Pipe sections on lorries	95	30
1862	100dh. Gaddafi in robes holding "Green Book"	95	30
1863	100dh. Boy giving Gaddafi bowl of fruit	95	30
1864	100dh. Boy drinking from tap	95	30
1865	100dh. Gaddafi praying	95	30

379 Gaddafi with Children

1986. Colonel Gaddafi, "Man of Peace". Multicoloured.
1866	100dh. Type **379**	1·10	30
1867	100dh. Reading book in tent	1·10	30
1868	100dh. With his mother	1·10	30
1869	100dh. Praying in tent with his sons	1·10	30
1870	100dh. Talking to hospital patient	1·10	30
1871	100dh. Driving tractor	1·10	30

380 General Dynamics F-111 Exploding above Man with injured Child

1986. Battle of the U.S.S. "Philadelphia" and American Attack on Libya. Multicoloured. (a) As T 380.
1872	50dh. Type **380**	40	25
1873	50dh. American aircraft carrier and escaping family	60	25
1874	100dh. "Philadelphia" exploding (59×38 mm)	1·25	50

381 Gaddafi, Ruined buildings and Stretcher-bearers

(b) As T 381.
1875	70dh. Type **381**	80	20
1876	70dh. Burning wreckage of car and man and boy in rubble	80	20
1877	70dh. Woman and child by burning ruin	80	20
1878	70dh. Men running from bomb strike	80	20
1879	70dh. Covered body and rescue workers searching ruins	80	20
1880	70dh. Libyans and General Dynamics F-111 airplane tail and wing	80	25
1881	70dh. Libyans waving fists	80	20
1882	70dh. Rescue workers lifting child from rubble	80	20
1883	70dh. Weeping women and soldier carrying baby	80	20
1884	70dh. Libyans and glare of explosion	80	20
1885	70dh. Libyans and General Dynamics F-111 airplane wing and nose	80	25
1886	70dh. Man carrying girl	80	20
1887	70dh. Coffins held aloft by crowd	80	20
1888	70dh. Crowd carrying pictures of Gaddafi	80	20
1889	70dh. Wounded being tended	80	20

| 1890 | 70dh. Hands tending wounded baby | 80 | 20 |

(c) Size 89×32 mm.

| 1891 | 100dh. General Dynamics F-111 bombers, Gaddafi and anti-aircraft rockets | 1·25 | 35 |

Nos. 1872/4 were printed together in *se-tenant* strips of three within the sheet, each strip forming a composite design.

382 "The House must be served by its own Tenant"

1986. Quotations from the "Green Book".

1892	**382**	100dh. lt green, grn & blk	1·00	30
1893	-	100dh. multicoloured	1·00	30
1894	-	100dh. lt green, grn & blk	1·00	30
1895	-	100dh. lt green, grn & blk	1·00	30
1896	-	100dh. multicoloured	1·00	30
1897	-	100dh. lt green, grn & blk	1·00	30
1898	-	100dh. lt green, grn & blk	1·00	30
1899	-	100dh. multicoloured	1·00	30
1900	-	100dh. lt green, grn & blk	1·00	30

DESIGNS: No. 1893, Gaddafi; 1894, "The Child is raised by his mother"; 1895, "Democracy is the Supervision of the People by the People"; 1896, "Green Books"; 1897, "Representation is a Falsification of Democracy"; 1898, "The Recognition of Profit is an Acknowledgement of Exploitation"; 1899, Vase of roses, iris, lilies and jasmine; 1900, "Knowledge is a Natural Right of every Human Being which Nobody has the Right to deprive him of under any Pretext".

383 Map, Chrysanthemum and Health Services

1986. 17th Anniv of Revolution. Multicoloured.

1901	200dh. Type **383**	2·50	95
1902	200dh. Map, sunflower and agriculture programme	2·50	95
1903	200dh. "Sunflowers" (Van Gogh)	2·50	95
1904	200dh. Map, rose and defence programme	2·50	95
1905	200dh. Map, campanula and oil exploration programme	2·50	95

384 Moroccan and Libyan Women

1986. Arab–African Union. Multicoloured.

| 1906 | 250dh. Type **384** | 2·50 | 80 |
| 1907 | 250dh. Libyan and Moroccan horsemen | 2·50 | 80 |

385 Libyan Horseman

1986. Evacuation of Foreign Forces. Multicoloured.

1908	50dh. Type **385**	50	15
1909	100dh. Libyan horsemen trampling Italian soldiers	1·10	30
1910	150dh. Italian soldiers charging	1·50	50

386 Globe and Rose

1986. International Peace Year. Multicoloured, background colours given.

| 1911 | **386** | 200dh. green | 1·90 | 70 |
| 1912 | **386** | 200dh. blue | 1·90 | 70 |

387 Brick "Fists" and Maps within Laurel Wreath

1986. Solidarity with Palestinian People. Multicoloured, background colours given.

| 1913 | **387** | 250dh. blue | 2·50 | 80 |
| 1914 | **387** | 250dh. red | 2·50 | 80 |

388 Drummer

1986. Folk Music. Multicoloured.

1915	70dh. Type **388**	95	20
1916	70dh. Masked stick dancer	95	20
1917	70dh. Woman dancer with pot headdress	95	20
1918	70dh. Bagpipe player	95	20
1919	70dh. Tambour player	95	20

389 Gazelles

1987. Endangered Animals. Sand Gazelle. Multicoloured.

1920	100dh. Type **389**	1·25	30
1921	100dh. Mother and calf	1·25	30
1922	100dh. Gazelle drinking	1·25	30
1923	100dh. Gazelle lying down	1·25	30

390 Oil Derricks and Crowd

1987. People's Authority Declaration. Multicoloured.

1924	500dh. Type **390**	4·00	1·75
1925	500dh. Buildings and crowd	4·00	1·75
1926	1000dh. Gaddafi addressing crowd and globe (40×38 mm)	8·00	3·25

391 Sheep and Shepherd

1987. 18th Anniv of Revolution. Multicoloured.

1927	150dh. Type **391**	1·50	50
1928	150dh. Col. Gaddafi in robes	1·50	50
1929	150dh. Mosque	1·50	50
1930	150dh. Water flowing from irrigation pipe	1·50	50
1931	150dh. Combine harvester	1·50	50
1932	150dh. Col. Gaddafi in army uniform with microphone	1·50	50
1933	150dh. Harvesting crop	1·50	50
1934	150dh. Irrigation	1·50	50
1935	150dh. Soldier with rifle	1·50	50
1936	150dh. Buildings behind Libyan with rifle	1·50	50
1937	150dh. Fountain	1·50	50
1938	150dh. Buildings and beach	1·50	50
1939	150dh. Fort and girls	1·50	50
1940	150dh. Children and hand on rifle butt	1·50	50
1941	150dh. Theatre	1·50	50
1942	150dh. Couple	1·50	50

392 Omar Abed Anabi al Mansusri

1988. Personalities. Multicoloured.

1943	100dh. Type **392**	75	30
1944	200dh. Ahmed Ali al Emrayd	1·50	70
1945	300dh. Khalifa Said Ben Asker	2·50	1·00
1946	400dh. Mohamed Ben Farhat Azawi	3·00	1·10
1947	500dh. Mohamed Souf al Lafi al Marmori	3·75	1·50

393 Gaddafi and Crowd with Raised Fists around Earthmover Bucket

1988. Freedom Festival Day.

1948	**393**	100dh. multicoloured	95	30
1949	**393**	150dh. multicoloured	1·60	75
1950	**393**	250dh. multicoloured	2·50	1·25

394 Woman and Children running

1988. Second Anniv of American Attack on Libya. Multicoloured.

1951	150dh. Type **394**	1·40	50
1952	150dh. Gaddafi playing chess with boy	1·40	50
1953	150dh. Gaddafi and children	1·40	50
1954	150dh. Gaddafi in robes	1·40	50
1955	150dh. Gaddafi and boys praying	1·40	50
1956	150dh. Gaddafi and injured girl	1·40	50
1957	150dh. Gaddafi in robes with children (horiz)	1·40	50
1958	150dh. Gaddafi making speech (horiz)	1·40	50
1959	150dh. Gaddafi and family (horiz)	1·40	50
MS1960	Two sheets (a) 124×89 mm. 500dh. As No. 1954 (35×50 mm); (b) 89×124 mm. 500dh. As No. 1958 (50×35 mm)	7·75	7·75

395 Roses

1988. 19th Anniv of Revolution.

1961	**395**	100dh. multicoloured	75	30
1962	**395**	250dh. multicoloured	2·00	80
1963	**395**	300dh. multicoloured	2·25	1·00
1964	**395**	500dh. multicoloured	4·25	1·50

396 Relay

1988. Olympic Games, Seoul. Multicoloured.

1965	150dh. Type **396**	1·25	50
1966	150dh. Cycling	1·25	50
1967	150dh. Football	1·25	50
1968	150dh. Tennis	1·25	50
1969	150dh. Running	1·25	50
1970	150dh. Showjumping	1·25	50
MS1971	Two sheets (a) 107×84 mm. 100dh. Arab on horse (28×40 mm); 200dh. Woman show jumper; 200dh. Male show jumper. (b) 95×75 mm. 750dh. Football (28×39 mm)	8·25	8·25

397 Dates

1988. The Palm Tree. Multicoloured.

| 1972 | 500dh. Type **397** | 4·25 | 1·50 |
| 1973 | 1000dh. Tree | 8·00 | 3·75 |

398 Petrol Bomb, Sling and Map

1988. Palestinian "Intifada" Movement. Multicoloured

1974	100dh. Type **398**	95	30
1975	200dh. Boy holding stones (45×38 mm)	1·60	70
1976	300dh. Map and flag	2·50	1·00

399 Globe, Declaration and Dove

1989. People's Authority Declaration.

| 1977 | **399** | 260dh. multicoloured | 1·10 | 65 |
| 1978 | **399** | 500dh. multicoloured | 2·00 | 1·25 |

400 Crowd and Green Books

1989. 20th Anniv of Revolution. Multicoloured.

1979	150dh. Type **400**	1·25	40
1980	150dh. Soldiers, Colonel Gaddafi and water pipeline	1·25	40
1981	150dh. Military hardware, Gaddafi in uniform, education, communications and medicine	1·25	40
1982	150dh. Armed horsemen	1·25	40
1983	150dh. U.S.S. "Philadelphia" exploding	1·25	55
MS1984	101×101 mm. 250dh. Gaddafi in Arab robes (35×50 mm)	1·90	1·90

401 Execution Victims, Soldiers and Colonel Gaddafi

1989. 78th Anniv of Deportation of Libyans to Italy. Multicoloured.

1985	100dh. Type **401**	40	25
1986	100dh. Colonel Gaddafi and Libyans	40	25
1987	100dh. Soldiers, deportees and Gaddafi	40	25
1988	100dh. Deportees on jetty and in boats	55	25
1989	100dh. Gaddafi and corpses	40	25
MS1990	140×92 mm. 150dh. Gaddafi and men (67×34 mm)	60	60

402 Demoliton of Wall

1989. "Demolition of Borders".

| 1991 | **402** | 150dh. multicoloured | 1·60 | 1·60 |
| 1992 | **402** | 200dh. multicoloured | 2·10 | 2·10 |

403 Emblem of Committee for supporting "Intifida"

1989. Palestinian "Intifada" Movement. Multicoloured
1993		100dh. Type **403**	1·10	1·10
1994		300dh. Crowd of youths	3·00	3·00
1995		500dh. Emblem (1st anniv of declaration of state of Palestine)	4·75	4·75

404 Circulation Diagram and Annafis

1989. Ibn Annafis (physician) Commemoration.
1996	**404**	100dh. multicoloured	1·25	1·25
1997	**404**	150dh. multicoloured	1·90	1·90

405 Green Books and Fort

1990. People's Authority Declaration.
1998	**405**	300dh. multicoloured	2·75	2·75
1999	**405**	500dh. multicoloured	5·00	5·00

406 Libyan People and Soldier

1990. 20th Anniv of American Forces Evacuation.
2000	**406**	100dh. multicoloured	1·00	1·00
2001	**406**	400dh. multicoloured	4·00	4·00

407 Eagle

1990. 21st Anniv of Revolution.
2002	**407**	100dh. multicoloured	1·00	1·00
2003	**407**	400dh. multicoloured	4·00	4·00
2004	**407**	1000dh. multicoloured	10·50	10·50
MS2005 120×90 mm. 200dh. multi-coloured (enlarged motif as T **407**). Imperf			1·90	1·90

408 Anniversary Emblem

1990. 30th Anniv of Organization of Petroleum Exporting Countries.
2006	**408**	100dh. multicoloured	1·00	1·00
2007	**408**	400dh. multicoloured	4·00	4·00

409 I.L.Y. Emblem and Figures

1990. International Literacy Year.
2008	**409**	100dh. multicoloured	1·10	1·10
2009	**409**	300dh. multicoloured	3·00	3·00

410 Player, Globe and Ball

1990. World Cup Football Championship, Italy.
2010	**410**	100dh. multicoloured	1·00	1·00
2011	**410**	400dh. multicoloured	4·00	4·00
2012	**410**	500dh. multicoloured	5·00	5·00
MS2013 100×80 mm. 500dh. multi-coloured (Trophy, map and mascot) (38×32 mm)			5·00	5·00

411 Hand holding Ears of Wheat

1990. World Food Day. Multicoloured.
2014	**411**	500dh. Type **411**	5·00	5·00
2015		2000dh. Ploughing	20·00	20·00

412 Members' Flags

1991. Second Anniv of Union of Arab Maghreb.
2016	**412**	100dh. multicoloured	1·10	1·10
2017	**412**	300dh. multicoloured	3·00	3·00

413 Flame, Scroll and Koran

1991. People's Authority Declaration.
2018	**413**	300dh. multicoloured	2·75	2·75
2019	**413**	400dh. multicoloured	3·75	3·75

414 Girl and International Year of the Child Emblem

1991. Children's Day. Multicoloured.
2020	**414**	100dh. Type **414**	95	95
2021		400dh. Boy and Day of the African Child emblem	3·75	3·75

415 World Health Organization Emblem

1991. World Health Day. Multicoloured.
2022		100dh. Type **415**	95	95
2023		200dh. As Type **415** but with emblem additionally inscr "WHO OMS"	1·90	1·90

416 Wadi el Hayat

1991. Scenes from Libya. Multicoloured.
2024		100dh. Type **416**	95	95
2025		250dh. Mourzuk (horiz)	2·50	2·50
2026		500dh. Ghadames (horiz)	5·00	5·00

417 Digging Riverbed and laying Pipes

1991. Great Man-made River. Multicoloured.
2027		50dh. Type **417**	25	15
2028		50dh. Col. Gaddafi, agricultural projects and livestock (59×37 mm)	25	15
2029		50dh. Produce	25	15

Nos. 2027/9 were printed together, *se-tenant*, forming a composite design.

418 "22", Roses and Broken Chain

1991. 22nd Anniv of Revolution. Multicoloured.
2030		300dh. Type **418**	2·75	2·75
2031		400dh. "22" within wheat/cogwheel wreath and broken chain	3·75	3·75
MS2032 83×103 mm. Nos. 2030/1			6·50	6·50

419 Emblem and Globe

1991. "Telecom 91" International Telecom-munications Exhibition, Geneva. Multicoloured.
2033		100dh. Type **419**	95	95
2034		500dh. Buldings and dish aerial (horiz)	4·50	4·50

420 Monument and Soldier

1991. 80th Anniv of Deportation of Libyans to Italy. Multicoloured.
2035		100dh. Type **420**	95	95
2036		400dh. Naval transport, Libyans and soldiers	3·75	3·75
MS2037 84×103 mm. Nos. 2035/6			4·75	4·75

421 Map

1991. Arab Unity.
2038	**421**	50dh. multicoloured	20	10
2039	**421**	100dh. multicoloured	40	20

422 Lorry

1991. Paris–Dakar Trans-Sahara Rally. Multicoloured
2040		50dh. Type **422**	20	10
2041		50dh. Blue lorry	20	10
2042		50dh. African Product lorry	20	10
2043		50dh. Tomel lorry	20	10
2044		50dh. All-terrain vehicle No. 173	20	10
2045		50dh. Mitsusuki all-terrain vehicle	20	10
2046		50dh. Michedop all-terrain vehicle	20	10
2047		50dh. All-terrain vehicle No. 401	20	10
2048		50dh. Motor cycle No. 100	20	10
2049		50dh. Rider pushing red motor cycle	20	10
2050		50dh. Rider pushing white motor cycle	20	10
2051		50dh. Motor cycle No. 98	20	10
2052		50dh. Motor cycle No. 101	20	10
2053		50dh. Motor cycle No. 80	20	10
2054		50dh. Motor cycle No. 12	20	10
2055		50dh. Motor cycle No. 45	20	10

423 Gaddafi and Camels

1992. "Gaddafi, Man of Peace 1992". Multicoloured, colour of frame given.
2056	**423**	100dh. green	40	20
2057	**423**	100dh. grey	40	20
2058	**423**	100dh. red	40	20
2059	**423**	100dh. ochre	40	20
MS2060 158×121 mm. 4×150dh. As Nos. 2056/9			1·60	1·60

424 State Arms

1992
2061	**424**	100dh. green, brn & yell	40	20
2062	**424**	150dh. green, brn & grey	60	30
2063	**424**	200dh. green, brown & bl	85	45
2064	**424**	250dh. green, brn & orge	1·10	55
2065	**424**	300dh. green, brn & vio	1·25	65
2066	**424**	400dh. green, brn & mve	1·75	90
2067	**424**	450dh. emerald, brn & grn	1·90	95

425 1991 100dh. Stamp, Tweezers, Magnifying Glass and Stamps

1992. Third Anniv of Union of Arab Maghreb.
2068	**425**	75dh. multicoloured	30	15
2069	**425**	80dh. multicoloured	35	20

426 Horse-drawn Carriage

1992. International Trade Fair, Tripoli. Multicoloured

2070	50dh. Type **426**	20	10
2071	100dh. Horse-drawn cart	40	20

427 Emblem

1992. People's Authority Declaration.

2072	**427**	100dh. multicoloured	40	20
2073	**427**	150dh. multicoloured	60	30

428 Emblem and Camel Rider

1992. African Tourism Year.

2074	**428**	50dh. multicoloured	20	10
2075	**428**	100dh. multicoloured	40	20

429 Big-eyed Tuna

1992. Fish. Multicoloured.

2076	100dh. Type **429**	75	30
2077	100dh. Mackerel scad	75	30
2078	100dh. Little tuna (seven spines on back)	75	30
2079	100dh. Seabream (continuous dorsal fin)	75	30
2080	100dh. Spanish mackerel (four spines on back)	75	30
2081	100dh. Striped red mullet (with whiskers)	75	30

430 Horsewoman with Rifle

1992. Horse Riders. Multicoloured.

2082	100dh. Type **430**	40	20
2083	100dh. Man on rearing white horse	40	20
2084	100dh. Man on brown horse with ornate bridle	40	20
2085	100dh. Roman soldier on brown horse	40	20
2086	100dh. Man in blue coat on brown horse	40	20
2087	100dh. Arab on white horse	40	20
MS2088	110×82 mm. 250dh. Arabs on horses	1·00	1·00

431 Long Jumping

1992. Olympic Games, Barcelona. Multicoloured.

2089	50dh. Type **431**	20	10
2090	50dh. Throwing the discus	20	10
2091	50dh. Tennis	20	10
MS2092	106×82 mm. 100dh. Olympic torch and rings. Imperf	40	40

432 Palm Trees

1992. Achievements of the Revolution. Multicoloured.

2093	100dh. Type **432**	40	20
2094	150dh. Ingots and foundry	60	30
2095	250dh. Container ship	1·10	55
2096	300dh. Airplane	1·25	65
2097	400dh. Assembly hall	1·75	90
2098	500dh. Water pipes and Gaddafi	2·10	1·10

433 Gaddafi

1992. Multicoloured, background colours given.

2099	**433**	500dh. green	2·50	1·10
2100	**433**	1000dh. pink	5·00	2·50
2101	**433**	2000dh. blue	10·00	5·00
2102	**433**	5000dh. violet	25·00	12·50
2103	**433**	6000dh. orange	32·00	16·00

434 Laurel Wreath, Torch and "23"

1992. 23rd Anniv of Revolution.

2104	**434**	59dh. multicoloured	20	10
2105	-	100dh. multicoloured	40	20
MS2106		110×95 mm. 250dh. emerald, gold and black	1·00	1·00

DESIGNS: 100dh. Laurel wreath, flag. Sun and "23". 43×35 mm—250dh. Hawk and "23".

435 Antelope drinking

1992. Oases. Multicoloured.

2107	100dh. Type **435**	40	20
2108	200dh. Sun setting behind camel train (vert)	85	45
2109	300dh. Camel rider	1·25	65

436 Horse and Broken Chain

1992. Evacuation of Foreign Forces. Multicoloured.

2110	75dh. Type **436**	30	15
2111	80dh. Flag and broken chain	35	20

437 Monument and Dates

1992. 81st Anniv of Deportation of Libyans to Italy.

2112	**437**	100dh. multicoloured	40	20
2113	**437**	250dh. multicoloured	1·10	55

438 Dome of the Rock and Palestinian

1992. Palestinian "Intifada" Movement. Multicoloured

2114	100dh. Type **438**	40	20
2115	300dh. Map, Dome of the Rock, flag and fist (vert)	1·25	65

439 Red and White Striped Costume

1992. Women's Costumes. Multicoloured.

2116	50dh. Type **439**	20	10
2117	50dh. Large red hat with silver decorations, white tunic and red wrap	20	10
2118	50dh. Brown and orange striped costume with small gold necklace and horseshoe brooch	20	10
2119	50dh. Purple and white costume	20	10
2120	50dh. Orange striped costume	20	10

440 Mohamed Ali Imsek

1993. Physicians.

2121	**440**	40dh. black, yellow and silver	15	10
2122	-	60dh. black, green and gold	20	15

DESIGN: 60dh. Aref Adhani Arif.

441 Globe, Crops and Spoon-feeding Man

1993. International Nutrition Conference, Rome.

2123	**441**	70dh. multicoloured	35	25
2124	**441**	80dh. multicoloured	40	30

442 Gaddafi, Eagle and Oil Refinery

1993. People's Authority Declaration.

2125	**442**	60dh. multicoloured	20	15
2126	**442**	65dh. multicoloured	25	15
2127	**442**	75dh. multicoloured	25	15

443 Crowd with Tambours

1993. International Trade Fair, Tripoli. Multicoloured

2128	60dh. Type **443**	20	15
2129	60dh. Crowd with camel	20	15
2130	60dh. Dance of veiled men (horiz)	20	15
2131	60dh. Women preparing food (horiz)	20	15
MS2132	100×80 mm. 100dh. Horsemen (38×31 mm)	35	35

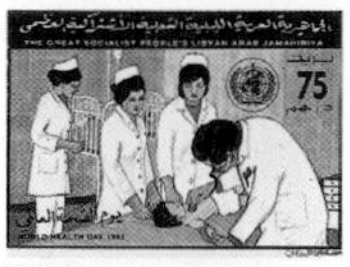

444 Examining Baby

1993. World Health Day. Multicoloured.

2133	75dh. Type **444**	25	15
2134	85dh. Medical staff attending patient	30	20

445 Girl

1993. Children's Day. Multicoloured.

2135	75dh. Type **445**	25	15
2136	75dh. Girl wearing blue and white veil and gold cuff	25	15
2137	75dh. Girl with white fluted collar and silver veil	25	15
2138	75dh. Girl with hands clasped	25	15
2139	75dh. Girl wearing blue scallop-edged veil	25	15

446 Phoenician Ship

1993. Ships. Multicoloured.

2140	50dh. Type **446**	20	15
2141	50dh. Arab galley	20	15
2142	50dh. Pharaonic ship	20	15
2143	50dh. Roman bireme	20	15
2144	50dh. Carvel	20	15
2145	50dh. Yacht (globe showing Italy)	20	15
2146	50dh. Yacht (globe showing Greece)	20	15
2147	50dh. Galeasse	20	15
2148	50dh. Nau	20	15
2149	50dh. Yacht (globe showing left half of Libya)	20	15
2150	50dh. Yacht (globe showing right half of Libya)	20	15
2151	50dh. "Santa Maria"	20	15
2152	50dh. "France" (liner)	20	15
2153	50dh. Schooner	20	15
2154	50dh. Sail/steam warship	20	15
2155	50dh. Modern liner	20	15

Nos. 2140/55 were issued together, *se-tenant*, the centre four stamps forming a composite design.

447 Combine Harvesters

1993. 24th Anniv of Revolution. Multicoloured.

2156	50dh. Type **447**	20	15
2157	50dh. Col. Gaddafi	20	15
2158	50dh. Cattle behind men filling sack with grain	20	15
2159	50dh. Chickens behind shepherd with flock	20	15
2160	50dh. Oil rig	20	15
2161	50dh. Eagle and camel	20	15
2162	50dh. Industrial plant	20	15
2163	50dh. Water pipeline	20	15
2164	50dh. Man harvesting dates	20	15
2165	50dh. Man in field and boxes of produce	20	15
2166	50dh. Pile of produce	20	15
2167	50dh. Man picking courgettes	20	15
2168	50dh. Children reading	20	15
2169	50dh. Typist and laboratory worker	20	15
2170	50dh. Hand-picking crop and ploughing with tractor	20	15
2171	50dh. Tractor towing circular harrow	20	15

Nos. 2156/71 were issued together, *se-tenant*, forming several composite designs.

448 Woman tending Youth

1993. 82nd Anniv of Deportation of Libyans to Italy. Multicoloured.

2172	50dh. Type **448**	20	15
2173	50dh. Soldiers and Libyan family	20	15
2174	50dh. Col. Gaddafi (in turban)	20	15
2175	50dh. Libyans in food queue	20	15
2176	50dh. Man being flogged	20	15
2177	50dh. Horseman charging between soldiers and Libyans	20	15
2178	50dh. Soldier with manacled Libyan before court	20	15
2179	50dh. Libyans gazing at hanged man	20	15
2180	50dh. Crowd of Libyans and two soldiers	20	15
2181	50dh. Soldiers guarding procession of Libyans	20	15
2182	50dh. Soldiers and manacled Libyans on quayside	20	15
2183	50dh. Deportees in boat	20	15
2184	50dh. Col. Gaddafi (bareheaded)	20	15
2185	50dh. Two Libyan families and branch of palm tree	20	15
2186	50dh. Soldiers in disarray (ruins in background)	20	15
2187	50dh. Libyan horsemen	20	15

Nos. 2172/87 were issued together, *se-tenant*, forming several composite designs.

449 Brooch

1994. Silver Jewellery. Multicoloured.

2188	55dh. Type **449**	20	15
2189	55dh. Armlet	20	15
2190	55dh. Pendant	20	15
2191	55dh. Pendants hanging from oblong	20	15
2192	55dh. Necklace	20	15
2193	55dh. Slippers	20	15

450 Gaddafi, Soldiers and Jet Fighters

1994. 25th Anniv of Revolution. Multicoloured.

2194	100dh. Type **450**	35	25
2195	100dh. Libyan tribesmen and Gaddafi in uniform (59×38 mm)	35	25
2196	100dh. Peaceful pursuits and elderly couple	35	25
MS2197	110×94 mm. 1000dh. Col. Gaddafi (39×49 mm)	1·75	1·75

Nos. 2194/6 were issued together, se-tenant, forming a composite design.

451 Player and Trophy

1994. World Cup Football Championship, U.S.A. Multicoloured.

2198	100dh. Type **451**	35	35
2199	100dh. Kicking ball with inside of foot	35	25
2200	100dh. Kicking ball in air	35	25
2201	100dh. Goalkeeper	35	25
2202	100dh. Running with ball	35	25
2203	100dh. Player taking ball on chest	35	25
MS2204	Two sheets (a) 128×86 mm. 500dh. Trophy between two players (41×50 mm); (b) 100×142 mm. 500dh. Ball, emblem, player and "1990" (50×41 mm)	3·50	3·50

452 Gaddafi

1994. 83rd Anniv of Deportation of Libyans to Italy. Multicoloured.

2205	95dh. Type **452**	35	25
2206	95dh. Light plane over rifleman	35	25
2207	95dh. Couple running from biplane	35	25
2208	95dh. Biplane flying over men and boy	35	25
2209	95dh. Man trapped beneath fallen horse	35	25
2210	95dh. Soldiers and Libyans fighting (camel's head and neck in foreground)	35	25
2211	95dh. Soldiers surrounding fallen Libyan	35	25
2212	95dh. Man carrying boy	35	25
2213	95dh. Soldier with whip raised	35	25
2214	95dh. Robed man shouting	35	25
2215	95dh. Tank and battle scene	35	25
2216	95dh. Women fleeing mounted soliers	35	25
2217	95dh. Man being flogged and woman cradling head of fallen Libyan	35	25
2218	95dh. Soldiers and Libyans fighting (camels in background)	35	25
2219	95dh. Women and soldiers on quayside	35	25
2220	95dh. Deportees in two boats	35	25

Nos. 2205/20 were issued together, *se-tenant*, forming several composite designs.

453 Darghut

1994. Mosques. Multicoloured.

2221	70dh. Type **453**	25	15
2222	70dh. Benghazi	25	15
2223	70dh. Kabao	25	15
2224	70dh. Gouzgu	25	15
2225	70dh. Siala	25	15
2226	70dh. El Kettani	25	15

454 Armed Forces

1994. People's Authority Declaration. Multicoloured.

2227	80dh. Type **454**	30	20
2228	80dh. Truck, hand holding Green Book and ears of wheat	30	20
2229	80dh. Pipes on trailers, water pipeline and family	30	20
2230	80dh. Crowd with Green Books	30	20
2231	80dh. Col. Gaddafi	30	20
2232	80dh. Youths and produce	30	20

Nos. 2227/32 were issued together, *se-tenant*, forming a composite design.

455 Sun over Cemetery, National Flag, Dove and Footprints

1994. Evacuation of Foreign Forces.

2233	**455**	65dh. multicoloured	25	15
2234	**455**	95dh. multicoloured	35	20

456 Men with Weapons and Troops in Background

1994. Gaddafi Prize for Human Rights. Multicoloured.

2235	95dh. Type **456**	35	20
2236	95dh. Men with weapons	35	20
2237	95dh. President Nelson Mandela of South Africa	35	20
2238	95dh. President Gaddafi	35	20
2239	95dh. Amerindian meditating	35	20
2240	95dh. Warriors on horseback	35	20
2241	95dh. Amerindian chief	35	20
2242	95dh. Amerindian	35	20
2243	95dh. Riflemen and aircraft	35	20
2244	95dh. Bomber, women, fire and left page of book	35	20
2245	95dh. Right page of book and surgeon operating	35	20
2246	95dh. Surgeons operating	35	20
2247	95dh. Masked revolutionaries with flag	35	20
2248	95dh. Revolutionaries raising arms with flag	35	20
2249	95dh. Young boys with stones	35	20
2250	95dh. Revolutionaries, fire and troops	35	20

Nos. 2235/50 were issued together, *se-tenant*, forming a composite design.

457 Declaration and Flowers

1995. People's Authority Declaration. Multicoloured, colour of background given.

2251	**457**	100dh. yellow	35	20
2252	**457**	100dh. blue	35	20
2253	**457**	100dh. green	35	20

458 Emblem, Members' Flags and Map showing Member Countries

1995. 50th Anniv of Arab League. Multicoloured, frame colour given.

2254	**458**	200f. blue	70	45
2255	**458**	200f. green	70	45
MS2256		147×120 mm. 458 1000dh.×2 as Nos. 2254/5 but with gold decoration	6·75	6·75

459 Messaud Zentuti

1995. 60th Anniv of National Football Team. Designs showing players. Multicoloured.

2257	100dh. Type **459**	35	20
2258	100dh. Salem Shermit	35	20
2259	100dh. Ottoman Marfua	35	20
2260	100dh. Ghaleb Siala	35	20
2261	100dh. Team, 1935	35	20
2262	100dh. Senussi Mresila	35	20

Nos. 2257/62 were issued together, *se-tenant*, forming a composite design.

460 Dromedary

1995. Libyan Zoo. Multicoloured.

2263	100dh. Type **460**	35	20
2264	100dh. Secretary bird	35	20
2265	100dh. African wild dog	35	20
2266	100dh. Oryx	35	20
2267	100dh. Baboon	35	20
2268	100dh. Golden jackal	35	20
2269	100dh. Crowned eagle	35	20
2270	100dh. Desert eagle owl ("Eagle Owl")	35	20
2271	100dh. Desert hedgehog	35	20
2272	100dh. Sand gerbil	35	20
2273	100dh. Addax	35	20
2274	100dh. Fennec fox	35	20
2275	100dh. Lanner falcon	35	20
2276	100dh. Desert wheatear	35	20
2277	100dh. Pin-tailed sandgrouse	35	20
2278	100dh. Jerboa	35	20

Nos. 2263/78 were issued together, *se-tenant*, the backgrounds forming a composite design.

461 Grapefruit

1995. Fruit. Multicoloured.

2279	100dh. Type **461**	35	20
2280	100dh. Wild cherry	35	20
2281	100dh. Mulberry	35	20
2282	100dh. Strawberry	35	20
2283	100dh. Plum	35	20
2284	100dh. Pear	35	20
2285	100dh. Apricot	35	20
2286	100dh. Almond	35	20
2287	100dh. Prickly pear	35	20
2288	100dh. Lemon	35	20
2289	100dh. Peach	35	20
2290	100dh. Dates	35	20
2291	100dh. Olive	35	20
2292	100dh. Orange	35	20
2293	100dh. Fig	35	20
2294	100dh. Grape	35	20

Nos. 2279/94 were issued together, *se-tenant*, the backgrounds forming a composite design.

462 Students

1995. 26th Anniv of Revolution. Multicoloured.

2295	100dh. Type **462**	35	20
2296	100dh. Mosque, teacher and students	35	20
2297	100dh. President Gaddafi	35	20
2298	100dh. Laboratory workers	35	20
2299	100dh. Hospital patient, doctor examining child, and nurse	35	20
2300	100dh. Surgeons operating	35	20
2301	100dh. Cobblers and keyboard operator	35	20
2302	100dh. Sound engineers and musician	35	20
2303	100dh. Crane and apartment block	35	20
2304	100dh. Silos	35	20
2305	100dh. Oil rig platform	35	20
2306	100dh. Airplane and ships	35	20
2307	100dh. Animals grazing and farmer	35	20
2308	100dh. Pipeline	35	20
2309	100dh. Camels at trough and crops	35	20
2310	100dh. Crops and farm vehicle	35	20

Nos. 2295/2310 were issued together, *se-tenant*, forming a composite design.

463 Scout Badge and Wildlife

1995. Scouting. Multicoloured.

2311	250dh. Type **463**		85	55
2312	250dh. Badge, butterflies and scouts with animals (59×39 mm)		85	55
2313	250dh. Badge and scouts		85	55

Nos. 2311/13 were issued together, *se-tenant*, forming a composite design.

464 Warships and Rocket

1995. Ninth Anniv of American Attack on Libya. Multicoloured.

2314	100dh. Type **464**		35	20
2315	100dh. Bombers, helicopters, warships and Libyans (59×49 mm)		35	20
2316	100dh. Bomber and woman holding baby		35	20

Nos. 2314/16 were issued together, *se-tenant*, forming a composite design.

465 Gaddafi on Horseback

1995. International Trade Fair, Tripoli. Multicoloured.

2317	100dh. Type **465**		35	20
2318	100dh. Horseman		35	20
2319	100dh. Horseman (horse galloping to right)		35	20
2320	100dh. Horsemen with whips (horiz)		35	20
2321	100dh. Horseman holding rifle (horiz)		35	20
2322	100dh. Horsewoman brandishing rifle in air (horiz)		35	20
MS2323	140×100 mm. 1000dh. Close-up of horsemen (79×49 mm)		1·75	1·75

466 Dromedary and Woman with Water Jars

1995. City of Ghadames. Multicoloured.

2324	100dh. Type **466**		35	20
2325	100dh. Making cheeses		35	20
2326	100dh. Woman holding jar		35	20
2327	100dh. Feeding chickens		35	20
2328	100dh. Spinning wool		35	20
2329	100dh. Woman in traditional costume		35	20
2330	100dh. Drying grain		35	20
2331	100dh. Milking goat		35	20
2332	100dh. Making shoes		35	20
2333	100dh. Weaving		35	20
2334	100dh. Engraving brass tabletops		35	20
2335	100dh. Harvesting dates		35	20
2336	100dh. Reading scriptures		35	20
2337	100dh. Potter		35	20
2338	100dh. Washing clothes in well		35	20
2339	100dh. Picking fruit		35	20

467 Family with Torch and National Flag

1995. Evacuation of Foreign Forces.

2340	**467**	50dh. multicoloured	20	10
2341	**467**	100dh. multicoloured	35	20
2342	**467**	200dh. multicoloured	70	45

468 Honeycomb and Bees on Flowers

1995. Arab Beekeepers' Association. Multicoloured, colour of border given.

2343	**468**	100dh. mauve	35	20
2344	**468**	100dh. lilac	35	20
2345	**468**	100dh. green	35	20

469 Stubbing out Cigarette and holding Rose

1995. World Health Day. Multicoloured, colour of central band given.

2346	**469**	100dh. yellow	35	20
2347	**469**	100dh. orange	35	20

470 Dr. Mohamed Feituri

1995

2348	**470**	200dh. multicoloured	70	45

471 Gaddafi and Horsemen

1995. 84th Anniv of Deportation of Libyans to Italy. Multicoloured.

2349	100dh. Type **471**		35	20
2350	100dh. Horsemen		35	20
2351	100dh. Battle scene		35	20
2352	100dh. Bomber over battle scene		35	20
2353	100dh. Libyans with rifles		35	20
2354	100dh. Soldiers fighting with Libyans		35	20
2355	100dh. Soldiers with weapons and man on ground		35	20
2356	100dh. Soldiers with rifles and building in background		35	20
2357	100dh. Libyans		35	20
2358	100dh. Soldiers charging men on ground		35	20
2359	100dh. Soldiers shooting at horseman		35	20
2360	100dh. Soldiers pushing Libyan to ground		35	20
2361	100dh. Horsemen charging		35	20
2362	100dh. Horses falling to ground		35	20
2363	100dh. Children		35	20
2364	100dh. Deportees in boats		35	20

Nos. 2349/64 were issued together, *se-tenant*, forming a composite design.

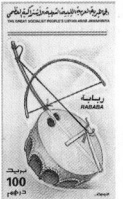

472 Rababa

1995. Musical Instruments. Multicoloured.

2365	100dh. Type **472**		35	20
2366	100dh. Nouba		35	20
2367	100dh. Clarinet		35	20
2368	100dh. Drums		35	20
2369	100dh. Magruna		35	20
2370	100dh. Zukra		35	20
2371	100dh. Zil		35	20
2372	100dh. Kaman		35	20
2373	100dh. Guitar		35	20
2374	100dh. Trumpet		35	20
2375	100dh. Tapla		35	20
2376	100dh. Gonga		35	20
2377	100dh. Saxophone		35	20
2378	100dh. Piano		35	20
2379	100dh. Ganoon		35	20
2380	100dh. Ood		35	20

473 Blue Door

1995. Doors from Mizda. Multicoloured.

2381	100dh. Type **473**		35	20
2382	100dh. Door with arch detail		35	20
2383	100dh. Door made of logs		35	20
2384	100dh. Arched door		35	20
2385	100dh. Wide door with bolts		35	20

474 Sports within Olympic Rings

1995. Centenary of International Olympic Committee. Multicoloured, colour of face value given.

2386	**474**	100dh. black	35	20
2387	**474**	100dh. red	35	20

475 Baryonyx

1995. Prehistoric Animals. Multicoloured.

2388	100dh. Type **475**		35	20
2389	100dh. Oviraptor		35	20
2390	100dh. Stenonychosaurus		35	20
2391	100dh. Tenontosaurus		35	20
2392	100dh. Yangchuanosaurus		35	20
2393	100dh. Stegotetrabelodon (facing right)		35	20
2394	100dh. Stegotetrabelodon (facing left)		35	20
2395	100dh. Psittacosaurus		35	20
2396	100dh. Heterodontosaurus		35	20
2397	100dh. "Loxodonta atlantica"		35	20
2398	100dh. "Mammuthus africanavus"		35	20
2399	100dh. Erlikosaurus		35	20
2400	100dh. Cynognathus		35	20
2401	100dh. Plateosaurus		35	20
2402	100dh. Staurikosaurus		35	20
2403	100dh. Lystrosaurus		35	20

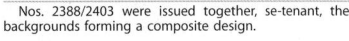

Nos. 2388/2403 were issued together, se-tenant, the backgrounds forming a composite design.

476 Child and Dinosaur walking with Stick

1995. Children's Day. Multicoloured.

2405	100dh. Type **476**		35	20
2406	100dh. Child on mammoth's back		35	20
2407	100dh. Child on way to school and tortoise under mushroom		35	20
2408	100dh. Dinosaur playing football		35	20
2409	100dh. Child pointing rifle at pteranodon		35	20

477 Helicopter, Soldier and Stone-thrower

1995. Palestinian "Intifada" Movement. Mult.

2410	100dh. Type **477**		35	20
2411	100dh. Dome of the Rock and Palestinian with flag		35	20
2412	100dh. Women with flag		35	20

Nos. 2410/12 were issued together, *se-tenant*, forming a composite design.

478 Airplane, Control Tower and Tailfin

1995. 50th Anniv of I.C.A.O. Multicoloured, colour of face value given.

2413	**478**	100dh. blue	35	20
2414	**478**	100dh. black	35	20

479 Headquarters, New York

1995. 50th Anniv of U.N.O. Multicoloured, colour of background given.

2415	**479**	100dh. pink	35	20
2416	**479**	100dh. lilac	35	20

480 "Iris germanica"

1995. Flowers. Multicoloured.

2417	200dh. Type **480**		35	20
2418	200dh. "Canna edulis"		35	20
2419	200dh. "Nerium oleander"		35	20
2420	200dh. Corn poppy ("Papaver rhoeas")		35	20
2421	200dh. Bird of Paradise flower ("Strelitzia reginae")		35	20
2422	200dh. "Amygdalus communis"		35	20

481 Open Hand

1996. People's Authority Declaration. Multicoloured.

2423	**481**	100dh. multicoloured	35	20
2424	**481**	150dh. multicoloured	50	30
2425	**481**	200dh. multicoloured	65	40

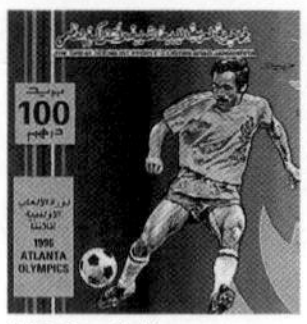

482 Football

1996. Olympic Games, Atlanta, U.S.A. Multicoloured.

2426	100dh. Type **482**	35	20
2427	100dh. Long jumping	35	20
2428	100dh. Tennis	35	20
2429	100dh. Cycling	35	20
2430	100dh. Boxing	35	20
2431	100dh. Equestrian show jumping	35	20
MS2432	Two sheets each 95×78 mm. (a) 500dh. Running; (b) 500dh. Dressage	1·75	1·75

Nos. 2426/31 were issued together, *se-tenant*, the background forming a composite design of the Games emblem.

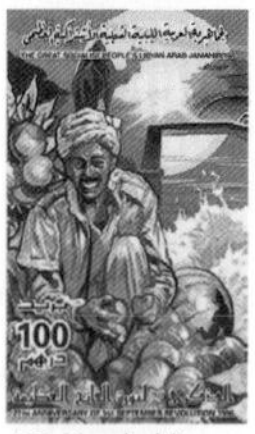

483 Man holding Fruit

1996. 27th Anniv of Revolution. Multicoloured.

2433	100dh. Type **483**	35	20
2434	100dh. Water flowing along chute and out of pipe	35	20
2435	100dh. Tractor, water and women with flowers	35	20
2436	100dh. Man working on pipe by water	35	20
2437	100dh. Man sewing	35	20
2438	100dh. Woman textile worker	35	20
2439	100dh. President Gaddafi in white shirt and red cape	35	20
2440	100dh. Women laboratory workers	35	20
2441	100dh. Anatomy instruction and man using microscope	35	20
2442	100dh. Child holding hand to face	35	20
2443	100dh. Woman praying before open Koran	35	20
2444	100dh. Man weaving	35	20
2445	100dh. Two aircraft	35	20
2446	100dh. Man on camel, liner and dish aerial	35	20
2447	100dh. Stern of liner and television camera	35	20
2448	100dh. Woman using microphone and woman being filmed	35	20

Nos. 2433/48 were issued together, *se-tenant*, forming a composite design.

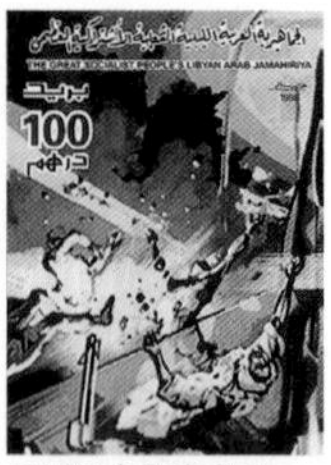

484 Bomb Exploding

1996. Tenth Anniv of American Attack on Libya. Multicoloured.

2449	100dh. Type **484**	35	20
2450	100dh. Man with raised arms	35	20
2451	100dh. Woman carrying child	35	20
2452	100dh. Injured man on ground and fighter plane	35	20
2453	100dh. Fireman hosing down burning car	35	20
2454	100dh. Exploding plane	35	20
2455	100dh. Head of President Gaddafi	35	20
2456	100dh. Airplane bombing tented camp	35	20
2457	100dh. Rescuers helping two women	35	20
2458	100dh. Man with bandaged head and hand	35	20
2459	100dh. Woman with handkerchief to mouth	35	20
2460	100dh. Stretcher bearers	35	20
2461	100dh. Explosion and man being carried away	35	20
2462	100dh. Explosion and man with injured hand	35	20
2463	100dh. Rescuers helping injured mother with baby	35	20
2464	100dh. Burning car and helpers tending injured boy	35	20

Nos. 2449/64 were issued together, *se-tenant*, forming a composite design.

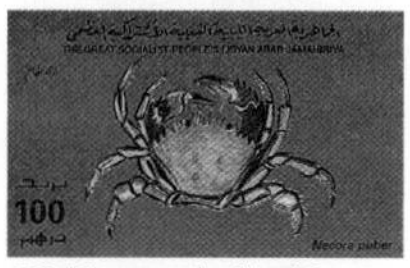

485 "Necora puber" (crab)

1996. Crustaceans. Multicoloured.

2465	100dh. Type **485**	35	20
2466	100dh. "Lissa chiragra" (crab)	35	20
2467	100dh. Rock lobster ("Palinurus elephas")	35	20
2468	100dh. "Scyllarus arctus"	35	20
2469	100dh. Green crab ("Carcinus maenas")	35	20
2470	100dh. Helmet crab ("Calappa granulata")	35	20
2471	100dh. "Parapenaeus longirostris" (prawn)	35	20
2472	100dh. Norway lobster ("Nephrops norvegicus")	35	20
2473	100dh. "Eriphia verrucosa" (crab)	35	20
2474	100dh. Edible crab ("Cancer pagurus")	35	20
2475	100dh. "Penaeus kerathurus" (prawn)	35	20
2476	100dh. Mantis shrimp ("Squilla mantis")	35	20
2477	100dh. Spider crab ("Maja squinado")	35	20
2478	100dh. "Pilumnus hirtellus" (crab)	35	20
2479	100dh. "Pagurus alatus" (crab)	35	20
2480	100dh. "Macropodia tenuirostris"	35	20

Nos. 2465/80 were issued together, *se-tenant*, the backgrounds forming a composite design.

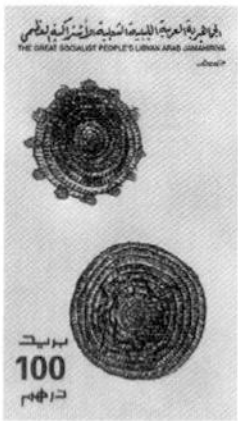

486 Mats

1996. Maghreb Handicrafts Day. Basketwork. Multicoloured.

2481	100dh. Type **486**	35	20
2482	100dh. Lidded storage vessel	35	20
2483	100dh. Bowl	35	20
2484	100dh. Mug and teapot	35	20
2485	100dh. Box with open lid	35	20
2486	100dh. Bird's-eye view of dish	35	20
2487	100dh. Pot with wide base and mouth and narrower neck	35	20
2488	100dh. Lidded pot with carrying handle	35	20
2489	100dh. Bulbous bottle-shaped carrier	35	20
2490	100dh. Large dish	35	20
2491	100dh. Oval dish with well in centre	35	20
2492	100dh. Straight-sided bottle-shaped carrier	35	20
2493	100dh. Vessel with double carrying handles and open lid	35	20
2494	100dh. Dish on stand	35	20
2495	100dh. Pot with wide base and narrow mouth	35	20
2496	100dh. Bag with lid	35	20

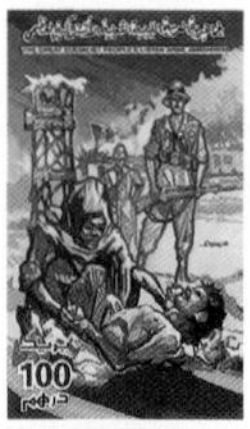

487 Woman kneeling over Boy

1996. 85th Anniv of Deportation of Libyans to Italy. Multicoloured.

2497	100dh. Type **487**	35	20
2498	100dh. Horseman leading prisoner	35	20
2499	100dh. President Gaddafi wearing turban	35	20
2500	100dh. Old man holding stick in camp	35	20
2501	100dh. Man being flogged	35	20
2502	100dh. Horseman, soldiers and crowd wearing fezzes	35	20
2503	100dh. Prisoner, advocate and man in tricolour sash	35	20
2504	100dh. Family and soldier	35	20
2505	100dh. Soldiers guarding prisoners (boy at front)	35	20
2506	100dh. Soldiers escorting woman on camel and man on donkey	35	20
2507	100dh. Prisoners being escorted through street	35	20
2508	100dh. Prisoners in boat	35	20
2509	100dh. President Gaddafi in white embroided shirt with open hand	35	20
2510	100dh. Group of prisoners including man with raised arm	35	20
2511	100dh. Horsemen charging and soldiers	35	20
2512	100dh. Horseman with rifle	35	20

Nos. 2497/2512 were issued together, *se-tenant*, forming several composite designs.

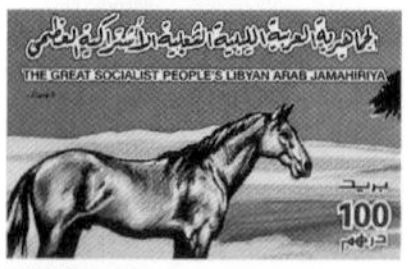

488 Bay

1996. Horses. Multicoloured.

2513	100dh. Type **488**	35	20
2514	100dh. Light brown horse under tree (branches at right of stamp)	35	20
2515	100dh. Light brown horse by lake under tree (branch at left)	35	20
2516	100dh. Dark brown horse (edge of lake at left)	35	20
2517	100dh. Black horse with hoof raised	35	20
2518	100dh. Chestnut horse	35	20
2519	100dh. Grey horse running	35	20
2520	100dh. Piebald	35	20
2521	100dh. Head of grey and tail of black horses	35	20
2522	100dh. Head of black and tail of chestnut horses	35	20
2523	100dh. Head and rump of chestnut horses	35	20
2524	100dh. Head of chestnut horse with white mane	35	20
2525	100dh. Head of black horse and parts of three other horses	35	20
2526	100dh. Head of chestnut horse with blond mane and parts of three other horses	35	20
2527	100dh. Head of dark brown horse and parts of three other horses	35	20
2528	100dh. Head of dark brown and part of chestnut horses	35	20

Nos. 2513/28 were issued together, *se-tenant*, forming a composite design.

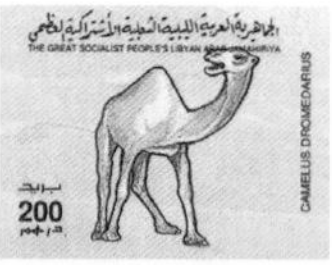

489 Camel

1996. Camels. Multicoloured.

2529	200dh. Type **489**	65	40
2530	200dh. Head of camel	65	40
2531	200dh. Dark brown dromedary	65	40
2532	200dh. Long-haired Bactrian camel	65	40
2533	200dh. Light brown Bactrian camel	65	40
2534	200dh. Brown Bactrian camel with white stripe and tail	65	40

Nos. 2529/34 were issued together, *se-tenant*, forming a composite design.

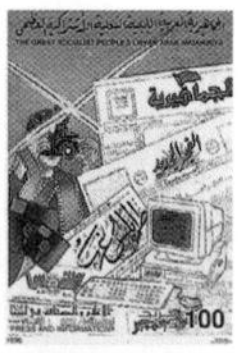

490 Photographer, Newspapers and Computer

1996. The Press and Information. Multicoloured.

2535	100dh. Type **490**	35	20
2536	200dh. Television, control desk, musicians, computer and dish aerial	65	40

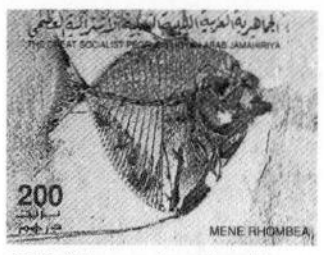

491 "Mene rhombea"

1996. Fossils. Multicoloured.

2537	200dh. Type **491**	65	40
2538	200dh. "Mesodon macrocephalus"	65	40
2539	200dh. "Eyron arctiformis"	65	40
2540	200dh. Stegosaurus	65	40
2541	200dh. Pteranodon	65	40
2542	200dh. Allosaurus	65	40

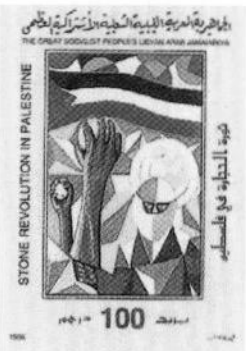

492 Palestinian Flag and Hands holding up Stones

1996. Palestinian "Intifada" Movement.

2543	**492**	100dh. multicoloured	35	20
2544	**492**	150dh. multicoloured	50	30
2545	**492**	200dh. multicoloured	65	40

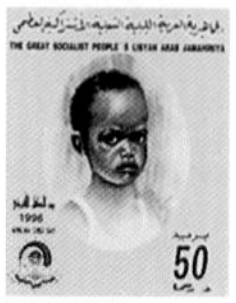

493 Child

1996. African Child Day. Multicoloured.

2546	50dh. Type **493**	10	10
2547	150dh. Type **493**	40	25
2548	200dh. Mother and child	50	35

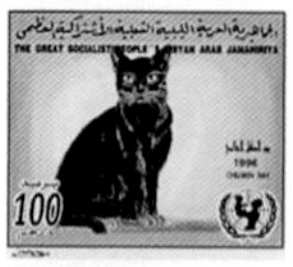

494 Cat

1996. Children's Day. Cats. Multicoloured.

2549	100dh. Type **494**	25	15
2550	100dh. Tabby (back view with head turned)	25	15
2551	100dh. Colourpoint (black and white)	25	15
2552	100dh. Tabby adult and kitten	25	15
2553	100dh. Tortoiseshell white (sitting)	25	15

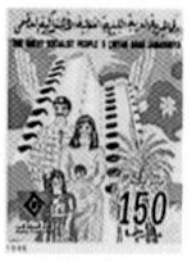

495 Family and Tower Block

1996. World Family Day. Multicoloured.

2554	150dh. Type **495**	40	25
2555	150dh. Family and car parked by palm trees	40	25
2556	200dh. Family, symbolic globe and flowers (45×26 mm)	50	35

Nos. 2554/6 were issued together, *se-tenant*, forming a composite design.

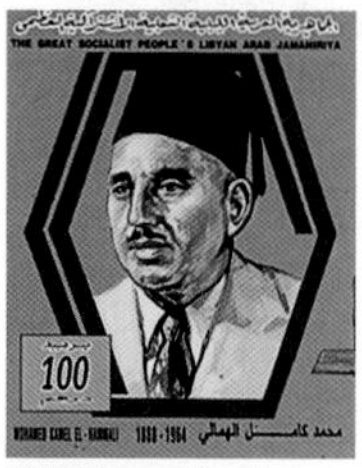

496 Mohamed Kamel el-Hammali

1996. Libyan Teachers. Multicoloured.

2557	100dh. Type **496**	25	15
2558	100dh. Mustafa Abdalla ben-Amer	25	15
2559	100dh. Mohamed Messaud Fesheka	25	15
2560	100dh. Kairi Mustafa Serraj	25	15

2561		100dh. Muftah el-Majri	25	15
2562		100dh. Mohamed Hadi Arafa	25	15

497 Mohamed Salim

1996. Libyan Singers. Multicoloured.

2563		100dh. Type **497**	25	15
2564		100dh. Mohamed M. Sayed Bumedyen	25	15
2565		100dh. Otman Najim	25	15
2566		100dh. Mahmud Sherif	25	15
2567		100dh. Mohamed Ferjani Marghani	25	15
2568		100dh. Mohamed Kabazi	25	15

498 Snake

1996. Reptiles. Multicoloured.

2569		100dh. Type **498**	25	15
2570		100dh. Diamond-back snake beside river	25	15
2571		100dh. Turtle on water (segmented shell and large flippers)	25	15
2572		100dh. Snake wrapped around tree branch	25	15
2573		100dh. Brown lizard on tree trunk	25	15
2574		100dh. Coiled snake with head raised and mouth open	25	15
2575		100dh. Snake with head raised beside water	25	15
2576		100dh. Turtle on water (flat shell, pointed snout and small flippers)	25	15
2577		100dh. Green lizard on tree trunk	25	15
2578		100dh. Snake with wavy pattern on ground	25	15
2579		100dh. Snake with horns	25	15
2580		100dh. Chameleon	25	15
2581		100dh. Tortoise on ground (facing right)	25	15
2582		100dh. Snake on rock with head raised	25	15
2583		100dh. Tortoise on ground (facing left)	25	15
2584		100dh. Grey lizard on rock	25	15

Nos. 2569/84 were issued together, *se-tenant*, forming a composite design.

499 Mirror and Clothes Brush

1996. International Trade Fair, Tripoli. Each silver, pink and black.

2585		100dh. Type **499**	25	15
2586		100dh. Decanter on tray	25	15
2587		100dh. Two round-bottomed flasks	25	15
2588		100dh. Two long-necked flasks	25	15
2589		100dh. Covered bowl	25	15
2590		100dh. Backs of hairbrush and mirror	25	15

500 Gaddafi and Symbolic Scenes

1997. People's Authority Declaration.

2591	**500**	100dh. multicoloured	25	15
2592	**500**	200dh. multicoloured	25	15
2593	**500**	300dh. multicoloured	25	15

501 Scouts and Stamp Album

1997. Postal Savings Bank. Multicoloured.

2594		50dh. Type **501**	10	10
2595		50dh. Two Girl Guides and albums	10	10
2596		100dh. Bank books and butterflies	25	15

Nos. 2594/6 were issued together, *se-tenant*, forming a composite design.

502 Scientist with Test Tubes

1997. World Health Day. Multicoloured.

2597		50dh. Type **502**	10	10
2598		50dh. Scientist at microscope	10	10
2599		100dh. Doctor and nurse examining baby	25	15

Nos. 2597/9 were issued together, *se-tenant*, forming a composite design.

503 Death enveloping Man's Head

1997. Anti-drugs Campaign.

2600	**503**	100dh. multicoloured	25	15
2601	**503**	150dh. multicoloured	40	25
2602	**503**	200dh. multicoloured	50	35

504 Library

1997. Arab National Central Library.

2603	**504**	100dh. multicoloured	25	15
2604	**504**	200dh. multicoloured	50	35
MS2605		168×118 mm. 100dh. Gaddafi, books, computer and library (105×48 mm)	30	30

505 Dancer and Local Crafts

1997. Arab Tourism Year.

2606	**505**	100dh. multicoloured	25	15
2607	**505**	200dh. multicoloured	50	25
2608	**505**	250dh. multicoloured	65	45

506 Mother and Child

1997. 28th Anniv of Revolution. Designs showing scenes from the life of Muammar al Qadhafi. Multicoloured.

2609–2621		100dh.×13, Type **506**; Student; Speaking at microphone; Tank and crew; Wearing uniform; With raised fist; Mother, child and book; With elderly couple; Writing; With child; Fly past; Wearing uniform with gold braid; 500d. Horseman (57×85 mm)		
		MS2622 125×87 mm. 500dh. Wearing brown robe (horiz)	10·50	10·50

Nos. 2609/21 and the stamps and margin of **MS**2622, respectively, each form composite designs.

507 Silverwork

1997. International Trade Fair, Tripoli. Multicoloured

2623–2628		500dh.×6, Type **507**; Circular brooch; Necklace and square pendant; Book shaped clasp; Necklace; Band	17·00	17·00

Nos. 2623/8 were issued together, *se-tenant*, with the background forming a composite design.

508 Ship and Crowd

1997. Evacuation of Foreign Troops.

2629	**508**	100dh. multicoloured	25	15
2630	**508**	150dh. multicoloured	40	25
2631	**508**	250dh. multicoloured	60	40

509 Slippers

1997. Maghreb Handicrafts Day. Multicoloured.

2632–2637		300dh.×6, Type **509**; Orange embroidered slippers with beads and tassels; Green and red leather slippers; Slippers with circular design on toes; Thong sandals; Red embroidered slippers with squared design	10·50	10·50

Nos. 2632/7 were issued together, *se-tenant*, with the background forming a composite design.

510 Woman carrying Pot

1997. 86th Anniv of Deportation of Libyans to Italy. Multicoloured.

2638–2653		200dh.×16, Type **510**; Muammar al Qadhafi; Mounted soldier; Soldier and couple; Flogging; Horseman; Leaders; Soldier and crowd; Woman with bowed head; Elderly man; Muammar al Qadhafi (different); Boats; Towers and hand; Horsemen; Horsemen (different); Horsemen and hand	16·00	16·00

Nos. 2638/53 were issued together, *se-tenant*, with the background forming a composite design.

511 Carrying Bird

1997. Endangered Species. *Felis lybica* (Asiatic desert cat) (2654/7) or Gazelles and Goat (MS2658).

2654		200dh. Type **511**	1·20	90
2655		200dh. Mother and cubs	1·20	90
2656		200dh. One cat seated	1·20	90
2657		200dh. Two cats	1·25	90
MS2658		147×81 mm. Size 36×42 mm. 100dh.×3, Gazelle; Goat; Gazelle (different)	9·00	9·00

512 Explosion

1997. 11th Anniv of American Attack on Libya. Multicoloured.

2659–2670		200dh.×16, Type **512**; Green book and aircraft; Towers and hand; Muammar al Qadhafi; Aircraft wing; Aircraft nose; Two aircraft; Aircraft tail and two men; Aircraft and missiles colliding; Qadhafi's left arm; Muammar al Qadhafi; Qadhafi's right arm; Missiles and crowd; Injured woman in bed; Qadhafi kissing girl's hand; Raised fists	22·00	22·00

Nos. 2659/70 were issued together, *se-tenant*, forming a composite design.

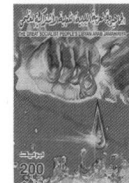

513 Hand and Droplet

1997. Man-made River (1st issue). Designs showing work on the pipeline and Muammar al Qadhafi. Multicoloured.

2671–2686		200dh.×16, Type **513**; Muammar al Qadhafi; Workmen looking at plans; Qadhafi on podium; Qadhafi facing right; Cranes; Pipes and Qadhafi; Qadhafi facing left; Looking at plans; Workman and wellhead; Pipeline and Qadhafi; Lorries carrying pipes; Turning valve; Qadhafi with clasped hands; Water falling from tap into hands; Qadhafi receiving bouquet	22·00	22·00

Nos. 2671/86 were issued together, *se-tenant*, forming a composite design. See also Nos. 2735/**MS**2737 and 2738/53.

514 Crowd and People's Authority Declaration

1998. People's Authority Declaration.

2687	**514**	150dh. multicoloured	1·40	90
2688	**514**	250dh. multicoloured	2·50	1·60
2689	**514**	300dh. multicoloured	2·75	1·80

515 Jar

1998. International Trade Fair, Tripoli. Multicoloured
2690- 400dh.×6, Type **515**; Stand;
2695 Vase; Lidded bowl on tray;
Lidded bowl on pedestal;
Egg-shaped container on
tripod 14·00 14·00

Nos. 2690/5 were issued together, *se-tenant* with the background forming a composite design.

516 Girl

1998. Children's Day (1st issue). Multicoloured.
2696 100dh. Type **516** 75 50
2697 100dh. Girl with arms by sides 75 50
2698 100dh. Girl with blue beaded headdress 75 50
2699 100dh. Girl facing right 75 50
2700 100dh. Girl with striped beaded headdress 75 50

See also Nos. 2754/9.

517 Emblem

1998. World Health Day.
2701 **517** 150dh. multicoloured 1·10 70
2702 **517** 250dh. multicoloured 1·80 1·20
2703 **517** 300dh. multicoloured 2·20 1·40

518 Ship, Aircraft and Crowd

1998. 12th Anniv of American Attack on Libya. Multicoloured.
2704- 100dh.×3, Type **518**; Muammar
2706 al Qadhafi (60×51 mm);
Aircraft, ship, man and boy 2·20 2·20

Nos. 2704/6 were issued together, *se-tenant*, forming a composite design.

519 Eye

1998. 35th Anniv of National Blind Association. Multicoloured.
2707 100dh. Type **519** 1·20 80
2708 250dh. Person with white cane, guitar and books 1·90

520 Bee and Clasped Hands

1998. Beekeeping.
2709 **520** 250dh. multicoloured 2·20 1·40
2710 **520** 300dh. multicoloured 3·00 2·00
2711 **520** 400dh. multicoloured 3·50 2·60

521 Footballer

1998. World Cup Football Championships, France. Multicoloured.
2712- 200dh.×6, Type **521**; Player
2717 preparing to kick ball; Player
kicking with leftt leg raised;
Player dribbling ball; Player
kicking with left leg; Player
racing towards ball 8·00 8·00

MS2718 Two sheets, each 145×104 mm. Size 42×51 mm. (a) 1000dh. Player with ball by right shoulder. (b) 1000dh. Ball passing player at head height Set of 2 sheets 8·00 8·00

522 Elderly Man and Child

1998. World Book Day. Multicoloured.
2719- 100dh.×16, Type **522**; Athletes;
2734 Teacher at blackboard;
Harvesting crops; Machine
workshop; News reader;
Child and teacher holding
compasses; Student using
microscope; Horseman and
girl student; Female teacher
and student; Music lesson;
Sewing machinist; Chemistry
lesson; Typist; Bread making;
Computer and users 11·00 11·00

523 Map of Pipeline

1998. Man-made River (2nd issue).
2735 **523** 300dh. multicoloured 2·30 1·50
2736 **523** 400dh. multicoloured 3·00 2·00
MS2737 90×115 mm. **523** 2000dh. multicoloured 14·00 14·00

524 Garlic

1998. Man-made River (3rd issue). Vegetables. Multicoloured.
2738- 100dh.×16, Type **524**; Broad
2753 beans; Potatoes; Maize;
Leeks; Tomatoes; Carrots
Beetroots; String beans; Pep-
pers; Aubergines; Cabbages;
Marrow; Squash; Onions;
Cauliflowers 13·00 13·00

Nos. 2738/53 were issued together, *se-tenant* with the background forming a composite design.

525 Girl Scout and Deer

1998. Children's Day (2nd issue). Scouts. Multicoloured.
2754- 400dh.×6, Type **525**; Emblem
2759 and scouts; Boy, tent, girl
and flag; Palm trees, ewe
and lamb; Scouts playing
music; Tent and campfire 25·00 25·00

Nos. 2754/9 were issued together, *se-tenant*, forming a composite design.

526 Muammar al Qadhafi

1998. 29th Anniv of Revolution. Multicoloured.
2760- 200dh.×16, Type **526**; Horse-
2775 man; Eagle; Eagle's wing
and minaret; Surgeon and
student; Left page of Koran;
Right page ; Mosque; Men
with raised arms and docks;
Ship; High rise building;
Youth; Left of building; Pool
and centre left of building;
Pool and centre right of
building; Right of building 21·00 21·00
MS2776 96×127 mm. 200dh. Muammar al Qadhafi (38×51 mm) 1·40 1·40

Nos. 2760/75, and the stamps and margin of **MS**2776, respectively, each form composite designs.

527 Troops, Ship and Flag

1998. Evacuation of Foreign Troops.
2777 **527** 100dh. multicoloured 75 50
2778 **527** 150dh. multicoloured 1·10 70
2779 **527** 200dh. Multicoloured 1·40 90

528 Stamps

1998. Stamp Day.
2780 **528** 300dh. multicoloured 2·75 1·80
2781 **528** 400dh. multicoloured 3·75 2·50

529 Ship and Trucks

1998. 87th Anniv of Deportation of Libyans to Italy. Multicoloured.
2782- 150dh.×16, Type **529**; Girl with
2797 bound arms; Older man;
Soldiers; Aircraft attacking;
Deportees; Soldier leading
child; Soldiers with raised
weapons and laden camel;
Water being given; Soldier
in boat prow; Boats; Boats
(different); Man carrying
woman; Horsemen; Horse-
man; Mother and baby 16·00 16·00

Nos. 2782/97 were issued together, *se-tenant*, forming a composite design.

530 White Mosque

1998. Libya and Islam. Multicoloured.
2798- 100dh.×8, Type **530**; Mosque
2807 with pink dome; Modern
mosque; Tower; Tower and
mosque; Entrance to deco-
rated mosque; Aerial view of
mosque; Mosque surrounded
by trees; 500dh.×2, Koran
and Mecca (57×85 mm);
Horseman (57×85 mm) 12·50 12·50

531 Scout and Wheelchair User

1998. Scouting and Disabilities. Multicoloured.
2808- 100dh.×16, Type **531**; Scouts;
2823 Scout and wheelchair user
photographers; Wheelchair
user and flags; Sawing wood;
Campfire; Cooking; Two
scouts painting; Wheelchair
football; Wheelchair
basketball; Amputees racing;
Wheelchair table tennis;
Wheelchair hockey; Wheel-
chair user with raised arm;
Amputee cycling; Amputee
throwing javelin 16·00 16·00

Nos. 2808/23 were issued together, *se-tenant*, with background forming a composite design.

533 "30" and Gazelles

1999. 30th Anniv of Revolution. Multicoloured.
2827- 100dh.×12, Type **533**; Mosque;
2839 Musician; Camel riders;
Combine harvester; Ship;
Ship and horse riders ;
Horse riders; Water pipe;
Shepherd; Waterside tower;
Dates; 200dh. Horseman
(57×85 mm) 7·00 7·00
MS2840 130×100 mm. 200dh. Muam-
mar al Qadhafi (38×51 mm) 1·20 1·20

Nos. 2827/39 were issued together, *se-tenant*, forming a composite design.

535 Flags and Tower

1999. Evacuation of Foreign Troops.
2848 **535** 150dh. multicoloured 1·20 80
2849 **535** 250dh. multicoloured 1·80 1·20
2850 **535** 300dh. multicoloured 2·20 1·40

536 Muammar al Qadhafi

2000. People's Authority Declaration. Mult.
2851- 100dh.×3, Type **536**; Family;
2853 Aircraft, high rise building
and satellite dish 1·50 1·50
2854- 100dh.×3, Gazelle and woman
2856 weaving; Water pipeline and
tap; Couple picking oranges 1·50 1·50
MS2857 Two sheets, each 110×72 mm.
Size 38×51 mm. (a) 300dh. Muammar al Qadhafi. (b) 300dh. Qadhafi
with raised fist 3·00 3·00

Nos. 2851/3 and 2854/6 were issued together, *se-ten-ant*, forming a composite design.

537 Camel Rider

2000. 31st Anniv of Revolution. Multicoloured.
2858- 100dh.×16, Type **537**; Couple
2873   seated and camels; Muam-
       mar al Qadhafi; Demonstra-
       tors; Welder; Student;
       Classroom; Chemist; Mother
       and child; Lecture; Palm tree
       and boy; Scanner; Mosque
       interior; Earth mover and
       high rise building; Refinery
       workers; Earth mover and
       dates   7·75   7·75
MS2874 Two sheets, each 120×90 mm.
   Size 38×51 mm. (a) 300dh. Muammar al Qadhafi. (b) 300dh. Muammar
   al Qadhafi and boy   2·50   2·50
   Nos. 2858/73 were issued together, se-tenant, with the
background forming a composite design.

538 Radio Operator

2000. Day of the Martyr. Multicoloured.
2875- 200dh.×6, Type **538**; Desert
2880   horsemen; Soldiers; Soldiers
       on foot and desert horse-
       men; Horseman with raised
       arm; Muammar al Qadhafi   5·50   5·50
MS2881 150×110 mm. 300dh. Reading
   Koran   1·50   1·50
   Nos. 2875/80 were issued together, se-tenant, forming
a composite design.

539 A. Castellano

2000. Espana 2000 International Stamp Exhibition. Sheet
   125×90 mm containing T **539** and similar vert
   design. Multicoloured. Imperf.
MS2882 250dh.×2, Type **539**; M. B.
   Karamanli   2·50   2·50

540 Muammar al
Qadhafi and
Symbols of Libya

2001. People's Authority Declaration.
2883 **540** 150dh. multicoloured   80   50
2884 **540** 200dh. multicoloured 1·10 70

541 Leaders

2001. Fifth Extraordinary Session of OAU Assembly of
   Heads of States and Governments. Multicoloured.
2885- 200dh.×6, Type **541**; Horsemen;
2890   Camel riders; Women danc-
       ing; Celebrations; Muammar
       al Qadhafi   5·50   5·50
MS2891 Two sheets, each 112×152
   mm. Size 42×51 mm. (a) 500dh.
   Muammar al Qadhafi (b) 500dh. Set
   of 2 sheets   5·00   5·00
   Nos. 2885/90 were issed together, froming a
composite design.

542 Saddle

2001. International Trade Fair, Tripoli. Multicoloured
2892- 300dh.×6, Type **542**; Saddle
2897   side view; Saddle front view;
       Stirrup; Saddle decorations;
       Oblong decorations   13·00   13·00
   Nos. 2892/7 were issued together, se-tenant, with the
background forming a composite design.

543 Aerial Explosion

2001. 15th Anniv of American Attack on Libya.
   Multicoloured.
2898- 100dh.×16, Type **543**; Aircraft;
2913   Pilot; Plane descending; Para-
       chute; Pillows; Girl crying;
       Fire and palm trees; Missiles;
       Falling vase; Teddy bear;
       Alarm clock; Ground explo-
       sion; Survivors; Man carrying
       child; Family fleeing   9·50   9·50
   Nos. 2898/913 were issued together, se-tenant, forming
a composite design.

544 Man hoeing

2001. Land Reclamation. Multicoloured.
2914- 250dh.×3, Type **544**; Men plant-
2916   ing (60×39 mm); Camels   2·75   2·75
   Nos. 2914/16 were issued together, se-tenant, forming
a composite design.

545 Chimney

2001. Man-made River (4th issue). Multicoloured.
2917- 200dh.×16, Type **545**; Pipe
2932   enclosing flags and crowd;
       Palm tree; Grapes; Rainbow
       enclosing man; Rainbow,
       bubbles and boy; Woman
       carrying fruit; Woman carry-
       ing jar; Woman; Woman in
       close up; Goose; Boy; Tabor
       player; Pipe player; Drum-
       mer; Tractors ploughing   19·00   19·00
   Nos. 2917/32 were issued together, se-tenant, forming
a composite design.

546 Muammar al
Qadhafi

2001. 32nd Anniv of Revolution. Multicoloured.
2933- 100dh.×4, Type **546**;
2936   pipeline and desert horse-
       men; Ship and camel rider;
       Elderly couple   1·75   1·75
2937- 100dh.×4, Boy and girl; Ruins
2940   and girl dancing; Camel
       rider; Camels and birds   1·75   1·75
2941- 100dh.×4, Jewellery and
2944   woman drummer; Sword
       fight; Desert dwellers;
       Woman driving tractor   1·75   1·75

2945- 100dh.×4, Artisans and musi-
2948   cians; Musicians and weaver;
       Workman; Qadhafi with
       clasped hands   1·75   1·75
MS2949 Two sheets, each 149×109
   mm. Size 42×51 mm. (a) 300dh.
   Muammar al Qadhafi. (b) 300dh. As
   No. MS2949a but silver background 5·50   5·50
   Nos. 2933/6, 2937/10, 2941/4 and 2945/8 were issued
together, se-tenant, forming a composite design.

547 Girl

2001. International Day for Orphans.
2950 **547** 100dh. multicoloured 1·20   80
2951 **547** 200dh. multicoloured 2·00 1·30
2952 **547** 300dh. multicoloured 2·75 1·80

548 Elderly Man,
Emblem and
Patient

2001. Welfare Services. Protection of Elderly and Infirm.
2953 **548** 200dh. multicoloured 1·70 1·10
2954 **548** 300dh. multicoloured 2·75 1·80

549 Doorways

2002. Tourism. Multicoloured.
2955- 200dh.×16, Type **549**; Palm
2970   trees; Arches; Mosque; Walls;
       Passage and sunbeam;
       Rooftop; Curved wall and
       arch; Aerial view; Tower;
       Interior with tented roof;
       Passage and bowl; Palms
       and ruins; Square tower and
       wall; Wall of narrow bricks;
       Building façade   30·00   30·00

550 Emblem,
Globe and "26"

2002
2971 **550** 200dh. multicoloured 1·70 1·10
2972 **550** 400dh. multicoloured 3·50 2·25

551 Muammar al
Qadhafi

2002. 33rd Anniv of Revolution. Multicoloured.
2973- 100dh.×16, Type **551**; Aircraft
2988   and engine; Camel rider and
       woman pouring tea; Crafts-
       men; Building and earth
       mover; Chemist and refinery;
       Ships; Hospital; Tower and
       control panel; Comput-
       ers and operator; Water
       pipeline and tap; Laboratory;
       Television studio; Fruit and
       vegetables; Arab musicians;
       African musicians   11·00   11·00
MS2989 Two sheets, each 149×117
   mm. Size 42×51 mm. (a) 300dh.
   Muammar al Qadhafi. (b) 300dh. As
   No. MS2989a but silver background
   Set of 2 sheets   5·00   5·00
   Nos. 2973/88 were issued together, se-tenant, forming
a composite background design.

552 Emblem

2002. 50th Anniv of Universal Declaration of Human
   Rights.
2990 **552** 250dh. multicoloured 2·20 1·40
2991 **552** 500dh. multicoloured 4·25 2·75

553 Emblem

2002. 125th Anniv of Universal Postal Union.
2992 **553** 200dh. multicoloured 1·70 1·10
2993 **553** 250dh. multicoloured 2·20 1·40

554 Muammar al Qadhafi

2003. People's Authority Declaration. Multicoloured
2994- 200dh.×6, Type **554**; Oil
2999   platform; Water pipeline, but-
       terflies and flowers; African
       musicians and dancer; Young
       couple; Camel riders   20·00   20·00
3000- 200dh.×6, As Type **554**; As
3005   No. 2995; As No. 2996; As
       No. 2997; As No. 2998; As
       No. 2999   20·00   20·00
MS3006 Two sheets, each 147×117
   mm. Size 42×51 mm. (a) 300dh.
   Muammar al Qadhafi. (b) 300dh. As
   No. MS3006a but silver background
   Set of 2 sheets   5·75   5·75

555 Women using
Microscope

2003. 34th Anniv of Revolution. Women in Society. Two
   sheets containing T **551** and similar multicoloured
   designs.
MS3007 151×151 mm. 300dh.×4,
   Type **555**; Anatomy lesson; Doctor
   and child; Soldiers; 500dh.×3,
   Embroiderer, business woman and
   teacher (60×40 mm); Helicopter and
   service women (60×40 mm); Service
   women in Army vehicle (60×40
   mm); 1000dh. Muammar al Qadhafi
   (60×40 mm)   14·00   14·00
MS3008 123×95 mm. 2000dh. Muam-
   mar al Qadhafi   16·00   16·00

556 Khairi Khaled Nuri (image scaled to 57% of original
size)

2004. Khairi Khaled Nuri Commemoration.
3009 **556** 500dh. multicoloured 4·25 2·75

   Nos. 3010/16 and Types **557/9** are left for the stamps
of 2005, not yet received.
   Nos. 3017/18 and Type **560** are left for Peoples' Authority Declaration issued on 2 March 2006, not yet received.
   Nos. 3019 and Type **561** are left for Total Eclipse issued
on 29 March 2006, not yet received.

562 '37'

2006. 37th Anniv of Revolution.
3020 **562** 1000dh. multicoloured   7·00   4·50

Nos. 3021 and Type **563** are left for Peoples' Authority Declaration issued on 2 March 2007, not yet received.
Nos. 3022 and Type **564** are left for African Leaders issued on 6 March 2007, not yet received.
Nos. 3023/8 and Type **565** are left for Tripoli Fair/Jewellery issued on 2 April 2007, not yet received.
Nos. 3029 and Type **566** are left for Telecommunications and IT Fair issued on 27 May 2007, not yet received.

567 Symbols of Drug Abuse

2007. International Day Against Drug Abuse.
3030 **567** 750dh. multicoloured   6·50   4·25

Nos. 3031 and Type **568** are left for Tripoli issued on 16 July 2007, not yet received.
Nos. 3032 and Type **569** are left for Confederation of African Football issued on 25 August 2007, not yet received.

570 '38' and Modern Technology

2007. 38th Anniv of Revolution.
3033 **570** 1000dh. multicoloured   7·00   4·50
MS3034 105×75 mm. As Type **570**   7·00   4·00

571 Child and Map of Africa

2007. Qadhafi Project for African Women, Children and Youth.
3035 **571** 500dh. multicoloured   4·25   2·75

Nos. 3036/7 and Type **572** are left for Quran Recital Competition issued on 24 September 2007, not yet received.
Nos. 3038/9 and Type **573** are left for 50th Anniv of Red Crescent issued on 29 October 2007, not yet received.

574 '31' and Emblem

2008. Peoples' Authority Declaration.
3040 **574** 500dh. multicoloured   3·75   2·40

Nos. 3041/3 and Type **575** are left for Tripoli Fair issued on 2 April 2008, not yet received.
Nos. 3044/7 and Type **576** are left for Fox issued on 1 May 2008, not yet received.
Nos. 3048 and Type **577** are left for Telecommunications and IT Fair issued on 27 May 2008, not yet received.
Nos. 3049 and Type **578** are left for 56th Anniv of 23 July Revolution issued on 23 July 2008, not yet received.
Nos. 3050 and Type **579** are left for Quadhafi Project issued on 27 July 2008, not yet received.
Nos. 3051 and Type **580** are left for Cen-Sad Session issued on 3 August 2008, not yet received.
Nos. 3052 and Type **581** are left for Olympic Games, Beijing issued on 18 August 2008, not yet received.
Nos. 3053/4 and Type **582** are left for 39th Anniv of Revolution issued on 1 September 2008, not yet received.

Nos. 3055 and Type **583** are left for Mobile Phones issued on 11 September 2008, not yet received.
Nos. 3056 and Type **584** are left for Memorizing Quran Competition issued on 23 September 2008, not yet received.
Nos. 3057 and Type **585** are left for Quran issued on 26 September 2008, not yet received.

586 Emblem

2009. Peoples' Authority Declaration.
3058 **586** 500dh. multicoloured   3·75   2·40

587 Injured Children, Raised Fist and Flag

2009. Support for Gaza.
3059 **587** 1000dh. multicoloured   7·00   4·50

588 Raised Fist

2009. Aggression.
3060 **588** 500dh. multicoloured   3·75   2·40

589 Symbols of Telecommunication and '5'

2009. Fifth Telecommunications and IT Fair.
3061 **589** 500dh. multicoloured   3·75   2·40

590 Omar Bongo Ondimba

2009. Omar Bongo Ondimba (president of Gabon) Commemoration.
3062 **590** 750dh. multicoloured   6·50   4·25

591 Emblems

2009. Mediterranean Games, Pescara. Libyan Olympic Committee.
3063 **591** 500dh. multicoloured   3·75   2·40

592 Emblem

2009. al-Quds—2009 Capital of Arab Culture.
3064 **592** 1000dh. multicoloured   7·00   4·50

593 Flags of Competing Nations and Competition Emblem

2009. Afrobasket 2009, Libya.
3065 **593** 500dh. multicoloured   3·75   2·40

594 Muammar al Qadhafi

2009. 40th Anniv of Revolution. Sheet 90×175 mm containing T **594** and similar horiz designs. Multicoloured.
MS3066 400dh. Type **594**; 600dh. As Type **594**; 750dh. As Type **594**   13·00   13·00

595 Map of Africa and Muammar al Qadhafi

2009. Muammar al Qadhafi, Founder and Chairman of African Union
3067 **595** 1000dh. multicoloured   7·00   4·50
MS3068 130×85 mm. 2000d. As Type **595**   13·00   13·00

596 Games Emblem

2009. Al-Fateh Futsal (indoor 5-a-side football) Continental Cup
3069 **596** 500dh. multicoloured   3·75   2·40

597 Symbols of Post

2010. 30th Anniv of Pan African Postal Union
3070 **597** 500dh. multicoloured   3·75   2·40

598 Chamber

2010. 33rd Anniv of People's Authority Declaration
3071 **598** 500dh. multicoloured   3·75   2·40

599 Flags of Member States

2010. 22nd Session of Council of League of Arab States, Sirte
3072 **599** 500h. multicoloured   3·75   2·40

600 Flags of Members and '50'

2010. 50th Anniv of OPEC (Organization of Petroleum Exporting Countries)
3073 **600** 1000dh. multicoloured   7·00   4·50

601 Airmen

2010. 40th Anniv of Evacuation of American Airbases
3074 **601** 1000dh. multicoloured   7·00   4·50

CONCESSIONAL LETTER POST

1929. No. CL227 of Italy optd LIBIA.
CL68 **CL93** 10c. blue   37·00   37·00

1941. No. CL267 of Italy optd LIBIA.
CL123 **CL109** 10c. brown   16·00   19·00

EXPRESS LETTER STAMPS.
A. ITALIAN ISSUES

1915. Express Letter stamps of Italy optd Libia.
E17 **E35** 25c. pink   40·00   32·00
E18 **E 41** 30c. blue and pink   8·50   45·00

E8

1921
E34 **E8** 30c. red and blue   3·25   9·50
E35 **E8** 50c. brown and red   4·75   15·00
E42 **E8** 60c. brown and red   13·00   27·00
E43 **E8** 2l. red and blue   21·00   45·00
Nos. E34 and E43 are inscribed "EXPRES".

1922. Nos. E17/18 surch.
E40 **E35** 60c. on 25c. pink   10·50   21·00
E41 **E 41** 11.60 on 30c. blue and pink   17·00   48·00

1926. Nos. E42/3 surch.
E62 **E 8** 70 on 60c. brown and red   10·50   24·00
E64 **E 8** 11.25 on 60c. brown and red   7·50   5·25
E63 **E 8** 2.50 on 2l. red and blue   17·00   45·00

B. INDEPENDENT ISSUES

1966. Design similar to T **74** inscr "EXPRES".
E368   90m. red and green   2·30   1·30
DESIGN—HORIZ: 90m. Saracen Castle, Zuela.

OFFICIAL STAMPS

1952. Optd Official in English and Arabic.
O192 **23** 2m. brown   40   35
O193 **23** 4m. grey   65   50
O194 **23** 5m. green   4·50   1·60
O195 **23** 8m. red   2·50   75
O196 **23** 10m. violet   3·75   1·25
O197 **23** 12m. red   6·75   2·50
O198 **23** 20m. blue   13·50   5·25
O199 **23** 25m. brown   17·00   6·75

PARCEL POST STAMPS

Unused prices are for complete pairs, used prices for a half

1915. Parcel Post stamps of Italy optd LIBIA on each half of the stamp.

P17	**P53**	5c. brown	2·75	10·50
P18	**P53**	10c. blue	2·75	10·50
P19	**P53**	20c. black	2·75	10·50
P20	**P53**	25c. red	4·25	13·00
P21	**P53**	50c. orange	5·25	13·00
P22	**P53**	1l. violet	5·25	13·00
P23	**P53**	2l. green	6·50	16·00
P24	**P53**	3l. yellow	8·00	16·00
P25	**P53**	4l. grey	8·00	16·00
P26	**P53**	10l. purple	70·00	85·00
P27	**P53**	12l. brown	£140	£250
P28	**P53**	15l. green	£140	£250
P29	**P53**	20l. purple	£200	£375

1927. Parcel Post stamps of Italy optd LIBIA on each half of the stamp.

P62	**P92**	5c. brown	£17000	
P63	**P92**	10c. blue	5·25	8·50
P64	**P92**	25c. red	5·25	8·50
P65	**P92**	30c. blue	2·10	5·25
P66	**P92**	50c. orange	£120	£225
P67	**P92**	60c. red	2·10	5·25
P68	**P92**	1l. violet	44·00	£110
P69	**P92**	2l. green	55·00	£110
P70	**P92**	3l. bistre	2·75	10·50
P71	**P92**	4l. black	2·75	16·00
P72	**P92**	10l. mauve	£375	£425
P73	**P92**	20l. purple	£375	£600

POSTAGE DUE STAMPS.

A. ITALIAN ISSUES

1915. Postage Due stamps of Italy optd Libia.

D17	**D12**	5c. mauve and orange	3·25	10·50
D18	**D12**	10c. mauve and orange	3·25	5·25
D19	**D12**	20c. mauve and orange	4·25	8·50
D20	**D12**	30c. mauve and orange	5·25	13·00
D21	**D12**	40c. mauve and orange	6·50	15·00
D22	**D12**	50c. mauve and orange	5·25	10·50
D23	**D12**	60c. mauve and orange	6·50	17·00
D24	**D12**	60c. brown and orange	85·00	£180
D25	**D12**	1l. mauve and blue	6·50	17·00
D26	**D12**	2l. mauve and blue	60·00	£110
D27	**D12**	5l. mauve and blue	85·00	£160

1934. Postage Due stamps of Italy optd LIBIA.

D68	**D141**	5c. brown	50	4·25
D69	**D141**	10c. blue	50	4·25
D70	**D141**	20c. red	1·90	2·10
D71	**D141**	25c. green	1·90	2·10
D72	**D141**	30c. red	1·90	7·50
D73	**D141**	40c. brown	1·90	5·25
D74	**D141**	50c. violet	3·00	60
D75	**D141**	60c. blue	3·00	17·00
D76	**D 142**	1l. orange	3·00	60
D77	**D 142**	2l. green	65·00	17·00
D78	**D 142**	5l. violet	£110	43·00
D79	**D 142**	10l. blue	16·00	65·00
D80	**D 142**	20l. red	16·00	85·00

B. INDEPENDENT ISSUES

1951. Postage Due stamps of Cyrenaica optd. (a) For use in Cyrenaica. Optd as T **20**.

D144	**D26**	2m. brown	5·00	5·00
D145	**D26**	4m. green	5·00	5·00
D146	**D26**	8m. red	6·75	6·25
D147	**D26**	10m. orange	7·50	6·25
D148	**D26**	20m. yellow	11·00	10·00
D149	**D26**	40m. blue	30·00	20·00
D150	**D26**	100m. black	40·00	23·00

(b) For use in Tripolitania. Surch as T **21**.

D161	**D 26**	1mal. on 2m. brown	5·50	5·00
D162	**D 26**	2mal. on 4m. green	7·50	5·50
D163	**D 26**	4mal. on 8m. red	12·50	10·00
D164	**D 26**	10mal. on 20m. yellow	27·00	20·00
D165	**D 26**	20mal. on 40m. blue	45·00	35·00

D25

1951

D188	**D25**	2m. brown	65	25
D189	**D25**	5m. green	95	50
D190	**D25**	10m. red	2·25	95
D191	**D25**	50m. blue	7·50	2·25

D53 Government Building, Tripoli 1952.

1964

D296	**D53**	2m. brown	10	10
D297	**D53**	6m. green	20	10
D298	**D53**	10m. red	70	45
D299	**D53**	50m. blue	1·25	85

D185 Men in Boat

1976. Ancient Mosaics. Multicoloured.

D725	5dh. Type D **185**	10	10
D726	10dh. Head of Medusa	10	10
D727	20dh. Peacock	10	10
D728	50dh. Fish	80	25

Pt. 8

LIECHTENSTEIN

A small independent principality lying between Austria and Switzerland.

1912. 100 heller = 1 krone.
1921. 100 rappen = 1 franc (Swiss).

1 Prince John II

1912

4	**1**	5h. green	14·50	22·00
2	**1**	10h. red	85·00	18·00
3	**1**	25h. blue	85·00	60·00

2

3

1917

7	**2**	3h. violet	2·20	2·20
8	**2**	5h. green	2·20	2·20
9	**3**	10h. purple	2·20	2·20
10	**3**	15h. brown	2·20	2·20
11	**3**	20h. green	2·20	2·20
12	**3**	25h. blue	2·20	2·20

1918. 60th Anniv of Prince John's Accession. As T **3** but dated "1858–1918" in upper corners.

13		20h. green	75	3·00

1920. Optd with a scroll pattern.

14	**2**	5h. green	3·00	9·00
15	**3**	10h. purple	3·00	9·75
16	**3**	25h. blue	3·00	9·75

1920. Surch.

17	**2**	40h. on 3h. violet	3·00	9·75
18	**3**	1k. on 15h. brown	3·00	9·75
19	**3**	2½k. on 20h. green	3·00	9·75

7

8 Castle of Vaduz

1920. Imperf.

20	**7**	5h. bistre	35	6·50
21	**7**	10h. orange	35	6·50
22	**7**	15h. blue	35	6·50
23	**7**	20h. brown	35	6·50
24	**7**	25h. green	35	6·50
25	**7**	30h. grey	35	6·50
26	**7**	40h. red	35	6·50
27	**8**	1k. blue	35	6·50

9 Prince John I

10 Arms

1920. Perf.

28	**7**	5h. bistre	35	75
29	**7**	10h. orange	35	75
30	**7**	15h. blue	35	75
31	**7**	20h. brown	35	75
32	-	25h. green	35	75
33	**7**	30h. grey	35	75
34	-	40h. purple	35	75
35	-	50h. green	35	75
36	-	60h. brown	35	75
37	-	80h. pink	35	75
38	**8**	1k. lilac	75	1·10
39	-	2k. blue	75	1·80
40	**9**	5k. black	75	2·50
41	-	7½k. grey	75	3·25
42	**10**	10k. brown	75	5·75

DESIGNS—As Type **8**: 25h. St. Mamertus Chapel; 40h. Gutenberg Castle; 50h. Courtyard, Vaduz Castle; 60h. Red House, Vaduz; 80h. Church Tower, Schaan; 2k. Bendern. As Type **9**: 7½k. Prince John II.

11 Madonna

1920. Prince John's 80th Birthday. Imperf or perf.

43A	**11**	50h. green	75	2·20
44A	**11**	80h. red	75	2·20
45A	**11**	2k. blue	75	3·00

1921. Surch 2 Rp. and bars.

47	**7**	2r. on 10h. orange (No. 21)	1·50	28·00

14 Arms

15 St. Mamertus Chapel

16 Vaduz

1921

47aB	**14**	2r. yellow	1·50	14·50
48A	**14**	2½r. brown	1·50	14·50
49A	**14**	3r. orange	1·50	14·50
50A	**14**	5r. green	14·50	2·20
51A	**14**	7½r. blue	7·25	20·00
53A	**14**	13r. brown	8·75	95·00
54B	**14**	15r. violet	28·00	25·00
55	**15**	20r. black and violet	75·00	2·20
56	-	25r. black and red	3·75	5·00
57	-	30r. black and green	85·00	22·00
58	-	35r. black and brown	7·25	17·00
59	-	40r. black and blue	11·00	6·50
60	-	50r. black and green	18·00	9·00
61	-	80r. black and grey	33·00	85·00
62	**16**	1f. black and red	60·00	60·00
65	**14**	10r. green	22·00	3·00
66	-	30r. black and blue	18·00	3·00

DESIGNS—As Type **15**: 25r. Vaduz Castle; 30r. Bendern; 35r. Prince John II; 40r. Church Tower at Schaan; 50r. Gutenberg Castle; 80r. Red House, Vaduz.

1924. Surch.

63A	**14**	5 on 7½r. blue	1·50	3·75
64B	**14**	10 on 13r. brown	1·50	3·75

19 Vine-dresser

21 Government Bldg. and Church, Vaduz

1924

67	**19**	2½r. mauve and green	1·50	7·25
68	**19**	5r. blue and brown	3·00	1·10
69	**19**	7½r. brown and green	2·20	7·25
70	-	10r. green	11·50	1·10
71	**19**	15r. green and purple	11·00	40·00
72	-	20r. red	44·00	1·50
73	**21**	1½f. blue	85·00	£120

DESIGN—As Type **19**: 10, 20r. Castle of Vaduz.

22 Prince John II

1925. 85th Birthday of Prince John.

74	**22**	10+5r. green	50·00	25·00
75	**22**	20+5r. red	29·00	25·00
76	**22**	30+5r. blue	7·25	7·25

23

1927. 87th Birthday of Prince. Arms multicoloured.

77	**23**	10+5r. green	11·00	29·00
78	**23**	20+5r. purple	11·00	29·00
79	**23**	30+5r. blue	7·25	22·00

24 Salvage Work by Austrian soldiers

1928. Flood Relief.

80	-	5r.+5r. brown and purple	18·00	29·00
81	-	10r.+10r. brown and green	25·00	36·00
82	**24**	20r.+10r. brown and red	25·00	40·00
83	-	30r.+10r. brown and blue	22·00	36·00

DESIGNS: 5r. Railway bridge between Buchs and Schaan; 10r. Village of Ruggell; 30r. Salvage work by Swiss soldiers.

26 Prince John II, 1858–1928

1928. 70th Anniv of Accession of Prince John II.

84		10r. green and brown	7·25	7·25
85		20r. green and red	11·00	14·50
86		30r. green and blue	36·00	25·00
87		60r. green and mauve	75·00	£110
88	**26**	1f.20 blue	60·00	£130
89	**26**	1f.50 brown	£110	£275
90	**26**	2f. red	£110	£275
91	**26**	5f. green	£110	£325

DESIGN—VERT: 10r. to 60r. Prince John II.

28 Prince Francis I

1929. Accession of Prince Francis I.

92	-	10r. green	60	4·25
93	**28**	20r. red	85	7·25
94	-	30r. blue	1·50	25·00
95	-	70r. brown	26·00	£150

PORTRAITS: 10r. Prince Francis I as a boy; 30r. Princess Elsa; 70r. Prince Francis and Princess Elsa.

31 Girl Vintager

32 Prince Francis I and Princess Elsa

1930

96A	**31**	3r. red	1·10	3·00
97B	-	5r. green	3·75	3·00
98B	-	10r. lilac	3·75	3·00
99B	-	20r. red	29·00	3·75
100A	-	25r. green	8·75	47·00
101B	-	30r. blue	8·75	5·00
102C	-	35r. green	11·00	22·00
103C	-	40r. brown	11·00	8·75
104C	-	50r. black	£110	21·00
105B	-	60r. green	£110	36·00
106B	-	90r. purple	£120	£150
107B	-	1f.20 brown	£160	£300
108B	-	1f.50 blue	60·00	75·00
109B	**32**	2f. brown and green	85·00	£150

DESIGNS—VERT: 5r. Mt. Three Sisters–Edelweiss; 10r. Alpine cattle-alpine roses; 20r. Courtyard of Vaduz Castle; 25r. Mt. Naafkopf; 30r. Valley of Samina; 35r. Rofenberg Chapel; 40r. St. Mamertus' Chapel; 50r. Kurhaus at Malbun; 60r. Gutenberg Castle; 90r. Schellenberg Monastery; 1f.20, Vaduz Castle; 1f.50, Pfaelzer club hut.

34 Monoplane over Vaduz Castle and Rhine Valley

1930. Air.

110	-	15r. brown	11·00	18·00
111	-	20r. green	25·00	25·00
112	-	25r. brown	14·50	47·00
113	-	35r. blue	22·00	44·00
114	**34**	45r. green	50·00	90·00
115	**34**	1f. purple	60·00	65·00

DESIGNS—VERT: 15, 20r. Biplane over snowy mountain peak. HORIZ: 25, 35r. Biplane over Vaduz Castle.

35 Airship LZ-127 "Graf Zeppelin" over Alps

1931. Air.

116	**35**	1f. green	75·00	£130
117	-	2f. blue	£150	£425

DESIGN: 2f. Airship "Graf Zeppelin" (different).

37 Princess Elsa

1932. Youth Charities.

118		10r.+5r. green	22·00	44·00
119	**37**	20r.+5r. red	22·00	44·00
120	-	30r.+10r. blue	29·00	60·00

DESIGNS—22×29 mm: 10r. Arms of Liechtenstein. As Type **37**: 30r. Prince Francis.

38 Mt. Naafkopf

1933

121	**38**	25r. orange	£275	90·00
122	-	90r. green	11·00	£110
123	-	1f.20 brown	£150	£375

DESIGNS: 90r. Gutenberg Castle; 1f.20, Vaduz Castle.

39 Prince Francis I

1933. Prince Francis's 80th Birthday.

124	**39**	10r. violet	29·00	50·00
125	**39**	20r. red	29·00	50·00
126	**39**	30r. blue	29·00	50·00

40

41 "Three Sisters"

42 Vaduz Castle

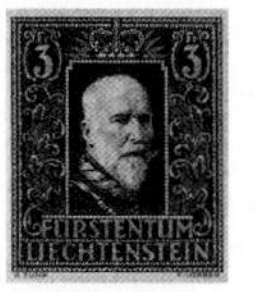

44 Prince Francis I

45 Arms of Liechtenstein

1933

127	**40**	3r. red	35	75
128	**41**	5r. green	5·75	2·20
129	-	10r. violet	3·00	1·50
130	-	15r. orange	35	1·50
131	-	20r. red	75	1·50
132	-	25r. brown	29·00	70·00
133	-	30r. blue	5·75	2·20
134	-	35r. green	8·75	18·00
135	-	40r. brown	1·80	7·25
136	**42**	50r. brown	25·00	22·00
137	-	60r. purple	2·20	9·50
138	-	90r. green	8·75	31·00
139	-	1f.20 blue	3·75	31·00
140	-	1f.50 brown	4·25	36·00
141	-	2f. brown	85·00	£250
142	**44**	3f. blue	£130	£250
143	**45**	5f. purple	£425	£1300

DESIGNS—As Type **41**: 10r. Schaan Church; 15r. Bendern am Rhein; 20r. Town Hall, Vaduz; 25r. Saminatal. As Type **44**: 2f. Princess Elsa. As Type **42**: 30r. Saminatal (different); 35r. Schellenberg ruins; 40r. Government Building, Vaduz; 60r. Vaduz Castle (different); 90r. Gutenberg Castle; 1f.20, Pfalzer Hut, Bettlerjoch; 1f.50, Valuna.

See also Nos. **MS**144, **MS**153, 174, 225/6 and 258.

1934. Vaduz First Liechtenstein Philatelic Exhibition. Sheet 105×125 mm.

MS144 **45** 5f. chocolate		£2000	£3000

46 Golden Eagle

1934. Air.

145a	**46**	10r. violet	7·25	25·00
146a	-	15r. orange	22·00	60·00
147a	-	20r. red	25·00	60·00
148a	-	30r. blue	25·00	60·00
149a	-	50r. green	22·00	44·00

DESIGNS: 10r. to 20r. Golden eagles in flight; 30r. Ospreys in nest; 50r. Golden eagle on rock.

1935. Air. No. 115 surch 60 Rp.

150	**34**	60r. on 1f. purple	44·00	75·00

49 LZ-129 "Hindenburg" and Schaan Church

1936. Air.

151	**49**	1f. red	55·00	£110
152	-	2f. violet	36·00	£110

DESIGN: 2f. LZ-127 "Graf Zeppelin" over Schaan Airport.

1936. Second Liechtenstein Philatelic Exhibition and Opening of Postal Museum, Vaduz. Sheet 165×119 mm containing two each of Nos. 131 and 133.

MS153 Sold at 2fr.		18·00	60·00

51 Masescha am Triesenberg

52 Schellenberg Castle

1937

154	-	3r. brown	35	75
155	**51**	5r. green and buff	35	35
156	-	10r. violet and buff	35	35
157	-	15r. black and buff	35	75
158	-	20r. red and buff	35	75
159	-	25r. brown and buff	75	3·75
160	-	30r. blue and buff	4·25	1·50
161	**52**	40r. green and buff	3·00	3·00
162	-	50c. brown and buff	3·75	7·25
163	-	60r. purple and buff	3·00	3·75
164	-	90r. violet and buff	22·00	44·00
165	-	1f. purple and buff	3·00	18·00
166	-	1f.20 brown and buff	11·00	33·00
167	-	1f.50 grey and buff	4·25	33·00

DESIGNS—As Type **51**: 3r. Schalun ruins; 10r. Knight and Vaduz Castle; 15r. Upper Saminatal; 20r. Church and Bridge at Bendern; 25r. Steg Chapel and girl. As Type **52**: 30r. Farmer and orchard, Triesenberg; 50r. Knight and Gutenberg Castle; 60r. Baron von Brandis and Vaduz Castle; 90r. "Three Sisters" mountain; 1f. Boundary-stone on Luziensteig; 1f.20, Minstrel and Gutenberg Castle; 1f.50, Lawena (Schwarzhorn).

53 Roadmakers at Triesenberg

1937. Workers' Issue.

168		10r. mauve	1·80	2·20
169	**53**	20r. red	1·80	3·00
170	-	30r. blue	1·80	3·75
171	-	50r. brown	1·80	4·25

DESIGNS: 10r. Bridge at Malbun; 30r. Binnen Canal Junction; 50r. Francis Bridge, near Planken.

1938. Third Liechtenstein Philatelic Exhibition, Vaduz. Sheet 100×135 mm containing stamps as No. 175 in different colour in a block of four.

MS173 **54** 50r. blue		29·00	29·00

1938. Death of Prince Francis I.

174	**44**	3f. black on yellow	14·50	£120

54 Josef Rheinberger

1939. Birth Centenary of Rheinberger (composer).

175	**54**	50r. grey	1·10	6·50

55 Black-headed Gulls

1939. Air.

176	-	10r. violet (Barn swallows)	1·50	1·80
177	**55**	15r. orange	75	3·75
178	-	20r. red (Herring gull)	3·00	1·50
179	-	30r. blue (Common buzzard)	1·80	3·00
180	-	50r. green (Northern goshawk)	4·25	5·00
181	-	1f. red (Lammergeier)	3·00	23·00
182	-	2f. violet Lammergeier	3·00	22·00

56 Offering Homage to First Prince

1939. Homage to Francis Joseph II.

183	**56**	20r. red	1·50	3·00
184	**56**	30r. blue	1·50	2·20
185	**56**	50r. green	1·50	3·00

57 Francis Joseph II

1939

186	-	2f. green on cream	11·00	55·00
187	-	3f. violet on cream	7·25	55·00
188	**57**	5f. brown on cream	22·00	£110

DESIGNS: 2f. Cantonal Arms; 3f. Arms of Principality.

58 Prince John when a Child

1940. Birth Centenary of Prince John II.

189	**58**	20r. red	75	3·00
190	-	30r. blue	75	4·25
191	-	50r. green	1·50	14·50
192	-	1f. violet	11·00	95·00
193	-	1f.50 black	21·00	85·00
194	-	3f. brown	5·00	29·00

DESIGNS—As Type **58**: Portraits of Prince John in early manhood (30r.), in middle age (50r.) and in later life (1f.), and Memorial tablet (1f.50). As Type **44**: 3f. Framed portrait of Prince John II.

60 Wine Press

1941. Agricultural Propaganda.

195		10r. brown	1·10	1·50
196	**60**	20r. purple	1·80	2·20
197	-	30r. blue	1·80	3·75
198	-	50r. green	3·00	22·00
199	-	90r. violet	3·25	25·00

DESIGNS: 10r. Harvesting maize; 30r. Sharpen-ing scythe; 50r. Milkmaid and cow; 90r. Girl wearing traditional headdress.

61 Madonna and Child

1941

200	**61**	10f. purple on stone	60·00	£150

62 Prince Hans Adam

1941. Princes (1st issue).

201	**62**	20r. red	75	2·20
202	-	30r. blue (Wenzel)	75	3·75
203	-	1f. grey (Anton Florian)	3·00	24·00
204	-	1f.50 green (Joseph)	75	25·00

See also Nos. 210/13 and 217/20.

63 St. Lucius preaching

1942. 600th Anniv of Separation from Estate of Montfort.

205	**63**	20r. red on pink	1·80	1·50
206	-	30r. blue on pink	1·10	3·75
207	-	50r. green on pink	3·25	11·00
208	-	1f. brown on pink	4·25	20·00
209	-	2f. violet on pink	4·75	20·00

DESIGNS: 30r. Count of Montfort replanning Vaduz; 50r. Counts of Montfort-Werdenberg and Sargans signing treaty; 1f. Battle of Gutenberg; 2f. Homage to Prince of Liechtenstein.

64 Prince John Charles

1942. Princes (2nd issue).

210	**64**	20r. pink	75	1·50
211	-	30r. blue (Francis Joseph I)	75	3·00
212	-	1f. purple (Alois I)	3·00	22·00
213	-	1f.50 brown (John I)	3·00	22·00

65 Princess Georgina

1943. Marriage of Prince Francis Joseph II and Countess Georgina von Wildczek.

214		10r. purple	75	1·80
215	**65**	20r. red	75	1·80
216	-	30r. blue	75	1·80

PORTRAITS—VERT: 10r. Prince Francis Joseph II. HORIZ (44×25 mm): 30r. Prince and Princess.

66 Alois II

1943. Princes (3rd issue).

217	**66**	20r. brown	75	1·50
218	-	30r. blue	1·50	2·20
219	-	1f. brown	2·20	11·00
220	-	1f.50 green	2·20	11·00

PORTRAITS: 30r. John II; 1f. Francis I; 1f.50, Francis Joseph II.

67 Marsh Land

1943. Completion of Irrigation Canal.

221	**67**	10r. violet	35	75
222	-	30r. blue	55	3·00
223	-	50r. green	2·00	12·50
224	-	2f. brown	3·75	20·00

DESIGNS: 30r. Draining the canal; 50r. Ploughing reclaimed land; 2f. Harvesting crops.

1943. Castles. As T **41**.

225	10r. grey (Vaduz)	55	75
226	20r. brown (Gutenberg)	90	1·50

69 Planken

1944. Various designs. Buff backgrounds.

227	**69**	3r. brown	35	35
228	-	5r. green (Bendern)	35	35
228a	-	5r. brown (Bendern)	55	75
229	-	10r. grey (Triesen)	35	35
230	-	15r. grey (Ruggell)	45	1·10
231	-	20r. red (Vaduz)	45	75
232	-	25r. brown (Triesenberg)	45	1·50
233	-	30r. blue (Schaan)	45	75
234	-	40r. brown (Balzers)	90	1·80
235	-	50r. blue (Mauren)	1·10	3·00
236	-	60r. green (Schellenberg)	6·25	8·75
237	-	90r. green (Eschen)	6·25	8·75
238	-	1f. purple (Vaduz Castle)	3·75	8·75
239	-	1f.20 brown (Valunatal)	3·75	10·00
240	-	1f.50 blue (Lawena)	3·75	10·00

70 Prince Francis Joseph II

1944

241	**70**	2f. brown and buff	9·00	25·00
242	-	3f. green and buff	5·50	18·00

DESIGN: 3f. Princess Georgina.

See also Nos. 302/3.

72

1945. Birth of Crown Prince Johann Adam Pius (known as Prince Hans Adam).

243	**72**	20r. red, yellow and gold	1·50	75
244	**72**	30r. blue, yellow and gold	1·50	2·20
245	**72**	100r. grey, yellow and gold	4·25	8·75

73

1945

246	**73**	5f. blue on buff	33·00	50·00
247	**73**	5f. brown on buff	40·00	65·00

74 First Aid

1945. Red Cross. Cross in red.

248	-	10r.+10r. purple and buff	2·20	3·00
249	**74**	20r.+20r. purple and buff	2·20	4·25
250	-	1f.+1f.40 blue and buff	14·00	40·00

DESIGNS: 10r. Mother and children; 1f. Nurse and invalid.

75 St. Lucius

1946

251	**75**	10f. grey on buff	65·00	50·00

1946. Fourth Liechtenstein Philatelic Exhibition, Vaduz and 25th Anniv of Postal Agreement with Switzerland. Sheet 84×60 mm.

MS251a 10r. (×2) Old Postal Coach (*horiz*), violet, brown and buff (sold at 3f.) 55·00 60·00

76 Red Deer Stag

1946. Wild Life.

252	**76**	20r. red	4·25	4·25
253	-	30r. blue (Arctic hare)	5·75	5·75
254	-	1f.50 green (Western capercaillie)	8·00	19·00
255	-	20r. red (Chamois)	7·25	7·25
256	-	30r. blue (Alpine marmot)	9·50	8·00
257	-	1f.50 brown (Golden eagle)	8·75	25·00
283	-	20r. red (Roebuck)	18·00	7·25
284	-	30r. green (Black grouse)	14·50	11·00
285	-	80r. brown (Eurasian badger)	60·00	75·00

1947. Death of Princess Elsa. As No. 141.

258	2f. black on yellow	7·25	22·00

79 Wilbur Wright

1948. Air. Pioneers of Flight.

259	-	10r. green	1·10	35
260	-	15r. violet	1·10	1·80
261	-	20r. brown	1·50	35
262	-	25r. red	2·20	3·00
263	-	40r. blue	2·50	3·00
264	-	50r. blue	3·00	3·00
265	-	1f. purple	4·75	6·25
266	-	2f. purple	7·25	8·00
267	**79**	5f. green	9·50	11·00
268	-	10f. black	60·00	31·00

PORTRAITS: 10r. Leoardo da Vinci; 15r. Joseph Montgolfier; 20r. Jakob Degen; 25r. Wilhelm Kress; 40r. Etienne Robertson; 50r. William Henson; 1f. Otto Lilienthal; 2f. Salomon Andree; 10f. Icarus.

80 "Ginevra de Benci" (Da Vinci)

1949. Paintings.

269	**80**	10r. green	1·50	55
270	-	20r. red	2·20	1·30
271	-	30r. brown	4·25	1·50
272	-	40r. blue	11·00	1·50
273	-	50r. violet	8·75	11·00
274	-	60r. grey	28·00	10·00
275	-	80r. brown	4·25	7·00
276	-	90r. green	20·00	9·50
277	-	120r. mauve	4·25	8·75

DESIGNS: 20r. "Portrait of a Young Girl" (Rubens); 30r. Self-portrait of Rembrandt in plumed hat; 40r. "Stephan Gardiner, Bishop of Winchester" (Quentin Massys); 50r. "Madonna and Child" (Hans Memling); 60r. "Franz Meister in 1456" (Jehan Fouquet); 80r. "Lute Player" (Orazio Gentileschi); 90r. "Portrait of a Man" (Bernhardin Strigel); 120r. "Portrait of a Man (Duke of Urbino)" (Raphael).

1949. No. 227 surch 5 Rp. and bars.

278	**69**	5r. on 3r. brown and buff	1·10	75

82 Posthorn and Map of World

1949. 75th Anniv of U.P.U.

279	**82**	40r. blue	5·75	7·25

1949. Fifth Liechtenstein Philatelic Exhibition, Vaduz. Sheet 122×70 mm containing paintings as 1949 issue in new colours.

MS279a 10r. green (as 10r.); 20r. mauve (as 80r.); 40r. blue (as 120r.). Sold at 3f. £180 £180

83 Rossauer Castle

1949. 250th Anniv of Acquisition of Domain of Schellenberg.

280	**83**	20r. purple	3·75	3·75
281	-	40r. blue	12·50	11·00
282	-	1f.50 red	16·00	16·00

DESIGN—HORIZ: 40r. Bendern Church. VERT: 1f.50, Prince Johann Adam I.

1950. Surch 100 100.

286	**82**	100r. on 40r. blue	44·00	75·00

86 Boy cutting Loaf

1951. Agricultural scenes.

287	**86**	5r. mauve	75	50
288	-	10r. green	75	75
289	-	15r. brown	8·75	8·75
290	-	20r. brown	1·80	1·10
291	-	25r. purple	8·75	8·75
292	-	30r. green	5·00	90
293	-	40r. blue	16·00	11·00
294	-	50r. purple	13·00	5·50
295	-	60r. brown	13·00	5·00
296	-	80r. brown	16·00	11·50
297	-	90r. green	33·00	11·50
298	-	1f. blue	£100	11·50

DESIGNS: 10r. Man whetting scythe; 15r. Mowing; 20r. Girl and sweet corn; 25r. Haywain; 30r. Gathering grapes; 40r. Man with scythe; 50r. Herdsman with cows; 60r. Ploughing; 80r. Girl carrying basket of fruit; 90r. Woman gleaning; 1f. Tractor hauling corn.

87 "Lock on the Canal" (Aelbert Cuyp)

88 "Willem von Heythuysen, Burgomaster of Haarlem" (Frans Hals)

1951. Paintings.

299	**87**	10r.+10r. green	14·50	11·00
300	**88**	20r.+10r. brown	14·50	22·00
301	-	40r.+10r. blue	14·50	14·50

DESIGN—As Type **87**: 40r. "Landscape" (Jacob van Ruysdael).

90 Vaduz Castle

1951

302A	**70**	2f. blue	22·00	60·00
303B	-	3f. brown	£180	£325
304	**90**	5f. green	£225	£225

DESIGN: 3f. Princess Georgina.

1952. No. 281 surch 1.20.

308	1f.20 on 40r. blue	36·00	85·00

1952. Paintings from Prince's Collection. (a) As T 80 but size 25×30 mm.

309	10r. green	3·75	1·50
305	20r. purple	65·00	4·25
307	40r. blue	22·00	9·50
312	40r. blue	55·00	75·00

PAINTINGS: No. 309, "Portrait of a Young Man" (A. G.); 305, "Portrait" (Giovanni Salvoldo); 307, "St. John" (Andrea del Sarto); 312, "Leonhard, Count of Hag" (Hans von Kulmbach).

(b) As T **88** (22½×24 mm).

306	30r. green	44·00	11·50
310	20r. brown	28·00	4·00
311	30r. brown	47·00	12·50

PAINTINGS: No. 310, "St. Nicholas" (Bartholomaus Zeitblom); 306, "Madonna and Child" (Sandro Botticelli); 311, "St. Christopher" (Lucas Cranach the elder).

96 Lord Baden-Powell

1953. 14th International Scout Conference.

313	**96**	10r. green	3·75	1·50
314	**96**	20r. brown	23·00	3·75
315	**96**	25r. red	18·00	29·00
316	**96**	40r. blue	17·00	9·50

97 Alemannic Ornamental Disc, (c. A.D. 600)

98 Prehistoric Walled Settlement, Borscht

1953. Opening of National Museum, Vaduz.

317	**97**	10r. brown	14·50	18·00
318	**98**	20r. green	14·50	18·00
319	-	1f.20 blue	80·00	50·00

DESIGN—VERT: 1f.20, Rossen jug (3000 B.C.).

99 Footballers

1954. Football.

320	**99**	10r. brown and red	4·25	1·50
321	-	20r. deep green and green	12·50	2·20
322	-	25r. deep brown and brown	29·00	50·00
323	-	40r. violet and grey	25·00	14·50

DESIGNS: 20r. Footballer kicking ball; 25r. Goalkeeper; 40r. Two footballers.

For stamps in similar designs see Nos. 332/5, 340/3, 351/4 and 363/6.

1954. Nos. 299/301 surch in figures.

324	**87**	35r. on 10r.+10r. green	5·75	3·75
325	**88**	60r. on 20r.+10r. brown	29·00	17·00
326	-	65r. on 40r.+10r. blue	8·75	11·50

100 Madonna and Child

1954. Termination of Marian Year.

327	**100**	20r. brown	5·75	3·75
328	**100**	40r. black	29·00	17·00
329	**100**	1f. brown	29·00	11·50

101 Princess Georgina

1955

330	-	2f. brown	£130	75·00
331	**101**	3f. green	£130	75·00

PORTRAIT: 2f. Prince Francis Joseph II.

1955. Mountain Sports. As T **99**.

332	10r. purple and blue	3·75	1·50
333	20r. green and bistre	9·50	1·50
334	25r. brown and blue	29·00	29·00
335	40r. green and red	29·00	11·00

DESIGNS: 10r. Slalom racer; 20r. Mountaineer hammering in piton; 25r. Skier; 40r. Mountaineer resting on summit.

102 Crown Prince John Adam Pius

1955. Tenth Anniv of Liechtenstein Red Cross. Cross in red.

336	**102**	10r. violet	4·25	1·10
337	-	20r. green	8·75	2·50
338	-	40r. brown	11·00	11·50
339	-	60r. red	11·00	6·50

PORTRAITS: 20r. Prince Philip; 40r. Prince Nicholas; 60r. Princess Nora.
See also No. 350.

1956. Athletics. As T **99**.

340	10r. green and brown	3·00	1·10
341	20r. purple and green	5·75	1·10
342	40r. brown and blue	8·75	7·25
343	1f. brown and red	20·00	25·00

DESIGNS: 10r. Throwing the javelin; 20r. Hurdling; 40r. Pole vaulting; 1f. Running.

103

1956. 150th Anniv of Sovereignty of Liechtenstein.

344	**103**	10r. purple and gold	5·75	1·50
345	**103**	1f.20 blue and gold	29·00	7·25

104 Prince Francis Joseph II

1956. 50th Birthday of Prince Francis Joseph II.

346	**104**	10r. green	3·00	75
347	**104**	15r. blue	19·00	4·75
348	**104**	25r. purple	19·00	4·75
349	**104**	60r. brown	17·00	4·25

1956. Sixth Philatelic Exhibition, Vaduz. As T **102** but inscr "6. BRIEFMARKEN-AUSSTELLUNG".

350	20r. green	4·75	1·10

1956. Gymnastics. As T **99**.

351	10r. green and pink	3·75	1·50
352	15r. purple and green	8·75	4·25
353	25r. green and drab	11·00	5·75
354	1f.50 brown and yellow	33·00	17·00

DESIGNS: 10r. Somersaulting; 15r. Vaulting; 25r. Exercising with rings; 1f.50, Somersaulting on parallel bars.

105 Norway Spruce

1957. Liechtenstein Trees and Bushes.

355	**105**	10r. purple	7·25	3·75
356	-	20r. red	7·25	1·50
357	-	1f. green	11·00	12·50

DESIGNS: 20r. Wild rose bush; 1f. Silver birch.
See also Nos. 369/71, 375/7 and 401/3.

106 Lord Baden-Powell

1957. 50th Anniv of Boy Scout Movement and Birth Centenary of Lord Baden-Powell (founder).

358		10r. blue	2·20	2·20
359	**106**	20r. brown	2·20	2·20

DESIGN: 10r. Torchlight procession.

107 St. Mamertus Chapel

1957. Christmas.

360	**107**	10r. brown	2·20	75
361	-	40r. blue	5·75	12·50
362	-	1f.50 purple	21·00	20·00

DESIGNS—(from St. Mamertus Chapel): 40r. Altar shrine; 1f.50, "Pieta" (sculpture).
See also Nos. 372/4 and 392/4.

1958. Sports. As T **99**.

363	15r. violet and blue	1·50	2·20
364	30r. green and purple	9·50	14·50
365	40r. green and orange	14·50	14·50
366	90r. brown and green	3·75	7·25

DESIGNS: 15r. Swimmer; 30r. Fencers; 40r. Tennis player; 90r. Racing cyclists.

108 Relief Map of Liechtenstein

1958. Brussels International Exhibition.

367	**108**	25r. violet, stone and red	1·50	1·10
368	**108**	40r. purple, blue and red	2·20	1·10

1958. Liechtenstein Trees and Bushes. As T **105**.

369	20r. brown (Sycamore)	5·50	1·50
370	50r. green (Holly)	22·00	9·50
371	90r. violet (Yew)	5·50	5·00

1958. Christmas. As T **107**.

372	20r. green	4·25	3·75
373	35r. violet	4·25	5·75
374	80r. brown	5·75	4·25

DESIGNS: 20r. "St. Maurice and St. Agatha"; 35r. "St. Peter"; 80r. St. Peter's Chapel, Mals-Balzers.

1959. Liechtenstein Trees and Bushes. As T **105**.

375	20r. lilac (Red-berried larch)	11·00	4·25
376	50r. red (Red-berried elder)	8·75	5·75
377	90r. green (Linden)	5·75	5·75

109

1959. Pope Pius XII Mourning.

378	**109**	30r. purple and gold	1·80	1·60

111 Harvester

110 Flags of Vaduz Castle and Rhine Valley

1959. Views.

379	-	5r. brown	35	35
380	**110**	10r. purple	35	35
381	-	20r. mauve	45	35
382	-	30r. red	60	45
383	-	40r. green	85	60
384	-	50r. blue	85	75
385	-	60r. blue	1·10	85
386	**111**	75r. brown	1·70	2·00
387	-	80r. green	1·50	1·10
388	-	90r. purple	1·60	1·20
389	-	1f. brown	1·80	1·30
390	-	1f.20 red	2·50	2·00
390a	-	1f.30 green	2·00	1·80
391	-	1f.50 blue	3·00	2·20

DESIGNS—HORIZ: 5r. Bendern Church; 20r. Rhine Dam; 30r. Gutenberg Castle; 40r. View from Schellenberg; 50r. Vaduz Castle; 60r. Naafkopf-Falknis Mountains (view from the Bettlerjoch); 1f.20, Harvesting apples; 1f.30, Farmer and wife; 1f.50, Saying grace at table. VERT: 80r. Alpine haymaker; 90r. Girl in vineyard; 1f. Mother in kitchen.

1959. Christmas. As T **107**.

392	5r. green	75	35
393	60r. brown	10·00	8·00
394	1f. purple	8·75	5·50

DESIGNS: 5r. Bendern Church belfry; 60r. Relief on bell of St. Theodul's Church; 1f. Sculpture on tower of St. Lucius's Church.

112 Bell 47J Ranger Helicopter

1960. Air. 30th Anniv of 1st Liechtenstein Air Stamps.

395	**112**	30r. red	3·75	4·25
396	-	40r. blue	6·50	4·25
397	-	50r. purple	16·00	8·75
398	-	75r. green	3·00	4·25

DESIGNS: 40r. Boeing 707 jetliner; 50r. Convair 990A Coronado jetliner; 75r. Douglas DC-8 jetliner.

1960. World Refugee Year. Nos. 367/8 surch WELTFLUCHTLINGSJAHR 1960, uprooted tree and new value.

399	**108**	30+10r. on 40r. purple, blue and red	1·90	1·90
400	**108**	50+10r. on 25r. violet, stone and red	3·25	3·25

1960. Liechtenstein Trees and Bushes. As T **105**.

401	20r. brown (Beech)	11·00	7·25
402	30r. purple (Juniper)	11·00	22·00
403	50r. turquoise (Mountain pines)	36·00	25·00

114 Europa "Honeycomb"

1960. Europa.

404	**114**	50r. multicoloured	£110	65·00

115 Princess Gina

1960

404a	-	1f.70 violet	2·50	1·50
405	**115**	2f. blue	3·75	2·20
406	-	3f. brown	4·25	2·20

PORTRAITS: 1f.70, Crown Prince Hans Adam; 3f. Prince Francis Joseph II.

116 Heinrich von Frauenberg

1961. Minnesingers (1st issue). Multicoloured. Reproduction from the Manessian Manuscript of Songs.

407	15r. Type **116**	25	55
408	25r. Ulrich von Liechtenstein	75	75
409	35r. Ulrich von Gutenberg	90	90
410	1f. Konrad von Altstatten	2·20	2·20
411	1f.50 Walther von der Vogelweide	11·50	18·00

See also Nos. 415/18 and 428/31.

117 "Power Transmission"

1961. Europa.

412	**117**	50r. multicoloured	55	55

117a Prince John II

1962. 50th Anniv of First Liechtenstein Postage Stamps. Sheet 133×118 mm. T **117a** and similar horiz design.
MS412a 5r. green; 10r. red; 25r. blue.
Sold at 2f.60 7·25 5·50
DESIGNS: 0r. Prince Francis I; 25r. Prince Francis Joseph I.

118 Clasped Hands

1962. Europa.

413	**118**	50r. red and blue	3·00	35

119 Campaign Emblem

1962. Malaria Eradication.

414	**119**	50r. blue	75	75

1962. Minnesingers (2nd issue). As T **116**. Mult.

415	20r. King Konradin	75	75
416	30r. Kraft von Toggenburg	1·50	1·50
417	40r. Heinrich von Veldig	1·50	1·50
418	2f. Tannhauser	1·80	1·80

120 Pieta

1962. Christmas.

419	**120**	30r. mauve	75	75
420	-	50r. red	1·10	1·10
421	-	1f.20 blue	1·80	1·80

DESIGNS: 50r. Fresco with angel; 1f.20, View of Mauren.
See also Nos. 438/40.

121 Prince Francis Joseph II

1963. 25th Anniv of Reign of Prince Francis Joseph II.

422	**121**	5f. green	7·25	5·50

122 Milk and Bread

1963. Freedom from Hunger.

423	**122**	50r. brown, purple and red	1·00	75

123 "Angel of Annunciation"

1963. Red Cross Cent. Cross in red; background grey.

424	**123**	20r. yellow and green	35	35
425	-	80r. violet and mauve	1·10	1·10
426	-	1f. blue and ultramarine	1·50	1·50

DESIGNS: 80r. "The Epiphany"; 1f. "Family".

124 "Europa"

1963. Europa.

427	**124**	50r. multicoloured	1·50	1·10

1963. Minnesingers (3rd issue). As T **116**. Mult.

428	25r. Heinrich von Sax	35	35
429	30r. Kristan von Hamle	75	75
430	75r. Werner von Teufen	1·10	1·10
431	1f.70 Hartmann von Aue	2·20	2·20

125 Olympic Rings and Flags

1964. Olympic Games, Tokyo.
| 432 | 125 | 50r. red, black and blue | 75 | 75 |

126 Arms of Counts of Werdenberg, Vaduz

1964. Arms (1st issue). Multicoloured.
433	20f. Type **126**		30	30
434	30f. Barons of Brandis		45	45
435	80r. Counts of Sulz		1·10	1·10
436	1f.50 Counts of Hohenems		1·80	1·80

See also Nos. 443/6.

127 Roman Castle, Schaan

1964. Europa.
| 437 | 127 | 50f. multicoloured | 1·80 | 1·10 |

1964. Christmas. As T **120**.
438	10r. purple		35	35
439	40r. blue		55	55
440	1f.30 purple		1·80	1·80

DESIGNS: 10r. Masescha Chapel; 40r. "Mary Magdalene" (altar painting); 1f.30, "St. Sebastian, Madonna and Child, and St. Rochus" (altar painting).

128 P. Kaiser

1964. Death Centenary of Peter Kaiser (historian).
| 441 | 128 | 1f. green on cream | 1·50 | 1·50 |

129 "Madonna" (wood sculpture, c. 1700)

1965
| 442 | 129 | 10f. red | 14·50 | 7·25 |

1965. Arms (2nd issue). As T **126**. Multicoloured.
443	20r. Von Schellenberg		30	30
444	30r. Von Gutenberg		45	45
445	80r. Von Frauenberg		1·10	1·10
446	1f. Von Ramschwag		1·10	1·10

130 Europa "Links" (ancient belt-buckle)

1965. Europa.
| 447 | 130 | 50r. brown, grey and blue | 75 | 75 |

131 "Jesus in the Temple"

1965. Birth Centenary of Ferdinand Nigg (painter).
448	-	10r. deep green and green	30	30
449	-	30r. brown and orange	35	35
450	131	1f.20 green and blue	1·20	1·30

DESIGNS—VERT: 10r. "The Annunciation"; 30r. "The Magi".

132 Princess Gina and Prince Franz (after painting by Pedro Leitao)

1965. Special Issue.
| 451 | 132 | 75r. multicoloured | 90 | 90 |

See also No. 457.

133 Telecommunications Symbols

1965. Centenary of I.T.U.
| 452 | 133 | 25r. multicoloured | 35 | 35 |

134 Tree ("Wholesome Earth")

1966. Nature Protection.
453	134	10r. green and yellow	20	20
454	-	20r. blue and light blue	20	20
455	-	30r. blue and green	20	20
456	-	1f.50 red and yellow	1·70	1·70

DESIGNS: 20r. Bird ("Pure Air"); 30r. Fish ("Clean Water"); 1f.50, Sun ("Protection of Nature").

1966. Prince Franz Joseph II's 60th Birthday. As T **132** but with portrait of Prince Franz and inscr "1906–1966".
| 457 | 1f. multicoloured | | 1·30 | 1·30 |

135 Arms of Herren von Richenstein

1966. Arms of Triesen Families. Multicoloured.
458	20r. Type **135**		35	35
459	30r. Jinker Vaistli		45	45
460	60r. Edle von Trisun		85	85
461	1f.20 Die von Schiel		1·30	1·30

136 Europa "Ship"

1966. Europa.
| 462 | 136 | 50r. multicoloured | 75 | 75 |

137 Vaduz Parish Church

1966. Restoration of Vaduz Parish Church.
463	137	5r. green and red	20	20
464	-	20r. purple and bistre	35	35
465	-	30r. blue and red	45	45
466	-	1f.70 brown and green	2·00	2·00

DESIGNS: 20r. St. Florin; 30r. Madonna; 1f.70, God the Father.

138 Cogwheels

1967. Europa.
| 467 | 138 | 50r. multicoloured | 75 | 60 |

139 "The Man from Malanser"

1967. Liechtenstein Sagas (1st series). Multicoloured.
468	20r. Type **139**		35	35
469	30r. "The Treasure of Gutenberg"		45	35
470	1f.20 "The Giant of Guflina"		1·50	1·20

See also Nos. 492/4 and 516/18.

140 Crown Prince Hans Adam

1967. Royal Wedding. Sheet 86×95 mm comprising T **140** and similar vert design.
| MS471 | 1f.50 indigo and blue (T **140**); 1f.50 brown and light brown (Princess Marie) | 4·25 | 3·75 |

141 "Alpha and Omega"

1967. Christian Symbols. Multicoloured.
472	20r. Type **141**		35	35
473	30r. "Tropaion" (Cross as victory symbol)		45	35
474	70r. Christ's monogram		1·10	85

142 Father J. B. Buchel (educator, historian and poet)

1967. Buchel Commemoration.
| 475 | 142 | 1f. red and green | 1·50 | 1·10 |

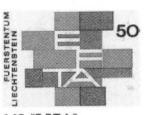
143 "E.F.T.A."

1967. European Free Trade Association.
| 476 | 143 | 50r. multicoloured | 75 | 60 |

144 "Peter and Paul", Mauren

1967. "Patrons of the Church". Multicoloured.
477	5r. "St. Joseph", Planken		15	15
478	10r. "St. Lawrence", Schaan		30	30
479	20r. Type **144**		35	35
480	40r. "St. Nicholas", Balzers		45	35
480a	40r. "St. Sebastian", Nendeln		75	50
481	50r. "St. George", Schellenberg		75	55
482	60r. "St. Martin", Eschen		85	65
483	70r. "St. Fridolin", Ruggell		95	80
484	80r. "St. Gallus", Triesen		1·10	85
485	1f. "St. Theodolus", Triesenberg		1·50	1·10
486	1f.20 "St. Anna", Vaduz Castle		1·60	1·30
487	1f.50 "St. Marie", Bendern-Camprin		2·20	1·60
488	2f. "St. Lucius", (patron saint of Liechtenstein)		3·00	2·20

145 Campaign Emblem

1967. "Technical Assistance".
| 489 | 145 | 50r.+20r. multicoloured | 1·10 | 1·10 |

146 Europa "Key"

1968. Europa.
| 490 | 146 | 50r. multicoloured | 75 | 60 |

147 Arms of Liechtenstein and Wilczek

1968. Silver Wedding Anniv of Prince Francis Joseph II and Princess Gina.
| 491 | 147 | 75r. multicoloured | 1·10 | 90 |

1968. Liechtenstein Sagas (2nd series). As T **139**. Multicoloured.
492	30r. "The Treasure of St. Mamerten"		45	35
493	50r. "The Hobgoblin in the Bergerwald"		75	55
494	80r. "The Three Sisters"		1·00	90

148 Sir Rowland Hill

1968. "Pioneers of Philately" (1st series).
495	148	20r. green	35	35
496	-	30r. brown	45	35
497	-	1f. black	1·50	1·20

PORTRAITS: 30r. Philippe de Ferrary; 1f. Maurice Burrus. See also Nos. 504/5 and 554/6.

150 Arms of Liechtenstein

1969
| 498 | 150 | 3f.50 brown | 4·25 | 2·50 |

151 Colonnade

1969. Europa.
| 499 | 151 | 50r. multicoloured | 75 | 60 |

152 "Biology"

1969. 250th Anniv of Liechtenstein. Multicoloured.
500	10r. Type **152**		35	35
501	30r. "Physics"		45	35
502	50r. "Astronomy"		80	60
503	80r. "Art"		1·20	1·10

1969. "Pioneers of Philately" (2nd series). As T **148**.
| 504 | 80r. brown | | 1·20 | 1·10 |
| 505 | 1f.20 blue | | 1·70 | 1·50 |

PORTRAITS: 80r. Carl Lindenberg; 1f.20, Theodore Champion.

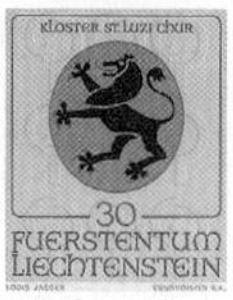
153 Arms of St. Luzi Monastery

1969. Arms of Church Patrons. Multicoloured.

506	20r. St. Johann's Abbey	35	35
507	30r. Type **153**	35	35
508	30r. Ladies' Priory, Schanis	45	35
509	30r. Knights Hospitallers, Feldkirch	45	45
510	50r. Pfafers Abbey	75	60
511	50r. Weingarten Abbey	75	65
512	75r. St. Gallen Abbey	1·10	85
513	1f.20 Ottobeuren Abbey	1·70	1·50
514	1f.50 Chur Episcopate	2·20	1·60

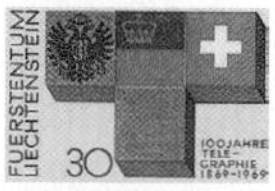
154 Symbolic "T"

1969. Centenary of Liechtenstein Telegraph System.

515	**154**	30r. multicoloured	45	35

1969. Liechtenstein Sagas (3rd series). As T 139. Multicoloured.

516	20r. "The Cheated Devil"	35	35
517	50r. "The Fiery Red Goat"	75	50
518	60r. "The Grafenberg Treasure"	80	65

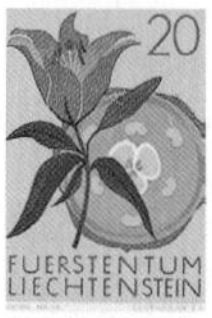
155 Orange Lily

1970. Nature Conservation Year. Multicoloured.

519	20r. Type **155**	35	35
520	30r. Wild orchid	60	45
521	50r. Ranunculus	85	80
522	1f.20 Bog bean	1·80	1·70

See also Nos. 532/5 and 548/51.

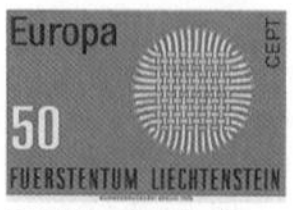
156 "Flaming Sun"

1970. Europa.

523	**156**	50r. yellow, blue and green	75	60

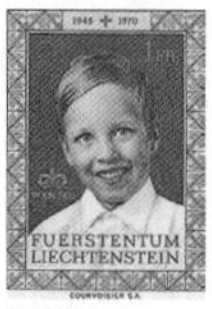
157 Prince Wenzel

1970. 25th Anniv of Liechtenstein Red Cross.

524	**157**	1f. multicoloured	1·50	1·10

1970. 800th Anniv of Wolfram von Eschenbach. Sheet 73×96 mm containing vert designs similar to T **116** from the "Codex Manaesse". Multicoloured.

MS525	30r. Wolfram von Eschenbach; 50r. Reinmar the Fiddler; 80r. Hartmann von Starkenberg; 1f.20 Friedrich von Hausen. Sold for 3f.	4·25	4·25

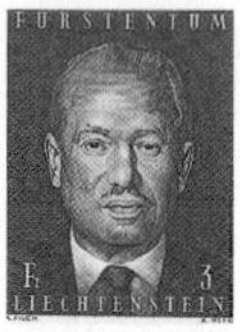
158 Prince Francis Joseph II

1970

526	-	1f.70 green	2·50	1·80
526a	-	2f.50 blue	3·75	2·50
527	**158**	3f. black	4·25	3·00

DESIGNS: 1f.70, Prince Hans Adam; 2f.50, Princess Gina.

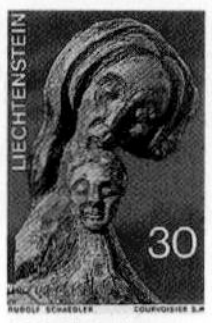
159 "Mother and Child" (R. Schadler)

1970. Christmas.

528	**159**	30r. multicoloured	45	35

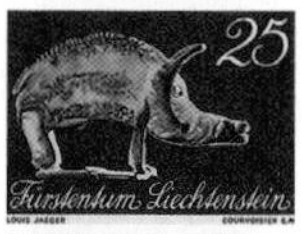
160 Bronze Boar (La Tene period)

1971. National Museum Inauguration.

529	**160**	25r. black, blue & ultram	35	35
530	-	30r. green and brown	45	35
531	-	75r. multicoloured	1·00	80

DESIGNS: 30r. Ornamental peacock (Roman, 2nd-century); 75r. Engraved bowl (13th-century).

1971. Liechtenstein Flowers (2nd series). As T **155**. Multicoloured.

532	10r. Cyclamen	35	35
533	20r. Moonwort	35	35
534	50r. Superb pink	75	65
535	1f.50 Alpine columbine	2·10	1·80

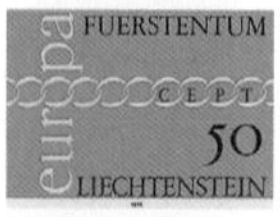
161 Europa Chain

1971. Europa.

536	**161**	50r. yellow, blue & black	75	60

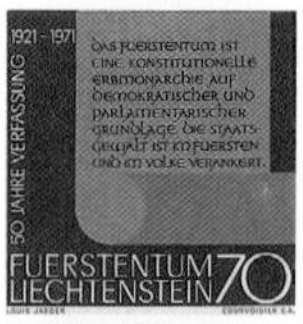
162 Part of Text

1971. 50th Anniv of 1921 Constitution. Mulicoloured.

537	70r. Type **162**	1·00	85
538	80r. Princely crown	1·20	95

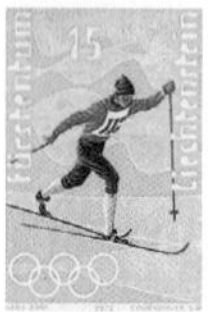
163 Cross-country Skiing

1971. Winter Olympic Games, Sapporo, Japan (1972). Multicoloured.

539	15r. Type **163**	35	35
540	40r. Ice hockey	60	55
541	65r. Downhill skiing	95	85
542	1f.50 Figure skating	2·20	2·00

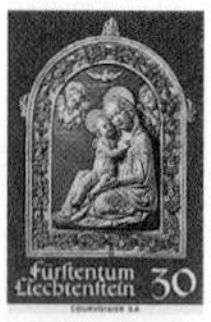
164 "Madonna and Child" (sculpture, Andrea della Robbia)

1971. Christmas.

543	**164**	30r. multicoloured	45	35

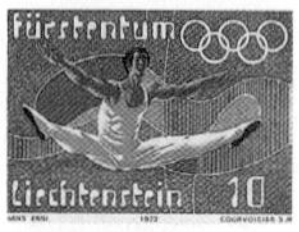
165 Gymnastics

1972. Olympic Games, Munich. Multicoloured.

544	10r. Type **165**	20	20
545	20r. High jumping	35	35
546	40r. Running	60	50
547	60r. Throwing the discus	80	75

1972. Liechtenstein Flowers (3rd series). As T **155**. Multicoloured.

548	20r. Sulphur anemone	35	35
549	30r. Turk's-cap lily	45	45
550	60r. Alpine centaury	85	75
551	1f.20 Reed-mace	1·70	1·50

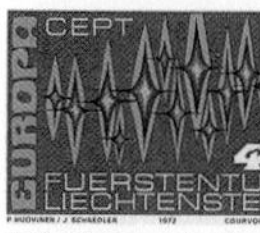
166 "Communications"

1972. Europa.

552	**166**	40r. multicoloured	75	50

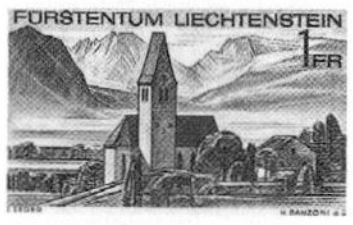
167 Bendern

1972. "Liba '72" Stamp Exhibition, Vaduz. Sheet 101×65 mm containing T **167** and similar horiz design.

MS553	1f. violet; 2f. red	4·25	4·25

DESIGN: 2f. Vaduz castle.

1972. "Pioneers of Philately" (3rd series). As T **148**.

554	30r. green	45	45
555	40r. purple	60	60
556	1f.30 blue	1·90	1·50

PORTRAITS: 30r. Emilio Diena; 40r. Andre de Cock; 1f.30, Theodore E. Steinway.

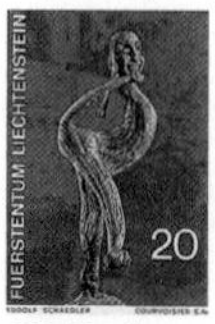
168 "Faun"

1972. "Natural Art". Motifs fashioned from roots and branches. Multicoloured.

557	20r. Type **168**	35	35
558	30r. "Dancer"	45	35
559	1f.10 "Owl"	1·50	1·30

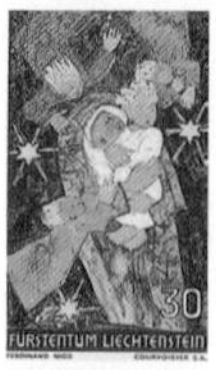
169 "Madonna with Angels" (F. Nigg)

1972. Christmas.

560	**169**	30r. multicoloured	45	35

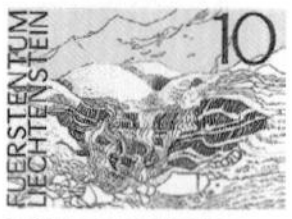
170 Lawena Springs

1972. Landscapes.

561	-	5r. purple and yellow	15	15
562	**170**	10r. green and light green	20	20
563	-	15r. brown and green	30	30
564	-	25r. purple and blue	35	35
565	-	30r. purple and brown	45	35
566	-	40r. purple and brown	60	45
567	-	50r. blue and lilac	75	55
568	-	60r. green and yellow	85	65
569	-	70r. blue and cobalt	1·00	80
570	-	80r. green and light green	1·20	85
571	-	1f. brown and green	1·50	1·10
572	-	1f.30 blue and green	1·90	1·50
573	-	1f.50 brown and blue	2·20	1·60
574	-	1f.80 brown & lt brown	2·50	2·00
575	-	2f. brown and blue	3·00	2·20

DESIGNS: 5r. Silum; 15r. Ruggeller Reed; 25r. Steg Kirchlispitz; 30r. Feld Schellenberg; 40r. Rennhof Mauren; 50r. Tidrufe; 60r. Eschner Riet; 70r. Mittagspitz; 80r. Schaan Forest; 1f. St. Peter's Chapel, Mals; 1f.30, Frommenhaus; 1f.50, Ochsenkopf; 1f.80, Hehlawangspitz; 2f. Saminaschlucht.

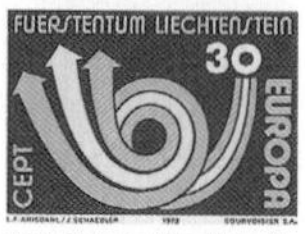
171 Europa "Posthorn"

1973. Europa.

576	**171**	30r. multicoloured	45	35
577	**171**	40r. multicoloured	60	50

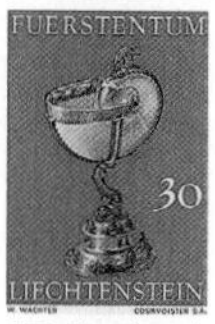
172 Chambered Nautilus Goblet

1973. Treasures from Prince's Collection (1st issue). Drinking Vessels. Multicoloured.

578	30r. Type **172**	45	45
579	70r. Ivory tankard	1·00	80
580	1f.10 Silver cup	1·60	1·30

See also Nos. 589/92.

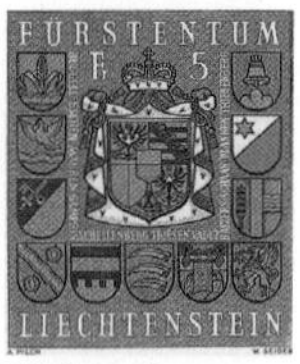
173 Arms of Liechtenstein

1973

581	**173**	5f. multicoloured	7·25	4·25

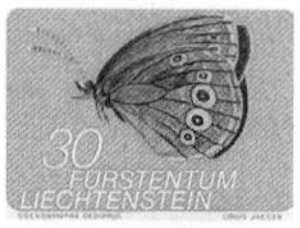
174 False Ringlet

1973. Small Fauna of Liechtenstein (1st series). Multicoloured.

582	30r. Type **174**	45	45
583	40r. Curlew	60	50
584	60r. Edible frog	80	75
585	80r. Grass snake	1·10	85

See also Nos. 596/9.

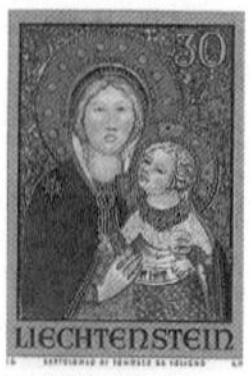
175 "Madonna" (Bartolomeo di Tommaso da Foligno)

1973. Christmas.

586	**175**	30r. multicoloured	45	35

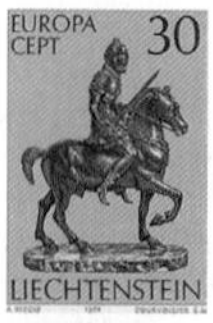
176 "Shouting Horseman" (sculpture, Andrea Riccio)

1974. Europa. Multicoloured.

587	30r. Type **176**	45	35
588	40r. "Squatting Aphrodite" (sculpture, Antonio Susini)	60	50

1974. Treasures from Prince's Collection (2nd issue). Porcelain. As T **172**. Multicoloured.

589	30r. Vase, 19th century	45	35
590	50r. Vase, 1740	75	55
591	60r. Vase, 1830	80	75
592	1f. Vase, c. 1700	1·30	1·30

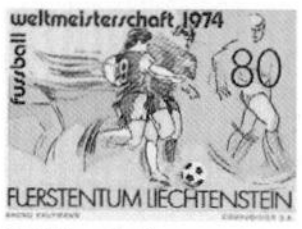
177 Footballers

1974. World Cup Football Championship, West Germany.

593	**177**	80f. multicoloured	1·20	1·10

178 Posthorn and U.P.U. Emblem

1974. Centenary of Universal Postal Union.

594	**178**	40r. black, green and gold	60	50
595	**178**	60r. black, red and gold	85	75

1974. Small Fauna of Liechtenstein (2nd series). As T **174**. Multicoloured.

596	15r. Mountain newt	30	30
597	25r. Adder	35	35
598	70r. Cynthia's fritillary (butterfly)	1·00	95
599	1f.10 Three-toed woodpecker	1·60	1·50

179 Bishop Marxer

1974. Death Centenary of Bishop Franz Marxer.

600	**179**	1f. multicoloured	1·50	1·10

180 Prince Francis Joseph II and Princess Gina

1974

601	**180**	10f. brown and gold	11·00	11·00

181 "St. Florian"

1974. Christmas. Glass Paintings. Multicoloured.

602	**181**	30r. Type **181**	45	35
603		50r. "St. Wendelin"	75	60
604		60r. "St. Mary, Anna and Joachim"	80	75
605		70r. "Jesus in Manger"	95	85

182 Prince Constantin

1975. Liechtenstein Princes.

606	**182**	70r. green and gold	1·00	95
607	-	80r. purple and gold	1·20	1·10
608	-	1f.20 blue and gold	1·70	1·60

PORTRAITS: 80r. Prince Maximilian; 1f.20, Prince Alois.

183 "Cold Sun" (M. Frommelt)

1975. Europa. Paintings. Multicoloured.

609	**183**	30r. Type **183**	45	35
610		60r. "Village" (L. Jager)	85	75

184 Imperial Cross

1975. Imperial Insignia (1st series). Multicoloured.

611	**184**	30r. Type **184**	45	35
612		60r. Imperial sword	85	75
613		1f. Imperial orb	1·50	1·30
614		1f.30 Imperial robe (50x32 mm)	3·00	3·00
615		2f. Imperial crown	3·00	2·75

See also Nos. 670/3.

185 "Red Cross Activities"

1975. 30th Anniv of Liechtenstein Red Cross.

616	**185**	60r. multicoloured	85	75

186 St. Mamerten, Triesen

1975. European Architectural Heritage Year. Multicoloured.

617		40r. Type **186**	60	55
618		50r. Red House, Vaduz	80	75
619		70r. Prebendary buildings, Eschen	1·00	90
620		1f. Gutenberg Castle, Balzers	1·60	1·50

187 Speed Skating

1975. Winter Olympic Games, Innsbruck (1976). Multicoloured.

621	20r. Type **187**	35	35
622	25r. Ice hockey	35	35
623	70r. Downhill skiing	1·10	95
624	1f.20 Slalom	1·80	95

188 "Daniel in the Lions' Den"

1975. Christmas and Holy Year. Capitals in Chur Cathedral.

625	**188**	30r. violet and gold	45	35
626	-	60r. green and gold	85	75
627	-	90r. red and gold	1·20	1·00

DESIGNS: 60r. "Madonna"; 90r. "St. Peter".

189 Mouflon

1976. Europa. Ceramics by Prince Hans von Liechtenstein. Multicoloured.

628	40r. Type **189**	60	45
629	80r. "Ring-necked Pheasant and Brood"	1·20	1·00

190 Crayfish

1976. World Wildlife Fund. Multicoloured.

630	25r. Type **190**	35	35
631	40r. Turtle	75	60
632	70r. European otter	1·10	1·00
633	80r. Northern lapwing	1·50	1·30

191 Roman Fibula

1976. 75th Anniv of National Historical Society.

634	**191**	90r. multicoloured	1·50	1·30

192 Obverse of 50f. Coin depicting portrait of Prince

1976. 70th Birthday of Prince Francis Joseph II. Sheet 102×65 mm containing T **192** and similar horiz design. Multicoloured.

MS635 1f. Type **192**; 1f. Reverse of 50f.
coin depicting Arms of Liechtenstein   3·00   3·00

193 Judo

1976. Olympic Games, Montreal. Multicoloured.

636	35r. Type **193**	50	45
637	50r. Volleyball	75	65
638	80r. Relay	1·20	1·10
639	1f.10 Long jumping	1·60	1·50

194 "Singing Angels"

1976. 400th Birth Anniv (1977) of Peter Paul Rubens (painter). Multicoloured.

640	50r. Type **194**	75	75
641	70r. "Sons of the Artist"	1·10	1·10
642	1f. "Daughters of Cecrops" (49×39 mm)	5·50	5·50

195 "Pisces"

1976. Signs of the Zodiac (1st series). Multicoloured.

643	20r. Type **195**	35	35
644	40r. "Aries"	50	50
645	80r. "Taurus"	1·20	1·00
646	90r. "Gemini"	1·30	1·10

See also Nos. 666/9 and 710/13.

196 "Child Jesus of Prague"

1976. Christmas. Monastic Wax Sculptures. Multicoloured.

647	20r. Type **196**	35	35
648	50r. "The Flight into Egypt" (vert)	75	50
649	80r. "Holy Trinity" (vert)	1·20	1·00
650	1f.50 "Holy Family"	2·20	3·50

197 Sarcophagus Statue, Chur Cathedral

1976. Bishop Ortlieb von Brandis of Chur Commemoration.

651	**197**	1f.10 brown and gold	1·60	1·50

199 Map of Liechtenstein, 1721 (J. Heber)

1977. Europa. Multicoloured.

664	**199**	40r. Type **199**	60	50
665		80r. "View of Vaduz, 1815" (F. Bachmann)	1·20	95

1977. Signs of the Zodiac (2nd series). As T **195**. Multicoloured.

666	40r. "Cancer"	60	50
667	70r. "Leo"	1·00	95
668	80r. "Virgo"	1·20	1·10
669	1f.10 "Libra"	1·60	1·50

1977. Imperial Insignia (2nd series). As T **184**. Multicoloured.

670	40r. Holy Lance and Reliquary with Particle of the Cross	60	50
671	50r. "St. Matthew" (Imperial Book of Gospels)	75	60
672	80r. St. Stephen's Purse	1·10	1·00
673	90r. Tabard of Imperial Herald	1·20	1·20

200 Coin of Emperor Constantine II

1977. Coins (1st series). Multicoloured.

674		35r. Type **200**	60	50
675		70r. Lindau Brakteat	1·10	95
676		80r. Coin of Ortlieb von Brandis	1·20	1·10

See also Nos. 707/9.

201 Frauenthal Castle, Styria

1977. Castles.

677	**201**	20r. green and gold	35	35
678	-	50r. red and gold	75	75
679	-	80r. lilac and gold	1·20	1·20
680	-	90r. blue and gold	1·50	1·50

DESIGNS: 50r. Gross-Ullersdorf, Moravia; 80r. Liechtenstein Castle, near Modling, Austria; 90r. Palais Liechtenstein, Alserbachstrasse, Vienna.

202 Children in Costume

1977. National Costumes. Multicoloured.

681		40r. Type **202**	60	50
682		70r. Two girls in traditional costume	1·10	95
683		1f. Woman in festive costume	1·60	1·50

203 Princess Tatjana

1977. Princess Tatjana.

684	**203**	1f.10 lt brn, brn & gold	1·80	1·50

204 "Angel"

1977. Christmas. Sculptures by Erasmus Kern. Multicoloured.

685	20r. Type **204**	35	35
686	50r. "St. Rochus"	75	65

| 687 | 80r. "Madonna" | 1·20 | 1·00 |
| 688 | 1f.50 "God the Father" | 3·00 | 2·75 |

205 Palais
Liechtenstein,
Bankgasse, Vienna

1978. Europa.

| 689 | **205** | 40r. blue and gold | 60 | 50 |
| 690 | - | 80r. red and gold | 1·20 | 95 |

DESIGN: 80r. Feldsberg Castle.

206 Farmhouse,
Triesen

1978. Buildings. Multicoloured.

691	10r. Type **206**	20	15
692	20r. Upper village of Triesen	35	30
693	35r. Barns at Balzers	50	35
694	40r. Monastery building, Bendern	60	45
695	50r. Rectory tower, Balzers-Mals	75	55
696	70r. Rectory, Mauren	95	80
697	80r. Farmhouse, Schellenberg	1·20	85
698	90r. Rectory, Balzers	1·30	1·00
699	1f. Rheinberger House, Vaduz	1·50	1·10
700	1f.10 Vaduz Mitteldorf	1·60	1·20
701	1f.50 Town Hall, Triesenberg	2·20	1·70
702	2f. National Museum and Administrator's residence, Vaduz	3·00	2·20

207 Vaduz Castle

1978. 40th Anniv of Prince Francis Joseph II's Accession. Royal Residence. Multicoloured.

703	40r. Type **207**	65	65
704	50r. Courtyard	75	75
705	70r. Hall	1·00	1·00
706	80r. High Altar, Castle Chapel	1·20	1·20

208 Coin of
Prince Charles

1978. Coins (2nd series). Multicoloured.

707	40r. Type **208**	60	50
708	50r. Coin of Prince John Adam	75	65
709	80r. Coin of Prince Joseph Wenzel	1·20	1·00

1978. Signs of the Zodiac (3rd series). As T **195**. Multicoloured.

710	40r. "Scorpio"	60	50
711	50r. "Sagittarius"	80	75
712	80r. "Capricorn"	1·20	1·10
713	1f.50 "Aquarius"	2·20	2·00

209 "Portrait of a
Piebald" (J. G. von
Hamilton and A.
Faistenberger)

1978. Paintings. Multicoloured.

| 714 | 70r. Type **209** | 95 | 95 |
| 715 | 80r. "Portrait of a Blackish-brown Stallion" (J. G. von Hamilton) | 1·10 | 1·10 |

| 716 | 1f.10 "Golden Carriage of Prince Joseph Wenzel" (Martin von Meytens) (48½×38 mm) | 1·60 | 1·60 |

210
"Adoration
of the
Shepherds"

1978. Christmas. Church Windows, Triesenberg. Multicoloured.

717	20r. Type **210**	35	35
718	50r. "Enthroned Madonna with St. Joseph"	75	65
719	80r. "Adoration of the Magi"	1·20	1·10

211 Comte AC-8 Mail
Plane "St. Gallen" over
Schaan

1979. Europa. Multicoloured.

| 720 | 40r. Type **211** | 60 | 60 |
| 721 | 80r. Airship LZ-127 "Graf Zeppelin" over Vaduz Castle | 1·20 | 1·20 |

212 Child
Drinking

1979. International Year of the Child. Multicoloured.

722	80r. Type **212**	1·20	1·10
723	90r. Child eating	1·30	1·20
724	1f.10 Child reading	1·50	1·40

213 Ordered
Wave-field

1979. 50th Anniv of International Radio Consultative Committee (CCIR).

| 725 | **213** | 50r. blue and black | 75 | 65 |

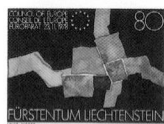

214 Abstract Composition

1979. Liechtenstein's Entry into Council of Europe.

| 726 | **214** | 80r. multicoloured | 1·20 | 1·00 |

215 Sun rising
over Continents

1979. Development Aid.

| 727 | **215** | 1f. multicoloured | 1·40 | 1·20 |

216 Arms of Carl
Ludwig von Sulz

1979. Heraldic Windows in the Liechtenstein National Museum. Multicoloured.

728	40r. Type **216**	60	50
729	70r. Arms of Barbara von Sulz	1·00	95
730	1f.10 Arms of Ulrich von Ramschwag and Barbara von Hallwil	1·70	1·50

217 Sts. Lucius and
Florian (fresco,
Waltensberg-Vuorz
Church)

1979. Patron Saints.

| 731 | **217** | 20f. multicoloured | 22·00 | 18·00 |

218 Base of Ski Slope,
Valuna

1979. Winter Olympic Games, Lake Placid (1980). Multicoloured.

732	40r. Type **218**	60	50
733	70r. Malbun and Ochsenkopf	1·00	95
734	1f.50 Ski-lift, Sareis	2·00	1·80

219 "The Annunciation"

1979. Christmas. Embroideries by Ferdinand Nigg. Multicoloured.

735	20r. Type **219**	35	35
736	50r. "Christmas"	75	65
737	80r. "Blessed are the Peacemakers"	1·20	95

220 Maria
Leopoldine von
Esterhazy (bust
by Canova)

1980. Europa.

| 738 | **220** | 40r. green, turq & gold | 45 | 50 |
| 739 | | 80r. brown, red and gold | 1·20 | 95 |

DESIGN: 80r. Maria Theresia von Liechtenstein (after Martin von Meytens).

221 Arms of Andreas
Buchel, 1690

1980. Arms of Bailiffs (1st series). Multicoloured.

740	40r. Type **221**	60	50
741	70r. Georg Marxer, 1745	1·00	95
742	80r. Luzius Frick, 1503	1·20	1·10
743	1f.10 Adam Oehri, 1634	1·60	1·50

See also Nos. 763/6, and 788/91.

222 3r. Stamp
of 1930

1980. 50th Anniv of Postal Museum.

| 744 | **222** | 80r. red, green and grey | 1·20 | 1·10 |

223 Milking Pail

1980. Alpine Dairy Farming Implements. Multicoloured.

745	20r. Type **223**	35	35
746	50r. Wooden heart dairy herd descent marker	75	65
747	80r. Butter churn	1·20	1·00

224 Crossbow

1980. Hunting Weapons.

748	**224**	80r. brown and lilac	1·20	1·10
749	-	90r. black and green	1·30	1·20
750	-	1f.10 black and stone	1·50	1·40

DESIGNS: 90r. Spear and knife; 1f.10, Rifle and powderhorn.

225 Triesenberg Costumes

1980. Costumes. Multicoloured.

751	40r. Type **225**	60	50
752	70r. Dancers, Schellenberg	1·10	95
753	80r. Brass band, Mauren	1·20	1·10

226 Beech Trees,
Matrula (spring)

1980. The Forest in the Four Seasons. Multicoloured.

754	40r. Type **226**	60	50
755	50r. Firs in the Valorsch (summer)	80	75
756	80r. Beech tree, Schaan (autumn)	1·20	1·10
757	1f.50 Edge of forest at Oberplanken (winter)	2·20	2·00

227 Angel
bringing
Shepherds
Good Tidings

1980. Christmas. Multicoloured.

758	20r. Type **227**	35	35
759	50r. Crib	75	65
760	80r. Epiphany	1·20	1·00

228 National
Day Procession

1981. Europa. Multicoloured.

761	40r. Fireworks at Vaduz Castle	60	50
762	80r. Type **228**	1·20	95

1981. Arms of Bailiffs (2nd series). As T **221**. Multicoloured.

763	40r. Anton Meier, 1748	60	50
764	70r. Kaspar Kindle, 1534	1·00	95
765	80r. Hans Adam Negele, 1600	1·20	1·10
766	1f.10 Peter Matt, 1693	1·60	1·50

229 Prince Alois and Princess Elisabeth with Francis Joseph

1981. 75th Birthday of Prince Francis Joseph II. Sheet 120×87 mm containing T **229** and similar vert designs. Multicoloured.

MS767 70r. Type **229**; 80r. Princes Alois and Francis Joseph; 150r. Prince Francis Joseph II   4·25   4·25

230 Scout Emblems

1981. 50th Anniv of Liechtenstein Boy Scout and Girl Guide Movements.

768	**230** 20r. multicoloured	45	40

231 Symbols of Disability

1981. International Year of Disabled Persons.

769	**231** 40r. multicoloured	60	50

232 St. Theodul (sculpture)

1981. 1600th Birth Anniv of St. Theodul.

770	**232** 80r. multicoloured	1·20	1·00

233 "Xanthoria parietina"

1981. Mosses and Lichens. Multicoloured.

771	40r. Type **233**	60	50
772	50r. "Parmelia physodes"	80	75
773	70r. "Sphagnum palustre"	1·00	95
774	80r. "Amblystegium serpens"	1·70	1·60

234 Gutenberg Castle

1981. Gutenberg Castle. Multicoloured.

775	20r. Type **234**	35	35
776	40r. Courtyard	65	65
777	50r. Parlour	75	75
778	1f.10 Great Hall	1·80	1·80

235 Cardinal Karl Borromaus von Mailand

1981. Famous Visitors to Liechtenstein (1st series). Multicoloured.

779	40r. Type **235**	60	60
780	70r. Johann Wolfgang von Goethe (writer)	1·00	95
781	89r. Alexander Dumas the younger (writer)	1·20	1·10
782	1f. Hermann Hesse (writer)	1·50	1·40

See also Nos. 804/7 and 832/5.

236 St. Nicholas blessing Children

1981. Christmas. Multicoloured.

783	20r. Type **236**	35	35
784	50r. Adoration of the Kings	75	65
785	80r. Holy Family	1·20	1·00

237 Peasant Revolt, 1525

1982. Europa. Multicoloured.

786	40r. Type **237**	60	50
787	80r. King Wenceslaus with Counts (Imperial direct rule, 1396)	1·20	95

1982. Arms of Bailiffs (3rd series). As T **221**. Multicoloured.

788	40r. Johann Kaiser, 1664	60	50
789	70r. Joseph Anton Kaufmann, 1748	1·00	95
790	80r. Christoph Walser, 1690	1·20	1·10
791	1f.10 Stephan Banzer, 1658	1·60	1·50

238 Triesenberg Sports Ground

1982. World Cup Football Championship, Spain. Multicoloured.

792	15r. Type **238**	20	20
793	25r. Eschen/Mauren playing fields	35	35
794	1f.80 Rheinau playing fields, Balzers	2·50	2·30

239 Crown Prince Hans Adam

1982. "Liba 82" Stamp Exhibition. Multicoloured.

795	1f. Type **239**	1·50	1·50
796	1f. Princess Marie Aglae	1·50	1·50

240 Tractor (agriculture)

1982. Rural Industries. Multicoloured.

797	30r. Type **240**	45	45
798	50r. Cutting flowers (horti-culture)	75	65
799	70r. Workers with logs (forestry)	1·00	95
800	150r. Worker and milk (dairy farming)	2·20	2·00

241 "Neu Schellenberg"

1982. 150th Birth Anniv of Mortiz Menzinger (artist). Multicoloured.

801	40r. Type **241**	60	50
802	50r. "Vaduz"	85	75
803	100r. "Bendern"	1·50	1·30

242 Angelika Kauffmann (artist, self-portrait)

1982. Famous Visitors to Liechtenstein (2nd series). Multicoloured.

804	40r. Emperor Maximilian I (after Benhard Strigel)	60	50
805	70f. Georg Jenatsch (liberator of Grisons)	1·00	95
806	80r. Type **242**	1·20	1·10
807	1f. St. Fidelis of Sigmaringen	1·60	1·50

243 Angel playing Lute

1982. Christmas. Details from High Altar by Jakob Russ, Chur Cathedral. Multicoloured.

808	20r. Type **243**	35	35
809	50r. Madonna and child	75	65
810	80r. Angel playing organ	1·20	1·00

244 Notker Balbulus of St. Gall

1983. Europa. Multicoloured.

811	40r. Type **244**	60	50
812	80r. Hildegard of Bingen	1·20	95

245 Shrove Thursday

1983. Shrovetide and Lent Customs. Multicoloured

813	40r. Type **245**	60	50
814	70r. Shrovetide carnival	1·10	95
815	1f.80 Lent Sunday bonfire	2·75	2·50

246 River Bank

1983. Anniversaries and Events. Multicoloured.

816	20r. Type **246**	50	35
817	40r. Montgolfier Brothers' balloon	60	50
818	50r. Airmail envelope	75	65
819	80r. Plant and hands holding spade	1·10	1·00

EVENTS: 20r. Council of Europe river and coasts protection campaign; 40r. Bicentenary of manned flight; 50r. World Communications Year; 80r. Overseas aid.

247 "Schaan"

1983. Landscape Paintings by Anton Ender. Multicoloured

820	40r. Type **247**	60	50
821	50r. "Gutenberg Castle"	85	75
822	200r. "Steg Reservoir"	3·00	2·75

248 Princess Gina

1983. Multicoloured.. Multicoloured.

823	2f.50 Type **248**	3·75	2·50
824	3f. Prince Francis Joseph II	4·25	3·00

249 Pope John Paul II

1983. Holy Year.

825	**249** 80r. multicoloured	1·20	1·10

250 Snowflakes and Stripes

1983. Winter Olympic Games, Sarajevo. Multicoloured.

826	40r. Type **250**	60	50
827	80r. Snowflake	1·20	1·10
828	1f.80 Snowflake and rays	2·50	2·40

251 Seeking Shelter

1983. Christmas. Multicoloured.

829	20r. Type **251**	35	35
830	50r. Infant Jesus	75	65
831	80r. Three Kings	1·20	1·00

252 Aleksandr Vassilievich Suvorov (Russian general)

1984. Famous Visitors to Liechtenstein (3rd series). Multicoloured.

832	40r. Type **252**	65	60
833	70r. Karl Rudolf von Buol-Schauenstein, Bishop of Chur	1·00	95
834	80r. Carl Zuckmayer (dramatist)	1·20	1·10
835	1f. Curt Goetz (actor)	1·50	1·40

253 Bridge

1984. Europa. 25th Anniv of E.P.T. Conference

836	**253** 50r. blue and deep blue	75	65
837	**253** 80r. pink and brown	1·10	1·00

254 The Warning Messenger

1984. Liechtenstein Legends. The Destruction of Trisona. Each brown, grey and blue.

838	35r. Type **254**	50	45
839	50r. The buried town	80	65
840	80r. The spared family	1·20	1·10

255 Pole Vaulting

1984. Olympic Games, Los Angeles. Multicoloured

841	70r. Type **255**	1·00	85
842	80r. Throwing the discus	1·20	1·10
843	1f. Putting the shot	1·50	1·30

256 Currency (trade and banking)

1984. Occupations. Multicoloured.

844	5r. Type **256**	15	15
845	10r. Plumber adjusting pipe (building trade)	20	20
846	20r. Operating machinery (industry—production)	35	35
847	35r. Draughtswoman (building trade—planning)	60	45
848	45r. Office worker and world map (industry—sales)	85	65
849	50r. Cook (tourism)	95	60
850	60r. Carpenter (building trade—interior decoration)	1·10	75
851	70r. Doctor injecting patient (medical services)	1·20	1·00
852	80r. Scientist (industrial research)	1·30	1·20
853	100r. Bricklayer (building trade)	1·60	1·30
854	120r. Flow chart (industry—administration)	2·00	1·60
855	150r. Handstamping covers (post and communications)	2·75	2·00

257 Princess Marie

1984. Multicoloured.

856	1f.70 Type **257**	2·20	50
857	2f. Crown Prince Hans Adam	3·00	75

258 Annunciation

1984. Christmas. Multicoloured.

858	35r. Type **258**	50	50
859	50r. Holy Family	80	75
860	80r. The Three Kings	1·20	1·10

259 Apollo and the Muses playing Music (detail from 18th-century harpsichord lid)

1985. Europa. Music Year. Multicoloured.

861	50r. Type **259**	75	75
862	80r. Apollo and the Muses playing music (different)	1·10	1·10

260 St. Elisabeth Convent, Schaan

1985. Monasteries. Multicoloured.

863	50r. Type **260**	75	75
864	1f. Schellenberg Convent	1·50	1·50

865	1f.70 Gutenberg Mission, Balzers	2·50	2·50

261 Princess Gina and handing out of Rations

1985. 40th Anniv of Liechtenstein Red Cross. Multicoloured.

866	20r. Type **261**	45	45
867	50r. Princess Gina and Red Cross ambulance	1·10	1·10
868	120r. Princess Gina with refugee children	2·10	2·10

262 Justice

1985. Cardinal Virtues. Multicoloured.

869	35r. Type **262**	50	50
870	50r. Temperance	75	75
871	70r. Prudence	95	95
872	1f. Fortitude	1·50	1·50

263 Papal Arms

1985. Papal Visit. Sheet 100×67 mm containing T **263** and similar vert designs. Multicoloured.

MS873	50r. Type **263**; 80r. St. Maria zum Trost Chapel; 170r. Our Lady of Liechtenstein (statue) (29×43 mm)	4·25	4·25

264 "Portrait of a Canon" (Quentin Massys)

1985. Paintings in Metropolitan Museum, New York. Multicoloured.

874	50r. Type **264**	85	85
875	1f. "Clara Serena Rubens" (Rubens)	2·00	2·00
876	1f.20 "Duke of Urbino" (Raphael)	1·80	1·80

265 Halberd used by Charles I's Bodyguard

1985. Guards' Weapons and Armour. Mult.

877	35r. Type **265**	50	35
878	50r. Morion used by Charles I's bodyguard	85	85
879	80r. Halberd used by Carl Eusebius's bodyguard	1·20	1·20

266 Frankincense

1985. Christmas. Multicoloured.

880	35r. Type **266**	60	60
881	50r. Gold	80	75
882	80r. Myrrh	1·20	1·20

267 Puppets performing Tragedy

1985. Theatre. Multicoloured.

883	50r. Type **267**	85	85
884	80r. Puppets performing comedy	1·20	1·20
885	1f.50 Opera	2·30	2·30

268 Courtyard

1986. Vaduz Castle. Multicoloured.

886	20r. Type **268**	30	20
887	25r. Keep	35	30
888	50r. Castle	75	60
889	90r. Inner gate	1·10	95
890	1f.10 Castle from gardens	1·50	1·30
891	1f.40 Courtyard (different)	1·80	1·60

269 Barn Swallows

1986. Europa. Birds. Multicoloured.

892	50r. Type **269**	75	75
893	90r. European robin	1·50	1·50

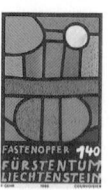

270 "Offerings"

1986. Lenten Fast.

894	**270** 1f.40 multicoloured	2·20	2·20

271 Palm Sunday

1986. Religious Festivals. Multicoloured.

895	35r. Type **271**	60	60
896	50r. Wedding	85	85
897	70r. Rogation Day procession	1·10	1·10

272 Karl Freiherr Haus von Hausen

1986. 125th Anniv of Liechtenstein Land Bank.

898	**272** 50r. brown, ochre and buff	75	75

273 Francis Joseph II

1986. 80th Birthday of Prince Francis Joseph II.

899	**273** 3f.50 multicoloured	4·25	3·75

274 Roebuck in Ruggeller Riet

1986. Hunting. Multicoloured.

900	35r. Type **274**	60	60
901	50r. Chamois at Rappenstein	85	85
902	1f.70 Stag in Lawena	3·00	3·00

275 Cabbage and Beetroot

1986. Field Crops. Multicoloured.

903	50r. Type **275**	85	85
904	80r. Red cabbages	1·30	1·30
905	90r. Potatoes, onions and garlic	1·50	1·50

276 Archangel Michael

1986. Christmas. Multicoloured.

906	35r. Type **276**	60	60
907	50r. Archangel Gabriel	85	85
908	90r. Archangel Raphael	1·50	1·50

277 Silver Fir

1986. Tree Bark. Multicoloured.

909	35r. Type **277**	45	45
910	90r. Norway spruce	1·60	1·60
911	1f.40 Pedunculate oak	2·30	2·30

278 Gamprin Primary School

1987. Europa. Multicoloured.

912	50r. Type **278**	80	80
913	90r. Schellenberg parish church	1·40	1·40

280 Niklaus von Flue

1987. 500th Death Anniv of Niklaus von Flue (martyr).

914	**280** 1f.10 multicoloured	1·80	1·60

281 Bullhead

1987. Fishes (1st series). Multicoloured.

915	50r. Type **281**	85	85
916	90r. Brown trout	1·50	1·50
917	1f.10 European grayling	2·00	2·00

See also Nos. 959/61.

282 Prince Alois (frame as in first stamps)

1987. 75th Anniv of First Liechtenstein Stamps.

918	**282**	2f. multicoloured	3·75	3·75

283 Staircase

1987. Liechtenstein City Palace, Vienna. Multicoloured.

919	35r. Type **283**	60	60
920	50r. Minoritenplatz doorway	85	85
921	90r. Staircase (different)	1·50	1·50

284 Arms

1987. 275th Anniv of Transfer of County of Vaduz to House of Liechtenstein.

922	**284**	1f.40 multicoloured	2·30	1·60

285 Constitution Charter, 1862

1987. 125th Anniv of Liechtenstein Parliament.

923	**285**	1f.70 multicoloured	2·75	2·75

286 St. Matthew

1987. Christmas. Illuminations from Golden Book of Pfafers Abbey. Multicoloured.

924	35r. Type **286**	60	60
925	50r. St. Mark	95	95
926	60r. St. Luke	1·10	1·10
927	90r. St. John	1·70	1·70

287 "The Toil of the Cross-country Skier"

1987. Winter Olympic Games, Calgary (1988). Multicoloured.

928	25r. Type **287**	45	45
929	90r. "The Courageous Pioneers of Skiing"	1·70	1·70
930	1f.10 "As our Grandfathers used to ride on a Bobsled"	2·20	2·20

288 Dish Aerial

1988. Europa. Transport and Communications. Multicoloured

931	50r. Type **288**	75	75
932	90r. Maglev monorail	1·50	1·50

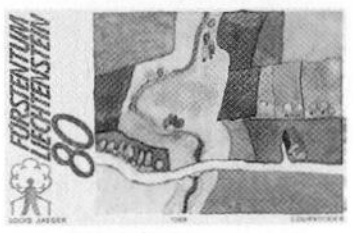

289 Agriculture

1988. European Campaign for Rural Areas. Multicoloured.

933	80r. Type **289**	1·50	1·50
934	90r. Village centre	1·80	1·80
935	1f.70 Road	2·50	2·50

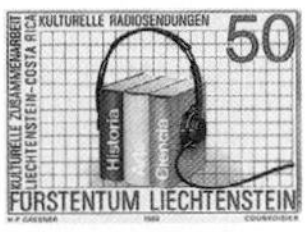

290 Headphones on Books (Radio Broadcasts)

1988. Costa Rica–Liechtenstein Cultural Co-operation.

936	**290**	50r. multicoloured	1·10	1·10
937	-	1f.40 red, brown and green	3·25	3·25

DESIGN: 1f.40, Man with pen and radio (Adult education).

291 Crown Prince Hans Adam

1988. 50th Anniv of Accesion of Prince Francis Joseph II. Sheet 100×68 mm containing T **291** and similar vert designs. Multicoloured.

MS938	50r. Type **291**; 50r. Prince Alois; 2f. Prince Francis Joseph II	6·50	6·50

292 St. Barbara's Shrine, Balzers

1988. Wayside Shrines. Multicoloured.

939	25r. Type **292**	50	50
940	35r. Shrine containing statues of Christ, St. Peter and St. Paul at Oberdorf, Vaduz	65	65
941	50r. St. Anthony of Egypt's shrine, Fallagass, Ruggel	1·00	1·00

293 Cycling

1988. Olympic Games, Seoul. Multicoloured.

942	50r. Type **293**	95	95
943	80r. Gymnastics	1·60	1·60
944	90r. Running	1·80	1·80
945	1f.40 Equestrian event	3·00	3·00

294 Joseph and Mary

1988. Christmas. Multicoloured.

946	35r. Type **294**	60	60
947	50r. Baby Jesus	85	85
948	90r. Wise Men presenting gifts to Jesus	1·50	1·50

295 Letter beside Footstool (detail)

1988. "The Letter" (portrait of Marie-Theresa, Princesse de Lamballe by Anton Hickel). Multicoloured.

949	50r. Type **295**	50	50
950	90r. Desk and writing materials (detail)	65	65
951	2f. "The Letter" (complete painting)	1·00	1·00

296 "Cat and Mouse"

1989. Europa. Children's Games. Multicoloured.

952	50r. Type **296**	1·10	75
953	90r. "Hide and Seek"	1·80	1·50

298 Rheinberger and Score

1989. 150th Birth Anniv of Josef Gabriel Rheinberger (composer).

954	**298**	2f.90 black, blue & purple	5·00	4·25

299 Little Ringed Plover

1989. Endangered Animals. Multicoloured.

955	25r. Type **299**	45	45
956	35r. Green tree frog	65	65
957	50r. "Libelloides coccajus" (lace-wing)	1·10	1·10
958	90r. Polecat	2·20	2·20

300 Northern Pike

1989. Fish (2nd series). Multicoloured.

959	50r. Type **300**	75	75
960	1f.10 Brown trout	1·80	1·60
961	1f.40 Stone loach	2·50	2·00

301 Return of Cattle from Alpine Pastures

1989. Autumn Customs. Multicoloured.

962	35r. Type **301**	60	60
963	50r. Peeling corn cobs	85	80
964	80r. Cattle market	1·50	1·20

302 Falknis

1989. Mountains. Watercolours by Josef Schadler.

965	-	5r. multicoloured	10	10
966	-	10r. multicoloured	15	15
967	-	35r. multicoloured	50	50
968	-	40r. multicoloured	60	60
969	-	45r. multicoloured	65	65
970	**302**	50r. multicoloured	75	75
971	-	60r. multicoloured	85	85
972	-	70r. multicoloured	1·00	1·00
973	-	75r. multicoloured	1·10	1·10
974	-	80r. violet, brown & black	1·20	1·20
975	-	1f. multicoloured	1·50	1·50
976	-	1f.20 multicoloured	1·80	1·80
977	-	1f.50 multicoloured	2·20	2·20
978	-	1f.60 multicoloured	3·00	3·00
979	-	2f. multicoloured	3·00	3·00

DESIGNS: 5r. Augstenberg; 10r. Hahenespiel; 35r. Nospitz; 40r. Ochsenkopf; 45r. Three Sisters; 60r. Kuhgrat; 70r. Galinakopf; 75r. Plassteikopf; 80pf. Naafkopf; 1f. Schonberg; 1f.20, Bleikaturm; 1f.50, Garselliturm; 1f.60, Schwarzhorn; 2f. Scheienkopf.

303 "Melchior and Balthasar"

1989. Christmas. Details of triptych by Hugo van der Goes. Multicoloured.

981	35r. Type **303**	60	50
982	50r. "Kaspar and Holy Family" (27×34 mm)	85	75
983	90r. "St. Stephen"	1·50	1·30

304 Mace Quartz

1989. Minerals. Multicoloured.

984	50r. Type **304**	85	75
985	1f.10 Globe pyrite	1·80	1·50
986	1f.50 Calcite	2·40	2·20

305 Nendeln Forwarding Agency, 1864

1990. Europa. Post Office Buildings. Multicoloured

987	50r. Type **305**	75	75
988	90r. Vaduz post office, 1976	1·50	1·50

306 Penny Black

1990. 150th Anniv of the Penny Black.

989	**306**	1f.50 multicoloured	3·00	3·00

307 Footballers

1990. World Cup Football Championship, Italy.

990	**307**	2f. multicoloured	3·75	3·75

308 Tureen, Oranges and Grapes

1990. Ninth Death Anniv of Benjamin Steck (painter). Multicoloured.

991	50r. Type **308**	1·10	85
992	80r. Apples and pewter bowl	1·50	1·30
993	1f.50 Basket, apples, cherries and pewter jug	3·00	3·00

309 Princess Gina

1990. Prince Francis Joseph II and Princess Gina Commemoration. Multicoloured.

994	2f. Type **309**	3·00	3·00
995	3f. Prince Francis Joseph II	4·25	4·25

310 Common
Pheasant

1990. Game Birds. Multicoloured.

996	25r. Type **310**		50	50
997	50r. Black grouse		95	95
998	2f. Mallard		3·75	3·75

311 Annunciation

1990. Christmas. Paintings. Multicoloured.

999	35r. Type **311**		75	75
1000	50r. Nativity		85	85
1001	90r. Adoration of the Magi		1·30	1·30

312 St. Nicholas

1990. Winter Customs. Multicoloured.

1002	35r. Type **312**		50	50
1003	50r. Awakening on New Year's Eve		80	80
1004	1f.50 Giving New Year greetings		2·30	2·30

313 Mounted Courier

1990. 500th Anniv of Regular European Postal Services.

1005	**313**	90r. multicoloured	1·80	1·80

314 "Olympus
1" Satellite

1991. Europa. Europe in Space. Multicoloured.

1006	50r. Type **314**		75	75
1007	90r. "Meteosat" satellite		1·50	1·50

315 St. Ignatius de
Loyola (founder of
Society of Jesus)

1991. Anniversaries. Multicoloured.

1008	80r. Type **315** (500th birth anniv)		1·10	1·10
1009	90r. Wolfgang Amadeus Mozart (composer, death bicentenary)		1·50	1·50

316 U.N. Emblem
and Dove

1991. Admission to U.N. Membership (1990).

1010	**316**	2f.50 multicoloured	3·75	3·75

317 Non-Commissioned
Officer and Private

1991. 125th Anniv of Last Mobilization of Liechtenstein's Military Contingent (to the Tyrol). Multicoloured.

1011	50r. Type **317**		75	75
1012	70r. Tunic, chest and portrait		1·10	1·10
1013	1f. Officer and private		1·50	1·50

318 "Near Maloja"
(Giovanni
Giacometti)

1991. 700th Anniv of Swiss Confederation. Paintings by Swiss artists. Multicoloured.

1014	50r. Type **318**		75	75
1015	80r. "Rhine Valley" (Ferdinand Gehr)		1·10	1·10
1016	90r. "Bergell" (Augusto Giacometti)		1·50	1·50
1017	1f.10 "Hoher Kasten" (Hedwig Scherrer)		2·20	2·20

319 Stampless and
Modern Covers

1991. "Liba 92" National Stamp Exhibition, Vaduz.

1018	**319**	90r. multicoloured	1·50	1·50

320 Princess
Marie

1991. Multicoloured

1019	3f. Type **320**		3·75	3·25
1020	3f.40 Prince Hans Adam II		4·25	4·00

321 Virgin of
the
Annunciation
(exterior of left
wing)

1991. Christmas. Details of the altar from St. Mamertus Chapel, Triesen. Multicoloured.

1021	50r. Type **321**		80	80
1022	80r. Madonna and Child (wood-carving attr. Jorg Syrlin, inner shrine)		1·20	1·20
1023	90r. Angel Gabriel (exterior of right wing)		1·30	1·30

322 Cross-country
Skiers and Testing
for Drug Abuse

1991. Winter Olympic Games, Albertville. Multicoloured.

1024	70r. Type **322**		1·50	1·50
1025	80r. Ice hockey player tackling opponent and helping him after fall		1·50	1·50
1026	1f.60 Downhill skier and fallen skier caught in safety net		2·50	2·50

323 Relay Race,
Drugs and
Shattered Medal

1992. Olympic Games, Barcelona. Multicoloured.

1027	50r. Type **323**		75	75
1028	70r. Cycling road race		1·50	1·50
1029	2f.50 Judo		4·25	4·25

324 Aztecs

1992. Europa. 500th Anniv of Discovery of America by Columbus. Multicoloured.

1030	80r. Type **324**		1·20	1·20
1031	90r. Statue of Liberty and New York skyline		1·40	1·40

325 Clown in
Envelope ("Good
Luck")

1992. Greetings Stamps. Multicoloured.

1032	50r. Type **325**		75	75
1033	50r. Wedding rings in envelope and harlequin violinist		75	75
1034	50r. Postman blowing horn (31×21 mm)		75	75
1035	50r. Flying postman carrying letter sealed with heart (31×21 mm)		75	75

326 Arms of
Liechtenstein—Kinsky
Alliance

1992. "Liba '92" National Stamp Exhibition. Silver Wedding Anniv of Prince Hans Adam and Princess Marie. Sheet 100×67 mm containing T **326** and similar vert design. Multicoloured.

MS1036	2f. Type **326**; 2f.50 Royal couple (photo by Anthony Buckley)		8·75	8·75

327 "Blechnum
spicant"

1992. Ferns. Multicoloured.

1037	40r. Type **327**		60	60
1038	50r. Maidenhair spleenwort		75	75
1039	70r. Hart's-tongue		1·00	1·00
1040	2f.50 "Asplenium ruta-muraria"		4·25	4·25

328 Reading Edict

1992. 650th Anniv of County of Vaduz.

1041	**328**	1f.60 multicoloured	3·00	3·00

329 Chapel of
St. Mamertus,
Triesen

1992. Christmas. Multicoloured.

1042	50r. Type **329**		75	75
1043	90r. Crib, St. Gallus's Church, Triesen		1·30	1·30
1044	1f.60 St. Mary's Chapel, Triesen		2·30	2·30

330 Crown
Prince Alois

1992

1045	**330**	2f.50 multicoloured	3·75	3·75

331 "Nafkopf and
Huts, Steg"

1993. 1400th Birth Anniv of Hans Gantner (painter). Multicoloured.

1046	50r. Type **331**		75	75
1047	60r. "Hunting Lodge, Sass"		85	85
1048	1f.80 "Red House, Vaduz"		2·75	2·75

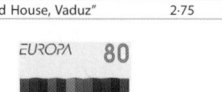

332 "910805"
(Bruno Kaufmann)

1993. Europa. Contemporary Art. Multicoloured.

1049	80r. Type **332**		1·30	1·30
1050	1f. "The Little Blue" (Evi Kliemand)		1·50	1·50

333 "Tale of the
Ferryman"
(painting)

1993. Tibetan Collection in the National Museum. Multicoloured.

1051	60r. Type **333**		1·10	1·10
1052	80r. Religious dance mask		1·30	1·30
1053	1f. "Tale of the Fish" (painting)		1·60	1·60

334 "Tree of Life"

1993. Missionary Work.

1054	**334**	1f.80 multicoloured	3·00	3·00

335 "The Black
Hatter"

1993. Homage to Liechtenstein.
| 1055 | **335** | 2f.80 multicoloured | 4·25 | 4·25 |

336 Crown Prince Alois and Duchess Sophie of Bavaria

1993. Royal Wedding. Sheet 100×67 mm.
| MS1056 | **336** | 4f. multicoloured | 7·25 | 7·25 |

337 Origanum

1993. Flowers. Illustrations from "Hortus Botanicus Liechtensteinsis". Multicoloured.
1057	50r. Type **337**	90	90
1058	60r. Meadow sage	1·10	1·10
1059	1f. "Seseli annuum"	1·60	1·60
1060	2f.50 Large self-heal	3·75	3·75

338 Eurasian Badger

1993. Animals. Multicoloured.
1061	60r. Type **338**	1·10	1·10
1062	80r. Beech marten	1·50	1·50
1063	1f. Red fox	1·80	1·80

339 "Now that the Quiet Days are Coming ..." (Rainer Maria Rilke)

1993. Christmas. Multicoloured.
1064	60r. Type **339**	90	90
1065	80r. "Can You See the Light ..." (Th. Friedrich)	1·30	1·30
1066	1f. "Christmas, Christmas ..." (R. A. Schroder)	1·50	1·50

340 Ski Jump

1993. Winter Olympic Games, Lillehammer, Norway (1994). Multicoloured.
1067	60r. Type **340**	1·30	1·30
1068	80r. Slalom	1·60	1·60
1069	2f.40 Bobsleighing	3·75	3·75

341 Seal and Title Page

1994. Anniversaries. Multicoloured.
| 1070 | 60r. Type **341** (275th anniv of Principality) | 1·10 | 1·10 |
| 1071 | 1f.80 State, Prince's and Olympic flags (centenary of International Olympic Committee) | 3·00 | 3·00 |

342 Andean Condor

1994. Europa. Discoveries of Alexander von Humboldt. Multicoloured.
| 1072 | 80r. Type **342** | 1·50 | 1·50 |
| 1073 | 1f. "Rhexia cardinalis" (plant) | 1·80 | 1·80 |

343 Football Pitch and Hopi Indians playing Kickball

1994. World Cup Football Championship, U.S.A.
| 1074 | **343** | 2f.80 multicoloured | 4·25 | 4·25 |

344 Elephant with Letter

1994. Greetings Stamps. Multicoloured.
1075	60r. Type **344**	1·10	1·10
1076	60r. Cherub with flower and hearts	1·10	1·10
1077	60r. Pig with four-leaf clover	1·10	1·10
1078	60r. Dog holding bunch of tulips	1·10	1·10

345 "Eulogy of Madness" (mobile, Jean Tinguely)

1994. Homage to Liechtenstein.
| 1079 | **345** | 4f. black, pink and violet | 7·25 | 7·25 |

346 Spring

1994. Seasons of the Vine. Multicoloured.
1080	60r. Type **346**	1·10	1·10
1081	60r. Vine leaves (Summer)	1·10	1·10
1082	60r. Trunk in snowy landscape (Winter)	1·10	1·10
1083	60r. Grapes (Autumn)	1·10	1·10

Nos. 1080/3 were issued together, se-tenant, forming a composite design.

347 Strontium

1994. Minerals. Multicoloured.
1084	60r. Type **347**	1·10	1·10
1085	80r. Quartz	1·50	1·50
1086	3f.50 Iron dolomite	5·50	5·50

348 "The True Light"

1994. Christmas. Multicoloured.
1087	60r. Type **348**	1·10	1·10
1088	80r. "Peace on Earth"	1·50	1·50
1089	1f. "Behold, the House of God"	1·80	1·80

349 Earth

1994. The Four Elements. Multicoloured.
1090	60r. Type **349**	1·10	1·10
1091	80r. Water	1·50	1·50
1092	1f. Fire	1·80	1·80
1093	2f.50 Air	4·25	4·25

350 "The Theme of all our Affairs must be Peace"

1995. Europa. Peace and Freedom. Quotations of Franz Josef II. Multicoloured.
| 1094 | 80r. Type **350** | 1·50 | 1·50 |
| 1095 | 1f. "Through Unity comes Strength and the Bearing of Sorrows" | 1·80 | 1·80 |

351 U.N. Flag and Bouquet of Flowers

1995. Anniversaries and Event. Multicoloured.
1096	60r. Princess Marie with children (50th anniv of Liechtenstein Red Cross) (horiz)	1·10	1·10
1097	1f.80 Type **351** (50th anniv of U.N.O.)	1·50	1·50
1098	3f.50 Alps (European Nature Conservation Year)	1·80	1·80

352 "Falknis Mountains"

1995. Birth Centenary of Anton Frommelt (painter). Multicoloured.
1099	60r. Type **352**	1·50	1·50
1100	80r. "Three Oaks"	1·80	1·80
1101	4f.10 "The Rhine"	7·00	7·00

353 "One Heart and One Soul"

1995. Greetings Stamps. Multicoloured.
1102	60r. Type **353**	1·10	1·10
1103	60r. Bandage round sunflower ("Get Well")	1·10	1·10
1104	60r. Baby arriving over rainbow ("Hurrah! Here I am")	1·10	1·10
1105	60r. Delivering letter by hot-air balloon ("Write again")	1·10	1·10

354 Coloured Ribbons woven through River

1995. Liechtenstein–Switzerland Co-operation.
| 1106 | **354** | 60r. multicoloured | 1·10 | 1·10 |

No. 1106 was valid for use in both Liechtenstein and Switzerland (see No. 1308 of Switzerland).

355 Arnica

1995. Medicinal Plants. Multicoloured.
1107	60r. Type **355**	1·50	1·50
1108	80r. Giant nettle	1·80	1·80
1109	1f.80 Common valerian	3·25	3·25
1110	3f.50 Fig-wort	5·75	5·75

356 Angel (detail of painting)

1995. Christmas. Painting by Lorenzo Monaco. Multicoloured.
1111	60r. Type **356**	85	85
1112	80r. "Virgin Mary with Infant and Two Angels"	1·20	1·20
1113	1f. Angel facing left (detail of painting)	1·50	1·50

357 "Lady with Lap-dog" (Paul Wunderlich)

1995. Homage to Liechtenstein. Multicoloured.
| 1114 | **357** | 4f. multicoloured | 7·25 | 7·25 |

358 Eschen

1996. Scenes. Multicoloured.
1115	10r. Type **358**	20	20
1116	20r. Planken	30	30
1117	50r. Ruggell	85	85
1117a	60r. Balzers	1·10	1·10
1117b	70r. Schellenberg	1·70	1·70
1118	80r. Ruggell	1·20	1·20
1120	1f. Nendeln	1·50	1·50
1120a	1f.10 Eschen	2·00	1·50
1122	1f.20 Triesen	1·70	1·70
1123	1f.30 Triesen	1·90	1·90
1124	1f.40 Mauren	2·40	2·40
1125	1f.70 Schaanwald	2·50	2·50
1125a	1f.80 Malbun	3·25	3·25
1125b	1f.90 Schaan	3·50	3·50
1126	2f. Gamprin	3·00	3·00
1126a	2f.20 Balzers	6·00	6·00
1127	4f. Triesenberg	5·75	5·75
1127a	4f.50 Bendern	7·00	7·00
1128	5f. Vaduz Castle	7·25	7·25

359 Crucible

1996. Bronze Age in Europe.
| 1130 | **359** | 90r. multicoloured | 1·80 | 1·80 |

360 Kinsky and Diary Extract, 7 March 1917

1996. Europa. Famous Women. Nora, Countess Kinsky (mother of Princess Gina of Liechtenstein).
| 1131 | 360 | 90r. grey, purple and blue | 1·80 | 1·80 |

1132 - 1f.10 grey, blue and
purple   1·80   1·80
DESIGN: 1f.10, Kinsky and diary extract for 28 February
1917.

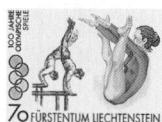

361 Gymnastics

1996. Centenary of Modern Olympic Games.
Multicoloured.
1133 70r. Type **361**   1·50   1·50
1134 90r. Hurdling   1·90   1·90
1135 1f.10 Cycling   1·90   1·90

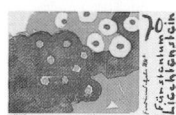

362 "Primroses"

1996. Birth Centenary of Ferdinand Gehr (painter).
Multicoloured.
1136 70r. Type **362**   1·90   1·90
1137 90r. "Daisies"   1·90   1·90
1138 1f.10 "Poppy"   1·90   1·90
1139 1f.80 "Buttercups" (33×23 mm) 3·50   3·50

363 State Arms

1996
1140 **363** 10f. multicoloured 15·00   15·00

364 Veldkirch, 1550

1996. Millenary of Austria.
1141 **364** 90r. multicoloured   1·50   1·50

365 "Poltava"

1996. 43rd Death Anniv of Eugen Zotow (painter).
Multicoloured.
1142 70r. Type **365**   1·50   1·50
1143 1f.10 "Three Bathers in a Berlin
Park"   2·30   2·30
1144 1f.40 "Vaduz"   3·00   3·00

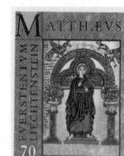

366 St. Matthew

1996. Christmas. Illustrations from Illuminated Manuscript
"Liber Viventium Fabariensis". Multicoloured.
1145 70r. Type **366**   1·50   1·50
1146 90r. Emblems of St. Mark 1·70   1·70
1147 1f.10 Emblems of St. Luke 1·90   1·90
1148 1f.80 Emblems of St. John 3·50   3·50

367 Schubert

1997. Birth Bicentenary of Franz Schubert (composer).
1149 **367** 70r. multicoloured 1·50   1·50

368 The Wild
Gnomes

1997. Europa. Tales and Legends. Multicoloured.
1150 90r. Type **368**   1·90   1·90
1151 1f.10 Man, pumpkin and rabbit
(The Foal of Planken)   2·30   2·30

369 "Madonna and Child
with St. Lucius and St.
Florinus" (Gabriel Dreher)

1997. National Patron Saints.
1152 **369** 20f. multicoloured 43·00   43·00

370 "Phaeolepiota
aurea"

1997. Fungi (1st series). Multicoloured.
1153 70r. Type **370**   1·50   1·50
1154 90r. "Helvella silvicola" 1·50   1·50
1155 1f.10 Orange peel fungus 2·30   2·30
See also Nos. 1238/40.

371 Steam Train,
Schaanwald Halt

1997. 125th Anniv of Liechtenstein Railways. Mult.
1156 70r. Type **371**   1·50   1·50
1157 90r. Diesel-electric train, Nendeln station   2·30   2·30
1158 1f.80 Electric train, Schaan-
Vaduz station   3·75   3·75

372 "Girl with
Flower" (Enrico
Baj)

1997. Homage to Liechtenstein.
1159 **372** 70r. multicoloured 1·50   1·50

373 Basket of Roses

1997. Christmas. Glass Tree Decorations. Multicoloured.
1160 70r. Type **373**   1·50   1·50
1161 90r. Bell   1·50   1·50
1162 1f.10 Bauble   2·30   2·30

374 Cross-country
skiing

1997. Winter Olympic Games, Nagano, Japan (1998).
Skiing. Multicoloured.
1163 70r. Type **374**   1·50   1·50
1164 90r. Slalom   1·90   1·90
1165 1f.80 Downhill   3·50   3·50

375 "Verano"
(The Summer)

1998. Homage to Liechtenstein. Paintings by Heinz Mack.
Multicoloured.
1166 70r. Type **375**   1·50   1·50
1167 70r. "Homage to Liechtenstein" 1·50   1·50
1168 70r. "Between Day and Dream" 1·50   1·50
1169 70r. "Salute Cirico!"   1·50   1·50

376 Prince's Festival
Procession, Vaduz

1998. Europa. National Festivals. Multicoloured.
1170 90r. Type **376**   1·90   1·90
1171 1f.10 Music Societies Festival,
Gutenberg Castle, Balzers 2·30   2·30

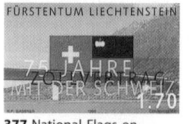

377 National Flags on
Bridge

1998. 75th Anniv of Liechtenstein–Switzerland Customs
Treaty.
1172 **377** 1f.70 multicoloured 3·00   3·00

378 Goalkeeper

1998. World Cup Football Championship, France.
1173 **378** 1f.80 multicoloured 3·00   3·00

379 Clown with
Queen of Hearts

1998. Greeting Stamps. Clowns. Multicoloured.
1174 70r. Type **379**   1·50   1·50
1175 70r. Clown holding four-leaf
clovers   1·50   1·50
1176 70r. Clown raising hat 1·50   1·50
1177 70r. Clown holding heart 1·50   1·50

380 Wooden Milk
Vat

1998. Traditional Crafts (1st series). Multicoloured.
1178 90r. Type **380**   2·50   2·50
1179 2f.20 Clog   4·25   4·25
1180 3f.50 Wheel   6·00   6·00
See also Nos. 1257/9.

381 Expelling Johann
Langer from Liechtenstein

1998. 150th Anniv of 1848 Revolutions in Europe.
1181 **381** 1f.80 multicoloured 3·75   3·75

382 Virgin Mary

1998. Christmas. Multicoloured.
1182 70r. Type **382**   1·50   1·50
1183 90r. "The Nativity" (35×26 mm) 1·90   1·90

1184 1f.10 Joseph   2·30   2·30
Nos. 1182 and 1184 show details of the complete relief
depicted on No. 1183.

383 Zum Lowen Guest
House

1998. Preservation of Historical Environment (1st series).
Hinterschellenberg. Multicoloured.
1185 90r. Type **383**   1·90   1·90
1186 1f.70 St. George's Chapel (vert) 3·00   3·00
1187 1f.80 Houses   3·50   3·50
See also Nos. 1250/2, 1274/5, 1292/3, 1358/9, 1386/7,
1428/9, 1462/3 and 1498.

384 Automatic
and Manual
Switchboards

1998. Centenary of Telephone in Liechtenstein.
1188 **384** 2f.80 multicoloured 5·25   5·25

385 Eschen

1999. 300th Anniv of Purchase of Unterland by Prince
Johann Adam. Sheet 107×68 mm containing T **385**
and similar horiz design. Multicoloured.
MS1189 90r. ×5 plus label, Composite
design of the Unterland showing the
villages of Eschen, Gamprin, Mauren,
Ruggell and Schellenberg   11·50   11·50

386 Smooth
Snake and
Schwabbrunnen-
Aescher Nature
Park

1999. Europa. Parks and Gardens. Multicoloured.
1190 90r. Type **386**   1·90   1·90
1191 1f.10 Corn crake and Ruggell
marsh   2·30   2·30

387 Council
Anniversary
Emblem and
Silhouettes

1999. Anniversaries and Event. Multicoloured.
1192 70r. Type **387** (50th anniv
of Council of Europe and
European Convention on
Human Rights)   1·50   1·50
1193 70r. Bird with envelope in beak
(125th anniv of U.P.U.) 1·50   1·50
1194 70r. Heart in hand (75th anniv
of Caritas Liechtenstein
(welfare organization)) 1·50   1·50

388 Judo

1999. Eighth European Small States Games,
Liechtenstein. Multicoloured.
1195 70r. Type **388**   1·50   1·50
1196 70r. Swimming   1·50   1·50
1197 70r. Throwing the javelin 1·50   1·50
1198 90r. Cycling   1·90   1·90
1199 90r. Shooting   1·90   1·90
1200 90r. Tennis   1·90   1·90
1201 90r. Squash   1·90   1·90

1202 90r. Table tennis 1·90 1·90
1203 90r. Volleyball 1·90 1·90

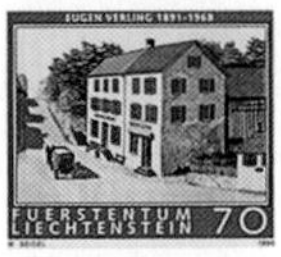

389 "Herrengasse"

1999. Paintings by Eugen Verling. Multicoloured.
1204 70r. Type **389** 1·50 1·50
1205 2f. "Old Vaduz with Castle" 3·75 3·75
1206 4f. "House in Furst-Franz-Josef Street, Vaduz" 7·50 7·50

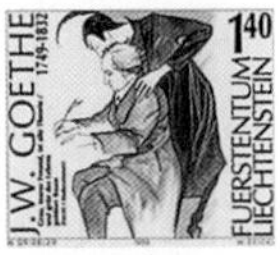

390 Scene from "Faust", Act I

1999. 250th Birth Anniv of Johann Wolfgang Goethe (poet and playwright). Multicoloured.
1207 1f.40 Type **390** 3·00 3·00
1208 1f.70 Faust and the Devil sealing wager 3·75 3·75

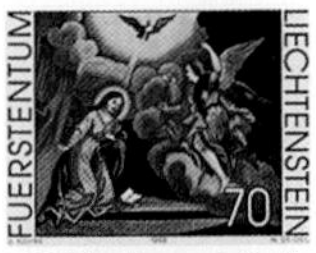

391 "The Annunciation"

1999. Christmas. Paintings by Joseph Walser from Chapel of Our Lady of Comfort, Dux. Mult.
1209 70r. Type **391** 1·50 1·50
1210 90r. "Nativity" 1·90 1·90
1211 1f.10 "Adoration" 2·30 2·30

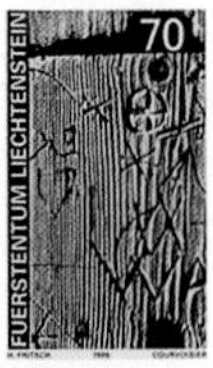

392 Identification Mark on Door, Ubersaxen

1999. Walser Identification Marks. Multicoloured.
1212 70r. Type **392** 1·50 1·50
1213 90r. Mark on mural 1·90 1·90
1214 1f.80 Mark on axe 3·50 3·50

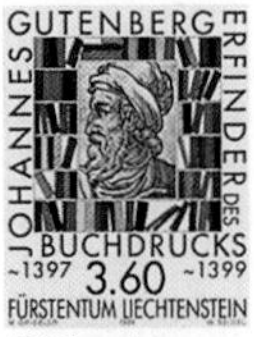

393 Gutenberg

1999. 600th Birth Anniv of Johannes Gutenberg (inventor of printing press).
1215 **393** 3f.60 multicoloured 7·50 7·50

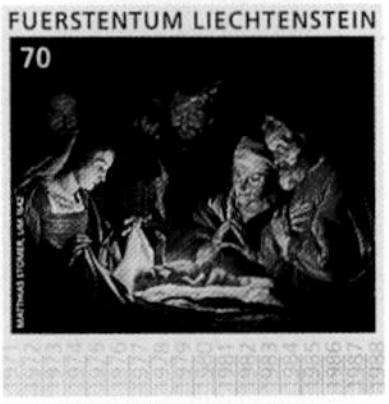

394 "The Adoration of the Shepheards" (Matthia Stomer)

2000. 2000 Years of Christianity. Sheet 108×68 mm containing T **394** and similar square design. Multicoloured.
MS1216 70r. Type **394**; 1f.10 "Three Kings" (Ferdinand Gehr) 4·50 4·50

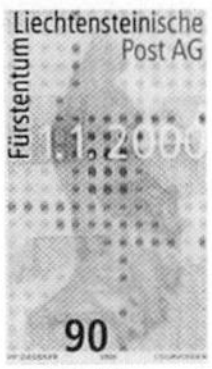

395 Emblem

2000. Provision of Postal Services by Liechtenstein Post in Partnership with Swiss Post.
1217 **395** 90r. multicoloured 1·70 1·70

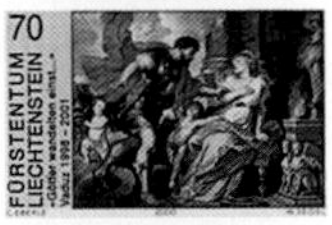

396 "Mars and Rhea Silvia" (Peter Paul Rubens)

2000. Paintings. Multicoloured.
1218 70r. Type **396** 1·40 1·40
1219 1f.80 "Cupid with Soap-Bubble" (Rembrandt) 3·50 3·50

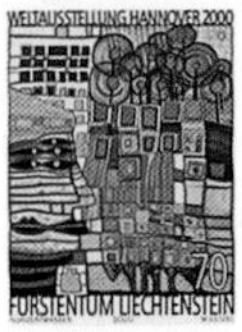

397 "Fragrance of Humus"

2000. "EXPO 2000" World's Fair, Hanover, Germany. Paintings by Friedensreich Hundertwasser. Multicoloured.
1220 70r. Type **397** 1·40 1·40
1221 90r. "Do Not Wait Houses-Move" 1·70 1·70
1222 1f.10 "The Car: a Drive Towards Nature and Creation" 2·00 2·10

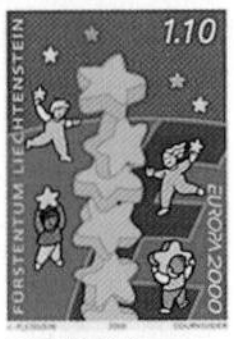

398 "Building Europe"

2000. Europa.
1223 **398** 1f.10 multicoloured 2·10 2·10

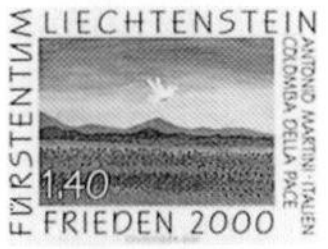

399 "Dove of Peace" (Antonio Martini)

2000. "Peace 2000". Paintings by members of Association of Mouth and Foot Painting Artists. Multicoloured
1224 1f.40 Type **399** 2·75 2·75
1225 1f.70 "World Peace" (Alberto Alvarez) 3·25 3·25
1226 2f.20 "Rainbow" (Eiichi Minami) 4·25 4·25

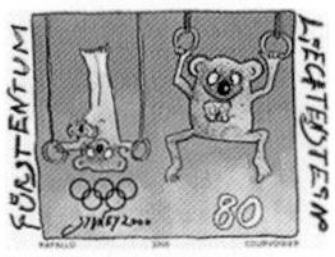

400 Koalas on Rings (Gymnastics)

2000. Olympic Games, Sydney. Multicoloured.
1227 80r. Type **400** 1·50 1·50
1228 1f. Joey leaping over crossbar (High jump) 1·90 1·90
1229 1f.30 Emus approaching finish line (Athletics) 2·40 2·40
1230 1f.80 Duckbill platypuses in swimming race 3·50 3·50

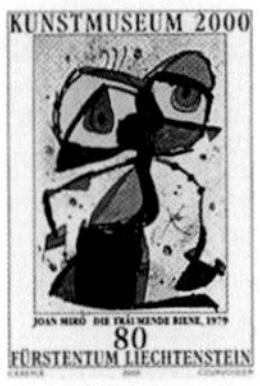

401 "The Dreaming Bee" (Joan Miro)

2000. Inauguration of Art Museum. Multicoloured.
1231 80r. Type **401** 1·50 1·50
1232 1f.20 "Cube" (Sol LeWitt) 2·30 2·30
1233 2f. "Bouquet of Flowers" (Raelant Savery) (31×46 mm) 3·75 3·75

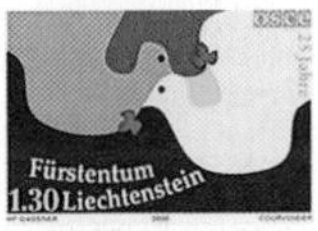

402 "Peace Doves"

2000. 25th Anniv of Organization for Security and Co-operation in Europe.
1234 **402** 1f.30 multicoloured 2·40 2·40

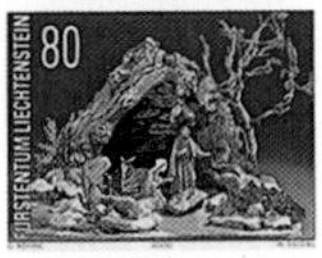

403 Root Crib

2000. Christmas. Cribs. Multicoloured.
1235 80r. Type **403** 1·50 1·50
1236 1f.30 Oriental crib 2·40 2·40
1237 1f.80 Crib with cloth figures 3·50 3·50

2000. Fungi (2nd series). As T **370**. Multicoloured.
1238 90r. Mycena adonis 1·70 1·70
1239 1f.10 Chalciporus amarellus 2·10 2·10
1240 2f. Pink waxcap 3·75 3·75

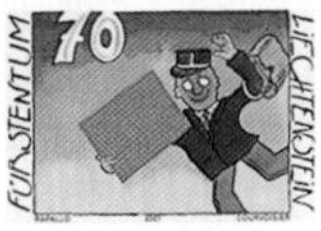

404 Postman delivering Parcel

2001. Greetings Stamps. Multicoloured.
1241 70r. Type **404** 1·40 1·40
1242 70r. Postman delivering flowers 1·40 1·40

Nos. 1241/2 are for the stamps with the parcel (1241) and flowers (1242) intact. The parcel and flowers can be scratched away to reveal a greetings message.

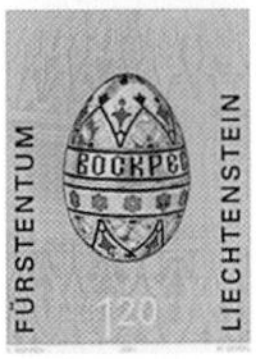

405 Silver Easter Egg

2001. Decorated Easter Eggs. Multicoloured.
1243 1f.20 Type **405** 2·30 2·30
1244 1f.80 Cloissonne egg 3·50 3·50
1245 2f. Porcelain egg 3·75 3·75

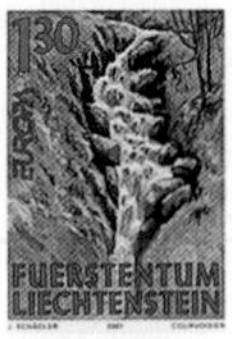

406 Mountain Spring

2001. Europa. Water Resources.
1246 **406** 1f.30 multicoloured 2·40 2·40

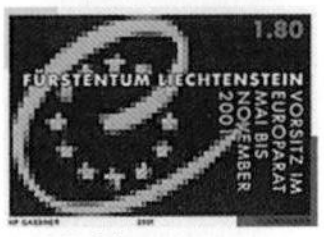

407 Emblem

2001. Liechtenstein Presidency of Council of Europe.
1247 **407** 1f.80 multicoloured 3·50 3·50

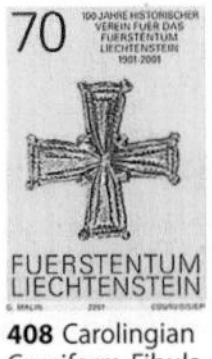

408 Carolingian Cruciform Fibula

2001. Centenary of Historical Association. Multicoloured.
1248 70r. Type **408** 1·40 1·40
1249 70r. "Mars of Gutenberg" (statue) 1·40 1·40

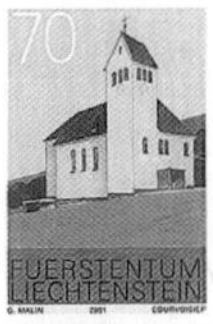

409 St. Theresa's Chapel, Schaanwald

2001. Preservation of Historical Environment (2nd series). Multicoloured.
1250 70r. Type **409** 1·40 1·40
1251 90r. St. Johann's Torkel (wine press), Mauren 1·70 1·70
1252 1f.10 Pirsch Transformer Station, Schaanwald 2·10 2·10

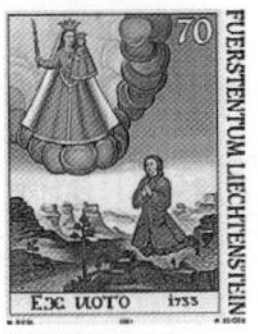

410 Mary and kneeling Votant (Chapel of Our Lady, Dux, Schann)

2001. Votive Paintings. Multicoloured.
1253 70r. Type **410** 1·50 1·50
1254 1f.20 Mary and Jesus, St. George among other Saints, and text of vow (St. George's Chapel, Schellenberg) 2·30 2·30
1255 1f.30 Mary, St. Joseph of Arimathea, St. Christopher, Johann Christoph Walser (votant) and text of vow (Chapel of Our Lady, Dux, Schann) 2·30 2·30

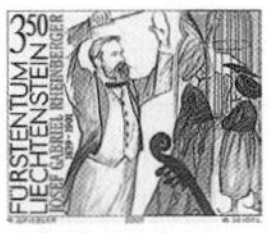

411 Rheinberger and Scene from *Zauberwort* (song cycle)

2001. Death Centenary of Josef Gabriel Rheinberger (composer).
1256 **411** 3f.50 multicoloured 6·75 6·75

2001. Traditional Crafts (2nd series). As T **380**. Multicoloured.
1257 70r. Agricultural implements and horseshoe 1·40 1·40
1258 90r. Rake 1·70 1·70
1259 1f.20 Harness 2·30 2·30

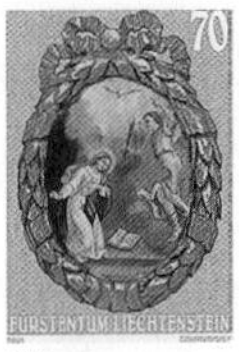

412 "Annunciation"

2001. Christmas. Medallions from The Joyful, Sorrowful and Glorious Rosary Cycle. Multicoloured.
1260 70r. Type **412** 1·40 1·40
1261 90r. Nativity 1·70 1·70
1262 1f.30 Presentation of Jesus at the Temple 2·40 2·40

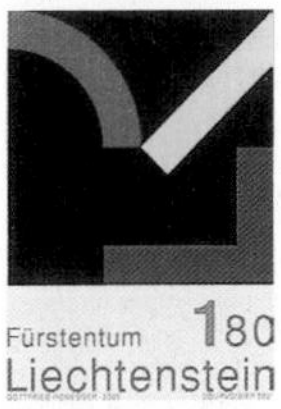

413 Square

2001. Paintings by Gottfried Honeggar. Multicoloured
1263 1f.80 Type **413** 3·50 3·50
1264 2f.20 Circle 4·25 4·25

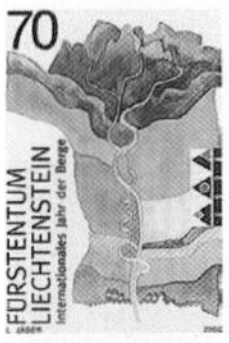

414 Mountains and River

2002. International Year of Mountains and 50th Anniv of the International Commission of Alpine Protection. Multicoloured.
1265 70r. Type **414** 90 90
1266 1f.20 Stylized mountains 2·30 2·30

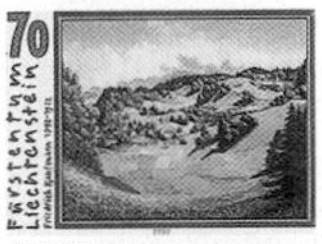

415 "Schellenberg"

2002. 30th Death Anniv of Friedrich Kaufmann (artist). Multicoloured.

1267	70r. Type **415**	1·40	1·40
1268	1f.30 "Schaan"	2·40	2·40
1269	1f.80 "Steg"	3·50	3·50

416 Space Shuttle and Bee

2002. Liechtenstein's participation in N.A.S.A. Space Technology and Research Students Project.

1270	**416**	90r. multicoloured	1·70	1·70

The project submitted by the Liechtenstein Gymnasium concerned the study of the effects of space on carpenter bees.

417 Man on Tightrope

2002. Europa. Circus. Multicoloured.

1271	90r. Type **417**	1·70	1·70
1272	1f.30 Juggler	2·40	2·40

418 Emblem

2002. "Liba '02" National Stamp Exhibition, Vaduz (1st issue).

1273	**418**	1f.20 multicoloured	2·30	2·30

See also Nos. 1282/3 and 1318/20.

419 Houses, Popers

2002. Preservation of Historical Environment (2nd series). Multicoloured.

1274	70r. Type **419**	1·40	1·40
1275	1f.20 House, Weiherring	3·25	3·00

420 Footballers

2002. World Cup Football Championship, Japan and South Korea.

1276	**420**	1f.80 multicoloured	3·75	3·50

421 Princess Marie

2002. The Royal Couple. Multicoloured.

1277	3f. Type **421**	5·75	5·75
1278	3f.50 Prince Hans-Adam II	6·75	6·75

422 Ghost Orchid (*Epipogium aphyllum*)

2002. Orchids. Multicoloured.

1279	70r. Type **422**	1·40	1·40
1280	1f.20 Fly orchid (*Ophrys insectifera*)	2·30	2·30
1281	1f.30 Black vanilla orchid (*Nigritella nigra*)	2·40	2·40

423 Stamps and Emblem

2002. "Liba '02" National Stamp Exhibition, Vaduz (2nd issue). 90th Anniv of First Liechtenstein Stamps. Multicoloured.

1282	90r. Type **423**	1·70	1·70
1283	1f.30 Stamps showing royal family	2·40	2·40

424 Princess Sophie

2002. Prince Alois and Princess Sophie. Multicoloured.

1284	2f. Type **424**	3·75	3·75
1285	2f.50 Prince Alois	4·75	4·75

425 Mary and Joseph

2002. Christmas. Batik. Multicoloured.

1286	70r. Type **425**	1·40	1·40
1287	1f.20 Nativity	1·50	1·50
1288	1f.80 Flight into Egypt	3·50	3·50

426 The Eagle, Vaduz

2002. Inn Signs. Multicoloured.

1289	1f.20 Type **426**	2·30	2·30
1290	1f.80 The Angel, Balzers	3·50	3·50
1291	3f. The Eagle, Bendern	5·75	5·75

427 St. Fridolin Parish Church

2003. Preservation of Historical Environment (3rd series). Multicoloured.

1292	70r. Type **427**	1·40	1·40
1293	2f.50 House, Spidach (horiz)	4·75	4·75

428 Postal Emblem

2003. Europa. Poster Art.

1294	**428**	1f.20 multicoloured	2·30	2·30

429 Pruning Vines

2003. Viticulture (1st issue). Multicoloured.

1295	1f.30 Type **429**	2·30	2·30
1296	1f.80 Tying up vines	3·50	3·50
1297	2f.20 Hoeing	6·75	6·75

See also Nos. 1301/3, 1304/6 and 1312/14.

430 Bridge

2003. 50th Anniv of Liechtenstein Association for the Disabled.

1298	**430**	70r. multicoloured	1·70	1·70

431 Renovated Buildings and Ammonite

2003. Renovation of National Museum. Multicoloured.

1299	1f.20 Type **431**	2·75	2·75
1300	1f.30 Verweserhaus building and bailiff's shield	3·00	3·00

2003. Viticulture (2nd issue). As T **429**. Multicoloured.

1301	1f.20 Looping the tendrils	2·75	2·75
1302	1f.80 Removing leaves from around grapes	4·25	4·25
1303	3f.50 Reducing top growth	8·50	8·50

2003. Viticulture (3rd issue). As T **429**. Multicoloured.

1304	70r. Thinning out	1·70	1·70
1305	90r. Harvesting	2·00	2·00
1306	1f.10 Pressing the grapes	2·75	2·75

432 St. George

2003. Saints (1st series). Multicoloured.

1307	1f.20 Type **432**	2·75	2·75
1308	1f.20 St. Blaise	2·75	2·75
1309	1f.30 St. Vitus	3·00	3·00
1310	1f.30 St. Erasmus	3·00	3·00

See also Nos. 1323/8.

433 Parents and Young on Nest

2003. Conservation of White Storks in Rhine Valley.

1311	**433**	2f.20 multicoloured	5·00	5·00

2003. Viticulture (4th issue). As T **429**. Multicoloured.

1312	70r. Tasting	1·70	1·70
1313	90r. Harvesting ice-wine grapes	2·00	2·00
1314	1f.20 Bottling	2·75	2·75

434 Archangel Gabriel appearing to Mary

2003. Christmas. Multicoloured.

1315	70r. Type **434**	1·70	1·70
1316	90r. Nativity	2·00	2·00
1317	1f.30 Three Kings	3·00	3·00

435 Cow (Laura Beck)

2003. "Liba '02" National Stamp Exhibition, Vaduz (3rd issue). Children's Drawing Competition Winners. Multicoloured.

1318	70r. Type **435**	1·70	1·70
1319	1f.80 Bee (Laura Lingg)	3·75	3·75
1320	1f.80 Apple tree (Patrick Marxer) (vert)	3·75	3·75

436 Hands enclosing Leaves

2004. 50th Anniv of AHV (retirement insurance).

1321	**436**	85r. multicoloured	1·80	1·80

437 Hot Air Balloon

2004. Europa. Holidays.

1322	**437**	1f.30 multicoloured	2·75	2·75

2004. Saints (2nd series). As T **432**. Multicoloured.

1323	1f. St. Achatius	2·10	2·10
1324	1f. St. Margaret	2·10	2·10
1325	1f.20 St. Christopher	2·75	2·75
1326	1f.20 St. Pantaleon	2·75	2·75
1327	2f.50 St. Cyriacus	5·00	5·00
1328	2f.50 St. Aegidius	5·00	5·00

438 Bendern

2004. Tourism. Aerial views of Liechtenstein. Multicoloured.

1329	15r. Type **438**	40	40
1330	85r. Gross-Teg	1·80	1·80
1331	1f. Tuass	2·00	2·00
1332	1f.50 Oberland	3·50	3·50
1333	1f.60 Ruggeller Riet	3·50	3·50
1334	2f.50 Canal	4·50	4·50
1335	3f. Naafkopf	5·50	5·50
1336	3f.50 Rhine Valley	6·50	6·50
1340	6f. Gutenberg	11·00	11·00

439 Olympic Torch

2004. Olympic Games, Athens 2004.

1350	**439**	85r. multicoloured	2·20	2·20

440 Bee Orchid (*Ophrys apifera*)

2004. Orchids. Multicoloured.

1351	85r. Type **440**	1·80	1·80
1352	1f. *Orchis ustulata*	2·00	2·00
1353	1f.20 *Epipactis purpurata*	2·40	2·40

441 Mathematical Symbols

2004. Science. Multicoloured.

1354	85r. Type **441**	1·80	1·80
1355	1f. Atomic diagram (physics)	2·00	2·00
1356	1f.30 Molecular structure (chemistry)	2·75	2·75
1357	1f.80 Star map and Saturn (astronomy)	3·75	3·75

442 Two-storied House on Unterdorfstrasse (street)

2004. Preservation of Historical Environment (4th series). Multicoloured.
| 1358 | 2f.20 Type **442** | 4·25 | 4·25 |
| 1359 | 2f.50 Unterdorfstrasse (street) | 4·50 | 4·50 |

443 The Annunciation

2004. Christmas. Multicoloured.
1360	85r. Type **443**	1·80	1·80
1361	1f. Nativity	2·10	2·10
1362	1f.80 Adoration of the Magi	4·25	4·25

444 Ammonite

2004. Fossils. Multicoloured.
1363	1f.20 Type **444**	2·75	2·75
1364	1f.30 Sea urchin	3·00	3·00
1365	2f.20 Shark's tooth	4·75	4·75

445 Map of Europe as Manuscript (emblem of Rinascimento Virtuale)

2004. Rinascimento Virtuale (Europe-wide co-operation in digital palimpsest (old manuscripts) research).
| 1366 | **445** | 2f.50 multicoloured | 5·50 | 5·50 |

2005. Saints (2nd issue). As T 432. Multicoloured.
1367	85r. St. Eustachius	1·80	1·80
1368	85r. St. Dionysius	1·80	1·80
1369	1f.80 St. Barbara	3·75	3·75
1370	1f.80 St. Katharina	3·75	3·75

446 Female Customer, Waiters and Chef

2005. Europa. Gastronomy.
| 1371 | **446** | 1f.30 multicoloured | 2·75 | 2·75 |

447 "Venus in Front of the Mirror" (Peter Paul Rubens)

2005. Liechtenstein Museum, Garden Palace, Vienna.
| 1372 | **447** | 2f.20 multicoloured | 5·50 | 5·50 |
A stamp of the same design was issued by Austria.

448 Triesenberg

2005. Tourism.
| 1373 | **448** | 3f.60 multicoloured | 7·75 | 7·75 |

449 "Flower Vase in a Window Niche" (Ambrosius Bosschaert)

2005. Paintings. Multicoloured.
| 1374 | 85r. Type **449** | 2·10 | 2·10 |
| 1375 | 85r. "Magnolias" (Chen Hongshou) | 2·10 | 2·10 |
Stamps of a similar design were issued by People's Republic of China.

450 Rossle, Schaan

2005. Inn Signs. Multicoloured.
1376	1f. Type **450**	2·10	2·10
1377	1f.40 Edelweiss, Triesenberg	3·00	3·00
1378	2f.50 Lowen, Bendern	5·25	5·25

451 Herman Sieger (founder)

2005. 75th Anniv of Postal Museum. Multicoloured.
1379	1f.10 Type **451**	2·40	2·40
1380	1f.30 Stamps	2·75	2·75
1381	1f.80 Postcard sent by Zeppelin mail	3·75	3·75

452 Bargalla

2005. Alpine Pastures. Multicoloured.
1382	85r. Type **452**	1·80	1·80
1383	1f. Pradamee	2·10	2·10
1384	1f.30 Gritsch	2·75	2·75
1385	1f.80 Valuna	4·00	4·00

453 Oberbendern

2005. Preservation of Historical Environment (5th series). Multicoloured.
| 1386 | 85r. Type **453** | 1·80 | 1·80 |
| 1387 | 2f.50 Schwurplatz | 4·75 | 4·75 |

454 *Plecotus auritus*

2005. Bats. Multicoloured.
| 1388 | 1f.80 Type **454** | 4·00 | 4·00 |
| 1389 | 2f. *Myotis myotis* | 4·25 | 4·25 |

455 Virgin and Child

2005. Christmas. Wood Carvings by Toni Gstohl. Multicoloured.
1390	85r. Type **455**	1·80	1·80
1391	1f. Holy family	2·10	2·10
1392	1f.30 Three Kings	3·00	3·00

456 Skier and Angel

2005. Winter Olympic Games, Turin. Multicoloured.
1393	1f.20 Type **456**	2·75	2·75
1394	1f.30 Cross country skier and wild boar	3·00	3·00
1395	1f.40 Slalom skier	3·25	3·25

457 "Peat Cutters"

2006. Eugen Wilhelm Schüepp (artist) Commemoration. Paintings. Multicoloured.
| 1396 | 1f. Type **457** | 2·10 | 2·10 |
| 1397 | 1f.80 "Neugut, Schaan" | 4·00 | 4·00 |

458 Bridge (Nadja Beck)

2006. Europa. Integration. Winning Entries in Children's Painting Competition. Multicoloured.
| 1398 | 1f.20 Type **458** | 3·00 | 2·75 |
| 1399 | 1f.30 Face (Elisabeth Mussner) | 2·75 | 2·75 |

459 "Lost in her Dreams" (Friedrich von Amerling)

2006. Liechtenstein Museum, Garden Palace, Vienna.
| 1400 | **459** | 2f.20 multicoloured | 4·75 | 4·75 |
A stamp of the same design was issued by Austria.

460 Prince Johann I

2006. Bicentenary of Sovereignty. Multicoloured.
1401	85r. Type **460**	1·80	1·80
1402	1f. National colours	2·10	2·10
1403	1f.20 Ruling house colours	2·75	2·75
1404	1f.80 State arms	4·00	4·00

461 Woman holding Base Clef (culture)

2006. Tourism. Multicoloured.
1405	85r. Type **461**	1·80	1·80
1406	1f. Hiker (summer)	2·10	2·10
1407	1f.20 Diner (hospitality)	2·75	2·75
1408	1f.80 Skier (winter)	4·00	4·00

462 Players on Field

2006. World Cup Football Championship, Germany.
| 1409 | **462** | 3f.30 multicoloured | 7·25 | 7·25 |

2006. Alpine Pastures. As T 452. Multicoloured.
1410	85r. Lawena	1·80	1·80
1411	1f.30 Gapfahl	2·75	2·75
1412	2f.40 Gafadura	5·25	5·25

463 "The Magic Flute" (Wolfgang Amadeus Mozart)

2006. Composers and Works. Multicoloured.
1413	1f. Type **463**	2·10	2·10
1414	1f. "Radetzky March" (Johann Strauss Sr.)	2·10	2·10
1415	1f. "Rhapsody in Blue" (George Gershwin)	2·10	2·10
1416	1f. "Water Music" (George Frideric Handel)	2·10	2·10
1417	1f. "Pastoral Symphony" (Ludwig van Beethoven)	2·10	2·10
1418	1f. "Waltz of the Flowers" (Pytor Ilyich Tchaikovsky)	2·10	2·10
1419	1f. "The Swan" (Camille Saint-Saens)	2·10	2·10
1420	1f. "Midsummer Night's Dream" (Felix Mendelssohn)	2·10	2·10

464 Mozart

2006. 250th Birth Anniv of Wolfgang Amadeus Mozart.
| 1421 | **464** | 1f.20 multicoloured | 2·75 | 2·75 |

465 The Annunciation

2006. Christmas. Paintings from Chapel of St. Mary, Dux. Multicoloured.
1422	85r. Type **465**	1·80	1·80
1423	1f. The Nativity	2·10	2·10
1424	1f.30 Presentation of Jesus	2·75	2·75

466 Curta Calculator

2006. Technical Innovations. Multicoloured.
1425	1f.30 Type **466**	2·75	2·75
1426	1f.40 Carrana narrow film camera	3·25	3·25
1427	2f.40 PVA sliding calliper	5·25	5·25

467 Governor's Residence and Liechtenstein Institute

2006. Preservation of Historical Environment (6th series). Multicoloured.
| 1428 | 1f.80 Type **467** | 4·00 | 4·00 |
| 1429 | 3f.50 Buhl, Gamprin | 7·50 | 7·50 |

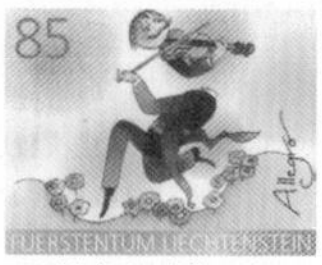

468 Violinist (Allegro)

2007. Music. Tempo and Temperament. Multicoloured

1430	85r. Type **468**	1·80	1·80
1431	1f.80 Gramophone and flying music sheets (Capriccio)	3·75	3·75
1432	2f. Brass players (Crescendo)	4·25	4·25
1433	3f.50 Pianist and flaming piano (Con fuoco)	7·00	7·00

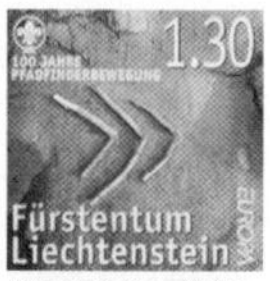

469 Trail Sign ("This Way")

2007. Europa. Centenary of Scouting.

1434	**469**	1f.30 multicoloured	2·75	2·75

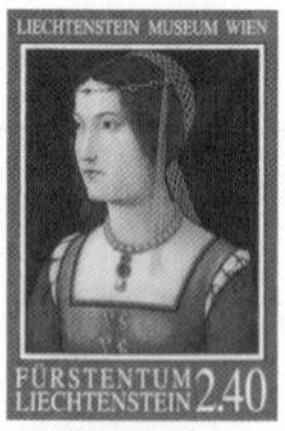

470 "Portrait of a Lady" (Bernardino Zaganelli da Cottignola)

2007. Liechtenstein Museum, Garden Palace, Vienna.

1435	**470**	2f.40 multicoloured	5·00	5·00

A stamp of a similar design was issued by Austria.

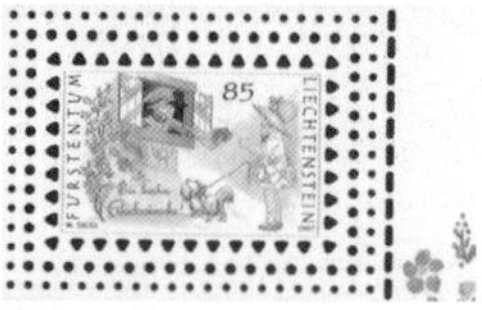

471 Letter Post

2007. Greetings Cards. Multicoloured.

1436	85r. Type **471**	1·80	1·80
1437	1f. Boys carrying bier containing envelope (courier post)	2·10	2·10
1438	1f.30 Swallow holding envelope (airmail)	2·75	2·75

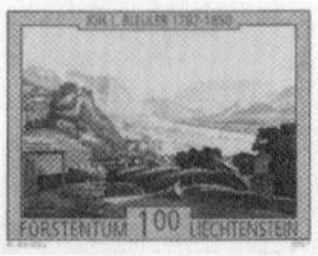

472 Castle and Vaduz

2007. Tourism. The Rhine. Paintings by Johann Ludwig Bleuler. Multicoloured.

1439	1f. Type **472**	2·10	2·10
1440	1f.30 Ratikon mountains	2·75	2·75
1441	2f.40 Confluence of Ill and Rhine	4·75	4·75

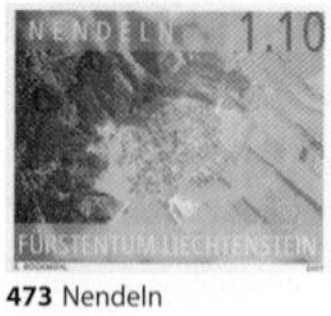

473 Nendeln

2007. Tourism. Liechtenstein from the Air. Multicoloured

1442	1f.10 Type **473**	2·40	2·40
1443	1f.80 Malbun	3·75	3·75
1444	2f.60 Arable land	5·50	5·50

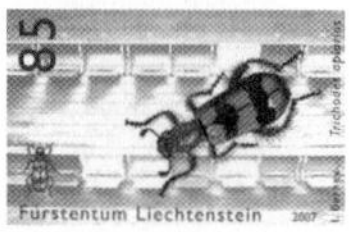

474 *Trichodes apiarius* (bee beetle)

2007. Insects. Multicoloured.

1445	85r. Type **474**	2·20	2·20
1446	1f. *Cetonia aurata* (rose chafer)	2·50	2·50
1447	1f.30 *Dytiscus marginalis* (great diving beetle)	3·25	3·25

2007. Alpine Pastures. As T **452**. Multicoloured.

1448	1f. Hintervalorsch	2·30	2·30
1449	1f.40 Sucka	3·00	3·00
1450	2f.20 Guschfiel	4·75	4·75

2007. Technical Innovations. As T **466**. Mult.

1451	1f.30 Hilti hammer and drill	3·00	3·00
1452	1f.80 Kaiser walking excavator	4·00	4·00
1453	2f.40 aluFer heating surface	5·50	5·50

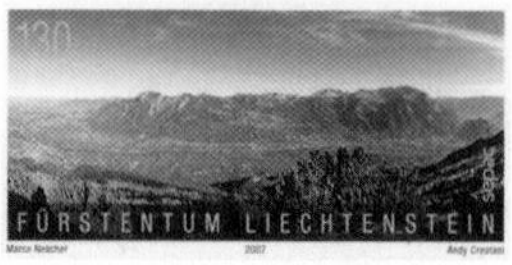

475 Liechtenstein from the Air

2007. SEPAC (small European mail services).

1454	**475**	1f.30 multicoloured	3·00	3·00

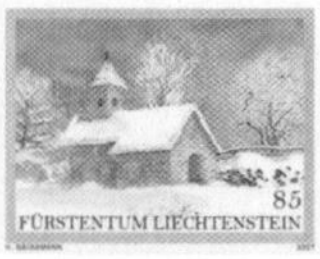

476 St Mary Chapel, Gamprin-Oberbuhl

2007. Christmas. Multicoloured.

1455	85r. Type **476**	2·00	2·00
1456	1f. Buel Chapel, Eschen	2·30	2·30
1457	1f.30 St Wolfgang Chapel, Triesen	3·00	3·00

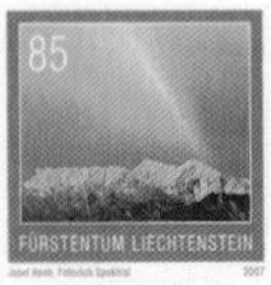

477 Rainbow over Three Sisters Massif

2007. Natural Phenomena. Multicoloured.

1458	85r. Type **477**	2·00	2·00
1459	1f. Lightning over Bendern	2·30	2·30
1460	1f.80 Halo over Malbun	4·00	4·00

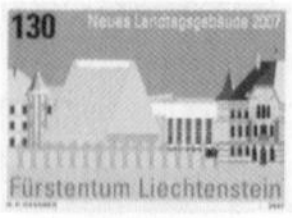

478 Landtagsgebaude (designed by Hansjorg Goritz)

2007. Architecture. New Parliament Building, Vaduz.

1461	**478**	1f.30 multicoloured	3·00	3·00

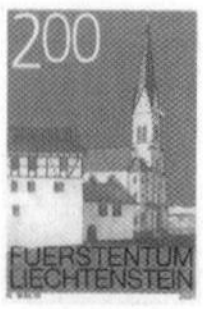

479 St Martin's Church

2007. Preservation of Historical Environment (7th series). Multicoloured.

1462	2f. Type **479**	4·50	4·50
1463	2f.70 Eschen Mill, St Martinsring (horiz)	6·00	6·00

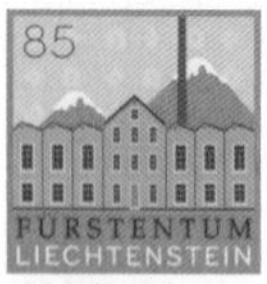

480 Industrial Buildings, Spoerry-Areal, Vaduz (industry)

2008. National Identity. Liechtenstein as Brand (1st series). Multicoloured.

1464	85r. Type **480**	2·20	2·20
1465	1f. St Mamertus Chapel, Triesen (homeland)	2·50	2·50
1466	1f.30 Vaduz Castle (monarchy)	3·25	3·25

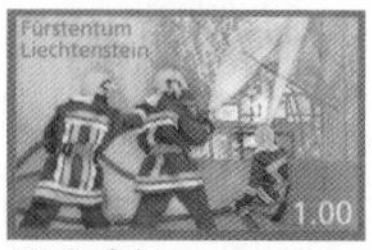

481 Firefighters

2008. Volunteer Civil Protection (1st issue). Volunteer Fire Service.

1467	**481**	1f. multicoloured	2·50	2·50

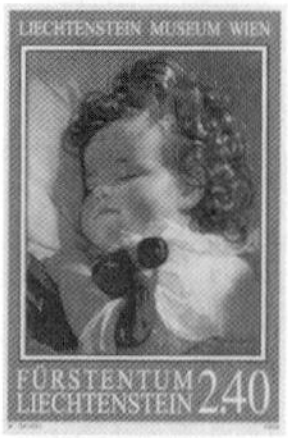

482 *Princess Marie Franziska von Liechtenstein* (Friedrich von Amerling)

2008. Liechtenstein Museum, Garden Palace, Vienna.

1468	**482**	2f.40 multicoloured	6·00	6·00

A stamp of a similar design was issued by Austria.

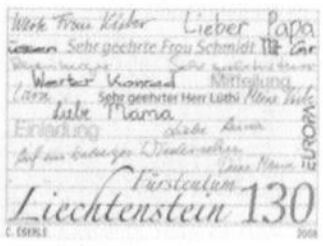

483 Script

2008. Europa. The Letter.

1469	**483**	1f.30 multicoloured	3·25	3·25

2008. Alpine Pastures. As T **452**. Multicoloured.

1470	2f.60 Schaan, Guschg	6·25	6·25
1471	3f. Balzers, Guschgle	7·50	7·50

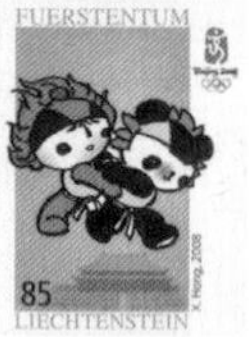

484 Huanhuan and Jingjing (martial arts)

2008. Olympic Games, Beijing. Multicoloured.

1472	85c. Type **484**	2·20	2·20
1473	1f. Huanhuan and Yingying (football and table tennis)	2·50	2·50

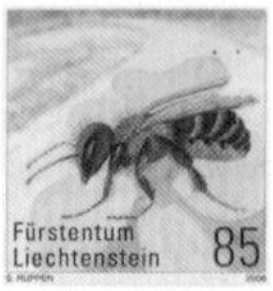

485 *Osmia brevicornis*

2008. Endangered Insects. Multicoloured.

1474	85c. Type **485**	2·20	2·20
1475	1f. *Epeoloides coecutiens*	2·50	2·50
1476	1f.30 *Odynerus spinipes*	3·25	3·25

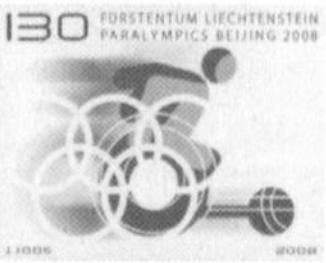

486 Marathon

2008. Paralympics, Beijing. Stylized athletes. Multicoloured.

1477	1f.30 Type **486**	3·25	3·25
1478	1f. 80 Table tennis	4·75	4·75

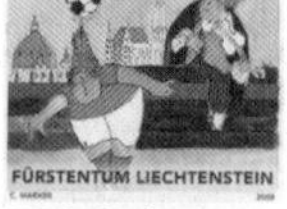

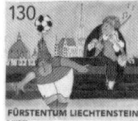

487 St. Stephen's Cathedral (Austria)

2008. EURO 2008 Football Championships. Multicoloured.

1479	1f.30 Type **487**	3·25	3·25
1480	1f.30 Flag, dancer and musician (Liechtenstein)	3·25	3·25
1481	1f.30 Alphorn and Matterhorn (Switzerland)	3·25	3·25

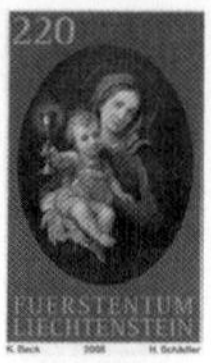

488 *Mother and Queen of the Precious Blood*

2008. 150th Anniv of Schellenberg Convent.

1482	**488**	2f.20 multicoloured	6·00	6·00

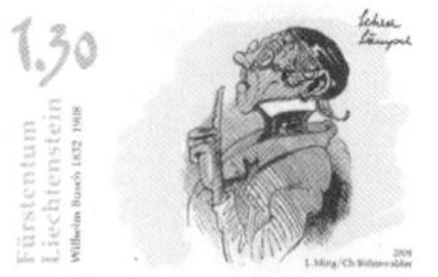

489 *Schoolmaster Lampel*

2008. Death Centenary of Heinrich Christian William Busch (writer and cartoonist). Multicoloured.

1483	1f.30 Type **489**	3·25	3·25
1484	1f.30 *Hans Huckebein*	3·25	3·25
1485	1f.30 *Max and Moritz*	3·25	3·25
1486	1f.30 *Widow Bolte*	3·25	3·25
1487	1f.30 *Pious Helen*	3·25	3·25
1488	1f.30 *Fips the Monkey*	3·25	3·25
1489	1f.30 *Tailor Bock*	3·25	3·25
1490	1f.30 *Balduin Bahlamm*	3·25	3·25

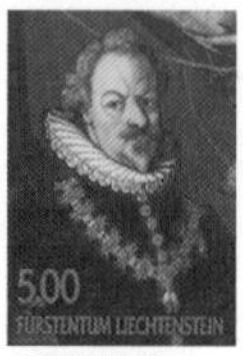

490 Karl I of Liechtenstein

2008. 400th Anniv of Princes of Liechtenstein. Sheet 58×77 mm.

MS1491	**490**	5f. multicoloured	13·00	13·00

The stamp and margin of **MS**1491 form a composite design of painting.

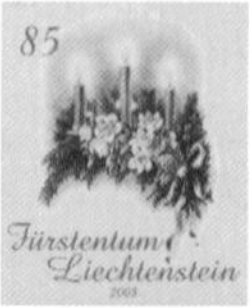

491 Candle Wreath

2008. Christmas. Multicoloured.

1492	85r. Type **491**	2·40	2·40
1493	1f. Children carrying holly (horiz)	2·75	2·75
1494	1f.30 Decorated tree	3·75	3·75

2008. Technical Innovations. As T 466. Multicoloured.

1495	1f.20 Neutrik XLR cable connector NC3MX	3·25	3·25
1496	1f.40 Ivoclar Vivadent blue phase polymerisation unit	3·50	3·50
1497	2f.20 ThyssenKrupp Presta DeltaValve control	6·50	6·50

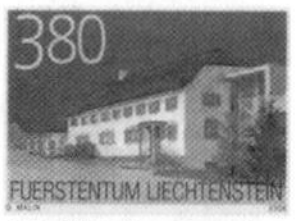

492 Schadler Ceramics Building, Nendeln

2008. Preservation of Historical Environment (8th series).

1498	**492**	3f.80 multicoloured	10·50	10·50

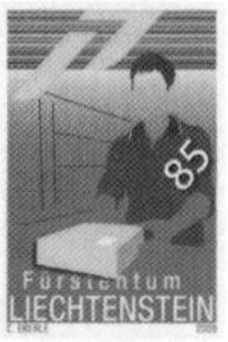

493 Postworker accepting Parcel

2009. Postal Service. Multicoloured.

1499	85c. Type **493**	2·75	2·75
1500	1f. Delivering	3·25	3·25
1501	1f.30 Sorting	4·25	4·25

494 First Aid

2009. Volunteer Civil Portection (2nd series). Association of Liechtenstein Samaritan Volunteers.
1502 **494** 1f. multicoloured 3·25 3·25

495 *Unfolding* (woman and butterfly)

2009. Artistic Techniques. Linocuts by Stephan Sude.
1503 1f. black and pink 3·25 3·25
1504 1f.30 black and olive 4·25 4·25
1505 2f.70 black and blue 8·00 8·00
DESIGNS: 1f. Type **495**; 1f.30 *Awareness* (man crying); 2f.70 *Fulfilment*(elderly man and mountains).

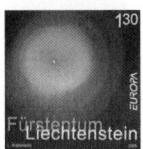

496 Super Nova (Leta Krahenbuhl)

2009. Europa. Astronomy.
1506 **496** 1f.30 multicoloured 4·25 4·25

497 Land Register

2009. Bicentenary of Land Register.
1507 **497** 3f.30 multicoloured 10·50 10·50

498 Ants and Forest

2009. Forest. Multicoloured.
1508 85c. Type **498** 2·75 1·90
1509 1f. Path through woods 3·25 2·50
1510 1f.40 Tree and rock 4·50 3·00
1511 1f.60 Mountain, lake and log pile 5·00 3·50

499 Summit Cross, Kuegrat

2009. Centenary of Alpine Association. Designs showing summit crosses. Multicoloured.
1512 1f. Type **499** 3·25 2·50
1513 1f.30 Langspitz (vert) 4·25 2·75
1514 2f.20 Rappastein (vert) 6·75 5·25
1515 2f.40 Jahn-Turm und Wolan 7·25 5·25

500 Vaduz Castle in Spring

2009. Vaduz Castle through the Seasons. Multicoloured.
1516 1f.30 Type **500** 4·25 2·75
1517 1f.80 In summer 5·50 3·75

501 *Pieris rapae*

2009. Butterflies. Multicoloured.
1518 85c. Type **501** 1·90 1·90
1519 1f. *Parnassius apollo* 2·50 2·50
1520 1f.30 *Melanargia galathea* 2·75 2·75
1521 2f. *Vanessa atlanta* 5·00 5·00

502 Emblem

2009. 75th Anniv of Liechtenstein Philatelic Society.
1522 **502** 1f.30 multicoloured 2·75 2·75

503 Badminton Cabinet (detail)

2009. Liechtenstein Museum, Garden Palace, Vienna. Designs showing details of Badminton Cabinet. Multicoloured.
1523 1f.30 Type **503** 2·75 2·75
1524 2f. Three birds and bouquet (detail centre) (34x49 mm) 4·50 4·50
1525 4f. Red-capped bird and lilies (detail left) 8·50 8·50

504 Chapel of St. Mamerta, Trisien

2009. SEPAC (small European mail services).
1526 **504** 1f.30 multicoloured 2·50 2·50

505 Lifestyle Museum, Schellenberg

2009. National Identity. Liechtenstein as Brand (2nd series). Multicoloured.
1527 20r. Type **505** (community) 70 70
1528 50r. Former Customs House, Vaduz (finance) 90 90
1529 60r. Parish House, Bendern (dialogue) 1·00 1·00

506 Annunciation

2009. Christmas. Advent Windows created by Pupils of Primary School, Gamprin. Multicoloured.
1530 85r. Type **506** 90 90
1531 1f. Journey to Bethlehem 1·50 1·50
1532 1f.30 The Nativity 1·70 1·70
1533 1f.80 The Three Magi 1·90 1·90

507 University of Applied Sciences (Karl+Probst), Vaduz

2009. Modern Architecture (1st issue). Multicoloured.
1534 85r. Type **507** 90 90
1535 2f.60 Art Museum (Morger, Degelo and Kerez), Vaduz 4·50 4·50

1536 3f.50 Ruggell–Nofels Border Crossing between Liechtenstein and Austria (EFFEFF) 5·50 5·50

508 Alpine Skier

2010. Winter Olympic Games, Vancouver. Multicoloured.
1537 1f. Type **508** 3·25 3·25
1538 1f.80 Nordic skier 3·75 3·75

509 Mountain Rescue (Liechtenstein Mountain Rescue (founded by Liechtenstein Alpine Association))

2010. Volunteer Civil Protection (3rd series). Volunteer Rescue Services. Multicoloured.
1539 85r. Type **509** 2·25 2·25
1540 1f.30 Water rescue (founded by 'Bubbles' diving club) 3·25 3·25

510 Hillside Farming

2010. Agriculture. Multicoloured.
1541 85r. Type **510** 1·50 1·50
1542 1f. Agriculture and the environment 2·50 2·50
1543 1f.10 Technology in farming 2·75 2·75
1544 1f.30 Farm animals 3·50 3·50

511 Natural Gas Filling Station (EFFEFF), Vaduz

2010. Modern Architecture (2nd issue). Multicoloured.
1545 2f.60 Type **511** 6·75 6·75
1546 3f.60 Liechtenstein Electric Power Authority Transformer Station (Marcel Ferrier) 8·25 8·25

512 Vaduz

2010. Expo 2010, Shanghai
MS1547 1f.60 Type **512**; 1f.90 Tidal bore on Qiantang river (32x60mm) 8·75 8·75

513 Ariadne giving Theseus the Thread

2010. Liechtenstein Museum, Garden Palace, Vienna. Multicoloured.
1548 1f. Type **513** 2·50 2·50
1549 1f.40 Surrender of Golden Fleece to Jason 3·50 3·50

 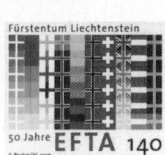

514 Figures supporting Roof   **515** Flags of Members

516 Finger Print

2011. 50th Anniversaries
1550 **514** 1f. olive-bistre and black (Disability Insurance) 2·50 2·50
1551 **515** 1f.40 multicoloured (EFTA) 3·50 3·50
1552 **516** 1f.90 pale yellow-olive and slate grey (Interpol in Vaduz) 3·75 3·75

517 *Coenonympha oedippus* (false ringlet)

2010. Butterflies. Multicoloured.
1553 1f.40 Type **517** 2·75 2·75
1554 1f.60 *Gonepteryx rhamni* (brimstone) 3·00 3·00
1555 2f.60 *Papilio machaon* (Old World swallowtail) 7·25 7·25

518 Roadway and Eschnerberg

2010. Liechtenstein Panorama
1556 1f. Type **518** 2·30 2·30
1557 1f. Field and Alvier mountains 2·30 33·00
Nos. 1556/7 were printed, *se-tenant*, forming a composite design

519 Hydropower

2010. Renewable Energy. Multicoloured.
1558 1f. Type **519** 2·50 2·50
1559 1f.40 Wood 3·50 3·50
1560 2f.80 Near-surface geothermal power 8·00 8·00

520 Children and Symbols of Magic and Fantasy

2010. Europa
1561 **520** 1f.40 multicoloured 4·00 4·00

521 Autumn

2010. Vaduz Castle through the Seasons. Multicoloured.
1562 1f.40 Type **521** 4·00 4·00
1563 1f.90 Winter 4·75 4·75

Nos. 1564/6 and Type **522** are left for Christmas; Nos. 1567/9 and Type **523** are left for Museum of Art and Nos. 1570/2 and Type **524** are left for Brand Liechtenstein, all issued on 15 November 2010 and not yet received.

525 Athletics, Volleyball and Cycling

2011. Small European States' Games 2011, Liechtenstein
1573 85r. bronze and black 1·50 1·50
1574 1f. silver and black 3·00 3·00
1575 1f.40 gold and black 5·00 5·00
Designs: Type 525; 1f. Judo, shooting and squash; 1f.40 Table tennis, tennis and swimming

526 Quick Response Code

2011. Anniversaries
1576 1f. multicoloured 3·00 3·00
1577 1f. black and gold (31×37 mm) 3·00 3·00
Designs: Type 526 (150th anniv of Landesbank); '50 Jahre Landesbibliothek' (50th anniv of national Library)

527 Photovoltaic Cells

2011. Renewable Energy. Multicoloured.
1578 1f. Type 527 3·00 3·00
1579 1f.10 Solar energy 3·25 3·35
1580 2f.90 Wind energy 7·75 7·75

528 Cloisonné Enamelled Egg from Moscow Workshop and Solemn Early Mass at Easter in St. Isaac's Cathedral, St. Petersburg (etching by Vasily Ivanovich Navozov)

2011. Decorated Easter Eggs, collected by Adulf Peter Goop. Multicoloured.
1581 1f. Type 528 3·00 3·00
1582 1f.40 Faberge egg with apple blossom and Anichkov Palace on Nevsky Prospekt in St. Petersburg (47×32 mm) 3·25 3·25
1583 2f.60 Egg with swan motif made by Pavel Akimovich Ovchinnikov and Red Square with St. Basil's Cathedral 7·75 7·75

529 Prince Nikolaus

2011. Children of Hereditary Prince and Princess. Multicoloured.
MS1584 1f. Type 529; 1f.80 Prince Georg; 2f. Princess Marie Caroline; 2f.60 Prince Joseph Wenzel 25·00 25·00

530 Tree as Ecosystem

2011. Europa. Forests
1585 530 1f.40 multicoloured 5·00 5·00

531 Inachis io (peacock)

2011. Butterflies. Multicoloured.
1586 2f.20 Type 531 8·00 8·00
1587 5f. Anthocharis cardamines (orange tip) 17·00 17·00

532 Fruit (Shirana Shahbazi)

2011. Art
1588 532 1f. multicoloured 3·00 3·00

533 Falco subbuteo (hobby)

2011. Engangered Bird Species. 50th Anniv of WWF. Multicoloured.
MS1589 1f.×8, Type 533; *Glaucidium passerinum* (pygmy owl); *Jynx torquilla* (wryneck); *Oriolus oriolus* (oriole); *Luscinia megarhynchos* (nightingale); *Phoenicurus phoenicurus* (redstart); *Lanius collurio* (red-backed shrike); *Saxicola rubetra* (whinchat); 25·00 25·00

534 Alpine Rhine

2011. 24 Hours in Liechtenstein. Paintings by Xiao Hui Wang. Multicoloured.
1590 1f.30 Type 534 3·50 3·50
1591 3f.70 Water Reflections, Gutenberg Castle, Balzers 8·50 8·50

535 Ruggell Marsh

2011. SEPAC (small European mail services)
1592 535 1f.40 multicoloured 4·50 4·50

536 Crib, Parish Church of St. Gallus, Triesen

2011. Christmas. Cribs. Multicoloured.
1593 85r. Type 536 1·50 1·50
1594 1f. St. Florin Parish Church, Vaduz (38×32 mm) 3·00 3·00
1595 1f.40 Parish Church cf the Assumption Bendern (32×38 mm) 5·00 5·00

537 Gutenberg Castle, Balzers

2011. Castles in Liechtenstein. Multicoloured.
1596 1f. Type 537 1·80 1·80
1597 1f.40 Schellenberg ruins 2·10 2·10
1598 2f. Schalun ruins 6·50 6·50
1599 2f.60 Vaduz Castle from north 7·25 7·25

538

2011. Chinese New Year. Year of the Dragon. Sheet 146×208 mm. Scarlet and gold.
MS1600 1f.90×4, Type 538×4 25·00 25·00

OFFICIAL STAMPS

1932. Stamps of 1930 optd REGIERUNGS DIENSTSACHE under crown.
O118B 5r. green 11·00 16·00
O119B 10r. lilac 75·00 16·00
O120B 20r. red 85·00 16·00
O121B 30r. blue 18·00 22·00
O122C 35r. green 14·50 36·00
O123C 50r. black 80·00 20·00
O124A 60r. green 14·50 50·00
O125B 1f.20 brown £150 £425

1933. Nos. 121 and 123 optd REGIERUNGS DIENSTSACHE in circle round crown.
O126 38 25r. orange 44·00 60·00
O127 - 1f.20 brown £100 £400

1934. Nos. 128 etc. optd REGIERUNGS DIENSTSACHE in circle round crown.
O150 41 5r. green 2·20 3·75
O151 - 10r. violet 4·25 3·75
O152 - 15r. orange 75 3·75
O153 - 20r. red 75 3·75
O155 - 25r. brown 3·75 22·00
O156 - 30r. blue 5·00 11·00
O157 42 50r. brown 1·50 5·00
O158 - 90r. green 11·00 60·00
O159 - 1f.50 brown 44·00 £300

1937. Stamps of 1937 optd REGIERUNGS DIENSTSACHE in circle round crown.
O174 51 5r. green and buff 35 75
O175 - 10r. violet and buff 75 2·20
O176 - 20r. red and buff 1·50 3·00
O177 - 25r. brown and buff 75 3·00
O178 - 30r. blue and buff 1·80 3·00
O179 - 50r. brown and buff 1·10 2·20
O180 - 1f. purple and buff 1·10 12·50
O181 - 1f.50 grey and buff 3·00 18·00

1947. Stamps of 1944 optd DIENSTMARKE and crown.
O255 5r. green 2·20 1·10
O256 10r. violet 2·20 1·50
O257 20r. red 3·00 1·50
O258 30r. blue 3·75 2·20
O259 50r. grey 3·75 4·25
O260 1f. red 14·50 16·00
O261 1f.50 blue 14·50 16·00

O86

1950. Buff paper.
O287 O86 5r. purple and grey 35 35
O288 O86 10r. green and mauve 35 35
O289 O86 20r. brown and blue 35 35
O290 O86 30r. purple and red 45 45
O291 O86 40r. blue and brown 60 60
O292 O86 55r. green and red 1·10 1·10
O293 O86 60r. grey and mauve 1·10 1·10
O294 O86 80r. orange and grey 1·20 1·20
O295 O86 90r. brown and blue 1·30 1·30
O296 O86 1f.20 turquoise and orange 1·80 1·80

1968. White paper.
O495 5r. brown and orange 15 15
O496 10r. violet and red 20 20
O497 20r. red and green 30 30
O498 30r. green and red 35 35
O499 50r. blue and red 60 60
O500 60r. orange and blue 75 75
O501 70r. purple and green 85 85
O502 80r. green and red 1·00 1·00
O503 95r. green and red 1·20 1·20
O504 1f. purple & turquoise 1·50 1·50
O505 1f.20 brown & turq 2·20 2·20
O506 2f. brown and orange 2·20 2·20

O198 Government Building, Vaduz

1976
O652 O198 10r. brown and violet 15 15
O653 O198 20r. red and blue 20 20
O654 O198 35r. blue and red 35 35
O655 O198 40r. violet and green 50 50
O656 O198 50r. green and mauve 55 55
O657 O198 70r. purple and green 75 75
O658 O198 80r. green and purple 85 85
O659 O198 90r. violet and blue 1·00 1·00
O660 O198 1f. grey and purple 1·10 1·10
O661 O198 1f.10 brown and blue 1·20 1·20
O662 O198 1f.50 green and red 1·60 1·60
O663 O198 2f. orange and blue 2·20 2·20
O664 O198 5f. purple and orange 14·50 11·00

POSTAGE DUE STAMPS

D11

1920
D43 D11 5h. red 35 45
D44 D11 10h. red 35 45
D45 D11 15h. red 35 45
D46 D11 20h. red 35 45
D47 D11 25h. red 35 60
D48 D11 30h. red 35 60
D49 D11 40h. red 35 60
D50 D11 50h. red 35 60
D51 D11 80h. red 35 60
D52 D11 1k. blue 45 1·50
D53 D11 2k. blue 45 1·50
D54 D11 5k. blue 45 1·50

D25

1928
D84 D25 5r. red and violet 1·50 3·75
D85 D25 10r. red and violet 1·80 3·75
D86 D25 15r. red and violet 3·00 16·00
D87 D25 20r. red and violet 3·00 3·75
D88 D25 25r. red and violet 3·00 11·00
D89 D25 30r. red and violet 9·50 17·00
D90 D25 40r. red and violet 10·00 18·00
D91 D25 50r. red and violet 12·00 22·00

D58

1940
D189 D58 5r. red and blue 1·80 4·25
D190 D58 10r. red and blue 75 1·50
D191 D58 15r. red and blue 1·10 7·25
D192 D58 20r. red and blue 1·10 2·20
D193 D58 25r. red and blue 2·20 4·75
D194 D58 30r. red and blue 4·75 8·00
D195 D58 40r. red and blue 4·75 7·25
D196 D58 50r. red and blue 5·50 8·25

Pt. 10

LITHUANIA

A country on the Baltic Sea, under Russian rule until occupied by the Germans in the first World War (see German Eastern Command). It was an independent republic from 1918 to 1940, when it was incorporated into the U.S.S.R.

Lithuania declared its independence in 1990, and the U.S.S.R. formally recognized the republic in 1991.

1918. 100 skatiku = 1 auksinas.
1922. 100 centu = 1 litas.
1990. 100 kopeks = 1 rouble.
1992. Talons.
1993. 100 centu = 1 litas.

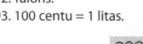

1

1918

3B	1	B 10s. black on buff	76·00	21·00
4B	1	B 15s. black on buff	38·00	23·00
5B	1	A 20s. black on buff	6·00	5·00
6B	1	A 30s. black on buff	6·00	5·00
7B	1	A 40s. black on buff	18·00	10·00
8B	1	A 50s. black on buff	6·00	5·00

2

1919

9	2	10s. black on buff	7·50	5·00
10	2	15s. black on buff	7·50	5·00
11	2	20s. black on buff	7·50	5·00
12	2	30s. black on buff	7·50	5·00

3

1919

13	3	10s. black on buff	3·75	2·20
14	3	15s. black on buff	3·75	2·20
15	3	20s. black on buff	3·75	2·20
16	3	30s. black on buff	3·75	2·20
17	3	40s. black on buff	3·75	2·50
18	3	50s. black on buff	3·75	2·50
19	3	60s. black on buff	3·75	2·75

4

1919

20	4	10s. black on buff	3·75	2·20
21	4	15s. black on buff	3·75	2·20
22	4	20s. black on buff	3·75	2·20
23	4	30s. black on buff	3·75	2·20
24	4	40s. black on buff	3·75	2·50
25	4	50s. black on buff	3·75	2·50
26	4	60s. black on buff	3·75	2·75

5 Arms

6

7

1919. "auksinas" in lower case letters on 1 to 5a.

40	5	10s. pink	35	40
50	5	10s. orange	35	15
51	5	15s. violet	35	15
52	5	20s. blue	35	15
43	5	30s. orange	35	40
53	5	30s. bistre	35	15
54	5	40s. brown	2·50	90
55	6	50s. green	35	15
56	6	60s. red and violet	35	15
57	6	75s. red and yellow	35	15
37	7	1a. red and grey	2·50	35
38	7	3a. red and brown	2·50	40
39	7	5a. red and green	2·50	75

1921. As T **7**, but "AUKSINAS" or "AUKSINAI" in capital letters.

58	7	1a. red and grey	35	15
59	7	3a. red and brown	35	20
60	7	5a. red and green	35	40

11 Lithuania receiving Independence

12 Lithuania arises

1920. Second Anniv of Independence.

65	11	10s. lake	3·50	2·50
66	11	15s. lilac	3·50	2·50
67	11	20s. blue	3·50	2·50
68	12	30s. brown	3·50	2·50
69	-	40s. green and brown	3·50	2·50
70	12	50s. red	3·50	2·50
71	12	60s. lilac	3·50	2·50
72	-	80s. red and violet	3·50	2·50
73	-	1a. red and green	3·50	2·50
74	-	3a. red and brown	3·50	2·50
75	-	5a. red and green	3·50	2·50

DESIGNS—VERT: 40s., 80s., 1a. Lithuania with chains broken; 3, 5a. (25×25 mm) Arms.

16 Arms

17 Vytautas

1920. National Assembly.

76	16	10s. red	85	40
77	16	15s. violet	85	40
78	17	20s. green	85	40
79	16	30s. brown	85	40
80	-	40s. violet and green	85	40
81	17	50s. brown and orange	2·10	85
82	17	60s. red and orange	85	40
83	-	80s. red, grey and black	85	40
84	-	1a. yellow and black	1·30	40
85	-	3a. green and black	1·30	85
86	-	5a. violet and black	3·50	1·70

DESIGNS—As Type **17**: 40s., 80s. Gediminas. As Type **16**: 1a. to 5a. Sacred Oak and Altar.

20 Sower

21 Kestutis

22 Reaper

23

1921

87A	20	10s. red	85	1·00
88A	20	15s. mauve	35	1·30
89A	20	20s. blue	25	15
90A	22	30s. brown	2·50	2·50
91A	21	40s. red	25	15
92A	22	50s. olive	35	15
93A	22	60s. mauve and green	2·50	4·50
94A	21	80s. red and orange	35	15
95A	21	1a. green and brown	35	15
96A	21	2a. red and blue	35	15
97A	23	3a. blue and brown	85	90
124	20	4a. blue and yellow	40	1·30
98A	23	5a. red and grey	85	2·00
125	20	8a black and green	40	1·60
99A	23	10a. mauve and red	85	40
100A	23	25a. green and brown	1·00	50
101A	23	100a. grey and red	12·00	9·75

24 Flying Posthorn

25 Junkers F-13 over River Niemen

1921. Air. Inauguration of Kaunas–Konigsberg Air Service.

102	24	20s. blue	85	80
103	24	40s. orange	85	80
104	24	60s. green	85	85
105	24	80s. red	85	85
106	25	1a. green and red	1·70	85
107	-	2a. brown and blue	1·70	85
108	-	5a. grey and yellow	1·70	1·60

DESIGNS—As Type **25**: 2a. Three Junkers F-13 monoplanes; 5a. Junkers F-13 over Gediminas Castle.

28 Allegory of Flight

1921. Air. Inauguration of Air Mail Service.

109	28	20s. lilac and orange	2·50	2·10
110	28	40s. red and blue	2·50	2·10
111	28	60s. olive and blue	2·50	2·10
112	28	80s. green and yellow	2·50	2·10
113	28	1a. blue and green	2·50	2·10
114	28	2a. red and grey	2·50	2·10
115	28	5a. green and purple	2·50	2·10

1922. Surch 4 AUKSINAI with or without frame.

116	6	4a. on 75s. red and yellow	85	1·30

30 Junkers F-13

1922. Air.

118	30	1a. red and brown	3·00	3·50
119	30	3a. green and violet	3·00	3·50
120	30	5a. yellow and blue	3·00	3·50

31 Junkers F-13 over Gediminas Castle

1922. Air.

121	31	2a. red and blue	1·70	1·70
122	31	4a. red and brown	1·70	1·70
123	31	10a. blue and black	1·70	1·70

33 Pte. Luksis

1922. "De jure" Recognition of Lithuania by League of Nations. Inscr "LIETUVA DE JURE".

126	33	20s. red and black	1·30	85
127	-	40s. violet and green	1·30	85
128	-	50s. blue and purple	1·30	85
129	-	60s. orange and violet	1·30	85
130	-	1a. blue and red	1·30	85
131	-	2a. brown and blue	1·30	85
132	-	3a. blue and brown	1·30	85
133	-	4a. purple and green	1·30	85
134	-	5a. red and brown	1·30	75
135	-	6a. blue	1·30	85
136	-	8a. yellow and blue	1·30	85
137	-	10a. green and violet	1·30	85

DESIGNS—VERT: 40s. Lt. Juozapavicius; 50s. Dr. Basanavicius; 60s. Mrs. Petkevicaite; 1a. Prof. Voldemaras; 2a. Dovidaitis; 3a. Dr. Slezevicius; 4a. Dr. Galvanauskas; 5a. Dr. Grinius; 6a. Dr. Stulginskis; 8a. Pres. Smetona. HORIZ: (39×27 mm): 10a. Stauguitis, Pres. Smetona and Silingas.

1922. Surch.

138	5	1c. on 10s. orange (postage)	3·00	6·00
139	5	1c. on 15s. violet	4·25	6·75
143	5	1c. on 20s. blue	4·25	5·25
144	5	1c. on 30s. orange	70·00	£120
145	5	1c. on 30s. bistre	40	70
146	5	1c. on 40s. brown	40	60
148	22	1c. on 50s. olive	25	15
149	6	2c. on 50s. green	3·50	5·00
150	6	2c. on 60s. red and violet	15	15
151	6	2c. on 75s. red and yellow	2·10	6·75
152	20	3c. on 10s. red	12·50	8·50
153	20	3c. on 15s. mauve	25	15
154	20	3c. on 20s. blue	40	5·00
155	22	3c. on 30s. brown	21·00	12·50
156	21	3c. on 40s. red	40	65
157	7	3c. on 1a. (No. 37)	£190	£190
158	7	3c. on 1a. (No. 58)	40	1·00
159	7	3c. on 3a. (No. 38)	£190	£190
160	7	3c. on 3a. (No. 59)	25	75
161	7	3c. on 5a. (No. 39)	£120	£120
162	7	3c. on 5a. (No. 60)	25	65
163	22	5c. on 50s. olive	15	15
164	22	5c. on 60s. mauve & green	21·00	21·00
165	21	5c. on 80s. red and orange	60	50
166	6	5c. on 4a. on 75s. red and yellow	1·70	13·50
168	21	10c. on 1a. green & brown	85	20
169	21	10c. on 2a. red and blue	25	15
170	20	15c. on 4a. blue and yellow	15	15
171	23	25c. on 3a. blue and green	21·00	34·00
172	23	25c. on 5a. red and grey	12·50	12·50
173	23	25c. on 10a. mauve and red	2·10	1·90
174	20	30c. on 8a. black and green	1·30	30
175	23	50c. on 25a. green & brown	4·25	3·75
176	23	1l. on 100 a grey and red	4·75	3·75
177	24	10c. on 20s. blue (air)	6·75	5·00
178	24	10c. on 40s. orange	3·50	6·00
179	24	10c. on 60s. green	3·50	6·00
180	24	10c. on 80s. red	3·50	6·00
181	25	20c. on 1a. green and red	21·00	17·00
182	-	20c. on 2a. (No. 107)	21·00	17·00
183	31	25c. on 2a. red and blue	1·70	1·10
184	31	30c. on 4a. red and brown	1·70	1·70
185	-	50c. on 5a. (No. 108)	3·50	1·70
186	31	50c. on 10a. blue and black	1·70	1·50
187	30	1l. on 5a. yellow and blue	30·00	17·00

38 Wayside Cross

39 Ruins of Kaunas Castle

40 Seminary Church

1923

201	38	2c. brown	85	25
202	38	3c. bistre	1·30	25
203	38	5c. green	1·30	20
204	38	10c. violet	2·50	10
189	38	15c. red	2·50	15
190	38	20c. green	2·50	15
191	38	25c. blue	2·50	15
206	38	36c. brown	10·00	65
192	39	50c. green	2·50	15
193	39	60c. red	2·50	25
194	40	1l. orange and green	10·00	15
195	40	3l. red and grey	15·00	75
196	40	5l. brown and blue	21·00	90

43 Arms of Memel

44 Ruins of Trakai

1923. Union of Memel with Lithuania.

210	43	1c. red and green	85	50
211	-	2c. mauve	85	85
212	-	3c. yellow	85	1·00
213	43	5c. buff and blue	2·50	2·50
214	-	10c. red	1·70	1·60
215	-	15c. green	1·70	1·60
216	44	25c. violet	1·70	1·80
217	-	30c. red	4·25	4·00
218	-	60c. green	1·70	1·70
219	-	1l. green	1·70	1·70
220	-	2l. red	8·50	9·75
221	44	3l. blue	8·50	8·25
222	-	5l. blue	8·50	8·50

DESIGNS—As Type **43**: 3c., 2l. Chapel of Biruta; 10c., 15c. War Memorial Kaunas; As Type **44**: 2, 30c. Arms of Lithuania; 60c., 5l. Memel Lighthouse; 1l. Memel Harbour.

45 Biplane

46 Biplane

1924. Air.

223	45	20c. yellow	1·20	65
224	45	40c. green	1·70	90
225	45	60c. red	1·70	90
226	46	1l. brown	3·50	85

1924. Charity. War Orphans Fund. Surch KARO NASLAICIAMS and premium.

227	38	2c.+2c. bistre (postage)	2·50	2·50
228	38	3c.+3c. bistre	2·50	2·50
229	38	5c.+5c. green	2·50	2·50
231	38	10c.+10c. violet	3·50	3·50
232	38	15c.+15c. red	4·25	4·25
233	38	20c.+20c. olive	5·00	5·00
235	38	25c.+25c. blue	12·50	12·50
236	38	36c.+34c. brown	12·50	12·50
237	39	50c.+50c. green	12·50	12·50
238	39	60c.+60c. red	17·00	17·00
239	40	1l.+1l. orange and green	17·00	17·00
240	40	3l.+2l. red and grey	34·00	34·00
241	40	5l.+3l. brown and blue	42·00	42·00
242	45	20c.+20c. yellow (air)	21·00	21·00
243	45	40c.+40c. green	21·00	21·00

244	45	60c.+60c. red	21·00	21·00
245	46	1l.+1l. brown	21·00	21·00

49 Barn Swallow carrying Letter

1926. Air.

246	49	20c. red	1·30	50
247	49	40c. orange and mauve	1·30	50
248	49	60c. black and blue	2·50	50

1926. Charity. War Invalids. Nos. 227/39 surch with new values and small ornaments.

249	38	1c.+1c. on 2c.+2c.	1·70	1·70
250	38	2c.+2c. on 3c.+3c.	1·70	1·70
251	38	2c.+2c. on 5c.+5c.	1·70	1·70
253	38	5c.+5c. on 10c.+10c.	3·50	3·50
254	38	5c.+5c. on 15c.+15c.	3·50	3·50
255	38	10c.+10c. on 20c.+20c.	3·50	3·50
257	38	10c.+10c. on 25c.+25c.	8·50	8·50
258	38	14c.+14c. on 36c.+34c.	10·00	10·00
259	39	20c.+20c. on 50c.+50c.	8·50	8·50
260	39	25c.+25c. on 60c.+60c.	17·00	17·00
261	40	30c.+30c. on 1l.+1l.	25·00	25·00

1926. Charity. War Orphans. Nos. 227/39 surch V.P. and new values in circular ornament.

262	38	1c.+1c. on 2c.+2c.	1·70	1·70
263	38	2c.+2c. on 3c.+3c.	1·70	1·70
264	38	2c.+2c. on 5c.+5c.	1·70	1·70
266	38	5c.+5c. on 10c.+10c.	3·50	3·50
267	38	10c.+10c. on 15c.+15c.	3·50	3·50
268	38	15c.+15c. on 20c.+20c.	3·50	3·50
270	38	15c.+15c. on 25c.+25c.	8·50	8·50
271	38	19c.+19c. on 36c.+34c.	8·50	8·50
272	39	25c.+25c. on 50c.+50c.	10·00	10·00
273	39	30c.+30c. on 60c.+60c.	17·00	17·00
274	40	50c.+50c. on 1l.+1l.	25·00	25·00

56

1927

275	56	2c. orange	1·70	10
276	56	3c. brown	1·70	10
277	56	5c. green	2·10	10
278	56	10c. violet	3·50	15
279	56	15c. red	3·50	15
280	56	25c. blue	1·70	15
283	56	30c. blue	30·00	3·00

57

1927. Dr. Basanavicius Mourning Issue.

285A	57	15c. red	2·50	1·70
286A	57	25c. blue	2·50	1·70
287A	57	50c. green	2·50	1·50
288A	57	60c. violet	5·00	3·00

58 "Vytis" of the Lithuanian Arms

1927

289	58	1l. green and grey	1·70	65
290	58	3l. violet and green	6·00	65
291	58	5l. brown and grey	6·75	1·30

59 President Antanas Smetona

60 Lithuania liberated

1928. 10th Anniv of Independence.

292	59	5c. green and brown	1·30	25
293	59	10c. black and violet	1·30	25
294	59	15c. brown and orange	1·30	20
295	59	25c. slate and blue	1·30	25
296	60	50c. purple and blue	1·30	25
297	60	60c. black and red	1·30	30
298	-	1l. brown	1·30	55

DESIGN—HORIZ: 1l. Lithuania's resurrection (angel and soldiers). Dated "1918-1928".

62

63

64 J. Tubelis

1930. 500th Death Anniv of Grand Duke Vytautas.

299	62	2c. brown (postage)	40	10
300	62	3c. violet and brown	40	10
301	62	5c. red and green	40	10
302	62	10c. green and violet	40	10
303	62	15c. violet and red	40	10
304	62	30c. purple and blue	85	10
305	62	36c. olive and purple	1·30	35
306	62	50c. blue and green	85	40
307	62	60c. red and blue	85	40
308	63	1l. purple, grey and green	3·50	95
309	63	3l. violet, pink and mauve	5·00	2·10
310	63	5l. red, grey and brown	12·50	3·00
311	63	10l. black and blue	34·00	17·00
312	63	25l. green and brown	70·00	60·00
313	64	5c. brown, yellow and black (air)	70	30
314	64	10c. black, drab and blue	70	30
315	64	15c. blue, grey and purple	70	30
316	-	20c. red, orange and brown	1·30	85
317	-	40c. violet, light blue & blue	1·70	90
318	-	60c. black, lilac and green	2·10	1·00
319	-	1l. black, lilac and red	3·75	1·70

DESIGNS—HORIZ: 20c., 40c. Vytautas and Kaunas; 60c., 1l. Vytautas and Smetona.

66 Railway Station, Kaunas

1932. Orphans' Fund. Imperf or perf.

320	66	5c. blue and brown	40	40
321	66	10c. purple and brown	40	40
322	-	15c. brown and green	85	75
323	-	25c. blue and green	1·30	1·10
324	-	50c. grey and olive	2·50	3·00
325	-	60c. grey and mauve	6·75	5·75
326	-	1l. blue and grey	6·75	5·75
327	-	3l. purple and green	6·75	5·75

DESIGNS—As Type **66**: 15, 25c. "The Two Pines" (painting); 50c. G.P.O. VERT: 60c., 1, 3l. Vilnius Cathedral.

68 Map of Lithuania, Memel and Vilna

1932. Air. Orphans' Fund. Imperf or perf.

328	68	5c. red and green	85	60
329	68	10c. purple and brown	85	60
330	-	15c. blue and buff	85	60
331	-	20c. black and brown	6·75	2·40
332	-	40c. purple and yellow	6·75	4·00
333	-	60c. blue and buff	8·50	7·50
334	-	1l. purple and green	8·50	7·25
335	-	2l. blue and green	8·50	7·75

DESIGNS: 15, 20c. Airplane over R. Niemen; 40, 60c. Town Hall, Kaunas; 1, 2l. Vytautas Church, Kaunas.

69 Vytautas escapes from Prison

71 Coronation of Mindaugas

1932. 15th Anniv of Independence. Imperf or perf.

336	69	5c. purple and red (postage)	85	50
337	69	10c. brown and grey	85	50
338	-	15c. green and red	85	50
339	-	25c. brown and purple	2·50	1·90
340	-	50c. brown and green	2·50	2·50
341	-	60c. red and green	6·00	5·50
342	-	1l. black and blue	6·00	3·50
343	-	3l. green and purple	6·00	6·50
344	-	5c. lilac and green (air)	85	35
345	-	10c. red and green	85	40
346	71	15c. brown and violet	85	65
347	-	20c. black and red	4·25	65
348	-	40c. black and purple	6·00	3·75
349	-	60c. black and orange	8·50	7·75
350	-	1l. green and violet	8·50	5·00
351	-	2l. brown and blue	8·50	5·75

DESIGNS—POSTAGE. As Type **69**: 15, 25c. Vytautas and Jagello preaching the gospel; 50, 60c. Battle of Grunewald; 1, 3l. Proclamation of Independence. AIR. As Type **71**: 5, 10c. Battle of Saules; 40c. Gediminas in Council; 60c. Founding of Vilnius; 1l. Russians surrendering to Gediminas; 2l. Algirdas before Moscow.

72 A. Visteliauskas

1933. 50th Anniv of Publication of "Ausra".

352	72	5c. red and green	85	40
353	72	10c. red and blue	85	40
354	-	15c. red and orange	85	40
355	-	25c. brown and blue	2·50	80
356	-	50c. blue and green	1·70	1·80
357	-	60c. deep brown & lt brown	12·00	6·00
358	-	1l. purple and red	12·00	6·00
359	-	3l. purple and blue	12·00	7·25

PORTRAITS: 15, 25c. P. Vileisis; 50, 60c. J. Sliupas; 1, 3l. J. Basanavicius.

73 Trakai Castle

1933. Air. 550th Death Anniv of Grand Duke Kestutis.

360	73	5c. blue and green	85	40
361	73	10c. brown and violet	85	40
362	-	15c. violet and blue	85	60
363	-	20c. purple and brown	4·25	80
364	-	40c. purple and blue	6·00	3·25
365	-	60c. blue and red	6·00	7·25
366	-	1l. blue and green	6·00	4·50
367	-	2l. green and violet	6·00	9·50

DESIGNS: 15, 20c. Kestutis encounters Birute; 40, 60c. Birute; 1, 2l. Kestutis and Algirdas.

74 Mother and Child

1933. Child Welfare. (a) Postage.

373	74	5c. brown and green	40	25
374	74	10c. blue and red	40	25
375	-	15c. purple and green	40	40
376	-	25c. black and orange	1·70	1·30
377	-	50c. red and green	1·70	2·00
378	-	60c. orange and black	7·25	6·25
379	-	1l. blue and brown	7·25	6·00
380	-	3l. green and purple	7·25	8·25

DESIGNS—VERT: 15, 25c. Boy reading a book; 50, 60c. Boy with building bricks; 1, 3l. Mother and child weaving.

75 J. Tumas Vaizgantas

(b) Air. Various medallion portraits in triangular frames.

381		5c. blue and red	40	20
382		10c. green and violet	40	20
383	75	15c. brown and green	40	25
384	75	20c. blue and red	85	45
385	-	40c. green and lake	2·50	2·00
386	-	60c. brown and blue	1·70	4·75
387	-	1l. blue and yellow	4·25	4·75
388	-	2l. lake and green	6·00	7·25

DESIGNS: 5, 10c. Maironis; 40, 60c. Vincas Kudirka; 1, 2l. Zemaite.

76 Captains S. Darius and S. Girenas

78 "Flight" mourning over Wreckage

1934. Air. Death of Darius and Girenas (trans-Atlantic airmen).

389	76	20c. red and black	10	10
390	-	40c. blue and red	10	10
391	76	60c. violet and black	10	10
392	78	1l. black and red	40	30
393	-	3l. orange and green	85	1·80
394	-	5l. blue and brown	3·50	3·50

DESIGNS—HORIZ: 40c. Bellanca monoplane "Lituanica" over Atlantic. VERT: 3l. "Lituanica" and globe; 5l. "Lituanica" and Vytis.

81 President A. Smetona

1934. President's 60th Birthday.

395	81	15c. red	10·00	10
396	81	30c. green	10·00	25
397	81	60c. blue	10·00	45

82

83

84 Gleaner

85

1934

398	82	2c. red and orange	40	15
399	82	5c. green	40	10
400	83	10c. brown	1·30	10
401	84	25c. brown and green	3·00	10
402	83	35c. red	3·00	10
403	84	50c. blue	6·25	10
404	85	1l. purple and red	42·00	15
405	85	3l. green	25	15
406	-	5l. purple and blue	25	15
407	-	10l. brown and yellow	2·10	4·00

DESIGNS—HORIZ: as Type **85**: 5l., 10l. Knight.

For design as Type **82** but smaller, see Nos. 411/12.

1935. Air. Honouring Atlantic Flyer Vaitkus. No. 390 optd F. VAITKUS nugalejo Atlanta 21-22-IX-1935.

407a		40c. blue and red	£425	£425

87 Vaitkus and Air Route

1936. Air. Felix Vaitkus's New York-Ireland Flight.

408	87	15c. purple	1·70	50
409	87	30c. green	3·50	50
410	87	60c. blue	4·25	1·50

1936. As T **82** but smaller (18×23 mm).

411	82	2c. orange	10	10
412	82	5c. green	15	10

88 President Smetona

1936

413	88	15c. red	6·75	10
414	88	30c. green	10·00	10
415	88	60c. blue	17·00	10

89

1937

416	89	10c. green	1·30	25
417	89	25c. mauve	10	10
418	89	35c. red	85	10
419	89	50c. brown	1·30	25
419a	89	1l. blue	40	80

90 Archer

1938. First National Olympiad Fund.

420	90	5c.+5c. green	6·75	8·00
421	-	15c.+5c. red	6·75	8·00
422	-	30c.+10c. blue	12·50	11·50
423	-	60c.+15c. brown	17·00	18·00

DESIGNS: 15c. Throwing the javelin; 30c. Diving; 60c. Relay runner breasting tape.

1938. Scouts' and Guides' National Camp Fund. Nos. 420/3 optd TAUTINE SKAUCIU (or SKAUTU) STOVYKLA and badge.

424	90	5c.+5c. green	8·50	8·50
425	-	15c.+5c. red	8·50	8·50
426	-	30c.+10c. blue	8·50	12·50
427	-	60c.+15c. brown	17·00	21·00

92 President Smetona

1939. 20th Anniv of Independence.

428		15c. red	40	20
429	92	30c. green	85	40
430	-	35c. mauve	85	45
431	92	60c. blue	1·30	75
MS431a	148×105 mm. Nos. 430/1		10·00	30·00
MS431b	Do. but imperf		75·00	£130

DESIGN: 15, 35c. Dr. Basanvicius proclaiming Lithuanian independence.

93 Scoring a Goal

1939. Third European Basketball Championship and Physical Culture Fund.

432	-	15c.+10c. brown	6·75	37·00
433	93	30c.+15c. green	6·75	37·00
434	-	60c.+40c. violet	12·50	21·00

DESIGNS—VERT: 15c. Scoring a goal. HORIZ: (40½×36 mm); 60c. International flags and ball.

1939. Recovery of Vilnius. Nos. 428/31 optd VILNIUS 1939-X-10 and trident.

435		15c. red	85	40
436	92	30c. green	85	40
437	-	35c. mauve	2·10	85
438	92	60c. blue	2·10	1·40

95 Vytis

1940. "Liberty" Issue.

439	95	5c. brown	10	25
440	-	10c. green	85	35
441	-	15c. orange	20	25
442	-	25c. brown	10	35
443	-	30c. green	10	25
444	-	35c. orange	25	35

DESIGNS: 10c. Angel; 15c. Woman releasing a dove; 25c. Mother and children; 30c. "Liberty Bell"; 35c. Mythical animal.

96 Vilnius

1940. Recovery of Vilnius.

445	96	15c. brown	40	35
446	-	30c. green	85	80
447	-	60c. blue	1·70	1·60
MS447a	140×106 mm. Nos. 445/7 with gold frames		10·00	13·50

DESIGNS—VERT: 30c. Portrait of Gediminas. HORIZ: 60c. Ruins of Trakai Castle.

1940. Incorporation of Lithuania in U.S.S.R. Optd LTSR 1940 VII 21.

448	82	2c. red and orange	15	25
449	95	5c. brown	15	25
450	-	10c. green (No. 440)	4·75	3·50
451	-	15c. orange (No. 441)	25	45
452	-	25c. brown (No. 442)	25	75
453	-	30c. green (No. 443)	40	80
454	-	35c. orange (No. 444)	40	1·20
455	89	50c. brown	40	1·30

From 1940 to 1990 Lithuania used stamps of Russia.

99 Angel and Map

1990. No gum. Imperf.

456	99	5k. green	25	25
457	99	10k. lilac	35	30
458	99	20k. blue	50	55
459	99	50k. red	1·90	1·90

1990. No gum. Imperf (simulated perfs).

460		5k. green and brown	10	15
461		10k. purple and brown	35	30
462		20k. blue and brown	35	50
463		50k. red and brown	40	40

100 Vytis

101 Hill of Crosses, Siauliai

1991

464	100	10k. black, gold and brown	10	10
465	100	15k. black, gold and green	40	35
466	100	20k. black, gold and blue	40	35
467	100	30k. black, gold and red	70	60
468	100	40k. black and gold	10	15
469	100	50k. black, gold and violet	10	15
470	101	50k. brown, chestnut & blk	85	75
471	100	100k. black, gold & green	10	25
472	-	200k. brown, chest & blk	1·70	1·80
473	100	500k. black, gold and blue	1·70	1·20

DESIGN: As T **101**—200k. Lithuanian Liberty Bell. See also Nos. 482 and 488/9.

102 Liberty Statue, Kaunas

1991. National Day.

480	102	20k. mauve, silver & black	40	35

103 Angel with Trumpet

1991. First Anniv of Declaration of Independence from U.S.S.R.

481	103	20k. deep green and green	40	40

1991. No gum. Imperf (simulated perfs).

482	100	15k. green and black	40	35

104 Wayside Crosses

1991

483	104	40k. green and silver	40	45
484	-	70k. brown, buff and gold	85	80
485	-	100k. brown, yellow & sil	1·30	1·30

DESIGNS: 70k. "Madonna" (icon from Pointed Gate Chapel, Vilnius); 100k. Towers of St. Anne's Church, Vilnius.

105 Candle

1991. 50th Anniv of Resistance to Soviet and German Occupations.

486	105	20k. yellow, black & bistre	25	30
487	-	50k. rose, black and red	60	90
488	-	70k. multicoloured	85	1·30

DESIGNS: 50k. Shield pierced by swords; 70k. Sword and wreath.

1991. No gum. Imperf.

489	100	25k. black and brown	35	35
490	100	30k. black and purple	50	45

106 World Map and Games Emblem

1991. Fourth International Lithuanians' Games.

491	106	20k. green, black & yellow	35	35
492	-	50k.+25k. green, black and yellow	1·40	1·20

DESIGN: 50k. Symbolic female athlete.

107 National Flag in Ice-axe and Mt. Everest

1991. Lithuanian Expedition to Mt. Everest.

493	107	20k. multicoloured	25	30
494	107	70k. multicoloured	1·00	1·30

108 Trakai Castle

1991. 650th Death Anniv of Grand Duke Gediminas. Each brown, ochre and green.

495		30k. Type **108**	40	40
496		50k. Gediminas	40	50
497		70k. Vilnius in 14th century	85	1·00

109 Black Storks

1991. Birds in the Red Book. Multicoloured.

498		30k.+15k. Type **109**	75	75
499		50k. Common cranes	95	90

110 U.N. and National Emblems and National Flag

1992. Admission to U.N.O.

500	110	100k. multicoloured	40	40

111 National Team Emblem and Colours

1992. Winter Olympic Games, Albertville, and Summer Games, Barcelona. Multicoloured.

501		50k.+25k. Type **111**	40	50
502		130k. Winter Games emblem	85	1·50
503		280k. Summer Games emblem	85	1·10

112 Slipper Orchid

1992. Plants in the Red Book. Multicoloured.

504		200k. Type **112**	1·00	1·00
505		300k. Sea holly	1·10	90

113 Goosander ("Mergus merganser")

1992. Birds of the Baltic. No value expressed.

506	113	B (15t.) black and green	60	60
507	-	B (15t.) brown, blk & grn	60	60
508	-	B (15t.) sepia, brown & grn	60	60
509	-	B (15t.) brown, blk & grn	60	60

DESIGNS: No. 506, Osprey ("Pandion haliaetus"); 507, Black-tailed godwit ("Limosa limosa"); 509, Common shelduck ("Tadorna tadorna").

114 Kedainiai

1992. Arms. Multicoloured.

510		2t. Type **114**	10	35
511		3t. Vilnius	25	25
512		10t. State arms	85	80

See also Nos. 531/3, 569/71, 594/5, 628/30, 663/5, 682/4, 712/14, 742/4, 769/71 and 781/3.

115 Couple

1992. Costumes of Suvalkija.

513	**115**	2t. multicoloured	25	25
514	-	5t. multicoloured	60	55
515	-	7t. multicoloured	85	65

DESIGNS: 5, 7t. Different costumes.

116 Zapyskis
Church

1993. Churches.

516	**116**	3t. black and stone	15	40
517	-	10t. black and blue	70	65
518	-	15t. black and grey	85	80

DESIGNS: 10t. Church of St. Peter and St. Paul, Vilnius; 15t. Church of the Resurrection, Kaunas.

1993. Nos. 467, 490 and 468 surch.

519	**100**	1t. on 30k. blk, gold & red	25	20
520	**100**	1t. on 30k. black & purple	25	20
521	**100**	3t. on 40k. black and gold	40	25

118 Jonas Basanavicius
(statesman)

1993. National Day. No value expressed.

522	**118**	A (3t.) red, cinn & brn	40	35
523	-	B (15t.) grn, stone & brn	85	1·00

DESIGN: No. 523, Jonas Vileisis (politician).

119 Vytautas

1993. 600th Anniv (1987) of Accession of Grand Duke Vytautas.

524		5t. gold, red and black	25	40
525	**119**	10t. green, black and red	60	55
526	-	15t. black, yellow and red	85	90
MS527	80×120 mm. 50t. olive, black and red		1·70	1·50

DESIGNS: 5t. Seal; 15t. "Battle of Grunwald" (Jan Matejka) 50t. Type **119**.

120 Simonas
Daukantas (historian)

1993. Birth Anniversaries. Each brown and yellow.

528		10t. Type **120** (bicent)	40	50
529		20t. Vydunas (125th anniv)	85	80
530		45t. Vincas Mykolaitis-Putinas (philosopher, centenary)	2·10	1·70

1993. Town Arms. As T 114. Multicoloured.

531		5c. Skuodas	15	15
532		30c. Telsiai	50	45
533		50c. Klaipeda	1·00	80

121 "Watchtower"
(M. K. Ciurlionis)

1993. World Unity Day (5c.) and Transatlantic Flight (80c.). Multicoloured.

534		5c. Type **121**	10	10
535		80c. Steponas Dariaus and Stasys Gireno	1·50	1·20

122 State
Arms

1993. No value expressed.

536	**122**	A, green, brown and red	10	10
537	**122**	B, red, green and bistre	75	70

123 Pope John Paul II
and View of Siluva

1993. Papal Visit. Multicoloured.

538	**123**	60c. Type **123**	70	60
539		60c. Pope and Hill of Crosses	70	60
540		80c. Pope and Kaunas	85	80
541		80c. Pope and Ausra Gates, Vilnius	85	80

124 Couple

1993. Costumes of Dzukai.

542	**124**	60c. multicoloured	75	65
543	-	80c. multicoloured	75	70
544	-	1l. multicoloured	75	75

DESIGNS: 80c. to 1l. Different costumes.

125 Klaipeda Post Office

1993. 75th Anniv of First Lithuanian Postage Stamps.

545	**125**	60c. multicoloured	40	50
546	-	60c. multicoloured	40	50
547	-	80c. multicoloured	50	75
548	-	1l. black, brown and green	85	80

DESIGNS: No. 546, Kaunas post office; 547, Ministry for Post and Information, Vilnius; 548, First Lithuanian stamp.

126 "The Ladle
Carver" (A. Gudaitis)

1993. Europa. Contemporary Art.

549	**126**	80c. multicoloured	1·00	95

127 European
Pond Turtle

1993. Pond Life. Multicoloured.

550		80c. Type **127**	40	75
551		1l. Running toad	85	90

128 Games
Emblem and
Team Colours

1994. Winter Olympic Games, Lillehammer, Norway.

552	**128**	1l.10 multicoloured	85	90

129 Antanas Smetona
(President 1919–22 and
1926–40)

1994. National Day.

553	**129**	1l. red and black	70	75
554	-	1l. brown and black	70	75

DESIGN: No. 554, Aleksandras Stulginskis (President 1922–26).

130 Kristijonas
Donelaitis

1994. Writers. Each cream, brown and orange.

555		60c. Type **130**	40	50
556		80c. Vincas Kudirka	50	65
557		1l. Jonas Maciulis Maironis	75	75

131 State
Arms

1994

558	**131**	5c. brown	10	10
559	**131**	10c. lilac	25	20
560	**131**	20c. green	25	25
612	**131**	40c. purple	25	25
613	**131**	50c. blue	25	25

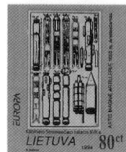

132 Rockets by
Kazimieras
Simonavicius (illus
from "Artis Magnae
Artilleriae")

1994. Europa. Inventions and Discoveries.

561	**132**	80c. multicoloured	1·30	1·00

1994. 100th Postage Stamp. Sheet 80×62 mm.

MS562	**99**	10l. green and red (sold at 12l.)	6·75	8·75

133 Couple

1994. 19th-century Costumes of Zemaiciai (Lowlands).

563	**133**	5c. multicoloured	10	10
564	-	80c. multicoloured	50	30
565	-	1l. multicoloured	60	75

DESIGNS: 80c., 1l., Different costumes from Zemaiciai.

134 Music Note,
Globe and Flag

1994. Lithuanians of the World Song Festival.

566	**134**	10c. multicoloured	25	1·00

135 State Arms

1994

567	**135**	2l. multicoloured	1·30	1·50
568	**135**	3l. multicoloured	1·70	95

See also MS580.

1994. Town Arms. As T 114 but size 25×32 mm. Multicoloured.

569		10c. Punia	10	10
570		60c. Alytus	40	50
571		80c. Perloja	70	65

136 Common
Bat

1994. Mammals. Multicoloured.

572		20c. Type **136**	25	25
573		20c. Fat dormouse	25	25

137 Kaunas Town
Hall

1994. Town Halls.

574	**137**	10c. black and mauve	10	25
575	-	60c. black and blue	35	40
576	-	80c. black and green	40	50

DESIGNS: 60c. Kedainiai; 80c. Vilnius.

138 Madonna and Child

1994. Christmas.

577	**138**	20c. multicoloured	25	25

139 Steponas Kairys

1995. National Day. Signatories to 1918 Declaration of Independence.

578	**139**	20c. lilac, grey and black	15	25
579	-	20c. blue, grey and black	25	25

DESIGN: No. 579, Pranas Dovydaitis (Head of Government, March–April 1919).

1995. Fifth Anniv of Independence. Sheet 75×105 mm.

MS580	**135**	4 ×1l. multicoloured	2·50	2·40

140 Kaunas
(Lithuania)

1995. Via Baltica Motorway Project. Multicoloured.

581		20c. Type **140**	25	25
MS582	100×110 mm. 1l. Beach Hotel, Parnu (Estonia); 1l. Bauska Castle (Latvia); 1l. Type **140**		2·50	2·20

141 "Lithuanian School, 1864–1904" (P. Rimsa)

1995. Europa. Peace and Freedom.
583 **141** 1l. multicoloured 1·30 1·30

142 Couple

1995. Costumes of the Highlands.
584 – 20c. multicoloured 25 25
585 – 70c. multicoloured 40 40
586 **142** 1l. multicoloured 60 60
DESIGNS: 70c. to 1l. Different 19th-century costumes.

143 Motiejus Valancius (120th death)

1995. Anniversaries.
587 **143** 30c. cream, pur & yell 15 25
588 – 40c. cream, grn & orge 25 30
589 – 70c. cream, dp bl & pink 40 45
DESIGNS: 40c. Zemaite (150th birth); 70c. Kipras Petrauskas (110th birth).

144 Pieta

1995. Day of Mourning and Hope.
590 **144** 20c. multicoloured 25 25

145 Torch-bearer

1995. Fifth World Lithuanians Games.
591 **145** 30c. multicoloured 25 25

146 "Baptria tibiale"

1995. Butterflies and Moths in "The Red Book". Multicoloured.
592 **146** 30c. Type **146** 40 35
593 – 30c. Cream-spot tiger moth ("Arctia villica") 40 35

1995. Town Arms. As T **114**. Multicoloured.
594 – 40c. Virbalis 40 35
595 – 1l. Kudirkos Naumiestis (horiz) 85 75

147 "Valerija Mesalina"

1995. 250th Birth Anniv of Pranciskus Smuglevicius (painter).
596 **147** 40c. multicoloured 25 25

148 Trakai Island Castle

1995. Castles.
597 – 40c. multicoloured 35 30
598 **148** 70c. blue, dp blue & black 60 50
599 – 1l. multicoloured 75 70
DESIGNS: 40c. Vilnius Upper Castle; 1l. Birzai Castle.

149 Star over Winter Scene

1995. Christmas. Multicoloured.
600 – 40c. Type **149** 40 40
601 – 1l. Churchgoers with lanterns 85 75

150 Bison

1996. The European Bison. Multicoloured.
602 – 30c. Type **150** 25 20
603 – 40c. Pair of bison 35 20
604 – 70c. Adult and calf 40 40
605 – 1l. Parents and calf 70 65

151 Kazys Grinius (130th)

1996. Birth Anniversaries.
606 **151** 40c. cream, brown & blue 25 25
607 – 1l. cream, bistre & yellow 50 65
608 – 1l. cream, blue and red 50 65
DESIGNS: No. 607, Antanas Zmuidzinavicius (120th); 608, Balys Sruoga (centenary).

152 Vladas Mironas

1996. National Day. Signatories to 1918 Declaration of Independence.
609 **152** 40c. cream, grey and black 35 20
610 – 40c. bistre, brown and black 35 20
DESIGN: No. 610, Jurgis Saulys.

153 Barbora Radvilaite

1996. Europa. Famous Women.
611 **153** 1l. multicoloured 1·30 1·30

154 Couple

1996. Costumes of Klaipeda. 19th-century costumes. Multicoloured.
618 – 40c. Type **154** 35 30
619 – 1l. Woman in red skirt and man in frock-coat 70 60

620 – 1l. Woman in black skirt and man in blue waistcoat 70 60

155 Angel

1996. Day of Mourning and Hope.
621 **155** 40c. blue, red and black 35 20
622 – 40c. green, red and black 35 20
DESIGN: No. 622, Head of crucifix.

156 "The Discus Thrower"

1996. Olympic Games, Atlanta. Multicoloured.
623 – 1l. Type **156** 70 60
624 – 1l. Basketball 70 60

157 "Sacrifice"

1996. 85th Death Anniv of Mikolajus Ciurlionis (artist). Multicoloured.
625 – 40c. Type **157** 40 35
626 – 40c. "Cemetery" 40 35
MS627 80×102 mm. 3l. "Sonata of the Andante" (25×36 mm); 3l. "Sonata of the Stars—Allegro" (25×36 mm) 3·00 2·75

1996. Town Arms. As T **114** but size 25×32 mm.
628 – 50c. multicoloured 35 30
629 – 90c. red, black and yellow 60 40
630 – 1l.20 multicoloured 75 70
DESIGN: 50c. Seduva; 90c. Panevezys; 1l.20, Zarasai.

158 Players

1996. Lithuanian Basketball Team, Bronze Medallist, Olympic Games, Atlanta. Sheet 50×72 mm.
MS631 **158** 4l.20 multicoloured 3·50 2·75

159 Angels heralding

1996. Christmas. Multicoloured.
632 – 50c. Type **159** 25 25
633 – 1l.20 Elf riding on "Pegasus" 60 60

160 Ieva Simonaityte (writer, birth centenary)

1997. Anniversaries.
634 **160** 50c. stone, brown and green 15 25
635 – 90c. stone, grey and yellow 40 40
636 – 1l.20 stone, grn & orge 70 60
MS638 94×56 mm. **161** 4l.80 brown and grey (26×36 mm) 2·50 2·30
DESIGNS: 90c. Jonas Sliupas (physician, 53rd death); 1l.20, Vladas Jurgutis (financier, 31st death).

161 Title Page

1997. 450th Anniv of Publication of "Catechism of Mazvydas" (first Lithuanian book).
637 **161** 50c. brown and grey 40 35

162 Mykolas Birziska

1997. National Day. Signatories to 1918 Declaration of Independence.
639 **162** 50c. green, lt grn & blk 40 40
640 – 50c. purple, stone and black 40 40
DESIGN: No. 640, Kazimieras Saulys.

163 Flag on Mountain Peak

1997. Completion of Ascent of World's Highest Mountains by Vladas Vitauskas. Sheet 80×60 mm.
MS641 **163** 4l.80 multicoloured 2·50 2·30

164 "Little Witch" (Jovita Jankeviciute)

1997. Europa. Tales and Legends. Multicoloured.
642 – 1l.20 Type **164** 85 75
643 – 1l.20 "Rainbow" (Ieva Staseviciute) (horiz) 85 75

165 Lecture

1997. 600th Anniv of First Lithuanian School.
644 **165** 50c. multicoloured 40 35

166 Kurshes Ship

1997. Baltic Sailing Ships. Multicoloured.
645 – 50c. Type **166** 40 40
MS646 110×70 mm. 1l.20 Kushes ship (as in T **166** but with frame etc); 1l.20 Maasilinn ship (Estonia); 1l.20 *Wappen der Herzogin von Kurland* (galleon) (Estonia) 2·50 2·10

167 Park

1997. Centenary of Palanga Botanical Park.
647 **167** 50c. yellow, black and brown 25 25

168 Ship of
Flags

1997. Second Baltic Sea Games, Lithuania.
648   **168**   90c. multicoloured   50   45

169 Elk's-horn Staff, 3000
B.C.

1997. Museum Exhibits. Multicoloured.
649   90c. Type **169**   50   45
650   1l.20 Silver coins of Grand
             Duke Kazimierz IV, 15th
             century A.D.   75   70

170 Vytis's
Cross

1997
651   **170**   5c. yellow & light yellow   10   10
652   **170**   10c. yellow and cream   10   10
653   **170**   20c. green and brown   10   10
654   **170**   35c. purple and lilac   25   25
655   **170**   50c. brown and cin-
                 namon   40   35
656   **170**   70c. yellow and cream   40   40

171 Black Morel

1997. Fungi in the Red Book. Multicoloured.
660   1l.20 Type **171**   85   75
661   1l.20 Bronze boletus   85   75

172 Letter and Seal

1997. 674th Anniv of Letters of Invitation for Migrants
sent by Grand Duke Gediminas to European Cities.
662   **172**   50c. multicoloured   40   40

1997. Town Arms. As T **114** but size 25×33 mm.
663   50c. Neringa   35   35
664   90c. Vilkaviskis   50   40
665   1l.20 Pasvalys   85   55

173 Cherub
holding Lantern
above Town

1997. Christmas. Multicoloured.
666   50c. Type **173**   40   35
667   1l.20 Snow-covered trees   85   85

174 Figure Skaters

1998. Winter Olympic Games, Nagano, Japan.
668   **174**   1l.20 ultramarine and
                 blue   85   85

175 Alfonsas Petrulis (priest)

1998. National Day. Signatories to 1918 Declaration of
Independence.
669   **175**   50c. green, grey and
                 black   35   65
670   -   90c. brown, lt brn & blk   50   90
DESIGN: No. 670, Jokubas Sernas (lawyer and politician).

176 Text of
Declaration and
State Emblem

1998. 80th Anniv of Declaration of Independence. Sheet
123×50 mm.
MS671 **176**   6l.60 multicoloured   3·50 3·50

177 Lyrics and
Kudirka's Memorial

1998. Centenary of Tautiskai giesmei (national anthem)
by Vincas Kudirka (lyricist). Sheet 90×64 mm.
MS672 **177**   5l.20 multicoloured   3·00 3·00

178 Gustaitis and
ANBO-41 (reconnaissance
plane)

1998. Birth Centenary of Antanas Gustaitis (pilot and
aircraft constructor). Multicoloured.
673   2l. Type **178**   1·30 80
674   3l. ANBO-VIII (light bomber)
             and diagrams   1·70 1·00

179 National Song
Festival

1998. Europa. National Festivals.
675   **179**   1l.20 multicoloured   1·30 95

180 Tadas Ivanauskas
(zoologist, 27th death
anniv)

1998. Anniversaries.
676   **180**   50c. green, lt yell & yell   35   50
677   -   90c. red, yellow & orge   50   50
678   -   90c. green, yellow &
                 orge   50   50
DESIGNS—45×25 mm: No. 677, Stasys Lozoraitis (diplomat, birth centenary) and Stasys Lozoraitis (diplomat,
10th death anniv); No. 678, Jurgis Baltrusaitis (writer and
diplomat, 125th birth anniv) and Jurgis Baltrusaitis (art
historian, 4th death anniv).

181 Long Jumping

1998. Sixth World Lithuanian Games and Second
National Games.
679   **181**   1l.35 multicoloured   85   55

182 Atlantic Salmon

1998. Fish in the Red Book. Multicoloured.
680   1l.40 Type **182**   75   75
681   1l.40 Whitefish ("Coregonus
             lavaretus")   75   70

1998. Town Arms. As T **114** but size 25×33 mm.
Multicoloured.
682   70c. Kernave   40   40
683   70c. Trakai   40   40
684   1l.35 Kaunas   85   80

183 Vilnius–Cracow
Postal Service, 1562

1998. Postal History. Multicoloured.
685   70c. Type **183**   40   40
MS686 55×86 mm. 13l. Hologram of
posthorn and map of Europe, Africa
and Asia (80th anniv of first Lithua-
nian stamps) (39×29 mm)   6·75 6·75

184 "All Night Long"
(Antanas Zmuidzinavicius)

1998. Paintings. Multicoloured.
687   70c. Type **184**   40   40
688   1l.35 "Vilnius: Bernardines' Gar-
             den" (Juozapas Marsevskis)   85   85

185 Girl holding
Church

1998. Christmas. Multicoloured.
689   70c. Type **185**   40   40
690   1l.35 Couple going into tree
             house   85   80

186 Mickiewicz
(statue, G. Jokuonis)

1998. Birth Bicentenary of Adam Mickiewicz (poet).
691   **186**   70c. multicoloured   40   40

187 Angwels
holding Title Page

1999. 400th Anniv of Publication of Translation
into Lithuanian by Mikalojus Dauksa of Postilla
Catholicka by Jacob Wujek. Sheet 60×67 mm.
MS692 **187**   5l.90 brown and silver   3·00 3·00

188 Petras Klimas (historian
and diplomat)

1999. National Day. Signatories to 1918 Declaration of
Independence.
693   **188**   70c. red and black   40   40
694   -   70c. blue and black   40   40
DESIGN: No. 694, Donatas Malinauskas (diplomat).

189 Augustinas
Gricius (dramatist)

1999. Birth Centenaries.
695   **189**   70c. black, cream & orge   40   40
696   -   70c. brown, cream
                 & pink   40   40
697   -   1l.35 green, cream and
                 orange   85   80
DESIGNS: No. 696, Juozas Matulis (chemist); 697, Pranas
Skardzius (philologian).

190 Emblem and
State Flag

1999. 50th Anniv of North Atlantic Treaty Organization.
698   **190**   70c. multicoloured   60   55

191 Aukstaitija National
Park

1999. Europa. Parks and Gardens. Multicoloured.
699   1l.35 Type **191**   85   80
700   1l.35 Curonian Spit National
             Park   85   80

192 Council Flag

1999. 50th Anniv of Council of Europe.
701   **192**   70c. multicoloured   60   55

193 Boarded Clay
Windmill, Melniai

1999. Windmills. Multicoloured.
702   70c. Type **193**   40   40
703   70c. Red-brick windmill,
             Pumpenai   40   40

194 "Dasypoda
argentata"

1999. Bumble Bees. Multicoloured.
704   70c. Type **194**   40   40
705   2l. "Bombus pomorum"   1·30 1·20

195 Sculpture of U.P.U.
Emblem, Berne

1999. 125th Anniv of Universal Postal Union.
706   **195**   70c. multicoloured   40   40

196 1918 and 1990 Stamps and Society Emblems

1999. 75th Anniv of Lithuanian Philatelic Society.
| 707 | **196** | 1l. multicoloured | 60 | 55 |

197 Cast and Producers

1999. Centenary of First Public Performance of Lithuanian Drama (America in the Bath by Keturakis). Sheet 99×59 mm containing T 197 and similar vert design. Multicoloured.
| MS708 | Type **197**; 4l. Playbill | 5·00 | 5·00 |

198 Family and State Flag

1999. Tenth Anniv of the Baltic Chain (human chain uniting the capitals of Lithuania, Estonia and Latvia). Multicoloured.
| 709 | 1l. Type **198** | 60 | 55 |

MS710 110×72 mm. 2l. Type **198**; 2l. Family and Estonian flag; 2l. Family and Latvian flag | 3·75 | 3·75

199 Emblem

1999. 50th Anniv of Establishment of Lithuanian Freedom Fight Movement.
| 711 | **199** | 70c. multicoloured | 40 | 40 |

1999. Town Arms. Designs as T 114 but size 25×33 mm. Multicoloured.
712	70c. Marijampole	50	50
713	1l. Siauliai	70	65
714	1l.40 Rokiskis	95	90

200 Sword of General S. Zukauskas, 1927

1999. Exhibits in Vytautas Magnus War Museum. Multicoloured.
| 715 | 70c. Type **200** | 70 | 65 |
| 716 | 3l. 17th-century Hussar's armour | 1·70 | 1·60 |

201 "Horse and Bear" (fable)

1999. Birth Bicentenary of Simonas Stanevicius (writer).
| 717 | **201** | 70c. multicoloured | 40 | 40 |

202 "Winter Symphony"

1999. Christmas. Multicoloured.
| 718 | 70c. Type **202** | 50 | 50 |
| 719 | 1l.35 Cathedral, candles and bell | 95 | 90 |

203 Top of Monument

2000. Ironwork.
720	**203**	10c. blue and brown	10	10
721	-	20c. blue and stone	25	25
722	-	1l. blue and pink	60	55
723	-	1l.30 blue and green	85	80
724	-	1l.70 blue and light blue	1·30	1·20

DESIGNS: 20c. to 1l.70, Different examples of ornamental ironwork.

204 Jonas Vailokaitis

2000. National Day. Signatories to 1918 Declaration of Independence.
| 725 | **204** | 1l.30 orange, stone & blk | 85 | 80 |
| 726 | - | 1l.70 brown, stone & blk | 1·30 | 1·20 |

DESIGN: 1l.70, Jonas Smilgevicius.

205 Declaration

2000. Tenth Anniv of Restoration of Independence. Sheet 86×71 mm.
| MS727 | **205** | 7l.40 multicoloured | 5·00 | 5·00 |

206 Vincas Pietaris (writer, 150th anniv)

2000. Birth Anniversaries.
728	**206**	1l. green, black and purple	70	65
729	-	1l.30 blue, black & brown	1·00	95
730	-	1l.70 brown, black & bl	1·30	1·20

DESIGNS:1l.30, Kanutas Ruseckas (painter, bicentenary); 1l.70, Povilas Visinskis (literary critic, 125th anniv). See also Nos. 753/5.

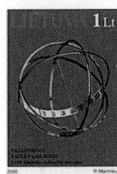

207 Equatorial Sundial

2000. Exhibits in Klaipeda Clock Museum. Multicoloured
| 731 | 1l. Type **207** | 70 | 65 |
| 732 | 2l. Renaissance-style clock case | 1·40 | 1·40 |

208 "Building Europe"

2000. Europa.
| 733 | **208** | 1l.70 multicoloured | 1·50 | 1·50 |

209 Osprey

2000. Birds of Prey. Multicoloured.
| 734 | 1l. Type **209** | 70 | 65 |
| 735 | 2l. Black kite | 1·40 | 1·40 |

210 Grey Seal

2000. Lithuanian Marine Museum, Kopgalis. Multicoloured
| 736 | 1l. Type **210** | 85 | 80 |
| 737 | 1l. Magellanic penguin (Spheniscus magellanicus) | 85 | 80 |

211 Cycling

2000. Olympic Games, Sydney. Multicoloured.
| 738 | 1l. Type **211** | 85 | 80 |
| 739 | 3l. Swimming | 2·50 | 2·40 |

212 "Fairy Tail Castle" (Ciurlionis)

2000. 125th Birth Anniv of Mikalojus Konstantinas Ciurlionis (artist and composer). Sheet 59×56 mm.
| MS740 | **212** | 4l. multicoloured | 3·00 | 3·00 |

213 Tree and Emblem

2000. Tenth Anniv of Lithuanian Postal Service.
| 741 | **213** | 1l. multicoloured | 85 | 80 |

2000. Town Arms. As T 114 but size 25×33 mm. Multicoloured.
742	1l. Raseiniai	75	75
743	1l. Taurage	75	75
744	1l.30 Utena	1·00	95

214 Snow-covered Village

2000. Christmas. Multicoloured.
| 745 | 1l. Type **214** | 85 | 80 |
| 746 | 1l.70 Snow-covered church | 1·30 | 1·20 |

215 The Nativity

2000. Holy Year (2000). Sheet 69×87 mm containing T 215 and similar vert designs. Multicoloured.
MS747 2l. Type **215**; 2l. Jesus with James and John; 2l. Crucifixion; 2l. Jesus entering Heaven | 6·00 | 6·00

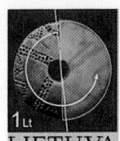

216 Neolithic Amber Artefact

2000. New Millennium.
| 748 | **216** | 1l. multicoloured | 1·00 | 95 |

217 Medals

2000. Lithuanian Victories in Olympic Games, Sydney. Sheet 65×102 mm.
| MS749 | **217** | 4l. multicoloured | 3·00 | 3·00 |

218 Vilnius Television Tower and Flag

2001. Tenth Anniv of Soviet Action in Vilnius.
| 750 | **218** | 1l. multicoloured | 70 | 65 |

219 Saliamonas Banaitis

2001. National Day. Signatories to 1918 Declaration of Independence.
| 751 | **219** | 1l. brown, grey and black | 85 | 80 |
| 752 | - | 2l. lilac, grey and black | 1·50 | 1·50 |

DESIGN: 2l. Justinas Staugaitis.

2001. Anniversaries. As T **206.**
753	1l. blue, red and black	85	80
754	1l. green, red and black	85	80
755	1l.70 brown, violet and black	1·30	1·20

DESIGNS: No. 753, Juozas MikEnas (artist, birth centenary); 754, Pranas Vaicaitis (poet, death centenary); 755, Petras Vileisis (civil engineer, 150th birth anniv).

220 Lake Galve

2001. Europa. Water Resources. Multicoloured.
| 756 | 1l.70 Type **220** | 1·10 | 1·10 |
| 757 | 1l.70 River Nemunas | 1·10 | 1·10 |

221 Floating Bogbean (Nymphoides peltata)

2001. Plants in the Red Book. Multicoloured.
| 758 | 2l. Type **221** | 1·50 | 1·50 |
| 759 | 3l. Crossleaf heather (Erica tetralix) | 2·40 | 2·30 |

222 Paplauja Bridge, Vilnius

2001. Bridges. Multicoloured.
| 760 | 1l. Type **222** | 85 | 80 |
| 761 | 1l.30 Pakruojis, Kruoja | 1·30 | 1·20 |

223 National Flag

2001. Millenary of Lithuania. Sheet 125×100 mm containing T **223** and similar horiz designs. Multicoloured.
MS762 2l. Type **223**; 2l. State emblem; 2l. Map of Lithuania; 2l. Map of Europe ... 6·00 6·00

224 Sand Dunes, Palanga, Lithuania

2001. Baltic Sea Coast. Multicoloured.
763   1l. Type **224**   85   80
MS764 125×60 mm. 2l. As **224** but with Palanga at left; 2l. Rocky coastline, Lahemaa, Estonia; 2l. Beach, Vidzeme, Latvia ... 4·75 4·75

225 19th-century Cottage, Kirdeikiai, Utena District

2001. 35th Anniv of Open Air Museum, Rumsiskes. Multicoloured.
765   1l. Type **225**   70   65
766   2l. Farmer's house, Darlenai, Kretinga district   1·40   1·40

226 "Sadness" (sculpture)

2001. 120th Birth Anniv of Juozas Zikaras (artist).
767   **226**   3l. multicoloured   2·10   2·00

227 Charter and King Stephan I Batory of Poland

2001. 418th Anniv of Introduction of Postal Rates based on Weight.
768   **227**   1l. multicoloured   85   80

2001. Town Arms. As T **114** but size 25×33 mm. Multicoloured.
769   1l. Lazdijai   85   80
770   1l.30 Birzai   95   90
771   1l.70 Veliuona   1·20   1·10

228 Birds on Straw and Pine Pyramid ("Winter troubles")

2001. Christmas and New Year. Multicoloured.
772   1l. Type **228**   85   80
773   1l.70 Birds and crib ("Jesus' cradle")   1·30   1·20

229 Basanavicius

2001. 150th Birth Anniv of Jonas Basanavicius (politician and signatory to 1918 Declaration of Independence). Sheet 82×60 mm.
MS774 **229** 5l. multicoloured   4·25   4·25

230 Skier

2002. Winter Olympic Games, Salt Lake City, U.S.A.
775   **230**   1l.30 multicoloured   1·30   1·20

231 Kazys Bizauskas

2002. National Day. Signatories to 1918 Declaration of Independence.
776   **231**   1l. sepia, brown and black   70   65
777   –   1l. violet, brown and black   70   65
DESIGN: No. 777 Stanislovas Narutavicius (politician).

232 Antanas Salys

2002. Birth Anniversaries. Multicoloured.
778   1l. Type **232** (linguist, centenary)   70   65
779   1l.30 Satrijos Ragana (writer, 125th anniv)   85   80
780   1l.70 Oskaras Milasius (poet, 125th anniv)   1·10   1·10

2002. Town Arms. As T **114** but size 25×33 mm. Multicoloured.
781   1l. Birstonas   70   65
782   1l. Anyksciai   70   65
783   1l.70 Prienai   1·30   1·20

233 Book, Archives and Seal

2002. 150th Anniv of State Archives.
784   **233**   1l. multicoloured   85   80

234 Stoat (*Mustela erminea*)

2002. Endangered Species. Multicoloured.
785   1l. Type **234**   70   65
786   3l. Lynx (*Lynx (Felis) lynx*)   2·30   2·20

235 Strongman

2002. Europa. Circus.
787   **235**   1l.70 multicoloured   1·30   1·20

236 Ford 350 Fire Engine

2002. Bicentenary of Vilnius Fire and Rescue Service.
788   **236**   1l. multicoloured   70   65

237 Diesel Locomotive TU 2

2002. Narrow-gauge Railway. Multicoloured.
789   1l.30 Type **237**   95   90
790   2l. Steam locomotive PT 4   1·40   1·30

238 Flint Tool

2002. Millenary of Lithuania (2009). Sheet 126×100 mm containing T **238** and similar horiz designs. Multicoloured.
MS791 2l. Type **238**; 2l. Publius Cornelius Tacitus (chronicler); 2l. Viking ship; 2l. Annals of Quedlinburg (manuscript containing first reference to Lithuania)   5·50   5·50

239 Rooftops

2002. 750th Anniv of Klaipeda. Sheet 88×59 mm.
MS792 **239** 5l. multicoloured   3·50   3·50

240 Script and Exhibits

2002. Maironis Literature Museum, Kaunas. Multicoloured.
793   1l. Type **240**   70   65
794   3l. Museum buildings   2·30   2·20

241 King Zigmantas Vaza (founder of postal system)

2002. Postal History.
795   **241**   1l. multicoloured   85   80

242 Star and Clock-face

2002. Christmas and New Year. Multicoloured.
796   1l. Type **242**   70   65
797   1l.70 Christmas tree   1·10   1·10

243 Mother and Child (Danielius Peciulis)

2002. European Children's Day.
798   **243**   1l. multicoloured   85   80

244 Laurynas Stuoka-Gucevicius (architect)

2003. Personalities. Multicoloured.
799   1l. Type **244**   75   75
800   1l. Juozas Eretas (writer)   95   90

245 Gargzdai

2003. Town Arms. Multicoloured.
801   1l. Type **245**   70   65
802   1l. Kretinga   70   65
803   1l. Palanga   70   65
804   1l. Papile   70   65
805   1l. Rietavas   70   65
See also Nos. 827/9, 855/6, 883/5, 907/9, 956/8 and 969/71.

246 Pervalka Lighthouse

2003. Lighthouses. Multicoloured.
806   1l. Type **246**   70   65
807   3l. Uostadvaris   2·30   2·20

247 Face and Pencils

2003. Europa. Poster Art.
808   **247**   1l.70 multicoloured   1·30   1·20

248 Royal Palace, Vilnius

2003. Royal Palace Restoration.
809   **248**   1l. multicoloured   85   80

249 Observatory Building

2003. 250th Anniv of Astronomical Observatory, Vilnius University.
810   **249**   1l. multicoloured   85   80

250 *Cerambyx cerdo*

2003. Endangered Species. Beetles. Multicoloured.
811   3l. Type **250**   2·10   2·00
812   3l. Stag beetle (*Lucanus cervus*)   2·10   2·00

251 Fortifications, 1183

2003. Lithuania Millenary (1st series). Sheet 125×100 mm containing T **251** and similar horiz designs. Multicoloured.
MS813 2l. Type **251**; 2l. The Battle of Shiauliai, 1236; 2l. The Coronation of King Mindaugas, 1253; 2l. Vilnius, 1323   5·00   5·00
See also No. **MS**862 and 886/9.

252 King
Mindaugas

2003. 750th Anniv of Coronation of King Mindaugas.
Sheet 87×58 mm.
MS814 **252** 5l. multicoloured   3·50   3·50

253 Hot Air Balloons

2003. 13th European Hot Air Balloon Championships,
Vilnius.
815   **253**   1l.30 multicoloured   85   80

254 Cardinal
Sladkevicius

2003. Third Death Anniv of Cardinal Vincentas
Sladkevicius.
816   **254**   1l. multicoloured   85   80

255 City Arms

2003. 500th Anniv of Panevezys City.
817   **255**   1l. multicoloured   85   80

256 Post Office, Map
and Postal Seal

2003. Postal History.
818   **256**   1l. multicoloured   85   80

257 Christmas Tree,
Church and Houses

2003. Christmas. Multicoloured.
819   **257**   1l. Type **257**   85   80
820   1l.70 Street lamps through
    houses   1·30   1·20

258 Trophy and
Basketball

2003. Lithuania, European Men's Basketball Champions,
2003. Sheet 62×75 mm.
MS821 **258** 5l. multicoloured   4·25   4·25

259 Plastic Glider BK-7

2003. Aviation Museum, Kaunas. Multicoloured
822   **259**   1l. Type **259**   95   65
823   1l. Training glider BRO-12   95   65

260 Jonas Aistis

2004. Anniversaries. Multicoloured.
824   1l. Type **260** (writer) (birth
    centenary)   1·10   80
825   1l. Kazimieras Buga (philologist)
    (80th death anniv)   1·10   80
826   1l. Adolfas Jucys (scientist)
    (birth centenary)   1·10   80

2004. Town Arms. As T **245**. Multicoloured.
827   1l. Mazeikiai   70   65
828   1l.30 Radviliskis   85   80
829   1l.40 Ukmerge Palanga   1·00   95

261 King
Steponas Batoras,
Petras Skarga

2004. 425th Anniv of Vilnius University.
830   **261**   1l. multicoloured   85   80

262 Parasol on
Beach and
University Building

2004. Europa. Holidays. Multicoloured.
831   1l.70 Type **262**   1·00   95
832   1l.70 Yacht at sea   1·00   95

263 Frontispieces

2004. Centenary of the Re-establishment of printing
using Latin Characters.
833   **263**   1l.30 multicoloured   1·50   1·20

264 Lithuania Flag, Map of
Europe, Stars and Shield

2004. Lithuania's Accession to the European Union.
Multicoloured.
834   1l.70 Type **264**   1·50   1·20
835   1l.70 Flags of new members   1·50   1·20

265 Football

2004. Centenary of FIFA (Federation Internationale de
Football Association).
836   **265**   3l. multicoloured   2·75   2·20

266 Chiune
Sugihara

2004. Chiune Sugihara (Japanese Consul 1939–40)
Commemoration.
837   **266**   1l. multicoloured   1·00   80

267 Burning of
Pilenai, 1336

2004. Lithuania Millenary. Sheet 125×100 mm containing
T **267** and similar vert designs.
MS838 2l. ×4, Type **267**; Algirdas
(leader of Siniye Vody battle), 1362;
Jagaila establishing Lithuania as
Catholic country; Battle of Zalgiris
(detail) (painting by Janas Mateika)   7·50   7·50

268 Iguana

2004. Tadas Ivanauskas Zoology Museum. Multicoloured.
839   1l. Type **268**   1·00   80
840   1l. Aquila chryaetos   1·00   80

269 Show Jumping

2004. Olympic Games, Athens. Multicoloured.
841   2l. Type **269**   2·00   1·60
842   3l. Canoeing   2·00   2·50

270 Northern
Eagle Owl (*Bubo
bubo*)

2004. Endangered Species. Owls. Multicoloured.
843   1l.30 Type **270**   1·50   1·20
844   3l. Short-eared owl (*Asio
    flammeus*)   3·50   3·00

271 Aleksotas Funicular
Railway

2004. Funicular Railways. Multicoloured.
845   1l. Type **271**   1·00   80
846   1l.30 Zaliakalnis   1·50   1·20

272 Snow-covered Tree

2004. Christmas. Multicoloured.
847   1l. Type **272**   1·50   1·20
848   1l.70 Bullfinch   1·00   80

273 Kazys Boruta

2005. Anniversaries. Multicoloured.
849   1l. Type **273** (writer) (birth
    centenary)   1·90   1·50
850   1l. Petras Kalpokas (artist) (60th
    death anniv)   1·20   1·00
851   1l. Jonas Puzinas (archaeologist)
    (birth centenary)   1·20   1·00

274 Pink and
Yellow Flowers

2005. Greetings Stamps. Multicoloured. Self-adhesive.
852   1l. Type **274**   1·20   1·00
853   1l. Orange flowers   1·20   1·00

275 Horses pulling
Sulkies

2005. Centenary of Horse Races, Sartai Lake, Dusetos.
854   **275**   1l. multicoloured   1·20   1·00

2005. Town Arms. As T **245**. Multicoloured.
855   1l. Druskininkai   1·20   1·00
856   1l. Vabalninkas   1·20   1·00

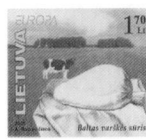

276 White Cheese
("Baltas varskes suris")

2005. Europa. Gastronomy. Multicoloured.
857   1l.70 Type **276**   1·90   1·50
858   1l.70 Black bread ("Juoda
    duona")   1·90   1·50

277 Early Exhibition Hall,
Vilnius University

2005. 150th Anniv of National Museum. Multicoloured.
859   1l. Type **277**   1·10   90
860   1l. Brass jewellery   1·10   90

278 Train emerging from
Tunnel

2005. Railway Tunnel between Vilnius and Kaunas.
861   **278**   3l. multicoloured   3·50   3·00

279 Pabaiskas Battle
(1435)

2005. Lithuania Millenary (2nd series). Sheet 125×100
mm containing T **279** and similar horiz designs.
Multicoloured.
MS862 2l.×4, Type **279**; Valakai reform
(1557); First statute (1529); Union of
Lublin (1569)   9·25   9·25
The stamps and margin of MS862 form a composite
design.

280 Ludovic Zamenhof
(creator of Esperanto)

2005. 90th World Esperanto Congress, Vilnius.
863   **280**   1l. multicoloured   1·20   90

281 Vilnius
Lutheran
Evangelical Church

2005. Churches. Multicoloured.
864   1l. Type **281**   1·10   90
865   1l.30 St. Casimir Church   1·50   1·20

282
Black-throated
Diver (*Gavia
arctica*)

2005. Endangered Species. Fauna and Flora.
Multicoloured.
866   1l. Type **282**   1·10   90
867   1l. *Trapa natans*   1·10   90
    Nos. 866/7 were issued together, se-tenant, forming a
composite design.

283 "Allegro"

2005. 130th Birth Anniv of Mikalojus Konstantinas
Ciurlionis (artist and composer). Sheet 126×66 mm
containing T **283** and similar vert designs showing
painting cycle "Sonata of the Sea". Multicoloured.
MS868 2l.×3, Type **283**; "Andante";
    "Finale"   7·00   7·00

284 Mail Coach
and Map

2005. Postal History.
869   **284**   1l. multicoloured   1·10   90

285 Snow covered Branch
and Candle

2005. Christmas. Multicoloured.
870   1l. Type **285**   1·10   90
871   1l.70 Father Christmas   1·90   1·50

286 City Hall (1905),
Jonas Basanavicius
(nationalist politician)
and Commemorative
Medal

2005. Centenary of the Congress of Lithuanians (Great
Seimas of Vilius) (beginning of independence and
democracy.
872   **286**   1l. multicoloured   1·10   90

287 Biathlon

2006. Winter Olympic Games, Turin.
873   **287**   1l.70 multicoloured   1·90   1·50

288 Petras Rimsa (artist
and sculptor)

2006. Personalities. Multicoloured.
874   1l. Type **288**   1·10   90
875   1l. Adolfas Sapoka (historian) 1·10   90
876   1l. Antanas Vaiculaitis (writer) 1·10   90

289 Street Scene

2006. 160th Anniv of First Publication "The Vilnius
Album" by Jonas Vilcinskis.
877   **289**   1l. multicoloured   1·10   90

290 Hands enclosing
People

2006. 80th Anniv of Social Insurance System.
878   **290**   1l. multicoloured   1·10   90

291 Cine Camera

2006. National Theatre, Music and Cinema Museum.
Multicoloured.
879   1l. Type **291**   1·10   90
880   1l. Polyphon   2·30   1·90

292 Wheelchair Dancer
and Partner

2006. Europa. Integration. Multicoloured.
881   1l.70 Type **292**   1·10   90
882   1l.70 Wheelchair race   1·90   1·50

2006. Town Arms. As T **245**. Multicoloured.
883   1l. Kupiskis   1·90   1·50
884   1l. Sakiai   1·10   90
885   1l. Silute   1·10   90

293 Establishment of
Vilnius University, 1579

2006. Lithuania Millenary (3rd series). Multicoloured.
886   2l. Type **293**   3·00   2·50
887   2l. Truce of Andrusov, 1667   4·50   3·75
888   2l. Establishment of four-years
        Seimas, 1788   2·20   1·80
889   2l. Uprising, 1794   4·50   3·75

294 Basilica, Vilnius
Cathedral

2006. Churches. Multicoloured.
890   1l. Type **294**   8·00   6·50
891   1l.70 Basilica, Kaunas Cathedral 1·10   90

295 *Polysticta stelleri*

2006. Endangered Species. Multicoloured.
892   1l. Type **295**   1·90   1·50
893   1l. *Acipenser sturio*   2·30   1·90

296 Document
establishing Post
Board

2006. Postal History.
894   **296**   1l. multicoloured   1·10   90

297 Score,
Performers, Mikas
Petraukas
(composer) and
Gabrielius
Landsberis-
Zemkalnis
(dramatist)

2006. Centenary of First Lithuania Opera—"Birute".
895   **297**   2l. multicoloured   2·20   1·80

298 Doves

2006. Christmas. Multicoloured.
896   1l. Type **298**   1·10   90
897   1l 70. Star and snow-covered
        trees   1·90   1·50

299 Pasvalys
Church Belfry

2007. Wooden Church Belfries. Designs showing 18th-
century church belfries. Self-adhesive.
898   **299**   10c. blue and black   10   10
899   -   20c. yellow and black 25   20
900   -   50c. green and black   65   40
901   -   1l. cinnamon and black 1·10   90
902   -   1l.30 lilac and black 1·50   1·20
903   -   1l.70 bistre and black 1·90   1·50
DESIGNS: 10c. Type **299**; 20c. Rozalimas; 50c. Tryskiai; 1l.
Saukenai; 1l.30 Vaiguva; 1l.70 Vajasiskis.
    See also Nos. 964/8.

300 Bernardas
Brazdzionis

2007. Personalities. Multicoloured.
904   1l. Type **300** (poet) (birth
        centenary)   1·10   90
905   1l. Vytautas Kazimierasv
        Jonynas (sculptor) (birth
        centenary)   1·10   90
906   3l. Leonas Sapiega (politician)
        (450th birth anniv)   3·50   3·25

2007. Town Arms. As T **245**. Multicoloured.
907   1l. Svencionys   1·10   90
908   1l.30 Kelme   1·50   1·20
909   2l. Moletai   2·20   1·80

301 Badge

2007. Europa. Centenary of Scouting. Multicoloured.
910   1l.70 Type **301**   1·90   1·50
911   1l.70 Flag   1·90   1·50

302 St.Anne's and
Bernardine Churches,
Vilnius

2007. Churches. Multicoloured.
912   1l. Type **302**   1·30   1·00
913   1l.30 Coming of the Blessed
        Virgin Mary and Camaldoli
        Monastery, Pazaislis   1·50   1·30

303 Jonas Basanavicius
(founder) and First
Lithuanian Newspaper
Ausra. 1883

2007. Lithuania Millenary. Sheet 125×100 mm containing
T **303** and similar horiz designs. Multicoloured.
MS914 3l×4. Type **303**; Knygnesys
    Jurgis Bielinis (clandestine nationalist
    book supplier) (prohibition on print-
    ing in Latin characters abolished,
    1904); Legislative building (the Great
    Seimas Of Vilnius, 1905); Building
    and signatures (declaration of
    independence, 1918)   12·50   11·50

304 15th-century Chess
Pieces

2007. Trakai History Museum. Multicoloured.
915   2l. Type **304**   1·90   1·50
916   2l. Naujieji Trakai 1600 (J.
        Kamarauskas)   1·90   1·50

2007. Wooden Church Belfries. As T **299**. Self-adhesive.
917   5c. green and black   30   10
918   35c. grey and black   70   50
919   1l.35 lemon and black   1·80   1·50
920   1l.55 orange and black   1·80   1·50
921   2l.15 claret and black   2·30   2·00
DESIGNS: 5c.Vabalninkas; 35c.Varputenai; 1l.35 DeguCiai;
1l.55 GeidZiai; 2l.15 Pavandene.

305 Juozas Miltinis

2007. Birth Centenary of Juozas Miltinis (actor and
theatrical producer).
922   **305**   2l.45 multicoloured   2·75   2·50

306 *Gallinago media*

2007. Cepkeliai and Kotra Nature Reserves. Multicoloured.
923   2l.90 Type **306**   3·25   3·00
924   2l.90 *Crex crex*   3·25   3·00
    Nos. 923/4 were issued in horizontal se-tenant strips of
two stamps surrounding a central stamp size label, each
strip forming a composite design.

307 Document
establishing Lithuania
Post and First Day
Covers

2007. Postal History. 15th Anniv of Lithuania Post State
Enterprise.
925   **307**   1l.35 multicoloured   1·50   1·30

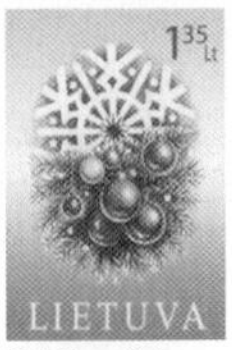

308 Snowflake and Baubles

2007. Christmas. Multicoloured.

926	1l.35 Type **308**	1·50	1·30
927	2l.45 Fir twig and globe as bauble	2·75	2·50

2008. Wooden Churches. As T **299**. Each orange and black. Self-adhesive.

928	5c. Antante	20	10
929	10c. Deguciai	30	15
930	20c. Inturke	50	30
931	35c. Prienai	80	50
932	1l.35 Siaudine	1·50	1·30
933	1l.55 Uzventis	1·80	1·50

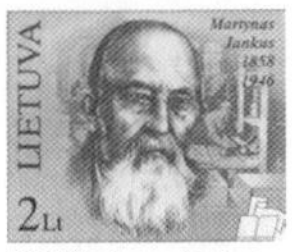

309 Martynas Jankus (publisher) (150th birth anniv)

2008. Personalities. Multicoloured.

934	2l. Type **309**	3·00	2·75
935	2l.15 Zenonas Ivinskis (historian and philosopher) (birth centenary)	3·25	3·00
936	2l.90 Antanas Maceina (philosopher and writer) (birth centenary)	3·50	3·25

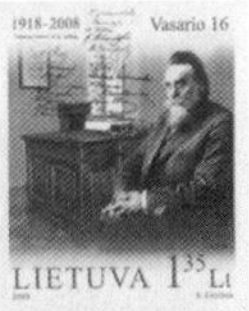

310 Jonas Basanavicius (Council chairman)

2008. 90th Anniv of Restored State of Lithuania.

937	**310**	1l.35 multicoloured	1·80	1·50

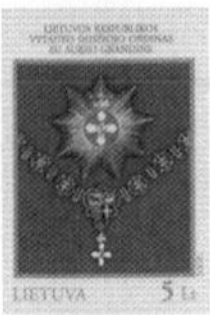

311 Order of Vytautas the Great with Golden when Act was signed) Chain (Lithuania)

2008. Baltic States' Orders. Sheet 116×51 mm containing T **311** and similar vert designs. Multicoloured.

MS938	Size 5l.×3, As Type **311**; Order of National Coat of Arms (Estonia); Order of Three Stars (Latvia)	5·50	5·00
939	7l. As Type **294**	7·75	7·25

Stamps of similar design were issued by Latvia and Estonia.

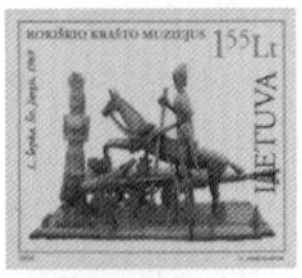

312 Wooden Carving (Lionginas sepka)

2008. Rokiskis Regional Museum. Multicoloured.

940	1l.55 Type **312**	1·80	1·50
941	1l.55 19th–centenary women's costumes	1·80	1·50

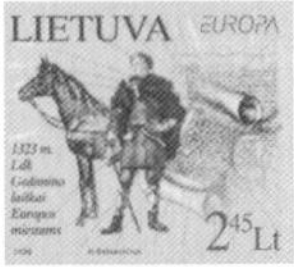

313 Letters from Gediminas (Grand Duke of Lithuania) to Pope John XXII, 1323

2008. Europa. The Letter. Multicoloured.

942	2l.45 Type **313**	3·25	3·00
943	2l.45 Vilnius, symbols of e-mail and written letter	3·25	3·00

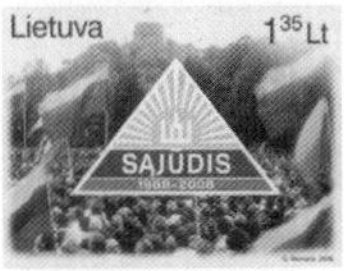

314 Emblem and Demonstrators

2008. 20th Anniv of Sajudis (reform movement).

944	**314**	1l.35 multicoloured	1·60	1·40

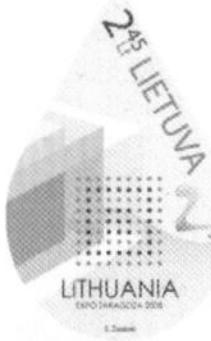

315 Emblem

2008. Zaragoza 2008 International Water and Sustainable Development Exhibition. Self adhesive.

945	**315**	2l.45 multicoloured	3·00	2·75

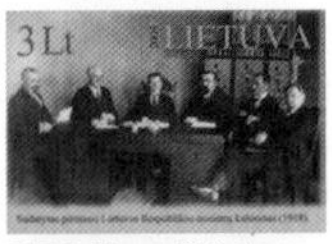

316 Cabinet of Ministers, 1918

2008. Lithuania Millennary (2009). Sheet 125×100 mm containing T **316** and similar horiz designs. Multicoloured.

MS946	3l×6, Type **316**; Constituent Assembly, 1920; Vytautas Magnus University (University of Lithuania), Kaunas, 1922; Klaipeda incorporated into Lithuania, 1923; Opening of road to Zemaiciu (place of pilgrimage), Samogitia, 1939; Return of Vilnius, 1939	19·00	19·00

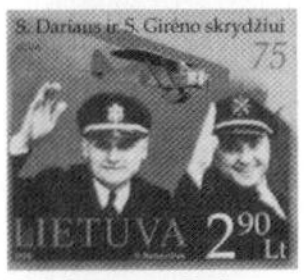

317 Steponas Darius, Stasys Girenas and Bellanca CH-300 *Lituanica*

2008. 75th Anniv of Steponas Darius and Stasys Girenas's Transatlantic Flight.

947	**317**	2l.90 multicoloured	3·75	3·50

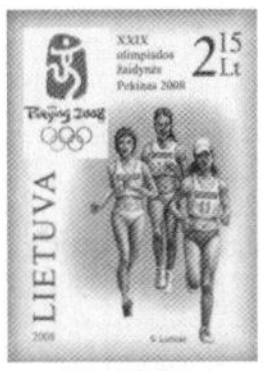

318 Runners

2008. Olympic Games, Beijing. Multicoloured.

948	2l.15 Type **318**	2·75	2·50
949	2l.45 Yachts	3·25	3·00

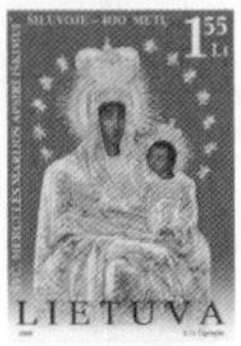

319 Virgin and Child

2008. 400th Anniv of Apparition of Our Lady of Siluva.

950	**319**	1l.55 multicoloured	7·00	6·75

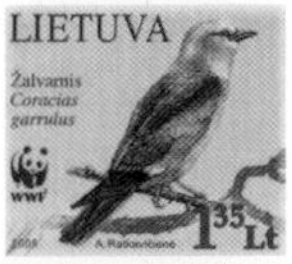

320 European Roller

2008. Endangered Species. European Roller (*Coracias garrulus*). Multicoloured.

951	1l.35 Type **320**	6·00	5·75
952	1l.35 In flight	6·00	5·75
953	1l.35 With open beak	6·00	5·75
954	1l.35 Looking over shoulder	6·00	5·75
MS955	97×81 mm. As Nos. 951/4	24·00	24·00

The stamps and margins of **MS**955 form a composite design.

2008. Town Arms. As T **245**. Multicoloured.

956	1l.35 Joniskis	1·80	1·60
957	1l.35 Jubarkas	1·80	1·60
958	3l. Sirvintos	3·25	3·00

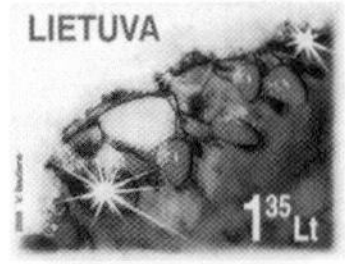

321 Hips

2008. Christmas and New Year. Multicoloured.

959	1l.35 Type **321**	2·00	1·80
960	2l.45 Snow covered branches	3·00	2·75

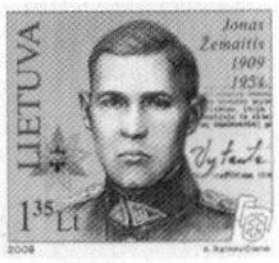

322 Jonas Zemaitis (soldier)

2009. Personalities. Multicoloured.

961	1l.35 Type **322**	2·00	1·80
962	2l. Vaclovas Birziska (bibliographer)	2·25	2·10
963	2l.15 Mecislovas Reinys (priest and psychologist)	2·50	2·25

2009. Wooden Churches. As T **299**. Self-adhesive.

964	10c. yellow, sepia and black	15	10
965	20c. yellow, sepia and black	15	10
966	50c. green and black	95	75
967	1l. cinnamon and black	1·20	1·00
968	1l.35 yellow, sepia and black	1·30	1·10

DESIGNS: 10c. As No. 929; 20c. As No. 930; 50c. As. No. 900; 1l. As No. 901; 1l.35 As No. 932.

2009. Town Arms. As T **245**. Multicoloured.

969	1l.35 Krekenava	1·75	1·50
970	1l.35 Pakruojis	1·75	1·50
971	3l. Salcininkai	3·50	3·25

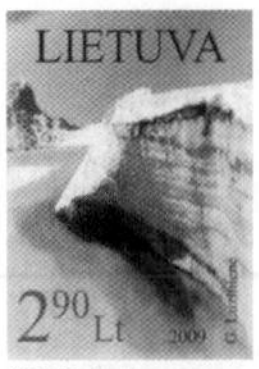

323 Polar Ice

2009. Preserve Polar Regions and Glaciers. Sheet 120×80 mm containing T **323** and similar vert design. Multicoloured.

MS972	2l.90×2, Type **323**; Ice cliffs	7·00	7·00

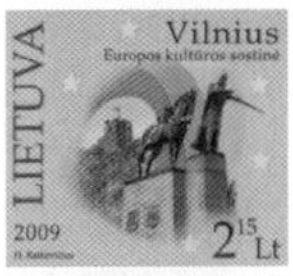

324 Statue

2009. Vilnius–European Capital of Culture.

973	**324**	2l.15 multicoloured	2·50	2·25

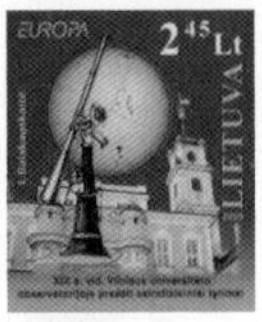

325 G. M. Dallmeyer's Photoheliograph and Vilnius University

2009. Europa. Astronomy. Multicoloured.

974	2l.45 Type **325**	3·50	3·25
975	2l.45 Galileo Galilei (astronomer)	3·50	3·25

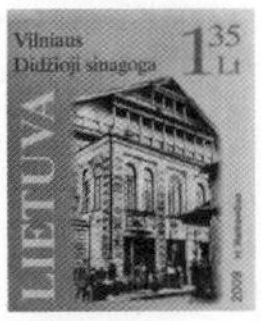

326 Great Synagogue, Vilnius

2009

976	**326**	1l.35 multicoloured	1·60	1·50

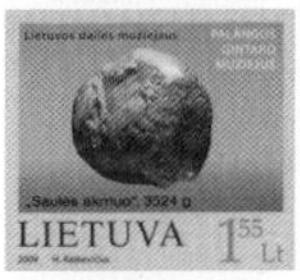

327 'Sun Stone' (3524 gm., one of world's largest amber pieces)

2009. Amber Museum, Palanga. Multicoloured.

977	1l.55 Type **327**	1·90	1·80
978	1l.55 Amber museum (Count Feliksas Tyskevichius's estate, built 1897)	1·90	1·80

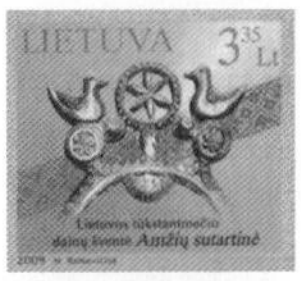

328 Spindle Fragment

2009. Millennium Song Festival of Lithuania. Song of Centuries.

979	**328**	3l.35 multicoloured	4·00	3·75

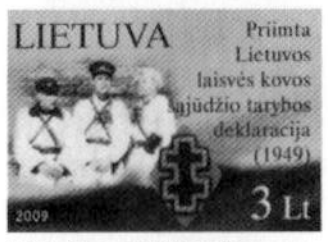

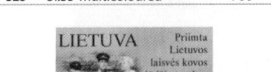

329 Council Members (Council of Struggle for Freedom of Lithuania Movement Declaration (1949))

2009. Millennary of Lithuania. Struggle for Independence. Sheet 125×100 mm containing T **329** and similar horiz designs. Multicoloured.

MS980	3l.×6, Type **329**; Front cover (launch of Chronicle of Catholic Church of Lithuania (illegal) (1972)); Crowds with flags (establishment of Lithuanian Reform Movement 'Sajudis' (1988)); Document (signing of Act of Independent State Reconstruction (1990)); European flag (membership of European Union (2004)); Map (membership of Schengen Area (2007))	22·00	22·00

The stamps and margins of **MS**980 form a common background design of the national flag.

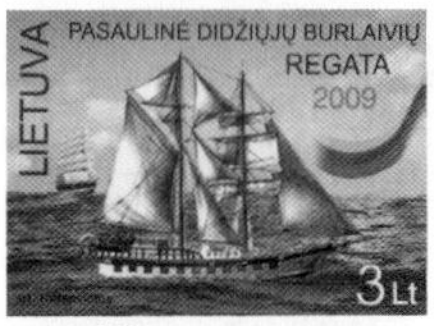

330 Sail Ship

2009. Tall Ships Race–2009, finishing in Klaipeda, Lithuania.

981	**330**	3l. multicoloured	3·50	3·25

No. 981 was printed, *se-tenant*, with a label showing an emblem for the occasion, the stamp and label forming a composite design.

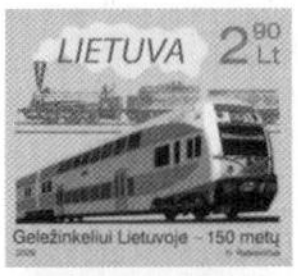

331 Commuter Train

2009. 150th Anniv of Lithuanian Railways.

982	**331**	2l.90 multicoloured	3·50	3·25

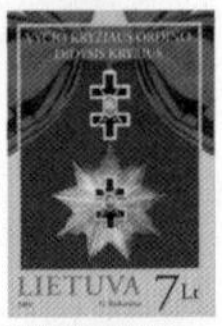

332 Grand Cross

2009. Grand Cross of the Order of Vytis (awarded for courage and bravery).

983	**332**	7l. multicoloured	8·50	8·25

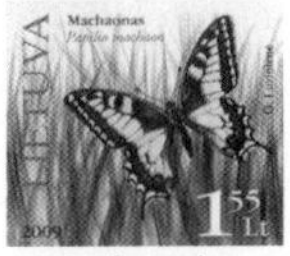

333 *Papilio machaon*

2009. Endangered Species. Multicoloured.
984		1l.55 Type **333**	1·90	1·80
985		1l.55 *Gentiana pneumonanthe*	1·90	1·80

Nos. 984/5 were printed, *se-tenant*, each pair forming a composite design.

334 George von Struve and Triagulation Chain of Struve Arc

2009. UNESCO World Heritage List. Struve Geodetic Arc. Multicoloured.
986		2l. Type **334**	2·10	2·00
987		2l. Struve's arc point in Meskonys	2·10	2·00

335 Church and Houses in Snow

2009. Christmas and New Year. Multicoloured.
988		1l.35 Type **335**	2·00	1·90
989		2l.45 Christmas baubles and house in snow	2·75	2·50

336 Jonas Karolis Chodkevichius

2010. Personalities. Multicoloured.
990		1l.35 Type **336** (courtier, military leader and founder of Kretinga Church and Monastery)	2·00	1·90
991		1l.35 Jonas Jablonskis (linguist)	2·00	1·90
992		3l. Mykolas Krupavichius (Ecclesiastic, politician and Minister of Agriculture)	3·50	3·25

337 Skier

2010. Winter Olympic Games, Vancouver.
993	**337**	2l.45 multicoloured	3·00	2·75

2010. Town Arms. As T **245**. Multicoloured.
994		1l.35 Silale	1·60	1·50
995		2l. Jonova	2·50	2·25
996		2l.15 Varena	2·75	2·50

338 Doves

2010. 20th Anniv of Restoration of Independence.
997	**338**	1l.35 multicoloured	2·00	1·90

339 Tree growing from Egg

2010. Easter.
998	**339**	1l.35 multicoloured	1·60	1·50

340 Balloon over Shanghai

2010. Expo 2010, Shanghai.
999	**340**	2l.90 multicoloured	3·50	3·25

341 Vladas Mikenas

2010. Birth Centenary of Vladas Mikenas (chess International Master).
1000	**341**	2l. multicoloured	2·50	2·25

342 Rabbit, Girl and Figures

2010. Europa. Children's Books. Multicoloured.
1001		2l.45 Type **342**	3·00	2·75
1002		2l.45 Letters, bird and boy	3·00	2·75

343 Oak Tree

2010. Natural Heritage. The Oak of Stelmuze. Sheet 70×70 mm
MS1003	**343**	8l.multicoloured	9·50	9·50

344 Crown and Shield with Swords and Battle of Zalgiris (engraving by M. Bielski)

2010. 600th Anniv of Battle of Grunvald (First Battle of Tannenberg), during the Polish–Lithuanian–Teutonic War
1004	**344**	2l.45 multicoloured	2·75	2·50

345

2010. 75th Anniv of Kretinga Museum. Multicoloured.
1005		1l.35 Type **345**	1·60	1·50
1006		1l.35 3rd-century buckle	1·60	1·50

346 Games Emblem and Basketball Player

2010. Youth Olympic Games, Singapore 2010
1007	**346**	2l.90 multicoloured	3·50	3·25

347 Kernavé within Landscape

2010. World Heritage Sites. Multicoloured.
1008		3l. Type **347**	3·50	3·25
1009		3l. Pathway and steps up earthwork	3·50	3·25

348 Stock Pigeon (*Columba oenas*)

2010. Endangered Species. Multicoloured.
1010		1l.35 Type **348**	2·00	1·90
1011		1l.35 Lesser Emperor dragonfly (*Anax parthenope*)	2·00	1·90

Nos. 1010/11 were printed, *se-tenant*, forming a composite design.

349 Christ's Transfiguration Cathedral, Kaisisdorys

2010. Churches. Multicoloured.
1012		1l.35 Type **349**	2·00	1·90
1013		1l.35 St. Anthony of Padua Cathedral, Telsiai	2·00	1·90

350 Snow-covered Houses

2010. Christmas and New Year
1014		1l.35 Type **350**	2·00	1·90
1015		2l.45 Winter sunset	2·00	1·90

351 Grand Cross of the Order of the Lithuanian Grand Duke Gediminas

2010. State Awards
1016	**351**	7l. multicoloured	8·50	8·25

2011. Wooden Churches and Belfries
1017		10c. orange-yellow, olive-sepia and black	15	10
1018		50c. light blue-green and black	60	55
1019		1l. cinnamon and black	1·20	1·00
1020		1l.35 cinnamon and black	2·00	1·90

Designs: 10c. Deguchiai Church, 1757; 50c. Tryshkiai Church, 18th century; 1l. Shaukenai Church, 1l.35 Shiaudine Church, 1775.

Square designs as T **299**.

352 Vilnius TV Tower (scene of defence)

2011. 13th January–Defenders of Freedom (unarmed resistors to military overthrow) Day
1021	**352**	1l.35 multicoloured	2·00	1·90

353 Ball and Hoop

2011. Men's European Basketball Championship 2011, Lithuania
1022	**353**	2l.45 multicoloured	3·50	3·25

354 Figures

2011. Population and Housing Census
1023	**354**	1l.35 multicoloured	2·00	1·90

355 Gabriele Petkevichaite-Bite (writer and philanthropist)

2011. Personalities. Multicoloured.
1024		1l.35 Type **355**	2·00	1·90
1025		2l.15 Justinas Vienozhinskis (writer)	2·75	2·50
1026		2l.90 Stasys Shalskausis (philosopher)	3·50	3·25

356 Town Hall

2011. 650th Anniv of Kaunas. Multicoloured.
MS1027		3l.×3, Type **356**; Central Post Office; Pekunas House	9·75	9·75

357 Fields and Forest

2011. Europa. Multicoloured.
1028		2l.45 Type **357**	3·00	2·75
1029		2l.45 River and forest	3·00	2·75

358 Pope John Paul II

2011. Pilgrim Route of Pope John Paul II (following John Paul II's route during his visit in 1993)
1030	**358**	2l.15 multicoloured	2·75	2·50

359 Giraffe

2011. Lithuanian Zoo. Multicoloured.
MS1031		4l.×4, Type **359**; Pelicans; *Cichiasoma octofasciatum*; Polar bear	9·50	9·50

360 Blacksmith's Bellows and Forge

2011. Exhibits in Alytus Ethnographic Museum. Multicoloured.
1032		2l. Type **360**	1·80	1·70
1033		2l. Ceramics	1·80	1·70

361 Czesław Miłosz

2011. Birth Centenary of Czesław Miłosz (writer)
1034	**361**	3l.35 multicoloured	3·00	2·75

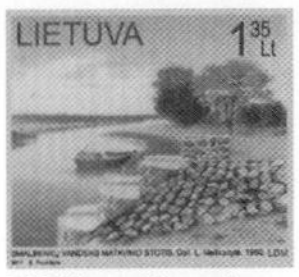

362 Water Measuring Station, Smalinkai (L. Meshkaityte)

2011. Bicentenary of Water Measuring (hydrometric) Station, Smalinkai

1035	**362**	1l.35 multicoloured	2·10	2·00

2011. Town Arms. Multicoloured.

1036	1l.35 Plungė	2·10	2·00
1037	2l.15 Kaišiadorys	3·00	2·75
1038	2l.90 Ignalina	3·75	3·50

Vert designs as T **245**

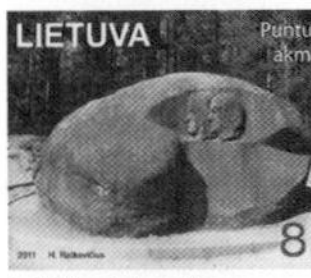

363 Puntukas Stone

2011. Natural Heritage. Puntukas Stone (second largest glacial erratic (rock) in Lithuania, engraved with portraits of pilots, Steponas Darius and Stasys Girėnas). Sheet 70×70 mm

MS1039	**363** 8l. multicoloured	9·00	9·50

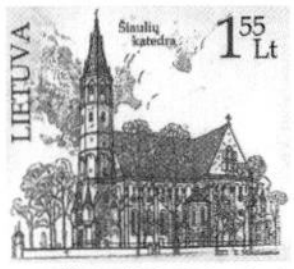

364 Šhiauliai Cathedral

2011. Churches. Multicoloured.

1040	1l.55 Type **364**	2·20	2·10
1041	1l.55 Trakai Parish Church	2·20	2·10

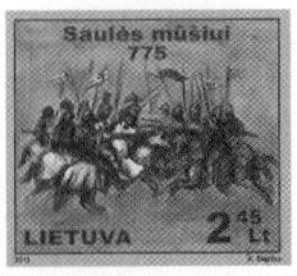

365 Cavalry

2011. 775th Anniv of Battle of Saule

1042	**365**	2l.45 multicoloured	3·75	3·50

2011. Wooden Churches and Belfries. Each cinnamon and black.

1043	5c. Antazavė Church, 1794	15	10
1044	20c. Inturkė Church, 1855	30	25
1045	35c. Prienai Church, 1750	55	50

Square designs as T **299**.

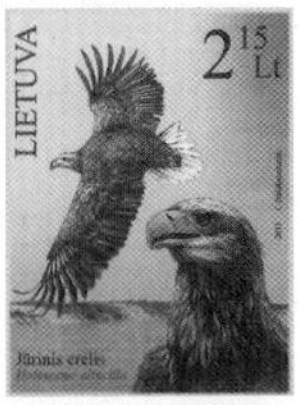

366 *Haliaeetus albicilla* (white-tailed sea eagle)

2011. Endangered Species. White-tailed Sea Eagle (*Haliaeetus albicilla*)

1046	**366**	2l.15 multicoloured	3·00	2·75

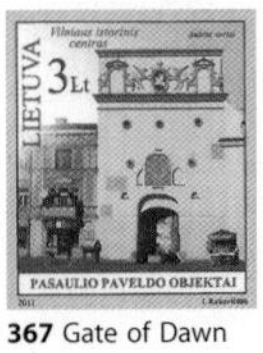

367 Gate of Dawn

2011. World Heritage Sites. Vilnius Historic Centre. Multicoloured.

1047	3l. Type **367**	3·25	3·00
1048	3l. St. John's Church	3·25	3·00

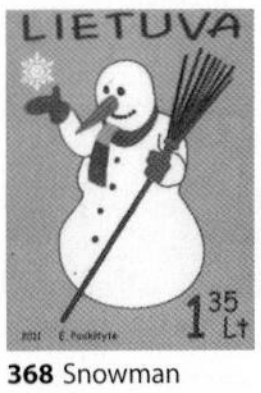

368 Snowman

2011. Christmas and New Year. Multicoloured.

1049	1l.35 Type **368**	1·10	1·00
1050	2l.45 Snowflake	2·25	2·25

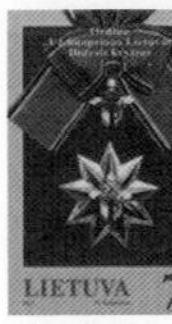

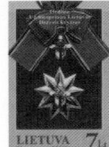

368a Grand Cross of the Order for Merits

2011. State Awards (2nd series)

1050a	**368a**	7l. multicoloured	8·00	7·75

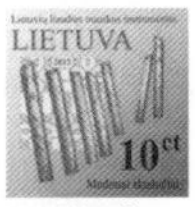

369 Wooden Panpipes

2012. Lithuanian Folk Music Instruments. Each dull scarlet and black.

1051	10c. Type **369**	25	20
1052	20c. Animal shaped clay pipes	30	25
1053	35c. Bladderbow bass	55	50
1054	1l. Alder bark trumpet	1·60	1·50
1055	1l.35 Kanklės (stringed instrument) from Suvalkija	1·10	1·00
1056	2l.15 Cowhorn reed-pipe	2·40	2·30

2012. Town Arms. Multicoloured.

1057	1l.35 Kalvarija	1·10	1·00
1058	1l.35 Kavarskas	1·10	1·00
1059	2l.45 Naujoji Akmene	2·75	2·50

Vert designs as T **245**

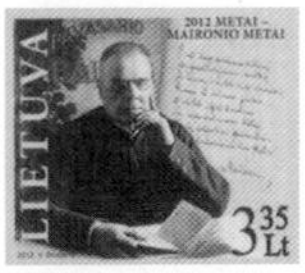

369a Jonas Mačiulis-Maironis

2012. Jonas Mačiulis-Maironis (priest, poet and author) Commemoration

1059a	**369a**	3l.35 multicoloured	4·00	3·75

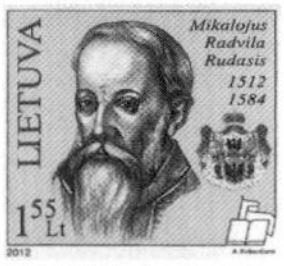

370 Mikalojus Radvila Rudasis

2012. Personalities. Multicoloured.

1060	1l.55 Type **370**	2·00	1·90
1061	2l. Domicelė Tarabildienė (artist)	2·75	2·50
1062	2l.90 Stasys Šimkus (composer and conductor)	3·50	3·25

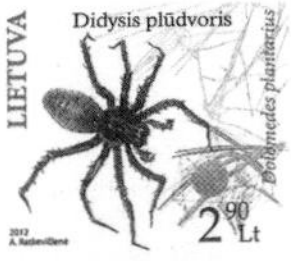

371 *Dolomedes plantarius* (Great Raft Spider)

2012. Endangered Species. Spiders. Multicoloured.

1063	2l.90 Type **371**	3·00	3·25
1064	2l.90 *Eresus cinnaberinus* (Ladybird Spider)	3·00	3·25

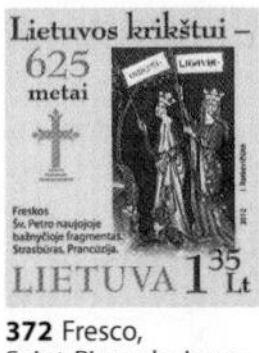

372 Fresco, Saint-Pierre-la-Jeune Church, Strasbourg (detail)

2012. 625th Anniv of Christianization of Lithuania

1065	**372**	1l.35 multicoloured	2·00	1·90

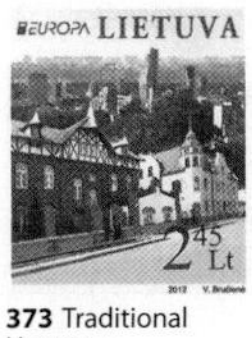

373 Traditional Houses

2012. Europa. Visit Lithuania. Multicoloured.

1066	2l.45 Type **373**	2·75	2·50
1067	2l.45 Woodland and lake	2·75	2·50

Pt. 2

LOMBARDY AND VENETIA

Formerly known as Austrian Italy. Although these provinces used a different currency the following issues were valid throughout Austria. Lombardy was annexed by Sardinia in 1859 and Venetia by Italy in 1866.

1850. 100 centesimi = 1 lira.
1858. 100 soldi = 1 florin. 100 kreuzer = 1 gulden.

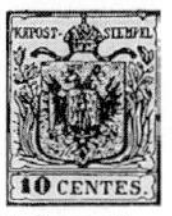

1 Arms of Austria

1850. Imperf.

1c	1	5c. orange	£1600	£120
2c	1	10c. black	£3000	£110
7	1	15c. red	£750	4·25
4c	1	30c. brown	£2750	8·50
5e	1	45c. blue	£7000	22·00

1859. As T **4** and **5** of Austria (Emperor Francis Joseph I) but value in soldi. Perf.

16B	5	2s. yellow	£600	£110
17A	4	3s. black	£2750	£300
18B	4	3s. green	£375	80·00
19B	5	5s. red	£300	5·50
20A	5	10s. brown	£450	60·00
21B	5	15s. blue	£1900	22·00

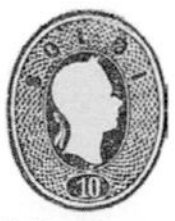

3 Emperor Francis Joseph I

1861

25	3	5s. red	£1600	2·75
26	3	10s. brown	£2750	27·00

4 Arms of Austria

1863

27	4	2s. yellow	£100	£190
33	4	3s. green	20·00	19·00
34	4	5s. red	3·25	1·60
35	4	10s. blue	19·00	6·00
36	4	15s. brown	80·00	60·00

JOURNAL STAMPS

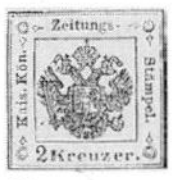

J5

1858. Imperf.

J22	J5	1k. black	£1800	£4750
J23	J5	2k. red	£275	95·00
J24	J5	4k. red	£17000	£4250

Pt. 9

LOURENCO MARQUES

A Portuguese colony in E. Africa, now part of Mozambique, whose stamps it uses.

1895. 1000 reis = 1 milreis.
1913. 100 centavos = 1 escudo.

1895. "Figures" key-type inscr "LOURENCO MARQUES".

1	R	5r. yellow	60	55
2	R	10r. mauve	60	55
3	R	15r. brown	1·40	1·00
4	R	20r. lilac	1·40	95
10	R	25r. green	1·10	55
12	R	50r. blue	2·75	2·10
18	R	75r. pink	2·50	1·70
14	R	80r. green	7·25	4·75
7	R	100r. brown on yellow	3·25	1·70
16	R	150r. red on pink	5·75	4·75
8	R	200r. blue on blue	5·50	3·50
9	R	300r. blue on brown	5·75	3·75

1895. 700th Death Anniv of St. Anthony. Optd L. MARQUES CENTENARIO DE S. ANTONIO MDCCCXCV on (a) "Embossed" key-type inscr "PROVINCIA DE MOCAMBIQUE".

19	Q	5r. black	25·00	21·00
20	Q	10r. green	28·00	21·00
21	Q	20r. red	31·00	23·00
22	Q	25r. purple	38·00	23·00
23	Q	40r. brown	38·00	23·00
27a	Q	50r. blue	25·00	23·00
25	Q	100r. brown	£120	£110
26	Q	200r. violet	50·00	41·00
27	Q	300r. orange	80·00	70·00

(b) "Figures" key-type inscr "MOCAMBIQUE".

28	R	5r. orange	2·30	1·60
29	R	10r. mauve	2·30	1·60
30	R	50r. blue	2·30	1·60
35	R	75r. pink	55	50
32	R	80r. green	1·60	1·20
33	R	100r. brown on yellow	55	50
35a	R	150r. red on pink	45	35

1897. No. 9 surch 50 reis.

36	50r. on 300r. blue on brown	£275	£250

1898. "King Carlos" key-type inscr "LOURENCO MARQUES". Name and value in black.

37	S	2½r. grey	50	50
38	S	5r. orange	50	50
39	S	10r. green	50	50
40	S	15r. brown	1·80	1·30
83	S	15r. green	1·20	80
41	S	20r. lilac	1·10	65
42	S	25r. green	1·10	65
84	S	25r. red	85	50
43	S	50r. blue	1·80	1·30
85	S	50r. brown	1·50	1·20
86	S	65r. blue	6·00	4·75
44	S	75r. pink	3·50	2·10
87	S	75r. purple	2·20	1·70
45	S	80r. mauve	3·00	2·00
46	S	100r. blue on blue	2·30	1·30
88	S	115r. brown on pink	7·00	6·25
89	S	130r. brown on yellow	7·00	6·25
47	S	150r. brown on yellow	3·50	2·10
48	S	200r. purple on pink	5·25	2·75
49	S	300r. blue on pink	3·75	2·75
90	S	400r. blue on yellow	7·75	6·75
50	S	500r. black on blue	7·50	4·00
51	S	700r. mauve on yellow	32·00	14·00

1899. Green and brown fiscal stamps of Mozambique, as T **9** of Macao, bisected and each half surch Correio de Lourenco Marques and value. Imperf.

55	5r. on half of 10r.	1·80	1·60
56	25r. on half of 10r.	2·10	1·60
57	50r. on half of 30r.	2·10	1·60
58	50r. on half of 800r.	1·80	1·30

1899. No. 44 surch 50 Reis.

59	S	50r. on 75r. pink	2·30	1·60

1902. "Figures" and "Newspaper" key-types surch.

60	V	65r. on 2½r. brown	3·75	3·25
62	R	65r. on 5r. yellow	3·75	3·00
63	R	65r. on 15r. brown	3·75	3·00
64	R	65r. on 20r. lilac	3·75	3·00
66	R	115r. on 10r. mauve	3·75	3·00
67	R	115r. on 200r. blue on blue	3·75	3·00
68	R	115r. on 300r. blue on brn	3·75	3·00
70	R	130r. on 25r. green	3·50	3·25
72	R	130r. on 80r. green	3·75	3·25
73	R	130r. on 150r. red on pink	3·75	3·25
74	R	400r. on 50r. blue	12·50	5·50
76	R	400r. on 75r. pink	10·00	5·50
78	R	400r. on 100r. brown on yellow	7·00	4·75

1902. "King Carlos" key-type inscr "LOURENCO MARQUES" optd PROVISORIO.

79	S	15r. brown	2·20	1·70
80	S	25r. green	2·20	1·20
81	S	50r. blue	3·25	1·80
82	S	75r. pink	4·25	2·75

1905. No. 86 surch 50 REIS.

91	50r. on 65r. blue	4·50	3·75

1911. "King Carlos" key-type inscr "LOURENCO MARQUES" optd REPUBLICA.

92	2½r. grey	50	35
93	5r. orange	50	35
94	10r. green	80	65
95	15r. green	80	65
96	20r. lilac	80	65
97	25r. red	1·50	90
98	50r. brown	1·30	90
99	75r. purple	2·10	90
100	100r. blue on blue	1·30	90
178	115r. brown on pink	2·10	1·80
102	130r. brown on yellow	1·50	90
103	200r. purple on pink	1·50	90
104	400r. blue on yellow	2·50	2·00
105	500r. black on blue	2·50	2·00
106	700r. mauve on yellow	3·25	2·00

1913. Surch REPUBLICA LOURENCO MARQUES and value on "Vasco da Gama" issues of (a) Portuguese Colonies.

107		¼c. on 2½r. green	2·20	1·80
108		½c. on 5r. red	2·20	1·80
109		1c. on 10r. purple	2·20	1·80
110		2½c. on 25r. green	2·20	1·80
111		5c. on 50r. blue	2·20	1·80
112		7½c. on 75r. brown	5·75	4·25
113		10c. on 100r. brown	3·25	1·80
114		15c. on 150r. brown	3·25	1·80

(b) Macao.

115		¼c. on ½a. green	1·40	1·10
116		½c. on 1a. red	1·90	1·10
117		1c. on 2a. purple	1·90	1·10
118		2½c. on 4a. green	1·90	1·40
119		5c. on 8a. blue	3·75	2·10
120		7½c. on 12a. brown	3·75	2·75
121		10c. on 16a. brown	5·00	3·50
122		15c. on 24a. brown	5·25	3·50

(c) Timor.

123		¼c. on ½a. green	5·25	3·50
124		½c. on 1a. red	7·00	5·75
125		1c. on 2a. purple	7·00	5·75
126		2½c. on 4a. green	7·00	6·50
127		5c. on 8a. blue	90	70
128		7½c. on 12a. brown	1·80	90
129		10c. on 16a. brown	1·30	1·10
130		15c. on 24a. brown	1·30	1·20

1914. "Ceres" key-type inscr "LOURENCO MARQUES".

147	U	¼c. green	45	35
148	U	½c. black	45	35
149	U	1c. green	45	35
150	U	1½c. brown	50	45
151	U	2c. red	50	45
152	U	2½c. violet	50	45
153	U	5c. blue	1·10	95
154	U	7½c. brown	1·10	95
155	U	8c. grey	1·10	95
140	U	10c. red	2·00	1·20
157	U	15c. purple	1·90	1·80
142	U	20c. green	2·20	1·80
143	U	30c. brown on green	2·00	1·70
144	U	40c. brown on pink	7·50	5·75
145	U	50c. orange on orange	3·50	2·75
146	U	1e. green on blue	3·50	2·75

1914. Provisionals of 1902 overprinted REPUBLICA.

166	R	115r. on 10r. mauve	1·20	95
167	R	115r. on 200r. blue on blue	1·40	95
168	R	115r. on 300r. blue on brn	1·40	95
161	R	130r. on 25r. green	2·00	1·80
164	R	130r. on 80r. green	2·00	1·80
169	R	130r. on 150r. red on pink	1·40	95
184	R	400r. on 50r. blue	2·20	1·70
185	R	400r. on 75r.	3·50	2·75

1915. Nos. 93 and 148 perf diagonally and each half surch ¼.

171	U	¼ on half of ½c. black	4·25	3·25
170	S	½ on half of 5r. orange	4·25	3·25

Prices for Nos. 170/1 are for whole stamps.

1915. Surch Dois centavos.

172	S	2c. on 15r. (No. 83)	1·90	1·40
173	S	2c. on 15c. (No. 95)	1·90	1·40

1918. Red Cross Fund. "Ceres" key-type inscr "LOURENCO MARQUES", optd 9-3-18 and Red Cross or surch with value in figures and bars also.

188	U	¼c. green	3·75	3·50
189	U	½c. black	3·75	3·50
190	U	1c. green	3·75	3·50
191	U	2½c. violet	3·75	3·50
192a	U	5c. blue	3·75	3·50
193	U	10c. red	4·50	4·00
194	U	20c. on 1½c. brown	4·50	4·00
195	U	30c. brown on green	5·00	4·75
196	U	40c. on 2c. red	5·00	4·75
197	U	50c. on 7½c. brown	5·00	4·75
198	U	70c. on 8c. grey	5·00	4·75
199	U	1e. on 15c. purple	5·00	4·75

1920. No. 166 surch Um quarto de centavo.

200	R	¼c. on 115r. on 10r. mauve	1·40	95

1920. No. 152 surch in figures or words.

201	U	1c. on 2½c. violet	1·10	65
202	U	1½c. on 2½c. violet	1·10	65
203	U	4c. on 2½c. violet	1·10	65

For other surcharges on "Ceres" key-type of Lourenco Marques, see Mozambique Nos. 309/10 and Nos. D44 and 46.

NEWSPAPER STAMPS

1893. "Newspaper" key-type inscr "LOURENCO MARQUES".

N1	V	2½r. brown	65	60

1895. 700th Death Anniv of St. Anthony. "Newspaper" key-type inscr "MOCAMBIQUE" optd L. MARQUES CENTENARIO DE S. ANTONIO MDCCCXCV.

N36		2½r. brown	9·50	6·50

Pt. 7

LUBECK

Formerly one of the free cities of the Hanseatic League. In 1868 joined the North German Confederation.

16 schilling = 1 mark.

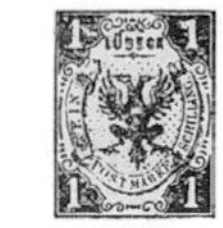
1

1859. Imperf.

9	1	½s. lilac	55·00	£2000
10	1	1s. orange	£120	£2000
3	1	2s. brown	£150	£325
4	1	2½s. red	£275	£1100
6	1	4s. green	£120	£800

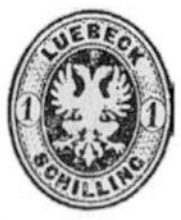
3

1863. Rouletted.

11	3	½s. green	65·00	£130
13	3	1s. orange	£170	£350
14	3	2s. red	37·00	85·00
16	3	2½s. blue	£170	£325
17	3	4s. bistre	75·00	£140

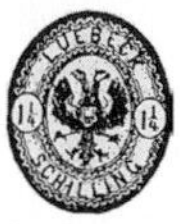
4

1864. Imperf.

18	4	1¼s. brown	42·00	£160

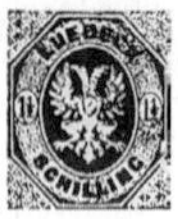
5

1865. Roul.

21	5	1½s. mauve	10·50	£120

Pt. 4

LUXEMBOURG

An independent Grand Duchy lying between Belgium and the Saar District. Under German Occupation from 1940 to 1944.

1852. 12½ centimes = 1 silver groschen.
100 centimes = 1 franc.
1940. 100 pfennig = 1 reichsmark.
1944. 100 centimes = 1 franc (Belgian).
2002. 100 cents = 1 euro.

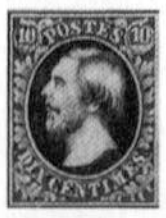
1 Grand Duke William III

1852. Imperf.

2	1	10c. black	£3250	85·00
3	1	1s. red	£2000	£110

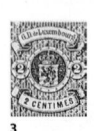

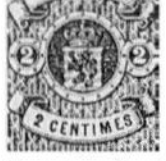
3

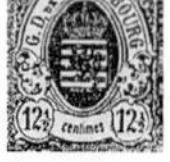
4

1859. Imperf or roul.

21	3	1c. orange	55·00	11·00
23	3	1c. brown	55·00	11·00
17	3	2c. black	28·00	22·00
8	3	4c. yellow	£275	£250
20	3	4c. green	55·00	33·00
10	4	10c. blue	£275	28·00
24	4	10c. purple	£170	5·50
25	4	10c. lilac	£200	5·50
28	4	12½c. red	£250	11·00
30	4	20c. brown	£200	11·00
12	4	25c. brown	£550	£400
32	4	25c. blue	£1100	17·00
13	4	30c. purple	£450	£325
14	4	37½c. green	£500	£275
35	4	37½c. bistre	£1100	£375
39	4	40c. orange	55·00	£110

1872. Surch UN FRANC. Roul.

37		1f. on 37½c. bistre	£1300	£110

1874. Perf.

57	3	1c. brown	5·50	2·75
58	3	2c. black	11·00	5·50
42	3	4c. green	5·50	14·00
43	3	5c. yellow	£250	39·00
60	4	10c. lilac	28·00	5·50
61a	4	12½c. red	17·00	17·00
62	4	20c. brown	8·25	5·50
63	4	25c. blue	28·00	2·75
64a	4	30c. red	8·25	22·00
55	4	40c. orange	5·50	14·00

1879. Surch Un Franc. Perf.

56		1f. on 37½c. bistre	11·00	39·00

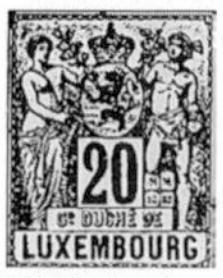
7 Agriculture and Trade

1882

81c	7	1c. grey	1·10	85
82c	7	2c. brown	20	55
83c	7	4c. bistre	75	2·75
84c	7	5c. green	1·10	85
85c	7	10c. red	11·00	85
86a	7	12½c. blue	1·80	42·00
87c	7	20c. orange	4·50	3·25
88c	7	25c. blue	£250	2·75
89a	7	30c. green	33·00	20·00
90c	7	50c. brown	1·70	17·00
91	7	1f. lilac	2·20	£250
92	7	5f. orange	47·00	£250

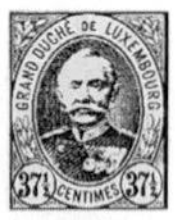
8 Grand Duke Adolf

1891

125c	8	10c. red	1·10	45
126b	8	12½c. green	1·70	1·10
128b	8	20c. orange	11·00	1·70
129c	8	25c. blue	1·10	1·10
130b	8	30c. green	2·20	1·70
131b	8	37½c. green	4·50	4·50
132b	8	50c. brown	10·00	5·50
133b	8	1f. purple	20·00	9·00
134	8	2½f. black	2·20	31·00
135	8	5f. lake	40·00	£100

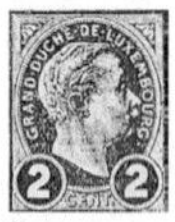
9

1895

152	9	1c. grey	8·25	1·10
153	9	2c. brown	2·20	55
154	9	4c. bistre	2·20	1·70
155	9	5c. green	17·00	55
156	9	10c. red	28·00	55

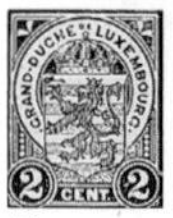
10

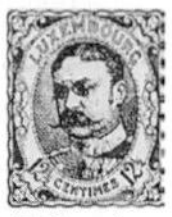
11 Grand Duke William IV

1906

157	10	1c. grey	20	30
158	10	2c. brown	20	30
159	10	4c. bistre	20	55
160	10	5c. green	35	30
231	10	5c. mauve	10	55
161	10	6c. lilac	20	85
161a	10	7½c. orange	20	4·50
162	11	10c. red	1·70	20
163	11	12½ slate	2·20	55
164	11	15c. brown	2·20	90
165	11	20c. orange	2·75	80
166	11	25c. blue	£100	55
166a	11	30c. olive	1·10	80
167	11	37½c. green	1·10	1·10
168	11	50c. brown	3·00	1·10
169	11	87½c. blue	2·20	17·00
170	11	1f. purple	4·50	2·20
171	11	2½f. red	£100	£110
172	11	5f. purple	13·50	90·00

1912. Surch 62½ cts.

173	11	62½c. on 87½c. blue	5·50	3·25
173a	11	62½c. on 2½f. red	5·50	6·75
173b	11	62½c. on 5f. purple	3·25	5·50

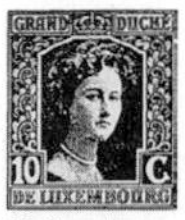
13 Grand Duchess Adelaide

1914

174	13	10c. purple	15	25
175	13	12½c. green	15	25
176	13	15c. brown	15	25
176a	13	17½c. brown	15	70
177	13	25c. blue	15	25
178	13	30c. brown	15	85
179	13	35c. blue	15	70
180	13	37½c. brown	15	70
181	13	40c. red	15	55
182	13	50c. grey	40	70
183	13	62½c. green	55	4·00
183a	13	87½c. orange	55	4·00
184	13	1f. brown	5·50	1·70
185	13	2½f. red	55	4·50
186	13	5f. violet	13·50	65·00

1916. Surch in figures and bars.

187	10	2½ on 5c. green	20	20
188	10	3 on 2c. brown	20	20
212	10	5 on 1c. grey	20	20
213	10	5 on 4c. bistre	20	55
214	10	5 on 7½c. orange	20	20
215	10	6 on 2c. brown	20	35
189	13	7½ on 10c. red	20	20
190	13	17½ on 30c. brown	20	55
191	13	20 on 17½c. brown	20	20
216	13	25 on 37½c. sepia	20	20
217	13	75 on 62½c. green	20	20
218	13	80 on 87½c. orange	20	20
192	13	87½ on 1f. brown	80	7·75

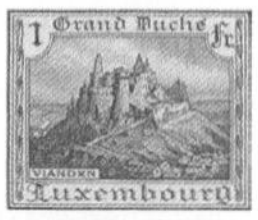
18 Vianden Castle

1921. Perf.

194	17	2c. brown	20	20
195	17	3c. green	20	20
196	17	6c. purple	20	20
197	17	10c. green	45	20
193a	17	15c. red*	15	20
198	17	15c. green	45	20
234	17	15c. orange	10	55
199	17	20c. orange	45	20
235	17	20c. green	10	55
200	17	25c. green	45	20
201	17	30c. red	45	20
202	17	40c. orange	45	20
203	17	50c. blue	1·10	65
236	17	50c. red	10	55
204	17	75c. red	65	1·70
237	17	75c. blue	10	55
205	17	80c. black	2·20	1·70
206a	18	1f. red	80	55
238	18	1f. blue	45	1·10
207	-	2f. blue	1·10	1·10
239	-	2f. brown	5·50	2·75
208	-	5f. violet	60·00	13·50

DESIGNS—As Type **18**: 2f. Factories at Esch; 5f. Railway viaduct over River Alzette.

*No. 193a was originally issued on the occasion of the birth of Crown Prince Jean.

See also Nos. 219/20.

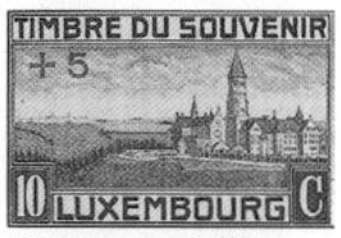
21 Monastery at Clervaux

1921. War Monument Fund.

209	21	10c.+5c. green	55	8·25
210	-	15c.+10c. orange	55	11·00
211	-	25c.+10c. green	55	8·25

DESIGNS—HORIZ: 15c. Pfaffenthal; 25c. as Type **26**.

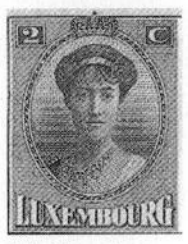

17 Grand Duchess Charlotte

1922. Philatelic Exhibition. Imperf.

219	**17**	25c. green	2·20	7·75
220	**17**	30c. red	2·20	7·75

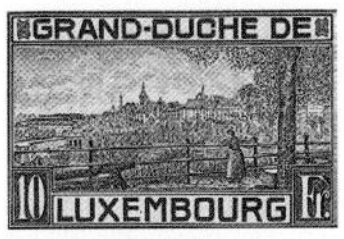

26 Luxembourg

1923. Birth of Princess Elisabeth. Sheet 78×59 mm to 79×61 mm.

MS221	**26**	10f. green	£1700	£2750

1923

222a	**26**	10f. black	11·00	17·00

1923. Unveiling of War Memorial by Prince Leopold of Belgium. Nos. 209/11 surch 27 mai 1923 and additional values.

223	**21**	10+5+25c. green	2·20	22·00
224	-	15+10+25c. orange	2·20	28·00
225	-	25+10+25c. green	2·20	22·00

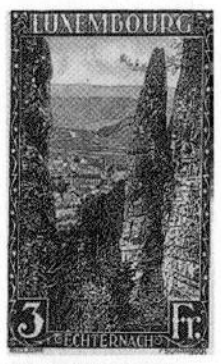

28 Echternach

1923

226	**28**	3f. blue	2·75	1·10

1924. Charity. Death of Grand Duchess Marie Adelaide. Surch CARITAS and new value.

227	**13**	12½c.+7½c. green	30	4·50
228	**13**	35c.+10c. blue	30	4·50
229	**13**	2½f.+1f. red	1·70	42·00
230	**13**	5f.+2f. violet	85	28·00

1925. Surch 5.

240	**17**	5 on 10c. green	45	45

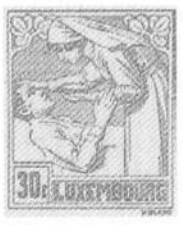

31

1925. Anti-T.B. Fund.

241	**31**	5c.+5c. violet	40	1·10
242	**31**	30c.+5c. orange	40	4·50
243	**31**	50c.+5c. brown	65	8·25
244	**31**	1f.+10c. blue	1·10	21·00

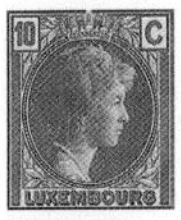

32 Grand Duchess Charlotte

1926

245	**32**	5c. mauve	10	30
246	**32**	10c. olive	10	30
246a	**32**	15c. black	30	55
247	**32**	20c. orange	45	55
248	**32**	25c. green	45	55
248a	**32**	25c. brown	30	55
248b	**32**	30c. green	30	55
248c	**32**	30c. violet	55	55
248d	**32**	35c. violet	5·50	55
248e	**32**	35c. green	30	55
249	**32**	40c. brown	10	30
250	**32**	50c. brown	10	30
250a	**32**	60c. green	5·50	30
251	**32**	65c. brown	30	2·75
251a	**32**	70c. violet	55	55
252	**32**	75c. red	30	1·10
252a	**32**	75c. brown	10	55
253	**32**	80c. brown	30	2·75
253a	**32**	90c. red	2·20	2·75
254	**32**	1f. black	2·20	55
254a	**32**	1f. red	85	55
255	**32**	1¼f. blue	30	1·10
255a	**32**	1¼f. yellow	17·00	2·20
255b	**32**	1¼f. green	85	55
255c	**32**	1¼f. red	17·00	2·75
255d	**32**	1½f. blue	2·75	2·20
255e	**32**	1¾f. blue	1·70	55

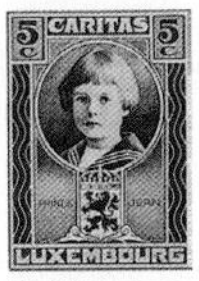

33 Prince Jean

1926. Child Welfare.

256	**33**	5c.+5c. black and mauve	70	1·10
257	**33**	40c.+10c. black & green	70	1·70
258	**33**	50c.+15c. black & yellow	70	1·70
259	**33**	75c.+20c. black and red	70	17·00
260	**33**	1f.50+30c. black & bl	70	20·00

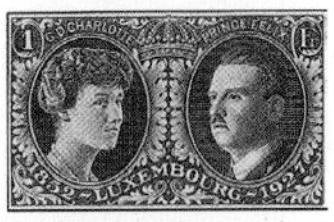

34 Grand Duchess and Prince Felix

1927. International Philatelic Exhibition.

261	**34**	25c. purple	1·70	16·00
262	**34**	50c. green	2·20	25·00
263	**34**	75c. red	1·70	16·00
264	**34**	1f. black	1·70	16·00
265	**34**	1½f. blue	1·70	16·00

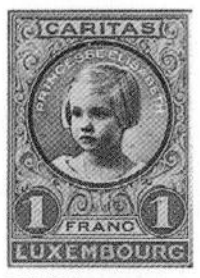

35 Princess Elisabeth

1927. Child Welfare.

266	**35**	10c.+5c. black and blue	30	1·10
267	**35**	50c.+10 black and brown	30	1·70
268	**35**	75c.+20c. black & orange	30	2·75
269	**35**	1f.+30c. black and red	30	17·00
270	**35**	1½f.+50c. black and blue	30	17·00

1927. Stamps of 1921 and 1926 surch.

270a	**32**	10 on 30c. green	55	55
271	**17**	15 on 20c. green	30	30
272	**32**	15 on 25c. green	30	85
273	**17**	35 on 40c. orange	30	30
274	**32**	60 on 65c. brown	30	55
275	**17**	60 on 75c. blue	30	55
276	**32**	60 on 75c. red	30	55
277	**17**	60 on 80c. black	30	85
278	**32**	60 on 80c. brown	30	55
278a	**32**	70 on 75c. brown	11·00	55
278b	**32**	75 on 90c. red	3·25	1·10
278c	**32**	1¾ on 1½f. blue	5·50	3·25

1928. Perf.

279a	**37**	2f. black	2·75	1·10

See also No. 339.

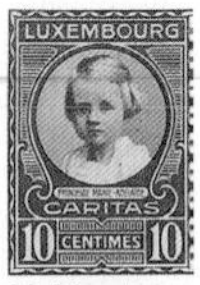

38 Princess Marie Adelaide

1928. Child Welfare.

280	**38**	10c.+5c. purple & green	55	1·70
281	**38**	60c.+10c. olive & brown	1·10	4·50
282	**38**	75c.+15c. green and red	1·70	11·00
283	**38**	1f.+25c. brown & green	2·75	33·00
284	**38**	1½f.+50c. blue & yellow	2·75	33·00

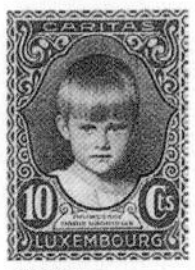

39 Princess Marie Gabrielle

1928. Child Welfare.

285	**39**	10c.+10c. green & brown	55	2·20
286	**39**	35c.+15c. brown & green	2·20	11·00
287	**39**	75c.+30c. black and red	2·75	14·00
288	**39**	1¼f.+50c. green and red	3·25	33·00
289	**39**	1¾f.+75c. black and blue	4·50	42·00

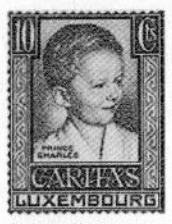

40 Prince Charles

1930. Child Welfare.

290	**40**	10c.+5c. brown & green	55	1·70
291	**40**	75c.+10c. green & brown	2·75	7·25
292	**40**	1f.+25c. violet and red	5·50	28·00
293	**40**	1¼f.+75c. black & yellow	8·25	36·00
294	**40**	1¾f.+1f.50 brown & blue	11·00	36·00

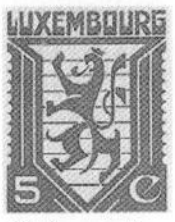

41 Arms of Luxembourg

1930

295	**41**	5c. red	1·10	55
296	**41**	10c. green	2·20	55

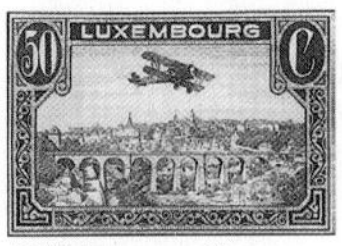

42 Biplane over River Alzette

1931. Air.

296a	**42**	50c. green	1·10	1·70
297	**42**	75c. brown	1·10	2·20
298	**42**	1f. red	1·10	2·20
299	**42**	1¼f. purple	1·10	2·20
300	**42**	1¾f. blue	1·10	2·20
300a	**42**	3f. black	2·20	9·00

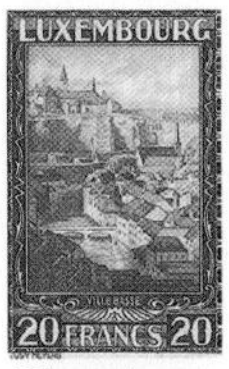

43 Luxembourg, Lower Town

1931

301	**43**	20f. green	5·50	28·00

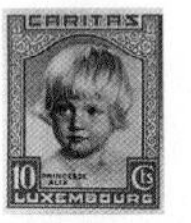

44 Princess Alix

1931. Child Welfare.

302	**44**	10c.+5c. grey and brown	55	1·70
303	**44**	75c.+10c. green and red	5·50	22·00
304	**44**	1f.+25c. grey and green	17·00	45·00
305	**44**	1¼f.+75c. green and violet	11·00	45·00
306	**44**	1¾f.+1f.50 grey and blue	22·00	85·00

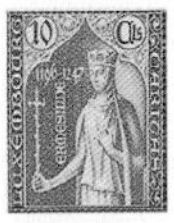

45 Countess Ermesinde

1932. Child Welfare.

307	**45**	10c.+5c. brown	55	1·70
308	**45**	75c.+10c. violet	5·50	22·00
309	**45**	1f.+25c. red	20·00	50·00
310	**45**	1¼f.+75c. lake	20·00	55·00
311	**45**	1¾f.+1f.50 blue	20·00	55·00

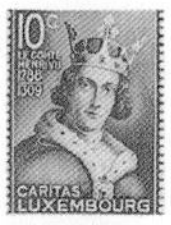

46 Emperor Henry VII

1933. Child Welfare.

312	**46**	10c.+5c. brown	55	1·70
313	**46**	75c.+10c. purple	8·25	22·00
314	**46**	1f.+25c. red	17·00	55·00
315	**46**	1¼f.+75c. brown	22·00	75·00
316	**46**	1¾f.+1f.50 blue	28·00	80·00

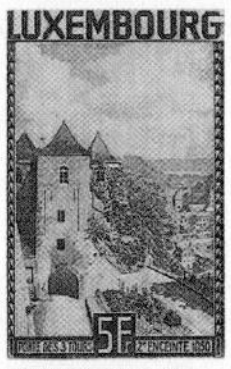

47 Gateway of the Three Towers

1934

317	**47**	5f. green	5·50	17·00

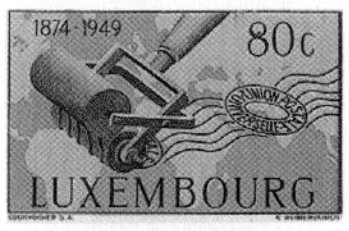

87 Date-stamp and Map

1949. 75th Anniv of U.P.U.

525	**87**	80c. green, lt green & black	95	95
526	**87**	2f.50 red, pink and black	4·00	2·50
527	**87**	4f. ultramarine, blue & black	7·75	8·25
528	**87**	8f. brown, buff and black	25·00	45·00

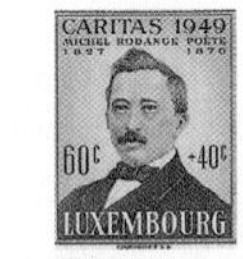

88 Michel Rodange

1949. National Welfare Fund.

529	**88**	60c.+40c. green and grey	95	95
530	**88**	2f.+1f. purple and claret	7·50	7·50
531	**88**	4f.+2f. blue and grey	13·00	15·00
532	**88**	10f.+5f. brown and buff	31·00	25·00

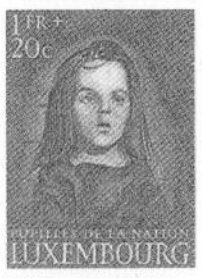

89 Young Girl

1950. War Orphans Relief Fund.

533	-	60c.+15c. turquoise	3·75	2·20
534	**89**	1f.+20c. red	8·25	2·20
535	-	2f.+30c. brown	6·25	2·20
536	**89**	4f.+75c. blue	22·00	25·00
537	-	8f.+3f. black	65·00	65·00
538	**89**	10f.+5f. purple	65·00	65·00

DESIGN: 60c., 2f., 8f. Mother and boy.

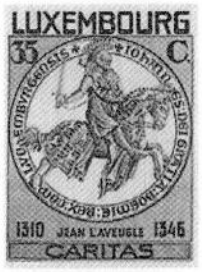

48 Arms of John the Blind

1934. Child Welfare.

318	**48**	10c.+5c. violet	1·10	2·75
319	**48**	35c.+10c. green	5·50	17·00
320	**48**	75c.+15c. red	5·50	17·00
321	**48**	1f.+25c. red	28·00	75·00
322	**48**	1¼f.+75c. orange	28·00	75·00
323	**48**	1¾f.+1½f. blue	28·00	75·00

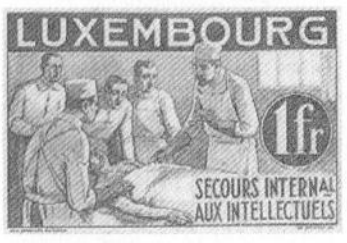

50 Surgeon

1935. International Relief Fund for Intellectuals.

324	-	5c. violet	1·10	1·70
325	-	10c. red	1·10	1·70
326	-	15c. olive	1·10	2·75
327	-	20c. orange	2·75	4·00
328	-	35c. green	2·75	5·00
329	-	50c. black	3·25	7·25
330	-	70c. green	5·50	8·25
331	**50**	1f. red	5·50	11·00
332	-	1f.25 turquoise	22·00	80·00
333	-	1f.75 blue	22·00	80·00
334	-	2f. brown	55·00	£170
335	-	3f. brown	65·00	£225
336	-	5f. blue	£110	£425
337	-	10f. purple	£275	£700
338	**50**	20f. green	£300	£850

DESIGNS—HORIZ: 5c., 10f. Schoolteacher; 15c., 3f. Journalist; 20c., 1f.75, Engineer; 35c., 1f.25, Chemist. VERT: 10c., 2f. "The Arts"; 50c., 5f. Barrister; 70c. University.
This set was sold at the P.O. at double face value.

1935. Esch Philatelic Exhibition. Imperf.

339	**37**	2f.(+50c.) black	8·25	28·00

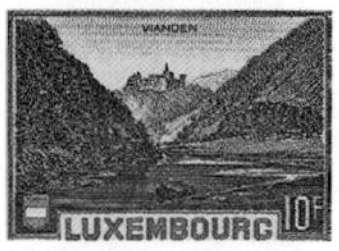

52 Vianden

1935

340	**52**	10f. green	5·50	22·00

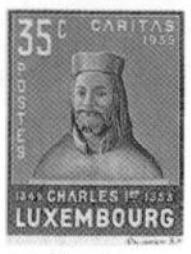

53 Charles I

1935. Child Welfare.

341	**53**	10c.+5c. violet	30	55
342	**53**	35c.+10c. green	85	1·10
343	**53**	70c.+20c. brown	1·70	2·20
344	**53**	1f.+25c. red	28·00	55·00
345	**53**	1f.25+75c. brown	28·00	55·00
346	**53**	1f.75+1f.50 blue	28·00	75·00

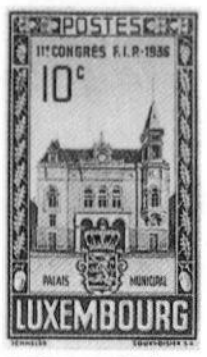

54 Town Hall

1936. 11th Int Philatelic Federation Congress.

347	**54**	10c. brown	55	1·10
348	**54**	35c. green	55	1·70
349	**54**	70c. orange	85	2·20
350	**54**	1f. red	2·20	13·50
351	**54**	1f.25 violet	4·00	17·00
352	**54**	1f.75 blue	2·20	14·00

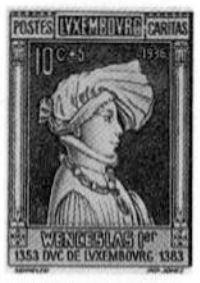
55 Wenceslas I

1936. Child Welfare.

353	**55**	10c.+5c. brown	55	55
354	**55**	35c.+10c. green	55	1·10
355	**55**	70c.+20c. slate	85	1·70
356	**55**	1f.+25c. red	4·50	25·00
357	**55**	1f.25+75c. violet	8·25	50·00
358	**55**	1f.75+1f.50 blue	8·25	31·00

1937. Dudelange Philatelic Exhibition. Sheet 125×85 mm. As No. 207 (pair) in new colour.

MS359 2f. (+3f.) brown	9·50	14·00

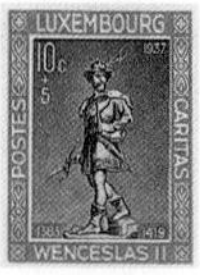

56 Wenceslas II

1937. Child Welfare.

360	**56**	10c.+5c. black and red	40	55
361	**56**	35c.+10c. green & purple	40	1·10
362	**56**	70c.+20c. red and blue	70	85
363	**56**	1f.+25c. red and green	4·25	25·00
364	**56**	1f.25+75c. purple & brn	5·50	25·00
365	**56**	1f.75+1f.50 blue & blk	8·25	28·00

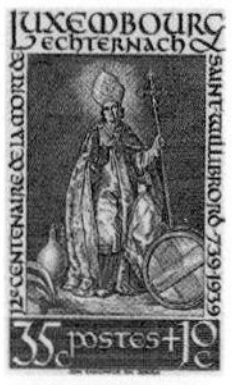
57 St. Willibrord

1938. Echternach Abbey Restoration Fund (1st issue). 1200th Death Anniv of St. Willibrord.

366	**57**	35c.+10c. green	55	85
367	-	70c.+10c. black	1·10	85
368	-	1f.25+25c. red	2·75	4·00
369	-	1f.75+50c. blue	5·50	4·50
370	-	3f.+2f. red	11·00	14·00
371	-	5f.+5f. violet	11·00	32·00

DESIGNS—As Type **57**: 70c. Town Hall, Echternach; 1f.25, Pavilion, Echternach Municipal Park. 31×51 mm: 1f.75, St. Willibrord (from miniature). 42×38 mm: 3f. Echternach Basilica; 5f. Whitsuntide dancing procession.
See also Nos. 492/7 and 569/70.

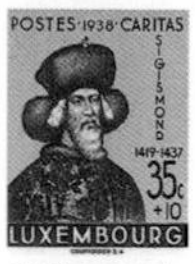

61 Sigismond of Luxembourg

1938. Child Welfare.

372	**61**	10c.+5c. black & mauve	30	55
373	**61**	35c.+10c. black & green	30	85
374	**61**	70c.+20c. black & brown	55	85
375	**61**	1f.+25c. black and red	4·50	22·00
376	**61**	1f.25+75c. black & grey	4·50	22·00
377	**61**	1f.75+1f.50 black & bl	14·00	33·00

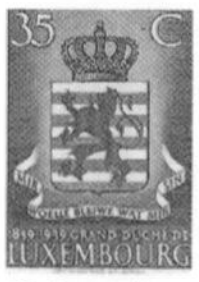
62 Arms of Luxembourg

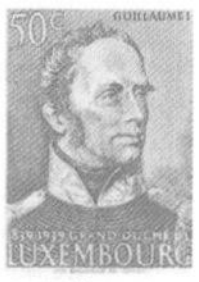
63 William I

1939. Centenary of Independence.

378	**62**	35c. green	30	55
379	**63**	50c. orange	30	55
380	-	70c. green	30	55
381	-	75c. olive	85	1·70
382	-	1f. red	1·70	2·75
383	-	1f.25 violet	30	1·10
384	-	1f.75 blue	30	1·10
385	-	3f. brown	45	1·70
386	-	5f. black	45	11·00
387	-	10f. red	1·70	17·00

PORTRAITS—As Type **63**: 70c. William II; 75c. William III; 1f. Prince Henry; 1f.25 Grand Duke Adolphe; 1f.75 William IV; 3f. Marie-Anne, wife of William IV; 5f. Grand Duchess Marie Adelaide; 10f. Grand Duchess Charlotte.

1939. Surch in figures.

388	**32**	30c. on 60c. green	30	2·20

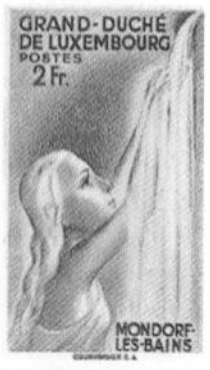

65 Allegory of Medicinal Spring

1939. Mondorf-les-Bains Propaganda.

389	**65**	2f. red	55	5·50

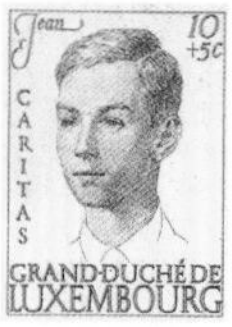

66 Prince Jean

1939. 20th Anniv of Reign and of Royal Wedding.

390	**66**	10c.+5c. brn on cream	30	55
391	-	35c.+10c. green on cream	55	1·70
392	-	70c.+20c. black on cream	1·70	2·20
393	**66**	1f.+25c. red on cream	5·50	50·00
394	-	1f.25+75c. violet on cream	8·25	80·00
395	-	1f.75+1f.50 blue on cream	11·00	£100

PORTRAITS: 35c., 1f.25, Prince Felix; 70c., 1f.75, Grand Duchess Charlotte.

1939. Twentieth Year of Reign of Grand Duchess Charlotte. Sheet 144×163 mm with designs as T **66** but without "CARITAS".

MS395a 2f. red (T **66**); 3f. green (Prince Felix); 5f. blue (Grand Duchess Charlotte)	80·00	£170

1940. Anti-T.B. Fund. Surch with Cross of Lorraine and premium.

396	**65**	2f.+50c. grey	2·75	31·00

1940–44. GERMAN OCCUPATION.

1940. T **94** of Germany optd Luxemburg.

397	**94**	3pf. brown	15	45
398	**94**	4pf. blue	15	55
399	**94**	5pf. green	15	55
400	**94**	6pf. green	15	45
401	**94**	8pf. red	15	45
402	**94**	10pf. brown	15	55
403	**94**	12pf. red	15	30
404	**94**	15pf. purple	45	85
405	**94**	20pf. blue	45	1·70
406	**94**	25pf. blue	55	1·70
407	**94**	30pf. green	55	1·10
408	**94**	40pf. mauve	55	1·70
409	**94**	50pf. black and green	55	2·20
410	**94**	60pf. black and purple	1·40	8·25
411	**94**	80pf. black and blue	5·50	31·00
412	**94**	100pf. black and yellow	2·00	8·25

1940. Types of Luxembourg surch.

413	**32**	3 Rpf. on 15c. black	15	85
414	**32**	4 Rpf. on 20c. orange	15	85
415	**32**	5 Rpf. on 35c. green	15	85
416	**32**	6 Rpf. on 10c. green	15	85
417	**32**	8 Rpf. on 25c. brown	15	85
418	**32**	10 Rpf. on 40c. brown	15	85
419	**32**	12 Rpf. on 60c. green	15	85
420	**32**	15 Rpf. on 1f. red	15	5·50
421	**32**	20 Rpf. on 50c. brown	15	1·70
422	**32**	25 Rpf. on 5c. mauve	1·40	5·50
423	**32**	30 Rpf. on 70c. violet	30	1·70
424	**32**	40 Rpf. on 75c. brown	30	1·70
425	**32**	50 Rpf. on 1¼f. green	30	1·70
426	**65**	60 Rpf. on 2f. red	4·25	35·00
427	**47**	80 Rpf. on 5f. green	85	5·50
428	**52**	100 Rpf. on 10f. green	85	5·50

1941. Nos. 739/47 of Germany optd Luxemburg.

429	3pf.+2pf. brown	55	1·10
430	4pf.+3pf. blue	55	1·10
431	5pf.+3pf. green	55	1·10
432	6pf.+4pf. green	55	1·10
433	8pf.+4pf. orange	55	1·10
434	12pf.+6pf. red	55	1·10
435	15pf.+10pf. purple	2·75	13·50
436	25pf.+15pf. blue	2·75	13·50
437	40pf.+35pf. purple	2·75	13·50

1944. INDEPENDENCE REGAINED.

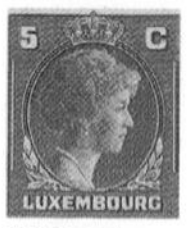

70 Grand Duchess Charlotte

1944

438	**70**	5c. brown	15	30
439	**70**	10c. slate	15	30
440	**70**	20c. orange	30	30
441	**70**	25c. brown	15	55
442	**70**	30c. red	55	5·50
443	**70**	35c. green	15	45
444	**70**	40c. blue	55	55
445	**70**	50c. violet	15	30
445a	**70**	60c. orange	4·00	30
446	**70**	70c. red	15	30
447	**70**	70c. green	1·10	1·70
448	**70**	75c. brown	55	45
449	**70**	1f. olive	15	30
450	**70**	1¼f. orange	15	75
451	**70**	1½f. orange	55	55
452	**70**	1¾f. blue	30	55
453	**70**	2f. red	5·50	55
454	**70**	2½f. mauve	8·25	7·25
455	**70**	3f. green	1·10	85
456	**70**	3½f. blue	1·10	1·10
457	**70**	5f. green	30	55
458	**70**	10f. red	30	2·20
459	**70**	20f. blue	85	28·00

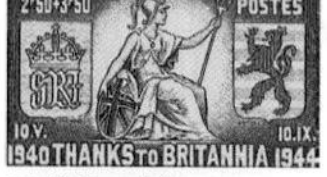

71 "Britannia"

1945. Liberation.

460	-	60c.+1f.40 green	45	30
461	-	1f.20+1f.80 red	45	30
462	**71**	2f.50+3f.50 blue	45	30
463	-	4f.20+4f.80 violet	45	30

DESIGNS: 60c. Ship symbol of Paris between Cross of Lorraine and Arms of Luxembourg; 1f.20, Man killing snake between Arms of Russia and Luxembourg; 4f.20, Eagle between Arms of U.S.A. and Luxembourg.

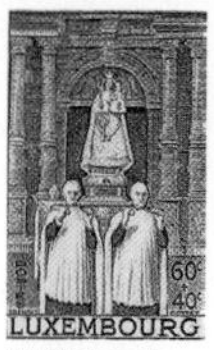

72 Statue of the Madonna in Procession

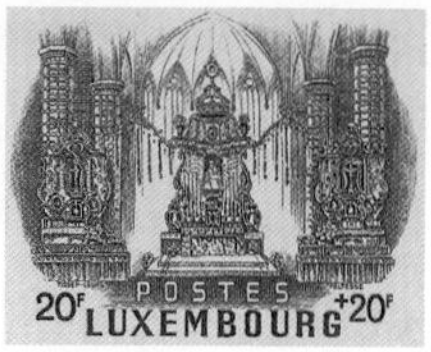

73 Altar and Shrine of the Madonna

1945. Our Lady of Luxembourg.

464	**72**	60c.+40c. green	40	3·75
465	-	1f.20+80c. red	45	3·75
466	-	2f.50+2f.50 blue	70	12·50
467	-	5f.50+6f.50 violet	2·00	£150
468	**73**	20f.+20f. brown	2·00	£150

MS468a 83×96 mm. 50f+50f. grey (as 1f.20)	2·50	55·00

DESIGNS: As Type **72**: 1f.20, The Madonna; 2f.50, The Madonna and Luxembourg; 5f.50, Portal of Notre Dame Cathedral.

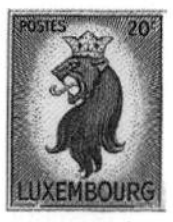

74 Lion of Luxembourg

1945

469	**74**	20c. black	40	25
470	**74**	30c. green	40	40
470a	**74**	60c. violet	40	25
471	**74**	75c. brown	40	25
472	**74**	1f.20 red	40	25
473	**74**	1f.50 violet	40	25
474	**74**	2f.50 blue	60	50

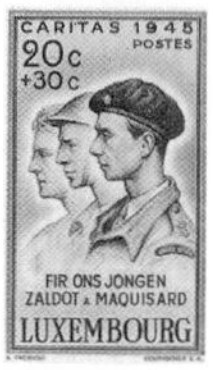

75 Members of the Maquis

1945. National War Victims Fund.

475	**75**	20c.+30c. green and buff	40	1·70
476	-	1f.50+1f. red and buff	45	1·70
477	-	3f.50+3f.50 blue & buff	85	16·00
478	-	5f.+10f. brown and buff	85	16·00

MS478a 100×110 mm. Designs and colours as Nos. 475/8 but values changed; 2f.50+2f.50, 3f.50+6f.50, 5f.+15f., 20f.+20f.	36·00	£450

DESIGNS: 1f.50, Mother and children; 3f.50, Political prisoner; 5f. Executed civilian.

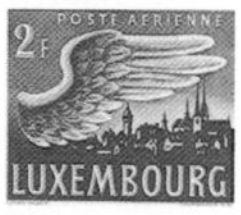

76

1946. Air.

479		1f. green and blue	45	25
480	**76**	2f. brown and yellow	45	35
481	-	3f. brown and yellow	45	35
482	-	4f. violet and grey	55	50
483	**76**	5f. purple and yellow	55	40
484	-	6f. purple and blue	55	65
485	-	10f. brown and yellow	2·10	65
486	**76**	20f. blue and grey	2·50	2·20
487	-	50f. green and light green	5·50	2·50

DESIGNS: 1, 4, 10f. Airplane wheel; 3, 6, 50f. Airplane engine and castle.

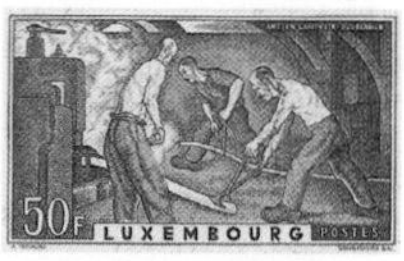

76a Old Rolling Mill, Dudelange

1946. National Stamp Exhibition, Dudelange. Sheet 100×80 mm.

MS487a **76a** 50f. (+5f.) blue on buff	22·00	55·00

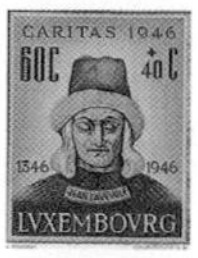

77 John the Blind, King of Bohemia

1946. 600th Death Anniv of John the Blind.

488	**77**	60c.+40c. green and grey	65	2·75
489	**77**	1f.50+50c. red and buff	75	4·25
490	**77**	3f.50+3f.50 blue & grey	3·00	44·00
491	**77**	5f.+10f. brown and grey	2·00	36·00

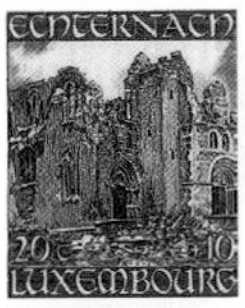

78 Exterior Ruins of St. Willibrord Basilica

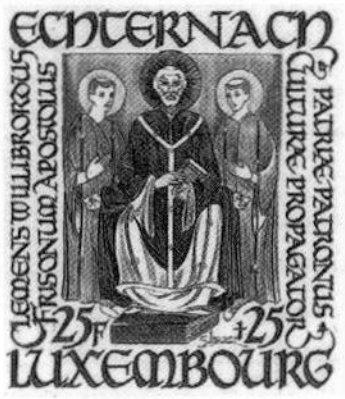

79 St. Willibrord

1947. Echternach Abbey Restoration (2nd issue). Inscr "ECHTERNACH".

492	**78**	20c.+10c. black	45	50
493	-	60c.+10c. green	80	1·00
494	-	75c.+25c. red	1·40	1·40
495	-	1f.50c.+50c. brown	1·70	1·40
496	-	3f.50c.+ 2f.50 blue	8·00	7·50
497	**79**	25f.+25f. purple	45·00	36·00

DESIGNS—As Type **78**: 60c. Statue of Abbot Bertels; 75c. Echternach Abbey emblem; 1f.50, Ruined interior of Basilica; 3f.50, St. Irmine and Pepin II carrying model of Abbey.

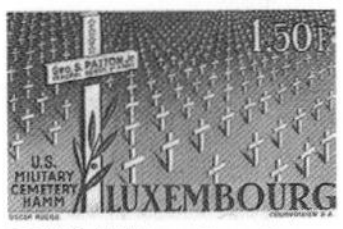

80 U.S. Military Cemetery, Hamm

1947. Honouring Gen. George S. Patton.

498	**80**	1f.50 red and buff	85	40
499	-	3f.50 blue and buff	4·25	3·75
500	**80**	5f. green and grey	4·25	4·25
501	-	10f. purple and grey	16·00	60·00

PORTRAIT: 3f.50, 10f. Gen. G. S. Patton.

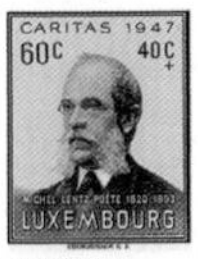

82 Michel Lentz (national poet)

1947. National Welfare Fund.

502	**82**	60c.+40c. brown & buff	1·10	1·70
503	**82**	1f.50+50c. pur & buff	1·70	1·70
504	**82**	3f.50+3f.50 blue & grey	10·00	29·00
505	**82**	10f.+5f. green and grey	8·25	29·00

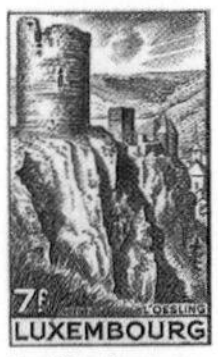

83 L'Oesling

1948. Tourist Propaganda.

505a	-	2f.50 brown and chocolate	2·75	80
505b	-	3f. violet	10·00	1·70
505c	-	4f. blue	8·00	1·70
506	**83**	7f. brown	28·00	1·10
507	-	10f. green	4·50	40
508	-	15f. red	4·50	1·10
509	-	20f. blue	4·50	1·10

DESIGNS—HORIZ: 2f.50, Television transmitter, Dudelange; 3f. Radio Luxembourg; 4f. Victor Hugo's house, Vianden; 10f. River Moselle; 15f. Mining district. VERT: 20f. Luxembourg.

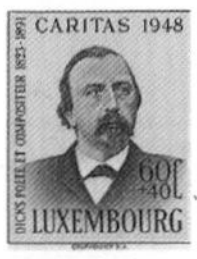

85 "Dicks" (Edmund de la Fontaine)

1948. National Welfare Fund.

510	**85**	60c.+40c. brown & bistre	85	1·40
511	**85**	1f.50+50c. red and pink	1·10	1·40
512	**85**	3f.50+3f.50 blue & grey	14·50	31·00
513	**85**	10f.+5f. green and grey	13·00	31·00

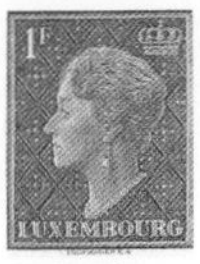

86 Grand Duchess Charlotte

1948

513a	**86**	5c. orange	55	30
513b	**86**	10c. blue	55	30
514	**86**	15c. olive	55	30
514a	**86**	20c. purple	55	30
515	**86**	25c. grey	55	30
515a	**86**	30c. olive	55	30
515b	**86**	40c. red	55	85
515c	**86**	50c. orange	85	30
516	**86**	60c. bistre	55	30
517	**86**	80c. green	55	30
518	**86**	1f. red	1·70	30
518a	**86**	1f.20 black	1·70	45
518b	**86**	1f.25 brown	1·70	55
519	**86**	1f.50 turquoise	1·70	30
520	**86**	1f.60 grey	2·20	2·20
521	**86**	2f. purple	1·70	30
521a	**86**	2f.50 red	2·75	30
521b	**86**	3f. blue	20·00	55
521c	**86**	3f.50 red	6·75	85
522	**86**	4f. blue	6·75	85
522a	**86**	5f. violet	16·00	1·10
523	**86**	6f. purple	14·00	1·10
524	**86**	8f. green	11·00	2·20

1949. 30th Year of Reign of Grand Duchess Charlotte. Sheet 110×75 mm.

MS524a **86** 8f.+3f. blue; 12f.+5f. green; 15f.+7f. brown £180 55·00

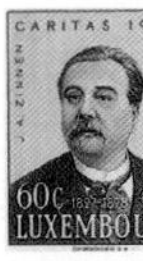

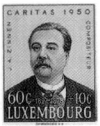

90 J. A. Zinnen (composer)

1950. National Welfare Week.

539	**90**	60c.+10c. violet and grey	1·00	55
540	**90**	2f.+15c. red and buff	1·00	70
541	**90**	4f.+15c. blue and grey	10·50	10·50
542	**90**	8f.+5f. brown and buff	33·00	42·00

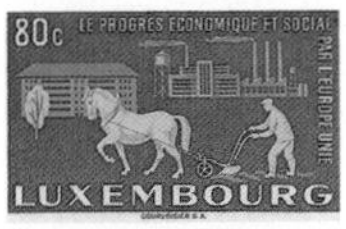

91 Ploughman and Factories

1951. To Promote United Europe.

543	**91**	80c. green and light green	21·00	15·00
544	-	1f. violet and light violet	14·50	95
545	-	2f. brown and grey	50·00	95
546	**91**	2f.50 red and orange	50·00	28·00
547	-	3f. brown and yellow	80·00	37·00
548	-	4f. blue and light blue	£120	60·00

DESIGNS: 1, 3f. Map, people and "Rights of Man" Charter; 2, 4f. Scales balancing "United Europe" and "Peace".

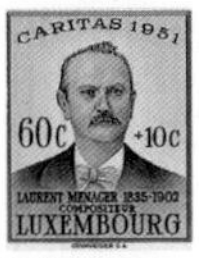

92 L. Menager (composer)

1951. National Welfare Fund.

549	**92**	60c.+10c. black and grey	85	55
550	**92**	2f.+15c. green and grey	85	55
551	**92**	4f.+15c. blue and grey	8·25	7·00
552	**92**	8f.+5f. purple and grey	39·00	50·00

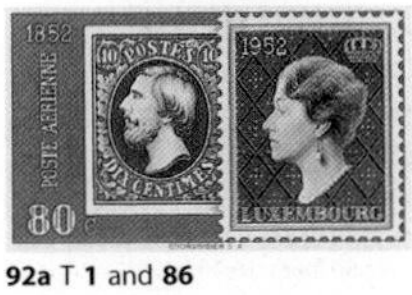

92a T **1** and **86**

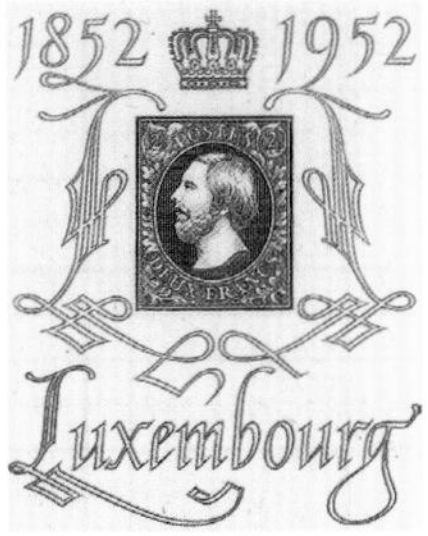

92b T **1**

1952. National Philatelic Exhibition ("CENTILUX") and Stamp Centenary.

552f	**92b**	2f. blk & grn (postage)	55·00	50·00
552g	**92b**	4f. red and green	55·00	50·00
552a	**92a**	80c. black, pur & grn (air)	90	85
552b	**92a**	2f.50 black, purple & red	2·30	2·20
552c	**92a**	4f. black, purple and blue	5·50	5·50
552d	**92a**	8f. black, purple and red	70·00	80·00
552e	**92a**	10f. black, purple & brn	55·00	65·00

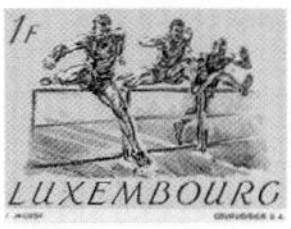

93 Hurdling

1952. 15th Olympic Games, Helsinki.

553	**93**	1f. black and green	95	85
554	-	2f. blk & lt brn (Football)	4·25	85
555	-	2f.50 blk & pink (Boxing)	5·50	2·20
556	-	3f. blk & drab (Water polo)	7·25	2·50
557	-	4f. black and blue (Cycling)	35·00	11·00
558	-	8f. black and lilac (Fencing)	22·00	5·00

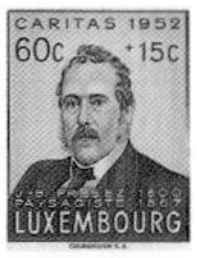

94 J. B. Fresez (painter)

1952. National Welfare Fund.

559	**94**	60c.+15c. green and blue	85	55
560	**94**	2f.+25c. brown & orange	85	55
561	**94**	4f.+25c. violet and grey	6·25	5·50
562	**94**	8f.+4f.75 purple & lt pur	45·00	55·00

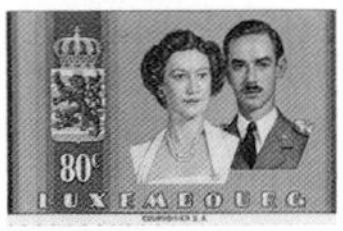

95 Prince Jean and Princess Josephine Charlotte

1953. Royal Wedding.

563	**95**	80c. violet and deep mauve	1·10	55
564	**95**	1f.20 deep brown & brown	1·10	55
565	**95**	2f. deep green and green	2·75	55
566	**95**	3f. deep purple and purple	2·75	95
567	**95**	4f. deep blue and blue	13·50	2·00
568	**95**	9f. brown and red	13·50	2·00

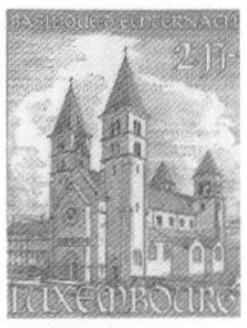

96 Echternach Basilica

1953. Echternach Abbey Restoration (3rd issue).

569	**96**	2f. red	5·50	55
570	-	2f.50 olive	8·25	8·25

DESIGN: 2f.50, Interior of Basilica.

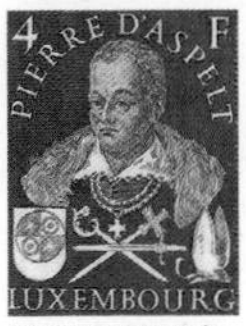

97 Pierre D'Aspelt

1953. Seventh Birth Centenary of Pierre D'Aspelt.

571	**97**	4f. black	13·00	7·25

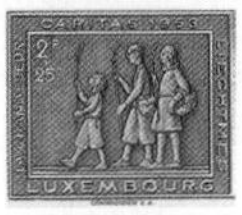

98 "Candlemas Singing"

1953. National Welfare Fund.

572	**98**	25c.+15c. carmine and red	85	55
573	-	80c.+20c. blue and brown	85	55
574	-	1f.20+30c. green & turq	1·70	1·30
575	**98**	2f.+25c. brown and red	1·70	55
576	-	4f.+50c. blue & turquoise	12·50	12·50
577	-	7f.+3f.35 lilac and violet	29·00	31·00

DESIGNS: 80c., 4f. "The Rattles"; 1f.20, 7f. "The Easter-eggs".

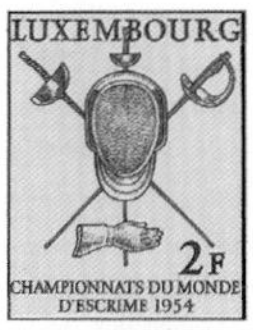

99 Foils, Mask and Gauntlet

1954. World Fencing Championships.

578	**99**	2f. deep brown and brown on cream	8·00	1·70

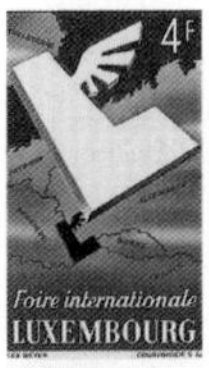

100 Fair Emblem

1954. Luxembourg International Fair.

579	**100**	4f. multicoloured	16·00	8·00

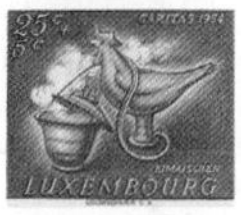

101 Earthenware Whistle

1954. National Welfare Fund.

580	**101**	25c.+5c. red and orange	95	75
581	-	80c.+20c. grey & black	95	75
582	-	1f.20+30c. green and cream	2·20	2·30
583	**101**	2f.+25c. brown and buff	1·10	85
584	-	4f.+50c. dp blue & blue	10·00	10·50
585	-	7f.+3f.45 violet & mve	32·00	39·00

DESIGNS: 80c., 4f. Sheep and drum; 1f.20, 7f. Merry-go-round horses.

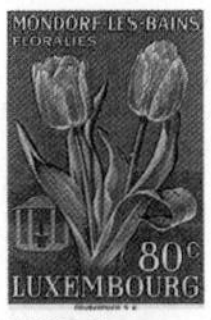

102 Tulips

1955. Mondorf-les-Bains Flower Show.

586	**102**	80c. red, green and brown	40	40
587	-	2f. yellow, green and red	45	45
588	-	3f. purple, green & emer	5·25	5·00
589	-	4f. orange, green and blue	7·25	7·25

FLOWERS: 2f. Daffodils; 3f. Hyacinths; 4f. Parrot tulips.

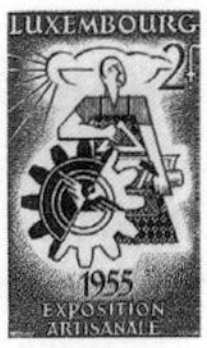

103

1955. First National Crafts Exhibition.

590	**103**	2f. black and grey	2·20	55

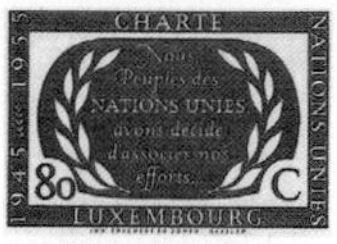

104 "Charter"

1955. 10th Anniv of U.N.

591	**104**	80c. blue and black	1·00	1·00
592	-	2f. brown and red	7·75	55
593	-	4f. red and blue	6·50	5·50
594	-	9f. green and brown	3·00	1·50

SYMBOLIC DESIGNS: 2f. "Security"; 4f. "Justice"; 9f. "Assistance".

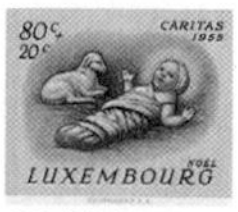

105 "Christmas Day"

1955. National Welfare Fund.

595		25c.+5c. red and pink	55	55
596	**105**	80c.+20c. black and grey	55	55
597	-	1f.20+30c. deep green and green	1·10	1·40
598	-	2f.+25c. deep brown and brown	85	55
599	**105**	4f.+50c. blue & lt blue	9·75	16·00
600	-	7f.+3f.45 purple & mve	22·00	23·00

ALLEGORICAL DESIGNS: 25c., 2f. "St. Nicholas's Day"; 1f.20, 7f. "Twelfth Night".

1956. Mondorf-les-Bains Flower Show. As T **102** but inscription at top in one line. Multicoloured.

601	2f. Anemones	1·10	55
602	3f. Crocuses	4·00	3·75

1956. Roses. As T **102** but inscr at top "LUXEMBOURG-VILLE DES ROSES". Multicoloured.

603	2f.50 Yellow roses	7·75	7·00
604	4f. Red roses	4·00	3·75

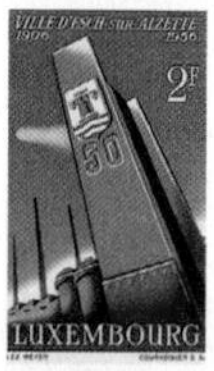

108 Steel Plant and Girder

1956. 50th Anniv of Esch-sur-Alzette.

605	**108**	2f. red, black & turquoise	4·50	90

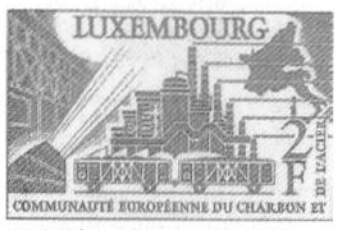

109 Blast Furnaces and Map

1956. European Coal and Steel Community. Inscr as in T **109**.

606	**109**	2f. red	39·00	55
607	-	3f. blue	39·00	32·00
608	-	4f. green	7·50	6·50

DESIGNS—VERT: 3f. Girder supporting City of Luxembourg. HORIZ: 4f. Chain and miner's lamp.

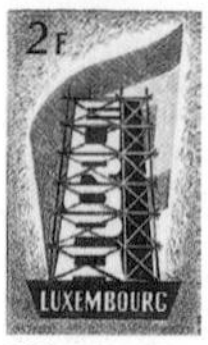

110

1956. Europa.

609	**110**	2f. black and brown	£325	85
610	**110**	3f. red and orange	£130	85·00
611	**110**	4f. deep blue and blue	11·00	7·00

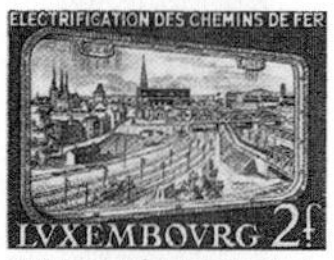

111 Luxembourg Central Station

1956. Electrification of Luxembourg Railways.

612	**111**	2f. sepia and black	4·50	90

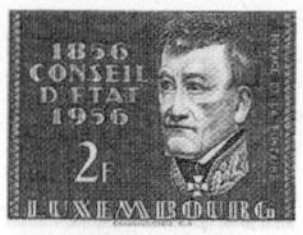

112 I. de la Fontaine

1956. Council of State Centenary. Inscr as in T **112**.

613	**112**	2f. sepia	2·20	55
614	-	7f. purple	4·00	1·10

DESIGN: 7f. Grand Duchess Charlotte.

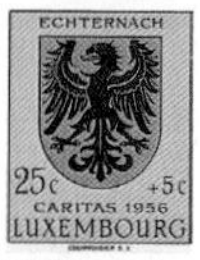

113 Arms of Echternach

1956. National Welfare Fund. Inscr "CARITAS 1956". Arms. Multicoloured.

615	25c.+5c. Type **113**	55	55
616	80c.+20c. Esch-sur-Alzette	55	55
617	1f.20+30c. Grevenmacher	85	1·10
618	2f.+25c. Type **113**	85	55
619	4f.+50c. Esch-sur-Alzette	7·00	7·25
620	7f.+3f.45 Grevenmacher	12·50	18·00

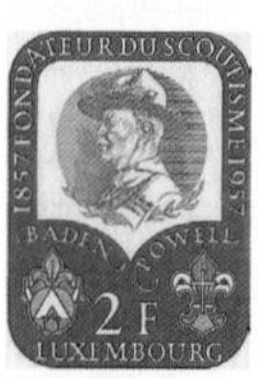

114 Lord Baden-Powell and Scout Emblems

1957. Birth Centenary of Lord Baden-Powell, and 50th Anniv of Scouting Movement.

621	**114**	2f. brown and green	1·80	50
622	-	2f.50 red and violet	3·75	3·00

DESIGN: 2f.50, as Type **114** but showing Girl Guide emblems.

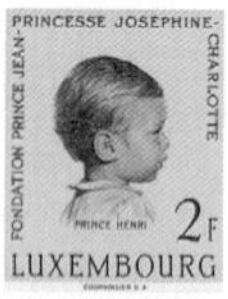

115 Prince Henri

1957. "Prince Jean and Princess Josephine-Charlotte Foundation" Child Welfare Clinic.

623	**115**	2f. deep brown and brown	1·40	40
624	-	3f. deep green and green	6·00	6·00
625	-	4f. deep blue and blue	3·75	4·25

DESIGNS—HORIZ: 3f. Children's Clinic Project. VERT: 4f. Princess Marie-Astrid.

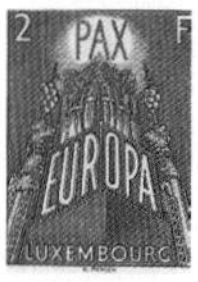

116 "Peace"

1957. Europa.

626	**116**	2f. brown	8·25	4·50
627	**116**	3f. red	£120	29·00
628	**116**	4f. purple	£110	28·00

1957. National Welfare Fund. Arms as T **113** inscr "CARITAS 1957". Multicoloured.

629	25c.+5c. Luxembourg	55	55
630	80c.+20c. Mersch	55	55
631	1f.20+30c. Vianden	85	95
632	2f.+25c. Luxembourg	55	55
633	4f.+50c. Mersch	7·00	7·75
634	7f.+3f.45 Vianden	8·25	11·50

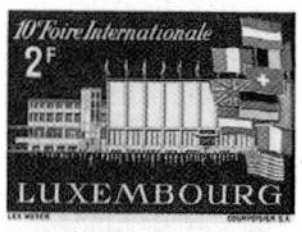

117 Fair Entrance and Flags

1958. Tenth Anniv of Luxembourg Int Fair.

635	**117**	2f. multicoloured	55	40

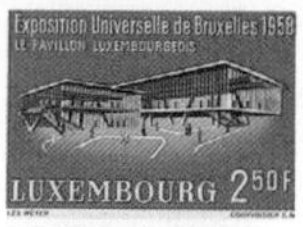

118 Luxembourg Pavilion

1958. Brussels Exhibition.

636	**118**	2f.50 blue and red	55	40

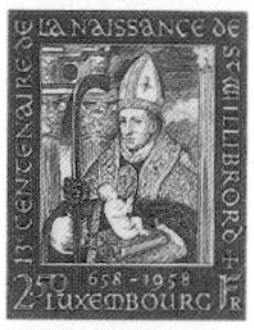

119 St. Willibrord holding Child (after Puseel)

1958. 1300th Birth Anniv of St. Willibrord.

637	-	1f. red	55	45
638	**119**	2f.50 sepia	55	30
639	-	5f. blue	1·50	1·00

DESIGNS: 1f. St. Willibrord and St. Irmina holding inscribed plaque; 5f. St. Willibrord and suppliant. (Miracle of the wine-cask).

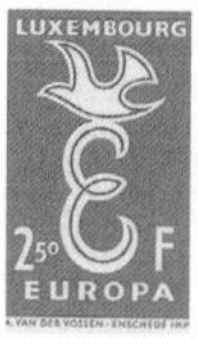

119a Europa

1958. Europa.

640	**119a**	2f.50 blue and red	55	25
641	**119a**	3f.50 brown and green	1·10	55
642	**119a**	5f. red and blue	2·00	1·10

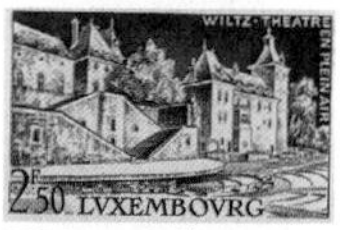

120 Open-air Theatre at Wiltz

1958. Wiltz Open-air Theatre Commemoration.

643	**120**	2f.50 sepia and grey	85	30

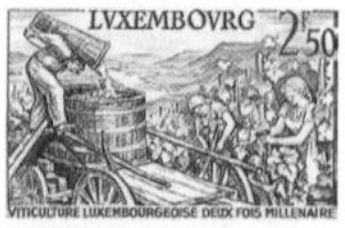

121 Vineyard

1958. Bimillenary of Moselle Wine Industry.

644	**121**	2f.50 brown and green	85	30

1958. National Welfare Fund. Arms as T **113** inscr "CARITAS 1958". Multicoloured.

645	30c.+10c. Capellen	55	55
646	1f.+25c. Diekirch	55	55
647	1f.50+25c. Redange	85	70
648	2f.50+50c. Capellen	55	55
649	5f.+50c. Diekirch	7·00	7·50
650	8f.50+4f.60 Redange	7·75	11·50

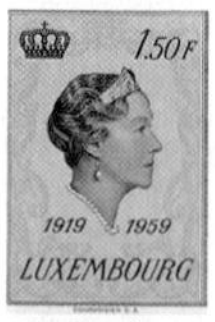

122 Grand Duchess Charlotte

1959. 40th Anniv of Accession of Grand Duchess Charlotte.

651	**122**	1f.50 deep green & green	1·40	70
652	**122**	2f.50 brown & lt brown	1·40	70
653	**122**	5f. lt blue and ultramarine	2·75	2·00

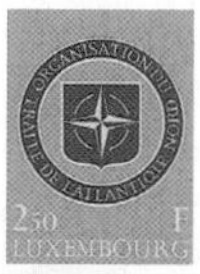

123 N.A.T.O. Emblem

1959. Tenth Anniv of N.A.T.O.

654	**123**	2f.50 blue and olive	25	25
655	**123**	8f.50 blue and brown	75	70

1959. Mondorf-les-Bains Flower Show. As T **102** but inscr "1959".

656	1f. violet, yellow and turquoise	55	45
657	2f.50 red, green and blue	70	50
658	3f. blue, green and purple	1·00	95

FLOWERS: 1f. Iris; 2f.50, Peony; 3f. Hortensia.

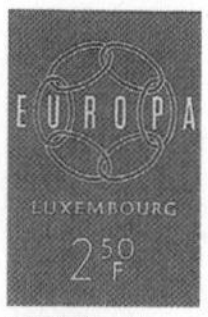

123a Europa

1959. Europa.

659	**123a**	2f.50 green	2·20	30
660	**123a**	5f. blue	4·00	1·70

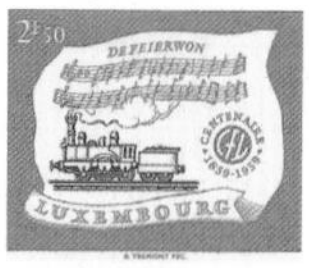

124 Steam Locomotive and First Bars of Hymn "De Feierwon"

1959. Railways Centenary.

661	**124**	2f.50 blue and red	2·75	55

1959. National Welfare Fund. Arms as T **113** inscr "CARITAS 1959". Multicoloured.

662	30c.+10c. Clervaux	55	45
663	1f.+25c. Remich	55	45
664	1f.50+25c. Wiltz	85	85
665	2f.50+50c. Clervaux	55	45
666	5f.+50c. Remich	2·20	3·00
667	8f.50+4f.60 Wiltz	10·50	17·00

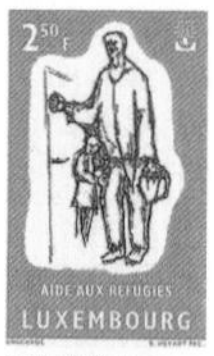

125 Refugees seeking Shelter

1960. World Refugee Year.

668	**125**	2f.50 blue and salmon	40	30
669	-	5f. blue and violet	55	55

DESIGN—HORIZ: 5f. "The Flight into Egypt" (Biblical scene).

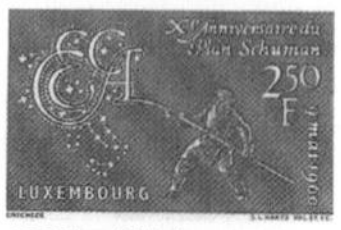

126 Steel Worker

1960. Tenth Anniv of Schuman Plan.

670	**126**	2f.50 lake	55	30

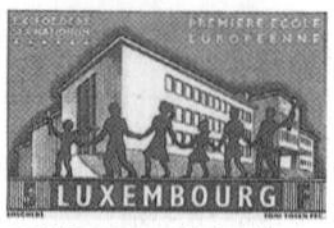

127 European School, Luxembourg

1960. European School Commemoration.

671	**127**	5f. black and blue	1·50	1·40

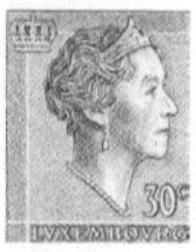

128 Grand Duchess Charlotte

1960

672	**128**	10c. red	40	25
673	**128**	20c. red	40	25
673a	**128**	25c. orange	40	25
674	**128**	30c. drab	35	25
675	**128**	50c. green	90	25
676	**128**	1f. violet	90	25
677	**128**	1f.50 mauve	90	25
678	**128**	2f. turquoise	1·30	25
679	**128**	2f.50 purple	1·80	25
680	**128**	3f. dull purple	4·50	25
680a	**128**	3f.50 turquoise	6·25	1·80
681	**128**	5f. brown	3·25	25
681a	**128**	6f. turquoise	5·25	25

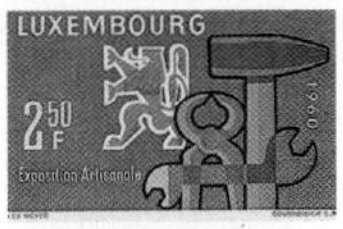

129 Heraldic Lion, and Tools

1960. Second National Crafts Exhibition.

682	**129**	2f.50 multicoloured	2·20	55

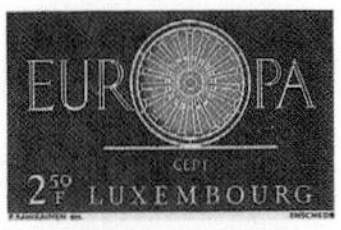

129a Conference Emblem

1960. Europa.

683	**129a**	2f.50 green and black	1·70	30
684	**129a**	5f. black and red	2·20	55

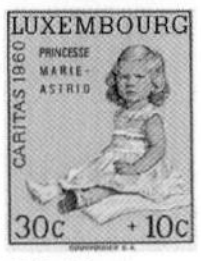

130 Princess Marie-Astrid

1960. National Welfare Fund. Inscr "CARITAS 1960". Centres and inscr in sepia.

685	**130**	30c.+10c. blue	45	40
686	-	1f.+25c. pink	45	40
687	-	1f.50+25c. turquoise	95	95
688	**130**	2f.50+50c. yellow	85	70
689	-	5f.+50c. lilac	1·50	4·25
690	-	8f.50+4f.60 sage	14·50	19·00

DESIGNS: Princess Marie-Astrid standing (1, 5f.), sitting with book on lap (1f.50, 8f.50).

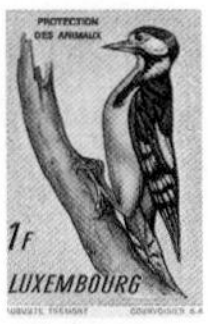

131 Great Spotted Woodpecker

1961. Animal Protection Campaign. Inscr "PROTECTION DES ANIMAUX".

691	**131**	1f. multicoloured	40	30
692	-	1f.50 buff, blue and black	45	45
693	-	3f. brown, buff and violet	55	50
694	-	8f.50 multicoloured	1·10	1·00

DESIGNS—VERT: 8f.50, Dachshund. HORIZ: 1f.50, Cat; 3f. Horse.

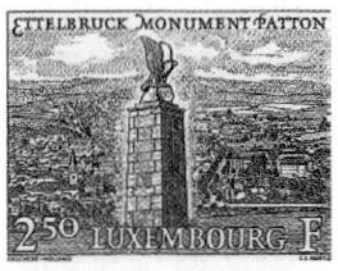

132 Patton Monument, Ettelbruck

1961. Tourist Publicity.

695	**132**	2f.50 blue and black	95	35
696	-	2f.50 green	95	35

DESIGN—VERT: No. 696, Clervaux.

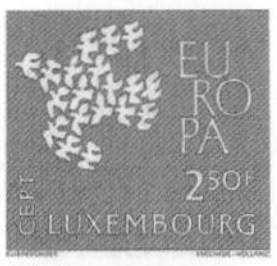

133 Doves

1961. Europa.

697	**133**	2f.50 red	55	30
698	**133**	5f. blue	85	35

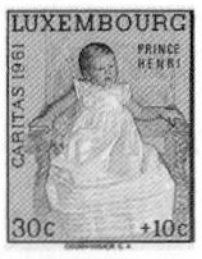

134 Prince Henri

1961. National Welfare Fund. Inscr "CARITAS 1961". Centres and inscr in sepia.

699	**134**	30c.+10c. mauve	70	55
700	-	1f.+25c. lavender	70	55
701	-	1f.50+25c. salmon	1·00	85
702	**134**	2f.50+50c. green	1·00	55
703	-	5f.+50c. yellow	5·00	4·75
704	-	8f.50+4f.60 grey	7·50	12·00

DESIGNS: Prince Henri when young boy (1, 5f.); youth in formal dress (1f.50, 8f.50).

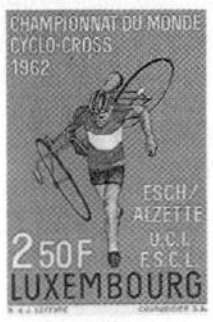

135 Cyclist carrying Cycle

1962. World Cross-country Cycling Championships, Esch-sur-Alzette.

705	**135**	2f.50 multicoloured	40	25
706	-	5f. multicoloured (Emblem)	50	55

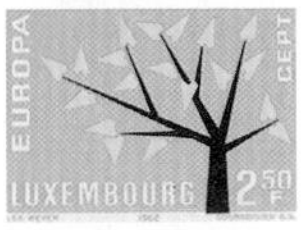

136 Europa "Tree"

1962. Europa.

707	**136**	2f.50 multicoloured	85	30
708	**136**	5f. brown, green & purple	1·10	55

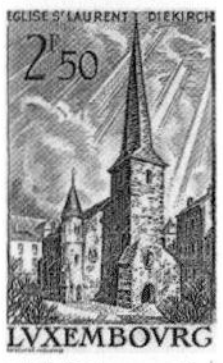

137 St. Laurent's Church, Diekirch

1962

709	**137**	2f.50 black and brown	75	35

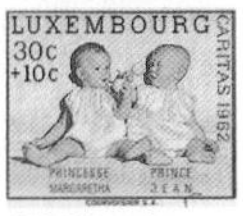

138 Prince Jean and Princess Margaretha as Babies

1962. National Welfare Fund. inscr "CARITAS 1962". Centres and inscr in sepia.

710	**138**	30c.+10c. buff	40	40
711	-	1f.+25c. blue	40	40
712	-	1f.50+25c. olive	85	55
713	-	2f.50+50c. pink	85	40
714	-	5f.+50c. green	2·50	4·00
715	-	8f.50+4f.60 violet	6·50	7·50

PORTRAITS—VERT: 1f., 2f.50, Prince Jean and: 2f.50, 5f. Princess Margaretha, at various stages of childhood. HORIZ: 8f.50, The Royal Children.

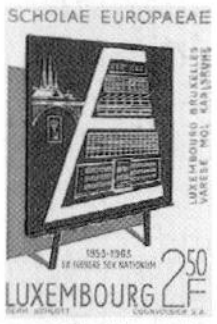

139 Blackboard

1963. Tenth Anniv of European Schools.

716	**139**	2f.50 green, red and grey	45	30

140 Benedictine Abbey, Munster

1963. Millenary of City of Luxembourg and International Philatelic Exhibition. (a) Horiz views.

717	-	1f. blue	60	30
718	**140**	1f.50 red	60	30
719	-	2f.50 green	60	30
720	-	3f. brown	60	30
721	-	5f. violet	1·00	65
722	-	11f. blue	2·75	2·40

VIEWS: 1f. Bock Rock; 2f.50, Rham Towers; 3f. Grand Ducal Palace; 5f. Castle Bridge; 11f. Millenary Buildings.

(b) Vert multicoloured designs.

723		1f. "Three Towers" Gate	60	40
724		1f.50 Great Seal	60	40
725		2f.50 "The Black Virgin" (statue), St. John's Church	60	40
726		3f. Citadel	75	40
727		5f. Town Hall	75	55

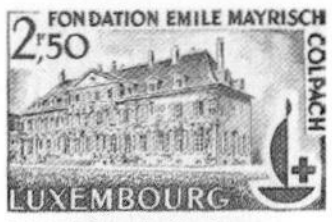

141 Colpach Castle

1963. Red Cross Centenary.

728	**141**	2f.50 red and slate	50	30

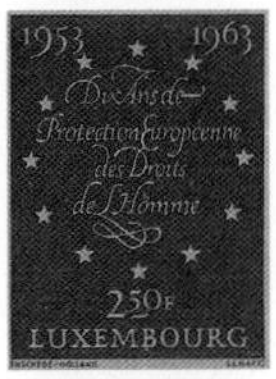

142 "Human Rights"

1963. Tenth Anniv of European "Human Rights" Convention.

729	**142**	2f.50 blue on gold	40	30

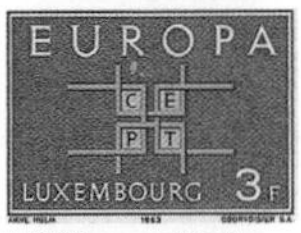

143 "Co-operation"

1963. Europa.

730	**143**	3f. green, orange & turq	85	30
731	**143**	6f. orange, red and brown	1·70	65

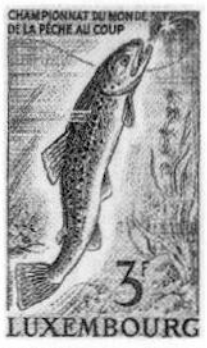

144 Brown trout snapping Bait

1963. World Fishing Championships, Wormeldange.

732	**144**	3f. slate	45	30

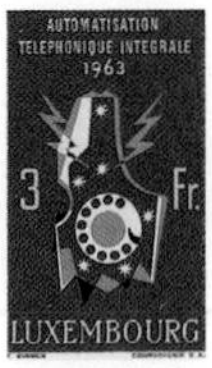

145 Telephone Dial

1963. Inauguration of Automatic Telephone System.

733	**145**	3f. green, black and blue	45	30

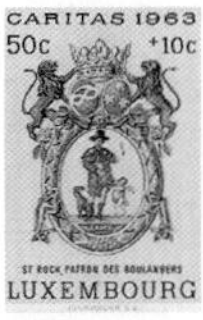

146 St. Roch (patron saint of bakers)

1963. National Welfare Fund. Patron Saints of Crafts and Guilds. Inscr "CARITAS 1963". Multicoloured.

734	50c.+10c. Type **146**	35	25
735	1f.+25c. St. Anne (tailors)	35	25
736	2f.+25c. St. Eloi (smiths)	35	40
737	3f.+50c. St. Michel (haberdashers)	40	25
738	6f.+50c. St. Barthelemy (butchers)	1·70	2·50
739	10f.+5f.90 St. Thibaut (seven crafts)	2·50	4·50

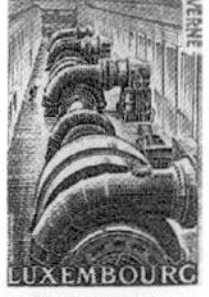

147 Power House

1964. Inauguration of Vianden Reservoir.

740	**147**	2f. blue, brown and red	30	30
741	-	3f. blue, turq & red	30	30
742	-	6f. brown, blue and green	40	40

DESIGNS—HORIZ: 3f. Upper reservoir. VERT: 6f. Lohmuhle Dam.

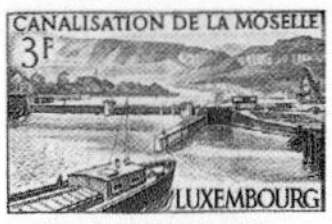

148 Barge entering Canal

1964. Inauguration of Moselle Canal.

743	**148**	3f. indigo and blue	45	30

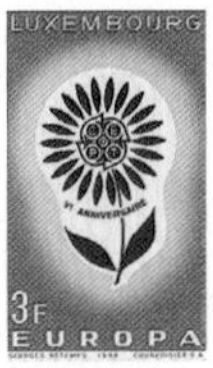

149 Europa "Flower"

1964. Europa.

744	**149**	3f. blue, brown and cream	85	30
745	**149**	6f. sepia, green and yellow	1·70	55

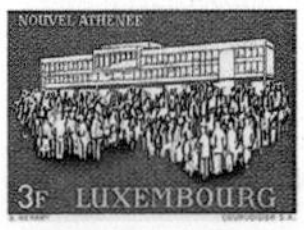

150 Students thronging "New Athenaeum"

1964. Opening of "New Athenaeum" (education centre).

746	**150**	3f. black and green	45	35

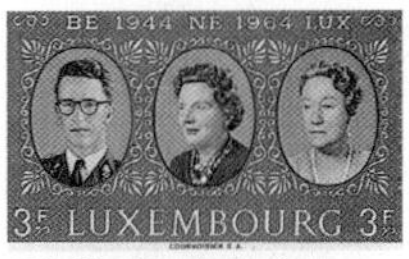

150a King Baudouin, Queen Juliana and Grand Duchess Charlotte

1964. 20th Anniv of "BENELUX".

747	**150a**	3f. brown, yellow & blue	45	30

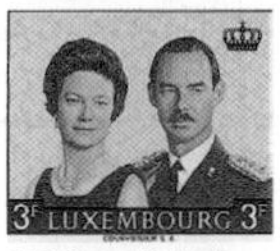

151 Grand Duke Jean and Princess Josephine-Charlotte

1964. Accession of Grand Duke Jean.

748	**151**	3f. deep blue and light blue	40	25
749	**151**	6f. sepia and light brown	55	40

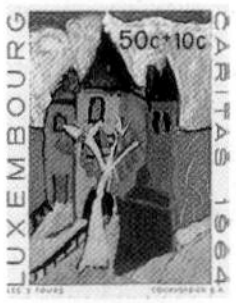

152 Three Towers

1964. National Welfare Fund. Inscr "CARITAS 1964". Multicoloured.

750	50c.+10c. Type **152**	25	25
751	1f.+25c. Grand Duke Adolphe Bridge	25	25
752	2f.+25c. Lower Town	25	25
753	3f.+50c. Type **152**	25	25
754	6f.+50c. Grand Duke Adolphe Bridge	1·50	2·50
755	10f.+5f.90 Lower Town	2·10	3·75

153 Rotary Emblem and Cogwheels

1965. 60th Anniv of Rotary International.

756	**153**	3f. multicoloured	45	30

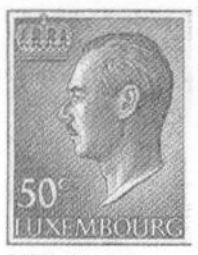

154 Grand Duke Jean

1965

757	**154**	25c. brown	55	10
758	**154**	50c. red	55	10
759	**154**	1f. blue	85	10
760	**154**	1f.50 purple	85	10
761	**154**	2f. red	1·10	10
762	**154**	2f.50 orange	1·10	45
763	**154**	3f. green	1·10	10
763b	**154**	3f.50 brown	1·70	75
764a	**154**	4f. purple	1·70	15
764ba	**154**	5f. green	1·70	10
765	**154**	6f. lilac	1·70	10
765b	**154**	7f. orange	1·10	55
765c	**154**	8f. blue	2·20	30
766	**154**	9f. green	2·20	30
766a	**154**	10f. black	2·20	20
767	**154**	12f. red	2·75	30
767a	**154**	14f. blue	2·20	85
767b	**154**	16f. green	2·20	55
767c	**154**	18f. green	2·00	85
767d	**154**	20f. blue	2·75	30
767e	**154**	22f. brown	2·20	1·70

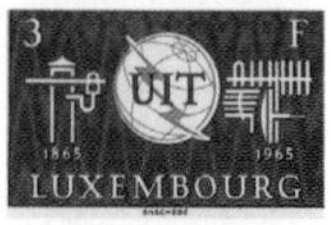

155 I.T.U. Emblem and Symbols

1965. Centenary of I.T.U.

768	**155**	3f. blue, lake and violet	45	30

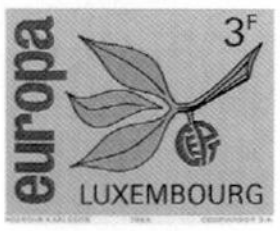

156 Europa "Sprig"

1965. Europa.

769	**156**	3f. turquoise, red and black	85	30
770	**156**	6f. brown, blue and green	1·70	55

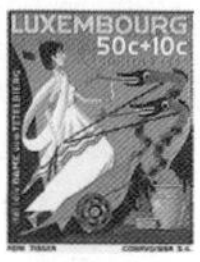

157 "The Roman Lady of the Titelberg"

1965. National Welfare Fund. Fairy Tales. Inscr "CARITAS 1965". Multicoloured.

771	50c.+10c. Type **157**	15	25
772	1f.+25c. "Schappchen, the Huntsman"	15	25
773	2f.+25c. "The Witch of Koerich"	25	25
774	3f.+50c. "The Goblins of Schoendels"	25	30
775	6f.+50c. "Tollchen, Watchman of Hesperange"	55	1·70
776	10f.+5f.90 "The Old Spinster of Heispelt"	1·80	4·25

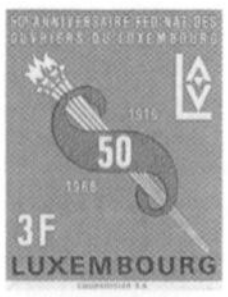

158 "Flag" and Torch

1966. 50th Anniv of Luxembourg Workers' Union.

777	**158**	3f. red and grey	45	45

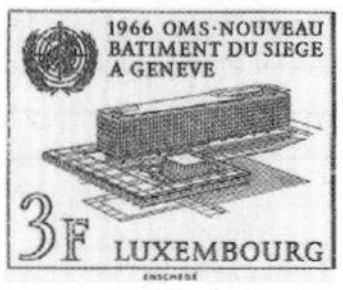

159 W.H.O. Building

1966. Inauguration of W.H.O. Headquarters, Geneva.

778	**159**	3f. green	45	45

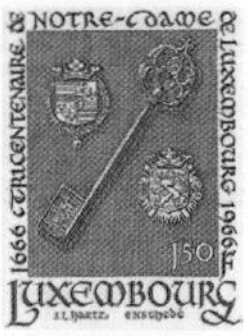

160 Golden Key

1966. Tercentenary of Solemn Promise to Our Lady of Luxembourg.

779	**160**	1f.50 green	30	25
780	-	2f. red	30	25
781	-	3f. blue	30	25
782	-	6f. brown	50	45

DESIGNS: 2f. Interior of Luxembourg Cathedral (after painting by J. Martin); 3f. Our Lady of Luxembourg (after engraving by R. Collin); 6f. Gallery pillar, Luxembourg Cathedral (after sculpture by D. Muller).

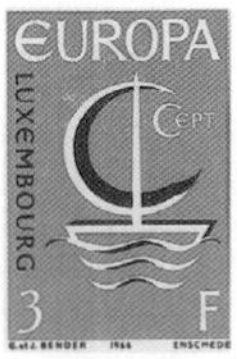

161 Europa "Ship"

1966. Europa.

783	**161**	3f. blue and grey	85	30
784	**161**	6f. green and brown	1·70	55

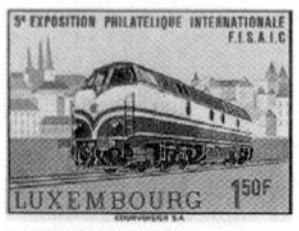

162 Class 1800 Diesel-electric Locomotive

1966. Luxembourg Railwaymen's Philatelic Exhibition. Multicoloured.

785	1f.50 Type **162**	90	25
786	3f. Class 3600 electric locomotive	90	40

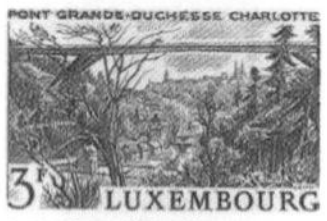

163 Grand Duchess Charlotte Bridge

1966. Tourism.

787	**163**	3f. lake	30	30

See also Nos. 807/8, 828 and 844/5.

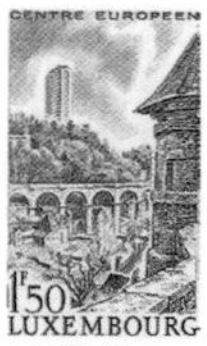

164 Kirchberg Building and Railway Viaduct

1966. "Luxembourg-European Centre".

788	**164**	1f.50 green	25	25
789	-	13f. blue (Robert Schuman monument)	85	40

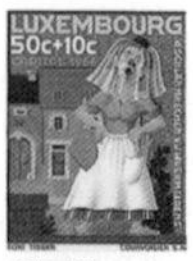

165 "Mary, Veiled Matron of Wormeldange"

1966. National Welfare Fund. Luxembourg Fairy Tales. Multicoloured.

790	50c.+10c. Type **165**	20	25
791	1f.50+25c. "Jekel Warden of the Wark"	20	25
792	2f.+25c. "The Black Gentleman of Vianden"	20	40
793	3f.+50c. "The Gracious Fairy of Rosport"	30	25
794	6f.+1f. "The Friendly Shepherd of Donkolz"	85	1·40
795	13f.+6f.90 "The Little Sisters of Trois-Vierges"	1·10	3·50

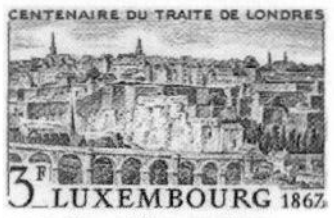

166 City of Luxembourg, 1850 (after engraving by N. Liez)

1967. Centenary of Treaty of London.

796	**166**	3f. brown, blue and green	40	25
797	-	6f. red, brown and blue	60	40

DESIGN—VERT: 6f. Plan of Luxembourg fortress c. 1850 (after T. de Cederstolpe).

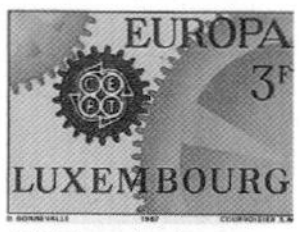

167 Cogwheels

1967. Europa.

798	**167**	3f. purple, grey and buff	2·20	30
799	**167**	6f. sepia, purple and blue	2·75	55

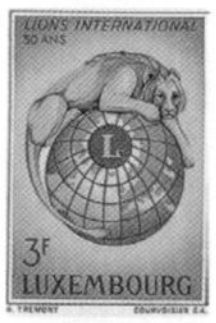

168 Lion on Globe

1967. 50th Anniv of Lions International.

800	**168**	3f. yellow, purple & black	35	30

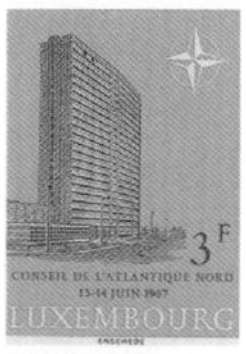

169 European Institutions Building, Luxembourg

1967. N.A.T.O. Council Meeting, Luxembourg.

801	**169**	3f. turquoise and green	40	40
802	**169**	6f. red and pink	65	65

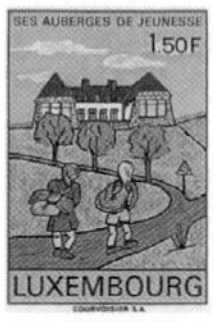

170 Hikers and Hostel

1967. Luxembourg Youth Hostels.

803	**170**	1f.50 multicoloured	35	35

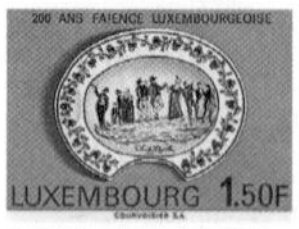

171 Shaving-dish (after Degrotte)

1967. "200 Years of Luxembourg Pottery".

804	**171**	1f.50 multicoloured	35	35
805	-	3f. multicoloured	35	35

DESIGN—VERT: 3f. Vase, c. 1820.

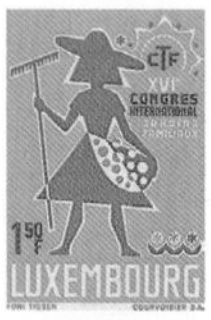

172 "Gardener"

1967. "Family Gardens" Congress, Luxembourg.

806	**172**	1f.50 orange and green	35	35

1967. Tourism. As T **163**.

807	3f. indigo and blue	75	30
808	3f. purple, green and blue	90	30

DESIGNS—HORIZ: No. 807, Moselle River and quayside, Mertert. VERT: No. 808, Moselle, Church and vines, Wormeldange.

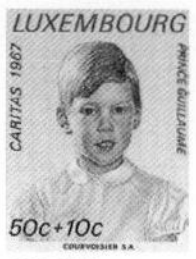

173 Prince Guillaume

1967. National Welfare Fund. Royal Children and Residence.

809	**173**	50c.+10c. brown & buff	30	30
810	-	1f.50+25c. brown & bl	30	30
811	-	2f.+25c. brown and red	30	30
812	-	3f.+50c. brown & yell	1·30	30
813	-	6f.+1f. brown & lav	85	1·80
814	-	13f.+6f.90 brn, grn & bl	1·10	5·00

DESIGNS: 1f.50, Princess Margaretha; 2f. Prince Jean; 3f. Prince Henri; 6f. Princess Marie-Astrid; 13f. Berg Castle.

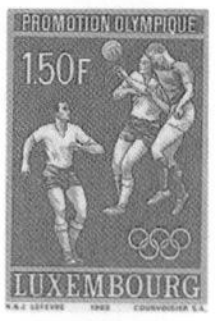

174 Football

1968. Olympic Games, Mexico.

815		50c. light blue and blue	45	30
816	**174**	1f.50 green and emerald	45	30
817	-	2f. yellow and green	65	30
818	-	3f. light orange and orange	45	30
819	-	6f. green and blue	65	55
820	-	13f. red and crimson	1·30	70

DESIGNS: 50c. Diving; 2f. Cycling; 3f. Running; 6f. Walking; 13f. Fencing.

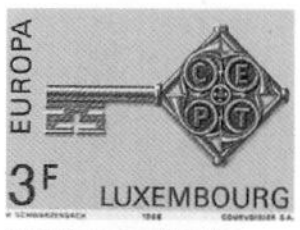

175 Europa "Key"

1968. Europa.

821	**175**	3f. brown, black and green	2·00	35
822	**175**	6f. green, black and orange	2·75	65

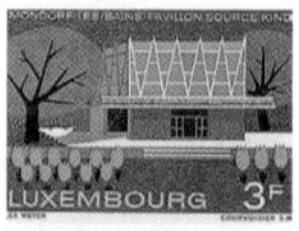

176 Thermal Bath Pavilion, Mondorf-les-Bains

1968. Mondorf-les-Bains Thermal Baths.

823	**176**	3f. multicoloured	55	35

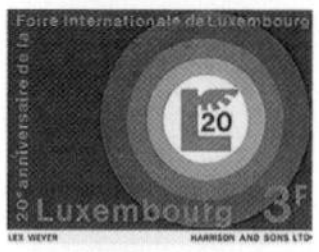

177 Fair Emblem

1968. 20th Anniv of Luxembourg Int Fair.

824	**177**	3f. multicoloured	55	35

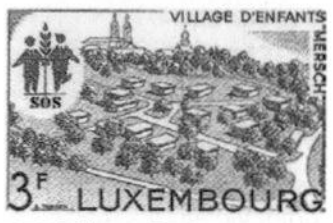

178 Village Project

1968. Luxembourg SOS Children's Village.

825	**178**	3f. purple and green	55	30
826	-	6f. black, blue and purple	65	45

DESIGN—VERT: 6f. Orphan with foster-mother.

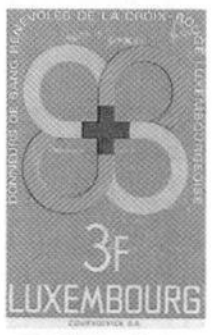

179 "Blood Transfusion"

1968. Blood Donors of Luxembourg Red Cross.

827	**179**	3f. red and blue	65	35

180 Fokker F.27 Friendship
over Luxembourg

1968. Tourism.
| 828 | **180** | 50f. dp blue, brown & blue | 6·00 | 35 |

181 Cap
Institute

1968. National Welfare Fund. Luxembourg Handicapped
Children.
829	**181**	50c.+10c. brown and blue	30	30
830	-	1f.50+25c. brn & grn	30	30
831	-	2f.+25c. brown & yell	40	55
832	-	3f.+50c. brown and blue	40	30
833	-	6f.+1f. brown and buff	1·00	1·70
834	-	13f.+6f.90 brown and pink	2·75	5·75

DESIGNS: 1f.50, Deaf and dumb child; 2f. Blind child; 3f. Nurse supporting handicapped child; 6f. and 13f. Mentally handicapped children (different).

182

1969. "Juventus 1969" Junior International Philatelic Exhibition. Sheet 111×70 mm containing T **182** and similar vert designs. Multicoloured.
| MS835 | 3f. Type **182**; 6f. "Sport"; 13f. Sun, open book and ball | 6·00 | 7·00 |

183 Colonnade

1969. Europa.
| 836 | **183** | 3f. multicoloured | 2·00 | 35 |
| 837 | **183** | 6f. multicoloured | 2·75 | 65 |

184 "The Wooden Horse"
(Kutter)

1969. 75th Birth Anniv of Joseph Kutter (painter). Multicoloured.
| 838 | **184** | 3f. Type **184** | 90 | 30 |
| 839 | - | 6f. "Luxembourg" (Kutter) | 90 | 65 |

185 ILO Emblem

1969. 50th Anniv of Int Labour Organization.
| 840 | **185** | 3f. gold, violet and green | 45 | 35 |

186 National
Colours

1969. 25th Anniv of "BENELUX" Customs Union.
| 841 | **186** | 3f. multicoloured | 55 | 35 |

187 N.A.T.O. Emblem

1969. 20th Anniv of N.A.T.O.
| 842 | **187** | 3f. orange and brown | 65 | 35 |

188 Ear of
Wheat and
Agrocentre,
Mersch

1969. "Modern Agriculture".
| 843 | **188** | 3f. grey and green | 45 | 35 |

189 Echternach

1969. Tourism.
| 844 | **189** | 3f. indigo and blue | 60 | 35 |
| 845 | - | 3f. blue and green | 60 | 35 |

DESIGN: No. 845, Wiltz.

190 Vianden Castle

1969. National Welfare Fund. Castles (1st series). Multicoloured.
846	**190**	50c.+10c. Type **190**	30	30
847	-	1f.50+25c. Lucilinburhuc	30	30
848	-	2f.+25c. Bourglinster	30	30
849	-	3f.+50c. Hollenfels	30	30
850	-	6f.+1f. Ansembourg	1·10	2·30
851	-	13f.+6f.90 Beaufort	1·70	5·75

See also Nos. 862/7.

191 Pasque
Flower

1970. Nature Conservation Year. Multicoloured.
| 852 | **191** | 3f. Type **191** | 45 | 30 |
| 853 | - | 6f. West European hedgehogs | 65 | 65 |

192 Firecrest

1970. 50 Years of Bird Protection.
| 854 | **192** | 1f.50 green, black & orge | 55 | 35 |

193 "Flaming Sun"

1970. Europa.
| 855 | **193** | 3f. multicoloured | 2·00 | 35 |
| 856 | **193** | 6f. multicoloured | 2·75 | 65 |

194 Road Safety Assoc.
Emblem and Traffic

1970. Road Safety.
| 857 | **194** | 3f. black, red and lake | 40 | 35 |

195 "Empress Kunegonde and
Emperor Henry II"
(stained-glass windows,
Luxembourg Cathedral)

1970. Centenary of Luxembourg Diocese.
| 858 | **195** | 3f. multicoloured | 40 | 40 |

196 Population
Pictograph

1970. Population Census.
| 859 | **196** | 3f. red, blue and green | 40 | 35 |

197 Facade of Town
Hall, Luxembourg

1970. 50th Anniv of Union of Four Suburbs with Luxembourg City.
| 860 | **197** | 3f. brown, ochre and blue | 40 | 35 |

199 Monks in the
Scriptorium

1970. 25th Anniv of United Nations.
| 861 | **198** | 1f.50 violet and blue | 40 | 35 |

1970. National Welfare Fund. Castles (2nd series). Designs as T **190**.
862	50c.+10c. Clervaux	30	30
863	1f.50+25c. Septfontaines	30	30
864	2f.+25c. Bourscheid	30	30
865	3f.+50c. Esch-sur-Sure	30	30
866	6f.+1f. Larochette	90	2·30
867	13f.+6f.90 Brandenbourg	1·70	5·75

198 U.N. Emblem

1971. Medieval Miniatures produced at Echternach. Multicoloured.
868	**199**	1f.50 Type **199**	45	30
869	-	3f. Vine-growers going to work	45	30
870	-	6f. Vine-growers at work and returning home	55	30
871	-	13f. Workers with spades and hoe	1·50	90

200 Europa Chain

1971
| 872 | **200** | 3f. black, brown and red | 2·00 | 35 |
| 873 | **200** | 6f. black, brown and green | 2·75 | 1·00 |

201 Olympic
Rings and Arms
of Luxembourg

1971. Int Olympic Committee Meeting, Luxembourg.
| 874 | **201** | 3f. red, gold and blue | 55 | 35 |

202 "50" and Emblem

1971. 50th Anniv of Luxembourg's Christian Workers' Union (L.C.G.B.).
| 875 | **202** | 3f. purple, orange & yell | 55 | 35 |

203 Artificial Lake, Upper
Sure Valley

1971. Man-made Landscapes.
876	**203**	3f. blue, grey and brown	85	35
877	-	3f. brown, green and blue	85	55
878	-	15f. black, blue and brown	1·70	35

DESIGNS: No. 877, Water-processing plant, Esch-sur-Sure; No. 878, ARBED (United Steelworks) Headquarters Building, Luxembourg.

204 Child with
Coin

1971. Schoolchildren's Saving Campaign.
| 879 | **204** | 3f. multicoloured | 55 | 35 |

205 "Bethlehem
Children"

1971. National Welfare Fund. "The Nativity"—wood-carvings in Beaufort Church. Multicoloured.
880	1f.+25c. Type **205**	55	35
881	1f.50+25c. "Shepherds"	55	35
882	3f.+50c. "Virgin, Child Jesus and St. Joseph"	70	35
883	8f.+1f. "Herdsmen"	2·10	4·00
884	18f.+6f.50 "One of the Magi"	3·25	9·00

206 Coins of
Belgium and
Luxembourg

1972. 50th Anniv of Belgium–Luxembourg Economic Union.
| 885 | **206** | 1f.50 silver, black & green | 55 | 35 |

207 Bronze Mask
(1st cent)

1972. Gallo-Roman Exhibits from Luxembourg State Museum. Multicoloured.
886	1f. Samian bowl (2nd century) (horiz)	65	25
887	3f. Type **207**	95	30
888	8f. Limestone head (2nd/3rd century)	2·00	1·30
889	15f. Glass "head" flagon (4th century)	1·90	1·00

208 "Communications"

1972. Europa.

890	**208**	3f. multicoloured	2·00	35
891	**208**	8f. multicoloured	3·25	2·00

209 Archer

1972. Third European Archery Championships, Luxembourg.

892	**209**	3f. multicoloured	75	35

210 R. Schuman (after bronze by R. Zilli)

1972. 20th Anniv of Establishment of European Coal and Steel Community in Luxembourg.

893	**210**	3f. green and grey	85	35

211 National Monument

1972. Monuments and Buildings.

894	**211**	3f. brown, green and violet	1·00	35
895	-	3f. brown, green and blue	1·40	35

DESIGN: No. 895, European Communities' Court of Justice.

212 "Renert"

1972. Centenary of Publication of Michel Rodange's "Renert" (satirical poem).

896	**212**	3f. multicoloured	60	35

213 "Angel"

1972. National Welfare Fund. Stained Glass Windows in Luxembourg Cathedral. Multicoloured.

897		1f.+25c. Type **213**	30	30
898		1f.50+25c. "St. Joseph"	30	30
899		3f.+50c. "Holy Virgin with Child Jesus"	30	30
900		8f.+1f. "People of Bethlehem"	1·70	4·00
901		18f.+6f.50 "Angel" (facing left)	5·00	11·50

214 "Epona on Horseback"

1973. Archaeological Relics. Multicoloured.

902		1f. Type **214**	65	30
903		4f. "Panther attacking swan" (horiz)	70	35
904		8f. Celtic gold coin	2·50	1·80
905		15f. Bronze boar (horiz)	1·90	1·00

215 Europa "Posthorn"

1973. Europa.

906	**215**	4f. orange, blue and violet	2·00	40
907	**215**	8f. green, yellow & purple	3·25	1·70

216 Bee on Honeycomb

1973. Bee-keeping.

908	**216**	4f. multicoloured	90	35

217 Nurse and Child

1973. Day Nurseries in Luxembourg.

909	**217**	4f. multicoloured	65	35

218 Capital, Vianden Castle

1973. Romanesque Architecture in Luxembourg.

910	**218**	4f. purple and green	55	35
911	-	8f. blue and brown	1·50	1·30

DESIGN: 8f. Detail of altar, St. Irmina's Chapel, Rosport.

219 Labour Emblem

1973. 50th Anniv of Luxembourg Board of Labour.

912	**219**	3f. multicoloured	55	35

220 J. de Busleyden

1973. 500th Anniv of Great Council of Malines.

913	**220**	4f. purple and brown	60	35

221 Monument, Wiltz

1973. National Strike Monument.

914	**221**	4f. green, brown and grey	85	35

222 Joachim and St. Anne

1973. National Welfare Fund. "The Nativity". Details from 16th-century reredos, Hachiville Hermitage. Multicoloured.

915		1f.+25c. Type **222**	30	35
916		3f.+25c. "Mary meets Elizabeth"	30	35
917		4f.+50c. "Magus presenting gift"	35	35
918		8f.+1f. "Shepherds at the manger"	1·80	4·25
919		15f.+7f. "St. Joseph with Candle"	5·25	11·50

223 Princess Marie-Astrid, Association President

1974. Luxembourg Red Cross Youth Association.

920	**223**	4f. multicoloured	2·75	65

224 Flame Emblem

1974. 50th Anniv of Luxembourg Mutual Insurance Federation.

921	**224**	4f. multicoloured	95	60

225 Seal of Henry VII, King of the Romans

1974. Seals in Luxembourg State Archives.

922	**225**	1f. brown, yellow & purple	45	30
923	-	3f. brown, yellow & green	55	45
924	-	4f. dk brown, yellow & brn	75	30
925	-	19f. brown, yellow & blue	2·00	1·30

DESIGNS: 3f. Equestrian seal of John the Blind, King of Bohemia; 4f. Municipal seal of Diekirch; 19f. Seal of Marienthal Convent.

226 "Hind" (A. Tremont)

1974. Europa. Sculptures. Multicoloured.

926		4f. Type **226**	4·00	35
927		8f. "Abstract" (L. Wercollier)	6·75	3·00

227 Churchill Memorial, Luxembourg

1974. Birth Centenary of Sir Winston Churchill.

928	**227**	4f. multicoloured	65	40

228 Diagram of Fair

1974. New International Fair, Luxembourg-Kirchberg.

929	**228**	4f. multicoloured	65	40

229 "Theis the Blind" (artist unknown)

1974. 150th Death Anniv of "Theis the Blind" (Mathias Schou, folk singer).

930	**229**	3f. multicoloured	65	65

230 "Crowning of St. Cecily and St. Valerien" (Hollenfels Church)

1974. Gothic Architecture.

931	**230**	4f. brown, green and violet	75	45
932	-	4f. black, brown and blue	75	45

DESIGN: No. 932, Interior of Septfontaines Church.

231 U.P.U. Emblem on "100"

1974. Centenary of Universal Postal Union.

933	**231**	4f. multicoloured	70	35
934	**231**	8f. multicoloured	1·70	1·20

232 "Benelux"

1974. 30th Anniv of Benelux (Customs Union).

935	**232**	4f. turquoise, green & blue	1·70	40

233 Differdange

1974. Tourism.

936	**233**	4f. purple	2·00	40

234 "Annunciation"

1974. National Welfare Fund. Illustrations from "Codex Aureus Epternacensis". Multicoloured.

937		1f.+25c. Type **234**	30	30
938		3f.+25c. "Visitation"	30	30
939		4f.+50c. "Nativity"	35	30
940		8f.+1f. "Adoration of the Magi"	2·00	4·25
941		15f.+7f. "Presentation at the Temple"	4·00	10·50

235 "Crucifixion"

1974. 50th Anniv of Christmas Charity Stamps. Detail of cover from "Codex Aureus Epternacensis". Sheet 80×90 mm.

MS942	**235**	20f.+10f. multicoloured	6·75	17·00

236 The Fish Market, Luxembourg

1975. European Architectural Heritage Year.

943	**236**	1f. green	95	35
944	-	3f. brown	2·30	65
945	-	4f. lilac	2·50	35
946	-	19f. red	2·75	1·70

DESIGNS—HORIZ: 3f. Bourglinster Castle; 4f. Market Square, Echternach. VERT: 19f. St. Michael's Square, Mersch.

237 "Joseph Kutter" (self-portrait)

1975. Luxembourg Culture, and Europa. Paintings. Multicoloured.

947	**237**	1f. Type **237**	65	30
948		4f. "Remich Bridge" (N. Klopp) (horiz)	2·75	55
949		8f. "Still Life" (J. Kutter) (horiz)	4·75	2·75
950		20f. "The Dam" (D. Lang)	3·00	85

238 Dr. Albert Schweitzer

1975. Birth Centenary of Dr. Albert Schweitzer (medical missionary).

951	**238**	4f. blue	1·10	40

239 Robert Schuman, G. Martino and P.-H. Spaak

1975. 25th Anniv of Robert Schuman Declaration for European Unity.

952	**239**	4f. black, gold and green	1·10	40

240 Civil Defence Emblem

1975. 15th Anniv of Civil Defence Reorganization.

953	**240**	4f. multicoloured	1·10	40

241 Ice Skating

1975. Sports. Multicoloured.

954	**241**	3f. purple, blue and green	1·00	55
955	-	4f. brown, green & dp brn	1·50	30
956	-	15f. blue, brown and green	2·75	95

DESIGNS—HORIZ: 4f. Water-skiing. VERT: 15f. Rock-climbing.

242 Fly Orchid

1975. National Welfare Fund. Protected Plants (1st series). Multicoloured.

957		1f.+25c. Type **242**	35	30
958		3f.+25c. Pyramid orchid	65	45
959		4f.+50c. Marsh helleborine	90	30
960		8f.+1f. Pasque flower	2·10	3·25
961		15f.+7f. Bee orchid	4·75	10·00

See also Nos. 976/80 and 997/1001.

243 Grand Duchess Charlotte (80th)

1976. Royal Birthdays. Multicoloured.

962	**243**	6f. Type **243**	2·75	60
963		6f. Prince Henri (21st)	2·75	60

244 7th-century Disc-shaped Brooch

1976. Luxembourg Culture. Ancient Treasures from Merovingian Tombs. Multicoloured.

964	**244**	2f. Type **244**	45	30
965		5f. 5th-6th century glass beaker (horiz)	55	55
966		6f. Ancient pot (horiz)	55	40
967		12f. 7th century gold coin	1·80	1·60

245 Soup Tureen

1976. Europa. 19th-century Pottery. Multicoloured.

968	**245**	6f. Type **245**	4·00	35
969		12f. Bowl	6·75	2·75

246 Independence Hall, Philadelphia

1976. Bicentenary of American Revolution.

970	**246**	6f. multicoloured	85	45

247 Symbol representing "Strength and Impetus"

1976. Olympic Games, Montreal.

971	**247**	6f. gold, magenta and mauve	85	45

249 "Virgin and Child"

1976. 30th Anniv of "Jeunesses Musicales" (Youth Music Association).

972	**248**	6f. multicoloured	85	45

248 Association Emblem and "Sound Vibrations"

1976. Renaissance Art. Multicoloured.

973		6f. Type **249**	85	40
974		12f. Bernard de Velbruck, Lord of Beaufort (funeral monument)	1·80	1·50

250 Alexander Graham Bell

1976. Telephone Centenary.

975	**250**	6f. green	85	45

1976. National Welfare Fund. Protected Plants (2nd series). As T **242**. Multicoloured.

976		2f.+25c. Gentian	30	45
977		5f.+25c. Wild daffodil	30	45
978		6f.+50c. Red helleborine (orchid)	45	45
979		12f.+1f. Late spider orchid	1·80	4·25
980		20f.+8f. Twin leaved squill	5·00	12·00

251 Johann von Goethe (poet)

1977. Luxembourg Culture. Famous Visitors to Luxembourg.

981	**251**	2f. purple	55	30
982	-	5f. violet	65	40
983	-	6f. black	1·10	40
984	-	12f. violet	1·30	1·30

DESIGNS: 5f. Joseph Mallard William Turner (painter); 6f. Victor Hugo (writer); 12f. Franz Liszt (musician).

252 Fish Market, Luxembourg

1977. Europa. Multicoloured.

985	**252**	6f. Type **252**	3·25	65
986		12f. Grand Duke Adolphe railway bridge and European Investment Bank	5·25	2·75

253 Esch-sur-Sure

1977. Tourism.

987	**253**	5f. blue	90	40
988	-	6f. brown	85	40

DESIGNS 6f. Ehnen.

254 Marguerite de Busbach (founder)

1977. Anniversaries. Multicoloured.

989		6f. Type **254**	85	40
990		6f. Louis Braille (after Filippi)	85	40

ANNIVERSARIES: No. 989, 350th anniv of foundation of Notre Dame Congregation; No. 990, 125th death anniv.

255 10c. and 1sgr. Stamps of 1852

1977. 125th Anniv of Luxembourg Stamps. Sheet 90×60 mm.

MS991	**255**	40f. black, chestnut and grey	9·50	9·50

256 St. Gregory the Great

1977. Baroque Art. Sculpture from Feulen Parish Church pulpit attributed to J.-G. Scholtus.

992	**256**	6f. purple	65	45
993	-	12f. grey	1·30	1·30

DESIGN: 12f. St. Augustine.

257 Head of Medusa

1977. Roman Mosaic at Diekirch.

994	**257**	6f. multicoloured	1·70	40

258 Scene from "Orpheus and Eurydice" (Gluck)

1977. 25th Wiltz International Festival.

995	**258**	6f. multicoloured	1·20	40

259 Map of E.E.C. and "Europa" (R. Zilli)

1977. 20th Anniv of Rome Treaties.

996	**259**	6f. multicoloured	1·10	40

1977. National Welfare Fund. Protected Plants (3rd series). As T **242**. Multicoloured.

997		2f.+25c. Lily of the valley	35	45
998		5f.+25c. Columbine	55	55
999		6f.+50c. Mezereon	1·00	55
1000		12f.+1f. Early spider orchid	2·75	5·25
1001		20f.+8f. Spotted orchid	4·50	11·00

260 Grand Duke Jean and Duchess Josephine-Charlotte

1978. Royal Silver Wedding. Sheet 116×67 mm.

MS1002	**260**	6f., 12f. multicoloured	3·25	3·25

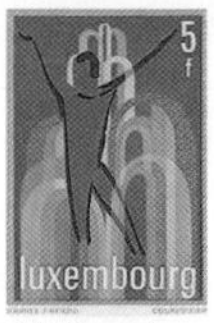

261 Fountain and Youth

1978. "Juphilux 78" Junior International Philatelic Exhibition. Sheet 103×72 mm containing T **261** and similar vert designs. Multicoloured.

MS1003	5f. Type **261**; 6f. Streamer; 20f. Dancing youths	5·25	6·25

MS1003 was on sale at 60f., including entrance fee of 29f., at the Exhibition, by postal application and at post offices.

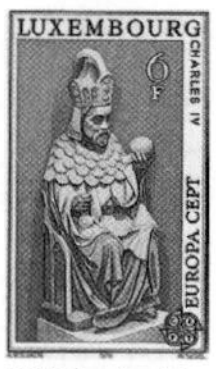

262 Charles IV

1978. Europa.

1004	**262**	6f. lilac	1·70	45
1005	-	12f. red	4·00	2·00

DESIGN: 12f. Pierre d'Aspelt (funeral monument, Mainz Cathedral).

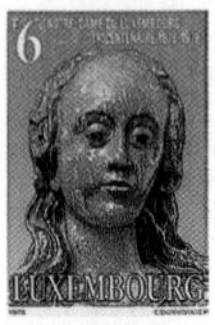

263 Head of Our Lady of Luxembourg

1978. Anniversaries. Multicoloured.

1006	6f. Type **263** (300th anniv of election as patron saint)	70	40
1007	6f. Trumpeters (135th anniv of Grand Ducal Military Band)	70	40

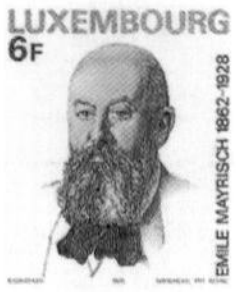

264 Emile Mayrisch (after T. van Rysselberghe)

1978. 50th Death Anniv of Emile Mayrisch (iron and steel magnate).

1008	**264**	6f. multicoloured	1·40	35

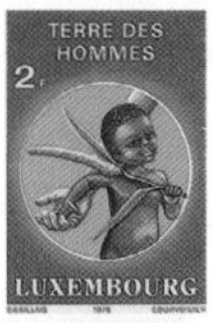

265 Child with Ear of Millet

1978. "Solidarity 1978". Multicoloured.

1009	2f. Type **265** (Terre des Hommes)	40	35
1010	5f. Flower and lungs (70th anniv of Luxembourg Anti-tuberculosis League)	50	35
1011	6f. Open cell (Amnesty International and 30th anniv of Declaration of Human Rights)	65	40

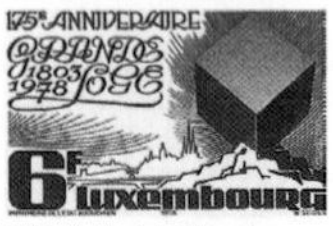

266 Perfect Ashlar

1978. 175th Anniv of Luxembourg Grand Lodge.

1012	**266**	6f. blue	85	40

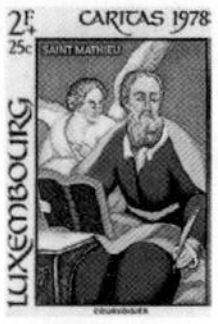

267 "St. Matthew"

1978. National Welfare Fund. Glass Paintings (1st series). Multicoloured.

1013	2f.+25c. Type **267**	25	25
1014	5f.+25c. "St. Mark"	40	40
1015	6f.+50c. "Nativity"	55	45
1016	12f.+1f. "St. Luke"	2·00	1·50
1017	20f.+8f. "St. John"	2·75	6·25

See also Nos. 1035/9 and 1055/8.

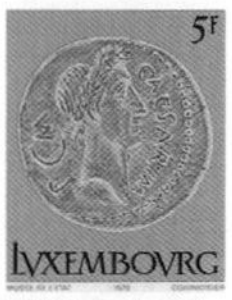

268 Denarius of Gaius Julius Caesar

1979. Luxembourg Culture. Roman Coins in the State Museum. Multicoloured.

1018	5f. Type **268**	45	35
1019	6f. Sestertius of Faustina 1	80	25
1020	9f. Follis of Helena	1·10	70
1021	26f. Solidus of Valens	2·20	1·70

See also Nos. 1040/3 and 1060/3.

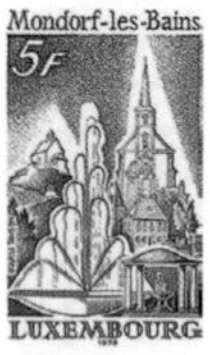

269 Mondorf-les-Bains

1979. Tourism.

1022	**269**	5f. green, brown and blue	85	35
1023	-	6f. red	1·40	35

DESIGN: 6f. Luxembourg Central Station.

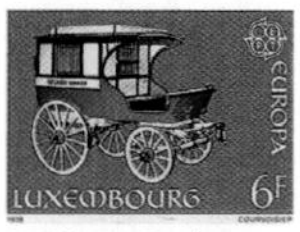

270 Stage Coach

1979. Europa. Multicoloured.

1024	6f. Type **270**	6·75	55
1025	12f. Old wall telephone (vert)	6·75	2·20

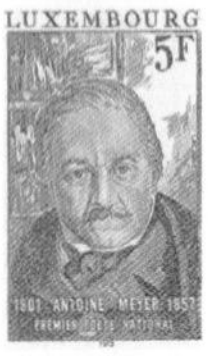

271 Antoine Meyer (poet)

1979. Anniversaries.

1026	-	2f. purple	75	35
1027	**271**	5f. red	60	35
1028	-	6f. turquoise	60	35
1029	-	9f. grey-black	2·30	60

DESIGNS—36×36 mm: 2f. Michel Pintz on trial (after L. Piedboeuf) and monument to rebels (180th anniv of peasant uprising against French). 22×36 mm: 5f. Type **271** (150th anniv of first publication in Luxembourg dialect); 6f. S. G. Thomas (cent of purchase of Thomas patent for steel production); 9f. "Abundance crowning Work and Saving" (ceiling painting by August Vinet) (50th anniv of Stock Exchange).

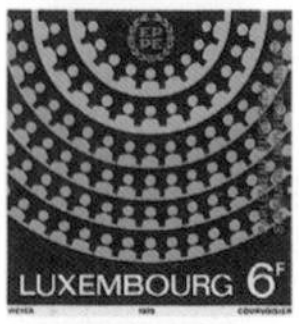

272 "European Assembly"

1979. First Direct Elections to European Assembly.

1030	**272**	6f. multicoloured	1·70	1·00

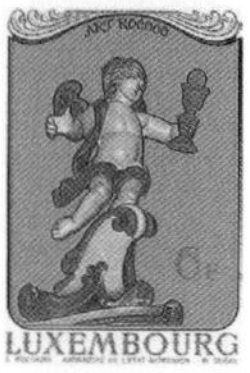

273 Blindfolded Cherub with Chalice

1979. Rococo Art. Details from altar of St. Michael's Church by Barthelemy Namur. Multicoloured.

1031	6f. Type **273**	55	40
1032	12f. Cherub with anchor	1·00	1·00

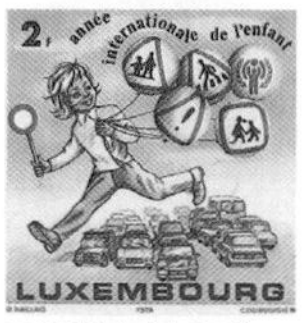

274 Child with Traffic Symbol Balloons jumping over Traffic

1979. International Year of the Child.

1033	**274**	2f. blue, brown and red	60	30

1979. 50th Anniv of Broadcasting in Luxembourg.

1034	**275**	6f. blue and red	90	35

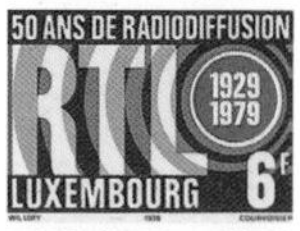

275 Radio Waves, "RTL" and Dates

1979. National Welfare Fund. Glass Paintings (2nd series). As T 267. Multicoloured.

1035	2f.+25c. "Spring"	30	30
1036	5f.+25c. "Summer"	40	35
1037	6f.+50c. "Charity"	55	40
1038	12f.+1f. "Autumn"	1·10	2·10
1039	20f.+8f. "Winter"	2·10	7·00

1980. Luxembourg Culture. Medieval Coins in the State Museum. As T 268. Multicoloured.

1040	2f. Grosso of Emperor Henry VII	40	25
1041	5f. Grosso of John the Blind of Bohemia	40	40
1042	6f. "Mouton d'or" of Wenceslas I and Jeanne, Duke and Duchess of Brabant	1·10	25
1043	20f. Grosso of Wenceslas II, Duke of Luxembourg	2·50	1·10

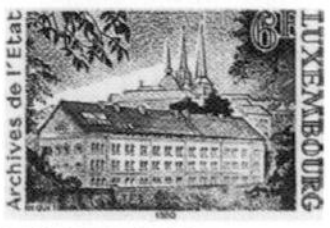

276 State Archives Building

1980. Tourism.

1044	**276**	6f. purple, ultram & bl	1·20	30
1045	-	6f. red and brown	1·30	30

DESIGN—VERT: No. 1045, Ettelbruck Town Hall.

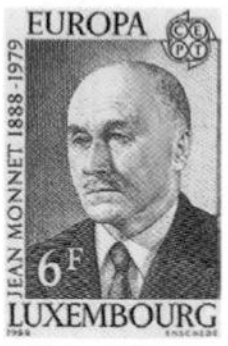

277 Jean Monnet (statesman)

1980. Europa.

1046	**277**	6f. black	2·75	30
1047	-	12f. olive	4·00	1·40

DESIGN: 12f. St. Benedict of Nursia (founder of Benedictine Order) (statue in Echternach Abbey).

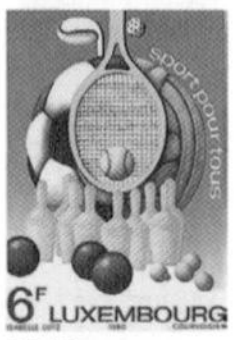

278 Sports Equipment

1980. "Sports for All".

1048	**278**	6f. black, orange & green	1·70	55

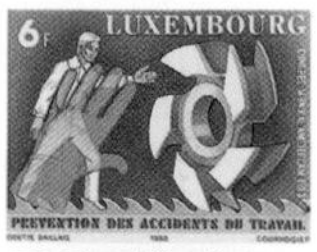

279 Gloved Hand protecting Worker from Machinery

1980. Ninth World Congress on the Prevention of Accidents at Work and Occupational Diseases, Amsterdam.

1049	-	2f. multicoloured	55	25
1050	**279**	6f. brown, grey and red	70	40

DESIGN—VERT: 2f. Worker pouring molten iron.

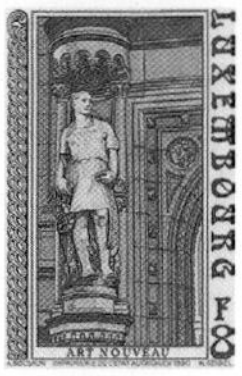

280 "Mercury" (Jean Mich)

1980. Art Nouveau Sculpture. Statues beside entrance to State Savings Bank.

1051	**280**	8f. lilac	90	40
1052	-	12f. blue	1·10	1·00

DESIGN: 12f. "Ceres" (Jean Mich).

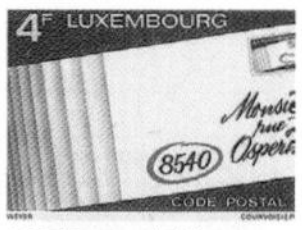

281 Postcoded Letter

1980. Postcode Publicity.

1053	**281**	4f. brown, ochre and red	95	40

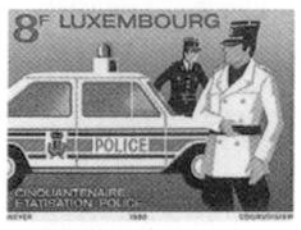

282 Policemen and Patrol Car

1980. 50th Anniv of National Police Force.

1054	**282**	8f. multicoloured	95	40

1980. National Welfare Fund. Glass Paintings (3rd series). As T **267**. Multicoloured.

1055	4f.+50c. "St. Martin"	55	30
1056	6f.+50c. "St. Nicholas"	55	35
1057	8f.+1f. "Virgin and child"	85	1·40
1058	30f.+10f. "St. George"	3·75	6·75

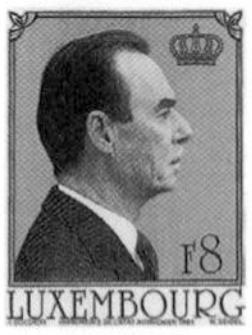

283 Grand Duke Jean

1981. Grand Duke Jean's 60th Birthday. Sheet 115×73 mm containing T **283** and similar vert design.

MS1059	8f. Type **283**; 12f. Grand Duke Jean's coat of arms; 30f. Type **283**	3·25	2·75

1981. Luxembourg Culture. Coins in the State Museum. As T 268.

1060	4f. Patagon of Philip IV of Spain, 1635	40	25
1061	6f. 12 sols coin of Maria Theresa, 1775	65	40
1062	8f. 12 sols coin of Emperor Joseph II, 1789	65	40
1063	30f. Siege crown of Emperor Francis II, 1795	2·20	1·50

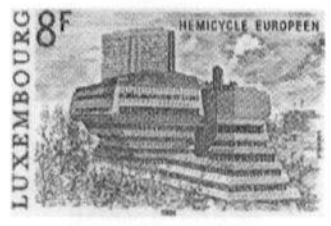

284 European Parliament Building, Luxembourg

1981. Tourism.

1064	**284**	8f. brown and blue	70	45
1065	-	8f. red and blue	70	45

DESIGN: No. 1065, National Library.

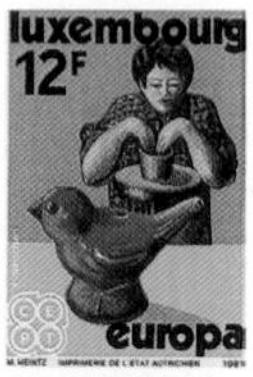

285 Cock-shaped Whistle sold at Easter Monday Market

1981. Europa. Multicoloured.

1066	8f. Procession of beribboned sheep and town band to local fair	2·20	40
1067	12f. Type **285**	3·25	85

286 Staunton
Knight on
Chessboard

1981. Anniversaries.
1068	**286**	4f. multicoloured	85	40
1069	-	8f. ochre, brown & silver	85	40
1070	-	8f. multicoloured	85	40

DESIGNS—VERT: 4f. Type **286** (50th anniv of Luxembourg Chess Federation); 8f. (1070), Pass-book and State Savings Bank (125th anniv of State Savings Bank). HORIZ: 8f. (1069), First Luxembourg banknote (125th anniv of International Bank of Luxembourg's issuing rights).

287 Prince Henri and
Princess Maria Teresa

1981. Royal Wedding.
| 1071 | **287** | 8f. multicoloured | 75 | 55 |

288 Gliders over
Useldange

1981. Aviation. Multicoloured.
1072		8f. Type **288**	85	45
1073		16f. Cessna 172F Skyhawk LX-AIZ and 182H Skylane sports planes	1·40	1·10
1074		35f. Boeing 747-200F over Luxembourg-Findel airport terminal	2·50	1·30

289 Flame

1981. Energy Conservation.
| 1075 | **289** | 8f. multicoloured | 85 | 45 |

290 Arms of
Petange

1981. National Welfare Fund. Arms of Local Authorities (1st series). Multicoloured.
1076		4f.+50c. Type **290**	30	30
1077		6f.+50c. Larochette	35	35
1078		8f.+1f. "Adoration of the Magi" (School of Rubens)	55	45
1079		16f.+2f. Stadtbredimus	1·10	2·50
1080		35f.+12f. Weiswampach	3·75	7·00

See also Nos. 1097/1101 and 1119/23.

291 "Apple Trees in
Blossom" (Frantz
Seimetz)

1982. Luxembourg Culture. Landscapes through the Four Seasons. Multicoloured.
1081		4f. Type **291**	40	35
1082		6f. "Landscape" (Pierre Blanc)	55	45
1083		8f. "The Larger Hallerbach" (Guido Oppenheim)	75	35
1084		16f. "Winter Evening" (Eugene Mousset)	1·50	1·00

292 Cross of
Hinzert and
Statue "Political
Prisoner" (Lucien
Wercollier)

1982. National Monument of the Resistance and Deportation, Notre-Dame Cemetery.
| 1085 | **292** | 8f. multicoloured | 70 | 40 |

293 Treaty of
London, 1867,
and
Luxembourg
Fortress

1982. Europa. Multicoloured.
| 1086 | | 8f. Type **293** | 2·75 | 55 |
| 1087 | | 16f. Treaty of Paris, 1951, and European Coal and Steel Community Building, Luxembourg | 3·25 | 1·10 |

294 St. Theresa
of Avila (wood
statue, Carmel
Monastery)

1982. Anniversaries. Multicoloured.
| 1088 | | 4f. Type **294** (400th death anniv) | 45 | 30 |
| 1089 | | 8f. Raoul Follereau (social worker for lepers, 5th death anniv) | 55 | 35 |

295 State Museum

1982. Tourism.
| 1090 | **295** | 8f. brown, blue and black | 55 | 40 |
| 1091 | - | 8f. buff, black and blue | 55 | 40 |

DESIGN: No. 1091, Luxembourg Synagogue.

296 Bourscheid
Castle

1982. Classified Monuments (1st series).
| 1092 | **296** | 6f. blue | 80 | 40 |
| 1093 | - | 8f. red | 90 | 40 |

DESIGN—HORIZ: 8f. Vianden Castle.
See also Nos. 1142/3 and 1165/6.

297 Key in Lock

1982. Anniversaries. Multicoloured.
| 1094 | | 4f. Type **297** (50th anniv of International Youth Hostel Federation) | 90 | 40 |
| 1095 | | 8f. Scouts holding hands around globe (75th anniv of Scouting Movement) (vert) | 1·10 | 40 |

298 Monument
to Civilian and
Military
Deportation

1982. Civilian and Military Deportation Monument, Hollerich Station.
| 1096 | **298** | 8f. multicoloured | 85 | 45 |

1982. National Welfare Fund. Arms of Local Authorities (2nd series) and Stained Glass Window (8f.). As T **290**. Multicoloured.
1097		4f.+50c. Bettembourg	30	20
1098		6f.+50c. Frisange	40	35
1099		8f.+1f. "Adoration of the Shepherds" (Gustav Zanter, Hoscheid parish church)	70	45
1100		16f.+2f. Mamer	1·40	2·50
1101		35f.+12f. Heinerscheid	3·75	7·00

299 Modern Fire
Engine

1983. Centenary of National Federation of Fire Brigades. Multicoloured.
| 1102 | | 8f. Type **299** | 1·40 | 55 |
| 1103 | | 16f. Hand fire-pump (18th century) | 1·70 | 1·10 |

300 "Mercury"
(Auguste
Tremont)

1983. Anniversaries and Events.
1104	**300**	4f. multicoloured	45	40
1105	-	6f. multicoloured	45	40
1106	-	8f. brown, black and blue	55	40
1107	-	8f. deep blue and blue	55	40

DESIGNS: No. 1104, Type **300** (25th Congress of International Association of Foreign Exchange Dealers); 1105, N.A.T.O. emblem surrounded by flags of member countries (25th anniv of N.A.T.O.); 1106, Echternach Cross of Justice (30th Congress of International Union of Barristers); 1107, Globe and customs emblem (30th anniv of Customs Co-operation Council).

301 Robbers attacking
Traveller

1983. Europa. Miniatures from "Codex Aureus Escorialensis", illustrating Parable of the Good Samaritan. Multicoloured.
| 1108 | | 8f. Type **301** | 4·50 | 75 |
| 1109 | | 16f. Good Samaritan helping traveller | 6·75 | 2·20 |

302 Initial "H" from
"Book of Baruch"

1983. Luxembourg Culture. Echternach Abbey Giant Bible. Multicoloured.
| 1110 | | 8f. Type **302** | 75 | 45 |
| 1111 | | 35f. Initial "B" from letter of St. Jerome to Pope Damasius I | 2·20 | 1·50 |

303 Despatch
Rider and
Postcode

1983. World Communications Year. Mult.
| 1112 | | 8f. Type **303** | 1·50 | 35 |
| 1113 | | 8f. Europan Communications Satellite (horiz) | 3·00 | 40 |

304 St. Lawrence's
Church, Diekirch

1983. Tourism.
| 1114 | **304** | 7f. orange, brown and blue | 70 | 40 |
| 1115 | - | 10f. orange, brown & bl | 80 | 40 |

DESIGN—HORIZ: 10f. Dudelange Town Hall.

305 Basketball

1983. Anniversaries and Events. Multicoloured.
1116		7f. Type **305** (50th anniv of Luxembourg basketball Federation)	90	50
1117		10f. Sheepdog (European Working Dog Championships)	1·10	50
1118		10f. City of Luxembourg ("The Green Heart of Europe")	1·80	50

1983. National Welfare Fund. Arms of Local Authorities (3rd series) and Painting. As T **290**. Multicoloured.
1119		4f.+1f. Winseler	45	45
1120		7f.+1f. Beckerich	55	45
1121		10f.+1f. "Adoration of the Shepherds" (Lucas Bosch)	85	45
1122		16f.+2f. Feulen	1·50	2·75
1123		40f.+13f. Mertert	3·75	7·25

306 Lion and
First
Luxembourg
Stamp

1984. Anniversaries. Each black, red and blue.
1124	**306**	10f. Type **306**	1·10	45
1125		10f. Lion and ministry buildings	1·10	45
1126		10f. Lion and postman's bag	1·10	45
1127		10f. Lion and diesel locomotive	1·10	45

ANNIVERSARIES: No. 1124, 50th anniv of Federation of Luxembourg Philatelic Societies; 1125, 75th anniv of Civil Service Trade Union Movement; 1126, 75th anniv of Luxembourg Postmen's Trade Union; 1127, 125th anniv of Luxembourg Railways.

307 Pedestrian Precinct

1984. Environmental Protection. Multicoloured.
| 1128 | | 7f. Type **307** | 1·00 | 55 |
| 1129 | | 10f. City of Luxembourg sewage treatment plant | 1·00 | 55 |

308 Hands
supporting
European
Parliament
Emblem

1984. Second Direct Elections to European Parliament.
| 1130 | **308** | 10f. multicoloured | 1·10 | 45 |

309 Bridge

1984. Europa. 25th Anniv of European Post and Telecommunications Conference.

1131	**309**	10f. green, dp green & blk	5·50	55
1132	**309**	16f. orange, brown & blk	8·25	2·20

310 "The Smoker" (David Teniers the Younger)

1984. Paintings. Multicoloured.

1133	4f. Type **310**	85	40
1134	7f. "Young Turk caressing his Horse" (Eugene Delacroix) (horiz)	1·10	45
1135	10f. "Ephiphany" (Jan Steen) (horiz)	1·60	45
1136	50f. "The Lacemaker" (Pieter van Slingelandt)	5·50	4·00

311 "The Race" (Jean Jacoby)

1984. Olympic Games, Los Angeles.

1137	**311**	10f. orange, black & blue	1·00	55

312 "Pecten sp."

1984. Luxembourg Culture. Fossils in the Natural History Museum. Multicoloured.

1138	4f. Type **312**	70	35
1139	7f. Devil's toe-nail	80	50
1140	10f. "Coeloceras raquinianum" (ammonite)	1·40	40
1141	16f. Dapedium (fish)	1·70	1·30

1984. Classified Monuments (2nd series). As T 296.

1142	7f. turquoise	85	50
1143	10f. brown	85	50

DESIGNS: 7f. Hollenfels Castle; 10f. Larochette Castle.

313 "American Soldier" (statue by Michel Heitz at Clervaux)

1984. 40th Anniv of Liberation.

1144	**313**	10f. black, red and blue	2·50	50

314 Infant astounded by Surroundings

1984. National Welfare Fund. The Child. Multicoloured

1145	4f.+1f. Type **314**	55	55
1146	7f.+1f. Child dreaming	85	85
1147	10f.+1f. "Nativity (crib, Steinsel church)	1·40	85
1148	16f.+2f. Child sulking	3·25	4·25
1149	40f.+13f. Girl admiring flower	9·50	11·00

315 Jean Bertels (abbot of Echternach Abbey)

1985. Luxembourg Culture. Portrait Medals in State Museum (1st series). Multicoloured.

1150	4f. Type **315** (steatite medal, 1595)	55	35
1151	7f. Emperor Charles V (bronze medal, 1537)	70	50
1152	10f. King Philip II of Spain (silver medal, 1555)	90	40
1153	30f. Maurice of Orange-Nassau (silver medal, 1615)	2·75	1·50

See also Nos. 1173/6.

316 Fencing

1985. Anniversaries. Multicoloured.

1154	10f. Type **316** (50th anniv of Luxembourg Fencing Federation)	1·00	50
1155	10f. Benz "Velo" (centenary of automobile)	1·00	50
1156	10f. Telephone within concentric circles (centenary of Luxembourg telephone service)	1·00	50

317 Papal Arms

1985. Visit of Pope John Paul II.

1157	**317**	10f. multicoloured	95	45

318 Treble Clef within Map of National Anthem

1965. Europa. Music Year. Multicoloured.

1158	10f. Type **318** (Grand Duke Adolphe Union of choral, instrumental and folklore societies)	5·50	55
1159	16f. Neck of violin, music school and score of Beethoven's Violin Concerto opus 61	9·00	2·75

319 Maquisards Badge and "Wounded Soldiers" (sculpture, Rene Weyland)

1985. 40th Anniv of V.E. (Victory in Europe) Day. Sheet 120×72 mm containing T **319** and similar vert designs.

MS1160 10f. multicoloured (Type **319**); 10f. brown, black and blue (War medal); 10f. multicoloured (Union of Resistance Movements badge); 10f. black, red and blue (dove and barbed wire hands) (liberation of prison camps) 5·50 5·00

320 Little Owl

1985. Endangered Animals. Multicoloured.

1161	4f. Type **320**	1·40	55
1162	7f. European wildcat (horiz)	2·50	85
1163	10f. Red admiral (horiz)	3·75	85
1164	50f. European tree frog	7·75	3·00

1985. Classified Monuments (3rd series). As T **296**.

1165	7f. red	70	40
1166	10f. green	70	40

DESIGNS—HORIZ: 7f. Echternach orangery. VERT: 10f. Mohr de Waldt house.

321 Mansfeld Arms (book binding)

1985. Luxembourg Culture.

1167	**321**	10f. multicoloured	95	45

322 Application

1985. National Welfare Fund. Multicoloured.

1168	4f.+1f. Type **322**	55	55
1169	7f.+1f. Friendship	85	85
1170	10f.+1f. "Adoration of the Magi" (16th century alabaster sculpture)	1·50	85
1171	16f.+2f. Child identifying with his favourite characters	3·75	4·50
1172	40f.+13f. Shame	11·00	14·00

1986. Luxembourg Culture. Portrait Medals in State Museum (2nd series). As T **315**.

1173	10f. multicoloured	1·00	55
1174	12f. multicoloured	1·00	40
1175	18f. black, grey and blue	1·10	95
1176	20f. multicoloured	1·70	1·10

DESIGNS: 10f. Count of Monterey (silver medal, 1675); 12f. Louis XIV of France (silver medal, 1684); 18f. Pierre de Weyms (president of Provincial Council) (pewter medal, 1700); 20f. Duke of Marlborough (silver medal, 1706).

323 Bee on Flower

1986. Anniversaries. Multicoloured.

1177	12f. Type **323** (centenary of Federation of Luxembourg Beekeeper's Associations)	1·30	55
1178	12f. Table tennis player (50th anniv of Luxembourg Table Tennis Federation)	1·30	55
1179	11f. Mosaic of woman with water jar (centenary of Mondorf State Spa)	1·30	55

324 Forest and City

1986. Europa. Multicoloured.

1180	12f. Type **324**	4·00	55
1181	20f. Mankind, industry and countryside	5·00	2·00

325 Fort Thungen

1986. Luxembourg Town Fortifications. Multicoloured.

1182	15f. Type **325**	2·30	70
1183	18f. Invalids' Gate (vert)	2·30	70
1184	50f. Malakoff Tower (vert)	3·75	1·00

326 Schuman

1986. Birth Centenary of Robert Schuman (politician).

1185	**326** 2f. black and red	20	20
1186	**326** 10f. black and blue	55	45

327 Road through Red Triangle on Map

1986. European Road Safety Year.

1187	**327**	10f. multicoloured	85	45

328 Ascent to Chapel of the Cross, Grevenmacher

1986. Tourism.

1188	**328** 12f. multicoloured	1·40	40
1189	- 12f. brown, stone and red	1·40	40

DESIGN: No. 1189, Relief from Town Hall facade, Esch-sur-Alzette.

329 Presentation of Letter of Freedom to Echternach (after P. H. Witkamp)

1986. 800th Birth Anniv of Countess Ermesinde of Luxembourg.

1190	**329** 12f. brown and stone	95	35
1191	- 30f. buff, black and grey	2·10	1·40

DESIGN: 30f. Seal, 1238.

330 Annunciation

1986. National Welfare Fund. Illustrations from 15th-century "Book of Hours". Multicoloured.

1192	6f.+1f. Type **330**	1·40	55
1193	10f.+1f. Angel appearing to shepherds	85	55
1194	12f.+2f. Nativity	1·50	75
1195	18f.+2f. Adoration of the Magi	4·00	4·50
1196	20f.+8f. Flight into Egypt	7·00	8·75

331 Garden Dormouse

1987. Endangered Animals. Multicoloured.

1197	6f. Type **331**	1·10	55
1198	10f. Banded agrion (vert)	1·70	70
1199	12f. White-throated dipper (vert)	2·50	55
1200	25f. Salamander	3·75	2·00

332 Network Emblem

1987. 50th Anniversaries. Multicoloured.

1201	12f. Type **332** (Amateur Short Wave Network)	1·10	40
1202	12f. Anniversary Emblem (International Fair)	1·10	40

333 "St. Bernard of Siena and St. John the Baptist"

1987. Paintings by Giovanni Ambrogio Bevilacqua in State Museum. Multicoloured.

1203	10f. Type **333**		1·00	55
1204	18f. "St. Jerome and St. Francis of Assisi"		1·60	1·10

334 National Swimming Centre (Roger Taillibert)

1987. Europa. Architecture. Multicoloured.

1205	12f. Type **334**		4·50	75
1206	20f. European Communities' Court of Justice		6·75	2·20

335 "Consecration" (stained glass window by Gustav Zanter)

1987. Millenary of St. Michael's Church. Multicoloured.

1207	12f. Type **335**		1·20	55
1208	20f. Baroque organ-chest		2·10	1·10

336 Charles Metz (first President) (after Jean-Baptiste Fresez)

1987. Chamber of Deputies.

1209	**336**	6f. brown	60	35
1210	–	12f. blue	95	55

DESIGN: 12f. Chamber of Deputies building.

337 Hennesbau, Niederfeulen

1987. Rural Architecture. Each ochre, brown and blue.

1211	10f. Type **337**		1·10	60
1212	12f. 18th-century dwelling house converted to health centre, Mersch		1·10	45
1213	100f. 18th-century house converted to Post Office, Bertrange		7·00	1·40

338 Annunciation

1987. National Welfare Fund. Illustrations from 15th-century Paris "Book of Hours". Multicoloured.

1214	6f.+1f. Type **338**		1·40	1·10
1215	10f.+1f. Visitation		1·80	1·70
1216	12f.+2f. Adoration of the Magi		2·50	1·70
1217	18f.+2f. Presentation in the Temple		4·50	4·00
1218	20f.+8f. Flight into Egypt		8·00	7·75

339 Lilies and Water-lily

1988. Luxembourg Culture. Flower Illustrations by Pierre-Joseph Redoute. Multicoloured.

1219	6f. Type **339**		1·10	55
1220	10f. Primulas and double narcissus		1·10	55
1221	12f. Tulips and chrysanthemums		2·50	75
1222	50f. Irises and gorterias		5·50	4·00

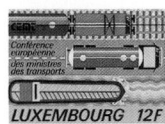

340 Rail, Road and Water Transport

1988. European Conference of Ministers of Transport, Luxembourg (1223) and 25th Anniv of Eurocontrol (air safety organization) (1224). Multicoloured.

1223	12f. Type **340**		1·40	55
1224	20f. Boeing 747 airplane		2·00	1·40

341 Princess Maria Teresa

1988. "Juvalux 88" Ninth Youth Philately Exhibition, Luxembourg. Sheet 11×72 mm containing T **341** and similar vert designs. Multicoloured.

MS1225	12f. Type **341**; 18f. Princes Guillaume, Felix and Louis; 50f. Crown Prince Henri		9·50	9·50

342 Wiltz Town Hall and Cross of Justice

1988. Tourism. Multicoloured.

1226	10f. Type **342**		1·50	45
1227	12f. Differdange Castle (vert)		1·50	65

See also Nos. 1254/5 and 1275/6.

343 Athletes

1988. 50th Anniv of League of Luxembourg Student Sports Associations.

1228	**343**	12f. multicoloured	1·40	65

344 Automated Mail Sorting

1988. Europa. Transport and Communications. Multicoloured.

1229	12f. Type **344**		8·25	55
1230	20f. Electronic communications		8·25	2·75

345 Jean Monnet (statesman, birth centenary)

1988. European Anniversaries.

1231	**345**	12f. pink, brn & lt brn	1·20	50
1232	–	12f. brown and green	1·60	50

DESIGN: No. 1232, European Investment Bank headquarters, Kirchberg (30th anniv).

346 Emblem and Flame

1988. Olympic Games, Seoul.

1233	**346**	12f. multicoloured	1·10	55

347 Septfontaines Castle

1988. Doorways.

1234	**347**	12f. black and brown	90	45
1235	–	25f. black and green	1·80	1·40
1236	–	50f. black and brown	3·75	2·10

DESIGNS: 25f. National Library; 50f. Holy Trinity Church.

348 Annunciation to Shepherds

1988. National Welfare Fund. Illustrations from 16th-century "Book of Hours". Multicoloured.

1237	9f.+1f. Type **348**		65	55
1238	12f.+2f. Adoration of the Magi		70	55
1239	18f.+2f. Madonna and Child		3·75	3·75
1240	20f.+8f. Pentecost		4·25	4·25

349 C. M. Spoo (promoter of Luxembourgish)

1989. Anniversaries.

1241	**349**	12f. black, red and brown	85	45
1242	–	18f. multicoloured	1·40	90
1243	–	20f. red, black and grey	2·20	1·50

DESIGNS: 12f. Type **349** (75th death anniv); 18f. Stylized inking pad (125th anniv of Book Workers' Federation); 20f. Henri Dunant (founder of International Red Cross) (75th anniv of Luxembourg Red Cross).

350 Grand Ducal Family Vault Bronze (Auguste Tremont)

1989. 150th Anniv of Independence.

1244	**350**	12f. multicoloured	1·30	50

351 "Astra" Satellite and Map on T.V. Screens

1989. Launch of 16-channel T.V. Satellite.

1245	**351**	12f. multicoloured	1·30	55

352 Cyclist

1989. Start in Luxembourg of Tour de France Cycling Race.

1246	**352**	9f. multicoloured	1·70	70

353 Assembly and Flag

1989. 40th Anniv of Council of Europe.

1247	**353**	12f. multicoloured	1·30	45

354 Emblem

1989. Centenary of Interparliamentary Union.

1248	**354**	12f. yellow, blue & indigo	1·30	45

355 Hands

1989. Third Direct Elections to European Parliament.

1249	**355**	12f. multicoloured	1·40	55

356 "Three Children in a Park" (anon)

1989. Europa. Children's Games and Toys. Multicoloured.

1250	12f. Type **356**		4·00	55
1251	20f. "Child with Drum" (anon)		5·00	1·70

357 Grand Duke Jean

1989. 25th Anniv of Accession of Grand Duke Jean.

1252	**357**	3f. black and orange	3·00	3·00
1253	**357**	9f. black and green	2·20	2·20

1989. Tourism. As T **342**. Multicoloured.

1254	12f. Clervaux Castle		1·20	45
1255	18f. 1st-century bronze wild boar, Titelberg		1·70	1·00

358 Charles IV

1989. Luxembourg History. Stained Glass Windows by Joseph Oterberger, Luxembourg Cathedral. Multicoloured.

1256	12f. Type **358**		85	55
1257	20f. John the Blind		1·70	1·30
1258	25f. Wenceslas II		2·00	1·70

359 St. Lambert and St. Blase, Fennange

1989. National Welfare Fund. Restored Chapels (1st series). Multicoloured.

1259		9f.+1f. Type **359**	70	45
1260		12f.+2f. St. Quirinus, Luxembourg (horiz)	95	80
1261		18f.+3f. St. Anthony the Hermit, Reisdorf (horiz)	2·20	3·00
1262		25f.+8f. The Hermitage, Hachiville	4·75	4·50

See also Nos. 1280/3 and 1304/7.

360 Funfair (650th anniv of Schueberfouer)

1990. Anniversaries.

1263	**360**	9f. multicoloured	1·10	55
1264	–	12f. brown, pink & black	95	45
1265	–	18f. multicoloured	1·50	1·70

DESIGNS: 12f. Batty Weber (writer, 50th death anniv); 18f. Dish aerial (125th anniv of International Telecommunications Union).

361 Troops at Fortress

1990. Luxembourg Culture. Etchings of the Fortress by Christoph Wilhelm Selig. Multicoloured.

1266	**361**	9f. Type **361**	90	55
1267		12f. Soldiers by weir	95	55
1268		20f. Distant view of fortress	2·30	1·40
1269		25f. Walls	3·00	1·50

362 Paul Eyschen (75th anniv)

1990. Statesmen's Death Anniversaries.

1270	**362**	9f. brown and blue	75	55
1271	–	12f. blue and brown	95	55

DESIGN: 12f. Emmanuel Servais (centenary).

363 "Psallus pseudoplatini" (male and female) on Maple

1990. Centenary of Luxembourg Naturalists' Society.

1272	**363**	12f. multicoloured	1·00	50

364 General Post Office, Luxembourg City

1990. Europa. Post Office Buildings.

1273	**364**	12f. black and brown	5·50	55
1274	–	20f. black and blue	6·75	2·20

DESIGN—VERT: 20f. Esch-sur-Alzette Post Office.

1990. Tourism. As T **342**. Multicoloured.

1275		12f. Mondercange administrative offices	1·60	40
1276		12f. Schifflange town hall and church	1·60	40

365 Hammelsmarsch Fountain (Will Lofy)

1990. Fountains. Multicoloured.

1277		12f. Type **365**	1·20	55
1278		25f. Doves Fountain	2·20	1·40
1279		50f. Maus Ketty Fountain, Mondorf-les-Bains (Will Lofy)	4·50	2·50

366 Congregation of the Blessed Virgin Mary, Vianden

1990. National Welfare Fund. Restored Chapels (2nd series). Multicoloured.

1280		9f.+1f. Type **366**	85	65
1281		12f.+2f. Notre Dame, Echternach (horiz)	1·40	85
1282		18f.+3f. Consoler of the Afflicted, Grentzingen (horiz)	2·50	2·30
1283		25f.+8f. St. Pirmin, Kaundorf	4·75	4·50

367 Grand Duke Adolf

1990. Centenary of Nassau-Weilbourg Dynasty. Sheet 115×160 mm containing T **367** and similar vert designs. Multicoloured.

MS1284	12f. Type **367**; 12f. Grand Duchess Marie Adelaide; 18f. Grand Ducal arms; 18f. Grand Duchess Charlotte; 20f. Grand Duke William IV; 20f. Grand Duke Jean	12·50	12·50

368 "Geastrum varians"

1991. Fungi. Illustrations by Pierre-Joseph Redoute. Multicoloured.

1285		14f. Type **368**	1·00	75
1286		14f. "Agaricus (Gymnopus) thiebautii"	1·00	75
1287		18f. "Agaricus (Lepiota) lepidocephalus"	1·80	1·30
1288		25f. "Morchella favosa"	2·10	1·40

369 "View from the Trier Road"

1991. Luxembourg Culture. 50th Death Anniv of Sosthene Weis (painter). Multicoloured.

1289		14f. Type **369**	1·40	65
1290		18f. "Vauban Street and the Viaduct"	1·40	1·00
1291		25f. "St. Ulric Street" (vert)	2·50	1·50

370 Dicks (after Jean Goedert)

1991. Death Centenary of Edmond de la Fontaine (penname Dicks) (poet).

1292	**370**	14f. multicoloured	1·40	70

371 Claw grasping Piece of Metal (after Emile Kirscht)

1991. 75th Anniv of Trade Union Movement in Luxembourg.

1293	**371**	14f. multicoloured	1·40	70

372 National Miners' Monument, Kayl

1991. Tourism. Multicoloured.

1294		14f. Type **372**	1·40	70
1295		14f. Magistrates' Court, Redange-sur-Attert (horiz)	1·40	70

373 Earth and Orbit of "Astra 1A" and "1B" Satellites

1991. Europa. Europe in Space. Multicoloured.

1296		14f. Type **373**	4·50	85
1297		18f. Betzdorf Earth Station	5·50	2·20

374 Telephone

1991. Posts and Telecommunications.

1298	**374**	4f. brown	4·00	2·50
1299	–	14f. blue	1·10	85

DESIGN: 14f. Postbox.

375 1936 International Philatelic Federation Congress Stamp

1991. 50th Stamp Day.

1300	**375**	14f. multicoloured	1·40	55

The stamp illustrated on No. 1300 incorrectly shows a face value of 10f.

376 Girl's Head

1991. Mascarons (stone faces on buildings) (1st series).

1301	**376**	14f. black, buff & brown	1·10	55
1302	–	25f. black, buff and pink	1·60	1·30
1303	–	50f. black, buff and blue	3·00	2·40

DESIGNS: 25f. Woman's head; 50f. Man's head.
See also Nos. 1320/22.

377 Chapel of St. Donatus, Arsdorf

1991. National Welfare Fund. Restored Chapels (3rd series). Multicoloured.

1304		14f.+2f. Type **377**	1·50	85
1305		14f.+2f. Chapel of Our Lady of Sorrows, Brandenbourg (horiz)	1·50	1·10
1306		18f.+3f. Chapel of Our Lady, Luxembourg (horiz)	2·40	2·50
1307		22f.+7f. Chapel of the Hermitage, Wolwelange	4·25	4·25

378 Jean-Pierre Pescatore Foundation

1992. Buildings. Multicoloured.

1308		14f. Type **378**	1·10	70
1309		14f. Higher Technology Institute, Kirchberg	1·10	70
1310		14f. New Fairs and Congress Centre, Kirchberg	1·10	70

379 Inner Courtyard, Bettembourg Castle

1992. Tourism. Multicoloured.

1311		18f. Type **379**	1·40	95
1312		25f. Walferdange railway station	2·00	1·30

380 Athlete (detail of mural, Armand Strainchamps)

1992. Olympic Games, Barcelona.

1313	**380**	14f. multicoloured	2·10	65

381 Luxembourg Pavilion

1992. "Expo '92" World's Fair, Seville.

1314	**381**	14f. multicoloured	1·10	65

382 Lions Emblem

1992. 75th Anniv of Lions International.

1315	**382**	14f. multicoloured	1·60	55

383 Memorial Tablet (Lucien Wercollier)

1992. 50th Anniv of General Strike.

1316	**383**	18f. brown, grey and red	1·60	1·00

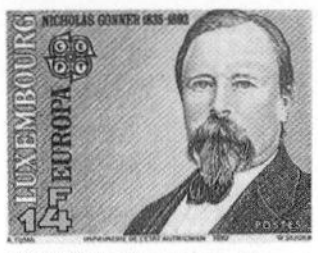

384 Nicholas Gonner (editor)

1992. Europa. 500th Anniv of Discovery of America by Columbus. Luxembourg Emigrants to America.

1317	**384**	14f. brown, black & green	4·50	85
1318	-	22f. blue, black & orange	4·50	2·20

DESIGN: 22f. Nicolas Becker (writer).

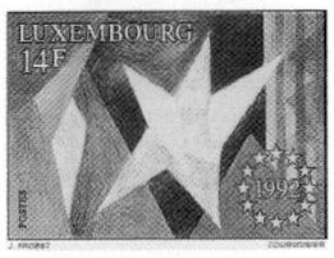

385 Star and European Community Emblem

1992. Single European Market.

1319	**385**	14f. multicoloured	1·10	55

1992. Mascarons (2nd series). As T **376**.

1320	14f. black, buff and green	1·20	55
1321	22f. black, buff and blue	1·80	1·40
1322	50f. black, buff and purple	3·00	2·40

DESIGNS: 14f. Ram's head; 22f. Lion's head; 50f. Goat's head.

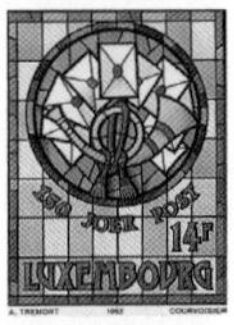

386 Posthorn and Letters

1992. 150th Anniv of Post and Telecommunications Office. Designs showing stained glass windows by Auguste Tremont. Multicoloured

1323	14f. Type **386**	95	70
1324	22f. Post rider	2·10	1·70
1325	50f. Telecommunications	3·00	4·50

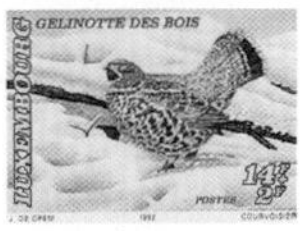

387 Hazel Grouse

1992. National Welfare Fund. Birds (1st series). Multicoloured.

1326	14f.+2f. Type **387**	1·40	1·40
1327	14f.+2f. Golden oriole (vert)	1·40	1·40
1328	18f.+3f. Black stork	4·00	3·50
1329	22f.+7f. Red kite (vert)	7·00	6·25

See also Nos. 1364/7 and 1383/6.

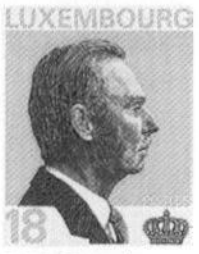

388 Grand Duke Jean

1993

1330	**388**	1f. black and yellow	40	10
1331	**388**	2f. black and green	40	25
1332	**388**	5f. black and yellow	55	25
1333	**388**	7f. black and brown	55	25
1334	**388**	8f. black and green	1·10	45
1335	**388**	9f. black and mauve	70	45
1336	**388**	10f. black and blue	85	50
1337	**388**	14f. black and purple	2·00	55
1338	**388**	15f. black and green	1·30	75
1339	**388**	16f. black and orange	1·80	1·20
1340	**388**	18f. black and yellow	1·20	55
1341	**388**	20f. black and red	1·70	85
1342	**388**	22f. black and green	1·60	1·20
1343	**388**	25f. black and blue	1·70	1·30
1344	**388**	100f. black and brown	6·25	4·00

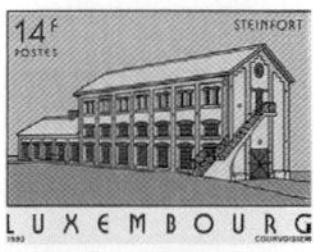

389 Old Ironworks Cultural Centre, Steinfort

1993. Tourism. Multicoloured.

1350	14f. Type **389**	1·30	55
1351	14f. "Children with Grapes" Fountain, Schwebsingen	1·30	55

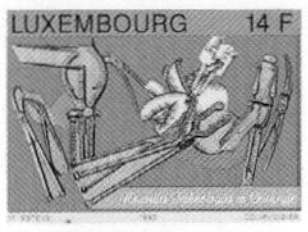

390 Collage by Maurice Esteve

1993. New Surgical Techniques.

1352	**390**	14f. multicoloured	1·20	65

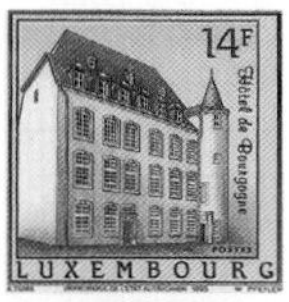

391 Hotel de Bourgogne (Prime Minister's offices)

1993. Historic Houses. Multicoloured.

1353	14f. Type **391**	1·30	75
1354	20f. Simons House (now Ministry of Agriculture)	2·10	1·00
1355	50f. Cassal House	4·50	2·50

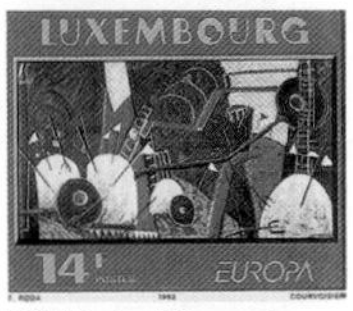

392 "Rezlop" (Fernand Roda)

1993. Europa. Contemporary Art. Multicoloured.

1356	14f. Type **392**	1·50	75
1357	22f. "So Close" (Sonja Roef)	4·00	1·70

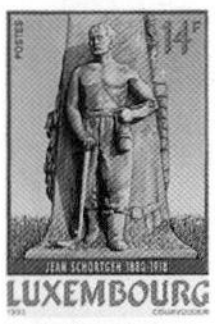

393 Monument (detail, D. Donzelli), Tetange Cemetery

1993. 75th Death Anniv of Jean Schortgen (first worker elected to parliament).

1358	**393**	14f. multicoloured	1·30	60

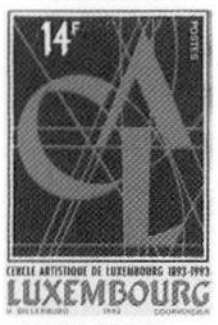

394 Emblem

1993. Centenary of Artistic Circle of Luxembourg.

1359	**394**	14f. mauve and violet	1·30	60

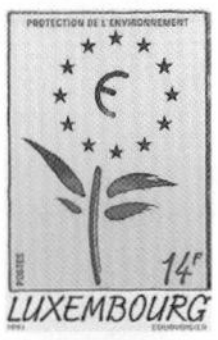

395 European Community Ecological Label

1993. Protection of Environment.

1360	**395**	14f. blue, green & emerald	1·20	85

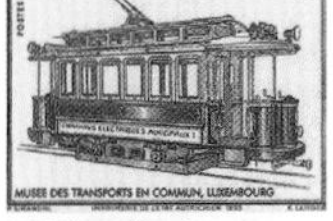

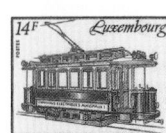

396 Tram No. 1 (Transport Museum, Luxembourg)

1993. Museum Exhibits (1st series). Multicoloured.

1361	14f. Type **396**	1·30	60
1362	22f. Iron ore tipper wagon (National Mining Museum, Rumelange)	1·90	1·60
1363	60f. Horse-drawn carriage (Arts and Ancient Crafts Museum, Wiltz)	4·75	3·75

See also Nos. 1404/6 and 1483/4.

1993. National Welfare Fund. Birds (2nd series). As T **387**. Multicoloured.

1364	14f.+2f. Common snipe ("Becassine")	2·10	1·80
1365	14f.+2f. River kingfisher ("Martin-Pecheur") (vert)	2·10	1·80
1366	18f.+3f. Little ringed plover ("Petit Gravelot")	3·50	4·00
1367	22f.+7f. Sand martin ("Hirondelle de Rivage") (vert)	6·50	6·00

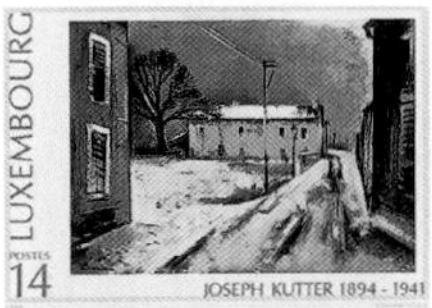

397 "Snow-covered Landscape" (Joseph Kutter)

1994. Artists' Birth Centenaries. Multicoloured.

1368	14f. Type **397**	1·60	70
1369	14f. "The Moselle" (Nico Klopp)	1·60	70

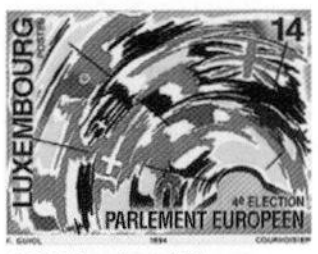

398 Members' Flags

1994. Fourth Direct Elections to European Parliament.

1370	**398**	14f. multicoloured	1·40	1·30

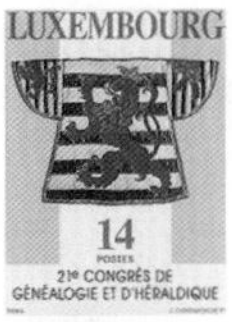

399 17th-century Herald's Tabard

1994. Congresses. Multicoloured.

1371	14f. Type **399** (21st International Genealogy and Heraldry Congress)	2·30	90
1372	18f. International Police Association emblem on map (14th World Congress)	2·40	1·10

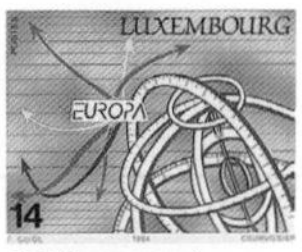

400 Arrows and Terrestrial Globe

1994. Europa. Discoveries. Multicoloured.

1373	14f. Type **400**	2·75	1·30
1374	22f. Chart, compass rose and sails	4·75	2·75

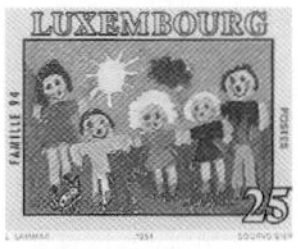

401 "Family" (Laura Lammar)

1994. International Year of the Family.

1375	**401**	25f. multicoloured	4·00	2·00

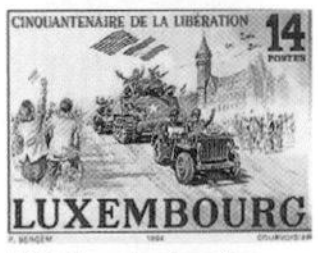

402 Crowds cheering American Soldiers

1994. 50th Anniv of Liberation.

1376	**402**	14f. multicoloured	1·40	1·10

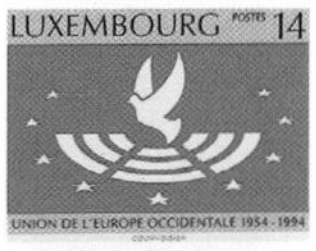

403 Western European Union Emblem (40th anniv)

1994. Anniversaries and Campaign.

1377	**403**	14f. blue, lilac and ultramarine	2·10	90
1378	-	14f. multicoloured	2·10	90
1379	-	14f. multicoloured	5·25	2·10

DESIGNS—No. 1378, Emblem (25th anniv in Luxembourg of European Communities' Office for Official Publications); 1379, 10th-century B.C. ceramic bowl from cremation tomb, Bigelbach (European Bronze Age Campaign).

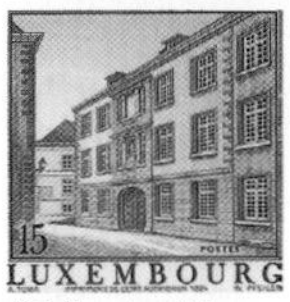

404 Munster Abbey (General Finance Inspectorate)

1994. Former Refuges now housing Government Offices. Multicoloured.

1380	15f. Type **404**	1·60	1·40
1381	25f. Holy Spirit Convent (Ministry of Finance)	2·30	1·80
1382	60f. St. Maximine Abbey of Trier (Ministry of Foreign Affairs)	5·00	3·50

1994. National Welfare Fund. Birds (3rd series). As T **387**. Multicoloured.

1383	14f.+2f. Common stonechat ("Traquet Patre") (vert)	2·50	2·10
1384	14f.+2f. Grey partridge ("Perdix Grise")	2·50	2·10
1385	18f.+3f. Yellow wagtail ("Bergeronnette Printaniere")	4·25	4·25
1386	22f.+7f. Great grey shrike ("Pie-Grieche Grise") (vert)	7·25	5·00

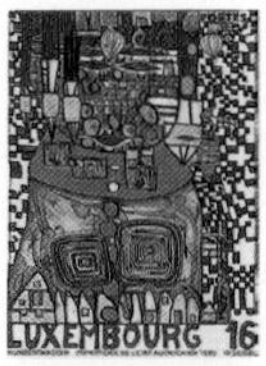

405 "King of the Antipodes"

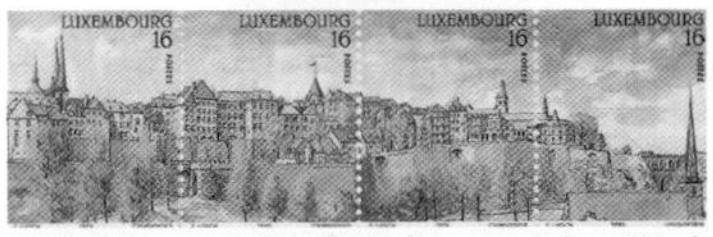

406/409 Panoramic View of City (image scaled to 43% of original size)

1995. Luxembourg, European City of Culture.

1387	**405**	16f. multicoloured	2·50	1·40
1388	-	16f. multicoloured	2·50	1·40
1389	-	16f. multicoloured	2·50	1·40
1390	**406**	16f. multicoloured	1·80	95
1391	**407**	16f. multicoloured	1·80	95
1392	**408**	16f. multicoloured	1·80	95
1393	**409**	16f. multicoloured	1·80	95
1394	-	16f. multicoloured	1·80	95

DESIGNS—As T **405**: No. 1388, "House with Arcades and Yellow Tower"; 1389, "Small Path" (maze). 35×26 mm: No. 1394, Emblem.

Nos. 1390/3 were issued together, *se-tenant*, forming the composite design illustrated.

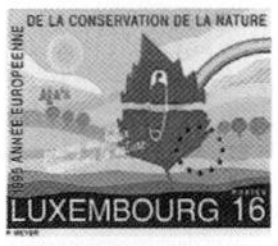

410 Landscape and Slogan

1995. European Nature Conservation Year.

1395	**410**	16f. multicoloured	1·80	1·30

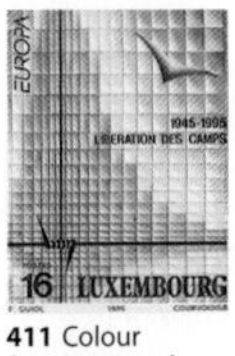

411 Colour Spectrum and Barbed Wire

1995. Europa. Peace and Freedom. 50th Anniv of Liberation of Concentration Camps. Mult.

1396	16f. Type **411**	2·75	1·40
1397	25f. Wire barbs breaking through symbolic sky and earth	3·50	2·75

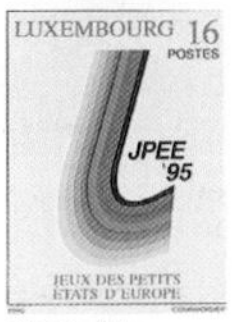

412 Emblem

1995. Anniversaries and Event. Multicoloured.

1398	16f. Type **412** (6th Small European States Games, Luxembourg)		1·60	1·10
1399	32f. Diagram of section through Earth (27th anniv of underground Geodynamics Laboratory, Walferdange) (33×34 mm)		3·50	2·75
1400	80f. Anniversary emblem (50th anniv of U.N.O.)		7·25	5·75

413 Boeing 757

1995. 40th Anniv of Luxembourg–Iceland Air Link.

1401	**413**	16f. multicoloured	1·40	1·10

414 Erpeldange Castle

1995. Tourism. Multicoloured.

1402	16f. Type **414**	1·80	1·10
1403	16f. Schengen Castle	1·80	1·10

1995. Museum Exhibits (2nd series). Vert designs as T 396. Multicoloured.

1404	16f. Churn (Country Art Museum, Vianden)	1·60	90
1405	32f. Wine-press (Wine Museum, Ehnen)	3·50	2·10
1406	80f. Sculpture of potter (Leon Nosbusch) (Pottery Museum, Nospelt)	8·25	4·75

415 Stained Glass Window from Alzingen Church

1995. Christmas.

1407	**415**	16f.+2f. multicoloured	3·25	3·25

416 Broad-leaved Linden ("Tilia platyphyllos")

1995. National Welfare Fund. Trees (1st series). Multicoloured.

1408	16f.+2f. Type **416**	1·80	1·40
1409	16f.+2f. Horse chestnut ("Aesculus hippocastanum") (horiz)	1·80	1·40
1410	20f.+3f. Pedunculate oak (horiz)	2·75	2·50
1411	32f.+7f. Silver birch	5·25	5·00

See also Nos. 1432/5 and 1458/61.

417 Mayrisch (after Theo van Rysselberghe)

1996. 68th Death Anniv of Emile Mayrisch (engineer).

1412	**417**	A (16f.) multicoloured	1·80	1·10

418 Mounument, Place Clairefontaine (Jean Cardot)

1996. Birth Centenary of Grand Duchess Charlotte.

1413	**418**	16f. multicoloured	2·30	1·40

419 Electric Railcar

1996. 50th Anniv of Luxembourg National Railway Company. Multicoloured.

1414	16f. Type **419**	2·75	1·10
1415	16f. Linked cars	2·75	1·10
1416	16f. Train (right-hand detail)	2·75	1·10

Nos. 1414/16 were issued together, se-tenant, forming a composite design of a Series 2000 electric railcar set.

420 "Marie Munchen"

1996. 96th Death Anniv of Mihaly Munkacsy (painter). Multicoloured.

1417	16f. Type **420**	1·60	1·10
1418	16f. Munkacsy (after Edouard Charlemont) (horiz)	1·60	1·10

421 Workers and Emblem

1996. Anniversaries.

1419	**421**	16f. green, orge & blk	1·60	1·10
1420	-	20f. multicoloured	1·90	1·40
1421	-	25f. multicoloured	2·40	1·90
1422	-	32f. multicoloured	3·50	2·50

DESIGNS—HORIZ: 16f. Type **421** (75th anniv of Luxembourg Confederation of Christian Trade Unions); 32f. Film negative (centenary of motion pictures). VERT: 20f. Transmitter and radio waves (centenary of Guglielmo Marconi's patented wireless telegraph); 25f. Olympic flame and rings (centenary of modern Olympic Games).

422 Marie de Bourgogne

1996. Europa. Famous Women. Duchesses of Luxembourg. Multicoloured.

1423	16f. Type **422**	2·50	1·40
1424	25f. Maria-Theresa of Austria	4·00	2·75

423 Handstamp

1996. Bicentenary (1995) of Registration and Property Administration.

1425	**423** 16f. multicoloured	1·80	1·10

424 Children of different Cultures (Michele Dockendorf)

1996. "Let us Live Together". Multicoloured.

1426	16f. Type **424**	1·30	1·10
1427	16f. "L'Abbraccio" (statue, Marie-Josee Kerschen) (vert)	1·30	1·10

425 Eurasian Badger

1996. Mammals. Multicoloured.

1428	16f. Type **425**	1·80	90
1429	20f. Polecat	2·75	1·40
1430	80f. European otter	7·25	5·75

426 "The Birth of Christ" (icon, Eva Mathes)

1996. Christmas.

1431	**426**	16f.+2f. multicoloured	5·00	5·00

1996. National Welfare Fund. Trees (2nd series). As T **416**. Multicoloured.

1432	16f.+2f. Willow ("Salix sp.") (horiz)	1·80	1·40
1433	16f.+2f. Ash ("Fraxinus excelsior")	1·80	1·40
1434	20f.+3f. Mountain ash (horiz)	3·50	3·25
1435	32f.+7f. Common beech	6·00	5·75

427 John the Blind

1996. 700th Birth Anniv of John the Blind (King of Bohemia and Count of Luxembourg).

1436	**427**	32f. multicoloured	3·25	2·10

428 Koerich Church

1997. Tourism. Multicoloured.

1437	16f. Type **428**	1·60	1·10
1438	16f. Servais House, Mersch (horiz)	1·60	1·10

429 Birthplace of Robert Schuman (politician), Luxembourg-Clausen

1997. Anniversaries. Multicoloured.

1439	16f. Type **429** (40th anniv of Treaties of Rome establishing European Economic Community and European Atomic Energy Community)	1·80	1·10
1440	20f. National colours forming wing of Mercury (75th anniv of Belgium–Luxembourg Economic Union)	2·10	1·40

430 "Grand Duchess Charlotte"

1997. 11th World Federation of Rose Societies Congress, Belgium, Mondorf (Luxembourg) and the Netherlands. Roses. Multicoloured.

1441	16f. Type **430**	2·75	1·10
1442	20f. "The Beautiful Sultana" (33×26 mm)	2·75	1·80
1443	80f. "In Memory of Jean Soupert" (33×26 mm)	8·50	6·00

431 Badge, Luxembourg Fortress, Shako and Sword

1997. Anniversaries.

1444	**431** 16f. multicoloured	1·80	1·10
1445	- 16f. black, blue and red	1·80	1·10
1446	- 16f. brown, green and pink	1·80	1·10

DESIGNS—As T **431**: No. 1444, Type **431** (bicentenary of Grand Ducal Gendarmerie Corps); 1445, Cock and rabbit (75th anniv of Luxembourg Union of Small Domestic Animals Farming Societies). 33×33 mm: No. 1446, Bather and attendant, early 1900s (150th anniv of Mondorf spa).

432 The Beautiful Melusina

1997. Europa. Tales and Legends. Multicoloured.

1447	16f. Type **432**	2·75	1·10
1448	25f. The Hunter of Hollenfels	4·25	2·75

433 Face on Globe

1997. "Juvalux 98" Youth Stamp Exhibition (1st issue). Multicoloured.

1449	16f. Type **433**	2·10	1·10
1450	80f. Postmen (painting, Michel Engels)	7·50	6·50

See also Nos. 1475/8.

434 Emblem

1997. Sar–Lor–Lux (Saarland–Lorraine–Luxembourg) European Region.

1451	**434** 16f. multicoloured	1·80	1·10

Stamps in similar designs were issued by France and Germany.

435 Wall Clock by Dominique Nauens, 1816

1997. Clocks. Multicoloured.

1452	16f. Type **435**	2·10	1·10
1453	32f. Astronomical clock by J. Lebrun, 1850 (26×44 mm)	4·75	2·30
1454	80f. Wall clock by Mathias Hebeler, 1815	8·25	5·25

436 "Kalborn Mill" (Jean-Pierre Gleis)

1997. Water Mills. Multicoloured.

1455	16f. Type **436**	2·10	95

1456 50f. Interior of Ramelli mill, 1588 (from book "The Water Wheel" by Wilhelm Wolfel) (vert) 5·00 3·50

437 Holy Family

1997. Christmas.
1457 **437** 16f.+2f. multicoloured 4·25 4·25

1997. National Welfare Fund. Trees (3rd series). As T 416. Multicoloured.
1458 16f.+2f. Wych elm ("Ulmus glabra") 1·80 1·80
1459 16f.+2f. Norway maple ("Acer platanoides") 1·80 1·80
1460 20f.+3f. Wild cherry 3·50 3·50
1461 32f.+7f. Walnut (horiz) 5·00 5·00

438 Count Henri V

1997. 750th Anniv of Accession of Henri V, Count of Luxembourg.
1462 **438** 32f. multicoloured 3·50 2·10

439 Rodange Church

1998. Tourism. Multicoloured.
1463 16f. Type **439** 1·80 1·10
1464 16f. Back of local authority building, Hesperange (horiz) 1·80 1·10

440 Cog and "50"

1998. Anniversaries.
1465 **440** 16f. multicoloured 2·30 1·10
1466 – 16f. multicoloured 2·30 1·10
1467 – 20f. multicoloured 2·30 1·30
1468 – 50f. black, red and stone 5·75 3·50
DESIGNS: No. 1465, Type **440** (50th anniv of Independent Luxembourg Trade Union); 1466, Festival poster (Rene Wismer) (50th anniv of Broom Festival, Wiltz); 1467, Memorial (death centenary of Jean Antoine Zinnen (composer of national anthem)); 1468, Typewriter keys and page from first issue of "Luxemburger Wort" (150th anniv of abolition of censorship).

441 Brown Trout

1998. Freshwater Fishes. Multicoloured.
1469 16f. Type **441** 2·75 1·30
1470 25f. Bullhead 5·00 2·75
1471 50f. Riffle minnow 6·50 4·00

442 Henri VII and Flags outside Fair Venue, Kirchberg

1998. 700th Anniv of Granting to Count Henri VII of Right to Hold a Fair. Value indicated by letter.
1472 **442** A (16f.) multicoloured 2·10 1·10

443 Fireworks over Adolphe Bridge (National Day)

1998. Europa. National Festivals. Multicoloured.
1473 16f. Type **443** 3·50 1·10
1474 25f. Stained-glass window and flame (National Remembrance Day) 4·25 2·75

444 Town Postman, 1880

1998. "Juvalux '98" Youth Stamp Exhibition (2nd issue). Multicoloured.
1475 16f. Type **444** 2·10 1·10
1476 25f. Letter, 1590 (horiz) 2·75 2·10
1477 50f. Rural postman, 1880 4·25 3·25
MS1478 125×76 mm 16f., 80f. Railway viaduct and city (composite design) 13·50 13·50

445 Masonic Symbols (Paul Moutschen)

1998. 150th Anniv of St. John of Hope Freemason Lodge.
1479 **445** 16f. multicoloured 2·10 1·30

698-1998 ECHTERNACH
446 Echternach

1998. 1300th Anniv of Echternach Abbey. Multicoloured.
1480 16f. Type **446** 2·10 1·10
1481 48f. Buildings in Echternach 4·75 3·75
1482 60f. Echternach Abbey 5·00 4·00

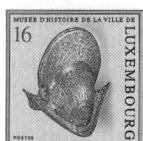
447 Spanish Morion (late 16th century)

1998. Museum Exhibits (3rd series). City of Luxembourg History Museum. Multicoloured.
1483 16f. Type **447** 2·50 1·10
1484 80f. Wayside Cross from Hollerich (1718) 5·75 5·50

448 "Nativity" (altarpiece by Georges Saget, St. Mauritius Abbey, Clervaux)

1998. Christmas.
1485 **448** 16f.+2f. multicoloured 4·25 4·25

449 "Bech"

1998. National Welfare Fund (1st series). Villages. 16th-century drawings by Jean Bertels. Multicoloured.
1486 16f.+2f. Type **449** 2·50 1·90
1487 16f.+2f. "Ermes Turf" (now Ermsdorf) 2·50 1·90

1488 20f.+3f. "Itsich" (now Itzig) 3·25 2·30
1489 32f.+7f. "Stein Hem" (now Steinheim) 4·75 5·25
See also Nos. 1510/13 and 1550/3.

450 Globe and Jigsaw

1998. 40th Anniv of North Atlantic Maintenance and Supply Agency.
1490 **450** 36f. multicoloured 4·75 3·25

451 Council Building and Emblem

1999. 50th Anniv of Council of Europe.
1491 **451** 16f. multicoloured 2·10 1·40

452 Euro Coin and Map

1999. Introduction of the Euro (European currency). Value expressed by letter.
1492 **452** A (16f.) multicoloured 2·10 1·10

453 Tawny Owl

1999. Owls. Multicoloured.
1493 A (16f.) Type **453** 2·10 1·30
1494 32f. Eagle owl (horiz) 3·25 3·00
1495 60f. Barn owl (horiz) 6·50 5·25

454 Globe and Emblem

1999. 50th Anniv of N.A.T.O.
1496 **454** 80f. multicoloured 7·25 5·75

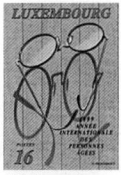
455 Spectacles

1999. International Year of the Elderly.
1497 **455** 16f. multicoloured 1·80 1·10

456 Emblem and Envelopes

1999. 125th Anniv of Universal Postal Union.
1498 **456** 16f. multicoloured 1·80 1·10

457 Haute-Sure National Park

1999. Europa. Parks and Gardens. Multicoloured.
1499 16f. Type **457** 3·50 1·40
1500 25f. Ardennes-Eifel National Park 4·25 2·50

458 Emblem

1999. Anniversaries. Multicoloured.
1501 16f. Type **458** (75th anniv of National Federation of Mutual Societies) 1·80 1·10
1502 32f. Camera and roll of film (50th anniv of Luxembourg Federation of Amateur Photographers) 2·75 2·75
1503 80f. Gymnasts (centenary of Luxembourg Gymnastics Federation) 7·25 5·75

460 Cars on Motorway

1999. 18th Birthday of Prince Guillaume.
1504 **459** 16f. multicoloured 1·40 1·10

459 Prince Guillaume

1999. Communications of the Future. Multicoloured.
1505 16f. Type **460** 1·60 1·30
1506 20f. Earth and satellite 2·10 2·00
1507 80f. Planets and spacecraft 7·25 5·75

461 A. Mayrisch de Saint-Hubert

1999. 125th Birth Anniv of Aline Mayrisch de Saint-Hubert (President of Luxembourg Red Cross).
1508 **461** 20f. multicoloured 2·40 1·40

462 Decorated Church Tower

1999. Christmas.
1509 **462** 16f.+2f. multicoloured 3·25 2·75

1999. National Welfare Fund. Villages (2nd series). As T 449, showing 6th-century drawings by Jean Bertels. Multicoloured.
1510 16f.+2f. "Oswiler" (now Osweiler) 2·75 2·10
1511 16f.+2f. "Bettem Burch" (now Bettembourg) 2·75 2·10
1512 20f.+3f. "Cruchte auf der Alset" (now Cruchten) 3·25 3·25
1513 32f.+7f. "Berchem" 5·25 5·25

463 "Gateway" (sketch by Goethe)

1999. 250th Birth Anniv of Johann Wolfgang von Goethe (poet and playwright).
1514 **463** 20f. chestnut, cream & brn 2·40 1·40

464 "2000"

2000. New Millennium. Value expressed by letter. Multicoloured. Self-adhesive.

1515		A (16f.) Type **464** (blue streaks emanating from bottom right)	2·00	1·40
1516		A (16f.) Blue streaks emanating from bottom left	2·00	1·40
1517		A (16f.) Blue streaks emanating from top right	2·00	1·40
1518		A (16f.) Blue streaks emanating from top left	2·00	1·40

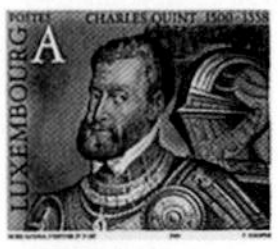

465 Charles V

2000. 500th Birth Anniv of Emperor Charles V. Value expressed by letter.

1519	**465**	A (16f.) multicoloured	1·80	1·10

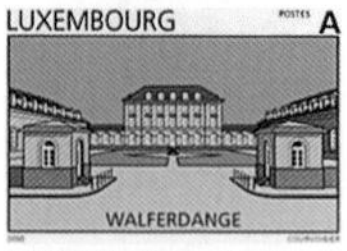

466 Walferdange Castle

2000. Tourism. Value expressed by letter. Multicoloured.

1520		A (16f.) Type **466**	1·30	1·10
1521		A (16f.) Local government offices, Wasserbillig (vert)	1·30	1·10

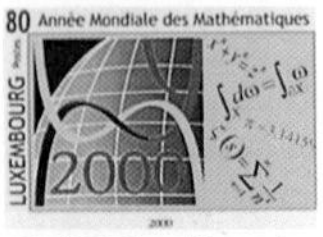

467 "2000" and Formulae

2000. World Mathematics Year.

1522	**467**	80f. multicoloured	6·25	4·50

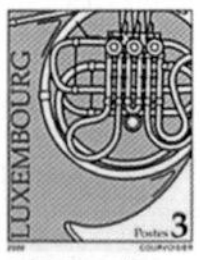

468 French Horn

2000. Musical Instruments.

1523	**468**	3f. black and violet	50	25
1524	-	9f. black and green	1·40	90
1525	-	12f. black and yellow	1·10	95
1526	-	21f. black and pink	1·90	1·40
1527	-	24f. black and blue	2·75	2·00
1528	-	30f. black and pink	2·50	2·00

DESIGNS: 9f. Electric guitar; 12f. Saxophone; 21f. Violin; 24f. Accordion; 30f. Grand piano.

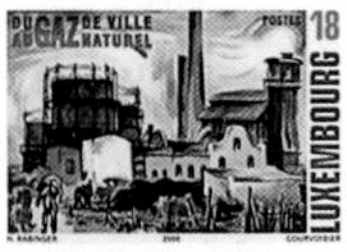

469 Production and Storage Facilities, 1930s (Harry Rabinger)

2000. Centenary (1999) of Esch-sur-Alzette Gas Works.

1535	**469**	18f. multicoloured	2·50	1·60

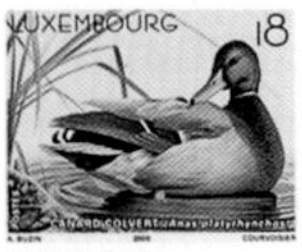

470 Mallard

2000. Ducks. Multicoloured.

1536		18f. Type **470**	2·50	1·80
1537		24f. Common pochard (vert)	3·25	2·50
1538		30f. Tufted duck (vert)	4·25	3·25

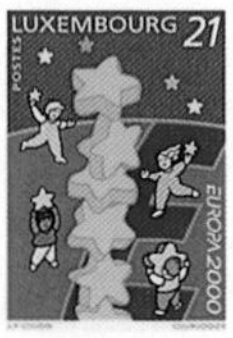

471 "Building Europe"

2000. Europa.

1539	**471**	21f. multicoloured	2·50	1·80

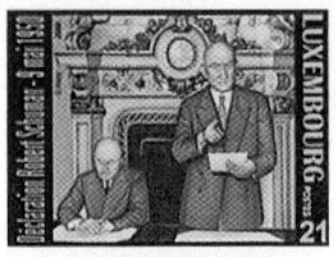

472 Jean Monnet and Robert Schuman

2000. 50th Anniv of Schuman Plan (proposal for European Coal and Steel Community).

1540	**472**	21f. black, blue & yellow	2·50	2·00

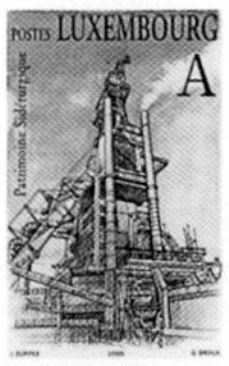

473 Blast Furnace

2000. 20th Anniv of Blast Furnace "B", Esch-Belval.

1541	**473**	A (18f.) multicoloured	2·50	1·10

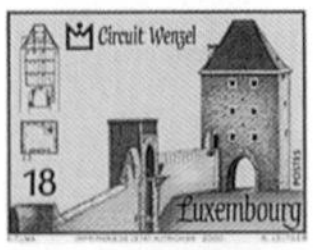

474 Castle Walls and Tower (Wenzel Walk)

2000. Circular City Walks. Multicoloured.

1542		18f. Type **474**	2·10	1·20
1543		42f. Bridge and tower (Vauban walk)	5·00	3·75

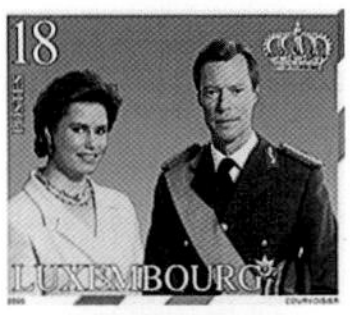

475 Will Kesseler

2000. Swearing in of Prince Henri as Head of State of Grand Duchy of Luxembourg. Multicoloured.

1544		18f. Type **475**	1·80	2·00
MS1545		125×90 mm. 100f. Prince Henri in civilian clothes and Princess Maria	19·00	6·50

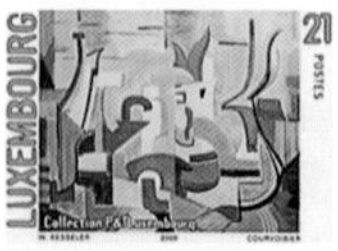

476 Prince Henri in Uniform and Princess Maria

2000. Modern Art (1st series). Showing paintings by artist named. Multicoloured.

1546		21f. Type **476**	2·30	1·80
1547		24f. Joseph Probst (vert)	2·40	1·20
1548		36f. Mett Hoffmann	3·25	1·40

See also Nos. 1612/14.

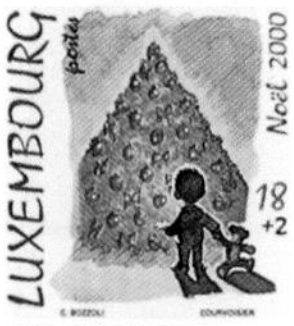

477 Child before Christmas Tree

2000. Christmas.

1549	**477**	18f.+2f. multicoloured	2·75	2·75

2000. National Welfare Fund. Villages (3rd series). As T **449** showing 16th-century drawings by Jean Bertels. Multicoloured.

1550		18f.+2f. "Lorentzwiller" (now dorentzweiler)	2·10	2·00
1551		21f.+3f. "Coosturf" (now Consdorf)	2·75	2·75
1552		24f.+3f. "Elfingen" (now Elvange)	3·25	2·75
1553		36f.+7f. "Sprenckigen" (now Sprinkange)	4·75	4·75

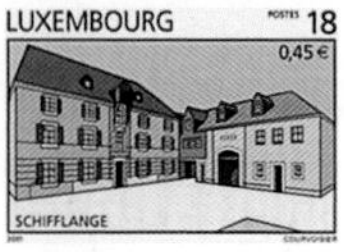

478 Bestgensmillen Mill, Schifflange

2001. Tourism. Multicoloured.

1554		18f. Type **478**	1·80	1·40
1555		18f. Vineyard, Wormeldange (vert)	1·80	1·40

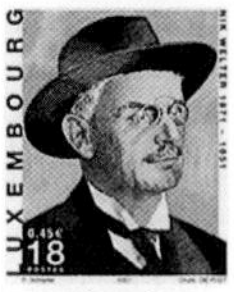

479 Nik Welter

2001. Writers' Death Anniversaries. Multicoloured.

1556		18f. Type **479** (50th anniv)	1·70	1·40
1557		24f. Andre Gide (50th anniv)	2·30	1·90
1558		30f. Michel Rodange (125th anniv)	2·75	2·50

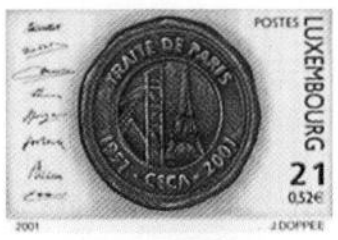

480 Signatures and Seal

2001. 50th Anniv of Treaty of Paris.

1559	**480**	21f. multicoloured	2·50	1·80

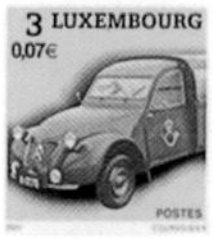

481 Citroen 2CV Mini-Van

2001. Postal Vehicles. Mult. Self-adhesive.

1560		3f. Type **481**	50	30
1561		18f. Volkswagen Beetle	2·10	1·30

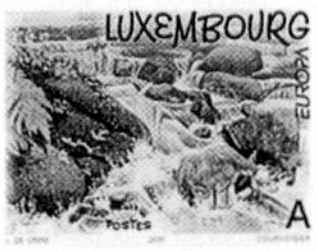

482 Stream, Mullerthal

2001. Europa. Water Resources. Multicoloured. Value expressed by letter (No. 1562) or with face value (No. 1563).

1562		A (18f.) Type **482**	2·10	1·40
1563		21f. Pond and Kaltreis water tower (vert)	2·75	1·80

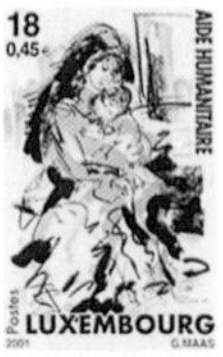

483 "Mother and Child" (Ger Maas)

2001. Humanitarian Projects. Multicoloured.

1564		18f. Type **483** (humanitarian aid)	2·10	1·40
1565		24f. International Organization for Migration emblem	3·25	2·50

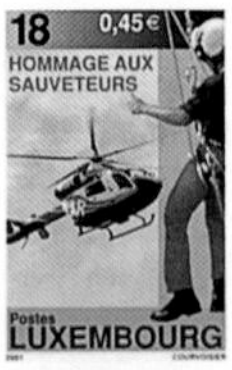

484 MD Helicopters MD Explorer and Rescuer

2001. Rescue Services. Multicoloured.

1566		18f. Type **484**	2·10	1·40
1567		30f. Divers and rubber dinghy	2·75	2·50
1568		45f. Fire engine and fireman wearing protective clothing	4·75	3·50

DENOMINATION. From No. 1569 Luxembourg stamps are denominated in euros only.

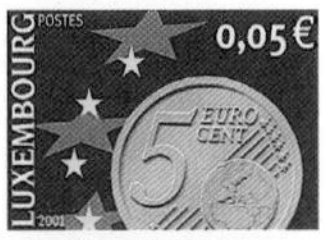

485 Five Cent Coin

2001. Euro Currency. Coins. Multicoloured.

1569		5c. Type **485**	50	50
1570		10c. Ten cent coin	55	55
1571		20c. Twenty cent coin	1·10	70
1572		50c. Fifty cent coin	1·80	1·40
1573		€1 One euro coin	3·25	2·75
1574		€2 Two euro coin	6·50	5·75

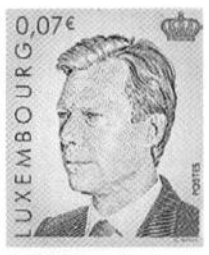

486 Grand Duke Henri

2001. Grand Duke Henri.

1575		1c. indigo, blue and ultramarine	25	25
1576		3c. olive, green and ultramarine	30	30
1580	**486**	7c. dp blue, blue & red	25	25
1583	**486**	22c. sepia, brown & red	60	45
1584	**486**	25c. lilac and ultramarine	60	45
1585	**486**	30c. dp green, grn & red	70	60
1588	**486**	45c. dp violet, vio & red	1·10	70
1589	**486**	50c. black and ultramarine	1·20	1·00
1590	**486**	52c. brown, buff and red	1·30	1·20
1591	**486**	59c. deep blue, blue and red	1·40	1·20
1592	**486**	60c. black, green and blue	1·40	1·20
1592a	**486**	70c. lilac ultramarine	1·80	1·60
1593	**486**	74c. brown, stone and red	1·80	1·50
1594	**486**	80c. agate, green and blue	1·90	1·60
1595	**486**	89c. mauve, brown and red	2·20	1·70
1595a	**486**	90c. brown, ochre and ultramarine	2·30	1·90
1595b	**486**	€1 blue, azuree and ultramarine	2·75	2·40

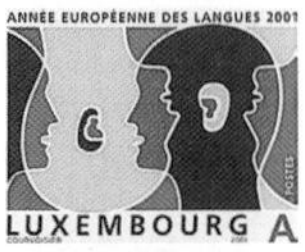

487 Emblem

2001. European Year of Languages. Value expressed by letter.

1596	**487**	A (45c.) multicoloured	1·20	85

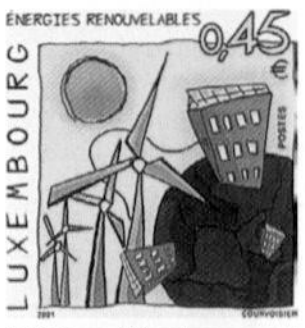

488 Sun, Wind-powered Generators and Houses (renewable energy)

2001. Environment and Medicine of the Future. Multicoloured.

1597		45c. Type **488**	1·20	1·20
1598		59c. Tyre, tins, bottle and carton (recycling)	1·80	1·70
1599		74c. Microscope and test-tubes (biological research)	1·80	1·70

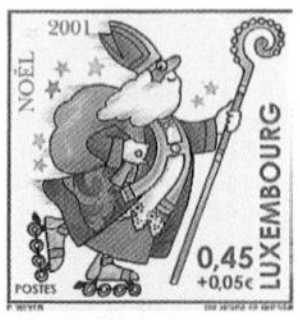

489 St. Nicholas

2001. Christmas.

1600	**489**	45c.+5c. multicoloured	1·80	1·70

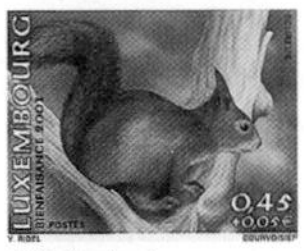

490 Squirrel

2001. National Welfare Fund. Animals (1st issue). Multicoloured.

1601		45c.+5c. Type **490**	1·60	1·40
1602		52c.+8c. Wild boar	1·80	1·60
1603		59c.+11c. Hare (vert)	2·10	1·90
1604		89c.+21c. Wood pigeon (vert)	3·00	2·75

See also Nos. 1632/5 and 1660/3.

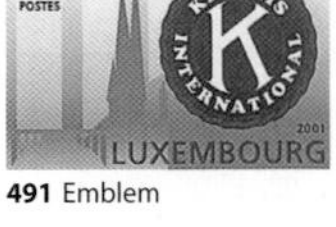

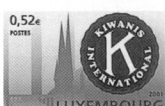

491 Emblem

2001. Kiwanis International (community organization).

| 1605 | 491 | 52c. dp blue, bl & gold | 1·80 | 1·50 |

492 Snowboarding

2002. Sports. Self-adhesive. Multicoloured.

1606	7c. Type **492**	25	25
1607	7c. Skateboarding	25	25
1608	7c. Inline skating	25	25
1609	45c. BMX biking	1·20	1·20
1610	45c. Beach volleyball	1·20	1·20
1611	45c. Street basketball	1·20	1·20

493 Mortiz Ney

2002. Modern Art (2nd series). Showing works by artist named. Multicoloured.

1612	22c. Type **493**	60	60
1613	45c. Dany Prum (horiz)	1·20	1·20
1614	59c. Christiane Schmit	1·80	1·70

494 Map of Europe and "1977"

2002. Anniversaries. Multicoloured.

| 1615 | 45c. Type **494** (25th anniv of European Court of Auditors) | 1·20 | 1·20 |
| 1616 | 52c. Scales of Justice and map of Europe (50th anniv of European Communities Court of Justice) | 1·80 | 1·70 |

495 Tightrope Walker

2002. Europa. The Circus. Multicoloured.

| 1617 | 45c. Type **495** | 1·20 | 1·20 |
| 1618 | 52c. Clown juggling | 1·80 | 1·70 |

496 Emblem

2002. 2002 Tour de France (starting in Luxembourg). Multicoloured.

1619	45c. Type **496**	1·20	60
1620	52c. Francois Faber (winner of 1909 Tour de France) (vert)	1·80	1·70
1621	€2.45 "The Champion" (Joseph Kutter) (vert)	6·75	6·50

497 Orchestra on Stage (50th Anniv of Festival of Wiltz)

2002. Cultural Anniversaries. Value expressed by letter (No. 1622) or face value (No. 1623). Multicoloured.

| 1622 | A (45c.) Type **497** | 1·20 | 1·20 |
| 1623 | €1.12 Victor Hugo and signature (birth bicentenary) | 3·50 | 3·50 |

498 Grand Duke William III of Netherlands

2002. 150th Anniv of First Luxembourg Stamp (1st issue). Sheet 121×164 mm, containing T **498** and similar horiz designs. Multicoloured.

| MS1624 | 45c. Type **498**; 45c. Grand Duke Adolphe; 45c. Grand Duchess Charlotte; 45c. Grand Duke Henri | 6·00 | 5·75 |

See also Nos. 1630/1.

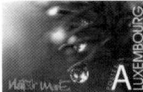

499 Water Droplet on Spruce

2002. Natural History Museum. Multicoloured. Value expressed by letter. Self-adhesive.

1625	A (45c.) Type **499**	1·20	1·20
1626	A (45c.) Mocker swallowtail	1·20	1·20
1627	A (45c.) Houseleek	1·20	1·20
1628	A (45c.) Blackthorn berries	1·20	1·20

500 Emblem

2002. 750th Anniv of Grevenmacher City Charter.

| 1629 | **500** | 74c. multicoloured | 1·80 | 1·70 |

501 Postmen in Flying Vehicles (Clare Nothumb)

2002. 150th Anniv of First Luxembourg Stamp (2nd issue). Winning Entries in Stamp Design Competition. (a) With face value.

| 1630 | 22c. Type **501** | 60 | 60 |

(b) Value expressed by letter.

| 1631 | A (45c.) Symbols of communications and flying saucer orbiting planet (Christine Hengen) (horiz) | 1·20 | 1·20 |

502 Fox

2002. National Welfare Fund. Animals (2nd series). Multicoloured.

1632	45c.+5c. Type **502**	1·20	1·20
1633	52c.+8c. Hedgehog (vert)	1·40	1·40
1634	59c.+11c. Pheasant	1·70	1·60
1635	89c.+21c. Deer (vert)	3·00	2·75

503 Place d'Armes

2002. Christmas.

| 1636 | **503** | 45c.+5c. multicoloured | 1·20 | 1·20 |

No. 1636 was issued in *se-tenant* sheetlets of 12 stamps, the margins of which were impregnated with the scent of cinnamon.

504 Grand Duke Jean and Grand Duchess Josephine-Charlotte

2003. Golden Wedding Anniversary of Grand Duke Jean and Grand Duchess Josephine-Charlotte.

| 1637 | **504** | 45c. multicoloured | 1·20 | 1·20 |

505 Catherine Schleimer-Kill

2003. 30th Death Anniversaries. Multicoloured.

| 1638 | 45c. Type **505** (political pioneer) | 1·20 | 1·20 |
| 1639 | 45c. Lou Koster (composer) | 1·20 | 1·20 |

506 Citeaux Abbey, Differdange

2003. Tourism. Multicoloured.

1640	50c. Type **506**	1·20	1·20
1641	€1 Mamer Castle	2·40	2·30
1642	€2.50 St. Joseph Church, Esch-sur-Alzette (vert)	6·00	5·75

507 Pamphlets and Compact Discs

2003. 50th Anniv of Official Journal of European Communities (daily publication of official reports).

| 1643 | **507** | 52c. multicoloured | 1·80 | 1·70 |

508 Head and Symbols

2003. 400th Anniv of the Athenee (secondary school), Luxembourg.

| 1644 | **508** | 45c. multicoloured | 1·20 | 1·00 |

509 1952 National Lottery Poster (Roger Gerson)

2003. Europa. Poster Art. Multicoloured.

| 1645 | 45c. Type **509** | 1·20 | 1·00 |
| 1646 | 52c. Tiger (1924 Commercial Fair poster) (Auguste Tremont) | 1·30 | 1·10 |

510 Adolphe Bridge

2003. Bridges and Viaducts. Multicoloured.

1647	45c. Type **510** (centenary)	1·20	1·00
1648	59c. Stierchen bridge (14th-century) (38×28 mm)	1·40	1·20
1649	89c. Victor Bodson bridge (Hesperange viaduct) (38×28 mm)	2·20	1·80

511 Woman Hoeing

2003. 75th Anniv of Gaart an Heem (gardening association). Multicoloured.

1650	25c. Type **511**	60	50
1651	A (45c.) Woman holding rake	1·20	1·00
1652	€2 Children	4·75	4·00

512 Baby at Breast

2003. Breastfeeding Campaign.

| 1653 | **512** | A (45c.) brown, chestnut and black | 1·20 | 1·00 |

513 Light Bulb

2003. 75th Anniv of Electricity.

| 1654 | **513** | A (45c.) multicoloured | 1·20 | 1·00 |

514 Engineering Steel Sheet Piles

2003. Made in Luxembourg. Multicoloured.

1655	60c. Type **514**	1·40	1·20
1656	70c. Medical valve	1·70	1·40
1657	80c. Technician and polyester film	1·90	1·60

515 Church and Cloud containing Buildings

2003. Christmas. Multicoloured.

| 1658 | 50c.+5c. Type **515** | 1·90 | 1·50 |
| 1659 | 50c.+5c. Child, church and Christmas tree | 1·90 | 1·50 |

516 Roe-deer

2003. Fauna (3rd series). Multicoloured.

1660	50c.+5c. Type **516**	1·40	1·10
1661	60c.+10c. Raccoon (horiz)	1·80	1·40
1662	70c.+10c. Weasel	2·00	1·60
1663	€1 +25c. Goshawk (horiz)	3·25	2·50

517 *Cantharellus tubaeformis*

2004. Fungi. Multicoloured. Self-adhesive.

1664	10c. Type **517**	30	25
1665	10c. *Ramaria flava*	30	25
1666	10c. *Stropharia cynea*	30	25
1667	50c. *Helvella lacunose*	1·60	1·30
1668	50c. *Anthurus archeri*	1·60	1·30
1669	50c. *Clitopilus prunulus*	1·60	1·30

518 Annual Street Market, Luxembourg-Ville

2004. Anniversaries. Multicoloured.

| 1670 | 50c. Type **518** (75th anniv) | 1·60 | 1·30 |
| 1671 | 50c. Haberdashery (centenary of Esch-sur-Alzette Commercial Union) | 1·60 | 1·30 |

519 Edward Steichen

2004. Birth Anniversaries. Multicoloured.

| 1672 | **519** | 50c. lilac, brown and black | 1·60 | 1·30 |
| 1673 | – | 70c. blue, buff and black | 2·20 | 1·80 |

DESIGNS: 50c. Type **519** (photographer) (125th); 70c. Hugo Gernsback (science fiction writer) (120th and centenary of his emigration to USA).

520 Stylized Figures

2004. European Elections.

| 1674 | **520** | 50c. multicoloured | 1·60 | 1·30 |

521 Hikers on Bridge, Mullerthal

2004. Europa. Holidays. Multicoloured.

| 1675 | | 50c. Type **521** | 1·60 | 1·30 |
| 1676 | | 60c. Camp site, Bourscheid-Beach | 1·90 | 1·50 |

522 Runners carrying Olympic Flame (A. Bilska)

2004. Sport. Winning Entries in Children's Drawing Competition. Multicoloured.

| 1677 | | 50c. Type **522** (Olympic Games, Athens, 2004) | 1·60 | 1·30 |
| 1678 | | 60c. Basketball (L. Eyschen) (European Year of Education through Sport) | 1·90 | 1·50 |

523 Building and Anniversary Emblem

2004. 50th Anniv of European School, Luxembourg.

| 1679 | **523** | 70c. multicoloured | 2·40 | 1·80 |

524 Breads and Beer

2004. Made in Luxembourg. Food. Multicoloured.

1680		35c. Type **524**	1·20	90
1681		60c. Meat products	2·00	1·60
1682		70c. Dairy products	2·40	1·80

525 Bull and Bear

2004. 75th Anniv of Luxembourg Stock Exchange.

| 1683 | **525** | 50c. multicoloured | 1·70 | 1·30 |

526 Museum Building (Marc Angel)

2004. National Museum of History and Art. Multicoloured.

| 1684 | | 50c. Type **526** | 1·70 | 1·30 |
| 1685 | | €1.10 "Young Woman with a Fan" (Luigi Rubio) | 3·75 | 2·75 |

| 1686 | | €3 "Charity" (Lucas Cranach) | 10·00 | 7·75 |

527 Carol Singers

2004. Christmas.

| 1687 | **527** | 50c.+5c. multicoloured | 2·00 | 1·60 |

528 Skiing

2004. Sport (1st series). Multicoloured.

1688		50c.+5c. Type **528**	1·90	1·40
1689		60c.+10c. Running (vert)	2·40	1·80
1690		70c.+10c. Swimming	2·75	2·10
1691		€1+25c. Football (vert)	4·25	3·25

See also Nos. 1729/32.

529 Tank, Soldiers and Liberation Monument, Schumannseck (Carlo Losch)

2004. Liberation of Luxembourg (1944–45).

| 1692 | **529** | 70c. multicoloured | 2·50 | 1·90 |

530 Building

2005. Luxembourg's Presidency of European Parliament. Value expressed by letter. Multicoloured. Self-adhesive.

1693		A (50c.) Type **530**	1·70	1·30
1694		A (50c.) Roman arch, Echternach Basilica	1·70	1·30
1695		A (50c.) Moselle river, Remich	1·70	1·30
1696		A (50c.) Riveted iron plate	1·70	1·30

Nos. 1693/6 were for use on first class mail within Luxembourg.

531 Woman (painting) (A. Huberty)

2005. 150th Anniv of Ettelbruck Neuro-Psychiatric Medical Centre.

| 1697 | **531** | 50c. multicoloured | 1·80 | 1·40 |

532 Emblem

2005. Centenary of Rotary International.

| 1698 | **532** | 50c. multicoloured | 1·80 | 1·40 |

533 Shoe Factory, Kayl-Tetange

2005. Tourism (1st series). Multicoloured.

1699		50c. Type **533**	1·80	1·40
1700		60c. Rooftops (75th anniv of National Tourism Office)	2·10	1·70
1701		€1 St. Eloi (statue), Rodange	3·50	2·75

See also Nos. 1721/4 and 1737/8.

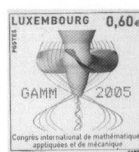
534 Turbine Air-stream Diagram

2005. GAMM 2005 International Congress of Applied Mathematics and Mechanics.

| 1702 | **534** | 60c. multicoloured | 2·10 | 1·70 |

535 Parliament Building

2005. 50th Anniv of Benelux Parliament.

| 1703 | **535** | 60c. multicoloured | 2·10 | 1·70 |

536 Fingers peeling back Label

2005. Business Stamps. Multicoloured, background colour given. Self-adhesive.

1704	**536**	25c. brown	90	70
1705	**536**	25c. red	90	70
1706	**536**	25c. salmon	90	70
1707	**536**	25c. yellow	90	70
1708	**536**	50c. bronze green	1·80	1·40
1709	**536**	50c. light green	1·80	1·40
1710	**536**	50c. bright green	1·80	1·40
1711	**536**	50c. apple green	1·80	1·40

537 Facade

2005. Opening of Grand Duchess Josephine-Charlotte Concert Hall (the Philharmonie).

| 1712 | **537** | 50c. multicoloured | 1·80 | 1·40 |

538 "judd mat gaardebounen" (pork and beans)

2005. Europa. Gastronomy. Multicoloured.

| 1713 | | 50c. Type **538** | 1·80 | 1·40 |
| 1714 | | 60c. "feierstengszalot" (diced beef and vinaigrette) | 2·10 | 1·70 |

539 Rail Car CVE 357, De Jhangeli Narrow Guage Railway

2005. Railways. Multicoloured.

1715		50c. Type **539**	1·70	1·40
1716		60c. Locomotive AL-T3	2·10	1·70
1717		€2.50 Rail car PH 408	8·75	7·00

540 Papilio machaon

2005. Butterflies. Multicoloured.

1718		35c. Type **540**	1·20	95
1719		70c. Argynnis paphia (vert)	2·40	1·90
1720		€1.80 Lysandra coridon	6·25	5·00

541 Schist, Eislek

2005. Tourism (2nd issue). Minerals. Value expressed by letter. Multicoloured. Self-adhesive.

1721		A (50c.) Type **541**	1·80	1·40
1722		A (50c.) Iron ore	1·80	1·40
1723		A (50c.) Sandstone	1·80	1·40
1724		A (50c.) Conglomerate, Folschette	1·80	1·40

Nos. 1721/4 were for use on first class mail within Luxembourg.

542 Jean Pierre Pescatore

2005. Anniversaries.

1725	**542**	50c. violet and grey	1·80	1·40
1726	–	90c. deep brown, brown and bistre brown	3·25	2·50
1727	–	€1 bistre brown and deep brown (vert)	3·50	2·75

DESGNS: 50c. Type **542** (philanthropist) (150th death); 90c. Marcel Reuland (writer) (birth centenary); €1 Marie-Henriette Steil (writer) (75th death).

543 Shoppers

2005. Christmas.

| 1728 | **543** | 50c.+5c. multicoloured | 2·00 | 1·50 |

544 Ice Skating

2005. Sport (2nd series). Multicoloured.

1729		50c.+5c. Type **544**	2·00	1·50
1730		60c.+10c. Basketball	2·75	2·20
1731		90c.+10c. Judo	3·50	2·75
1732		€1+25c. Tennis	4·50	3·50

545 Guide Dog

2005. Guide Dogs for the Blind.

| 1733 | **545** | 70c. ultramarine and yellow | 2·50 | 1·90 |

No. 1733 was embossed with the value in Braille.

546 Grand Duke and Duchess

2006. 25th Wedding Anniv of Grand Duke Henri and Grand Duchess Maria Teresa. Multicoloured.

| 1734 | | 50c. Type **546** | 1·80 | 1·40 |

MS1735 74×102 mm. €2.50 As No. 1734 (30×40 mm.) ... 9·00 9·00

547 Hands

2006. Blood Donation Campaign.

| 1736 | **547** | 50c. multicoloured | 1·80 | 1·40 |

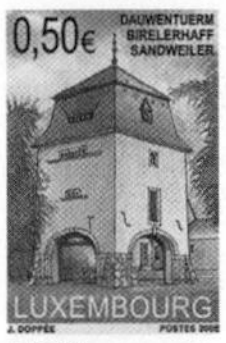

548 Pigeon Tower, Birelerhaff, Sandweiler

2006. Tourism (3rd series). Multicoloured.

1737	50c. Type **548**	1·80	1·40
1738	50c. Parc Merveilleux, Bettembourg (50th anniv) (horiz)	1·80	1·40

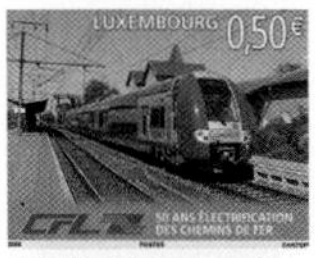

549 Electric Locomotive

2006. 50th Anniv of Electrification of Luxembourg Rail Network. Multicoloured.

1739	50c. Type **549**	1·80	1·40
1740	70c. Train on viaduct	2·50	1·90
1741	€1 Repairs to overhead cables (vert)	3·50	2·75

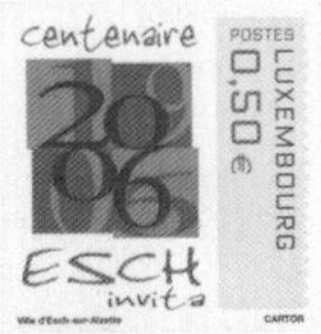

550 "2006"

2006. Centenary of Esch-sur-Alzette (town).

1742	**550**	50c. multicoloured	1·80	1·40

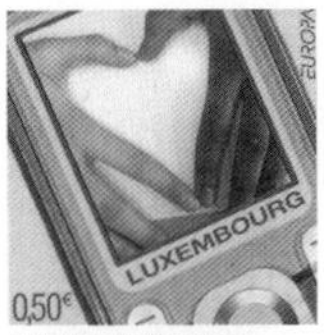

551 Hands forming Heart-shape (Anne Marie Simon)

2006. Europa. Integration. Winning entries in MMS Photograph Competition. Multicoloured.

1743	50c. Type **551**	1·80	1·40
1744	70c. Hands holding globe (Tamara da Silva)	2·50	1·90

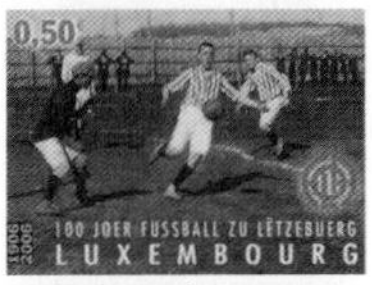

552 Early Match (centenary of first Luxembourg football club)

2006. Football. Multicoloured.

1745	50c. Type **552**	1·80	1·40
1746	90c. Emblem and football (World Cup Football Championship, Germany)	3·25	2·50

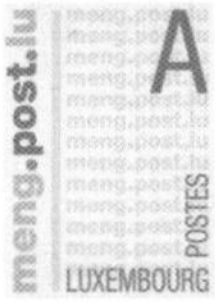

553 "meng.post.lu"

2006. Personal Stamp.

1747	**553 A**	(50c.) multicoloured	1·80	1·40

No. 1747 was for use on standard first class mail within Luxembourg.

554 Building

2006. 150th Anniv of State Council.

1748	**554**	50c. grey, red and slate	1·80	1·40

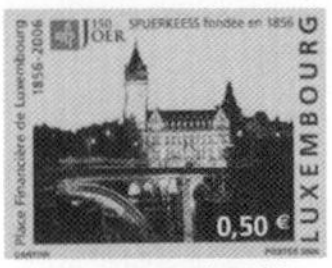

555 Savings Bank Building

2006. 150th Anniv of Financial Centre.

1749	**555**	50c. grey, ultramarine and vermilion	1·80	1·40
1750	-	50c. ultramarine and vermilion	1·80	1·40

DESIGNS: Type **555**; No. 1750, Dexia-BIL building.

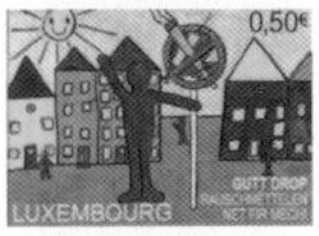

556 Figure holding Stop Drugs Sign (Victor Tesch)

2006. "Drugs are not for me" Campaign. Winning Designs in Children's Drawing Competition. Multicoloured.

1751	50c. Type **556**	1·80	1·40
1752	€1 Ashtray containing vegetables (Paul Hoffmann) (vert)	3·50	2·75

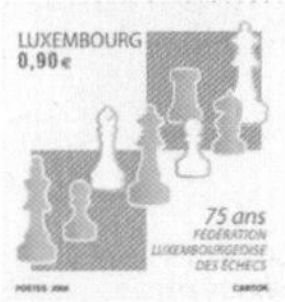

557 Chess Pieces

2006. 75th Anniv of National Chess Federation.

1753	**557**	90c. orange, light green and green	3·25	2·50

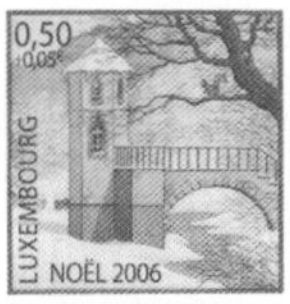

558 Yolande Tower, Marienthal

2006. Christmas. Marienthal Cultural Heritage.

1754	**558**	50c.+5c. multicoloured	1·90	1·50

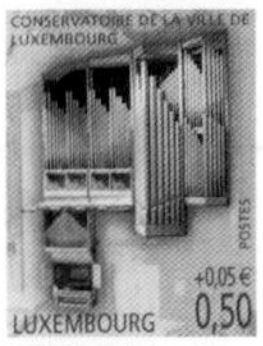

559 Grand Auditorium, Luxembourg Music Conservatory

2006. Pipe Organs. Designs showing pipe organs. Multicoloured.

1755	50c.+5c. Type **559**	1·90	1·50
1756	70c.+10c. Bridel	2·75	2·20
1757	90c.+10c. Mondercange Parish Church	3·50	2·75
1758	€1+25c. Luxembourg Grund	4·50	3·50

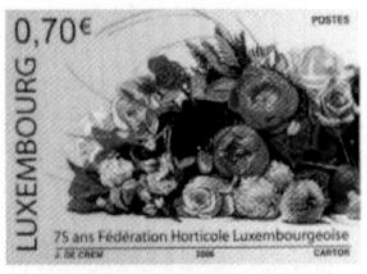

560 Flowers

2006. 75th Anniv of Horticultural Association. Multicoloured.

1759	70c. Type **560**	2·50	1·90
1760	70c. Vegetables	2·50	1·90

Nos. 1759/60 were issued together, se-tenant, forming a composite design.

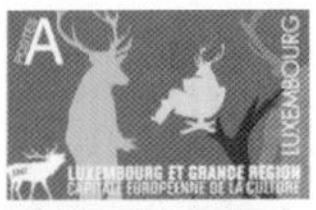

561 Men with Antlered Deer Heads

2007. Luxembourg—European Capital of Culture—2007. Multicoloured. Self-adhesive.

1761	A (50c.) Type **561**	1·80	1·40
1762	A (50c.) Antlered man and deer	1·80	1·40
1763	A (50c.) Antlered men with arm raised	1·80	1·40
1764	A (50c.) Base of chair, legs and antlered man with raised arm	1·80	1·40

562 "Postes"

563 "€0,25"

2007. Self-adhesive.

1765	**562**	25c. multicoloured	90	70
1766	**562**	25c. multicoloured	90	70
1767	**563**	25c. multicoloured	90	70
1768	**563**	25c. multicoloured	90	70
1769	**562**	50c. multicoloured	1·80	1·40
1770	**562**	50c. multicoloured	1·80	1·40
1771	**563**	50c. multicoloured	1·80	1·40
1772	**563**	50c. multicoloured	1·80	1·40

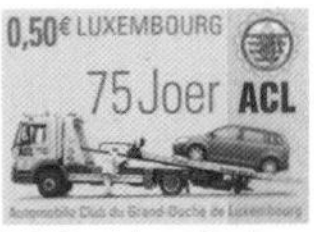

564 Breakdown Truck

2007. 75th Anniv of Automobile Club du Luxembourg (ACL).

1773	**564**	50c. multicoloured	1·80	1·40

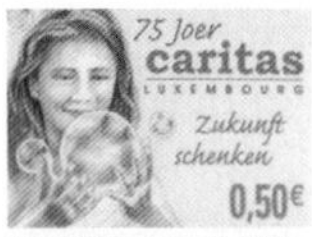

565 Girl holding Bubble

2007. 75th Anniv of Caritas Luxembourg Foundation.

1774	**565**	50c. multicoloured	1·80	1·40

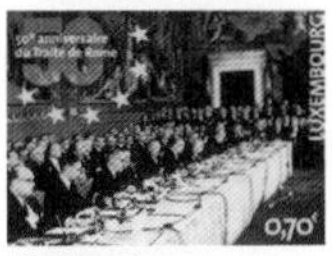

566 Signatories

2007. 50th Anniv of Treaty of Rome. Multicoloured.

1775	70c. Type **566**	2·50	1·90
1776	€1 List of signatories	3·50	2·75

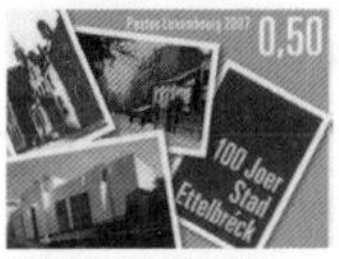

567 Early and Modern Buildings, Ettelbreck

2007. Centenary of "Law of 4 August 1907" conferring Town Status on Ettelbreck, Deifferdang, Diddeleng and Remeleng. Multicoloured.

1777	50c. Type **567**	1·80	1·40
1778	50c. Early buildings and gardens, Deifferdang	1·80	1·40
1779	50c. Early buildings and tower, Diddeleng	1·80	1·40
1780	50c. Early buildings, miner and modern machinery, Remeleng	1·80	1·40

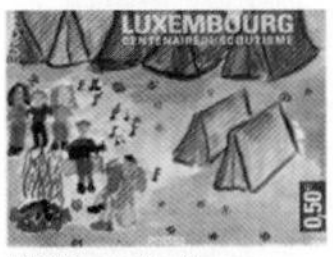

568 Campsite (Jenny Spielmann)

2007. Europa. Centenary of Scouting. Winning designs in Children's Painting Competition. Multicoloured.

1781	50c. Type **568**	1·80	1·40
1782	70c. Children and globe (Jean Heuschling)	2·50	1·90

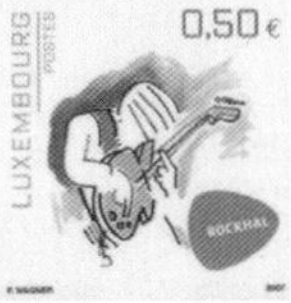

569 Musician (Rockhal)

2007. Cultural Centres. Multicoloured.

1783	50c. Type **569**	1·80	1·40
1784	70c. Grand Duke Jean Museum of Modern Art	2·50	1·90
1785	€1 Neumunster Abbey Meeting Centre	3·50	2·75

570 Letters (Stephanie Rausch)

2007. Luxembourg and Greater Regions Joint European Capital of Culture–2007. Winning Entry in Stamp Design Competition (1786).

1786	50c. Type **570**	1·80	1·40
1787	70c. Rotunda, Luxembourg Train Station	2·50	1·90

Stamps of a similar design were issued by Belgium.

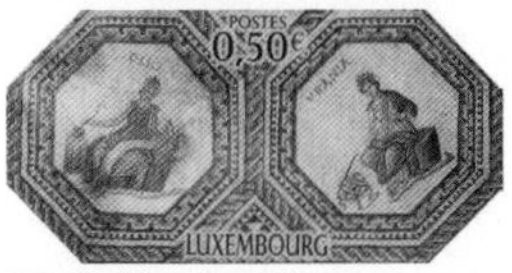

571 Clio (history) and Urania (astronomy)

2007. Roman Mosaic, Vichten. Nine Muses. Sheet 111×111 mm containing T **571** and similar multicoloured designs showing muses.

MS1788	50c. Type **571**; 50c. Polyhymnia (choral singing) and Erato (lyrical poetry); 50c. Terpsichore (dance) and Melpomene (tragedy); 50c. Thalia (comedy) and Euterpe (music); €1 Calliope (epic poetry) and Homer (diamond shaped) (55×55 mm)	10·50	10·50

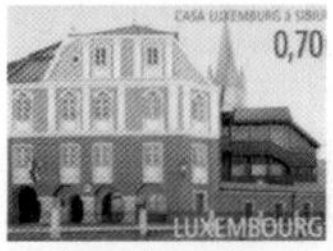

572 Luxembourg House, Sibiu

2007. Sibiu Joint European Capital of Culture–2007.

1789	**572**	70c. multicoloured	2·50	1·90

Stamps of a similar design were issued by Romania.

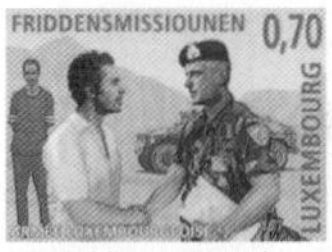

573 Soldier and Local Inhabitant

2007. Peace Keeping Missions of Luxembourg Army.

1790	**573**	70c. multicoloured	2·50	1·90

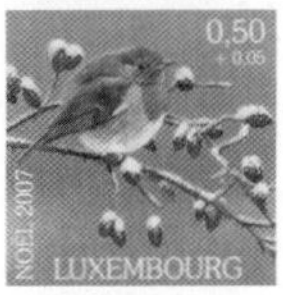

574 Robin

2007. Christmas.

1791	**574**	50c.+5c. multicoloured	1·90	1·50

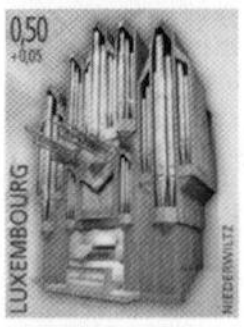

575 Niederwilz Church

2007. Pipe Organs. Multicoloured.

1792	50c.+5c. Type **575**	1·90	1·50
1793	70c.+10c. Sandweiler (horiz)	2·75	2·20
1794	90c.+10c. St Joseph Church, Esch-sur-Alzette (horiz)	3·50	2·75
1795	€1+25c. Echternach Basilica	4·50	3·50

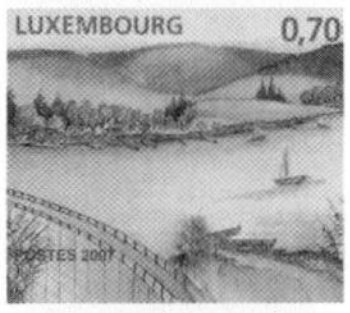

576 Dam and Reservoir (left)

2007. 50th Anniv of Esch-sur-Sure Dam. Self-adhesive. Multicoloured.

1796	70c. Type **576**	2·50	1·90
1797	70c. Reservoir (right)	2·50	1·90

Nos. 796/7 were issued together, *se-tenant*, a composite design of the reservoir and environs.

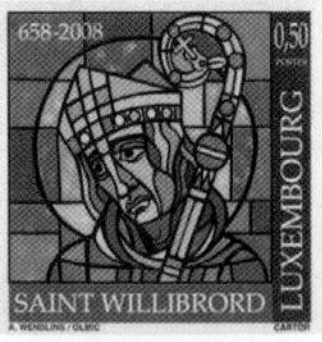

577 St. Willibrord

2008. 1350th Birth Anniv of St. Willibrord.

1798	**577**	50c. multicoloured	2·00	1·60

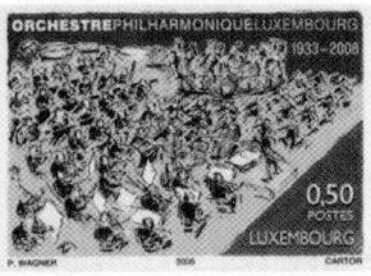

578 Orchestra

2008. 75th Anniv of Philharmonic Orchestra. 50th Death Anniv of Henri Pensis (composer). Multicoloured.

1799	50c. Type **578**	2·00	1·60
1800	70c. Henri Pensis	2·75	2·20

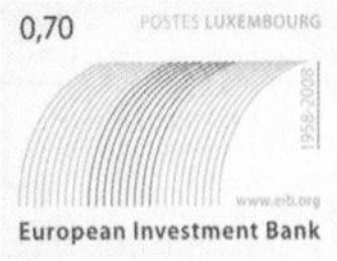

579 Emblem

2008. 50th Anniv of European Investment Bank.

1801	**579**	70c. ultramarine and silver	2·75	2·20

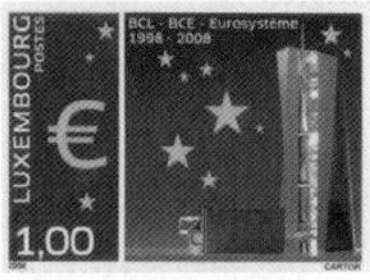

580 Stars and 'Eurotower' (New headquarters of ECB) (designed by COOP HIMMELB(L)AU)

2008. Tenth Anniv of Eurosysteme (unitary system of European Central Bank and EU members using the euro).

1802	**580**	€1 multicoloured	4·00	3·25

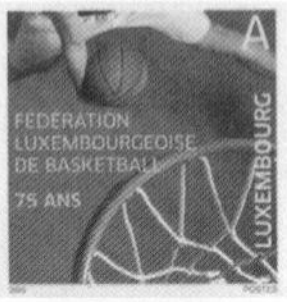

581 Ball and Basket

2008. Sport 2008. Multicoloured.

1803	A (50c.) Type **581** (75th anniv of National Basketball Federation)	2·00	1·60
1804	A (50c.) Football and player's foot (centenary of National Football Federation)	2·00	1·60

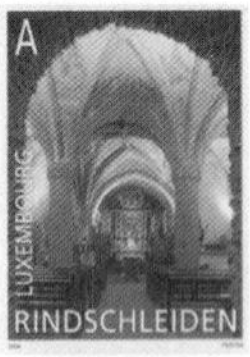

582 10th-century Church, Rindschleiden

2008. Tourism. Multicoloured.

1805	A (50c.) Type **582**	2·00	1·60
1806	A (50c.) Leudelange (150th anniv) (horiz)	2·00	1·60
1807	A (50c.) Diekirch (125th anniv) (horiz)	2·00	1·60

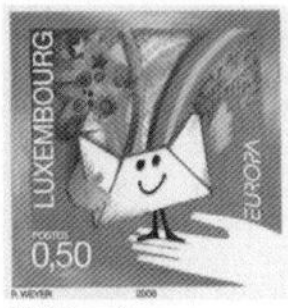

583 Envelope containing Rainbow

2008. Europa. The Letter. Multicoloured.

1808	50c. Type **583**	2·00	1·60
1809	70c. Envelope with wings	2·75	2·20

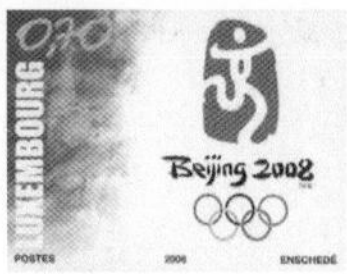

584 Emblems

2008. Olympic Games, Beijing.

1810	**584**	70c. multicoloured	2·75	2·20

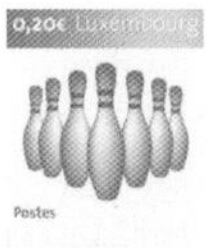

585 Skittles

2008. Happy. Multicoloured. Self-adhesive.

1811	20c. Type **585**	80	65
1811a	20c. As Type **585**	80	65
1812	20c. Parcel	80	65
1812a	20c. As No. 1812	80	65
1813	20c. Sweets	80	65
1813a	20c. As No. 1813	80	65
1814	A (50c.) Dice	2·00	1·60
1814a	A (50c.) As No. 1814	2·00	1·60
1815	A (50c.) Drum	2·00	1·60
1815a	A (50c.) As No. 1815	2·00	1·60
1816	A (50c.) Four leafed clover	2·00	1·60
1816a	A (50c.) As No. 1816	2·00	1·60

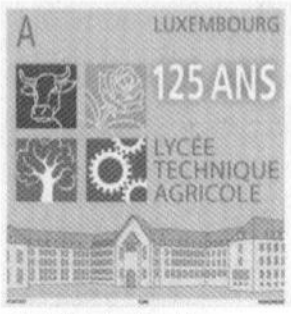

586 Symbols of Agriculture

2008. Anniversaries. Multicoloured.

1817	A (50c.) Type **586** (125th anniv of Agricultural College, Ettelbruck)	2·00	1·60
1818	A (50c.) Stylized flower (centenary of Ligue Medico-Sociale (medical and social league))	2·00	1·60

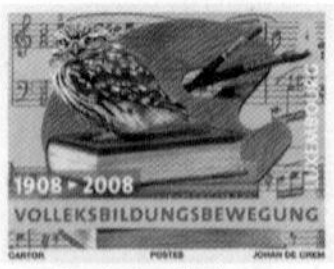

587 Symbols of Education and Culture

2008. Centenaries. Multicoloured.

1819	A (50c.) Type **587** (Volleksbildungsbewegung (cultural and educational association))	2·00	1·60
1820	A (50c.) Dog and cat (centenary of Letzebuerger Deiereschutliga (protection of animals association))	2·00	1·60

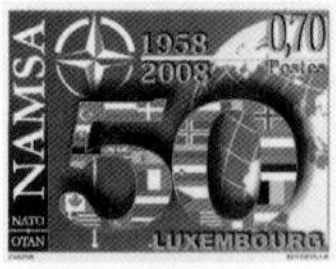

588 Flags as '50'

2008. 50th Anniv of NAMSA (NATO Maintenance and Supply Agency).

1821	**588**	70c. multicoloured	3·00	2·50

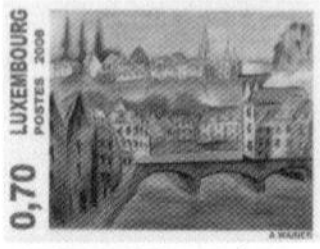

589 Town, River and Bridge (A. Wainer)

2008. Greetings from Luxembourg. Winning Designs in Children's Drawing Competition. Multicoloured.

1822	70c. Type **589**	3·00	2·50
1823	€1 Bridge and valley (S. Rauschenberger)	4·00	3·50

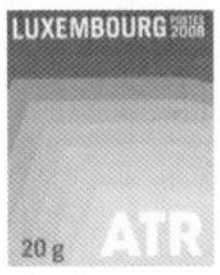

590 'ATR'

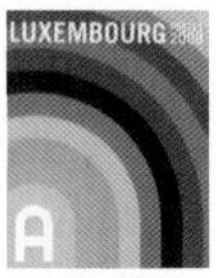

591 'A'

2008. Self-adhesive. Multicoloured.

1824	(25c.) Type **590**	1·00	90
1825	(25c.) ATR at top left (purple)	1·00	90
1826	(25c.) ATR at bottom left (green)	1·00	90
1827	(25c.) ATR at top right (red)	1·00	90
1828	A (50c.) Type **591**	2·10	1·80
1829	A (50c.) A top left	2·10	1·80
1830	A (50c.) A bottom right	2·10	1·80
1831	A (50c.) A top right	2·10	1·80

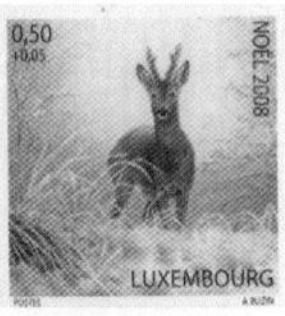

592 Buck

2008. Christmas.

1832	**592**	50c.+5c. multicoloured	2·30	2·00

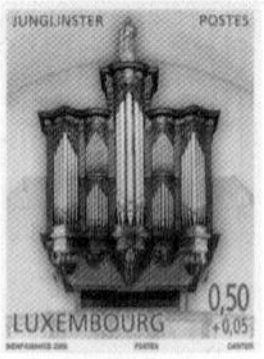

593 Junglinster

2008. Pipe Organs. Multicoloured.

1833	50c.+5c. Type **593**	2·30	2·00
1834	70c.+10c. Mondorf-les-Bains (horiz)	3·25	2·75
1835	90c.+10c. Vianden	4·00	3·50
1836	€1+25c. Cathedral	5·25	4·50

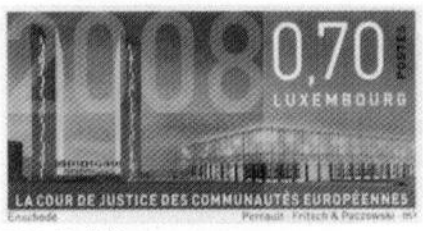

594 Building

2008. Court of Justice of the European Communities.

1837	**594**	70c. multicoloured	3·00	2·50

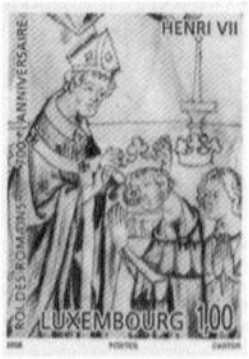

595 Coronation

2008. 700th Death Anniv (2009) of Henry VII.

1838	**595**	€1 multicoloured	4·25	3·75

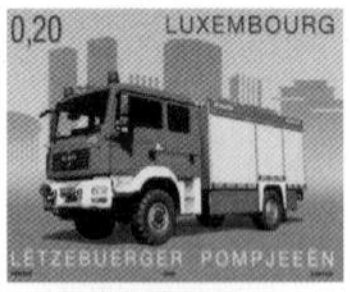

596 Fire Appliance

2009. Firefighters. Multicoloured.

1839	20c. Type **596**	95	80
1840	A (50c.) Firefighter carrying child	2·30	2·00
1841	€2 Early fire appliance	9·25	7·75

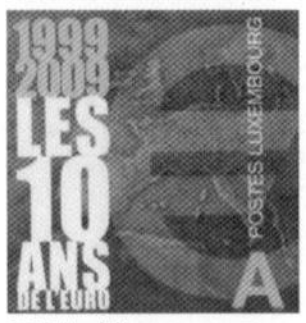

597 Emblem

2009. Tenth Anniv of the Euro.

1842	**597**	A (50c.) multicoloured	2·40	2·10

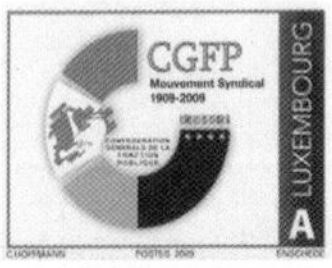

598 CGFP (General Confederation of Civil Service) Emblem

2009. Trade Union Centenaries. Multicoloured.

1843	A (50c.) Type **598**	2·50	2·10
1844	A (50c.) FNCTTFEL (National Federation of Railway Workers, Transport Workers and Employees) emblem	2·50	2·10
1845	50c. Postman (Postman's Federation)	2·50	2·10

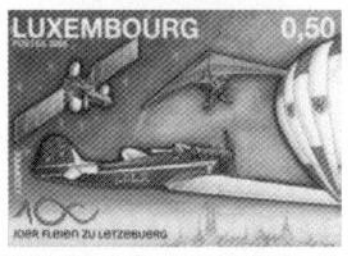

599 Aircraft and Air Balloon

2009. Centenary of Areo-Club Luxembourgeois. Multicoloured.

1846	50c. Type **599**	2·50	2·10
1847	50c. Air balloon and aircraft (right)	2·50	2·10
1848	90c. Airport	4·50	3·75

Nos. 1846/7 were printed together, *se-tenant*, forming a composite design.

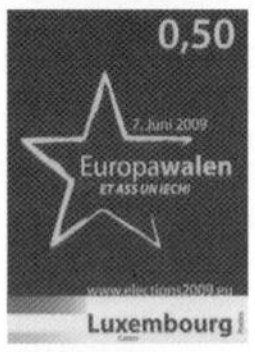

600 Emblem

2009. European Parliamentary Elections.

1849	**600**	50c. multicoloured	2·30	2·25

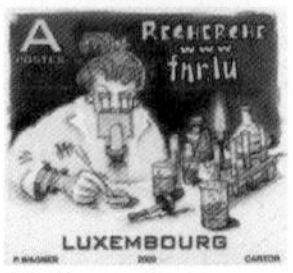

601 Researcher

2009. Tenth Anniv of National Research Fund.

1850	**601**	A (50c.) multicoloured	2·30	2·25

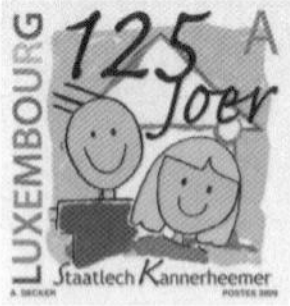

602 Children

2009. 125th Anniv of Children's Houses.

1851	**602**	A (50c.) multicoloured	2·30	2·25

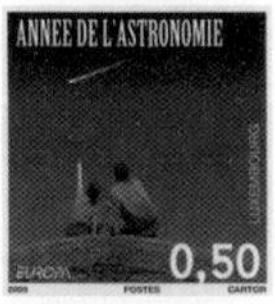

603 Shooting Star

2009. Europa. Astronomy. Multicoloured.

1852	50c. Type **603**	2·30	2·25
1853	70c. Galileo and satellite	2·75	2·75

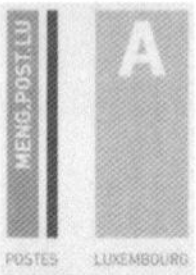

604 Red Line

2009. Personalised Stamps. New Designs for www.meng.post.lu.

1854	A (50c.) deep rose-red and grey	2·30	2·25
1855	A (70c.) bright blue and grey	2·75	2·75

DESIGNS: (50c.) Type **604**: (70c.) Blue line

No. 1854 was for use on domestic mail and No. 1855 was for use on mail within Europe.

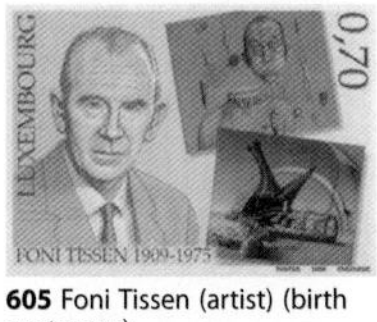

605 Foni Tissen (artist) (birth centenary)

2009. Personalities. Multicoloured.

1856	70c. Type **605**	3·25	3·00
1857	90c. Charles Bernhoeft (photographer) (150th birth anniv)	4·25	3·75
1858	€1 Henri Tudor (electrical engineer) (150th birth anniv)	4·75	4·25

606 1934 5f. Stamp (As Type 47)

2009. 75th Anniv of FSPL (federation of philatelic societies). Sheet 120×80 mm containing T **606** and similar horiz design. Multicoloured.

MS1859 50c. Type **606**; 70c. Gateway
of the Three Towers .... 5·25 5·25

607 Modern Electric Locomotive

2009. 150th Anniv of Railways. Multicoloured.
1860	50c. Type **607**	2·25	2·25
1861	€1 Electric goods train	4·25	4·25
1862	€3 Early steam locomotive	12·50	12·50

608 Vanden Castle

2009. SEPAC (small European mail services).
| 1863 | **608** | 70c. multicoloured | 3·00 | 3·00 |

609 Louis Braille and Fingerprint

2009. Birth Bicentenary of Louis Braille (inventor of Braille writing for the blind).
| 1864 | **609** | 90c. claret and new blue | 4·00 | 4·00 |

No. 1864 is embossed with Braille letters.

610 Johannes Gutenberg (inventor of movable type printing)

2009. Communication–From Gutenberg to the Internet. Multicoloured.
| 1865 | 50c. Type **610** | 2·25 | 2·25 |
| 1866 | 70c. @ | 3·00 | 3·00 |

611 Fox decorating Tree

2009. Christmas.
| 1867 | **611** | 50c.+5c. multicoloured | 2·25 | 2·25 |

612 Philharmonie

2009. Pipe Organs. Designs showing pipe organs. Multicoloured.
1868	50c.+5c. Type **612**	2·25	2·25
1869	70c.+10c. Dudelange	3·00	3·00
1870	90c.+10c. Nommern	3·75	3·75
1871	€1+25c. Heiderscheid	4·50	4·50

613 Grand Duke Henri

2010. Tenth Anniv of Accession of Grand Duke Henri. 25th Death Anniv of Grand Duchess Charlotte. Multicoloured.
| 1872 | 50c. Type **613** | 2·25 | 2·25 |
| 1873 | €1 Grand Duchess Charlotte | 4·25 | 4·25 |

614 Schengen Monument

2010. 25th Anniv of Schengen Accord (setting area of free movement between countries).
| 1874 | **614** | 70c. multicoloured | 3·25 | 3·25 |

615 Septfontaines Castles

2010. Tourism. Eisch Valley. Value expressed by letter. Multicoloured. Self-adhesive.
| 1875 | (70c.) Type **615** | 3·25 | 3·25 |
| 1876 | (70c.) Hollenfels | 3·25 | 3·25 |

The two stamps and margins form a composite design

616 Arnica montana

2010. International Year of Biodiversity. Countdown 2010 (conservation and restoration project). Multicoloured.
| 1877 | 70c. Type **616** | 3·00 | 3·00 |
| 1878 | €1 Freshwater pearl mussel (inscr 'Moule perliere') | 4·25 | 4·25 |

617 Luxembourg Pavillion

2010. World Expo 2010, Shanghai, China.
| 1879 | **617** | 90c. multicoloured | 4·00 | 4·00 |

618 Grand Duke Henri and Grand Duchess Maria Teresa

2010. The Grand Ducal Family. Sheet 200×138 mm.
MS1880 **681** €3 multicoloured .... 13·00 13·00

619 Boy and Dragon reading

2010. Europa . Multicoloured.
| 1881 | 50c. Type **619** | 2·25 | 2·25 |
| 1882 | 70c. Girl riding book lassoing horse as book | 3·25 | 3·25 |

620

2010. Philalux 2011 International Stamp Exhibition. Multicoloured.

MS1883 50c. Type **620**; 70c. Red Bridge (Grand Duchess Charlotte Bridge) and skyscrapers; €3 New buildings (60×38 mm) .... 17·00 17·00

621 Motorcycling

2010. Leisure and Liberty. Multicoloured.
| 1884 | A (60c.) Type **621** | 2·25 | 2·25 |
| 1885 | A (85c.) Camping | 3·25 | 3·25 |

No. !884 was for use on mail within Luxembourg and No. 1885 was for use on mail within Europe

622 Bernie

2010. Cartoons. Multicoloured.
MS1886 A (60c.)×5, Type **622**; Police Chief Harespel; Leonie Lamesch (vert); Superjhemp; Leandre Schro-biltgen .... 12·50 12·50

623 John of Luxembourg and Elisabeth of Bohemia

2010. 700th Anniv of Accession of House of Luxembourg to Czech Throne
| 1887 | **623** | 70c. multicoloured | 3·00 | 3·00 |

A stamp of a similar design was issued by Czech Republic

624 Grand-Duc Adolphe de Luxembourg

2010. Roses. Multicoloured.
1888	A (60c.) Type **624**	2·40	2·40
1889	A (60c.) Bagatelle (white single)	2·40	2·40
1890	A (60c.) Bordeaux (small pink double)	2·40	2·40
1891	A (60c.) Duc de Constantine (pink, three blooms)	2·40	2·40
1892	A (60c.) Prince Jean de Luxembourg (double white)	2·40	2·40
1893	A (60c.) Clothilde Soupert (double apricot)	2·40	2·40
1894	A (60c.) Mrs E G Hill (large bright pink)	2·40	2·40
1895	A (60c.) Pierre Watine (pale pink large bloom)	2·40	2·40
1896	A (60c.) Souvenir de Maria de Zayas (rich pink)	2·40	2·40
1897	A (60c.) Yvan Misson (pale pink two blooms)	2·40	2·40

625 Symbols of Education (fight against poverty in developing countries) (Timothy Clement)

2010. European Year of Fight against Poverty and Social Exclusion. Multicoloured.
| 1898 | A (60c.) Type **625** | 2·50 | 2·50 |
| 1899 | A (85c.) Offering tools to work (fight against poverty in industrialised countries) (Cinthya Goncalves Guerriro) | 3·50 | 3·50 |

626 Anne Beffort (educationalist and writer)

2010. Personalities. Multicoloured.
1900	70c. Type **626**	2·75	2·75
1901	90c. Duc de Constantine (rose) and Jean Soupert (rose breeder)	3·50	3·50
1902	€1 Nicolas Frantz (cyclist)	4·75	4·75

627 Liner and Yacht

2010. Ships and Navigation. Multicoloured.
| 1903 | A (60c.) Type **627** | 3·50 | 3·50 |
| 1904 | A (60c.) Yacht and container ship | 3·50 | 3·50 |

Nos. 1903/4 were printed, *se-tenant*, forming a composite design

628 Boy and Dog Sledding

2010. Christmas
| 1905 | **628** | 60c.+5c. multicoloured | 3·00 | 3·00 |

629 Farrier

2010. Trades of Yesteryear. Multicoloured.
1906	60c.+5c. Type **629**	3·00	3·00
1907	85c.+10c. Basket weaver	3·75	3·75
1908	€1.10+10c. Knife grinder (horiz)	5·00	5·00
1909	€1.20+25c. Cooper (horiz)	6·25	6·25

630 Hands grasping Arms

2011. European Year of Volunteering
| 1910 | **630** | A (60c.) multicoloured | 2·75 | 2·75 |

631 Bowlers, Pins and Alley

2011. 50th Anniv of Fédération luxembourgeoise des Quilleurs (nine pin bowlers)
| 1911 | **631** | 60c. multicoloured | 2·75 | 2·75 |

632 Clock Tower and Perforated Edges

2011. 75th Anniv of 'Journée du Timbre' (Stamp Day)
| 1912 | **632** | 60c. multicoloured | 2·75 | 2·75 |

633 Figures with Arms raised, Pen and 'sign'

2011. 50th Anniv of Amnesty International

1913	**633**	60c. multicoloured	2·75	2·75

634 Prince Guillaume

2011. House of Luxembourg Dynasty. Multicoloured.

1914		85c. Type **634**	3·25	3·25
1915		€1.10 Grand Duke Jean	5·25	5·25

635 Sun draped with Grapes holding Wine Glass and Bottle

2011. Centenary of Wënzerverband (wine growers federation) (60c.) or 20th Anniv of Appellation contrôlée Crémant de Luxembourg (85c.). Multicoloured.

1916		60c. Type **635**	2·75	2·75
1917		85c. Cork and wire	3·75	3·75

636 Girl blowing Bubbles

2011. Personalised Stamps. Multicoloured.

1918		60c. Type **636**	2·75	2·75
1919		85c. Boy dozing (vert)	3·75	3·75

637 Deciduous Forest

2011. Europa. Multicoloured.

1920		60c. Type **637**	2·75	2·75
1921		85c. Wooded valley	3·75	3·75

638 Maloo

2011. *De leschte Ritter* cartoon created by Lucien Czuga and illustrated by Andy "ND!" Genen. Multicoloured.

MS1922 A (60c.)×4, Type **638**; Jean, The Last Knight (horiz); Pedro (horiz); Pixel the Galago	10·50	10·50

639 AIDS Ribbon

2011. 30th Anniv of Discovery of AIDS

1923	**639**	60c. multicoloured	2·50	2·50

640 Emblem and Stars

2011. 50th Anniv of Luxembourg Consumers Union

1924	**640**	60c. multicoloured	2·50	2·50

641 Buildings and Walkway

2011. Cercle Cité, Luxembourg

1925	**641**	A (60c.) multicoloured	2·75	2·75

642 Franz Liszt

2011. Birth Bicentenary of Franz Liszt (composers)

1826	**642**	85c. multicoloured	3·75	3·75

643 Chemin de la Corniche

2011. Small European Postal Administration Cooperation (SEPAC)

1927	**643**	85c. multicoloured	3·75	3·75

644 Globe and Chip

2011. Centenary of Comptes Chèques Postaux (CCP) (Postchèque) Service

1928	**644**	60c. multicoloured	2·50	2·50

645 Christmas Table

2011. Christmas

1929	**645**	60c. multicoloured	2·75	2·75

646 Eisleck

2011. Architecture. Booklet Stamps. Multicoloured.

1930		A (60c.) Type **646**	2·50	2·50
1931		A (60c.) 'Red' farm, Rédange region	2·50	2·50
1932		A (60c.) Decorated buildings, Echternach region	2·50	2·50
1933		A (60c.) Brick houses of local marl, Minette	2·50	2·50

647 Scarf

2011. Cultural Heritage. UNESCO Intangible Representation of Humanity. Dancing Procession of Echternach. Multicoloured.

MS1934 60c. Type **647**; 85c. Scarf, right	6·00	6·00

2011. Trades of Yesteryear. Multicoloured.

1935		60c.+5c. Joiner	2·50	2·50
1936		85c.+10c. Potter	3·75	3·75
1937		€1.10+10c. Stonemason (horiz)	5·25	5·25
1938		€1.20+25c. Printer (horiz)	5·75	5·75

648 Radio Waves

2012. 75th Anniv of Réseau Luxembourgeois des Amateurs d'Ondes Courtes (Luxembourg Amateur Radio Society)

1939	**648**	60c. multicoloured	2·50	2·50

649 Sculpture (Pit Nicolas)

2012. 50th Anniv of Institut Grand-Ducal - Section Arts et Lettres

1940	**649**	60c. multicoloured	2·50	2·50

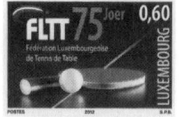

650 Paddle and Ball

2012. 75th Anniv of 'Fédération Luxembourgeoise de Tennis de Table (FLT)

1941	**650**	60c. multicoloured	2·50	2·50

651 '10'

2012. Tenth Anniv of the Euro

1942	**651**	85c. multicoloured	3·75	3·75

652 Graph

2012

1943	**652**	60c. multicoloured	2·50	2·50

653 Mil

654 Friends and Villains (image scaled to 33% of original size)

2012. Mil's Adventures

1944	A (75c.)×5, Type **653** (Mil) and friends and villians	16·00 16·00

655 Monument au Souvenir (Gëlle Fra) and Traditional Buildings

2012. Europa. Visit Luxembourg. Multicoloured.

1945		60c. Type **655**	2·50	2·50
1946		85c. Mudam (Grand Duke Jean Museum of Modern Art), Philharmonie, Centre des Arts Pluriels d'Ettelbrück and Leudelange Water Tower (modern buildings)	3·75	3·75

656 COSL Emblem

2012. Olympic Games, London (No. 1948) or Centenary of Luxembourg Olympic Committee (COSL) (No. 1947). Multicoloured.

1947		60c. Type **656**	2·50	2·50
1948		€1.10 British flag and games emblem	5·25	5·25

OFFICIAL STAMPS

1875. Stamps of 1859–72 optd OFFICIEL. Roul.

O79	**3**	1c. brown	60·00	55·00
O80	**3**	2c. black	60·00	55·00
O81	**4**	10c. lilac	£3250	£3250
O82	**4**	12½c. red	£750	£850
O83	**4**	20c. brown	60·00	85·00
O84	**4**	25c. blue	£400	£225
O85	**4**	30c. purple	60·00	£110
O88b	**4**	40c. orange	£325	£325
O87	**4**	1f. on 37½c. bistre (No. 37)	£250	39·00

1875. Stamps of 1874–79 optd OFFICIEL. Perf.

O89	**3**	1c. brown	14·00	42·00
O90	**3**	2c. black	17·00	50·00
O91	**3**	4c. green	£140	£225
O92	**3**	5c. yellow	£110	£110
O93a	**4**	10c. lilac	£140	£170
O111	**4**	12½c. red	£110	£170
O99a	**4**	25c. blue	4·50	5·50
O96	**4**	1f. on 37½c. bistre (No. 56)	55·00	85·00

1881. Stamp of 1859 optd S. P. Roul.

O116	**3**	40c. orange	55·00	£110

1881. Stamps of 1874–79 optd S. P. Perf.

O121a	**3**	1c. brown	17·00	14·00
O122a	**3**	2c. black	17·00	14·00
O118	**3**	4c. green	£250	£275
O123a	**3**	5c. yellow	£225	£275
O124a	**4**	10c. lilac	£225	£275
O125a	**4**	12½c. red	£250	£325
O126a	**4**	20c. brown	£100	£140
O127a	**4**	25c. blue	£110	£140
O128	**4**	30c. red	£110	£170
O120	**4**	1f. on 37½c. bistre (No. 56)	55·00	85·00

7 Agriculture and Trade

1882. Stamps of 1882 optd S. P.

O141	**7**	1c. grey	55	55
O142	**7**	2c. brown	55	55
O143	**7**	4c. olive	55	75
O144	**7**	5c. green	55	85
O145	**7**	10c. red	20·00	22·00
O146	**7**	12½c. blue	2·20	7·25
O147	**7**	20c. orange	2·20	7·25
O148	**7**	25c. blue	33·00	35·00
O149	**7**	30c. olive	5·50	13·00
O150	**7**	50c. brown	1·70	4·25
O151	**7**	1f. lilac	1·70	4·25
O152	**7**	5f. orange	20·00	55·00

1891. Stamps of 1891 optd S. P.

O188	**8**	10c. red	30	85
O189	**8**	12½c. green	10·00	10·00

O190	8	20c. orange	17·00	13·00
O191a	8	25c. blue	45	85
O192	8	30c. green	10·00	13·00
O193a	8	37½c. green	10·00	13·00
O194	8	50c. brown	8·25	14·00
O195a	8	1f. purple	8·25	17·00
O196	8	2½f. black	55·00	£110
O197	8	5f. lake	50·00	80·00

1898. Stamps of 1895 optd **S. P.**

O213	9	1c. grey	2·75	2·75
O214	9	2c. brown	2·20	2·75
O215	9	4c. bistre	2·20	2·20
O216	9	5c. green	11·00	5·50
O217	9	10c. red	39·00	50·00

1908. Stamps of 1906 optd **Officiel**.

O218	10	1c. grey	20	55
O219	10	2c. brown	20	55
O220	10	4c. bistre	20	55
O221	10	5c. green	20	55
O271	10	5c. mauve	15	55
O222	10	6c. lilac	20	55
O223	10	7½c. yellow	20	55
O224	10	10c. red	30	55
O225	10	12½c. slate	30	85
O226	10	15c. brown	45	85
O227	10	20c. orange	45	1·10
O228	10	25c. blue	45	1·10
O229	10	30c. olive	8·25	11·00
O230	10	37½c. green	1·10	1·10
O231	10	50c. brown	1·10	2·20
O232	10	87½c. blue	2·75	5·50
O233	10	1f. purple	4·50	5·50
O234	10	2½f. red	£140	£110
O235	10	5f. purple	85·00	80·00

1915. Stamps of 1914 optd **Officiel**.

O236	13	10c. purple	30	85
O237	13	12½c. green	30	85
O238	13	15c. brown	30	85
O239	13	17½c. brown	30	85
O240	13	25c. blue	30	85
O241	13	30c. brown	2·20	8·25
O242	13	35c. blue	30	1·70
O243	13	37½c. brown	30	2·20
O244	13	40c. red	45	1·70
O245	13	50c. grey	45	1·70
O246	13	62½c. green	45	2·20
O247	13	87½c. orange	45	2·75
O248	13	1f. brown	45	2·20
O249	13	2½f. red	45	4·50
O250	13	5f. violet	45	5·50

1922. Stamps of 1921 optd **Officiel**.

O251	17	2c. brown	10	20
O252	17	3c. green	10	20
O253	17	6c. purple	20	55
O272	17	10c. green	15	55
O273	17	15c. green	15	55
O274	17	15c. orange	15	55
O256	17	20c. orange	20	55
O275	17	20c. green	15	55
O257	17	25c. green	20	55
O258	17	30c. red	20	55
O259	17	40c. orange	20	55
O260	17	50c. blue	35	80
O276	17	50c. red	30	85
O261	17	75c. red	35	80
O277	17	75c. blue	30	85
O266	17	80c. black	45	65
O263	18	1f. red	1·10	2·75
O278	18	1f. blue	45	2·20
O267	-	2f. blue	2·20	2·75
O279	-	2f. brown	2·10	7·75
O269	-	5f. violet	12·50	13·50

26 Luxembourg

28 Echternach

1922. Stamps of 1923 optd **Officiel**.

O268a	28	3f. blue	1·70	2·00
O270	26	10f. black	40·00	33·00

1926. Stamps of 1926 optd **Officiel**.

O280	32	5c. mauve	10	30
O281	32	10c. green	10	30
O298	32	15c. black	45	1·70
O282	32	20c. orange	10	30
O283	32	25c. green	10	30
O300	32	25c. brown	40	1·10
O301	32	30c. green	65	2·75
O302	32	30c. violet	45	1·70
O303	32	35c. violet	45	1·70
O304	32	35c. green	45	1·70
O286	32	40c. brown	10	30
O287	32	50c. brown	10	30
O307	32	60c. green	45	1·10
O288	32	65c. brown	10	55
O308	32	70c. violet	4·25	9·50
O289	32	75c. red	10	55
O309	32	75c. brown	45	1·10
O291	32	80c. brown	15	55
O292	32	90c. red	30	1·10
O293	32	1f. black	30	85
O312	32	1f. red	55	3·25
O294	32	1¼f. blue	15	85
O313	32	1¼f. yellow	2·75	9·50
O314	32	1¼f. green	2·50	6·75
O315	32	1½f. blue	45	2·20
O316	32	1¾f. blue	55	2·20

1928. Stamp of 1928 optd **Officiel**.

O317	37	2f. black	1·10	2·75

43 Luxembourg, Lower Town

1931. Stamp of 1931 optd **Officiel**.

O318	43	20f. green	2·75	14·00

47 Gateway of the Three Towers

1934. Stamp of 1934 optd **Officiel**.

O319	47	5f. green	2·20	8·25

52 Vianden

1935. No. 340 optd **Officiel**.

O341	52	10f. green	2·20	11·00

POSTAGE DUE STAMPS

1907

D173	D12	5c. black and green	30	45
D174	D12	10c. black and green	1·70	45
D175	D12	12½c. black and green	55	1·40
D176	D12	20c. black and green	1·10	1·10
D177	D12	25c. black and green	22·00	1·70
D178	D12	50c. black and green	1·70	6·25
D179	D12	1f. black and green	55	5·50

D12 Arms of Luxembourg

1920. Surch.

D193	D 12	15 on 12½c. blk & grn	2·20	11·00
D194	D 12	30 on 25c. black & grn	2·20	14·00

1922

D221	D12	5c. red and green	30	55
D222	D12	10c. red and green	30	55
D223	D12	20c. red and green	30	55
D224	D12	25c. red and green	30	55
D225	D12	30c. red and green	55	1·10
D226	D12	35c. red and green	55	45
D227	D12	50c. red and green	55	1·10
D228	D12	60c. red and green	45	55
D229	D12	70c. red and green	55	45
D230	D12	75c. red and green	55	30
D231	D12	1f. red and green	55	2·75
D232	D12	2f. red and green	55	10·00
D233	D12	3f. red and green	2·20	20·00

D77

1946

D488	D77	5c. green	2·00	85
D489	D77	10c. green	2·00	70
D490	D77	20c. green	2·00	70
D491	D77	30c. green	2·00	70
D492	D77	50c. green	2·00	70
D493	D77	70c. green	2·00	1·10
D494	D77	75c. green	5·75	55
D495	D77	1f. red	2·00	55
D496	D77	1f.50 red	2·00	55
D497	D77	2f. red	2·00	55
D498	D77	3f. red	4·00	70
D499	D77	5f. red	4·00	70
D500	D77	10f. red	6·75	5·00
D501	D77	20f. red	11·50	42·00

Pt. 9, Pt. 17

MACAO

A former Portuguese territory in China at the mouth of the Canton River.

1884. 1000 reis = 1 milreis.
1894. 78 avos = 1 rupee.
1913. 100 avos = 1 pataca.

1884. "Crown" key-type inscr "MACAU".

10	P	5r. black	21·00	14·00
2	P	10r. orange	40·00	21·00
21	P	10r. green	28·00	14·00
12	P	20r. bistre	55·00	29·00
27	P	20r. red	50·00	28·00
13	P	25r. red	22·00	8·50
22	P	25r. lilac	40·00	21·00
14	P	40r. blue	£225	75·00
23	P	40r. buff	50·00	24·00
15	P	50r. green	£250	85·00
24	P	50r. blue	55·00	30·00
31	P	80r. grey	90·00	48·00
16	P	100r. lilac	55·00	28·00
17	P	200r. orange	65·00	28·00
9	P	300r. brown	70·00	28·00

1885. "Crown" key type of Macao surch 80 reis in circle. No gum.

19	80r. on 100r. lilac	£110	65·00

1885. "Crown" key type of Macao surch in Reis. With gum (43, 44, 45), no gum (others).

32	5r. on 25r. pink	26·00	14·00
43	5r. on 80r. grey	39·00	14·00
46	5r. on 100r. lilac	£110	60·00
33	10r. on 25r. pink	49·00	23·00
38	10r. on 50r. green	£225	£180
44	10r. on 80r. grey	70·00	28·00
47	10r. on 200r. orange	£225	£110
35	20r. on 50r. green	49·00	16·00
45	20r. on 80r. grey	£100	40·00
40	40r. on 50r. green	£250	£120

1885. "Crown" key-type of Macao surch with figure of value only and bar. No gum.

41	5 on 25r. red	39·00	26·00
42a	10 on 50r. green	39·00	26·00

9

1887. Fiscal stamps as T **9** surch **CORREIO** and new value. No gum.

50	5r. on 10r. green and brown	£110	£110
51	5r. on 20r. green and brown	£110	£110
52	5r. on 60r. green and brown	£110	£110
53	10r. on 10r. green and brown	£110	£110
54	10r. on 60r. green and brown	£140	£130
55	40r. on 20r. green and brown	£160	£140

1888. "Embossed" key-type inscr "PROVINCIA DE MACAU".

56	Q	5r. black	20·00	8·00
57	Q	10r. green	22·00	8·00
58	Q	20r. red	36·00	14·00
59	Q	25r. mauve	39·00	14·00
60	Q	40r. brown	39·00	17·00
61	Q	50r. blue	48·00	16·00
62	Q	80r. grey	75·00	29·00
63	Q	100r. brown	70·00	28·00
71	Q	200r. lilac	£130	40·00
72	Q	300r. orange	£140	40·00

1892. No. 71 surch **3030**.

73	30 on 200r. lilac	65·00	29·00

1894. "Embossed" key-type of Macao surch **PROVISORIO**, value and Chinese characters. No gum.

75b	1a. on 5r. black	12·00	5·75
76	3a. on 20r. red	14·00	7·00
77	4a. on 25r. violet	23·00	12·00
89	5a. on 30 on 200r. lilac (No. 73)	£200	£100
78	6a. on 40r. brown	23·00	11·00
79	8a. on 50r. blue	50·00	21·00
80	13a. on 80r. grey	28·00	14·00
81	16a. on 100r. brown	46·00	18·00
82	31a. on 200r. lilac	70·00	42·00
83	47a. on 300r. orange	80·00	40·00

1894. "Figures" key-type inscr "MACAU".

91	R	5r. yellow	14·00	5·25
92	R	10r. mauve	14·00	5·25
93	R	15r. brown	21·00	7·50
94	R	20r. lilac	28·00	8·00
95	R	25r. green	55·00	16·00
96	R	50r. blue	55·00	20·00
97	R	75r. pink	75·00	46·00
98	R	80r. green	48·00	31·00
99	R	100r. brown on buff	47·00	25·00
100	R	150r. red on pink	47·00	25·00
101	R	200r. blue on blue	70·00	34·00
102	R	300r. blue on brown	£100	46·00

1898. As Vasco da Gama types of Portugal but inscr "MACAU".

104	½a. green	7·00	4·25
105	1a. red	8·00	5·75
106	2a. purple	14·00	5·75
107	4a. green	18·00	7·00
108	8a. blue	30·00	16·00
109	12a. brown	40·00	24·00
110	16a. brown	46·00	23·00
111	24a. brown	50·00	34·00

1898. "King Carlos" key-type inscr "MACAU". Name and value in black.

112	S	½a. grey	3·25	1·10
113	S	1a. yellow	3·25	1·10
114	S	2a. green	4·50	1·40
115	S	2½a. brown	9·25	4·25
116	S	3a. lilac	9·25	4·25
174	S	3a. grey	5·50	3·00
117	S	4a. green	12·50	8·00
175	S	4a. red	5·50	3·00
176	S	5a. brown	8·50	5·00
177	S	6a. brown	11·00	5·00
119	S	8a. blue	13·00	6·25
178	S	8a. brown	13·50	7·50
120	S	10a. blue	11·50	6·50
121	S	12a. pink	17·00	10·50
179	S	12a. purple	60·00	28·00
122	S	13a. mauve	20·00	10·50
180	S	13a. lilac	25·00	15·00
123	S	15a. green	£110	29·00
124	S	16a. blue on blue	21·00	10·50
181	S	18a. brown on pink	43·00	22·00
125	S	20a. brown on cream	46·00	15·00
126	S	24a. brown on yellow	25·00	12·00
127	S	31a. purple	34·00	16·00
182	S	31a. purple on pink	43·00	22·00
128	S	47a. blue on pink	48·00	20·00
183	S	47a. blue on yellow	60·00	31·00
129	S	78a. black on blue	75·00	28·00

1900. "King Carlos" key-type of Macao surch **PROVISORIO** and new value.

132	5 on 13a. mauve	16·00	5·25
133	10 on 16a. blue on blue	20·00	8·00
134	15 on 24a. brown on yellow	26·00	10·50
135	20 on 31a. purple	36·00	15·00

1902. Various types of Macao surch.

138	Q	6a. on 5r. black	9·25	5·25
142	R	6a. on 5r. yellow	8·00	4·50
136	P	6a. on 10r. yellow	30·00	12·50
137	P	6a. on 10r. green	20·00	8·00
139	Q	6a. on 10r. green	8·00	5·25
143	R	6a. on 10r. mauve	23·00	8·50
144	R	6a. on 15r. brown	21·00	8·00
145	R	6a. on 25r. green	9·25	4·50
140	Q	6a. on 40r. brown	9·25	5·25
146	R	6a. on 80r. green	9·25	4·50
148	R	6a. on 100r. brown on buff	15·00	6·00
149	R	6a. on 200r. blue on blue	10·50	4·50
151	V	18a. on 2½r. brown	10·50	7·00
153	Q	18a. on 20r. red	21·00	7·50
162	R	18a. on 20r. lilac	25·00	10·50
154	Q	18a. on 25r. mauve	£200	75·00
163	R	18a. on 50r. blue	25·00	10·50
165	R	18a. on 75r. pink	25·00	10·50
155	Q	18a. on 80r. grey	£200	90·00
156	Q	18a. on 100r. brown	48·00	30·00
166	R	18a. on 150r. red on pink	25·00	10·50
158	Q	18a. on 200r. lilac	£170	80·00
160	Q	18a. on 300r. orange	42·00	21·00
167	R	18a. on 300r. blue on brn	25·00	10·50

1902. "King Carlos" type of Macao optd **PROVISORIO**.

168	S	2a. green	15·00	6·25
169	S	4a. green	40·00	14·00
170	S	8a. blue	21·00	11·50

171	**S**	10a. blue	22·00	12·50
172	**S**	12a. pink	80·00	30·00

1905. No. 179 surch **10 AVOS** and bar.

184	10a. on 12a. purple	37·00	18·00

1910. "Due" key-type of Macao, but with words "PORTEADO" and "RECEBER" cancelled.

185	**W**	½a. green	16·00	9·50
186	**W**	1a. green	20·00	9·50
187	**W**	2a. grey	34·00	11·00

1911. "King Carlos" key-type of Macao optd REPUBLICA.

188	**S**	½a. grey	3·75	1·40
189	**S**	1a. orange	3·00	1·00
190	**S**	2a. green	3·00	1·00
191	**S**	3a. grey	5·00	1·50
192	**S**	4a. red	7·50	2·30
193	**S**	5a. brown	7·50	3·50
194	**S**	6a. brown	7·50	3·50
195	**S**	8a. brown	7·50	3·50
196	**S**	10a. blue	7·50	3·50
197	**S**	13a. lilac	12·50	4·25
198	**S**	16a. blue on blue	12·50	5·75
199	**S**	18a. brown on pink	20·00	7·50
200	**S**	20a. brown on cream	20·00	7·50
201	**S**	31a. purple on pink	25·00	8·00
202	**S**	47a. blue on yellow	37·00	13·50
203	**S**	78a. black on blue	49·00	20·00

30

1911. Fiscal stamp surch **POSTAL 1 AVO** and bar.

204	**30**	1a. on 5r. brown, yellow and black	27·00	11·00

1911. Stamps bisected and surch.

205	**S**	2a. on half of 4a. red (No. 175)	75·00	55·00
206	**S**	5a. on half of 10a. blue (No. 120)	£600	£375
207	**S**	5a. on half of 10a. blue (No. 171)	£160	£110

32

1911

210	**32**	1a. black	£600	£500
211	**32**	2a. black	£650	£550

1913. Provisionals of 1902 surch in addition with new value and bars over old value and optd REPUBLICA.

212	**R**	2a. on 18a. on 20r. lilac (No. 162)	13·50	5·50
213	**R**	2a. on 18a. on 50r. blue (No. 163)	13·50	5·50
215	**R**	2a. on 18a. on 75r. pink (No. 165)	13·50	5·50
216	**R**	2a. on 18a. on 150r. red on pink (No. 166)	13·50	5·50

1913. Provisionals of 1902 and 1905 optd **REPUBLICA**.

218	**Q**	6a. on 5r. (No. 138)	18·00	10·00
284	**R**	6a. on 5r. (No. 142)	15·00	6·25
217	**P**	6a. on 10r. (No. 137)	55·00	11·00
285	**Q**	6a. on 10r. (No. 139)	49·00	31·00
286	**R**	6a. on 10r. (No. 143)	15·00	7·50
287	**R**	6a. on 15r. (No. 144)	12·50	6·25
288	**R**	6a. on 25r. (No. 145)	13·50	7·50
220	**Q**	6a. on 40r. (No. 140)	13·50	6·75
289	**R**	6a. on 80r. (No. 146)	13·50	7·50
291	**R**	6a. on 100r. (No. 148)	13·50	7·50
292	**R**	6a. on 200r. (No. 149)	18·00	10·50
281	**S**	8a. (No. 170)	21·00	11·00
282	**S**	10a. (No. 171)	21·00	11·00
283	**S**	10a. on 12a. (No. 184)	22·00	11·50
293	**V**	18a. on 2½r. (No. 151)	21·00	10·50
229	**Q**	18a. on 20r. (No. 153)	21·00	9·75
295	**R**	18a. on 20r. (No. 162)	21·00	10·50
296	**R**	18a. on 50r. (No. 163)	22·00	11·50
298	**R**	18a. on 75r. (No. 165)	23·00	11·50
230	**Q**	18a. on 100r. (No. 156)	£110	50·00
299	**R**	18a. on 150r. (No. 166)	31·00	15·00
233	**Q**	18a. on 300r. (No. 160)	47·00	22·00
300	**R**	18a. on 300r. (No. 167)	49·00	18·00

1913. Stamps of 1911 issue surch.

252	**S**	½a. on 5a. brown	21·00	5·50
255	**S**	1a. on 13a. lilac	22·00	8·50
253	**S**	4a. on 8a. brown	44·00	9·25

1913. Vasco da Gama stamps of Macao optd **REPUBLICA**, and the 12a. surch **10 A**.

256	½a. green	6·25	2·75
257	1a. red	8·50	2·75
258	2a. purple	8·50	2·75
259	4a. green	18·00	7·50
260	8a. blue	23·00	8·00
261	10a. on 12a. brown	43·00	22·00
262	16a. brown	37·00	18·00
263	24a. brown	38·00	16·00

1913. "Ceres" key-type inscr "MACAU".

264	**U**	½a. green	2·75	1·40
310	**U**	1a. black	6·25	2·50
311	**U**	1½a. green	4·00	1·80
280	**U**	2a. green	9·75	6·25
313	**U**	3a. orange	12·50	4·00
267	**U**	4a. red	6·75	2·75
315	**U**	4a. yellow	16·00	6·25
268	**U**	5a. brown	7·50	4·25
269	**U**	6a. violet	7·50	4·25
270	**U**	8a. brown	7·50	4·25
271	**U**	10a. blue	9·75	4·25
272	**U**	12a. brown	11·00	4·25
320	**U**	14a. mauve	42·00	22·00
321	**U**	16a. grey	37·00	27·00
274	**U**	20a. red	21·00	11·00
322	**U**	24a. green	37·00	25·00
323	**U**	32a. brown	43·00	32·00
275	**U**	40a. purple	21·00	11·00
324	**U**	56a. pink	60·00	34·00
276	**U**	58a. brown on green	33·00	21·00
325	**U**	72a. brown	80·00	37·00
277	**U**	76a. brown on pink	36·00	22·00
278	**U**	1p. orange on orange	60·00	28·00
326	**U**	1p. orange	£100	70·00
279	**U**	3p. green on blue	£160	85·00
327	**U**	3p. turquoise	£425	£180
328	**U**	5p. red	£250	£150

1919. Surch.

301		½a. on 5a. brown (No. 268)	£100	43·00
330	**U**	1a. on 24a. grn (No. 322)	8·00	4·00
304	**S**	2a. on 6a. (No. 177)	£275	£120
302	**R**	2 on 6a. on 25r. green (No. 288)	£600	£250
303	**R**	2 on 6a. on 80r. green (No. 289)	£375	£180
331	**U**	2a. on 32a. (No. 323)	8·00	4·00
332	**U**	4a. on 12a. (No. 272)	8·00	4·25
329	**U**	5a. on 6a. violet (No. 269)	11·00	6·25
334	**U**	7a. on 8a. brn (No. 270)	11·00	6·75
335	**U**	12a. on 14a. (No. 320)	11·00	6·75
336	**U**	15a. on 16a. (No. 321)	11·00	6·75
337	**U**	20a. on 56a. pink (No. 324)	90·00	50·00

50 "Portugal" and Galeasse

1934

338	**50**	½a. brown	1·40	60
339	**50**	1a. brown	1·40	60
340	**50**	2a. green	2·20	75
341	**50**	3a. mauve	2·20	75
342	**50**	4a. black	2·50	90
343	**50**	5a. grey	2·50	90
344	**50**	6a. brown	3·00	90
345	**50**	7a. red	3·75	1·40
346	**50**	8a. blue	3·75	1·40
347	**50**	10a. red	5·50	2·10
348	**50**	12a. blue	5·50	2·10
349	**50**	14a. green	5·50	2·10
350	**50**	15a. purple	5·50	2·10
351	**50**	20a. orange	6·25	2·10
352	**50**	30a. green	13·50	4·00
353	**50**	40a. violet	13·50	4·00
354	**50**	50a. brown	23·00	8·00
355	**50**	1p. blue	60·00	20·00
356	**50**	2p. brown	80·00	26·00
357	**50**	3p. green	£225	60·00
358	**50**	5p. mauve	£275	80·00

1936. Air. Stamps of 1934 optd **Aviao** and with Greek characters or surch also.

359	**40**	2a. green	5·25	2·00
360	**40**	3a. mauve	6·75	2·75
361	**40**	5a. on 6a. brown	8·00	3·25
362	**40**	7a. red	8·00	3·25
363	**40**	8a. blue	11·00	7·50
364	**40**	15a. purple	37·00	17·00

54 Vasco da Gama

56 Airplane over Globe

1938. Name and value in black.

365	**54**	1a. green (postage)	2·30	1·20
366	**54**	2a. brown	2·50	1·40
367	**54**	3a. violet	2·50	1·40
368	**54**	4a. green	2·50	1·40
369	-	5a. red	2·50	1·40
370	-	6a. grey	3·75	2·20
371	-	8a. purple	4·00	2·50
372	-	10a. mauve	5·00	3·00
373	-	12a. red	5·25	3·25
374	-	15a. orange	6·75	4·25
375	-	20a. blue	8·00	4·25
376	-	40a. black	20·00	9·25
377	-	50a. brown	23·00	10·50
378	-	1p. red	70·00	26·00
379	-	2p. green	£100	39·00
380	-	3p. blue	£140	49·00
381	-	5p. brown	£250	60·00
382	**56**	1a. red (air)	1·40	60
383	**56**	2a. violet	2·50	1·40
384	**56**	3a. orange	5·25	2·00
385	**56**	5a. blue	6·75	4·00
386	**56**	10a. red	8·00	5·25
387	**56**	20a. green	16·00	9·25
388	**56**	50a. brown	25·00	13·50
389	**56**	70a. red	41·00	17·00
390	**56**	1p. mauve	70·00	25·00

DESIGNS: Nos. 369/71, Mousinho de Albuquerque; 372/4, Henry the Navigator; 375/7, Dam; 378/81, Afonso de Albuquerque.

1940. Surch.

391	**50**	1a. on 6a. brown (No. 344)	7·50	5·00
394	**50**	2a. on 6a. brown (No. 344)	4·00	3·00
395	**50**	3a. on 6a. brown (No. 344)	4·00	3·00
401	-	3a. on 6a. grey (No. 370)	80·00	47·00
396	**50**	5a. on 7a. red (No. 345)	12·50	8·50
397	**50**	5a. on 8a. blue (No. 346)	16·00	9·75
398	**50**	8a. on 30a. (No. 352)	12·50	6·25
399	**50**	8a. on 40a. (No. 353)	13·50	7·00
400	**50**	8a. on 50a. (No. 354)	13·50	8·25

61 Mountain Fort

1948

410		1a. brown and orange	7·50	60
427	-	1a. violet and pink	5·00	1·50
411	**61**	2a. purple	7·50	60
428	**61**	2a. brown and yellow	5·00	1·50
412	-	3a. purple	10·50	2·00
429	-	3a. orange	12·50	2·50
413	-	8a. red	8·00	2·50
430	-	8a. grey	16·00	2·50
414	-	10a. purple	12·50	2·50
431	-	10a. brown and orange	22·00	6·25
415	-	20a. blue	31·00	6·25
416	-	30a. grey	50·00	9·75
432	-	30a. blue	25·00	6·75
417	-	50a. brown and buff	85·00	11·00
433	-	50a. olive and green	60·00	8·50
418	-	1p. green	£180	25·00
419	-	1p. blue	£225	
434	-	1p. brown	£180	31·00
420	-	2p. red	£200	25·00
421	-	3p. green	£200	25·00
422	-	5p. violet	£300	25·00

DESIGNS—HORIZ: 1a. Macao house; 3a. Port of Macao; 8a. Praia Grande Bay; 10a. Leal Senado Sq; 20a. Sao Jerome Hill; 30a. Street scene, Macao; 50a. Relief of goddess of Ma (allegory); 5p. Forest road. VERT: 1p. Cerco Gateway; 2p. Barra Pagoda, Ma-Cok-Miu; 3p. Post Office.

62 Our Lady of Fatima

1948. Honouring the Statue of Our Lady of Fatima.

423	**62**	8a. red	70·00	22·00

64 Globe and Letter

1949. 75th Anniv of U.P.U.

424	**64**	32a. purple	£150	37·00

65 Bells and Dove

1950. Holy Year.

425	**65**	32a. black	42·00	11·50
426	-	50a. red	43·00	12·50

DESIGN: 50a. Angel holding candelabra.

66 Arms and Dragon

1950

435	**66**	1a. yellow on cream	4·25	1·80
436	**66**	2a. green on green	4·25	1·80
437	**66**	10a. purple on green	15·00	3·75
438	**66**	10a. mauve on green	12·50	3·75

67 F. Mendes Pinto

1951

439	**67**	1a. indigo and blue	1·20	90
440	-	2a. brown and green	2·50	90
441	-	3a. green and light green	4·00	1·60
442	-	6a. violet and blue	5·25	1·80
443	-	10a. brown and orange	12·50	2·20
444	**67**	20a. purple and light purple	22·00	5·00
445	-	30a. brown and green	33·00	6·25
446	-	50a. red and orange	85·00	17·00

DESIGNS: 2, 10a. St. Francis Xavier; 3, 50a. J. Alvaras; 6, 30a. L. de Camoens.

68 Junk

1951

447		1p. ultramarine and blue	49·00	4·00
448		3p. black and blue	£180	31·00
449	**68**	5p. brown and orange	£250	34·00

DESIGNS—HORIZ: 1p. Sampan. VERT: 3p. Junk.

69 Our Lady of Fatima

1951. Termination of Holy Year.

450	**69**	60a. mauve and pink	75·00	13·50

71 St. Raphael Hospital

1952. First Tropical Medicine Congress, Lisbon.

451	**71**	6a. lilac and black	15·00	5·50

72 St. Francis
Xavier Statue

1952. 400th Death Anniv of St. Francis Xavier.
452	72	3a. black on cream	7·50	1·50
453	–	16a. brown on buff	23·00	5·00
454	–	40a. black on blue	34·00	7·50

DESIGNS: 16a. Miraculous Arm of St. Francis; 40a. Tomb of St. Francis.

73 The Virgin

1953. Missionary Art Exhibition.
455	73	8a. brown and drab	6·25	1·80
456	73	10a. blue and brown	25·00	6·25
457	73	50a. green and drab	33·00	8·50

74 Honeysuckle

1953. Indigenous Flowers.
458	74	1a. yellow, green and red	1·20	45
459	–	3a. purple, green and yellow	1·20	45
460	–	5a. red, green and brown	1·20	45
461	–	10a. multicoloured	1·20	45
462	–	16a. yellow, green & brown	2·50	60
463	–	30a. pink, brown and green	5·00	1·20
464	–	39a. multicoloured	6·25	1·60
465	–	1p. yellow, green and purple	11·00	2·10
466	–	3p. red, brown and grey	25·00	3·75
467	–	5p. yellow, green and red	43·00	8·00

FLOWERS: 3a. Myosotis; 5a. Dragon claw; 10a. Nunflower; 16a. Narcissus; 30a. Peach blossom; 39a. Lotus blossom; 1p. Chrysanthemum; 3p. Plum blossom; 5p. Tangerine blossom.

75 Portuguese
Stamp of 1853 and
Arms of Portuguese
Overseas Provinces

1954. Portuguese Stamp Centenary.
468	75	10a. multicoloured	16·00	3·75

76 Father M. de
Nobrega and View of
Sao Paulo

1954. Fourth Centenary of Sao Paulo.
469	76	39a. multicoloured	21·00	5·25

77 Map of
Macao

1956. Map multicoloured. Values in red, inscr in brown. Colours given are of the backgrounds.
470	77	1a. drab	1·20	60
471	77	3a. slate	2·50	85
472	77	5a. brown	3·75	1·20
473	77	10a. buff	6·25	1·50
474	77	30a. blue	9·25	1·80
475	77	40a. green	12·50	2·50
476	77	90a. grey	31·00	4·25
477	77	1p.50 pink	37·00	5·75

78 Exhibition
Emblem and
Atomic
Emblems

1958. Brussels International Exhibition.
478	78	70a. multicoloured	7·50	3·00

79 "Cinnamomum
camphora"

1958. Sixth International Congress of Tropical Medicine.
479	79	20a. multicoloured	11·00	5·00

1960. 500th Death Anniv of Prince Henry the Navigator.
480	80	2p. multicoloured	15·00	5·00

80 Globe girdled
by Signs of the
Zodiac

1960. Air. Multicoloured.
481		50a. Praia Grande Bay	4·25	85
482		76a. Type 81	9·25	2·50
483		3p. Macao	21·00	3·75
484		5p. Mong Ha	27·00	3·75
485		10p. Shore of Praia Grande Bay	43·00	4·25

82 Hockey

1962. Sports. Multicoloured.
486		10a. Type 82	3·75	85
487		16a. Wrestling	5·00	2·75
488		20a. Table tennis	7·50	2·30
489		50a. Motor cycle racing	6·75	3·50
490		1p.20 Relay racing	27·00	6·00
491		2p.50 Badminton	55·00	11·00

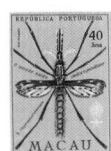

83 "Anopheles
hycranus
sinensis"

1962. Malaria Eradication.
492	83	40a. multicoloured	8·50	3·00

84 Bank Building

1964. Centenary of National Overseas Bank.
493	84	20a. multicoloured	15·00	3·75

85 I.T.U. Emblem
and St. Gabriel

1965. Centenary of I.T.U.
494	85	10a. multicoloured	7·50	2·75

86 Infante Dom Henrique
Academy and Visconde de
Sao Januario Hospital

1966. 40th Anniv of Portuguese National Revolution.
495	86	10a. multicoloured	7·50	2·75

87 Drummer,
1548

1966. Portuguese Military Uniforms. Multicoloured.
496		10a. Type 87	3·00	60
497		15a. Soldier, 1548	5·50	1·20
498		20a. Arquebusier, 1649	6·25	1·20
499		40a. Infantry officer, 1783	8·50	1·40
500		50a. Infantryman, 1783	11·00	2·50
501		60a. Infantryman, 1902	25·00	3·00
502		1p. Infantryman, 1903	31·00	5·00
503		3p. Infantryman, 1904	49·00	9·75

88 O. E. Carmo and Patrol
Boat "Vega"

1967. Centenary of Military Naval Assn. Multicoloured.
504	88	10a. Type 88	5·00	1·30
505		20a. Silva Junior and sail frigate "Don Fernando"	9·75	2·50

89 Arms of Pope
Paul VI, and
"Golden Rose"

1967. 50th Anniv of Fatima Apparitions.
506	89	50a. multicoloured	11·00	2·50

90 Cabral
Monument,
Lisbon

1968. 500th Birth Anniv of Pedro Cabral (explorer). Multicoloured.
507	90	20a. Type 90	8·50	1·80
508		70a. Cabral's statue, Belmonte	10·50	3·25

91 Adm. Gago
Coutinho with
Sextant

1969. Birth Centenary of Admiral Gago Coutinho.
509	91	20a. multicoloured	5·50	2·00

92 Church and
Convent of Our
Lady of the
Reliquary,
Vidigueira

1969. 500th Birth Anniv of Vasco da Gama (explorer).
510	92	1p. multicoloured	16·00	2·50

93 L. A. Rebello
da Silva

1969. Centenary of Overseas Administrative Reforms.
511	93	90a. multicoloured	9·75	1·60

94 Bishop D.
Belchoir Carneiro

1969. 400th Anniv of Misericordia Monastery, Macao.
512	94	50a. multicoloured	6·25	1·40

95 Facade of
Mother Church,
Golega

1969. 500th Birth Anniv of King Manoel I.
513	95	30a. multicoloured	9·75	1·50

96 Marshal
Carmona

1970. Birth Centenary of Marshal Carmona.
514	96	5a. multicoloured	2·50	1·40

97 Dragon Mask

1971. Chinese Carnival Masks. Multicoloured.
515		5a. Type 97	2·00	60
516		10a. Lion mask	3·75	1·20

98 Portuguese
Traders at the
Chinese Imperial
Court

1972. 400th Anniv of Camoens' "The Lusiads" (epic poem).
517	98	20a. multicoloured	17·00	6·25

99 Hockey

1972. Olympic Games, Munich.

| 518 | **99** | 50a. multicoloured | 5·50 | 1·40 |

100 Fairey IIID Seaplane "Santa Cruz" arriving at Rio de Janeiro

1972. 50th Anniv of First Flight from Lisbon to Rio de Janeiro.

| 519 | **100** | 5p. multicoloured | 31·00 | 9·75 |

101 Lyre Emblem and Theatre Facade

1972. Centenary of Pedro V Theatre, Macao.

| 520 | **101** | 2p. multicoloured | 16·00 | 3·75 |

102 W.M.O. Emblem

1973. Centenary of W.M.O.

| 521 | **102** | 20a. multicoloured | 9·75 | 2·50 |

103 Visconde de Sao Januario

1974. Centenary of Visconde de Sao Januario Hospital. Multicoloured.

| 522 | 15a. Type **103** | | 1·40 | 60 |
| 523 | 60a. Hospital buildings of 1874 and 1974 | | 6·25 | 1·40 |

104 Chinnery (self-portrait)

1974. Birth Bicent of George Chinnery (painter).

| 524 | **104** | 30a. multicoloured | 6·25 | 2·20 |

105 Macao–Taipa Bridge

1975. Inauguration of Macao–Taipa Bridge. Multicoloured.

| 525 | 20a. Type **105** | | 2·50 | 1·00 |
| 526 | 2p.20 View of Bridge from below | | 22·00 | 3·00 |

106 Man waving Banner

1975. First Anniv of Portuguese Revolution.

| 527 | **106** | 10a. multicoloured | 4·00 | 3·50 |
| 528 | **106** | 1p. multicoloured | 20·00 | 7·50 |

107 Pou Chai Pagoda

1976. Pagodas. Multicoloured.

| 529 | 10p. Type **107** | | 21·00 | 7·50 |
| 530 | 20p. Tin Hau Pagoda | | 41·00 | 9·75 |

108 Symbolic Figure

1977. Legislative Assembly.

531	**108**	5a. blue, dp blue & black	12·50	6·25
532	**108**	2p. brown and black	£180	12·50
533	**108**	5p. yellow, green and black	60·00	15·00

1979. Nos. 462, 464, 469, 482, 523 and 526 surch.

536	–	10a. on 16a. yellow, green and brown	9·75	5·50
537	–	30a. on 39a. multicoloured	10·50	5·50
538	**76**	30a. on 39a. multicoloured	50·00	25·00
539	–	30a. on 60a. multicoloured	7·50	6·25
540	**81**	70a. on 76a. multicoloured	39·00	9·75
541	–	2p. on 2p.20 multicoloured	11·00	8·00

111 Camoes and Macao Harbour

1981. 400th Death Anniv (1980) of Camoes (Portuguese poet).

542	**111**	10a. multicoloured	1·50	1·20
543	**111**	30a. multicoloured	2·75	2·50
544	**111**	1p. multicoloured	6·75	3·75
545	**111**	3p. multicoloured	9·75	5·00

113 Buddha and Macao Cathedral

1981. Transcultural Psychiatry Symposium.

547	**113**	15a. multicoloured	60	50
548	**113**	40a. multicoloured	1·00	55
549	**113**	50a. multicoloured	1·20	60
550	**113**	60a. multicoloured	2·00	75
551	**113**	1p. multicoloured	3·75	1·00
552	**113**	2p.20 multicoloured	9·75	2·00

115 Health Services Buildings

1982. Buildings.

554	–	10a. grey, blue and yellow	50	35
555	–	20a. black, green & lt grn	60	35
556	**115**	30a. green, grey and stone	60	35
557	–	40a. yellow, lt green & grn	75	35
558	–	60a. orange, chocolate and brown	60	35
559	–	80a. pink, green & brown	1·50	50
560	–	90a. purple, blue and red	85	60
561	–	1p. multicoloured	1·60	60
562	–	1p.50 yellow, brn & grey	5·00	2·00
563	–	2p. purple, ultramarine and blue	3·00	1·40
564	–	2p.50 ultramarine, pink and blue	2·75	1·80
565	–	3p. yellow, green and olive	2·50	1·00
566	–	7p.50 lilac, blue and red	7·50	3·00
567	–	10p. grey, lilac and mauve	11·00	5·00
568	–	15p. yellow, brown and red	11·00	6·25

DESIGNS: 10a. Social Welfare Institute; 20a. Holy House of Mercy; 40a. Guia lighthouse; 60a. St. Lawrence's Church; 80a. St. Joseph's Seminary; 90a. Pedro V Theatre; 1p. Cerco city gate; 1p.50, St. Domenico's Church; 2p. Luis de Camoes Museum; 2p.50, Ruins of St. Paul's Church; 3p. Palace of St. Sancha (Governor's residence); 7p.50, Senate House; 10p. Schools Welfare Service building; 15p. Barracks of the Moors (headquarters of Port Captaincy and Maritime Police).

116 Heng Ho (Moon goddess)

1982. Autumn Festival. Multicoloured.

569	40a. Type **116**		2·50	1·20
570	1p. Decorated gourds		7·50	2·50
571	2p. Paper lantern		9·75	5·00
572	5p. Warrior riding lion		20·00	7·50

117 Aerial View of Macao, Taipa and Coloane Islands

1982. Macao's Geographical Situation. Multicoloured.

| 573 | 50a. Type **117** | | 12·50 | 2·00 |
| 574 | 3p. Map of South China | | 25·00 | 8·50 |

118 "Switchboard Operators" (Lou Sok Man)

1983. World Communications Year. Children's Drawings. Multicoloured.

575	60a. Type **118**		2·30	1·10
576	3p. Postman and pillar box (Lai Sok Pek)		5·25	3·50
577	6p. Globe with methods of communication (Loi Chak Keong)		9·75	4·50

119 "Asclepias curassavica"

1983. Medicinal Plants. Multicoloured.

578	20a. Type **119**		1·10	80
579	40a. "Acanthus ilicifolius"		2·30	80
580	60a. "Melastoma sanguineum"		3·50	1·00
581	70a. Indian lotus ("Nelumbo nucifera")		4·50	1·40
582	1p.50 "Bombax malabaricum"		5·75	2·30
583	2p.50 "Hibiscus mutabilis"		10·50	5·25
MS584	143×90 mm. Nos. 578/83 (sold at 6p.50)		£170	£140

120 Galleon and Map of Macao (left)

1983. 16th Century Portuguese Discoveries. Multicoloured.

| 585 | 4p. Type **120** | | 8·00 | 4·50 |
| 586 | 4p. Galleon, astrolabe and map of Macao (right) | | 8·00 | 4·50 |

Nos. 585/6 were printed together, *se-tenant*, forming a composite design.

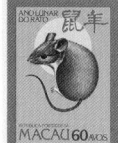

121 Rat

1984. New Year. "Year of the Rat".

| 587 | **121** | 60a. multicoloured | 8·00 | 5·75 |

122 Detail of First Macao Stamp, 1884

1984. Centenary of Macao Stamps.

588	**122**	40a. black and red	2·30	55
589	**122**	3p. black and red	4·50	1·80
590	**122**	5p. black and brown	10·50	3·75
MS591	116×139 mm. Nos. 588/90		55·00	55·00

123 Jay

1984. "Ausipex 84" International Stamp Exhibition, Melbourne. Birds. Multicoloured.

592	30a. White-throated and river kingfishers		1·70	70
593	40a. Type **123**		1·70	70
594	50a. Japanese white-eye		2·30	70
595	70a. Hoopoe		4·50	80
596	2p.50 Pekin robin		10·50	2·30
597	6p. Mallard		11·50	4·00

124 Hok Lou T'eng

1984. "Philakorea 84" International Stamp Exhibition, Seoul. Fishing Boats. Multicoloured.

598	20a. Type **124**		1·10	55
599	60a. Tai Tong		2·30	1·10
600	2p. Tai Mei Chai		5·75	2·30
601	5p. Ch'at Pong T'o		11·50	4·00

126 Open Hand with Stylized Doves

1985. New Year. Year of the Ox.

| 602 | **125** | 1p. multicoloured | 10·50 | 3·50 |

125 Ox and Moon

1985. International Youth Year. Multicoloured.

| 603 | 2p.50 Type **126** | | 6·25 | 80 |
| 604 | 3p. Open hands and plants | | 8·50 | 2·75 |

127 Pres. Eanes

1985. Visit of President Ramalho Eanes of Portugal.

| 605 | **127** | 1p.50 multicoloured | 5·25 | 2·30 |

128 Riverside Scene

1985. 25th Anniv of Luis de Camoes Museum. Paintings by Cheng Chi Yun. Multicoloured.
606	2p.50 Type **128**	8·50	2·30
607	2p.50 Man on seat and boy filling jar from river	8·50	2·30
608	2p.50 Playing harp in sum-merhouse	8·50	2·30
609	2p.50 Three men by river	8·50	2·30

129 "Euploea midamus"

1985. World Tourism Day. Butterflies. Multicoloured.
610	30a. Type **129**	2·30	55
611	50a. Great orange-tip	2·30	55
612	70a. "Lethe confusa"	3·75	70
613	2p. Purple sapphire	4·75	1·10
614	4p. "Euthalia phemius seitzi"	9·75	4·75
615	7p.50 Common birdwing	12·50	4·75
MS616	95×120 mm. Nos. 610/15	£160	£110

130 Tou (sailing barge)

1985. "Italia '85" International Stamp Exhibition, Rome. Cargo Boats. Multicoloured.
617	50a. Type **130**	1·10	35
618	70a. "Veng Seng Lei" (motor junk)	3·50	45
619	1p. "Tong Heng Long No. 2" (motor junk)	5·75	1·10
620	6p. "Fong Vong San" (container ship)	9·25	5·25

131 Tiger and Moon

1986. New Year. Year of the Tiger.
621	**131**	1p.50 multicoloured	8·50	1·40

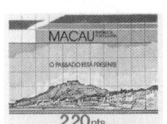

132 View of Macao

1986. Macao, "the Past is still Present".
622	**132**	2p.20 multicoloured	7·00	2·75

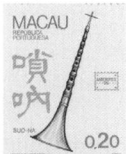

133 Suo-na

1986. "Ameripex '86" International Stamp Exn, Chicago. Musical Instruments. Multicoloured.
623	20a. Type **133**	4·00	1·40
624	50a. Sheng (pipes)	5·00	1·60
625	60a. Er-hu (bowed instrument)	7·00	2·00
626	70a. Ruan (string instrument)	8·25	2·20
627	5p. Cheng (harp)	26·00	3·50
628	8p. Pi-pa (lute)	30·00	5·75
MS629	119×111 mm. Nos. 623/8	£200	£140

134 "Flying Albatros" (hydrofoil)

1986. "Stockholmia 86" International Stamp Exhibition. Passenger Ferries. Multicoloured.
630	10a. Type **134**	55	55
631	40a. "Tejo" (hovercraft)	5·25	1·10
632	3p. "Tercera" (jetfoil)	5·75	1·80
633	7p.50 "Cheung Kong" (high speed ferry)	11·50	3·75

135 Taipa Fortress

1986. Tenth Anniv of Security Forces. Fortresses. Multicoloured.
634	2p. Type **135**	11·50	5·75
635	2p. St. Paul on the Mount	11·50	5·75
636	2p. St. Francis	11·50	5·75
637	2p. Guia	11·50	5·75

Nos. 634/7 were printed together, *se-tenant*, forming a composite design.

136 Sun Yat-sen

1986. 120th Birth Anniv of Dr. Sun Yat-sen. Multicoloured.
638	70a. Type **136**	5·75	2·75
MS639	95×70 mm. 1p.30 Dr. Sun Yat-sen (*different*)	70·00	50·00

137 Hare and Moon

1987. New Year. Year of the Hare.
640	**137**	1p.50 multicoloured	8·00	1·70

138 Wa To (physician)

1987. Shek Wan Ceramics. Multicoloured.
641	2p.20 Type **138**	9·25	4·50
642	2p.20 Choi San, God of Fortune	9·25	4·50
643	2p.20 Yi, Sun God	9·25	4·50
644	2p.20 Cung Kuei, Keeper of Demons	9·25	4·50

139 Boats

1987. Dragon Boat Festival. Multicoloured.
645	50a. Type **139**	4·50	1·10
646	5p. Dragon boat prow	10·50	3·75

140 Circular Fan

1987. Fans. Multicoloured.
647	30a. Type **140**	5·75	1·80
648	70a. Folding fan with tree design	11·50	2·75
649	1p. Square-shaped fan with peacock design	29·00	3·75
650	6p. Heart-shaped fan with painting of woman and tree	32·00	9·75
MS651	113×139 mm. Nos. 647/50	£275	£140

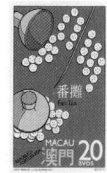

141 Fantan

1987. Casino Games. Multicoloured.
652	20a. Type **141**	9·25	4·25
653	40a. Cussec	10·50	4·75
654	4p. Baccarat	14·00	5·25
655	7p. Roulette	17·00	5·75

142 Goods Hand-cart

1987. Traditional Vehicles. Multicoloured.
656	10a. Type **142**	1·10	1·10
657	70a. Open sedan chair	3·50	1·70
658	90a. Rickshaw	6·25	2·30
659	10p. Cycle rickshaw	17·00	4·00
MS660	90×65 mm. 7p.50 Covered sedan chair	55·00	29·00

143 Dragon and Moon

1988. New Year. Year of the Dragon.
661	**143**	2p.50 multicoloured	8·00	4·50

144 West European Hedgehog

1988. Protected Mammals. Multicoloured.
662	3p. Type **144**	8·00	2·30
663	3p. Eurasian badger	8·00	2·30
664	3p. European otter	8·00	2·30
665	3p. Chinese pangolin	8·00	2·30

145 Breastfeeding

1988. 40th Anniv of W.H.O. Multicoloured.
666	60a. Type **145**	3·50	90
667	80a. Vaccinating child	4·50	1·10
668	2p.40 Donating blood	9·25	3·50

146 Bicycles

1988. Transport. Multicoloured.
669	20a. Type **146**	1·10	55
670	50a. Lambretta and Vespa	2·30	1·10
671	3p.30 Open-sided motor car	7·00	1·70
672	5p. Renault delivery truck, 1912	9·25	3·50
MS673	68×57 mm. 7p.50 Rover (1907)	70·00	34·00

147 Hurdling

1988. Olympic Games, Seoul. Multicoloured.
674	40a. Type **147**	1·60	55
675	60a. Basketball	2·40	75
676	1p. Football	4·00	1·70
677	8p. Table tennis	8·00	3·50
MS678	112×140 mm. Nos. 673/6; 5p. Taekwondo	55·00	40·00

148 Intelpost (electronic mail)

1988. New Postal Services. Multicoloured.
679	13p.40 Type **148**	9·25	2·75
680	40p. Express Mail Service (EMS)	12·00	8·00

149 B.M.W. Saloon Car

1988. 35th Macao Grand Prix. Multicoloured.
681	80a. Type **149**	1·70	55
682	2p.80 Motor cycle	5·75	1·40
683	7p. Formula 3 car	12·50	4·00
MS684	115×139 mm. Nos. 681/3	75·00	46·00

150 Snake and Moon

1989. New Year. Year of the Snake.
685	**150**	3p. multicoloured	9·75	2·75

151 Water Carrier

1989. Traditional Occupations (1st series). Multicoloured.
686	50a. Type **151**	1·10	35
687	1p. Tan-kya (boat) woman	2·30	55
688	4p. Tin-tin man (pedlar)	3·50	1·90
689	5p. Tao-fu-fa (soya bean cheese) vendor	5·75	2·50

See also Nos. 714/17 and 743/6.

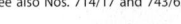

152 White Building

1989. Paintings by George Vitalievich Smirnoff in Luis Camoes Museum. Multicoloured.
690	2p. Type **152**	2·75	1·10
691	2p. Building with railings	2·75	1·10
692	2p. Street scene	2·75	1·10
693	2p. White thatched cottage	2·75	1·10

153 Common Cobra

1989. "Philexfrance 89" International Stamp Exhibition, Paris. Snakes of Macao. Mult.

694	2p.50 Type **153**	3·50	1·50
695	2p.50 Banded krait ("Bungarus fasciatus")	3·50	1·50
696	2p.50 Bamboo pit viper ("Trimeresurus alboabris")	3·50	1·50
697	2p.50 Rat snake ("Elaphe radiata")	3·50	1·50

154 Talu

1989. Traditional Games. Multicoloured.

698	10a. Type **154**	1·10	70
699	60a. Triol (marbles)	2·75	85
700	3p.30 Chiquia (shuttlecock)	5·75	1·70
701	5p. Chinese chequers	7·00	2·75

155 Piaggio P-136L Flying Boat

1989. Aircraft. Multicoloured.

702	50a. Type **155**	80	45
703	70a. Martin M-130 flying boat	1·40	55
704	2p.80 Fairey 111D seaplane	1·80	1·10
705	4p. Hawker Osprey seaplane	3·50	1·80
MS706	105×82 mm. 7p.50 De Havilland D.H.80A Puss Moth	34·00	17·00

156 Malacca

1989. "World Stamp Expo '89" International Stamp Exhibition, Washington D.C. Portuguese Presence in Far East. Multicoloured.

707	40a. Type **156**	55	35
708	70a. Thailand	1·10	45
709	90a. India	1·70	70
710	2p.50 Japan	3·50	90
711	7p.50 China	5·75	2·50
MS712	147?×130 mm. Nos. 707/11; 3p. Macao	46·00	29·00

157 Horse and Moon

1990. New Year. Year of the Horse.

| 713 | **157** | 4p. multicoloured | 5·25 | 1·80 |

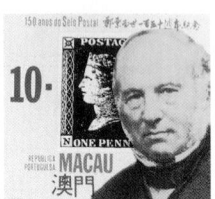

158 Penny Black and Sir Rowland Hill (postal reformer)

1990. Traditional Occupations (2nd series). As T 151. Multicoloured.

714	30a. Long-chau singer	1·30	80
715	70a. Cobbler	2·50	1·30
716	1p.50 Travelling penman	3·75	1·70
717	7p.50 Fisherman with wide nets	11·00	3·50

1990. 150th Anniv of the Penny Black. Sheet 91×130 mm.

| MS718 | **158** 10p. multicoloured | 29·00 | 17·00 |

159 Long-finned Grouper ("Epinephelus megachir")

1990. Fishes. Multicoloured.

719	2p.40 Type **159**	2·50	1·30
720	2p.40 Malabar snapper ("Lutianus malabaricus")	2·50	1·30
721	2p.40 Spotted snakehead ("Ophiocepalus maculatus")	2·50	1·30
722	2p.40 Paradise fish ("Macropodus opercularis")	2·50	1·30

160 Porcelain

1990. "New Zealand 1990" International Stamp Exhibition, Auckland. Industrial Diversification. Multicoloured.

723	3p. Type **160**	2·75	1·40
724	3p. Furniture	2·75	1·40
725	3p. Toys	2·75	1·40
726	3p. Artificial flowers	2·75	1·40
MS727	131×95 mm. Nos. 723/6	39·00	17·00

161 Cycling

1990. 11th Asian Games, Peking. Multicoloured.

728	80a. Type **161**	1·10	35
729	1p. Swimming	1·40	55
730	3p. Judo	4·00	1·40
731	4p.20 Shooting	6·25	2·30
MS732	95×140 mm. Nos. 728/31; 6p. Athlete with bamboo pole	40·00	34·00

162 Rose by Lazaro Luis

1990. Compass Roses. Designs showing roses from ancient charts by cartographer named. Multicoloured.

733	50a. Type **162**	1·30	55
734	1p. Diogo Homem	2·40	70
735	3p.50 Diogo Homem (different)	4·25	1·70
736	6p.50 Fernao Vaz Dourado	8·50	2·30
MS737	107×100 mm. 5p. Luiz Teixeira (29×39 mm)	47·00	29·00

163 Cricket Fight

1990. Betting on Animals. Multicoloured.

738	20a. Type **163**	1·10	45
739	80a. Melodious laughing thrush fight	2·75	90
740	1p. Greyhound racing	3·50	1·40
741	10p. Horse racing	10·00	2·50

164 Goat and Moon

1991. New Year. Year of the Goat.

| 742 | **164** | 4p.50 multicoloured | 5·25 | 1·30 |

1991. Traditional Occupations (3rd series). As T **151**. Multicoloured.

743	80a. Knife-grinder	1·10	55
744	1p.70 Flour-puppets vendor	2·30	70
745	3p.50 Street barber	5·25	1·40
746	4p.20 Fortune-teller	7·50	2·50

165 True Harp ("Harpa harpa")

1991. Sea Shells. Multicoloured.

747	3p. Type **165**	3·50	1·70
748	3p. Oil-lamp tun ("Tonna zonata")	3·50	1·70
749	3p. Bramble murex ("Murex pecten")	3·50	1·70
750	3p. Rose-branch murex ("Chicoreus rosarius")	3·50	1·70

The Latin names on Nos. 749/50 are incorrect.

166 Character and Backcloth

1991. Chinese Opera. Multicoloured.

751	**166**	60a. multicoloured	1·80	45
752	-	80a. multicoloured	2·75	55
753	-	1p. multicoloured	4·50	1·10
754	-	10p. multicoloured	13·00	2·75

DESIGNS: Nos. 752/4, Different backcloths and costumes.

167 "Delonix regia" and Lou Lim Ioc Garden

1991. Flowers and Gardens (1st series). Multicoloured.

755	1p.70 Type **167**	1·80	70
756	3p. "Ipomoea cairica" and Sao Francisco Garden	2·75	1·40
757	3p.50 "Jasminum mesyi" and Sun Yat Sen Park	4·50	2·00
758	4p.20 "Bauhinia variegata" and Seac Pai Van Park	5·50	2·75
MS759	95×137 mm. Nos. 755/8	55·00	29·00

See also Nos. 815/**MS**19.

168 Portuguese Traders unloading Boats

1991. Cultural Exchange. Nambam Paintings attr. Kano Domi. Multicoloured.

760	4p.20 Type **168**	2·75	1·40
761	4p.20 Portuguese traders displaying goods to buyers	2·75	1·40
MS762	107×74 mm. Nos. 760/1	37·00	23·00

169 Firework Display

1991. Christmas. Multicoloured.

763	1p.70 Type **169**	1·40	55
764	3p. Father Christmas	2·10	80
765	3p.50 Man dancing	3·50	1·30
766	4p.20 January 1st celebrations	7·00	2·30

170 Concertina Door

1992. Doors and Windows. Multicoloured.

767	1p.70 Type **170**	1·40	80
768	3p. Window with four shutters	2·75	1·50
769	3p.50 Window with two shutters	4·00	2·10
770	4p.20 Louvred door	5·75	2·75

171 Monkey and Moon

1992. New Year. Year of the Monkey.

| 771 | **171** | 4p.50 multicoloured | 5·00 | 2·50 |

172 T'it Kuai Lei

1992. Gods of Chinese Mythology (1st series). Multicoloured.

772	3p.50 (1) Type **172**	8·00	3·50
773	3p.50 (2) Chong Lei Kun	8·00	3·50
774	3p.50 (3) Cheong Kuo Lou on donkey	8·00	3·50
775	3p.50 (4) Loi Tong Pan	8·00	3·50

See also Nos. 796/9.

173 Lion Dance

1992. "World Columbian Stamp Expo '92", Chicago. Chinese Dances. Multicoloured.

776	1p. Type **173**	1·10	70
777	2p.70 Lion dance (different)	2·20	80
778	6p. Dragon dance	4·25	1·70

174 High Jumping

1992. Olympic Games, Barcelona. Multicoloured.

779	80a. Type **174**	75	45
780	4p.20 Badminton	1·40	90
781	4p.70 Roller hockey	2·20	1·10
782	5p. Yachting	2·75	1·60
MS783	137×95 mm. Nos. 779/82	21·00	11·50

175 Na Cha Temple

1992. Temples (1st series). Multicoloured.

784	1p. Type **175**	1·10	70
785	1p.50 Kun lam	1·60	80
786	1p.70 Hong Kon	2·30	1·50
787	6p.50 A Ma	4·25	2·50

See also Nos. 792/5 and 894/8.

176 Tung Sin Tong Services

1992. Centenary of Tung Sin Tong (medical and educational charity).

| 788 | **176** | 1p. multicoloured | 2·10 | 55 |

177 Rooster and Dragon

1992. Portuguese–Chinese Friendship.
789	**177**	10p. multicoloured	3·75	2·30
MS790		109×74 mm. **177** 10p. multi-coloured	17·00	14·00

178 Red Junglefowl

1992. New Year. Year of the Cock.
791	**178**	5p. multicoloured	3·75	1·30

See also No. **MS**917.

1993. Temples (2nd series). As T **175**. Multicoloured.
792	50a. T'am Kong	55	35
793	2p. T'in Hau	1·10	45
794	3p.50 Lin Fong	1·70	90
795	8p. Pau Kong	2·50	2·10

1993. Gods of Chinese Mythology (2nd series). As T **172**. Multicoloured.
796	3p.50 (1) Lam Ch'oi Wo flying on crane	3·25	2·30
797	3p.50 (2) Ho Sin Ku (goddess) on peach blossom	3·25	2·30
798	3p.50 (3) Hon Seong Chi crossing sea on basket of flowers	3·25	2·30
799	3p.50 (4) Ch'ou Kuok K'ao crossing river on plank	3·25	2·30

179 Children carrying Banners

1993. Chinese Wedding. Multicoloured.
800	**179**	3p. Type **179**	1·70	85
801		3p. Bride	1·70	85
802		3p. Bridegroom	1·70	85
803		3p. Wedding guests	1·70	85
MS804		124×106 mm. 8p. Bride and groom (50×40 mm)	16·00	12·50

Nos. 800/3 were issued together, *se-tenant*, forming a composite design.

180 Bird perched on Hand

1993. Environmental Protection.
805	**180**	1p. multicoloured	1·80	55

181 Eurasian Scops Owl

1993. Birds of Prey. Multicoloured.
806	3p. Type **181**	1·40	80
807	3p. Barn owl ("Tyto alba")	1·40	80
808	3p. Peregrine falcon ("Falco peregrinus")	1·40	80
809	3p. Golden eagle ("Aquila obrysaetos")	1·40	80
MS810	107×128 mm. Nos. 806/9	23·00	11·50

182 Town Hall

1993. Union of Portuguese-speaking Capital Cities.
811	**182**	1p.50 green, blue and red	1·10	70

183 Portuguese Missionaries

1993. 450th Anniv of First Portuguese Visit to Japan. Multicoloured.
812	50a. Japanese man with musket	70	35
813	3p. Type **183**	1·40	80
814	3p.50 Traders carrying goods	2·20	1·10

184 "Spathodea campanulata" and Luis de Camoes Garden

1993. Flowers and Gardens (2nd series). Multicoloured.
815	1p. Type **184**	70	35
816	2p. "Tithonia diversifolia" and Montanha Russa Garden	1·30	55
817	3p. "Rhodomyrtus tomentosa" and Cais Garden	1·40	80
818	8p. "Passiflora foetida" and Flora Garden	2·40	2·30
MS819	90×120 mm. Nos. 815/18	21·00	14·00

185 Caravel

1993. 16th-century Sailing Ships. Multicoloured.
820	1p. Type **185**	50	25
821	2p. Caravel (different)	1·10	55
822	3p.50 Nau	1·40	90
823	4p.50 Galleon	1·70	1·40
MS824	160×105 mm. Nos. 820/3	14·00	8·00

186 Saloon Car

1993. 40th Anniv of Macao Grand Prix. Multicoloured.
825	1p.50 Type **186**	70	70
826	2p. Motor cycle	1·30	80
827	4p.50 Racing car	2·40	2·00

187 Chow-chow and Moon

1994. New Year. Year of the Dog.
828	**187**	5p. multicoloured	3·50	1·40

See also No. **MS**917.

188 Map and Prince Henry (½-size illustration)

1994. 600th Birth Anniv of Prince Henry the Navigator.
829	**188**	3p. multicoloured	2·75	1·60

189 Lakeside Hut

1994. Birth Bicentenary of George Chinnery (artist). Multicoloured.
830	3p.50 Type **189**	1·40	1·10
831	3p.50 Fisherman on sea wall	1·40	1·10
832	3p.50 Harbour	1·40	1·10
833	3p.50 Sao Tiago Fortress	1·40	1·10
MS834	138×87 mm. Nos. 830/3	17·00	10·50

190 Lai Sis Exchange

1994. Spring Festival of Lunar New Year. Multicoloured.
835	1p. Type **190**	55	35
836	2p. Flower and tangerine tree decorations	1·40	55
837	3p.50 Preparing family meal	1·50	90
838	4p.50 Paper decorations bearing good wishes	2·20	1·40

191 "Longevity"

1994. Legends and Myths (1st series). Chinese Gods. Multicoloured.
839	3p. Type **191**	2·75	1·70
840	3p. "Prosperity"	2·75	1·70
841	3p. "Happiness"	2·75	1·70
MS842	138×90 mm. Nos. 839/41	17·00	11·50

See also Nos. 884/**MS**888, 930/**MS**933 and 994/**MS**998.

192 Footballer

1994. World Cup Football Championship, U.S.A. Multicoloured.
843	2p. Type **192**	70	45
844	3p. Tackling	1·30	80
845	3p.50 Heading ball	1·40	90
846	4p.50 Goalkeeper saving goal	1·80	1·50
MS847	138×90 mm. Nos. 843/6	17·00	10·50

193 Rice Shop

1994. Traditional Chinese Shops. Multicoloured.
848	1p. Type **193**	80	35
849	1p.50 Medicinal tea shop	90	45
850	2p. Salt-fish shop	1·70	70
851	3p.50 Pharmacy	2·75	90

194 Astrolabe

1994. Nautical Instruments. Multicoloured.
852	3p. Type **194**	1·00	70
853	3p.50 Quadrant	1·40	90
854	4p.50 Sextant	2·10	1·30

195 Fencing

1994. 12th Asian Games, Hiroshima, Japan. Multicoloured.
855	1p. Type **195**	70	45
856	2p. Gymnastics	90	55
857	3p. Water-polo	1·70	80
858	3p.50 Pole vaulting	2·00	1·40

196 Nobre de Carvalho Bridge

1994. Bridges. Multicoloured.
859	1p. Type **196**	1·10	25
860	8p. Friendship Bridge	3·50	2·10

197 Carp

1994. Good Luck Signs. Multicoloured.
861	3p. Type **197**	1·70	1·40
862	3p.50 Peaches	2·30	1·50
863	4p.50 Water lily	3·25	2·30

198 Angel's Head (stained glass window, Macao Cathedral)

1994. Religious Art. Multicoloured.
864	50a. Type **198**	35	30
865	1p. Holy Ghost (stained glass window, Macao Cathedral)	45	40
866	1p.50 Silver sacrarium	80	45
867	2p. Silver salver	1·10	55
868	3p. "Escape into Egypt" (ivory statuette)	1·80	80
869	3p.50 Gold and silver cup	2·30	1·00

199 Pig and Moon

1995. New Year. Year of the Pig.
870	**199**	5p.50 multicoloured	3·50	1·40

200 "Lou Lim Iok Garden"

1995. Paintings of Macao by Lio Man Cheong. Multicoloured.
871	50a. Type **200**	40	35
872	1p. "Guia Fortress and Lighthouse"	50	45
873	1p.50 "Barra Temple"	70	55
874	2p. "Avenida da Praia, Taipa"	90	70
875	2p.50 "Kun lam Temple"	1·40	1·10
876	3p. "St. Paul's Seminary"	2·10	1·40
877	3p.50 "Penha Hill"	2·75	1·50
878	4p. "Gates of Understanding Monument"	2·75	2·10

201 Magnifying Glass over Goods

1995. World Consumer Day.
| 879 | **201** | 1p. multicoloured | 1·40 | 45 |

202 Pangolin

1995. Protection of Chinese ("Asian") Pangolin. Multicoloured.
880	1p.50 In fork of tree	1·70	70
881	1p.50 Hanging from tree by tail	1·70	70
882	1p.50 On leafy branch	1·70	70
883	1p.50 Type **202**	1·70	70

203 Kun Sai Iam

1995. Legends and Myths (2nd series). Kun Sai Iam (Buddhist god). Multicoloured.
884	3p. Type **203**	3·25	1·40
885	3p. Holding baby	3·25	1·40
886	3p. Sitting behind water lily	3·25	1·40
887	3p. With water lily and dragonfish	3·25	1·40
MS888	138×90 mm. 8p. Kun Sai Iam (different)	23·00	14·00

204/7 Senado Square (½-size illustration)

1995. Senado Square.
889	**204**	2p. multicoloured	1·70	80
890	**205**	2p. multicoloured	1·70	80
891	**206**	2p. multicoloured	1·70	80
892	**207**	2p. multicoloured	1·70	80
MS893		138×90 mm. 8p. multicoloured (Leal Senado building and Post Office Clock tower) (horiz)	16·00	8·50

Nos. 889/92 were issued together, *se-tenant*, forming the composite design illustrated.

1995. Temples (3rd series). As T **175**. Multicoloured.
894	50a. Kuan Tai	40	15
895	1p. Pak Tei	55	25
896	1p.50 Lin K'ai	80	35
897	3p. Se Kam Tong	1·50	70
898	3p.50 Fok Tak	1·80	80

208 Pekin Robin ("Leiothrix lutea")

1995. "Singapore'95" International Stamp Exhibition. Birds. Multicoloured.
899	2p.50 Type **208**	2·30	1·00
900	2p.50 Japanese white-eye ("Zosterops japonica")	2·30	1·00
901	2p.50 Island canary ("Serinus canarius canarius")	2·30	1·00
902	2p.50 Melodious laughing thrush ("Gurrulax canonus")	2·30	1·00
MS903	137×90 mm. 10p. Magpie robin (Copyschus saularis)	21·00	9·75

209 Pipa

1995. International Music Festival. Musical Instruments. Multicoloured.
904	1p. Type **209**	1·70	45
905	1p. Erhu (string instrument)	1·70	45
906	1p. Gong (hand-held drum)	1·70	45
907	1p. Sheng (string instrument)	1·70	45
908	1p. Xiao (flute)	1·70	45
909	1p. Tambor (drum)	1·70	45
MS910	137×90 mm. 8p. Two players with instruments (40×29 mm)	14·00	5·75

210 Anniversary Emblem, World Map and U.N. Headquarters, New York

1995. 50th Anniv of United Nations Organization.
| 911 | **210** | 4p.50 multicoloured | 2·50 | 1·40 |

211 Terminal Building

1995. Inauguration of Macao International Airport. Multicoloured.
912	1p. Type **211**	45	35
913	1p.50 Terminal (different)	90	45
914	2p. Loading airplane and cargo building	1·50	70
915	3p. Control tower	2·10	1·00
MS916	137×90 mm. 8p. Airplane taking off	17·00	8·00

1995. Lunar Cycle. Sheet 180×216 mm containing previous New Year designs.
| MS917 | 12×1p.50. As Nos. 791, 828, 870, 587, 771, 602, 742, 621, 713, 685, 661 and 640 | 23·00 | 10·50 |

212 Rat

1996. New Year. Year of the Rat.
| 918 | **212** | 5p. multicoloured | 5·75 | 3·50 |
| MS919 | 137×90 mm. **212** 10p. multicoloured | 14·00 | 8·00 |

213 Cage

1996. Traditional Chinese Cages.
920	**213**	1p. multicoloured	45	30
921	-	1p.50 multicoloured	70	45
922	-	3p. multicoloured	1·30	80
923	-	4p.50 multicoloured	2·10	1·10
MS924	137×90 mm. 10p. multicoloured	16·00	8·00
DESIGNS: 1p.50 to 10p., Different cages.

214 Street

1996. Paintings of Macao by Herculano Estorninho. Multicoloured.
925	50a. Fishing boats (horiz)	45	25
926	1p. Town square	90	35
927	3p. Type **214**	1·50	70
928	5p. Townscape (horiz)	2·75	1·40
MS929	137×90 mm. 10p. Colonnaded entrance	11·50	5·25

215 Tou Tei (God of Earth)

1996. Legends and Myths (3rd series). Multicoloured.
930	3p.50 Type **215**	1·80	1·30
931	3p.50 Choi San (God of Fortune)	1·80	1·30
932	3p.50 Chou Kuan (God of the Kitchen)	1·80	1·30
MS933	137×89 mm. Nos. 930/2	15·00	7·75

216 Customers

1996. Traditional Chinese Tea Houses. Multicoloured.
934	2p. Type **216**	2·10	85
935	2p. Waiter with tray of steamed stuffed bread	2·10	85
936	2p. Newspaper vendor	2·10	85
937	2p. Waiter pouring tea at table	2·10	85
MS938	138×90 mm. 8p. Jar and food snacks	16·00	8·00

Nos. 934/7 were issued together, se-tenant, forming a composite design.

217 Get Well Soon

1996. Greetings stamps. Multicoloured.
939	50a. Type **217**	45	25
940	1p.50 Congratulations on new baby	1·00	45
941	3p. Happy birthday	1·40	80
942	4p. Wedding congratulations	2·10	1·10

218 Swimming

1996. Olympic Games, Atlanta, U.S.A. Multicoloured.
943	2p. Type **218**	55	45
944	3p. Football	90	70
945	3p.50 Gymnastics	1·40	90
946	4p.50 Sailboarding	1·70	1·10
MS947	137×90 mm. 10p. Boxing	9·25	4·00

219 Crane (civil, 1st rank)

1996. Civil and Military Insignia of the Mandarins (1st series). Multicoloured.
948	2p. Type **219**	2·10	80
949	2p.50 Lion (military, 2nd rank)	2·10	80
950	2p.50 Golden pheasant (civil, 2nd rank)	2·10	80
951	2p.50 Leopard (military, 3rd rank)	2·10	80

See also Nos. 1061/4.

220 Trawler with Multiple Nets

1996. Nautical Sciences: Fishing Nets. Multicoloured.
952	3p. Type **220**	2·20	90
953	3p. Modern trawler with net from stern	2·20	90
954	3p. Two sailing junks with common net	2·20	90
955	3p. Junk with two square nets at sides	2·20	90

Nos. 952/5 were issued together, se-tenant, forming a composite design.

221 National Flag and Statue (½-size illustration)

1996. 20th Anniv of Legislative Assembly.
| 956 | **221** | 2p.80 multicoloured | 1·40 | 70 |
| MS957 | 138×90 mm. **221** 8p. multicoloured | 12·50 | 5·25 |

222 Dragonfly

1996. Paper Kites. Multicoloured.
958	3p.50 Type **222**	2·30	90
959	3p.50 Butterfly	2·30	90
960	3p.50 Owl	2·30	90
961	3p.50 Swallow	2·30	90
MS962	138×90 mm. 8p. Chinese dragon (50×37 mm)	15·00	7·00

223 Doll

1996. Traditional Chinese Toys. Multicoloured.
963	50a. Type **223**	70	40
964	1p. Fish	1·50	75
965	3p. Painted doll	3·75	1·40
966	4p.50 Dragon	4·50	2·00

224 Ox

1997. New Year. Year of the Ox.
| 967 | **224** | 5p.50 multicoloured | 4·00 | 2·75 |
| MS968 | 137×89 mm. **224** 10p. multicoloured | 11·50 | 7·00 |

225 Colourful and Gold Twos

1997. Lucky Numbers. Multicoloured.
969	2p. Type **225**	1·00	50
970	2p.80 Eights	1·40	70
971	3p. Threes	1·50	75
972	3p.90 Nines	1·80	1·00
MS973	137×90 mm. 9p. Numbers around doorway of café	7·00	6·50

No. MS973 also commemorates "Hong Kong '97" International Stamp Exhibition.

226 "Sail Boats"

1997. Paintings of Macao by Kwok Se. Multicoloured.
974	2p. Type **226**	1·30	55
975	3p. "Fortress on the Hill"	1·70	80
976	3p.50 "Asilum"	2·10	1·00
977	4p.50 "Portas do Cerco"	2·75	1·40
MS978	138×90 mm. 8p. "Rua de Sao Paulo" (detail) (horiz)	9·75	8·50

227 Elderly Woman

1997. Tan-Ka (boat) People. Multicoloured.
979	1p. Type **227**	55	35
980	1p.50 Elderly woman holding tiller	70	45
981	2p.50 Woman with child on back	1·40	70
982	5p.50 Man mending fishing nets	2·50	1·50

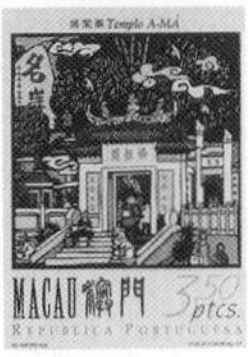

228 Entrance to Temple

1997. A-Ma Temple. Multicoloured.

983	3p.50 Type **228**	1·00	80
984	3p.50 Wall and terraces of Temple	1·00	80
985	3p.50 View of incense smoke through gateway	1·00	80
986	3p.50 Incense smoke emanating from pagoda	1·00	80
MS987	138×90 mm. Ship (representative of land reclamation in front of temple)	6·25	6·25

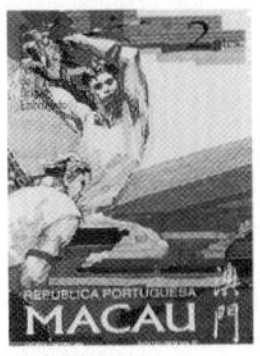

229 Dragon Dancers

1997. Drunken Dragon Festival. Multicoloured.

988	2p. Type **229**	55	45
989	3p. Dragon dancer	90	70
990	5p. Dancer holding "tail" of dragon	1·70	1·40
MS991	138×90 mm. Dancer with dragon's head (horiz)	5·75	5·75

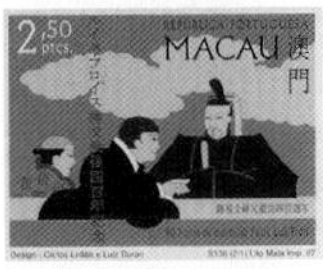

230 Frois with Japanese Man

1997. 400th Death Anniv of Father Luis Frois (author of "The History of Japan"). Multicoloured.

992	2p.50 Type **230**	85	70
993	2p.50 Father Frois and church (vert)	85	70

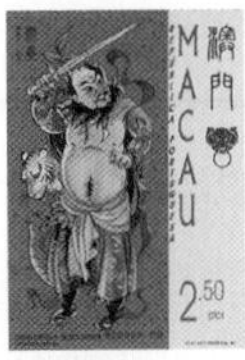

231 Wat Lot

1997. Legends and Myths (4th series). Door Gods. Multicoloured.

994	2p.50 Type **231**	90	55
995	2p.50 San Su	90	55
996	2p.50 Chon Keng	90	55
997	2p.50 Wat Chi Kong	90	55
MS998	138×39 mm. 10p. Chon Keng and Wat Chi Kong on doors (39×39 mm)	5·25	5·25

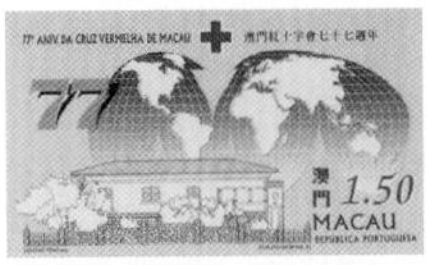

232 Globe and First Aid and Family Health School

1997. 77th Anniv of Macao Red Cross.

999	**232**	1p.50 multicoloured	55	55

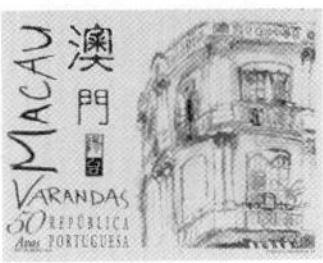

233 Balconies

1997. Balconies.

1000	**233**	50a. multicoloured	25	25
1001	-	1p. multicoloured	30	25
1002	-	1p.50 multicoloured	45	35
1003	-	2p. multicoloured	65	45
1004	-	2p.50 multicoloured	80	70
1005	-	3p. multicoloured	1·10	80
MS1006		137×90 mm. 8p. multicoloured (29×39 mm)	2·75	2·75

DESIGNS: 1p. to 8p. Various balcony styles.

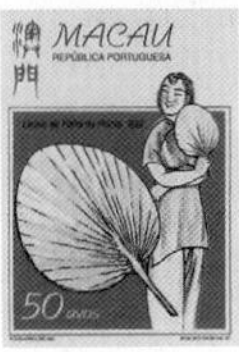

234 Plant Leaf Fan

1997. Fans. Multicoloured.

1007	50a. Type **234**	25	25
1008	1p. Paper fan	30	25
1009	3p.50 Silk fan	1·10	90
1010	4p. Feather fan	1·40	1·10
MS1011	138×90 mm. 9p. Woman holding sandalwood fan	5·75	5·25

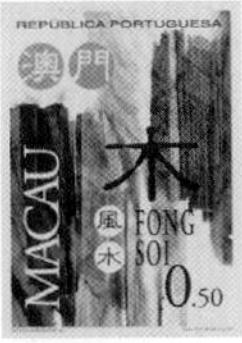

235 Wood

1997. Feng Shui. The Five Elements. Multicoloured.

1012	50a. Type **235**	35	25
1013	1p. Fire	45	30
1014	1p.50 Earth	55	35
1015	2p. Metal	70	45
1016	2p.50 Water	1·00	70
MS1017	138×90 mm. 10p. Centre of geomancer's chart	6·00	5·50

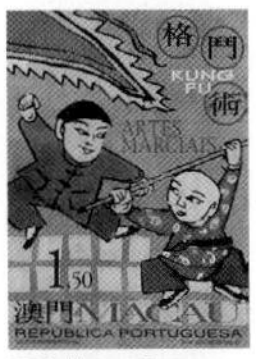

236 Kung Fu

1997. Martial Arts. Multicoloured.

1018	1p.50 Type **236**	55	35
1019	3p.50 Judo	1·10	80
1020	4p. Karate	1·70	1·10

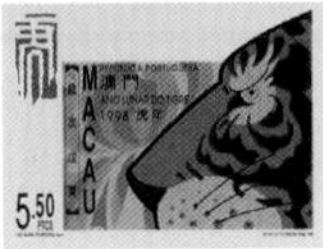

237 Tiger

1998. New Year. Year of the Tiger.

1021	**237**	5p.50 multicoloured	2·10	1·70
MS1022		138×90 mm. **237** 10p. multicoloured	3·75	3·75

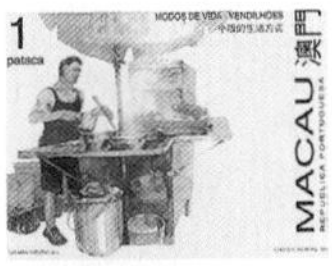

238 Soup Stall

1998. Street Traders. Multicoloured.

1023	1p. Type **238**	30	25
1024	1p.50 Snack stall	45	35
1025	2p. Clothes stall	65	45
1026	2p.50 Balloon stall	80	65
1027	3p. Flower stall	1·00	80
1028	3p.50 Fruit stall	1·30	1·00
MS1029	138×90 mm. 6p. Fruit stall (different)	2·50	2·50

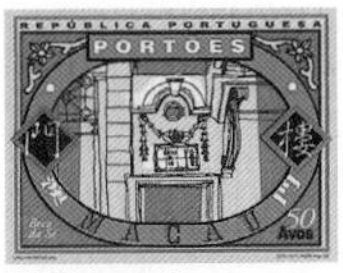

239 Beco da Se

1998. Gateways. Multicoloured.

1030	50a. Type **239**	25	25
1031	1p. Patio da Ilusao	40	35
1032	3p.50 Travessa das galinhas	1·40	1·30
1033	4p. Beco das Felicidades	1·80	1·60
MS1034	138×90 mm. 9p. St. Joseph's Seminary	4·00	4·00

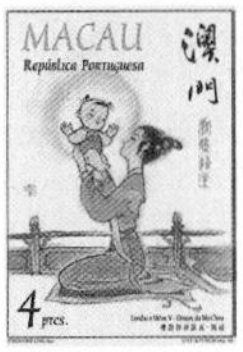

240 Woman and Child

1998. Legends and Myths (5th series). Gods of Ma Chou. Multicoloured.

1035	4p. Type **240**	1·60	1·00
1036	4p. Woman and man's face in smoke	1·60	1·00
1037	4p. Woman with children playing instruments	1·60	1·00
1038	4p. Goddess and sailing barges	1·60	1·00
MS1039	138×90 mm. 10p. Head of goddess	4·00	4·00

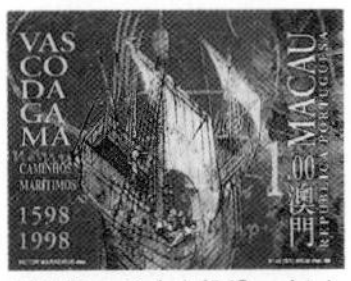

241 "Sao Gabriel" (flagship)

1998. 500th Anniv of Vasco da Gama's Voyage to India via Cape of Good Hope. Multicoloured. (a) Wrongly dated "1598 1998".

1040	1p. Type **241**	65	35
1041	1p.50 Vasco da Gama	90	45
1042	2p. "Sao Gabriel" and map of India	1·20	70
MS1043	138×90 mm. 8p. Compass rose	5·75	5·75

(b) Correctly dated "1498 1998".

1044	1p. Type **241**	50	25
1045	1p.50 As No. 1041	80	35
1046	2p. As No. 1042	1·10	55
MS1047	138×90 mm. 8p. As No. **MS**1043	3·50	3·50

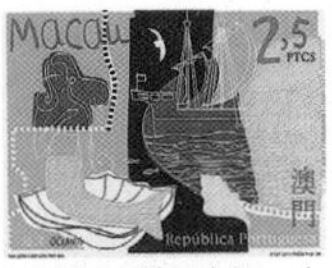

242 Mermaid and Caravel

1998. International Year of the Ocean. Multicoloured.

1048	2p.50 Type **242**	90	70
1049	3p. Whale and oil-rig	1·10	80
MS1050	138×90 mm. Caravel and whale	3·50	3·50

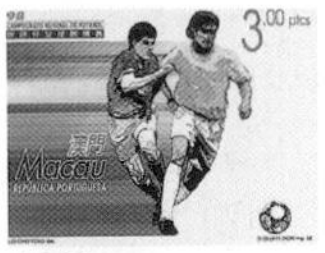

243 Players

1998. World Cup Football Championship, France. Multicoloured.

1051	3p. Type **243**	1·10	90
1052	3p.50 Players competing for ball	1·30	1·10
1053	4p. Player kicking ball clear while being tackled	1·60	1·40
1054	4p.50 Player beating another to ball	2·00	1·70
MS1055	138×90 mm. 9p. Players and ball	4·50	4·00

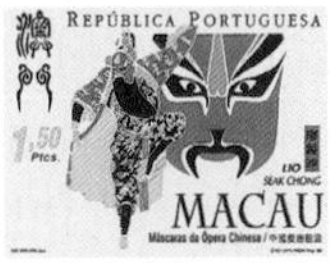

244 Lio Seak Chong Mask

1998. Chinese Opera Masks. Multicoloured.

1056	1p.50 Type **244**	50	35
1057	2p. Wat Chi Kong	65	45
1058	3p. Kam Chin Pao	90	70
1059	5p. Lei Kwai	1·60	1·30
MS1060	138×90 mm. Opera mask	3·50	2·75

1998. Civil and Military Insignia of the Mandarins (2nd series). As T **219**. Multicoloured.

1061	50a. Lion (military, 2nd rank)	25	10
1062	1p. Bear (military, 5th rank)	40	25
1063	1p.50 Golden pheasant (civil, 2nd rank)	50	35
1064	2p. Silver pheasant (civil, 5th rank)	65	45
MS1065	138×90 mm. 9p. Crane (civil, 1st rank)	4·00	3·75

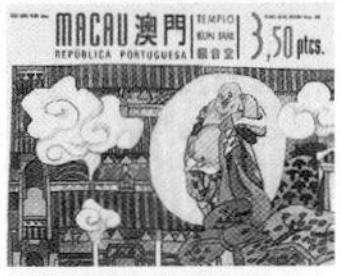

245 Smiling Buddha

1998. Kun Iam Temple. Multicoloured.

1066	3p.50 Type **245**	1·10	80
1067	3p.50 Pavilion and temple gardens	1·10	80
1068	3p.50 Temple gateway	1·10	80
1069	3p.50 Pagoda, stream and gardens	1·10	80
MS1070	138×90 mm. 10p. Temple	4·00	3·75

Nos. 1066/9 were issued together, *se-tenant*, forming a composite design.

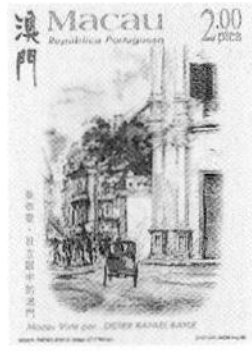

246 Carriage in Street

1998. Paintings of Macao by Didier Rafael Bayle. Multicoloured.

1071	2p. Type **246**	80	70
1072	3p. Street (horiz)	1·20	1·00
1073	3p.50 Building (horiz)	1·30	1·10
1074	4p.50 Kiosk in square	2·00	1·70
MS1075	138×90 mm. 8p. Balcony (horiz)	3·25	3·25

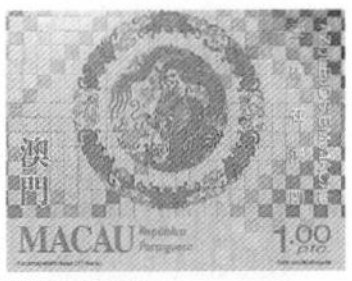

247 Dragon

1998. Tiles by Eduardo Nery (from panel at Departure Lounge of Macao Airport). Multicoloured.

1076	1p. Type **247**	40	25
1077	1p.50 Galleon	50	40
1078	2p.50 Junk	80	55
1079	5p.50 Phoenix	1·70	1·40
MS1080	138×90 mm. 10p. Guia Lighthouse	4·00	3·75

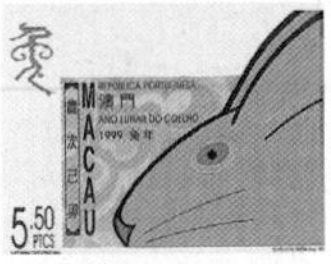

248 Rabbit

1999. New Year. Year of the Rabbit.

1081	**248**	5p.50 multicoloured	2·10	1·80
MS1082		138×90 mm. **248** 10p. multicoloured	4·25	4·00

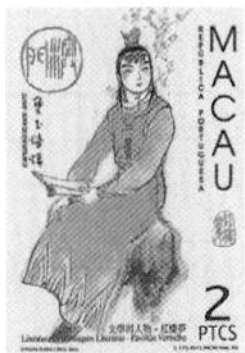

249 Jia Bao Yu

1999. Literature. Characters from "A Dream of Red Mansions" by Cao Xue Qin. Multicoloured.

1083	2p. Type **249**	65	50
1084	2p. Lin Dai Yu holding pole and cherry blossom	65	50
1085	2p. Bao Chai holding fan	65	50
1086	2p. Wang Xi Feng sitting in chair	65	50
1087	2p. You San Jie holding sword	65	50
1088	2p. Qing Wen sewing "peacock" cloak	65	50
MS1089	138×90 mm. 8p. Jia Bao Yu and Lin Dai Yu	3·25	3·25

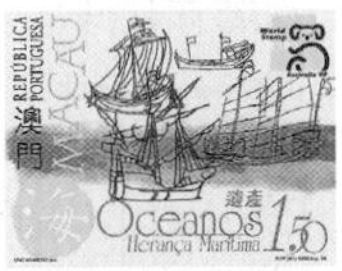

250 Sailing Ships

1999. "Australia'99" International Stamp Exhibition, Melbourne. Oceans and Maritime Heritage. Multicoloured.

1090	1p.50 Type **250**	50	45

1091	2p.50 Marine life	90	80
MS1092	138×90 mm. 6p. Head of whale (vert)	2·40	2·20

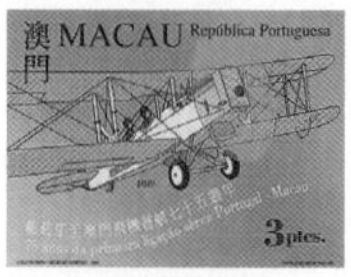
251 de Havilland D.H.9 Biplane

1999. 75th Anniv of Sarmento de Beires and Brito Pais's Portugal–Macao Flight. Multicoloured.

1093	3p. Breguet 16 Bn2 Patria	1·60	1·40
1094	3p. Type **251**	1·60	1·40
MS1095	137×104 mm. Nos. 1093/4	3·25	3·00

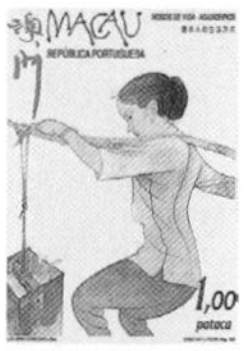
252 Carrying Containers on Yoke

1999. The Water Carrier. Multicoloured.

1096	1p. Type **252**	40	25
1097	1p.50 Filling containers from pump	50	35
1098	2p. Lowering bucket down well	65	45
1099	2p.50 Filling containers from tap	1·00	70
MS1100	138×90 mm. 7p. Woman with containers on yoke climbing steps	3·00	2·75

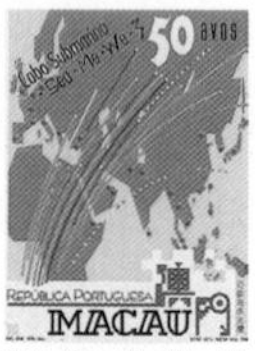
253 "Sea-Me-We-3" Undersea Fibre Optic Cable

1999. Telecommunications Services. Multicoloured.

1101	50a. Type **253**	20	10
1102	1p. Dish aerial at Satellite Earth Station	35	30
1103	3p.50 Analogue mobile phone	1·10	90
1104	4p. Televisions	1·30	1·10
1105	4p.50 Internet and e-mail	1·60	1·40
MS1106	138×90 mm. 8p. Emblem and computer mouse (horiz)	3·25	3·25

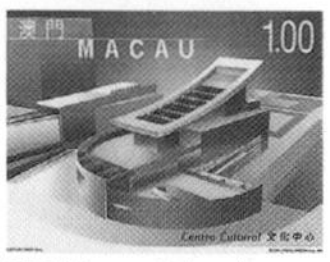
254 Macao Cultural Centre

1999. Modern Buildings. Multicoloured.

1107	1p. Type **254**	35	25
1108	1p.50 Museum of Macao	40	35
1109	2p. Macao Maritime Museum	80	70
1110	2p.50 Ferry Terminal	1·10	90
1111	3p. Macao University	1·20	1·00
1112	3p.50 Public Administration building (vert)	1·30	1·10
1113	4p.50 Macao World Trade Centre (vert)	1·70	1·50
1114	5p. Coloane kart-racing track (vert)	1·80	1·60
1115	8p. Bank of China (vert)	2·50	2·30
1116	12p. National Overseas Bank (vert)	4·00	3·50

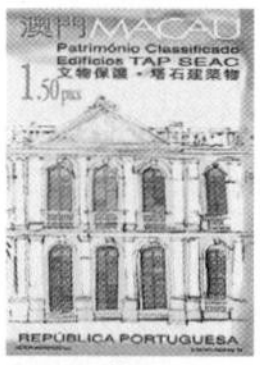
255 Health Department

1999. Classified Buildings in Tap Seac District. Multicoloured.

1117	1p.50 Type **255**	50	45
1118	1p.50 Central Library (face value in salmon)	50	45
1119	1p.50 Centre of Modern Art of the Orient Foundation (face value in yellow)	50	45
1120	1p.50 Portuguese Institute of the Orient (face value in light blue)	50	45
MS1121	138×90 mm. 10p. I.P.O.R. building	4·00	3·75

Nos. 1117/20 were issued together, *se-tenant*, forming a composite design.

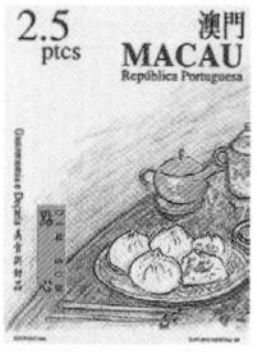
256 Teapot and Plate of Food

1999. Dim Sum. Multicoloured.

1122	2p.50 Type **256**	80	70
1123	2p.50 Plates of food, chopsticks and left half of bowls	80	70
1124	2p.50 Plates of food, glass, cups and right half of bowls	80	70
1125	2p.50 Plates of food and large teapot	80	70
MS1126	138×90 mm. 9p. Plates of food	3·50	3·00

Nos. 1122/5 were issued together, *se-tenant*, forming a composite design.

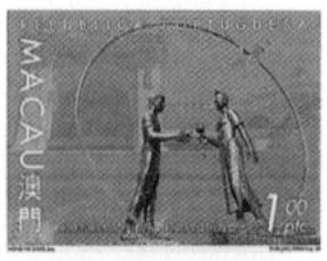
257 "Portuguese Sailor and Chinese Woman" (Lagoa Henriques), Company of Jesus Square

1999. Contemporary Sculptures (1st series). Multicoloured.

1127	1p. Type **257**	40	35
1128	1p.50 "The Gate of Understanding" (Charters de Almeida), Praia Grande Bay (vert)	50	45
1129	2p.50 "Statue of the Goddess Kun Iam" (Cristina Leiria), Macao Cultural Centre (vert)	1·10	90
1130	3p.50 " Taipa Viewing Point" (Dorita Castel-Branco), Nobre de Carvalho Bridge, Taipa	1·30	1·10
MS1131	138×90 mm. 10p. "The Pearl" (Jose Rodrigues), Amizade rounderbout	4·00	3·75

See also Nos. 1186/MS1190.

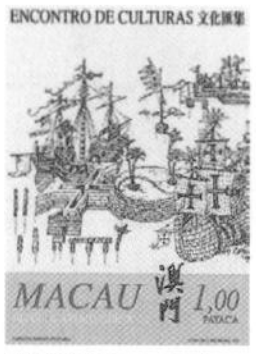
258 Chinese and Portuguese Ships, Christ's Cross and Yin Yang

1999. Portuguese–Chinese Cultural Mix. Multicoloured.

1132	1p. Type **258**	35	30
1133	1p.50 Ah Mah Temple and Portuguese and Macanese architecture	50	45
1134	2p. Bridge, steps and Chinese architecture	70	65
1135	3p. Macanese architecture and Portuguese terrace	1·10	90
MS1136	138×90 mm. Enlargement of right-hand part of design in No. 1135	4·00	3·75

Nos. 1132/5 were issued together, *se-tenant*, forming a composite design.

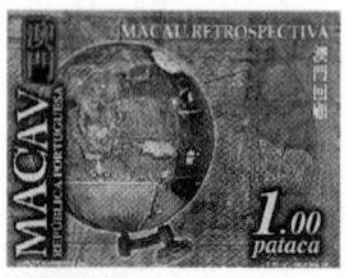
259 Globe

1999. Macao Retrospective. Multicoloured.

1137	1p. Type **259**	40	35
1138	1p.50 Roof terrace	65	55
1139	2p. Portuguese and Chinese people	90	80
1140	3p.50 Modern Macao	1·40	1·30
MS1141	138×90 mm. 9p. City coat of arms	3·50	3·00

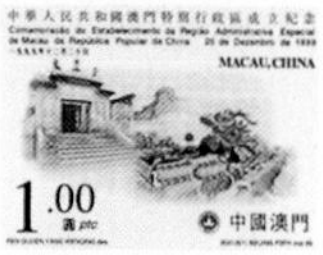
260 Gateway

1999. Establishment of Macao as Special Administrative Region of People's Republic of China. Multicoloured.

1142	1p. Type **260**	50	35
1143	1p.50 Bridge and boat race	60	50
1144	2p. Wall of ruined church	85	75
1145	2p.50 Lighthouse and racing cars	1·00	85
1146	3p. Building facade	1·10	1·00
1147	3p.50 Stadium and orchestra	1·20	1·10
MS1148	138×90 mm. 8p. Pink flower	3·00	2·75

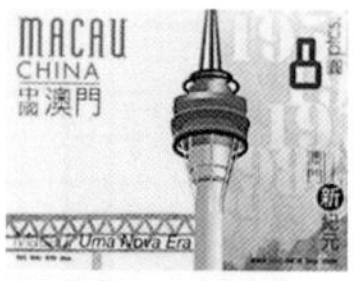
261 Sight-seeing Tower

2000. A New Era. Sheet 138×90 mm.

MS1149	**261** 8p. multicoloured	3·50	3·00

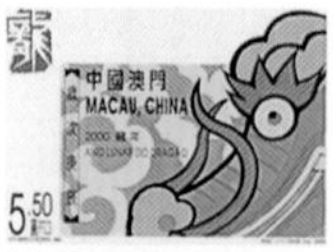
262 Dragon

2000. New Year. Year of the Dragon.

1150	**262** 5p.50 multicoloured	2·20	1·80
MS1151	138×90 mm. **262** 10p. multicoloured	3·75	3·75

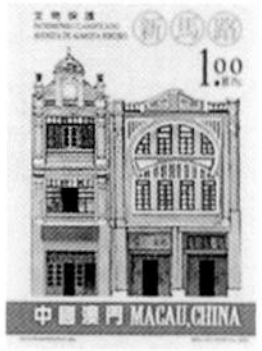
263 Buildings

2000. Classified Buildings in Almeida Ribeiro Avenue, Macao City. Multicoloured.

1152	1p. Type **263**	35	25
1153	1p.50 Yellow and pink buildings	60	50
1154	2p. Yellow building	75	60
1155	3p. Purple, green and pink buildings	1·10	1·00
MS1156	138×90 mm. 9p. Beige building	4·25	3·50

SERIAL NUMBERS. In sets containing several stamps of the same denomination, the serial number is quoted in brackets to assist identification. This is the last figure in the bottom right corner of the stamp.

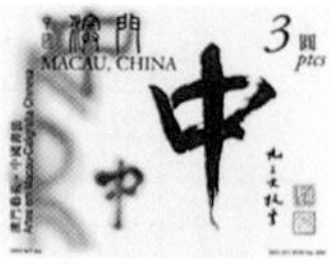
264 Zhong (Leong Pai Wan)

2000. Arts in Macao. Chinese Calligraphy. Showing Chinese characters by named calligraphy masters. Each black and red.

1157	3p. (1) Type **264**	1·20	1·00
1158	3p. (2) Guo (Lin Ka Sang)	1·20	1·00
1159	3p. (3) Shu (Lok Hong)	1·20	1·00
1160	3p. (4) Fa (Sou Su Fai)	1·20	1·00
MS1161	138×90 mm. 8p. Zhong, guo, shu and fa	3·50	3·00

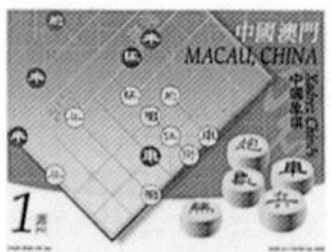
265 Chinese Chess

2000. Board Games. Multicoloured.

1162	1p. Type **265**	35	35
1163	1p.50 Chess	60	60
1164	2p. Go	85	75
1165	2p.50 Flying chess	1·10	95
MS1166	138×90 mm. 9p. Chinese checkers	3·75	3·00

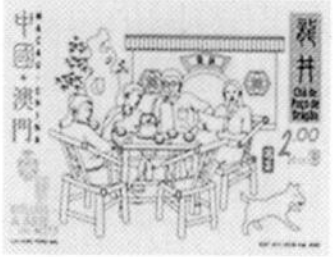
266 Group of Friends

2000. Tea. Multicoloured.

1167	2p. Type **266**	75	75
1168	3p. Family drinking tea	1·10	1·10
1169	3p.50 Women drinking tea	1·40	1·40
1170	4p.50 Men drinking tea	1·75	1·75
MS1171	138×90 mm. 8p. Woman making tes	3·50	3·50

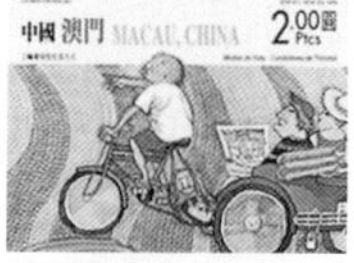
267 Tricycle Driver and Foreign Tourists

2000. Tricycle Drivers. Multicoloured.

1172	2p. (1) Type **267**	75	75
1173	2p. (2) With couple in carriage	75	75
1174	2p. (3) With empty carriage	75	75
1175	2p. (4) With feet resting on saddle	75	75
1176	2p. (5) Sitting in carriage	75	75
1177	2p. (6) Mending tyre	75	75
MS1178	138×90 mm. 8p. Standing beside tricycle (vert)	3·50	3·00

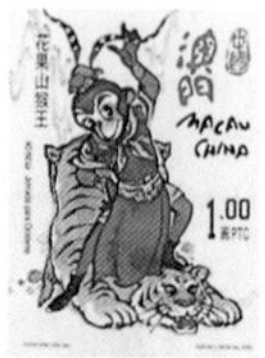
268 Monkey King standing on Tiger Skin

2000. Classical Literature. Journey to the West (Ming dynasty novel). Multicoloured.

1179	1p. Type **268**	35	35
1180	1p.50 Monkey King tasting the heavenly peaches	50	50
1181	2p. Monkey King, Prince Na Zha and flaming wheels	75	75
1182	2p.50 Erlang Deity with spear	1·00	1·00
1183	3p. Heavenly Father Lao Jun	1·25	1·25
1184	3p.50 Monkey King in Buddha's hand	1·40	1·40
MS1185	138×90 mm. 9p. Monkey King holding baton (horiz)	4·00	3·25

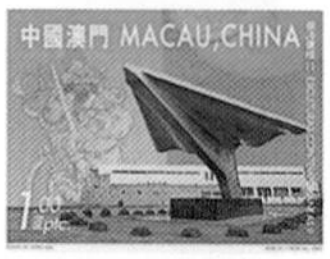
269 "Wing of Good Winds" (Augusto Cid), Pac On Roundabout, Taipa

2000. Contemporary Sculptures (2nd series). Multicoloured.

1186	1p. Type **269**	50	35
1187	2p. "The Embrace" (Irene Vilar), Luis de Camoes Garden (vert)	85	75
1188	3p. Monument (Soares Branco), Guia's Tunnel, Outer Harbour (vert)	1·40	1·20
1189	4p. "The Arch of the Orient" (Zulmiro de Carvalho), Avienda Rodrigo Rodrigues Viaduct	1·70	1·60
MS1190	90×138 mm. 10p. "Goddess A-Ma" (Leong Man Lin). Coloane lland	4·75	4·50

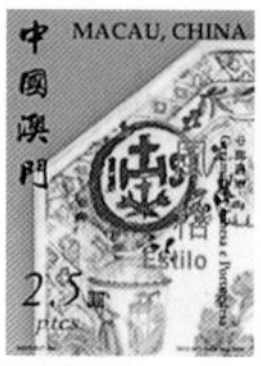
270 Decorated Pot

2000. Ceramics. Multicoloured.

1191	2p.50 (1) Type **270**	1·00	1·00
1192	2p.50 (2) Vase, dish and teapot	1·00	1·00
1193	2p.50 (3) Blue vase	1·00	1·00
1194	2p.50 (4) Cabbage-shaped pot and leaf-shaped dish	1·00	1·00
1195	2p.50 (5) Plate and fishes	1·00	1·00

1196	2p.50 (6) Blue and white vase	1·00	1·00

MS1197 138×90 mm. 8p. Decorated plate (round-design) — 4·25 3·50

Nos. 1191/6 were issued together, *se-tenant*, with the backgrounds forming a composite design.

271 Phoenix crouching, Shang Dynasty

2000. Jade Ornaments. Multicoloured.
1198	1p.50 Type 271	60	50
1199	2p. Archer's white jade ring, Warring States period	85	75
1200	2p.50 Dragon and phoenix, Six Dynasties	1·10	1·00
1201	3p. Pendant with dragon decoration, Western Han Dynasty	1·20	1·10

MS1202 138×90 mm. 9p. Medallion (detail) (vert) — 4·00 3·25

272 Dancers with National and Special Administrative Flags

2000. First Anniv of Macau as Special Administrative Region of People's Republic of China. Multicoloured.
1203	2p. Type 272	85	90
1204	3p. Chinese dragons and lotus flower	1·20	1·10

MS1205 138×90 mm. 18p. Flags, statesmen and lotus flower (59×39 mm) — 6·75 6·75

Nos. 1203/4 were issued together, *se-tenant*, forming a composite design.

273 Snake

2001. New Year. Year of the Snake.
1206	273 5p.50 multicoloured	2·50	1·80

MS1207 138×90 mm. 272 10p. multicoloured — 4·00 3·75

274 Man holding Bottle ("Nursing Vengeance despite Hardships")

2001. Ancient Proverbs. Multicoloured.
1208	2p. (1) Type 274	1·00	80
1209	2p. (2) Man waiting for a rabbit ("Trusting to Chance and Windfalls")	1·00	80
1210	2p. (3) Fox and tiger ("Bullying Others by Flaunting One's Powerful Connections")	1·00	80
1211	2p. (4) Mother with child ("Selecting a Proper Surrounding to Bring up Children")	1·00	80

MS1212 138×90 mm. 8p. Man stealing bell ("Burying Ones' Head in the Sand") — 3·50 3·00

275 Abacus

2001. Traditional Tools. Multicoloured.
1213	1p. Type 275	50	35
1214	2p. Plane	85	75
1215	3p. Iron	1·20	1·10
1216	4p. Scales	1·70	1·50

MS1217 138×90 mm. 8p. Text, scales and iron — 4·25 3·50

276 Buddha

2001. Religions. Multicoloured.
1218	1p. Type 276	35	35
1219	1p.50 Worshippers	60	60
1220	2p. Man carrying Cross and religious procession	85	75
1221	2p.50 Procession	1·10	1·00

MS1222 138×90 mm. 8p. Religious Symbols (circular design) (59×59 mm) — 3·75 3·25

Nos. 1218/19 and 1220/1 respectively were issued together, *se-tenant*, forming a composite design.

277 Fireman and Platform Car

2001. Fire Brigade. Multicoloured.
1223	1p.50 Type 277	1·10	60
1224	2p.50 Fireman wearing chemical protection suit using portable flammable gases detector and Pumping Tank vehicle	1·10	1·00
1225	3p. Foam car and fireman wearing asbestos suit using foam hose	1·25	1·10
1226	4p. Fire officers in dress uniforms and ambulance	1·70	1·50

MS1227 138×90 mm. 8p. Fireman (59×39 mm) — 5·00 3·75

278 Electronic Keys

2001. E-Commerce. Multicoloured.
1228	1p.50 Type 278	75	60
1229	2p. Hands passing letter (e-mail)	85	75
1230	2p.50 Mobile phone	1·20	1·00
1231	3p. Palm hand-held computer	1·50	1·10

MS1232 138×90 6p. Laptop computers (59×39 mm) — 3·00 2·50

279 Emblem

2001. Choice of Beijing as 2008 Olympic Games Host City.
1233	279 1p. multicoloured	1·20	35

280 Praying

2001. Classical Literature. Romance of the Three Kingdoms (novel by Luo Guanzhong). Multicoloured.
1234	3p. (1) Type 280	1·20	1·10
1235	3p. (2) Soldier and man fighting	1·20	1·10
1236	3p. (3) Men talking	1·20	1·10
1237	3p. (4) Man dreaming	1·20	1·10

MS1238 138×90 mm. 7p. Head of Soldier (horiz) — 4·00 2·75

281 Baby, Doctor and Schoolchildren

2001. National Census. Multicoloured.
1239	1p. Type 281	60	50
1240	1p.50 Street scene	60	60

1241	2p.50 Suspension bridge and crowd	1·00	85

MS1242 137×90 mm. 6p. Subjects as Nos. 1239/41 (86×37 mm) — 2·75 2·20

282 Municipal Market

2001. Macau Markets. Multicoloured.
1243	1p.50 Type 282	60	60
1244	2p.50 Building and road-side stall	1·00	1·00
1245	3p.50 Covered market	1·40	1·40
1246	4p.50 Multi-storey building	1·70	1·70

MS1247 138×90 mm. 7p. Bus station building (59×38 mm) — 3·50 2·75

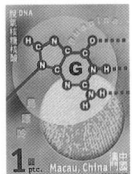
283 DNA Helix containing Guanine Base

2001. Science and Technology. Composition and Structure of DNA. Showing chemical bases of DNA. Multicoloured.
1248	1p. Type 283	60	35
1249	2p. Helix containing cytosine base	1·00	75
1250	3p. Helix containing adenine base	1·40	1·10
1251	4p. Helix containing thymine base	1·80	1·50

MS1252 137×90 mm. 8p. Helix containing adenine base (different) (44×29 mm) — 4·00 3·00

284 Commander Ho Yin's Garden

2001. Parks and Gardens. Multicoloured.
1253	1p.50 Type 284	60	60
1254	2p.50 Mong Há Hill municipal park	1·00	1·00
1255	3p. City of Flowers Garden	1·20	1·20
1256	4p.50 Great Taipa Natural Park	1·70	1·70

MS1257 138×90 mm. 8p. Garden of Art — 4·00 4·00

285 Trigrams and Dragons

2001. Pa Kua (martial art) (1st series). Multicoloured.
1258	2p. (1) Type 285	85	80
1259	2p. (4) Trigrams, couple and deer	85	80
1260	2p. (7) Trigrams, fields and buffaloes	85	80
1261	2p. (3) Trigrams and volcano	85	80
1262	2p. (6) Trigrams and three men crawling	85	80
1263	2p. (2) Trigrams, man and donkey	85	80
1264	2p. (5) Trigrams, horse and carriage	85	80
1265	2p. (8) Trigrams, men with gifts and potentate	85	80

MS1266 15×90 mm. 8p. Yu Fu (Pa Kua master) (59×27 mm) — 3·75 3·00

See also Nos. 1323/**MS**1331, 1367/**MS**1375, 1386/**MS**1394, 1552/**MS**1560 AND 1629/**MS**1637.

286 Horse's Head

2002. New Year. Year of the Horse. Multicoloured.
1267	5p.50 Type 286	2·75	2·00

MS1268 138×91 mm. 10p. As No. 1267 but design enlarged — 4·50 4·00

287 Lao Lao visiting Fidalgo's House

2002. Classical Literature. Dream of Red Mansions. Multicoloured.
1269	2p. Type 287	85	85
1270	2p. Jin Chuan suffering injustice	85	85
1271	2p. Proof of Dada's love for Zi Juan	85	85
1272	2p. Xiang Yun adorned with peony flowers	85	85
1273	2p. Liu Lang combing her hair	85	85
1274	2p. Miao Yu offering tea	85	85

MS1275 139×90 mm. 8p. Woman reading (The wonderful dream of love) — 4·50 3·75

288 Cantao San Kong Opera Performers

2002. Festivals. Tou-Tei (God of Earth) Festival. Multicoloured.
1276	1p.50 Type 288	60	60
1277	2p.50 Respected elders dinner	1·00	1·00
1278	3p.50 Burning of cult objects	1·50	1·50
1279	4p.50 Cooking suckling pig	1·80	1·80

MS1280 139×90 mm. 8p. Bearded man with sword (vert) — 4·00 3·25

289 Facade and bas-relief of St. Paul

2002. 400th Anniv St. Paul's Church, Macao. Multicoloured.
1281	1p. Type 289	60	45
1282	3p.50 Corner of façade and ornament	1·70	1·50

MS1283 139×90 mm. 8p. Statue in alcove (30×40 mm) — 4·00 3·25

290 Goalkeeper diving for Ball

2002. World Cup Football Championships, Japan and South Korea. Multicoloured.
1284	1p. Type 290	60	35
1285	1p.50 Players tackling for ball	1·50	90

291 Underwater Animals and Oil Refinery

2002. Environmental Protection. Multicoloured.
1286	1p. Type 291 (marine conservation)	50	35
1287	1p.50 Boy planting tree (reforestation)	60	55
1288	2p. Emblem and bins (recycling)	85	75
1289	2p.50 Spoonbills (wetland conservation)	1·10	1·00
1290	3p. Energy plant and waste truck (energy regeneration)	1·40	1·25
1291	3p.50 Boy sweeping leaves (clean urban environment)	1·50	1·40

1292	4p. Girl blowing bubbles (air purification)	1·60	1·50
1293	4p.50 Nurse and elderly patient (health and hygiene)	1·80	1·70
1294	8p. Owl (improving city living)	3·25	3·00

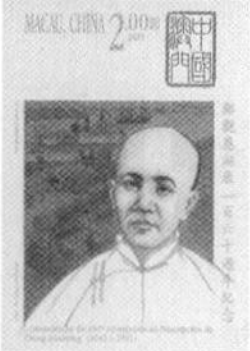

292 Zheng Guanying at Home

2002. 160th Birth Anniv of Zheng Guanying (industrialist, reformer and philanthropist). Multicoloured.

1295	1p. Type **292**	35	35
1296	2p. As young man and docks	75	75
1297	3p. As young man and alms giving	1·10	1·10
1298	3p.50 As older man and writing	1·70	1·60
MS1299 138×90 mm. 6p. Seated at table (40×60 mm)		3·00	2·30

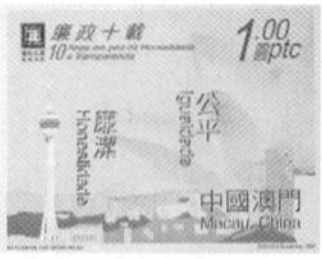

293 Macau Tower and Skyline

2001. Honesty and Transparency. Multicoloured.

1300	1p. Type **293**	60	35
1301	3p.50 Macau skyline from Monte Fort	1·50	1·40

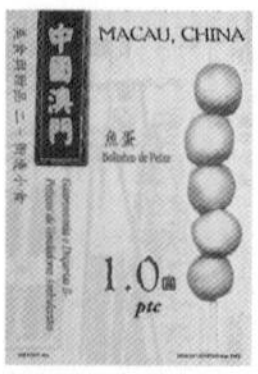

294 Fish Balls

2002. Street Vendor's Food. Multicoloured.

1302	1p. Type **294**	35	35
1303	1p.50 Dried beef	60	55
1304	2p. Tongue roll	85	75
1305	2p.50 Sat Kei Ma	1·10	1·00
MS1306 138×91 mm. 7p. Cookie (50×50 mm)		3·00	2·75

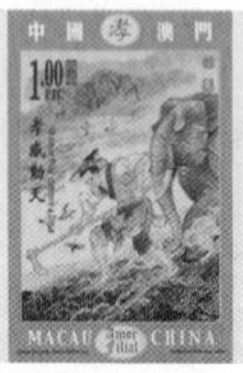

295 Shun ploughing

2002. The Twenty-four Paragons of Filial Devotion (book by Guo Jujing). Multicoloured.

1307	1p. Type **295**	60	35
1308	1p.50 Huang Xiang cooling his father's bed with fan	85	60
1309	2p. Meng Zong crying over bamboo shoots for mother	1·00	75
1310	2p.50 Wang Xiang melting ice to get fish for stepmother	1·10	85
1311	4p.50 Min Ziqian pleading for cruel stepmother	2·00	1·80
1312	4p.50 Jiang Shi, wife and bubbling spring	2·00	1·80
1313	4p.50 Bin Chen surrendering to be with mother	2·00	1·80
1314	4p.50 Wang Gang pleading for father's body	2·00	1·80
MS1315 95×139 mm. 7p. Tanzi bringing deer milk to his parents		3·25	2·50

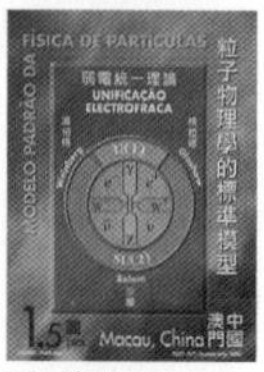

296 Electroweak Unification with the help of Elephant Diagram

2002. Science and Technology. Particle Physics. Multicoloured.

1316	1p.50 Type **296**	75	60
1317	1p.50 Scales (spontaneous symmetry breaking)	75	60
1318	1p.50 Higgs boson diagram	75	60
1319	1p.50 Three families Z decay curve diagram	75	60
1320	1p.50 Quark groups (quantum cromodynamics)	75	60
1321	1p.50 Graph showing interactions and predicted interactions	75	60
MS1322 138×90 mm. 8p. DELPHI detector		3·75	3·00

2002. Pa Kua (martial art) (2nd series). As T **285**. Multicoloured.

1323	2p. (1) Trigrams, stream and tiger	75	75
1324	2p. (4) Trigrams, man and woman	75	75
1325	2p. (7) Trigrams, couple feeding elderly person	75	75
1326	2p. (3) Trigrams, birds, men and path	75	75
1327	2p. (6) Trigrams and man sat in tree	75	75
1328	2p. (2) Trigrams and two men bowing	75	75
1329	2p. (5) Trigrams, yin/yang symbols and storks	75	75
1330	2p. (8) Trigrams and potentate	75	75
MS1331 135×90 mm. 8p. Woman with jug (59×27 mm)		3·50	2·75

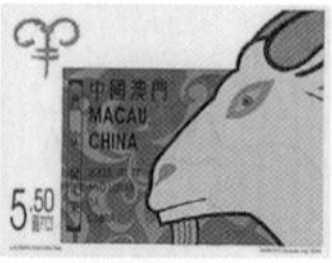

297 Goat's Head

2003. Year of the Goat. Multicoloured.

1332	5p.50 Type **297**	2·50	2·00
MS1333 138×90 mm. Goat's head (detail)		4·00	3·50

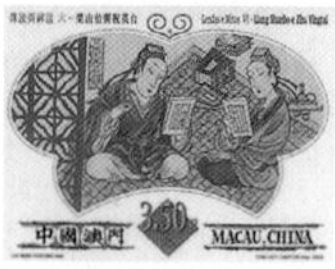

298 Classmates

2003. Folk Tales. Liang Shanbo and Zhu Yingtai. Multicoloured.

1334	3p.50 (1) Type **298**	1·10	1·10
1335	3p.50 (2) Saying goodbye	1·10	1·10
1336	3p.50 (3) On terrace	1·10	1·10
1337	3p.50 (4) Yingtai's parents arranging marriage	1·10	1·10
MS1338 138×90 mm. 9p.Turning into butterflies (40×60 mm)		4·00	3·00

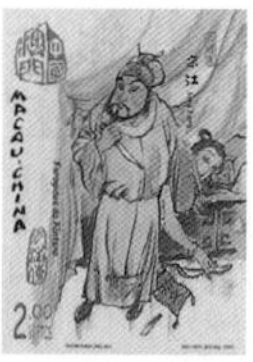

299 Song Jiang

2003. Classical Literature. Outlaws of the Marsh. Multicoloured.

1339	2p. (1) Type **299**	85	75
1340	2p. (2) Lin Chong	85	75
1341	2p. (3) Wu Song	85	75
1342	2p. (4) Lu Zhishen	85	75
1343	2p. (5) Wu Yong	85	75
1344	2p. (6) Hua Rong	85	75
MS1345 138×90 mm. 8p. Two outlaws		3·50	2·75

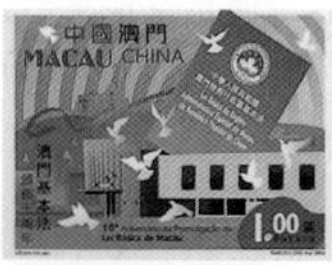

300 Administrative Building and Doves

2003. Tenth Anniv of Proclamation of Basic Law of Macao. Multicoloured.

1346	1p. Type **300**	60	35
1347	4p.50 Flags, children, book and doves	1·80	1·60

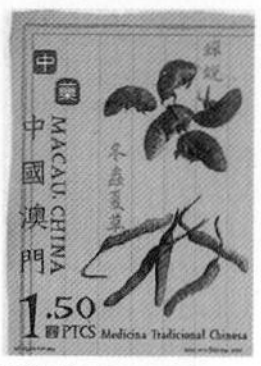

301 Fungus and Chrysalis

2003. Traditional Chinese Medicine. Multicoloured.

1348	1p.50 Type **301**	60	50
1349	2p. Flowers and fruit	75	60
1350	3p. Gingko leaves and dried stems	1·00	90
1351	3p.50 Liquorice root and angelica	1·20	1·10
MS1352 139×90 mm. 8p. Seated man holding tea cup (horiz)		3·00	2·50

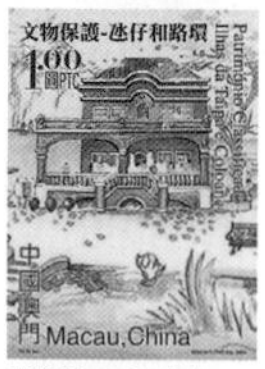

302 Two-storied Building

2003. Cultural Heritage. Architecture of Taipa and Coloane Islands. Multicoloured.

1353	1p. Type **302**	35	30
1354	1p.50 Single-storied building	60	50
1355	2p. Two buildings and dog	75	60
1356	3p.50 Dog, tree, buildings and fish	1·20	1·10
MS1357 139×90 mm. 9p. Building with bell tower (horiz)		3·25	2·75

Nos. 1353/6 were issued together, *se-tenant*, forming a composite design.

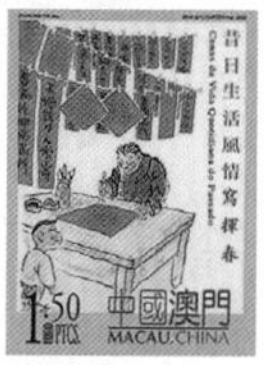

303 Scribe

2003. Traditional Scenes from Everyday Life. Multicoloured.

1358	1p.50 Type **303**	50	50
1359	1p.50 Puppeteer	50	50
1360	1p.50 Street vendor and children	50	50
1361	1p.50 Washer woman	50	50
1362	1p.50 Lantern seller	50	50
1363	1p.50 Man carrying tray on head	50	50
1364	1p.50 Photographer	50	50
1365	1p.50 Man wearing cockerel costume	50	50
MS1366 138×90 mm. 8p. Barber		3·50	2·50

See also Nos. 1444/**MS**1452.

2003. Pa Kua (martial art) (3rd series). As T **285**. Multicoloured.

1367	2p. (1) Trigrams, people and castle	75	60
1368	2p. (4) Trigrams and women with raised arms	75	60
1369	2p. (7) Trigrams and horsemen	75	60
1370	2p. (3) Trigrams and ox	75	60
1371	2p. (6) Trigrams and water wheels	75	60
1372	2p. (2) Trigrams, masked figures and leopard	75	60
1373	2p. (5) Trigrams and seated men and women	75	60
1374	2p. (8) Trigrams, bird and sunset	75	60
MS1375 135×90 mm. 8p. Woman and child (59×27 mm)		3·25	2·50

Nos. 1367/74 were issued together, *se-tenant*, each showing two trigrams and a descriptive painting.

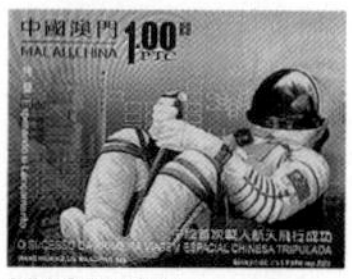

304 Astronaut

2003. First Chinese Manned Space Flight. Multicoloured.

1376	1p. Type **304**	75	25
1377	1p.50 Ship and satellite	1·00	50

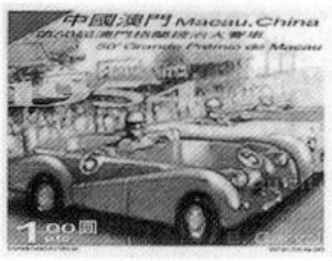

305 Triumph TR2

2003. 50th Anniv of Macao Grand Prix. Two sheets containing T 305 and similar multicoloured designs.

MS1378 (a) 225×156 mm. 1p. Type **305**; 1p.50 Early Brabham race car; 2p. Formula 3 race car; 3p. Grand Prix motorcyclist; 3p.50 Saloon car; 4p.50 Dallara race car. (b) 138×91 mm.12p. Anniversary emblem (38×38 mm) (circular)		4·25	3·75

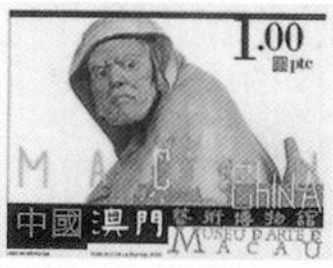

306 Hua Tuo (detail, ceramic sculpture) (Pan Yushu)

2003. Macao Museum of Art. Multicoloured.

1379	1p. Type **306**	35	25
1380	1p.50 "View of Praia Grande and Penha Hill at Sunset" (George Smirnoff)	50	35
1381	2p. "Ruins of S. Paulo" (George Chinnery)	75	60
1382	2p.50 "Music in the Garden" (Su Liupeng)	85	75
MS1383 138×90 mm. 7p. "Macao, The Praia Grande" (58×55 mm)		2·75	2·00

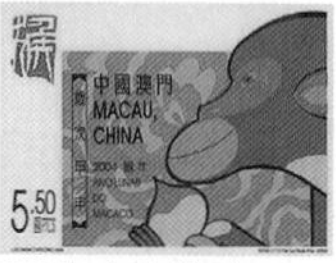

307 Monkey's Head

2004. Year of the Monkey. Multicoloured.

1384	5p.50 Type **307**	2·10	1·50
MS1385 138×90 mm. 10p. Monkey's head (detail)		3·50	2·75

2004. Pa Kua (martial art) (4th series). As T **285**. Multicoloured.

1386	2p. (1) Trigrams, men and sack	75	60
1387	2p. (4) Trigrams and storm over hill	75	60
1388	2p. (7) Trigrams and men eating	75	60
1389	2p. (3) Trigrams and imprisoned animal	75	60
1390	2p. (6) Trigrams, waterfall and family on horseback	75	60
1391	2p. (2) Trigrams and climbers	75	60
1392	2p. (5) Trigrams and junks (boats)	75	60
1393	2p. (8) Trigrams counting	75	60
MS1394 135×90 mm. 8p. Stone carver (59×27 mm)		3·50	2·50

Nos. 1386/93 were issued together, *se-tenant*, each showing two trigrams and a descriptive painting.

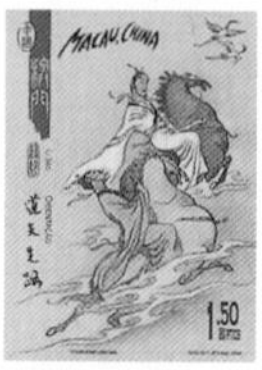

309 Li Sao and Chariot Steeds

2004. Classical Literature. Li Sao (poem by Qu Yuan). Showing scenes from poem. Multicoloured.

1395	1p.50 Type **309**	60	50
1396	1p.50 Cultivating orchids	60	50
1397	1p.50 With sister	60	50
1398	1p.50 With phoenix	60	50
1399	1p.50 With cart drawn by dragons	60	50
1400	1p.50 In garden	60	50
MS1401 138×90 mm. 8p. With arm outstretched (vert)		3·50	2·50

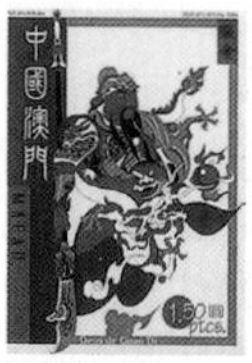

310 Guan Di

2004. Myths and Legends. Guan Di (war god). Multicoloured.

1402	1p.50 Type **310**	60	50
1403	1p.50 Wearing armour	85	75
1404	1p.50 On horseback	1·10	1·00
1405	1p.50 Wearing robes	1·40	1·20
MS1406	138×90 mm. 9p. Facing left	3·50	2·75

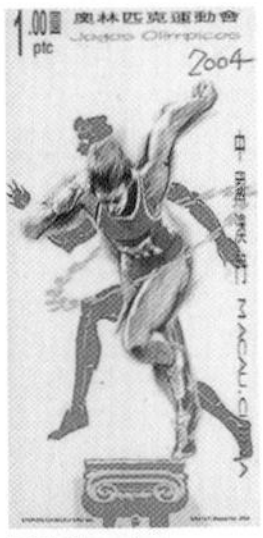

311 Running

2004. Olympic Games, Athens. Multicoloured.

1407	1p. Type **311**	50	25
1408	1p.50 Long jump	60	35
1409	2p. Discus	85	60
1410	3p.50 Javelin	1·20	1·00

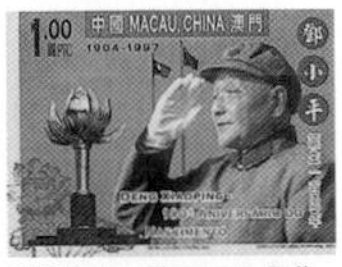

312 "Lotus Flower in Full Bloom" (statue) and Deng Xiaoping wearing Uniform

2004. Birth Centenary of Deng Xiaoping (leader of China, 1978–89). Multicoloured.

1411	1p. Type **312**	35	25
1412	1p.50 Deng Xiaoping and St. Paul's Church	50	35
MS1413	138×90 mm. 8p. As young man and lotus flower (40×40 mm) (circular)	3·00	2·50

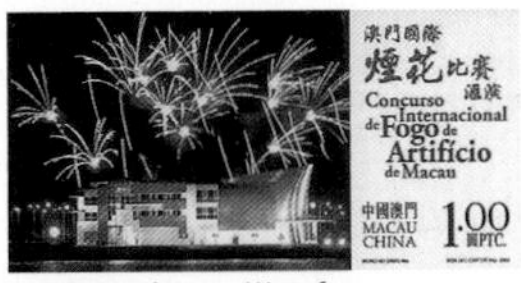

313 Fireworks over Waterfront

2004. International Firework Display Competition. Multicoloured.

1414	1p. Type **313**	35	25
1415	1p.50 Large burst and Macao Tower	50	35
1416	2p. Two large bursts and Macao Bridge	60	50
1417	4p.50 Large burst over Monte Hill	1·40	1·20
MS1418	138×90 mm. 9p. Trophy (vert)	3·00	2·50

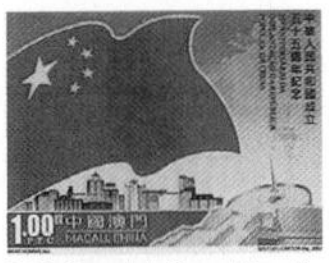

314 People's Republic of China Flag

2004. 55th Anniv of People's Republic of China. Multicoloured.

1419	1p. Type **314**	35	25
1420	1p.50 Macao flag	50	35
1421	2p. People's Republic emblem	60	50
1422	3p. Macao emblem	85	75
MS1423	138×90 mm. 7p. Imperial Palace, Beijing (59×39 mm)	3·00	1·70

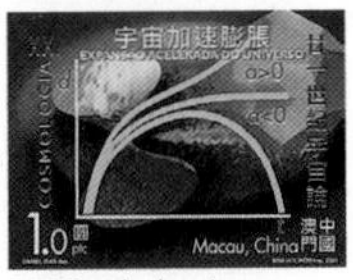

315 Graph showing Expanding Universe

2004. Science and Technology. Cosmology. Multicoloured.

1424	1p. Type **315**	35	25
1425	1p.50 Graph showing cosmic radiation	50	35
1426	2p. Galaxies (fluctuating galaxies)	60	50
1427	3p.50 Tetrahedron divided into dark matter, dark energy and the known universe	1·00	85
MS1428	138×90 mm. 8p. Mathematical shapes (Big Bang theory)	3·00	2·00

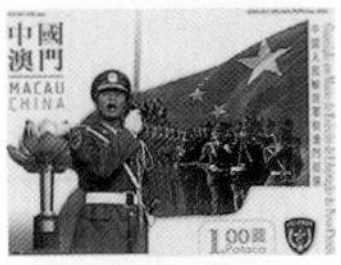

316 Soldier and Flag

2004. People's Republic of China Garrison, Macao. Multicoloured.

1429	1p. Type **316**	35	25
1430	1p. Tank soldier saluting	35	25
1431	1p.50 St. Paul's Church and convoy	35	35
1432	1p.50 Nursing corps	35	35
1433	3p.50 Soldier at attention	85	85
1434	3p.50 Soldier charging	85	85
MS1435	138×90 mm. 8p. Soldiers carrying Flag (39×60 mm)	3·00	2·00

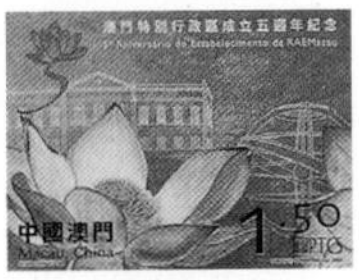

317 Lotus Blossom

2004. Fifth Anniv of Macao Special Administrative Region. Multicoloured.

1436	1p.50 Type **317**	50	35
1437	2p. Blossoms and Cultural Centre	60	50
1438	2p.50 Blossoms and Monte Hill buildings	75	60
1439	3p. Blossoms, Macao Tower and Lisboa Hotel	85	75
MS1440	138×90 mm. 10p. Lotus blossom (different)	4·25	4·25

Nos. 1436/9 were issued together, *se-tenant*, forming a composite design.

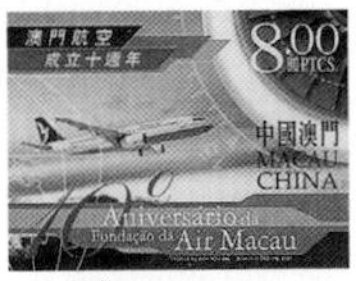

318 Airliner

2004. 10th Anniv of Air Macao. Sheet 138×90 mm.

MS1441	**318** 8p. multicoloured	3·00	2·00

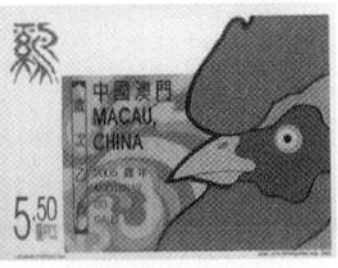

319 Rooster

2005. New Year. "Year of the Rooster".

1442	**319** 5p. multicoloured	2·10	1·40
MS1443	138×90 mm. **319** $10 multicoloured	3·50	2·50

2005. Traditional Scenes from Everyday Life. As T **303**. Multicoloured.

1444	1p.50 Cooking food on brazier	50	35
1445	1p.50 Man carrying pole of glass bowls	50	35
1446	1p.50 Craftsman working at table	50	35
1447	1p.50 Making bundles	50	35
1448	1p.50 Coconut vendor	50	35
1449	1p.50 Man cooking on griddle	50	35
1450	1p.50 Serving food under lantern	50	35
1451	1p.50 Hair braiding	50	35
MS1452	138×90 mm. 8p. Postman	3·00	2·00

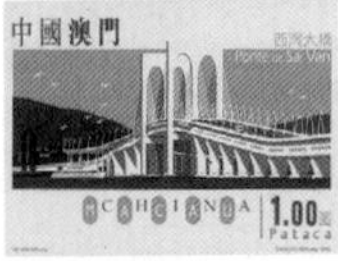

320 Sai Van Bridge

2005. Opening of Sai Van Bridge linking Macao Peninsula to Taipa Island. Multicoloured.

1453	1p. Type **320**	50	25
1454	3p.50 Approach to bridge	1·10	85
MS1455	138×91 mm. 8p. Tower, bridge and boat (vert)	3·00	2·00

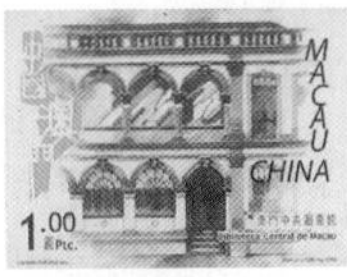

321 Central Library

2005. Libraries. Multicoloured.

1456	1p. Type **321**	35	25
1457	1p.50 Sir Robert Ho Tung library	50	35
1458	2p. Coloane library	60	50
1459	3p.50 Mong Ha library	1·00	85
MS1460	138×90 mm. 8p. Commercial Association Public Library (60×40 mm)	3·00	2·00

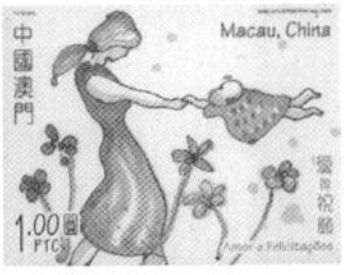

322 Mother and Child

2005. Greetings Stamps. Multicoloured.

1461	1p. Type **322**	35	25
1462	1p.50 Kangaroo with young in pocket	50	35
1463	2p. Bird and chicks in nest	60	50
1464	3p.50 Duck and ducklings	1·00	85

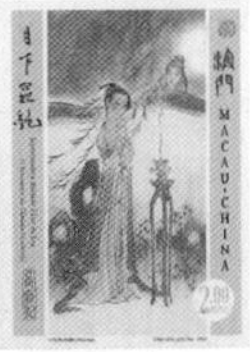

323 Chang Hung sees Ying Ying

2005. Classical Literature. The Romance of the Western Chamber. Multicoloured.

1465	1p.50 Type **323**	60	50
1466	1p.50 Reciting poems to each other	60	50
1467	1p.50 Chang Hung made ill	60	50
1468	1p.50 Huang Niang petitioning Madam Ts'ui	60	50
1469	1p.50 Chang Hung sleeping	60	50
1470	1p.50 Chang Hung and Ying Ying together	60	50
MS1471	139×90 mm. 8p. Ying Ying	3·00	2·00

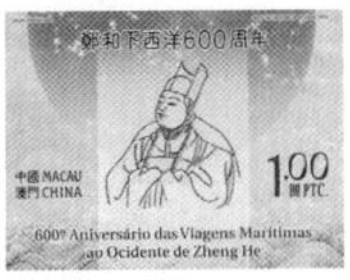

324 Zheng He

2005. 600th Anniv of the Voyages of Zheng He (Ma Sanbao). Multicoloured.

1472	1p. Type **324**	1·10	60
1473	1p.50 Giraffe	1·20	60
1474	1p.50 Ships and compass	1·40	60
MS1475	139×90 mm. 8p. Ship (50×30 mm)	4·25	2·50

Stamps of a similar design were issued by Hong Kong and People's Republic of China.

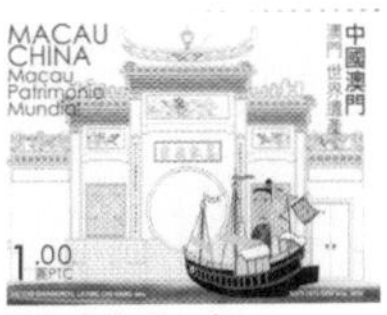

324a A Ma Temple

2005. World Heritage Sites. Multicoloured.

1476	1p. Type **324a**	50	35
1477	1p.50 St. Joseph's Seminar	60	50
1478	2p. Mandarin's House	75	60
1479	3p.50 Dom Pedro V Theatre	1·10	1·00
MS1480	138×90 mm. 8p. St. Paul's Church	3·00	2·50

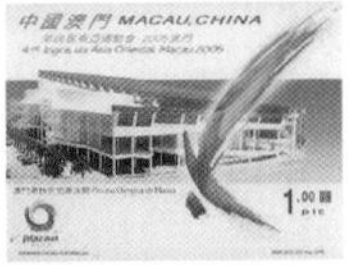

325 Olympic Swimming Pool

2005. East Asian Games, Macao. Multicoloured.

1481	1p. Type **325**	35	35
1482	1p.50 Grand Beach	50	50
1483	2p. Tennis Academy	60	60
1484	2p.50 IPM Sports Pavilion	85	85
1485	3p.50 Macao Stadium	1·00	1·00
1486	4p.50 Tap Seac Sports Pavilion	1·20	1·20
MS1487	138×90 mm. 8p. Stadium (55×38 mm) (oval)	3·00	2·50

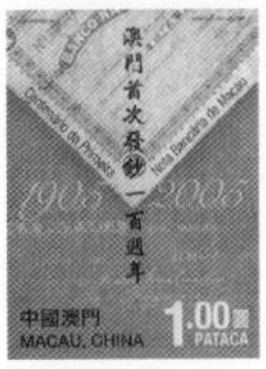

326 Banknote

2005. Centenary of First Macao Banknote. Multicoloured.

1488	1p. Type **326**	50	35
1489	1p.50 $5 note	60	50
1490	2p. $10 note	1·00	85
1491	2p.50 $50 note	1·40	1·20
MS1492	138×90 mm. 8p. $100 note	3·00	2·20

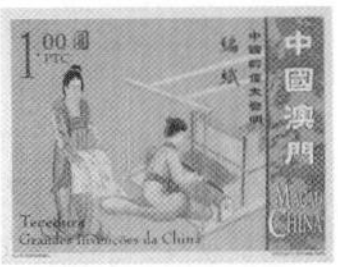

327 Weaving

2005. Chinese Inventions. Multicoloured.

1493	1p. Type **327**	50	35
1494	1p.50 Papermaking	60	50
1495	2p. Metal work	75	60
1496	4p.50 Calendar	1·40	1·20
MS1497	138×90 mm. 8p. Seismograph	3·00	2·20

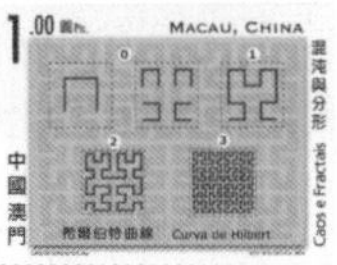

328 Hilbert's Curve

2005. Science and Technology. Chaos and Fractals. Multicoloured.

1498	1p. Type **328**	35	25
1499	1p. Tree fractal	35	25
1500	1p.50 Sierpinskis triangles	50	35
1501	1p.50 Chaos game	50	35
1502	2p. Von Koch's curve	75	60
1503	2p. Cantor set	75	60
MS1504	139×91 mm. 8p. Julia set	3·00	2·20

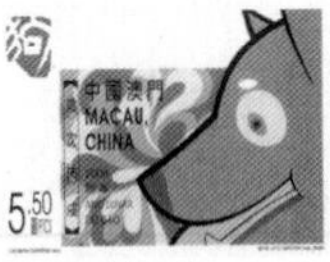

329 Dog's Head

2006. New Year. Year of the Dog. Multicoloured.

1505	5p.50 Type **329**	2·10	1·60
MS1506	138×90 mm. 10p. As No. 1505	3·50	3·00

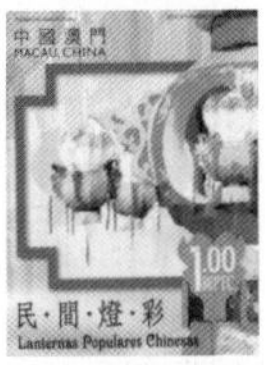

330 Circular Lantern with Roosters

2006. Chinese Lanterns. Multicoloured.

1507	1p. Type **330**	50	35
1508	1p. Lantern with crowned top and small lanterns	50	35
1509	1p.50 Phoenix lantern	50	35
1510	1p.50 Fringed lantern with tassels	50	35
MS1511	138×90 mm. 8p. Circular lantern with tassels	3·00	2·20

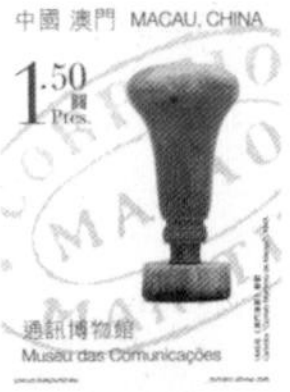

331 Hand Stamp (1845)

2006. Traditional Scenes from Everyday Life. As T **303**. Multicoloured.

1512	1p.50 Cook	50	50
1513	1p.50 Tea seller and boy	50	50
1514	1p.50 Serving food	50	50
1515	1p.50 Boy and craftsman working at circular table	50	50

1515a	1p.50	50	50
1515b	1p.50 Potter	50	50
1515d	1p.50 Man using yoke to carry pots	50	50
1515c	1p.50 Tinsmith	50	50
MS1516	138×90 mm. 8p. Making tea	3·00	2·50

2006. Museum Exhibits. Communications Museum. Multicoloured.

1517	1p.50 Type **331**	50	50
1518	1p.50 Scales	50	50
1519	1p.50 Post box (1910)	50	50
1520	1p.50 Sorting shelves	50	50
1521	1p.50 Telephone (1925)	50	50
1522	1p.50 Telephone exchange (1929)	50	50
1523	1p.50 Radio transmitter (1950)	50	50
1524	1p.50 Submarine cables (1953)	50	50
MS1525	138×90 mm. 10p. 1884 5r. stamp (first Macao stamp) (horiz)	3·00	3·00

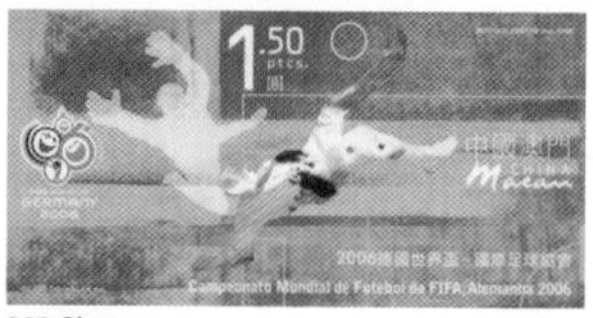

332 Player

2006. World Cup Football Championship, Germany. Multicoloured.

1526	1p.50 Type **332**	50	50
1527	2p.50 Player running forward	75	75
1528	3p.50 Player on knees	1·00	1·00
1529	4p. Player running left	1·10	1·10

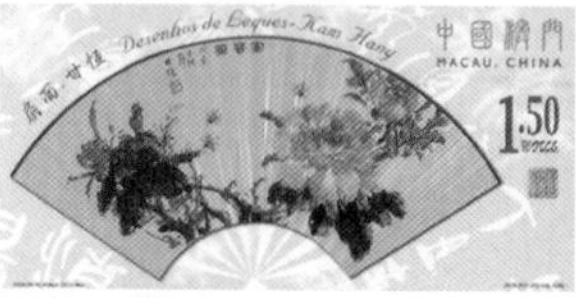

333 Peony Flowers

2006. Fans. Showing designs on fans. Multicoloured.

1530	1p.50 Type **333**	50	50
1531	1p.50 Warrior holding fan	50	50
1532	2p.50 Laughing Buddha	75	75
1533	2p.50 Snail and bamboo	75	75
1534	3p.50 Eagle	1·00	1·00
MS1535	138×90 mm. 10p. Children (detail) (40×30 mm)	3·00	3·00

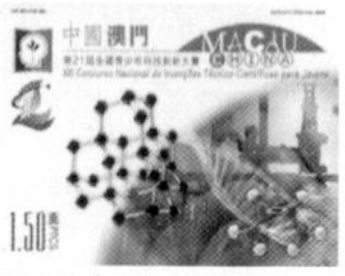

334 Molecular Diagram and DNA Strand

2006. XXI China Adolescents Science and Technology Invention Contest, Macau. Multicoloured.

1536	1p.50 Type **334**	20	20
1537	2p. Satellite dish and wind turbines	25	25
1538	2p.50 Cog and protractors	50	50
1539	3p.50 Laboratory equipment and computer mouse	75	75
MS1540	138×90 mm. 10p. Statue, building entrance and atomic symbol (40×60 mm)	2·00	2·00

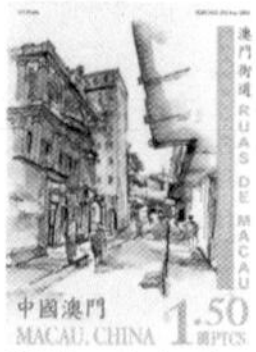

335 Rua de Camilo Pessanha

2006. Streets of Macao. Multicoloured.

1541	1p.50 Type **335**	20	2·20
1542	1p.50 Rua de St. Domingos	20	20
1543	2p.50 Calcada de St. Francisco Xavier	50	50
1544	3p.50 Travessa da Paixao	75	75
MS1545	138×90 mm. 10p. Largo de Santo Agostinho	2·00	2·00

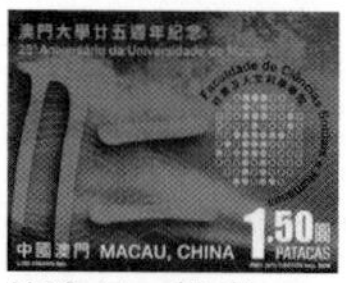

336 Script and Emblem

2006. 25th Anniv of University of Macau. Multicoloured, background colour given.

1546	1p.50 Type **336**	20	20
1547	1p.50 Script and emblem (magenta)	20	20
1548	1p.50 Script and emblem (blue)	20	20
1549	1p.50 Script and emblem (orange)	20	20
1550	1p.50 Script and emblem (grey)	20	20
MS1551	138×90 mm. 10p. University arms	2·00	2·00

2006. Pa Kua (martial art) (5th series). As T **285**. Multicoloured.

1552	2p. (1) Trigrams, women brushing hair	25	25
1553	2p. (4) Trigrams, elderly couple and dragon	25	25
1554	2p. (7) Trigrams and lovers	25	25
1555	2p. (3) Trigrams three-legged pot and people	25	25
1556	2p. (6) Trigrams, carriage and well	25	25
1557	2p. (2) Trigrams and supported log	25	25
1558	2p. (5) Trigrams and women seated on carpet	25	25
1559	2p. (8) Trigrams, sage and followers	25	25
MS1560	135×90 mm. 8p. Women fishing (59×27 mm)	2·20	2·20

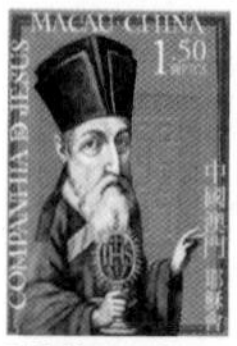

337 Matteo Ricci

2006. Society of Jesus. Multicoloured.

1561	1p.50 (1) Type **337**	20	20
1562	1p.50 (2) Francis Xavier	20	20
1563	3p.50 (3) Alessandro Valignano	70	70
1564	3p.50 (4) Melchior Carneiro	70	70
MS1565	138×90 mm. 10p. Inigo Loyola	2·00	2·00

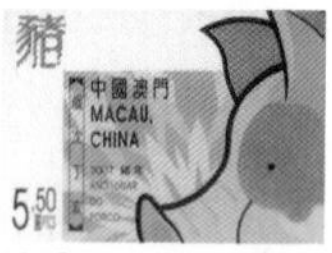

338 Pig

2007. New Year. "Year of the Pig".

1566	**338** 5p.50 multicoloured	1·40	1·40
MS1567	138×90 mm. **338** $10 multicoloured	2·20	2·20

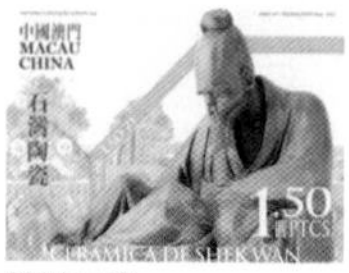

339 Lao Zi

2007. Shek Wan Ceramics. Multicoloured.

1568	1p.50 (1) Type **339**	40	40
1569	1p.50 (2) Lu Yu	40	40
1570	1p.50 (3) Philosopher	40	40
1571	2p.50 (4) Luo Han	60	60
MS1572	138×90 mm. 8p. "Concubine after Bathing"	2·00	2·00

2007. Traditional Scenes from Everyday Life. As T **303**. Multicoloured.

1573	1p.50 Porter	40	40
1574	1p.50 Tea seller	40	40
1575	1p.50 Rickshaw	40	40
1576	1p.50 Cricket fighting	40	40
1577	1p.50 Decorating cloth	40	40
1578	1p.50 Cobbler	40	40
1579	1p.50 Parasol making	40	40
1580	1p.50 Seamstress	40	40
MS1581	138×90 mm. 10p. Dragon procession	2·20	2·20

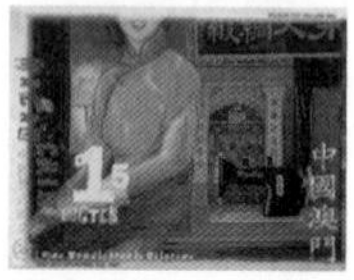

340 Seamstress

2007. Traditional Shops. Multicoloured.

1582	1p.50 Type **340**	40	40
1583	1p.50 Herbalist	40	40
1584	2p.50 Calligrapher	55	55
1585	3p.50 Food shop	70	70
MS1586	138×90 mm.10p. Street	1·90	1·90

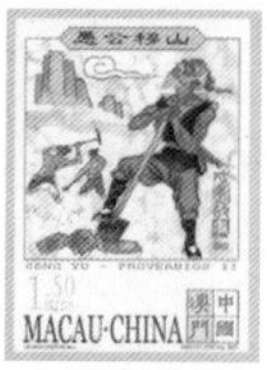

341 Man leaning on Shovel ('The Foolish Old Man moved Mountain')

2007. Ancient Proverbs. Multicoloured. (a) Ordinary or self-adhesive gum.

1587	1p.50 (1) Type **341**	30	30
1588	1p.50 (2) Two seated men ('A Friendship between Guan and Bao')	30	30
1589	3p.50 (3) Masked men and deer ('Calling Black White')	65	65
1590	3p.50 (4) Man holding clam and bird ('The Quarrel between Snipe and Clam')	65	65

(b) Miniature Sheet. Ordinary gum.

MS1595	138×90 mm. 8p. Horse riders	2·20	2·20

See also Nos. 1208/**MS**1212.

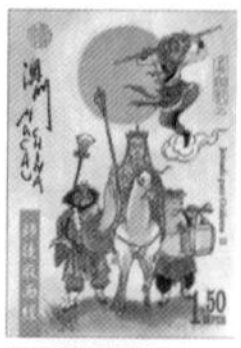

342 Tripitaka, Sandy, Pigsy and Monkey King

2007. Classical Literature. The Journey to the West. Multicoloured.

1596	1p.50 Type **342**	30	30
1597	1p.50 Iron Fan Princess	30	30
1598	2p. Red Boy impaled on swords	40	40
1599	2p. Subduing monkeys	40	40
1600	2p.50 Sandy, Pigsy and Monkey King	45	45
1601	2p.50 Pigsy and Seven-spider demon	45	45
MS1602	139×90 mm.10p. Monkey king	2·20	2·20

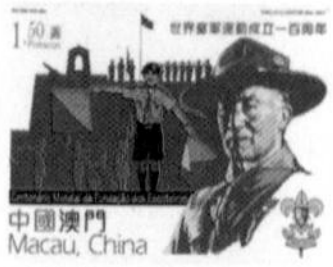

343 Robert Baden Powell (founder) and Scout using Semaphore

2007. Centenary of Scouting. Designs showing Robert Baden Powell and scouts. Multicoloured.

1603	1p.50 Type **343**	30	30
1604	2p. Scouts saluting	50	50
1605	2p.50 Scouts and campfire	55	55
1606	3p.50 Scouts building tripod	70	70
1607	3p.50 Scouts orienteering	70	70
MS1608	138×90 mm. 10p. Monument (vert)	2·20	2·20

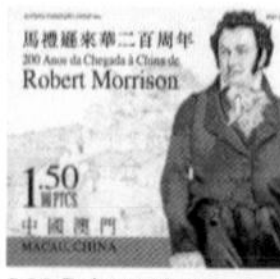

344 Robert Morrison as Young Man

2007. Bicentenary of Robert Morrison's Arrival in China (missionary and translator of Bible into Chinese). Multicoloured.

1609	1p.50 Type **344**	30	30
1610	3p.50 As older man	85	85

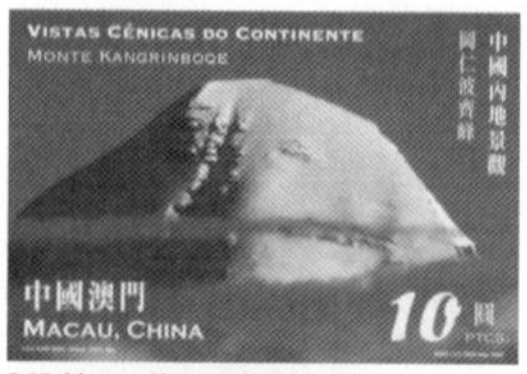

345 Mount Kangrinboqe

2007. Mainland Scenery. Sheet 138×90 mm.

MS1611	**345**0p. multicoloured	2·20	2·20

The stamp and margins of **MS**1611 form a composite design.

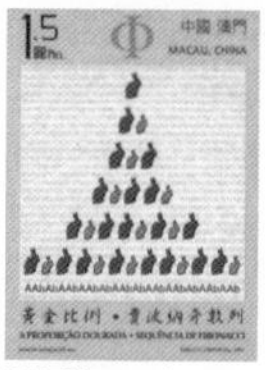

346 Fibonacci Sequence

2007. Science and Technology. The Golden Ratio. Multicoloured.

1612	1p.50 Type **346**	30	30
1613	2p. Sunflower spiral	45	45
1614	2p.50 Penrose tiles	50	50
1615	3p.50 Nautilus	65	65
MS1616	138×90 mm. 10p.Greek letter phi (symbol of golden ratio)	1·90	1·90

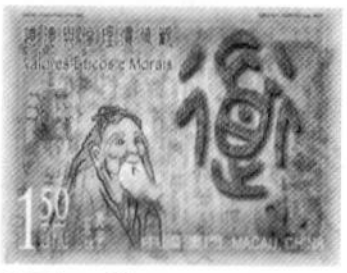

347 Lao Zi

2007. Ethics and Moral Values. Philosophers. Multicoloured.

1617	1p.50 Type **347**	30	30
1618	2p.50 Zhuang Zi	50	50
1619	3p.50 Confucius	65	65
1620	4p. Mencius	90	90
MS1621	138×90 mm. 10p. Lao Zi, Zhuang Zi, Confucius and Mencius (circular) (41×41 mm)	1·90	1·90

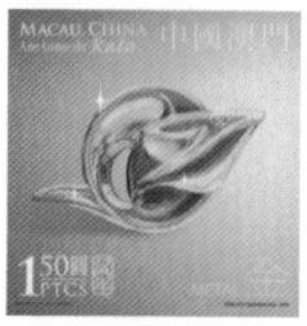

348 Rat shaped Brooch (metal)

2008. New Year. 'The Year of the Rat'. Multicoloured.

1622	1p.50 Type **348**	30	30
1623	1p.50 Carving (wood)	30	30
1624	1p.50 Rat in water (water)	30	30
1625	1p.50 Rat outlined in fireworks (fire)	30	30
1627	5p. Rat shaped teapot (earth)	1·20	1·20
MS1628	139×90 mm. 10p. As No. 1627 (49×49 mm) (diamond)	1·90	1·90

2008. Pa Kua (martial art) (6th series). As T **285**. Multicoloured.

1629	2p. (1) Trigrams and women kneeling	50	50
1630	2p. (2) Trigrams and woman on shore	50	50
1631	2p. (3) Trigrams and watermill	50	50
1632	2p. (4) Trigrams and figure with arms raised	50	50
1633	2p. (5) Trigrams and bearded man seated	50	50
1634	2p. (6) Trigrams, waterfalls and men with poles	50	50
1635	2p. (7) Trigrams and grass skirted figure holding bow	50	50
1636	2p. (8) Trigrams, banners and figure wearing armour	50	50
MS1637	135×90 mm. 10p. Fisherman (60×30 mm)	2·20	2·20

The stamp and margins of **MS**1637 form a composite design.

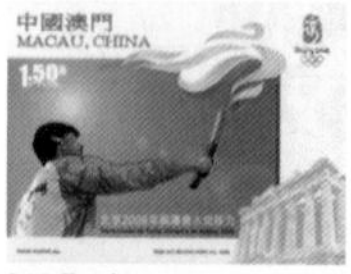

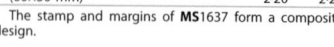

349 Torch

2008. Olympic Torch Relay. Multicoloured.

1638	1p.50 Type **349**	30	30
1639	3p.50 Huanhuan	60	60
MS1640	90×139 mm. 10p. Torch (40×70 mm)	2·00	2·00

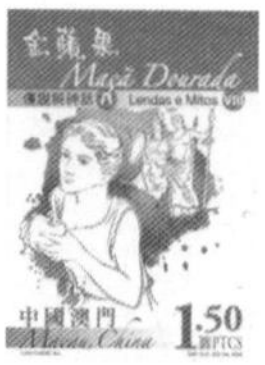

350 Golden Apple

2008. Legends and Myths. Multicoloured.
1641 1p.50 Type **350** 25 25
1642 2p.50 Gordian knot 45 45
1643 3p.50 Trojan horse 60 60
1644 4p. Riddle of the sphinx 70 70
MS1645 138×90 mm. 10p. Cupid and Psyche (40×70 mm) 1·90 1·90

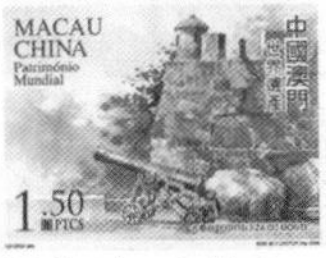

352 Fortaleza do Monte (Fortaleza de Nossa Senhora do Monte de Sao Paulo)

2008. World Heritage Sites. Multicoloured.
1655 1p.50 Type **352** 30 30
1656 2p. Largo do Lilau (Lilau Square) 40 40
1657 2p.50 Casa de Lou Kau (Lou Kau Mansion) 45 45
1658 3p. Largo do Senado (Senado Square) 55 55
1659 3p.50 Sam Kai Vui Kun temple 65 65
1660 4p. Igreja da Se (Cathedral Church) 75 75
1661 4p.50 Quartel dos Mouros (Moorish quarter) 80 80
1662 5p. Igreja de Santo Antonio (Church of St. Anthony) 85 85

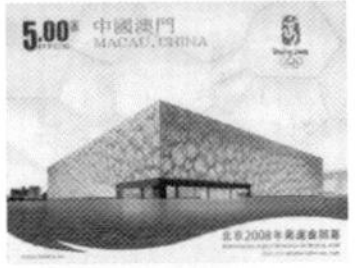

353 National Aquatic Center, Beijing

2008. Olympic Games, Beijing. Multicoloured.
1663 5p. Type **353** 1·10 1·10
MS1664 138×90 mm. 10p. National Stadium (72×55 mm) 2·20 2·20

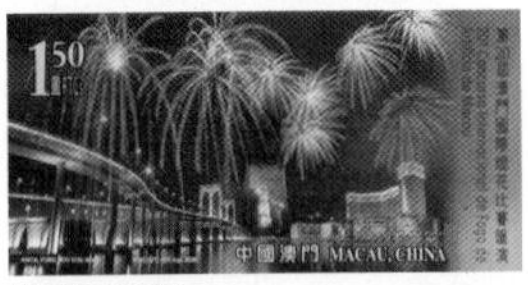

354 Fireworks

2008. 20th International Firework Competition. Two sheets containing T **354** and similar horiz designs showing firework displays. Multicoloured.
MS1665 160×110 mm. 1p.50 Type **354**; 2p.50 Orange central burst amongst magenta; 3p.50 Shades of gold; 5p. Large multicoloured burst at right 2·75 2·75
MS1666 137×90 mm. 10p. Fireworks 2·20 2·20

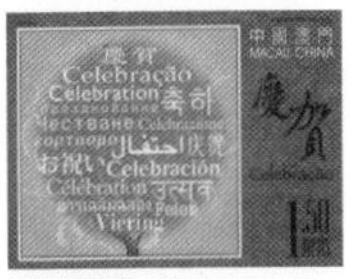

355 'Celebration'

2008. World Post Day. Multicoloured.
1667 1p.50 Type **355** 30 30
1668 3p.50 UPU emblem 65 65

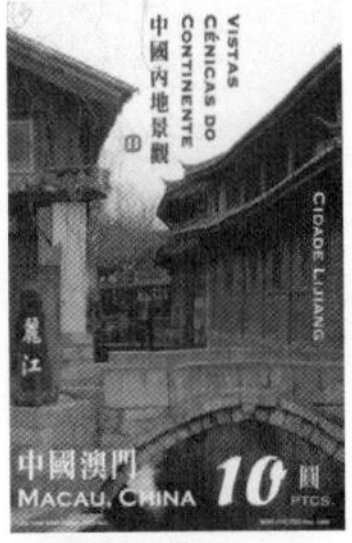

356 Bridge, Lijiang

2008. Mainland Scenery. Sheet 138×90 mm.
MS1669 **356** 10p. multicoloured 2·20 2·20

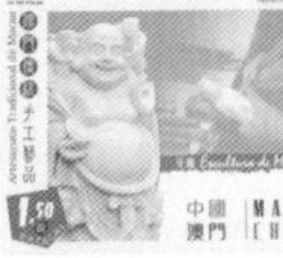

357 Carved Ivory Buddha

2008. Traditional Handicrafts. Multicoloured.
1670 1p.50 Type **357** 30 30
1671 2p. Ceramic jar 40 40
1672 2p.50 Basket 45 45
1673 3p50. Wooden carving 55 55
MS1674 138×90 mm. 10p. Beaded bag (60×40 mm) 2·20 2·20

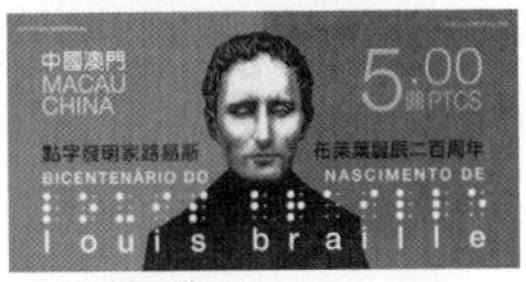

358 Louis Braille

2009. Birth Bicentenary of Louis Braille (inventor of Braille writing for the blind).
1675 **358** 5p. multicoloured 95 95

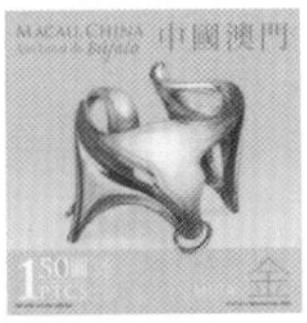

359 Metal Ox

2009. Chinese New Year. Year of the Ox. Multicoloured.
1676 1p.50 Type **359** 30 30
1677 1p.50 Ox's head (carving) 30 30
1678 1p.50 Ox's head (painting) 30 30
1679 1p.50 Fireworks 30 30
1680 5p. Ox as teapot 95 95
MS1681 138×90 mm. As No. 1680 (50×50 mm) (diamond shape) 1·50 1·50

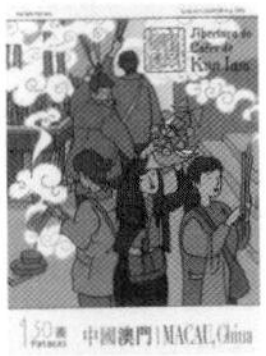

360 People holding Incense

2009. Opening of Kun Iam Treasury. Multicoloured.
1682 1p.50 Type **360** 30 30
1683 2p.50 Woman carrying paper house, woman and gong, people holding incense 45 45
1684 3p.50 Mother with baby, people, incense and shrine 65 65
1685 4p. People, incense and stalls 75 75
MS1686 138×90 mm. 10p. Elderly woman (horiz) 1·90 1·90

Nos. 1682/5 were printed together, *se-tenant*, forming a composite design.

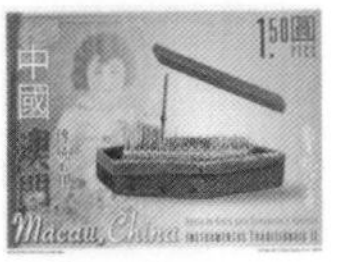

361 Compactor

2009. Traditional Tools. Multicoloured.
1687 1p.50 Type **361** 30 30
1688 2p.50 Whetstone 40 40
1689 3p.50 Mill stone 65 65
1690 4p. Biscuit press 75 75
MS1691 138×90 mm. 10p. Tools (60×41 mm) 1·90 1·90

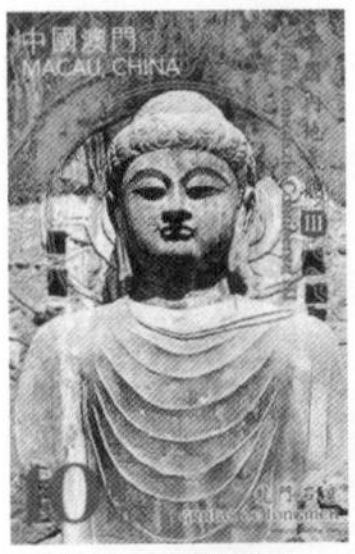

362 Vairocana Buddha, Longmen Caves, Luoyang

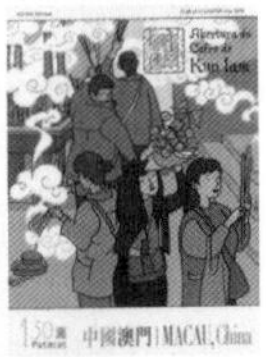
360 People holding Incense

2009. Mainland Scenery. Sheet 138×90 mm.
MS1692 **362** 10p. multicoloured 2·20 2·20

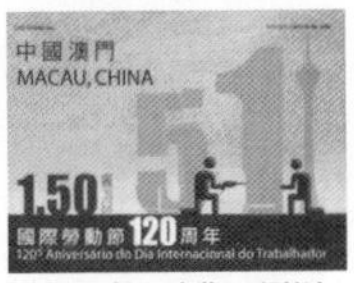

363 Workers drilling '5.' '1.'

2009. 120th Anniv of Labour Day (1st May). Multicoloured.
1693 1p.50 Type **363** 30 30
1694 5p. Workers digging '5.' '1.' 90 90
MS1695 138×90 mm. 10p. Workers supporting '5.' '1.' 1·90 1·90

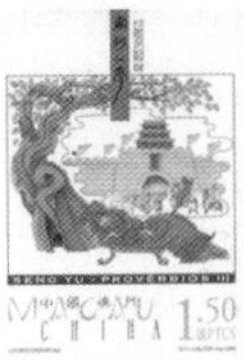

364 Mantis stalking Cicada

2009. Ancient Proverbs. Multicoloured. Ordinary or self-adhesive gum.
1696 1p.50 Type **364** 30 30
1697 1p.50 Bird in tree ('A Fond Dream of Nanke') 30 30
1698 3p.50 Swordsman ('Songs of Chu on All Sides') 65 65
1699 3p.50 Scribe ('Give the Last Measure of Devotion') 65 65
MS1700 138×90 mm. 10p. Men on boat ('Marking the Boat to find the Sword') 1·90 1·90

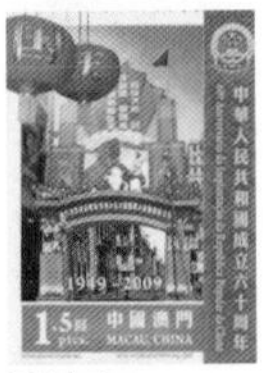

365 Archway

2009. 60th Anniv of People's Republic of China. Multicoloured.
1705 1p.50 Type **365** 30 30
1706 2p.50 Tanks 45 45
1707 3p.50 Children exercising 65 65
1708 4p. Flag and parade 75 75
MS1709 138×90 mm. 10p. As Nos. 1707/8 (59×39 mm) 1·90 1·90

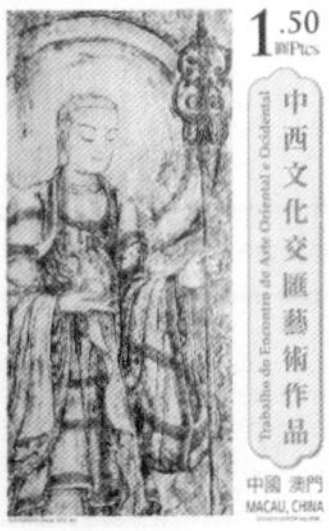

366 Bodhisattva Avalokitsvara

2009. Artwork from Cultural Mix of East and West. Paintings from Porcelain Plate. Multicoloured.
1710 1p.50 Type **366** 30 30
1711 5p. Bodhisattva Ksitigarbha 90 90

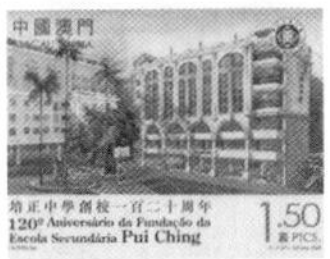

367 School Campus

2009. 120th Anniv of Pui Ching Middle School. Multicoloured.
1712 1p.50 Type **367** 30 30
1713 2p. School buildings 40 40
1714 2p.50 School chapel 45 45
1715 3p.50 Bust and fireplace 65 65
MS1716 138×90 mm. 10p. Original building 1·90 1·90

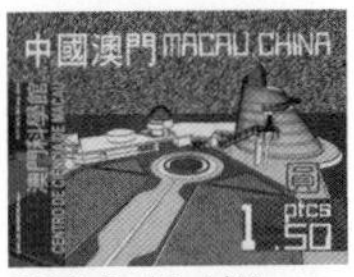

368 Stylized Aerial View

2009. Science Centre. Multicoloured.
1717 1p.50 Type **368** 30 30
1718 2p.50 Aerial view, Exhibition Centre at left 45 45
1719 3p.50 Exhibition Centre 65 65
1720 4p. Planetarium at left 75 75
MS1721 138×90 mm. 10p. Stylized Exhibition Centre 1·90 1·90

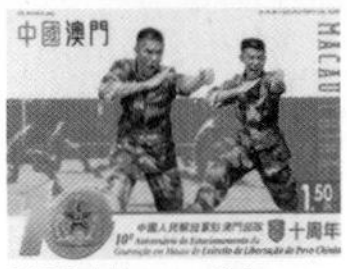

369 Soldiers practising Martial Arts

2009. Tenth Anniv of Chinese Army in Macau. Multicoloured.
1722 1p.50 Type **369** 30 30
1723 1p.50 Service women 30 30
1724 1p.50 Soldiers with weapons 30 30
1725 1p.50 Soldiers with children 30 30
1726 1p.50 Soldiers and children planting tree 30 30
1727 1p.50 Soldiers and tank 30 30
MS1728 105×125 mm. 10p. Soldiers on parade (40×60 mm) 1·90 1·90

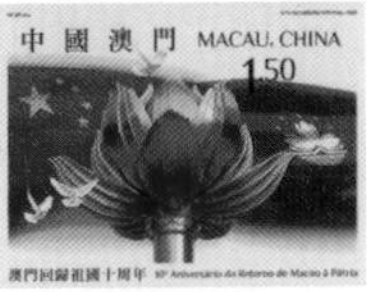

370 Lotus Flower

2009. Tenth Anniv of Re-integration of Macau. Multicoloured.
1729 1p.50 Type **370** 30 30
1730 1p.50 Senado Square and Macau Tower 30 30
1731 1p.50 Waterside skyline 30 30
MS1732 138×90 mm. 10p. Lotus flower and gateway (40×60 mm) 1·90 1·90

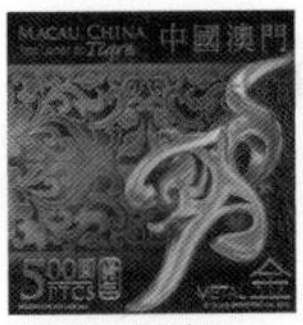

371 Tiger (Madeira (Wood))

2010. Chinese New Year. Multicoloured.
1733 1p.50 Type **371** 35 35
1734 1p.50 Tiger head and shoulders (Agua (water)) 35 35
1735 1p.50 Stylized multicoloured tiger (Fogo (fire)) 35 35
1736 1p.50 Clay tiger and cub (Terra (earth)) 35 35
1737 5p. Stylized golden tiger (Metal) 1·10 1·10
MS1738 139×90 mm. 1p.50 Stylized golden tiger (different) (diamond shaped) 1·90 1·90

2010. Pa Kua (martial art) (7th series). As T **285**. Multicoloured.
1739 2p. (1) Trigrams, mountains and man with pack 40 40
1740 2p. (2) Trigrams and couple by lake 40 40
1741 2p. (3) Trigrams and pack-horse 40 40
1742 2p. (4) Trigrams and figure crouched on rock 40 40
1743 2p. (5) Trigrams, couple and houses 40 40
1744 2p. (6) Trigrams, waterfall and figure watching from above 40 40
1745 2p. (7) Trigrams and figure looking up 40 40
1746 2p. (8) Trigrams and two men greeting 40 40
MS1747 135×90 mm. 10p. Child with rattle (60×30 mm) 1·90 1·90

Nos. 1739/46 were issued in *se-tenant* sheetlets of eight stamps each showing two trigrams and a descriptive painting.

The stamp and margins of **MS**1747 form a composite design.

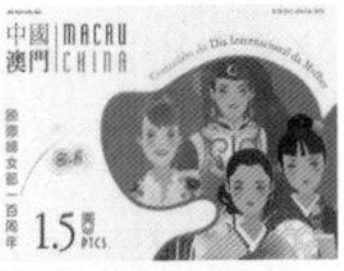

372 Women

2010. Centenary of Women's Day. Multicoloured.
1748 1p.50 (1) Type **372** 30 30
1749 2p.50 (2) Women 45 45
1750 3p.50 (3) Women 65 65
1751 4p. (4) Women 75 75
MS1752 138×90 mm. 10p. Women of different professions (40×60 mm) 1·90 1·90

Nos. 1748/51 were printed, *se-tenant*, forming a composite design of women of the world.

373 Rabbits

2010. Expo 2010, Shanghai. Multicoloured.

1753	3p.50 Type **373**	65	65
1754	4p. Lanterns	75	75
MS1755 138×90 mm. 10p. Large pink rabbit		1·90	1·90

374 Ruins of St Paul Cathedral

2010. 60th Anniv Bank of China, Macau Branch. Multicoloured.

1756	1p.50 Type **374**	30	30
1757	2p.50 Modern HQ	45	45
1758	3p.50 Banknote details and inverted skyline	65	65
1759	4p. Clasped hands and inverted skyline	75	75
MS1760 138×90 mm. 10p. Modern HQ and lotus flower (60×40 mm)		1·90	1·90

375 Dom Pedro V Theatre

2010. St. Augustine's Square. Multicoloured.

1761	1p.5 Type **375**	30	30
1762	2p.50 Sir Robert Ho Tung Library	45	45
1763	3p.50 St. Augustine Church	65	65
1764	4p. St. Joseph's Seminary and Church	70	70
MS1765 138×90 mm. St. Augustine Church tower		1·90	1·90

376 St. Lawrence receiving Deaconship from Pope Sixtus II (stained glass window (detail), St. Lawrence Church)

2010. Church Interiors. Multicoloured.

1766	5p.50 Type **376**	1·10	1·10
MS1767 105×70 mm. 10p. Stained glass window (horiz)		1·90	1·90

Stamps of a similar design were issued by Åland.

377 Buddha

2010. Woodcarving. Multicoloured.

1768	1p.50 Type **377**	30	30
1769	2p.50 Na Tcha (or Nezha)	45	45
1770	2p.50 Kun lam (Kun Sai lam) (Avalokitasvara Bodhisattva)	65	65
1771	4p. Mazu (Tin Hau) (goddess)	75	75
MS1772 138×90 mm. 10p. The Eight Immortals (60×30 mm)		1·90	1·90

378 Hand-cranked Bakelite and 1960's Single Unit Handsets

2010. Antique Telephones. Multicoloured.

1773	1p.50 Type **378**	30	30
1774	2p.50 Modern public telephone and early box handset	45	45
1775	3p.50 Early rotary handset and 1960's public telephone	65	65
1776	4p. Bakelite wall-mounted and metal hand-cranked box handsets	75	75
MS1777 139×90 mm. 10p. Early 1900's wall mounted telephone (60×40 mm)		1·90	1·90

379 Noodle Soup from Van Tan (Sopa de Fitas com Van-Tan)

2010. Tenth Anniv of Macau Food Festival. Multicoloured.

1778	1p.50 Type **379**	30	30
1779	2p.50 Steamed buns (Xiao-longbao)	45	45
1780	3p.50 Sushi	65	65
1781	4p. Custard tart (Pastel de Nata)	75	75
MS1782 138×90 mm. 10p. Portuguese chicken (Galinha a portuguesa)		1·90	1·90

380 Tangzhuang (Tang suit)

2010. Traditional Costumes. Multicoloured.

1783	1p.50 Type **380**	30	30
1784	2p.50 Qipao (traditional Chinese woman's dress)	45	45
1785	3p.50 Duanyichangqun (blouse and long skirt) (traditional Han woman's costume)	65	75
1786	4p. Zhongsanzhuang (Chinese tunic suit) (Chinese 'National Costume')	75	75
MS1787 139×90 mm. 10p. Qipao and Duanyichangqun (60×40 mm)		1·90	1·90

381 Panda

2011. Pandas. Multicoloured.

1788	1p.50 Type **381**	30	30
1789	5p. Panda, facing forward	1·10	1·10
MS1790 138×90 mm. 10p. Two pandas (40×60 mm)		2·20	2·20

382 Rabbit (Madeira (wood))

2011. Chinese New Year. Year of the Rabbit. Multicoloured.

1791	1p.50 Type **382**	30	30
1792	1p.50 Rabbit (Agua (water))	30	30
1793	1p.50 Fireworks as rabbit (Fogo (fire))	30	30
1794	1p.50 Rabbit (Terra (earth))	30	30
1795	5p. Stylized rabbit (metal)	1·10	1·10
MS1796 138×90 mm. 10p. Stylized rabbit (different) (35×35 mm (diamond-shaped))		1·10	1·10

383 Ancient City of Fenghuang

2011. Mainland Scenery. Sheet 138×90 mm

MS1797 **383** 10p. multicoloured	1·10	1·10

384 Seat of Government

2011. Public Buildings and Monuments. Multicoloured.

1798	1p.50 Type **384**	30	30
1799	2p.50 Monetory Authority	45	45
1800	3p.50 Albergue da Santa Casa (old inn, now creative industries centre)	65	65
1801	4p. Macau Foundation	75	75

385 Singer with Yehu

2011. Cantonese Naamyam Singers. Multicoloured.

1802	1p.50 Type **385**	30	30
1803	2p.50 Singer on dockside with sails behind	45	45
1804	3p.50 Blind singer with stick, carrying instruments	65	65
1805	4p. Singer with guzheng on dockside with boats behind	75	75
MS1806 138×90 mm. 10p. Singer with yehu, facing left		1·10	1·10

386 Meeting when Travelling the Lake

2011. Legend of the White Snake. Multicoloured.

1807	1p.50 Type **386**	30	30
1808	1.50p. White snake exposed during Duanyang Festival	30	30
1809	2p. Lady Bai stealing herb to save Xu Xian	40	40
1810	2p. Fight between dragon and snake	40	40
1811	2p.50 Lady Bai captured in pagoda	45	45
1812	2p.50 Xu Shilin (Lady Bai's son) meets his mother at the pagoda	45	45
MS1813 138×90 mm. 10p. Flooding of Jinshan Temple (60×30 mm)		1·10	1·10

387 Pycnonotus sinensis (Light-vented Bulbul)

2011. 50th Anniv of WWF. Multicoloured.

1814	1p.50 Type **387**	30	30
1815	2p.50 Streptopelia chinensis (Spotted turtle dove)	45	45
1816	3p.50 Ixobrychus sinensis (Yellow bittern)	65	65
1817	4p.50 Centropus sinensis (Greater coucal)	75	75
MS1818 138×90 mm. Nos. 1814/17		1·10	1·10

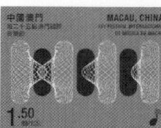

388 Piano

2011. 25th Macao International Music Festival. Each grey, black and scarlet-vermilion.

1819	1p.50 Type **388**	30	30
1820	2p.50 Trumpet	45	45
1821	3p.50 Drums	65	65
1822	4p. Strings	75	75
MS1823 138×90 mm. 10p. Sound waves		1·10	1·10

389 Lin Zexu (anti-opium campaigner)

2011. Personalities. Multicoloured.

1824	1p.50 Type **389**	30	30
1825	2p.50 Ye Ting (army commander)	45	45
1826	3p.50 Xian Xinghai (musician)	65	65
1827	4p. Ho Yin (industrialist and social activist)	75	75
MS1828 138×90 mm. 10p. Lin Zexu, Ye Ting, Xian Xinghai, Ho Yin, golden lotus flower and stars (40×60 mm)		1·10	1·10

390 Gao Jianfu (Chairman of Tongmenghui, Guangdong Branch) and 41, Nanwan Street

2011. Centenary of Xinhai Revolution (Revolution of 1911). Multicoloured.

1829	1p.50 Type **390**	30	30
1830	2p.50 Huang Xing (founder of Huaxinghui) and Monument to 72 Martyrs of Huang-huagang	45	45
1831	3p.50 Xiong Bingkun (leader Wuchung Uprising) and Wuchung Gate	65	65
1832	4p. Sun-Yat Sen (provisional president) and 292 Changjiang Road, Nanjing City	75	75
MS1833 138×90 mm. 10p. 1912 20c. stamp (As Type **41**) (60×40 mm)		1·10	1·10

391 Early Building and Stele

2011. 140th Anniv of Kiang Wu Hospital Charitable Association

1834	1p.50 Type **391**	30	30
1835	2p.50 Sun Yat-Sen (introduces western style medicine) (statue)	45	45
1836	3p.50 Traditional wooden medicine grinder and boat-shaped vessel	65	65
1837	4p. CAT scanner	75	75
MS1838 138×90 mm. 10p. Sun Yat-Sen (statue) in close up (40×40 mm)		1·10	1·10

CHARITY TAX STAMPS

The notes under this heading in Portugal also apply here.

43

1919. Fiscal stamp optd **TAXA DE GUERRA**.

C305	**43**	2a. green	9·75	6·25
C306	**43**	11a. green	37·00	18·00

The above was for use in Timor as well as Macao.

1925. As Marquis de Pombal issue of Portugal but inscr "MACAU".

C329	**C73**	2a. red	5·00	2·20
C330	–	2a. red	5·00	2·20
C331	**C75**	2a. red	6·25	3·00

1930. No gum.

C332	**C48**	5a. brown and buff	60·00	34·00

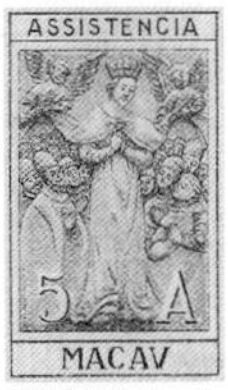

C48 Our Lady of Charity (altarpiece, Macao Cathedral)

1945. As Type **C48** but values in Arabic and Chinese numerals left and right, at bottom of design. No gum.

C486	1a. olive and green	2·10	1·80
C487	2a. purple and grey	2·10	1·80
C415	5a. brown and yellow	20·00	16·00
C416	5a. blue and light blue	55·00	37·00
C417	10a. green and light green	37·00	25·00
C488	10a. blue and green	2·10	1·80
C418	15a. orange and light orange	37·00	25·00
C419	20a. red and orange	55·00	31·00
C489	20a. brown and yellow	2·50	2·10
C420	50a. lilac and buff	70·00	43·00
C472	50a. red and pink	25·00	13·50

1981. No. C487 and similar higher (fiscal) values surch **20 avos** and Chinese characters.

C546	20a. on 2a. purple on grey	3·00	2·50
C534	20a. on 1p. green & lt green	3·75	2·00
C535	20a. on 3p. black and pink	3·50	1·50
C536	20a. on 5p. brown & yellow		

1981. No. C418 surch 10 avos and Chinese characters.

C553	10a. on 15a. orange and light orange	3·00	2·50

NEWSPAPER STAMPS

1892. "Embossed" key-type of Macao surch JORNAES and value. No gum.

N73	**Q**	2½r. on 10r. green	11·50	9·25
N74	**Q**	2½r. on 40r. brown	11·00	4·00
N75	**Q**	2½r. on 80r. grey	14·00	8·00

1893. "Newspaper" key-type inscr "Macau".

N80	**V**	2½r. brown	8·00	5·25

1894. "Newspaper" key-type of Macao surch ½ **avo PROVISORIO** and Chinese characters.

N82	½a. on 2½r. brown	7·00	4·50

POSTAGE DUE STAMPS

1904. "Due" key-type inscr "MACAU". No gum (12a. to 1p.), with or without gum (others).

D184	**W**	½a. green	1·80	1·40
D185	**W**	1a. green	2·50	1·40
D186	**W**	2a. grey	3·00	1·40
D187	**W**	4a. brown	3·75	1·70
D188	**W**	5a. orange	5·00	2·75
D189	**W**	8a. brown	5·75	3·00
D190	**W**	12a. brown	8·50	4·25
D191	**W**	20a. blue	16·00	7·50
D192	**W**	40a. red	30·00	11·00
D193	**W**	50a. orange	37·00	16·00
D194	**W**	1p. lilac	75·00	25·00

1911. "Due" key-types of Macao optd **REPUBLICA**.

D204	½a. green	1·70	60
D205	1a. green	2·50	1·20
D206	2a. grey	3·75	1·80
D207	4a. brown	5·00	1·80
D208	5a. orange	6·25	2·50
D209	8a. brown	6·75	2·75
D287	12a. brown	15·00	6·25
D211	20a. blue	14·00	4·50
D212	40a. red	21·00	6·25
D290	50a. orange	41·00	13·50
D291	1p. lilac	60·00	21·00

1925. Marquis de Pombal issue, as Nos. C329/31 optd **MULTA**.

D329	**C73**	4a. red	5·00	3·00
D330	-	4a. red	5·00	3·00
D331	**C 75**	4a. red	5·00	3·00

1947. As Type D **1** of Portuguese Colonies, but inscr "MACAU".

D410	**D1**	1a. black and purple	6·25	2·10
D411	**D1**	2a. black and violet	6·25	2·50
D412	**D1**	4a. black and blue	6·25	3·75
D413	**D1**	5a. black and brown	7·75	5·00
D414	**D1**	8a. black and purple	11·00	6·25
D415	**D1**	12a. black and brown	16·00	6·25
D416	**D1**	20a. black and green	18·00	11·50
D417	**D1**	40a. black and red	25·00	12·50
D418	**D1**	50a. black and yellow	43·00	15·00
D419	**D1**	1p. black and blue	75·00	18·00

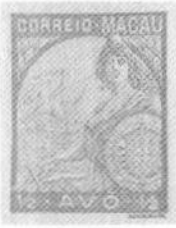

50 "Portugal" and Galeasse

1949. Postage stamps of 1934 surch **PORTEADO** and new value.

D424	**50**	1a. on 4a. black	4·25	2·30
D425	**50**	2a. on 6a. brown	4·25	2·30
D426	**50**	4a. on 8a. blue	4·25	2·30
D427	**50**	5a. on 10a. red	5·00	2·50
D428	**50**	8a. on 12a. blue	8·00	4·00
D429	**50**	12a. on 30a. green	11·50	5·00
D430	**50**	20a. on 40a. violet	16·00	8·00

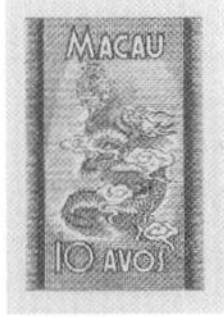

66 Arms and Dragon

1951. Optd **PORTEADO** or surch also.

D439	**66**	1a. yellow on cream	2·50	1·70
D440	**66**	2a. green on green	2·50	1·70
D441	**66**	7a. on 10a. mauve on green	3·00	1·80

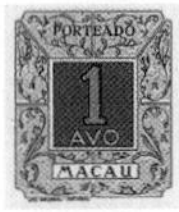

D70

1952. Numerals in red. Name in black.

D451	**D70**	1a. blue and green	1·00	75
D452	**D70**	3a. brown and salmon	1·30	85
D453	**D70**	5a. slate and blue	1·80	85
D454	**D70**	10a. red and blue	2·50	1·70
D455	**D70**	30a. blue and brown	6·25	2·50
D456	**D70**	1p. brown and grey	12·50	5·00

Pt. 3

MACEDONIA

Part of Austro-Hungarian Empire until 1918 when it became part of Yugoslavia. Separate stamps were issued during German Occupation in the Second World War. In 1991 Macedonia became an independent republic.

German Occupation.
100 stotinki = 1 lev.

Independent Republic.
1991. 100 paras = 1 dinar.
1992. 100 deni (de.) = 1 denar (d.).

A. GERMAN OCCUPATION

Македония

8. IX. 1944

1 лв.

(G1)

1944. Stamps of Bulgaria, 1940–44. (a) Surch as Type **G1**.

G1	1l. on 10st. orange	2·75	19·00
G2	3l. on 15st. blue	2·75	19·00

(b) Surch similar to Type G 1 but larger.

G3	6l. on 10st. blue	4·25	32·00
G4	9l. on 15st. green	4·25	32·00
G5	9l. on 15st. green	5·25	37·00
G6	15l. on 4l. black	21·00	75·00
G7	20l. on 7l. blue	32·00	75·00
G8	30l. on 14l. brown	37·00	£140

B. INDEPENDENT REPUBLIC

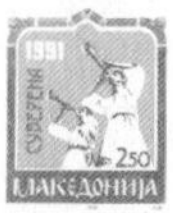

1 Trumpeters

1991. Obligatory Tax. Independence.

1	**1**	2d.50 black and orange	35	35

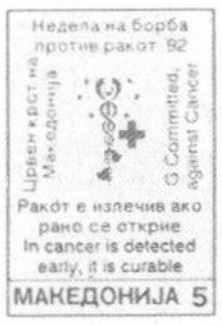

2 Emblems and Inscriptions

1992. Obligatory Tax. Anti-cancer Week. (a) T **2** showing Red Cross symbol at bottom left.

2	**2**	5d. mauve, black and blue	70	70
3	-	5d. multicoloured	70	70
4	-	5d. multicoloured	70	70
5	-	5d. multicoloured	70	70

DESIGNS: No. 3, Flowers, columns and scanner; 4, Scanner and couch; 5, Computer cabinet.

(b) As T **2** but with right-hand inscr reading down instead of up and without Red Cross symbol.

6	5d. mauve, black & blue (as No. 2)	25	25
7	5d. multicoloured (as No. 3)	25	25
8	5d. multicoloured (as No. 4)	25	25
9	5d. multicoloured (as No. 5)	25	25

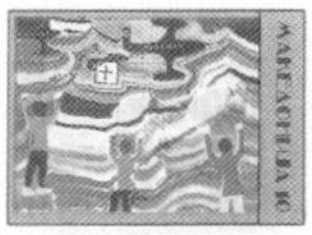

3 Red Cross Aircraft dropping Supplies

1992. Obligatory Tax. Red Cross Week. Multicoloured.

10	10d. Red Cross slogans (dated "08–15 MAJ 1992")	15	15
11	10d. Type **3**	15	15
12	10d. Treating road accident victim	15	15
13	10d. Evacuating casualties from ruined building	15	15

The three pictorial designs are taken from children's paintings.

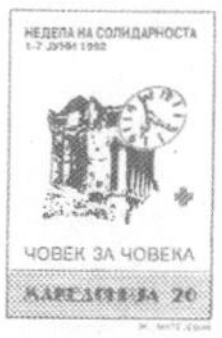

4 "Skopje Earthquake"

1992. Obligatory Tax. Solidarity Week.

14	**4**	20d. black and mauve	15	15
15	-	20d. multicoloured	15	15
16	-	20d. multicoloured	15	15
17	-	20d. multicoloured	15	15

DESIGNS: No. 15, Red Cross nurse with child; 16, Mothers carrying toddlers at airport; 17, Family at airport.

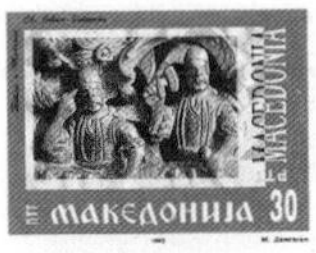

5 "Wood-carvers Petar and Makarie" (icon), St. Joven Bigorsk Monastery, Debar

1992. First Anniv of Independence.

18	**5**	30d. multicoloured	55	55

For 40d. in same design see No. 33.

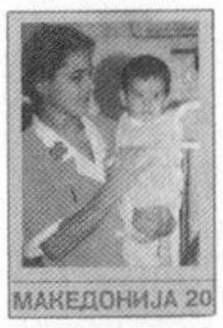

6 Nurse with Baby

1992. Obligatory Tax. Anti-tuberculosis Week. Multicoloured.

19	20d. Anti-tuberculosis slogans (dated "14–21.IX.1992")	15	15
20	20d. Type **6**	15	15
21	20d. Nurse giving oxygen	15	15
22	20d. Baby in cot	15	15

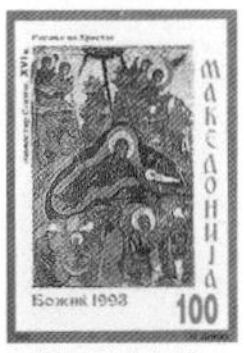

7 "The Nativity" (fresco, Slepce Monastery)

1992. Christmas. Multicoloured.

23	100d. Type **7**	1·40	1·40
24	500d. "Madonna and Child" (fresco), Zrze Monastery	3·25	3·25

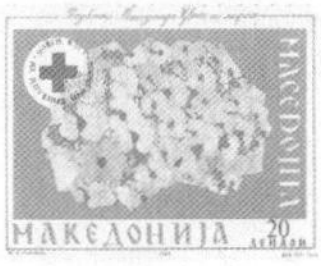

8 Mixed Bouquet

1993. Obligatory Tax. Red Cross Fund. Multicoloured.

25	20d. Red Cross slogans	15	15
26	20d. Marguerites	15	15
27	20d. Carnations	15	15
28	20d. Type **8**	15	15

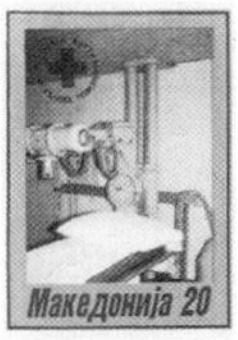

9 Radiography Equipment

1993. Obligatory Tax. Anti-cancer Week. Multicoloured.

29	20d. Anti-cancer slogans (dated "1–8 MART 1993")	15	15
30	20d. Type **9**	15	15
31	20d. Overhead treatment unit	15	15
32	20d. Scanner	15	15

1993. As No. 18 but changed value.

33	40d. multicoloured	60	60

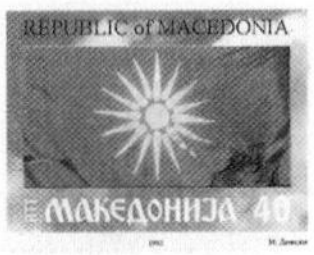

10 Macedonian Flag

1993

34	**10**	10d. multicoloured	35	35
35	**10**	40d. multicoloured	1·40	1·40
36	**10**	50d. multicoloured	1·80	1·80

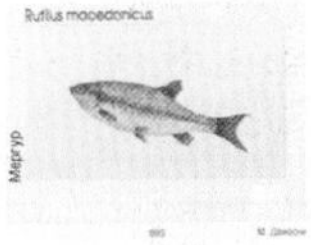

11 Macedonian Roach

1993. Fishes from Lake Ohrid. Multicoloured.

37	50d. Type **11**	25	25
38	100d. Lake Ohrid salmon	35	35
39	1000d. Type **11**	3·50	3·50
40	2000d. As No. 38	4·75	4·75

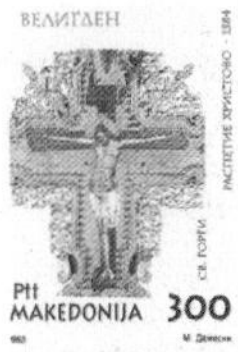

12 Crucifix, St. George's Monastery

1993. Easter.

41	**12**	300d. multicoloured	3·00	3·00

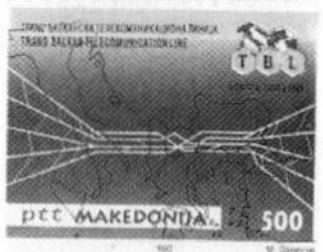

13 Diagram of Telecommunications Cable and Map

1993. Opening of Trans-Balkan Telecommunications Line.

42	**13**	500d. multicoloured	1·80	1·80

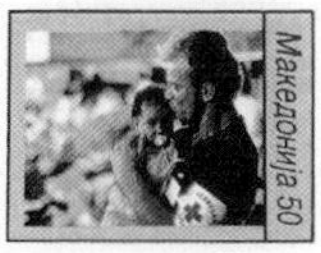

14 Red Cross Worker with Baby

1993. Obligatory Tax. Red Cross Week. Multicoloured.

43	50d. Red Cross inscriptions (dated "08–15 MAJ 1993")	15	15
44	50d. Type **14**	15	15
45	50d. Physiotherapist and child in wheelchair	15	15

| 46 | | 50d. Stretcher party | 15 | 15 |

See also No. 73.

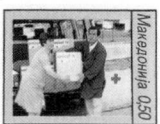

15 Unloading UNICEF Supplies from Lorry

1993. Obligatory Tax. Solidarity Week.

47	-	50de. black, mauve and silver	15	15
48	**15**	50de. multicoloured	15	15
49	-	50de. multicoloured	15	15
50	-	50de. multicoloured	15	15

DESIGNS: No. 47, "Skopje Earthquake"; 49, Labelling parcels in warehouse; 50, Consignment of parcels on fork-lift truck.

See also No. 72.

16 U.N. Emblem and Rainbow

1993. Admission to United Nations Organization.

| 51 | **16** | 10d. multicoloured | 1·40 | 1·40 |

17 "Insurrection" (detail), (B. Lazeski)

1993. 90th Anniv of Macedonian Insurrection.

| 52 | **17** | 10d. multicoloured | 1·40 | 1·40 |
| MS53 | | 116×73 mm. 30d. multicoloured | 4·25 | 4·25 |

18 Children in Meadow

1993. Obligatory Tax. Anti-tuberculosis Week. Multicoloured.

54		50de. Anti-tuberculosis slogans (dated "14–21.09.1993")	15	15
55		50de. Type 18	15	15
56		50de. Bee on flower	15	15
57		50de. Goat behind boulder	15	15

See also No. 71.

19 Tapestry

1993. Centenary of Founding of Inner Macedonia Revolutionary Organization.

| 58 | | 4d. Type 19 | 60 | 60 |
| MS59 | | 90×75 mm. 40d. Two motifs as Type 19 | 4·25 | 4·25 |

20 "The Nativity" (fresco from St. George's Monastery, Rajcica)

1993. Christmas. Multicoloured.

| 60 | | 2d. Type 20 | 50 | 50 |
| 61 | | 20d. "The Three Kings" (fresco from Slepce Monastery) | 3·50 | 3·50 |

21 Lily

1994. Obligatory Tax. Anti-cancer Week. Multicoloured.

62		1d. Red Cross and anti-cancer emblems	15	15
63		1d. Type 21	15	15
64		1d. Caesar's mushroom	15	15
65		1d. Mute swans on lake	15	15

1994. Nos. 1, 18 and 34 surch.

66	**5**	2d. on 30d. multicoloured	25	25
67	**1**	8d. on 2d.50 black and orange	95	95
68	**6**	15d. on 10d. multicoloured	1·90	1·90

23 Decorated Eggs

1994. Easter.

| 69 | **23** | 2d. multicoloured | 60 | 60 |

1994. Obligatory Tax. Red Cross Week. As previous designs but values, and date (70), changed. Multicoloured.

70		1d. Red Cross inscriptions (dated "8–15 MAJ 1994")	15	15
71		1d. Type 18	15	15
72		1d. As No. 50	15	15
73		1d. Type 14	15	15

24 Kosta Racin (writer)

1994. Revolutionaries. Portraits by Dimitar Kondovski. Multicoloured.

74		8d. Type 24	60	60
75		15d. Grigor Prlicev (writer)	1·20	1·20
76		20d. Nikola Vaptsarov (Bulgarian poet)	1·80	1·80
77		50d. Goce Delcev (founder of Internal Macedonian–Odrin Revolutionary– Organization)	4·25	4·25

25 "Skopje Earthquake"

1994. Obligatory Tax. Solidarity Week.

| 78 | **25** | 1d. black, red and silver | 35 | 35 |

26 Tree and Family

1994. Census.

| 79 | **26** | 2d. multicoloured | 60 | 60 |

27 St. Prohor Pcinski Monastery (venue)

1994. 50th Anniv of Macedonian National Liberation Council. Multicoloured.

| 80 | | 5d. Type 27 | 60 | 60 |
| MS81 | | 108×73 mm. 50d. Aerial view of Monastery | 4·25 | 4·25 |

28 Swimmer

1994. Swimming Marathon, Ohrid.

| 82 | **28** | 8d. multicoloured | 85 | 85 |

29 Turkish Cancellation and 1992 30d. Stamp on Cover

1994. 150th Anniv (1993) of Postal Service in Macedonia.

| 83 | **29** | 2d. multicoloured | 60 | 60 |

30 Mastheads

1994. 50th Anniversaries of "Nova Makedonija", "Mlad Borec" and "Makedonka" (newspapers).

| 84 | **30** | 2d. multicoloured | 60 | 60 |

31 Open Book

1994. 50th Anniv of St. Clement of Ohrid Library. Multicoloured.

| 85 | | 2d. Type 31 | 25 | 25 |
| 86 | | 10d. Page of manuscript (vert) | 1·60 | 1·60 |

32 Globe

1994. Obligatory Tax. Anti-AIDS Week.

87	-	2d. red and black	15	15
88	**32**	2d. black, red and blue	15	15
89	-	2d. black, yellow and red	15	15
90	-	2d. black and red	15	15

DESIGNS: No. 87, Inscriptions in Cyrillic (dated "01-08.12.1994"); 89, Exclamation mark in warning triangle; 90, Safe sex campaign emblem.

33 Wireless and Gramophone Record

1994. 50th Anniv of Macedonian Radio.

| 91 | **33** | 2d. multicoloured | 60 | 60 |

34 Macedonian Pine

1994. Flora and Fauna. Multicoloured.

| 92 | | 5d. Type 34 | 60 | 60 |
| 93 | | 10d. Lynx | 1·20 | 1·20 |

1995. Nos. 35 and 33 surch.

| 94 | **10** | 2d. on 40d. multicoloured | 1·20 | 1·20 |
| 96 | **5** | 5d. on 40d. multicoloured | 70 | 70 |

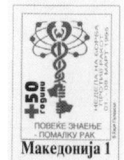

36 Emblems and Inscriptions

1995. Obligatory Tax. Anti-cancer Week. Multicoloured.

97		1d. Type 36	15	15
98		1d. White lilies	15	15
99		1d. Red lilies	15	15
100		1d. Red roses	15	15

37 Fresco

1995. Easter.

| 101 | **37** | 4d. multicoloured | 60 | 60 |

38 Voluntary Workers

1995. Obligatory Tax. Red Cross. Multicoloured.

102		1d. Cross and inscriptions in Cyrillic (dated "8–15 MAJ 1995")	15	15
103		1d. Type 38	15	15
104		1d. Volunteers in T-shirts	15	15
105		1d. Globe, red cross and red crescent	15	15

39 Troops on Battlefield

1995. 50th Anniv of End of Second World War.

| 106 | **39** | 2d. multicoloured | 1·20 | 1·20 |

40 Anniversary Emblem

1995. 50th Anniv of Macedonian Red Cross.

| 107 | **40** | 2d. multicoloured | 1·20 | 1·20 |

41 Rontgen and X-Ray Lamp

1995. Centenary of Discovery of X-Rays by Wilhelm Rontgen.

| 108 | **41** | 2d. multicoloured | 1·40 | 1·40 |

42 "Skopje Earthquake"

1995. Obligatory Tax. Solidarity Week.

| 109 | **42** | 1d. black, red and gold | 15 | 15 |

43 Cernodrinski
(dramatist)

1995. 50th Anniv of Vojdan Cernodrinski Theatre Festival.
110	**43**	10d. multicoloured	1·20	1·20

44 Kraljevic (fresco,
Markov Monastery, Skopje)

1995. 600th Death Anniv of Marko Kraljevic (Serbian Prince).
111	**44**	20d. multicoloured	1·60	1·60

45 Puleski

1995. Death Centenary of Gorgi Puleski (linguist and revolutionary).
112	**45**	2d. multicoloured	1·20	1·20

46 Manuscript, Bridge and
Emblem

1995. Writers' Festival, Struga.
113	**46**	2d. multicoloured	1·20	1·20

47 Robert Koch (discoverer
of tubercule bacillus)

1995. Obligatory Tax. Anti-tuberculosis Week.
114	**47**	1d. brown, black and red	35	35

48 Child
holding
Parents' Hands

1995. Obligatory Tax. Childrens' Week. Self-adhesive. Imperf.
115	**48**	2d. blue	35	35

49 Maleshevija

1995. Buildings. Multicoloured.
116		2d. Type **49**	20	20
117		20d. Krakornica	1·40	1·40

50 Interior of
Mosque

1995. Tetovo Mosque.
118	**50**	15d. multicoloured	1·20	1·20

51 Lumiere Brothers
(inventors of cine-camera)

1995. Centenary of Motion Pictures. Multicoloured.
119		10d. Type **51**	1·20	1·20
120		10d. Milton and Janaki Manaki (Macedonian cinematographers)	1·20	1·20

Nos. 119/20 were issued together, *se-tenant*, forming a composite design.

52 Globe in Nest within
Frame

1995. 50th Anniv of U.N.O. Multicoloured.
121		20d. Type **52**	95	95
122		50d. Sun within frame	2·75	2·75

53 Male and Female
Symbols

1995. Obligatory Tax. Anti-AIDS Week.
123	**53**	1d. multicoloured	35	35

54 Madonna and Child

1995. Christmas.
124	**54**	15d. multicoloured	1·40	1·40

55 Dalmatian Pelican

1995. Birds. Multicoloured.
125		15d. Type **55**	1·20	1·20
126		40d. Lammergeier	2·40	2·40

56 Letters of
Alphabet and
Jigsaw Pieces

1995. 50th Anniv of Alphabet Reform.
127	**56**	5d. multicoloured	60	60

57 St. Clement of Ohrid
(detail of fresco)

1995. 700th Anniv of Fresco, St. Bogorodica's Church, Ohrid.
128	**57**	8d. multicoloured	70	70
MS129	85×67 mm. **57** 50d. multicoloured. Imperf		60·00	60·00

58 Postal Headquarters,
Skopje

1995. Second Anniv of Membership of U.P.U.
130	**58**	10d. multicoloured	70	70

59 Zip joining Flags

1995. Entry to Council of Europe and Organization for Security and Co-operation in Europe.
131	**59**	20d. multicoloured	1·60	1·60

60 Hand holding out
Apple

1996. Obligatory Tax. Anti-cancer Week.
132	**60**	1d. multicoloured	35	35

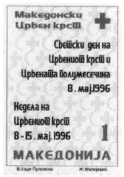

61 Inscriptions

1996. Obligatory Tax. Red Cross Week. Each red, black and yellow.
133		1d. Type **61**	15	15
134		1d. Red Cross principles in Macedonian	15	15
135		1d. Red Cross principles in English	15	15
136		1d. Red Cross principles in French	15	15
137		1d. Red Cross principles in Spanish	15	15

62 Canoeing

1996. Olympic Games, Atlanta. Designs showing statue of discus thrower and sport. Multicoloured.
138		2d. Type **62**	35	35
139		8d. Basketball (vert)	50	50
140		15d. Swimming	85	85
141		20d. Wrestling	1·30	1·30
142		40d. Boxing (vert)	2·75	2·75
143		50d. Running (vert)	3·25	3·25

63 "Skopje
Earthquake"

1996. Obligatory Tax. Solidarity Week.
144	**63**	1d. gold, red and black	35	35

64 Scarecrow Drug
Addict

1996. United Nations Anti-drugs Decade.
145	**64**	20d. multicoloured	1·20	1·20

65 Boy

1996. Children's Week. Children's Drawings. Multicoloured.
146		2d. Type **65**	25	25
147		8d. Girl	60	60

66 Fragment from Tomb
and Tsar Samuel (after
Dimitar Kondovski)

1996. Millenary of Crowning of Tsar Samuel (ruler of Bulgaria and Macedonia).
148	**66**	40d. multicoloured	2·20	2·20

67 Petrov

1996. 75th Death Anniv of Gorce Petrov (revolutionary).
149	**67**	20d. multicoloured	1·20	1·20

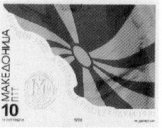

68 Ohrid Seal, 1903, and
State Flag

1996. Fifth Anniv of Independence.
150	**68**	10d. multicoloured	60	60

69 Lungs on
Globe

1996. Obligatory Tax. Anti-tuberculosis Week.
151	**69**	1d. red, blue and black	50	50

70 Vera
Ciriviri-Trena
(freedom fighter)

1996. Europa. Famous Women. Multicoloured.
152		20d. Type **70**	8·50	8·50
153		40d. Mother Teresa (Nobel Peace Prize winner and founder of Missionaries of Charity)	12·00	12·00

71 Hand holding Syringe

1996. Obligatory Tax. Anti-AIDS Week.
154	**71**	1d. black, red and yellow	35	35

72 Candle, Nuts
and Fruit

1996. Christmas. Multicoloured.
155		10d. Type **72**	70	70
156		10d. Tree and carol singers	70	70

73 "Daniel in the Lions' Den"

1996. Early Christian Terracotta Reliefs. (a) Green backgrounds.

157	4d. Type **73**	25	25
158	8d. St. Christopher and St. George	50	50
159	20d. Joshua and Caleb	1·20	1·20
160	50d. Unicorn	3·00	3·00

(b) Blue backgrounds.

161	4d. Type **73**	25	25
162	8d. As No. 158	50	50
163	20d. As No. 159	1·20	1·20
164	50d. As No. 160	3·00	3·00

74 Nistrovo

1996. Traditional Houses. Multicoloured.

165	2d. Type **74**	25	25
166	8d. Brodec	70	70
167	10d. Niviste	85	85

75 "Pseudochazara cingovskii"

1996. Butterflies. Multicoloured.

168	4d. Type **75**	25	25
169	40d. Danube clouded yellow	3·00	3·00

76 UNICEF Coach

1996. 50th Anniversaries. Multicoloured.

170	20d. Type **76** (UNICEF)	1·20	1·20
171	40d. Church in Mtskheta, Georgia (UNESCO)	2·40	2·40

77 Skier

1997. 50 Years of Ski Championships at Sar Planina.

172	**77**	20d. multicoloured	1·40	1·40

78 Bell

1997. 150th Birth Anniv of Alexander Graham Bell (telephone pioneer).

173	**78**	40d. multicoloured	2·40	2·40

79 Family and Healthy Foodstuffs

1997. Obligatory Tax. Anti-cancer Week.

174	**79**	1d. multicoloured	1·80	1·80

80 Hound

1997. Roman Mosaics from Heraklia. Mult.

175	2d. Type **80**	25	25
176	8d. Steer	50	50
177	20d. Lion	1·10	1·10
178	40d. Leopard with prey	2·40	2·40

MS179 85×60 mm. 50d. Deer and plant tub. Imperf ... 4·75　4·75

81 Red Cross on Globe

1997. Obligatory Tax. Red Cross Week.

180	**81**	1d. mult	35	35

82 Gold Plate

1997. 1100th Anniv of Cyrillic Alphabet. Mult.

181	10d. Type **82**	70	70
182	10d. Sts. Cyril and Methodius	70	70

83 Schoolchildren

1997. Obligatory Tax. Solidarity Week.

183	**83**	1d. multicoloured	35	35

84 Mountain Flowers

1997. Fifth Anniv of Ecological Association.

184	**84**	15d. multicoloured	1·20	1·20

85 Itar Pejo

1997. Europa. Tales and Legends. Multicoloured.

185	20d. Type **85**	7·25	7·25
186	40d. Stork-men	13·00	13·00

86 St. Naum and St. Naum's Church, Ohrid

1997. 1100th Birth Anniv of St. Naum.

187	**86**	15d. multicoloured	1·20	1·20

87 Diseased Lungs

1997. Obligatory Tax. Anti-tuberculosis Week.

188	**87**	1d. multicoloured	35	35

88 Stibnite

1997. Minerals. Multicoloured.

189	27d. Type **88**	1·80	1·80
190	40d. Lorandite	2·40	2·40

89 Dove and Sun above Child in Open Hand

1997. International Children's Day.

191	**89**	27d. multicoloured	1·70	1·70

90 Chanterelle

1997. Fungi. Multicoloured.

192	2d. Type **90**	35	35
193	15d. Bronze boletus	85	85
194	27d. Caesar's mushroom	1·60	1·60
195	50d. "Morchella conica"	2·75	2·75

91 Group of Children

1998. Obligatory Tax. Anti-AIDS Week.

196	**91**	1d. multicoloured	35	35

92 Gandhi

1998. 50th Death Anniv of Mahatma Gandhi (Indian independence campaigner).

197	**92**	30d. multicoloured	1·40	1·40

93 Formula of Pythagoras's Theory

1998. 2500th Death Anniv of Pythagoras (philosopher and mathematician).

198	**93**	16d. multicoloured	85	85

94 Alpine Skiing

1998. Winter Olympic Games, Nagano, Japan. Multicoloured.

199	4d. Type **94**	10	10
200	30d. Cross-country skiing	1·40	1·40

95 Novo Selo

1998. Traditional Houses. Multicoloured.

201	1d. Bogomila	10	10
202	2d. Type **95**	10	10
203	3d. Jachintse	20	20
204	4d. Jablanica	25	25
205	4d. Svekani	30	30
206	5d. Teovo	30	30
207	6d. Zdunje	35	35
208	6d. Mitrasinci	35	35
209	9d. Ratevo	50	50
210	16d. Kiselica	65	65
211	20d. Konopnica	85	85
212	30d. Ambar	1·40	1·40
213	50d. Galicnik	2·40	2·40

96 "Exodus" (Kole Manev)

1998. 50th Anniv of Exodus of Children during Greek Civil War.

215	**96**	30d. multicoloured	1·40	1·40

97 "Proportions of Man" (Leonardo da Vinci)

1998. Obligatory Tax. Anti-cancer Week.

216	**97**	1d. multicoloured	50	50

98 Bowl supported by Animal

1998. Archaeological Finds from Nedit. Multicoloured.

217	4d. Carafes	25	25
218	18d. Type **98**	70	70
219	30d. Sacred female figurine	1·40	1·40
220	60d. Stemmed cup	2·75	2·75

99 Football Pitch

1998. World Cup Football Championship, France. Multicoloured.

221	4d. Type **99**	25	25
222	30d. Globe and football pitch	1·60	1·60

100 Folk Dance

1998. Europa. National Festivals. Multicoloured.

223	30d. Type **100**	3·00	3·00
224	40d. Carnival	4·25	4·25

101 Profiles

1998. Obligatory Tax. Red Cross Week.

225	**101**	2d. multicoloured	50	50

102 Carnival
Procession

1998. 18th Congress of Carnival Towns, Strumica.
226 **102** 30d. multicoloured 1·40 1·40

103 Hands and
Red Cross

1998. Obligatory Tax. Solidarity Week.
227 **103** 2d. multicoloured 50 50

104 Flower

1998. Environmental Protection. Multicoloured.
228 **104** 4d. Type **104** 25 25
229 30d. Polluting chimney uproot-
ing tree 1·30 1·30

105 Cupovski

1998. 120th Birth Anniv of Dimitrija Cupovski.
230 **105** 16d. multicoloured 70 70

106 Steam
Locomotive and
Station

1997. 150th Anniv of Railways in Macedonia.
Multicoloured.
231 **106** 30d. Type **106** 1·80 1·80
232 60d. Steam locomotive, 1873
(horiz) 3·50 3·50

107 Doctor and
Patient

1998. Obligatory Tax. Anti-tuberculosis Week.
233 **107** 2d. multicoloured 50 50

108 "Ursus spelaeus"

1998. Fossilized Skulls. Multicoloured.
234 **108** 4d. Type **108** 25 25
235 8d. "Mesopithecus pentelici" 35 35
236 18d. "Tragoceros" 95 95
237 30d. "Aceratherium incsivum" 1·40 1·40

109 Atanos Badev
(composer) and Score

1998. Centenary of "Zlatoustova Liturgy".
238 **109** 25d. multicoloured 1·20 1·20

110 Child with
Kite

1998. Children's Day.
239 **110** 30d. multicoloured 1·40 1·40

111 "Cerambyx cerdo"
(longhorn beetle)

1998. Insects. Multicoloured.
240 **111** 4d. Type **111** 25 25
241 8d. Alpine longhorn beetle 50 50
242 20d. European rhinoceros
beetle 95 95
243 40d. Stag beetle 1·90 1·90

112 Reindeer and
Snowflakes

1998. Christmas and New Year. Multicoloured.
244 **112** 4d. Type **112** 25 25
245 30d. Bread and oak leaves 1·60 1·60

113 Ribbon and
Gender Symbols

1998. Obligatory Tax. Anti-AIDS Week.
246 **113** 2d. multicoloured 50 50

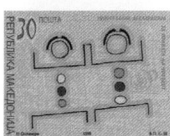

114 Stylized Couple

1998. 50th Anniv of Universal Declaration of Human
Rights.
247 **114** 30d. multicoloured 1·40 1·40

115 Sharplaninec

1999. Dogs.
248 **115** 15d. multicoloured 1·20 1·20

116 Girl's Face

1999. Obligatory Tax. Anti-cancer Week.
249 **116** 2d. multicoloured 50 50

117 "The
Annunciation"
(Demir Hisar,
Slepce
Monastery)

1999. Icons. Multicoloured.
250 4d. Type **117** 35 35
251 8d. "Saints" (St. Nicholas's
Church, Ohrid) 50 50
252 18d. "Madonna and Child"
(Demir Hisar, Slepce
Monastery) 85 85
253 30d. "Christ the Redeemer"
(Zrze Monastery, Prilep) 1·30 1·30
MS254 53×74 mm. 50d. "Christ and
Archangels" (Archangel Michael
Church, Lesnovo Monastery,
Probiotip) 3·00 3·00

118 Pandilov and "Hay
Harvest"

1999. Birth Centenary of Dimitar Pandilov (painter).
255 **118** 4d. multicoloured 25 25

119 Telegraph Apparatus

1999. Centenary of the Telegraph in Macedonia.
256 **119** 4d. multicoloured 25 25

120 University and Sts.
Cyril and Methodius

1999. 50th Anniv of Sts. Cyril and Methodius University.
257 **120** 8d. multicoloured 35 35

121 Anniversary Emblem
and Map of Europe

1999. 50th Anniv of Council of Europe.
258 **121** 30d. multicoloured 1·40 1·40

122 Pelister National Park

1999. Europa. Parks and Gardens. Multicoloured.
259 30d. Type **122** 3·00 3·00
260 40d. Mavrovo National Park 4·25 4·25

123 Figures linking
Raised Arms

1999. Obligatory Tax. Red Cross Week.
261 **123** 2d. multicoloured 60 60

124 People
running round
Globe

1999. Obligatory Tax. Solidarity Week.
262 **124** 2d. multicoloured 60 60

125 Tree

1999. Environmental Protection.
263 **125** 30d. multicoloured 1·40 1·40

126 Tsar Petur Delyan

1999. Medieval Rulers of Macedonia. Multicoloured.
264 **126** 4d. Type **126** 10 10
265 8d. Prince Gjorgji Vojteh 35 35
266 18d. Prince Dobromir Hrs 85 85
267 30d. Prince Strez 1·40 1·40
Nos. 264/7 were issued together, *se-tenant*, forming a
composite design.

127 Kuzman Shaikarev
(author)

1999. 125th Anniv of First Macedonian Language Primer.
268 **127** 4d. multicoloured 25 25

128 Faces in
Outline of Lungs

1999. Obligatory Tax. Anti-tuberculosis Week.
269 **128** 2d. multicoloured 60 60

129 "Crocus
scardicus"

1999. Flowers. Multicoloured.
270 **129** 4d. Type **129** 25 25
271 8d. "Astragalus mayeri" 35 35
272 18d. "Campanula formanekiana" 95 95
273 30d. "Viola kosaninii" 1·40 1·40

130 Child

1999. Children's Week.
274 **130** 30d. multicoloured 1·40 1·40

131 Emblem

1999. 125th Anniv of Universal Postal Union. Multicoloured.
275		5d. Type 131	25	25
276		30d. Emblem (different)	1·60	1·60

132 Men on Horseback

1999. 1400th Anniv of Slavs in Macedonia.
277	**132**	5d. multicoloured	25	25

133 Misirkov

1999. 125th Birth Anniv (2000) of Krste Petkov Misirkov (writer).
278	**133**	5d. multicoloured	25	25

134 Pine Needles

1999. Christmas. Multicoloured.
279		5d. Type 134	35	35
280		30d. Traditional pastry (vert)	1·40	1·40

135 Stylized Figures supporting Globe

1999. Obligatory Tax. Anti-AIDS Week.
281	**135**	2d.50 multicoloured	60	60

136 Altar Cross (19th-century), St. Nikita Monastery

2000. Bimillenary of Christianity. Multicoloured.
282		5d. Type 136	35	35
283		10d. "Akathist of the Holy Mother of God" (14th-century fresco), Marko's Monastery (horiz)	60	60
284		15d. "St. Clement" (14th-century icon), Ohrid	70	70
285		30d. "Paul the Apostle" (14th-century fresco), St. Andrew's Monastery	1·30	1·30
MS286		70×50 mm. 50d. Cathedral Church of St. Sophia (11th-century), Ohrid (29×31 mm)	2·40	2·40

137 "2000"

2000. New Year. Multicoloured.
287		5d. Type 137	25	25
288		30d. Religious symbols	1·20	1·20

139 Jewelled Brooch with Icon, Ohrid

2000. Obligatory Tax. Anti-cancer Week.
289	**138**	2d.50 multicoloured	60	60

138 Globe Unravelling and Medical Symbols

2000. Jewellery. Multicoloured.
290		5d. Type 139	25	25
291		10d. Bracelet, Bitola	35	35
292		20d. Earrings, Ohrid	95	95
293		30d. Butterfly brooch, Bitola	1·40	1·40

140 Magnifying Glass and Perforation Gauge

2000. 50th Anniv of Philately in Macedonia.
294	**140**	5d. multicoloured	25	25

141 Globe and Emblem

2000. 50th Anniv of World Meteorological Organization.
295	**141**	30d. multicoloured	1·40	1·40

142 Men with Easter Eggs

2000. Easter.
296	**142**	5d. multicoloured	25	25

143 Stylized Figures

2000. Obligatory Tax. Red Cross Week.
297	**143**	2d.50 multicoloured	60	60

144 "Building Europe"

2000. Europa.
298	**144**	30d. multicoloured	3·00	3·00

145 Running

2000. Olympic Games, Sydney. Multicoloured.
299		5d. Type 145	25	25
300		30d. Wrestling	1·60	1·60

146 Cupped Hands

2000. Obligatory Tax. Solidarity Week.
301	**146**	2d.50 multicoloured	60	60

147 Flower and Globe

2000. International Environmental Protection Day.
302	**147**	5d. multicoloured	25	25

149 Teodosija Sinaitski (printing pioneer)

2000. Printing. Multicoloured.
303		6d. Type 148	25	25
304		30d. Johannes Gutenberg (inventor of printing press)	1·40	1·40

148 Mother Teresa

2000. Third Death Anniv of Mother Teresa (Order of Missionaries of Charity).
305	**149**	6d. multicoloured	25	25

150 Faces and Hands

2000. Obligatory Tax. Red Cross Week.
306	**150**	3d. multicoloured	60	60

151 Little Egret

2000. Birds. Multicoloured.
307		6d. Type 151	35	35
308		10d. Grey heron	50	50
309		20d. Purple heron	1·10	1·10
310		30d. Glossy ibis	1·70	1·70

152 Children and Tree

2000. Children's Week.
311	**152**	6d. multicoloured	25	25

153 Dimov

2000. 125th Birth Anniv of Dimo Hadzi Dimov (revolutionary).
312	**153**	6d. multicoloured	25	25

154 Emblem

2000. 50th Anniv of Faculty of Economics, St. Cyril and St. Methodius University, Skopje.
313	**154**	6d. multicoloured	25	25

155 Church and Frontispiece

2000. 250th Birth Anniv of Joakim Krcovski (writer).
314	**155**	6d. multicoloured	1·00	1·00

156 Nativity

2000. Christmas.
315	**156**	30d. multicoloured	1·50	1·50

157 Hand holding Condom

2000. Obligatory Tax. Anti-AIDS. Week.
316	**157**	3d. multicoloured	65	65

158 Handprints and Emblem

2001. 50th Anniv of United Nations Commissioner for Human Rights. Multicoloured.
317		6d. Type 158	25	25
318		30d. Hands forming Globe (vert)	1·70	1·70

159 Imperial Eagle on Branch

2001. Endangered Species. The Imperial Eagle (Aquila heliaca). Multicoloured.
319		6d. Type 159	25	25
320		8d. With chick	40	40
321		10d. Flying	50	50
322		30d. Head	1·40	1·40

160 Zografski

2001. 125th Death Anniv of Partenja Zografski (historian).
323	**160**	6d. multicoloured	25	25

161 Emblem

2001. Obligatory Tax. Anti-Cancer Week.
324 **161** 3d. multicoloured 65 65

162 Woman in Costume

2001. Regional Costumes. Multicoloured.
325 6d. Type **162** 40 40
326 12d. Couple in costume 65 65
327 18d. Woman in costume 90 90
328 30d. Couple in costume 1·40 1·40
MS329 76×64 mm. 50d. Women working (30×30 mm). Imperf 2·50 2·50

163 Landscape

2001. Birth Centenary of Lazar Licenoski (artist).
330 **163** 6d. multicoloured 40 40

164 Text

2001. 50th Anniv of State Archives.
331 **164** 6d. multicoloured 40 40

165 Jesus and Sick Man

2001. Easter.
332 **165** 6d. multicoloured 40 40

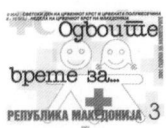

166 Children

2001. Obligatory Tax. Red Cross Week.
333 **166** 3d. multicoloured 65 65

167 Lake and Island

2001. Europa. Water Resources. Multicoloured.
334 18d. Type **167** 1·00 1·00
335 36d. Right-side of lake and
island 2·20 2·20
Nos. 334/5 were issued together, *se-tenant*, forming a
composite design.

168 Dimitri Berovski
(nationalist leader) and
Flag

2001. 125th Anniversary of Razlovci Village Uprising.
336 **168** 6d. multicoloured 40 40

169 Man carrying
Red Cross Boxes

2001. Obligatory Tax. Red Cross Week.
337 **169** 3d. multicoloured 65 65

170 Championship
Emblem

2001. Second Individual Chess Championship, Ohrid.
338 **170** 36d. multicoloured 1·90 1·90

171 Boats on Lake

2001. Environment Protection. Lake Dojran.
339 **171** 6d. multicoloured 40 40

172 Emblem

2001. Tenth Anniv of Independence.
340 **172** 6d. multicoloured 40 40

173 Juniper (*Juniperus
exelsa*)

2001. Trees. Multicoloured.
341 6d. Type **173** 40 40
342 12d. Macedonian oak (*Quercus
macedonica*) 65 65
343 24d. Strawberry tree (*Arbutus
andrachne*) 1·20 1·20
344 36d. Kermes oak (*Quercus
coccifera*) 1·70 1·70

174 Man with
raised Arms

2001. Obligatory Tax. Anti-Tuberculosis Week.
345 **174** 3d. multicoloured 65 65

175 Stylized
Woman with Basket

2001. Children's Day.
346 **175** 6d. multicoloured 40 40

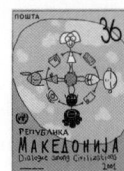

176 Children
encircling Globe

2001. United Nations Year of Dialogue among
Civilizations.
347 **176** 36d. multicoloured 2·20 2·20

177 Fox and Cubs

2001. 75th Anniv of Zoological Museum.
348 **177** 6d. multicoloured 50 50

178 Icon

2001. Christmas.
349 **178** 6d. multicoloured 50 5·00

179 Faces

2001. Obligatory Tax. Anti-AIDS Week.
350 **179** 3d. multicoloured 65 65

180 Alfred Nobel

2001. Centenary of First Nobel Prize.
351 **180** 36d. multicoloured 1·90 1·90

181 Skier

2002. Winter Olympic Games, Salt Lake City, USA.
Multicoloured.
352 6d. Type **181** 40 40
353 36d. Skier (different) 1·50 1·50

182 Sunrise

2002. Obligarory Tax. Anti-Cancer Week.
354 **182** 3d. multicoloured 65 65

183 Likej (coin)

2002. Ancient Coins. Coins. Multicoloured.
355 6d. Type **183** 40 40
356 12d. Alexander III tetradrachm 65 65
357 24d. Lichnidos 1·20 1·20
358 36d. Philip II gold coin (stater) 1·70 1·70
MS359 85×62 mm. 50d. Coin 3·25 3·25

184 Painting and Petar
Mazev

2002. Artists Birth Anniversaries. Multicoloured.
360 6d. Type **184** (75th anniv) 50 50
361 6d. Triptych, 1978 (Dimitar
Kondovski, 75th anniv) 50 50
362 36d. Mona Lisa (La Gioconda)
and Leonardo da Vinci
(550th anniv) 1·90 1·90

185 "The Risen
Christ"

2002. Easter.
363 **185** 6d. multicoloured 50 50

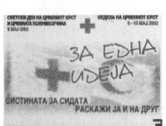

186 Red Cross and Red
Crescent Flags

2002. Obligatory Tax. Red Cross Week.
364 **186** 3d. multicoloured 65 65

187 Acrobat, Bicycle, Sea
Lion and Ball

2002. Europa. Circus. Multicoloured.
365 6d. Type **187** 65 65
366 36d. Circles, bicycle and ball 1·90 1·90

188
Championship
Emblem, Ball and
Player

2002. World Cup Football Championships, Japan and
South Korea.
367 **188** 6d. multicoloured 2·30 2·30

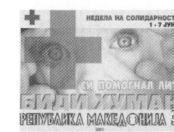

189 Red Cross and Face

2002. Obligatory Tax. Solidarity Week.
368 **189** 3d. multicoloured 65 65

190 Tree containing
Shapes

2002. Environment Protection.
369 **190** 6d. multicoloured 50 50

191 1595 Korenic
Neonic Coat of
Arms

2002. National Arms. Multicoloured.
370   10d. Type **191**   65   65
371   36d. 1620 Coat of Arms   1·90   1·90

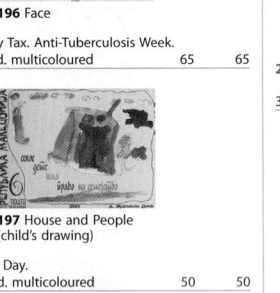

192 House, Krusevo

2002. City Architecture. Multicoloured.
372   36d. Type **192**   1·30   1·30
373   50d. House, Bitola   2·50   2·50

193 Metodija
Andonov-Cento

2002. Birth Centenary of Metodija Andonov-Cento (first
Macedonian president).
374   **193**   6d. multicoloured   50   50

194 Nikola Karev

2002. 125th Birth Anniv of Nikola Karev (revolutionary
leader).
375   **194**   18d. multicoloured   1·00   1·00

195 Grey Partridge (*Perdix
perdix*)

2002. Fauna. Multicoloured.
376   6d. Type **195**   25   25
377   12d. Wild Pig (*Sus scrofa*)   50   50
378   24d. Chamois (*Rupicapra
      rupicapra*)   1·00   1·00
379   36d. Rock Partridge (*Alectoris
      graeca*)   1·50   1·50

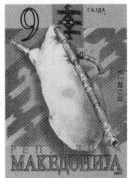

196 Face

2002. Obligatory Tax. Anti-Tuberculosis Week.
380   **196**   3d. multicoloured   65   65

197 House and People
(child's drawing)

2002. Children's Day.
381   **197**   6d. multicoloured   50   50

198 Mary and
Jesus
(14th-century icon)

2002. Christmas.
382   **198**   9d. multicoloured   50   50

199 Clock, Numbers and
Face

2002. Obligatory Tax. Anti-AIDS Week.
383   **199**   3d. multicoloured   65   65

200 Andreja Damjanov and
Building Facade

2003. 125th Death Anniv of Andreja Damjanov
(architect).
384   **200**   36d. multicoloured   1·90   1·90

201 Gajga

2003. Traditional Musical Instruments. Multicoloured.
385   9d. Type **201**   40   40
386   10d. Tambura   40   40
387   20d. Kemene   1·30   1·30
388   50d. Tapan   2·50   2·50

202 Scouts and Campsite

2003. 50th Anniv of Scouting in Macedonia.
389   **202**   9d. multicoloured   60   60

203 Face
surrounded by
Petals

2003. Obligatory Tax. Anti-Cancer Week.
390   **203**   4d. multicoloured   75   75

204 Krste Petkov Misirkov
(founder)

2003. 50th Anniv of Krste Petkov Misirkov Macedonian
Language Institute.
391   **204**   9d. multicoloured   60   60

205 Red Ribbon
with Red Cross and
Red Crescent
Emblems

2003. Obligatory Tax. Red Cross Week.
392   **205**   3d. multicoloured   75   75

206 International
Graphic Art
Triennial, Bitola
(1994)

2003. Europa. Poster Art. Multicoloured.
393   36d. Type **206**   2·30   2·30
394   36d. "Ohrider Sommer" (1966)   2·30   2·30

207 Outstretched
Hand

2003. Obligatory Tax. Solidarity Week. Litho.
395   **207**   4d. multicoloured   75   75

208 Brown Bear (*Ursus
arctos*)

2003.
396   **208**   9d. multicoloured   60   60

2003. City Architecture. As T **192**. Multicoloured.
397   10d. House, Skopje   60   60
398   20d. House, Resen   1·20   1·20

2003. National Arms. As T **191**. Multicoloured.
399   9d. 17th-century arms   60   60
400   36d. 1694 Coat of Arms   2·40   2·40

209 Handball Player

2003. World Youth Handball Championships.
401   **209**   36d. multicoloured   2·30   2·30

210 Seal and
Revolutionaries

2003. Centenary of Ilinden Uprising. Multicoloured.
402   9d. Type **210**   60   60
403   36d. Leaders and Mechen Ka-
      men monument   2·40   2·40
MS404 60×75 mm. 50d. Revolutionar-
    ies (different)   3·00   3·00

211 "Self Portrait" (Nikola
Martinovski)

2003. Artists' Anniversaries. Multicoloured.
405   9d. Type **211** (birth centenary)   60   60
406   36d. "Moulin de Galette" (Vin-
      cent van Gogh) (150th birth
      anniv) (horiz)   2·10   2·10

212 Stylized Figure

2003. Obligatory Tax. Anti-Tuberculosis Week.
407   **212**   4d. multicoloured   75   75

213 Colchicum
(*Colchicum
macedonicum*)

2003. Flowers. Multicoloured.
408   9d. Type **213**   80   80
409   20d. Viola (*Viola allchariensis*)   1·60   1·60
410   36d. *Tulipa mariannae*   2·75   2·75
411   50d. *Thymus oehmianus*   4·00   4·00

214 Said Najdeni

2003. Death Centenaries. Multicoloured.
412   9d. Type **214** (Albanian writer
      and reformer)   70   70
413   9d. Jeronim de Rada (Italian-
      Albanian writer)   70   70

215 Family
sheltering under
Umbrella

2003. Children's Day.
414   **215**   9d. multicoloured   1·00   1·00

216 Seal and Armed
Revolutionaries

2003. 125th Anniv of Kresna Uprising.
415   **216**   9d. multicoloured   1·00   1·00

217 Dimitir Vlahov

2003. 50th Death Anniv of Dimitir Vlahov (politician).
416   **217**   9d. multicoloured   1·00   1·00

218 Mary and Jesus (fresco)

2003. Christmas.
417   **218**   9d. multicoloured   1·00   1·00

219 Ribbon

2003. Obligatory Tax. Anti-AIDS Week.
418   **219**   4d. vermilion   1·00   1·00

220 19th-century
Jug, Smojmirovo

2003. Cultural Artifacts. Multicoloured.

419	3d. Amphora	40	40
420	3d. 18th-19th century lid-ded jug	40	40
421	4d. 19th century coffee pot (horiz)	50	50
422	5d. Tassel, Vrutok	60	60
423	5d. 20th century circular flask	60	60
424	6d. 18th–19th century jug and ewer	70	70
425	9d. Type **220**	80	80
426	10d. Kettle, Ohrid	80	80
427	10d. 18th–century hand-bell	80	80
428	12d. Albastron (alabaster incense pot)	1·00	1·00
429	12d. 18th–19th century pot with cover	1·40	1·40
430	20d. Chest decoration, Galicnik	2·30	2·30

221 Wilbur and Orville Wright and *Wright Flyer*

2003. Centenary of Powered Flight.

440	**221**	50d. multicoloured	3·75	3·75

222 Street Scene (Tomo Vladimirski)

2004. Artists' Birth Centenaries. Multicoloured.

441	9d. Type **222**	65	65
442	9d. Ohrid Street (Vangel Kodzoman)	65	65

223 Breast Examination

2004. Obligatory Tax. Anti-Cancer Week.

443	**223**	4d. multicoloured	1·00	1·00

224 Knives and Armour

2004. Cultural Heritage. Weapons. Multicoloured.

444	10d. Type **224**	1·00	1·00
445	20d. 19th-century sword	1·80	1·80
446	36d. 18th-century pistol	2·75	2·75
447	50d. 18th-century rifle	3·75	3·75

225 Carpet

2004. Traditional Carpets. Multicoloured.

448	36d. Type **225**	2·50	2·50
449	50d. Carpet (different)	3·75	3·75

226 Kostandin Kristoforidhi (writer)

2004. Centenary of Publication of First Albanian Dictionary in Macedonia.

450	**226**	36d. multicoloured	2·50	2·50

227 House, Kratovo

2004. City Architecture.

451	**227**	20d. multicoloured	1·50	1·50

228 Parasol and Woman Reading

2004. Europa. Holidays. Multicoloured.

452	50d. Type **228**	3·50	3·50
453	50d. Yacht and island	3·50	3·50

Nos. 452/3 were issued together, *se-tenant*, forming a composite design of a beach scene.

229 Profiles

2004. Obligatory Tax. Red Cross Week.

454	**229**	4d. multicoloured	1·00	1·00

230 Stars

2004. Application to join European Union.

455	**230**	36d. multicoloured	2·50	2·50

231 Hands enclosing Globe

2004. Obligatory Tax. Solidarity Week.

456	**231**	6d. multicoloured	1·00	1·00

232 Pelican and Lake

2004. Prespa National Park.

457	**232**	36d. multicoloured	2·50	2·50

233 Flags as Interlocking Rings

2004. Olympic Games, Athens. Multicoloured.

458	50d. Type **233**	3·50	3·50
459	50d. Rings (different)	3·50	3·50

Nos. 458/9 were issued together, *se-tenant*, forming a composite design of Olympic rings.

234 Sami Frasheri

2004. Death Centenary of Sami Frasheri (Albanian writer).

460	**234**	12d. multicoloured	1·00	1·00

235 Emblem, Feet and Ball

2004. Centenary of FIFA (Federation Internationale de Football Association).

461	**235**	100d. multicoloured	7·25	7·25

236 Marko Cepenkov

2004. Anniversaries. Multicoloured.

462	12d. Type **236** (writer) (175th birth)	1·00	1·00
463	12d. Vasil Glavinov (politician) (75th death) (vert)	1·00	1·00

237 Child blowing Bubbles

2004. Obligatory Tax. Anti-Tuberculosis Week.

464	**237**	4d. multicoloured	1·00	1·00

238 Bohemian Waxwing (*Bombycilla garrulous*)

2004. Birds. Multicoloured.

465	12d. Type **238**	1·00	1·00
466	24d. Woodchat shrike (*Lanius senato*)	2·10	2·10
467	36d. Rock thrush (*Monticola saxatilis*)	2·75	2·75
468	48d. Northern bullfinch (*Pyrrhula pyrrhula*)	4·00	4·00
MS469	86×61 mm. 60d. Wall creeper (*Tichodroma muraria*). Imperf	4·50	4·50

239 Children

2004. Children's Day.

470	**239**	12d. multicoloured	1·00	1·00

240 Binary Code

2004. World Summit on Information Technology Society (WSIS).

471	**240**	36d. multicoloured	2·50	2·50

241 Manuscript

2004. Millenary of Publication of Asseman Gospel (Glagolitic (early Slavonic language) liturgical gospel).

472	**241**	12d. multicoloured	1·00	1·00

242 Marco Polo

2004. 750th Birth Anniv of Marco Polo (traveller).

473	**242**	36d. multicoloured	2·50	2·50

243 Star, Ribbons, Snowflakes and Holly

2004. Christmas.

474	**243**	12d. multicoloured	1·00	1·00

244 Hands

2004. Obligatory Tax. AIDS Week.

475	**244**	6d. multicoloured	1·00	1·00

245 Konstantin Miladinov

2005. 175th Birth Anniv of Konstantin Miladinov (writer).

476	**245**	36d. multicoloured	2·50	2·50

246 Ash Tray

2005. Obligatory Tax. Anti-Cancer Week.

477	**246**	6d. multicoloured	1·00	1·00

247 Manuscript (16th–17th century)

2005. Illuminated Manuscripts. Multicoloured.

478	12d. Type **247**	1·00	1·00
479	24d. Illustration (16th century)	1·80	1·80

248 Embroidered Cloth (19th century)

2005. Embroidery. Multicoloured.

480	36d. Type **248**	2·50	2·50
481	50d. Embroidery (20th century)	3·75	3·75

249 Woman's Head
(sculpture) (Ivan Mestrovic)

2005. Art. Multicoloured.
482	**249**	36d. Type **249**	2·50	2·50
483		50d. Portrait of Woman (painting) (Paja Jovanovic) (horiz)	3·75	3·75

250 Fragment

2005. 450th Anniv of "The Missal" by Gjon Buzuku (first book written and published in Albanian).
484	**250**	12d. multicoloured	1·00	1·00

251 Skanderbeg

2005. 600th Birth Anniv of Gjergj Kastrioti (Skanderbeg) (Albanian leader).
485	**251**	36d. multicoloured	2·50	2·50

252 Henry Dunant (Red Cross founder)

2004. Obligatory Tax. Red Cross Week.
486	**252**	6d. multicoloured	1·00	1·00

253 Grain, Cake and Bread

2005. Europa. Gastronomy. Multicoloured.
487	**253**	36d. Type **253**	2·50	2·50
488		60d. Roasted meat with peppers	4·00	4·00

254 Building and Script

2005. Centenary of National Day of Vlachs (Aromanians) (imperial decree, issued by Ottoman Sultan Abdual Hamid II, which gave Vlachs their first collective rights).
489	**254**	12d. multicoloured	1·00	1·00

256 Globe as Tree

2005. Environmental Protection.
491	**256**	36d. multicoloured	2·50	2·50

257 Figure (16th century)

2005. Carvings. Multicoloured.
492		3d. Type **257**	20	20
493		4d. Ten-sided stars shape (15th century)	40	40
494		6d. Winged serpents (16th century)	60	60
495		8d. Diamond shaped design (1883–4)	80	80
496		12d. Figure, snake and animals (16th century)	1·00	1·00

258 Ford (1905)

2005. Transport Anniversaries. Multicoloured.
497		12d. Type **258** (centenary of first car)	1·00	1·00
498		36d. Glider (50th anniv of Macedonia aircraft)	2·50	2·50

259 Albert Einstein and Emblem

2005. International Year of Physics. Centenary of Publication of "Theory of Special Relativity".
499	**259**	60d. multicoloured	4·50	4·50

260 Cross of Lorraine

2005. Obligatory Tax. Anti-Tuberculosis Week.
500	**260**	6d. multicoloured	1·00	1·00

261 Malus (apples)

2005. Fruit. Multicoloured.
501		12d. Type **261**	1·00	1·00
502		24d. *Prunus persica* (peaches)	2·10	2·10
503		36d. *Prunus avium*	3·00	3·00
504		48d. *Prunus* (plums)	3·75	3·75
MS505	97×65 mm. 100d. *Pyrus* (pears) (vert)		7·25	7·25

262 Smolarski Waterfall

2005
506	**262**	24d. multicoloured	1·80	1·80

263 Hans Christian Andersen

2005. Birth Bicentenary of Hans Christian Andersen (writer).
507	**263**	12d. multicoloured	1·00	1·00

264 Kozjak Dam

2005
508	**264**	12d. multicoloured	1·00	1·00

265 "1880–8"

2005. 125th Anniv of Brsjai Rebellion.
509	**265**	12d. multicoloured	1·00	1·00

266 Delegates

2005. Centenary of Rila Congress.
510	**266**	12d. multicoloured	1·00	1·00

267 2002 36d. Stamp (as Type **187**)

2005. 50th Anniv of Europa Stamps. Multicoloured.
511	**267**	60d. Type **267**	4·00	4·00
512		170d. 1999 30d. stamp (as Type **122**)	11·50	11·50
513		250d. 1997 20d. stamp (as Type **85**)	17·00	17·00
514		350d. 1996 40d. stamp (as No. 153)	24·00	24·00
MS515	66×132 mm. Nos. 511/14		80·00	80·00

268 Candle

2005. Christmas. Litho.
516	**268**	12d. multicoloured	1·00	1·00

269 White Water Kayaking

2005
517	**269**	36d. multicoloured	2·75	2·75

270 Hand holding Condom

2005. Obligatory Tax. Anti-AIDS Week.
518	**270**	6d. multicoloured	1·00	1·00

271 Postal Emblem

2005
519	**271**	12d. multicoloured	1·00	1·00

272 Skier

2006. Winter Olympic Games, Turin. Multicoloured.
520		36d. Type **272**	2·50	2·50
521		60d. Ice hockey player	4·00	4·00

273 Woman examining Breast

2006. Obligatory Tax. Anti-Cancer Week.
522	**273**	6d. multicoloured	1·00	1·00

274 Fresco, Monastic Church, Matejce

2006. Cultural Heritage. Multicoloured.
523		12d. Type **274**	80	80
524		24d. Isaac Celebi Mosque, Bitola	1·60	1·60

275 Leopold Senghor

2006. Birth Centenary of Leopold Sedar Senghor (Senegalese politician).
525	**275**	36d. multicoloured	2·75	2·75

276 Wooden Pattens

2006. Craftwork. Mother of Pearl Inlays. Multicoloured.
526		12d. Type **276**	1·00	1·00
527		24d. Pipes	2·10	2·10

277 Woodcarving, Church of the Holy Saviour, Skopje

2006. Birth Bicentenary of Makarie Negriev Frckovski.
528	**277**	12d. multicoloured	1·00	1·00

278 Cupola

2006. 450th Anniv of Cupola, Church of St Peter, Rome.
529	**278**	36d. multicoloured	2·75	2·75

279 Zhivko Firfov

2006. Birth Centenary of Zhivko Firkov (composer).
530 **279** 24d. multicoloured 1·80 1·80

280 Mozart, Score and Violins

2006. 250th Birth Anniv of Wolfgang Amadeus Mozart (composer).
531 **280** 60d. multicoloured 4·50 4·50

281 Stylized Figure

2006. Obligatory Tax. Red Cross Week.
532 **281** 6d. multicoloured 1·00 1·00

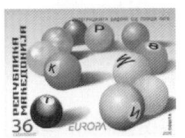

282 Coloured Balls

2006. Europa. Integration. Multicoloured.
533 36d. Type **282** 2·50 2·50
534 60d. Coloured building blocks 4·50 4·50

283 Pope John Paul II

2006. Tenth Anniv of Europa Stamps in Macedonia. Sheet 80×70 mm containing T **283** and similar vert design. Multicoloured.
MS535 60d.×2, Type **283**; Mother Teresa 8·75 8·75

284 Greenery running to Sand through Hourglass

2006. International Year of Deserts and Desertification.
536 **284** 12d. multicoloured 1·00 1·00

285 Chequered Flag

2006. Centenary of Grand Prix Motor Race.
537 **285** 36d. multicoloured 2·75 2·75

286 Nikola Tesla

2006. 150th Birth Anniv of Nikola Tesla (inventor).
538 **286** 24d. multicoloured 1·80 1·80

287 Santa Maria

2006. 500th Death Anniv of Christopher Columbus.
539 **287** 36d. multicoloured 2·75 2·75

288 Ancylus scalariformis

2006. Shells. Multicoloured.
540 12d. Type **288** 1·10 1·10
541 24d. Macedopyrgula pavlovici 2·00 2·00
542 36d. Gyraulus trapezoids 3·00 3·00
543 48d. Valvata hirsutecostata 4·00 4·00
MS544 80×70 mm. 72d. Ochridopyrgula macedonica 5·75 5·75

289 Child

2006. Obligatory Tax. Anti-Tuberculosis Week.
545 **289** 6d. multicoloured 1·00 1·00

290 Girl drawing

2006. 60th Anniv of UNICEF.
546 **290** 12d. multicoloured 1·00 1·00

291 National Park, Galicica

2006
547 **291** 24d. multicoloured 1·80 1·80

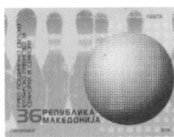

292 Ball and Pins

2006. World Ten-Pin Bowling Championship, Skopje.
548 **292** 36d. multicoloured 2·75 2·75

293 Frang Bardhi (author of the first Albanian dictionary)

2006. Personalities. Multicoloured.
549 12d. Type **293** 90 90
550 24d. Boris Trajkovski (president, 1999–2004) 90 90
551 36d. Mustafa Kemel Attaturk (founder of Turkish Republic) 2·00 2·00
552 48d. Dositheus II (Metropolitan of Macedonia) 2·00 2·00

294 Stars

2006. Christmas.
553 **294** 12d. multicoloured 1·00 1·00

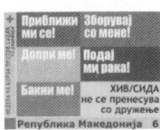

295 Emblem

2006. Obligatory Tax. Anti-AIDS Week.
554 **295** 6d. multicoloured 1·00 1·00

296 Carved Stone

2007. Kokino Megalithic Observatory. Multicoloured.
555 12d. Type **296** 90 90
556 36d. Sunrise 2·75 2·75

297 Slivnik Monastery (400th anniv)

2007. Monasteries' Anniversaries. Multicoloured.
557 12d. Type **297** 90 90
558 36d. St. Nikita (700th anniv) (vert) 2·75 2·75

298 18th–19th century Metal Cap

2007. Crafts. Multicoloured.
559 12d. Type **298** 90 90
560 36d. 19th century decorated box 2·75 2·75

299 Cobitis vardarensis

2006. Fish. Multicoloured.
561 12d. Type **299** 1·10 1·10
562 36d. Zingel balcanicus 2·75 2·75
563 60d. Chondrostoma vardarense 4·50 4·50
564 100d. Barbus macedonicus 7·50 7·50
MS565 60×71 mm. 100d. Leuciscus cephalus 7·50 7·50

299a Woman

2007. Obligatory Tax. Anti-Cancer Week.
565a **299a** 6d. multicoloured 1·00 1·00

300 "Epos of Freedom" (mosaic, detail) (Borko Lazeski)

2007. Art. Centenary of Cubism. Multicoloured.
566 36d. Type **300** 2·75 2·75
567 100d. "Head of a Woman" (Pablo Picasso) (vert) 7·50 7·50

301 Emblem and People talking

2007. International Day of Francophonie (organization of French speaking communities).
568 **301** 12d. multicoloured 1·00 1·00

302 Cat

2007. Pets.
569 **302** 12d. multicoloured 1·00 1·00

302a Hands and Globe

2007. Obligatory Tax. Red Cross Week.
569a **302a** 6d. multicoloured 1·00 1·00

303 Camp

2007. Europa. Centenary of Scouting. Multicoloured.
570 60d. Type **303** 5·00 5·00
571 100d. Scout (vert) 7·75 7·75
MS572 60×70 mm. 160d. Emblem 32·00 32·00

303a Fresco, Basilica of San Clemente (detail)

2007. 150th Anniv of Discovery of St Cyril's Grave.
572a **303a** 50d. multicoloured 1·00 1·00

304 Globe, Chimneys and Clock

2007. Pollution Awareness.
573 **304** 12d. multicoloured 1·00 1·00

305 Dimitri Ivanovich Mendeleev

2007. Scientific Personalities. Multicoloured.
574 36d. Type **305** (chemist and creator of first periodic tables) (death centenary) 3·00 3·00
575 36d. Carl von Linne (Linnaeus) (scientist and plant and animal classification deviser) (300th birth anniv) (vert) 3·00 3·00

306 NATO and EPAC Emblems

2007. Euro–Atlantic Security Forum, Ohrid.
576	**306**	60d. multicoloured	5·50	5·50

307 Yachts

2007. Centenary of Yacht Racing Union.
577	**307**	36d. multicoloured	3·00	3·00

308 Child and Dandelion

2007. Obligatory Tax. Anti-Tuberculosis Week.
578	**308**	6d. multicoloured	1·00	1·00

309 Maminska River Waterfall

2007. Natural Heritage.
579	**309**	12d. multicoloured	1·00	1·00

310 Dhimiter Pasko (Mitrush Kuteli)

2007. Personalities. Multicoloured.
580		12d. Type **310** (writer) (birth centenary)	1·00	1·00
581		12d. Theofan (Fan) Stilian Noli (nationalist) (125th birth anniv)	1·00	1·00

311 Drawings and Child

2007. Children's Day.
582	**311**	12d. multicoloured	1·00	1·00

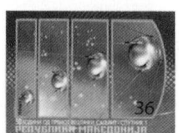

312 *Sputnik*

2007. 50th Anniv of Space Exploration.
583	**312**	36d. multicoloured	3·00	3·00

313 Petre Prlicko

2007. Petre Prlicko (actor) Commemoration.
584	**313**	12d. multicoloured	1·00	1·00

314 Jordan Dzinot

2007. Jordan Hadzi-Konstantinov Dzinot (educator) Commemoration.
585	**314**	12d. multicoloured	1·00	1·00

315 Textile

2007
586	**315**	12d. multicoloured	1·00	1·00

316 Santa Claus

2007. Christmas.
587	**316**	12d. multicoloured	1·00	1·00

317 AIDS Ribbon

2007. Obligatory Tax. Anti-AIDS Week.
588	**317**	6d. multicoloured	1·00	1·10

318 Tose Proeski

2007. Tose Proeski (singer) Commemoration.
589	**318**	12d. multicoloured	1·00	1·00

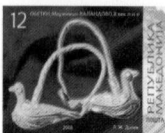

319 Earrings

2008. Cultural Heritage. Jewellery. Multicoloured.
590		12d. Type **319**	1·00	1·00
591		24d. Lion headed earring (vert)	2·00	2·00

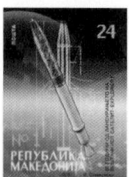

320 Launching of Satellite Explorer 1

2008. 50th Anniv of Space Exploration.
592	**320**	24d. multicoloured	2·50	2·50

321 Train

2008. Transportation.
593	**321**	100d. multicoloured	7·50	7·50

322 Child and Cigarette

2008. Obligatory Tax. Anti-Cancer Week.
594	**322**	6d. multicoloured	1·00	1·00

323 Hoopoe

2008. Hoopoe (*Upupa epops*). Multicoloured.
595		12d. Type **323**	1·00	1·00
596		24d. Head	2·00	2·00
597		48d. Facing left	3·75	3·75
598		60d. Facing right	5·00	5·00

324 Bull Dog

2008. Pets.
599	**324**	30d. multicoloured	2·30	2·30

325 Envelope and Globe

2008. Europa. The Letter. Multicoloured, background colours given.
600		50d. Type **325**	1·20	1·20
601		50d. Envelopes and globe	1·20	1·20
602		50d. As Type **325** (cobalt)	1·20	1·20
603		50d. As No. 601 (cobalt)	1·20	1·20
604		50d. As Type **325** (deep blue)	1·20	1·20
605		100d. As No. 601 (deep blue)	2·40	2·40

Nos. 600/1 602/3 and 604/5, respectively were printed together, *se-tenant*, each pair forming a composite design.

326 Stylized Figures and Globe as Jigsaw Puzzle

2008. Obligatory Tax. Red Cross Week.
606	**326**	6d. multicoloured	1·00	1·00

327 Robert Schuman (one of founders of EU)

2008. European Union. Multicoloured.
607		36d. Type **327**	3·00	3·00
608		50d. Eiffel Tower (horiz)	4·00	4·00
609		50d. Ljublijana (horiz)	4·00	4·00

329 Cupped Hands and Water

2008. Environmental Protection.
610	**328**	12d. multicoloured	3·75	3·75

328 Rudolf Diesel

2008. 150th Birth Anniv of Rudolf Diesel (German engineer and inventor of the diesel engine).
611	**329**	30d. multicoloured	8·00	8·00

330 Sailing

2008. Olympic Games, Beijing. Designs showing stylized athletes. Multicoloured.
612		12d. Type **330**	3·75	3·75
613		18d. Gymnastics	5·75	5·75
614		20d. Tennis	6·00	6·00
615		36d. Equestrian	6·50	6·50

331 Eqrem Cabej

2008. Birth Centenary of Eqrem Cabej.
616	**331**	12d. multicoloured	3·75	3·75

332 *Helichrysum zivojinii*

2008. Flora. Multicoloured.
617		1d. Type **332**	1·00	1·00
618		12d. *Pulsatilla halleri* (horiz)	1·00	1·00
619		50d. *Stachys* (horiz)	4·00	4·00
620		72d. *Fritillaria macedonica*	5·50	5·50
MS621		59×70 mm. 72d. *Centaurea grbavacensis*	5·50	5·50

333a Figure

2008. Obligatory Tax. TAX. Anti-Tuberculosis Week.
622a	**333a**	6d. multicoloured	1·90	1·90

334 Ubava Cave

2008
623	**334**	12d. multicoloured	1·00	1·00

335 Child and Jigsaw

2008. Children's Day.
624	**335**	12d. multicoloured	1·00	1·00

336 Stylized Players

2008. European Women's Handball Championship, Macedonia.
625	**336**	30d. multicoloured	2·40	2·40

337 Annotation

2008. 700th Anniv of Eucharistic Song by Saint John Kukuzel.

| 626 | **337** | 12d. multicoloured | 1·00 | 1·00 |

338 Giacomo Puccini and Score

2008. 150th Birth Anniv of Giacomo Puccini (composer).

| 627 | **338** | 100d. multicoloured | 6·75 | 6·75 |

339 Kosta Racin

2008. Birth Centenary of Kosta Solev (Kosta Racin) (revolutionary and poet).

| 628 | **339** | 12d. multicoloured | 1·00 | 1·00 |

No. 629 and Type **340** are left for Centenary of Congress of Monastir (to decide on the use of Latin script for written Albanian), issued on 14 November 2008, not yet received.

341 Baubles

2008. Christmas and New Year.

| 630 | **341** | 12d. multicoloured | 1·00 | 1·00 |

341a Emblem

2008. Obligatory Tax. Anti-Cancer Week.

| 630a | **341a** | 6d. multicoloured | 1·00 | 1·00 |

342 Street, Ohrid

2008. Architecture.

631	**342**	12d. brown, salmon and black	1·10	1·10
632	–	12d. indigo, new blue and black	1·10	1·10
633	–	12d. indigo, greenish slate and black	1·10	1·10
634	–	12d. deep yellow-green and scarlet-vermilion	1·10	1·10
635	–	12d. black and bright green	1·10	1·10

DESIGNS: 631 Type **342**; 632 Street, Bitola; 633 Bridge, Skopje; 634 Building, Tetobo; 635 Building, Stip.

343 Lech Walesa

2008. Macedonia–Poland Friendship.

| 636 | **343** | 50d. multicoloured | 3·75 | 3·75 |

343a St. Sava

2008

| 636a | **343a** | 12d. multicoloured | 1·00 | 1·00 |

344 Anvil

2009. Cultural Heritage. Multicoloured.

| 637 | | 10d. Type **344** | 1·00 | 1·00 |
| 638 | | 20d. Hand made horse shoe | 1·90 | 1·90 |

345 Yuri Gagarin

2009. 75th Birth Anniv of Yuri Alekseyevich Gagarin (cosmonaut and first man in space).

| 639 | **345** | 50d. multicoloured | 3·75 | 3·75 |

345a Figure

2009. Obligatory Tax. AIDS Awareness Week.

| 639a | **345a** | 6d. multicoloured | 1·00 | 1·00 |

346 Diana, the Huntress

2009. Breast Cancer Awareness.

| 640 | **346** | 15d. multicoloured | 1·70 | 1·70 |

DESIGN: As Type **2342** of USA.

347 Trajko Prokopiev and Todor Skalovski

2009. Composers Anniversaries. Multicoloured.

| 641 | | 12d. Type **347** (birth centenaries) | 1·10 | 1·10 |
| 642 | | 60d. George Frideric Handel (150th death anniv) and Franz Josef Haydn (death bicentenary) | 4·50 | 4·50 |

348 Chestnut

2009. Horses. Multicoloured.

| 643 | | 20d. Type **348** | 7·00 | 7·00 |
| 644 | | 50d. Bay cantering | 17·00 | 17·00 |

348a Battle

2009. Obligatory Tax. 150th Anniv of Battle of Solferino (witnessed by Henry Dunant who instigated campaign resulting in establishment of Geneva Conventions and Red Cross).

| 644a | **348a** | 6d. multicoloured | 1·00 | 1·00 |

349 Macedonian Folklore Constellations (hen and chicks)

2009. Europa. Astronomy. Multicoloured.

645		50d. Type **349**	7·00	7·00
646		100d. Macedonian folklore constellations (plough)	13·00	13·00
MS647		57×77 mm 150d. Macedonian folklore constellations (rooster) (vert)	20·00	20·00

350 Prague

2009. Macedonia in Europe. Multicoloured.

| 648 | | 10d. Type **350** | 1·00 | 1·00 |
| 649 | | 60d. Pippi Longstocking (Swedish children's book character) and European flag (vert) | 4·50 | 4·50 |

351 Vrelo

2009. Caves.

| 650 | **351** | 12d. multicoloured | 1·00 | 1·00 |

352 Charles Darwin (evolutionary theorist) and Anthropoid Progress

2009. Science. Birth Bicentenaries.

| 651 | | 18d. multicoloured | 1·10 | 1·10 |
| 652 | | 18d. black, scarlet-vermilion and orange | 1·10 | 1·10 |

DESIGNS: 651 Type **352**; 652 Louis Braille (inventor of Braille writing for the blind) and Braille letters.

353 Galeb

2009

| 653 | **353** | 18d. multicoloured | 1·10 | 1·10 |

354 Ship's Prow

2009

| 654 | **354** | 18d. multicoloured | 1·10 | 1·10 |

355 Bell Tower, Prilep

2009. Cities.

| 655 | **355** | 18d. brown-purple, azure and black | 1·10 | 1·10 |

2009. Cities. As T **355**. Grey-black, dull orange and black.

| 656 | | 16d. Town Hall, Strumica | 1·10 | 1·10 |

356 Player, Emblem and Flag

2009. Centenary of Football in Macedonia.

| 657 | **356** | 18d. multicoloured | 1·10 | 1·10 |

357 Cyclist

2009. Centenary of Giro d'Italia (cycle race). Multicoloured.

| 658 | | 18d. Type **357** | 1·10 | 1·10 |
| 659 | | 18d. Chain wheel and pedal (horiz) | 1·10 | 1·10 |

358 Pelobates syriacus balcanicus (Balkan spadefoot toad)

2009. Fauna. Multicoloured.

660		2d. Type **358**	1·00	1·00
661		3d. Salmo letnica (ohrid trout)	1·00	1·00
662		6d. Austropotamobius torrentium macedonicus (Macedonian stone crab)	1·00	1·00
663		8d. Triturus macedonicus (Macedonian crested newt)	1·00	1·00
MS664		60×70 mm. 100d. Dr. Stanko Karaman and crustaceans (vert)	2·20	2·20

358a Stethoscope and Lungs

2009. OBLIGATORY TAX. Anti-Tuberculosis Week

| 665 | **358a** | 6d. multicoloured | 1·00 | 1·00 |

359 Paintings

2009. 150th Birth Anniv of Dimitar Andonov Papradishki (artist).

| 666 | **359** | 16d. multicoloured | 1·10 | 1·10 |

360 Charter

2009. Centenary of Elbasan High School

| 667 | **360** | 16d. multicoloured | 1·00 | 1·00 |

361 Filip Shiroka

2008. 150th Birth Anniv of Filip Shiroka (poet).

| 668 | **361** | 16d. multicoloured | 1·10 | 1·10 |

362 Krume Kepeski

2009. Birth Centenary of Krume Kepeski (linguist).

| 669 | **362** | 16d. multicoloured | 1·10 | 1·10 |

363 Petre M. Andreevski

2009. 75th Birth Anniv of Petre M. Andreevski (poet, novelist, short story writer and playwright).

| 670 | **363** | 16d. multicoloured | 1·10 | 1·10 |

2009. Cities. Vert designs as T **355**.

671	16d. olive-green and turquoise-blue	1·40	1·40
672	16d. orange-brown and dull ultramarine	1·40	1·40
673	16d. deep turquoise-green and bistre-brown	1·40	1·40
674	16d. dull ultramarine and bright crimson	1·40	1·40
675	16d. olive-sepia and black	1·60	1·60
676	16d. orange-brown and black	1·60	1·60

Designs: 671 Kicevo; 672 Gostivar; 673 Delcevo; 674 Struga; 675 Kumanovo; 676 Resen

364 The Nativity

2009. Christmas

| 677 | **364** | 16d. multicoloured | 1·50 | 1·50 |

365 Profiles and Emblem

2009. OBLIGATORY TAX. AIDS Awareness Week

| 678 | **365** | 8d. muulticoloured | 1·00 | 1·00 |

366 Helicopter

2010. Transport

| 679 | **366** | 50d. multicoloured | 3·75 | 3·75 |

367 Ski Jump and Stone Emblem

2010. Winter Olympic Games, Vancouver. Multicoloured.

| 680 | **367** | 50d. Type **367** | 3·75 | 3·75 |
| 681 | | 100d. Hockey and emblem | 6·50 | 6·50 |

367a Profile, Hands and Emblem

2010. OBLIGATORY TAX. AIDS Awareness Week

| 681a | **367a** | 8d. multicoloured | 1·00 | 1·00 |

368 Deep Pink Peony

2010. Centenary of International Women's Day. Multicoloured.

| **MS**682 | 18d.×2, Type **368**; Pale pink peony from below | 2·40 | 2·40 |

369 Frescoes

2010. 650th Anniv of St Peter's Church, Golem Grad

| 683 | **369** | 18d. multicoloured | 1·20 | 1·20 |

370 Budgerigar

2010. Pets. Birds. Multicoloured.

| 684 | 20d. Type **370** | 1·40 | 1·40 |
| 685 | 40d. Macaw (horiz) | 2·75 | 2·75 |

370a Globe and Symbols of Habitation

2010. OBLIGATORY TAX. Red Cross–Urban Life

| 685a | **370a** | 8d. multicoloured | 1·00 | 1·00 |

371 Peter Pan

2010. Europa

| 686 | **371** | 100d. multicoloured | 6·50 | 6·50 |

372 Map of Europe and Silhouettes

2010. Macedonian Chairmanship of Council of Europe

| 687 | **372** | 18d. multicoloured | 1·50 | 1·50 |

373 EU Headquarters, Brussels

2010. European Union. Cities

| 688 | 20d. Type **373** | 1·75 | 1·75 |
| 689 | 50d. Palacio de Comunicaciones, Madrid | 4·50 | 4·50 |

2010. Cities. Vert designs as T **355**. Multicoloured.

689a	16d. House, Debar	1·90	1·90
689b	16d. Terrace, Gevgelija	1·90	1·90
689c	16d. Bridge, Kratovo	1·90	1·90
689d	18d. Clock Tower, Veles	1·90	1·90
689e	18d. House, Kruševo	1·90	1·90

374 Chestnut and Tree

2010. Environmental Protection. Sweet Chestnut (*Castanea sativa*)

| 690 | **374** | 20d. muulticoloured | 1·75 | 1·75 |

375 Robert Schumann, Piano Keys and Musical Score

2010. Birth Bicentenary of Robert Alexander Schumann (composer)

| 691 | **375** | 50d. black, azure and orange-vermilion | 4·50 | 4·50 |

376 Frédéric Chopin

2010. Birth Bicentenary of Frédéric François Chopin (composer)

| 692 | **376** | 60d. multicoloured | 4·50 | 4·50 |

377 Football in Net

2010. World Cup Football Championships, South Africa. Multicoloured.

693	693	Type **377**	4·50	4·50
694		100d. Football on centre line (vert)	8·00	8·00
MS695	70×60 mm. 150d. Championship emblem and football	12·00	12·00

378 Church St. Sophia, Ohrid

2010. 50th Ohrid Summer Festival

| 696 | **378** | 18d. multicoloured | 1·50 | 1·50 |

379 Mother Teresa

2010. Birth Centenary of Mother Teresa (Agnes Gonxha Bojaxhiu) (founder of Missionaries of Charity in Calcutta)

| 697 | **379** | 60d. multicoloured | 4·75 | 4·75 |

380 Crescent Moon and Mosque

2010. Bayram Festival

| 698 | **380** | 50d. multicoloured | 4·25 | 4·25 |

381 *Chara ohridana* (algae)

2010. Flora and Fauna of Lake Ohrid. Multicoloured.

699	18d. Type **381**	1·75	1·75
700	20d. *Gocea ohridana* (water snail)	2·00	2·00
701	44d. *Surirella spiralis* (algae)	3·25	3·25
702	100d. *Ochridaspongia Arndt* (sponge)	8·25	8·25

382 Laurel Wreath and Hand writing Poem

2010. 150th Anniv of Award of Laurel Wreath to Grigor Prlicev (first prize for best poem in literary competition held every year in Athens) for his Poem

| 703 | **382** | 100d. multicoloured | 8·00 | 8·00 |

383 Joyful Figures

2010. OBLIGATORY TAX. Anti-Tuberculosis Week

| 704 | **383** | 8d. multicoloured | 1·00 | 1·00 |

384 Henry Dunant

2010. Death Centenary of Henry Dunant (instigator of Red Cross movement)

| 705 | **384** | 10d. scarlet-vermilion and black | 1·50 | 1·50 |

385 Jacques Cousteau

2010. Birth Centenary of Jacques-Yves Cousteau (marine explorer, ecologist, filmmaker, and writer)

| 706 | **385** | 20d. multicoloured | 1·50 | 1·50 |

386 Robert Koch

2010. Death Centenary of Heinrich Hermann Robert Koch (isolator of anthrax, cholera and TB bacilli and winner of 1905, Nobel Prize for Medicine)

| 707 | **386** | 20d. multicoloured | 1·50 | 1·50 |

387 St Naum (icon)

2010. 1100th Death Anniv of St. Naum of Ohrid (educator and one of founders of Macedonian Orthodox Church)
708 **387** 18d. multicoloured   1·50   1·50

388 Dimitar Miladinov

2010. Birth Bicentenary of Dimitar Miladinov (poet and folklorist)
709 **388** 18d. multicoloured   1·50   1·50

389 Skyline, Family and Voting Form

2010. 20th Anniv of Multi-Party Elections
710 **389** 16d. multicoloured   1·50   1·50

390 Marin Barleti

2010. 550th Birth Anniv of Marin Barleti (historian and Catholic priest)
711 **390** 20d. multicoloured   1·50   1·50

391 Seated Figure

2010. Birth Centenary of Dimce Koco (artist)
712 **391** 50d. multicoloured   3·75   3·75

392 Emaciated Figures

2010. Birth Centenary of Dimo Todorovski (sculptor)
713 **392** 50d. multicoloured   3·75   3·75

393 Christmas Baskets

2010. Christmas
714 **393** 16d. multicoloured   1·50   1·50

2010. OBLIGATORY TAX. AIDS Awareness Week
714a **393a** 8d. multicoloured   90   90

2010. Cities. Vert designs as T **355**. Multicoloured.
715   16d. Kavadarci   1·90   1·80
716   16d. Kriva Planka   1·90   1·80
717   16d. Negotin   1·90   1·80
718   16d. Probištip   1·90   1·80
719   18d Koščani   1·90   1·80
720   18d Radoviš (horiz)   1·90   1·80
721   18d Sveti Nikole   1·90   1·80

394 Prince Konstantin Dragaš Coin, 1371-1395

2011. Cultural Heritage. Coins
722 **394** 50d. multicoloured   3·50   3·50

394a Face, Flower and AIDS Ribbon

2011. OBLIGATORY TAX. AIDS Awareness Week
722a **394a** 8d. multicoloured   90   90

395 Space Walk

2011. 50th Anniv of First Manned Space Flight
723 **395** 40d. multicoloured   3·50   3·50

396 Menorah

2011. Holocaust Memorial Center for Jews of Macedonia, Skopje
724 **396** 100d. ultramarine, chrome yellow and black   7·75   7·75

397 Karaman (Macedonian shepherd dog)

2011. Pets. Dog
725 **397** 50d. multicoloured   3·75   3·75

398 Princess Diana

2011. 50th Birth Anniv of Princess Diana
726 **398** 100d. multicoloured   8·25   8·25

399 Distillation and Periodic Tables

2011. International Year of Chemistry
727 **399** 60d. multicoloured   5·00   5·00

400 Benz Patent-Motorwagen, 1886

2011. Transport. 125th Anniv of First Automobile (20d.) or Centenary of First Automobile in Skopje (70d.). Multicoloured.
728   20d. Type **400**   1·75   1·75
729   70d. First car in Skopje (vert)   5·75   5·75

401 James Watt and Low-pressure Steam Engine

2011. Science. 275th Birth Anniv of James Watt
730 **401** 40d. multicoloured   5·00   5·00

402 Warsaw

2011. Macedonia in EU. Multicoloured.
731   40d. Type **402**   3·50   3·50
732   40d. Budapest   3·50   3·50

403 Woods in Autumn

2011. Europa. Forests. Multicoloured.
733   50d. Type **403**   2·75   2·75
734   100d. Woods in winter   5·75   5·75
MS735 70×60 mm. 100d. Woods in spring   12·00   12·00

404 Heart-shaped Labyrinth containing Red Cross

2011. OBLIGATORY TAX. Red Cross
736 **404** 8d. scarlet-vermilion and black   90   90

405 Front Page of Shkupi

2011. Centenary of *Shkupi* Newspaper
737 **405** 60d. multicoloured   5·00   5·00

406 Book

2011. 50th Anniv of Poetry Evenings
738 **406** 40d. multicoloured   3·50   3·50

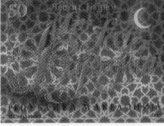

407 Emperor Justinian

2011. 60th Anniv of Faculty of Law. Sheet 110×42 mm
MS739 **407** 100d. multicoloured   8·25   8·25

408 Emblem

2011. Bayram Festival
740 **408** 50d. multicoloured   3·50   3·50

No. 741 and Type **409** are left for Basketball Championships, issued on 31 August 2011, not yet received.

410 Sunrise

2011. 20th Anniv of Independence
742 **410** 20d. multicoloured   1·75   1·75

No. 743 and Type **411** are left for Birth Centenary of L. Belogaski, issued on 14 September 2011, not yet received.

No. 744 and Type **412** are left for Birth Bicentenary of Liszt, issued on 21 September 2011, not yet received.

413 Ernest Hemingway

2011. 50th Death Anniv of Ernest Miller Hemingway (writer)
745 **413** 50d. multicoloured   3·75   3·75

414 Migjeni

2011. Birth Centenary of Millosh Gjergj Nikolla (Migjeni) (writer)
746 **414** 20d. multicoloured   1·75   1·75

415 Archbishop Angelarios

2011. Birth Centenary of Archbishop Angelarios
747 **415** 40d. multicoloured   3·50   3·50

Pt. 6

MADAGASCAR

A large island in the Indian Ocean off the east coast of Africa. French Post Offices operated there from 1885.

In 1896 the island was declared a French colony, absorbing Diego-Suarez and Ste. Marie de Madagascar in 1898 and Nossi-Be in 1901.

Madagascar became autonomous as the Malagasy Republic in 1958; it reverted to the name of Madagascar in 1992.

100 centimes = 1 franc.
2005 5 old francs = 1 ariary.

A. FRENCH POST OFFICES

1889. Stamps of French Colonies "Commerce" type surch with value in figures.

1	J	05 on 10c. black on lilac	£600	£200
2	J	05 on 25c. black on red	£600	£200
4	J	05 on 40c. red on yellow	£170	£120
5	J	5 on 10c. black on lilac	£200	£130
6	J	5 on 25c. black on red	£200	£140
7	J	15 on 25c. black on red	£160	£120
3	J	25 on 40c. red on yellow	£550	£180

5

1891. No gum. Imperf.

9	5	5c. black on green	£170	18·00
10	5	10c. black on blue	£130	32·00
11	5	15c. blue on blue	£130	28·00
12	5	25c. brown on buff	50·00	16·00
13	5	1f. black on yellow	£1100	£275
14	5	5f. black and lilac on lilac	£2250	£900

1895. Stamps of France optd **POSTE FRANCAISE Madagascar**.

15	10	5c. green	7·25	4·50
16	10	10c. black on lilac	50·00	55·00
17	10	15c. blue	75·00	11·00
18	10	25c. black on red	75·00	7·25
19	10	40c. red on yellow	60·00	14·50
20	10	50c. red	£130	19·00
21	10	75c. brown on orange	£130	65·00
22	10	1f. olive	£130	55·00
23	10	5f. mauve on lilac	£170	£100

1896. Stamps of France surch with value in figures in oval.

29	5c. on 1c. black on blue	£6000	£2250
30	15c. on 2c. brown on yellow	£2250	£1000
31	25c. on 3c. grey	£3250	£1100
32	25c. on 4c. red on grey	£6500	£1800
33	25c. on 40c. red on yellow	£1400	£800

B. FRENCH COLONY OF MADAGASCAR AND DEPENDENCIES

1896. "Tablet" key-type inscr "MADAGASCAR ET DEPENDANCES".

1	D	1c. black and red on blue	1·40	1·00
2	D	2c. brown and blue on buff	1·20	1·20
2a	D	2c. brown & blk on buff	16·00	18·00
3	D	4c. brown and blue on grey	1·40	1·80
17	D	5c. green and red	5·75	30
6	D	10c. black and blue on lilac	19·00	1·50
18	D	10c. red and blue	5·00	30
7	D	15c. blue and red	23·00	1·30
19	D	15c. grey and red	6·25	65
8	D	20c. red and blue on green	8·00	1·90
9	D	25c. black and red on pink	16·00	20
20	D	25c. blue and red	42·00	65·00
10	D	30c. brown & bl on drab	10·00	2·75
21	D	35c. black and red on yellow	65·00	3·50
11	D	40c. red and blue on yellow	9·25	1·30
12	D	50c. red and blue on pink	24·00	1·60
22	D	50c. brown and red on blue	50·00	60·00
13	D	75c. violet & red on orge	2·75	4·50
14	D	1f. green and red	24·00	2·50
15	D	1f. green and blue	50·00	42·00
16	D	5f. mauve and blue on lilac	60·00	65·00

1902. "Tablet" key-type stamps as above surch.

27	0.01 on 2c. brown and blue on buff	10·00	9·75
27a	0.01 on 2c. brown and black on buff	9·00	23·00
29	0.05 on 30c. brown and blue on drab	6·00	6·50
23	05 on 50c. red and blue on pink	3·25	2·75
31	0.10 on 50c. red and blue on pink	3·50	4·50
24	10 on 5f. mauve and blue on lilac	22·00	10·00
32	0.15 on 75c. violet and red on orange	1·70	1·80
33	0.15 on 1f. green and red	4·00	3·00
25	15 on 1f. green and red	3·00	1·90

1902. Nos. 59 and 61 of Diego-Suarez surch.

34	0.05 on 30c. brown and blue on drab	£140	£140
36	0.10 on 50c. red and blue on pink	£5000	£5000

4 Zebu and Lemur

1903

38	4	1c. purple	90	20
39	4	2c. brown	55	25
40	4	4c. brown	65	80
41	4	5c. green	8·25	30
42	4	10c. red	12·00	35
43	4	15c. red	19·00	45
44	4	20c. orange	2·75	1·20
45	4	25c. blue	46·00	2·30
46	4	30c. red	55·00	13·00
47	4	40c. lilac	60·00	4·00
48	4	50c. brown	75·00	30·00
49	4	75c. yellow	70·00	27·00
50	4	1f. green	70·00	60·00
51	4	2f. blue	85·00	40·00
52	4	5f. black	75·00	£120

5 Transport in Madagascar

1908

53a	5	1c. green and violet	35	50
54	5	2c. green and red	10	35
55	5	4c. brown and green	80	1·30
56	5	5c. olive and green	3·00	35
90	5	5c. red and black	85	1·30
57	5	10c. brown and pink	3·25	30
91	5	10c. olive and green	75	1·10
92	5	10c. purple and brown	40	90
58	5	15c. red and lilac	90	60
93	5	15c. green and olive	1·00	4·25
94	5	15c. red and blue	1·00	9·50
59	5	20c. brown and orange	1·70	1·50
60	5	25c. black and blue	9·25	90
95	5	25c. black and violet	1·80	35
61	5	30c. black and brown	8·50	9·50
96	5	30c. brown and red	1·50	2·00
97	5	30c. purple and green	1·00	65
98	5	30c. light green and green	4·25	7·50
62	5	35c. black and red	2·75	1·60
63	5	40c. black and brown	2·00	1·60
64	5	45c. black and green	1·90	4·00
99	5	45c. red and scarlet	1·10	2·75
100	5	45c. purple and lilac	4·50	6·50
65	5	50c. black and violet	1·00	1·30
101	5	50c. black and blue	1·00	50
102	5	50c. yellow and black	1·10	35
103	5	60c. violet on pink	1·20	2·30
104	5	65c. blue and black	2·50	4·50
66	5	75c. black and red	1·80	1·40
105	5	85c. red and green	2·75	8·50
67	5	1f. green and brown	1·00	45
106	5	1f. blue	90	1·60
107	5	1f. green and mauve	11·50	22·00
108	5	1f.10 green and brown	2·30	4·75
68	5	2f. green and blue	4·25	1·80
69	5	5f. brown and violet	16·00	20·00

1912. "Tablet" key-type surch.

70A	D	05 on 15c. grey and red	45	70
71A	D	05 on 20c. red and blue on green	90	1·60
72A	D	05 on 30c. brown and blue on drab	1·40	5·50
73A	D	10 on 75c. violet and red on orange	3·75	36·00
81	D	0.60 on 75c. violet and red on orange	20·00	28·00
82	D	1f. on 5f. mauve and blue on lilac	1·70	3·00

1912. Surch.

74	4	05 on 2c. brown	70	6·50
75	4	05 on 20c. orange	75	1·60
76	4	05 on 30c. red	90	4·00
77	4	10 on 40c. lilac	1·50	6·25
78	4	10 on 50c. brown	2·00	5·50
79	4	10 on 75c. brown	5·00	28·00
83	4	1f. on 5f. black	£130	£130

1915. Surch **5c** and red cross.

80	5	10c.+5c. brown and pink	1·20	2·75

1921. Surch **1 cent**.

84	1c. on 15c. red and lilac	35	2·75

1921. Type **5** (some colours changed) surch.

109	25c. on 15c. red and lilac	1·00	7·50
85	0.25 on 35c. black and red	11·50	17·00
86	0.25 on 40c. black and brown	7·00	8·00
87	0.25 on 45c. black and green	5·00	11·50
111	25c. on 2f. green and blue	1·90	1·80
112	25c. on 5f. brown and violet	70	7·25
88	0.30 on 40c. black and brown	1·70	3·25
113	50c. on 1f. green and brown	2·00	45
89	0.60 on 75c. black and red	5·00	7·25
114	60 on 75c. violet on pink	55	45
115	65c. on 75c. black and red	2·75	7·50
116	85c. on 45c. black and green	2·50	7·75
117	90c. on 75c. pink and red	75	2·30
118	1f.25 on 1f. blue	1·20	4·25
119	1f.50 on 1f. lt blue & blue	2·75	20
120	3f. on 5f. violet and green	3·25	4·00
121	10f. on 5f. mauve and red	9·75	10·50
122	20f. on 5f. blue and mauve	14·00	9·75

14 Sakalava Chief

15 Zebus

17 Betsileo Woman

18 General Gallieni

1930

123	18	1c. blue	80	3·00
124	15	1c. green and blue	20	35
125	14	2c. brown and red	20	1·20
177	18	3c. blue	35	3·00
126a	14	4c. mauve and brown	90	80
127	15	5c. red and green	50	35
128	-	10c. green and red	45	35
129	17	15c. red	50	35
130	15	20c. blue and brown	55	75
131	-	25c. brown and lilac	70	10
132	17	30c. green	55	1·30
133	14	40c. red and green	75	30
134	17	45c. lilac	2·75	3·25
178	18	45c. green	1·20	2·75
179	18	50c. brown	65	10
180	18	60c. mauve	10	4·00
136a	15	65c. mauve and brown	2·25	10
181	18	70c. red	2·30	5·50
137	17	75c. brown	2·75	50
138	15	90c. red	4·25	1·70
182	18	90c. brown	60	45
139	-	1f. blue and brown	4·00	2·75
140	-	1f. red and scarlet	1·40	1·50
140a	-	1f.25 brown and blue	4·50	2·00
183	18	1f.40 orange	3·00	7·25
141	14	1f.50 ultramarine and blue	9·75	55
142	14	1f.50 red and brown	1·80	1·60
278	14	1f.50 brown and red	40	2·50
184	18	1f.60 violet	2·75	7·00
143	14	1f.75 red and brown	7·50	75
185	18	2f. red	1·20	55
186a	18	3f. green	1·10	2·75
146	14	5f. brown and mauve	3·00	3·75
147	18	10f. orange	10·00	8·50
148	14	20f. blue and brown	3·75	10·00

DESIGN—VERT: 10c., 25c., 1f., 1f.25, Hova girl.

1931. "Colonial Exhibition" key-types inscr "MADAGASCAR".

149	E	40c. black and green	4·00	4·75
150	F	50c. black and mauve	4·50	5·00
151	G	90c. black and red	3·00	4·75
152	H	1f.50 black and blue	4·25	4·00

19 Bloch 120 over Madagascar

1935. Air.

153	19	50c. red and green	3·00	3·00
154	19	90c. red and green	1·10	7·25
155	19	1f.25 red and lake	3·50	5·50
156	19	1f.50 red and blue	2·75	3·50
157	19	1f.60 red and blue	1·20	6·00
158	19	1f.75 red and orange	14·50	6·00
159	19	2f. red and blue	3·25	3·50
160	19	3f. red and orange	1·20	2·75
161	19	3f.65 red and black	1·90	1·70
162	19	3f.90 red and green	80	4·50
163	19	4f. red and carmine	50·00	4·25
164	19	4f.50 red and black	20·00	2·00
165	19	5f.50 red and green	1·00	5·25
166	19	6f. red and mauve	1·00	3·25
167	19	6f.90 red and purple	85	3·50
168	19	8f. red and mauve	3·75	7·25
169	19	8f.50 red and green	4·00	5·25
170	19	9f. red and green	1·20	4·00
171	19	12f. red and brown	65	3·00
172	19	12f.50 red and violet	3·50	7·75
173	19	15f. red and orange	65	3·00
174	19	16f. red and green	3·75	9·25
175	19	20f. red and brown	6·50	8·25
176	19	50f. red and blue	8·25	17·00

1937. International Exhibition, Paris. As T **12a** of Ivory Coast.

187	20c. violet	1·40	4·00
188	30c. green	1·80	4·50
189	40c. red	90	1·80
190	50c. brown and agate	45	75
191	90c. red	55	2·00
192	1f.50 blue	55	2·00
MS192a	120×100 mm. 3f. red (as No. 139). Imperf	18·00	40·00

20 J. Laborde and Tananarivo Palace

1938. 60th Death Anniv of Jean Laborde (explorer).

193	20	35c. green	1·20	1·50
194	20	55c. violet	85	1·30
195	20	65c. red	1·90	50
196	20	80c. purple	1·00	75
197	20	1f. red	1·30	60
198	20	1f.25 red	2·30	7·00
199	20	1f.75 blue	75	1·10
200	20	2f.15 brown	2·75	5·50
201	20	2f.25 blue	2·00	5·25
202	20	2f.50 brown	90	90
203	20	10f. green	75	2·30

1938. Int Anti-cancer Fund. As T **16a** of Ivory Coast.

204	1f.75+50c. blue	6·50	21·00

1939. New York World's Fair. As T **16c** of Ivory Coast.

205	1f.25 red	2·00	2·00
206	2f.25 blue	2·30	3·00

1939. 150th Anniv of French Revolution. As T **16d** of Ivory Coast.

207	45c.+25c. green and black (postage)	9·25	25·00
208	70c.+30c. brown and black	9·25	25·00
209	90c.+35c. orange and black	9·25	25·00
210	1f.25+1f. red and black	9·25	25·00
211	2f.25+2f. blue and black	9·25	25·00
212	4f.50+4f. black and orange (air)	18·00	42·00

1942. Surch **50** and bars.

213	15	50 on 65c. mauve and brown	5·25	65

1942. Free French Administration. Optd **FRANCE LIBRE** or surch also.

214	14	2c. brown and red (postage)	4·00	7·25
215	18	3c. blue	£130	£130
216	15	0.05 on 1c. green and blue	1·80	2·50

217	20	0.10 on 55c. violet	90	7·75
218	17	15c. red	27·00	36·00
219	20	0.30 on 65c. red	1·00	4·50
220	15	0f.50 on 0.05 on 1c. green and blue	2·30	8·00
221	15	50 on 65c. mauve and brown	1·40	10
222	18	50 on 90c. brown	1·70	45
223	15	65c. mauve and brown	4·75	8·25
224	18	70c. red	2·75	7·00
225	20	80c. purple	5·75	9·00
226	-	1.00 on 1f.25 brown and blue (No. 140a)	5·00	6·25
227	20	1.00 on 1f.25 red	11·00	13·50
228	18	1f.40 orange	4·25	6·75
229	5	1f.50 on 1f. blue	4·00	4·50
230	14	1f.50 ultramarine and blue	3·00	6·50
231	14	1f.50 red and brown	5·00	8·25
232	18	1.50 on 1f.60 violet	2·30	6·50
233	14	1.50 on 1f.75 red and brown	3·00	2·00
234	20	1.50 on 1f.75 blue	3·00	3·50
235	18	1f.60 violet	4·00	4·00
236	20	2.00 on 2f.15 brown	2·30	2·30
237	20	2f.25 blue	4·25	7·25
238	-	2f.25 blue (No. 206)	3·75	6·75
239	20	2f.50 brown	6·25	9·75
240	5	10f. on 5f. mauve and red	22·00	27·00
241	20	10f. green	6·50	7·50
242	5	20f. on 5f. blue and mauve	25·00	38·00
243	14	20f. blue and brown	£800	£900
244	19	1.00 on 1f.25 red and lake (air)	14·50	16·00
245	19	1f.50 red and blue	19·00	22·00
246	19	1f.75 red and orange	£130	£130
247	19	3.00 on 3f.65 red and black	2·75	90
248	19	8f. red and purple	5·75	8·25
249	19	8.00 on 8f.50 red and green	4·75	3·00
250	19	12f. red and brown	7·00	7·75
251	19	12f.50 red and violet	6·25	4·75
252	19	16f. red and green	11·50	14·00
253	19	50f. red and blue	7·25	8·00

24 Traveller's Tree

1943. Free French Issue.

254	24	5c. brown	10	5·75
255	24	10c. mauve	10	1·00
256	24	25c. green	10	4·75
257	24	30c. orange	30	80
258	24	40c. blue	55	2·30
259	24	80c. purple	55	2·30
260	24	1f. blue	1·00	90
261	24	1f.50 red	90	30
262	24	2f. yellow	75	1·00
263	24	2f.50 blue	65	75
264	24	4f. blue and red	1·40	1·30
265	24	5f. green and black	65	1·50
266	24	10f. red and blue	85	70
267	24	20f. violet and brown	1·40	90

24a Fairy FC-1 Airliner

1943. Free French Administration. Air.

268	24a	1f. orange	35	2·00
269	24a	1f.50 red	20	1·80
270	24a	5f. purple	35	1·50
271	24a	10f. black	60	2·50
272	24a	25f. blue	80	4·50
273	24a	50f. green	55	75
274	24a	100f. red	75	1·50

24b

1944. Mutual Aid and Red Cross Funds.

275	24b	5f.+20f. green	55	7·75

1944. Surch **1f.50.**

276	24	1f.50 on 5c. brown	1·10	1·00
277	24	1f.50 on 10c. mauve	1·60	3·75

25a Felix Eboue

1945. Eboue.

279	25a	2f. black	55	45
280	25a	25f. green	75	7·00

25b "Victory"

1946. Air. Victory.

281	25b	8f. red	90	90

1945. Surch with new value.

282	24	50c. on 5c. brown	50	35
283	24	60c. on 5c. brown	65	4·50
284	24	70c. on 5c. brown	55	2·75
285	24	1f.20 on 5c. brown	45	4·50
286	24	2f.40 on 25c. green	1·00	1·70
287	24	3f. on 25c. green	1·00	1·30
288	24	4f.50 on 25c. green	1·10	2·75
289	24	15f. on 2f.50 blue	75	2·50

25c Legionaries by Lake Chad

1946. Air. From Chad to the Rhine.

290	25c	5f. blue	1·80	7·25
291	-	10f. red	1·80	7·25
292	-	15f. green	1·80	7·25
293	-	20f. brown	1·80	7·25
294	-	25f. violet	1·80	7·25
295	-	50f. red	1·80	7·25

DESIGNS: 10f. Battle of Koufra; 15f. Tank Battle, Mareth; 20f. Normandy Landings; 25f. Liberation of Paris; 50f. Liberation of Strasbourg.

29 Gen. Gallieni

1946

296		10c. green (postage)	10	1·40
297		30c. orange	10	50
298		40c. olive	10	1·60
299		50c. purple	10	35
300		60c. blue	55	4·00
301		80c. green	65	4·00
302		1f. sepia	65	35
303		1f.20 green	80	4·00
304	29	1f.50 red	60	35
305	-	2f. black	70	35
306	-	3f. purple	75	45
307	-	3f.60 red	1·10	3·50
308	-	4f. blue	1·20	90
309	-	5f. orange	1·40	50
310	-	6f. blue	60	20
311	-	10f. lake	80	20
312	-	15f. brown	90	30
313	-	20f. blue	75	35
314	-	25f. brown	1·00	35
315	-	50f. blue and red (air)	2·30	2·00
316	-	100f. brown and red	1·50	65
317	-	200f. brown and green	3·50	3·75

DESIGNS—As T **29**. VERT: 10 to 50c. Native with spear; 6, 10f. Gen. Duchesne; 15, 20, 25f. Lt.-Col. Joffre. HORIZ: 60, 80c. Zebus; 1f., 1f.20, Sakalava man and woman; 3f.60, 4, 5f. Betsimisaraka mother and child. 49×28 mm: 50f. Aerial view of Port of Tamatave. 28×51 mm: 100f. Allegory of flight. 51×28 mm: Douglas DC-2 airplane and map of Madagascar.

36 Gen. Gallieni and View

1946. 50th Anniv of French Protectorate.

318	36	10f.+5f. purple	45	7·75

1948. Air. Discovery of Adelie Land, Antarctic. No. 316 optd **TERRE ADELIE DUMONT D'URVILLE 1840.**

319		100f. brown and red	28·00	60·00

37a People of Five Races, Bomber and Globe

1949. Air. 75th Anniv of U.P.U.

320	37a	25f. multicoloured	1·80	2·75

37b Doctor and Patient

1950. Colonial Welfare Fund.

321	37b	10f.+2f. purple and green	4·00	22·00

38 Cacti and Succulents

39 Long-tailed Ground Roller

40 Woman and Forest Road

1952

322	38	7f.50 green and blue (postage)	45	35
323	39	8f. lake	1·20	40
324	39	15f. blue and green	90	50
325	-	50f. green and blue (air)	4·00	1·00
326	-	100f. black, brown and blue	12·00	1·60
327	-	200f. brown and green	22·00	10·50
328	40	500f. brown, sepia and green	23·00	8·50

DESIGNS—As Type **40**: 50f. Palm trees; 100f. Antsirabe Viaduct; 200f. Ring-tailed lemurs.

40a

1952. Military Medal Centenary.

329	40a	15f. turquoise, yellow and green	1·40	1·60

40b Normandy Landings, 1944

1954. Air. Tenth Anniv of Liberation.

330	40b	15f. purple and violet	4·50	1·60

41 Marshal Lyautey

1954. Birth Centenary of Marshal Lyautey.

331	41	10f. indigo, blue and ultram	1·10	60
332	41	40f. lake, grey and black	1·20	45

42 Gallieni School

1956. Economic and Social Development Fund.

333	-	3f. brown and grey	1·80	85
334	42	5f. brown and chestnut	1·20	75
335	-	10f. blue and grey	1·30	80
336	-	15f. green and turquoise	1·60	45

DESIGNS: 3f. Tamatave and tractor; 10f. Dredging canal; 15f. Irrigation.

42a Coffee

1956. Coffee.

337	42a	20f. sepia and brown	65	20

43 Cassava

1957. Plants.

338	43	2f. green, brown and blue	40	35
339	-	4f. red, brown and green	1·30	35
340	-	12f. green, brown and violet	1·40	50

DESIGNS: 4f. Cloves; 12f. Vanilla.

Issues of 1958–92. For issues between these dates, see under MALAGASY REPUBLIC.

362 Children with Mascot

1992. School Sports Festival (1990).

910	362	140f. multicoloured	35	10

363 Environmental Projects

1992. Air. World Environment Day.

911	363	140f. multicoloured	10	10

364 Post Box and Globe

1992. Air. World Post Day.

912	364	500f. multicoloured	75	25

365 Basenji

1992. Domestic Animals. Multicoloured.

913	140f. Type **365**	10	10
914	500f. Anglo-Arab horse	90	25
915	640f. Tortoiseshell cat and kitten	1·10	30
916	1025f. Siamese and colourpoint (cats)	1·60	50
917	1140f. Holstein horse	2·25	60
918	5000f. German shepherd dogs	6·50	75
MS919	104×72 mm. 1000f. Hanovarian horse, Maine coon cat and Maltese terrier (32×47 mm)	12·00	12·00

366 Foodstuffs

1992. International Nutrition Conference, Rome.

920	**366**	500f. multicoloured	1·10	25

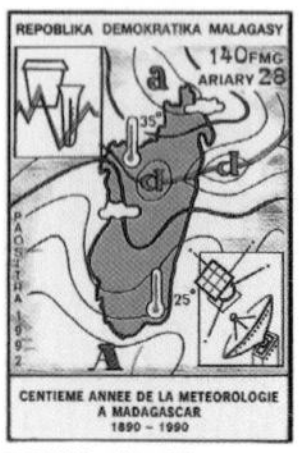

367 Weather Map

1992. Centenary of Meteorological Service.

921	**367**	140f. multicoloured	35	10

368 *Eusemia bisma*

1992. Butterflies and Moths. Multicoloured.

922	15f. Type **368**	10	10
923	35f. Tailed comet moth (vert)	10	10
924	65f. *Alcides aurora*	10	10
925	140f. *Agarista agricola*	35	10
926	600f. *Trogonoptera croesus*	1·40	30
927	850f. *Trogonodtera priamus*	1·75	45
928	1300f. *Pereute leucodrosime*	2·25	70
MS929	70×90 mm. 1500f. Sunset moth. Imperf	2·75	2·75

369 Barn Swallow

1992. Birds. Multicoloured.

930	40f. Type **369**	10	10
931	55f. Pied harrier (vert)	10	10
932	60f. European cuckoo (vert)	10	10
933	140f. Sacred ibis	10	10
934	210f. Purple swamphen	45	10
935	500f. Common roller	1·10	25
936	2000f. Golden oriole	4·00	1·10
MS937	69×90 mm. 1500f. Hoopoe. Imperf	3·25	3·25

370 Gymnastics

1992. Olympic Games, Barcelona. Multicoloured.

938	65f. Type **370**	10	10
939	70f. High jumping	10	10
940	120f. Archery	10	10
941	140f. Cycling	35	10
942	675f. Weightlifting	1·10	30
943	720f. Boxing	1·40	35
944	1200f. Two-man kayak	1·75	60
MS945	90×70 mm. 1600f. Olympic rings and volleyball. Imperf	2·25	2·25

371 Pusher-tug, Pangalanes Canal

1993

946	**371**	140f. multicoloured	35	10

372 BMW

1993. Motor Cars. Multicoloured.

947	20f. Type **372**	10	10
948	40f. Toyota "Carina"	10	10
949	60f. Cadillac	10	10
950	65f. Volvo	10	10
951	140f. Mercedes-Benz	10	10
952	640f. Ford "Sierra"	1·00	30
953	3000f. Honda "Concerto"	4·50	90
MS954	90×70 mm. 2000f. Renault 23. Imperf	3·00	3·00

373 Hyacinth Macaw

1993. Parrot Family. Multicoloured.

955	50f. Type **373**	10	10
956	60f. Cockatiel	10	10
957	140f. Budgerigar	10	10
958	500f. Jandaya conure	60	25
959	675f. Budgerigar (different)	1·10	35
960	800f. Red-fronted parakeet	1·40	45
961	1750f. Kea	2·75	65
MS962	71×91 mm. 2000f. Military macaw. Imperf	5·75	5·75

374 Broad-nosed Gentle Lemur

1993. World Post Day (1992). National Stamp Exhibition, Antananarivo. Lemurs. Sheet 90×115 mm containing T 374 and similar vert designs.

MS963	60f. Type **374**; 150f. Diadem sifaka; 250f. Indri, 350f. Ruffled lemur	1·40	1·40

375 Albert Einstein (physics, 1921) and Niels Bohr (physics, 1922)

1993. Nobel Prize Winners. Multicoloured.

964	500f. Type **375**	60	25
965	500f. Wolfgang Pauli (physics, 1945) and Max Born (physics, 1954)	60	25
966	500f. Joseph Thomson (physics, 1906) and Johannes Stark (physics, 1919)	60	25
967	500f. Otto Hahn (physics, 1944) and Hideki Yukawa (physics, 1949)	60	25
968	500f. Owen Richardson (physics, 1928) and William Shockley (physics, 1956)	60	25
969	500f. Albert Michelson (physics, 1907) and Charles Townes (physics, 1964)	60	25
970	500f. Wilhelm Wien (physics, 1911) and Lev Landau (physics, 1962)	60	25
971	500f. Carl Braun (physics, 1909) and Sir Edward Appleton (physics, 1947)	60	25
972	500f. Percy Bridgman (physics, 1946) and Nikolai Semyonov (physics, 1956)	60	25
973	500f. Sir William Ramsay (chemistry, 1904) and Glenn Seaborg (chemistry, 1951)	60	25
974	500f. Otto Wallach (chemistry, 1910) and Hermann Staudinger (chemistry, 1953)	60	25
975	500f. Richard Synge (chemistry, 1952) and Axel Theorell (chemistry, 1955)	60	25
976	500f. Thomas Morgan (medicine, 1933) and Hermann Muller (medicine, 1946)	60	25
977	500f. Allvar Gullstrand (medicine, 1911) and Willem Einthoven (medicine, 1924)	60	25
978	500f. Sir Charles Sherrington (medicine, 1932) and Otto Loewi (medicine, 1936)	60	25
979	500f. Jules Bordet (medicine, 1936) and Sir Alexander Fleming (medicine, 1945)	60	25

376 1956 Bugatti

1993. Racing Cars and Railway Locomotives. Multicoloured.

980	20f. Type **376**	10	10
981	20f. 1968 Ferrari	10	10
982	20f. 1948 Class C62 steam locomotive, 1948, Japan	10	10
983	20f. Electric train, 1975, Russia	10	10
984	140f. 1962 Lotus Mk 25	10	10
985	140f. 1970 Matra	10	10
986	140f. Diesel locomotive, 1954, Norway	10	10
987	140f. Class 26 steam locomotive, 1982, South Africa	10	10
988	1250f. 1963 Porsche	90	65
989	1250f. 1980 Ligier JS 11	90	65
990	1250f. Metroliner electric train, 1967, U.S.A.	90	65
991	1250f. Diesel train, 1982, Canada	90	65
992	3000f. 1967 Honda	2·10	1·50
993	3000f. 1992 Benetton B 192	2·10	1·50
994	3000f. Union Pacific Railroad diesel-electric locomotive, 1969, U.S.A.	2·10	2·10
995	3000f. TGV Atlantique express train, 1990, France	2·10	2·10

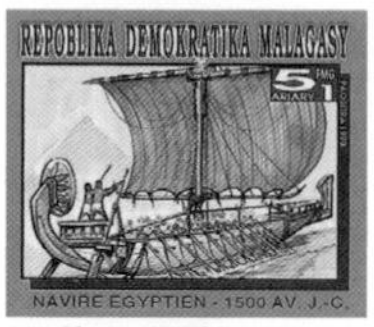

377 Pharaonic Ship

1993. Ships. Multicoloured.

996	5f. Type **377**	10	10
997	5f. Mediterranean carrack	10	10
998	5f. *Great Western* (sail paddle-steamer), 1837	10	10
999	5f. *Mississippi* (paddle-steamer), 1850	10	10
1000	15f. Phoenician bireme	10	10
1001	15f. Viking ship	10	10
1002	15f. *Clermont* (first commercial paddle-steamer), 1806	10	10
1003	15f. *Pourquoi Pas?* (Charcot's ship), 1936	10	10
1004	140f. *Santa Maria* (Columbus's ship), 1492	10	10
1005	140f. H.M.S. *Victory* (ship of the line), 1765	10	10
1006	140f. Motor yacht	10	10
1007	140f. *Bremen* (liner), 1950	10	10
1008	10000f. *Sovereign of the Seas* (galleon), 1637	9·25	80
1009	10000f. *Cutty Sark* (clipper)	9·25	80
1010	10000f. *Savannah* (nuclear-powered freighter)	9·25	80
1011	10000f. *Condor* (hydrofoil)	9·25	80

No. 999 is wrongly inscribed "Missisipi".

378 Johannes Gutenberg and Printing Press

1993. Inventors. Multicoloured.

1012	500f. Type **378**	60	25
1013	500f. Sir Isaac Newton and telescope	60	25
1014	500f. John Dalton and atomic theory	60	25
1015	500f. Louis Jacques Daguerre and camera	60	25
1016	500f. Michael Faraday and electric motor	60	25
1017	500f. Wright brothers and "Flyer"	60	25
1018	500f. Alexander Bell and telephone	60	25
1019	500f. Thomas Edison and telegraph	60	25
1020	500f. Karl Benz and motor vehicle	60	25
1021	500f. Sir Charles Parsons and "Turbina"	60	25
1022	500f. Rudolf Diesel and diesel locomotive	60	35
1023	500f. Guglielmo Marconi and early radio	60	25
1024	500f. Lumiere brothers and cine-camera	60	35
1025	500f. Herman Oberth and space rocket	60	25
1026	500f. John Mauchly, J. Prosper Eckert and computer	60	25
1027	500f. Arthur Shawlow, compact disc and laser	60	25

379 Leonardo da Vinci and *Virgin of the Rocks*

1993. Painters. Multicoloured.

1028	50f. Type **379**	10	10
1029	50f. Titian and *Sacred and Profane Love*	10	10
1030	50f. Rembrandt and *Jeremiah crying*	10	10
1031	50f. J. M. W. Turner and *Ulysses*	10	10
1032	640f. Michelangelo and the Doni Tondo	70	30
1033	640f. Peter Paul Rubens and *Self-portrait*	70	30
1034	640f. Francisco Goya and *Don Manuel Osorio de Zuniga*	70	30
1035	640f. Eugene Delacroix and *Christ on Lake Gennesaret*	70	30
1036	1000f. Claude Monet and *Poppyfield*	95	50
1037	1000f. Paul Gauguin and *Two Tahitians*	95	50
1038	1000f. Henri Marie de Toulouse-Lautrec and *Woman with a Black Boa*	95	50
1039	1000f. Salvador Dali and *St. James of Compostela*	95	50
1040	2500f. Pierre Auguste Renoir and *Child carrying Flowers*	2·75	90
1041	2500f. Vincent Van Gogh and *Dr. Paul Gachet*	2·75	90
1042	2500f. Pablo Picasso and *Crying Woman*	2·75	90
1043	2500f. Andy Warhol and *Portrait of Elvis*	2·75	90

380 Sunset Moth (*Chrysiridia madagascariensis*)

1993. Butterflies, Moths and Birds. Multicoloured.

1044	45f. Type **380**	10	10
1045	45f. African monarch (*Hypolimnas misippus*)	10	10
1046	45f. Southern crested Madagascar coucal (*Coua verreauxi*)	10	10
1047	45f. African marsh owl (*Asio helvola*)	10	10
1048	60f. *Charaxes antamboulou*	10	10
1049	60f. *Papilio antenor*	10	10
1050	60f. Crested Madagascar coucal (*Coua cristata*)	10	10
1051	60f. Helmet bird (*Euryceros prevostii*)	10	10
1052	140f. *Hypolimnas dexithea*	10	10
1053	140f. *Charaxes andronodorus*	10	10
1054	140f. Giant Madagascar coucal (*Couca gigas*)	10	10

1055	140f. Madagascar red fody (*Foudia madagascarensis*)	10	10
1056	3000f. *Euxanthe madagascarensis*	3·25	45
1057	3000f. *Papilio grosesmithi*	3·25	45
1058	3000f. Sicklebill (*Falculea palliata*)	3·25	45
1059	3000f. Madagascar serpent eagle (*Eutriorchis astur*)	3·25	45

Nos. 1044/59 were issued together, se-tenant, the butterfly and bird designs respectively forming composite designs.

381 Henri Dunant and Volunteers unloading Red Cross Lorry

1993. Anniversaries and Events. Multicoloured.

1060	500f. Type **381** (award of first Nobel Peace Prize, 1901)	35	25
1061	640f. Charles de Gaulle and battlefield (50th anniv of Battle of Bir-Hakeim (1992))	45	30
1062	1025f. Crowd at Brandenburg Gate (bicentenary (1991) and fourth anniv of breach of Berlin Wall)	1·10	55
1063	1500f. Doctors giving health instruction to women (Rotary International and Lions International)	1·60	55
1064	3000f. Konrad Adenauer (German chancellor 1949–63, 24th death anniv (1991))	3·25	60
1065	3500f. "LZ-4" (airship), 1908, and Count Ferdinand von Zeppelin (75th death anniv (1992))	4·00	60
MS1066	92×81 mm. 7500f. Wolfgang Mozart at piano and Salzburg (death bicentenary (1991))	8·00	8·00

382 Guides and Anniversary Emblem

1993. Air. 50th Anniv of Madagascan Girl Guides.

1067	**382** 140f. multicoloured	10	10

383 Player, Trophy and Ficklin Home, Macon

1993. World Cup Football Championship, United States (1992). Multicoloured.

1068	140f. Type **383**	10	10
1069	640f. Player, trophy and Herndon Home, Atlanta	65	35
1070	1025f. Player, trophy and Cultural Centre, Augusta	1·40	55
1071	5000f. Player, trophy and Old Governor's Mansion, Milledgeville	6·00	1·00
MS1072	117×80 mm. 7500f. Player on US flag	8·00	8·00

1993. Various stamps optd with emblem and inscription.

(a) Germany, World Cup Football Champion, 1990. Nos. 778/81 optd **VAINQEUR:ALLEMAGNE.**

1073	328	350f. multicoloured	25	15
1074	-	1000f. multicoloured	90	50
1075	-	1500f. multicoloured	1·50	80
1076	-	2500f. multicoloured	2·75	1·00

(b) Gold Medallists at Winter Olympic Games, Albertville (1992). Nos. 812/15 optd with Olympic rings, **"MEDAILLE D'OR"** and further inscr as below.

1077	350f. **BOB A QUATRE (AUT) INGO APPELT HARALD WINKLER GERHARD HAIDACHER THOMAS SCROLL**	25	15
1078	1000f. **1000 M. - OLAF ZINKE (GER)**	90	50
1079	1500f. **50 KM LIBRE BJOERN DAEHLIE (NOR)**	1·50	80
1080	2500f. **SUPER G MESSIEURS KJETIL-ANDRE AAMODT (NOR)**	2·75	1·25
MS1081	92×77 mm. 3000f. **GEANT MESSIEURS ALBERT TOMBA (ITA)**	3·25	3·25

(c) Anniversaries. Nos. 1060, 675 and 707 optd as listed below.

1082	500f. Red Cross and **130e ANNIVERSAIRE DE LA CREATION DE LA CROIX-ROUGE 1863–1993**	2·25	1·10
1083	550f. Lions emblem and **75eme ANNIVERSAIRE LIONS**	2·25	1·10
1084	1500f. Guitar and **THE ELVIS'S GUITAR 15TH ANNIVERSARY OF HIS DEATH 1977–1992**	1·75	80
1085	1500f. Guitar and **GUITARE ELVIS 15eme ANNIVERSAIRE DE SA MORT 1977–1992**	1·75	80

(d) 50th Death Anniv of Robert Baden-Powell (founder of Boy Scouts). Optd **50eme ANNIVERSAIRE DE LA MORT DE BADEN POWEL** and emblem. (i) On Nos. 870/5 with scout badge in wreath.

1086	**354**	140f. multicoloured	10	10
1087	-	500f. multicoloured	35	25
1088	-	640f. multicoloured	45	30
1089	-	1025f. multicoloured	1·10	30
1090	-	1140f. multicoloured	1·10	35
1091	-	3500f. multicoloured	3·25	1·10
MS1092		119×94 mm. 4500f. multicoloured	3·75	3·75

(ii) On No. 676 with profile of Baden-Powell.

1093	1500f. multicoloured	1·75	80

(e) Bicentenary of French Republic. Nos. 761/5 optd **Republique Francaise** and emblem within oval and **BICENTENAIRE DE L'AN I DE LA REPUBLIQUE FRANCAISE.**

1094	250f. multicoloured	20	15
1095	350f. multicoloured	25	15
1096	1000f. multicoloured	1·10	50
1097	1500f. multicoloured	1·75	50
1098	2500f. multicoloured	2·75	90
MS1099	113×79 mm. 3000f. multicoloured	3·25	3·25

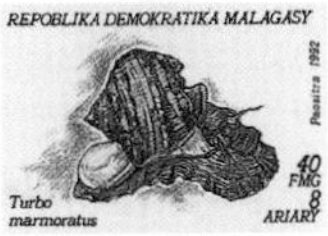

385 Great Green Turban

1993. Molluscs. Multicoloured.

1100	40f. Type **385**	10	10
1101	60f. Episcopal mitre	10	10
1102	65f. Common paper nautilis	10	10
1103	140f. Textile cone	10	10
1104	500f. European sea hare	90	25
1105	675f. "Harpa amouretta"	1·10	35
1106	2500f. Tiger cowrie	3·50	70
MS1107	70×91 mm. 2000f. Giant sundial. Imperf	3·00	3·00

386 Tiger Shark

1993. Sharks. Multicoloured.

1108	10f. Type **386**	10	10
1109	45f. Japanese sawshark	10	10
1110	140f. Whale shark	15	10
1111	270f. Smooth hammerhead	30	20
1112	600f. Oceanic white-tipped shark	65	35
1113	1200f. Zebra shark	1·25	80
1114	1500f. Goblin shark	1·90	1·10
MS1115	70×90 mm. 2000f. "Galeorhinus zyopterus". Imperf	5·25	5·25

387 Map of Africa and Industry

1993. Air. African Industrialization Day.

1116	**387** 500f. red, yellow and blue	80	50

388 "Superviem Odoriko" Express Train

1993. Locomotives. Multicoloured.

1117	5f. Type **388**	10	10
1118	15f. Morrison Knudsen diesel locomotive No. 801	10	10
1119	140f. ER-200 diesel train, Russia	10	10
1120	265f. General Motors GP60 diesel-electric locomotive No. EKD-5, U.S.A.	20	15
1121	300f. New Jersey Transit diesel locomotive, U.S.A.	20	15
1122	575f. ICE high speed train, Germany	40	30
1123	2500f. X2000 high speed train, Sweden	1·75	1·25
MS1124	91×71 mm. 2000f. Alstham's TGV	1·50	1·50

389 "Paphiopedilum siamense"

1993. Orchids. Multicoloured.

1125	50f. Type **389** (wrongly inscr "Paphpiopedilum")	10	10
1126	65f. "Cypripedium calceolus"	10	10
1127	70f. "Ophrys oestrifera"	10	10
1128	140f. "Cephalanthera rubra"	10	10
1129	300f. "Cypripedium macranthon"	20	15
1130	640f. "Calanthe vestita"	80	30
1131	2500f. "Cypripedium guttatum"	3·25	90
MS1132	90×70 mm. 2000f. "Oncidium tigrinum". Imperf	2·75	2·75

390 "Necrophorus tomentosus"

1994. Beetles. Multicoloured.

1133	20f. Type **390**	10	10
1134	60f. "Dynastes tityus"	10	10
1135	140f. "Megaloxanta bicolor"	10	10
1136	605f. Searcher	40	10
1137	720f. "Chrysochroa mirabilis"	50	15
1138	1000f. "Crioceris asparaqi"	70	25
1139	1500f. Rose chafer	1·10	35
MS1140	95×70 mm. 2000f. Goliath beetle. Imperf	1·40	1·40

391 Lufthansa Airliner, Germany

1994. Aircraft. Multicoloured.

1141	10f. Type **391**	10	10
1142	10f. British Aerospace/Aerospatiale Concorde supersonic jetliner of Air France	10	10
1143	10f. Air Canada airliner	10	10
1144	10f. ANA airliner, Japan	10	10
1145	60f. Boeing 747 jetliner of British Airways	10	10
1146	60f. Dornier Do-X flying boat, Germany	10	10
1147	60f. Shinmeiwa flying boat, Japan	10	10
1148	60f. Royal Jordanian airliner	10	10
1149	640f. Alitalia airliner	45	15
1150	640f. French-European Development Project Hydro 2000 flying boat	45	15
1151	640f. Boeing 314 flying boat	45	15
1152	640f. Air Madagascar airliner	45	15
1153	5000f. Emirates Airlines airliner, United Arab Emirates	3·50	1·10
1154	5000f. Scandinavian Airways airliner	3·50	1·10
1155	5000f. KLM airliner, Netherlands	3·50	1·10
1156	5000f. Air Caledonie airliner, New Caledonia	3·50	1·10

Nos. 1141/56 were issued together, *se-tenant*, Nos. 1146/7 and 1150/1 forming a composite design.

392 Fork and Spoon, Sakalava

1994. Traditional Crafts. Multicoloured.

1157	30f. Silver jewellery, Mahafaly	10	10
1158	60f. Type **392**	10	10
1159	140f. Silver jewellery, Antandroy	10	10
1160	430f. Silver jewellery on table, Sakalava	30	10
1161	580f. Frames of decorated paper, Ambalavao	40	10
1162	1250f. Silver jewellery, Sakalava	90	30
1163	1500f. Marquetry table, Ambositra	1·10	35
MS1164	70×90 mm. 2000f. Carpet, Ampanihy. Imperf	1·25	1·25

393 "Chicoreus torrefactus" (shell)

1994. Marine Life. Multicoloured.

1165	15f. Type **393**	10	10
1166	15f. "Fasciolaria filamentosa" (shell)	10	10
1167	15f. Regal angelfish ("Pigopytes diacanthus")	10	10
1168	15f. Coelacanth ("Latimeria chalumnae")	10	10
1169	30f. "Stellaria solaris" (shell)	10	10
1170	30f. Ventral harp ("Harpa ventricosa")	10	10
1171	30f. Blue-tailed boxfish ("Ostracion cyanurus")	10	10
1172	30f. Clown wrasse ("Coris gaimardi")	10	10
1173	1250f. Lobster ("Panulirus sp.")	90	30
1174	1250f. "Stenopus hispidus" (crustacean)	90	30
1175	1250f. Undulate triggerfish ("Balistapus undulatus")	90	30
1176	1250f. Forceps butterflyfish ("Forcipiger longirostris")	90	30
1177	1500f. Hermit crab ("Pagure")	1·10	35
1178	1500f. Hermit crab ("Bernard l'Hermite")	1·10	35
1179	1500f. Diadem squirrelfish ("Adioryx diadema")	1·10	35
1180	1500f. Lunulate lionfish ("Pterois lunulata")	1·10	35

Nos. 1165/80 were issued together, *se-tenant*, the backgrounds forming a composite design.

394 Arms

1994. Air. Junior Economic Chamber Zone A (Africa, Middle East and Indian Ocean) Conference, Antananarivo. Multicoloured.

1181	140f. Type **394**	10	10
1182	500f. Arms as in Type **394** but with inscriptions differently arranged (vert)	70	20

395 Troops landing on Beach

1994. 50th Anniv of Allied Landings at Normandy. Multicoloured.

1183	1500f. Type **395**	1·10	35
1184	3000f. German troops defending ridge and allied troops (as T **397**)	2·25	75
1185	3000f. Airplanes over battle scene, trooper with U.S. flag and German officer (as T **397**)	2·25	75

Nos. 1183/5 were issued together, *se-tenant*, forming a composite design.

396 Emperor Angelfish

1994. Aquarium Fish. Multicoloured.

1186	10f. Type **396**	10	10
1187	30f. Siamese fighting fish	10	10
1188	45f. Pearl gourami	10	10
1189	95f. Cuckoo-wrasse	10	10
1190	140f. Blotched upsidedown catfish ("Synodontis nigreventris")	10	10
1191	140f. Jack Dempsey ("Cichlasoma biocellatum")	10	10
1192	3500f. Mummichog	2·50	80
MS1193	70×90 mm. 2000f. Goldfish (29×41 mm)	75	75

397 Notre Dame Cathedral, Armed Resistance Fighters and Rejoicing Crowd

1994. 50th Anniv of Liberation of Paris by Allied Forces. Multicoloured.

1194	1500f. Crowd and Arc de Triomphe (as T **395**)	55	15
1195	3000f. Type **397**	1·10	35
1196	3000f. Eiffel Tower and tank convoy	1·10	35

Nos. 1194/6 were issued together, *se-tenant*, forming a composite design.

398 Emblem and "75"

1994. 75th Anniv of I.L.O.

1197	**398**	140f. multicoloured	10	10

399 Biathlon

1994. Winter Olympic Games, Lillehammer, Norway. Multicoloured. (a) Without overprints.

1198	140f. Type **399**	10	10
1199	1250f. Ice hockey	45	15
1200	2000f. Figure skating	75	25
1201	2500f. Skiing (downhill)	95	30
MS1202	116×112 mm. 5000f. Skiing (slalom)	1·90	1·90

(b) Gold Medal Winners. Nos. 1198/1201 optd.

1203	140f. Optd M. BEDARD CANADA	10	10
1204	1250f. Optd MEDAILLE D'OR SUEDE	45	15
1205	2000f. Optd O. BAYUL UKRAINE	75	25
1206	2500f. Optd M. WASMEIER ALLEMAGNE	95	30
MS1207	116×112 mm. 5000f. D. COMPAGNONI ITALIE	1·90	1·90

401 Majestic performing Dressage Exercise and Windsor Hotel, 1892

1994. Olympic Games, Atlanta, U.S.A. Multicoloured.

1208	640f. Type **401**	25	10
1209	1000f. Covington Courthouse, 1884, and putting the shot	35	10

1210	1500f. Table tennis and Carolton Community Activities Centre	55	15
1211	3000f. Newman Commercial Court Square, 1800, and footballer	1·10	35
MS1212	120×112 mm. 7500f. Games emblem and relay runner	2·75	2·75

402 Spider on Map of Madagascar

1994. *Archaea workmani* (spider).

1213	**402**	500f. multicoloured	20	15

403 "Oceonia oncidiflora"

1994. Flowers, Fruit, Fungi and Vegetables. Multicoloured.

1214	45f. Type **403**	10	10
1215	45f. Breadfruit ("Artocarpus altilis")	10	10
1216	45f. "Russula annulata"	10	10
1217	45f. Sweet potato	10	10
1218	60f. "Cymbidella rhodochica"	10	10
1219	60f. "Eugenia malaceensis"	10	10
1220	60f. "Lactarius claricolor"	10	10
1221	60f. Yam	10	10
1222	140f. Vanilla orchid ("Vanilla planifolia")	10	10
1223	140f. "Jambosa domestica"	10	10
1224	140f. "Russula tuberculosa"	10	10
1225	140f. Avocado	10	10
1226	3000f. "Phaius humblotii"	1·10	35
1227	3000f. Papaya	1·10	35
1228	3000f. "Russula fistulosa"	1·10	35
1229	3000f. Manioc	1·10	35

Nos. 1214/29 were issued together, *se-tenant*, the backgrounds forming a composite design.

Nos. 1230/1310 and Types **404/411** are vacant.

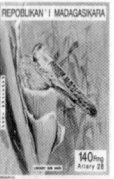

412 Locusts

1995. Locusts. Multicoloured.

1311	140f. Type **412**	10	10
1312	140f. Robber fly (*Asilidae*) (predator) (horiz)	10	10
1313	140f. Harvesting locusts for food (horiz)	10	10

413 Emblem

1995. Air. 20th Anniv of Francophone.

1314	**413**	500f. multicoloured	25	25

414 Emblem

1995. 160th Anniv of Malagasy Bible Translation.

1315	**414**	140f. multicoloured	10	10

415 'HILTON' and '25'

1995. 25th Anniv of Hilton Hotel, Madagascar.

1316	**415**	500f. indigo, black and gold	25	25

416 Messengers

1995. World Post Day.

1317	**416**	500f. multicoloured	25	25

417 Emblem and Map

1996. 30th Anniv of United Nations Industrial Development Organization (ONUDI).

1318	**417**	140f. blue, brown and black	10	10

418 Symbols of Drug Abuse

1996. International Day against Drug Abuse.

1319	**418**	140f. grey, green and black	10	10

419 Tennis

1996. Olympic Games, Atlanta. Multicoloured.

1320	140f. Type **419**	10	10
1321	140f. Judo	10	10

420 Fredy Rajaofera

1997. Personalities. Multicoloured.

1322	140f. Type **420**	10	10
1323	140f. Andrianary Ratianarivo	10	10
1324	140f. Odeam Rakoto	10	10

421 '25'

1997. 25th Anniv of Radio Nederland in Madagascar.

1325	**421**	500f. orange, black and blue	25	25

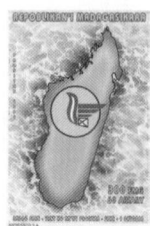

422 Map and Postal Emblem

1997. World Post Day.

1326	**422**	300f. multicoloured	20	20

423 Emblem

1997. Third Francophonie Games, Madagascar.

1327	**423**	300f. multicoloured	20	20
1328	**423**	1850f. multicoloured	55	55

424 Emblem

1999. 15th Anniv of Indian Ocean Commission.

1329	**424**	500f. blue, black and vermilion	25	25

(424a)

1999. Various stamps surcharged as T **424a**.

1329a	300f. on 430f. multicoloured (1160)	30	30
1329b	500f. on 170f. multicoloured (468)	45	45
1329c	500f. on 555f. multicoloured (896)	45	45
1329d	500f. on 580f. multicoloured (1161)	45	45
1329e	500f. on 1850f. multicoloured (1328)	45	45

(424b)

1999. No. 820 surcharged as T **424b**.

1329f	60f. on 350f.+20f. on 250f.+20f. multicoloured (820)	15	15

425 Rasalama (Christian martyr)

2000. Personalities. Multicoloured.

1330	900f. Type **425**	35	35
1331	900f. Razafindrakotohasina Rahantravololona (first Malagasy woman engineer and Ministry of Economy and Commerce Water Division Chief)	35	35
1332	900f. Ralivao Ramiaramanana (first Malagasy woman doctor)	35	35
1333	900f. Cardinal Jerome-Henri Rakotomalala	35	35
1334	900f. Rakotovao Razakaboana (Minister of Finance and Planning)	35	35
1335	900f. General Gabriel Ramanantsoa (president 1972–1975)	35	35

426 'Eclipse 2001'

2001. Total Solar Eclipse.

1336	**426**	5600f. multicoloured	1·90	1·90

427 Children surrounding Globe

2001. International Year of Dialogue among Civilizations.
1337	**427**	3500f. multicoloured	1·20	1·20

428 Rice Fronds and Map

2001. Rice.
1338	**428**	450f. multicoloured	25	25
1339	**428**	900f. multicoloured	35	35

Nos. 1340/1 have been left for stamps not yet received.

429 *Chorisia ventricosa*

2002. Flora and Fauna. Multicoloured.
1342		100f. Type **429**	10	10
1343		350f. *Eichhornia crassipes* (common water hyacinth) (vert)	15	15
1344		400f. *Didieraceae*	15	15
1345		500f. Palms, Nosy Iranja beach (vert)	20	20
1346		900f. *Ravinala* (travellers' tree) (national tree) (vert)	35	35
1347		1000f. *Propithecus verreauxi* (inscr 'Prophiteque deverreaux') (vert)	35	35
1348		2500f. *Lemur catta* (ring-tailed lemur) (vert)	80	80
1349		3000f. *Furcifer pardalis* (chameleon)	1·10	1·10
1350		4400f. *Takhtajania perrieri*	1·30	1·30
1351		6800f. *Ravinala* (vert)	2·75	2·75

430 Albert Rakoto Ratsimamanga (scientist and diplomat)

2002. Personalities. Multicoloured.
1352		1500f. Type **430**	45	45
1353		1500f. Rakoto Frah (flautist)	45	45

431 Mahamasina Stadium

2002. 30th Anniv of Madagascar—China Diplomatic Relations.
1354	**431**	2500f. multicoloured	85	85

432 *Xyloolaena perrieri*

2003. Indigenous Plants. Multicoloured.
1355		100f. Type **432**	10	10
1356		500f. *Megistostegium microphyllum*	20	20
1357		600f. *Tambourissa* (horiz)	20	20
1358		1000f. *Leptolaena diospyroidea*	35	35
1359		1500f. *Ochna greveanum*	40	40
1360		7500f. *Schizolaena tampoketsana*	2·75	2·75

433 Landscape, Madagascar and Japan Flags

2003. Japan International Cooperation Agency (JICA) Office in Madagascar.
1361	**433**	1500f. multicoloured	40	40

434 *Indri indri* (lemur)

2003
1362	**434**	2500f. multicoloured	65	65
1363	**434**	15000f. multicoloured	2·75	2·75

435 First Catholic Church in Madagascar, Sainte-Marie

2003. Tourism. Multicoloured.
1364		4000f. Type **435**	1·20	1·20
1365		4500f. House made of falafa, Coastal region	1·20	1·20
1366		5500f. House, High Plateau region	1·30	1·30
1367		10000f. Pirates graveyard, Sainte-Marie	2·40	2·40

436 Emblem

2003. 20th Anniv of Indian Ocean Commission.
1368	**436**	6000f. multicoloured	1·40	1·40

437 Emblem

2004. World for Health and Road Safety.
1369	**437**	1500f. multicoloured	35	35

438 Ranavalona I

2004. Rulers. Multicoloured.
1370		100f. Type **438**	10	10
1371		400f. Ranavalona III	15	15
1372		500f. Radama I	15	15
1373		1000f. Radama II	35	35
1374		2500f. Rasoherina	80	80
1375		4000f. Andrian-ampoinimerina	1·30	1·30
1376		7500f. Ranavalona II	1·50	1·50

439 Wolf-shaped Rock, Isalo

2004. Tourism. Multicoloured.
1377		2000f. Type **439**	65	65
1378		3000f. Nosy Mitsio (vert)	70	70

1379		5000f. Beach, Fort Dauphin	1·30	1·30
1381		10000f. Traditional dancers, Ambohimanga Palace (rova)	2·40	2·40
1382		25000f. Red Tsingy (limestone peaks) Irodo	2·75	2·75

No. 1380 has been left for stamp not yet received.

440 Ostriches and Lemur

2004. Morondava Fauna.
1383	**440**	50000f. multicoloured	1·90	1·90

441 Map enclosing Canoeists and Lemur

2005. Centenary of Rotary International.
1384	**441**	2100a. multicoloured	20	20

Change of Currency on Stamps (values remain unchanged).
1 Ariary (a)=5 Francs (f)

Nos. 1385/6 and Type **442** have been left for '30th Anniversary of the Medical Cooperation between China and Madagascar' issued on 8 December 2005, not yet received.

443 *Aerangis cryptodon*

2005. Indigenous Orchids. Multicoloured.
1387		1500a. Type **442**	15	15
1388		1500a. *Aeranthes grandiflora*	15	15
1389		1500a. *Aeranthes henrici*	15	15
1390		1500a. *Aeranthes peyrotii*	15	15
1391		1500a. *Oeceoclades spathulifera* (Inscr 'Oeccoclades spathulifera')	15	15
1392		1500a. *Angraecum sesquipedale*	15	15
1393		1500a. Inscr 'Cynorchis elata'	15	15
1394		1500a. *Angraecum viguieri*	15	15
1395		1500a. *Gastrorchis humblotii*	15	15
1396		1500a. *Gastrorchis lutea*	15	15
1397		1500a. *Gastrorchis pulcher*	15	15
1398		1500a. *Jumellea sagittata*	15	15
1399		1500a. *Microcoelia gilpinae*	15	15
1400		1500a. *Angraecum praestans*	15	15

444 Map and AIDS Ribbon

2006. AIDS Awareness Campaign.
1401	**444**	300a. multicoloured	10	10

445 Pastor Rainmamonjisoa

2006. Birth Bicentenary of Mpitandrina Rainmamonjisoa.
1402	**445**	300a. pale blue and black	10	10

446 Emblem, Philatelic Tools and Stamps

2006. 20th Anniv of Stamp Collectors Association (APM).
1403	**446**	300a. multicoloured	10	10

447 Leopold Senghor

2006. Birth Centenary of Leopold Sedar Senghor (poet and first president of Senegal (1960–1980)).
1404	**447**	2000a. multicoloured	25	25

448 Emblem

2007. Seventh Indian Ocean Games, Madagascar.
1405	**448**	300a. multicoloured	10	10

449 Whale

2007. Whales Festival, Sainte Marie. Multicoloured.
1406		1100a. Type **449**)	15	15
1407		3000a. Whale and two small fish (vert)	40	40

450 Regis Rajemisa-Raolison

2008. Regis Rajemisa-Raolison (writer and founder of Havatsa UPEM (Union of Writers and Poets in Malagasy)) Commemoration.
1408	**450**	300a. black and carmine-vermilion	10	10

300 ARIARY

(451)

2008. Nos. 1340 and 1371 surcharged as T **451**.
1409		300f. on 100f. multicoloured (1371)	10	10
1410		300f. on 5600f. multicoloured (1340)	10	10

452 Postman delivering Letter

2008. Postal Service–Part of Developement.
1411	**452**	100a. multicoloured	10	10

PARCEL POST STAMPS

1919. Receipt stamp of France surch **MADAGASCAR ET DEPENDANCES 0fr.10 COLIS POSTAUX.**
P81	0f.10 on 10c. grey	9·50	9·75

1919. Fiscal stamp of Madagascar surch **COLIS POSTAUX 0f.10.**

P82	0f.10 on 1f. pink	£130	£110

1919. Fiscal stamps surch **Madagascar et Dependances** (in capitals on No. P83) **COLIS POSTAUX 0f.10.**

P83	0f.10 pink	27·00	13·00
P84	0f.10 red and green	8·25	6·75
P85	0f.10 black and green	8·00	7·00

POSTAGE DUE STAMPS

1896. Postage Due stamps of Fr. Colonies optd **Madagascar et DEPENDANCES.**

D17	U	5c. blue	10·50	20·00
D18	U	10c. brown	8·50	9·25
D19	U	20c. yellow	5·00	9·75
D20	U	30c. red	8·50	10·50
D21	U	40c. mauve	65·00	70·00
D22	U	50c. violet	8·75	6·00
D23	U	1f. green	£120	80·00

D6 Governor's Palace, Tananarive

1908

D70	D 6	2c. red	10	35
D71	D 6	4c. violet	35	35
D72	D 6	5c. green	35	90
D73	D 6	10c. red	35	10
D74	D 6	20c. olive	10	2·30
D75	D 6	40c. brown on cream	20	5·00
D76	D 6	50c. brown on blue	20	2·50
D77	D 6	60c. red	80	5·00
D78	D 6	1f. blue	65	3·50

1924. Surch in figures.

D123	60c. on 1f. red	1·40	7·25
D124	2f. on 1f. purple	30	4·25
D125	3f. on 1f. blue	35	6·25

1942. Free French Administration. Optd **FRANCE LIBRE** or surch also.

D254	10c. red	1·90	4·50
D255	20c. green	85	4·50
D256	0,30 on 5c. green	3·25	5·25
D257	40c. brown on cream	2·50	4·00
D258	50c. brown and blue	2·30	3·75
D259	60c. red	2·50	4·00
D260	1f. blue	90	3·25
D261	1f. on 2c. purple	10·50	17·00
D262	2f. on 4c. violet	4·75	6·25
D263	2f. on 1f. mauve	2·50	3·75
D264	3f. on 1f. blue	2·75	4·00

D37

1947

D319	D 37	10c. mauve	10	6·00
D320	D 37	30c. brown	10	6·50
D321	D 37	50c. green	20	6·75
D322	D 37	1f. brown	30	4·75
D323	D 37	2f. red	1·10	4·00
D324	D 37	3f. brown	1·30	5·00
D325	D 37	4f. blue	1·30	6·50
D326	D 37	5f. red	1·80	5·75
D327	D 37	10f. green	1·10	2·75
D328	D 37	20f. blue	2·30	9·00

APPENDIX

The following stamps have either been issued in excess of postal needs or have not been available to the public in reasonable quantities at face value.

1990

Birth Centenary of General Charles de Gaulle. 5000f.×2

1992

Olympic Games, Barcelona. 500f. (on gold foil).

1993

Bicentenary of French Republic. 1989 "Philexfrance 89" issue optd. 5000f.

1994

Elvis Presley (entertainer). 10000f. (on gold foil).
World Cup Football Championship, U.S.A. 10000f. (on gold foil).
Winter Olympic Games, Lillehammer, Norway. 10000f. (on gold foil).
Olympic Games, Atlanta, U.S.A. 5000f. (on gold foil).
Centenary of Olympic Committee. 2500×2, 3500f.
Stuff of Heroes by Phillip Kaufman. 140×2, 5000f.
Sculpture and Architecture. 350f.×20
Big Cats. 10, 30, 60, 120, 140×2, 350f.
Philakorea '94, Seoul. 100, 140, 550f.
Cathedrals. 10, 100,120, 140, 525, 605f.
Pre-historic Animals. 35, 40, 140, 525, 640, 755, 1800f.
Sport. 5, 140, 525, 550, 640, 720, 1500f.

1995

Cinema. 100×2,140×2, 550, 1250, 5000×2, 10000f.×2
Ships. 45, 50, 60, 100, 140, 350, 3000f.

1996

25th Anniv of Greenpeace. 1500, 3000, 3500, 5000f.
20th Anniv of Concorde. 2000f.×4
50th Anniv of UNICEF. 140×3, 7500f.
Personalities. 1500, 1750, 2000, 2500, 3000, 3500, 5000, 7500f.

1997

Winter Olympics, Nagano. 160, 350, 5000, 7500f.

1998

World Cup Football championship, France. 300×3, 1350×3, 3000×3, 10000f.×3
Transport. 1700×9 a. Sheetlet of 9, 2000×9 a. Sheetlet of 9, 2500×9 a. Sheetlet of 9, 3000×9 a. Sheetlet of 9, 4000×9 a. Sheetlet of 9
Pre-historic Animals. 3500×9 a. Sheetlet of 9, 3500f.×9 a. Sheetlet of 9

1999

Birds. 250×9 a. Sheetlet of 9,
Chinese New Year. Year of the Rabbit. 1500f.×4 a. Sheetlet of 4
Comic Book Heroes. 1800×9 a. Sheetlet of 9, 1800×9 a. Sheetlet of 9, 3200f.×9 a. Sheetlet of 9
Betty Boop 2500f.×9 a. Sheetlet of 9
Garfield. 3200f.×9 a. Sheetlet of 9
Trains. 2000×9 a. Sheetlet of 9, 3000×9 a. Sheetlet of 9, 3000f.×9 a. Sheetlet of 9, 4000×9 a. Sheetlet of 9, 4000×9 a. Sheetlet of 9, 4000f.×9 a. Sheetlet of 9
Fauna. 300, 1700, 2050, 2400f. a. Block of 4
Personalities. 1950f.×6 a. Sheetlet of 6
Princess Diana Commemoration. 1350f.
Fauna. 1950f.×6
25th Death Anniv of Pablo Picasso. 2750, 7200, 7500f.
Scouts. 1350×4 a. Sheetlet of 4, 1500×4 a. Sheetlet of 4, 1950f.×4 a. Sheetlet of 4, 2000×4 a. Sheetlet of 4, 2500×4 a. Sheetlet of 4, 3000×4 a. Sheetlet of 4, 5000×4 a. Sheetlet of 4, 7500f.×4 a. Sheetlet of 4
30th Anniv of Concorde. 2000f.9 a. Sheetlet of 9
125th Anniv of UPU. 1000, 1200, 1800, 3200, 3500, 5000, 5600, 7500f.
Space Exploration. 1500×8, 12500f.
Animals of the World. Elephants. 2000f.×9 a. Sheetlet of 9
Railways. 3000×9 a. Sheetlet of 9, 3500×4 a. Sheetlet of 4, 5000×4 a. Sheetlet of 4, 7500f.×4 a. Sheetlet of 4
Insects. 2000f.×9 a. Sheetlet of 9
Philex France 99. 1500f.×9 a. Sheetlet of 9
Birds. 2000×9 a. Sheetlet of 9, 2000f.×9 a. Sheetlet of 9
Flora and Fauna. 2000×4 a. Sheetlet of 4, 2000×9 a. Sheetlet of 9, 2000×9 a. Sheetlet of 9, 4000×4 a. Sheetlet of 4, 5000×4 a. Sheetlet of 4, 5000×4 a. Sheetlet of 4, 7500f.×4 a. Sheetlet of 4,
Motor Cycle Racing. 2000f.×9 a. Sheetlet of 9
Art. 2000×9 a. Sheetlet of 9, 2000×9 a. Sheetlet of 9, 2500×9 a. Sheetlet of 9, 5000×9 a. Sheetlet of 9
Antonio Gaudi. 2000f.×9 a. Sheetlet of 9
Marilyn Monroe. 1750f.×9 a. Sheetlet of 9
Albert Einstein. 4000f.×4 a. Sheetlet of 4

Pt. 9

MADEIRA

A Portuguese island in the Atlantic Ocean off the N.W. coast of Africa. From 1868 to 1929 and from 1980 separate issues were made.

1868. 1000 reis = 1 milreis.
1912. 100 centavos = 1 escudo.
2002. 100 cents = 1 euro.

Nos. 1/78b are stamps of Portugal optd **MADEIRA**.

1868. With curved value label. Imperf.

1	14	20r. bistre	£275	£200
2	14	50r. green	£275	£200
3	14	80r. orange	£300	£200
4	14	100r. lilac	£300	£200

1868. With curved value label. Perf.

10	5r. black	80·00	55·00
13	10r. yellow	£130	£110
14	20r. bistre	£200	£160
15	25r. red	85·00	16·00
16	50r. green	£250	£200
17	80r. orange	£250	£200
19	100r. mauve	£250	£200
20	120r. blue	£170	£110
21	240r. mauve	£700	£600

1871. With straight value label.

30	15	5r. black	12·00	8·50
47	15	10r. yellow	40·00	29·00
72a	15	10r. green	95·00	75·00
48	15	15r. brown	28·00	16·00
49	15	20r. bistre	44·00	29·00
34	15	25r. pink	16·00	6·00
51	15	50r. green	90·00	39·00
71	15	50r. blue	£170	90·00
36	15	80r. orange	£110	95·00
53	15	100r. mauve	£120	70·00
38	15	120r. blue	£170	£110
55	15	150r. blue	£250	£200
74	15	150r. yellow	£400	£350
39	15	240r. lilac	£1000	£700
67	15	300r. lilac	£110	95·00

1880. Stamps of 1880.

79	16	5r. black	37·00	28·00
77	17	25r. grey	40·00	28·00
78	16	25r. grey	40·00	15·00
78b	16	25r. brown	40·00	15·00

1898. Vasco da Gama. As Nos. 378/85 of Portugal.

134	17	2½r. green	3·75	1·90
135	17	5r. red	3·75	1·90
136	17	10r. purple	4·75	2·20
137	17	25r. green	4·50	2·00
138	17	50r. blue	13·50	5·00
139	17	75r. brown	17·00	11·50
140	17	100r. brown	18·00	11·50
141	17	150r. brown	26·00	19·00

For Nos. 134/41 with **REPUBLICA** overprint, see Nos. 455/62 of Portugal.

6 Ceres

1929. Funchal Museum Fund. Value in black.

148	6	3c. violet	95	80
149	6	4c. yellow	95	80
150	6	5c. blue	95	80
151	6	6c. brown	1·30	1·10
152	6	10c. red	1·30	1·10
153	6	15c. green	1·30	1·10
154	6	16c. brown	1·30	1·10
155	6	25c. purple	1·40	1·20
156	6	32c. green	1·40	1·20
157	6	40c. brown	1·40	1·20
158	6	50c. grey	1·40	1·20
159	6	64c. blue	1·40	1·20
160	6	80c. brown	1·40	1·20
161	6	96c. red	5·50	5·25
162	6	1e. black	1·10	1·10
163	6	1e.20 pink	1·10	1·10
164	6	1e.60 blue	1·10	1·10
165	6	2e.40 yellow	1·70	1·60
166	6	3e.36 green	2·40	2·10
167	6	4e.50 red	2·40	2·10
168	6	7e. blue	8·50	8·50

7 20r. Stamp, 1868

1980. 112th Anniv of First Overprinted Madeira Stamps.

169	7	6e.50 black, bistre and green	45	25
170	-	19e.50 black, purple and red	1·50	1·00

MS171	140×115 mm. Nos. 169/70 (sold at 30e.)	6·75	6·75

DESIGN: 19e.50, 100r. stamp, 1868.

8 Ox Sledge

1980. World Tourism Conference, Manila, Philippines. Multicoloured.

172	50c. Type **8**	20	15
173	1e. Wine and grapes	30	20
174	5e. Map of Madeira	75	40
175	6e.50 Basketwork	95	45
176	8e. Orchid	1·40	65
177	30e. Fishing boat	2·75	1·10

9 O Bailinho (folk dance)

1981. Europa.

178	9	22e. multicoloured	1·90	95

MS179	141×115 mm. No. 178 ×2	8·50	8·50

10 Portuguese Caravel approaching Madeira

1981. 560th Anniv (1980) of Discovery of Madeira. Multicoloured.

180	8e.50 Type **10**	70	45
181	33e.50 Prince Henry the Navigator and map of Atlantic Ocean	2·75	1·00

11 "Dactylorhiza foliosa"

1981. Regional Flowers. Multicoloured.

182	7e. Type **11**	50	30
183	8e.50 "Geranium maderense"	55	30
184	9e. "Goodyera macrophylla"	65	20
185	10e. "Armeria maderensis"	65	25
186	12e.50 "Matthiola maderensis"	45	20
187	20e. "Isoplexis sceptrum"	1·10	70
188	27e. "Viola paradoxa"	1·90	1·20
189	30e. "Erica maderensis"	1·20	75
190	33e.50 "Scilla maderensis"	2·00	1·40
191	37e.50 "Cirsium latifolium"	1·70	1·00
192	50e. "Echium candicans"	2·75	1·50
193	100e. "Clethra arborea"	3·50	1·60

12 First Sugar Mill

1982. Europa.

199	12	33e.50 multicoloured	3·25	1·50

MS200	139×115 mm. No. 199 ×3	17·00	17·00

13 Dancer holding Dolls on Staff

1982. O Brinco Dancing Dolls. Multicoloured.

201	27e. Type **13**	2·20	1·30
202	33e.50 Dancers	3·50	1·80

14 Los Levadas Irrigation Channels

1983. Europa.

203	14	37e.50 multicoloured	3·25	1·30

MS204	114×140 mm. No. 203 ×3	21·00	21·00

15 Flag of Madeira

1983. Flag.

205	15	12e.50 multicoloured	1·30	45

1984. Europa. As T 398 of Portugal but additionally inscr "MADEIRA".

206	51e. multicoloured	4·50	2·20
MS207	113×140 mm. No. 206 ×3	19·00	19·00

16 Rally Car

1984. 25th Anniv of Madeira Rally. Multicoloured.

208	16e. Type **16**	90	45
209	51e. Rally car (different)	3·25	1·60

17 Basket Sledge

1984. Transport (1st series). Multicoloured.
210	16e. Type **17**	80	45
211	35e. Hammock	1·70	1·10
212	40e. Borracheiros (wine carriers)	2·40	1·10
213	51e. Carreira local sailing boat	3·00	1·70

See also Nos. 218/21.

18 Braguinha Player

1985. Europa.
214	**18** 60e. multicoloured	4·50	1·90
MS215	140×115 mm. No. 214 ×3	23·00	23·00

19 Black Scabbardfish

1985. Fish (1st series). Multicoloured.
216	40e. Type **19**	2·40	1·30
217	60e. Opah	3·25	1·90

See also Nos. 222/3 and 250/3.

1985. Transport (2nd series). As T **17**. Multicoloured.
218	20e. Ox sledge	80	45
219	40e. Mountain railway	1·90	1·10
220	46e. Fishing boat and basket used by pesquitos (itinerant fish sellers)	2·50	1·80
221	60e. Coastal ferry	3·00	1·50

1986. Fish (2nd series). As T **19**. Multicoloured.
222	20e. Big-eyed tuna	1·10	45
223	75e. Alfonsino	5·25	2·10

20 Cory's Shearwater and Tanker

1986. Europa.
224	**20** 68e.50 multicoloured	5·25	2·10
MS225	140×114 mm. No. 224 ×3	21·00	21·00

21 Sao Lourenco Fort, Funchal

1986. Fortresses. Multicoloured.
226	22e.50 Type **21**	1·10	55
227	52e.50 Sao Joao do Pico Fort, Funchal	3·25	1·60
228	68e.50 Sao Tiago Fort, Funchal	4·25	2·10
229	100e. Nossa Senhora do Amparo Fort, Machico	5·25	1·80

22 Firecrest

1987. Birds (1st series). Multicoloured.
230	25e. Type **22**	1·10	45
231	57e. Trocaz pigeon	3·25	1·80
232	74e.50 Barn owl	4·25	2·40
233	125e. Soft-plumaged petrel	5·25	2·75

See also Nos. 240/3.

23 Social Services Centre, Funchal (Raul Chorao Ramalho)

1987. Europa. Architecture.
234	**23** 74e.50 multicoloured	4·75	2·10
MS235	140×113 mm. No. 234 ×4	21·00	21·00

24 Funchal Cathedral

1987. Historic Buildings. Multicoloured.
236	51e. Type **24**	3·00	1·50
237	74e.50 Old Town Hall, Santa Cruz	3·50	1·50

25 "Maria Cristina" (mail boat)

1988. Europa. Transport and Communications.
238	**25** 80e. multicoloured	5·75	2·10
MS239	139×112 mm. As No. 238 ×4 but with cream background	21·00	21·00

1988. Birds (2nd series). As T **22** but horiz. Multicoloured.
240	27e. European robin	1·10	30
241	60e. Streaked rock sparrow	2·75	1·70
242	80e. Chaffinch	3·75	1·80
243	100e. Northern sparrowhawk	4·25	1·80

26 Columbus and Funchal House

1988. Christopher Columbus's Houses in Madeira. Multicoloured.
244	55e. Type **26**	3·00	1·30
245	80e. Columbus and Porto Santo house (horiz)	3·25	1·70

27 Child flying Kite

1989. Europa. Children's Games and Toys. Multicoloured.
246	80e. Type **27**	5·25	2·75
MS247	139×112 mm. 80e. ×2, Type **27**; 80e. ×2, Child flying kite (different)	21·00	21·00

28 Church of St. John the Evangelist

1989. Brasiliana 89 Stamp Exhibition, Rio de Janeiro. Madeiran Churches. Multicoloured.
248	29e. Type **28**	85	45
249	87e. St. Clara's Church and Convent	3·75	2·10

29 Spiny Hatchetfish

1989. Fish (3rd series). Multicoloured.
250	29e. Type **29**	85	20
251	60e. Dog wrasse	2·50	1·50
252	87e. Rainbow wrasse	3·75	2·00
253	100e. Madeiran scorpionfish	4·00	2·75

30 Zarco Post Office

1990. Europa. Post Office Buildings. Multicoloured.
254	80e. Type **30**	2·50	1·70
MS255	139×111 mm. 80e. ×2, Type **30**; 80e. ×2, Porto da Cruz Post Office	18·00	18·00

31 Bananas

1990. Sub-tropical Fruits. Multicoloured.
256	5e. Type **31**	25	15
257	10e. Thorn apple	25	15
258	32e. Avocado	90	50
259	35e. Mangoes	90	50
260	38e. Tomatoes	1·00	50
261	60e. Sugar apple	2·30	1·40
262	65e. Surinam cherries	2·20	1·30
263	70e. Brazilian guavas	2·40	1·40
264	85e. Delicious fruits	2·75	1·60
265	100e. Passion fruit	3·50	2·10
266	110e. Papayas	3·50	2·10
267	125e. Guava	3·50	2·10

32 Tunny Boat

1990. Boats. Multicoloured.
270	32e. Type **32**	70	25
271	60e. Desert Islands boat	1·70	1·00
272	70e. Maneiro	2·00	1·40
273	95e. Chavelha	3·00	2·00

33 Trocaz Pigeon

1991. The Trocaz Pigeon. Multicoloured.
274	35e. Type **33**	1·60	55
275	35e. Two pigeons	1·60	55
276	35e. Pigeon on nest	1·60	55
277	35e. Pigeon alighting on twig	1·60	55

Nos. 264/7 were issued together, *se-tenant*, forming a composite design.

34 European Remote Sensing ("ERS1") Satellite

1991. Europa. Europe in Space. Multicoloured.
278	80e. Type **34**	3·25	2·10
MS279	140×112 mm. 80e. ×2, Type **34**; 80e. ×2, "Spot" satellite	18·00	18·00

35 Columbus and Funchal House

1992. Europa. 500th Anniv of Discovery of America by Columbus.
280	**35** 85e. multicoloured	3·25	1·30

36 "Gaviao" (ferry)

1992. Inter-island Ships. Multicoloured.
281	38e. Type **36**	85	35
282	65e. "Independencia" (catamaran ferry)	1·70	1·20
283	85e. "Madeirense" (car ferry)	2·10	1·40
284	120e. "Funchalense" (freighter)	3·00	1·60

37 "Shadow thrown by Christa Maar" (Lourdes Castro)

1993. Europa. Contemporary Art. Multicoloured.
285	50e. Type **37**	3·00	1·40
MS286	140×112 mm. 90e. ×2, Type **37**; 90e. ×2, "Shadow thrown by Dahlia"	13·00	13·00

38 Seals Swimming

1993. Mediterranean Monk Seal. Multicoloured.
287	42e. Type **38**	1·40	70
288	42e. Seal basking	1·40	70
289	42e. Two seals on rocks	1·40	70
290	42e. Mother suckling young	1·40	70

Nos. 287/90 were issued together, se-tenant, forming a composite design.

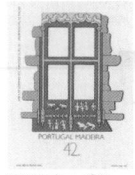

39 Window of St. Francis's Convent, Funchal

1993. Regional Architecture. Multicoloured.
291	42e. Type **39**	85	55
292	130e. Window of Mercy, Old Hospital, Funchal	3·00	1·90

40 Native of Cape of Good Hope and Explorer with Model Caravel

1992. Europa. Discoveries. Multicoloured.
293	90e. Type **40**	2·10	1·60
MS294	140×112 mm. 100e. ×2, Type **40**; 100e. ×2, Palm tree and explorer with model caravel	10·50	10·50

41 Embroidery

1994. Traditional Crafts (1st series). Multicoloured.
295	45e. Type **41**	75	35
296	75e. Tapestry	1·50	95
297	100e. Boots	2·00	1·30
298	140e. Wicker chair back	3·00	1·90

See also Nos. 301/4.

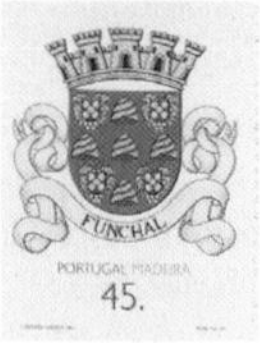

42 Funchal

1994. District Arms. Multicoloured.

299	45e. Type **42**	75	35
300	140e. Porto Santo	2·75	1·60

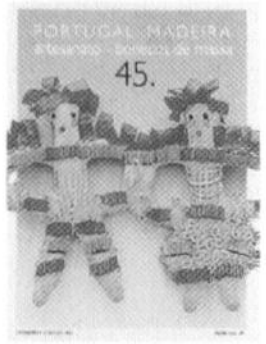

43 Bread Dough Figures

1995. Traditional Crafts (2nd series). Multicoloured.

301	45e. Type **43**	85	50
302	80e. Inlaid wooden box	1·50	85
303	95e. Bamboo cage	1·70	1·20
304	135e. Woollen bonnet	2·30	1·50

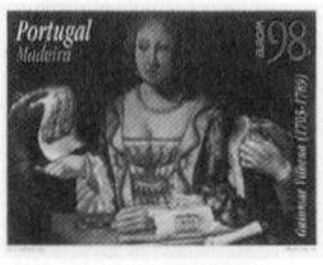

44 Guiomar Vilhena (entrepreneur)

1996. Europa. Famous Women. Multicoloured.

305	98e. Type **44**	2·10	1·10
MS306	140×112 mm. No. 305 ×3	6·50	6·50

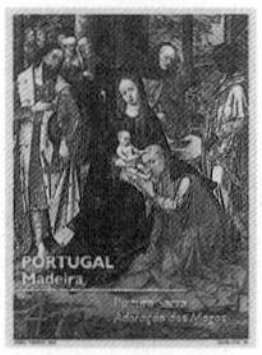

45 "Adoration of the Magi"

1996. Religious Paintings by Flemish Artists. Multicoloured.

307	47e. Type **45**	80	35
308	78e. "St. Mary Magdalene"	1·40	95
309	98e. "The Annunciation" (horiz)	1·70	1·20
310	140e. "Saints Peter, Paul and Andrew" (horiz)	2·10	1·50

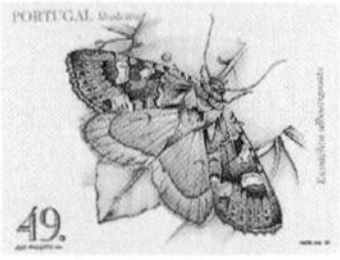

46 "Eumichtis albostigmata" (moth)

1997. Butterflies and Moths. Multicoloured.

311	49e. Type **46**	75	35
312	80e. Menophra maderae (moth)	1·30	65
313	100e. Painted lady	1·50	1·20
314	140e. Large white	2·75	2·50

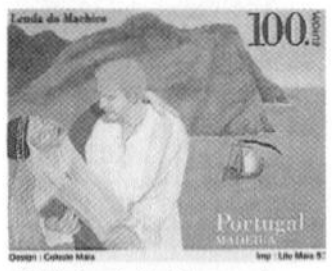

47 Robert Achim and Anne of Arfet (Legend of Machico)

1997. Europa. Tales and Legends. Multicoloured.

315	100e. Type **47**	2·10	1·10
MS316	140×106 mm. No. 315 ×3	6·50	6·50

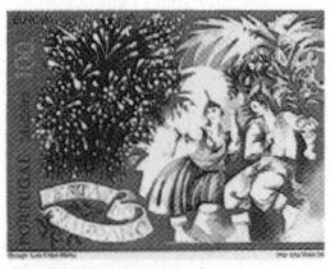

48 New Year's Eve Fireworks Display, Funchal

1998. Europa. National Festival. Multicoloured.

317	100e. Type **48**	1·90	95
MS318	140×109 mm. No. 317 ×3	6·25	6·25

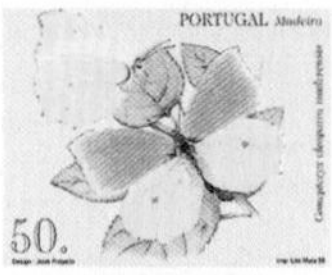

49 "Gonepteryx cleopatra"

1998. Butterflies and Moths. Multicoloured.

319	50e. Type **49**	75	35
320	85e. "Xanthorhoe rupicola"	1·10	75
321	100e. "Noctua teixeirai"	1·50	95
322	140e. "Xenochlorodes nubigena"	2·10	1·50

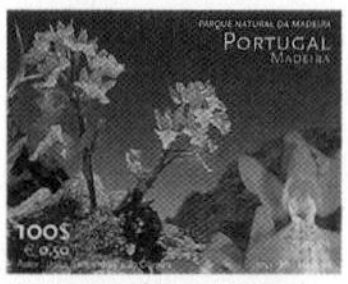

50 Madeira Island Nature Park

1999. Europa. Parks and Gardens. Multicoloured.

323	100e. Type **50**	1·50	95
MS324	153×108 mm. No. 323 ×3	5·25	5·25

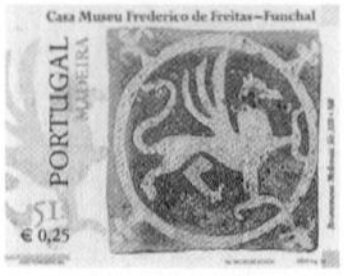

51 Medieval Floor Tile

1999. Tiles from Frederico de Freitas Collection, Funchal. Multicoloured.

325	51e. Type **51**	75	35
326	80e. English art-nouveau tile (19th–20th century)	1·20	85
327	95e. Persian tile (14th century)	1·50	95
328	100e. Spanish Moor tile (13th century)	1·60	1·10
329	140e. Dutch Delft tile (18th century)	2·10	1·50
330	210e. Syrian tile (13th–14th century)	3·00	2·10

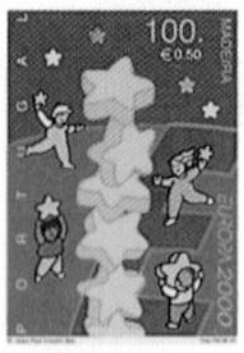

52 "Building Europe"

2000. Europa. Multicoloured.

332	100e. Type **52**	2·75	2·10
MS333	154×108 mm. Nos. 332 ×3	8·50	8·50

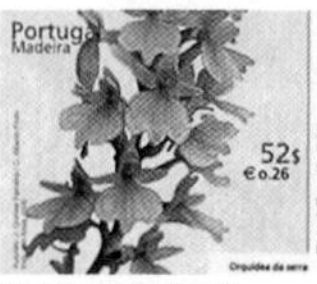

53 Mountain Orchid

2000. Plants of Laurissilva Forest. Multicoloured.

334	52e. Type **53**	70	35
335	85e. White orchid	1·20	80
336	100e. Leafy plant	1·40	90
337	100e. Laurel	1·40	90
338	140e. Barbusano	2·10	1·50
339	350e. Visco	4·75	3·75

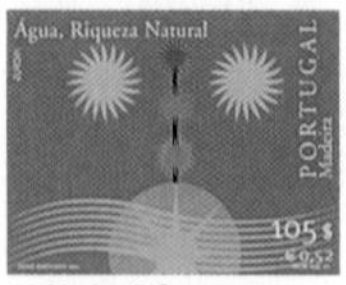

54 Marine Life

2001. Europa. Water Resources. Multicoloured.

341	105e. Type **54**	3·25	2·10
MS342	140×110 mm. No. 341 ×3	7·50	7·50

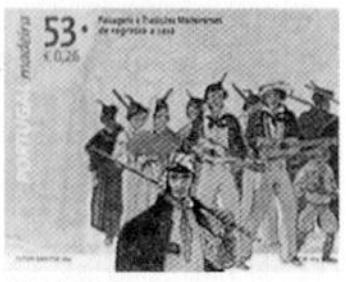

55 Musicians

2001. Traditions of Madeira. Multicoloured.

343	53e. Type **55**	70	55
344	85e. Couple carrying produce	1·20	95
345	105e. Couple selling goods	1·60	1·20
MS346	140×112 mm. 350e. Man carrying birds	5·00	5·00

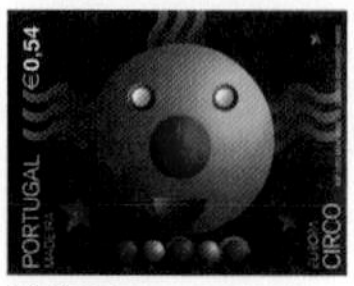

56 Clown

2002. Europa. Circus.

347	**56** 54c. multicoloured	3·00	2·75
MS348	140×110 mm. No. 347 ×3	8·50	8·50

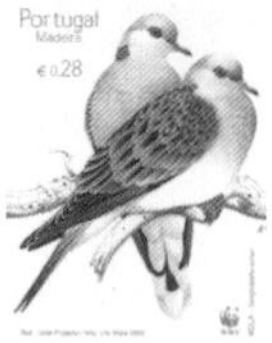

57 Turtle Doves (*Streptopelia turtur*)

2002. Birds. Multicoloured.

349	28c. Type **57**	1·00	65
350	28c. Perching dove	1·00	65
351	28c. Dove with raised wings	1·00	65
352	28c. Dove with chicks	1·00	65

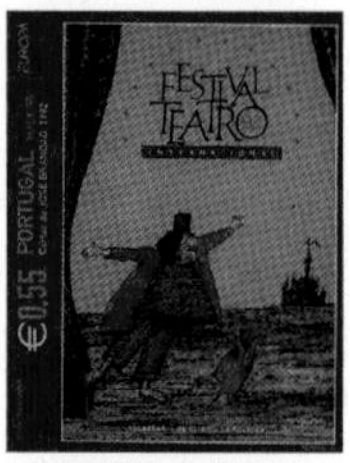

58 1992 Theatre Festival Poster (José Brandao)

2003. Europa. Poster Art.

353	**58** 55c. multicoloured	2·50	1·80
MS354	140×113 mm. No. 353 ×2	4·75	4·75

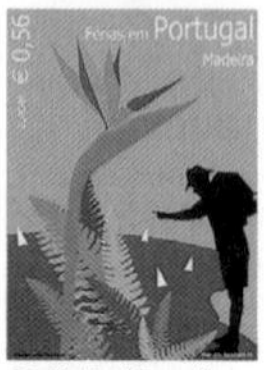

59 Bird of Paradise Flower, Figure and Yachts

2004. Europa. Holidays.

355	**59** 56c. multicoloured	2·50	1·80
MS356	141×112 mm. No. 355 ×2	4·75	4·75

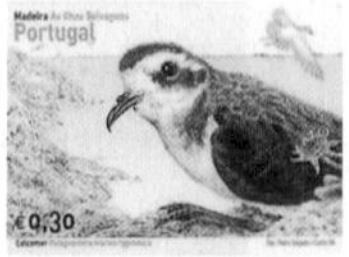

60 Selvagens White-faced Storm-Petrel (*Pelagodroma marina hypoleuca*)

2004. Selvagens Islands. Multicoloured.

357	30c. Type **60**	1·00	70
358	45c. *Monathes lowei* (plant) and beetle	1·60	1·10
359	72c. *Tarentola bischoffi*	2·75	1·80
MS360	140×112 mm. Nos. 357/9	5·75	5·75

No. **MS**360 has the stamps arranged so as to make a composite design with a description of the islands below.

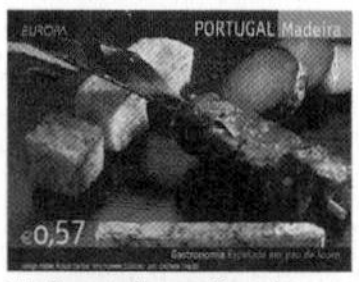

61 Espetada em Pau de Louro (skewered meat)

2005. Europa. Gastronomy. Multicoloured.

361	57c. Type **61**	2·10	1·30
MS362	125×95 mm. 57c.×2, Filete de espada (fish)×2	5·50	5·50

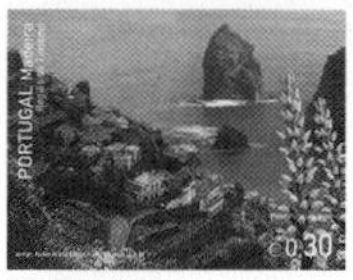

62 Coastline

2005. Tourism. Multicoloured.

363	30c. Type **62**	85	65
364	30c. Chaffinch	85	65
365	45c. Hikers	1·30	1·00
366	45c. Windmill	1·30	1·00
367	57c. Horse riders and scuba divers	1·50	1·20
368	74c. Flowers and fireworks	2·10	1·70
MS369	125×96 mm. 30c. Girl carrying basket; €1.55 Lace and tower	5·25	5·25

Nos. 363/8 were issued together, *se-tenant*, forming a composite design.

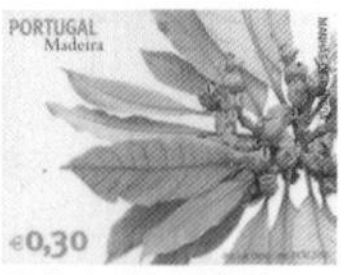

63 *Euphorbia pulcherrima*

2006. Flowers. Multicoloured.

370	30c. Type **63**	85	65
371	45c. *Aloe arborescens*	1·30	1·00
372	57c. *Senna didymobotrya*	1·50	1·20
373	74c. *Anthurium andraeanum*	2·10	1·70
374	€1 *Strelitzia reginae*	2·75	2·20
375	€2 *Hydrangea macrophylla*	5·50	4·50
MS376	Two sheets, each 124×95 mm. (a) 45c.×4, *Rosa*; *Leucospermum nutans*; *Paphiopedilum insigne*; *Hippeastrum vittatum*. (b) 45c.×4, *Bougainvillea*; *Cymbidium*; *Hibiscus rosa-sinesis*; *Erythrina crista-galli*	10·00	10·00

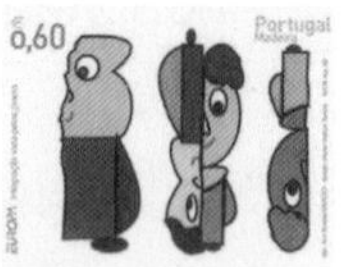

64 Figures (Ana Soares)

2006. Europa. Integration. Winning Entries in ANACED (association for art and creativity by and for people with disabilities) Painting Competition. Multicoloured.

377	60c. Type **64**	1·70	1·30
MS378	125×95 mm. 60c.×2, Swimming pool (Pedro Fonseca); Blind figure with dog (Andre Gaspar)	3·25	2·75

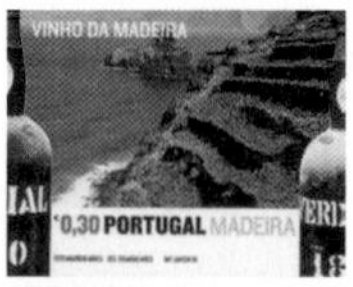

65 Terraces

2006. Madeira Wine. Multicoloured.

379	30c. Type **65**	85	65
380	52c. Workers and baskets of grapes	1·30	1·00
381	60c. Barrels in cellar	1·70	1·30
382	75c. Barrels and glass of wine	2·10	1·70
MS383	125×95 mm. 45c. Vines; 60c. Worker amongst vines; 75c. Bottles; €1 Barrels	7·75	7·75

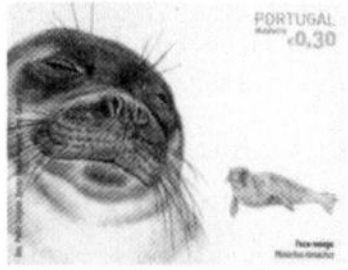

66 *Monachus monachus* (Mediterranean monk seal)

2007. Marine Fauna. Multicoloured.

384	30c. Type **66**	85	65
385	45c. *Caretta caretta* (loggerhead sea turtle)	85	65
386	61c. *Calonectris diomedea borealis* (Cory's shearwater)	85	65
387	75c. *Aphanopus carbo* (black scabbard fish)	85	65
MS388	126×95 mm 61c.×4, *Telmatactis cricoides* (sea anemone); *Charonia lampas*; *Patella aspera* (limpet); *Sparisoma cretense* (parrotfish)	7·00	7·00

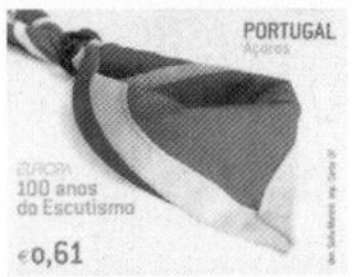

67 Scarf

2007. Europa. Centenary of Scouting. Multicoloured.

389	61c. Type **67**	1·70	1·30
MS390 125×95 mm. 61c.×2, Robert Baden Powell (founder); Hat		3·25	2·75

The stamps of **MS**390 form a composite design.

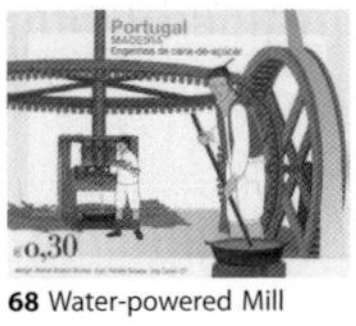

68 Water-powered Mill

2007. Sugar Cane Mills. Multicoloured.

391	30c. Type **68**	85	65
392	75c. Cattle and crushing	2·10	1·70
MS393 125×95 mm. €2.45 Ox driven mill (60×40 mm)		7·00	7·00

The stamp and margin of **MS**393 form a composite design.

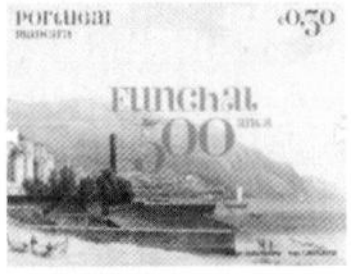

69 Early City

2008. 500th Anniv of Funchal City. Multicoloured.

394	30c. Type **69**	90	70
395	61c. Early map of city and environs	1·80	1·40
396	75c. Arms	2·20	1·70
397	€1 Ship and city from the sea	3·00	2·30
MS398 125×95 mm. (a) €2.45 King Manuel I of Portugal; (b) €2.45 Ships and harbour		13·50	13·00

The stamps and margins of **MS**398a/b, each form a composite design.

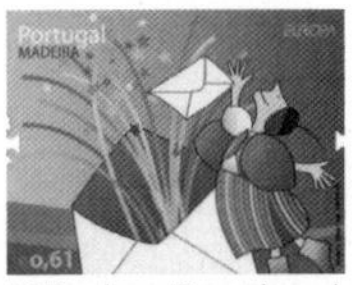

70 Envelope, Fireworks and Woman

2008. Europa. The Letter. Multicoloured.

399	61c. Type **70**	1·80	1·40
MS400 125×95 mm. 61c.×2, Houses and envelopes; As Type **70**		3·50	3·50

The stamps of **MS**400 form a composite design.

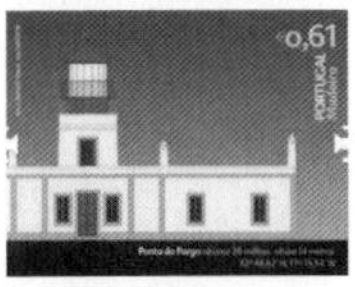

71 Ponta do Pargo

2008. Lighthouse.

401	**71**	61c. multicoloured	1·80	1·40

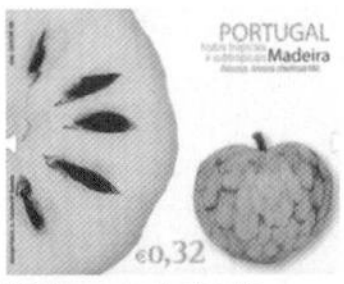

72 *Annona cherimola*

2009. Fruit. Multicoloured.

402	32c. Type **72**	1·10	85
403	68c. *Eugenia uniflora*	2·20	1·70
404	80c. *Persea americana*	2·50	2·00
405	€2 *Psidium guajava*	6·25	5·00
MS406 125×95 mm. €2.50 *Passiflora edulis* (80×31 mm)		7·75	7·75
MS407 125×95 mm. €2.50 *Musa* Dwarf Cavendish (80×31 mm)		7·75	7·75

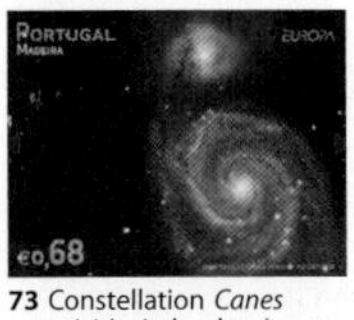

73 Constellation *Canes venatici* (spiral galaxy)

2009. Europa. Astronomy. Multicoloured.

408	68c. Type **73**	2·20	1·70
MS409 125×95 mm. 68c.×2, Telescope (built by University of Madeira student); As Type **73**		4·25	4·25

The stamps and margins of **MS**409 form a composite design.

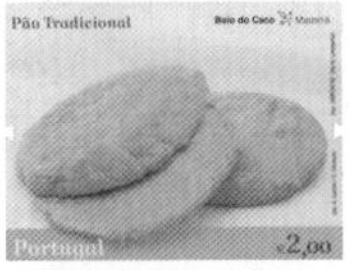

74 Bolo do Caco (rolls)

2009. Bread. Sheet 125×95 mm.

MS410 $2 multicoloured		6·25	6·25

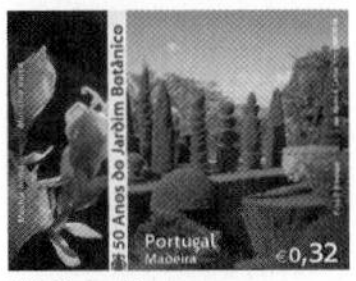

75 *Musschia aurea*

2010. 50th Anniv of Botanic Gardens, Rui Veira. Multicoloured.

411	32c. Type **75**	1·10	85
412	68c. *Geranium maderense*	2·20	1·70
413	80c. *Ranunculus cortusifolius*	2·50	2·00
414	€2 *Convolvulus massonii*	6·25	5·00
MS415 125×96 mm. €2 Topiary garden (80×30 mm)		6·25	5·00
MS416 125×96 mm. €2 Building, laboratory, climber and seeds (80×30 mm)		6·25	5·00

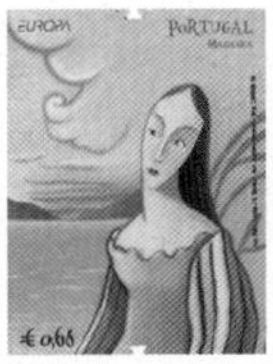

76 Girl

2010. Europa. Children's Books. Multicoloured.

417	68c. Type **76**	2·20	1·70
MS418 125×96 mm. 68c.×2, Man seated wearing hat (Father); As Type **76**		4·25	4·25

CHARITY TAX STAMPS

The note under this heading in Portugal also applies here.

1925. As Marquis de Pombal stamps of Portugal but inscr "MADEIRA".

C142	**C73**	15c. grey	2·50	2·10
C143	-	15c. grey	2·50	2·10
C144	**C 75**	15c. grey	2·50	2·10

NEWSPAPER STAMPS

1876. Newspaper stamp of Portugal optd **MADEIRA**.

N69	**N17**	2½r. green	12·00	6·00

POSTAGE DUE STAMPS

1925. Marquis de Pombal stamps as Nos. C1/3 optd **MULTA**.

D145	**C73**	30c. grey	2·00	1·90
D146	-	30c. grey	2·00	1·90
D147	**C 75**	30c. grey	2·00	1·90

Pt. 1

MAFEKING

A town in the Cape of Goog Hope. Special stamps issued by British garrison during Boer War.

12 pence = 1 shilling; 20 shillings = 1 pound.

1900. Surch MAFEKING, BESIEGED. and value. (a) On Cape of Good Hope stamps.

1	**6**	1d. on ½d. green	£300	85·00
2	**17**	1d. on ½d. green	£350	£110
3	**17**	3d. on 1d. red	£300	65·00
4	**6**	6d. on 3d. mauve	£42000	£325
5	**6**	1s. on 4d. olive	£8000	£425

(b) On stamps of Bechuanaland Protectorate (opts on Great Britain).

6	**71**	1d. on ½d. red (No. 59)	£300	80·00
7	**57**	3d. on 1d. lilac (No. 61)	£1000	£120
13	**73**	6d. on 2d. green and red (No. 62)	£1500	£100
9	**75**	6d. on 3d. purple on yellow (No. 63)	£7000	£400
14	**79**	1s. on 6d. purple on red (No. 65)	£7000	£120

(c) On stamps of British Bechuanaland (opts on Great Britain).

10	**3**	6d. on 3d. lilac and black (No. 12)	£500	90·00
11	**76**	1s. on 4d. green and brown (No. 35)	£1600	£100
15	**79**	1s. on 6d. purple on red (No. 36)	£32000	£850
16	**82**	2s. on 1s. green (No. 37)	£14000	£600

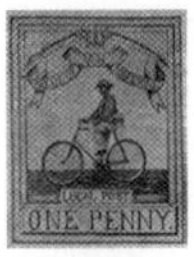

3 Cadet Sgt.-Major Goodyear

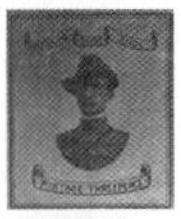

4 General Baden-Powell

1900

17	**3**	1d. blue on blue	£1100	£300
20	**4**	3d. blue on blue	£1600	£400

Pt. 1

MAHRA SULTANATE OF QISHN AND SOCOTRA

The National Liberation Front took control on 1 October 1967, and full independence was granted by Great Britain on 30 November 1967. Subsequently part of South Yemen.

1000 fils = 1 dinar.

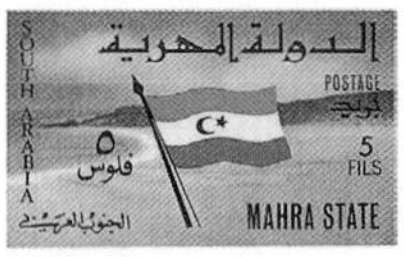

1 Mahra Flag

1967

1	**1**	5f. multicoloured	2·75	45
2	**1**	10f. multicoloured	2·75	45
3	**1**	15f. multicoloured	2·75	45
4	**1**	20f. multicoloured	2·75	45
5	**1**	25f. multicoloured	2·75	45
6	**1**	35f. multicoloured	2·75	45
7	**1**	50f. multicoloured	2·75	45
8	**1**	65f. multicoloured	3·00	45
9	**1**	100f. multicoloured	3·00	45
10	**1**	250f. multicoloured	3·00	45
11	**1**	500f. multicoloured	3·00	45

APPENDIX

The National Liberation Front took control on 1 October 1967, and full independence was granted by Great Britain on 30 November 1967. Subsequently part of Southern Yemen.

1967

Scout Jamboree, Idahoo. 15, 75, 100, 150f.

President Kennedy Commemoration. Postage 10, 15, 25, 50, 75, 100, 150f.; Air 250, 500f.

Olympic Games, Mexico (1968). Postage 10, 25, 50f.; Air 250, 500f.

Fot later issues see **SOUTHERN YEMEN** and **YEMEN PEOPLE'S DEMOCRATIC REPUBLIC** in Volume 6.

Pt. 1

MALACCA

A British Settlement on the Malay Peninsula which became a state of the Federation of Malaya, incorporated in Malaysia in 1963.

100 cents = 1 dollar (Malayan).

1948. Silver Wedding. As T **59b/c** of Jamaica.

1	10c. violet	30	1·75
2	$5 brown	32·00	48·00

1949. As T 58 of Straits Settlements.

3	1c. black	30	70
4	2c. orange	80	45
5	3c. green	30	1·75
6	4c. brown	30	10
6a	5c. purple	3·00	1·50
7	6c. grey	75	85
8	8c. red	75	6·00
8a	8c. green	7·00	5·00
9	10c. mauve	30	10
9a	12c. red	7·00	12·00
10	15c. blue	3·00	60
11	20c. black and green	75	7·00
11a	20c. blue	8·50	2·75
12	25c. purple and orange	75	70
12a	35c. red and purple	8·00	3·00
13	40c. red and purple	1·50	11·00
14	50c. black and blue	1·50	1·25
15	$1 blue and purple	17·00	28·00
16	$2 green and red	28·00	28·00
17	$5 green and brown	65·00	60·00

1949. U.P.U. As T **59d/g** of Jamaica.

18	10c. purple	30	50
19	15c. blue	2·00	2·75
20	25c. orange	40	10·50
21	50c. black	60	4·75

1953. Coronation. As T **61a** of Jamaica.

22	10c. black and purple	1·50	1·50

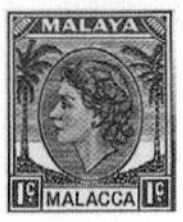

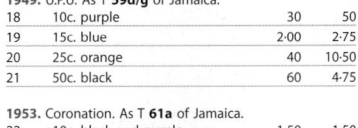

1 Queen Elizabeth II

1954

23	1c. black	10	60
24	2c. orange	30	1·25
25	4c. brown	1·75	10
26	5c. mauve	30	2·50
27	6c. grey	10	40
28	8c. green	40	2·75
29	10c. purple	2·25	10
30	12c. red	30	3·00
31	20c. blue	30	1·25
32	25c. purple and orange	30	1·50
33	30c. red and purple	30	30
34	35c. red and purple	30	1·50
35	50c. black and blue	5·00	2·50
36	$1 blue and purple	7·00	14·00
37	$2 green and red	24·00	50·00
38	$5 green and brown	24·00	55·00

1957. As Nos. 92/102 of Kedah but inset portrait of Queen Elizabeth II.

39	1c. black	10	50
40	2c. red	10	50
41	4c. sepia	50	10
42	5c. lake	50	10
43	8c. green	2·50	2·50
44	10c. sepia	40	10
45	20c. blue	2·75	1·50
46	50c. black and blue	1·50	1·25
47	$1 blue and purple	8·00	6·00
48	$2 green and red	24·00	35·00
49	$5 brown and green	26·00	48·00

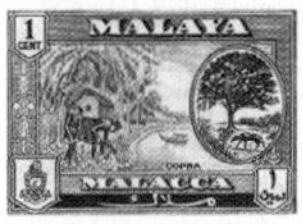

2 Copra

1960. As Nos. 39/49 but with inset picture of Melaka tree and Pelandok (mouse-deer) as in T **2**.

50	1c. black	10	30
51	2c. red	10	65
52	4c. sepia	10	10
53	5c. lake	10	10
54	8c. green	4·50	3·00
55	10c. purple	30	10
56	20c. blue	2·75	80
57	50c. black and blue	1·50	1·00
58	$1 blue and purple	6·50	2·75
59	$2 green and red	7·00	16·00
60	$5 brown and green	16·00	14·00

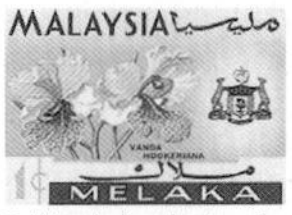

3 "Vanda hookeriana"

1965. As Nos. 115/21 of Kedah but with Arms of Malacca inset and inscr "MELAKA" as in T **3**.

61	**3**	1c. multicoloured	10	2·25
62	-	2c. multicoloured	10	1·75
63	-	5c. multicoloured	55	40
64	-	6c. multicoloured	50	1·00
65	-	10c. multicoloured	30	10
66	-	15c. multicoloured	1·75	40
67	-	20c. multicoloured	2·25	1·00

The higher values used in Malacca were Nos. 20/7 of Malaysia.

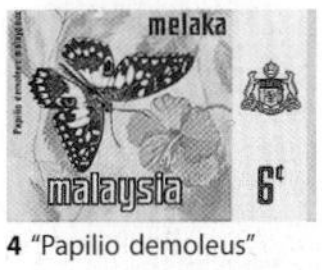

4 "Papilio demoleus"

1971. Butterflies. As Nos. 124/30 of Kedah but with Arms of Malacca as in T **4**. Inscr "melaka".

70		1c. multicoloured	60	2·25
71		2c. multicoloured	1·00	2·25
72		5c. multicoloured	1·50	1·00
73	**4**	6c. multicoloured	1·50	3·00
74	-	10c. multicoloured	1·50	60
75	-	15c. multicoloured	2·25	20

76 - 20c. multicoloured 2·25 2·50

The higher values in use with this issue were Nos. 64/71 of Malaysia.

5 "Durio zibethinus"

1979. Flowers. As Nos. 135/41 of Kedah but with Arms of Malacca and inscr "melaka" as in T **5**.

82 1c. "Rafflesia hasseltii" 10 1·25
83 2c. "Pterocarpus indicus" 10 1·25
84 5c. "Lagerstroemia speciosa" 15 1·00
85 10c. Type **5** 20 35
86 15c. "Hibiscus rosa-sinesis" 20 10
87 20c. "Rhododendron scorte-chinii" 25 10
88 25c. "Etlingera elatior" (inscr "Phaeomeria speciosa") 45 80

6 Rubber

1986. As Nos. 152/8 of Kedah but with Arms of Malacca and inscr "MELAKA" as in T **6**.

96 1c. Coffee 10 25
97 2c. Coconuts 10 30
98 5c. Cocoa 15 10
99 10c. Black pepper 20 10
100 15c. Type **6** 30 10
101 20c. Oil palm 30 15
102 30c. Rice 40 15

7 *Nelumbium nelumbo* (sacred lotus)

2007. Garden Flowers. As Nos. 210/15 of Johore, but with Arms of Malacca as in T **7**. Multicoloured.

103 5s. Type **7** 10 10
104 10s. *Hydrangea macrophylla* 15 10
105 20s. *Hippeastrum reticulatum* 25 15
106 30s. *Bougainvillea* 40 20
107 40s. *Ipomoea indica* 50 30
108 50s. *Hibiscus rosa-sinensis* 65 35
MS109 100×85 mm. Nos. 103/8 1·50 1·50

Pt. 6, Pt. 13

MALAGASY REPUBLIC

The former areas covered by Madagascar and Dependencies were renamed the Malagasy Republic within the French Community on 14 October 1958. It became independent on 26 June 1960. In 1992 it reverted to the name of Madagascar.

1958. 100 centimes = 1 franc.
1976. 5 francs = 1 ariary.

1 "Human Rights"

1958. Tenth Anniv of Declaration of Human Rights.
1 **1** 10f. brown and blue 65 55

2 "Datura"

1959. Tropical Flora.
2 **2** 6f. green, brown and yellow 30 30
3 - 25f. multicoloured 1·00 45
DESIGN—VERT: 25f. Poinsettia.

2a Malagasy Flag and Assembly Hall

1959. Proclamation of Malagasy Republic and "French Community" Commemorative (60f.).
4 **2a** 20f. red, green and purple 45 30
5 - 25f. red, green and grey 65 45
6 - 60f. multicoloured 1·70 75
DESIGNS—VERT: 25f. Malagasy flag on map of Madagascar; 60f. Natives holding French and Malagasy flags.

3 "Chionaema pauliani" (butterfly)

1960
7 30c. multicoloured (postage) 90 30
8 40c. brown, chocolate & green 90 30
9 50c. turquoise and purple 90 30
10 **3** 1f. red, purple and black 90 30
11 - 3f. black, red and olive 90 30
12 - 5f. green, brown and red 35 20
13 - 6f. yellow and green 55 30
14 - 8f. black, green and red 55 30
15 - 10f. green, brown & turquoise 1·00 30
16 - 15f. green and brown 1·20 30
17 - 30f. multicoloured (air) 1·80 10
18 - 40f. brown and turquoise 1·80 30
19 - 50f. multicoloured 3·25 45
20 - 100f. multicoloured 5·50 65
21 - 200f. yellow and violet 7·25 1·80
22 - 500f. brown, blue and green 14·00 3·25

OTHER DESIGNS—As Type **2**: HORIZ: 5f. Sisal; 8f. Pepper; 15f. Cotton. VERT: 6f. Ylang ylang (flower); 10f. Rice. 48½×27 mm: 30f. Sugar cane trucks; 40f. Tobacco plantation; 500f. Mandrare Bridge.

3a Reafforestation

1960. Trees Festival.
23 **3a** 20f. brown, green and ochre 90 45

4

1960. Tenth Anniv of African Technical Co-operation Commission.
24 **4** 25f. lake and green 65 35

5 Pres. Philibert Tsiranana

1960
25 **5** 20f. brown and green 35 10

6 Young Athletes

1960. First Youth Games, Tananarive.
26 **6** 25f. brown, chestnut and blue 65 35

7 Pres. Tsiranana

1960
27 **7** 20f. black, red and green 45 10

1960. Independence. Surch **+10 F FETES DE L'INDEPENDANCE**.
28 20f.+10f. black, red & grn 70 40

9 Ruffed Lemur

1961. Lemurs.
29 - 2f. purple & turq (postage) 20 15
30 **9** 4f. black, brown and myrtle 40 15
31 - 12f. brown and green 95 25
32 - 65f. brown, sepia and myrtle (air) 2·75 90
33 - 85f. black, sepia and green 3·00 1·30
34 - 250f. purple, black & turq 8·75 3·50
LEMURS—VERT: As Type **9**: 2f. Grey gentle lemur; 12f. Mongoose-lemur. 48×27 mm: 65f. Diadem sifaka; 85f. Indris; 250f. Verreaux's sifaka.

10 Diesel Train

1962
35 **10** 20f. myrtle 1·10 35
36 - 25f. blue 85 15
DESIGN: 25f. President Tsirianana Bridge.

11 U.N. and Malagasy Flags, and Govt. Building, Tananarive

1962. Admission into U.N.O.
37 **11** 25f. multicoloured 50 25
38 **11** 85f. multicoloured 1·80 70

11a

1962. Malaria Eradication.
39 **11a** 25f.+5f. green 95 90

12 Ranomafana

1962. Tourist Publicity.
40 **12** 10f. purple, myrtle and blue (postage) 25 15
41 - 30f. purple, blue and myrtle 60 25
42 - 50f. blue, myrtle and purple 90 40
43 - 60f. myrtle, purple and blue 1·10 55
44 - 100f. brown, myrtle and blue (air) 1·90 1·20
MS44a 150×85 mm. For Tananarive Philatelic Exhibition. Nos. 40/4 5·75 5·50

DESIGNS—As Type **12**: 30f. Tritriva Lake; 50f. Foulpointe; 60f. Fort Dauphin. 27×47½ mm: 100f. Boeing 707 airliner over Nossi-Be.

13 G.P.O., Tamatave

1962. Stamp Day.
45 **13** 25f.+5f. brn, myrtle & bl 70 70

14 Malagasy and UNESCO. Emblems

1962. UNESCO. Conference on Higher Education in Africa, Tananarive.
46 **14** 20f. black, green and red 50 25

14a

1962. First Anniv of Union of African and Malagasy States.
47 **14a** 30f. green 85 55

15 Hydro-electric Station

1962. Malagasy Industrialization.
48 **15** 5f. multicoloured 10 10
49 - 8f. multicoloured 30 10
50 - 10f. multicoloured 35 25
51 - 15f. brown, black and blue 45 25
52 - 20f. multicoloured 55 25
DESIGNS—HORIZ: 8f. Atomic plant; 15f. "Esso Gasikara" (tanker); 20f. Hertzian aerials at Tananarive-Fianarantsoa. VERT: 10f. Oilwell.

16 Globe and Factory

1963. International Fair, Tamatave.
53 **16** 25f. orange and black 45 25

16a

1963. Freedom from Hunger.
54 **16a** 25f.+5f. lake, brown and red 95 80

17 Douglas DC-8 Airliner

1963. Air. Malagasy Commercial Aviation.
55 **17** 500f. blue, red and green 9·75 4·25

18 Central Post Office, Tananarive

1963. Stamp Day.
56 **18** 20f.+5f. brown & turq 75 70

19 Madagascar
Blue Pigeon

1963. Malagasy Birds and Orchids (8f. to 12f.).
Multicoloured. (a) Postage as T **19**.

57		1f. Type **19**	55	45
58		2f. Blue Madagascar coucal	55	45
59		3f. Madagascar red fody	80	45
60		6f. Madagascar pygmy kingfisher	1·00	45
61		8f. "Gastrorchis humblotii"	85	30
62		10f. "Eulophiella roempleriana"	1·30	50
63		12f. "Angraceum sesquipedale"	1·40	50

(b) Air. Horiz: 49½×28 mm.

64		40f. Helmet bird	2·30	80
65		100f. Pitta-like ground roller	4·75	1·60
66		200f. Crested wood ibis	8·75	3·00

20 Centenary
Emblem and
Map

1963. Red Cross Centenary.

67	**20**	30f. multicoloured	95	65

20a

1963. Air. African and Malagasy Posts and
Telecommunications Union.

68	**20a**	85f. multicoloured	1·80	1·10

21 U.P.U. Monument,
Berne, and Map of
Malagasy

1963. Air. Second Anniv of Malagasy's Admission to U.P.U.

69	**21**	45f. blue, red and turquoise	70	25
70	**21**	85f. blue, red and violet	1·20	60

22 Arms of
Fianarantsoa

1963. Town Arms (1st series). Multicoloured.

71	1f.50 Antsirabe	10	10
72	5f. Antalaha	10	10
73	10f. Tulear	30	20
74	15f. Majunga	30	15
75	20f. Type **22**	55	25
75a	20f. Manajary	30	15
76	25f. Tananarive	55	25
76a	30f. Nossi Be	55	25
77	50f. Diego-Suarez	1·60	70
77a	90f. Antsohihy	1·90	1·30

See also Nos. 174/7 and 208/9.

23 Flame, Globe
and Hands

1963. 15th Anniv of Declaration of Human Rights.

78	**23**	60f. ochre, bronze and mauve	95	55

24 Meteorological Station,
Tananarive

1964. Air. World Meteorological Day.

79	**24**	90f. brown, blue and grey	1·90	1·40

25 Postal
Cheques and
Savings Bank
Building,
Tananarive

1964. Stamp Day.

80	**25**	25f.+5f. brown, bl & grn	85	80

26 Scouts beside Campfire

1964. 40th Anniv of Malagasy Scout Movement.

81	**26**	20f. multicoloured	75	45

27 Symbolic Bird and
Globe within "Egg"

1964. "Europafrique".

82	**27**	45f. brown and green	90	55

28 Statuette of
Woman

1964. Malagasy Art.

83	**28**	6f. brown, blue and indigo (postage)	45	25
84	-	30f. brown, bistre & green	85	40
85	-	100f. brown, red & vio (air)	2·10	1·20

DESIGNS: 30f. Statuette of squatting vendor. 27×48½ mm:
100f. Statuary of peasant family, ox and calf.

1964. French, African and Malagasy Co-operation. As T
41a of Ivory Coast.

86	25f. brown, chestnut and black	75	35

29 Tree on Globe

1964. University of Malagasy Republic.

87	**29**	65f. black, red and green	75	45

30 Cithern

1965. Malagasy Musical Instruments.

88	-	3f. brown, blue and mauve (postage)	45	10
89	**30**	6f. sepia, purple and green	60	10
90	-	8f. brown, black and green	75	25
91	-	25f. multicoloured	1·80	80
92	-	200f. brown, orange and green (air)	5·75	2·75

DESIGNS—As Type **30**: 3f. Kabosa (lute); 8f. Hazolahy
(sacred drum). LARGER—VERT: 35½×48 mm: 25f. "Valiha
Player" (after E. Ralambo). 27×48 mm: 200f. Bara violin.

31 Foulpointe Post Office

1965. Stamp Day.

93	**31**	20f. brown, green and orange	45	25

32 I.T.U. Emblem

1965. I.T.U. Centenary.

94	**32**	50f. green, blue and red	1·20	60

33 J.-J.
Rabearivelo
(poet)

1965. Rabearivelo Commemorative.

95	**33**	40f. brown and orange	75	40

34 Nurse weighing Baby

1965. Air. International Co-operation Year.

96	**34**	50f. black, bistre and blue	95	40
97	-	100f. purple, brown and blue	1·50	70

DESIGN: 100f. Boy and girl.

35 Pres.
Tsiranana

1965. Pres. Tsiranana's 55th Birthday.

98	**35**	20f. multicoloured	30	15
99	**35**	25f. multicoloured	65	25
MS100	Two sheets each 78×120 mm. (a) No. 98×4; (b) No. 99×4		3·50	3·25

36 Bearer

1965. Postal Transport.

102	-	3f. violet, blue and brown	60	40

103	-	4f. blue, brown and green	35	25
104	**36**	10f. multicoloured	45	25
105	-	12f. multicoloured	40	25
106	-	20f. multicoloured	1·20	40
107	-	25f. multicoloured	1·00	40
108	-	30f. red, brown and blue	1·80	70
109	-	65f. brown, blue and violet	1·90	85

DESIGNS—HORIZ: 3f. Early car; 4f. Filanzane (litter); 12f.
Pirogue; 20f. Horse-drawn mail-cart; 25f. Bullock cart; 30f.
Early railway postal carriage; 65f. Hydrofoil, "Porthos", Bet-
siboka.

37 Diseased Hands

1966. World Leprosy Day.

110	**37**	20f. purple, red and green	75	40

38 Planting Trees

1966. Reafforestation Campaign.

111	**38**	20f. violet, brown & turq	55	25

39 "Cicindelidae
chaetodera andriana"

1966. Malagasy Insects. Multicoloured.

112	1f. Type **39**	55	20
113	6f. "Mantodea tisma freiji"	80	20
114	12f. "Cerambycini mastododera nodicollis"	1·70	40
115	45f. "Trachelophoru giraffa"	2·50	75

40 Madagascar
1c. Stamp of
1903

1966. Stamp Day.

116	**40**	25f. bistre and red	60	40

41 Betsileo Dance

1966. Folk Dances. Multicoloured.

117	2f. Bilo Sakalava dance (vert) (postage)	10	10
118	5f. Type **41**	30	10
119	30f. Antandroy dance (vert)	60	25
120	200f. Southern Malagasy dancer (air)	4·75	1·80
121	250f. Sakalava Net Dance	5·75	3·00

Nos. 120/1 are size 27×48 mm.

43 "Tree" of Emblems

1966. O.C.A.M. Conference, Tananarive.

122	**43**	25f. multicoloured	55	25

The above was issued with "Janvier 1966" obliterated
by bars, and optd JUIN 1966.

44 Singing
Anthem

1966. National Anthem.
123   **44**   20f. brown, mauve &
green   45   25

45 UNESCO. Emblem

1966. 20th Anniv of UNESCO.
124   **45**   30f. blue, bistre and red   55   25

46 Lions
Emblem

1967. 50th Anniv of Lions Int.
125   **46**   30f. multicoloured   55   40

47 Harvesting Rice

1967. International Rice Year.
126   **47**   20f. multicoloured   55   25

48 Adventist Temple,
Tanambao-Tamatave

1967. Religious Buildings (1st series).
127   **48**   3f. ochre, blue and green   10   10
128   -   5f. lilac, purple and
green   10   10
129   -   10f. purple, blue and
green   45   20
BUILDINGS—VERT: 5f. Catholic Cathedral, Tananarive.
HORIZ: 10f. Mosque, Tamatave.
    See also Nos. 148/50.

49 Raharisoa at Piano

1967. Fourth Death Anniv of Norbert Raharisoa
(composer).
130   **49**   40f. multicoloured   95   45

50 Jean Raoult's Bleriot XI,
1911

1967. "History of Malagasy Aviation".
131   **50**   5f. brown, blue and
green (postage)   70   35
132   -   45f. black, blue and
brown   1·40   65
133   -   500f. black, blue and
ochre (air)   10·50   5·00
DESIGNS: 45f. Bernard Bougault and flying boat, 1926.
48×27 mm: 500f. Jean Dagnaux and Breguet 19A2 biplane, 1927.

51 Ministry of
Communications,
Tananarive

1967. Stamp Day.
134   **51**   20f. green, blue and
orange   55   25

1967. Air. Fifth Anniv of U.A.M.P.T. As T **64a** of Ivory
Coast.
135   100f. mauve, bistre and red   1·80   85

52 Church, Torch
and Map

1967. Centenary of Malagasy Lutheran Church.
136   **52**   20f. multicoloured   55   25

53 Map and
Decade Emblem

1967. Int Hydrological Decade.
137   **53**   90f. brown, red and blue   1·20   55

54 Woman's Face and
Scales of Justice

1967. Women's Rights Commission.
138   **54**   50f. blue, ochre and
green   75   45

55 Human
Rights Emblem

1968. Human Rights Year.
139   **55**   50f. red, green and black   75   45

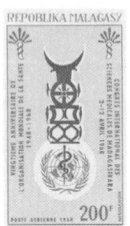

56 Congress and
W.H.O. Emblems

1968. Air. 20th Anniv of W.H.O. and Int Medical Sciences
Congress, Tananarive.
140   **56**   200f. red, blue and ochre 2·75   1·50

57 International Airport,
Tananarive-Ivato

1968. Air. Stamp Day.
141   **57**   500f. blue, green and
brown   8·75   4·25

1968. Nos. 33 and 38 surch.
142   **11**   20f. on 85f. (postage)   75   55
143   -   20f. on 85f. (No. 33) (air) 70   45

59 "Industry and
Construction"

1968. Five-year Plan (1st issue).
144   **59**   10f. plum, red and green   30   10
145   -   20f. black, red and green   30   10
146   -   40f. blue, brown &
ultram   75   25
DESIGNS—VERT: 20f. "Agriculture". HORIZ: 40f. "Transport".
    See also Nos. 156/7.

60 Church and Open Bible

1968. 150th Anniv of Christianity in Madagascar.
147   **60**   20f. multicoloured   55   25

61 Isotry
Protestant
Church,
Fitiavana,
Tananarive

1968. Religious Buildings (2nd series).
148   **61**   4f. brown, green and red   10   10
149   -   12f. brown, blue and
violet   30   15
150   -   50f. indigo, blue and
green   75   25
DESIGNS: 12f. Catholic Cathedral, Fianarantsoa; 50f. Aga
Khan Mosque, Tananarive.

62 President Tsiranana
and Wife

1968. Tenth Anniv of Republic.
151   **62**   20f. brown, red and
yellow   45   10
152   **62**   30f. brown, red and blue   50   20
MS153 161×120 mm. Nos. 151/2×2 2·00   1·90

63 Cornucopia,
Coins and Map

1968. 50th Anniv of Malagasy Savings Bank.
154   **63**   20f. multicoloured   45   10

64 "Dance of the
Whirlwind"

1968. Air.
155   **64**   100f. multicoloured   1·90   85

65 Malagasy Family

1968. Five-year Plan (2nd issue).
156   **65**   15f. red, yellow and blue   30   10
157   -   45f. multicoloured   65   25
DESIGN—VERT: 45f. Allegory of "Achievement".

1968. Air. "Philexafrique" Stamp Exn, Abidjan (1969) (1st
issue). As T **74a** of Ivory Coast.
158   100f. multicoloured   3·75   80
DESIGN—VERT: 100f. "Young Woman sealing a Letter" (J.
B. Santerre).

1969. Air. "Philexafrique" Stamp Exn, Abidjan, Ivory Coast
(2nd issue). As T **74b** of Ivory Coast.
159   50f. red, green and drab   2·20   1·40
DESIGN: 50f. Malagasy Arms, map and Madagascar stamp
of 1946.

68 "Queen Adelaide receiving
Malagasy Mission, London"
(1836–37)

1969
160   **68**   250f. multicoloured   5·50   4·00

69 Hand with Spanner,
Cogwheels and I.L.O.
Emblem

1969. 50th Anniv of I.L.O.
161   **69**   20f. multicoloured   45   25

70 Post and
Telecommunications
Building, Tananarive

1969. Stamp Day.
162   **70**   30f. multicoloured   75   25

71 Map, Steering
Wheel and
Vehicles

1969. 20th Anniv of Malagasy Motor Club.
163   **71**   65f. multicoloured   1·00   45

72 President
Tsiranana making
Speech

1969. Tenth Anniv of President Tsiranana's Assumption
of Office.
164   **72**   20f. multicoloured   45   10

73 Bananas

1969. Fruits.
165   **73**   5f. green, brown and
blue   45   10
166   -   15f. red, myrtle and
green   95   25
DESIGN: 15f. Lychees.

74 Start of Race and
Olympic Flame

1969. Olympic Games, Mexico (1968).
167   **74**   15f. brown, red and
green   50   20

75 "Malagasy Seashore, East Coast" (A. Razafinjohany)

1969. Air. Paintings by Malagasy Artists. Multicoloured.
168		100f. Type **75**	1·70	1·50
169		150f. "Sunset on the High Plateaux" (H. Ratovo)	3·75	1·90

76 Imerino House, High Plateaux

1969. Malagasy Traditional Dwellings (1st series).
170	–	20f. red, blue and green	30	15
171	–	20f. brown, red and blue	30	15
172	**76**	40f. red, blue and indigo	55	25
173	–	60f. purple, green and blue	90	35

HOUSES—HORIZ: 20f. (No. 170), Tsimihety hut, East Coast; 60f. Betsimisaraka dwellings, East Coast. VERT: 20f. (No. 171), Betsileo house, High Plateaux.
  See also Nos. 205/6.

77 Ambalavao Arms

1970. Town Arms (2nd series). Multicoloured.
174		10f. Type **77**	40	10
175		25f. Morondava	55	10
176		25f. Ambatondrazaka	55	10
177		80f. Tamatave	1·20	45

  See also Nos. 208/9.

78 Agate

1970. Semi-precious Stones. Multicoloured.
178		5f. Type **78**	4·00	1·90
179		20f. Ammonite	13·00	3·75

1970. New U.P.U. Headquarters Building, Berne. As T **81** of New Caledonia.
180		20f. blue, brown and mauve	50	25

80 U.N. Emblem and Symbols

1970. 25th Anniv of United Nations.
181	**80**	50f. black, blue and orange	80	40

81 Astronaut and Module on Moon

1970. Air. First Anniv of "Apollo 11" Moon-landing.
182	**81**	75f. green, slate and blue	1·50	55

82 Malagasy Fruits

1970
183	**82**	20f. multicoloured	1·20	35

83 Delessert's Lyria

1970. Sea Shells (1st series). Multicoloured.
184		5f. Type **83**	65	30
185		10f. Bramble murex	95	35
186		20f. Thorny oyster	2·00	45

84 Aye-aye

1970. International Nature Conservation Conference, Tananarive.
187	**84**	20f. multicoloured	1·50	40

85 Boeing 737 in Flight

1970. Air.
188	**85**	200f. red, green and blue	3·25	1·40

86 Pres. Tsiranana

1970. Pres. Tsiranana's 60th Birthday.
189	**86**	30f. brown and green	60	25

87 Calcite

1971. Minerals. Multicoloured.
190		12f. Type **87**	2·50	55
191		15f. Quartz	3·50	80

88 Soap Works, Tananarive

1971. Malagasy Industries.
192	**88**	5f. multicoloured	25	10
193	–	15f. black, brown and blue	45	10
194	–	50f. multicoloured	80	20

DESIGNS: 15f. Chrome works, Comina-Andriamena; 50f. Textile complex, Sotema-Majunga.

89 Globe and Emblems

1971. Council Meeting of Common Market Countries with African and Malagasy Associated States, Tananarive.
195	**89**	5f. multicoloured	30	25

90 Rural Mobile Post Office

1971. Stamp Day.
196	**90**	25f. multicoloured	55	25

91 Gen. De Gaulle

1971. Death (1970) of Gen. Charles de Gaulle.
197	**91**	30f. black, red and blue	1·00	55

92 Palm Beach Hotel, Nossi-Be

1971. Malagasy Hotels.
198	**92**	25f. multicoloured	45	25
199	–	65f. brown, blue and green	1·00	40

DESIGN: 65f. Hilton Hotel, Tananarive.

93 Forestry Emblem

1971. Forest Preservation Campaign.
200	**93**	3f. multicoloured	30	20

94 Jean Ralaimongo

1971. Air. Malagasy Celebrities.
201	**94**	25f. brown, red and orange	45	25
202	–	65f. brown, myrtle & green	65	25
203	–	100f. brown, ultram & bl	1·70	40

CELEBRITIES: 65f. Albert Sylla; 100f. Joseph Ravoahangy Andrianavalona.

1971. Air. Tenth Anniv of African and Malagasy Posts and Telecommunications Union. As T **101a** of Ivory Coast.
204		100f. U.A.M.P.T. H.Q., Brazzaville, and painting "Mpisikidy" (G. Rakotovao)	1·50	70

96 Vezo Dwellings, South-east Coast

1971. Malagasy Traditional Dwellings (2nd series). Multicoloured.
205		5f. Type **96**	25	10
206		10f. Antandroy hut, South coast	45	10

97 "Children and Cattle in Meadow" (G. Rasoaharijaona)

1971. 25th Anniv of UNICEF.
207	**97**	50f. multicoloured	1·60	45

1972. Town Arms (3rd series). As T **77**. Multicoloured.
208		1f. Maintirano Arms	55	10
209		25f. Fenerive-Est	1·10	25

99 Cable-laying train

1972. Co-axial Cable Link, Tananarive–Tamatave.
210	**99**	45f. brown, green and red	1·20	55

100 Telecommunications Station

1972. Inauguration of Philibert Tsiranana Satellite Communications Station.
211	**100**	85f. multicoloured	95	55

101 Pres. Tsiranana and Voters

1972. Presidential Elections.
212	**101**	25f. multicoloured	55	40

102 "Moped" Postman

1972. Stamp Day.
213	**102**	10f. multicoloured	75	25

1972. De Gaulle Memorial. No. 197 surch **MEMORIAL +20F**.
214	**91**	30f.+20f. black, red & bl	95	85

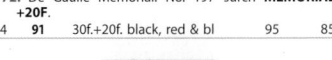

104 Exhibition Emblem and Stamps

1972. Second National Stamp Exn, Antanarive.
215	**104**	25f. multicoloured	45	25
216	**104**	40f. multicoloured	75	40
217	**104**	100f. multicoloured	1·70	70
MS218		151×116 mm. Nos. 215/17	4·50	4·50

106 Petroleum Refinery, Tamatave

1972. Malagasy Economic Development.
220	**106**	2f. blue, green and yellow	45	10
221	–	100f. multicoloured	4·75	90

DESIGN: 100f. 3600 CV diesel locomotive.

107 R. Rakotobe

1972. Air. First Death Anniv of Rene Rakotobe (poet).
222	**107**	40f. brown, purple & orge	75	25

108 College Buildings

1972. 150th Anniv of Razafindrahety College, Tananarive.
223	**108**	10f. purple, brown & blue	30	20

109 Volleyball

1972. African Volleyball Championships.
224	**109**	12f. black, orange & brn	45	15

110 Runners breasting Tape

1972. Air. Olympic Games, Munich. Multicoloured.
225	**110**	100f. Type **110**	1·70	90
226		200f. Judo	3·25	1·10

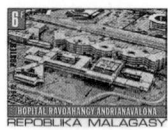

111 Hospital Complex

1972. Inauguration of Ravoahangy Andrianavalona Hospital.
227	**111**	6f. multicoloured	30	15

112 Mohair Goat

1972. Air. Malagasy Wool Production.
228	**112**	250f. multicoloured	5·25	2·75

113 Ploughing with Oxen

1972. Agricultural Expansion.
229	**113**	25f. multicoloured	1·50	45

114 "Virgin and Child" (15th-cent Florentine School)

1972. Air. Christmas. Religious Paintings. Multicoloured.
230		85f. Type **114**	1·20	70
231		150f. "Adoration of the Magi" (A. Mantegna) (horiz)	2·50	1·10

115 Betsimsarka Women

1972. Traditional Costumes. Multicoloured.
232		10f. Type **115**	30	10
233		15f. Merina mother and child	45	20

116 Astronauts on Moon

1973. Air. Moon Flight of "Apollo 17".
234	**116**	300f. purple, brown & grey	4·50	2·20

117 "Natural Produce"

1973. Tenth Anniv of Malagasy Freedom from Hunger Campaign Committee.
235	**117**	25f. multicoloured	1·10	50

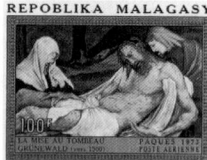

118 "The Entombment" (Grunewald)

1973. Air. Easter. Multicoloured.
236		100f. Type **118**	1·50	70
237		200f. "The Resurrection" (Grune-wald) (vert)	3·00	1·40

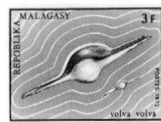

119 Shuttlecock Volva

1973. Sea Shells (2nd series). Multicoloured.
238		3f. Type **119**	20	10
239		10f. Arthritic spider conch	45	25
240		15f. Common harp	65	25
241		25f. Type **119**	95	50
242		40f. As 15f.	1·30	50
243		50f. As 10f.	2·10	65

120 Postal Courier, Tsimandoa

1973. Stamp Day.
244	**120**	50f. blue, green and brown	75	40

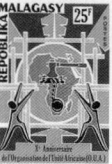

121 "Africa" within Scaffolding

1973. Tenth Anniv of Organization of African Unity.
245	**121**	25f. multicoloured	55	25

122 "Cameleon campani"

1973. Malagasy Chameleons. Multicoloured.
246		1f. Type **122**	25	10
247		5f. "Cameleon nasutus" (male)	25	10
248		10f. "Cameleon nasutus" (female)	45	20
249		40f. As 5f.	1·20	30
250		60f. Type **122**	1·70	55
251		85f. As 10f.	2·40	95

123 Excursion Carriage

1973. Air. Early Malagasy Railways. Multicoloured.
252		100f. Type **123**	2·00	1·40
253		150f. Mallet steam locomotive No. 24, 1907	3·00	1·60

124 "Cypripedium"

1973. Orchids. Multicoloured.
254		10f. Type **124**	55	10
255		25f. "Nepenthes pervillei"	80	35
256		40f. As 25f.	1·70	50
257		100f. Type **124**	3·50	1·00

1973. Pan African Drought Relief. No. 235 surch **SECHERESSE SOLIDARITE AFRICAINE** and value.
258	**117**	100f. on 25f. multicol-oured	1·50	70

126 Dish Aerial and Meteorological Station

1973. Air. W.M.O. Centenary.
259	**126**	100f. orange, blue & black	1·70	80

1973. 12th Anniv of African and Malagasy Posts and Telecommunications. As T **129a** of Ivory Coast.
260		100f. red, violet and green	1·50	70

128 Greater Dwarf Lemur

1973. Malagasy Lemurs.
261	**128**	5f. brown, green and purple (postage)	95	45
262	-	25f. brown, sepia & green	2·00	90
263	-	150f. brn, grn & sepia (air)	3·75	1·50
264	**128**	200f. brown, turq & blue	5·25	2·30

DESIGN—VERT: 25f., 150f. Weasel-lemur.

129 Pres. Kennedy

1973. Air. Tenth Death Anniv of Pres. John Kennedy.
265	**129**	300f. multicoloured	4·00	2·10

130 Footballers

1973. Air. World Cup Football Championship. West Germany.
266	**130**	500f. mauve, brown and light brown	7·50	3·00

CURRENCY. Issues from No. 267 to No. 389 have face values shown as "Fmg". This abbreviation denotes the Malagasy Franc which was introduced in 1966.

131 Copernicus, Satellite and Diagram

1974. Air. 500th Birth Anniv of Copernicus.
267	**131**	250f. blue, brown & green	4·50	1·70

1974. No. 76a surch.
268		25f. on 30f. multicoloured	45	25

133 Agricultural Training

1974. 25th World Scouting Conference, Nairobi, Kenya.
269	**133**	4f. grey, blue and green (postage)	10	10
270	-	15f. purple, green and blue	45	25
271	-	100f. ochre, red & blue (air)	1·10	55
272	-	300f. brown, blue & black	3·75	1·50

DESIGNS—VERT: 15f. Building construction. HORIZ: 100f. First Aid training; 300f. Fishing.

134 Male Player, and Hummingbird on Hibiscus

1974. Air. Asia, Africa and Latin America Table-Tennis Championships, Peking.
273	**134**	50f. red, blue and brown	1·20	45
274	-	100f. red, blue and violet	2·50	95

DESIGN: 100f. Female player and stylized bird.

135 Family and House

1974. World Population Year.
275	**135**	25f. red, orange and blue	45	10

136 Micheline Railcar

1974. Air. Malagasy Railway Locomotives.

276	**136**	50f. green, red and brown	85	50
277	-	85f. red, blue and green	1·50	70
278	-	200f. blue, lt blue & brown	3·75	1·60

DESIGNS: 85f. Track-inspection trolley; 200f. Garratt steam locomotive, 1926.

1974. Air. Centenary of U.P.U.

279	**137**	250f. red, blue and violet	4·25	1·70

138 Rainibetsimisaraka

1974. Rainibetsimisaraka Commemoration.

280	**138**	25f. multicoloured	55	40

1974. Air. West Germany's Victory in World Cup Football Championship. No. 266 optd **R.F.A. 2 HOLLANDE 1**.

281	**130**	500f. mauve, brown and light brown	6·50	3·50

105 Road and Monument

1972. Opening of Andapa–Sambava Highway.

219	**105**	50f. multicoloured	55	40

140 "Apollo" and "Soyuz" spacecraft

1974. Air. Soviet–U.S. Space Co-operation.

282	**140**	150f. orange, green & blue	1·50	80
283	-	250f. green, blue & brown	2·75	1·20

DESIGN: No. 283, As Type **140** but different view.

141 Marble Slabs

1974. Marble Industry. Multicoloured.

284	4f. Type **141**	75	25
285	25f. Quarrying	2·20	65

1974. Air. Universal Postal Union Centenary (2nd issue). No. 279 optd **100 ANS DE COLLABORATION INTERNATIONALE**.

286	**137**	250f. red, blue and violet	2·20	1·10

143 Faces and Maps

1974. Europafrique.

287	**143**	150f. brown, red & orange	2·00	85

144 "Food in Hand"

1974. "Freedom from Hunger".

288	**144**	80f. blue, brown and grey	1·00	55

145 "Coton"

1974. Malagasy Dogs. Multicoloured.

289	50f. Type **145**	2·40	70
290	100f. Hunting dog	3·50	1·40

146 Malagasy People

1974. Founding of "Fokonolona" Commune.

291	**146**	5f. multicoloured	30	10
292	**146**	10f. multicoloured	30	10
293	**146**	20f. multicoloured	35	10
294	**146**	60f. multicoloured	95	30

147 "Discovering Talent"

1974. National Development Council.

295	**147**	25f. multicoloured	30	10
296	**147**	35f. multicoloured	45	25

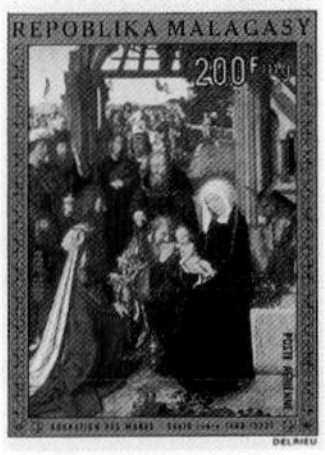

148 "Adoration of the Magi" (David)

1974. Air. Christmas. Multicoloured.

297	200f. Type **148**	3·00	1·10
298	300f. "Virgin of the Cherries and Child" (Metzys)	4·50	1·80

149 Malagasy Girl and Rose

1975. International Women's Year.

299	**149**	100f. brown, orange & grn	1·20	55

150 Colonel Richard Ratsimandrava (Head of Government)

1975

300	**150**	15f. brown, black & yellow	30	10
301	**150**	25f. brown, black and blue	35	25
302	**150**	100f. brown, black & green	1·30	45

151 Sofia Bridge

1975

303	**151**	45f. multicoloured	75	40

152 U.N. Emblem and Part of Globe

1975. Air. 30th Anniv of U.N. Charter.

304	**152**	300f. multicoloured	3·75	1·40

153 De Grasse (after Mauzaisse) and "Randolph"

1975. Bicentenary of American Revolution (1st issue). Multicoloured.

305	40f. Type **153** (postage)	70	25
306	50f. Lafayette, "Lexington" and H.M.S. "Edward"	95	40
307	100f. D'Estaing and "Languedoc" (air)	1·30	45
308	200f. Paul Jones, "Bonhomme Richard" and H.M.S. "Serapis"	2·50	1·00
309	300f. Benjamin Franklin, "Millern" and "Montgomery"	4·00	1·40
MS310	127×91 mm. 500f. George Washington (after Peale) and "Hanna". Imperf	7·50	2·30

See also Nos. 371/**MS**376.

154 "Euphorbia viguieri"

1975. Malagasy Flora. Multicoloured.

311	15f. Type **154** (postage)	40	25
312	25f. "Hibiscus rosesinensis"	55	25
313	30f. "Plumeria rubra acutitolia"	80	40
314	40f. "Pachypodium rosulatum"	1·20	40
315	85f. "Turraea sericea" (air)	2·30	1·40

1975. Air. "Apollo"–"Soyuz" Space Link. Nos. 282/3 optd **JONCTION 17 JUILLET 1975**.

316	**140**	150f. orange, green & blue	1·50	70
317	-	250f. green, blue & brown	3·00	1·40

156 Temple Frieze

1975. Air. "Save Borobudur Temple" (in Indonesia) Campaign.

318	**156**	50f. red, orange and blue	1·50	70

157 "Racial Unity"

1975. Namibia Day.

319	**157**	50f. multicoloured	75	25

158 Pryer's Woodpecker

1975. International Exposition, Okinawa. Fauna. Multicoloured.

320	25f. Type **158** (postage)	65	25
321	40f. Ryukyu rabbit	1·00	25
322	50f. Toad	1·40	40
323	75f. Tortoise	2·50	70
324	125f. Sika deer (air)	2·50	80
MS325	101×82 mm. 300f. Jay	5·50	1·40

159 Lily Waterfall

1975. Lily Waterfall. Multicoloured.

326	25f. Type **159**	45	25
327	40f. Lily Waterfall (distant view)	75	25

160 Hurdling

1975. Air. "Pre-Olympic Year". Olympic Games, Montreal (1976). Multicoloured.

328	75f. Type **160**	1·00	45
329	200f. Weightlifting (vert)	2·75	1·00

161 Bobsleigh "Fours"

1975. Winter Olympic Games, Innsbruck. Multicoloured.

330	75f. Type **161** (postage)	75	25
331	100f. Ski-jumping	1·20	45
332	140f. Speed-skating	1·80	55
333	200f. Cross-country skiing (air)	2·75	75
334	245f. Downhill skiing	3·00	1·10
MS335	116×79 mm. 450f. Pairs figure skating	4·50	2·10

162 Pirogue

1975. Malagasy Sailing-vessels. Multicoloured.

336	8f. Type **162**	95	25
337	45f. Malagasy schooner	2·30	65

163 Canoeing

1976. Olympic Games, Montreal. Multicoloured.

338	40f. Type **163** (postage)	45	25
339	50f. Sprinting and hurdling	55	25
340	100f. Putting the shot, and long-jumping (air)	1·20	25
341	200f. Gymnastics-horse and parallel bars	2·30	70
342	300f. Trampoline-jumping and high-diving	3·50	1·30
MS343	117×91 mm. 500f. Swimming	5·50	2·00

164 "Apollo 14"
Lunar Module and
Flight Badge

1976. Air. Fifth Anniv of "Apollo 14" Mission.
344	**164**	150f. blue, red and green	1·80	80

1976. Air. Fifth Anniv of "Apollo 14" Mission. No. 344 optd
5e Anniversaire de la mission APOLLO XIV.
345	150f. blue, red and green	1·80	1·00

166 "Graf Zeppelin" over Fujiyama

1976. 75th Anniv of Zeppelin. Multicoloured.
346	**166**	40f. Type **166** (postage)	55	25
347		50f. "Graf Zeppelin" over Rio de Janeiro	80	25
348		75f. "Graf Zeppelin" over New York	1·30	40
349		100f. "Graf Zeppelin" over Sphinx and pyramids	1·60	55
350		200f. "Graf Zeppelin" over Berlin (air)	3·25	90
351		300f. "Graf Zeppelin" over London	4·75	1·10
MS352	130×103 mm. 450f. Vatican		5·50	2·20

167 "Prevention of Blindness"

1976. World Health Day.
353	**167**	100f. multicoloured	1·50	70

168 Aragonite

1976. Minerals and Fossils. Multicoloured.
354	25f. Type **168**		2·20	45
355	50f. Fossilized wood		3·75	90
356	150f. Celestyte		11·00	3·00

169 Alexander Graham Bell and
Early Telephone

1976. Telephone Centenary. Multicoloured.
357	25f. Type **169**		30	10
358	50f. Cable maintenance, 1911		45	25
359	100f. Telephone operator and switchboard, 1895		95	25
360	200f. "Emile Baudot" cable ship		2·00	55
361	300f. Man with radio-telephone		3·00	80
MS362	133×104 mm. 500f. Telecommunications satellite		5·25	2·00

170 Children reading
Book

1976. Children's Books Promotion. Multicoloured.
363	10f. Type **170**		30	10
364	25f. Children reading book (vert)		45	25

1976. Medal winners, Winter Olympic Games, Innsbruck.
Nos. 330/4 optd **VAINQUEUR** and medal winner.
365	75f. Type **161** (postage)		75	45
366	100f. Ski-jumping		1·20	70
367	140f. Skating		1·80	90
368	200f. Cross-country skiing (air)		2·00	95
369	245f. Downhill skiing		2·50	1·20
MS370	116×79 mm. 450f. multicoloured		5·00	4·50

OPTS: 75f. **ALLEMAGNE FEDERALE**; 100f. **KARL SCHNABL, AUTRICHE**; 140f. **SHEILA YOUNG, ETATS-UNIS**; 200f. **IVAR FORMO, NORVEGE**; 245f. **ROSI MITTERMAIER, ALLEMAGNE DE L'OUEST**; 450f. **VIANQUEUR IRINA RODNINA ALEXANDER ZAITSEV URSS**.
  The subject depicted on No. 367 is speed-skating, an event in which the gold medal was won by J. E. Storholt, Norway.

1976. Bicentenary of American Revolution (2nd issue).
Nos. 305/9 optd **4 JUILLET 1776–1976** in frame.
371	**153**	40f. multicoloured (postage)	75	35
372	-	50f. multicoloured	1·10	55
373	-	100f. multicoloured (air)	1·20	90
374	-	200f. multicoloured	2·75	1·10
375	-	300f. multicoloured	4·00	1·80
MS376	127×91 mm. 500f. multicoloured		5·00	4·50

173 Descent Trajectory

1976. "Viking" Landing on Mars. Multicoloured.
377	75f. Type **173**		55	25
378	100f. "Viking" landing module separation		95	40
379	200f. "Viking" on Martian surface		1·80	55
380	300f. "Viking" orbiting Mars		2·75	85
MS381	133×90 mm. 500f. "Viking" spacecraft and Sun		5·25	2·10

174
Rainandriamampandry

1976. 30th Anniv of Treaties signed by
Rainandriamampandry (Foreign Minister).
382	**174**	25f. multicoloured	55	40

175 Doves over
Globe

1976. Indian Ocean—"Zone of Peace". Multicoloured.
383	60f. Type **175**		55	25
384	160f. Doves flying across Indian Ocean (horiz)		40	70

1976. Olympic Games Medal Winners. Nos. 338/42 optd
with names of two winners on each stamp.
385	**163**	40f. multicoloured (postage)	40	25
386	-	50f. multicoloured	55	40
387	-	100f. multicoloured (air)	1·00	55
388	-	200f. multicoloured	2·00	90
389	-	300f. multicoloured	3·00	1·00
MS390	117×91 mm. 500f.		5·25	4·75

OVERPRINTS: 40f. **V. DIBA, A. ROGOV**; 50f. **H. CRAWFORD, J. SCHALLER**; 100f. **U. BEYER, A. ROBINSON**; 200f. **N. COMANECI, N. ANDRIANOV**; 300f. **K. DIBIASI, E. VAYTSEKHOVSKAIA**; 500f. **J. MONTGOMERY and H. ANKE**.

177 Malagasy Arms

1976. First Anniv of Malagasy Democratic Republic.
391	**177**	25f. multicoloured	45	10

178 Rabezavana
(Independence
Movement Leader)

1977. National Heroes. Multicoloured.
392	25f. Type **178**		30	10
393	25f. Lt. Albert Randriamaromanana		30	10
394	25f. Ny Avana Ramanantoanina (politician)		45	10
395	100f. Fasam-Pirenena National Mausoleum, Tananarive (horiz)		1·30	55

179 Family

1977. World Health Day.
396	**179**	5f. multicoloured	30	10

180 Medical School, Antananarivo

1977. 80th Anniv of Medical School, Antananarivo.
397	**180**	250f. multicoloured	2·75	1·10

181 Rural Post Van

1977. Rural Mail.
398	**181**	35f. multicoloured	45	25

182 Morse Key and Man with
Headphones

1977. 90th Anniv of Antananarivo–Tamatave Telegraph.
399	**182**	15f. multicoloured	30	20

183 Academy Emblem

1977. 75th Anniv of Malagasy Academy.
400	**183**	10f. multicoloured	30	10

184 Lenin and Russian Flag

1977. 60th Anniv of Russian Revolution.
401	**184**	25f. multicoloured	2·50	45

185 Raoul Follereau

1978. 25th Anniv of World Leprosy Day.
402	**185**	5f. multicoloured	1·50	45

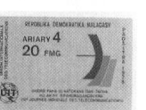

186 Microwave Antenna

1978. World Telecommunications Day.
403	**186**	20f. multicoloured	30	20

187
"Co-operation"

1978. Anti-Apartheid Year.
404	**187**	60f. red, black and yellow	75	30

188 Children
with
Instruments of
Revolution

1978. "Youth—Pillar of the Revolution".
405	**188**	125f. multicoloured	1·20	55

189 Tractor,
Factory and
Labourers

1978. Socialist Co-operatives.
406	**189**	25f. multicoloured	30	10

190 Women at
Work

1979. "Women, Pillar of the Revolution".
407	**190**	40f. multicoloured	45	10

191 Children with Books, Instruments and Fruit

1979. International Year of the Child.
408	**191**	10f. multicoloured	30	10

192 Ring-tailed Lemur

1979. Animals. Multicoloured.
409	25f. Type **192** (postage)		60	10
410	125f. Black lemur		2·40	25
411	1000f. Malagasy civet		11·50	2·20
412	20f. Tortoise (air)		50	35
413	95f. Black lemur (different)		1·50	55

193 J. V. S. Razakandraina

1979. J. V. S. Razakandraina (poet) Commem.
414	**193**	25f. multicoloured	35	10

194 "Centella asiatica"

1979. Medicinal Plant.
415	**194**	25f. multicoloured	70	25

195 Map of Malagasy and Ste. Marie Telecommunications Station

1979. Telecommunications.
416	**195**	25f. multicoloured	30	10

196 Post Office, Antsirabe

1979. Stamp Day.
417	**196**	500f. multicoloured	4·50	1·40

197 Palestinians with Flag

1979. Air. Palestinian Solidarity.
418	**197**	60f. multicoloured	55	25

198 Concorde and Map of Africa

1979. 20th Anniv of ASECNA (African Air Safety Organization).
419	**198**	50f. multicoloured	75	25

199 Lenin addressing Meeting

1980. 110th Birth Anniv of Lenin.
420	**199**	25f. multicoloured	75	25

200 Taxi-bus

1980. Fifth Anniv of Socialist Revolution.
421	**200**	30f. multicoloured	45	10

201 Map illuminated by Sun

1980. 20th Anniv of Independence.
422	**201**	75f. multicoloured	75	25

202 Military Parade

1980. 20th Anniv of Army.
423	**202**	50f. multicoloured	55	25

203 Joseph Raseta

1980. Dr. Joseph Raseta Commemoration.
424	**203**	30f. multicoloured	45	10

204 Anatirova Temple

1980. Anatirova Temple Centenary.
425	**204**	30f. multicoloured	45	25

205 Boxing

1980. Olympic Games, Moscow. Multicoloured.
426	30f. Hurdling		75	10
427	75f. Type **205**		1·20	40
428	250f. Judo		2·50	1·10
429	500f. Swimming		4·50	2·20

206 Emblem, Map and Sun

1980. Fifth Anniv of Malagasy Democratic Republic.
430	**206**	30f. multicoloured	45	10

207 Skier

1981. Winter Olympic Games, Lake Placid (1980).
431	**207**	175f. multicoloured	1·70	80

208 "Angraecum leonis"

1981. Flowers. Multicoloured.
432	5f. Type **208**		30	10
433	80f. "Angraecum famosum"		1·40	50
434	170f. "Angraecum sesquipedale"		2·30	1·00

209 Handicapped Student

1981. International Year of Disabled People. Multicoloured.
435	25f. Type **209**		35	10
436	80f. Disabled carpenter		95	40

210 Ribbons forming Caduceus, I.T.U. and W.H.O. Emblems

1981. World Telecommunications Day.
437	**210**	15f. blue, black and yellow	30	10
438	**210**	45f. multicoloured	65	30

211 Valentina Tereshkova (first woman in space)

1981. Space Achievements. Multicoloured.
439	30f. Type **211**		30	10
440	80f. Astronaut on Moon		80	25
441	90f. Yuri Gagarin (first man in space)		95	50

212 Raphael-Louis Rafiringa

1981. Raphael-Louis Rafiringa Commemoration.
442	**212**	30f. multicoloured	45	10

213 Child writing Alphabet

1981. World Literacy Day.
443	**213**	30f. multicoloured	45	10

214 Ploughing and Sowing

1981. World Food Day.
444	**214**	200f. multicoloured	1·80	70

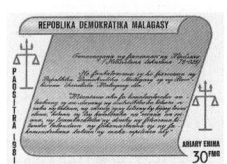

215 Magistrates' Oath

1981. Renewal of Magistrates' Oath.
445	**215**	30f. mauve and black	45	15

216 "Dove"

1981. Birth Centenary of Pablo Picasso.
446	**216**	80f. multicoloured	1·30	45

217 U.P.U. Emblem and Malagasy Stamps

1981. 20th Anniv of Admission to U.P.U.
447	**217**	5f. multicoloured	10	10
448	**217**	30f. multicoloured	35	10

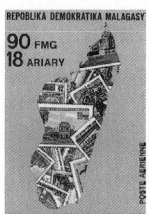

218 Stamps forming Map of Malagasy

1981. Stamp Day.
449	**218**	90f. multicoloured	95	45

219 Hook-billed Vanga

1982. Birds. Multicoloured.
450	25f. Type **219**		90	20
451	30f. Courol		1·10	20
452	200f. Madagascar fish eagle (vert)		4·75	1·00

220 Vaccination

1982. Centenary of Discovery of Tubercule Bacillus.
453	**220**	30f. multicoloured	55	10

221 Jeannette Mpihira

1982. Jeannette Mpihira Commemoration.
454	**221**	30f. multicoloured	45	25

222 Woman's Head formed from Map of Africa

1982. Air. 20th Anniv of Pan-African Women's Organization.
455	**222**	80f. multicoloured	95	25

223 Pierre Louis Boiteau

1982. Pierre Louis Boiteau Commemoration.
456	**223**	30f. multicoloured	45	10

224 Andekaleka Dam

1982. Air. Andekaleka Hydro-electric Complex.
457	**224**	80f. multicoloured	95	35

225 "Sputnik I"

1982. 25th Anniversary of First Artificial Satellite. Multicoloured.
458	10f. Type **225**		25	10
459	80f. Yuri Gagarin		75	30
460	100f. "Soyuz"–"Salyut" space station		1·00	45

226 Heading Ball

1982. World Cup Football Championship, Spain. Multicoloured.
461	30f. Type **226**		30	10
462	40f. Running with ball		45	10
463	80f. Tackle		75	30
MS464	101×71 mm. 450f. Saving goal		4·50	2·75

227 Ploughing, Sowing and F.A.O. Emblem

1982. World Food Day.
465	**227**	80f. multicoloured	75	45

228 Bar Scene

1982. 150th Anniv of Edouard Manet (artist). Multicoloured.
466	5f. Type **228**		75	25
467	30f. Woman in white		1·10	45
468	170f. Man with pipe		5·00	1·10
MS469	101×81 mm. 400f. Fifer		8·50	3·00

229 Emperor Snapper

1982. Fish. Multicoloured.
470	5f. Type **229**		10	10
471	20f. Sailfish		30	10
472	30f. Lionfish		50	25
473	50f. Yellow-finned tuna		90	30
474	200f. Black-tipped grouper		3·00	85
MS475	100×80 mm. 450f. "Latimeria chalumnae" (horiz 37×26 mm)		5·00	3·25

230 Fort Mahavelona

1982. Landscapes. Multicoloured.
476	10f. Type **230** (postage)		10	10
477	30f. Ramena coast		30	10
478	400f. Jacarandas in flower (air)		4·00	1·60

231 Flags of Russia and Malagasy, Clasped Hands and Tractors

1982. 60th Anniv of U.S.S.R. Multicoloured.
479	10f. Type **231**		10	10
480	15f. Flags, clasped hands and radio antenna		10	10
481	30f. Map of Russia, Kremlin and Lenin		35	10
482	150f. Flags, clasped hands, statue and arms of Malagasy		1·60	70

232 Television, Drums, Envelope and Telephone

1983. World Communications Year. Multicoloured.
483	30f. Type **232**		30	10
484	80f. Stylized figures holding cogwheel		95	40

233 Axe breaking Chain on Map of Africa

1983. 20th Anniv of Organization of African Unity.
485	**233**	30f. multicoloured	30	10

234 Henri Douzon

1983. Henri Douzon (lawyer) Commemoration.
486	**234**	30f. multicoloured	30	10

235 Montgolfier Balloon

1983. Bicentenary of Manned Flight. Sheet 110×80 mm.
MS487	**235**	500f. multicoloured	6·00	3·00

236 "Madonna and Child"

1983. 500th Birth Anniv of Raphael. Sheet 108×80 mm.
MS488	**236**	500f. multicoloured	6·50	3·00

237 Ruffed Lemur

1984. Lemurs. Multicoloured.
489	30f. Type **237**		65	25
490	30f. Verreaux's sifaka		65	25
491	30f. Lesser mouse-lemur (horiz)		65	25
492	30f. Aye-aye (horiz)		65	25
493	200f. Indri (horiz)		4·25	1·20
MS494	80×98 mm. 500f. "Perodicticus potto"		7·50	3·00

238 Ski Jumping

1984. Winter Olympic Games, Sarajevo. Mult.
495	20f. Type **238**		10	10
496	30f. Ice hockey		30	10
497	30f. Downhill skiing		30	10
498	30f. Speed skating		30	10
499	200f. Ice dancing		2·20	85
MS500	81×101 mm. 500f. Cross-country skiing (horiz 47×32 mm)		4·50	3·00

239 Renault, 1907

1984. Early Motor Cars. Multicoloured.
501	15f. Type **239**		25	10
502	30f. Benz, 1896		45	10
503	30f. Baker, 1901		45	10
504	30f. Blake, 1901		45	10
505	200f. F.I.A.L., 1908		2·40	85
MS506	81×101 mm. 450f. Russo–Baltique, 1909		5·50	3·00

240 Pastor Ravelojaona

1984. Pastor Ravelojaona (encylopaedist) Commemoration.
507	**240**	30f. multicoloured	30	10

241 "Noli me Tangere"

1984. 450th Death Anniv of Correggio. Paintings by Artist.
508	**241**	5f. multicoloured	10	10
509	-	20f. multicoloured	30	10
510	-	30f. multicoloured	45	10
511	-	80f. multicoloured	80	40
512	-	200f. multicoloured	2·20	85
MS513	81×102 mm. 400f. multicoloured		5·50	3·00

242 Paris Landmarks and Emblem

1984. 60th Anniv of International Chess Federation. Multicoloured.
514	5f. Type **242**		10	10
515	20f. Wilhelm Steinitz and stylized king		35	10
516	30f. Vera Menchik and stylized queen		75	30
517	30f. Anatoly Karpov and trophy		75	30
518	215f. Nona Gaprindashvili and trophy		3·50	90
MS519	101×80 mm. 400f. Children playing chess		6·00	3·00

243 Football

1984. Olympic Games, Los Angeles.
520	**243**	100f. multicoloured	95	45

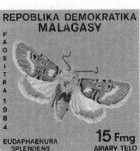

244 "Eudaphaenura splendens"

1984. Butterflies. Multicoloured.
521	15f. Type **244**		55	10
522	50f. "Acraea hova"		1·10	25
523	50f. "Othreis boesae"		1·10	25
524	50f. "Pharmocophagus antenor"		1·10	25
525	200f. "Epicausis smithii"		3·25	1·00
MS526	101×81 mm. 400f. "Papilio delalandi" (32×47 mm)		5·50	3·00

245 Ralaimongo

1984. Birth Centenary of Jean Ralaimongo (politician).
527	**245**	50f. multicoloured	30	10

246 Children in Brief-case

1984. 25th Anniv of Children's Rights Legislation.
528	**246**	50f. multicoloured	45	25

247 "Disa incarnata"

1984. Orchids. Multicoloured.
529	20f. Type **247** (postage)		30	10
530	235f. "Eulophiella roempleriana"		2·50	1·00
531	50f. "Eulophiella roempleriana" (horiz) (air)		80	25
532	50f. "Grammangis ellisii" (horiz)		80	25
533	50f. "Grammangis spectabilis"		80	25
MS534	101×80 mm. 400f. "Gasrrorchis tuberculosa" (26×38 mm)		4·75	3·00

248 U.N. Emblem and Cotton Plant

1984. 20th Anniv of United Nations Conference on Commerce and Development.
535	**248**	100f. multicoloured	95	45

249 "Sun Princess" (Sadio Diouf)

1984. 40th Anniv of International Civil Aviation Organization.
536	**249**	100f. multicoloured	95	45

250 Bible, Map and Gothic Letters

1985. 150th Anniv of First Bible in Malagasy Language.
537	**250**	50f. brown, pink and black	45	20

251 Farming Scenes, Census-taker and Farmer

1985. Agricultural Census.
538	**251**	50f. grey, black and mauve	45	20

252 Lap-dog

1985. Cats and Dogs. Multicoloured.
539	20f. Type **252**		30	10
540	20f. Siamese cat		30	10
541	50f. Abyssinian cat (vert)		75	25
542	100f. Cocker spaniel (vert)		1·40	50
543	235f. Poodle		3·25	1·20
MS544	100×80 mm. 400f. White cat (41×27 mm)		5·50	2·75

253 Russian Soldiers in Berlin

1985. 40th Anniv of Victory in Second World War.
545	20f. Type **253**		30	10
546	50f. Arms of French squadron and fighter planes		1·10	45
547	100f. Victory parade, Red Square, Moscow		1·60	50
548	100f. French troops entering Paris (vert)		2·00	55

254 Parade in Stadium

1985. Tenth Anniv of Malagasy Democratic Republic.
549	**254**	50f. multicoloured	45	20

255 Medal and Independence Obelisk

1985. 25th Anniv of Independence.
550	**255**	50f. multicoloured	90	25

256 Peace Dove and Stylized People

1985. 12th World Youth and Students' Festival, Moscow.
551	**256**	50f. multicoloured	45	10

257 I.Y.Y. Emblem and Map of Madagascar

1985. International Youth Year.
552	**257**	100f. multicoloured	1·00	45

258 Red Cross Centres and First Aid Post

1985. 70th Anniv of Malagasy Red Cross.
553	**258**	50f. multicoloured	70	20

259 "View of Sea at Saintes-Maries" (Vincent van Gogh)

1985. Impressionist Paintings. Multicoloured.
554	20f. Type **259**		65	10
555	20f. "Rouen Cathedral in the Evening" (Claude Monet) (vert)		65	10
556	45f. "Young Girls in Black" (Pierre-Auguste Renoir) (vert)		1·10	30
557	50f. "Red Vineyard at Arles" (van Gogh)		1·50	30
558	100f. "Boulevard des Capucines, Paris" (Monet)		3·00	75
MS559	80×101 mm. 400f. "In the Garden" (Renoir) (vert)		6·75	4·50

260 Indira Gandhi

1985. Indira Gandhi (Indian Prime Minister) Commemoration.
560	**260**	100f. multicoloured	1·10	45

261 Figures and Dove on Globe and Flag

1985. 40th Anniv of U.N.O.
561	**261**	100f. multicoloured	95	45

262 "Aeranthes grandiflora"

1985. Orchids. Multicoloured.
562	20f. Type **262**		65	20
563	45f. "Angraecum magdalenae" and "Nephele oenopion" (insect) (horiz)		1·10	30
564	50f. "Aerangis stylosa"		1·30	40
565	100f. "Angraecum eburneum longicalcar" and "Hippotion batschi" (insect)		2·30	70
566	100f. "Angraecum sesquipedale" and "Xanthopan morgani-predicta" (insect)		2·30	75

MS567	100×80 mm. 400f. "Angraecum eburneum superbum" and "Deilephila neri" (insect) (29×41 mm)		5·50	3·50

263 Russian and Czechoslovakian Cosmonauts

1985. Russian "Interkosmos" Space Programme. Multicoloured.
568	20f. Type **263**		30	10
569	20f. Russian and American flags and "Apollo"–"Soyuz" link		30	10
570	50f. Russian and Indian cosmonauts		50	25
571	100f. Russian and Cuban cosmonauts		95	45
572	200f. Russian and French cosmonauts		1·80	90
MS573	99×89 mm. 400f. Satellite (41×39 mm)		4·25	2·75

264 Emblem in "10"

1985. Tenth Anniv of Malagasy Democratic Republic.
574	**264**	50f. multicoloured	45	20

265 Headquarters

1986. Tenth Anniv of ARO (State insurance system).
575	**265**	50f. yellow and brown	45	25

266 "David and Uriah" (Rembrandt)

1986. Foreign Paintings in Hermitage Museum, Leningrad. Multicoloured.
576	20f. Type **266**		35	10
577	50f. "Portrait of Old Man in Red" (Rembrandt)		1·00	35
578	50f. "Danae" (Rembrandt) (horiz)		1·00	35
579	50f. "Marriage of Earth and Water" (Rubens)		1·00	35
580	50f. "Portrait of Infanta Isabella's Maid" (Rubens)		1·00	35
MS581	100×80 mm. 50f. "Holy Family" (Raphael)		5·75	3·75

267 Comet

1986. Air. Appearance of Halley's Comet.
582	**267**	150f. multicoloured	1·70	75

1986. Russian Paintings in the Tretyakov Gallery, Moscow. As T 266. Multicoloured.
583	20f. "Fruit and Flowers" (I. Khroutsky) (horiz)		40	10
584	50f. "The Rooks have Returned" (A. Savrasov)		80	35
585	50f. "Unknown Woman" (I. Kramskoi) (horiz)		85	35
586	50f. "Aleksandr Pushkin" (O. Kiprenski)		85	35
587	100f. "March, 1895" (I. Levitan) (horiz)		1·90	70
MS588	80×101 mm. 450f. Pavel Tretyakov (I. Repine)		5·50	3·25

268 Sombrero, Football and Player

1986. World Cup Football Championship, Mexico.
| 589 | **268** | 150f. multicoloured | 1·50 | 50 |

269 Child Care

1986. UNICEF Child Survival Campaign.
| 590 | **269** | 60f. multicoloured | 55 | 25 |

270 Jungle Cat

1986. Wild Cats. Multicoloured.
591	10f. Type **270**	35	10
592	10f. Wild cat	35	10
593	60f. Caracal	80	30
594	60f. Leopard cat	80	30
595	60f. Serval	75	30
MS596	81×100 mm. 450f. African golden cat	5·50	3·00

271 Dove above Hands holding Globe

1986. International Peace Year. Multicoloured.
| 597 | 60f. Type **271** | 55 | 25 |
| 598 | 150f. Doves above emblem and map | 1·40 | 65 |

272 U.P.U. Emblem on Dove

1986. World Post Day.
| 599 | **272** | 60f. multicoloured (postage) | 70 | 25 |
| 600 | **272** | 150f. blue, black and red (air) | 1·50 | 70 |

273 U.P.U. Emblem on Globe

1986. Air. 25th Anniv of Admission to U.P.U.
| 601 | **273** | 150f. multicoloured | 1·50 | 70 |

274 Giant Madagascar Coucal

1986. Birds. Multicoloured.
602	60f. Type **274**	80	25
603	60f. Crested Madagascar coucal	80	25
604	60f. Rufous vangas (vert)	80	25
605	60f. Red-tailed vangas (vert)	80	25
606	60f. Sicklebill	70	25

| MS607 | 80×100 mm. 450f. Cattle egret (41×29 mm) | 5·50 | 3·00 |

275 Tortoise

1987. Endangered Animals. Multicoloured.
608	60f. Type **275**	85	30
609	60f. Crocodile	85	30
610	60f. Crested wood ibis (vert)	85	30
611	60f. Vasa parrot	85	30
MS612	80×100 mm. 450f. Black coucal (horiz)	5·50	2·50

276 Crowd in "40"

1987. 40th Anniv of Anti-colonial Uprising.
| 613 | **276** | 60f. brown, red and yellow | 55 | 10 |
| 614 | - | 60f. multicoloured | 55 | 10 |

DESIGN: No. 614, Hands in broken manacles, map, rifleman and spearman.

277 Emblems, Map and Pictogram

1987. First Indian Ocean Towns Games.
| 615 | **277** | 60f. multicoloured | 55 | 25 |
| 616 | **277** | 150f. multicoloured | 1·40 | 55 |

278 "Sarimanok"

1987. The "Sarimanok" (replica of early dhow). Multicoloured.
| 617 | 60f. Type **278** | 75 | 25 |
| 618 | 150f. "Sarimanok" (different) | 1·50 | 55 |

279 Coffee Plant

1987. 25th Anniv of African and Malagasy Coffee Producers Organization. Multicoloured.
| 619 | 60f. Type **279** | 55 | 25 |
| 620 | 150f. Map showing member countries | 1·70 | 65 |

280 Rifle Shooting and Satellite

1987. Winter Olympic Games, Calgary (1988). Multicoloured.
621	60f. Type **280**	45	10
622	150f. Slalom	1·00	25
623	250f. Luge	1·70	55
624	350f. Speed skating	2·40	75
625	400f. Ice hockey	2·75	80
626	450f. Ice skating (pairs)	3·25	90
MS627	88×68 mm. 600f. Downhill (41×29 mm)	4·50	4·50

281 "Giotto" Space Probe

1987. Appearance of Halley's Comet (1986). Space Probes. Multicoloured.
628	60f. Type **281**	45	10
629	150f. "Vega 1"	1·00	25
630	250f. "Vega 2"	1·70	55
631	350f. "Planet A 1"	2·40	75
632	400f. "Planet B 1"	2·75	80
633	450f. "I.C.E."	3·25	90
MS634	88×68 mm. 600f. Sir Edmund Halley and "Giotto" (43×32 mm)	4·25	4·25

282 Piper Aztec

1987. Air. 25th Anniv of Air Madagascar. Multicoloured.
635	60f. Type **282**	55	25
636	60f. De Havilland Twin Otter	55	25
637	150f. Boeing 747-200	1·30	55

283 Rabearivelo

1987. 50th Death Anniv of Jean-Joseph Rabearivelo (poet).
| 638 | **283** | 60f. multicoloured | 45 | 25 |

284 Communications Equipment Robot and Print-out Paper

1987. National Telecommunications Research Laboratory.
| 639 | **284** | 60f. green, black and red | 45 | 25 |

285 Emblem

1987. 150th Anniv of Execution of Rafaravavy Rasalama (Christian martyr).
| 640 | **285** | 60f. black, deep blue and blue | 40 | 25 |

286 Hand using Key and Telegraphist

1987. Cent of Antananarivo–Tamatave Telegraph.
| 641 | **286** | 60f. multicoloured | 45 | 25 |

287 Bartholomeu Dias and Departure from Palos, 1492

1987. 500th Anniv (1992) of Discovery of America by Columbus. Multicoloured.
642	60f. Type **287**	40	10
643	150f. Route around Samana Cay and Henry the Navigator	75	25
644	250f. Columbus and crew disembarking, 1492, and A. de Marchena	1·60	40

645	350f. Building Fort Navidad and Paolo del Pozzo Toscanelli	2·00	55
646	400f. Columbus in Barcelona, 1493, and Queen Isabella of Spain	2·20	70
647	450f. Columbus and "Nina"	2·40	70
MS648	91×81 mm. 600f. Columbus landing with soldiers (41×29 mm)	5·00	5·00

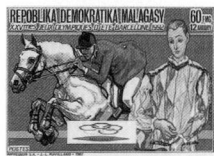

288 Showjumping and "Harlequin" (Picasso)

1987. Olympic Games, Barcelona (1992). Multicoloured.
649	60f. Type **288** (postage)	30	10
650	150f. Weightlifting and Barcelona Cathedral	70	25
651	250f. Hurdling and Canaletas Fountain	1·40	40
652	350f. High jumping and Parc d'Attractions	1·90	55
653	400f. Gymnast on bar and church (air)	2·20	70
654	450f. Gymnast with ribbon and Triumphal Arch	2·50	70
MS655	123×89 mm. 600f. Cross-country rider and Columbus monument	4·00	1·60

289 Anniversary Emblem, T.V. Tower and Interhotel "Berlin"

1987. 750th Anniv of Berlin.
| 656 | **289** | 150f. multicoloured | 50 | 30 |

290 Musician and Dancers

1987. Schools Festival.
| 657 | **290** | 60f. multicoloured | 30 | 10 |

291 Madagascar Pasteur Institute and Pasteur

1987. Centenary of Pasteur Institute, Paris.
| 658 | **291** | 250f. multicoloured | 1·20 | 50 |

292 "After the Shipwreck" (Eugene Delacroix)

1987. Paintings in Pushkin Museum of Fine Arts, Moscow. Multicoloured.
659	10f. Type **292**	45	10
660	60f. "Jupiter and Callisto" (Francois Boucher) (vert)	50	10
661	60f. "Still Life with Swan" (Frans Snyders)	50	10
662	60f. "Chalet in the Mountains" (Gustave Courbet)	50	10
663	150f. "At the Market" (Joachim Bueckelaer)	1·20	25
MS664	80×100 mm. 1000f. "Minerva" (Paolo Veronese) (horiz)	7·00	4·25

293 Emblem

1987. Tenth Anniv of Pan-African Telecommunications Union.
665 **293** 250f. multicoloured 55 25

294 Family and House on Globe

1988. International Year of Shelter for the Homeless (1987). Multicoloured.
666 80f. Type **294** 15 10
667 250f. Hands forming house protecting family from rain 60 30

295 Lenin addressing Crowd

1988. 70th Anniv of Russian Revolution. Multicoloured.
668 60f. Type **295** 55 10
669 60f. Revolutionaries 55 10
670 150f. Lenin in crowd 1·10 20

296 Broad-nosed Gentle Lemur

1988. Endangered Species. Multicoloured.
671 60f. Type **296** 40 10
672 150f. Diadem sifaka 50 25
673 250f. Indri 95 25
674 350f. Ruffed lemur 1·80 40
675 550f. Purple herons (horiz) 1·50 55
676 1500f. Nossi-be chameleon (horiz) 4·25 1·10
MS677 110×58 mm. 1500f. Long-tailed ground roller ("Uratelornis chinaera) (horiz) 5·50 5·50

297 Ice Skating

1988. Winter Olympic Games, Calgary. Multicoloured.
678 20f. Type **297** 10 10
679 60f. Speed-skating 10 10
680 60f. Slalom 10 10
681 100f. Cross-country skiing 35 10
682 250f. Ice hockey 80 30
MS683 80×65 mm. 800f. Ski-jumping 3·00 1·50

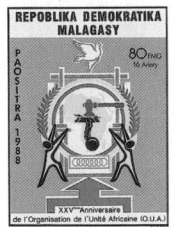

298 Dove, Axe breaking Chain and Map

1988. 25th Anniv of Organization of African Unity.
684 **298** 80f. multicoloured 30 10

299 Institute Building

1988. 20th Anniv of National Posts and Telecommunications Institute.
685 **299** 80f. multicoloured 30 10

300 College

1988. Centenary of St. Michael's College.
686 **300** 250f. multicoloured 45 25

301 Pierre and Marie Curie in Laboratory

1988. 90th Anniv of Discovery of Radium.
687 **301** 150f. brown and mauve 45 15

302 Emblem

1988. Tenth Anniv of Alma-Ata Declaration (on health and social care).
688 **302** 60f. multicoloured 30 15

303 Emblem

1988. 40th Anniv of W.H.O.
689 **303** 150f. brown, blue and black 30 15

304 Ring-tailed Lemurs on Island

1988. 50th Anniv of Tsimbazaza Botanical and Zoological Park. Multicoloured.
690 20f. Type **304** 30 15
691 80f. Ring-tailed lemur with young (25×37 mm) 40 20
692 250f. Palm tree and ring-tailed lemur within "Zoo" (47×32 mm) 90 40
MS693 80×100 mm. 1000f. Grey gentle lemur with baby (36×51 mm) 5·00 1·80

305 Hoopoe and Blue Madagascar Coucal

1988. Scouts, Birds and Butterflies. Multicoloured.
694 80f. Type **305** 10 10
695 250f. "Chrysiridia croesus" (butterfly) 50 10
696 270f. Nelicourvi weaver and red forest fody 70 10
697 350f. "Papilio dardanus" (butterflies) 95 25
698 550f. Crested Madagascar coucal 1·50 25
699 1500f. "Argema mittrei" (butterfly) 3·75 1·10
MS700 80×114 mm. 1500f. "Anteva" (butterfly) and blue-cheeked bee eater (35×50 mm) 4·00 1·40

306 Cattle grazing

1988. Tenth Anniv of International Fund for Agricultural Development.
701 **306** 250f. multicoloured 45 25

307 Karl Bach and Clavier

1988. Musicians' Anniversaries. Multicoloured.
702 80f. Type **307** (death bicentenary) 15 10
703 250f. Franz Schubert and piano (160th death) 55 20
704 270f. Georges Bizet and scene from "Carmen" (150th birth) 65 25
705 350f. Claude Debussy and scene from "Pelleas et Melisande" (70th death) 90 40
706 550f. George Gershwin at piano writing score of "Rhapsody in Blue" (90th birth) 1·30 55
707 1500f. Elvis Presley (10th death (1987)) 4·00 1·60
MS708 93×74 mm. 1500f. Nikolai Rimsky-Korsakov and "The Golden Cockerel" (80th death) (35×50 mm) 4·25 2·30

308 Books

1988. "Ecole en Fete" Schools Festival.
709 **308** 80f. multicoloured 30 10

309 "Black Sea Fleet at Feodosiya" (Ivan Aivazovski)

1988. Paintings of Sailing Ships. Multicoloured.
710 20f. Type **309** 20 10
711 80f. "Lesnoie" (N. Semenov) 35 15
712 80f. "Seascape with Sailing Ships" (Simon de Vlieger) 35 15
713 100f. "Orel" (N. Golitsine) (horiz) 50 20
714 250f. "Naval Battle Exercises" (Adam Silo) 95 30
MS715 91×71 mm. 550f. "On the River" (Abraham Beerstraten) (36×51 mm) 3·25 1·10

310 "Tragocephala crassicornis"

1988. Endangered Beetles. Multicoloured.
716 20f. Type **310** 60 25
717 80f. "Polybothris symptuosagema" 1·80 45
718 250f. "Euchroea auripigmenta" 3·50 90
719 350f. "Stellognata maculata" 4·75 1·10

311 Stretcher Bearers and Anniversary Emblem

1988. 125th Anniv of International Red Cross. Multicoloured.
720 80f. Type **311** 20 10
721 250f. Red Cross services, emblem and Henri Dunant (founder) 50 30

312 Symbols of Human Rights

1988. 40th Anniv of Declaration of Human Rights. Multicoloured.
722 80f. Type **312** 30 10
723 250f. Hands with broken manacles holding "40" 65 30

313 Mercedes-Benz "Blitzen-Benz", 1909

1989. Cars and Trains. Multicoloured.
724 80f. Type **313** 10 10
725 250f. Micheline diesel railcar "Tsikirity", 1952, Tananarive–Moramanga line 45 10
726 270f. Bugatti coupe binder, "41" 45 10
727 350f. Class 1020 electric locomotive, Germany 75 25
728 1500f. Souleze 701 diesel train, Malagasy 2·75 1·00
729 2500f. Opel racing car, 1913 4·25 1·80
MS730 98×76 mm. 2500f. Bugatti "Presidential" autorail and Bugatti Type 57 "Atalante" (39×28 mm) 6·00 2·30

314 Tyrannosaurus

1989. Prehistoric Animals. Multicoloured.
731 20f. Type **314** 10 10
732 80f. Stegosaurus 35 10
733 250f. Arsinoitherium 85 25
734 450f. Triceratops 1·30 35
MS735 91×73 mm. 600f. Sauralophus (vert) 3·75 1·40

315 "Tahitian Girls"

1989. Woman in Art. Multicoloured.
736 20f. Type **315** 10 10
737 80f. "Portrait of a Girl" (Jean-Baptiste Greuze) 30 10
738 80f. "Portrait of a Young Woman" (Titian) 30 10
739 100f. "Woman in Black" (Auguste Renoir) 40 20
740 250f. "The Lace-maker" (Vasily Tropinine) 95 55
MS741 100×80 mm. 550f. "The Annunciation" (Cima da Conegliano) 2·00 1·00

316
"Sobennikoffia
robusta"

1989. Orchids. Multicoloured.

742	5f. Type **316**		10	10
743	10f. "Grammangis fallax" (horiz)		10	10
744	80f. "Angraecum sororium"		45	25
745	80f. "Cymbidiella humblotii"		45	25
746	250f. "Oenia oncidiiflora"		1·10	45
MS747	100×80 mm. 1000f. "Aerangis curnowiana"		2·75	1·50

317 Nehru

1989. Birth Centenary of Jawaharlal Nehru (Indian statesman).

748	**317**	250f. multicoloured	45	25

318 Mahamasina Sports
Complex, Lake Anosy
and Ampefiloha Quarter

1989. Antananarivo. Multicoloured.

749	5f. Type **318**		10	10
750	20f. Andravoahangy and Anjanahary Quarters		10	10
751	80f. Zoma market and Faravohi-tra Quarter		30	10
752	80f. Andohan' Analekely Quarter and 29 March Column		30	10
753	250f. Avenue de l'Independance and Jean Ralaimongo Column		55	25
754	550f. Lake Anosy, Queen's Palace and Andohalo School		1·00	45

319 Rose Quartz

1989. Ornamental Minerals. Multicoloured.

755	80f. Type **319**		40	10
756	250f. Fossilized wood		1·10	50

320 Pope and
Rasoamanarivo

1989. Visit of Pope John Paul II and Beatification of Victoire Rasoamanarivo. Multicoloured.

757	80f. Type **320**		30	10
758	250f. Map and Pope		70	30

321 Map and
Runner with
Torch

1989. Town Games.

759	**321**	80f.+20f. multicoloured	30	10

322 "Storming the
Bastille"

1989. Bicentenary of French Revolution (1st issue).

760	**322**	250f. multicoloured	70	25

See also Nos. 773/5.

323 Mirabeau and Gabriel Riqueti at
Meeting of States General

1989. "Philexfrance 89" International Stamp Exhibition, Paris. Multicoloured.

761	250f. Type **323**		50	15
762	350f. Camille Desmoulins' call to arms		85	15
763	1000f. Lafayette and crowd demanding bread		2·00	40
764	1500f. Trial of King Louis XVI		3·50	70
765	2500f. Assassination of Marat		5·75	1·10
MS766	113×79 mm. 3000f. Robespi-erre, Couthon, Collot d'Herbois and Prieur (59×41 mm)		14·50	5·50

324 "Mars 1"

1989. Space Probes. Multicoloured.

767	20f. Type **324**		10	10
768	80f. "Mars 3"		30	10
769	80f. "Zond 2"		30	10
770	250f. "Mariner 9"		55	25
771	270f. "Viking 2"		70	40
MS772	100×80 mm. 550f. "Phobos" (41×28 mm)		1·50	90

325 "Liberty guiding the People"
(Eugene Delacroix)

1989. Bicentenary of French Revolution (2nd issue). Multicoloured.

773	5f. Type **325** (postage)		10	10
774	80f. "La Marseillaise" (Francois Rude)		50	25
775	250f. "Oath of the Tennis Court" (Jacques Louis David) (air)		85	35

326 Rene Cassin
(founder)

1989. 25th Anniv of International Human Rights Institute for French Speaking Countries.

776	**326**	250f. multicoloured	45	10

327 Mother and Young
on Bamboo

1989. Golden Gentle Lemur.

777	**327**	250f. multicoloured	95	45

328 Footballer and
Cavour Monument,
Turin

1989. World Cup Football Championship, Italy. Multicoloured.

778	350f. Type **328**		75	25
779	1000f. Footballer and Christopher Columbus monument, Genoa		1·80	40
780	1500f. Florentine footballer, 1530, and "David" (sculpture, Michelangelo)		2·75	55
781	2500f. Footballer and "Rape of Proserpina" (sculpture, Bernini), Rome		4·75	1·30
MS782	110×77 mm. 3000f. Leonardo de Vinci monument, Milan, footballer and trophy (29×41 mm)		4·50	1·40

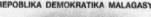

329 Pennant Coralfish

1990. Fish. Multicoloured.

783	5f. Type **329**		10	10
784	20f. Snub-nosed parasitic eel (vert)		10	10
785	80f. Manta ray (vert)		20	10
786	250f. Black-tipped grouper		75	35
787	320f. Smooth hammerhead		1·00	50
MS788	90×70 mm. 550f. Coelacanth		3·00	1·80

330 Long Jumping

1990. Olympic Games, Barcelona (1992). Multicoloured.

789	80f. Type **330**		10	10
790	250f. Pole vaulting		45	10
791	550f. Hurdling		95	25
792	1500f. Cycling		3·00	40
793	2000f. Baseball		4·00	70
794	2500f. Tennis		4·50	1·10
MS795	90×66 mm. 3000f. Football		4·50	4·50

331 "Queen of the
Isalo" (rock)

1990. Natural Features. Multicoloured.

796	70f. Type **331**		20	15
797	150f. Lonjy Island (as T **332**)		35	15

332 Pipe

1990. Sakalava Craft. Multicoloured.

798	70f. Type **332**		20	15
799	150f. Combs (as T **331**)		35	15

333 Emblem and
Projects

1990. 25th Anniv of African Development Bank.

800	**333**	80f. multicoloured	40	10

334 "Voyager II" and Neptune

1990. 20th Anniv of First Manned Landing on Moon. Multicoloured.

801	80f. Type **334**		10	10
802	250f. Hughes Hercules flying boat, Boeing 747 airliner and flying boat "of the future"		45	10
803	550f. "Noah" satellite tracking elephants		95	25
804	1500f. Venus and "Magellan" space probe		1·20	25
805	2000f. Halley's Comet and Concorde		2·30	40
806	2500f. "Apollo 11" landing capsule and crew		4·25	80
MS807	94×63 mm. 3000f. Astronaut, mission emblem and crew		4·50	1·40

335 Liner on
Globe

1990. 30th Anniv of International Maritime Organization.

808	**335**	250f. ultramarine, bl & blk	45	20

336 Maps showing
Development
between 1975 and
1990

1990. Air. 15th Anniv of Malagasy Socialist Revolution.

809	**336**	100f. multicoloured	40	10
810	–	350f. black and grey	75	40

DESIGN: 350f. Presidential Palaces, 1975 and 1990.

337 Oral
Vaccination

1990. Anti-Polio Campaign.

811	**337**	150f. multicoloured	40	20

338 Four-man
Bobsleigh

1990. Winter Olympic Games, Albertville (1992) (1st issue). Multicoloured.

812	350f. Type **338**		55	15
813	1000f. Speed skating		1·60	45
814	1500f. Cross-country skiing		2·50	55
815	2500f. Super G		4·00	1·10
MS816	92×77 mm. 3000f. Giant slalom		4·50	1·40

See also Nos. 862/**MS**869.

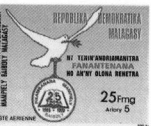

339 Society Emblem

1990. Air. 25th Anniv of Malagasy Bible Society.

817	**339**	25f. multicoloured	10	10
818		100f. blue, black and green	35	10

DESIGN—VERT: 100f. Society emblem.

340 Mascot

1990. Third Indian Ocean Island Games, Malagasy (1st issue).

819	**340**	100f.+20f. on 80f.+20f. multicoloured	45	25
820	**340**	350f.+20f. on 250f.+20f. multicoloured	1·00	65

The games were originally to be held in 1989 and the stamps were printed for release then. The issued stamps are handstamped with the correct date and new value. See also Nos. 822/3.

341 Symbols of Agriculture and Industry

1990. 30th Anniv of Independence.

821	**341**	100f. multicoloured	30	10

342 Torch

1990. Third Indian Ocean Island Games, Malagasy (2nd issue).

822	**342**	100f. multicoloured	40	10
823	**342**	350f. multicoloured	80	40

343 Envelopes forming Map and Mail Transportation

1990. Air. World Post Day.

824	**343**	350f. multicoloured	1·90	35

344 Ho Chi Minh

1990. Birth Centenary of Ho Chi Minh (President of North Vietnam, 1945–69).

825	**344**	350f. multicoloured	75	40

345 "Avahi laniger"

1990. Lemurs. Multicoloured.

826		10f. Type **345**	10	10
827		20f. "Lemur fulvus albifrons"	25	20
828		20f. "Lemur fulvus sanfordi"	25	20
829		100f. "Lemur fulvus collaris"	85	20
830		100f. "Lepulemur ruficaudatus"	90	25
MS831		70×90 mm. 350f. "Lemur fulvus fulvus"	3·00	1·50

346 Fluted Giant Clam

1990. Shells. Multicoloured.

832		40f. Type **346**	70	20
833		50f. Dimidiate and subulate augers	90	25

347 Letters in Book

1990. International Literacy Year. Multicoloured.

834		20f. Type **347**	35	20
835		100f. Open book and hand holding pen (horiz)	85	50

348 Cep

1991. Fungi. Multicoloured.

836		25f. Type **348**	10	10
837		100f. Butter mushroom	35	10
838		350f. Fly agaric	95	20
839		450f. Scarlet-stemmed boletus	1·20	30
840		680f. Flaky-stemmed witches' mushroom	1·70	45
841		800f. Brown birch bolete	2·00	60
842		900f. Orange birch bolete	2·10	80
MS843		71×90 mm. 1500f. Common puffball. Imperf	3·75	2·75

349 De Gaulle, Leclerc and Parod under Arc de Triomphe, 1944

1991. Multicoloured

844		100f. Type **349**	25	20
845		350f. "Galileo" space probe near Jupiter	75	25
846		800f. Crew of "Apollo 11" on Moon	1·40	40
847		900f. De Gaulle and Free French emblem, 1942	2·00	65
848		1250f. Concorde aircraft and German ICE high speed train	2·20	70
849		2500f. Gen. Charles de Gaulle (French statesman)	4·75	90
MS850		144×93 mm. 3000f. Crew of "Apollo 11". Imperf	4·50	1·40

350 Industrial and Agricultural Symbols and Arms

1991. 15th Anniv (1990) of Republic.

851	**350**	100f. multicoloured	30	10

351 Baobab Tree

1991. Trees. Multicoloured.

852		140f. Type **351**	55	10
853		500f. "Dideria madagascariensis"	1·30	55

352 Whippet

1991. Dogs. Multicoloured.

854		30f. Type **352**	40	10
855		50f. Japanese spaniel	55	10
856		140f. Toy terrier	1·30	25
857		350f. Chow-chow	95	25
858		500f. Chihuahua	1·20	40
859		800f. Afghan hound	1·60	65
860		1140f. Papillon	2·30	90
MS861		70×91 mm. 1500f. Shih-tzu. Imperf	9·50	1·90

353 Cross-country Skiing

1991. Winter Olympic Games, Albertville (2nd issue). Multicoloured.

862		5f. Type **353**	10	10
863		15f. Biathlon	10	10
864		60f. Ice hockey	45	10
865		140f. Skiing	55	25
866		640f. Ice skating	55	25
867		1000f. Ski jumping	2·75	40
868		1140f. Speed skating	3·75	90
MS869		90×70 mm. 1500f. Ice hockey (different). Imperf	3·75	2·00

354 "Helictopleurus splendidicollis"

1992. Scouts, Insects and Fungi. Multicoloured.

870		140f. Type **354**	35	10
871		500f. "Russula radicans" (mushroom)	1·20	25
872		640f. "Cocles contemplator" (insect)	1·50	40
873		1025f. "Russula singeri" (mushroom)	2·00	55
874		1140f. "Euchroea oberthurii" (beetle)	2·50	55
875		3500f. "Lactariopsis pandani" (mushroom)	7·50	80
MS876		119×94 mm. 4500f. "Euchroea spininasuta" (beetle) and "Russula aureotacta" (mushroom)	7·25	2·10

355 Former and Present Buildings

1992. 90th Anniv (1991) of Paul Minault College.

877	**355**	140f. multicoloured	70	25

356 Repairing Space Telescope

1992. Space. Multicoloured.

878		140f. Type **356**	25	10
879		500f. "Soho" sun probe	95	25
880		640f. "Topex-Poseidon" oceanic survey satellite	1·20	25
881		1025f. "Hipparcos" planetary survey satellite	1·60	40
882		1140f. "Voyager 2" Neptune probe	2·00	40
883		5000f. "ETS-VI" Japanese test communications satellite	8·75	1·20
MS884		85×103 mm. 7500f. "Apollo 11" crew	11·50	11·50

357 Ryuichi Sakamoto

1992. Entertainers. Multicoloured.

885		100f. Type **357**	25	10
886		350f. John Lennon	60	15
887		800f. Bruce Lee	2·00	25
888		900f. Sammy Davis jun	2·20	55
889		1250f. John Wayne	2·20	40
890		2500f. James Dean	4·00	1·20
MS891		117×79 mm. 3000f. Vivien Leigh (wrongly inscr "Vivian Leight") and Clark Gable	4·75	4·75

358 Lychees

1992. Fruits. Multicoloured.

892		10f. Type **358**	10	10
893		50f. Oranges	10	10
894		60f. Apples	20	10
895		140f. Peaches	45	25
896		555f. Bananas (vert)	1·50	40
897		800f. Avocados (vert)	1·80	55
898		1400f. Mangoes (vert)	3·25	95
MS899		89×70 mm. 1600f. Mango, pineapple, peach, apple and grapes in dish	4·00	1·80

359 9th-century Galley

1992. Sailing Ships. Multicoloured.

900		15f. Type **359**	10	10
901		65f. Full-rigged sailing ship, 1878	30	10
902		140f. "Golden Hind" (Drake's flagship)	55	10
903		500f. 18th-century dhow	1·40	40
904		640f. "Ostrust" (galleon), 1721 (vert)	1·60	45
905		800f. Dutch caravel, 1599 (vert)	2·00	50
906		1025f. "Santa Maria" (Columbus's flagship), 1492	2·40	85
MS907		91×70 mm. 1500f. Columbus and fleet	4·50	1·60

360 Couple in Heart

1992. Anti-AIDS Campaign.

908	**360**	140f. black and mauve	45	10

361 Tending Trees

1992. Reforestation.

909	**361**	140f. dp green, black & grn	40	10

POSTAGE DUE STAMPS

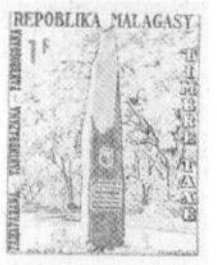

D13 Independence Obelisk

1962

D45	**D13**	1f. green	10	10
D46	**D13**	2f. brown	10	10
D47	**D13**	3f. violet	10	10
D48	**D13**	4f. slate	10	10
D49	**D13**	5f. red	30	25
D50	**D13**	10f. green	30	25
D51	**D13**	20f. purple	30	25
D52	**D13**	40f. blue	75	75
D53	**D13**	50f. red	95	90
D54	**D13**	100f. black	1·80	1·60

APPENDIX

The following stamps have either been issued in excess of postal needs or have not been available to the public in reasonable quantities at face value.

1987

Winter Olympic Games, Calgary (1988). 1500f. (on gold foil).

1989

Scout and Butterfly. 5000f. (on gold foil).
"Philexfrance 89" Int Stamp Exhibition, Paris. 5000f. (on gold foil).
World Cup Football Championship, Italy. 5000f. (on gold foil).

1990

Winter Olympic Games, Albertville (1992). 5000f. (on gold foil).

1991

Birth Centenary of De Gaulle. 5000f. (on gold foil).

1992

Olympic Games, Barcelona. 500f. (on gold foil).

1993

Bicentenary of French Republic. 1989 "Philexfrance 89" issue optd. 5000f.

1994

Elvis Presley (entertainer). 10000f. (on gold foil).
World Cup Football Championship, U.S.A. 10000f. (on gold foil).
Winter Olympic Games, Lillehammer, Norway. 10000f. (on gold foil).
Olympic Games, Atlanta, U.S.A. 5000f. (on gold foil).

For further issues see under **MADAGASCAR**.

Pt. 1

MALAWI

Formerly Nyasaland, became an independent Republic within the Commonwealth on 6 July 1966.

1964. 12 pence = 1 shilling; 20 shillings = 1 pound.
1970. 100 tambalas = 1 kwacha.

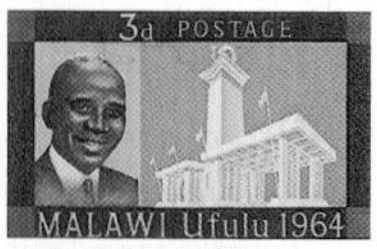

44 Dr. H. Banda (Prime Minister) and Independence Monument

1964. Independence.

211	**44**	3d. olive and sepia	10	10
212	-	6d. multicoloured	10	10
213	-	1s.3d. multicoloured	45	10
214	-	2s.6d. multicoloured	45	1·25

DESIGNS—each with Dr. Hastings Banda: 6d. Rising sun; 1s.3d. National flag; 2s.6d. Coat of arms.

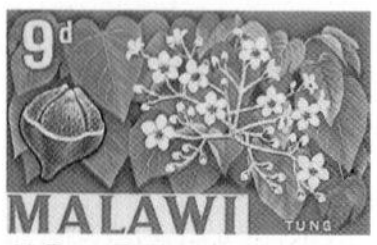

48 Tung Tree

1964. As Nos. 199/210 of Nyasaland but inscr "MALAWI" as in T **48**. The 9d., 1s.6d. and £2 are new values and designs.

252	½d. violet	10	10
216	1d. black and green	10	10
217	2d. brown	10	10
218	3d. brown, green and bistre	15	10
219	4d. blue and yellow	85	15
220	6d. purple, green and blue	75	10
221	9d. brown, green and yellow	30	15
258	1s. brown, blue and yellow	25	10
223	1s.3d. green and brown	50	60
259	1s.6d. brown and green	55	10
224	2s.6d. brown and blue	1·10	1·00
225	5s. multicoloured (I)	65	3·25
225a	5s. multicoloured (II)	10·00	1·00
226	10s. green, salmon and black	1·50	2·00
227	£1 brown and yellow	6·00	5·50
262	£2 multicoloured	27·00	24·00

DESIGNS (New): 1s.6d. Burley tobacco; £2 "Cyrestis camillus" (butterfly).

Two types of 5s. I, inscr "LAKE NYASA". II, inscr "LAKE MALAWI".

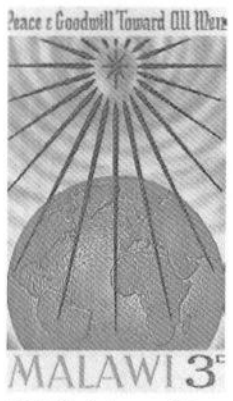

49 Christmas Star and Globe

1964. Christmas.

228	**49**	3d. green and gold	10	10
229	**49**	6d. mauve and gold	10	10
230	**49**	1s.3d. violet and gold	10	10
231	**49**	2s.6d. blue and gold	20	50
MS231a 83×126 mm. Nos. 228/31. Imperf			1·00	1·75

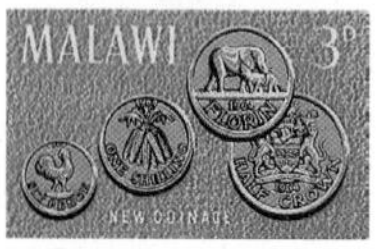

50 Coins

1964. Malawi's First Coinage. Coins in black and silver.

232	**50**	3d. green	10	10
233	**50**	9d. mauve	20	10
234	**50**	1s.6d. purple	25	10
235	**50**	3s. blue	35	1·10
MS235a 126×104 mm. Nos. 232/5. Imperf			1·40	1·10

1965. Nos. 223/4 surch.

236	1s.6d. on 1s.3d. green & brown	10	10
237	3s. on 2s.6d. brown and blue	20	20

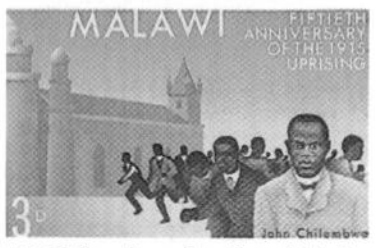

52 Chilembwe leading Rebels

1965. 50th Anniv of 1915 Rising.

238	**52**	3d. violet and green	10	10
239	**52**	9d. olive and orange	10	10
240	**52**	1s.6d. brown and blue	15	10
241	**52**	3s. turquoise and blue	20	25
MS241a 127×83 mm. Nos. 238/41			5·00	6·00

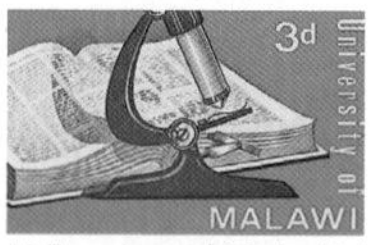

53 "Learning and Scholarship"

1965. Opening of Malawi University.

242	**53**	3d. black and green	10	10
243	**53**	9d. black and mauve	10	10
244	**53**	1s.6d. black and violet	10	10
245	**53**	3s. black and blue	15	40
MS246 127×84 mm. Nos. 242/5			2·50	2·50

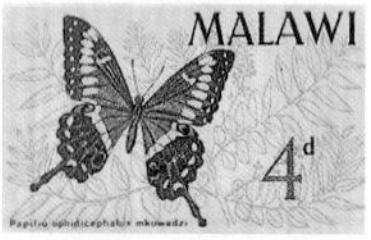

54 "Papilio ophidicephalus"

1966. Malawi Butterflies. Multicoloured.

247	4d. Type **54**	80	10
248	9d. "Papilio desmondi" (magdae)	1·25	10
249	1s.6d. "Epamera handmani"	1·75	30
250	3s. "Amauris crawshayi"	2·75	6·00
MS251 130×100 mm. Nos. 247/50		17·00	11·00

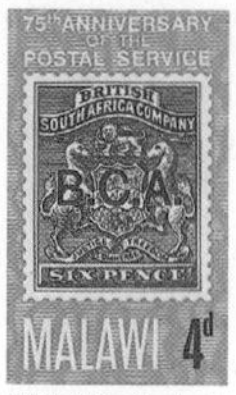

58 British Central Africa 6d. Stamp of 1891

1966. 75th Anniv of Postal Services.

263	**58**	4d. blue and green	10	10
264	**58**	9d. blue and red	15	10
265	**58**	1s.6d. blue and lilac	20	10
266	**58**	3s. grey and blue	30	70
MS267 83×127 mm. Nos. 263/6			5·00	3·25

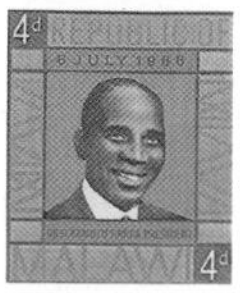

59 President Banda

1966. Republic Day.

268	**59**	4d. brown, silver and green	10	10
269	**59**	9d. brown, silver and mauve	10	10
270	**59**	1s.6d. brown, silver & violet	15	10
271	**59**	3s. brown, silver and blue	25	15
MS272 83×127 mm. Nos. 268/71			2·00	3·25

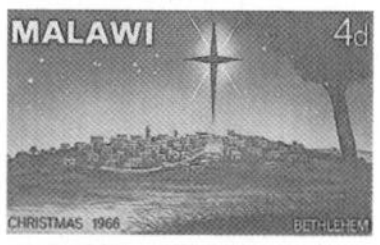

60 Bethlehem

1966. Christmas.

273	**60**	4d. green and gold	10	10
274	**60**	9d. purple and gold	10	10
275	**60**	1s.6d. red and gold	15	10
276	**60**	3s. blue and gold	40	80

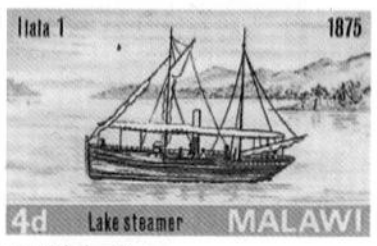

61 "Ilala I"

1967. Lake Malawi Steamers.

277	**61**	4d. black, yellow and green	40	10
278	-	9d. black, yellow and mauve	45	10
279	-	1s.6d. black, red and violet	65	20
280	-	3s. black, red and blue	1·25	1·75

DESIGNS: 9d. "Dove"; 1s.9d. "Chauncy Maples I" (wrongly inscr "Chauncey"); 3s. "Gwendolen".

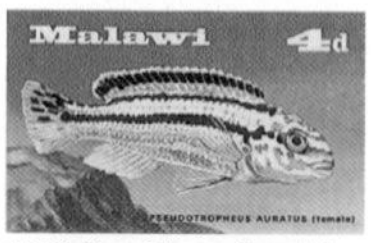

62 Golden Mbuna (female)

1967. Lake Malawi Cichlids. Multicoloured.

281	4d. Type **62**	30	10
282	9d. Scraped-mouthed mbuna	45	10
283	1s.6d. Zebra mbuna	60	25
284	3s. Orange mbuna	1·25	2·00

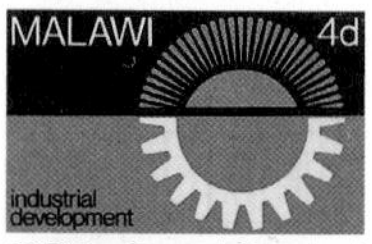

63 Rising Sun and Gearwheel

1967. Industrial Development.

285	**63**	4d. black and green	10	10
286	**63**	9d. black and red	10	10
287	**63**	1s.6d. black and violet	10	10
288	**63**	3s. black and blue	15	30
MS289 134×108 mm. Nos. 285/8			1·00	1·75

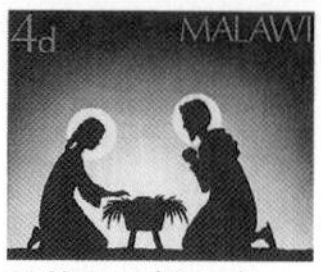

64 Mary and Joseph beside Crib

1967. Christmas.

290	**64**	4d. blue and green	10	10
291	**64**	9d. blue and red	10	10
292	**64**	1s.6d. blue and yellow	10	10
293	**64**	3s. deep blue and blue	15	30
MS294 114×100 mm. Nos. 290/3			1·00	3·00

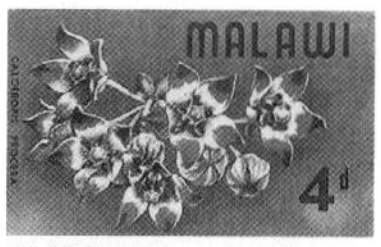

65 "Calotropis procera"

1968. Wild Flowers. Multicoloured.

295	4d. Type **65**	15	10
296	9d. "Borreria dibrachiata"	15	10
297	1s.6d. "Hibiscus rhodanthus"	15	10
298	3s. "Bidens pinnatipartita"	20	95
MS299 135×91 mm. Nos. 295/8		1·25	3·25

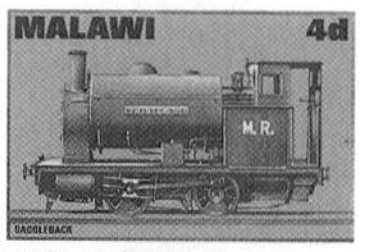

66 Bagnall Steam Locomotive No. 1 "Thistle"

1968. Malawi Locomotives.

300	**66**	4d. green, blue and red	25	10
301	-	9d. red, blue and green	30	15
302	-	1s.6d. multicoloured	40	30
303	-	3s. multicoloured	70	3·00
MS304 120×88 mm. Nos. 300/3			1·50	6·00

DESIGNS: 9d. Class G steam locomotive No. 49; 1s.6d. Class "Zambesi" diesel locomotive No. 202; 3s. Diesel railcar No. DR1.

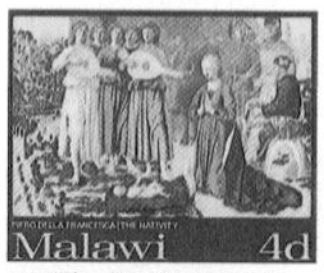

67 "The Nativity" (Piero della Francesca)

1968. Christmas. Multicoloured.

305	4d. Type **67**	10	10
306	9d. "The Adoration of the Shepherds" (Murillo)	10	10
307	1s.6d. "The Adoration of the Shepherds" (Reni)	10	10
308	3s. "Nativity, with God the Father and Holy Ghost" (Pittoni)	15	15
MS309 115×101 mm. Nos. 305/8		35	1·60

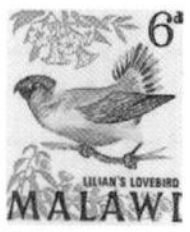

69 Nyassa Lovebird

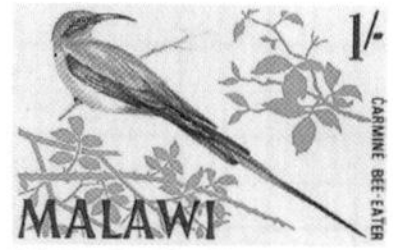

70 Carmine Bee Eater

1968. Birds (1st series). Multicoloured.

310	1d. Scarlet-chested sunbird (horiz)	15	50
311	2d. Violet starling (horiz)	30	20
312	3d. White-browed robin chat (horiz)	30	10
313	4d. Red-billed fire finch (horiz)	50	40
314	6d. Type **69**	2·50	15
315	9d. Yellow-rumped bishop	2·50	60
316	1s. Type **70**	1·00	15
317	1s.6d. Grey-headed bush shrike	5·00	8·00
318	2s. Paradise whydah	5·00	8·00
319	3s. African paradise flycatcher (vert)	8·50	4·25
320	5s. Bateleur (vert)	6·00	4·25
321	10s. Saddle-bill stork (vert)	4·50	7·50
322	£1 Purple heron (vert)	8·00	18·00
323	£2 Green turaco ("Livingstone's Loerie")	42·00	48·00

SIZES: 1d. to 9d. as Type **69**; 1s.6d. to £2 as Type **70**.

See also Nos. 473/85.

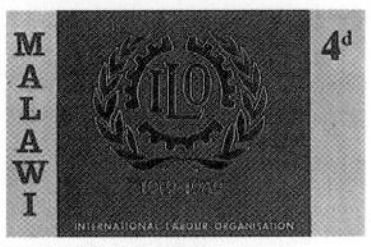

71 I.L.O. Emblem

1969. 50th Anniv of Int Labour Organization.

324	**71**	4d. gold and green	10	10
325	**71**	9d. gold and brown	10	10
326	**71**	1s.6d. gold and brown	10	10
327	**71**	3s. gold and blue	15	15
MS328 127×89 mm. Nos. 324/7			1·00	4·75

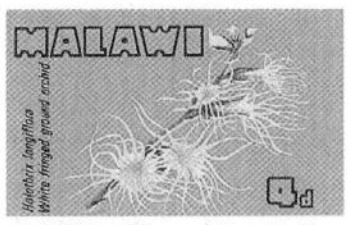

72 White-fringed Ground Orchid

1969. Orchids of Malawi. Multicoloured.

329	4d. Type **72**	15	10
330	9d. Red ground orchid	20	10
331	1s.6d. Leopard tree orchid	30	20
332	3s. Blue ground orchid	60	2·00
MS333 118×86 mm. Nos. 329/32		1·10	3·75

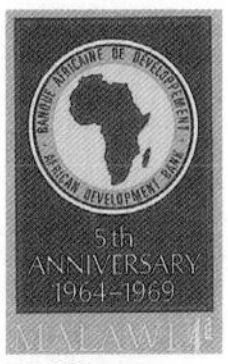

73 African Development Bank Emblem

1969. Fifth Anniv of African Development Bank.

334	**73**	4d. yellow, brown and ochre	10	10
335	**73**	9d. yellow, ochre and green	10	10
336	**73**	1s.6d. yellow, ochre & brn	10	10
337	**73**	3s. yellow, ochre and blue	15	15
MS338 102×137 mm. Nos. 334/7			50	1·00

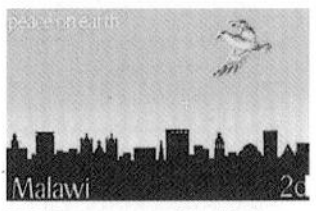

74 Dove over Bethlehem

1969. Christmas.

339	**74**	2d. black and yellow	10	10
340	**74**	4d. black and turquoise	10	10
341	**74**	9d. black and red	10	10
342	**74**	1s.6d. black and violet	10	10
343	**74**	3s. black and blue	15	15
MS344 130×71 mm. Nos. 339/43			1·00	1·75

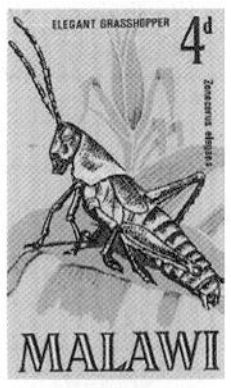

75 "Zonocerus elegans" (grasshopper)

1970. Insects of Malawi. Multicoloured.

345	4d. Type **75**	15	10
346	9d. "Mylabris dicincta" (beetle)	15	10
347	1s.6d. "Henosepilachna elaterii" (ladybird)	20	15
348	3s. "Sphodromantis speculabunda" (mantid)	35	1·40
MS349 86×137 mm. Nos. 345/8		1·25	2·50

1970. Rand Easter Show. No. 317 optd **Rand Easter Show 1970.**

350	1s.6d. multicoloured	50	2·25

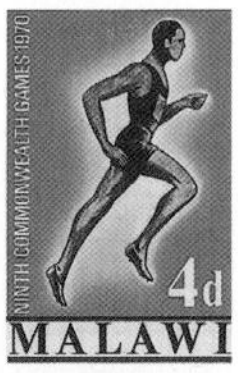

77 Runner

1970. Ninth Commonwealth Games, Edinburgh.

351	**77**	4d. blue and green	10	10
352	**77**	9d. blue and red	10	10
353	**77**	1s.6d. blue and yellow	10	10
354	**77**	3s. deep blue and blue	15	15
MS355 146×96 mm. Nos. 351/4			55	1·00

1970. Decimal Currency. Nos. 316 and 318 surch.

356	10t. on 1s. multicoloured	3·00	25
357	20t. on 2s. multicoloured	3·00	4·50

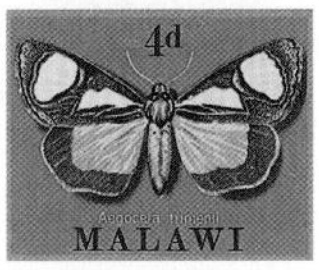

79 "Aegocera trimeni"

1970. Moths. Multicoloured.

358	4d. Type **79**	20	10
359	9d. "Faidherbia bauhiniae"	30	10
360	1s.6d. "Parasa karschi"	50	20
361	3s. "Teracotona euprepia"	1·25	3·50
MS362 112×92 mm. Nos. 358/61		4·25	6·50

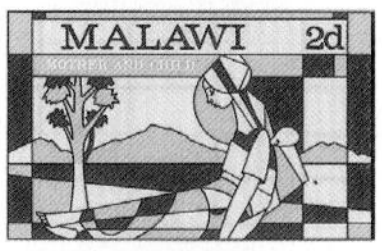

80 Mother and Child

1970. Christmas.

363	**80**	2d. black and yellow	10	10
364	**80**	4d. black and green	10	10
365	**80**	9d. black and red	10	10
366	**80**	1s.6d. black and purple	10	10
367	**80**	3s. black and blue	15	15
MS368 166×100 mm. Nos. 363/7			1·00	2·50

1971. No. 319 surch 30t **Special United Kingdom Delivery Service.**

369	30t. on 3s. multicoloured	50	2·25

No. 369 was issued for use on letters carried by an emergency airmail service from Malawi to Great Britain during the British postal strike. The fee of 30t. was to cover the charge for delivery by a private service, and ordinary stamps to pay the normal airmail postage had to be affixed as well. These stamps were in use from 8 February to 8 March.

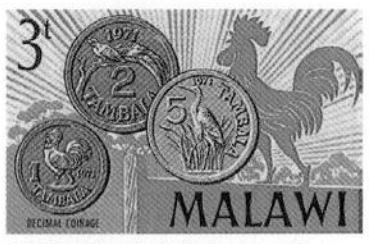

82 Decimal Coinage and Cockerel

1971. Decimal Coinage.

370	**82**	3t. multicoloured	15	10
371	**82**	8t. multicoloured	20	10
372	**82**	15t. multicoloured	25	20
373	**82**	30t. multicoloured	35	1·50
MS374 140×101 mm. Nos. 370/3			1·00	2·50

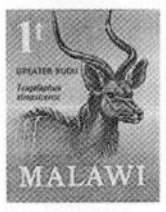

83 Greater Kudu

1971. Decimal Currency. Antelopes. Multicoloured.

375	1t. Type **83**	10	10
376	2t. Nyala	15	15
377	3t. Mountain reedbuck	20	50
378	5t. Puku	40	1·25
379	8t. Impala	45	1·00
380	10t. Eland	60	10
381	15t. Klipspringer	1·00	20
382	20t. Suni	1·50	90
383	30t. Roan antelope	11·00	1·40
384	50t. Waterbuck	1·00	65
385	1k. Bushbuck	1·50	85
386	2k. Red forest duiker	2·75	1·50
387	4k. Common duiker	21·00	24·00

Nos. 380/7 are larger, size 25×42 mm.
No. 387 is incorrectly inscr "Gray Duiker".

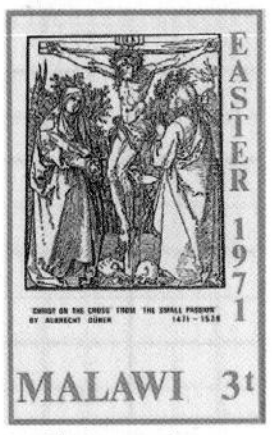

85 Christ on the Cross

1971. Easter. Multicoloured.

388	**85**	3t. black and green	10	25
389	-	3t. black and green	10	25
390	**85**	8t. black and red	10	25
391	-	8t. black and red	10	25
392	**85**	15t. black and violet	15	30
393	-	15t. black and violet	15	30
394	**85**	30t. black and blue	20	45
395	-	30t. black and blue	20	45
MS396 Two sheets, each 95×145 mm. (a) Nos. 388, 390, 392 and 394. (b) Nos. 389, 391, 393 and 395 Set of 2 sheets			1·50	4·00

DESIGN: Nos. 389, 391, 393, 395, The Resurrection. Both designs from "The Small Passion" (Durer).

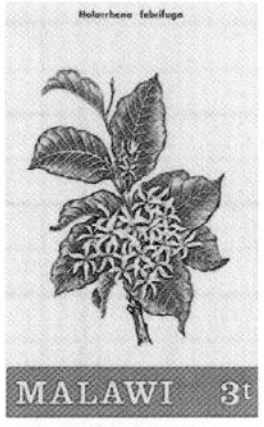

87 "Holarrhena febrifuga"

1971. Flowering Shrubs and Trees. Multicoloured.

397	3t. Type **87**	10	10
398	8t. "Brachystegia spiciformis"	10	10
399	15t. "Securidaca longepedunculata"	15	15
400	30t. "Pterocarpus rotundifolius"	30	1·25
MS401 102×135 mm. Nos. 397/400		1·00	2·50

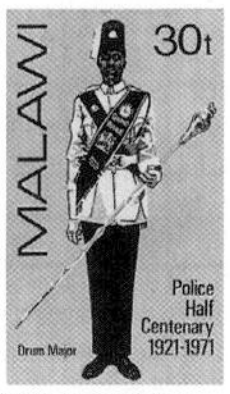

88 Drum Major

1971. 50th Anniv of Malawi Police Force.

402	**88**	30t. multicoloured	65	1·50

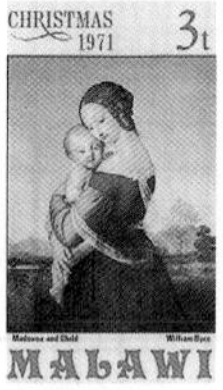

89 "Madonna and Child" (William Dyce)

1971. Christmas. Multicoloured.

403	3t. Type **89**	10	10
404	8t. "The Holy Family" (M. Schongauer)	15	10
405	15t. "The Holy Family with St. John" (Raphael)	20	20
406	30t. "The Holy Family" (Bronzino)	50	1·40
MS407 101×139 mm. Nos. 403/6		1·10	2·75

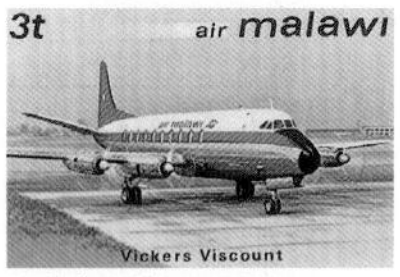

90 Vickers Viscount 700

1972. Air. Malawi Aircraft. Multicoloured.

408	3t. Type **90**	40	10
409	8t. Hawker Siddeley H.S.748	60	10
410	15t. Britten Norman Islander	85	30
411	30t. B.A.C. One Eleven	1·40	2·75
MS412 143×94 mm. Nos. 408/11		8·00	6·00

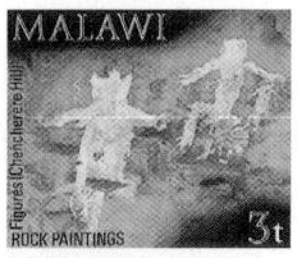

91 Figures (Chencherere Hill)

1972. Rock Paintings.

413	**91**	3t. green and black	25	10
414	-	8t. red, grey and black	30	10
415	-	15t. multicoloured	35	30
416	-	30t. multicoloured	45	1·00
MS417 121×97 mm. Nos. 413/16			2·75	2·75

DESIGNS: 8t. Lizard and cat (Chencherere Hill); 15t. Schematics (Diwa Hill); 30t. Sun through rain (Mikolongwe Hill).

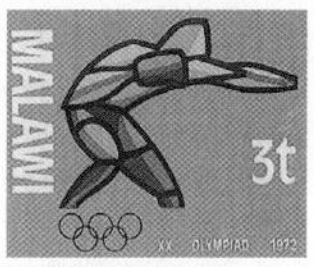

92 Boxing

1972. Olympic Games, Munich.

418	**92**	3t. multicoloured	10	10
419	**92**	8t. multicoloured	15	10
420	**92**	15t. multicoloured	20	10
421	**92**	30t. multicoloured	35	45
MS422 110×92 mm. Nos. 418/21			1·25	1·75

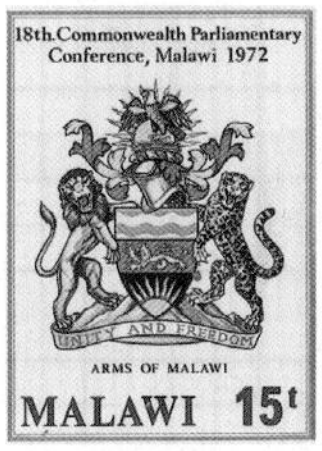

93 Arms of Malawi

1972. Commonwealth Parliamentary Conf.

423	**93**	15t. multicoloured	30	35

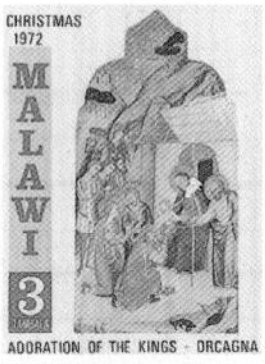

94 "Adoration of the Kings" (Orcagna)

1972. Christmas. Multicoloured.

424	3t. Type **94**	10	10
425	8t. "Madonna and Child Enthroned" (Florentine School)	10	10
426	15t. "Virgin and Child" (Crivelli)	20	10
427	30t. "Virgin and Child with St. Anne" (Flemish School)	45	70
MS428 95×121 mm. Nos. 424/7		1·10	2·00

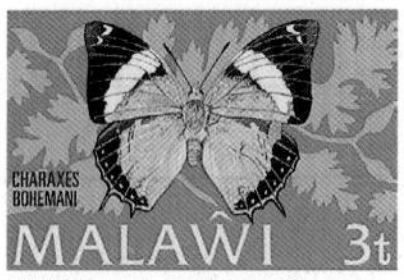

95 "Charaxes bohemani"

1973. Butterflies. Multicoloured.

429	3t. Type **95**	50	10
430	8t. "Uranothauma crawshayi"	75	10
431	15t. "Charaxes acuminatus"	1·00	30
432	30t. "Amauris ansorgei" (inscr in error "EUPHAEDRA ZADDACHI")	4·00	8·50
433	30t. "Amauris ansorgei" (inscr corrected)	5·50	8·50
MS434 145×95 mm. Nos. 429/32		7·00	12·00

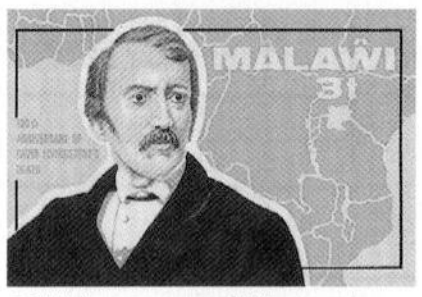

96 Livingstone and Map

1973. Death Cent of David Livingstone (1st issue).

435	**96**	3t. multicoloured	10	10
436	**96**	8t. multicoloured	15	10
437	**96**	15t. multicoloured	20	10
438	**96**	30t. multicoloured	35	60
MS439 144×95 mm. Nos. 435/8			1·00	1·75

See also No. 450/**MS**451.

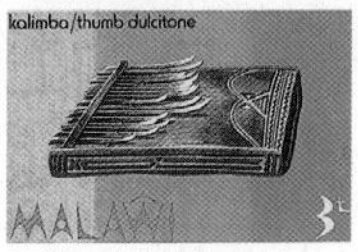

97 Thumb Dulcitone

1973. Musical Instruments. Multicoloured.

440	3t. Type **97**	10	10
441	8t. Hand zither (vert)	15	10
442	15t. Hand drum (vert)	25	10
443	30t. One-stringed fiddle	45	60
MS444 120×103 mm. Nos. 440/3		2·75	2·00

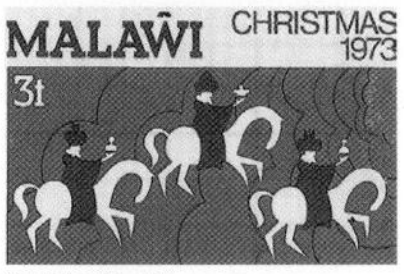

98 The Magi

1973. Christmas.

445	98	3t. blue, lilac & ultramarine	10	10
446	98	8t. red, lilac and brown	10	10
447	98	15t. mauve, blue & dp mve	15	10
448	98	30t. yellow, lilac and brown	30	70
MS449		165×114 mm. Nos. 445/8	75	1·40

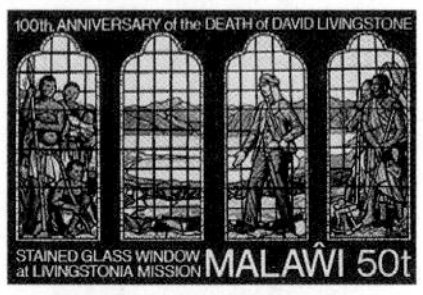

99 Stained-glass Window, Livingstonia Mission

1973. Death Cent of David Livingstone (2nd issue).

450	99	50t. multicoloured	45	1·25
MS451		71×77 mm. No. 450	80	1·60

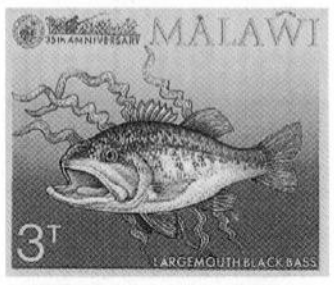

100 Large-mouthed Black Bass

1974. 35th Anniv of Malawi Angling Society. Multicoloured.

452	3t. Type **100**	20	10
453	8t. Rainbow trout	25	10
454	15t. Silver alestes ("Lake salmon")	40	20
455	30t. Tigerfish	70	1·90
MS456	169×93 mm. Nos. 452/5	2·50	3·00

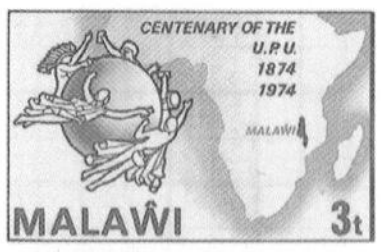

101 U.P.U. Monument and Map of Africa

1974. Centenary of U.P.U.

457	101	3t. green and brown	10	10
458	101	8t. red and brown	10	10
459	101	15t. violet and brown	15	10
460	101	30t. blue and brown	30	1·10
MS461		115×146 mm. Nos. 457/60	65	2·00

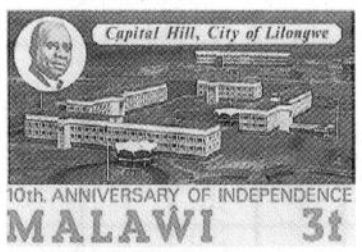

102 Capital Hill, Lilongwe

1974. 10th Anniv of Independence.

462	102	3t. multicoloured	10	10
463	102	8t. multicoloured	10	10
464	102	15t. multicoloured	10	10
465	102	30t. multicoloured	25	35
MS466		120×86 mm. Nos. 462/5	45	1·25

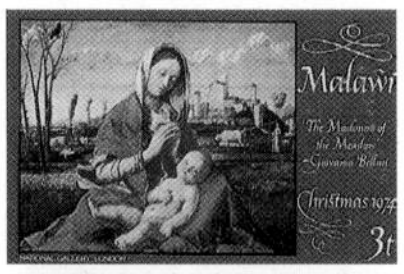

103 "Madonna of the Meadow" (Bellini)

1974. Christmas. Multicoloured.

467	3t. Type **103**	10	10
468	8t. "The Holy Family with Sts. John and Elizabeth" (Jordaens)	10	10
469	15t. "The Nativity" (Pieter de Grebber)	15	10
470	30t. "Adoration of the Shepherds" (Lorenzo di Credi)	30	50
MS471	163×107 mm. Nos. 467/70	60	1·50

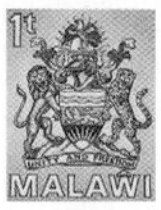

104 Arms of Malawi

1975

472	104	1t. blue	20	40
472a	104	5t. red	65	2·25

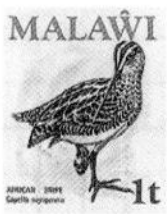

105 African Snipe

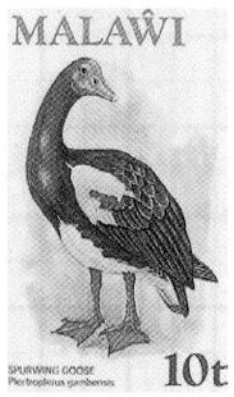

106 Spur-winged Goose ("Spurwing Goose")

1975. Birds (2nd series). Multicoloured. (a) As T **105**.

473	1t. Type **105**	1·50	2·50
474	2t. Double-banded sandgrouse (horiz)	1·50	2·25
475	3t. Indian blue quail ("Blue Quail") (horiz)	1·50	1·75
476	5t. Red-necked spurfowl ("Red-necked Francolin")	3·50	1·25
477	8t. Harlequin quail (horiz)	4·75	1·00

(b) As T **106**.

480	20t. Comb duck ("Knob-billed Duck")	1·00	2·25
481	30t. Helmeted guineafowl ("Crowned Guinea Fowl")	1·25	70
482	50t. African pygmy goose ("Pigmy Goose") (horiz)	2·00	1·60
483	1k. Garganey	3·00	8·50
485	4k. African green pigeon ("Green Pigeon")	13·00	16·00
502	10t. Type **106**	2·00	1·50
503	15t. Denham's bustard ("Stanley Bustard")	2·00	2·00
504	2k. White-faced whistling duck ("White Face Tree Duck")	5·00	11·00

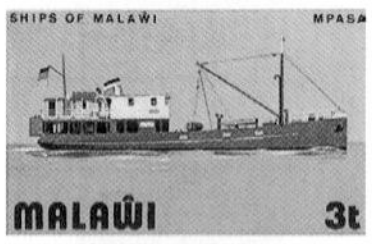

107 M.V. "Mpasa"

1975. Ships of Lake Malawi. Multicoloured.

486	3t. Type **107**	30	10
487	8t. M.V. "Ilala II"	40	10
488	15t. M.V. "Chauncy Maples II"	75	30
489	30t. M.V. "Nkwazi"	1·00	3·50
MS490	105×142 mm. Nos. 486/9	2·25	4·25

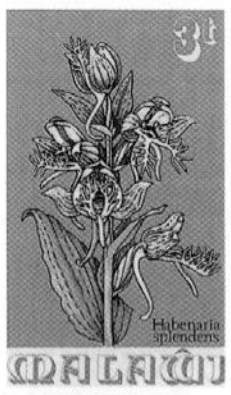

108 "Habenaria splendens"

1975. Malawi Orchids. Multicoloured.

491	3t. Type **108**	50	10
492	10t. "Eulophia cucullata"	60	10
493	20t. "Disa welwitschii"	90	25
494	40t. "Angraecum conchiferum"	1·25	2·25
MS495	127×111 mm. Nos. 491/4	7·00	8·50

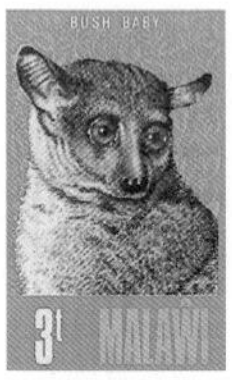

109 Thick-tailed Bushbaby

1976. Malawi Animals. Multicoloured.

496	3t. Type **109**	10	10
497	10t. Leopard	35	10
498	20t. Roan antelope	55	35
499	40t. Common zebra	1·00	3·25
MS500	88×130 mm. Nos. 496/9	2·50	3·50

1975. Tenth Africa, Caribbean and Pacific Ministerial Conference. No. 482 optd **10th ACP Ministerial Conference 1975**.

514	50t. African pygmy goose	1·00	2·50

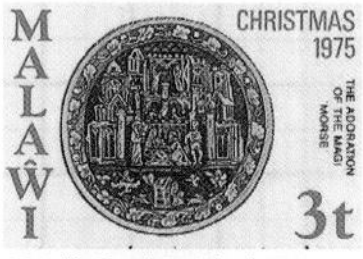

111 "A Castle with the Adoration of the Magi"

1975. Christmas. Religious Medallions. Multicoloured.

515	3t. Type **111**	10	10
516	10t. "The Nativity"	15	10
517	20t. "Adoration of the Magi" (different)	20	10
518	40t. "Angel appearing to Shepherds"	50	2·50
MS519	98×168 mm. Nos. 515/18	1·50	3·75

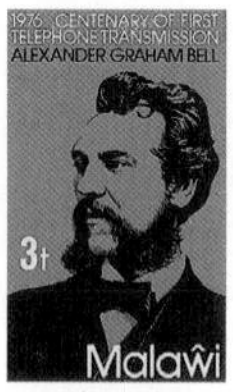

112 Alexander Graham Bell

1976. Centenary of Telephone.

520	112	3t. green and black	10	10
521	112	10t. purple and black	10	10
522	112	20t. violet and black	20	10
523	112	40t. blue and black	50	1·40
MS524		137×114 mm. Nos. 520/3	1·10	1·75

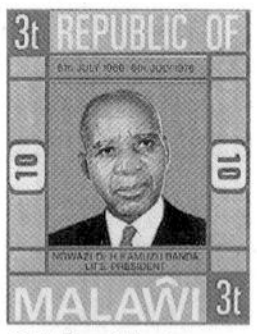

113 President Banda

1976. Tenth Anniv of Republic. Multicoloured.

525	113	3t. green	10	10
526	113	10t. purple	10	10
527	113	20t. blue	20	10
528	113	40t. blue	50	1·40
MS529		102×112 mm. Nos. 524/8	1·00	2·50

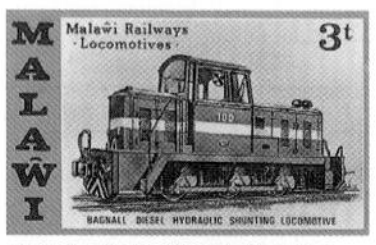

114 Bagnall Diesel Shunter No. 100

1976. Malawi Locomotives. Multicoloured.

530	3t. Type **114**	40	15
531	10t. Class "Shire" diesel locomotive No. 503	70	15
532	20t. Nippon Sharyo diesel-hydraulic locomotive No. 301	1·40	45
533	40t. Hunslet diesel-hydraulic locomotive No. 110	2·10	6·50
MS534	130×118 mm. Nos. 530/3	4·25	7·00

1976. Centenary of Blantyre Mission. Nos. 479 and 481 optd **Blantyre Mission Centenary 1876–1976**.

535	15t. Denham's bustard	1·50	1·50
536	30t. Helmeted guineafowl	1·75	3·75

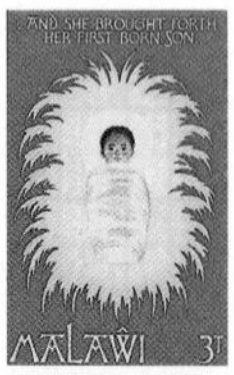

116 Child on Bed of Straw

1976. Christmas.

537	116	3t. multicoloured	10	10
538	116	10t. multicoloured	10	10
539	116	20t. multicoloured	20	10
540	116	40t. multicoloured	40	60
MS541		135×95 mm. Nos. 537/40	1·60	2·50

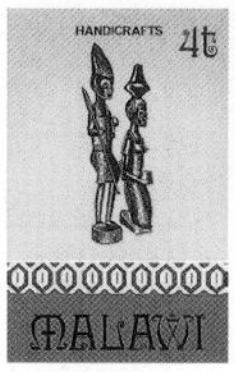

117 Man and Woman

1977. Handicrafts. Wood-carvings. Multicoloured.

542	4t. Type **117**	10	10
543	10t. Elephant (horiz)	15	10
544	20t. Rhinoceros (horiz)	20	10
545	40t. Antelope	50	70
MS546	153×112 mm. Nos. 542/5	1·50	2·75

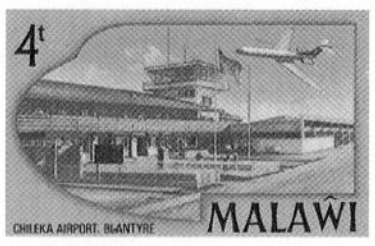

118 Chileka Airport

1977. Transport. Multicoloured.

547	4t. Type **118**	40	10
548	10t. Blantyre–Lilongwe Road	40	10
549	20t. M.V. "Ilala II"	1·00	35
550	40t. Blantyre–Nacala rail line	1·50	4·75
MS551	127×83 mm. Nos. 547/50	3·00	4·75

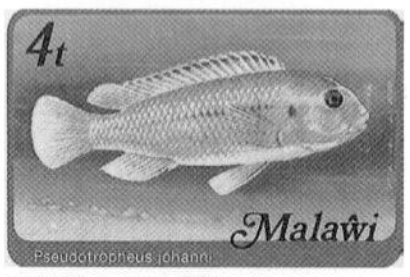

119 Blue-grey Mbuna

1977. Fish of Lake Malawi. Multicoloured.

552B	4t. Type **119**	30	10
553B	10t. Livingston mbuna	50	20
554A	20t. Zebra mbuna	1·40	45
555B	40t. Malawi scale-eater	1·50	1·25
MS556A	147×99 mm. Nos. 552A/5B	3·00	5·00

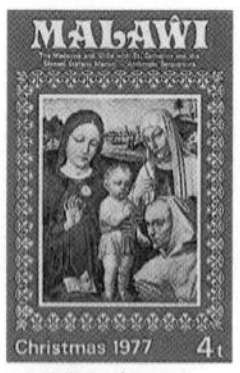

120 "Madonna and Child with St. Catherine and the Blessed Stefano Maconi" (Borgognone)

1977. Christmas.

557	120	4t. multicoloured	10	10
558	-	10t. multicoloured	15	10
559	-	20t. multicoloured	25	10
560	-	40t. multicoloured	60	1·50
MS561		150×116 mm. Nos. 557/60	2·50	3·00

DESIGNS: 10t. "Madonna and Child with the Eternal Father and Angels" (Borgognone); 20t. Bottigella altarpiece (detail, Foppa); 40t. "Madonna of the Fountain" (van Eyck).

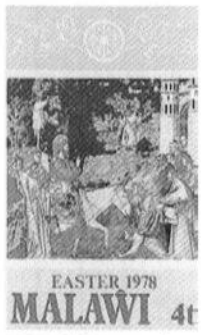

121 "Entry of Christ into Jerusalem" (Giotto)

1978. Easter. Paintings by Giotto. Multicoloured.

562	4t. Type **121**	10	10
563	10t. "The Crucifixion"	15	10
564	20t. "Descent from the Cross"	30	10
565	40t. "Jesus appears before Mary"	50	55
MS566	150×99 mm. Nos. 562/5	1·90	2·40

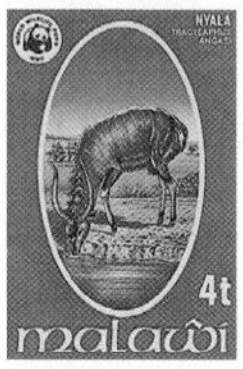

122 Nyala

1978. Wildlife. Multicoloured.

567	4t. Type **122**	2·75	10
568	10t. Lion (horiz)	7·50	40
569	20t. Common zebra (horiz)	11·00	1·00
570	40t. Mountain reedbuck	12·00	7·50
MS571	173×113 mm. Nos. 567/70	35·00	12·00

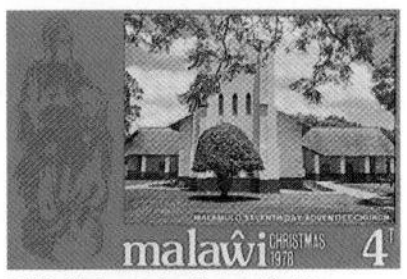

123 Malamulo Seventh Day Adventist Church

1978. Christmas. Multicoloured.

572	4t. Type **123**	10	10
573	10t. Likoma Cathedral	10	10
574	20t. St. Michael's and All Angels', Blantyre	20	10
575	40t. Zomba Catholic Cathedral	40	1·50
MS576	190×105 mm. Nos. 572/5	70	1·75

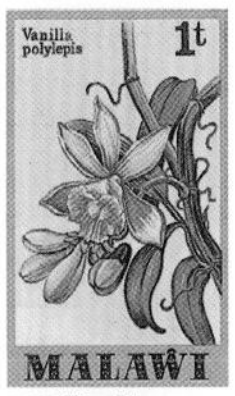

124 "Vanilla polylepis"

1979. Orchids. Multicoloured.

577	1t. Type **124**	50	40
578	2t. "Cirrhopetalum umbellatum"	50	40
579	5t. "Calanthe natalensis"	50	10
580	7t. "Ansellia gigantea"	50	60
581	8t. "Tridactyle bicaudata"	50	40
582	10t. "Acampe pachyglossa"	50	10
583	15t. "Eulophia quartiniana"	50	15
584	20t. "Cyrtorchis arcuata"	50	60
585	30t. "Eulophia tricristata"	1·25	30
586	50t. "Disa hamatopetala"	85	60
587	75t. "Cynorchis glandulosa"	2·00	6·50
588	1k. "Aerangis kotschyana"	1·60	1·75
589	1k.50 "Polystachya dendrobiiflora"	1·75	6·00
590	2k. "Disa ornithantha"	1·25	2·00
591	4k. "Cyrtorchis praetermissa"	1·50	5·00

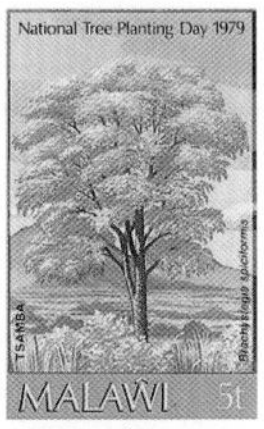

125 Tsamba

1979. National Tree Planting Day. Multicoloured.

592	5t. Type **125**	20	10
593	10t. Mulanje cedar	25	10
594	20t. Mlombwa	40	20
595	40t. Mbawa	70	2·75
MS596	118×153 mm. Nos. 592/5	1·40	3·00

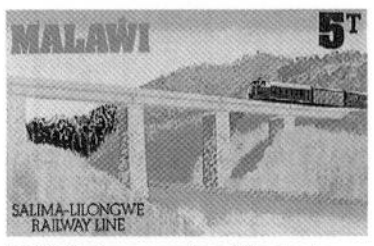

126 Train crossing Viaduct

1979. Opening of Salima–Lilongwe Railway Line. Multicoloured.

597	5t. Type **126**	25	15
598	10t. Diesel railcar at station	40	15
599	20t. Diesel train rounding bend	60	30
600	40t. Diesel train passing through cutting	85	2·50
MS601	153×103 mm. Nos. 597/600	3·25	4·50

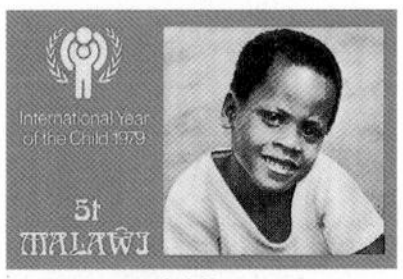

127 Young Child

1979. International Year of the Child. Designs showing young children. Multicoloured; background colours given.

602	127	5t. green	10	10
603	-	10t. red	10	10
604	-	20t. mauve	25	10
605	-	40t. blue	45	1·60

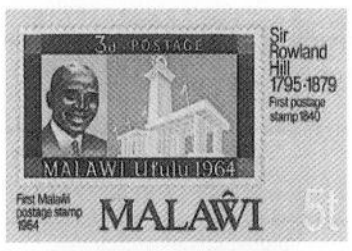

128 1964 3d. Independence Commemorative Stamp

1979. Death Centenary of Sir Rowland Hill. Designs showing 1964 Independence Commemorative Stamps. Multicoloured.

606	5t. Type **128**	10	10
607	10t. 6d. value	10	10
608	20t. 1s.3d. value	20	10
609	40t. 2s.6d. value	35	85
MS610	163×108 mm. Nos. 606/9	75	1·40

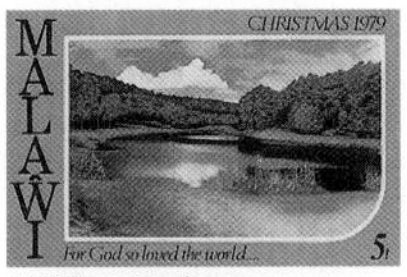

129 River Landscape

1979. Christmas. Multicoloured.

611	5t. Type **129**	10	10
612	10t. Sunset	10	10
613	20t. Forest and hill	25	15
614	40t. Plain and mountains	50	2·25

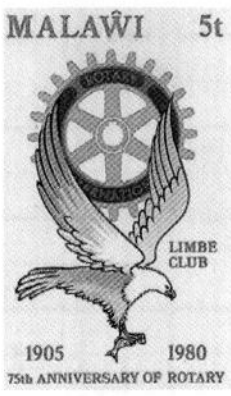

130 Limbe Rotary Club Emblem

1980. 75th Anniv of Rotary International.

615	130	5t. multicoloured	10	10
616	-	10t. multicoloured	10	10
617	-	20t. blue, gold and red	30	15
618	-	40t. gold and blue	75	2·25
MS619		105×144 mm. Nos. 615/18	1·10	2·50

DESIGNS: 10t. Blantyre Rotary Club pennant; 20t. Lilongwe Rotary Club pennant; 40t. Rotary International emblem.

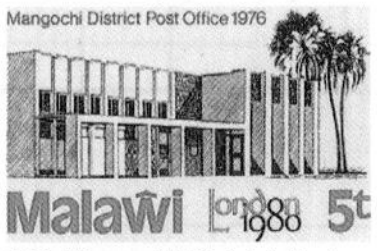

131 Mangochi District Post Office

1980. "London 1980" International Stamp Exhibition.

620	131	5t. black and green	10	10
621	-	10t. black and red	10	10
622	-	20t. black and violet	15	10
623	-	1k. black and blue	65	1·10
MS624		114×89 mm. Nos. 620/3	1·25	2·25

DESIGNS: 10t. New Blantyre Sorting Office; 20t. Mail transfer hut, Walala; 1k. First Nyasaland Post Office, Chiromo.

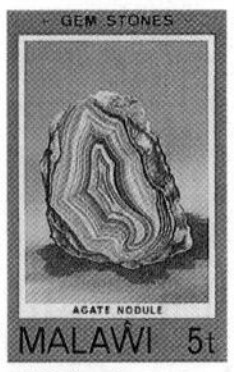

132 Agate Nodule

1980. Gemstones. Multicoloured.

625	5t. Type **132**	60	10
626	10t. Sunstone	80	10
627	20t. Smoky quartz	1·40	30
628	1k. Kyanite crystal	3·50	6·00

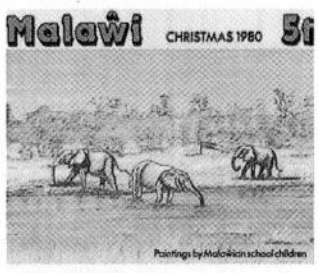

133 Elephants

1980. Christmas. Children's Paintings. Multicoloured.

629	5t. Type **133**	40	10
630	10t. Flowers	30	10
631	20t. Class "Shire" diesel train	75	20
632	1k. Malachite kingfisher	1·60	2·00

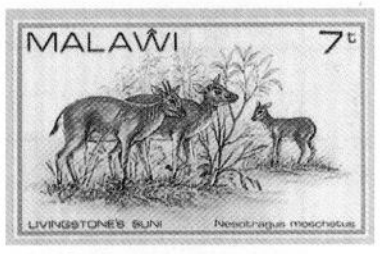

134 Suni

1981. Wildlife. Multicoloured.

633	7t. Type **134**	15	10
634	10t. Blue duiker	20	10
635	20t. African buffalo	30	15
636	1k. Lichtenstein's hartebeest	1·25	1·60

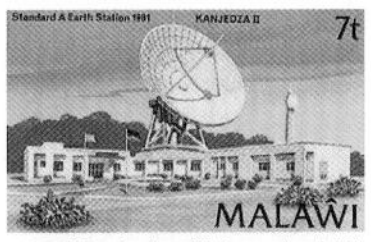

135 "Kanjedza II" Standard "A" Earth Station

1981. International Communications. Multicoloured.

637	7t. Type **135**	10	10
638	10t. Blantyre International Gateway Exchange	15	10
639	20t. "Kanjedza I" standard "B" earth station	25	15
640	1k. "Satellite communications"	1·50	1·90
MS641	101×151 mm. Nos. 637/40	1·75	3·25

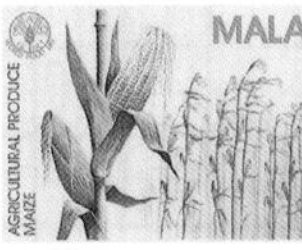

136 Maize

1981. World Food Day. Agricultural Produce. Multicoloured.

642	7t. Type **136**	15	10
643	10t. Rice	20	10
644	20t. Finger-millet	30	20
645	1k. Wheat	1·00	1·40

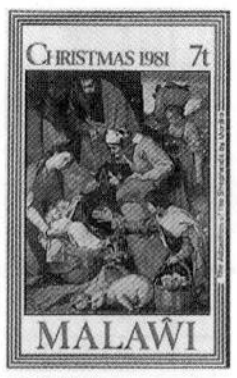

137 "The Adoration of the Shepherds" (Murillo)

1981. Christmas. Paintings. Multicoloured.

646	7t. Type **137**	20	10
647	10t. "The Holy Family" (Lippi) (horiz)	25	10
648	20t. "The Adoration of the Shepherds" (Louis le Nain) (horiz)	45	15
649	1k. "The Virgin and Child, St. John the Baptist and an Angel" (Paolo Morando)	1·10	2·25

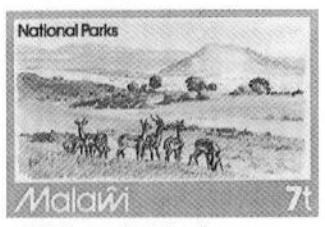

138 Impala Herd

1982. National Parks. Wildlife. Multicoloured.

650	7t. Type **138**	20	10
651	10t. Lions	35	10
652	20t. Greater kudu	50	20
653	1k. Greater flamingoes	1·75	5·50

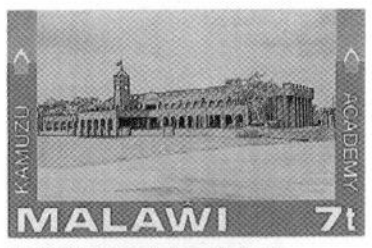

139 Kamuzu Academy

1982. Kamuzu Academy.

654	139	7t. multicoloured	15	10
655	-	20t. multicoloured	20	10
656	-	30t. multicoloured	30	45
657	-	1k. multicoloured	1·00	3·75

DESIGNS: 20t. to 1k. Various views of the Academy.

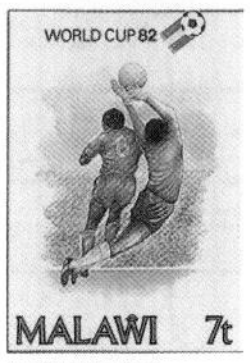

140 Attacker challenging Goalkeeper

1982. World Cup Football Championship, Spain. Multicoloured.

658	7t. Type **140**	75	25
659	20t. FIFA World Cup trophy	1·60	1·25
660	30t. Football stadium	1·90	3·25
MS661	80×59 mm. 1k. Football	1·75	1·75

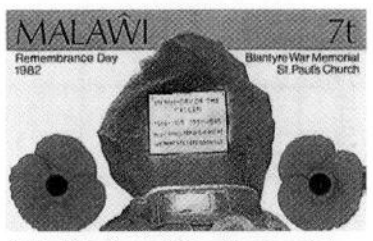

141 Blantyre War Memorial, St. Paul's Church

1982. Remembrance Day. Multicoloured.

662	7t. Type **141**	10	10
663	20t. Zomba war memorial	15	10
664	30t. Chichiri war memorial	20	30
665	1k. Lilongwe war memorial	65	4·25

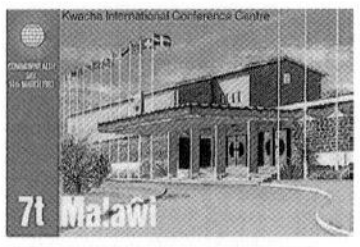

142 Kwacha International Conference Centre

1983. Commonwealth Day. Multicoloured.

666	7t. Type **142**	10	10
667	20t. Tea-picking, Mulanje	20	10
668	30t. World map showing position of Malawi	25	30
669	1k. Pres. Dr. H. Kamuzu Banda	60	1·50

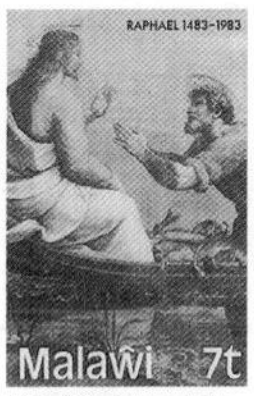

143 "Christ and St. Peter"

1983. 500th Birth Anniv of Raphael. Details from the cartoon for "The Miraculous Draught of Fishes" Tapestry. Multicoloured.

670	7t. Type **143**	25	10
671	20t. "Hauling in the Catch"	55	80
672	30t. "Fishing Village" (horiz)	60	2·50
MS673	110×90 mm. 1k. "Apostle"	1·75	1·75

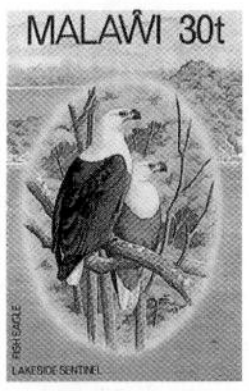

144 Pair by Lake

1983. African Fish Eagle. Multicoloured.

674	30t. Type **144**	1·60	2·00
675	30t. Making gull-like call	1·60	2·00
676	30t. Diving on prey	1·60	2·00
677	30t. Carrying fish	1·60	2·00
678	30t. Feeding on catch	1·60	2·00

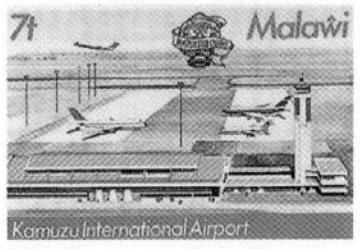

145 Kamuzu International Airport

1983. Bicentenary of Manned Flight. Multicoloured.

679	7t. Type **145**	10	10
680	20t. Kamuzu International Airport (different)	25	15
681	30t. B.A.C. One Eleven	40	45
682	1k. Short Empire "C" Class flying boat at Cape Maclear	1·10	2·75
MS683	100×121 mm. Nos. 679/82	2·00	4·00

146
"Clerodendrum
myricoides"

1983. Christmas. Flowers. Multicoloured.
684	7t. Type **146**	40	10
685	20t. "Gloriosa superba"	90	15
686	30t. "Gladiolus laxiflorus"	1·00	60
687	1k. "Aframomum angustifolium"	2·25	7·00

147 Golden Mbuna

1984. Fishes. Multicoloured.
688	1t. Type **147**	30	1·00
689	2t. Malawi eyebiter	30	1·00
690	5t. Blue mbuna	30	1·00
691	7t. Lombardo's mbuna	30	30
692	8t. Golden zebra mbuna	30	30
693	10t. Fairy cichlid	30	10
694	15t. Crabro mbuna	30	10
695	20t. Marbled zebra mbuna	30	10
696	30t. Sky-blue mbuna	50	20
697	40t. Venustus cichlid	60	30
698	50t. Thumbi emperor cichlid	2·50	3·25
699	75t. Purple mbuna	3·00	5·50
700	1k. Zebra mbuna	3·50	50
701	2k. Fairy cichlid (different)	4·00	7·00
702	4k. Mbenje emperor cichlid	5·00	11·00

Nos. 688 and 691/7 exist with different imprint dates at foot.

148 Smith's Red Hare

1984. Small Mammals. Multicoloured.
703	7t. Type **148**	20	10
704	20t. Gambian sun squirrel	35	50
705	30t. South African hedgehog	35	1·10
706	1k. Large-spotted genet	50	5·50

149 Running

1984. Olympic Games, Los Angeles. Multicoloured.
707	7t. Type **149**	15	10
708	20t. Boxing	35	20
709	30t. Cycling	75	70
710	1k. Long jumping	1·00	4·00
MS711	90×128 mm. Nos. 707/10	2·40	5·00

150 "Euphaedra
neophron"

1984. Butterflies.
712	**150**	7t. multicoloured	75	30
713	–	20t. yellow, brown and red	1·75	45
714	–	30t. multicoloured	2·00	1·10
715	–	1k. multicoloured	3·25	9·00

DESIGNS: 20t. "Papilio dardanus"; 30t. "Antanartia schaeneia"; 1k. "Spindasis nyassae".

151 "Virgin and
Child" (Duccio)

1984. Christmas. Religious Paintings. Multicoloured.
716	7t. Type **151**	45	10
717	20t. "Madonna and Child" (Raphael)	1·10	20
718	30t. "Virgin and Child" (ascr to Lippi)	1·40	70
719	1k. "The Wilton Diptych"	2·50	8·00

152 "Leucopaxillus
gracillimus"

1985. Fungi. Multicoloured.
720	7t. Type **152**	1·00	30
721	20t. "Limacella guttata"	2·00	45
722	30t. "Termitomyces eurrhizus"	2·50	1·25
723	1k. "Xerulina asprata"	4·00	9·50

153 Map showing Member
States and Lumberjack
(Forestry)

1985. Fifth Anniv of Southern African Development Co-ordination Conference. Designs showing map and aspects of development.
724	**153**	7t. black, green and light green	75	10
725	–	15t. black, red and pink	1·25	20
726	–	20t. black, violet and mauve	4·00	1·75
727	–	1k. black, blue and light blue	4·50	10·00

DESIGNS: 15t. Radio mast (Communications); 20t. Diesel locomotive (Transport); 1k. Trawler and net (Fishing).

154 M.V. "Ufulu"

1985. Ships of Lake Malawi (2nd series). Multicoloured.
728	7t. Type **154**	90	10
729	15t. M.V. "Chauncy Maples II"	1·75	20
730	20t. M.V. "Mtendere"	2·25	65
731	1k. M.V. "Ilala II"	4·50	6·00
MS732	120×84 mm. Nos. 728/31	8·00	9·00

155 Stierling's
Woodpecker

1985. Birth Bicentenary of John J. Audubon (ornithologist). Multicoloured.
733	7t. Type **155**	1·00	30
734	15t. Lesser seedcracker	1·75	30
735	20t. East coast akalat ("Gunning's Akalat")	1·75	65
736	1k. Boehm's bee eater	3·25	7·00
MS737	130×90 mm. Nos. 733/6	8·00	10·00

156 "The Virgin
of Humility"
(Jaime Serra)

1985. Christmas. Nativity Paintings. Multicoloured.
738	7t. Type **156**	30	10

739	15t. "The Adoration of the Magi" (Stefano da Zevio)	75	15
740	20t. "Madonna and Child" (Gerard van Honthorst)	85	25
741	1k. "Virgin of Zbraslav" (Master of Vissy Brod)	2·25	5·50

157 Halley's Comet
and Path of "Giotto"
Spacecraft

1986. Appearance of Halley's Comet. Multicoloured.
742	8t. Type **157**	60	10
743	15t. Halley's Comet above Earth	65	15
744	20t. Comet and dish aerial, Malawi	1·00	30
745	1k. "Giotto" spacecraft	2·00	6·50

158 Two Players
competing for Ball

1986. World Cup Football Championship, Mexico. Multicoloured.
746	8t. Type **158**	70	10
747	15t. Goalkeeper saving goal	95	20
748	20t. Two players competing for ball (different)	1·10	35
749	1k. Player kicking ball	4·00	5·50
MS750	108×77 mm. Nos. 746/9	10·00	12·00

159 President
Banda

1986. 20th Anniv of Republic. Multicoloured.
751	8t. Type **159**	1·50	2·75
752	15t. National flag	80	15
753	20t. Malawi coat of arms	85	25
754	1k. Kamuzu International Airport and emblem of national airline	3·50	6·00

160 "Virgin and
Child" (Botticelli)

1986. Christmas. Multicoloured.
755	8t. Type **160**	45	10
756	15t. "Adoration of the Shepherds" (Guido Reni)	80	15
757	20t. "Madonna of the Veil" (Carlo Dolci)	1·25	35
758	1k. "Adoration of the Magi" (Jean Bourdichon)	3·75	9·00

161 Wattled Crane

1987. Wattled Crane. Multicoloured.
759	8t. Type **161**	1·50	40
760	15t. Two cranes	2·25	50
761	20t. Cranes at nest	2·25	80
762	75t. Crane in lake	4·50	12·00

162 Bagnall Steam
Locomotive No. 2
"Shamrock"

767	10t. Type **162**	2·00	45
768	25t. Class D steam locomotive No. 8, 1914	2·75	70
769	30t. Bagnall steam locomotive No. 1 "Thistle"	3·00	85
770	1k. Kitson steam locomotive No. 6, 1903	6·00	13·00

1987. Steam Locomotives. Multicoloured.

163
Hippopotamus
grazing

1987. Hippopotamus. Multicoloured.
771	10t. Type **163**	1·50	40
772	25t. Hippopotami in water	2·25	50
773	30t. Female and calf in water	2·25	75
774	1k. Hippopotami and cattle egret	6·00	12·00
MS775	78×101 mm. Nos. 771/4	11·00	12·50

164
"Stathmostelma
spectabile"

1987. Christmas. Wild Flowers. Multicoloured.
776	10t. Type **164**	65	10
777	25t. "Pentanisia schweinfurthii"	1·50	25
778	30t. "Chironia krebsii"	1·75	55
779	1k. "Ochna macrocalyx"	3·00	9·50

165 African and
Staunton Knights

1988. Chess. Local and Staunton chess pieces. Multicoloured.
780	15t. Type **165**	1·25	30
781	35t. Bishops	1·75	70
782	50t. Rooks	2·00	1·50
783	2k. Queens	6·00	12·00

166 High
Jumping

1988. Olympic Games, Seoul. Multicoloured.
784	15t. Type **166**	30	10
785	35t. Javelin throwing	50	20
786	50t. Tennis	75	50
787	2k. Shot-putting	1·60	3·75
MS788	91×121 mm. Nos. 784/7	3·50	4·00

167 Evergreen
Forest Warbler
("Eastern Forest
Scrub Warbler")

1988. Birds. Multicoloured.
789	1t. Type **167**	50	1·50
790	2t. Yellow-throated woodland warbler ("Yellow-throated Warbler")	70	1·50
791	5t. Moustached green tinkerbird	70	1·50
792	7t. Waller's red-winged starling ("Waller's Chestnut-wing Starling")	70	1·50
793	8t. Oriole-finch	70	1·50

794	10t. White starred robin ("Starred Robin")	2·75	1·50
795	15t. Bar-tailed trogon	1·00	20
796	20t. Green-backed twin-spot ("Green Twinspot")	70	20
797	30t. African grey cuckoo shrike ("Grey Cuckoo Shrike")	70	20
798	40t. Black-fronted bush shrike	70	20
799	50t. White-tailed crested flycatcher	3·25	1·50
800	75t. Green barbet	70	1·25
801	1k. Lemon dove ("Cinnamon Dove")	70	1·25
802	2k. Silvery-cheeked hornbill	1·00	1·60
803	4k. Crowned eagle	1·25	2·50
804	10k. Anchieta's sunbird ("Red and Blue Sunbird")	12·00	14·00
804a	10k. As 10t.	9·00	3·75

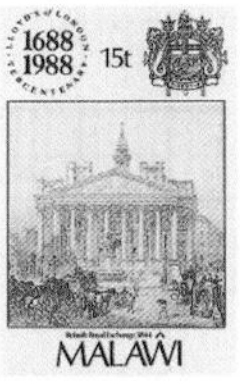

167a Rebuilt Royal Exchange, 1844

1988. 300th Anniv of Lloyd's of London. Multicoloured.

805	15t. Type **167a**	30	10
806	35t. Opening ceremony, Nkula Falls Hydro-electric Power Station (horiz)	70	20
807	50t. Air Malawi B.A.C. One Eleven airliner (horiz)	3·00	75
808	2k. "Seawise University" (formerly "Queen Elizabeth") on fire, Hong Kong, 1972	7·00	5·00

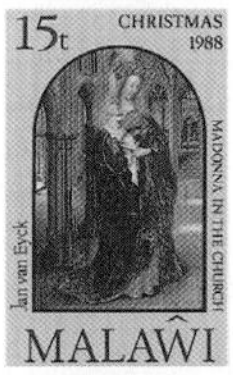

168 "Madonna in the Church" (Jan van Eyck)

1988. Christmas. Multicoloured.

809	15t. Type **168**	60	10
810	35t. "Virgin, Infant Jesus and St. Anna" (da Vinci)	90	25
811	50t. "Virgin and Angels" (Cimabue)	1·25	70
812	2k. "Virgin and Child" (Baldovinetti Apenio)	3·00	6·50

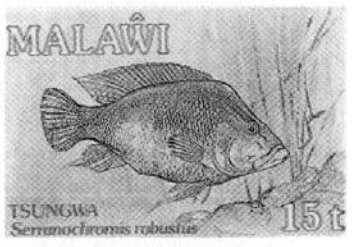

169 Robust Cichlid

1989. 50th Anniv of Malawi Angling Society. Multicoloured.

813	15t. Type **169**	60	20
814	35t. Small-scaled minnow ("Mpasa")	1·10	35
815	50t. Long-scaled yellowfish	1·50	1·40
816	2k. Tigerfish	4·00	9·50

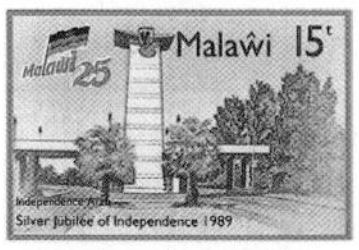

170 Independence Arch, Blantyre

1989. 25th Anniv of Independence. Multicoloured.

817	15t. Type **170**	80	20
818	35t. Grain silos	1·50	35
819	50t. Capital Hill, Lilongwe	2·00	1·50
820	2k. Reserve Bank Headquarters	5·00	10·00

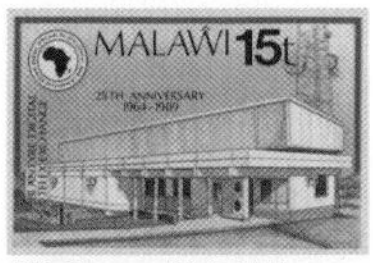

171 Blantyre Digital Telex Exchange

1989. 25th Anniv of African Development Bank. Multicoloured.

821	15t. Type **171**	80	20
822	40t. Dzalanyama steer	1·50	35
823	50t. Mikolongwe heifer	2·00	1·50
824	2k. Zebu bull	5·00	10·00

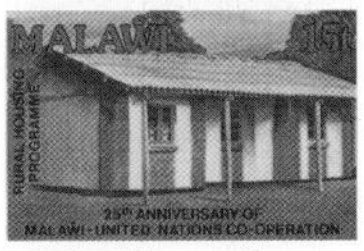

172 Rural House with Verandah

1989. 25th Anniv of Malawi–United Nations Co-operation. Multicoloured.

825	15t. Type **172**	80	20
826	40t. Rural house	1·50	35
827	50t. Traditional hut and modern houses	2·00	1·50
828	2k. Tea plantation	5·00	10·00

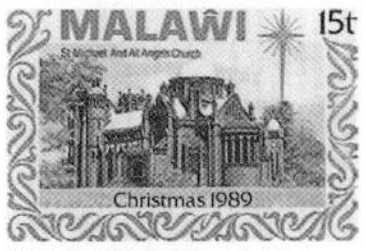

173 St. Michael and All Angels Church

1989. Christmas. Churches of Malawi. Multicoloured.

829	15t. Type **173**	80	20
830	40t. Catholic Cathedral, Limbe	1·50	35
831	50t. C.C.A.P. Church, Nkhoma	2·00	1·50
832	2k. Cathedral, Likoma Island	5·00	11·00

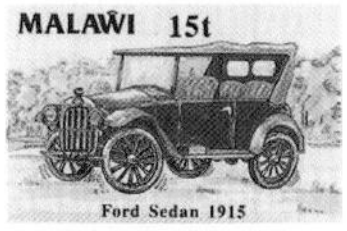

174 Ford "Sedan", 1915

1990. Vintage Vehicles. Multicoloured.

833	15t. Type **174**	80	20
834	40t. Two-seater Ford, 1915	1·50	35
835	50t. Ford pick-up, 1915	2·00	1·50
836	1k. Chevrolet bus, 1930	5·00	11·00
MS837	120×85 mm. Nos. 833/6	15·00	15·00

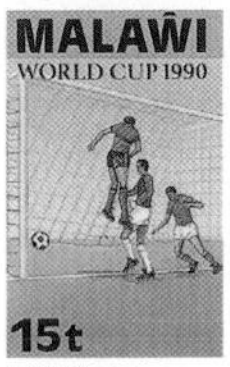

175 Player heading Ball into Net

1990. World Cup Football Championship, Italy. Multicoloured.

838	15t. Type **175**	1·00	20
839	40t. Player tackling	1·60	35
840	50t. Player scoring goal	2·00	1·50
841	2k. World Cup	5·50	11·00
MS842	88×118 mm. Nos. 838/41	11·00	13·00

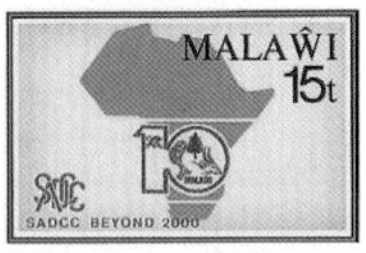

176 Anniversary Emblem on Map

1990. Tenth Anniv of Southern Africa Development Co-ordination Conference. Multicoloured.

843	15t. Type **176**	1·00	20
844	40t. Tilapia	1·60	40
845	50t. Cedar plantation	2·00	1·50
846	2k. Male nyala (antelope)	5·00	11·00
MS847	174×116 mm. Nos. 843/6	14·00	16·00

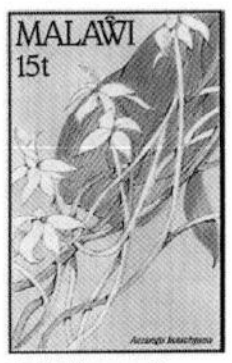

177 "Aerangis kotschyana"

1990. Orchids. Multicoloured.

848	15t. Type **177**	1·75	25
849	40t. "Angraecum eburneum"	2·75	80
850	50t. "Aerangis luteo-alba rhodostica"	2·75	1·60
851	2k. "Cyrtorchis arcuata whytei"	6·50	12·00
MS852	85×120 mm. Nos. 848/51	15·00	15·00

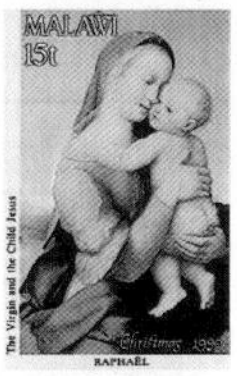

178 "The Virgin and the Child Jesus" (Raphael)

1990. Christmas. Paintings by Raphael. Multicoloured.

853	15t. Type **178**	1·00	20
854	40t. "Transfiguration" (detail)	1·75	35
855	50t. "St. Catherine of Alexandrie" (detail)	1·75	90
856	2k. "Transfiguration"	5·50	12·00
MS857	85×120 mm. Nos. 853/6	14·00	16·00

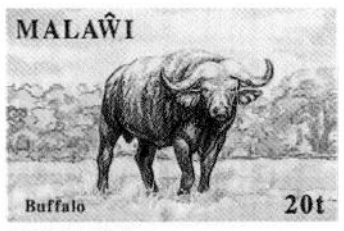

179 Buffalo

1991. Wildlife. Multicoloured.

858	20t. Type **179**	1·00	25
859	60t. Cheetah	2·25	1·00
860	75t. Greater kudu	2·25	1·00
861	2k. Black rhinoceros	9·00	11·00
MS862	120×85 mm. Nos. 858/61	13·00	15·00

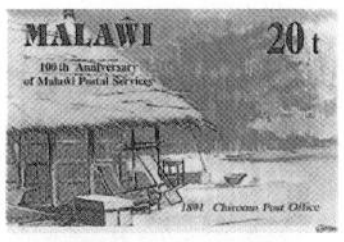

180 Chiromo Post Office, 1891

1991. Centenary of Postal Services. Multicoloured.

863	20t. Type **180**	1·25	20
864	60t. Re-constructed mail exchange hut at Walala	2·25	85
865	75t. Mangochi post office	2·25	95
866	2k. Satellite Earth station	8·00	12·00
MS867	119×83 mm. Nos. 863/6	12·00	14·00

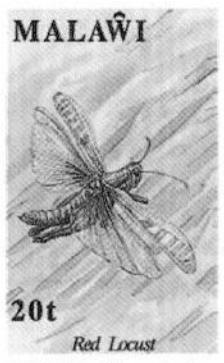

181 Red Locust

1991. Insects. Multicoloured.

868	20t. Type **181**	1·00	25
869	60t. Weevil	2·25	1·10
870	75t. Cotton stainer bug	2·25	1·40
871	2k. Pollen beetle	6·50	11·00

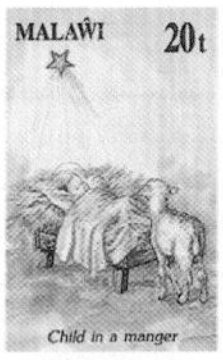

182 Child in a Manger

1991. Christmas. Multicoloured.

872	20t. Type **182**	80	20
873	60t. Adoration of the Kings and Shepherds	1·75	55
874	75t. Nativity	2·00	75
875	2k. Virgin and Child	4·75	12·00

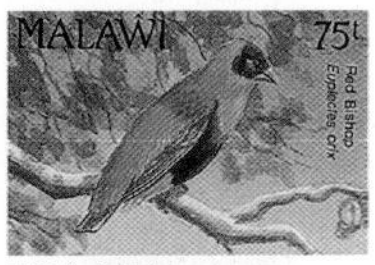

183 Red Bishop

1992. Birds. Multicoloured.

876	75t. Type **183**	2·25	2·25
877	75t. Lesser striped swallow	2·25	2·25
878	75t. Long-crested eagle	2·25	2·25
879	75t. Lilac-breasted roller	2·25	2·25
880	75t. African paradise flycatcher	2·25	2·25
881	75t. White-fronted bee eater	2·25	2·25
882	75t. White-winged black tern	2·25	2·25
883	75t. African fire finch ("Brown-backed Fire-finch")	2·25	2·25
884	75t. White-browed robin chat	2·25	2·25
885	75t. African fish eagle	2·25	2·25
886	75t. Malachite kingfisher	2·25	2·25
887	75t. Lesser masked weaver ("Cabani's Masked Weaver")	2·25	2·25
888	75t. Barn owl ("African Barn Owl")	2·25	2·25
889	75t. Variable sunbird ("Yellow-bellied Sunbird")	2·25	2·25
890	75t. Lesser flamingo	2·25	2·25
891	75t. South African crowned crane ("Crowned Crane!")	2·25	2·25
892	75t. African pitta	2·25	2·25
893	75t. African darter	2·25	2·25
894	75t. White-faced whistling duck ("White-faced Tree-duck")	2·25	2·25
895	75t. African pied wagtail	2·25	2·25

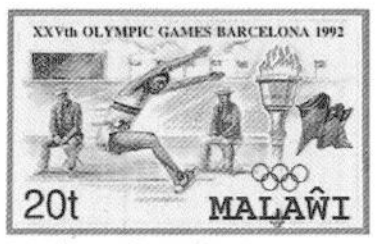

184 Long Jumping

1992. Olympic Games, Barcelona. Multicoloured.

896	20t. Type **184**	80	20
897	60t. High jumping	1·25	60
898	75t. Javelin	1·50	90
899	2k. Running	3·50	7·00
MS900	110×100 mm. Nos. 896/9	6·50	9·00

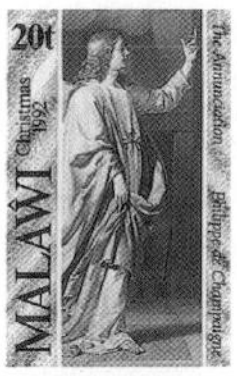

185 "The Angel Gabriel" (detail, "The Annunciation") (Philippe de Champaigne)

1992. Christmas. Religious Paintings. Multicoloured.

901	20t. Type **185**	70	20
902	75t. "Virgin and Child" (Bernandino Luini)	1·50	50
903	95t. "Virgin and Child" (Sassoferrato)	1·75	90
904	2k. "Virgin Mary" (detail, "The Annunciation") (De Champaigne)	4·50	9·00

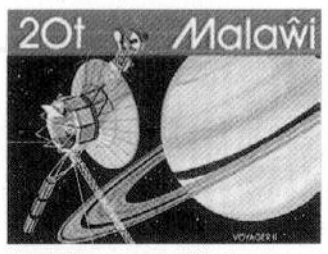

186 "Voyager 2" passing Saturn

1992. International Space Year. Multicoloured.

905	20t. Type **186**	1·00	30
906	75t. Centre of galaxy	2·00	90
907	95t. Kanjedza II Standard A Earth Station	2·00	1·00
908	2k. Communications satellite	4·50	8·00

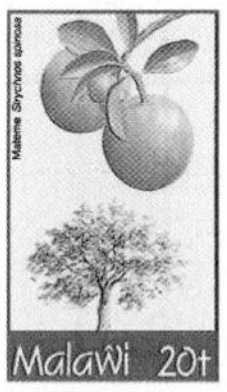

187 "Strychnos spinosa"

1993. World Forestry Day. Indigenous Fruit Trees. Multicoloured.

909	20t. Type **187**	70	20
910	75t. "Adansonia digitata"	1·50	80
911	95t. "Ximenia caffra"	1·60	1·00
912	2k. "Uapaca kirkiana"	3·25	6·50

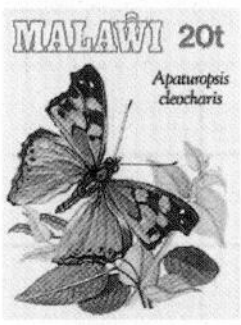

188 "Apaturopsis cleocharis"

1993. Butterflies. Multicoloured.

913	20t. Type **188**	90	30
914	75t. "Euryphura achlys"	1·75	85

| 915 | 95t. "Cooksonia aliciae" | 2·00 | 1·25 |
| 916 | 2k. "Charaxes protoclea azota" | 3·00 | 5·50 |

189 The Holy
Family

1993. Christmas. Multicoloured.

917	20t. Type **189**	15	10
918	75t. Shepherds and star	30	20
919	95t. Three Kings	30	30
920	2k. Adoration of the Kings	75	2·50

190 Kentrosaurus

1993. Prehistoric Animals. Multicoloured.

921	20t. Type **190**	55	30
922	75t. Stegosaurus	90	90
923	95t. Sauropod	1·00	1·00

MS924 157×97 mm. 2k. Tyrannosaurus;
2k. Dilophosaurus; 2k. Brachiosaurus;
2k. Gallimimus; 2k. Triceratops; 2k.
Velociraptor   11·00   12·00

191 Socolof's Mbuna

1994. Fishes. Multicoloured.

925	20t. Type **191**	25	10
926	75t. Golden mbuna	60	30
927	95t. Lombardo's mbuna	65	35
928	1k. Scraper-mouthed mbuna	65	70
929	2k. Zebra mbuna	1·40	2·25
930	4k. Elongate mbuna	2·25	4·50

192 "Ilala II" (lake vessel)

1994. Ships of Lake Malawi. Multicoloured.

931	20t. Type **192**	40	10
932	75t. "Ufulu" (tanker)	1·00	35
933	95t. "Pioneer" (steam launch)	1·10	40
934	2k. "Dove" (paddle-steamer)	1·75	3·00

MS935 85×51 mm. 5k. "Monteith"
(lake vessel)   3·50   5·00

193 "Virgin and
Child" (detail)
(Durer)

1994. Christmas. Religious Paintings. Multicoloured.

936	20t. Type **193**	60	10
937	75t. "Wise Men present Gifts" (Franco-Flemish Book of Hours)	1·10	15
938	95t. "The Nativity" (detail) (Fra Filippo Lippi) (horiz)	1·25	15
939	2k. "Nativity Scene with Wise Men" (Rogier van der Weyden) (horiz)	2·25	3·50

194 Pres. Bakili
Muluzi
(C.O.M.E.S.A.
chairman,
1994–95)

1995. Establishment of C.O.M.E.S.A. (Common Market for
Eastern and Southern African States).

940	**194**	40t. multicoloured	15	10
941	**194**	1k.40 multicoloured	30	20
942	**194**	1k.80 multicoloured	30	55
943	**194**	2k. multicoloured	40	1·00

195 Telecommunications
Training

1995. 50th Anniv of the United Nations. Multicoloured.

944	40t. Type **195**	50	10
945	1k.40 Village women collecting water	1·00	35
946	1k.80 Mt. Mulanje	1·10	1·25
947	2k. Villagers in field	1·25	2·00
MS948	123×77 mm. Nos. 944/7	3·50	4·00

196 Teacher and Class

1995. Christmas. Multicoloured.

949	40t. Type **196**	30	10
950	1k.40 Dispensing medicine	70	25
951	1k.80 Crowd at water pump	80	1·00
952	2k. Refugees on ferries	1·00	1·60

197 "Precis tugela"

1996. Butterflies. Multicoloured.

953	60t. Type **197**	40	10
954	3k. "Papilio pelodorus"	90	45
955	4k. "Acrea acrita"	1·00	75
956	10k. "Melanitis leda"	2·25	3·50

198 Children's
Party

1996. Christmas. Multicoloured.

957	10t. Type **198**	50	25
958	20t. Nativity play	75	25
959	30t. Children wearing party hats	90	25
960	60t. Mother and child	1·50	2·25

199 Map of
Malawi

1997. 50th Death Anniv of Paul Harris (founder of Rotary
International). Multicoloured.

961	60t. Type **199**	50	15
962	3k. African fish eagle	1·50	80
963	4k.40 Leopard	1·00	1·25
964	5k. Rotary International emblem	1·00	1·50

200 Mother and Child

1997. 50th Anniv of UNICEF. Multicoloured.

965	60t. Type **200**	30	10
966	3k. Children in class	65	35
967	4k.40 Boy with fish	1·25	1·50
968	5k. Nurse inoculating child	1·40	1·75

201 The Nativity

1997. Christmas. Multicoloured.

969	60t. Type **201**	30	10
970	3k. The Nativity (different)	60	30
971	4k.40 Adoration of the Magi	1·25	1·25
972	5k. The Holy Family	1·40	1·75

1998. Diana, Princess of Wales Commemoration. As T **91**
of Kiribati. Multicoloured.

973	60t. Wearing red dress	20	10
974	6k. Wearing lilac jacket	40	35
975	7k. With head scarf	50	70
976	8k. Wearing blue evening dress	55	80
MS977	145×70 mm. Nos. 973/6	1·25	1·75

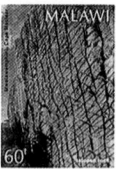

202 Tattooed
Rock,
Mwalawamphini,
Cape Maclear

1998. Monuments. Multicoloured.

978	60t. Type **202**	20	10
979	6k. War Memorial Tower, Zomba	70	65
980	7k. Mtengatenga Postal Hut, Walala (horiz)	85	1·00
981	8k. P.I.M. Church, Chiradzulu (horiz)	95	1·10

No. 978 is inscribed "tatooed" and No. 979 "Memoral",
both in error.

203 Woman voting

1998. 50th Anniv of Declaration of Human Rights.
Multicoloured.

982	60t. Type **203**	25	10
983	6k. Books, pens and pencils ("Education")	70	65
984	7k. Man and woman on scales ("Justice")	85	1·00
985	8k. Person hugging house and land ("Property")	95	1·10

204 "Madonna
and Child with
Book"

1998. Christmas. Religious Paintings. Multicoloured.

986	60t. Type **204**	3·00	20
987	6k. Madonna and Child	14·00	1·75
988	7k. Angel	14·00	2·50
989	8k. Adoration of the Magi	14·00	3·00

205 "Madonna
and Child"

1999. Christmas. Religious Paintings. Multicoloured.

990	60t. Type **205**	60	10
991	6k. "The Nativity"	1·75	55
992	7k. "Adoration of the Magi"	1·75	1·00
993	8k. "Flight into Egypt"	1·75	1·40

206 Ng'oma (hand
drum)

2000. 50th Anniv of the Commonwealth. Musical
Instruments. Multicoloured.

994	60t. Type **206**	30	10
995	6k. Kaligo (single stringed fiddle)	70	55
996	7k. Kalimba (thumb dulcitone)	85	90
997	8k. Chisekese (rattle)	95	1·10

207 Map of Africa
and S.A.D.C.
Emblem

2000. South African Development Community.
Multicoloured.

998	60t. Type **207**	40	10
999	6k. Bottles of Malambe fruit juice	65	55
1000	7k. Ndunduma (fisheries research ship) (horiz)	1·50	1·25
1001	8k. Class "Shire" diesel locomotive and goods train (horiz)	2·00	1·75

208 "Madonna
and Child"

2000. Christmas. Religious Paintings. Multicoloured.

1002	5k. Type **208**	45	10
1003	18k. "Adoration of the Shepherds"	1·50	1·75
1004	20k. "Madonna and Child"	1·50	1·75

209 Euxanthe
wakefieldi

2002. Butterflies. Multicoloured.

1005	1k. Type **209**	30	70
1006	2k. Pseudacraea boisdurali	30	70
1007	4k. Catacroptera cloanthe	30	70
1008	5k. Myrina silenus ficedula	50	30
1009	10k. Cymothoe zombana	70	60
1010	20k. Charaxes castor	1·00	1·00
1011	50k. Charaxes pythoduras ventersi	1·75	2·00
1012	100k. Iolaus lalos	3·00	4·00

210 Puku

2003. Endangered Species. Puku (Kobus vardonii).
Multicoloured.

| 1013 | 50k. Type **210** | 1·50 | 2·00 |

1014	50k. Two males	1·50	2·00
1015	50k. Male and female	1·50	2·00
1016	50k. Herd	1·50	2·00
MS1017	204×138 mm. Nos. 1013/16, each ×2	10·00	13·00

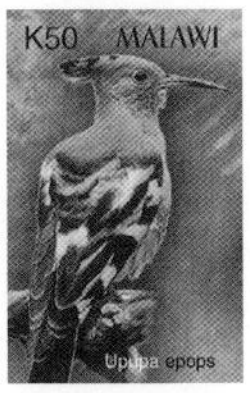

211 Hoopoe (*Upupa epops*)

2003. Fauna and Flora of Africa. Multicoloured.

MS1018	118×137 mm. 50k. Type **211**; 50k. Grey parrot (*Psittacus erithacus*); 50k. Bateleur (*Terathopius ecaudatus*) 50k. Martial eagle (*Polemaetus bellicosus*); 50k. Masked lovebird (*Agapornis personatus*); 50k. Pel's pishing owl (*Scotopelia peli*)	7·50	8·50
MS1019	113×138 mm. 50k. *Bebearia octogramma*; 50k. *Charaxes nobilis*; 50k. *Cymothoe beckeri*; 50k. *Salamis anteva*; 50k. *Charaxes xiphares*; 50k. *Bebearia arcadius Fabricius* (all horiz)	7·50	8·50
MS1020	137×117 mm. 50k. *Pleurotus ostreatus*; 50k. *Macrolepiota procera*; 50k. *Amanita vaginata*; 50k.*Cantharellus tubaeformis*; 50k. *Hydnum repandum*; 50k.*Trametes versicolor* (all horiz)	7·50	8·50
MS1021	95×135 mm. 50k. *Angraecum eburneum*; 50k.*Ancistrochilus rothschildianus*; 50k. *Angraecum infundibulare*; 50k. *Ansellia Africana*; 50k. *Disa veitchii*; 50k.*Angraecum compactum*	7·50	8·50
MS1022	Four sheets. (a) 105×71 mm. 180k. Grey heron (*Arde cinerea*) (horiz). (b) 72×98 mm. 180k. *Carterocephalus palaemon* (horiz). (c) 68×94 mm. 180k. *Auricularia auricula*. (d) 93×66 mm. 180k. *Aerangis kotschyana* (horiz) Set of 4	13·00	15·00

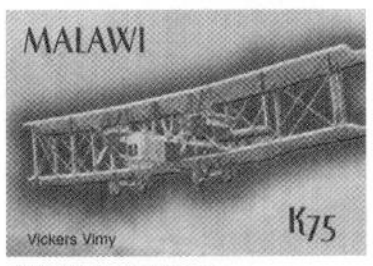

212 Vickers Vimy

2004. Centenary of Powered Flight. Multicoloured.

MS1023	174×97 mm. 75k. Type **212**; 75k. D.H.9A; 75k. Messerschmitt Bf; 75k. Mitsubishi A6M3	4·00	4·50
MS1024	96×67 mm. 180k. Fiat CR.2	3·00	3·25

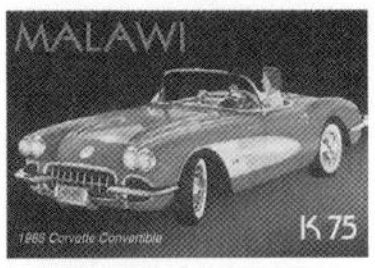

213 Corvette Convertible (1965)

2004. 50th Anniv of the Corvette. Multicoloured.

MS1025	116×156 mm. 75k. Type **213**; 75k. Corvette Stingray (1965); 75k. Corvette (1979); 75k. Corvette (1998)	4·00	4·50
MS1026	110×83 mm. 180k. Corvette (1998)	3·00	3·25

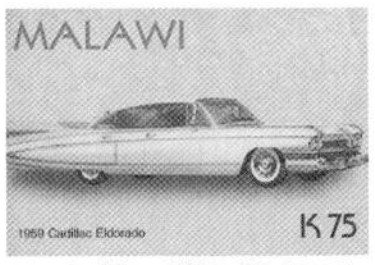

214 Cadillac Eldorado (1959)

2004. Centenary of the Cadillac. Multicoloured.

MS1027	116×156 mm. 75k. Type **214**; 75k. Cadillac Series 62 (1962); 75k. Cadillac Sedan DeVille (1961); 75k. Cadillac V-16 (1930)	4·00	4·50
MS1028	110×85 mm. 180k. Cadillac Eldorado (1954)	3·00	3·25

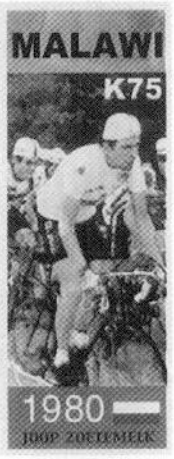

215 Joop Zoetemelk (1980)

2004. Centenary of Tour de France Cycle Race. T 215 and similar vert designs showing winners. Multicoloured.

MS1029	157×96 mm. 75k. Type **215**; 75k. Bernard Hinault (1981); 75k. Bernard Hinault (1982); 75k. Laurent Fignon (1983)	5·00	5·50
MS1030	95×67 mm. 180k. Miguel Indurain (199–5)	3·50	4·00

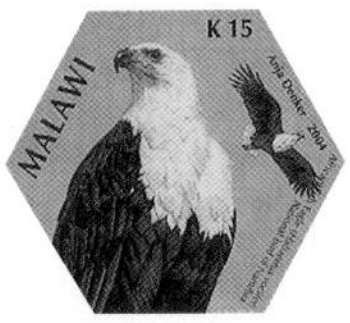

216 African Fish Eagle (Namibia)

2004. 1st Joint Issue of Southern Africa Postal Operators Association Members. Sheet 170×95 mm containing T 216 and similar hexagonal designs showing national birds of Association members. Multicoloured.

MS1031	15k. Type **216**; 15k. Two African fish eagles perched (Zimbabwe); 15k. Peregrine falcon (Angola); 15k. Cattle egret (Botswana); 15k. Purple-crested turaco ("Lourie") (Swaziland); 15k. Stanley ("Blue") crane (South Africa); 15k. Bar-tailed trogon (Malawi); 15k. Two African fish eagles in flight (Zambia)	4·50	5·00

The stamp depicting the bar-tailed trogon is not inscribed with the name of the country of which the bird is a national symbol.

Miniature sheets of similar designs were also issued by Angola, Botswana, Namibia, South Africa, Swaziland, Zambia and Zimbabwe.

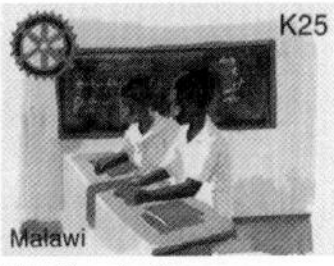

217 Boys in Classroom

2005. Centenary of Rotary International. Sheet 150×131 mm containing T 217 and similar horiz designs. Multicoloured.

MS1032	25k. Type **217**; 55k. Boy in wheelchair; 60k. Boys and teacher in classroom; 65k. Nurse and newborn baby in incubator	4·50	5·00

2007. Butterflies . Multicoloured.

1032*a*	5k. *Myrena silenus ficedula*	10	10
1032*b*	10k. *Cymothoe zombana*	20	15
1032*c*	20k. *Charaxes castor*	35	25
1032*d*	40k. *Papilio pelodorus*	60	60
1032*e*	50k. *Charaxes pythoduras ventersi*	60	60
1032*f*	65k. *Papilio pelodorus*	70	70
1032*g*	75k. *Acrea acrita*	1·00	1·00
1032*h*	100k. *Iolaus lalos*	80	80
1032*i*	105k. *Acrea acrita*	1·10	1·10
1032*j*	110k. *Euxanthe wakefieldi*	1·25	1·25
1032*k*	115k. *Pseudacraea boisdurali*	1·40	1·40

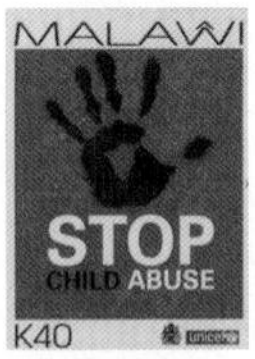

218 Handprint

2008. UNICEF 'STOP CHILD ABUSE'. Day of the African Child. Multicoloured.

1033	40k. Type **218**	75	75
MS1034	141×160 mm. 40k. Type **218**	75	75

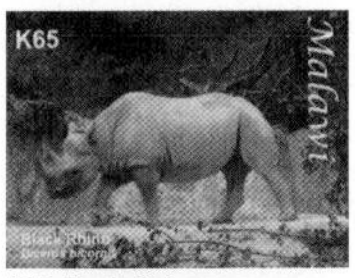

219 Black Rhinoceros (*Diceros bicornis*)

2009. Endangered Animals of Malawi. Multicoloured.

MS1035	100×110 mm. 65k.×4 Type **219**; Sable antelope (*Hippotragus niger*); Zebra (*Equus zebra*); African buffalo (*Syncerus caffer*)	2·75	2·75
MS1036	100×70 mm. 325k. Roan antelope (*Hippotragus equinus*)	2·25	2·25

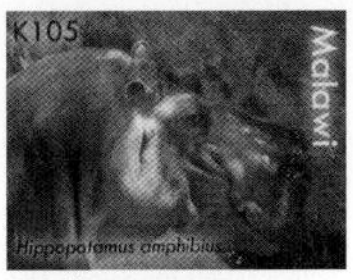

220 Hippopotamus

2009. Hippopotamuses of Malawi (*Hippopotamus amphibius*). Multlcoloured.

MS1037	120×100 mm. 105k.×4 Type **220**; Hippos laying in mud; Hippo standing; Two hippos in water	3·50	3·50
MS1038	100×71 mm. 325k. Hippos in water (vert)	2·25	2·25

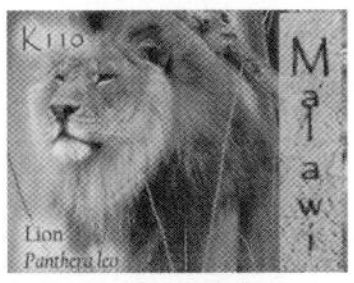

221 Lion (*Panthera leo*)

2009. Wildlife of Malawi. Multicoloured.

MS1039	145×110 mm. 110k.×6 Type **221**; Elephant shrew (*Macroscelides proboscideus*); Black-backed jackal (*Canis mesomelas*); Reedbuck (*Redunca redunca*); African elephant (*Loxodonta africana*); Warthog (*Phacochoerus africanus*)	8·00	8·00
MS1040	70×100 mm. 325k. Leopard (*Panthera pardus*)	2·25	2·25

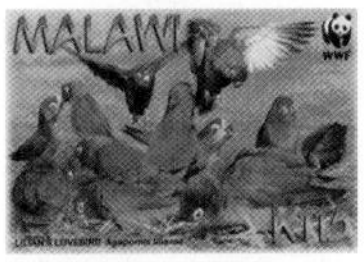

222 Flock of Lovebirds

2009. Endangered Species. Lilian's Lovebird (*Agapornis lilianae*). Multicoloured.

1041	115k. Type **222**	1·40	1·50
1042	115k. Six lovebirds perched on branches	1·40	1·50
1043	115k. Seven lovebirds in flight	1·40	1·50
1044	115k. Pair perched on branch and four others in flight	1·40	1·50
MS1045	112×165 mm. Nos. 1041/4, each ×2	11·50	11·50

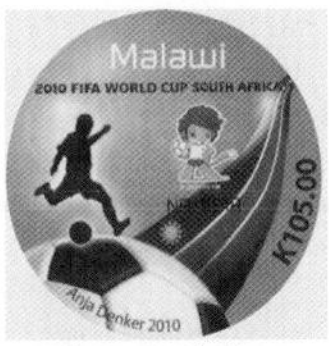

223 Player, Football, Namibian Flag and Zakumi Mascot

2010. Third Joint Issue of Southern Africa Postal Operators Association Members. World Cup Football Championship, South Africa. Multicoloured.

1046	105k. Type **223**	1·10	1·10
1047	105k. South Africa	1·10	1·10
1048	105k. Zimbabwe	1·10	1·10
1049	105k. Malawi	1·10	1·10
1050	105k. Swaziland	1·10	1·10
1051	105k. Botswana	1·10	1·10
1052	105k. Mauritius	1·10	1·10
1053	105k. Lesotho	1·10	1·10
1054	105k. Zambia	1·10	1·10
MS1055	188×167 mm. Nos. 1046/54	9·00	9·00

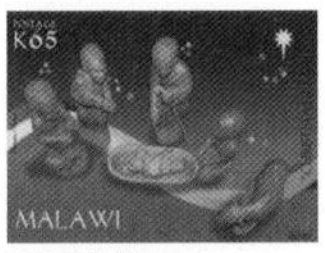

224 Crib Figures

2010. Christmas. Multicoloured: colour of lower background given.

1056	**224**	65k. orange-red	80	80
1057		65k. Indian red	80	80
1058		65k. Royal blue	80	80
1059		65k. yellowish green	80	80

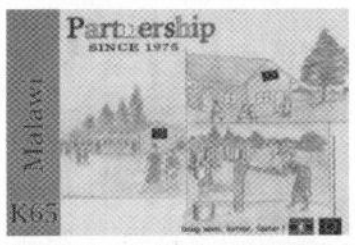

225 School, Clinic and Water Pump

2011. 35th Anniv of EU Aid Projects in Malawi. Multicoloured.

1060	65k. Type **225**	80	80
1061	65k. '35' in circle of stars and family (vert)	80	80

POSTAGE DUE STAMPS

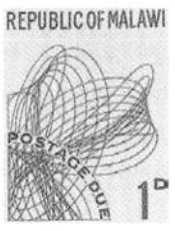

D2

1967

D6	**D2**	1d. red	15	4·50
D7	**D2**	2d. brown	20	4·50
D8	**D2**	4d. violet	25	4·75
D9	**D2**	6d. blue	25	5·00
D10	**D2**	8d. green	35	5·50
D11	**D2**	1s. black	45	6·00

1971. Values in tambalas. No accent over "W" of "MALAWI".

D12	2t. brown	30	5·00
D13	4t. mauve	50	3·00
D14	6t. blue	50	3·25
D15	8t. green	50	3·25
D16	10t. brown	60	3·25

1975. With circumflex over "W" of "MALAWI".

D27	2t. brown	3·75	5·50
D28	4t. purple	3·75	5·50
D29	6t. blue	3·75	5·50
D21	8t. green	1·50	4·00
D31	10t. black	3·75	5·50

Pt. 1

MALAYA (BRITISH MILITARY ADMINSTRATION)

The following stamps were for use throughout the Malayan States and in Singapore during the period of the British Military Administration and were gradually replaced by individual issues for each state.

100 cents = 1 dollar.

1945. Straits Settlements stamps optd B M A MALAYA.

1a	**58**	1c. black	10	30
2a	**58**	2c. orange	20	10
4	**58**	3c. green	4·00	50
5	**58**	5c. brown	70	1·00
6a	**58**	6c. grey	30	20
7	**58**	8c. red	30	10
8a	**58**	10c. purple	50	10
10	**58**	12c. blue	1·75	16·00
12a	**58**	15c. blue	75	20
13a	**58**	25c. purple and red	1·40	30
14a	**58**	50c. black on green	1·00	10
15	**58**	$1 black and red	2·00	10
16	**58**	$2 green and red	2·75	75
17	**58**	$5 green and red on green	£100	£150
18	**58**	$5 purple and orange	4·75	3·00

For stamps inscribed "MALAYA" at top and with Arabic characters at foot see under Kelantan, Negri Sembilan, Pahang, Perak, Selangor or Trengganu.

Pt. 1

MALAYA (JAPANESE OCCUPATION)

Japanese forces invaded Malaya on 8 December 1941 and the conquest of the Malay peninsula was completed by the capture of Singapore on 15 February.

The following stamps were used in Malaya until the defeat of Japan in 1945.

100 cents = 1 dollar.

(a) JOHORE

POSTAGE DUE STAMPS

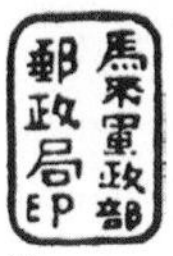

(1)

1942. Nos. D1/5 of Johore optd with T **1**.

JD1a	**D1**	1c. red	20·00	70·00
JD2a	**D1**	4c. green	65·00	80·00
JD3a	**D1**	8c. orange	80·00	95·00
JD4a	**D1**	10c. brown	16·00	50·00
JD5a	**D1**	12c. purple	48·00	55·00

大日本郵便

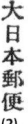

(2)

1943. Postage Due stamps of Johore optd with T **2**.

JD6		1c. red	10·00	32·00
JD7		4c. green	8·00	38·00
JD8		8c. orange	10·00	38·00
JD9		10c. brown	9·50	48·00
JD10		12c. purple	11·00	65·00

(b) KEDAH

1942. Stamps of Kedah optd **DAI NIPPON 2602**.

J1	**1**	1c. black	8·50	12·00
J2	**1**	2c. green	27·00	30·00
J3	**1**	4c. violet	8·50	4·00
J4	**1**	5c. yellow	5·50	6·50
J5	**1**	6c. red	5·00	20·00
J6	**1**	8c. black	6·00	4·50
J7	**6**	10c. blue and brown	18·00	20·00
J8	**6**	12c. black and violet	42·00	60·00
J9	**6**	25c. blue and purple	14·00	22·00
J10	**6**	30c. green and red	70·00	80·00
J11	**6**	40c. black and purple	40·00	50·00
J12	**6**	50c. brown and blue	40·00	50·00
J13	**6**	$1 black and green	£140	£150
J14	**6**	$2 green and brown	£170	£170
J15	**6**	$5 black and red	75·00	£110

(c) KELANTAN

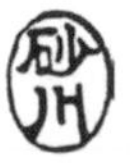

(5) Sunagawa Seal

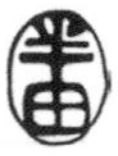

(6) Handa Seal

1942. Stamps of Kelantan surch. (a) With T **5**. (i) New value in **CENTS**.

J16	**4**	1c. on 50c. green and orange	£425	£250
J17	**4**	2c. on 40c. orange and green	£1100	£400
J18	**4**	4c. on 30c. violet and red	£3000	£1600
J19	**4**	5c. on 12c. blue	£400	£250
J20	**4**	6c. on 25c. red and violet	£425	£250
J21	**4**	8c. on 5c. brown	£600	£160
J22	**4**	10c. on 6c. red	90·00	£140
J23	**4**	12c. on 8c. green	65·00	£130
J24	**4**	25c. on 10c. purple	£2000	£1800
J25	**4**	30c. on 4c. red	£3000	£2750
J26	**4**	40c. on 2c. green	75·00	£100
J27	**4**	50c. on 1c. green and yellow	£2250	£1700
J28	**4**	$1 on 4c. black and red	50·00	90·00
J29	**4**	$2 on 5c. green & red on yell	50·00	90·00
J30	**4**	$5 on 6c. red	50·00	90·00

(ii) New Value in Cents.

J32		1c. on 50c. green and orange	£275	£130
J33		2c. on 40c. orange and green	£350	£180
J34		5c. on 12c. blue	£225	£250
J35		8c. on 5c. brown	£180	90·00
J36		10c. on 6c. red	£550	£600

(b) With T **6** and new value.

J41		1c. on 50c. green and orange	£180	£250
J42		2c. on 40c. orange and green	£200	£250
J43		8c. on 5c. brown	90·00	£170
J44		10c. on 6c. red	£140	£250
J31		12c. on 8c. green	£250	£425

(d) PENANG

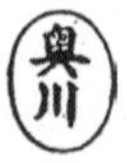

(11) Okugawa Seal

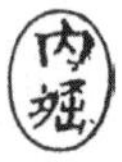

(12) Ochiburi Seal

1942. Straits Settlements stamps optd. (a) As T **11**.

J56	**58**	1c. black	10·00	14·00
J57	**58**	2c. orange	24·00	25·00
J58	**58**	3c. green	20·00	25·00
J59	**58**	5c. brown	24·00	32·00
J60	**58**	8c. grey	32·00	45·00
J61	**58**	10c. purple	50·00	50·00
J62	**58**	12c. blue	48·00	50·00
J63	**58**	15c. blue	50·00	50·00
J64	**58**	40c. red and purple	£100	£110
J65	**58**	50c. black on green	£225	£225
J66	**58**	$1 black and red on blue	£275	£300
J67	**58**	$2 green and red	£900	£750
J68	**58**	$5 green and red on green	£2750	£1600

(b) With T **12**.

J69		1c. black	£190	£160
J70		2c. orange	£190	£130
J71		3c. green	£120	£120
J72		5c. brown	£3250	£3250
J73		8c. grey	£110	£110
J74		10c. purple	£200	£225
J75		12c. blue	£130	£140
J76		15c. blue	£150	£150

1942. Stamps of Straits Settlements optd **DAI NIPPON 2602 PENANG**.

J77		1c. black	9·00	3·75
J78		2c. orange	8·00	5·00
J79		3c. green	8·00	9·00
J80		5c. brown	4·50	9·00
J81		8c. grey	2·75	1·40
J82		10c. purple	1·50	2·25
J83		12c. blue	5·50	19·00
J84		15c. blue	1·75	4·75
J85		40c. red and purple	7·50	19·00
J86		50c. black on green	3·75	35·00
J87		$1 black and red on blue	6·00	48·00
J88		$2 green and red	60·00	£100
J89		$5 green and red on green	£750	£800

(e) SELANGOR

1942. Agri-horticultural Exhibition. Stamps of Straits Settlements optd **SELANGOR EXHIBITION DAI NIPPON 2602 MALAYA**.

J90		2c. orange	12·00	24·00
J91		8c. grey	13·00	24·00

(f) SINGAPORE

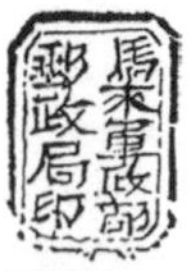

(15) "Malay Military Government Division Postal Services Bureau Seal"

1942. Stamps of Straits Settlements optd with T **15**.

J92		1c. black	20·00	21·00
J93		2c. orange	14·00	13·00
J94		3c. green	55·00	70·00
J95		8c. grey	25·00	18·00
J96		15c. blue	19·00	15·00

(g) TRENGGANU

1942. Stamps of Trengganu optd with T **1**.

J97	**4**	1c. black	90·00	95·00
J98	**4**	2c. green	£140	£140
J99	**4**	2c. on 5c. pur & yell (No. 59)	40·00	40·00
J100	**4**	3c. brown	£100	90·00
J101	**4**	4c. red	£190	£150
J102	**4**	5c. purple on yellow	10·00	19·00
J103	**4**	6c. orange	11·00	25·00
J104	**4**	8c. grey	9·00	13·00
J105	**4**	8c. on 10c. blue (No. 60)	13·00	50·00
J106	**4**	10c. blue	35·00	50·00
J107	**4**	12c. blue	8·00	50·00
J108	**4**	20c. purple and orange	12·00	50·00
J109	**4**	25c. green and purple	8·00	55·00
J110	**4**	30c. purple and black	15·00	50·00
J111	**4**	35c. red on yellow	35·00	60·00
J112	**4**	50c. green and red	85·00	£100
J113	**4**	$1 purple and blue on blue	£5000	£5000
J114	**4**	$3 green and red on green	80·00	£130
J115	-	$5 green and red on yellow (No. 31)	£275	£350
J116	-	$25 purple and blue (No. 40)	£2000	
J117	-	$50 green and yellow (No. 41)	£16000	
J118	-	$100 green and red (No. 42)	£1900	

1942. Stamps of Trengganu optd **DAI NIPPON 2602 MALAYA**.

J119	**4**	1c. black	17·00	12·00
J120	**4**	2c. green	£325	£250
J121	**4**	2c. on 5c. pur on yell (No. 59)	6·50	8·00
J122	**4**	3c. brown	18·00	28·00
J123	**4**	4c. red	18·00	11·00
J124	**4**	5c. purple on yellow	5·50	13·00
J125	**4**	6c. orange	7·50	13·00
J126	**4**	8c. grey	90·00	29·00
J127	**4**	8c. on 10c. blue (No. 60)	7·50	10·00
J128	**4**	12c. blue	7·50	40·00
J129	**4**	20c. purple and orange	21·00	20·00
J130	**4**	25c. green and purple	9·00	50·00
J131	**4**	30c. purple and black	10·00	48·00
J132	**4**	$3 green and red on green	£100	£190

1942. Stamps of Trengganu optd with T **2**.

J133		1c. black	22·00	24·00
J134		2c. green	19·00	45·00
J135		2c. on 5c. pur on yell (No. 59)	12·00	26·00
J136		5c. purple on yellow	17·00	45·00
J137		6c. orange	18·00	50·00
J138		8c. grey	85·00	£120
J139		8c. on 10c. blue (No. 60)	35·00	55·00
J140		10c. blue	£110	£250
J141		12c. blue	21·00	50·00
J142		20c. purple and orange	28·00	50·00
J143		25c. green and purple	23·00	55·00
J144		30c. purple and black	29·00	55·00
J145		35c. red on yellow	29·00	75·00

POSTAGE DUE STAMPS

1942. Postage Due stamps of Trengganu optd with T **2**.

JD17	**D1**	1c. red	55·00	90·00
JD18a	**D1**	4c. green	50·00	90·00
JD19	**D1**	8c. yellow	14·00	50·00
JD20	**D1**	10c. brown	14·00	50·00

(h) GENERAL ISSUES

1942. Stamps of various states optd with T **1**. (a) Straits Settlements.

J146	**58**	1c. black	3·50	3·25
J147	**58**	2c. green	£3500	£2500
J148	**58**	2c. orange	3·25	2·25
J149	**58**	3c. green	3·25	2·25
J150	**58**	5c. brown	27·00	30·00
J151	**58**	8c. grey	8·00	2·25
J152	**58**	10c. purple	65·00	48·00
J153	**58**	12c. blue	95·00	£150
J154	**58**	15c. blue	3·50	3·75
J155	**58**	30c. purple and orange	£4000	£4000
J156	**58**	40c. red and purple	£140	£100
J157	**58**	50c. black and green	75·00	48·00
J158	**58**	$1 black and red on blue	£100	75·00
J159	**58**	$2 green and red	£170	£200
J160	**58**	$5 green and red on green	£225	£275

There also exists a similar overprint with double-lined frame.

(b) Negri Sembilan.

J161	**6**	1c. black	19·00	13·00
J162	**6**	2c. orange	38·00	24·00
J163	**6**	3c. green	50·00	24·00
J164b	**6**	5c. brown	17·00	15·00
J165	**6**	6c. grey	£170	£130
J166	**6**	8c. red	£200	£180
J167	**6**	10c. purple	£300	£275
J168	**6**	12c. blue	£2000	£2000
J169	**6**	15c. blue	32·00	8·00
J170	**6**	25c. purple and red	28·00	38·00
J171	**6**	30c. purple and orange	£325	£275
J172a	**6**	40c. red and purple	£1500	£1100
J173	**6**	50c. black on green	£1800	£1600
J174a	**6**	$1 black and red on blue	£180	£200
J175	**6**	$5 green and red on green	£800	£900

(c) Pahang.

J176	**15**	1c. black	55·00	50·00
J177a	**15**	3c. green	£225	£275
J178	**15**	5c. brown	20·00	13·00
J179	**15**	8c. grey	£1500	£950
J180	**15**	8c. red	25·00	8·00
J181a	**15**	10c. purple	£375	£225
J182a	**15**	12c. blue	£1200	£1200
J183	**15**	15c. blue	£170	£120
J184	**15**	25c. purple and red	25·00	29·00
J185	**15**	30c. purple and orange	20·00	32·00
J186	**15**	40c. red and purple	29·00	38·00
J187	**15**	50c. black on green	£1700	£1700
J188	**15**	$1 black and red on blue	£170	£180
J189	**15**	$5 green and red on green	£850	£950

(d) Perak.

J190	**51**	1c. black	70·00	45·00
J191	**51**	2c. orange	38·00	20·00
J192	**51**	3c. green	35·00	32·00
J193	**51**	5c. brown	10·00	6·00
J194	**51**	8c. grey	£100	60·00
J195	**51**	8c. red	48·00	48·00
J196	**51**	10c. purple	26·00	24·00
J197	**51**	12c. blue	£275	£250
J198	**51**	15c. blue	24·00	32·00
J199	**51**	25c. purple and red	14·00	28·00
J200	**51**	30c. purple and orange	17·00	32·00
J201	**51**	40c. red and purple	£750	£375
J202	**51**	50c. black on green	48·00	50·00
J203	**51**	$1 black and red on blue	£600	£400
J204	**51**	$2 green and red	£4750	£4750
J205	**51**	$5 green and red on green	£550	

(e) Selangor.

J206	**46**	1c. black	14·00	28·00
J207	**46**	2c. green	£2500	£1400
J208	**46**	2c. orange	£100	60·00
J210c	**46**	3c. green	18·00	15·00
J211	**46**	5c. brown	6·50	5·50
J212a	**46**	6c. red	£225	£275
J213	**46**	8c. grey	27·00	17·00
J214	**46**	10c. purple	20·00	21·00
J215	**46**	12c. blue	70·00	80·00
J216	**46**	15c. blue	17·00	24·00
J217a	**46**	25c. purple and red	65·00	85·00
J218	**46**	30c. purple and orange	11·00	24·00
J219	**46**	40c. red and purple	£170	£150
J220	**46**	50c. black on green	£180	£190
J221	**48**	$1 black and red on blue	38·00	55·00
J222	**48**	$2 green and red	42·00	65·00
J223	**48**	$5 green and red on green	85·00	£100

1942. Various stamps optd **DAI NIPPON 2602 MALAYA**. (a) Stamps of Straits Settlements.

J224	**58**	2c. orange	3·50	60
J225	**58**	3c. green	50·00	65·00
J226	**58**	8c. grey	10·00	4·50
J227	**58**	15c. blue	24·00	15·00

(b) Stamps of Negri Sembilan.

J228	**6**	1c. black	3·00	60
J229	**6**	2c. orange	11·00	50
J230	**6**	3c. green	9·00	50
J231	**6**	5c. brown	1·75	5·50
J232	**6**	6c. grey	5·50	4·75
J233	**6**	8c. red	9·00	1·25
J234	**6**	10c. purple	3·25	2·50
J235	**6**	15c. blue	22·00	2·50
J236	**6**	25c. purple and red	7·00	24·00
J237	**6**	30c. purple and orange	11·00	4·50
J238	**6**	$1 black and red on blue	85·00	£110

(c) Stamps of Pahang.

J239	**15**	1c. black	3·50	5·00
J240	**15**	5c. brown	1·25	70
J241	**15**	8c. red	32·00	3·50
J242	**15**	10c. purple	16·00	10·00
J243	**15**	12c. blue	4·50	21·00
J244	**15**	25c. purple and red	9·00	35·00
J245	**15**	30c. purple and orange	3·75	16·00

(d) Stamps of Perak.

J246	**51**	2c. orange	4·50	4·00
J247	**51**	3c. green	1·50	1·50
J248	**51**	8c. red	1·25	50
J249	**51**	10c. purple	22·00	9·50
J250	**51**	15c. blue	12·00	2·00
J251	**51**	50c. black on green	4·00	7·50
J252	**51**	$1 black and red on blue	£550	£600
J253	**51**	$5 green and red on green	60·00	90·00

(e) Stamps of Selangor.

J254	**46**	3c. green	2·25	6·00
J255	**46**	12c. blue	2·00	21·00
J256	**46**	15c. blue	9·00	1·50
J257	**46**	40c. red and purple	2·25	7·50
J258	**48**	$2 green and red	11·00	55·00

1942. No. 108 of Perak surch **DAI NIPPON 2602 MALAYA 2 Cents**.

J259	**88**	2c. on 5c. brown	1·75	4·50

1942. Stamps of Perak optd **DAI NIPPON YUBIN** ("Japanese Postal Service") or surch also in figures and words.

J260	**51**	1c. black	7·00	11·00
J261	**51**	2c. on 5c. brown	2·25	6·50
J262	**51**	8c. red	10·00	3·50

1943. Various stamps optd vert or horiz with T **2** or surch in figures and words. (a) Stamps of Straits Settlements.

J263	**58**	8c. grey	1·40	50
J264	**58**	12c. blue	1·75	15·00
J265	**58**	40c. red and purple	4·00	7·50

(b) Stamps of Negri Sembilan.

J266	**6**	1c. black	75	5·00
J267	**6**	2c. on 5c. brown	1·00	2·75
J268	**6**	6c. on 5c. brown	40	3·00
J269	**6**	25c. purple and red	1·75	22·00

(c) Stamp of Pahang.

J270	**7**	6c. on 5c. brown	50	75

(d) Stamps of Perak.

J272	**51**	1c. black	1·25	1·50
J274	**51**	2c. on 5c. brown	60	50
J275	**51**	5c. brown	55	65
J276	**51**	8c. red	1·25	3·25
J277	**51**	10c. purple	75	1·50
J278	**51**	30c. purple and orange	5·50	9·50
J279	**51**	50c. black on green	4·50	26·00
J280	**51**	$5 green and red on green	80·00	£140

(e) Stamps of Selangor.

J288	**46**	1c. black	50	60
J289	**46**	2c. on 5c. brown	2·00	50
J282	**46**	3c. green	40	1·50
J290	**46**	3c. on 5c. brown	30	5·00

J291	46	5c. brown	2·50	6·50
J293	46	6c. on 5c. brown	50	70
J283	46	12c. blue	45	2·00
J284	46	15c. blue	4·50	3·75
J285	48	$1 black and red on blue	3·00	27·00
J295	46	$1 on 10c. purple	40	1·25
J296	46	$1.50 on 30c. purple and orange	40	1·25
J286	48	$2 green and red	10·00	55·00
J287	48	$5 green and red on green	22·00	85·00

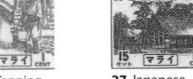

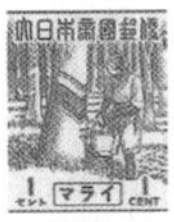
25 Tapping Rubber

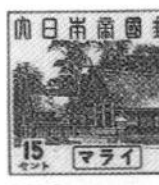
27 Japanese Shrine, Singapore

1943

J297	25	1c. green	1·75	55
J298	-	2c. green	1·00	20
J299	25	3c. grey	1·00	20
J300	-	4c. red	3·00	20
J301	-	8c. blue	50	20
J302	-	10c. purple	1·25	20
J303	27	15c. violet	1·75	5·00
J304	-	30c. olive	1·50	35
J305	-	50c. blue	5·00	5·00
J306	-	70c. blue	25·00	14·00

DESIGNS—VERT: 2c. Fruit; 4c. Tin dredger; 8c. War Memorial, Bukit Batok, Singapore; 10c. Fishing village; 30c. Sago palms; 50c. Straits of Johore. HORIZ: 70c. Malay Mosque, Kuala Lumpur.

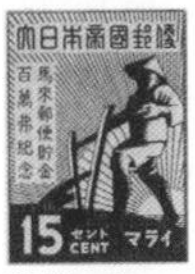
28 Ploughman

1943. Savings Campaign.

J307	28	8c. violet	9·50	2·75
J308	28	15c. red	6·50	2·75

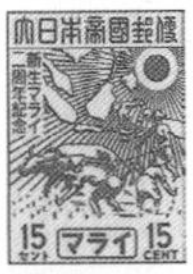
29
Rice-planting

1944. "Re-birth of Malaya".

J309	29	8c. red	17·00	3·25
J310	29	15c. mauve	4·00	3·25

大日本
マライ郵便
50 セント
(30)

1944. Stamps intended for use on Red Cross letters. Surch with T **30**. (a) On Straits Settlements.

J311	58	50c. on 50c. black on grn	10·00	24·00
J312	58	$1 on $1 black & red on bl	22·00	35·00
J313	58	$1.50 on $2 green on red	40·00	70·00

(b) On Johore.

J314	24	50c. on 50c. purple & red	7·00	20·00
J315	24	$1.50 on $2 green and red	4·00	12·00

(c) On Selangor.

J316	48	$1 on $2 black & red on bl	3·50	14·00
J317	48	$1.50 on $2 green and red	7·00	20·00

POSTAGE DUE STAMPS

1942. Postage Due stamps of Malayan Postal Union optd with T **1**.

JD21	D1	1c. violet	12·00	35·00
JD22	D1	3c. green	90·00	£100
JD23	D1	4c. green	90·00	55·00
JD24	D1	8c. red	£160	£130
JD25	D1	10c. orange	38·00	65·00
JD26	D1	12c. blue	25·00	60·00
JD27	D1	50c. black	80·00	£120

1942. Postage Due stamps of Malayan Postal Union optd **DAI NIPPON 2602 MALAYA**.

JD28	1c. violet	3·50	10·00
JD29	3c. green	24·00	29·00
JD30	4c. green	22·00	11·00
JD31	8c. red	35·00	25·00
JD32	10c. orange	2·00	17·00
JD33	12c. blue	1·75	45·00

1943. Postage Due stamps of Malayan Postal Union optd with T **2**.

JD34	1c. violet	2·25	5·00
JD35	3c. green	2·25	4·50
JD36	4c. green	60·00	50·00
JD37	5c. red	1·50	5·00
JD38	9c. orange	80	8·50
JD39	10c. orange	2·25	9·00
JD40	12c. blue	2·25	21·00
JD41	15c. blue	2·25	9·00

Pt. 1

MALAY (THAI OCCUPATION)

Stamps issued for use in the four Malay states of Kedah, Kelantan, Perlis and Trengganu ceded by Japan to Thailand on 19 October 1943 and restored to British rule on the defeat of the Japanese.

100 cents = 1 dollar.

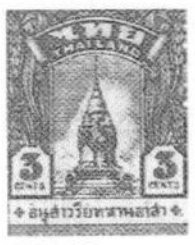
TM1 War Memorial

1943

TM1	TM1	1c. yellow	30·00	32·00
TM2	TM1	2c. brown	12·00	20·00
TM3	TM1	3c. green	20·00	38·00
TM4	TM1	4c. purple	14·00	28·00
TM5	TM1	8c. red	14·00	20·00
TM6	TM1	15c. blue	38·00	60·00

Pt. 1

MALAYAN FEDERATION

An independent country within the British Commonwealth, comprising all the Malay States (except Singapore) and the Settlements of Malacca and Penang. The component units retained their individual stamps. In 1963 the Federation became part of Malaysia (q.v).

100 cents (sen) = 1 Malayan dollar.

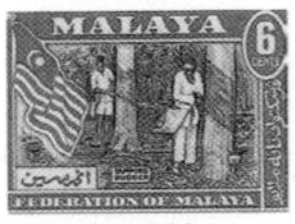
1 Tapping Rubber

1957

1	1	6c. blue, red and yellow	50	10
2	-	12c. multicoloured	1·75	1·00
3	-	25c. multicoloured	4·25	20
4	-	30c. red and lake	1·50	20

DESIGNS—HORIZ: 12c. Federation coat of arms; 25c. Tin dredge. VERT: 30c. Map of the Federation.

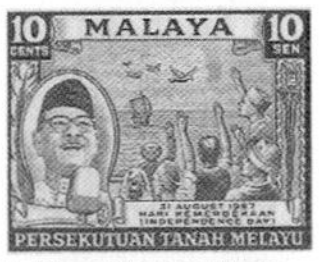
5 Prime Minister Tunku Abdul Rahman and Populace greeting Independence

1957. Independence Day.

5	5	10c. brown	80	10

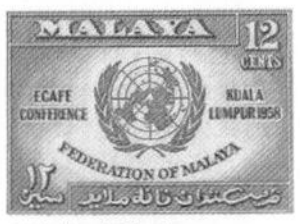
6 United Nations Emblem

1958. U.N. Economic Commission for Asia and Far East Conference, Kuala Lumpur.

6	6	12c. red	30	80
7	-	30c. purple	40	80

DESIGN: 30c. As Type **6** but vert.

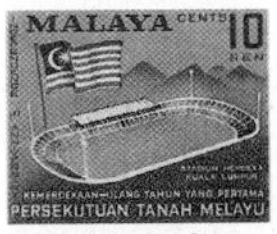
8 Merdeka Stadium, Kuala Lumpur

1958. First Anniv of Independence.

8	8	10c. multicoloured	15	10
9	-	30c. multicoloured	40	70

DESIGN—VERT: 30c. Portrait of the Yang di-Pertuan Agong (Tuanku Abdul Rahman).

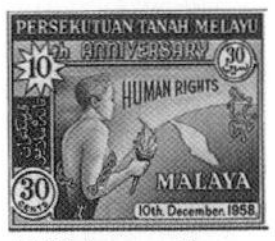
11 Malayan with "Torch of Freedom"

1958. Tenth Anniv of Declaration of Human Rights.

10		10c. multicoloured	15	10
11	11	30c. green	45	60

DESIGN—VERT: 10c. "Human Rights".

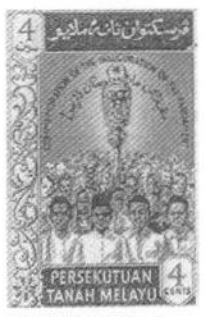
12 Mace and Malayan Peoples

1959. Inauguration of Parliament.

12	12	4c. red	10	10
13	12	10c. violet	10	10
14	12	25c. green	75	20

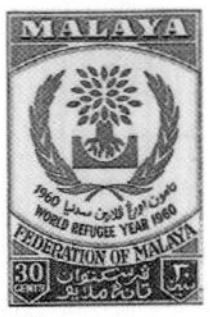
14

1960. World Refugee Year.

15	-	12c. purple	10	60
16	14	30c. green	10	10

DESIGN: 12c. As Type **14** but horiz.

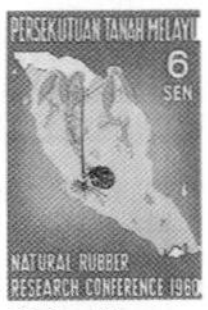
15 Seedling Rubber Tree and Map

1960. Natural Rubber Research Conf and 15th Int Rubber Study Group Meeting, Kuala Lumpur.

17	15	6c. multicoloured	20	1·25
18	15	30c. multicoloured	50	75

No. 18 is inscr "INTERNATIONAL RUBBER STUDY GROUP 15th MEETING KUALA LUMPUR" at foot.

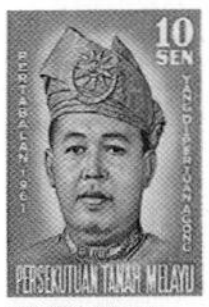
16 The Yang di-Pertuan Agong (Tuanku Syed Putra)

1961. Installation of Yang di-Pertuan Agong, Tuanku Syed Putra.

19	16	10c. black and blue	10	10

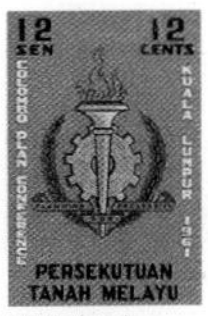
17 Colombo Plan Emblem

1961. Colombo Plan Conf, Kuala Lumpur.

20	17	12c. black and mauve	35	3·00
21	17	25c. black and green	80	2·50
22	17	30c. black and blue	70	1·00

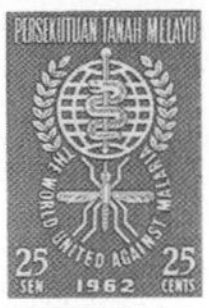
18 Malaria Eradication Emblem

1962. Malaria Eradication.

23	18	25c. brown	20	40
24	18	30c. lilac	20	15
25	18	50c. blue	40	80

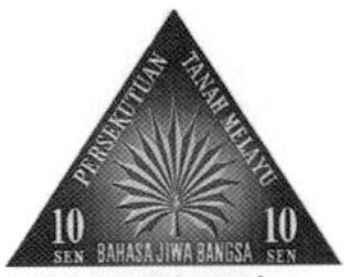
19 Palmyra Palm Leaf

1962. National Language Month.

26	19	10c. brown and violet	25	10
27	19	20c. brown and green	1·00	1·25
28	19	50c. brown and mauve	2·25	1·75

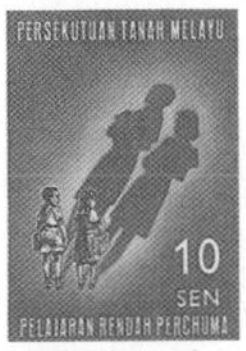
20 "Shadows of the Future"

1962. Introduction of Free Primary Education.

29	20	10c. purple	10	10
30	20	25c. ochre	50	1·25
31	20	30c. green	2·75	10

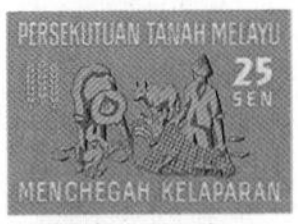
21 Harvester and Fisherman

1963. Freedom from Hunger.

32	21	25c. pink and green	2·75	3·00
33	21	30c. pink and lake	3·00	1·50
34	21	50c. pink and blue	2·50	3·00

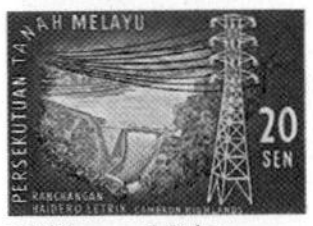
22 Dam and Pylon

1963. Cameron Highlands Hydro-electric Scheme.

35	22	20c. green and violet	60	10
36	22	30c. turquoise and blue	1·00	1·50

Pt. 1

MALAYAN POSTAL UNION

In 1936 postage due stamps were issued in Type D 1 for use in Negri Sembilan, Pahang, Perak, Selangor and Straits Settlements but later their use was extended to the whole of the Federation and Singapore, and from 1963 throughout Malaysia.

POSTAGE DUE STAMPS

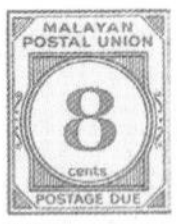
D1

1936

D7	D1	1c. purple	4·75	2·00
D14	D1	1c. violet	70	1·60
D15	D1	2c. slate	1·25	2·25
D8	D1	3c. green	9·00	2·25
D17	D1	4c. sepia	70	7·00
D2	D1	4c. green	35·00	1·00
D9	D1	5c. red	6·00	2·00
D3	D1	8c. red	17·00	2·75
D19	D1	8c. orange	2·50	7·00
D11	D1	9c. orange	40·00	50·00
D4	D1	10c. orange	24·00	30
D5	D1	12c. blue	35·00	14·00
D20	D1	12c. mauve	1·25	6·00
D12	D1	15c. blue	£110	29·00
D21	D1	20c. blue	7·00	6·50
D6	D1	50c. black	30·00	4·50

1965. Surch **10 cents.**

D29	10c. on 8c. orange	60	3·00

Pt. 1

MALAYSIA

Issues for use by the new Federation comprising the old Malayan Federation (Johore ("JOHOR"), Kedah, Kelantan, Malacca ("MELAKA"), Negri Sembilan ("NEGERI SEMBILAN"), Pahang, Penang ("PULAU PINANG"), Perak, Perlis, Selangor and Trengganu), Sabah (North Borneo), Sarawak and Singapore, until the latter became an independent state on 9 August 1965.

Stamps inscr "MALAYSIA" and state name are listed under the various states, as above.

1963. 100 cents (sen) = 1 Malaysian dollar.
1996. 100 sen = 1 ringgit.

A. NATIONAL SERIES

General issues for use throughout the Federation.

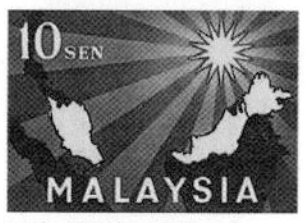

1 Federation Map

1963. Inauguration of Federation.

1	**1**	10c. yellow and violet	1·00	10
2	**1**	12c. yellow and green	1·40	60
3	**1**	50c. yellow and brown	1·40	10

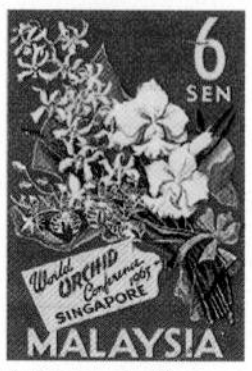

2 Bouquet of Orchids

1963. Fourth World Orchid Congress, Singapore.

4	**2**	6c. multicoloured	1·25	1·25
5	**2**	25c. multicoloured	1·25	25

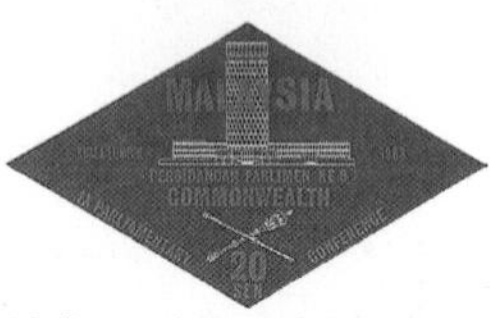

4 Parliament House, Kuala Lumpur

1963. Ninth Commonwealth Parliamentary Conf, Kuala Lumpur.

7	**4**	20c. mauve and gold	1·25	40
8	**4**	30c. green and gold	1·75	15

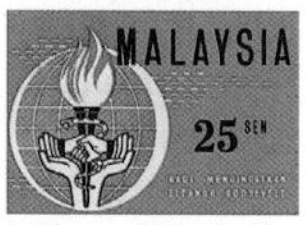

5 "Flame of Freedom" and Emblems of Goodwill, Health and Charity

1964. Eleanor Roosevelt Commemoration.

9	**5**	25c. black, red and turquoise	20	10
10	**5**	30c. black, red and lilac	20	15
11	**5**	50c. black, red and yellow	20	10

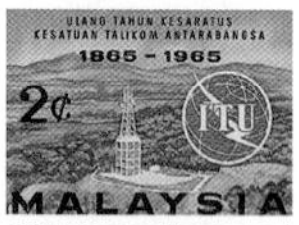

6 Microwave Tower and I.T.U. Emblem

1965. Centenary of I.T.U.

12	**6**	2c. multicoloured	75	2·10
13	**6**	25c. multicoloured	2·00	60
14	**6**	50c. multicoloured	2·75	10

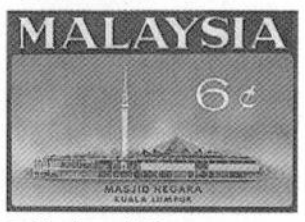

7 National Mosque

1965. Opening of National Mosque, Kuala Lumpur.

15	**7**	6c. red	10	10
16	**7**	15c. brown	20	10
17	**7**	20c. green	20	15

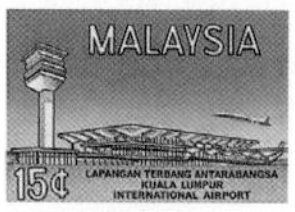

8 Air Terminal

1965. Opening of Int Airport, Kuala Lumpur.

18	**8**	15c. black, green and blue	40	10
19	**8**	30c. black, green and mauve	60	20

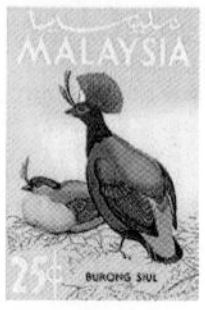

9 Crested Wood Partridge

1965. Birds. Multicoloured.

20	25c. Type **9**	50	10
21	30c. Blue-backed fairy bluebird	60	10
22	50c. Black-naped oriole	1·25	10
23	75c. Rhinoceros hornbill	1·00	10
24	$1 Zebra dove	1·50	10
25	$2 Great argus pheasant	6·50	30
26	$5 Asiatic paradise flycatcher	20·00	3·25
27	$10 Blue-tailed pitta	48·00	13·00

For the lower values see the individual sets listed under each of the states which form Malaysia.

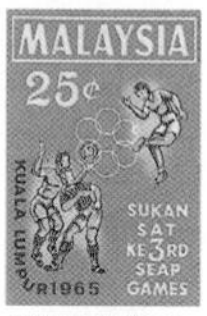

17 Sepak Raga (ball game) and Football

1965. Third South East Asian Peninsular Games.

28	**17**	25c. black and green	40	1·25
29	-	30c. black and purple	40	20
30	-	50c. black and blue	70	30

DESIGNS: 30c. Running; 50c. Diving.

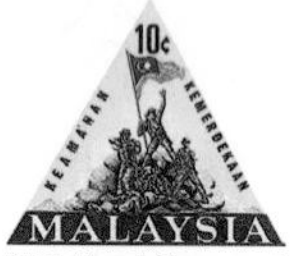

20 National Monument

1966. National Monument, Kuala Lumpur.

31	**20**	10c. multicoloured	50	10
32	**20**	20c. multicoloured	1·00	40

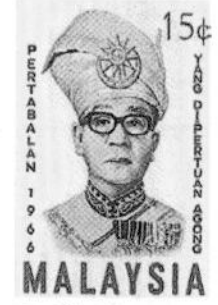

21 The Yang di-Pertuan Agong (Tuanku Ismail Nasiruddin Shah)

1966. Installation of Yang di-Pertuan Agong, Tuanku Ismail Nasiruddin Shah.

33	**21**	15c. black and yellow	10	10
34	**21**	50c. black and blue	20	20

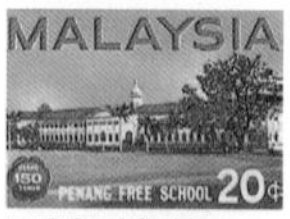

22 School Building

1966. 150th Anniv of Penang Free School.

35	**22**	20c. multicoloured	70	10
36	**22**	50c. multicoloured	90	10

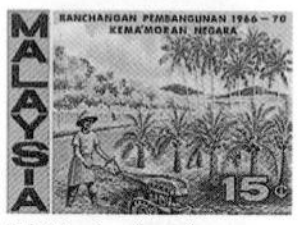

23 "Agriculture"

1966. First Malaysia Plan. Multicoloured.

37	15c. Type **23**	20	10
38	15c. "Rural Health"	20	10
39	15c. "Communications"	1·90	15
40	15c. "Education"	20	10
41	15c. "Irrigation"	20	10

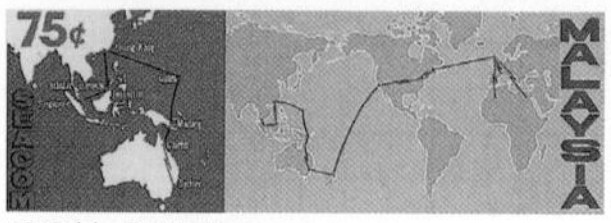

28 Cable Route Maps

1967. Completion of Malaysia–Hong Kong Link of SEACOM Telephone Cable.

42	**28**	30c. multicoloured	80	50
43	**28**	75c. multicoloured	2·50	4·25

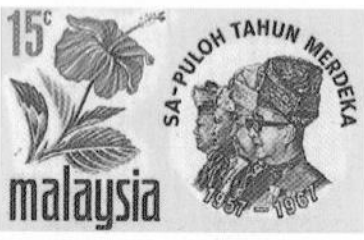

29 Hibiscus and Paramount Rulers

1967. Tenth Anniv of Independence.

44	**29**	15c. multicoloured	20	10
45	**29**	50c. multicoloured	1·25	80

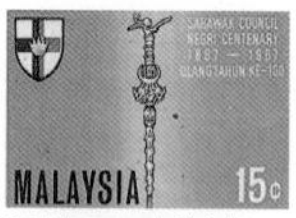

30 Mace and Shield

1967. Centenary of Sarawak Council.

46	**30**	15c. multicoloured	10	10
47	**30**	50c. multicoloured	30	60

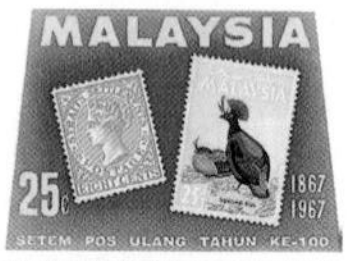

31 Straits Settlements 1867 8c. Stamp and Malaysian 1965 25c. Stamp

1967. Stamp Centenary.

48	**31**	25c. multicoloured	1·60	3·25
49	-	30c. multicoloured	1·60	2·75
50	-	50c. multicoloured	2·50	3·50

DESIGNS: 30c. Straits Settlements 1867 24c. stamp and Malaysian 1965 30c. stamp; 50c. Straits Settlements 1867 32c. stamp and Malaysian 1965 50c. stamp.

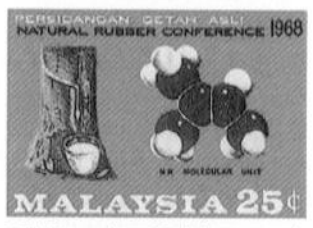

34 Tapping Rubber, and Molecular Unit

1968. Natural Rubber Conf, Kuala Lumpur. Multicoloured.

51	25c. Type **34**	30	10
52	30c. Tapping rubber and export consignment	40	20
53	50c. Tapping rubber and aircraft tyres	40	10

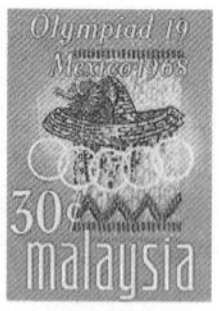

37 Mexican Sombrero and Blanket with Olympic Rings

1968. Olympic Games, Mexico. Multicoloured.

54	30c. Type **37**	20	10
55	75c. Olympic Rings and Mexican embroidery	55	20

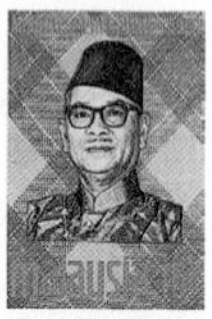

39 Tunku Abdul Rahman against background of Pandanus Weave

1969. Solidarity Week.

56	**39**	15c. multicoloured	15	10
57	-	20c. multicoloured	45	1·25
58	-	50c. multicoloured	50	20

DESIGNS—VERT: 20c. As Type **39** (different). HORIZ: 50c. Tunku Abdul Rahman with pandanus pattern.

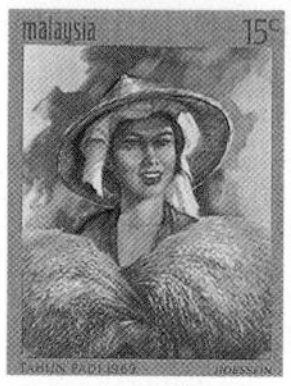

42 Peasant Girl with Sheaves of Paddy

1969. National Rice Year.

59	**42**	15c. multicoloured	15	10
60	**42**	75c. multicoloured	55	1·50

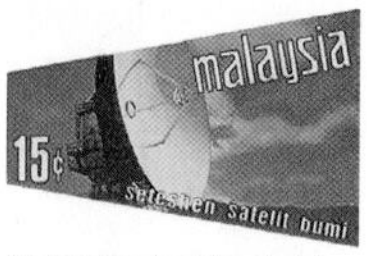

43 Satellite-tracking Aerial

1970. Satellite Earth Station.

61	**43**	15c. drab, black and blue	1·00	15
62	-	30c. multicoloured	1·00	2·50
63	-	30c. multicoloured	1·00	2·50

DESIGN—40×27 mm: Nos. 62/3, "Intelstat III" in Orbit.

No. 62 has inscriptions and value in white and No. 63 has them in gold.

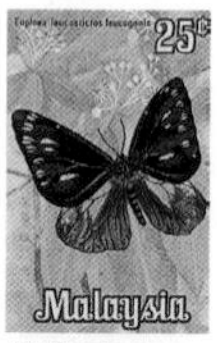

45 "Euploea leucostictus"

1970. Butterflies. Multicoloured.

64	25c. Type **45**	1·00	10
65	30c. "Zeuxidia amethystus"	1·50	10
66	50c. "Polyura athamas"	2·00	10
67	75c. "Papilio memnon"	2·00	10
68	$1 "Appias nero"	3·00	10
69	$2 "Trogonoptera brookiana"	3·50	10
70	$5 "Narathura centaurus"	5·00	3·75
71	$10 "Terinos terpander"	17·00	5·00

Lower values were issued for use in the individual States.

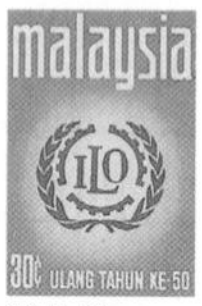

46 Emblem

1970. 50th Anniv of Int Labour Organization.

72	**46**	30c. grey and blue	10	20
73	**46**	75c. pink and blue	20	30

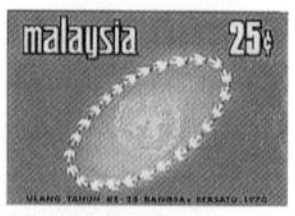

47 U.N. Emblem encircled by Doves

1970. 25th Anniv of United Nations.

74	**47**	25c. gold, black and brown	35	40
75	-	30c. multicoloured	35	35
76	-	50c. black and green	40	75

DESIGNS: 30c. Line of doves and U.N. emblem; 50c. Doves looping U.N. emblem.

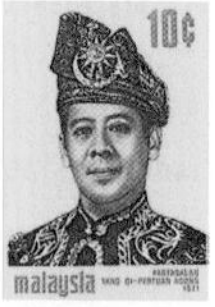

50 The Yang di-Pertuan Agong (Tuanku Abdul Halim Shah)

1971. Installation of Yang di-Pertuan Agong (Paramount Ruler of Malaysia).

77	**50**	10c. black, gold and yellow	20	30
78	**50**	15c. black, gold and mauve	20	30
79	**50**	50c. black, gold and blue	70	1·60

51 Bank Negara Complex

1971. Opening of Bank Negara Building.

80	**51**	25c. black and silver	2·50	2·75
81	**51**	50c. black and gold	1·75	1·25

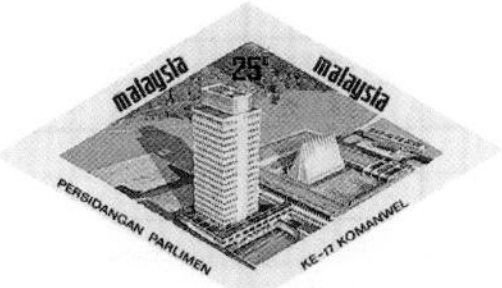

52 Aerial View of Parliament Buildings

1971. 17th Commonwealth Parliamentary Association Conference, Kuala Lumpur. Multicoloured.

82	25c. Type **52**	1·25	50
83	75c. Ground view of Parliament Buildings (horiz, 73×23½ mm)	2·75	1·75

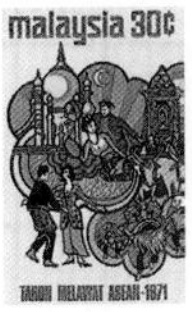

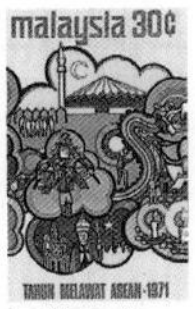

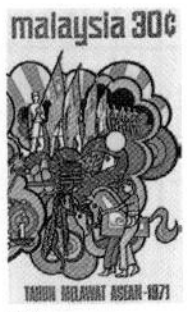

53 **54** Malaysian Carnival **55**

1971. Visit ASEAN Year.

84	**53**	30c. multicoloured	1·60	55
85	**54**	30c. multicoloured	1·60	55
86	**55**	30c. multicoloured	1·60	55

ASEAN = Association of South East Asian Nations.

Nos. 84/6 form a composite design of a Malaysian Carnival, as illustrated.

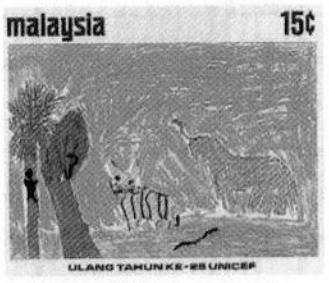

56 Trees, Elephant and Tiger

1971. 25th Anniv of UNICEF. Multicoloured.

87	15c. Type **56**	2·50	60
88	15c. Cat and kittens	2·50	60
89	15c. Sun, flower and bird (22×29 mm)	2·50	60
90	15c. Monkey, elephant and lion in jungle	2·50	60
91	15c. Spider and butterflies	2·50	60

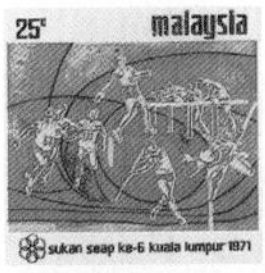

57 Athletics

1971. Sixth S.E.A.P. Games, Kuala Lumpur. Multicoloured.

92	25c. Type **57**	45	40
93	30c. Sepak Raga players	60	50
94	50c. Hockey	1·75	95

S.E.A.P. = South East Asian Peninsula.

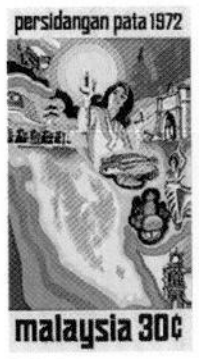

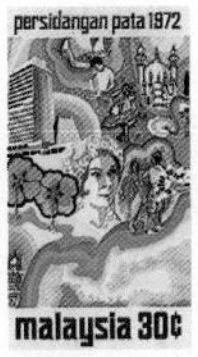

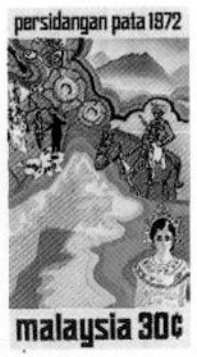

58 **59** Map and Tourist Attractions **60**

1971. Pacific Area Tourist Association Conference.

95	**58**	30c. multicoloured	3·00	1·50
96	**59**	30c. multicoloured	3·00	1·50
97	**60**	30c. multicoloured	3·00	1·50

Nos. 95/7 form a composite design of a map showing tourist attractions, as illustrated.

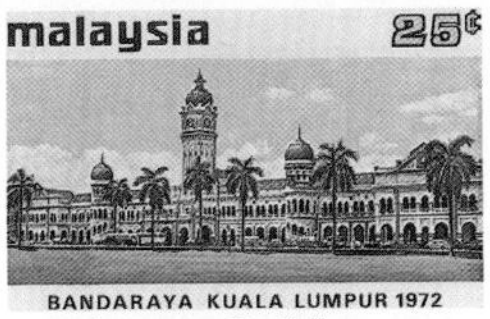

61 Kuala Lumpur City Hall

1972. City Status for Kuala Lumpur. Multicoloured.

98	25c. Type **61**	1·25	1·25
99	50c. City Hall in floodlights	2·00	1·25

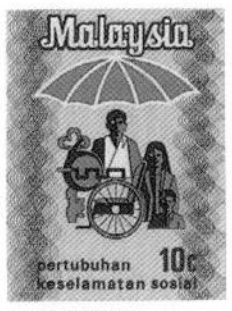

62 SOCSO Emblem

1973. Social Security Organization.

100	**62**	10c. multicoloured	15	15
101	**62**	15c. multicoloured	15	10
102	**62**	50c. multicoloured	40	1·40

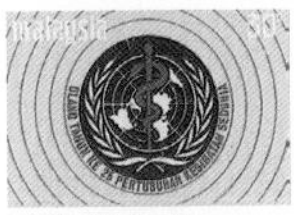

63 W.H.O. Emblem

1973. 25th Anniv of W.H.O.

103	**63**	30c. multicoloured	50	25
104	-	75c. multicoloured	1·00	2·75

The 75c. is similar to Type **63**, but vertical.

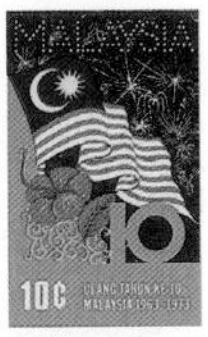

64 Fireworks, National Flag and Flower

1973. Tenth Anniv of Malaysia.

105	**64**	10c. multicoloured	40	25
106	**64**	15c. multicoloured	55	15
107	**64**	50c. multicoloured	1·90	1·60

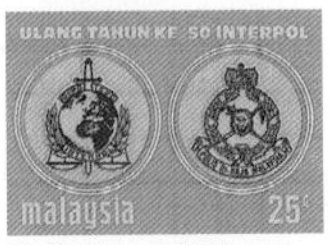

65 Emblems of Interpol and Royal Malaysian Police

1973. 50th Anniv of Interpol. Multicoloured.

108	25c. Type **65**	1·00	50
109	75c. Emblems within "50"	2·25	2·00

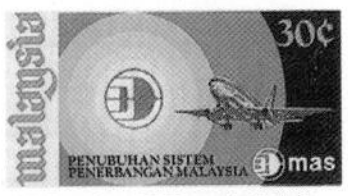

66 Boeing 737 and M.A.S. Emblem

1973. Foundation of Malaysian Airline System.

110	**66**	15c. multicoloured	35	10
111	**66**	30c. multicoloured	65	60
112	**66**	50c. multicoloured	95	1·60

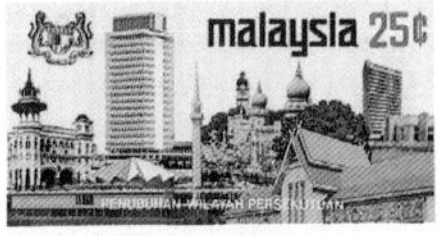

67 Kuala Lumpur

1974. Establishment of Kuala Lumpur as Federal Territory.

113	**67**	25c. multicoloured	50	85
114	**67**	50c. multicoloured	1·00	1·75

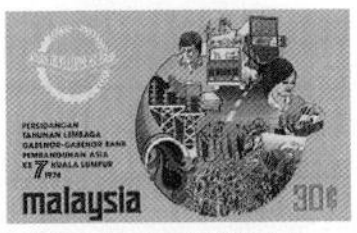

68 Development Projects

1974. Seventh Annual Meeting of Asian Development Bank's Board of Governors, Kuala Lumpur.

115	**68**	30c. multicoloured	25	50
116	**68**	75c. multicoloured	80	1·75

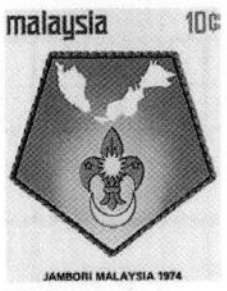

69 Scout Badge and Map

1974. Malaysian Scout Jamboree. Multicoloured.

117	10c. Type **69**	60	1·00
118	15c. Scouts saluting and flags (46×24 mm)	95	30
119	50c. Scout badge	1·75	3·00

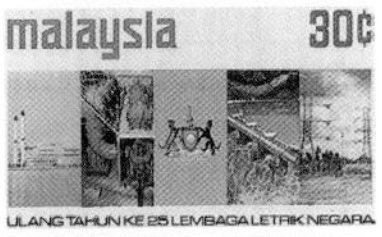

70 Coat of Arms and Power Installations

1974. 25th Anniv of National Electricity Board. Multicoloured.

120	30c. Type **70**	30	50
121	75c. National Electricity Board building (37×27 mm)	1·00	2·50

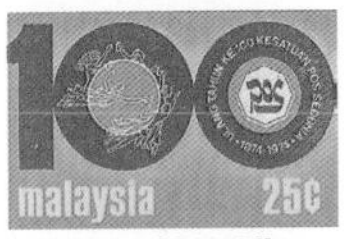

71 U.P.U. and Post Office Emblems within "100"

1974. Centenary of U.P.U.

122	**71**	25c. green, yellow and red	20	35
123	**71**	30c. blue, yellow and red	25	35
124	**71**	75c. orange, yellow and red	65	1·75

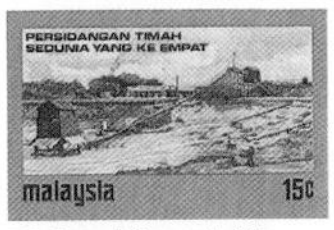

72 Gravel Pump in Tin Mine

1974. Fourth World Tin Conf, Kuala Lumpur. Multicoloured.

125	15c. Type **72**	1·75	20
126	20c. Open-cast mine	2·00	2·50
127	50c. Dredger within "ingot"	3·75	5·50

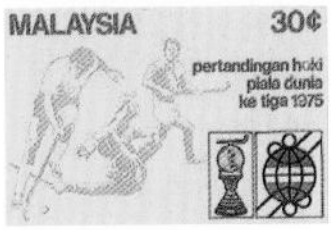

73 Hockey-players, World Cup and Federation Emblem

1975. Thrid World Cup Hockey Championships.

128	**73**	30c. multicoloured	90	60
129	**73**	75c. multicoloured	2·10	2·25

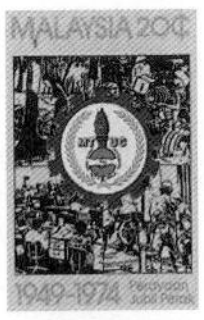

74 Congress Emblem

1975. 25th Anniv of Malaysian Trade Union Congress.

130	**74**	20c. multicoloured	20	25
131	**74**	25c. multicoloured	25	30
132	**74**	30c. multicoloured	65	60

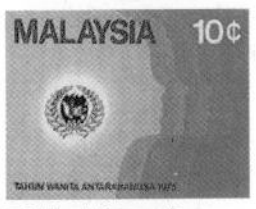

75 Emblem of M.K.P.W. (Malayan Women's Organization)

1975. International Women's Year.

133	**75**	10c. multicoloured	15	25
134	**75**	15c. multicoloured	30	25
135	**75**	50c. multicoloured	1·25	2·25

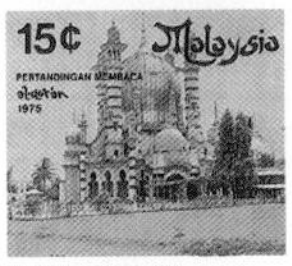

76 Ubudiah Mosque, Kuala Kangsar

1975. Koran Reading Competition. Multicoloured.

136	15c. Type **76**	1·75	60
137	15c. Zahir Mosque, Alor Star	1·75	60
138	15c. National Mosque, Kuala Lumpur	1·75	60
139	15c. Sultan Abu Bakar Mosque, Johore Bahru	1·75	60
140	15c. Kuching State Mosque, Sarawak	1·75	60

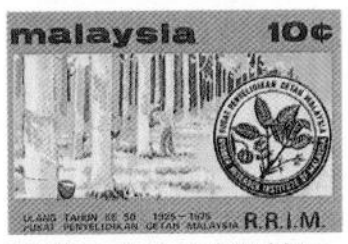

77 Plantation and Emblem

1975. 50th Anniv of Malaysian Rubber Research Institute. Multicoloured.

141	10c. Type **77**	40	15
142	30c. Latex cup and emblem	1·10	70
143	75c. Natural rubber in test-tubes	2·25	2·25

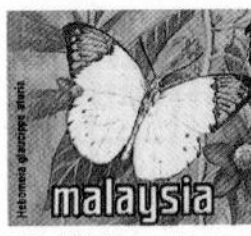

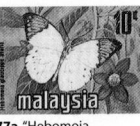

77a "Hebomoia glaucippe"

1976. Multicoloured

144	10c. Type **77a**	2·75	7·00
145	15c. "Precis orithya"	2·75	7·00

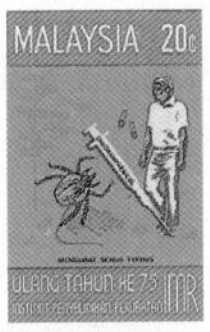

78 Scrub Typhus

1976. 75th Anniv of Institute of Medical Research. Multicoloured.

146	20c. Type **78**	40	15
147	25c. Malaria diagnosis	45	20
148	$1 Beri-beri	1·60	2·50

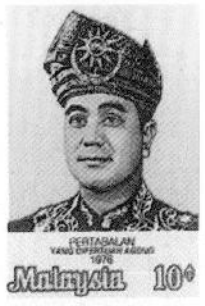

79 The Yang di-Pertuan Agong (Tuanku Yahya Petra)

1976. Installation of Yang di-Pertuan Agong.

149	**79**	10c. black, brown & yellow	25	10
150	**79**	15c. black, brown & mauve	40	10
151	**79**	50c. black, brown and blue	2·25	2·50

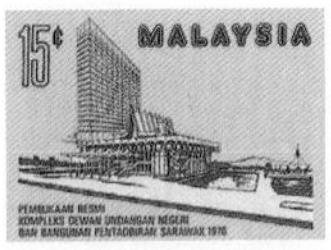

80 State Council Complex

1976. Opening of State Council Complex and Administrative Building, Sarawak.

152	**80**	15c. green and yellow	35	10
153	**80**	20c. green and mauve	45	40
154	**80**	50c. green and blue	1·00	1·40

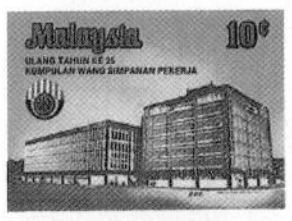

81 E.P.F. Building

1976. 25th Anniv of Employees' Provident Fund. Multicoloured.

155	10c. Type **81**	15	10
156	25c. E.P.F. emblems (27×27 mm)	35	75
157	50c. E.P.F. Building at night	60	1·40

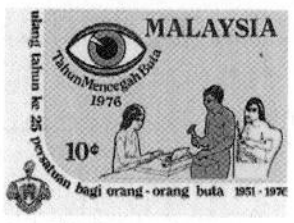

82 Blind People at Work

1976. 25th Anniv of Malayan Assn for the Blind. Multicoloured.

158	10c. Type **82**	15	15
159	75c. Blind man and shadow	1·25	2·75

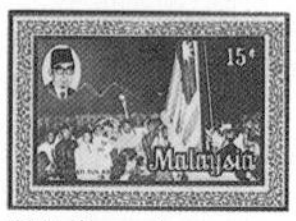

83 Independence Celebrations, 1957

1977. First Death Anniv of Tun Abdul Razak (Prime Minister).

160	15c. Type **83**	1·50	60
161	15c. "Education"	1·50	60
162	15c. Tun Razak and map ("Development")	1·50	60
163	15c. "Rukunegara" (National Philosophy)	1·50	60
164	15c. A.S.E.A.N. meeting	1·50	60

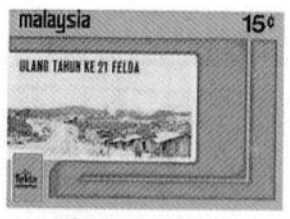

84 F.E.L.D.A. Village Scheme

1977. 21st Anniv of Federal Land Development Authority (F.E.L.D.A.). Multicoloured.

165	15c. Type **84**	30	10
166	30c. Oil palm settlement	80	2·00

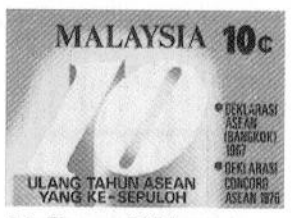

85 Figure "10"

1977. Tenth Anniv of Association of South East Asian Nations (A.S.E.A.N.). Multicoloured.

167	10c. Type **85**	10	10
168	75c. Flags of members	1·25	1·00

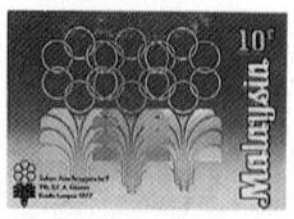

86 Games Logos

1977. Ninth South East Asia Games, Kuala Lumpur. Multicoloured.

169	10c. Type **86**	15	15
170	20c. "Ball"	20	15
171	75c. Symbolic athletes	75	1·75

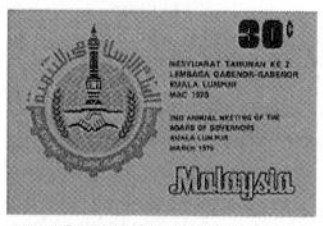

87 Islamic Development Bank Emblem

1978. Islamic Development Bank Board of Governors' Meeting, Kuala Lumpur.

172	**87**	30c. multicoloured	25	15
173	**87**	75c. multicoloured	75	85

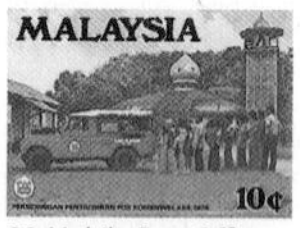

88 Mobile Post Office

1978. Fourth Commonwealth Postal Administrations Conference, Kuala Lumpur. Multicoloured.

174	10c. Type **88**	30	10
175	25c. G.P.O., Kuala Lumpur	75	2·00
176	50c. Rural delivery by motorcycle	2·00	3·00

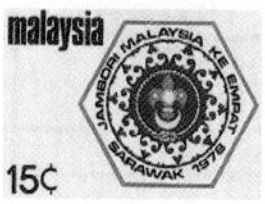

89 Boy Scout Emblem

1978. Fourth Malaysian Scout Jamboree, Sarawak. Multicoloured.

177	15c. Type **89**	75	10
178	$1 Bees and honeycomb	2·75	3·25

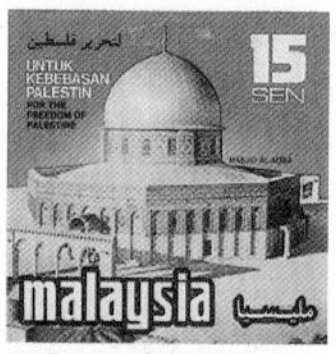

90 Dome of the Rock, Jerusalem

1978. Palestinian Welfare.

179	**90**	15c. multicoloured	1·00	25
180	**90**	30c. multicoloured	1·75	2·50

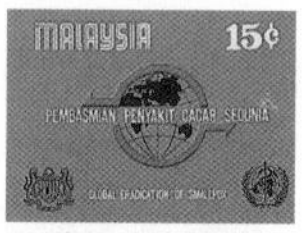

91 Globe and Emblems

1978. Global Eradication of Smallpox.

181	**91**	15c. black, red and blue	25	10
182	**91**	30c. black, red and green	40	30
183	**91**	50c. black, red and pink	70	95

92 "Seratus Tahun Getah Asli" and Tapping Knives Symbol

1978. Centenary of Rubber Industry.

184	**92**	10c. gold and green	10	10
185	-	20c. blue, brown and green	15	10
186	-	75c. gold and green	65	1·00

DESIGNS: 20c. Rubber tree seedling and part of "maxi stump"; 75c. Graphic design of rubber tree, latex cup and globe arranged to form "100".

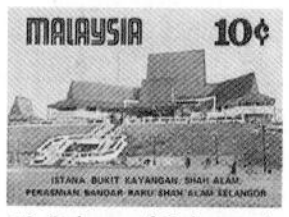

93 Sultan of Selangor's New Palace

1978. Inauguration of Shah Alam New Town as State Capital of Selangor. Multicoloured.

187	10c. Type **93**	15	10
188	30c. Aerial view of Shah Alam	30	15
189	75c. Shah Alam	65	2·00

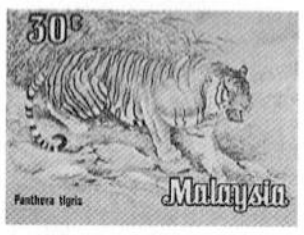

94 Tiger

1979. Animals. Multicoloured.

190	30c. Type **94**	1·75	10
191	40c. Malayan flying lemur	80	10
192	50c. Lesser Malay chevrotain	1·75	10
193	75c. Leathery pangolin	1·00	10
194	$1 Malayan turtle	1·50	10
195	$2 Malayan tapir	1·50	10
196	$5 Gaur	4·50	2·00
197	$10 Orang-utang (vert)	7·00	3·50

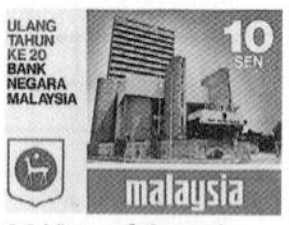

96 View of Central Bank of Malaysia

1979. 20th Anniv of Central Bank of Malaysia. Multicoloured.

198	10c. Type **96**	10	10
199	75c. Central Bank (vert)	40	1·50

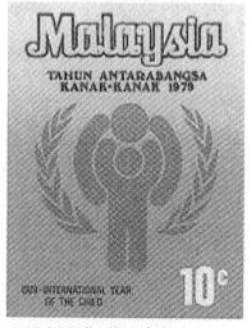

97 I.Y.C. Emblem

1979. International Year of the Child.

200	**97**	10c. gold, blue and salmon	35	20
201	-	15c. multicoloured	60	10
202	-	$1 multicoloured	3·00	4·00

DESIGNS: 15c. Children holding hands in front of globe; $1 Children playing.

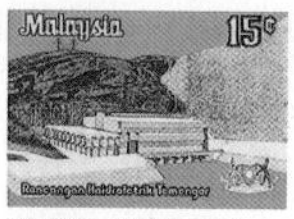

98 Dam and Power Station

1979. Opening of Hydro-electric Power Station, Temengor.

203	**98**	15c. multicoloured	20	15
204	-	25c. multicoloured	35	70
205	-	50c. multicoloured	55	1·40

DESIGNS: 25c., 50c. Different views of dam.

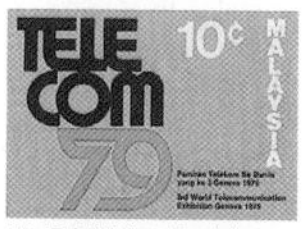

99 Exhibition Emblem

1979. Third World Telecommunications Exhibition, Geneva.

206	**99**	10c. orange, blue and silver	15	50
207	-	15c. multicoloured	20	10
208	-	50c. multicoloured	75	2·50

DESIGNS—34×24 mm: 15c. Telephone receiver joining the one half of World to the other. 39×28 mm: 50c. Communications equipment.

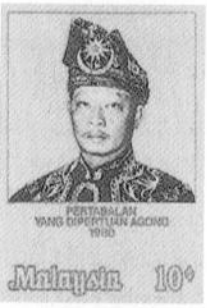

100 Tuanku Haji Ahmad Shah

1980. Installation of Tuanku Haji Ahmad Shah as Yang di-Pertuan Agong.

209	**100**	10c. black, gold and yellow	15	40
210	**100**	15c. black, gold and purple	20	10
211	**100**	50c. black, gold and blue	75	2·00

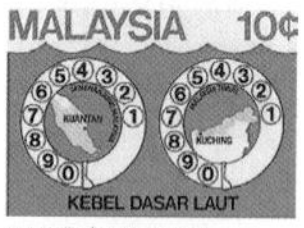

101 Pahang and Sarawak Maps within Telephone Dials

1980. Kuantan–Kuching Submarine Cable Project. Multicoloured.

212	10c. Type **101**	15	40
213	15c. Kuantan and Kuching views within telephone dials	20	10
214	50c. Pahang and Sarawak maps within telephone receiver	45	1·75

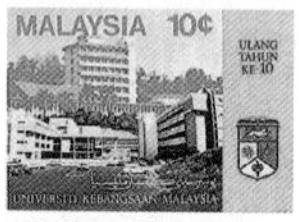

102 Bangi Campus

1980. 10th Anniv of National University of Malaysia. Multicoloured.

215	10c. Type **102**	15	20
216	15c. Jalan Pantai Baru campus	20	10
217	75c. Great Hall	80	3·00

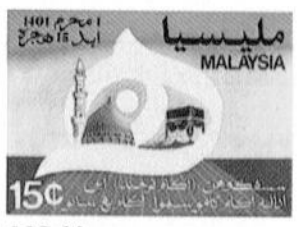

103 Mecca

1980. Moslem Year 1400 A.H. Commemoration.

218	**103**	15c. multicoloured	10	10
219	**103**	50c. multicoloured	30	1·50

No. 219 is inscribed in Roman lettering.

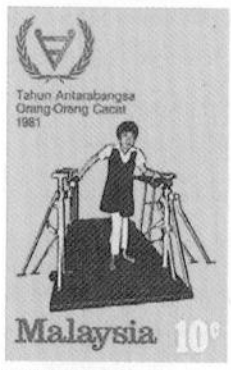

104 Disabled Child learning to Walk

1981. International Year for Disabled Persons. Multicoloured.

220	10c. Type **104**	30	30
221	15c. Girl sewing	55	10
222	75c. Disabled athlete	1·50	3·50

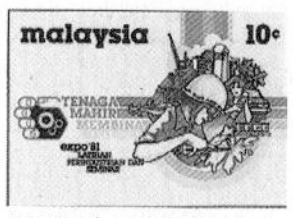

105 Industrial Scene

1981. Expo "81" Industrial Training Exposition, Kuala Lumpur and Seminar, Genting Highlands. Multicoloured.

223	10c. Type **105**	10	10
224	15c. Worker and bulldozer	15	10
225	30c. Workers at shipbuilding plant	25	35
226	75c. Agriculture and fishing produce, workers and machinery	65	2·25

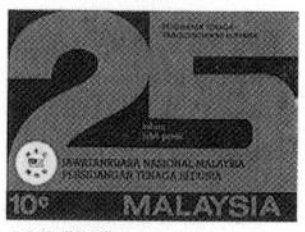

106 "25"

1981. 25th Anniv of Malaysian National Committee for World Energy Conferences. Multicoloured.

227	10c. Type **106**	20	20
228	15c. Drawings showing importance of energy sources in industry	45	10
229	75c. Symbols of various energy sources	2·50	3·75

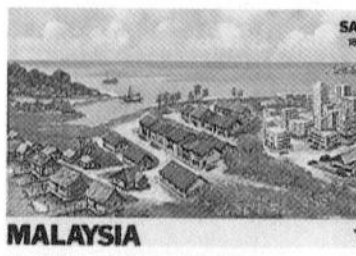

107 Drawing showing development of Sabah from Village to Urbanized Area

1981. Centenary of Sabah. Multicoloured.

230	15c. Type **107**	50	15
231	80c. Drawing showing traditional and modern methods of agriculture	2·00	4·25

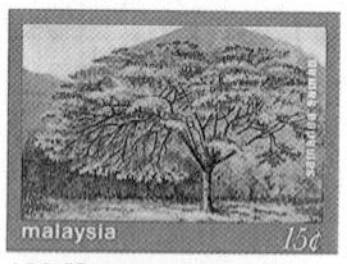

108 "Samanea saman"

1981. Trees. Multicoloured.

232	15c. Type **108**	55	10
233	50c. "Dyera costulata" (vert)	1·75	1·40
234	80c. "Dryobalanops aromatica" (vert)	2·00	4·25

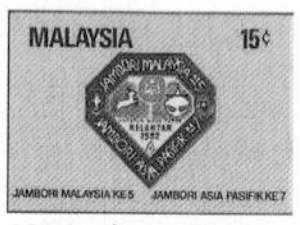

109 Jamboree Emblem

1982. Fifth Malaysian/7th Asia–Pacific Boy Scout Jamboree. Multicoloured.

235	15c. Type **109**	35	10
236	50c. Malaysian flag and scout emblem	80	85
237	80c. Malaysian and Asia–Pacific scout emblem	1·25	4·25

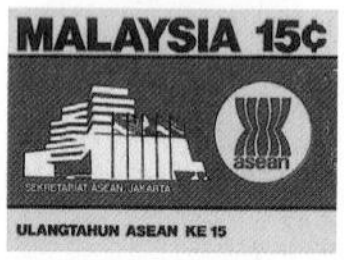

110 A.S.E.A.N. Building and Emblem

1982. 15th Anniv of Ministerial Meeting of A.S.E.A.N. (Association of South East Asian Nations). Multicoloured.

238	15c. Type **110**	15	10
239	$1 Flags of members	2·00	3·75

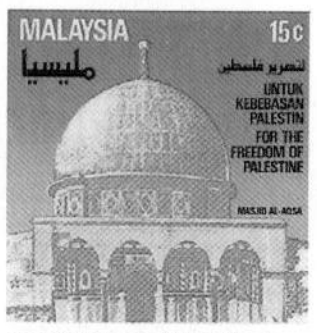

111 Dome of the Rock, Jerusalem

1982. "Freedom for Palestine".

240	**111**	15c. gold, green and black	1·50	25
241	**111**	$1 silver, green and black	4·50	5·25

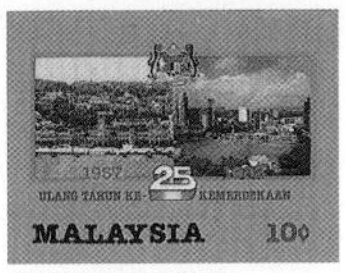

112 Views of Kuala Lumpur in 1957 and 1982

1982. 25th Anniv of Independence. Multicoloured.

242	10c. Type **112**	10	10
243	15c. Malaysian industries	15	15
244	50c. Soldiers on parade	40	55
245	80c. Independence ceremony	70	3·00
MS246a	120×190 mm. Nos. 242/5	12·00	12·00

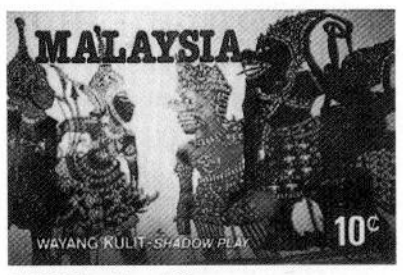

113 Shadow Play

1982. Traditional Games. Multicoloured.

247	10c. Type **113**	55	30
248	15c. Cross top	55	15
249	75c. Kite flying	2·25	4·75

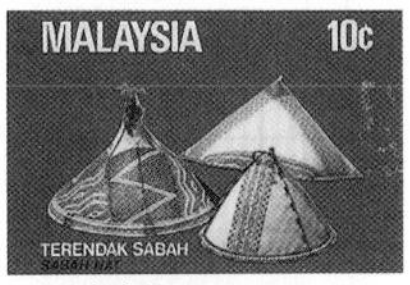

114 Sabah Hats

1982. Malaysian Handicrafts. Multicoloured.

250	10c. Type **114**	25	30
251	15c. Gold-threaded cloth	25	20
252	75c. Sarawak pottery	1·25	3·75

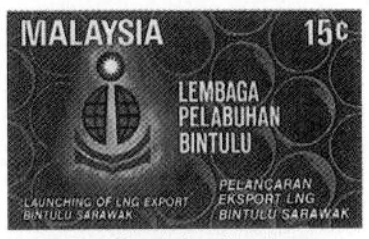

115 Gas Exploitation Logo

1983. Export of Liquefied Natural Gas from Bintulu Field, Sarawak. Multicoloured.

253	15c. Type **115**	75	15
254	20c. "Tenaga Satu" (liquid gas tanker)	1·50	70
255	$1 Gas drilling equipment	3·50	6·50

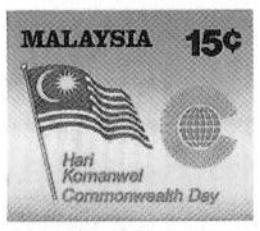

116 Flag of Malaysia

1983. Commonwealth Day. Multicoloured.

256	15c. Type **116**	20	10
257	20c. The King of Malaysia	20	20
258	40c. Oil palm tree and refinery	25	45
259	$1 Satellite view of Earth	60	2·75

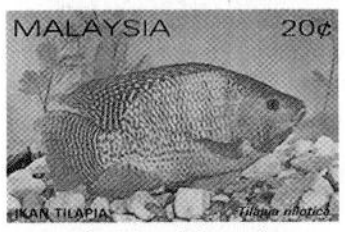

117 Nile Mouthbrooder

1983. Freshwater Fish (1st series). Multicoloured.

260	20c. Type **117**	1·25	2·00
261	20c. Common carp	1·25	2·00
262	40c. Lampan barb	1·75	2·75
263	40c. Grass carp	1·75	2·75

See also Nos. 753/62 and 1333/**MS**1337.

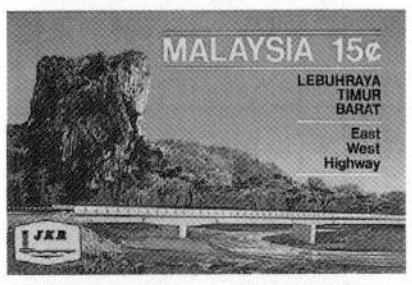

118 Lower Pergau River Bridge

1983. Opening of East–West Highway. Multicoloured.

264	15c. Type **118**	80	15
265	20c. Perak river reservoir bridge	1·00	75
266	$1 Map showing East–West highway	3·75	6·50

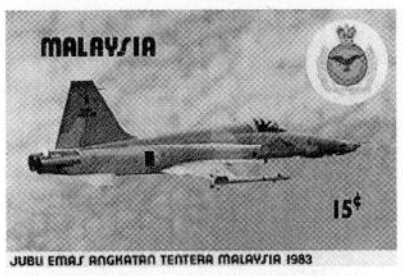

119 Northrop Tiger II Fighter

1983. 50th Anniv of Malaysian Armed Forces. Multicoloured.

267	15c. Type **119**	1·25	15
268	20c. Missile boat	1·75	45
269	40c. Battle of Pasir Panjang	2·25	2·50
270	80c. Trooping the Colour	3·25	6·00
MS271	130×85 mm. Nos. 267/70	13·00	14·00

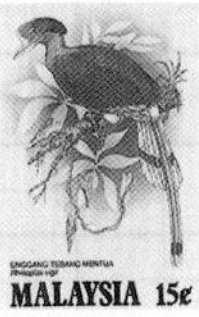

120 Helmeted Hornbill

1983. Hornbills of Malaysia. Multicoloured.

280	15c. Type **120**	1·00	15
281	20c. Wrinkled hornbill	1·25	50
282	50c. Long-crested hornbill	2·00	2·00
283	$1 Rhinoceros hornbill	3·25	5·50

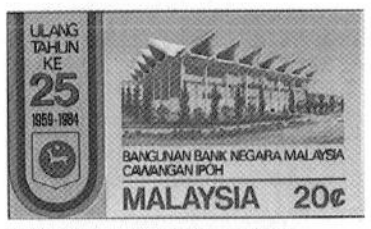

121 Bank Building, Ipoh

1984. 25th Anniv of Bank Negara. Multicoloured.

284	20c. Type **121**	40	30
285	$1 Bank building, Alor Setar	2·00	3·75

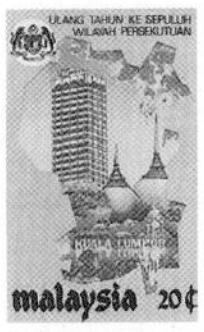

122 Sky-scraper and Mosque, Kuala Lumpur

1984. Tenth Anniv of Federal Territory of Kuala Lumpur. Multicoloured.

286	20c. Type **122**	80	20
287	40c. Aerial view	1·60	1·40
288	80c. Gardens and clock-tower (horiz)	2·50	6·50

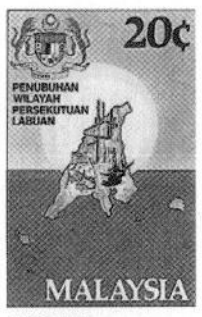

123 Map showing Industries

1984. Formation of Labuan Federal Territory. Multicoloured.

289	20c. Type **123**	75	25
290	$1 Flag and map of Labuan	4·25	6·00

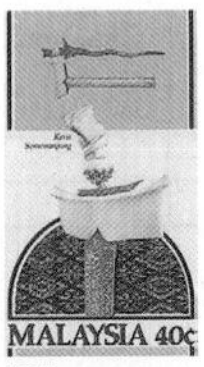

124 Semenanjung Keris

1984. Traditional Malay Weapons. Multicoloured.

291	40c. Type **124**	1·25	2·10
292	40c. Pekakak keris	1·25	2·10
293	40c. Jawa keris	1·25	2·10
294	40c. Lada tumbuk	1·25	2·10

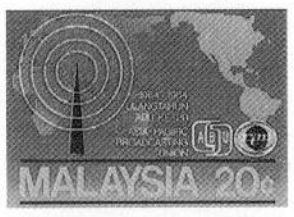

125 Map of World and Transmitter

1984. 20th Anniv of Asia–Pacific Broadcasting Union. Multicoloured.

295	20c. Type **125**	40	25
296	$1 Clasped hands within "20"	2·00	5·00

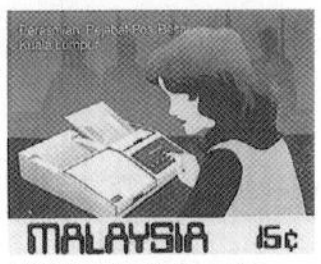

126 Facsimile Service

1984. Opening of New General Post Office, Kuala Lumpur. Multicoloured.

297	15c. Type **126**	35	20
298	20c. New G.P.O. building	45	45
299	$1 Mailbag conveyor	2·00	4·75

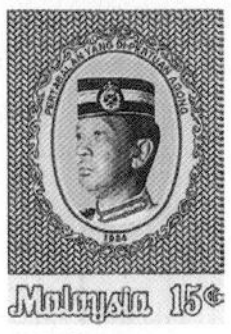

127 Yang di-Pertuan Agong (Tuanku Mahmood)

1984. Installation of Yang di-Pertuan Agong (Tuanku Mahmood).

300	**127**	15c. multicoloured	60	20
301	**127**	20c. multicoloured	65	20
302	-	40c. multicoloured	1·25	1·00
303	-	80c. multicoloured	2·50	5·00

DESIGN—HORIZ: 40c., 80c. Yang di-Pertuan Agong and federal crest.

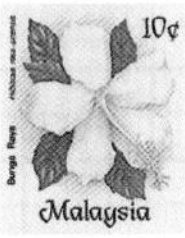

128 White Hibiscus

1984. Hibiscus. Multicoloured.

304	10c. Type **128**	50	30
305	20c. Red hibiscus	1·00	20
306	40c. Pink hibiscus	1·75	2·00
307	$1 Orange hibiscus	2·75	5·75

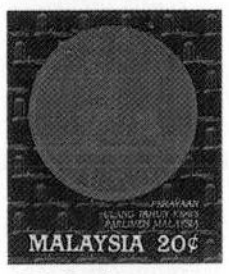

129 Parliament Building

1985. 25th Anniv of Federal Parliament. Multicoloured.

308	20c. Type **129**	30	15
309	$1 Parliament Building (different) (horiz)	1·75	3·50

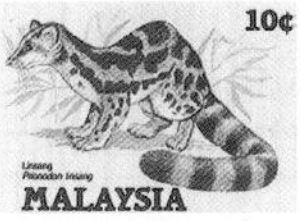

130 Banded Linsang

1985. Protected Animals of Malaysia (1st series). Multicoloured.

310	10c. Type **130**	60	10
311	40c. Slow loris (vert)	2·00	1·40
312	$1 Spotted giant flying squirrel (vert)	4·00	6·50

See also Nos. 383/6.

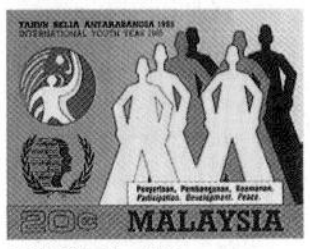

131 Stylized Figures

1985. International Youth Year. Multicoloured.

313	20c. Type **131**	40	15
314	$1 Young workers	3·50	5·50

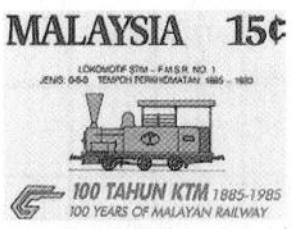

132 Steam Locomotive No. 1, 1885

1985. Centenary of Malayan Railways.

315	**132**	15c. black, red and orange	1·60	50
316	-	20c. multicoloured	1·75	60
317	-	$1 multicoloured	4·25	7·00
MS318		119×59 mm. 80c. multicoloured	8·00	9·00

DESIGNS—HORIZ: 20c. Class 20 diesel-electric locomotive, 1957; $1 Hitachi Class 23 diesel-electric locomotive, 1983. 48×31 mm: 80c. Class 56 steam locomotive No. 564.18, "Seletar", 1938.

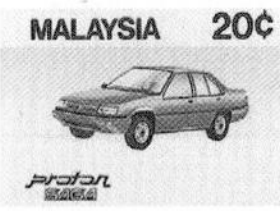

133 Blue Proton "Saga 1.3s" Car

1985. Production of Proton "Saga" (Malaysian national car). Multicoloured.

319	20c. Type **133**	80	15
320	40c. White Proton "Saga 1.3s"	1·40	1·00
321	$1 Red Proton "Saga 1.5s"	2·50	6·50

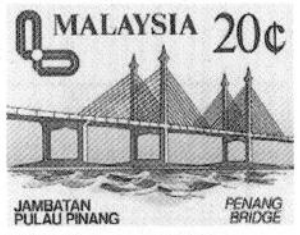

134 Penang Bridge

1985. Opening of Penang Bridge. Multicoloured.

322	20c. Type **134**	90	15
323	40c. Penang Bridge and location map	1·75	90
324	$1 Symbolic bridge linking Penang to mainland (40×24 mm)	3·50	6·00

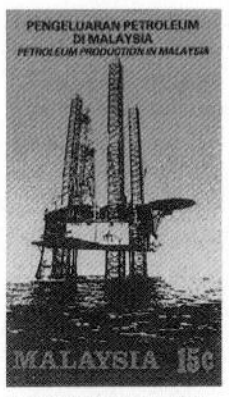

135 Offshore Oil Rig

1985. Malaysian Petroleum Production. Multicoloured.

325	15c. Type **135**	1·25	20
326	20c. Malaysia's first oil refinery (horiz)	1·40	50
327	$1 Map of Malaysian offshore oil and gas fields (horiz)	3·75	6·00

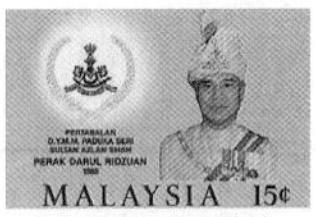

136 Sultan Azlan Shah and Perak Royal Crest

1985. Installation of the Sultan of Perak.

328	**136**	15c. multicoloured	65	10
329	**136**	20c. multicoloured	75	25
330	**136**	$1 multicoloured	3·75	7·00

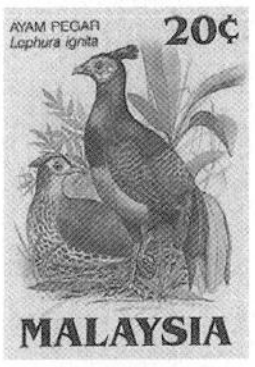

137 Crested Fireback Pheasant

1986. Protected Birds of Malaysia (1st series). Multicoloured.

331	20c. Type **137**	2·50	3·25
332	20c. Malay peacock-pheasant	2·50	3·25
333b	40c. Bulwer's pheasant (horiz)	2·00	3·50
334b	40c. Great argus pheasant (horiz)	2·00	3·50

See also Nos. 394/7.

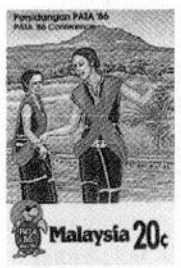

139 Two Kadazan Dancers, Sabah

1986. Pacific Area Travel Association Conference, Malaysia. Multicoloured.

335	20c. Type **139**	85	1·25
336	20c. Dyak dancer and longhouse, Sarawak	85	1·25
337	20c. Dancers and fortress, Malacca	85	1·25

338	40c. Malay dancer and Kuala Lumpur	1·25	1·50
339	40c. Chinese opera dancer and Penang Bridge	1·25	1·50
340	40c. Indian dancer and Batu Caves	1·25	1·50

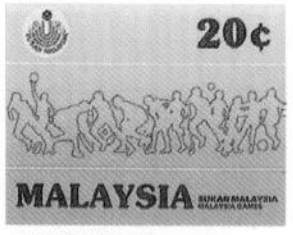

140 Stylized Competitors

1986. Malaysia Games. Multicoloured.

341	20c. Type **140**	1·25	20
342	40c. Games emblems (vert)	2·25	2·00
343	$1 National and state flags (vert)	9·00	7·75

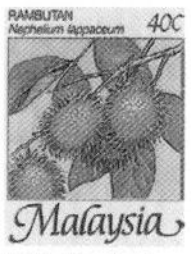

141 Rambutan

1986. Fruits of Malaysia. Multicoloured.

344	40c. Type **141**	1·00	10
345	50c. Pineapple	1·00	10
346	80c. Durian	1·25	10
347	$1 Mangosteen	1·50	10
348	$2 Star fruit	2·00	10
349	$5 Banana	4·50	50
350	$10 Mango	7·00	1·25
351	$20 Papaya	12·00	3·25

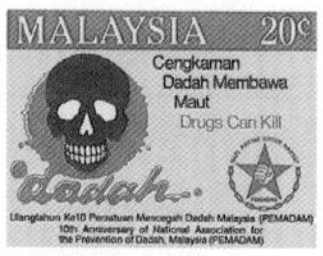

142 Skull and Slogan "Drugs Can Kill"

1986. Tenth Anniv of National Association for Prevention of Drug Addiction. Multicoloured.

352	20c. Type **142**	1·50	30
353	40c. Bird and slogan "Stay Free From Drugs"	2·50	1·10
354	$1 Addict and slogan "Drugs Can Destroy" (vert)	3·75	5·00

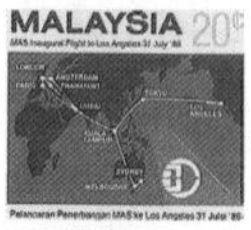

143 MAS Logo and Map showing Routes

1986. Inaugural Flight of Malaysian Airlines Kuala Lumpur–Los Angeles Service. Multicoloured.

355	20c. Type **143**	2·50	20
356	40c. Logo, stylized aircraft and route diagram	3·50	80
357	$1 Logo and stylized aircraft	5·00	4·50

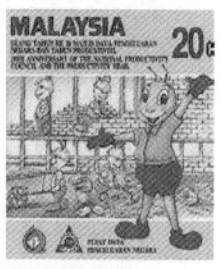

144 Building Construction

1986. 20th Anniv of National Productivity Council and 25th Anniv of Asian Productivity Organization (40c., $1). Multicoloured.

358	20c. Type **144**	85	25
359	40c. Planning and design (horiz)	1·40	1·25
360	$1 Computer-controlled car assembly line (horiz)	3·75	6·50

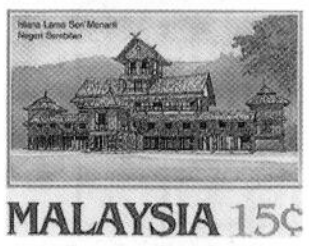

145 Old Seri Menanti Palace, Negri Sembilan

1986. Historic Buildings of Malaysia (1st series). Multicoloured.

361	15c. Type **145**	1·00	20
362	20c. Old Kenangan Palace, Perak	1·10	20
363	40c. Old Town Hall, Malacca	2·00	80
364	$1 Astana, Kuching, Sarawak	3·50	5·00

See also Nos. 465/8.

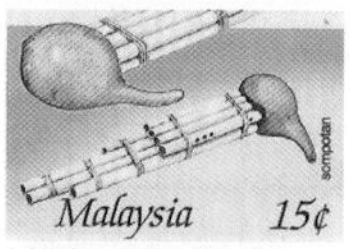

146 Sompotan (bamboo pipes)

1987. Malaysian Musical Instruments. Multicoloured.

365	15c. Type **146**	1·40	10
366	20c. Sapih (four-stringed chordophone)	1·50	20
367	50c. Serunai (pipes) (vert)	2·50	60
368	80c. Rebab (three-stringed fiddle) (vert)	3·50	2·50

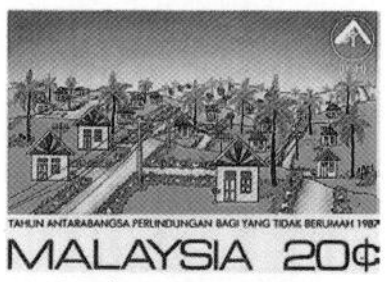

147 Modern Housing Estate

1987. International Year of Shelter for the Homeless. Multicoloured.

369	20c. Type **147**	1·25	15
370	$1 Stylized families and houses	3·50	1·75

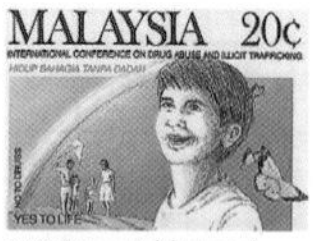

148 Drug Addict and Family

1987. International Conference on Drug Abuse, Vienna. Multicoloured.

371	20c. Type **148**	2·00	1·50
372	20c. Hands holding drugs and damaged internal organs	2·00	1·50
373	40c. Healthy boy and broken drug capsule	2·75	1·75
374	40c. Drugs and healthy internal organs	2·75	1·75

Nos. 371/2 and 373/4 were printed together, *se-tenant*, forming composite designs.

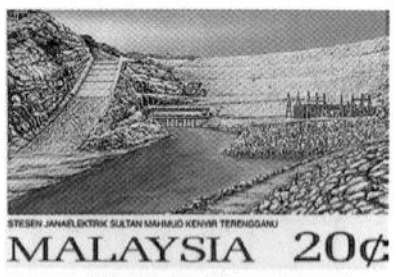

149 Spillway and Power Station

1987. Opening of Sultan Mahmud Hydro-electric Scheme, Kenyir, Trengganu. Multicoloured.

375	20c. Type **149**	75	10
376	$1 Dam, spillway and reservoir	2·75	2·00

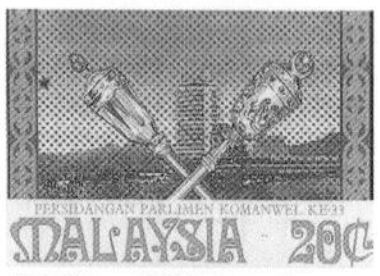

150 Crossed Maces and Parliament Building, Kuala Lumpur

1987. 33rd Commonwealth Parliamentary Conf. Multicoloured.

377	20c. Type **150**	25	10
378	$1 Parliament building and crossed mace emblem	1·25	1·25

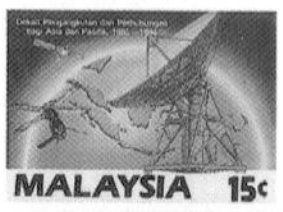

151 Dish Aerial, Satellite and Globe

1987. Asia/Pacific Transport and Communications Decade. Multicoloured.

379	15c. Type **151**	65	10
380	20c. Diesel train and car	2·00	75
381	40c. Container ships and lorry	2·50	1·60
382	$1 Malaysian Airlines Boeing 747, Kuala Lumpur Airport	4·75	7·00

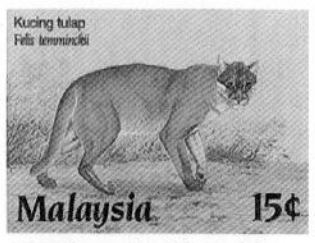

152 Temminck's Golden Cat

1987. Protected Animals of Malaysia (2nd series). Multicoloured.

383	15c. Type **152**	2·75	50
384	20c. Flatheaded cat	2·75	50
385	40c. Marbled cat	4·00	1·75
386	$1 Clouded leopard	7·50	7·50

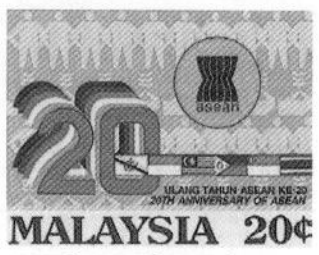

153 Flags of Member Nations and "20"

1987. 20th Anniv of Association of South East Asian Nations. Multicoloured.

387	20c. Type **153**	35	10
388	$1 Flags of member nations and globe	1·25	1·50

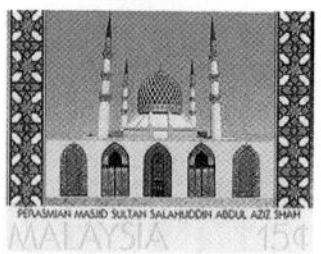
154 Mosque and Portico

1988. Opening of Sultan Salahuddin Abdul Aziz Shah Mosque. Multicoloured.

389	15c. Type **154**	30	10
390	20c. Dome, minarets and Sultan of Selangor	30	20
391	$1 Interior and dome (vert)	1·50	3·00

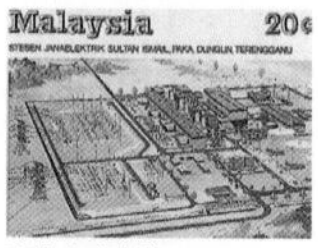

155 Aerial View

1988. Sultan Ismail Hydro-electric Power Station, Paka, Trengganu. Multicoloured.

392	20c. Type **155**	30	10
393	$1 Power-station and pylons	1·40	1·50

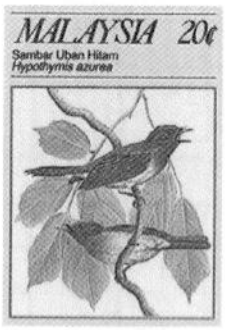

156 Black-naped Blue Monarch

1988. Protected Birds of Malaysia (2nd series). Multicoloured.

394	20c. Type **156**	1·75	2·25
395	20c. Scarlet-backed flower-pecker	1·75	2·25
396	50c. Yellow-backed sunbird	2·50	3·00
397	50c. Black and red broadbill	2·50	3·00

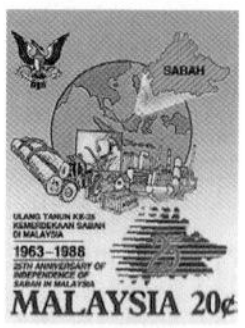

157 Outline Map and Products of Sabah

1988. 25th Anniv of Sabah and Sarawak as States of Malaysia. Multicoloured.

398	20c. Type **157**	65	80
399	20c. Outline map and products of Sarawak	65	80
400	$1 Flags of Malaysia, Sabah and Sarawak (30×40 mm)	2·00	3·50

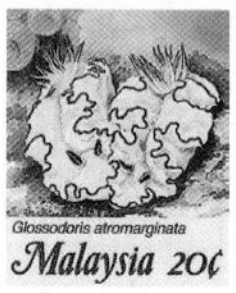

158 "Glossodoris atromarginata"

1988. Marine Life (1st series). Multicoloured.

401	20c. Type **158**	85	1·10
402	20c. Ocellate nudibranch	85	1·10
403	20c. "Chromodoris annae"	85	1·10
404	20c. "Flabellina macassarana"	85	1·10
405	20c. Ruppell's nudibranch	85	1·10
MS406	100×75 mm. $1 Blue-ringed angelfish (50×40 mm)	3·00	1·75

Nos. 401/5 were printed together, *se-tenant*, forming a composite background design.

See also Nos. 410/13, 450/3, 492/6 and 559/62.

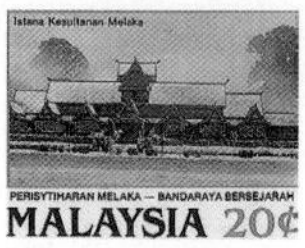

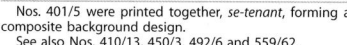

159 Sultan's Palace, Malacca

1989. Declaration of Malacca as Historic City. Multicoloured.

407	20c. Type **159**	35	30
408	20c. Independence Memorial Building	35	30
409	$1 Porta De Santiago Fortress (vert)	1·40	2·00

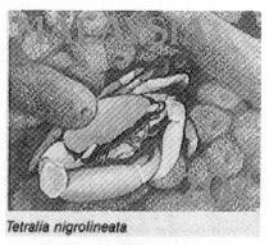
160 "Tetralia nigrolineata"

1989. Marine Life (2nd series). Crustaceans. Multicoloured.

410	20c. Type **160**	45	90
411	20c. "Neopetrolisthes maculatus" (crab)	45	90
412	40c. "Periclimenes holthuisi" (shrimp)	55	1·10
413	40c. "Synalpheus neomeris" (shrimp)	55	1·10

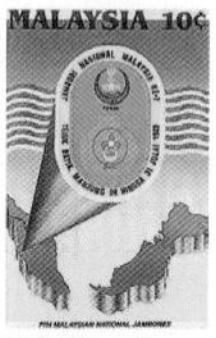

161 Map of Malaysia and Scout Badge

1989. Seventh National Scout Jamboree. Multicoloured.

414	10c. Type **161**	30	10
415	20c. Saluting national flag	60	25
416	80c. Scouts around camp fire (horiz)	1·40	3·00

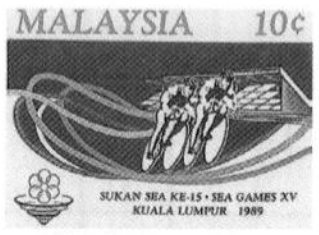

162 Cycling

1989. 15th South East Asian Games, Kuala Lumpur. Multicoloured.

417	10c. Type **162**	1·50	70
418	20c. Athletics	55	20
419	50c. Swimming (vert)	1·00	1·00
420	$1 Torch bearer (vert)	1·75	4·00

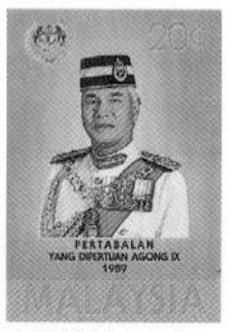
163 Sultan Azlan Shah

1989. Installation of Sultan Azlan Shah as Yang di-Pertuan Agong.

421	**163**	20c. multicoloured	20	15
422	**163**	40c. multicoloured	35	35
423	**163**	$1 multicoloured	1·00	2·75

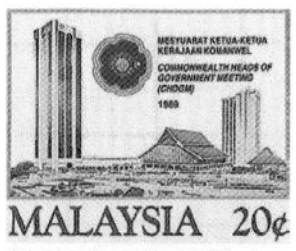

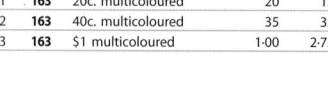

164 Putra World Trade Centre and Pan-Pacific Hotel

1989. Commonwealth Heads of Government Meeting, Kuala Lumpur. Multicoloured.

424	20c. Type **164**	20	10
425	50c. Traditional dancers (vert)	1·00	75
426	$1 National flag and map showing Commonwealth countries	2·25	3·00

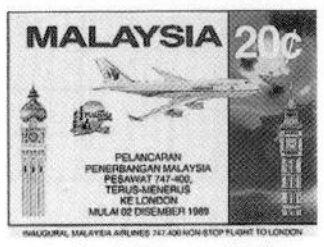

165 Clock Tower, Kuala Lumpur City Hall and Big Ben

1989. Inaugural Malaysia Airlines "747" Non-stop Flight to London. Each showing Malaysia Airlines Boeing "747-400". Multicoloured.

427	20c. Type **165**	2·25	2·25
428	20c. Parliament Buildings, Kuala Lumpur, and Palace of Westminster	2·25	2·25
429	$1 World map showing route	5·50	5·50

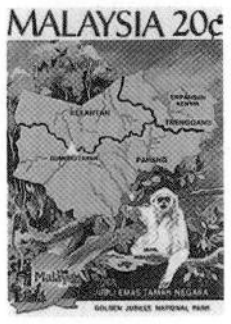

166 Sloth and Map of Park

1989. 50th Anniv of National Park. Multicoloured.

430	20c. Type **166**	1·50	30
431	$1 Pair of crested argus	4·50	5·00

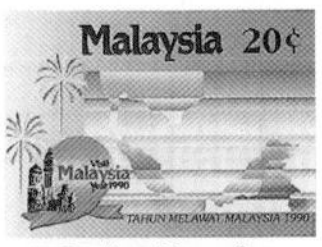

167 Outline Map of South-east Asia and Logo

1990. "Visit Malaysia Year". Multicoloured.

432	20c. Type **167**	1·00	25
433	50c. Traditional drums	1·25	1·25
434	$1 Scuba diving, windsurfing and yachting	2·50	3·50

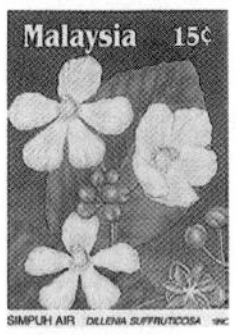

168 "Dillenia suffruticosa"

1990. Wildflowers (1st series). Multicoloured.

435	15c. Type **168**	25	15
436	20c. "Mimosa pudica"	30	20
437	50c. "Ipmoea carnea"	60	90
438	$1 "Nymphaea pubescens"	80	2·75

See also Nos. 505/8.

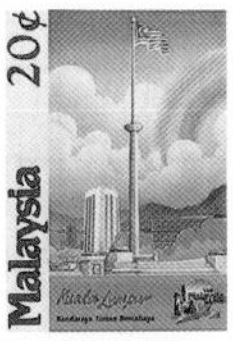

169 Monument and Rainbow

1990. Kuala Lumpur, Garden City of Lights. Multicoloured.

439	20c. Type **169**	25	20
440	40c. Mosque and skyscrapers at night (horiz)	55	55
441	$1 Kuala Lumpur skyline (horiz)	1·40	3·50

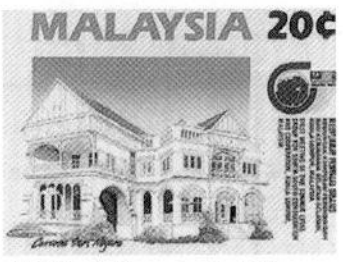

170 Seri Negara Building

1990. First Summit Meeting of South–South Consultation and Co-operation Group, Kuala Lumpur. Multicoloured.

442	20c. Type **170**	40	15
443	80c. Summit logo	1·40	2·50

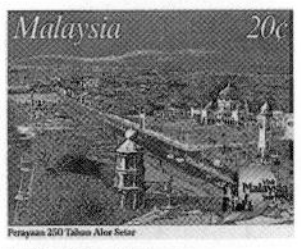

171 Alor Setar

1990. 250th Anniv of Alor Setar. Multicoloured.

444	20c. Type **171**	40	20
445	40c. Musicians and monument (vert)	50	40
446	$1 Zahir Mosque (vert)	1·25	3·75

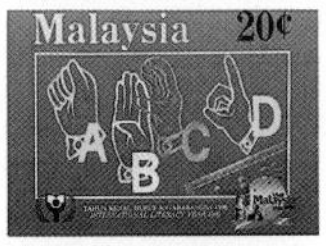

172 Sign Language Letters

1990. International Literacy Year. Multicoloured.

447	20c. Type **172**	70	10
448	40c. People reading	1·00	40
449	$1 Symbolic person reading (vert)	2·50	3·50

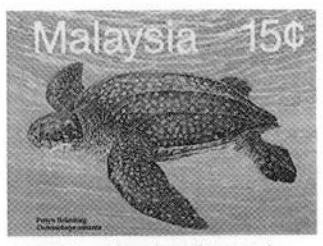

173 Leatherback Turtle

1990. Marine Life (3rd series). Sea Turtles. Multicoloured.

450	15c. Type **173**	60	10
451	20c. Common green turtle	60	15
452	40c. Olive Ridley turtle	1·25	80
453	$1 Hawksbill turtle	2·25	3·75

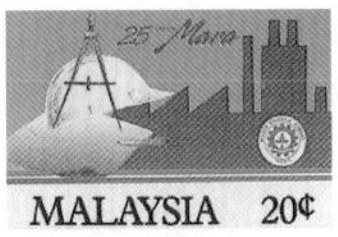

174 Safety Helmet, Dividers and Industrial Skyline

1991. 25th Anniv of MARA (Council of the Indigenous People). Multicoloured.

454	20c. Type **174**	15	10
455	40c. Documents and graph	30	35
456	$1 25th Anniversary logo	75	2·25

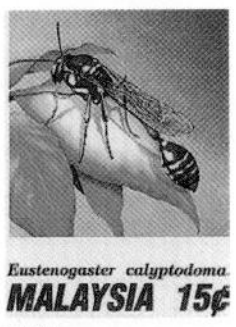

175 "Eustenogaster calyptodoma"

1991. Insects. Wasps. Multicoloured.

457	15c. Type **175**	25	30
458	20c. "Vespa affinis indonensis"	25	20
459	50c. "Sceliphorn javanum"	60	70
460	$1 "Ampulex compressa"	1·00	2·50
MS461	130×85 mm. Nos. 457/60	4·25	5·50

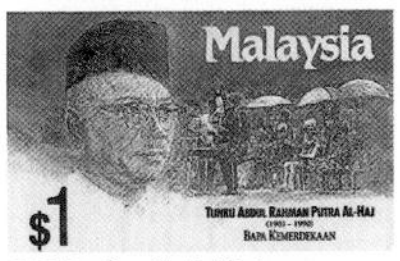

176 Tunku Abdul Rahman Putra and Independence Rally

1991. Former Prime Ministers of Malaysia. Multicoloured.

462	$1 Type **176**	70	1·25
463	$1 Tun Abdul Razak Hussein and jungle village	70	1·25
464	$1 Tun Hussein Onn and standard-bearers	70	1·25

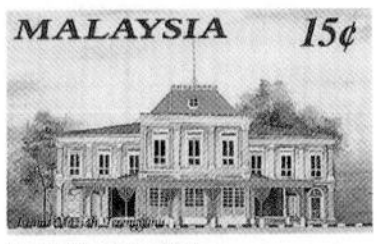

177 Maziah Palace, Trengganu

1991. Historic Buildings of Malaysia (2nd series). Multicoloured.

465	15c. Type **177**	25	10
466	20c. Grand Palace, Johore	25	15
467	40c. Town Palace, Kuala Langat, Selangor	50	50
468	$1 Jahar Palace, Kelantan	1·00	2·75

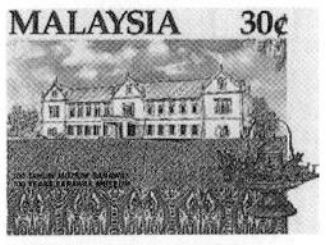

178 Museum Building in 1891, Brass Lamp and Fabric

1991. Centenary of Sarawak Museum. Multicoloured.

469	30c. Type **178**	30	15
470	$1 Museum building in 1991, vase and fabric	1·00	2·00

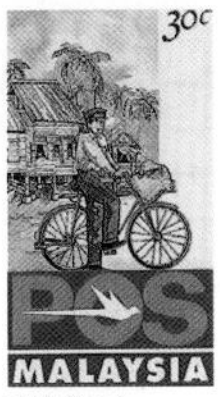

179 Rural Postman on Cycle

1992. Inauguration of Post Office Corporation. Multicoloured.

471	30c. Type **179**	60	85
472	30c. Urban postman on motorcycle	60	85
473	30c. Inner city post van	60	85
474	30c. Industrial post van	60	85
475	30c. Malaysian Airlines Boeing 747 and globe	60	85

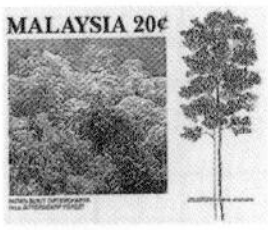

180 Hill Forest and Jelutong Tree

1992. Tropical Forests. Multicoloured.

476	20c. Type **180**	35	10
477	50c. Mangrove swamp and Bakau Minyak tree	65	50
478	$1 Lowland forest and Chengal tree	1·10	2·50

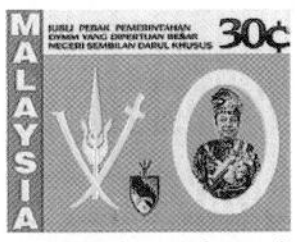

181 Tuanku Ja'afar and Coat of Arms

1992. 25th Anniv of Installation of Tuanku Ja'afar as Yang di-Pertuan Besar of Negri Sembilan. Multicoloured.

479	30c. Type **181**	30	20
480	$1 Palace, Negri Sembilan	1·00	2·25

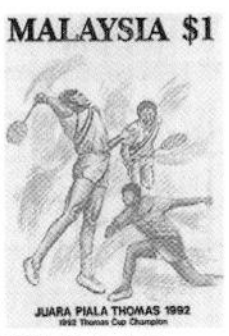

182 Badminton Players

1992. Malaysian Victory in Thomas Cup Badminton Championship. Multicoloured.

481	$1 Type **182**	90	1·40
482	$1 Thomas Cup and Malaysian flag	90	1·40
MS483	105×80 mm. $2 Winning team (76×28 mm)	1·75	2·75

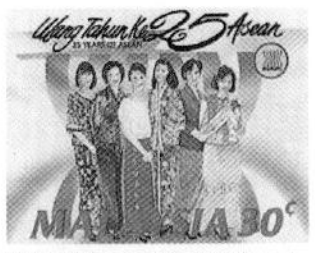

183 Women in National Costumes

1992. 25th Anniv of A.S.E.A.N. (Association of South East Asian Nations). Multicoloured.

484	30c. Type **183**	40	30
485	50c. Regional flowers	65	75
486	$1 Traditional architecture	1·25	2·25

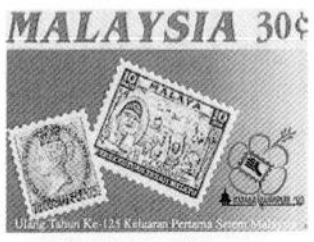

184 Straits Settlements 1867 1½c. and Malaysian Federation 1957 10c. Stamps

1992. 125th Anniv of Postage Stamps and "Kuala Lumpur '92" Int Stamp Exn. Multicoloured.

487	30c. Type **184**	45	90
488	30c. Straits Settlements 1867 2c. and Malaysia 1963 Federation Inauguration 12c.	45	90
489	50c. Straits Settlements 1868 4c. and Malaysia 1990 Kuala Lumpur 40c.	70	1·10
490	50c. Straits Settlements 1867 12c. and Malaysia "Kuala Lumpur '92" $2	70	1·10
MS491	120×92 mm. $2 "Kuala Lumpur '92" logo on Malaysian flag	1·75	2·75

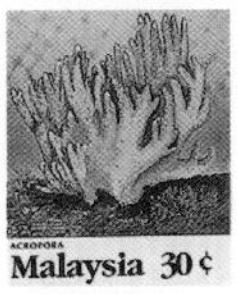

185 "Acropora"

1992. Marine Life (4th series). Corals. Multicoloured.

492	30c. Type **185**	80	1·10
493	30c. "Dendronephthya"	80	1·10
494	30c. "Dendrophyllia"	80	1·10
495	30c. "Sinularia"	80	1·10
496	30c. "Melithaea"	80	1·10
MS497	100×70 mm. $2 "Subergorgia" (38×28 mm)	2·50	4·00

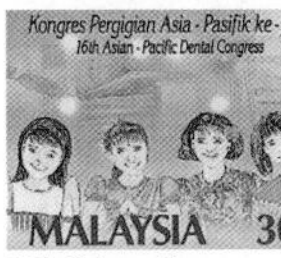

186 Girls smiling

1993. 16th Asian–Pacific Dental Congress. Multicoloured.

498	30c. Type **186**	50	75
499	30c. Girls smiling with koala bear	50	75
500	50c. Dentists with Japanese, Malaysian and South Korean flags	1·00	1·00
501	$1 Dentists with New Zealand, Thai, Chinese and Indonesian flags	1·25	2·00

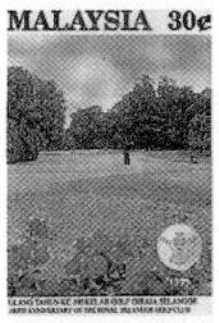

187 View of Golf Course

1993. Cent of Royal Selangor Golf Club. Multicoloured.

502	30c. Type **187**	60	20
503	50c. Old and new club houses	90	80
504	$1 Bunker on course (horiz)	2·00	3·50

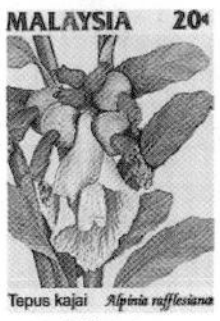

188 "Alpinia rafflesiana"

1993. Wildflowers (2nd series). Gingers. Multicoloured.

505	20c. Type **188**	40	10
506	30c. "Achasma megalocheilos"	50	20
507	50c. "Zingiber spectabile"	90	80
508	$1 "Costus speciosus"	1·75	3·00

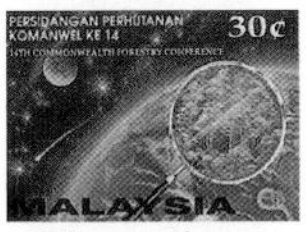

189 Forest under Magnifying Glass

1993. 14th Commonwealth Forestry Conference, Kuala Lumpur. Multicoloured.

509	30c. Type **189**	40	20
510	50c. Hand holding forest	65	70
511	$1 Forest in glass dome (vert)	1·40	2·75

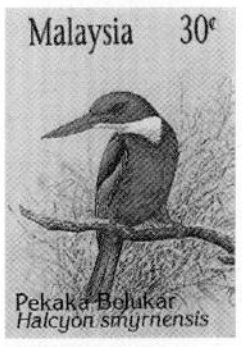

190 White-throated Kingfisher

1993. Kingfishers. Multicoloured.

512	30c. Type **190**	1·75	2·00

513	30c. Pair of blue-eared kingfishers	1·75	2·00
514	50c. Chestnut-collared kingfisher	2·00	2·25
515	50c. Pair of three-toed kingfishers	2·00	2·25

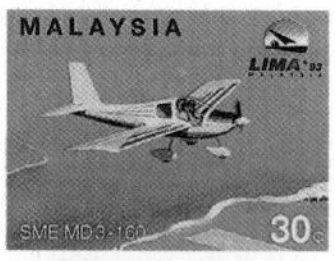

191 SME MD3-160m Light Aircraft

1993. Langkawi International Maritime and Aerospace Exhibition '93. Multicoloured.

516	30c. Type **191**	50	20
517	50c. Eagle X-TS light aircraft	80	90
518	$1 "Kasturi" (frigate)	1·50	2·75
MS519	120×80 mm. $2 Map of Langkawi	1·60	2·50

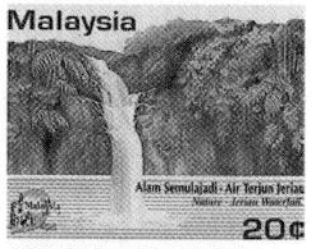

192 Jeriau Waterfalls

1994. Visit Malaysia. Multicoloured.

520	20c. Type **192**	50	10
521	30c. Flowers	50	25
522	50c. Turtle and fishes	75	65
523	$1 Orang-utan and other wildlife	1·60	2·50

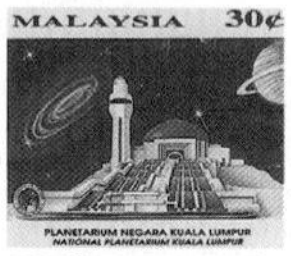

193 Planetarium and Planets

1994. National Planetarium, Kuala Lumpur. Multicoloured.

524	30c. Type **193**	50	25
525	50c. Static displays	65	80
526	$1 Planetarium auditorium	1·50	2·50

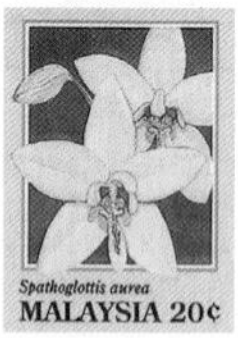

194 "Spathoglottis aurea"

1994. Orchids. Multicoloured.

527	20c. Type **194**	40	15
528	30c. "Paphiopedilum barbatum"	50	25
529	50c. "Bulbophyllum lobbii"	85	90
530	$1 "Aerides odorata"	1·40	2·75
MS531	120×82 mm. $2 "Grammatophyllum speciosum" (horiz)	2·50	4·00

No. **MS**531 also commemorates the "Hong Kong '94" International Stamp Exhibition.

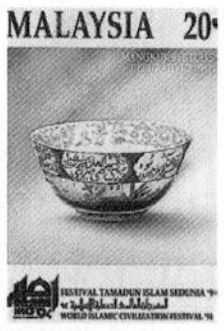

195 Decorative Bowl

1994. World Islamic Civilisation Festival '94, Kuala Lumpur. Multicoloured.

532	20c. Type **195**	20	10
533	30c. Celestial globe	30	20
534	50c. Dinar coins	50	65
535	$1 Decorative tile	95	2·00

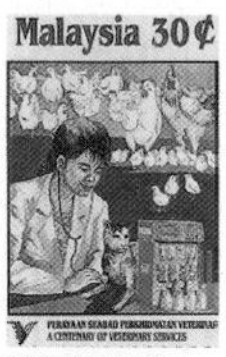

196 Flock of Chickens and Vet examining Cat

1994. Centenary of Veterinary Services. Multicoloured.

536	30c. Type **196**	50	25
537	50c. Vet in abattoir	70	55
538	$1 Herd of cows and veterinary equipment	1·00	2·25

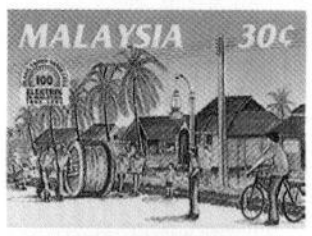

197 Workers laying Electric Cable

1994. Centenary of Electricity Supply. Multicoloured.

539	30c. Type **197**	40	65
540	30c. Illuminated city	40	65
541	$1 City of the future	1·00	2·00

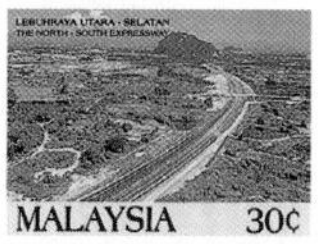

198 Expressway from the Air

1994. Opening of North–South Expressway. Multicoloured.

542	30c. Type **198**	30	20
543	50c. Expressway junction	45	50
544	$1 Expressway bridge	90	2·00

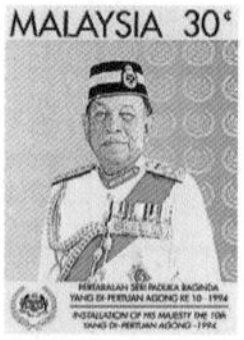

199 Sultan Tuanku Ja'afar

1994. Installation of Sultan Tuanku Ja'afar as Yang di-Pertuan Agong.

545	**199**	30c. multicoloured	30	20
546	**199**	50c. multicoloured	50	50
547	**199**	$1 multicoloured	85	2·00

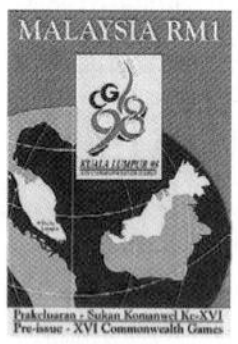

200 Map of Malaysia and Logo

1994. 16th Commonwealth Games, Kuala Lumpur (1998) (1st issue). Multicoloured.

548	$1 Type **200**	90	1·50
549	$1 Wira (games mascot) holding national flag	90	1·50

See also Nos. 575/6, 627/30, 668/71, **MS**678, 693/708 and **MS**715/16.

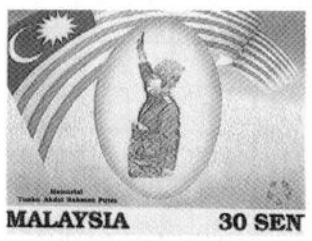

201 Tunku Abdul Rahman Putra and National Flag

1994. Fifth Death Anniv of Tunku Abdul Rahman Putra (former Prime Minister). Multicoloured.

550	30c. Type **201**	30	20
551	$1 The Residency, Kuala Lumpur	1·00	1·75

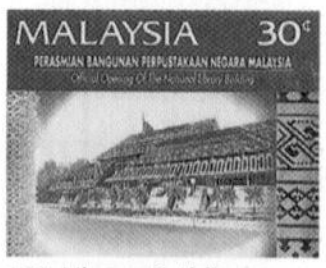

202 Library Building

1994. Opening of New National Library Building. Multicoloured.

552	30c. Type **202**	20	25
553	50c. Computer plan on screen	45	50
554	$1 Ancient Koran	1·00	2·00

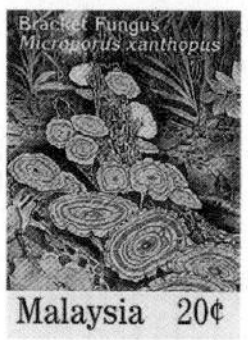

203 "Microporus xanthopus"

1995. Fungi. Multicoloured.

555	20c. Type **203**	15	10
556	30c. "Cookeina tricholoma"	25	20
557	50c. "Phallus indusiatus" ("Dictyophora phalloidea")	45	55
558	$1 "Ramaria sp."	90	2·75

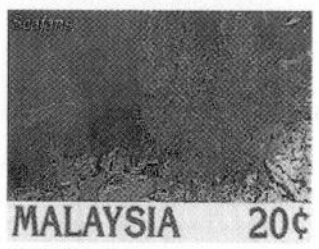

204 Seafans

1995. Marine Life (5th series). Corals. Mult.

559	20c. Type **204**	1·00	1·50
560	20c. Feather stars	1·00	1·50
561	30c. Cup coral	1·00	1·50
562	30c. Soft coral	1·00	1·50

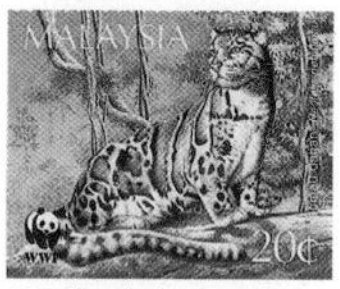

205 Clouded Leopard on Branch

1995. Endangered Species. Clouded Leopard. Multicoloured.

563	20c. Type **205**	70	35
564	30c. With cubs	80	40
565	50c. Crouched on branch	1·00	90
566	$1 Climbing tree	1·50	2·25

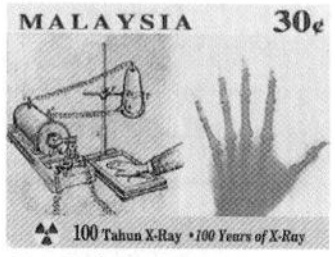

206 Early X-Ray Equipment and X-Ray of Hand

1995. Centenary of Discovery of X-Rays by Wilhelm Conrad Rontgen. Multicoloured.

567	30c. Type **206**	65	80
568	30c. Body scanner and brain scan	65	80
569	$1 Chest X-rays	1·50	2·00

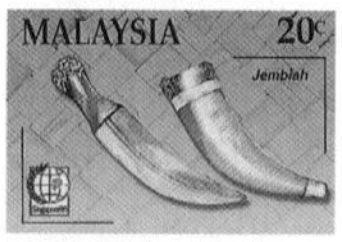

207 Jembiah (curved dagger)

1995. "Singapore '95" International Stamp Exhibition. Traditional Malay Weapons. Multicoloured.

570	20c. Type **207**	15	10
571	30c. Keris panjang (sword)	25	20
572	50c. Kerambit (curved dagger)	40	50
573	$1 Keris sundang (sword)	80	2·00
MS574	100×70 mm. $2 Ladig terus (dagger)	3·00	3·50

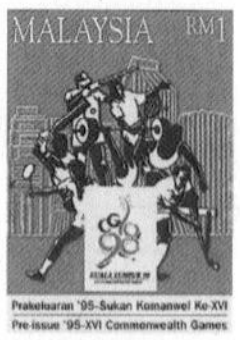

208 Badminton, Cricket, Shooting, Tennis, Hurdling, Hockey and Weightlifting

1995. 16th Commonwealth Games, Kuala Lumpur (1998) (2nd issue). Multicoloured.

575	$1 Type **208**	2·50	2·50
576	$1 Cycling, bowls, boxing, basketball, rugby, gymnastics and swimming	2·50	2·50

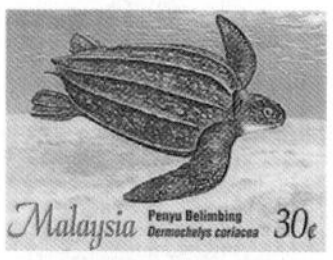

209 Leatherback Turtle ("Dermochelys coriacea")

1995. Turtles. Multicoloured.

577	30c. Type **209**	1·25	1·25
578	30c. Green turtle ("Chelonia mydas")	1·25	1·25

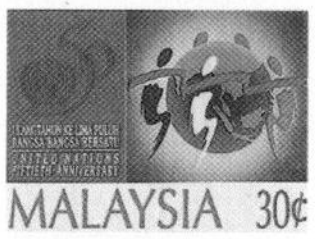

210 Anniversary Emblem and Symbolic People around Globe

1995. 50th Anniv of United Nations. Multicoloured.

579	30c. Type **210**	30	20
580	$1 United Nations emblem	70	1·50

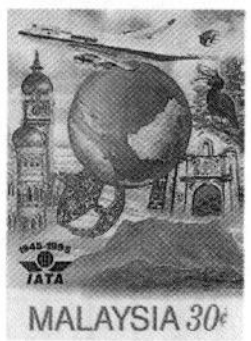

211 Boeing 747, Globe, Emblem and Malaysian Scenes

1995. 50th Anniv of International Air Transport Association. Designs each showing Boeing 747 and Globe. Multicoloured.

581	30c. Type **211**	60	70
582	30c. Asian and Australasian scenes	60	70
583	50c. European and African scenes	80	1·00
584	50c. North and South American scenes	80	1·00

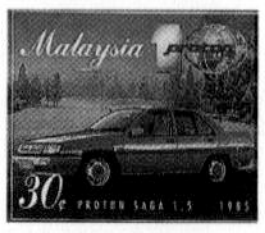

212 Proton "Saga 1.5" Saloon, 1985

1995. Tenth Anniv of Proton Cars. Multicoloured.

585	30c. Type **212**	70	90
586	30c. "Iswara 1.5" aeroback, 1992	70	90
587	30c. "Iswara 1.5" saloon, 1992	70	90
588	30c. "Wira 1.6" saloon, 1993	70	90
589	30c. "Wira 1.6" aeroback, 1993	70	90
590	30c. Proton rally car, 1994	70	90
591	30c. "Satria 1.6" hatchback, 1994	70	90
592	30c. "Perdana 2.0" saloon, 1995	70	90
593	30c. "Wira 1.6" aeroback, 1995	70	90
594	30c. "Wira 1.8" saloon, 1995	70	90

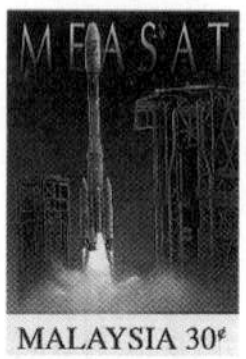

213 "Ariane 4" Launch Rocket

1996. Launch of MEASAT I (Malaysia East Asia Satellite). Multicoloured.

595	30c. Type **213**	25	20
596	50c. Satellite over Eastern Asia	40	45
597	$1 Satellite Earth station, Langkawi	90	2·00
MS598	100×70 mm. $5 Satellite orbiting Globe (hologram) (horiz)	7·00	8·00

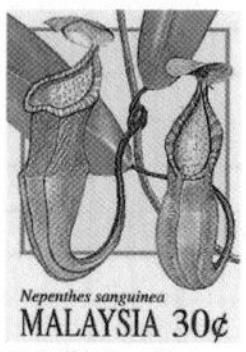

214 "Nepenthes sanguinea"

1996. Pitcher Plants. Multicoloured.

599	30c. Type **214**	25	45
600	30c. "Nepenthes macfarlanei"	25	45
601	50c. "Nepenthes rajah"	35	55
602	50c. "Nepenthes lowii"	35	55

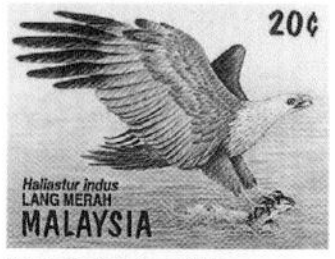

215 Brahminy Kite

1996. Birds of Prey. Multicoloured.

603	20c. Type **215**	45	20
604	30c. Crested serpent eagle	60	25

605	50c. White-bellied sea eagle	90	75
606	$1 Crested hawk eagle	1·40	2·50
MS607	100×70 mm. $2 Blyth's Hawk Eagle (vert)	3·50	4·00

No. **MS**607 also includes the "CHINA '96" 9th Asian International Stamp Exhibition logo on the sheet margin.

216 Family, Globe and Burning Drugs

1996. International Day against Drug Abuse and Illicit Trafficking. Multicoloured.

608	30c. Type 216	65	70
609	30c. Sporting activities	65	70
610	$1 Family and rainbow	1·25	2·00

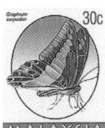

217 "Graphium sarpedon"

1996. "ISTANBUL '96" International Stamp Exhibition. Butterflies. Multicoloured.

611	30c. Type 217	1·25	1·25
612	30c. "Terinos terpander"	1·25	1·25
613	30c. "Melanocyma faunula"	1·25	1·25
614	30c. "Trogonoptera brookiana"	1·25	1·25
615	30c. "Delias hyparete"	1·25	1·25

218 Kuala Lumpur Tower

1996. Opening of Kuala Lumpur Telecommunications Tower. Multicoloured.

616	30c. Type 218	20	20
617	50c. Diagram of top of tower	30	35
618	$1 Kuala Lumpur Tower at night	80	1·75
MS619	70×100 mm. $2 Top of Kuala Lumpur Tower (different) (vert)	1·50	2·50

219 C.A.P.A. Logo on Kite

1996. 14th Conference of the Confederation of Asian and Pacific Accountants. Multicoloured.

| 620 | 30c. Type 219 | 25 | 20 |
| 621 | $1 Globe and C.A.P.A. logo | 75 | 1·40 |

1996. "TAIPEI '96" 10th Asian International Stamp Exhibition. As No. **MS**619, but with exhibition logo added to bottom right-hand corner of sheet.

| MS622 | 70×100 mm. $2 Top of Kuala Lumpur Tower (vert) | 1·50 | 2·25 |

220 Model of D.N.A. Molecule

1996. Opening of National Science Centre, Kuala Lumpur. Multicoloured.

623	30c. Type 220	25	20
624	50c. Planetary model and Science Centre	40	40
625	$1 National Science Centre	90	1·50

221 Slow Loris

1996. Stamp Week. Wuildlife. Sheet 165×75 mm, containing T 221 and similar multicoloured designs.

| MS626 | 20s. Type 221; 50s. Prevost's squirrel; 50s. Atlas moth; 1r. Rhinoceros hornbill (60×30 mm); 1r. White-handed gibbon (30×60 mm); 2r. Banded palm civet (60×30 mm) | 3·25 | 4·00 |

222 Running

1996. 16th Commonwealth Games, Kuala Lumpur (1998) (3rd issue). Multicoloured.

627	30s. Type 222	35	55
628	30s. Hurdling	35	55
629	50s. High jumping	45	65
630	50s. Javelin	45	65

223 Pygmy Blue Flycatcher

1997. Highland Birds. Multicoloured.

631	20s. Type 223	45	20
632	30s. Silver-eared mesia	55	25
633	50s. Black-sided flower-pecker	70	70
634	1r. Scarlet sunbird	1·10	1·75

1997. "HONG KONG '97" International Stamp Exhibition. As No. **MS**626, but with exhibition logo added to top sheet margin.

| MS635 | 165×75 mm. 20s. Type 221; 30s. Prevost's squirrel; 50s. Atlas moth; 1r. Rhinoceros hornbill (60×30 mm); 1r. White-handed gibbon (30×60 mm); 2r. Banded palm civet (60×30 mm) | 5·50 | 6·50 |

224 Transit Train leaving Station

1997. Opening of Kuala Lumpur Light Rail Transit System. Multicoloured.

| 636 | 30s. Type 224 | 1·25 | 1·00 |
| 637 | 30s. Trains in central Kuala Lumpur | 1·25 | 1·00 |

225 Bowler

1997. International Cricket Council Trophy, Kuala Lumpur. Multicoloured.

638	30s. Type 225	45	15
639	30s. Batsman	60	55
640	1r. Wicket-keeper	1·10	1·75

226 Boeing 747-400 over World Map

1997. 50th Anniv of Aviation in Malaysia. Multicoloured.

641	30s. Type 226	65	15
642	50s. Boeing 747-400 over Kuala Lumpur	1·10	60
643	1r. Tail fins of four airliners	1·50	2·25

227 "Schima wallichii"

1997. Highland Flowers. Multicoloured.

644	30s. Type 227	65	80
645	30s. "Aeschynanthus longicalyx"	65	80
646	30s. "Aeschynanthus speciosa"	65	80
647	30s. "Phyllagathis tuberculata"	65	80
648	30s. "Didymocarpus quinquevulnerus"	65	80

228 World Youth Football Championship Mascot

1997. Ninth World Youth Football Championship, Malaysia. Multicoloured.

649	30s. Type 228	30	10
650	50s. Football and players	45	35
651	1r. Map of Malaysia and football	1·00	1·75

229 Members of First Conference, 1897

1997. Centenary of Rulers' Conference. Multicoloured.

652	30s. Type 229	20	10
653	50s. State emblem	40	45
654	1r. Seal and press	80	1·75

230 A.S.E.A.N. Logo and Ribbons

1997. 30th Anniv of Association of South-east Asian Nations. Multicoloured.

655	30s. Type 230	65	10
656	50s. "30" enclosing logo	1·00	55
657	1r. Chevrons and logo	1·50	2·00

231 "Tubastrea sp."

1997. International Year of the Coral Reefs. Multicoloured.

658	20s. Type 231	30	15
659	30s. "Melithaea sp."	35	15
660	50s. "Aulostomus chinensis"	45	40
661	1r. "Symphillia sp."	70	1·40
MS662	70×100 mm. 2r. Green Turtle (horiz)	2·00	3·00

232 Women Athletes, Scientist and Politician

1997. 20th International Pan-Pacific and South-east Asia Women's Association Conference, Kuala Lumpur. Multicoloured.

| 663 | 30s. Type 232 | 40 | 50 |
| 664 | 30s. Family and house | 40 | 50 |

233 1867 12c. on 4 anna with Malacca Postmark

1997. "Malpex '97" Stamp Exhibition, Kuala Lumpur. 50th Anniv of Organised Philately. Sheet 120×70 mm, containing T 233 and similar diamond-shaped designs. Multicoloured.

| MS665 | 20s. Type 233; 30s. 1997 Highland Birds set; 50s. 1996 Wildlife miniature sheet seen through magnifying glass; 1r. 1867 cover to Amoy | 3·00 | 3·50 |

234 Group of 15 Emblem

1997. Seventh Summit Conference of the Group of 15, Kuala Lumpur. Multicoloured.

| 666 | 30s. Type 234 | 15 | 10 |
| 667 | 1r. Flags of member countries | 1·25 | 1·50 |

235 Hockey

1997. 16th Commonwealth Games, Kuala Lumpur (1998) (4th issue). Multicoloured.

668	30s. Type 235	85	85
669	30s. Netball	85	85
670	50s. Cricket	1·25	1·25
671	50s. Rugby	1·25	1·25

236 False Gharial

1997. Stamp Week '97. Endangered Wildlife. Sheet 165×75 mm, containing T **236** and similar multicoloured designs.

| MS672 | 20s. Type 236; 30s. Western tarsier (vert); 50s. Indian sambar (vert); 2r. Crested wood partridge; 2r. Malayan bony-tongue (fish) | 2·50 | 3·25 |

1997. "INDEPEX '97" International Stamp Exhibition, New Delhi. As No. **MS**665, but with exhibition logo added to the sheet margin, in gold, at bottom right.

| MS673 | 120×70 mm. 20s. Type 233; 30s. 1997 Highlands Bird set; 50s. 1996 Wildlife miniature sheet seen through magnifying glass; 1r. 1867 cover to Amoy | 1·25 | 2·00 |

237 Kundang

1998. Fruit. Multicoloured.

674	20s. Type 237	15	15
675	30s. Sentul	20	15
676	50s. Pulasan	30	25
677	1r. Asam gelugur	70	1·60

238 Swimming Complex

1998. 16th Commonwealth Games, Kuala Lumpur (5th issue). Venues. Sheet 120×80 mm, containing T **238** and similar horiz designs. Multicoloured.

| MS678 | 20s. Type 238; 30s. Hockey Stadium; 50s. Indoor Stadium; 1r. Main Stadium | 1·75 | 2·50 |

239 Mas (coin) from Trengganu, 1793–1808

1998. Gold coins. Multicoloured.

679	20s. Type 239	25	15
680	30s. Kupang from Kedah, 1661–1687	25	15
681	50s. Kupang from Johore, 1597–1615	45	35
682	1r. Kupang from Kelantan, 1400–1780	60	1·50

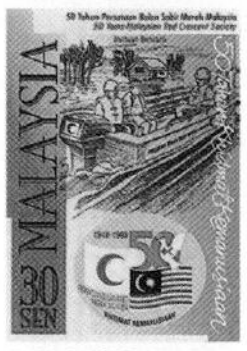

240 Red Crescent Ambulance Boat and Emblem

1998. 50th Anniv of Malaysian Red Crescent Society. Multicoloured.

683	30s. Type **240**	40	10
684	1r. Ambulance and casualty	1·25	1·60

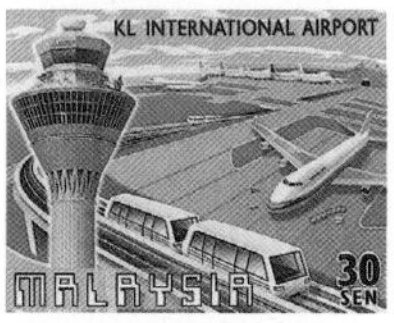

241 Transit Train and Boeing 747-400 at Airport

1998. Opening of Kuala Lumpur International Airport. Designs showing control tower. Multicoloured.

685	30s. Type **241**	50	10
686	50s. Airport Terminals	85	60
687	1r. Airliner in flight	1·75	2·25
MS688	119×70 mm. 2r. Globe and control tower (22×32 mm)	2·25	2·75

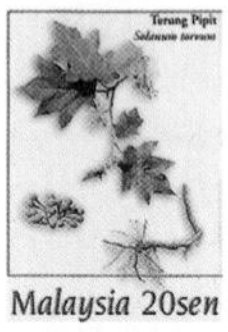

242 "Solanum torvum"

1998. Medicinal Plants. Multicoloured.

689	20s. Type **242**	20	15
690	30s. "Tinospora crispa"	25	10
691	50s. "Jatropha podagrica"	45	35
692	1r. "Hibiscus rosa-sinensis"	80	1·60

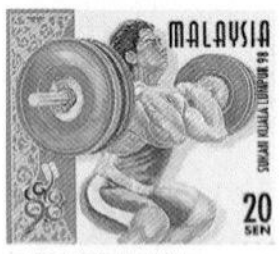

243 Weightlifting

1998. 16th Commonwealth Games, Kuala Lumpur, Malaysia (5th issue). Sports. Multicoloured.

693	20s. Type **243**	35	40
694	20s. Badminton	35	40
695	20s. Netball	35	40
696	20s. Shooting	35	40
697	30s. Men's hockey	40	45
698	30s. Women's hockey	40	45
699	30s. Cycling	40	45
700	30s. Bowls	40	45
701	50s. Gymnastics	40	45
702	50s. Cricket	40	45
703	50s. Rugby	40	45
704	50s. Running	40	45
705	1r. Swimming	40	55
706	1r. Squash	40	55
707	1r. Boxing	40	55
708	1r. Ten-pin bowling	40	55

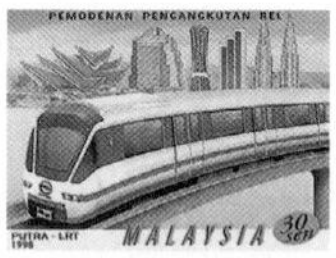

244 L.R.T. "Putra" Type Train

1998. Modern Kuala Lumpur Rail Transport. Multicoloured.

709b	30s. Type **244**	65	15
710b	50s. L.R.T. "Star" type train	55	35
711	1r. K.T.M. commuter train	75	1·50

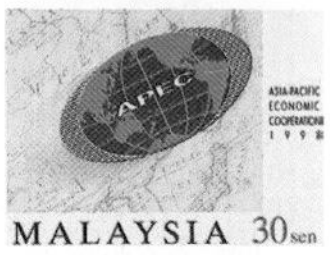

245 Globe and A.P.E.C. Logo

1998. Asia–Pacific Econmic Co-operation Conf. Multicoloured.

712b	30s. Type **245**	30	10
713	1r. Business meeting and computer office	70	1·25

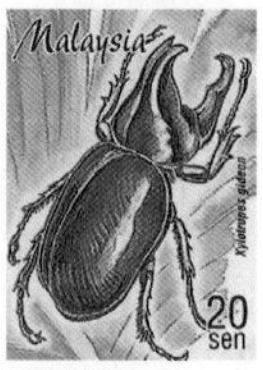

246 "Xylotrupes gideon"

1998. Stamp Week '98. Malaysian Insects. Sheet 165×75 mm, containing T **246** and similar multicoloured designs.

MS714	20s. Type **246**; 30s. "Pomponia imperatoria"; 50s. "Phyllium pulchrifolium"; 2r. "Hymenopus coronatus" (43×27 mm); 2r. "Macrolyristes corporalis" (43×27 mm)	3·00	3·75

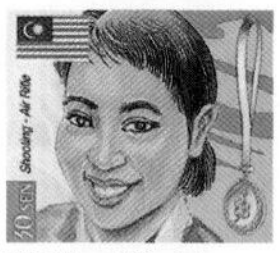

247 Nural Hudda (Women's Air Rifle Shooting)

1998. 16th Commonwealth Games, Kuala Lumpur (7th issue). Malaysian Gold Medal Winners. Two miniature sheets, each 160×125 mm, containing multicoloured designs as T **247**.

MS715	2r. Malaysian badminton team celebrating (128×80 mm)	3·50	4·00
MS716	30s. Type **247**; 30s. Sapok Biki (48kg Boxing); 30s. G. Saravanan (50km Walk); 30s. Muhamad Hidayat Hamidon (69kg Weightlifting); 50s. Kenny Ang and Ben Heng (Tenpin Bowling Men's Doubles); 50s. Kenny Ang (Tenpin Bowling Men's Singles); 50s. Choong Tan Fook and Lee Wan Wah (Badminton Men's Doubles); 50s. Wong Choon Hann (Badminton Men's Singles); 1r. Women's Rhythmic Gymnastics team (63×26 mm)	6·00	7·50

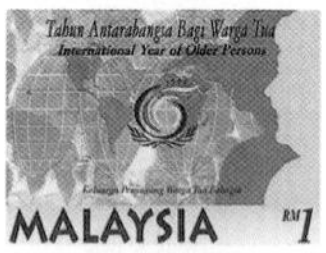

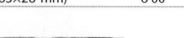

248 Profile of Elderly Couple, World Map and Emblem

1999. International Year of the Older Person. Multicoloured.

717	1r. Type **248**	70	1·00
718	1r. Four silhouettes of elderly people, world map and emblem	70	1·00

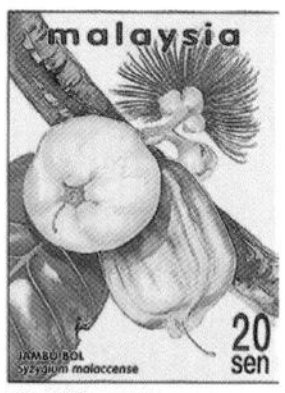

249 "Syzygium malaccense"

1999. Rare Fruits of Malaysia. Multicoloured.

719	20s. Type **249**	25	15
720	30s. "Garcinia prainiana"	30	15
721	50s. "Mangifera caesia"	40	30
722	1r. "Salacca glabrescens"	70	1·25

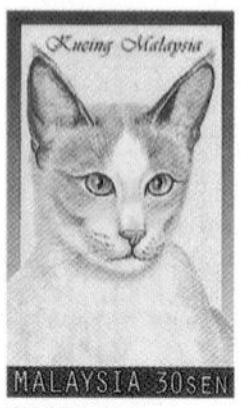

250 Kucing Malaysia Cat

1999. Malaysian Cats. Multicoloured.

727	30s. Type **250**	30	15
728	50s. Siamese	45	35
729	1r. Abyssinian	80	1·25
MS730	Two sheets, each 81×90 mm. (a) 1r. British shorthair; 1r. Scottish fold. (B) 1r. Birman; 1r. Persian Set of 2 sheets	2·00	2·50

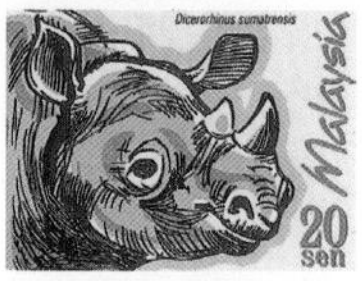

251 Sumatran Rhinoceros

1999. Protected Mammals of Malaysia (1st series). Multicoloured.

731	20s. Type **251**	50	15
732	30s. Panther	20	15
733	50s. Sun bear	25	25
734	1r. Indian elephant	65	1·00
739	2r. Orang-utan	1·50	2·00
MS740	119×80 mm. 2r. No. 739	1·50	2·00

See also Nos. 923/31.

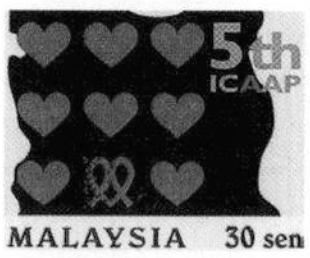

252 Hearts and AIDS Ribbons

1999. Fifth International Conference on AIDS in Asia and the Pacific. Each red, blue and black.

741	30s. Type **252**	35	15
742	50s. Fragmenting and stylized AIDS ribbons	55	45
743	1r. Two AIDS ribbons	90	1·50

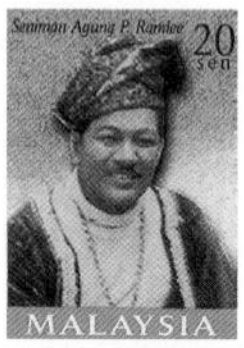

253 P. Ramlee in Traditional Dress

1999. 70th Birth Anniv of P. Ramlee (actor and film director) Commemoration. (a) Multicoloured.

744	20s. Type **253**	55	15
745	30s. Receiving an award	65	15
746	50s. Playing part of soldier in film	85	55
747	1r. Using film camera	1·40	1·60
MS748a	Two sheets, each 100×70 mm. (a) 1r. Wearing check shirt. (b) 1r. In traditional dress Set of 2 sheets	15·00	15·00

(b) Each brown, light brown and black.

749	30s. In traditional dress	1·25	1·40
750	30s. With hands raised	1·25	1·40
751	30s. Singing into microphone	1·25	1·40
752	30s. Wearing army uniform	1·25	1·40

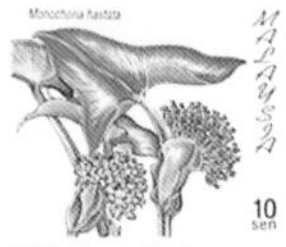

254 *Monochoria hastoria* (water plant)

1999. Freshwater Fish (2nd series). Multicoloured.

753	10s. Type **254**	20	30
754	10s. *Trichopsis vittatus*	20	30
755	15s. *Limnocharis flava* (water plant)	20	30
756	15s. *Betta imbellis*	20	30
757	25s. *Nymphaea pubescens* (water plant)	30	40
758	25s. *Trichogaster trichopterus*	30	40
759	50s. *Eichhornia crassipes* (water plant)	45	50
760	50s. *Sphaerichthys osphromenoides*	45	50
761	50s. *Ipomea aquatica* (water plant)	45	50
762	50s. *Helostoma temmincki*	45	50

No. 760 is inscribed "Sphaerichthys osphronemodies" in error.

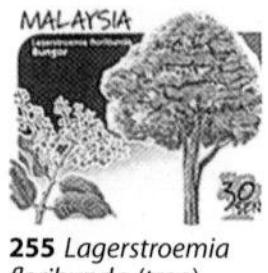

255 *Lagerstroemia floribunda* (tree)

1999. Trees of Malaysia. Multicoloured.

763	30s. Type **255**	45	70
764	30s. *Elateriospermum tapos*	45	70
765	30s. *Dryobalanops aromatica*	45	70
766	30s. *Alstonia angustiloba*	45	70
767	30s. *Fagraea fragrans*	45	70

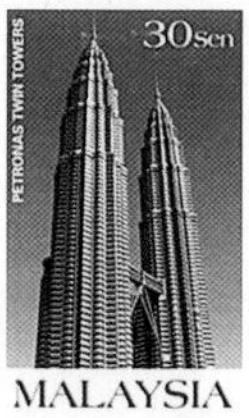

256 Petronas Twin Towers, Kuala Lumpur

1999. Completion of Petronas Twin Towers Building, Kuala Lumpur. Multicoloured (except 50c.).

768	30s. Type **256**	35	15
769	50s. Construction sketches (blue, violet and black)	45	40
770	1r. Twin Towers at night	80	1·25
MS771	100×75 mm. 5r. Hologram of Twin Towers (30×50 mm)	4·00	4·50

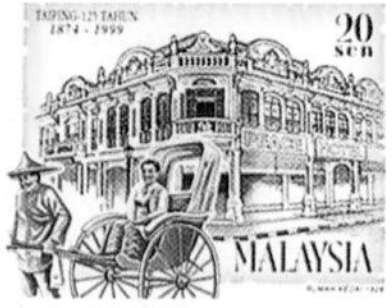

257 Peace Hotel and Rickshaw

1999. 125th Anniv of Taiping, Perak. Multicoloured.

772	20s. Type **257**	30	15
773	30s. Town Hall and 1930s car	30	15
774	50s. Railway Station	1·25	65
775	1r. Airport	1·50	1·75
MS776	120×69 mm. 2r. Perak Museum and horse-drawn carriage	4·50	5·00

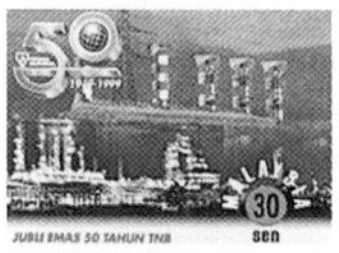

258 Power Station at Night

1999. 50th Anniv of Tenaga Nasional Berhad (electricity generating company). Multicoloured.

777	30s. Type **258**	35	15
778	50s. Control room and pylon	50	35
779	1r. Kuala Lumpur skyline at night	90	1·50
MS780	Two sheets, each 69×99 mm. (a) 1r. Electric cart. (b) 1r. Pylon Set of 2 sheets	2·00	2·50

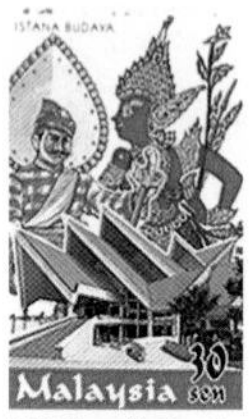

259 New National Theatre and Traditional Characters

1999. Opening of New National Theatre, Kuala Lumpur. Multicoloured.

781	30s. Type **259**	30	15
782	50s. New National Theatre and horseman	55	40
783	1r. New National Theatre and traditional musician	90	1·25

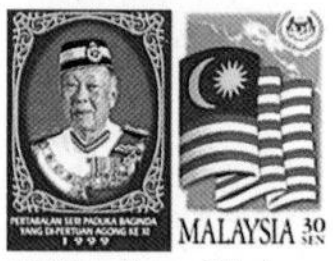

260 New Yang di-Pertuan Agong and Malaysian Flag

1999. Installation of Sultan Salahuddin Abdul Aziz Shah of Selangor as Yang di-Pertuan Agong. (a) Horiz designs as T 260. Multicoloured.

784	30s. Type **260**	30	15
785	50s. Yang di-Pertuan Agong and Palace	45	30
786	1r. Yang di-Pertuan Agong and Parliament Buildings	90	1·25

(b) Vert designs, 24×29 mm, showing portrait only.

787	(30s.) multicoloured (purple frame)	75	90
788	(30s.) multicoloured (yellow frame)	75	90
789	(30s.) multicoloured (blue frame)	75	90

Nos. 787/9 are inscribed "BAYARAN POS TEMPATAN HINGGA 20GM" and were valid on local mail weighing no more than 20 gm.

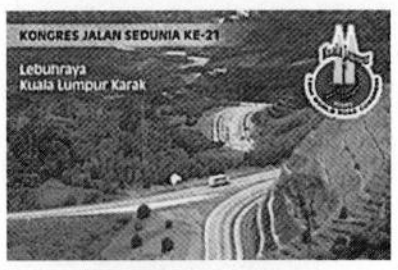

261 Motorway Junction outside Kuala Lumpur

1999. 21st World Road Congress, Kuala Lumpur. Multicoloured.

790	30s. Type **261**	35	15
791	50s. Damansara Puchong Bridge at night	50	30
792	1r. Aerial view of motorway junction, Selatan	90	1·25

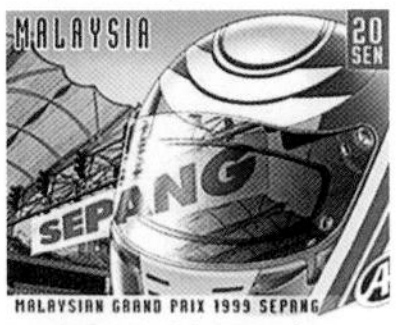

262 Driver's Helmet and Canopy Tower, Formula 1 Circuit, Sepang

1999. Malaysian Grand Prix, Sepang. Multicoloured. (a) Designs including driver's helmet.

793	20s. Type **262**	40	20
794	30s. Central Grandstand	50	20
795	50s. Formula 1 racing car	75	50
796	1r. Formula 1 racing car from Red Bull team	1·25	1·50

(b) Scenes from Sepang Formula 1 Circuit.

797	20s. Canopy Tower and Central Grandstand	40	50
798	30s. Pit building	50	50
799	50s. Wheel-change in pits	75	90
800	1r. Race in progress	1·25	1·40

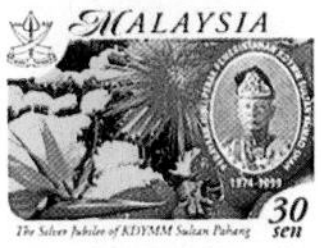

263 Sultan Haji Ahmad Shah and Flowers

1999. 25th Anniv of Installation of Sultan of Pahang. Multicoloured.

801	30s. Type **263**	55	60
802	30s. Butterfly and motorway	55	60
803	30s. Diver and beach	55	60
804	30s. Power station	55	60
805	30s. Mosque	55	60

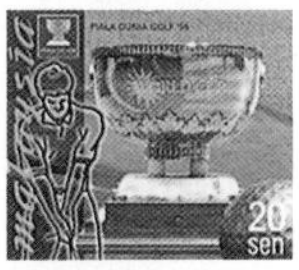

264 World Cup

1999. World Cup Golf Championship, Mines Resort City. Multicoloured.

806	20s. Type **264**	35	15
807	30s. Emblem on golf ball	35	15
808	50s. Fairway	60	45
809	1r. First hole and club house	1·10	1·40

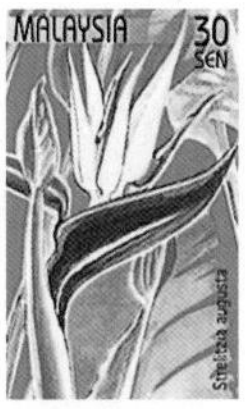

265 *Strelitzia augusta*

1999. Stamp Week '99. Heliconias. Multicoloured.

814	30s. Type **265**	55	55
815	30s. *Heliconia rostrata*	55	55
816	30s. *Heliconia psittacorum* (yellow)	55	55
817	30s. *Heliconia stricta*	55	55
818	30s. *Musa violascens*	55	55
819	30s. *Strelitzia reginae*	55	55
820	30s. *Heliconia colganta*	55	55
821	30s. *Heliconia psittacorum* (white and pink)	55	55
822	30s. *Heliconia latispatha*	55	55
823	30s. *Phaeomeria speciosa*	55	55
MS824	198×136 mm. Nos. 814/23	5·00	5·50

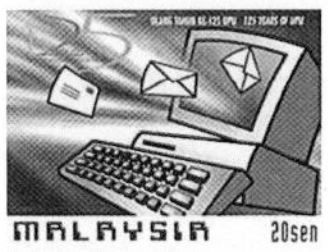

266 Letters and Computer Screen

1999. 125th Anniv of Universal Postal Union. Multicoloured.

825	20s. Type **266**	20	10
826	30s. Globe and Malaysian stamps	40	10
827	50s. World map and mail plane	1·00	70
828	1r. POS Malaysia emblem	1·25	1·60

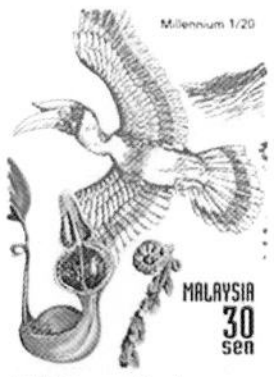

267 Fern, Pitcher Plant and Great Indian Hornbill

1999. New Millennium (1st issue). Land and History. Multicoloured (except No. MS839).

829	30s. Type **267**	50	60
830	30s. Ceramic pots and Mt. Kinabalu	50	60
831	30s. Frog and tualang (tree)	50	60
832	30s. Rolling rubber and palm trees	50	60
833	30s. Angelfish and sailing barge	50	60
834	30s. Mousedeer and traditional Malay building	50	60
835	30s. Ruler on elephant and Straits of Malacca	50	60
836	30s. Malay kris (sword) and junks	50	60
837	30s. Clock Tower, Kuala Lumpur, and A Famosa ruins	50	60
838	30s. Sailing boat and palm trees	50	60
MS839	120×80 mm. 1r. Traditional Malay sailing ship (horiz) (black and red)	2·50	2·75

2000. New Millennium (2nd issue). People and Achievements. As T **267**. Multicoloured.

840	30s. Iban playing sape and traditional costumes from East Malaysia	60	60
841	30s. Hurricane lamp, shell and couple from fishing village	60	60
842	30s. Doctor with patient and toddler with mother	60	60
843	30s. Badminton player and young Malaysians	60	60
844	30s. Man with kite and traditional dancers	60	60
845	30s. Motor cycle, car and motorway	60	60
846	30s. Butterfly, Sepang motor racing circuit and airport	60	60
847	30s. High speed train and Kuala Lumpur skyline	60	60
848	30s. Computer operator and mosque	60	60
849	30s. Lorry and container port	60	60
MS850	120×80 mm. 1r. Modern airliner (horiz)	2·50	2·75

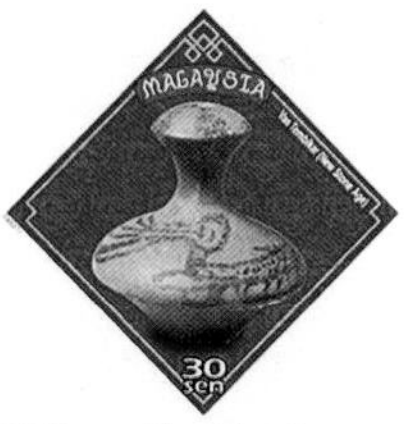

268 Pottery Vase (New Stone Age)

2000. Chinese New Year ("Year of the Dragon"). Artefacts and Fish. Multicoloured.

851	30s. Type **268**	60	60
852	30s. Dragon eaves tile (Western Han Dynasty)	60	60
853	30s. Bronze knocker base (Tang Dynasty)	60	60
854	30s. Jade sword pommel (Western Han Dynasty)	60	60
855	30s. Dragon statue (Tang Dynasty)	60	60
856	30s. Arawana (*Osteoglossum bicirrhosum*)	60	60
857	30s. Spotted barramundi (*Scleropages leichardti*)	60	60
858	30s. Asian bonytongue (red) (Scleropages formosus)	60	60
859	30s. Black arawana (*Osteoglossum ferrerirai*)	60	60
860	30s. Asian bonytongue (gold) (*Scleropages formosus*)	60	60
MS861	Two sheets, each 120×65 mm. (a) 1r. Dragon dance (square). (b) 1r. Dragon boat (square) Set of 2 sheets	2·25	3·00

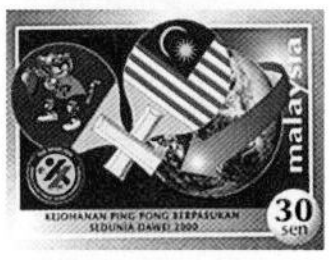

269 Table Tennis Bats and Globe

2000. World Table Tennis Championships, Bukit Jalil. Multicoloured.

862	30s. Type **269**	25	10
863	50s. Mascot and logo	45	35
864	1r. Table tennis bats and ball	75	1·10
MS865	100×70 mm. 1r. Mascot and table tennis table; 1r. Bats and table tennis table	1·25	1·75

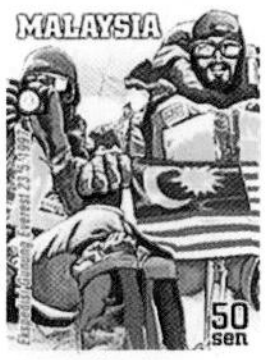

270 Malaysian Climbers on Mt. Everest

2000. New Millennium (3rd issue). Malaysian Triumphs. Two sheets, each 120×80 mm, containing T **270** and similar vert designs. Multicoloured.

MS866	(a) 50s. Type **270**; 50s. Hikers; 50s. Arctic expedition and Proton car. (B) 50s. Solo yachtsman Set of 2 sheets	3·25	3·50

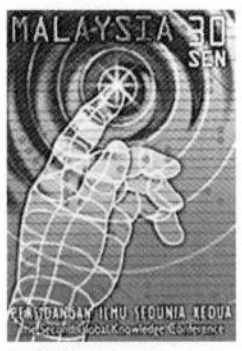

271 Outline Hand on Button

2000. Second Global Knowledge Conference, Kuala Lumpur. Multicoloured.

867	30s. Type **271**	55	60
868	30s. Outline globe	55	60
869	50s. Woman's silhouette	80	90
870	50s. Man's silhouette	80	90

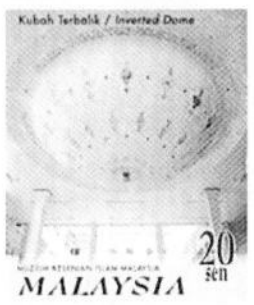

272 Internal Inverted Dome

2000. Islamic Arts Museum, Kuala Lumpur. Multicoloured.

871	20s. Type **272**	40	15
872	30s. Main dome of Museum	45	15
873	50s. Ottoman panel	65	45
874	1r. Ornate Mihrab	1·25	1·75

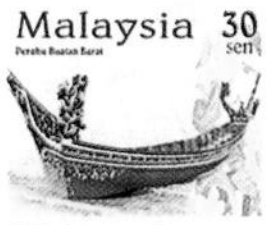

273 Buatan Barat Prahu

2000. Traditional Malaysian Prahus (canoes). Multicoloured.

875	30s. Type **273**	35	45
876	30s. Payang prahu (red and blue hull)	35	45
877	30s. Payang prahu (red, white and green hull)	35	45
878	30s. Burung prahu	35	45

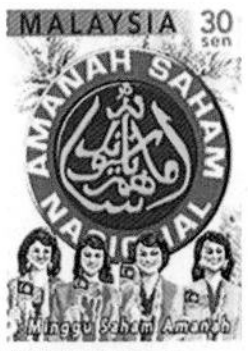

274 Unit Trust Emblem and Women with Flags

2000. Unit Trust Week. Multicoloured.

879	30s. Type **274**	50	10
880	50s. City skyline and Malaysians in traditional costume	70	50
881	1r. Map of South East Asia and Malaysians in traditional costume	1·40	1·75

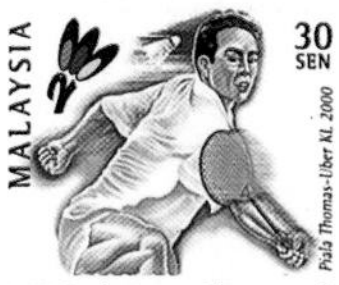

275 Badminton Player and Cup Logo

2000. Thomas Cup Badminton Championships, Bukit Jalil. Multicoloured.

882	30s. Type **275**	60	60
883	30s. Thomas Cup and flags	60	60
884	30s. Championship logo and mascot	60	60
885	30s. Uber Cup and flags	60	60
886	30s. Badminton player and mascot	60	60
MS887	120×80 mm. 1r. Thomas Cup (vert)	1·75	2·25

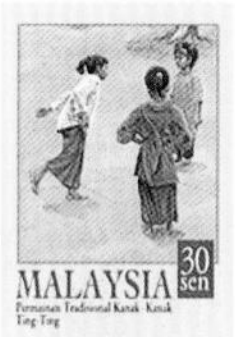

276 Children playing Ting Ting

2000. Children's Traditional Games (1st series). Multicoloured.

888	30s. Type **276**	80	80
889	30s. Tarik Upih	80	80
890	30s. Kite flying	80	80
891	30s. Marbles	80	80
892	30s. Bicycle rim racing	80	80

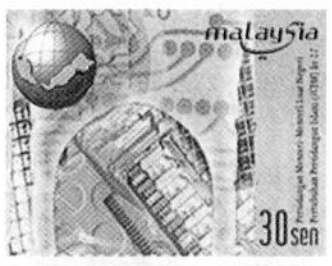

277 Aspects of Computer Technology

2000. 27th Islamic Foreign Ministers' Conference, Kuala Lumpur. Multicoloured.

898	30s. Type **277**	55	60
899	30s. Traditonal Islamic scrollwork	55	60
900	30s. Conference logo	55	60
901	30s. Early coin	55	60
902	30s. Pens and satellite photograph	55	60

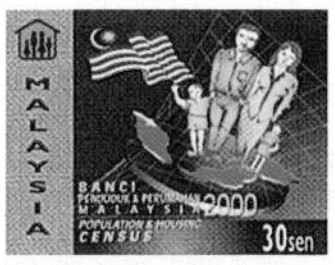

278 Malaysian Family on Map

2000. Population and Housing Census. Multicoloured.

903	30s. Type **278**	55	60
904	30s. Symbolic house	55	60
905	30s. People on pie-chart	55	60
906	30s. Diplomas and workers	55	60
907	30s. Male and female symbols	55	60

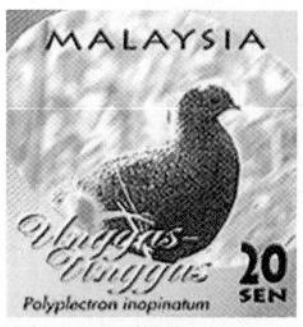

279 Rothchild's Peacock-pheasant

2000. Pheasants and Partridges. Multicoloured.

908	20s. Type **279**	40	20
909	30s. Crested argus (female)	45	20
910	50s. Great argus pheasant	65	50
911	1r. Crestless fireback pheasant	1·10	1·50
MS912	100×40 mm. 2r. Crested argus (male) (31×26 mm)	2·00	2·75

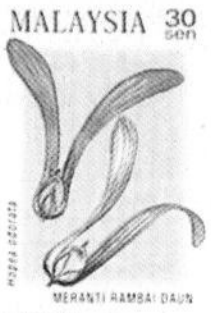

280 *Hopea odorata* (fruit)

2000. International Union of Forestry Research Organisations Conference, Kuala Lumpur. Multicoloured.

913	30s. Type **280**	75	75
914	30s. *Adenanthera pavonina* (seeds)	75	75
915	30s. *Shorea macrophylla* (seeds)	75	75
916	30s. *Dyera costulata* (fruits)	75	75
917	30s. *Alstonia angustiloba* (seeds)	75	75
MS918	Four sheets, each 92×71 mm. (a) Trees. 10s. *Fagraea fragrans*; 10s. *Dryobalanops aromatica*; 10s. *Terminalia catappa*; 10s. *Samanea saman*; 10s. *Dracontomelon dao*. (b) Leaves. 15s. *Heritiera javanica*; 15s. *Johannesteijsmannia altifrons*; 15s. *Macaranga gigantea*; 15s. *Licuala grandis*; 15s. *Endospermum diadenum*. (c). Bark. 25s. *Pterocymbium javanicum*; 25s. *Dryobalanops aromatica*; 25s. *Dipterocarpus costulatus*; 25s. *Shorea leprosula*; 25s. *Ochanostachys amentacea*. (d) Forest fauna. 50s. Indian flycatcher; 50s. Slow loris; 50s. Marbled cat; 50s. Common carp; 50s. Pit viper Set of 4 sheets	6·50	7·50

No. **MS**918 contains four sheets each of five 18×22 mm designs, and a label showing the Conference logo.

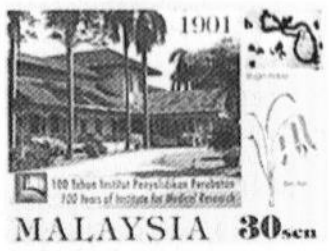

281 Institute in 1901, *Brugia malayi* and Beri-Beri

2000. Centenary of Institute for Medical Research. Multicoloured.

919	30s. Type **281**	60	10
920	50s. Institute in 1953, bacteria and mosquito	85	60
921	1r. Institute in 1976, chromatogram and Eurycoma longifolia	1·75	2·00
MS922	120×65 mm. 2r. DNA molecule	2·75	3·00

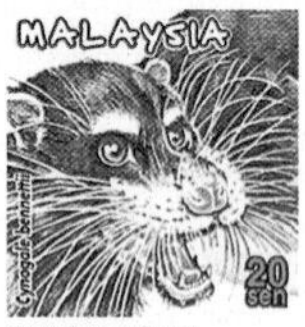

282 Otter Civet

2000. Protected Mammals of Malaysia (2nd series). Multicoloured.

923	20s. Type **282**	60	25
924	30s. Young otter civet	60	30
925	50s. Binturong on bank	75	50
926	1r. Head of binturong	1·40	1·60
927	30s. Hose's palm civet (*Hemigalus hosei*)	60	70
928	30s. Common palm civet (*Paradoxurus hermaphroditus*)	60	70
929	30s. Masked palm civet (Paguma larvata)	60	70
930	30s. Malay civet (Viverra tangalunga)	60	70
931	30s. Three-striped palm civet (*Arctogalidia trivirgata*)	60	70
MS932	140×80 mm. 1r. Banded palm civet; 1r. Banded linsang	2·75	3·00

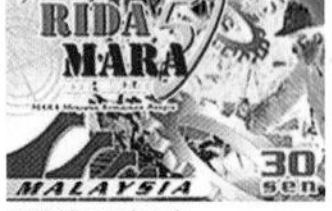

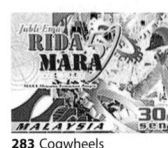

283 Cogwheels

2000. 50th Anniv of RIDA-MARA (Rural and Industrial Development Authority – Council for Indigenous People). Multicoloured.

933	30s. Type **283**	40	10
934	50s. Compasses and stethoscope	55	40
935	1r. Computer disk, book and mouse	1·00	1·40

2000. Children's Traditional Games (2nd series). As T **276**. Multicoloured.

936	20s. Bailing tin	50	60
937	20s. Top-spinning	50	60
938	30s. Sepak Raga	60	70
939	30s. Letup-Letup	60	70

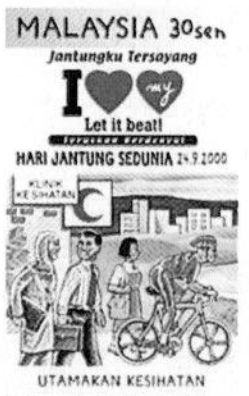

284 Cyclist and Pedestrians

2000. World Heart Day. Multicoloured.

940	30s. Type **284**	60	60
941	30s. Family at play	60	60
942	30s. Kite flying, football and no smoking sign	60	60
943	30s. Keep fit class	60	60
944	30s. Farmer, animals and food	60	60

Nos. 940/4 were printed together, se-tenant, with the backgrounds forming a composite design.

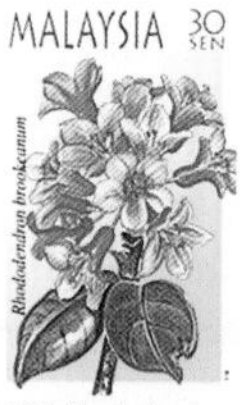

285 *Rhododendron brookeanum*

2000. Stamp Week 2000. Highland Flowers (2nd series). Multicoloured.

945	30s. Type **285**	40	50
946	30s. *Rhododendron jasminiflorum*	40	50
947	30s. *Rhododendron scortechinii*	40	50
948	30s. *Rhododendron pauciflorum*	40	50
949	30s. *Rhododendron crassifolium*	40	50
950	30s. *Rhododendron longiflorum*	40	50
951	30s. *Rhododendron javanicum*	40	50
952	30s. *Rhododendron variolosum*	40	50
953	30s. *Rhododendron acuminatum*	40	50
954	30s. *Rhododendron praetervisum*	40	50
955	30s. *Rhododendron himantodes*	40	50
956	30s. *Rhododendron maxwellii*	40	50
957	30s. *Rhododendron erocoides*	40	50
958	30s. *Rhododendron fallacinum*	40	50
MS959	55×90 mm. 1r. *Rhododendron malayanum*	1·25	1·75

No. 955 is inscribed "Rhodadendron", No. 957 "Ericoides", both in error.

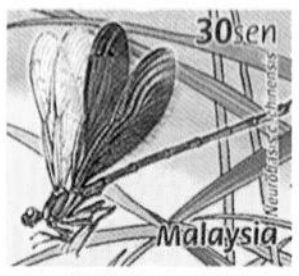

286 *Neurobasis c. chinensis*

2000. Dragonflies and Damselflies. Multicoloured.

960	30s. Type **286**	45	45
961	30s. *Aristocypha fenestrella* (blue markings on tail)	45	45
962	30s. *Vestalis gracilis*	45	45
963	30s. *Nannophya pymaea*	45	45
964	30s. *Aristocypha fenestrella* (white markings on tail)	45	45
965	30s. *Rhyothemis p. phyllis*	45	45
966	30s. *Crocothemis s. servilia*	45	45
967	30s. *Euphaea ochracea* (male)	45	45
968	30s. *Euphaea ochracea* (female)	45	45
969	30s. *Ceriagrion cerinorubellum*	45	45
970	(30s.) *Vestalis gracilis*	40	50
971	(30s.) *Crocothemis s. servilia* (male)	40	50
972	(30s.) *Trithemis aurora*	40	50
973	(30s.) *Pseudothemis jorina*	40	50
974	(30s.) *Diplacodes nebulosa*	40	50
975	(30s.) *Crocothemis s. servilia* (female)	40	50
976	(30s.) *Neurobasis c. chinensis* (male)	40	50
977	(30s.) *Burmagomphus divaricatus*	40	50
978	(30s.) *Ictinogomphus d. melaenops*	40	50
979	(30s.) *Orthetrum testaceum*	40	50
980	(30s.) *Trithemis festiva*	40	50
981	(30s.) *Brachythemis contaminata*	40	50
982	(30s.) *Neurobasis c. chinensis* (female)	40	50
983	(30s.) *Neurothemis fluctuans*	40	50
984	(30s.) *Acisoma panorpoides*	40	50
985	(30s.) *Orthetrum s. sabina*	40	50
986	(30s.) *Rhyothemis p. phyllis*	40	50
987	(30s.) *Rhyothemis obsolescens*	40	50
988	(30s.) *Neurothemis t. tulia*	40	50
989	(30s.) *Lathrecista a. asiatica*	40	50
990	(30s.) *Aethriamanta gracilis*	40	50
991	(30s.) *Diplacodes trivialis*	40	50
992	(30s.) *Neurothemis fulvia*	40	50
993	(30s.) *Rhyothemis triangularis*	40	50
994	(30s.) *Orthetrum glaucum*	40	50

Nos. 960/9 were issued togetther, *se-tenant*, and show the backgrounds forming a composite design.

Nos. 970/94 are inscribed "Bayaran Pos Tempatan Hingga 20gm". They were valid at 30s. for local mail up to 20 g.

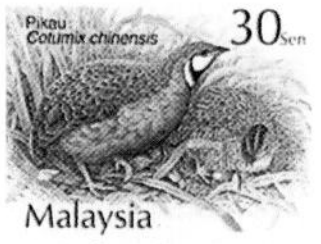

287 Indian Blue Quail

2001. Quails and Partridges. Multicoloured.

995	30s. Type **287**	60	20
996	50s. Sumatran hill partridge	1·00	65
997	1r. Bustard quail	1·75	2·00
MS998	100×170 mm. 2r. Chestnut-breasted tree partridge; 2r. Crimson-headed wood partridge	4·00	4·25

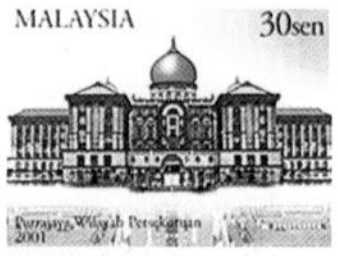

288 Federal Government Administrative Centre

2001. Formation of Putrajaya Federal Territory. Multicoloured.

999	30s. Type **288**	50	10
1000	1r. Government buildings and motorway bridge	2·00	2·25

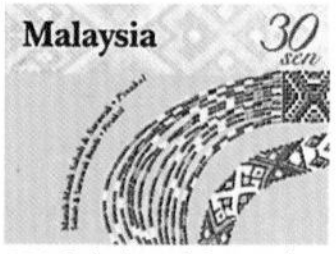

289 Sabah and Sarawak Beadwork

2001. Sabah and Sarawak Beadwork. Mult, background colours given.

1001	**289**	30s. green	50	55
1002	-	30s. blue	50	55
1003	-	30s. buff	50	55
1004	-	30s. red	50	55

DESIGN: Nos. 1001/4 Showing different styles of beadwork.

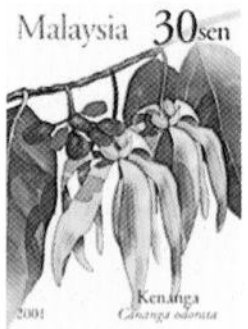

290 *Cananga odorata*

2001. Scented Flowers. Multicoloured.

1005	30s. Type **290**	50	10
1006	50s. *Mimusops elengi*	70	50
1007	1r. *Mesua ferrea*	1·40	1·75
MS1008	70×100 mm. 2r. *Muchelia champaca*	2·75	3·00

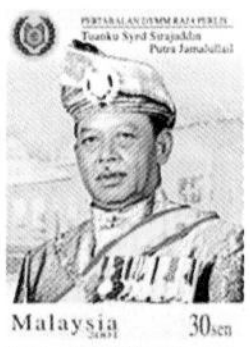

291 Raja Tuanku Syed Sirajuddin

2001. Installation of Tuanku Syed Sirajuddin as Raja of Perlis.

1009	**291**	30s. multicoloured	50	15
1010	**291**	50s. multicoloured	70	50
1011	**291**	1r. multicoloured	1·40	1·75
MS1012		100×70 mm. 2r. Raja Tuanku Syed Sirajuddin and Tengku Fauziah (horiz). Multicoloured	2·75	3·00

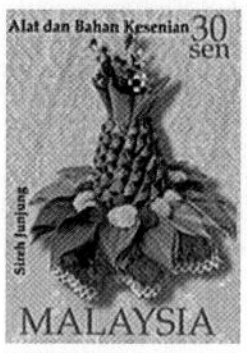

292 Beetlenut Leaf Arrangement

2001. Traditional Malaysian Artefacts. Multicoloured.

1013	30s. Type **292**	50	60
1014	30s. Baby carrier	50	60
1015	50s. Quail trap	80	90
1016	50s. Ember container	80	90

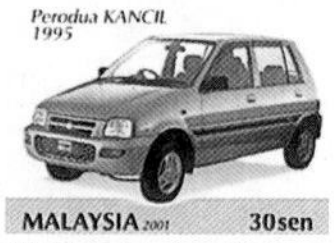

293 Perodua Kancil Car, 1995

2001. Malaysia-made Motor Vehicles. Multicoloured.

1017	30s. Type **293**	60	60
1018	30s. Proton Tiara, 1995	60	60
1019	30s. Perodua Rusa, 1995	60	60
1020	30s. Proton Putra, 1997	60	60
1021	30s. Inokom Permas, 1999	60	60
1022	30s. Perodua Kembara, 1999	60	60
1023	30s. Proton GTI, 2000	60	60
1024	30s. TD 2000, 2000	60	60
1025	30s. Perodua Kenari, 2000	60	60
1026	30s. Proton Waja, 2000	60	60

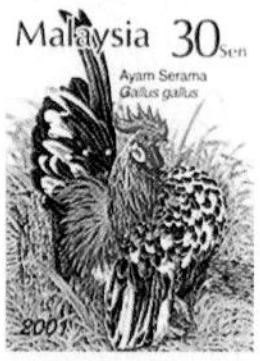

294 Serama Bantam Cock

2001. Malaysian Bantams. Multicoloured.

1027	30s. Type **294**	50	15
1028	50s. Kapan bantam cock	90	60
1029	1r. Serama bantam hen	1·60	1·75
MS1030	98×70 mm. 3r. Red junglefowl hens and chicks (44×34 mm)	4·50	4·75

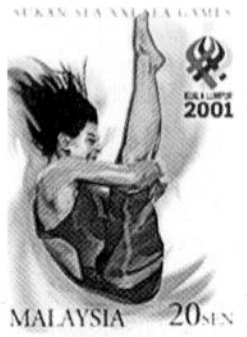

295 Diving

2001. 21st South East Asian Games, Kuala Lumpur. Multicoloured.

1031	20s. Type **295**	30	35
1032	30s. Rhythmic gymnastics	35	35
1033	50s. Bowling	50	70
1034	1r. Weightlifting	85	1·25
1035	2r. Cycling	2·00	2·25
MS1036	110×90 mm. 5r. Running	5·50	6·00

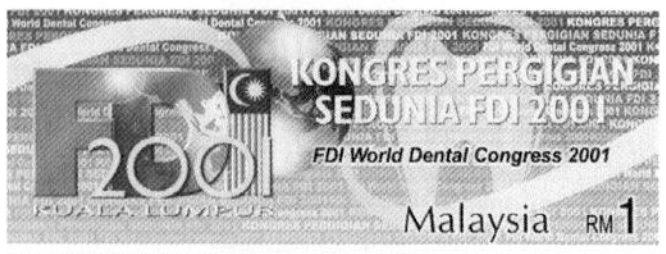

296 "F.D.I. 2001" Logo

2001. "F.D.I. 2001" World Dental Congress, Kuala Lumpur.

1037	**296**	1r. multicoloured	1·75	1·75

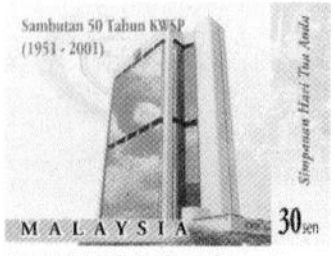

297 K.W.S.P. Headquarters, Kuala Lumpur

2001. 50th Anniv of Employees' Provident Fund ("Kumpulan Wang Simpanan Pekerja"). Multicoloured.

1038	30s. Type **297**	30	15
1039	50s. Column chart on coins and banknotes	45	40
1040	1r. Couple with K.W.S.P. logo	90	1·25

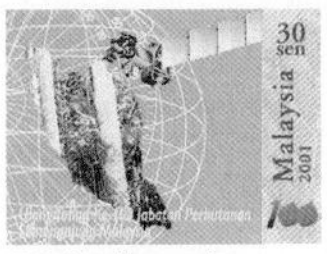

298 Satellite and Rainforest in Shape of Malaya Peninsula

2001. Centenary of Peninsular Malaysia Forestry Department. Multicoloured.

1041	30s. Type **298**	55	15
1042	50s. Cross-section through forest and soil	75	50
1043	1r. Newly-planted forest	1·50	2·00

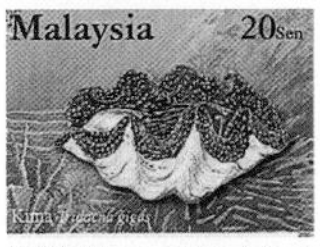

299 *Tridacna gigas* (clam)

2001. Stamp Week. Endangered Marine Life. Multicoloured.

1044	20s. Type **299**	40	15
1045	30s. *Hippocampus sp.* (seahorse)	50	15
1046	50s. *Oreaster occidentalis* (starfish)	70	50
1047	1r. *Cassis cornu* (shell)	1·40	2·00
MS1048	100×70 mm. 3r. Dugong	2·75	3·25

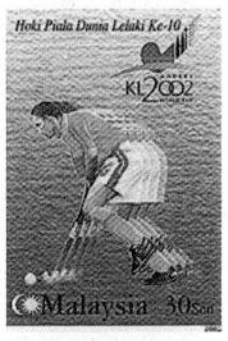

300 Hockey Player in Orange

2002. Tenth Hockey World Cup, Kuala Lumpur. Multicoloured.

1049	30s. Type **300**	50	15
1050	50s. Goalkeeper	70	55
1051	1r. Hockey player in yellow	1·50	1·50
MS1052	100×70 mm. 3r. Hockey player in blue (30×40 mm)	3·50	3·50

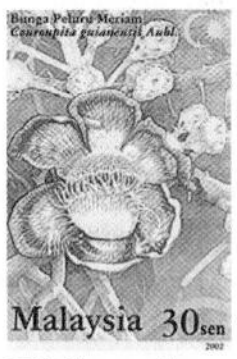

301 *Couroupita guianensis*

2002. Malaysia–China Joint Issue. Rare Flowers. Multicoloured.

1053	30s. Type **301**	45	10
1054	1r. *Couroupita guianensis*	90	1·25
1055	1r. *Camellia nitidissima*	90	1·25
MS1056	108×79 mm. 2r. *Schima brevifolia* buds (horiz); 2r. *Schima brevifolia* blossom	2·25	2·75

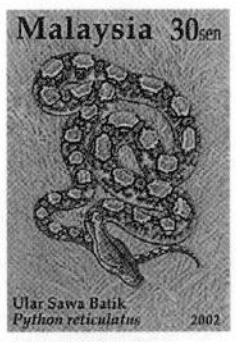

302 *Python reticulatus*

2002. Malaysian Snakes. Multicoloured.

1057	30s. Type **302**	60	30
1058	30s. *Gonyophis margaritatus*	60	30
1059	50s. *Bungarus candidus*	85	60
1060	1r. *Maticora bivirgata*	1·60	1·75
MS1061	108×78 mm. 2r. *Ophiophagus hannah* (head of adult); 2r. *Ophiophagus hannah* (juvenile)	3·50	4·00

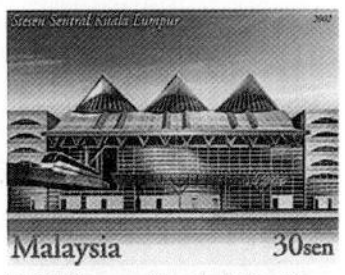

303 Stesen Sentral Station, Kuala Lumpur

2002. Express Rail Link from Central Kuala Lumpur to International Airport. Multicoloured.

1062	30s. Type **303**	75	25
1063	50s. Train and Central Station	1·40	1·50
1064	50s. Train and International Airport	1·40	1·50
MS1065	Two sheets, each 106×76 mm. (a) 1r. KLIA Express and high speed train; 1r. Express and local trains. (b) 2r. KLIA Express Set of 2 sheets	5·50	6·00

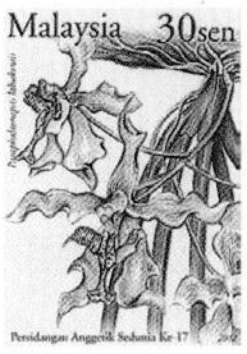

304 *Paraphalaenopsis labukensis*

2002. 17th World Orchid Conference. Multicoloured.

1066	30s. Type **304**	65	65
1067	30s. *Renanthera bella*	65	65
1068	50s. *Paphiopedilum sanderianum*	1·00	40
1069	1r. *Coelogyne pandurata*	1·50	1·75
1070	1r. *Phalaenopsis amabilis*	1·50	1·25
MS1071	76×105 mm. 5r. *Cleisocentron merillianum* (45×40 mm)	5·00	6·00

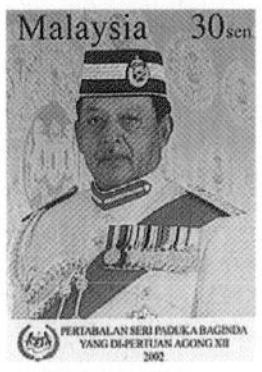

305 Raja Tuanku Syed Sirajuddin of Perlis

2002. Installation of Raja Tuanku Syed Sirajuddin as Yang di-Pertuan Agong.

1072	**305**	30s. multicoloured	65	10
1073	**305**	50s. multicoloured	90	50
1074	**305**	1r. multicoloured	1·75	2·00

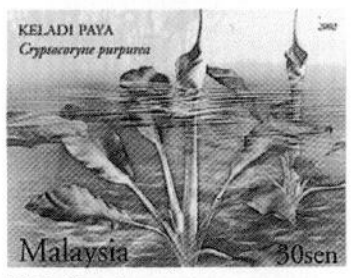

306 *Cryptocoryne purpurea*

2002. Aquatic Plants. Multicoloured.

1075	30s. Type **306**	55	10
1076	50s. *Barclaya kunstleri*	85	30
1077	1r. *Neptunia oleracea*	1·50	2·00
1078	1r. *Monochoria hastata*	1·50	2·00
MS1079	110×80 mm. 1r. *Eichhornia crassipes* (vert); 2r. *Nymphaea pubescens*	5·50	6·00

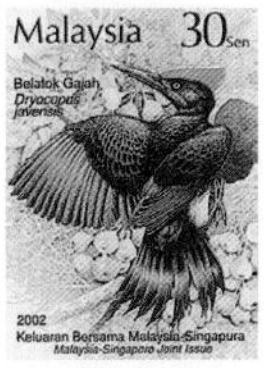

307 White-bellied Woodpecker (*Dryocopus javensis*)

2002. Malaysia–Singapore Joint Issue. Birds. Multicoloured.

1080	30s. Type **307**	75	75
1081	30s. Black-naped oriole (*Oriolus chinensis*)	75	75
1082	1r. Red-throated sunbird (*Anthreptes rhodolaema*)	2·00	2·25
1083	1r. Asian fairy bluebird (*Irena puella*)	2·00	2·25
MS1084	99×70 mm. 5r. Orange-bellied flowerpecker (*Dicaeum trigonostigma*) (60×40 mm)	6·50	7·00

Stamps with similar designs were issued by Singapore.

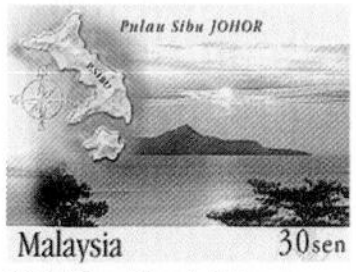

308 Sibu Island, Johore

2002. Tourist Beaches (1st series). Multicoloured.

1085	30s. Type **308**	70	60
1086	30s. Perhentian Islands, Trengganu	70	60
1087	50s. Manukan Island, Sabah	85	85
1088	50s. Tioman Island, Pahang	85	85
1089	1r. Singa Besar Island, Kedah	1·60	1·75
1090	1r. Pangkor Island, Perak	1·60	1·75
MS1091	110×80 mm. 1r. Ferringhi Bay, Penang; 1r. Port Dickson, Negri Sembilan	3·75	4·00

See also Nos. 1143/**MS**1153.

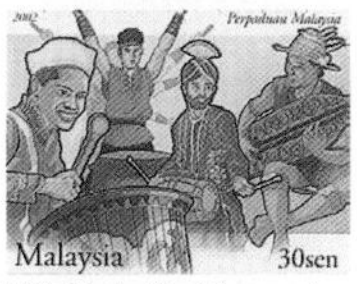

309 Ethnic Musicians and Dancers

2002. Malaysian Unity. Multicoloured.

1092	30s. Type **309**	70	70
1093	30s. Children playing mancala (game)	70	70
1094	50s. Children from different races (82×30 mm)	1·00	1·00
MS1095	68×99 mm. 1r. Children playing tug-of-war	2·50	2·75

2002. Fruits of Malaysia. As T **141** and similar vert designs but redenominated in "sen" and "RM". Multicoloured.

1095a	40s. Type **141**	1·00	10
1095b	50s. Pineapple	1·00	10
1095g	10r. Mango	6·00	1·50
1095h	20r. Papaya	9·00	2·75

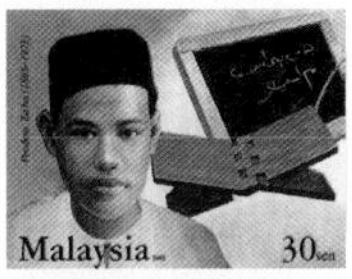

310 Zainal Abidin bin Ahmad ("Za'ba") as a Student

2002. 30th Death Anniv of Zainal Abidin bin Ahmad ("Za'ba") (2003) (scholar). Multicoloured.

1096	30s. Type **310**	55	10
1097	50s. Za'ba with typewriter	85	95
1098	50s. Za'ba and traditional Malay building	85	95
MS1099	100×70 mm. 1r. Za'ba at desk (vert)	2·50	3·00

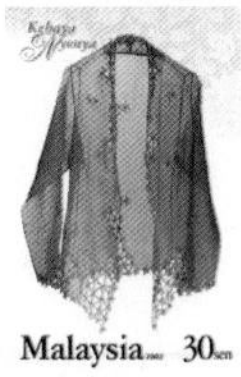

311 Green Kebaya, Nyonya

2002. The Kebaya Nyonya (traditional Malay women's blouse). Multicoloured.

1100	30s. Type **311**	60	45
1101	30s. Red kebaya nyonya	60	45
1102	50s. Yellow kebaya nyonya	90	1·00
1103	50s. Pink kebaya nyonya	90	1·00
MS1104	70×100 mm. 2r. Kebaya nyonya and sarong (34×69 mm)	3·00	3·25

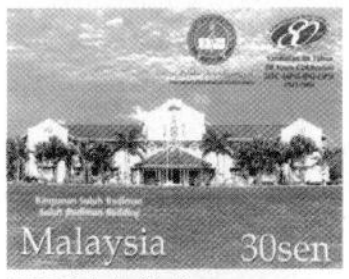

312 Suluh Budiman Building, Sultan Idris University of Education

2002. 80th Anniv of Sultan Idris University of Education. Multicoloured.

1105	30s. Type **312**	60	10
1106	50s. Tadahan Selatan Building	90	1·00
1107	50s. Chancellery Building	90	1·00

No. 1107 is inscribed "Chancellory" in error.

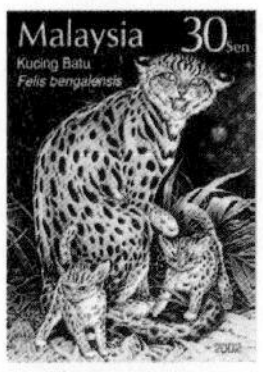

313 Leopard Cat with Kittens

2002. Stamp Week. Wild and Domesticated Animals. Multicoloured.

1108	30s. Type **313**	70	70
1109	30s. Domestic cat and kittens	70	70
1110	1r. Lesser sulphur-crested cockatoo	1·90	2·25
1111	1r. Malay fish owl	1·90	2·25
MS1112	Two sheets, each 105×76 mm. (a) 1r. Goldfish (horiz); 1r. Porcupine-fish (horiz); (b) 1r. Giant squirrel; 1r. Domestic rabbit with young Set of 2 sheets	5·00	5·50

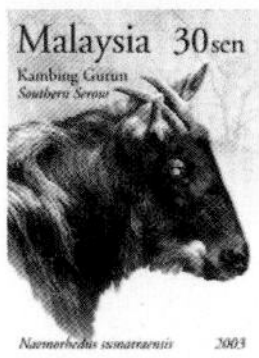

314 Southern Serow

2003. Southern Serow. Multicoloured.

1113	30s. Type **314**	80	10
1114	50s. Southern serow lying down	1·00	1·25
1115	50s. Young southern serow	1·00	1·25

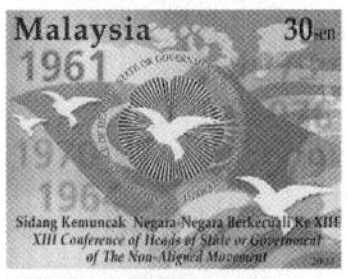

315 Peace Doves and Emblem

2003. 13th Conference of Heads of State or Government of the Non-Aligned Movement, Kuala Lumpur. Multicoloured.

1116	30s. Type **315**	50	50
1117	30s. Conference emblem in cupped hands	50	50
1118	50s. Emblem and outline map of Malaysia	1·00	1·00
1119	50s. "2003" with noughts containing Malaysian flag and emblem	1·00	1·00

Nos. 1116/17 and 1118/19 were each printed together, *se-tenant*, each pair forming a composite background design of a Malaysian flag and world map (Nos. 1116/17) or a globe (Nos. 1118/19).

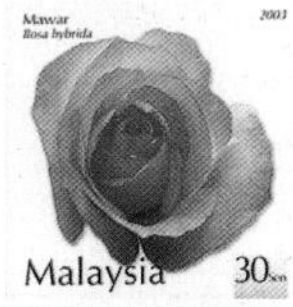

316 Pale Pink Hybrid Tea Rose

2003. Roses in Malaysia. Multicoloured.

1120	30s. Type **316**	55	40
1121	30s. Red hybrid tea	55	40
1122	50s. Apricot hybrid tea	90	1·25
1123	50s. Pink and white striped floribunda	90	1·25
MS1124	70×100 mm. 1r. Miniature floribunda (29×40 mm); 2r. *Rosa centifolia* (29×81 mm)	2·75	3·25

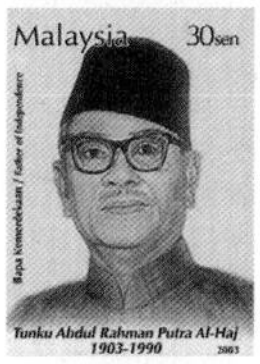

317 Tunku Abdul Rahman

2003. Birth Centenary of Tunku Abdul Rahman (first Prime Minister of Federation of Malaya (1957–63) and of Malaysia (1963–70)). Multicoloured.

1125	30s. Type **317**	55	15
1126	50s. Tunku Abdul Rahman (different)	85	30
1127	1r. Tunku Abdul Rahman in ceremonial dress	1·25	1·50
1128	1r. Tunku Abdul Rahman wearing topi hat	1·25	1·50
MS1129	100×70 mm. 1r. Tunku Abdul Rahman reading Proclamation of Independence, 1957	2·00	2·00

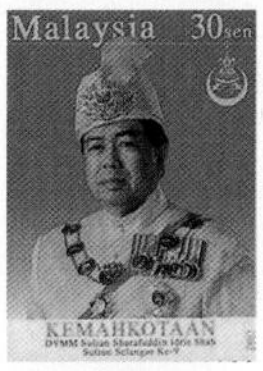

318 Sultan Sharafuddin Idris Shah

2003. Coronation of Sultan of Selangor. Multicoloured.

1130	30s. Type **318**	60	15
1131	50s. Sultan in uniform	1·00	45

1132	1r. Sultan of Selangor (wearing crown)	1·75	2·00

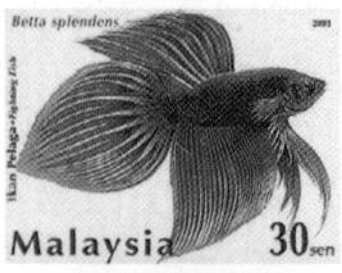

319 Siamese Fighting Fish

2003. Siamese Fighting Fish (Betta splendens). Multicoloured.

1133	30s. Type **319**	60	15
1134	50s. Siamese Fighting fish (yellow)	3·00	30
1135	1r. Siamese Fighting fish (blue)	1·40	1·75
1136	1r. Siamese Fighting fish (red with fringed fins)	1·40	1·75
MS1137	99×70 mm. 50s. *Betta imbellis* (Local Fighting Fish) (33×28 mm); 50s. *Betta coccina* (Red Fighting Fish) (33×28 mm)	2·00	2·25

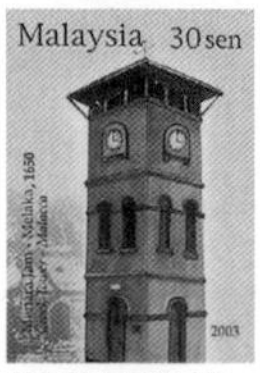

320 Christ Church Clock

2003. Clock Towers (1st series). Multicoloured.

1138	30s. Type **320**	55	55
1139	30s. Jubilee Clock Tower, Penang	55	55
1140	30s. Sungai Petani Clock Tower, Jalan Ibrahim	55	55
1141	30s. Teluk Intan Clock Tower	55	55
1142	30s. Sarawak State Council Monument	55	55
MS1143	99×70 mm. 1r. Sultan Abdul Samad Building; 1r. Taiping Clock Tower, Perak	2·25	2·50

See also Nos. 1404/6.

2003. Islands and Beaches of Malaysia (2nd series). As T **308**. Multicoloured.

1149	30s. Aerial view of Ligitan Island	55	55
1150	30s. Outline map of Ligitan Island	55	55
1151	50s. Sipadan Island	90	1·00
1152	50s. Outline map of Sipadan Island	90	1·00
MS1153	70×100 mm. 50c. Aerial view of Sipadan Island (vert); 50c. Relief map of Ligitan Island (vert)	2·25	2·50

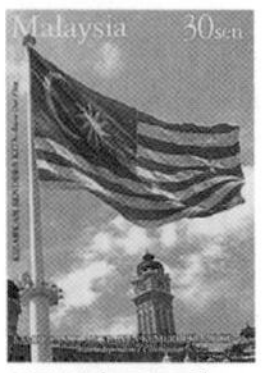

321 Malaysian Flag and Sultan Tower, Malacca Abdul Samad Building, Kuala Lumpur

2003. 46th Independence Celebration.

1154	**321**	30s. multicoloured	65	15
1155	-	1r. multicoloured	1·75	1·75
MS1156		70×100 mm. 1r. black and grey	2·25	2·50

DESIGNS—59×40 mm No. 1155, Malaysian flag; No. **MS**1156, Independence delegation in motorcade, Malacca, 1956.

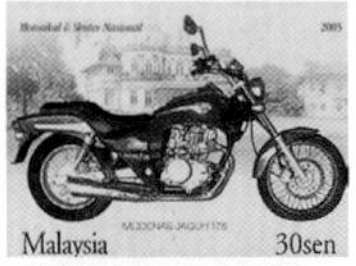

322 Modenas Jaguh 175

2003. Malaysian made Motorcycles and Scooters. Multicoloured.

1157	30s. Type **322**	70	15
1158	50s. Modenas Karisma 125	90	1·00
1159	50s. Modenas Kriss 1	90	1·00
1160	50s. Modenas Kriss 2	90	1·00
1161	50s. Modenas Kriss SG	90	1·00
MS1162	Four sheets, each 100×70 mm. (a) 1r. Comel Turbulence RG125; 1r. Comel Cyclone GP150. (b) 1r. Demak Adventurer; 1r. Demak Beetle. (c) 1r. MZ 125SM; 1r. MZ Perintis 120S Classic. (d) 1r. Gagiva Momos 125R; 1r. Nitro NE150 Windstar	6·50	7·00

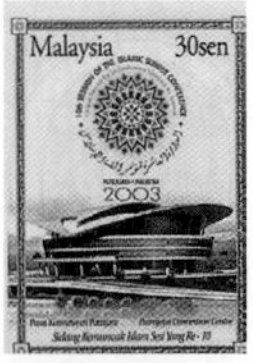

323 Putrajaya Convention Centre

2003. Tenth Session of Islamic Summit Conference, Putrajaya. Multicoloured.

1163	30s. Type **323**	50	50
1164	30s. Emblem	50	50
1165	50s. Putrajaya Mosque, modern Kuala Lumpur buildings and flag	90	1·00
1166	50s. Sultan Abdul Samad Building, Kuala Lumpur and Federal Government Administrative Centre, Putrajaya	90	1·00

Nos. 1165/6 were each printed together, *se-tenant*, forming a composite design.

2003. "Bangkok 2003" World Stamp Exhibition, Thailand. Nos. 1157/61 additionally inscr with "Bangkok" and exhibition logo.

1167	30s. Type **322**	60	20
1168	50s. Modenas Karisma 125	80	1·00
1169	50s. Modenas Kriss 1	80	1·00
1170	50s. Modenas Kriss 2	80	1·00
1171	50s. Modenas Kriss SG	80	1·00

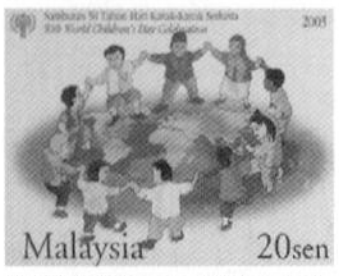

324 Children in Circle and World Map

2003. 50th World Children's Day. Multicoloured.

1172	20s. Type **324**	50	10
1173	30s. Family outside their home	70	75
1174	30s. Girl flying kite and children with computer	70	75
1175	30s. "Sambutan 50 tahun Hari kanak-kanak Sedunia" in child's writing	70	75
1176	30s. Open book, house, Malaysian flag, rainbow, car and flower	70	75

Nos. 1173/4 were printed together, *se-tenant*, forming a composite design.

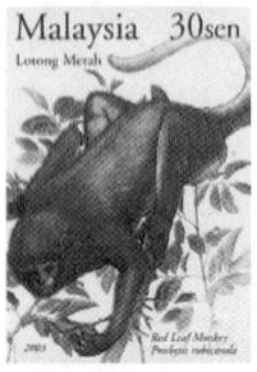

325 Red Leaf Monkey feeding

2003. Stamp Week. Primates of Malaysia. Multicoloured.

1177	30s. Type **325**	60	60
1178	30s. Red leaf monkey sat on branch	60	60
1179	50s. Proboscis monkey	90	90
1180	50s. Female proboscis monkey with baby	90	90

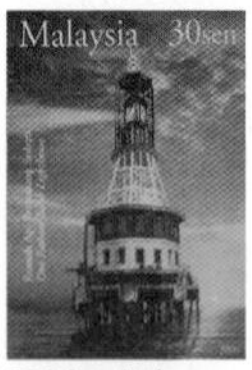

326 One Fathom Bank Lighthouse

2004. Lighthouses. Multicoloured.

1181	30s. Type **326**	70	60
1182	30s. Muka Head Lighthouse, Pulau Pinang	70	60
1183	30s. Pulau Undan Lighthouse, Melaka	70	60
1184	30s. Althingsburg Lighthouse, Selangor	70	60
MS1185	70×100 mm. 1r. Tanjung Tuan Lighthouse	2·75	3·00

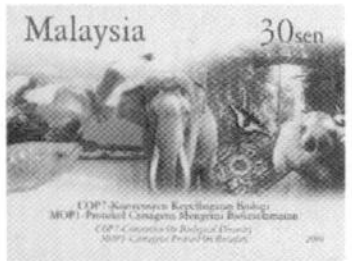

327 Fauna at Seashore and in Forest

2004. Seventh Conference of Convention on Biological Diversity and First Meeting of Cartagena Protocol on Biosafety. Multicoloured.

1186	30s. Type **327**	70	15
1187	50s. Conference logo	90	95
1188	50s. DNA, leaf and test tube	90	95

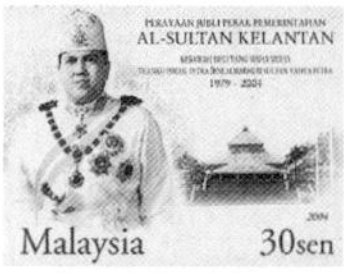

328 Sultan of Kelantan

2004. Silver Jubilee of Sultan Ismail Petra Ibni Almarhum of Kelantan. Multicoloured.

1189	30s. Type **328**	60	15
1190	50s. Sultan and Istana Jahar, Museum of Royal Traditions and Customs	90	40
1191	1r. Sultan and Khota Bharu	1·75	2·00

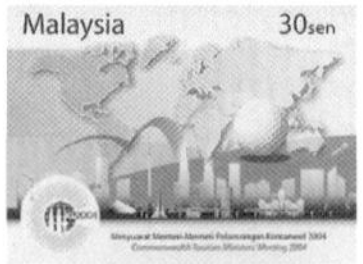

329 Golf Ball, City Skyline and World Map

2004. First Commonwealth Tourism Ministers Meeting, Kuala Lumpur. Multicoloured.

1192	30s. Type **329**	65	20
1193	50s. World map and seashore	90	40
1194	1r. Logo and montage of images of Malaysia (vert)	1·60	1·75

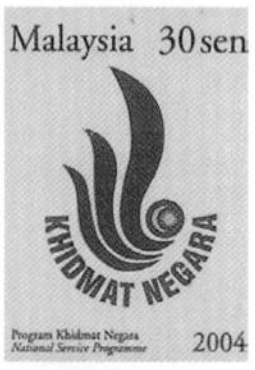

330 Emblem

2004. National Service Programme. Multicoloured.

1195	30s. Type **330**	20	15
1196	50s. Abseiling	55	30
1197	1r. Three youths with Malaysian flag	1·25	1·50
MS1198	70×100 mm. 2r. Saluting	2·25	2·50
MS1198a	70×100 mm. 2r. As No. **MS**1198	2·25	2·50

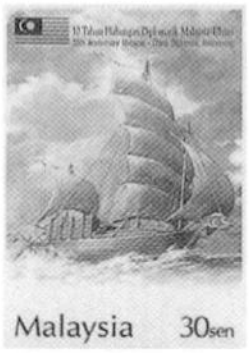

331 *Lanchara* (Malayan sailing ship)

2004. 30th Anniv of Malaysia—China Diplomatic Relations. Multicoloured.

1199	30s. Type **331**	30	30
1200	30s. Chinese junk	30	30
1201	1r. Handshake and sailing ship	1·00	1·40
1202	1r. Sailing ship and flags of Malaysia and China	1·00	1·40
MS1203	100×70 mm. 2r. Niujie Mosque, Beijing and Kampung Hulu Mosque, Malacca (59×39 mm)	1·90	2·50

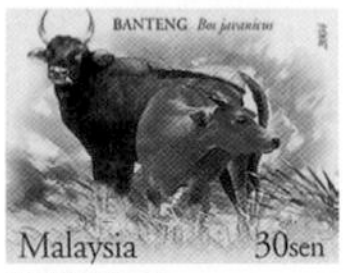

332 Banteng

2004. Wildlife in the Malaysian Forest. Multicoloured.

1204	30s. Type **332**	50	50
1205	30s. Gaur ("SELADANG")	50	50
1206	1r. Tiger	1·75	1·75
1207	1r. Indian elephant	1·75	1·75
MS1208	101×70 mm. 2r. Malayan tapir (vert)	2·00	2·50

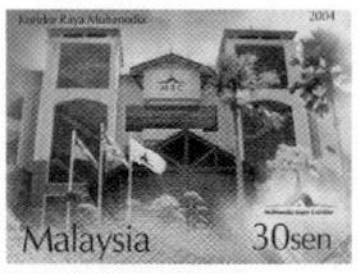

333 Multimedia Super Corridor Entrance

2004. Multimedia Super Corridor. Multicoloured.

1209	30s. Type **333**	30	15
1210	50s. Globe, binary code and Petronas Towers	50	30
1211	1r. ID card, computer terminals and brain linked to Multimedia Super Corridor	90	1·25
MS1212	70×100 mm. 2r. Map of Multimedia Super Corridor	2·75	3·00

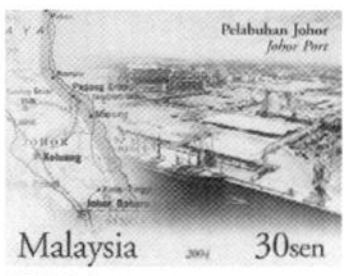

334 Johor

2004. Ports of Malaysia. Multicoloured.

1213	30s. Type **334**	60	40
1214	30s. Kota Kinabalu	60	40
1215	50s. Kuantan	90	90
1216	50s. Penang	90	90
1217	1r. Bintulu	1·75	1·75
MS1218	100×70 mm. 2r. Northpor	2·75	3·00

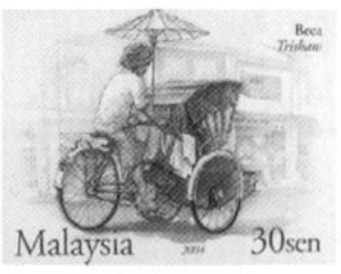

335 Trishaw

2004. Traditional Transportation. Multicoloured.

1219	30s. Type **335**	45	15
1220	50s. Rickshaw	65	30
1221	1r. Padi horse	1·10	1·40
MS1222	100×70 mm. 2r. Bullock cart (39×49 mm)	2·75	3·00

2004. World Stamp Championship, Singapore. As No. **MS**1203 but with exhibition logo and numbering added to the sheet margin.

MS1224	100×70 mm. 2r. Niujie Mosque, Beijing and Kampung Hulu Mosque, Malacca (59×39 mm)	2·50	3·00

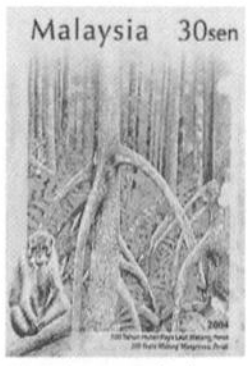

336 Long-tailed Macaque

2004. Centenary of Matang Mangroves, Perak. Multicoloured.

1225	30s. Type **336**	50	45
1226	30s. *Sonneratia ovata* (Mangrove apple) and moth	50	45
1227	1r. Fishing boat at jetty and cockle	1·50	1·75
1228	1r. Lesser adjutant stork and Brahminy kite	1·50	1·75
MS1229	100×69 mm. 2r. Tall-stilted Mangrove	2·25	2·75

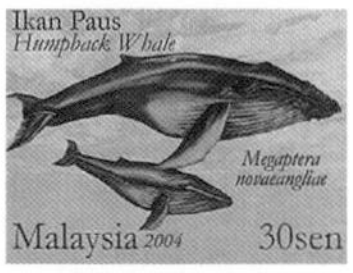

337 Humpback Whales

2004. Marine Life. Multicoloured.

1230	30s. Type **337**	60	25
1231	50s. Octopus	80	35
1232	1r. Bottlenose dolphins	1·50	1·75
MS1233	101×71 mm. 2r. Thornback ray	2·75	3·00

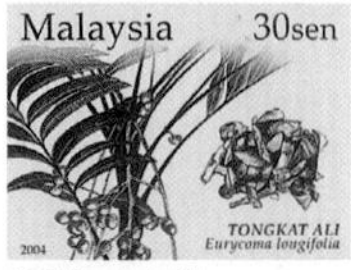

338 Tongkat Ali

2004. Medicinal Plants. Multicoloured.

1234	30s. Type **338**	40	20
1235	50s. Kacip Fatimah	60	30
1236	1r. Kerdas	1·10	1·40
1237	1r. Buah Keras	1·10	1·40
MS1238	100×71 mm. 2r. Mas Cotek	2·50	3·00

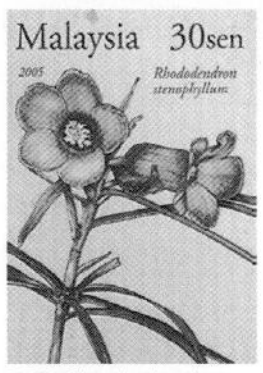

339 *Rhododendron stenophyllum*

2005. Rare Flowers. Multicoloured.

1239	30s. Type **339**	50	30
1240	30s. *Rhododendron nervulosum*	50	30
1241	50s. *Rhododendron rugosum*	90	50
1242	1r. *Rhododendron stapfianum*	1·75	1·90
MS1243	100×70 mm. 2r. *Rhododendron lowii* (horiz)	2·50	3·00

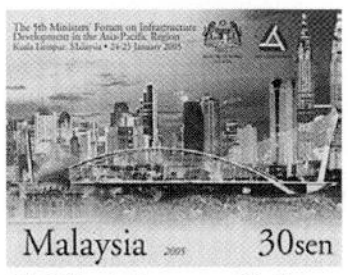

340 Kuala Lumpur Skyline

2005. Fifth Ministers Forum in the Asia Pacific. Multicoloured.

1244	30s. Type **340**	40	15
1245	50s. Putrajaya International Convention Centre and Parliament Building	70	40
1246	1r. Kuala Lumpur International Airport	2·00	2·00

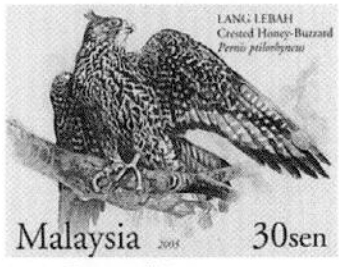

341 Crested Honey Buzzard

2005. Migratory Birds. Multicoloured.

1247	30s. Type **341**	60	25
1248	50s. Purple heron	95	50
1249	1r. Lesser Crested tern	1·75	1·90
MS1250	70×100 mm. 2r. Dunlin	3·25	3·25

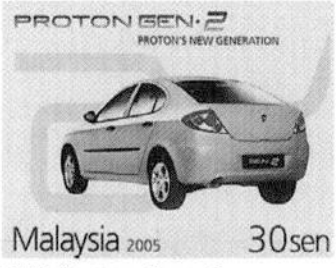

342 Proton Gen. 2

2004. Proton Gen. 2. Multicoloured.

1251	30s. Type **342**	40	20
1252	50s. Proton Gen. 2 (blue)	65	35
1253	2r. Proton Gen. 2 (red)	1·60	2·00
MS1254	100×70 mm. 2r. Proton Gen. 2 (purple) (vert)	2·25	2·75

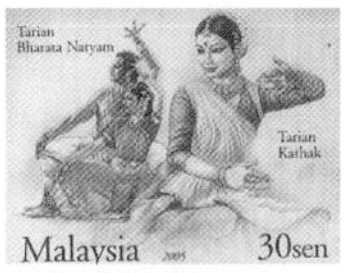

343 Bharata Natyam and Kathak

2005. Traditional Dances. Multicoloured.

1255	30s. Type **343**	35	15
1256	50s. Kipas and Payung	55	35
1257	1r. Zapin and Asyik	1·00	1·40
MS1258	100×70 mm. 2r. Datun julud and Sumazau	2·75	3·00

2005. Pacific Explorer 2005 World Stamp Expo, Sydney. No. **MS**1249 additionally inscr with "PACIFIC EXPLORER 2005 WORLD STAMP EXPO 21-24 APR II SYDNEY CONVENTION AND EXHIBITION CENTRE" and emblem on sheet margin.

MS1259	70×100 mm. 2r. Dunlin	2·50	3·00

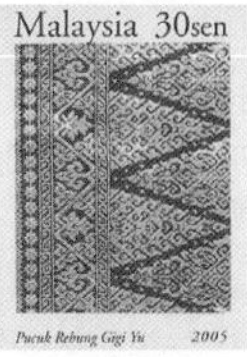

344 Pucuk Rebung Gigi Yu

2005. Songket (designs on brocade textiles). Multicoloured.

1260	30s. Type **344**	35	10
1261	50s. Bunga Bertabur Pecah Lapan	55	35
1262	1r. Pucuk Rebung Gigi Yu dan Bunga Kayohan	90	1·25
1263	1r. Teluk Berantai Bunga Pecah Empat	90	1·25
MS1263a	100×70 mm. 2r. Potong Wajik Bertabur	2·00	2·50

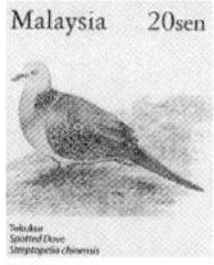

345 Spotted-necked Dove

2005. Birds. Multicoloured.

1264	20s. Type **345**	35	10
1265	30s. Ochraceous bulbul	40	10
1266	40s. Long-tailed parakeet	50	20
1267	50s. White-rumped shama	60	25
1268	75s. Yellow-bellied ("Olive-backed") sunbird	80	40
1269	1r. Emerald dove ("Green-winged Pigeon)	90	55
1270	2r. Blue-tailed ("Banded") pitta	1·75	1·50
1271	5r. Imperial pigeon	3·50	3·50

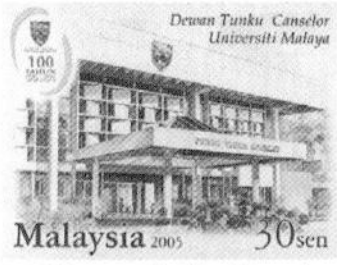

346 Dewan Tunku Canselor University

2005. Centenary of University of Malaya. Multicoloured.

1272	30s. Type **346**	30	10
1273	50s. Perpustakaan University	50	30
1274	1r. Pusat Perubatan University	90	1·25
MS1275	70×100 mm. 1r. Rimba Ilmu University; 1r. Koleksi Muzium Seni Asia University	1·75	2·25

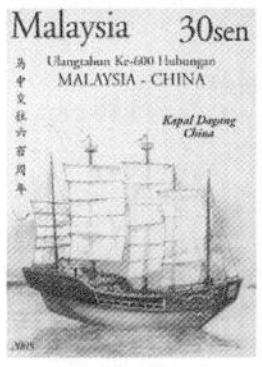

347 *Kapal Dagang* (Merchant Ship)

2005. 600th Anniv of Trade between Malaysia and China. Multicoloured.

1276	30s. Type **347**	30	20
1277	30s. Royal Seal of the Emperor of China	30	20
1278	50s. Merchants	45	30
1279	1r. Nyonya cerami plate	85	1·10
MS1280	100×70 mm. 2r. Tin animal and copper coins	1·50	2·00

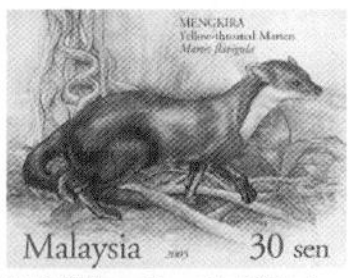

348 Yellow-throated Marten

2005. Protected Mammals of Malaysia (3rd series). Multicoloured.

1281	30s. Type **348**	40	25
1282	40s. Malay weasel	40	25
1283	50s. Hairy-nosed otter	70	35
1284	1r. Large Spotted civet	1·25	1·50
MS1285	100×70 mm. 2r. Long-tailed porcupine (vert)	2·00	2·25

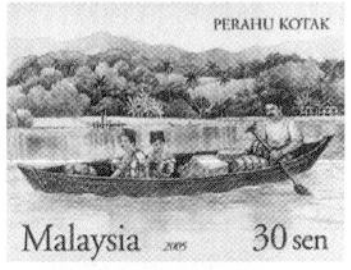

349 Box Boat (Perahu Kotak)

2005. Traditional Water Transport. Multicoloured.

1286	30s. Type **349**	35	10
1287	50s. Sampan	60	35
1288	1r. Bamboo raft (Rakit buluh)	1·00	1·25
MS1289	70×100 mm. 2r. Long boat (Perahu batang) (40×50 mm)	2·25	2·50
MS1289a	70×100 mm. 2r. As No. **MS**1289	2·25	2·50
MS1289b	70×100 mm. 2r. As No. **MS**1289a	1·25	1·40

2005. Taipei 2005 International Stamp Exhibition. No. **MS**1285 additionally inscr with "TAIPEI 2005" and emblem on sheet margin.

MS1290	100×70 mm. 2r. Long-tailed porcupine (vert)	1·50	2·00

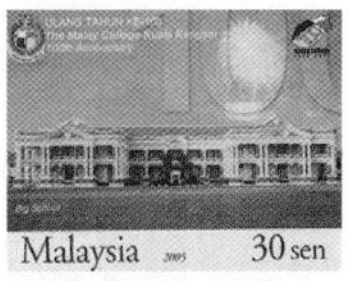

350 Big School and Playing Field

2005. Centenary of Malay College, Kuala Kangsar. Multicoloured.

1291	30s. Type **350**	35	10
1292	50s. Prep School	65	70
1293	50s. Big Tree	65	70
MS1294	100×70 mm. 50s.×4 (22×51 mm), Sultan Idris Murshidul'Adzam Shah; Sultan Alaiddin Sulaiman Shah; Yam Tuan Tuanku Muhamad Shah; Sultan Ahmad Al-Mu'adzam Shah	1·75	2·25

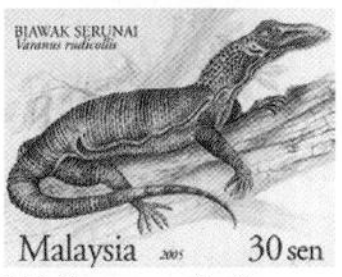

351 *Varanus rudicollis*

2005. Endangered Reptiles. Multicoloured.

1295	30s. Type **351**	35	25
1296	30s. *Varanus dumerilii*	35	25
1297	50s. *Gonocephalus grandis*	65	35
1298	1r. *Crocodylus porosus*	1·25	1·50
MS1299	70×100 mm. 2r. *Draco quinquefasciatus* (40×50 mm)	1·75	2·25

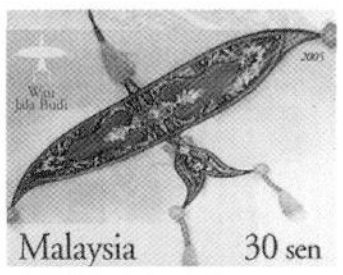

352 Wau Jala Budi

2005. Traditional Kites. Multicoloured.

1300	30s. Type **352**	35	10
1301	50s. Wau Bulan	65	35
1302	1r. Wau Kucing	1·25	1·40
MS1303	100×70 mm. 2r. Wau Merak	1·75	2·25

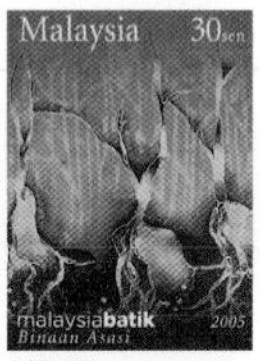

353 "Binaan Asasi" (Masrina Abdullah)

2005. Stamp Week. Malaysian Batik Designs. T **353** and similar vert designs showing motifs produced by winners of Piala Seri Endon Batik Design Competition. Multicoloured.

1304	30s. Type **353**	25	10
1305	50s. "Pesona Sutera" (Nazari Maarus)	45	35
1306	1r. "Malaysia Bersatu" (Mohd Nizamuddin Ambia)	80	1·10
MS1307	100×70 mm. 2r. "Penyatuan" (Mohd Azizi Hassan)	1·50	2·00

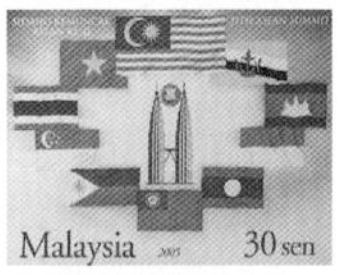

354 Flags of Member Countries

2005. 11th ASEAN Summit, Kuala Lumpur. Each showing summit emblem. Multicoloured.

1308	30s. Type **354**	25	10
1309	50s. "ONE VISION IDENTITY COMMUNITY"	45	35
1310	1r. Petronas Twin Towers and city of Kuala Lumpur	80	1·10

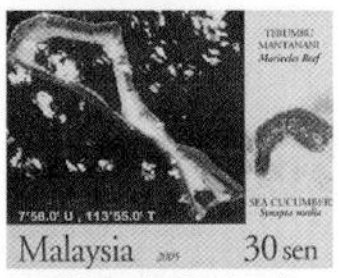

355 Mariveles Reef and *Synapta media* (sea cucumber)

2005. Malaysia's Five Islands and Reefs in the South China Sea. Multicoloured.

1311	30s. Type **355**	25	20
1312	30s. Erica Reef and *Chromodoris magnifica* (nudibranch)	25	20
1313	1r. Investigator Reef and *Chlamys rastellum* (bivalve)	80	1·10
1314	1r. Swallow Island and *Echinaster callosus* (sea star)	80	1·10
MS1315	100×70 mm. 2r. Aerial view of Malaysia's five islands and reefs, South China Sea (50×40 mm)	2·25	2·50

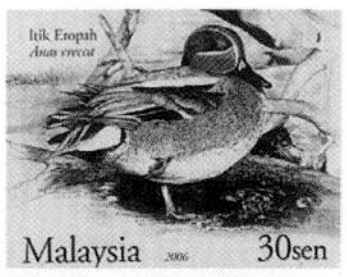

356 Green-winged Teal (*Anas crecca*)

2006. Wild Duck Species. Multicoloured.

1316	30s. Type **356**	50	30
1317	30s. White-winged wood duck (*Cairina scutulata*)	50	30
1318	50s. Northern pintail (*Anas acuta*)	90	90
1319	50s. Northern shoveller (*Anas clypeata*)	90	90
MS1320	100×70 mm. 2r. Great cormorant (*Phalacrocorax carbo*)	3·00	3·25

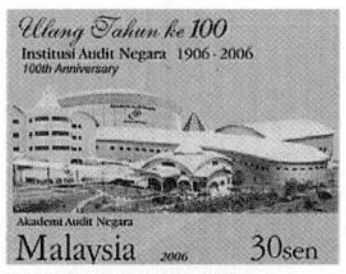

357 National Audit Academy, Negri Sembilan

2006. Centenary of National Audit Institution. Multicoloured.

1321	30s. Type **357**	30	20
1322	50s. Arms and logo of National Audit Department	55	55
1323	50s. Auditor General's reports	55	55

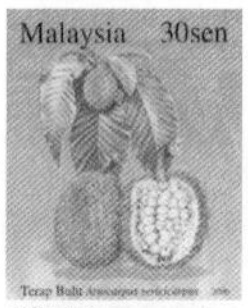

358 *Artocarpus sericicarpus*

2006. Rare Fruits of Malaysia (3rd series). Multicoloured.

1324	30s. Type **358**	30	20
1325	50s. *Phyllanthus acidus*	50	35
1326	1r. *Garcinia hombroniana*	90	1·25
MS1327	100×70 mm. 1r. *Lepisanthes alata*; 1r. *Baccaurea polyneura*	1·75	1·90

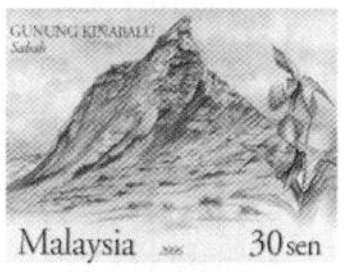

359 Mount Kinabalu, Sabah and Orchid

2006. Mountains of Malaysia. Multicoloured.

1328	30s. Type **359**	55	45
1329	30s. Mount Ledang, Johor and pitcher plant	55	45
1330	50s. Mount Jerai, Kedah and orchid	90	1·00
1331	50s. Mount Mulu and the Pinnacles, Sarawak	90	1·00
MS1332	100×70 mm. 2r. Mount Tahan, Pahang (49×39 mm)	1·75	2·25

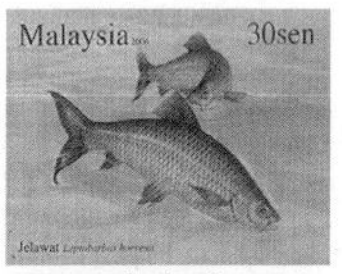

360 *Leptobarbus hoevenii* (carp)

2006. Freshwater Fish (3rd series). Multicoloured.

1333	30s. Type **360**	35	15
1334	50s. *Hampala macrolepidota*	65	65
1335	50s. *Pangasius* sp.	65	65
1336	1r. *Probarbus jullieni*	1·10	1·40
MS1337	100×70 mm. 5r. *Clarias batrachus* and *Mystus nemurus* (silver foil hologram) (69×33 mm)	4·00	5·00

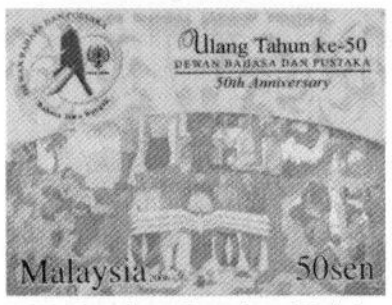

361 Mural on Facade of Balai Budaya Tun Syed Nasir

2006. 50th Anniv of Dewan Bahasa dan Pustaka (Malay language organization). Multicoloured.

1338	50s. Type **361**	55	40
1339	50s. Palmyra palm frond and emblem	55	40
1340	1r. Books and laptop computer	95	1·25

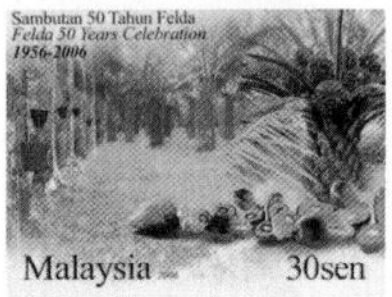

362 Oil Palm and Rubber Trees

2006. 50th Anniv of FELDA (Federal Land Development Authority). Multicoloured.

1341	30s. Type **362**	35	15
1342	50s. Settler's houses, c. 1956, modern bungalow house and aerial view of oil palm estate	60	35
1343	1r. Old and new FELDA offices and new office tower, Kuala Lumpur	1·00	1·25

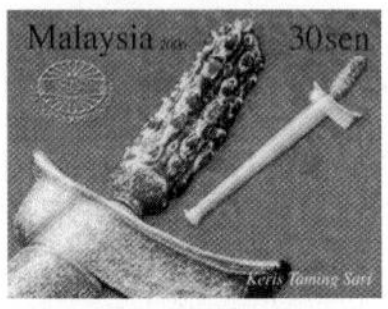

363 Keris Taming Sari (sword from Perak State Regalia)

2006. Galeri Sultan Azlan Shah. Multicoloured.

1344	30s. Type **363**	35	15
1345	50s. Galeri Sultan Azlan Shah	60	35
1346	1r. Royal aigrette	1·00	1·25

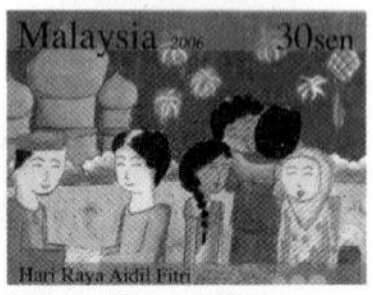

364 Hari Raya Aidil Fitri

2006. Festivals. Children's Paintings. Multicoloured.

1347	30s. Type **364**	35	15
1348	50s. Tahun Baru Cina (Chinese New Year)	60	35
1349	1r. Deepavali	1·00	1·25
MS1350	70×100 mm. 1r. Tadau Kaamatan (vert); 1r. Pesta Gawai (vert)	1·75	2·00

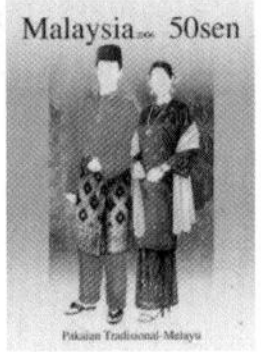

365 Malaysian Traditional Costume

2006. Traditional Costumes. Multicoloured.

1351	50s. Type **365**	65	65
1352	50s. Chinese	65	65
1353	50s. Indian	65	65
MS1354	70×100 mm. 1r. Iban; 1r. Kadazan	2·50	2·75

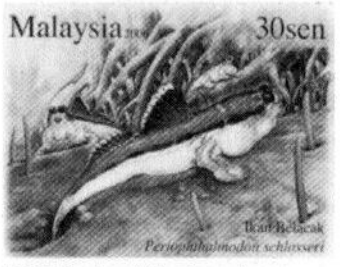

366 *Periophthalmodon schlosseri* (mudskipper)

2006. Stamp Week. Semi Aquatic Animals. Multicoloured.

1355	30s. Type **366**	40	15
1356	50s. *Pagurus bernhardus* (hermit crab)	65	35
1357	1r. *Cnora amboinensis* (Asian box turtle)	1·10	1·40
MS1358	119×69 mm. 1r. *Polypedates leucomystax* (four-lined tree frog); 1r. *Varanus salvator* (common monitor); 1r. *Cynogale bennettii* (otter civet); 1r. *Xenochrophistrianguligera* (triangle keelback snake) (all 29×34 mm)	2·75	3·25

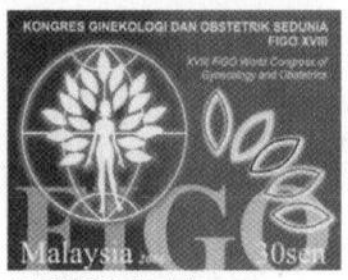

367 FIGO Emblem

2006. 18th FIGO World Congress of Gynecology and Obstetrics, Kuala Lumpur. Multicoloured.

1359	30s. Type **367**	40	15
1360	50s. Congress emblem and map of the Americas	75	75
1361	50s. Silhouette of foetus, map of Asia and Congress emblem	75	75

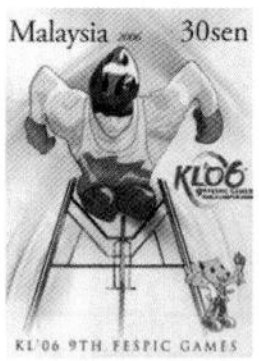

368 Wheelchair Race

2006. Ninth Far East and South Pacific Games for the Disabled (FESPIC), Kuala Lumpur. Multicoloured.

1362	30s. Type **368**	40	15
1363	50s. Swimming	65	35
1364	1r. Wheelchair tennis	1·10	1·40
MS1365	100×70 mm. 2r. Wheelchair basketball	3·00	3·00

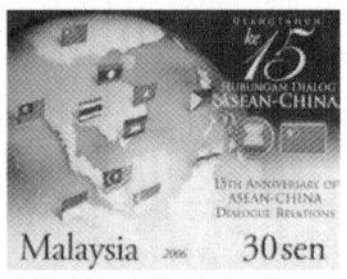

369 Map with Flags of China and ASEAN Countries

2006. 15th Anniv of Dialogue between ASEAN Countries and China. Multicoloured.

1366	30s. Type **369**	45	15
1367	50s. Great Wall of China and motorway intersection	65	35
1368	1r. Red ribbons tied in knot	1·10	1·40

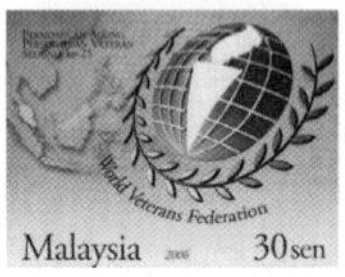

370 Emblem

2006. 25th General Assembly of the World Veterans Association, Kuala Lumpur. Multicoloured.

1369	30s. Type **370**	35	15
1370	50s. "25" and Kuala Lumpur Convention Centre	65	35
1371	1r. Tugu Negara Independence memorial	1·10	1·40

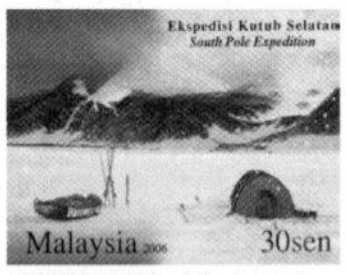

371 Expedition Tent and Sled in Antarctic

2006. Sharifah Mazlina Syed Abdul Kadir's South Pole Expedition (2004). Multicoloured.

1372	30s. Type **371**	50	20
1373	50s. Sharifah Mazlina Syed Abdul Kadir on skis with sled	90	50
1374	1r. Ski sailing from Hercules Inlet to South Pole	1·40	1·60

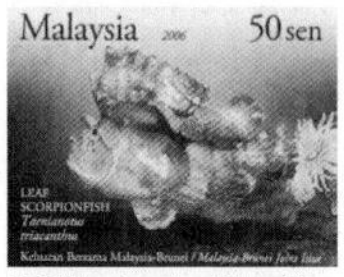

372 *Taenianotus triacanthus* (leaf scorpionfish)

2007. Marine Life. Multicoloured.

1375	50s. Type **372**	75	65
1376	50s. *Balistapus undulatus* (orange-striped triggerfish)	75	65
MS1377	100×70 mm. 1r. *Nautilus pompilius* (chambered nautilus); 1r. *Ostracionmeleagris* (spotted boxfish)	2·25	2·50

Stamps in similar designs were issued by Brunei.

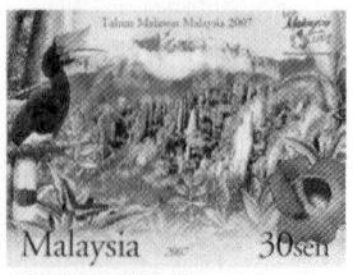

373 Hornbill, Flower and Rain Forest

2007. Visit Malaysia Year. Multicoloured.

1378	30s. Type **373**	45	45
1379	30s. Coral reef	45	45
1380	50s. Malaysian buildings	80	80
1381	50s. Malaysian crafts	80	80
MS1382	100×70 mm. 2r. Petronas Twin Towers (29×49 mm)	2·00	2·50

(b) Horiz designs as T **373** showing national costumes and dishes.

1383	30s. Malay (dancer with headdress)	40	50
1384	30s. Chinese (dancer with fans)	40	50
1385	30s. Indian (dancer in turquoise)	40	50
1386	30s. Kadazandusun of Sabah (black and gold dress)	40	50
1387	30s. Iban of Sarawak (woman wearing elaborate headdress)	40	50
1388	30s. Satay	40	50
1389	30s. Yee Sang	40	50
1390	30s. Banana leaf rice	40	50
1391	30s. Hinava (raw fish salad)	40	50
1392	30s. Manok Pansuh (chicken meat stuffed in bamboo)	40	50

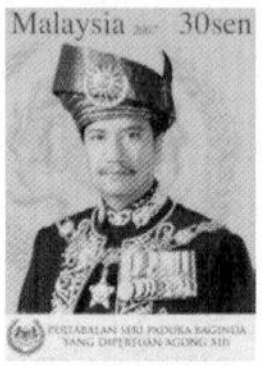

374 Tuanku Mizan Zainal Abidin

2007. Installation of Tuanku Mizan Zainal Abidin, Sultan of Terengganu as Yang di-Pertuan Agong. Multicoloured.

1393	30s. Type **374**	35	10
1394	50s. Wearing white uniform	65	40
1395	1r. As Type **374** (bright mauve background)	1·10	1·40

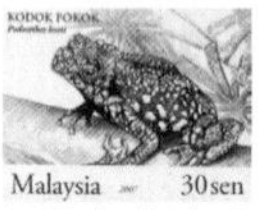

375 *Pedostibes hosii* (brown tree toad)

2007. Frogs and Toads of Malaysia. Multicoloured.

1396	30s. Type **375**	35	10
1397	50s. *Megophrys nasuta* (horned toad)	65	40
1398	50s. *Nyctixalus pictus* (spotted tree frog)	1·10	1·40
MS1399	100×70 mm. 1r. *Rana laterimaculata* (lesser swamp frog) (34×33 mm)	1·50	1·75

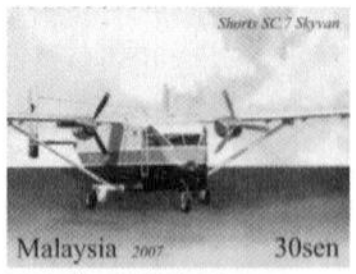

376 Shorts SC.7 Skyvan

2007. Air Transportation in Malaysia. Multicoloured.

1400	30s. Type **376**	40	15
1401	50s. De Havilland Canada DHC 7-110	75	75
1402	50s. GAF N22 Nomad	75	75
MS1403	100×70 mm. 1r. Airspeed Consul; 1r. Douglas DC-3	2·00	2·25

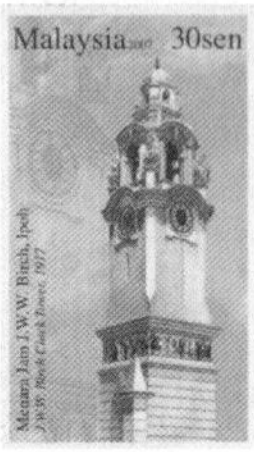

377 J.W.W. Birch Clock Tower, Ipoh, 1917

2007. Clock Towers (2nd series). Multicoloured.

1404	30s. Type **377**	35	10
1405	50s. Atkinson Clock Tower, Kota Kinabalu, 1905	65	50
1406	1r. Alor Setar Clock Tower, 1912	1·10	1·40

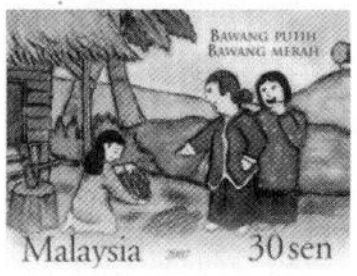

378 Bawang Merah put to work by her Stepmother and Stepsister

2007. Traditional Children's Folk Tales. Multicoloured.

1407	30s. Type **378**	50	55
1408	30s. Badang carrying rock	50	55
1409	30s. Sang Kancil crossing river on backs of crocodiles	50	55
1410	30s. Crocodile Sang Bedal seizing Sang Kerbau's leg	50	55
1411	30s. Mat Jenin daydreaming	50	55
1412	50s. Type **378**	70	70
1413	50s. As No. 1408	70	70
1414	50s. As No. 1409	70	70
1415	50s. As No. 1410	70	70
MS1416	100×70 mm. 5r. Ship's captain Si Tanggang and his rejected mother (59×38 mm)	4·25	4·50

Nos. 1407/8, 1409/10, 1412/13 and 1414/15 each form composite background designs.

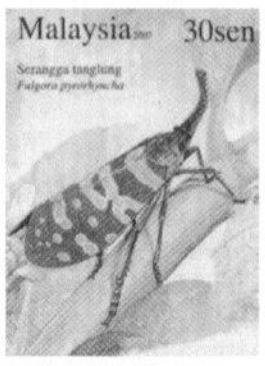

379 *Fulgora pyrorhyncha* (lantern fly)

2007. Insects. Multicoloured.

1417	30s. Type **379**	35	35
1418	30s. *Dysdercus cingulatus* (fruit bug)	35	35
1419	50s. *Valanga nigricornis* (grasshopper)	65	65
1420	50s. *Rhaphipodus hopei* (long-horn beetle)	65	65

No. **MS**1421 is left for miniature sheet not yet received.

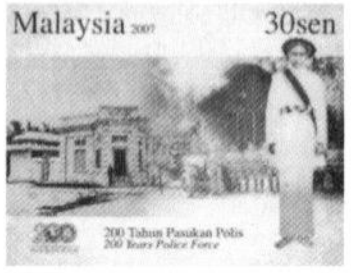

380 Peon, Fire Brigade and Hutton Lane Police Station, Penang, 1880

2007. Bicentenary of the Establishment of the Police Force. Multicoloured.

1422	30s. Type **380**	50	15
1423	50s. Royal Federation of Malaya Policeman, 1958 and 'Flying Squad' anti-terrorist police in jungle, 1948	90	90
1424	50s. Modern police officers, police vehicles and Putrajaya District Police Headquarters	90	90

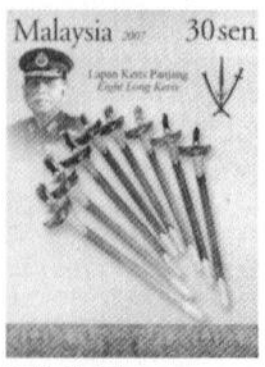

381 Eight Long Keris

2007. Royal Heritage of Negri Sembilan. Multicoloured.

1425	30s. Type **381**	35	10
1426	50s. Audience Hall	65	50
1427	1r. Raja of Negri Sembilan	1·10	1·40
MS1428	100×70 mm. 2r. Tuanku Ja'afar and Tuanku Najihah Binti Tuanku Besar Burhanudin	2·00	2·25

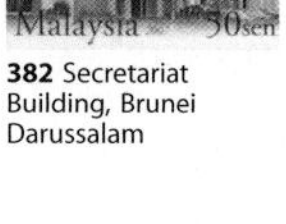

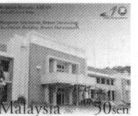

382 Secretariat Building, Brunei Darussalam

2007. 40th Anniv of ASEAN (Association of South-east Asian Nations). Ancient and Modern Architecture. Multicoloured.

1429	50s. Type **382**	65	65
1430	50s. National Museum of Cambodia	65	65
1431	50s. Fatahillah Museum, Jakarta, Indonesi	65	65
1432	50s. Typical Lao house	65	65
1433	50s. Malayan Railway Headquarters Building, Kuala Lumpur, Malaysia	65	65
1434	50s. Yangon Post Office, Myanmar	65	65
1435	50s. Malacañang Palace, Philippines	65	65
1436	50s. National Museum of Singapore	65	65
1437	50s. Vimanmek Mansion, Bangkok, Thailand	65	65
1438	50s. Presidential Palace, Hanoi, Vietnam	65	65

Similar designs were issued on the same day by the ten member countries, Indonesia, Philippines, Singapore, Thailand, Brunei, Vietnam, Laos, Myanmar and Cambodia.

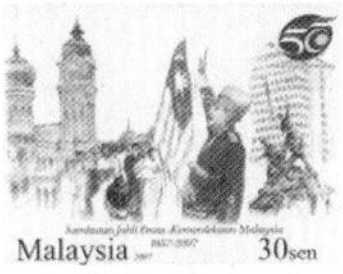

383 Tunku Abdul Rahman Putra Al-Haj declaring Independence, 31 August 1957

2007. 50th Anniv of Independence. Multicoloured.

1439	30s. Type **383**	35	35
1440	30s. Petronas Twin Towers, Kuala Lumpur Tower, Government administrative building at Putrajaya, Proton car and Penang Bridge	35	35
1441	50s. Tunku Abdul Rahman Putra Al-Haj signing Declaration of Independence	65	65
1442	50s. Golden Jubilee logo	65	65
1443	30s. Dato' Onn Jafar (founder of United Malays National Organization)	50	50
1444	30s. Tunku Abdul Rahman Putra Al-Haj (Prime Minister 1957–70)	50	50
1445	30s. Tun Abdul Razak (Prime Minister 1970–6)	50	50
1446	30s. Tun Tan Cheng Lock (founder of Malaysian Chinese Association)	50	50
1447	30s. Tun V. T. Sambanthan (President of Malaysian Indian Congress 1955–73)	50	50

DESIGNS: 1439/47, showing Malaysian leaders and national flag.

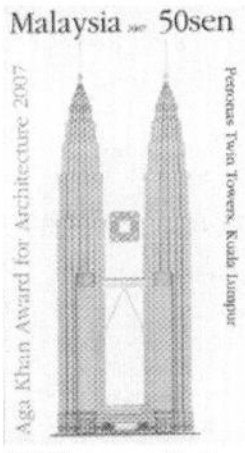

384 Petronas Twin Towers, Kuala Lumpur

2007. Aga Khan Award for Architecture.

1448	**384**	50s. grey, black and gold	4·50	1·75

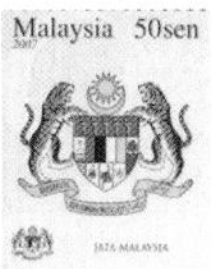

385 Arms of Malaysia

2007. State Emblems. Designs showing arms. Multicoloured.

1449	50s. Type **385**	50	50
1450	50s. Kedah	50	50
1451	50s. Negeri Sembilan	50	50
1452	50s. Pahang	50	50
1453	50s. Kelantan	50	50
1454	50s. Johor	50	50
1455	50s. Perak	50	50
1456	50s. Perlis	50	50
1457	50s. Selangor	50	50
1458	50s. Terengganu	50	50
1459	50s. Sarawak	50	50
1460	50s. Pulau Pinang	50	50
1461	50s. Sabah	50	50
1462	50s. Melaka	50	50

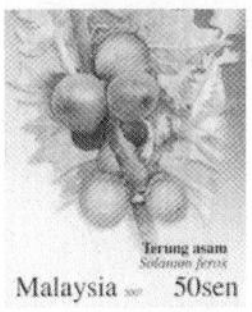

386 *Solanum ferox*

2007. Stamp Week. Rare Vegetables. Multicoloured.

1463	50s. Type **386**	50	50
1464	50s. *Momordica charantia* (bitter melon)	50	50
1465	50s. *Etlingera elatior* (torch ginger)	50	50
MS1466	120×70 mm. 1r.×4 *Luffa aegyptiaca* (smooth petola); *Psophocarpustetragonolobus* (winged bean); *Sesbania grandiflora*; *Solanum torvum*	3·00	3·25

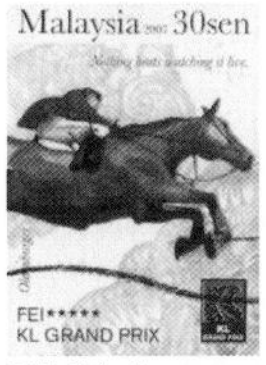

387 Oldenburger

2007. KL Grand Prix (show-jumping), Kuala Lumpur. Designs showing horse breeds as show-jumpers. Multicoloured.

1467	30s. Type **387**	40	20
1468	50s. Hanoverian	70	70
1469	50s. Dutch warmblood	70	70

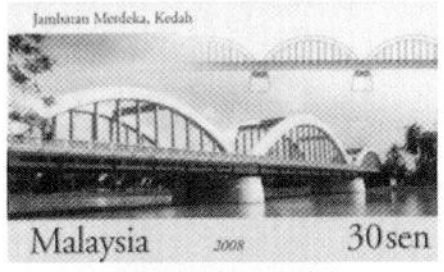

388 Merdeka Bridge, Kedah

2008. Bridges of Malaysia. Multicoloured.

1470	30s. Type **388**	30	10
1471	50s. Victoria Bridge, Perak	55	55
1472	50s. Kota Bridge, Selangor	55	55
1473	1r. Sungai Segamat Bridge, Johor	80	1·00

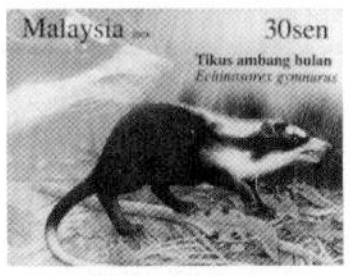

389 *Echinosorex gymnurus* (moonrat)

2008. Nocturnal Animals. Multicoloured.

1474	30s. Type **389**	30	20
1475	30s. *Mydaus javanensis* (Malay badger)	30	20
1476	50s. *Catopuma temminckii* (golden cat)	55	45
1477	1r. *Pteropus vampyrus* (flying fox)	80	1·00
MS1478	120×70 mm. 2r. *Tarsius bancanus* (tarsier) (vert); 3r. *Nycticebus coucang* (slow loris) (59×39 mm)	4·00	4·25

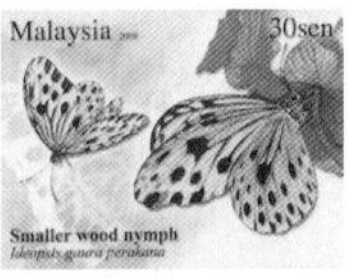

390 Smaller Wood Nymph (*Ideopsis gaura perakana*)

2008. Butterflies of Malaysia. Multicoloured.

1479	30s. Type **390**	40	45
1480	30s. Malayan lacewing (*Cethosia hypsea hypsina*)	40	45
1481	30s. Common rose (*Atrophaneura aristolochiae*)	40	45
1482	30s. Blue glassy tiger (*Ideopsis vulgaris*)	40	45
1483	30s. Green dragontail (*Lamproptera meges*)	40	45
1484	50s. Malay red harlequin (*Paralaxita damajanti damajanti*)	65	65
1485	1r. Glorious begum (*Agatasa calydonia calydonia*)	90	1·00
MS1486	114×66 mm. 5r. Five-bar swordtail (*Graphium antiphates*) (49×38 mm)	4·25	4·25

Nos. 1479/80 were printed together, *se-tenant*, forming a composite design of butterflies on a hibiscus flower.

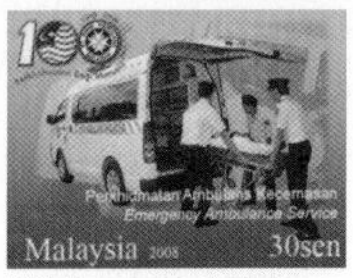

391 Emergency Ambulance Service

2008. Centenary of St. John Ambulance in Malaysia. Multicoloured.

1487	30s. Type **391**	50	20
1488	50s. First aid	95	70
1489	1r. Cardio pulmonary resuscitation	1·60	1·60

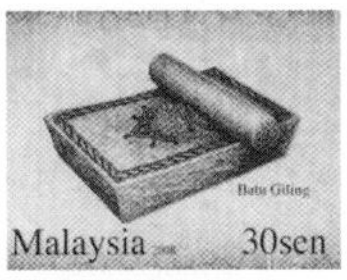

392 Batu Giling (stone grinder for chilli or spices)

2008. Traditional Malaysian Artefacts (2nd series). Multicoloured.

1490	30s. Type **392**	40	20
1491	50s. Supu (silver tobacco container)	65	65
1492	50s. Kukur Kelapa (wooden coconut grater with metal spur) (triangular 62×31 mm)	65	65

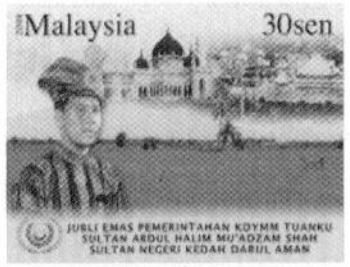

393 Sultan of Kedah, Paddy Field, Zahir Mosque and Alor Setar in early 1950s

2008. Golden Jubilee of Sultan Abdul Halim Mu'Adzam Shah of Kedah. Multicoloured.

1493	30s. Type **393**	40	20
1494	50s. Sultan, Jalan Telok Wanjah Water Fountain and old State Secretary's office	65	50
1495	1r. Sultan, Jubilee emblem and modern Alor Setar	90	1·25

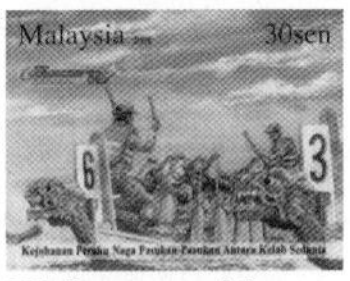

394 Drummer and Crew on Boat No. 6

2008. Sixth IDBF Club Crew World Championship, Penang. Designs showing dragon boats. Multicoloured.

1496	30s. Type **394**	40	20
1497	50s. Boats No. 2 and No. 5	65	50
1498	1r. Boat No. 4 and steerer in stern of other boat	90	1·25
MS1499	120×60 mm. 2r. Dragon boat No. 5 (79×29 mm)	1·75	1·75

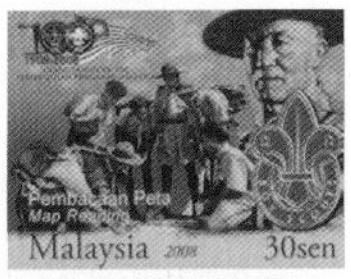

395 Scouts Map reading and Lord Baden-Powell (founder of World Scouting)

2008. Centenary of the Scouts Association of Malaysia. Multicoloured.

1500	30s. Type **395**	40	20
1501	50s. Scouts crossing Monkey Bridge	65	65
1502	50s. Sea scouts diving, kayaking and in launch	65	65

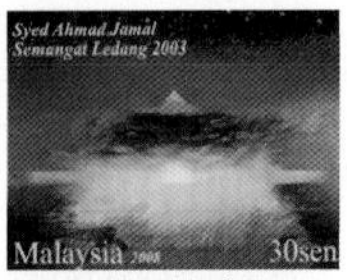

396 *Semangat Ledang* (Spirit of Ledang) (Syed Ahmad Jamal) (acrylic on canvas), 2003

2008. 'Treasures of the Nation's Visual Arts'. Artwork from the National Art Gallery of Malaysia. Multicoloured.

1503	30s. Type **396**	40	20
1504	50s. *Chuah Thean Teng* (Fruits Season) (Musim Buah) (batik), 1968 (vert)	65	65
1505	1r. *Pago-pago* (Latiff Mohidin) (oil on canvas), 1965 (35×35 mm)	90	1·00

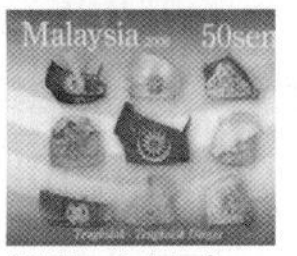

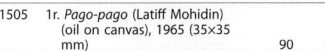

397 Tengkoloks for Yang Di-Pertuan Agong and Sultans of the Nine Malaysian States

2008. Royal Headgear. Designs showing official tengkoloks of the Sultans of the Malaysian states. Multicoloured.

1506	50s. Type **397**	65	65
1507	50s. Black tengkolok with gold embroidery and platinum star and crescent (Yang Di-Pertuan Agong at his Coronation)	65	65
1508	50s. Black tengkolok with gold thread design and Kedah crest with diamond paddy stalks (Kedah)	65	65
1509	50s. Yellow songket destar (Negri Sembilan)	65	65
1510	50s. Purple tengkolok with embroidery (Pahang)	65	65
1511	50s. Pale blue destar with crest (Kelantan)	65	65
1512	50s. White destar with silver embroidery and crest (Perak)	65	65
1513	50s. Embroidered tengkolok with white and yellow crest (Perlis)	65	65
1514	50s. Yellow songket destar with crest (Selangor)	65	65
1515	50s. Embroidered yellow songket destar with crest (Trengganu)	65	65

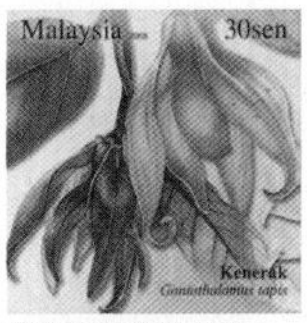

398 *Goniothalamus tapis*

2008. Unique Flowers. Multicoloured.

1516	50s. Type **398**	65	65
1517	50s. *Gloriosa superba*	65	65
1518	50s. *Quisqualis indica*	65	65
1519	50s. *Michelia figo*	65	65
MS1520	100×70 mm. 5r. *Epiphyllum oxypetalum* (38×49 mm)	4·25	4·25

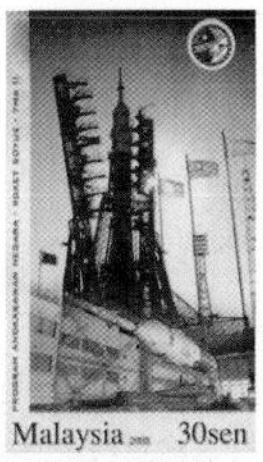

399 *Soyuz TMA II* Rocket

2008. National Astronaut Programme. Multicoloured.

1521	30s. Type **399**	40	20
1522	50s. Dr. Sheikh Muszaphar Syukor Al-Masrie conducting experiments in microgravity	65	50
1523	1r. International Space Station	90	1·25
MS1524	100×70 mm. 1r. Launch of Dr. Al-Masrie aboard rocket, Baikonur Cosmodrome, 2007; 1r. *Soyuz TMA II* rocket in flight	2·00	2·00

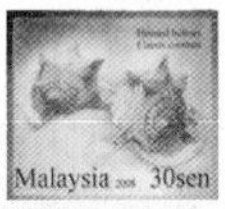

400 Horned Helmet (*Cassis cornuta*)

2008. Seashells of Malaysia. Multicoloured.

1525	30s. Type **400**	40	35
1526	30s. Burnt murex (*Chicoreus brunneus*)	40	35
1527	50s. Frog shell (*Tutufa rubeta*)	65	75
1528	50s. Triton's trumpet (*Charonia tritonis*)	65	75
MS1529	90×60 mm. 2r. Venus comb murex (*Murex pecten*) (60×40 mm)	2·00	2·00

No. **MS**1529 also exists imperforate.

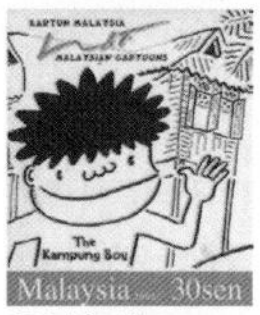

401 'The Kampung Boy'

2008. Malaysian Cartoons by Lat (Dato' Mohd. Nor Khalid). Nos. 1530/8 black and red (Nos. 1530/8) or black and silver (MS1539) designs.

1530 30s. Type **401** 40 45
1531 30s. Riding the pinang frond ('Permainen Anak Kampung') (58×33 mm) 40 45
1532 30s. Drawing caricature of teacher Mrs. Hew on blackboard ('Guru Sekolah Yang Garang') (58×33 mm) 40 45
1533 30s. Mat and Frankie playing at rock musicians with brush and racket ('Town Boy') 40 45
1534 30s. Lat at easel painting, spilling paint everywhere 40 45
1535 50s. As Type **401** 65 65
1536 50s. As No. 1531 65 65
1537 50s. As No. 1532 65 65
1538 50s. As No. 1533 65 65
MS1539 120×70 mm. 5r. People on pedestrian crossing ('Malaysian daily life') (60×40 mm) 4·25 4·25

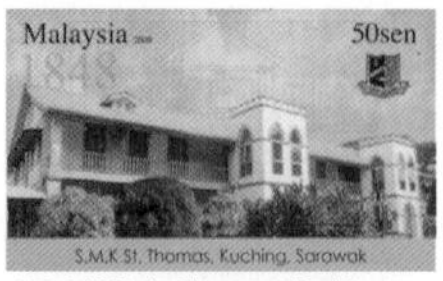

402 S.M.K. St. Thomas, Kuching, Sarawak

2008. Premier Schools. Multicoloured.

1540 50s. Type **402** 65 65
1541 50s. SMK Victoria (Victoria Institution), Kuala Lumpur 65 65
1542 50s. SMK Convent Bukit Nanas, Kuala Lumpur 65 65
1543 50s. SM All Saints, Kota Kinabalu, Sabah 65 65

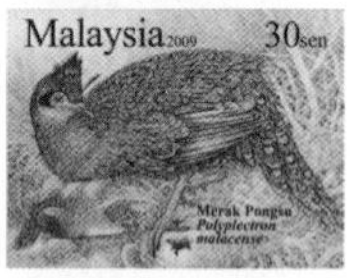

403 *Polyplectron malacense* (Malaysian peacock-pheasant)

2009. Unique Birds of Malaysia. Multicoloured.

1544 30s. Type **403** 50 25
1545 50s. *Mycteria cinerea* (milky stork) 90 90
1546 50s. *Myophonus robinsoni* (Malaysian whistling thrush) 90 90
MS1547 110×70 mm. 5r. *Aceros subruficollis* (wreathed hornbill) 4·75 4·75

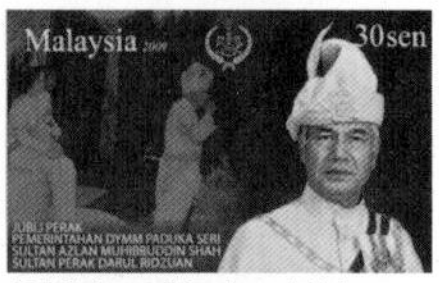

404 Sultan of Perak and Sultan kissing Ceremonial Sword during Installation Ceremony, 1985

2009. Silver Jubilee of Sultan Azlan Muhibbuddin Shah of Perak. Multicoloured.

1548 30s. Type **404** 40 20
1549 50s. Sultan of Perak and Ubudiah Mosque 65 50
1550 1r. Sultan Azlan Muhibbuddin Shah and Raja Permaisuri Perak Tuanku Bainun 90 1·25

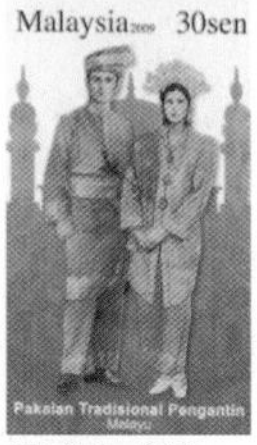

405 Malay Bride and Groom and Mosque

2009. Traditional Wedding Costumes. Multicoloured. (a) As T **405**.

1551 30s. Type **405** 40 45
1552 30s. Chinese bride and groom, and temple columns with dragons and phoenix 40 45
1553 30s. Indian bride and groom and temple 40 45
1554 30s. Orang Ulu bride and groom and traditional house 40 45
1555 30s. Bajau bride and groom and traditional house 40 45

(b) Designs as Nos. 1551/5 but with different backgrounds.

1556 50s. Malay bride and groom and Bunga telur (wedding decoration) 65 65
1557 50s. Chinese bride and groom and red "double happiness" symbols 65 65
1558 50s. Indian bride and groom and garland 65 65
1559 50s. Orang Ulu bride and groom and Bunga Jarau (wooden wedding ornament) 65 65
1560 50s. Bajau bride and groom and Tipo serisir (woven silk material and beadwork wedding mat) 65 65

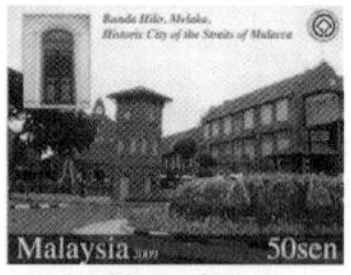

406 Stadthuys (former Dutch governor's residence) and Old Town Square, Banda Hilir, Malacca

2009. UNESCO World Heritage Sites. Multicoloured.

1561 50s. Type **406** 65 65
1562 50s. Old City Hall (now Municipal Council building), George Town, Penang 65 65
1563 50s. Pinnacles of Gunung Api, Mulu National Park and tarsier 65 65
1564 50s. Kinabalu National Park and scarlet minivet (bird) 65 65
MS1565 70×110 mm. 50s.×4 Banda Hilir, Malacca; Lenticular cloud over mountain peak, Kinabalu National Park; Clock tower and colonial corner building, George Town, Penang; Cave, Mulu National Park (all 59×25 mm) 1·75 1·75

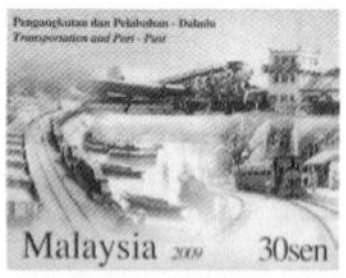

407 Railway, Harbour, Aircraft and Steam Locomotive ('Transportation and Port – Past')

2009. 'Engineering Excellence in Nation Building'. Multicoloured.

1566 30s. Type **407** 55 55
1567 30s. Modern buildings ('Transportation and Ports – Present') 55 55
1568 30s. Switchboard and pylon ('Telecommunication and Power – Past') 55 55
1569 30s. Satellite dish and pylons ('Telecommunication and Power – Present') 55 55
1570 50s. Bridge and dam ('Road, Bridge and Dam – Past') 75 75
1571 50s. Reservoir, roads and bridge ('Road, Bridge and Dam – Present') 75 75

Nos. 1566/7, 1568/9 and 1570/1 were each printed together, *se-tenant*, each pair forming a composite design.

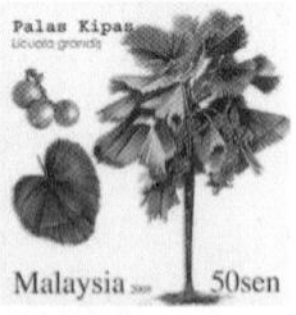

408 *Licuala grandis*

2009. Palm Trees. Multicoloured.

1572 50s. Type **408** 65 65
1573 50s. *Caryota mitis* 65 65
1574 50s. *Livistona saribus* 65 65
MS1575 80×80 mm. 3r. *Livistona endauensis* and *Johannesteijsmannia altifrons* (69×49 mm) 2·75 2·75

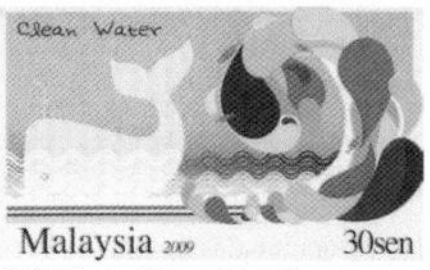

409 Whale (Clean Water)

2009. Conservation of Nature. Multicoloured.

1577 30s. Type **409** 55 55
1578 50s. Rainforest trees ('Go Green') 75 75
1579 50s. Chimneys emitting pollution ('Fresh Air') 75 75

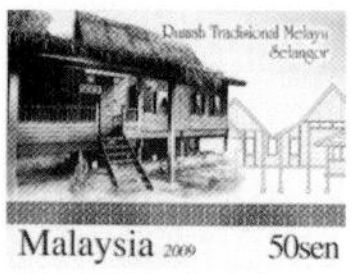

410 Malay Traditional House, Selangor

2009. Traditional Houses. Multicoloured.

1580 50s. Type **410** 75 75
1581 50s. Dusun Lotud traditional house, Sabah 75 75
1582 50s. Kutai house, Perak 75 75
1583 50s. Twelve Pillars house, Kota Bharu, Kelantan 75 75
1584 50s. Iban long house, Sarawak 75 75
1585 50s. Semai house, Pahang 75 75
1586 50s. Limas house, Pontian, Johor 75 75
1587 50s. Long house, Kedah 75 75
1588 50s. Limas Bungkus house, Besut, Terengganu 75 75
1589 50s. Adat Minangkabau house, Negeri Sembilan 75 75
1590 50s. 'Gajah Menyusu' verandah house, Pulau Pinang 75 75
1591 50s. Long roofed house, Perlis 75 75
1592 50s. Malay house, Melaka 75 75
1593 50s. Bajau Laut, Sabah 75 75
1594 50s. Verandah house, Pahang 75 75
1595 50s. Bidayuh headhouse, Sarawak 75 75

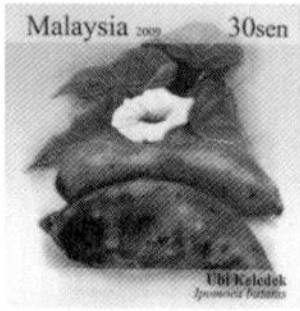

411 *Ipomoea batatas* (sweet potato)

2009. Tuber Plants. Multicoloured.

1596 30s. Type **411** 55 55
1597 30s. *Manihot esculenta crantz* (cassava or tapioca) 55 55
1598 50s. *Pachyrrhizus erosus* (yam bean) 75 75
1599 50s. *Dioscorea alataL.* (yam) 75 75
MS1600 100×71 mm. 3r. *Colocasia esculenta* (taro) (diamond 62×63 mm) 2·75 2·75

2009. Philakorea 2009 International Stamp Exhibition, Seoul. As No. **MS**1575 additionally inscr with 'PHILAKOREA 2009 24th Asian International Stamp Exhibition' and emblem on upper right sheet margin.

MS1601 80×80 mm. 3r. *Livistona endauensis* and *Johannesteijsmannia altifrons* (69×49 mm) 2·75 2·75

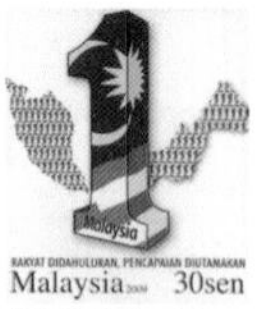

412 '1 Malaysia' Logo

2009. '1 Malaysia People First Performance Now'. Multicoloured.

1602 30s. Type **412** 55 55
1603 30s. National flag in heart surrounded by Malaysians of different races 55 55
1604 30s. Malaysian citizens and light bulb 55 55
MS1605 70×100 mm. 5r. Citizens of different races surrounding 'Malaysia 1' logo 4·50 4·50

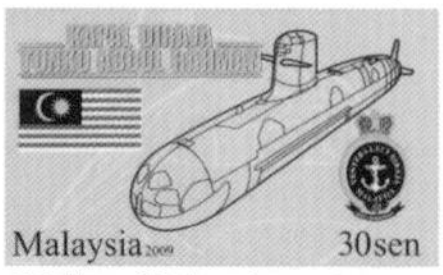

413 Plan of Submarine

2009. First Malaysian Submarine. Multicoloured.

1611 30s. Type **413** 55 55
1612 50s. New Scorpene submarine *KD Tunku Abdul Rahman* (seen from above) 75 75
1613 50s. New submarine (side view) 75 75

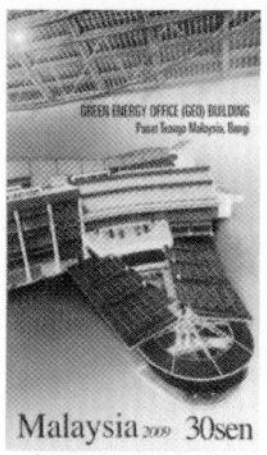

414 Green Energy Office at the Green Energy Centre, Bangi

2009. Energy Efficient Buildings. Multicoloured.

1614 30s. Type **414** 55 55
1615 50s. Green Technology and Water Ministry's Low Energy Office, Putrajaya 75 75
1616 1r. Energy Commission's Diamond Building, Putrajaya 90 90

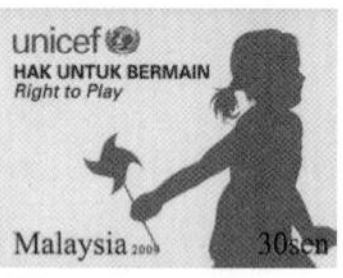

415

2010. 'Caring Society'. Multicoloured.

1616a 30s. Type **415** 55 55
1617 30s. Boy drinking ('Right to Food') 55 55
1618 30s. Boy with backpack ('Right to Education') 55 55
1619 30s. Girl with umbrella (Right to Protection) 55 55
1620 1r. Children and rainbow ('Convention on the Rights of the Child') 10 1·00

No. 1620 is embossed with Braille.

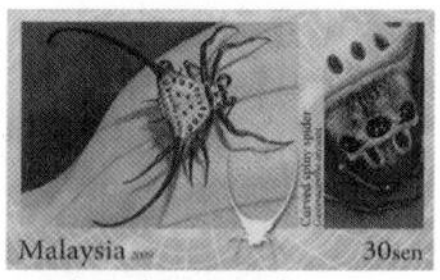

416 Curved Spiny Spider (*Gasteracantha arcuata*)

2010. Stamp Week

1621 30s. Type **416** 60 60
1622 30s. Fighting spider (*Thiania bhamoensis*) 60 60
1623 50s. St. Andrew's Cross spider (*Argiope versicolor*) 60 60
1624 1r. Golden orb-web spider (*Nephila maculata*) 60 60
MS1625 100×65 mm. 5r. Black scorpion (*Heterometrus longimanus*) (hexagon 64×32 mm). Wmk sideways. P 13½ 1·00 1·00

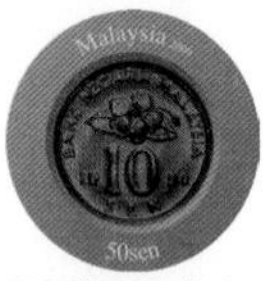

417 Obverse of 10s. Coin showing Hibiscus Flower

2010. Malaysian Currency

1626 50s. Type **417** 60 60
1627 50s. Reverse of 10s. coin showing congkak board (for indoor games with marbles) 60 60
1628 50s. Obverse of 20s. coin showing hibiscus flower 60 60
1629 50s. Reverse of 20s. coin showing tepak sirih (box for storing betel leaves) 60 60
1630 50s. Obverse of 50s. coin showing hibiscus flower 60 60
1631 50s. Reverse of 50s. coin showing kite 60 60
MS1632 120×80 mm. 5r. New 50r. bank note (50×40 mm) 4·50 4·50

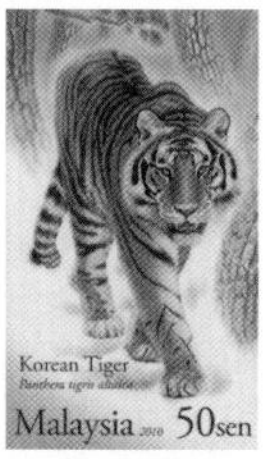

418 Korean Tiger (Panthera tigris altaica)

2010. Tigers. Multicoloured.

1633	50s. Type **418**	75	75
1634	50s. Malayan tiger (*Panthera tigris jacksoni*)	75	75

Nos. 1633/34 were printed together *se-tenant* as horizontal pairs in sheets of 20.

Nos. 1633/34 commemorate the 50th anniversary of diplomatic relations between Malaysia and Korea.

Stamps in a similar designs were issued by Korea.

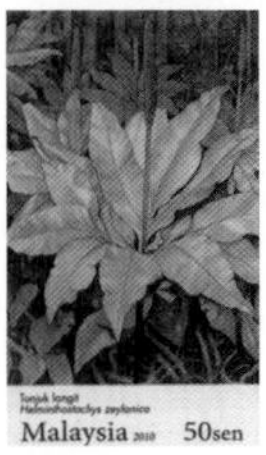

419 *Helminthostachys zeylanica*

2010. Ferns. Multiocoloured.

1635	50s. Type **419**	60	60
1636	50s. *Stenochlaena palustris*	60	60
1637	50s. *Platycerium coronarium*	60	60
1638	50s. *Dicranopteris linearis*	60	60
1639	50s. *Diplazium esculentum*	60	60
MS1640	120x70 mm. 3r. *Asplenium nidus*; *Matonia pectinata* and *Dipteris conjugata* (100x45 mm). P 14	3·50	3·50

Nos. 1635/9 were printed together *setenant*, forming a composite design of ferns in a rainforest.

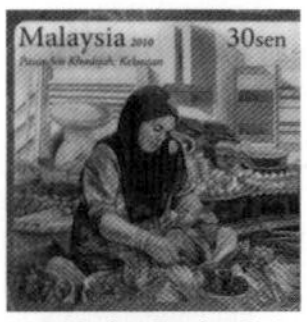

420 Market Trader, Siti Khadijah Market, Kelantan

2010. Local Markets. Multicoloured.

1641	30s. Type **420**	50	50
1642	30s. Vegetable stalls on ground floor, Siti Khadijah Market, Kelantan	50	50
1643	50s. Food stalls, Kraf Tangan Market, Kota Kinabalu	60	60
1644	Handicraft stalls, Kraf Tangan Market, Kota Kinabalu	60	60
MS1645	110×80 mm. 1r. Handicrafts stall, Pekan Rabu Market, Kedah; Stall at Pekan Rabu Market, Kedah.	3·75	3·75
MS1646	110×80 mm. 1r. Vegetable and fish stall, Pasar Minggu Satok Market; 1r. Flower and herb stall, Pasar Minggu Satok Market.	3·75	3·75

Nos. 1641/2 and 1643/4 were each printed together, *se-tenant*, each pair forming a composite design of a market.

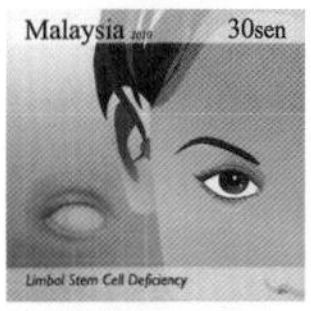

421 Limbal Stem Cell Deficiency

2010. Medical Excellence. Multicoloured.

1647	30s. Type **421**	55	55
1648	50s. Premaxilla retractor	60	60
1649	1r. Arm transplant	1·10	1·10

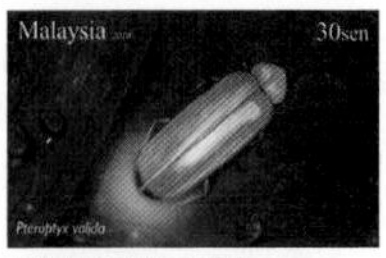

422 Pteroptyx valida

2010. Fireflies. Multicoloured.

1650	30s. Type **422**	40	40
1651	30s. *Pteroptx bearni*	40	40
1652	50s. *Diaphanes* sp.	55	55
1653	50s. *Lychnuris* sp.	55	55
MS1654	110×80 mm. 5r. *Pteroptx tener* (60×40 mm)	6·50	6·50

No. **MS**1654 has light reflecting ink die-stamped onto firefly's tail.

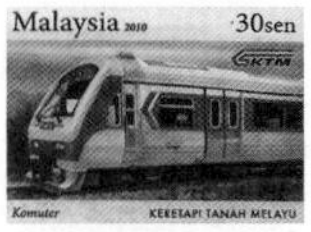

423 Komuter Locomotive

2010. 125th Anniv of KTM (Keretapi Tanah Melayu) Railways

(a) Sheet stamps

1655	30s. Type **423**	50	50
1656	30s. ETS locomotive	50	50
1657	50s. *Blue Tiger* locomotive (70×25 mm)	75	75
1658	1r. 56 Class steam locomotive (70×25 mm)	1·00	1·00
MS1659	120×70 mm. 3r. FMSR Class T steam locomotive (in shed) (30×50 mm)	4·00	4·00

(b) Booklet stamps

1660	30s. 20 Class locomotives (70×25 mm)	50	50
1661	30s. Designs as Nos. 1655/6 (70×25 mm)	50	50
1662	30s. As No. 1657	50	50
1663	30s. As No. 1658	50	50
1664	30s. FMSR Class T steam locomotive	50	50

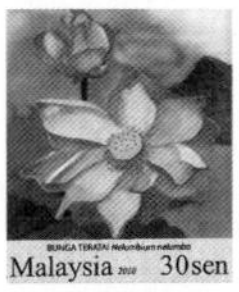

424 Nelumbium nelumbo (sacred lotus)

2010. Garden Flowers. Multicoloured.

A. With imprint date '2010' at foot

1668A	30s. Type **424**	45	45
1669A	50s. *Hydrangea macrophylla*	55	55
1670A	60s. Bougainvillea	75	75
1671A	70s. *Hippeastrum reticulatum*	85	85
1672A	80s. *Hibiscus rosa-sinensis*	90	90
1673A	90s. *Ipomoea indica*	1·00	1·00
1674A	1r. *Canna orientalis*	1·40	1·40
1675A	2r. *Allamanda cathartica*	2·40	2·40

B. Without imprint date

1671B	70s. *Hippeastrum reticulatum*	85	85
1672B	80s. *Hibiscus rosa-sinensis*	90	90
1673B	90s. *Ipomoea indica*	1·10	1·10
1674B	1r. *Canna orientalis*	1·40	1·40

Nos. 1665/7 and 1676/8 are left for possible additions to this definitive series.

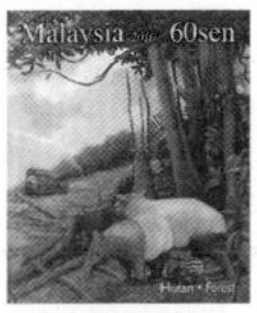

425 Tapirs and Decimated Forest

2010. Threatened Habitats. Multicoloured.

1679	60s. Type **425**	60	60
1680	70s. Turtle and damaged coral reef	1·25	1·25
1681	80s. Otter on bank and dead fish in polluted river	1·25	1·25

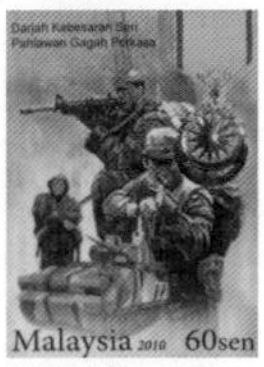

426 Soldiers and Tank

2010. Grand Knight of Valour Award. Multicoloured.

1682	60s. Type **426**	60	60
1683	70s. Recipients	85	85
1684	80s. Soldiers	1·25	1·25

2010. Bangkok 2010 25th Asian International Stamp Exhibition, Thailand

MS1685	120×70 mm. 3r. FMSR Class T steam locomotive (in shed) (30×50 mm)	2·75	2·75

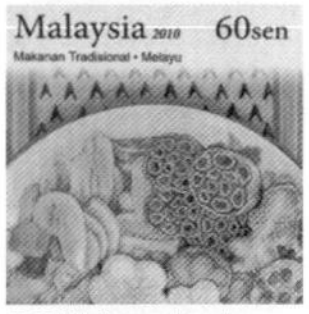

427 Malayan Food

2010. Traditional Festive Food

(a) Booklet stamps

1691	60s. Malayan (bottom portion)	50	50
1692	60s. Chinese (bottom portion)	50	50
1693	60s. Indian (bottom portion)	50	50
1694	60s. Sabah (bottom portion)	50	50
1695	60s. Sarawak (bottom portion)	50	50

(b) Sheet stamps

1696	80s. Malayan (top portion)	70	70
1697	80s. Chinese (top portion)	70	70
1698	80s. Indian (top portion)	70	70
1699	80s. Sabah (top portion)	70	70
1700	80s. Sarawak (top portion)	70	70
1702	80s. Malayan (bottom portion)	70	70
1702	80s. Chinese (bottom portion)	70	70
1703	80s. Indian (bottom portion)	70	70
1704	80s. Sabah (bottom portion)	70	70
1705	80s. Sarawak (bottom portion)	70	70
MS1706	130×100 mm. 1r. Indian; 1r. Chinese; 1r. Malayan (all diamond shape, 48×48 mm). Wmk sideways	4·00	4·00

Nos. 1686 and 1691, 1687 and 1692, 1688 and 1693, 1689 and 1694, 1690 and 1695, 1696 and 1701, 1697 and 1702, 1698 and 1703, 1699 and 1704 and 1700 and 1705 each form composite designs showing the complete plate of food.

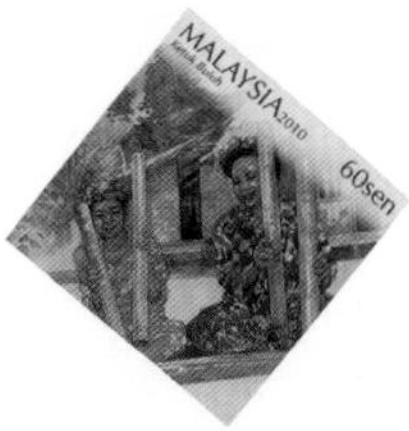

428 Ketuk Buluh

2010. Lifestyles of the Aboriginal People. Multicoloured.

1707	60s. Type **428**	65	65
1708	70s. Menyumpit hunter with blowpipe	90	90
1709	80s. Mengukir wood carver	1·40	1·40

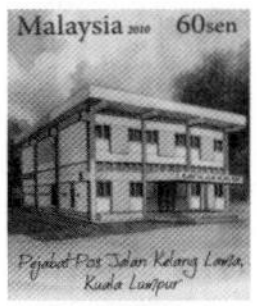

426 Post Office, Jalan Kelang Lama, Kuala Lumpur

2010. Post Office Buildings. Multicoloured.

1710	60s. Type **429**	60	60
1711	60s. Layang-Layang, Johor	60	60
1712	60s. Jalan Raja, Kedah	60	60
1713	60s. Temangan, Kelantan	60	60
1714	60s. Mertimau, Malaka	60	60
1715	60s. Seremban, Negri Sembilan	60	60
1716	60s. Bukit Fraser, Pahang	60	60
1717	60s. Kuala Kangsar, Perak	60	60
1718	60s. Kaki Bukit, Perlis	60	60
1719	60s. Jalan Bagan Luar, Penang	60	60
1720	60s. Kudat, Sabah	60	60
1721	60s. Kuching, Sarawak	60	60
1722	60s. Kajang, Selangor	60	60
1723	60s. Kuala Terengganu, Trengganu	60	60
1724	60s. Kuala Lumpur and Federal Territories flag	60	60
1725	60s. Johor Bahru, and Johore flag	60	60
1726	60s. Sungai Petani and Kedah flag	60	60
1727	60s. Rantau Panjang and Kelantan flag	60	60
1728	60s. Alor Gajah and Malacca flag	60	60
1729	60s. Bandar Baru Serting and Negri Sembilan flag	60	60
1730	60s. Ringlet and Pahang flag	60	60
1731	60s. Tronoh and Perak flag	60	60
1732	60s. Kangar and Perlis flag	60	60
1733	60s. Bukit Mertajam and Penang flag	60	60
1734	60s. Kota Kinabalu and Sabah flag	60	60
1735	60s. Sarikei and Sarawak flag	60	60
1736	60s. Bukit Rotan and Selangor flag	60	60
1737	60s. Jerteh and Trengganu flag	60	60

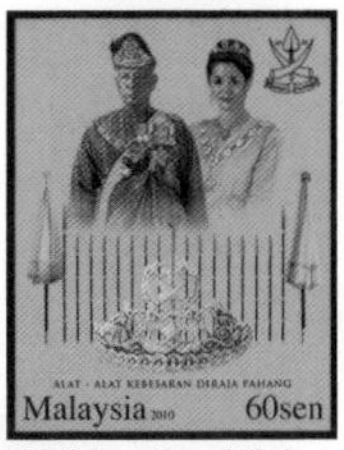

430 Sultan Ahmad Shah, Sultanah Kalsom and Pahang Crown

2010. Heritage of Pahang. Multicoloured.

1738	60s. Type **430**	90	90
1739	80s. Sultan (in military uniform), woven cloth and handicrafts	1·10	1·10
1740	1r. Sultan Ahmad Shah and thrones	1·25	1·25

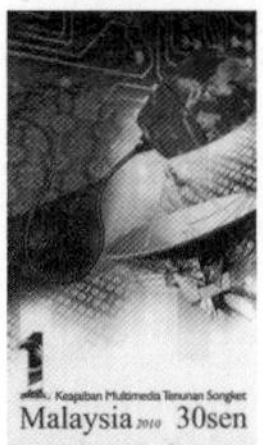

431 Satellite Image in Computer Mouse, Satellite Dish and Songket Textile Designs

2010. '1 Malaysia' (2nd series). Multicoloured.

1741	30s. Type **431**	45	45
1742	30s. Traditional kite, astronaut and space shuttle	45	45
1743	50s. Petronas Twin Towers, other modern buildings and carved wood panel	65	65
1744	50s. Woven basket and bio-technology	65	65

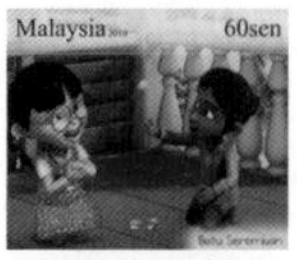

432 Mei Mei and Devi

2010. Stamp Week. Traditional Games of the Past with Upin, Ipin and Friends (characters from TV programme). Multicoloured.

1745	60s. Type **432**	90	90
1746	60s. Grandmother Opah and Susanti	90	90
1747	60s. Upin, Ipin and Ehsan playing war game	90	90
1748	60s. Fizi and Mail playing with tin can 'telephones'	90	90
1749	60s. Upin, Jarjah and Mei Mei	90	90
1750	60s. Ipin, Jarjah and Susanti	90	90
MS1751	100×80 mm. 5r. Upin and Ipin with elder sister Ros making shadow puppets	6·50	6·50

Nos. 1745/6, 1747/8 and 1749/50 were each printed together, *se-tenant*, as horizontal pairs in sheets of 20 stamps, each pair forming a composite design.

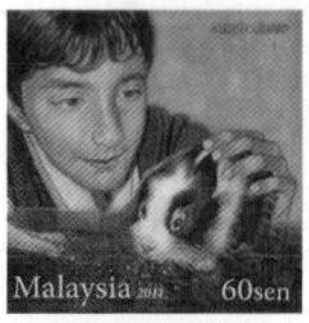

433 Boy with Rabbit

2011. Children's Pets. Multicoloured.

1752	60s. Type **433**	80	80
1753	80s. Girl with cat	1·10	1·10
1754	1r. Girl with dog	1·40	1·40
MS1755	Circular 95×95 mm. 5r. Rabbit	6·50	6·50

2011. Indipex 2011 World Philatelic Exhibition, New Delhi. No. **MS**1755 additionally inscr with INDIPEX 2011 emblem at top left of stamp

MS1755a	Circular 95×95 mm. 5r. Rabbit	6·75	6·75

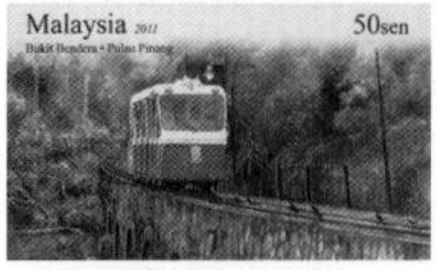

434 Funicular Railway, Bukit Pendera (Penang Hill)

2011. Highland Tourist Spots. Multicoloured.

1756	50s. Type **434**	65	65
1757	60s. Tea picking, Cameron Highlands, Pahang	90	90
1758	90s. Cable car, Gunung Mat Cincang, Langkawi, Kedah	1·10	1·10
1759	1r. Field of cabbages, Kundasang, Sabah	1·40	1·40

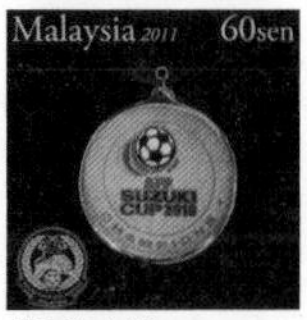

435 Medallion

2011. Suzuki Cup (football tournament for south-east Asian nations), Vietnam and Indonesia

1760	60s. Type **435**	90	90
1761	60s. Trophy (30×50 mm)	90	90

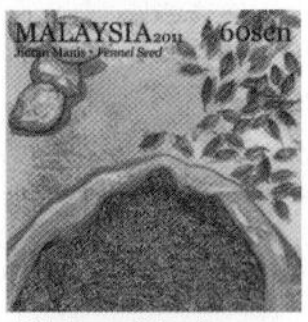

436 Fennel Seed

2011. Spices. Micoloured.

1762	60s. Type **436**	90	90
1763	60s. Sack of tumeric (top portion)	90	90
1764	60s. Sack of chilli (top portion)	90	90
1765	60s. Sack of coriander (top portion)	90	90
1766	60s. White pepper (top portion)	90	90
1767	60s. Sack of fennel seed (bottom portion)	90	90
1768	60s. Sack of tumeric (bottom portion)	90	90
1769	60s. Sack of chilli (bottom portiion)	90	90
1770	60s. Sack of coriander (bottom portion)	90	90
1771	60s. Sack of white pepper (bottom portion)	90	90
1772	60s. Cinnamon sticks	90	90
1773	90s. Star anise	1·10	1·10
1774	1r. Cardamom pods	1·25	1·25
MS1775	121×80 mm. 1r. White peppers, chillis,coriander and fennel seed (50×60 mm); 1r. Cinnamon sticks, star anise and tumeric (50×60 mm)	3·75	3·75

Nos. 1762 and 1767, 1763 and 1768, 1764 and 1769, 1765 and 1770 and 1766 and 1771 each form composite designs showing the complete sack of spices. Nos. 1762/71 form a composite background design

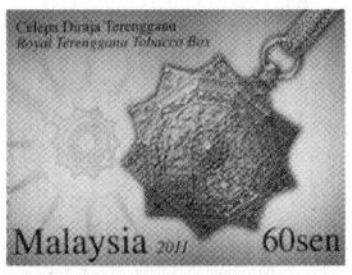

437 18th Century Tobacco Box

2011. Artifacts of National Heritage. Multicoloured.

1776	60s. Type **437**	90	90
1777	60s. Sultan Alau'uddin Riayat Shah gold coin	90	90
1778	60s. 15th century bronze bell from Dong S'on, Vietnaml	90	90
1779	60s. Sultan Zainal Abidin II of Terengganu gold coin	90	90
1780	60s. Bronze statue of Avalokitesvara, 7-12th century AD (inscr 'Statute')	90	90
1781	60s. Malay belt buckle	90	90
1782	60s. 16th century gold coin showing deer	90	90
1783	60s. Sultan Abdul Samad of Selangor's set of sireh	90	90
1784	60s. Sultan Muzaffar Shah of Johore gold coin	90	90
1785	60s. Arch of sitting Buddha, 1000-1100 AD	90	90

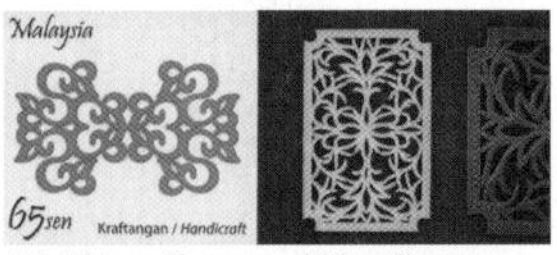

438 Hibiscus Flowers and Silver Flower

2011. Personalised Stamps. Silverwork. Multicoloured (except No. 1786).

1786	35s. Type **438** (bright green, deep green and black)	80	80
1787	35s. Silver durian fruit and pink pattern	80	80
1788	65s. Pattern and screen	1·75	1·75
1789	65s. Silverwork Wau Bulan (moon kite) and blue pattern	1·75	1·75

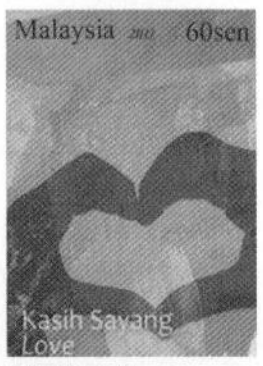

439 'Love'

2011. Virtues. Multicoloured.

1790	60s. Type **439**	75	75
1791	60s. Bee and honeycomb ('Hardworking')	75	75
1792	60s. Smiling face ('Courteous')	75	75
1793	60s. Man bowing and taking off hat ('Mutual Respect')	75	75
1794	60s. Mountaineer on summit with flag ('Independent')	75	75
1795	60s. Green ribbon ('Awareness')	75	75
1796	60s. Outstretched hand and hand holding walking stick ('Kind Hearted')	75	75
1797	60s. 'Thank You' in seven languages ('Thankful')	75	75
1798	60s. Raised hands with smiley faces on fingertips ('Living in Harmony')	75	75
1799	60s. Raised hand ('Integrity')	75	75

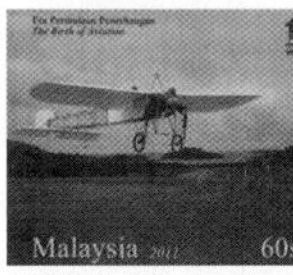

440 G. P. Fuller landing Monoplane at Ampang Race Course, Kuala Lumpur, 1911

2011. Centenary of Malaysian Aviation. Multicoloured.

1800	60s. Type **440** ('The Birth of Aviation')	90	90
1801	80s. Malayan Airways aircraft on ground ('Era of Aviation Development')	1·10	1·10
1802	1r. Modern aircraft on ground ('Era of Aviation Excellence')	1·40	1·40

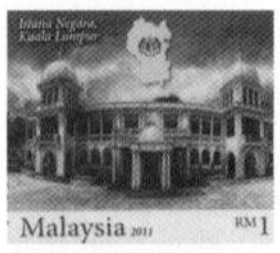

441 Negara Palace, Kuala Lumpur

2011. Royal Palaces. Multicoloured.

1803	1r. Type **441**	1·25	1·25
1804	1r. Seri Menanti Palace, Negri Sembilan	1·25	1·25
1805	1r. Alam Shah Palace, Klang, Selangor	1·25	1·25
1806	1r. Arau Palace, Perlis	1·25	1·25
1807	1r. Maziah Palace, Kuala Terengganu	1·25	1·25
1808	1r. Anak Bukit Palace, Kedah	1·25	1·25
1809	1r. Balai Besar Palace, Kelantan	1·25	1·25
1810	1r. Abu Bakar Palace, Pekan, Pahang	1·25	1·25
1811	1r. Besar Palace, Johore	1·25	1·25
1812	1r. Iskandariah Palace, Perak	1·25	1·25

2011. Philanippon '11 World Stamp Exhibition, Yokohama, Japan. As No. **MS**1659 additionally inscr 'PHILA NIPPON '11 2011' and emblem on upper left sheet margin

MS1813	120×70 mm. 3r. FMSR Class T steam locomotive (in shed) (30×50 mm)	9·25	9·25

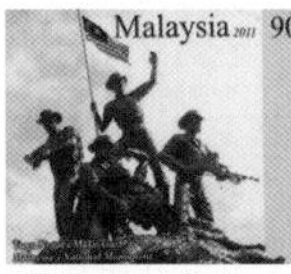

442 Malaysia's National Monument

2011. Malaysia - Indonesia Joint Issue. Multicoloured.

1814	90s. Type **442**	1·00	1·00
1815	90s. Proclamation Monument	1·00	1·00
1816	90s. Malaysia's first currency issued after Independence	1·00	1·00
1817	90s. ORI (Oeang Republik Indonesia) banknote	1·00	1·00
1818	90s. Malaya 1957 Independence Day stamp	1·00	1·00
1819	90s. Indonesia 1949 Surakarta Military Stamp	1·00	1·00
1820	90s. *Gallus gallus* (red junglefowl)	1·00	1·00
1821	90s. *Gallus varius* (green junglefowl)	1·00	1·00

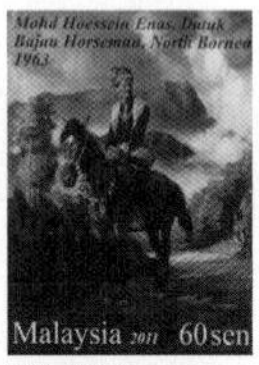

443 *Bajau Horseman, North Borneo* (Mohammed Hoessein Enas), 1963

2011. Visual Arts (2nd series). Multicoloured.

1822	60s. Type **443**	95	95
1823	90s. *The Rooster* (Anthony Lau), 1963 (horiz)	1·25	1·25
1824	1r. *Flag* (Nik Zainal Abidin Nik Salleh), 1970 (horiz)	1·50	1·50

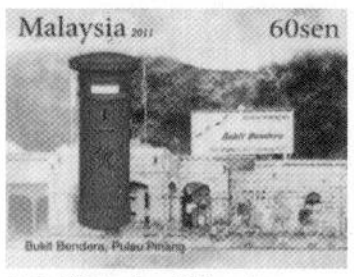

444 Victorian Pillar Box, Bukit Bendera, Penang

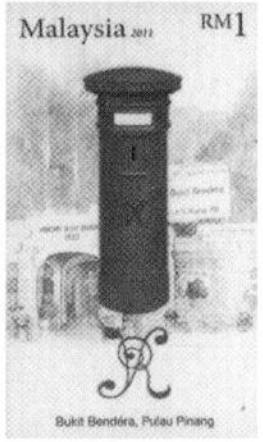

445 Victorian Pillar Box, Bukit Bendera, Penang

2011. Stamp Week. Postboxes. Multicoloured.

(a) Self-adhesive booklet stamps as T **444**

1825	60s. Type **444**	1·40	1·40
1826	60s. Wall box, Bukit Fraser, Pahang	1·40	1·40
1827	60s. Pillar box on pole, Bandaraya Bersejarah, Melaka	1·40	1·40
1828	60s. Pillar box, Seremban, Negri Sembilan	1·40	1·40
1829	60s. Wall box, Pejabat Pos Besar, Kuala Lumpur	1·40	1·40

(b) Ordinary gum. Sheet stamps as T **445**

1830	1r. Type **445**	2·25	2·25
1831	1r. Wall box, Bukit Fraser, Pahang	2·25	2·25
1832	1r. Pillar box on pole, Bandaraya Bersejarah, Melaka	2·25	2·25
1833	1r. Pillar box, Seremban, Negri Sembilan	2·25	2·25
1834	1r. Wall box, Pejabat Pos Besar, Kuala Lumpur	2·25	2·25

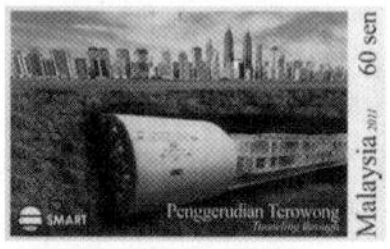

446 Excavating Tunnel

2011. Underground Engineering Excellence. SMART Tunnel (Stormwater Management and Road Tunnel), Kuala Lumpur. Multicoloured.

(a) Ordinary gum

1835	60s. Type **446**	80	80
1836	60s. TBM after breakthrough	80	80
1837	60s. Tunnel breakthrough	80	80
1838	60s. Construction gantry	80	80
1839	60s. Road tunnel	80	80
1840	60s. Cross section of SMART tunnel	80	80

(b) Self-adhesive

MS1841	81×90 mm. 2r. Nos. 1835 and 1837/8; 2r. Nos. 1836 and 1839/40 (all 35×40 mm)	6·50	6·50

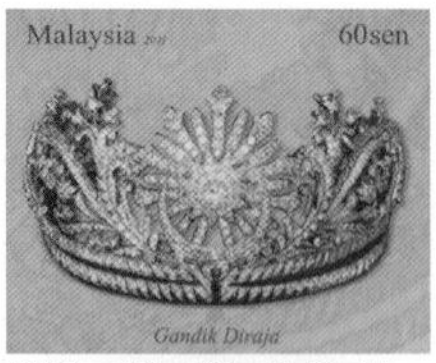

447 Royal Tiara ('Gandik Diraja')

2011. Royal Institution (of the Monarchy). Multicoloured.

1842	60s. Type **446**	90	90
1843	80s. Royal Waist-Buckle ('Pending Diraja')	1·00	1·00
1844	90s. Royal Throne ('Singgahsana')	1·25	1·25

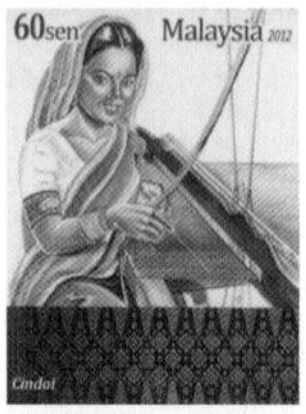

448 Cindai

2012. 'Legacy of the Loom' (traditional textiles). Multicoloured.

1845	60s. Type **447**	90	90
1846	60s. Songket	90	90
1847	60s. Pua Kumbu	90	90
1848	60s. Ci Xiu	90	90
1849	60s. Rangkit	90	90
MS1850	115×100 mm. 3r. Ming Express robe with dragon design (normal colours)	4·50	4·50
MS1851	115×100 mm. 5r. Ming Express robe with dragon design (dragon in gold)	7·50	7·50

POSTAGE DUE STAMPS

Until 15 August 1966, the postage due stamps of Malaysian Postal Union were in use throughout Malaysia.

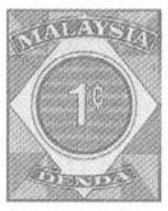

D1

1966

D1	**D1**	1s. red	20	6·50
D2	**D1**	2s. blue	25	2·75
D3	**D1**	4s. green	1·00	12·00
D18	**D1**	8s. green	80	6·50
D19	**D1**	10s. blue	80	3·00
D6	**D1**	12s. violet	60	4·50
D20	**D1**	20s. brown	1·00	3·50
D21	**D1**	50s. bistre	1·50	4·25

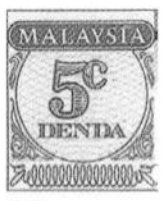

D2

1986

D22	**D2**	5s. mauve and lilac	20	1·25
D23	**D2**	10s. black and grey	25	60
D24	**D2**	20s. red and brown	45	75
D25	**D2**	50s. green and blue	70	1·00
D26	**D2**	1r. blue and cobalt	1·25	2·25

B. FEDERAL TERRITORY ISSUES

For use in the Federal Territories of Kuala Lumpur, Labuan (from 1984) and Putrajaya (from 2001).

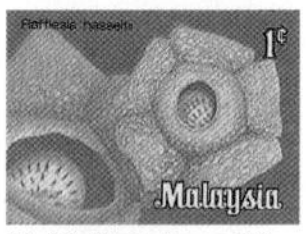

K1 "Rafflesia hasseltii"

1979. Flowers. Multicoloured.

K1	1c. Type K **1**	10	40
K2	2c. "Pterocarpus indicus"	10	40
K3	5c. "Lagerstroemia speciosa"	15	40
K4	10c. "Durio zibethinus"	15	10
K5	15c. "Hibiscus rosa-sinensis"	30	10
K6	20c. "Rhododendron scortechinii"	30	10
K7	25c. "Etlingera elatior" (inscr "Phaeomeria speciosa")	70	10

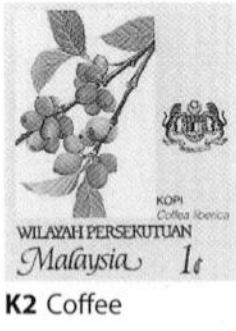

K2 Coffee

1986. Agricultural Products of Malaysia. Multicoloured.

K15	1c. Type K **2**	10	30
K16	2c. Coconuts	10	30
K17	5c. Cocoa	10	10
K18	10c. Black pepper	15	10
K19	15c. Rubber	20	10
K20	20c. Oil palm	20	10
K21	30c. Rice	30	15
K22	50c. Coco	2·00	10

Nos. K17, K18, K20, K21 also come redominated in 'sen'.

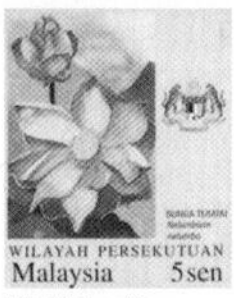

K3 *Nelumbium nelumbo* (sacred lotus)

2007. Garden Flowers. Multicoloured.

K25	5s. Type K **3**	1·50	10
K26	10sc *Hydrangea macrophylla*	10	10
K27	20s. *Hippeastrum reticulatum*	15	10
K28	3s. Bougainvillea	25	15
K29	40s. *Ipomoea indica*	40	20
K30	50s. *Hibiscus rosa-sinensis*	50	30
MSK32	100×85 mm. Nos. K26/31	1·00	3·00
MSK32	100×85 mm. Nos. K26/31	1·00	3·00

Pt. 1

MALDIVE ISLANDS

A group of islands W. of Ceylon. A republic from 1 January 1953, but reverted to a sultanate in 1954. Became independent on 26 July 1965 and left the British Commonwealth, but was re-admitted as an Associate Member on 9 July 1982.

1906. 100 cents = 1 rupee.
1951. 100 larees = 1 rupee.

1906. Nos. 268, 277/9 and 283/4 of Ceylon optd MALDIVES.

1	**44**	2c. brown	22·00	50·00
2	**45**	3c. green	32·00	50·00
3	**45**	4c. orange and blue	50·00	90·00
4	-	5c. purple	4·00	6·50
5	**45**	15c. blue	£100	£180
6	**45**	25c. brown	£110	£190

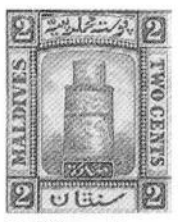
2 Minaret, Juma Mosque, Male

1909

7a	**2**	2c. brown	2·50	90
11A	**2**	2c. grey	2·75	2·00
8	**2**	3c. green	50	70
12A	**2**	3c. brown	70	2·75
9	**2**	5c. purple	50	35
15A	**2**	6c. red	1·50	5·50
10	**2**	10c. red	7·50	80
16A	**2**	10c. green	85	55
17A	**2**	15c. black	6·50	24·00
18A	**2**	25c. brown	6·50	24·00
19A	**2**	50c. purple	6·50	28·00
20B	**2**	1r. blue	16·00	3·25

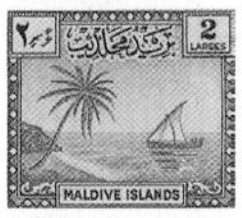

5 Palm Tree and Dhow

1950

21	**5**	2l. olive	2·75	4·25
22	**5**	3l. blue	14·00	1·50
23	**5**	5l. green	14·00	1·50
24	**5**	6l. brown	1·25	1·25
25	**5**	10l. red	1·25	1·00
26	**5**	15l. orange	1·25	1·00
27	**5**	25l. purple	1·25	3·25
28	**5**	50l. violet	1·50	4·75
29	**5**	1r. brown	14·00	40·00

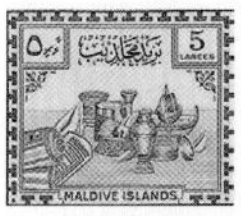
8 Native Products

1952

30	-	3l. blue (Fish)	2·00	60
31	**8**	5l. green	1·00	2·00

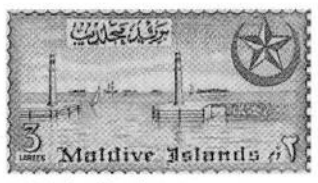
9 Male Harbour

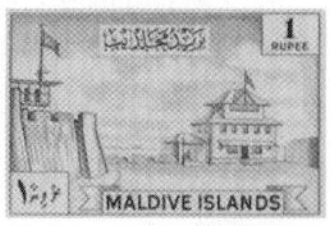

10 Fort and Building

1956

32	**9**	2l. purple	10	10
33	**9**	3l. slate	10	10
34	**9**	5l. brown	10	10
35	**9**	6l. violet	10	10
36	**9**	10l. green	10	10
37	**9**	15l. brown	10	85
38	**9**	25l. red	10	10
39	**9**	50l. orange	10	10
40	**10**	1r. green	15	10
41	**10**	5r. blue	1·75	30
42	**10**	10r. mauve	2·75	1·25

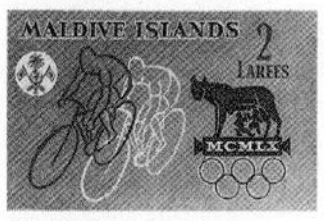

11 Cycling

1960. Olympic Games.

43	**11**	2l. purple and green	15	75
44	**11**	3l. slate and purple	15	75
45	**11**	5l. brown and blue	15	25
46	**11**	10l. green and brown	15	25
47	**11**	15l. sepia and blue	15	25
48	-	25l. red and olive	15	25
49	-	50l. orange and violet	20	40
50	-	1r. green and purple	40	1·25

DESIGN—VERT: 25l. to 1r. Basketball.

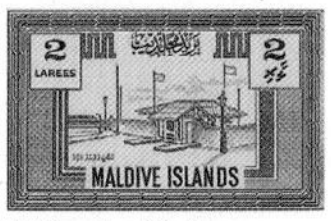

13 Tomb of Sultan

1960

51	**13**	2l. purple	10	10
52	-	3l. green	10	10
53	-	5l. brown	3·75	4·00
54	-	6l. blue	10	10
55	-	10l. red	10	10
56	-	15l. sepia	10	10
57	-	25l. violet	10	10
58	-	50l. grey	10	10
59	-	1r. orange	15	10
60	-	5r. blue	7·50	60
61	-	10r. green	13·00	1·25

DESIGNS: 3l. Custom House; 5l. Cowrie shells; 6l. Old Royal Palace; 10l. Road to Juma Mosque, Male; 15l. Council House; 25l. New Government Secretariat; 50l. Prime Minister's Office; 1r. Old Ruler's Tomb; 5r. Old Ruler's Tomb (distant view); 10r. Maldivian port.

Higher values were also issued, intended mainly for fiscal use.

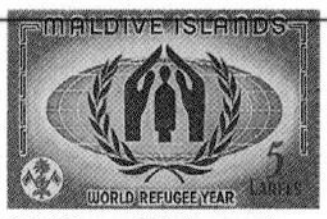

24 "Care of Refugees"

1960. World Refugee Year.

62	**24**	2l. violet, orange and green	10	15
63	**24**	3l. brown, green and red	10	15
64	**24**	5l. green, sepia and red	10	10
65	**24**	10l. green, violet and red	10	10
66	**24**	15l. violet, green and red	10	10
67	**24**	25l. blue, brown and green	10	10
68	**24**	50l. olive, red and blue	10	10
69	**24**	1r. red, slate and violet	15	35

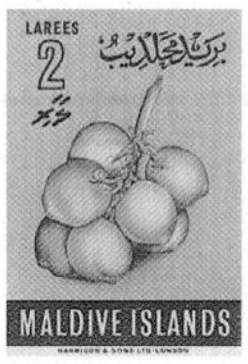

25 Coconuts

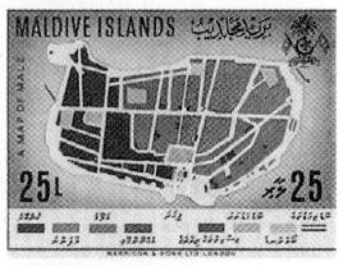

26 Map of Male

1961

70	**25**	2l. brown and green	10	65
71	**25**	3l. brown and blue	10	65
72	**25**	5l. brown and mauve	10	10
73	**25**	10l. brown and orange	15	10
74	**25**	15l. brown and black	20	15
75	**26**	25l. multicoloured	45	20
76	**26**	50l. multicoloured	45	40
77	**26**	1r. multicoloured	50	70

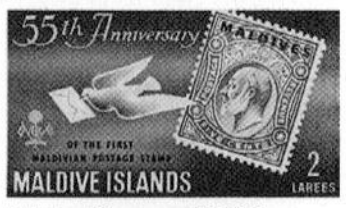

27 5c. Stamp of 1906

1961. 55th Anniv of First Maldivian Stamp.

78	**27**	2l. purple, blue and green	10	1·10
79	**27**	3l. purple, blue and green	10	1·10
80	**27**	5l. purple, blue and green	10	15
81	**27**	6l. purple, blue and green	10	1·40
82	-	10l. green, red and purple	10	15
83	-	15l. green, red and purple	15	15
84	-	20l. green, red and purple	15	20
85	-	25l. red, green and black	15	20
86	-	50l. red, green and black	25	80
87	-	1r. red, green and black	40	2·00
MS87a		114×88 mm. No. 87 (block of four). Imperf	1·50	7·00

DESIGNS: 10l. to 20l. Posthorn and 3c. stamp of 1906; 25l. to 1r. Olive sprig and 2c. stamp of 1906.

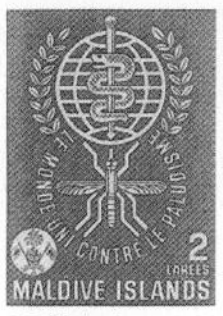

30 Malaria Eradication Emblem

1962. Malaria Eradication.

88	**30**	2l. brown	10	1·50
89	**30**	3l. green	10	1·50
90	**30**	5l. turquoise	10	15
91	**30**	10l. red	10	15
92	-	15l. sepia	15	15
93	-	25l. blue	20	20
94	-	50l. myrtle	25	55
95	-	1r. purple	55	80

Nos. 92/5 are as Type **30**, but have English inscriptions at the side.

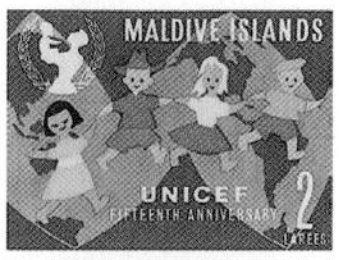

31 Children of Europe and America

1962. 15th Anniv of UNICEF.

96	**31**	2l. multicoloured	10	1·50
97	**31**	6l. multicoloured	10	1·50
98	**31**	10l. multicoloured	10	15
99	**31**	15l. multicoloured	10	15
100	-	25l. multicoloured	15	15
101	-	50l. multicoloured	20	15
102	-	1r. multicoloured	25	20
103	-	5r. multicoloured	1·25	5·00

DESIGN: Nos. 100/3, Children of Middle East and Far East.

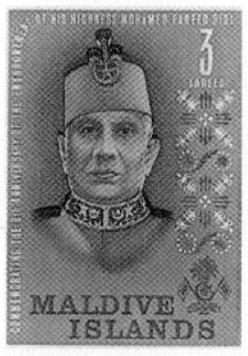

33 Sultan Mohamed Farid Didi

1962. Ninth Anniv of Enthronement of Sultan.

104	**33**	3l. brown and green	10	1·50
105	**33**	5l. brown and blue	15	20
106	**33**	10l. brown and blue	20	20
107	**33**	20l. brown and olive	30	25
108	**33**	50l. brown and mauve	35	45
109	**33**	1r. brown and violet	45	65

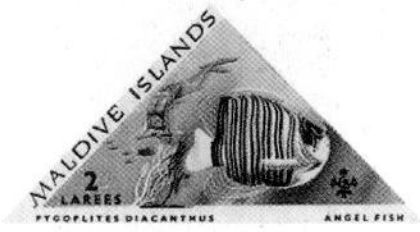

34 Royal Angelfish

1963. Tropical Fish. Multicoloured.

110		2l. Type **34**	10	1·50
111		3l. Type **34**	10	1·50
112		5l. Type **34**	15	55
113		10l. Moorish idol (fish)	25	55
114		25l. As 10l.	65	55
115		50l. Diadem soldierfish	90	70
116		1r. Powder-blue surgeonfish	1·25	75
117		5r. Racoon butterflyfish	6·25	11·00

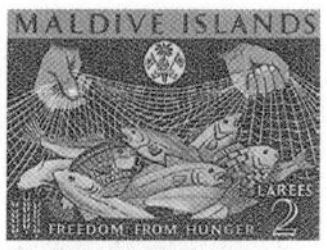

39 Fishes in Net

1963. Freedom from Hunger.

118	**39**	2l. brown and green	30	3·25
119	-	5l. brown and red	50	1·75
120	**39**	7l. brown and turquoise	70	1·75
121	-	10l. brown and blue	85	1·75
122	**39**	25l. brown and red	2·50	4·00
123	-	50l. brown and violet	3·75	8·00
124	**39**	1r. brown and mauve	6·00	12·00

DESIGN—VERT: 5l., 10l., 50l. Handful of grain.

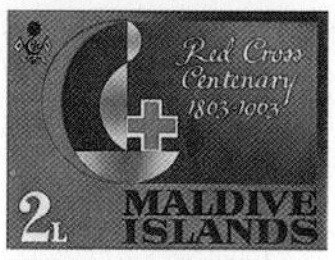

41 Centenary Emblem

1963. Centenary of Red Cross.

125	**41**	2l. red and purple	30	2·00
126	**41**	15l. red and green	1·00	1·00
127	**41**	50l. red and brown	1·60	1·75
128	**41**	1r. red and blue	2·25	2·00
129	**41**	4r. red and olive	4·75	21·00

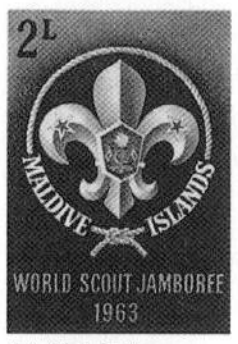

42 Maldivian Scout Badge

1964. World Scout Jamboree, Marathon (1963).

130	**42**	2l. green and violet	10	65
131	**42**	3l. green and brown	10	65
132	**42**	25l. green and blue	15	15
133	**42**	1r. green and red	55	1·50

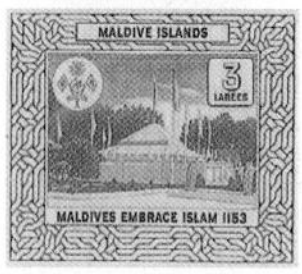
43 Mosque, Male

1964. "Maldives Embrace Islam".

134	**43**	2l. purple	10	60
135	**43**	3l. green	10	60
136	**43**	10l. red	10	10
137	**43**	40l. purple	30	25
138	**43**	60l. blue	50	40
139	**43**	85l. brown	60	60

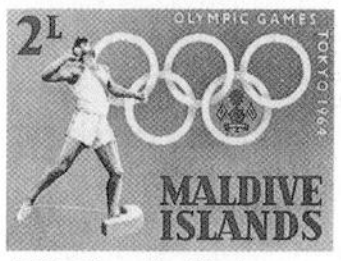

44 Putting the Shot

1964. Olympic Games, Tokyo.

140	**44**	2l. purple and blue	10	1·60
141	**44**	3l. red and brown	10	1·60
142	**44**	5l. bronze and green	15	30
143	**44**	10l. violet and purple	20	30
144	-	15l. sepia and brown	30	30
145	-	25l. indigo and blue	50	30
146	-	50l. bronze and olive	75	35
147	-	1r. purple and grey	1·25	75
MS147a		126×140 mm. Nos. 145/7. Imperf	2·25	4·50

DESIGN: 15l. to 1r. Running.

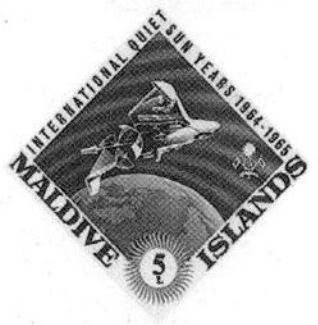
46 Telecommunications Satellite

1965. International Quiet Sun Years.

148	**46**	5l. blue	20	75
149	**46**	10l. brown	25	75
150	**46**	25l. green	50	75
151	**46**	1r. mauve	1·00	1·25

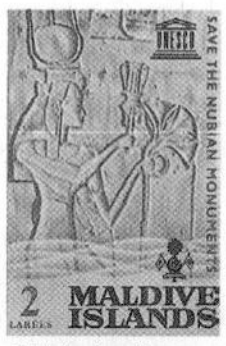

47 Isis (wall carving, Abu Simbel)

1965. Nubian Monuments Preservation.

152	**47**	2l. green and purple	15	1·00
153	-	3l. lake and green	15	1·00
154	**47**	5l. green and purple	20	15
155	-	10l. blue and orange	30	15
156	**47**	15l. brown and violet	50	15

157	-	25l. purple and blue	80	15
158	47	50l. green and sepia	95	45
159	-	1r. ochre and green	1·40	55

DESIGN: 3, 10, 25l., 1r. Rameses II on throne (wall carving, Abu Simbel).

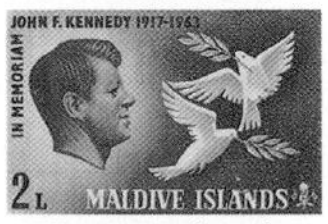

48 Pres. Kennedy and Doves

1965. Second Death Anniv of Pres. Kennedy.

160	48	2l. black and mauve	10	1·00
161	48	5l. brown and mauve	10	10
162	48	25l. blue and mauve	20	10
163	-	1r. purple, yellow and green	35	25
164	-	2r. bronze, yellow and green	50	1·10
MS164a		150×130 mm. No. 164 in block of four. Imperf	2·75	3·25

DESIGN: 1r., 2r. Pres. Kennedy and hands holding olive-branch.

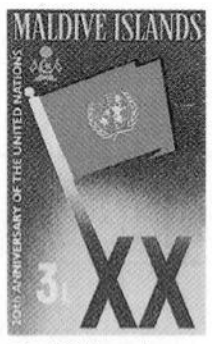

49 "XX" and U.N. Flag

1965. 20th Anniv of U.N.

165	49	3l. blue and brown	15	50
166	49	10l. blue and violet	40	10
167	49	1r. blue and green	1·25	35

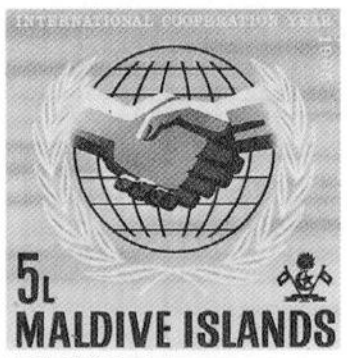

50 I.C.Y. Emblem

1965. International Co-operation Year.

168	50	5l. brown and bistre	20	20
169	50	15l. brown and lilac	35	20
170	50	50l. brown and olive	75	30
171	50	1r. brown and red	1·40	1·50
172	50	2r. brown and blue	2·00	4·50
MS173		101×126 mm. Nos. 170/2. Imperf	6·50	9·50

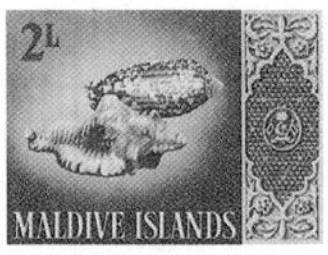

51 Princely Cone Shells

1966. Multicoloured.. Multicoloured..

174		2l. Type **51**	20	1·50
175		3l. Yellow flowers	20	1·50
176		5l. Reticulate distorsio and leopard shells	30	15
177		7l. Camellias	30	15
178		10l. Type **51**	1·00	15
179		15l. Crab plover and seagull	3·75	30
180		20l. As 3l.	80	30
181		30l. Type **51**	2·75	35
182		50l. As 15l.	6·00	55
183		1r. Type **51**	4·00	70
184		1r. As 7l.	3·50	70
185		1r.50 As 3l.	3·75	3·75
186		2r. As 7l.	5·00	4·25
187		5r. As 15l.	23·00	16·00
188		10r. As 5l.	23·00	23·00

The 3l., 7l., 20l., 1r. (No. 184), 1r.50 and 2r. are DIAMOND (43½×43½ mm).

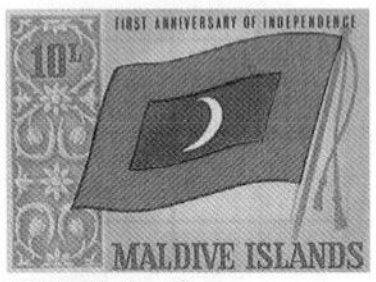

52 Maldivian Flag

1966. First Anniv of Independence.

189	52	10l. green, red and turquoise	3·50	75
190	52	1r. multicoloured	8·00	1·25

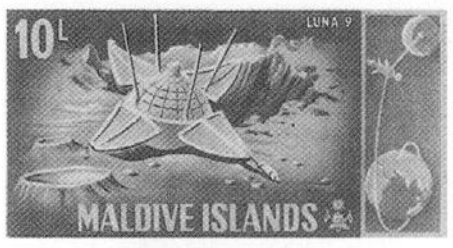

53 "Luna 9" on Moon

1966. Space Rendezvous and Moon Landing.

191	53	10l. brown, indigo and blue	30	10
192	-	25l. green and red	40	10
193	53	50l. brown and green	60	15
194	-	1r. turquoise and brown	1·00	35
195	-	2r. green and violet	1·75	65
196	-	5r. pink and turquoise	2·50	1·60
MS197		108×126 mm. Nos. 194/6. Imperf	3·75	6·00

DESIGNS: 25l., 1r., 5r. "Gemini 6" and "7" rendezvous in space; 2r. "Gemini" spaceship as seen from the other spaceship.

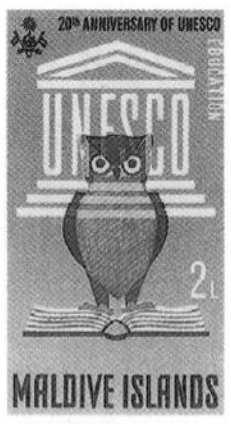

54 UNESCO Emblem and Owl on Book

1966. 20th Anniv of UNESCO. Multicoloured.

198		2l. Type **54**	40	2·00
199		3l. UNESCO emblem and globe and microscope	40	2·00
200		5l. UNESCO emblem and mask, violin and palette	80	40
201		50l. Type **54**	7·00	65
202		1r. Design as 3l.	8·00	90
203		5r. Design as 5l.	22·00	23·00

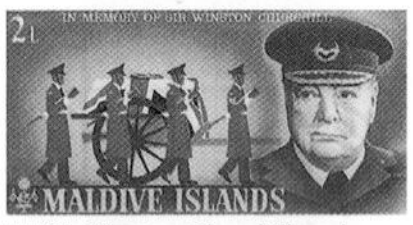

55 Sir Winston Churchill and Cortege

1966. Churchill Commem. Flag in red and blue.

204	55	2l. brown	40	3·25
205	-	10l. turquoise	2·75	50
206	55	15l. green	3·50	50
207	-	25l. violet	5·00	50
208	-	1r. brown	13·00	1·75
209	55	2r.50 red	22·00	21·00

DESIGN: 10l., 25l., 1r. Churchill and catafalque.

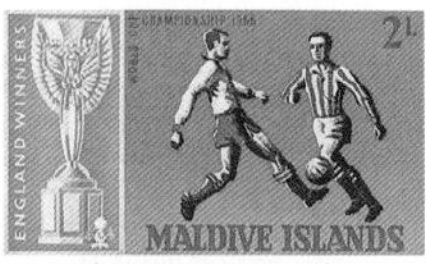

56 Footballers and Jules Rimet Cup

1967. England's Victory in World Cup Football Championship. Multicoloured.

210		2l. Type **56**	30	1·60
211		3l. Player in red shirt kicking ball	30	1·75
212		5l. Scoring goal	30	50
213		25l. As 3l.	1·75	50
214		50l. Making a tackle	2·50	50
215		1r. Type **56**	4·25	80
216		2r. Emblem on Union Jack	6·50	6·00
MS217		100×121 mm. Nos. 214/16. Imperf	15·00	12·00

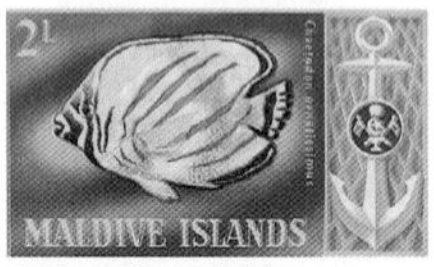

57 Ornate Butterflyfish

1967. Tropical Fishes. Multicoloured.

218		2l. Type **57**	15	1·00
219		3l. Black-saddled pufferfish	20	1·00
220		5l. Blue boxfish	30	20
221		6l. Picasso triggerfish	30	30
222		50l. Semicircle angelfish	3·75	40
223		1r. As 3l.	5·50	80
224		2r. As 50l.	9·00	8·50

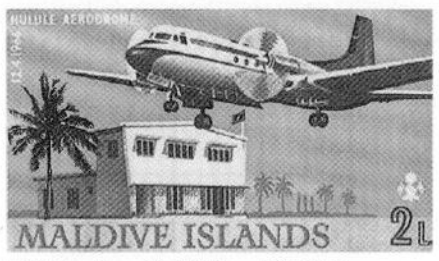

58 Hawker Siddeley H.S.748 over Hulule Airport Building

1967. Inauguration of Hulule Airport.

225	58	2l. violet and olive	20	75
226	-	5l. green and lavender	30	10
227	58	10l. violet and green	40	10
228	-	15l. green and ochre	65	10
229	58	30l. ultramarine and blue	1·25	10
230	-	50l. brown and mauve	2·00	20
231	58	5r. blue and orange	5·50	5·50
232	-	10r. brown and blue	7·50	9·00

DESIGN: 5, 15, 50l., 10r. Airport building and Hawker Siddeley H.S.748.

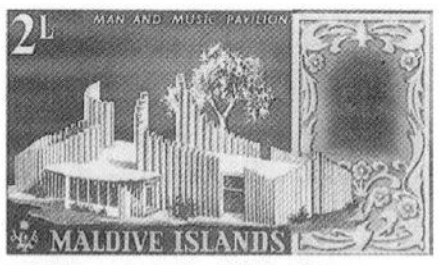

59 "Man and Music" Pavilion

1967. World Fair, Montreal. Multicoloured.

233		2l. Type **59**	10	1·00
234		5l. "Man and His Community" Pavilion	10	10
235		10l. Type **59**	10	10
236		50l. As 5l.	50	30
237		1r. Type **59**	85	50
238		2r. As 5l.	2·00	2·25
MS239		102×137 mm. Nos. 237/8. Imperf	2·50	4·25

1968. International Tourist Year (1967). Nos. 225/32 optd **International Tourist Year 1967**.

240	58	2l. violet and olive	10	85
241	-	5l. green and lavender	15	20
242	58	10l. violet and green	20	20
243	-	15l. green and ochre	20	20
244	58	30l. ultramarine and blue	30	25
245	-	50l. brown and mauve	45	30
246	58	5r. blue and orange	3·50	4·50
247	-	10r. brown and blue	5·00	7·00

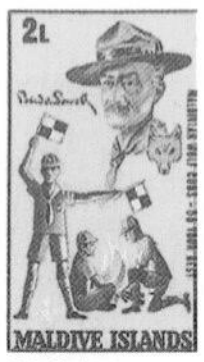

61 Cub signalling and Lord Baden-Powell

1968. Maldivian Scouts and Cubs.

248	61	2l. brown, green and yellow	10	1·00
249	-	3l. red, blue and light blue	10	1·00
250	61	25l. violet, lake and red	1·50	40
251	-	1r. green, brown and light green	3·50	1·60

DESIGN: 3l. and 1r. Scouts and Lord Baden-Powell.

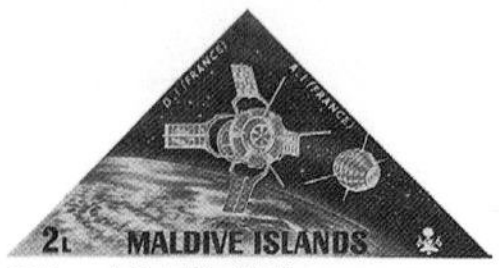

62 French Satellite "A 1"

1968. Space Martyrs.

252	62	2l. mauve and blue	15	80
253	-	3l. violet and brown	15	80
254	-	7l. brown and lake	20	80
255	-	10l. blue, drab and black	20	20
256	-	25l. green and violet	50	20
257	62	50l. blue and brown	85	30
258	-	1r. purple and green	1·25	50
259	-	2r. brown, blue and black	2·00	2·25
260	-	5r. mauve, drab and black	3·00	3·50
MS261		110×155 mm. Nos. 258/9. Imperf	6·00	7·00

DESIGNS: 3l., 25l. "Luna 10"; 7l., 1r. "Orbiter" and "Mariner"; 10l., 2r. Astronauts White, Grissom and Chaffee; 5r. Cosmonaut V. M. Komarov.

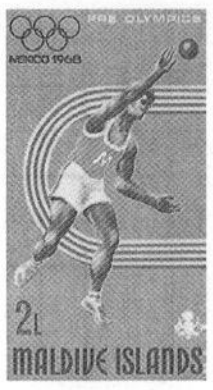

63 Putting the Shot

1968. Olympic Games, Mexico (1st Issue). Multicoloured.

262		2l. Type **63**	10	75
263		6l. Throwing the discus	15	75
264		10l. Type **63**	20	10
265		25l. As 6l.	25	10
266		1r. Type **63**	75	35
267		2r.50 As 6l.	2·00	2·00

See also Nos. 294/7.

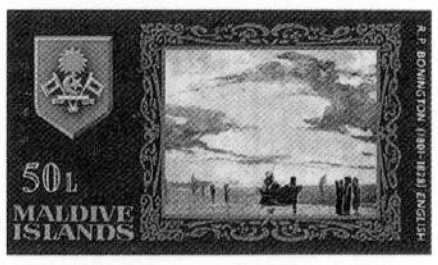

64 "Adriatic Seascape" (Bonington)

1968. Paintings. Multicoloured.

268		50l. Type **64**	2·25	30
269		1r. "Ulysses deriding Polyphemus" (Turner)	2·75	45
270		2r. "Sailing Boat at Argenteuil" (Monet)	3·50	2·75
271		5r. "Fishing Boat at Les Saintes-Maries" (Van Gogh)	6·00	7·00

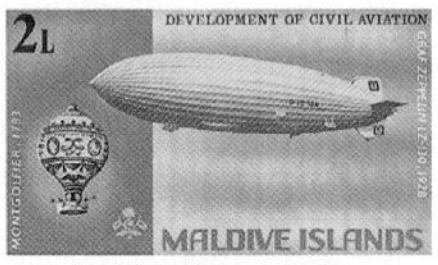

65 LZ-130 "Graf Zeppelin II" and Montgolfier's Balloon

1968. Development of Civil Aviation.

272	65	2l. brown, green and blue	20	1·00
273	-	3l. blue, violet and brown	20	1·00
274	-	5l. green, red and blue	20	20
275	-	7l. blue, purple and orange	3·00	1·50
276	65	10l. brown, blue and purple	45	20
277	-	50l. red, green and olive	1·50	30
278	-	1r. green, blue and red	2·25	50
279	-	2r. purple, bistre and blue	20·00	11·00

DESIGNS: 3l., 1r. Boeing 707-420 and Douglas DC-3; 5l., 50l. Wright Type A and Lilienthal's glider; 7l., 2r. Projected Boeing 733 and Concorde.

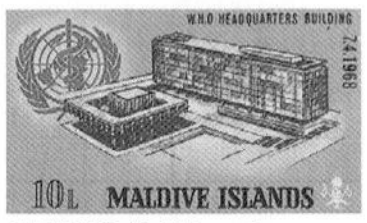

66 W.H.O. Building, Geneva

1968. 20th Anniv of World Health Organization.

280	66	10l. violet, turquoise & blue	60	20
281	66	25l. green, brown & yellow	1·00	20
282	66	1r. brown, emerald & green	3·25	90
283	66	2r. violet, purple and mauve	5·25	6·00

1968. First Anniv of Scout Jamboree, Idaho. Nos. 248/51 optd International Boy Scout Jamboree, Farragut Park, Idaho, U.S.A. August 1–9, 1967.

284	61	2l. brown, green and yellow	10	75
285	-	3l. red, blue and light blue	10	75
286	61	25l. violet, lake and red	1·50	55
287	-	1r. green, brown and light green	4·50	2·10

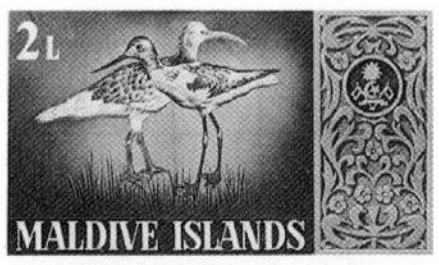

68 Curlew and Common Redshank

1968. Multicoloured

288		2l. Type **68**	50	1·00
289		10l. Pacific grinning tun and Papal mitre shells	1·25	20
290		25l. Oriental angel wing and tapestry turban shells	1·75	25
291		50l. Type **68**	8·00	1·10

292	1r. As 10l.		4·50	1·10
293	2r. As 25l.		5·00	5·00

69 Throwing the Discus

1968. Olympic Games, Mexico (2nd issue). Multicoloured.

294	10l. Type **69**		10	10
295	50l. Running		20	20
296	1r. Cycling		5·00	1·00
297	2r. Basketball		7·00	3·50

70 Fishing Dhow

1968. Republic Day.

298	**70**	10l. brown, blue and green	1·50	50
299	–	1r. green, red and blue	9·50	1·75

DESIGN: 1r. National flag, crest and map.

71 "The Thinker" (Rodin)

1969. UNESCO. "Human Rights". Designs showing sculptures by Rodin. Multicoloured.

300	6l. Type **71**		50	25
301	10l. "Hands"		50	20
302	1r.50 "Eve"		3·25	3·25
303	2r.50 "Adam"		3·50	3·50
MS304	112×130 mm. Nos. 302/3. Imperf		13·00	13·00

72 Module nearing Moon's Surface

1969. First Man on the Moon. Multicoloured.

305	6l. Type **72**		40	35
306	10l. Astronaut with hatchet		40	20
307	1r.50 Astronaut and module		3·00	2·25
308	2r.50 Astronaut using camera		3·50	2·75
MS309	101×130 mm. Nos. 305/8. Imperf		6·50	7·50

1969. Gold Medal Winner, Olympic Games, Mexico (1968). Nos. 295/6 optd **Gold Medal Winner Mohamed Gammoudi 5000m. run Tunisia REPUBLIC OF MALDIVES** or similar opt.

310	50l. multicoloured		60	60
311	1r. multicoloured		1·40	90

The overprint on No. 310 honours P. Trentin (cycling, France).

74 Racoon Butterflyfish

1970. Tropical Fish. Multicoloured.

312	2l. Type **74**		40	70
313	5l. Clown triggerfish		65	40
314	25l. Broad-barred lionfish		1·25	40
315	50l. Long-nosed butterflyfish		1·50	1·00
316	1r. Emperor angelfish		1·75	1·00
317	2r. Royal angelfish		2·25	6·50

75 Columbia Dauman Victoria, 1899

1970. "75 Years of the Automobile". Multicoloured.

318	2l. Type **75**		20	50
319	5l. Duryea phaeton, 1902		25	30
320	7l. Packard S-24, 1906		30	30
321	10l. Autocar Runabout, 1907		35	30
322	25l. Type **75**		1·00	30
323	50l. As 5l.		1·25	55
324	1r. As 7l.		1·50	90
325	2r. As 10l.		1·90	5·50
MS326	95×143 mm. Nos. 324/5		3·25	7·50

76 U.N. Headquarters, New York

1970. 25th Anniv of United Nations. Multicoloured.

327	2l. Type **76**		10	1·00
328	10l. Surgical operation (W.H.O.)		2·25	40
329	25l. Student, actress and musician (UNESCO)		3·75	50
330	50l. Children at work and play (UNICEF)		2·00	70
331	1r. Fish, corn and farm animals (F.A.O.)		2·00	1·00
332	2r. Miner hewing coal (I.L.O.)		7·50	7·50

77 Ship and Light Buoy

1970. Tenth Anniv of I.M.C.O. Multicoloured.

333	50l. Type **77**		1·25	50
334	1r. Ship and lighthouse		6·50	1·50

78 "Guitar-player and Masqueraders" (A. Watteau)

1970. Famous Paintings showing the Guitar. Multicoloured.

335	3l. Type **78**		15	80
336	7l. "Spanish Guitarist" (Manet)		25	80
337	50l. "Costumed Player" (Watteau)		1·00	40
338	1r. "Mandolin-player" (Roberti)		1·75	55
339	2r.50 "Guitar-player and Lady" (Watteau)		3·25	3·75
340	5r. "Mandolin-player" (Frans Hals)		6·00	7·00
MS341	132×80 mm. Nos. 339/40		9·00	11·00

79 Australian Pavilion

1970. "EXPO 70" World Fair, Osaka, Japan. Multicoloured.

342	2l. Type **79**		15	1·00
343	3l. West German Pavilion		15	1·00
344	10l. U.S. Pavilion		65	10
345	25l. British Pavilion		2·00	15
346	50l. Soviet Pavilion		2·50	45
347	1r. Japanese Pavilion		2·75	65

80 Learning the Alphabet

1970. Int Education Year. Multicoloured.

348	5l. Type **80**		50	60
349	10l. Training teachers		60	40
350	25l. Geography lesson		2·75	60
351	50l. School inspector		2·75	80
352	1r. Education by television		3·00	1·00

1970. "Philympia 1970" Stamp Exn, London. Nos. 306/8 optd **Philympia London 1970**.

353	10l. multicoloured		10	10
354	1r.50 multicoloured		1·00	1·00
355	2r.50 multicoloured		1·25	1·50
MS356	101×130 mm. Nos. 305/8 optd. Imperf		6·50	8·50

82 Footballers

1970. World Cup Football Championship, Mexico.

357	**82**	3l. multicoloured	15	1·00
358	–	6l. multicoloured	20	65
359	–	7l. multicoloured	20	40
360	–	25l. multicoloured	90	20
361	–	1r. multicoloured	2·50	90

DESIGNS: 6l. to 1r. Different designs showing footballers in action.

83 Little Boy and UNICEF Flag

1970. 25th Anniv of UNICEF. Multicoloured.

362	5l. Type **83**		10	15
363	10l. Little girl with UNICEF "balloon"		10	15
364	1r. Type **83**		1·75	85
365	2r. As 10l.		2·75	3·00

84 Astronauts Lovell, Haise and Swigert

1971. Safe Return of "Apollo 13". Multicoloured.

366	5l. Type **84**		35	35
367	20l. Explosion in Space		65	25
368	1r. Splashdown		1·40	50

85 "Multiracial Flower"

1971. Racial Equality Year.

369	**85**	10l. multicoloured	15	15
370	**85**	25l. multicoloured	20	15

86 "Mme. Charpentier and her Children" (Renoir)

1971. Famous Paintings showing "Mother and Child". Multicoloured.

371	5l. Type **86**		25	20
372	7l. "Susanna van Collen and her Daughter" (Rembrandt)		30	20
373	10l. "Madonna nursing the Child" (Titian)		40	20
374	20l. "Baroness Belleli and her Children" (Degas)		1·00	20
375	25l. "The Cradle" (Morisot)		1·00	20
376	1r. "Helena Fourment and her Children" (Reubens)		3·00	85
377	3r. "On the Terrace" (Renoir)		5·50	6·50

87 Alan Shepard

1971. Moon Flight of "Apollo 14". Multicoloured.

378	6l. Type **87**		40	40
379	10l. Stuart Roosa		45	30
380	1r.50 Edgar Mitchell		5·50	3·50
381	5r. Mission insignia		11·00	11·00

88 "Ballerina" (Degas)

1971. Famous Paintings showing "Dancers". Multicoloured.

382	5l. Type **88**		20	20
383	10l. "Dancing Couple" (Renoir)		25	20
384	2r. "Spanish Dancer" (Manet)		2·75	2·50
385	5r. "Ballerinas" (Degas)		5·00	5·00
386	10r. "La Goulue at the Moulin Rouge" (Toulouse-Lautrec)		7·50	8·00

1972. Visit of Queen Elizabeth II and Prince Philip. Nos. 382/6 optd **ROYAL VISIT 1972**.

387	**88**	5l. multicoloured	20	10
388	–	10l. multicoloured	25	10
389	–	2r. multicoloured	5·00	4·00
390	–	5r. multicoloured	9·00	8·00
391	–	10r. multicoloured	10·00	10·00

90 Book Year Emblem

1972. International Book Year.

392	**90**	25l. multicoloured	15	15
393	**90**	5r. multicoloured	1·60	2·25

91 Scottish Costume

1972. National Costumes of the World. Multicoloured.

394	10l. Type **91**		1·00	10
395	15l. Netherlands		1·25	15

396	25l. Norway	2·25	15
397	50l. Hungary	3·00	55
398	1r. Austria	3·50	80
399	2r. Spain	4·50	3·50

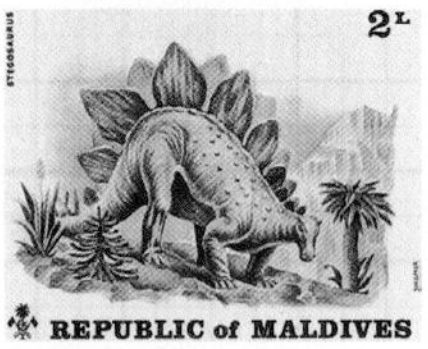

92 Stegosaurus

1972. Prehistoric Animals. Multicoloured.

400	2l. Type **92**	75	75
401	7l. Dimetrodon (inscr "Edaphosaurus")	1·50	60
402	25l. Diplodocus	2·25	50
403	50l. Triceratops	2·50	75
404	2r. Pteranodon	5·50	5·00
405	5r. Tyrannosaurus	9·50	9·50

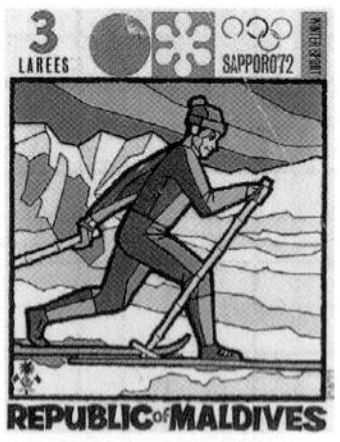

93 Cross-country Skiing

1972. Winter Olympic Games, Sapporo, Japan. Multicoloured.

406	3l. Type **93**	10	50
407	6l. Bobsleighing	10	50
408	15l. Speed skating	20	20
409	50l. Ski jumping	1·00	45
410	1r. Figure skating (pair)	1·75	70
411	2r.50 Ice hockey	5·50	3·25

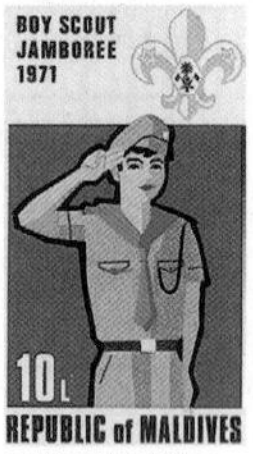

94 Scout Saluting

1972. 13th Boy Scout Jamboree, Asagiri, Japan (1971). Multicoloured.

412	10l. Type **94**	75	20
413	15l. Scout signalling	95	20
414	50l. Scout blowing bugle	3·25	1·25
415	1r. Scout playing drum	4·50	2·25

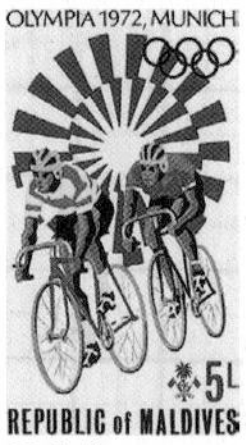

95 Cycling

1972. Olympic Games, Munich. Multicoloured.

416	5l. Type **95**	1·25	30
417	10l. Running	20	20
418	25l. Wrestling	30	20
419	50l. Hurdling	50	35
420	2r. Boxing	1·50	2·00
421	5r. Volleyball	3·00	3·75
MS422 92×120 mm. 3r. As 50l.; 4r. As 10l.		5·75	8·00

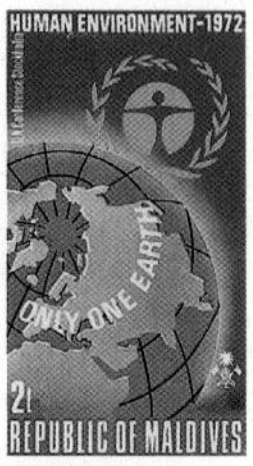

96 Globe and Conference Emblem

1972. U.N. Environmental Conservation Conference, Stockholm.

423	**96**	2l. multicoloured	10	40
424	**96**	3l. multicoloured	10	40
425	**96**	15l. multicoloured	30	15
426	**96**	50l. multicoloured	75	45
427	**96**	2r.50 multicoloured	3·25	4·25

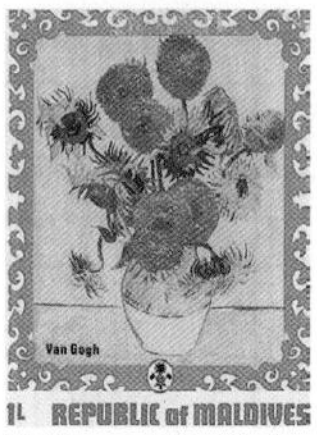

97 "Flowers" (Van Gogh)

1973. Floral Paintings. Multicoloured.

428	1l. Type **97**	10	60
429	2l. "Flowers in Jug" (Renoir)	10	60
430	3l. "Chrysanthemums" (Renoir)	10	60
431	50l. "Mixed Bouquet" (Bosschaert)	1·50	30
432	1r. As 3l.	2·00	40
433	5r. As 2l.	4·25	5·50
MS434 120×94 mm. 2r. As 50l.; 3r. Type **97**		7·00	8·50

1973. Gold-medal Winners, Munich Olympic Games. Nos. 420/1 optd as listed below.

435	2r. multicoloured	3·25	2·50
436	5r. multicoloured	4·25	3·75
MS437 92×120 mm. 3r. multicoloured; 4r. multicoloured		7·50	8·50

OVERPRINTS: 2r. **LEMECHEV MIDDLE-WEIGHT GOLD MEDALLIST;** 5r. **JAPAN GOLD MEDAL WINNERS**. Miniature sheet: 3r. **EHRHARDT 100 METER HURDLES GOLD MEDALLIST**; 4r. **SHORTER MARATHON GOLD MEDAL-LIST**.

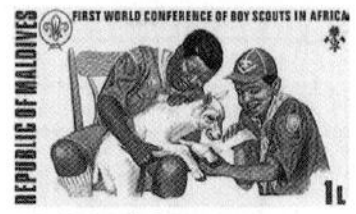

99 Animal Care

1973. International Scouting Congress, Nairobi and Addis Ababa. Multicoloured.

438	1l. Type **99**	10	30
439	2l. Lifesaving	10	30
440	3l. Agricultural training	10	30
441	4l. Carpentry	10	30
442	5l. Playing leapfrog	10	30
443	1r. As 2l.	2·75	75
444	2r. As 4l.	4·00	4·75
445	3r. Type **99**	4·50	7·00
MS446 101×79 mm. 5r. As 3l.		8·00	14·00

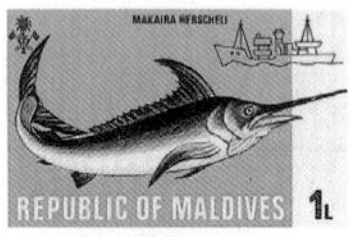

100 Blue Marlin

1973. Fish. Multicoloured.

447	1l. Type **100**	10	40
448	2l. Skipjack tuna	10	40
449	3l. Blue-finned tuna	10	40
450	5l. Dolphin (fish)	10	40
451	60l. Humpbacked snapper	80	40
452	75l. As 60l.	1·00	40
453	1r.50 Yellow-edged lyretail	1·75	2·00
454	2r.50 As 5l.	2·25	3·00
455	3r. Spotted coral grouper	2·25	3·25
456	10r. Spanish mackerel	4·75	8·00
MS457 119×123 mm. 4r. As 2l. 5r. Type **100**		17·00	20·00

Nos. 451/2 are smaller, size 29×22 mm.

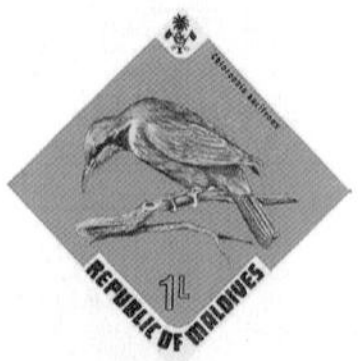

101 Golden-fronted Leafbird

1973. Fauna. Multicoloured.

458	1l. Type **101**	10	50
459	2l. Indian flying fox	10	50
460	3l. Land tortoise	10	50
461	4l. Butterfly ("Kallima inachus")	30	50
462	50l. As 3l.	60	40
463	2r. Type **101**	5·50	4·50
464	3r. As 2l.	3·50	4·50
MS465 66×74 mm. 5r. As 4l.		18·00	20·00

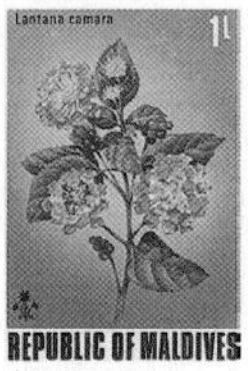

102 "Lantana camara"

1973. Flowers of the Maldive Islands. Multicoloured.

466	1l. Type **102**	10	50
467	2l. "Nerium oleander"	10	50
468	3l. "Rosa polyantha"	10	50
469	4l. "Hibiscus manihot"	10	50
470	5l. "Bougainvillea glabra"	10	20
471	10l. "Plumera alba"	15	20
472	50l. "Poinsettia pulcherrima"	70	30
473	5r. "Ononis natrix"	3·75	5·50
MS474 110×100 mm. 2r. As 3l.; 3r. As 10l.		3·25	5·25

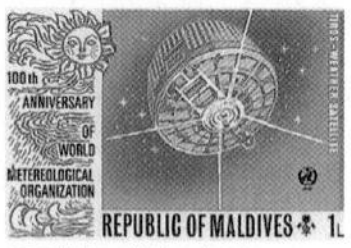

103 "Tiros" Weather Satellite

1974. Centenary of World Meteorological Organization. Multicoloured.

475	1l. Type **103**	10	30
476	2l. "Nimbus" satellite	10	30
477	3l. "Nomad" (weather ship)	10	30
478	4l. Scanner, A.P.T. Instant Weather Picture equipment	10	30
479	5l. Richard's wind-speed recorder	10	20
480	2r. Type **103**	3·50	3·75
481	3r. As 3l.	3·75	4·00
MS482 110×79 mm. 10r. As 2l.		8·50	14·00

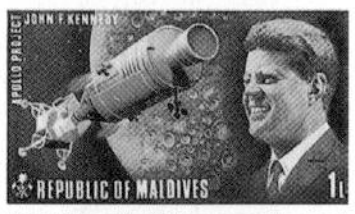

104 "Apollo" Spacecraft and Pres. Kennedy

1974. American and Russian Space Exploration Projects. Multicoloured.

483	1l. Type **104**	10	35
484	2l. "Mercury" capsule and John Glenn	10	35
485	3l. "Vostok 1" and Yuri Gagarin	10	35
486	4l. "Vostok 6" and Valentina Tereshkova	10	35
487	5l. "Soyuz 11" and "Salyut" space-station	10	25
488	2r. "Skylab" space laboratory	3·75	3·75
489	3r. As 2l.	4·25	4·25
MS490 103×80 mm. 10r. Type **104**		12·00	14·00

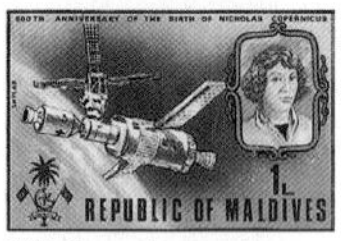

105 Copernicus and "Skylab" Space Laboratory

1974. 500th Birth Anniv of Nicholas Copernicus (astronomer). Multicoloured.

491	1l. Type **105**	10	35
492	2l. Orbital space-station of the future	10	35
493	3l. Proposed "Space-shuttle" craft	10	35
494	4l. "Mariner 2" Venus probe	10	35
495	5l. "Mariner 4" Mars probe	10	20
496	25l. Type **105**	1·25	20
497	1r.50 As 2l.	2·75	3·25
498	5r. As 3l.	4·50	11·00
MS499 106×80 mm. 10r. "Copernicus" orbital observatory		15·00	18·00

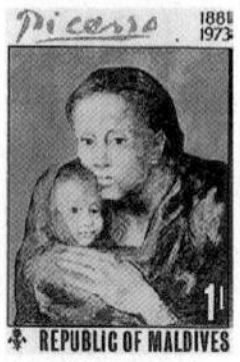

106 "Maternity" (Picasso)

1974. Paintings by Picasso. Multicoloured.

500	1l. Type **106**	10	40
501	2l. "Harlequin and Friend"	10	40
502	3l. "Pierrot Sitting"	10	40
503	20l. "Three Musicians"	50	20
504	75l. "L'Aficionado"	1·25	80
505	5r. "Still Life"	4·75	6·50
MS506 100×101 mm. 2r. As 20l.; 3r. As 5r.		8·50	11·00

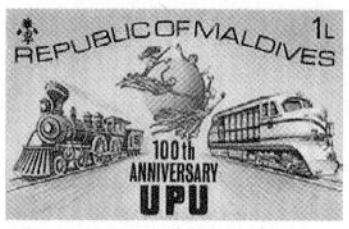

107 U.P.U. Emblem, Steam and Diesel Locomotives

1974. Cent of Universal Postal Union. Multicoloured.

507	1l. Type **107**	10	30
508	2l. Paddle-steamer and modern mailboat	10	30
509	3l. Airship "Graf Zeppelin" and Boeing 747 airliner	10	30
510	1r.50 Mailcoach and motor van	1·10	1·10
511	2r.50 As 2l.	1·40	1·75
512	5r. Type **107**	2·00	3·25
MS513 126×105 mm. 4r. Type **107**		5·50	7·00

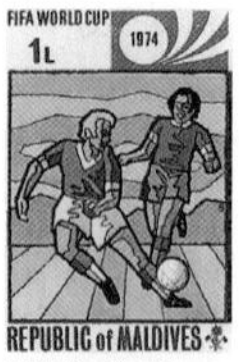

108 Footballers

1974. World Cup Football Championship, West Germany.

514	**108**	1l. multicoloured	15	20
515	-	2l. multicoloured	15	20
516	-	3l. multicoloured	15	20
517	-	4l. multicoloured	15	20
518	-	75l. multicoloured	1·25	75
519	-	4r. multicoloured	2·50	4·00
520	-	5r. multicoloured	2·50	4·00
MS521 88×95 mm. 10r. multicoloured			10·00	12·00

DESIGNS: Nos. 515/**MS**521 show football scenes similar to Type **108**.

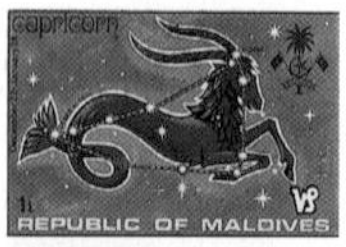

109 "Capricorn"

1974. Signs of the Zodiac. Multicoloured.

522	1l. Type **109**	25	50
523	2l. "Aquarius"	25	50
524	3l. "Pisces"	25	50
525	4l. "Aries"	25	50
526	5l. "Taurus"	25	50
527	6l. "Gemini"	25	50
528	7l. "Cancer"	25	50
529	10l. "Leo"	40	50
530	15l. "Virgo"	40	50
531	20l. "Libra"	40	50
532	25l. "Scorpio"	40	50
533	5r. "Sagittarius"	6·50	12·00
MS534 119×99 mm. 10r. "The Sun" (49×37 mm)		20·00	22·00

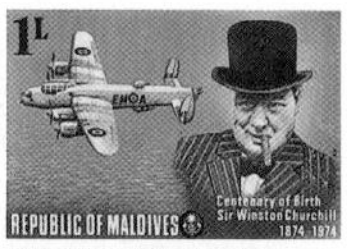

110 Churchill and Avro Type 683 Lancaster

1974. Birth Cent of Sir Winston Churchill. Multicoloured.

535	1l. Type **110**	30	60
536	2l. Churchill as pilot	30	60
537	3l. Churchill as First Lord of the Admiralty	30	60
538	4l. Churchill and H.M.S. "Eagle" (aircraft carrier)	30	60
539	5l. Churchill and de Havilland Mosquito bombers	30	35
540	60l. Churchill and anti-aircraft battery	3·50	2·00
541	75l. Churchill and tank in desert	3·75	2·00
542	5r. Churchill and Short S.25 Sunderland flying boat	14·00	14·00
MS543 113×83 mm. 10r. As 4l.		20·00	21·00

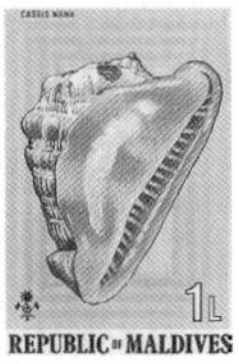

111 Bullmouth Helmet

1975. Sea Shells and Cowries. Multicoloured.

544	1l. Type **111**	10	30
545	2l. Venus comb murex	10	30
546	3l. Common or major harp	10	30
547	4l. Chiragra spider conch	10	30
548	5l. Geography cone	10	30
549	60l. Dawn cowrie (22×30 mm)	3·00	2·00
550	75l. Purplish clanculus (22×30 mm)	3·50	2·00
551	5r. Ramose murex	8·50	11·00
MS552	152×126 mm. 2r. As 3l.; 3r. As 2l.	13·00	16·00

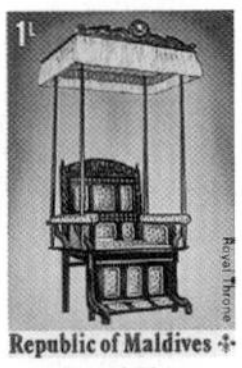

112 Royal Throne

1975. Historical Relics and Monuments. Multicoloured.

553	1l. Type **112**	10	10
554	10l. Candlesticks	10	10
555	25l. Lamp-tree	15	10
556	60l. Royal umbrellas	30	30
557	75l. Eid-Miskith Mosque (horiz)	35	35
558	3r. Tomb of Al-Hafiz Abu-al Barakath-al Barubari (horiz)	1·60	2·75

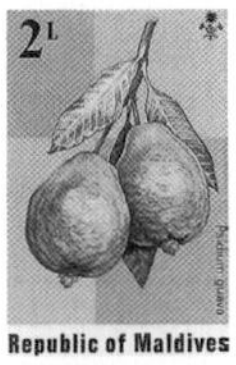

113 Guavas

1975. Exotic Fruits. Multicoloured.

559	2l. Type **113**	10	40
560	4l. Maldive mulberry	15	40
561	5l. Mountain apples	15	40
562	10l. Bananas	20	15
563	20l. Mangoes	40	25
564	50l. Papaya	1·00	60
565	1r. Pomegranates	1·75	70
566	5r. Coconut	5·50	11·00
MS567	136×102 mm. 2r. As 10l.; 3r. As 2l.	11·00	15·00

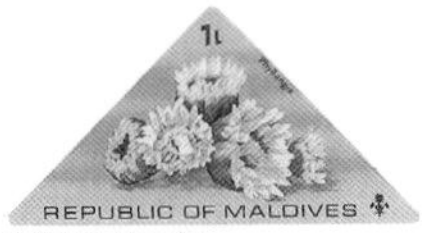

114 "Phyllangia"

1975. Marine Life. Corals, Urchins and Sea Stars. Multicoloured.

568	1l. Type **114**	10	40
569	2l. "Madrepora oculata"	10	40
570	3l. "Acropora gravida"	10	40
571	4l. "Stylotella"	10	40
572	5l. "Acrophora cervicornis"	10	40
573	60l. "Strongylocentrotus purpuratus"	75	65
574	75l. "Pisaster ochraceus"	85	75
575	5r. "Marthasterias glacialis"	5·00	6·50
MS576	155×98 mm. 4r. As 1l. Imperf	11·00	14·00

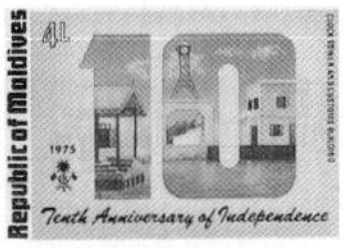

115 Clock Tower and Customs Building within "10"

1975. 10th Anniv of Independence. Multicoloured.

577	4l. Type **115**	10	30
578	5l. Government offices	10	15
579	7l. Waterfront	10	20
580	15l. Mosque and minaret	10	15
581	10r. Sultan Park and museum	2·25	6·00

1975. "Nordjamb 75" World Scout Jamboree, Norway. Nos. 443/5 and MS446 optd **14th Boy Scout Jamboree July 29–August 7, 1975.**

582	-	1r. multicoloured	85	60
583	-	2r. multicoloured	1·25	80
584	**99**	3r. multicoloured	1·75	1·60
MS585		101×79 mm. 5r. multicoloured	7·00	8·00

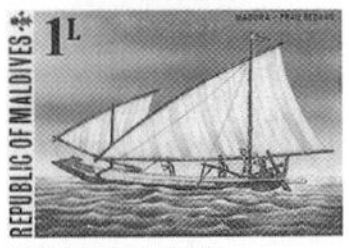

117 Madura Prau

1975. Ships. Multicoloured.

586	1l. Type **117**	10	20
587	2l. Ganges patela	10	20
588	3l. Indian palla (vert)	10	20
589	4l. Odhi (dhow) (vert)	10	20
590	5l. Maldivian schooner	10	20
591	25l. "Cutty Sark" (British tea clipper)	1·50	40
592	1r. Maldivian baggala (vert)	1·75	70
593	5r. "Maldive Courage" (freighter)	3·00	6·00
MS594	99×85 mm. 10r. As 1r.	10·00	14·00

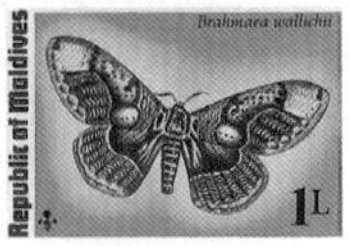

118 "Brahmophthalma wallichi" (moth)

1975. Butterflies and Moth. Multicoloured.

595	1l. Type **118**	15	30
596	2l. "Teinopalpus imperialis"	15	30
597	3l. "Cethosia biblis"	15	30
598	4l. "Idea jasonia"	15	30
599	5l. "Apatura ilia"	15	30
600	25l. "Kallima horsfieldi"	1·25	35
601	1r.50 "Hebomoia leucippe"	3·50	3·75
602	5r. "Papilio memnon"	8·00	10·00
MS603	134×97 mm. 10r. As 25l.	20·00	20·00

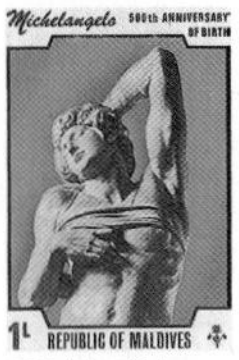

119 "The Dying Captive"

1975. 500th Birth Anniv of Michelangelo. Multicoloured.

604	1l. Type **119**	10	20
605	2l. Detail of "The Last Judgement"	10	20
606	3l. "Apollo"	10	20
607	4l. Detail of Sistine Chapel ceiling	10	20
608	5l. "Bacchus"	10	20
609	1r. Detail of "The Last Judgement" (different)	1·25	30
610	2r. "David"	1·50	2·00
611	5r. "Cumaean Sibyl"	2·25	5·00
MS612	123×113 mm. 10r. As 2r.	5·00	11·00

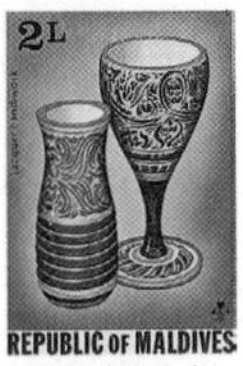

120 Beaker and Vase

1975. Maldivian Lacquerware. Multicoloured.

613	2l. Type **120**	10	50
614	4l. Boxes	10	50
615	50l. Jar with lid	30	20
616	75l. Bowls with covers	40	30
617	1r. Craftsman at work	50	40

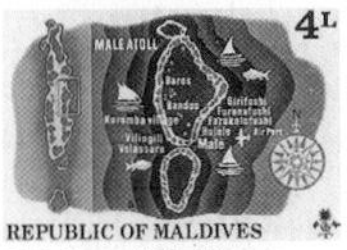

121 Map of Maldives

1975. Tourism. Multicoloured.

618	4l. Type **121**	40	50
619	5l. Motor launch and small craft	40	50
620	7l. Sailing-boats	40	50
621	15l. Underwater fishing	40	40
622	3r. Hulule Airport	5·00	3·00
623	10r. Motor cruisers	7·00	8·50

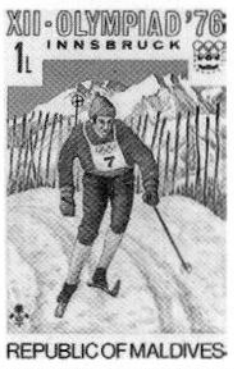

122 Cross-country Skiing

1976. Winter Olympic Games, Innsbruck. Multicoloured.

624	1l. Type **122**	10	20
625	2l. Speed-skating (pairs)	10	20
626	3l. Figure-skating (pairs)	10	20
627	4l. Four-man bobsleighing	10	20
628	5l. Ski-jumping	10	20
629	25l. Figure-skating (women's)	35	20
630	1r.15 Skiing (slalom)	90	1·25
631	4r. Ice-hockey	1·50	4·00
MS632	93×117 mm. 10r. Downhill Skiing	6·50	12·00

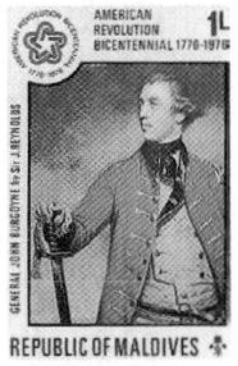

123 "General Burgoyne" (Reynolds)

1976. Bicent of American Revolution. Multicoloured.

633	1l. Type **123**	10	10
634	2l. "John Hancock" (Copley)	10	10
635	3l. "Death of Gen. Montgomery" (Trumbull) (horiz)	10	10
636	4l. "Paul Revere" (Copley)	10	10
637	5l. "Battle of Bunker Hill" (Trumbull) (horiz)	10	10
638	2r. "The Crossing of the Delaware" (Sully) (horiz)	1·75	2·50
639	3r. "Samuel Adams" (Copley)	2·00	3·00
640	5r. "Surrender of Cornwallis" (Trumbull) (horiz)	2·25	3·25
MS641	147×95 mm. 10r. "Washington at Dorchester Heights" (Stuart)	16·00	19·00

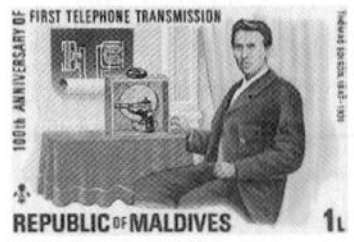

124 Thomas Edison

1976. Centenary of Telephone. Multicoloured.

642	1l. Type **124**	10	30
643	2l. Alexander Graham Bell	10	30
644	3l. Telephone of 1919, 1937 and 1972	10	30
645	10l. Cable entrance into station	20	20
646	20l. Equalizer circuit assembly	30	20
647	1r. "Salernum" (cable ship)	1·75	55
648	10r. "Intelsat IV-A" and Earth Station	4·75	7·50
MS649	156×105 mm. 4r. Early telephones	7·50	9·00

1976. "Interphil 76" International Stamp Exhibition, Philadelphia. Nos. 638/**MS**641 optd **MAY 29TH–JUNE 6TH "INTERPHIL" 1976.**

650	2r. multicoloured	1·50	1·75
651	3r. multicoloured	2·00	2·25
652	5r. multicoloured	2·50	2·75
MS653	147×95 mm. 10r. multicoloured	10·00	12·00

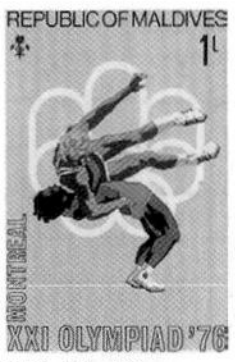

126 Wrestling

1976. Olympic Games, Montreal. Multicoloured.

654	1l. Type **126**	10	20
655	2l. Putting the shot	10	20
656	3l. Hurdling	10	20
657	4l. Hockey	10	20
658	5l. Running	10	20
659	6l. Javelin-throwing	10	20
660	1r.50 Discus-throwing	1·25	1·75
661	5r. Volleyball	2·75	5·25
MS662	135×106 mm. 10r. Throwing the hammer	8·50	12·00

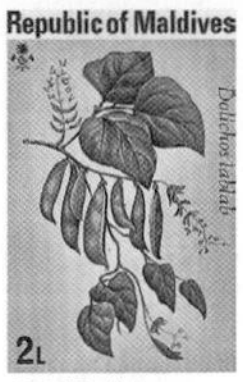

127 "Dolichos lablab"

1976. Vegetables. Multicoloured.

663	2l. Type **127**	10	40
664	4l. "Moringa pterygosperma"	10	40
665	10l. "Solanum melongena"	15	15
666	20l. "Moringa pterygosperma"	3·25	2·25
667	50l. "Cucumis sativus"	50	65
668	75l. "Trichosanthes anguina"	55	75
669	1r. "Momordica charantia"	65	85
670	2r. "Trichosanthes anguina"	4·75	8·00

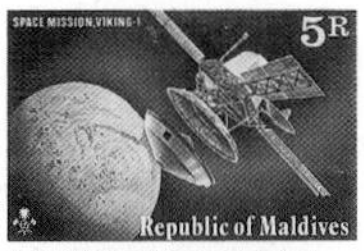

128 "Viking" approaching Mars

1977. "Viking" Space Mission. Multicoloured.

671	5r. Type **128**	1·90	2·75
MS672	121×89 mm. 20r. Landing module on Mars	10·00	14·00

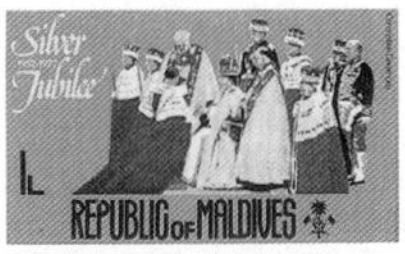

129 Coronation Ceremony

1977. Silver Jubilee of Queen Elizabeth II. Multicoloured.

673	1l. Type **129**	10	30
674	2l. Queen and Prince Philip	10	30
675	3l. Royal couple with Princes Andrew and Edward	10	30
676	1r.15 Queen with Archbishops	65	35
677	3r. State coach in procession	1·25	75
678	4r. Royal couple with Prince Charles and Princess Anne	1·25	1·25
MS679	120×77 mm. 10r. Queen and Prince Charles	5·00	3·75

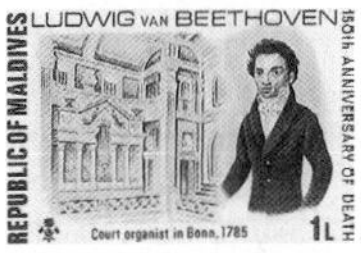

130 Beethoven and Organ

1977. 150th Death Anniv of Ludwig van Beethoven. Multicoloured.

680	1l. Type **130**	25	30
681	2l. Portrait and manuscript of "Moonlight Sonata"	25	30
682	3l. With Goethe at Teplitz	25	30
683	4l. Beethoven and string instruments	25	30
684	5l. Beethoven's home, Heiligenstadt	25	30
685	25l. Hands and gold medals	1·50	20
686	2r. Portrait and "Missa solemnis"	4·00	3·75
687	5r. Composer's hearing-aids	6·50	7·00
MS688	121×92 mm. 4r. Death mask and room where composer died	9·00	11·00

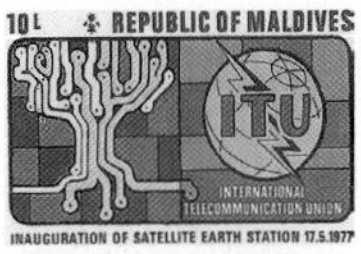

131 Printed Circuit and I.T.U. Emblem

1977. Inauguration of Satellite Earth Station. Multicoloured.

689	10l. Type **131**	10	10
690	90l. Central Telegraph Office	45	45
691	10r. Satellite Earth Station	3·00	6·00
MS692	100×85 mm. 5r. "Intelsat IV-A" satellite over Maldives	4·50	5·50

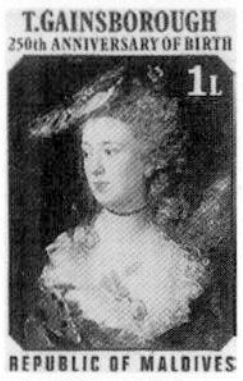

132 "Miss Anne Ford" (Gainsborough)

1977. Artists' Birth Anniversaries. Multicoloured.

693	1l. Type **132** (250th anniv)	10	30
694	2l. Group painting by Rubens (400th anniv)	10	30
695	3l. "Girl with Dog" (Titian) (500th Anniv)	10	30
696	4l. "Mrs. Thomas Graham" (Gainsborough)	10	30
697	5l. "Artist with Isabella Brant" (Rubens)	10	30
698	95l. Portrait by Titian	1·25	30
699	1r. Portrait by Gainsborough	1·25	30
700	10r. "Isabella Brant" (Rubens)	4·50	7·00
MS701	152×116 mm. 5r. "Self-portrait" (Titian)	3·75	5·50

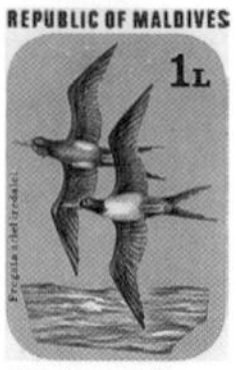

133 Lesser Frigate Birds

1977. Birds. Multicoloured.

702	1l. Type **133**	20	40
703	2l. Crab plover	20	40
704	3l. White-tailed tropic bird	20	40
705	4l. Wedge-tailed shearwater	20	40
706	5l. Grey heron	20	40
707	20l. White tern	90	30
708	95l. Cattle egret	2·25	1·60
709	1r.25 Black-naped tern	2·50	2·50
710	5r. Pheasant coucal	6·50	8·00
MS711	124×117 mm. 10r. Green-backed heron	25·00	25·00

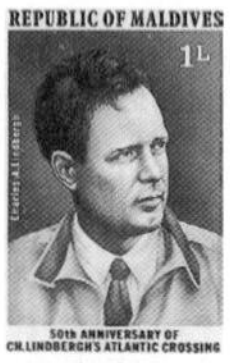

134 Charles Lindbergh

1977. 50th Anniv of Lindbergh's Transatlantic Flight and 75th Anniv of First Navigable Airships. Multicoloured.

712	1l. Type **134**	25	30
713	2l. Lindbergh and "Spirit of St. Louis"	25	30
714	3l. Lindbergh's Miles Mohawk aircraft (horiz)	25	30
715	4l. Lebaudy-Juillot airship "Morning Post" (horiz)	25	30
716	5l. Airship "Graf Zeppelin" and portrait of Zeppelin	25	30
717	1r. Airship "Los Angeles" (horiz)	1·25	30
718	3r. Lindbergh and Henry Ford	2·00	2·00
719	10r. Vickers airship R-23 rigid airship	2·75	6·00
MS720	148×114 mm. 5r. Ryan NYP Special "Spirit of St. Louis", Statue of Liberty and Eiffel Tower; 7r.50, Airship L-31 over "Ostfriesland" (German battleship)	13·00	18·00

No. 715 is inscr "Lebaudy I built by H. Juillot 1902".

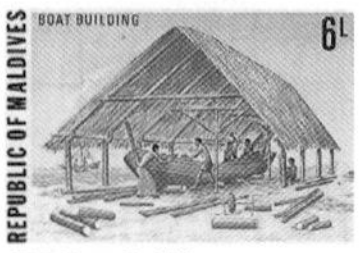

135 Boat Building

1977. Occupations. Multicoloured.

721	6l. Type **135**	65	45
722	15l. Fishing	1·10	20
723	20l. Cadjan weaving	1·40	20
724	90l. Mat-weaving	3·25	1·60
725	2r. Lace-making (vert)	5·00	4·75

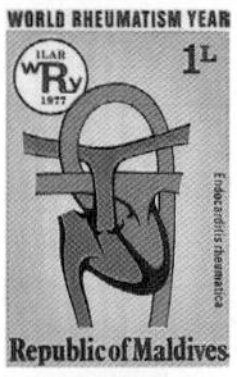

136 Rheumatic Heart

1977. World Rheumatism Year. Multicoloured.

726	1l. Type **136**	10	30
727	50l. Rheumatic shoulder	40	20
728	2r. Rheumatic hands	75	1·25
729	3r. Rheumatic knees	85	1·40

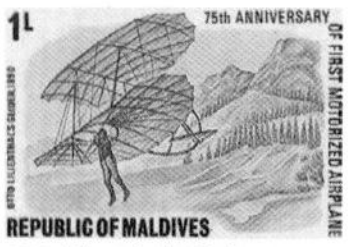

137 Lilienthal's Biplane Glider

1978. 75th Anniv of First Powered Aircraft. Multicoloured.

730	1l. Type **137**	20	40
731	2l. Chanute's glider	20	40
732	3l. Wright glider No. II, 1901	20	40
733	4l. A. V. Roe's Triplane I	20	40
734	5l. Wilbur Wright demonstrating Wright Type A for King Alfonso of Spain	20	40
735	10l. A. V. Roe's Avro Type D biplane	70	40
736	20l. Wright Brothers and A. G. Bell at Washington	2·00	40
737	95l. Hadley's triplane	5·00	2·25
738	5r. Royal Aircraft Factory B.E.2A biplanes at Upavon, 1914	11·00	11·00
MS739	98×82 mm. 10r. Wright Brothers' Wright Type A	14·00	16·00

No. 732 is wrongly dated "1900".

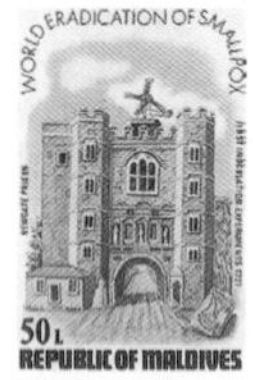

138 Newgate Prison

1978. World Eradication of Smallpox. Multicoloured.

740	15l. Foundling Hospital, London (horiz)	50	30
741	50l. Type **138**	1·25	60
742	2r. Edward Jenner (discoverer of smallpox vaccine)	2·25	4·00

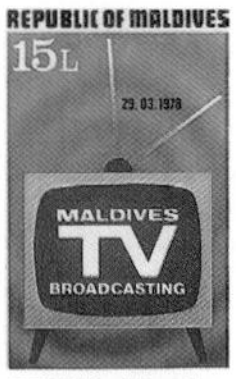

139 Television Set

1978. Inaug of Television in Maldive Islands. Multicoloured.

743	15l. Type **139**	40	30
744	25l. Television aerials	55	30
745	1r.50 Control desk (horiz)	2·25	2·75

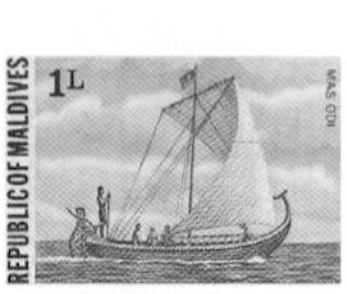

140 Mas Odi

1978. Ships. Multicoloured.

746	1l. Type **140**	10	35
747	2l. Battela	10	35
748	3l. Bandu odi (vert)	10	35
749	5l. "Maldive Trader" (freighter)	20	35
750	1r. "Fath-hul Baaree" (brigantine)	65	30
751	1r.25 Mas dhoni	85	1·00
752	3r. Baggala (vert)	1·10	1·75
753	4r. As 1r.25	1·10	1·75
MS754	152×138 mm. 1r. As No. 747; 4r. As No. 751	2·00	3·75

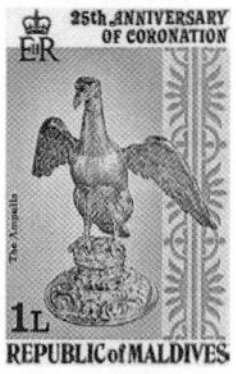

141 Ampulla

1978. 25th Anniv of Coronation. Multicoloured.

755	1l. Type **141**	10	20
756	2l. Sceptre with Dove	10	20
757	3l. Golden Orb	10	20
758	1r.15 St. Edward's Crown	30	20
759	2r. Sceptre with Cross	40	35
760	5r. Queen Elizabeth II	60	80
MS761	108×106 mm. 10r. Annointing spoon	1·75	2·25

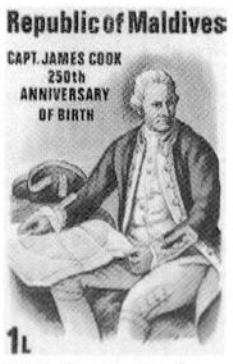

142 Capt. Cook

1978. 250th Birth Anniv of Capt. James Cook and Bicent of Discovery of Hawaiian Islands. Multicoloured.

762	1l. Type **142**	10	25
763	2l. Statue of Kamehameha I of Hawaii	10	25
764	3l. H.M.S. "Endeavour"	10	25
765	25l. Route of third voyage	45	45
766	75l. H.M.S. "Discovery", H.M.S. "Resolution" and map of Hawaiian Islands (horiz)	1·25	1·25
767	1r.50 Cook meeting Hawaiian islanders (horiz)	2·00	2·25
768	10r. Death of Capt. Cook (horiz)	4·00	10·00
MS769	100×92 mm. 5r. H.M.S. "Endeavour" (different)	15·00	20·00

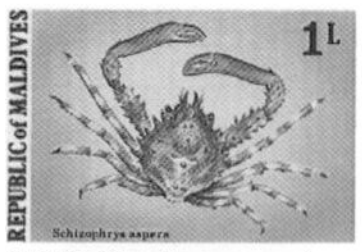

143 "Schizophrys aspera"

1978. Crustaceans. Multicoloured.

770	1l. Type **143**	10	25
771	2l. "Atergatis floridus"	10	25
772	3l. "Perenon planissimum"	10	25
773	90l. "Portunus granulatus"	50	40
774	1r. "Carpilius maculatus"	50	40
775	2r. "Huenia proteus"	1·00	1·40
776	25r. "Etisus laevimanus"	4·50	13·00
MS777	147×146 mm. 2r. "Panulirus longipes" (vert)	2·00	2·50

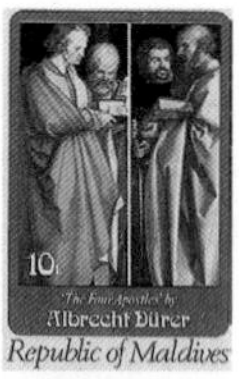

144 "Four Apostles"

1978. 450th Death Anniv of Albrecht Durer (artist).

778	**144**	10l. multicoloured	10	10
779	-	20l. multicoloured	15	10
780	-	55l. multicoloured	20	20
781	-	1r. black, brown and buff	30	30
782	-	1r.80 multicoloured	45	60
783	-	3r. multicoloured	70	1·25
MS784		141×122 mm. 10r. multicoloured	4·00	6·00

DESIGNS—VERT: 20l. "Self-portrait at 27"; 55l. "Madonna and Child with a Pear"; 1r.80, "Hare"; 3r. "Great Piece of Turf"; 10r. "Columbine". HORIZ: 1r. "Rhinoceros".

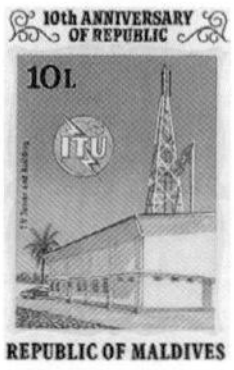

145 T.V. Tower and Building

1978. Tenth Anniv of Republic. Multicoloured.

785	1l. Fishing boat (horiz)	10	60
786	5l. Montessori School (horiz)	10	40
787	10l. Type **145**	10	10
788	25l. Islet (horiz)	20	15
789	50l. Boeing 737 aircraft (horiz)	80	25
790	95l. Beach scene (horiz)	60	30
791	1r.25 Dhow at night (horiz)	75	55
792	3r. President's residence (horiz)	80	1·25
793	5r. Masjidh Afeefuddin Mosque (horiz)	1·00	3·00
MS794	119×88 mm. 3r. Fisherman casting net	2·25	4·00

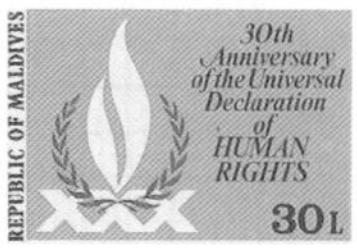

146 Human Rights Emblem

1978. 30th Anniv of Declaration of Human Rights.

795	**146**	30l. pink, lilac and green	15	15
796	**146**	90l. yellow, brown and green	40	60
797	**146**	1r.80 blue, deep blue and green	70	1·00

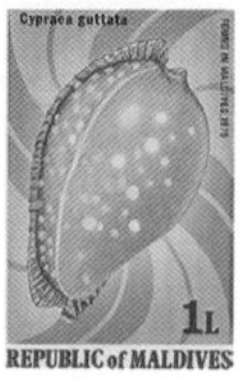

147 Great Spotted or Rare Spotted Cowrie

1979. Shells. Multicoloured.

798	1l. Type **147**	10	20
799	2l. Imperial cone	10	20
800	3l. Great green turban	10	20
801	10l. Giant spider conch	45	10
802	1r. White-toothed cowrie	2·00	40
803	1r.80 Fig cone	3·00	2·50
804	3r. Glory of the sea cone	4·50	3·75
MS805	141×110 mm. 5r. Common Pacific vase	13·00	12·00

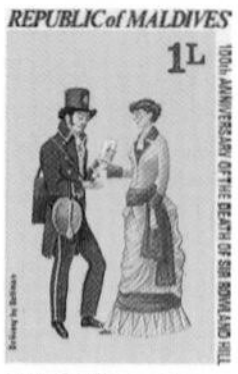

148 Delivery by Bellman

1979. Death Cent of Sir Rowland Hill. Multicoloured.

806	1l. Type **148**	10	20
807	2l. Mail coach, 1840 (horiz)	10	20
808	3l. First London letter box, 1855	10	20
809	1r.55 Penny Black	40	50
810	5r. First Maldive Islands stamp	70	1·25
MS811	132×107 mm. 10r. Sir Rowland Hill	1·25	3·00

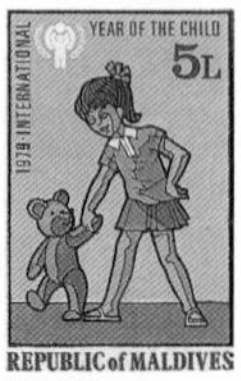

149 Girl with Teddy Bear

1979. Int Year of the Child (1st issue). Multicoloured.

812	5l. Type **149**	10	10
813	1r.25 Boy with sailing boat	40	50
814	2r. Boy with toy rocket	45	55
815	3r. Boy with toy airship	60	75
MS816	108×109 mm. 5r. Boy with toy train	1·25	2·00

See also Nos. 838/**MS**847.

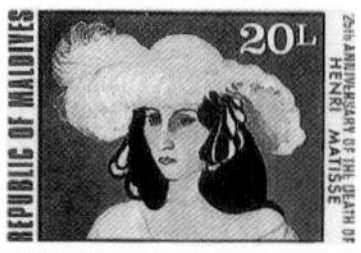

150 "White Feathers"

1979. 25th Death Anniv of Henri Matisse (artist). Multicoloured.

817	20l. Type **150**	15	15
818	25l. "Joy of Life"	15	15
819	30l. "Eggplants"	15	15
820	1r.50 "Harmony in Red"	45	65

821	5r. "Still-life"	70	2·25
MS822	135×95 mm. 4r. "Water Pitcher"	4·25	4·50

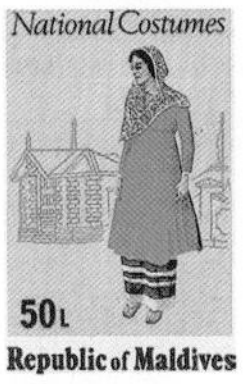

151 Sari with Overdress

1979. National Costumes. Multicoloured.

823	50l. Type **151**	20	15
824	75l. Sashed apron dress	25	20
825	90l. Serape	30	25
826	95l. Ankle-length printed dress	35	30

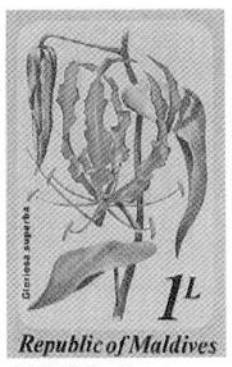

152 "Gloriosa superba"

1979. Flowers. Multicoloured.

827	1l. Type **152**	10	10
828	3l. "Hibiscus tiliaceus"	10	10
829	50l. "Barringtonia asiatica"	20	15
830	1r. "Abutilon indicum"	40	25
831	5r. "Guettarda speciosa"	1·00	2·00
MS832	94×85 mm. 4r. "Pandanus odoratissimus"	1·75	2·75

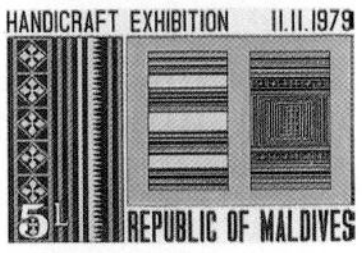

153 Weaving

1979. Handicraft Exhibition. Multicoloured.

833	5l. Type **153**	10	10
834	10l. Lacquerwork	10	10
835	1r.30 Tortoiseshell jewellery	45	55
836	2r. Carved woodwork	60	90
MS837	125×85 mm. 5r. Gold and silver jewellery	1·25	2·25

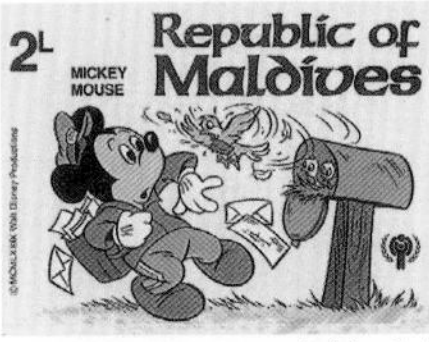

154 Mickey Mouse attacked by Bird

1979. International Year of the Child (2nd issue). Disney Characters. Multicoloured.

838	1l. Goofy delivering parcel on motor-scooter (vert)	10	10
839	2l. Type **154**	10	10
840	3l. Goofy half-covered with letters	10	10
841	4l. Pluto licking Minnie Mouse's envelopes	10	10
842	5l. Mickey Mouse delivering letters on roller skates (vert)	10	10
843	10l. Donald Duck placing letter in mail-box	10	10
844	15l. Chip and Dale carrying letter	10	10
845	1r.50 Donald Duck on monocycle (vert)	75	95
846	5r. Donald Duck with ostrich in crate (vert)	2·25	3·25
MS847	127×102 mm. 4r. Pluto putting parcel in mail-box	5·50	7·00

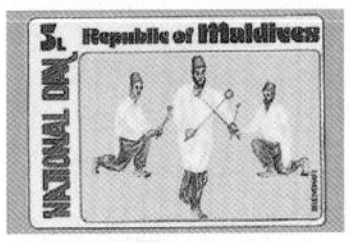

155 Post-Ramadan Dancing

1980. National Day. Multicoloured.

848	5l. Type **155**	10	10
849	15l. Musicians and dancer, Eeduu Festival	10	10
850	95l. Sultan's ceremonial band	35	30
851	2r. Dancer and drummers Circumcision Festival	60	85
MS852	131×99 mm. 5r. Swordsmen	1·90	2·50

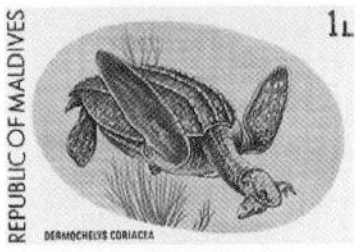

156 Leatherback Turtle

1980. Turtle Conservation Campaign. Multicoloured.

853	1l. Type **156**	15	30
854	2l. Flatback turtle	15	30
855	5l. Hawksbill turtle	20	30
856	10l. Loggerhead turtle	25	30
857	75l. Olive Ridley turtle	1·00	45
858	10r. Atlantic Ridley turtle	3·00	4·25
MS859	85×107 mm. 4r. Green turtle	2·00	2·75

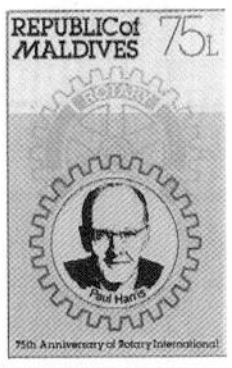

157 Paul Harris (founder)

1980. 75th Anniv of Rotary Int. Multicoloured.

860	75l. Type **157**	45	10
861	90l. Humanity	50	20
862	1r. Hunger	50	25
863	10r. Health	2·75	4·50
MS864	109×85 mm. 5r. Globe	1·75	2·50

1980. "London 1980" International Stamp Exhibition. Nos. 809/**MS**811 optd **LONDON 1980.**

865	1r.55 Penny Black	2·50	1·00
866	5r. First Maldives stamp	4·00	2·75
MS867	132×107 mm. 10r. Sir Rowland Hill	7·50	8·00

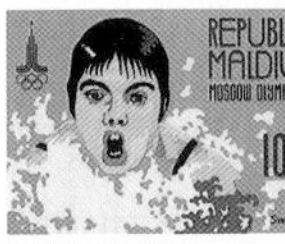

159 Swimming

1980. Olympic Games, Moscow. Multicoloured.

868	10l. Type **159**	10	10
869	50l. Running	20	20
870	3r. Putting the shot	70	1·10
871	4r. High jumping	80	1·40
MS872	105×85 mm. 5r. Weightlifting	1·25	2·25

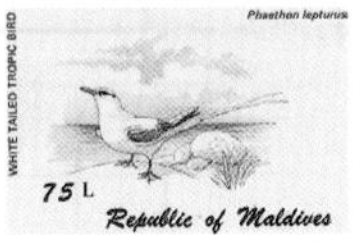

160 White-tailed Tropic Bird

1980. Birds. Multicoloured.

873	75l. Type **160**	25	15
874	95l. Sooty tern	35	30
875	1r. Common noddy	35	30
876	1r.55 Curlew	50	70
877	2r. Wilson's storm petrel ("Wilson's Petrel")	60	85
878	4r. Caspian tern	1·10	1·60
MS879	124×85 mm. 5r. Red-footed booby and brown booby	8·00	9·00

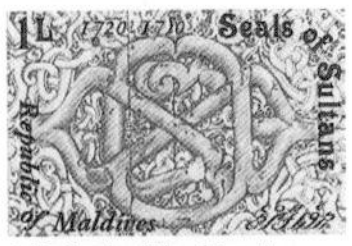

161 Seal of Ibrahim II

1980. Seals of the Sultans.

880	**161**	1l. brown and black	10	10
881	-	2l. brown and black	10	10
882	-	5l. brown and black	10	10
883	-	1r. brown and black	40	30
884	-	2r. brown and black	50	70
MS885		131×95 mm. 3r. brown and black	85	1·60

DESIGNS: 2l. Mohammed Imadudeen II; 5l. Bin Haji Ali; 1r. Kuda Mohammed Rasgefaanu; 2r. Ibrahim Iskander I; 3r. Ibrahim Iskander I (different).

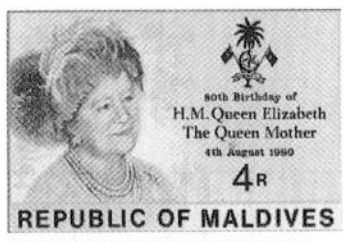

162 Queen Elizabeth the Queen Mother

1980. 80th Birthday of the Queen Mother.

886	**162**	4r. multicoloured	1·00	1·25
MS887		85×110 mm. **162** 5r. multicoloured	1·90	2·25

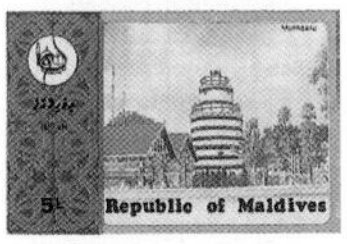

163 Munnaru

1980. 1400th Anniv of Hegira. Multicoloured.

888	5l. Type **163**	20	10
889	10l. Hukuru Miskiiy mosque	25	10
890	30l. Medhuziyaaraiy (shrine of saint)	30	30
891	55l. Writing tablets with verses of Koran	40	35
892	90l. Mother teaching child Koran	60	70
MS893	124×101 mm. 2r. Map of Maldives and coat of arms	80	1·60

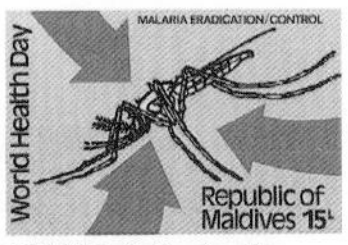

164 Malaria Eradication

1980. World Health Day.

894	**164**	15l. black, brown and red	20	10
895	-	25l. multicoloured	20	10
896	-	1r.50 brown, light brown and black	2·00	1·00
897	-	5r. multicoloured	3·25	3·00
MS898		68×85 mm. 4r. black, blue and light blue	1·25	2·50

DESIGNS: 25l. Nutrition; 1r.50, Dental health; 4, 5r. Clinics.

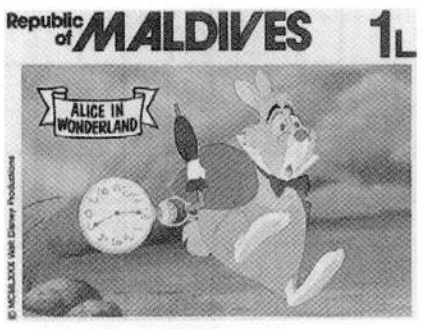

165 White Rabbit

1980. Walt Disney's "Alice in Wonderland". Multicoloured.

899	1l. Type **165**	10	10
900	2l. Alice falling into Wonderland	10	10
901	3l. Alice too big to go through door	10	10
902	4l. Alice with Tweedledum and Tweedledee	10	10
903	5l. Alice and caterpillar	10	10
904	10l. The Cheshire cat	10	10
905	15l. Alice painting the roses	10	10
906	2r.50 Alice and the Queen of Hearts	2·50	2·50
907	4r. Alice on trial	2·75	2·75
MS908	126×101 mm. 5r. Alice at the Mad Hatter's tea-party	4·50	6·50

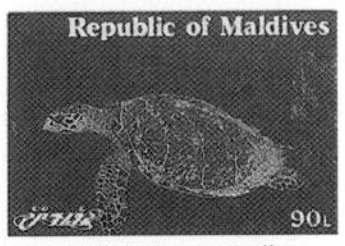

166 Indian Ocean Ridley Turtle

1980. Marine Animals. Multicoloured.

909	90l. Type **166**	2·25	60
910	1r.25 Pennant coralfish	2·75	1·25
911	2r. Spiny lobster	3·25	1·75
MS912	140×94 mm. 4r. Oriental sweetlips and scarlet-finned squirrelfish	3·00	3·25

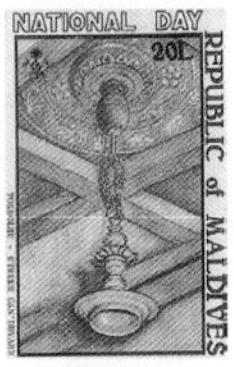

167 Pendant Lamp

1981. National Day. Multicoloured.

913	10l. Tomb of Ghaazee Muhammad Thakurufaan (horiz)	15	10
914	20l. Type **167**	20	10
915	30l. Chair used by Muhammad Thakurufaan	25	10
916	95l. Muhammad Thakurufaan's palace (horiz)	60	30
917	10r. Cushioned divan	2·75	4·50

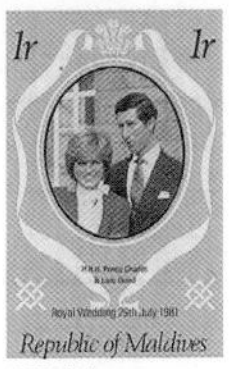

168 Prince Charles and Lady Diana Spencer

1981. British Royal Wedding. Multicoloured.

918	1r. Type **168**	15	15
919	2r. Buckingham Palace	25	25
920	5r. Prince Charles, polo player	40	50
MS921	95×83 mm. 10r. State coach	75	1·10

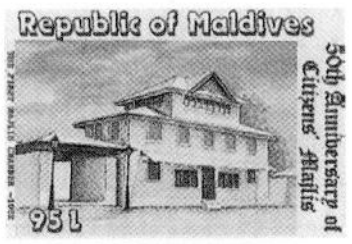

169 First Majlis Chamber

1981. 50th Anniv of Citizens' Majlis (grievance rights). Multicoloured.

922	95l. Type **169**	30	30
923	1r. Sultan Muhammed Shamsuddin III	35	35
MS924	137×94 mm. 4r. First written constitution (horiz)	2·00	4·00

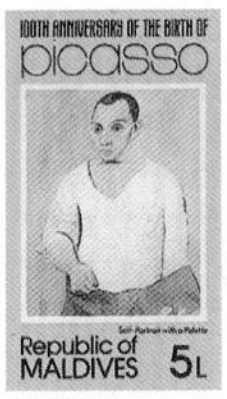

170 "Self-portrait with a Palette"

1981. Birth Centenary of Pablo Picasso. Multicoloured.

925	5l. Type **170**	15	10
926	10l. "Woman in Blue"	20	10
927	25l. "Boy with Pipe"	30	10
928	30l. "Card Player"	30	10
929	90l. "Sailor"	50	40
930	3r. "Self-portrait"	80	1·00
931	5r. "Harlequin"	1·00	1·25
MS932	106×130 mm. 10r. "Child holding a Dove". Imperf	2·50	3·50

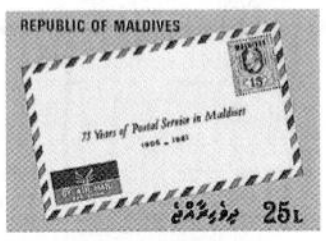

171 Airmail Envelope

1981. 75th Anniv of Postal Service.

933	**171**	25l. multicoloured	15	10
934	**171**	75l. multicoloured	25	25
935	**171**	5r. multicoloured	70	1·25

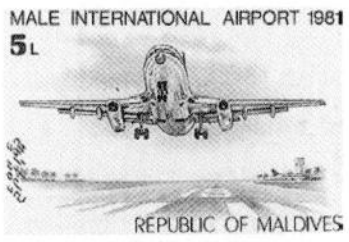

172 Boeing 737 taking off

1981. Male International Airport. Multicoloured.

936	5l. Type **172**	30	20
937	20l. Passengers leaving Boeing 737	55	20
938	1r.80 Refuelling	90	1·25
939	4r. Plan of airport	1·10	2·25
MS940	106×79 mm. 5r. Aerial view of airport	2·50	3·00

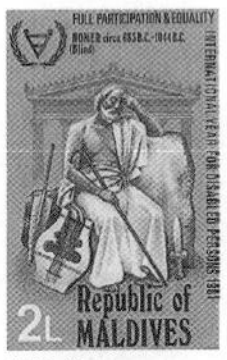

173 Homer

1981. International Year of Disabled People. Multicoloured.

941	2l. Type **173**	10	10
942	5l. Miguel Cervantes	10	10
943	1r. Beethoven	2·75	85
944	5r. Van Gogh	3·25	5·00
MS945	116×91 mm. 4r. Helen Keller and Anne Sullivan	3·25	5·50

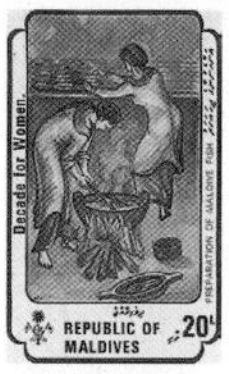

174 Preparation of Maldive Fish

1981. Decade for Women. Multicoloured.

946	20l. Type **174**	10	10
947	90l. 16th-century Maldive women	25	25
948	1r. Farming	30	30
949	2r. Coir rope-making	55	1·10

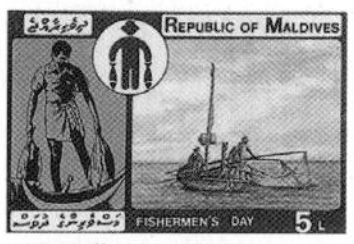

175 Collecting Bait

1981. Fishermen's Day. Multicoloured.

950	5l. Type **175**	45	15
951	15l. Fishing boats	85	25
952	90l. Fisherman with catch	1·60	60
953	1r.30 Sorting fish	2·00	1·10
MS954	147×101 mm. 3r. Loading fish for export	1·50	2·50

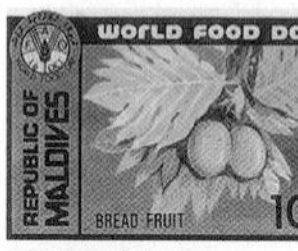

176 Bread Fruit

1981. World Food Day. Multicoloured.

955	10l. Type **176**	40	10
956	25l. Hen with chicks	80	15
957	30l. Maize	80	20
958	75l. Skipjack tuna	2·50	65
959	1r. Pumpkin	3·00	70
960	2r. Coconuts	3·25	3·25
MS961	110×85 mm. 5r. Eggplant	2·50	3·50

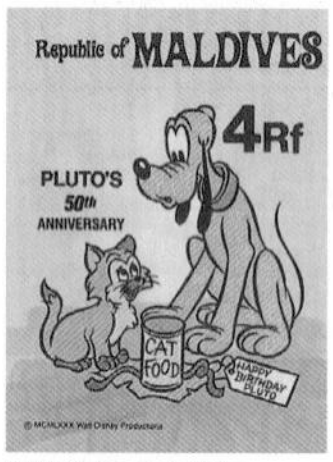

177 Pluto and Cat

1982. 50th Anniv of Pluto (Walt Disney Cartoon Character). Multicoloured.

962	4r. Type **177**	2·00	2·75
MS963	127×101 mm. 6r. Pluto (scene from "The Pointer")	3·25	4·00

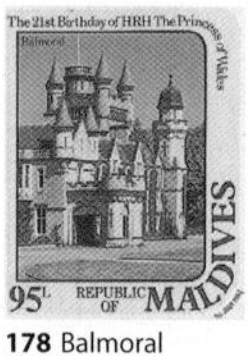

178 Balmoral

1982. 21st Birthday of Princess of Wales. Multicoloured.

964	95l. Type **178**	50	20
965	3r. Prince and Princess of Wales	1·25	65
966	5r. Princess on aircraft steps	1·75	95
MS967	103×75 mm. 8r. Princess of Wales	1·75	1·75

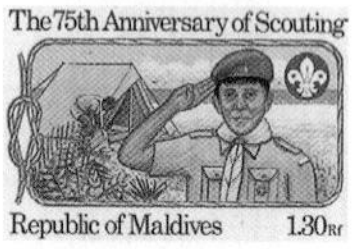

179 Scout saluting and Camp-site

1983. 75th Anniv of Boy Scout Movement. Multicoloured.

968	1r.30 Type **179**	40	45
969	1r.80 Lighting a fire	50	60
970	4r. Life-saving	1·10	1·40
971	5r. Map-reading	1·40	1·75
MS972	128×66 mm. 10r. Scout emblem and flag of the Maldives	2·00	3·00

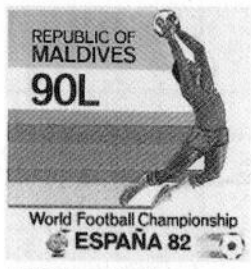

180 Footballer

1982. World Cup Football Championship, Spain.

973	**180**	90l. multicoloured	1·50	60
974	-	1r.50 multicoloured	2·00	1·10
975	-	3r. multicoloured	2·75	1·75
976	-	5r. multicoloured	3·25	2·50
MS977		94×63 mm. 10r. multicoloured	4·50	6·00

DESIGNS: 1r.50 to 10r. Various footballers.

1982. Birth of Prince William of Wales. Nos. 964/**MS**967 optd **ROYAL BABY 21.6.82.**

978	95l. Type **178**	30	20
979	3r. Prince and Princess of Wales	1·00	65
980	5r. Princess on aircraft steps	1·00	95
MS981	103×75 mm. 8r. Princess of Wales	3·50	2·50

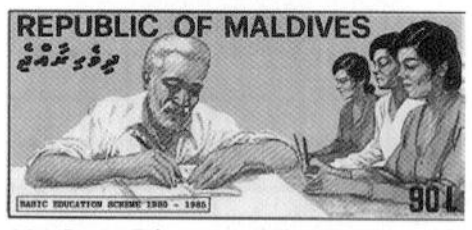

181 Basic Education Scheme

1983. National Education. Multicoloured.

982	90l. Type **181**	20	30
983	95l. Primary education	20	30
984	1r.30 Teacher training	25	30
985	2r.50 Printing educational material	45	75
MS986	100×70 mm. 6r. Thaana typewriter keyboard	1·00	2·00

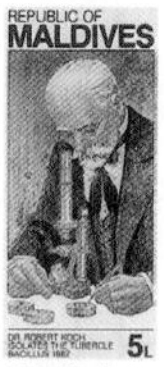

182 Koch isolates the Bacillus

1983. Centenary of Robert Koch's Discovery of Tubercle Bacillus. Multicoloured.

987	5l. Type **182**	15	20
988	15l. Micro-organism and microscope	20	20
989	95l. Dr. Robert Koch in 1905	45	45
990	3r. Dr. Koch and plates from publication	85	1·75
MS991	77×61 mm. 5r. Koch in his laboratory (horiz)	1·00	2·00

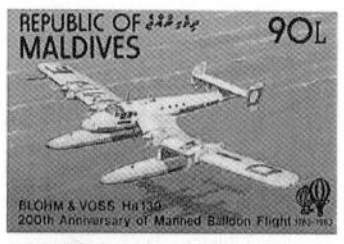

183 Blohm and Voss Seaplane "Nordsee"

1983. Bicentenary of Manned Flight. Multicoloured.

992	90l. Type **183**	2·25	70
993	1r.45 Macchi Castoldi MC.72 seaplane	2·75	1·75
994	4r. Boeing F4B-3 biplane fighter	4·50	3·25
995	5r. Renard and Krebs airship "La France"	4·50	3·50
MS996	110×85 mm. 10r. Nadar's balloon "Le Geant"	3·00	4·00

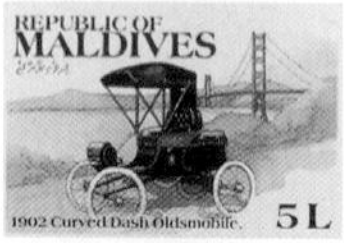

184 "Curved Dash" Oldsmobile, 1902

1983. Classic Motor Cars. Multicoloured.

997	5l. Type **184**	20	40
998	30l. Aston Martin "Tourer", 1932	60	40
999	40l. Lamborghini "Muira", 1966	60	45
1000	1r. Mercedes-Benz "300SL", 1945	1·00	70
1001	1r.40 Stutz "Bearcat", 1913	1·25	2·00
1002	5r. Lotus "Elite", 1958	2·00	4·25
MS1003	132×103 mm. 10r. Grand Prix "Sunbeam", 1924	5·50	10·00

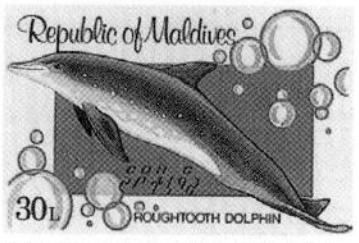

185 Rough-toothed Dolphin

1983. Marine Mammals. Multicoloured.

1004	30l. Type **185**	1·60	60
1005	40l. Indo-Pacific hump-backed dolphin	1·60	65
1006	4r. Finless porpoise	5·00	4·00
1007	6r. Pygmy sperm whale	10·00	7·00
MS1008	82×90 mm. 5r. Striped dolphin	6·00	5·50

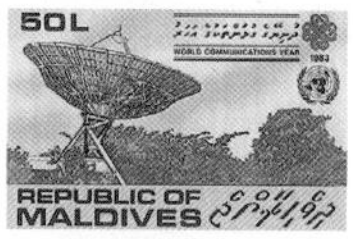

186 Dish Aerial

1983. World Communications Year. Multicoloured.

1009	50l. Type **186**	50	20
1010	1r. Land, sea and air communications	1·75	60
1011	2r. Ship-to-shore communications	2·50	1·75
1012	10r. Air traffic controller	4·75	7·50
MS1013	91×76 mm. 20r. Telecommunications	3·75	4·75

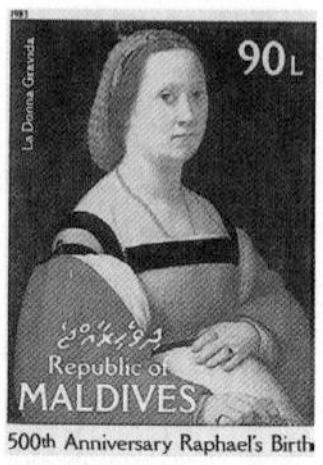

187 "La Donna Gravida"

1983. 500th Birth Anniv of Raphael. Multicoloured.

1014	90l. Type **187**	25	25
1015	3r. "Giovanna d'Aragona" (detail)	75	1·40
1016	4r. "Woman with Unicorn"	75	1·90
1017	6r. "La Muta"	1·00	2·50
MS1018	121×97 mm. 10r. "The Knight's Dream" (detail)	2·50	5·50

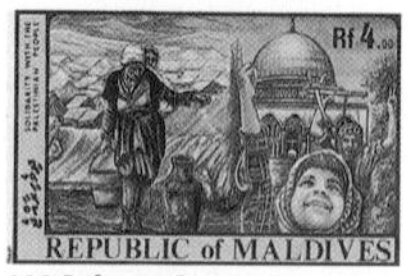

188 Refugee Camp

1983. Solidarity with the Palestinian People. Multicoloured.

1019	4r. Type **188**	2·25	2·00
1020	5r. Refugee holding dead child	2·25	2·00
1021	6r. Child carrying food	2·75	2·50

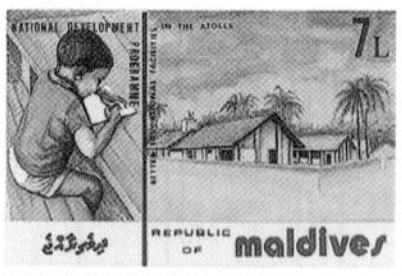

189 Education Facilities

1983. National Development Programme. Multicoloured.

1022	7l. Type **189**	20	10
1023	10l. Health service and education	50	10
1024	5r. Growing more food	1·50	1·25
1025	6r. Fisheries development	2·25	1·50
MS1026	134×93 mm. 10r. Air transport	2·25	2·75

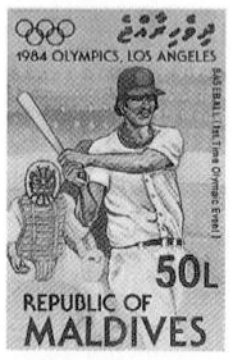

190 Baseball

1984. Olympic Games, Los Angeles. Multicoloured.

1027	50l. Type **190**	30	15
1028	1r.55 Backstroke swimming	65	40
1029	3r. Judo	1·40	90
1030	4r. Shot-putting	1·60	1·40
MS1031	85×105 mm. 10r. Team handball	2·40	2·75

1984. U.P.U. Congress, Hamburg. Nos. 994/**MS**996 optd **19th UPU CONGRESS HAMBURG.**

1032	4r. Boeing "F4B-3"	1·75	1·40
1033	5r. "La France" airship	1·75	1·60
MS1034	110×85 mm. 10r. Nadar's balloon "Le Geant"	2·75	4·50

1984. Surch **Rf.1.45.** (a) Nos. 964/**MS**967.

1035	1r.45 on 95l. Type **178**	2·00	1·50
1036	1r.45 on 3r. Prince and Princess of Wales	2·00	1·50
1037	1r.45 on 5r. Princess on aircraft steps	2·00	1·50
MS1038	103×75 mm. 1r.45 on 8r. Princess of Wales	2·00	3·75

(b) Nos. 978/**MS**981.

1039	1r.45 on 95l. Type **178**	2·00	1·50
1040	1r.45 on 3r. Prince and Princess of Wales	2·00	1·50
1041	1r.45 on 5r. Princess on aircraft steps	2·00	1·50
MS1042	103×75 mm. 1r.45 on 8r. Princess of Wales	2·00	3·75

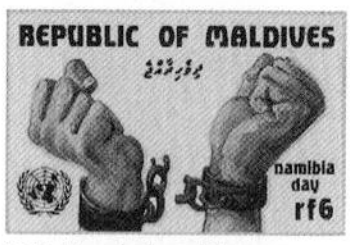

193 Hands breaking Manacles

1984. Namibia Day. Multicoloured.

1043	6r. Type **193**	1·00	1·25
1044	8r. Namibian family	1·00	1·75
MS1045	129×104 mm. 10r. Map of Namibia	1·75	2·50

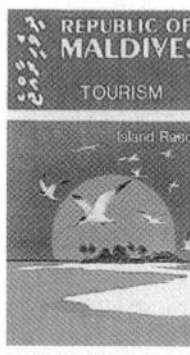

194 Island Resort and Common Terns

1984. Tourism. Multicoloured.

1046	7l. Type **194**	1·75	80
1047	15l. Dhow	90	15
1048	20l. Snorkelling	70	15
1049	2r. Wind-surfing	2·00	50
1050	4r. Aqualung diving	2·50	1·10
1051	6r. Night fishing	3·50	1·75
1052	8r. Game fishing	4·00	2·00
1053	10r. Turtle on beach	4·50	2·25

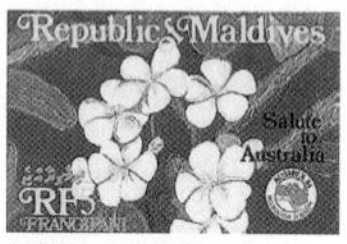

195 Frangipani

1984. "Ausipex" International Stamp Exhibition, Melbourne. Multicoloured.

1054	5r. Type **195**	2·25	1·75
1055	10r. Cooktown orchid	4·75	3·75
MS1056	105×77 mm. 15r. Sun orchid	10·00	5·50

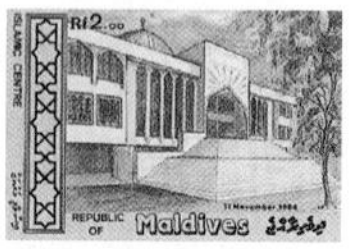

196 Facade of Male Mosque

1984. Opening of Islamic Centre. Multicoloured.

1057	2r. Type **196**	45	50
1058	5r. Male Mosque and minaret (vert)	1·10	1·25

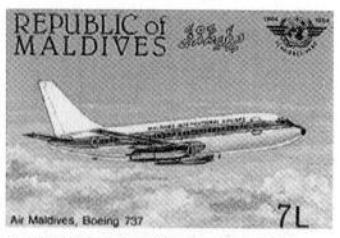

197 Air Maldives Boeing 737

1984. 40th Anniv of I.C.A.O. Multicoloured.

1059	7l. Type **197**	85	45
1060	4r. Air Lanka Lockheed L-1011 TriStar	3·25	2·00
1061	6r. Alitalia Douglas DC-10-30	4·00	3·50
1062	8r. L.T.U. Lockheed L-1011 TriStar	4·25	4·50
MS1063	110×92 mm. 15r. Air Maldives Short S.7 Skyvan	3·75	4·00

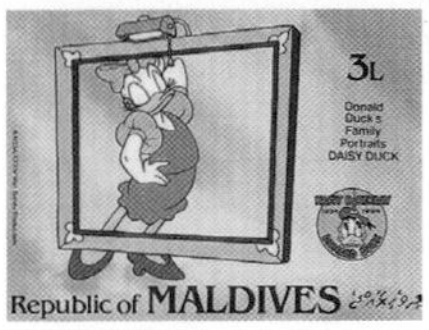

198 Daisy Duck

1984. 50th Birthday of Donald Duck. Walt Disney Cartoon Characters. Multicoloured.

1064	3l. Type **198**	10	10
1065	4l. Huey, Dewey and Louie	10	10
1066	5l. Ludwig von Drake	10	10
1067	10l. Gyro Gearloose	10	10
1068	15l. Uncle Scrooge painting self-portrait	15	10
1069	25l. Donald Duck with camera	15	10
1070	5r. Donald Duck and Gus Goose	2·25	1·25
1071	8r. Gladstone Gander	2·50	2·00
1072	10r. Grandma Duck	3·00	2·50
MS1073	102×126 mm. 15r. Uncle Scrooge and Donald Duck in front of camera	4·75	5·00
MS1074	126×102 mm. 15r. Uncle Scrooge	4·75	5·00

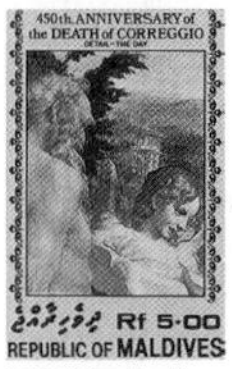

199 "The Day" (detail)

1984. 450th Death Anniv of Correggio (artist). Multicoloured.

1075	5r. Type **199**	1·00	1·50
1076	10r. "The Night" (detail)	1·50	1·75
MS1077	60×80 mm. 15r. "Portrait of a Man"	3·50	3·25

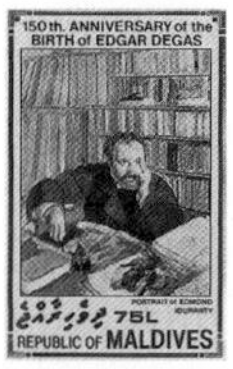

200 "Edmond Iduranty" (Degas)

1984. 150th Birth Anniv of Edgar Degas (artist). Multicoloured.

1078	75l. Type **200**	20	20
1079	2r. "James Tissot"	50	50
1080	5r. "Achille de Gas in Uniform"	1·00	1·00
1081	10r. "Lady with Chrysanthemums"	1·75	2·00
MS1082	100×70 mm. 15r. "Self-portrait"	3·25	3·75

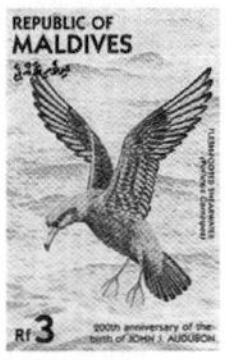

201 Pale-footed Shearwater ("Flest-footed Shearwater")

1985. Birth Bicentenary of John J. Audubon (ornithologist) (1st issue). Designs showing original paintings. Multicoloured.

1083	3r. Type **201**	1·75	80
1084	3r.50 Little grebe (horiz)	2·00	90
1085	4r. Great cormorant	2·00	1·00
1086	4r.50 White-faced storm petrel (horiz)	2·00	1·10
MS1087	108×80 mm. 15r. Red-necked phalarope (horiz)	4·50	4·50

See also Nos. 1192/200.

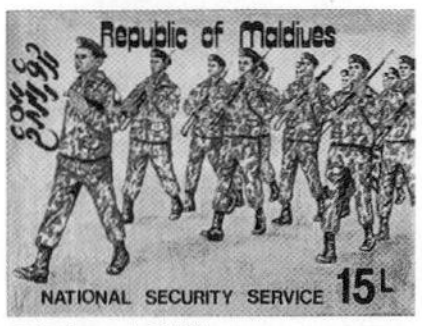

202 Squad Drilling

1985. National Security Service. Multicoloured.

1088	15l. Type **202**	50	10
1089	20l. Combat patrol	50	10
1090	1r. Fire fighting	2·00	40
1091	2r. Coastguard cutter	2·50	1·00
1092	10r. Independence Day Parade (vert)	3·25	3·50
MS1093	128×85 mm. 10r. Cannon on saluting base and National Security Service badge	2·25	2·25

1985. Olympic Games Gold Medal Winners, Los Angeles. Nos. 1027/31 optd.

1094	50l. Type **190** (optd **JAPAN**)	30	15
1095	1r.55 Backstroke swimming (optd **GOLD MEDALIST THERESA ANDREWS USA**)	60	55
1096	3r. Judo (optd **GOLD MEDALIST FRANK WIENEKE USA**)	1·25	1·25
1097	4r. Shot-putting (optd **GOLD MEDALIST CLAUDIA LOCH WEST GERMANY**)	1·25	1·40
MS1098	85×105 mm. 10r. Team handball (optd **U.S.A.**)	1·90	2·00

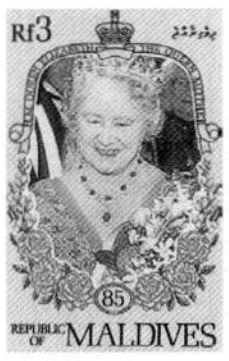

204 Queen Elizabeth the Queen Mother, 1981

1985. Life and Times of Queen Elizabeth the Queen Mother. Multicoloured.

1099	3r. Type **204**	45	60
1100	5r. Visiting the Middlesex Hospital (horiz)	65	1·00
1101	7r. The Queen Mother	85	1·25
MS1102	56×85 mm. 15r. With Prince Charles at Garter Ceremony	4·25	3·25

Stamps as Nos. 1099/1101 but with face values of 1r., 4r. and 10r. exist from additional sheetlets with changed background colours.

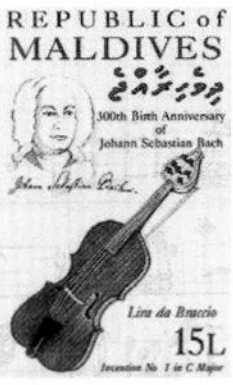

204a Lira da Braccio

1985. 300th Birth Anniversary of Johann Sebastian Bach (composer). Multicoloured (except No. **MS**1107).

1103	15l. Type **204a**	10	10
1104	2r. Tenor oboe	50	45
1105	4r. Serpent	90	85
1106	10r. Table organ	1·90	2·25
MS1107	104×75 mm. 15r. Johann Sebastian Bach (black and orange)	3·00	3·50

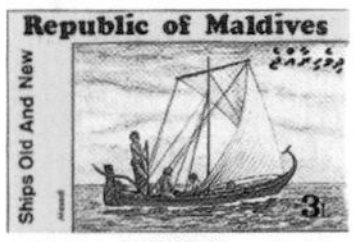

205 Mas Odi (fishing boat)

1985. Maldives Ships and Boats. Multicoloured.

1108	3l. Type **205**	10	30
1109	5l. Battela (dhow)	10	30
1110	10l. Addu odi (dhow)	10	30
1111	2r.60 Modern dhoni (fishing boat)	2·00	1·75
1112	2r.70 Mas dhoni (fishing boat)	2·00	1·75
1113	3r. Baththeli dhoni	2·25	1·75
1114	5r. "Inter I" (inter-island vessel)	3·50	3·00
1115	10r. Dhoni-style yacht	5·00	6·00

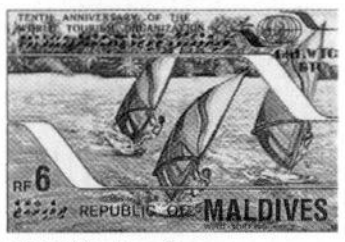

206 Windsurfing

1985. Tenth Anniv of World Tourism Organization. Multicoloured.

1116	6r. Type **206**	3·00	2·75
1117	8r. Scuba diving	3·25	3·00
MS1118	171×114 mm. 15r. Kuda Hithi Resort	2·75	3·00

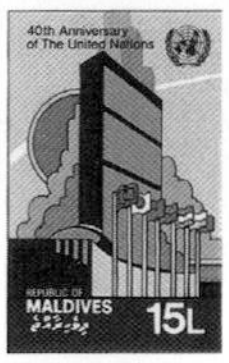

207 United Nations Building, New York

1985. 40th Anniv of U.N.O. and International Peace Year. Multicoloured.

1119	15l. Type **207**	10	10
1120	2r. Hands releasing peace dove	40	45
1121	4r. U.N. Security Council meeting (horiz)	70	85
1122	10r. Lion and lamb	1·25	2·00
MS1123	76×92 mm. 15r. U.N. building and peace dove	2·25	2·75

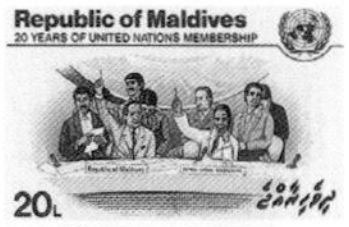

208 Maldivian Delegate voting in U.N. General Assembly

1985. 20th Anniv of United Nations Membership. Multicoloured.

1124	20l. Type **208**	10	10
1125	15r. U.N. and Maldivian flags, and U.N. Building, New York	2·00	3·00

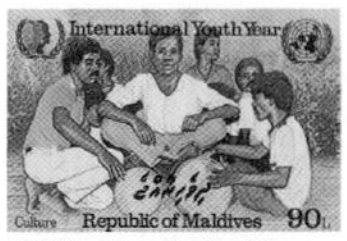

209 Youths playing Drums

1985. International Youth Year. Multicoloured.

1126	90l. Type **209**	15	20
1127	6r. Tug-of-war	80	1·10
1128	10r. Community service (vert)	1·25	2·00
MS1129	85×84 mm. 15r. Raising the flag at youth camp (vert)	2·25	3·00

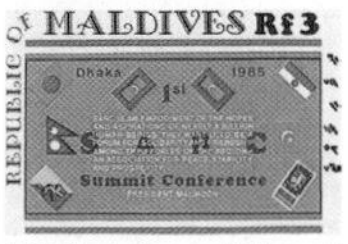

210 Quotation and Flags of Member Nations

1985. First Summit Meeting of South Asian Association for Regional Co-operation, Dhaka, Bangladesh.

1130	**210** 3r. multicoloured	1·50	1·50

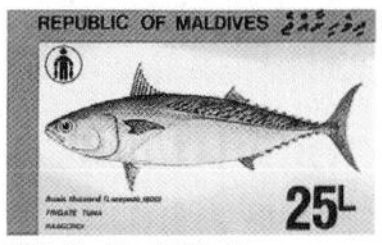

211 Mackerel Frigate

1985. Fishermen's Day. Species of Tuna. Multicoloured.

1131	25l. Type **211**	35	10
1132	75l. Kawakawa ("Little tuna")	65	15
1133	3r. Dog-toothed tuna	2·00	1·00
1134	5r. Yellow-finned tuna	2·50	1·50
MS1135	130×90 mm. 15r. Skipjack tuna	3·50	3·50

1985. 150th Birth Anniv of Mark Twain. Designs as T 160a of Lesotho, showing Walt Disney cartoon characters illustrating various Mark Twain quotations. Multicoloured.

1136	2l. Winnie the Pooh (vert)	10	20
1137	3l. Gepetto and Figaro the cat (vert)	10	20
1138	4l. Goofy and basket of broken eggs (vert)	10	20
1139	20l. Goofy as doctor scolding Donald Duck (vert)	25	10
1140	4r. Mowgli and King Louis (vert)	1·40	1·75
1141	13r. The wicked Queen and mirror (vert)	5·00	7·00
MS1142	126×101 mm. 15r. Mickey Mouse as Tom Sawyer on comet's tail	6·50	7·00

1985. Birth Bicentenaries of Grimm Brothers (folklorists). Designs as T **160b** of Lesotho, showing Walt Disney cartoon characters in scenes from "Dr. Knowall". Multicoloured.

1143	1l. Donald Duck as Crabb driving oxcart (horiz)	10	10
1144	5l. Donald Duck as Dr. Knowall (horiz)	10	10
1145	10l. Dr. Knowall in surgery (horiz)	10	10
1146	15l. Dr. Knowall with Uncle Scrooge as a lord (horiz)	10	10
1147	3r. Dr. and Mrs. Knowall in pony and trap (horiz)	1·10	1·50
1148	15r. Dr. Knowall and thief (horiz)	5·50	7·00
MS1149	126×101 mm. 15r. Donald and Daisy Duck as Dr. and Mrs. Knowall	6·50	7·00

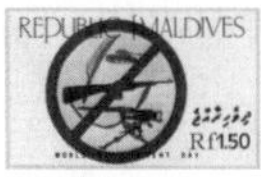

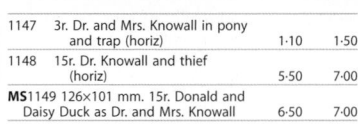

211c Weapons on Road Sign

1986. World Disarmament Day. Multicoloured.

1149a	1r.50 Type **211c**		
1149b	10r. Peace dove		

1986. Appearance of Halley's Comet (1st issue). As T **162a** of Lesotho. Multicoloured.

1150	20l. N.A.S.A. space telescope and Comet	50	25
1151	1r.50 E.S.A. "Giotto" spacecraft and Comet	1·25	1·50
1152	2r. Japanese "Planet A" spacecraft and Comet	1·50	1·75
1153	4r. Edmond Halley and Stonehenge	2·25	3·00
1154	5r. Russian "Vega" spacecraft and Comet	2·25	3·00
MS1155	101×70 mm. 15r. Halley's Comet	8·00	10·00

See also Nos. 1206/11.

1986. Centenary of Statue of Liberty. Multicoloured. As T **163b** of Lesotho, showing the Statue of Liberty and immigrants to the U.S.A.

1156	50l. Walter Gropius (architect)	40	30
1157	70l. John Lennon (musician)	2·00	1·25
1158	1r. George Balanchine (choreographer)	2·00	1·25
1159	10r. Franz Werfel (writer)	4·00	7·00
MS1160	100×72 mm. 15r. Statue of Liberty (vert)	7·50	8·50

1986. "Ameripex" International Stamp Exhibition, Chicago. As T **163c** of Lesotho, showing Walt Disney cartoon characters and U.S.A. stamps. Multicoloured.

1161	3l. Johnny Appleseed and 1966 Johnny Appleseed stamp	10	10
1162	4l. Paul Bunyan and 1958 Forest Conservation stamp	10	10
1163	5l. Casey and 1969 Professional Baseball Centenary stamp	10	10
1164	10l. Ichabod Crane and 1974 "Legend of Sleepy Hollow" stamp	10	10
1165	15l. John Henry and 1944 75th Anniv of completion of First Transcontinental Railroad stamp	15	15
1166	20l. Windwagon Smith and 1954 Kansas Territory Centenary stamp	15	15
1167	13r. Mike Fink and 1970 Great Northwest stamp	7·00	7·00
1168	14r. Casey Jones and 1950 Railroad Engineers stamp	8·00	8·00
MS1169	Two sheets, each 127×101 mm. (a) 15r. Davy Crockett and 1967 Davy Crockett stamp. (b) 15r. Daisy Duck as Pocahontas saving Captain John Smith (Donald Duck) Set of 2 sheets	13·00	16·00

1986. 60th Birthday of Queen Elizabeth II. As T **163** of Lesotho.

1170	1r. black and yellow	30	25
1171	2r. multicoloured	40	55
1172	12r. multicoloured	1·50	2·50
MS1173	120×85 mm. 15r. black and brown	4·00	4·25

DESIGNS: 1r. Royal Family at Girl Guides Rally, 1938; 2r. Queen in Canada; 12r. At Sandringham, 1970; 15r. Princesses Elizabeth and Margaret at Royal Lodge, Windsor, 1940.

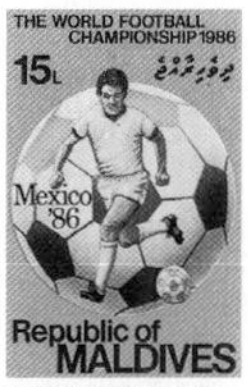

212 Player running with Ball

1986. World Cup Football Championship, Mexico. Multicoloured.

1174	15l. Type **212**	75	30
1175	2r. Player gaining control of ball	2·50	1·75
1176	4r. Two players competing for ball	4·00	3·50
1177	10r. Player bouncing ball on knee	7·50	8·00
MS1178	95×114 mm. 15r. Player kicking ball	5·00	6·00

1986. Royal Wedding. As T **170a** of Lesotho. Multicoloured.

1179	10l. Prince Andrew and Miss Sarah Ferguson	20	10
1180	2r. Prince Andrew	85	70
1181	12r. Prince Andrew in naval uniform	3·75	3·75
MS1182	88×88 mm. 15r. Prince Andrew and Miss Sarah Ferguson (different)	5·00	4·75

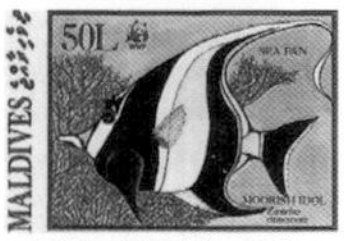

213 Moorish Idol and Sea Fan

1986. Marine Wildlife. Multicoloured.

1183	50l. Type **213**	1·50	40
1184	90l. Regal angelfish	2·00	55
1185	1r. Maldive anemonefish	2·00	55
1186	2r. Tiger cowrie and stinging coral	2·50	1·60
1187	3r. Emperor angelfish and staghorn coral	2·50	2·00
1188	4r. Black-naped tern	3·00	3·00
1189	5r. Fiddler crab and staghorn coral	2·50	3·00
1190	10r. Hawksbill turtle	3·00	5·00
MS1191	Two sheets, each 107×76 mm. (a) 15r. Long-nosed butterflyfish. (b) 15r. Oriental trumpetfish Set of 2 sheets	12·00	15·00

1986. Birth Bicentenary (1985) of John J. Audubon (ornithologist) (2nd issue). As T **201** showing original paintings. Multicoloured.

1192	3l. Little blue heron (horiz)	40	60
1193	4l. White-tailed kite	40	60
1194	5l. Greater shearwater (horiz)	40	60
1195	10l. Magnificent frigate bird	45	40
1196	15l. Black-necked grebe ("Eared Grebe")	85	40
1197	20l. Goosander ("Common Merganser")	90	40
1198	13r. Peregrine falcon ("Great Footed Hawk") (horiz)	7·50	7·50
1199	14r. Prairie chicken ("Greater Prairie Chicken") (horiz)	7·50	7·50
MS1200	Two sheets, each 74×104 mm. (a) 15r. Fulmar ("Northern Fulmar"). (b) 15r. White-fronted goose (horiz) Set of 2 sheets	23·00	21·00

1986. World Cup Football Championship Winners, Mexico. Nos. 1174/7 optd **WINNERS Argentina 3 W. Germany 2**.

1201	15l. Type **212**	40	30
1202	2r. Player gaining control of ball	1·25	1·10
1203	4r. Two players competing for ball	2·00	2·00
1204	10r. Player bouncing ball on knee	3·25	4·25
MS1205	95×114 mm. 15r. Player kicking ball	3·00	4·25

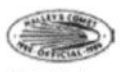

(213b)

1986. Appearance of Halley's Comet (2nd issue). Nos. 1150/4 optd with T **213b**.

1206	20l. N.A.S.A. space telescope and Comet	65	40
1207	1r.50 E.S.A. "Giotto" spacecraft and Comet	1·25	1·25
1208	2r. Japanese "Planet A" spacecraft and Comet	1·50	1·50
1209	4r. Edmond Halley and Stonehenge	2·00	2·50
1210	5r. Russia "Vega" spacecraft and Comet	2·00	2·50
MS1211	101×70 mm. 15r. Halley's Comet	6·00	7·00

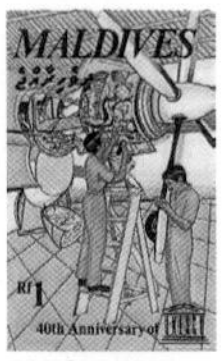

214 Servicing Aircraft

1986. 40th Anniv of UNESCO. Multicoloured.

1212	1r. Type **214**	80	30
1213	2r. Boat building	90	1·00
1214	3r. Children in classroom	1·00	1·40
1215	5r. Student in laboratory	1·10	2·50
MS1216	77×100 mm. 15r. Diving bell on sea bed	2·75	4·25

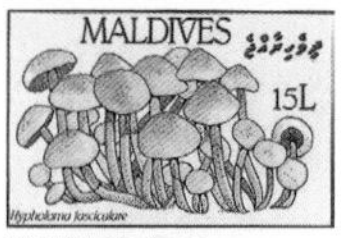

215 "Hypholoma fasciculare"

1986. Fungi of the Maldives. Multicoloured.

1217	15l. Type **215**	80	25
1218	50l. "Kuehneromyces mutabilis" (vert)	1·50	45
1219	1r. "Amanita muscaria" (vert)	1·75	60
1220	2r. "Agaricus campestris"	2·00	1·50
1221	3r. "Amanita pantherina" (vert)	2·00	1·75
1222	4r. "Coprinus comatus" (vert)	2·00	2·25
1223	5r. "Gymnopilus junonius" ("Pholiota spectabilis")	2·00	2·75
1224	10r. "Pluteus cervinus"	2·50	4·50
MS1225	Two sheets, each 100×70 mm. (a) 15r. "Armillaria mellea". (b) 15r. "Stropharia aeruginosa" (vert) Set of 2 sheets	13·00	14·00

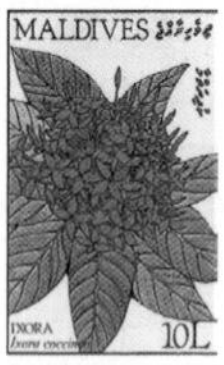

216 Ixora

1987. Flowers. Multicoloured.

1226	10l. Type **216**	10	10
1227	20l. Frangipani	10	10
1228	50l. Crinum	2·00	60
1229	2r. Pink rose	40	80
1230	4r. Flamboyant flower	60	1·50
1231	10r. Ground orchid	6·00	8·00
MS1232	Two sheets, each 100×70 mm. (a) 15r. Gardenia. (b) 15r. Oleander Set of 2 sheets	4·75	6·50

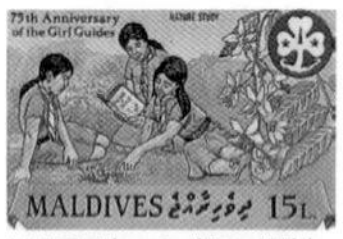

217 Guides studying Wild Flowers

1987. 75th Anniv (1985) of Girl Guide Movement. Multicoloured.

1233	15l. Type **217**	30	20
1234	2r. Guides with pet rabbits	50	80
1235	4r. Guide observing white spoonbill	2·50	2·25
1236	12r. Lady Baden-Powell and Guide flag	2·50	6·50
MS1237	104×78 mm. 15r. Guides in sailing dinghy	2·25	3·75

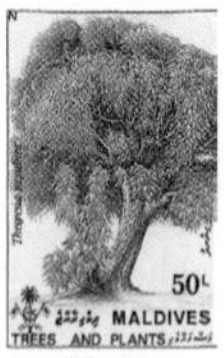

218 "Thespesia populnea"

1987. Trees and Plants. Multicoloured.

1238	50l. Type **218**	15	10
1239	1r. "Cocos nucifera"	25	20
1240	2r. "Calophyllum mophyllum"	40	40
1241	3r. "Xanthosoma indica" (horiz)	60	65
1242	5r. "Ipomoea batatas" (horiz)	1·00	1·40
1243	7r. "Artocarpus altilis"	1·25	2·25
MS1244	75×109 mm. 15r. "Cocos nucifera" (different)	2·25	3·25

No. 1241 is inscr "Xyanthosomaindica" in error.

1987. America's Cup Yachting Championship. As T **218a** of Lesotho. Multicoloured.

1245	15l. "Intrepid", 1970	10	10
1246	1r. "France II", 1974	20	20
1247	2r. "Gretel", 1962	40	60
1248	12r. "Volunteer", 1887	2·00	3·00
MS1249	113×83 mm. 15r. Helmsman and crew on deck of "Defender", 1895 (horiz)	2·25	3·25

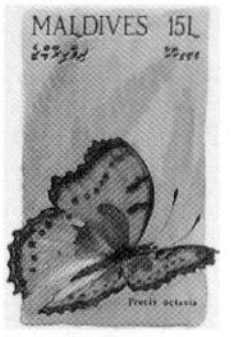

219 "Precis octavia"

1987. Butterflies. Multicoloured.

1250	15l. Type **219**	45	30
1251	20l. "Atrophaneura hector"	45	30
1252	50l. "Teinopalpus imperialis"	75	40
1253	1r. "Kallima horsfieldi"	1·00	45
1254	2r. "Cethosia biblis"	1·60	1·25
1255	4r. "Idea jasonia"	2·50	2·25
1256	7r. "Papilio memnon"	3·50	4·00
1257	10r. "Aeropetes tulbaghia"	4·00	5·00
MS1258	Two sheets, each 135×102 mm. (a) 15r. "Acraea violae". (b) 15r. "Hebomoia leucippe" Set of 2 sheets	9·00	11·00

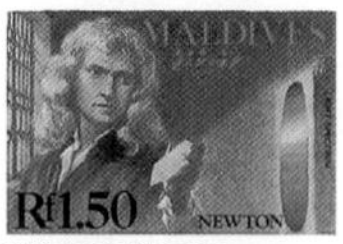

220 Isaac Newton experimenting with Spectrum

1988. Great Scientific Discoveries. Multicoloured.

1259	1r.50 Type **220**	1·25	1·00
1260	3r. Euclid composing "Principles of Geometry" (vert)	1·60	1·75
1261	4r. Mendel formulating theory of Genetic Evolution (vert)	1·75	2·00
1262	5r. Galileo and moons of Jupiter	3·00	3·00
MS1263	102×72 mm. 15r. "Apollo" lunar module (vert)	4·50	5·50

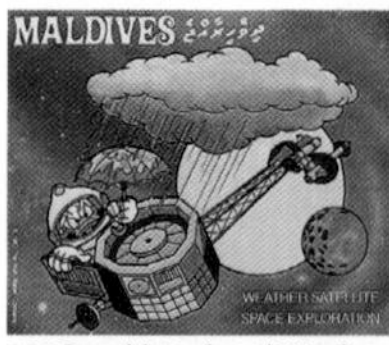

221 Donald Duck and Weather Satellite

1988. Space Exploration. Walt Disney cartoon characters. Multicoloured.

1264	3l. Type **221**	10	10
1265	4l. Minnie Mouse and navigation satellite	10	10
1266	5l. Mickey Mouse's nephews talking via communication satellite	10	10
1267	10l. Goofy in lunar rover (vert)	10	10
1268	20l. Minnie Mouse delivering pizza to flying saucer (vert)	10	10
1269	13r. Mickey Mouse directing spacecraft docking (vert)	5·00	5·00
1270	14r. Mickey Mouse and "Voyager 2"	5·00	5·00
MS1271	Two sheets, each 127×102 mm. (a) 15r. Mickey Mouse at first Moon landing, 1969. (b) 15r. Mickey Mouse and nephews in space station swimming pool (vert) Set of 2 sheets	13·00	13·00

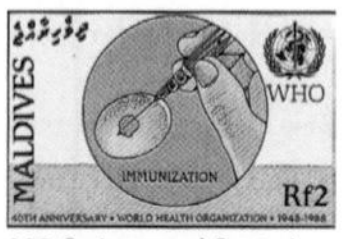

222 Syringe and Bacterium ("Immunization")

1988. 40th Anniv of W.H.O. Multicoloured.

1272	2r. Type **222**	40	40
1273	4r. Tap ("Clean Water")	60	85

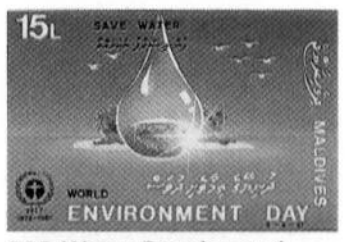

223 Water Droplet and Atoll

1988. World Environment Day (1987). Multicoloured.

1274	15l. Type **223**	10	10
1275	75l. Coral reef	20	40
1276	2r. Audubon's shearwaters in flight	85	1·40
MS1277	105×76 mm. 15r. Banyan tree (vert)	4·00	5·50

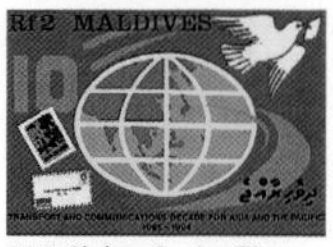

224 Globe, Carrier Pigeon and Letter

1988. Transport and Telecommunications Decade. Each showing central globe. Multicoloured.

1278	2r. Type **224**	75	65
1279	3r. Dish aerial and girl using telephone	1·25	1·10
1280	5r. Satellite, television, telephone and antenna tower	2·00	2·00
1281	10r. Car, ship and Lockheed TriStar airliner	11·00	6·50

1988. Royal Ruby Wedding. Nos. 1170/3 optd **40TH WEDDING ANNIVERSARY H.M. QUEEN ELIZABETH II H.R.H. THE DUKE OF EDINBURGH**.

1282	1r. black and yellow	50	25
1283	2r. multicoloured	75	60
1284	12r. multicoloured	3·00	3·50
MS1285	120×85 mm. 15r. black and brown	4·50	4·50

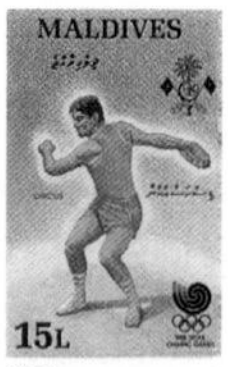

226 Discus-throwing

1988. Olympic Games, Seoul. Multicoloured.

1286	15l. Type **226**	10	10
1287	2r. 100 m race	40	40
1288	4r. Gymnastics (horiz)	70	80
1289	12r. Three-day equestrian event (horiz)	2·25	3·25
MS1290	106×76 mm. 20r. Tennis (horiz)	4·00	4·75

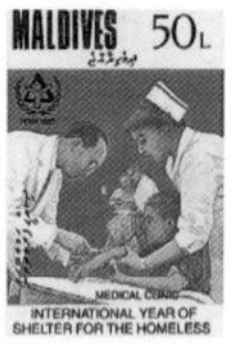

227 Immunization at Clinic

1988. Int Year of Shelter for the Homeless. Multicoloured.

1291	50l. Type **227**	30	30
1292	3r. Prefab housing estate	1·10	1·40
MS1293	63×105 mm. 15r. Building site	1·75	2·50

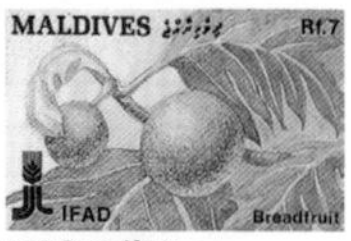

228 Breadfruit

1988. Tenth Anniv of International Fund for Agricultural Development. Multicoloured.

1294	7r. Type **228**	1·00	1·40
1295	10r. Mangoes (vert)	1·50	1·90
MS1296	103×74 mm. 15r. Coconut palm, fishing boat and yellowtail tuna	2·50	3·00

1988. World Aids Day. Nos. 1272/3 optd **WORLD AIDS DAY** and emblem.

1297	2r. Type **222**	35	45
1298	4r. "Tap" ("Clean Water")	65	80

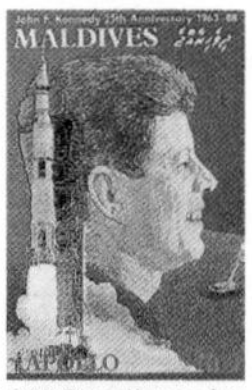

230 Pres. Kennedy and Launch of "Apollo" Spacecraft

1989. 25th Death Anniv (1988) of John F. Kennedy (American statesman). U.S. Space Achievements. Multicoloured.

1299	5r. Type **230**	2·50	2·75
1300	5r. Lunar module and astronaut on Moon	2·50	2·75
1301	5r. Astronaut and buggy on Moon	2·50	2·75
1302	5r. President Kennedy and spacecraft	2·50	2·75

MS1303 108×77 mm. 15r. President Kennedy making speech 4·00 5·00

1989. Olympic Medal Winners, Seoul. Nos. 1286/90 optd.

1304 15l. Type **226** (optd **J. SCHULT DDR**) 20 20
1305 2r. 100 m race (optd **C. LEWIS USA**) 65 65
1306 4r. Gymnastics (horiz) (optd **MEN'S ALL AROUND V. ARTEMOV USSR**) 1·40 1·40
1307 12r. Three-day equestrian event (horiz) (optd **TEAM SHOW JUMPING W. GERMANY**) 5·00 5·50
MS1308 106×76 mm. 20r. Tennis (horiz) (optd **OLYMPIC WINNERS MEN'S SINGLES GOLD M. MECIR CZECH SILVER T. MAYOTTE USA BRONZE B. GILBERT USA**) 6·50 7·50

On No. **MS**1308 the overprint appears on the sheet margin.

1989. 500th Birth Anniv of Titian (artist). As T **186a** of Lesotho, showing paintings. Multicoloured.

1309 15l. "Benedetto Varchi" 10 10
1310 1r. "Portrait of a Young Man" 20 15
1311 2r. "King Francis I of France" 40 40
1312 5r. "Pietro Aretino" 1·10 1·25
1313 15r. "The Bravo" 3·50 5·50
1314 20r. "The Concert" (detail) 3·50 6·00
MS1315 Two sheets. (a) 112×96 mm. 20r. "An Allegory of Prudence" (detail). (b) 96×110 mm. 20r. "Francesco Maria della Rovere" Set of 2 sheets 8·50 9·50

1989. Tenth Anniversary of Asia–Pacific Telecommunity. Nos. 1279/80 optd **ASIA-PACIFIC TELECOMMUNITY 10 YEARS** and emblem. Multicoloured.

1316 3r. Dish aerial and girl using telephone 1·25 1·50
1317 5r. Satellite, television, telephone and antenna tower 1·75 2·00

1989. Japanese Art. Paintings by Hokusai. As T **187a** of Lesotho. Multicoloured.

1318 15l. "Fuji from Hodogaya" (horiz) 10 10
1319 50l. "Fuji from Lake Kawaguchi" (horiz) 15 15
1320 1r. "Fuji from Owari" (horiz) 25 15
1321 2r. "Fuji from Tsukudajima in Edo" (horiz) 50 40
1322 4r. "Fuji from a Teahouse at Yoshida" (horiz) 80 90
1323 6r. "Fuji from Tagonoura" (horiz) 90 1·25
1324 10r. "Fuji from Mishima-goe" (horiz) 2·25 2·75
1325 12r. "Fuji from the Sumida River in Edo" (horiz) 2·25 2·75
MS1326 Two sheets, each 101×77 mm. (a) 18r. "Fuji from Inume Pass". (b) 18r. "Fuji from Fukagawa in Edo" Set of 2 sheets 8·50 9·00

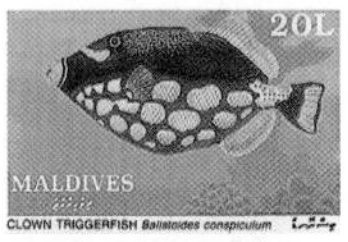

233 Clown Triggerfish

1989. Tropical Fishes. Multicoloured.

1327 20l. Type **233** 25 20
1328 50l. Blue-striped snapper 35 25
1329 1r. Powder-blue surgeonfish 45 30
1330 2r. Oriental sweetlips 75 65
1331 3r. Six-barred wrasse 1·00 85
1332 8r. Thread-finned butterflyfish 2·00 2·50
1333 10r. Bicoloured parrotfish 2·40 2·75
1334 12r. Scarlet-finned squirrelfish 2·40 2·75
MS1335 Two sheets, each 101×73 mm. (a) 15r. Butterfly perch. (b) 15r. Semicircle angelfish Set of 2 sheets 13·00 12·00

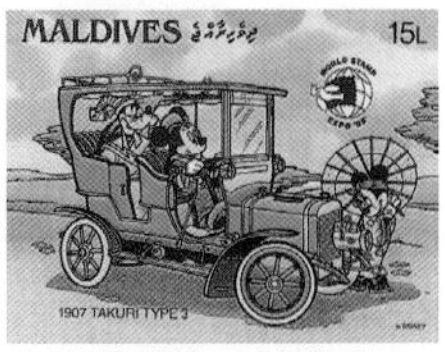

234 Goofy, Mickey and Minnie Mouse with Takuri "Type 3", 1907

1989. "World Stamp Expo '89" International Stamp Exhibition, Washington (1st issue). Designs showing Walt Disney cartoon characters with Japanese cars. Multicoloured.

1336 15l. Type **234** 20 15
1337 50l. Donald and Daisy Duck in Mitsubishi "Model A", 1917 40 30
1338 1r. Goofy in Datsun "Roadstar", 1935 70 50
1339 2r. Donald and Daisy Duck with Mazda, 1940 1·00 75
1340 4r. Donald Duck with Nissan "Bluebird 310", 1959 1·50 1·25
1341 6r. Donald and Daisy Duck with Subaru "360", 1958 1·75 1·75
1342 10r. Mickey Mouse and Pluto in Honda "5800", 1966 3·25 3·75
1343 12r. Mickey Mouse and Goofy in Daihatsu "Fellow", 1966 3·75 4·25
MS1344 Two sheets, each 127×102 mm. (a) 20r. Daisy Duck with Chip n'Dale and Isuzu "Trooper II", 1981. (b) 20r. Mickey Mouse with tortoise and Toyota "Supra", 1985 Set of 2 sheets 11·00 13·00

1989. "World Stamp Expo '89" International Stamp Exhibition, Washington (2nd issue). Landmarks of Washington. Sheet 62×78 mm, containing multicoloured designs as T **193a** of Lesotho, but vert.

MS1345 8r. Marine Corps Memorial, Arlington National Cemetery 2·50 3·00

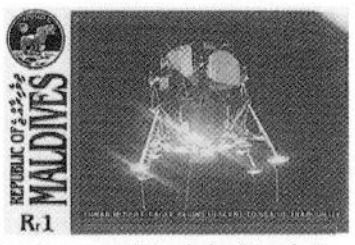

235 Lunar Module "Eagle"

1989. 20th Anniv of First Manned Landing on Moon. Multicoloured.

1346 1r. Type **235** 30 20
1347 2r. Astronaut Aldrin collecting dust samples 50 60
1348 6r. Aldrin setting up seismometer 1·25 1·75
1349 10r. Pres. Nixon congratulating "Apollo 11" astronauts 1·90 2·50
MS1350 107×75 mm. 18r. Television picture of Armstrong about to step onto Moon (34×47 mm) 7·50 8·00

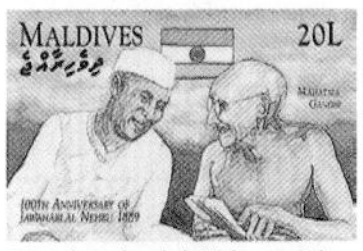

236 Jawaharlal Nehru with Mahatma Gandhi

1989. Anniversaries and Events. Multicoloured.

1351 20l. Type **236** (birth cent) 3·50 1·00
1352 50l. Opium poppies and logo (anti-drugs campaign) (vert) 1·50 45
1353 1r. William Shakespeare (425th birth anniv) 1·25 45
1354 2r. Storming the Bastille (bicent of French Revolution) (vert) 1·25 1·25
1355 3r. Concorde (20th anniv of first flight) 5·00 4·25
1356 8r. George Washington (bicent of inauguration) 2·00 3·00
1357 10r. William Bligh (bicent of mutiny on the "Bounty") 8·00 5·00
1358 12r. Hamburg harbour (800th anniv) (vert) 4·00 4·50
MS1359 Two sheets. (a) 115×85 mm. 18r. Baseball players (50th anniv of first televised game) (vert). (b) 110×80 mm. 18r. Franz von Taxis (500th anniv of regular European postal services) (vert) Set of 2 sheets 14·00 16·00

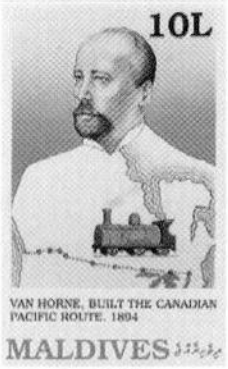

237 Sir William van Horne (Chairman of Canadian Pacific), Locomotive and Map, 1894

1989. Railway Pioneers. Multicoloured.

1360 10l. Type **237** 25 15
1361 25l. Matthew Murray (engineer) with Blenkinsop and Murray's rack locomotive, 1810 35 20
1362 50l. Louis Favre (railway engineer) and steam locomotive entering tunnel 40 25
1363 2r. George Stephenson (engineer) and "Locomotion", 1825 75 55
1364 6r. Richard Trevithick and "Catch-Me-Who-Can", 1808 1·50 1·50
1365 8r. George Nagelmackers and "Orient Express" dining car 1·75 1·75
1366 10r. William Jessop and horse-drawn wagon, Surrey Iron Railway, 1770 2·50 2·50
1367 12r. Isambard Brunel (engineer) and GWR steam locomotive, 1833 3·00 3·00
MS1368 Two sheets, each 71×103 mm. (a) 18r. George Pullman (inventor of sleeping cars), 1864. (b) 18r. Rudolf Diesel (engineer) and first oil engine Set of 2 sheets 11·00 12·00

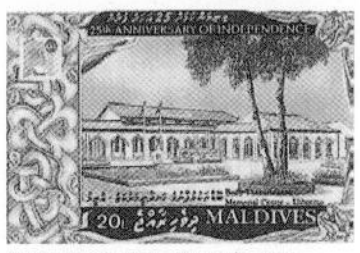

238 Bodu Thakurufaanu Memorial Centre, Utheemu

1990. 25th Anniv of Independence. Multicoloured.

1369 20l. Type **238** 10 10
1370 25l. Islamic Centre, Male 10 10
1371 50l. National flag and logos of international organizations 10 10
1372 2r. Presidential Palace, Male 30 40
1373 5r. National Security Service 85 1·25
MS1374 128×90 mm. 10r. National emblem 4·75 5·00

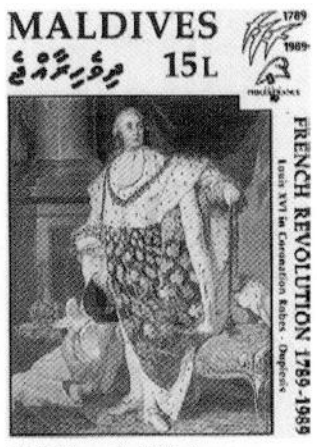

239 "Louis XVI in Coronation Robes" (Duplessis)

1990. Bicentenary of French Revolution and "Philexfrance '89" International Stamp Exhibi-tion, Paris. French Paintings. Multicoloured.

1375 15l. Type **239** 20 15
1376 50l. "Monsieur Lavoisier and his Wife" (David) 45 25
1377 1r. "Madame Pastoret" (David) 65 35
1378 2r. "Oath of Lafayette, 14 July 1790" (anon) 1·00 70
1379 4r. "Madame Trudaine" (David) 1·75 1·50
1380 6r. "Chenard celebrating the Liberation of Savoy" (Boilly) 2·50 2·50
1381 10r. "An Officer swears Allegiance to the Constitution" (anon) 4·00 4·50
1382 12r. "Self Portrait" (David) 4·00 4·75
MS1383 Two sheets. (a) 104×79 mm. 20r. "The Oath of the Tennis Court, 20 June 1789" (David) (horiz). (b) 79×104 mm. 20r. "Rousseau and Symbols of the Revolution" (Jeaurat) Set of 2 sheets 13·00 14·00

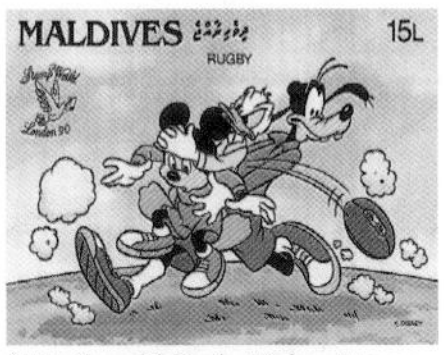

239a Donald Duck, Mickey Mouse and Goofy Playing Rugby

1990. "Stamp World London '90" International Stamp Exhibition. Walt Disney cartoon characters playing British sports. Multicoloured.

1384 15l. Type **239a** 30 15
1385 50l. Donald Duck and Chip-n-Dale curling 45 25
1386 1r. Goofy playing polo 65 40
1387 2r. Mickey Mouse and nephews playing soccer 90 70
1388 4r. Mickey Mouse playing cricket 1·75 1·50
1389 6r. Minnie and Mickey Mouse at Ascot races 2·25 1·90
1390 10r. Mickey Mouse and Goofy playing tennis 3·50 3·50
1391 12r. Donald Duck and Mickey Mouse playing bowls 3·50 3·50
MS1392 Two sheets, each 126×101 mm. (a) 20r. Minnie Mouse fox-hunting. (b) 20r. Mickey Mouse playing golf Set of 2 sheets 15·00 15·00

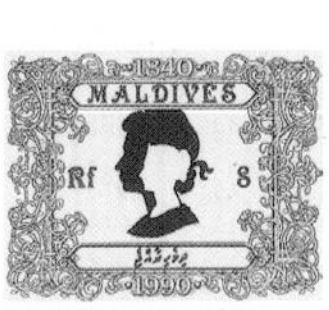

240 Silhouettes of Queen Elizabeth II and Queen Victoria

1990. 150th Anniv of the Penny Black.

1393 **240** 8r. black and green 3·00 3·00
1394 - 12r. black and blue 3·50 3·50
MS1395 109×84 mm. 18r. black and brown 6·00 7·00

DESIGN: 12r. As Type **240**, but with position of silhouettes reversed; 18r. Penny Black.

1990. 90th Birthday of Queen Elizabeth the Queen Mother. As T 198a of Lesotho.

1396 6r. black, mauve and blue 1·10 1·40
1397 6r. black, mauve and blue 1·10 1·40
1398 6r. black, mauve and blue 1·10 1·40
MS1399 90×75 mm. 18r. multicoloured 3·25 3·50

DESIGNS: No. 1396, Lady Elizabeth Bowes-Lyon; 1397, Lady Elizabeth Bowes-Lyon wearing headband; 1398, Lady Elizabeth Bowes-Lyon leaving for her wedding; **MS**1399, Lady Elizabeth Bowes-Lyon wearing wedding dress.

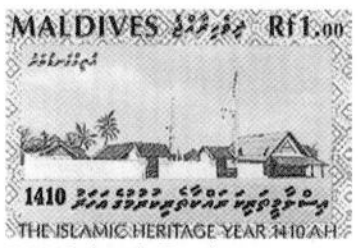

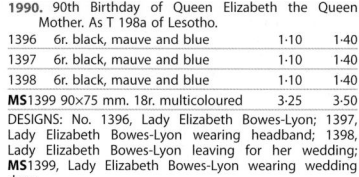

241 Sultan's Tomb

1990. Islamic Heritage Year. Each black and blue.

1400 1r. Type **241** 35 45
1401 1r. Thakurufaan's Palace 35 45
1402 1r. Male Mosque 35 45
1403 2r. Veranda of Friday Mosque 45 55
1404 2r. Interior of Friday Mosque 45 55
1405 2r. Friday Mosque and Monument 45 55

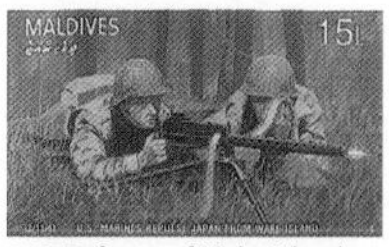

242 Defence of Wake Island, 1941

1990. 50th Anniv of Second World War. Multicoloured.

1406 15l. Type **242** 25 20
1407 25l. Stilwell's army in Burma, 1944 30 20
1408 50l. Normandy offensive, 1944 40 25
1409 1r. Capture of Saipan, 1944 55 40
1410 2r.50 D-Day landings, 1944 90 80
1411 3r.50 Allied landings in Norway, 1940 1·10 1·10
1412 4r. Lord Mountbatten, Head of Combined Operations, 1943 1·40 1·40
1413 6r. Japanese surrender, Tokyo Bay, 1945 2·75 3·25
1414 10r. Potsdam Conference, 1945 2·75 3·00
1415 12r. Allied invasion of Sicily, 1943 3·00 3·25
MS1416 115×87 mm. 18r. Atlantic convoy 5·50 6·50

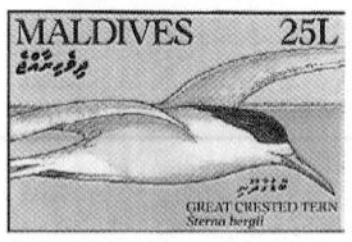

243 Crested Tern ("Great Crested Tern")

1990. Birds. Multicoloured.

1417 25l. Type **243** 15 15
1418 50l. Koel 25 25
1419 1r. White tern 35 35
1420 3r.50 Cinnamon bittern 90 1·00
1421 6r. Sooty tern 1·40 1·60
1422 8r. Audubon's shearwater 1·60 2·00
1423 12r. Common noddy ("Brown Noddy") 2·50 3·00
1424 15r. Lesser frigate bird 2·75 3·25
MS1425 Two sheets, each 100×69 mm. (a) 18r. Grey heron. (b) 18r. White-tailed tropic bird Set of 2 sheets 8·00 10·00

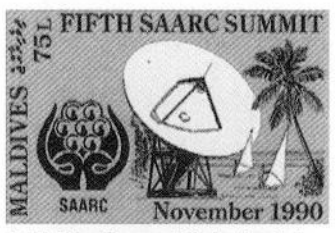

244 Emblem, Dish Aerial and Sailboards

1990. 5th South Asian Association for Regional Co-operation Summit.

1426 **244** 75l. black and orange 30 25
1427 - 3r.50 multicoloured 2·00 1·50
MS1428 112×82 mm. 20r. multicoloured 5·50 6·50

DESIGN: 3r.50, Flags of member nations; 20r. Global warming diagram.

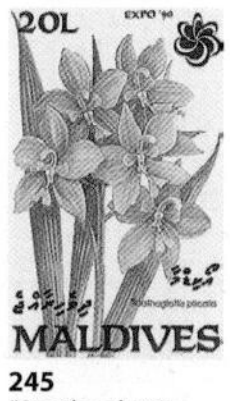

245 "Spathoglottis plicata"

1990. "EXPO '90" International Garden and Greenery Exhibition, Osaka. Flowers. Mult.

1429	20l. Type **245**	1·25	40
1430	75l. "Hippeastrum puniceum"	1·50	50
1431	2r. "Tecoma stans" (horiz)	1·60	90
1432	3r.50 "Catharanthus roseus" (horiz)	1·60	1·60
1433	10r. "Ixora coccinea" (horiz)	3·00	3·25
1434	12r. "Clitorea ternatea" (horiz)	3·25	3·50
1435	15r. "Caesalpinia pulcherrima"	3·25	3·75
MS1436	Four sheets, each 111×79 mm. (a) 20r. "Plumeria obtusa" (horiz). (b) 20r. "Jasminum grandiflorum" (horiz). (c) 20r. "Rosa" sp (horiz). (d) 20r. "Hibiscus tiliaceous" (horiz) Set of 4 sheets	13·00	13·00

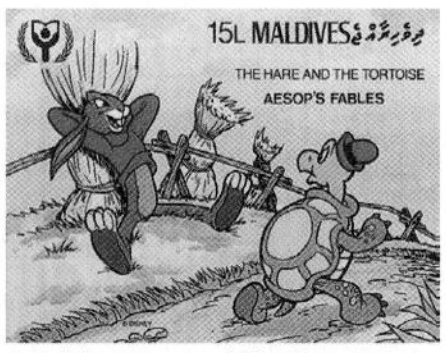

246 "The Hare and the Tortoise"

1990. International Literacy Year. Walt Disney cartoon characters illustrating fables by Aesop. Multicoloured.

1437	15l. Type **246**	35	15
1438	50l. "The Town Mouse and the Country Mouse"	60	25
1439	1r. "The Fox and the Crow"	90	35
1440	3r.50 "The Travellers and the Bear"	1·75	1·60
1441	4r. "The Fox and the Lion"	1·90	1·75
1442	6r. "The Mice Meeting"	2·50	2·50
1443	10r. "The Fox and the Goat"	3·00	3·25
1444	12r. "The Dog in the Manger"	3·00	3·50
MS1445	Two sheets, each 127×102 mm. (a) 20r. "The Miller, his Son and the Ass" (vert). (b) 20r. "The Miser's Gold" (vert) Set of 2 sheets	13·00	13·00

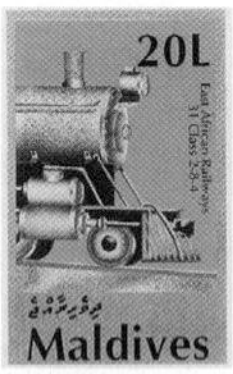

247 East African Railways Class 31 Steam Locomotive

1990. Railway Steam Locomotives. Multicoloured.

1446	20l. Type **247**	85	30
1447	50l. Steam locomotive, Sudan	1·10	45
1448	1r. Class GM Garratt, South Africa	1·60	60
1449	3r. 7th Class, Rhodesia	2·50	2·00
1450	5r. Central Pacific Class No. 229, U.S.A.	3·00	2·25
1451	8r. Reading Railroad No. 415, U.S.A.	3·50	3·00
1452	10r. Porter narrow gauge, Canada	3·50	3·00
1453	12r. Great Northern Railway No. 515, U.S.A.	3·50	3·50
MS1454	Two sheets, each 90×65 mm. (a) 20r. 19th-century standard American locomotive No. 315. (b) 20r. East African Railways Garratt locomotive No. 5950 Set of 2 sheets	17·00	16·00

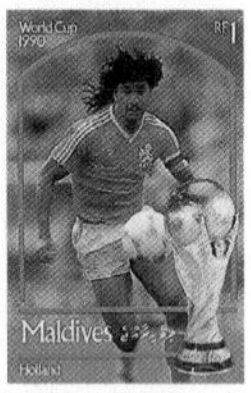

248 Ruud Gullit of Holland

1990. World Cup Football Championship, Italy. Multicoloured.

1455	1r. Type **248**	1·50	50
1456	2r.50 Paul Gascoigne of England	2·25	1·25
1457	3r.50 Brazilian challenging Argentine player	2·25	1·60
1458	5r. Brazilian taking control of ball	2·50	2·00
1459	7r. Italian and Austrian jumping for header	3·25	3·25
1460	10r. Russian being chased by Turkish player	3·50	3·50
1461	15r. Andres Brehme of West Germany	4·00	4·50
MS1462	Four sheets, each 77×92 mm. (a) 18r. Head of an Austrian player (horiz). (b) 18r. Head of a South Korean player (horiz). (c) 20r. Diego Maradona of Argentina (horiz). (d) 20r. Schilacci of Italy (horiz) Set of 4 sheets	17·00	17·00

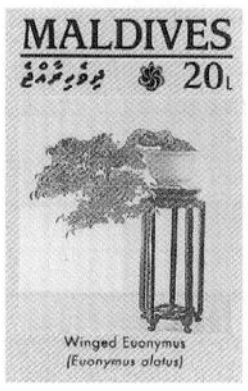

249 Winged Euonymus

1991. Bonsai Trees and Shrubs. Multicoloured.

1463	20l. Type **249**	50	20
1464	50l. Japanese black pine	65	35
1465	1r. Japanese five needle pine	90	55
1466	3r.50 Flowering quince	2·00	1·75
1467	5r. Chinese elm	2·50	2·50
1468	8r. Japanese persimmon	2·75	3·00
1469	10r. Japanese wisteria	2·75	3·00
1470	12r. Satsuki azalea	2·75	3·25
MS1471	Two sheets, each 89×88 mm. (a) 20r. Trident maple. (b) 20r. Sargent juniper Set of 2 sheets	12·00	14·00

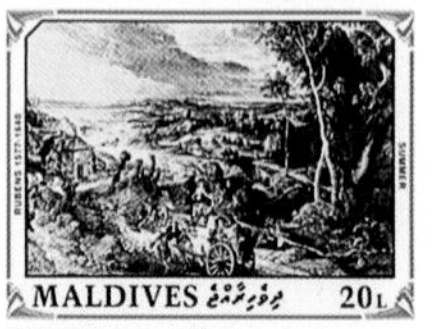

250 "Summer" (Rubens)

1991. 350th Death Anniv of Rubens. Multicoloured.

1472	20l. Type **250**	25	15
1473	50l. "Landscape with Rainbow" (detail)	40	25
1474	1r. "Wreck of Aeneas"	65	40
1475	2r.50 "Chateau de Steen" (detail)	1·25	1·00
1476	3r.50 "Landscape with Herd of Cows"	1·50	1·25
1477	7r. "Ruins on the Palantine"	2·50	2·75
1478	10r. "Landscape with Peasants and Cows"	2·75	3·00
1479	12r. "Wagon fording Stream"	3·00	3·50
MS1480	Four sheets, each 100×71 mm. (a) 20r. "Landscape at Sunset". (b) 20r. "Peasants with Cattle by a Stream". (c) 20r. "Shepherd with Flock". (d) 20r. "Wagon in Stream" Set of 4 sheets	15·00	16·00

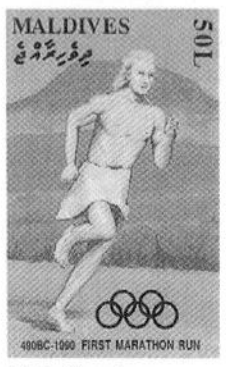

251 Greek Messenger from Marathon, 490 B.C. (2480th Anniv)

1991. Anniversaries and Events (1990). Multicoloured.

1481	50l. Type **251**	45	25
1482	1r. Anthony Fokker in Haarlem Spin monoplane (birth centenary)	1·00	45
1483	3r.50 "Early Bird" satellite (25th anniv)	1·50	1·50
1484	7r. Signing Reunification of Germany agreement (horiz)	1·75	2·50
1485	8r. King John signing Magna Carta (775th anniv)	2·75	2·50
1486	10r. Dwight D. Eisenhower (birth centenary)	2·25	2·75
1487	12r. Sir Winston Churchill (25th death anniv)	5·00	4·50
1488	15r. Pres. Reagan at Berlin Wall (German reunification) (horiz)	3·00	4·50
MS1489	Two sheets. (a) 180×81 mm. 20r. German Junkers Ju88 bomber (50th anniv of Battle of Britain) (horiz). (b) 160×73 mm. 20r. Brandenburg Gate (German reunification) (horiz) Set of 2 sheets	14·00	14·00

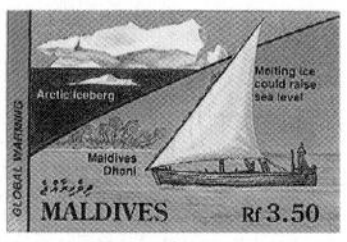

252 Arctic Iceberg and Maldives Dhoni

1991. Global Warming. Multicoloured.

1490	3r.50 Type **252**	2·00	1·25
1491	7r. Antarctic iceberg and "Maldive Trader" (freighter)	4·50	4·25

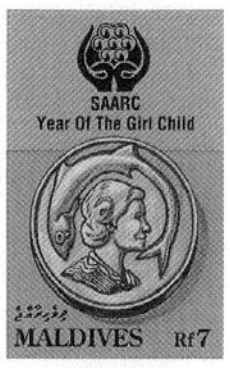

253 S.A.A.R.C. Emblem and Medal

1991. Year of the Girl Child.

1492	**253**	7r. multicoloured	1·75	2·00

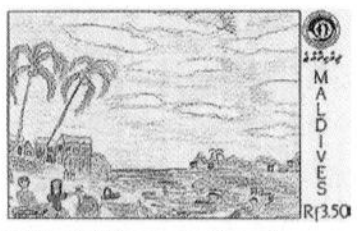

254 Children on Beach

1991. Year of the Maldivian Child. Children's Paintings. Multicoloured.

1493	3r.50 Type **254**	2·25	1·40
1494	5r. Children in a park	2·75	2·25
1495	10r. Hungry child dreaming of food	3·75	4·00
1496	25r. Scuba diver	7·00	11·00

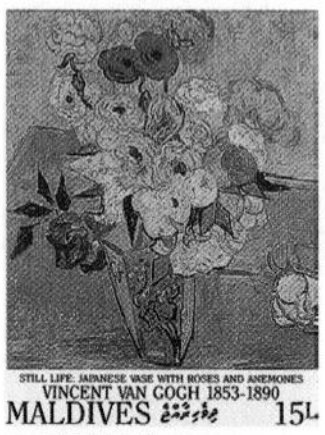

255 "Still Life: Japanese Vase with Roses and Anemones"

1991. Death Centenary (1990) of Vincent van Gogh (artist). Multicoloured.

1497	15l. Type **255**	60	25
1498	20l. "Still Life: Red Poppies and Daisies"	60	25
1499	2r. "Vincent's Bedroom in Arles" (horiz)	2·00	90
1500	3r.50 "The Mulberry Tree"	2·25	1·25
1501	7r. "Blossoming Chestnut Branches" (horiz)	3·25	3·25
1502	10r. "Peasant Couple going to Work" (horiz)	3·75	3·75
1503	12r. "Still Life: Pink Roses" (horiz)	4·00	4·25
1504	15r. "Child with Orange"	4·25	4·75
MS1505	Two sheets. (a) 77×101 mm. 25r. "Houses in Auvers" (70×94 mm). (b) 101×77 mm. 25r. "The Courtyard of the Hospital at Arles" (94×70 mm). Imperf Set of 2 sheets	13·00	14·00

1991. 65th Birthday of Queen Elizabeth II. As T **201** of Lesotho. Multicoloured.

1506	2r. Queen at Trooping the Colour, 1990	1·60	60
1507	5r. Queen with Queen Mother and Princess Margaret, 1973	2·75	1·75
1508	8r. Queen and Prince Philip in open carriage, 1986	3·25	3·00
1509	12r. Queen at Royal Estates Ball	3·50	3·75
MS1510	68×90 mm. 25r. Separate photographs of Queen and Prince Philip	5·75	6·50

1991. Tenth Wedding Anniv of Prince and Princess of Wales. As T **210** of Lesotho. Multicoloured.

1511	1r. Prince and Princess skiing, 1986	1·00	20
1512	3r.50 Separate photographs of Prince, Princess and sons	2·00	1·10
1513	7r. Prince Henry in Christmas play and Prince William watching polo	2·50	2·00
1514	15r. Princess Diana at Ipswich, 1990, and Prince Charles playing polo	3·75	3·75
MS1515	68×90 mm. 25r. Prince and Princess of Wales in Hungary, and Princes William and Harry going to school	6·25	6·50

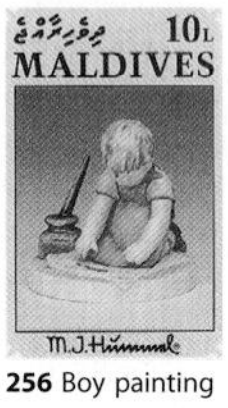

256 Boy painting

1991. Hummel Figurines. Multicoloured.

1516	10l. Type **256**	15	15
1517	25l. Boy reading at table	20	20
1518	50l. Boy with school satchel	30	30
1519	2r. Girl with basket	70	70
1520	3r.50 Boy reading	1·00	1·00
1521	8r. Girl and young child reading	2·25	2·50
1522	10r. School girls	2·25	2·50
1523	25r. School boys	4·75	6·50
MS1524	Two sheets, each 97×127 mm. (a) 5r. As No. 1519; 5r. As No. 1520; 5r. As No, 1521; 5r. As No. 1522. (b) 8r. As Type **256**; 8r. As No. 1517; 8r. As No. 1518; 8r. As No. 1523 Set of 2 sheets	9·00	11·00

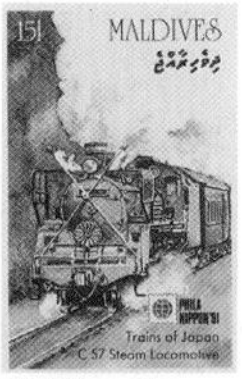

257 Class C57 Steam Locomotive

1991. "Phila Nippon '91" International Stamp Exn, Tokyo. Japanese Steam Locomotives. Mult.

1525	15l. Type **257**	50	20
1526	25l. Class 6250 locomotive, 1915 (horiz)	75	30
1527	1r. Class D51 locomotive, 1936	1·25	40
1528	3r.50 Class 8620 locomotive, 1914 (horiz)	2·00	1·25
1529	5r. Class 10 locomotive, 1889 (horiz)	2·25	1·75
1530	7r. Class C61 locomotive, 1947	2·50	2·75
1531	10r. Class 9600 locomotive, 1913 (horiz)	2·50	3·00
1532	12r. Class D52 locomotive, 1943 (horiz)	2·75	3·50
MS1533	Two sheets, each 118×80 mm. (a) 20r. Class C56 locomotive, 1935 (horiz). (b) 20r. Class 1080 locomotive, 1925 (horiz) Set of 2 sheets	8·00	9·00

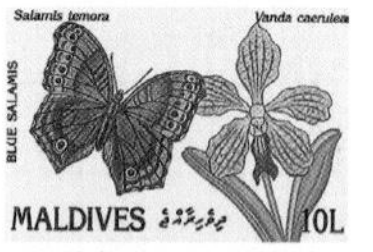

258 "Salamis temora" and "Vanda caerulea"

1991. Butterflies and Flowers. Multicoloured.

1534	10l. Type **258**	40	40
1535	25l. "Meneris tulbaghia" and "Incarvillea younghusbandii"	55	30
1536	50l. "Polyommatus icarus" and "Campsis grandiflora"	75	40
1537	2r. "Danaus plexippus" and "Thunbergia grandiflora"	1·25	90
1538	3r.50 "Colias interior" and "Medinilla magnifica"	1·75	1·75
1539	5r. "Ascalapha ordorata" and "Meconopsis horridula"	2·00	2·00
1540	8r. "Papilio memnon" and "Dillenia obovata"	2·50	3·00
1541	10r. "Precis octavia" and "Thespesia populnea"	2·50	3·00
MS1542	Two sheets, each 100×70 mm. (a) 20r. "Bombax ceiba" and "Plyciodes tharos". (b) 20r. "Amauris niavius" and "Bombax insigne" Set of 2 sheets	10·00	12·00

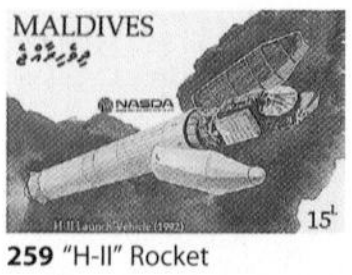

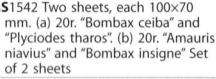

259 "H-II" Rocket

1991. Japanese Space Programme. Multicoloured.

1543	15l. Type **259**	50	30
1544	20l. Projected "H-II" orbiting plane	50	30
1545	2r. Satellite "GMS-5"	1·25	75
1546	3r.50 Satellite "MOMO-1"	1·60	1·40
1547	7r. Satellite "CS-3"	2·50	2·75
1548	10r. Satellite "BS-2a, 2b"	2·75	3·00
1549	12r. "H-I" Rocket (vert)	3·00	3·50
1550	15r. Space Flier unit and U.S. Space shuttle	3·00	3·50
MS1551	Two sheets. (a) 116×85 mm. 20r. Dish aerial, Katsura Tracking Station (vert). (b) 85×116 mm. 20r. "M-3SII" rocket (vert) Set of 2 sheets	13·00	13·00

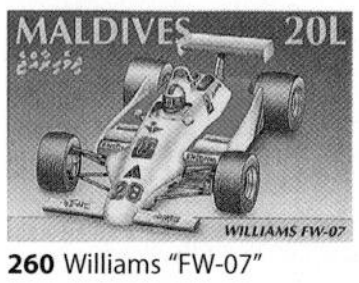

260 Williams "FW-07"

1991. Formula 1 Racing Cars. Multicoloured.

1552	20l. Type **260**	30	20
1553	50l. Brabham/BMW "BT50" turbo	45	30
1554	1r. Williams/Honda "FW-11"	60	45
1555	3r.50 Ferrari "312 T3"	1·25	1·25
1556	5r. Lotus/Honda "99T"	1·75	1·75
1557	7r. Benetton/Ford "B188"	2·00	2·25
1558	10r. Tyrrell "P34" six-wheeler	2·25	2·50
1559	21r. Renault "RE-30B" turbo	4·00	5·00
MS1560	Two sheets, each 84×56 mm. (a) 25r. Brabham/BMW "BT50" turbo (different). (b) 25r. Ferrari "F189" Set of 2 sheets	16·00	13·00

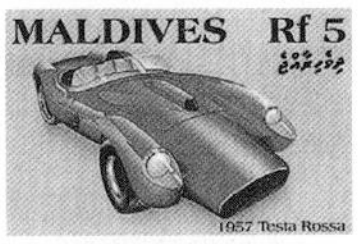
261 "Testa Rossa", 1957

1991. Ferrari Cars. Multicoloured.

1561	5r. Type **261**	2·00	2·00
1562	5r. "275GTB", 1966	2·00	2·00
1563	5r. "Aspirarta", 1951	2·00	2·00
1564	5r. "Testarossa"	2·00	2·00
1565	5r. Enzo Ferrari	2·00	2·00
1566	5r. "Dino 246", 1958	2·00	2·00
1567	5r. "Type 375", 1952	2·00	2·00
1568	5r. Nigel Mansell's Formula 1 racing car	2·00	2·00
1569	5r. "312T", 1975	2·00	2·00

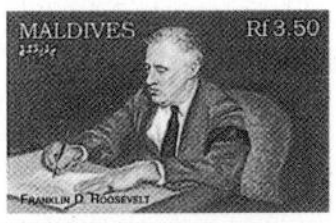
262 Franklin D. Roosevelt

1991. 50th Anniv of Japanese Attack on Pearl Harbor. American War Leaders. Multicoloured.

1570	3r.50 Type **262**	1·75	1·50
1571	3r.50 Douglas MacArthur and map of Philippines	1·75	1·50
1572	3r.50 Chester Nimitz and Pacific island	1·75	1·50
1573	3r.50 Jonathan Wainwright and barbed wire	1·75	1·50
1574	3r.50 Ernest King and U.S.S. "Hornet" (aircraft carrier)	1·75	1·50
1575	3r.50 Claire Chennault and Curtiss Tomahawk II fighters	1·75	1·50
1576	3r.50 William Halsey and U.S.S. "Enterprise" (aircraft carrier)	1·75	1·50
1577	3r.50 Marc Mitscher and U.S.S. "Hornet" (aircraft carrier)	1·75	1·50
1578	3r.50 James Doolittle and North American B-25 Mitchell bomber	1·75	1·50
1579	3r.50 Raymond Spruance and Douglas Dauntless dive bomber	1·75	1·50

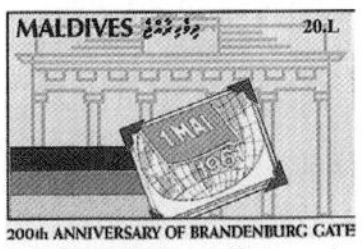
263 Brandenburg Gate and Postcard Commemorating Berlin Wall

1992. Anniversaries and Events. Multicoloured.

1580	20l. Type **263**	15	10
1581	50l. Schwarzenburg Palace	80	40
1582	1r. Spa at Baden	1·10	50
1583	1r.75 Berlin Wall and man holding child	50	50
1584	2r. Royal Palace, Berlin	2·00	1·00
1585	4r. Demonstrator and border guards	1·10	1·25
1586	5r. Viennese masonic seal	4·00	2·25
1587	6r. De Gaulle and Normandy landings, 1944 (vert)	2·50	2·25
1588	6r. Lilienthal's signature and "Flugzeug Nr. 16"	2·50	2·25
1589	7r. St. Marx	3·75	2·50
1590	7r. Trans-Siberian Railway Class VL80T electric locomotive No. 1406 (vert)	3·75	2·50
1591	8r. Kurt Schwitters (artist) and Landesmuseum	2·50	2·50
1592	9r. Map of Switzerland and man in Uri traditional costume	3·00	2·75
1593	10r. De Gaulle in Madagascar, 1958	2·50	2·75
1594	10r. Scouts exploring coral reef	2·50	2·75
1595	11r. Scout salute and badge (vert)	2·50	2·75
1596	12r. Trans-Siberian Railway steam locomotive	4·00	3·75
1597	15r. Imperial German badges	2·50	3·75
1598	20r. Josepsplatz, Vienna	5·00	5·00
MS1599	Eight sheets. (a) 76×116 mm. 15r. General de Gaulle during Second World War (vert). (b) 101×72 mm. 18r. Ancient German helmet. (c) 101×72 mm. 18r. 19th-century shako. (d) 101×72 mm. 18r. Helmet of 1939. (e) 90×117 mm. 18r. Postcard of Lord Baden-Powell carried by rocket, 1937 (grey, black and mauve) (vert). (f) 75×104 mm. 20r. Bust of Mozart (vert). (g) 115×85 mm. 20r. Trans-Siberian Railway Class P36 steam locomotive stopped at signal (57×43 mm). (h) 117×90 mm. 20r. Czechoslovakia 1918 10h. "Scout Post" stamp (vert) Set of 8 sheets	42·00	45·00

ANNIVERSARIES AND EVENTS: Nos. 1580, 1583, 1585, 1597, **MS**1599b/d, Bicentenary of Brandenburg Gate, Berlin; 1581/2, 1584, 1586, 1589, 1598, **MS**1599f, Death bicentenary of Mozart (1991); 1587, 1593, **MS**1599a, Birth centenary of Charles de Gaulle (French statesman) (1990); 1588, Centenary of Otto Lilienthal's first gliding experiments; 1590, 1596, **MS**1599g, Centenary of Trans-Siberian Railway; 1591, 750th anniv of Hannover; 1592, 700th anniv of Swiss Confederation; 1594/5, **MS**1599e,h, 17th World Scout Jamboree, Korea.

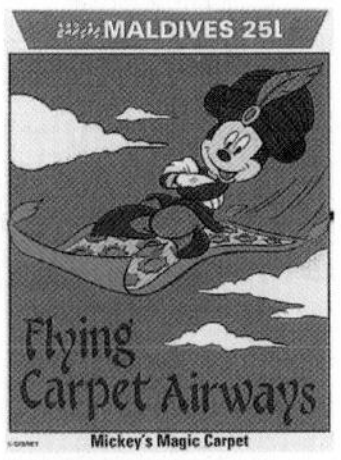

264 Mickey Mouse on Flying Carpet, Arabia

1992. Mickey's World Tour. Designs showing Walt Disney cartoon characters in different countries. Multicoloured.

1600	25l. Type **264**	45	20
1601	50l. Goofy and Big Ben, Great Britain	55	25
1602	1r. Mickey wearing clogs, Netherlands	75	35
1603	2r. Pluto eating pasta, Italy	1·25	75
1604	3r. Mickey and Donald doing Mexican hat dance	1·40	1·25
1605	3r.50 Mickey, Goofy and Donald as tiki, New Zealand	1·40	1·40
1606	5r. Goofy skiing in Austrian Alps	1·50	1·50
1607	7r. Mickey and city gate, Germany	1·75	2·00
1608	10r. Donald as samurai, Japan	2·00	2·25
1609	12r. Mickey as heroic statue, Russia	2·25	2·75
1610	15r. Mickey, Donald, Goofy and Pluto as German band	2·50	3·00
MS1611	Three sheets, each 83×104 mm. (a) 25r. Donald chasing leprechaun, Ireland (horiz). (b) 25r. Baby kangaroo surprising Pluto, Australia. (c) 25r. Mickey and globe Set of 3 sheets	13·00	14·00

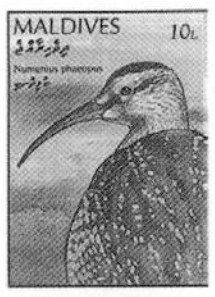
265 Whimbrel

1992. Birds. Multicoloured.

1612	10l. Type **265**	60	60
1613	25l. Great egret	70	40
1614	50l. Grey heron	75	50
1615	2r. Shag	1·60	75
1616	3r.50 Roseate tern	1·75	85
1617	5r. Greater greenshank	2·25	1·10
1617a	6r.50+50l. Egyptian vulture	3·50	3·50
1618	8r. Hoopoe	2·75	2·50
1619	10r. Black-shouldered kite	2·75	2·50
1620	25r. Scarlet ibis	4·50	4·25
1620a	30r. Peregrine falcon	5·50	4·75
1620b	40r. Black kite	6·50	6·00
1621	50r. Grey plover	6·50	7·00
1621a	100r. Common shoveler	16·00	16·00

Nos. 1617a, 1620a/b and 1621a are larger, 23×32 mm.

1992. 40th Anniv of Queen Elizabeth II's Accession. As T **214** of Lesotho. Multicoloured.

1622	1r. Palm trees on beach	60	25
1623	3r.50 Path leading to jetty	2·00	1·00
1624	7r. Tropical plant	2·75	2·75
1625	10r. Palm trees on beach (different)	3·00	3·25
MS1626	Two sheets, each 74×97 mm. (a) 18r. Dhow. (b) 18r. Palm trees on beach (different) Set of 2 sheets	14·00	12·00

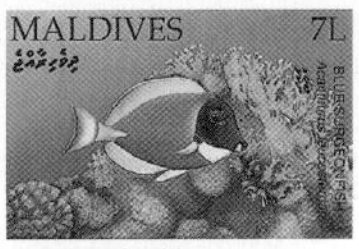
266 Powder-blue Surgeonfish

1992. Fishes. Multicoloured.

1627	7l. Type **266**	30	20
1628	20l. Catalufa	40	25
1629	50l. Yellow-finned tuna	55	30
1630	1r. Twin-spotted red snapper	75	35
1631	3r.50 Hawaiian squirrelfish	1·50	1·25
1632	5r. Picasso triggerfish	2·00	2·00
1633	8r. Bennet's butterflyfish	2·25	2·50
1634	10r. Parrotfish	2·50	2·75
1635	12r. Coral hind	2·75	3·00
1636	15r. Skipjack tuna	2·75	3·00
MS1637	Four sheets, each 116×76 mm. (a) 20r. Thread-finned butterflyfish. (b) 20r. Oriental sweetlips. (c) 20r. Two-banded anemonefish ("Clown-fish"). (d) 20r. Clown triggerfish Set of 4 sheets	13·00	15·00

1992. International Stamp Exhibitions. As T **215** of Lesotho showing Walt Disney cartoon characters. Multicoloured. (a) "Granada '92", Spain. The Alhambra.

1638	2r. Minnie Mouse in Court of the Lions	90	70
1639	5r. Goofy in Lions Fountain	1·75	1·75
1640	8r. Mickey Mouse at the Gate of Justice	2·25	2·75
1641	12r. Donald Duck serenading Daisy at the Vermilion Towers	2·75	3·50
MS1642	127×102 mm. 25r. Goofy pushing Mickey in wheelbarrow	5·50	6·00

(b) "World Columbian Stamp Expo '92". Chicago Landmarks.

1643	1r. Mickey meeting Jean Baptiste du Sable (founder)	1·00	40
1644	3r.50 Donald Duck at Old Chicago Post Office	2·00	1·25
1645	7r. Donald at Old Fort Dearborn	3·00	2·75
1646	15r. Goofy in Museum of Science and Industry	4·00	4·50
MS1647	127×102 mm. 25r. Mickey and Minnie Mouse at Columbian Exposition, 1893 (horiz)	5·50	6·00

On No. 1646 the design is wrongly captioned as the Science and Industry Museum.

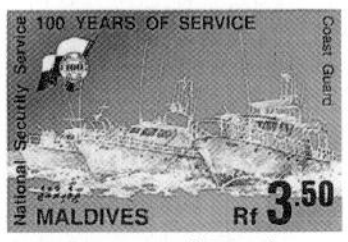

267 Coastguard Patrol Boats

1992. Cent of National Security Service. Multicoloured.

1648	3r.50 Type **267**	2·50	1·25
1649	5r. Infantry in training	2·50	1·75
1650	10r. Aakoatey fort	2·75	3·00
1651	15r. Fire Service	11·00	10·00
MS1652	100×68 mm. 20r. Ceremonial procession, 1892	7·00	9·00

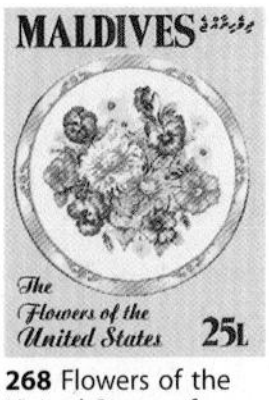

268 Flowers of the United States of America

1992. National Flowers. Multicoloured.

1653	25l. Type **268**	50	30
1654	50l. Australia	70	30
1655	2r. England	1·60	1·10
1656	3r.50 Brazil	2·00	1·50
1657	5r. Holland	2·25	2·00
1658	8r. France	2·50	3·00
1659	10r. Japan	2·75	3·00
1660	15r. Africa	3·50	4·50
MS1661	Two sheets, each 114×85 mm. (a) 25r. "Plumieria rubra", "Classia fistula" and "Eugenia malaccensis" (57×43 mm). (b) 25r. "Bauhinia variegata", "Catharanthus roseus" and "Plumieria alba" (57×43 mm) Set of 2 sheets	9·00	10·00

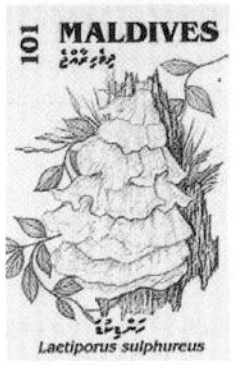
269 "Laetiporus sulphureus"

1992. Fungi. Multicoloured.

1662	10l. Type **269**	30	30
1663	25l. "Coprinus atramentarius"	40	30
1664	50l. "Ganoderma lucidum"	60	40
1665	3r.50 "Russula aurata"	1·25	1·00
1666	5r. "Grifola umbellata" ("Polyporus umbellatus")	1·75	1·75
1667	8r. "Suillus grevillei"	2·25	2·50
1668	10r. "Clavaria zollingeri"	2·50	2·50
1669	25r. "Boletus edulis"	5·00	6·00
MS1670	Two sheets, each 100×70 mm. (a) 25r. "Marasmius oreades". (b) 25r. "Pycnoporus cinnabarinus" ("Trametes cinnabarina") Set of 2 sheets	12·00	13·00

1992. Olympic Games, Albertville and Barcelona (1st issue). As T **216** of Lesotho. Multicoloured.

1671	10l. Pole vault	20	10
1672	25l. Men's pommel horse (horiz)	25	15
1673	50l. Men's shot put	30	25
1674	1r. Men's horizontal bar (horiz)	35	30
1675	2r. Men's triple jump (horiz)	80	65
1676	3r.50 Table tennis	1·10	1·10
1677	5r. Two-man bobsled	1·40	1·40
1678	7r. Freestyle wrestling (horiz)	1·75	2·00
1679	8r. Freestyle ski-jump	1·75	2·00
1680	9r. Baseball	2·00	2·25
1681	10r. Women's cross-country Nordic skiing	2·00	2·25
1682	12r. Men's 200 m backstroke (horiz)	2·00	2·25
MS1683	Three sheets. (a) 100×70 mm. 25r. Decathalon (horiz). (b) 100×70 mm. 25r. Women's slalom skiing (horiz). (c) 70×100 mm. 25r. Men's figure skating Set of 3 sheets	12·00	13·00

See also Nos. 1684/92.

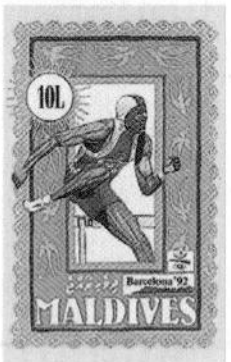
270 Hurdling

1992. Olympic Games, Barcelona (2nd issue). Multicoloured.

1684	10l. Type **270**	10	10
1685	1r. Boxing	30	30
1686	3r.50 Women's sprinting	1·00	70
1687	5r. Discus	1·50	1·25
1688	7r. Basketball	4·50	2·75
1689	10r. Long-distance running	2·50	2·75
1690	12r. Aerobic gymnastics	2·50	3·25
1691	20r. Fencing	3·25	4·50
MS1692	Two sheets, each 70×100 mm. (a) 25r. Olympic symbol and national flags. (b) 25r. Olympic symbol and flame Set of 2 sheets	8·50	9·00

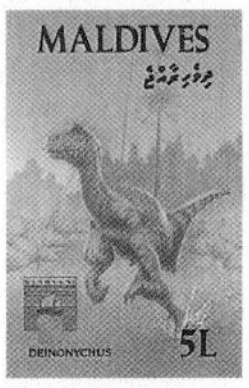

271 Deinonychus

1992. "Genova '92" International Thematic Stamp Exhibition. Prehistoric Animals. Multicoloured.

1693	5l. Type **271**	40	20
1694	10l. Styracosaurus	40	20
1695	25l. Mamenchisaurus	50	30
1696	50l. Stenonychosaurus	60	30
1697	1r. Parasaurolophus	75	40
1698	1r.25 Scelidosaurus	85	50
1699	1r.75 Tyrannosaurus	1·10	55
1700	2r. Stegosaurus	1·25	60
1701	3r.50 Iguanodon	1·50	80
1702	4r. Anatosaurus	1·50	1·00
1703	5r. Monoclonius	1·60	1·10
1704	7r. Tenontosaurus	1·90	1·90
1705	8r. Brachiosaurus	1·90	1·90
1706	10r. Euoplocephalus	2·00	2·00
1707	25r. Triceratops	3·25	4·50
1708	50r. Apatosaurus	6·00	8·00

MS1709 Four sheets, each 116×85 mm. (a) 25r. Hadrosaur hatchling. (b) 25r. Iguanodon fighting Allosaurus. (c) 25r. Tyrannosaurus attacking Triceratops. (d) 25r. Brachiosaurus and Iguanodons Set of 4 sheets 14·00 15·00

1992. Postage Stamp Mega Event, New York. Sheet 100×70 mm, containing multicoloured design as T **219** of Lesotho, but horiz.

MS1710 20r. New York Public Library 2·50 3·50

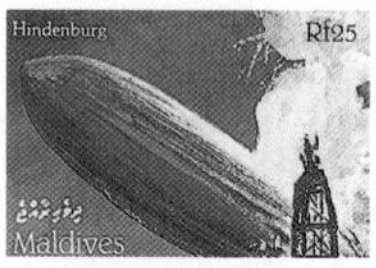

272 Destruction of LZ-129 "Hindenburg" (airship), 1937

1992. Mysteries of the Universe. T **272** and similar multicoloured designs, each in separate miniature sheet.

MS1711 Sixteen sheets, each 100×71 mm. (a) 25r. Type **272**. (b) 25r. Loch Ness Monster. (c) 25r. Crystal skull. (d) 25r. Space craft in Black Hole. (e) 25r. Ghosts (vert). (f) 25r. Flying saucer, 1947 (vert). (g) 25r. Bust of Plato (Atlantis). (h) 25r. U.F.O., 1973. (i) 25r. Crop circles. (j) 25r. Mil Mi-26 Russian helicopter at Chernobyl nuclear explosion. (k) 25r. Figure from Plain of Nazca. (l) 25r. Stonehenge (vert). (m) 25r. Yeti footprint (vert). (n) 25r. The Pyramid of Giza. (o) 25r. "Marie Celeste" (brigantine) (vert). (p) 25r. American Grumman TBF Avenger fighter aircraft (Bermuda Triangle) Set of 16 sheets 55·00 55·00

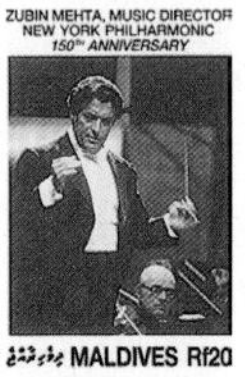

273 Zubin Mehta (musical director)

1992. 150th Anniv of New York Philharmonic Orchestra. Sheet 100×70 mm.

MS1712 **273** 20r. multicoloured 6·00 6·00

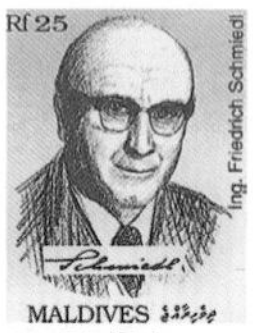

274 Friedrich Schmiedl

1992. 90th Birth Anniv of Friedrich Schmiedl (rocket mail pioneer). Sheet 104×69 mm.

MS1713 **274** 25r. multicoloured 5·50 6·50

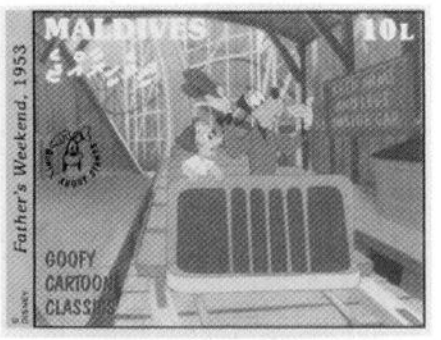

275 Goofy in "Father's Weekend", 1953

1992. 60th Anniv of Goofy (Disney cartoon character). Goofy in various cartoon films. Multicoloured.

1714 10l. Type **275** 10 10
1715 50l. "Symphony Hour", 1942 35 20
1716 75l. "Frank Duck Brings 'Em Back Alive", 1946 45 20
1717 1r. "Crazy with the Heat", 1947 45 20
1718 2r. "The Big Wash", 1948 70 60
1719 3r.50 "How to Ride a Horse", 1950 1·25 1·25
1720 5r. "Two Gun Goofy", 1952 1·50 1·50
1721 8r. "Saludos Amigos", 1943 (vert) 2·00 2·25
1722 10r. "How to be a Detective", 1952 2·00 2·25
1723 12r. "For Whom the Bulls Toil", 1953 2·25 2·50
1724 15r. "Double Dribble", 1946 (vert) 2·25 2·50

MS1725 Three sheets, each 127×102 mm. (a) 20r. "Double Dribble", 1946 (different) (vert). (b) 20r. "The Goofy Success Story", 1955 (vert). (c) 20r. "Mickey and the Beanstalk", 1947 Set of 3 sheets 10·00 10·50

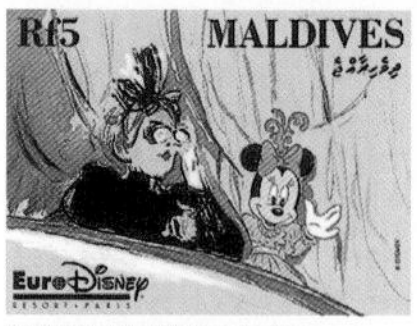

276 Minnie Mouse in "Le Missioner" (Toulouse-Lautrec)

1992. Opening of Euro-Disney Resort, France. Disney cartoon characters superimposed on Impressionist paintings. Multicoloured.

1726 5r. Type **276** 1·50 1·75
1727 5r. Goofy in "The Card Players" (Cezanne) 1·50 1·75
1728 5r. Mickey and Minnie Mouse in "The Cafe Terrace, Place du Forum" (Van Gogh) 1·50 1·75
1729 5r. Mickey in "The Bridge at Langlois" (Van Gogh) 1·50 1·75
1730 5r. Goofy in "Chocolate Dancing" (Toulouse-Lautrec) 1·50 1·75
1731 5r. Mickey and Minnie in "The Seine at Asnieres" (Renoir) 1·50 1·75
1732 5r. Minnie in "Ball at the Moulin Rouge" (Toulouse-Lautrec) 1·50 1·75
1733 5r. Mickey in "Wheatfield with Cypresses" (Van Gogh) 1·50 1·75
1734 5r. Minnie in "When will you Marry?" (Gauguin) 1·50 1·75

MS1735 Four sheets. (a) 128×100 mm. 20r. Minnie as can-can dancer. (b) 128×100 mm. 20r. Goofy as cyclist. (c) 100×128 mm. 20r. Mickey as artist. (d) 100×128 mm. 20r. Donald as Frenchman (vert) Set of 4 sheets 12·00 14·00

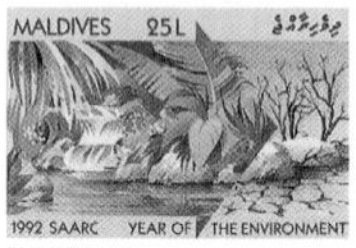

277 Rivers

1992. South Asian Association for Regional Co-operation Year of the Environment. Natural and Polluted Environments. Multicoloured.

1736 25l. Type **277** 15 10
1737 50l. Beaches 25 10
1738 5r. Oceans 80 1·00
1739 10r. Weather 1·50 2·25

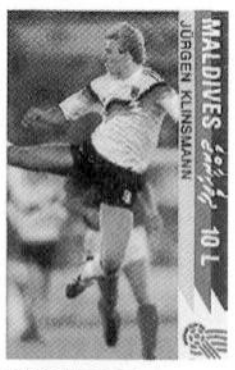

278 Jurgen Klinsmann (Germany)

1993. World Cup Football Championship, U.S.A. (1994) (1st issue). German Players and Officials. Multicoloured.

1740 10l. Type **278** 40 20
1741 25l. Pierre Littbarski 45 20
1742 50l. Lothar Matthaus 55 20
1743 1r. Rudi Voller 75 25
1744 2r. Thomas Hassler 1·25 60
1745 3r.50 Thomas Berthold 1·60 1·00
1746 4r. Jurgen Kohler 1·75 1·25
1747 5r. Berti Vogts 1·90 1·40
1748 6r. Bodo Illgner 2·25 2·25
1749 7r. Klaus Augenthaler 2·25 2·25
1750 8r. Franz Beckenbauer 2·25 2·25
1751 10r. Andreas Brehme 2·50 2·75
1752 12r. Guido Buchwald 2·50 3·25

MS1753 Two sheets, each 103×73 mm. (a) 35r. German players celebrating (horiz). (b) 35r. Rudi Voller (horiz) Set of 2 sheets 13·00 14·00

See also Nos. 1990/7 and 2089/2100.

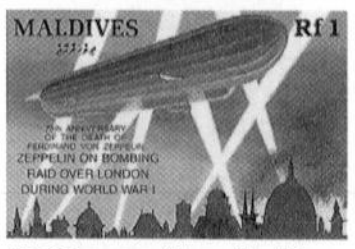

279 German Navy Airship L-13 bombing London, 1914–18

1993. Anniversaries and Events. Multicoloured.

1754 1r. Type **279** 1·00 40
1755 3r.50 Radio telescope 70 1·00
1756 3r.50 Chancellor Adenauer and Pres. de Gaulle 70 1·00
1757 6r. Indian rhinoceros 5·50 2·50
1758 6r. Columbus and globe 3·25 2·00
1759 7r. Conference emblems 1·50 2·00
1760 8r. Green seaturtle 1·75 2·00
1761 10r. "America" (yacht), 1851 1·75 2·25
1762 10r. Melvin Jones (founder) and emblem 1·75 2·25
1763 12r. Columbus landing on San Salvador 3·75 3·75
1764 15r. "Voyager I" approaching Saturn 6·00 6·00
1765 15r. Adenauer, N.A.T.O. flag and Lockheed Starfighter aircraft 6·00 6·00
1766 20r. "Graf Zeppelin" over New York, 1929 6·00 6·00

MS1767 Five sheets, each 111×80 mm. (a) 20r. Count Ferdinand von Zeppelin. (b) 20r. "Landsat" satellite. (c) 20r. Konrad Adenauer. (d) 20r. Scarlet macaw. (e) 20r. "Santa Maria" Set of 5 sheets 25·00 30·00

ANNIVERSARIES AND EVENTS: 1754, 1766, **MS**1767a, 75th death anniv of Count Ferdinand von Zeppelin; 1755, 1764, **MS**1767b, International Space Year; 1756, 1765, **MS**1767c, 25th death anniv of Konrad Adenauer; 1757, 1760, **MS**1767d, Earth Summit '92, Rio; 1758, 1763, **MS**1767e, 500th anniv of discovery of America by Columbus; 1759, International Conference on Nutrition, Rome; 1761, Americas Cup Yachting Championship; 1762, 75th anniv of International Association of Lions Clubs.

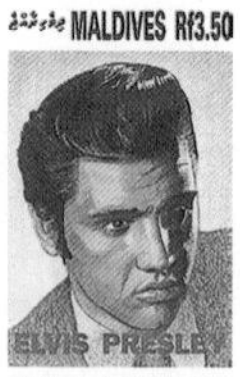

280 Elvis Presley

1993. 15th Death Anniv of Elvis Presley (singer). Multicoloured.

1768 3r.50 Type **280** 90 70
1769 3r.50 Elvis with guitar 90 70
1770 3r.50 Elvis with microphone 90 70

1993. Bicentenary of the Louvre, Paris. As T **221a** of Lesotho. Multicoloured.

1771 8r. "The Study" (Fragonard) 95 1·10
1772 8r. "Denis Diderot" (Fragonard) 95 1·10
1773 8r. "Marie-Madelaine Guimard" (Fragonard) 95 1·10
1774 8r. "Inspiration" (Fragonard) 95 1·10
1775 8r. "Waterfalls, Tivoli" (Fragonard) 95 1·10
1776 8r. "The Music Lesson" (Fragonard) 95 1·10
1777 8r. "The Bolt" (Fragonard) 95 1·10
1778 8r. "Blind-man's Buff" (Fragonard) 95 1·10
1779 8r. "Self-portrait" (Corot) 95 1·10
1780 8r. "Woman in Blue" (Corot) 95 1·10
1781 8r. "Woman with a Pearl" (Corot) 95 1·10
1782 8r. "Young Girl at her Toilet" (Corot) 95 1·10
1783 8r. "Haydee" (Corot) 95 1·10
1784 8r. "Chartres Cathedral" (Corot) 95 1·10
1785 8r. "The Belfry of Douai" (Corot) 95 1·10
1786 8r. "The Bridge of Mantes" (Corot) 95 1·10
1787 8r. "Madame Seriziat" (David) 95 1·10
1788 8r. "Pierre Seriziat" (David) 95 1·10
1789 8r. "Madame De Verninac" (David) 95 1·10
1790 8r. "Madame Recamier" (David) 95 1·10
1791 8r. "Self-portrait" (David) 95 1·10
1792 8r. "General Bonaparte" (David) 95 1·10
1793 8r. "The Lictors bringing Brutus his Son's Body" (David) (left detail) 95 1·10
1794 8r. "The Lictors bringing Brutus his Son's Body" (David) (right detail) 95 1·10

MS1795 Two sheets, each 100×70 mm. (a) 20r. "Gardens of the Villa D'Este, Tivoli" (Corot) (85×52 mm). (b) 20r. "Tiger Cub playing with its Mother" (Delacroix) (85×52 mm) Set of 2 sheets 8·50 8·50

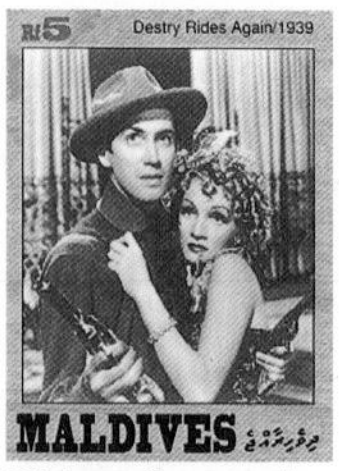

281 James Stewart and Marlene Dietrich ("Destry Rides Again")

1993. Famous Western Films. Multicoloured.

1796 5r. Type **281** 1·50 1·10
1797 5r. Gary Cooper ("The Westerner") 1·50 1·10
1798 5r. Henry Fonda ("My Darling Clementine") 1·50 1·10
1799 5r. Alan Ladd ("Shane") 1·50 1·10
1800 5r. Kirk Douglas and Burt Lancaster ("Gunfight at the O.K. Corral") 1·50 1·10
1801 5r. Steve McQueen ("The Magnificent Seven") 1·50 1·10
1802 5r. Robert Redford and Paul Newman ("Butch Cassidy and The Sundance Kid") 1·50 1·10
1803 5r. Jack Nicholson and Randy Quaid ("The Missouri Breaks") 1·50 1·10

MS1804 Two sheets, each 134×120 mm. (a) 20r. John Wayne ("The Searchers") (French poster). (b) 20r. Clint Eastwood ("Pale Rider") (French poster) Set of 2 sheets 8·50 7·50

1993. 40th Anniv of Coronation. As T **224** of Lesotho.

1805 3r.50 multicoloured 1·00 1·10
1806 5r. multicoloured 1·25 1·40
1807 10r. blue and black 1·50 1·75
1808 10r. blue and black 1·50 1·75

DESIGNS: No. 1805, Queen Elizabeth II at Coronation (photograph by Cecil Beaton); 1806, St. Edward's Crown; 1807, Guests in the Abbey; 1808, Queen Elizabeth II and Prince Philip.

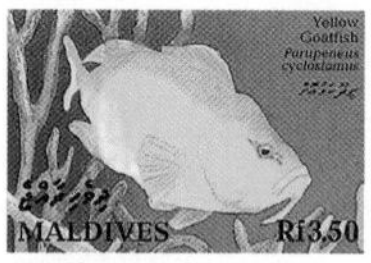

282 Blue Goatfish

1993. Fish. Multicoloured.

1809 3r.50 Type **282** 60 70
1810 3r.50 Emperor angelfish 60 70
1811 3r.50 Madagascar butterflyfish 60 70
1812 3r.50 Regal angelfish 60 70
1813 3r.50 Forceps fish ("Longnose butterflyfish") 60 70
1814 3r.50 Racoon butterflyfish 60 70
1815 3r.50 Harlequin filefish 60 70
1816 3r.50 Rectangle triggerfish 60 70
1817 3r.50 Yellow-tailed anemonefish 60 70
1818 3r.50 Clown triggerfish 60 70
1819 3r.50 Zebra lionfish 60 70
1820 3r.50 Maldive anemonefish ("Clownfish") 60 70
1821 3r.50 Black-faced butterflyfish 60 70
1822 3r.50 Bird wrasse 60 70
1823 3r.50 Checkerboard wrasse 60 70
1824 3r.50 Yellow-faced angelfish 60 70
1825 3r.50 Masked bannerfish 60 70
1826 3r.50 Thread-finned butterflyfish 60 70
1827 3r.50 Painted triggerfish 60 70
1828 3r.50 Coral hind 60 70
1829 3r.50 Pennant coralfish 60 70
1830 3r.50 Black-backed butterflyfish 60 70
1831 3r.50 Red-toothed triggerfish 60 70
1832 3r.50 Melon butterflyfish 60 70

MS1833 Two sheets. (a) 69×96 mm. 25r. Klein's butterflyfish (vert). (b) 96×69 mm. 25r. Brown anemonefish (vert) Set of 2 sheets 8·00 8·50

Nos. 1809/20 and 1821/32 were printed together, *se-tenant*, with the backgrounds forming composite designs.

Nos. 1810 and 1824 are both inscribed "Angelfish" in error.

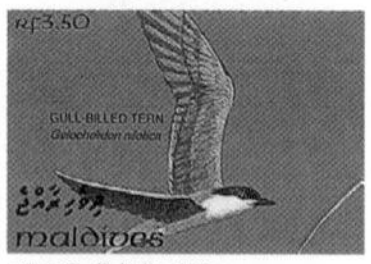

283 Gull-billed Tern

1993. Birds. Multicoloured.

1834 3r.50 Type **283** 65 70
1835 3r.50 White-tailed tropic bird ("Long-tailed Tropicbird") 65 70
1836 3r.50 Great frigate bird ("Frigate Bird") 65 70
1837 3r.50 Wilson's storm petrel ("Wilson's Petrel") 65 70
1838 3r.50 White tern 65 70
1839 3r.50 Brown booby 65 70
1840 3r.50 Marsh harrier 65 70
1841 3r.50 Common noddy 65 70
1842 3r.50 Green-backed heron ("Little Heron") 65 70
1843 3r.50 Ruddy turnstone ("Turnstone") 65 70
1844 3r.50 Curlew 65 70
1845 3r.50 Crab plover 65 70
1846 3r.50 Pallid harrier (vert) 65 70
1847 3r.50 Cattle egret (vert) 65 70
1848 3r.50 Koel (vert) 65 70
1849 3r.50 Tree pipit (vert) 65 70
1850 3r.50 Short-eared owl (vert) 65 70
1851 3r.50 Common kestrel ("European Kestrel") (vert) 65 70
1852 3r.50 Yellow wagtail (vert) 65 70
1853 3r.50 Grey heron ("Common Heron") (vert) 65 70
1854 3r.50 Black bittern (vert) 65 70

1855	3r.50 Common snipe (vert)	65	70
1856	3r.50 Little egret (vert)	65	70
1857	3r.50 Little stint (vert)	65	70
MS1858	Two sheets, each 105×75 mm. (a) 25r. Caspian tern. (b) 25r. Audubon's shearwater Set of 2 sheets	8·50	9·00

Nos. 1834/45 and 1846/57 were printed together, *se-tenant*, with the backgrounds forming composite designs.

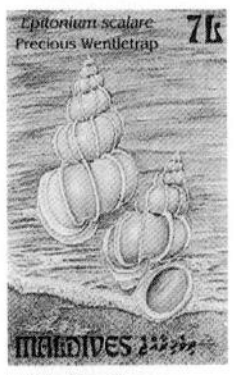

284 Precious Wentletrap

1993. Shells. Multicoloured.

1859	7l. Type **284**	30	30
1860	15l. Common purple janthina	35	30
1861	50l. Asiatic arabian cowrie	45	30
1862	3r.50 Common or major harp	1·50	1·00
1863	4r. Amplustre or royal paper bubble	1·75	1·25
1864	5r. Sieve cowrie	1·75	1·40
1865	6r. Episcopal mitre	2·00	2·00
1866	7r. Camp pitar venus	2·00	2·25
1867	8r. Spotted or eyed auger	2·25	2·50
1868	10r. Exposed cowrie	2·50	2·50
1869	12r. Geographic map cowrie	2·75	3·50
1870	20r. Bramble murex	3·50	4·50
MS1871	Three sheets, each 104×75 mm. (a) 25r. Black-striped triton. 25r. Scorpion conch. (c) 25r. Bull-mouth helmet Set of 3 sheets	50	30

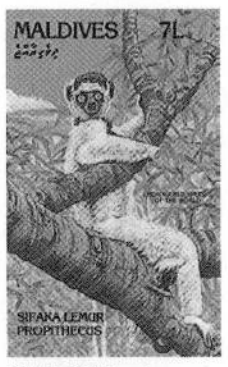

285 Sifaka Lemur

1993. Endangered Species. Multicoloured.

1872	7l. Type **285**	50	30
1873	10l. Snow leopard	50	30
1874	15l. Numbat	90	40
1875	25l. Gorilla	1·10	70
1876	2r. Koala	1·25	1·10
1877	3r.50 Cheetah	1·40	1·40
1878	5r. Yellow-footed rock wallaby	2·25	2·25
1879	7r. Orang-utan	2·25	2·25
1880	8r. Black lemur	3·50	3·00
1881	10r. Black rhinoceros	4·50	4·00
1882	15r. Humpback whale	5·00	4·50
1883	20r. Mauritius parakeet	17·00	19·00
MS1884	Three sheets, each 104×75 mm. (a) 25r. Giant panda. (b) 25r. Tiger. (c) 25r. Indian elephant Set of 3 sheets	1·25	1·40

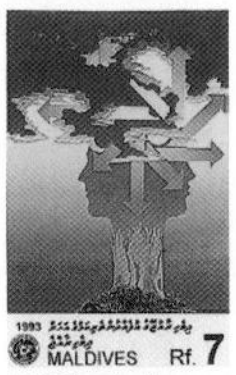

286 Symbolic Heads and Arrows

1993. Productivity Year. Multicoloured.

1885	7r. Type **286**	1·60	1·75
1886	10r. Abstract	1·00	1·00

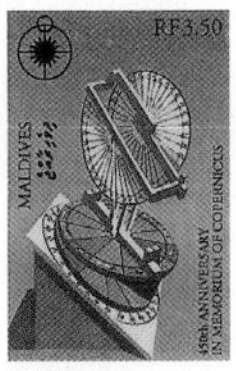

287 Early Astronomical Equipment

1993. Anniversaries and Events. Multicoloured.

1887	3r.50 Type **287**	1·00	1·00
1888	3r.50 "Still Life with Pitcher and Apples" (Picasso)	1·00	1·00
1889	3r.50 "Zolte Roze" (Menasze Seidenbeurel)	1·00	1·00
1890	3r.50 Prince Naruhito and engagement photographs (horiz)	1·25	1·25
1891	5r. "Bowls and Jug" (Picasso)	1·25	1·25
1892	5r. Krysztofory Palace, Cracow	1·75	1·90
1893	8r. "Jabtka i Kotara" (Waclaw Borowski)	1·75	1·90
1894	8r. Marina Kiehl (Germany) (women's downhill skiing)	1·90	2·00
1895	10r. "Bowls of Fruit and Loaves on a Table" (Picasso)	1·90	2·00
1896	10r. Masako Owada and engagement photographs (horiz)	2·75	3·00
1897	15r. American astronaut in space	2·75	3·00
1898	15r. Vegard Ulvang (Norway) (30km cross-country skiing)	2·75	3·00
MS1899	Five sheets. (a) 105×75 mm. (a) 20r. Copernicus. (b) 105×75 mm. 20r. "Green Still Life" (detail) (Picasso) (horiz). (c) 105×75 mm. 25r. "Pejzaz Morski-Port z DoplywajacymStstkiem" (detail (Roman Sielski) (horiz). (d) 75×105 mm. 25r. Masako Owada. (e) 105×75 mm. 25r. Ice hockey goalkeeper Set of 5 sheets	21·00	23·00

ANNIVERSARIES AND EVENTS: Nos. 1887, 1897, **MS**1899a, 450th death anniv of Copernicus (astronomer); 1888, 1891, 1895, **MS**1899b, 20th death anniv of Picasso (artist); 1889, 1892/3, **MS**1899c, "Polska '93" International Stamp Exhibition, Poznan; 1890, 1896, **MS**1899d, Marriage of Crown Prince Naruhito of Japan; 1894, 1898, **MS**1899e, Winter Olympic Games '94, Lillehammer.

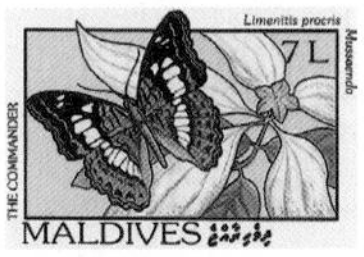

288 "Limenitis procris" and "Mussaenda"

1993. Butterflies and Flowers. Multicoloured.

1900	7l. Type **288**	40	20
1901	20l. "Danaus limniace" and "Thevetia neriifolia"	55	20
1902	25l. "Amblypodia centaurus" and "Clitoria ternatea"	55	20
1903	50l. "Papilio crino" and "Crossandra infundibuliformis"	90	20
1904	5r. "Mycalesis patnia" and "Thespesia populnia"	2·00	1·40
1905	6r.50+50l. "Idea jasonia" and "Cassia glauca"	2·25	2·50
1906	7r. "Catopsilia pomona" and "Calotropis"	2·25	2·50
1907	10r. "Precis orithyia" and "Thunbergia grandiflora"	2·50	2·75
1908	12r. "Vanessa cardui" and "Caesalpinia pulcherrima"	2·75	3·25
1909	15r. "Papilio polymnestor" and "Nerium oleander"	3·00	3·50
1910	18r. "Cirrochroa thais" and "Vinca rosea"	3·25	3·75
1911	20r. "Pachliopta hector" and "Ixora coccinea"	3·25	3·75
MS1912	Three sheets, each 105×72 mm. (a) 25r. "Cheritra freja" and "Bauhinia purpurea" (vert). (b) 25r. "Rohana parisatis" and "Plumeria acutifolia" (vert). (c) 25r. "Hebomoia glaucippe" and "Punica granatum" (vert) Set of 3 sheets	15·00	17·00

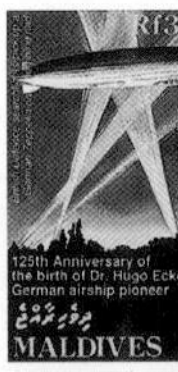

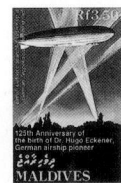

289 Airship "Graf Zeppelin" in Searchlights

1993. Aviation Anniversaries. Multicoloured.

1913	3r.50 Type **289**	2·00	65
1914	5r. Homing pigeon and message from Santa Catalina mail service, 1894	2·25	1·10
1915	10r. Eckener and airship "Graf Zeppelin"	2·75	2·50
1916	15r. Pilot's badge and loading Philadelphia–Washington mail, 1918	4·00	4·25
1917	20r. U.S.S. "Macon" (airship) and mooring mast, 1933	4·00	4·25
MS1918	Two sheets. (a) 70×100 mm. 25r. Santos Dumont's airship "Ballon No. 5" and Eiffel Tower, 1901. (b) 100×70 mm. 25r. Jean-Pierre Blanchard's balloon, 1793 (vert) Set of 2 sheets	8·00	8·50

ANNIVERSARIES: Nos. 1913, 1915, 1917, **MS**1918a, 125th birth anniv of Hugo Eckener (airship pioneer); 1914, 1916, **MS**1918b, Bicent of first airmail flight.

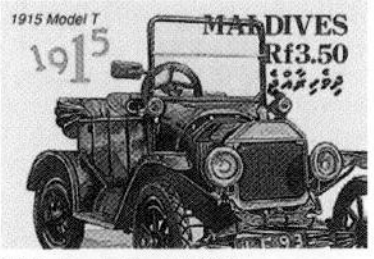

290 Ford Model "T"

1993. Centenaries of Henry Ford's First Petrol Engine (Nos. 1919/30) and Karl Benz's First Four-wheeled Car (others).

1919	**290**	3r.50 multicoloured	90	1·00
1920	-	3r.50 multicoloured	90	1·00
1921	-	3r.50 black and violet	90	1·00
1922	-	3r.50 multicoloured	90	1·00
1923	-	3r.50 multicoloured	90	1·00
1924	-	3r.50 multicoloured	90	1·00
1925	-	3r.50 multicoloured	90	1·00
1926	-	3r.50 multicoloured	90	1·00
1927	-	3r.50 multicoloured	90	1·00
1928	-	3r.50 multicoloured	90	1·00
1929	-	3r.50 multicoloured	90	1·00
1930	-	3r.50 black, brn & vio	90	1·00
1931	-	3r.50 multicoloured	90	1·00
1932	-	3r.50 multicoloured	90	1·00
1933	-	3r.50 green, blk & vio	90	1·00
1934	-	3r.50 multicoloured	90	1·00
1935	-	3r.50 multicoloured	90	1·00
1936	-	3r.50 multicoloured	90	1·00
1937	-	3r.50 multicoloured	90	1·00
1938	-	3r.50 multicoloured	90	1·00
1939	-	3r.50 multicoloured	90	1·00
1940	-	3r.50 multicoloured	90	1·00
1941	-	3r.50 multicoloured	90	1·00
1942	-	3r.50 black, brn and violet	90	1·00
MS1943		Two sheets, each 100×70 mm. (a) 25r. multicoloured. (b) 25r. multicoloured Set of 2 sheets	9·00	10·00

DESIGNS: No. 1920, Henry Ford; 1921, Plans of first petrol engine; 1922, Ford "Probe GT", 1993; 1923, Front of Ford "Sportsman", 1947; 1924, Back of Ford "Sportsman"; 1925, Advertisement of 1915; 1926, Ford "Thunderbird", 1955; 1927, Ford logo; 1928, Ford "Edsel Citation", 1958; 1929, Ford half-ton pickup, 1941; 1930, Silhouette of early Ford car; 1931, Daimler-Benz "Straight 8", 1937; 1932, Karl Benz; 1933, Mercedes-Benz poster; 1934, Mercedes "38-250SS", 1929; 1935, Benz "Viktoria", 1893; 1936, Benz logo; 1937, Plan of Mercedes engine; 1938, Mercedes-Benz "300SL Gullwing", 1952; 1939, Mercedes-Benz "SL", 1993; 1940, Front of Benz 4-cylinder car, 1906; 1941, Back of Benz 4-cylinder car and advertisement; 1942, Silhouette of early Benz car; **MS**1943a, Ford Model "Y", 1933; **MS**1943b, Mercedes "300S", 1955.

Nos. 1919/30 and 1931/42 were printed together, se-tenant, forming a composite design.

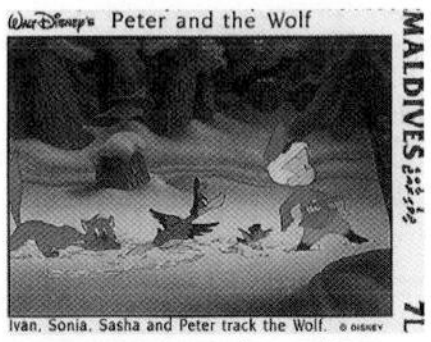

291 Ivan, Sonia, Sasha and Peter in the Snow

1993. "Peter and the Wolf". Scenes from Walt Disney's cartoon film. Multicoloured.

1944	7l. Type **291**	25	25
1945	15l. Grandpa and Peter	30	25
1946	20l. Peter on bridge	30	25
1947	25l. Yascha, Vladimir and Mischa	30	25
1948	50l. Sasha on lookout	45	30
1949	1r. The wolf	60	35
1950	3r.50 Peter dreaming	70	80
1951	3r.50 Peter taking gun	70	80
1952	3r.50 Peter with gun in snow	70	80
1953	3r.50 Sasha and Peter	70	80
1954	3r.50 Sonia and Peter	60	60
1955	3r.50 Peter with Ivan and Sasha	70	80
1956	3r.50 Ivan warning Peter of the wolf	70	80
1957	3r.50 Ivan, Peter and Sasha in tree	70	80
1958	3r.50 Wolf below tree	70	80
1959	3r.50 Wolf and Sonia	70	80
1960	3r.50 Sasha attacking the wolf	70	80
1961	3r.50 Sasha walking into wolf's mouth	70	80
1962	3r.50 Peter firing pop gun at wolf	70	80
1963	3r.50 Wolf chasing Sonia	70	80
1964	3r.50 Ivan tying rope to wolf's tail	70	80
1965	3r.50 Peter and Ivan hoisting wolf	70	80
1966	3r.50 Sasha and the hunters	70	80
1967	3r.50 Ivan and Peter on wolf hanging from tree	70	80
MS1968	Two sheets. (a) 102×127 mm. 25r. Sonia as an angel. (b) 127×102 mm. 25r. Ivan looking proud Set of 2 sheets	8·00	8·50

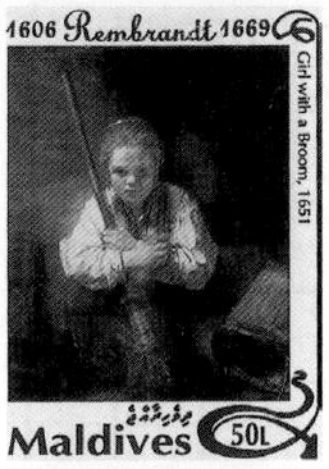

292 "Girl with a Broom" (Rembrandt)

1994. Famous Paintings by Rembrandt and Matisse. Multicoloured.

1969	50l. Type **292**	40	25
1970	2r. "Girl with Tulips" (Matisse)	90	70
1971	3r.50 "Young Girl at half-open Door" (Rembrandt)	1·25	1·10
1972	3r.50 "Portrait of Greta Moll" (Matisse)	1·25	1·10
1973	5r. "The Prophetess Hannah" (Rembrandt)	1·50	1·25
1974	6r.50 "The Idol" (Matisse)	1·75	1·75
1975	7r. "Woman with a Pink Flower" (Rembrandt)	1·75	1·75
1976	9r. "Mme Matisse in a Japanese Robe" (Matisse)	2·00	2·25
1977	10r. "Portrait of Mme Matisse" (Matisse)	2·00	2·25
1978	12r. "Lucretia" (Rembrandt)	2·25	2·50
1979	15r. "Lady with a Ostrich Feather Fan" (Rembrandt)	2·25	2·75
1980	15r. "The Woman with the Hat" (Matisse)	2·25	2·75
MS1981	Three sheets. (a) 106×132 mm. 25r. "The Music-makers" (detail) (Rembrandt). (b) 132×106 mm. 25r. "Married Couple with Three Children" (detail) (Rembrandt) (horiz). (c) 132×106 mm. 25r. "The Painter's Family" (detail) (Matisse) Set of 3 sheets	16·00	16·00

No. 1979 is inscribed "The Lady with an Ostich Feather Fan" in error.

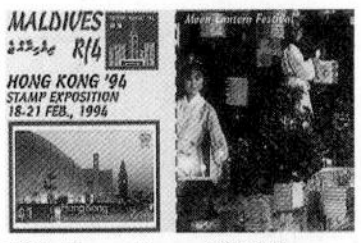

293 Hong Kong 1983 Space Museum Stamp and Moon-lantern Festival

1994. "Hong Kong '94" International Stamp Exn (1st issue). Multicoloured.

1982	4r. Type **293**	65	80
1983	4r. Maldive Islands 1976 5r. "Viking" space mission stamp and Moon-lantern festival	65	80

Nos. 1982/3 were printed together, *se-tenant*, forming a composite design.

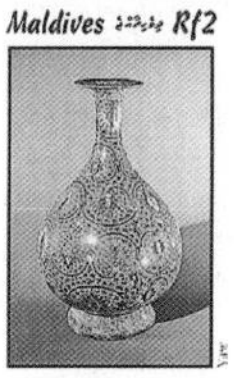

294 Vase

1994. "Hong Kong '94" International Stamp Exhibition (2nd issue). Ching Dynasty Cloisonne Enamelware. Multicoloured.

1984	2r. Type **294**	90	85
1985	2r. Flower holder	90	85
1986	2r. Elephant with vase on back	90	85
1987	2r. Tibetan style lama's teapot	90	85
1988	2r. Fo-Dog	90	45
1989	2r. Teapot with swing handle	90	85

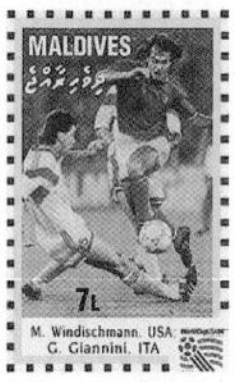

295 Windischmann (U.S.A.) and Giannini (Italy)

1994. World Cup Football Championship, U.S.A. (2nd issue). Multicoloured.

1990	7l. Type **295**	30	25
1991	20l. Carnevale (Italy) and Gascoigne (England)	50	25
1992	25l. England players congratulating Platt	50	25
1993	3r.50 Koeman (Holland) and Klinsmann (Germany)	1·25	80

1994	5r. Quinn (Ireland) and Maldini (Italy)	1·40	1·00
1995	7r. Lineker (England)	2·00	1·50
1996	15r. Hassam (Egypt) and Moran (Ireland)	3·00	3·50
1997	18r. Canniggia (Argentina)	3·25	3·50
MS1998	Two sheets, each 103×73 mm. 25r. Ogris (Austria). (b) 25r. Conejo (Costa Rica) (horiz) Set of 2 sheets	13·00	12·00

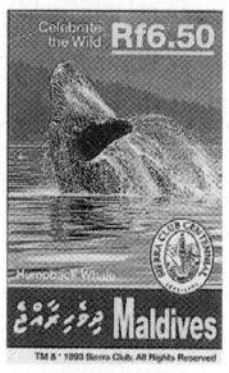

296 Humpback Whale

1994. Centenary (1992) of Sierra Club (environmental protection society). Endangered Species. Multicoloured.

1999	6r.50 Type **296**	1·60	1·60
2000	6r.50 Ocelot crouched in grass	1·60	1·60
2001	6r.50 Ocelot sitting	1·60	1·60
2002	6r.50 Snow monkey	1·60	1·60
2003	6r.50 Prairie dog	1·60	1·60
2004	6r.50 Golden lion tamarin	1·60	1·60
2005	6r.50 Prairie dog eating (horiz)	1·60	1·60
2006	6r.50 Prairie dog outside burrow (horiz)	1·60	1·60
2007	6r.50 Herd of woodland caribou (horiz)	1·60	1·60
2008	6r.50 Woodland caribou facing left (horiz)	1·60	1·60
2009	6r.50 Woodland caribou facing right (horiz)	1·60	1·60
2010	6r.50 Pair of Galapagos penguins (horiz)	1·60	1·60
2011	6r.50 Galapagos penguin facing right	1·60	1·60
2012	6r.50 Galapagos penguin looking straight ahead	1·60	1·60
2013	6r.50 Bengal tiger looking straight ahead	1·60	1·60
2014	6r.50 Bengal tiger looking right	1·60	1·60
2015	6r.50 Philippine tarsier with tree trunk at left	1·60	1·60
2016	6r.50 Philippine tarsier with tree trunk at right	1·60	1·60
2017	6r.50 Head of Philippine tarsier	1·60	1·60
2018	6r.50 Sierra Club centennial emblem (black, buff and green)	1·60	1·60
2019	6r.50 Golden lion tamarin between two branches (horiz)	1·60	1·60
2020	6r.50 Golden lion tamarin on tree trunk (horiz)	1·60	1·60
2021	6r.50 Tail fin of humpback whale and coastline (horiz)	1·60	1·60
2022	6r.50 Tail fin of humpback whale at night (horiz)	1·60	1·60
2023	6r.50 Bengal tiger (horiz)	1·60	1·60
2024	5r.50 Ocelot (horiz)	1·60	1·60
2025	6r.50 Snow monkey in water climbing out of pool (horiz)	1·60	1·60
2026	6r.50 Snow monkey swimming (horiz)	1·60	1·60

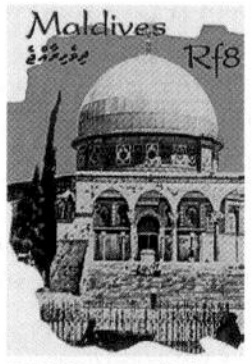

297 Dome of the Rock, Jerusalem

1994. Solidarity with the Palestinians.

2027	**297**	8r. multicoloured	1·60	1·60

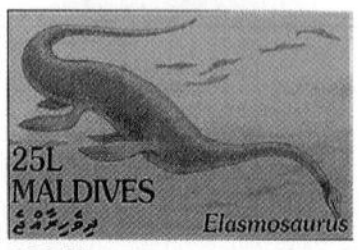

298 Elasmosaurus

1994. Prehistoric Animals. Multicoloured.

2028-2059	25l., 50l., 1r., 3r.×24, 5r., 8r., 10r., 15r., 20r.		
2028-2059	Set of 32, 2028-2059	30·00	28·00
MS2060	Two sheets, each 106×76 mm. (a) 25r. Gallimimus. (b) 25r. Plateosaurus (vert) Set of 2 sheets	8·00	8·50

Nos. 2031/42 and 2043/54 respectively were printed together, se-tenant, forming composite designs. The species depicted are, in addition to Type **298**, Dilophosaurus, Avimimus, Dimorphodon, Megalosaurus, Kuehneosaurus, Dryosaurus, Kentro- saurus, Baraposaurus, Tenontosaurus, Elaphrosaurus, Maiasaura, Huayangosaurus, Rutiodon, Pianitzkysaurus, Quetzalcoatlus, Daspleto- saurus, Pleurocoelus, Baryonyx, Pentaceratops, Kritosaurus, Microvenator, Nodosaurus, Montanaceratops, Dromiceiomimus, Dryptosaurus, Parkosaurus, Chasmosaurus, Edmontonia, Anatosaurus, Velociraptor and Spinosaurus.

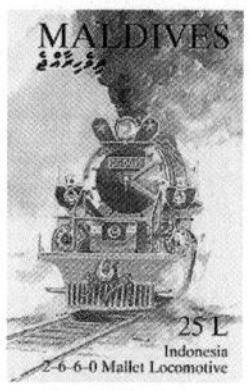

299 Mallet Steam Locomotive, Indonesia

1994. Railway Locomotives of Asia. Multicoloured.

2061	25l. Type **299**	20	20
2062	50l. Class C62 steam locomotive, Japan, 1948	25	20
2063	1r. Class D51 steam locomotive, Japan, 1936 (horiz)	30	20
2064	5r. Steam locomotive, India (horiz)	90	90
2065	6r.50+50l. Class W steam locomotive, India (horiz)	1·25	1·50
2066	6r.50+50l. Class C53 steam locomotive, Indonesia (horiz)	1·25	1·50
2067	6r.50+50l. Class C10 steam locomotive, Japan (horiz)	1·25	1·50
2068	6r.50+50l. Hanomag steam locomotive, India (horiz)	1·25	1·50
2069	6r.50+50l. "Hikari" express train, Japan (horiz)	1·25	1·50
2070	6r.50+50l. Class C55 steam locomotive, Japan, 1935 (horiz)	1·25	1·50
2071	8r. Class 485 electric locomotive, Japan (horiz)	1·50	1·75
2072	10r. Class WP steam locomotive, India (horiz)	1·75	2·00
2073	15r. Class RM steam locomotive, China (horiz)	2·00	2·25
2074	20r. Class C57 steam locomotive, Japan, 1937	2·25	2·50
MS2075	Two sheets, each 110×80 mm. (a) 25r. Steam locomotive pulling goods train, Indonesia (horiz). (b) 25r. Class 8620 steam locomotive, Japan, 1914 (horiz) Set of 2 sheets	9·00	9·50

No. 2069 is inscribed "Hakari" in error.

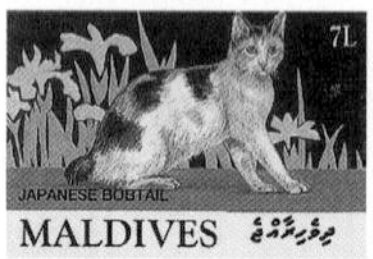

300 Japanese Bobtail

1994. Cats. Multicoloured.

2076	7l. Type **300**	30	20
2077	20l. Siamese (vert)	45	20
2078	25l. Persian longhair	45	20
2079	50l. Somali (vert)	55	20
2080	3r.50 Oriental shorthair	1·25	80
2081	5r. Burmese	1·50	1·00
2082	7r. Bombay carrying kitten	1·75	1·50
2083	10r. Turkish van (vert)	1·75	1·75
2084	12r. Javanese (vert)	2·00	2·00
2085	15r. Singapura	2·25	2·75
2086	18r. Turkish angora (vert)	2·50	3·25
2087	20r. Egyptian mau (vert)	2·50	3·25
MS2088	Three sheets. (a) 70×100 mm. 25r. Birman (vert). (b) 70×100 mm. 25r. Korat (vert). (c) 100×70 mm. 25r. Abyssinian (vert) Set of 3 sheets	13·00	15·00

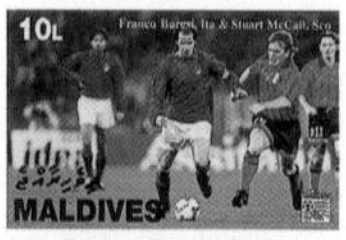

301 Franco Baresi (Italy) and Stuart McCall (Scotland)

1994. World Cup Football Championship, U.S.A. (3rd issue). Multicoloured. (a) Horiz designs.

2089	10l. Type **301**	40	40
2090	25l. Mick McCarthy (Ireland) and Gary Lineker (England)	50	50
2091	50l. J. Helt (Denmark) and R. Gordillo (Spain)	50	50
2092	5r. Martin Vasquez (Spain) and Enzo Scifo (Belgium)	1·25	1·25
2093	10r. Championship emblem	1·60	1·60
2094	12r. Tomas Brolin (Sweden) and Gordon Durie (Scotland)	1·75	1·75

(b) Vert designs.

2095	6r.50 Bebeto (Brazil)	1·25	1·25
2096	6r.50 Lothar Matthaus (Germany)	1·25	1·25
2097	6r.50 Diego Maradona (Argentina)	1·25	1·25
2098	6r.50 Stephane Chapuisat (Switzerland)	1·25	1·25
2099	6r.50 George Hagi (Rumania)	1·25	1·25
2100	6r.50 Carlos Valderama (Colombia)	1·25	1·25
MS2101	100×70 mm. 10r. Egyptian players	4·25	4·25

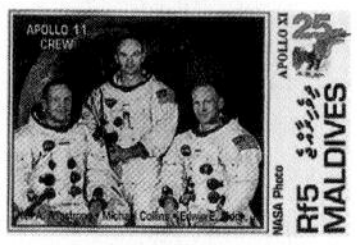

302 Crew of "Apollo 11"

1994. 25th Anniv of First Manned Moon Landing. Multicoloured.

2102	5r. Type **302**	1·00	1·00
2103	5r. "Apollo 11" mission logo	1·00	1·00
2104	5r. Edwin Aldrin (astronaut) and "Eagle"	1·00	1·00
2105	5r. Crew of "Apollo 12"	1·00	1·00
2106	5r. "Apollo 12" mission logo	1·00	1·00
2107	5r. Alan Bean (astronaut) and equipment	1·00	1·00
2108	5r. Crew of "Apollo 16"	1·00	1·00
2109	5r. "Apollo 16" mission logo	1·00	1·00
2110	5r. Astronauts with U.S. flag	1·00	1·00
2111	5r. Crew of "Apollo 17"	1·00	1·00
2112	5r. "Apollo 17" mission logo	1·00	1·00
2113	5r. Launch of "Apollo 17"	1·00	1·00
MS2114	100×76 mm. 25r. Launch of Russian rocket from Baikonur (vert)	4·00	4·75

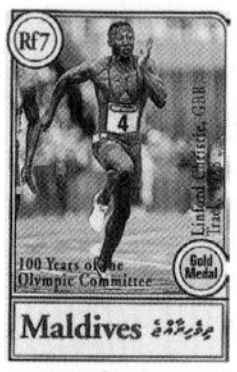

303 Linford Christie (Great Britain) (100 m), 1992

1994. Centenary of International Olympic Committee. Gold Medal Winners. Multicoloured.

2115	7r. Type **303**	1·50	1·25
2116	12r. Koji Gushiken (Japan) (gymnastics), 1984	1·75	2·00
MS2117	106×71 mm. 25r. George Hackl (Germany) (single luge), 1994	4·50	5·00

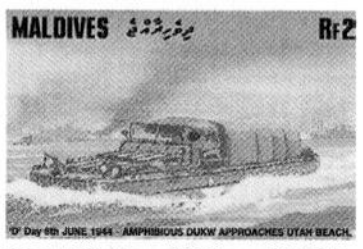

304 U.S. Amphibious DUKW

1994. 50th Anniv of D-Day. Multicoloured.

2118	2r. Type **304**	60	30
2119	4r. Tank landing craft unloading at Sword Beach	1·00	60
2120	18r. Infantry landing craft at Omaha Beach	4·00	4·75
MS2121	105×76 mm. 25r. Landing craft with Canadian commandos	5·50	6·00

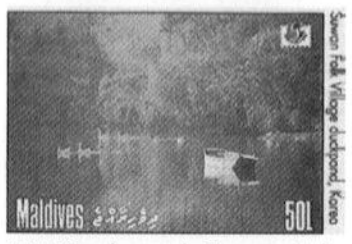

305 Duckpond, Suwan Folk Village

1994. "Philakorea '94" International Stamp Exn, Seoul. Multicoloured.

2122	50l. Type **305**	50	30
2123	3r. Pear-shaped bottle (vert)	60	70
2124	3r. Vase with dragon decoration (vert)	60	70
2125	3r. Vase with repaired lip (vert)	60	70
2126	3r. Stoneware vase with floral decoration (vert)	60	70
2127	3r. Celadon-glazed vase (vert)	60	70
2128	3r. Unglazed stone vase (vert)	60	70
2129	3r. Ritual water sprinkler (vert)	60	70
2130	3r. Long-necked celadon-glazed vase (vert)	60	70
2131	3r.50 Yongduson Park	70	75
2132	20r. Ploughing with ox, Hahoe	3·50	4·50
MS2133	70×102 mm. 25r. "Hunting" (detail from eight-panel painted screen) (vert)	4·50	5·50

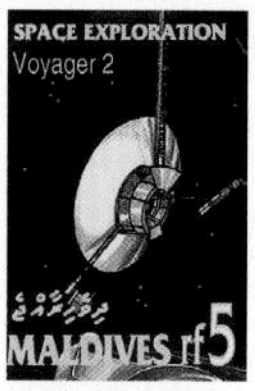

306 U.S. "Voyager 2" Satellite

1994. Space Exploration. Multicoloured.

2134	5r. Type **306**	1·50	1·25
2135	5r. Russian "Sputnik" satellite	1·50	1·25
2136	5r. "Apollo-Soyuz" mission	1·50	1·25
2137	5r. "Apollo 10" on parachutes	1·50	1·25
2138	5r. "Apollo 11" mission flag	1·50	1·25
2139	5r. Hubble space telescope	1·50	1·25
2140	5r. Edwin "Buzz" Aldrin (astronaut)	1·50	1·25
2141	5r. RCA lunar camera	1·50	1·25
2142	5r. Lunar Rover (space buggy)	1·50	1·25
2143	5r. Jim Irwin (astronaut)	1·50	1·25
2144	5r. "Apollo 12" lunar module	1·50	1·25
2145	5r. Astronaut holding equipment	1·50	1·25
MS2146	Two sheets. (a) 70×100 mm. 25r. David Scott (astronaut) in open hatch of "Apollo 9". (b) 100×70 mm. 25r. Alan Shepherd Jr. (astronaut) (horiz) Set of 2 sheets	13·00	12·00

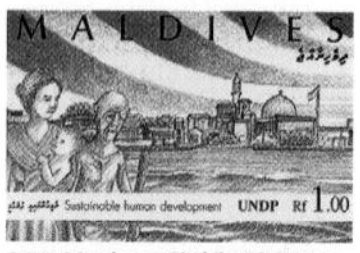

307 Mother, Child, Old Man and Town Skyline

1994. United Nations Development Programme. Multicoloured.

2147	1r. Type **307**	25	10
2148	8r. Fisherman with son and island	1·60	2·25

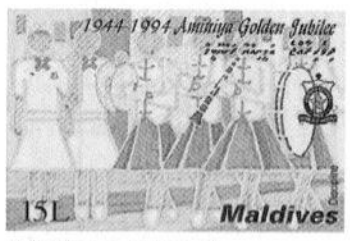

308 School Band

1994. 50th Anniv of Aminiya School. Children's Paintings. Multicoloured.

2149	15l. Type **308**	15	10
2150	50l. Classroom	25	15
2151	1r. School emblem and hand holding book (vert)	35	15
2152	8r. School girls holding books (vert)	2·00	2·25
2153	10r. Sporting activities	2·00	2·25
2154	11r. School girls holding crown (vert)	2·00	2·75
2155	13r. Science lesson	2·25	2·75

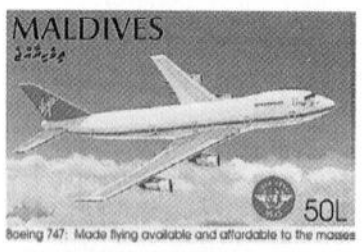

309 Boeing 747

1994. 50th Anniv of I.C.A.O. Multicoloured.

2156	50l. Type **309**	65	25
2157	1r. Hawker Siddeley ("de Havilland") Comet 4	90	25
2158	2r. Male International Airport	1·40	55
2159	3r. Lockheed L.1649 Super Star	1·50	85
2160	8r. European Airbus	2·50	2·75
2161	10r. Dornier Do-228	2·50	2·75
MS2162	100×70 mm. 25r. Concorde	5·00	6·00

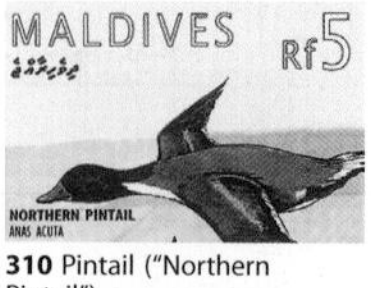

310 Pintail ("Northern Pintail")

1995. Ducks. Multicoloured.

2163	5r. Type **310**	90	1·00
2164	5r. Comb duck	90	1·00
2165	5r. Ruddy shelduck	90	1·00
2166	5r. Garganey	90	1·00
2167	5r. Indian whistling duck ("Lesser Whistling Duck")	90	1·00
2168	5r. Green-winged teal	90	1·00
2169	5r. Fulvous whistling duck	90	1·00
2170	5r. Common shoveler ("Northern Shoveler")	90	1·00

2171	5r. Cotton teal ("Cotton Pygmy Goose")	90	1·00
2172	6r.50+50l. Common pochard ("Pochard") (vert)	90	1·00
2173	6r.50+50l. Mallard (vert)	90	1·00
2174	6r.50+50l. European wigeon ("Wigeon") (vert)	90	1·00
2175	6r.50+50l. Common shoveler ("Northern Shoveler") (vert)	90	1·00
2176	6r.50+50l. Pintail ("Northern Pintail") (vert)	90	1·00
2177	6r.50+50l. Garganey (vert)	90	1·00
2178	6r.50+50l. Tufted duck (vert)	90	1·00
2179	6r.50+50l. Red-crested pochard ("Ferruginous Duck") (vert)	90	1·00
2180	6r.50+50l. Ferruginous duck ("Red-crested Pochard") (vert)	90	1·00
MS2181	Two sheets. (a) 100×71 mm. 25r. Spotbill duck ("Garganey"). (b) 73×100 mm. 25r. Cotton teal ("Cotton Pygmy Goose") (vert) Set of 2 sheets	7·50	8·50

Nos. 2163/71 and 2172/80 were printed together, *se-tenant*, forming composite designs.

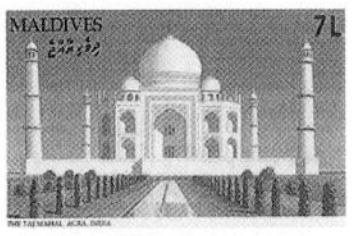

311 Taj Mahal, India

1995. Famous Monuments of the World. Multicoloured.

2182	7l. Type **311**	50	25
2183	10l. Washington Monument, U.S.A.	10	10
2184	15l. Mount Rushmore, U.S.A.	10	10
2185	25l. Arc de Triomphe, Paris (vert)	10	10
2186	50l. Sphinx, Egypt (vert)	50	20
2187	5r. El Castillo, Toltec pyramid, Yucatan	85	1·00
2188	8r. Toltec statue, Tula, Mexico (vert)	1·25	2·00
2189	12r. Victory Column, Berlin (vert)	1·60	2·50
MS2190	Two sheets, each 112×85 mm. (a) 25r. Easter Island statue (42×56 mm). (b) 25r. Stonehenge, Wiltshire (85×28 mm) Set of 2 sheets	7·50	8·50

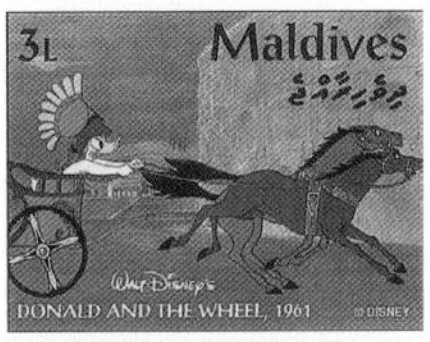

312 Donald Duck driving Chariot

1995. History of Wheeled Transport. Scenes from Disney cartoon film "Donald and the Wheel". Multicoloured.

2191	3l. Type **312**	10	10
2192	4l. Donald with log	10	10
2193	5l. Donald driving Stephenson's "Rocket"	10	10
2194	10l. Donald pondering over circle (vert)	10	10
2195	20l. Donald in crashed car (vert)	10	10
2196	25l. Donald listening to early gramophone	10	10
2197	5r. Donald on mammoth	1·25	1·25
2198	20r. Donald pushing early car	3·75	4·75

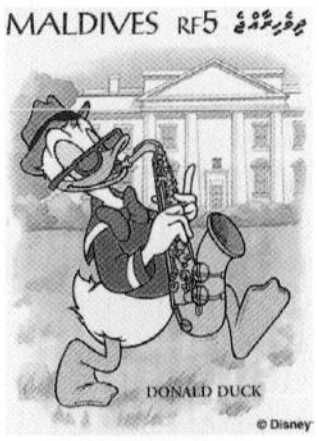

313 Donald Duck playing Saxophone

1995. 60th Birthday of Donald Duck. Walt Disney cartoon characters. Multicoloured.

2199	5r. Type **313**	90	90
2200	5r. Moby Duck playing fiddle	90	90
2201	5r. Feathry Duck with banjo and drum	90	90
2202	5r. Daisy Duck playing harp	90	90
2203	5r. Gladstone Gander with clarinet	90	90
2204	5r. Huey, Dewey and Louie with bassoon	90	90
2205	5r. Gus Goose playing flute	90	90
2206	5r. Prof. Ludwig von Drake playing trombone	90	90
2207	5r. Daisy picking flowers	90	90
2208	5r. Donald with backpack	90	90
2209	5r. Grandma Duck with kitten	90	90
2210	5r. Gus Goose and pie	90	90
2211	5r. Gyro Gearloose in space	90	90
2212	5r. Huey, Dewey and Louie photographing porcupine	90	90
2213	5r. Prof. Ludwig von Drake	90	90
2214	5r. Scrooge McDuck with money	90	90
MS2215	Four sheets. (a) 108×130 mm. 25r. Donald playing banjo. (b) 133×108 mm. 25r. Donald posing for photo. (c) 108×130 mm. 25r. Donald conducting (horiz). (d) 102×121 mm. 25r. Huey, Dewey and Louie (horiz) Set of 4 sheets	14·00	15·00

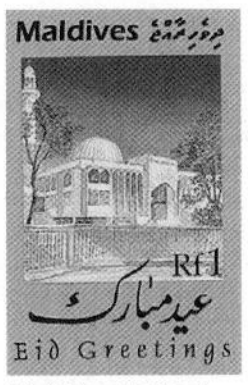

314 Islamic Centre, Male

1995. Eid Greetings. Multicoloured.

2216	1r. Type **314**	15	15
2217	1r. Rose	15	15
2218	8r. Orchid	1·50	1·50
2219	10r. Orchid (different)	1·50	1·50

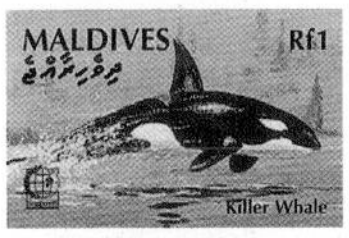

315 Killer Whale

1995. "Singapore '95" International Stamp Exhibition (1st issue). Whales, Dolphins and Porpoises. Multicoloured.

2220	1r. Type **315**	40	30
2221	2r. Bottlenose dolphins	45	35
2222	3r. Right whale	60	70
2223	3r. Pair of killer whales	60	70
2224	3r. Humpback whale	60	70
2225	3r. Pair of belugas	60	70
2226	3r. Narwhal	60	70
2227	3r. Head of blue whale	60	70
2228	3r. Bowhead whale	60	70
2229	3r. Head of fin whale	60	70
2230	3r. Pair of pilot whales	60	70
2231	3r. Grey whale	60	70
2232	3r. Sperm whale	60	70
2233	3r. Pair of goosebeaked whales	60	70
2234	3r. Hourglass dolphin	60	70
2235	3r. Bottlenose dolphin (different)	60	70
2236	3r. Dusky dolphin	60	70
2237	3r. Spectacled porpoise	60	70
2238	3r. Fraser's dolphin	60	70
2239	3r. Camerson's dolphin	60	70
2240	3r. Pair of spinner dolphins	60	70
2241	3r. Pair of Dalls dolphins	60	70
2242	3r. Spotted dolphin	60	70
2243	3r. Indus River dolphin	60	70
2244	3r. Hector's dolphin	60	70
2245	3r. Amazon River dolphin	60	70
2246	8r. Humpback whale and calf	1·25	1·50
2247	10r. Common dolphin	1·40	1·60
MS2248	Two sheets, each 100×70 mm. (a) 25r. Sperm whale (different). (b) 25r. Pair of hourglass dolphins Set of 2 sheets	9·00	9·00

See also Nos. 2302/10.

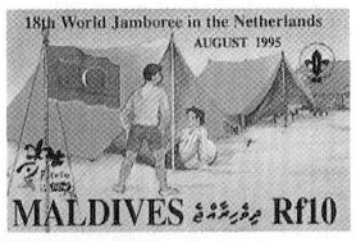

316 Scout Camp and National Flag

1995. 18th World Scout Jamboree, Netherlands. Multicoloured.

2249	10r. Type **316**	1·75	2·00
2250	12r. Campfire cooking	1·90	2·25
2251	15r. Scouts erecting tent	2·00	2·40
MS2252	102×72 mm. 25r. Scouts around camp fire (vert)	3·50	4·00

Nos. 2249/51 were printed together, *se-tenant*, forming a composite design.

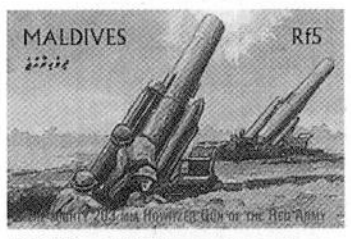

317 Soviet Heavy Howitzer Battery

1995. 50th Anniv of End of Second World War in Europe. Multicoloured.

2253	5r. Type **317**	95	85
2254	5r. Ruins of Berchtesgaden	95	85
2255	5r. U.S. Boeing B-17 Flying Fortress dropping food over the Netherlands	95	85
2256	5r. Soviet Ilyushin Il-1 bomber	95	85
2257	5r. Liberation of Belsen	95	85
2258	5r. Supermarine Spitfire and V-1 flying bomb	95	85
2259	5r. U.S. tanks advancing through Cologne	95	85
2260	5r. Reichstag in ruins	95	85
MS2261	107×76 mm. 25r. Soviet and U.S. troops celebrating	3·50	4·00

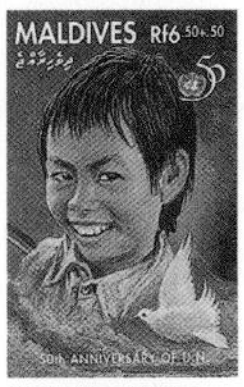

318 Asian Child and Dove

1995. 50th Anniv of United Nations (1st issue). Multicoloured.

2262	6r.50+50l. Type **318**	90	1·25
2263	8r. Globe and dove	1·00	1·40
2264	10r. African child and dove	1·10	1·50
MS2265	72×102 mm. 25r. United Nations emblem and dove	2·75	3·75

Nos. 2262/4 were printed together, *se-tenant*, forming a composite design.

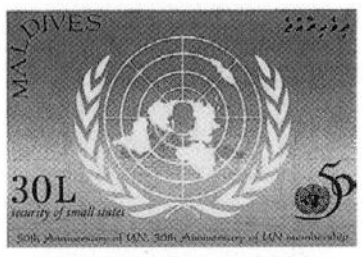

319 United Nations Emblem

1995. 50th Anniv of United Nations (2nd issue).

2266	**319**	30l. black, blue & grn	10	10
2267	-	8r. multicoloured	1·00	1·25
2268	-	11r. multicoloured	1·25	1·75
2269	-	13r. black, grey and red	1·60	2·25

DESIGNS: 8r. Symbolic women, flag and map; 11r. U.N. soldier and symbolic dove; 13r. Gun barrels, atomic explosion and bomb sight.

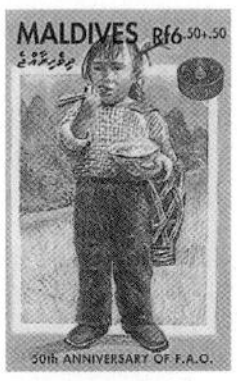

320 Asian Child eating Rice

1995. 50th Anniv of F.A.O. (1st issue). Multicoloured.

2270	6r.50+50l. Type **320**	1·00	1·25
2271	8r. F.A.O. emblem	1·00	1·25
2272	10r. African mother and child	1·00	1·25
MS2273	72×102 mm. 25r. African child and symbolic hand holding maize	5·00	6·00

See also Nos. 2311/12.

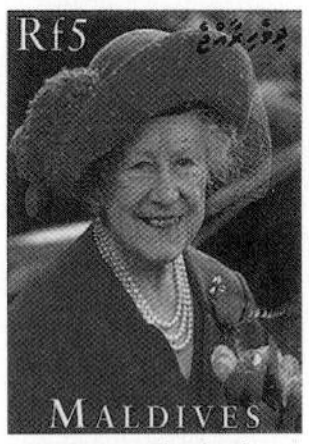

321 Queen Elizabeth the Queen Mother

1995. 95th Birthday of Queen Elizabeth the Queen Mother.

2274	**321**	5r. brown, lt brn & blk	1·00	1·10
2275	-	5r. multicoloured	1·00	1·10
2276	-	5r. multicoloured	1·00	1·10
2277	-	5r. multicoloured	1·00	1·10
MS2278		125×100 mm. 25r. multicoloured	6·00	6·00

DESIGNS: No. 2275, Without hat; 2276, At desk (oil painting); 2277, Queen Elizabeth the Queen Mother; **MS**2278, Wearing lilac hat and dress.

1995. 50th Anniv of End of Second World War in the Pacific. As T **317**. Multicoloured.

2279	6r.50+50l. Grumman F6F-3 Hellcat aircraft	1·50	1·50
2280	6r.50+50l. F4-U1 fighter aircraft attacking beach	1·50	1·50
2281	6r.50+50l. Douglas SBD Dauntless aircraft	1·50	1·50
2282	6r.50+50l. American troops in landing craft, Guadalcanal	1·50	1·50
2283	6r.50+50l. U.S. marines in Alligator tanks	1·50	1·50
2284	6r.50+50l. U.S. landing ship	1·50	1·50
MS2285	106×74 mm. 25r. F4-U1 fighter aircraft	4·00	4·50

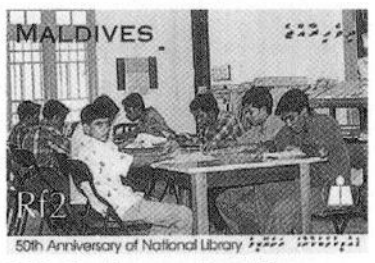

322 Students using Library

1995. 50th Anniv of National Library. Multicoloured.

2286	2r. Type **322**	25	25
2287	8r. Students using library (different)	1·00	1·50
MS2288	105×75 mm. 10r. Library entrance (100×70 mm). Imperf	1·40	1·60

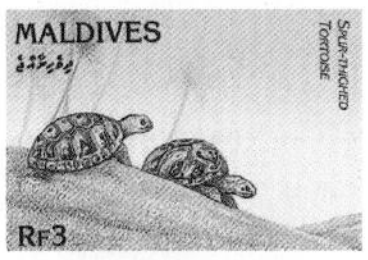

323 Spur-thighed Tortoise

1995. Turtles and Tortoises. Multicoloured.

2289	3r. Type **323**	70	80
2290	3r. Aldabra turtle	70	80
2291	3r. Loggerhead turtle	70	80
2292	3r. Olive Ridley turtle	70	80
2293	3r. Leatherback turtle	70	80
2294	3r. Green turtle	70	80
2295	3r. Atlantic Ridley turtle	70	80
2296	3r. Hawksbill turtle	70	80
2297	10r. Hawksbill turtle on beach	1·50	1·75
2298	10r. Pair of hawksbill turtles	1·50	1·75
2299	10r. Hawksbill turtle climbing out of water	1·50	1·75
2300	10r. Hawksbill turtle swimming	1·50	1·75
MS2301	100×70 mm. 25r. Green turtle	3·75	4·50

Nos. 2289/96 were printed together, *se-tenant*, forming a composite design.

Nos. 2297/2300 include the W.W.F. Panda emblem.

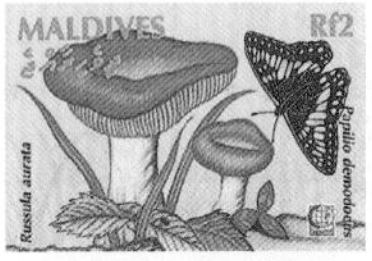

324 "Russula aurata" (fungi) and "Papilio demodocus" (butterfly)

1995. "Singapore '95" International Stamp Exhibition. Butterflies and Fungi. Multicoloured.

2302	2r. Type **324**	75	75
2303	2r. "Lepista saeva" and "Kallimoides rumia"	75	75
2304	2r. "Lepista nuda" and "Hypolimnas salmacis"	75	75
2305	2r. "Xerocomus subtomentosus" ("Boletus subtomentosus" and "Precis octavia")	75	75
2306	5r. "Gyroporus castaneus" and "Hypolimnas salmacis"	1·10	1·10
2307	8r. "Gomphidius glutinosus" and "Papilio dardanus"	1·25	1·25
2308	10r. "Russula olivacea" and "Precis octavia"	1·40	1·40
2309	12r. "Boletus edulis" and "Prepona praeneste"	1·40	1·40
MS2310	Two sheets, each 105×76 mm. (a) 25r. "Amanita muscaria" and "Kallimoides rumia" (vert). (b) 25r. "Boletus rhodoxanthus" and "Hypolimnas salmacis" (vert) Set of 2 sheets	8·00	8·00

Nos. 2302/5 and 2306/9 respectively were printed together, *se-tenant*, forming composite designs.

No. 2304 is inscribed "Lapista" in error.

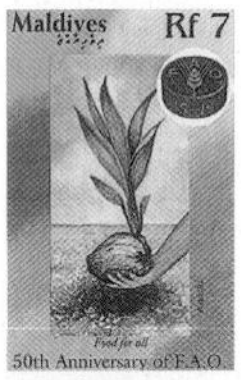

325 Planting Kaashi

1995. 50th Anniv of F.A.O. (2nd issue). Multicoloured.

2311	7r. Type **325**	90	1·10
2312	8r. Fishing boat	1·10	1·25

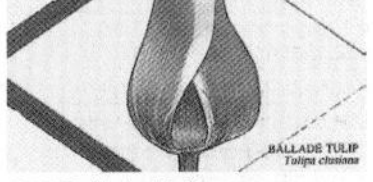

326 Ballade Tulip

1995. Flowers. Multicoloured.

2313	1r. Type **326**	20	15
2314	3r. White mallow	50	50
2315	5r. Regale trumpet lily	1·00	1·00
2316	5r. "Dendrobium Waipahu Beauty"	1·00	1·00
2317	5r. "Brassocattleya Jean Murray"	1·00	1·00
2318	5r. "Cymbidium Fort George"	1·00	1·00
2319	5r. "Paphiopedilum malipoense"	1·00	1·00
2320	5r. "Cycnoches chlorochilon"	1·00	1·00
2321	5r. "Rhyncholaelia digbgana"	1·00	1·00
2322	5r. "Lycaste deppei"	1·00	1·00
2323	5r. "Masdevallia constricta"	1·00	1·00
2324	5r. "Paphiopedilum Clair de Lune"	1·00	1·00
2325	7r. "Lilactime dahlia"	1·25	1·25
2326	8r. Blue ideal iris	1·25	1·25
2327	10r. Red crown imperial	1·40	1·40
MS2328	Two sheets, each 106×76 mm. (a) 25r. "Encyclia cochleata" (vert). (b) 25r. "Psychopsis kramerina" (vert) Set of 2 sheets	8·00	9·50

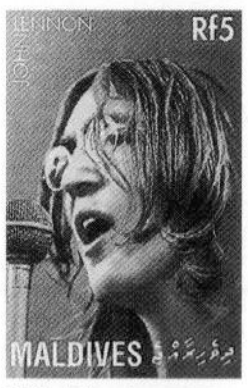
LENNON
Rf5
MALDIVES
327 John Lennon with Microphone

1995. 15th Death Anniv of John Lennon (musician). Multicoloured.

2329	5r. Type **327**	1·50	1·25
2330	5r. With glasses and moustache	1·50	1·25
2331	5r. With guitar	1·50	1·25
2332	5r. With guitar and wearing glasses	1·50	1·25
2333	5r. Wearing sun glasses and red jacket	1·50	1·25
2334	5r. Wearing headphones	1·50	1·25
MS2335	88×117 mm. 2, 3, 8, 10r. Different portraits of John Lennon	5·50	5·50
MS2336	102×72 mm. 25r. John Lennon performing	5·50	5·50

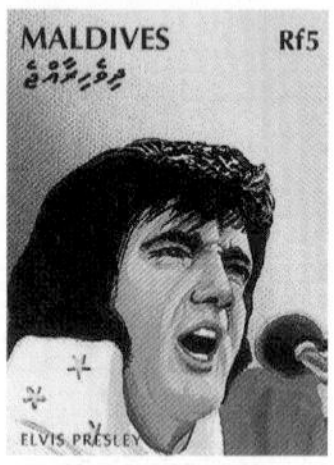
MALDIVES
Rf5
ELVIS PRESLEY
328 Elvis Presley with Microphone

1995. 60th Birth Anniv of Elvis Presley (entertainer). Multicoloured.

2337	5r. Type **328**	5·50	5·50
2338	5r. Wearing red jacket	90	80
2339	5r. Wearing blue jacket	90	80
2340	5r. With microphone and wearing blue jacket	90	80
2341	5r. In army uniform	90	80
2342	5r. Wearing yellow bow tie	90	80
2343	5r. In yellow shirt	90	80
2344	5r. In light blue shirt	90	80
2345	5r. Wearing red and white high-collared jacket	90	80
MS2346	80×110 mm. 25r. Elvis Presley (horiz)	4·25	4·50

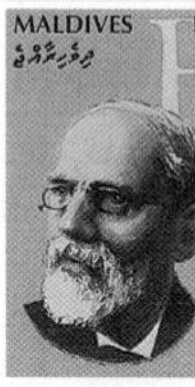
MALDIVES
Rf5
329 Johannes van der Waals (1919 Physics)

1995. Cent of Nobel Prize Trust Fund. Multicoloured.

2347-2355	5r.×9 (Type **329**; Charles Guillaume (1920 Physics); Sir James Chadwick (1935 Physics); Willem Einthoven (1924 Medicine); Henrik Dam (1943 Medicine); Sir Alexander Fleming (1945 Medicine); Hermann Muller (1946 Medicine); Rodney Porter (1972 Medicine); Werner Arber (1978 Medicine))	6·25	
2356-2664	5r.×9 (Niels Bohr (1922 Physics); Ben Mottelson (1975 Physics); Patrick White (1973 Literature); Elias Canetti (1981 Literature); Theodor Kocher (1909 Medicine); August Krogh (1920 Medicine); William Murphy (1934 Medicine); John Northrop (1946 Chemistry); Luis Leloir (1970 Chemistry))	6·25	
2365-2373	5r.×9 (Dag Hammarskjold (1961 Peace); Alva Myrdal (1982 Peace); Archbishop Desmond Tutu (1984 Peace); Rudolf Eucken (1908 Literature); Aleksandr Solzhenitsyn (1970 Literature); Gabriel Marquez (1982 Literature); Chen Yang (1957 Physics); Karl Muller (1987 Physics); Melvin Schwartz (1988 Physics))	6·25	
2374-2382	5r.×9 (Robert Millikan (1923 Physics); Louis de Broglie (1929 Physics); Ernest Walton (1951 Physics); Richard Willstatter (1915 Chemistry); Lars Onsager (1968 Chemistry); Gerhard Herzberg (1971 Chemistry); William B. Yeats (1923 Literature); George Bernard Shaw (1925 Literature); Eugene O'Neill (1936 Literature))	6·25	
2383-2391	5r.×9 (Bernardo Houssay (1947 Medicine); Paul Muller (1948 Medicine); Walter Hess (1949 Medicine); Sir MacFarlane Burnet (1960 Medicine); Baruch Blumberg (1976 Medicine); Daniel Nathans (1978 Medicine); Glenn Seaborg (1951 Chemistry); Ilya Prigogine (1977 Chemistry); Kenichi Fukui (1981 Chemistry))	6·25	
2392-2400	5r.×9 (Carl Spitteler (1919 Literature); Henri Bergson (1927 Literature); Johannes Jensen (1944 Literature); Antoine-Henri Becquerel (1903 Physics); Sir William H. Bragg (1915 Physics); Sir William L. Bragg (1915 Physics); Frederik Bajer (1908 Peace); Leon Bourgeois (1920 Peace); Karl Branting (1921 Peace))	6·25	
MS2401	Six sheets. (a) 80×110 mm. 25r. Konrad bloch (1964 Medicine). (b) 80×110 mm. 25r. Samuel Beckett (1969 Literature). (c) 80×110 mm. 25r. Otto Wallach (1910 Chemistry). (d) 110×80 mm. 25r. Hideki Yukawa (1949 Physics). (e) 110×80 mm. 25r. Eisaku Sato (1974 Peace). (f) 110×80 mm. 25r. Robert Koch (1905 Medicine) Set of 6 sheets	16·00	18·00

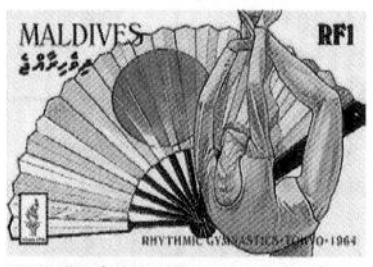
MALDIVES
RF1
330 Rythmic Gymnast and Japanese Fan

1996. Olympic Games, Atlanta (1st issue). Multicoloured.

2402	1r. Type **330**	25	10
2403	3r. Archer and Moscow Olympics logo	50	35
2404	5r. Diver and Swedish flag	1·00	1·00
2405	5r. Canadian Maple Leaf	1·00	1·00
2406	5r. Shot putting (decathlon)	1·00	1·00
2407	5r. Moscow Olympic medal and ribbon	1·00	1·00
2408	5r. Fencer	1·00	1·00
2409	5r. Gold medal	1·00	1·00
2410	5r. Equestrian competitor	1·00	1·00
2411	5r. Sydney Opera House	1·00	1·00
2412	5r. Athlete on starting blocks	1·00	1·00
2413	5r. South Korean flag	1·00	1·00
2414	7r. High jumper and Tower Bridge, London	1·10	1·10
2415	10r. Athlete on starting blocks and Brandenburg Gate, Germany	1·40	1·60
2416	12r. Hurdler and Amsterdam Olympic logo	1·60	1·90
MS2417	Two sheets, each 113×80 mm. (a) 25r. Red Olympic Flame (vert). (b) 25r. Multicoloured Olympic Flame (vert) Set of 2 sheets	8·00	9·00

See also Nos. 2469/87.

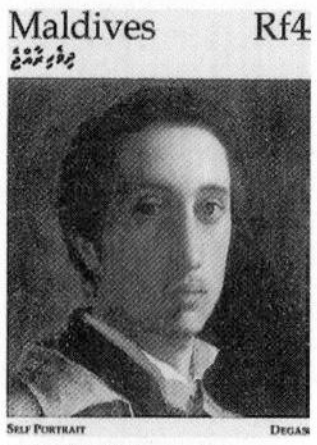
Maldives
Rf4
SELF PORTRAIT
DEGAS
331 "Self Portrait" (Degas)

1996. 125th Anniv of Metropolitan Museum of Art, New York. Multicoloured.

2418-2425	4r.×8 ("Self-Portrait" (Degas); "Andromache and Astyanax" (Prud'hon); "Rene Grenier" (Toulouse-Lautrec); "The Banks of the Bievre near Bicetre" (Rousseau); "The Repast of the Lion" (Rousseau); "Portrait of Yves Gobillard-Morisot" (Degas); "Sunflowers" (Van Gogh); "The Singer in Green" (Degas))	7·00	
2426-2433	4r.×8 ("Still Life" (Fantin-Latour); "Portrait of a Lady in Grey" (Degas); "Apples and Grapes" (Monet); "The Englishman" (Toulouse-Lautrec); "Cypresses" (Van Gogh); "Flowers in a Chinese Vase" (Redon); "The Gardener" (Seurat); "Large Sunflowers I" (Nolde))	7·00	
2434-2441	4r.×8 (All by Manet: "The Spanish Singer"; "Young Man in Costume of Majo"; "Mademoiselle Victorine"; "Boating"; "Peonies"; "Woman with a Parrot"; "George Moore"; "The Monet Family in their Garden")	7·00	
2442-2449	4r.×8 ("Goldfish" (Matisse); "Spanish Woman: Harmony in Blue" (Matisse); "Nasturtiums and the "Dance" II" (Matisse); "The House behind Trees" (Braque); "Mada Primavesi" (Klimt); "Head of a Woman" (Picasso); "Woman in White" (Picasso); "Harlequin" (Picasso))	7·00	
MS2450	Four sheets, each 95×70 mm, containing horiz designs, 81×53 mm. (a) 25r. "Northeaster" (Homer). (b) 25r. "The Fortune Teller" (De La Tour). (c) 25r. "Santo (Sanzio), Ritratto de Andrea Navagero e Agostino Beazzano" (Raphael). (d) 25r. "Portrait of a Woman" (Rubens) Set of 4 sheets	17·00	20·00

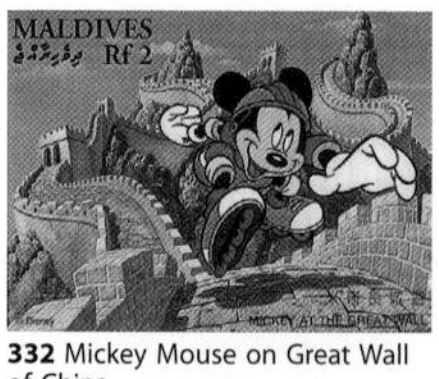
MALDIVES
Rf 2
332 Mickey Mouse on Great Wall of China

1996. "CHINA '96" 9th Asian International Stamp Exhibition, Peking. Walt Disney cartoon characters in China. Multicoloured.

2451	2r. Type **332**	80	80
2452	2r. Pluto with temple guardian	80	80
2453	2r. Minnie Mouse with pandas	80	80
2454	2r. Mickey windsurfing near junks	80	80
2455	2r. Goofy cleaning grotto statue	80	80
2456	2r. Donald and Daisy Duck at Marble Boat	80	80
2457	2r. Mickey with terracotta warriors	80	80
2458	2r. Goofy with geese and masks	80	80
2459	2r. Donald and Goofy on traditional fishing boat	80	80
2460	2r. Mickey and Minnie in dragon boat	80	80
2461	2r. Donald at Peking opera	80	80
2462	2r. Mickey and Minnie in Chinese garden	80	80
2463	3r. Mickey and Minnie at the Ice Pagoda (vert)	1·00	1·00
2464	3r. Donald and Mickey flying Chinese kites (vert)	1·00	1·00
2465	3r. Goofy playing anyiwu (vert)	1·00	1·00
2466	3r. Paper cutouts of Mickey and Goofy (vert)	1·00	1·00
2467	3r. Donald and Mickey in dragon dance (vert)	1·00	1·00
MS2468	Three sheets. (a) 108×133 mm. 5r. Mickey pointing. (b) 133×108 mm. 7r. Mickey and Minnie watching Moon. (c) 133×108 mm. 8r. Donald using chopsticks Set of 3 sheets	5·50	6·00

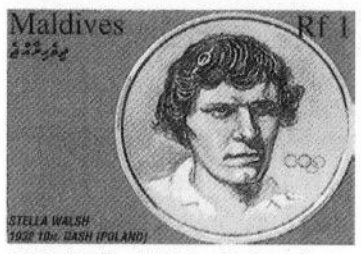
Maldives
Rf 1
STELLA WALSH
333 Stella Walsh (Poland) (100 m sprint, 1932) on Medal

1996. Olympic Games, Atlanta (2nd issue). Previous Gold Medal Winners. Multicoloured.

2469	1r. Type **333**	25	15
2470	3r. Emile Zatopek (Czechoslovakia) (10,000 m running, 1952) and Olympic torch (vert)	50	35
2471	5r. Yanko Rousseu (Bulgaria) (lightweight, 1980) (vert)	85	85
2472	5r. Peter Baczako (Hungary) (middle heavyweight, 1980) (vert)	85	85
2473	5r. Leonid Taranenko (Russia) (heavyweight, 1980) (vert)	85	85
2474	5r. Aleksandr Kurlovich (Russia) (heavyweight, 1988) (vert)	85	85
2475	5r. Assen Zlateu (Bulgaria) (middleweight, 1980) (vert)	85	85
2476	5r. Zeng Guoqiang (China) (flyweight, 1984) (vert)	85	85
2477	5r. Yurik Vardanyan (Russia) (heavyweight, 1980) (vert)	85	85
2478	5r. Sultan Rakhmanov (Russia) (super heavyweight, 1980) (vert)	85	85
2479	5r. Vassily Alexeev (Russia) (super heavyweight, 1972) (vert)	85	85
2480	5r. Ethel Catherwood (Canada) (high jump, 1928)	85	85
2481	5r. Mildred Didrikson (U.S.A.) (javelin, 1932)	85	85
2482	5r. Francina Blankers-Koen (Netherlands) (80 m hurdles, 1948)	85	85
2483	5r. Tamara Press (Russia) (shot put, 1960)	85	85
2484	5r. Lia Manoliu (Rumania) (discus, 1968)	85	85
2485	5r. Rosa Mota (Portugal) (marathon, 1988)	85	85
2486	10r. Olga Fikotova (Czechoslovakia) (discus, 1956) on medal	1·40	1·60
2487	12r. Joan Benoit (U.S.A.) (marathon, 1984) on medal	1·60	1·90
MS2488	Two sheets. (a) 76×106 mm. 25r. Naeem Suleymanoglu (Turkey) (weightlifting, 1988) (vert). (b) 105×75 mm. 25r. Irena Szewinska (Poland) (400 m running, 1976) on medal Set of 2 sheets	8·00	9·00

No. 2469 identifies the event as 10 metres in error.

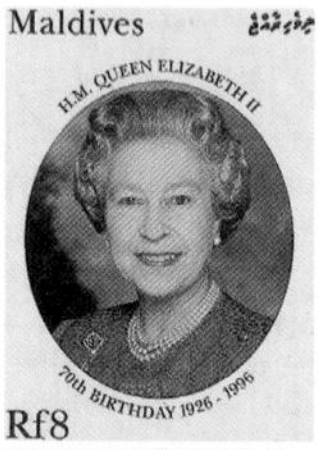
Maldives
H.M. QUEEN ELIZABETH II
70th BIRTHDAY 1926-1996
Rf8
334 Queen Elizabeth II

1996. 70th Birthday of Queen Elizabeth II. Multicoloured.

2489	8r. Type **334**	1·75	1·75
2490	8r. Wearing hat	1·75	1·75
2491	8r. At desk	1·75	1·75
MS2492	125×103 mm. 25r. Queen Elizabeth and Queen Mother on Buckingham Palace balcony	6·50	6·00

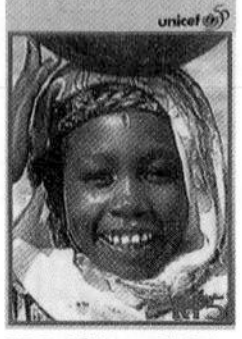
MALDIVES
unicef
335 African Child

1996. 50th Anniv of UNICEF. Multicoloured.

2493	5r. Type **335**	75	55
2494	7r. European girl	1·00	1·25
2495	7r. Maldivian boy	1·00	1·25
2496	10r. Asian girl	1·40	1·50
MS2497	114×74 mm. 25r. Baby with toy	3·50	4·50

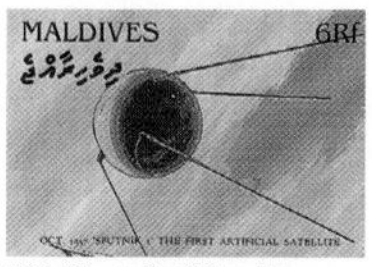
MALDIVES
6Rf
336 "Sputnik 1" Satellite

1996. Space Exploration. Multicoloured.

2498	6r. Type **336**	1·10	1·10
2499	6r. "Apollo 11" command module	1·10	1·10
2500	6r. "Skylab"	1·10	1·10
2501	6r. Astronaut Edward White walking in space	1·10	1·10
2502	6r. "Mariner 9"	1·10	1·10
2503	6r. "Apollo" and "Soyuz" docking	1·10	1·10
MS2504	104×74 mm. 25r. Launch of "Apollo 8" (vert)	4·50	5·00

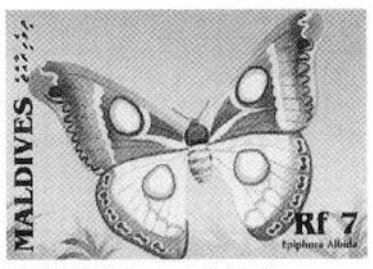

337 "Epiphora albida"

1996. Butterflies. Multicoloured.

2505	7r. Type **337**	1·25	1·25
2506	7r. "Satyrus dryas"	1·25	1·25
2507	7r. "Satyrus lena"	1·25	1·25
2508	7r. "Papilio tynderaeus"	1·25	1·25
2509	7r. "Urota suraka"	1·25	1·25
2510	7r. "Satyrus nercis"	1·25	1·25
2511	7r. "Papilio troilus" (vert)	1·25	1·25
2512	7r. "Papilio cresphontes" (vert)	1·25	1·25
2513	7r. Lime swallowtail caterpillar (vert)	1·25	1·25
2514	7r. "Cynthia virginiensis" (vert)	1·25	1·25
2515	7r. Monarch caterpillar (vert)	1·25	1·25
2516	7r. "Danaus plexippus" (vert)	1·25	1·25
2517	7r. Monarch caterpillar and pupa (vert)	1·25	1·25
2518	7r. "Chlosyne harrisii" (vert)	1·25	1·25
2519	7r. "Cymothoe coccinata" (vert)	1·25	1·25
2520	7r. "Morpho rhetenor" (vert)	1·25	1·25
2521	7r. "Callicore lidwina" (vert)	1·25	1·25
2522	7r. "Heliconius erato reducti-macula" (vert)	1·25	1·25
MS2523	Two sheets, each 106×76 mm. (a) 25r. "Heliconius charitonius" (vert). (b) 25r. "Heliconius cydno" (vert) Set of 2 sheets	8·50	9·00

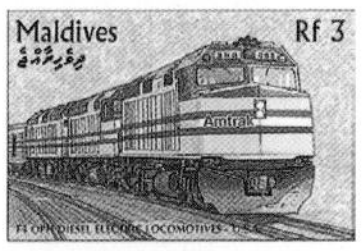

338 Amtrak F40H Diesel-electric Locomotive, U.S.A.

1996. Trains of the World. Multicoloured.

2524	3r. Type **338**	80	80
2525	3r. Stephenson's "Experiment"	80	80
2526	3r. Indian-Pacific Intercontinental, Australia	80	80
2527	3r. Stephenson's Killingworth type steam locomotive, 1815	80	80
2528	3r. George Stephenson	80	80
2529	3r. Stephenson's "Rocket", 1829	80	80
2530	3r. High Speed Train 125, Great Britain	80	80
2531	3r. First rail passenger coach "Experiment", 1825	80	80
2532	3r. Union Pacific Class U25B diesel locomotive (inscr "Tofac"), U.S.A.	80	80
2533	3r. Southern Pacific's "Daylight" express, 1952, U.S.A.	80	80
2534	3r. Timothy Hackworth's "Sans Pareil", 1829	80	80
2535	3r. Chicago and North Western diesel locomotive, U.S.A.	80	80
2536	3r. Richard Trevithick's "Pen-y-Darren" locomotive, 1804	80	80
2537	3r. Isambard Kingdom Brunel	80	80
2538	3r. Great Western locomotive, 1838	80	80
2539	3r. Vistadome observation car, Canada	80	80
2540	3r. Mohawk and Hudson Railroad "Experiment", 1832	80	80
2541	3r. ICE high speed train, Germany	80	80
2542	3r. Electric container locomotive, Germany	80	80
2543	3r. John Blenkinsop's rack locomotive, 1811	80	80
2544	3r. Diesel-electric locomotive, Western Australia	80	80
2545	3r. Timothy Hackworth's "Royal George", 1827	80	80
2546	3r. Robert Stephenson	80	80
2547	3r. Trevithick's "Newcastle"	80	80
2548	3r. Deltic diesel-electric locomotive, Great Britain	80	80
2549	3r. Stockton and Darlington Railway locomotive No. 5 "Stockton", 1826	80	80
2550	3r. Channel Tunnel "Le Shuttle" train	80	80
MS2551	Three sheets, each 96×91 mm. (a) 25r. Peter Cooper's "Tom Thumb", 1829. (b) 25r. John Jarvis's "De Witt Clinton", 1831. (c) 25r. William Hudson's "The General", 1855 Set of 3 sheets	13·00	13·00

No. 2524 is inscribed "F4 OPH" in error.

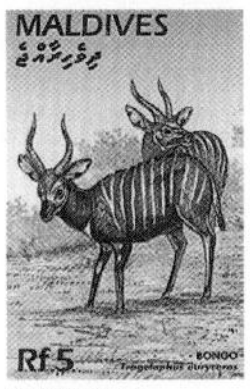

339 Bongo

1996. Wildlife of the World. Multicoloured.

2552	5r. Type **339**	1·25	1·25
2553	5r. Bushbuck	1·25	1·25
2554	5r. Namaqua dove	1·25	1·25
2555	5r. Hoopoe	1·25	1·25
2556	5r. African fish eagle	1·25	1·25
2557	5r. Egyptian goose	1·25	1·25
2558	5r. Saddle-bill stork	1·25	1·25
2559	5r. Blue-breasted kingfisher	1·25	1·25
2560	5r. Yellow baboon	1·25	1·25
2561	5r. Banded duiker ("Zebra Duiker")	1·25	1·25
2562	5r. Yellow-backed duiker	1·25	1·25
2563	5r. Pygmy hippopotamus	1·25	1·25
2564	5r. Large-spotted genet	1·25	1·25
2565	5r. African spoonbill	1·25	1·25
2566	5r. White-faced whistling duck	1·25	1·25
2567	5r. Helmeted guineafowl	1·25	1·25
2568	7r. Cotton-headed tamarin (horiz)	1·50	1·50
2569	7r. European bison (horiz)	1·50	1·50
2570	7r. Tiger (horiz)	1·50	1·50
2571	7r. Western capercaillie (horiz)	1·50	1·50
2572	7r. Giant panda (horiz)	1·50	1·50
2573	7r. "Trogonoptera brookiana" (butterfly) (horiz)	1·50	1·50
2574	7r. American beaver (horiz)	1·50	1·50
2575	7r. "Leiopelma hamiltoni" (frog) (horiz)	1·50	1·50
2576	7r. Manatee (horiz)	1·50	1·50
MS2577	106×76 mm. 25r. Chimpanzee (horiz)	4·25	5·00

Nos. 2552/9, 2560/7 and 2568/76 respectively were printed together, *se-tenant*, with the backgrounds forming composite designs.

No. 2553 is inscribed "BUSHBACK" in error.

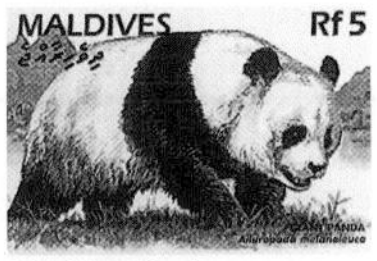

340 Giant Panda

1996. Endangered Species. Multicoloured.

2578	5r. Type **340**	1·25	1·25
2579	5r. Indian elephant	1·25	1·25
2580	5r. Arrow-poison frog	1·25	1·25
2581	5r. Mandrill	1·25	1·25
2582	5r. Snow leopard	1·25	1·25
2583	5r. California condor	1·25	1·25
2584	5r. Whale-headed stork ("Shoe-bill Stork")	1·25	1·25
2585	5r. Red-billed hornbill	1·25	1·25
2586	5r. Hippopotamus	1·25	1·25
2587	5r. Gorilla	1·25	1·25
2588	5r. Lion	1·25	1·25
2589	5r. South African crowned crane ("Gray Crowned Crane")	1·25	1·25
MS2590	Two sheets, each 110×80 mm. (a) 25r. Tiger (vert). (b) 25r. Leopard Set of 2 sheets	9·50	11·00

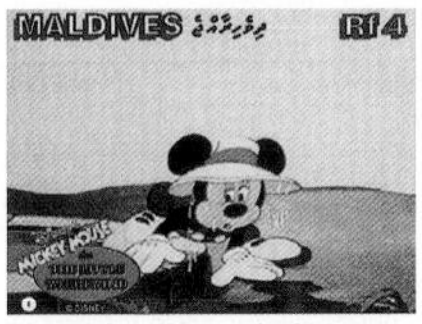

341 Mickey Mouse climbing out of Puddle

1996. Centenary of the Cinema. Cartoon Frames from "The Little Whirlwind" (Nos. 2591/2607) or "Pluto and the Flypaper" (Nos. 2608/24). Multicoloured.

2591	4r. Type **341**	1·25	1·25
2592	4r. Frame 2	1·25	1·25
2593	4r. Frame 3	1·25	1·25
2594	4r. Frame 4	1·25	1·25
2595	4r. Frame 5	1·25	1·25
2596	4r. Frame 6	1·25	1·25
2597	4r. Frame 7	1·25	1·25
2598	4r. Frame 8	1·25	1·25
2599	4r. Frame 9	1·25	1·25
2600	4r. Frame 10	1·25	1·25
2601	4r. Frame 11	1·25	1·25
2602	4r. Frame 12	1·25	1·25
2603	4r. Frame 13	1·25	1·25
2604	4r. Frame 14	1·25	1·25
2605	4r. Frame 15	1·25	1·25
2606	4r. Frame 16 (Mickey holding fish above head)	1·25	1·25
2607	4r. Frame 17 (Mickey throwing fish into pool)	1·25	1·25
2608	4r. Frame 1 (Pluto)	1·25	1·25
2609	4r. Frame 2	1·25	1·25
2610	4r. Frame 3	1·25	1·25
2611	4r. Frame 4	1·25	1·25
2612	4r. Frame 5	1·25	1·25
2613	4r. Frame 6	1·25	1·25
2614	4r. Frame 7	1·25	1·25
2615	4r. Frame 8	1·25	1·25
2616	4r. Frame 9	1·25	1·25
2617	4r. Frame 10	1·25	1·25
2618	4r. Frame 11	1·25	1·25
2619	4r. Frame 12	1·25	1·25
2620	4r. Frame 13	1·25	1·25
2621	4r. Frame 14	1·25	1·25
2622	4r. Frame 15	1·25	1·25
2623	4r. Frame 16	1·25	1·25
2624	4r. Frame 17	1·25	1·25
MS2625	Two sheets, 111×131 mm. (a) 25r. Frame 18 ("The Little Whirlwind"). (b) 25r. Frame 18 ("Pluto and the Flypaper") Set of 2 sheets	14·00	15·00

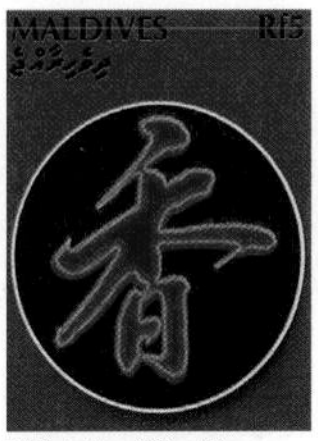

342 Letter "O" with Chinese Character

1997. "HONG KONG '97" International Stamp Exhibition. Multicoloured.

2626	5r. Letter "H" and Chinese couple	85	85
2627	5r. Type **342**	85	85
2628	5r. Letter "N" and Chinese dragon	85	85
2629	5r. Letter "G" and carnival dragon	85	85
2630	5r. Letter "K" and modern office block	85	85
2631	5r. Letter "O" and Chinese character (different)	85	85
2632	5r. Letter "N" and Chinese fan cases	85	85
2633	5r. Letter "G" and Chinese junk	85	85
MS2634	106×125 mm. 25r. "HONG KONG" as on Nos. 2626/33 (76×38 mm)	3·75	4·50

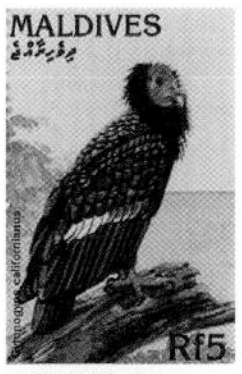

343 California Condor

1997. Birds of the World. Multicoloured.

2635	5r. Type **343**	1·00	1·00
2636	5r. Audouin's gull	1·00	1·00
2637	5r. Atlantic puffin	1·00	1·00
2638	5r. Resplendent quetzal	1·00	1·00
2639	5r. Puerto Rican amazon	1·00	1·00
2640	5r. Lesser bird of paradise	1·00	1·00
2641	5r. Japanese crested ibis	1·00	1·00
2642	5r. Mauritius kestrel	1·00	1·00
2643	5r. Kakapo	1·00	1·00
MS2644	76×106 mm. 25r. Ivory-billed woodpecker	5·50	6·00

Nos. 2635/43 were printed together, *se-tenant*, with the backgrounds forming a composite design.

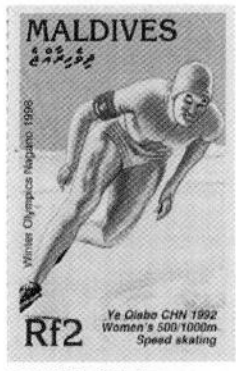

344 Ye Qiabo (China) (women's 500/1000 m speed skating, 1992)

1997. Winter Olympic Games, Nagano, Japan (1998). Multicoloured.

2645	2r. Type **344**	40	25
2646	3r. Leonhard Stock (Austria) (downhill skiing, 1980)	55	35
2647	5r. Herma von Szabo-Planck (Austria) (figure skating, 1924)	85	85
2648	5r. Katarina Witt (Germany) (figure skating, 1988)	85	85
2649	5r. Natalia Bestemianova and Andrei Bukin (Russia) (pairs ice dancing, 1988)	85	85
2650	5r. Jayne Torvill and Christopher Dean (Great Britain) (pairs ice dancing, 1984)	85	85
2651	8r. Bjorn Daehlie (Norway) (cross-country skiing, 1992)	1·25	1·25
2652	12r. Wolfgang Hoppe (Germany) (bobsleigh, 1984)	1·75	2·00
MS2653	Two sheets, each 76×106 mm. (a) 25r. Sonja Henie (Norway) (figure skating, 1924). (b) 25r. Andree Joly and Pierre Brunet (France) (pairs ice dancing, 1932) Set of 2 sheets	8·00	9·00

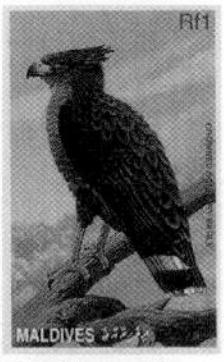
345 Crowned Solitary Eagle

1997. Eagles. Multicoloured.

2654	1r. Type **345**	55	25
2655	2r. African hawk eagle (horiz)	75	35
2656	3r. Lesser spotted eagle	1·00	65
2657	5r. Stellar's sea eagle	1·25	1·25
2658	5r. Bald eagle attacking	1·25	1·25
2659	5r. Bald eagle on branch	1·25	1·25
2660	5r. Bald eagle looking left	1·25	1·25
2661	5r. Bald eagle looking right	1·25	1·25
2662	5r. Bald eagle sitting on branch with leaves	1·25	1·25
2663	5r. Bald eagle soaring	1·25	1·25
2664	8r. Imperial eagle ("Spanish Imperial Eagle") (horiz)	1·75	2·00
2665	10r. Harpy eagle	1·75	2·00
2666	12r. Crested serpent eagle (horiz)	2·00	2·50
MS2667	Two sheets. (a) 73×104 mm. 25r. Bald eagle. (b) 104×73 mm. 25r. American bald eagle (horiz) Set of 2 sheets	9·00	10·00

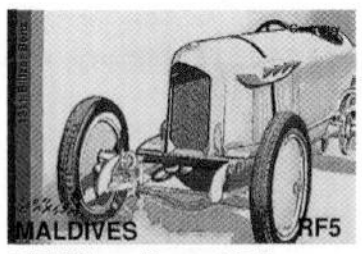

346 Blitzer Benz, 1911

1997. Classic Cars. Multicoloured.

2668	5r. Type **346**	80	85
2669	5r. Datsun, 1917	80	85
2670	5r. Auburn 8-120, 1929	80	85
2671	5r. Mercedes-Benz C280, 1996	80	85
2672	5r. Suzuki UR-1	80	85
2673	5r. Chrysler Atlantic	80	85
2674	5r. Mercedes-Benz 190SL, 1961	80	85
2675	5r. Kwaishinha D.A.T., 1916	80	85
2676	5r. Rolls-Royce Roadster 20/25	80	85
2677	5r. Mercedes-Benz SLK, 1997	80	85
2678	5r. Toyota Camry, 1996	80	85
2679	5r. Jaguar MK 2, 1959	80	85
MS2680	Two sheets, each 100×70 mm. (a) 25r. Volkswagen, 1939. (b) 25r. Mazda RX-01 Set of 2 sheets	7·50	8·50

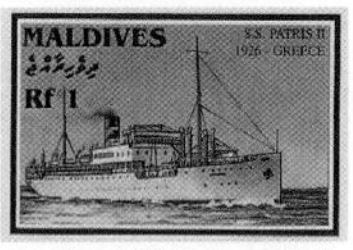

347 "Patris II", Greece (1926)

1997. Passenger Ships. Multicoloured.

2681	1r. Type **347**	45	15
2682	2r. "Infanta Beatriz", Spain (1928)	60	25
2683	3r. "Vasilefs Constantinos", Greece (1914)	75	75
2684	3r. "Cunene", Portugal (1911)	75	75
2685	3r. "Selandia", Denmark (1912)	75	75
2686	3r. "President Harding", U.S.A. (1921)	75	75
2687	3r. "Ulster Monarch", Great Britain (1929)	75	75
2688	3r. "Matsonia", U.S.A. (1913)	75	75
2689	3r. "France", France (1911)	75	75
2690	3r. "Campania", Great Britain (1893)	75	75

2691 3r. "Klipfontein", Holland (1922) 75 75
2692 3r. "Eridan", France (1929) 75 75
2693 3r. "Mount Clinton", U.S.A. (1921) 75 75
2694 3r. "Infanta Isabel", Spain (1912) 75 75
2695 3r. "Suwa Maru", Japan (1914) 75 75
2696 3r. "Yorkshire", Great Britain (1920) 75 75
2697 3r. "Highland Chieftain", Great Britain (1929) 75 75
2698 3r. "Sardinia", Norway (1920) 75 75
2699 3r. "San Guglielmo", Italy (1911) 75 75
2700 3r. "Avila", Great Britain (1927) 75 75
2701 8r. "Stavangerfjord", Norway (1918) 1·50 1·75
2702 12r. "Baloeran", Netherlands (1929) 2·00 2·25
MS2703 Four sheets. (a) 69×69 mm. 25r. "Mauritania", Great Britain (1907). (b) 69×69 mm. 25r. "United States", U.S.A. (1952). (c) 69×69 mm. 25r. "Queen Mary", Great Britain (1930). (d) 91×76 mm. 25r. Royal Yacht "Britannia" amd Chinese junk, Hong Kong (56×42 mm) Set of 4 sheets 18·00 18·00

No. **MS**2703d is inscribed "BRITTANIA" in error.

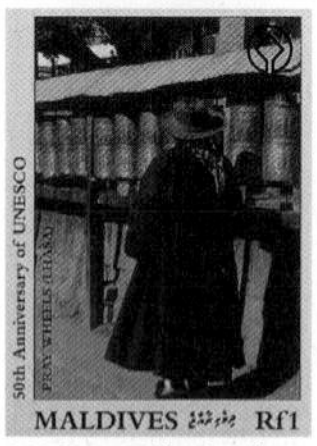

348 Prayer Wheels, Lhasa

1997. 50th Anniv of UNESCO. Multicoloured.
2704 1r. Type **348** 20 15
2705 2r. Ruins of Roman Temple of Diana, Portugal (horiz) 30 25
2706 3r. Santa Maria Cathedral, Hildesheim, Germany (horiz) 45 35
2707 5r. Vivunga National Park, Zaire 75 75
2708 5r. Valley of Mai Nature Reserve, Seychelles 75 75
2709 5r. Kandy, Sri Lanka 75 75
2710 5r. Taj Mahal, India 75 75
2711 5r. Istanbul, Turkey 75 75
2712 5r. Sana'a, Yemen 75 75
2713 5r. Bleinheim Palace, England 75 75
2714 5r. Grand Canyon National Park, U.S.A. 75 75
2715 5r. Tombs, Gondar, Ethiopia 75 75
2716 5r. Bwindi National Park, Uganda 75 75
2717 5r. Bemaraha National Reserve, Madagascar 75 75
2718 5r. Buddhist ruins at Takht-I-Bahi, Pakistan 75 75
2719 5r. Anuradhapura, Sri Lanka 75 75
2720 5r. Cairo, Egypt 75 75
2721 5r. Ruins, Petra, Jordan 75 75
2722 5r. Volcano, Ujung Kulon National Park, Indonesia 75 75
2723 5r. Terrace, Mount Taishan, China 75 75
2724 5r. Temple, Mount Taishan, China 75 75
2725 5r. Temple turret, Mount Taishan, China 75 75
2726 5r. Standing stones, Mount Taishan, China 75 75
2727 5r. Courtyard, Mount Taishan, China 75 75
2728 5r. Staircase, Mount Taishan, China 75 75
2729 5r. Terracotta Warriors, China 75 75
2730 5r. Head of Terracota Warrior, China 75 75
2731 7r. Doorway, Abu Simbel, Egypt 90 95
2732 8r. Mandraki, Rhodes, Greece (horiz) 1·25 1·25
2733 8r. Agios Stefanos Monastery, Meteora, Greece (horiz) 1·25 1·25
2734 8r. Taj Mahal, India (horiz) 1·25 1·25
2735 8r. Cistercian Abbey of Fontenay, France (horiz) 1·25 1·25
2736 8r. Yarushima, Japan (horiz) 1·25 1·25
2737 8r. Cloisters, San Gonzalo Convent, Portugal (horiz) 1·25 1·25
2738 8r. Olympic National Park, U.S.A. (horiz) 1·25 1·25
2739 8r. Waterfall, Nahanni National Park, Canada (horiz) 1·25 1·25
2740 8r. Mountains, National Park, Argentina (horiz) 1·25 1·25
2741 8r. Bonfin Salvador Church, Brazil (horiz) 1·25 1·25
2742 8r. Convent of the Companions of Jesus, Morelia, Mexico (horiz) 1·25 1·25
2743 8r. Two-storey temple, Horyu Temple, Japan (horiz) 1·25 1·25
2744 8r. Summer house, Horyu Temple, Japan (horiz) 1·25 1·25
2745 8r. Temple and cloister, Horyu Temple, Japan (horiz) 1·25 1·25
2746 8r. Single storey temple, Horyu Temple, Japan (horiz) 1·25 1·25
2747 8r. Well, Horyu Temple, Japan (horiz) 1·25 1·25
2748 10r. Scandola Nature Reserve, France (horiz) 1·25 1·40
2749 12r. Temple on the Lake, China (horiz) 1·50 1·75
MS2750 Four sheets, each 127×102 mm. (a) 25r. Fatehpur Sikri Monument, India (horiz). (b) 25r. Temple, Chengde, China (horiz). (c) 25r. Serengeti National Park, Tanzania (horiz). (d) 25r. Buddha, Anuradhapura, Sri Lanka (horiz) Set of 4 sheets 13·00 14·00

No. 2717 is inscribed "MADAGASGAR" and 2737 "COVENT", both in error.

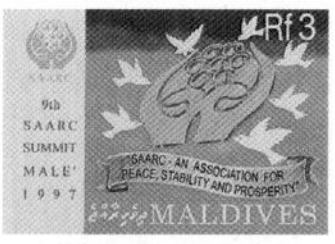

349 White Doves and S.A.A.R.C. Logo

1997. Ninth South Asian Association for Regional Cooperation Summit, Male. Multicoloured.
2751 3r. Type **349** 40 35
2752 5r. Flags of member countries 1·00 75

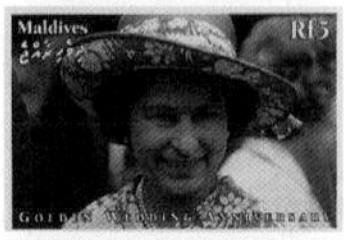

350 Queen Elizabeth II

1997. Golden Wedding of Queen Elizabeth and Prince Philip. Multicoloured.
2753 5r. Type **350** 1·00 1·00
2754 5r. Royal coat of arms 1·00 1·00
2755 5r. Queen Elizabeth and Prince Philip at opening of Parliament 1·00 1·00
2756 5r. Queen Elizabeth and Prince Philip with Prince Charles, 1948 1·00 1·00
2757 5r. Buckingham Palace from the garden 1·00 1·00
2758 5r. Prince Philip 1·00 1·00
MS2759 100×70 mm. 25r. Queen Elizabeth II 4·00 4·50

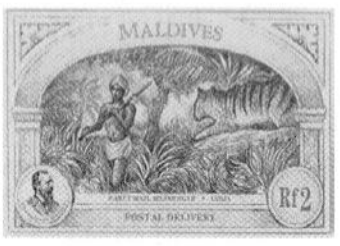

351 Early Indian Mail Messenger

1997. "Pacific '97" International Stamp Exhibition, San Francisco. Death Centenary of Heinrich von Stephan (founder of the U.P.U.).
2760 **351** 2r. green and black 55 60
2761 - 2r. brown and black 55 60
2762 - 2r. violet 55 60

DESIGNS: No. 2761, Von Stephan and Mercury; 2762, Autogyro, Washington.

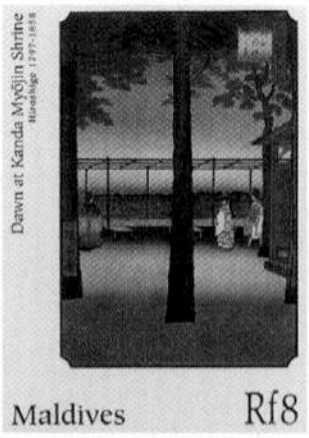

352 "Dawn at Kanda Myojn Shrine"

1997. Birth Bicentenary of Hiroshige (Japanese painter). "One Hundred Famous Views of Edo". Multicoloured.
2763 8r. Type **352** 1·25 1·25
2764 8r. "Kiyomizu Hall and Shinobazu Pond at Ueno" 1·25 1·25
2765 8r. "Ueno Yamashita" 1·25 1·25
2766 8r. "Moon Pine, Ueno" 1·25 1·25
2767 8r. "Flower Pavilion, Dango Slope, Sendagi" 1·25 1·25
2768 8r. "Shitaya Hirokoji" 1·25 1·25
MS2769 Two sheets, each 102×127 mm. (a) 25r. "Hilltop View, Yushima Tenjin Shrine". (b) 25r. "Seido and Kanda River from Shohei Bridge" Set of 2 sheets 7·50 8·50

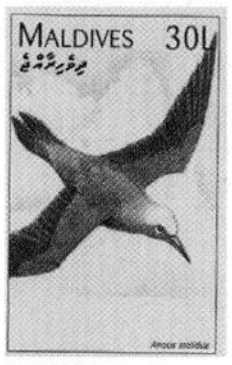

353 Common Noddy

1997. Birds. Multicoloured.
2770 30l. Type **353** 30 45
2771 1r. Spectacled owl 75 40
2772 2r. Malay fish owl 1·25 65
2773 3r. Peregrine falcon 1·50 1·00
2774 5r. Golden eagle 1·50 1·10
2775 7r. Ruppell's parrot 1·50 1·50
2776 7r. Blue-headed parrot 1·50 1·50
2777 7r. St Vincent amazon ("St Vincent Parrot") 1·50 1·50
2778 7r. Grey parrot 1·50 1·50
2779 7r. Masked lovebird 1·50 1·50
2780 7r. Sun conure ("Sun Parakeet") 1·50 1·50
2781 8r. Bateleur 1·50 1·50
2782 10r. Whiskered tern with chicks 1·50 1·75
2783 10r. Common caracara 1·50 1·75
2784 15r. Red-footed booby 2·25 2·50
MS2785 Two sheets, each 67×98 mm. (a) 25r. American bald eagle. (b) 25r. Secretary bird Set of 2 sheets 11·00 12·00

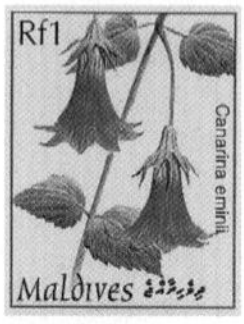

354 "Canarina eminii"

1997. Flowers. Multicoloured.
2786 1r. Type **354** 25 15
2787 2r. "Delphinium macrocentron" 40 25
2788 3r. "Leucadendron discolor" 55 40
2789 5r. "Nymphaea caerulea" 75 60
2790 7r. "Rosa multiflora polyantha" (20×23 mm) 1·00 1·00
2791 8r. "Bulbophyllum barbigerum" 1·50 1·50
2792 8r. "Acacia seyal" (horiz) 1·50 1·50
2793 8r. "Gloriosa superba" (horiz) 1·50 1·50
2794 8r. "Gnidia subcordata" (horiz) 1·50 1·50
2795 8r. "Platycelyphium voense" (horiz) 1·50 1·50
2796 8r. "Aspilia mossambicensis" (horiz) 1·50 1·50
2797 8r. "Adenium obesum" (horiz) 1·50 1·50
2798 12r. "Hibiscus vitifolius" 2·00 2·50
MS2799 Two sheets, each 105×76 mm. (a) 25r. "Aerangis rhodosticta" (horiz). (b) 25r. "Dichrostachys cinerea" and two sailing boats (horiz) Set of 2 sheets 16·00 16·00

Nos. 2792/7 were printed together, se-tenant, with the backgrounds forming a composite design.

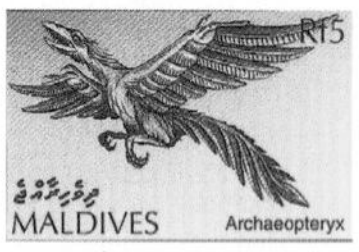

355 Archaeopteryx

1997. Prehistoric Animals. Multicoloured. (a) Horiz designs.
2800 5r. Type **355** 1·00 65
2801 7r. Diplodocus 1·10 1·10
2802 7r. Tyrannosaurus rex 1·10 1·10
2803 7r. Pteranodon 1·10 1·10
2804 7r. Montanceratops 1·10 1·10
2805 7r. Dromaeosaurus 1·10 1·10
2806 7r. Oviraptor 1·10 1·10
2807 8r. Mosasaurus 1·25 1·25
2808 12r. Deinonychus 1·60 1·75
2809 15r. Triceratops 1·75 2·00

(b) Square designs, 31×31 mm.
2810 7r. Troodon 1·10 1·10
2811 7r. Brachiosaurus 1·10 1·10
2812 7r. Saltasaurus 1·10 1·10
2813 7r. Oviraptor 1·10 1·10
2814 7r. Parasaurolophus 1·10 1·10
2815 7r. Psittacosaurus 1·10 1·10
2816 7r. Triceratops 1·10 1·10
2817 7r. Pachycephalosaurus 1·10 1·10
2818 7r. Iguanodon 1·10 1·10
2819 7r. Tyrannosaurus rex 1·10 1·10
2820 7r. Corythosaurus 1·10 1·10
2821 7r. Stegosaurus 1·10 1·10
2822 7r. Euophlocephalus 1·10 1·10
2823 7r. Compsognathus 1·10 1·10
2824 7r. Herrerasaurus 1·10 1·10
2825 7r. Styracosaurus 1·10 1·10
2826 7r. Baryonyx 1·10 1·10
2827 7r. Lesothosaurus 1·10 1·10
MS2828 Two sheets. (a) 99×79 mm. 25r. Tyrannosaurus rex (42×28 mm). (b) 73×104 mm. 25r. Archaeopteryx (31×31 mm) Set of 2 sheets 20·00 20·00

Nos. 2801/6, 2810/15, 2816/21 and 2822/7 respectively were printed together, se-tenant, with the backgrounds of Nos. 2801/6 and 2810/15 forming composite designs.

1997. World Cup Football Championship, France. As T **246** of Lesotho.
2829 1r. black 30 15
2830 2r. black 45 25
2831 3r. multicoloured 55 35
2832-2839 3r.×8 (black; black; multicoloured; multi- coloured; black; multicoloured; black; multicoloured) 3·75 4·00
2840-2847 3r.×8 (multicoloured; multicoloured; black; black; black; multicoloured; multicoloured; black) 3·75 4·00
2848-2855 3r.×8 (multicoloured; multicoloured; multi-coloured; black; black; multicoloured; multi-coloured; multicoloured) 3·75 4·00
2856 7r. black 1·10 1·10
2857 8r. black 1·40 1·40
2858 10r. multicoloured 1·50 1·60
MS2859 Three sheets. (a) 103×128 mm. 25r. multicoloured. (b) 103×128 mm. 25r. multicoloured. (c) 128×103 mm. 25r. multicoloured Set of 3 sheets 12·00 13·00

DESIGNS—HORIZ: No. 2829, Brazilian team, 1994; 2830, German player, 1954; 2831, Maradona holding World Cup, 1986; 2832, Brazilian team, 1958; 2833, Luis Bellini, Brazil, 1958; 2834, Brazilian team, 1962; 2835, Carlos Alberto, Brazil, 1970; 2836, Mauro, Brazil, 1962; 2837, Brazilian team, 1970; 2838, Dunga, Brazil, 1994; 2839, Brazilian team, 1994; 2840, Paulo Rossi, Italy, 1982; 2841, Zoff and Gentile, Italy, 1982; 2842, Angelo Schavio, Italy; 2843, Italian team, 1934; 2844, Italian team with flag, 1934; 2845, Italian team, 1982; 2846, San Paolo Stadium, Italy; 2847, Italian team, 1938; 2848, English player with ball, 1966; 2849, Wembley Stadium, London; 2850, English player heading ball, 1966; 2851, English players celebrating, 1966; 2852, English and German players chasing ball, 1966; 2853, English player wearing No. 21 shirt, 1966; 2854, English team with Jules Rimet trophy, 1966; 2855, German player wearing No. 5 shirt, 1966; 2856, Argentine player holding trophy, 1978; 2857, English players with Jules Rimet trophy, 1966; 2858, Brazilian player with trophy, 1970; **MS**2859c, Klinsmann, Germany. VERT: No. **MS**2859a, Ronaldo, Brazil; **MS**2892b, Schmeichel, Denmark.

1998. Diana, Princess of Wales Commemoration. As T **249** of Lesotho. Multicoloured (except Nos. 2864, 2870, 2872, 2877 and MS2878b).
2860 7r. Laughing 80 85
2861 7r. With Prince William and Prince Harry 80 85
2862 7r. Carrying bouquets 80 85
2863 7r. In white evening dress 80 85
2864 7r. Wearing bow tie (brown and black) 80 85
2865 7r. Wearing black jacket 80 85
2866 7r. With Indian child on lap 80 85
2867 7r. Wearing blue evening dress 80 85
2868 7r. Wearing blue jacket and poppy 80 85
2869 7r. Wearing cream jacket 80 85
2870 7r. Wearing blouse and jacket (brown and black) 80 85
2871 7r. Wearing red jacket 80 85
2872 7r. Wearing hat (blue and black) 80 85
2873 7r. Wearing red evening dress 80 85
2874 7r. With Sir Richard Attenborough 80 85
2875 7r. Wearing jeans and white shirt 80 85
2876 7r. Wearing white jacket 80 85
2877 7r. Carrying bouquet (brown and black) 80 85
MS2878 Three sheets. (a) 100×70 mm. 25r. On ski-lift. (b) 100×70 mm. 25r. Wearing polkadot dress (brown and black). (c) 70×100 mm. 25r. Wearing garland of flowers Set of 3 sheets 12·00 13·00

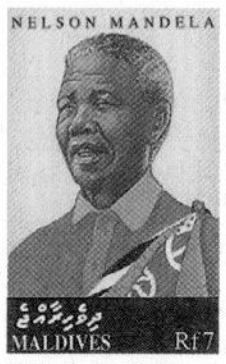

356 Pres. Nelson Mandela

1998. 80th Birthday of Nelson Mandela (President of South Africa).
2879 **356** 7r. multicoloured 1·75 1·40

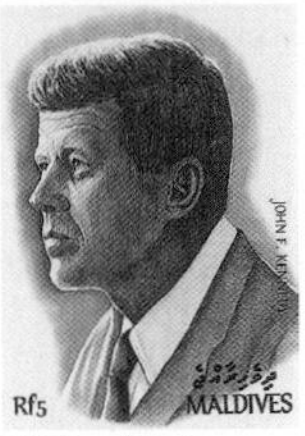

357 Pres. John F. Kennedy

1998. Pres. John F. Kennedy Commemoration. Multicoloured, background colours given.

2880	**357**	5r. green	75	80
2881	-	5r. green	75	80
2882	-	5r. brown (inscr at right)	75	80
2883	-	5r. yellow	75	80
2884	-	5r. violet	75	80
2885	-	5r. blue	75	80
2886	-	5r. grey	75	80
2887	-	5r. brown (inscr at left)	75	80
2888	-	5r. blue (value at bottom right)	75	80

DESIGNS: Nos. 2881/8, Various portraits.

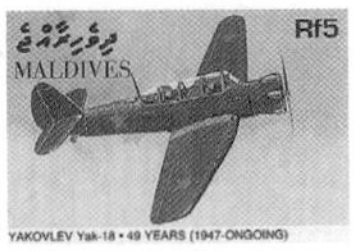

358 Yakovlev Yak-18 (from 1947)

1998. Aircraft in Longest Continuous Production. Multicoloured.

2889	5r. Type **358**	95	95
2890	5r. Beechcraft Bonanza (from 1947)	95	95
2891	5r. Piper Cub (1937–82)	95	95
2892	5r. Tupolev Tu-95 (1954–90)	95	95
2893	5r. Lockheed C-130 Hercules (from 1954)	95	95
2894	5r. Piper PA-28 Cherokee (from 1961)	95	95
2895	5r. Mikoyan Gurevich MiG-21 (from 1959)	95	95
2896	5r. Pilatus PC-6 Turbo Porter (from 1960)	95	95
2897	5r. Antonov An-2 (from 1949)	95	95
MS2898	120×90 mm. 25r. Boeing KC-135E (from 1956) (84×28 mm)	4·25	4·50

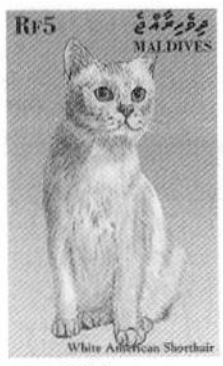

359 White American Shorthair

1998. Cats. Multicoloured.

2899	5r. Type **359**	1·25	65
2900	7r. American curl and Maine coon (horiz)	1·25	1·25
2901	7r. Maine coon (horiz)	1·25	1·25
2902	7r. Siberian (horiz)	1·25	1·25
2903	7r. Somali (horiz)	1·25	1·25
2904	7r. European Burmese (horiz)	1·25	1·25
2905	7r. Nebelung (horiz)	1·25	1·25
2906	7r. Bicolour British shorthair (horiz)	1·25	1·25
2907	7r. Manx (horiz)	1·25	1·25
2908	7r. Tabby American shorthair (horiz)	1·25	1·25
2909	7r. Silver tabby Persian (horiz)	1·25	1·25
2910	7r. Oriental white (horiz)	1·25	1·25
2911	7r. Norwegian forest cat (horiz)	1·25	1·25
2912	8r. Sphynx cat	1·25	1·25
2913	10r. Tabby American shorthair	1·25	1·25
2914	12r. Scottish fold	1·40	1·60
MS2915	Two sheets, each 98×68 mm. (a) 30r. Norwegian forest cat. (b) 30r. Snowshoe Set of 2 sheets	8·50	9·00

Nos. 2900/5 and 2906/11 respectively were printed together, *se-tenant*, forming composite designs.

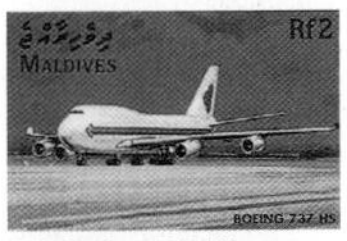

360 Boeing 737 HS

1998. Aircraft. Multicoloured.

2916	2r. Type **360**	60	30
2917	5r. CL-215 (flying boat)	1·00	1·00
2918	5r. Orion	1·00	1·00
2919	5r. Yakolev Yak-54	1·00	1·00
2920	5r. Cessna sea plane	1·00	1·00
2921	5r. CL-215 (amphibian)	1·00	1·00
2922	5r. CL-215 SAR (amphibian)	1·00	1·00
2923	5r. Twin Otter	1·00	1·00
2924	5r. Rockwell Quail	1·00	1·00
2925	5r. F.S.W. fighter	1·00	1·00
2926	5r. V-Jet II	1·00	1·00
2927	5r. Pilatus PC-12	1·00	1·00
2928	5r. Citation Exel	1·00	1·00
2929	5r. Stutz Bearcat	1·00	1·00
2930	5r. Cessna T-37 (B)	1·00	1·00
2931	5r. Peregrine Business Jet	1·00	1·00
2932	5r. Beech 58 Baron	1·00	1·00
2933	7r. Boeing 727	1·25	1·40
2934	8r. Boeing 747-400	1·40	1·50
2935	10r. Boeing 737	1·50	1·60
MS2936	Two sheets, each 98×68 mm. (a) 25r. Beechcraft Model 18. (b) 25r. Falcon Jet Set of 2 sheets	9·00	10·00

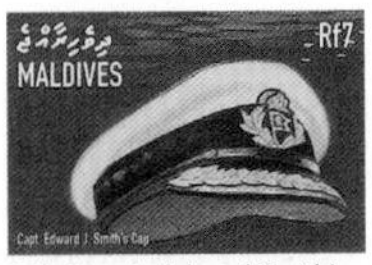

361 Captain Edward Smith's Cap

1998. "Titanic" Commemoration. Multicoloured.

2937	7r. Type **361**	1·40	1·40
2938	7r. Deck chair	1·40	1·40
2939	7r. Fifth Officer Harold Lowe's coat button	1·40	1·40
2940	7r. Lifeboat	1·40	1·40
2941	7r. "Titanic's" wheel	1·40	1·40
2942	7r. Passenger's lifejacket	1·40	1·40
MS2943	110×85 mm. 25r. "Titanic" from newspaper picture	5·00	5·50

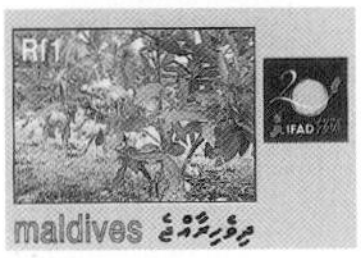

362 Guava Tree

1998. 20th Anniv of International Fund of Agriculture. Multicoloured.

2944	1r. Type **362**	30	15
2945	5r. Selection of fruit	1·00	75
2946	7r. Fishing boat	1·25	1·25
2947	8r. Papaya tree	1·25	1·50
2948	10r. Vegetable produce	1·50	1·75

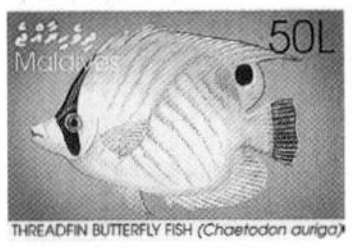

363 Thread-finned Butterflyfish

1998. Fish. Multicoloured.

2949	50l. Type **363**	20	20
2950	50l. Queen angelfish	20	20
2951	1r. Oriental sweetlips	30	15
2952	3r. Mandarin fish	50	50
2953	3r. Copper-banded butterflyfish	50	50
2954	3r. Harlequin tuskfish	50	50
2955	3r. Yellow-tailed demoiselle	50	50
2956	3r. Wimplefish	50	50
2957	3r. Red emperor snapper	50	50
2958	3r. Clown triggerfish	50	50
2959	3r. Common clown	50	50
2960	3r. Palette surgeonfish ("Regal Tang")	50	50
2961	5r. Emperor angelfish	80	80
2962	5r. Common squirrelfish ("Diadem Squirrelfish")	80	80
2963	5r. Lemon-peel angelfish	80	80
2964	5r. Powder-blue surgeonfish	80	80
2965	5r. Moorish idol	80	80
2966	5r. Bicolor angelfish ("Bicolor Cherub")	80	80
2967	5r. Duboulay's angelfish ("Scribbled Angelfish")	80	80
2968	5r. Two-banded anemonefish	80	80
2969	5r. Yellow tang	80	80
2970	7r. Red-tailed surgeonfish ("Achilles Tang")	1·00	1·10
2971	7r. Bandit angelfish	1·00	1·10
2972	8r. Hooded butterflyfish ("Red-headed Butterflyfish")	1·10	1·25
2973	50r. Blue-striped butterflyfish	5·50	6·50
MS2974	Two sheets, each 110×85 mm. (a) 25r. Long-nosed butterflyfish. (b) 25r. Porkfish Set of 2 sheets	7·50	8·00

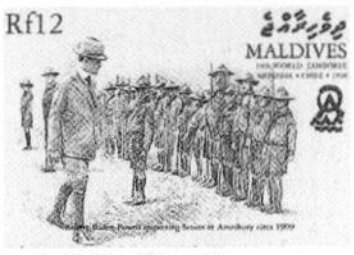

364 Baden-Powell inspecting Scouts, Amesbury, 1909

1998. 19th World Scout Jamboree, Chile. Multicoloured.

2975	12r. Type **364**	1·75	2·00
2976	12r. Sir Robert and Lady Baden-Powell with children, 1927	1·75	2·00
2977	12r. Sir Robert Baden-Powell awarding merit badges, Chicago, 1926	1·75	2·00

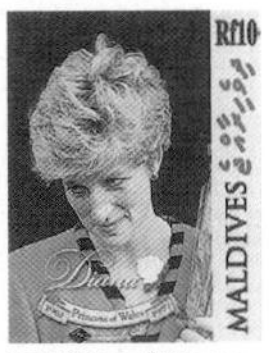

365 Diana, Princess of Wales

1998. First Death Anniv of Diana, Princess of Wales.

2978	**365**	10r. multicoloured	1·25	1·50

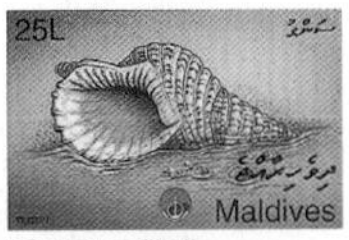

366 Triton Shell

1999. International Year of the Ocean. Marine Life. Multicoloured.

2979	25l. Type **366**	60	60
2980	50l. Napoleon wrasse	75	75
2981	1r. Whale shark	1·00	1·00
2982	3r. Grey reef shark	1·25	1·25
2983	5r. Harp seal	1·10	1·10
2984	5r. Killer whale	1·10	1·10
2985	5r. Sea otter	1·10	1·10
2986	5r. Beluga	1·10	1·10
2987	5r. Narwhal	1·10	1·10
2988	5r. Walrus	1·10	1·10
2989	5r. Sea lion	1·10	1·10
2990	5r. Humpback salmon	1·10	1·10
2991	5r. Emperor penguin	1·10	1·10
2992	7r. Blue whale	1·75	1·75
2993	7r. Skipjack tuna	1·10	1·10
2994	8r. Ocean sunfish	1·25	1·25
2995	8r. Opalescent squid	1·25	1·25
2996	8r. Electric ray	1·25	1·25
2997	8r. Corded neptune	1·25	1·25
MS2998	Three sheets, each 110×85 mm. (a) 25r. Horseshoe crab. (b) 25r. Blue whale. (c) 25r. Triton shell Set of 3 sheets	11·00	12·00

Nos. 2983/91 were printed together, *se-tenant*, with the backgrounds forming a composite design.

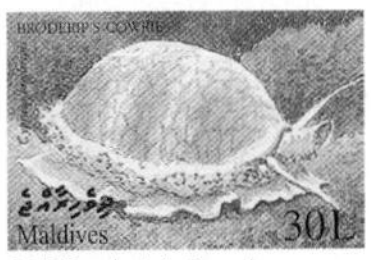

367 Broderip's Cowrie

1999. Marine Life. Multicoloured.

2999	30l. Type **367**	25	25
3000	1r. White tern ("Fairy Tern")	1·00	40
3001	3r. Green-backed heron ("Darker Maldivian Green Heron")	1·50	1·10
3002	5r. Manta ray	1·10	1·10
3003	5r. Green turtle	1·10	1·10
3004	5r. Spotted dolphins	1·10	1·10
3005	5r. Moorish idols	1·10	1·10
3006	5r. Threadfin anthias	1·10	1·10
3007	5r. Goldbar wrasse	1·10	1·10
3008	5r. Palette surgeonfish	1·10	1·10
3009	5r. Three-spotted angelfish	1·10	1·10
3010	5r. Oriental sweetlips	1·10	1·10
3011	5r. Brown booby	1·10	1·10
3012	5r. Red-tailed tropic bird	1·10	1·10
3013	5r. Sooty tern	1·10	1·10
3014	5r. Striped dolphin	1·10	1·10
3015	5r. Spinner dolphin	1·10	1·10
3016	5r. Crab plover	1·10	1·10
3017	5r. Hawksbill turtle	1·10	1·10
3018	5r. Indo-Pacific sergeant	1·10	1·10
3019	5r. Yellow-finned tuna	1·10	1·10
3020	7r. Blackflag sandperch	1·25	1·25
3021	8r. Coral hind	1·40	1·40
3022	10r. Olive Ridley turtle	1·60	1·60
MS3023	Two sheets, each 110×85 mm. (a) 25r. Cinnamon bittern. (b) 25r. Blue-faced angelfish Set of 2 sheets	8·00	9·00

Nos. 3002/10 and 3011/19 were each printed together, *se-tenant*, with the backgrounds forming composite designs.

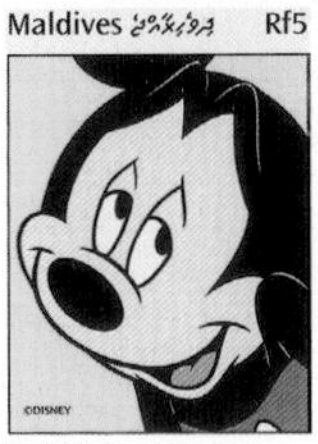

368 Mickey Mouse

1999. 70th Anniv of Mickey Mouse (Disney cartoon character). Multicoloured.

3024-3029	5r.×6 (Mickey Mouse: Type **368**; laughing; looking tired; frowning; smiling; winking)	5·50	5·50
3030-3035	5r.×6 (Minnie Mouse: facing left and smiling; with eyes closed; with hand on head; looking surprised; smiling; looking cross)	5·50	5·50
3036-3041	7r.×6 (Donald Duck: facing left and smiling; laughing; looking tired; looking cross; smiling; winking)	6·00	6·00
3042-3047	7r.×6 (Daisy Duck: with half closed eyes; laughing; looking shocked; looking cross; facing forwards; with head on one side)	6·00	6·00
3048-3053	7r.×6 (Goofy: facing right and smiling; with eyes closed; with half closed eyes; looking shocked; looking puzzled; looking thoughtful)	6·00	6·00
3054-3059	7r.×6 (Pluto: looking shocked; with eyes closed; smiling; scowling; with tongue out (orange background); with tongue out (green background)	6·00	6·00
MS3060	Six sheets, each 127×102 mm. (a) 25r. Minnie Mouse wearing necklace. (b) 25r. Mickey with hand on head. (c) 25r. Mickey wearing baseball hat. (d) 25r. Mickey facing right (horiz). (e) 25r. Minnie looking left (includes label showing Mickey with bouquet). (f) 25r. Minnie drinking through straw Set of 6 sheets	23·00	23·00

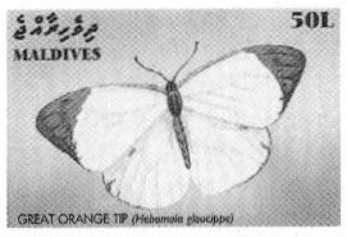

369 Great Orange Tip

1999. Butterflies. Multicoloured.

3061	50l. Type **369**	15	25
3062	1r. Large green aporandria	25	20
3063	2r. Common mormon	40	30
3064	3r. African migrant	55	40
3065	5r. Common pierrot	85	60
3066	7r. Crimson tip (vert)	1·10	1·10
3067	7r. Tawny rajah (vert)	1·10	1·10
3068	7r. Leafwing butterfly (vert)	1·10	1·10
3069	7r. Great egg-fly (vert)	1·10	1·10
3070	7r. Blue admiral (vert)	1·10	1·10
3071	7r. African migrant (vert)	1·10	1·10
3072	7r. Common red flash (vert)	1·10	1·10
3073	7r. Burmese lascar (vert)	1·10	1·10
3074	7r. Common perriot (vert)	1·10	1·10
3075	7r. Baron (vert)	1·10	1·10
3076	7r. Leaf blue (vert)	1·10	1·10
3077	7r. Great orange tip (vert)	1·10	1·10
3078	10r. Giant red-eye	1·25	1·60
MS3079	Two sheets, each 70×100 mm. (a) 25r. Crimson tip. (b) 25r. Large oak blue Set of 2 sheets	7·50	8·00

Nos. 3066/71 and 3072/7 were each printed together, *se-tenant*, with the backgrounds forming composite designs.

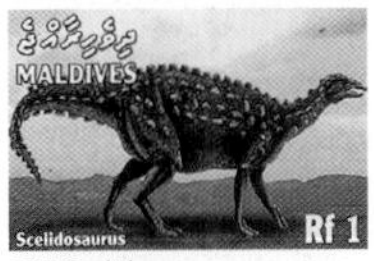

370 Scelidosaurus

1999. Prehistoric Animals. Multicoloured.

3080	1r. Type **370**	25	15
3081	3r. Yansudaurus	45	40
3082	5r. Ornitholestes	85	70
3083	7r. Dimorphodon (vert)	1·10	1·10
3084	7r. Rhamphorhynchus (vert)	1·10	1·10
3085	7r. Allosaurus (vert)	1·10	1·10
3086	7r. Leaellynasaura (vert)	1·10	1·10
3087	7r. Troodon (vert)	1·10	1·10
3088	7r. Syntarsus (vert)	1·10	1·10
3089	7r. Anchisaurus (vert)	1·10	1·10
3090	7r. Pterenodon (vert)	1·10	1·10

3091	7r. Barosaurus (vert)	1·10	1·10
3092	7r. Iguanodon (vert)	1·10	1·10
3093	7r. Archaeopteryx (vert)	1·10	1·10
3094	7r. Ceratosaurus (vert)	1·10	1·10
3095	7r. Stegosaurus	1·10	1·10
3096	7r. Corythosaurus	1·10	1·10
3097	7r. Cetiosaurus	1·10	1·10
3098	7r. Avimimus	1·10	1·10
3099	7r. Styracosaurus	1·10	1·10
3100	7r. Massospondylus	1·10	1·10
3101	8r. Astrodon	1·10	1·25
MS3102	Two sheets, each 116×81 mm. (a) 25r. Megalosaurus (vert). (b) 25r. Brachiosaurus (vert) Set of 2 sheets	7·50	8·00

Nos. 3083/8, 3089/94 and 3095/100 were each printed together, *se-tenant*, forming composite designs.

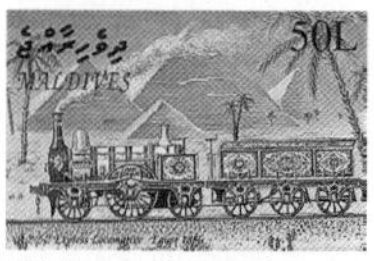

371 Express Locomotive, Egypt, 1856

1999. Trains of the World. Multicoloured.

3103	50l. Type **371**	35	25
3104	1r. Channel Tunnel Le Shuttle, France, 1994	40	15
3105	2r. Gowan and Marx loco-motive, U.S.A., 1839	60	25
3106	3r. TGV train, France, 1981	75	35
3107	5r. "Ae 6/6" electric loco-motive, Switzerland, 1954	1·00	65
3108	7r. Stephenson's long-boilered locomotive, Great Britain, 1846 (red livery)	1·25	1·25
3109	7r. "Cornwall", Great Britain, 1847	1·25	1·25
3110	7r. First locomotive, Germany, 1848	1·25	1·00
3111	7r. Great Western locomotive, Great Britain, 1846	1·25	1·25
3112	7r. Standard Stephenson loco-motive, France, 1837	1·25	1·25
3113	7r. "Meteor", Great Britain, 1843	1·25	1·25
3114	7r. Class 4T diesel-electric locomotive, Great Britain, 1940–65	1·25	1·25
3115	7r. Mainline diesel-electric lo-comotive No. 20101, Malaya, 1940–65	1·25	1·25
3116	7r. Class 7000 high-speed elec-tric locomotive, France, 1949	1·25	1·25
3117	7r. Diesel hydraulic express lo-comotive, Thailand, 1940–65	1·25	1·25
3118	7r. Diesel hydraulic locomotive, Burma, 1940–65	1·25	1·25
3119	7r. "Hikari" super express train, Japan, 1940–65	1·25	1·25
3120	8r. Stephenson's long-boilered locomotive, Great Britain, 1846 (orange and green livery)	1·40	1·40
3121	10r. "Philadelphia", Austria, 1838	1·40	1·40
3122	15r. S.E. and C.R. Class E steam locomotive, Great Britain, 1940	2·00	2·25
MS3123	Two sheets, each 110×85 mm. (a) 25r. Passenger locomotive, France, 1846. (b) 25r. Southern Railway Class "King Arthur", steam locomotive, Great Britain, 1940 Set of 2 sheets	9·50	10·00

1999. "Queen Elizabeth the Queen Mother's Century". As T **267** of Lesotho.

3124	7r. black and gold	1·25	1·25
3125	7r. black and gold	1·25	1·25
3126	7r. multicoloured	1·25	1·25
3127	7r. multicoloured	1·25	1·25
MS3128	153×157 mm. 25r. multi-coloured	5·00	5·00

DESIGNS: No. 3124, King George VI and Queen Elizabeth, 1936; 3125, Queen Elizabeth, 1941; 3126, Queen Elizabeth in evening dress, 1960; 3127, Queen Mother at Ascot, 1981. 37×50 mm: No. **MS**3128, Queen Mother in Garter robes.

1999. "iBRA '99" International Stamp Exhibition, Nuremberg. As T **262** of Lesotho. Multicoloured.

3129	12r. "Adler" (first German rail-way locomotive), 1833	2·00	2·50
3130	15r. "Drache" (Henshell and Sohn's first locomotive), 1848	2·25	2·75

The captions on Nos. 3129/30 are transposed.

1999. 150th Death Anniv of Katsushika Hokusai (Japanese artist). As T **263** of Lesotho. Multicoloured (except No. 3133).

3131	7r. "Haunted House"	1·25	1·25
3132	7r. "Juniso Shrine at Yotsuya"	1·25	1·25
3133	7r. Drawing of bird (black, green and gold)	1·25	1·25
3134	7r. Drawing of two women	1·25	1·25
3135	7r. "Lover in the Snow"	1·25	1·25
3136	7r. "Mountain Tea House"	1·25	1·25
3137	7r. "A Coastal View"	1·25	1·25
3138	7r. "Bath House by a Lake"	1·25	1·25
3139	7r. Drawing of a horse	1·25	1·25
3140	7r. Drawing of two birds on branch	1·25	1·25
3141	7r. "Evening Cool at Ryogoku"	1·25	1·25
3142	7r. "Girls boating"	1·25	1·25
MS3143	Two sheets, each 100×70 mm. (a) 25r. "Girls gathering Spring Herbs" (vert). (b) 25r. "Scene in the Yoshiwara" (vert) Set of 2 sheets	9·00	9·50

1999. Tenth Anniv of United Nations Rights of the Child Convention. As T **264** of Lesotho. Multicoloured.

3144	10r. Baby boy and young mother	1·60	2·00
3145	10r. Young girl laughing	1·60	2·00
3146	10r. Three children	1·60	2·00
MS3147	110×85 mm. 25r. Sir Peter Ustinov (Goodwill ambassador for UNICEF)	4·00	4·75

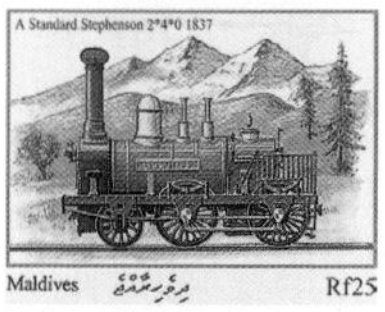

372 Standard Stephenson Railway Locomotive "Versailles", 1837

1999. "PhilexFrance '99" International Stamp Exhibition, Paris. Railway Locomotives. Two sheets, each 106×81 mm, containing T **372** and similar horiz design. Multicoloured.

MS3148	(a) 25r. Type **372**. (b) 25r. Stephenson long-boilered locomo-tive, 1841 Set of 2 sheets	8·50	9·50

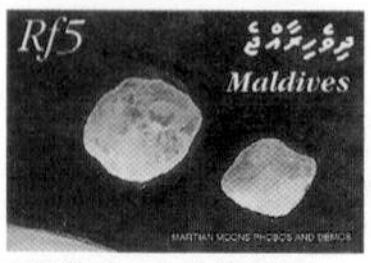

373 Phobos and Demos (Martian Moons)

2000. Future Colonization of Mars. Multicoloured.

3149	5r. Type **373**	1·00	1·00
3150	5r. Improved Hubble Telescope	1·00	1·00
3151	5r. Passenger shuttle	1·00	1·00
3152	5r. Skyscrapers on Mars	1·00	1·00
3153	5r. Martian taxi	1·00	1·00
3154	5r. Martian landing facilities	1·00	1·00
3155	5r. Vegetation in Martian biosphere	1·00	1·00
3156	5r. Walking on Mars and biosphere	1·00	1·00
3157	5r. Mars rover	1·00	1·00
3158	5r. Russian Phobos 25 satellite	1·00	1·00
3159	5r. Earth and Moon	1·00	1·00
3160	5r. Space shuttle leaving Earth	1·00	1·00
3161	5r. Lighthouse on Mars	1·00	1·00
3162	5r. Mars excursion space liner	1·00	1·00
3163	5r. Mars shuttle and skyscrapers	1·00	1·00
3164	5r. Viking Lander	1·00	1·00
3165	5r. Mars air and water purifica-tion plant	1·00	1·00
3166	5r. Family picnic on Mars	1·00	1·00
MS3167	Two sheets, each 110×85 mm. (a) 25r. Astronaut with jet-pack. (b) 25r. Mars Set of 2 sheets	9·50	10·00

Nos. 3149/57 and 3158/66 were each printed together, *se-tenant*, with the backgrounds forming composite designs.

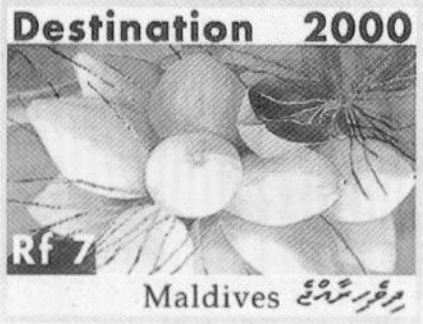

374 Coconuts

2000. "Destination 2000 – Maldives" Campaign. Multicoloured.

3168	7r. Type **374**	1·75	1·75
3169	7r. Shoal of skipjack tuna	1·75	1·75
3170	7r. Seaplane and traditional dhow	1·75	1·75
3171	7r. "Plumeria alba"	1·75	1·75
3172	7r. Lionfish	1·75	1·75
3173	7r. Windsurfers	1·75	1·75

2000. New Millennium. People and Events of Eighteenth Century (1750–1800). As T **268** of Lesotho. Multicoloured.

3174	3r. American bald eagle and American Declaration of Independence, 1776	80	80
3175	3r. Montgolfier brothers and first manned hot- air balloon flight, 1783	80	80
3176	3r. Napoleon and mob (French Revolution, 1789)	80	80
3177	3r. James Watt and drawing of steam engine, 1769	80	80
3178	3r. Wolfgang Amadeus Mozart (born 1756)	80	80
3179	3r. Front cover of The Dream of the Red Chamber (Chinese novel, published 1791)	80	80
3180	3r. Napoleon and pyramid (conquest of Egypt, 1798)	80	80
3181	3r. Empress Catherine the Great of Russia and St. Petersburg, 1762	80	80
3182	3r. Joseph Priestley (discovery of oxygen, 1774)	80	80
3183	3r. Benjamin Franklin (publica-tion of work on electricity, 1751)	80	80
3184	3r. Edward Jenner (develop-ment of smallpox vaccine, 1796)	80	80
3185	3r. Death of General Wolfe, 1759	80	80
3186	3r. "The Swing" (Jean Honore Fragonard), 1766	80	80
3187	3r. Ludwig von Beethoven (born 1770)	80	80
3188	3r. Marriage of Louis XVI of France and Marie Antoinette, 1770	80	80
3189	3r. Captain James Cook (ex-ploration of Australia, 1770) (59×39 mm)	80	80
3190	3r. Luigi Galvani and frog (experiments into the effect of electricity on nerves and muscles, 1780)	80	1·00

The main design on No. 3184 may depict Sir William Jenner who undertook research into typhus.

On No. 3185 the uniforms are incorrectly shown as blue instead of red.

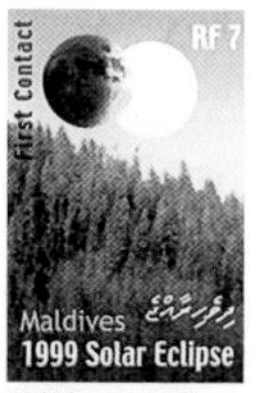

375 Sun and Moon over Forest

2000. Solar Eclipse Showing varying stages of eclipse as seen from Earth (Nos. 3191/6) or Space (Nos. 3197/202). Multicoloured.

3191	7r. Type **375**	1·25	1·25
3192	7r. "Second Contact"	1·25	1·25
3193	7r. "Totality"	1·25	1·25
3194	7r. "Third Contact"	1·25	1·25
3195	7r. "Fourth Contact"	1·25	1·25
3196	7r. Observatory	1·25	1·25
3197	7r. "First Contact"	1·25	1·25
3198	7r. "Second Contact"	1·25	1·25
3199	7r. "Totality"	1·25	1·25
3200	7r. "Third Contact"	1·25	1·25
3201	7r. "Fourth Contact"	1·25	1·25
3202	7r. Solar and heliospheric observatory	1·25	1·25

Nos. 3191/6 and 3197/202 were each printed together, se-tenant, with the backgrounds forming composite designs.

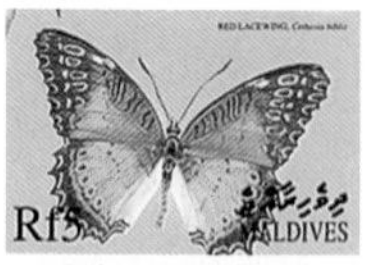

376 Red Lacewing

2000. Butterflies of the Maldives. Multicoloured.

3203	5r. Type **376**	1·10	1·10
3204	5r. Large oak blue	1·10	1·10
3205	5r. Yellow coster	1·10	1·10
3206	5r. Great orange-tip	1·10	1·10
3207	5r. Common pierrot	1·10	1·10
3208	5r. Cruiser	1·10	1·10
3209	5r. Hedge blue	1·10	1·10
3210	5r. Common eggfly	1·10	1·10
3211	5r. Plain tiger	1·10	1·10
3212	5r. Common wall butterfly	1·10	1·10
3213	5r. Koh-i-Noor butterfly	1·10	1·10
3214	5r. Painted lady ("Indian Red Admiral")	1·10	1·10
3215	5r. Tawny rajah	1·10	1·10
3216	5r. Blue triangle	1·10	1·00
3217	5r. Orange albatross	1·10	1·10
3218	5r. Common rose swallowtail	1·10	1·10
3219	5r. Jewelled nawab	1·10	1·10
3220	5r. Striped blue crow	1·10	1·10
MS3221	Two sheets. (a) 85×110 mm. 25r. Large tree nymph. (b) 110×85 mm. 25r. Blue pansy Set of 2 sheets	10·00	11·00

Nos. 3203/11 and 3212/20 were each printed together, *se-tenant*, with the backgrounds forming composite designs.

No. 3219 is inscribed "JEWELED NAWAB" in error.

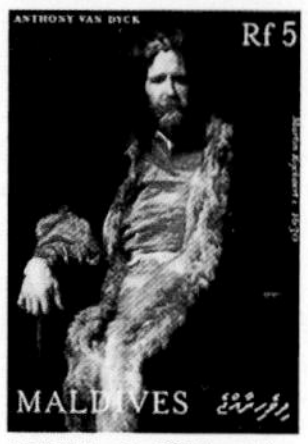

377 "Martin Rijckaert"

2000. 400th Birth Anniv of Sir Anthony Van Dyck (Flemish painter). Multicoloured.

3222	5r. Type **377**	1·40	1·40
3223	5r. "Frans Snyders"	1·40	1·40
3224	5r. "Quentin Simons"	1·40	1·40
3225	5r. "Lucas van Uffel", 1632	1·40	1·40
3226	5r. "Nicolaes Rockox"	1·40	1·40
3227	5r. "Nicholas Lamier"	1·40	1·40
3228	5r. "Inigo Jones"	1·40	1·40
3229	5r. "Lucas van Uffel", c. 1622–25	1·40	1·40
3230	5r. Detail of "Margaretha de Vos, Wife of Frans Snyders"	1·40	1·40
3231	5r. "Peter Brueghel the Younger"	1·40	1·40
3232	5r. "Cornelis van der Geest"	1·40	1·40
3233	5r. "Francois Langlois as a Savoyard"	1·40	1·40
3234	5r. "Portrait of a Family"	1·40	1·40
3235	5r. "Earl and Countess of Denby and Their Daughter"	1·40	1·40
3236	5r. "Family Portrait"	1·40	1·40
3237	5r. "A Genoese Nobleman with his Children"	1·40	1·40
3238	5r. "Thomas Howard, Earl of Arundel, and His Grandson"	1·40	1·40
3239	5r. "La dama d'oro"	1·40	1·40
MS3240	Six sheets. (a) 102×127 mm. 25r. "The Painter Jan de Wael and his Wife Gertrude de Jode". (b) 102×127 mm. 25r. "John, Count of Nassau-Siegen, and His Family". (c) 102×127 mm. 25r. "The Lomellini Family". (d) 102×127 mm. 25r. "Lucas and Cor-nelis de Wael". (e) 127x102 mm. 25r. "Sir Kenelm and Lady Digby with their two Eldest Sons". (f) 127×102 mm. 25r. "Sir Philip Herbert, 4th Earl of Pembroke, and His Family" (horiz) Set of 6 sheets	24·00	26·00

No. 3230 is inscribed "Margaretha de Vos, Wife of Frans Snders" in error.

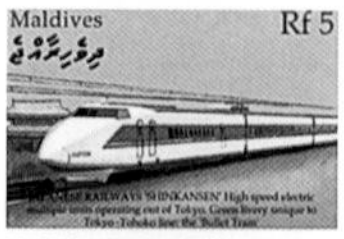

378 Japanese Railways "Shinkansen", High Speed Electric Train

2000. "The Stamp Show 2000" International Stamp Exhibition, London. Asian Railways. Multicoloured.

3241	5r. Type **378**	1·50	85
3242	8r. Japanese Railways "Super Azusa", twelve-car train	1·75	1·75
3243	10r. Tobu Railway "Spacia", ten-car electric train, Japan	2·00	2·00
3244	10r. Shanghai-Nanking Railway passenger tank locomotive, China, 1909	2·00	2·00
3245	10r. Shanghai–Nanking Railway "Imperial Yellow" express mail locomotive, China, 1910	2·00	2·00
3246	10r. Manchurian Railway "Pa-cific" locomotive, China, 1914	2·00	2·00
3247	10r. Hankow Line mixed traffic locomotive, China, 1934	2·00	2·00
3248	10r. Chinese National Railway freight locomotive, 1949	2·00	2·00
3249	10r. Chinese National Railway mixed traffic locomotive, 1949	2·00	2·00
3250	10r. East Indian Railway pas-senger tank locomotive Fawn, 1856	2·00	2·00
3251	10r. East Indian Railway express locomotive, 1893	2·00	2·00
3252	10r. Bengal–Nagpur Railway Atlantic Compound loco-motive, India, 1909	2·00	2·00
3253	10r. Great Peninsular Railway passenger and mail locomo-tive, India, 1924	2·00	2·00
3254	10r. North Western Class XS2 Pacific locomotive, India, 1932	2·00	2·00
3255	10r. Indian National Railway Class YP Pacific locomotive, India, 1949–70	2·00	2·00
3256	15r. Japanese Railway "Nozomi", high-speed electric train	2·75	3·25
MS3257	Two sheets, each 100×70 mm. (a) 25r. Indian National Railways Class WP locomotive (57×41 mm). (b) 25r. Chinese National Railway Class JS locomotive (57×41 mm) Set of 2 sheets	11·00	12·00

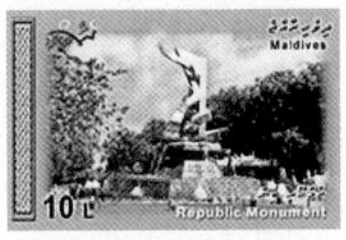

379 Republic Monument

2000. New Millennium (2nd issue). Multicoloured.

3258	10l. Type **379**	15	20
3259	30l. Bodu Thakurufaanu Memorial Centre	20	15
3260	1r. Modern medical facilities and new hospital	50	15
3261	7r. Male International Airport	1·40	1·75
3262	7r. Hukuru Miskiiy	1·40	1·75
3263	10r. Computer room, science lab and new school	1·75	2·00
MS3264	Three sheets, each 106×77 mm. (a) 25r. Tourist resort and fish packing factory. (b) 25r. Islamic Centre. (c) 25r. People's Majlis (assembly) Set of 3 sheets	11·00	13·00

2000. 25th Anniv of "Apollo–Soyuz" Joint Project. As T **271** of Lesotho. Multicoloured.

3265	13r. "Apollo 18" and "Soyuz 19" docking (vert)	2·50	2·50
3266	13r. "Soyuz 19" (vert)	2·50	2·50
3267	13r. "Apollo 18" (vert)	2·50	2·50
MS3268	105×76 mm. 25r. "Soyuz 19"	5·00	5·50

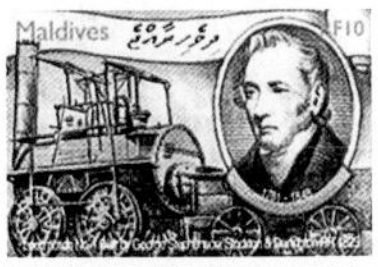

380 George Stephenson and *Locomotion No. 1*, 1825

2000. 175th Anniv of Stockton and Darlington Line (first public railway). Multicoloured.

3269	10r. Type **380**	2·25	2·25
3270	10r. William Hedley's *Puffing Billy* locomotive	2·25	2·25

2000. Centenary of First Zeppelin Flight. As T **276** of Lesotho. Multicoloured.

3271	13r. LZ-127 *Graf Zeppelin*, 1928	1·75	1·90
3272	13r. LZ-130 *Graf Zeppelin II*, 1938	1·75	1·90
3273	13r. LZ-9 *Ersatz*, 1911	1·75	1·90
MS3274	115×80 mm. 25r. LZ-88 (L-40), 1917 (37×50 mm)	3·75	4·00

No. 3272 is inscribed "LZ-127" in error.

2000. Olympic Games, Sydney. As T **277** of Lesotho. Multicoloured.

3275	10r. Suzanne Lenglen, (French tennis player), 1920	2·00	2·00
3276	10r. Fencing	2·00	2·00
3277	10r. Olympic Stadium, Tokyo, 1964, and Japanese flag	2·00	2·00
3278	10r. Ancient Greek long jumping	2·00	2·00

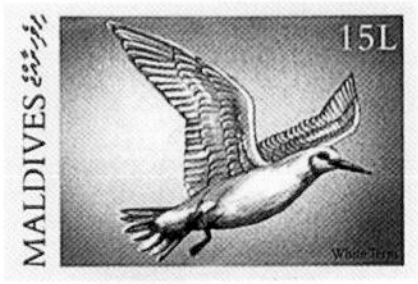

381 White Tern

2000. Tropical Birds. Multicoloured.

3279	15l. Type **381**	35	50
3280	25l. Brown booby	40	50
3281	30l. White-collared kingfisher (vert)	40	50
3282	1r. Black-winged stilt (vert)	60	25
3283	10r. White-collared kingfisher (different) (vert)	2·00	2·00
3284	10r. Island thrush (vert)	2·00	2·00
3285	10r. Red-tailed tropic bird (vert)	2·00	2·00
3286	10r. Peregrine falcon (vert)	2·00	2·00
3287	10r. Black-crowned night heron ("Night Heron") (vert)	2·00	2·00
3288	10r. Great egret (vert)	2·00	2·00
3289	10r. Great frigate bird	2·00	2·00
3290	10r. Common noddy	2·00	2·00
3291	10r. Common tern	2·00	2·00
3292	10r. Red-footed booby ("Sula Sula")	2·00	2·00
3293	10r. Sooty tern	2·00	2·00
3294	10r. White-tailed tropic bird (*Phaethon lepturus*)	2·00	2·00
3295	13r. Ringed plover	2·00	2·00
3296	13r. Ruddy turnstone ("Turnstone")	2·00	2·00
3297	13r. Australian stone-curlew	2·00	2·00
3298	13r. Grey plover ("Black-bellied Plover")	2·00	2·00
3299	13r. Crab plover	2·00	2·00
3300	13r. Western curlew ("Curlew")	2·00	2·00
MS3301	Two sheets, each 77×103 mm. (a) 25r. Great cormorant (vert). (b) 25r. Cattle egret (vert) Set of 2 sheets	11·00	12·00

Nos. 3283/8, 3289/4 and 3295/300 were each printed together, *se-tenant*, with the backgrounds forming composite designs.

No. 3294 is inscribed "Leturus" in error.

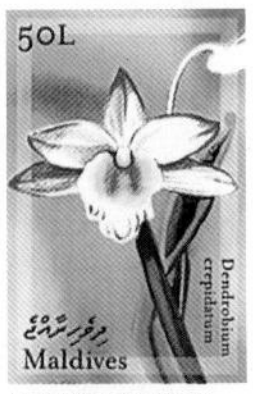

382 *Dendrobium crepidatum*

2000. Orchids. Multicoloured.

3302	50l. Type **382**	45	50
3303	1r. *Eulophia guineensis*	55	25
3304	2r.50 *Cymbidium finlaysonianum*	85	60
3305	3r.50 *Paphiopedilum druryi*	1·00	75
3306	10r. *Angraecum germinyanum*	1·75	1·75
3307	10r. *Phalaenopsis amabilis*	1·75	1·75
3308	10r. *Thrixspermum cantipeda*	1·75	1·75
3309	10r. *Phaius tankervilleae*	1·75	1·75
3310	10r. *Rhynchostylis gigantea*	1·75	1·75
3311	10r. *Papilionanthe teres*	1·75	1·75
3312	10r. Aerides odorata	1·75	1·75
3313	10r. *Dendrobium chrysotoxum*	1·75	1·75
3314	10r. *Dendrobium anosmum*	1·75	1·75
3315	10r. *Calypso bulbosa*	1·75	1·75
3316	10r. *Paphiopedilum fairrieanum*	1·75	1·75
3317	10r. *Cynorkis fastigiata*	1·75	1·75
MS3318	Two sheets, each 96×72 mm. (a) 25r. *Cymbidium dayanum*. (b) 25r. *Spathoglottis plicata* Set of 2 sheets	8·00	9·00

Nos. 3306/11 and 3312/17 were each printed together, *se-tenant*, with the backgrounds forming composite designs.

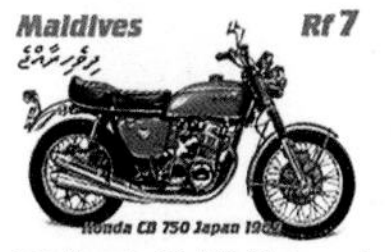

383 Honda CB 750 Motorcycle, 1969

2000. A Century of Motorcycles. Multicoloured.

3319	7r. Type **383**	1·10	1·10
3320	7r. Pioneer Harley Davidson, 1913	1·10	1·10
3321	7r. Bohmerland, 1925	1·10	1·10
3322	7r. American Indian, 1910	1·10	1·10
3323	7r. Triumph Trophy 1200, 1993	1·10	1·10
3324	7r. Moto Guzzi 500S, 1928	1·10	1·10
3325	7r. Matchless, 1907	1·10	1·10
3326	7r. Manch 4 1200 TTS, 1966	1·10	1·10
3327	7r. Lambretta LD-150, 1957	1·10	1·10
3328	7r. Yamaha XJP 1200, 1990's	1·10	1·10
3329	7r. Daimler, 1885	1·10	1·10
3330	7r. John Player Norton, 1950s–60's	1·10	1·10
MS3331	Two sheets, each 62×46 mm. (a) 25r. Harley Davidson, 1950. (b) 25r. Electra Glide, 1960 Set of 2 sheets	8·00	9·00

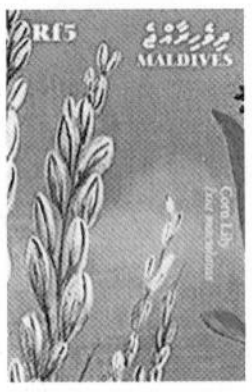

384 Corn Lily

2000. Flowers of the Indian Ocean. Multicoloured.

3332	5r. Type **384**	1·00	1·00
3333	5r. Clivia	1·00	1·00
3334	5r. Red hot poker	1·00	1·00
3335	5r. Crown of Thorns	1·00	1·00
3336	5r. Cape daisy	1·00	1·00
3337	5r. Geranium	1·00	1·00
3338	5r. Fringed hibiscus (horiz)	1·00	1·00
3339	5r. *Erica vestita* (horiz)	1·00	1·00
3340	5r. Bird-of-paradise flower (horiz)	1·00	1·00
3341	5r. Peacock orchid (horiz)	1·00	1·00
3342	5r. Mesembryanthemums (horiz)	1·00	1·00
3343	5r. African violets (horiz)	1·00	1·00
MS3344	Two sheets, each 112×80 mm. (a) 25r. Gladiolus. (b) 25r. Calla lily (horiz) Set of 2 sheets	8·50	9·50

Nos. 3332/7 and 3338/43 were each printed together, *se-tenant*, with the backgrounds forming composite designs.

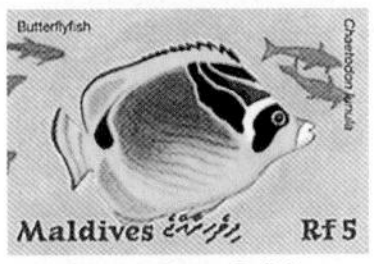

385 Racoon Butterflyfish (*Chaetodon lunula*)

2000. Marine Life of the Indian Ocean. Multicoloured.

3345	5r. Type **385**	85	85
3346	5r. Wrasse (*Stethojulis albovittata*)	85	85
3347	5r. Green turtle	85	85
3348	5r. Jobfish	85	85
3349	5r. Damsel fish	85	85
3350	5r. Meyer's butterflyfish (*Chaetodon meyeri*)	85	85
3351	5r. Wrasse (*Cirrhilabrus exquisitus*)	85	85
3352	5r. Maldive anemonefish	85	85
3353	5r. Hind (*Cephalopholis* sp)	85	85
3354	5r. Regal angelfish (*Pygopolites diacanthus*) (red face value)	85	85
3355	5r. Forceps butterflyfish (*Forcipiger flavissimus*)	85	85
3356	5r. Goatfish	85	85
3357	5r. Trumpet fish	85	85
3358	5r. Butterfly perch (*Pseudanthias squamipinnis*)	85	85
3359	5r. Two-spined angelfish (*Centropyge bispinosus*)	85	85
3360	5r. Sweetlips	85	85
3361	5r. Twin-spotted wrasse (*Coris aygula*)	85	85
3362	5r. Snapper	85	85
3363	5r. Sea bass	85	85
3364	5r. Bennett's butterflyfish (*Chaetodon bennetti*)	85	85
3365	5r. Pelagic snapper	85	85
3366	5r. Cardinalfish	85	85
3367	5r. Six-barred wrasse (*Thalassoma hardwicke*)	85	85
3368	5r. Surgeonfish	85	85
3369	5r. Longnosed filefish	85	85
3370	5r. Hawaiian squirrelfish	85	85
3371	5r. Freckled hawkfish	85	85
3372	5r. McCosker's flasher wrasse	85	85
3373	5r. Regal angelfish (*Pygoplites diacanthus*) (white face value)	85	85
3374	5r. Angelfish (*Parseentzopyge venusta*)	85	85
MS3375	Four sheets, each 108×80 mm. (a) 25r. Moray eel. (b) 25r. Yellow-bellied hamlet (*Hypoplectrus aberrans*). (c) 25r. Yellow-banded angelfish (*Pomacanthus maculosus*). (d) 25r. Spiny butterflyfish (*Pygoplites diacanthus*) Set of 4 sheets	15·00	17·00

Nos. 3345/52, 3353/60, 3361/8 and 3369/74 were each printed together, *se-tenant*, with the backgrounds forming composite designs.

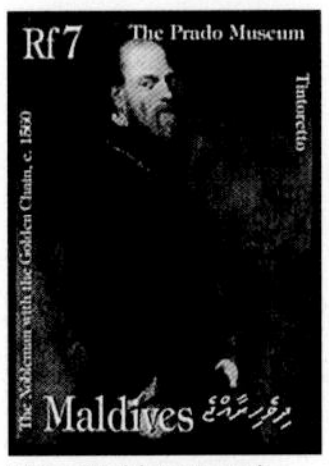

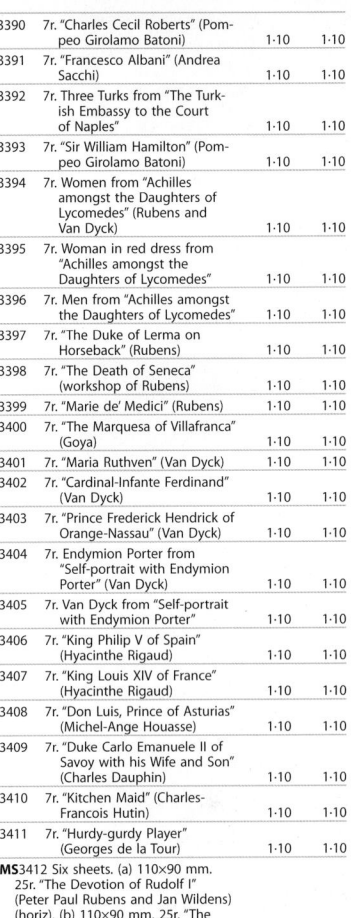

385a "Nobleman with Golden Chain" (Tintoretto)

2000. "Espana 2000" International Stamp Exhibition, Madrid. Paintings from the Prado Museum. Multicoloured.

3376	7r. Type **385a**	1·10	1·10
3377	7r. "Triumphal Arch" (Domenichino)	1·10	1·10
3378	7r. "Don Garzia de'Medici" (Bronzino)	1·10	1·10
3379	7r. Man from "Micer Marsilio and his Wife" (Lorenzo Lotto)	1·10	1·10
3380	7r. "The Infanta Maria Antonieta Fernanda" (Jacopo Amigoni)	1·10	1·10
3381	7r. Woman from "Micer Marsilio and his Wife"	1·10	1·10
3382	7r. "Self-portrait" (Albrecht Durer)	1·10	1·10
3383	7r. "Woman and her Daughter" (Adriaen van Cronenburch)	1·10	1·10
3384	7r. "Portrait of a Man" (Albrecht Durer)	1·10	1·10
3385	7r. Wife and daughters from "The Artist and his Family" (Jacob Jordaens)	1·00	1·00
3386	7r. "Artemisia" (Rembrandt)	1·10	1·10
3387	7r. Man from "The Artist and his Family"	1·10	1·10
3388	7r. "The Painter Andrea Sacchi" (Carlo Maratta)	1·10	1·10
3389	7r. Two Turks from "The Turkish Embassy to the Court of Naples" (Giuseppe Bonito)	1·10	1·10
3390	7r. "Charles Cecil Roberts" (Pompeo Girolamo Batoni)	1·10	1·10
3391	7r. "Francesco Albani" (Andrea Sacchi)	1·10	1·10
3392	7r. Three Turks from "The Turkish Embassy to the Court of Naples"	1·10	1·10
3393	7r. "Sir William Hamilton" (Pompeo Girolamo Batoni)	1·10	1·10
3394	7r. Women from "Achilles amongst the Daughters of Lycomedes" (Rubens and Van Dyck)	1·10	1·10
3395	7r. Woman in red dress from "Achilles amongst the Daughters of Lycomedes"	1·10	1·10
3396	7r. Men from "Achilles amongst the Daughters of Lycomedes"	1·10	1·10
3397	7r. "The Duke of Lerma on Horseback" (Rubens)	1·10	1·10
3398	7r. "The Death of Seneca" (workshop of Rubens)	1·10	1·10
3399	7r. "Marie de' Medici" (Rubens)	1·10	1·10
3400	7r. "The Marquesa of Villafranca" (Goya)	1·10	1·10
3401	7r. "Maria Ruthven" (Van Dyck)	1·10	1·10
3402	7r. "Cardinal-Infante Ferdinand" (Van Dyck)	1·10	1·10
3403	7r. "Prince Frederick Hendrick of Orange-Nassau" (Van Dyck)	1·10	1·10
3404	7r. Endymion Porter from "Self-portrait with Endymion Porter" (Van Dyck)	1·10	1·10
3405	7r. Van Dyck from "Self-portrait with Endymion Porter"	1·10	1·10
3406	7r. "King Philip V of Spain" (Hyacinthe Rigaud)	1·10	1·10
3407	7r. "King Louis XIV of France" (Hyacinthe Rigaud)	1·10	1·10
3408	7r. "Don Luis, Prince of Asturias" (Michel-Ange Houasse)	1·10	1·10
3409	7r. "Duke Carlo Emanuele II of Savoy with his Wife and Son" (Charles Dauphin)	1·10	1·10
3410	7r. "Kitchen Maid" (Charles-Francois Hutin)	1·10	1·10
3411	7r. "Hurdy-gurdy Player" (Georges de la Tour)	1·10	1·10
MS3412	Six sheets. (a) 110×90 mm. 25r. "The Devotion of Rudolf I" (Peter Paul Rubens and Jan Wildens) (horiz). (b) 110×90 mm. 25r. "The Artist and his Family" (Jacob Jordaens) (horiz). (c) 90×110 mm. 25r. "The Turkish Embassy to the Court of Naples" (Guiseppe Bonito). (d) 90×110 mm. 25r. "Camilla Gonzaga, Countess of San Segundo, with her Three Children" (Parmigianino). (e) 90×110 mm. 25r. "Elizabeth of Valois" (Sofonisba Anguisciola). (f) 110×90 mm. 25r. "Duke Carlo Emanuele II of Savoy with his Wife and Son" (Charles Dauphin) Set of 6 sheets	24·00	26·00

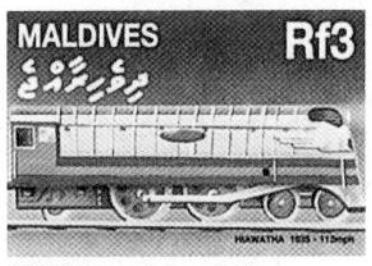

386 Steam Locomotive *Hiawatha*, 1935

2000. Milestones in Twentieth-century Transport. Multicoloured.

3413	2r. 50 Steam locomotive *Papyrus*, 1934 (vert)	75	50
3414	3r. Type **386**	75	50
3415	5r. Thrust SSC rocket car, 1997	1·00	1·00
3416	5r. Curtiss R3C-2 seaplane, 1925	1·00	1·00
3417	5r. Steam locomotive *Rocket*, 1829	1·00	1·00
3418	5r. BB-9004 electric train, 1955	1·00	1·00
3419	5r. Steam locomotive *Mallard*, 1938	1·00	1·00
3420	5r. T.G.V. electric train, 1980	1·00	1·00
3421	5r. Lockheed XP-80 aircraft, 1947	1·00	1·00
3422	5r. Mikoyan Mig 23 Foxbat aircraft, 1965	1·00	1·00
3423	5r. Hawker Tempest aircraft, 1943	1·00	1·00
3424	5r. *Bluebird* car, 1964	1·00	1·00
3425	5r. *Blue Flame* car, 1970	1·00	1·00
3426	5r. *Thrust 2* car, 1983	1·00	1·00
3427	12r. Supermarine S.B.G. seaplane, 1931	2·00	2·25
3428	13r. MLX01 train, 1998	2·00	2·25
MS3429	Two sheets. (a) 100×75 mm. 25r. Lockheed SR-71 Blackbird airplane, 1976 (vert). (b) 75×100 mm. 25r. Bell X-1 aircraft, 1947 Set of 2 sheets	9·50	10·00

Nos. 3415/20 and 3421/6 were each printed together, *se-tenant*, with the backgrounds forming composite designs.

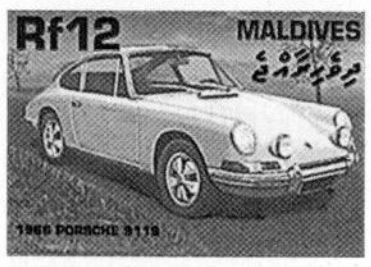

387 Porsche 911S, 1966

2000. "The World of Porsche". Multicoloured.

3430	12r. Type **387**	1·75	2·00
3431	12r. Model 959, 1988	1·75	2·00
3432	12r. Model 993 Carrera, 1995	1·75	2·00
3433	12r. Model 356 SC, 1963	1·75	2·00
3434	12r. Model 911 Turbo, 1975	1·75	2·00
3435	12r. Contemporary model	1·75	2·00
MS3436	110×85 mm. 25r. Model Boxter, 2000 (56×42 mm)	4·00	4·50

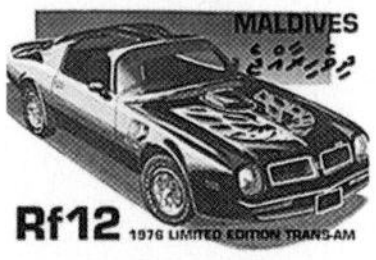

388 Limited Edition Trans-Am, 1976

2000. "The World of the Pontiac". Multicolourd.

3437	12r. Type **388**	1·75	2·00
3438	12r. Trans-Am, 1988	1·75	2·00
3439	12r. Trans-Am Coupe, 1988	1·75	2·00
3440	12r. Yellow Trans-Am, 1970–72	1·75	2·00
3441	12r. 25th Anniv Trans-Am, 1989	1·75	2·00
3442	12r. Trans-Am GT convertible, 1994	1·75	2·00
MS3443	110×85 mm. 25r. Trans-Am model, 1999 (56×42 mm)	4·00	4·50

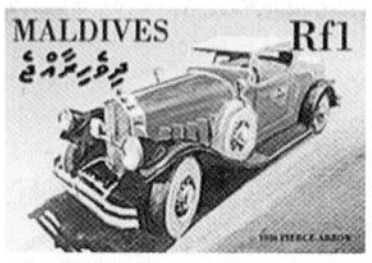

389 Pierce-Arrow (1930)

2000. Twentieth-century Classic Cars. Multicoloured.

3444	1r. Type **389**	40	15
3445	2r. Mercedes-Benz 540K (1938)	60	30
3446	7r. Auburn Convertible Sedan (1931)	1·40	1·40
3447	7r. Mercedes SSKL (1931)	1·40	1·40
3448	7r. Packard Roadster (1929)	1·40	1·40
3449	7r. Chevrolet (1940)	1·40	1·40
3450	7r. Mercer (1915)	1·40	1·40
3451	7r. Packard Sedan (1941)	1·40	1·40
3452	7r. Chevrolet Roadster (1932)	1·40	1·40
3453	7r. Cadillac Fleetwood Roadster (1929)	1·40	1·40
3454	7r. Bentley Speed Six (1928)	1·40	1·40
3455	7r. Cadillac Fleetwood (1930)	1·40	1·40
3456	7r. Ford Convertible (1936)	1·40	1·40
3457	7r. Hudson Phaeton (1929)	1·40	1·40
3458	8r. Duesenberg J (1934)	1·40	1·40
3459	10r. Bugatti Royale (1931)	1·50	1·75
MS3460	Two sheets, each 106×81 mm. (a) 25r. Rolls Royce P-1 (1931). (b) 25r. Cord Brougham (1930) Set of 2 sheets	8·50	9·50

No. 3457 is inscribed "HUDSIN" in error.

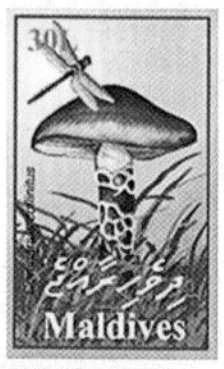

390 *Cortinarius collinitus*

2001. Fungi. Multicoloured.

3461	30l. Type **390**	25	35
3462	50l. *Russula ochroleuca*	25	35
3463	2r. *Lepiota acutesquamosa*	66	30
3464	3r. *Hebeloma radicosum*	70	35
3465	7r. *Tricholoma aurantium*	1·10	1·10
3466	7r. *Pholiota spectabilis*	1·10	1·10
3467	7r. *Russula caerulea*	1·10	1·10
3468	7r. *Amanita phalloides*	1·10	1·10
3469	7r. *Mycena strobilinoides*	1·10	1·10
3470	7r. *Boletus satanas*	1·10	1·10
3471	7r. *Amanita muscaria*	1·10	1·10
3472	7r. *Mycena lilacifolia*	1·10	1·10
3473	7r. *Coprinus comatus*	1·10	1·10
3474	7r. *Morchella crassipes*	1·10	1·10
3475	7r. *Russula nigricans*	1·10	1·10
3476	7r. *Lepiota procera*	1·10	1·10
3477	13r. *Amanita echinocephala*	1·75	1·75
3478	15r. *Collybia iocephala*	1·90	1·90
MS3479	Two sheets, each 112×82 mm. (a) 25r. *Tricholoma aurantium*. (b) 25r. *Lepiota procera* Set of 2 sheets	8·00	9·00

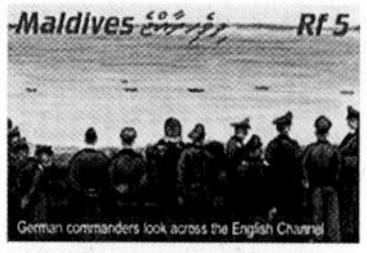

390a German Commanders looking across English Channel

2001. 60th Anniv of Battle of Britain. Multicoloured.

3480	5r. Type **390a**	1·40	1·40
3481	5r. Armourers with German bomber	1·40	1·40
3482	5r. German Stuka dive-bombers	1·40	1·40
3483	5r. Bombing the British coast	1·40	1·40
3484	5r. German bomber over Greenwich	1·40	1·40
3485	5r. St. Paul's Cathedral surrounded by fire	1·40	1·40
3486	5r. British fighter from German bomber	1·40	1·40
3487	5r. Spitfire on fire	1·40	1·40
3488	5r. Prime Minister Winston Churchill	1·40	1·40
3489	5r. British fighter pilots running to planes	1·40	1·40
3490	5r. R.A.F. planes taking off	1·40	1·40
3491	5r. British fighters in formation	1·40	1·40
3492	5r. German bomber crashing	1·40	1·40
3493	5r. British fighters attacking	1·40	1·40
3494	5r. German bomber in sea	1·40	1·40
3495	5r. Remains of German bomber in flames	1·40	1·40
MS3496	Two sheets, each 103×66 mm. (a) 25r. Hawker Hurricane. (b) 25r. Messerschmitt ME 109 Set of 2 sheets	8·00	9·00

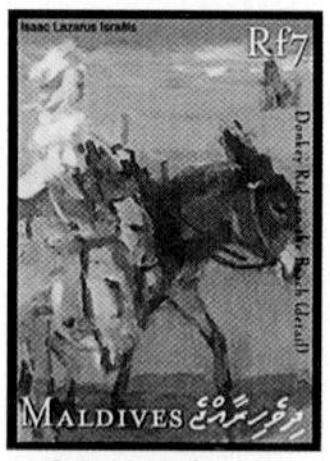

390b Donkeys from "Donkey Ride on the Beach" (Isaac Lazarus Israels)

2001. Bicentenary of Rijksmuseum, Amsterdam. Dutch Paintings. Multicoloured.

3497	7r. Type **390b**	1·10	1·10
3498	7r. "The Paternal Admonition" (Gerard ter Borch)	1·10	1·10
3499	7r. "The Sick Woman" (Jan Havicksz Steen)	1·10	1·10
3500	7r. Girls from "Donkey Ride on the Beach"	1·10	1·10
3501	7r. "Pompejus Occo" (Dick Jacobsz)	1·10	1·10
3502	7r. "The Pantry" (Pieter de Hooch)	1·10	1·10
3503	7r. Woman in doorway from "The Little Street" (Johannes Vermeer)	1·10	1·10
3504	7r. Woman with maid from "The Love Letter" (Johannes Vermeer)	1·10	1·10
3505	7r. "Woman in Blue Reading a Letter" (Johannes Vermeer)	1·10	1·10
3506	7r. Woman from "The Love Letter"	1·10	1·10
3507	7r. "The Milkmaid" (Johannes Vermeer)	1·10	1·10
3508	7r. Woman in alley from "The Little Street"	1·10	1·10
3509	7r. "Rembrandt's Mother" (Gerard Dou)	1·10	1·10
3510	7r. "Girl dressed in Blue" (Johannes Verspronck)	1·10	1·10
3511	7r. "Old Woman at Prayer" (Nicolaes Maes)	1·10	1·10
3512	7r. "Feeding the Hungry" (De Meester van Alkmaar)	1·10	1·10
3513	7r. "The Threatened Swan" (Jan Asselyn)	1·10	1·10
3514	7r. "The Daydreamer" (Nicolaes Maes)	1·10	1·10
3515	7r. "The Holy Kinship" (Geertgen Tot Sint Jans)	1·10	1·10
3516	7r. "Sir Thomas Gresham" (Anthonis Mor Vas Dashorst)	1·10	1·10
3517	7r. "Self portrait as St. Paul" (Rembrandt)	1·10	1·10
3518	7r. "Cleopatra's Banquet" (Gerard Lairesse)	1·10	1·10
3519	7r. "Flowers in a Glass" (Jan Brueghel the elder)	1·10	1·10
3520	7r. "Nicolaes Hasselaer" (Frans Hals)	1·10	1·10
MS3521	Four sheets. (a) 118×78 mm. 25r. "The Syndics" (Rembrandt). (b) 88×118 mm. 25r. "Johannes Wtenbogaert" (Rembrandt). (c) 118×88 mm. 25r. "The Night Watch" (Rembrandt). (d) 118×88 mm. 25r. "Shipwreck on a Rocky Coast" (Wijnandus Johannes Nuyen) (horiz) Set of 4 sheets	16·00	19·00

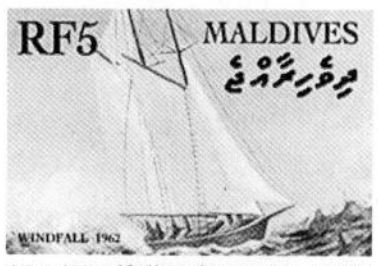

391 *Windfall* (schooner), 1962

2001. Maritime Disasters. Multicoloured.

3522	5r. Type **391**	1·00	1·00
3523	5r. *Kobenhavn* (barque), 1928	1·00	1·00
3524	5r. *Pearl* (schooner), 1874	1·00	1·00
3525	5r. H.M.S. *Bulwark* (battleship), 1914	1·00	1·00
3526	5r. *Patriot* (brig), 1812	1·00	1·00
3527	5r. *Lusitania* (liner), 1915	1·00	1·00
3528	5r. *Milton Iatrides* (coaster), 1970	1·00	1·00
3529	5r. *Cyclops* (freighter), 1918	1·00	1·00
3530	5r. *Marine Sulphur Queen* (tanker), 1963	1·00	1·00
3531	5r. *Rosalie* (full-rigged ship), 1840	1·00	1·00
3532	5r. *Mary Celeste* (sail merchantman), 1872	1·00	1·00
3533	5r. *Atlanta* (brig), 1880	1·00	1·00
MS3534	Two sheets, each 110×85 mm. (a) 25r. *L'Astrolabe* and *La Boussole* (La Perouse, 1789). (b) 25r. *Titanic* (liner), 1912 Set of 2 sheets	12·00	12·00

Nos. 3522/7 and 3528/33 were printed together, *se-tenant*, with the backgrounds forming composite designs. No. 3530 is inscribed "SULPHER" and No. **MS**3517a "LA BAUSSOLE", both in error.

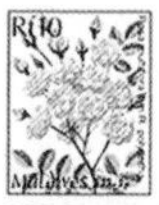
392 Roses

2001

3535	**392**	10r. multicoloured	1·25	1·25

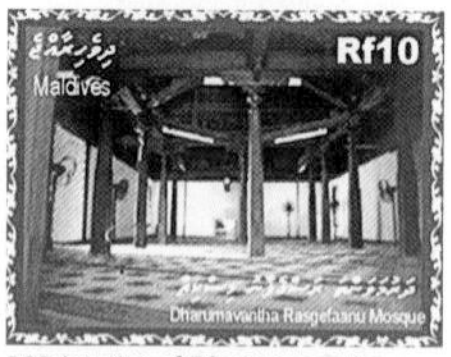

393 Interior of Dharumavantha Rasgefaanu Mosque

2001. 848th Anniv of Introduction of Islam to the Maldives. Multicoloured (except Nos. 3537/8).

3536	10r. Type **393**	1·40	1·60
3537	10r. Plaque of Hukurumiskiiy (black and green)	1·40	1·60
3538	10r. Family studying the Holy Quran (black)	1·40	1·60
3539	10r. Class at Institute of Islamic Studies	1·40	1·60
3540	10r. Centre for the Holy Quran	1·40	1·60
3541	10r. Islamic Centre, Male	1·40	1·60
MS3542	116×90 mm. 25r. Tomb of Sultan Abdul Barakaat	3·75	4·50

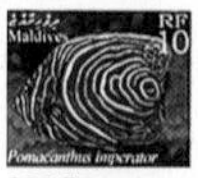
394 Emperor Angelfish

2001. Fish. Multicoloured.

3543	10r. Type **394**	2·25	2·25
3544	10r. Indian Ocean lionfish ("*Pterois miles*")	2·25	2·25

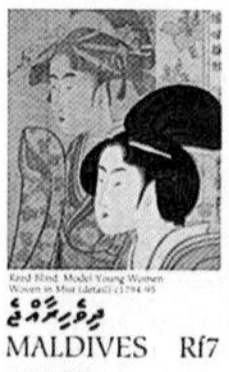

395 "Young Women in Mist"

2001. "Philanippon '01" International Stamp Exhibition, Tokyo. Japanese Art. Multicoloured.

3545	7r. Type **395**	1·00	1·00
3546	7r. "Woman with Parasol"	1·00	1·00
3547	7r. "Courtesan"	1·00	1·00
3548	7r. "Comparison of Beauties"	1·00	1·00
3549	7r. "Barber"	1·00	1·00
3550	7r. Ichikawa Danjuro V in black robes (20×81 mm)	1·00	1·00
3551	7r. Ichikawa Danjuro V in brown robes with sword (20×81 mm)	1·00	1·00
3552	7r. Ichikawa Danjuro V with arms folded (20×81 mm)	1·00	1·00
3553	7r. Ichikawa Danjuro V seated in brown robes (20×81 mm)	1·00	1·00
3554	7r. Otani Tomoeman I and Bando Mitsugaro I (53×81 mm)	1·00	1·00
MS3555	Two sheets, each 88×124 mm. (a) 25r. "Courtesan Hinazuru" (Kitagawa Utamaro). (b) 25r. "Tsutsui Jōmyō and the Priest Ichirai" (Torii Kiyomasu I) Set of 2 sheets	8·00	9·00

Nos. 3545/9 show paintings of women by Kitagawa Utamaro, and Nos. 3550/4 show famous actors by Katsukawa Shunsho.

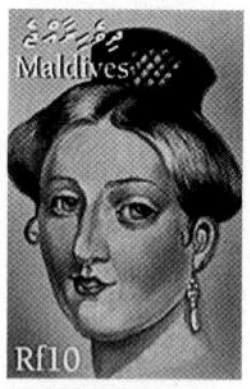

395a Victoria as a Young Girl (face value bottom left)

2001. Death Centenary of Queen Victoria. Multicoloured.

3556	10r. Type **395a**	1·40	1·60
3557	10r. Victoria in old age	1·40	1·60
3558	10r. Victoria as a young girl (face value top right)	1·40	1·60
3559	10r. Queen Victoria in mourning	1·40	1·60
MS3560	125×87 mm. 25r. Young Queen Victoria in evening dress	3·75	4·25

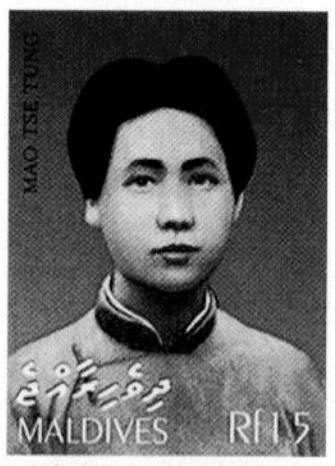

395b Mao as a teenager (brown background)

2001. 25th Death Anniv of Mao Tse-tung (Chinese leader). Multicoloured.

3561	15r. Type **395b**	1·50	1·75
3562	15r. Mao as leader of Communist Party in 1930s (violet background)	1·50	1·75
3563	15r. Mao in 1940s (grey background)	1·50	1·75
MS3564	139×132 mm. 25r. Mao as leader of China in 1960s	3·50	4·00

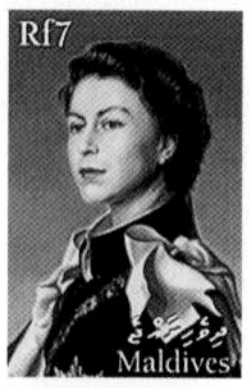

395c Portrait in Garter robes

2001. 75th Birthday of Queen Elizabeth II. Multicoloured.

3565	7r. Type **395c**	1·75	1·75
3566	7r. Queen at Coronation	1·25	1·75
3567	7r. In evening gown and tiara	1·25	1·75
3568	7r. In uniform for Trooping the Colour	1·25	1·75
3569	7r. In Garter robes and hat	1·25	1·75
3570	7r. Queen wearing cloak of kiwi feathers	1·75	1·75
MS3571	112×138 mm. 25r. Young Queen Elizabeth	5·00	4·00

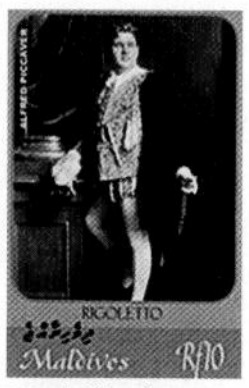

395d Alfred Piccaver (opera singer) after Annigoni as Duke of Mantua

2001. Death Centenary of Giuseppe Verdi (Italian composer). Multicoloured.

3572	10r. Type **395d**	2·25	2·25
3573	10r. Heinrich's costume from Rigoletto (opera)	2·25	2·25
3574	10r. Cologne's costume from Rigoletto	2·25	2·25
3575	10r. Cornell MacNeil (opera singer) as Rigoletto	2·25	2·25
MS3576	79×119 mm. 25r. Matteo Manvgerri (opera singer) as Rigoletto	6·00	6·50

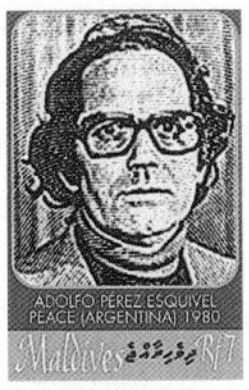

396 Adolfo Perez Esquivel (Peace Prize, 1980)

2001. Centenary of Nobel Prizes. Prize Winners. Multicoloured.

3577	7r. Type **396**	85	90
3578	7r. Mikhail Gorbachev (Peace, 1990)	85	90
3579	7r. Betty Williams (Peace, 1976)	85	90
3580	7r. Alfonso Garcia Robles (Peace, 1982)	85	90
3581	7r. Paul d'Estournelles de Constant (Peace, 1909)	85	90
3582	7r. Louis Renault (Peace, 1907)	85	90
3583	7r. Ernesto Moneta (Peace, 1907)	85	90
3584	7r. Albert Luthuli (Peace, 1960)	85	90
3585	7r. Henri Dunant (Peace, 1901)	85	90
3586	7r. Albert Gobat (Peace, 1902)	85	90
3587	7r. Sean MacBride (Peace, 1974)	85	90
3588	7r. Elie Ducommun (Peace, 1902)	85	90
3589	7r. Simon Kuznets (Economics, 1971)	85	90
3590	7r. Wassily Leontief (Economics, 1973)	85	90
3591	7r. Lawrence Klein (Economics, 1980)	85	90
3592	7r. Friedrich von Hayek (Economics, 1974)	85	90
3593	7r. Leonid Kantorovich (Economics, 1975)	85	90
MS3594	Three sheets, each 108×127 mm. (a) 25r. Trygve Haavelmo (Economics, 1989). (b) 25r. Octavio Paz (Literature, 1990). (c) 25r. Vicente Aleixandre (Literature, 1977) Set of 3 sheets	11·00	14·00

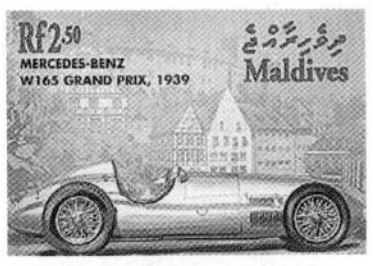

397 Mercedes-Benz W165 Racing Car, 1939

2001. Centenary of Mercedes-Benz Cars. Multicoloured.

3595	2r.50 Type **397**	45	35
3596	5r. 460 Nurburg Sport-roadster, 1928	85	65
3597	7r. 680S racing car, 1927	1·00	1·10
3598	7r. 150, 1934	1·00	1·10
3599	7r. 540K Roadster, 1936	1·00	1·10
3600	7r. 770 "Grosser Mercedes", 1932	1·00	1·10
3601	7r. 220SE, 1958	1·00	1·10
3602	7r. 500SL, 1990	1·00	1·10
3603	7r. 290, 1933	1·00	1·10
3604	7r. Model 680S, 1927	1·00	1·10
3605	7r. 300SL Coupe, 1953	1·00	1·10
3606	7r. Benz Victoria, 1911	1·00	1·10
3607	7r. 280SL, 1968	1·00	1·10
3608	7r. W125 racing car, 1937	1·00	1·10
3609	8r. Boattail Speedster, 1938	1·10	1·25
3610	15r. "Blitzen Benz", 1909	1·60	1·75
MS3611	Two sheets, each 109×96 mm. (a) 25r. 370S, 1931. (b) 25r. 300SLR racing car, 1955 Set of 2 sheets	8·50	9·50

Nos. 3600 and 3606 are inscribed "GROBERMERCEDES" or "BENA", both in error.

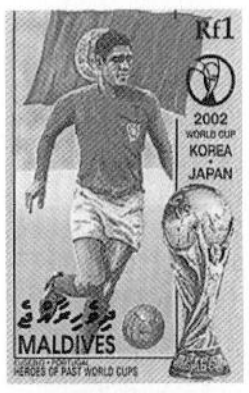

398 Eusebio and Portuguese Flag

2001. World Cup Football Championship, Japan and Korea (2002). Multicoloured.

3612	1r. Type **398**	20	15
3613	3r. Johan Cruyff and Dutch flag	45	35
3614	7r. Footballer and French flag	1·00	90
3615	10r. Footballer and Japanese flag	1·25	1·25
3616	12r. World Cup Stadium, Seoul, Korea (horiz)	1·50	1·75
3617	15r. Poster for first World Cup Championship, Uruguay, 1930	1·75	2·25
MS3618	70×100 mm. 25r. Gerd Muller, 1974 World Cup Final (43×57 mm)	5·50	6·00

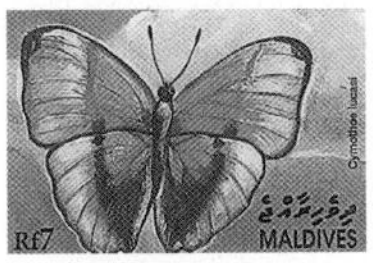

399 *Cymothoe lucasi*

2001. Moths and Butterflies. Multicoloured.

3619	7r. Type **399**	90	95
3620	7r. *Milionia grandis*	90	95
3621	7r. *Ornithoptera croesus*	90	95
3622	7r. *Hyantis hodeva*	90	95
3623	7r. *Ammobiota festiva*	90	95
3624	7r. *Salamis temora*	90	95
3625	7r. *Zygaena occitanica*	90	95
3626	7r. *Campylotes desgodinsi*	90	95
3627	7r. *Bhutanitis thaidina*	90	95
3628	7r. *Helicopsis endymion*	90	95
3629	7r. *Parnassius charitonius*	90	95
3630	7r. *Acaca ecucogiap*	90	95
3631	10r. *Papilio dardanus*	1·25	1·40
3632	10r. *Baomisa hieroglyphica*	1·25	1·40
3633	10r. *Troides prattorum*	1·25	1·40
3634	10r. *Funonia rhadama*	1·25	1·40
MS3635	Two sheets. (a) 83×108 mm. 25r. *Hypolera cassotis*. (b) 108×83 mm. 25r. *Euphydryas maturna* (vert)	9·50	10·00

Nos. 3621 and 3629 are inscribed "eroesus" or "charltonius", both in error.

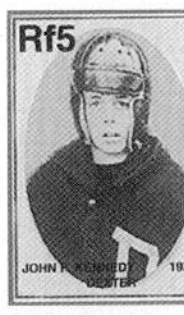

400 John F. Kennedy in American Football Kit, 1927

2001. John F. Kennedy (American President) Commemoration. Multicoloured.

3636	5r. Type **400**	75	85
3637	5r. John Kennedy at Harvard, 1935	75	85
3638	5r. As U.S. Navy officer, Solomon Islands, 1943	75	85
3639	5r. On wedding day, 1953	75	85
3640	5r. With brother, Robert, 1956	75	85
3641	5r. Presidential Inauguration, 1961	75	85
3642	5r. With First Secretary Nikita Khrushchev of U.S.S.R., 1961	75	85
3643	5r. With Prime Minister Harold MacMillan of Great Britain	75	85
3644	5r. With Pres. Charles de Gaulle of France, 1961	75	85
3645	5r. With Prime Minister Jawaharlal Nehru of India, 1962	75	85
3646	5r. With Chancellor Konrad Adenauer of West Germany, 1963	75	85
3647	5r. With Martin Luther King (Civil Rights campaigner) 1963	75	85
MS3648	Two sheets, each 82×112 mm. (a) 25r. John Kennedy. (b) 25r. With wife, Paris, 1961	8·00	9·00

No. 3642 is inscribed "PRIMIER" in error.

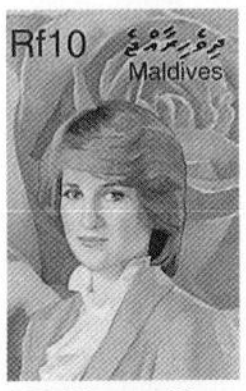

401 Princess Diana wearing Pink Jacket

2001. 40th Birth Anniv of Diana, Princess of Wales. Multicoloured.

3649	10r. Type **401**	1·25	1·75
3650	10r. In evening dress with tiara	1·25	1·75
3651	10r. Wearing matching yellow hat and coat	1·23	1·75
3652	10r. In beige dress	1·25	1·75
MS3653	73×109 mm. 25r. Princess Diana wearing pearls	3·75	4·25

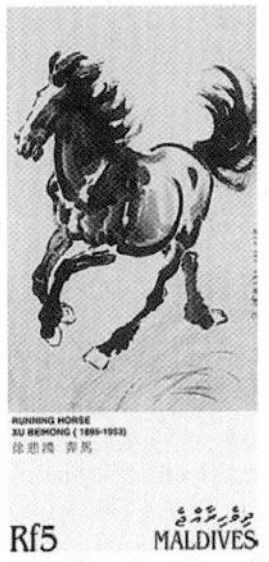

402 "Running Horse" (Xu Beihong)

2001. Chinese New Year ("Year of the Horse"). Paintings by Xu Beihong. Multicoloured.

3654	5r. Type **402**	1·50	1·50
3655	5r. "Standing Horse" (from back, with head up)	1·50	1·50
3656	5r. "Running Horse" (different)	1·50	1·50
3657	5r. "Standing Horse" (with head down)	1·50	1·50
3658	5r. "Horse" (with head up, from front)	1·50	1·50
MS3659	110×70 mm. 15r. "Six Horses running" (57×37 mm)	2·50	2·75

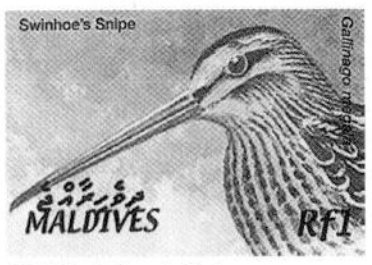

403 Swinhoe's Snipe

2002. Birds. Multicoloured.

3660	1r. Type **403**	75	40
3661	2r. Oriental honey buzzard	65	40
3662	3r. Asian koel	80	55
3663	5r. Red-throated pipet	1·00	80
3664	5r. Cattle egret	1·00	1·00
3665	5r. Barn swallow	1·00	1·00
3666	5r. Osprey	1·00	1·00
3667	5r. Green-backed heron ("Little Heron")	1·00	1·00
3668	5r. Ruddy turnstone	1·00	1·00
3669	5r. Sooty tern	1·00	1·00
3670	5r. Lesser noddy	1·00	1·00
3671	5r. Roseate tern	1·00	1·00
3672	5r. Great frigate bird ("Frigate Minor")	1·00	1·00
3673	5r. Black-shafted tern ("Saunder's Tern")	1·00	1·00
3674	5r. White-bellied storm petrel	1·00	1·00
3675	5r. Red-footed booby	1·00	1·00
3676	7r. Rose-ringed parakeet	1·25	1·25
3677	7r. Common swift	1·40	1·40
3678	7r. Lesser kestrel	1·40	1·40
3679	7r. Golden oriole	1·40	1·40
3680	7r. Asian paradise flycatcher	1·40	1·40
3681	7r. Indian roller	1·40	1·40
3682	7r. Pallid harrier	1·40	1·40
3683	7r. Grey heron	1·40	1·40
3684	7r. Blue-tailed bee eater	1·40	1·40
3685	7r. White-breasted water hen	1·40	1·40
3686	7r. Cotton teal ("Cotton Pygmy Goose")	1·40	1·40
3687	7r. Maldivian pond heron	1·40	1·40
3688	7r. Short-eared owl	1·40	1·40
3689	10r. White spoonbill ("Eurasian Spoonbill")	1·50	1·50
3690	12r. Pied wheatear	1·75	2·00
3691	15r. Oriental pratincole	2·25	2·75
MS3692	Four sheets, each 114×57 mm. (a) 25r. White tern. (b) 25r. Greater flamingo. (c) 25r. Cinnamon bittern. (d) 25r. White-tailed tropicbird	28·00	28·00

Nos. 3664/9, 3670/5, 3676/81 and 3682/7 were each printed together, se-tenant, with the backgrounds forming composite designs.

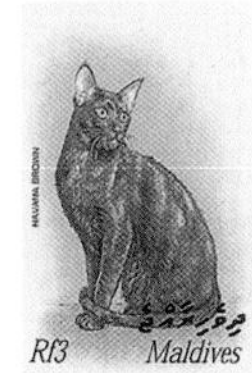

404 Havana Brown

2002. Cats. Multicoloured.

3693	3r. Type **404**	70	35
3694	5r. American wirehair	91	60
3695	7r. Persian (horiz)	1·10	1·10
3696	7r. Exotic shorthair (horiz)	1·10	1·10
3697	7r. Ragdoll (horiz)	1·10	1·10
3698	7r. Manx (horiz)	1·10	1·10
3699	7r. Tonkinese (horiz)	1·10	1·10
3700	7r. Scottish fold (horiz)	1·10	1·10
3701	7r. British blue	1·10	1·10
3702	7r. Red mackerel manx	1·10	1·10
3703	7r. Scottish fold	1·10	1·10
3704	7r. Somali	1·10	1·10
3705	7r. Balinese	1·10	1·10
3706	7r. Exotic shorthair	1·10	1·10
3707	8r. Norwegian forest cat	1·10	1·25
3708	10r. Seal point siamese	1·25	1·60
MS3709	110×85 mm. 25r. Blue mackerel tabby cornish rex	4·00	4·50

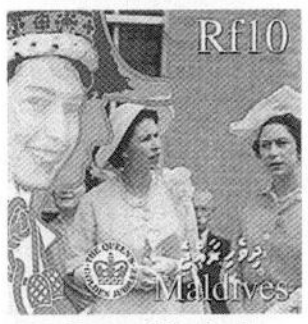

405 Queen Elizabeth with Princess Margaret

2002. Golden Jubilee. Multicoloured.

3710	10r. Type **405**	2·50	2·50
3711	10r. Princess Elizabeth wearing white hat and coat	2·50	2·50
3712	10r. Queen Elizabeth in evening dress	2·50	2·50
3713	10r. Queen Elizabeth on visit to Canada	2·50	2·50
MS3714	76×108 mm. 25r. Paying homage, at Coronation, 1953	4·50	4·75

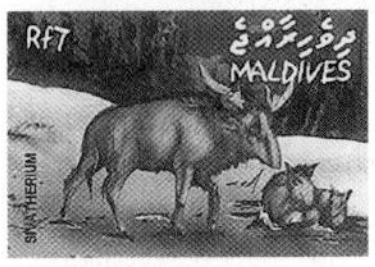

406 Sivatherium

2002. Prehistoric Animals. Multicoloured.

3715	7r. Type **406**	1·25	1·25
3716	7r. Flat-headed peccary	1·25	1·25
3717	7r. Shasta ground sloth	1·25	1·25
3718	7r. Harlan's ground sloth	1·25	1·25
3719	7r. European woolly rhinoceros	1·25	1·25
3720	7r. Dwarf pronghorn	1·25	1·25
3721	7r. Macrauchenia	1·25	1·25
3722	7r. Glyptodon	1·25	1·25
3723	7r. Nesodon	1·25	1·25
3724	7r. Imperial tapir and calf	1·25	1·25
3725	7r. Short-faced bear	1·25	1·25
3726	7r. Mastodon	1·25	1·25
MS3727	Two sheets, each 94×67 mm. (a) 25r. Sabre-toothed cat. (b) 25r. Mammoth	8·50	9·00

Nos. 3715/20 and 3721/6 were each printed together, *se-tenant*, with the backgrounds forming composite designs.

Nos. 3722 and 3726 are inscribed "GIYPTODON" and "MAMMOTH", both in error.

2002. International Year of Mountains. As T **219** of Lesotho, but vert. Multicoloured.

3728	15r. Ama Dablam, Nepal	1·75	2·25
3729	15r. Mount Clements, U.S.A.	1·75	2·25
3730	15r. Mount Artesonraju, Peru	1·75	2·25
3731	15r. Mount Cholatse, Nepal	1·75	2·25
MS3732	96×65 mm. 25r. Mount Jefferson, U.S.A., and balloon	3·75	4·25

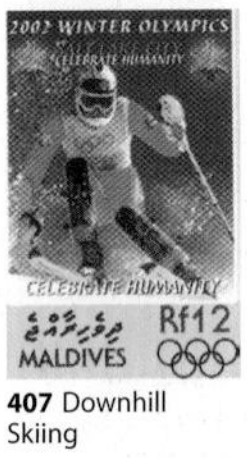

407 Downhill Skiing

2002. Winter Olympic Games, Salt Lake City. Multicoloured.

3733	12r. Type **407**	1·75	2·00
3734	12r. Ski jumping	1·75	2·00
MS3735	82×103 mm. Nos. 3733/4	3·75	4·25

2002. 20th World Scout Jamboree, Thailand. As T **295** of Lesotho. Multicoloured.

3736	15r. Buddhist pagoda, Thailand (vert)	2·00	2·50
3737	15r. Thai scout (vert)	2·00	2·50
3738	15r. Scout badges on Thai flag (vert)	2·00	2·50
MS3739	106×78 mm. 25r. Mountain-climbing badge and knot diagrams	3·75	4·00

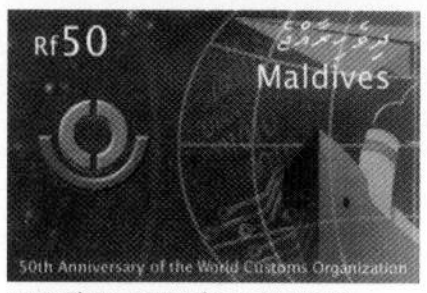

408 Ship, Aircraft and W.C.O. Logo

2002. 50th Anniv of World Customs Organization. Sheet 135×155 mm.

MS3740	**408** 50r. multicoloured	7·50	9·00

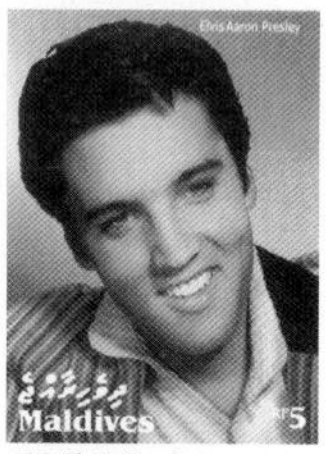

409 Elvis Presley

2002. 25th Death Anniv of Elvis Presley (American entertainer).

3741	**409** 5r. multicoloured	1·00	1·00

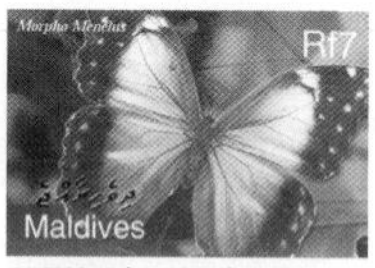

410 *Morpho menelaus*

2002. Flora and Fauna. Multicoloured.

3742	7r. Type **410**	1·25	1·25
3743	7r. *Heliconius erato*	1·25	1·25
3744	7r. *Thecla coronata*	1·25	1·25
3745	7r. *Battus philenor*	1·25	1·25
3746	7r. *Ornithoptera priamus*	1·25	1·25
3747	7r. *Danaus gilippus berenice*	1·25	1·25
3748	7r. *Ipomoea tricolor* Morning Glory	1·25	1·25
3749	7r. *Anemone coronaria* Wedding Bell	1·25	1·25
3750	7r. *Narcissus* Barrett Browning	1·25	1·25
3751	7r. *Nigella* Persian Jewel	1·25	1·25
3752	7r. *Osteospermum* Whirligig Pink	1·25	1·25
3753	7r. *Iris* Brown Lasso	1·25	1·25
3754	7r. *Laelia gouldiana*	1·25	1·25
3755	7r. *Cattleya* Louise Georgiana	1·25	1·25
3756	7r. *Laeliocattleya* Christopher Gubler	1·25	1·25
3757	7r. *Miltoniopsis* Bert Field Crimson Glow	1·25	1·25
3758	7r. *Lemboglossum bictoniense*	1·25	1·25
3759	7r. *Derosara* Divine Victor	1·25	1·25
MS3760	Three sheets. (a) 72×50 mm. 25r. *Cymothoe lurida* (butterfly). (b) 66×45 mm. 25r. Perennial Aster Little Pink Beauty. (c) 50×72 mm. 25r. *Angraecum veitchii* (vert)	9·00	10·00

Nos. 3742/7 (butterflies), 3748/53 (flowers) and 3754/9 (orchids) were each printed together, *se-tenant*, with the backgrounds forming composite designs.

Nos. 3742 and 3748 are inscribed "Menelus" or "Impomoea", both in error.

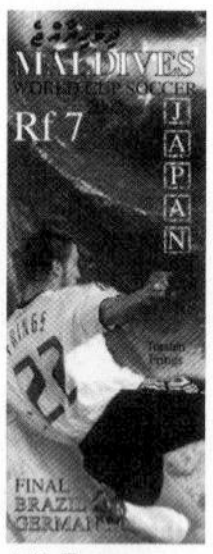

411 Torsten Frings (Germany)

2002. World Cup Football Championship, Japan and Korea. Multicoloured.

3761	7r. Type **411**	1·00	1·00
3762	7r. Roberto Carlos (Brazil)	1·00	1·00
3763	7r. Torsten Frings (Germany) (different)	1·00	1·00
3764	7r. Ronaldo (Brazil), with one finger raised	1·00	1·00
3765	7r. Oliver Neuville (Germany)	1·00	1·00
3766	7r. Ronaldo (Brazil), heading ball	1·00	1·00
3767	7r. Eul Yong Lee (South Korea) and Alpay Ozalan (Turkey)	1·00	1·00
3768	7r. Myung Bo Hong (South Korea) and Hakan Sukur (Turkey)	1·00	1·00
3769	7r. Chong Gug Song (South Korea) and Emre Belozoglu (Turkey)	1·00	1·00
3770	7r. Chong Gug Song (South Korea) and Ergun Penbe (Turkey)	1·00	1·00
3771	7r. Ki Hyeon Seol (South Korea) and Ergun Penbe (Turkey)	1·00	1·00
3772	7r. Chong Gug Song (South Korea) and Hakan Unsal (Turkey)	1·00	1·00
MS3773	Four sheets, each 82×82 mm. (a) 15r. Cafu (Brazil) and Oliver Neuville (Germany); 15r. World Cup Trophy. (b) 15r. Dietmar Hamann (Germany); 15r. Cafu (Brazil), holding Trophy. (c) 15r. Hakan Sukur (Turkey); 15r. Sang Chul Yoo (South Korea). (d) 15r. Ilhan Mansiz (Turkey); 15r. Young Pyo Lee (South Korea)	14·00	15·00

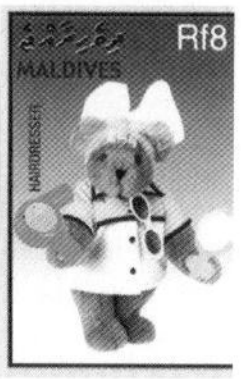

412 Hairdresser Bear

2002. Centenary of the Teddy Bear. Multicoloured.

3774	8r. Type **412**	1·00	1·10
3775	8r. Construction worker bear	1·00	1·10
3776	8r. Gardener bear	1·00	1·10
3777	8r. Chef bear	1·00	1·10
3778	12r. Nurse bear	1·40	1·50
3779	12r. Doctor bear	1·40	1·50
3780	12r. Dentist bear	1·40	1·50
3781	12r. Bride ("MOTHER") bear	1·40	1·50
3782	12r. Brother and sister bears	1·40	1·50
3783	12r. Groom ("FATHER") bear	1·40	1·50
MS3784	Three sheets, each 110×105 mm. (a) 30r. Golfer bear. (b) 30r. Footballer bear. (c) 30r. Skier bear ("SNOW BOARDER")	11·00	12·00

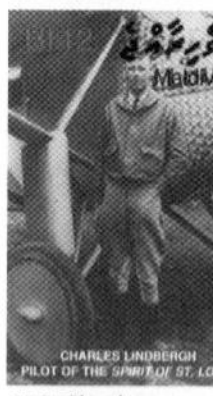

413 Charles Lindbergh and *Spirit of St. Louis*

2002. 75th Anniv of First Solo Transatlantic Flight. Multicoloured.

3785	12r. Type **413**	2·25	2·25
3786	12r. Lindbergh in flying helmet and *Spirit of St. Louis*	2·25	2·25
3787	12r. Lindbergh holding propeller	2·25	2·25
3788	12r. Lindbergh in overalls and *Spirit of St. Louis*	2·25	2·25
3789	12r. Donald Hall (designer)	2·25	2·25
3790	12r. Charles Lindbergh (pilot)	2·25	2·25
3791	12r. Lindbergh under wing of *Spirit of St. Louis*	2·25	2·25
3792	12r. Lindbergh, Mahoney and Hall at Ryan Airlines	2·25	2·25

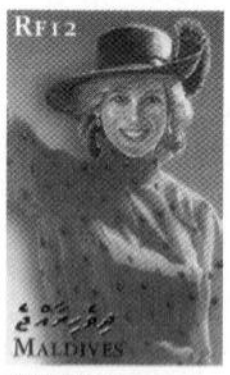

414 Princess Diana

2002. Fifth Death Anniv of Diana, Princess of Wales. Multicoloured.

3793	12r. Type **414**	1·75	2·00
3794	12r. In evening dress and tiara	1·75	2·00

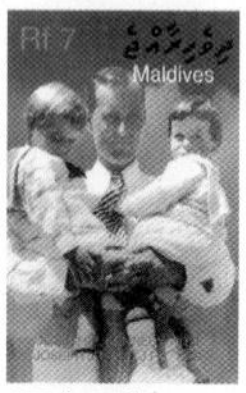

415 Joseph Kennedy with Sons Joseph Jr. and John, 1919

2002. Presidents John F. Kennedy and Ronald Reagan Commemoration. Multicoloured.

3795	7r. Type **415**	1·00	1·25
3796	7r. John F. Kennedy aged 11	1·00	1·25
3797	7r. Kennedy inspecting Boston waterfront, 1951	1·00	1·25
3798	7r. Kennedy in naval ensign uniform, 1941	1·00	1·25
3799	7r. With sister Kathleen in London, 1939	1·00	1·25
3800	7r. Talking to Eleanor Roosevelt, 1951	1·00	1·25
3801	12r. Ronald Reagan facing right	1·50	1·75
3802	12r. Ronald Reagan (full-face portrait)	1·50	1·75

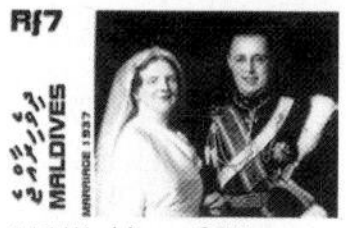

416 Wedding of Princess Juliana and Prince Bernhard, 1937

2002. "Amphilex '02" International Stamp Exhibition, Amsterdam. Dutch Royal Family.

3803	**416** 7r. blue and black	1·00	1·00
3804	- 7r. brown and black	1·00	1·00
3805	- 7r. red and black	1·00	1·00
3806	- 7r. brown and black	1·00	1·00
3807	- 7r. violet and black	1·00	1·00
3808	- 7r. green and black	1·00	1·00
3809	- 7r. multicoloured	1·00	1·00
3810	- 7r. brown and black	1·00	1·00
3811	- 7r. multicoloured	1·00	1·00
3812	- 7r. multicoloured	1·00	1·00
3813	- 7r. multicoloured	1·00	1·00
3814	- 7r. multicoloured	1·00	1·00

DESIGNS: No. 3804, Princess Juliana and Prince Bernhard with baby Princess Beatrix, 1938; 3805, Princess Juliana with her daughters in Canada, 1940–45; 3806, Inauguration of Queen Juliana, 1948; 3807, Royal Family inspecting Zeeland floods, 1953; 3808, Queen Juliana and Prince Bernhard; 3809, "Princess Beatrix as a Baby" (Pauline Hille); 3810, "Princess Beatrix in Flying Helmet" (John Klinkenberg); 3811, "Princess Beatrix" (Beatrice Filius); 3812, "Princess Beatrix and Prince Claus" (Will Kellermann); 3813, "Queen Beatrix in Royal Robes" (Graswinkel); 3814, "Queen Beatrix" (Marjolijn Spreeuwenberg).

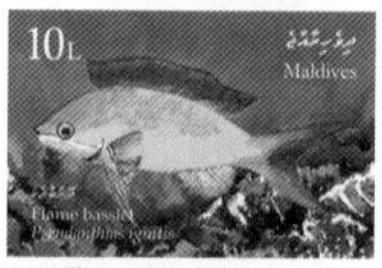

417 Flame Basslet

2002. Marine Life. Multicoloured.

3815	10l. Type **417**	15	50
3816	15l. Teardrop butterflyfish	20	50
3817	20l. White-tailed damselfish ("Hambug Damselfish")	20	50
3818	25l. Bridled tern (23×27 mm)	50	50
3819	50l. Clown surgeonfish ("Blue-lined Surgeonfish")	25	30
3820	1r. Common tern (23×27 mm)	65	30
3821	2r. Common noddy (23×27 mm)	1·00	50
3822	2r.50 Yellow-breasted wrasse	70	80
3823	2r.50 Blue shark (23×27 mm)	70	80
3824	4r. Harlequin filefish	1·00	1·00
3825	5r. Masked unicornfish ("Orang-espine Unicornfish")	1·00	1·00
3826	10r. Emperor angelfish	1·75	1·75
3827	12r. Catalufa ("Bullseye")	2·00	2·25
3828	20r. Scalloped hammerhead shark (23×27 mm)	3·50	4·25

No. 3822 is inscribed "wrass" in error.

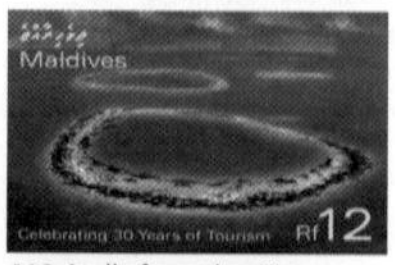

418 Atolls from the Air

2002. 30 Years of Maldives' Tourism Promotion. Multicoloured.

3829	12r. Type **418**	2·50	2·50
3830	12r. Island beach	2·50	2·50
3831	12r. Surfing	2·50	2·50
3832	12r. Scuba diving	2·50	2·50

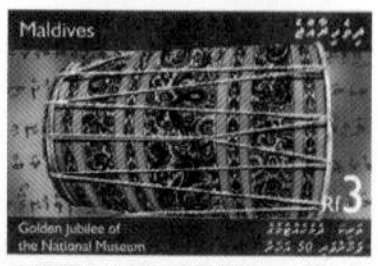

419 Decorated Drum

2003. 50th Anniv of National Museum. Multicoloured.

3835	3r. Type **419**	55	40
3836	3r.50 Carved covered bowl	55	50
3837	6r.50 Ceremonial sunshade	85	85
3838	22r. Ceremonial headdress	3·00	4·00

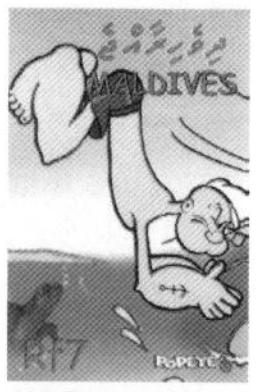

420 Popeye diving

2003. "Popeye" (cartoon character). Multicoloured. Summer sports.

3839	7r. Type **420**	85	95
3840	7r. Surfing	85	95
3841	7r. Sailboarding	85	95
3842	7r. Baseball	85	95
3843	7r. Hurdling	85	95
3844	7r. Tennis	85	95
MS3845	120×90 mm. 25r. Volleyball (horiz)	3·25	3·75

Nos. 3839/45 were printed together, *se-tenant*, with the backgrounds forming a composite design.

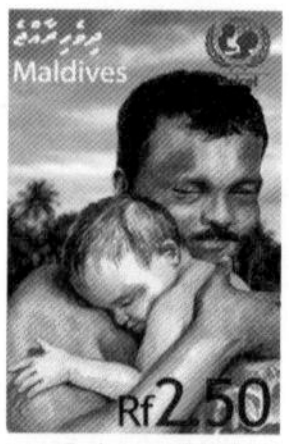

421 Father with Baby

2003. UNICEF. "First Steps" Campaign. Multicoloured.

3846	2r.50 Type **420**	60	35
3847	5r. Mother and baby	1·00	75
3848	20r. Campaign emblem	3·50	4·50

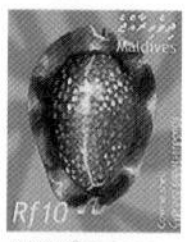

422 *Cypraea caputserpentis* (Cowrie)

2003. Sea Shells. Multicoloured.

3849	10r. Type **422**	1·75	2·00
3850	10r. *Trachycardium orbita* (Cardita clam)	1·75	2·00
3851	10r. *Architectonica perspective* (Sundial shell)	1·75	2·00
3852	10r. *Conus capitaneus* (Corn shell)	1·75	2·00

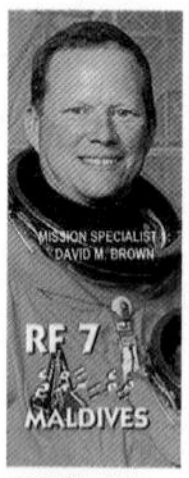

423 David Brown

2003. Columbia Space Shuttle Commemoration. Sheet 184×145 mm, containing T **423** and similar vert designs showing crew members. Multicoloured.

MS3853	7r. Type **423**; 7r. Commander Rick Husband; 7r. Laurel Clark; 7r. Kalpana Chawla; 7r. Michael Anderson; 7r. William McCool; 7r. Ilan Ramon	7·00	8·00

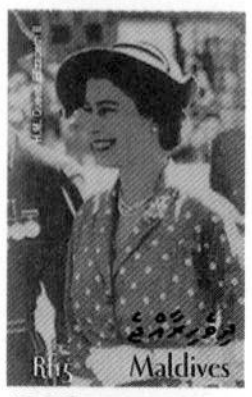

424 Queen wearing Polka Dot Jacket

2003. 50th Anniv of Coronation.

MS3854	147×85 mm.15r. Type **424**; 15r. Queen after Coronation wearing Imperial State Crown; 15r. Queen wearing tiara (all black, deep brown and brown)	7·50	8·50
MS3855	68×98 mm. 25r. Queen wearing tiara and blue sash (multicoloured)	4·40	5·00

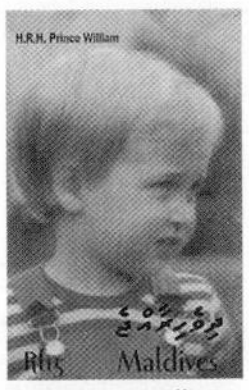

425 Prince William as Toddler

2003. 21st Birthday of Prince William. Multicoloured.

MS3856	148×78 mm. 15r. Type **425**; 15r. As teenager (looking forward); 15r. As teenager (looking right)	7·50	8·00
MS3857	68×98 mm. 25r. As young boy, wearing school cap	4·50	5·00

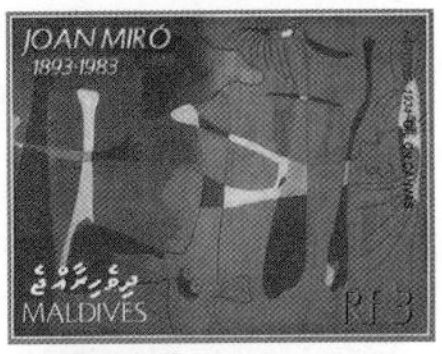

426 "Painting"

2003. 20th Death Anniv of Joan Miro (artist). Multicoloured.

3858	3r. Type **426**	55	35
3859	5r. "Hirondelle Amour"	90	60
3860	10r. "Two Women"	1·50	1·60
3861	15r. "Women listening to Music"	2·00	2·50
MS3862	176×134 mm. 12r. "Woman and Birds"; 12r. "Nocturne"; 12r. "Morning Star"; 12r. "The Escape Ladder"	6·50	7·50
MS3863	Two sheets, each 83×104 mm. (a) 25r. "Women encircled by the Flight of a Bird". (b) 25r. "Rhythmic Personages". Both imperf Set of 2 sheets	7·00	8·00

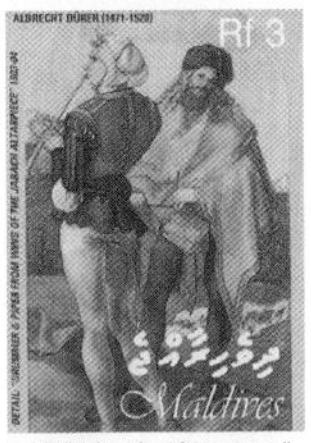

427 "Jabach Altarpiece" (detail of drummer and piper)

2003. 475th Death Anniv of Albrecht Dürer (artist). Multicoloured.

3864	3r. Type **427**	55	45
3865	5r. "Portrait of a Young Man"	90	65
3866	7r. "Wire-drawing Mill" (horiz)	1·25	1·40
3867	10r. "Innsbruck from the North" (horiz)	1·50	1·75
MS3868	174×157 mm. 12r. "Portrait of Jacob Muffel"; 12r. "Portrait of Hieronymus Holzschuher"; 12r. "Portrait of Johannes Kleburger"; 12r. "Self-portrait"	6·50	7·50
MS3869	145×105 mm. 25r. "The Weiden Mill"	3·00	3·25

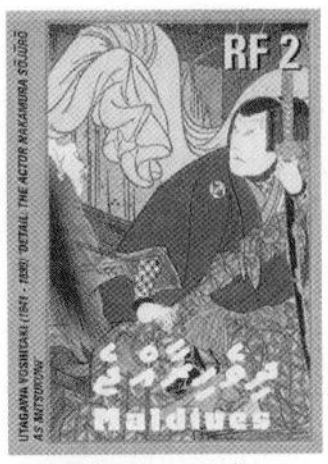

428 "The Actor Nakamura Sojuro as Mitsukuni" (detail) (Utagawa Yoshitaki)

2003. Japanese Art. Ghosts and Demons. Multicoloured.

3870	2r. Type **428**	45	20
3871	5r. "The Actor Nakamura Sojuro as Mitsukuni" (detail of ghosts) (Utagawa Yoshitaki)	90	65
3872	7r. "The Ghost of Kohada Koheiji" (Shunkoosai Hokuei)	1·10	1·00
3873	15r. "Ariwara no Narihira as Seigen" (Utagawa Kunisada)	1·90	2·50
MS3874	149×145 mm. 10r. "The Ghost of Shikibunojo Mitsumune" (Utagawa Kunisada); 10r. "Fuwa Bansakui" (Tsukioka Yoshitoshi); 10r. "The Lantern Ghost of Oiwa" (Shunkosai Hokuei); 10r. "The Greedy Hag" (Tsukioka Yoshitoshi)	5·50	6·50
MS3875	116×86 mm. 25r. "The Spirit of Sakura Sogoro haunting Hotta Kozuke" (Utagawa Kuniyoshi)	3·25	3·50

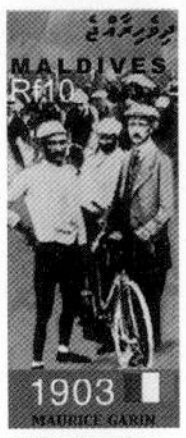

429 Maurice Garin (1903)

2003. Centenary of Tour de France Cycle Race. Past winners. Multicoloured.

MS3876	160×100 mm. 10r. Type **429**; 10r. Henri Cornet (1904); 10r. Louis Trousselier (1905); 10r. Rene Pottier (1906)	6·50	7·00
MS3877	160×100 mm. 10r. Lucien Petit-Breton on cycle (1907); 10r. Close up of Lucien Petit-Breton (1907); 10r. Francois Faber (1909); 10r. Octave Lapize (1910)	6·50	7·00
MS3878	160×100 mm. 10r. Eddy Merckx (1974); 10r. Bernard Thevenet (1975); 10r. Lucien van Impe (1976); 10r. Bernard Thevenet (1977)	6·50	7·00
MS3879	Three sheets, each 100×70 mm. (a) 25r. Start of first Tour De France at Le Reveil Matin cafe, Montgeron. (b) 25r. Henri Desgranges (editor of L'Auto). (c) 25r. Bernard Hinault (1979) Set of 3 sheets	1·00	12·00

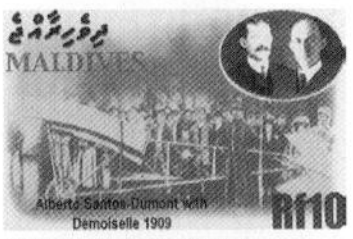

430 Santos-Dumont Monoplane No. 20 Demoiselle on Ground, 1909

2003. Centenary of Powered Flight. Multicoloured.

MS3880	176×97 mm. 10r. Type **430**; 10r. Santos-Dumont monoplane No. 20 Demoiselle taking off, 1909; 10r. Voisin-Farman No. 1 biplane, 1908; 10r. Glenn Curtiss' *Gold Bug*, 1909	6·50	7·00
MS3881	176×97 mm. 10r. Santos-Dumont's *Airship No. 1*; 10r. Santos-Dumont's *Airship No. 4*; 10r. Santos Dumont's *Ballon No. 14 and 14 bis* biplane, 1906; 10r. Santos-Dumont's *Airship No. 16*	6·50	7·00
MS3882	Two sheets, each 105×75 mm. (a) 25r. Santos-Dumont's *Ballon No. 6* circling Eiffel Tower, Paris, 1901. (b) 25r. Santos-Dumont's *14 bis* biplane,1906 Set of 2 sheets	7·50	8·00

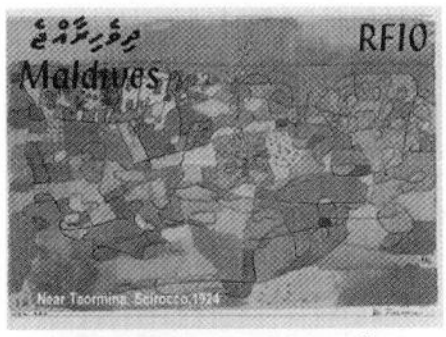

431 "Near Taormina, Scirocco" (1924)

2003. Paul Klee (artist) Commemoration. Multicoloured.

MS3883	162×135 mm. 10r. Type **431**; 10r. "Small Town Among the Rocks" (1932);10r. "Still Life with Props" (1924); 10r. "North Room", (1932)	4·50	5·50
MS3884	70×103 mm. 25r. "Dame Demon" (1935) (vert)	3·25	3·50

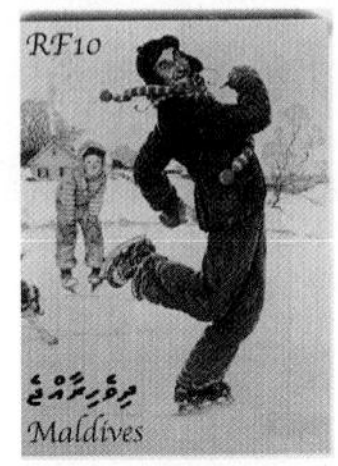

432 Man Ice-skating

2003. 25th Death Anniv of Norman Rockwell (artist). Multicoloured.

MS3885	10r. Type **432**; 10r. Man lying on back and boy with dog; 10r. Man and boy going fishing; 10r. Man and boy sweeping leaves	4·50	5·50
MS3886	45×81 mm. 25r. Illustration for Hallmark Cards (1957). Imperf	3·25	3·50

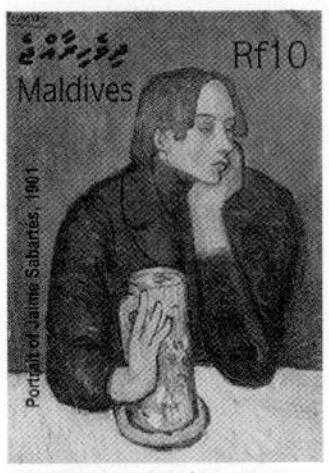

433 "Portrait of Jaime Sabartes" (1901)

2003. 30th Death Anniv of Pablo Picasso (artist). Multicoloured.

MS3887	133×167 mm. 10r. Type **433**; 10r. "Portrait of the Artist's Wife (Olga)" (1923); 10r. "Portrait of Olga" (1923); 10r. "Portrait of Jaime Sabartes" (1904)	7·00	7·00
MS3888	67×100 mm. 30r. "The Tragedy" (1903). Imperf	6·50	6·50

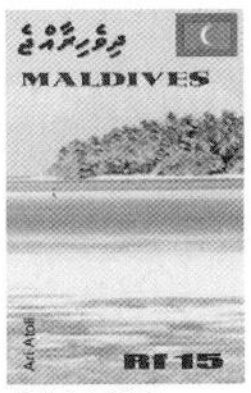

434 Ari Atoll

2003. International Year of Freshwater. Multicoloured.

MS3889	147×85 mm. 15r. Type **434**; 15r. Running tap; 15r. Desalination plant, Male	7·00	8·00
MS3890	96×66 mm. 25r. Community rain water tank	3·50	4·00

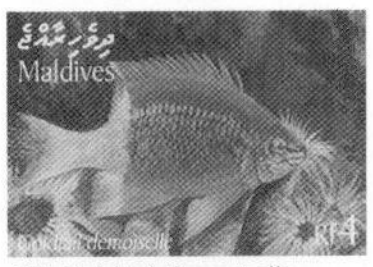

435 Goldtail Demoiselle

2003. Marine Life. Sheet 147×105 mm containing T **435** and similar horiz designs. Multicoloured.

MS3891	4r. Type **435**; 4r. Queen coris; 4r. Eight-banded butterflyfish; 4r. Meyer's butterflyfish; 4r. Exquisite butterflyfish; 4r. Yellowstripe snapper; 4r. Yellowback anthias; 4r. Black-spotted moray; 4r. Clown anemonefish	5·00	5·50

The stamps in No. **MS**3891 were printed together, *se-tenant*, with the backgrounds forming a composite design.

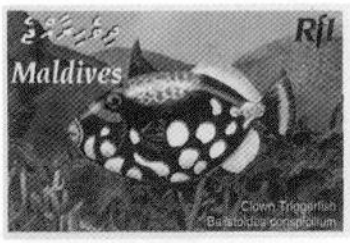

436 Clown Triggerfish

2003. Tropical Fish. Multicoloured.

3892	1r. Type **436**	15	10
3893	7r. Sixspot grouper	1·10	1·00
3894	10r. Long-nosed butterflyfish	1·50	1·50
3895	15r. Longfin bannerfish	2·25	2·50
MS3896	116×134 mm. 7r. Bluestreak cleaner wrasse; 7r. Threeband demoiselle; 7r. Palette surgeonfish; 7r. Emperor snapper; 7r. Bicolor angelfish; 7r. Picasso triggerfish	6·00	7·00
MS3897	72×102 mm. 25r. Chevron butterflyfish	3·50	4·00

2003. Tropical Butterflies. As T **436**. Multicoloured.

3898	3r. Yamfly (vert)	55	35
3899	5r. Striped blue crow (vert)	90	65
3900	8r. Indian red admiral (vert)	1·40	1·40
3901	15r. Great eggfly (vert)	2·50	3·00
MS3902	116×134 mm. 7r. Blue triangle; 7r. Monarch; 7r. Broad-bordered grass yellow; 7r. Red lacewing; 7r. African migrant; 7r. Plain tiger	6·50	7·50
MS3903	102×72 mm. 25r. Beak butterfly (vert)	4·00	4·50

2003. Birds. As T **436**. Multicoloured.

3904	15l. Great frigate bird	50	40
3905	20l. Ruddy turnstone	50	40
3906	25l. Hoopoe	65	45
3907	1r. Cattle egret	1·00	50
MS3908	116×134 mm. 7r. Red-billed tropic bird; 7r. Red-footed booby; 7r. Common tern; 7r. Caspian tern; 7r. Western ("Common") curlew; 7r. Grey ("Black-bellied") plover	6·50	7·50
MS3909	72×102 mm. 25r. Grey heron	4·00	4·50

2003. Flowers. As T **436**. Multicoloured.

3910	30l. *Coelogyne asperata* (vert)	20	15
3911	75l. *Calanthe rosea* (vert)	40	20
3912	2r. *Eria javanica* (vert)	1·00	55
3913	10r. *Spathoglottis affinis* (vert)	2·00	2·25
MS3914	116×134 mm. 7r. *Strelitzia reginae*; 7r. *Anthurium andreanum*; 7r. *Alpinia Purpurata*; 7r. *Dendrobium phalaenopsis*; 7r. *Vanda tricolo*; 7r. *Hibiscus rosa-Sinensis*	6·50	7·50
MS3915	72×102 mm. 25r. *Ipomoea crassicaulis* (vert)	3·50	3·75

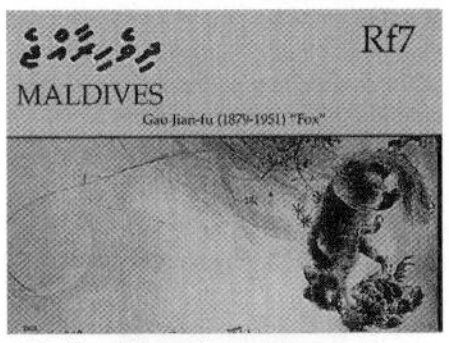

437 "Landscape"

2004. Hong Kong 2004 International Stamp Exhibition. 125th Birth Anniv of Gao Jian-fu (artist). T 437 and similar vert designs. Multicoloured.

MS3916	170×149 mm. 7r. Type **437**; 7r. "Moon Night"; 7r. "Fox"; 7r. Chinese ink and colour on paper (spider and web); 7r. Chinese ink and colour on paper (girl); 7r. Chinese ink and colour on paper (man)	6·50	7·50
MS3917	108×129 mm. 12r. "Eagle"; 12r. "Sunset"	3·50	4·00

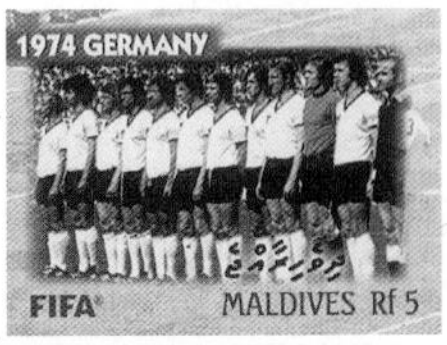

438 German Team (1974)

2004. Centenary of FIFA (Federation Internationale de Football Association). T 438 and similar horiz designs showing winning football teams. Multicoloured.

3918	5r. Type **438**	85	85
3919	5r. Argentina (1978)	85	85
3920	5r. Italy (1982)	85	85
3921	5r. Argentina (1986)	85	85
3922	5r. Germany (1990)	85	85
3923	5r. Brazil (1994)	85	85
3924	5r. France (1998)	85	85
3925	5r. Brazil (2002)	85	85

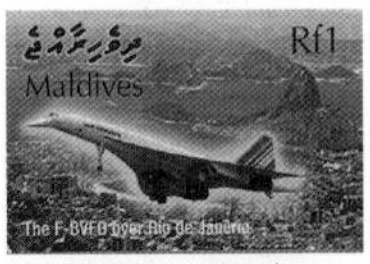

439 F-BVFD over Rio de Janeiro

2004. Last Flight of Concorde (2003). Multicoloured.

MS3926	147×150 mm. 1r. Type **439**; 1r. F-BVFC over New York; 1r. F-BTSD over Honolulu; 1r. F-BTDS over Lisbon; 1r. F-BVFA over Washington; 1r. F-BVFD over Dakar; 1r. G-BOAC over Singapore; 1r. G-BOAA over Sydney; 1r. G-BOAD over Hong Kong; 1r. G-BOAD over Amsterdam; 1r. G-BOAE over Tokyo; 1r. G-BOAF over Madrid	3·00	3·25
MS3927	Three sheets, each 70×100 mm. (a) 25r. G-BOAC against Union Jack. (b) 25r. G-BOAG over London. (c) 25r. G-BOAG against museum exhibits Set of 3 sheets	15·00	16·00

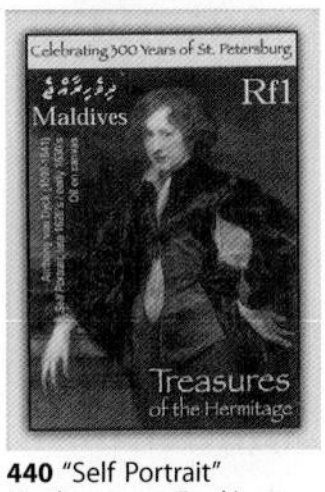

440 "Self Portrait" (Anthony van Dyck)

2004. 300th Anniv of St. Petersburg. "Treasures of the Hermitage". Multicoloured.

3928	1r. Type **440**	20	15
3929	3r. "Self Portrait" (Michael Sweets)	55	40
3930	7r. "Anna Dalkeith, Countess of Morton" (Anthony van Dyck)	1·10	1·00
3931	12r. "Lady Anna Kirk" (Anthony van Dyck)	1·75	2·10

MS3932 116×180 mm. 10r. "Portrait of Prince Alexander Kurakin" (Louis-Elisabeth Vigee-Lebrun); 10r. "Portrait of a Lady in Waiting to the Infanta Isabella" (Peter Paul Rubens); 10r. "Portrait of a Lady in Blue" (Thomas Gainsborough); 10r. "The Actor Pierre Jeliolte in the Role of Apollo" (Louis Tocque) 5·50 6·00

MS3933 Two sheets, each 102×72 mm. (a) 25r. "A Scene from Corneille's Tragedy Le Comte d'Essex" (Nicolas Lancret) (horiz). (b) 25r. "The Stolen Kiss" (Jean-Honore Fragonard) (horiz) Set of 2 sheets 7·00 8·00

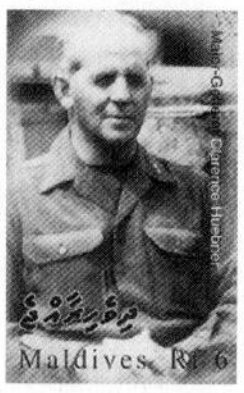

441 Major General Clarence Huebner

2004. 60th Anniv of D-Day Landings. Ten sheets containing T **441** and similar multicoloured designs.

MS3934 Five sheets. (a) 137×117 mm. 6r. Type **441**; 6r. Brig. General Anthony McAuliffe; 6r. Major General Leonard Gerow; 6r. General Adolf Galland; 6r. Brig. General W. M. Hoge; 6r. Major General Sir Percy Hobart. (b) 127×127 mm. 6r. Rear Admiral Kirk; 6r. General Field Marshal Erwin Rommel; 6r. General George Marshal; 6r. General Jan Smuts; 6r. General Lieutenant Gunther Blumentritt; 6r. Major General J. Lawton Collins. (c) 138×137 mm. 6r. Winston Churchill; 6r. Admiral Sir Bertram Ramsey; 6r. General Lieutenant Dietrich Kraiss; 6r. Major General Richard Gale; 6r. General George Patton; 6r. Major General Maxwell Taylor. (d) 138×137 mm. 6r. General Dwight Eisenhower; 6r. Field Marshal Guenther von Kluge; 6r. Air Marshal Sir Trafford Leigh-Mallory; 6r. Field Marshal Walter Model; 6r. Field Marshal Gerd von Rundstedt; 6r. Sir Arthur Tedder. (e) 137×127 mm. 6r. Lieutenant General Omar Bradley (horiz); 6r. Rear Admiral Hall (horiz); 6r. Major General Huebner (horiz); 6r. Grossadmiral Karl Donitz (horiz); 6r. Rear Admiral Wilkes (horiz); 6r. Capt. Chauncey Camp (horiz) Set of 10 sheets 35·00 35·00

MS3935 Five sheets. (a) 68×98 mm. 30r. Rear Admiral Donald Moon. (b) 68×98 mm. 30r. Lieutenant General Sir Frederick Morgan. (c) 68×98 mm. 30r. General Henry Arnold. (d) 69×99 mm. 30r. General Sir Bernard Montgomery. (e) 98×68 mm. 30r. Rear Admiral Carlton Bryant (horiz) Set of 5 sheets 29·00 29·00

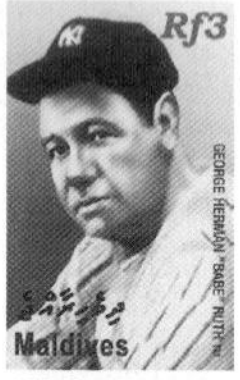

442 George Herman Ruth Jr

2004. Centenary of Baseball World Series. George Herman Ruth Jr. ("Babe Ruth"). Multicoloured.

3936	3r. Type **442**	30	40
3937–3940	10r.×4, Swinging bat; Looking sombre; Carrying two bats; Looking left	3·75	4·25

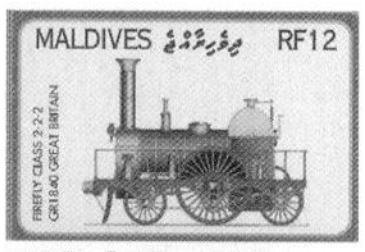

443 Firefly Class 2-2-2 GR1840

2004. Bicentenary of Steam Trains. Multicoloured.

MS3941 Six sheets. (a) 105×150 mm. 12r.×4, Type **443**; French 'Single' (1854); Medoc Class 2-4-0 Swiss (1857); German 4-4-0 (1893). (b) 105×150 mm.12r.×4, Planet Class 2-2-0 (1830); American 4-4-0 (1855); Newmar (1846); Class 500 4-6-0 (1900). (c) 105×150 mm. 12r.×4, Adler 2-2-2 (1835); Beuth 2-2-2 (1843); Northumbrian 0-2-2 (1830); Class 4-6-2 (1901). (d) 150×105 mm.12r.×4, *The Evening Star*; *The Britannia*; *The George Stephenson*; Sudan Railways 310 2-8-2. (e) 150×105 mm. 12r.×4, East African Railways Garratt; Rhodesian Railways 12th Class; Class 2-6-2; Class 19d 4-8-2. (f) 150×105 mm. 12r.×4, Woodburning Beyer Garratt; Double-headed train over Kaaiman River; Garratt 4-8-2+2-8-2; Class 15 Garratt 45·00 45·00

MS3942 Six sheets. (a) 100×70 mm. 30r. *Lord Nelson*. (b) 100×70 mm. 30r. *The Americani*. (c) 100×70 mm. 30r. *Flying Scotsman*. (d) 100×70 mm. 30r. *Vauxhall* 2-2-0 (1834). (e) 70×102 mm.30r. Claud Hamilton Class 4-4-0. (f) 70×102 mm. 30r. Class P8 4-6-0 (1906) 35·00 35·00

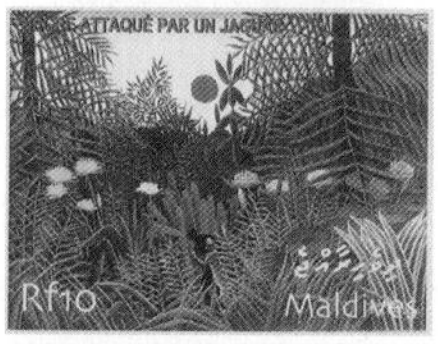

444 "Negre Attaque par un Jaguar"

2004. 160th Birth Anniv of Henri Rousseau (French artist). Multicoloured.

MS3943 127×127 mm. 10r.×4, Type **444**; "Paysage Exotique"; "La Cascade"; "Le Repas du Lion" 5·00 5·50

MS3944 75×92 mm. 25r. "Le Reeve" (detail). Imperf 3·50 3·75

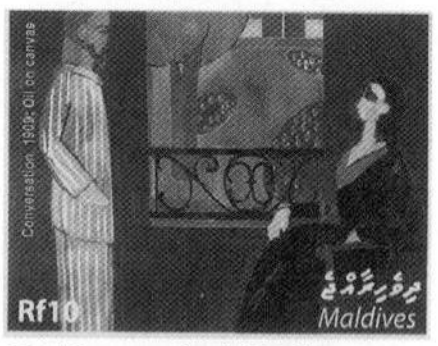

445 "Conversation" (1909)

2004. 50th Death Anniv of Henri Matisse (French artist). Multicoloured.

MS3945 126×128 mm. 10r.×4, Type **445**; "Still Life with a Blue Tablecloth" (1909); "Seville Still Life II" (1910–11); "Woman before an Aquarium" (1921–23) 5·00 5·50

MS3946 62×93 mm. 25r. "Interior at Nice" (1921). Imperf 3·50 3·75

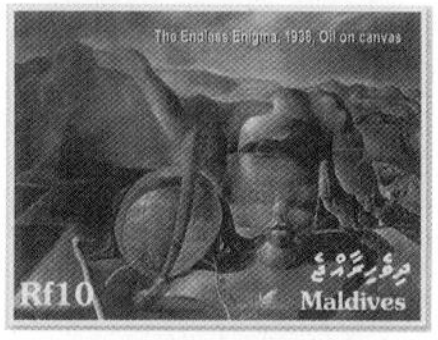

446 "The Endless Enigma" (1938)

2004. Birth Centenary of Salvador Dali (Spanish artist). Multicoloured.

MS3947 126×127 mm. 10r.×4, Type **446**; "The Persistence of Memory (1931)"; "Soft Construction with Boiled Beans – Premonition of Civil War" (1936); "Still Life moving Fast" (1956) 5·00 5·50

MS3948 100×65 mm. 25r. "Figure on the Rocks" (1926). Imperf 3·50 3·75

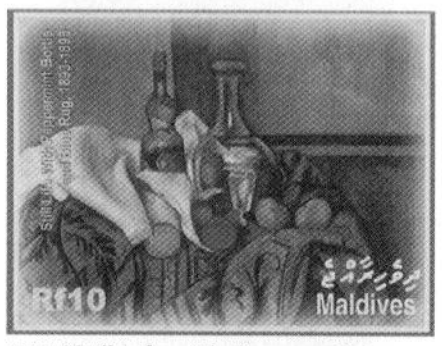

447 "Still Life with Peppermint Bottle and Blue Rug" (1893–95)

2004. 165th Birth Anniv of Paul Cezanne (French artist). Multicoloured.

MS3949 127×127 mm. 10r.×4, Type **447**; "House in Provence" (1880); "Le Chateau Noir" (1900–04); "Basket of Apples" (1895) 6·50 7·00

MS3950 75×92 mm. 25r. "Boy in a Red Waistcoat leaning on his Elbow". Imperf 4·75 5·00

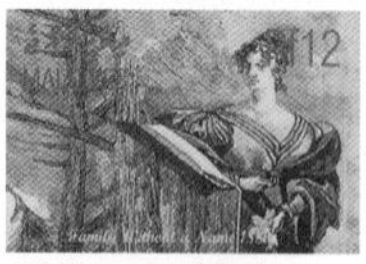

448 Woman and Book

2004. 176th Birth Anniv of Jules Verne (French writer). Designs showing scenes from novels.

MS3951 Five sheets, each 150×100 mm. (a) 12r.×4, agate; lemon and scarlet; lilac, lemon and scarlet; brown; lemon and scarlet; green, lemon and scarlet. (b) 12r.×4, blue; lemon and scarlet; blue, lemon and scarlet; black; lemon and scarlet; black, lemon and scarlet. (c) 12r.×4,lemon and scarlet; green, lemon and scarlet; blue and scarlet; green and scarlet. (d) 12r.×4,brown, ultramarine and scarlet; multicoloured; purple and scarlet; lilac and scarlet. (e)green and scarlet; sepia and scarlet; green, lemon and scarlet; purple, lemon and scarlet 38·00 38·00

MS3952 Five sheets, each 98×67 mm. (a) 25r. brown and scarlet. (b) 25r. blue and scarlet. (c) 25r. blue, lemon and scarlet. (d) 25r. purple, lemon and scarlet. (e) 25r. brown, lemon and scarlet 23·00 23·00

DESIGNS: **MS**3951 (a) "Family without a Name", Type **448**; Soldier; Battle scene on dockside; Men with rifles. (b) "The Lighthouse at the End of the World", Crew on ship; Man on rocks and waves; Rocks on coastline; Man wearing hat and coastline. (c) "Michael Strogoff, Courier of the Czar", Man held at gunpoint; Man and woman in tall grass; Two men and robed characters; Man and dog in flattened grass. (d) "Archipelago on Fire"; "Clovis Dardentor"; "The Golden Volcano"; "Le Superbe Orenoque". (e) "Cesar Cascabel", Men in snow storm; Moustached man; Man caught in gust; Crowd reading poster. **MS**3952 (a) 25r. "The Survivors of the Chancellor". (b) 25r. "Cesar Cascabel". (c) 25r. "The Lighthouse at the End of the World". (d) 25r. "Family without a Name". (e) 25r. "Keraban the Inflexible".

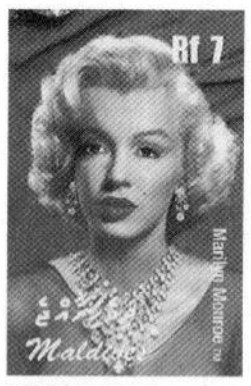

449 Marilyn Monroe

2004. Marilyn Monroe (actress) Commemoration.

3953	**449**	7r. multicoloured	70	80

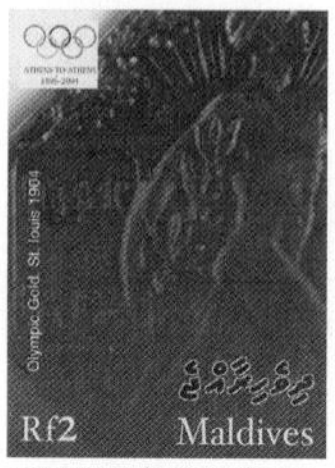

450 Olympic Gold Medal, St Louis (1904)

2004. Olympic Games, Athens. Multicoloured.

3954	2r. Type **450**	40	25
3955	5r. Greek art	70	60
3956	7r. Comte Jean de Beaumont	1·10	1·00
3957	12r. The pommel horse (horiz)	1·75	2·25

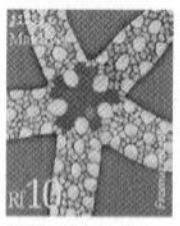

451 *Fromia monilis*

2004. Star Fish. Multicoloured.

3958	10r. Type **451**	1·75	2·00
3959	10r. *Nardoa novaecaledoniae*	1·75	2·00
3960	10r. *Fromia monilis* (red background)	1·75	2·00
3961	10r. *Linckia laevigata*	1·75	2·00

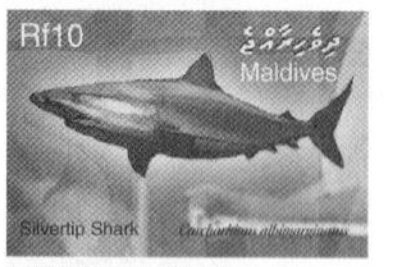

452 Silvertip Shark

2004. Sharks. Multicoloured.

MS3962 136×115 mm. 10r.×4, Type **452**; Silky shark; Great white shark; Gray reef shark 7·00 7·50

MS3963 96×65 mm. 25r. Starry smoothhound 3·75 4·00

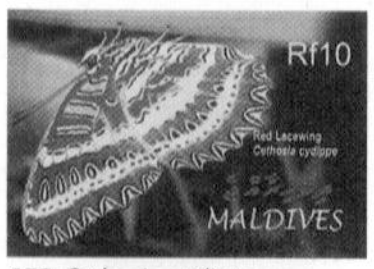

453 *Cethosia cydippe*

2004. Butterflies. Multicoloured.

MS3964 180×111 mm. 10r.×4, Type **453**; *Amesia sanguiflua*; *Pericallia galactina*; *Limenitis dudu dudu* 7·50 8·00

MS6965 98×68 mm. 25r. *Papilio demoleus malayanus* (vert) 4·25 4·50

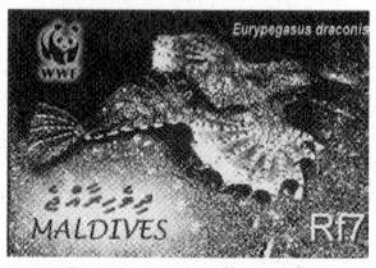

454 *Eurypegasus draconis*

2004. Endangered Species. Eurypegasus draconis (Little Dragonfish). Multicoloured.

3966	7r. Type **454**	1·10	1·25
3967	7r. Orange *Eurypegasus draconis*	1·10	1·25
3968	7r. White *Eurypegasus draconis*	1·10	1·25
3969	7r. *Eurypegasus draconis* on sandy sea bed	1·10	1·25

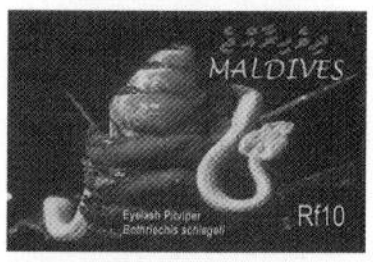

455 Eyelash Pit Viper

2004. Reptiles and Amphibians. Multicoloured.

MS3970 180×111 mm. 10r.×4, Type **455**; Basilisk lizard; Calico snake; Maki frog 6·00 6·50

MS3971 66×96 mm. 25r. *Naja melanoleuca* (vert) 3·50 3·75

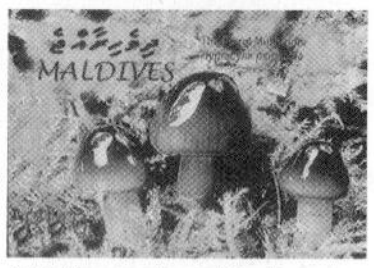

456 *Hygrocybe psittacina*

2004. Mushrooms. Multicoloured.

MS3972 181×111 mm. 10r.×4, Type **456**; *Hygrocybe miniata*; *Aleuria aurantia*; *Thaxterogaster porphyreum* 6·50 7·00

MS3973 98×68 mm. 25r. *Galerina autumnalis* (vert) 3·50 3·75

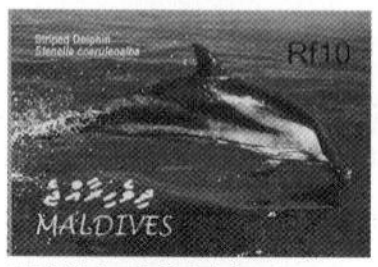

457 Striped Dolphin

2004. Dolphins. Multicoloured.

MS3974 181×111 mm. 10r.×4, Type **457**; Amazon River dolphin; Bottlenose dolphin; Spinner dolphin 6·00 6·50

MS3975 97×66 mm. 25r. Long-snouted Spinner dolphin 3·50 4·00

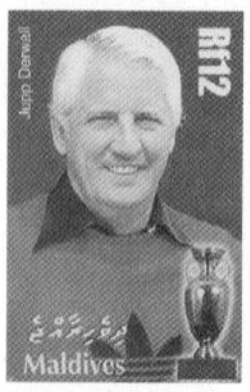

458 Jupp Derwall

2005. European Football Championship 2004, Portugal. Commemoration of 1980 Cup Final between Germany and Belgium. Multicoloured.

MS3976 148×86 mm. 12r.×4, Type **458**; Rene Vandereycken; Horst Hrubesch; Estadio Olimpico 5·50 6·50

MS3977 97×86 mm. 25r. German team, 1980 (50×37 mm) 3·50 4·00

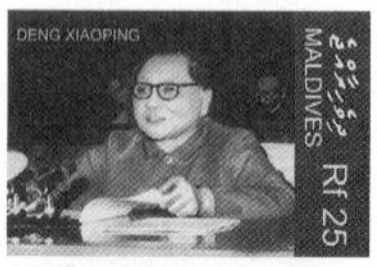

459 Deng Xiaoping

2005. Birth Centenary (2004) of Deng Xiaoping (Chinese Leader, 1978–89). Sheet 96×67 mm.

MS3978 **459** 25r. multicoloured 2·25 3·75

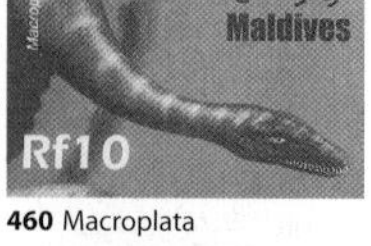

460 Macroplata

2005. Prehistoric Animals. Multicoloured.

MS3979 Four sheets, each 148×111 mm. (a) 10r.×4, Type **460**; Ichthyosaurus; Shonisaurus; Archelon. (b) 10r.×4 (vert), Pterodactyl; Cearadactylus; Pterosaur; Sordes. (c) 10r.×4 (vert), Deinonychus; Styracosaurus (from front); Ornitholestes; Euoplocephalus. (d) 10r.×4 (vert), Albertosaurus; Iguanodon; Deinonychus; Baryonyx 24·00 25·00

MS3980 Four sheets, each 96×67 mm. (a) 25r. Muraeonosaurus. (b) 25r. Archaeopteryx. (c) 25r. Styracosaurus (from side). (d) 25r. Leptoceratops 16·00 17·00

461 Albert Einstein

2005. 50th Death Anniv of Albert Einstein (physicist). Multicoloured.
MS3981 110×135 mm. 15r.×4, Type **461**; Smiling; With pipe in mouth; With raised eyebrows   6·50   7·50
MS3982 55×85 mm. 25r. Albert Einstein (vert)   3·25   3·75

462 Oscar (Brazil)

2005. 75th Anniv of First World Cup Football Championship, Uruguay. Multicoloured.
MS3983 175×130 mm. 15r.×3, Type **462**; Karl-Heinz Rummenigge (Germany); Oliver Kahn (Germany)   6·50   7·50
MS3984 124×105 mm. 25r. Karlheinz Forster (Germany)   4·50   3·75

463 Chicago Skyline

2005. Centenary of Rotary International. Mult.
MS3985 151×68 mm. 15r.×3, Type **463**; Skyline with Sears Tower; Skyline (different)   6·50   7·50
MS3986 102×67 mm. 25r. Telecommunications tower   3·50   4·00
   The stamps of No. MS3985 form a composite design showing a panoramic view of Chicago's skyline.

464 Hans Christian Andersen (statue)

2005. Birth Bicentenary of Hans Christian Andersen (writer). Multicoloured.
MS3987 70×151 mm. 15r.×3, Type **464**; Hans Christian Andersen; Statue facing left   6·50   7·50
MS3988 71×101 mm. 25r. The Little Mermaid   3·50   4·00

465 Admiral Cuthbert Collingwood

2005. Bicentenary of the Battle of Trafalgar. Multicoloured.
3989   10r. Type **465**   2·25   2·25
3990   10r. Napoleon Bonaparte   2·25   2·25
3991   10r. Admiral Lord Horatio Nelson   2·25   2·25
3992   10r. Captain Thomas Masterman Hardy   2·25   2·25
MS3993 99×70 mm. 25r. Ships engaged in battle   6·50   7·00

466 Elvis Presley, 1956

2005. 70th Birth Anniv of Elvis Presley. Multicoloured.
3994   7r. Type **466**   1·10   1·10
3995   7r. On Frank Sinatra Show, 1960   1·10   1·10
3996   7r. In 1962   1·10   1·10
3997   7r. Performing in Las Vegas, 1969   1·10   1·10
3998   7r. Arriving in Hawaii, 1973   1·10   1·10
3999   7r. In concert, 1975   1·10   1·10
4000   7r. In "Love Me Tender", 1956   1·10   1·10
4001   7r. In "Loving You", 1957   1·10   1·10
4002   7r. In "King Creole", 1958   1·10   1·10
4003   7r. Riding motorcycle in "Roustabout", 1964   1·10   1·10
4004   7r. In "Double Trouble", 1967   1·10   1·10
4005   7r. In "Live a Little, Love a Little", 1968   1·10   1·10

467 "Purple Bird" (Anna Badger)

2006. "Kids-Did-It!" Showing children's paintings. Multicoloured.
4006   10r. Type **467**   1·25   1·25
4007   10r. "Parrots" (Nick Abrams)   1·25   1·25
4008   10r. "Pretty Bird" (Jessie Abrams)   1·25   1·25
4009   10r. "Royal Parrot" (Ashley Mondfrans)   1·25   1·25
4010   10r. "Orange Sunflower" (Brett Walker)   1·25   1·25
4011   10r. "Red Flower Pot" (Jessica Shutt)   1·25   1·25
4012   10r. "Flower Pot" (Nick Abrams)   1·25   1·25
4013   10r. "Blue Flower Vase" Trevor Nielsen)   1·25   1·25
4014   10r. "Bubbles" (Raquel Bobolia)   1·25   1·25
4015   10r. "Bubble Fish" (Sarah Bowen)   1·25   1·25
4016   10r. "Lipfish" (Elsa Fleischer)   1·25   1·25
4017   10r. "Flounder" (Erica Malchowski)   1·25   1·25

468 Himantura uamak

2006. Rays. Multicoloured.
4018   20l. Type **468**   25   25
4019   1r. Manta birostris   40   25
4020   2r. Taeniura lymma   70   40
4021   20r. Aetobatus narinari   3·40   4·00

469 Emblem

2006. 20th Anniv of SAARC (South Asian Association for Regional Co-operation). Sheet 115×125 mm.
MS4032 **469** 25r. multicoloured   4·00   5·00

470 Mozart

2006. 250th Birth Anniv of Wolfgang Amadeus Mozart (composer). Multicoloured.
4033   12r. Type **470**   2·50   2·50
4034   12r. Portrait of Mozart (facing left)   2·50   2·50
4035   12r. Young Mozart   2·50   2·50
4036   12r. Bust of Mozart   2·50   2·50

471 Queen Elizabeth II and Pres. John F. Kennedy

2006. 80th Birthday of Queen Elizabeth II. Multicoloured.
4037   15r. Type **471**   2·50   2·50
4038   15r. With Pres. Reagan, riding horses   2·50   2·50
4039   15r. Dancing with Pres. Ford   2·50   2·50
4040   15r. With Pres. Bush   2·50   2·50
MS4041 126×126 mm. 25r. "Horse in a Field" (detail) (George Stubbs)   4·75   5·00
   The stamp within No. MS4041 is incorrectly inscribed "QUEEN ELIZABETH II".

472 Norway 1951 Winter Olympics 55ore+20ore Stamp

2006. Winter Olympic Games, Turin. Multicoloured.
4042   7r. Type **472**   1·10   1·10
4043   8r. Poster for Winter Olympic Games, Oslo, 1952 (vert)   1·40   1·40
4044   10r. Poster for Winter Olympic Games, Garmisch-Partenkirchen, Germany, 1936 (vert)   1·50   1·50
4045   12r. Germany 1935 Winter Olympics 6pf.+4pf. skating stamp (vert)   1·75   2·00

473 "100"

2006. Centenary of Postal Service in the Maldives. Sheet 135×175 mm.
MS4046 **473** 12r. multicoloured   2·00   2·25

474 Elvis Presley

2006. 50th Anniv of Purchase of Gracelands by Elvis Presley. Multicoloured, background tint given.
4047   12r. Type **474** (grey)   2·25   2·25
4048   12r. Elvis Presley singing (brownish grey)   2·25   2·25
4049   12r. As No. 4048 (lavender-grey)   2·25   2·25
4050   12r. As Type **474** (greenish grey)   2·25   2·25

475 International Airship Exhibition, Frankfurt, Germany, 1909

2006. 50th Death Anniv of Ludwig Durr (Zeppelin engineer). Multicoloured.
4051   15r. Type **475**   2·25   2·25
4052   15r. Hot air balloons at International Airship Exhibition, Frankfurt, 1909   2·25   2·25
4053   15r. Airship LZ-129 Hindenburg   2·25   2·25

476 R-7 Missile (Sputnik 1 launcher)

2006. Space Anniversaries. Multicoloured.
4054   8r. Type **476**   1·75   1·75
4055   8r. Sputnik 1   1·75   1·75
4056   8r. Inside Sputnik 1   1·75   1·75
4057   8r. Sputnik 2   1·75   1·75
4058   8r. Sputnik 1 orbits over the Earth   1·75   1·75
4059   8r. Sputnik 3   1·75   1·75

    (b) 20th Anniv of Giotto Comet Probe.
4060   12r. Nucleus of Halley's Comet   2·25   2·25
4061   12r. Halley's Comet   2·25   2·25
4062   12r. Giotto Space Probe and Halley's Comet   2·25   2·25
4063   12r. Image of Halley's Comet by Giotto Probe   2·25   2·25
MS4064 150×100 mm. 12r.×4 Calipso Satellite; CloudSat Satellite; Aqua Satellite; Aura Satellite   7·00   7·25
MS4065 Two sheets, each 100×70 mm. (a) 25r. Stardust Satellite, 2004. (b) 25r. Giotto Comet Probe   6·50   7·00
   The stamps and margins of No. MS4064 form a composite design showing satellites above the Earth.

477 Pomacanthus imperator

2007. Fish. Multicoloured.
4066   10r. Type **477**   2·00   2·00
4067   10r. Balistoides conspicillum   2·00   2·00
4068   10r. Chaetodon meyeri   2·00   2·00
4069   10r. Dascyllus arnanus   2·00   2·00

478 Ragged-finned Lion Fish

2007. Fish of the Maldives. Multicoloured.
4070   1r. Type **478**   35   20
4071   2r. Vlaming's unicornfish   50   30
4072   10r. White-spotted grouper   2·00   2·00
4073   10r. Bicolour parrotfish   2·00   2·00
4074   10r. Blue-barred parrotfish   2·00   2·00
4075   10r. Bullethead parrotfish   2·00   2·00
4076   10r. Dusky parrotfish   2·00   2·00
4077   10r. Imperial angelfish   2·00   2·00
4078   10r. Clown triggerfish   2·00   2·00
4079   10r. Black-saddled coral trout   2·00   2·00
4080   10r. Slender grouper   2·00   2·00
4081   20r. Maldive anemonefish   3·50   4·00
MS4082 Three sheets, each 93×63 mm. (a) 30r. Picasso triggerfish. (b) 30r. Blue-faced angelfish. (c) 30r. Shadow soldierfish   12·00   12·00

479 Bar-tailed Godwit

2007. Migratory Birds of the Maldives. Multicoloured.
4083   1r. Type **479**   35   20
4084   2r. Black-headed gull   50   30
4085   10r. Masked booby (vert)   2·00   2·00
4086   10r. Common swifts   2·00   2·00
4087   10r. Sooty tern   2·00   2·00
4088   10r. Yellow wagtail   2·00   2·00
4089   10r. House sparrow   2·00   2·00
4090   10r. Tufted duck   2·00   2·00
4091   10r. Caspian tern   2·00   2·00
4092   10r. Southern giant petrel   2·00   2·00
4093   10r. Glossy ibis   2·00   2·00
4094   20r. Kentish plover   3·50   4·00
MS4095 Three sheets. (a) 64×94 mm. 30r. Golden-throated barbet (vert). (b) 94×64 mm. 30r. Purple herons. (c) 64×94 mm. 30r. Osprey (vert)   12·00   13·00

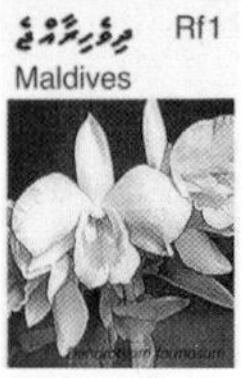

480 *Dendrobium formosum*

2007. Orchids of Asia. Multicoloured.

4096	1r. Type **480**	35	20
4097	2r. *Bulbophyllum* Elizabeth Ann	50	30
4098	10r. *Dendrobium bigibbum*	2·00	2·00
4099	10r. *Cymbidium erythrostylum*	2·00	2·00
4100	10r. *Phaius humboldtii×Phaius tuberculosis*	2·00	2·00
4101	10r. *Dendrobium farmeri*	2·00	2·00
4102	10r. *Dendrobium junceum*	2·00	2·00
4103	10r. *Bulbophyllum lasiochilum*	2·00	2·00
4104	10r. *Phaius* Microburst	2·00	2·00
4105	10r. *Coelogyne mooreana*	2·00	2·00
4106	10r. *Bulbophyllum nasseri*	2·00	2·00
4107	20r. *Spathoglottis gracilis*	3·50	3·00
MS4108	Three sheets, each 66×97 mm. (a) 30r. *Coelogyne cristata* (horiz). (b) 30r. *Dendrobium crocatum* (horiz). (c) 30r. *Bulbophyllum graveolens* (horiz)	12·00	13·00

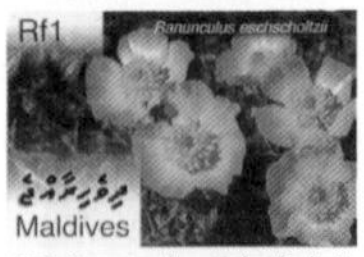

481 *Ranunculus eschscholtzii*

2007. Flowers of the World. Multicoloured.

4109	1r. Type **481**	35	20
4110	2r. *Ratibida columnaris*	50	30
4111	10r. *Mentzelia laevicaulis*	2·00	2·00
4112	10r. *Ipomopsis aggregate*	2·00	2·00
4113	10r. *Rosa woodsii*	2·00	2·00
4114	10r. *Lewisia rediviva*	2·00	2·00
4115	10r. *Penstemon rydbergii*	2·00	2·00
4116	10r. *Machaeranthera tanacetifolia*	2·00	2·00
4117	10r. *Aquilegia coerulea*	2·00	2·00
4118	10r. *Gentiana detonsa*	2·00	2·00
4119	10r. *Linum perenne*	2·00	2·00
4120	20r. *Clintonia unifloria*	3·50	4·00
MS4121	Three sheets, each 95×67 mm. (a) 30r. *Encelia farinosa*. (b) 30r. *Epilobiumangustifolium*. (c) 30r. *Ipomoea purpurea*	12·00	13·00

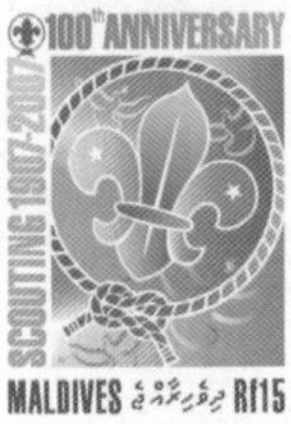

482 Scout Badge

2007. Centenary of World Scouting.

4122	**482** 15r. multicoloured	2·50	2·75
MS4123	110×80 mm. **482** 25r. blue and violet	3·75	4·00

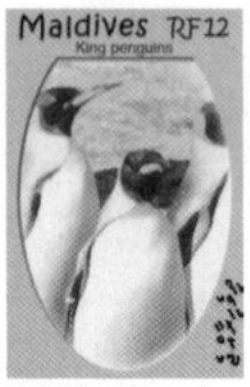

483 King Penguins

2007. International Polar Year. Penguins. Multicoloured.

4124	12r. Type **483**	2·50	2·50
4125	12r. King penguin preening	2·50	2·50
4126	12r. King penguins (green background)	2·50	2·50
4127	12r. Two king penguin chicks	2·50	2·50
4128	12r. King penguin chick with wings raised	2·50	2·50
4129	12r. King penguin chick huddled against adult	2·50	2·50
MS4130	100×70 mm. 25r. African penguin wearing party hat	5·00	5·50

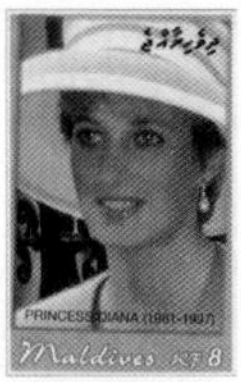

484 Diana, Princess of Wales

2007. Tenth Death Anniv of Diana, Princess of Wales. Multicoloured.

4131	8r. Type **484**	1·40	1·40
4132	8r. Wearing white hat and pearls	1·40	1·40
4133	8r. Wearing white hat and white coat with pinstripes	1·40	1·40
4134	8r. Wearing white hat and green dress with white pinstripes	1·40	1·40
4135	8r. Carrying bouquet, wearing white hat and white coat with pinstripes	1·40	1·40
4136	8r. Wearing grey jacket and grey and white hat	1·40	1·40
MS4137	100×70 mm. 25r. Wearing black jacket with white lapels and white and black hat	4·50	4·75

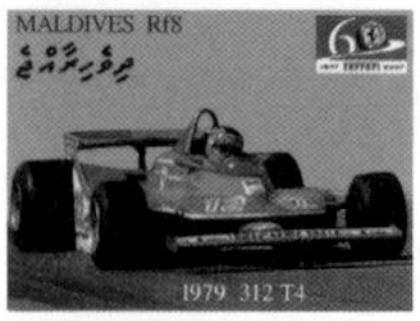

485 Ferrari 312 T 4

2007. 60th Anniv of Ferrari. Multicoloured.

4138	8r. Type **485**	1·25	1·25
4139	8r. 456 GT, 1992	1·40	1·40
4140	8r. 250 GT Berlinetta, 1959	1·40	1·40
4141	8r. F1 89, 1989	1·40	1·40
4142	8r. 456M GTA, 1998	1·40	1·40
4143	8r. 735 LM, 1955	1·40	1·40
4144	8r. DINO 308 GT4, 1973	1·40	1·40
4145	8r. F 200l, 2001	1·40	1·40

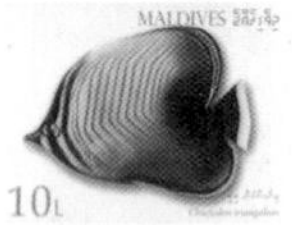

486 *Chaetodon triangulum*

2007. Fish. Multicoloured.

4146	10l. Type **486**	15	25
4147	50l. *Chaetodon kleinii*	25	25
4148	12r. *Chaetodon trifasciatus*	2·25	2·25
4149	15r. *Chaetodon madagascariensis*	2·50	2·50
4150	20r. *Chaetodon lunula*	3·00	3·00

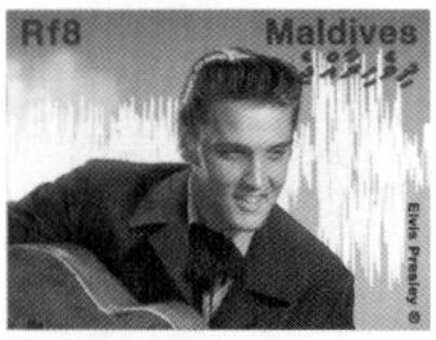

487 Elvis Presley

2008. 30th Death Anniv of Elvis Presley (2007). Multicoloured.

4151	8r. Type **487**	1·40	1·40
4152	8r. Wearing bright blue jacket, playing guitar	1·40	1·40
4153	8r. Wearing red jacket	1·40	1·40
4154	8r. Wearing grey collarless jacket and black shirt	1·40	1·40
4155	8r. Wearing blue shirt, singing	1·40	1·40
4156	8r. Wearing red shirt, holding microphone	1·40	1·40

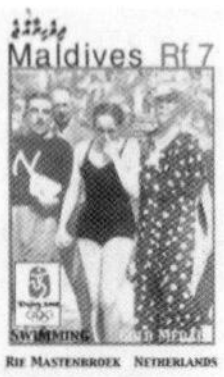

488 Rie Mastenbroek (Netherlands) (swimming triple gold medallist)

2008. Olympic Games, Beijing. Designs showing scenes from Olympic Games, Berlin, 1936. Multicoloured.

4157	7r. Type **488**	1·40	1·40
4158	7r. Poster for Olympic Games, Berlin, 1936	1·40	1·40
4159	7r. Jesse Owens (USA) (field and track gold medallist)	1·40	1·40
4160	7r. Jack Beresford (Great Britain) (double scull gold medallist)	1·40	1·40
MS4161	177×101 mm. Nos. 4157/60	5·00	5·50

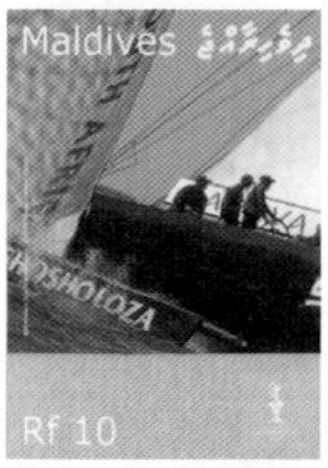

489 Americas Cup Yachts

2008. America's Cup Yachting Championship. Multicoloured.

4162	10r. Type **489**	1·50	1·75
4163	12r. Two yachts (green yacht in background)	1·75	2·00
4164	15r. Two yachts (*Prada* in foreground)	2·25	2·50
4165	20r. Two yachts (yellow yacht in foreground)	2·75	3·00

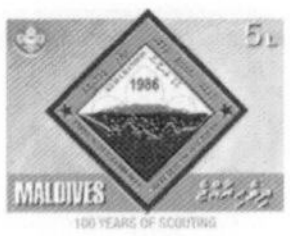

490 Emblem of First Scout Jamboree, Kuda Bandos, 1986

2008. 50th Anniv of Scouting in the Maldives (5l. to 5r.) and Centenary of World Scouting (8r.). Multicoloured.

4166	5l. Type **490**	25	25
4167	10l. Second Scout Jamboree, Kuda Bandos, 1988	30	30
4168	15l. Third Scout Jamboree, Huraa, 1990	35	35
4169	20l. Fourth National Scout Jamboree, Villingili, December 1992	35	35
4170	25l. Fifth National Scout Jamboree, Villingili, September 1993	35	35
4171	30l. Jamboree '98 badge	35	35
4172	95l. Scout Jamboree 2002	50	50
4173	5r. Eighth National (Golden Jubilee) Jamboree, Hulhumale', 15–19 April, 2007	1·00	1·00
MS4174	130×172 mm. 8r. Lord Baden-Powell	1·40	1·40

Nos. 4166/73 all show emblems.

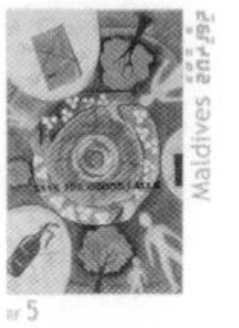

491 Rose in Ozone Layer and Pollutants

2008. International Day for the Preservation of the Ozone Layer. Sheet 177×127 mm containing T **491** and similar vert designs showing posters drawn by Maldivian students for International Ozone Day 2002. Multicoloured.

MS4175	5r. Type **491**; 12r. Two people, trees and sea with fish in ozone bubble; 15r. People standing on globe holding up ozone layer; 18r. Four people standing on island holding up ozone layer	7·00	8·00

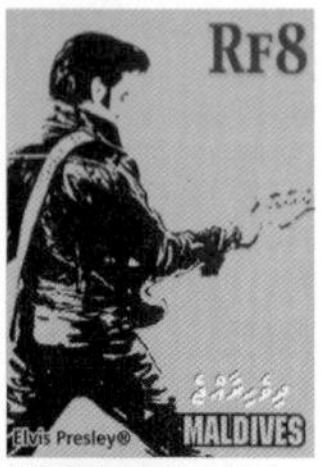

492 Elvis Presley

2008. Elvis Presley Commemoration. Multicoloured.

4176	8r. Type **492**	1·40	1·40
4177	8r. With hand close-up in right foreground of picture	1·40	1·40
4178	8r. Wearing jumpsuit, shown in yellow with blue background	1·40	1·40
4179	8r. Holding microphone, lemon background	1·40	1·40
4180	8r. Wearing white	1·40	1·40
4181	8r. Wearing stetson, sitting on car bonnet	1·40	1·40

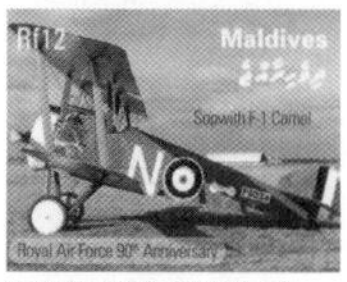

493 Sopwith F-1 Camel

2008. 90th Anniv of the Royal Air Force. Multicoloured.

4182	12r. Type **493**	2·75	2·75
4183	12r. Aerospatiale Puma HC1 helicopter	2·75	2·75
4184	12r. Wessex helicopter	2·75	2·75
4185	12r. Armstrong Whitworth Atlas seaplane	2·75	2·75

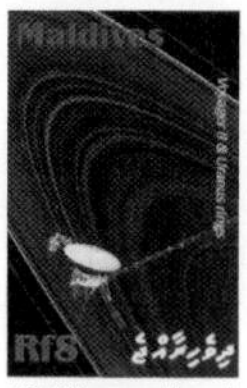

494 Voyager II and Uranus Rings

2008. 50 Years of Space Exploration and Satellites. Multicoloured.

4186	8r. Type **494**	1·25	1·25
4187	8r. Titan 3E Centaur rocket launches Voyager II, 1977	1·25	1·25
4188	8r. Voyager II and Neptune's Great Dark Spot	1·25	1·25
4189	8r. Voyager II and Jupiter's Great Red Spot	1·25	1·25
4190	8r. Technician places Voyager's Gold Record	1·25	1·25
4191	8r. Voyager II and Saturn's Rings	1·25	1·25
4192	12r. Sputnik I in space, 1957	2·00	2·00
4193	12r. Components of Sputnik I	2·00	2·00
4194	12r. Technician and Sputnik I	2·00	2·00
4195	12r. Sputnik I above Moon	2·00	2·00
4196	12r. Explorer I atop launcher Juno I, 1958	2·00	2·00
4197	12r. Explorer I and Planet Earth	2·00	2·00
4198	12r. Explorer I above Earth	2·00	2·00
4199	12r. Dr. James Van Allen and the Van Allen radiation belt	2·00	2·00
4200	12r. Vanguard I in orbit below Earth, 1953	2·00	2·00
4201	12r. Two technicians with Vanguard I	2·00	2·00
4202	12r. Vanguard I satellite and rocket	2·00	2·00
4203	12r. Vanguard I above Earth	2·00	2·00
4204	12r. Spitzer Space Telescope (bright star in gas cloud at right)	2·00	2·00
4205	12r. Spitzer Space Telescope (gas cloud only at foot and left of telescope)	2·00	2·00
4206	12r. Spitzer Space Telescope (bright stars in gas cloud below telescope)	2·00	2·00
4207	12r. Spitzer Space Telescope (with solar panels visible)	2·00	2·00

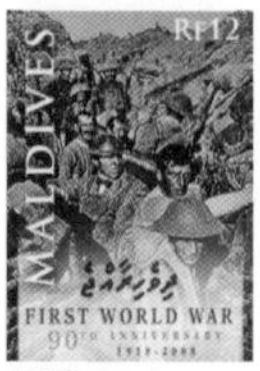

495 Troops in Trench

2008. 90th Anniv of the End of World War One. Multicoloured.

MS4208	91×140 mm. 12r.×4 Type **495**; Two soldiers looking out from trench (side view); Soldiers in trench (seen from back); ANZAC soldier carrying wounded comrade	7·00	7·50
MS4209	195×178 mm. 12r.×4 Motorcycle despatch riders studying map; ANZAC troops ascending hill; Tank; Two soldiers looking out from trench (seen from back)	7·00	7·50

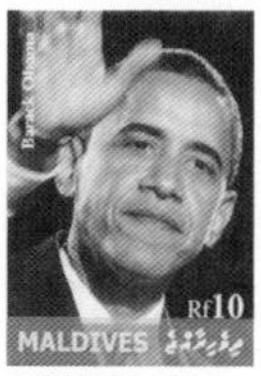

496 Pres. Barack Obama

2009. Inauguration of President Barack Obama. Multicoloured.

MS4210 165×140 mm. 10r.×6 Type 496; Pres. Obama facing right; Michelle Obama; Pres. Obama facing left; Michelle Obama clapping; Pres. Obama facing camera, smiling — 9·00 10·00

MS4211 85×110 mm. 30r. Pres. Barack Obama and Michelle Obama (50×37 mm) — 6·00 7·00

497 Abraham Lincoln

2009. Birth Bicentenary of Abraham Lincoln (US President 1861–5). Sheet 136×175 mm containing T 497 and similar vert designs. Multicoloured.

MS4212 Type 497; Seated by desk; Seated by desk, holding book; Abraham Lincoln (head turned to left) — 6·00 7·00

498 Black-saddled Coralgrouper (*Plectropomus laevis*)

2009. Fish. Multicoloured.
4213	12r. Type 498	2·00	2·00
4214	12r. Sixblotch hind (*Cephalopholis sexmaculata*)	2·00	2·00
4215	12r. Foursaddle grouper (*Epinephelus spilotoceps*)	2·00	2·00
4216	12r. Peacock hind (*Cephalopholis argus*)	2·00	2·00

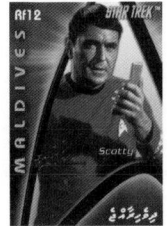

499 Scotty (James Doohan)

2009. *Star Trek.* Multicoloured.

MS4217 178×127 mm. 12r.×4 Type 499; Dr. McCoy (DeForest Kelly) (looking left); Captain Kirk (William Shatner); Mr. Spock (Leonard Nimoy) (in profile) — 7·00 7·50

MS4218 127×178 mm. 12r.×4 Fleet crew; Uhura (Nichelle Nichols); Mr. Spock (speaking); Dr. McCoy (all horiz) — 7·00 7·50

500 Prince Harry at Official Naming of the British Garden

2009. Visit of Prince Harry to New York. Sheet 140×100 mm.

MS4219 Type 500; With little girl at World Trade Center site; Prince Harry speaking; Competing in Polo Classic — 8·50 8·50

501 Marilyn Monroe

2009. Marilyn Monroe Commemoration.

MS4220 Type 501; Sitting in open-top car; Wearing print blouse; Laying down (head and shoulders portrait) — 7·50 8·50

502 Crimson Rose (*Atrophaneura hector*)

2009. Butterflies of Maldives. Multicoloured.
4221	10l. Type 502	20	30
4222	16r. Common mormon (*Papilio polytes*)	2·75	2·75
4223	18r. Common jay (*Graphium dosun*)	3·00	3·00
4224	20r. Common tiger (*Danaus genutia*)	3·25	2·25

MS4225 176×75 mm. 12r.×4 Small salmon arab (*Colotis amata*); Lemon pansy (*Junonia lemonias*); Tamil yeoman (*Cirrochroa thais*); Dark blue tiger (*Tirumala septentrionis*) (all horiz) — 7·50 8·00

MS4226 100×70 mm. 15r.×2 Common jezebel (*Delias eucharis*); Common gull (*Cepora nerissa*) — 4·75 5·00

503 Beluga Whale

2009. Whales. Multicoloured.
4227	10l. Type 503	25	35
4228	12r. Hector's beaked whale (*Mesoplodon hectori*)	2·50	2·50
4229	16r. Beaked whale (*Mesoplodon layardii*)	3·00	3·00
4230	18r. Baird's beaked whale (*Berardius bairdii*)	3·25	3·25

MS4231 150×110 mm. 12r.×6 Dwarf sperm whale (*Kogia sima*); Pygmy sperm whale (*Kogia breviceps*); Baird's beaked whale (*Berardius bairdii*); Sperm whale (*Physeter catodon*); Shepherd's beaked whale (*Tasmacetus shepherdi*); Cuvier's beaked whale (*Ziphius cavirostris*) (all horiz) — 14·00 15·00

504 Y-5

2009. Centenary of Chinese Aviation and Aeropex 2009 Exhibition, Beijing. Designs showing aircraft. Multicoloured.

MS4232 145×95 mm. 9r.×4 Type 504; Y-7; Y-8; Y-12 — 5·00 5·50

MS4233 120×79 mm. 25r. Xian Y7-MA60 (50×38 mm) — 3·75 4·00

505 Melon-headed Whales

2009. Endangered Species. Melon-headed Whale (*Peponocephala electra*). Multicoloured.
4234	8r. Type 505	1·75	1·75
4235	8r. Melon-headed whale	1·75	1·75
4236	8r. Four whales	1·75	1·75
4237	8r. Six whales	1·75	1·75

MS4238 112×165 mm. Nos. 4234/7, each ×2 — 12·00 13·00

506 Copelandia bispora

2009. Fungi. Multicoloured.

MS4239 180×80 mm. 8r.×4 Type 506; *Copelandia cyanescens*; *Psilocybe semilanceata*; *Volvariella vovvacea* — 6·00 6·50

2009. 40th Anniv of First Manned Landing on Moon. Multicoloured.

MS4240 120×110 mm. 8r.×6 Dark grey fungi; Two round-headed chestnut fungi; Yellow-brown fungi with prominent gills around edge of cap; White fungi with prominent gills; Dark chestnut fungi; Two bracket fungi — 7·50 8·00

507 Apollo 11 Command Module

2009. 40th Anniv of First Manned Landing on Moon. Multicoloured.

MS4241 130×100 mm. 12r.×4 Type 507; Apollo 11; Astronaut Neil Armstrong; Apollo 11 Lunar Module — 6·50 7·00

MS4242 100×70 mm. 30r. Astronauts Michael Collins, Edwin E. Aldrin and Neil Armstrong (horiz) — 4·75 5·00

508 Nelumbo nucifera

2009. Flowers. Multicoloured.

MS4243 150×110 mm. 10r.×6 Type 508; *Rosa bracteata*; *Freycinetia cumingiana*; *Thespesia lampas*; *Plumeria champa*; *Plumeria cubensis* — 9·00 10·00

MS4244 110×80 mm. 15r.×2 *Plumeria rubra*; *Hibiscus tilaceus* — 4·75 5·50

MS4245 110×80 mm. 15r.×2 *Lagerstroemia speciosa*; *Plumeria alba* — 4·75 5·50

508a Tiger Symbol

2010. Chinese New Year. Year of the Tiger. Multicoloured.

MS4245a 25r. Type 508a; 25r. Tiger — 6·00 7·00

508b Rat

2010. Chinese Lunar Calendar. 30th Anniv of Chinese Zodiac Stamps. Multicoloured.

MS4245b 3r.×12 Type 508b; Ox; Tiger; Rabbit; Dragon; Snake; Horse; Ram; Monkey; Rooster; Dog; Pig — 7·00 7·00

509 White-tailed Tropicbird (*Phaethon lepturus*)

2010. Birds of the Maldives. Multicoloured.

MS4246 170×106 mm. 8r.×6 Type 509; Common tern (*Sterna hirundo*); Bar-tailed godwit (*Limosa lapponica*); Crab plover (*Dromas ardeola*); Whimbrel (*Numenius phaeopus hudsonicus*); Black-winged stilt (*Himantopus himantopus*) — 7·50 7·50

MS4247 100×70 mm. 30r. Asian koel or Dhivehi kovel (*Eudynamys scolopacea*) — 4·75 5·00

510 Conus abbas

2010. Seashells of Maldives. Multicoloured.
4248	10l. Type 510	25	25
4249	12r. *Conus amadis*	1·60	1·60
4250	16r. *Conus bengalensis*	2·25	2·25
4251	18r. *Pinctada margaritifera*	2·50	2·50

MS4252 150×100 mm. 15r.×4 *Harpa costata*; *Phalium fimbria*; *Zoila friendii friendii*; *Cyprae leucodon tenuidon* — 8·00 8·80

511 Olive Ridley Turtle (*Lepidochelys olivacea*)

2010. Reptiles of the Maldives. Multicoloured.

MS4253 150×100 mm. 15r.×4 Type 511; Good sucker lizard (*Calotes versicolar*); Indian wolf snake (*Lycodon aulicus*); Green turtle (*Chelonia mydas*) — 8·00 8·50

MS4254 100×70 mm. 15r. Common house gecko (*Hemidactylus frenatus*); 15r. Loggerhead turtle (*Caretta caretta gigas*) — 4·25 4·50

512 Lyndon B. Johnson

2010. 50th Anniv of Election of Pres. John F. Kennedy. Multicoloured.

MS4255 $15r.×4 Type 512; John F. Kennedy; Election campaign leaflets; Campaign badge — 8·00 8·50

MS4256 15r.×4 President John F. Kennedy; 1955 Pulitzer Prize medal (won for book *Profiles in Courage*); Civil Rights Act, 1964; Peace Corps emblem (established by JFK, 1961) — 8·00 8·50

513 Elvis Presley as Ross Carpenter

2010. Elvis Presley in Film *Girls! Girls! Girls!*, 1962. Multicoloured.
MS4257 90×125 mm. 25r. Type 513	3·25 3·25
MS4258 125×90 mm. 25r. Wearing cap and mauve and white spotted pyjamas	3·25 3·25
MS4259 90×125 mm. 25r. Wearing white shirt, singing	3·25 3·25
MS4260 125×90 mm. 25r. Poster for *Girls! Girls! Girls!*	3·25 3·25

514 Brownies

2010. Centenary of Girlguiding. Multicoloured.

MS4261 150×100 mm. 16r.×4 Type 514; Two guides; Guide rock climbing; Two guides jumping for joy — 8·00 8·50

MS4262 71×100 mm. 30r. Brownie saluting (vert) — 3·75 4·00

MS4263 173×240 mm. 12r. 'girls worldwide say 100 YEARS of changing lives'; 12r. '58 YEARS OF GUIDING MALDIVES' (both 34×26 mm) — 6·50 6·50

515 Girl standing in Corner (Aishath Shamha Nizam) (1st)

2010. Human Rights Commission of the Maldives. Prevention of Child Abuse. Winning Entries in Children's Poster Drawing Competition. Multicoloured.

MS4264 10l. Type **515**; 20l. Girl sitting on floor, silhouettes and 'Join your hands to protect us not to abuse us!!' (Shaulann Shafeeq) (3rd) ; 95l. Man and crying woman and boy (Sameen Moosa) (3rd); 5r. Children and 'we dont bully' in speech bubbles (Zaha Mohamed Ziyad) (2nd) 95   95

MS4265 25l. Blindfolded girl and gagged girl ('Open Your eyes! And Break our silence') (Emau Ahmed Saleem) (3rd); 50l. Three silhouettes (Rishwan Naseem) (Special Prize); 1r. Child's hand and 'THIS CHILD NEEDS HOPE' (Ahmed Nafiu) (Special Prize); 2r. Boy holding drawing and 'It Shouldn't HURT to be a CHILD' (Sam'aan Abdul Raheem) (Special Prize); 3r. Family and heart (Ummu Haanee Hussain) (1st); 4r. Wounded girl (Fathimath Shaufa Easa (2nd); 6r. Girl and 'Stop Child Abuse' (Hussain Hazim (3rd); 7r. Child fallen from bed (Fathimath Afaaf Bushree) (2nd) (all vert) .... 3·50   3·50

Pt. 6, Pt. 13

MALI

Federation of French Sudan and Senegal, formed in 1959 as an autonomous republic within the French Community. In August 1960 the Federation was split up and the French Sudan part became the independent Mali Republic.

100 centimes = 1 franc.

A. FEDERATION

1 Map, Flag, Mali and Torch

1959. Establishment of Mali Federation.
1   **1**   25f. multicoloured .... 1·50   1·10

2

1959. Air. 300th Anniv of St. Louis, Senegal.
2   **2**   85f. multicoloured .... 3·50   2·30

3 West African Parrotfish   **4** Violet Starling

1960. (a) Postage. Fish as T **3**.
3	**3**	5f. orange, blue and bronze	55	25
4	-	10f. black, brown and turquoise	70	35
5	-	15f. brown, slate and blue	70	45
6	-	20f. black, bistre and green	1·00	55
7	-	25f. yellow, sepia and green	1·70	90
8	-	30f. red, purple and blue	2·30	1·60
9	-	85f. red, blue and green	5·25	3·50

(b) Air. Birds as T **4**.
10	**4**	100f. multicoloured	4·50	2·30
11	-	200f. multicoloured	11·50	5·75
12	-	500f. multicoloured	30·00	17·00

DESIGNS—HORIZ: 10f. West African triggerfish; 15f. Guinean fingerfish; 20f. Threadfish; 25f. Shining butterflyfish; 30f. Monrovian surgeonfish; 85f. Pink dentex; 200f. Bateleur. VERT: 500f. Common gonolek.

1960. Tenth Anniv of African Technical Co-operation Commission. As T **4** of Malagasy Republic.
13	25f. purple and violet	1·80	1·10

B. REPUBLIC

1960. Nos. 6, 7, 9 and 10/12 optd REPUBLIQUE DU MALI and bar or bars or surch also.
14	20f. black, bistre and green (postage)	1·50	85
15	25f. red, purple and blue	2·10	85
16	85f. red, blue and green	3·75	2·10
17	100f. multicoloured (air)	5·00	2·10
18	200f. multicoloured	8·50	4·25
19	300f. on 500f. multicoloured	12·00	6·50
20	500f. multicoloured	20·00	11·00

7 Pres. Mamadou Konate

1961
21	**7**	20f. sepia and green (postage)	40	25
22	-	25f. black and purple	55	25
23	**7**	200f. sepia and red (air)	4·00	1·20
24	-	300f. black and green	5·75	1·70

DESIGN: 25, 300f. President Keita. Nos. 23/4 are larger, 27×38 mm.

8 U.N. Emblem, Flag and Map

1961. Air. Proclamation of Independence and Admission into U.N.
25	**8**	100f. multicoloured	2·10	1·20

MS25a 160×100 mm. Nos. 21/2 and 25 ...... 3·00   3·00

9 Sankore Mosque, Timbuktu

1961. Air.
26	**9**	100f. brown, blue and sepia	1·90	70
27	-	200f. brown, red and green	5·25	2·30
28	-	500f. green, brown and blue	13·50	4·50

DESIGN: 200f. View of Timbuktu; 500f. Arms and view of Bamako.

10 Africans learning Vowels

1961. First Anniv of Independence.
29	**10**	25f. multicoloured	85	55

11 Sheep at Pool

1961
30	**11**	50c. sepia, myrtle and red	10	10
31	A	1f. bistre, green and blue	10	10
32	B	2f. red, green and blue	10	10
33	C	3f. brown, green and blue	10	10
34	D	4f. blue, green and bistre	10	10
35	**11**	5f. purple, green and blue	10	10
36	A	10f. brown, myrtle and blue	30	20
37	B	15f. brown, green and blue	30	20
38	C	20f. red, green and blue	45	25
39	D	25f. brown and blue	50	25
40	**11**	30f. brown, green and violet	75	40
41	A	40f. brown, green and blue	1·40	40
42	B	50f. lake, green and blue	70	40
43	C	60f. brown, green and blue	1·50	45

44	D	85f. brown, bistre and blue	2·30	55

DESIGNS: A, Oxen at pool; B, House of Arts, Mali; C, Land tillage; D, Combine-harvester in rice field.

12 African Map and King Mohammed V of Morocco

1962. First Anniv of African Conf, Casablanca.
45	**12**	25f. multicoloured	35	10
46	**12**	50f. multicoloured	70	30

13 Patrice Lumumba

1962. First Death Anniv of Patrice Lumumba (Congo leader).
47	**13**	25f. brown and bistre	35	25
48	**13**	100f. brown and green	1·20	70

1962. Malaria Eradication. As T **11a** of Malagasy.
49	25f.+5f. blue	1·20	1·00

14 Pegasus and U.P.U. Emblem

1962. 1st Anniv of Admission into U.P.U.
50	**14**	85f. multicoloured	1·60	1·00

14a Posthorn on Map of Africa

1962. African Postal Union Commem.
51	**14a**	25f. green and brown	45	25
52	**14a**	85f. orange and green	1·20	55

15 Sansanding Dam

1962
53	**15**	25f. black, green and blue	45	25
54	-	45f. multicoloured	1·60	70

DESIGN—HORIZ: 45f. Cotton plant.

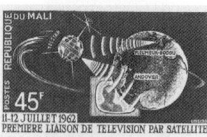

16 "Telstar" Satellite, Globe and Television Receiver

1962. First Trans-Atlantic Telecommunications Satellite Link.
55	**16**	45f. brown, violet and lake	1·10	70
56	**16**	55f. violet, olive and green	1·20	80

17 Soldier and Family

1962. Mali–Algerian Solidarity.
57	**17**	25f.+5f. multicoloured	65	55

18 Bull's Head, Laboratory Equipment and Chicks

1963. Zoological Research Centre, Sobuta.
58	**18**	25f. turq & brn (postage)	55	40
59	-	200f. turquoise, purple and bistre (air)	4·50	2·00

DESIGN: 200f. As Type **18** but horiz, 47×27 mm.

19 Tractor and Campaign Emblem

1963. Freedom from Hunger.
60	**19**	25f. purple, black and blue	60	25
61	**19**	45f. brown, green & turq	1·10	50

20 Balloon and W.M.O. Emblem

1963. Atmospheric Research.
62	**20**	25f. multicoloured	45	25
63	**20**	45f. multicoloured	80	50
64	**20**	60f. multicoloured	1·20	65

21 Race Winners

1963. Youth Week. Multicoloured.
65	**21**	5f. Type **21**	10	10
66	**21**	10f. Type **21**	20	25
67	**21**	20f. Acrobatic dance (horiz)	65	35
68	**21**	85f. Football (horiz)	1·50	70

22 Centenary Emblem and Globe

1963. Red Cross Centenary. Inscr in black.
69	**22**	5f. multicoloured	25	15
70	**22**	10f. red, yellow and grey	40	30
71	**22**	85f. red, yellow and grey	1·90	1·00

23 Stretcher case entering Aero 145 Ambulance Airplane

1963. Air.

72	23	25f. brown, blue and green	45	25
73	-	55f. blue, ochre and brown	1·20	55
74	-	100f. blue, brown and green	2·10	95

DESIGNS: 55f. Douglas DC-3 airliner on tarmac; 100f. Illyushin Il-18 airliner taking off.

24 South African Crowned Crane standing on Giant Tortoise

1963. Air. Fauna Protection.

75	24	25f. brown, red and orange	1·30	70
76	24	200f. multicoloured	6·25	2·75

25 U.N. Emblem, Doves and Banner

1963. Air. 15th Anniv of Declaration of Human Rights.

77	25	50f. yellow, red and green	1·20	60

26 "Kaempferia aethiopica"

1963. Tropical Flora. Multicoloured.

78		30f. Type 26	55	25
79		70f. "Bombax costatum"	1·70	80
80		100f. "Adenium honghel"	3·75	95

27 Pharaoh and Cleopatra, Philae

1964. Air. Nubian Monuments Preservation.

81	27	25f. brown and purple	85	35
82	27	55f. olive and purple	1·70	80

28 Locust on Map of Africa

1964. Anti-locust Campaign.

83	28	5f. brown, green and purple	45	20
84	-	10f. brown, green and olive	80	30
85	-	20f. brown, green and bistre	1·50	55

DESIGNS: VERT: 10f. Locust and map. HORIZ: 20f. Airspraying, locust and village.

29 Football

1964. Olympic Games, Tokyo.

86	29	5f. purple, green and red	10	10
87	-	10f. brown, blue and sepia	35	25
88	-	15f. red and violet	55	40
89	-	85f. green, brown and violet	2·30	1·50
MS89a		190×100 mm. Nos. 86/9	5·00	5·00

DESIGNS: VERT: 10f. Boxing; 15f. Running and Olympic Flame. HORIZ: 85f. Hurdling. Each design has a stadium in the background.

30 Solar Flares

1964. International Quiet Sun Years.

90	30	45f. olive, red and blue	1·00	55

31 President Kennedy

1964. Air. First Death Anniv of Pres. Kennedy.

91	31	100f. multicoloured	2·40	1·60
MS91a		120×90 mm. No. 91 in block of four	9·00	8·50

32 Map of Vietnam

1964. Mali–South Vietnam Workers' Solidarity Campaign.

92	32	30f. multicoloured	65	30

33 Greater Turacos ("Touraco")

1965. Air. Birds.

93	33	100f. green, blue and red	2·40	90
94	-	200f. black, red and blue	8·25	2·10
95	-	300f. black, ochre and green	12·00	3·25
96	-	500f. red, brown and green	21·00	6·25

BIRDS—VERT: 200f. Abyssinian ground hornbills; 300f. Egyptian vultures. HORIZ: 500f. Goliath herons.

34 I.C.Y. Emblem and U.N. Headquarters

1965. Air. International Co-operation Year.

97	34	55f. ochre, purple and blue	1·10	55

35 African Buffalo

1965. Animals.

98	-	1f. brown, blue and green	10	10
99	35	5f. brown, orange and green	30	25
100	-	10f. brown, mauve & green	50	25
101	-	30f. brown, green and red	1·00	45
102	-	90f. brown, grey and green	2·75	1·10

ANIMALS—VERT: 1f. Waterbuck; 10f. Scimitar oryx; 90f. Giraffe. HORIZ: 30f. Leopard.

36 Abraham Lincoln

1965. Death Centenary of Abraham Lincoln.

103	36	45f. multicoloured	95	65
104	36	55f. multicoloured	1·30	90

37 Hughes' Telegraph

1965. Centenary of I.T.U.

105	-	20f. black, blue and orange	45	25
106	37	30f. green, brown & orange	65	50
107	-	50f. green, brown & orange	1·30	75

DESIGNS—VERT: 20f. Denis's pneumatic tube; 50f. Lescurre's heliograph.

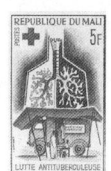

38 "Lungs" and Mobile X-Ray Unit (Anti-T.B.)

1965. Mali Health Service.

108	38	5f. violet, red and crimson	10	10
109	-	10f. green, bistre and red	45	10
110	-	25f. green and brown	65	35
111	-	45f. green and brown	1·40	75

DESIGNS: 10f. Mother and children (Maternal and Child Care); 25f. Examining patient (Marchoux Institute); 45f. Nurse (Biological Laboratory).

39 Diving

1965. First African Games, Brazzaville, Congo.

112	39	5f. red, brown and blue	30	10
113	-	15f. turquoise, brown and red (Judo)	75	50

40 Pope John XXIII

1965. Air. Pope John Commemoration.

114	40	100f. multicoloured	2·30	1·40

41 Sir Winston Churchill

1965. Air. Churchill Commemoration.

115	41	100f. blue and brown	2·30	1·40

42 Dr. Schweitzer and Young African

1965. Air. Dr. Albert Schweitzer Commemoration.

116	42	100f. multicoloured	2·75	1·50
MS116a		160×140 mm. No. 116 in block of four	10·50	9·50

43 Leonov

1966. International Astronautic Conference, Athens (1965). Multicoloured.

117	43	100f. Type 43	2·00	1·10
118	-	100f. White	2·00	1·10
119	-	300f. Cooper, Conrad, Leonov and Beliaiev (vert)	5·25	2·75

44 Vase, Quill and Cornet

1966. World Festival of Negro Arts, Dakar, Cameroun.

120	44	30f. black, red and ochre	45	25
121	-	55f. red, black and green	95	50
122	-	90f. brown, orange and blue	1·80	75

DESIGNS: 55f. Mask, brushes and palette, microphones; 90f. Dancers, mask and patterned cloth.

45 W.H.O. Building

1966. Inaug of W.H.O. Headquarters, Geneva.

123	45	30f. green, blue and yellow	60	30
124	45	45f. red, blue and yellow	85	50

46 Fisherman with Net

1966. River Fishing.

125	46	3f. brown and blue	10	10
126	-	4f. purple, blue and brown	30	10
127	-	20f. purple, green and blue	50	20
128	46	25f. purple, blue and green	65	30
129	-	60f. purple, lake and green	1·20	50
130	-	85f. plum, green and blue	1·80	80

DESIGNS: 4f., 60f. Collective shore fishing; 20f., 85f. Fishing pirogue.

47 Papal Arms, U.N. and Peace Emblems

1966. Air. Pope Paul's Visit to U.N.

131	47	200f. blue, green & turq	3·25	1·80

48 Initiation Ceremony

1966. Mali Pioneers. Multicoloured.

132	48	5f. Type 48	30	10
133		25f. Pioneers dancing	80	35

49 People and
UNESCO Emblem

1966. Air. 20th Anniv of UNESCO.
134   **49**   100f. red, green and blue   2·30   1·20

50 Footballers, Globe, Cup and
Football

1966. Air. World Cup Football Championship, England.
135   **50**   100f. multicoloured   2·40   1·30

51 Cancer ("The
Crab")

1966. Air. Ninth International Cancer Congress, Tokyo.
136   **51**   100f. multicoloured   2·00   90

52 UNICEF Emblem
and Children

1966. 20th Anniv of UNICEF.
137   **52**   45f. blue, purple and
brown   1·00   55

53 Inoculating Cattle

1967. Campaign for Preventing Cattle Plague.
138   **53**   10f. multicoloured   45   10
139   **53**   30f. multicoloured   95   40

54 Desert Vehicles in Pass

1967. Air. Crossing of the Hoggar (1924).
140   **54**   200f. green, brown &
violet   6·50   3·25

55 "Diamant" Rocket
and Francesco de
Lana-Terzis's "Aerial
Ship"

1967. Air. French Space Rockets and Satellites.
141   **55**   50f. blue, turquoise
& pur   95   45

---

142   -   100f. lake, purple & turq   2·00   80
143   -   200f. purple, olive and
blue   3·50   1·60
DESIGNS: 100f. Satellite "A 1" and Jules Verne's "rocket";
200f. Satellite "D 1" and Da Vinci's "bird-powered" flying
machine.

56 Ancient City

1967. International Tourist Year.
144   **56**   25f. orange, blue and
violet   60   30

57 Amelia Earhart and Mail
Route-map

1967. Air. 30th Anniv of Amelia Earhart's Flight, via Gao.
145   **57**   500f. multicoloured   11·00   4·75

58 "The Bird Cage"

1967. Air. Picasso Commemoration. Designs showing
paintings. Multicoloured.
146   **58**   50f. Type **58**   1·30   60
147   **58**   100f. "Paul as Harlequin"   2·75   1·10
148   **58**   250f. "The Pipes of Pan"   5·50   2·50
See also Nos. 158/9 and 164/7.

59 Scout Emblems
and Rope Knots

1967. Air. World Scout Jamboree, Idaho.
149   **59**   70f. red and green   1·20   40
150   **59**   100f. black, lake and
green   1·80   55
DESIGN: 100f. Scout with "walkie-talkie" radio.

60 "Chelorrhina
polyphemus"

1967. Insects.
151   **60**   5f. green, brown and
blue   75   30
152   -   15f. purple, brown &
green   1·20   50
153   -   50f. red, brown and
green   3·00   1·10
INSECTS—HORIZ: 15f. "Ugada grandicollis"; 50f. "Phyma-
teus cinctus".

61 School Class

1967. International Literacy Day.
154   **61**   50f. black, red and green   1·00   35

62 "Europafrique"

1967. Europafrique.
155   **62**   45f. multicoloured   1·10   50

63 Lions
Emblem and
Crocodile

1967. 50th Anniv of Lions International.
156   **63**   90f. multicoloured   1·70   1·00

64 "Water Resources"

1967. International Hydrological Decade.
157   **64**   25f. black, blue and
bistre   65   25

1967. Air. Toulouse-Lautrec Commemoration. Paintings as
T **58**. Multicoloured.
158   100f. "Gazelle" (horse's head)
(horiz)   3·00   1·60
159   300f. "Gig drawn by Cob" (vert)   7·50   3·25

65 Block of Flats,
Grenoble

1968. Air. Winter Olympic Games, Grenoble.
160   **65**   50f. brown, green and
blue   95   55
161   -   150f. brown, blue and
ultramarine   2·30   1·10
DESIGN: 150f. Bobsleigh course, Huez mountain.

66 W.H.O. Emblem

1968. 20th Anniv of W.H.O.
162   **66**   90f. blue, lake and green   1·30   60

67 Human Figures and
Entwined Hearts

1968. World "Twin Towns" Day.
163   **67**   50f. red, violet and green   85   35

1968. Air. Flower Paintings. As T **58**. Multicoloured.
164   50f. "Roses and Anemones"
(Van Gogh)   85   30
165   150f. "Vase of Flowers" (Manet)   2·30   75
166   300f. "Bouquet of Flowers"
(Delacroix)   4·50   1·50
167   500f. "Marguerites" (Millet)   7·25   2·50
SIZES: 50f., 300f. 40×41½ mm; 150f. 36×47½ mm; 500f.
50×36 mm.

68 Dr. Martin
Luther King

1968. Air. Martin Luther King Commemoration.
168   **68**   100f. black, pink and
purple   1·30   65

69 "Draisienne" Bicycle,
1809

1968. Veteran Bicycles and Motor Cars.
169   **69**   2f. brown, mauve and
green (postage)   45   15
170   -   5f. red, blue and bistre   80   40
171   -   10f. blue, brown and
green   1·30   55
172   -   45f. black, green and
brown   2·20   90
173   -   50f. red, green & brn (air)   1·50   45
174   -   100f. blue, mauve and
bistre   3·00   90
DESIGNS—HORIZ: 5f. De Dion-Bouton, 1894; 45f. Pan-
hard-Levassor, 1914; 100f. Mercedes-Benz, 1927. VERT: 10f.
Michaux Bicycle, 1861; 50f. "Bicyclette", 1918".

70 Books, Graph and
A.D.B.A. Emblem

1968. Tenth Anniv of International African Libraries and
Archives Development Association.
175   **70**   100f. red, black and
brown   1·10   45

71 Football

1968. Air. Olympic Games, Mexico. Multicoloured.
176   **71**   100f. Type **71**   1·60   75
177   150f. Long-jumping (vert)   2·75   1·10

1968. Air. "Philexafrique" Stamp Exhibition, Abidjan, Ivory
Coast, 1969 (1st issue). As T **74a** of Ivory Coast.
Multicoloured.
178   200f. "The Editors" (F. M. Granet)   3·50   2·30

1969. Air. "Philexafrique" Stamp Exn, Abidjan, Ivory Coast
(2nd issue). As T **74b** of Ivory Coast.
179   100f. purple, red and violet   2·20   2·10
DESIGN: 100f. Carved animal and French Sudan stamp of
1931.

72 "Napoleon Bonaparte,
First Consul" (Gros)

1969. Air. Birth Bicentenary of Napoleon Bonaparte.
Multicoloured.
180   150f. Type **72**   4·00   1·60
181   200f. "The Bivouac – Battle of
Austerlitz" (Lejeune) (horiz)   6·25   2·40

73 Montgolfier Balloon

1969. Air. Aviation History. Multicoloured.
182	50f. Type **73**		85	30
183	150f. Ferdinand Ferber's Glider No. 5		2·50	75
184	300f. Concorde		5·50	1·90

74 African Tourist Emblem

1969. African Tourist Year.
185	**74**	50f. red, green and blue	65	25

75 "O.I.T." and I.L.O. Emblem

1969. 50th Anniv of I.L.O.
186	**75**	50f. violet, blue and green	50	25
187	**75**	60f. slate, red and brown	75	40

76 Panhard of 1897 and Model "24-CT"

1969. French Motor Industry.
188	**76**	25f. lake, black and bistre (postage)	1·00	45
189	-	30f. green and black	1·30	45
190	-	55f. red, black and purple (air)	1·40	35
191	-	90f. blue, black and red	2·10	55

DESIGNS: 30f. Citroen of 1923 and Model "DS-21"; 55f. Renault of 1898 and Model "16"; 90f. Peugeot of 1893 and Model "404".

77 Clarke (Australia), 10,000 m (1965)

1969. Air. World Athletics Records.
192	**77**	60f. brown and blue	45	40
193	-	90f. brown and red	75	45
194	-	120f. brown and green	1·00	65
195	-	140f. brown and slate	1·20	70
196	-	150f. black and red	1·40	75

DESIGNS: 90f. Lusis (Russia), Javelin (1968); 120f. Miyake (Japan), Weightlifting (1967); 140f. Matson (U.S.A.), Shotputting (1968); 150f. Keino (Kenya), 3,000 m (1965).

78 Hollow Blocks

1969. International Toy Fair, Nuremberg.
197	**78**	5f. red, yellow and grey	10	10
198	-	10f. multicoloured	30	10
199	-	15f. green, red and pink	35	20
200	-	20f. orange, blue and red	45	30

DESIGNS: 10f. Toy donkey on wheels; 15f. "Ducks"; 20f. Model car and race-track.

79 "Apollo 8", Earth and Moon

1969. Air. Moon Flight of "Apollo 8".
201	**79**	2,000f. gold	26·00	26·00

This stamp is embossed on gold foil.

1969. Air. First Man on the Moon. Nos. 182/4 optd L'HOMME SUR LA LUNE JUILLET 1969 and Apollo 11.
202	50f. multicoloured	95	80
203	150f. multicoloured	3·00	1·80
204	300f. multicoloured	4·50	3·25

81 Sheep

1969. Domestic Animals.
205	**81**	1f. olive, brown and green	25	10
206	-	2f. brown, grey and red	25	10
207	-	10f. olive, brown and blue	45	20
208	-	35f. slate and red	1·50	60
209	-	90f. brown and blue	2·40	90

ANIMALS: 2f. Goat; 10f. Donkey; 35f. Horse; 90f. Dromedary.

1969. Fifth Anniv of African Development Bank. As T **122a** of Mauritania.
210	50f. brown, green and purple	45	25
211	90f. orange, green and brown	70	35

83 "Mona Lisa" (Leonardo da Vinci)

1969. Air. 450th Death Anniv of Leonardo da Vinci.
212	**83**	500f. multicoloured	8·50	4·50

84 Vaccination

1969. Campaign against Smallpox and Measles.
213	**84**	50f. slate, brown and green	85	35

85 Mahatma Gandhi

1969. Air. Birth Centenary of Mahatma Gandhi.
214	**85**	150f. brown and green	2·40	90

1969. Tenth Anniv of Aerial Navigation Security Agency for Africa and Madagascar (A.S.E.C.N.A.). As T **94a** of Niger.
215	100f. green	1·00	50

87 West African Map and Posthorns

1970. Air. 11th Anniv of West African Postal Union (C.A.P.T.E.A.O.).
216	**87**	100f. multicoloured	1·00	50

1970. Air. Religious Paintings. As T **83**. Multicoloured.
217	100f. "Virgin and Child" (Van der Weydan School)		1·00	50
218	150f. "The Nativity" (The Master of Flamalle)		1·60	1·00
219	250f. "Virgin, Child and St. John the Baptist" (Low Countries School)		3·75	1·90

89 Franklin D. Roosevelt

1970. Air. 25th Death Anniv of Franklin D. Roosevelt.
220	**89**	500f. black, red and blue	5·00	3·00

90 Women of Mali and Japan

1970. "EXPO 70" World Fair, Osaka, Japan.
221	**90**	100f. orange, brown & blue	95	40
222	-	150f. red, green and yellow	1·30	55

DESIGN: 150f. Flags and maps of Mali and Japan.

91 Lenin

1970. Air. Birth Centenary of Lenin.
223	**91**	300f. black, green and flesh	4·50	1·70

92 Verne and Moon Rockets

1970. Air. Jules Verne "Prophet of Space Travel". Multicoloured.
224	**92**	50f. Type **92**	1·00	45
225		150f. Moon orbit	2·20	90
226		300f. Splashdown	4·00	1·90

93 I.T.U. Emblem and Map

1970. World Telecommunications Day.
227	**93**	90f. red, brown and sepia	1·00	40

1970. New U.P.U. Headquarters Building, Berne. As Type **87a** of Ivory Coast.
228	50f. brown, green and red	45	25
229	60f. brown, blue and mauve	65	2·00

1970. Air. Space Flight of "Apollo 13". Nos. 224/6 optd APOLLO XIII EPOPEE SPATIALE 11-17 AVRIL 1970 in three lines.
230	50f. multicoloured	50	30
231	150f. multicoloured	1·60	85
232	300f. multicoloured	3·25	1·80

96 "Intelstat 3" Satellite

1970. Air. Space Telecommunications.
233	**96**	100f. indigo, blue & orange	95	50
234	-	200f. purple, grey and blue	1·80	70

235	-	300f. brown, orange & slate	3·25	1·60
236	-	500f. brown, blue & indigo	5·00	2·30

DESIGNS: 200f. "Molnya I" satellite; 300f. Dish aerial, Type PB 2; 500f. "Symphony Project" satellite.

97 Auguste and Louis Lumiere, Jean Harlow and Marilyn Monroe

1970. Air. Lumiere Brothers (inventors of the cine camera) Commemoration.
237	**97**	250f. multicoloured	5·00	2·40

98 Footballers

1970. Air. World Cup Football Championship, Mexico.
238	**98**	80f. green, brown and red	85	45
239	**98**	200f. red, brown and blue	2·00	70

99 Rotary Emblem, Map and Antelope

1970. Air. Rotary International.
240	**99**	200f. multicoloured	2·75	1·30

100 "Supporting United Nations"

1970. Air. 25th Anniv of U.N.O.
241	**100**	100f. blue, brown & violet	1·10	60

101 Page from 11th century Baghdad Koran

1970. Air. Ancient Muslim Art. Multicoloured.
242	**101**	50f. Type **101**	85	25
243		200f. "Tree and wild Animals" (Jordanian mosaic, c.730)	1·80	70
244		250f. "The Scribe" (Baghdad miniature, 1287)	2·75	1·10

1970. Air. Moon Landing of "Luna 16". Nos. 234/5 surch LUNA 16 PREMIERS PRELEVEMENTS AUTOMATIQUES SUR LA LUNE SEPTEMBRE 1970 and new values.
245	150f. on 200f. purple, grey and blue	1·50	75
246	250f. on 300f. brown, orange and grey	2·30	1·10

103 G.P.O., Bamako

1970. Public Buildings.
247	**103**	30f. olive, green and brown	45	35
248	-	40f. purple, brown & green	55	35
249	-	60f. grey, green and red	75	35
250	-	80f. brown, green and grey	1·10	40

BUILDINGS: 40f. Chamber of Commerce, Bamako; 60f. Ministry of Public Works, Bamako; 80f. Town Hall, Segou.

104 Pres. Nasser

1970. Air. Pres. Gamal Nasser of Egypt. Commemoration.
251	**104**	1000f. gold	12·00	12·00

105 "The Nativity"
(Antwerp School 1530)

1970. Air. Christmas. Paintings. Multicoloured.
252		100f. Type **105**	1·20	55
253		250f. "Adoration of the Shepherds" (Memling)	2·75	1·20
254		300f. "Adoration of the Magi" (17th-century Flemish school)	3·50	1·70

106 Gallet Steam
Locomotive, 1882

1970. Mali Railway Locomotives from the Steam Era (1st series).
255	**106**	20f. black, red and green	1·50	60
256	-	40f. black, green & brown	2·00	75
257	-	50f. black, green & brown	3·00	95
258	-	80f. black, red and green	3·75	1·30
259	-	100f. black, green & brn	5·75	1·90

LOCOMOTIVES: 40f. Felou, 1882; 50f. Bechevel, 1882; 80f. Series 1100, 1930 (inscr "Type 23"); 100f. Class 40, 1927 (incr "Type 141" and "vers 1930").
See also Nos. 367/70.

107 Scouts crossing
Log-bridge

1970. Scouting in Mali. Multicoloured.
260		5f. Type **107**	40	10
261		30f. Bugler and scout camp (vert)	55	25
262		100f. Scouts canoeing	1·40	45

108 Bambara de
San Mask

1971. Mali Masks and Ideograms. Multicoloured.
263		20f. Type **108**	30	10
264		25f. Dogon de Bandiagara mask	40	20
265		50f. Kanaga ideogram	75	30

266		80f. Bambara ideogram	1·00	35

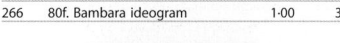

109 General De Gaulle

1971. Air. Charles De Gaulle Commem. Die-stamped on gold foil.
267	**109**	2000f. gold, red and blue	75·00	70·00

110 Alfred Nobel

1971. Air. 75th Death Anniv of Alfred Nobel (philanthropist).
268	**110**	300f. red, brown and green	3·50	1·60

111 Tennis Player
(Davis Cup)

1971. Air. World Sporting Events.
269	**111**	100f. slate, purple and blue	1·70	75
270	-	150f. olive, brown & green	2·50	1·10
271	-	200f. brown, olive and blue	3·75	1·60

DESIGNS—HORIZ: 150f. Steeplechase (inscr "Derby at Epsom" but probably represents the Grand National). VERT: 200f. Yacht (Americas Cup).

112 Youth, Sun and
Microscope

1971. 50th Anniv of 1st B.C.G. Vaccine Innoculation.
272	**112**	100f. brown, green and red	1·50	60

113 "The Thousand and One
Nights"

1971. Air. "Tales of the Arabian Nights". Multicoloured.
273		120f. Type **113**	1·70	70
274		180f. "Ali Baba and the Forty Thieves"	2·30	90
275		200f. "Aladdin's Lamp"	3·25	1·10

114 Scouts, Japanese
Horseman and Mt. Fuji

1971. 13th World Scout Jamboree, Asagiri, Japan.
276	**114**	80f. plum, green and blue	85	35

115 Rose between Hands

1971. 25th Anniv of UNICEF.
277	**115**	50f. brown, red and orange	45	25
278	-	60f. blue, green and brown	65	30

DESIGN—VERT: 60f. Nurses and children.

116 Rural Costume

1971. National Costumes. Multicoloured.
279		5f. Type **116**	10	10
280		10f. Rural costume (female)	35	25
281		15f. Tuareg	40	25
282		60f. Embroidered "boubou"	65	30
283		80f. Women's ceremonial costume	1·00	45

117 Olympic Rings and Events

1971. Air. Olympic Games Publicity.
284	**117**	80f. blue, purple and green	85	35

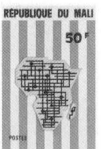

118 Telecommunications
Map

1971. Pan-African Telecommunications Network Year.
285	**118**	50f. multicoloured	50	25

119 "Mariner 4" and Mars

1971. Air. Exploration of Outer Space.
286	**119**	200f. green, blue & brown	1·80	75
287	-	300f. blue, plum & purple	2·75	1·10

DESIGN: 300f. "Venera 5" and Venus.

120 "Santa Maria" (1492)

1971. Air. Famous Ships.
288	**120**	100f. brown, violet & blue	1·20	40
289	-	150f. violet, brown & grn	1·90	80
290	-	200f. green, blue and red	2·50	90
291	-	250f. red, blue and black	3·50	1·30

DESIGNS: 150f. "Mayflower" (1620); 200f. Battleship "Potemkin" (1905); 250f. Liner "Normandie" (1935).

121 "Hibiscus
rosa-sinensis"

1971. Flowers. Multicoloured.
292		20f. Type **121**	45	20
293		50f. "Euphorbia pulcherrima"	90	25
294		60f. "Adenium obesum"	1·20	40
295		80f. "Allamanda cathartica"	1·60	55
296		100f. "Satancrater berhautii"	2·10	65

122 Allegory of Justice

1971. 25th Anniv of Int Court of Justice, The Hague.
297	**122**	160f. chocolate, red & brn	1·30	60

123 Nat King Cole

1971. Air. Famous Negro Musicians. Multicoloured.
298		130f. Type **123**	2·75	50
299		150f. Erroll Garner	3·25	70
300		270f. Louis Armstrong	4·50	1·00

124 Statue of
Olympic Zeus (by
Pheidias)

1971. Air. "The Seven Wonders of the Ancient World".
301	**124**	70f. blue, brown & purple	65	25
302	-	80f. black, brown and blue	90	30
303	-	100f. blue, red and violet	1·00	35
304	-	130f. black, purple & blue	1·30	45
305	-	150f. brown, green & blue	1·60	65
306	-	270f. blue, brown & pur	2·75	90
307	-	280f. blue, purple & brn	2·75	1·10

DESIGNS—VERT: 80f. Pyramid of Cheops, Egypt; 130f. Pharos of Alexandria; 270f. Mausoleum of Halicarnassos; 280f. Colossus of Rhodes. HORIZ: 100f. Temple of Artemis, Ephesus; 150f. Hanging Gardens of Babylon.

125 "Family Life" (carving)

1971. 15th Anniv of Social Security Service.
308	**125**	70f. brown, green and red	85	35

126 Slalom-skiing and
Japanese Girl

1972. Air. Winter Olympic Games, Sapporo, Japan.
309	**126**	150f. brown, green & orge	1·30	65
310	-	200f. green, brown and red	1·80	85
MS311		160×100 mm. Nos. 309/10	3·75	3·50

DESIGNS: 200f. Ice-hockey and Japanese actor.

127 "Santa Maria della Salute"
(Caffi)

1972. Air. UNESCO "Save Venice" Campaign. Multicoloured.
312		130f. Type **127**	1·10	55
313		270f. "Rialto Bridge"	2·00	85
314		280f. "St. Mark's Square" (vert)	2·40	1·00

128 Hands clasping
Flagpole

1972. Air. Int Scout Seminar, Cotonou, Dahomey.
315 **128** 200f. green, orange
& brn   2·00   80

129 Heart and Red Cross Emblems

1972. Air. World Heart Month.
316 **129** 150f. red and blue   1·70   75

130 Football

1972. Air. Olympic Games, Munich (1st issue). Sports and Munich Buildings.
317 **130** 50f. blue, brown and
green   45   25
318 - 150f. blue, brown &
green   1·30   50
319 - 200f. blue, brown &
green   1·60   70
320 - 300f. blue, brown &
green   2·40   95
MS321 191×100 mm. Nos. 317/20 6·00 6·00
DESIGNS—VERT: 150f. Judo; 200f. Hurdling. HORIZ: 300f. Running.
See also Nos. 357/62.

131 "Apollo 15" and Lunar Rover

1972. Air. History of Transport Development.
322 **131** 150f. red, green and lake 1·70   75
323 - 250f. red, blue and green 4·00 1·60
DESIGN: 250f. Montgolfier's balloon and Cugnot's steam car.

132 "UIT" on T.V. Screen

1972. World Telecommunications Day.
324 **132** 70f. black, blue and red 90   35

133 Clay Funerary Statue

1972. Mali Archaeology. Multicoloured.
325 30f. Type **133**   35   15
326 40f. Female Figure (woodcarving)   55   25
327 50f. "Warrior" (stone-painting) 75   40
328 100f. Wrought-iron ritual figures 1·40   65

134 Samuel Morse and
Early Telegraph

1972. Death Centenary of Samuel Morse (inventor of telegraph).
329 **134** 80f. purple, green
and red   1·40   45

135 "Cinderella"

1972. Air. Charles Perrault's Fairy Tales.
330 **135** 70f. green, red and
brown   1·40   40
331 - 80f. brown, red and
green   1·50   55
332 - 150f. violet, purple
& blue   2·75   80
DESIGNS: 80f. "Puss in Boots"; 150f. "The Sleeping Beauty".

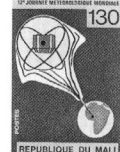

136 Weather
Balloon

1972. World Meteorological Day.
333 **136** 130f. multicoloured   1·70   75

137 Astronauts and Lunar Rover

1972. Air. Moon Flight of "Apollo 16".
334 **137** 500f. brown, violet & grn 4·25 1·70

138 Book Year Emblem

1972. Air. International Book Year.
335 **138** 80f. gold, green and blue 1·70   70

139 Sarakole
Dance, Kayes

1972. Traditional Dances. Multicoloured.
336 10f. Type **139**   45   25
337 20f. Malinke dance, Bamako 55   25
338 50f. Hunter's dance, Bougouni 75   30
339 70f. Bambara dance, Segou 95   35
340 80f. Dogon dance, Sanga   1·20   50
341 120f. Targuie dance, Timbukto 1·70   65

140 Learning the
Alphabet

1972. International Literacy Day.
342 **140** 80f. black and green   85   30

141 Statue and
Musical Instruments

1972. First Anthology of Mali Music.
343 **141** 100f. multicoloured   1·10   55

142 Club Banner

1972. Air. Tenth Anniv of Bamako Rotary Club.
344 **142** 170f. purple, blue
and red   1·70   75

143 Aries the Ram

1972. Signs of the Zodiac.
345 **143** 15f. brown and purple   30   25
346 - 15f. black and brown   30   25
347 - 35f. blue and red   55   25
348 - 35f. red and green   55   25
349 - 40f. brown and blue   65   30
350 - 40f. brown and purple   65   30
351 - 45f. red and blue   80   45
352 - 45f. green and red   80   45
353 - 65f. blue and violet   1·20   50
354 - 65f. brown and violet   1·20   50
355 - 90f. blue and mauve   1·70   80
356 - 90f. green and mauve   1·70   80
DESIGNS: No. 346, Taurus the Bull; No. 347, Gemini the Twins; No. 348, Cancer the Crab; No. 349, Leo the Lion; No. 350, Virgo the Virgin; No. 351, Libra the Scales; No. 352, Scorpio the Scorpion; No. 353, Sagittarius the Archer; No. 354, Capricornus the Goat; No. 355, Aquarius the Water-carrier; No. 356, Pisces the Fish.

1972. Air. Olympic Games, Munich (2nd issue). Sports and Locations of Games since 1952. As Type **130**.
357 70f. blue, brown and red   40   25
358 90f. green, red and blue   50   25
359 140f. olive, green and brown 95   25
360 150f. brown, green and red   1·20   25
361 170f. blue, brown and purple 1·20   40
362 210f. blue, red and green   1·40   55
DESIGNS—VERT: 70f. Boxing, Helsinki Games (1952); 150f. Weightlifting, Tokyo Games (1964). HORIZ: 90f. Hurdling, Melbourne Games (1956); 140f. 200 metres, Rome Games (1960); 170f. Swimming, Mexico Games (1968); 210f. Throwing the javelin, Munich Games (1972).

1972. Medal Winners, Munich Olympic Games. Nos. 318/20 and 362 optd with events and names, etc.
363 150f. blue, brown and green 1·00   50
364 200f. blue, brown and green 1·50   65
365 210f. blue, red and green   1·60   70
366 300f. blue, brown and green 2·20 1·00
OVERPRINTS: 150f. **JUDO RUSKA 2 MEDAILLES D'OR**; 200f. **STEEPLE KEINO MEDAILLE D'OR**; 210f. **MEDAILLE D'OR 90m. 48**; 300f. **100m. - 200m. BORZOV 2 MEDAILLES D'OR**.

1972. Mali Locomotives (2nd series). As T **106**.
367 10f. blue, green and red   1·50   60
368 30f. blue, green and brown 3·00 1·00
369 60f. blue, brown and green 4·75 1·60
370 120f. purple, green and black 6·25 2·20
LOCOMOTIVES: 10f. First Locomotive to arrive at Bamako, 1906; 30f. Steam locomotive, Thies–Bamako line, 1920; 60f. Class 40 steam locomotive, Thies–Bamako line, 1927 (inscr "141");. 120f. Alsthom series BB 100 coupled diesel, Dakar–Bamako line, 1947.

146 Emperor Haile
Selassie

1972. Air. 80th Birth Anniv of Emperor Haile Selassie.
371 **146** 70f. multicoloured   65   30

147 Balloon, Breguet 14T Biplane
and Map

1972. Air. First Mali Airmail Flight by Balloon, Bamako to Timbukto. Multicoloured.
372 200f. Type **147**   1·30   65
373 300f. Balloon, Concorde and
map   2·30   95

148 High Jumping

1973. Second African Games, Lagos, Nigeria. Multicoloured.
374 70f. Type **148**   50   30
375 270f. Throwing the discus 1·60   80
376 280f. Football   2·00 1·00

149 14th-century
German Bishop

1973. Air. World Chess Championship, Reykjavik, Iceland.
377 **149** 100f. lt blue, blue &
brown   1·70   70
378 - 200f. red, light red &
black   3·50 1·40
DESIGN: 200f. 18th-century Indian knight (elephant).

150 Interpol
Headquarters, Paris

1973. 50th Anniv of International Criminal Police Organization (Interpol).
379 **150** 80f. multicoloured   85   30

151 Emblem and Dove with
letter

1973. Tenth Anniv (1971) of African Postal Union.
380 **151** 70f. multicoloured   65   40

152 "Fauna
Protection" Stamp
of 1963

1973. Air. Stamp Day.
381 **152** 70f. orange, red and
brown   1·70   70

153 Astronauts on Moon

1973. Moon Mission of "Apollo" 17.
382 **153** 250f. brown and blue   2·50 1·10
MS383 130×101 mm. **153** 350f. ultramarine, brown and black 2·75 2·75

154 Copernicus

1973. 500th Birth Anniv of Copernicus.
384	**154**	300f. purple and blue	3·50	1·60

155 Handicapped
Africans

1973. "Help the Handicapped".
385	**155**	70f. orange, black and red	75	30

156 Dr. G. A. Hansen

1973. Centenary of Hansen's Identification of the Leprosy Bacillus.
386	**156**	200f. green, black and red	2·20	1·00

157 Bentley and Alfa Romeo, 1930

1973. 50th Anniv of Le Mans 24-hour Endurance Race.
387	**157**	50f. green, orange and blue	50	1·40
388	-	100f. green, blue and red	1·00	35
389	-	200f. blue, green and red	2·50	80

DESIGNS: 100f. Jaguar and Talbot, 1953; 200f. Matra and Porsche, 1952.

158 Scouts around Campfire

1973. International Scouting Congress, Addis Ababa and Nairobi.
390	**158**	50f. brown, red and blue	40	20
391	-	70f. brown, red and blue	55	25
392	-	80f. red, brown and green	60	30
393	-	130f. green, blue & brown	1·00	50
394	-	270f. red, violet and grey	90	85

DESIGNS—VERT: 70f. Scouts saluting flag; 130f. Lord Baden-Powell. HORIZ: 80f. Standard-bearers; 270f. Map of Africa and Scouts and Guides in ring.

159 Swimming and National Flags

1973. First Afro-American Sports Meeting, Bamako.
395	**159**	70f. green, red and blue	45	25
396	-	80f. green, red and blue	60	30
397	-	330f. blue and red	2·30	1·00

DESIGNS—VERT: 80f. Throwing the discus and javelin. HORIZ: 330f. Running.

1973. Pan-African Drought Relief. No. 296 surch SECHERESSE SOLIDARITE AFRICAINE and value.
398		200f. on 100f. multicoloured	2·00	90

161 African Mask and Old Town Hall, Brussels

1973. Air. African Fortnight, Brussels.
399	**161**	70f. violet, blue and brown	75	30

162 "Perseus" (Cellini)

1973. Air. Famous Sculptures.
400	**162**	100f. green and red	1·10	45
401	-	150f. purple and red	1·50	65
402	-	250f. green and red	2·75	95

DESIGNS: 150f. "Pieta" (Michelangelo); 250f. "Victory of Samothrace".

163 Stephenson's "Rocket" (1829) and French Buddicom Locomotive

1973. Air. Famous Locomotives.
403	**163**	100f. black, blue & brown	1·10	45
404	-	150f. multicoloured	1·60	75
405	-	200f. blue, slate and brown	2·40	1·00

DESIGNS: 150f. Union Pacific steam locomotive No. 119 (1890) and Santa Fe Railroad steam locomotive "Blue Goose" (1937), U.S.A.; 200f. "Mistral" express (France) and "Hikari" express train (Japan).

164 "Apollo 11" First Landing

1973. Conquest of the Moon.
406	**164**	50f. purple, red and brown	35	25
407	-	75f. grey, blue and red	50	30
408	-	100f. slate, brown and blue	75	45
409	-	280f. blue, green and red	1·80	80
410	-	300f. blue, red and green	2·30	1·00

DESIGNS: 75f. "Apollo 13" Recovery capsule; 100f. "Apollo 14" Lunar trolley; 280f. "Apollo 15" Lunar rover; 300f. "Apollo 17" lift off from Moon.

165 Picasso

1973. Air. Pablo Picasso (artist). Commem.
411	**165**	500f. multicoloured	4·75	2·30

166 Pres. John Kennedy

1973. Air. Tenth Death Anniv of Pres. Kennedy.
412	**166**	500f. black, purple & gold	4·25	2·00

1973. Air. Christmas. As T **105** but dated "1973". Multicoloured.
413		100f. "The Annunciation" (V. Carpaccio) (horiz)	80	45
414		200f. "Virgin of St. Simon" (F. Baroccio)	1·70	75
415		250f. "Flight into Egypt" (A. Solario)	2·10	90

167 Player and Football

1973. Air. World Football Cup Championship, West Germany.
416	**167**	150f. red, brown and green	1·20	55
417	-	250f. green, brown & violet	2·20	80
MS418		110×85 mm. 500f. multicoloured	4·50	4·50

DESIGNS——VERT: 250f. Goalkeeper and ball. HORIZ: 500f. Football, Arms and Church of Our Lady, Munich.

168 Cora

1973. Musical Instruments.
419	**168**	5f. brown, red and green	40	10
420	-	10f. brown and blue	45	20
421	-	15f. brown, red and yellow	55	25
422	-	20f. brown and red	65	25
423	-	25f. brown, red and yellow	75	30
424	-	30f. black and blue	95	25
425	-	35f. sepia, brown and red	95	45
426	-	40f. brown and red	1·40	50

DESIGNS—HORIZ: 10f. Balafon. VERT: 15f. Djembe; 20f. Guitar; 25f. N'Djarka; 30f. M'Bolon; 35f. Dozo N'Goni; 40f. N'Tamani.

169 "Musicians" (mosaic)

1974. Roman Frescoes and Mosaics from Pompeii.
427	**169**	150f. red, brown and grey	1·30	45
428	-	250f. brown, red & orange	1·80	65
429	-	350f. brown, orange and olive	2·50	95

DESIGNS—VERT: 250f. "Alexander the Great" (mosaic); 350f. "Bacchante" (fresco).

170 Corncob, Worker and "Kibaru" Newspaper

1974. Second Anniv of Rural Press.
430	**170**	70f. brown and green	75	30

171 Sir Winston Churchill

1974. Air. Birth Cent of Sir Winston Churchill.
431	**171**	500f. black	3·75	1·80

172 Chess-pieces on Board

1974. Air. 21st Chess Olympiad, Nice.
432	**172**	250f. indigo, red and blue	3·50	1·50

173 "The Crucifixion" (Alsace School c. 1380)

1974. Air. Easter. Multicoloured.
433	**173**	400f. Type **173**	2·50	1·30
434	-	500f. "The Entombment" (Titian) (horiz)	3·50	1·60

174 Lenin

1974. Air. 50th Death Anniv of Lenin.
435	**174**	150f. purple and violet	2·30	80

175 Goalkeeper and Globe

1974. World Cup Football Championship, West Germany.
436	**175**	270f. red, green and lilac	2·00	1·10
437	-	280f. blue, brown and red	2·40	1·10

DESIGN: 280f. World Cup emblem on football.

176 Horse-jumping Scenes

1974. Air. World Equestrian Championships, La Baule.
438	**176**	130f. brown, lilac and blue	2·00	85

177 Full-rigged Sailing Ship and Modern Liner

1974. Centenary of Universal Postal Union.
439	**177**	80f. purple, lilac & brown	45	35
440	-	90f. orange, grey and blue	70	50
441	-	270f. purple, olive & green	2·10	1·10

DESIGNS: 90f. Breguet 14T biplane and Douglas DC-8; 270f. Steam and electric mail trains.
See also Nos. 463/4.

178 "Skylab" over Africa

1974. Air. Survey of Africa by "Skylab" Space Station.

442	**178**	200f. indigo, blue & orge	1·30	65
443	-	250f. blue, purple & orge	2·10	95

DESIGN: 250f. Astronaut servicing cameras.

1974. Air. 11th Arab Scout Jamboree, Lebanon. Nos. 391/2 surch 130f. 11e JAMBOREE ARABE AOUT 1974 LIBAN or 170f. CONGRES PAN-ARABE LIBAN AOUT 1974.

444	130f. on 70f. brown, red & bl	1·40	65
445	170f. on 80f. blue, green & red	1·70	85

1974. Air. Fifth Anniv of First Landing on Moon. Nos. 408/9 surch 130f. 1er DEBARQUEMENT SUR LA LUNE 20-VII-69 or 300f. 1er PAS SUR LA LUNE 21-VII-69.

446	130f. on 100f. slate, brown and blue	95	55
447	300f. on 280f. blue, grn & red	2·40	1·80

1974. West Germany's Victory in World Cup Football Championship. Nos. 436/7 surch R.F.A. 2 HOLLANDE 1 and value.

448	**175**	300f. on 270f. red, green and lilac	2·30	1·20
449	-	330f. on 280f. blue, brown and red	2·75	1·30

182 Weaver

1974. Crafts and Craftsmen. Multicoloured.

450	50f. Type **182**	45	25
451	60f. Potter	55	25
452	70f. Smith	75	30
453	80f. Wood-carver	1·00	35

183 River Niger near Gao

1974. Mali Views. Multicoloured.

454	10f. Type **183**	15	10
455	20f. "The Hand of Fatma" (rock formation, Hombori) (vert)	20	15
456	40f. Waterfall, Gouina	50	25
457	70f. Hill-dwellings, Dogon (vert)	80	35

184 Class C No. 3 (1906) and Class P (1939) Steam Locomotives, France

1974. Air. Steam Locomotives.

458	**184**	90f. indigo, red and blue	90	45
459	-	120f. brown, orange & bl	1·30	55
460	-	210f. brown, orange & bl	2·10	90
461	-	330f. black, green and blue	3·00	1·30

DESIGNS: 120f. Baldwin (1870) and Pacific (1920) steam locomotives, U.S.A.; 210f. Class A1 (1925) and Buddicom (1847) steam locomotives; 330f. Hudson steam locomotive, 1938 (U.S.A.) and steam locomotive "Gironde", 1839.

185 Skiing

1974. Air. 50th Anniv of Winter Olympics.

462	**185**	300f. red, blue and green	2·30	1·10

1974. Berne Postal Convention. Cent, Nos. 439 and 441 surch 9 OCTOBRE 1974 and value.

463	**177**	250f. on 80f. purple, lilac and brown	2·00	1·10
464	-	300f. on 270f. purple, olive and green	2·50	1·20

187 Mao Tse-tung and Great Wall of China

1974. 25th Anniv of Chinese People's Republic.

465	**187**	100f. blue, red and green	2·20	70

188 "The Nativity" (Memling)

1974. Air. Christmas. Multicoloured.

466	290f. Type **188**	2·00	80
467	310f. "Virgin and Child" (Bourgogne School)	2·30	1·00
468	400f. "Adoration of the Magi" (Schongauer)	2·75	1·40

189 Raoul Follereau (missionary)

1974. Air. Raoul Follereau, "Apostle of the Lepers".

469	**189**	200f. blue	2·75	1·30
469a	**189**	200f. brown	2·75	1·30

190 Electric Train and Boeing 707

1974. Air. Europafrique.

470	**190**	100f. green, brown & blue	95	55
471	**190**	110f. blue, violet & brown	95	55

191 Dr. Schweitzer

1975. Birth Centenary of Dr Albert Schweitzer.

472	**191**	150f. turquoise, green & bl	1·60	80

192 Patients making Handicrafts and Lions International Emblem

1975. Fifth Anniv of Samanko (Leprosy rehabilitation village). Multicoloured.

473	90f. Type **192**	85	35
474	100f. View of Samanko	1·10	40

193 "The Pilgrims at Emmaus" (Champaigne)

1975. Air. Easter. Multicoloured.

475	200f. Type **193**	1·40	55
476	300f. "The Pilgrims at Emmaus" (Veronese)	2·20	80
477	500f. "Christ in Majesty" (Limoges enamel) (vert)	4·00	1·40

194 "Journey to the Centre of the Earth"

1975. Air. 70th Death Anniv of Jules Verne.

478	**194**	100f. green, blue & brown	75	40
479	-	170f. brown, blue & lt brn	1·10	50
480	-	190f. blue, turquoise & brn	1·30	65
481	-	220f. brown, purple & blue	1·60	75

DESIGNS: 170f. Jules Verne and "From the Earth to the Moon"; 190f. Giant octopus–"Twenty Thousand Leagues Under the Sea"; 220f. "A Floating City".

195 Head of "Dawn" (Tomb of the Medici)

1975. Air. 500th Birth Anniv of Michelangelo (artist). Multicoloured.

482	400f. Type **195**	2·75	1·40
483	500f. "Moses" (marble statue, Rome)	3·50	1·60

196 Nile Pufferfish

1975. Fish (1st series).

484	**196**	60f. brown, yellow & grn	1·00	40
485	-	70f. black, brown and grey	1·30	50
486	-	80f. multicoloured	1·50	55
487	-	90f. blue, grey and green	2·00	70
488	-	110f. black and blue	3·00	80

DESIGNS: 70f. Electric catfish; 80f. Deep-sided citharinid; 90f. Lesser tigerfish; 110f. Nile perch.

See also Nos. 544/8.

197 Astronaut

1975. Air. Soviet–U.S. Space Co-operation.

489	**197**	290f. red, blue and black	1·20	70
490	-	300f. red, blue and black	1·50	90
491	-	370f. green, purple & black	2·00	1·10

DESIGNS: 300f. "America and Russia"; 370f. New York and Moscow landmarks.

198 Einstein and Equation

1975. Air. 20th Death Anniv of Albert Einstein.

492	**198**	90f. blue, purple & brown	1·00	50

See also Nos. 504, 507 and 519.

199 Woman with Bouquet

1975. International Women's Year.

493	**199**	150f. red and green	1·10	55

200 Morris "Oxford", 1913

1975. Early Motor-cars.

494	**200**	90f. violet, brown and blue	80	40
495	-	130f. red, grey and blue	1·00	40
496	-	190f. deep blue, green and blue	1·90	55
497	-	230f. brown, blue and red	1·90	70

DESIGNS—MOTOR-CARS: 130f. Franklin "E", 1907; 190f. Daimler, 1900; 230f. Panhard & Levassor, 1895.

201

1975. Air. "Nordjamb 75" World Scout Jamboree, Norway.

498	**201**	100f. blue, brown and lake	75	45
499	-	150f. green, brown & blue	1·00	45
500	-	290f. lake, brown and blue	2·00	95

DESIGNS: 150f., 290f. Scouts and emblem (different).

202 Lafayette and Battle Scene

1975. Air. Bicentenary of American Revolution. Multicoloured.

501	290f. Type **202**	2·00	85
502	300f. Washington and battle scene	2·00	85
503	370f. De Grasse and Battle of the Chesapeake, 1781	2·75	1·20

1975. 20th Death Anniv of Sir Alexander Fleming (scientist). As T **198**.

504	150f. brown, purple and blue	1·30	55

204 Olympic Rings

1975. Air. "Pre-Olympic Year".

505	**204**	350f. violet and blue	2·20	95
506	-	400f. blue	2·50	1·10

DESIGNS: 400f. Emblem of Montreal Olympics (1976).

1975. Birth Bicentenary of Andre-Marie Ampere. As T **198**.

507	90f. brown, red and violet	1·00	45

205 Tristater of Carthage

1975. Ancient Coins.

508	**205**	130f. black, blue & purple	75	35
509	-	170f. black, green & brn	1·00	55
510	-	190f. black, green and red	1·70	80
511	-	260f. black, blue & orange	2·20	1·20

COINS: 170f. Decadrachm of Syracuse; 190f. Tetradrachm of Acanthe; 260f. Didrachm of Eretrie.

1975. Air. "Apollo–Soyuz" Space Link. Nos. 489/91 optd ARRIMAGE 17 Juil. 1975.

512	**197**	290f. red, blue and black	2·20	80
513	-	300f. red, blue and black	2·20	80
514	-	370f. green, purple & black	2·75	1·10

207 U.N. Emblem and Names of Agencies forming "ONU"

1975. 30th Anniv of United Nations Charter.

515	**207**	200f. blue and green	1·10	60

208 "The Visitation" (Ghirlandaio)

1975. Air. Christmas. Religious Paintings.. Multicoloured.

516	**208**	290f. Type **208**	2·20	80
517		300f. "Nativity" (Fra Filippo Lippi School)	2·20	95
518		370f. "Adoration of the Magi" (Velasquez)	2·50	1·50

1975. Air. 50th Death Anniv of Clement Ader (aviation pioneer). As T **198**.

519		100f. purple, red and blue	1·00	45

209 Concorde in Flight

1976. Air. Concorde's First Commercial Flight.

520	**209**	500f. multicoloured	4·75	2·00

210 Figure-Skating

1976. Air. Winter Olympic Games, Innsbruck. Multicoloured.

521	**210**	120f. Type **210**	75	30
522		420f. Ski-jumping	2·30	75
523		430f. Skiing (slalom)	2·50	1·00

211 Alexander Graham Bell

1976. Telephone Centenary.

524	**211**	180f. blue, brown and light brown	1·30	55

212 Chameleon

1976. Reptiles. Multicoloured.

525	**212**	20f. Type **212**	45	20
526		30f. Lizard	65	25
527		40f. Tortoise	80	35
528		90f. Python	1·90	60
529		120f. Crocodile	2·50	90

213 Nurse and Patient

1976. Air. World Health Day.

530	**213**	130f. multicoloured	85	30

214 Dr. Adenauer and Cologne Cathedral

1976. Birth Centenary Dr. Konrad Adenauer.

531	**214**	180f. purple and brown	1·30	60

215 Constructing Orbital Space Station

1976. Air. "The Future in Space".

532	**215**	300f. deep blue, blue and orange	1·80	80
533	-	400f. blue, red and purple	2·75	1·10

DESIGN: 400f. Sun and space-ship with solar batteries.

216 American Bald Eagle and Liberty Bell

1976. Air. American Revolution Bicentenary and "Interphil '76" Int Stamp Exn, Philadelphia.

534	**216**	100f. blue, purple & black	75	45
535	-	400f. brown, blue & black	2·75	90
536	-	440f. violet, green & black	2·75	1·10

DESIGNS—HORIZ: 400f. Warships and American bald eagle. VERT: 440f. Red Indians and American bald eagle.

217 Running

1976. Air. Olympic Games, Montreal.

537	**217**	200f. black, brown and red	1·20	45
538	-	250f. brown, green & blue	1·40	50
539	-	300f. black, blue and green	2·20	65
540	-	400f. black, blue and green	2·75	95

DESIGNS: 250f. Swimming; 300f. Handball; 440f. Football.

218 Scouts marching

1976. Air. First All-African Scout Jamboree, Nigeria.

541	**218**	140f. brown, blue & green	95	40
542	-	180f. brown, green & grey	1·30	60
543	-	200f. violet and brown	1·30	90

DESIGNS—HORIZ: 180f. Scouts tending calf. VERT: 200f. Scout surveying camp at dusk.

1976. Fishes (2nd series). As T **196**.

544	100f. black and blue	95	30
545	120f. yellow, brown and green	1·10	35
546	130f. turquoise, brown & black	1·30	40
547	150f. yellow, drab and green	1·40	55
548	220f. black, green and brown	2·00	70

DESIGNS: 100f. African bonytongue; 120f. Budgett's upside-down catfish; 130f. Double-dorsal catfish; 150f. Monod's tilapia; 220f. Big-scaled tetra.

220 Scenes from Children's Book

1976. Literature for Children.

549	**220**	130f. grey, green and red	90	45

221 "Roi de L'Air"

1976. First Issue of *L'Essor* Newspaper.

550	**221**	120f. multicoloured	1·60	55

222 Fall from Scaffolding

1976. 20th Anniv of National Social Insurance.

551	**222**	120f. multicoloured	75	30

223 Moenjodaro

1976. Air. UNESCO "Save Moenjodaro" (Pakistan) Campaign.

552	**223**	400f. purple, blue & black	2·50	90
553	-	500f. red, yellow and blue	3·25	1·40

DESIGN: 500f. Effigy, animals and remains.

224 Freighter, Vickers Viscount 800 and Map

1976. Air. Europafrique.

554	**224**	200f. purple and blue	1·70	80

225 Cascade of Letters

1976. 25th Anniv of U.N. Postal Administration.

555	**225**	120f. orange, green & lilac	75	25

226 Moto Guzzi "254" (Italy)

1976. Motorcycling.

556	**226**	90f. red, grey and brown	75	40
557	-	120f. violet, blue and black	95	25
558	-	130f. red, grey and green	1·30	45
559	-	140f. blue, green and grey	1·30	50

DESIGNS: 120f. B.M.W. "900" (Germany); 130f. Honda "Egli" (Japan); 140f. Motobecane "LT3" (France).

227 "The Nativity" (Taddeo Gaddi)

1976. Air. Christmas. Religious Paintings. Multicoloured.

560	**227**	280f. Type **227**	1·80	65
561		300f. "Adoration of the Magi" (Hans Memling)	2·00	80
562		320f. "The Nativity" (Carlo Crivelli)	2·20	95

228 Muscat Fishing Boat

1976. Ships.

563	**228**	160f. purple, green & blue	80	40
564	-	180f. green, red and blue	90	45
565	-	190f. purple, blue & green	1·00	45
566	-	200f. green, red and blue	1·20	55

DESIGNS: 180f. Cochin Chinese junk; 190f. Dunkirk lightship "Ruytingen"; 200f. Nile felucca.

229 Rocket in Flight

1976. Air. Operation "Viking".
567	229	500f. blue, red and lake	2·75	1·60
568	-	1000f. lake, blue and deep blue	4·50	2·50

MS569 119×90 mm. 500f. deep blue, blue and brown; 1000f. violet, mauve and black   8·75   4·75

DESIGN: 1000f. Spacecraft on Mars.

230 Pres. Giscard d'Estaing and Sankore Mosque, Timbuktu

1977. Air. Visit of Pres. Giscard d'Estaing of France.
570	230	430f. multicoloured	4·00	1·40

231 Rocket on Launch-pad, Newton and Apple

1977. Air. 250th Death Anniv of Isaac Newton.
571	231	400f. purple, red and green	3·00	1·10

232 Prince Philip and Queen Elizabeth II

1977. Air. "Personalities of Decolonization". Multicoloured.
572		180f. Type 232	1·10	50
573		200f. General De Gaulle (vert)	1·70	65
574		250f. Queen Wilhelmina of the Netherlands (vert)	1·50	70
575		300f. King Baudouin and Queen Fabiola of Belgium	1·80	85
576		480f. Crowning of Queen Elizabeth II (vert)	3·50	1·30

233 Lindbergh and "Spirit of St. Louis"

1977. Air. 50th Anniv of Lindbergh's Transatlantic Flight.
577	233	420f. orange and violet	2·50	1·10
578	-	430f. blue, orange & violet	3·00	1·10

DESIGN: 430f. "Spirit of St. Louis" crossing the Atlantic.

234 Village Indigobird

1977. Mali Birds. Multicoloured.
579		15f. Type 234	55	20
580		25f. Yellow-breasted barbet	90	25
581		30f. Vitelline masked weaver	1·00	30
582		40f. Carmine bee eater	1·30	50
583		50f. Senegal parrot	1·80	65

235 Louis Braille and Hands reading Book

1977. 125th Death Anniv of Louis Braille (inventor of "Braille" system of reading and writing for the blind).
584	235	200f. blue, red and green	1·50	65

236 Printed Circuit

1977. World Telecommunications Day.
585	236	120f. red and brown	60	25

236a Chateau Sassenage, Grenoble

1977. Air. Tenth Anniv of International French Language Council.
586	236a	300f. multicoloured	1·70	75

237 Airship LZ-1 over Lake Constance

1977. Air. History of the Zeppelin.
587	237	120f. green, brown & blue	75	40
588	-	130f. deep blue, brown and blue	85	40
589	-	350f. red, blue and deep blue	2·30	85
590	-	500f. deep blue, green and blue	3·00	95

DESIGNS: 130f. "Graf Zeppelin" over Atlantic; 350f. Burning of "Hindenburg" at Lakehurst; 500f. Count Ferdinand von Zeppelin and "Graf Zeppelin" at mooring mast.

238 "Anaz imperator"

1977. Insects. Multicoloured.
591		5f. Type 238	45	20
592		10f. "Sphadromantis viridis"	50	20
593		20f. "Vespa tropica"	60	25
594		35f. "Melolontha melolantha"	1·10	40
595		60f. Stag beetle	1·40	45

239 Knight and Rook

1977. Chess Pieces.
596	239	120f. black, green & brn	1·30	50
597	-	130f. green, red and black	1·60	60
598	-	300f. green, red and blue	3·50	1·40

DESIGNS—VERT: 130f. Pawn and Bishop. HORIZ: 300f. King and Queen.

240 Henri Dunant

1977. Air. Nobel Peace Prize Winners. Multicoloured.
599		600f. Type 240 (founder of Red Cross)	2·30	90
600		700f. Martin Luther King	3·25	1·10

241 Ship

1977. Europafrique.
601	241	400f. multicoloured	2·30	1·00

242 "Head of Horse"

1977. 525th Birth Anniv of Leonardo da Vinci.
602	242	200f. brown and black	1·50	70
603	-	300f. brown	2·00	80
604	-	500f. red	3·00	1·30

DESIGNS: 300f. "Head of Young Girl"; 500f. Self-portrait.

243 Footballers

1977. Air. Football Cup Elimination Rounds.
605		180f. brown, green & orge	65	45
606	243	200f. brown, green & orge	95	45
607	-	420f. grey, green and lilac	2·00	1·00

DESIGNS—HORIZ: 180f. Two footballers; 420f. Tackling.

244 Friendship Hotel

1977. Inauguration of Friendship Hotel, Bamako.
608	244	120f. multicoloured	65	30

245 Dome of the Rock

1977. Palestinian Welfare.
609	245	120f. multicoloured	60	30
610	245	180f. multicoloured	1·00	45

246 Mao Tse-tung and "Comatex" Hall, Bamako

1977. Air. Mao Tse-tung Memorial.
611	246	300f. red	4·50	1·10

1977. Air. First Commercial Paris–New York Flight by Concorde. Optd PARIS NEW - YORK 22.11.77.
612	209	500f. multicoloured	12·00	7·25

248 "Adoration of the Magi" (Rubens)

1977. Air. Christmas. Details from "Adoration of the Magi" by Rubens.
613	248	400f. multicoloured	2·00	90
614	-	500f. multicoloured	2·50	1·10
615	-	600f. multicoloured (horiz)	3·00	1·50

249 "Hercules and the Nemean Lion"

1978. 400th Birth Anniv of Peter Paul Rubens. Multicoloured.
616		200f. "Battle of the Amazons" (horiz)	1·00	45
617		300f. "Return from Labour in the Fields" (horiz)	1·60	70
618		500f. Type 249	2·75	1·00

250 Schubert and Mute Swans

1978. Air. 150th Death Anniv of Franz Schubert (composer). Multicoloured.
619		300f. Schubert and bars of music (vert)	1·60	70
620		420f. Type 250	2·50	1·00

251 Cook and Shipboard Scene

1978. Air. 250th Birth Anniv of Captain James Cook.
621	251	200f. blue, red and violet	1·50	50
622	-	300f. brown, blue & green	2·20	75

DESIGN: 300f. Capt. Cook meeting natives.

252 African and Chained Building

1978. World Anti-Apartheid Year.
623	252	120f. violet, brown & blue	60	25
624	-	130f. violet, blue & orange	70	30
625	-	180f. brown, pur & orge	1·10	50

DESIGNS: 130f. Statue of Liberty and Africans walking to open door; 180f. African children and mule in fenced enclosure.

253 Players and Ball

1978. Air. World Cup Football Championship, Argentina.

626	**253**	150f. red, green and brown	1·00	45
627	-	250f. red, brown and green	1·60	65
628	-	300f. red, brown and blue	2·10	80

MS629 190×100 mm. 150f. emerald, chocolate and red; 250f. red, chocolate and emerald; 300f. blue, chocolate and red   5·25   4·00

DESIGNS——VERT: 250f. Player heading ball. HORIZ: 300f. Goalkeeper clearing ball over head of player.

254 "Head of Christ"

1978. Air. Easter. Works by Durer.

630	**254**	420f. green and brown	3·00	80
631	-	430f. blue and brown	3·00	80

DESIGN: 430f. "The Resurrection".

255 Red-cheeked Cordon-bleu

1978. Birds. Multicoloured.

632	**255**	20f. Type **255**	70	25
633	-	30f. Masked fire finch	90	25
634	-	50f. Red-billed fire finch	1·00	30
635	-	70f. African collared dove	1·50	50
636	-	80f. White-billed buffalo weaver	2·00	65

256 C-3 "Trefle"

1978. Air. Birth Centenary of Andre Citroen (automobile pioneer).

637	**256**	120f. brown, lake & green	1·20	25
638	-	130f. grey, orange and blue	1·40	45
639	-	180f. blue, green and red	2·00	45
640	-	200f. black, red and lake	2·30	65

DESIGNS: 130f. B-2 "Croisiere Noir" track-laying vehicle, 1924; 180f. B-14 G Saloon, 1927; 200f. Model-11 front-wheel drive car, 1934.

1978. 20th Anniv of Bamako Lions Club. Nos. 473/4 surch XXe ANNIVERSAIRE DU LIONS CLUB DE BAMAKO 1958-1978 and value.

641		120f. on 90f. Type **192**	70	30
642		130f. on 100f. View of Samanko	1·00	30

258 Names of 1978 U.P.U. members forming Map of the World

1978. Centenary of U.P.U. Foundation Congress, Paris.

643	**258**	120f. green, orange & mve	80	30
644	-	130f. yellow, red and green	90	30

DESIGN: 130f. Names of 1878 member states across globe.

259 Desert Scene

1978. Campaign against Desertification.

645	**259**	200f. multicoloured	1·30	55

260 Mahatma Gandhi

1978. 30th Anniv of Gandhi's Assassination.

646	**260**	140f. brown, red and black	1·10	45

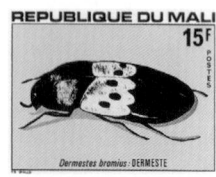

261 "Dermestes bromius"

1978. Insects. Multicoloured.

647	**261**	15f. Type **261**	45	20
648	-	25f. "Calosoma sp."	55	20
649	-	90f. "Lopocerus variegatus"	1·00	40
650	-	120f. "Coccinella septempunctata"	1·10	40
651	-	140f. "Goliathus giganteus"	1·50	50

262 Dominoes

1978. Social Games.

652	**262**	100f. black, green and red	85	25
653	-	130f. red, black and blue	1·50	45

DESIGN: 130f. Bridge hand.

263 Ostrich on Nest (Syrian Manuscript)

1978. Air. Europafrique. Multicoloured.

654	**263**	100f. Type **263**	1·90	60
655	-	110f. Common zebra (Mansur miniature)	1·90	60

1978. Air. World Cup Football Championship Finalists. Nos. 626/8 optd with results.

656	**253**	150f. red, green and brown	1·00	40
657	-	250f. red, brown and green	1·60	65
658	-	300f. red, brown and blue	2·10	75

MS659 190×100 mm. As Nos. 656/8 multicoloured   5·50   3·00

OPTS: 150f. **CHAMPION 1978 ARGENTINE**; 250f. **2e HOLLANDE**; 300f. **3e BRESIL 4e ITALIE; FINALE ARGENTINA 3 HOLLANDE 1**.

265 Coronation Coach

1978. Air. 25th Anniv of Coronation of Queen Elizabeth II. Multicoloured.

660		500f. Type **265**	2·50	90
661		1000f. Queen Elizabeth II	5·00	1·70

266 Aristotle and African Animals

1978. 2300th Death Anniv of Aristotle (Greek philosopher).

662	**266**	200f. brown, red and green	1·30	50

267 Douglas DC-3 and U.S.A. 1918 24c. stamp

1978. Air. History of Aviation.

663	**267**	80f. deep blue, red & blue	45	15
664	-	100f. multicoloured	55	25
665	-	120f. black, blue and red	75	25
666	-	130f. green, red and black	75	40
667	-	320f. violet, blue and red	1·70	70

DESIGNS: 100f. Stampe and Renard SV-4 and Belgium Balloon stamp of 1932; 120f. Clement Ader's Avion III and France Concorde stamp of 1976; 130f. Junkers Ju-52/3m and Germany Biplane stamp of 1919; 320f. Mitsubishi A6M Zero-Sen and Japan Pagoda stamp of 1951.

268 "The Annunciation"

1978. Air. Christmas. Works by Durer.

668	**268**	420f. brown and black	2·00	70
669	-	430f. brown and green	2·00	80
670	-	500f. black and brown	2·50	90

DESIGNS: 430f. "Virgin and Child"; 500f. "Adoration of the Magi".

269 Launch of "Apollo 8" and Moon

1978. Air. Tenth Anniv of First Manned Flight around the Moon.

671	**269**	200f. red, green and violet	1·40	50
672	-	300f. violet, green and red	2·20	75

DESIGN: 300f. "Apollo 8" in orbit around the Moon.

270 U.N. and Human Rights Emblems

1978. 30th Anniv of Declaration of Human Rights.

673	**270**	180f. red, blue and brown	1·10	35

271 Concorde and Clement Ader's "Eole"

1979. Air. Third Anniv of First Commercial Concorde Flight. Multicoloured.

674		120f. Type **271**	75	40
675		130f. Concorde and Wright Flyer I	95	45
676		200f. Concorde and "Spirit of St. Louis"	1·50	70

271a Ruff (bird) and Lubeck 1859 ½s. stamp

1979. Air. "Philexafrique" Stamp Exhibition, Libreville, Gabon (1st issue) and International Stamp Fair, Essen, West Germany. Multicoloured.

677		200f. Type **271a**	3·00	1·40
678		200f. Dromedary and Mali 1965 200f. stamp	3·00	1·40

See also Nos. 704/5.

1979. Air. Birth Centenary of Albert Einstein (physicist). No. 492 surch "1879-1979" 130F.

679	**198**	130f. on 90f. blue, purple and brown	1·30	65

273 "Christ carrying the Cross"

1979. Air. Easter. Works by Durer.

680	**273**	400f. black and turquoise	2·40	70
681	-	430f. black and red	2·75	80
682	-	480f. black and blue	3·25	1·10

DESIGNS: 430f. "Christ on the Cross"; 480f. "The Great Lamentation".

274 Basketball and St. Basil's Cathedral, Moscow

1979. Air. Pre-Olympic Year. Multicoloured.

683	**274**	420f. Type **274**	2·30	95
684	-	430f. Footballer and Kremlin	2·30	95

275 African Manatee

1979. Endangered Animals. Multicoloured.
685	100f. Type **275**	85	20
686	120f. Chimpanzee	1·00	25
687	130f. Topi	1·10	30
688	180f. Gemsbok	1·50	45
689	200f. Giant eland	1·70	50

276 Child and I.Y.C. Emblem

1979. International Year of the Child.
690	**276**	120f. green, red and brown	65	25
691	-	200f. purple and green	1·20	50
692	-	300f. brown, mauve and deep brown	1·80	70

DESIGNS: 200f. Girl and scout with birds; 300f. Children with calf.

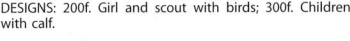

277 Judo

1979. World Judo Championships, Paris.
693	**277**	200f. sepia, red and ochre	1·30	55

278 Wave Pattern and Human Figures

1979. World Telecommunications Day.
694	**278**	120f. multicoloured	65	20

279 Goat's Head and Lizard Fetishes

1979. World Museums Day. Multicoloured.
695	90f. Type **279**	50	25
696	120f. Seated figures (wood carving)	70	30
697	130f. Two animal heads and figurine (wood carving)	90	35

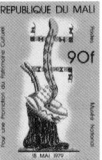

280 Rowland Hill and Mali 1961 25f. stamp

1979. Death Centenary of Sir Rowland Hill.
698	**280**	120f. multicoloured	60	20
699	-	130f. red, blue and green	80	20
700	-	180f. black, green and blue	95	40
701	-	200f. black, red and purple	1·20	40
702	-	300f. blue, deep blue and red	1·90	70

DESIGNS: 130f. Airship "Graf Zeppelin" and Saxony stamp of 1850; 180f. Concorde and France stamp of 1849; 200f. Stage coach and U.S.A. stamp of 1849; 300f. U.P.U. emblem and Penny Black.

281 Cora Players

1979
703	**281**	200f. multicoloured	1·70	65

282 Sankore Mosque and "Adenium obesum"

1979. "Philexafrique" Exhibition, Libreville, Gabon (2nd issue).
704	**282**	120f. multicoloured	1·70	95
705	-	300f. red, blue and orange	3·25	1·90

DESIGN: 300f. Horseman and satellite.

283 Map of Mali showing Conquest of Desert

1979. Operation "Sahel Vert". Multicoloured.
706	200f. Type **283**	1·10	50
707	300f. Planting a tree	1·90	90

284 Lemons

1979. Fruit (1st series). Multicoloured.
708	10f. Type **284**	20	10
709	60f. Pineapple	50	15
710	100f. Papaw	75	25
711	120f. Sweet-sops	95	30
712	130f. Mangoes	1·10	35

See also Nos. 777/81.

285 Sigmund Freud

1979. 40th Death Anniv of Sigmund Freud (psychologist).
713	**285**	300f. sepia and violet	1·70	80

286 Caillie and Camel approaching Fort

1979. 180th Birth Anniv of Rene Caillie (explorer).
714	**286**	120f. sepia, brown & blue	85	35
715	-	130f. blue, green & brown	1·00	45

DESIGN: 130f. Rene Caillie and map of route across Sahara.

287 "Eurema brigitta"

1979. Butterflies and Moths (1st series). Multicoloured.
716	100f. Type **287**	90	20
717	120f. "Papilio pylades"	1·10	35
718	130f. "Melanitis leda satyridae"	1·30	40
719	180f. "Gonimbrasis belina occidentalis"	1·80	60
720	200f. "Bunaea alcinoe"	1·70	65

See also Nos. 800/4.

288 Mali 1970 300f. Stamp and Modules orbiting Moon

1979. Air. Tenth Anniv of First Moon Landing.
721	430f. Type **288**	2·20	95
722	500f. 1973 250f. stamp and rocket launch	2·50	1·20

289 Capt. Cook and H.M.S. "Resolution" off Kerguelen Islands

1979. Air. Death Bicent of Captain James Cook.
723	300f. Type **289**	1·70	75
724	400f. Capt. Cook and H.M.S. "Resolution" off Hawaii	2·50	1·10

290 Menaka Greyhound

1979. Dogs. Multicoloured.
725	20f. Type **290**	55	25
726	50f. Water spaniel	85	25
727	70f. Beagle	95	30
728	80f. Newfoundland	1·20	45
729	90f. Sheepdog	1·40	50

291 David Janowski

1979. Air. Chess Grand-masters.
730	**291**	100f. red and brown	80	25
731	-	140f. red, brown and blue	1·30	30
732	-	200f. blue, violet and green	1·80	50
733	-	300f. brown, ochre and red	2·75	70

DESIGNS: 140f. Alexander Alekhine; 200f. Willi Schlage; 300f. Efim Bogoljubow.

292 "The Adoration of the Magi" 1511 (detail, Durer)

1979. Air. Christmas. Works by Durer.
734	**292**	300f. brown and orange	1·70	65
735	-	400f. brown and blue	2·30	95
736	-	500f. brown and green	3·00	1·30

DESIGNS: 400f. "Adoration of the Magi" (1503); 500f. "Adoration of the Magi" (1511, different).

1979. Air. 20th Anniv of ASECNA (African Air Safety Organization). As T **198** of Malagasy but 36×27 mm.
737	120f. multicoloured	85	35

293 Globe, Rotary Emblem and Diesel-electric Train

1980. Air. 75th Anniv of Rotary International. Multicoloured.
738	220f. Type **293**	1·40	55
739	250f. Globe, Rotary emblem and Douglas DC-10 airliner	1·60	60
740	430f. Bamako Rotary Club and emblem	2·50	10

294 African Ass

1980. Protected Animals. Multicoloured.
741	90f. Type **294**	80	25
742	120f. Addax	1·00	25
743	130f. Cheetahs	1·10	35
744	140f. Barbary sheep	1·20	45
745	180f. African buffalo	1·70	55

295 Speed Skating

1980. Air. Winter Olympic Games, Lake Placid. Multicoloured.
746	200f. Type **295**	1·00	45
747	300f. Ski jump	1·80	70
MS748	93×93 mm. As Nos. 746/7 but colours changed	3·00	2·20

296 Stephenson's "Rocket" (1829) and Mali 30f. Stamp, 1972

1980. Air. 150th Anniv of Liverpool and Manchester Railway.
749	**296**	200f. blue, brown & green	1·20	45
750	-	300f. black, brown & turq	1·80	90

DESIGN: 300f. "Rocket" (1829) and Mali 50f. railway stamp, 1970.

297 Horse Jumping

1980. Air. Olympic Games, Moscow.
751	**297**	200f. green, brown & blue	1·20	45
752	-	300f. blue, brown & green	1·50	70
753	-	400f. red, green & lt green	2·30	95
MS754	180×118 mm. Nos. 751/3 plus three labels		4·50	3·50

DESIGNS: 300f. Sailing; 400f. Football.

298 Solar Pumping Station, Koni

1980. Solar Energy. Multicoloured.
755	90f. Type **298**	50	15
756	100f. Solar capture tables, Dire	60	20
757	120f. Solar energy cooker	80	25
758	130f. Solar generating station, Dire	95	30

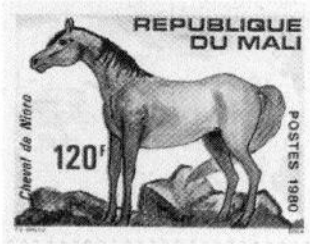

299 Nioro Horse

1980. Horses. Multicoloured.

759	100f. Mopti	70	10
760	120f. Type **299**	85	10
761	130f. Koro	1·00	20
762	180f. Lake zone horse	1·10	45
763	200f. Banamba	1·30	70

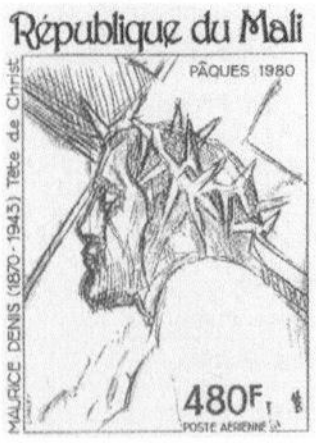

300 "Head of Christ" (Maurice Denis)

1980. Air. Easter.

764	**300**	480f. red and brown	3·00	1·00
765	-	500f. brown and red	3·00	1·10

DESIGN: 500f. "Christ before Pilate" (Durer).

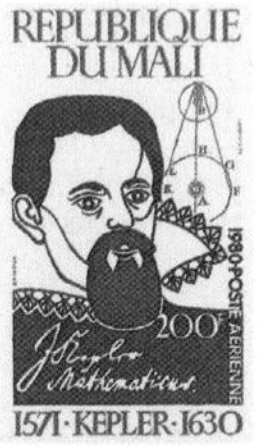

301 Kepler and Diagram of Earth's Orbit

1980. Air. 350th Death Anniv of J. Kepler (astronomer).

766	**301**	200f. light blue, blue & red	1·50	55
767	-	300f. mauve, violet & grn	1·80	80

DESIGN: 300f. Kepler, Copernicus and diagram of solar system.

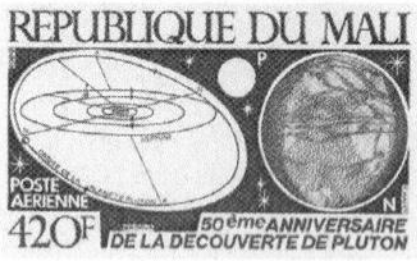

302 Pluto and Diagram of Orbit

1980. Air. 50th Anniv of Discovery of Planet Pluto.

768	**302**	402f. blue, grey and mauve	2·20	90

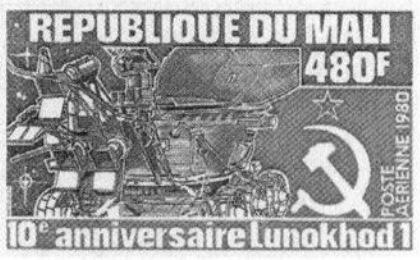

303 "Lunokhod 1" (10th Anniv)

1980. Air. Space Events.

769	**303**	480f. black, red and blue	2·50	90
770	-	500f. grey, blue and red	2·50	90

DESIGN: 500f. "Apollo"–"Soyuz" link-up.

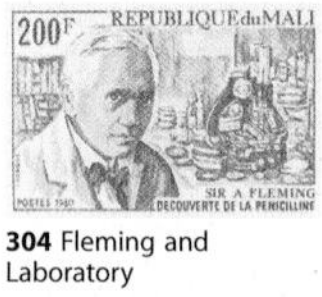

304 Fleming and Laboratory

1980. Sir Alexander Fleming (discoverer of penicillin). Commemoration.

771	**304**	200f. green, sepia & brown	1·90	60

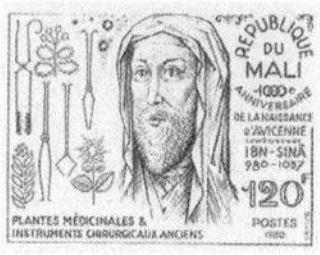

305 Avicenna, Medical Instruments and Herbs

1980. Birth Millenary of Avicenna (Arab physician and philosopher).

772	**305**	120f. blue, red and brown	75	30
773	-	180f. dp brn, turq & brn	1·00	50

DESIGN: 180f. Avicenna as teacher.

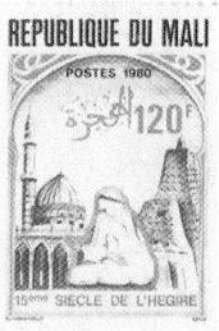

306 Pilgrim at Mecca

1980. 1400th Anniv of Hegira. Multicoloured.

774	120f. Type **306**	60	25
775	130f. Praying hands	75	25
776	180f. Pilgrims (horiz)	95	40

1980. Fruit (2nd series). As T **284**. Multicoloured.

777	90f. Guavas	60	15
778	120f. Cashews	75	15
779	130f. Oranges	90	25
780	140f. Bananas	1·00	25
781	180f. Grapefruit	1·20	40

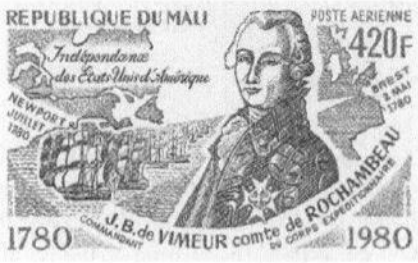

307 Rochambeau and French Fleet at Rhode Island, 1780

1980. Air. French Support for American Independence.

782	**307**	420f. brown, turq & red	2·30	1·00
783	-	430f. black, blue and red	2·75	1·10

DESIGN: 430f. Rochambeau, Washington and Eagle.

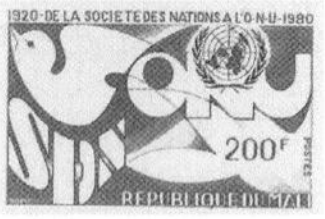

308 Dove and U.N. Emblem

1980. 60th Anniv of League of Nations.

784	**308**	200f. blue, red and violet	95	45

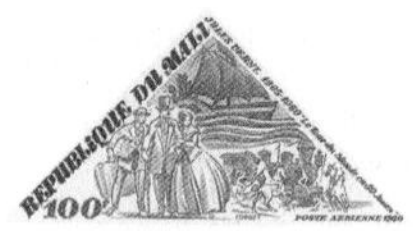

309 Scene from "Around the World in 80 Days"

1980. Air. 75th Death Anniv of Jules Verne (writer).

785	**309**	100f. red, green and brown	95	30
786	-	100f. brown, chestnut and turquoise	95	30
787	-	150f. green, brn & dp brn	1·30	45
788	-	150f. blue, violet & dp bl	1·30	45

DESIGNS: No. 786, Concorde; No. 787, "From the Earth to the Moon"; No. 788, Astronaut on Moon.

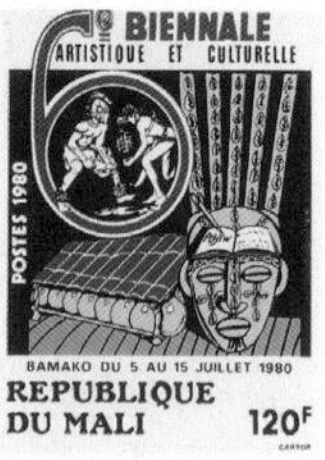

310 Xylophone, Mask and Emblem

1980. Sixth Arts and Cultural Festival, Bamako.

789	**310**	120f. multicoloured	75	30

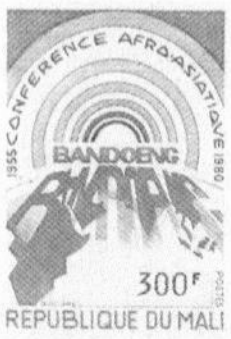

311 Map of Africa and Asia

1980. 25th Anniv of Afro-Asian Bandung Conference.

790	**311**	300f. green, red and blue	1·40	60

1980. Air. Olympic Medal Winners. Nos. 751/3 optd.

791	200f. green, brown and blue	1·20	70
792	300f. blue, brown and green	1·50	90
793	400f. red, green and light green	2·30	1·10
MS794	180×118 mm. Nos. 791/3 plus three labels	5·25	5·25

OVERPRINTS: 200f. **CONCOURS COMPLET INDIVIDUEL ROMAN (It.) BLINOV (Urss) SALNIKOV (Urss)**; 300f. **FINN RECHARDT (Fin.) MAYRHOFER (Autr.) BALACHOV (Urss)**; 400f. **TCHECOSLOVAQUIE ALLEMAGNE DE L'EST URSS**.

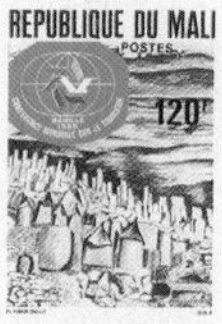

313 Conference Emblem

1980. World Tourism Conference, Manila. Multicoloured.

795	120f. Type **313**	60	25
796	180f. Encampment outside fort and Conference emblem	1·00	45

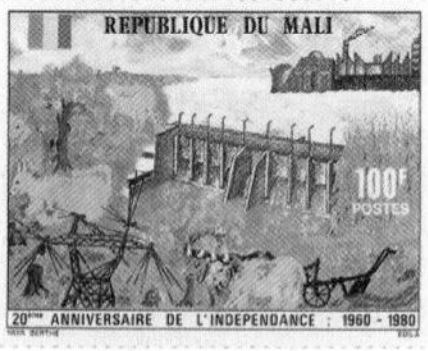

314 Dam and Rural Scene

1980. 20th Anniv of Independence. Multicoloured.

797	100f. Type **314**	55	25
798	120f. National Assembly Building	65	30
799	130f. Independence Monument (vert)	90	35

1980. Butterflies. (2nd series). As T **287** but dated "1980". Multicoloured.

800	50f. "Uterheisa pulchella" (postage)	75	25
801	60f. "Mylothis chloris pieridae"	85	25
802	70f. "Hypolimnas mishippus"	1·10	30
803	80f. "Papilio demodocus"	95	35
804	420f. "Denaus chrysippus" (48×36 mm) (air)	2·30	75

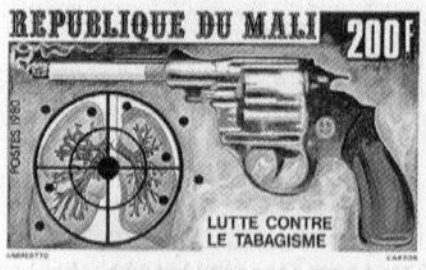

315 Pistol firing Cigarette and Target over Lungs

1980. Anti-smoking Campaign.

805	**315**	200f. multicoloured	1·10	60

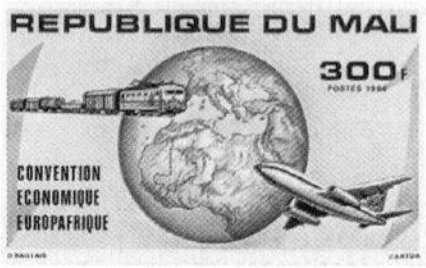

316 Electric Train, Boeing 737 and Globe

1980. Europafrique.

806	**316**	300f. multicoloured	2·00	80

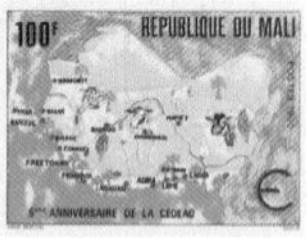

317 Map of West Africa and Agricultural Symbols

1980. Fifth Anniv of West African Economic Council. Multicoloured.

807	100f. Type **317**	55	20
808	120f. "Transport"	60	25
809	130f. "Industry"	75	30
810	140f. "Energy"	80	35

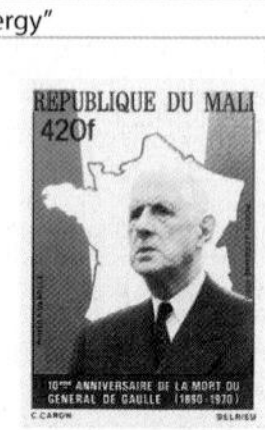

318 Gen. de Gaulle and Map of France

1980. Air. Tenth Death Anniv of Gen. Charles de Gaulle. Multicoloured.

811	420f. Type **318**	3·75	1·30
812	430f. De Gaulle and Cross of Lorraine	3·75	1·30

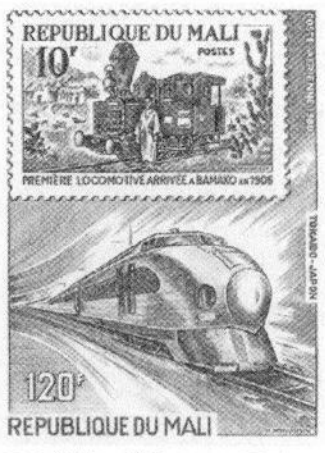

319 "Hikari" Express Train (Japan) and Mali 1972 10f. Stamp

1980. Air. Locomotives.

813	**319**	120f. blue, green and red	80	25
814	-	130f. green, blue and red	85	30
815	-	200f. orange, black & grn	1·30	50
816	-	480f. black, red and green	3·50	1·20

DESIGNS—HORIZ: 130f. RTG train, U.S.A. and 20f. locomotive stamp of 1970; 200f. "Rembrandt" express, Germany, and 100f. locomotive stamp of 1970. VERT: 480f. TGV 001 turbotrain, France, and 80f. locomotive stamp of 1970.

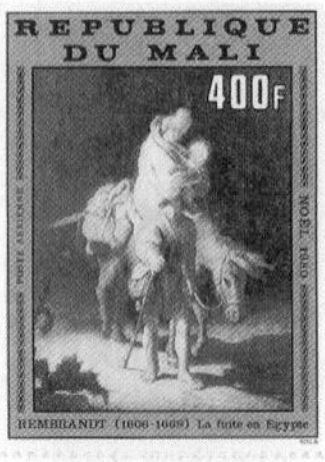

320 "Flight into Egypt" (Rembrandt)

1980. Air. Christmas. Multicoloured.

817	300f. "St. Joseph showing the infant Jesus to St. Catherine" (Lorenzo Lotto) (horiz)	1·60	70
818	400f. Type **320**	2·20	1·00
819	500f. "Christmas Night" (Gauguin) (horiz)	2·75	1·20

1980. Fifth Anniv of African Posts and Telecommunications Union. As T **292** of Niger.

820	130f. multicoloured	85	35

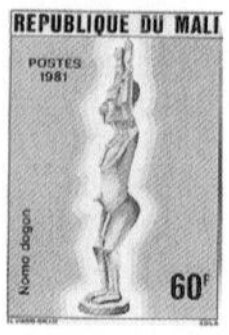

321 Nomo Dogon

1981. Statuettes. Multicoloured.

821	60f. Type **321**	35	10
822	70f. Senoufo fertility symbol	45	15
823	90f. Bamanan fertility statuette	60	20
824	100f. Senoufo captives snuff-box	65	30
825	120f. Dogon fertility statuette	90	35

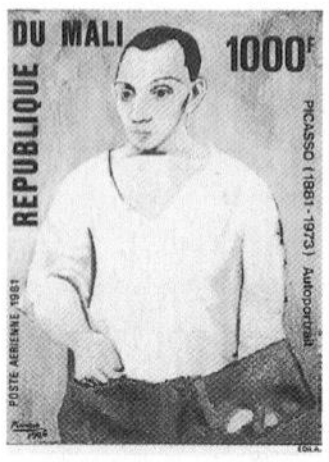

322 "Self-portrait" (Blue Period)

1981. Birth Bicentenary of Pablo Picasso (artist).

826	**322**	1000f. multicoloured	6·50	2·40

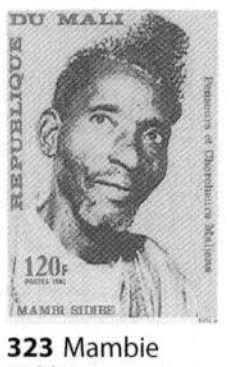

323 Mambie Sidibe

1981. Mali Thinkers and Savants.

827	**323**	120f. brown, buff and red	65	30
828	-	130f. brown, buff & black	70	30

DESIGN: 130f. Amadou Hampate Ba.

324 Mosque and Ka'aba

1981. 1400th Anniv of Hejira.

829	**324**	120f. multicoloured	60	25
830	**324**	180f. multicoloured	1·10	45

325 Tackle

1981. Air. World Cup Football Championship Eliminators. Multicoloured.

831	100f. Type **325**	75	30
832	200f. Heading the ball	1·20	50
833	300f. Running for ball	1·80	70
MS834	90×101 mm. 600f. Goalkeeper reaching for ball	3·75	2·40

326 Kaarta Zebu

1981. Cattle. Multicoloured.

835	20f. Type **326**	45	10
836	30f. Peul du Macina sebu	50	15
837	40f. Maure zebu	65	20
838	80f. Touareg zebu	1·10	35
839	100f. N'Dama cow	1·10	40

327 Crinum de Moore "Crinum moorei"

1981. Flowers. Multicoloured.

840	50f. Type **327**	35	10
841	100f. Double rose hibiscus "Hibiscus rosa-sinensis"	65	15
842	120f. Pervenche "Catharanthus roseus"	85	30
843	130f. Frangipani "Plumeria rubra"	1·00	35
844	180f. Orgueil de Chine "Caesalpinia pulcherrima"	1·50	55

328 Mozart and Musical Instruments

1981. Air. 225th Birth Anniv of Mozart. Multicoloured.

845	420f. Type **328**	2·40	1·10
846	430f. Mozart and musical instruments (different)	2·40	1·10

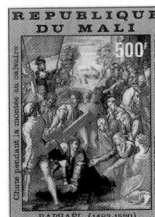

329 "The Fall on the Way to Calvary" (Raphael)

1981. Air. Easter.

847	500f. Type **329**	2·40	1·10
848	600f. "Ecce Homo" (Rembrandt)	3·25	1·60

330 Yuri Gagarin

1981. Air. Space Anniversaries and Events.

849	200f. blue, black and red	1·00	45
850	200f. blue, black & lt blue	1·00	45
851	380f. multicoloured	1·90	70
852	430f. violet, black and blue	2·30	85

DESIGNS—VERT: No. 849, Type **330**: first man in space (20th anniv); No. 850, Alan Shepard, first American in space (20th anniv); No. 851, Saturn and moons (exploration of Saturn). HORIZ: No. 852, Sir William Herschel, and diagram of Uranus (discovery bicentenary).

331 Blind and Sighted Faces

1981. International Year of Disabled People.

853	**331** 100f. light brown, brown and green	55	25
854	120f. violet, blue and purple	75	30

DESIGN: 120f. Mechanical hand and human hand with spanner.

332 Caduceus (Tele-communications and Health)

1981. World Telecommunications Day.

855	**332** 130f. multicoloured	90	35

333 Pierre Curie and Instruments

1981. 75th Death Anniv of Pierre Curie (discoverer of radioactivity).

856	**333** 180f. blue, black & orange	2·10	55

334 Scouts at Well and Dorcas Gazelle

1981. Fourth African Scouting Conference, Abidjan. Multicoloured.

857	110f. Type **334**	90	35
858	160f. Scouts signalling and patas monkey	1·30	50
859	300f. Scouts saluting and cheetah (vert)	2·40	80
MS860	120×90 mm. 500f. Lord Baden Powell (vert)	5·75	3·50

1981. Air. World Railway Speed Record. No. 816 optd 26 fevrier 1981 Record du monde de vitesse–380 km/h.

861	480f. black, red and blue	3·25	95

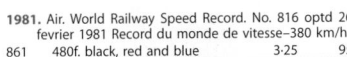

336 Columbus, Fleet and U.S. Columbus Stamp of 1892

1981. Air. 475th Death Anniv of Christopher Columbus.

862	**336**	180f. brown, black & blue	1·20	45
863	-	200f. green, blue & brown	1·50	55
864	-	260f. black, violet and red	1·80	70
865	-	300f. lilac, red and green	2·10	90

DESIGNS—VERT: 200f. "Nina" and 1c. Columbus stamp of Spain; 260f. "Pinta" and 5c. Columbus stamp of Spain. HORIZ: 300f. "Santa Maria" and U.S. 3c. Columbus stamp.

1981. 23rd World Scouting Conference, Dakar. Nos. 857/MS860 optd DAKAR 8 AOUT 1981 28e CONFERENCE MONDIALE DU SCOUTISME.

866	**334**	110f. multicoloured	90	35
867	-	160f. multicoloured	1·20	55
868	-	300f. multicoloured	2·50	90
MS869		120×90 mm. 500f. multicoloured	5·75	3·50

338 Space Shuttle after Launching

1981. Air. Space Shuttle. Multicoloured.

870	200f. Type **338**	1·00	45
871	500f. Space Shuttle in orbit	2·75	1·10
872	600f. Space Shuttle landing	3·25	1·40
MS873	86×67 mm. 700f. Space shuttle on carrier aeroplane	4·75	2·50

339 "Harlequin on a Horse"

1981. Air. Birth Centenary of Pablo Picasso. Multicoloured.

874	600f. Type **339**	4·25	1·40
875	750f. "Child with Pigeon"	5·00	1·60

340 Prince Charles, Lady Diana Spencer and St. Paul's Cathedral

1981. Air. British Royal Wedding. Multicoloured.

876	500f. Type **340**	2·50	1·00
877	700f. Prince Charles, Lady Diana Spencer and coach	3·50	1·50

342 Maure Sheep

1981. Sheep. Multicoloured.

886	10f. Type **342**	20	10
887	25f. Peul sheep	35	20
888	100f. Sahel sheep	1·00	30
889	180f. Touareg sheep	1·40	45
890	200f. Djallonke ram	1·70	50

343 Heinrich von Stephan (founder of U.P.U.), Latecoere 28 and Concorde

1981. Universal Postal Union Day.

891	**343**	400f. red and green	2·50	90

344 Woman drinking from Bowl

1981. World Food Day.

892	**344**	200f. brown, orge & mve	1·30	50

345 "The Incarnation of the Son of God" (detail, Grunewald)

1981. Air. Christmas. Multicoloured.

893	500f. Type **345**	2·75	1·00
894	700f. "The Campori Madonna" (Correggio)	3·75	1·50

1981. Air. Second Flight of Space Shuttle. MS873 optd JOE ENGLE RICHARD TRULY 2eme VOL SPATIAL.

MS895	700f. multicoloured	5·50	3·25

347 Transport and Hands holding Map of Europe and Africa

1981. Europafrique.

896	**347**	700f. blue, brown & orge	3·50	1·30

348 Guerin, Calmette, Syringe and Bacillus

1981. 60th Anniv of First B.C.G. Inoculation.

897	**348**	200f. brown, violet & blk	1·40	55

1982. Air. World Chess Championship, Merano. Nos. 731 and 733 optd.

898	140f. red, brown and blue	1·30	50
899	300f. brown, ochre and red	2·50	80

OPTS: 140f. **ANATOLI KARPOV VICTOR KORTCHNOI MERANO (ITALIE) Octobre-Novembre 1981**; 300f. Octobre-Novembre 1981 ANATOLI KARPOV Champion du Monde 1981.

350 "Nymphaea lotus"

1982. Flowers. Multicoloured.

900	170f. Type **350**	1·00	25
901	180f. "Bombax costatum"	1·00	30
902	200f. "Parkia biglobosa"	1·30	35
903	220f. "Gloriosa simplex"	1·40	50
904	270f. "Satanocrater berhautii"	1·60	60

351 Lewis Carroll and Characters from "Alice" Books

1982. Air. 150th Birth Anniv of Lewis Carroll (Revd. Charles Dodgson).

905	110f. Type **351**	1·70	65
906	130f. Characters from "Alice" books	1·70	85
907	140f. Characters from "Alice" books (different)	1·90	1·10

352 "George Washington" (Gilbert Stuart)

1982. Air. 250th Birth Anniv of George Washington.
908	**352**	700f. multicoloured	3·50	1·50

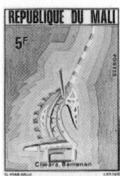

353 Ciwara Bamanan

1982. Masks. Multicoloured.
909	5f. Type **353**	15	10
910	35f. Kanga Dogon	30	10
911	180f. N Domo Bamanan	1·00	40
912	200f. Cimier (Sogoninkum Bamanan)	1·30	45
913	250f. Kpelie Senoufo	1·50	50

354 Football

1982. Air. World Cup Football Championship, Spain.
914	**354**	220f. multicoloured	1·00	45
915	-	420f. multicoloured	2·00	80
916	-	500f. multicoloured	2·40	1·00
MS917	105×85 mm. 680f. multicoloured		6·00	2·75

DESIGNS: 420f. to 680f. Football scenes.

355 "Sputnik 1"

1982. 25th Anniv of First Artificial Satellite.
918	**355**	270f. violet, blue and red	1·50	60

356 Lord Baden-Powell, Tent and Scout Badge

1982. Air. 125th Birth Anniv of Lord Baden-Powell. Multicoloured.
919	300f. Type **356**	1·20	60
920	500f. Saluting scout	2·40	1·00

357 "The Transfiguration" (Fra Angelico)

1982. Air. Easter. Multicoloured.
921	680f. Type **357**	3·00	1·20
922	1000f. "Pieta" (Giovanni Bellini)	4·75	1·70

358 Doctor giving Child Oral Vaccine

1982. Anti-polio Campaign.
923	**358**	180f. multicoloured	1·00	40

359 Lions Emblem and Blind Person

1982. Lions Club Blind Day.
924	**359**	260f. orange, blue and red	1·50	35

360 "En Bon Ami" (N'Teri)

1982. Hairstyles. Multicoloured.
925	140f. Type **360**	55	25
926	150f. Tucked-in pony tail	65	25
927	160f. "Pour l'Art"	85	40
928	180f. "Bozo Kun"	1·30	40
929	270f. "Fulaw Kun"	2·00	70

361 Arms Stamp of Mali and France

1982. Air. "Philexfrance 82" International Stamp Exhibition, Paris. Multicoloured.
930	180f. Type **361**	1·00	30
931	200f. Dromedary caravan and 1979 "Philexafrique II" stamp	1·30	50

362 Fire-engine, 1850

1982. Fire-engines. Multicoloured.
932	180f. Type **362**	1·20	30
933	200f. Fire-engine, 1921	1·50	45
934	270f. Fire-engine, 1982	1·80	70

363 Gobra

1982. Zebu Cattle. Multicoloured.
935	10f. Type **363**	25	10
936	60f. Azaouak	60	15
937	110f. Maure	90	30
938	180f. Toronke	1·30	40
939	200f. Peul Sambourou	1·50	55

1982. Air. World Cup Football Championship Winners. Nos. 914/16 optd.
940	**354**	220f. multicoloured	1·20	45
941	-	420f. multicoloured	2·00	75
942	-	500f. multicoloured	2·50	1·10
MS943	105×85 mm. 680f. multicoloured		4·00	2·50

OPTS: 220f. **1 ITALIE 2 RFA 3 POLOGNE**; 420f. **POLOGNE FRANCE 3-2**; 500f. **ITALIE RFA 3-1**; 680f. **ITALIE CHAMPION 1982**.

365 "Urchin with Cherries"

1982. Air. 150th Birth Anniv of Edouard Manet (painter).
944	**365**	680f. multicoloured	4·50	1·60

366 "Virgin and Child" (detail) (Titian)

1982. Air. Christmas. Multicoloured.
945	500f. Type **366**	2·30	1·00
946	1000f. "Virgin and Child" (Giovanni Bellini)	4·75	1·80

367 Wind-surfing

1982. Air. Introduction of Wind-surfing as Olympic Event. Multicoloured.
947	200f. Type **367**	1·20	35
948	270f. Wind-surfer	1·50	55
949	300f. Wind-surfer (different)	1·80	70

368 Goethe

1982. Air. 150th Death Anniv of Goethe (poet).
950	**368**	500f. brown, light brown and black	3·00	1·10

369 Valentina Tereshkova

1983. Air. 20th Anniv of Launching of Vostok VI.
951	**369**	400f. multicoloured	2·00	80

370 Transatlantic Balloon "Double Eagle II"

1983. Air. Bicentenary of Manned Flight. Multicoloured.
952	500f. Type **370**	3·75	1·00
953	700f. Montgolfier balloon	4·00	1·50

371 Football

1983. Air. Olympic Games, Los Angeles. Multicoloured.
954	180f. Type **371**	95	35
955	270f. Hurdles	1·30	60
956	300f. Windsurfing	2·00	75

372 "The Transfiguration" (detail)

1983. Air. Easter. Multicoloured.
957	400f. Type **372**	2·00	90
958	600f. "The Entombment" (detail from Baglioni Retable)	3·00	1·30

373 Martin Luther King

1983. Celebrities.
959	**373**	800f. brown, blue & pur	4·00	1·40
960	-	800f. brown, red & dp red	4·00	1·40

DESIGN: No. 960, President Kennedy.

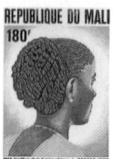

374 Oua Hairstyle

1983. Hairstyles. Multicoloured.
961	180f. Type **374**	1·10	25
962	200f. Nation (Diamani)	1·30	25
963	270f. Rond Point	1·60	40
964	300f. Naamu-Naamu	1·80	40
965	500f. Bamba-Bamba	3·25	70

375 "Family of Acrobats with Monkey"

1983. Air. Tenth Death Anniv of Picasso.
966	**375**	680f. multicoloured	3·50	1·70

376 Lions Club Emblem and Lions

1983. Air. Lions and Rotary Clubs. Multicoloured.
967	700f. Type **376**	6·50	1·80
968	700f. Rotary Club emblem, container ship, diesel railcar and Boeing 737 airliner	6·50	1·80

377 Satellite, Antenna and Telephone

1983. World Communications Year.
969 **377** 180f. multicoloured 1·00 50

378 Lavoisier and Apparatus

1983. Bicent of Lavoisier's Analysis of Water.
970 **378** 300f. green, brown & blue 1·70 65

379 Banzoumana Sissoko

1983. Mali Musicians. Multicoloured.
971 200f. Type **379** 1·00 30
972 300f. Batourou Sekou Kouyate 1·60 50

380 Nicephore Niepce and Camera

1983. 150th Death Anniv of Nicephore Niepce (pioneer of photography).
973 **380** 400f. blue, green & dp grn 2·20 70

381 Space Shuttle "Challenger"

1983. Air. Space Shuttle.
974 **381** 1000f. multicoloured 4·50 1·90

382 Young People and Map of Africa

1983. Second Pan-African Youth Festival. Multicoloured.
975 240f. Type **382** 1·30 45
976 270f. Hands reaching for map of Africa 1·40 50

383 Mercedes, 1914

1983. Air. Paris–Dakar Rally. Multicoloured.
977 240f. Type **383** 1·50 50

978 270f. Mercedes SSK, 1929 1·60 55
979 500f. Mercedes W 196, 1954 3·75 80
MS980 124×93 mm. 1000f. Modern Mercedes 8·75 80

384 Liner and U.P.U. Emblem

1983. U.P.U. Day.
981 **384** 240f. red, black and blue 1·30 45

385 Pawn and Bishop

1983. Air. Chess Pieces.
982 **385** 300f. grey, violet and green 2·10 50
983 - 420f. green, pink and grey 2·75 80
984 - 500f. blue, dp blue & green 3·50 1·10
MS985 119×89 mm. 700f. brown, green and black 5·50 2·40
DESIGNS: 420f. Castle and knight; 500f. King and queen. 36×47 mm: 700f. chess pieces.

386 "Canigiani Madonna"

1983. Air. Christmas. 500th Birth Anniv of Raphael. Multicoloured.
986 700f. Type **386** 3·75 1·10
987 800f. "Madonna of the Lamb" 3·75 1·50

387 Sahara Goat

1984. Goats. Multicoloured.
988 20f. Type **387** 15 10
989 30f. Billy goat 35 10
990 50f. Billy goat (different) 50 20
991 240f. Kaarta goat 1·60 45
992 350f. Southern goat 2·30 60

388 "Leopold Zborowski" (Modigliani)

1984. Air. Birth Centenary of Modigliani (painter).
993 **388** 700f. multicoloured 5·00 1·70

389 Henri Dunant (founder of Red Cross)

1984. Air. Celebrities.
994 **389** 400f. deep blue, red & blue 2·20 65
995 - 540f. deep blue, red & blue 3·75 85
DESIGN: 540f. Abraham Lincoln.

390 Sidney Bechet

1984. Air. Jazz Musicians. Multicoloured.
996 470f. Type **390** 4·25 1·00
997 500f. Duke Ellington 4·75 1·00

391 Microlight Aircraft

1984. Air. Microlight Aircraft. Multicoloured.
998 270f. Type **391** 1·60 55
999 350f. Lazor Gemini motorized hang-glider 1·90 80

392 Weightlifting

1984. Air. Olympic Games, Los Angeles. Multicoloured.
1000 265f. Type **392** 1·60 55
1001 440f. Show jumping 2·40 80
1002 500f. Hurdles 3·00 1·10
MS1003 130×99 mm. 700f. Sailing (vert) 5·25 2·40

393 "Crucifixion" (Rubens)

1984. Air. Easter.
1004 **393** 940f. brown & dp brown 6·00 1·70
1005 - 970f. brown and red 6·00 1·70
DESIGN—HORIZ: 970f. "The Resurrection" (Mantegna).

1984. Currency revaluation. Various stamps surch. (i) U.P.U. Day (No. 981).
1006 **384** 120f. on 240f. red, black and blue (postage) 1·40 50

(ii) Goats (Nos. 988/92).
1007 **387** 10f. on 20f. mult 20 10
1008 - 15f. on 30f. mult 20 10
1009 - 25f. on 50f. mult 35 20
1010 - 125f. on 240f. mult 1·70 50
1011 - 175f. on 350f. mult 2·20 65

(iii) Paris–Dakar Rally (No. 977).
1012 **383** 120f. on 240f. mult (air) 2·20 80

395 Mercedes "Simplex"

1984. Air. 150th Birth Anniv of Gottlieb Daimler (motor car designer).
1035 **395** 350f. olive, blue and mauve 3·75 1·30
1036 - 470f. green, violet and plum 5·25 1·70
1037 - 485f. blue, violet and plum 5·25 1·80
DESIGNS: 470f. Mercedes-Benz Type "370 S"; 485f. Mercedes-Benz "500 S EC".

396 Farm Workers

1984. Progress in Countryside and Protected Essences. Multicoloured.
1038 5f. Type **396** 10 10
1039 90f. Carpentry 95 30
1040 100f. Tapestry making 95 35
1041 135f. Metal work 1·40 50
1042 515f. "Borassus flabelifer" 4·75 1·90
1043 1225f. "Vitelaria paradoxa" 11·50 2·75

397 Emblem and Child

1984. United Nations Children's Fund.
1044 **397** 120f. red, brown and green 1·30 50
1045 - 135f. red, blue and brown 1·40 60
DESIGN: 135f. Emblem and two children.

398 U.P.U. Emblem, Anchor and Hamburg

1984. Universal Postal Union Congress, Hamburg.
1046 **398** 135f. mauve, green and blue 1·30 50

1984. Air. Olympic Winners, Los Angeles. No. 1000/1002 optd.
1047 135f. on 265f. Optd **HALTERES 56 KGS / 1. WU (CHINE). 2. LAI (CHINE). 3. KOTAKA (JAPON)** 1·20 65
1048 220f. on 440f. Optd **DRESSAGE / PAR EQUIPES / 1. RFA 2. SUISSE / 3. SUEDE** 1·80 1·10
1049 250f. on 500f. Optd **ATHLETISME 3000 METRES STEEPLE / 1. KORIR (KENYA). / 2. MAHMOUD (FRANCE). / 3. DIEMER (E-U)** 2·50 1·60

400 Emblem

1984. Tenth Anniv of Economic Community of West Africa.
1051 **400** 350f. multicoloured 3·25 1·50

401 Dimetrodon

1984. Prehistoric Animals. Multicoloured.
1052 10f. Type **401** 15 10
1053 25f. Iguanodon (vert) 40 15
1054 30f. Archaeopteryx (vert) 50 20
1055 120f. Type **401** 2·00 55
1056 175f. As No. 1053 2·75 80
1057 350f. As No. 1054 5·25 1·60
1058 470f. Triceratops 7·75 2·20

402 "Virgin and Child between St. Joseph and St. Jerome" (detail, Lorenzo Lotto)

1984. Air. Christmas.
1059	**402**	500f. multicoloured	4·75	2·50

1984. Drought Aid. No. 758 surch.
1060	**298**	470f. on 130f. mult	4·25	2·40

404 Horse Galloping

1985. Horses. Multicoloured.
1061	90f. Type **404**	1·00	40
1062	135f. Beledougou horse	1·50	55
1063	190f. Nara horse	2·10	90
1064	530f. Trait horse	6·50	2·20

405 "Clitocybe nebularis"

1985. Fungi. Multicoloured.
1065	120f. Type **405**	1·60	55
1066	200f. "Lepiota cortinarius"	2·30	85
1067	485f. "Agaricus semotus"	6·00	2·40
1068	525f. "Lepiota procera"	6·75	2·50

406 Emile Marchoux and Marchoux Institute

1985. Health. Multicoloured.
1069	120f. Type **406** (World Lepers' Day and 40th anniv of Marchoux Institute) (postage)	1·20	50
1070	135f. Lions' emblem and Samanto Village (15th anniv)	1·80	75
1071	470f. Laboratory technicians and polio victim (anti-polio campaign) (air)	3·75	1·60

407 Profiles and Emblem

1985. 15th Anniv of Technical and Cultural Co-operation Agency.
1072	**407**	540f. green and brown	5·50	2·30

408 River Kingfisher

1985. Air. Birth Bicentenary of John J. Audubon (ornithologist). Multicoloured.
1073	180f. Type **408**	2·20	80
1074	300f. Great bustard (vert)	3·50	1·30
1075	470f. Ostrich (vert)	6·00	2·40
1076	540f. Ruppell's griffon	6·25	2·50

409 National Pioneers Movement Emblem

1985. International Youth Year. Multicoloured.
1077	120f. Type **409**	1·20	55
1078	190f. Boy leading oxen	2·00	80
1079	500f. Sports motifs and I.Y.Y. emblem	5·25	1·80

410 Sud Aviation Caravelle, Boeing 727-200 and Agency Emblem

1985. Air. 25th Anniv of Aerial Navigation Security Agency for Africa and Madagascar (ASECNA).
1080	**410**	700f. multicoloured	6·75	3·50

411 Lion, and Scouts collecting Wood

1985. Air. "Philexafrique" Stamp Exhibition, Lome. Multicoloured.
1081	200f. Type **411**	2·30	1·60
1082	200f. Satellite, dish aerial and globe	2·30	1·60

412 U.P.U. Emblem, Computer and Reservoir (Development)

1985. "Philexafrique" Stamp Exhibition, Lome, Togo (2nd issue). Multicoloured.
1083	250f. Type **412**	2·75	1·80
1084	250f. Satellite, girls writing and children learning from television (Youth)	2·75	1·80

413 Grey Cat

1986. Cats. Multicoloured.
1085	150f. Type **413**	1·90	70
1086	200f. White cat	2·75	1·00
1087	300f. Tabby cat	3·75	1·40

414 Hands releasing Doves and Globe

1986. Anti-apartheid Campaign. Multicoloured.
1088	100f. Type **414**	1·00	50
1089	120f. People breaking chain around world	1·30	55

415 Comet and Diagram of Orbit

1986. Air. Appearance of Halley's Comet.
1090	**415**	300f. multicoloured	3·00	1·40

416 Internal Combustion Engine

1986. Air. Centenaries of First Motor Car with Internal Combustion Engine and Statue of Liberty. Multicoloured.
1091	400f. Type **416**	4·50	1·80
1092	600f. Head of statue, and French and American flags	6·25	2·75

417 Robeson

1986. Air. Tenth Death Anniv of Paul Robeson (singer).
1093	**417**	500f. multicoloured	6·50	2·40

418 Women tending Crop

1986. World Communications Day.
1094	**418**	200f. multicoloured	1·80	80

419 Players

1986. World Cup Football Championship, Mexico. Multicoloured.
1095	160f. Type **419**	1·70	65
1096	225f. Player capturing ball	2·30	95
MS1097	120×80 mm. 500f. Goalkeeper failing to save goal	5·25	3·00

420 Watt

1986. 250th Birth Anniv of James Watt (inventor).
1098	**420**	110f. multicoloured	1·50	50

421 Eberth and Microscope

1986. Air. 60th Death Anniv of Karl Eberth (discoverer of typhoid bacillus).
1099	**421**	550f. multicoloured	5·50	2·10

422 Chess Pieces on Board

1986. Air. World Chess Championship, London and Leningrad. Multicoloured.
1100	400f. Type **422**	5·00	1·80
1101	500f. Knight and board	6·50	2·40

1986. World Cup Winners. Nos. 1095/MS1097 optd ARGENTINE 3 R.F.A. 2.
1102	160f. multicoloured	2·00	1·10
1103	225f. multicoloured	2·50	1·80
MS1104	120×80 mm. 500f. multicoloured	5·50	5·50

424 Head

1986. Endangered Animals. Giant Eland. Multicoloured.
1105	5f. Type **424**	1·00	25
1106	20f. Standing by dead tree	2·30	45
1107	25f. Stepping over fallen branch	2·50	45
1108	200f. Mother and calf	15·00	3·00

425 Mermoz and "Croix du Sud"

1986. Air. 50th Anniv of Disappearance of Jean Mermoz (aviator). Multicoloured.
1109	150f. Type **425**	1·70	70
1110	600f. CAMS 53 flying boat and monoplane	6·00	2·50
1111	625f. Map and seaplane "Comte de la Vaulx"	6·25	3·00

1986. Tenth Anniv of Concorde's First Commercial Flight. Nos. 674/6 surch 1986—10e Anniversaire du 1er Vol Commercial Supersonique.
1112	175f. on 120f. Type **271**	1·70	90
1113	225f. on 130f. Concorde and Wright Flyer I	2·00	1·10
1114	300f. on 200f. Concorde and Lindbergh's "Spirit of St. Louis"	3·25	1·60

427 Hansen and Follereau

1987. Air. 75th Death Anniv of Gerhard Hansen (discoverer of bacillus) and 10th Death Anniv of Raoul Follereau (leprosy pioneer).
1115	**427**	500f. multicoloured	5·00	2·20

428 Model "A", 1903

1987. 40th Death Anniv of Henry Ford (motor car manufacturer). Multicoloured.
1116	150f. Type **428**	1·60	65
1117	200f. Model "T", 1923	2·20	95
1118	225f. "Thunderbird", 1968	2·40	1·20
1119	300f. "Continental", 1963	2·75	1·60

429 Konrad Adenauer

1987. Air. 20th Death Anniv of Konrad Adenauer (German statesman).
1120	**429**	625f. stone, brown and red	6·50	2·75

430 Runners and Buddha's Head

1987. Air. Olympic Games, Seoul (1988) (1st issue).
1121	**430**	400f. black and brown	4·00	1·80

1122	-	500f. dp green, grn & red	4·75	2·30

DESIGN: 500f. Footballers.
See also Nos. 1133/4.

431 Scenes from "The Jazz Singer"

1987. Air. 60th Anniv of First Talking Picture.
| 1123 | **431** | 550f. red, brn & dp brn | 7·25 | 3·00 |

432 "Apis florea"

1987. Bees. Multicoloured.
1124		100f. Type **432**	1·10	60
1125		150f. "Apis dorsata"	1·70	75
1126		175f. "Apis adonsonii"	1·90	90
1127		200f. "Apis mellifera"	2·50	1·10

433 Map, Dove and Luthuli

1987. Air. 20th Death Anniv of Albert John Luthuli (Nobel Peace Prize winner).
| 1128 | **433** | 400f. mauve, blue & brn | 3·75 | 1·60 |

434 Profiles and Lions Emblem

1987. Air. Lions International and Rotary International. Multicoloured.
| 1129 | **434** | 500f. Type **434** | 4·75 | 2·10 |
| 1130 | | 500f. Clasped hands and Rotary emblem | 4·75 | 2·10 |

435 Anniversary Emblem and Symbols of Activities

1988. 30th Anniv of Lions International in Mali.
| 1131 | **435** | 200f. multicoloured | 1·80 | 95 |

436 Emblem and Doctor examining Boy

1988. 40th Anniv of W.H.O.
| 1132 | **436** | 150f. multicoloured | 1·50 | 70 |

437 Coubertin and Ancient and Modern Athletes

1988. Air. Olympic Games, Seoul (2nd issue). 125th Birth Anniv of Pierre de Coubertin (founder of modern games). Multicoloured.
| 1133 | **437** | 240f. Type **437** | 3·00 | 1·20 |
| 1134 | | 400f. Stadium, Olympic rings and sports pictograms | 4·00 | 2·40 |

438 "Harlequin"

1988. Air. 15th Death Anniv of Pablo Picasso (painter).
| 1135 | **438** | 600f. multicoloured | 6·75 | 2·50 |

439 Concorde and Globe

1988. Air. 15th Anniv of First North Atlantic Crossing by Concorde.
| 1136 | **439** | 500f. multicoloured | 4·75 | 2·30 |

440 Pres. Kennedy

1988. 25th Death Anniv of John Fitzgerald Kennedy (American President).
| 1137 | **440** | 640f. multicoloured | 6·00 | 2·50 |

1988. Mali Mission Hospital, Mopti. No. 1132 surch MISSION MALI HOPITAL de MOPTI 300F and MEDECINS DU MONDE emblem.
| 1138 | **436** | 300f. on 150f. mult | 3·00 | 2·10 |

442 Map

1988. 25th Anniv of Organization of African Unity.
| 1139 | **442** | 400f. multicoloured | 3·75 | 1·80 |

443 Map, Leaf and Stove

1989. Air. "Improved Stoves: For a Green Mali". Multicoloured.
1140		5f. Type **443**	10	10
1141		10f. Tree and stove	20	10
1142		25f. Type **443**	35	25
1143		100f. As No. 1141	1·50	50

444 Astronauts on Moon

1989. Air. 20th Anniv of First Manned Moon Landing.
| 1144 | **444** | 300f. blue, purple & grn | 1·60 | 60 |
| 1145 | - | 500f. purple, blue & brn | 3·00 | 1·50 |

DESIGN: 500f. Astronauts on Moon (different).

445 Emblem and Crossed Syringes

1989. Vaccination Programme. Multicoloured.
1146		20f. Type **445**	4·75	2·30
1147		30f. Doctor vaccinating woman	35	10
1148		50f. Emblem and syringes	55	25
1149		175f. Doctor vaccinating child	1·80	95

446 Emblem

1989. 25th Anniv of International Law Institute of French-speaking Countries.
| 1150 | **446** | 150f. multicoloured | 1·60 | 60 |
| 1151 | **446** | 200f. multicoloured | 2·00 | 90 |

447 Crowd

1989. Air. Bicentenary of French Revolution and "Philexfrance 89" International Stamp Exn, Paris.
| 1152 | **447** | 400f. red, blue and purple | 4·50 | 1·80 |
| 1153 | - | 600f. violet, pur & mve | 6·50 | 2·50 |

DESIGN: 600f. Marianne and Storming of Bastille.

448 U.P.U. Emblem and Hands holding Envelopes

1989. World Post Day.
| 1154 | **448** | 625f. multicoloured | 6·25 | 2·75 |

449 Pope and Cathedral

1990. Visit of Pope John Paul II.
| 1155 | **449** | 200f. multicoloured | 2·20 | 1·10 |

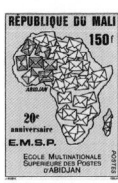

450 Envelopes on Map

1990. 20th Anniv of Multinational Postal Training School, Abidjan.
| 1156 | **450** | 150f. multicoloured | 1·70 | 70 |

451 Footballers

1990. Air. World Cup Football Championship, Italy. Multicoloured.
1157		200f. Type **451**	2·00	90
1158		225f. Footballers (different)	2·20	95
MS1159		100×75 mm. 500f. Type **451**	5·25	3·00

1990. World Cup Result. Nos. 1157/8 optd. Mult.
1160		200f. **ITALIE : 2 / ANGLETERRE : 1**	2·10	1·30
1161		225f. **R.F.A. : 1 / ARGENTINE : 0**	2·20	1·40
MS1162		100×75 mm. 500f. **1er : R.F.A. 2eme : ARGENTINE 3me : ITALIE**	5·50	5·00

453 Pres. Moussa Traore and Bamako Bridge

1990. 30th Anniv of Independence.
| 1163 | **453** | 400f. multicoloured | 4·00 | 2·00 |

454 Man writing and Adults learning to Read

1990. International Literacy Year.
| 1164 | **454** | 150f. multicoloured | 1·70 | 65 |
| 1165 | **454** | 200f. multicoloured | 2·10 | 95 |

455 Woman carrying Water and Cattle at Well

1991. Lions Club (1166) and Rotary International (1167) Projects. Multicoloured.
| 1166 | | 200f. Type **455** (6th anniv of wells project) | 2·10 | 1·10 |
| 1167 | | 200f. Bamako branch emblem and hand (30th anniv of anti-polio campaign) | 2·10 | 1·10 |

456 Sonrai Dance, Takamba

1991. Dances. Multicoloured.
1168		50f. Type **456**	50	30
1169		100f. Malinke dance, Mandiani	1·00	55
1170		150f. Bamanan dance, Kono	1·50	80
1171		200f. Dogon dance, Songho	2·00	1·10

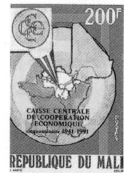

457 Bank Emblem and Map of France

1991. 50th Anniv of Central Economic Co-operation Bank.
| 1172 | **457** | 200f. multicoloured | 1·80 | 80 |

458 Women with Torch and Banner

1992. National Women's Movement for the Safeguarding of Peace and National Unity.
| 1173 | **458** | 150f. multicoloured | 1·60 | 80 |

1992. Various stamps surch.
1174	-	25f. on 470f. mult (No. 1058) (postage)	30	25
1175	**420**	30f. on 110f. mult	30	25
1176	-	50f. on 300f. mult (No. 1087)	45	40
1177	-	50f. on 1225f. mult (No. 1043)	45	40
1178	-	150f. on 135f. mult (No. 1070)	1·40	70
1179	-	150f. on 190f. mult (No. 1063)	1·40	70

1180 - 150f. on 190f. mult (No. 1078) 1·40 70
1181 400 150f. on 350f. mult 1·40 70
1182 - 150f. on 485f. mult (No. 1067) 1·40 70
1183 - 150f. on 525f. mult (No. 1068) 1·40 70
1184 - 150f. on 530f. mult (No. 1064) 1·40 70
1185 440 200f. on 640f. mult 1·80 1·60
1186 - 240f. on 350f. mult (No. 1057) 2·40 1·60
1187 448 240f. on 625f. mult 2·50 1·60
1188 410 20f. on 700f. mult (air) 30 10
1189 415 20f. on 300f. mult 30 10
1190 - 25f. on 470f. mult (No. 1071) 30 10
1191 408 30f. on 180f. mult 30 10
1192 - 30f. on 500f. purple, blue and brown (No. 1145) 30 10
1193 - 100f. on 540f. mult (No. 1076) 95 55
1194 438 100f. on 600f. mult 95 55
1195 444 150f. on 300f. blue, purple and green 1·50 80
1196 447 150f. on 400f. red, blue and purple 1·50 80
1197 - 200f. on 300f. mult (No. 1074) 2·00 1·10
1198 - 240f. on 600f. violet, purple and mauve (No. 1153) 2·75 1·80

1992. (a) Postage. No. 1095 surch 150 f "Euro 92".
1199 419 150f. on 160f. mult 1·50 80

(b) Air. No. 1134 surch 150F "Barcelone 92".
1200 150f. on 400f. multicoloured 1·70 80

461 Map of Africa

1993. First Anniv of Third Republic.
1201 461 150f. multicoloured 7·00 1·80

462 Blood, Memorial and Martyrs

1993. Second Anniv of Martyrs' Day.
1203 462 150f. multicoloured 2·20 1·10
1204 462 160f. multicoloured 2·20 1·10

463 Polio Victims

1993. Vaccination Campaign.
1205 463 150f. multicoloured 7·00 1·80

464 Lecture on Problem Issues

1993. 35th Anniv of Lions International in Mali.
1207 464 200f. multicoloured 1·50 80
1208 464 225f. multicoloured 1·50 80

465 Place de la Liberte

1993. Multicoloured, background colour of top panel given.
1209 465 20f. blue 10 10
1210 465 25f. yellow 10 10
1211 465 50f. pink 45 25
1212 465 100f. grey 95 25
1213 465 110f. yellow 95 40
1214 465 150f. green 1·20 40
1215 465 200f. yellow 1·90 70
1216 465 225f. flesh 1·90 80
1217 465 240f. lilac 2·40 80
1218 465 260f. lilac 2·50 80

466 Figure Skating

1994. Winter Olympic Games, Lillehammer. Multicoloured.
1219 150f. Type **466** 90 60
1220 200f. Giant slalom 1·20 80
1221 225f. Ski jumping 1·50 1·00
1222 750f. Speed skating 4·00 2·20
MS1223 100×69 mm. 2000f. Special slalom 6·50 6·50

467 Juan Schiaffino (Uruguay)

1994. World Cup Football Championship, U.S.A. Players from Different Teams. Multicoloured.
1224 200f. Type **467** 90 60
1225 240f. Diego Maradona (Argentine Republic) 1·20 85
1226 260f. Paolo Rossi (Italy) 1·40 95
1227 1000f. Franz Beckenbauer (Germany) 4·75 3·25
MS1228 97×68 mm. 2000f. Just Fontaine (France) 9·75 5·50

468 Scaphonyx

1994. Prehistoric Animals. Multicoloured.
1229 5f. Type **468** 10 10
1230 10f. Cynognathus 10 10
1231 15f. Lesothosaurus 10 10
1232 20f. Scutellosaurus 10 10
1233 25f. Ceratosaurus 10 10
1234 30f. Dilophosaurus 10 10
1235 40f. Dryosaurus 10 10
1236 50f. Heterodontosaurus 10 10
1237 60f. Anatosaurus 10 10
1238 70f. Saurornithoides 30 10
1239 80f. Avimimus 30 10
1240 90f. Saltasaurus 45 10
1241 300f. Dromaeosaurus 1·60 40
1242 400f. Tsintaosaurus 2·10 55
1243 600f. Velociraptor 3·25 70
1244 700f. Ouranosaurus 3·75 80
MS1245 105×130 mm. 2000f. Daspletosaurus and Iguanodon fighting 10·50 6·50

Nos. 1229/44 were issued together, se-tenant, forming a composite design.

469 "Sternuera castanea"

1994. Insects. Multicoloured.
1246 40f. Type **469** 25 20
1247 50f. "Eudicella gralli" (horiz) 45 25
1248 100f. "Homoderus mellyi" 70 50
1249 200f. "Kraussaria angulifera" (horiz) 1·30 80

470 Vaccinating Child

1994. Vaccination Campaign.
1250 470 150f. green and black 75 75
1251 470 200f. blue and black 1·30 1·30

471 Feral Rock Pigeons

1994. Birds. Multicoloured.
1252 25f. Type **471** 10 10
1253 30f. Helmeted guineafowl 10 10
1254 150f. South African crowned cranes (vert) 70 25
1255 200f. Red junglefowl (vert) 1·00 25

472 Family

1994. International Year of the Family.
1256 472 200f. multicoloured 45 25

473 Kirk Douglas in "Spartacus"

1994. Film Stars. Multicoloured.
1257 100f. Type **473** (postage) 50 10
1258 150f. Elizabeth Taylor in "Cleopatra" 90 25
1259 225f. Marilyn Monroe in "The River of No Return" 1·00 25
1260 500f. Arnold Swarzenegger in "Conan the Barbarian" 1·80 70
1261 1000f. Elvis Presley in "Loving You" 3·75 1·10
MS1262 149×90 mm. 1500f. Charlton Heston in "The Ten Commandments" 6·50 6·50

1263 200f. Clint Eastwood in "A Mule for Sister Sara" (inscr "SIERRA TORRIDE") (air) 2·10 25

474 Ella Fitzgerald

1994. Jazz Singers. Multicoloured.
1264 200f. Type **474** 80 25
1265 225f. Lionel Hampton 95 25
1266 240f. Sarah Vaughan 1·20 25
1267 300f. Count Basie 1·60 55
1268 400f. Duke Ellington 1·90 70
1269 600f. Miles Davis 2·75 70
MS1270 120×81 mm. 1500f. Louis Armstrong 6·75 6·75

475 Soldiers caught in Explosion

1994. 50th Anniv of Second World War D-Day Landings. Multicoloured. (a) Villers-Bocage.
1271 200f. Type **475** 95 25
1272 200f. Tank (29×47 mm) 95 25
1273 200f. Troops beside tank 95 25

(b) Beaumont-sur-Sarthe.
1274 300f. Bombers and troops under fire 1·40 40
1275 300f. Bombers and tanks (29×47 mm) 1·40 40
1276 300f. Tank and soldier with machine gun 1·40 40

(c) Utah Beach (wrongly inscr "Utha").
1277 300f. Wounded troops and bow of boat 1·40 40
1278 300f. Troops in boat (29×47 mm) 1·40 40
1279 300f. Troops in boats 1·80 45

(d) Air Battle.
1280 400f. Bombers 1·80 45
1281 400f. Aircraft (29×47 mm) 1·80 45
1282 400f. Airplane on fire 1·80 45

(e) Sainte-Mere-Eglise.
1283 400f. Troops firing at paratrooper 1·80 45
1284 400f. Church and soldier (29×47 mm) 1·80 45
1285 400f. Paratroopers and German troops 1·80 45

Nos. 1271/3, 1274/6, 1277/9, 1280/2 and 1283/5 respectively were issued together, se-tenant, forming composite designs.

476 Olympic Rings on National Flag

1994. Centenary of International Olympic Committee (1st issue).
1286 476 150f. multicoloured 75 35
1287 476 200f. multicoloured 95 55

See also Nos. 1342/5.

477 Couple holding Condoms

1994. Anti-AIDS Campaign. Multicoloured.
1288 150f. Type **477** 75 35
1289 225f. Nurse treating patient and laboratory worker 1·20 55

478 "Venus of Brassempoury"

1994. Ancient Art. Multicoloured.
1290 15f. Type **478** 10 10
1291 25f. Cave paintings, Tanum 10 10
1292 45f. Prehistoric men painting mural 30 10
1293 50f. Cave paintings, Lascaux (horiz) 30 10
1294 55f. Painting from tomb of Amonherkhopeshef 30 10
1295 65f. God Anubis laying out Pharaoh (horiz) 30 10
1296 75f. Sphinx and pyramid, Mycerinus (horiz) 30 10
1297 85f. Bust of Nefertiti 30 10
1298 95f. Statue of Shibum 45 10
1299 100f. Cavalry of Ur (horiz) 45 10
1300 130f. Head of Mesopotamian harp 55 25
1301 135f. Mesopotamian tablet (horiz) 55 25
1302 140f. Assyrian dignitary 55 25
1303 180f. Enamel relief from Babylon (horiz) 75 25
1304 190f. Assyrians hunting 95 25
1305 200f. "Mona Lisa of Nimrod" 95 25
1306 225f. Phoenician coins (horiz) 95 25
1307 250f. Phoenician sphinx 1·20 25
1308 275f. Persian archer 1·20 25
1309 280f. Glass paste mask 1·80 25

479 "Polyptychus roseus"

1994. Multicoloured. (a) Butterflies and Moths.

1310	20f. Type **479**	10	10
1311	30f. "Elymniopsis bammakoo"	10	10
1312	40f. Silver-striped hawk moth	10	10
1313	150f. Crimson-speckled moth	75	25
1314	180f. Foxy charaxes	75	25
1315	200f. Common dotted border	80	25

(b) Plants.

1316	25f. "Disa kewensis"	10	10
1317	50f. "Angraecum eburneum"	10	10
1318	100f. "Ansellia africana"	45	10
1319	140f. Sorghum	70	10
1320	150f. Onion	75	25
1321	190f. Maize	95	25
1322	200f. Clouded agaric	95	25
1323	225f. Parasol mushroom	1·20	25
1324	500f. "Lepiota aspera"	2·10	80

(c) Insects.

1325	225f. Goliath beetle	95	35
1326	240f. Cricket	1·20	35
1327	350f. Praying mantis	1·50	40

1994. Winter Olympic Games Medal Winners, Lillehammer. Nos. 1219/MS1223 optd.

1328	150f. **O GRISHSHUK Y. PLATOV RUSSIE**	55	10
1329	150f. **Y. GORDEYEVA S. GRINKOV RUSSIE**	55	10
1330	200f. **M. WASMEIER ALLEMAGNE**	95	25
1331	200f. **D. COMPAGNONI ITALIE**	95	25
1332	225f. **T. WEISSFLOG ALLEMAGNE**	1·20	25
1333	225f. **E. BREDESEN NORVEGE**	1·20	25
1334	750f. **J.O. KOSS NORVEGE**	3·00	70
1335	750f. **B. BLAIR U.S.A.**	3·00	70
MS1336	Two sheets each 100×69 mm. (a) 2000f. Optd **L. KJUS NORVEGE**; (b) Optd **P. WIBERG SUEDE**	10·00	10·00

A sheetlet also exists containing Nos. 1219/22 each optd with both of the inscriptions for that value.

1994. Results of World Cup Football Championship. Nos. 1224/**MS**1228 optd 1. BRESIL 2. ITALIE 3. SUEDE.

1337	200f. multicoloured	95	25
1338	240f. multicoloured	95	25
1339	260f. multicoloured	1·30	25
1340	1000f. multicoloured	4·50	1·20
MS1341	87×68 mm. 2000f. multicoloured	6·50	6·50

482 Pierre de Coubertin (founder) and Torchbearer

1994. Centenary of International Olympic Committee (2nd issue). Multicoloured.

1342	225f. Type **482**	95	25
1343	240f. Coubertin designing Olympic rings	95	25
1344	300f. Athlete bearing torch and Coubertin (horiz)	1·30	25
1345	500f. Olympic rings and Coubertin at desk (horiz)	2·20	80
MS1346	117×80 mm. 600f. First Olympic ceremony and Coubertin at desk	3·00	3·00

483 Statue and Village

1994. 20th International Tourism Day. Multicoloured.

1347	150f. Type **483**	75	35
1348	200f. Sphinx, pyramids and Abu Simbel temple (horiz)	95	55

484 Reiner Klimker (dressage)

1995. Olympic Games, Atlanta (1996). Multicoloured.

1349	25f. Type **484**	10	10
1350	50f. Kristin Otto (swimming)	10	10
1351	100f. Gunther Winkler (show jumping)	45	10
1352	150f. Birgit Fischer-Schmidt (single kayak)	55	10
1353	200f. Nicole Uphoff (dressage) (vert)	95	25
1354	225f. Renate Stecher (athletics) (vert)	95	25
1355	230f. Michael Gross (swimming)	95	25
1356	240f. Karin Janz (gymnastics)	1·20	25
1357	550f. Anja Fichtel (fencing) (vert)	2·50	70
1358	700f. Heide Rosendahl-Ecker (long jump) (vert)	3·00	1·10

485 Ernst Opik, "Galileo" Probe, Shoemaker-Levy Comet and Jupiter

1995. Anniversaries and Events. Multicoloured.

1359	150f. Type **485**	55	10
1360	200f. Clyde Tombaugh (discoverer of Pluto, 1930) and "Pluto" probe	95	25
1361	500f. Henri Dunant (founder of Red Cross)	2·20	70
1362	650f. Astronauts and lunar rover (first manned moon landing, 1969)	2·75	55
1363	700f. Emblems of Lions International and Rotary International and child drinking from pump	3·00	55
1364	800f. Gary Kasparov (world chess champion, 1993)	3·50	70

486 Agriculture and Fishing (regional integration)

1995. 20th Anniv of Economic Community of West African States. Multicoloured.

1365	150f. Type **486**	55	25
1366	200f. Emblem and handshake (co-operation) (vert)	95	25
1367	220f. Emblem and banknotes (proposed common currency)	95	40
1368	225f. Emblem and doves (peace and security)	1·00	40

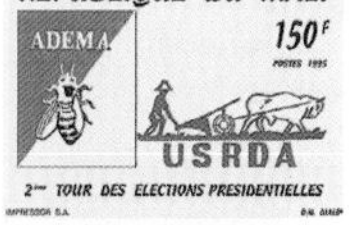

487 Emblems of Alliance for Democracy in Mali and Sudanese Union-RDA

1995. Third Anniv of New Constitution. Multicoloured.

1369	150f. Type **487** (second round of Presidential election)	55	25
1370	200f. President Alpha Oumar Konare (vert)	80	25
1371	225f. Emblems of competing parties (first round of Presidential election)	95	40
1372	240f. Map, flag and initials of parties (multi-party democracy) (vert)	1·10	40

488 Scout and Viennese Emperor Moth

1995. Scout Jamboree, Netherlands. Designs showing scouts and insects or fungi. Multicoloured.

1373	150f. Type **488**	55	10
1374	225f. Brimstone	95	25
1375	240f. Fig-tree blue	95	25
1376	500f. Clouded agaric	2·20	55
1377	650f. "Agaricus semotus"	3·00	70
1378	725f. Parasol mushroom	3·25	80
MS1379	124×85 mm. 1500f. Blue morpho	6·75	6·75

489 Paul Harris (founder) and Emblem

1995. 90th Anniv of Rotary International. Multicoloured.

1380	1000f. Type **489**	5·00	1·40
MS1381	76×106 mm. 1500f. 1905 and present-day emblems	6·75	6·75

490 Imperial Woodpecker ("Campephilus imperialis")

1995. Birds and Butterflies. Multicoloured.

1382	50f. Type **490**	40	20
1383	50f. Blue-crowned motmot ("Momotus momota")	40	20
1384	50f. Keel-billed toucan ("Ramphastos sulfuratus")	40	20
1385	50f. Blue-breasted kingfisher ("Halycon malimbica")	40	20
1386	50f. Streamertail ("Trochilus polytmus")	40	20
1387	50f. Common cardinal ("Cardinalis cardinalis")	40	20
1388	50f. Resplendent quetzal ("Pharomachrus mocinno")	40	20
1389	50f. Sun conure ("Aratinga solstitialis")	40	20
1390	50f. Red-necked amazon ("Amazona arausiaca")	40	20
1391	50f. Scarlet ibis ("Eudocimus ruber")	40	20
1392	50f. Red siskin ("Carduelis cucullatus")	40	20
1393	50f. Hyacinth macaw ("Anodorhynchus hyacinthinus")	40	20
1394	50f. Orange-breasted bunting ("Passerina leclancherii")	40	20
1395	50f. Red-capped manakin ("Pipra mentalis")	40	20
1396	50f. Guianan cock of the rock ("Rupicola rupicola")	40	20
1397	50f. Saffron finch ("Sicalis flaveola")	40	20
1398	100f. Black-spotted barbet ("Capito niger")	55	25
1399	100f. Amazon kingfisher ("Chloroceryle amazona")	55	25
1400	100f. Swallow tanager ("Tersina viridis")	55	25
1401	100f. Blue-crowned motmot ("Momotus momota")	55	25
1402	100f. Crimson-crested woodpecker ("Campephilus melanoleucos")	55	25
1403	100f. Red-breasted blackbird ("Leistes militaris")	55	25
1404	100f. King vulture ("Sarcorhamphus papa")	55	25
1405	100f. Capped heron ("Pilherodius pileatus")	55	25
1406	100f. Black-tailed tityra ("Tityra cayana")	55	25
1407	100f. Paradise tanager ("Tangara chilensis")	55	25
1408	100f. Yellow-crowned amazon ("Amazona ochrocephala")	55	25
1409	100f. Buff-throated saltator ("Saltator maximus")	55	25
1410	100f. Red-cowled cardinal ("Paroaria dominicana")	55	25
1411	100f. Louisiana heron ("Egretta tricolor")	55	25
1412	100f. Black-bellied cuckoo ("Piaya melanogaster")	55	25
1413	100f. Barred antshrike ("Thamnophilus doliatus")	55	25
1414	150f. Paradise whydah	75	25
1415	150f. Red-necked spurfowl ("Red-necked Francolin")	75	25
1416	150f. Whale-headed stork (inscr "Shoebill")	75	25
1417	150f. Ruff	75	25
1418	150f. Marabou stork	75	25
1419	150f. Eastern white pelican ("White Pelican")	75	25
1420	150f. Western curlew	75	25
1421	150f. Scarlet ibis	75	25
1422	150f. Great crested grebe	75	25
1423	150f. White spoonbill	75	25
1424	150f. African jacana	75	25
1425	150f. African pygmy goose	75	25
1426	200f. Ruby-throated hummingbird	1·00	30
1427	200f. Grape shoemaker and blue morpho butterflies	1·00	30
1428	200f. Northern hobby	1·00	30
1429	200f. Black-mandibled toucan ("Cuvier Toucan")	1·00	30
1430	200f. Black-necked red cotinga and green-winged macaw	1·00	30
1431	200f. Green-winged macaws and blue and yellow macaw	1·00	30
1432	200f. Greater flamingo ("Flamingo")	1·00	30
1433	200f. Malachite kingfisher	1·00	30
1434	200f. Bushy-crested hornbill	1·00	30
1435	200f. Purple swamphen	1·00	30
1436	200f. Striped body	1·00	30
1437	200f. Painted lady	1·00	30
MS1438	Two sheets each 114×91 mm. (a) 1000f. Crimson topaz ("Topaza pella"); (b) 1000f. Lined seedeater ("Sporophila lineola")	5·00	4·75

Stamps of the same value were issued together, in se-tenant sheetlets, each sheetlet forming a composite design.

491 Emblem and Scales of Justice

1995. 50th Anniv of U.N.O. Multicoloured.

1439	20f. Type **491**	10	10
1440	170f. Type **491**	75	40
1441	225f. Emblem, doves and men with linked arms (horiz)	95	40
1442	240f. As No. 1441	1·10	70

492 Food Jar

1995. Cooking Utensils. Multicoloured.

1443	5f. Type **492**	10	10
1444	50f. Pestle and mortar	45	15
1445	150f. Bowl (horiz)	95	25
1446	200f. Grain sack	1·30	30
MS1447	80×110 mm. 500f. Mat	3·25	3·25

493 Lennon

1995. 15th Death Anniv of John Lennon (musician).

1448	**493** 150f. multicoloured	95	25

494 Justus Barnes

1995. 40th Anniv of Rock Music (1461/6) and Centenary of Motion Pictures (others). Multicoloured. (a) Actors in Western Films.

1449	150f. Type **494**	95	55
1450	150f. William S. Hart	95	55
1451	150f. Tom Mix	95	55
1452	150f. Wallace Beery	95	55
1453	150f. Gary Cooper	95	55
1454	150f. John Wayne	95	55

(b) Leading Ladies and their Directors.

1455	200f. Marlene Dietrich and Josef von Sternberg ("The Blue Angel")	1·30	90
1456	200f. Jean Harlow and George Cukor ("Dinner at Eight")	1·30	90
1457	200f. Mary Astor and John Houston ("The Maltese Falcon")	1·30	90
1458	200f. Ingrid Bergman and Alfred Hitchcock ("Spellbound")	1·30	90
1459	200f. Claudette Colbert and Cecil B. de Mille ("Cleopatra")	1·30	90
1460	200f. Marilyn Monroe and Billy Wilder ("Some Like it Hot")	1·30	90

(c) Female Singers.

1461	225f. Connie Francis	1·40	90
1462	225f. The Ronettes	1·40	90
1463	225f. Janis Joplin	1·40	90
1464	225f. Debbie Harry	1·40	90
1465	225f. Cyndi Lauper	1·40	90
1466	225f. Carly Simon	1·40	90

(d) Musicals.

1467	240f. Gene Kelly in "Singin' in the Rain"	1·60	1·10
1468	240f. Cyd Charisse and Fred Astaire in "The Bandwagon"	1·60	1·10
1469	240f. Liza Minelli in "Cabaret"	1·60	1·10
1470	240f. Julie Andrews in "The Sound of Music"	1·60	1·10
1471	240f. Ginger Rogers and Fred Astaire in "Top Hat"	1·60	1·10
1472	240f. John Travolta and Karen Lynn Gorney in "Saturday Night Fever"	1·60	1·10

MS1473 Four sheets. (a) 104×74 mm. 1000f. Robert Redford; (b) 73×102 mm. 1000f. Liv Ullman and Ingmar Bergman ("Shame"); (c) 76×106 mm. 1000f. Bette Midler; (d) 76×106 mm. 1000f. Judy Garland in "The Wizard of Oz"   23·00   23·00

No. 1449 is wrongly inscribed George Barnes.

495 Charles de Gaulle (French statesman, 25th death anniv)

1995. Anniversaries. Multicoloured.

1474	150f. Type **495**	70	25
1475	200f. General de Gaulle (50th anniv of liberation of France)	80	25
1476	240f. Enzo Ferrari (car designer, 7th death anniv)	95	25
1477	500f. Ayrton Senna (racing driver, 1st death anniv)	2·00	40
1478	650f. Paul Emile Victor (explorer, 88th birthday)	2·50	40
1479	725f. Paul Harris (founder, 90th anniv of Rotary International)	3·25	55
1480	740f. Michael Schumacher (racing driver, 26th birth anniv) (wrongly dated "1970")	3·25	55
1481	1000f. Jerry Garcia (popular singer, death commemoration)	4·50	70

Nos. 1482/90 and Types **496/505** are left for possible issues not seen.

506 Djenne Mosque

1996. Mosques. Multicoloured.

1491	250f. Type **506**	2·75	1·30
1492	310f. Sankoré Mosque	3·20	1·60

507 Nanking Bridge

1996. Centenary of Chinese Postal Service.

1493	**507**	270f. multicoloured	2·50	1·30

508 Fire and Crowd

1996. Peace Bonfire, Timbuktu.

1494	**508**	180f. multicoloured	2·30	1·10
1495	**508**	250f. mullticoloured	3·00	1·50

509 Delivery

1996. Tenth Anniv of EMS

1496	30f. Type **509**	75	35
1497	40f. Eagle carrying parcel and envelope	75	40
1498	90f. Emblem and woman taking phone call (horiz)	1·00	75
1499	320f. Delivery van and emblem (horiz)	3·75	2·00

510 Kara

1996. Exhibits from National Museum. Multicoloured.

1500	5f. Type **510**	30	10
1501	10f. Hambe	30	15
1502	180f. Pinge	2·00	1·40
1503	250f. Merenkun	3·00	1·80

511 Dounouba

1996. Traditional Dances. Muulticoloured.

1504	150f. Type **511**	1·30	60
1505	170f. Gomba	1·50	65
1506	225f. Sandia	2·00	85
1507	230f. Sabar	2·30	90

512 Cotton

1996. Cotton Production

1508	20f. Type **512**	25	15
1509	25f. Picking cotton (horiz)	30	20
1510	50f. Hand holding cotton	60	30
1511	310f. Emptying basket of cotton onto trailer (horiz)	3·50	2·00

513 Student

1996. Year of African Education

1512	100f. Type **513**	75	45
1513	150f. Children in classroom (horiz)	1·20	60
1514	180f. Adult literacy class (horiz)	1·40	75
1515	250f. Map enclosing uses of literacy	1·90	1·10

514 Cabral

1996. 16th Death Anniv of Abdoul Karim (Cabral) Camara (general secretary of student union).

1516	180f. multicoloured	1·50	95
1517	250f. mutlicoloured	2·00	1·40

515 Kita Basilica

1997. Churches. Multicoloured.

1518	5f. Type **515**	20	10
1519	10f. San Cathedral	25	10
1520	150f. Bamako Cathedral	1·60	75
1521	370f. Mandiakuy Church	4·00	1·80

516 Traditional Dance Headdress

1997. Exhibits from National Museum. Multicoloured.

1522	20f. Type **516**	20	15
1523	25f. Couple (statuette)	25	20
1524	250f. Saddlebag key	2·00	1·20
1525	310f. Oil lamp	2·75	1·50

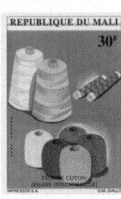

517 Yarn

1997. Cotton Industry. Multicoloured.

1526	30f. Type **517**	30	15
1527	50f. Clothes	45	25
1528	180f. Bolts of cloth	1·60	90
1529	320f. Textile printing machine	2·75	1·60

518 Addax

1998. 18th Anniv of Pan African Postal Union.

1530	**518**	250f. multicoloured	2·50	1·30

519 Mofti Mosque

1998. Art and Culture

1531	5f. Type **519**	10	30
1532	10f. La Tanga (vert)	15	30
1533	15f. Fishermen	20	30
1534	20f. Fula woman (inscr 'La Femme Peulh') (vert)	30	30
1535	25f. Friendship Hotel (vert)	35	35
1536	30f. Hill, Sikasso (inscr 'La Mamelon de Sikasso') (vert)	40	40
1537	40f. Azalai caravan camel rider (vert)	55	55
1538	50f. Kassonike woman (vert)	70	70
1539	60f. Dogon drummer (vert)	85	1·00
1540	70f. Cattle herders (vert)	1·00	1·00
1541	80f. Doson n'goni (lute-harp) player (vert)	1·20	1·30
1542	90f. Male antelope shaped hair comb (vert)	1·30	1·40

520 Senufo Traditional House

1998. Traditional Houses. Multicoloured.

1543	25f. Type **520**	25	60
1544	180f. Sarakole (Soninke) (horiz)	1·80	1·00
1545	310f. Minianka	3·00	1·70
1546	320f. Boo	3·25	1·80

521 Tamarindus indica (tamarind)

1998. Trees. Multicoloured.

1547	100f. Type **521**	1·00	60
1548	150f. Adansonia digitata (baobab)	1·50	90
1549	180f. Acacia	1·80	1·10
1550	310f. Parkia biglobosa (néré)	3·25	1·80

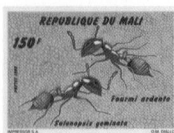

522 Solenopsis geminata

1998. Ants. Multicoloured.

1551	150f. Type **522**	1·50	75
1552	180f. Camponotus pensylvanicus (vert)	1·70	95
1553	250f. Monorium minimum	2·30	1·10
1554	310f. Lasius niger	2·75	1·60

523 Wasamba

1998. Exhibits from National Museum. Multicoloured.

1555	50f. Type **523**	40	20

1556	150f. Receptacle	1·30	55
1557	250f. Seated figure (statuette)	2·10	1·10
1558	320f. Rattle	2·75	1·60

Nos. 1559/70 and Types **524/6** are left for possible issues not yet seen.

527 Baladji Cisse

1999. 75th Birth Anniv of Baladji Cisse (boxer). Multicoloured.
| 1571 | 150f. Type **527** | 1·50 | 1·50 |
| 1572 | 250f. Wearing suit and tie | 2·50 | 1·50 |

528 Cultivating Gardens

1999. Combating Poverty Campaign. Multicoloured.
1573	150f. Type **528**	85	35
1574	180f. Building work	1·00	40
1575	750f. Nutrition (vert)	4·25	1·60
1576	1000f. Clean drinking water	5·50	2·20

529 Teacher using Blackboard

1999. Teachers' Day. Multicoloured.
1577	150f. Type **529**	90	40
1578	250f. Teacher and older students	1·50	60
1579	370f. Woman teaching adults	2·20	90
1580	390f. Classroom, girl using blackboard (horiz)	2·40	1·10

530 Airplane, Ship and Train

1999. 125th Anniv of Universal Postal Union. Multicoloured.
1581	150f. Type **530**	2·00	80
1582	250f. Emblem and stylized figures holding envelopes	2·00	90
1583	310f. Emblem, eagles and antelope hair combs holding envelopes	2·50	1·00
1584	320f. Eagle holding envelope and emblem (vert)	2·75	1·10

531 Building Façade

1999. Sikasso Cathedral. Multicoloured.
| 1585 | 150f. Type **531** | 1·50 | 80 |
| 1586 | 150f. Stylized cathedral | 1·00 | 80 |

532 No Needle Symbol, Instructions and Doctor

2000. Combating Malaria Campaign. Multicoloured.
1587	150f. Type **532**	1·20	50
1588	150f. Two patients and no needle symbol	1·20	50
1589	150f. Child receiving interrectal infusion	1·20	50
1590	430f. Mother giving child Coprim syrup	3·25	1·80

533 Emblem and Map

2000. International Year of Volunteering
| 1591 | **533** | 250f. light green, chrome yellow and scarlet vermilion | 1·50 | 60 |

534 Sirigue (Dogon mask)

2001. Exhibits from National Museum. Multicoloured.
1596	75f. Type **534** (2004)	50	50
1597	195f. As Type **534** (2005)	1·00	1·00
1602	325f. As Type **534**	1·50	1·00

Numbers have been left for possible additions to this series.

535 Manantali Dam

2002. Regional Integration Organization for Flow from Senegal River
1606	30f. multicoloured (2004)	1·00	1·00
1607	100f. multicoloured (2003)	1·00	1·00
1608	5000f. multicoloured	25·00	15·00

Numbers have been left for possible additions to this series.

Nos. 1613/14 and Type **536** are left for AIDS issued on 10 January 2002, not yet received.
Nos. 1615/16 and Type **537** are left for African Cup issued on 19 January 2002, not yet received.

538 Songhoi Woman

2003. African Women. Multicoloured.
| 1617 | 50f. Type **538** | 50 | 30 |
| 1618 | 385f. Fula woman | 3·00 | 2·00 |

539 Musicians

2003. Balafon Festival.
| 1619 | **539** | 565f. multicoloured | 4·00 | 2·50 |

540 Tuareg

2005. Tourism. Multicoloured.
| 1620 | 10f. Type **540** | 50 | 40 |
| 1621 | 20f. Djenne Fair | 1·00 | 80 |

541 Emblem, Map and Water Droplet

2005. Water for Africa
| 1622 | **541** | 465f. multicoloured | 5·00 | 4·00 |

OFFICIAL STAMPS

O9 Dogon Mask

1961
O26	O9	1f. violet	10	10
O27	O9	2f. red	10	10
O28	O9	3f. slate	10	10
O29	O9	5f. turquoise	25	25
O30	O9	10f. brown	30	25
O31	O9	25f. blue	45	25
O32	O9	30f. red	60	25
O33	O9	50f. myrtle	1·00	40
O34	O9	85f. purple	1·60	80
O35	O9	100f. green	1·90	95
O36	O9	200f. purple	4·00	1·90

O30 Mali Flag and Emblems

1964. Centre and flag mult; frame colour given.
O90	O30	1f. green	10	10
O91	O30	2f. lavender	10	10
O92	O30	3f. slate	10	10
O93	O30	5f. purple	10	10
O94	O30	10f. blue	30	10
O95	O30	25f. ochre	30	10
O96	O30	30f. green	45	20
O97	O30	50f. orange	55	25
O98	O30	85f. brown	80	25
O99	O30	100f. red	1·00	40
O100	O30	200f. blue	2·10	55

O341 Arms of Gao

1981. Town Arms. Multicoloured.
O878	5f. Type O **341**	10	10
O879	15f. Tombouctou	20	10
O880	50f. Mopti	35	10
O881	180f. Segou	1·00	35
O882	200f. Sikasso	1·40	50
O883	680f. Koulikoro	3·25	1·30
O884	700f. Kayes	4·25	1·50
O885	1000f. Bamako	6·00	2·10

1984. Nos. O878/85 surch.
O1013	15f. on 5f. Type O **341**	10	10
O1014	50f. on 15f. Tombouctou	45	20
O1015	120f. on 50f. Mopti	1·00	30
O1016	295f. on 180f. Segou	2·75	85
O1017	470f. on 200f. Sikasso	4·00	1·30
O1018	515f. on 680f. Koulikoro	5·00	1·60
O1019	845f. on 700f. Kayes	7·50	2·75
O1020	1225f. on 1000f. Bamako	11·50	3·25

POSTAGE DUE STAMPS

D9 Bambara Mask

1961
D26	D9	1f. black	10	10
D27	D9	2f. blue	10	10
D28	D9	5f. mauve	30	10
D29	D9	10f. orange	45	25
D30	D9	20f. turquoise	75	30
D31	D9	25f. purple	95	45

D28 "Polyptychus roseus"

1964. Butterflies and Moths. Multicoloured.
D83	1f. Type D **28**	10	10
D84	1f. "Deilephila nerii"	10	10
D85	2f. "Bunaea alcinoe"	30	25
D86	2f. "Gynanisa maja"	30	25
D87	3f. "Teracolus eris"	30	25
D88	3f. "Colotis antevippe"	30	25
D89	5f. "Manatha microcera"	30	25
D90	5f. "Charaxes epijasius"	30	25
D91	10f. "Hypokopelates otraeda"	55	55
D92	10f. "Lipaphnaeus leonina"	55	55
D93	20f. "Lobobunaea christyi"	1·20	1·10
D94	20f. "Gonimbrasia hecate"	1·20	1·10
D95	25f. "Hypolimnas misippus"	1·40	1·40
D96	25f. "Catopsilia florella"	1·50	1·40

1984. Nos. D83/96 surch.
D1021	5f. on 1f. Type D **28**	10	10
D1022	5f. on 1f. "Deilephila nerii"	10	10
D1023	10f. on 2f. "Bunaea alcinoe"	10	10
D1024	10f. on 2f. "Gynanisa maja"	10	10
D1025	15f. on 3f. "Teracolus eris"	30	25
D1026	15f. on 3f. "Colotis antevippe"	30	25
D1027	25f. on 5f. "Manatha microcera"	30	25
D1028	25f. on 5f. "Charaxes epijasius"	30	25
D1029	50f. on 10f. "Hypokopelates otraeda"	50	50
D1030	50f. on 10f. "Lipaphnaeus leonina"	50	50
D1031	100f. on 20f. "Lobobunaea christyi"	1·00	1·00
D1032	100f. on 20f. "Gonimbrasia hecate"	1·00	1·00
D1033	125f. on 25f. "Hypolimnas misippus"	1·40	1·40
D1034	125f. on 25f. "Catopsilia florella"	1·50	1·50

APPENDIX

The following stamps have either been issued in excess of postal needs or have not been available to the public in reasonable quantities at face value. Such stamps may later be given full listing if there is evidence of regular postal use.

All on gold foil.

1994

World Cup Football Championship, U.S.A. Air. 3000f.
Film Stars. Air 3000f.

1996

Bridges. 100f.; 150f.; 180f.; 250f.
World Cup Football championship, France. 180f.; 250f.; 320f.; 1060f.
Winter Olympic Games, Nagano. 250f.; 310f.; 750f.; 900f.
70th Birth Anniv of Queen Elizabeth II. 370f.×3
Symbols of China. 180f.×3
ENDA. 250f.×2

1997

Scouting. 150f.; 180f.; 250f.; 310f.; 320f.; 460f.; 490f.; 530f.; 750f.; 900f.; 1060f.

1998

Transport. 180f.×3; 250f.×3; 320f.×3; 370f.×3; 460f.×3; 490f.×3; 530f.×3; 750f.×3
Chinese Ceramics. 500f.×2
Crested Porcupine. 250f.×4

2002

Tomb of Tutankamun. 3000f.×8

2003

Eagle. 3000f.
Yugi Gagarin Commemoration. 3000f.

2004

Personalities.300f.; 350f.; 400f.×2; 750f.×2; 1000f.×2

Pt. 1

MALTA

An island in the Mediterranean Sea, south of Italy. After a period of self-government under various Constitutions, independence was attained on 21 September 1964. The island became a republic on 13 December 1974.

1860. 12 pence = 1 shilling; 20 shillings = 1 pound.
1972. 10 mils = 1 cent; 100 cents = M£1.
2008. 100 cents = 1 euro.

1

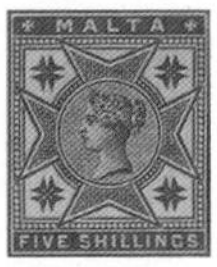
5

1860. Various frames.

18	**1**	½d. yellow	40·00	35·00
20	**1**	½d. green	4·25	50
22	-	1d. red	10·00	35
23	-	2d. grey	8·50	2·25
26	-	2½d. blue	50·00	1·00
27	-	4d. brown	11·00	3·00
28	-	1s. violet	48·00	12·00
30	**5**	5s. red	£110	80·00

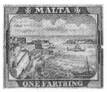

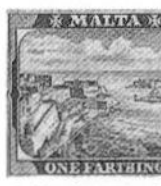
6 Harbour of Valletta

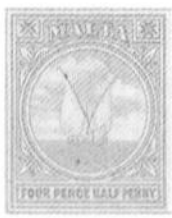
7 Gozo Fishing Boat

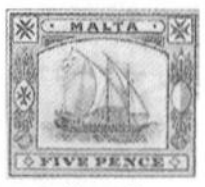
8 Galley of Knights of St. John

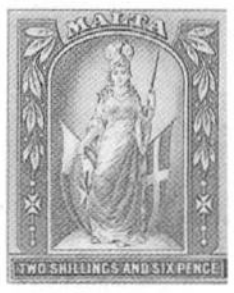
9 Emblematic Figure of Malta

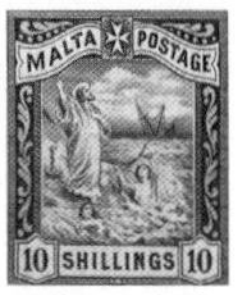
10 Shipwreck of St. Paul

1899

31a	**6**	¼d. brown	1·50	40
79	**6**	4d. black	15·00	7·00
32	**7**	4½d. brown	23·00	16·00
58	**7**	4½d. orange	4·75	4·00
59	**8**	5d. red	38·00	7·00
60	**8**	5d. green	4·25	3·75
34	**9**	2s.6d. olive	45·00	15·00
35	**10**	10s. black	£100	65·00

1902. No. 26 surch One Penny.

37	**10**	1d. on 2½d. blue	1·00	2·00

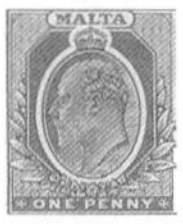
12

1903

47	**12**	½d. green	5·50	30
39	**12**	1d. black and red	15·00	40
49	**12**	1d. red	3·50	10
50	**12**	2d. purple and grey	13·00	3·25
51	**12**	2d. grey	4·50	5·50
52	**12**	2½d. purple and blue	32·00	60
53	**12**	2½d. blue	5·50	4·25
42	**12**	3d. grey and purple	2·00	50
54	**12**	4d. black and brown	11·00	8·00
55	**12**	4d. black and red on yellow	4·00	4·50
44	**12**	1s. grey and violet	27·00	7·00
62	**12**	1s. black on green	7·50	4·25
63	**12**	5s. green and red on yellow	65·00	75·00

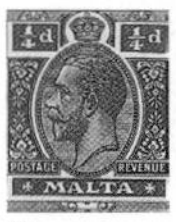
13

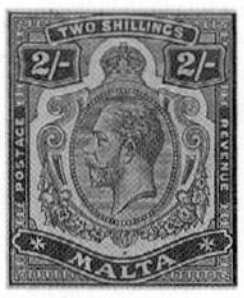
15

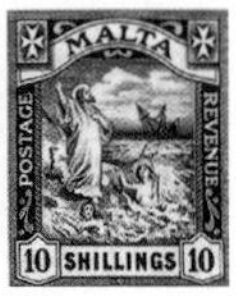
17

1914

69	**13**	¼d. brown	1·00	10
71	**13**	½d. green	2·50	30
73	**13**	1d. red	1·50	10
75	**13**	2d. grey	12·00	6·00
77	**13**	2½d. blue	2·25	50
78	**13**	3d. purple on yellow	2·50	17·00
80	**13**	6d. purple	11·00	21·00
81a	**13**	1s. black on green	12·00	23·00
86	**15**	2s. purple and blue on blue	50·00	38·00
88	**15**	5s. green and red on yellow	£100	£110
104	**17**	10s. black	£350	£800

1918. Optd WAR TAX.

92	**13**	½d. green	2·00	15
93	**12**	3d. grey and purple	2·00	12·00

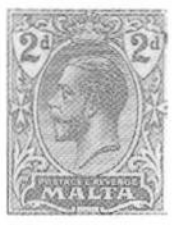
18

1921

100	**18**	2d. grey	8·00	1·75

1922. Optd SELF-GOVERNMENT.

114	**13**	¼d. brown	30	75
106	**13**	½d. green	1·25	3·00
116	**13**	1d. red	1·00	20
117	**18**	2d. grey	4·25	45
118	**13**	2½d. blue	1·10	1·75
108	**13**	3d. purple on yellow	4·50	27·00
109	**13**	6d. purple	4·50	24·00
110	**13**	1s. black on green	4·75	24·00
120	**15**	2s. purple and blue on blue	50·00	95·00
112	**9**	2s.6d. olive	32·00	55·00
113	**15**	5s. green and red on yellow	55·00	£100
105	**10**	10s. black	£225	£400
121	**17**	10s. black	£140	£250

1922. Surch One Farthing.

122	**18**	¼d. on 2d. grey	85	30

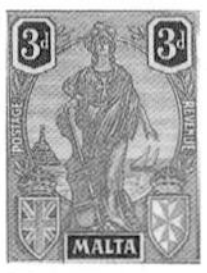
22

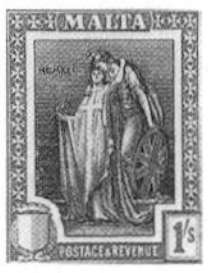
23

1922

123	**22**	¼d. brown	2·50	60
124	**22**	½d. green	2·50	15
125	**22**	1d. orange and purple	4·75	20
126	**22**	1d. violet	4·25	80
127	**22**	1½d. red	5·50	15
128	**22**	2d. brown and blue	3·25	1·25
129	**22**	2½d. blue	4·50	14·00
130	**22**	3d. blue	6·50	2·75
131	**22**	3d. black on yellow	4·25	21·00
132	**22**	4d. yellow and blue	3·00	4·50
133	**22**	6d. green and violet	5·00	4·00
134	**23**	1s. blue and brown	11·00	3·75
135	**23**	2s. brown and blue	14·00	19·00
136	**23**	2s.6d. purple and black	12·00	15·00
137	**23**	5s. orange and blue	21·00	50·00
138	**23**	10s. grey and brown	65·00	£160
140	**22**	£1 black and red	£110	£325

1925. Surch Two pence halfpenny.

142		2½d. on 3d. blue	1·75	5·00

1926. Optd POSTAGE.

143		¼d. brown	70	6·00
144		½d. green	70	15
145		1d. violet	1·00	25
146		1½d. red	1·25	60
147		2d. brown and blue	75	2·00
148		2½d. blue	1·25	1·00
149		3d. black on yellow	75	80
150		4d. yellow and blue	18·00	30·00
151		6d. green and violet	2·75	6·00
152	**23**	1s. blue and brown	5·50	19·00
153	**23**	2s. brown and blue	55·00	£150
154	**23**	2s.6d. purple and black	17·00	50·00
155	**23**	5s. orange and blue	10·00	50·00
156	**23**	10s. grey and brown	7·00	21·00

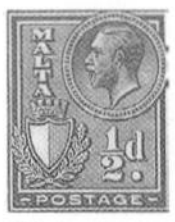
26

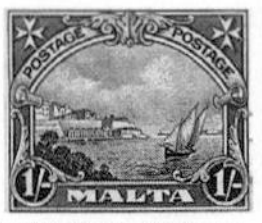
27 Valletta Harbour

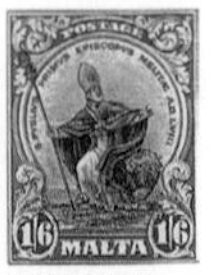
28 St. Publius

1926. Inscr "POSTAGE".

157	**26**	¼d. brown	80	15
158	**26**	½d. green	60	15
159	**26**	1d. red	3·00	1·00
160	**26**	1½d. brown	2·00	10
161	**26**	2d. grey	4·50	16·00
162	**26**	2½d. blue	4·00	1·50
162a	**26**	3d. violet	4·25	4·50
163	**26**	4d. black and red	3·50	17·00
164	**26**	4½d. violet and yellow	3·50	4·75
165	**26**	6d. violet and red	4·25	6·50
166	**27**	1s. black	6·50	9·00
167	**28**	1s.6d. black and green	8·00	19·00
168	-	2s. black and purple	8·00	24·00
169	-	2s.6d. black and red	20·00	55·00
170	-	3s. black and blue	20·00	38·00
171	-	5s. black and green	24·00	70·00
172	-	10s. black and red	65·00	£100

DESIGNS—As Type **27**: 2s. Mdina (Notabile); 5s. Neolithic temple, Mnajdra. As Type **28**: 2s.6d. Gozo boat; 3s. Neptune; 10s. St. Paul.

1928. Air. Optd AIR MAIL.

173	**26**	6d. violet and red	1·75	1·00

1928. Optd POSTAGE AND REVENUE.

174		¼d. brown	1·50	10
175		½d. green	1·50	10
176		1d. red	1·75	3·25
177		1d. brown	4·50	10
178		1½d. brown	2·00	85
179		1½d. red	4·25	10
180		2d. grey	4·25	9·00
181		2½d. blue	2·00	10
182		3d. violet	2·00	80
183		4d. black and red	2·00	1·75
184		4½d. violet and yellow	2·25	1·00
185		6d. violet and red	2·25	1·50
186	**27**	1s. black	5·50	2·50
187	**28**	1s.6d. black and green	12·00	9·50
188	-	2s. black and purple	27·00	70·00
189	-	2s.6d. black and red	17·00	21·00
190	-	3s. black and blue	22·00	24·00
191	-	5s. black and green	38·00	70·00
192	-	10s. black and red	70·00	£100

1930. As Nos. 157/72, but inscr "POSTAGE & REVENUE".

193	¼d. brown	60	10
194	½d. green	60	10
195	1d. brown	60	10
196	1½d. red	70	10
197	2d. grey	1·25	50
198	2½d. blue	2·00	10
199	3d. violet	1·50	20
200	4d. black and red	1·25	5·50
201	4½d. violet and yellow	3·25	1·25
202	6d. violet and red	2·75	1·50
203	1s. black	10·00	20·00
204	1s.6d. black and green	8·50	26·00
205	2s. black and purple	13·00	27·00
206	2s.6d. black and red	17·00	60·00
207	3s. black and blue	42·00	60·00
208	5s. black and green	50·00	75·00
209	10s. black and red	£100	£180

1935. Silver Jubilee. As Nos. 144/7 of Cyprus.

210	½d. black and green	50	70
211	2½d. brown and blue	2·50	4·50
212	6d. blue and olive	7·00	9·50
213	1s. grey and purple	18·00	26·00

1937. Coronation. As Nos. 148/50 of Cyprus.

214	½d. green	10	20
215	1½d. red	1·50	65
216	2½d. blue	1·50	80

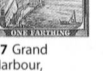

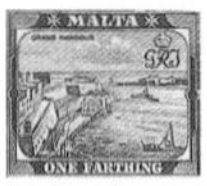
37 Grand Harbour, Valletta

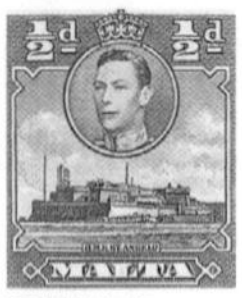
38 H.M.S. *St. Angelo*

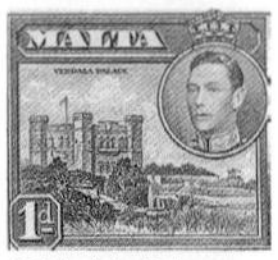
39 Verdala Palace

1938. Various designs with medallion King George VI.

217	**37**	¼d. brown	10	10
218	**38**	½d. green	4·25	30
218a	**38**	½d. brown	55	30
219	**39**	1d. brown	6·50	40
219a	**39**	1d. green	60	10
220	-	1½d. red	3·00	30
220b	-	1½d. black	30	15
221	-	2d. black	3·00	2·00
221b	-	2d. red	40	30
222	-	2½d. blue	6·50	60
222a	-	2½d. violet	60	10
223	-	3d. violet	3·50	80
223a	-	3d. blue	30	20
224	-	4½d. olive and brown	50	30
225	-	6d. olive and red	2·75	30
226	-	1s. black	2·50	30
227	-	1s.6d. black and olive	8·50	4·00
228	-	2s. green and blue	4·50	7·50
229	-	2s.6d. black and red	9·00	6·00
230	-	5s. black and green	4·75	9·00
231	-	10s. black and red	19·00	18·00

DESIGNS—As Types **38/9**. VERT: 1½d. Hypogeum, Hal Saflieni; 3d. St. John's Co-Cathedral; 6d. Statue of Manoel de Vilhena; 1s. Maltese girl wearing faldetta; 5s. Palace Square, Valletta; 10s. St. Paul. HORIZ: 2d. Victoria and Citadel, Gozo; 2½d. De l'Isle Adam entering Mdina; 4½d. Ruins at Mnajdra; 1s.6d. St. Publius; 2s. Mdina Cathedral; 2s.6d. Statue of Neptune.

1946. Victory. As Nos. 164/5 of Cyprus.

232	1d. green	15	10
233	3d. blue	50	2·00

1948. Self-government. As 1938 issue optd SELF-GOVERNMENT 1947.

234	¼d. brown	30	20
235	½d. brown	30	10
236	1d. green	30	10
236a	1d. grey	75	10
237	1½d. black	1·25	10
237b	1½d. green	30	10
238	2d. red	1·25	10
238c	2d. yellow	30	10
239	2½d. violet	80	10
239a	2½d. red	75	1·50
240	3d. blue	3·00	15
240a	3d. violet	50	15
241	4½d. olive and brown	2·75	1·50
241a	4½d. olive and blue	50	90
242	6d. olive and red	3·25	15
243	1s. black	3·75	40
244	1s.6d. black and olive	2·50	50
245	2s. green and blue	5·00	2·50
246	2s.6d. black and red	12·00	2·50
247	5s. black and green	30·00	3·50
248	10s. black and red	30·00	24·00

1949. Silver Wedding. As 34a of Cyprus.

249	1d. green	50	10
250	£1 blue	38·00	48·00

1949. U.P.U. As 38d/g of Cyprus.

251	2½d. violet	30	10
252	3d. blue	3·00	1·00
253	6d. red	60	1·00
254	1s. black	60	2·50

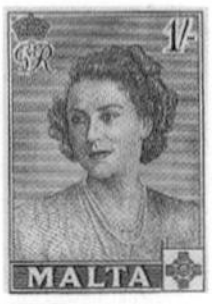
53 Queen Elizabeth II when Princess

1950. Visit of Princess Elizabeth.

255	**53**	1d. green	10	15
256	**53**	3d. blue	20	20
257	**53**	1s. black	80	2·25

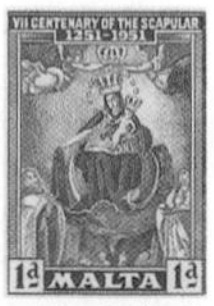
54 "Our Lady of Mount Carmel" (attrib Palladino)

1951. Seventh Centenary of the Scapular.

258	**54**	1d. green	20	30
259	**54**	3d. violet	50	10
260	**54**	1s. black	1·75	1·60

1953. Coronation. As **38h** of Cyprus.

261	1½d. black and green	70	10

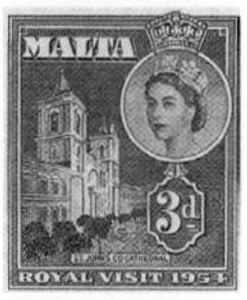
55 St. John's Co-Cathedral

1954. Royal Visit.

262	**55**	3d. violet	45	10

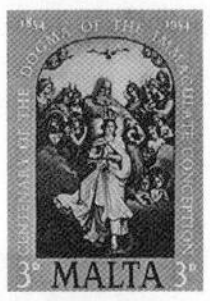

56 "Immaculate Conception" (Caruana) (altar-piece, Cospicua)

1954. Centenary of Dogma of the Immaculate Conception.

263	**56**	1½d. green	15	10
264	**56**	3d. blue	15	10
265	**56**	1s. grey	35	20

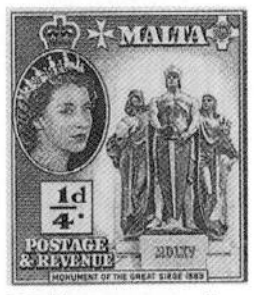

57 Monument of the Great Siege, 1565

1956

266	**57**	¼d. violet	20	10
267	-	½d. orange	50	10
314	-	1d. black	50	30
269	-	1½d. green	30	10
270	-	2d. sepia	2·25	10
271	-	2½d. brown	2·25	30
272	-	3d. red	1·50	10
273	-	4½d. blue	2·50	1·00
274	-	6d. indigo	75	10
275	-	8d. ochre	4·50	1·00
276	-	1s. violet	1·75	10
277	-	1s.6d. turquoise	15·00	35
278	-	2s. olive	13·00	4·50
279	-	2s.6d. brown	11·00	2·50
280	-	5s. green	17·00	3·25
281	-	10s. red	38·00	16·00
282	-	£1 brown	38·00	35·00

DESIGNS—VERT: ½d. Wignacourt aqueduct horsetrough; 1d. Victory church; 1½d. Second World War memorial; 2d. Mosta Church; 3d. The King's Scroll; 4½d. Roosevelt's Scroll; 8d. Vedette (tower); 1s. Mdina Gate; 1s.6d. "Les Gavroches" (statue); 2s. Monument of Christ the King; 2s.6d. Monument of Grand Master Cottoner; 5s. Grand Master Perellos's monument; 10s. St. Paul (statue); £1 Baptism of Christ (statue). HORIZ: 2½d. Auberge de Castile; 6d. Neolithic Temples at Tarxien.

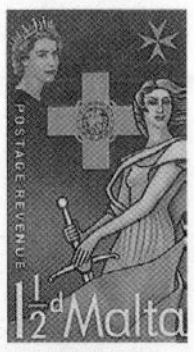

74 "Defence of Malta"

1957. George Cross Commem. Cross in Silver.

283	**74**	1½d. green	15	10
284	-	3d. red	15	10
285	-	1s. brown	15	10

DESIGNS—HORIZ: 3d. Searchlights over Malta. VERT: 1s. Bombed buildings.

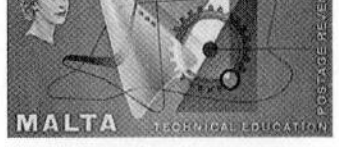

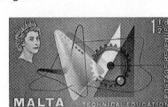

77 "Design"

1958. Technical Education in Malta. Inscr "TECHNICAL EDUCATION".

286	**77**	1½d. black and green	15	10
287	-	3d. black, red and grey	15	10
288	-	1s. grey, purple and black	25	10

DESIGNS—VERT: 3d. "Construction". HORIZ: 1s. Technical School, Paola.

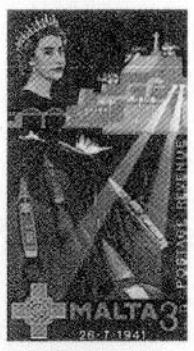

81 Sea Raid on Grand Harbour, Valletta

1958. George Cross Commem. Cross in first colour outlined in silver.

289		1½d. green and black	20	10
290	**81**	3d. red and black	20	10
291	-	1s. mauve and black	35	10

DESIGNS—HORIZ: 1½d. Bombed-out family; 1s. Searchlight crew.

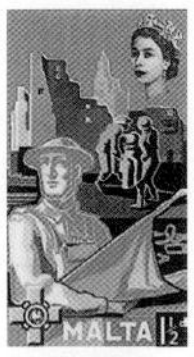

83 Air Raid Casualties

1959. George Cross Commemoration.

292	**83**	1½d. green, black and gold	30	10
293	-	3d. mauve, black and gold	30	10
294	-	1s. grey, black and gold	1·40	1·50

DESIGNS—HORIZ: 3d. "For Gallantry". VERT: 1s. Maltese under bombardment.

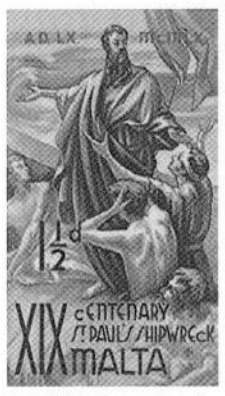

86 Shipwreck of St. Paul (after Palombi)

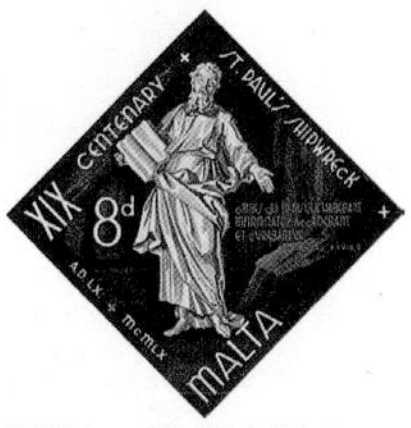

87 Statue of St. Paul, Rabat, Malta

1960. 19th Centenary of the Shipwreck of St. Paul. Inscr as in T **86/7**.

295	**86**	1½d. blue, gold and brown	15	10
296	-	3d. purple, gold and blue	15	10
297	-	6d. red, gold and grey	25	10
298	**87**	8d. black and gold	40	60
299	-	1s. purple and gold	30	10
300	-	2s.6d. blue, green and gold	1·25	2·50

DESIGNS—As Type **88**: 3d. Consecration of St. Publius, First Bishop of Malta; 6d. Departure of St. Paul (after Palombi). As Type **87**: 1s. Angel with the "Acts of the Apostles"; 2s.6d. St. Paul with the "Second Epistle to the Corinthians".

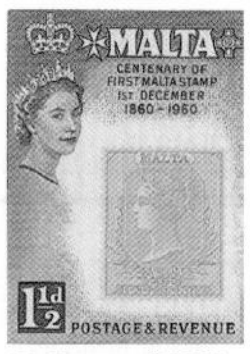

92 Stamp of 1860

1960. Centenary of Malta Stamps. Stamp in buff and blue.

301	**92**	1½d. green	25	10
302	**92**	3d. red	30	10
303	**92**	6d. blue	80	1·00

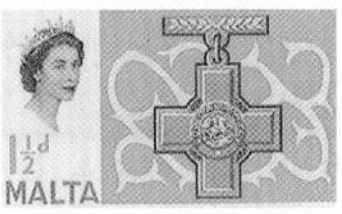

93 George Cross

1961. George Cross Commemoration.

304	**93**	1½d. black, cream and bistre	30	10
305	-	3d. brown and blue	30	10
306	-	1s. green, lilac and violet	1·40	2·25

DESIGNS: 3d. and 1s. show George Cross as Type **93** over backgrounds with different patterns.

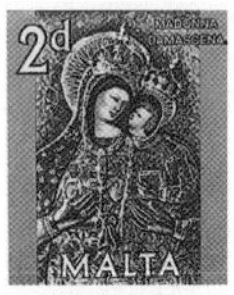

96 "Madonna Damascena"

1962. Great Siege Commemoration.

307	**96**	2d. blue	10	10
308	-	3d. red	10	10
309	-	6d. bronze	30	10
310	-	1s. purple	30	40

DESIGNS: 3d. Great Siege Monument; 6d. Grand Master La Valette; 1s. Assault on Fort St. Elmo.

1963. Freedom from Hunger. As T **41** of Gibraltar.

311		1s.6d. sepia	1·75	2·50

1963. Cent of Red Cross. As T **42** of Gibraltar.

312		2d. red on black	25	15
313		1s.6d. red and blue	1·75	4·50

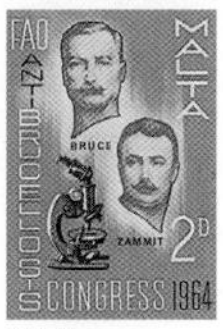

100 Bruce, Zammit and Microscope

1964. Anti-brucellosis Congress.

316	**100**	2d. brown, black and green	10	10
317	-	1s.6d. black and purple	90	1·25

DESIGN: 1s.6d. Goat and laboratory equipment.

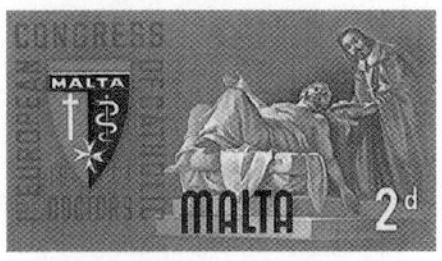

102 "Nicola Cotoner tending Sick Man" (M. Preti)

1964. First European Catholic Doctors' Congress, Valletta. Multicoloured.

318		2d. Type **102**	20	10
319		6d. St. Luke and hospital	50	15
320		1s.6d. Sacra Infermeria, Valletta	1·10	1·90

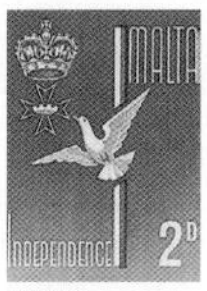

106 Dove and British Crown

1964. Independence.

321	**106**	2d. olive, red and gold	30	10
322	-	3d. brown, red and gold	30	10
323	-	6d. slate, red and gold	70	15
324	**106**	1s. blue, red and gold	70	15
325	-	1s.6d. blue, red and gold	1·50	1·00
326	-	2s.6d. blue, red and gold	1·75	3·00

DESIGNS: 3d., 1s.6d. Dove and Pope's tiara; 6d., 2s.6d. Dove and U.N. emblem.

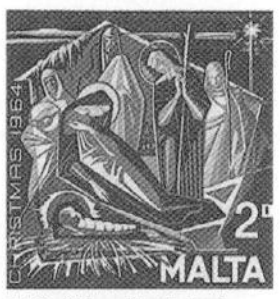

109 "The Nativity"

1964. Christmas.

327	**109**	2d. purple and gold	10	10
328	**109**	4d. blue and gold	20	15
329	**109**	8d. green and gold	45	45

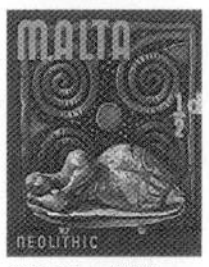

110 Neolithic Era

1965. Multicoloured.

330		½d. Type **110**	10	10
331		1d. Punic era (vert)	10	10
332		1½d. Roman era (vert)	30	10
333		2d. Proto Christian era (vert)	10	10
334		2½d. Saracenic era (vert)	1·50	10
335		3d. Siculo Norman era (vert)	10	10
336		4d. Knights of Malta (vert)	1·50	10
337		4½d. Maltese Navy (vert)	1·50	75
337b		5d. Fortifications (vert)	30	20
338		6d. French occupation (vert)	30	10
339		8d. British rule	70	10
339c		10d. Naval Arsenal	50	1·90
340		1s. Maltese Corps of the British Army	30	10
341		1s.3d. International Eucharistic Congress, 1913	2·00	1·40
342		1s.6d. Self-government, 1921	60	20
343		2s. Gozo Civic Council	70	10
344		2s.6d. State of Malta	70	50
345		3s. Independence, 1964	1·75	75
346		5s. HAFMED (Allied Forces, Mediterranean)	6·00	1·00
347		10s. The Maltese Islands (map)	3·00	5·00
348		£1 Patron Saints	4·25	5·50

Nos. 339/48 are larger, 41×29 mm from perf to perf, and include portrait of Queen Elizabeth II.

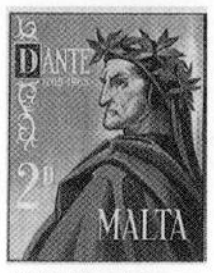

129 "Dante" (Raphael)

1965. 700th Birth Anniv of Dante.

349	**129**	2d. blue	10	10
350	**129**	6d. green	25	10
351	**129**	2s. brown	1·10	1·50

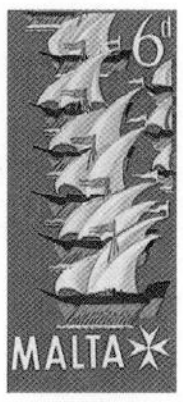

131 Turkish Fleet

1965. 400th Anniv of Great Siege. Multicoloured.

352		2d. Turkish camp	30	10
353		3d. Battle scene	30	10
354		6d. Type **131**	40	10
355		8d. Arrival of relief force	80	90
356		1s. Grand Master J. de La Valette's arms	40	10
357		1s.6d. "Allegory of Victory" (from mural by M. Preti)	80	30
358		2s.6d. Victory medal	1·50	3·25

SIZES—As Type **131**: 1s. SQUARE (32½×32½ mm): others.

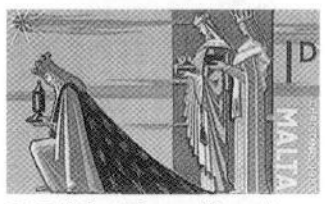

137 "The Three Kings"

1965. Christmas.

359	**137**	1d. purple and red	10	10
360	**137**	4d. purple and blue	30	30
361	**137**	1s.3d. slate and purple	30	30

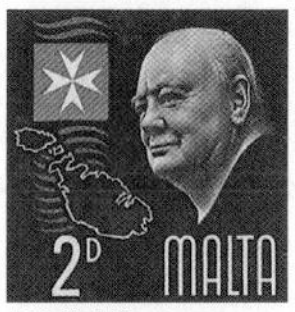

138 Sir Winston Churchill

1966. Churchill Commemoration.

362	**138**	2d. black, red and gold	25	10
363	-	3d. green, olive and gold	25	10
364	**138**	1s. purple, red and gold	40	10
365	-	1s.6d. blue, ultram & gold	50	1·10

DESIGN : 3d., 1s.6d. Sir Winston Churchill and George Cross.

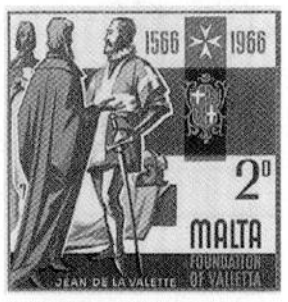

140 Grand Master La Valette

1966. 400th Anniv of Valletta. Multicoloured.

366		2d. Type **140**	10	10
367		3d. Pope Pius V	15	10
368		6d. Map of Valletta	20	10
369		1s. F. Laparelli (architect)	25	10
370		2s.6d. G. Cassar (architect)	75	60

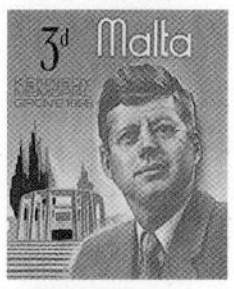

145 President Kennedy and Memorial

1966. Pres. Kennedy Commemoration.

371	**145**	3d. olive, gold and black	10	10
372	**145**	1s.6d. blue, gold and black	10	10

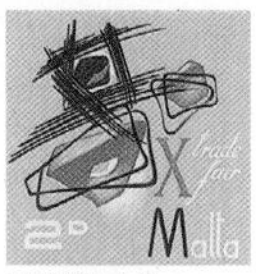

146 "Trade"

1966. Tenth Malta Trade Fair.

373	**146**	2d. multicoloured	10	10
374	**146**	8d. multicoloured	30	95
375	**146**	2s.6d. multicoloured	30	1·00

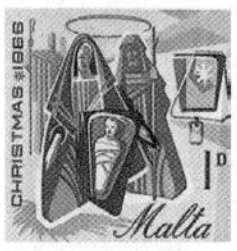

147 "The Child in the Manger"

1966. Christmas.

376	**147**	1d. multicoloured	10	10
377	**147**	4d. multicoloured	10	10
378	**147**	1s.3d. multicoloured	10	10

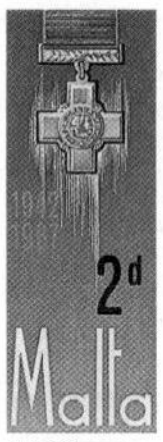

148 George Cross

1967. 25th Anniv of George Cross Award to Malta.

379	**148**	2d. multicoloured	10	10
380	**148**	4d. multicoloured	10	10
381	**148**	3s. multicoloured	15	20

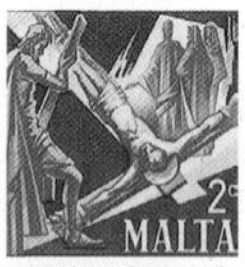

149 Crucifixion of St. Peter

1967. 1900th Anniv of Martyrdom of Saints Peter and Paul.

382	**149**	2d. brown, orange & black	10	10
383	-	8d. olive, gold and black	15	10
384	-	3s. blue and black	20	20

DESIGNS—As Type **149**: 3s. Beheading of St. Paul. HORIZ (47×25 mm): 8d. Open Bible and episcopal emblems.

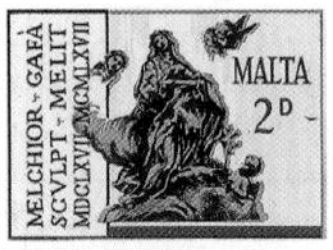

152 "St. Catherine of Siena"

1967. 300th Death Anniv of Melchior Gafa (sculptor). Multicoloured.

385	2d. Type **152**	10	10
386	4d. "St. Thomas of Villanova"	10	10
387	1s.6d. "Baptism of Christ" (detail)	25	10
388	2s.6d. "St. John the Baptist" (from "Baptism of Christ")	30	20

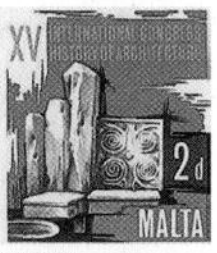

156 Temple Ruins, Tarxien

1967. 15th International Historical Architecture Congress, Valletta. Multicoloured.

389	2d. Type **156**	10	10
390	6d. Facade of Palazzo Falzon, Notabile	10	10
391	1s. Parish Church, Birkirkara	10	10
392	3s. Portal, Auberge de Castille	25	25

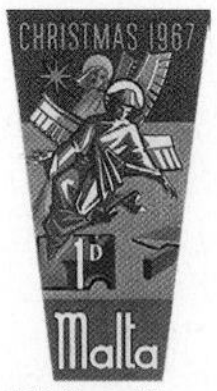

160 "Angels"

1967. Christmas. Multicoloured.

393	1d. Type **160**	10	10
394	8d. "Crib"	20	10
395	1s.4d. "Angels"	20	10

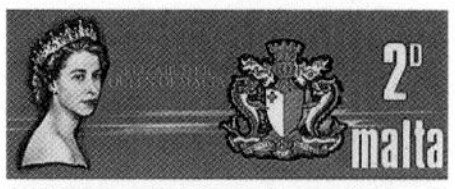

163 Queen Elizabeth II and Arms of Malta

1967. Royal Visit.

396	**163**	2d. multicoloured	10	10
397	-	4d. black, purple and gold	10	10
398	-	3s. multicoloured	20	30

DESIGNS—VERT: 4d. Queen in Robes of Order of St. Michael and St. George. HORIZ: 3s. Queen and outline of Malta.

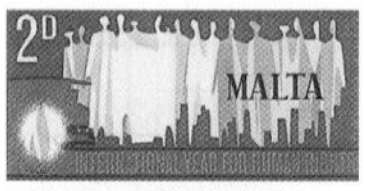

166 Human Rights Emblem and People

1968. Human Rights Year. Multicoloured.

399	2d. Type **166**	10	10
400	6d. Human Rights emblem and people (different)	10	10
401	2s. Type **166** (reversed)	10	15

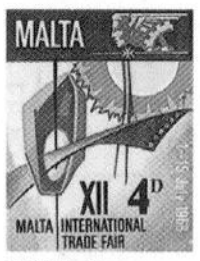

169 Fair "Products"

1968. Malta International Trade Fair.

402	**169**	4d. multicoloured	10	10
403	**169**	8d. multicoloured	10	10
404	**169**	3s. multicoloured	15	15

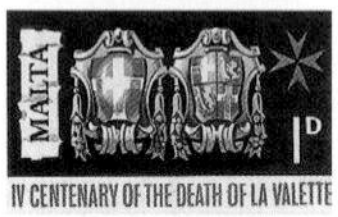

170 Arms of the Order of St. John and La Valette

1968. Fourth Death Cent of Grand Master La Valette. Multicoloured.

405	1d. Type **170**	10	10
406	8d. "La Valette" (A. de Favray) (vert)	15	10
407	1s.6d. La Valette's tomb (28×23 mm)	15	10
408	2s.6d. Angels and scroll bearing date of death (vert)	20	25

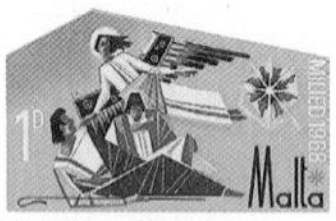

174 Star of Bethlehem and Angel waking Shepherds

1968. Christmas. Multicoloured.

409	1d. Type **174**	10	10
410	8d. Mary and Joseph with shepherd watching over Cradle	15	10
411	1s.4d. Three Wise Men and Star of Bethlehem	15	20

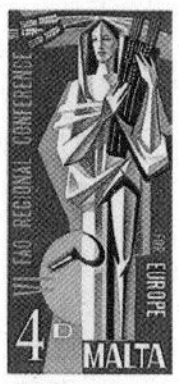

177 "Agriculture"

1968. Sixth Food and Agricultural Organization Regional Conference for Europe. Multicoloured.

412	4d. Type **177**	10	10
413	1s. F.A.O. emblem and coin	10	10
414	2s.6d. "Agriculture" sowing Seeds	10	15

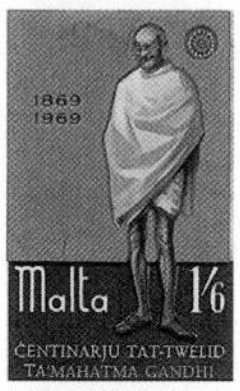

180 Mahatma Gandhi

1969. Birth Centenary of Mahatma Gandhi.

415	**180**	1s.6d. brown, black & gold	50	10

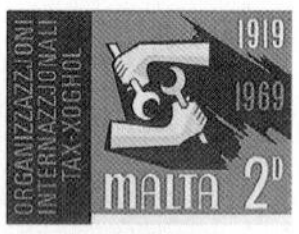

181 ILO Emblem

1969. 50th Anniv of Int Labour Organization.

416	**181**	2d. blue, gold & turquoise	10	10
417	**181**	6d. sepia, gold and brown	10	10

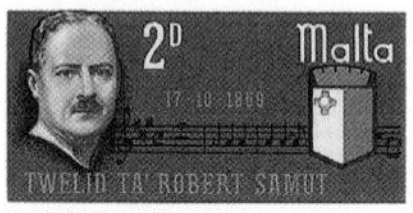

182 Robert Samut

1969. Birth Centenary of Robert Samut (composer of Maltese National Anthem).

418	**182**	2d. multicoloured	10	10

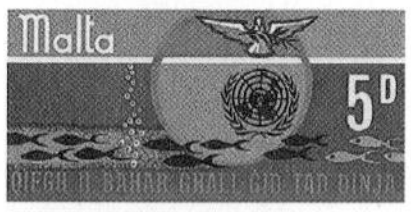

183 Dove of Peace, U.N. Emblem and Sea-bed

1969. United Nations Resolution on Oceanic Resources.

419	**183**	5d. multicoloured	10	10

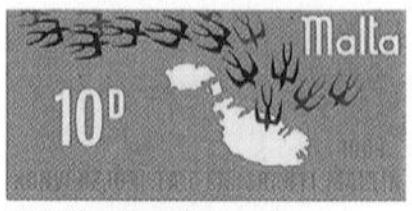

184 "Swallows" returning to Malta

1969. Maltese Migrants' Convention.

420	**184**	10d. black, gold and olive	10	10

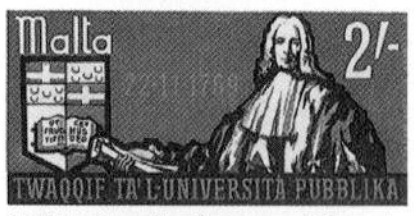

185 University Arms and Grand Master de Fonseca (founder)

1969. Bicentenary of University of Malta.

421	**185**	2s. multicoloured	15	20

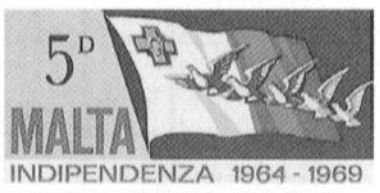

187 Flag of Malta and Birds

1969. Fifth Anniv of Independence.

422	-	2d. multicoloured	10	10
423	**187**	5d. black, red and gold	10	10
424	-	10d. black, blue and gold	10	10
425	-	1s.6d. multicoloured	20	40
426	-	2s.6d. black, brown & gold	25	50

DESIGNS—SQUARE (31×31 mm): 2d. 1919 War Monument. VERT: 10d. "Tourism"; 1s.6d. U.N. and Council of Europe emblems; 2s.6d. "Trade and Industry".

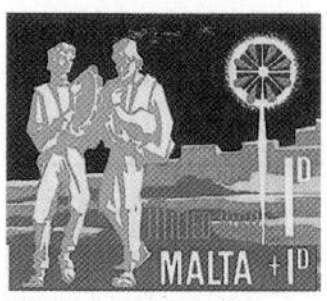

191 Peasants playing Tambourine and Bagpipes

1969. Christmas. Children's Welfare Fund. Multicoloured.

427	1d.+1d. Type **191**	10	20
428	5d.+1d. Angels playing trumpet and harp	15	20
429	1s.6d.+3d. Choir boys singing	15	45

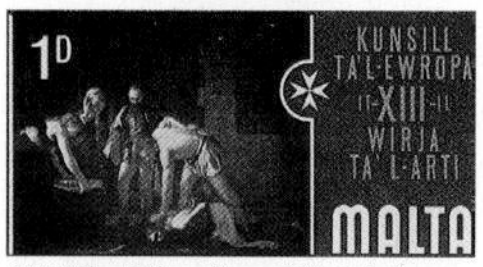

194 "The Beheading of St. John" (Caravaggio)

1970. 13th Council of Europe Art Exn. Multicoloured.

430	1d. Type **194**	10	10
431	2d. "St. John the Baptist" (M. Preti)	10	10
432	5d. Interior of St. John's Co-Cathedral, Valletta	10	10
433	6d. "Allegory of the Order" (Neapolitan school)	15	10
434	8d. "St. Jerome" (Caravaggio)	15	50
435	10d. Articles from the Order of St. John in Malta	15	10
436	1s.6d. "The Blessed Gerard receiving Godfrey de Bouillon" (A. de Favray)	25	40
437	2s. Cape and Stolone (16th cent)	25	55

SIZES—HORIZ: 1d., 8d. 56×30 mm; 2d., 6d. 45×32 mm; 10d., 2s. 63×21 mm; 1s.6d. 45×34 mm. SQUARE: 5d. 39×39 mm.

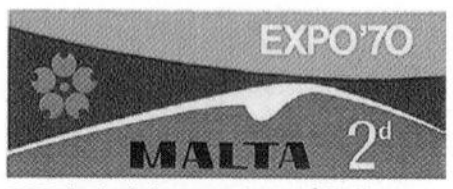

202 Artist's Impression of Fujiyama

1970. World Fair, Osaka.

438	**202**	2d. multicoloured	10	10
439	**202**	5d. multicoloured	10	10
440	**202**	3s. multicoloured	15	15

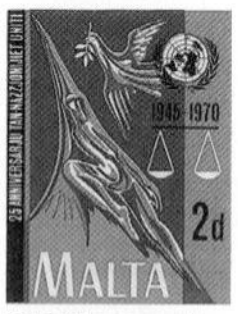

203 "Peace and Justice"

1970. 25th Anniv of United Nations.

441	**203**	2d. multicoloured	10	10
442	**203**	5d. multicoloured	10	10
443	**203**	2s.6d. multicoloured	15	15

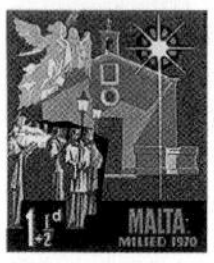

204 Carol-singers, Church and Star

1970. Christmas. Multicoloured.

444	1d.+½d. Type **204**	10	10
445	10d.+2d. Church, star and angels with Infant	15	20
446	1s.6d.+3d. Church, star and nativity scene	20	40

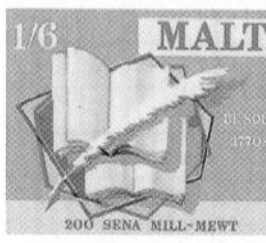

207 Books and Quill

1971. Literary Anniversaries. Multicoloured.

447	1s.6d. Type **207** (De Soldanis (historian) death bicent)	10	10
448	2s. Dun Karm (poet), books, pens and lamp (birth cent)	10	15

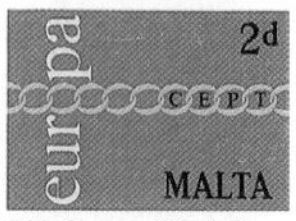

209 Europa "Chain"

1971. Europa.

449	**209**	2d. orange, black and olive	10	10
450	**209**	5d. orange, black and red	10	10
451	**209**	1s.6d. orange, blk & slate	60	90

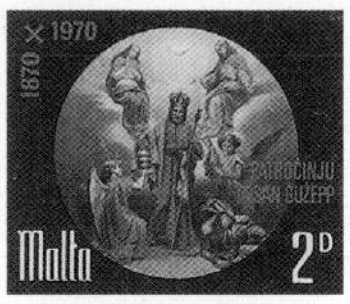

210 "St. Joseph, Patron of the Universal Church" (G. Calì)

1971. Centenary of Proclamation of St. Joseph as Patron Saint of Catholic Church, and 50th Anniv of Coronation of the Statue of "Our Lady of Victories". Multicoloured.

452	2d. Type **210**	10	10
453	5d. Statue of "Our Lady of Victories" and galley	10	10
454	10d. Type **210**	15	10
455	1s.6d. As 5d.	30	40

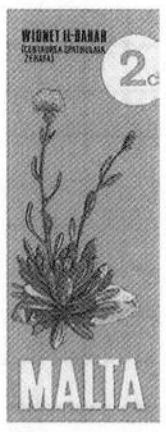

211 "Centaurea spathulata"

1971. National Plant and Bird of Malta. Multicoloured.

456	2d. Type **211**	10	10
457	5d. Blue rock thrush (horiz)	20	10
458	10d. As 5d.	30	15
459	1s.6d. Type **211**	30	1·25

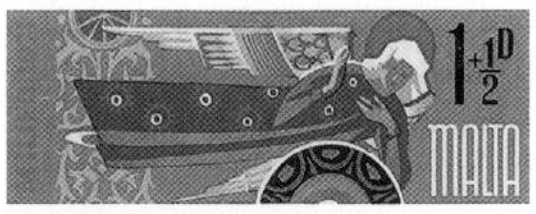

212 Angel

1971. Christmas. Multicoloured.

460	1d.+½d. Type **212**	10	10
461	10d.+2d. Mary and the Child Jesus	15	25
462	1s.6d.+3d. Joseph lying awake	20	40
MS463	131×113 mm. Nos. 460/2	75	2·50

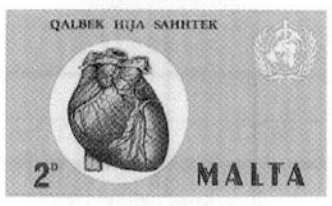

213 Heart and W.H.O. Emblem

1972. World Health Day.

464	**213**	2d. multicoloured	10	10
465	**213**	10d. multicoloured	15	10
466	**213**	2s.6d. multicoloured	40	80

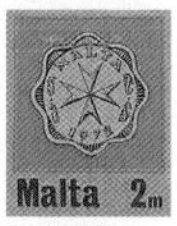

214 Maltese Cross

1972. Decimal Currency. Coins. Multicoloured.

467	2m. Type **214**	10	10
468	3m. Bee on honeycomb	10	10
469	5m. Earthen lampstand	10	10
470	1c. George Cross	10	10
471	2c. Classical head	10	10
472	5c. Ritual altar	10	10
473	10c. Grandmaster's galley	20	10
474	50c. Great Siege Monument	1·25	1·25

SIZES: 3m., 2c. As Type **214**: 5m., 1c., 5c. 25×30 mm; 10c., 50c. 31×38 mm.

1972. Nos. 337a, 339 and 341 surch.

475	1c.3 on 5d. multicoloured	10	10
476	3c. on 8d. multicoloured	15	10
477	5c. on 1s.3d. multicoloured	15	20

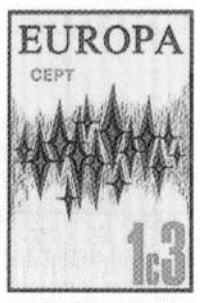

216 "Communications"

1972. Europa.

478	**216**	1c.3 multicoloured	10	10
479	**216**	3c. multicoloured	10	10
480	**216**	5c. multicoloured	15	35
481	**216**	7c.5 multicoloured	20	75

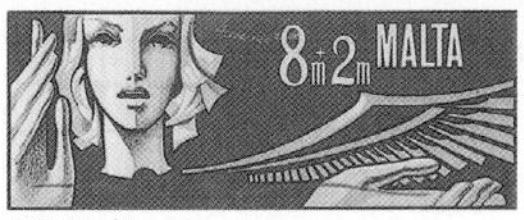

217 Angel

1972. Christmas.

482	**217**	8m.+2m. brown, grey and gold	10	10
483	-	3c.+1c. purple, violet and gold	15	40
484	-	7c.5+1c.5 indigo, blue and gold	20	50
MS485		137×113 mm. Nos. 482/4	1·75	4·25

DESIGNS: No. 483, Angel with tambourine; No. 484, Singing angel.

See also Nos. 507/9.

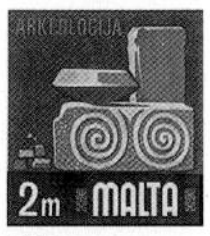

218 Archaeology

1973. Multicoloured.

486	2m. Type **218**	10	10
487	4m. History	10	10
488	5m. Folklore	10	10
489	8m. Industry	10	10
490	1c. Fishing industry	10	10
491	1c.3 Pottery	10	10
492	2c. Agriculture	10	10
493	3c. Sport	10	10
494	4c. Yacht marina	15	10
495	5c. Fiesta	15	10
496	7c.5 Regatta	25	10
497	10c. Voluntary service	25	10
498	50c. Education	2·00	50
499	£1 Religion	2·75	2·00
500	£2 Coat of arms (32×27 mm)	14·00	19·00
500b	£2 National Emblem (32×27 mm)	9·00	14·00

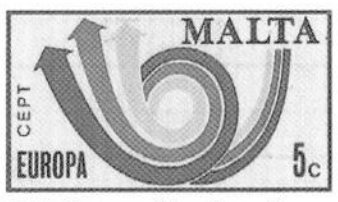

219 Europa "Posthorn"

1973. Europa.

501	**219**	3c. multicoloured	15	10
502	**219**	5c. multicoloured	15	35
503	**219**	7c.5 multicoloured	25	65

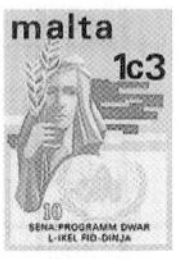

220 Emblem, and Woman holding Corn

1973. Anniversaries.

504	**220**	1c.3 multicoloured	10	10
505	-	7c.5 multicoloured	25	40
506	-	10c. multicoloured	30	50

ANNIVERSARIES: 1c.3, 10th anniv of World Food Programme; 7c.5, 25th anniv of W.H.O.; 10c. 25th anniv of Universal Declaration of Human Rights.

1973. Christmas. As T **217**. Multicoloured.

507	8m.+2m. Angels and organ pipes	15	10
508	3c.+1c. Madonna and Child	25	60
509	7c.5+1c.5 Buildings and Star	45	1·50
MS510	137×112 mm. Nos. 507/9	4·75	7·50

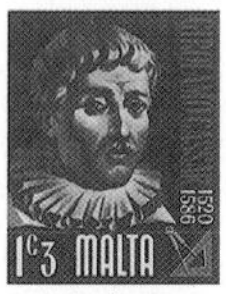

221 Girolamo Cassar (architect)

1974. Prominent Maltese.

511	**221**	1c.3 deep green, green and gold	10	10
512	-	3c. green, blue and gold	15	10
513	-	5c. brown, green and gold	20	15
514	-	7c.5 blue, lt blue & gold	20	30
515	-	10c. deep purple, purple and gold	20	40

DESIGNS: 3c. Giuseppe Barth (ophthalmologist); 5c. Nicolo' Isouard (composer); 7c.5, John Borg (botanist); 10c. Antonio Sciortino (sculptor).

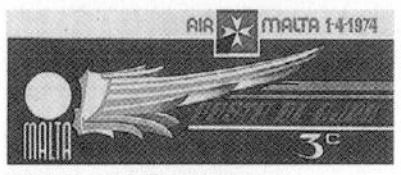

222 "Air Malta" Emblem

1974. Air. Multicoloured.

516	3c. Type **222**	15	10
517	4c. Boeing 720B	15	10
518	5c. Type **222**	15	10
519	7c.5 As 4c.	20	10
520	20c. Type **222**	35	60
521	25c. As 4c.	35	60
522	35c. Type **222**	45	1·40

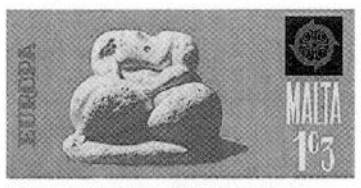

223 Prehistoric Sculpture

1974. Europa.

523	**223**	1c.3 blue, black and gold	15	10
524	-	3c. brown, black and gold	20	15
525	-	5c. purple, black and gold	25	50
526	-	7c.5 green, black and gold	35	1·00

DESIGNS—VERT: 3c. Old Cathedral Door, Mdina; 7c.5, "Vetlina" (sculpture by A. Sciortino). HORIZ: 5c. Silver monstrance.

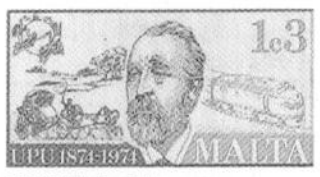

224 Heinrich von Stephan (founder) and Land Transport

1974. Centenary of U.P.U.

527	**224**	1c.3 green, blue & orange	30	10
528	-	5c. brown, red and green	30	10
529	-	7c.5 blue, violet and green	35	20
530	-	50c. purple, red and orange	1·00	1·25
MS531		126×91 mm. Nos. 527/30	4·75	7·50

DESIGNS (each containing portrait as Type **224**): 5c. "Washington" (paddle-steamer) and "Royal Viking Star" (liner); 7c.5, Balloon and Boeing 747-100; 50c. U.P.U. Buildings, 1874 and 1974.

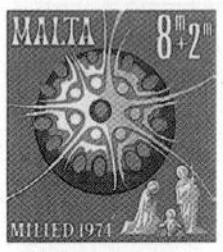

225 Decorative Star and Nativity Scene

1974. Christmas. Multicoloured.

532	8m.+2m. Type **225**	10	10
533	3c.+1c. "Shepherds"	15	20
534	5c.+1c. "Shepherds with gifts"	20	35
535	7c.5+1c.5 "The Magi"	30	45

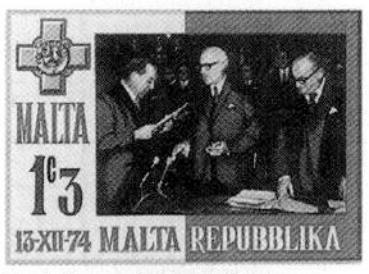

226 Swearing-in of Prime Minister

1975. Inauguration of Republic.

536	**226**	1c.3 multicoloured	10	10
537	-	5c. red and black	20	10
538	-	25c. multicoloured	60	1·00

DESIGNS: 5c. National flag; 25c. Minister of Justice, President and Prime Minister.

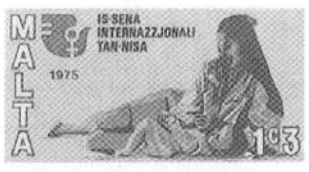

227 Mother and Child ("Family Life")

1975. International Women's Year.

539	**227**	1c.3 violet and gold	15	10
540	-	3c. blue and gold	15	10
541	**227**	5c. brown and gold	25	15
542	-	20c. brown and gold	80	2·50

DESIGN: 3c., 20c. Office secretary ("Public Life").

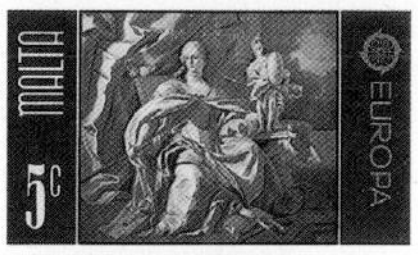

228 "Allegory of Malta" (Francesco de Mura)

1975. Europa. Multicoloured.

543	5c. Type **228**	30	10
544	15c. "Judith and Holofernes" (Valentin de Boulogne)	50	75

The 15c. is smaller, 47×23 mm.

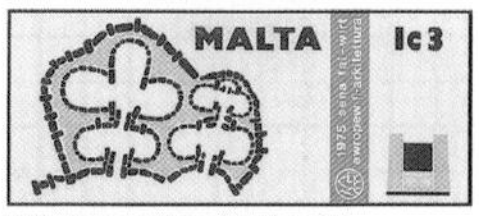

229 Plan of Ggantija Temple

1975. European Architectural Heritage Year.

545	**229**	1c.3 black and red	10	10
546	-	3c. purple, red and brown	20	10
547	-	5c. brown and red	30	25
548	-	25c. green, red and black	1·10	3·00

DESIGNS: 3c. Mdina skyline; 5c. View of Victoria, Gozo; 25c. Silhouette of Fort St. Angelo.

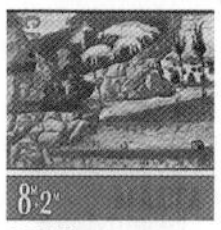

230 Farm Animals

1975. Christmas. Multicoloured.

549	8m.+2m. Type **230**	25	25
550	3c.+1c. Nativity scene (50×23 mm)	40	75
551	7c.5+1c.5 Approach of the Magi	45	1·40

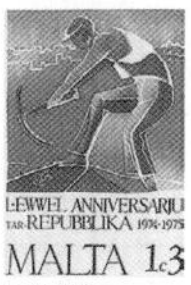

231 "The Right to Work"

1975. First Anniv of Republic.

552	**231**	1c.3 multicoloured	10	10
553	-	5c. multicoloured	20	10
554	-	25c. red, blue and black	70	1·10

DESIGNS: 5c. "Safeguarding the Environment"; 25c. National flag.

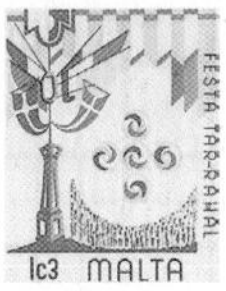

232 "Festa Tar-Rahal"

1976. Maltese Folklore. Multicoloured.

555	1c.3 Type **232**	10	10
556	5c. "L-Imnarja" (horiz)	15	10
557	7c.5 "Il-Karnival" (horiz)	35	70
558	10c. "Il-Gimgha L-Kbira"	55	1·40

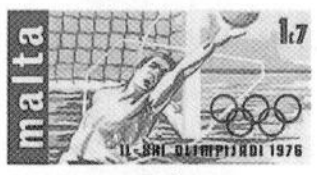

233 Water Polo

1976. Olympic Games, Montreal. Multicoloured.

559	1c.7 Type **233**	10	10
560	5c. Sailing	25	10
561	30c. Athletics	85	1·50

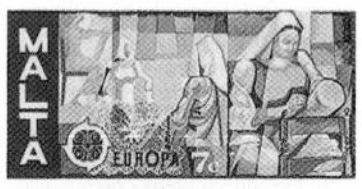

234 Lace-making

1976. Europa. Multicoloured.

562	7c. Type **234**	20	35
563	15c. Stone carving	25	60

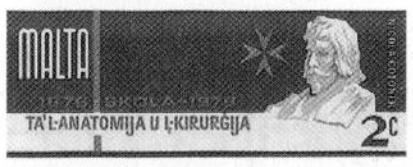

235 Nicola Cotoner

1976. 300th Anniv of School of Anatomy and Surgery. Multicoloured.

564	2c. Type **235**	10	10

565	5c. Arm	15	10
566	7c. Giuseppe Zammit	20	10
567	11c. Sacra Infermeria	35	65

236 St. John the Baptist and St. Michael

1976. Christmas. Multicoloured.

568	1c.+5m. Type **236**	10	20
569	5c.+1c. Madonna and Child	15	60
570	7c.+1c.5 St. Christopher and St. Nicholas	20	80
571	10c.+2c. Complete painting (32×27 mm)	30	1·25

Nos. 568/71 show portions of "Madonna and Saints" by Domenico di Michelino.

237 Jean de la Valette's Armour

1977. Suits of Armour. Multicoloured.

572	2c. Type **237**	10	10
573	7c. Aloph de Wignacourt's armour	20	10
574	11c. Jean Jacques de Verdelin's armour	25	50

1977. No. 336 surch 1c7.

575	1c.7 on 4d. multicoloured	25	25

239 "Annunciation"

1977. 400th Birth Anniv of Rubens. Flemish Tapestries. Multicoloured.

576	2c. Type **239**	10	10
577	7c. "Four Evangelists"	25	10
578	11c. "Nativity"	45	45
579	20c. "Adoration of the Magi"	80	1·00

See also Nos. 592/5, 615/18 and 638/9.

240 Map and Radio Aerial

1977. World Telecommunications Day.

580	**240**	1c. black, green and red	10	10
581	**240**	6c. black, blue and red	20	10
582	-	8c. black, brown and red	30	10
583	-	17c. black, mauve and red	60	40

DESIGN—HORIZ: 8, 17c. Map, aerial and airplane tail-fin.

241 Ta' L-Isperanza

1977. Europa. Multicoloured.

584	7c. Type **241**	30	15
585	20c. Is-Salini	35	1·00

242 "Aid to Handicapped Workers" (detail from Workers' Monument)

1977. Maltese Worker Commemoration.

586	**242**	2c. orange and brown	10	10
587	-	7c. light brown and brown	15	10
588	-	20c. multicoloured	40	60

DESIGNS—VERT: 7c. "Stoneworker, modern industry and ship-building" (monument detail). HORIZ: 20c. "Mother with Dead Son" and Service Medal.

243 The Shepherds

1977. Christmas. Multicoloured.

589	1c.+5m. Type **243**	10	35
590	7c.+1c. The Nativity	15	55
591	11c.+1c.5 The Flight into Egypt	20	70

1978. Flemish Tapestries. (2nd series). As T 239. Multicoloured.

592	2c. "The Entry into Jerusalem"	10	10
593	7c. "The Last Supper" (after Poussin)	25	10
594	11c. "The Raising of the Cross" (after Rubens)	30	25
595	25c. "The Resurrection" (after Rubens)	70	80

244 "Young Lady on Horseback and Trooper"

1978. 450th Death Anniv of Albrecht Durer.

596	**244**	1c.7 black, red and blue	10	10
597	-	8c. black, red and grey	15	10
598	-	17c. black, red and grey	40	45

DESIGNS: 8c. "The Bagpiper"; 17c. "The Virgin and Child with a Monkey".

245 Monument to Grand Master Nicola Cotoner (Foggini)

1978. Europa. Monuments. Multicoloured.

599	7c. Type **245**	15	10
600	25c. Monument to Grand Master Ramon Perellos (Mazzuoli)	35	90

246 Goalkeeper

1978. World Cup Football Championship, Argentina. Multicoloured.

601	2c. Type **246**	10	10
602	11c. Players heading ball	15	10
603	15c. Tackling	25	35
MS604	125×90 mm. Nos. 601/3	2·00	3·25

247 Boeing 707 over Megalithic Temple

1978. Air. Multicoloured.

605	5c. Type **247**	20	10
606	7c. Air Malta Boeing 720B	20	10
607	11c. Boeing 747 taking off from Luqa Airport	35	10
608	17c. Type **247**	45	30
609	20c. As 7c.	40	40
610	75c. As 11c.	1·25	2·75

248 Folk Musicians and Village Church

1978. Christmas. Multicoloured.

611	1c.+5m. Type **248**	10	10
612	5c.+1c. Choir of Angels	15	20
613	7c.+1c.5 Carol singers	20	35
614	11c.+3c. Folk musicians, church, angels and carol singers (58×22 mm)	25	45

1979. Flemish Tapestries (3rd series) showing paintings by Rubens. As T 239. Multicoloured.

615	2c. "The Triumph of the Catholic Church"	10	10
616	7c. "The Triumph of Charity"	20	10
617	11c. "The Triumph of Faith"	30	25
618	25c. "The Triumph of Truth"	95	80

249 Fishing Boat and Aircraft Carrier

1979. End of Military Facilities Agreement. Multicoloured.

619	2c. Type **249**	10	10
620	5c. Raising the flag ceremony	10	10
621	7c. Departing soldier and olive sprig	15	10
622	8c. Type **249**	30	30
623	17c. As 5c.	40	45
624	20c. As 7c.	40	45

250 Speronara (fishing boat) and Tail of Air Malta Boeing 707

1979. Europa. Communications. Multicoloured.

625	7c. Type **250**	20	10
626	25c. Coastal watch tower and radio link towers	40	75

251 Children on Globe

1979. International Year of the Child. Multicoloured.

627	2c. Type **251**	10	10
628	7c. Children flying kites (27×33 mm)	15	10
629	11c. Children in circle (27×33 mm)	20	35

252 Shells

1979. Marine Life. Multicoloured.

630	2c. Type **252**	10	10
631	5c. Loggerhead turtle	20	10
632	7c. Dolphin (fish)	25	10
633	25c. Noble pen shell	90	1·25

253 "The Nativity" (detail)

1979. Christmas. Paintings by Giuseppe Cali. Multicoloured.

634	1c.+5m. Type **253**	10	10
635	5c.+1c. "The Flight into Egypt" (detail)	15	15
636	7c.+1c.5 "The Nativity"	20	20
637	11c.+3c. "The Flight into Egypt"	30	50

1980. Flemish Tapestries (4th series). As T 239. Multicoloured.

638	2c. "The Institution of Corpus Domini" (Rubens)	10	10
639	8c. "The Destruction of Idolatry" (Rubens)	20	20
MS640	114×86 mm. 50c. "Grand Master Perelles with St. Jude and St. Simon (unknown Maltese artist) (vert)	80	1·60

254 Hal Saflieni Hypogeum, Paola

1980. Int Restoration of Monuments Campaign. Multicoloured.

641	2c.5 Type **254**	10	15
642	6c. Vilhena Palace, Mdina	15	20
643	8c. Citadel of Victoria, Gozo (horiz)	20	40
644	12c. Fort St. Elmo, Valletta (horiz)	30	60

255 Dun Gorg Preca

1980. Birth Centenary of Dun Gorg Preca (founder of Society of Christian Doctrine).

645	**255**	2c. 5 grey and black	10	10

256 Ruzar Briffa (poet)

1980. Europa.

646	**256**	8c. yellow, brown & green	20	10
647	-	30c. green, brown and lake	55	1·25

DESIGN: 30c. Nikiol Anton Vassalli (scholar and patriot).

257 "Annunciation"

1980. Christmas. Paintings by A. Inglott. Multicoloured.

648	2c.+5m. Type **257**	10	10
649	6c.+1c. "Conception"	20	20
650	8c.+1c.5 "Nativity"	25	40
651	12c.+3c. "Annunciation", "Conception" and "Nativity" (47×38 mm)	30	70

258 Rook and Pawn

1980. 24th Chess Olympiad and International Chess Federation Congress. Multicoloured.

652	2c.5 Type **258**	20	20
653	8c. Bishop and pawn	45	20
654	30c. King, queen and pawn (vert)	70	1·50

259 Barn Owl

1981. Birds. Multicoloured.
655	3c. Type **259**	30	25
656	8c. Sardinian warbler	50	25
657	12c. Woodchat shrike	60	80
658	23c. British storm petrel	1·10	1·75

260 Traditional Horse Race

1981. Europa. Folklore. Multicoloured.
659	8c. Type **260**	20	10
660	30c. Attempting to retrieve flag from end of "gostra" (greasy pole)	40	65

261 Stylized "25"

1981. 25th Maltese International Trade Fair.
661	**261** 4c. multicoloured	15	15
662	**261** 25c. multicoloured	50	60

262 Disabled Artist at Work

1981. International Year for Disabled Persons. Multicoloured.
663	3c. Type **262**	20	10
664	35c. Disabled child playing football	90	75

263 Wheat Ear in Conical Flask

1981. World Food Day.
665	**263** 8c. multicoloured	15	15
666	**263** 23c. multicoloured	60	50

264 Megalithic Building

1981. History of Maltese Industry. Multicoloured.
667	5m. Type **264**	10	85
668	1c. Cotton production	10	10
669	2c. Early ship-building	85	10
670	3c. Currency minting	30	10
671	5c. "Art"	30	25
672	6c. Fishing	1·25	25
673	7c. Agriculture	30	1·50
674	8c. Stone quarrying	1·00	35
675	10c. Grape pressing	35	50
676	12c. Modern ship-building	2·00	2·25
677	15c. Energy	70	2·00
678	20c. Telecommunications	70	75
679	25c. "Industry"	1·00	2·25
680	50c. Drilling for Water	2·50	2·75
681	£1 Sea transport	7·00	7·50
682	£3 Air transport	13·00	18·00

265 Children and Nativity Scene

1981. Christmas. Multicoloured.
683	2c.+1c. Type **265**	25	10
684	8c.+2c. Christmas Eve procession (horiz)	35	20
685	20c.+3c. Preaching midnight sermon	50	1·10

266 Shipbuilding

1982. Shipbuilding Industry.
686	**266**	3c. multicoloured	15	10
687	-	8c. multicoloured	30	30
688	-	13c. multicoloured	55	55
689	-	27c. multicoloured	1·25	1·25
DESIGNS: 8c. to 27c. Differing shipyard scenes.

267 Elderly Man and Has-Serh (home for elderly)

1982. Care of Elderly. Multicoloured.
690	8c. Type **267**	30	20
691	30c. Elderly woman and Has-Zmien (hospital for elderly)	1·10	1·40

268 Redemption of Islands by Maltese, 1428

1982. Europa. Historical Events. Multicoloured.
692	8c. Type **268**	40	20
693	30c. Declaration of rights by Maltese, 1802	70	1·40

269 Stylized Footballer

1982. World Cup Football Championship, Spain.
694	**269** 3c. multicoloured	20	10
695	- 12c. multicoloured	60	55
696	- 15c. multicoloured	70	65
MS697	125×90 mm. Nos. 694/6	3·50	4·50
DESIGNS: 12c., 15c. Various stylized footballers.

270 Angel appearing to Shepherds

1982. Christmas. Multicoloured.
698	2c.+1c. Type **270**	15	20
699	8c.+2c. Nativity and Three Wise Men bearing gifts	40	60
700	20c.+3c. Nativity scene (45×37 mm)	80	1·25

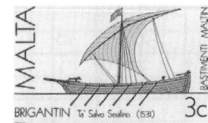
271 "Ta Salvo Serafino" (oared brigantine), 1531

1982. Maltese Ships (1st series). Multicoloured.
701	3c. Type **271**	25	10
702	8c. "La Madonna del Rosaria" (tartane), 1740	50	30
703	12c. "San Paulo" (xebec), 1743	70	55
704	20c. "Ta' Pietro Saliba" (xprunara), 1798	90	90

See also Nos. 725/8, 772/5, 792/5 and 809/12.

272 Locomotive "Manning Wardle", 1883

1983. Centenary of Malta Railway. Multicoloured.
705	3c. Type **272**	45	15
706	13c. Locomotive "Black Hawthorn", 1884	85	1·00
707	27c. Beyer Peacock locomotive, 1895	1·50	3·25

273 Peace Doves leaving Malta

1983. Commonwealth Day. Multicoloured.
708	8c. Type **273**	20	30
709	12c. Tourist landmarks	30	60
710	15c. Holiday beach (vert)	35	75
711	23c. Ship-building (vert)	55	1·00

274 Ggantija Megalithic Temples, Gozo

1983. Europa. Multicoloured.
712	8c. Type **274**	40	40
713	30c. Fort St. Angelo	70	2·40

275 Dish Aerials (World Communications Year)

1983. Anniversaries and Events. Multicoloured.
714	3c. Type **275**	30	15
715	7c. Ships' prows and badge (25th anniv of I.M.O. Convention)	50	55
716	13c. Container lorries and badge (30th anniv of Customs Co-operation Council)	80	90
717	20c. Stadium and emblem (9th Mediterranean Games)	90	2·25

276 Monsignor Giuseppe de Piro

1983. 50th Death Anniv of Monsignor Giuseppe de Piro.
718	**276** 3c. multicoloured	15	15

277 Annunciation

1983. Christmas. Multicoloured.
719	2c.+1c. Type **277**	30	15
720	8c.+2c. The Nativity	70	60
721	20c.+3c. Adoration of the Magi	1·25	2·25

278 Workers at Meeting

1983. 40th Anniv of General Workers' Union. Multicoloured.
722	3c. Type **278**	25	10
723	8c. Worker with family	45	40
724	27c. Union H.Q. Building	1·25	1·75

1983. Maltese Ships (2nd series). As T 271. Multicoloured.
725	2c. "Strangier" (full-rigged ship), 1813	30	25
726	12c. "Tigre" (topsail schooner), 1839	80	1·25
727	13c. "La Speranza" (brig), 1844	80	1·25
728	20c. "Wignacourt" (barque), 1844	1·25	2·75

279 Boeing 737 9H-ABA

1984. Air. Multicoloured.
729	7c. Type **279**	50	30
730	8c. Boeing 720B	60	35
731	16c. Vickers 953 Vanguard G-APED	1·25	70
732	23c. Vickers Viscount 700	1·50	70
733	27c. Douglas DC-3 G-AGHH	1·75	80
734	38c. Armstrong Whitworth A.W.15 Atalanta G-ABTJ "Artemis"	2·25	2·75
735	75c. Marina Fiat MF.5 flying boat I-AZDL	3·25	5·00

280 Bridge

1984. Europa. 25th Anniv of C.E.P.T.
736	**280** 8c. green, black and yellow	35	35
737	**280** 30c. red, black and yellow	1·00	1·25

281 Early Policeman

1984. 170th Anniv of Malta Police Force. Multicoloured.
738	3c. Type **281**	65	15
739	8c. Mounted police	1·25	65
740	11c. Motorcycle policeman	1·50	2·00
741	25c. Policeman and firemen	2·25	3·75

282 Running

1984. Olympic Games, Los Angeles. Multicoloured.
742	7c. Type **282**	25	30
743	12c. Gymnastics	50	70
744	23c. Swimming	85	1·25

283 "The Visitation" (Pietru Caruana)

1984. Christmas. Paintings from Church of Our Lady of Porto Salvo, Valletta. Multicoloured.
745	2c.+1c. Type **283**	55	65
746	8c.+2c. "The Epiphany" (Rafel Caruana) (horiz)	1·00	1·40
747	20c.+3c. "Jesus among the Doctors" (Rafel Caruana) (horiz)	2·00	4·00

284 Dove on Map

1984. Tenth Anniv of Republic. Multicoloured.

748	3c. Type **284**	30	20
749	8c. Fort St. Angelo	60	65
750	30c. Hands	2·10	4·75

285 1885 ½d. Green Stamp

1985. Centenary of Malta Post Office. Multicoloured.

751	3c. Type **285**	45	15
752	8c. 1885 1d. rose	65	45
753	12c. 1885 2½d. blue	90	1·40
754	20c. 1885 4d. brown	1·40	3·00
MS755	165×90 mm. Nos. 751/4	3·75	6·50

286 Boy, and Hands planting Vine

1985. International Youth Year. Multicoloured.

756	2c. Type **286**	15	15
757	13c. Young people and flowers (vert)	70	60
758	27c. Girl holding flame in hand	1·40	1·40

287 Nicolo Baldacchino (tenor)

1985. Europa. European Music Year. Multicoloured.

759	8c. Type **287**	1·50	50
760	30c. Francesco Azopardi (composer)	2·75	5·00

288 Guzeppi Bajada and Manwel Attard (victims)

1985. 66th Anniv of 7 June 1919 Demonstrations. Multicoloured.

761	3c. Type **288**	30	15
762	7c. Karmnu Abela and Wenzu Dyer (victims)	60	40
763	35c. Model of projected Demonstration monument by Anton Agius (vert)	1·90	2·75

289 Stylized Birds

1985. 40th Anniv of United Nations Organization. Multicoloured.

764	4c. Type **289**	25	15
765	11c. Arrow-headed ribbons	60	1·25
766	31c. Stylized figures	1·40	3·25

290 Giorgio Mitrovich (nationalist) (death centenary)

1985. Celebrities' Anniversaries. Multicoloured.

767	8c. Type **290**	75	35
768	12c. Pietru Caxaru (poet and administrator) (400th death anniversary)	1·25	2·50

291 The Three Wise Men

1985. Christmas. Designs showing details of terracotta relief by Ganni Bonnici. Multicoloured.

769	2c.+1c. Type **291**	45	60
770	8c.+2c. Virgin and Child	1·00	1·50
771	20c.+3c. Angels	2·00	3·50

1985. Maltese Ships (3rd series). Steamships. As T **271**. Multicoloured.

772	3c. "Scotia" (paddle-steamer), 1844	85	20
773	7c. "Tagliaferro" (screw-steamer), 1822	1·25	75
774	15c. "Gleneagles" (screw-steamer), 1885	1·75	2·75
775	23c. "L'Isle Adam" (screw-steamer), 1886	2·00	3·75

292 John XXIII Peace Laboratory and Statue of St. Francis of Assisi

1986. International Peace Year. Multicoloured.

776	8c. Type **292**	1·25	50
777	11c. Dove and hands holding olive branch (40×19 mm)	1·50	2·50
778	27c. Map of Africa, dove and two heads	3·25	4·75

293 Symbolic Plant and "Cynthia cardui", "Vanessa atalanta" and "Polyommatus icarus"

1986. Europa. Environmental Conservation. Multicoloured.

779	8c. Type **293**	1·25	50
780	35c. Island, Neolithic frieze, sea and sun	2·25	6·00

294 Heading the Ball

1986. World Cup Football Championship, Mexico. Multicoloured.

781	3c. Type **294**	50	20
782	7c. Saving a goal	1·00	1·00
783	23c. Controlling the ball	3·50	6·50
MS784	125×90 mm. Nos. 781/3	7·00	8·50

295 Father Diegu

1986. Maltese Philanthropists. Multicoloured.

785	2c. Type **295**	40	30
786	3c. Adelaide Cini	50	30
787	8c. Alfonso Maria Galea	1·25	60
788	27c. Vincenzo Bugeja	3·25	6·00

296 "Nativity"

1986. Christmas. Paintings by Giuseppe D'Arena. Multicoloured.

789	2c.+1c. Type **296**	1·25	1·75
790	8c.+2c. "Nativity" (detail) (vert)	2·75	3·50
791	20c.+3c. "Epiphany"	3·75	7·00

1986. Maltese Ships (4th series). As T **271**. Multicoloured.

792	7c. "San Paul" (freighter), 1921	1·00	50
793	10c. "Knight of Malta" (mail steamer), 1930	1·25	1·75
794	12c. "Valetta City" (freighter), 1948	1·50	2·75
795	20c. "Saver" (freighter), 1959	2·25	4·50

297 European Robin

1987. 25th Anniv of Malta Ornithological Society. Multicoloured.

796	3c. Type **297**	1·25	50
797	8c. Peregrine falcon (vert)	2·50	1·00
798	13c. Hoopoe (vert)	3·25	4·00
799	23c. Cory's shearwater	3·75	6·00

298 Aquasun Lido

1987. Europa. Modern Architecture. Multicoloured.

800	8c. Type **298**	1·00	75
801	35c. Church of St. Joseph, Manikata	2·50	4·75

299 16th-century Pikeman

1987. Maltese Uniforms (1st series). Multicoloured.

802	3c. Type **299**	85	40
803	7c. 16th-century officer	1·60	90
804	10c. 18th-century standard bearer	1·75	2·25
805	27c. 18th-century General of the Galleys	3·75	4·75

See also Nos. 832/5, 851/4, 880/3 and 893/6.

300 Maltese Scenes, Wheat Ears and Sun

1987. Anniversaries and Events. Multicoloured.

806	5c. Type **300** (European Environment Year)	1·25	50
807	8c. Esperanto star as comet (Centenary of Esperanto)	2·00	60
808	23c. Family at house door (International Year of Shelter for the Homeless)	3·00	3·00

1987. Maltese Ships (5th series). As T **271**. Multicoloured.

809	2c. "Medina" (freighter), 1969	70	60
810	11c. "Rabat" (container ship), 1974	2·50	2·50
811	13c. "Ghawdex" (passenger ferry), 1979	2·75	2·75
812	20c. "Pinto" (car ferry), 1987	3·75	4·00

301 "The Visitation"

1987. Christmas. Illuminated illustrations, score and text from 16th-century choral manuscript. Multicoloured.

813	2c.+1c. Type **301**	50	65
814	8c.+2c. "The Nativity"	1·75	2·50
815	20c.+3c. "The Adoration of the Magi"	3·25	4·50

302 Dr. Arvid Pardo (U.N. representative)

1987. 20th Anniv of United Nations Resolution on Peaceful Use of the Seabed. Multicoloured.

816	8c. Type **302**	1·00	75
817	12c. U.N. emblem and sea	1·75	3·00
MS818	125×90 mm. Nos. 816/17	3·00	4·50

303 Ven. Nazju Falzon (Catholic catechist)

1988. Maltese Personalities. Multicoloured.

819	2c. Type **303**	30	30
820	3c. Mgr. Sidor Formosa (philanthropist)	30	30
821	4c. Sir Luigi Preziosi (ophthalmologist)	60	30
822	10c. Fr. Anastasju Cuschieri (poet)	80	85
823	25c. Mgr. Pietru Pawl Saydon (Bible translator)	2·00	3·25

304 "St. John Bosco with Youth" (statue)

1988. Religious Anniversaries. Multicoloured.

824	10c. Type **304** (death centenary)	1·00	75
825	12c. "Assumption of Our Lady" (altarpiece by Perugino, Ta' Pinu, Gozo) (Marian Year)	1·25	1·25
826	14c. "Christ the King" (statue by Sciortino) (75th anniv of International Eucharistic Congress, Valletta)	1·50	2·00

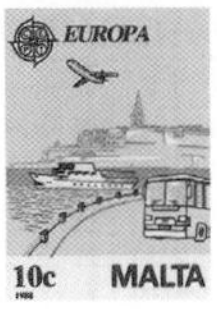

305 Bus, Ferry and Airliner

1988. Europa. Transport and Communications. Multicoloured.

827	10c. Type **305**	1·25	75
828	35c. Control panel, dish aerial and pylons	2·00	3·75

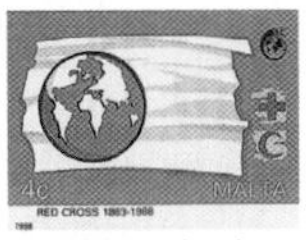

306 Globe and Red Cross Emblems

1988. Anniversaries and Events. Multicoloured.

829	4c. Type **306** (125th anniv of Int Red Cross)	60	50
830	18c. Divided globe (Campaign for North–South Interdependence and Solidarity)	1·50	2·50
831	19c. Globe and symbol (40th anniv of W.H.O.)	1·50	2·50

1988. Maltese Uniforms (2nd series). As T **299**. Multicoloured.

832	3c. Private, Maltese Light Infantry, 1800	50	30
833	4c. Gunner, Malta Coast Artillery, 1802	55	35
834	10c. Field Officer, 1st Maltese Provincial Battalion, 1805	1·40	1·25
835	25c. Subaltern, Royal Malta Regiment, 1809	2·75	4·25

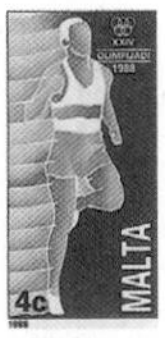

307 Athletics

1988. Olympic Games, Seoul. Multicoloured.

836	4c. Type **307**	30	30
837	10c. Diving	70	80
838	35c. Basketball	2·00	3·00

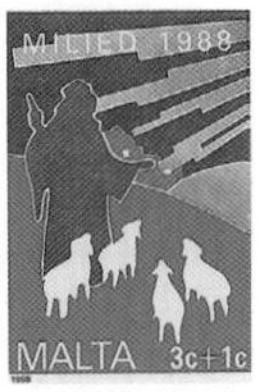

308 Shepherd with Flock

1988. Christmas. Multicoloured.

839	3c.+1c. Type **308**	30	30
840	10c.+2c. The Nativity	75	1·00
841	25c.+3c. Three Wise Men	1·75	2·50

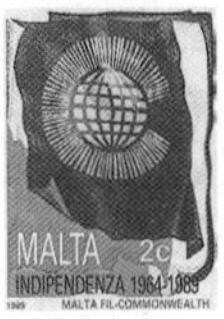

309 Commonwealth Emblem

1989. 25th Anniv of Independence. Multicoloured.

842	2c. Type **309**	25	35
843	3c. Council of Europe flag	25	35
844	4c. U.N. flag	30	35
845	10c. Workers, hands gripping ring and national flag	75	95
846	12c. Scales and allegorical figure of Justice	90	1·40
847	25c. Prime Minister Borg Olivier with Independence constitution (42×28 mm)	1·90	3·25

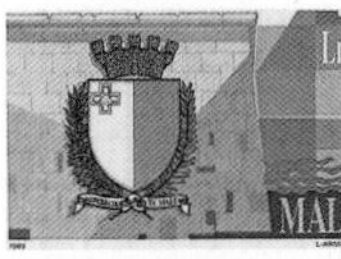

310 New State Arms

1989

848	**310**	£1 multicoloured	4·00	4·50

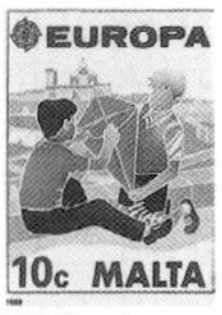

311 Two Boys flying Kite

1989. Europa. Children's Games. Multicoloured.

849	10c. Type **311**	1·00	75
850	35c. Two girls with dolls	2·50	4·50

1989. Maltese Uniforms (3rd series). As T **299**. Multicoloured.

851	3c. Officer, Maltese Veterans, 1815	45	45
852	4c. Subaltern, Royal Malta Fencibles, 1839	50	50
853	10c. Private, Malta Militia, 1856	1·50	1·50
854	25c. Colonel, Royal Malta Fencible Artillery, 1875	2·75	3·75

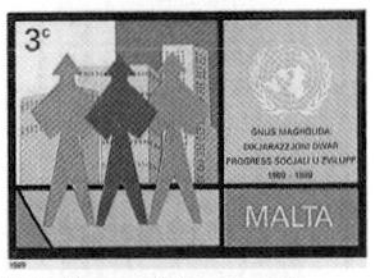

312 Human Figures and Buildings

1989. Anniversaries and Commemorations. Designs showing logo and stylized human figures. Multicoloured.

855	3c. Type **312** (20th anniv of U.N. Declaration on Social Progress and Development)	30	30
856	4c. Workers and figure in wheelchair (Malta's Ratification of European Social Charter)	35	35
857	10c. Family (40th anniv of Council of Europe)	80	1·25
858	14c. Teacher and children (70th anniv of Malta Union of Teachers)	1·00	1·75
859	25c. Symbolic knights (Knights of the Sovereign Military Order of Malta Assembly)	2·25	3·50

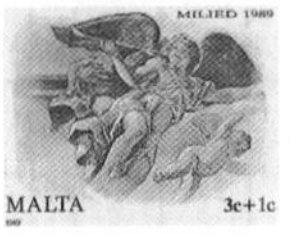

313 Angel and Cherub

1989. Christmas. Vault paintings by Mattia Preti from St. John's Co-Cathedral, Valletta.

860	3c.+1c. Type **313**	60	60
861	10c.+2c. Two angels	1·40	1·90
862	20c.+3c. Angel blowing trumpet	2·00	4·00

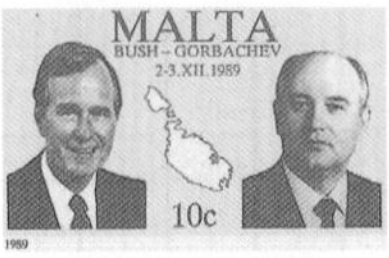

314 Presidents George H. Bush and Mikhail Gorbachev

1989. U.S.A.–U.S.S.R. Summit Meeting, Malta.

863	**314**	10c. multicoloured	1·00	1·25

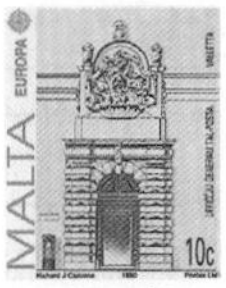

315 General Post Office, Auberge d'Italie, Valletta

1990. Europa. Post Office Buildings. Multicoloured.

864	10c. Type **315**	1·00	50
865	35c. Branch Post Office, Zebbug (horiz)	2·00	3·75

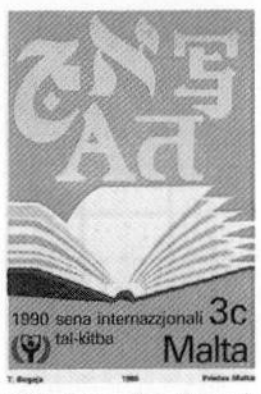

316 Open Book and Letters from Different Alphabets (International Literacy Year)

1990. Anniversaries and Events. Multicoloured.

866	3c. Type **316**	25	25
867	4c. Count Roger of Sicily and Norman soldiers (900th anniv of Sicilian rule) (horiz)	60	30
868	19c. Communications satellite (25th anniv of I.T.U.) (horiz)	2·25	2·50
869	20c. Football and map of Malta (Union of European Football Association 20th Ordinary Congress, Malta)	2·25	2·50

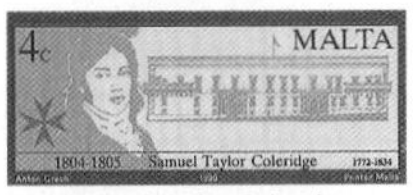

317 Samuel Taylor Coleridge (poet) and Government House

1990. British Authors. Multicoloured.

870	4c. Type **317**	50	30
871	10c. Lord Byron (poet) and map of Valletta	90	70
872	12c. Sir Walter Scott (novelist) and Great Siege	1·00	95
873	25c. William Makepeace Thackeray (novelist) and Naval Arsenal	2·00	2·25

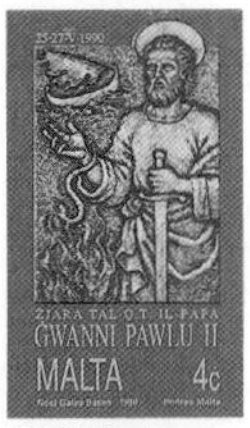

318 St. Paul

1990. Visit of Pope John Paul II. Bronze Bas-reliefs.

874	**318**	4c. black, flesh and red	50	1·50
875	-	25c. black, flesh and red	1·50	1·75

DESIGN: 25c. Pope John Paul II.

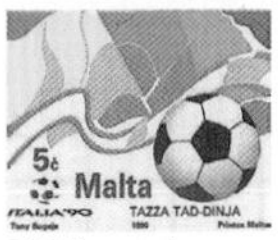

319 Flags and Football

1990. World Cup Football Championship, Italy. Multicoloured.

876	5c. Type **319**	35	30
877	10c. Football in net	65	1·00
878	14c. Scoreboard and football	1·00	1·75
MS879	123×90 mm. Nos. 876/8	3·00	4·25

1990. Maltese Uniforms (4th series). As T **299**. Multicoloured.

880	3c. Captain, Royal Malta Militia, 1889	1·25	55
881	4c. Field officer, Royal Malta Artillery, 1905	1·40	60
882	10c. Labourer, Malta Labour Corps, 1915	2·50	1·50
883	25c. Lieutenant, King's Own Malta Regiment of Militia, 1918	3·75	4·50

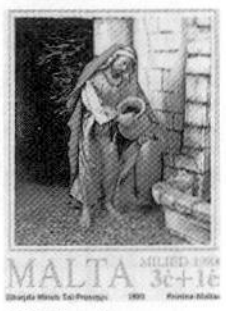

320 Innkeeper

1990. Christmas. Figures from Crib by Austin Galea, Marco Bartolo and Rosario Zammit. Multicoloured.

884	3c.+1c. Type **320**	30	50
885	10c.+2c. Nativity (41×28 mm)	70	1·25
886	25c.+3c. Shepherd with sheep	1·60	2·50

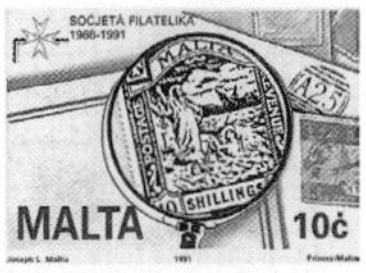

321 1919 10s. Stamp under Magnifying Glass

1991. 25th Anniv of Philatelic Society of Malta.

887	**321**	10c. multicoloured	60	70

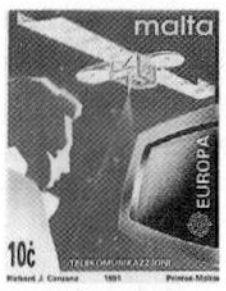

322 "Eurostar" Satellite and V.D.U. Screen

1991. Europa. Europe in Space. Multicoloured.

888	10c. Type **322**	1·00	70
889	35c. "Ariane 4" rocket and projected HOTOL aerospace-plane	1·75	2·75

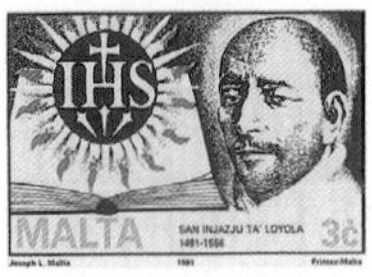

323 St. Ignatius Loyola (founder of Jesuits) (500th birth anniv)

1991. Religious Commemorations. Multicoloured.

890	3c. Type **323**	30	20
891	4c. Abbess Venerable Maria Adeodata Pisani (185th birth anniversary) (vert)	35	25
892	30c. St. John of the Cross (400th death anniversary)	2·00	2·75

1991. Maltese Uniforms (5th series). As T **299**. Multicoloured.

893	3c. Officer with colour, Royal Malta Fencibles, 1860	50	25
894	10c. Officer with colour, Royal Malta Regiment of Militia, 1903	1·00	60
895	19c. Officer with Queen's colour, King's Own Malta Regiment, 1968	1·90	1·75
896	25c. Officer with colour, Malta Armed Forces, 1991	2·25	2·00

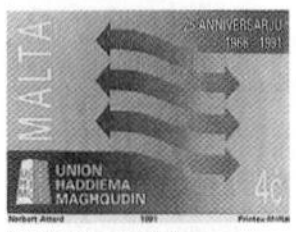

324 Interlocking Arrows

1991. 25th Anniv of Union Haddiema Maghqudin (public services union).

897	**324**	4c. multicoloured	30	30

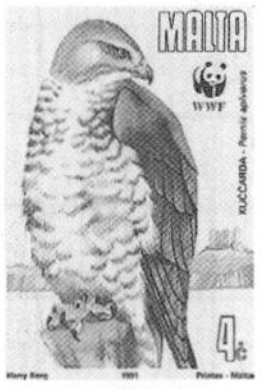

325 Western Honey Buzzard

1991. Endangered Species. Birds. Multicoloured.

898	4c. Type **325**	2·50	2·50
899	4c. Marsh harrier	2·50	2·50
900	10c. Eleonora's falcon	2·50	2·50
901	10c. Lesser kestrel	2·50	2·50

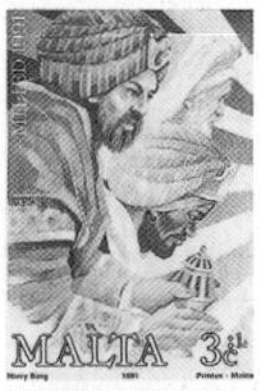

326 Three Wise Men

1991. Christmas. Multicoloured.

902	3c.+1c. Type **326**	55	50
903	10c.+2c. Holy Family	1·25	1·40
904	25c.+3c. Two shepherds	2·25	3·25

327 Ta' Hagrat Neolithic Temple

1991. National Heritage of the Maltese Islands. Multicoloured.

905	1c. Type **327**	35	50
906	2c. Cottoner Gate	35	50
907	3c. St. Michael's Bastion, Valletta	35	50
908	4c. Spinola Palace, St. Julian's	40	15
909	5c. Birkirkara Church	50	20
910	10c. Mellieha Bay	90	35
911	12c. Wied iz-Zurrieq	1·25	40
912	14c. Mgarr harbour, Gozo	1·50	45
913	20c. Yacht marina	2·00	65
914	50c. Gozo Channel	3·25	1·60
915	£1 "Arab Horses" (sculpture by Antonio Sciortino)	5·50	3·25
916	£2 Independence Monument (Ganni Bonnici) (vert)	10·00	8·00

328 Aircraft Tailfins and Terminal

1992. Opening of Int Air Terminal. Multicoloured.

917	4c. Type **328**	75	30
918	10c. National flags and terminal	1·25	70

329 Ships of Columbus

1992. Europa. 500th Anniv of Discovery of America by Columbus. Multicoloured.

919	10c. Type **329**	1·25	55
920	35c. Columbus and map of Americas	2·50	2·25

330 George Cross and Anti-aircraft Gun Crew

1992. 50th Anniv of Award of George Cross to Malta. Multicoloured.

921	4c. Type **330**	1·00	30
922	10c. George Cross and memorial bell	1·50	1·00
923	50c. Tanker "Ohio" entering Grand Harbour	7·00	8·50

331 Running

1992. Olympic Games, Barcelona. Multicoloured.

924	3c. Type **331**	65	20
925	10c. High jumping	1·25	1·00
926	30c. Swimming	2·50	4·50

332 Church of the Flight into Egypt

1992. Rehabilitation of Historical Buildings.

927	**332**	3c. black, stone and grey	55	30
928	-	4c. black, stone and pink	60	30
929	-	19c. black, stone and lilac	2·75	3·75

930	-	25c. black, stone and green	3·00	3·75

DESIGNS—HORIZ: 4c. St. John's Co-Cathedral; 25c. Auberge de Provence. VERT: 19c. Church of Madonna del Pillar.

333 "The Nativity" (Giuseppe Cali)

1992. Christmas. Religious Paintings by Giuseppe Cali from Mosta Church. Multicoloured.

931	3c.+1c. Type **333**	1·00	1·10
932	10c.+2c. "Adoration of the Magi"	2·25	2·50
933	25c.+3c. "Christ with the Elders in the Temple"	3·75	4·50

334 Malta College Building, Valletta

1992. 400th Anniv of University of Malta. Multicoloured.

934	4c. Type **334**	75	25
935	30c. Modern University complex, Tal-Qroqq (horiz)	2·75	4·25

335 Lions Club Emblem

1993. 75th Anniv of International Association of Lions Club. Multicoloured.

936	4c. Type **335**	50	25
937	50c. Eye (Sight First Campaign)	2·75	4·00

336 Untitled Painting by Paul Carbonaro

1993. Europa. Contemporary Art. Multicoloured.

938	10c. Type **336**	1·25	50
939	35c. Untitled painting by Alfred Chircop (horiz)	3·00	5·00

337 Mascot holding Flame

1993. Fifth Small States of Europe Games. Multicoloured.

940	3c. Type **337**	20	20
941	4c. Cycling	1·75	30
942	10c. Tennis	1·50	1·00
943	35c. Yachting	2·75	3·50
MS944	120×80 mm. Nos. 940/3	5·50	5·50

338 Learning First Aid

1993. 50th Anniv of Award of Bronze Cross to Maltese Scouts and Guides. Multicoloured.

945	3c. Type **338**	50	20
946	4c. Bronze Cross	50	20
947	10c. Scout building camp fire	1·10	90
948	35c. Governor Lord Gort presenting Bronze Cross, 1943	2·75	4·00

339 "Papilio machaon"

1993. European Year of the Elderly. Butterflies. Multicoloured.

949	5c. Type **339**	35	20
950	35c. "Vanessa atalanta"	1·75	2·25

340 G.W.U. Badge and Interlocking "50"

1993. 50th Anniv of General Workers Union.

951	**340**	4c. multicoloured	35	40

341 Child Jesus and Star

1993. Christmas. Multicoloured.

952	3c.+1c. Type **341**	30	35
953	10c.+2c. Christmas tree	85	1·25
954	25c.+3c. Star in traditional window	1·60	2·75

342 Council Arms (face value top left)

1993. Inauguration of Local Community Councils. Sheet 110×93 mm, containing T 342 and similar horiz designs showing different Council Arms. Multicoloured.

MS955	5c. Type **342**; 5c. Face value top right; 5c. Face value bottom left; 5c. Face value bottom right	1·50	2·25

343 Symbolic Tooth and Probe

1994. 50th Anniv of Maltese Dental Association. Multicoloured.

956	5c. Type **343**	35	30
957	44c. Symbolic mouth and dental mirror	3·00	3·00

344 Sir Themistocles Zammit (discoverer of Brucella microbe)

1994. Europa. Discoveries. Multicoloured.

958	14c. Type **344**	50	30
959	30c. Bilingually inscribed candelabrum of 2nd century B.C. (deciphering of ancient Phoenician language)	1·90	3·25

345 Family in Silhouette (International Year of the Family)

1994. Anniversaries and Events. Multicoloured.

960	5c. Type **345**	30	20
961	9c. Stylized Red Cross (International recognition of Malta Red Cross Society)	60	50
962	14c. Animals and crops (150th anniv of Agrarian Society)	90	80
963	20c. Worker in silhouette (75th anniv of I.L.O.)	1·25	1·60
964	25c. St. Paul's Anglican Cathedral (155th anniv) (vert)	1·40	1·75

346 Football and Map

1994. World Cup Football Championship, U.S.A. Multicoloured.

965	5c. Type **346**	40	20
966	14c. Ball and goal	1·00	80
967	30c. Ball and pitch superimposed on map	2·00	4·25
MS968	123×88 mm. Nos. 965/7	3·75	4·50

347 Falcon Trophy, Piper PA-30 Twin Commanche and Auster J-5 Autocar (25th anniv of Malta International Rally)

1994. Aviation Anniversaries and Events. Multicoloured.

969	5c. Type **347**	50	20
970	14c. Aerospatiale (Sud) Alouette helicopter, display teams and logo (Malta International Airshow)	1·75	85
971	20c. de Havilland DH.104 Dove "City of Valetta" and Avro Type 685 York aircraft with logo (50th anniv of I.C.A.O.)	1·90	1·75
972	25c. Airbus 320 "Nicolas Cottoner" and de Havilland DH.106 Comet aircraft with logo (50th anniv of I.C.A.O.)	1·90	1·90

348 National Flags and Astronaut on Moon

1994. 25th Anniv of First Manned Moon Landing. Multicoloured.

973	**348**	14c. multicoloured	1·10	1·25

349 Virgin Mary and Child with Angels

1994. Christmas. Multicoloured.

974	5c. Type **349**	25	10
975	9c.+2c. Angel in pink (vert)	65	70
976	14c.+3c. Virgin Mary and Child (vert)	90	1·25
977	20c.+3c. Angel in green (vert)	1·60	2·50

Nos. 975/7 are larger, 28×41 mm, and depict details from Type **349**.

350 Helmet-shaped
Ewer

1994. Maltese Antique Silver Exhibition. Multicoloured.
978	5c. Type **350**	50	20
979	14c. Balsamina	1·10	80
980	20c. Coffee pot	1·50	2·00
981	25c. Sugar box	1·75	2·75

351 "60 plus"
and Hands
touching

1995. Anniversaries and Events. Multicoloured.
982	2c. Type **351** (25th anniv of National Association of Pensioners)	15	15
983	5c. Child's drawing (10th anniv of National Youth Council)	25	20
984	14c. Conference emblem (4th World Conference on Women, Peking, China)	70	80
985	20c. Nurse and thermometer (50th anniv of Malta Memorial District Nursing Association)	1·25	1·40
986	25c. Louis Pasteur (biologist) (death centenary)	1·50	1·75

352 Hand holding
Leaf and Rainbow

1995. Europa. Peace and Freedom. Multicoloured.
987	14c. Type **352**	1·00	55
988	30c. Peace doves (horiz)	1·50	2·50

353 Junkers Ju 87B Stuka
Dive Bombers over Valletta
and Anti-aircraft Gun

1995. Anniversaries. Multicoloured.
989	5c. Type **353** (50th anniv of end of Second World War)	25	25
990	14c. Silhouetted people holding hands (50th anniv of United Nations)	55	60
991	35c. Hands holding bowl of wheat (50th anniv of F.A.O.) (vert)	1·60	2·25

354 Light Bulb

1995. Maltese Electricity and Telecommunications. Multicoloured.
992	2c. Type **354**	15	15
993	5c. Symbolic owl and binary codes	25	25
994	9c. Dish aerial	45	50
995	14c. Sun and rainbow over trees	70	80
996	20c. Early telephone, satellite and Moon's surface	1·25	1·50

355 Rock Wall and Girna

1995. European Nature Conservation Year. Multicoloured.
997	5c. Type **355**	75	25
998	14c. Maltese wall lizards	2·25	80
999	44c. Aleppo pine	3·50	3·00

356 Pinto's Turret
Clock

1995. Treasures of Malta. Antique Maltese Clocks. Multicoloured.
1000	1c. Type **356**	15	60
1001	5c. Michelangelo Sapiano (horologist) and clocks	50	25
1002	14c. Arlogg tal-lira clock	1·50	80
1003	25c. Sundials	2·50	3·50

357 Children's Christmas Eve Procession

1995. Christmas. Multicoloured.
1004	5c. Type **357**	25	10
1005	5c.+2c. Children with crib (vert)	30	50
1006	14c.+3c. Children with lanterns (vert)	1·00	1·25
1007	25c.+3c. Boy with lantern and balustrade (vert)	1·75	2·75

Nos. 1005/7 are 27×32 mm and depict details from Type **357**.

358 Silhouetted Children and
President's Palace, San Anton

1996. Anniversaries. Multicoloured.
1008	5c. Type **358** (35th anniv of the President's Award)	25	25
1009	14c. Nazzareno Camilleri (priest) and St. Patrick's Church, Salesjani (90th birth anniv)	65	65
1010	20c. St. Mary Euphrasia and convent (birth bicentenary)	1·00	1·10
1011	25c. Silhouetted children and fountain (50th anniv of UNICEF)	1·25	1·40

359 Carved Figures from
Skorba

1996. Maltese Prehistoric Art Exhibition. Multicoloured.
1012	5c. Type **359**	30	20
1013	14c. Temple carving, Gozo	80	85
1014	20c. Carved figure of a woman, Skorba (vert)	1·10	1·25
1015	35c. Ghar Dalam pot (vert)	1·90	2·50

360 Mabel
Strickland (politician
and journalist)

1996. Europa. Famous Women. Multicoloured.
1016	14c. Type **360**	75	55
1017	30c. Inez Soler (artist, musician and writer)	2·00	2·00

361 Face and
Emblem (United
Nations Decade
against Drug Abuse)

1996. Anniversaries and Events. Multicoloured.
1018	5c. Type **361**	25	25
1019	5c. "Fi" and emblem (50th anniv of Malta Federation of Industry)	25	25
1020	14c. Commemorative plaque and national flag (75th anniv of self-government)	80	80
1021	44c. Guglielmo Marconi and early radio equipment (centenary of radio)	2·25	2·50

362 Judo

1996. Olympic Games, Atlanta. Multicoloured.
1022	2c. Type **362**	10	10
1023	5c. Athletics	30	25
1024	14c. Diving	80	80
1025	25c. Rifle-shooting	1·40	1·60

363 "Harvest Time" (Cali)

1996. 150th Birth Anniv of Guiseppe Cali (painter). Multicoloured.
1026	5c. Type **363**	30	25
1027	14c. "Dog" (Cali)	70	70
1028	20c. "Countrywoman in a Field" (Cali) (vert)	90	1·10
1029	25c. "Cali at his Easel" (Edward Dingli) (vert)	1·00	1·25

364 Bus No. 1990 "Diamond
Star", 1920s

1996. Buses. Multicoloured.
1030	2c. Type **364**	40	10
1031	5c. No. 434 "Tom Mix", 1930s	70	25
1032	14c. No. 1764 "Verdala", 1940s	1·40	80
1033	30c. No. 3495, 1960s	2·00	2·00

365 Stained Glass Window

1996. Christmas. Multicoloured.
1034	5c. Type **365**	35	10
1035	5c.+2c. Madonna and Child (29×35 mm)	40	60
1036	14c.+3c. Angel facing right (29×35 mm)	80	1·40
1037	25c.+3c. Angel facing left (29×35 mm)	1·25	2·50

Nos. 1035/7 show details from Type **365**.

366 Hompesch Arch
and Arms, Zabbar

1997. Bicentenary of Maltese Cities. Multicoloured.
1038	6c. Type **366**	30	25
1039	16c. Statue, church and arms, Siggiewi	70	70
1040	26c. Seated statue and arms, Zejtun	1·10	1·25
MS1041	125×90 mm. Nos. 1038/40	5·50	4·50

367 Captain-General of the
Galleys' Sedan Chair

1997. Treasures of Malta. Sedan Chairs. Multicoloured.
1042	2c. Type **367**	15	15
1043	6c. Cotoner Grandmasters' chair	30	30
1044	16c. Chair from Cathedral Museum, Mdina (vert)	70	70
1045	27c. Chevalier D'Arezzo's chair (vert)	1·10	1·10

368 Gahan
carrying Door

1997. Europa. Tales and Legends. Multicoloured.
1046	16c. Type **368**	1·00	75
1047	35c. St. Dimitrius appearing from painting	1·75	2·50

369 Modern
Sculpture (Antonio
Sciortino)

1997. Anniversaries. Multicoloured.
1048	1c. Type **369**	10	15
1049	6c. Joseph Calleia and film reel (horiz)	40	40
1050	6c. Gozo Cathedral (horiz)	40	40
1051	11c. City of Gozo (horiz)	60	50
1052	16c. Sculpture of head (Sciortino)	80	70
1053	22c. Joseph Calleia and film camera (horiz)	1·00	1·00

ANNIVERSARIES: 1, 16c. 50th death anniv of Antonio Sciortino (sculptor); 6 (No. 1049), 22c. Birth centenary of Joseph Calleia (actor); 6 (No. 1050), 11c. 300th anniv of construction of Gozo Cathedral.

370 Dr. Albert
Laferla

1997. Pioneers of Education. Multicoloured.
1054	6c. Type **370**	30	25
1055	16c. Sister Emilie de Vialar	70	70
1056	19c. Mgr. Paolo Pullicino	80	80
1057	26c. Mgr. Tommaso Gargallo	1·00	1·10

371 The Nativity

1997. Christmas. Multicoloured.
1058	6c. Type **371**	30	10
1059	6c.+2c. Mary and baby Jesus (vert)	35	50
1060	16c.+3c. Joseph with donkey (vert)	1·00	1·40
1061	26c.+3c. Shepherd with lamb (vert)	1·50	2·50

Nos. 1059/61 show details from Type **371**.

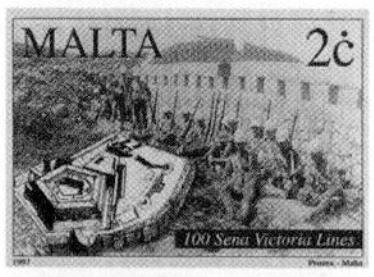

372 Plan of Fort and Soldiers in Victoria Lines

1997. Anniversaries. Multicoloured (except 6c.).

1062	2c. Type **372**	20	10
1063	6c. Sir Paul Boffa making speech (black and red)	30	25
1064	16c. Plan of fort and gun crew	90	65
1065	37c. Queue of voters	1·50	2·00

ANNIVERSARIES: 2, 16c. Centenary of Victoria Lines; 6, 37c. 50th anniv of 1947 Self-government Constitution.

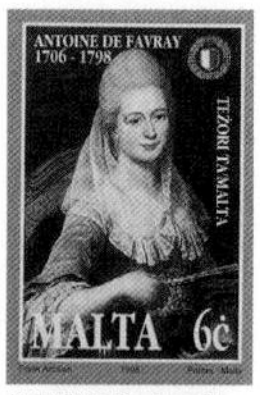

373 "Maria Amelia Grognet" (Antonine de Favray)

1998. Treasures of Malta. Costumes and Paintings.

1066	6c. Type **373**	80	50
1067	6c. Gentleman's waistcoat, c.1790–1810	80	50
1068	16c. Lady's dinner dress, c.1880	1·10	90
1069	16c. "Veneranda, Baroness Abela, and her Grandson" (De Favray)	1·10	90
MS1070	123×88 mm. 26c. City of Valletta from old print (39×47 mm)	1·60	1·60

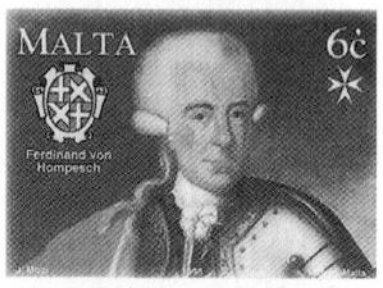

374 Grand Master Ferdinand von Hompesch

1998. Bicentenary of Napoleon's Capture of Malta. Multicoloured.

1071	6c. Type **374**	60	80
1072	6c. French fleet	60	80
1073	16c. French landing	1·10	1·60
1074	16c. General Napoleon Bonaparte	1·10	1·60

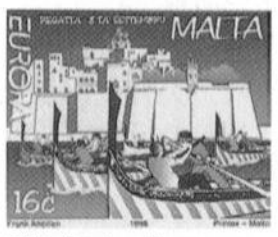

375 Racing Two-man Luzzus

1998. Europa. Sailing Regatta, Grand Harbour. Multicoloured.

1075	16c. Type **375**	1·10	55
1076	35c. Racing four-man luzzus	1·50	2·50

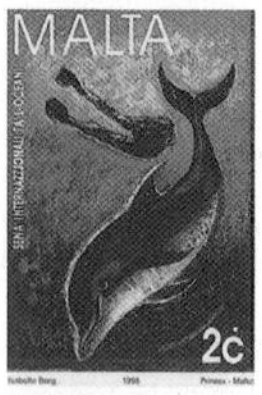

376 Dolphin and Diver

1998. International Year of the Ocean. Multicoloured.

1077	2c. Type **376**	40	25
1078	6c. Diver and sea-urchin	65	25
1079	16c. Jacques Cousteau and diver (horiz)	1·60	80
1080	27c. Two divers (horiz)	2·00	2·25

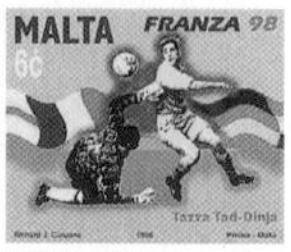

377 Goalkeeper saving Goal

1998. World Cup Football Championship, France. Players and flags. Multicoloured.

1081	6c. Type **377**	70	25
1082	16c. Two players and referee	1·40	70
1083	22c. Two footballers	1·60	2·00
MS1084	122×87 mm. Nos. 1081/3	3·50	3·25

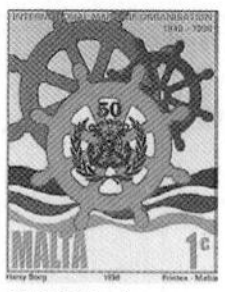

378 Ships' Wheels (50th anniv of Int Maritime Organization)

1998. Anniversaries. Multicoloured.

1085	1c. Type **378**	10	30
1086	6c. Symbolic family (50th anniv of Universal Declaration of Human Rights)	40	25
1087	11c. "GRTU" and cogwheels (50th anniv of General Retailers and Traders Union)	70	40
1088	19c. Mercury (50th anniv of Chamber of Commerce)	1·10	1·40
1089	26c. Aircraft tailfins (25th anniv of Air Malta)	2·40	2·50

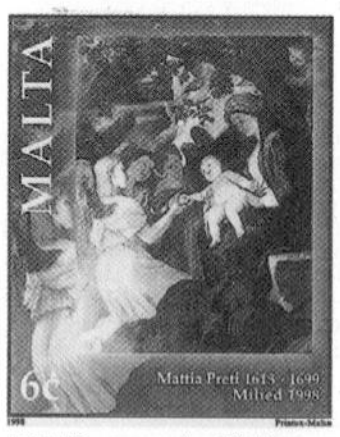

379 "Rest on the Flight to Egypt"

1998. Christmas. Paintings by Mattia Preti. Multicoloured.

1090	6c. Type **379**	40	10
1091	6c.+2c. "Virgin and Child with Sts. Anthony and John the Baptist"	50	70
1092	16c.+3c. "Virgin and Child with Sts. Raphael, Nicholas and Gregory"	1·25	1·75
1093	26c.+3c. "Virgin and Child with Sts. John the Baptist and Nicholas"	1·75	3·00

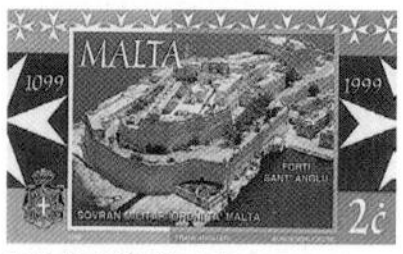

380 Fort St. Angelo

1999. 900th Anniv of the Sovereign Military Order of Malta. Multicoloured.

1094	2c. Type **380**	50	10
1095	6c. Grand Master De l'Isle Adam (vert)	80	25
1096	16c. Grand Master La Valette (vert)	1·50	65
1097	27c. Auberge de Castille et Leon	2·50	3·00

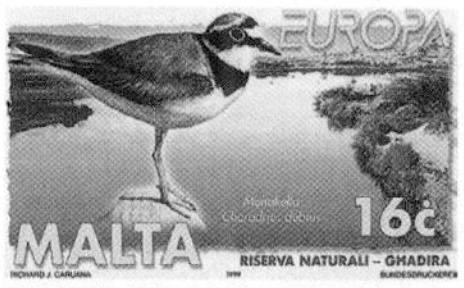

381 Little Ringed Plover, Ghadira Nature Reserve

1999. Europa. Parks and Gardens. Multicoloured.

1098	16c. Type **381**	2·00	55
1099	35c. River kingfisher, Simar Nature Reserve	2·50	3·00

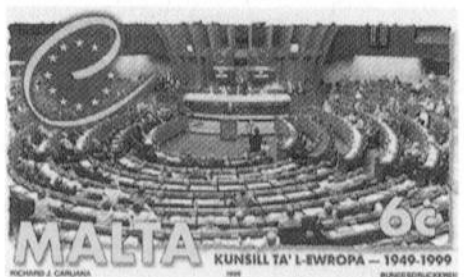

382 Council of Europe Assembly

1999. 50th Anniv of Council of Europe. Multicoloured.

1100	6c. Type **382**	60	25
1101	16c. Council of Europe Headquarters, Strasbourg	1·00	1·25

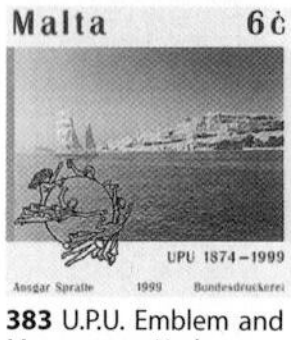

383 U.P.U. Emblem and Marsamxett Harbour, Valletta

1999. 125th Anniv of Universal Postal Union. Multicoloured.

1102	6c. Type **383**	1·25	1·50
1103	16c. Nuremberg and "iBRA '99" International Stamp Exhibition emblem	1·50	1·75
1104	22c. Paris and "Philexfrance '99" International Stamp Exhibition emblem	1·60	1·90
1105	27c. Peking and "China '99" International Stamp Exhibition emblem	1·75	2·00
1106	37c. Melbourne and "Australia '99" International Stamp Exhibition emblem	1·90	2·50

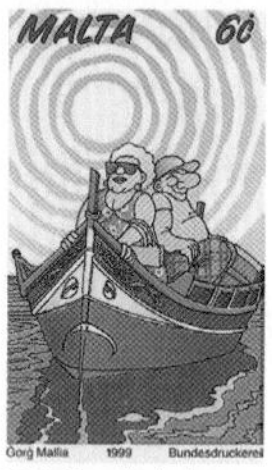

384 Couple in Luzzu

1999. Tourism. Multicoloured.

1107	6c. Type **384**	50	25
1108	16c. Tourist taking photograph	95	55
1109	22c. Man sunbathing (horiz)	1·25	1·00
1110	27c. Couple with horse-drawn carriage (horiz)	1·90	1·40
1111	37c. Caveman at Ta' Hagrat Neolithic temple (horiz)	2·50	3·25

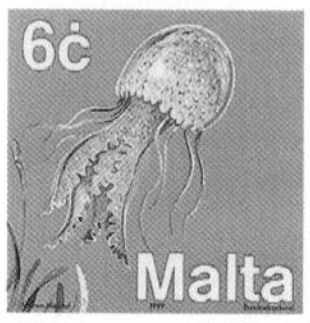

385 Common Jellyfish

1999. Marine Life of the Mediterranean. Multicoloured.

1112	6c. Type **385**	70	75
1113	6c. Peacock wrasse	70	75
1114	6c. Common cuttlefish	70	75
1115	6c. Violet sea-urchin	70	75
1116	6c. Dusky grouper	70	75
1117	6c. Common two-banded seabream	70	75
1118	6c. Star-coral	70	75
1119	6c. Spiny spider crab	70	75
1120	6c. Rainbow wrasse	70	75
1121	6c. Octopus	70	75
1122	6c. Atlantic trumpet triton	70	75
1123	6c. Mediterranean parrotfish	70	75
1124	6c. Long-snouted seahorse	70	75
1125	6c. Deep-water hermit crab	70	75
1126	6c. Mediterranean moray	70	75
1127	6c. Common starfish	70	75

Nos. 1112/27 were printed together, *se-tenant*, forming a composite design.

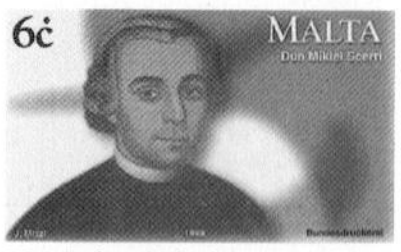

386 Father Mikiel Scerri

1999. Bicentenary of Maltese Uprising against the French. Multicoloured.

1128	6c. Type **386**	90	90
1129	6c. "L-Eroj Maltin" (statue)	90	90
1130	16c. General Belgrand de Vaubois (French commander)	1·75	1·75
1131	16c. Captain Alexander Ball R.N.	1·75	1·75

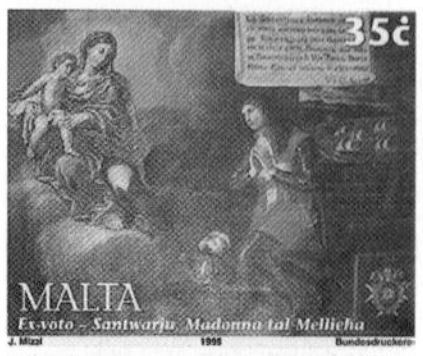

387 "Wolfgang Philip Guttenberg interceding with The Virgin" (votive painting)

1999. Mellieha Sanctuary Commemoration. Multicoloured.

1132	**387** 35c. multicoloured	2·25	2·75
MS1133	123×88 mm. 6c. "Mellieha Virgin and Child" (rock painting) (vert)	1·00	1·10

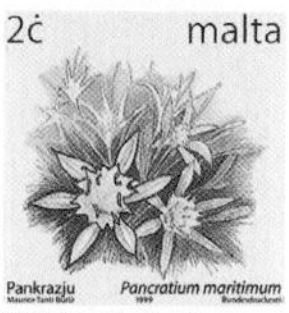

388 Sea Daffodil

1999. Maltese Flowers. Multicoloured.

1134	1c. *Helichrysum melitense*	10	10
1135	2c. Type **388**	10	10
1136	3c. *Cistus creticus*	10	15
1137	4c. Southern dwarf iris	15	20
1138	5c. *Papaver rhoeas*	30	25
1139	6c. French daffodil	25	25
1139a	7c. *Vitex angus-castus*	50	65
1140	10c. *Rosa sempervirens*	40	35
1141	11c. *Silene colorata*	60	40
1142	12c. *Cynara cardunculus*	50	45
1143	16c. Yellow-throated crocus	65	55
1144	19c. *Anthemis arvensis*	1·00	65
1145	20c. *Anacamptis pyramidalis*	1·00	70
1145a	22c. *Spartium junceum*	1·75	75
1146	25c. Large Star of Bethlehem	1·10	85
1147	27c. *Borago officinalis*	1·75	90
1147a	28c. *Crataegus azalorus*	1·75	95
1147b	37c. *Cercis siliquastrum*	2·00	1·40
1147c	45c. *Myrtus communis*	2·25	1·75
1148	46c. Wild tulip	2·25	1·75
1149	50c. *Chrysanthemum coronarium*	2·00	1·90
1149a	76c. *Pistacia lentiscus*	5·00	3·25
1150	£1 *Malva sylvestris*	4·50	4·25
1151	£2 *Adonis microcarpa*	8·00	8·50

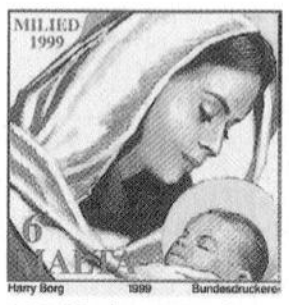

389 Madonna and Child

1999. Christmas. Multicoloured.

1152	6c. Type **389**	60	10
1153	6c.+3c. Carol singers	65	80
1154	16c.+3c. Santa Claus	1·60	2·00
1155	26c.+3c. Christmas decorations	2·00	3·00

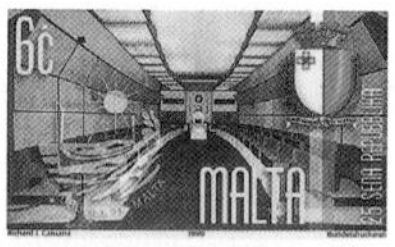

390 Parliament Chamber and Symbolic Luzzu

1999. 25th Anniv of Republic. Multicoloured.

1156	6c. Type **390**	40	25
1157	11c. Parliament in session and Council of Europe emblem	60	35
1158	16c. Church and Central Bank of Malta building	80	55
1159	19c. Aerial view of Gozo and emblems	1·10	1·00
1160	26c. Computer and shipyard	1·40	1·60

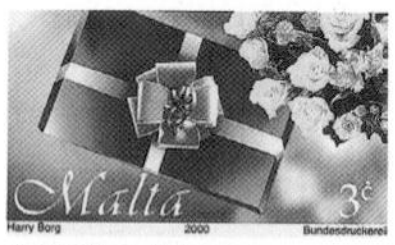

391 Gift and Flowers

2000. Greetings Stamps. Multicoloured.

1161	3c. Type **391**	30	15
1162	6c. Photograph, envelope and rose	50	25
1163	16c. Flowers and silver heart	1·00	55
1164	20c. Champagne and pocket watch	1·25	1·00
1165	22c. Wedding rings and roses	1·25	1·40

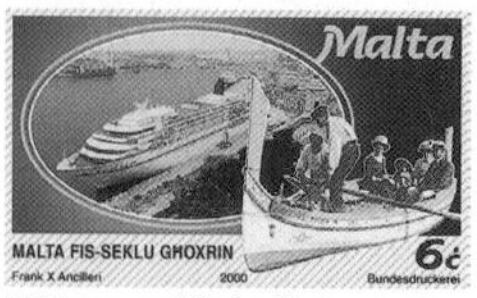

392 Luzzu and Cruise Liner

2000. Malta during the 20th Century. Multicoloured.

1166	6c. Type **392**	65	25
1167	16c. Street musicians and modern street carnival	90	65
1168	22c. Family in 1900 and illuminated quayside	1·25	1·25
1169	27c. Rural occupations and Citadel, Victoria	1·75	2·50

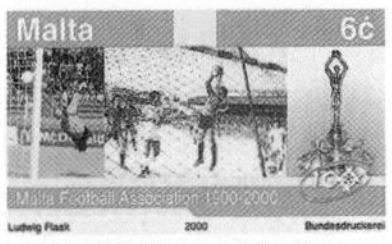

393 Footballers and Trophy (Centenary of Malta Football Association)

2000. Sporting Events. Multicoloured.

1170	6c. Type **393**	55	25
1171	16c. Swimming and sailing (Olympic Games, Sydney)	85	55
1172	26c. Judo, shooting and running (Olympic Games, Sydney)	1·40	1·10
1173	37c. Football (European Championship)	1·75	2·50

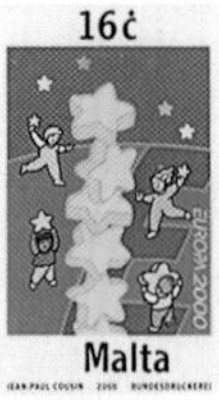

394 "Building Europe"

2000. Europa.

1174	**394**	16c. multicoloured	1·25	65
1175	**394**	46c. multicoloured	2·75	3·25

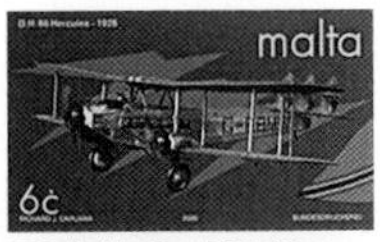

395 de Havilland DH.66 Hercules, 1928

2000. Century of Air Transport, 1900–2000. Multicoloured.

1176	6c. Type **395**	85	1·10
1177	6c. LZ 127 *Graf Zeppelin*, 1933	85	1·10
1178	16c. Douglas DC-3 Dakota of Air Malta Ltd, 1949	1·60	1·90
1179	16c. Airbus Industries Airbus A320 of Air Malta	1·60	1·90
MS1180	122×87 mm. Nos. 1176/9	4·50	5·50

Nos. 1176/7 and 1178/9 were each printed together, se-tenant, with the backgrounds forming composite designs.

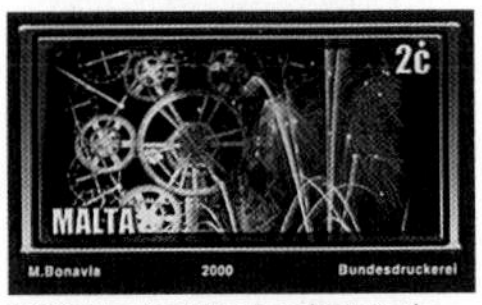

396 Catherine Wheel and Fireworks

2000. Fireworks. Multicoloured.

1181	2c. Type **396**	30	10
1182	6c. Exploding multicoloured fireworks	65	25
1183	16c. Catherine wheel	1·25	55
1184	20c. Exploding green fireworks	1·40	1·00
1185	50c. Numbered rockets in rack	3·00	5·00

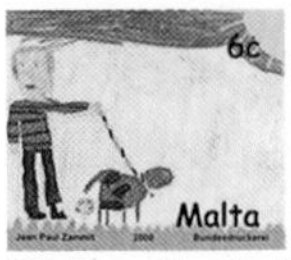

397 "Boy walking Dog" (Jean Paul Zammit)

2000. "Stampin' the Future" (Children's stamp design competition winners). Multicoloured.

1186	6c. Type **397**	55	65
1187	6c. "Stars and Woman in Megalithic Temple" (Chiara Borg)	55	65
1188	6c. "Sunny Day" (Bettina Paris)	55	65
1189	6c. "Hands holding Heart" (Roxana Caruana)	55	65

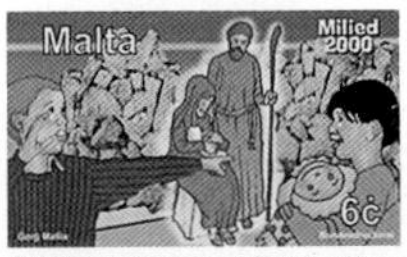

398 Boy's Sermon, Nativity Play and Girl with Doll

2000. Christmas. Multicoloured.

1190	6c. Type **398**	65	10
1191	6c.+3c. Three Wise Men (23×27 mm)	75	75
1192	16c.+3c. Family with Father Christmas	1·75	2·00
1193	26c.+3c. Christmas tree, church and family	2·25	3·25
MS1194	174×45 mm. Nos. 1190/3	4·75	6·00

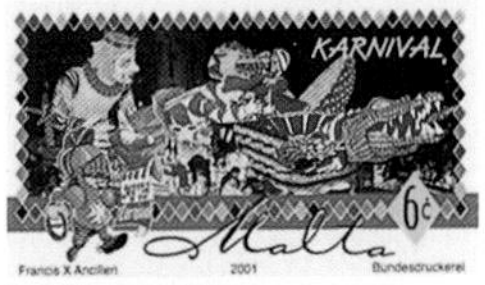

399 Crocodile Float

2001. Maltese Carnival. Multicoloured.

1195	6c. Type **399**	50	25
1196	11c. King Karnival in procession (vert)	75	40
1197	16c. Woman and children in costumes (vert)	90	55
1198	19c. Horseman carnival float (vert)	1·10	1·40
1199	27c. Carnival procession	1·50	2·00
MS1200	127×92 mm. 12c. Old-fashioned clowns; 37c. Women dressed as clowns (both 32×32 mm)	2·75	4·00

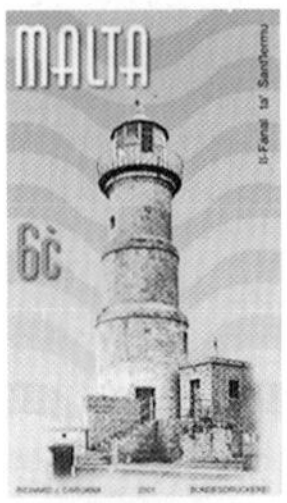

400 St. Elmo Lighthouse

2001. Maltese Lighthouses. Multicoloured.

1201	6c. Type **400**	65	25
1202	16c. Gurdan Lighthouse	1·25	70
1203	22c. Delimara Lighthouse	1·75	2·25

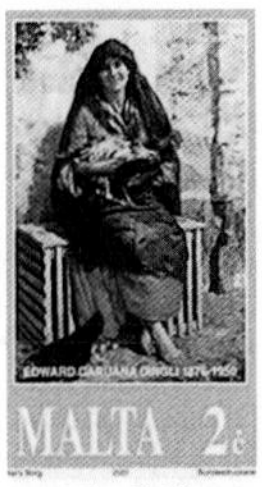

401 "The Chicken Seller" (E. Caruana Dingli)

2001. Edward Caruana Dingli (painter) Commemoration. Multicoloured.

1204	2c. Type **401**	20	30
1205	4c. "The Village Beau"	35	15
1206	6c. "The Faldetta"	50	25
1207	10c. "The Guitar Player"	80	60
1208	26c. "Wayside Orange Seller"	2·00	2·75

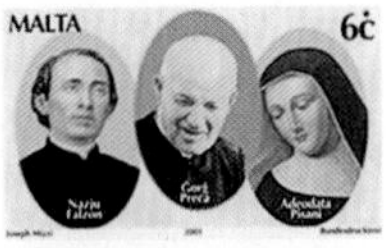

402 Nazju Falzon, Gorg Preca and Adeodata Pisani (candidates for Beatification)

2001. Visit of Pope John Paul II. Multicoloured.

1209	6c. Type **402**	1·00	25
1210	16c. Pope John Paul II and statue of St. Paul	1·75	1·50
MS1211	123×87 mm. 75c. Pope John Paul with Nazju Falzon, Gorg Preca and Adeodata Pisani	5·00	5·50

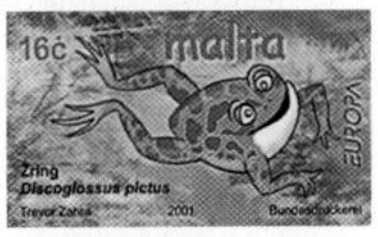

403 Painted Frog

2001. Europa. Pond Life. Multicoloured.

1212	16c. Type **403**	1·75	65
1213	46c. Red-veined darter (dragonfly)	3·25	3·75

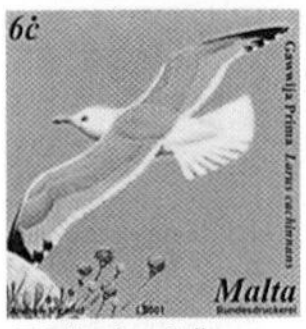

404 Herring Gull ("Yellow-legged Gull") (*Larus cachinnans*)

2001. Maltese Birds. Multicoloured.

1214	6c. Type **404**	85	85
1215	6c. Common kestrel (*Falco tinnunculus*)	85	85
1216	6c. Golden oriole (*Oriolus oriolus*)	85	85
1217	6c. Chaffinch (*Fringilla coelebs*) and Eurasian goldfinch (*Carduelis carduelis*)	85	85
1218	6c. Blue rock thrush (*Monticola solitarius*)	85	85
1219	6c. European bee-eater (*Merops apiaster*)	85	85
1220	6c. House martin (*Delichon urbica*) and barn swallow (*Hirundo rustica*)	85	85
1221	6c. Spanish sparrow (*Passer hispaniolensis*)	85	85
1222	6c. Spectacled warbler (*Sylvia conspicillata*)	85	85
1223	6c. Turtle dove (*Streptopelia turtur*)	85	85
1224	6c. Northern pintail (*Anas acuta*)	85	85
1225	6c. Little bittern (*Ixobrychus minutus*)	85	85
1226	6c. Eurasian woodcock (*Scolopax rusticola*)	85	85
1227	6c. Short-eared owl (*Asio flammeus*)	85	85
1228	6c. Northern lapwing (*Vanellus vanellus*)	85	85
1229	6c. Moorhen (*Gallinula chloropus*)	85	85

Nos 1214/29 were printed together, se-tenant, with the backgrounds forming a composite design.

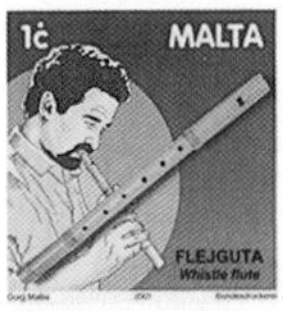

405 Whistle Flute

2001. Traditional Maltese Musical Instruments. Multicoloured.

1230	1c. Type **405**	15	50
1231	3c. Reed pipe	30	40
1232	14c. Maltese bagpipe	85	50
1233	20c. Friction drum	1·25	1·50
1234	25c. Frame drum	1·50	2·00

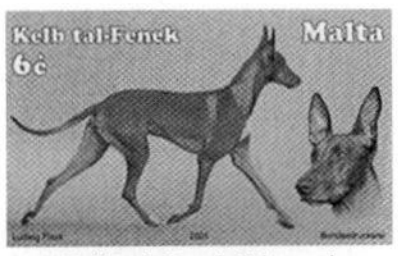

406 Kelb tal-Fenek (Pharaoh Hound)

2001. Maltese Dogs. Multicoloured.

1235	6c. Type **406**	75	25
1236	16c. Kelb tal-Kacca	1·50	55
1237	19c. Maltese	1·50	1·25
1238	35c. Kelb tal-But	2·25	3·50

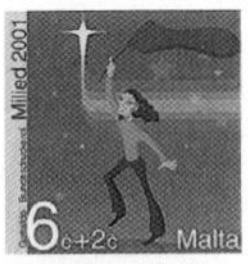

407 Man with Net chasing Star

2001. Christmas. Multicoloured.

1239	6c.+2c. Type **407**	80	50
1240	15c.+2c. Father and children	1·50	1·75
1241	16c.+2c. Mother and daughter	1·50	1·75
1242	19c.+3c. Young woman with shopping bags	1·75	2·25

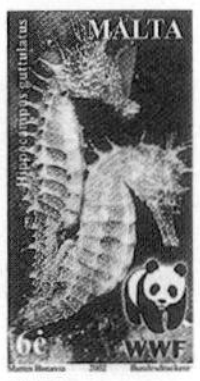

408 *Hippocampus guttulatus*

2002. Endangered Species. Mediterranean Seahorses. Multicoloured.

1243	6c. Type **408**	80	80
1244	6c. *Hippocampus hippocampus*	80	80
1245	16c. Close-up of *Hippocampus guttulatus*	1·60	1·75
1246	16c. *Hippocampus hippocampus* on seabed	1·60	1·75

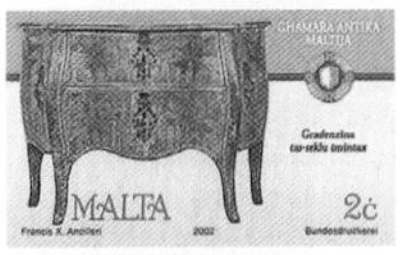

409 Sideboard

2002. Antique Furniture. Multicoloured.

1247	2c. Type **409**	25	40
1248	4c. Bureau (vert)	45	30
1249	11c. Inlaid table (vert)	85	40
1250	26c. Cabinet (vert)	1·50	85
1251	60c. Carved chest	3·00	5·00

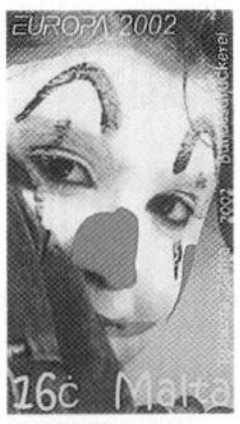

410 Child's Face painted as Clown

2002. Europa. Circus.

1252	**410**	16c. multicoloured	1·25	1·00

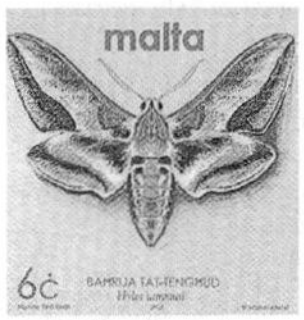

411 *Hyles sammuti*

2002. Moths and Butterflies. Multicoloured.

1253	6c. Type **411**	50	55
1254	6c. *Utetheisa pulchella*	50	55
1255	6c. *Ophiusa tirhaca*	50	55
1256	6c. *Phragmatobia fulginosa melitensis*	50	55
1257	6c. *Vanessa cardui*	50	55
1258	6c. *Polyommatus icarus*	50	55
1259	6c. *Gonepteryx cleopatra*	50	55
1260	6c. *Vanessa atlanta*	50	55
1261	6c. *Eucrostes indigenata*	50	55
1262	6c. *Macroglossum stellatarum*	50	55
1263	6c. *Lasiocampa quercus*	50	55
1264	6c. *Catocala electa*	50	55
1265	6c. *Maniola jurtina hyperhispulla*	50	55
1266	6c. *Pieris brassicaei*	50	55
1267	6c. *Papilio machaon melitensis*	50	55
1268	6c. *Dainaus chrysippus*	50	55

No. 1260 is inscribed "atalania" and 1264 "elocata", both in error.

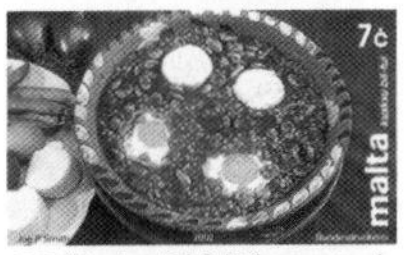

412 "Kusksu Bil-ful" (bean stew)

2002. Maltese Cookery. Multicoloured.

1269	7c. Type **412**	70	25
1270	12c. "Qaqocc mimli" (stuffed artichoke)	1·25	50
1271	16c. "Lampuki" (dorada with aubergines)	1·40	75
1272	27c. "Qaghqd Tal-kavatelli" (chestnut dessert)	2·25	2·75
MS1273	125×90 mm. 75c. "Stuffat Tal-fenek" (rabbit stew)	4·50	5·50

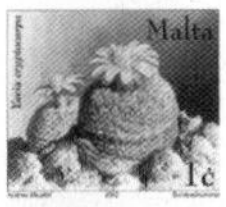

413 *Yavia cryptocarpa* (cactus)

2002. Cacti and Succulents. Multicoloured.

1274	1c. Type **413**	15	50
1275	7c. *Aztekium hintonii* (cactus) (vert)	65	25
1276	28c. *Pseudolithos migiurtinus* (succulent)	1·75	70
1277	37c. *Pierrebraunia brauniorum* (cactus) (vert)	2·25	1·50

1278	76c. *Euphorbia turbiniformis* (succulent)	4·00	6·00

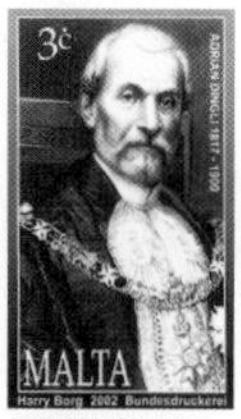

414 Chief Justice Adrian Dingli,

2002. Personalities.

1279	**414**	3c. green and black	30	40
1280	-	7c. green and black	60	25
1281	-	15c. brown and agate	1·00	60
1282	-	35c. brown and sepia	2·00	1·75
1283	-	50c. light blue and blue	2·50	4·00

DESIGNS: 7c. Oreste Kirkop (opera singer); 15c. Athanasius Kircher (Jesuit scholar); 35c. Archpriest Saverio Cassar; 50c. Emmanuele Vitali (notary).

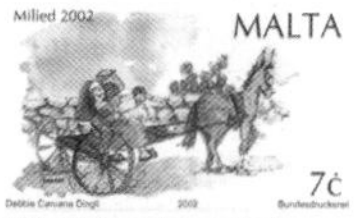

415 Mary and Joseph in Donkey Cart

2002. Christmas. Multicoloured.

1284	7c. Type **415**	70	25
1285	16c. Shepherds and Kings on a bus	1·25	55
1286	22c. Holy Family and angels in luzzu (boat)	1·60	75
1287	37c. Holy Family in horse-drawn carriage	2·00	1·50
1288	75c. Nativity on Maltese fishing boat	3·75	6·00

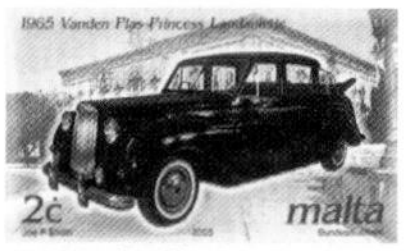

416 Vanden Plas Princess Landaulette, 1965

2003. Vintage Cars. Multicoloured.

1289	2c. Type **416**	25	60
1290	7c. Allard "M" type, 1948	65	25
1291	10c. Cadillac Model "B", 1904	85	35
1292	26c. Fiat Cinquecento Model "A" Topolino, 1936	1·60	1·60
1293	35c. Ford Anglia Super, 1965	2·25	3·00

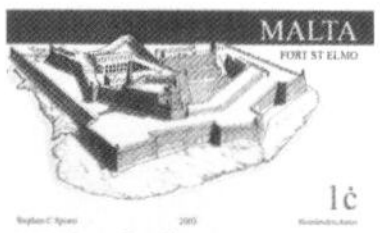

417 Fort St. Elmo

2003. Maltese Military Architecture. Multicoloured.

1294	1c. Type **417**	15	40
1295	4c. Rinella Battery	40	30
1296	11c. Fort St. Angelo	85	40
1297	16c. Section through Reserve Post R15	1·25	60
1298	44c. Fort Tigne	2·75	4·25

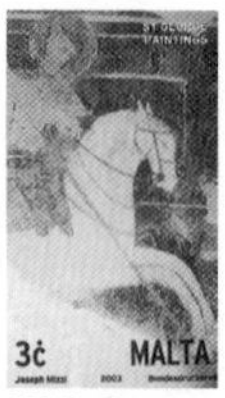

418 St. George on Horseback

2003. Paintings of St. George.

1299	**418**	3c. multicoloured	30	30
1300	-	7c. multicoloured	60	30
1301	-	14c. multicoloured	95	60
1302	-	19c. multicoloured	1·40	1·40
1303	-	27c. multicoloured	1·75	2·25

DESIGNS: 7c. to 27c. Various paintings of St. George.

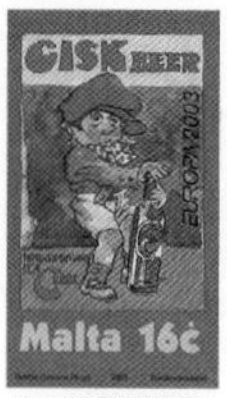

419 "CISKBEER"

2003. Europa. Poster Art. Multicoloured.

1304	16c. Type **419**	1·10	55
1305	46c. "CARNIVAL 1939"	2·75	3·50

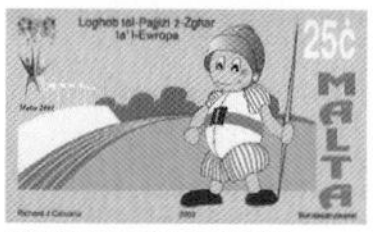

420 Games Mascot with Javelin

2003. Games of Small European States, Malta. Multicoloured.

1306	25c. Type **420**	1·25	85
1307	50c. Mascot with gun	2·25	1·75
1308	75c. Mascot with ball and net	3·75	2·75
1309	£3 Mascot with rubber ring at poolside	14·00	17·00

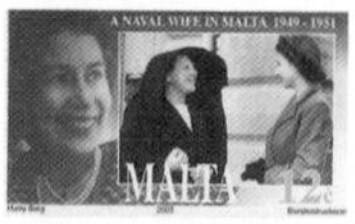

421 Princess Elizabeth in Malta, c. 1950

2003. 50th Anniv of Coronation. Multicoloured (except No. 1312).

1310	12c. black, grey and cinnamon	70	45
1311	15c. multicoloured	75	50
1312	22c. black, deep grey and grey	1·00	90
1313	60c. black, grey and deep ultramarine	2·50	3·50
MS1314	100×72 mm. £1 multicoloured	6·50	7·50

DESIGNS: 15c. Princess Elizabeth with crowd of children, Malta, c. 1950; 22c. Queen Elizabeth II in evening dress with Duke of Edinburgh, Malta; 60c. Queen Elizabeth II (receiving book) and Duke of Edinburgh, Malta; £1 Queen on walkabout with crowd.

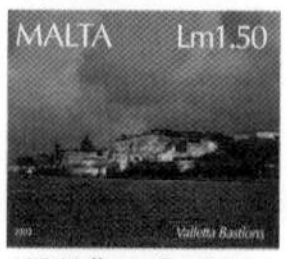

422 Valletta Bastions at Night

2003. Elton John, The Granaries, Floriana. Sheet 125×90 mm.

MS1315	**422** £1.50 multicoloured	9·00	10·00

No. **MS**1315 also contains four labels showing different portraits of Elton John.

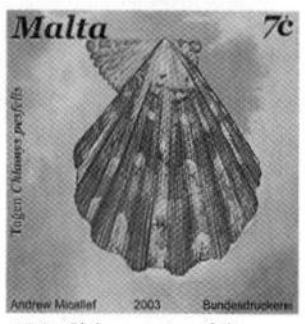

423 *Chlamys pesfelis*

2003. Sea Shells. Multicoloured.

1316	7c. Type **423**	50	55
1317	7c. *Gyroscala lamellose*	50	55
1318	7c. *Phalium granulatum*	50	55
1319	7c. *Fusiturris similes*	50	55
1320	7c. *uria lurida*	50	55
1321	7c. *Bolinus brandaris*	50	55
1322	7c. *Charonia tritonis variegate*	50	55
1323	7c. *Clanculus corallinus*	50	55
1324	7c. *Fusinus syracusanus*	50	55
1325	7c. *Pinna nobilis*	50	55
1326	7c. *Acanthocardia tuberculata*	50	55
1327	7c. *Aporrhais pespelecani*	50	55
1328	7c. *Haliotis tuberculata lamellose*	50	55
1329	7c. *Tonna galea*	50	55
1330	7c. *Spondylus gaederopus*	50	55
1331	7c. *Mitra zonata*	50	55

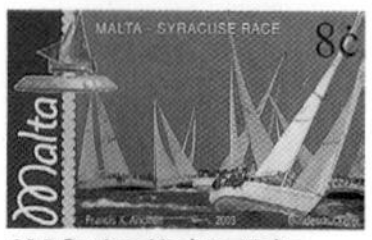

424 Racing Yachts, Malta–Syracuse Race

2003. Yachting. Multicoloured.

1332	8c. Type **424**	60	35
1333	22c. Yacht, Middle Sea Race (vert)	1·25	1·00
1334	35c. Racing yachts, Royal Malta Yacht Club (vert)	2·00	3·00

2003. As Nos. 1139a and 1143 but smaller, 23×23 mm. Self-adhesive.

1335	7c. *Vitex agnus-castus*	50	40
1336	16c. *Crocus longiflorus*	1·25	1·25

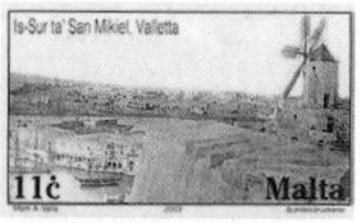

425 Is-Sur ta' San Mikiel, Valletta

2003. Windmills. Each black.

1337	11c. Type **425**	85	40
1338	27c. Ta' Kola, Xaghra (vert)	2·00	1·25
1339	45c. Tax-Xarolla, Zurrieq (vert)	2·75	4·50

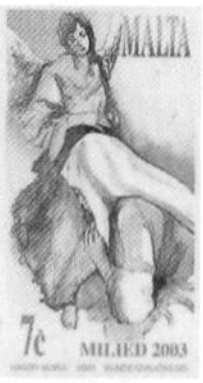

426 The Annunciation

2003. Christmas. Multicoloured.

1340	7c. Type **426**	70	30
1341	16c. Holy Family	1·00	35
1342	22c. The Shepherds following the Star (horiz)	1·40	85
1343	50c. The Three Kings with gifts (horiz)	2·75	4·00

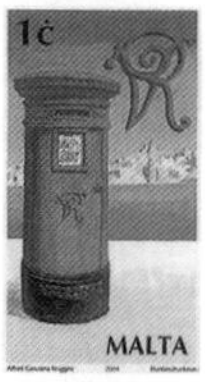

427 Pillar Box on Seafront

2004. Letter Boxes. Multicoloured.

1344	1c. Type **427**	10	30
1345	16c. Pillar box on pavement	1·50	55
1346	22c. Wall pillar boxes	1·75	90
1347	37c. Pillar box inside post office	2·50	1·75
1348	76c. Square pillar box and statue	6·00	8·00

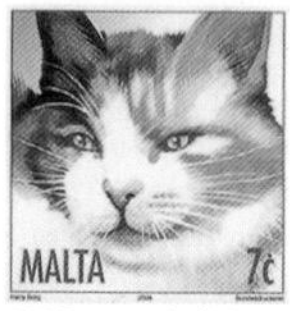

428 Tortoiseshell Cat

2004. Cats. Multicoloured.

1349	7c. Type **428**	70	30
1350	27c. Tabby	1·90	1·25
1351	28c. Silver tabby	1·90	1·25
1352	50c. Ginger tabby	3·50	4·00
1353	60c. Black and white cat	3·75	4·75

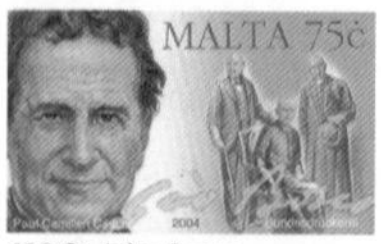

429 St. John Bosco

2004. Centenary of Salesians in Malta. Sheet 124×89 mm.

MS1354	**429** 75c. multicoloured	4·25	5·50

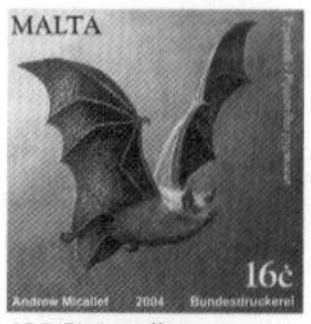

430 Pipistrelle (*Pipistrellus pygmaeus*)

2004. Mammals and Reptiles. Multicoloured.

1355	16c. Type **430**	85	90
1356	16c. Lesser mouse-eared bat (*Myotis blythi punicus*)	85	90
1357	16c. Weasel (*Mustela nivalis*)	85	90
1358	16c. Algerian hedgehog (*Atelerix algirus fallax*)	85	90
1359	16c. Mediterranean chameleon (*Chamaeleo chamaeleon*)	85	90
1360	16c. Sicilian shrew (*Crocidura sicula*)	85	90
1361	16c. Ocellated skink (*Chalcides ocellatus*)	85	90
1362	16c. Filfla Maltese wall lizard (*Podarcis filfolensis filfolensis*)	85	90
1363	16c. Moorish gecko (*Tarentola mauritanica*)	85	90
1364	16c. Turkish gecko (*Hemidactylus turcicus*)	85	90
1365	16c. Leopard snake (*Elaphe situla*)	85	90
1366	16c. Western whip snake (*Coluber viridiflavus*)	85	90
1367	16c. Common dolphin (*Delphinus delphis*)	85	90
1368	16c. Striped dolphin (*Stenella coeruleoalba*)	85	90
1369	16c. Mediterranean donk seal (*Monachus monachus*)	85	90
1370	16c. Green turtle (*Chelonia mydas*)	85	90

Nos. 1355/70 were printed together, se-tenant, in sheetlets of 16 with the background of each horizontal pair (1355/6, 1357/8, 1359/60, 1361/2, 1363/4, 1365/6, 1367/8 and 1369/70) forming a composite design.

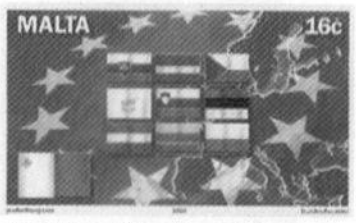

431 New Members Flags inside E.U. Stars

2004. Accession to European Union. Multicoloured.

1371	16c. Type **431**	1·00	55
1372	28c. Former Prime Minister Eddie Fenech Adami and former Foreign Minister Joe Borg signing Accession Treaty	1·50	2·00

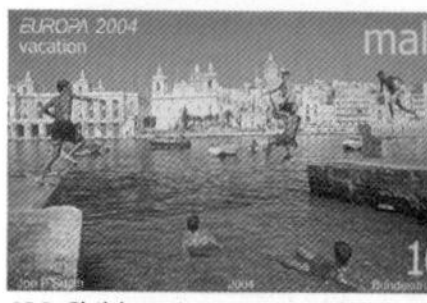

432 Children Jumping into Water

2004. Europa. Holidays. Multicoloured.

1373	16c. Type **432**	1·00	55
1374	51c. Hagar Qim prehistoric temples	2·75	3·50

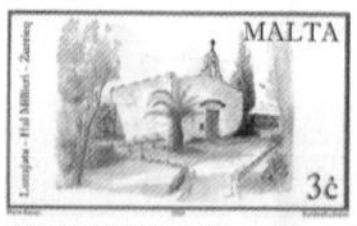

433 Hal Millieri Chapel, Zurrieq

2004. Chapels. Multicoloured.

1375	3c. Type **433**	30	30
1376	7c. San Basilju, Mqabba	60	30
1377	39c. San Cir, Rabat	2·25	1·75
1378	48c. Santa Lucija, Mtarfa	2·50	2·75
1379	66c. Ta' Santa Marija, Kemmuna	4·25	6·00

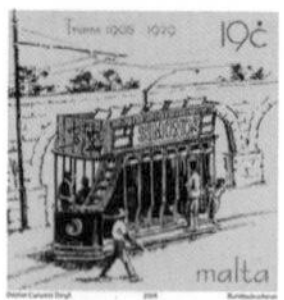

434 Tram

2004. Trams.

1380	**434**	19c. green and black	1·25	65
1381	-	37c. orange and black (25×42 mm)	2·25	1·40
1382	-	50c. yellow and black (25×42 mm)	3·25	3·50
1383	-	75c. blue and black	4·50	6·00

DESIGNS: 19c. Type **434**; 37c. Tram driver; 50c. Ticket; 75c. Tram under bridge.

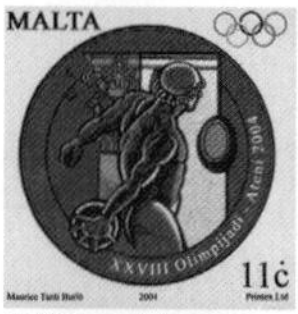

435 Discus Thrower

2004. Olympic Games, Athens. Multicoloured.

1384	11c. Type **435**	80	40
1385	16c. Greek column and laurel wreath	1·10	55
1386	76c. Javelin thrower	5·00	6·50

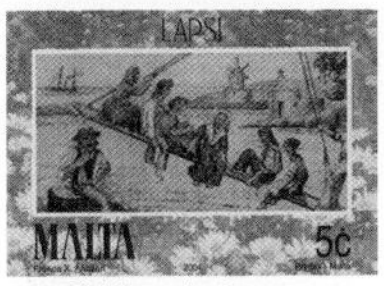

436 Children playing on Ascension Day (Luigi Brocktorff painting) (Lapsi)

2004. Festivals. Multicoloured.

1387	5c. Type **436**	45	30
1388	15c. Votive Penitentiary General Procession, Zejtun (San Girgor)	1·25	50
1389	27c. Pilgrimage in front of the Sanctuary of Our Lady of Graces, Zabbar (painting, Italo Horatio Serge) (Hadd In-Nies)	2·00	1·00
1390	51c. Children with St. Martin's Bags of nuts (Michele Bellanti lithograph) (San Martin) (vert)	3·50	3·75
1391	£1 Peasants in traditional costumes singing and dancing (painting, Antoine Favray) (Mnarja) (vert)	6·50	8·50

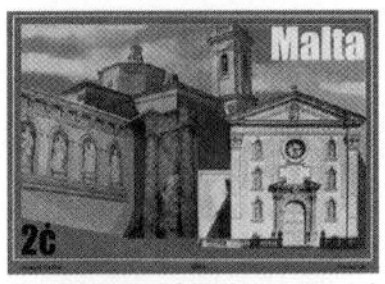

437 Church of St. Mary, Attard

2004. Art. Multicoloured.

1392	2c. Type **437**	30	35
1393	20c. Mdina Cathedral organ and music score (vert)	1·40	70
1394	57c. Statue of St. Agatha (vert)	4·25	5·00
1395	62c. Il-Gifen Tork (poem) and books (vert)	4·75	6·00
MS1396	93×100 mm. 72c. Medieval painting of St. Paul (vert)	4·50	6·00

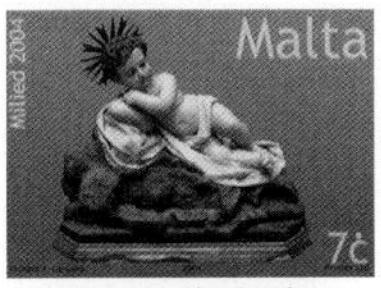

438 Papier mache Bambino on rocks, Lecce

2004. Christmas. Bambino Models. Multicoloured.

1397	7c. Type **438**	55	25
1398	16c. Wax Bambino inside glass dome (vert)	1·10	55
1399	22c. Wax Bambino on back, Lija (vert)	1·50	75
1400	50c. Beeswax Bambino under tree (vert)	3·25	4·50

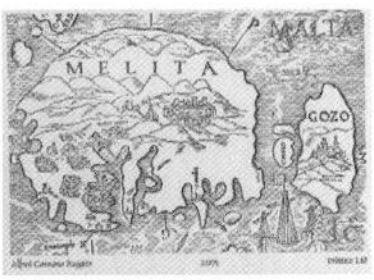

439 Quintinus Map

2005. Old Maps.

1401	**439**	1c. black and scarlet	15	40
1402	-	12c. multicoloured	90	50
1403	-	37c. multicoloured	2·75	2·00
1404	-	£1 multicoloured	6·50	8·25

DESIGNS: 1c. Type **439**; 12c. Copper-engraved map; 37c. Fresco map; £1 Map of Gozo.

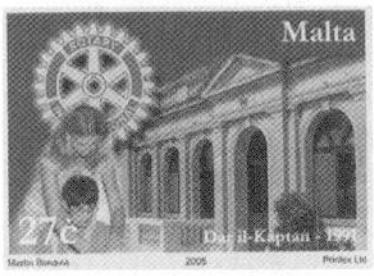

440 Dar il-Kaptan (Respite Home)

2005. Centenary of Rotary International (humanitarian organisation). Multicoloured.

1405	27c. Type **440**	1·50	90
1406	76c. Outline of Malta and Gozo and "CELEBRATE ROTARY"	4·75	6·00

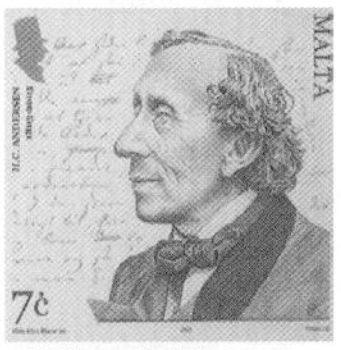

441 Hans Christian Andersen

2005. Birth Bicentenary of Hans Christian Andersen (artist and children's writer).

1407	**441**	7c. black and silver	55	25
1408	-	22c. multicoloured	1·50	75
1409	-	60c. multicoloured	3·75	4·50
1410	-	75c. multicoloured	4·50	6·00

DESIGNS: 7c. Type **441**; 20×38 mm—22c. Scissors and paper cutting; 60c. Ugly Duckling, pen and inkwell; 75c. Moroccan travelling boots and drawing of Villa Borghese, Rome.

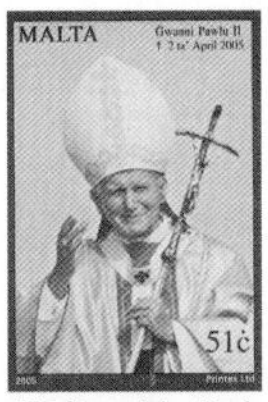

442 Pope John Paul II

2005. Pope John Paul II Commemoration.

1411	**442**	51c. multicoloured	4·25	4·00

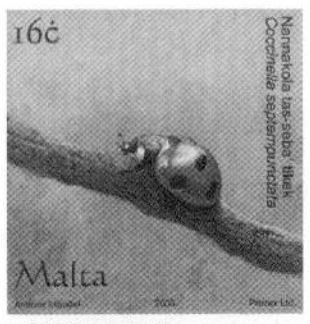

443 *Coccinella septempunctata*

2005. Insects. Multicoloured.

1412	16c. Type **443**	1·10	1·25
1413	16c. *Chrysoperla carnea*	1·10	1·25
1414	16c. *Apis mellifera*	1·10	1·25
1415	16c. *Crocothemis erythraea*	1·10	1·25
1416	16c. *Anax imperator*	1·10	1·25
1417	16c. *Lampyris pallida*	1·10	1·25
1418	16c. *Henosepilachna elaterii*	1·10	1·25
1419	16c. *Forficula decipiens*	1·10	1·25
1420	16c. *Mantis religiosa*	1·10	1·25
1421	16c. *Eumenes lunulatus*	1·10	1·25
1422	16c. *Cerambyx cerdo*	1·10	1·25
1423	16c. *Gryllus bimaculatus*	1·10	1·25
1424	16c. *Xylocopa violacea*	1·10	1·25
1425	16c. *Cicada orni*	1·10	1·25
1426	16c. *Acrida ungarica*	1·10	1·25
1427	16c. *Oryctes nasicornis*	1·10	1·25

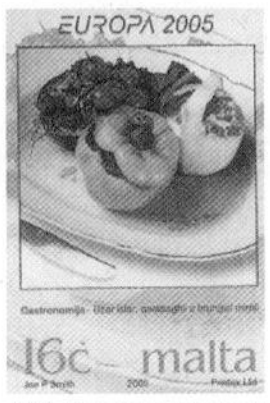

444 Cayenne Pepper, Baked, Stuffed Courgettes and Stuffed Eggplant

2005. Europa. Gastronomy. Multicoloured.

1428	16c. Type **444**	1·00	60
1429	51c. Roast rabbit	3·00	3·75

2005. Flowers. Personalised Stamps. As Nos. 1139a and 1143. Multicoloured.

1430	7c. *Vitex agnus-castus*	45	15
1431	16c. Yellow-throated crocus	80	55

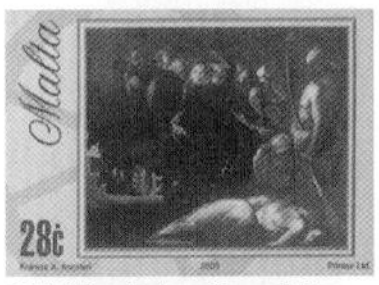

446 "The Beheading of St Catherine"

2005. St Catherine in Art. Multicoloured.

1432	28c. Type **446**	1·40	1·40
1433	28c. "Martyrdom of St Catherine" (Mattia Preti) (vert)	1·40	1·40
1434	45c. "Mystic Marriage" (Francesco Zahra) (vert)	2·00	2·75
1435	45c. "St Catherine Disputing the Philosophers" (Francesco Zahra)	2·00	2·75

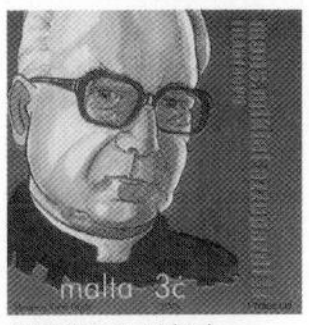

447 Mons. Mikiel Azzopardi (philanthropist)

2005. Personalities. Multicoloured.

1436	3c. Type **447**	30	20
1437	19c. Egidio Lapira (professor of dental surgery)	1·25	1·00
1438	20c. Letter and shield of Order of the Knights (Guzeppi Callus, doctor)	1·25	1·00
1439	46c. Hand writing musical score (Geronimo Abos, composer)	2·50	2·75
1440	76c. Gann Frangisk Abela (historian)	4·00	5·50

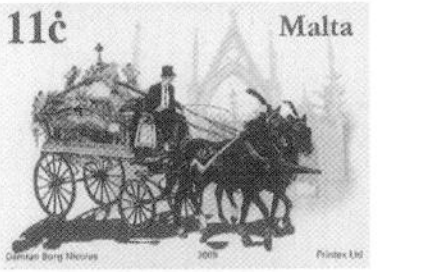

448 Horse-drawn Hearse

2005. Equines in Malta. Multicoloured.

1441	11c. Type **448**	1·00	40
1442	15c. Mule pulling traditional wooden plough	1·25	50
1443	62c. Mule on treadmill grinding flour	3·75	4·50
1444	66c. Horse-drawn water sprinkler cart	3·75	4·50

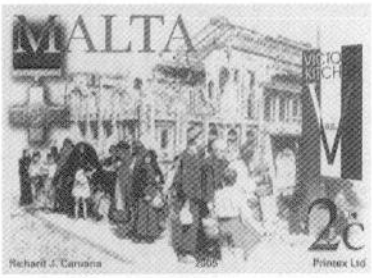

449 Queue outside "Victory Kitchen" and Ruins of Royal Opera House, Valletta

2005. 60th Anniv of End of Second World War. Battle of Malta. All showing George Cross. Multicoloured.

1445	2c. Type **449**	50	30
1446	5c. Royal Navy convoy under air attack from Savoia Marchetti S-73 Sparviero	75	25
1447	25c. Anti aircraft guns and St. Publius Church, Floriana	2·00	95
1448	51c. Pilots scrambling, Hawker Hurricane, Supermarine Spitfire and Gloster Sea Gladiators	3·75	3·75
1449	£1 Tanker Ohio and unloading of supplies at Grand Harbour, August 1943	7·00	8·50

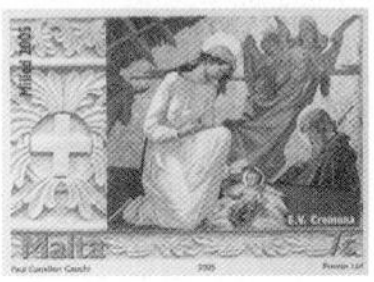

450 "The Nativity"

2005. Christmas. Paintings by Emvin Cremona from Sanctuary of Our Lady of Ta' Pinu, Gozo. Multicoloured.

1450	7c. Type **450**	60	25
1451	16c. "The Annunciation" (vert)	1·10	55
1452	22c. "The Adoration of the Magi"	1·50	75
1453	50c. "The Flight to Egypt" (69×30 mm)	3·50	4·50

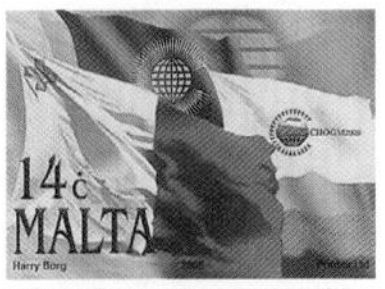

451 Maltese, Commonwealth and CHOGM Flags

2005. Commonwealth Heads of Government Meeting (CHOGM), Valletta. Each showing Maltese and Commonwealth flags. Multicoloured.

MS1454	Four sheets, each 75×63 mm. (a) 14c. Type **451**. (b) 28c. Peace doves. (c) 37c. Maltese cross. (d) 75c. Silhouettes shaking hands	7·00	9·50

452 1986 8c. Butterflies Stamp

2006. 50th Anniv of Europa Stamps. Showing Maltese Europa stamps. Multicoloured.

MS1455	120×85 mm. 5c. Type **452**; 13c. 1983 30c. Fort St. Angelo stamp; 23c. 1977 20c. Is-Salini stamp; 24c. 1989 35c. Girls with dolls stamp	4·00	5·00

No. **MS**1455 has a composite background design.

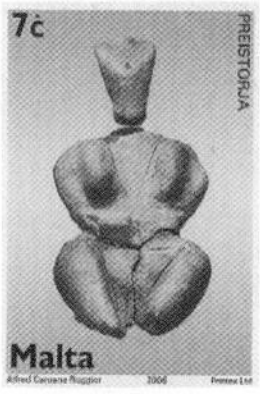

453 Female Terracotta Female Figurine, c. 4100 B.C.

2006. Ceramics in Maltese Collections. Multicoloured.

1456	7c. Type **453**	50	25
1457	16c. Roman terracotta head, c. 1st-3rd century B.C	1·00	55
1458	28c. Terracotta oil lamp holder, 14th-15th century A.D	1·25	1·40
1459	37c. Sicilian maiolica display plate, 18th century	2·25	2·40
1460	60c. Modern stylized figure in Maltese costume (Ianni Bonniçi)	3·00	4·25

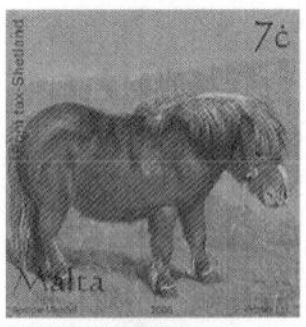

454 Shetland Pony

2006. Pets. Multicoloured.

1461	7c. Type **454**	85	90
1462	7c. Kelb tal-But (Maltese pocket dog)	85	90
1463	7c. Goldfish	85	90
1464	7c. Siamese cat	85	90
1465	7c. Siamese fighting fish	85	90
1466	7c. Ferret	85	90
1467	7c. Canary	85	90
1468	7c. Terrapin	85	90
1469	22c. Chinchilla	85	90
1470	22c. Budgerigar	85	90
1471	22c. Rabbit	85	90
1472	22c. Zebra finch	85	90
1473	22c. Kelb tal-Kacca (Maltese hunting dog)	85	90
1474	22c. Pigeon	85	90
1475	22c. Guinea pig	85	90
1476	22c. Cat	85	90

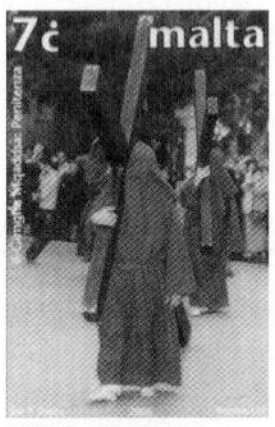

455 Penitents carrying Crosses

2006. Holy Week. Multicoloured.

1477	7c. Type **455**	50	15
1478	15c. Crucifixion tableau in procession	1·00	30
1479	22c. Burial of Christ tableau in procession	1·25	75
1480	27c. Statue of the Risen Christ paraded on Easter Sunday	1·50	1·10
1481	82c. Altar of Repose, Collegiate Church of St. Lawrence, Vittoriosa	4·50	6·50

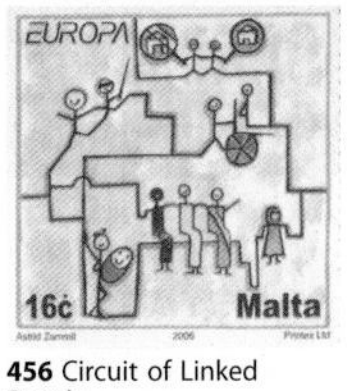

456 Circuit of Linked People

2006. Europa. Integration. Multicoloured.

1482	16c. Type **456**	1·00	50
1483	51c. Four rows of linked people (30×43 mm)	2·50	3·50

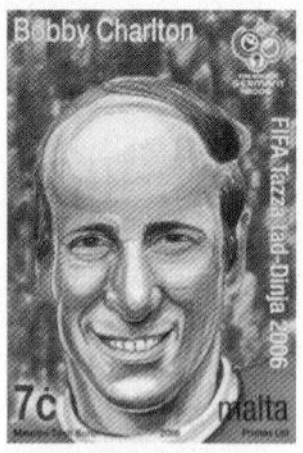

457 Bobby Charlton

2006. World Cup Football Championship, Germany. Multicoloured.

1484	7c. Type **457**	50	15
1485	16c. Pele	1·00	30
1486	27c. Franz Beckenbauer	1·60	1·10
1487	76c. Dino Zoff	4·25	6·00
MS1488	160×86 mm	6·50	7·50

2006. Sting Concert, Luxol Grounds. Sheet 121×86 mm containing design as No. 1188.

MS1489	£1.50 "Sunny Day" (Bettina Paris)	7·50	8·50

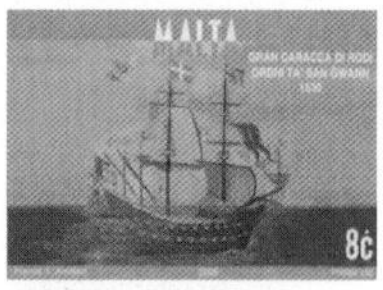

458 *Santa Anna* ("Gran Caracca di Rodi"), 1530

2006. Naval Vessels. Multicoloured.

1490	8c. Type **458**	80	20
1491	29c. *Guillaume Tell* (French) dismasted by HMS *Penelope*, *Lion* and *Foudroyant*, Malta, 1800 (Edwin Galea)	2·00	1·10
1492	51c. USS *Constitution*, 1837 (J. G. Evans)	3·25	3·00
1493	76c. HMS *Dreadnought* leaving Grand Harbour, November 1913	5·00	6·00
1494	£1 USS *Belknap* (frigate) and *Slava* (Soviet cruiser) providing communications support for Malta Summit, December 1989	6·00	7·50

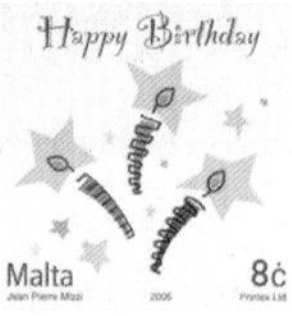

459 Candles ("Happy Birthday")

2006. Occasions. Multicoloured.

1495	8c. Type **459**	55	15
1496	16c. Heart ("Happy Anniversary")	1·00	35
1497	27c. Stars holding parcel, balloon and candle ("Congratulations")	1·60	1·25
1498	37c. Balloons ("Best Wishes")	2·00	2·75

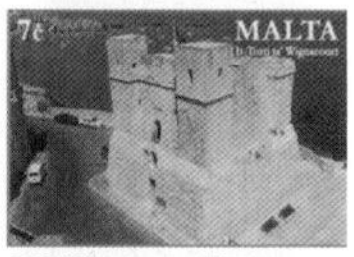

460 Wignacourt Tower

2006. Maltese Castles and Towers. Multicoloured.

1499	7c. Type **460**	65	15
1500	16c. Verdala Castle	1·25	35
1501	27c. San Lucjan Tower	1·90	1·10
1502	37c. Kemmuna Tower	2·50	1·75
1503	£1 Selmun Castle	6·00	8·50

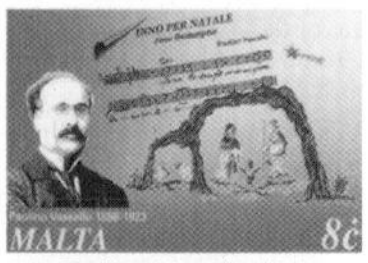

461 Paolino Vassallo, "Inno per Natale" and Nativity

2006. Christmas Music. Showing composer and score. Multicoloured.

1504	8c. Type **461**	55	15
1505	16c. Carmelo Pace, "They Heard the Angels" and Three Magi	1·00	30
1506	22c. Paul Nani, "Maltese Christmas" and angels	1·40	1·25
1507	27c. Carlo Diacono, "Notte di Natale", shepherds and angel	1·60	1·60
MS1508	120×86 mm. 50c. Wolfgang Amadeus Mozart (250th birth anniv) and "Alma di Creatoris"	3·00	3·50

2006. Bob Geldof Concert for YMCA, Manoel Island. Sheet 121×86 mm containing design as No. 1189.

MS1509	£1.50 "Hands holding Heart" (Roxana Caruana)	7·50	8·50

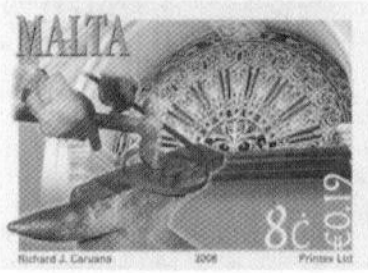

462 Wrought Iron Work

2006. Crafts. Multicoloured.

1510	8c. Type **462**	55	15
1511	16c. Glass making	1·00	35
1512	22c. Filigree work	1·40	70
1513	37c. Pottery	2·00	1·75
1514	60c. Reed basketwork	3·75	5·00

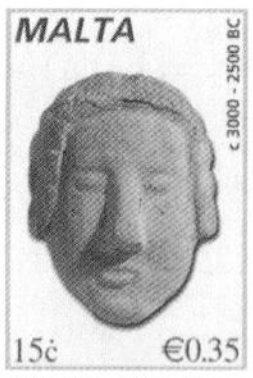

463 Stone Head

2007. Prehistoric Sculptures, c. 3000–2500 BC. Multicoloured.

1515	15c. Type **463**	1·00	30
1516	29c. Stone bas-relief of animals (horiz)	1·75	1·10
1517	60c. Stone-carved spiral pattern (horiz)	3·75	4·25
1518	£1.50 Clay statuette of female figure	7·50	9·00

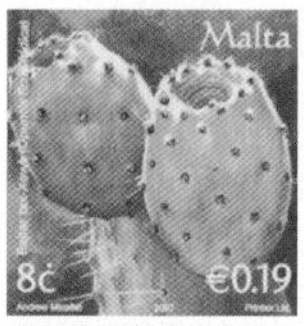

464 *Opuntia ficus-indica* (prickly pear)

2007. Maltese Fruits. Multicoloured.

1519	8c. Type **464**	45	50
1520	8c. *Vitis vinifera* (grapes)	45	50
1521	8c. *Eriobotrya japonica* (loquat)	45	50
1522	8c. *Morus nigra* (black mulberry)	45	50
1523	8c. *Ficus carica* (figs)	45	50
1524	8c. *Citrus limonum* (lemons)	45	50
1525	8c. *Pyrus communis* (pear)	45	50
1526	8c. *Prunus persica* (peaches)	45	50
1527	8c. *Punica granatum* (pomegranate)	45	50
1528	8c. *Prunus salicina* (Japanese plum)	45	50
1529	8c. *Citrullus vulgaris* (watermelon)	45	50
1530	8c. *Citrus sinensis* (orange)	45	50
1531	8c. *Olea europaea* (olives)	45	50
1532	8c. *Lycopersicon esculentum* (tomatoes)	45	50
1533	8c. *Malus domestica* (apples)	45	50
1534	8c. *Cucumis melo* (melon)	45	50

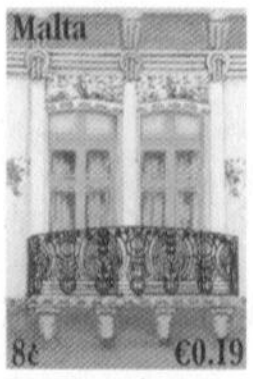

465 Wrought-iron Balcony

2007. Maltese Balconies. Multicoloured.

1535	8c. Type **465**	50	40
1536	22c. Ornate open stone balcony and recessed doorway, Gozo	1·25	1·10
1537	27c. Balustraded balcony, National Library of Malta	1·60	1·40
1538	29c. Carved stone balcony with glazed timber enclosure, Gozo	1·75	1·50
1539	46c. Two balconies on Art Deco 1930's building	2·75	3·50
MS1540	123×86 mm. 51c. Detail of balcony on Hostel de Verdelin, Valletta (horiz)	2·75	3·25

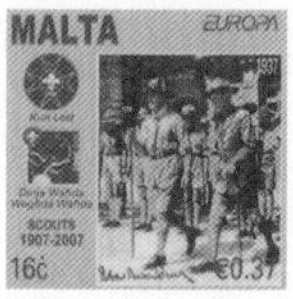

466 Lord Baden-Powell (founder) and District Commissioner Capt J. V. Abela, Malta, 1937

2007. Europa. Centenary of Scouting. Multicoloured.

1541	16c. Type **466**	1·00	60
1542	51c. Malta scouts marching, Golden Jubilee Jamboree, near Birmingham, 1957	3·00	3·50

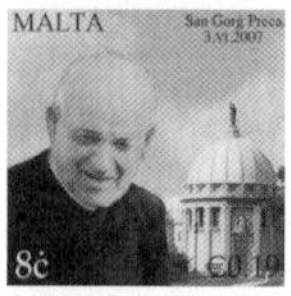

467 St. Gorg Preca

2007. Canonization of Dun Gorg Preca. Multicoloured.

1543	8c. Type **467**	50	50
1544	£1 As Type **467** but sun rising behind Basilica	5·00	6·00

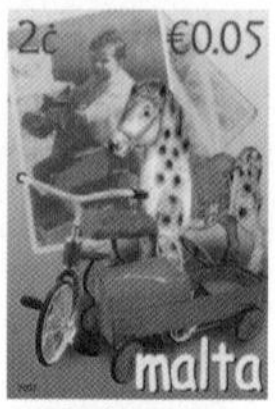

468 Rocking Horse, Tricycle and Car, all Triang (1950s)

2007. Toys from Days Gone By. Multicoloured.

1545	2c. Type **468**	10	10
1546	3c. Pedigree dolls pram (1950s), drums and skipping rope	15	15
1547	16c. Japanese tin cabin cruiser (1960s), sand pails, spade and Triang sailing boat	90	80
1548	22c. Lenci doll, Pedigree doll and 1930s Armand Marseille doll	1·25	1·10
1549	50c. Alps clockwork racing car (1950s), P.N. motorcycle (1950s) and Chad Valley delivery van (1930s)	3·25	4·00

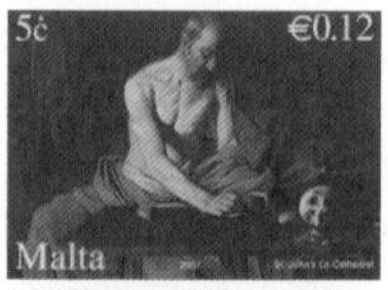

469 'St. Jerome' (Caravaggio)

2007. 400th Anniv of the Arrival of Michelangelo Merisi (Caravaggio) in Malta. Paintings. Multicoloured.

1550	5c. Type **469**	35	35
1551	29c. 'The Beheading of St. John the Baptist' (detail)	1·75	1·75
MS1552	130×86 mm. £2 'The Beheading of St. John the Baptist' (vert)	14·00	16·00

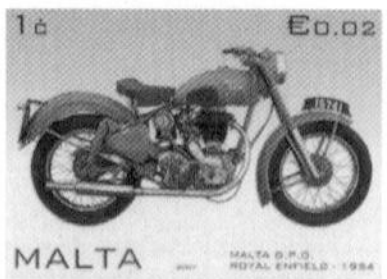

470 Malta GPO Royal Enfield Motorcycle, 1954

2007. Motorcycles. Multicoloured.

1553	1c. Type **470**	15	30
1554	16c. Malta Garrison Matchless G3/L, 1941	1·25	85
1555	27c. Civilian Minerva, 1903	2·00	1·40
1556	50c. Malta Police Triumph Speed Twin, 1965	4·00	4·50

471 Heart and 'LOVE'

2007. Occasions Greetings Stamps. Multicoloured.

1557	8c. Type **471**	55	55
1558	8c. Teddy bears	55	55
1559	8c. Star decorations ('Congratulations!')	55	55
1560	8c. Pink roses ('GREETINGS')	55	55
1561	8c. Balloons	55	55
1562	8c. Champagne glasses	55	55

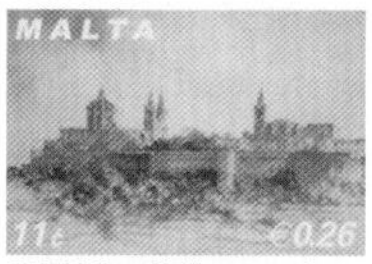

472 Mdina Skyline seen from Mtarfa

2007. Maltese Scenery. Designs showing watercolours by John Martin Borg. Multicoloured.

1563	11c. Type **472**	90	65
1564	16c. Farmhouse, windmill and church, Qrendi	1·25	85
1565	37c. Vittoriosa waterfront	2·50	2·25
1566	46c. Mgarr Harbour, Gozo	3·00	3·00
1567	76c. Xlendi Bay, Gozo	4·75	6·00

No. 1564 is inscr 'sepac'.

2007. 34U (Tree for You) Campaign. Sheet 100×66 mm containing design as No. 1531.

MS1568	75c. *Olea europaea* (olives)	4·00	5·00

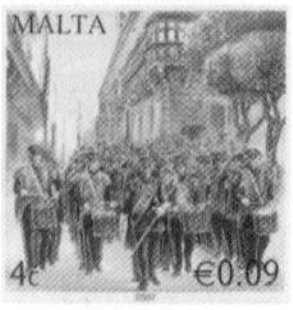

473 Military Band

2007. Maltese Bands. Multicoloured.

1569	4c. Type **473**	45	40
1570	15c. Police band	1·50	85
1571	21c. Band playing at carnival	1·75	1·25
1572	22c. Band playing at Christmas	1·75	1·25
1573	£1 Band and conductor	7·00	8·50

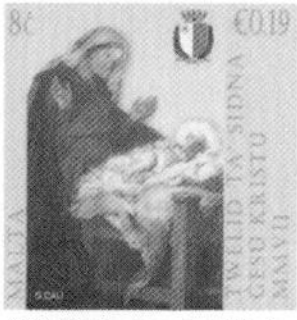

474 Madonna and Baby Jesus

2007. Christmas. Showing details from painting The Nativity by Giuseppe Cali in St. Andrew's parish church, Luqa. Multicoloured.

1574	8c. Type **474**	60	30
1575	16c. Holy Family with two countrywomen and young girl	1·25	85
1576	27c. Baby Jesus and young girl	2·00	2·25

Similar stamps were issued by the Vatican City.

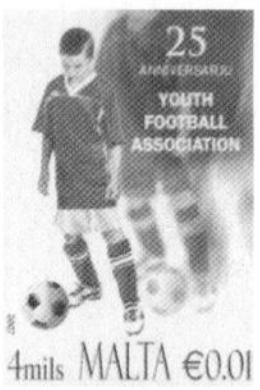

475 Boys playing Football

2007. Anniversaries and Personalities. Multicoloured.

1577	4mils Type **475** (25th anniv of Youth Football Association)	10	10
1578	9c. Children receiving religious instruction (centenary of Society of Christian Doctrine)	65	30
1579	16c. Canon Monsignor Professor Francesco Bonnici (founder of St. Joseph Institute for orphan boys)	1·25	85
1580	43c. Father Manwel Magri (ethnographer, archaeologist and educator)	3·00	3·00
1581	86c. Carolina Cauchi (founder of Dominican order at Lunzjata Monastery, Gozo)	5·50	6·50
MS1582	100×70 mm. 76c. Signatories (50th anniv of Treaty of Rome) (horiz)	4·50	5·50

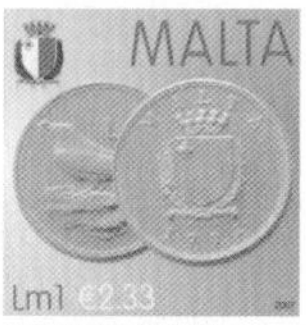

476 Malta £1 Coin

2007. Coins of Malta 1972–2007. Sheet 100×66 mm.

MS1583 **476** €2.33 multicoloured — 6·00 / 7·00

2008. Adoption of the Euro Currency (1st issue). Sheet 100×66 mm containing square design as T **476**. Multicoloured.

MS1584 €2.33 Obverse and reverse of one euro coin — 3·50 / 4·00

477 'Aphrodite' State of Cyprus

2008. Adoption of the Euro Currency (2nd issue). Sheet 100×62 mm containing T **477** and similar square design. Multicoloured.

MS1585 €1 Type **477**; €1 'Sleeping Lady' statuette, Malta — 5·50 / 7·00

A similar miniature sheet was issued by Cyprus.

478 Door Knocker from Ministry of Finance, Valletta

2008. Door Knockers. Multicoloured.

1586	26c. Type **478**	1·00	65
1587	51c. Fish door knocker from Museum of Fine Arts, Valletta	1·60	1·25
1588	63c. Door knocker from Department of Industrial & Employment Relations, Valletta	1·75	2·00
1589	€1.77 Door knocker from Museum of Archaeology, Valletta	5·00	6·00

479 Shooting

2008. Olympic Games, Beijing. Multicoloured.

1590	5c. Type **479**	15	10
1591	12c. Swimming	30	20
1592	€1.57 Running	4·75	5·50

480 Postman and Mail Room (in sepia)

2008. Europa. The Letter. Multicoloured.

1593	37c. Type **480**	1·25	85
1594	€1.19 As Type **480** (in monochrome)	4·00	4·25

481 Woodcarving by Xandru Farrugia, Conversion of St. Paul Church, Hal Safi

2008. Annus Paulinus 2008–2009 (2000th Birth Anniv of St. Paul). Showing statues of St. Paul. Multicoloured.

1595	19c. Type **481**	70	30
1596	68c. Papier mache statue by Agostino Camilleri, St. Paul's Shipwreck Church, Munxar, Gozo	2·25	2·25
1597	€1.08 Wooden statue by Giovanni Caruana, St. Paul's Shipwreck Church, Rabat	3·75	4·25
MS1598	120×86 mm. €3 Wooden statue by Melchiorre Gafà, St. Paul's Shipwreck Church, Valletta	8·50	9·50

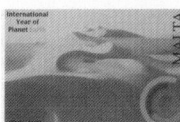

482 Sand Dunes

2008. International Year of Planet Earth. Multicoloured.

1599	7c. Type **482**	30	20
1600	86c. Single tree growing in field	3·00	3·00
1601	€1 Globe	3·50	3·75
1602	€1.77 Rocky coast	6·00	7·00

483 MSC Musica

2008. Cruise Liners. Multicoloured.

1603	63c. Type **483**	2·50	1·50
1604	€1.16 MS Voyager of the Seas	4·00	4·00
1605	€1.40 MS Westerdam	4·50	4·50
1606	€3 RMS Queen Elizabeth II	10·00	12·00

484 Madonna and Child with Infant St. John the Baptist (detail) (Francesco Trevisani)

2008. Christmas. Nativity Paintings from the National Museum of Fine Arts, Valletta. Multicoloured.

1607	19c. Type **484**	60	30
1608	26c. Nativity (detail of Virgin and Christ Child from panel by Maestro Alberto)	90	60
1609	37c. Virgin and Child with Infant St. John the Baptist (Carlo Maratta)	1·25	1·25

485 Laetiorus sulphureus

2009. Fungi. Multicoloured.

1610	5c. Type **485**	15	15
1611	12c. Montagnea arenaria	35	30
1612	19c. Pleurotus eryngii	65	40
1613	26c. Inonotus indicus	90	70
1614	€1.57 Suillus collinitus	5·25	5·75

486 Dornier Wal SANA Seaplane

2009. Vintage Postal Transport. Multicoloured.

1615	9c. Type **486**	40	25
1616	35c. Postmen on BSA motorcycles	1·75	1·00
1617	€2.50 Postmen with Raleigh bicycles	8·00	9·00
1618	€3 Gozo Mail Boat	9·00	10·00

487 Emblem

2009. Tenth Anniv of the Euro.

1619	**487** €2 multicoloured	6·00	7·00

488 Galileo Galilei, his Sketch of Moon and Apollo 11 Lunar Module Eagle

2009. Europa. Astronomy. Multicoloured.

1620	37c. Type **488**	1·50	1·10
1621	€1.19 William Lassell's telescope (set up in Malta 1861–5) and Nebula M42	3·00	3·50

489 Sailing

2009. 13th Games of the Small States of Europe, Nicosia and Limassol, Cyprus. Multicoloured.

1622	10c. Type **489**	35	25
1623	19c. Judo	65	40
1624	37c. Shooting	1·40	1·10
1625	67c. Swimming	2·50	2·50
1626	€1.77 Athletics	5·00	6·00

2009. Cruise Liners (2nd series). As T **483**. Multicoloured.

1627	37c. Seabourn Pride	1·75	1·10
1628	68c. Brilliance of the Seas	2·50	1·90
1629	91c. Costa Magica and Costa Atlantica	3·25	3·25
1630	€2 MSC Splendida	6·00	7·00

490 Headland

2009. Scenery. Multicoloured.

1631	2c. Type **490**	15	25
1632	7c. Watchtower of Knights of the Sovereign Military Order of Malta	35	20
1633	37c. Stone salt pans, Qbajjar, Gozo	1·50	70
1634	€1.02 Segment of the Ggantija Temples, Gozo	3·50	4·50

No. 1633 is inscr 'sepac'.

491 Mater Admirablis (in the manner of Botticelli)

2009. Christmas. Multicoloured.

1635	19c. Type **491**	65	30
1636	37c. Madonna and Child (Corrado Giacquinto)	1·25	60
1637	63c. The Madonna and Child (follower of Simone Cantarini)	2·00	2·50

492 Skeleton of Prehistoric Animal (Pleistocene Period)

2009. History of Malta. Multicoloured.

1638	1c. Type **492**	15	30
1639	2c. Ruins of stone temple (Early Temple Period)	20	30
1640	5c. Carved stone pattern (Late Temple Period)	30	25
1641	7c. Pair of pots (Bronze Age)	35	25
1642	9c. Gold statue (Phoenician and Punic Period) (vert)	40	40
1643	10c. Mosaic (Roman Period)	40	40
1644	19c. Gold coin (Byzantine Period) (stone background) (vert)	65	30

1644a	20c. As No. 1644 (grey background) (vert) (7.3.12)	65	30
1645	26c. Fragment of carved stone (Arab Period)	90	60
1646	37c. Painting (Norman and Hohenstaufen Period) (vert)	1·25	75
1647	50c. Stone tablet carved with shield (Angevin and Aragonese) (vert)	1·75	1·75
1648	51c. Gold pattern with central Maltese Cross (Knights of St. John)	1·75	1·75
1649	63c. Painting of officers and crew disembarking in rowing boats from ships (French Period)	1·75	1·75
1650	68c. George Cross (British Period) (lavender background) (vert)	2·00	2·00
1650a	69c. As No. 1650 (stone background) (vert) (7.3.12)	2·00	2·00
1651	86c. Independence (vert)	2·75	2·75
1652	€1 Republic (vert)	3·50	3·50
1653	€1.08 EU Accession (vert)	3·50	3·50
1654	€5 Arms of Malta (vert)	16·00	17·00
MS1655	170×263 mm. Nos. 1638/54. Wmk upright	35·00	37·00

493 100 Ton Gun, Fort Rinella, Malta, 2010

2010. 100 Ton Guns. Multicoloured.

MS1656 75c.×4 Type **493**; '100 ton' gun, Fort Rinella, Malta, 1882; '100 ton' gun, Napier of Magdala Battery, Gibraltar, 1880; '100 ton' gun, Napier of Magdala Battery, Gibraltar, 2010 — 7·00 / 8·00

A miniature sheet containing the same designs was issued by Gibraltar.

494 Balloons

2010. Occasions Greetings Stamps. Multicoloured.

1657	19c. Type **494**	65	65
1658	19c. Aerial view of coastline and offshore rocks	65	65
1659	19c. Mortarboard and scroll	65	65
1660	19c. Woman greeting man and crowd (painting)	65	65
1661	19c. Two glasses of champagne and bottle in ice bucket (vert)	65	65
1662	19c. St. John's Co-Cathedral, Valletta and fireworks (vert)	65	65
1663	19c. Hand holding trophy (vert)	65	65
1664	37c. Outline map of Malta and Gozo	1·10	1·10

495 Pope Benedict XVI

2010. Visit of Pope Benedict XVI to Malta

MS1665 **495** €3 multicoloured — 9·75 / 9·75

496 Puttinu u Toninu (Dr. Philip Farrugia Randon)

2010. Europa. Children's Books. Multicoloured.

1666	37c. Type **496**	1·50	1·10
1667	€1.19 Meta l-Milied ma giex (Clare Azzopardi)	3·00	3·25

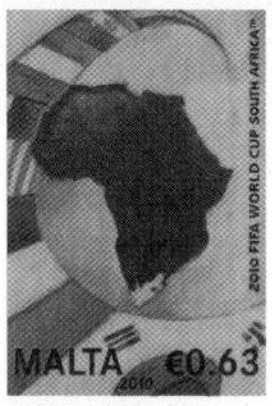

497 Globe and National Flags

2010. World Cup Football Championship, South Africa. Multicoloured.

1668	63c. Type **497**	1·75	1·75
1669	€2.50 Zakumi the leopard mascot	7·00	7·50
MS1669a	131×80 mm. As Nos. 1668/9	8·75	9·25

498 Maltese Wall Lizard

2010. Biodiversity. Multicoloured.

1670	19c. Type **498**	75	40
1671	68c. Storm petrel (vert)	2·50	2·00
1672	86c. Maltese pyramidal orchid (vert)	3·00	3·00
1673	€1.40 Freshwater crab	3·75	4·50

499 Azure Window, Gozo

2010. Natural Treasures. Multicoloured.

1674	37c. Type **499**	1·60	1·10
1675	51c. Blue Grotto, Zurrieq (vert)	2·25	2·00
1676	67c. Ta' Cenc, Gozo (vert)	2·50	2·50
1677	€1.16 Filfla	3·00	3·75

500 *The Adoration of the Magi* (Valerio Castello)

2010. Christmas. Multicoloured.

1678	19c. Type **500**	65	30
1679	37c. *The Flight into Egypt* (Filippo Paladini)	1·75	2·00
1680	63c. *Madonna di Maggio* (Pierre Guillemin) (vert)	3·50	3·00

501 Cancelled 1860 ½d. Buff Stamp

2010. 150th Anniv of the First Malta Stamp

MS1681	**501** €2.80 multicoloured	8·50	9·00

502 *Valletta*

2011. Treasures of Malta. Landscapes. Multicoloured.

1682	19c. Type **502**	65	30
1683	37c. *Manoel Island*	1·50	1·10
1684	€1.57 *Cittadella* (Gozo)	4·25	4·25

503 *Chimaera monstrosa* (Rabbit fish)

2011. 50th Anniv of WWF (Worldwide Fund for Nature). *Chimaera monstrosa* (Rabbit fish). Multicoloured.

MS1685	51c. Type **503**; 63c. Rabbit fish (swimming towards top right); 67c. Rabbit fish (seen from front); 97c. Rabbit fish (with fins outstretched)	8·50	8·50

504 Trees, Pine Cones, Flowers and Butterfly (Nicole Sciberras)

2011. Europa. Forests. Multicoloured.

1686	37c. Type **504**	1·50	1·10
1687	€1.19 Trees, fallen tree and fungi	3·25	4·00

505 Reo Bus, Birkirkara

2011. Malta Buses of the 1950s and 1960s. Make of Bus and Route given. Multicoloured.

1688	20c. Type **505**	70	45
1689	20c. Dodge T110L, Zabbar	70	45
1690	20c. Leyland Comet, Zurrieq	70	45
1691	20c. Ford V8, Zebbug-Siggiewi	70	45
1692	20c. Bedford SLD, Gudja-Ghaxaq	70	45
1693	20c. Gozo mail bus	70	45
1694	20c. Federal bus, Kalafrana	70	45
1695	20c. Dodge T110L, Siggiewi	70	45
1696	20c. Indiana bus, Rabat	70	45
1697	20c. Austin CXD, Zejtun	70	45
1698	69c. Ford V8, Sliema	2·00	2·40
1699	69c. Commer Q4, Lija	2·00	2·40
1700	69c. Fordson BB, Mosta - Naxxar	2·00	2·40
1701	69c. Thorneycroft Sturdy ZE, Mellieha	2·00	2·40
1702	69c. Bedford QL, Cospicua	2·00	2·40
1703	69c. Magirus Deutz, all routes	2·00	2·40
1704	69c. Commer Q4, Naxxar	2·00	2·40
1705	69c. Bedford SB8, Gozo	2·00	2·40
1706	69c. Thames ET7, Birkirkara - St. Julians	2·00	2·40
1707	69c. Bedford QL, private hire	2·00	2·40

506 MV *Ta' Pinu* (Gozo Channel Company passenger and car ferry)

2011. Maritime Malta. Multicoloured.

1708	26c. Type **506**	80	30
1709	37c. MV *Jean De La Valette* (Virtu Ferries catamaran)	1·50	1·10
1710	67c. P23 (Maritime Squadron patrol boat)	2·50	2·50
1711	91c. MV *Spinola* (Tug Malta Bollard Pull Terminal/Escort VSP tractor tug)	2·75	3·00

507 Mgarr, Gozo

2011. Fishing Villages. Sheet 120×81 mm

MS1712	**507** €2.07 multicoloured	6·25	6·50

508 *The Holy Family in an Interior* (follower of Marcello Venusti, 1510-79)

2011. Christmas. Multicoloured.

1713	20c. Type **508**	55	30
1714	37c. *The Madonna and Child with Infant St. John the Baptist* (Tuscan school, c. 1600)	95	50
1715	63c. *The Rest on the Flight into Egypt* (16th-century Flemish)	2·00	1·25

509 Malta 1922 £1 Stamp

2011. 90th Anniv of Malta Senate and Legislative Assembly. Sheet 130×85 mm

MS1716	**509** €4.16 multicoloured	12·00	12·00

510 *Marsalforn* (H. M. Bateman)

2012. International Artists and Malta. Paintings of Maltese Landscapes by H. M. Bateman and Edward Lear. Multicoloured.

1717	20c. Type **510**	55	30
1718	26c. *Qala* (H. M. Bateman)	60	45
1719	37c. *Ghajnsielem* ((H. M. Bateman) (vert)	95	50
1720	67c. *Inquisitor's Palace* (Edward Lear)	2·00	1·25
1721	97c. *Gran Fontana* (Edward Lear)	3·00	2·25

POSTAGE DUE STAMPS

D1

1925. Imperf.

D1	**D1**	½d. black	1·25	8·00
D2	**D1**	1d. black	3·25	3·25
D3	**D1**	1½d. black	3·00	3·75
D4	**D1**	2d. black	13·00	22·00
D5	**D1**	2½d. black	2·75	2·75
D6	**D1**	3d. black on grey	9·00	15·00
D7	**D1**	4d. black on yellow	5·00	9·50
D8	**D1**	6d. black on yellow	5·00	24·00
D9	**D1**	1s. black on yellow	6·50	24·00
D10	**D1**	1s. 6d. black on yellow	17·00	65·00

D2

1925. Perf.

D11	**D2**	½d. green	1·25	60
D12	**D2**	1d. violet	1·25	45
D13	**D2**	1½d. brown	1·50	80
D14	**D2**	2d. grey	11·00	1·00
D35	**D2**	2d. brown	85	70
D36	**D2**	2½d. orange	60	70
D37	**D2**	3d. blue	60	60
D38	**D2**	4d. green	1·00	80
D39	**D2**	6d. purple	75	1·50
D40	**D2**	1s. black	90	1·50
D41	**D2**	1s.6d. red	2·75	7·00

D3 Maltese Lace

1973

D42	**D3**	2m. brown and red	10	10
D43	**D3**	3m. orange and red	10	15
D44	**D3**	5m. pink and red	15	20
D45	**D3**	1c. blue and green	30	35
D46	**D3**	2c. grey and black	40	35
D47	**D3**	3c. light brown & brown	40	35
D48	**D3**	5c. dull blue and blue	65	70
D49	**D3**	10c. lilac and plum	85	1·00

D4

1993

D50	**D4**	1c. magenta and mauve	20	30
D51	**D4**	2c. blue and light blue	25	40
D52	**D4**	5c. green and turquoise	35	45
D53	**D4**	10c. orange and yellow	55	55

Pt. 19

MANAMA

A dependency of Ajman.

100 dirhams = 1 riyal.

1966. Nos. 10, 12, 14 and 18 of Ajman surch Manama in English and Arabic and new value.

1	40d. on 40n.p. multicoloured	60	60
2	70d. on 70n.p. multicoloured	60	60
3	1r.50 on 1r.50 multicoloured	1·20	1·20
4	10r. on 10r. multicoloured	7·25	7·25

1967. Nos. 140/8 of Ajman optd MANAMA in English and Arabic. (a) Postage.

5	15d. blue and brown	10	10
6	30d. brown and black	25	25
7	50d. black and brown	50	50
8	70d. violet and black	50	50
	(b) Air.		
9	1r. green and brown	70	70
10	2r. mauve and black	1·40	1·40
11	3r. black and brown	2·10	2·10
12	5r. brown and black	4·00	4·00
13	10r. blue and brown	7·25	7·25

APPENDIX

The following stamps have either been issued in excess of postal needs or have not been available to the public in reasonable quantities at face value. Such stamps may later be given full listing if there is evidence of regular postal use.

1966. New Currency Surcharges. Stamps of Ajman surch Manama in English and Arabic and new value.

(a) Nos. 19/20 and 22/4 (Kennedy). 10d. on 10n.p., 15d. on 15n.p., 1r. on 1r., 2r. on 2r., 3r. on 3r.
(b) Nos. 27, 30 and 35/6 (Olympics). 5d. on 5n.p., 25d. on 25n.p., 3r. on 3r., 5r. on 5r.
(c) Nos. 80/2 and 85 (Churchill). 50d. on 50n.p., 75d. on 75n.p., 1r. on 1r., 5r. on 5r.
(d) Nos. 95/8 (Space). Air 50d. on 50n.p., 1r. on 1r., 3r. on 3r., 5r. on 5r.

1967

World Scout Jamboree, Idaho. Postage 30, 70d., 1r.; Air 2, 3, 4r.
Olympic Games, Mexico (1968). Postage 35, 65, 75d., 1r.; Air 1r.25, 2, 3, 4r.
Winter Olympic Games, Grenoble (1968). Postage 5, 35, 60, 75d.; Air 1, 1r.25, 2, 3r.
Paintings by Renoir and Terbrugghen. Air 35, 65d., 1, 2r.×3.

1968

Paintings by Velazquez. Air 1r.×2, 2r.×2.
Costumes. Air 30d.×2, 70d.×2, 1r.×2, 2r.×2.
Olympic Games, Mexico. Postage 1r.×4; Air 2r.×4.
Satellites and Spacecraft. Air 30d.×2, 70d.×2, 1r.×2, 2r.×2, 3r.×2.
Human Rights Year. Kennedy Brothers and Martin Luther King. Air 1r.×3, 2r.×3.
Sports Champions, Famous Footballers. Postage 15, 20, 50, 75d., 1r.; Air 10r.
Heroes of Humanity. Circular designs on gold or silver foil. 60d.×12.
Olympic Games, Mexico. Circular designs on gold or silver foil. Air 3r.×8.
Mothers' Day. Paintings. Postage 1r.×6.
Kennedy Brothers Commem. Postage 2r.; Air 5r.
Cats (1st series). Postage 1, 2, 3d.; Air 2, 3r.
5th Death Anniv of Pres. Kennedy. Air 10r.
Space Exploration. Postage 5, 10, 15, 20, 25d.; Air 15r.
Olympic Games, Mexico. Gold Medals. Postage 2r.×4; Air 5r.×4.
Christmas. Air 5r.

1969

Sports Champions. Cyclists. Postage 1, 2, 5, 10, 15, 20d.; Air 12r.
Sports Champions. German Footballers. Postage 5, 10, 15, 20, 25d.; Air 10r.
Sports Champions. Motor-racing Drivers. Postage 1, 5, 10, 15, 25d.; Air 10r.
Motor-racing Cars. Postage 1, 5, 10, 15, 25d.; Air 10r.
Sports Champions. Boxers. Postage 5, 10, 15, 20d.; Air 10r.
Sports Champions. Baseball Players. Postage 1, 2, 5, 10, 15d.; Air 10r.
Birds. Air 1r.×11.
Roses. Postage 1r.×6.
Animals. Air 1r.×6.
Paintings by Italian Artists. 5, 10, 15, 20d., 10r.
Great Composers. Air 5, 10, 25d., 10r.
Paintings by French Artists. 1r.×4.
Nude Paintings. Air 2r.×4.
Kennedy Brothers. Air 2, 3, 10r.
Olympic Games, Mexico. Gold Medal Winners. Postage 1, 2d., 10r.; Air 10d., 5, 10r.
Paintings of the Madonna. Postage 10d.; Air 10r.
Space Flight of "Apollo 9". Optd on 1968 Space Exploration issue. Air 15r.
Space Flight of "Apollo 10". Optd on 1968 Space Exploration issue. Air 15r.

1st Death Anniv of Gagarin. Optd on 1968 Space Exploration issue. 5d.
2nd Death Anniv of Edward White (astronaut). Optd on 1968 Space Exploration issue. 10d.
1st Death Anniv of Robert Kennedy. Optd on 1969 Kennedy Brothers issue. Air 2r.
Olympic Games, Munich (1972). Optd on 1969 Mexico Gold Medal Winners issue. Air 10d., 5, 10r.
Moon Mission of "Apollo 11". Air 1, 2, 3r.
Christmas. Paintings by Brueghel. Postage 1, 2, 4, 5, 10d.; Air 6r.

1970

"Soyuz" and "Apollo" Space Programmes. Postage 1, 2, 4, 5, 10d.; Air 3, 5r.
Kennedy and Eisenhower Commem. Embossed on gold foil. Air 20r.
Lord Baden-Powell Commem. Embossed on gold foil. Air 20r.
World Cup Football Championship, Mexico. Postage 20, 40, 60, 80d., 1r.; Air 3r.
Brazil's Victory in World Cup Football Championship. Optd on 1970 World Cup issue. Postage 20, 40, 60, 80d., 1r.; Air 3r.
Paintings by Michelangelo. Postage 1, 2, 4, 5, 10d.; Air 6r.
World Fair "Expo 70", Osaka, Japan. Air 25, 50, 75d., 1, 2, 3, 12r.
Paintings by Renoir. Postage 1, 2, 5, 6, 10d.; Air 5, 12r.
Olympic Games, Rome, Tokyo, Mexico and Munich. Postage 15, 30, 50, 70d.; Air 2, 5r.
Winter Olympic Games, Sapporo (1972) (1st issue). Postage 2, 3, 4, 10d.; Air 2, 5r.
Christmas. Flower Paintings by Brueghel. Postage 5, 20, 25, 30, 50d.; Air 60d., 1, 2r.

1971

Winter Olympic Games, Sapporo (2nd issue). Postage 1, 2, 3, 4, 5, 6, 8, 10, 12, 15, 20, 25, 30, 35, 40, 50d.; Air 75 d, 1, 2, 2r.50.
Roses. Postage 5, 20, 25, 30, 50d.; Air 60d., 1, 2r.
Birds. Postage 5, 20, 25, 30, 50d.; Air 60d., 1, 2r.
Paintings by Modigliani. Air 25, 50, 60, 75d., 1r.50, 3r.
Paintings by Rubens. Postage 1, 2, 3, 4, 5, 10d.; Air 2, 3r.
"Philatokyo '71" Stamp Exhibition, Paintings by Hokusai and Hiroshige. Postage 10, 15, 20, 25, 50, 75d.; Air 1, 2r.
25th Anniv of United Nations. Optd on 1970 Christmas issue. Postage 5, 20, 25, 30, 50d.; Air 60d., 1, 2r.
British Military Uniforms. Postage 5, 20, 25, 30, 50d.; Air 60d., 1, 2r.
Space Flight of "Apollo 14". Postage 15, 25, 50, 60, 70d.; Air 5r.
Space Flight of "Apollo 15". Postage 25, 40, 50, 60d.; Air 1, 6r.
13th World Scout Jamboree, Asagiri, Japan (1st issue). Postage 1, 2, 3, 5, 7, 10, 12, 15, 20, 25, 30, 35, 40, 50, 65, 80d.; Air 1, 1r.25, 1r.50, 2r.
World Wild Life Conservation. Postage 1, 2, 3, 5, 7, 10, 12, 15, 20, 25, 30, 35, 40, 50, 65, 80d.; Air 1r., 1r.25, 1r.50, 2r.
13th World Scout Jamboree, Asagiri, Japan (2nd issue). Stamps. Postage 10, 15, 20, 25, 50, 75d.; Air 1, 2r.
Winter Olympic Games, Sapporo (3rd issue). Postage 1, 2, 3, 4, 5, 10d.; Air 2, 3r.
Cats (2nd series). Postage 15, 25, 40, 60d.; Air 3, 10r.
Lions International Clubs. Optd on 1971 Uniforms issue. Postage 5, 20, 25, 30, 50d.; Air 60d., 1, 2r.
Paintings of Ships. Postage 15, 20, 25, 30, 50d.; Air 60d., 1, 2r.
Great Olympic Champions. Postage 25, 50, 75d., 1r.; Air 5r.
Prehistoric Animals. Postage 15, 20, 25, 30, 50, 60d.; Air 1, 2r.
Footballers. Postage 5, 10, 15, 20, 40d.; Air 5r.
Royal Visit of Queen Elizabeth II to Japan. Postage 10, 20, 30, 40, 50d.; Air 2, 3r.
Fairy Tales. Stories by Hans Andersen. Postage 1, 2, 4, 5, 10d.; Air 3r.
World Fair, Philadelphia (1976). American Paintings. Postage 20, 25, 50, 60, 75d.; Air 3r.
Fairy Tales. Well-known stories. Postage 1, 2, 4, 5, 10d.; Air 3r.
Space Flight of "Apollo 16". Postage 20, 30, 40, 50, 60d.; Air 3, 4r.
Tropical Fishes. Postage 1, 2, 3, 4, 5, 10d.; Air 2, 3r.
European Tour of Emperor Hirohito of Japan. Postage 1, 2, 4, 5, 10d.; Air 6r.
Meeting of Pres. Nixon and Emperor Hirohito of Japan in Alaska. Optd on 1971 Emperor's Tour issue. Air 6r.
2500th Anniv of Persian Empire. Postage 10, 20, 30, 40, 50d.; Air 3r.
Space Flight of "Apollo 15" and Future Developments in Space. Postage 10, 15, 20, 25, 50d.; Air 1, 2r.

1972

150th Death Anniv (1971) of Napoleon. Postage 10, 20, 30, 40d.; Air 1, 2, 3, 4r.
1st Death Anniv of Gen. de Gaulle. Postage 10, 20, 30, 40d.; Air 1, 2, 3, 4r.
Paintings from the "Alte Pinakothek", Munich. Postage 5, 10, 15, 20, 25d.; Air 5r.
"Tour de France" Cycle Race. Postage 5, 10, 15, 20, 25, 30, 35, 40, 45, 50, 55, 60d.; Air 65, 70, 75, 80, 85, 90, 95d., 1r.
Cats and Dogs. Postage 10, 20, 30, 40, 50d.; Air 1r.
25th Anniv of U.N.I.C.E.F. Optd on 1971 World Scout Jamboree, Asagiri (2nd issue). Postage 10, 15, 20, 25, 50, 75d.; Air 1, 2r.
Past and Present Motorcars. Postage 10, 20, 30, 40, 50d.; Air 1r.
Military Uniforms. 1r.×11.

The United Arab Emirates Ministry of Communications took over the Manama postal service on 1 August 1972. Further stamps inscribed "Manama" issued after that date were released without authority and had no validity.

Pt. 17

MANCHUKUO

Issues for the Japanese puppet Government set up in 1932 under President (later Emperor) Pu Yi.

100 fen = 1 yuan.

1 White Pagoda, Liaoyang

2 Pu Yi, later Emperor Kang-teh

1932. (a) With five characters in top panel as T **1** and **2**.

1	**1**	½f. brown	3·00	75
2	**1**	1f. red	3·75	30
24	**1**	1f. brown	4·50	1·00
25	**1**	1½f. violet	6·50	3·25
4	**1**	2f. grey	7·50	90
26	**1**	2f. blue	8·50	3·00
27	**1**	3f. brown	5·00	1·00
6	**1**	4f. green	5·00	40
28	**1**	4f. brown	75·00	5·50
7	**1**	5f. green	6·50	1·00
8	**1**	6f. red	15·00	3·25
9	**1**	7f. grey	5·00	1·50
10	**1**	8f. brown	25·00	20·00
11	**1**	10f. orange	8·50	65
12	**2**	13f. brown	20·00	8·50
13	**2**	15f. red	30·00	3·25
14	**2**	16f. blue	38·00	10·00
15	**2**	20f. brown	15·00	1·50
16	**2**	30f. orange	20·00	2·75
17	**2**	50f. green	45·00	3·50
31	**2**	1y. violet	50·00	22·00

(b) With six characters in top panel.

40	**1**	½f. brown	1·00	60
41	**1**	1f. brown	1·10	40
42	**1**	1½f. violet	1·25	90
43	**1**	3f. brown	1·50	40
44	**1**	5f. blue	25·00	1·50
45	**1**	5f. slate	8·50	2·50
46	**1**	6f. red	4·25	1·40
47	**1**	7f. grey	4·25	2·25
48	**1**	9f. orange	5·00	1·00
55	**1**	10f. blue	25·00	1·25
56	**2**	13f. brown	22·00	25·00
49	**2**	15f. red	6·50	1·25
50	**2**	18f. green	45·00	6·50
51	**2**	20f. brown	6·50	1·50
52	**2**	30f. brown	6·75	1·50
53	**2**	50f. green	11·00	2·50
54	**2**	1y. violet	35·00	12·00

3 Map and Flags

1933. First Anniv of Republic.

19	**3**	1f. orange	8·50	3·25
20	-	2f. green	32·00	25·00
21	**3**	4f. red	8·50	3·25
22	-	10f. blue	50·00	50·00

DESIGN: 2, 10f. Council Hall, Hsinking.

6 Emperor's Palace

1934. Enthronement of Emperor.

32	**6**	1½f. brown	7·25	5·00
33	-	3f. red	6·50	3·25
34	**6**	6f. green	20·00	15·00
35	-	10f. blue	28·00	25·00

DESIGN: 3f., 10f. Phoenixes.

1934. Stamps of 1932 surch with four Japanese characters.

36	**1**	1f. on 4f. green (No. 6)	18·00	9·00
37	**1**	3f. on 4f. green	£150	£140
38	**1**	3f. on 4f. brown (No. 28)	20·00	10·00
39	**2**	3f. on 16f. blue (No. 14)	32·00	28·00

In No. 38 the left hand upper character of the surcharge consists of three horizontal lines.

12 Orchid Crest of Manchukuo

13 Changpai Mountain and Sacred Lake

1935. China Mail.

64	**12**	2f. green	2·25	75
65	**12**	2½f. violet	1·00	75
66	**13**	4f. green	5·50	1·00
67	**13**	5f. blue	50	50
68	**12**	8f. yellow	7·50	1·75
60	**13**	12f. red	38·00	20·00
70	**13**	13f. brown	2·00	1·50

15 Mt. Fuji

16 Phoenixes

1935. Visit of Emperor Kang-teh to Japan.

71	**15**	1½f. green	5·00	4·25
72	**16**	3f. orange	5·50	5·00
73	**15**	6f. red	10·00	10·00
74	**16**	10f. blue	18·00	15·00

17 Symbolic of Accord

1936. Japan–Manchukuo Postal Agreement.

75	**17**	1½f. brown	7·50	7·50
76	-	3f. purple	8·00	5·00
77	**17**	6f. red	18·00	16·00
78	-	10f. blue	28·00	22·00

DESIGN—HORIZ: 3f., 10f. Department of Communications.

19 State Council Building, Hsinking

20 Chengte Palace, Jehol

1936

79	**19**	½f. brown	75	50
80	**19**	1f. red	50	15
81	**19**	1½f. lilac	7·50	7·50
82	**A**	2f. green	75	15
83	**19**	3f. brown	1·50	50
84	**B**	4f. green	80	15
149	**19**	5f. black	80	4·00
86	**A**	6f. red	1·25	50
87	**B**	7f. black	2·25	80
88	**B**	9f. red	2·25	75
89	**20**	10f. blue	2·75	35
90	**B**	12f. orange	2·25	30
91	**B**	13f. brown	85·00	£100
92	**B**	15f. red	7·25	1·00
93	**C**	18f. green	38·00	38·00
94	**C**	19f. green	10·00	5·00
95	**A**	20f. brown	3·25	75
96	**20**	30f. brown	3·50	75
97	**D**	38f. blue	38·00	38·00
98	**D**	39f. blue	3·50	4·00
99	**A**	50f. green	4·25	75
154	**20**	1y. purple	3·50	5·00

DESIGNS: A, Carting soya-beans; B. Peiling Mausoleum; C, Airplane and grazing sheep (domestic and China air mail); D, Nakajima-built Fokker F.VIIb/3m airplane over Sungari River railway bridge (air mail to Japan).

21 Sun rising over Fields

22 Shadowgraph of old and new Hsinking

1937. Fifth Anniv of Founding of State.

101	**21**	1½f. red	25·00	25·00
102	**22**	3f. green	7·50	6·50

1937. China Mail. Surch in Chinese characters.

108	**12**	2½f. on 2f. green	6·00	5·50
110	**13**	5f. on 4f. green	18·00	15·00
111	**13**	13f. on 12f. brown	38·00	32·00

27 Pouter Pigeon and Hsinking

1937. Completion of Five Year Reconstruction Plan for Hsinking.

112	**27**	2f. purple	8·50	6·50
113	-	4f. red	10·00	3·75
114	**27**	10f. green	20·00	12·00
115	-	20f. blue	28·00	20·00

DESIGN: 4, 20f. Flag over Imperial Palace.

29 Manchukuo

30 Japanese Residents Assn. Building

1937. Japan's Relinquishment of Extra-territorial Rights.

116	**29**	2f. red	2·50	1·75
117	**30**	4f. green	6·50	3·00
118	**30**	8f. orange	12·00	9·00
119	-	10f. blue	14·00	10·00
120	-	12f. violet	18·00	12·00
121	-	20f. brown	25·00	15·00

DESIGNS—As Type **30**: 10, 20f. Dept. of Communications Bldg. HORIZ: 12f. Ministry of Justice.

32 "Twofold Happiness"

1937. New Year's Greetings.

122	**32**	2f. red and blue	7·50	1·50

33 Red Cross on Map and Globe

1938. Inaug of Manchukuo Red Cross Society.

123	**33**	2f. red	2·50	2·50
124	**33**	4f. green	2·50	2·50

34 Map of Railway Lines

35 "Asia" Express

1939. Completion of 10,000 Kilometres of Manchurian Railways.

125	**34**	2f. blue and orange	3·50	3·50
126	**35**	4f. deep blue and blue	3·50	3·50

36 Manchurian Cranes over Shipmast

1940. Second Visit of Emperor Kang-teh to Japan.

127	**36**	2f. purple	1·50	2·50
128	**36**	4f. green	1·50	2·50

37 Census Official and Manchukuo

38 Census Slogans in Chinese and Mongolian

1940. National Census.

129	**37**	2f. brown and yellow	1·00	2·50
130	**38**	4f. deep green and green	1·00	2·50

39 Message of Congratulation

40 Dragon Dance

1940. 2600th Anniv of Founding of Japanese Empire.

131	**39**	2f. red	1·00	2·25
132	**40**	4f. blue	1·00	2·25

41 Recruit

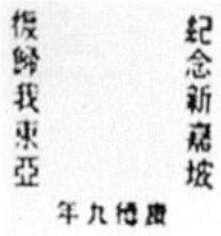

(42)

1941. Enactment of Conscription Law.

133	**41**	2f. red	1·00	2·50
134	**41**	4f. blue	1·00	2·50

1942. Fall of Singapore. Stamps of 1936 optd with T 42.

135	**A**	2f. green	1·25	3·25
136	**B**	4f. green	1·25	3·25

43 Kenkoku Shrine

44 Achievement of Fine Crops

45 Women of Five Races Dancing

46 Map of Manchukuo

1942. Tenth Anniv of Founding of State.

137	**43**	2f. red	70	2·25
138	**44**	3f. orange	2·50	3·75
139	**43**	4f. lilac	75	2·50
140	**45**	6f. green	1·50	3·25
141	**46**	10f. red on yellow	2·00	3·50
142	-	20f. blue on yellow	3·25	4·00

DESIGN—HORIZ: 20f. Flag of Manchukuo.

1942. First Anniv of "Greater East Asia War". Stamps of 1936 optd with native characters above date 8.12.8.

143	**19**	3f. brown	1·00	3·00
144	**A**	6f. red	1·00	3·00

1943. Labour Service Law Proclamation. Stamps of 1936 optd with native characters above heads of pick and shovel.

145	**19**	3f. brown	1·00	3·25
146	**A**	6f. red	1·00	3·25

49 Nurse and Stretcher

1943. Fifth Anniv of Manchukuo Red Cross Society.

147	**49**	6f. green	1·25	3·25

50 Furnace at Anshan Plant

1943. Second Anniv of "Greater East Asia War".

148	**50**	6f. red	1·50	4·00

51 Chinese characters

52 Japanese characters

1944. Friendship with Japan. (a) Chinese characters.

155	**51**	10f. red	1·00	2·00
156	**51**	40f. green	3·75	4·50

(b) Japanese characters.

157	**52**	10f. red	1·00	2·00
158	**52**	40f. green	3·75	4·50

53 "One Heart One Soul"

1945. Tenth Anniv of Emperor's Edict.

159	**53**	10f. red	1·25	5·00

Pt. 7

MARIANA ISLANDS

A group of Spanish islands in the Pacific Ocean of which Guam was ceded to the U.S.A. and the others to Germany. The latter are now under U.S. Trusteeship.

100 pfennig = 1 mark.

1899. German stamps optd **Marianen**.

7	**8**	3pf. brown	15·00	38·00
8	**8**	5pf. green	20·00	40·00
9	**9**	10pf. red	23·00	60·00
10	**9**	20pf. blue	32·00	£160
11	**9**	25pf. orange	80·00	£200
12	**9**	50pf. brown	80·00	£275

1901. "Yacht" key-type inscr "MARIANEN".

13	**N**	3pf. brown	1·40	2·10
14	**N**	5pf. green	1·40	2·30
15	**N**	10pf. red	1·40	5·25
16	**N**	20pf. blue	1·60	9·00
17	**N**	25pf. black & red on yellow	2·10	16·00
18	**N**	30pf. black & orge on buff	2·10	17·00
19	**N**	40pf. black and red	2·10	17·00
20	**N**	50pf. black & pur on buff	2·50	19·00
21	**N**	80pf. black and red on rose	3·25	32·00
22	**O**	1m. red	5·25	90·00
23	**O**	2m. blue	7·50	£120
24	**O**	3m. black	10·50	£170
25	**O**	5m. red and black	£180	£650

Pt. 7

MARIENWERDER

A district of E. Prussia where a plebiscite was held in 1920. As a result the district remained part of Germany. After the War of 1939–45 it was returned to Poland and reverted to its original name of Kwidzyn.

100 pfennig = 1 mark.

1

1920

1	**1**	5pf. green	85	2·10
2	**1**	10pf. red	85	2·10
3	**1**	15pf. grey	85	2·10
4	**1**	20pf. brown	85	2·10
5	**1**	25pf. blue	85	2·10
6	**1**	30pf. orange	1·20	2·10
7	**1**	40pf. brown	85	2·10
8	**1**	50pf. violet	85	2·10
9	**1**	60pf. brown	5·25	3·75
10	**1**	75pf. brown	1·20	2·10
11	**1**	1m. brown and green	95	2·10
12	**1**	2m. purple	2·75	3·75
13	**1**	3m. red	6·25	7·50
14	**1**	5m. blue and red	32·00	26·00

1920. Stamps of Germany inscr "DEUTSCHES REICH" optd or surch Commission Interalliee Marienwerder.

15	**10**	5pf. green	19·00	37·00
16	**10**	20pf. blue	7·50	32·00
17	**10**	50pf. black & purple on buff	£475	£1100
18	**10**	75pf. black and green	5·25	9·50
19	**10**	80pf. black and red on rose	95·00	£150
25	**12**	1m. red	3·25	8·50
21	**24**	1m. on 2pf. grey	27·00	60·00
26	**12**	1m.25 green	4·25	8·50
27	**12**	1m.50 brown	5·25	10·50
22	**24**	2m. on 2½pf. grey	12·50	21·00
28	**13**	2m.50 purple	3·25	9·50
23	**10**	3m. on 3pf. brown	16·00	21·00
24	**24**	5m. on 7½pf. orange	12·50	26·00

1920. As T 1, with inscription at top changed to "PLEBISCITE".

29	**24**	5pf. green	4·25	2·75
30	**24**	10pf. red	4·25	2·75
31	**24**	15pf. grey	15·00	16·00
32	**24**	20pf. brown	2·40	2·75
33	**24**	25pf. blue	16·00	21·00
34	**24**	30pf. orange	2·10	1·60
35	**24**	40pf. brown	1·10	2·10
36	**24**	50pf. violet	2·10	2·75
37	**24**	60pf. brown	6·25	5·25
38	**24**	75pf. brown	7·50	6·25
39	**24**	1m. brown and green	2·10	1·60
40	**24**	2m. purple	2·10	1·90
41	**24**	3m. red	2·75	2·40
42	**24**	5m. blue and red	4·25	3·25

Pt. 7, Pt. 22

MARSHALL ISLANDS

A group of islands in the Pacific Ocean, a German protectorate from 1885. From 1920 to 1947 it was a Japanese mandated territory and from 1947 part of the United States Trust Territory of the Pacific Islands, using United States stamps. In 1984 it assumed control of its postal services, and became independent in 1991.

A. German Protectorate.
100 pfennig = 1 mark.

B. Republic.
100 cents = 1 dollar.

A. GERMAN PROTECTORATE

1897. Stamps of Germany (a) optd Marschall-Inseln.

G1	**8**	3pf. brown	£4750	£2750
G2	**8**	5pf. green	£700	£600
G3	**9**	10pf. red	80·00	£120
G4	**9**	20pf. blue	80·00	£130

(b) optd Marshall-Inseln.

G5	**8**	3pf. brown	5·75	6·75
G6	**8**	5pf. green	11·50	16·00
G7	**9**	10pf. red	16·00	20·00
G8	**9**	20pf. blue	20·00	32·00
G9	**9**	25pf. orange	23·00	55·00
G10	**9**	50pf. brown	37·00	60·00

1901. "Yacht" key-type inscr "MARSHALL INSELN".

G11	**N**	3pf. brown	85	2·10
G12	**N**	5pf. green	85	2·10
G13	**N**	10pf. red	85	5·75
G14	**N**	20pf. blue	1·20	11·50
G15	**N**	25pf. black & red on yell	1·30	20·00
G16	**N**	30pf. black & orge on buff	1·30	20·00
G17	**N**	40pf. black and red	1·30	20·00
G18	**N**	50pf. black & pur on buff	1·80	30·00
G19	**N**	80pf. black & red on rose	3·25	44·00
G20	**O**	1m. red	4·75	£110
G21	**O**	2m. blue	6·75	£150
G22	**O**	3m. black	10·50	£250
G23	**O**	5m. red and black	£180	£650

B. REPUBLIC

1 Canoe

1984. Inauguration of Postal Independence. Multicoloured.

1	20c. Type **1**	65	60
2	20c. Fishes and net	65	60
3	20c. Navigational stick-chart	65	60
4	20c. Islet with coconut palms	65	60

2 Mili Atoll

1984. Maps. Multicoloured.

5	1c. Type **2**	15	10
6	3c. Likiep Atoll	15	10
7	5c. Ebon Atoll	20	10
8	10c. Jaluit Atoll	25	10
9	13c. Ailinginae Atoll	25	25
10	14c. Wotho Atoll	30	30
11	20c. Kwajalein and Ebeye Atolls	50	45
12	22c. Enewetak Atoll	55	50
13	28c. Ailinglaplap Atoll	70	65
14	30c. Majuro Atoll	75	70
15	33c. Namu Atoll	80	75
16	37c. Rongelap Atoll	95	85
16a	39c. Taka and Utirik Atolls	1·00	90
16b	44c. Ujelang Atoll	1·10	1·00
16c	50c. Aur and Maloclap Atolls	1·30	1·20
17	$1 Arno Atoll	2·50	2·30
18	$2 Wotje and Erikub Atolls	5·75	5·25
19	$5 Bikini Atoll	12·00	11·00
20	$10 Mashallese stick chart (31×31 mm)	20·00	18·00

3 German Marshall Islands 1900 3pf. Optd Stamp

1984. 19th Universal Postal Union Congress Philatelic Salon, Hamburg.

21	**3**	40c. brown, black and yellow	75	70
22	-	40c. brown, black and yellow	75	70
23	-	40c. blue, black and yellow	75	70
24	-	40c. multicoloured	75	70

DESIGNS: No. 22, German Marshall Islands 1901 3pf. "Yacht" stamp; 23, German Marshall Islands 1897 20pf. stamp; 24, German Marshall Islands 1901 5m. "Yacht" stamp.

4 Common Dolphin

1984. "Ausipex 84" International Stamp Exhibition, Melbourne. Dolphins. Multicoloured.

25	20c. Type **4**	50	45
26	20c. Risso's dolphin	50	45
27	20c. Spotter dolphins	50	45
28	20c. Bottle-nosed dolphin	50	45

5 Star over Bethlehem and Text

1984. Christmas. Multicoloured.

29	20c. Type **5**	65	60
30	20c. Desert landscape	65	60
31	20c. Two kings on camels	65	60
32	20c. Third king on camel	65	60

6 Traditional Chief and German and Marshallese Flags

1984. Fifth Anniv of Constitution. Multicoloured.

33	20c. Type **6**	50	45
34	20c. Pres. Amata Kabua and American and Marshallese flags	50	45
35	20c. Admiral Chester W. Nimitz and Japanese and Marshallese flags	50	45
36	20c. Trygve H. Lie (first Secretary-General of United Nations) and U.N. and Marshallese flags	50	45

7 Leach's Storm Petrel ("Forked-tailed Petrel")

1985. Birth Bicentenary of John J. Audubon (ornithologist). Multicoloured.

37	22c. Type **7** (postage)	75	70
38	22c. Pectoral sandpiper	75	70
39	44c. Brown booby ("Booby Gannet") (air)	1·10	1·00
40	44c. Whimbrel ("Great Esquimaux Curlew")	1·10	1·00

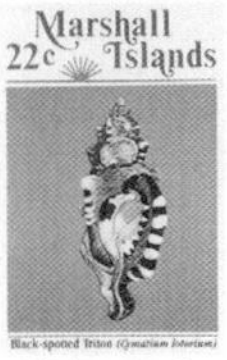

8 Black-spotted Triton

1985. Sea Shells (1st series). Multicoloured.

41	22c. Type **8**	55	50
42	22c. Monodon murex	55	50
43	22c. Diana conch	55	50
44	22c. Great green turban	55	50
45	22c. Rose-branch murex	55	50

See also Nos. 85/9, 131/5 and 220/4.

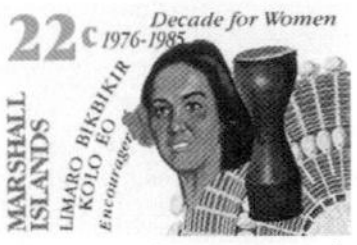

9 Woman as Encourager and Drum

1985. International Decade for Women. Multicoloured.

46	22c. Type **9**	50	45
47	22c. Woman as Peacemaker and palm branches	50	45
48	22c. Woman as Nurturer and pounding stone	50	45
49	22c. Woman as Benefactress and lesser frigate bird	50	45

Nos. 46/9 were printed together in se-tenant blocks of four within the sheet, each block forming a composite design.

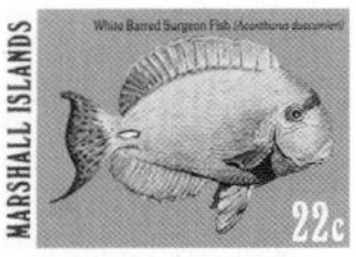

10 Palani ("White Barred Surgeon Fish")

1985. Lagoon Fishes. Multicoloured.

50	22c. Type **10**	55	50
51	22c. Silver-spotted squirrelfish ("White Blotched Squirrel Fish")	55	50
52	22c. Spotted boxfish	55	50
53	22c. Saddle butterflyfish	55	50

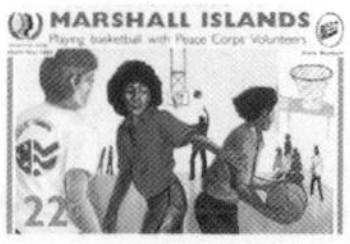

11 Basketball

1985. International Youth Year. Multicoloured.

54	22c. Type **11**	55	50
55	22c. Elderly woman recording for oral history project	55	50
56	22c. Islander explaining navigational stick charts	55	50
57	22c. Dancers at inter-atoll music and dance competition	55	50

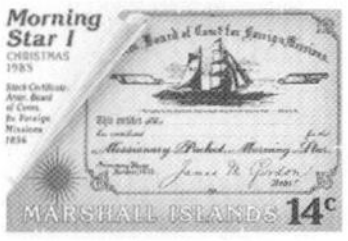

12 American Board of Commissions for Foreign Missions Stock Certificate

1985. Christmas. "Morning Star I" (first Christian missionary ship to visit Marshall Islands). Multicoloured.

58	14c. Type **12**	30	30
59	22c. Launching of "Morning Star I", 1856	55	50
60	33c. Departure from Honolulu, 1857	80	75
61	44c. Entering Ebon Lagoon, 1857	1·10	1·00

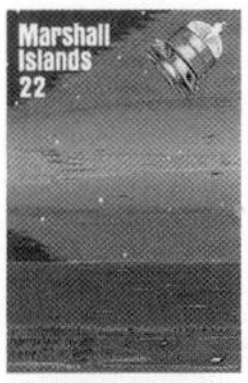

13 "Giotto" and Section of Comet Tail

1985. Appearance of Halley's Comet. Designs showing comet over Roi-Namur Island. Multicoloured.

62	22c. Space shuttle and comet	1·30	1·20
63	22c. "Planet A" space probe and dish aerial	1·30	1·20
64	22c. Type **13**	1·30	1·20
65	22c. "Vega" satellite and buildings on island	1·30	1·20
66	22c. Sir Edmund Halley, satellite communications ship and airplane	1·30	1·20

Nos. 62/6 were printed together, se-tenant, forming a composite design.

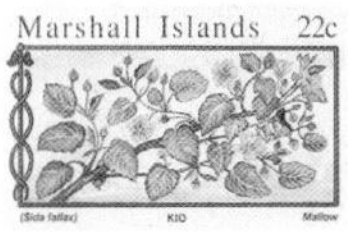

14 Mallow

1985. Medicinal Plants. Multicoloured.

67	22c. Type **14**	55	50
68	22c. Half-flower	55	50
69	22c. "Guettarda speciosa"	55	50
70	22c. Love-vine	55	50

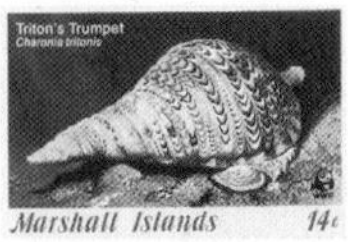

15 Trumpet Triton

1986. World Wildlife Fund. Marine Life. Multicoloured.

71	14c. Type **15**	1·90	1·70
72	14c. Giant clam	1·90	1·70
73	14c. Small giant clam	1·90	1·70
74	14c. Coconut crab	1·90	1·70

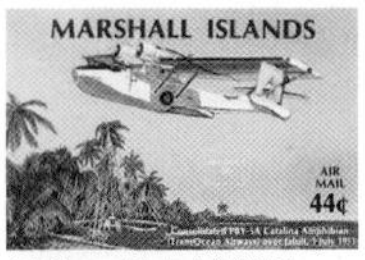

16 Consolidated PBY-5A Catalina Amphibian

1986. Air. "Ameripex 86" International Stamp Exhibition, Chicago. Mail Planes. Multicoloured.

75	44c. Type **16**	1·10	1·00
76	44c. Grumman SA-16 Albatross	1·10	1·00
77	44c. Douglas DC-6B	1·10	1·00
78	44c. Boeing 727-100	1·10	1·00
MS79	89×63 mm. $1 Douglas C-54 Globester	3·50	3·25

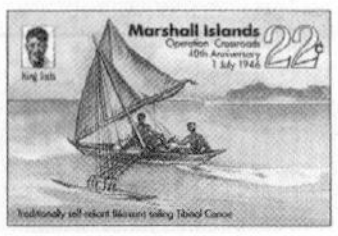

17 Islanders in Outrigger Canoe

1986. 40th Anniv of Operation Crossroads (atomic bomb tests on Bikini Atoll). Multicoloured.

80	22c. Type **17** (postage)	60	55
81	22c. Advance landing of amphibious DUKW from U.S.S. "Sumner"	60	55
82	22c. Loading "L.S.T. 1108" (tank landing ship) for islanders' departure	60	55
83	22c. Man planting coconuts as part of reclamation programme	60	55
MS84	101×77 mm. 44c. U.S.S. "Saratoga" (bomb target) (air)	5·25	4·75

1986. Sea Shells (2nd series). As T **8**. Multicoloured.

85	22c. Ramose ("Rose") murex	60	55
86	22c. Orange spider conch	60	55
87	22c. Red-mouth frog shell	60	55
88	22c. Laciniate conch	60	55
89	22c. Giant frog shell	60	55

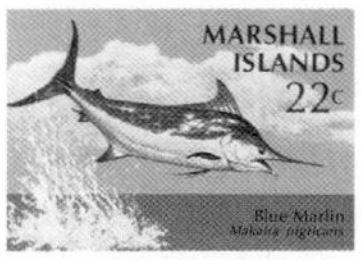

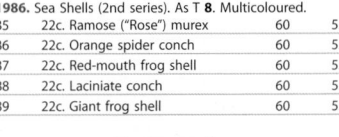

18 Blue Marlin

1986. Game Fishes. Multicoloured.

90	22c. Type **18**	55	50
91	22c. Wahoo	55	50
92	22c. Dolphin	55	50
93	22c. Yellow-finned tuna	55	50

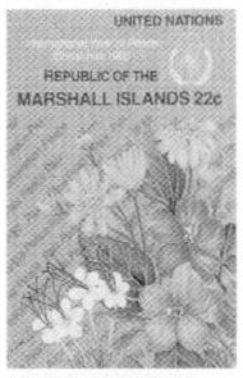

19 Flowers (top left)

1986. International Peace Year. Multicoloured.

94	22c. Type **19** (Christmas) (postage)	80	70
95	22c. Flowers (top right)	80	70
96	22c. Flowers (bottom left)	80	70
97	22c. Flowers (bottom right)	80	70
98	44c. Head of Statue crowned with flowers (24×39 mm) (cent of Statue of Liberty) (air)	1·60	1·40

Nos. 94/7 were issued together, se-tenant, in blocks of four within the sheet, each block forming a composite design of mixed flower arrangement.

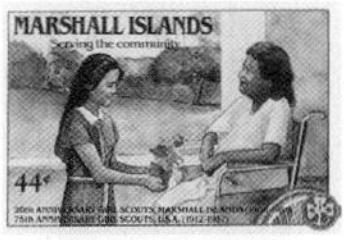

20 Girl Scout giving Plant to Patient

1986. Air. 20th Anniv of Marshall Island Girl Scouts and 75th Anniv (1987) of United States Girl Scout Movement. Multicoloured.

99	44c. Type **20**	1·00	90
100	44c. Giving salute	1·00	90
101	44c. Girl scouts holding hands in circle	1·00	90
102	44c. Weaving pandana and palm branch mats	1·00	90

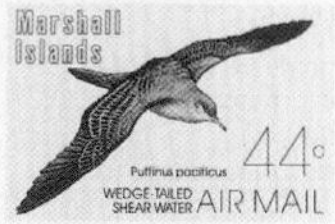

21 Wedge-tailed Shearwater

1987. Air. Sea Birds. Multicoloured.

103	44c. Type **21**	1·00	90
104	44c. Red-footed booby	1·00	90
105	44c. Red-tailed tropic bird	1·00	90
106	44c. Lesser frigate bird ("Great Frigatebird")	1·00	90

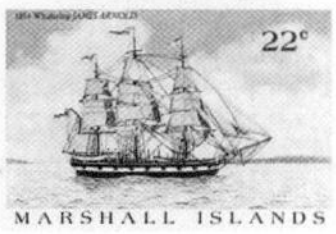

22 "James T. Arnold", 1854

1987. Whaling Ships. Multicoloured.

107	22c. Type **22**	65	60
108	22c. "General Scott", 1859	65	60
109	22c. "Charles W. Morgan", 1865	65	60
110	22c. "Lucretia", 1884	65	60

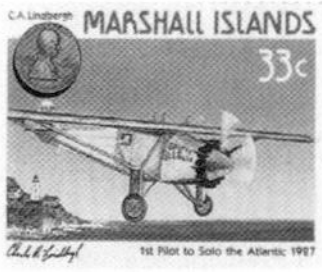

23 Lindbergh's "Spirit of St. Louis" and Congressional Medal of Honour, 1927

1987. Aviators. Multicoloured.

111	33c. Type **23**	95	85
112	33c. Charles Lindbergh and Chance Vought F4U Corsair fighter, Marshall Islands, 1944	95	85
113	39c. William Bridgeman and Consolidated B-24 Liberator bomber, Kwajalein, 1944	1·00	90
114	39c. Bridgeman and Douglas Skyrocket, 1951	1·00	90
115	44c. John Glenn and Chance Vought F4U Corsair fighters, Marshall Islands, 1944	1·10	95
116	44c. Glenn and "Friendship 7" space capsule	1·10	95

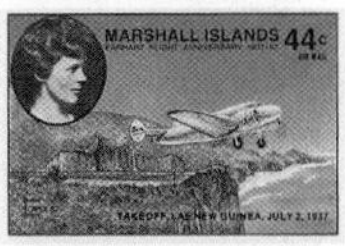

24 Earhart's Lockheed 10E Electra taking off from Lae, New Guinea

1987. Air. "Capex '87" International Stamp Exhibition, Toronto. 50th Anniv of Amelia Earhart's Round the World Flight Attempt. Multicoloured.

117	44c. Type **24**	1·00	90
118	44c. U.S. Coastguard cutter "Itasca" waiting off Howland Island for Electra	1·00	90
119	44c. Islanders and crashed Electra on Mili Atoll	1·00	90
120	44c. Japanese patrol boat "Koshu" recovering Electra	1·00	90
MS121	88×62 mm. $1 Earhat's flight route (41×8 mm)	3·25	3·00

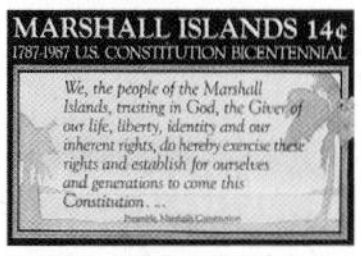

25 "We, the people of the Marshall Islands ..."

1987. Bicentenary of United States of America Constitution. Multicoloured.

122	14c. Type **25**	40	35
123	14c. Marshall Is. and U.S.A. emblems	40	35
124	14c. "We the people of the United States ..."	40	35
125	22c. "All we have and are today as a people ..."	55	50
126	22c. Marshall Is. and U.S.A. flags	55	50
127	22c. "... to establish Justice ..."	55	50
128	44c. "With this Constitution ..."	1·10	95
129	44c. Marshall Is. stick chart and U.S. Liberty Bell	1·10	95
130	44c. "... to promote the general Welfare ..."	1·10	95

The three designs of each value were printed together, se-tenant, the left hand stamp of each strip bearing quotations from the preamble to the Marshall Islands Constitution and the right hand stamp, quotations from the United States Constitution preamble.

1987. Sea Shells (3rd series). As T **8**. Multicoloured.

131	22c. Magnificent cone	55	50
132	22c. Pacific partridge tun	55	50
133	22c. Scorpion spider conch	55	50
134	22c. Common hairy triton	55	50
135	22c. Arthritic ("Chiragra") spider conch	55	50

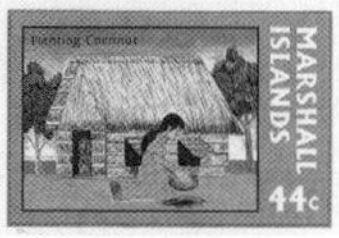

26 Planting Coconut

1987. Copra Industry. Multicoloured.

136	44c. Type **26**	90	85
137	44c. Making copra	90	85
138	44c. Bottling extracted coconut oil	90	85

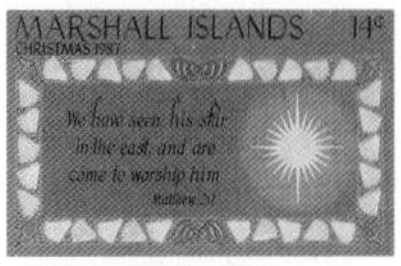

27 "We have seen his star in the east ..."

1987. Christmas. Multicoloured.

139	14c. Type **27**	35	30
140	22c. "Glory to God in the highest; ..."	55	50
141	33c. "Sing unto the Lord a new song ..."	85	75
142	44c. "Praise him in the cymbals and dances; ..."	1·10	95

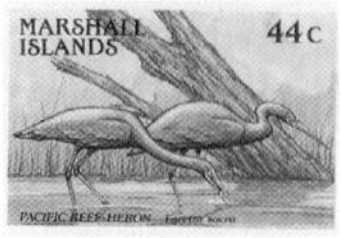

28 Reef Heron ("Pacific Reef Heron")

1988. Shore and Water Birds. Multicoloured.

143	44c. Type **28**	1·10	95
144	44c. Bar-tailed godwit	1·10	95
145	44c. Blue-faced booby ("Masked Booby")	1·10	95
146	44c. Northern shoveler	1·10	95

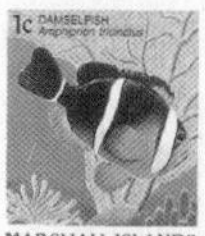

29 Maroon Anemonefish ("Damselfish")

1988. Fish. Multicoloured.

147	1c. Type **29**	15	15
148	3c. Black-faced butterflyfish	15	15
149	14c. Stocky hawkfish	35	30
150	15c. White-spotted puffer ("Balloonfish")	35	30
151	17c. Starry pufferfish ("Trunk Fish")	40	40
152	22c. Moon ("Lyretail") wrasse	50	45
153	25c. Six-banded parrotfish	55	50
154	33c. Spotted ("White-spotted") boxfish	85	75
155	36c. Yellow ("Spotted") boxfish	90	85
156	39c. Red-tailed surgeonfish	1·10	95
157	44c. Forceps ("Long-snouted") butterflyfish	1·10	1·00
158	45c. Oriental trumpetfish	1·10	1·00
159	56c. False-eyed pufferfish ("Sharp-nosed Puffer")	1·40	1·30
160	$1 Yellow seahorse	2·75	2·40
161	$2 Ghost pipefish	5·00	4·50
162	$5 Clown triggerfish ("Big-spotted Triggerfish")	11·00	10·00
163	$10 Blue-finned trevally ("Blue Jack") (50×28 mm)	22·00	20·00

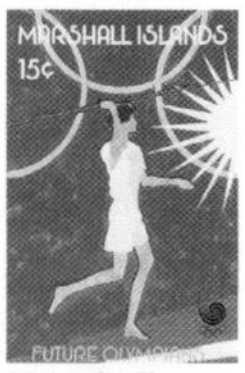

30 Javelin Thrower

1988. Olympic Games, Seoul. Multicoloured.

166	15c. Type **30**	50	45
167	15c. Drawing javelin back and star	50	45
168	15c. Javelin drawn back fully (value at left)	50	45
169	15c. Commencing throw (value at right)	50	45
170	15c. Releasing javelin	50	45
171	25c. Runner and star (left half)	65	60
172	25c. Runner and star (right half)	65	60
173	25c. Runner (value at left)	65	60
174	25c. Runner (value at right)	65	60
175	25c. Finish of race	65	60

Nos. 166/70 were printed together, se-tenant, forming a composite design of a javelin throw with background of the Marshallese flag. Nos. 171/5 were similarly arranged forming a composite design of a runner and flag.

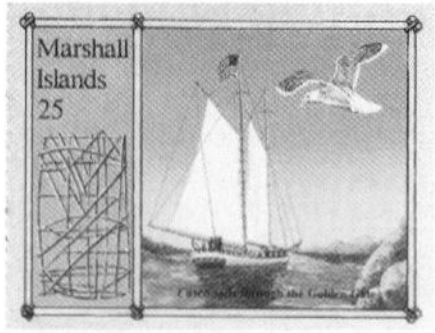

31 "Casco" sailing through Golden Gate of San Francisco

1988. Centenary of Robert Louis Stevenson's Pacific Voyages. Multicoloured.

176	25c. Type **31**	90	85
177	25c. "Casco" at the Needles of Ua-Pu, Marquesas	90	85
178	25c. "Equator" leaving Honolulu	90	85
179	25c. Chieftain's canoe, Majuro Lagoon	90	85
180	25c. Bronze medallion depicting Stevenson by Augustus St. Gaudens, 1887	90	85
181	25c. "Janet Nicoll" (inter-island steamer), Majuro Lagoon	90	85
182	25c. Stevenson's visit to maniap of King Tembinoka of Gilbert Islands	90	85
183	25c. Stevenson in Samoan canoe, Apia Harbour	90	85
184	25c. Stevenson on horse Jack at Valima (Samoan home)	90	85

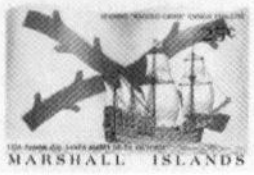

32 Spanish Ragged Cross Ensign (1516–1785) and Magellan's Ship "Vitoria"

1988. Exploration Ships and Flags. Multicoloured.

185	25c. Type **32**	70	65
186	25c. British red ensign (1707–1800), "Charlotte" and "Scarborough" (transports)	70	65
187	25c. American flag and ensign (1837–45), U.S.S. "Flying Fish" (schooner) and U.S.S. "Peacock" (sloop)	70	65
188	25c. German flag and ensign (1867–1919) and "Planet" (auxiliary schooner)	70	65

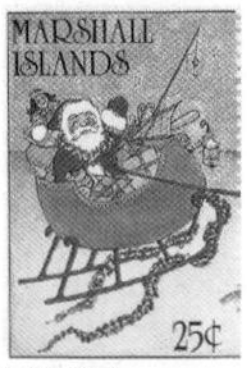

33 Father Christmas in Sleigh

1988. Christmas. Multicoloured.

189	25c. Type **33**	70	65
190	25c. Reindeer over island with palm huts and trees	70	65
191	25c. Reindeer over island with palm trees	70	65
192	25c. Reindeer and billfish	70	65
193	25c. Reindeer over island with outrigger canoe	70	65

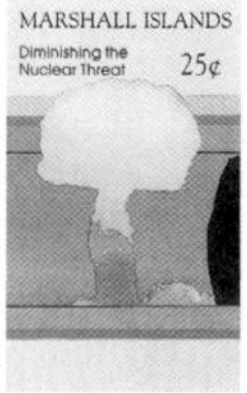

34 Nuclear Test on Bikini Atoll

1988. 25th Anniv of Assassination of John F. Kennedy (American President). Multicoloured.

194	25c. Type **34**	70	65
195	25c. Kennedy signing Test Ban Treaty	70	65
196	25c. Kennedy	70	65
197	25c. Kennedy using hot-line between Washington and Moscow	70	65
198	25c. Peace Corps volunteers	70	65

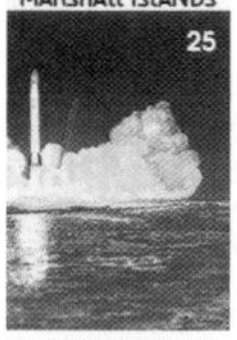

35 "SV-5D PRIME" Vehicle Launch from Vandenberg Air Force Base

1988. Kwajalein Space Shuttle Tracking Station. Multicoloured.

199	25c. Type **35** (postage)	70	65
200	25c. Re-entry of "SV-5D"	70	65
201	25c. Recovery of "SV-5D" off Kwajalein	70	65
202	25c. Space shuttle "Discovery" over Kwajalein	70	65
203	45c. Shuttle and astronaut over Rongelap (air)	1·20	1·10

Nos. 199/202 were printed together, se-tenant, forming a composite design.

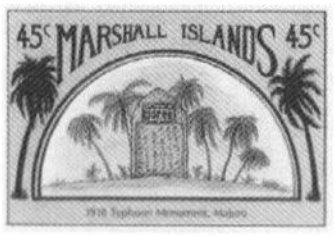

36 1918 Typhoon Monument, Majuro

1989. Links with Japan. Multicoloured.

204	45c. Type **36**	1·10	95
205	45c. Japanese seaplane base and railway, Djarret Islet, 1940s	1·10	95
206	45c. Japanese fishing boats	1·10	95
207	45c. Japanese skin-divers	1·10	95

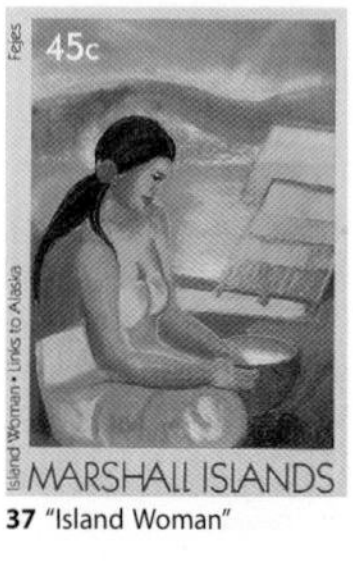

37 "Island Woman"

1989. Links with Alaska. Oil Paintings by Claire Fejes. Multicoloured.

208	45c. Type **37**	1·20	1·10
209	45c. "Kotzebue, Alaska"	1·20	1·10
210	45c. "Marshallese Madonna"	1·20	1·10

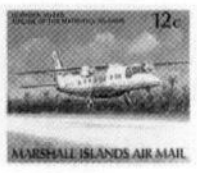

38 Dornier Do-228

1989. Air. Airplanes. Multicoloured.

211	12c. Type **38**	35	30
212	36c. Boeing 737	1·10	95
213	39c. Hawker Siddeley H.S. 748	1·30	1·20
214	45c. Boeing 727	1·40	1·30

1989. Sea Shells (4th series). As T **8**. Multicoloured.

220	25c. Pontifical mitre	70	65
221	25c. Tapestry turban	70	65
222	25c. Flame mouthed ("Bull-mouth") helmet	70	65
223	25c. Prickly Pacific drupe	70	65
224	25c. Blood-mouth conch	70	65

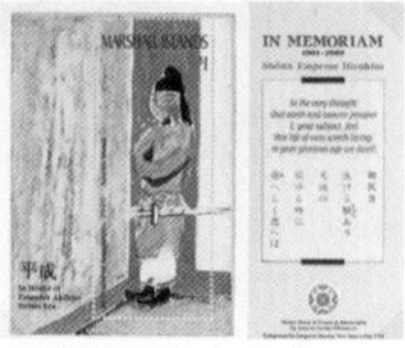

39 39 Illustration by Sanko Inoue of "In Praise of Sovereigns" (poem)

1989. Emperor Hirohito of Japan Commemoration. Sheet 106×88 mm.

MS225	**39** $1 multicoloured	2·75	2·50

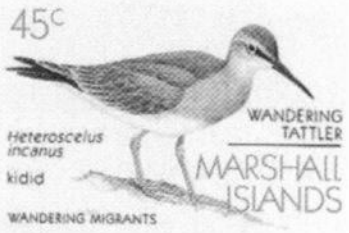

40 Wandering Tattler

1989. Birds. Multicoloured.

226	45c. Type **40**	1·20	1·10
227	45c. Ruddy turnstone	1·20	1·10
228	45c. Pacific golden plover	1·20	1·10
229	45c. Sanderling	1·20	1·10

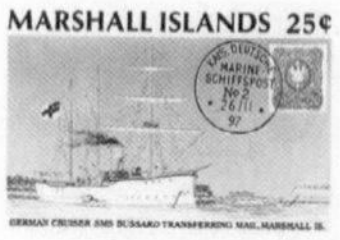

41 "Bussard" (German cruiser) and 1897 Ship's Post Cancellation

1989. "Philexfrance 89" International Stamp Exhibition, Paris. Marshall Islands Postal History. Multicoloured.

230	25c. Type **41**	2·10	1·90
231	25c. First day cover bearing first Marshall Islands stamps and U.S. 10c. stamp	2·10	1·90
232	25c. Consolidated PBY-5 Catalina flying boats, floating Fleet Post Office ("L.S.T. 119"), Majuro, and 1944 U.S. Navy cancellation	2·10	1·90
233	25c. Nakajima A6M2 "Rufe" seaplane, mailboat off Mili Island and Japanese cancellation	2·10	1·90
234	25c. Majuro Post Office	2·10	1·90
235	25c. Consolidated PBY-5A Catalina amphibian, outrigger canoe and 1951 U.S. civilian mail cancellation	2·10	1·90
236	45c. "Morning Star V" (missionary ship) and 1905 Jaluit cancellation	1·10	1·00
237	45c. 1906 registered cover with Jaluit cancellation	1·10	1·00
238	45c. "Prinz Eitel Freiderich" (auxiliary cruiser) and 1914 German ship's post cancellation	1·10	1·00
239	45c. "Scharnhorst" (cruiser) leading German Asiatic Squadron and 1914 ship's post cancellation	1·10	1·00
MS240	93×80 mm. $1 German 20pf. stamp with 1889 Jaluit cancellation	14·00	6·50

Nos. 230/5 were printed together, se-tenant, Nos. 231 and 234 forming a composite design to commemorate the 5th anniversary of Marshall Islands Independent Postal Service.

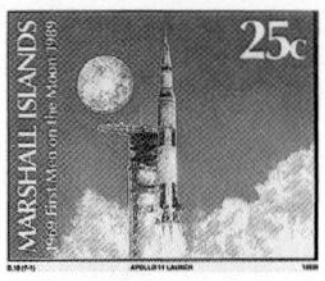

42 Launch of Apollo "11"

1989. 20th Anniv of First Manned Moon Landing. Multicoloured.

241	25c. Type **42**	1·80	1·60
242	25c. Neil Armstrong	1·80	1·60
243	25c. Descent of lunar module to moon's surface	1·80	1·60
244	25c. Michael Collins	1·80	1·60
245	25c. Planting flag on Moon	1·80	1·60
246	25c. Edwin "Buzz" Aldrin	1·80	1·60
MS247	114×87 mm. $1 Astronaut on lunar surface (70×29 mm)	9·75	6·50

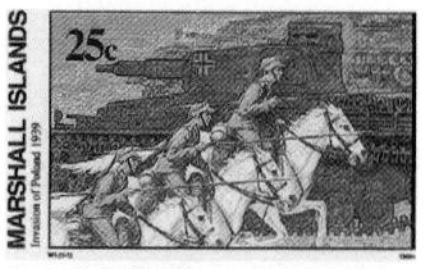

43 Polish Cavalry and German Tanks

1989. History of Second World War. Multicoloured. (a) 1st issue. Invasion of Poland, 1939.

248	25c. Type **43**	85	75

(b) 2nd issue. Sinking of H.M.S. "Royal Oak", 1939.

249	45c. U-boat and burning battleship	1·40	1·30

(c) 3rd issue. Invasion of Finland, 1939.

250	45c. Troops on skis and tanks	1·40	1·30

(d) 4th issue. Battle of the River Plate, 1939.

251	45c. H.M.S. "Exeter" (cruiser)	1·40	1·30
252	45c. H.M.S. "Ajax" (cruiser)	1·40	1·30
253	45c. "Admiral Graf Spee" (German battleship)	1·40	1·30
254	45c. H.M.N.Z.S. "Achilles" (cruiser)	1·40	1·30

See also Nos. 320/44, 359/84, 409/40, 458/77, 523/48 and 575/95.

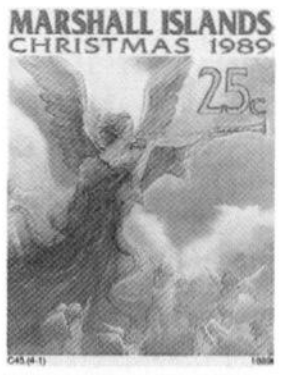

44 Angel with Horn

1989. Christmas. Multicoloured.

255	25c. Type **44**	1·10	1·00
256	25c. Angel singing	1·10	1·00
257	25c. Angel with lute	1·10	1·00
258	25c. Angel with lyre	1·10	1·00

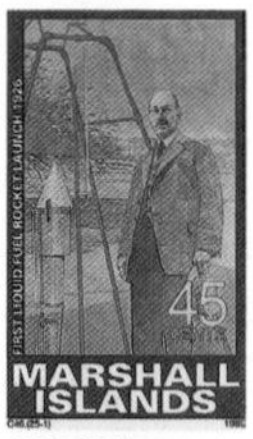

45 Dr. Robert Goddard

1989. Milestones in Space Exploration. Multicoloured.

259	45c. Type **45** (first liquid fuel rocket launch, 1926)	1·40	1·30
260	45c. "Sputnik 1" (first man-made satellite, 1957)	1·40	1·30
261	45c. Rocket lifting off (first American satellite, 1958)	1·40	1·30
262	45c. Yuri Gagarin (first man in space, 1961)	1·40	1·30
263	45c. John Glenn (first American in Earth orbit, 1962)	1·40	1·30
264	45c. Valentina Tereshkova (first woman in space, 1963)	1·40	1·30
265	45c. Aleksei Leonov (first space walk, 1965)	1·40	1·30
266	45c. Edward White (first American space walk, 1965)	1·40	1·30
267	45c. "Gemini 6" and "7" (first rendezvous in space, 1965)	1·40	1·30
268	45c. "Luna 9" (first soft landing on the Moon, 1966)	1·40	1·30
269	45c. "Gemini 8" (first docking in space, 1966)	1·40	1·30
270	45c. "Venera 4" (first successful Venus probe, 1967)	1·40	1·30
271	45c. Moon seen from "Apollo 8" (first manned orbit of Moon, 1968)	1·40	1·30

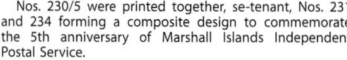

272 45c. Neil Armstrong and U.S. flag (first man on Moon, 1969) 1·40 1·30
273 45c. "Soyuz 11" and "Salyut 1" space station (first space station crew, 1971) 1·40 1·30
274 45c. Lunar rover of "Apollo 15" (first manned lunar vehicle, 1971) 1·40 1·30
275 45c. "Skylab 1" (first American space station, 1973) 1·40 1·30
276 45c. "Pioneer 10" and Jupiter (first flight past Jupiter, 1973) 1·40 1·30
277 45c. "Apollo" and "Soyuz" craft approaching each other (first international joint space flight, 1975) 1·40 1·30
278 45c. "Viking 1" on Mars (first landing on Mars, 1976) 1·40 1·30
279 45c. "Voyager 1" and Saturn's rings (first flight past Saturn, 1979) 1·40 1·30
280 45c. "Columbia" (first space shuttle flight, 1981) 1·40 1·30
281 45c. Satellite in outer space (first probe beyond the solar system, 1983) 1·40 1·30
282 45c. Astronaut (first untethered space walk, 1984) 1·40 1·30
283 45c. Launch of space shuttle "Discovery", 1988 1·40 1·30

46 White-capped Noddy ("Black Noddy")

1990. Birds. Multicoloured.
284 1c. Type **46** 20 15
285 5c. Red-tailed tropic bird 20 15
286 9c. Whimbrel 20 20
287 10c. Sanderling 30 25
288 12c. Black-naped tern 35 30
289 15c. Wandering tattler 40 40
290 20c. Bristle-thighed curlew 55 50
291 22c. Greater scaup 65 60
292 23c. Common (inscr "Northern") shoveler 65 60
293 25c. Common (inscr "Brown") noddy 70 65
294 27c. Sooty tern 75 70
295 28c. Sharp-tailed sandpiper 75 70
296 29c. Wedge-tailed shearwater 85 75
297 30c. Pacific golden plover 85 75
298 35c. Brown booby 1·00 90
299 36c. Red-footed booby 1·10 95
300 40c. White tern 1·10 1·00
301 45c. Green-winged (inscr "Common") teal 1·30 1·20
302 50c. Great frigate bird 1·40 1·30
303 52c. Crested tern (inscr "Great Crested Tern") 1·40 1·30
304 65c. Lesser sand plover 1·80 1·60
305 75c. Little tern 2·10 1·90
306 $1 Reef heron (inscr "Pacific") 2·75 2·50
307 $2 Blue-faced (inscr "Masked") booby 5·50 5·00
MS308 92×119 mm. Nos. 285, 289, 293 and 302 3·25 3·00

47 Lodidean (coconut-palm leaf windmill)

1990. Children's Games. Multicoloured.
309 25c. Type **47** 1·10 1·00
310 25c. Lejonjon (juggling green coconuts) 1·10 1·00
311 25c. Etobobo (coconut leaf musical instrument) 1·10 1·00
312 25c. Didmakol (pandanus leaf flying-toy) 1·10 1·00

48 Penny Black

1990. 150th Anniv of the Penny Black. Multicoloured.
313 25c. Type **48** 1·40 1·30
314 25c. Essay of James Chalmers's cancellation 1·40 1·30
315 25c. Stamp essay by Robert Sievier 1·40 1·30
316 25c. Stamp essay by Charles Whiting 1·40 1·30
317 25c. Stamp essay by George Dickinson 1·40 1·30
318 25c. "City" medal by William Wyon (struck to commemorate Queen Victoria's first visit to City of London) 1·40 1·30
MS319 114×86 mm. $1 Charles Heath and original engraving for master die (71×29 mm) 5·50 5·00

1990. History of Second World War. As T **43**. Multicoloured. (a) 5th issue. Invasions of Denmark and Norway, 1940.
320 25c. German soldier and "Stuka" dive bombers in Copenhagen 85 75
321 25c. Norwegian soldiers, burning building and German column 85 75

(b) 6th issue. Katyn Forest Massacre of Polish Prisoners, 1940.
322 25c. Bound hands and grave (vert) 85 75

(c) 7th issue. Appointment of Winston Churchill as Prime Minister of Great Britain, 1940.
323 45c. Union Jack, Churchill and war scenes 1·40 1·30

(d) 8th issue. Invasion of Low Countries, 1940.
324 25c. Bombing of Rotterdam 85 75
325 25c. Invasion of Belgium 85 75

(e) 9th issue. Evacuation at Dunkirk, 1940.
326 45c. British bren-gunner on beach 1·40 1·30
327 45c. Soldiers queueing for boats 1·40 1·30
Nos. 326/7 were issued together, se-tenant, forming a composite design.

(f) 10th issue. German Occupation of Paris, 1940.
328 45c. German soldiers marching through Arc de Triomphe (vert) 1·40 1·30

(g) 11th issue. Battle of Mers-el-Kebir, 1940.
329 25c. Vice-Admiral Sir James Somerville, Vice-Admiral Marcel Gensoul and British and French battleships 85 75

(h) 12th issue. The Burma Road, 1940.
330 25c. Allied and Japanese forces (vert) 85 75

(i) 13th issue. British Bases and American Destroyers Lend-lease Agreement, 1940.
331 45c. H.M.S. "Georgetown" (formerly U.S.S. "Maddox") 1·40 1·30
332 45c. H.M.S. "Banff" (formerly U.S.C.G.C. "Saranac") 1·40 1·30
333 45c. H.M.S. "Buxton" (formerly U.S.S. "Edwards") 1·40 1·30
334 45c. H.M.S. "Rockingham" (formerly U.S.S. "Swasey") 1·40 1·30

(j) 14th issue. Battle of Britain, 1940.
335 45c. Supermarine Spitfire Mk 1A fighters 1·40 1·30
336 45c. Hawker Hurricane Mk 1 and Spitfire fighters 1·40 1·30
337 45c. Messerschmitt Bf 109E fighters 1·40 1·30
338 45c. Junkers Ju 87B-2 "Stuka" dive bomber 1·40 1·30
Nos. 335/8 were issued together, se-tenant, forming a composite design.

(k) 15th issue. Tripartite Pact, 1940.
339 45c. Officers' caps of Germany, Italy and Japan (vert) 1·40 1·30

(l) 16th issue. Election of Franklin D. Roosevelt for Third United States Presidential Term, 1940.
340 25c. Roosevelt (vert) 85 75

(m) 17th issue. Battle of Taranto, 1940.
341 25c. H.M.S. "Illustrious" (aircraft carrier) 85 75
342 25c. Fairey Swordfish bomber 85 75
343 25c. "Andrea Doria" (Italian battleship) 85 75
344 25c. "Conte di Cavour" (Italian battleship) 85 75
Nos. 341/4 were issued together, se-tenant, forming a composite design.

49 Pacific Green Turtles

1990. Endangered Turtles. Multicoloured.
345 25c. Type **49** 1·10 1·00
346 25c. Pacific green turtle swimming 1·10 1·00
347 25c. Hawksbill turtle hatching 1·10 1·00
348 25c. Hawksbill turtle swimming 1·10 1·00

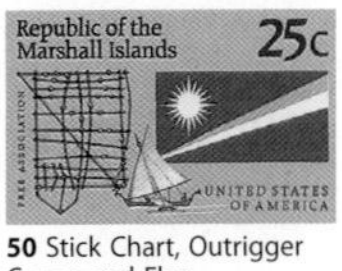

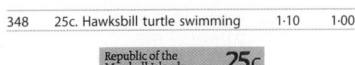

50 Stick Chart, Outrigger Canoe and Flag

1990. 4th Anniv of Ratification of Compact of Free Association with United States.
349 **50** 25c. multicoloured 1·30 75

51 Brandenburg Gate, Berlin

1990. Re-unification of Germany.
350 **51** 45c. multicoloured 1·80 1·30

52 Outrigger Canoe and Stick Chart

1990. Christmas. Multicoloured.
351 25c. Type **52** 1·10 95
352 25c. Missionary preaching and "Morning Star" (missionary ship) 1·10 95
353 25c. British sailors dancing 1·10 95
354 25c. Electric guitar and couple dancing 1·10 95

53 Harvesting Breadfruit

1990. Breadfruit. Multicoloured.
355 25c. Type **53** 1·10 95
356 25c. Peeling breadfruit 1·10 95
357 25c. Soaking breadfruit 1·10 95
358 25c. Kneading dough 1·10 95

1991. History of Second World War. As T **43**. Multicoloured. (a) 18th issue. Four Freedoms Speech to U.S. Congress by President Franklin Roosevelt, 1941.
359 30c. Freedom of Speech 90 85
360 30c. Freedom from Want 90 85
361 30c. Freedom of Worship 90 85
362 30c. Freedom from Fear 90 85

(b) 19th issue. Battle of Beda Fomm, 1941.
363 30c. Tank battle 90 85

(c) 20th issue. German Invasion of Balkans, 1941.
364 29c. German Dornier DO-17Z bombers over Acropolis, Athens (Greece) (vert) 85 75
365 29c. German tank and Yugoslavian Parliament building (vert) 85 75

(d) 21st issue. Sinking of the "Bismarck" (German battleship), 1941.
366 50c. H.M.S. "Prince of Wales" (battleship) 1·40 1·30
367 50c. H.M.S. "Hood" (battle cruiser) 1·40 1·30
368 50c. "Bismarck" 1·40 1·30
369 50c. Fairey Swordfish torpedo bombers 1·40 1·30

(e) 22nd issue. German Invasion of Russia, 1941.
370 30c. German tanks 85 75

(f) 23rd issue. Declaration of Atlantic Charter by United States and Great Britain, 1941.
371 29c. U.S.S. "Augusta" (cruiser) and Pres. Roosevelt of United States (vert) 85 75
372 29c. H.M.S. "Prince of Wales" (battleship) and Winston Churchill (vert) 85 75
Nos. 371/2 were issued together, se-tenant, forming a composite design.

(g) 24th issue. Siege of Moscow, 1941.
373 29c. German tanks crossing snow-covered plain 85 75

(h) 25th issue. Sinking of U.S.S. "Reuben James", 1941.
374 30c. U.S.S. "Reuben James" (destroyer) 85 75
375 30c. German U-boat 562 (submarine) 85 75
Nos. 374/5 were issued together, se-tenant, forming a composite design.

(i) 26th issue. Japanese Attack on Pearl Harbor, 1941.
376 50c. American airplanes (inscr "Peal Harbor") (vert) 1·40 1·30
376b As No. 376 but inscr "Pearl Harbor" 2·75 2·50
377 50c. Japanese dive bombers (vert) 1·40 1·30
378 50c. U.S.S. "Arizona" (battleship) (vert) 1·40 1·30
379 50c. "Akagi" (Japanese aircraft carrier) (vert) 1·40 1·30
Nos. 376/9 were issued together, se-tenant, forming a composite design.

(j) 27th issue. Japanese Capture of Guam, 1941.
380 29c. Japanese troops (vert) 85 75

(k) 28th issue. Fall of Singapore to Japan, 1941.
381 29c. Japanese soldiers with Japanese flag, Union Jack and white flag 85 75

(l) 29th issue. Formation of "Flying Tigers" (American volunteer group), 1941.
382 50c. American Curtiss Tomahawk fighters 1·40 1·30
383 50c. Japanese Mitsubishi Ki-21 "Sally" bombers 1·40 1·30
Nos. 382/3 were issued together, se-tenant, forming a composite design.

(m) 30th issue. Fall of Wake Island to Japan, 1941.
384 29c. American Grumman Wildcat fighters and Japanese Mitsubishi G3M "Nell" bombers over Wake Island 85 75

54 Boeing 747 carrying "Columbia" to Launch Site

1991. Ten Years of Space Shuttle Flights. Multicoloured.
385 50c. Type **54** 1·30 1·20
386 50c. Orbital release of Long Duration Exposure Facility from "Challenger", 1984 1·30 1·20
387 50c. Shuttle launch at Cape Canaveral 1·30 1·20
388 50c. Shuttle landing at Edwards Air Force Base 1·30 1·20
Nos. 385/8 were issued together, se-tenant, the backgrounds forming a composite design.

55 "Ixora carolinensis"

1991. Native Flowers. Multicoloured.
389 52c. Type **55** 1·50 1·40
390 52c. Glory-bower ("Clerodendum inerme") 1·50 1·40
391 52c. "Messerschmidia argentea" 1·50 1·40
392 52c. "Vigna marina" 1·50 1·40
MS393 92×120 mm. Nos. 389/92 6·75 6·00
No. **MS**393 commemorates Phila Nippon'91 International Stamp Exhibition, Tokyo.

56 American Bald Eagle and Marshall Islands and U.S. Flags

1991. United States Participation in Operation Desert Storm (campaign to liberate Kuwait).
394 **56** 29c. multicoloured 1·10 1·00

57 Red-footed Booby

1991. Birds. Multicoloured.
395 29c. Type **57** 1·80 1·60
396 29c. Great frigate bird (facing right) 1·80 1·60
397 29c. Brown booby 1·80 1·60
398 29c. White tern 1·80 1·60

399 29c. Great frigate bird (facing left) 1·80 1·60
400 29c. White-capped noddy ("Black Noddy") 1·80 1·60
MS401 113×87 mm. $1 White-tailed tropic birds (74×32 mm) 9·00 8·25

58 Dornier Do-228

1991. Passenger Aircraft. Multicoloured.
402 12c. Type **58** 35 30
403 29c. Douglas DC-8 jetliner 90 85
404 50c. Hawker Siddeley H.S. 748 airliner 1·50 1·40
405 50c. Saab 2000 1·50 1·40

59 U.N. and State Emblems and Outrigger Canoe

1991. Admission of Marshall Islands to the United Nations.
406 **59** 29c. multicoloured 1·00 90

60 Dove and Glory-bower Flowers

1991. Christmas.
407 **60** 30c. multicoloured 1·10 95

61 State Flag and Dove

1991. 25th Anniv of Peace Corps in Marshall Islands.
408 **61** 29c. multicoloured 1·10 95

1992. History of Second World War. As T **43**. Multicoloured. (a) 31st issue. Arcadia Conference, Washington D.C., 1942.
409 29c. Pres. Franklin Roosevelt of U.S.A., Winston Churchill of Great Britain, White House and United Nations emblem 85 75

(b) 32nd issue. Fall of Manila to Japan, 1942.
410 50c. Japanese tank moving through Manila 1·40 1·30

(c) 33rd issue. Capture of Rabaul by Japan, 1942.
411 29c. Japanese flag, Admiral Yamamoto, General Douglas MacArthur and U.S. flag 85 75

(d) 34th issue. Battle of the Java Sea, 1942.
412 29c. Sinking of the "De Ruyter" (Dutch cruiser) 85 75

(e) 35th issue. Capture of Rangoon by Japan, 1942.
413 50c. Japanese tank and soldiers in Rangoon (vert) 1·40 1·30

(f) 36th issue. Japanese Landing on New Guinea, 1942.
414 29c. Japanese soldiers coming ashore 85 75

(g) 37th issue. Evacuation of General Douglas MacArthur from Corregidor, 1942.
415 29c. MacArthur 85 75

(h) 38th issue. British Raid on Saint Nazaire, 1942.
416 29c. H.M.S. "Campbeltown" (destroyer) and motor torpedo boat 85 75

(i) 39th issue. Surrender of Bataan, 1942.
417 29c. Prisoners on "death" march (vert) 85 75

(j) 40th issue. Doolittle Raid on Tokyo, 1942.
418 50c. North American B-25 Mitchell bomber taking off from U.S.S. "Hornet" (aircraft carrier) (vert) 1·40 1·30

(k) 41st issue. Fall of Corregidor to Japan, 1942.
419 29c. Lt.-Gen. Jonathan Wainwright 85 75

(l) 42nd issue. Battle of the Coral Sea, 1942.
420 50c. U.S.S. "Lexington" (aircraft carrier) and Grumman F4F-3 Wildcat fighter (inscr "U.S.S. Lexington") 1·40 1·30
420b As No. 420 but additionally inscr with aircraft name 2·75 2·50
421 50c. Japanese Aichi D3A 1 "Val" and Nakajima B5N2 "Kate" dive bombers (wrongly inscr `Mitsubishi A6M2 "Zero"') 1·40 1·30
421a As No. 421 but inscr corrected 2·75 2·50
422 50c. American Douglas TBD-1 Devastator torpedo bombers (wrongly inscr "U.S. Douglas SBD Dauntless") 1·40 1·30
422a As No. 422 but with inscr corrected 2·75 2·50
423 50c. "Shoho" (Japanese aircraft carrier) and Mitsubishi A6M2 Zero-Sen fighters (inscr "Japanese carrier Shoho") 1·40 1·30
423a As No. 423 but additionally inscr with aircraft name 2·75 2·50

The four designs were issued together, se-tenant, each pair forming a composite design.

(m) 43rd issue. Battle of Midway, 1942.
424 50c. "Akagi" (Japanese aircraft carrier) 1·40 1·30
425 50c. U.S.S. "Yorktown" (aircraft carrier) 1·40 1·30
426 50c. American Douglas SBD Dauntless dive bombers 1·40 1·30
427 50c. Japanese Nakajima B5N2 "Kate" dive bombers 1·40 1·30

Nos. 424/7 were issued together, se-tenant, forming a composite design.

(n) 44th issue. Destruction of Lidice (Czechoslovakian village), 1942.
428 29c. Cross and memorial at Lidice 85 75

(o) 45th issue. German Capture of Sevastopol, 1942.
429 29c. German siege gun "Dora" (vert) 85 75

(p) 46th issue. Destruction of Convoy PQ-17, 1942.
430 29c. British merchant ship 85 75
431 29c. German U-boat 85 75

(q) 47th issue. Marine Landing on Guadalcanal, 1942.
432 29c. American marines landing on beach 85 75

(r) 48th issue. Battle of Savo Island, 1942.
433 29c. Admiral Mikawa of Japan (vert) 85 75

(s) 49th issue. Dieppe Raid, 1942.
434 29c. Soldiers landing at Dieppe 85 75

(t) 50th issue. Battle of Stalingrad, 1942.
435 50c. Heroes monument and burning buildings (vert) 1·80 1·30

(u) 51st issue. Battle of Eastern Solomon Islands, 1942.
436 29c. Aircraft over U.S.S. "Enterprise" (aircraft carrier) 85 75

(v) 52nd issue. Battle of Cape Esperance, 1942.
437 50c. American cruiser firing guns at night 1·80 1·30

(w) 53rd issue. Battle of El Alamein, 1942.
438 29c. Gen. Bernard Montgomery of Great Britain and Gen. Erwin Rommel of Germany 85 75

(x) 54th issue. Battle of Barents Sea, 1942.
439 29c. H.M.S. "Sheffield" (cruiser) 85 75
440 29c. "Admiral Hipper" (German cruiser) 85 75

62 "Emlain" (bulk carrier)

1992. Ships flying the Marshall Islands Flag. Multicoloured.
441 29c. Type **62** 1·10 1·00
442 29c. "CSK Valiant" (tanker) 1·10 1·00
443 29c. "Ionmeto" (fisheries protection vessel) 1·10 1·00
444 29c. "Micro Pilot" (inter-island freighter) 1·10 1·00

63 Northern Pintail

1992. Nature Protection.
445 **63** 29c. multicoloured 85 75

64 Tipnol (outrigger canoe)

1992. Legends of Discovery. Multicoloured.
446 50c. Type **64** 1·40 1·30
447 50c. "Santa Maria" (reconstruction of Columbus's flagship) 1·40 1·30
448 50c. Constellation Argo Navis 1·40 1·30
449 50c. Sailor and tipnol 1·40 1·30
450 50c. Christopher Columbus and "Santa Maria" 1·40 1·30
451 50c. Astronaut and Argo Navis constellation 1·40 1·30
MS452 114×87 mm. $1 Columbus, sailor and astronaut (74×31 mm) 5·50 5·00

65 Basket Making

1992. Handicrafts. Multicoloured.
453 29c. Type **65** 85 75
454 29c. Boy holding model outrigger canoe 85 75
455 29c. Man carving boat 85 75
456 29c. Fan making 85 75

66 Christmas Offering

1992. Christmas.
457 **66** 29c. multicoloured 1·00 90

1993. History of Second World War. As T **43**. Multicoloured. (a) 55th issue. Casablanca Conference, 1943.
458 29c. Pres. Franklin Roosevelt and Winston Churchill 90 85

(b) 56th issue. Liberation of Kharkov, 1943.
459 29c. Russian tank in Kharkov 90 85

(c) 57th issue. Battle of the Bismarck Sea, 1943.
460 50c. Japanese Mitsubishi A6M Zero-Sen fighters and "Arashio" (Japanese destroyer) 1·40 1·30
461 50c. American Lockheed P-38 Lightnings and Australian Bristol Beaufighter fighters 1·40 1·30
462 50c. "Shirayuki" (Japanese destroyer) 1·40 1·30
463 50c. American A-20 Havoc and North American B-52 Mitchell bombers 1·40 1·30

Nos 460/63 were issued together, se-tenant, forming a composite design.

(d) 58th issue. Interception of Yamamoto, 1943.
464 50c. Admiral Yamamoto 1·40 1·30

(e) 59th issue. Battle of Kursk, 1943.
465 29c. German "Tiger 1" tank 1·20 1·10
466 29c. Soviet "T-34" tank 1·20 1·10

Nos. 465/6 were issued together, se-tenant, forming a composite design.

(f) 60th issue. Allied Invasion of Sicily, 1943.
467 52c. Gen. George Patton, Jr 1·50 1·40
468 52c. Gen. Bernard Montgomery 1·50 1·40
469 52c. Americans landing at Licata 1·50 1·40
470 52c. British landing south of Syracuse 1·50 1·40

(g) 61st issue. Raids on Schweinfurt, 1943.
471 50c. American Boeing B-17F Flying Fortress bombers and German Messerschmitt Bf 109 fighter 1·40 1·30

(h) 62nd issue. Liberation of Smolensk, 1943.
472 29c. Russian soldier and burning buildings (vert) 85 75

(i) 63rd issue. Landing at Bougainville, 1943.
473 29c. American Marines on beach at Empress Augusta Bay 85 75

(j) 64th issue. U.S. Invasion of Tarawa, 1943.
474 50c. American Marines 1·40 1·30

(k) 65th issue. Teheran Allied Conference, 1943.
475 52c. Winston Churchill of Great Britain, Pres. Franklin Roosevelt of U.S.A. and Josef Stalin of Russia (vert) 1·50 1·40

(l) 66th issue. Battle of North Cape, 1943.
476 29c. H.M.S. "Duke of York" (British battleship) 85 75
477 29c. "Scharnhorst" (German battleship) 85 75

67 Atoll Butterflyfish

1993. Reef Life. Multicoloured.
478 50c. Type **67** 2·00 1·80
479 50c. Brick soldierfish 2·00 1·80
480 50c. Caerulean damselfish 2·00 1·80
481 50c. Japanese inflator-filefish 2·00 1·80
482 50c. Arc-eyed hawkfish 2·00 1·80
483 50c. Powder-blue surgeonfish 2·00 1·80
MS484 114×87 mm. $1 Bridled parrotfish (74×32 mm) 7·75 7·00

68 "Britannia" (full-rigged ship)

1993. Ships. Multicoloured. (a) Size 35×20 mm.
485 10c. "San Jeronimo" (Spanish galleon) 30 25
486 14c. U.S.C.G. "Cape Corwin" (fisheries patrol vessel) 40 40
487 15c. Type **68** 40 40
488 19c. "Micro Palm" (inter-island freighter) 55 50
489 20c. "Eendracht" (Dirk Hartog's ship) 55 50
490 23c. H.M.S "Cornwallis" (sail frigate) 65 60
491 24c. U.S.S. "Dolphin" (schooner) 70 65
492 29c. "Morning Star I" (missionary brigantine) 85 75
493 30c. "Rurik" (Otto von Kotzebue's brig) (inscr "Rurick") 85 75
494 32c. "Vitoria" (Magellan's flagship) 90 85
495 35c. "Nautilus" (German gunboat) 1·00 90
496 40c. "Nautilus" (British brig) 1·10 1·00
497 45c. "Nagara" and "Isuzu" (Japanese cruisers) 1·30 1·20
498 46c. "Equator" (schooner) 1·30 1·20
499 50c. U.S.S. "Lexington" (aircraft carrier) 1·40 1·30
500 52c. H.M.S. "Serpent" (brig) 1·50 1·40
501 55c. "Potomac" (whaling ship) 1·60 1·90
502 60c. U.S.C.G. "Assateague" (cutter) 1·80 1·60
503 75c. "Scarborough" (transport) 2·10 1·90
504 78c. "Charles W. Morgan" (whaling ship) 2·30 2·10
505 95c. "Tanager" (inter-island steamer) 2·75 2·40
506 $1 "Tole Mour" (hospital schooner) 2·75 2·50
507 $2.90 Fishing vessels 8·00 7·25
508 $3.00 "Victoria" (whaling ship) 8·50 7·75
669 32c. As Type **68** 85 75
670 32c. U.S.S. "Dolphin" (schooner) 85 75
671 32c. "Morning Star I" (missionary brigantine) 85 75
672 32c. U.S.S. "Lexington" (aircraft carrier) 85 75
673 32c. "Micro Palm" (inter-island freighter) 85 75
674 32c. H.M.S. "Cornwallis" (sail frigate) 85 75
675 32c. H.M.S. "Serpent" (brig) 85 75
676 32c. "Scarborough" (transport) 85 75
677 32c. "San Jeronimo" (Spanish galleon) 85 75
678 32c. "Rurik" (Otto von Kotzebue's brig) (inscr "Rurick") 85 75
679 32c. "Nautilus" (German gunboat) 85 75
680 32c. Fishing vessels 85 75
681 32c. Malmel outrigger canoe 85 75
682 32c. "Eendracht" (Dirk Hartog's ship) 85 75
683 32c. "Nautilus" (brig) 85 75
684 32c. "Nagara" and "Isuzu" (Japanese cruisers) 85 75
685 32c. "Potomac" (whaling ship) 85 75
687 32c. U.S.C.G. "Assateague" (cutter) 85 75
688 32c. "Charles W. Morgan" (whaling ship) 85 75
689 32c. "Victoria" (whaling ship) 85 75
690 32c. U.S.C.G. "Cape Corwin" (fisheries patrol vessel) 85 75
691 32c. "Equator" (schooner) 85 75
692 32c. "Tanager" (inter-island steamer) 85 75
693 32c. "Tole Mour" (hospital schooner) 85 75

(b) Size 46×26 mm.

509	$1 Enewetak outrigger canoe	2·75	2·50
510	$2 Jaluit outrigger canoe	5·50	5·00
511	$5 Ailuk outrigger canoe	14·00	13·00
512	$10 Racing outrigger canoes	28·00	26·00

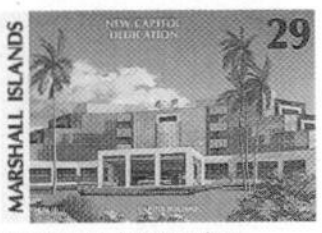

69 Capitol Complex

1993. Inauguration of New Capitol Complex, Majuro. Multicoloured.

513	29c. Type **69**	70	65
514	29c. Parliament building	70	65
515	29c. National seal (vert)	70	65
516	29c. National flag (vert)	70	65

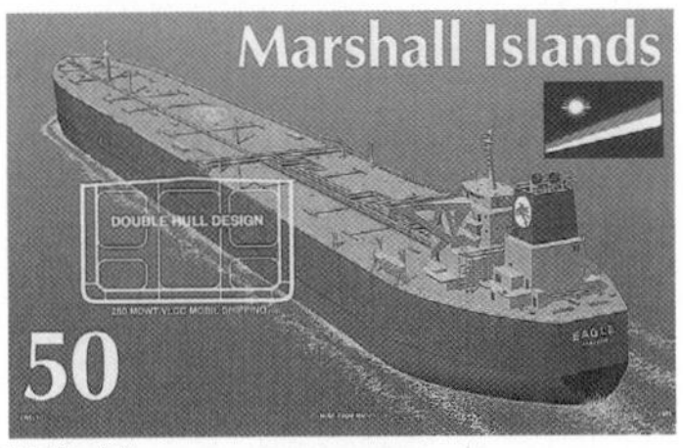

70 "Eagle"

1993. Marshall Islands Registration of "Eagle" (oil tanker). Sheet 115×87 mm.

MS517	**70** 50c. multicoloured	1·20	1·10

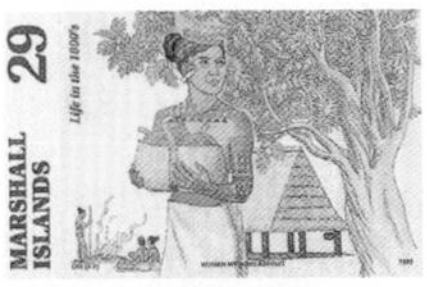

71 Woman with Breadfruit

1993. Marshallese Life in the 1800s. Designs adapted from sketches by Louis Choris. Multicoloured.

518	29c. Type **71**	85	75
519	29c. Canoes and warrior	85	75
520	29c. Chief and islanders	85	75
521	29c. Drummer and dancers	85	75

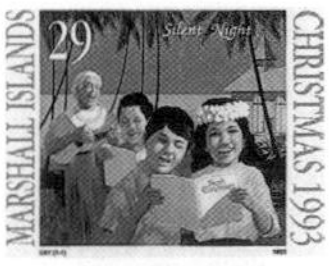

72 Singing Silent Night

1993. Christmas.

522	**72** 29c. multicoloured	85	75

1994. History of Second World War. As T **43**. Multicoloured. (a) 67th issue. Appointment of Gen. Dwight D. Eisenhower as Commander of Supreme Headquarters, Allied Expeditionary Force, 1944.

523	29c. Eisenhower	85	75

(b) 68th issue. Invasion of Anzio, 1944.

524	50c. Troops landing	1·40	1·30

(c) 69th issue. Lifting of Siege of Leningrad, 1944.

525	52c. St. Isaac's Cathedral and soldier with Soviet flag	1·50	1·40

(d) 70th issue. U.S. Liberation of Marshall Islands, 1944.

526	29c. Douglas SBD Dauntless dive bombers	85	75

(e) 71st issue. Japanese Defeat at Truk, 1944.

527	29c. Admirals Spruance and Marc Mitscher (vert)	85	75

(f) 72nd issue. U.S. Bombing of Germany, 1944.

528	52c. Boeing B-17 Flying Fortress bombers	1·50	1·40

(g) 73rd issue. Allied Liberation of Rome, 1944.

529	50c. Lt.-Gen. Mark Clark and flowers in gun barrel (vert)	1·40	1·30

(h) 74th issue. Allied Landings in Normandy, 1944.

530	75c. Airspeed A.S.51 Horsa gliders (inscr "Horsa Gliders")	2·20	2·00
530b	As No. 530 but inscr "Horsa Gliders, Parachute Troops"	4·50	4·25
531	75c. Hawker Typhoon 1B and North American P-51B Mustang fighters (wrongly inscr "U.S. P51B Mustangs, British Hurricanes")	2·20	2·00
531a	As No. 531 but inscr corrected	4·50	4·25
532	75c. German gun defences (inscr "German Gun Defenses")	2·20	2·00
532a	As No. 523 but inscr "German Gun Defenses, Pointe du Hoc"	4·50	4·25
533	75c. Allied amphibious landing	2·20	2·00

The four designs were issued together, se-tenant, forming a composite design.

(i) 75th issue. V-1 Bombardment of England, 1944.

534	50c. V-1 flying bomb over River Thames	1·40	1·30

(j) 76th issue. U.S. Marines Land on Saipan, 1944.

535	29c. U.S. and Japanese troops	85	75

(k) 77th issue. First Battle of the Philippine Sea, 1944.

536	50c. Grumman F6F-3 Hellcat fighter	1·40	1·30

(l) 78th issue. U.S. Liberation of Guam, 1944.

537	29c. Naval bombardment	85	75

(m) 79th issue. Warsaw Uprising, 1944.

538	50c. Polish Home Army fighter	1·40	1·30

(n) 80th issue. Liberation of Paris, 1944.

539	50c. Allied troops marching along Champs Elysee	1·40	1·30

(o) 81st issue. U.S. Marines Land on Peleliu, 1944.

540	29c. Amphibious armoured tracked vehicle	85	75

(p) 82nd issue. General Douglas MacArthur's Return to Philippines, 1944.

541	52c. McArthur and soldiers	1·50	1·40

(q) 83rd issue. Battle of Leyte Gulf, 1944.

542	52c. American motor torpedo boat and Japanese warships	1·50	1·40

(r) 84th issue. Sinking of the "Tirpitz" (German battleship), 1944.

543	50c. Avro Lancaster bombers	1·40	1·30
544	50c. Tirpitz burning	1·40	1·30

(s) 85th issue. Battle of the Bulge, 1944.

545	50c. Infantrymen	1·40	1·30
546	50c. Tank driver and tanks	1·40	1·30
547	50c. Pilot and aircraft	1·40	1·30
548	50c. Lt.-Col. Creighton Abrams and Brig.-Gen. Anthony McAuliffe shaking hands	1·40	1·30

1994. "Hong Kong '94" International Stamp Exhibition. British Ships. Sheet 131×93 mm containing horiz designs as Nos. 487, 490, 500 and 503 but size 46×27 mm.

MS549	15c. "Britannia"; 23c. H.M.S. "Cornwallis"; 52c. H.M.S. "Serpent"; 75c. "Scarborough"	5·25	4·75

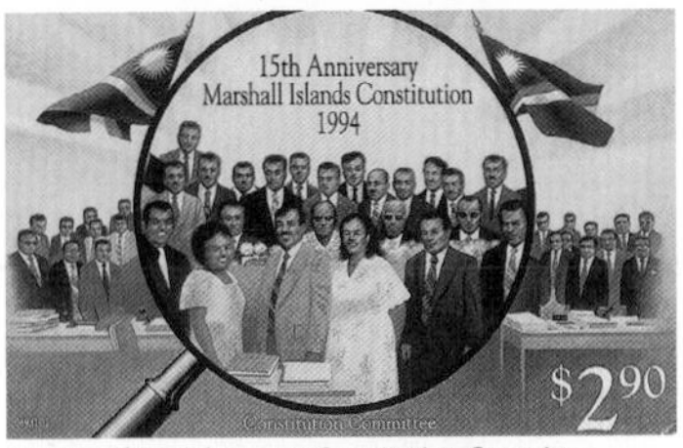

73 Magnifying Glass over Constitution Committee

1994. 15th Anniv of Marshall Islands Constitution. Sheet 100×87 mm.

MS550	**73** $2.90 multicoloured	6·25	5·75

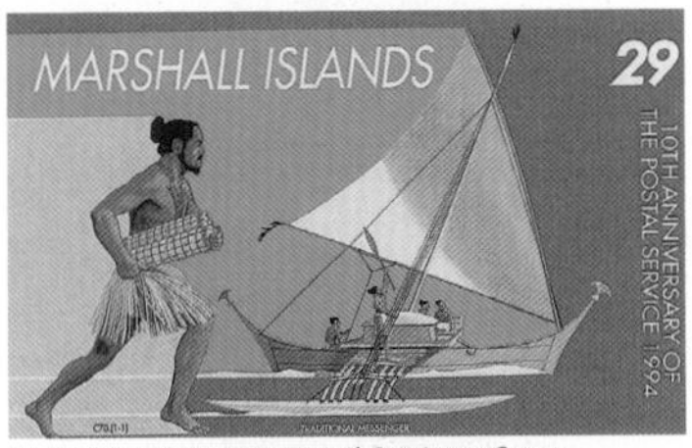

74 Traditional Messenger and Outrigger Canoe

1994. Tenth Anniv of Independent Postal Service. Sheet 115×87 mm.

MS551	**74** 29c. multicoloured	85	75

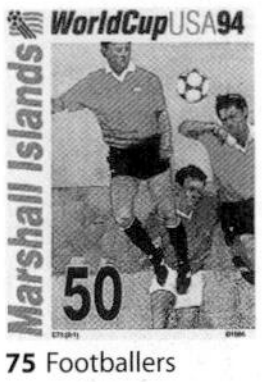

75 Footballers

1994. World Cup Football Championship, U.S.A. Multicoloured.

552	50c. Type **75**	2·20	2·00
553	50c. Footballers (different)	2·20	2·00

Nos. 552/53 were issued together, se-tenant, forming a composite design.

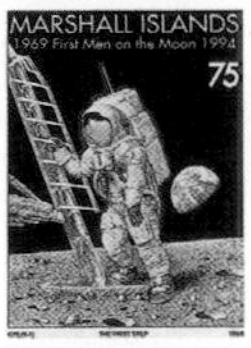

76 Neil Armstrong stepping onto Moon

1994. 25th Anniv of First Manned Moon Landing. Multicoloured.

554	75c. Type **76**	1·50	1·40
555	75c. Planting U.S. flag on Moon	1·50	1·40
556	75c. Astronauts saluting	1·50	1·40
557	75c. Pres. John F. Kennedy and Armstrong	1·50	1·40
MS558	93×120 mm. Nos. 554/7	6·25	5·75

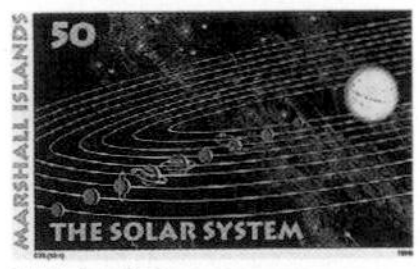

77 Solar System

1994. The Solar System. Multicoloured.

559	50c. Type **77**	1·40	1·30
560	50c. Sun	1·40	1·30
561	50c. Moon	1·40	1·30
562	50c. Mercury	1·40	1·30
563	50c. Venus	1·40	1·30
564	50c. Earth	1·40	1·30
565	50c. Mars	1·40	1·30
566	50c. Jupiter	1·40	1·30
567	50c. Saturn	1·40	1·30
568	50c. Uranus	1·40	1·30
569	50c. Neptune	1·40	1·30
570	50c. Pluto	1·40	1·30

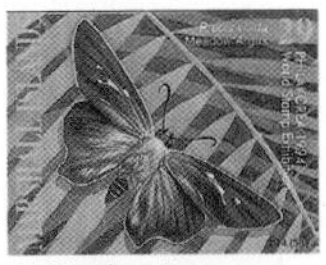

78 Meadow Argus

1994. "Philakorea 1994" International Stamp Exhibition, Seoul. Butterflies. Sheet 160×62 mm containing T 78 and similar horiz designs. Multicoloured.

MS571	29c. Type **78**; 52c. Brown awl; $1 Common (inscr "Great") eggfly	5·25	4·75

1994. 50th Anniv of General Douglas MacArthur's Return to Philippines. Sheet 150×62 mm containing previous designs.

MS572	50c. As No. 415; 50c. As No. 541 but with inscription at right-hand sideways	2·75	2·50

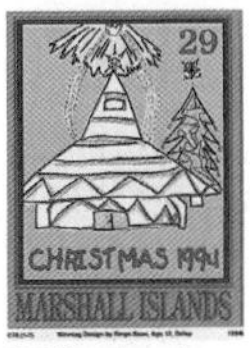

79 Church and Christmas Tree (Ringo Baso)

1994. Christmas.

573	**79** 29c. multicoloured	85	75

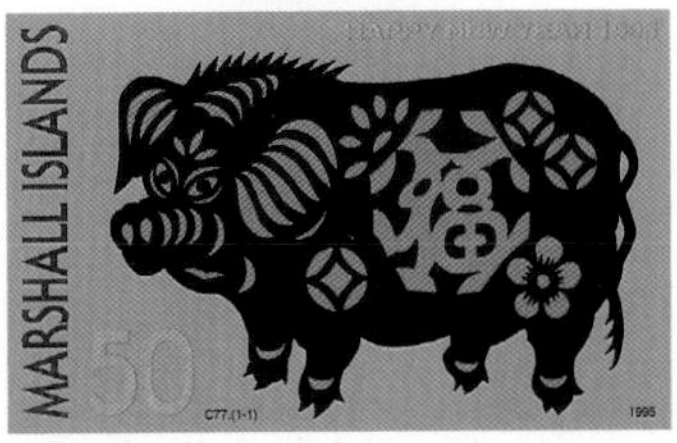

80 Pig

1995. New Year. Year of the Pig. Sheet 115×87 mm.

MS574	**80** 50c. multicoloured	1·40	1·30

1995. History of Second World War. As T **43**. Multicoloured. (a) 86th issue. Yalta Conference, 1945.

575	32c. Josef Stalin of U.S.S.R., Winston Churchill of Great Britain and Franklin Roosevelt of U.S.A. (vert)	90	85

(b) 87th issue. Allied Bombing of Dresden, 1945.

576	55c. "Europe" (Meissen porcelain statuette), flames and bombers (vert)	1·50	1·40

(c) 88th issue. U.S. Marine Invasion of Iwo Jima, 1945.

577	$1 Marines planting flag on Mt. Suribachi (vert)	3·25	3·00

(d) 89th issue. U.S. Capture of Remagen Bridge, Germany, 1945.

578	32c. Troops and tanks crossing bridge (vert)	90	85

(e) 90th issue. U.S. Invasion of Okinawa, 1945.

579	55c. Soldiers throwing grenades (vert)	1·50	1·40

(f) 91st issue. Death of Franklin D. Roosevelt, 1945.

580	50c. Funeral cortege	1·40	1·30

(g) 92nd issue. U.S. and U.S.S.R. Troops meet at Elbe, 1945.

581	32c. American and Soviet troops	90	85

(h) 93rd issue. Capture of Berlin by Soviet Troops, 1945.

582	60c. Soviet Marshal Georgi Zhukov and Berlin landmarks	1·80	1·60

(i) 94th issue. Allied Liberation of Concentration Camps, 1945.

583	55c. Inmates and soldier cutting barbed-wire fence	1·50	1·40

(j) 95th issue. V-E (Victory in Europe) Day, 1945.

584	75c. Signing of German surrender, Rheims	2·20	2·00
585	75c. Soldier kissing girl, Times Square, New York	2·20	2·00
586	75c. Victory Parade, Red Square, Moscow	2·20	2·00
587	75c. Royal Family and Churchill on balcony of Buckingham Palace, London	2·20	2·00

(k) 96th issue. Signing of United Nations Charter, 1945.

588	32c. U.S. President Harry S. Truman and Veterans' Memorial Hall, San Francisco	90	85

(l) 97th issue. Potsdam Conference, 1945.

589	55c. Pres. Harry S. Truman of U.S.A., Winston Churchill and Clement Attlee of Great Britain and Josef Stalin of U.S.S.R.	1·50	1·40

(m) 98th issue. Resignation of Winston Churchill, 1945.

590	60c. Churchill leaving 10 Downing Street (vert)	1·80	1·60

(n) 99th issue. Dropping of Atomic Bomb on Hiroshima, 1945.

591	$1 Boeing B-29 Superfortress bomber "Enola Gay" and mushroom cloud	3·25	3·00

(o) 100th issue. V-J (Victory in Japan) Day, 1945.

592	75c. Mount Fuji and warships in Tokyo Bay	2·50	2·20
593	75c. U.S.S. "Missouri" (battleship)	2·50	2·20
594	75c. Admiral Chester Nimitz signing Japanese surrender watched by Gen. Douglas MacArthur and Admirals William Halsey and Forest Sherman	2·50	2·20
595	75c. Japanese Foreign Minister Shigemitsu, General Umezu and delegation	2·50	2·20

Nos. 592/5 were issued together, se-tenant, each pair forming a composite design.

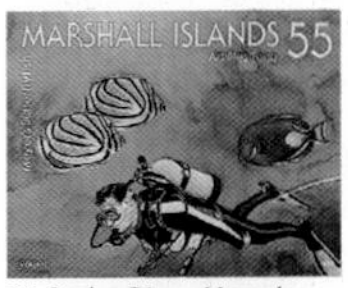

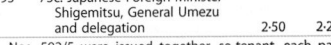

81 Scuba Diver, Meyer's Butterflyfish and Red-tailed Surgeonfish ("Achilles Tang")

1995. Undersea World (1st series). Multicoloured.

596	55c. Type **81**	1·50	1·30
597	55c. Moorish idols and scuba diver	1·50	1·30
598	55c. Pacific green turtle and anthias ("Fairy Basslet")	1·50	1·30
599	55c. Anthias ("Fairy Basslet"), emperor angelfish and orange-finned anemonefish	1·50	1·30

Nos. 596/9 were issued together, se-tenant, forming a composite design.

See also Nos. 865/8.

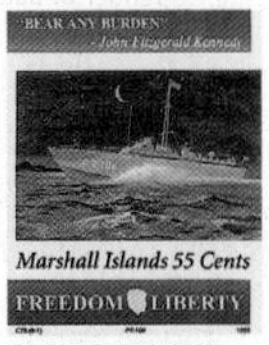

82 U.S.S. "PT 109" (motor torpedo boat)

1995. 35th Anniv of Election of John F. Kennedy as U.S. President. Multicoloured.

600	55c. Type **82** (Second World War command)	1·10	1·00
601	55c. Presidential inauguration	1·10	1·00
602	55c. Peace corps on agricultural project in Marshall Islands	1·10	1·00
603	55c. US Boeing B-29 Superfortress and warships superintending removal of Soviet missiles from Cuba	1·10	1·00
604	55c. Kennedy signing Nuclear Test Ban Treaty, 1963	1·10	1·00
605	55c. Eternal flame on Kennedy's grave, Arlington National Cemetery, Washington D.C.	1·10	1·00

83 Marilyn Monroe

1995. 69th Birth Anniv of Marilyn Monroe (actress). Multicoloured.

606	75c. Type **83**	1·80	1·60
607	75c. Monroe (face value top right)	1·80	1·60
608	75c. Monroe (face value bottom left)	1·80	1·60
609	75c. Monroe (face value bottom right)	1·80	1·60

84 Pres. Harry Truman and Veteran's Memorial Hall, San Francisco

1995. 50th Anniv of United Nations Organization. Sheet 111×86 mm.

MS610	**84** $1 multicoloured	2·50	2·30

85 "Mir" (Soviet space station)

1995. Docking of Atlantis with "Mir" Space Station (611/12) and 20th Anniv of "Apollo"–"Soyuz" Space Link (613/14). Multicoloured.

611	75c. Type **85**	1·50	1·40
612	75c. "Atlantis" (U.S. space shuttle)	1·50	1·40
613	75c. "Apollo" (U.S. spacecraft)	1·50	1·40
614	75c. "Soyuz" (Soviet spacecraft)	1·50	1·40

Nos. 611/14 were issued together, se-tenant, forming a composite design.

86 Siamese and Exotic Shorthair

1995. Cats. Multicoloured.

615	32c. Type **86**	85	75
616	32c. American shorthair tabby and red Persian	85	75
617	32c. Maine coon and Burmese	85	75
618	32c. Himalayan and Abyssinian	85	75

87 Sailfish and Tuna

1995. Pacific Game Fish. Multicoloured.

619	60c. Type **87**	1·80	1·60
620	60c. Albacores	1·80	1·60
621	60c. Wahoo	1·80	1·60
622	60c. Blue marlin	1·80	1·60
623	60c. Yellow-finned tunas	1·80	1·60
624	60c. Giant trevally	1·80	1·60
625	60c. Dolphin (fish)	1·80	1·60
626	60c. Short-finned mako	1·80	1·60

Nos. 619/26 were issued together, se-tenant, forming a composite design.

88 Inedel's Magic Kite

1995. Folk Legends (1st series). Multicoloured.

627	32c. Type **88**	85	75
628	32c. Lijebake rescues her granddaughter	85	75
629	32c. Jebro's mother invents the sail	85	75
630	32c. Limajnon escapes to the moon	85	75

See also Nos. 727/30 and 861/4.

89 "Paphiopedilum armenaicum"

1995. "Singapore'95" International Stamp Exhibition. Orchids. Sheet 93×120 mm containing T 89 and similar vert designs. Multicoloured.

MS631	32c. Type **89**; 32c. "Masdevallia veitchiana"; 32c. "Cattleya francis"; 32c. "Cattleya x guatemalensis"	3·00	2·75

90 Suzhou Gardens

1995. International Stamp and Coin Exhibition, Peking. Sheet 110×87 mm.

MS632	**90** 50c. multicoloured	1·10	1·00

91 Shepherds gazing at Sky

1995. Christmas.

633	**91** 32c. multicoloured	70	65

92 Messerschmit Me 262-la Schwalbe

1995. Jet Fighters. Multicoloured.

634	32c. Type **92**	85	75
635	32c. Gloster Meteor F Mk 8	85	75
636	32c. Lockheed F-80 Shooting Star	85	75
637	32c. North American F-86 Sabre	85	75
638	32c. F9F-2 Panther	85	75
639	32c. Mikoyan Gurevich MiG-15	85	75
640	32c. North American F-100 Super Sabre	85	75
641	32c. Convair TF-102A Delta Dagger	85	75
642	32c. Lockheed F-104 Starfighter	85	75
643	32c. Mikoyan Gurevich MiG-21 MT	85	75
644	32c. F8U Crusader	85	75
645	32c. Republic F-105 Thunderchief	85	75
646	32c. Saab J35 Draken	85	75
647	32c. Fiat G-91Y	85	75
648	32c. McDonnell Douglas F-4 Phantom II	85	75
649	32c. Saab JA 37 Viggen	85	75
650	32c. Dassault Mirage F1C	85	75
651	32c. Grumman F-14 Tomcat	85	75
652	32c. F-15 Eagle	85	75
653	32c. General Dynamics F-16 Fighting Falcon	85	75
654	32c. Panavia Tornado F Mk 3	85	75
655	32c. Sukhoi Su-27UB	85	75
656	32c. Dassault Mirage 2000C	85	75
657	32c. Hawker Siddeley Sea Harrier FRS.MK1	85	75
658	32c. F-117 Nighthawk	85	75

93 Rabin

1995. Yitzhak Rabin (Israeli Prime Minister) Commemoration.

659	**93** 32c. multicoloured	70	65

94 Rat

1996. New Year. Year of the Rat. Sheet 110×84 mm.

MS660	**94** 50c. multicoloured	1·10	1·00

95 Blue-grey Noddy

1996. Birds. Multicoloured.

661	32c. Type **95**	85	75
662	32c. Spectacled tern ("Gray-backed Tern")	85	75
663	32c. Blue-faced booby ("Masked Booby")	85	75
664	32c. Black-footed albatross	85	75

96 Cheetah

1996. Big Cats. Multicoloured.

665	55c. Type **96**	1·20	1·10
666	55c. Tiger	1·20	1·10
667	55c. Lion	1·20	1·10
668	55c. Jaguar	1·20	1·10

97 5l. Stamp

1996. Centenary of Modern Olympic Games. Designs reproducing 1896 Greek Olympic stamps. Multicoloured.

694	60c. Type **97**	1·30	1·20
695	60c. 60l. stamp	1·30	1·20
696	60c. 40l. stamp	1·30	1·20
697	60c. 1d. stamp	1·30	1·20

98 Undersea Eruptions form Islands

1996. History of Marshall Islands. Multicoloured.

698	55c. Type **98**	1·10	1·00
699	55c. Coral reefs grow around islands	1·10	1·00
700	55c. Storm-driven birds carry seeds to atolls	1·10	1·00
701	55c. First human inhabitants arrive, 1500 B.C.	1·10	1·00
702	55c. Spanish explorers discover islands, 1527	1·10	1·00
703	55c. John Marshall charts islands, 1788	1·10	1·00
704	55c. German Protectorate, 1885	1·10	1·00
705	55c. Japanese soldier on beach, 1914	1·10	1·00
706	55c. American soldiers liberate islands, 1944	1·10	1·00
707	55c. Evacuation of Bikini Atoll for nuclear testing, 1946	1·10	1·00
708	55c. Marshall Islands becomes United Nations Trust Territory, 1947	1·10	1·00
709	55c. People and national flag (independence, 1986)	1·10	1·00

99 Presley

1996. 40th Anniv of Elvis Presley's First Number One Hit Record "Heartbreak Hotel".

710	**99** 32c. multicoloured	85	75

100 Palace Museum, Shenyang

1996. "China 96" International Stamp Exhibition, Peking. Sheet 110×88 mm.

MS711	**100** 50c. multicoloured	1·30	1·20

101 Dean

1996. 65th Birth Anniv of James Dean (actor).

712	**101** 32c. multicoloured	85	75

102 1896 Quadricycle

1996. Centenary of Ford Motor Vehicle Production. Multicoloured.

713	60c. Type **102**	95	85
714	60c. 1903 Model A Roadster	95	85
715	60c. 1909 Model T touring car	95	85
716	60c. 1929 Model A station wagon	95	85
717	60c. 1955 "Thunderbird"	95	85
718	60c. 1964 "Mustang" convertible	95	85
719	60c. 1995 "Explorer"	95	85
720	60c. 1996 "Taurus"	95	85

103 Evacuees boarding "L.S.T. 1108" (tank landing ship)

1996. 50th Anniv of Operation Crossroads (nuclear testing) at Bikini Atoll. Multicoloured.

721	32c.+8c. Type **103**	1·00	95
722	32c.+8c. U.S. Navy preparation of site	1·00	95
723	32c.+8c. Explosion of "Able" (first test)	1·00	95

724	32c.+8c. Explosion of "Baker" (first underwater test)	1·00	95
725	32c.+8c. Ghost fleet (targets)	1·00	95
726	32c.+8c. Bikinian family	1·00	95

1996. Folk Legends (2nd series). As T **88**. Multicoloured.

727	32c. Letao gives gift of fire	75	70
728	32c. Mennin Jobwodda flying on giant bird	75	70
729	32c. Koko chasing Letao in canoe	75	70
730	32c. Mother and girl catching Kouj (octopus) to cook	75	70

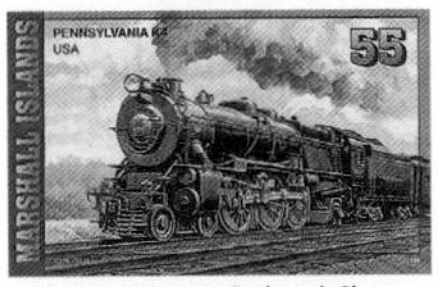

104 Pennsylvania Railroad Class K4, U.S.A.

1996. Steam Railway Locomotives. Multicoloured.

731	55c. Type **104**	1·10	1·00
732	55c. Big Boy, U.S.A.	1·10	1·00
733	55c. Class A4 "Mallard", Great Britain	1·10	1·00
734	55c. Class 242, Spain	1·10	1·00
735	55c. Class 01 No. 052, Germany	1·10	1·00
736	55c. Class 691 No. 031, Italy	1·10	1·00
737	55c. "Royal Hudson", Canada	1·10	1·00
738	55c. "Evening Star", Great Britain	1·10	1·00
739	55c. Class 520, South Australia	1·10	1·00
740	55c. Class 232.U.2, France	1·10	1·00
741	55c. Class QJ "Advance Forward", China	1·10	1·00
742	55c. Class C62 "Swallow", Japan	1·10	1·00

1996. Tenth Asian International Stamp Exhibition, Taipeh. Sheet 120×92 mm containing designs as Nos. 596/9 but values changed, inscriptions rearranged and with additional inscr in Chinese or English.

MS743	32c. Scuba diver, Meyer's butterflyfish and red-tailed surgeonfish ("Achilles tang"); 32c. Moorish idols and scuba diver; 32c. Pacific green turtle and anthias ("Fairy Basslet"); 32c. Anthias ("Fairy Basslet"), emperor angelfish and orange-finned anemonefish	3·00	2·75

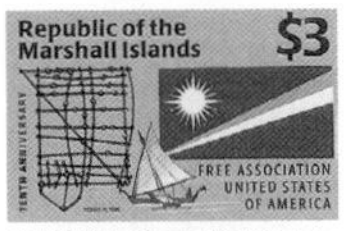

105 Stick Chart, Outrigger Canoe and Flag

1996. Tenth Anniv of Ratification of Compact of Free Association with U.S.A.

744	**105**	$3 multicoloured	7·75	7·00

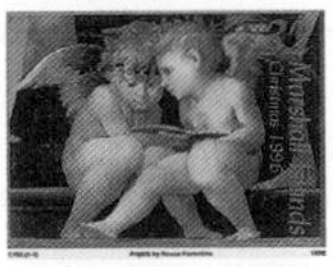

106 "Madonna and Child with Four Saints" (detail, Rosso Fiorentino)

1996. Christmas.

745	**106**	32c. multicoloured	70	65

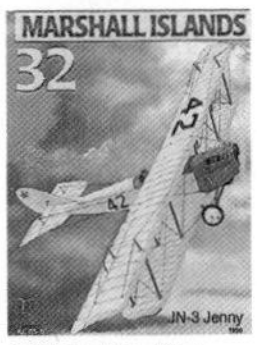

107 Curtiss JN-4 "Jenny"

1996. Biplanes. Multicoloured.

746	32c. Type **107**	85	75
747	32c. SPAD XIII	85	75
748	32c. Albatros	85	75
749	32c. de Havilland D.H.4 Liberty	85	75
750	32c. Fokker Dr-1	85	75
751	32c. Sopwith Camel	85	75
752	32c. Martin MB-2	85	75
753	32c. Martin MB-3A Tommy	85	75
754	32c. Curtiss TS-1	85	75
755	32c. P-1 Hawk	85	75
756	32c. Boeing PW-9	85	75
757	32c. Douglas O-2-H	85	75
758	32c. LB-5 Pirate	85	75
759	32c. O2U-1 Corsair	85	75
760	32c. Curtiss F8C Helldiver	85	75
761	32c. Boeing F4B-4	85	75
762	32c. J6B Gerfalcon	85	75
763	32c. Martin BM	85	75
764	32c. FF-1 Fifi	85	75
765	32c. C.R.32 Cricket	85	75
766	32c. Polikarpov I-15 Gull	85	75
767	32c. Fairey Swordfish	85	75
768	32c. Aichi D1A2	85	75
769	32c. Grumman F3F	85	75
770	32c. SOC-3 Seagull	85	75

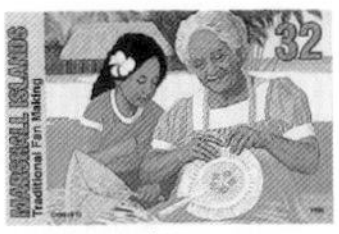

108 Fan-making

1996. Traditional Crafts. Multicoloured. Self-adhesive gum (780, 782); ordinary or self-adhesive gum (others).

771	32c. Type **108**	55	50
772	32c. Boys sailing model outrigger canoes (country name at right)	55	50
773	32c. Carving canoes	55	50
774	32c. Weaving baskets (country name at right)	55	50
780	32c. As No. 772 but with country name at left	85	75
782	32c. As No. 774 but with country name at left	85	75

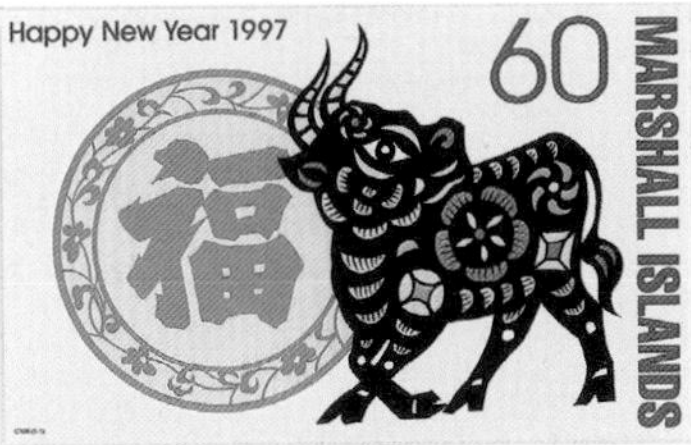

109 Chinese Character and Ox

1997. New Year. Year of the Ox. Sheet 110×87 mm.

MS783	**109**	60c. multicoloured	1·60	1·50

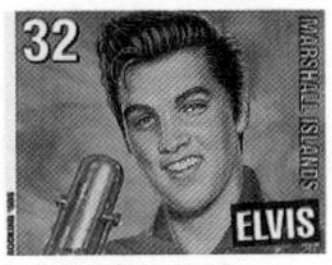

110 "Rocking '50s"

1997. 20th Death Anniv of Elvis Presley (entertainer). Different portraits. Multicoloured.

784	32c. Type **110**	85	75
785	32c. "Soaring '60s"	85	75
786	32c. "Sensational '70s"	85	75

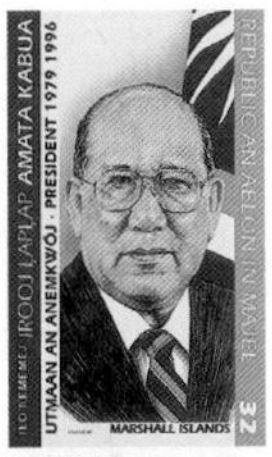

111 Kabua

1997. President Amata Kabua Commemoration. Multicoloured.

787	32c. Type **111**	85	75
788	60c. As Type **111** but inscr in English at left and right and in Marshallese at foot	1·60	1·50

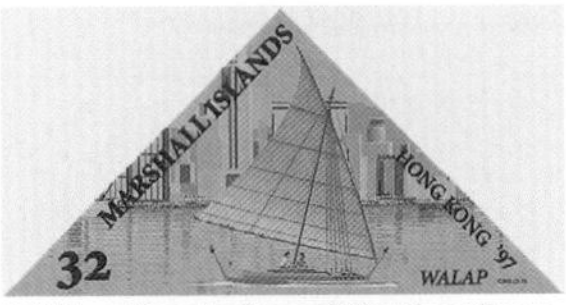

112 Hong Kong by Day and Outrigger Canoe

1997. "Hong Kong '97" International Stamp Exhibition. Two sheets, each 168×66 mm containing triangular designs as T **112**. Multicoloured.

MS789	Two sheets. (a) 32c. Type **112**; 32c. Hong Kong by day and junk. (b) 32c. Hong Kong at night and outrigger canoe; 32c. Hong Kong at night and junk	3·25	3·00

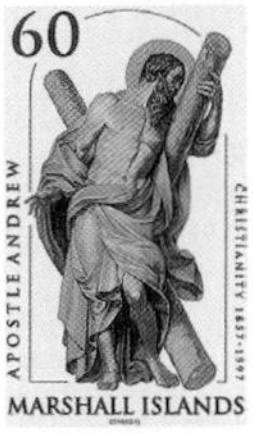

113 St. Andrew

1997. Easter. 140th Anniv of Introduction of Christianity to the Marshall Islands. The Twelve Disciples. Multicoloured.

790	60c. Type **113**	1·50	1·40
791	60c. St. Matthew	1·50	1·40
792	60c. St. Philip	1·50	1·40
793	60c. St. Simon	1·50	1·40
794	60c. St. Thaddeus	1·50	1·40
795	60c. St. Thomas	1·50	1·40
796	60c. St. Bartholomew	1·50	1·40
797	60c. St. John	1·50	1·40
798	60c. St. James the Lesser	1·50	1·40
799	60c. St. James the Greater	1·50	1·40
800	60c. St. Paul	1·50	1·40
801	60c. St. Peter	1·50	1·40
MS802	110×87 mm. $3 "The Last Supper" (Peter Paul Rubens) (78×48 mm)	7·75	7·00

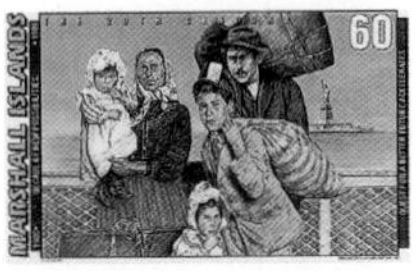

114 Immigrants arriving at Ellis Island, New York, 1900

1997. The Twentieth Century (1st series). "Decade of New Possibilities, 1900–1909". Multicoloured.

803	60c. Type **114**	1·50	1·40
804	60c. Chinese and Dowager Empress Ci Xi, 1900 (Boxer Rebellion)	1·50	1·40
805	60c. George Eastman (inventor of box camera) photographing family, 1900	1·50	1·40
806	60c. Walter Reed (discoverer of yellow fever transmission by mosquito), 1900	1·50	1·40
807	60c. Sigmund Freud (pioneer of psychoanalysis) (publication of "Interpretation of Dreams", 1900)	1·50	1·40
808	60c. Guglielmo Marconi sending first transatlantic wireless message, 1901	1·50	1·40
809	60c. Enrico Caruso (opera singer) (first award of Gold Disc for one million record sales, 1903)	1·50	1·40
810	60c. Wright Brothers' "Flyer I" (first powered flight, Kitty Hawk, 1903)	1·50	1·40
811	60c. Albert Einstein and formula (development of Theory of Relativity, 1905)	1·50	1·40
812	60c. White ensign and H.M.S. "Dreadnought" (battleship), 1906	1·50	1·40
813	60c. San Francisco earthquake, 1906	1·50	1·40
814	60c. Mohandas Gandhi and protestors, Johannesburg, South Africa, 1906	1·50	1·40
815	60c. Pablo Picasso and "Les Demoiselles d'Avignon", 1907	1·50	1·40
816	60c. First Paris–Peking motor car race, 1907	1·50	1·40
817	60c. Masjik-i-Salaman oil field, Persia, 1908	1·50	1·40

See also Nos. 872/86, 948/62, 975//89, 1067/81, 1165/79, 1218/32, 1239/55, 1256/70 and 1303/17.

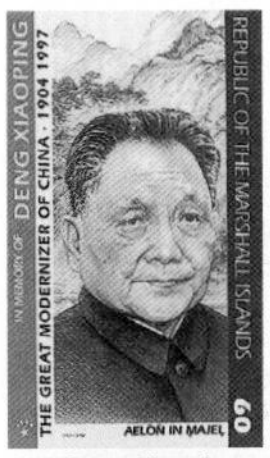

115 Deng Xiaoping

1997. Deng Xiaoping (Chinese statesman) Commemoration.

818	**115**	60c. multicoloured	1·60	1·50

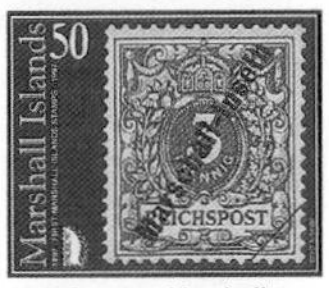

116 German Marshall Islands 1899 3pf. Stamp

1997. "Pacific 97" International Stamp Exhibition, San Francisco. Centenary of Marshall Islands Postage Stamps. Multicoloured.

819	50c. Type **116**	1·30	1·20
820	50c. German Marshall Islands 1899 5pf. stamp	1·30	1·20
821	50c. German Marshall Islands 1897 10pf. stamp	1·30	1·20
822	50c. German Marshall Islands 1897 20pf. stamp	1·30	1·20
823	50c. Unissued German Marshall Islands 25pf. stamp	1·30	1·20
824	50c. Unissued German Marshall Islands 50pf. stamp	1·30	1·20
MS825	114×88 mm. $1 United States 1847 5c. Franklin and 10c. Washington stamps (73×31 mm)	2·50	2·30

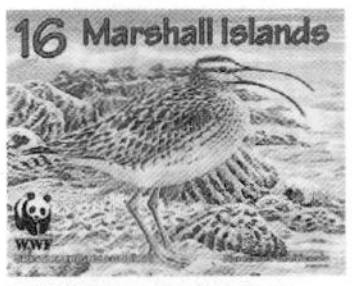

117 Curlew on Seashore

1997. The Bristle-thighed Curlew. Multicoloured.

826	16c. Type **117**	50	45
827	16c. Flying	50	45
828	16c. Running	50	45
829	16c. Standing on branch	50	45

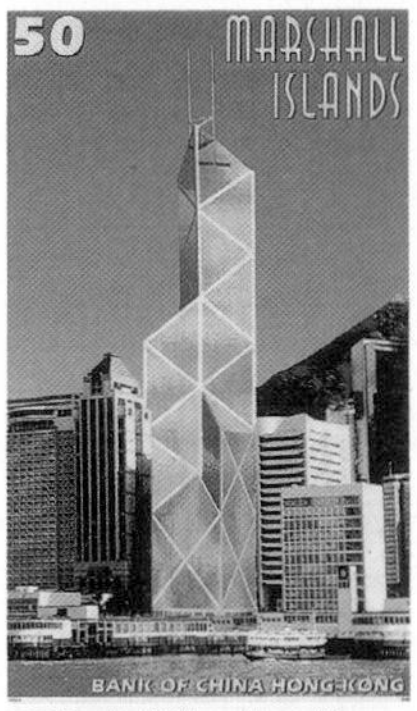

118 Bank of China, Hong Kong

1997. Return of Hong Kong to China. Sheet 87×110 mm.

MS830	**118**	50c. multicoloured	1·30	1·20

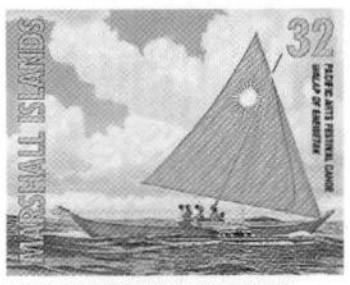

119 Pacific Arts Festival Canoe, Enewetak

1997. Traditional Outrigger Canoes. Multicoloured.

831	32c. Type **119**	85	75
832	32c. Kor Kor racing canoes	85	75
833	32c. Large voyaging canoe, Jaluit	85	75
834	32c. Sailing canoe, Ailuk	85	75

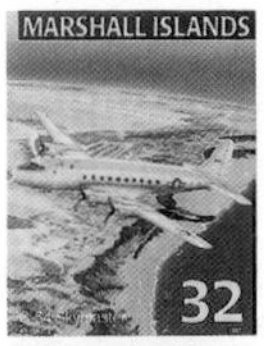

120 Douglas C-54 Skymaster Transport

1997. Aircraft of United States Air Force (1st series). Multicoloured.

835	32c. Type **120**	85	75
836	32c. Boeing B-36 Peacemaker	85	75
837	32c. North American F-86 Sabre jet fighter	85	75
838	32c. Boeing B-47 Stratojet jet bomber	85	75
839	32c. Douglas C-124 Globemaster II transport	85	75
840	32c. Lockheed C-121 Constellation	85	75
841	32c. Boeing B-52 Stratofortress jet bomber	85	75

842 32c. North American F-100 Super Sabre jet fighter 85 75
843 32c. Lockheed F-104 Starfighter jet fighter 85 75
844 32c. Lockheed C-130 Hercules transport 85 75
845 32c. Republic F-105 Thunderchief jet fighter 85 75
846 32c. KC-135 Stratotanker 85 75
847 32c. Convair B-58 Hustler jet bomber 85 75
848 32c. McDonnell Douglas F-4 Phantom II jet fighter 85 75
849 32c. Northrop T-38 Talon trainer 85 75
850 32c. Lockheed C-141 StarLifter jet transport 85 75
851 32c. General Dynamics F-111 Aardvark jet fighter 85 75
852 32c. SR-71 Blackbird 85 75
853 32c. Lockheed C-5 Galaxy jet transport 85 75
854 32c. A-10 Thunderbolt II bomber 85 75
855 32c. F-15 Eagle fighter 85 75
856 32c. General Dynamics F-16 Fighting Falcon jet fighter 85 75
857 32c. Lockheed F-117 Nighthawk Stealth bomber 85 75
858 32c. B-2 Spirit 85 75
859 32c. C-17 Globemaster III transport 85 75

See also Nos. 1272/96.

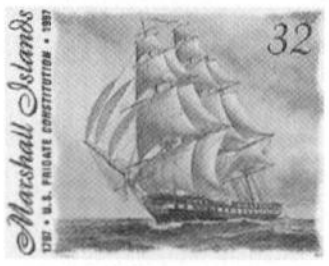

121 U.S.S. "Constitution"

1997. Bicentenary of Launch of U.S.S. "Constitution" (frigate).

860 **121** 32c. multicoloured 85 75

1997. Folk Legends (3rd series). As T **88**. Multicoloured.

861 32c. The Large Pool of Mejit 85 75
862 32c. The Beautiful Woman of Kwajalein 85 75
863 32c. Sharks and Lowakalle Reef 85 75
864 32c. The Demon of Adrie 55 45

1997. Undersea World (2nd series). As T **81**. Multicoloured.

865 60c. Watanabe's angelfish, blue-finned trevallys ("Bluefin Jack"), grey reef shark and scuba diver 1·50 1·40
866 60c. Scuba diver, anchor and racoon butterflyfish 1·50 1·40
867 60c. Lionfish and flame angelfish 1·50 1·40
868 60c. Square-spotted anthias ("Fairy Basslet"), anchor, scuba diver with torch and orange-finned anemonefish 1·50 1·40

Nos. 865/8 were issued together, *se-tenant*, forming a composite design.

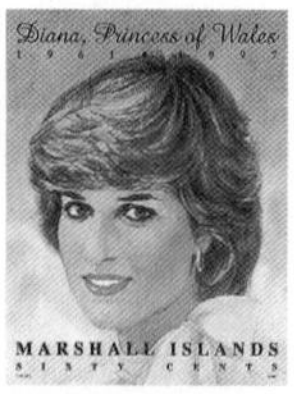

122 Diana, Princess of Wales, aged 20

1997. Diana, Princess of Wales Commemoration. Multicoloured.

869 60c. Type **122** 1·50 1·40
870 60c. Wearing pearl drop ear-rings (aged 27) 1·50 1·40
871 60c. Wearing pearl choker (aged 36) 1·50 1·40

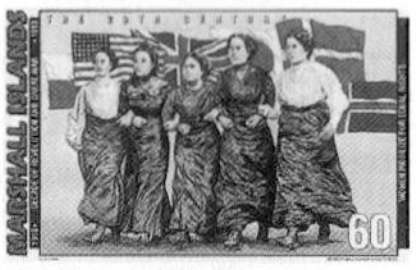

123 Flags and Suffragettes

1997. The Twentieth Century (2nd series). "Decade of Revolution and Great War, 1910–1919". Multicoloured.

872 60c. Type **123** 1·50 1·40
873 60c. Nobel Prize medal, Ernest Rutherford and diagram of atom, 1911 1·50 1·40
874 60c. Sun Yat-Sen (Chinese Revolution, 1911–12) 1·50 1·40
875 60c. Sinking of the "Titanic" (liner), 1912 1·50 1·40
876 60c. Igor Stravinsky (composer) and score of "The Rite of Spring", 1913 1·50 1·40
877 60c. Building motor car (introduction of assembly line construction of motor vehicles by Ford Motor Company), 1913 1·50 1·40
878 60c. Countess Sophie Chotek and Archduke Franz Ferdinand of Austria, 1914 (assassination in Sarajevo leads to First World War) 1·50 1·40
879 60c. Torpedo striking "Lusitania" (liner), 1915 1·50 1·40
880 60c. Battle of Verdun, 1916 1·50 1·40
881 60c. Patrick Pearse and proclamation of Irish Republic (Easter Rebellion, 1916) 1·50 1·40
882 60c. Western wall, Jerusalem (Balfour Declaration of Jewish Homeland, 1917) 1·50 1·40
883 60c. "Aurora" (cruiser) signals start of Russian Revolution, 1917 1·50 1·40
884 60c. Fokker Dr.1 Biplanes and "Red" Baron Manfred von Richthofen (fighter pilot), 1918 1·50 1·40
885 60c. Armed revolutionaries, Berlin, 1918 1·50 1·40
886 60c. Meeting of heads of state (Treaty of Versailles, 1919) 1·50 1·40

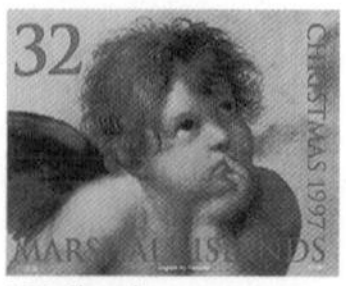

124 Cherub

1997. Christmas. Details of "Sistine Madonna" by Raphael. Multicoloured.

887 32c. Type **124** 75 70
888 32c. Cherub resting head on folded arms 75 70

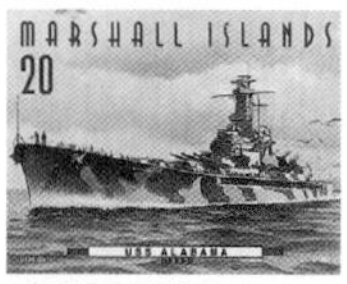

125 U.S.S. "Alabama" (battleship), 1942

1997. Ships named after U.S. States. Multicoloured.

889 20c. Type **125** 50 45
890 20c. U.S.S. "Alaska" (cruiser), 1869, and junk 50 45
891 20c. U.S.S. "Arizona" (battleship), 1916 50 45
892 20c. U.S.S. "Arkansas" (battleship), 1912 50 45
893 20c. U.S.S. "California" (cruiser), 1974 50 45
894 20c. U.S.S. "Colorado" (battleship), 1921, and landing craft 50 45
895 20c. U.S.S. "Connecticut" (gunboat), 1776, with fleet 50 45
896 20c. U.S.S. "Delaware" (ship of the line), 1828 50 45
897 20c. U.S.S. "Florida" (cruiser), 1967 50 45
898 20c. U.S.S. "Georgia" (battleship), 1906 50 45
899 20c. U.S.S. "Honolulu" (cruiser), 1938 50 45
900 20c. U.S.S. "Idaho" (battleship), 1919 50 45
901 20c. U.S.S. "Illinois" (battleship), 1901 50 45
902 20c. U.S.S. "Indiana" (battleship), 1895 50 45
903 20c. U.S.S. "Iowa" (battleship), 1943 50 45
904 20c. U.S.S. "Kansas" (battleship), 1907 50 45
905 20c. U.S.S. "Kentucky" (battleship), 1900 50 45
906 20c. U.S.S. "Louisiana" (frigate), 1812 50 45
907 20c. U.S.S. "Maine" (battleship), 1895 50 45
908 20c. U.S.S. "Maryland" (frigate), 1799 50 45
909 20c. U.S.S. "Massachusetts" (battleship), 1942 50 45
910 20c. U.S.S. "Michigan" (paddle gunboat), 1843 50 45
911 20c. U.S.S. "Minnesota" (corvette), 1857 50 45
912 20c. U.S.S. "Mississippi" (paddle gunboat), 1841, and junk 50 45
913 20c. U.S.S. "Missouri" (battleship), 1944, in Tokyo Bay 50 45
914 20c. U.S.S. "Montana" (battleship), 1908 50 45
915 20c. U.S.S. "Nebraska" (battleship), 1907 50 45
916 20c. U.S.S. "Nevada" (battleship), 1916, at Pearl Harbor 50 45
917 20c. U.S.S. "New Hampshire" (battleship), 1908, and Statue of Liberty 50 45
918 20c. U.S.S. "New Jersey" (battleship), 1943 50 45
919 20c. U.S.S. "New Mexico" (battleship), 1918, in Tokyo Bay 50 45
920 20c. U.S.S. "New York" (frigate), 1800, and felucca 50 45
921 20c. U.S.S. "North Carolina" (battleship), 1941 50 45
922 20c. U.S.S. "North Dakota" (battleship), 1910 50 45
923 20c. U.S.S. "Ohio" (ship of the line), 1838 50 45
924 20c. U.S.S. "Oklahoma" (battleship), 1916 50 45
925 20c. U.S.S. "Oregon" (battleship), 1896 50 45
926 20c. U.S.S. "Pennsylvania" (battleship), 1905 50 45
927 20c. U.S.S. "Rhode Island" (paddle gunboat), 1861 50 45
928 20c. U.S.S. "South Carolina" (frigate), 1783 50 45
929 20c. U.S.S. "South Dakota" (battleship), 1942 50 45
930 20c. U.S.S. "Tennessee" (battleship), 1906 50 45
931 20c. U.S.S. "Texas" (battleship), 1914 50 45
932 20c. U.S.S. "Utah" (battleship), 1911 50 45
933 20c. U.S.S. "Vermont" (battleship), 1907 50 45
934 20c. U.S.S. "Virginia" (schooner), 1798 50 45
935 20c. U.S.S. "Washington" (battleship), 1941 50 45
936 20c. U.S.S. "West Virginia" (battleship), 1923 50 45
937 20c. U.S.S. "Wisconsin" (battleship), 1944 50 45
938 20c. U.S.S. "Wyoming" (monitor), 1902 50 45

Dates given are those of either launch or commission.

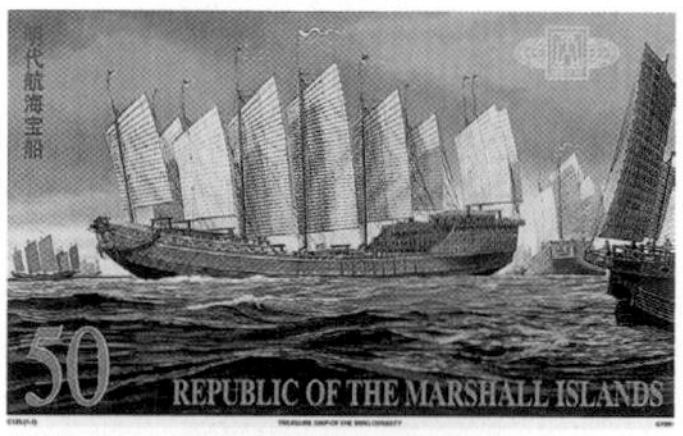

126 Treasure Junks, Ming Dynasty

1997. "Shanghai 1997" International Stamp and Coin Exhibition. Sheet 110×87 mm.

MS939 **126** 50c. multicoloured 1·30 1·20

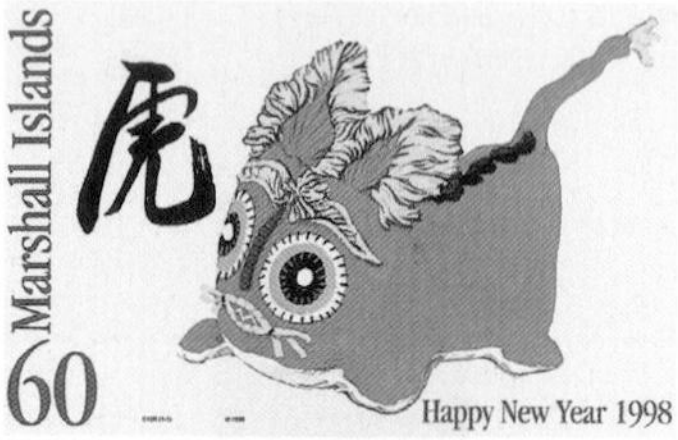

127 Chinese Character and Tiger

1998. New Year. Year of the Ox. Sheet 110×87 mm.

MS940 **127** 60c. multicoloured 1·60 1·50

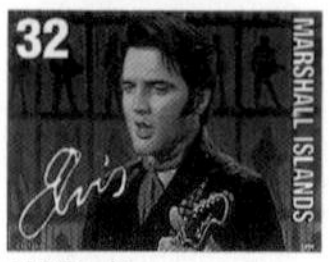

128 Presley

1998. 30th Anniv of First Television Special by Elvis Presley (entertainer). Multicoloured.

941 32c. Type **128** 75 70
942 32c. Presley in black leather jacket 75 70
943 32c. Presley in white suit in front of "ELVIS" in lights 75 70

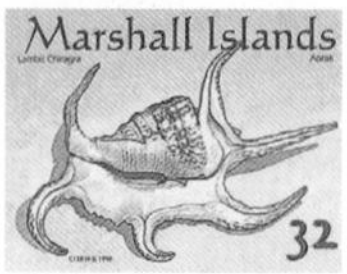

129 Chiragra Spider Conch ("Lambis chiragra")

1998. Sea Shells. Multicoloured.

944 32c. Type **129** 85 75
945 32c. Fluted giant clam ("Tridacna squamosa") 85 75
946 32c. Adusta murex ("Chicoreus brunneus") 85 75
947 32c. Golden cowrie ("Cypraea aurantium") 85 75

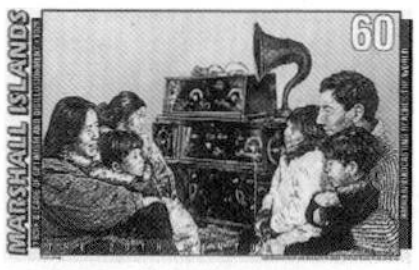

130 Family listening to Radio

1998. The Twentieth Century (3rd series). "Decade of Optimism and Disillusionment, 1920–1929". Multicoloured.

948 60c. Type **130** 1·50 1·40
949 60c. Leaders from Japan, United States, France, Great Britain and Italy (Washington Conference, 1920) 1·50 1·40
950 60c. Ludwig Mies van der Rohe (architect), 1922 1·50 1·40
951 60c. Mummiform coffin of Tutankhamun (discovery of tomb, 1922) 1·50 1·40
952 60c. Workers from U.S.S.R., 1923 (emergence of U.S.S.R. as communist state) 1·50 1·40
953 60c. Kemal Ataturk (first president of modern Turkey, 1923) (break-up of Turkish Empire) 1·50 1·40
954 60c. Bix Beiderbecke (trumpeter) and flappers (dancers), 1924 (Jazz Age) 1·50 1·40
955 60c. Robert Goddard demonstrates first liquid-propelled rocket, 1926 1·50 1·40
956 60c. Poster for "The Jazz Singer" (second talking picture, 1926) 1·50 1·40
957 60c. Benito Mussolini assumes total power in Italy, 1926 1·50 1·40
958 60c. Explosive glare and Leonardo da Vinci's "Proportion of Man" (Big Bang Theory of beginning of Universe, 1927) 1·50 1·40
959 60c. Sir Alexander Fleming discovers penicillin, 1928 1·50 1·40
960 60c. John Logie Baird invents television, 1926 1·50 1·40
961 60c. Airship "Graf Zeppelin" above Mt. Fuji, Japan (first round the world flight, 1929) 1·50 1·40
962 60c. U.S. stock market crash, 1929 (economic depression) 1·50 1·40

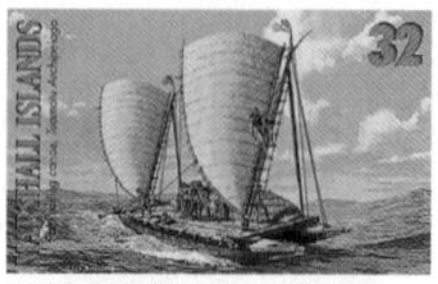

131 Pahi Sailing Canoe, Tuamotu Archipelago

1998. Canoes of the Pacific. Multicoloured.

963 32c. Type **131** 85 75
964 32c. Maori war canoe, New Zealand 85 75
965 32c. Wa'a Kaukahi fishing canoe, Hawaii 85 75
966 32c. Amatasi sailing canoe, Samoa 85 75
967 32c. Ndrua sailing canoe, Fiji Islands 85 75
968 32c. Tongiaki voyaging canoe, Tonga 85 75
969 32c. Tipairua travelling canoe, Tahiti 85 75
970 32c. Walap sailing canoe, Marshall Islands 85 75

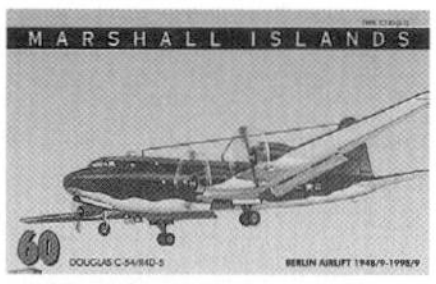

132 Douglas C-54 Skymaster Transport

1998. 50th Anniv of Berlin Airlift (relief of Berlin during Soviet blockade). Multicoloured.

971 60c. Type **132** 1·50 1·40
972 60c. Avro Type 685 York transport 1·50 1·40
973 60c. Crowd and building 1·50 1·40
974 60c. Crowd 1·50 1·40

Nos. 971/4 were issued together, se-tenant, forming a composite design.

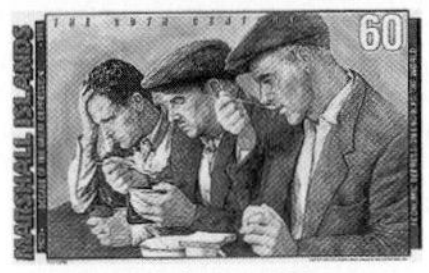

133 Soup Kitchens, 1930 (depression)

1998. The Twentieth Century (4th series). "Decade of the Great Depression, 1930–1939". Multicoloured.

975 60c. Type **133** 1·50 1·40
976 60c. Ernest Lawrence and first cyclotron, 1931 (splitting of atom) 1·50 1·40
977 60c. Forced collectivization of farms in Soviet Union, 1932 (Stalin era) 1·50 1·40
978 60c. Torchlight Parade celebrates rise of Hitler to power, 1933 (fascism) 1·50 1·40
979 60c. Dneproges Dam on Dnepr River, 1933 (harnessing of nature) 1·50 1·40
980 60c. Streamlined locomotive "Zephyr" (record-breaking run, Denver to Chicago, 1934) 1·50 1·40
981 60c. Douglas DC-3 airliner (first all-metal airliner, 1936) 1·50 1·40
982 60c. Pablo Picasso (artist) and "Guernica" (German bombing during Spanish Civil War, 1937) 1·50 1·40
983 60c. "Hindenburg" (airship disaster), 1937 (media reporting) 1·50 1·40
984 60c. Families fleeing ruins (Japanese assault on Nanjing, 1937) 1·50 1·40
985 60c. Neville Chamberlain declares "Peace in our Time", 1938 (appeasement) 1·50 1·40
986 60c. Chester Carlson (invention of xerography, 1938) 1·50 1·40
987 60c. Jew and Star of David (Kristallnacht (Nazi violence against Jews), 1938) 1·50 1·40
988 60c. Junkers Stuka bombers over Poland, 1939 (start of Second World War) 1·50 1·40
989 60c. Audience (premiere of "Gone with the Wind", 1939) (movies) 1·50 1·40

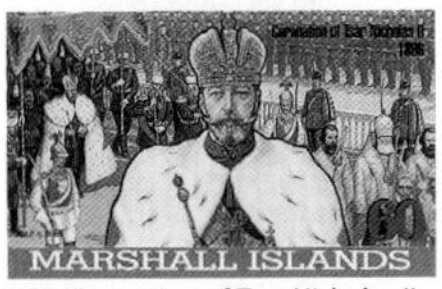

134 Coronation of Tsar Nicholas II, 1896

1998. 80th Death Anniv of Tsar Nicholas II and his Family. Multicoloured.

990 60c. Type **134** 1·60 1·50
991 60c. "Varyag" (cruiser) and Tsar (Russo-Japanese war, 1904–05) 1·60 1·50
992 60c. Troops firing on crowd, Tsar and October manifesto, 1905 1·60 1·50
993 60c. Peasant sowing, Tsar and Rasputin, 1905 1·60 1·50
994 60c. Mounted troops, Tsar and Nicholas II at strategy meeting, 1915 1·60 1·50
995 60c. Abdication, Tsar and Ipateva House, Ekaterinburg, 1917 1·60 1·50
MS996 87×61 mm. $3 Royal Family. Imperf 7·75 7·00

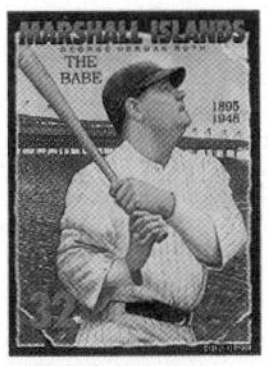

135 Babe Ruth

1998. 50th Death Anniv of Babe Ruth (baseball player).

997 **135** 132c. multicoloured 85 75

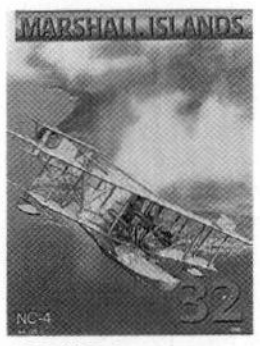

136 NC-4

1998. Aircraft of United States Navy. Multicoloured.

998 32c. Type **136** 85 75
999 32c. Consolidated PBY-5 Catalina flying boat 85 75
1000 32c. TBD Devastator 85 75
1001 32c. SB2U Vindicator 85 75
1002 32c. Grumman F4F Wildcat fighter 85 75
1003 32c. Vought-Sikorsky OS2U Kingfisher seaplane 85 75
1004 32c. Douglas SBD Dauntless bomber 85 75
1005 32c. Chance Vought F4U Corsair fighter 85 75
1006 32c. Curtiss SB2C Helldiver bomber 85 75
1007 32c. Lockheed PV-1 Ventura bomber 85 75
1008 32c. Grumman TBM Avenger bomber 85 75
1009 32c. Grumman F6F Hellcat fighter 85 75
1010 32c. PB4Y-2 Privateer 85 75
1011 32c. A-1J Skyraider 85 75
1012 32c. McDonnell F2H-2P Banshee 85 75
1013 32c. F9F-2B Panther 85 75
1014 32c. P5M Marlin 85 75
1015 32c. F-8 Crusader 85 75
1016 32c. McDonnell Douglas F-4 Phantom II fighter 85 75
1017 32c. A-6 Intruder 85 75
1018 32c. Lockheed P-3 Orion reconnaissance 85 75
1019 32c. Vought A-70 Corsair II 85 75
1020 32c. Douglas A-4 Skyhawk bomber 85 75
1021 32c. S-3 Viking 85 75
1022 32c. F/A-18 Hornet 85 75

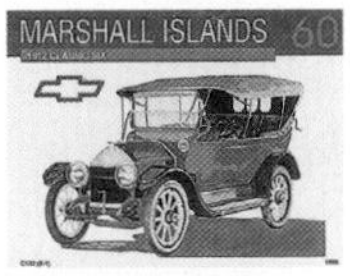

137 Classic Six, 1912

1998. Chevrolet Vehicles. Multicoloured.

1023 60c. Type **137** 1·50 1·40
1024 60c. Sport Roadster, 1931 1·50 1·40
1025 60c. Special Deluxe, 1941 1·50 1·40
1026 60c. Cameo Carrier Fleetside, 1955 1·50 1·40
1027 60c. Corvette, 1957 1·50 1·40
1028 60c. Bel Air, 1957 1·50 1·40
1029 60c. Camaro, 1967 1·50 1·40
1030 60c. Chevelle SS 454, 1970 1·50 1·40

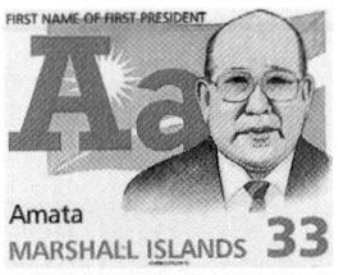

138 Letter "A" and Pres. Amata Kabua

1998. Marshallese Alphabet and Language. Multicoloured.

1031 33c. Type **138** 85 75
1032 33c. Letter "A" and woman weaving 85 75
1033 33c. Letter "B" and butterfly 85 75
1034 33c. Letter "D" and woman wearing garland of flowers 85 75
1035 33c. Letter "E" and fish 85 75
1036 33c. Letter "I" and couple in front of rainbow 85 75
1037 33c. Letter "J" and woven mat 85 75
1038 33c. Letter "K" and Government House 85 75
1039 33c. Letter "L" and night sky 85 75
1040 33c. Letter "L" and red-tailed tropicbird 85 75
1041 33c. Letter "M" and breadfruit 85 75
1042 33c. Letter "M" and arrowroot plant 85 75
1043 33c. Letter "N" and coconut tree 85 75
1044 33c. Letter "N" and wave 85 75
1045 33c. Letter "N" and shark 85 75
1046 33c. Letter "O" and fisherman 85 75
1047 33c. Letter "O" and tattooed woman 85 75
1048 33c. Letter "O" and lionfish 85 75
1049 33c. Letter "P" and visitor's hut 85 75
1050 33c. Letter "R" and whale 85 75
1051 33c. Letter "T" and outrigger sailing canoe 85 75
1052 33c. Letter "U" and fire 85 75
1053 33c. Letter "U" and whale's fin 85 75
1054 33c. Letter "W" and woven leaf sail 85 75

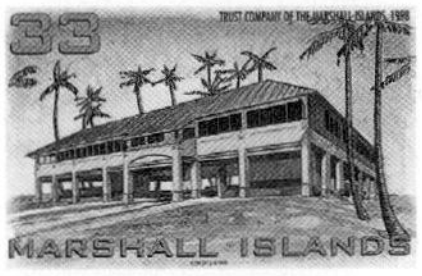

139 Trust Company of the Marshall Islands Offices, 1998

1998. New Buildings. Multicoloured.

1055 33c. Type **139** 85 75
1056 33c. Embassy of the People's Republic of China, 1996 85 75
1057 33c. Outrigger Marshall Islands Resort, 1996 85 75

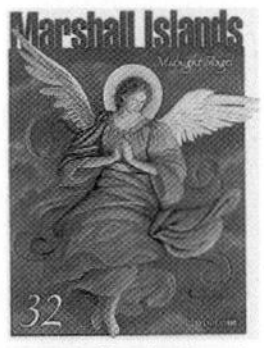

140 Midnight Angel

1998. Christmas.

1058 **140** 33c. multicoloured 85 75

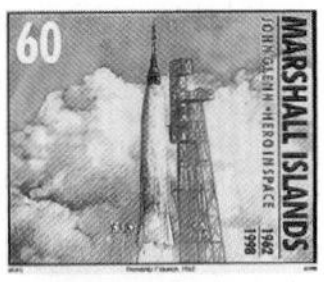

141 Launch of "Friendship 7", 1962

1998. John Glenn's (astronaut) Return to Space. Multicoloured.

1059 60c. Type **141** 1·60 1·50
1060 60c. John Glenn, 1962, and Earth 1·60 1·50
1061 60c. "Friendship 7" orbiting Earth 1·60 1·50
1062 60c. Launch of space shuttle "Discovery", 1998 1·60 1·50
1063 60c. John Glenn, 1998, and flag 1·60 1·50
1064 60c. "Discovery" orbiting Earth, 1998 1·60 1·50
MS1065 115×87 mm. $3 U.S. 4c. Project Mercury stamp, 1962 (74×32 mm) 7·75 7·00

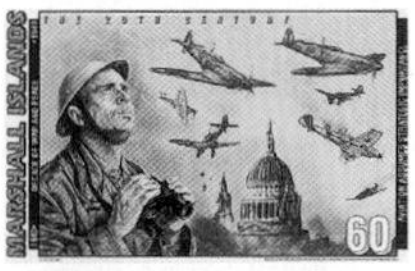

143 British and German Planes over St. Paul's Cathedral (Battle of Britain, 1940)

1998. The Twentieth Century (5th series). "Decade of War and Peace, 1940–1949". Multicoloured.

1067 60c. Type **143** 1·50 1·40
1068 60c. Japanese aircraft attack American battleship (Pearl Harbor, 1941) (global warfare) 1·50 1·40
1069 60c. Wernher von Braun and missiles (first surface to surface guided missile, 1942) 1·50 1·40
1070 60c. The Dorsey Brothers (Big Bands, 1942) 1·50 1·40
1071 60c. Soviet worker building weaponry (fight for survival against Germans, 1943) 1·50 1·40
1072 60c. Concentration camp prisoners (the Holocaust, 1945) 1·50 1·40
1073 60c. Mushroom cloud and skull (first atomic bomb tested, Alamogordo, New Mexico, 1945) 1·50 1·40
1074 60c. Families reunited (end of war, 1945) 1·50 1·40
1075 60c. Eniac computer and worker (first electronic digital computer goes into operation, 1946) 1·50 1·40
1076 60c. American delegate (United Nations, 1946) 1·50 1·40
1077 60c. Nuremberg Tribunal (trials of Germans for war crimes 1946) 1·50 1·40
1078 60c. George Marshall (U.S. Secretary of State) and Europeans (Marshall Plan, 1947) 1·50 1·40
1079 60c. William Shockley, John Bardeen and Walter Brattain (development of transistor, 1948) 1·50 1·40
1080 60c. Berlin Airlift, 1948–49 (Cold War) 1·50 1·40
1081 60c. Mao Tse-tung proclaiming People's Republic of China, 1949 1·50 1·40

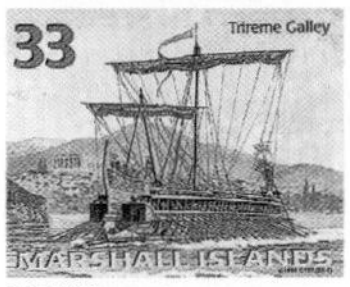

144 Trireme

1998. Warships. Multicoloured.

1082 33c. Type **144** 85 75
1083 33c. Roman galley ("Trireme Romano") 85 75
1084 33c. Viking longship 85 75
1085 33c. Ming treasure ship 85 75
1086 33c. "Mary Rose" (English galleon) 85 75
1087 33c. "Nuestra Senora del Rosario" (Spanish galleon) 85 75
1088 33c. Korean "turtle" ship 85 75
1089 33c. "Brederode" (Dutch ship of the line) 85 75
1090 33c. Venetian galley 85 75
1091 33c. "Santissima Trinidad" (Spanish ship of the line) 85 75
1092 33c. "Ville de Paris" (French ship of the line) 85 75
1093 33c. H.M.S. "Victory" (ship of the line) 85 75
1094 33c. "Bonhomme Richard" (American sail frigate) 85 75
1095 33c. U.S.S. "Constellation" (sail frigate) 85 75
1096 33c. U.S.S. "Hartford" (steam frigate) 85 75
1097 33c. Fijian Ndrua canoe 85 75
1098 33c. H.M.S. "Dreadnought" (battleship) 85 75
1099 33c. H.M.A.S. "Australia" (battle cruiser) 85 75
1100 33c. H.M.S. "Dorsetshire" (cruiser) 85 75
1101 33c. "Admiral Graf Spee" (German battleship) 85 75
1102 33c. "Yamato" (Japanese battleship) 85 75
1103 33c. U.S.S. "Tautog" (submarine) 85 75
1104 33c. "Bismarck" (German battleship) 85 75
1105 33c. U.S.S. "Hornet" (aircraft carrier) 85 75
1106 33c. U.S.S. "Missouri" (battleship) 85 75

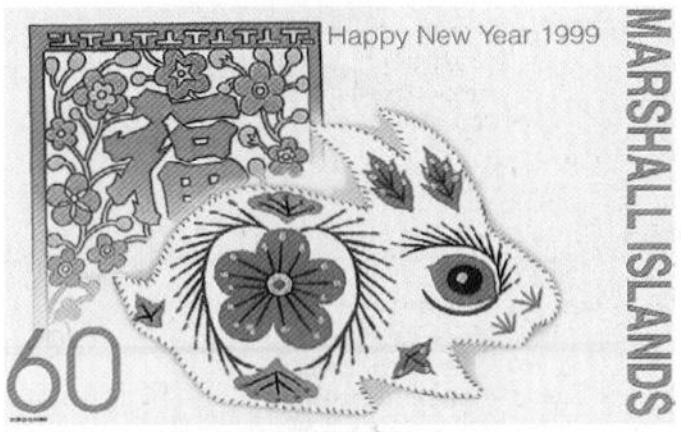

145 Chinese Character and Rabbit

1999. New Year. Year of the Rabbit. Sheet 110×87 mm.

MS1107 **145** 60c. multicoloured 1·60 1·50

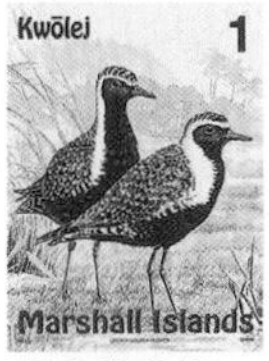

146 Pacific Golden Plover ("Lesser Golden Plover")

1999. Birds. Multicoloured.

1108 1c. Type **146** 15 10
1109 3c. Grey-rumped sandpiper ("Siberian (gray-tailed) Tattler") 15 10
1110 5c. Black-tailed godwit 15 10
1113 20c. Common noddy ("Brown Noddy") 50 45
1114 22c. White tern ("Common Fairy Tern") 55 50
1116 33c. Micronesian pigeon 85 75
1117 40c. Franklin's gull 1·00 95
1118 45c. Rufous-necked sandpiper ("Rufous-necked Stint") 1·10 1·00
1119 55c. Long-tailed koel ("Long-tailed Cuckoo") 1·40 1·30
1121 75c. Kermadec petrel 1·90 1·70
1122 $1 Christmas Island shearwater ("Christmas Shearwater") 2·50 2·30
1123 $1.20 Purple-capped fruit dove 3·00 2·75
1124 $2 Lesser sand plover ("Mongolian Plover") 5·00 4·75
1125 $3.20 Cattle egret 8·25 7·50
1127 $5 Dunlin 12·50 11·50
1129 $10 Eurasian tree sparrow 19·00 17·00

1999. Canoes of the Pacific. Multicoloured. (a) Size 49×30 mm.

1130	33c. Type **131**	85	75
1131	33c. As No. 964	85	75
1132	33c. As No. 965	85	75
1133	33c. As No. 966 but inscr changed to "Tongiaki voyaging canoe, Tonga"	85	75
1134	33c. As No. 967	85	75
1135	33c. As No. 968 but inscr changed to "Amatasi sailing canoe, Samoa"	85	75
1136	33c. As No. 969	85	75
1137	33c. As No. 970	85	75

(b) Size 39×24 mm.

1138	33c. Type **131**	75	70
1139	33c. As No. 1131	75	70
1140	33c. As No. 1132	75	70
1141	33c. As No. 1133	75	70
1142	33c. As No. 1134	75	70
1143	33c. As No. 1135	75	70
1144	33c. As No. 1136	75	70
1145	33c. As No. 1137	75	70

Nos. 1138/45 were self-adhesive.

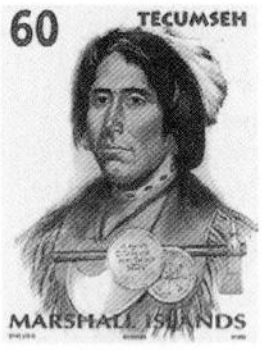

147 Tecumseh

1999. Great American Indian Chiefs. Multicoloured.

1146	60c. Type **147**	1·50	1·40
1147	60c. Powhatan	1·50	1·40
1148	60c. Hiawatha	1·50	1·40
1149	60c. Dull Knife	1·50	1·40
1150	60c. Sequoyah	1·50	1·40
1151	60c. Sitting Bull	1·50	1·40
1152	60c. Cochise	1·50	1·40
1153	60c. Red Cloud	1·50	1·40
1154	60c. Geronimo	1·50	1·40
1155	60c. Chief Joseph	1·50	1·40
1156	60c. Pontiac	1·50	1·40
1157	60c. Crazy Horse	1·50	1·40

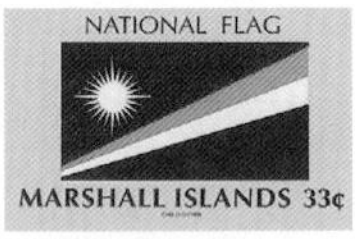

148 State Flag

1999

1158	**148**	33c. multicoloured	85	75

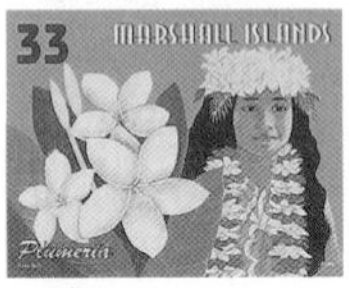

149 Plumeria

1999. Flowers of the Pacific. Multicoloured.

1159	33c. Type **149**	85	75
1160	33c. Vanda	85	75
1161	33c. Ilima	85	75
1162	33c. Tiare	85	75
1163	33c. White ginger	85	75
1164	33c. Hibiscus	85	75

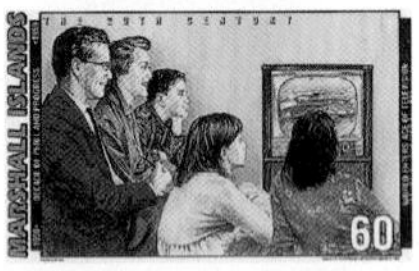

150 Family watching Television

1999. The Twentieth Century (6th series). "Decade of Peril and Progress, 1950–1959". Multicoloured.

1165	60c. Type **150**	1·50	1·40
1166	60c. U.N. landing at Inchon, Korea, 1950 (Cold War)	1·50	1·40
1167	60c. Vaccination against polio, 1952	1·50	1·40
1168	60c. American hydrogen bomb test, Enewetak Atoll, 1952 (Arms race)	1·50	1·40
1169	60c. James Watson and Francis Crick (scientists) and DNA double helix, 1953 (unravelling of genetic code)	1·50	1·40
1170	60c. Sir Edmund Hillary, Tenzing Norgay and Mt. Everest, 1953	1·50	1·40
1171	60c. Coronation of Queen Elizabeth II, Westminster Abbey, 1953	1·50	1·40
1172	60c. Singer and dancers, 1954 (rock 'n' roll music)	1·50	1·40
1173	60c. Ho Chi Minh and Vietnamese troops celebrating victory over French garrison at Dien Bien Phu, 1954 (end of colonial empires)	1·50	1·40
1174	60c. People of different races on bus, 1955 (condemnation of racial discrimination)	1·50	1·40
1175	60c. Hungarians firing on Russian tanks, Budapest, 1956 (challenge to Communism)	1·50	1·40
1176	60c. Signing of Treaty of Rome, 1957 (European union)	1·50	1·40
1177	60c. Launch of Russian sputnik, 1957 (space race)	1·50	1·40
1178	60c. de Havilland DH.106 Comet (first commercial jet airline service, 1958)	1·50	1·40
1179	60c. Jack Kilby (inventor) and first microchip, 1959	1·50	1·40

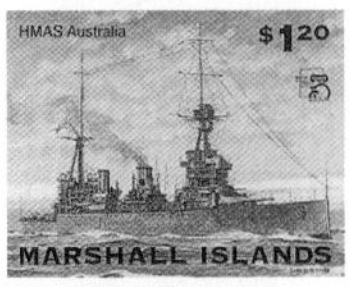

151 H.M.A.S. "Australia" (battle Cruiser)

1999. "Australia 99" International Stamp Exhibition, Melbourne. Sheet 190×116 mm.

MS1180 **151** $1.20 multicoloured	3·25	3·00

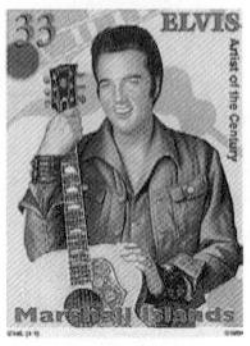

152 Presley

1999. Elvis Presley, "Artist of the Century".

1181	**152**	33c. multicoloured	85	75

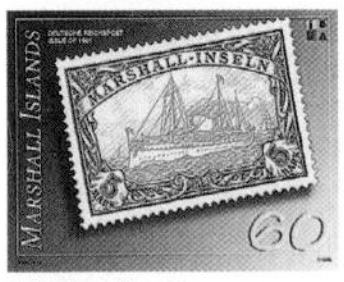

153 5m. Stamp

1999. "iBRA '99" International Stamp Exhibition, Nuremberg, Germany. Multicoloured.

1182	60c. Type **153**	1·50	1·40
1183	60c. 3m. stamp	1·50	1·40
1184	60c. 2m. stamp	1·50	1·40
1185	60c. 1m. stamp	1·50	1·40

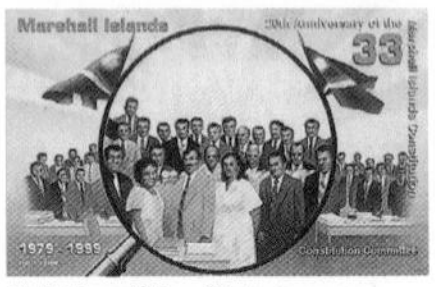

154 Magnifying Glass over Committee Members

1999. 20th Anniv of Marshall Islands Constitution.

1186	**154**	33c. multicoloured	85	75

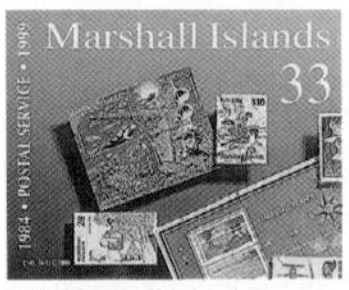

155 Marshall Island Stamps

1999. 15th Anniv of Marshall Islands Postal Service. Multicoloured.

1187	33c. Type **155**	85	75
1188	33c. Butterfly, fish, canoe and flower stamps	85	75
1189	33c. Pres. Amata Kabua, flower and legend stamps	85	75
1190	33c. Stamps and magnifying glass	85	75

Nos. 1187/90 were issued together, se-tenant, forming a composite design.

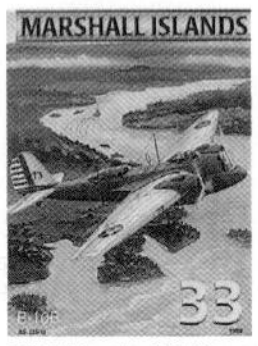

156 Martin B-10B

1999. Legendary Aircraft. Multicoloured.

1191	33c. Type **156**	85	75
1192	33c. A-17A Nomad	85	75
1193	33c. Douglas B-18 Bolo bomber	85	75
1194	33c. Boeing B-17F Flying Fortress bomber	85	75
1195	33c. A-20 Havoc	85	75
1196	33c. North American B-25B Mitchell bomber	85	75
1197	33c. Consolidated B-24D Liberator bomber	85	75
1198	33c. North American P-51B Mustang fighter	85	75
1199	33c. Martin B-26 Marauder bomber	85	75
1200	33c. A-26B Invader	85	75
1201	33c. P-59 Airacomet	85	75
1202	33c. KC-97 Stratofreighter	85	75
1203	33c. A-1J Skyraider	85	75
1204	33c. P2V-7 Neptune	85	75
1205	33c. B-45 Tornado	85	75
1206	33c. Boeing B-50 Superfortress	85	75
1207	33c. AJ-2 Savage	85	75
1208	33c. F9F Cougar	85	75
1209	33c. Douglas A-3 Skywarrior jet bomber	85	75
1210	33c. English Electric B-57E Canberra jet bomber	85	75
1211	33c. EB-66 Destroyer	85	75
1212	33c. E-2A Hawkeye	85	75
1213	33c. Northrop F-5E Tiger II jet fighter	85	75
1214	33c. AV-8B Harrier II	85	75
1215	33c. B-1B Lancer	85	75

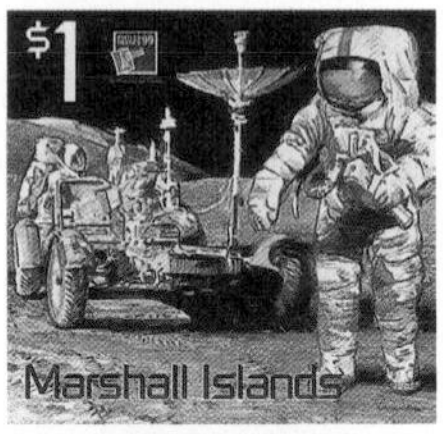

157 Astronaut on Moon

1999. "Philexfrance 99" International Stamp Exhibition, Paris. Sheet 131×70 mm.

MS1216 **157** $1 multicoloured	2·50	2·30

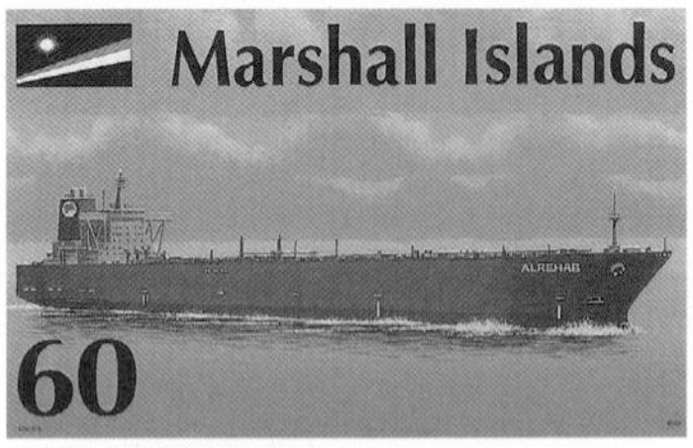

158 "Alrehab" (gas tanker)

1999. Marshall Islands Maritime Administration. Sheet 110×87 mm.

MS1217 **158** 60c. multicoloured	1·60	1·50

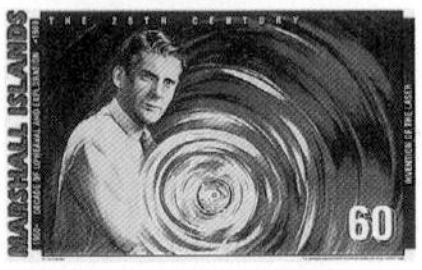

159 T. H. Maiman and Ruby Crystal Laser, 1960

1999. The Twentieth Century (7th series). "Decade of Upheaval and Exploration 1960–1969". Multicoloured.

1218	60c. Type **159**	1·50	1·40
1219	60c. Young couple (birth control pill, 1960)	1·50	1·40
1220	60c. Yuri Gagarin (first man in space, 1961)	1·50	1·40
1221	60c. John F. Kennedy (President of U.S.A., 1960–63) making speech in Berlin, 1961 (failures of Communism)	1·50	1·40
1222	60c. Rachel Carson and endangered species (publication of "Silent Spring", 1962)	1·50	1·40
1223	60c. John F. Kennedy and Russian President Nikita Khrushchev (Cuban missile crisis, 1962)	1·50	1·40
1224	60c. Pope John XXIII and crowds (Spirit of Ecumenism)	1·50	1·40
1225	60c. "Hikari" express train, Japan (new railway record speeds, 1964)	1·50	1·40
1226	60c. Chinese workers waving banners (Chinese cultural revolution, 1965)	1·50	1·40
1227	60c. Soldier with gun (Arab–Israeli six-day war, 1967)	1·50	1·40
1228	60c. Surgeons (first human heart transplants, 1967)	1·50	1·40
1229	60c. American soldiers in jungle (Vietnam war)	1·50	1·40
1230	60c. Robert F. Kennedy (U.S. presidential candidate) and statue of Abraham Lincoln (political assassinations)	1·50	1·40
1231	60c. British Aerospace/Aerospatiale Concorde supersonic jetliner (maiden flight, 1969)	1·50	1·40
1232	60c. Neil Armstrong and Buzz Aldrin planting American flag (first men on Moon, 1969)	1·50	1·40

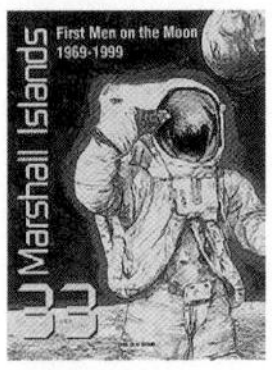

160 Astronaut Saluting

1999. 30th Anniv of First Manned Moon Landing. Sheet 110×97 mm containing T **160** and similar vert designs. Multicoloured.

MS1233 33c. Type **160**; 33c. American flag and Lunar Rover; 33c. Astronaut (different)	2·50	2·30

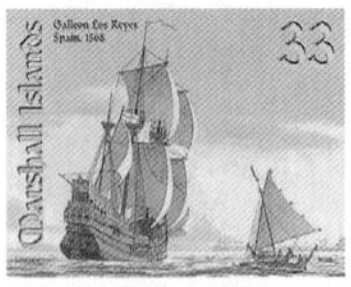

161 "Los Reyes" (Alvarao de Menana de Neyra's galleon, 1568)

1999. European Exploration of Marshall Islands. Multicoloured.

1234	33c. Type **161**	90	80
1235	33c. H.M.S. "Dolphin" (Samuel Wallis's frigate, 1767)	90	80
1236	33c. "Scarborough" (John Marshall's transport, 1788)	90	80
1237	33c. "Rurik" (Otto van Kotzebue's brig, 1817)	90	80

No. 1236 is wrongly inscribed "Scarsborough" and No. 1237 "Rurick".

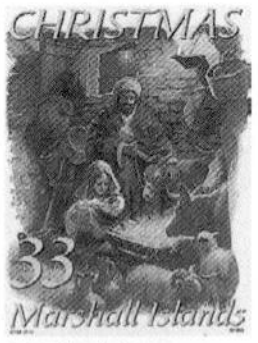

162 Nativity

1999. Christmas.

1238	**162**	33c. multicoloured	85	75

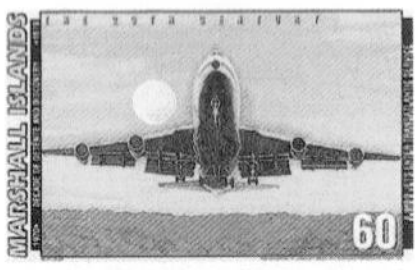

163 First Scheduled Transatlantic Flight of Boeing 747 Jetliner, 1970

1999. The Twentieth Century (8th series). "Decade of Detente and Discovery 1970–1979". Multicoloured.

1239	60c. Type **163**	1·50	1·40
1240	60c. Mao Tse Tung and U.S. President Richard Nixon (visit to China, 1972)	1·50	1·40
1241	60c. Terrorist with gun (murder of Israeli athletes at Munich Olympics, 1972)	1·50	1·40
1242	60c. U.S. "Skylab" and U.S.S.R. "Salyut" space stations orbiting Earth	1·50	1·40
1243	60c. Cars queueing for petrol (oil crisis, 1973)	1·50	1·40
1244	60c. Terracotta warriors (discovery of Qin Shi Huang's tomb at Xian, China, 1974)	1·50	1·40
1245	60c. Skulls and Cambodians in paddy fields	1·50	1·40
1246	60c. "Apollo"–"Soyuz" link-up, 1975 (era of detente)	1·50	1·40
1247	60c. "Eagle" (cadet ship) in New York Harbour (bicentenary of U.S. Independence, 1976)	1·50	1·40
1248	60c. Computer and family (personal computers reach markets, 1977)	1·50	1·40
1249	60c. Scanner and scanned images (diagnostic tools revolutionize medicine, 1977)	1·50	1·40
1250	60c. Volkswagen Beetle motor car, 1978	1·50	1·40
1251	60c. Pres. Anwar Sadat of Egypt, U.S. President Jimmy Carter and Israeli Prime Minister Menachim Begin, 1978 (peace in Middle East)	1·50	1·40

1252	60c. Compact disc, 1979	1·50	1·40
1253	60c. Ayatollah Khomeini becomes Iran's leader, 1979	1·50	1·40

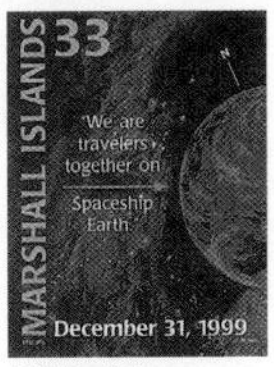

164 Earth in Darkness, December 31, 1999

1999. Year 2000. Multicoloured.

1254	33c. Type **164**	85	75
1255	33c. Earth in sunlight, 1 January 2000	85	75

Nos. 1254/5 were issued together, se-tenant, forming a composite design.

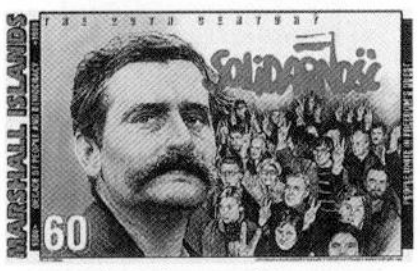

165 Lech Walesa and Protestors at Gdansk Shipyard, Poland, 1980

2000. The Twentieth Century (9th series). "Decade of People and Democracy, 1980–1989". Multicoloured.

1256	60c. Type **165**	1·50	1·40
1257	60c. Doctor treating AIDS patient, 1981	1·50	1·40
1258	60c. Prince and Princess of Wales (Royal wedding, 1981)	1·50	1·40
1259	60c. Man and computer (IBM personal computers introduced 1981)	1·50	1·40
1260	60c. British Aerospace Sea Harrier and warships (Falkland Islands war, 1982)	1·50	1·40
1261	60c. Man using mobile phone (first commercial wireless cellular system, Chicago, 1983)	1·50	1·40
1262	60c. Girl playing football (camcorders, 1983)	1·50	1·40
1263	60c. Astronauts (space shuttle *Challenger* explodes, 1986)	1·50	1·40
1264	60c. Power station and man wearing protective clothing (Chernobyl Nuclear Power Station disaster, 1986)	1·50	1·40
1265	60c. Mikhail Gorbachev and workers (era of Glasnost (openness) and Perestroika (restructuring) in U.S.S.R., 1987)	1·50	1·40
1266	60c. Northrop B-24 Spirit, 1988	1·50	1·40
1267	60c. Boeing 747 wreckage (bombing of Pan-American flight 103 over Lockerbie, Scotland, 1988)	1·50	1·40
1268	60c. *Exxon Valdez* (oil-tanker) and whales (oil spill off Alaskan Coast, 1989)	1·50	1·40
1269	60c. Student demonstrators and police in Tiananmen Square, China, 1989	1·50	1·40
1270	60c. German breaking down wall (dismantling of Berlin Wall, 1989)	1·50	1·40

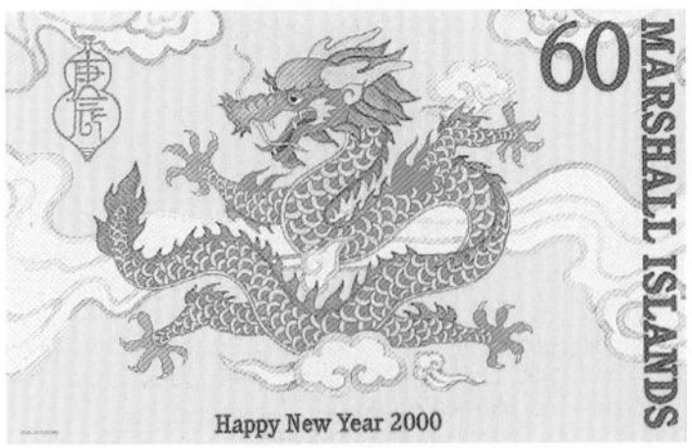

166 Chinese Dragon

2000. New Year. Year of the Dragon. Sheet 110×87 mm.

MS1271	**166** 60c. multicoloured	1·60	1·50

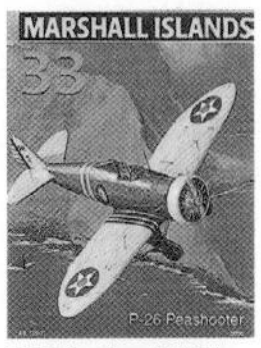

167 Boeing P-26A "Peashooter" fighter

2000. Legendary Aircraft (2nd series). Multicoloured.

1272	33c. Type **167**	85	75
1273	33c. Stearman N2S-1 Kaydett biplane	85	75
1274	33c. Seversky P-35A	85	75
1275	33c. Curtiss P-36A Hawk	85	75
1276	33c. Curtiss P-40B Warhawk fighter	85	75
1277	33c. Lockheed P-38 Lightning fighter	85	75
1278	33c. Bell P-39D Airacobra fighter	85	75
1279	33c. Curtiss C-46 Commando airliner	85	75
1280	33c. Republic P-47D Thunderbolt fighter	85	75
1281	33c. Northrop P-61A Black Widow	85	75
1282	33c. Boeing B-29 Superfortress bomber	85	75
1283	33c. Grumman F7F-3N Tigercat	85	75
1284	33c. Grumman F8F-2 Bearcat	85	75
1285	33c. North American F-82 Twin Mustang	85	75
1286	33c. Republic F-84G Thunderjet jet fighter	85	75
1287	33c. North American FJ-1 Fury	85	75
1288	33c. Fairchild C-119C Flying Boxcar	85	75
1289	33c. Douglas F3D-2 Skynight	85	75
1290	33c. Northrop F-89D Scorpion	85	75
1291	33c. Lockheed F-94B Starfire	85	75
1292	33c. Douglas F4D Skyray	85	75
1293	33c. McDonnell F3H-2 Demon	85	75
1294	33c. McDonnell RF-101A/C Voodoo	85	75
1295	33c. Lockheed U-2F Dragon Lady	85	75
1296	33c. Rockwell OV-10 Bronco	85	75

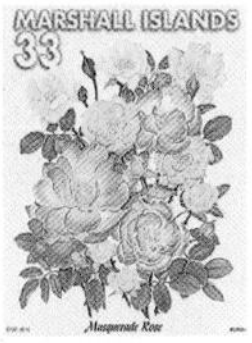

168 "Masquerade"

2000. Garden Roses. Multicoloured.

1297	33c. Type **168**	85	75
1298	33c. "Tuscany Superb"	85	75
1299	33c. "Frau Dagmar Hastrup"	85	75
1300	33c. "Ivory Fashion"	85	75
1301	33c. "Charles de Mills"	85	75
1302	33c. "Peace"	85	75

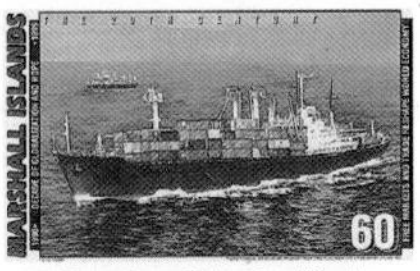

169 Container Ships (political reform in Poland, 1990)

2000. The Twentieth Century (10th series). "Decade of Globalization and Hope, 1990–1999". Multicoloured.

1303	60c. Type **169**	1·50	1·40
1304	60c. Fighter planes over burning oil wells, 1991	1·50	1·40
1305	60c. Nelson Mandela and F. W. de Klerk (abolition of apartheid, 1991)	1·50	1·40
1306	60c. Tim Berners-Lee and computer (creator of World Wide Web, 1991)	1·50	1·40
1307	60c. Boris Yeltsin (President of Russian Federation, 1991)	1·50	1·40
1308	60c. Yitzhak Rabin, Bill Clinton and Yasir Arafat (signing of Middle East Peace Accord, Washington D.C., 1993)	1·50	1·40
1309	60c. High-speed train (inauguration of the "Channel Tunnel" between United Kingdom and France, 1994)	1·50	1·40
1310	60c. Family (Bosnian civil war, 1995)	1·50	1·40
1311	60c. Athletes (Atlanta Olympic Games, 1996)	1·50	1·40
1312	60c. Sheep (researchers clone Dolly, 1997)	1·50	1·40
1313	60c. Hong Kong and Chinese flag (return of Hong Kong to Chinese rule, 1997)	1·50	1·40
1314	60c. Sojourner (roving vehicle) (Mars "Pathfinder" mission, 1997)	1·50	1·40
1315	60c. Deaths of Diana, Princess of Wales and Mother Teresa, 1997	1·50	1·40
1316	60c. Rebuilding of German Reichstag, 1999	1·50	1·40
1317	60c. People of different races (birth of World's sixth billionth inhabitant, 1999)	1·50	1·40

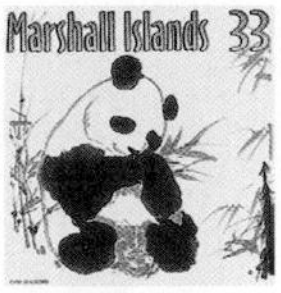

170 Panda

2000. Giant Pandas. Multicoloured.

1318	33c. Type **170**	85	75
1319	33c. Adult facing cub	85	75
1320	33c. Adult holding cub	85	75
1321	33c. Two adults	85	75
1322	33c. Moving rock	85	75
1323	33c. Cub beside adult eating bamboo	85	75

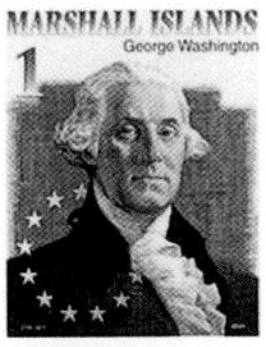

171 George Washington

2000. American Presidents. Multicoloured.

1324	1c. Type **171**	15	10
1325	2c. John Adams	15	10
1326	3c. Thomas Jefferson	15	10
1327	4c. James Madison	15	10
1328	5c. James Monroe	15	10
1329	6c. John Quincy Adams	15	10
1330	7c. Andrew Jackson	25	25
1331	8c. Martin van Buren	25	25
1332	9c. William Henry Harrison	25	25
1333	10c. John Tyler	25	25
1334	11c. James K. Polk	25	25
1335	12c. Zachary Taylor	25	25
1336	13c. Millard Filmore	30	30
1337	14c. Franklin Pierce	30	30
1338	15c. James Buchanan	30	30
1339	16c. Abraham Lincoln	30	30
1340	17c. Andrew Johnson	30	30
1341	18c. Ulysses S. Grant	30	30
1342	19c. Rutherford B. Hayes	50	45
1343	20c. James A. Garfield	50	45
1344	21c. Chester A. Arthur	50	45
1345	22c. Grover Cleveland	50	45
1346	23c. Benjamin Harrison	50	45
1347	24c. The White House	50	45
1348	25c. William McKinley	65	60
1349	26c. Theodore Roosevelt	65	60
1350	27c. William H. Taft	65	60
1351	28c. Woodrow Wilson	65	60
1352	29c. Warren G. Harding	65	60
1353	30c. Calvin Coolidge	65	60
1354	31c. Herbert C. Hoover	75	70
1355	32c. Franklin D. Roosevelt	75	70
1356	33c. Harry S. Truman	75	70
1357	34c. Dwight D. Eisenhower	75	70
1358	35c. John F. Kennedy	75	70
1359	36c. Lyndon B. Johnson	75	70
1360	37c. Richard M. Nixon	90	80
1361	38c. Gerald R. Ford	90	80
1362	39c. James E. Carter	90	80
1363	40c. Ronald W. Reagan	90	80
1364	41c. George H. Bush	90	80
1365	42c. William J. Clinton	90	80

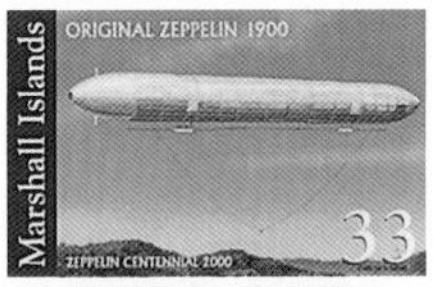

172 LZ-1 (first Zeppelin airship), 1900

2000. Centenary of Zeppelin Airships. Multicoloured.

1366	33c. Type **172**	90	80
1367	33c. *Graf Zeppelin I*, 1928	90	80
1368	33c. *Hindenburg*, 1936	90	80
1369	33c. *Graf Zeppelin II*, 1937	90	80

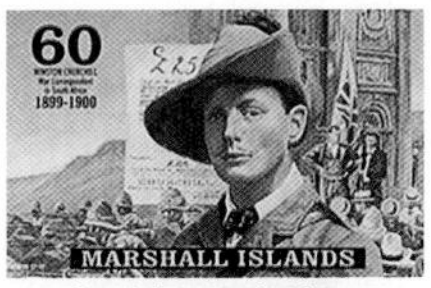

173 Churchill in South Africa as War Correspondent, 1899–1900

2000. 35th Death Anniv of Winston Churchill (British Prime Minister, 1940–45 and 1951–55). Multicoloured.

1370	60c. Type **173**	1·60	1·50
1371	60c. Churchill and Clementine Hozier on wedding day, 1908	1·60	1·50
1372	60c. Kaiser Wilhelm II, Churchill and clock tower, Houses of Parliament	1·60	1·50
1373	60c. Various portraits of Churchill between 1898 and 1960	1·60	1·50
1374	60c. Wearing naval cap (First Lord of the Admiralty, 1939–40)	1·60	1·50
1375	60c. Churchill giving "Victory" sign and St. Paul's Cathedral (Prime Minister, 1940–45)	1·60	1·50
MS1376	87×61 mm. $1 Winston Churchill receiving knighthood, 1946. Imperf	2·50	2·30

The top edge of **MS**1376 is perforated.

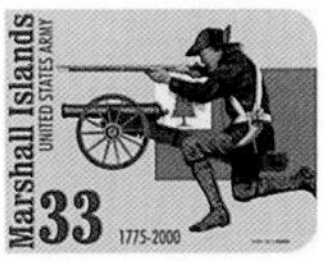

174 Cannon, Flag and Soldier preparing to Fire (Army)

2000. 225th Anniv of United States Military Forces. Multicoloured.

1377	33c. Type **174**	85	75
1378	33c. Ship, flag and officer looking through telescope (Navy)	85	75
1379	33c. Ship, cannon and mariner drawing sword (Marines)	85	75

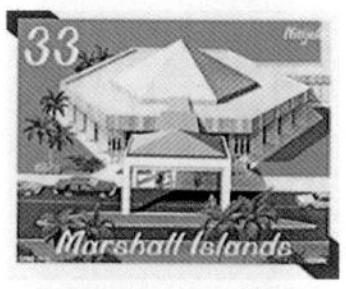

175 Nitijela (elected lower house) Complex

2000. Multicoloured.

1380	33c. Type **175**	85	75
1381	33c. Capitol building	85	75
1382	33c. National Seal and Nitijela Complex (vert)	85	75
1383	33c. National Flag and Nitijela Complex (vert)	85	75

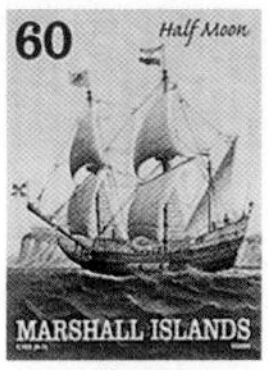

176 *Half Moon* (Hudson)

2000. Sailing Ships. Multicoloured.

1384	60c. Type **176**	1·50	1·40
1385	60c. *Grande Hermine* (Cartier)	1·50	1·40
1386	60c. *Golden Hind* (Drake)	1·50	1·40
1387	60c. *Matthew* (Cabot) (wrongly inscr "Mathew")	1·50	1·40
1388	60c. *Vitoria* (Magellan) (inscr "Victoria")	1·50	1·40
1389	60c. *Sao Gabriel* (Vasco da Gama)	1·50	1·40

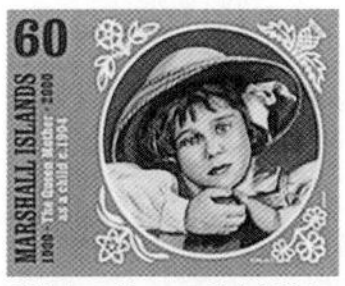

177 As a Young Girl, 1904

2000. "Queen Elizabeth the Queen Mother's Century". Multicoloured.

1390	60c. Type **177**	1·50	1·40
1391	60c. Wearing a turquoise hat, 1923	1·50	1·40
1392	60c. Wearing pearl necklace, 1940	1·50	1·40
1393	60c. Wearing purple hat, 1990	1·50	1·40

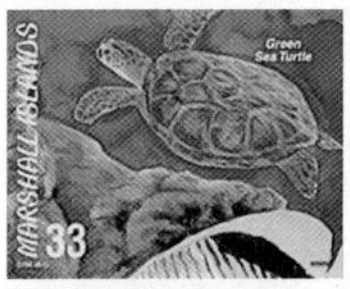

178 Green Sea Turtle

2000. Marine Life. Multicoloured.

1394	33c. Type **178**	85	75
1395	33c. Blue-girdled angelfish	85	75
1396	33c. Clown triggerfish	85	75
1397	33c. Harlequin tuskfish	85	75

1398	33c. Lined butterflyfishes	85	75
1399	33c. Whitebonnet anemonefish	85	75
1400	33c. Long-nose filefish	85	75
1401	33c. Emperor angelfish	85	75

Nos. 1394/1401 were issued together, se-tenant, forming the composite design of the reef.

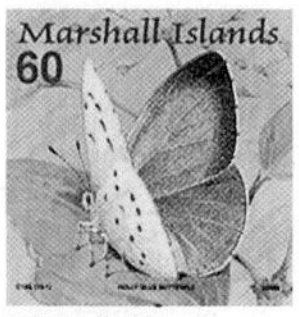

179 Holly Blue Butterfly

2000. Butterflies. Multicoloured.

1402	60c. Type **179**	1·50	1·40
1403	60c. Swallowtail butterfly	1·50	1·40
1404	60c. Clouded yellow butterfly	1·50	1·40
1405	60c. Small tortoiseshell butterfly	1·50	1·40
1406	60c. Nettle-tree butterfly	1·50	1·40
1407	60c. Long tailed blue butterfly	1·50	1·40
1408	60c. Cranberry blue butterfly	1·50	1·40
1409	60c. Small heath butterfly	1·50	1·40
1410	60c. Pontic blue butterfly	1·50	1·40
1411	60c. Lapland fritillary butterfly	1·50	1·40
1412	60c. Large blue butterfly	1·50	1·40
1413	60c. Monarch butterfly	1·50	1·40

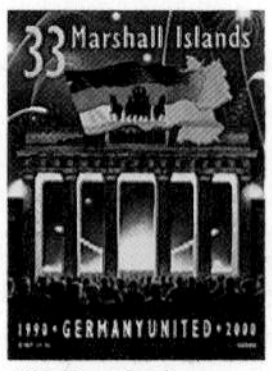

180 Brandenburg Gate, Berlin and Flag

2000. Tenth Anniv of Reunification of Germany.

1414	**180**	33c. multicoloured	85	75

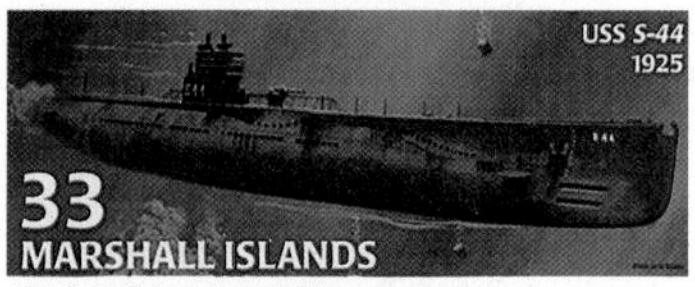

181 S-44 Submarine, 1925

2000. Centenary of United States Submarine Fleet. Multicoloured.

1415	33c. Type **181**	85	75
1416	33c. Gato, 1941	85	75
1417	33c. Wyoming, 1996	85	75
1418	33c. Cheyenne, 1997	85	75

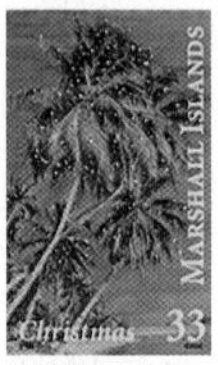

182 Decorated Trees

2000. Christmas.

1419	**182**	33c. multicoloured	85	75

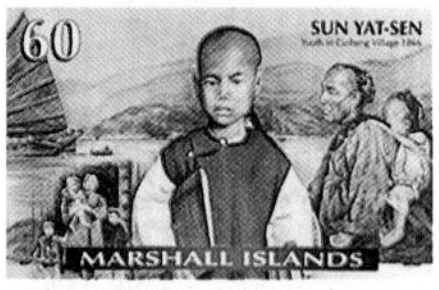

183 Sun Yat-sen as Young Boy, 1866

2000. 75th Death Anniv of Dr. Sun Yat-sen (President of Republic of China, 1912–25). Multicoloured.

1420	60c. Type **183**	1·60	1·50
1421	60c. With family in Honolulu, 1879 and amongst other students in Hong Kong	1·60	1·50
1422	60c. As President of Tong Meng Hui, 1905	1·60	1·50
1423	60c. Empress Dowager (Revolution, 1911)	1·60	1·50
1424	60c. As President of Republic of China, 1912	1·60	1·50
1425	60c. Flag and various portraits of Sun Yat-sen	1·60	1·50

MS1426 87×61 mm. $1 Memorial, Nanjing, Sun Yat-sen and Great Wall of China. Imperf 2·50 2·30

The top edge of **MS**1426 is perforated.

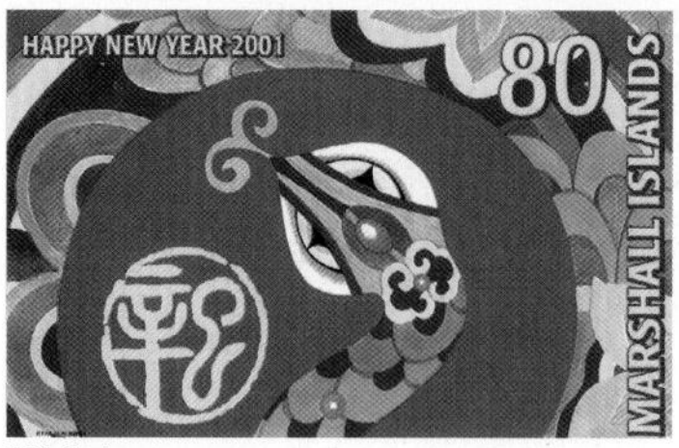

184 Snake

2001. New Year. Year of the Snake. Sheet 111×88 mm.

MS1427 **184** 80c. multicoloured 2·20 2·00

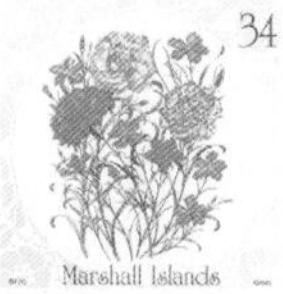

185 Carnations

2001. Flowers. Multicoloured.

1428	34c. Type **185**	90	80
1429	34c. Violet	90	80
1430	34c. Jonquil	90	80
1431	34c. Sweet pea	90	80
1432	34c. Lily of the valley	90	80
1433	34c. Rose	90	80
1434	34c. Larkspur	90	80
1435	34c. Poppy	90	80
1436	34c. Aster	90	80
1437	34c. Marigold	90	80
1438	34c. Chrysanthemum	90	80
1439	34c. Poinsettia	90	80

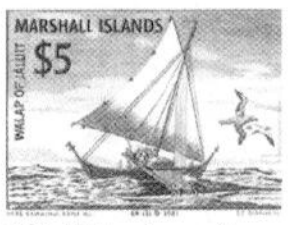

186 Walap (canoe), Jaluitt

2001. Sailing Canoes.

1440	**186**	$5 green	12·50	11·50
1441	-	$10 blue	25·00	23·00

DESIGN: $10 Walap, Enewetak.

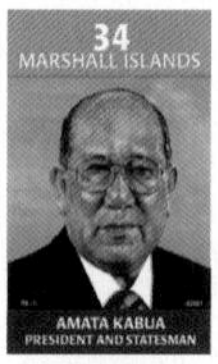

187 Amata Kabua (first President)

2001. Personalities. Multicoloured.

1442	34c. Type **187**	90	80
1442a	37c. Oscar Debrum (statesman)	95	85
1443	55c. Robert Reimers (entrepreneur)	1·40	1·30
1444	57c. Atlan Anien (legislator)	1·40	1·30
1445	80c. Father Leonard Hacker (humanitarian)	2·00	1·90
1446	$1 Dwight Heine (educator)	2·50	2·30
1447	$3.85 Tipne Philippo (senator)	9·75	9·00
1448	$13.65 Henchi Balos (senator)	32·00	29·00

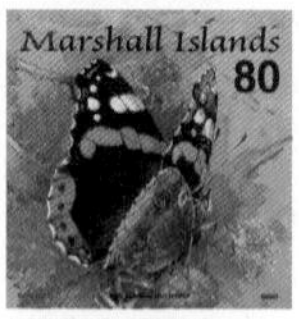

188 Red Admiral

2001. Butterflies (1st series). Multicoloured.

1450	80c. Type **188**	2·20	2·00
1451	80c. Moroccan orange tip	2·20	2·00
1452	80c. Silver-studded blue	2·20	2·00
1453	80c. Marbled white	2·20	2·00
1454	80c. False Apollo	2·20	2·00
1455	80c. Ringlet	2·20	2·00
1456	80c. Map	2·20	2·00
1457	80c. Fenton's wood white	2·20	2·00
1458	80c. Grecian copper	2·20	2·00
1459	80c. Pale Arctic clouded yellow	2·20	2·00
1460	80c. Great banded greyling	2·20	2·00
1461	80c. Cardinal	2·20	2·00

See also Nos. 1565/76, 1698/1709 and 1947/58.

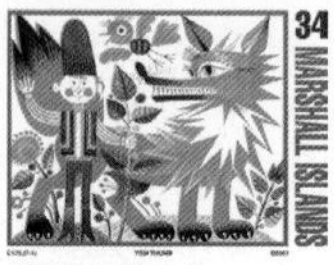

189 *Tom Thumb*

2001. Fairytales. Multicoloured.

1462	34c. Type **189**	90	80
1463	34c. *Three Little Pigs*	90	80
1464	34c. *Gulliver's Travels*	90	80
1465	34c. *Cinderella*	90	80
1466	34c. *Gallant John*	90	80
1467	34c. *The Ugly Duckling*	90	80
1468	34c. *Fisher and the Goldfish*	90	80

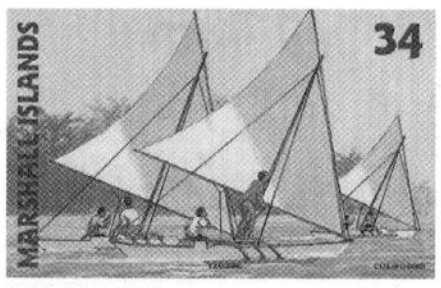

190 Pirogues

2001. Racing Watercraft. Multicoloured.

1469	34c. Type **190**	90	80
1470	34c. Windsurfers	90	80
1471	34c. Yachts	90	80
1472	34c. Sailing dinghies	90	80

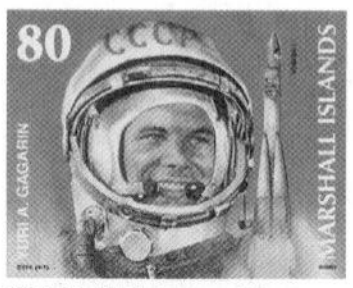

191 Yuri Alekseyevich Gagarin

2001. 40th Anniv of First Manned Space Flight. Multicoloured.

1473	80c. Type **191**	2·00	1·90
1474	80c. Alan Bartlett Shepard	2·00	1·90
1475	80c. Virgil Ivan (Gus) Grissom	2·00	1·90
1476	80c. Gherman Stepanovich Titov	2·00	1·90

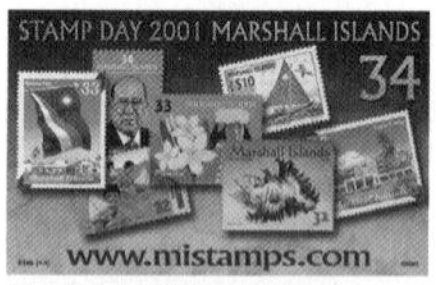

192 2000–1 Marshall Island Stamps

2001. Stamp Day.

1477	**192**	34c. multicoloured	90	80

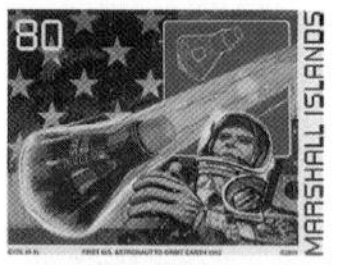

193 Friendship 7 Spacecraft and John Glenn (first USA manned orbit of Earth, 1962)

2001. Space Exploration. Multicoloured.

1478	80c. Type **193**	2·00	1·90
1479	80c. First space walk, 1965	2·00	1·90
1480	80c. First man on moon, 1969	2·00	1·90
1481	80c. First space shuttle voyage, 1977	2·00	1·90

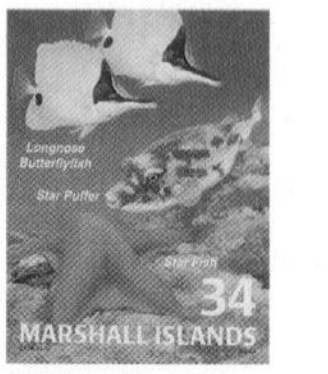

194 Longnose Butterflyfish, Star Puffer and Star Fish

2001. Coral Reef Fauna. Multicoloured.

1482	34c. Type **194**	90	80
1483	34c. Nautilus	90	80
1484	34c. Raccoon butterflyfish	90	80
1485	34c. Porkfish and grouper	90	80

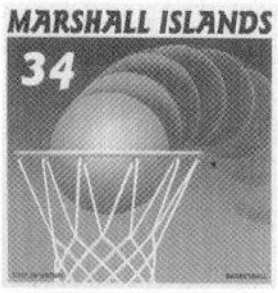

195 Basketball

2001. Sport. Multicoloured.

1486	34c. Type **195**	90	80
1487	34c. Bowling	90	80
1488	34c. Table tennis	90	80
1489	34c. Kayaking	90	80

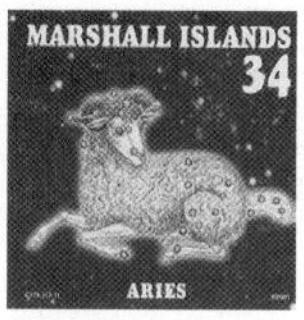

196 Aries

2001. Signs of the Zodiac. Multicoloured.

1490	34c. Type **196**	90	80
1491	34c. Taurus	90	80
1492	34c. Gemini	90	80
1493	34c. Cancer	90	80
1494	34c. Leo	90	80
1495	34c. Virgo	90	80
1496	34c. Libra	90	80
1497	34c. Scorpio	90	80
1498	34c. Sagittarius	90	80
1499	34c. Capricorn	90	80
1500	34c. Aquarius	90	80
1501	34c. Pisces	90	80

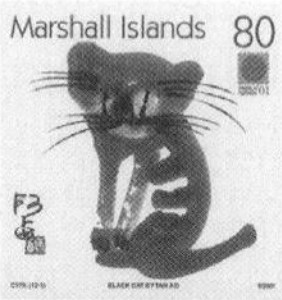

197 Black Cat (Tan Axi)

2001. Philanippon 2001 International Stamp Exhibition. Children's Paintings. Multicoloured.

1502	34c. Type **197**	2·20	2·00
1503	34c. Brown cat (Tan Axi)	2·20	2·00
1504	34c. Cliffs (Wang Xihai)	2·20	2·00
1505	34c. Boat and bridge (Li Yan)	2·20	2·00
1506	34c. Rooster (Wang Xinlan)	2·20	2·00
1507	34c. Great Wall of China (Lui Zhong)	2·20	2·00
1508	34c. Crane (Wang Lynn)	2·20	2·00
1509	34c. Baboon with basket (Wang Yani)	2·20	2·00
1510	34c. Baboon in tree (Wang Yani)	2·20	2·00
1511	34c. Umbrella (Sun Yuan)	2·20	2·00
1512	34c. Baboon with fruit (Wang Yani)	2·20	2·00
1513	34c. Baboon riding ox (Wang Yani)	2·20	2·00

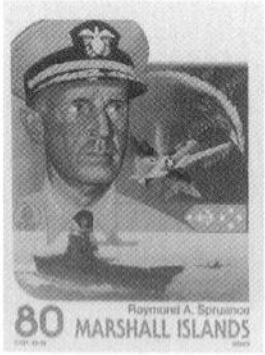

198 Raymond Spruance (head of Cruiser Division 5)

2001. Naval Heroes of World War II in the Pacific. Sheet 117×144 mm containing T **198** and similar vert designs. Multicoloured.

MS1514 80c. ×9, Type **198**; Arleigh Burke (destroyer fleet commander); Ernest King (Commander in Chief of the USA Fleet); Richmond Turner (Amphibious Forces commander); Marc Mitscher (Fleet Air commander, Solomon Islands); Chester Nimitz (Pacific Fleet commander); Edward O'Hare (naval pilot); William Halsey Jr. (Guadalcanal campaign commander); Albert, Francis, George, Joseph and Madison Sullivan (brothers) 18·00 17·00

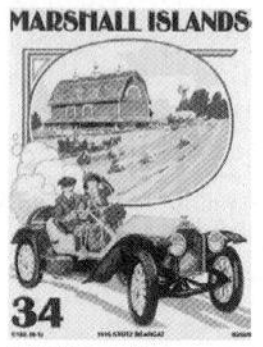

199 Stutz Bearcat (1916)

2001. Vintage Cars (1st series). Multicoloured.

1515	34c. Type **199**	90	80
1516	34c. Stanley Steamer (1909)	90	80
1517	34c. Citroen 7CV (1934)	90	80
1518	34c. Rolls-Royce Silver Ghost (1910)	90	80
1519	34c. Daimler (1927)	90	80
1520	34c. Hispano Suiza (1935)	90	80
1521	34c. Lancia Lambda V4 (1928)	90	80
1522	34c. Volvo OV4 (1927)	90	80

See also Nos. 1553/60, 1660/8, 1720/7, 1744/51 and 1884/91.

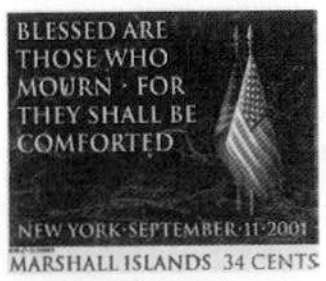

200 USA Flag and "Blessed are those who mourn for they shall be comforted"

2001. Support for Victims of Attack on World Trade Centre, New York (1st issue). Multicoloured.

1523	34c. Type **200**	90	80
1524	34c. Statue of Liberty, New York and script	90	80
1525	34c. "An attack on freedom anywhere is an attack on freedom everywhere"	90	80
1526	34c. "In the great struggle of good versus evil good will prevail"	90	80
1527	34c. Statue of Freedom, Washington and script	90	80
1528	34c. "In the face of terrorism we remain one nation under God indivisible"	90	80
MS1529	$1 Rescue workers, service personnel and New York citizens (75×34 mm)	2·50	2·30

See also No. 1552.

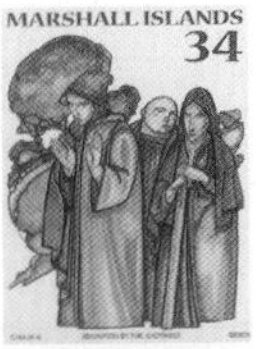

201 Adoration of the Shepherds

2001. Christmas. Multicoloured.

1530	34c. Type **201**	90	80
1531	34c. Angel on high	90	80
1532	34c. Adoration of the Magi	90	80
1533	34c. Nativity	90	80

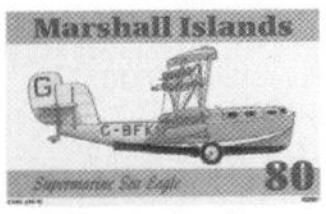

202 Supermarine Sea Eagle

2001. Classic Aircraft. Multicoloured.

1534	80c. Type **202**	2·00	1·90
1535	80c. Gloster Sea Gladiator	2·00	1·90
1536	80c. de Havilland DHC-6 Twin Otter	2·00	1·90
1537	80c. Shorts 350 airliner	2·00	1·90
1538	80c. Sandringham Flying Boat	2·00	1·90
1539	80c. de Havilland DHC-7	2·00	1·90
1540	80c. Beech Duke B60	2·00	1·90
1541	80c. Fokker/Fairchild Friendship F27	2·00	1·90
1542	80c. Consolidated B-24J Liberator	2·00	1·90
1543	80c. Vickers 953C Merchantman	2·00	1·90

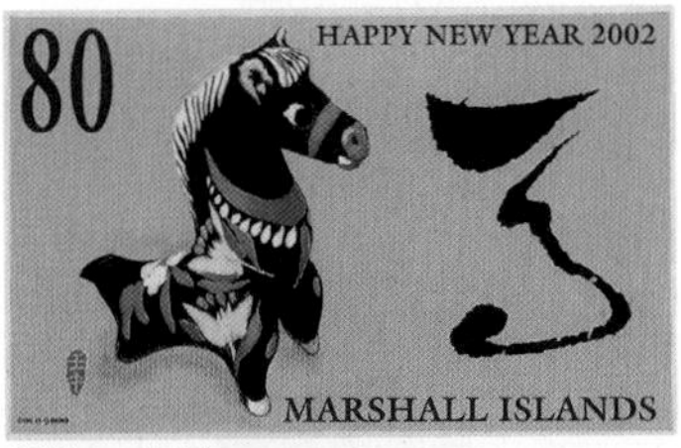

203 Decorated Horse

2002. New Year. "Year of the Horse". Sheet 110×86 mm.
MS1544 **203** 80c. multicoloured 2·20 2·00

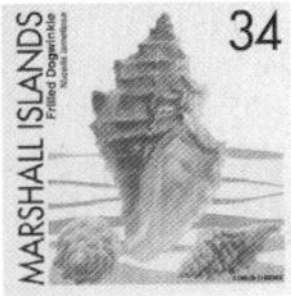

204 Frilled Dog Winkle (*Nucella lamellose*)

2002. Sea Shells. Multicoloured.

1545	34c. Type **204**	90	80
1546	34c. Reticulated cowrie-helmet (*Cypraecassis testiculus*)	90	80
1547	34c. New England neptune (*Neptunea decemcostata*)	90	80
1548	34c. Calico scallop (*Argopecten gibbus*)	90	80
1549	34c. Lightning whelk (*Busycon contrarium*)	90	80
1550	34c. Hawk-wing conch (*Strombus raninus*) (inscr "ranius")	90	80

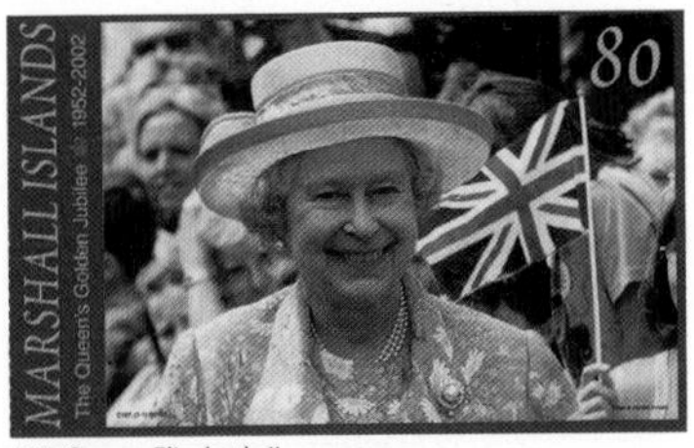

205 Queen Elizabeth II

2002. Golden Jubilee. 50th Anniv of Queen Elizabeth II's Accession to the Throne. Sheet 110×87 mm.
MS1551 **205** 80c. multicoloured 2·20 2·00

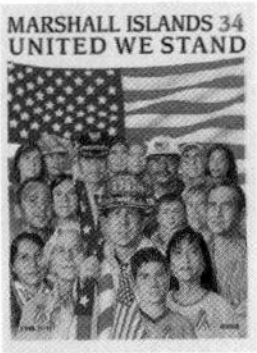

206 Rescue Workers, Service Personnel and New York Citizens

2002. Support for Victims of Attack on World Trade Centre, New York (2nd issue).

1552	**206**	34c. multicoloured	90	80

2002. Vintage Cars (2nd series). As T **199**. Multicoloured.

1553	34c. Le Zebre (1909)	90	80
1554	34c. Hammel (1886)	90	80
1555	34c. Wolseley (1902)	90	80
1556	34c. Eysink (1899)	90	80
1557	34c. Dansk (1903)	90	80
1558	34c. Spyker (1907)	90	80
1559	34c. Fiat Zero (1913)	90	80
1560	34c. Weber (1902)	90	80

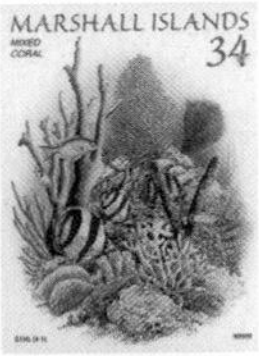

207 Mixed Coral

2002. Marine Life (1st series). Showing corals and fish. Multicoloured.

1561	34c. Type **207**	90	80
1562	34c. Chalice coral	90	80
1563	34c. Elkhorn coral	90	80
1564	34c. Finger coral	90	80

See also Nos. 1763/4.

2002. Butterflies (2nd series). As T **88**. Multicoloured.

1565	80c. Grayling	2·20	2·00
1566	80c. Eastern festoon	2·20	2·00
1567	80c. Speckled wood	2·20	2·00
1568	80c. Cranberry fritillary	2·20	2·00
1569	80c. Bath white	2·20	2·00
1570	80c. Meadow brown	2·20	2·00
1571	80c. Two-tailed pasha	2·20	2·00
1572	80c. Scarce swallowtail	2·20	2·00
1573	80c. Dusky grizzled skipper	2·20	2·00
1574	80c. Provencal short-tailed blue	2·20	2·00
1575	80c. The dryal	2·20	2·00
1576	80c. Comma	2·20	2·00

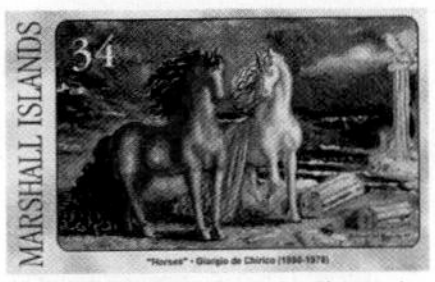

208 "Horses" (Giorgio de Chiroco)

2002. Horse Paintings. Multicoloured.

1577	34c. Type **208**	90	80
1578	34c. "Tartar Envoys giving Horse to Qianlong" (Guiseppe Castiglione)	90	80
1579	34c. "Gathering Seaweed" (Anton Mauve)	90	80
1580	34c. "Mares and Foals" (George Stubbs)	90	80
1581	34c. "Mare and Foal in spring Meadow" (Wilson Hepple)	90	80
1582	34c. "Horse with Child and Dog" (Natale Attanasio)	90	80
1583	34c. "The Horse" (Waterhouse Hawkins)	90	80
1584	34c. "Attendants and Horse" (Edgar Degas)	90	80
1585	34c. "Mares and Foals in Landscape" (George Stubbs)	90	80
1586	34c. "The Horse" (Guliemo Clardi)	90	80
1587	34c. "Little Blue Horse" (Franz Marc)	90	80
1588	34c. Sketch for "Firebird" (ballet) (Pavel Kuznetsov)	90	80
MS1589	110×87 mm. 80c. "Emperor Qianlong leaving for his Summer Residence" (Guiseppe Castiglione) (inscr "Casiglione")	2·20	2·00

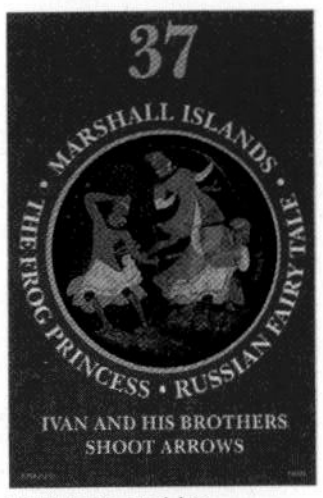

209 Ivan and his Brothers shoot Arrows

2002. "The Frog Princess" (fairytale). Multicoloured.

1590	37c. Type **209**	95	85
1591	37c. First brother finds a wife	95	85
1592	37c. Second brother finds a wife	95	85
1593	37c. Ivan and the frog princess	95	85
1594	37c. Ivan presents shirt to king	95	85
1595	37c. Ivan presents bread to king	95	85
1596	37c. Princess arrives at ball	95	85
1597	37c. Princess dances for king	95	85
1598	37c. Princess says goodbye to Ivan	95	85
1599	37c. Ivan and little hut	95	85
1600	37c. Ivan and princess re-united	95	85
1601	37c. Ivan and princess on magic carpet	95	85

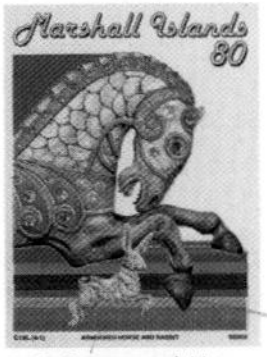

210 Armoured Horse and Rabbit

2002. Carousel Animals. Multicoloured.

1602	80c. Type **210**	2·00	1·90
1603	80c. Zebra and camel	2·00	1·90
1604	80c. Horse, angel and reindeer	2·00	1·90
1605	80c. Horse, frog and tiger	2·00	1·90

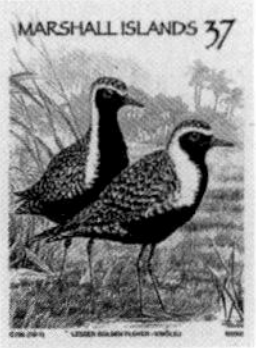

211 Lesser Golden Plover

2002. Birds. Multicoloured.

1606	37c. Type **211**	95	85
1607	37c. Siberian tattler	95	85
1608	37c. Brown noddy	95	85
1609	37c. Fairy tern	95	85
1610	37c. Micronesian pigeon	95	85
1611	37c. Long-tailed cuckoo	95	85
1612	37c. Christmas shearwater	95	85
1613	37c. Eurasian tree sparrow	95	85
1614	37c. Black-tailed godwit	95	85
1615	37c. Franklin's gull	95	85
1616	37c. Rufous-necked stint	95	85
1617	37c. Kermadec petrel	95	85
1618	37c. Purple-capped fruit dove	95	85
1619	37c. Mongolian plover	95	85
1620	37c. Cattle egret	95	85
1621	37c. Dunlin	95	85

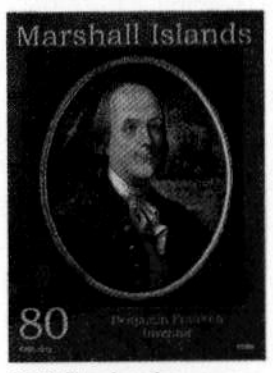

212 Benjamin Franklin, Inventor (Gherman Komlev)

2002. Benjamin Franklin, Commemoration. Multicoloured.

1622	80c. Type **212**	2·00	1·90
1623	80c. Benjamin Franklin, scholar (David Martin)	2·00	1·90

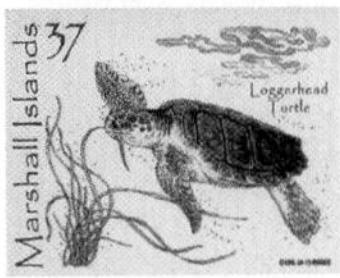

213 Loggerhead Turtle

2002. Sea Turtles. Multicoloured.

1624	37c. Type **213**	95	85
1625	37c. Leatherback	95	85
1626	37c. Hawksbill	95	85
1627	37c. Green	95	85

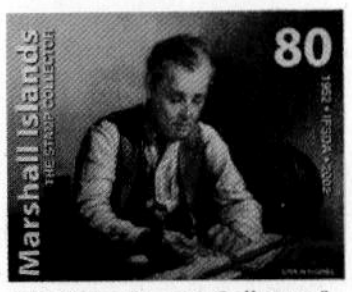

214 "The Stamp Collector"

2002. 50th Anniv of International Federation of Stamp Dealers' Association (IFSDA). Paintings by Lyle Tayson. Multicoloured.

1628	80c. Type **214**	2·00	1·90
1629	80c. "The First Day of Issue"	2·00	1·90
1630	80c. "Father and Daughter Collectors"	2·00	1·90
1631	80c. "The Young Collector"	2·00	1·90
1632	80c. "Sharing Dad's Stamp Collection"	2·00	1·90
1633	80c. "The New Generation"	2·00	1·90

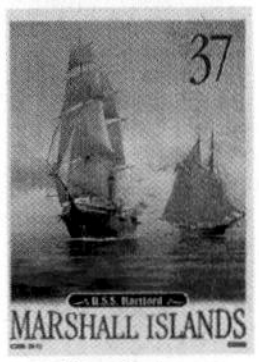

215 *Hartford*

2002. USA Naval Sail Ships. Multicoloured.

1634	37c. Type **215**	95	85
1635	37c. *Bon Homme Richard*	95	85
1636	37c. *Prince de Neufchatel*	95	85
1637	37c. *Ohio*	95	85
1638	37c. *Onkahye*	95	85
1639	37c. *Oneida*	95	85

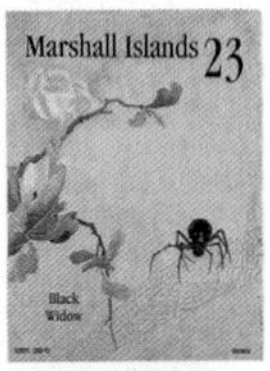

216 Black Widow Spider

2002. Insects. Multicoloured.

1640	23c. Type **216**	55	50
1641	23c. Elderberry longhorn	55	50
1642	23c. Lady beetle	55	50
1643	23c. Yellow garden spider	55	50
1644	23c. Dogbane beetle	55	50
1645	23c. Flower fly	55	50
1646	23c. Assassin bug	55	50
1647	23c. Ebony jewel wing	55	50

1648	23c. Velvet ant	55	50
1649	23c. Monarch caterpillar	55	50
1650	23c. Monarch butterfly	55	50
1651	23c. Eastern Hercules beetle	55	50
1652	23c. Bombardier beetle	55	50
1653	23c. Dung beetle	55	50
1654	23c. Spotted water beetle	55	50
1655	23c. True katydid	55	50
1656	23c. Spiny-backed spider	55	50
1657	23c. Periodical cicada	55	50
1658	23c. Scorpion fly	55	50
1659	23c. Jumping spider	55	50

2002. Vintage Cars (3rd series). As T **199**. Multicoloured.

1660	34c. Hotchkiss (1934)	2·00	1·90
1661	34c. De Dion Bouton (1909)	2·00	1·90
1662	34c. Renault (1922)	2·00	1·90
1663	34c. Amilcar "Surbaisse" (1927)	2·00	1·90
1664	34c. Austin (1943)	2·00	1·90
1665	34c. Peugeot "Bebe" (1927)	2·00	1·90
1666	34c. O.M. "Superba" (1913)	2·00	1·90
1667	34c. Elizade-Tipo (1922)	2·00	1·90

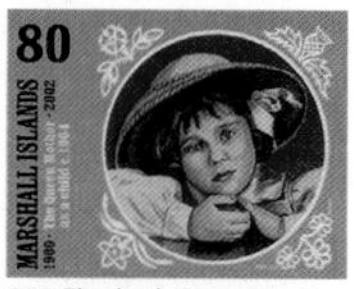

218 Elizabeth Bowes-Lyon (1904)

2002. Queen Elizabeth the Queen Mother Commemoration. Multicoloured.

1668	80c. Type **218**	2·00	1·90
1669	80c. Duchess of York (1923)	2·00	1·90
1670	80c. Queen Elizabeth wearing pearl necklace (1940)	2·00	1·90
1671	80c. Queen Elizabeth the Queen Mother wearing blue outfit (1990)	2·00	1·90

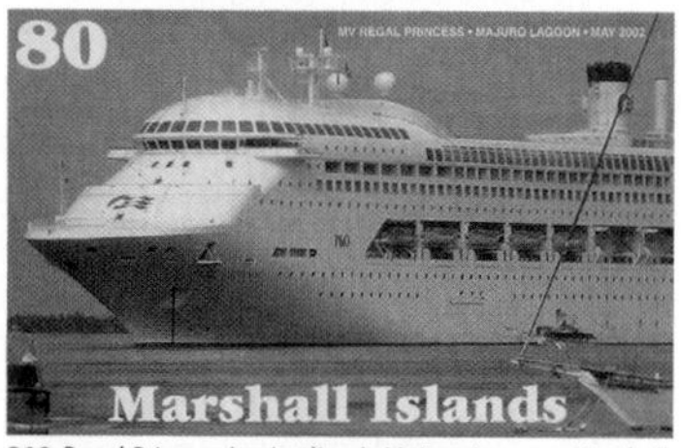

219 *Regal Princess* (cruise liner), Majuro Lagoon, Marshall Islands

2002. World War II Veterans Visit Sites in the South Pacific. Sheet 110×88 mm.
MS1672 **219** 80c. multicoloured 2·20 2·00

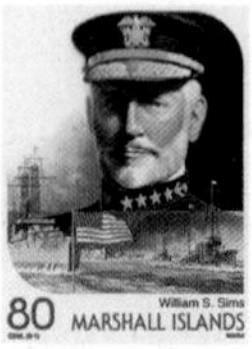

220 William Sims (commander USA Navy in Europe)

2002. World War I Military Heroes. Multicoloured.

1673	80c. Type **220**	2·00	1·90
1674	80c. William Mitchell (senior aviation officer) and de Havilland D.H.4	2·00	1·90
1675	80c. Freddie Stowers (posthumous Medal of Honor)	2·00	1·90
1676	80c. Smedley Butler (United States Marine Corps)	2·00	1·90
1677	80c. Edward Rickenbacker (USA flying ace) and SPAD S.X.III	2·00	1·90
1678	80c. Alvin York (French Medaille Militaire, Croix de Guerre, Italian Groce de Guerra and Medal of Honor)	2·00	1·90
1679	80c. John Lejeune (division commander)	2·00	1·90
1680	80c. John Pershing (Commander-in-Chief American expeditionary force in Europe)	2·00	1·90

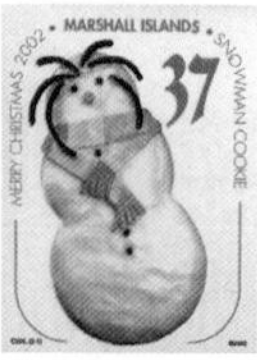

221 Snowman Cookie

2002. Christmas. Multicoloured.

1681	37c. Type **221**	95	85
1682	37c. Snowman cookie wearing hat	95	85

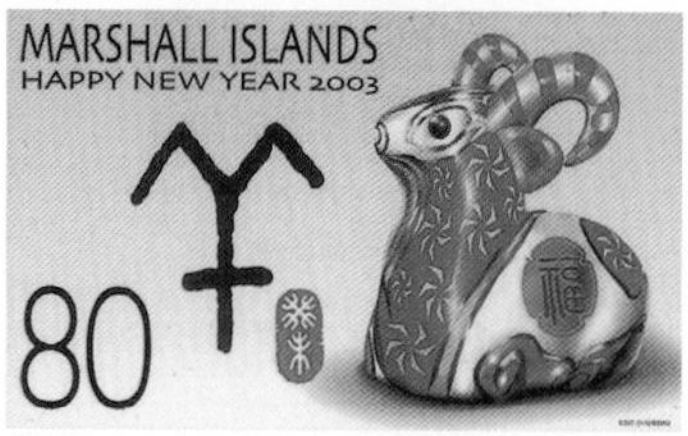

222 Decorated Ram

2003. New Year. "Year of the Ram".
MS1683 **222** 80c. multicoloured 2·00 1·90

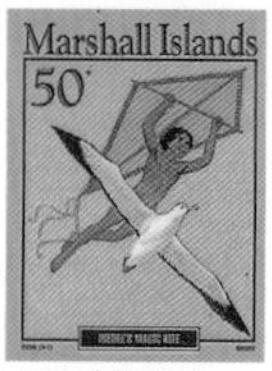

223 Indel's Magic Kite

2003. Folktales. Multicoloured.

1684	50c. Type **223**	1·30	1·20
1685	50c. Lijebake rescues her Granddaughter	1·30	1·20
1686	50c. Jebro's Mother invents the Sail	1·30	1·20
1687	50c. Limajnon escapes to the Moon	1·30	1·20

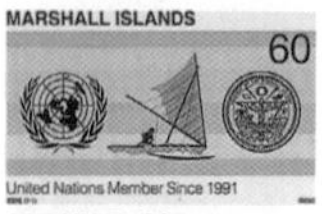

224 UN Emblem, Outrigger Canoe and Marshall Islands Emblem

2003. 12th Anniv of Marshall Islands' Membership of United Nations.
1688 **224** 60c. multicoloured 1·60 1·50

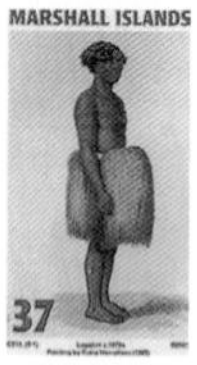

225 Lagajimi (Franz Hernsheim)

2003. Cultural Heritage (1st issue). Multicoloured.

1689	37c. Type **225**	95	85
1690	37c. Traditional house (50×42 mm)	95	85
1691	37c. Lake, Jabwor, Jaluit Atoll (50×42 mm)	95	85
1692	37c. Kabua (Franz Hernsheim)	95	85
1693	37c. Children wearing traditional dress	95	85
1694	37c. Jaluit Pass (Franz Hernsheim) (50×42 mm)	95	85
1695	37c. Traditional Canoe (Franz Hernsheim) (50×42 mm)	95	85
1696	37c. Fisherman	95	85

See also Nos. 1727/34, 1931/5, 1978/82 and 2053/7.

2003. Butterflies (3rd series). As T **188**. Multicoloured.

1697	80c. False grayling	2·20	2·00
1698	80c. Green hairstreak	2·20	2·00
1699	80c. Purple-shot copper	2·20	2·00
1700	80c. Black-veined white	2·20	2·00
1701	80c. Arctic grayling	2·20	2·00
1702	80c. Greek clouded yellow	2·20	2·00
1703	80c. American painted lady	2·20	2·00
1704	80c. Wall brown	2·20	2·00
1705	80c. Polar fritillary	2·20	2·00
1706	80c. Mountain clouded yellow	2·20	2·00
1707	80c. Camberwell beauty	2·20	2·00
1708	80c. Large white	2·20	2·00

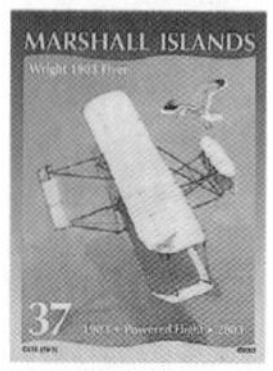

226 *Wright Flyer I*

2003. Centenary of Powered Flight. Multicoloured.

1709	37c. Type **226**	95	85
1710	37c. Curtiss JN-3	95	85
1711	37c. Douglas World Cruiser	95	85
1712	37c. Ryan NYP *Spirit of St Louis*	95	85
1713	37c. Lockheed Vega 5	95	85
1714	37c. Boeing 314 Clipper	95	85
1715	37c. Douglas C-47 Skytrain	95	85
1716	37c. Boeing B-50 Superfortress	95	85
1717	37c. Antonov An-225 Mriya	95	85
1718	37c. B-2 Spirit	95	85

2003. Vintage Cars (4th series). As T **199**. Multicoloured.

1719	37c. Alfa Romeo (1927)	95	85
1720	37c. Austro-Daimler "Prince Henry" (1912)	95	85
1721	37c. Mors 14/20 Tourer (1923)	95	85
1722	37c. AC Tourer (1926)	95	85
1723	37c. Scania (1903) and Vabis (1897)	95	85
1724	37c. Graf und Stift (1914)	95	85
1725	37c. Pic-Pic (1919)	95	85
1726	37c. Hispano Suiza-Alfonso XIII (1911)	95	85

2003. Cultural Heritage (2nd issue) As T **225**. Multicoloured.

1727	37c. Kabua's daughter	95	85
1728	37c. Walap (50×42 mm)	95	85
1729	37c. Jabwor, Jaluit Atoll (50×42 mm)	95	85
1730	37c. Traditional and modern dress	95	85
1731	37c. Nemedj	95	85
1732	37c. Typhoon damage, 1905 (50×42 mm)	95	85
1733	37c. Marshallese kor kor (50×42 mm)	95	85
1734	37c. Grandfather	95	85

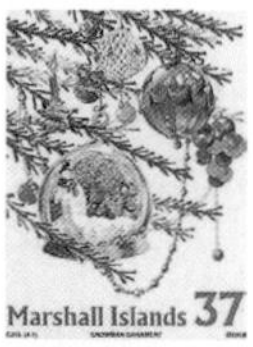

227 Bauble containing Snow Scene

2003. Christmas. Multicoloured.

1735	37c. Type **227**	95	85
1736	37c. Jack-in-the-box	95	85
1737	37c. Toy soldier	95	85
1738	37c. Reindeer	95	85

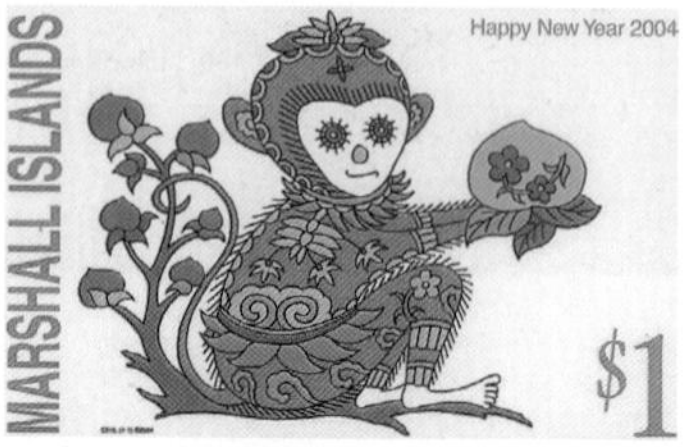

228 Decorated Monkey

2004. New Year. "Year of the Monkey".
MS1739 **228** 80c. multicoloured 2·50 2·30

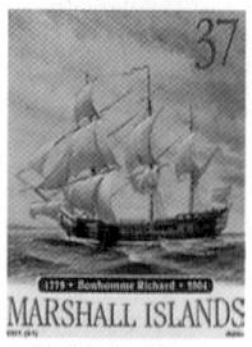

229 *Bonhomme Richard*

2004. 225th Anniversaries. Multicoloured.

1740	37c. Type **229** (American revolution sea battle)	95	85
1741	37c. HMS *Resolution* (Captain Cook's final voyages)	95	85
1742	37c. HMS *Resolution* (different) (Captain Cook's final voyages)	95	85

2004. Vintage Cars (5th series). As T **199**. Multicoloured.

1743	37c. Wolseley-Siddeley (1906)	95	85
1744	37c. Mors (1901)	95	85
1745	37c. Hutton (1908)	95	85
1746	37c. Metallurgique (1907)	95	85
1747	37c. Benz (1902)	95	85
1748	37c. Cudell (1900)	95	85
1749	37c. Peugeot (1906)	95	85
1750	37c. Inscr "The 60 Mercedes"	95	85

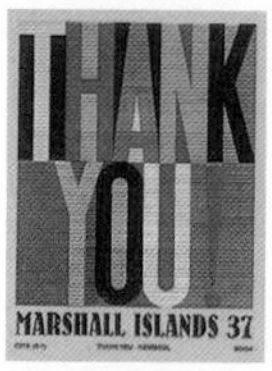

230 "THANK YOU"

2004. Greetings Stamps. Sheet 148×104 mm containing T **230** and similar vert designs. Multicoloured.
MS1751 37c. ×8, Type **230**; "CONGRATULATIONS"; "HAPPY BIRTHDAY"; "Best Wishes"; "Get Well Soon"; "LOVE YOU DAD"; "Love you Mom"; Bouquet of greetings 7·75 7·00

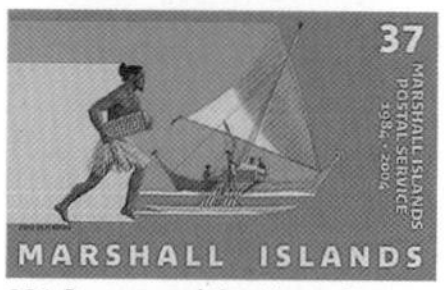

231 Runner and Outrigger Canoe

2004. 20th Anniv of Marshall Islands Postal Service.

1752	**231** 37c. multicoloured	95	85
1753	**231** 60c. multicoloured	1·50	1·40
1754	**231** $2.30 multicoloured	5·75	5·25

No. 1752 was for use on first class mail, No. 1753 was for use on international mail and No. 1754 was for use on certified mail.

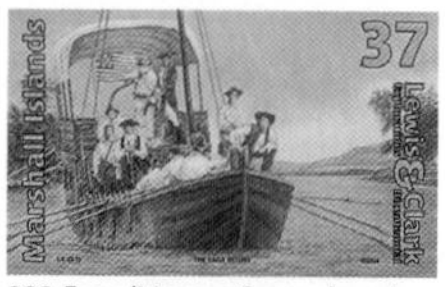

232 Expeditionary Corps aboard Boat

2004. Bicentenary of Meriwether Lewis and William Clark's Expedition to Explore the West Coast of America (1st issue). Multicoloured.

1755	37c. Type **232**	95	85
1756	37c. Clark and Sacagawea (Shoshone guide)	95	85
1757	37c. Lewis and Clark and bison herd	95	85

See also Nos. 1831/3, 1838/40, 1856/8, 1895/7, 1928/30 and 1976/7.

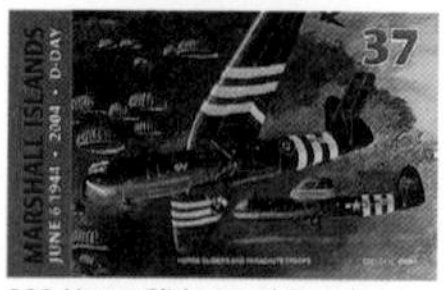

233 Horsa Gliders and Parachute Troops

2004. 60th Anniv of D-Day (invasion of German occupied French coast). Multicoloured.

1758	37c. Type **233**	95	85
1759	37c. Typhoon-1B and P518 Mustangs	95	85
1760	37c. Gun emplacements	95	85
1761	37c. Allied craft and soldiers landing	95	85

Nos. 1758/61 were issued together, se-tenant, forming a composite design.

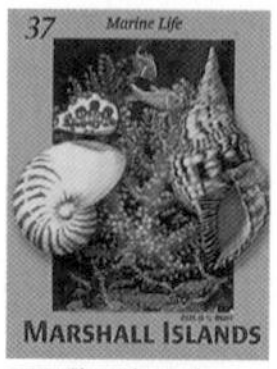

234 Chambered Nautilus, Map Cowrie and Trumpet Triton

2004. Marine Life (2nd series). Multicoloured.

1762	37c. Type **234**	95	85
1763	37c. Marlin spike, turban shell and Toulerei's cowrie	95	85

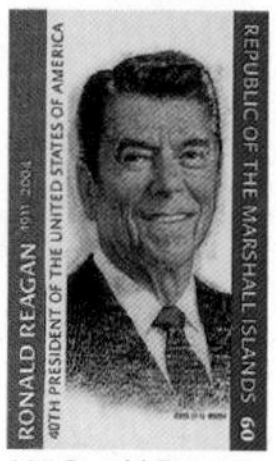

235 Ronald Reagan

2004. Ronald Reagan (president of USA, 1980–88) Commemoration.

1764	**235** 60c. multicoloured	95	85

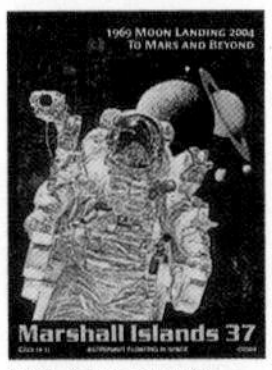

236 Astronaut in Space

2004. 35th Anniv of First Moon Walk. Multicoloured.

1765	37c. Type **236**	95	85
1766	37c. Astronaut and Saturn	95	85
1767	37c. Astronaut and Space Shuttle	95	85
1768	37c. Two astronauts	95	85

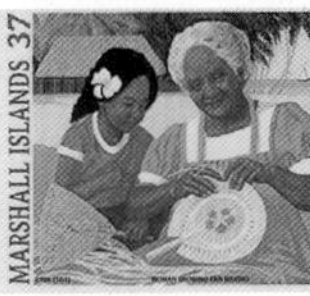

237 Making Fans

2004. Festival of Pacific Arts, Koror, Palau. Multicoloured.

1769	37c. Type **237**	95	85
1770	37c. Basket makers	95	85
1771	37c. Carving canoes	95	85
1772	37c. Boys and toy outrigger canoes	95	85
1773	37c. Older woman and white ginger flowers	95	85
1774	37c. Boy and vandal flower	95	85
1775	37c. Man and tiare flower	95	85
1776	37c. Young woman and hibiscus flower	95	85
1777	37c. Woman carrying breadfruit	95	85
1778	37c. Canoes and tattooed man	95	85
1779	37c. Men in traditional dress	95	85
1780	37c. Drummer and dancers	95	85

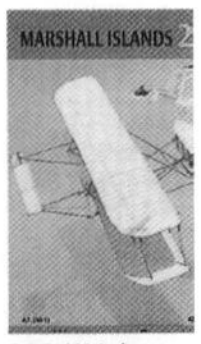

238 *Wright Flyer I*

2004. Aircraft. Multicoloured.

1781	23c. Type **238**	55	50
1782	23c. Bleriot XI	55	50
1783	23c. Curtiss *Golden Flyer*	55	50
1784	23c. Curtiss Flying Boat	55	50
1785	23c. Deperdussin Racer	55	50
1786	23c. Sikorsky Ilya Muromets	55	50
1787	23c. Fokker EI	55	50
1788	23c. Junkers JI	55	50
1789	23c. S.E.5a	55	50
1790	23c. Handley Page O/400	55	50
1791	23c. Fokker D.VII	55	50
1792	23c. Junkers F.13	55	50
1793	23c. Lockheed Vega	55	50
1794	23c. M-130 Pan Am Clipper	55	50
1795	23c. Messerschmitt Bf.109	55	50
1796	23c. Spitfire	55	50
1797	23c. Junkers Ju88	55	50
1798	23c. A6M Zero	55	50
1799	23c. Ilyushin Il-2	55	50
1800	23c. Heinkel He-178	55	50
1801	23c. C-47 Skytrain	55	50
1802	23c. Piper Cub	55	50
1803	23c. Avro Lancaster	55	50
1804	23c. B-17F Flying Fortress	55	50
1805	23c. Messrschmitt Me-262	55	50
1806	23c. B-29 Superfortress	55	50
1807	23c. P-51 Mustang	55	50
1808	23c. Yak 9	55	50
1809	23c. Bell Model 47	55	50
1810	23c. Bell X-1	55	50
1811	23c. Beechcraft Bonanza	55	50
1812	23c. AN-225 Mriya	55	50
1813	23c. B-47 Stratojet	55	50
1814	23c. MIG-15	55	50
1815	23c. Saab J35 Draken	55	50
1816	23c. B-52 Stratofortress	55	50
1817	23c. Boeing 367-80	55	50
1818	23c. U-2	55	50
1819	23c. C-130 Hercules	55	50
1820	23c. F-4 Phantom II	55	50
1821	23c. North American X-15	55	50
1822	23c. Sikorsky S-61 helicopter	55	50
1823	23c. Learjet 23	55	50
1824	23c. SR-71 Blackbird	55	50
1825	23c. Boeing 747	55	50
1826	23c. Concorde	55	50
1827	23c. Airbus A300	55	50
1828	23c. MIG-29	55	50
1829	23c. F-117A Nighthawk	55	50
1830	23c. F/A-22 Raptor	55	50

2004. Bicentenary of Meriwether Lewis and William Clark's Expedition to Explore the West Coast of America (2nd issue). As T **232**. Multicoloured.

1831	37c. Celebrating July 4th	95	85
1832	37c. Corps surrounding flag (burial of Charles Floyd)	95	85
1833	37c. Smoking peace pipe	95	85

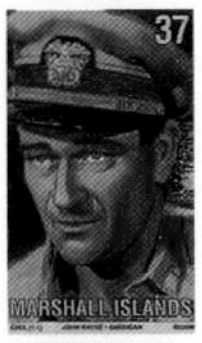

239 John Wayne

2004. 25th Death Anniv of John Wayne (actor).

1834	**239** 37c. multicoloured	95	85

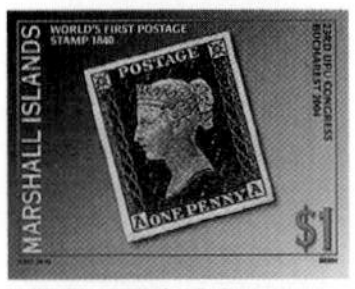

240 Penny Black Stamp

2004. 23rd Universal Postal Union Congress, Bucharest. Sheet 100×92 mm containing T **240** and similar horiz designs.

MS1835	$1 ×4, Type **240** (first postage stamp); First Romanian stamp (1858); First Marshall Islands' stamp (1897); First Republic of Marshall Islands' stamp (1984)	10·00	9·25

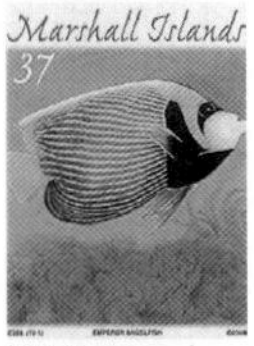

241 Emperor Angelfish

2004. Pacific Coral Reef. Sheet 179×104 mm containing T **241** and similar vert designs. Multicoloured.

MS1836	37c. ×10, Type **241**; Pink anemone fish; Humphead wrasse and moorish idol; Black-spotted puffer; Snowflake moray eel; Lionfish; Bumphead parrotfish and threadfin butterfly fish; Hawksbill turtle; Triton's trumpet; Oriental sweetlips.	9·50	8·75

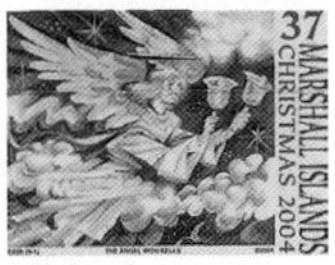

242 Angel

2004. Christmas. Sheet 144×118 mm containing T **242** and similar horiz designs. Multicoloured.

MS1837	37c. ×9, Type **242**; God crowned; Adoration of the kings; Three wise men; Procession of poor people; Shepherds; Flight into Egypt; Nativity; Jesus and animals	8·50	7·75

2004. Bicentenary of Meriwether Lewis and William Clark's Expedition to Explore the West Coast of America (3rd issue). As T **232**. Multicoloured.

1838	37c. Interpreters	95	85
1839	37c. Hunting bison	95	85
1840	37c. Attack by Sioux	95	85

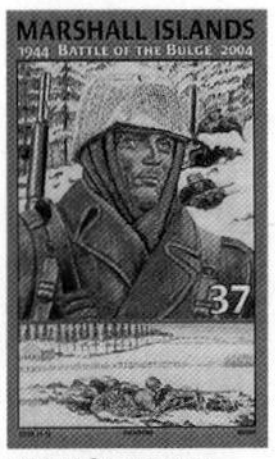

243 Infantryman

2004. 60th Anniv of Battle of the Bulge. Multicoloured.

1841	37c. Type **243**	95	85
1842	37c. Tank division soldier	95	85
1843	37c. Aviator	95	85
1844	37c. Lt. Colonel Creighton Abrams and General Anthony McAuliffe (inscr "Anathony")	95	85

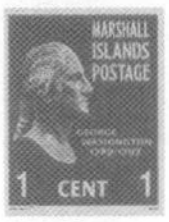

244 George Washington

2005. Presidents of USA. Sheet 214×150 mm containing T **244** and similar vert designs. Colours given.

MS1845	1c. green (Type **244**); 2c. rose (John Adams); 3c. violet (Thomas Jefferson); 4c. purple (James Madison); 5c. blue (James Monroe); 6c. red (John Quincy Adams); 7c. brown (Andrew Jackson); 8c. green (Martin van Buren); 9c. claret (William Henry Harrison); 10c. brown (John Tyler); 11c. blue (James K. Polk); 12c. mauve (Zachary Taylor); 13c. green (Millard Fillmore); 14c. blue (Franklin Pierce); 15c. blue (James Buchanan); 16c. green (Abraham Lincoln); 17c. vermilion (Andrew Johnson); 18c. chestnut (Ulysses S. Grant); 19c. green (Rutherford B. Hayes); 20c. rose (James A. Garfield); 21c. violet (Chester A. Arthur); 22c. purple (Grover Cleveland); 23c. turquoise blue (Benjamin Harrison); 24c. red (Grover Cleveland (2nd term)); 25c. brown (William McKinley); 26c. green (Theodore Roosevelt); 27c. claret (William Howard Taft); 28c. brown (Woodrow Wilson); 29c. blue (Warren G. Harding); 30c. mauve (Calvin Coolidge); 31c. green (Herbert Hoover); 32c. blue (Franklin D. Roosevelt); 33c. blue (Harry S. Truma); 34c. green (Dwight D. Eisenhower); 35c. vermilion (John F. Kennedy); 36c. chestnut (Lyndon B. Johnson); 37c. green (Richard M. Nixon); 38c. rose (Gerald R. Ford); 39c. violet (Jimmy Carter); 40c. purple (Ronald W. Reagan); 41c. blue (George H. W. Bush); 42c. red (William J. Clinton); 43c. brown (George W. Bush); 60c. green (The White House); $1 claret (The White House)	39·00	36·00

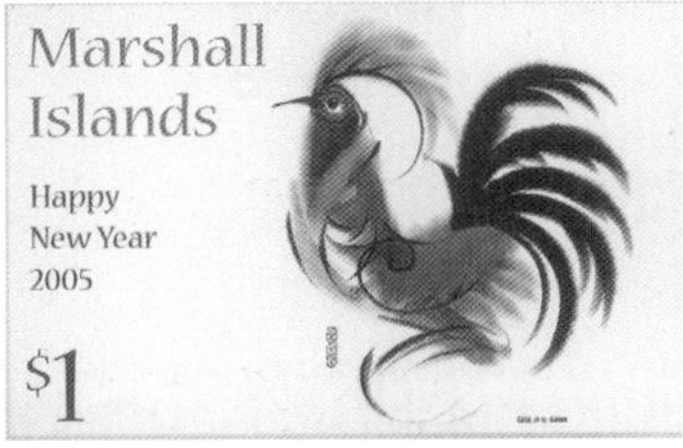

245 Rooster

2005. New Year. "Year of the Rooster". Sheet 111×87 mm.

MS1846	**245** $1 multicoloured	2·50	2·30

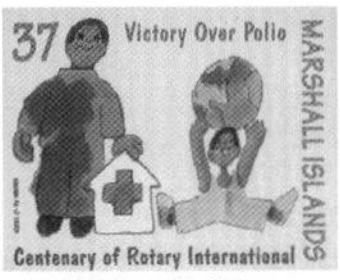

246 Children, Red Cross and Globe

2005. Centenary of Rotary International.

1847	**246** 37c. multicoloured	95	85

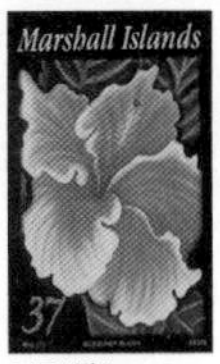

247 Hibiscus "Burgundy Blush"

2005. Hibiscus (1st issue). Designs showing cultivated varieties of Hibiscus. Multicoloured.

1848	37c. Type **247**	95	85
1849	60c. "Fiesta"	1·60	1·50
1850	80c. "June's Joy"	2·00	1·90
1851	$1 "Norman Lee"	2·50	2·30

See also Nos. 1874/7 and 1960/3.

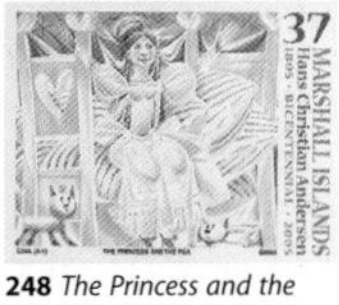

248 *The Princess and the Pea*

2005. Birth Bicentenary of Hans Christian Andersen (writer). Multicoloured.

1852	37c. Type **248**	95	85
1853	37c. *Thumbelina*	95	85
1854	37c. *The Little Mermaid*	95	85
1855	37c. *The Emperor's New Suit*	95	85

2005. Bicentenary of Meriwether Lewis and William Clark's Expedition to Explore the West Coast of America (4th issue). As T **232**. Multicoloured.

1856	37c. Grizzly bear	95	85
1857	37c. Lewis reaches the Great Falls	95	85
1858	37c. Sacagawea reunited with her brother	95	85

249 Modern Cover

2005. Stamp Day. 50th Anniv of American First Day Cover Society (AFDCS). Multicoloured.

1859	37c. Type **249**	95	85
1860	37c. First Marshall Islands' Postal Service issue	95	85
1861	37c. US First Man on the Moon cancellation	95	85
1862	37c. Marshall Island Stamp Day 2005 issue	95	85

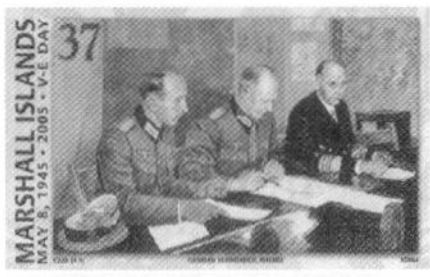

250 German Surrender, Rheims

2005. 60th Anniv of Victory in Europe. Mult.

1863	37c. Type **250**	95	85
1864	37c. Celebrating, Times Square, New York	95	85
1865	37c. Victory Parade, Moscow	95	85
1866	37c. Royal family and Winston Churchill, Buckingham Palace	95	85

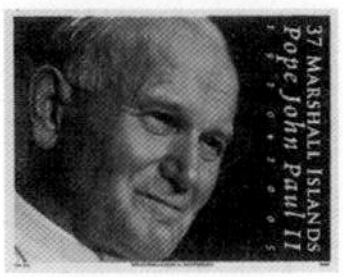

251 Pope John Paul II

2005. Pope John Paul II Commemoration. Mult.

1867	37c. Type **251**	95	85
1868	37c. Wearing mitre, red cape and holding staff	95	85
1869	37c. Facing right	95	85
1870	37c. Facing left with raised hand	95	85
1871	37c. Wearing mitre and green cape with raised hand	95	85

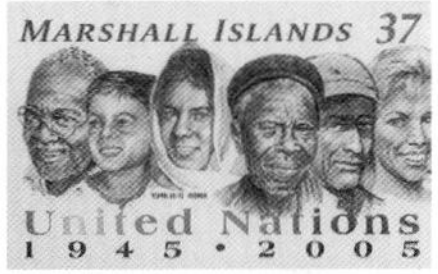

252 People of Many Nations

2005. 60th Anniv of United Nations. Multicoloured.

1872	37c. Type **252**	95	85
1873	80c. People of many nations (different)	2·00	1·90

Nos. 1872/3 were issued together, se-tenant, forming a composite design.

2005. Hibiscus (2nd issue). Multicoloured.

1874	1c. "Margaret Okano"	25	25
1875	24c. "Cameo Queen"	65	60
1876	39c. "Madonna"	1·00	95
1877	$4 "Estrella Red"	10·00	9·25

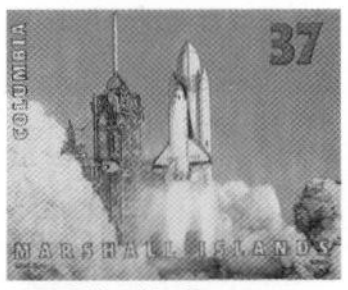

253 *Columbia* Space Shuttle

2005. Re-start of Space Shuttle Flights—26 July 2005. Multicoloured.

1878	37c. Type **253**	95	85
1879	37c. *Discovery*	95	85
1880	37c. *Endeavour*	95	85
1881	37c. *Challenger*	95	85
1882	37c. *Atlantis*	95	85

2005. Vintage Cars (6th series). As T **199**. Multicoloured.

1883	37c. Excelsior (1925)	95	85
1884	37c. Adler K (1912)	95	85
1885	37c. Thulin (19203)	95	85
1886	37c. Palladium (1913)	95	85
1887	37c. Minerva (1926)	95	85
1888	37c. Elizalde (1922)	95	85
1889	37c. Rolls Royce Silver Ghost (1911)	95	85
1890	37c. Invicta (1931)	95	85

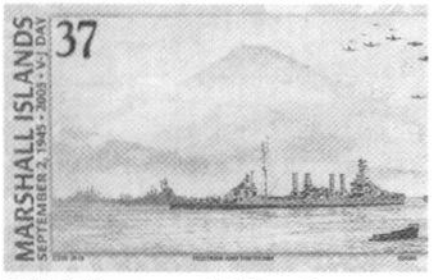

254 *Fujiyama* and Tokyo Bay

2005. 60th Anniv of Victory in Japan. Multicoloured.

1891	37c. Type **254**	95	85
1892	37c. *Missouri*	95	85
1893	37c. USA signing treaty	95	85
1894	37c. Japanese delegation	95	85

Nos. 1891/2 and 1893/4, respectively were issued together, in se-tenant pairs, forming composite design.

2005. Bicentenary of Meriwether Lewis and William Clark's Expedition to Explore the West Coast of America (5th issue). As T **232**. Multicoloured.

1895	37c. Crossing the Bitterroots	95	85
1896	37c. Peace agreement	95	85
1897	37c. Reaching the ocean	95	85

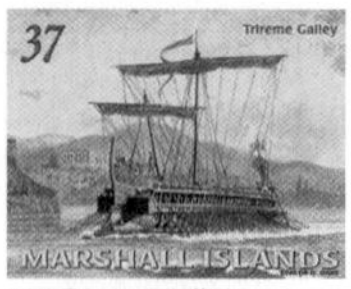

255 Trireme Galley

2005. Bicentenary of Battle of Trafalgar. Multicoloured.

1898	37c. Type **255**	95	85
1899	37c. Trireme Romano	95	85
1900	37c. Viking longship	95	85
1901	37c. Ming dynasty treasure ship	95	85
1902	37c. *Mary Rose*	95	85
1903	37c. *Nuestra Senora del Rosario*	95	85
1904	37c. Korean turtle ship	95	85
1905	37c. *Brederode*	95	85
1906	37c. *Galera Veneziana*	95	85
1907	37c. *Santisima Trinidad*	95	85
1908	37c. *Ville de Paris*	95	85
1909	37c. HMS *Victory*	95	85
1910	37c. *Bonhomme Richard*	95	85
1911	37c. USS *Constellation*	95	85
1912	37c. USS *Hartford*	95	85
1913	37c. *Fijian Ndrua*	95	85
1914	37c. HMS *Dreadnought*	95	85
1915	37c. HMAS *Australia*	95	85
1916	37c. HMS *Dorsetshire*	95	85
1917	37c. Admiral *Graf Spee*	95	85
1918	37c. *Yamato*	95	85
1919	37c. USS *Tautog*	95	85
1920	37c. *Bismarck*	95	85
1921	37c. USS *Hornet*	95	85
1922	37c. USS *Missouri*	95	85
MS1923	110×87 mm. $2 HMS *Victory*. Imperf	5·00	4·75

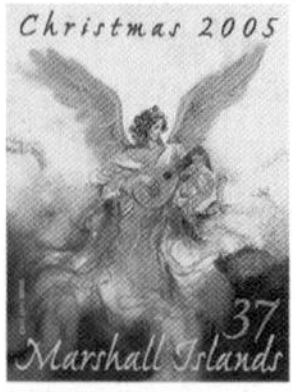

256 Angel

2005. Christmas. Multicoloured.

1924	37c. Type **256**	95	85
1925	37c. Three angels	95	85
1926	37c. Angel blowing horn	95	85
1927	37c. Angel playing harp	95	85

2005. Bicentenary of Meriwether Lewis and William Clark's Expedition to Explore the West Coast of America (6th issue). As T **232**. Multicoloured.

1928	37c. First universal voter	95	85
1929	37c. Leaving Fort Clatsop	95	85
1930	37c. At Pompey's Pillar	95	85

2005. Cultural Heritage (3rd issue). As T **225**. Multicoloured.

1931	37c. First Catholic Church, Jabwor, Jaluit Atoll	95	85
1932	37c. Women, Jaluit Atoll	95	85
1933	37c. Canoes, Jaluit harbour	95	85
1934	37c. Nelu and his wife Ledagoba	95	85
1935	37c. Old man, Ebon Atoll	95	85

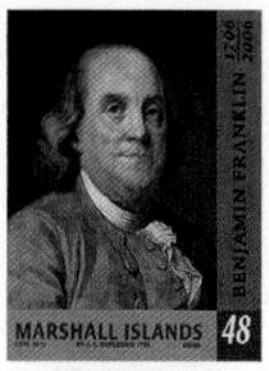

257 Benjamin Franklin (J. S. Duplessis)

2006. 300th Birth Anniv of Benjamin Franklin (scientist and statesman). Portraits of Benjamin Franklin, Artist given. Multicoloured.

1936	48c. Type **257**	1·30	1·20
1937	48c. David K. Stone	1·30	1·20
1938	48c. Mason Chamberlain	1·30	1·20
1939	48c. John Trumbull	1·30	1·20
1940	48c. Bust (James Earle Fraser)	1·30	1·20
1941	48c. David Martin	1·30	1·20
1942	48c. Benjamin West	1·30	1·20
1943	48c. J. B. Greuze	1·30	1·20
1944	48c. After C. N. Cochin	1·30	1·20

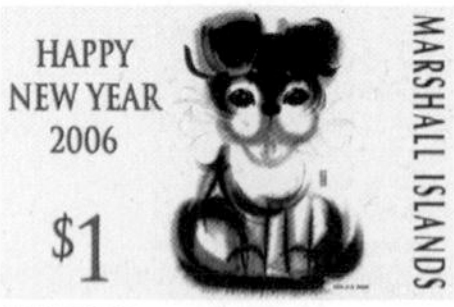

258 258 Dog

2006. New Year. Year of the Dog. Sheet 110×87 mm.

MS1945	**258** $1 multicoloured	2·50	2·30

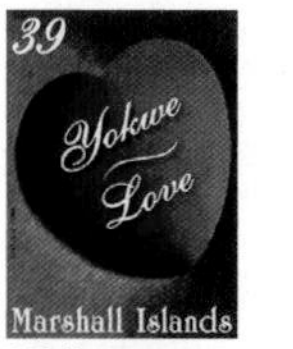

259 Heart

2006. St. Valentine's Day.

1946	**259**	39c. multicoloured	1·00	95

2006. Butterflies (4th series). As T **188**. Multicoloured.

1947	84c. Peacock	2·20	2·00
1948	84c. Southern comma	2·20	2·00
1949	84c. Pale clouded yellow	2·20	2·00
1950	84c. Common blue	2·20	2·00
1951	84c. Wood white	2·20	2·00
1952	84c. Baltic grayling	2·20	2·00
1953	84c. Purple emperor	2·20	2·00
1954	84c. Silky ringlet	2·20	2·00
1955	84c. Peak white	2·20	2·00
1956	84c. Idas blue	2·20	2·00
1957	84c. Camberwell beauty	2·20	2·00
1958	84c. Chequered skipper	2·20	2·00

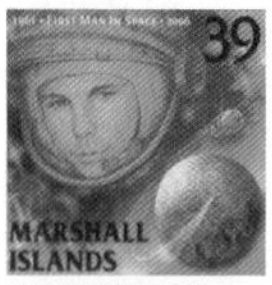

260 Yuri Gagarin, Vostok I and Earth

2006. 45th Anniv of First Manned Space Flight.

1959	**260**	39c. multicoloured	1·00	95

2006. Hibiscus (3rd issue). As T **247** showing cultivated varieties of Hibiscus. Multicoloured.

1960	10c. "Butterscotch Sundae"	25	25
1961	63c. "Magic Moments"	1·60	1·50
1962	84c. "Joanne Boulin"	2·20	2·00
1963	$4.05 "Capsicum Red"	10·00	9·25

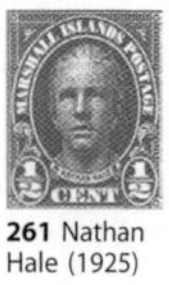

261 Nathan Hale (1925)

2006. Historical Stamps, 1922–25. Sheet 114×155 mm containing T **261** and similar designs showing stamps of America inscr "Marshall Island Postage". Colours given.

MS1964	½c. sepia (Type **261**); 1c. green (Benjamin Franklin) (1923); 1½c. brown (Warren G. Harding) (1925); 2c. carmine (George Washington) (1923); 3c. violet (Abraham Lincoln) (1923); 4c. brown (Martha Washington) (1923); 5c. blue (Theodore Roosevelt) (1922); 6c. red (James Garfield) (1922); 7c. black (William McKinley) (1922); 8c. green (Ulysses S. Grant) (1923); 9c. rose (Thomas Jefferson) (1923); 10c. orange (James Monroe) (1923); 11c. blue (Rutherford B. Hayes) (1922); 12c. plum (Grover Cleveland) (1923); 14c. indigo (Indian Chief) (1923); 15c. grey (Statue of Liberty); 20c. carmine (Golden Gate) (1923) (horiz); 25c. green (Niagara Falls) (1922) (horiz); 30c. brown (American bison) (1923) (horiz); 50c. green (Arlington Amphitheatre and Unknown Soldier's Tomb) (1922) (horiz)	6·00	5·50

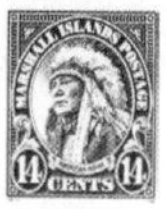

262 American 1923 14c. Stamp inscr "Marshall Island Postage"

2006. WASHINGTON 2006 International Stamp Exhibition. Sheet 115×90 mm containing T **262** and similar design showing stamps of America inscr "Marshall Island Postage". Imperf.

MS1965	14c. indigo; 30c. brown	1·30	1·20

DESIGNS: Type **262**; 30c. 1923 30c. stamp (bison).

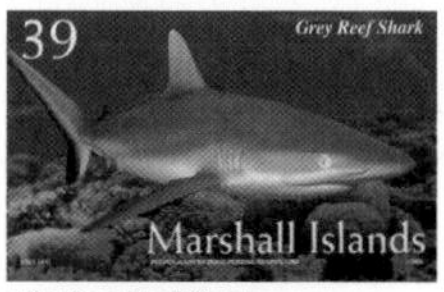

263 Grey Reef Shark

2006. Sharks. Multicoloured.

1966	39c. Type **263**	1·00	95
1967	39c. Silvertip	1·00	95
1968	39c. Blacktip	1·00	95
1969	39c. Whitetip	1·00	95

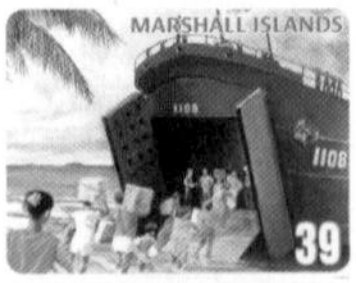

264 Evacuation (As Type **103**)

2006. 60th Anniv of Operation Crossroads (nuclear testing on Bikini Atoll). Multicoloured.

1970	39c. Type **264**	1·00	95
1971	39c. As No. 722	1·00	95
1972	39c. As No. 723	1·00	95
1973	39c. As No. 724	1·00	95
1974	39c. As No. 725	1·00	95
1975	39c. As No. 726	1·00	95

2006. Bicentenary of Meriwether Lewis and William Clark's Expedition to Explore the West Coast of America (7th issue). As T **232**. Multicoloured.

1976	37c. Leaving Sacagawea and Charbonneau	1·00	95
1977	37c. Returning to St. Louis	1·00	95

2006. Cultural Heritage (4th issue). As T **225** Multicoloured.

1978	39c. Harbour, Jabwor, Jaluit Atol	1·00	95
1979	39c. Irooj and family, Jabwor, Jaluit Atoll	1·00	95
1980	39c. Traditional voyaging canoe, Jaluit Atoll	1·00	95
1981	39c. Mission sisters and girls washing clothes, Jaluit	1·00	95
1982	39c. Traditional homes on Mile Atoll	1·00	95

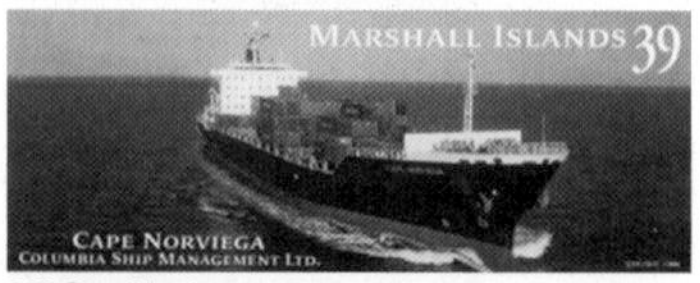

265 Cape Norviega

2006. Maritime and Corporate Registry. Multicoloured.

1983	39c. Type **265**	1·00	95
1984	39c. Front Century	1·00	95
1985	39c. Ashley	1·00	95
1986	39c. Ti Africa	1·00	95
1987	39c. Discoverer Enterprise	1·00	95
1988	39c. Genmar Spyridon	1·00	95
1989	39c. Rickmers New Orleans	1·00	95
1990	39c. Lng Aquarius	1·00	95
1991	39c. Centurion	1·00	95
1992	39c. Barkald	1·00	95

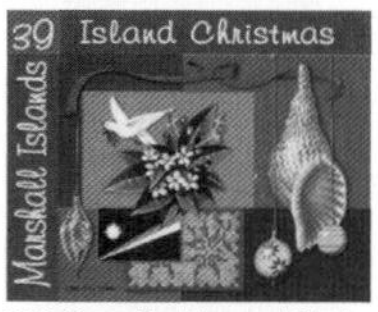

266 Dove, Baubles and Shell

2006. Christmas.

1993	**266**	39c. multicoloured	1·00	95

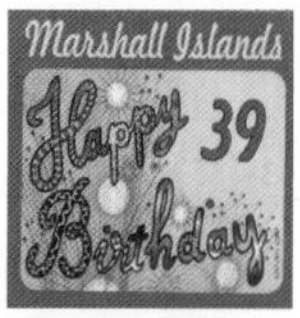

267 'Happy Birthday'

2007. Greetings Stamps. Multicoloured.

1994	39c. Type **267**	1·00	95
1995	39c. 'CONGRATULATIONS'	1·00	95
1996	39c. 'THANK YOU'	1·00	95
1997	39c. 'Best Wishes'	1·00	95

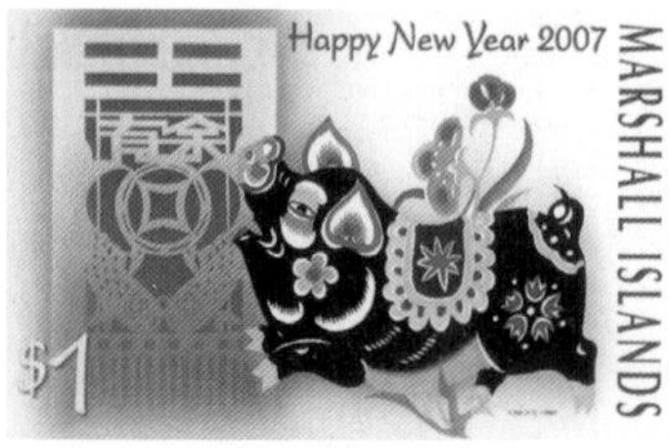

268 Pig

2007. New Year.Year of the Pig. Sheet 110×87 mm.

MS1998	**268** $1 multicoloured	2·50	2·30

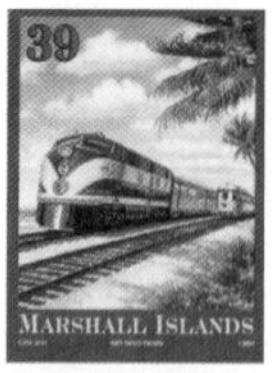

269 Inscr 'Art Deco Train'

2007. Trains. Multicoloured.

1999	39c. Type **269**	1·00	95
2000	39c. Pennsylvania electric locomotive GG1 4800	1·00	95
2001	39c. General Motors EMD E1 (Atchison, Topeka and Santa Fe Railway' No2A) pulling *Super Chief* streamliner (Inscr 'Santa Fe 'Chief')	1·00	95
2002	39c. Streamlined 4-4-2 class A steam locomotive pulling *Hiawatha* (Inscr 'Hiawatha')	1·00	95
2003	39c. 20th Century Limited	1·00	95
2004	39c. Southern Pacific GS-4 4-8-4 steam locomotive *Daylight*	1·00	95

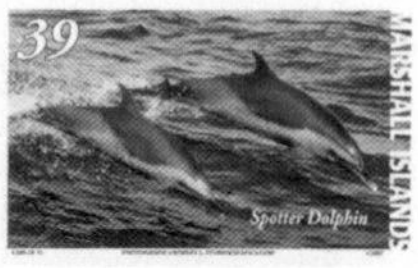

270 Spotted Dolphin (Inscr 'Spotter Dolphin')

2007. Dolphins. Multicoloured.

2005	39c. Type **270**	1·00	95
2006	39c. Bottlenose dolphin	1·00	95
2007	39c. Risso's dolphin	1·00	95
2008	39c. Common dolphin	1·00	95

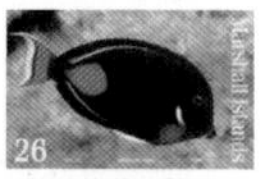

271 Achilles Tang

2007. Fish. Multicoloured.

2009	26c. Type **271**	70	65
2010	41c. Regal angelfish	1·10	1·00
2011	52c. Saddled butterflyfish	1·40	1·30
2012	61c. Tinker's butterflyfish	1·60	1·50

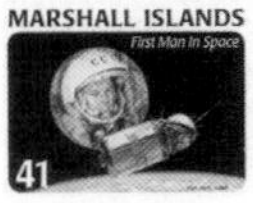

272 Yuri Gagarin (1st man in space)

2007. 50th Anniv of Space Exploration. Multicoloured.

2013	41c. Type **272**	1·00	95
2014	41c. *Sputnik* (1st man made satellite)	1·00	95
2015	41c. Neil Armstrong and Buzz Aldrin (1st men on the moon)	1·00	95
2016	41c. *Apollo-Soyuz* docking (1st joint USA—Soviet Union space programme)	1·00	95
2017	41c. Valentina Tereshkova (1st woman in space)	1·00	95
2018	41c. Lunar roving vehicle	1·00	95
2019	41c. Alexey Leonov (1st space walk)	1·00	95
2020	41c. *Viking 1* (1st landing on Mars)	1·00	95
2021	41c. *Venera 4* (1st probe on Venus)	1·00	95
2022	41c. John Glenn aboard *Friendship 7* (1st American in orbit)	1·00	95

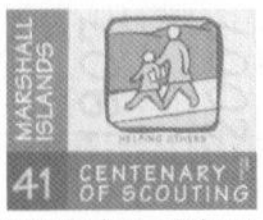

273 'Helping Others'

2007. Centenary of Scouting. Multicoloured.

2023	41c. Type **273**	1·00	95
2024	41c. 'Physically Strong'	1·00	95
2025	41c. 'Mentally Awake'	1·00	95
2026	41c. 'Fun and Adventure'	1·00	95

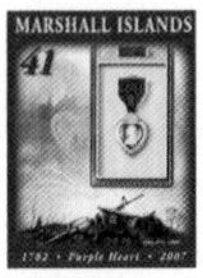

274 Purple Heart

2007. 225th Anniv of Purple Heart.

2027	**274** 41c. multicoloured	1·00	95

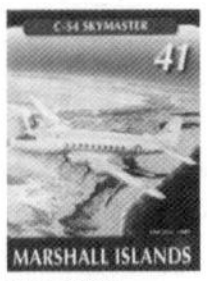

275 C-54 Skymaster

2007. 60th Anniv of USA Airforce. Multicoloured.

2028	41c. Type **275**	1·00	95
2029	41c. B-36 Peacemaker	1·00	95
2030	41c. F-86 Sabre	1·00	95
2031	41c. B-47 Stratojet	1·00	95
2032	41c. C-124 Globemaster	1·00	95
2033	41c. C-121 Constellation	1·00	95
2034	41c. B-52 Stratofortress	1·00	95
2035	41c. F-100 Super Sabre	1·00	95
2036	41c. F-104 Starfighter	1·00	95
2037	41c. C-130 Hercules	1·00	95
2038	41c. F-105 Thunderchief	1·00	95
2039	41c. KC-135 Stratotanker	1·00	95
2040	41c. B-58 Hustler	1·00	95
2041	41c. F-4 Phantom II	1·00	95
2042	41c. T-38 Talon	1·00	95
2043	41c. C-141 Starlifter	1·00	95
2044	41c. F-111 Aardvark	1·00	95
2045	41c. SR-71 *Blackbird*	1·00	95
2046	41c. C-5 Galaxy	1·00	95
2047	41c. A-10 Thunderbolt II	1·00	95
2048	41c. F-15 Eagle	1·00	95
2049	41c. F-16 Fighting Falcon	1·00	95
2050	41c. F-117 Nighthawk	1·00	95
2051	41c. B-2 Spirit	1·00	95
2052	41c. C-17 Globemaster III	1·00	95

2007. Cultural Heritage (5th issue). As T **225**. Multicoloured.

2053	41c. Lonkwon getting fish from his fish trap	1·00	95
2054	41c. Alele style fishing, Bilarek	1·00	95
2055	41c. Lanju and family	1·00	95
2056	41c. Outrigger with sail	1·00	95
2057	41c. Lien and Litublan collecting shells	1·00	95

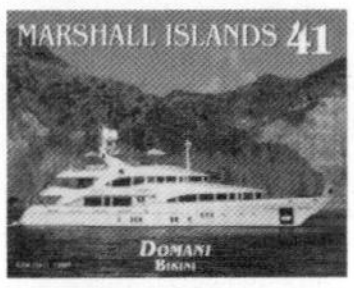

276 *Domani*, Bikini

2007. Marshall Island Maritime Registry. Yachts. Multicoloured.

2058	41c. Type **276**	1·00	95
2059	41c. *Excellence III*, Jaluit	1·00	95
2060	41c. *Aquasition*, Bikini	1·00	95
2061	41c. *Perfect Symmetry* 5, Jaluit	1·00	95
2062	41c. *Happy Days*, Bikini	1·00	95
2063	41c. *Mystique*, Jaluit	1·00	95
2064	41c. *Halcyon Days*, Jaluit	1·00	95
2065	41c. *Man of Steel*, Jaluit	1·00	95
2066	41c. *Marathon*, Bikini	1·00	95
2067	41c. *Sinbad*, Jaluit	1·00	95

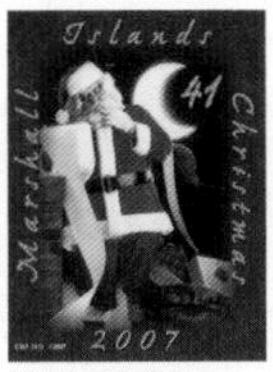

277 Santa Claus

2007. Christmas. Showing Santa Claus. Multicoloured.

2068	41c. Type **277**	1·00	95
2069	41c. Waving by fireplace	1·00	95
2070	41c. Holding present	1·00	95
2071	41c. Waving from sleigh	1·00	95

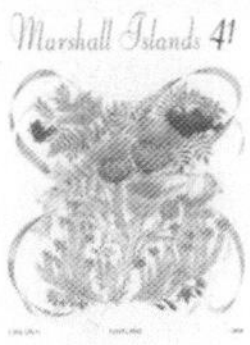

278 Scotland

2008. Greetings Stamps. Designs showing bouquets and country names. Multicoloured.

2072	41c. Type **278**	1·00	95
2073	41c. Jersey	1·00	95
2074	41c. Gibraltar	1·00	95
2075	41c. Dominica	1·00	95
2076	41c. Canada	1·00	95
2077	41c. Cyprus	1·00	95
2078	41c. Turks and Cacos Islands	1·00	95
2079	41c. Bahamas	1·00	95
2080	41c. Montserrat	1·00	95
2081	41c. Cayman Islands	1·00	95
2082	41c. Bangladesh	1·00	95
2083	41c. Falkland Islands	1·00	95
2084	41c. Grenada	1·00	95
2085	41c. Nevis	1·00	95
2086	41c. Jamaica	1·00	95
2087	41c. Australia	1·00	95
2088	41c. Fiji	1·00	95
2089	41c. New Hebrides	1·00	95
2090	41c. Pitcairn Islands	1·00	95
2091	41c. Cook Islands	1·00	95
2092	41c. Tonga	1·00	95
2093	41c. Seychelles	1·00	95
2094	41c. Zimbabwe	1·00	95
2095	41c. Christmas Island	1·00	95
2096	41c. Antigua	1·00	95

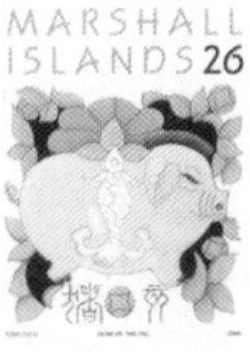

279 Year of the Pig

2008. Chinese New Year. Designs showing animals. Multicoloured.

2097	26c. Type **279**	65	60
2098	26c. Ram	65	60
2099	26c. Horse	65	60
2100	26c. Tiger	65	60
2101	26c. Dog	65	60
2102	26c. Rabbit	65	60
2103	26c. Dragon	65	60
2104	26c. Ox	65	60
2105	26c. Rooster	65	60
2106	26c. Monkey	65	60
2107	26c. Snake	65	60
2108	26c. Rat	65	60

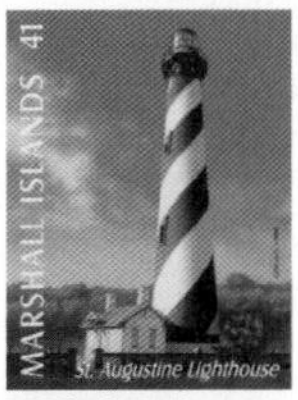

280 St. Augustine

2008. Lighthouses. Multicoloured.

2109	41c. Type **280**	1·00	95
2110	41c. Old Cape Henry	1·00	95
2111	41c. Cape Lookout	1·00	95
2112	41c. Tybee Island	1·00	95
2113	41c. Morris Island	1·00	95
2114	41c. Hillsboro Inlet	1·00	95

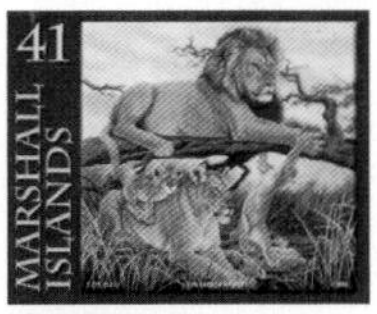

281 Lions

2008. Big Cats. Multicoloured.

2115	41c. Type **281**	1·00	95
2116	41c. Ocelots	1·00	95
2117	41c. White Siberian tigers	1·00	95
2118	41c. Tigers	1·00	95
2119	41c. Servals	1·00	95
2120	41c. Cougars	1·00	95
2121	41c. Lynx	1·00	95
2122	41c. Jaguars	1·00	95
2123	41c. Panthers	1·00	95
2124	41c. Clouded leopards	1·00	95
2125	41c. Cheetahs	1·00	95
2126	41c. Snow leopards	1·00	95

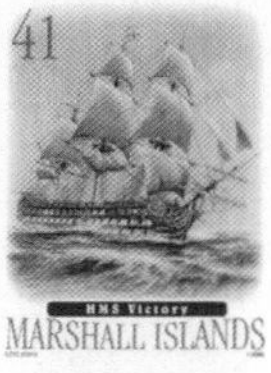

282 HMS *Victory*

2008. Sailing Ships. Multicoloured.

2127	41c. Type **282**	1·00	95
2128	41c. *La Grande Hermine*	1·00	95
2129	41c. *Constitution*	1·00	95
2130	41c. *Fram*	1·00	95
2131	41c. *Tovarisch I*	1·00	95
2132	41c. *Ark* and *Dove*	1·00	95
2133	41c. *Rainbow*	1·00	95
2134	41c. *Great Republic*	1·00	95
2135	41c. HMS *Resolution*	1·00	95
2136	41c. *La Dauphine*	1·00	95
2137	41c. *Kruzenshtern*	1·00	95
2138	41c. *Golden Hind*	1·00	95

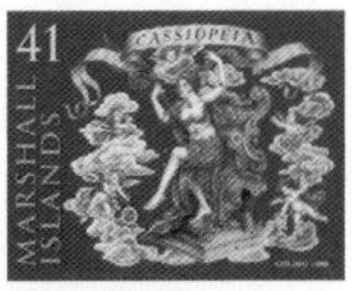

283 Cassiopeia

2008. Constellations. Multicoloured.

2139	41c. Type **283**	1·00	95
2140	41c. Ursa Major	1·00	95
2141	41c. Corvus	1·00	95
2142	41c. Camelopardalis	1·00	95
2143	41c. Cygnus	1·00	95
2144	41c. Andromeda	1·00	95
2145	41c. Capricornus	1·00	95
2146	41c. Canis Major	1·00	95
2147	41c. Dorado	1·00	95
2148	41c. Libra	1·00	95
2149	41c. Lynx	1·00	95
2150	41c. Serpentarius	1·00	95
2151	41c. Eridanus	1·00	95
2152	41c. Pavo	1·00	95
2153	41c. Orion	1·00	95
2154	41c. Leo Minor	1·00	95
2155	41c. Pegasus	1·00	95
2156	41c. Corona Borealis	1·00	95
2157	41c. Phoenix	1·00	95
2158	41c. Aquarius	1·00	95

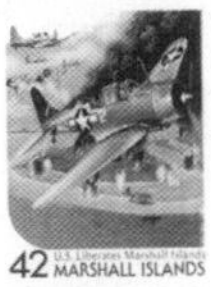

284 Aircraft ('USA liberates Marshall Islands')

2008. Marine Corps Heroes. Multicoloured.

2159	42c. Type **284**	1·00	95
2160	42c. John Lejune	1·00	95
2161	42c. Holland Smith	1·00	95
2162	42c. Smedley D. Butler	1·00	95
2163	42c. Daniel J. Daly	1·00	95
2164	42c. Lewis 'Chesty' Puller	1·00	95
2165	42c. John Basilone	1·00	95
2166	42c. Alexander Vandergrift	1·00	95
2167	42c. Gregory 'Pappy' Boyington	1·00	95
2168	42c. Marines raising flag on Iwo Jima	1·00	95

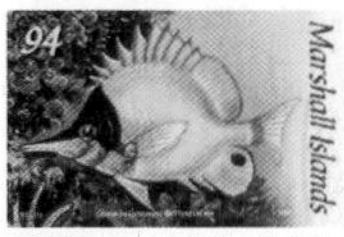

285 Longnose Butterflyfish

2008. Tropical Fish. Multicoloured.

2169	94c. Type **285**	2·40	2·20
2170	$4.80 Longfin bannerfish	12·50	11·50
2171	$16.50 Emperor butterflyfish	38·00	35·00

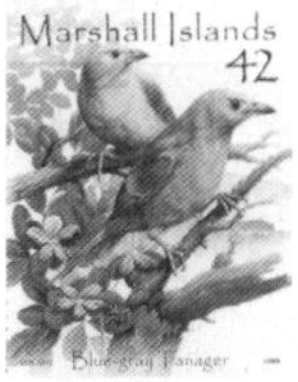

286 Blue-grey Tanager

2008. Birds. Multicoloured.

2172	42c. Type **286**	1·00	95
2173	42c. St. Vincent parrot	1·00	95
2174	42c. Green-throated carib	1·00	95
2175	42c. Yellow oriole	1·00	95
2176	42c. Blue-hooded euphonia	1·00	95
2177	42c. Crested honeycreeper	1·00	95
2178	42c. Purple-capped fruit dove	1·00	95
2179	42c. Green magpie	1·00	95
2180	42c. Bay-headed tanager	1·00	95
2181	42c. Bananaquit	1·00	95
2182	42c. Cardinal honeyeater	1·00	95
2183	42c. Toucan	1·00	95
2184	42c. Cattle egret	1·00	95
2185	42c. Ringed kingfisher	1·00	95
2186	42c. Red-necked parrot	1·00	95
2187	42c. Purple gallinule	1·00	95
2188	42c. Copper-rumped hummingbird	1·00	95
2189	42c. Micronesian pigeon	1·00	95
2190	42c. Painted bunting	1·00	95
2191	42c. Black-naped oriole	1·00	95
2192	42c. Channel-billed toucan	1·00	95
2193	42c. Saddle-billed stork	1·00	95
2194	42c. Blood pheasant	1·00	95
2195	42c. Grey crowned crane	1·00	95
2196	42c. Little blue heron	1·00	95

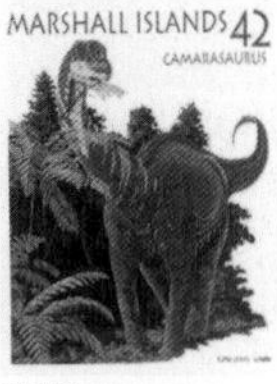

287 Camasaurus

2008. Dinosaurs. Multicoloured.

2197	42c. Type **287**	1·00	95
2198	42c. Allosaurus	1·00	95
2199	42c. Parasaurolophus	1·00	95
2200	42c. Ornithomimus	1·00	95
2201	42c. Goniopholis	1·00	95
2202	42c. Camptosaurus	1·00	95
2203	42c. Edmontia	1·00	95
2204	42c. Ceratosaurus	1·00	95
2205	42c. Stegosaurus	1·00	95
2206	42c. Einiosaurus	1·00	95
2207	42c. Brachiosaurus	1·00	95
2208	42c. Corythosaurus	1·00	95

2008. Tropical Fish. As T **285**. Multicoloured.

2209	27c. Copperband butterflyfish	70	65

2210	42c. Threadfin butterflyfish	1·00	95

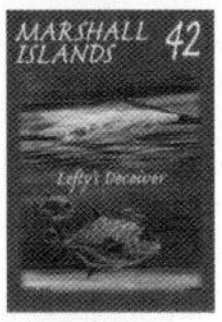

288 Lefty's Deceiver

2008. Fishing Flies. Sheet 70×134 mm containing T **288** and similar multicoloured designs.

MS2211	42c.×5, Type **288**; Apte Tarpon; Royal Wulff (50×47 mm); Muddler Minnow; Jock Scott	5·50	5·00

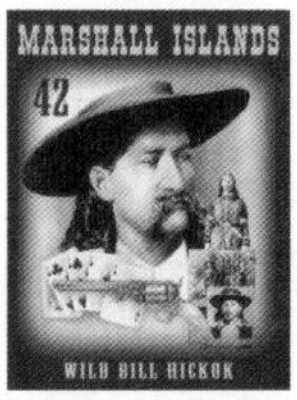

289 Wild Bill Hickok (gunfighter and scout)

2008. Wild West Characters. Multicoloured.

2212	42c. Type **289**	1·00	95
2213	42c. Jim Bridger (frontiersman)	1·00	95
2214	42c. Geronimo (leader of the Chiricahua Apache)	1·00	95
2215	42c. Charles Goodnight (cattle rancher)	1·00	95
2216	42c. Chief Joseph (humanitarian and peacemaker)	1·00	95
2217	42c. Kit Carson (frontiersman)	1·00	95
2218	42c. Jim Beckwourth (writer of *The Life and Adventures of James P. Beckwourth*)	1·00	95
2219	42c. Wyatt Earp (law officer known for his participation in the Gunfight at the O.K. Corral)	1·00	95
2220	42c. Bat Masterson (buffalo hunter, U.S. Marshal and columnist for New York Morning Telegraph)	1·00	95
2221	42c. Bill Pickett (cowboy and rodeo performer)	1·00	95
2222	42c. Bill Tilghman (lawman and gunslinger)	1·00	95
2223	42c. Annie Oakley (Phoebe Ann Mosey) (sharpshooter and exhibition shooter)	1·00	95
2224	42c. Buffalo Bill (William Frederick Cody) (soldier, bison hunter and showman)	1·00	95
2225	42c. Nellie Cashman (Angel of Tombstone) (philanthropist)	1·00	95
2226	42c. Sacagawea (Shoshone woman who accompanied the Lewis and Clark expedition to explore Western United States)	1·00	95
2227	42c. John Fremont (military officer, explorer, the first candidate of the Republican Party for the office of President)	1·00	95

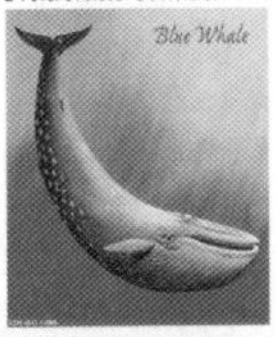

290 Blue Whale

2008. Endangered Species. Multicoloured.

2228	42c. Type **290**	1·00	95
2229	42c. Amazonian manatee	1·00	95
2230	42c. Hawaiian monk seal	1·00	95
2231	42c. Green turtle	1·00	95
2232	42c. Giant clam	1·00	95
2233	42c. Killer whale	1·00	95

2008. Tropical Fish. As T **285**. Multicoloured.

2234	1c. Banded butterflyfish	15	10
2235	3c. Damsel	15	10
2236	5c. Pink skunk clownfish	20	15
2237	60c. Beau gregory damsel	1·60	1·50
2238	61c. Porkfish	1·60	1·50
2239	63c. Goatfish	1·60	1·50
2240	$1 Royal gramma	2·50	2·30
2241	$4.05 Blue striped blenny	12·50	11·50

2008. Cultural Heritage (6th issue). As T **225**. Multicoloured.

2242	42c. Lokeinlik wearing traditional mat for men	1·00	95
2243	42c. Limekto weaving hat from kimej	1·00	95
2244	42c. Unfinished outrigger	1·00	95
2245	42c. Boys in Mejit	1·00	95
2246	42c. Lonkoon with fish trap	1·00	95

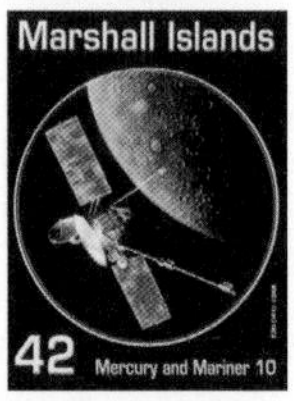

291 *Mariner 10* and Mercury

2008. Space Exploration. 50th Anniv of NASA. Multicoloured.

2247	42c. Type **291**	1·00	95
2248	42c. *Voyager 2* and Uranus	1·00	95
2249	42c. *Mariner 2* and Venus	1·00	95
2250	42c. *Voyager 2* and Pluto	1·00	95
2251	42c. *Pioneer 11* and Jupiter	1·00	95
2252	42c. *Landsat* and Earth	1·00	95
2253	42c. *Lunar Orbiter* and Moon	1·00	95
2254	42c. *Voyager 2* and Saturn	1·00	95
2255	42c. *Viking Orbiter* and Mars	1·00	95
2256	42c. *Voyager 2* and Neptune	1·00	95

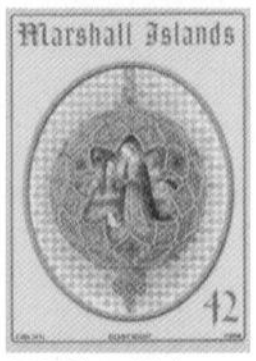

292 *Silent Night*

2008. Christmas Ornaments. Designs showing illustrations of Christmas carols and songs. Multicoloured.

2257	42c. Type **292**	1·00	95
2258	42c. *We Three Kings*	1·00	95
2259	42c. *Deck the Halls*	1·00	95
2260	42c. *Hark the Herald Angels Sing*	1·00	95
2261	42c. *O Little Town of Bethlehem*	1·00	95
2262	42c. *Joy to the World*	1·00	95
2263	42c. *Jingle Bells*	1·00	95
2264	42c. *O Come All Ye Faithful*	1·00	95

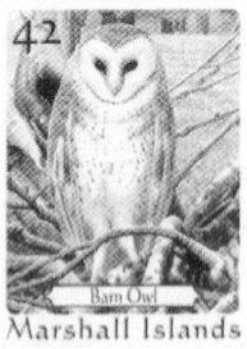

293 Barn Owl

2008. Owls. Multicoloured.

2265	42c. Type **293**	1·00	95
2266	42c. Barred owl	1·00	95
2267	42c. Burrowing owl	1·00	95
2268	42c. Snowy owl	1·00	95
2269	42c. Great horned owl	1·00	95
2270	42c. Spotted owl	1·00	95

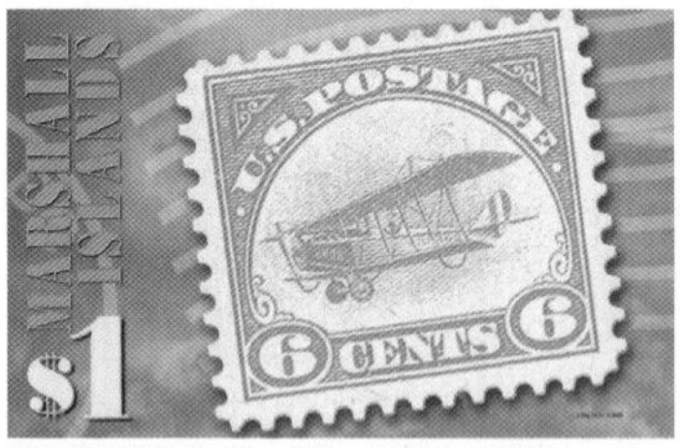

294 USA 1918 6c. Airmail Stamp (As Type **139**)

2008. 90th Anniv of First USA Airmail Stamp. Sheet 110×87 mm.

MS2271	**294** $1multicoloured	2·50	2·30

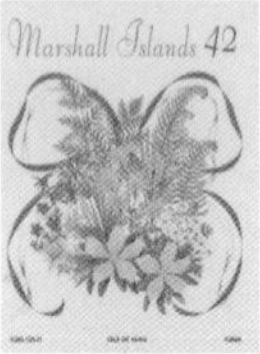

295 Isle of Man

2009. Greetings Stamps. Designs showing bouquets and country names. Multicoloured.

2272	42c. Type **295**	1·00	95
2273	42c. St Lucia	1·00	95
2274	42c. Grenada	1·00	95
2275	42c. Bermuda	1·00	95
2276	42c. Anguilla	1·00	95
2277	42c. Barbados	1·00	95
2278	42c. Belize	1·00	95
2279	42c. St Kitts	1·00	95
2280	42c. Hong Kong	1·00	95
2281	42c. British Virgin Islands	1·00	95
2282	42c. St Vincent	1·00	95
2283	42c. Tristan da Cunha	1·00	95
2284	42c. St Helena	1·00	95
2285	42c. British Antarctic Territory	1·00	95
2286	42c. St Vincent and the Grenadines	1·00	95
2287	42c. New Zealand	1·00	95
2288	42c. Papua New Guinea	1·00	95
2289	42c. Western Samoa	1·00	95
2290	42c. Solomon Islands	1·00	95
2291	42c. Brunei	1·00	95
2292	42c. Swaziland	1·00	95
2293	42c. Botswana	1·00	95
2294	42c. Maldives	1·00	95
2295	42c. Ghana	1·00	95
2296	42c. Sierra Leone	1·00	95

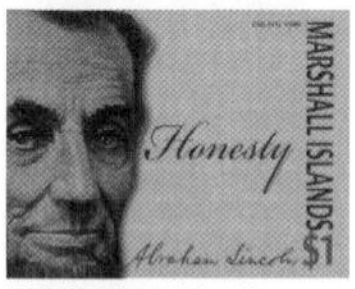

296 Abraham Lincoln (Honesty)

2009. Birth Bicentenary of Abraham Lincoln (USA president 1861–5). Multicoloured.

2297	$1 Type **296**	2·50	2·30
2298	$1 As Type **296** (Equality)	2·50	2·30
2299	$1 As Type **296** (Unity)	2·50	2·30
2300	$1 As Type **296** (Liberty)	2·50	2·30

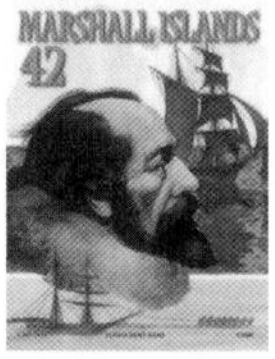

297 Elisha Kent Kane

2009. Centenary of Robert Peary's Expedition to North Pole. Multicoloured.

2301	42c. Type **297**	1·00	95
2302	42c. Robert Peary and Matthew Henson	1·00	95
2303	42c. Vilhjalmur Stefansson	1·00	95
2304	42c. Adolphus Washington Greely	1·00	95

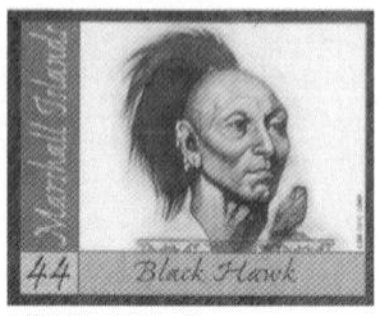

298 Black Hawk

2009. Native Americans. Multicoloured.

2305	44c. Type **298**	1·10	1·00
2306	44c. Colorow	1·10	1·00
2307	44c. Looking Glass	1·10	1·00
2308	44c. Dull Knife	1·10	1·00
2309	44c. Mangas Coloradas	1·10	1·00
2310	44c. Red Cloud	1·10	1·00
2311	44c. Little Raven	1·10	1·00
2312	44c. Black Kettle	1·10	1·00
2313	44c. Standing Bear	1·10	1·00
2314	44c. Little Crow	1·10	1·00
2315	44c. Seattle	1·10	1·00
2316	44c. Washakie	1·10	1·00

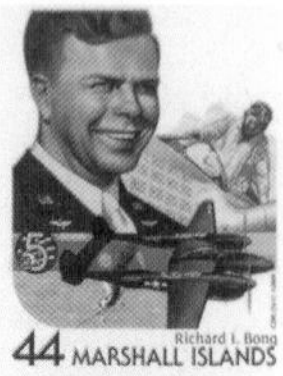

299 Richard I. Bong

2009. Military Heroes of the Air. Multicoloured.

2317	44c. Type **299**	1·10	1·00
2318	44c. Charles 'Chuck' Yeager	1·10	1·00
2319	44c. Lauris Norstad	1·10	1·00
2320	44c. William 'Billy' Mitchell	1·10	1·00
2321	44c. Curtis E. LeMay	1·10	1·00
2322	44c. Edward Henry O'Hare	1·10	1·00
2323	44c. Claire L. Chennault	1·10	1·00
2324	44c. George C. Kenney	1·10	1·00
2325	44c. James 'Jimmy' Doolittle	1·10	1·00
2326	44c. Paul W. Tibbets Jr.	1·10	1·00
2327	44c. Benjamin O. Davis Jr.	1·10	1·00
2328	44c. Carl 'Tooey' Spaatz	1·10	1·00
2329	44c. Ira C. Eaker	1·10	1·00
2330	44c. Edward 'Eddie' Rickenbacker	1·10	1·00
2331	44c. Henry 'Hap' Arnold	1·10	1·00
2332	44c. Outrigger canoe and Marshall Islands	1·10	1·00

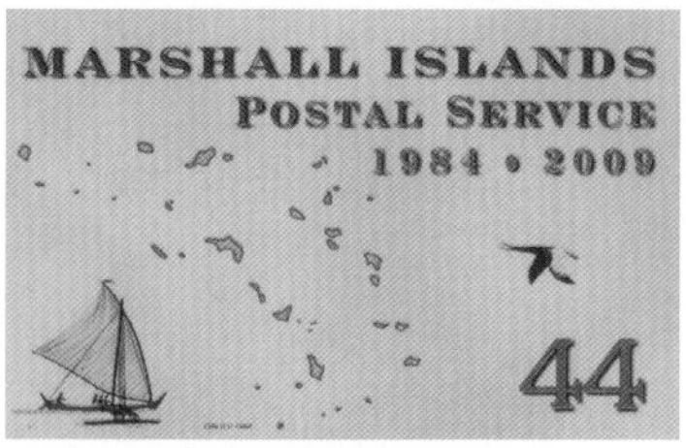

300 Outrigger Canoe and Islands

2009. 25th Anniv of Marshall Islands Postal Service. Sheet 110×87 mm.

MS2333	**300** 44c. multicoloured	1·10	1·00

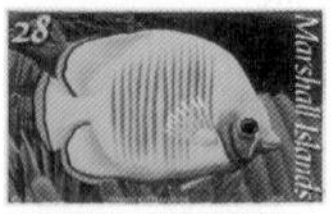

301 Masked Butterflyfish

2009. Marine Fauna. Multicoloured.

2334	28c. Type **301**	70	65
2335	44c. Queen angelfish	1·10	1·00
2336	88c. Clownfish	2·20	2·00
2337	98c. Starfish	2·50	2·30
2338	$1.22 Orca whales	3·00	2·75

2009. Constellations. As T **283**. Multicoloured.

2339	44c. Antinous	1·10	1·00
2340	44c. Aquilla	1·10	1·00
2341	44c. Cancer	1·10	1·00
2342	44c. Canis minor	1·10	1·00
2343	44c. Leo	1·10	1·00
2344	44c. Ara	1·10	1·00
2345	44c. Sextans uraniae	1·10	1·00
2346	44c. Cephus	1·10	1·00
2347	44c. Apus	1·10	1·00
2348	44c. Indus	1·10	1·00
2349	44c. Ursa minor	1·10	1·00
2350	44c. Grus	1·10	1·00
2351	44c. Centaurus	1·10	1·00
2352	44c. Cetus	1·10	1·00
2353	44c. Pisces volans	1·10	1·00
2354	44c. Lupus	1·10	1·00
2355	44c. Equuleus	1·10	1·00
2356	44c. Draco	1·10	1·00
2357	44c. Bootes		
2358	44c. Scorpius	1·10	1·00

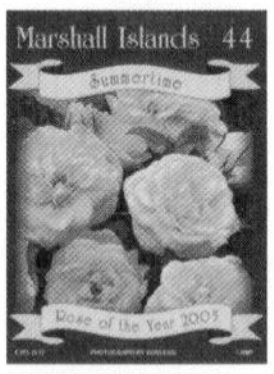

302 'Summertime'

2008. Roses. Multicoloured.

2359	44c. Type **302**	1·10	1·00
2360	44c. Champagne Moment	1·10	1·00
2361	44c. Tickled Pink	1·10	1·00
2362	44c. Sweet Haze	1·10	1·00
2363	44c. Lucky!	1·10	1·00

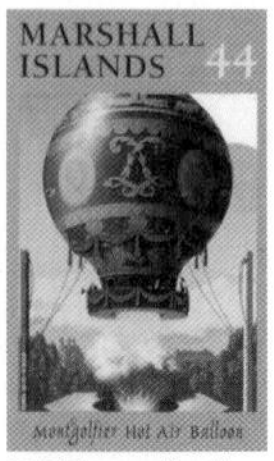

303 Montgolfier Hot Air Balloon

2009. Hot Air Balloons. Multicoloured.

2364	44c. Type **303**	1·10	1·00
2365	44c. *Intrepid*	1·10	1·00
2366	44c. *ExplorerII*	1·10	1·00
2367	44c. *Double Eagle*	1·10	1·00
2368	44c. Contemporary hot air balloons	1·10	1·00

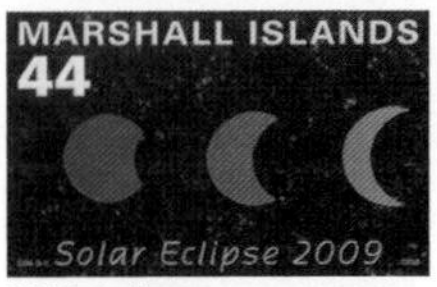

304 Early Phase

2009. Solar Eclipse–2009, Marshall Islands. Multicoloured.

2369	44c. Type **304**	1·10	1·00
2370	44c. Eclipse	1·10	1·00
2371	44c. Final phase		

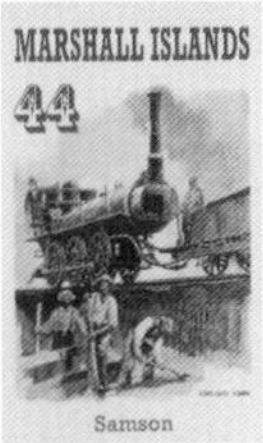

305 *Samson*

2009. Steam Locomotives. Multicoloured.

2372	44c. Type **305**	1·10	1·00
2373	44c. *Best Friend of Charleston*	1·10	1·00
2374	44c. *John Bull*	1·10	1·00
2375	44c. *Gowan & Marx*	1·10	1·00
2376	44c. *Stourbridge Lion*	1·10	1·00
2377	44c. *Brother Jonathan*		

2009. Cultural Heritage (7th issue). As T **225**. Multicoloured.

2378	44c. Making arrowroot	1·10	1·00
2379	44c. Boats and lagoon	1·10	1·00
2380	44c. Family in front of house with pandanus roof	1·10	1·00
2381	44c. Man carrying fish trap	1·10	1·00
2382	44c. Weaving baskets	1·10	1·00

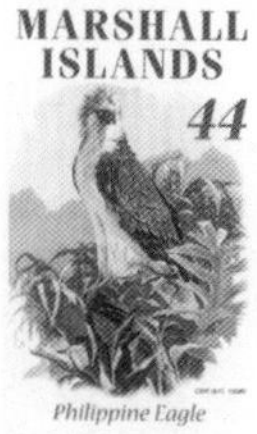

306 Philippine Eagle

2008. Eagles. Multicoloured.

2383	44c. Type **306**	1·10	1·00
2384	44c. Tawny eagle	1·10	1·00
2385	44c. Martial eagle	1·10	1·00
2386	44c. Bald eagle	1·10	1·00
2387	44c. African fish eagle	1·10	1·00
2388	44c. Bateleur eagle		
2389	44c. Golden eagle	1·10	1·00
2390	44c. Harpy eagle	1·10	1·00

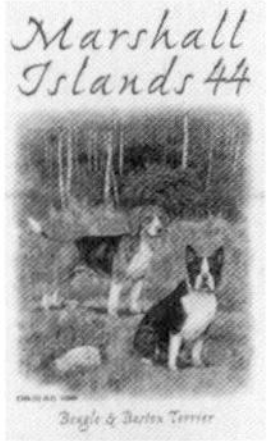

307 Beagle and Boston Terrier

2009. Dogs. Multicoloured.

2391	44c. Type **307**	1·10	1·00
2392	44c. Chesapeake Bay retriever and cocker spaniel	1·10	1·00
2393	44c. Alaskan malamute and collie	1·10	1·00
2394	44c. Water spaniel and basset hound	1·10	1·00
2395	44c. Coonhound and foxhound	1·10	1·00

MS2396 140×102 mm. All horiz. 98c.×4, Old English sheepdog; Irish setter; Welsh springer spaniel; West Highland terrier 5·00 4·75

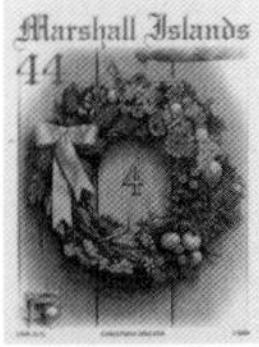

308 Christmas Wreath

2009. Christmas Wreaths. Designs showing wreaths. Multicoloured.

2397	44c. Type **308**	1·10	1·00
2398	44c. Traditional	1·10	1·00
2399	44c. Tropical	1·10	1·00
2400	44c. Colonial	1·10	1·00
2401	44c. Chilli	1·10	1·00

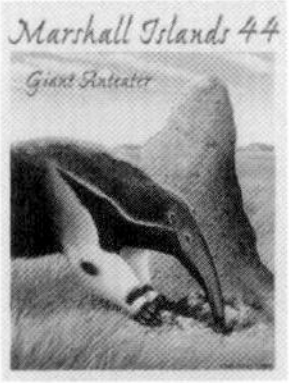

309 Giant Anteater

2009. Endangered Species. Multicoloured.

2402	44c. Type **309**	1·10	1·00
2403	44c. Caracal	1·10	1·00
2404	44c. Yak	1·10	1·00
2405	44c. Giant panda	1·10	1·00
2406	44c. Black-footed ferret	1·10	1·00
2407	44c. Black rhinoceros	1·10	1·00
2408	44c. Golden lion tamarin	1·10	1·00
2409	44c. African elephant	1·10	1·00
2410	44c. Persian fallow deer	1·10	1·00
2411	44c. Polar bear	1·10	1·00
2412	44c. Ocelot	1·10	1·00
2413	44c. Gorilla	1·10	1·00

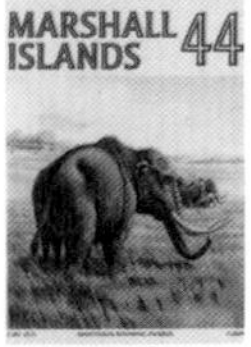

310 Mastodon in Grasslands

2009. Prehistoric Animals. Multicoloured.

2414	44c. Type **310**	1·10	1·00
2415	44c. Eohippus	1·10	1·00
2416	44c. Woolly mammoth	1·10	1·00
2417	44c. Sabre-toothed cat	1·10	1·00
2418	44c. Mastodon mother and calf drinking	1·10	1·00

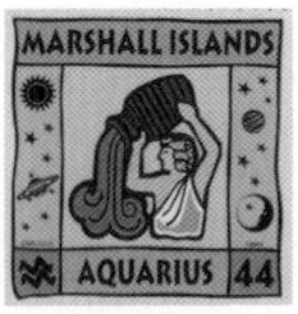

312 Aquarius

2010. Signs of the Zodiac. Multicoloured.

2423	44c. Type **312**	1·10	1·00
2424	44c. Pisces	1·10	1·00
2425	44c. Aries	1·10	1·00
2426	44c. Taurus	1·10	1·00
2427	44c. Gemini	1·10	1·00
2428	44c. Cancer	1·10	1·00
2429	44c. Leo	1·10	1·00
2430	44c. Virgo	1·10	1·00
2431	44c. Libra	1·10	1·00
2432	44c. Scorpio	1·10	1·00
2433	44c. Sagittarius	1·10	1·00
2434	44c. Capricorn	1·10	1·00

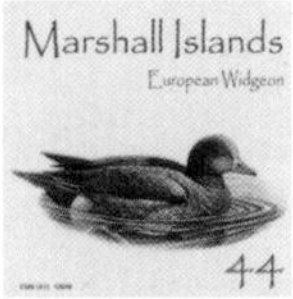

313 European Widgeon

2010. Waterfowl. Multicoloured.

2435	44c. Type **313**	1·10	1·00
2436	44c. Tufted duck	1·10	1·00
2437	44c. Mallard	1·10	1·00
2439	44c. Gadwall	1·10	1·00
2439	44c. Snow goose	1·10	1·00
2440	44c. Pintail	1·10	1·00
2441	44c. Northern shoveler	1·10	1·00
2442	44c. Canvasback	1·10	1·00

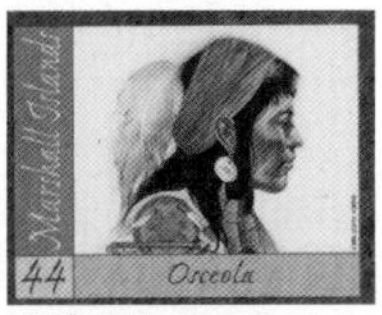

314 Osceola

2010. Native American Personalities. Multicoloured.

2443	44c. Type **314**	1·10	1·00
2444	44c. Lone Wolf	1·10	1·00
2445	44c. Menawa	1·10	1·00
2446	44c. Wabasha	1·10	1·00
2447	44c. Captain Jack	1·10	1·00
2448	44c. Quanah Parker	1·10	1·00
2449	44c. Ouray	1·10	1·00
2450	44c. Manuelito	1·10	1·00
2451	44c. Cochise	1·10	1·00
2452	44c Satanta	1·10	1·00
2453	44c. Massasoit	1·10	1·00
2454	44c. Red Eagle	1·10	1·00

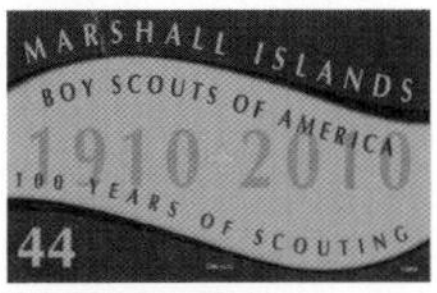

315 Anniversary Emblem

2010. Centenary of American Boy Scout Movement

2455	**315**	44c. multicoloured	1·10	1·00
2456		44c. multicoloured	1·10	1·00
2457		44c. multicoloured	1·10	1·00
2458		44c. multicoloured	1·10	1·00

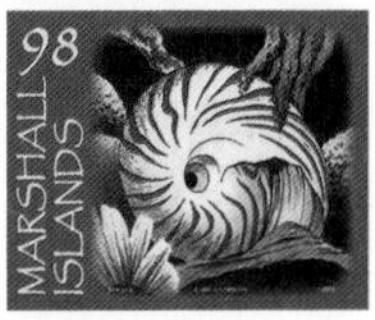

316 Gibbula Magus

2010. Sea Shells. Multicoloured.

2459	98c. Type **316**	2·00	1·90
2460	98c. Paper Nautilus	2·00	1·90
2460	98c. Giant Tun	2·00	1·90
2462	98c. Pilgrims Scallop	2·00	1·90

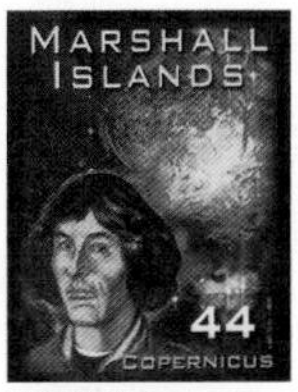

317 Nicolaus Copernicus

2010. Early Astronomers. Multicoloured.

2463	44c. Type **317**	1·10	1·00
2464	44c. Johannes Kepler	1·10	1·00
2465	44c. Galileo Galilei	1·10	1·00
2466	44c. Isaac Newton	1·10	1·00
2467	44c. Wilhelm Hirschel	1·10	1·00

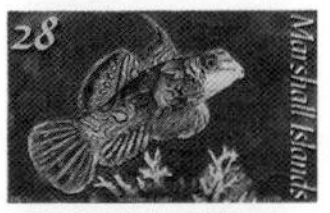

318 Mandarin Goby

2010. Fish

2468	**318**	28c. multicoloured	55	50

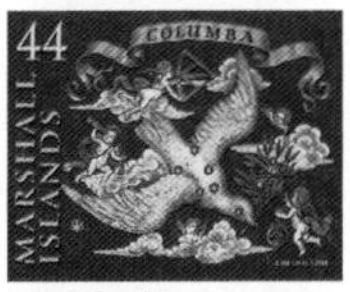

319 Columbia

2010. Constellations. Multicoloured.

2469	44c. Type **319**	1·10	1·00
2470	44c. Virgo	1·10	1·00
2471	44c. Argo Navis	1·10	1·00
2472	44c. Toucan	1·10	1·00
2473	44c. Aries	1·10	1·00
2474	44c. Coma Bernices	1·10	1·00
2475	44c. Delphinus	1·10	1·00
2476	44c. Perseus	1·10	1·00
2477	44c. Taurus	1·10	1·00
2478	44c. Monoceros	1·10	1·00
2479	44c. Gemini	1·10	1·00
2480	44c. Vulpecula	1·10	1·00
2481	44c. Lepus	1·10	1·00
2482	44c. Auriga	1·10	1·00
2483	44c. Pisces	1·10	1·00
2484	44c. Sagittarius	1·10	1·00
2485	44c. Crater	1·10	1·00
2486	44c. Lyra	1·10	1·00
2487	44c. Hercules	1·10	1·00
2488	44c. Canes Venatici	1·10	1·00

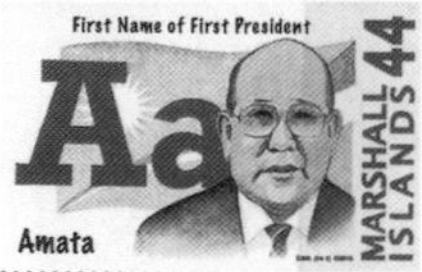

320 Aa Amata (first name of First President)

2010. Marshallese Alphabet. Multicoloured.

2489	44c. Type **320**	1·10	1·00
2490	44c. Āā Āj ('to weave')	1·10	1·00
2491	44c. Bb Babbub (butterfly)	1·10	1·00
2492	44c. Dd Deo ('beautiful young lady')	1·10	1·00
2493	44c. Ee Ek (fish)	1·10	1·00
2494	44c. Ii Iokwe ('you are a rainbow')	1·10	1·00
2495	44c. Jj Jaki (mat)	1·10	1·00
2496	44c. Kk Imon Kien (House of Government)	1·10	1·00
2497	44c. Ll Lokantur ('Capella, mother of all great stars')	1·10	1·00
2498	44c. Ll Lokwajek (red-tailed tropic bird)	1·10	1·00
2499	44c. Mm Ma (breadfruit)	1·10	1·00
2500	44c. Mm Makmok (arrowroot)	1·10	1·00
2501	44c. Nn Ni (coconut tree)	1·10	1·00
2502	44c. Nn No (ocean wave)	1·10	1·00
2503	44c. Nn Niin-pako (shark tooth)	1·10	1·00
2504	44c. Oo Ok (fish net)	1·10	1·00
2505	44c. Oo Eo (tattoo)	1·10	1·00
2506	44c. Ōō Ōō (lionfish)	1·10	1·00
2507	44c. Pp Pelak (visitor's hut)	1·10	1·00
2508	44c. Rr Raj (whale)	1·10	1·00
2509	44c. Tt Tipnōl (outrigger sailing canoe)	1·10	1·00
2510	44c. Uu Urur (fire)	1·10	1·00
2511	44c. Ūū Ūlin-raj (dorsal fin of whale)	1·10	1·00
2512	44c. Ww Wōjlā (woven pandanus leaf sail)	1·10	1·00

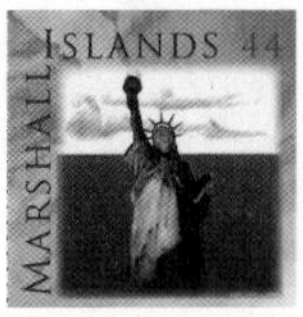

321 Statue of Liberty

2010. 125th Anniv of Statue of Liberty (designed by Frédéric-Auguste Bartholdi). Multicoloured.

MS2513 44c.×9, Type **321**; At night; With storm clouds behind; Head and arm with lights lit and flag behind; Head and arm, with close up of head and Frédéric-Auguste Bartholdi behind; Head, arm and book; Head only; Torch only; Head with lights lit 9·50 9·50

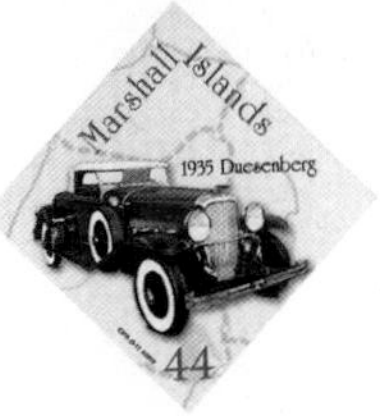

322 Duesenberg (1935)

2010. Classic Cars. Multicoloured.

MS2514 44c.×5, Type **322**; Packard (1932); Locomobile (1928); Cord (1931); Pierce Arrow (1929) 5·00 5·00

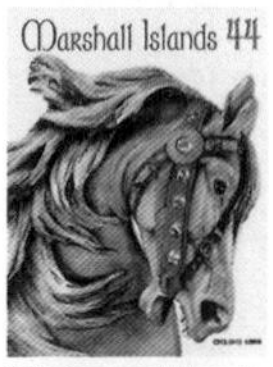

323 Carousel Horse's Head

2010. Carousel Horses. Multicoloured.

2515	44c. Type **323**	1·10	1·00
2516	44c. Dun, with black mane and red bridle	1·10	1·00
2517	44c. Palamino, with armoured head and neck covering	1·10	1·00
2518	44c. Palamino, with pale mane and blue acoutrements	1·10	1·00
2519	44c. Black, with red and yellow bridle	1·10	1·00
2520	44c. Grey, with yellow and red bridle	1·10	1·00

552 **Marshall Islands**

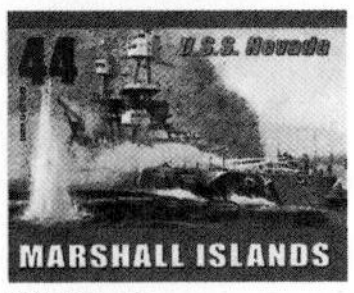
44
U.S.S. Nevada
MARSHALL ISLANDS

324 Nevada

2010. World War II Warships of the South Pacific. Multicoloured.

2521	44c. Type **324**	1·10	1·00
2522	44c. *Missouri*	1·10	1·00
2523	44c. *Wisconsin*	1·10	1·00
2524	44c. *Oregon*	1·10	1·00
2525	44c. *Massachusetts*	1·10	1·00
2526	44c. *North Carolina*	1·10	1·00
2527	44c. *Texas*	1·10	1·00
2528	44c. *Idaho*	1·10	1·00
2529	44c. *New Jersey*	1·10	1·00
2530	44c. *Colorado*	1·10	1·00
2531	44c. *South Dakota*	1·10	1·00
2532	44c. *New Mexico*	1·10	1·00
2533	44c. *Washington*	1·10	1·00
2534	44c. *Iowa*	1·10	1·00
2535	44c. *Iowa*	1·10	1·00

2010. Sea Shells. Multicoloured.

2536	28c. Pilgrim's scallop	55	50
2537	98c. *Gibbula magus*	2·00	1·90

As Type **316**.

2010. Cultural Heritage (8th issue). Multicoloured.

2538	44c. Church buildings, Likiep, c.1912	1·10	1·00
2539	44c. Ijuran ready to launch, c.1921	1·10	1·00
2540	44c. Islanders, c.1904	1·10	1·00
2541	44c. Lejek with fish trap on Korkor, Likiep Lagoon, c.1920	1·10	1·00
2542	44c. Landscape with outrigger and sailboat, c.1904	1·10	1·00

As Type **225**.

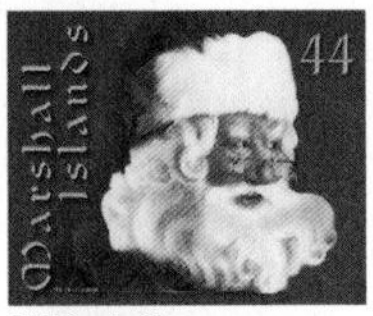
Marshall Islands
44

325 Santa Claus

2010. Christmas. Multicoloured.

2543	44c. Type **325**	1·10	1·00
2544	44c. Reading list	1·10	1·00
2545	44c. Facing left, head tilted to right	1·10	1·00
2546	44c. Facing left, laughing	1·10	1·00

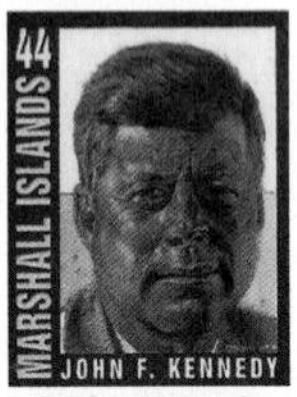
44
MARSHALL ISLANDS
JOHN F. KENNEDY

326 John F. Kennedy (Mark Sculer)

2010. 50th Anniv of John F. Kennedy's Election. Multicoloured.

2547	44c. Type **326**	1·10	1·00
2548	44c. Facing left (Mort Kunstler)	1·10	1·00
2549	44c. With eyes downcast (Ed Vebell)	1·10	1·00
2550	44c. Facing right (Paul and Chris Calle)	1·10	1·00
2551	44c. Facing front (Dean Ellis)	1·10	1·00
2552	44c. In profile (Paul Calle)	1·10	1·00

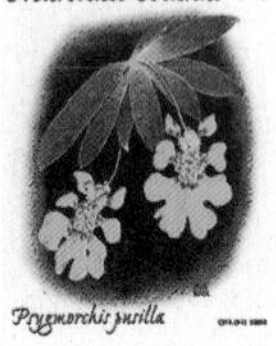
Marshall Islands 44

327 *Psygmorchis pusilla*

2010. Endangered Species. Multicoloured.

2553	44c. Type **327**	1·10	1·00
2554	44c. *Cycnoches*	1·10	1·00
2555	44c. *Aerangis modesta*	1·10	1·00
2556	44c. *Ansellia africana*	1·10	1·00
2557	44c. *Vanda coerulea*	1·10	1·00
2558	44c. *Dendrobium cruentum*	1·10	1·00
2559	44c. *Phragmipedium kovachii*	1·10	1·00
2560	44c. *Cymbidium ensifolium*	1·10	1·00
2561	44c. *Laelia milleri*	1·10	1·00

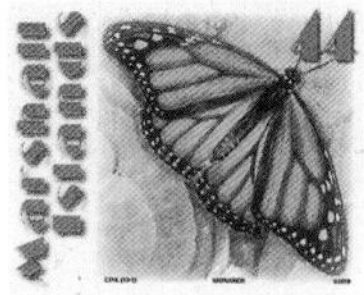
Marshall Islands
44

328 Monarch

2010. Butterflies. Multicoloured.

2562	44c. Type **328**	1·10	1·00
2563	44c. Brimstone	1·10	1·00
2564	44c. Blue-spotted hairstreak	1·10	1·00
2565	44c. Small tortoiseshell	1·10	1·00
2566	44c. Small skipper	1·10	1·00
2567	44c. Large blue	1·10	1·00
2568	44c. Large copper	1·10	1·00
2569	44c. Eastern orange tip	1·10	1·00
2570	44c. Red admiral	1·10	1·00
2571	44c. American painted lady	1·10	1·00
2572	44c. Great eggfly	1·10	1·00
2573	44c. Dark green fritillary	1·10	1·00

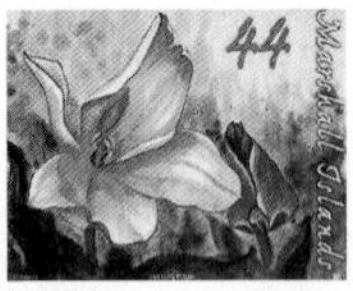
44
Marshall Islands

329 Tulips

2011. Tulips. Multicoloured.

2574	44c. Type **329**	1·10	1·00
2575	44c. Bowl of tulips	1·10	1·00
2576	44c. Mauve and purple tulips	1·10	1·00
2577	44c. Orange tulip	1·10	1·00
2578	44c. Orange and yellow tuips	1·10	1·00
2579	44c. Large orange and two smaller tulips	1·10	1·00

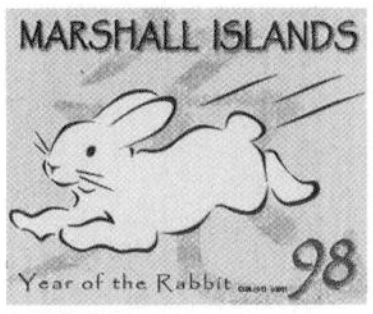
MARSHALL ISLANDS
Year of the Rabbit
98

330 Rabbit

2011. Chinese New Year. Year of the Rabbit. Multicoloured, background colour given.

2580	98c. Type **330**	2·20	2·00
2581	98c. As Type **330** (carmine)	2·20	2·00
2582	98c. As Type **330** (orange-brown)	2·20	2·00
2583	98c. AsType **330** (bottle-green)	2·20	2·00

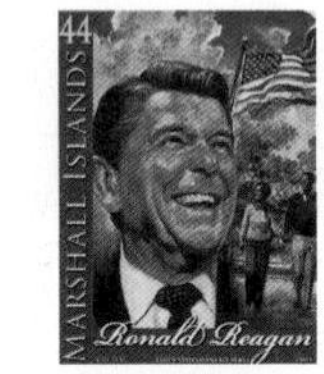
44
MARSHALL ISLANDS
Ronald Reagan

331 Ronald Reagan

2011. Birth Centenary of Ronald Reagan. Multicoloured.

2584	44c. Type **331**	1·10	1·00
2585	44c. As young man with radio microphone	1·10	1·00
2586	44c. As an cinema actor	1·10	1·00
2587	44c. As Governor of California	1·10	1·00
2588	44c. As President of USA	1·10	1·00

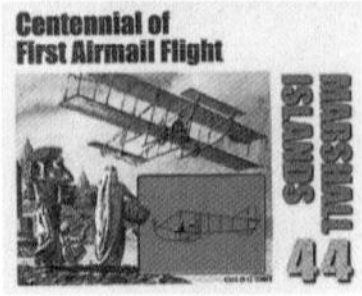
Centennial of
First Airmail Flight
MARSHALL ISLANDS
44

332 Centenary of First Airmail Flight

2011. Firsts in Flight (1st series). The Mail Takes Flight. Multicoloured.

2590	44c. Type **332**	1·10	1·00
2591	44c. First Airmail Service in America	1·10	1·00
2592	44c. First U.S. Coast-to-Coast Airmail Service	1·10	1·00
2593	44c. First Permanent U.S. Transcontinental Airmail Service	1·10	1·00
2594	44c. First International Airmail Service	1·10	1·00

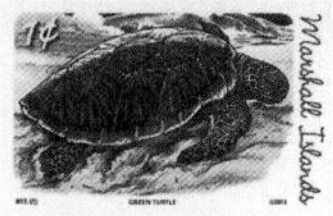
1c
Marshall Islands

333 Green Turtle

2011. Sea Turtles. Multicoloured.

2595	1c. Type **333**	25	20
2596	2c. Loggerhead turtle	30	25
2597	5c. Leatherhead turtle	35	30
2598	$10 Hawksbill turtle	14·00	13·00

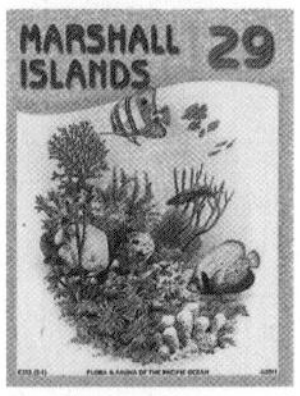
MARSHALL ISLANDS 29

334 Flora and Fauna of the Seabed

2011. Corals. Multicoloured.

2599	29c. Type **334**	80	75
2600	29c. Chalis coral	80	75
2601	29c. Elkhorn coral	80	75
2602	29c. Brain coral	80	75
2603	29c. Finger coral	80	75

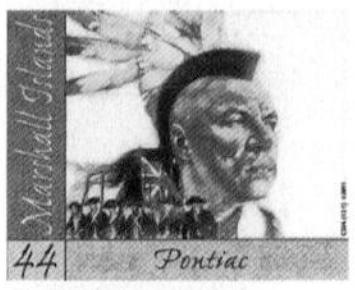
Marshall Islands
44
Pontiac

335 Pontiac

2011. Native American Personalities. Multicoloured.

2604	44c. Type **335**	1·10	1·00
2605	44c. Barboncito	1·10	1·00
2606	44c. Geronimo	1·10	1·00
2607	44c. Victorio	1·10	1·00
2608	44c. Sitting Bull	1·10	1·00
2609	44c. Cornplanter	1·10	1·00
2610	44c. Uncas	1·10	1·00
2611	44c. Little Wolf	1·10	1·00
2612	44c. Crazy Horse	1·10	1·00
2613	44c. Gall	1·10	1·00
2614	44c. Joseph	1·10	1·00
2615	44c. Tecumseh	1·10	1·00

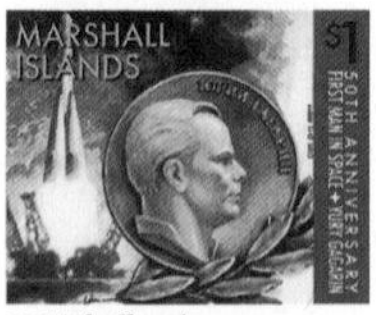
MARSHALL ISLANDS
$1

336 Liftoff and Commemorative Medal

2011. 50th Anniv of First Manned Space Flight. Multicoloured.

2616	$1 Type **336**	2·25	2·10
2617	$1 Yuri Gagarin and orbit of globe	2·25	2·10
2618	$1 Yuri Gagarin (statue), Moscow and medal	2·25	2·10

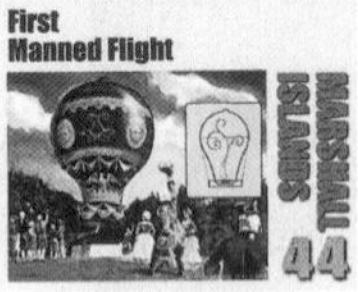
First
Manned Flight
MARSHALL ISLANDS
44

337 First Manned Flight

2011. Firsts in Flight (2nd series). Learning to Fly. Multicoloured.

2619	44c. Type **337**	1·10	1·00
2620	44c. First Manned Flight of Semi-Controlled Airship	1·10	1·00
2621	44c. First Powered Aircraft Leaves the Ground	1·10	1·00
2622	44c. First Manned Flight of Powered, Controlled Airship	1·10	1·00
2623	44c. First Controlled, Powered Flight	1·10	1·00

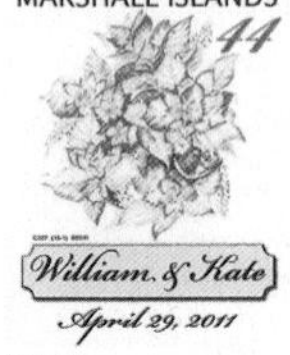
MARSHALL ISLANDS
44
William & Kate
April 29, 2011

338 Flowers

2011. Royal Wedding of Prince William and Catherine Middleton. Multicoloured.

2624	44c. Type **338**	1·10	1·00
2625	44c. Yellow flowers	1·10	1·00
2626	44c. Blue harebells	1·10	1·00
2627	44c. White convolvulus with dark centres	1·10	1·00
2628	44c. Reddish brown flowers	1·10	1·00
2629	44c. White hibiscus	1·10	1·00
2630	44c. Purple and white orchids	1·10	1·00
2631	44c. Datura flowers	1·10	1·00
2632	44c. Pink nerines	1·10	1·00
2633	44c. Bouquet of white flowers	1·10	1·00
2634	44c. Yellow and brown flowers	1·10	1·00
2635	44c. Pink pom-pom shaped flowers	1·10	1·00
2636	44c. White flowers and green and white sprays	1·10	1·00
2637	44c. Yellow trumpet shaped flowers	1·10	1·00
2638	44c. White datura flowers with pink edges	1·10	1·00

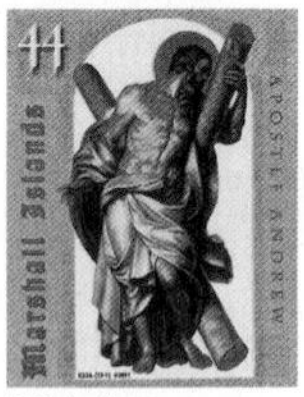
44
Marshall Islands
APOSTLE ANDREW

339 Andrew

2011. 400th Anniv of King James Bible. Multicoloured.

2639	44c. Type **339**	1·10	1·00
2640	44c. Philip	1·10	1·00
2641	44c. Simon	1·10	1·00
2642	44c. James (inscr 'the lesser')	1·10	1·00
2643	44c. Paul	1·10	1·00
2644	44c. Matthew	1·10	1·00
2645	44c. James (inscr 'the greater')	1·10	1·00
2646	44c. Jude (inscr 'Thaddeus')	1·10	1·00
2647	44c. Peter	1·10	1·00
2648	44c. John	1·10	1·00
2649	44c. Bartholomew	1·10	1·00
2650	44c. Thomas	1·10	1·00

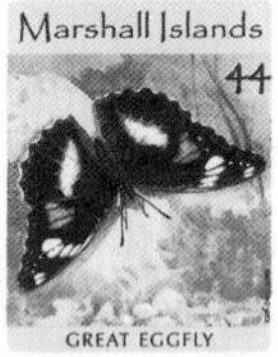
Marshall Islands
44
GREAT EGGFLY

340 Great Eggfly

2011. Garden Fauna and Flora. Multicoloured.

2651	44c. Type **340**	1·10	1·00
2652	44c. Passion flower	1·10	1·00
2653	44c. Ladybird (inscr 'Ladybug')	1·10	1·00
2654	44c. Emperor dragonfly	1·10	1·00
2655	44c. Sweet white violet	1·10	1·00
2656	44c. Magpie moth	1·10	1·00
2657	44c. Bluets	1·10	1·00
2658	44c. Katydid	1·10	1·00
2659	44c. Painted Lady	1·10	1·00
2660	44c. Bumble bee	1·10	1·00
2661	44c. Stag beetle	1·10	1·00
2662	44c. Large tortoiseshell	1·10	1·00

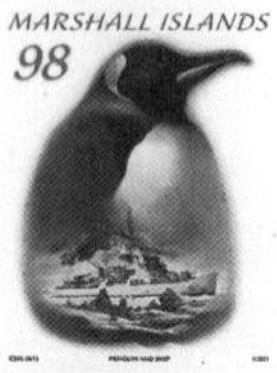
MARSHALL ISLANDS
98

341 King Penguin enclosing Research Ship

2011. 50th Anniv of Antarctic Treaty. Multicoloured.

2663	98c. Type **341** (6-1)	2·30	2·20
2664	98c. Emperor penguin looking down at chick (6-2)	2·30	2·20
2665	98c. As Type **341** (light bluish violet) (6-3)	2·30	2·20
2666	98c. Two King penguins (6-4)	2·30	2·20
2667	98c. Emperor penguin and chick, facing left (6-5)	2·30	2·20
2668	98c. Two King penguins with chicks at feet (6-6)	2·30	2·20
2669	98c. As Type **341** (bluish violet) (6-7)	2·30	2·20
2670	98c. Two King penguins with chick between (6-8)	2·30	2·20
2671	98c. As Type **341** (deep reddish violet) (6-9)	2·30	2·20

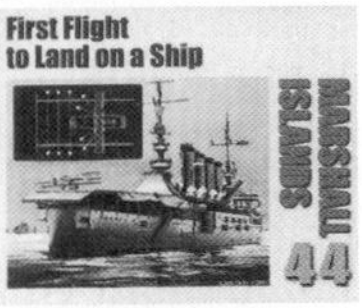

342 First Flight to Land on a Ship

2011. Firsts in Flight (3rd series). Multicoloured.

2672	44c. Type **342**	1·10	1·00
2673	44c. First Non-stop N. American Coast-to-Coast Flight	1·10	1·00
2674	44c. First Non-stop Transatlantic Flight	1·10	1·00
2675	44c. First Round the World Flight	1·10	1·00
2676	44c. First Flight Over the North Pole	1·10	1·00

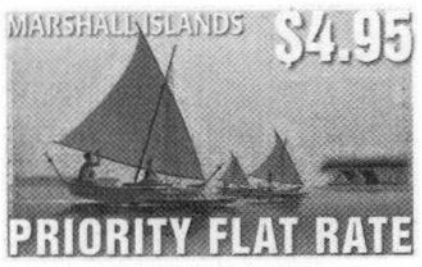

343 Pirogues and 'PRIORITY FLAT RATE'

2011. Special Rate Stamps. Multicoloured.

2677	$4.95 Type **343**	5·25	5·25
2678	$10.95 Frangipani and 'MEDIUM FLAT RATE'	9·50	
2679	$13.95 Flag and '*INTERNATIONAL FLAT RATE*'	12·00	12·00
2680	$14.95 Coconut palms and 'LARGE FLAT RATE'	13·00	13·00
2681	$18.30 Micronesian Imperial pigeons and '*EXPRESS FLAT RATE*'	17·00	17·00
2682	$29.95 Triton shell and 'INTERNATIONAL FLAT RATE'	28·00	28·00

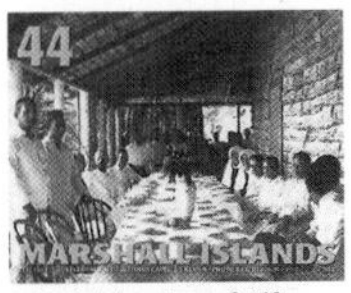

344 Celebration of Alfonso Capelle's Kemen (c.1910)

2011. Cultural Heritage (9th issue). Multicoloured.

2684	44c. Type **344**	1·10	1·00
2685	44c. Three women making pandanus thatch (c.1918)	1·10	1·00
2686	44c. Men spearfishing on reef oceanside Likiep (c.1914)	1·10	1·00
2687	44c. Men in boat house grinding arrowroot (c.1909)	1·10	1·00
2688	44c. Boat *Vilma* being launched at Likiep (c.1904)	1·10	1·00

SPECIAL DELIVERY STAMP

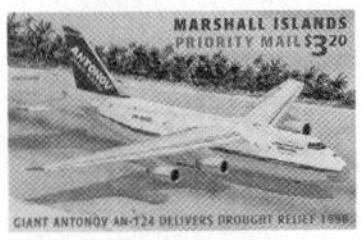

E142 Antonov An-124 delivering Supplies

1998. Drought Relief. Sheet 110×87 mm.

MSE1066	E **142** $3.20 multicoloured	8·25	7·50

Pt. 6

MARTINIQUE

An island in the West Indies, now an overseas department using the stamps of France.

100 centimes = 1 franc.

1886. Stamp of French Colonies, "Commerce" type. (a) Surch **MARTINIQUE** and new value.

3	**J**	01 on 20c. red on green	12·00	25·00
1	**J**	5 on 20c. red on green	60·00	75·00
2	**J**	5c. on 20c. red on green	£14000	£14000
4	**J**	05 on 20c. red on green	7·50	7·75
5	**J**	15 on 20c. red on green	£140	£130
6	**J**	015 on 20c. red on green	65·00	80·00

(b) Surch **MQE 15 c.**

7		15c. on 20c. red on green	85·00	£110

1888. Stamps of French Colonies, "Commerce" type, surch **MARTINIQUE** and value, thus **01 c.**

10	01c. on 4c. brown on grey	8·25	3·75
11	05c. on 4c. brown on grey	£1000	£850
12	05c. on 10c. black and lilac	75·00	65·00
13	05c. on 20c. red on green	20·00	20·00
14	05c. on 30c. brown on drab	14·50	40·00
15	05c. on 35c. black on yellow	40·00	22·00
16	05c. on 40c. red on yellow	55·00	44·00
17	15c. on 4c. brown on grey	£11000	£9000
18	15c. on 20c. red on green	£130	85·00
19	15c. on 25c. black on pink	11·00	6·50
20	15c. on 75c. red on pink	£150	£140

1891. Postage Due stamps of French Colonies surch **TIMBRE-POSTE MARTINIQUE** and value in figures.

21	**U**	05c. on 5c. black	13·00	21·00
25	**U**	05c. on 10c. black	6·50	4·50
22	**U**	05c. on 15c. black	7·75	6·00
23	**U**	15c. on 20c. black	21·00	14·00
24	**U**	15c. on 30c. black	29·00	13·00

1891. Stamp of French Colonies, "Commerce" type, surch **TIMBRE-POSTE 01c. MARTINIQUE.**

9	01c. on 2c. brown on buff	90	1·50

1892. Stamp of French Colonies, "Commerce" type, surch **1892 MARTINIQUE** and new value.

31	15c. on 25c. black on pink	36·00	48·00

1892. "Tablet" key-type inscr "MARTINIQUE", in red (1, 5, 15, 25, 75c., 1f.) or blue (others).

33	**D**	1c. black on blue	1·90	85
34	**D**	2c. brown on buff	1·40	1·40
35	**D**	4c. brown on grey	2·30	2·75
36	**D**	5c. green on green	4·50	90
37	**D**	10c. black on lilac	8·75	85
47	**D**	10c. red	7·25	65
38	**D**	15c. blue	55·00	1·80
48	**D**	15c. grey	18·00	1·50
39	**D**	20c. red on green	32·00	9·75
40	**D**	25c. black on pink	25·00	1·40
49	**D**	25c. blue	22·00	46·00
41	**D**	30c. brown on drab	11·00	22·00
50	**D**	35c. black on yellow	14·00	3·25
42	**D**	40c. red on yellow	48·00	26·00
43	**D**	50c. red on pink	13·00	10·00
51	**D**	50c. brown on blue	32·00	48·00
44	**D**	75c. brown on orange	35·00	23·00
45	**D**	1f. green	30·00	27·00
52	**D**	2f. violet on pink	75·00	85·00
53	**D**	5f. mauve on lilac	£110	£120

1903. Postage Due stamp of French Colonies surch **TIMBRE POSTE 5 F. MARTINIQUE COLIS POSTAUX.**

53a	**U**	5f. on 60c. brown on buff	£550	£600

Despite the surcharge No. 53a was for use on letters as well as parcels.

1904. Nos. 41 and 43 surch **10 c.**

54	10c. on 30c. brown and drab	9·50	22·00
55	10c. on 5f. mauve on lilac	10·00	38·00

1904. Surch **1904 0f10.**

56	0f.10 on 30c. brown on drab	14·00	44·00
57	0f.10 on 40c. red on yellow	24·00	26·00
58	0f.10 on 50c. red on pink	11·00	44·00
59	0f.10 on 75c. brown on orange	12·00	42·00
60	0f.10 on 1f. green	32·00	46·00
61	0f.10 on 5f. mauve on lilac	£180	£180

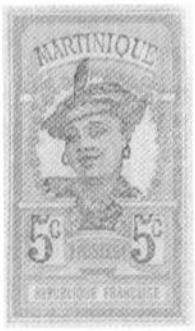

13 Martinique Woman

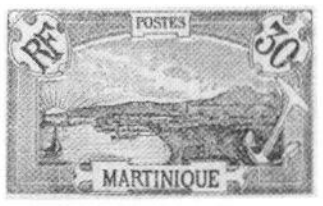

14 Fort-de-France

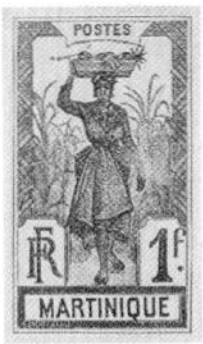

15 Woman and Sugar Cane

1908

62	**13**	1c. chocolate and brown	10	10
63	**13**	2c. brown and green	30	35
64	**13**	4c. brown and purple	90	55
65	**13**	5c. brown and green	1·80	40
87	**13**	5c. brown and orange	60	35
66	**13**	10c. brown and red	5·75	30
88	**13**	10c. olive and green	2·50	1·80
89	**13**	10c. red and purple	1·80	1·10
67	**13**	15c. red and purple	2·30	1·10
90	**13**	15c. olive and green	1·00	35
91	**13**	15c. red and blue	3·00	1·40
68	**13**	20c. brown and lilac	2·50	2·00
69	**14**	25c. brown and blue	4·50	1·30
92	**14**	25c. brown and orange	1·90	20
93	**14**	30c. brown and red	3·50	6·00
94	**14**	30c. red and carmine	1·30	6·50
95	**14**	30c. brown and light brown	1·50	1·80
96	**14**	30c. green and blue	3·25	1·20
71	**14**	35c. brown and lilac	1·70	1·60
72	**14**	40c. brown and green	1·60	60
73	**14**	45c. chocolate and brown	3·00	3·25
74	**14**	50c. brown and red	3·75	3·25
97	**14**	50c. brown and blue	3·00	4·25
98	**14**	50c. green and red	3·00	20
99	**14**	60c. pink and blue	2·50	6·75
100	**14**	65c. brown and violet	4·75	8·50
75	**14**	75c. brown and black	1·60	3·75
101	**14**	75c. blue and deep blue	3·75	2·75
102	**14**	75c. blue and brown	6·25	6·25
103	**14**	90c. carmine and red	11·00	19·00
76	**15**	1f. brown and red	3·75	3·25
104	**15**	1f. blue	3·75	3·25
105	**15**	1f. green and red	4·75	4·00
106	**15**	1f.10 brown and violet	6·75	12·50
107	**15**	1f.50 light blue and blue	12·00	13·00
77	**15**	2f. brown and grey	5·00	3·25
108	**15**	3f. mauve on pink	23·00	32·00
78	**15**	5f. brown and red	12·50	34·00

1912. Stamps of 1892 surch.

79A	05 on 15c. grey	55	20
80A	05 on 25c. black on pink	50	3·00
81A	10 on 40c. red on yellow	4·00	7·75
82A	10 on 5f. mauve on lilac	3·00	9·75

1915. Surch **5c** and red cross.

83	**13**	10c.+5c. brown and red	2·50	3·75

1920. Surch in figures.

115	**13**	0.01 on 2c. brown & green	3·50	10·50
109		0.01 on 15c. red and purple	80	6·50
110		0.02 on 15c. red and purple	1·10	6·50
84		05 on 1c. chocolate & brn	4·75	5·00
111		0.05 on 15c. red and purple	65	7·25
116	**13**	0.05 on 20c. brown and lilac	4·50	10·50
85		10 on 2c. brown and green	1·20	1·10
117	**14**	0.15 on 30c. brown and red	16·00	44·00
86		25 on 15c. red and purple	2·50	4·50
121	**13**	25c. on 15c. red and purple	65	5·50
119	**14**	0.25 on 50c. brown and red	£250	£250
120	**14**	0.25 on 50c. brown and blue	5·75	12·50
122	**15**	25c. on 2f. brown and grey	1·00	6·25
123	**15**	25c. on 5f. brown and red	2·00	6·50
112	**14**	60 on 75c. pink and blue	1·30	45
113	**14**	65 on 45c. brown & lt brn	2·75	6·50
114	**14**	85 on 75c. brown and black	2·50	8·75
124	**14**	90c. on 75c. carmine and red	3·25	4·75
125	**15**	1f.25 on 1f. blue	75	3·00
126	**15**	1f.50 on 1f. ultram & bl	2·75	2·00
127	**15**	3f. on 5f. green and red	3·50	5·25
128	**15**	10f. on 5f. red and green	12·00	38·00
129	**15**	20f. on 5f. violet & brown	20·00	55·00

1931. "Colonial Exhibition" key-types inscr "MARTINIQUE".

130	**E**	40c. black and green	6·50	12·50
131	**F**	50c. black and mauve	5·50	6·50
132	**G**	90c. black and red	7·75	13·00
133	**H**	1f.50 black and blue	7·00	10·00

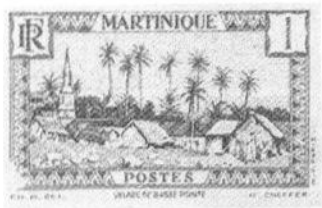

26 Basse Pointe Village

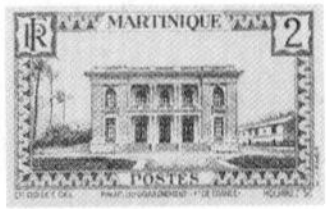

27 Government House, Fort-de-France

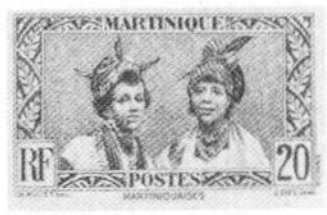

28 Martinique Woman

1933

134	**26**	1c. red on pink	65	2·30
135	**27**	2c. blue	25	4·00
136	**27**	3c. purple	1·10	6·50
137	**26**	4c. green	30	4·50
138	**27**	5c. purple	35	45
139	**26**	10c. black on pink	10	10
140	**27**	15c. black on red	35	45
141	**28**	20c. brown	35	45
142	**26**	25c. purple	65	35
143	**27**	30c. green	1·50	40
144	**27**	30c. blue	90	6·00
145	**28**	35c. green	1·30	2·00
146	**28**	40c. brown	45	65
147	**27**	45c. brown	4·00	4·50
148	**27**	45c. green	2·30	5·50
149	**27**	50c. red	1·20	35
150	**26**	55c. red	2·50	3·75
151	**26**	60c. blue	85	6·75
152	**28**	65c. red on blue	1·80	2·75
153	**28**	70c. purple	2·00	5·75
154	**26**	75c. brown	3·00	2·00
155	**27**	80c. violet	1·30	2·30
156	**26**	90c. red	4·25	1·50
157	**26**	90c. purple	2·00	4·00
158	**27**	1f. black on green	3·00	1·30
159	**27**	1f. red	90	2·75
160	**28**	1f.25 violet	3·00	3·75
161	**28**	1f.25 red	2·75	6·00
162	**28**	1f.40 blue	2·50	4·50
163	**27**	1f.50 blue	1·30	90
164	**27**	1f.60 brown	2·50	3·25
165	**28**	1f.75 green	21·00	7·00
166	**28**	1f.75 blue	3·00	2·50
167	**26**	2f. blue on green	2·75	1·50
168	**28**	2f.25 blue	3·25	7·25
169	**26**	2f.50 purple	2·75	3·75
170	**28**	3f. purple	2·75	1·60
171	**28**	5f. red on pink	2·75	1·90
172	**26**	10f. blue on blue	2·30	2·00
173	**27**	20f. red on yellow	2·50	2·50

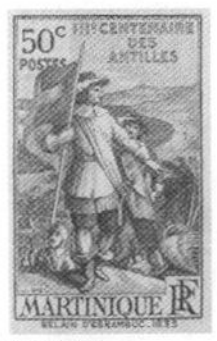

30 Belain d'Esnambuc, 1635

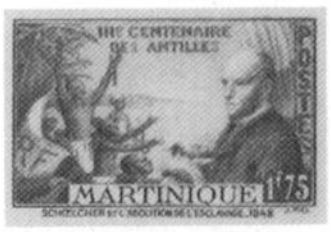

31 Schoelcher and Abolition of Slavery, 1848

1935. West Indies Tercentenary.

174	**30**	40c. brown	5·75	9·00
175	**30**	50c. red	6·00	9·25
176	**30**	1f.50 blue	14·50	21·00
177	**31**	1f.75 red	20·00	23·00
178	**31**	5f. brown	14·00	22·00
179	**31**	10f. green	14·00	13·00

1937. International Exhibition, Paris. As T **16** of Mauritania.

180	20c. violet	2·00	6·25
181	30c. green	2·00	5·25
182	40c. red	1·30	4·25
183	50c. brown and agate	1·30	1·80
184	90c. red	1·50	3·25
185	1f.50 blue	1·50	2·50
MS185a	120×100 mm. 3f. green (as T **16**) Imperf	14·00	34·00

1938. Int Anti-cancer Fund. As T **22** of Mauritania.

186	1f.75+50c. blue	9·50	28·00

1939. New York World's Fair. As T **28** of Mauritania.

187	1f.25 red	1·60	6·75
188	2f.25 blue	1·80	6·50

1939. 150th Anniv of French Revolution. As T **29** of Mauritania.

189	45c.+25c. green and black	9·25	20·00
190	70c.+30c. brown and black	9·25	20·00
191	90c.+35c. orange and black	9·25	20·00
192	1f.25+1f. red and black	9·25	20·00
193	2f.25+2f. blue and black	9·25	20·00

1944. Mutual Aid and Red Cross Funds. As T **19b** of Oceanic Settlements.

194	5f.+20f. violet	65	9·00

1945. Eboue. As T **20a** of Oceanic Settlements.

195	2f. black	30	50
196	25f. green	45	6·00

1945. Surch.

197	**27**	1f. on 2c. blue	2·50	1·20
198	**26**	2f. on 4c. olive	1·00	1·80
199	**27**	3f. on 2c. blue	2·75	1·40
200	**28**	5f. on 65c. red on blue	1·50	1·80
201	**28**	10f. (DIX f.) on 65c. red on blue	3·00	1·70
202	**27**	20f. (VINGT f.) on 3c. pur	3·00	3·00

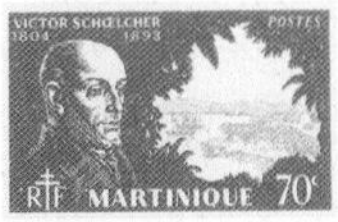

33 Victor Schoelcher

1945

203	**33**	10c. blue and violet	45	5·25

204	**33**	30c. brown and red	1·10	5·25
205	**33**	40c. blue and light blue	80	5·25
206	**33**	50c. red and purple	1·00	3·25
207	**33**	60c. orange and yellow	1·60	4·50
208	**33**	70c. purple and brown	1·60	7·50
209	**33**	80c. green and light green	1·70	7·00
210	**33**	1f. blue and light blue	75	1·60
211	**33**	1f.20 violet and purple	85	7·50
212	**33**	1f.50 red and orange	60	1·70
213	**33**	2f. black and grey	90	1·00
214	**33**	2f.40 red and pink	1·40	7·75
215	**33**	3f. pink and light pink	1·20	75
216	**33**	4f. ultramarine and blue	1·10	2·75
217	**33**	4f.50 turquoise and green	1·20	1·10
218	**33**	5f. light brown and brown	1·30	1·40
219	**33**	10f. purple and mauve	1·40	1·30
220	**33**	15f. red and pink	1·70	1·40
221	**33**	20f. olive and green	1·40	2·00

1945. Air. As No. 299 of New Caledonia.

222	50f. green	55	3·00
223	100f. red	75	6·25

1946. Air. Victory. As T **20b** of Oceanic Settlements.

224	8f. blue	55	6·25

1946. Air. From Chad to the Rhine. As T **25a** of Madagascar.

225	5f. orange	1·50	6·75
226	10f. green	1·00	7·00
227	15f. red	1·40	8·25
228	20f. brown	1·80	6·00
229	25f. blue	1·20	7·25
230	50f. grey	1·60	5·50

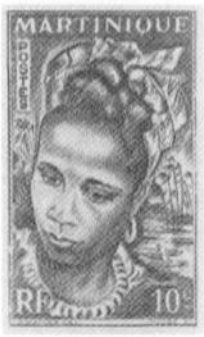

34 Martinique Woman

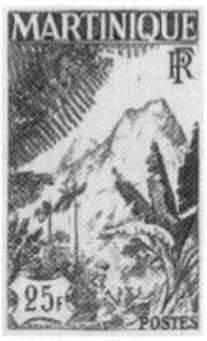

39 Mountains and Palms

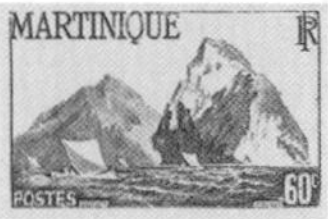

35 Local Fishing Boats and Rocks

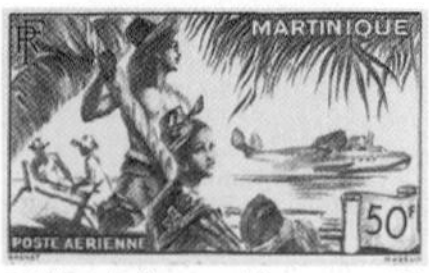

40 West Indians and Latecoere 611 (flying boat)

1947

231	**34**	10c. lake (postage)	10	5·50
232	**34**	30c. blue	10	5·75
233	**34**	50c. brown	25	7·00
234	**35**	60c. green	1·10	5·75
235	**35**	1f. lake	1·10	1·70
236	**35**	1f.50 violet	1·10	5·25
237	-	2f. green	2·00	4·25
238	-	2f.50 brown	2·00	7·50
239	-	3f. blue	2·50	3·75
240	-	4f. brown	2·50	4·75
241	-	5f. green	2·50	3·25
242	-	6f. mauve	2·30	1·50
243	-	10f. blue	2·75	3·00
244	-	15f. lake	3·00	3·00
245	-	20f. brown	2·75	3·00
246	**39**	25f. violet	3·50	3·50
247	**39**	40f. green	3·25	7·00
248	**40**	50f. purple (air)	8·50	9·50
249	-	100f. green	6·75	11·50
250	-	200f. violet	20·00	65·00

DESIGNS—HORIZ: As Type **35**: 2f. to 3f. Gathering sugar cane; 4f. to 6f. Mount Pele; 10f. to 20f. Fruit products. As Type **40**—VERT: 100f. Aeroplane over landscape. HORIZ: 200f. Wandering albatross in flight.

POSTAGE DUE STAMPS

1927. Postage Due stamps of France optd **MARTINIQUE.**

D130	**D11**	5c. blue	90	4·50
D131	**D11**	10c. brown	1·00	4·75
D132	**D11**	20c. olive	1·10	9·25
D133	**D11**	25c. red	1·20	11·00
D134	**D11**	30c. red	1·60	11·50
D135	**D11**	45c. green	2·00	12·00
D136	**D11**	50c. purple	1·50	23·00
D137	**D11**	60c. green	2·50	20·00
D138	**D11**	1f. red on yellow	5·00	28·00
D139	**D11**	2f. mauve	7·25	46·00
D140	**D11**	3f. red	4·50	50·00

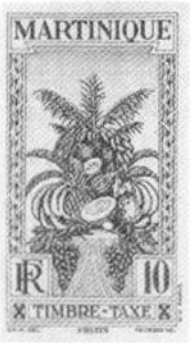

D29 Fruit

1933

D174	**D29**	5c. blue on green	35	3·75
D175	**D29**	10c. brown	1·00	6·25
D176	**D29**	20c. blue	1·70	7·75
D177	**D29**	25c. red on pink	1·50	7·50
D178	**D29**	30c. purple	1·00	7·25
D179	**D29**	45c. red on yellow	70	5·50
D180	**D29**	50c. brown	45	8·75
D181	**D29**	60c. green	1·10	8·75
D182	**D29**	1f. black on red	1·20	9·25
D183	**D29**	2f. purple	1·20	8·75
D184	**D29**	3f. blue on blue	1·30	9·25

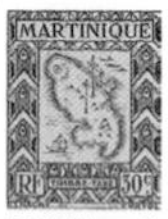

D43 Map of Martinique

1947

D251	**D43**	10c. blue	10	7·00
D252	**D43**	30c. green	10	7·25
D253	**D43**	50c. blue	45	7·50
D254	**D43**	1f. orange	75	7·00
D255	**D43**	2f. purple	2·00	7·00
D256	**D43**	3f. purple	1·80	6·75
D257	**D43**	4f. brown	2·75	8·50
D258	**D43**	5f. red	2·00	8·50
D259	**D43**	10f. black	2·30	8·75
D260	**D43**	20f. green	2·00	10·50

Pt. 6, Pt. 13

MAURITANIA

A French colony extending inland to the Sahara, incorporated in French West Africa from 1945 to 1959. In 1960 Mauritania became an independent Islamic republic.

1906. 100 centimes = 1 franc.
1973. 100 cents = 1 ouguiya (um).

1906. "Faidherbe", "Palms" and "Balay" key-types inscr "MAURITANIE" in blue (10, 40c., 5f.) or red (others).

1	**I**	1c. grey	1·00	80
2	**I**	2c. brown	1·50	90
3	**I**	4c. brown on blue	3·50	3·25
4	**I**	5c. green	3·00	3·25
5	**I**	10c. pink	15·00	11·00
6	**J**	20c. black on blue	13·00	42·00
7	**J**	25c. blue	9·75	18·00
8	**J**	30c. brown on pink	90·00	95·00
9	**J**	35c. black on yellow	5·00	14·00
10	**J**	40c. red on blue	7·00	20·00
11	**J**	45c. brown on green	9·75	21·00
12	**J**	50c. violet	10·00	19·00
13	**J**	75c. green on orange	7·50	16·00
14	**K**	1f. black on blue	25·00	46·00
15	**K**	2f. blue on pink	60·00	£110
16	**K**	5f. red on yellow	£130	£130

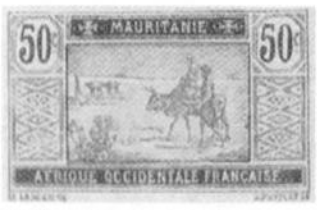

6 Merchants crossing Desert

1913

18	**6**	1c. brown and lilac	10	35
19	**6**	2c. blue and black	30	1·00
20	**6**	4c. black and violet	40	1·30
21	**6**	5c. green and light green	2·50	1·80
37	**6**	5c. red and purple	65	3·25
22	**6**	10c. orange and pink	3·25	4·50
38	**6**	10c. green and light green	75	3·50
39	**6**	10c. pink on blue	40	3·75
23	**6**	15c. black and brown	75	3·50
24	**6**	20c. orange and brown	2·75	4·00
25	**6**	25c. ultramarine and blue	5·50	7·50
40	**6**	25c. red and green	2·30	1·50
26	**6**	30c. pink and green	4·25	6·50
41	**6**	30c. orange and red	2·50	6·50
42	**6**	30c. yellow and black	55	3·25
43	**6**	30c. light green and green	4·00	9·50
27	**6**	35c. violet and brown	1·70	7·25
44	**6**	35c. light green and green	1·10	7·50
28	**6**	40c. green and brown	2·75	7·25
29	**6**	45c. brown and orange	1·60	5·00
30	**6**	50c. pink and lilac	2·00	7·00
45	**6**	50c. ultramarine and blue	1·40	4·25
46	**6**	50c. blue and green	2·30	2·50
47	**6**	60c. violet on pink	1·90	7·25
48	**6**	65c. blue and brown	2·00	6·25
31	**6**	75c. brown and blue	2·30	5·75
49	**6**	85c. brown and green	1·00	7·75
50	**6**	90c. pink and red	2·75	7·25
32	**6**	1f. black and red	1·80	3·25
51	**6**	1f.10 red and mauve	9·00	38·00
52	**6**	1f.25 brown and blue	5·25	8·50
53	**6**	1f.50 blue and light blue	2·30	7·75
54	**6**	1f.75 red and green	3·50	7·00
55	**6**	1f.75 ultramarine and blue	2·30	7·25
33	**6**	2f. violet and orange	2·30	5·00
56	**6**	3f. mauve on pink	2·50	5·50
34	**6**	5f. blue and violet	4·00	10·00

1915. Surch **5c** and red cross.

35	10c.+5c. orange and pink	1·70	3·25
36	15c.+5c. black and brown	1·50	7·50

1922. Surch in figures and bars (some colours changed).

60	25c. on 2f. violet and orange	2·00	8·00
57	60 on 75c. violet on pink	1·20	4·50
58	65 on 15c. black and brown	2·75	9·75
59	85 on 75c. brown and blue	2·75	9·75
61	90c. on 75c. pink and red	2·50	10·00
62	1f.25 on 1f. ultram & blue	1·80	8·50
63	1f.50 on 1f. blue & light blue	1·70	5·50
64	3f. on 5f. mauve and brown	7·50	29·00
65	10f. on 5f. green and mauve	7·50	23·00
66	20f. on 5f. orange and blue	6·50	24·00

1931. "Colonial Exhibition" key-types inscr "MAURITANIE".

67	**E**	40c. green and black	10·50	34·00
68	**F**	50c. purple and black	5·00	13·50
69	**G**	90c. red and black	5·25	16·00
70	**H**	1f.50 blue and black	9·00	16·00

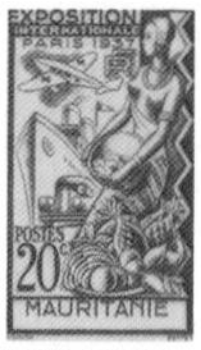

16 Commerce

1937. International Exhibition, Paris.

71	**16**	20c. violet	1·70	2·75
72	**16**	30c. green	1·50	4·25
73	**16**	40c. red	1·00	4·00
74	**16**	50c. brown	75	2·00
75	**16**	90c. red	75	2·50
76	**16**	1f.50 blue	1·00	3·00

MS76a 120× 100 mm. **18** 3f. blue. Imperf 13·00 26·00

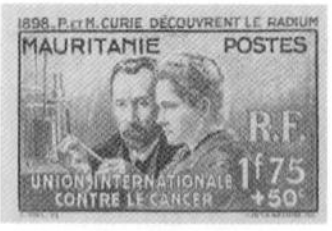

22 Pierre and Marie Curie

1938. International Anti-cancer Fund.

76b	**22**	1f.75+50c. blue	5·50	32·00

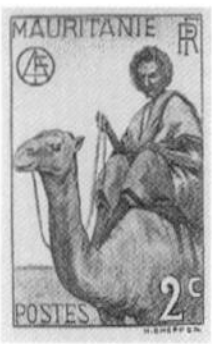

23 Man on Camel

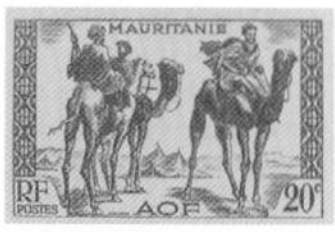

24 Warriors

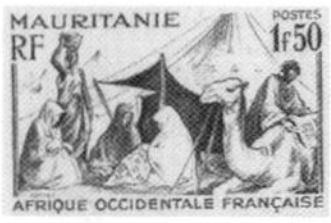

25 Encampment

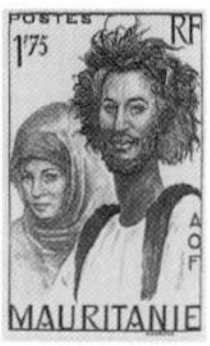

26 Mauritanians

1938

77	**23**	2c. purple	40	3·75
78	**23**	3c. blue	35	3·50
79	**23**	4c. lilac	55	3·75
80	**23**	5c. red	20	3·00
81	**23**	10c. red	35	3·75
82	**23**	15c. violet	1·00	6·75
83	**24**	20c. red	65	1·20
84	**24**	25c. blue	70	3·50
85	**24**	30c. purple	55	4·25
86	**24**	35c. green	65	7·25
87	**24**	40c. red	1·00	5·50
88	**24**	45c. green	1·60	4·50
89	**24**	50c. violet	45	6·50
90	**25**	55c. lilac	1·10	4·25
91	**25**	60c. violet	1·70	7·00
92	**25**	65c. green	1·10	7·50
93	**25**	70c. red	1·40	6·75
94	**25**	80c. blue	1·70	9·00
95	**25**	90c. lilac	1·50	6·00
96	**25**	1f. red	1·40	5·75
97	**25**	1f. green	65	2·30
98	**25**	1f.25 red	2·00	5·25
99	**25**	1f.40 blue	2·50	5·25
100	**25**	1f.50 violet	1·00	4·25
100a	**25**	1f.50 red	£120	£120
101	**25**	1f.60 brown	3·25	5·25
102	**26**	1f.75 blue	1·70	2·75
103	**26**	2f. lilac	1·10	4·00
104	**26**	2f.25 blue	2·30	6·75
105	**26**	2f.50 brown	2·30	4·25
106	**26**	3f. green	75	3·75
107	**26**	5f. red	2·00	6·25
108	**26**	10f. purple	1·50	6·00
109	**26**	20f. red	1·30	4·75

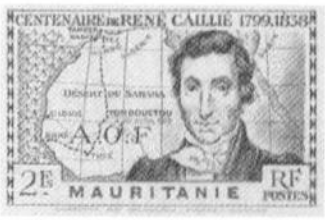

27 Rene Caillie (explorer)

1939. Death Centenary of Caillie.

110	**27**	90c. orange	1·00	4·50
111	**27**	2f. violet	85	2·30
112	**27**	2f.25 blue	1·00	5·25

28

1939. New York World's Fair.

113	**28**	1f.25 red	1·20	4·50
114	**28**	2f.25 blue	1·20	3·00

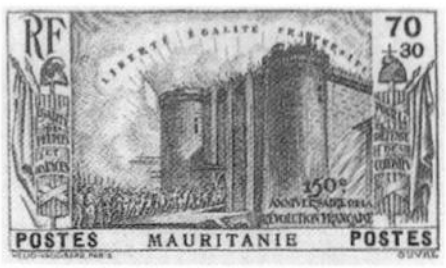

29 Storming the Bastille

1939. 150th Anniv of French Revolution.

115	**29**	45c.+25c. green and black	9·25	22·00
116	**29**	70c.+30c. brown and black	9·25	22·00
117	**29**	90c.+35c. orange and black	9·25	22·00
118	**29**	1f.25+1f. red and black	9·25	22·00
119	**29**	2f.25+2f. blue and black	9·25	22·00

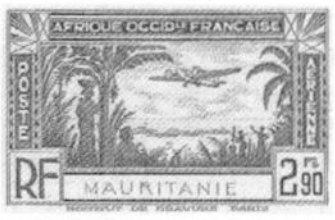

30 Twin-engine Airliner over Jungle

1940. Air.

120	**30**	1f.90 blue	1·70	6·50
121	**30**	2f.90 red	75	7·50
122	**30**	4f.50 green	1·20	6·00
123	**30**	4f.90 olive	1·40	3·75
124	**30**	6f.90 orange	1·60	5·00

1941. National Defence Fund. Surch **SECOURS NATIONAL** and value.

124a	+1f. on 50c. (No. 89)	6·00	9·00
124b	+2f. on 80c. (No. 94)	14·50	21·00
124c	+2f. on 1f.50 (No. 100)	14·00	23·00
124d	+3f. on 2f. (No. 103)	16·00	23·00

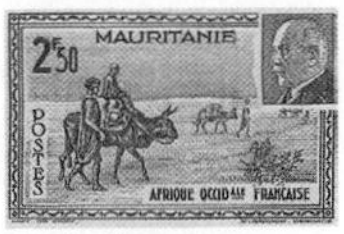

31a Ox Caravan

1942. Marshal Petain issue.

124e	**31a**	1f. green	1·70	4·00
124f	**31a**	2f.50 blue	65	4·25

1942. Air. Colonial Child Welfare Fund. As Nos. 98g/i of Niger.

124g	1f.50+3f.50 green	1·00	8·25
124h	2f.+6f. brown	1·00	8·25
124i	3f.+9f. red	85	7·25

1942. Air. Imperial Fortnight. As No. 98j of Niger.

124j	1f.20+1f.80 blue and red	85	8·25

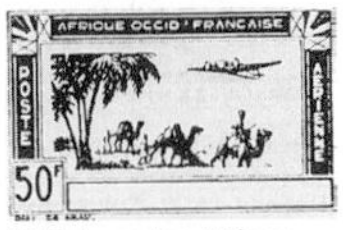

32 Twin-engine Airliner over Camel Caravan

1942. Air. T 32 inscr "MAURITANIE" at foot.

124k	**32**	50f. orange and yellow	3·00	9·25

1944. Surch.

125	**25**	3f.50 on 65c. green	1·10	30
126	**25**	4f. on 65c. green	1·40	70
127	**25**	5f. on 65c. green	1·50	85
128	**25**	10f. on 65c. green	1·50	45
129	**27**	15f. on 90c. orange	1·60	1·00

ISLAMIC REPUBLIC

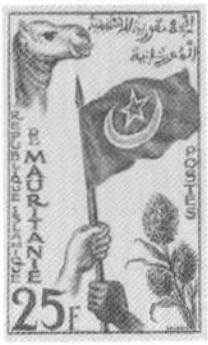

35 Flag of Republic

1960. Inauguration of Islamic Republic.

130	**35**	25f. bistre, green and brown on rose	4·25	5·00

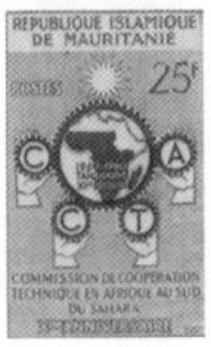

36

1960. Tenth Anniv of African Technical Co-operation Commission.

131	**36**	25f. blue and turquoise	3·00	3·75

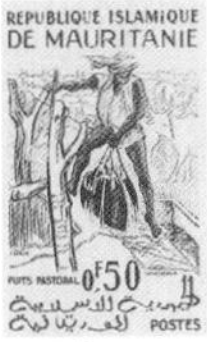

37 Well

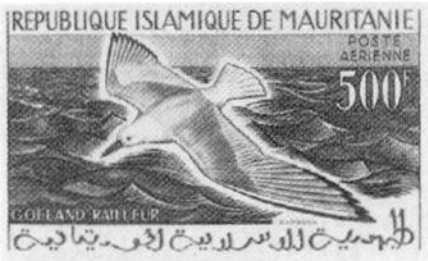

38 Slender-billed Gull

1960

132	**37**	50c. purple and brown (postage)	10	10
133	-	1f. bistre, brown and green	10	10
134	-	2f. brown, green and blue	10	10
135	-	3f. red, sepia and turquoise	55	25
136	-	4f. buff and green	75	40
137	-	5f. chocolate, brown and red	30	10
138	-	10f. blue, black and brown	30	10
139	-	15f. multicoloured	45	25
140	-	20f. brown and green	45	25
141	-	25f. blue and green	70	25
142	-	30f. blue, violet and bistre	85	25
143	-	50f. brown and green	1·20	55
144	-	60f. purple, red and green	1·80	70
145	-	85f. brown, sepia and blue	5·50	2·50
146	-	100f. brn, choc & bl (air)	4·25	2·75
147	-	200f. myrtle, brown & sepia	6·75	4·75
148	**38**	500f. sepia, blue and brown	22·00	10·50

DESIGNS—VERT: (As Type **37**) 2f. Harvesting dates; 5f. Harvesting millet; 25, 30f. Seated dance; 50f. "Telmidi" (symbolic figure); 60f. Metalsmith; 85f. Scimitar oryx; 100f. Greater flamingo; 200f. African spoonbill. HORIZ: 3f. Barbary sheep; 4f. Fennec foxes; 10f. Cordwainer; 15f. Fishing-boat; 20f. Nomad school.

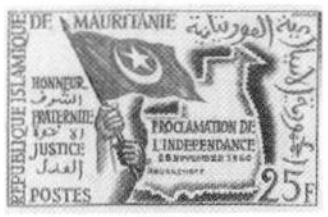

39 Flag and Map

1960. Proclamation of Independence.

149	**39**	25f. green, brown and chestnut	75	40

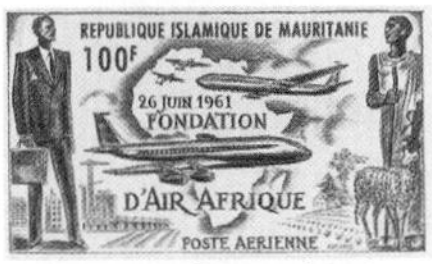

42 European, African and Boeing 707 Airliners

1962. Air. Air Afrique Airline.

150	**42**	100f. green, brown and bistre	3·00	1·60

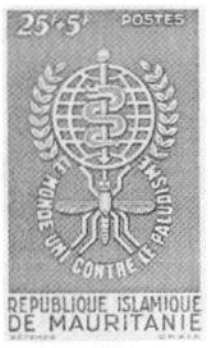

43 Campaign Emblem

1962. Malaria Eradication.

151	**43**	25f.+5f. olive	95	90

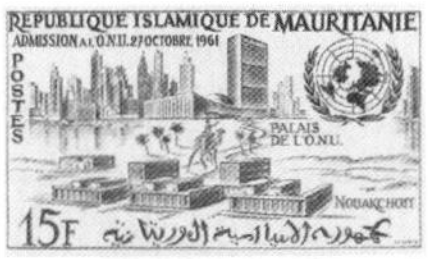

44 U.N. Headquarters and View of Nouakchott

1962. Admission to U.N.O.

152	**44**	15f. brown, black and blue	45	40
153	**44**	25f. brown, myrtle and blue	50	50
154	**44**	85f. brown, purple and blue	1·60	1·60

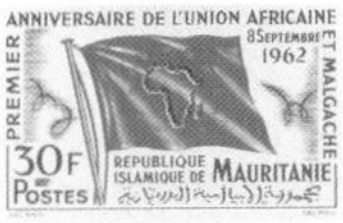

45 Union Flag

1962. First Anniv of Union of African and Malagasy States.

155	**45**	30f. blue	95	90

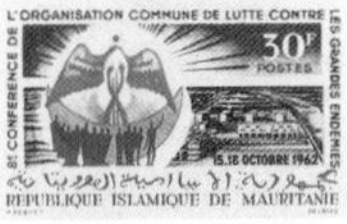

46 Eagle and Crescent over Nouakchott

1962. Eighth Endemic Diseases Eradication Conference, Nouakchott.

156	**46**	30f. green, brown and blue	80	65

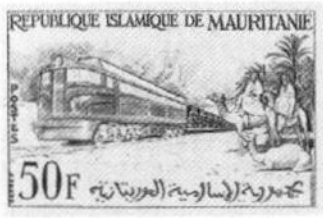

47 Diesel Mineral Train

1962

157	**47**	50f. multicoloured	3·00	1·40

1962. Air. First Anniv of Admission to U.N.O. As T **44** but views from different angles and inscr "1 er ANNIVERSAIRE 27 OCTOBRE 1962".

158	100f. blue, brown & turquoise	1·70	1·30

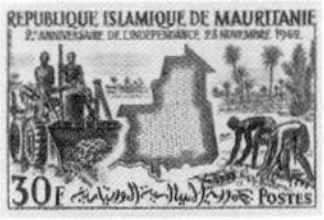

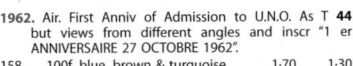

49 Map and Agriculture

1962. Second Anniv of Independence.

159	**49**	30f. green and purple	95	55

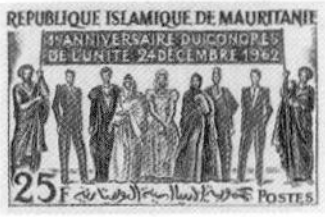

50 Congress Representatives

1962. First Anniv of Unity Congress.

160	**50**	25f. brown, myrtle and blue	55	35

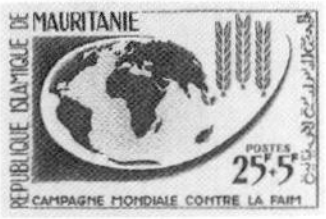

51 Globe and Emblem

1962. Freedom from Hunger.

161	**51**	25f.+5f. blue, brown and purple	95	90

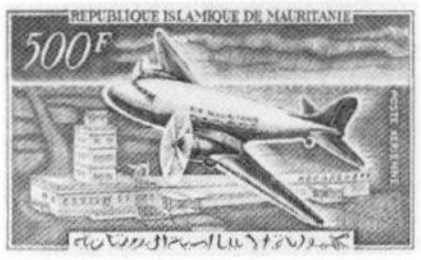

52 Douglas DC-3 Airliner over Nouakchott Airport

1963. Air. Creation of National Airline.

162	**52**	500f. myrtle, brown and blue	13·50	5·75

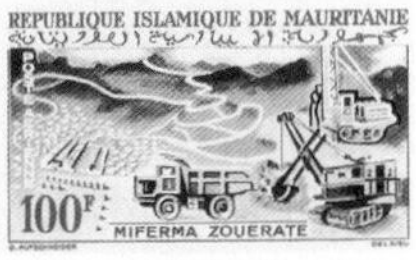

53 Open-cast Mining, Zouerate

1963. Air. Mining Development. Multicoloured.

163	100f. Type **53**	2·00	70
164	200f. Port-Etienne	5·00	1·40

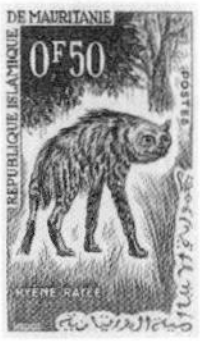

54 Striped Hyena

1963. Animals.

165	**54**	50c. black, brown and myrtle	10	10
166	-	1f. black, blue and buff	10	10
167	-	1f.50 brown, olive & pur	20	10
168	-	2f. purple, green and red	30	10
169	-	5f. bistre, blue and ochre	30	25
170	-	10f. black and ochre	55	25
171	-	15f. purple and blue	55	25
172	-	20f. bistre, purple and blue	75	40
173	-	25f. ochre, brown & turq	1·20	40
174	-	30f. bistre, brown and blue	1·70	40
175	-	50f. bistre, brown and green	2·40	85
176	-	60f. bistre, brown & turq	3·00	1·40

ANIMALS—HORIZ: 1f. Spotted hyena; 2f. Guinea baboons; 10f. Leopard; 15f. Bongos; 20f. Aardvark; 30f. North African crested porcupine; 60f. Chameleon. VERT: 1f.50, Cheetah; 5f. Dromedaries; 25f. Patas monkeys; 50f. Dorcas gazelle.

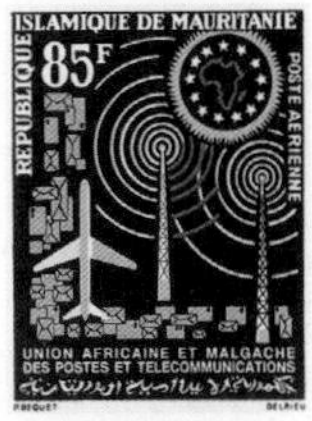

56 "Posts and Telecommunications"

1963. Air. African and Malagasy Posts and Telecommunications Union.

177	**56**	85f. multicoloured	1·50	85

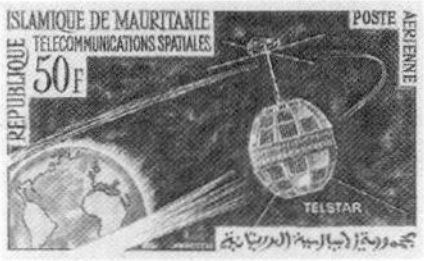

57 "Telstar" Satellite

1963. Air. Space Telecommunications.

178	**57**	50f. brown, purple and green	80	60
179	-	100f. blue, brown and red	1·70	80
180	-	150f. turquoise and brown	3·00	1·80

DESIGNS: 100f. "Syncom" satellite; 150f. "Relay" satellite.

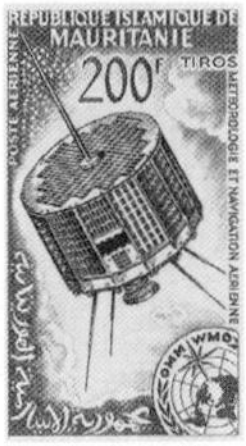

58 "Tiros" Satellite

1963. Air. World Meteorological Day.

181	**58**	200f. brown, blue and green	5·00	2·20

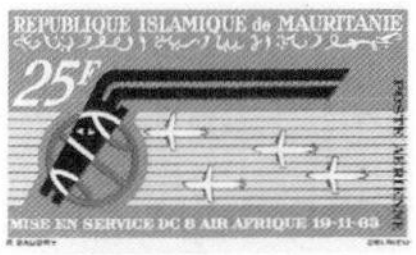

59 Airline Emblem

1963. Air. First Anniv of "Air Afrique" and DC-8 Service Inauguration.

182	**59**	25f. multicoloured	75	30

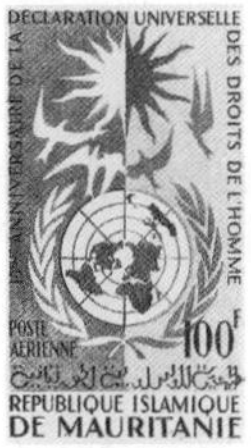

60 U.N. Emblem, Sun and Birds

1963. Air. 15th Anniv of Declaration of Human Rights.

183	**60**	100f. blue, violet and purple	2·00	1·10

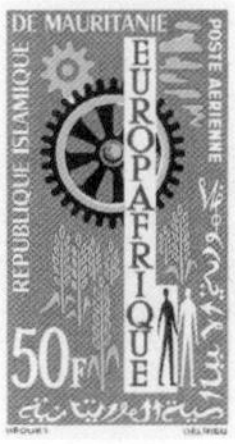

61 Cogwheels and Wheat

1964. Air. European-African Economic Convention.

184	**61**	50f. multicoloured	1·70	1·10

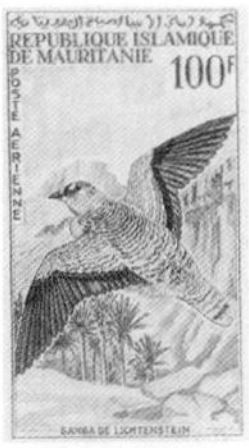

62 Lichtenstein's Sandgrouse

1964. Air. Birds.

185	**62**	100f. ochre, brown and green	3·50	1·40
186	-	200f. black, brown and blue	5·75	2·30
187	-	500f. slate, red and green	17·00	7·25

DESIGNS: 200f. Reed cormorant; 500f. Dark chanting goshawk.

63 Temple, Philae

1964. Air. Nubian Monuments Preservation.
188	**63**	10f. brown, black and blue	75	25
189	**63**	25f. slate, brown and blue	95	65
190	**63**	60f. chocolate, brown and blue	2·00	1·00

64 W.M.O. Emblem. Sun and Lightning

1964. World Meteorological Day.
191	**64**	85f. blue, orange and brown	1·80	1·00

65 Radar Antennae and Sun Emblem

1964. International Quiet Sun Years.
192	**65**	25f. red, green and blue	75	55

66 Bowl depicting Horse-racing

1964. Air. Olympic Games, Tokyo.
193	**66**	15f. brown and bistre	75	45
194	-	50f. brown and blue	1·30	70
195	-	85f. brown and red	2·30	1·50
196	-	100f. brown and green	2·75	1·70
MS196a	191×100 mm. Nos. 193/6		9·00	9·00

DESIGNS—VERT: 50f. Running (vase); 85f. Wrestling (vase). HORIZ: 100f. Chariot-racing (bowl).

67 Flat-headed Grey Mullet

1964. Marine Fauna.
197	**67**	1f. green, blue and brown	30	25
198	-	5f. purple, green and brown	30	25
199	-	10f. green, ochre and blue	45	25
200	-	60f. slate, green and brown	2·75	1·20

DESIGNS—VERT: 5f. Lobster ("Panulirus mauritanicus"); 10f. Lobster ("Panulirus regius"). HORIZ: 60f. Meagre.

68 "Co-operation"

1964. French, African and Malagasy Co-operation.
201	**68**	25f. brown, green and mauve	75	55

69 Pres. Kennedy

1964. Air. First Death Anniv of Pres. Kennedy.
202	**69**	100f. multicoloured	2·00	1·40
MS202a	90×130 mm. No. 202 in block of four		8·25	8·25

70 "Nymphaea lotus"

1965. Mauritanian Flowers.
203	**70**	5f. green, red and blue	30	25
204	-	10f. green, ochre and purple	30	25
205	-	20f. brown, red and sepia	60	30
206	-	45f. turquoise, purple and green	1·50	80

FLOWERS—VERT: 10f. "Acacia gommier"; 45f. "Caralluma retrospiciens". HORIZ: 20f. "Adenium obesum".

71 "Hardine"

1965. Musical Instruments and Musicians.
207	**71**	2f. brown, bistre and blue	30	25
208	-	8f. brown, bistre and red	45	25
209	-	25f. brown, black and green	75	25
210	-	40f. black, blue and violet	1·20	55

DESIGNS: 8f. "Tobol" (drums); 25f. "Tidinit" ("Violins"); 40f. Native band.

72 Abraham Lincoln

1965. Death Centenary of Abraham Lincoln.
211	**72**	50f. multicoloured	1·00	50

73 Early Telegraph and Relay Satellite

1965. Air. Centenary of I.T.U.
212	**73**	250f. green, mauve and blue	6·00	4·00

74 Palms in the Adrar

1965. "Tourism and Archaeology" (1st series).
213	**74**	1f. green, brown and blue	10	10
214	-	4f. brown, red and blue	30	10
215	-	15f. multicoloured	45	25
216	-	60f. sepia, brown and orange	1·40	70

DESIGNS—VERT: 4f. Chinguetti Mosque. HORIZ: 15f. Clay-pits; 60f. Carved doorway, Qualata.
See also Nos. 255/8.

75 "Attack on Cancer" (the Crab)

1965. Air. Campaign against Cancer.
217	**75**	100f. red, blue and ochre	1·80	85

76 Wooden Tea Service

1965. Native Handicrafts.
218	**76**	3f. brown, ochre and slate	10	10
219	-	7f. purple, orange and blue	30	25
220	-	25f. brown, black and red	55	40
221	-	50f. red, green and orange	1·20	55

DESIGNS—VERT: 7f. Snuff-box and pipe; 25f. Damascine dagger. HORIZ: 50f. Mederrda chest.

77 Nouakchott Wharf

1965. Mauritanian Development.
222		5f. green and brown	30	25
223	**77**	10f. red, turquoise and blue	30	10
224	-	30f. red, brown and purple	70	25
225	-	85f. violet, lake and blue	1·50	75

DESIGNS—VERT: 5f., 30f. Choum Tunnel. HORIZ: 85f. Nouakchott Hospital.

78 Sir Winston Churchill

1965. Air. Churchill Commemoration.
226	**78**	200f. multicoloured	3·50	1·60

79 Rocket "Diamant"

1966. Air. French Satellites.
227	**79**	30f. green, red and blue	75	45
228	-	60f. purple, blue and turquoise	1·30	70
229	-	90f. lake, violet and blue	2·20	1·00

DESIGNS—HORIZ: 60f. Satellite "A 1" and Globe; 90f. Rocket "Scout" and satellite "FR 1".

80 Dr. Schweitzer and Hospital Scene

1966. Air. Schweitzer Commemoration.
230	**80**	50f. multicoloured	1·70	85

81 Stafford, Schirra and "Gemini 6"

1966. Air. Space Flights. Multicoloured.
231	**81**	50f. Type **81**	80	45
232		100f. Borman, Lovell and "Gemini 7"	1·80	75
233		200f. Beliaiev, Leonov and "Voskhod 2"	3·50	1·70

82 African Woman and Carved Head

1966. World Festival of Negro Arts, Dakar.
234	**82**	10f. black, brown and green	30	10
235	-	30f. black, black and blue	45	25
236	-	60f. purple, red and orange	1·20	70

DESIGNS: 30f. Dancers and hands playing cornet; 60f. Cine-camera and village huts.

83 "Dove" over Map of Africa

1966. Air. Organization of African Unity (O.A.U.).
237	**83**	100f. multicoloured	1·20	60

84 Satellite "D 1"

1966. Air. Launching of Satellite "D 1".
238	**84**	100f. plum, brown and blue	1·70	1·10

85 Breguet 14T2 Salon

1966. Air. Early Aircraft.
239	**85**	50f. indigo, blue and bistre	1·20	30
240	-	100f. green, purple and blue	2·20	70
241	-	150f. turquoise, brown and blue	4·75	2·20
242	-	200f. indigo, blue and purple	6·75	3·25

AIRCRAFT: 100f. Farman Goliath; 150f. Couzinet "Arc en Ciel"; 200f. Latecoere 28-3 seaplane "Comte de la Vaulx".

86 "Acacia ehrenbergiana"

1966. Mauritanian Flowers. Multicoloured.
243		10f. Type **86**	35	10
244		15f. "Schouwia purpurea"	50	25
245		20f. "Ipomaea asarifolia"	60	25
246		25f. "Grewia bicolor"	95	30
247		30f. "Pancratium trianthum"	1·30	45
248		60f. "Blepharis linariifolia"	2·10	75

87 DC-8F and "Air Afrique" Emblem

1966. Air. Inauguration of Douglas DC-8F Air Services.
249   87   30f. grey, black and red   75   45

88 "Raft of the Medusa" (after Gericault)

1966. Air. 150th Anniv of Shipwreck of the "Medusa".
250   88   500f. multicoloured   13·00   8·75

89 "Myrina silenus"

1966. Butterflies. Multicoloured.
251   89   5f. Type 89   75   35
252   -   30f. "Colotis danae"   2·20   70
253   -   45f. "Hypolimnas misippus"   3·25   95
254   -   60f. "Danaus chrysippus"   4·75   1·60

90 "Hunting" (petroglyph from Tenses, Adrar)

1966. Tourism and Archaeology (2nd series).
255   90   2f. chestnut and brown   45   10
256   -   3f. brown and blue   60   25
257   -   30f. green and red   1·20   45
258   -   50f. brown, green and purple   2·20   1·20
DESIGNS—3f. "Fighting" (petroglyph from Tenses, Adrar); 30f. Copper jug (from Le Mreyer, Adrar); 50f. Camel and caravan.

91 Cogwheels and Ears of Wheat

1966. Air. Europafrique.
259   91   50f. multicoloured   1·20   50

92 UNESCO Emblem

1966. 20th Anniv of UNESCO.
260   92   30f. multicoloured   75   40

93 Olympic Village, Grenoble

1967. Publicity for Olympic Games (1968).
261   -   20f. brown, blue and green   50   30
262   93   30f. brown, green and blue   75   45
263   -   40f. brown, purple and blue   1·00   60
264   -   100f. brown, green and black   2·30   1·10
DESIGNS—VERT: 20f. Old and new buildings, Mexico City; 40f. Ice rink, Grenoble and Olympic torch. HORIZ: 100f. Olympic stadium, Mexico City.

94 South African Crowned Crane

1967. Air. Birds. Multicoloured.
265   94   100f. Type 94   3·00   1·10
266   -   200f. Great egret   5·25   1·70
267   -   500f. Ostrich   15·00   5·75

95 Globe, Rockets and Eye

1967. Air. World Fair, Montreal.
268   95   250f. brown, blue and black   4·50   1·90

96 Prosopis

1967. Trees.
269   96   10f. green, blue and brown   40   10
270   -   15f. green, blue and purple   55   20
271   -   20f. green, purple and blue   60   25
272   -   25f. brown and green   75   40
273   -   30f. brown, green and red   1·10   45
TREES: 15f. Jujube; 20f. Date palm; 25f. Peltophorum; 30f. Baobab.

97 Jamboree Emblem and Scout Kit

1967. World Scout Jamboree, Idaho.
274   97   60f. blue, green and brown   1·20   45
275   -   90f. blue, green and red   1·80   70
DESIGN—HORIZ: 90f. Jamboree emblem and scouts.

98 Weaving

1967. Advancement of Mauritanian Women.
276   98   5f. red, black and violet   30   10
277   -   10f. black, violet and green   30   10
278   -   20f. black, purple and blue   55   25
279   -   30f. blue, black and brown   80   40
280   -   50f. black, violet and indigo   1·10   45
DESIGNS—VERT: 10f. Needlework; 30f. Laundering. HORIZ: 20f. Nursing; 50f. Sewing (with machines).

99 Atomic Symbol

1967. Air. International Atomic Energy Agency.
281   99   200f. blue, green and red   3·50   1·50

100 Cattle

1967. Campaign for Prevention of Cattle Plague.
282   100   30f. red, blue and green   95   55

101 Map of Africa, Letters and Pylons

1967. Air. Fifth Anniv of U.A.M.P.T.
283   101   100f. green, brown & pur   1·50   75

102 "Francois of Rimini" (Ingres)

1967. Air. Death Centenary of Jean Ingres (painter). Multicoloured.
284   102   90f. Type 102   2·00   80
285   -   200f. "Ingres in his Studio" (Alaux)   3·75   1·50
See also Nos. 306/8.

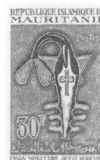

103 Currency Tokens

1967. Fifth Anniv of West African Monetary Union.
286   103   30f. grey and orange   55   25

104 "Hyphaene thebaica"

1967. Mauritanian Fruits.
287   104   1f. brown, green and purple   20   10
288   -   2f. yellow, green and brown   25   10
289   -   3f. olive, green and violet   40   20
290   -   4f. red, green and brown   45   20
291   -   5f. orange, brown and green   55   25
FRUITS—HORIZ: 2f. "Balanites aegyptiaca"; 4f. "Ziziphus lotus". VERT: 3f. "Adansonia digitata"; 5f. "Phoenix dactylifera".

105 Human Rights Emblem

1968. Human Rights Year.
292   105   30f. yellow, green and black   75   25
293   105   50f. yellow, brown and black   95   55

106 Chancellor Adenauer

1968. Air. Adenauer Commemoration.
294   106   100f. sepia, brown and blue   2·00   85
MS295   120×170 mm. No. 294×4   8·25   8·25

107 Skiing

1968. Air. Olympic Games, Grenoble and Mexico.
296   107   20f. purple, indigo & blue   45   10
297   -   30f. brown, green and plum   55   25
298   -   50f. green, blue and ochre   80   40
299   -   100f. green, red and brown   1·80   65
DESIGNS—VERT: 30f. Horse-vaulting; 50f. Ski-jumping. HORIZ: 100f. Hurdling.

108 Mosque, Nouakchott

1968. Tourism. Multicoloured.
300   108   30f. Type 108   45   25
301   -   45f. Amogjar Pass   60   30
302   -   90f. Cavaliers' Tower, Boutilimit   1·10   60

109 Man and W.H.O. Emblem

1968. Air. 20th Anniv of W.H.O.
303   109   150f. blue, purple and brown   2·50   1·10

110 UNESCO Emblem and "Movement of Water"

1968. International Hydrological Decade.
304   110   90f. green and lake   95   50

111 U.P.U. Building, Berne

1968. Admission of Mauritania to U.P.U.
305   111   30f. brown and red   55   25

1968. Air. Paintings by Ingres. As T 102. Multicoloured.
306   100f. "Man's Torso"   1·90   85
307   150f. "The Iliad"   3·00   1·30
308   250f. "The Odyssey"   5·00   2·20

112 Land-yachts
crossing Desert

1968. Land-yacht Racing.

309	**112**	30f. blue, yellow and orange	75	30
310	-	40f. purple, blue and orange	95	40
311	-	60f. green, yellow and orange	1·50	70

DESIGNS—HORIZ: 40f. Racing on shore. VERT: 60f. Crew making repairs.

113 Dr. Martin
Luther King

1968. Air. "Apostles of Peace".

312	**113**	50f. brown, blue and olive	95	45
313	-	50f. brown and blue	1·00	45
MS314		121×161 mm. Nos. 312/13×2 alternately se-tenant	4·25	4·25

DESIGN: No. 313, Mahatma Gandhi.

113a "Surprise Letter" (C.
A. Coypel)

1968. Air. Philexafrique Stamp Exn, Abidjan, Ivory Coast
(1969) (1st issue).

315	**113a**	100f. multicoloured	3·75	3·50

114 Donkey
and Foal

1968. Domestic Animals. Multicoloured.

316	5f. Type **114**	35	10
317	10f. Ewe and lamb	55	25
318	15f. Dromedary and calf	65	30
319	30f. Mare and foal	95	40
320	50f. Cow and calf	1·40	60
321	90f. Goat and kid	2·75	80

114a Forest Scene and Stamp of
1938

1969. Air. Philexafrique Stamp Exhibition, Abidjan, Ivory
Coast (2nd issue).

322	**114a**	50f. purple, green and brown	2·30	2·10

114b "Napoleon at
Council of Five Hundred"
(Bouchot)

1969. Air. Birth Bicentenary of Napoleon Bonaparte.
Multicoloured.

323	**114b**	50f. 114b	2·20	1·10
324		90f. "Napoleon's Installation by the Council of State" (Conder)	3·00	1·70
325		250f. "The Farewell of Fontainebleau" (Vernet)	7·50	4·25

115 Map and
I.L.O. Emblem

1969. 50th Anniv of I.L.O.

326	**115**	50f. multicoloured	75	40

116 Monitor
Lizard

1969. Reptiles. Multicoloured.

327	5f. Type **116**	55	25
328	10f. Horned viper	80	40
329	30f. Black-collared cobra	1·90	55
330	60f. Rock python	3·00	1·60
331	85f. Nile crocodile	5·25	1·90

117 Date Palm, "Parlatoria
blanchardi" and
"Pharoscymus anchorage"

1969. Date-palms. Protection Campaign.

332	**117**	30f. blue, red and green	1·90	90

118 Camel and Emblem

1969. Air. African Tourist Year.

333	**118**	50f. purple, blue and orange	1·20	60

119 Dancers and Baalbek Columns

1969. Baalbek Festival, Lebanon.

334	**119**	100f. brown, red and blue	1·80	70

120 "Apollo 8" and Moon

1969. Air. Moon Flight of "Apollo 8". Embossed on gold
foil.

335	**120**	1,000f. gold	24·00	24·00

121 Wolde
(marathon)

1969. Air. Gold Medal Winners, Mexico Olympic Games.

336	**121**	30f. red, brown and blue	45	25
337	-	70f. red, brown and green	95	50
338	-	150f. green, bistre and red	2·30	1·10

DESIGNS: 70f. Beamon (athletics); 150f. Vera Caslavska
(gymnastics).

122 London-Istanbul Route-Map

1969. Air. London–Sydney Motor Rally.

339	**122**	10f. brown, blue and purple	20	10
340	-	20f. brown, blue and purple	50	25
341	-	50f. brown, blue and purple	95	45
342	-	70f. brown, blue and purple	1·40	55
MS343		131×101 mm. Nos. 339/42	3·75	3·75

ROUTE—MAPS: 20f. Ankara–Teheran; 50f. Kandahar–Bombay; 70f. Perth–Sydney.

122a Bank
Emblem

1969. Fifth Anniv of African Development Bank.
Multicoloured.

344	**122a**	30f. brown, green & blue	55	25

123 Pendant

1969. Native Handicrafts.

345	**123**	10f. brown and purple	30	10
346	-	20f. red, black and blue	65	25

DESIGN—HORIZ: 20f. Rahla headdress.

124 Sea-water
Desalination Plant,
Nouakchott

1969. Economic Development.

347	**124**	10f. blue, purple and red	35	30
348	-	15f. black, lake and blue	35	30
349	-	30f. black, purple and blue	45	25

DESIGNS: 15f. Fishing quay, Nouadhibou; 30f. Meat-
processing plant, Kaedi.

125 Lenin

1970. Birth Centenary of Lenin.

350	**125**	30f. black, red and blue	2·10	70

126 "Sternocera
interrupta"

1970. Insects.

351	**126**	5f. black, buff and brown	40	35
352	-	10f. brown, yellow & lake	50	30
353	-	20f. olive, purple and brown	95	35
354	-	30f. violet, green and brown	1·70	50
355	-	40f. brown, blue and lake	3·00	95

INSECTS: 10f. "Anoplocnemis curvipes"; 20f. "Julodis ae-
quinoctialis"; 30f. "Thermophilum sexmaculatum margina-
tum"; 40f. "Plocaederus denticornis".

127 Footballers and
Hemispheres

1970. World Cup Football Championship, Mexico.

356	**127**	25f. multicoloured	45	25
357	-	30f. multicoloured	60	25
358	-	70f. multicoloured	1·20	60
359	-	150f. multicoloured	2·40	95

DESIGNS: 30, 70, 150f. As Type **127**, but with different
players.

1970. New U.P.U. Headquarters Building. As T **81** of New
Caledonia.

360	30f. red, brown and green	75	40

128 Japanese
Musician, Emblem
and Map on
Palette

1970. Air. EXPO 70 World Fair, Osaka, Japan.
Multicoloured.

361	50f. Type **128**	75	30
362	75f. Japanese fan	1·20	50
363	150f. Stylised bird, map and boat	2·20	1·00

129 U.N. Emblem and Examples of
Progress

1970. Air. 25th Anniv of U.N.O.

364	**129**	100f. green, brown and blue	1·50	80

130 Vladimir
Komarov

1970. Air. "Lost Heroes of Space" (1st series).

365	**130**	150f. brown, orge & slate	2·20	95
366	-	150f. brown, blue and slate	2·20	95
367	-	150f. brown, orge & slate	2·20	95
MS368		130×100 mm. Nos. 365/7	7·25	7·25

HEROES: No. 366, Elliott See; 376, Yuri Gagarin.
See also Nos. 376/MS379.

131 Descent of "Apollo 13"

1970. Air. Space Flight of "Apollo 13".
369 **131** 500f. red, blue and gold   8·75   8·75

132 Woman in Traditional Costume

1970. Traditional Costumes. As T **132**.
370 **132** 10f. orange and brown   60   35
371 − 30f. blue, red and brown   1·30   45
372 − 40f. brown, purple and red   1·60   45
373 − 50f. blue and brown   1·90   50
374 − 70f. brown, choc & bl   2·20   80

133 Arms and State House

1970. Air. Tenth Anniv of Independence.
375 **133** 100f. multicoloured   1·50   60

1970. Air. "Lost Heroes of Space" (2nd series). As T **130**.
376 150f. brown, blue & turquoise   2·20   90
377 150f. brown, blue & turquoise   2·20   90
378 150f. brown, blue and orange   2·20   90
MS379 130×100 mm. Nos. 376/8   7·25   6·75
HEROES: No. 376, Roger Chaffee; No. 377, Virgil Grissom; No. 378, Edward White.

134 Greek Wrestling

1971. Air. "Pre-Olympics Year".
380 **134** 100f. brown, purple & blue   2·20   1·10

135 People of Different Races

1971. Racial Equality Year.
381 **135** 30f. plum, blue and brown   70   25
382 − 40f. black, red and blue   1·00   30
DESIGN—VERT: 40f. European and African hands.

136 Pres. Nasser

1971. Air. Pres. Gamal Nasser of Egypt Commemoration.
383 **136** 100f. multicoloured   1·20   55

137 Gen. De Gaulle in Uniform

1971. De Gaulle Commemoration. Multicoloured.
384 40f. Type **137**   2·30   90
385 100f. De Gaulle as President of France   5·25   1·80

138 Scout Badge, Scout and Map

1971. Air. 13th World Scout Jamboree, Asagiri, Japan.
387 **138** 35f. multicoloured   50   25
388 **138** 40f. multicoloured   75   25
389 **138** 100f. multicoloured   1·50   55

139 Diesel Locomotive

1971. Miferma Iron-ore Mines. Multicoloured.
390 35f. Iron ore train   2·20   1·00
391 100f. Type **139**   5·50   2·30
Nos. 390/1 were issued together, *se-tenant*, forming a composite design.

139a Headquarters, Brazzaville, and Ardin Musicians

1971. Air. Tenth Anniv of African and Malagasy Posts and Telecommunications Union.
392 **139a** 100f. multicoloured   1·50   85

140 A.P.U. Emblem and Airmail Envelope

1971. Air. Tenth Anniv of African Postal Union.
393 **140** 35f. multicoloured   75   45

141 UNICEF Emblem and Child

1971. 25th Anniv of UNICEF.
394 **141** 35f. black, brown and blue   70   25

142 "Moslem King" (c. 1218)

1972. Air. Moslem Miniatures. Multicoloured.
395 35f. Type **142**   60   10
396 40f. "Enthroned Prince" (Egypt, c. 1334)   95   45
397 100f. "Pilgrims' Caravan" (Maq-uamat, Baghdad, 1237)   2·20   85

1972. Air. UNESCO "Save Venice" Campaign. As T **135a** of Niger. Multicoloured.
398 45f. "Quay and Ducal Palace" (Carlevaris) (vert)   95   45
399 100f. "Grand Canal" (Canaletto)   2·00   90
400 250f. "Santa Maria della Salute" (Canaletto)   4·75   2·10

143 Hurdling

1972. Air. Olympic Games, Munich.
401 **143** 75f. purple, orange & grn   95   40
402 **143** 100f. purple, blue & brn   1·50   60
403 **143** 200f. purple, lake & green   2·75   1·00
MS404 191×100 mm. Nos. 401/3   6·75   6·75

144 Nurse tending Baby

1972. Mauritanian Red Crescent Fund.
405 **144** 35f.+5f. multicoloured   95   90

145 Samuel Morse and Morse Key

1972. World Telecommunications Day. Multicoloured.
406 35f. Type **145**   65   25
407 40f. "Relay" satellite and hemispheres   80   25
408 75f. Alexander Graham Bell and early telephone   1·40   55

146 Spirifer Shell

1972. Fossil Shells. Multicoloured.
409 25f. Type **146**   3·25   95
410 75f. Trilobite   5·50   2·75

147 "Luna 16" and Moon Probe

1972. Air. Russian Exploration of the Moon.
411 **147** 75f. brown, blue and green   95   35
412 − 100f. brown, grey & violet   1·30   60
DESIGN—HORIZ: 100f. "Lunokhod 1".

1972. Air. Gold Medal Winners, Munich. Nos. 401/3 optd as listed below.
413 **143** 75f. purple, orange & grn   1·00   35
414 **143** 100f. purple, blue & brn   1·50   55
415 **143** 200f. purple, lake & green   3·00   90
OVERPRINTS: 75f. **110m. HAIES MILBURN MEDAILLE D'OR**; 100f. **400m. HAIES AKII-BUA MEDAILLE D'OR**; 200f. **3,000m. STEEPLE KEINO MEDAILLE D'OR**.

149 Africans and 500f. Coin

1972. Tenth Anniv of West African Monetary Union.
416 **149** 35f. grey, brown and green   70   30

1973. Air. Moon Flight of "Apollo 17". No. 267 surch **Apollo XVII Decembre 1972** and value.
417 250f. on 500f. multicoloured   3·75   1·80

151 Mediterranean Monk Seal with Young

1973. Seals. Multicoloured.
418 40f. Type **151** (postage)   3·75   95
419 135f. Head of Mediterranean monk seal (air)   5·00   2·75

152 "Lion and Crocodile" (Delacroix)

1973. Air. Paintings by Delacroix. Mult.
420 100f. Type **152**   2·30   1·10
421 250f. "Lion attacking Forest Hog"   5·25   2·75

153 "Horns of Plenty"

1973. Tenth Anniv of World Food Programme.
422 **153** 35f. multicoloured   55   30

154 U.P.U. Monument, Berne, and Globe

1973. World U.P.U. Day.
423 **154** 100f. blue, orange & green   1·80   95

155 Nomad Encampment and Eclipse

1973. Total Eclipse of the Sun.
424 **155** 35f. purple and green   70   25
425 − 40f. purple, red and blue   70   25
426 − 140f. purple and red   2·75   1·00
MS427 173×100 mm. As Nos. 424/6 but colours changed; 35f. ultramarine and purple; 40f. ultramarine, orange and purple; 140f. ultramarine and purple   4·50   4·25
DESIGNS—VERT: 40f. Rocket and Concorde. HORIZ: 140f. Observation team.

1973. "Drought Relief". African Solidarity. No. 320 surch **SECHERESSE SOLIDARITE AFRICAINE** and value.
428 20um. on 50f. multicoloured   95   55

155a Crane with Letter and Union Emblem

1973. 12th Anniv of African and Malagasy Posts and Telecommunications Union.
429 **155a** 20um. brown, lt brn & orge   1·20   55

157 Detective making Arrest and Fingerprint

1973. 50th Anniv of International Criminal Police Organization (Interpol).

430	**157**	15um. violet, red & brown	1·20	60

1974. Various stamps surch with values in new currency. (a) Postage. (i) Nos. 345/6.

431	**123**	27um. on 10f. brn & pur	1·70	80
432	-	28um. on 20f. red, blk & bl	2·00	1·20

(ii) Nos. 351/5.

433	**126**	5um. on 5f. black, buff and brown	60	25
434	-	7um. on 10f. brown, yellow and lake	75	25
435	-	8um. on 20f. olive, purple and brown	95	45
436	-	10um. on 30f. violet, purple and brown	1·50	55
437	-	20um. on 40f. brown, blue and lake	2·75	1·20

(iii) Nos. 409/10.

438	**146**	5um. on 25f. multicoloured	2·50	1·10
439	-	15um. on 75f. mult	4·25	2·30

(iv) No. 418.

440	**151**	8um. on 40f. multicoloured	1·20	55

(b) Air. (i) Nos. 395/7.

441	**142**	7um. on 35f. mult	45	25
442	-	8um. on 40f. mult	75	25
443	-	20um. on 100f. mult	2·00	80

(ii) No. 419.

444		27um. on 135f. mult	2·75	1·10

(iii) Nos. 420/1.

445	**152**	20um. on 100f. mult	2·00	90
446	-	50um. on 250f. mult	4·50	2·30

(iv) Nos. 424/6.

447	**155**	7um. on 35f. purple and green	45	25
448	-	8um. on 40f. pur, red and blue	75	25
449	-	28um. on 140f. pur & red	2·20	80

159 Footballers

1974. Air. World Cup Football Championship, West Germany.

450	**159**	7um. multicoloured	55	25
451	**159**	8um. multicoloured	75	25
452	**159**	20um. multicoloured	1·60	80
MS453		120×105 mm. 30um. multicoloured	2·75	2·75

160 Jules Verne and Scenes from Books

1974. Air. Jules Verne "Prophet of Space Travel" and "Skylab" Flights Commemoration.

454	**160**	70um. silver	7·25	7·25
455	-	70um. silver	7·25	7·25
456	**160**	250um. gold	22·00	22·00
457	-	250um. gold	22·00	22·00

DESIGNS: Nos. 455, 457, "Skylab" in Space.

161 Sir Winston Churchill

1974. Air. Birth Centenary of Sir Winston Churchill.

458	**161**	40um. red and purple	2·75	1·40

162 U.P.U. Monument and Globes

1974. Centenary of U.P.U.

459	**162**	30um. red, green & dp grn	2·50	1·10
460	**162**	50um. red, lt blue & blue	4·50	1·70

163 5 Ouguiya Coin and Banknote

1974. First Anniv of Introduction of Ouguiya Currency.

461	**163**	7um. black, green and blue	55	25
462	-	8um. black, mauve and green	60	25
463	-	20um. black, blue and red	1·50	65

DESIGNS: 8um. 10 ouguiya coin and banknote; 20um. 20 ouguiya coin and banknote.

164 Lenin

1974. Air. 50th Death Anniv of Lenin.

464	**164**	40um. green and red	4·00	1·80

1974. Treaty of Berne Centenary. Nos. 459/60 optd **9 OCTOBRE 100 ANS D'UNION POSTALE INTERNATIONALE.**

465	**162**	30um. red, green and deep green	2·50	1·40
466	**162**	50um. red, light blue and blue	4·50	1·80

1975. Nos. 287/91 surch in new currency.

467	-	1um. on 5f. orange, brown and green	10	10
468	-	2um. on 4f. red, green and brown	30	10
469	-	3um. on 2f. yellow, green and brown	30	25
470	**104**	10um. on 1f. brown, green and purple	80	30
471	-	12um. on 3f. olive, green and violet	1·20	45

166 Two Hunters

1975. Rock-carvings, Zemmour.

472	**166**	4um. red and brown	70	10
473	-	5um. purple	95	35
474	-	10um. blue and light blue	1·60	80

DESIGNS—VERT: 5um. Ostrich. HORIZ: 10um. Elephant.

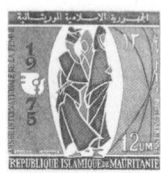

167 Mauritanian Women

1975. Air. International Women's Year.

475	**167**	12um. purple, brown and blue	75	25
476	-	40um. purple, brown and blue	2·75	1·10

DESIGNS: 40um. Head of Mauritanian woman.

168 Combined European and African Heads

1975. Europafrique.

477	**168**	40um. brown, red & bistre	2·75	1·10

169 Dr. Schweitzer

1975. Birth Centenary of Dr. Albert Schweitzer.

478	**169**	60um. olive, brown & green	4·00	2·30

1975. Pan-African Drought Relief. Nos. 301/2 surch **SECHERESSE SOLIDARITE AFRICAINE** and value.

479		15um. on 45f. multicoloured	1·50	70
480		25um. on 90f. multicoloured	2·30	1·10

171 Akoujt Plant and Man with Camel

1975. Mining Industry.

481	**171**	10um. brown, blue & orge	95	40
482	-	12um. blue, red and brown	1·30	60

DESIGN: 12um. Mining operations.

172 Fair Emblem

1975. Nouakchott National Fair.

483	**172**	10um. multicoloured	75	40

173 Throwing the Javelin

1975. Air. "Pre-Olympic Year". Olympic Games, Montreal (1976).

484	**173**	50um. red, green & brown	3·00	1·80
485	-	52um. blue, brown and red	3·00	1·80

DESIGN: 52um. Running.

174 Commemorative Medal

1975. 15th Anniv of Independence. Multicoloured.

486		10um. Type **174**	90	45
487		12um. Map of Mauritania	1·20	45

175 "Soyuz" Cosmonauts Leonov and Kubasov

1975. "Apollo–Soyuz" Space Link. Multicoloured.

488		8um. Type **175** (postage)	75	25
489		10um. "Soyuz" on launch-pad	95	40
490		20um. "Apollo" on launch-pad (air)	1·30	55
491		50um. Cosmonauts meeting astronauts	2·75	1·10
492		60um. Parachute splashdown	3·50	1·60
MS493		103×77 mm. 100um. Leonov Kubasov, Brand, Stafford and Slayton	5·50	2·50

176 Foot-soldier of Lauzun's Legion

1976. Bicentenary of American Independence. Multicoloured.

494		8um. Type **176** (postage)	85	25
495		10um. "Green Mountain" infantryman	1·20	45
496		20um. Lauzun Hussars officer (air)	1·20	50
497		50um. Artillery officer of 3rd Continental Regiment	3·50	1·10
498		60um. Grenadier of Gatinais' Regiment	4·25	1·60
MS499		100×125 mm. 100um. Soldier of Washington Guards	6·75	2·50

1976. Tenth Anniv of Arab Labour Charter. No. 408 surch **10e ANNIVERSAIRE DE LA CHARTE ARABE DU TRAVAIL** in French and Arabic.

500		12um. on 75f. blue, blk & grn	95	45

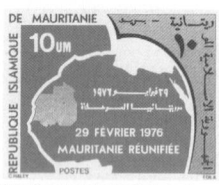

178 Commemorative Text on Map

1976. Reunification of Mauritania.

501	**178**	10um. green, lilac and deep green	95	45

181 Running

1976. Air. Olympic Games, Montreal.

514	**181**	10um. brown, green and violet	90	40
515	-	12um. brown, green and violet	1·10	60
516	-	52um. brown, green and violet	3·50	2·10

DESIGNS: 12um. Vaulting (gymnastics); 52um. Fencing.

182 LZ-4 at Friedrichshafen

1976. 75th Anniv of Zeppelin Airship. Multicoloured.

517		5um. Type **182** (postage)	30	10
518		10um. "Schwaben" over German Landscape	55	25
519		12um. "Hansa" over Heligoland	75	40
520		20um. "Bodensee" and Doctor H. Durr	1·40	55

521	50um. "Graf Zeppelin" over Capitol, Washington (air)	3·25	1·30
522	60um. "Graf Zeppelin II" crossing Swiss Alps	4·25	1·60
MS523	130×104 mm. 100um. "LZ-129" over Olympic Stadium, Berlin	7·50	2·30

183 Temple and Bas-relief

1976. UNESCO "Save Moenjodaro" (Pakistan) Campaign.

524	**183**	15um. multicoloured	1·20	55

184 Sacred Ibis and Yellow-billed Stork

1976. Air. Mauritanian Birds. Multicoloured.

525	50um. Type **184**	3·00	1·40
526	100um. Marabou storks (horiz)	6·00	2·30
527	200um. Long-crested and Martial eagles	13·00	5·50

185 Alexander Graham Bell, Early Telephone and Satellite

1976. Telephone Centenary.

528	**185**	10um. blue, lake and red	95	35

186 Mohammed Ali Jinnah

1976. Birth Centenary of Mohammed Ali Jinnah (first Governor-General of Pakistan).

529	**186**	10um. multicoloured	55	40

187 Capsule Assembly

1977. "Viking" Space Mission. Multicoloured.

530	10um. Misson Control (horiz) (postage)	60	25
531	12um. Type **187**	95	25
532	20um. "Viking" in flight (horiz) (air)	1·00	25
533	50um. "Viking" over Mars (horiz)	2·75	65
534	60um. Parachute descent	3·00	90
MS535	103×79 mm. 100um. "Viking" on Mars	5·50	1·80

188 Bush Hare

1977. Mauritanian Animals. Multicoloured.

536	5um. Type **188**	45	20
537	10um. Golden jackals	1·00	45

538	12um. Warthogs	1·40	60
539	14um. Lion and lioness	1·70	75
540	15um. African elephants	2·75	1·10

189 Frederic and Irene Joliot-Curie (Chemistry, 1935)

1977. Nobel Prize-winners. Multicoloured.

541	12um. Type **189** (postage)	1·40	25
542	15um. Emil von Behring and nurse inoculating patient (1901)	95	25
543	14um. George Bernard Shaw and scene from "Androcles and the Lion" (1925) (air)	95	25
544	55um. Thomas Mann and scene from "Joseph and his Brethren" (1929)	3·00	75
545	60um. International Red Cross and scene on Western Front (Peace Prize) (1917)	3·50	90
MS546	117×80 mm. 100um. General George C. Marshall (Peace, 1953)	8·00	2·20

190 A.P.U. Emblem

1977. 25th Anniv of Arab Postal Union.

547	**190**	12um. multicoloured	75	45

191 Oil Lamp

1977. Pottery from Tegdaoust.

548	**191**	1um. olive, brown and blue	10	10
549	-	2um. mauve, brown and blue	30	10
550	-	5um. orange, brown and blue	45	25
551	-	12um. brown, green and red	1·00	40

DESIGNS: 2um. Four-handled tureen; 5um. Large jar; 12um. Narrow-necked jug.

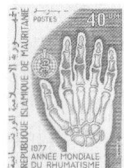

192 Skeleton of Hand

1977. World Rheumatism Year.

552	**192**	40um. orange, brown and green	3·00	1·60

193 Holy Kaaba, Mecca

1977. Air. Pilgrimage to Mecca.

553	**193**	12um. multicoloured	1·20	65

194 Charles Lindbergh and "Spirit of St. Louis"

1977. History of Aviation. Multicoloured.

554	12um. Type **194**	75	25
555	14um. Clement Ader and "Eole"	95	25
556	15um. Louis Bleriot and Bleriot XI	1·10	40
557	55um. General Italo Balbo and Savoia Marchetti S-55X flying boats	3·50	90
558	60um. Concorde	3·75	1·10
MS559	116×91 mm. 100um. Lindbergh standing beside "Spirit of St. Louis"	7·25	2·10

195 Dome of the Rock

1977. Palestinian Welfare.

560	**195**	12um. multicoloured	75	40
561	**195**	14um. multicoloured	95	55

196 Two Players

1977. World Cup Football Championship—Elimination Rounds. Multicoloured.

562	12um. Type **196** (postage)	60	10
563	14um. Sir Alf Ramsey and Wembley Stadium	75	25
564	15um. A "throw-in"	95	25
565	50um. Football and emblems (air)	2·75	85
566	60um. Eusebio Ferreira	3·25	1·30
MS567	119×81 mm. 100um. Players exchanging pennants	6·00	1·70

197 "Helene Fourment and Her Children" (Rubens)

1977. 400th Birth Anniv of Rubens. Paintings. Multicoloured.

568	12um. Type **197**	75	25
569	14um. "The Marquis of Spinola"	95	45
570	67um. "The Four Philosophers"	4·25	90
571	69um. "Steen Castle and Park" (horiz)	5·00	1·10
MS572	90×116 mm. 100um. "Rubens and Helene Fourment in the Garden"	6·75	2·10

198 Addra Gazelles

1978. Endangered Animals. Multicoloured.

573	5um. Scimitar oryx (horiz)	55	25
574	12um. Type **198**	1·40	25
575	14um. African manatee (horiz)	1·90	25
576	55um. Barbary sheep	5·00	90
577	60um. African elephant (horiz)	5·50	90
578	100um. Ostrich	7·50	1·50

199 Clasped Hands and President Giscard d'Estaing of France

1978. Air. Franco-African Co-operation. Embossed on foil.

579	199	250um. silver	13·00	13·00
580	199	500um. gold	28·00	28·00

199a Earth-mover and Route Map

1978. Nouakchott–Nema Highway. Multicoloured.

580a	12um. Type **199a**	10·00	7·00
580b	14um. Bulldozer and route map	12·00	8·00

200 Footballers

1978. World Cup Football Championship, Argentina. Multicoloured.

581	12um. Type **200**	70	30
582	14um. World Cup	80	45
583	20um. F.I.F.A. flag and football	1·40	50
MS584	82×70 mm. 50um. World Cup and football (horiz)	3·00	1·40

201 Raoul Follereau and St. George fighting Dragon

1978. 25th Anniv of Raoul Follereau Foundation.

585	**201**	12um. brown and green	1·90	90

202 Emblem and People holding Hands

1978. International Anti-Apartheid Year.

586	-	25um. brown, blue and red	1·30	80
587	**202**	30um. brown, blue & green	2·20	1·10

DESIGN—HORIZ: 25um. Emblem and people behind fence.

203 Charles de Gaulle

1978. Personalities. Multicoloured.

588	12um. Type **203**	1·50	45
589	14um. King Baudouin of Belgium	1·30	45
590	55um. Queen Elizabeth II (25th anniv of Coronation)	3·25	1·30

1978. Air. Philexafrique Stamp Exhibition, Libreville (Gabon) (1st issue), and Second International Stamp Fair, Essen (West Germany). As T **262** of Niger. Multicoloured.

591		20um. Water rail and Hamburg 1859 ½s. stamp	2·50	1·60
592		20um. Spotted hyena and Mauritania 1967 100f. South African crowned crane stamp	2·50	1·60

See also Nos. 619/20.

1978. Argentina's Victory in World Cup Football Championship. Nos. 562/6 optd ARGENTINE–PAYS BAS 3-1 in English and Arabic.

593	**196**	12um. mult (postage)	75	25
594	-	14um. multicoloured	95	40
595	-	1·20um. multicoloured	1·20	70
596	-	50um. multicoloured (air)	2·75	1·70
597	-	60um. multicoloured	3·25	2·10
MS598		119×81 mm. 100um. multicoloured	6·00	5·75

205 View of Nouakchott

1978. 20th Anniv of Nouakchott.

599	**205**	12um. multicoloured	75	50

206 Human Rights Emblem

1978. 30th Anniv of Declaration of Human Rights.

600	**206**	55um. red and blue	3·00	1·60

207 Wright Flyer I and Clement Ader's Avion III

1979. Air. 75th Anniv of First Powered Flight.

601	**207**	15um. grey, red and blue	95	55
602	-	40um. violet, blue & brn	2·75	1·50

DESIGN: 40um. Concorde and Wright Flyer I.

208 Key Chain

1979. Handicrafts. Multicoloured.

603		5um. Type **208**	45	25
604		7um. Tooth-brush case	55	30
605		10um. Knife sheath	75	40

209 "Market Peasant and Wife"

1979. 450th Birth Anniv of Albrecht Durer (artist). Each black and red.

606		12um. Type **209**	75	40
607		14um. "Young Peasant and his Wife"	1·30	75
608		55um. "Mercenary with Banner"	3·00	1·10
609		60um. "St. George and the Dragon"	3·75	1·30
MS610		114×107 mm. 100um. "Group of Mercenaries" (horiz)	6·50	4·00

210 Seated Buddha, Temple of Borobudur

1979. UNESCO Campaign for Preservation of Historic Monuments. Multicoloured.

611		12um. Type **210**	75	45
612		14um. Carthaginian warrior and hunting dog	95	45
613		55um. Erechtheum Caryatid, Acropolis	3·00	1·70

211 Rowland Hill and Paddle-steamer "Sirius"

1979. Death Centenary of Sir Rowland Hill. Multicoloured.

614		12um. Type **211**	60	10
615		14um. Hill and *Great Republic* (paddle-steamer)	95	25
616		55um. Hill and *Mauretania I* (liner)	2·75	80
617		60um. Hill and *Stirling Castle* (liner)	3·50	95
MS618		113×89 mm. 100um. Rowland Hill and Mauritanian 1906 25c. stamp	6·00	1·70

212 Satellite over Earth

1979. Philexafrique Exhibition, Libreville (2nd issue).

619	-	12um. multicoloured	1·30	70
620	**212**	30um. red, blue and lilac	3·25	1·90

DESIGN—HORIZ: 12um. Embossed leather cushion cover.

213 Mother and Children

1979. International Year of the Child. Multicoloured.

621		12um. Type **213**	60	30
622		14um. Mother with sleeping baby	95	55
623		40um. Children playing with ball	2·40	1·30

1979. Tenth Anniv of "Apollo 11" Moon Landing. Nos. 530/4 optd **ALUNISSAGE APOLLO XI JUILLET 1969**, with Lunar module, or surch also.

624		10um. Mission Control (horiz) (postage)	75	45
625		12um. Type **187**	70	45
626		14um. on 20um. "Viking" in flight (horiz) (air)	75	45
627		50um. "Viking" over Mars (horiz)	2·75	1·50
628		60um. Parachute descent	3·00	1·80
MS629		103×79 mm. 100um. multicoloured	6·00	5·75

215 Sprinter on Starting-blocks

1979. Pre-Olympic Year. Multicoloured.

630		12um. Type **215**	65	25
631		14um. Female runner	95	25
632		55um. Male runner leaving start	2·75	70
633		60um. Hurdling	3·25	80
MS634		102×78 mm. 100um. Male runner	6·00	1·70

215a Skipper

1979. Fish. Multicoloured.

634a		1um. Type **215a**	40	30
634b		2um. Swordfish		
634c		5um. Tub gurnard	55	25

216 Ice Hockey

1979. Winter Olympic Games, Lake Placid (1980). Ice Hockey. Multicoloured.

635		10um. Type **216**	55	10
636		12um. Saving a goal	65	10
637		14um. Goalkeeper and player	80	25
638		55um. Two players	2·50	75
639		60um. Goalkeeper	3·00	85
640		100um. Tackle	4·50	1·50

217 Woman pouring out Tea

1980. Taking Tea.

641	**217**	1um. multicoloured	10	10
642	**217**	5um. multicoloured	45	25
643	**217**	12um. multicoloured	75	45

218 Koran, World Map and Symbols of Arab Achievements

1980. The Arabs.

644	**218**	12um. multicoloured	60	45
645	**218**	15um. multicoloured	95	45

1980. Winter Olympics Medal Winners. Nos. 635/40 optd.

646		10um. Medaille de bronze SUEDE	55	25
647		12um. MEDAILLE DE BRONZE SUEDE	60	25
648		14um. Medaille d'argent U.R.S.S.	80	40
649		55um. MEDAILLE D'ARGENT U.R.S.S.	2·50	1·10
650		60um. MEDAILLE D'OR ETATS-UNIS	3·00	1·30
651		100um. Medaille d'or ETATS-UNIS	4·50	2·20

220 Holy Kaaba, Mecca

1980. Pilgrimage to Mecca. Multicoloured.

652		10um. Type **220**	1·20	45
653		50um. Pilgrims outside Mosque	3·50	1·70

221 Mother and Child

1980. World Red Cross Societies Day.

654	**221**	20um. multicoloured	7·50	1·30

222 Crowd greeting Armed Forces

1980. Armed Forces Festival.

655	**222**	12um. multicoloured	60	25
656	**222**	14um. multicoloured	95	40

223 Horse jumping Bar

1980. Olympic Games, Moscow. Multicoloured.

657		10um. Type **223**	55	10
658		20um. Water polo	1·20	25
659		50um. Horse jumping brick wall (horiz)	2·75	75
660		70um. Horse jumping stone wall	4·00	95
MS661		77×104 mm. 100um. Horse's head	6·50	2·30

224 Trees on Map of Mauritania

1980. Tree Day.

662	**224**	12um. multicoloured	1·20	60

225 "Rembrandt's Mother"

1980. Paintings by Rembrandt. Multicoloured.

663		10um. "Self-portrait"	75	25
664		20um. Type **225**	1·20	40
665		50um. "Portrait of a Man in Oriental Costume"	2·75	70
666		70um. "Titus Lisant"	3·50	1·20
MS667		104×79 mm. 100um. "The Polish Cavalier" (horiz)	6·00	2·10

226 Footballers

1980. Air. World Cup Football Championship, Spain (1982). Multicoloured.

668		10um. Type **226**	55	10
669		12um. Goalkeeper and players	60	25
670		14um. Goalkeeper catching ball	80	25
671		20um. Fighting for possession	1·00	45
672		67um. Tackle	3·50	90
MS673		103×81 mm. 100um. Match scene	6·00	2·10

1980. Olympic Medal Winners. Nos. 657/60 optd.

674		10um. VAINQUEUR KOWALLZYK (POL)	55	25
675		20um. VAINQUEUR THEURER (AUTR)	95	40
676		50um. VAINQUEUR URSS	2·50	90
677		70um. VAINQUEUR ROMAN (IT)	3·50	1·80
MS678		77×104 mm. 100um. VAINQUEUR/URSS	6·00	5·75

228 "Mastodonte del Giovi", 1853, Italy

1980. Steam Locomotives. Multicoloured.
679	10um. Type **228**		80	25
680	12um. Diesel ore train		95	25
681	14um. Chicago, Milwaukee and St. Paul Railway locomotive No. 810, U.S.A.		1·10	25
682	20um. Bury steam locomotive, 1837, Great Britain		1·50	40
683	67um. Locomotive No. 170, France		5·00	90
684	100um. Berlin–Potsdam line, Germany		7·25	1·40

229 Palm Tree, Crescent and Star, Maize and Map

1980. 20th Anniv of Independence.
685	**229**	12um. multicoloured	60	25
686	**229**	15um. multicoloured	95	45

230 El Haram Mosque

1981. 15th Century of Hegira. Multicoloured.
687	2um. Type **230**		10	10
688	12um. Medine Mosque		60	35
689	14um. Chinguetti Mosque		95	45

231 Space Shuttle in Orbit

1981. Air. Space Shuttle. Multicoloured.
690	12um. Type **231**		60	10
691	20um. Shuttle and space station		1·00	25
692	50um. Shuttle performing experiment		2·40	75
693	70um. Shuttle landing		3·50	1·00
MS694	103×78 mm. 100um. Shuttle and carrier plane		6·00	1·60

232 "The Harlequin"

1981. Air. Birth Centenary of Pablo Picasso. Multicoloured.
695	12um. Type **232**		75	15
696	20um. "Vase of Flowers"		1·20	40
697	50um. "Three Women at a Fountain" (horiz)		2·75	85
698	70um. "Dinard Landscape" (horiz)		3·75	1·20
699	100um. "Le Dejeuner sur l'Herbe" (horiz)		5·25	1·70

233 I.Y.D.P. Emblem

1981. International Year of Disabled People.
700	**233**	12um. violet, gold and blue	95	55

234 Open Landau

1981. British Royal Wedding. Multicoloured.
701	14um. Type **234**		80	25
702	18um. Light carriage		1·00	25
703	77um. Closed coupe		3·50	1·30
MS704	117×78 mm. 100um. Coach		6·50	1·70

235 George Washington

1981. Bicentenary of Battles of Yorktown and Chesapeake Bay. Multicoloured.
705	14um. Type **235**		60	25
706	18um. Admiral de Grasse		95	25
707	63um. Surrender of Cornwallis at Yorktown (horiz)		3·25	1·10
708	81um. Battle of Chesapeake Bay (horiz)		4·00	1·50

236 Columbus and "Pinta"

1981. 450th Death Anniv of Christopher Columbus. Multicoloured.
709	19um. Type **236**		1·70	55
710	55um. Columbus and "Santa Maria"		4·75	1·20

237 Wheat and F.A.O. Emblem

1981. World Food Day.
711	**237**	19um. multicoloured	95	55

238 Kemal Ataturk

1981. Birth Centenary of Kemal Ataturk (Turkish statesman).
712	**238**	63um. multicoloured	3·00	1·60

239 Eastern White Pelicans

1981. Birds of the Arguin. Multicoloured.
713	2um. Type **239**		80	30
714	18um. Greater flamingoes		2·75	1·10

240 Hand holding Torn Flag

1981. Battle of Karameh Commemoration.
715	**240**	14um. multicoloured	95	50

241 "Dermochelys coiacer"

1981. Turtles. Multicoloured.
716	1um. Type **241**		75	35
717	3um. "Chelonia mydas"		1·00	35
718	4um. "Eretmochelys imbricata"		1·40	55

242 Sea Scouts

1982. 75th Anniv of Boy Scout Movement. Multicoloured.
719	14um. Type **242**		95	45
720	19um. Scouts boarding rowing boat		1·20	40
721	22um. Scouts in rowing boat		1·40	55
722	92um. Scouts in yacht		4·75	1·50
MS723	105×80 mm. 100um. Lord Baden-Powell and Sea Scout		6·00	1·60

243 Deusenberg, 1921

1982. 75th Anniv of French Grand Prix Motor Race. Multicoloured.
724	7um. Type **243**		75	25
725	12um. Alfa Romeo, 1932		95	25
726	14um. Juan Fangio		1·20	40
727	18um. Renault, 1979		1·30	55
728	19um. Niki Lauda		1·30	55
MS729	114×89 mm. 100um. French Grand Prix, 1979		6·75	2·30

244 A.P.U. Emblem

1982. 30th Anniv of Arab Postal Union.
730	**244**	14um. orange and brown	75	45

245 Hexagonal Pattern

1982. World Telecommunications Day.
731	**245**	21um. multicoloured	95	60

246 Environmental Emblem on Map

1982. Tenth Anniv of U.N. Environmental Programme.
732	**246**	14um. blue and light blue	75	45

247 Princess of Wales

1982. 21st Birthday of Princess of Wales. Multicoloured.
733	21um. Type **247**		95	45
734	77um. Princess of Wales (different)		3·75	90
MS735	112×80 mm. 100um. Princess of Wales		5·25	1·50

248 Straw Hut

1982. Traditional Houses. Multicoloured.
736	14um. Type **248**		75	40
737	18um. Thatched hut		95	55
738	19um. Tent		1·00	65

1982. Birth of Prince William of Wales. Nos. 701/3 surch **NAISSANCE ROYALE 1982.**
739	14um. Type **234**		75	40
740	18um. Light carriage		95	45
741	77um. Closed coupe		3·50	1·70
MS742	117×78 mm. 100um. Coach		5·25	1·80

1982. Air. World Cup Football Championship Results. Nos. 668/72 optd **ITALIE 3 ALLEMAGNE (R.F.A.) 1.**
743	10um. Type **226**		55	25
744	12um. Goalkeeper punching ball		60	25
745	14um. Goalkeeper catching ball		80	40
746	20um. Three players		1·00	45
747	67um. Tackle		3·50	1·40
MS748	103×81 mm. 100um. Match scene		5·25	1·60

251 Cattle at Collinaire Dam, Hodh El Gharbi

1982. Agricultural Development.
749	14um. Type **251**		3·50	1·80
750	18um. Irrigation canal, Gorgol		4·75	2·10

252 Desert Rose

1982. Desert Rose.
751	**252**	21um. multicoloured	7·25	1·90

253 Montgolfier Balloon, 1783

1983. Bicent of Manned Flight. Multicoloured.
752	14um. Type **253**		1·00	25
753	18um. Charles's hydrogen balloon ascent, 1783 (horiz)		1·00	25
754	19um. Goodyear Aerospace airship		1·00	45

755	55um. Nieuport 11 "Bebe" biplane (horiz)	2·75	70
756	63um. Concorde (horiz)	3·00	80
757	77um. "Apollo 11" on Moon	3·50	95

No. 754 is wrongly inscribed "Zeppelin".

254 Ouadane

1983. Protection of Ancient Sites. Multicoloured.

758	14um. Type **254**	70	30
759	18um. Chinguetti	80	45
760	24um. Oualata	1·00	60
761	30um. Tichitt	1·50	80

255 Manuscript

1983. Ancient Manuscripts. Multicoloured.

762	2um. Type **255**	20	10
763	5um. Decorated manuscript	30	10
764	7um. Shield-shaped patterned manuscript	50	25

256 I.M.O. Emblem

1983. 25th Anniv of I.M.O.

765	**256** 18um. multicoloured	95	55

257 W.C.Y. Emblem

1983. World Communications Year.

766	**257** 14um. multicoloured	75	45

258 Customs Emblems

1983. 30th Anniv of Customs Co-operation Council.

767	**258** 14um. multicoloured	75	45

259 Pilatre de Rozier and Montgolfier Balloon

1983. Bicentenary of Manned Flight. Multicoloured.

768	10um. Type **259** (postage)	55	25
769	14um. John Wise and balloon "Atlantic"	1·10	25
770	25um. Charles Renard and Renard and Krebs' airship "La France" (horiz)	1·40	35
771	100um. Henri Juillot and Lebaudy-Juillot airship "Patrie" (horiz) (air)	6·00	1·40
MS772	101×81 mm. 100um. Joseph Montgolfier and balloon (46×37 mm)	6·00	1·70

260 Grinding Stone

1983. Prehistoric Grindstones. Multicoloured.

773	10um. Type **260**	1·00	55
774	14um. Pestle and mortar	1·50	65
775	18um. Grinding dish	2·10	1·10

261 Basketball

1983. Pre-Olympic Year. Multicoloured.

776	1um. Type **261** (postage)	20	10
777	20um. Wrestling	95	55
778	50um. Show-jumping	2·30	1·00
779	77um. Running (air)	4·25	1·30
MS780	85×85 mm. 100um. Football (41×35 mm)	5·25	1·60

262 Lord Baden-Powell (founder of Scout Movement)

1984. Celebrities. Multicoloured.

781	5um. Type **262** (postage)	30	10
782	14um. Goethe (poet)	75	35
783	25um. Rubens and detail of painting "The Virgin and Child"	1·30	45
784	100um. P. Harris (founder of Rotary International) (air)	5·50	1·40
MS785	85×75 mm. 100um. Rembrandt and painting "Arthemis" (38×47 mm)	5·50	1·60

263 Blue-finned Tuna

1984. Fishing Resources. Multicoloured.

786	1um. Type **263**	10	10
787	2um. Atlantic mackerel	10	10
788	5um. European hake	45	25
789	14um. Atlantic horse-mackerel	1·20	70
790	18um. Building a fishing boat	1·50	80

264 Durer and "Madonna and Child"

1984. Multicoloured.

791	10um. Type **264** (postage)	60	25
792	12um. "Apollo 11" and astronaut (15th anniv of first manned Moon landing)	75	35
793	50um. Chess pieces and globe	2·40	1·50
794	77um. Prince and Princess of Wales (air)	3·75	2·20
MS795	80×80 mm. 100um. Prince and Princess of Wales (38×41 mm)	6·00	4·00

265 Start of Race

1984. Olympic Games, Los Angeles. Multicoloured.

796	14um. Type **265**	75	40
797	18um. Putting the shot (vert)	1·00	55
798	19um. Hurdling (vert)	1·10	55
799	44um. Throwing the javelin (vert)	2·50	1·30
800	77um. High jumping	5·00	1·20
MS801	103×77 mm. 100um. Steeple-chase (vert)	6·50	6·50

266 Feeding Dehydrated Child from Glass

1984. Infant Survival Campaign. Multicoloured.

802	1um. Type **266**	10	10
803	4um. Breast-feeding baby	30	10
804	10um. Vaccinating baby	50	30
805	14um. Weighing baby	45	45

267 Aerial View of Complex

1984. Nouakchott Olympic Complex.

806	**267** 14um. multicoloured	95	55

268 Tents and Mosque Courtyard

1984. Pilgrimage to Mecca. Multicoloured.

807	14um. Type **268**	75	55
808	18um. Tents and courtyard (different)	1·20	80

269 Emblem

1984. Tenth Anniv of West African Economic Community.

809	**269** 14um. multicoloured	85	55

270 S. van den Berg (windsurfing)

1984. Air. Olympic Games Sailing Gold Medallists. Multicoloured.

810	14um. Type **270**	95	50
811	18um. R. Coutts ("Finn" class)	1·20	60
812	19um. Spain ("470" class)	1·50	70
813	44um. U.S.A. ("Soling" class)	3·25	1·50
MS814	110×80 mm. 100um. USA ("Flying Dutchman" class)	5·25	1·60

1984. Drought Relief. No. 537 surch **Aide au Sahel 84.**

815	18um. on 10um. multicoloured	1·20	70

272 Profiles and Emblem

1985. 15th Anniv of Technical and Cultural Co-operation Agency.

816	**272** 18um. blue, deep blue and red	95	70

273 Animal drinking in Water Droplet and Skeletons

1985. Campaign against Drought. Multicoloured.

817	14um. Type **273**	95	55
818	18um. Lush trees by river in water droplet and dead trees	1·40	80

274 Replanting Trees

1985. Anti-desertification Campaign. Multicoloured.

819	10um. Type **274**	60	45
820	14um. Animals fleeing from forest fire	95	55
821	18um. Planting grass to hold sand dunes	1·40	80

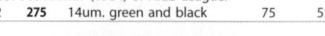

275 Emblem

1985. 30th Anniv (1984) of Arab League.

822	**275** 14um. green and black	75	55

276 Map, I.Y.Y. Emblem and Youths

1985. Air. Philexafrique Stamp Exhibition, Lome. Multicoloured.

823	40um. Type **276** (International Youth Year)	2·30	1·70
824	40um. Nouadhibou oil refinery	2·30	1·70

277 Bonaparte's Gulls

1985. Air. Birth Bicentenary of John J. Audubon (ornithologist). Multicoloured.

825	14um. Wester tanager and scarlet tanager	95	40
826	18um. Type **277**	1·30	50
827	19um. Blue jays	1·50	65
828	44um. Black skimmer	3·25	1·50
MS829	85×110 mm. 100um. American darters	7·75	5·25

278 Locomotive "Adler", 1835

1985. Anniversaries. Multicoloured.

830	12um. Type **278** (150th anniv of German railways)	75	25
831	18um. Class 10 steam locomotive, 1956 (150th anniv of German railways)	1·00	55
832	44um. Johann Sebastian Bach (composer, 300th birth anniv European Music Year)	2·00	1·30

833	77um. Georg Frederick Handel (composer, 300th birth anniv European Music Year)	3·50	2·20
834	90um. Statue of Liberty (centenary) (vert)	4·25	2·75
MS835	80×102 mm. 100um. Queen Elizabeth, the Queen Mother (85th birthday)	5·25	3·25

279 Globe and Emblem

1985. World Food Day.

836	**279**	18um. multicoloured	95	65

280 Tending Sheep and reading Book

1985. Air. Philexafrique Stamp Exhibition, Lome, Togo (2nd issue). Multicoloured.

837	50um. Type **280**	3·25	2·10
838	50um. Dock, iron ore mine and diesel train	3·25	2·10

281 Map showing Industries

1985. 25th Anniv of Independence.

839	**281**	18um. multicoloured	95	60

282 Development

1986. International Youth Year. Multicoloured.

840	18um. Type **282**	80	45
841	22um. Re-afforestation (voluntary work)	1·00	60
842	25um. Hands reaching from globe to dove (peace) (vert)	1·20	75

283 Latecoere Seaplane "Comte de la Vaulx" and Map

1986. Air. 55th Anniv (1985) of First Commercial South Atlantic Flight. Multicoloured.

843	18um. Type **283**	75	45
844	50um. Piper Twin Commanche airplanes crossing between maps of Africa and South America	2·20	1·40

284 Toujounine Earth Receiving Station

1986

845	**284**	25um. multicoloured	1·20	70

285 Heads of Mother and Pup

1986. World Wildlife Fund. Mediterranean Monk Seal. Multicoloured.

846	2um. Type **285**	1·20	50
847	5um. Mother and pup on land	1·80	70
848	10um. Mother and pup swimming	2·75	90
849	18um. Seal family	4·75	1·20
MS850	104×80 mm. 50um. Seal in water	8·25	2·75

286 Player and 1970 25f. Stamp

1986. Air. World Cup Football Championship, Mexico. Multicoloured.

851	8um. Type **286**	45	10
852	18um. Player and 1970 30f. stamp	80	40
853	22um. Player and 1970 70f. stamp	1·00	50
854	25um. Player and 1970 150f. stamp	1·20	70
855	40um. Player and World Cup trophy on "stamp"	2·00	1·00
MS856	194×80 mm. 100um. Players	4·75	2·50

287 Weaving

1986

857	**287**	18um. multicoloured	95	55

288 Emblem, Boeing 737, Douglas DC-10 and Map

1986. Air. 25th Anniv of Air Afrique.

858	**288**	26um. multicoloured	1·20	60

289 Indian, *Santa Maria* and Route Map

1986. 500th Anniv (1992) of Discovery of America by Christopher Columbus. Multicoloured.

859	2um. Type **289** (postage)	10	10
860	22um. Indian, *Nina* and map	90	55
861	35um. Indian, *Pinta* and map	1·50	80
862	150um. Indian, map and Christopher Columbus (air)	6·75	3·00
MS863	82×65 mm. 100um. Globe, Indian and Columbus (50×41 mm)	5·00	3·00

290 J. H. Dort, Comet Picture and Space Probe "Giotto"

1986. Appearance of Halley's Comet. Multicoloured.

864	5um. Type **290** (postage)	30	10

865	18um. William Huggins (astronomer) and "Ariane" space rocket	75	35
866	26um. E. J. Opik and space probes "Giotto" and "Vega"	1·20	60
867	80um. F. L. Whipple and "Planet A" space probe (air)	3·75	1·60
MS868	109×67 mm. 100um. Sir Edmund Halley, "Giotto" space probe and comet (50×35 mm)	4·50	3·00

291 Astronauts

1986. "Challenger" Astronauts Commemoration. Multicoloured.

869	7um. Type **291** (postage)	30	10
870	22um. Judith Resnik and astronaut	95	45
871	32um. Ellison Onizuka and Ronald McNair	1·30	75
872	43um. Christa Corrigan McAuliffe (air)	2·00	95
MS873	69×99 mm. 100um. Astronauts (different)	4·50	2·75

292 Red Seabream

1986. Fish and Birds. Multicoloured.

874	4um. Type **292**	25	25
875	22um. White spoonbills	1·50	80
876	32um. Bridled terns	1·80	1·10
877	98um. Sea-trout	5·25	3·50

See also Nos. 896/900.

293 Arrow through Victim

1986. Fourth Anniv of Massacre of Palestinian Refugees in Sabra and Shatila Camps, Lebanon.

878	**293**	22um. black, gold and red	95	60

294 Fisherman

1986. World Food Day.

879	**294**	22um. multicoloured	95	55

295 Dome of the Rock

1987. "Arab Jerusalem".

880	**295**	22um. multicoloured	95	55

296 Boxing

1987. Air. Olympic Games, Seoul (1988) (1st issue). Multicoloured.

881	30um. Type **296**	1·20	65
882	40um. Judo	1·80	85
883	50um. Fencing	2·30	1·00
884	75um. Wrestling	3·50	1·60
MS885	104×80 mm. 150um. Judo (different)	7·00	3·75

See also Nos. 902/MS906.

297 Cordoue Mosque

1987. 1200th Anniv of Cordoue Mosque.

886	**297**	30um. multicoloured	1·40	70

298 Women's Slalom

1987. Air. Winter Olympic Games, Calgary (1988). Multicoloured.

887	30um. Type **298**	1·40	65
888	40um. Men's speed skating	1·80	85
889	50um. Ice hockey	2·30	1·00
890	75um. Women's downhill skiing	3·50	1·60
MS891	104×79 mm. 150um. Men's cross-country skiing	7·00	3·00

299 Adults at Desk

1987. Literacy Campaign. Multicoloured.

892	18um. Type **299**	85	55
893	20um. Adults and children reading	1·20	80

300 People queueing for Treatment

1987. World Health Day.

894	**300**	18um. multicoloured	95	55

301 Map within Circle

1988. National Population and Housing Census.

895	**301**	20um. multicoloured	95	55

1988. Fish and Birds. Horiz designs as T **292**. Multicoloured.

896	1um. Small-horned blenny	45	25
897	7um. Grey triggerfish	1·90	50
898	15um. Skipjack tuna	3·25	1·10
899	18um. Great cormorants	1·30	70
900	80um. Royal terns	5·50	3·25

302 People with Candles

1988. 40th Anniv of W.H.O.

901	**302**	30um. multicoloured	1·40	65

303 Hammer Throwing

1988. Air. Olympic Games, Seoul (2nd issue). Multicoloured.

902	20um. Type **303**	95	35
903	24um. Discus	1·20	40
904	30um. Putting the shot	1·40	50
905	150um. Javelin throwing	6·50	2·75
MS906	107×83 mm. 170um. Javelin throwing (different)	7·50	4·00

1988. Winter Olympic Games Gold Medal Winners. Nos. 887/90 optd.

907	30um. Optd **Medaille d'or Vreni Schneider (Suisse)**	1·50	80
908	40um. Optd **Medaille d'or 1500m. Andre Hoffman (R.D.A.)**	2·00	1·20
909	50um. Optd **Medaille d'or U.R.S.S.**	2·30	1·40
910	75um. Optd **Medaille d'or Marina Kiehl (R.F.A.)**	3·75	2·20
MS911	150um. **Medaille d'or 15 km Mikhail Deviatiarov (USSR)**	7·25	3·75

305 Flags and Globe

1988. 75th Anniv of Arab Scout Movement.

912	**305**	35um. multicoloured	1·50	80

306 Men at Ballot Box

1988. First Municipal Elections. Multicoloured.

913	20um. Type **306**	95	40
914	24um. Woman at ballot box	1·30	55

307 Emblem

1988. 25th Anniv of Organization of African Unity.

915	**307**	40um. multicoloured	1·80	90

308 Ploughing with Oxen

1988. Tenth Anniv of International Agricultural Development Fund.

916	**308**	35um. multicoloured	2·00	1·00

309 Port Activities

1989. First Anniv of Nouakchott Free Port.

917	**309**	24um. multicoloured	1·50	85

310 "Heliothis armigera"

1989. Plant Pests. Multicoloured.

918	2um. Type **310**	10	10
919	6um. "Aphis gossypii"	30	10
920	10um. "Agrotis ypsilon"	55	25
921	20um. "Chilo" sp.	1·20	45
922	24um. "Plitella xylostella"	1·50	55
923	30um. "Henosepilachna elaterii"	1·70	55
924	42um. "Trichoplusia ni"	2·50	1·00

311 "Nomadacris septemfasciata"

1989. Locusts. Multicoloured.

925	5um. Type **311**	45	10
926	20um. Locusts mating	1·00	50
927	24um. Locusts emerging from chrysallis	1·30	50
928	40um. Locusts flying	2·30	1·00
929	88um. Locust (different)	5·00	2·00

312 Men of Different Races embracing

1989. Philexfrance '89 Int Stamp Exn, Paris, and Bicent of French Revolution.

930	**312**	35um. multicoloured	1·80	85

313 Footballers

1989. World Cup Football Championship, Italy (1990) (1st issue).

931	**313**	20um. multicoloured	1·20	55

See also Nos. 937/41.

314 Attan'eem Migat, Mecca

1989. Pilgrimage to Mecca.

932	**314**	20um. multicoloured	95	45

315 Emblem

1989. 25th Anniv of African Development Bank.

933	**315**	37um. black and mauve	1·50	70

316 Carpet

1989

934	**316**	50um. multicoloured	2·75	1·20

317 Youths

1989. Second Anniv of Palestinian "Intifada" Movement.

935	**317**	35um. multicoloured	1·80	75

318 Member Countries' Leaders

1990. First Anniv of Arab Maghreb Union.

936	**318**	50um. multicoloured	2·20	1·00

319 Players

1990. Air. World Cup Football Championship, Italy (2nd issue).

937	**319**	50um. multicoloured	2·30	95
938	-	60um. multicoloured	2·75	1·00
939	-	70um. multicoloured	3·50	1·20
940	-	90um. multicoloured	4·50	1·50
941	-	150um. multicoloured	7·00	2·40

DESIGNS: 60 to 150um. Show footballers.

320 Envelopes on Map

1990. 20th Anniv of Multinational Postal Training School, Abidjan.

942	**320**	50um. multicoloured	2·20	95

321 Books and Desk

1990. International Literacy Year.

943	**321**	60um. multicoloured	2·75	1·40

322 Maps and Earth-moving Vehicles

1990. Mineral Resources.

944	**322**	60um. multicoloured	3·25	1·70

323 Dressage

1990. Olympic Games, Barcelona (1992). Multicoloured.

945	5um. Type **323** (postage)	25	25
946	50um. Archery	2·00	80
947	60um. Throwing the hammer	2·30	1·30
948	75um. Football	3·00	1·20
949	90um. Basketball	4·00	1·40
950	220um. Table tennis (air)	9·00	3·25
MS951	120×84 mm. 150um. Running	7·00	2·75

324 Emblem

1990. Second Anniv of Declaration of State of Palestine.

952	**324**	85um. multicoloured	3·75	2·10

325 Camp

1990. Integration of Repatriates from Senegal. Multicoloured.

953	50um. Type **325**	2·50	1·40
954	75um. Women's sewing group	3·75	2·10
955	85um. Water collection	4·75	2·10

326 Map, Dove and Mandela

1990. Release from South African Prison of Nelson Mandela.

956	**326**	85um. multicoloured	4·00	2·30

327 Downhill skiing

1990. Winter Olympic Games, Albertville (1992). Multicoloured.

957	60um. Type **327** (postage)	2·40	95
958	75um. Cross-country skiing	3·25	1·20
959	90um. Ice hockey	4·00	1·50
960	220um. Figure skating (pairs) (air)	9·50	3·25
MS961	137×95 mm. 150um. Slalom	6·75	4·00

328 Blue Leg

1991. Scouts, Fungi and Butterflies. Multicoloured.

962	5um. Type **328** (postage)	40	10
963	50um. "Agaricus bitorquis edulis"	2·40	80
964	60um. "Bunea alcinoe" (butterfly)	2·75	1·00
965	90um. "Salamis cytora" (butterfly)	4·50	1·60
966	220um. "Bronze boletus"	10·00	3·50

967	75um. "Cyrestis camillus" (butterfly) (air)	3·00	1·60
MS968	85×107 mm. 150um. "Mesoacidalia aglaja" (butterfly) and "Clathrus rubber"	7·50	7·25

329 Dish Aerials and Transmitting Tower

1991. 30th Anniv of Independence. Multicoloured.

969	50um. Type **329**	1·00	65
970	60um. Container ship in dock	2·20	1·40
971	100um. Workers in field	3·25	1·80

330 Woman carrying Bucket of Water

1991. World Meteorological Day.

972	**330**	100um. multicoloured	5·00	2·75

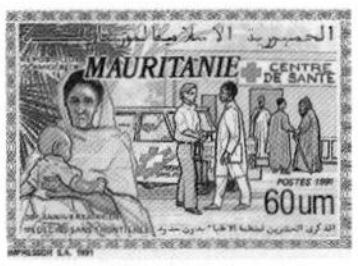

331 Health Centre

1991. 20th Anniv of Medecins sans Frontieres (international medical relief organization).

973	**331**	60um. multicoloured	3·00	1·60

332 Cats

1991. Domestic Animals. Multicoloured.

974	50um. Type **332**	2·20	1·40
975	60um. Basenji dog	3·50	2·10

333 Globe and Stylized Figures

1991. World Population Day.

976	**333**	90um. multicoloured	4·00	2·10

334 Blind Woman with Sight restored

1991. Anti-blindness Campaign.

977	**334**	50um. multicoloured	2·75	1·40

335 Nouakchott Electricity Station

1991. Second Anniv of Nouakchott Electricity Station.

978	**335**	50um. multicoloured	2·75	1·20

336 Quarrying

1993. Mineral Exploitation, Haoudat. Multicoloured.

979	50um. Type **336**	2·50	1·40
980	60um. Dry land	3·00	1·90

337 Camel Train

1993

981	**337**	50um. multicoloured	2·50	1·50
982	**337**	60um. multicoloured	2·75	1·90

338 Palestinians

1993. Palestinian "Intifada" Movement. Multicoloured.

983	50um. Type **338**	2·50	1·50
984	60um. Palestinian children by fire (horiz)	3·00	1·90

339 Four-man Bobsleighing

1993. Winter Olympic Games, Lillehammer. Multicoloured.

985	10um. Type **339** (postage)	45	20
986	50um. Luge	1·80	90
987	60um. Figure skating	2·20	1·00
988	80um. Skiing	3·00	1·60
989	220um. Cross-country skiing	9·00	4·25
MS990	121×82 mm. 150um. Ski jumping (air)	6·75	3·50

340 Soldier Field, Chicago

1994. World Cup Football Championship, U.S.A. Players and Stadiums. Multicoloured.

991	10um. Type **340**	45	20
992	50um. Foxboro Stadium, Boston	1·80	90
993	60um. Robert F. Kennedy Stadium, Washington D.C.	2·20	1·00
994	90um. Stanford Stadium, San Francisco	3·00	1·60
995	220um. Giant Stadium, New York	9·00	4·25
MS996	123×84 mm. 150um. Rose Bowl, Los Angeles	6·75	3·50

341 Anniversary Emblem and 1962 15f. Stamp

1995. 50th Anniv of U.N.O.

997	**341**	60um. multicoloured	1·50	90

342 Stabilizing Desert

1995. 50th Anniv of F.A.O. Multicoloured.

998	50um. Type **342**	1·20	75
999	60um. Fishermen launching boat	1·50	95
1000	90um. Planting crops	2·00	1·40

345 Weaving

1995. Crafts. Multicoloured.

1006	50um. Type **345**	
1007	60um. Metalwork	

346 Door

1995. Tourism. Re-vitalization of Ancient Towns. Multicoloured.

1008	10um. Type **346**
1009	20um. Arch and rubble
1010	40um. Town in desert
1011	50um. Door in ornate wall

347 Start of Race

1996. Olympic Games, Atlanta, U.S.A. Multicoloured.

1012	20um. Type **347**
1013	30um. Start of race (horiz)
1014	40um. Running in lane
1015	50um. Long-distance race (horiz)

348 Beaded Locks and Headdress

1996. Traditional Hairstyles. Multicoloured.

1016	50um. Type **348**
1017	60um. Woman with hair adornments

349 Ball-in-Pot Game

1996. Traditional Games. Multicoloured.

1018	50um. Type **349**
1019	60um. Strategy game with spherical and conical pieces (horiz)
1020	90um. Pegs-in-board game (horiz)

350 Family

1996. 50th Anniv of United Nations Children's Fund. The Rights of the Child. Showing children's drawings. Multicoloured.

1021	50um. Type **350**
1022	60um. Boy in wheelchair

OFFICIAL STAMPS

O41 Cross of Trarza

1961

O150	**O41**	1f. purple and blue	10	10
O151	**O41**	3f. myrtle and red	10	10
O152	**O41**	5f. brown and green	30	10
O153	**O41**	10f. blue and turquoise	30	10
O154	**O41**	15f. orange and blue	40	25
O155	**O41**	20f. green and myrtle	55	25
O156	**O41**	25f. red and orange	55	40
O157	**O41**	30f. green and purple	75	55
O158	**O41**	50f. sepia and red	1·20	70
O159	**O41**	100f. blue and orange	2·00	1·10
O160	**O41**	200f. red and green	4·50	2·30

O179

1976

O502	**O179**	1um. multicoloured	10	10
O503	**O179**	2um. multicoloured	10	10
O504	**O179**	5um. multicoloured	30	10
O505	**O179**	10um. multicoloured	55	25
O506	**O179**	12um. multicoloured	80	45
O507	**O179**	40um. multicoloured	2·50	1·40
O508	**O179**	50um. multicoloured	3·00	1·60

POSTAGE DUE STAMPS

1906. Stamps of 1906 optd **T** in a triangle.

D18	**I**	5c. green and red	60·00
D19	**I**	10c. pink and blue	60·00
D20	**J**	20c. black and red on blue	85·00
D21	**J**	25c. blue and red	85·00
D22	**J**	30c. brown & red on pink	£140
D23	**J**	40c. red on blue	£500
D24	**J**	50c. violet and red	£140
D25	**K**	1f. black and red on blue	£225

1906. "Natives" key-type inscr "MAURITANIE" in blue (10, 30c.) or red (others).

D25a	**L**	5c. green	1·40	90
D26	**L**	10c. purple	1·80	2·00
D27	**L**	15c. blue on blue	3·50	2·30
D28	**L**	20c. black on yellow	3·50	11·00
D29	**L**	30c. red on cream	5·50	13·00
D30	**L**	50c. violet	9·75	42·00
D31	**L**	60c. black on buff	7·00	23·00
D32	**L**	1f. black on pink	13·00	44·00

1914. "Figure" key-type inscr "MAURITANIE".

D35	**M**	5c. green	35	2·50
D36	**M**	10c. red	10	35
D37	**M**	15c. grey	10	4·75
D38	**M**	20c. brown	35	5·75
D39	**M**	30c. blue	45	5·75
D40	**M**	50c. black	75	5·00
D41	**M**	60c. orange	50	4·00
D42	**M**	1f. violet	80	5·00

1927. Surch in figures.

D67	2f. on 1f. purple	1·00	11·00
D68	3f. on 1f. brown	65	11·50

D40 Qualata Motif

1961

D150	**D40**	1f. yellow and purple	10	10
D151	**D40**	2f. grey and red	10	10
D152	**D40**	5f. pink and red	30	25
D153	**D40**	10f. green and myrtle	45	25
D154	**D40**	15f. brown and drab	45	25
D155	**D40**	20f. blue and red	60	25
D156	**D40**	25f. red and green	95	70

D55 Ruppell's Griffon

1963. Birds. Multicoloured.

D177	50c. Type D **55**	20	10
D178	50c. Common crane	20	10
D179	1f. Eastern white pelican	25	10
D180	1f. Garganey	25	10
D181	2f. Golden oriole	30	10
D182	2f. Variable sunbird	30	10
D183	5f. Great snipe	45	40
D184	5f. Common shoveler	45	40
D185	10f. Vulturine guineafowl	90	90
D186	10f. Black stork	90	90
D187	15f. Grey heron	1·10	1·10

D188	15f. White stork	1·10	1·10
D189	20f. Paradise whydah	1·60	1·60
D190	20f. Red-legged partridge	1·60	1·60
D191	25f. Little stint	2·10	2·10
D192	25f. Arabian bustard	2·10	2·10

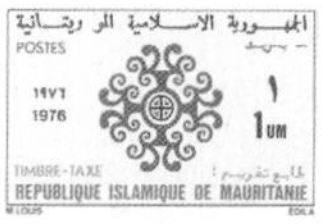
D180

1976

D509	**D180**	1um. multicoloured	10	10
D510	**D180**	3um. multicoloured	30	25
D511	**D180**	10um. multicoloured	55	55
D512	**D180**	12um. multicoloured	65	65
D513	**D180**	20um. multicoloured	1·00	95

APPENDIX

The following stamps have either been issued in excess of postal needs or have not been available to the public in a reasonable quantities at face value. Such stamps may later be given full listing if there is evidence of regular postal use.

1962

World Refugee Year (1960). Optd on 1960 Definitive issue, 30, 50, 60f.
Olympic Games in Rome (1960) and Tokyo (1964). Surch on 1960 Definitive issue 75f. on 15f., 75f. on 20f.
European Steel and Coal Community and Exploration of Iron-ore in Mauritania. Optd on 1960 Definitive issue. Air 500f.
Malaria Eradication. Optd on 1960 Definitive issue. Air. 100, 200f.

Pt. 1

MAURITIUS

An island in the Indian Ocean, east of Madagascar. Attained self-government on 1 September 1967, and became independent on 12 March 1968.

1847. 12 pence = 1 shilling; 20 shillings = 1 pound.
1878. 100 cents = 1 rupee.

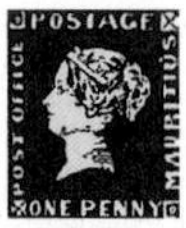
1 ("POST OFFICE")

1847. Imperf.

1	1	1d. red		£1100000
2	1	2d. blue		£1300000

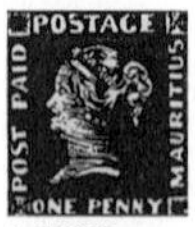
2 ("POST PAID")

1848. Imperf.

23	2	1d. red	£5000	£700
25	2	2d. blue	£6000	£1000

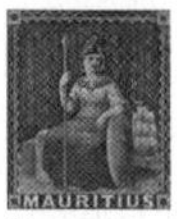
3

1854. Surch FOUR-PENCE. Imperf.

26	3	4d. green	£1600	£450

1858. No value on stamps. Imperf.

27		(4d.) green	£450	£200
28		(6d.) red	55·00	£120
29		(9d.) purple	£800	£200

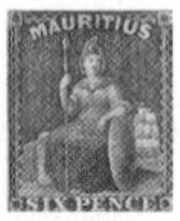
5

1859. Imperf.

32	5	6d. blue	£750	55·00
33	5	6d. black	35·00	65·00
34	5	1s. red	£3000	60·00
35	5	1s. green	£600	£150

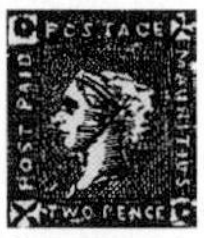
6

1859. Imperf.

39	6	2d. blue	£4000	£800

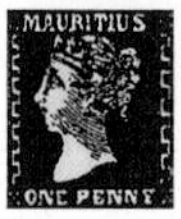
8

1859. Imperf.

42	**8**	1d. red	£7500	£1300
44	**8**	2d. blue	£4250	£800

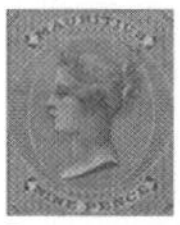
9

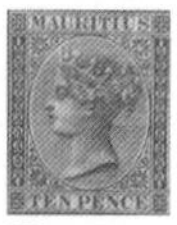
10

1860

56	**9**	1d. purple	75·00	17·00
57	**9**	1d. brown	90·00	12·00
59	**9**	2d. blue	70·00	12·00
61a	**9**	3d. red	85·00	19·00
62	**9**	4d. red	90·00	3·75
50	**9**	6d. grey	£400	£110
63	**9**	6d. violet	£400	42·00
65	**9**	6d. green	£225	6·50
51	**9**	9d. purple	£180	42·00
66	**9**	9d. green	£180	£350
67	**10**	10d. red	£350	55·00
53	**9**	1s. green	£850	£190
69	**9**	1s. blue	£130	25·00
70	**9**	1s. yellow	£275	12·00
71	**9**	5s. mauve	£250	55·00

1862. Perf.

54	**5**	6d. black	32·00	£100
55	**5**	1s. green	£2750	£325

HALF
PENNY
(11)

1876. Surcharged with T 11.

76	**9**	½d. on 9d. purple	23·00	21·00
77	**10**	½d. on 10d. red	4·00	26·00

HALF PENNY
(13)

1877. Surch with T 13.

79		½d. on 10d. red	9·50	45·00

1877. Surch in words.

80	**9**	1d. on 4d. red	22·00	24·00
81	**9**	1s. on 5s. mauve	£325	£120

1878. Surch.

83	**10**	2c. red	15·00	9·50
84	**9**	4c. on 1d. brown	24·00	8·50
85	**9**	8c. on 2d. blue	80·00	3·75
86	**9**	13c. on 3d. red	23·00	42·00
87	**9**	17c. on 4d. red	£190	4·00
88	**9**	25c. on 6d. blue	£275	7·00
89	**9**	38c. on 9d. purple	42·00	95·00
90	**9**	50c. on 1s. green	90·00	4·50
91	**9**	2r.50 on 5s. mauve	19·00	23·00

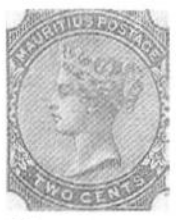
18

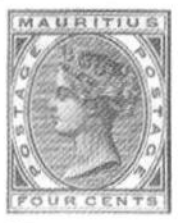
19

1879. Various frames.

101	**18**	1c. violet	1·75	45
102	**18**	2c. red	35·00	5·50
103	**18**	2c. green	4·00	60
93	**19**	4c. orange	60·00	3·50
105	**19**	4c. red	4·25	1·00
106	-	8c. blue	4·00	1·50
95	-	13c. grey	£170	£300
107	-	15c. brown	8·50	1·25
108	-	15c. blue	9·50	1·25
109	-	16c. brown	9·00	2·50
96	-	17c. red	85·00	9·00
110	-	25c. olive	11·00	3·50
98	-	38c. purple	£190	£350
99	-	50c. green	5·00	4·25
111	-	50c. orange	40·00	17·00
100	-	2r.50 purple	55·00	80·00

1883. No. 96 surch 16 CENTS.

112	16c. on 17c. red	£170	55·00

1883. No. 96 surch SIXTEEN CENTS.

115	16c. on 17c. red	£110	2·00

1885. No. 98 surch 2 CENTS with bar.

116	2c. on 38c. purple	£160	45·00

1887. No. 95 surch 2 CENTS without bar.

117	2c. on 13c. grey	75·00	£120

1891. Surch in words with or without bar.

123	**18**	1c. on 2c. violet	2·50	1·25
124	-	1c. on 16c. brown (No. 109)	2·50	3·75
118	**19**	2c. on 4c. red	1·75	80
119	-	2c. on 17c. red (No. 96)	£140	£150
120	**9**	2c. on 38c. on 9d. purple (No. 89)	12·00	6·50
121	-	2c. on 38c. purple (No. 98)	10·00	14·00

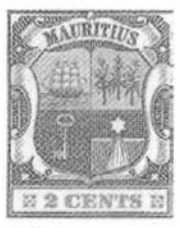
36

1895

127	**36**	1c. purple and blue	75	1·50
128	**36**	2c. purple and orange	6·50	50
129	**36**	3c. purple	70	50
130	**36**	4c. purple and green	4·25	50
131	**36**	6c. green and red	5·50	4·00
132	**36**	18c. green and blue	18·00	3·50

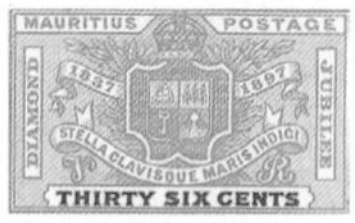
37

1898. Diamond Jubilee.

133	**37**	36c. orange and blue	12·00	24·00

1899. Surch in figures and words.

137	-	4c. on 16c. brown (No. 109)	13·00	22·00
134	**36**	6c. on 18c. (No. 132)	1·25	1·00
156	**36**	12c. on 18c. (No. 132)	2·75	8·50
163	**37**	12c. on 36c. (No. 133)	1·75	1·25
135	**37**	15c. on 36c. (No. 133)	2·75	1·75

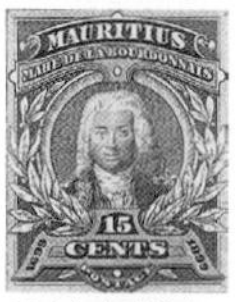
40 Admiral Mahe de Labourdonnais, Governor of Mauritius 1735–46

1899. Birth Bicentenary of Labourdonnais.

136	**40**	15c. blue	27·00	4·25

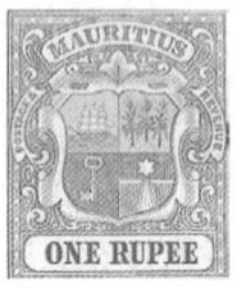
42

1900

138	**36**	1c. grey and black	50	10
139	**36**	2c. purple	75	20
140	**36**	3c. green & red on yellow	3·75	1·25
141	**36**	4c. purple & red on yellow	1·75	40
142	**36**	4c. green and violet	1·75	2·00
167a	**36**	4c. black and red on blue	14·00	10
144	**36**	5c. purple on buff	9·50	80·00
145	**36**	5c. purple & black on buff	2·50	2·50
146	**36**	6c. purple and red on red	3·25	80
147	**36**	8c. green & black on buff	3·75	12·00
148	**36**	12c. black and red	2·50	2·25
149	**36**	15c. green and orange	25·00	9·50
171	**36**	15c. black & blue on blue	4·00	35
151a	**36**	25c. green & red on green	4·75	24·00
174	**36**	50c. green on yellow	2·75	5·00
175	**42**	1r. grey and red	45·00	60·00
154	**42**	2r.50 green & blk on blue	32·00	£150
155	**42**	5r. purple and red on red	95·00	£160

1902. Optd Postage & Revenue.

157	**36**	4c. purple and red on yellow	1·25	20
158	**36**	6c. green and red	1·25	2·75
159	**36**	15c. green and orange	6·00	1·25
160	-	25c. olive (No. 110)	7·50	2·75
161	-	50c. green (No. 99)	19·00	6·00
162	-	2r.50 purple (No. 100)	£120	£200

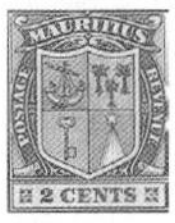
46

1910

205	**46**	1c. black	1·00	1·00
206	**46**	2c. brown	1·00	10
207	**46**	2c. purple on yellow	3·25	1·75
183	**46**	3c. green	3·00	10
209	**46**	4c. green and red	1·50	1·75
210	**46**	4c. green	1·00	10
211	**46**	4c. brown	4·25	2·25
186	**46**	6c. red	5·00	20
213	**46**	6c. mauve	1·25	10
187	**46**	8c. orange	3·00	1·50
215	**46**	10c. grey	2·00	3·25
216	**46**	10c. red	11·00	6·50
217	**46**	12c. red	1·50	40
218	**46**	12c. grey	1·75	4·75
219b	**46**	15c. blue	1·00	25
220	**46**	20c. blue	2·00	80
221	**46**	20c. purple	8·50	15·00

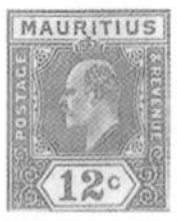
47

1910

185	**47**	5c. grey and red	2·75	3·00
188	**47**	12c. grey	3·50	2·75
190	**47**	25c. black & red on yellow	2·00	12·00
191	**47**	50c. purple and black	2·50	18·00
192	**47**	1r. black on green	17·00	12·00
193	**47**	2r.50 black and red on blue	26·00	70·00
194	**47**	5r. green and red on yellow	40·00	95·00
195	**47**	10r. green and red on green	£160	£250

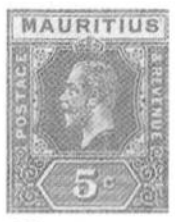
48

1913

223	**48**	1c. black	2·25	2·75
224	**48**	2c. brown	1·00	10
225	**48**	3c. green	2·00	40
226	**48**	4c. green and red	3·00	30
226c	**48**	4c. green	13·00	45
227	**48**	5c. grey and red	1·00	10
228	**48**	6c. brown	5·00	60
229	**48**	8c. orange	2·00	15·00
230	**48**	10c. red	4·00	20
232	**48**	12c. red	65	3·50
198	**48**	12c. grey	7·50	1·00
233	**48**	15c. blue	4·50	20
234	**48**	20c. purple	4·50	40
235	**48**	20c. blue	10·00	2·50
236	**48**	25c. black & red on yellow	1·00	15
237	**48**	50c. purple and black	7·50	4·00
238	**48**	1r. black on green	6·50	50
239	**48**	2r.50 black & red on blue	20·00	18·00
240	**48**	5r. green and red on yellow	45·00	50·00
204d	**48**	10r. green & red on green	45·00	£170

1924. As T 42 but Arms similar to T 46.

222	50r. purple and green	£900	£2500

1925. Surch with figures, words and bar.

242	**46**	3c. on 4c. green	7·50	6·00
243	**46**	10c. on 12c. red	45	1·50
244	**46**	15c. on 20c. blue	60	1·50

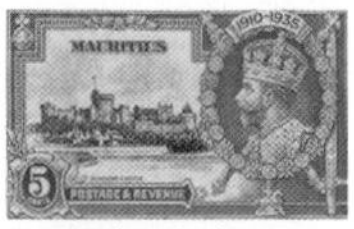
50a Windsor Castle

1935. Silver Jubilee.

245	**50a**	5c. blue and grey	50	10
246	**50a**	12c. green and blue	4·50	10
247	**50a**	20c. brown and blue	5·50	20
248	**50a**	1r. grey and purple	29·00	50·00

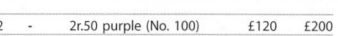

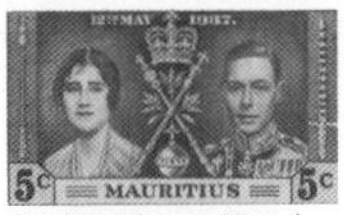

50b King George VI and Queen Elizabeth

1937. Coronation.

249	**50b**	5c. violet	40	20
250	**50b**	12c. red	75	2·25
251	**50b**	20c. blue	1·75	1·00

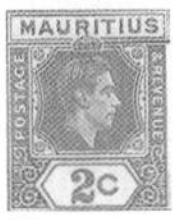

51

1938

252	**51**	2c. grey	30	10
253	**51**	3c. purple and red	2·00	2·00
254b	**51**	4c. green	2·00	2·25
255a	**51**	5c. violet	3·25	20
256b	**51**	10c. red	2·50	20
257	**51**	12c. orange	1·00	20
258	**51**	20c. blue	1·00	10
259b	**51**	25c. purple	8·50	10
260b	**51**	1r. brown	19·00	1·75
261a	**51**	2r.50 violet	35·00	25·00
262a	**51**	5r. olive	35·00	40·00
263a	**51**	10r. purple	15·00	40·00

1946. Victory. As T 8a of Pitcairn Islands.

264	5c. violet	10	75
265	20c. blue	20	25

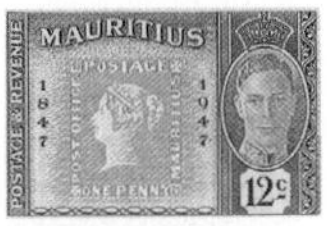

52 1d. "Post Office" Mauritius and King George VI

1948. Cent of First British Colonial Stamp.

266	**52**	5c. orange and mauve	10	50
267	**52**	12c. orange and green	15	25
268	-	20c. blue	15	10
269	-	1r. blue and brown	25	30

DESIGN: 20c., 1r. As Type **52**, but showing 2d. "Post Office" Mauritius.

1948. Silver Wedding. As T 8b/c of Pitcairn Islands.

270	5c. violet	10	10
271	10r. mauve	17·00	42·00

1949. U.P.U. As T 8d/g of Pitcairn Islands.

272	12c. red	50	2·00
273	20c. blue	2·25	2·50
274	35c. purple	60	1·50
275	1r. brown	50	20

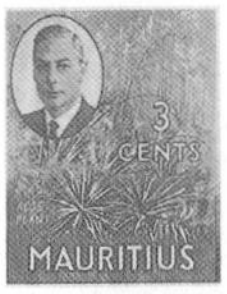

55 Aloe Plant

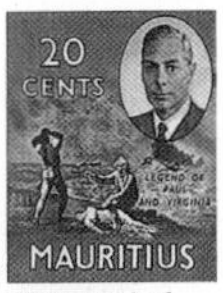

60 Legend of Paul and Virginie

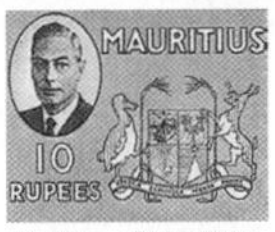

67 Arms of Mauritius

1950

276	-	1c. purple	10	50
277	-	2c. red	15	10
278	**55**	3c. green	60	4·25
279	-	4c. green	20	3·00
280	-	5c. blue	15	10
281	-	10c. red	30	75
282	-	12c. green	1·50	3·00
283	**60**	20c. blue	1·00	15
284	-	25c. red	2·00	40
285	-	35c. violet	40	10
286	-	50c. green	2·75	50
287	-	1r. brown	9·00	10
288	-	2r.50 orange	21·00	18·00
289	-	5r. brown	22·00	18·00
290	**67**	10r. blue	17·00	42·00

DESIGNS—HORIZ: 1c. Labourdonnais sugar factory; 2c. Grand Port; 5c. Rempart Mountain; 10c. Transporting cane; 12c. Mauritius dodo and map; 35c. Government House, Reduit; 1r. Timor deer; 2r.50, Port Louis; 5r. Beach scene. VERT: 4c. Tamarind Falls; 25c. Labourdonnais statue; 50c. Pieter Both Mountain.

1953. Coronation. As T 8i of Pitcairn Islands.

291	10c. black and green	1·50	15

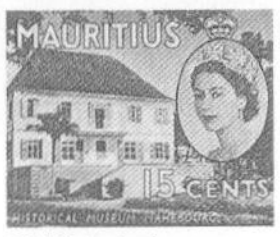

69 Historical Museum, Mahebourg

1953. As 1950 but portrait of Queen Elizabeth II. Designs as for corresponding values except where stated.

293	-	2c. red	10	10
294	-	3c. green	30	40
295	-	4c. purple (as 1c.)	10	1·00
296	-	5c. blue	10	10
314	-	10c. green (as 4c.)	15	10
298	**69**	15c. red	10	10
299	-	20c. red (as 25c.)	15	20
300	-	25c. blue (as 20c.)	1·50	10
301	-	35c. violet	20	10
302	-	50c. green	55	85
315	-	60c. green (as 12c.)	4·00	10
303	-	1r. sepia	30	10
316	-	2r.50 orange	13·00	8·50
305	-	5r. brown	22·00	10·00
306	-	10r. blue	13·00	2·00

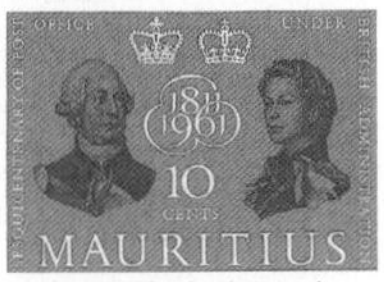

70 Queen Elizabeth II and King George III (after Lawrence)

1961. 150th Anniv of British Post Office in Mauritius.

307	**70**	10c. black and red	10	10
308	**70**	20c. ultramarine and blue	30	50
309	**70**	35c. black and yellow	40	50
310	**70**	1r. purple and green	60	30

1963. Freedom from Hunger. As T 21a of Pitcairn Islands.

311	60c. violet	40	10

1963. Cent of Red Cross. As T 20b of Pitcairn Islands.

312	10c. red and black	15	10
313	60c. red and blue	60	20

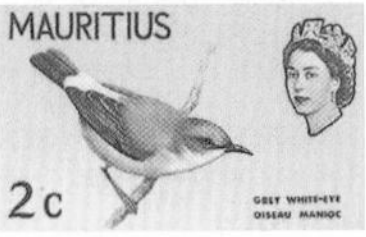

71 Bourbon White-eye

1965. Birds. Multicoloured.

317	2c. Type **71** (yellow background)	40	15
318	3c. Rodriguez fody ("Rodrigues Fody") (brown background)	1·00	15
319	4c. Mauritius olive white-eye ("Olive White-Eye")	30	15
340	5c. Mascarene paradise flycatcher ("Paradise Flycatcher")	70	15
321	10c. Mauritius fody	30	10
322	15c. Mauritius parakeet ("Parakeet") (grey background)	2·00	40
323	20c. Mauritius greybird ("Cuckoo-Shrike") (yellow background)	2·00	10
324	25c. Mauritius kestrel ("Kestrel")	2·00	30
341	35c. Pink pigeon	30	15
326	50c. Reunion bulbul ("Mascarene Bul-Bul")	50	40
327	60c. Mauritius blue pigeon (extinct) ("Dutch Pigeon") (yellow background)	60	10
328	1r. Mauritius dodo (extinct) (olive background)	9·50	10
329	2r.50 Rodriguez solitaire (extinct) ("Rodrigues Solitaire")	5·00	9·00
330	5r. Mauritius red rail (extinct) ("Red Rail")	15·00	16·00
331	10r. Broad-billed parrot (extinct)	35·00	38·00

For some values with background colours changed see Nos. 370/5.

1965. Centenary of I.T.U. As T 24a of Pitcairn Islands.

332	10c. orange and green	20	10
333	60c. yellow and violet	70	20

1965. I.C.Y. As T 24b of Pitcairn Islands.

334	10c. purple and turquoise	15	10
335	60c. green and violet	30	20

1966. Churchill Commemoration. As T 24c of Pitcairn Islands.

336	2c. blue	10	3·25
337	10c. green	30	10
338	60c. brown	1·25	20
339	1r. violet	1·40	20

1966. 20th Anniv of UNESCO. As T 25b/d of Pitcairn Islands.

342	5c. multicoloured	25	30
343	10c. yellow, violet and green	30	10
344	60c. black, purple and orange	1·40	15

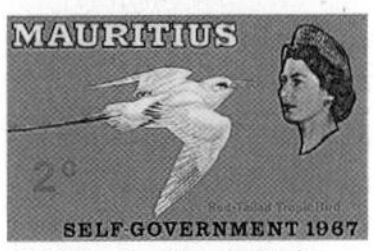

86 Red-tailed Tropic Bird

1967. Self-Government. Multicoloured.

345	2c. Type **86**	20	2·50
346	10c. Rodriguez brush warbler	70	10
347	60c. Rose-ringed parakeet (extinct) ("Rodrigues Parakeet")	80	10
348	1r. Grey-rumped swiftlet ("Mauritius Swiftlet")	80	10

1967. Self-Government. Nos. 317/31 optd SELF GOVERNMENT 1967.

349	**71**	2c. multicoloured	10	50
350	-	3c. multicoloured	10	50
351	-	4c. multicoloured	10	50
352	-	5c. multicoloured	10	10
353	-	10c. multicoloured	10	10
354	-	15c. multicoloured	10	30
355	-	20c. multicoloured	15	10
356	-	25c. multicoloured	15	10
357	-	35c. multicoloured	20	10
358	-	50c. multicoloured	30	15
359	-	60c. multicoloured	30	10
360	-	1r. multicoloured	1·50	10
361	-	2r.50 multicoloured	1·00	2·25
362	-	5r. multicoloured	6·00	3·25
363	-	10r. multicoloured	9·00	15·00

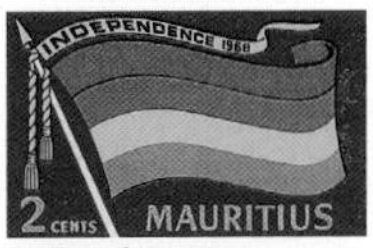

91 Flag of Mauritius

1968. Independence. Multicoloured.

364	2c. Type **91**	10	1·50
365	3c. Arms and Mauritius dodo emblem	20	1·50
366	15c. Type **91**	60	10
367	20c. As 3c.	60	10
368	60c. Type **91**	1·10	10
369	1r. As 3c.	1·10	10

1968. As Nos. 317/8, 322/3 and 327/8 but background colours changed as below.

370	**71**	2c. olive	20	4·25
371	-	3c. blue	1·75	8·00
372	-	15c. brown	55	20
373	-	20c. buff	3·50	4·00
374	-	60c. red	1·50	1·25
375	-	1r. purple	3·25	1·50

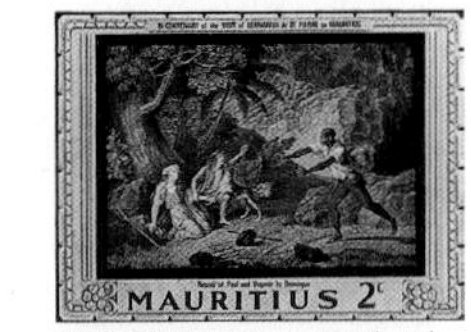

93 Dominique rescues Paul and Virginie

1968. Bicentenary of Bernardin de St. Pierre's Visit to Mauritius. Multicoloured.

376	2c. Type **93**	10	1·25
377	15c. Paul and Virginie crossing the river (vert)	55	10
378	50c. Visit of Labourdonnais to Madame de la Tour	1·00	10
379	60c. Meeting of Paul and Virginie in Confidence (vert)	1·00	10
380	1r. Departure of Virginie for Europe	1·00	20
381	2r.50 Bernardin de St. Pierre (vert)	1·75	3·75

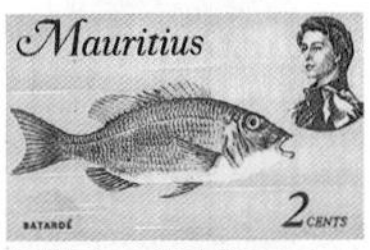

99 Black-spotted Emperor

1969. Multicoloured (except 10, 15, 25, 60c.).

382	2c. Type **99**	10	2·75
383	3c. Red reef crab	10	3·50
384	4c. Episcopal mitre	2·50	4·50
385	5c. Black-saddled pufferfish ("Bourse")	30	10
386	10c. Starfish (red, black and flesh)	2·00	10
387	15c. Sea urchin (brown, black and blue)	30	10
388	20c. Fiddler crab	65	70
389	25c. Spiny shrimp (red, black and green)	30	3·75
390	30c. Single harp shells and double harp shell	1·50	1·75
483	35c. Common paper nautilus	1·75	15
484	40c. Spanish dancer	1·00	60
448	50c. Orange spider conch and violet spider conch	45	10
449b	60c. Blue marlin (black, pink and blue)	65	10
487	75c. "Conus clytospira"	1·25	1·50
396	1r. Dolphin (fish)	60	10
452	2r.50 Spiny lobster	2·00	4·50
453	5r. Ruby snapper ("Sacre chien rouge")	2·00	2·00
399w	10r. Yellow-edged lyretail ("Croissant queue jaune")	1·50	1·50

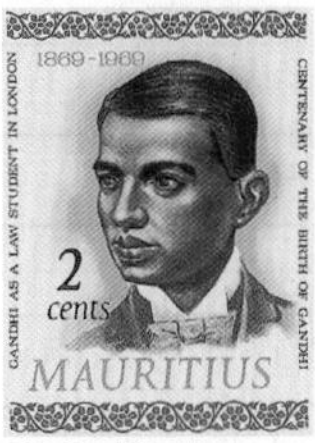

117 Gandhi as Law Student

1969. Birth Cent of Mahatma Gandhi. Mult.

400	2c. Type **117**	30	20
401	15c. Gandhi as stretcher-bearer during Zulu Revolt	65	10
402	50c. Gandhi as Satyagrahi in South Africa	80	50
403	60c. Gandhi at No. 10 Downing Street, London	80	10
404	1r. Gandhi in Mauritius, 1901	90	10
405	2r.50 Gandhi, the "Apostle of Truth and Non-Violence"	2·00	2·00
MS406	153×153 mm. Nos. 400/5	9·00	8·00

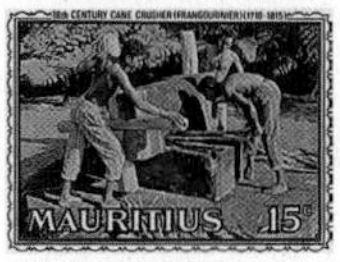

124 Frangourinier Cane-crusher (18th cent)

1969. 150th Anniv of Telfair's Improvements to the Sugar Industry. Multicoloured.

407	2c. Three-roller Vertical Mill	10	20
408	15c. Type **124**	10	10
409	60c. Beau Rivage Factory, 1867	10	10
410	1r. Mon Desert-Alma Factory, 1969	10	10
411	2r.50 Dr. Charles Telfair (vert)	25	1·25
MS412	159×88 mm. Nos. 407/11	1·50	2·25

1970. Expo '70. Nos. 394 and 396 optd EXPO '70' OSAKA.

413	60c. black, red and blue	10	10
414	1r. multicoloured	20	20

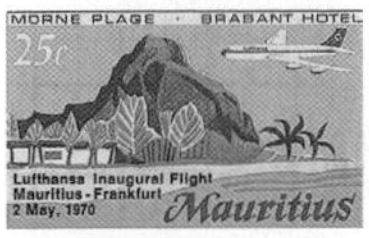

129 Morne Plage, Mountain and Boeing 707

1970. Inauguration of Lufthansa Flight, Mauritius–Frankfurt. Multicoloured.

415	25c. Type **129**	25	20
416	50c. Boeing 707 and map (vert)	25	20

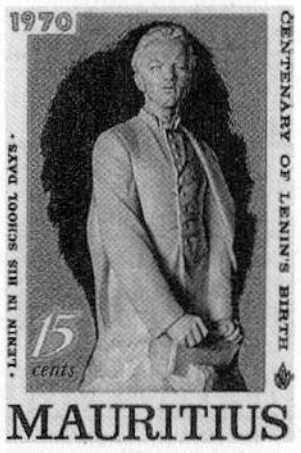

131 Lenin as a Student

1970. Birth Centenary of Lenin.

417	**131**	15c. green and silver	10	10
418	-	75c. brown	20	20

DESIGN: 75c. Lenin as founder of U.S.S.R.

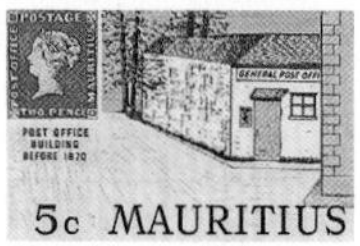

133 2d. "Post Office" Mauritius and original Post Office

1970. Port Louis, Old and New. Multicoloured.

419	5c. Type **133**	20	10
420	15c. G.P.O. Building (built 1870)	20	10
421	50c. Mail coach (c. 1870)	70	10
422	75c. Port Louis Harbour (1970)	85	10
423	2r.50 Arrival of Pierre A. de Suffren (1783)	90	70
MS424	165×95 mm. Nos. 419/23	4·50	8·00

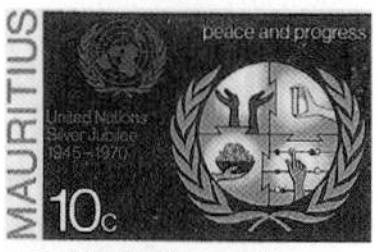

138 U.N. Emblem and Symbols

1970. 25th Anniv of U.N.

425	**138** 10c. multicoloured	10	10
426	**138** 60c. multicoloured	40	10

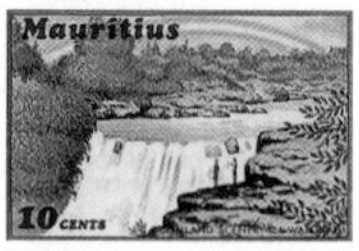

139 Rainbow over Waterfall

1971. Tourism. Multicoloured.

427	10c. Type **139**	25	10
428	15c. Trois Mamelles Mountains	25	10
429	60c. Beach scene	35	10
430	2r.50 Marine life	50	1·50

Nos. 427/30 have inscriptions on the reverse.

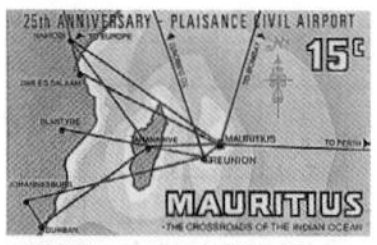

140 "Crossroads" of Indian Ocean

1971. 25th Anniv of Plaisance Airport. Multicoloured.

431	15c. Type **140**	45	10
432	60c. Boeing 707 and Terminal buildings	45	10
433	1r. Air hostesses on gangway	75	10
434	2r.50 Farman F.190, "Roland Garros" airplane, Choisy Airfield, 1937	75	10

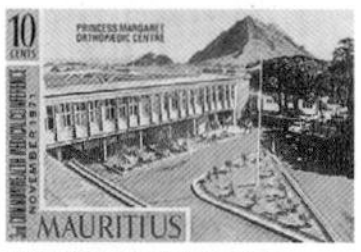

141 Princess Margaret Orthopaedic Centre

1971. 3rd Commonwealth Medical Conference. Multicoloured.

435	10c. Type **141**	10	10
436	75c. Operating theatre in National Hospital	50	20

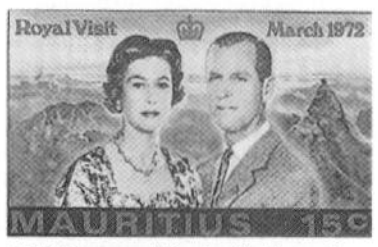

142 Queen Elizabeth II and Prince Philip

1972. Royal Visit. Multicoloured.

455	15c. Type **142**	15	10
456	2r.50 Queen Elizabeth II (vert)	2·00	2·00

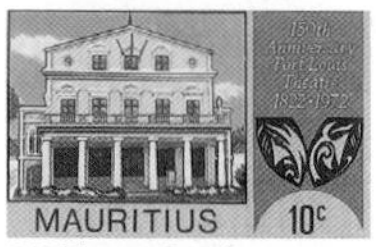

143 Theatre Facade

1972. 150th Anniv of Port Louis Theatre. Multicoloured.

457	10c. Type **143**	10	10
458	1r. Theatre auditorium	40	20

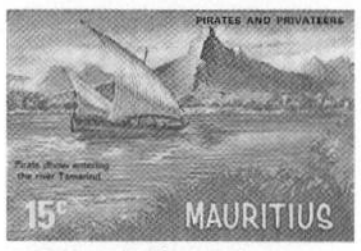

144 Pirate Dhow

1972. Pirates and Privateers. Multicoloured.

459	15c. Type **144**	65	15
460	60c. Treasure chest (vert)	1·00	20
461	1r. Lemene and "L'Hirondelle" (vert)	1·25	20
462	2r.50 Robert Surcouf	4·50	8·00

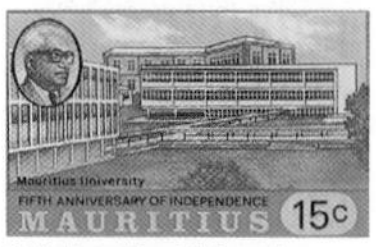

145 Mauritius University

1973. 5th Anniv of Independence. Multicoloured.

463	15c. Type **145**	10	10
464	60c. Tea development	15	15
465	1r. Bank of Mauritius	15	15

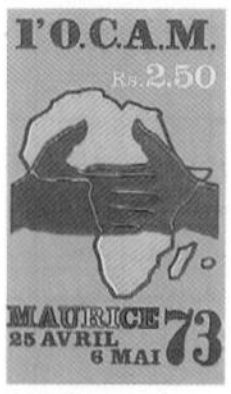

146 Map and Hands

1973. O.C.A.M. Conference. Multicoloured.

466	10c. O.C.A.M. emblem (horiz)	10	10
467	2r.50 Type **146**	40	45

O.C.A.M. = Organisation Commune Africaine Malgache et Mauricienne.

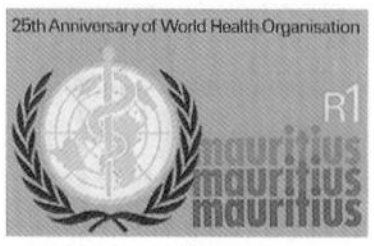

147 W.H.O. Emblem

1973. 25th Anniv of W.H.O.

468	**147** 1r. multicoloured	10	10

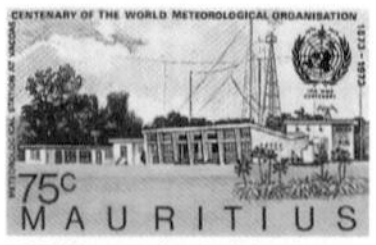

148 Meteorological Station, Vacoas

1973. Centenary of I.M.O./W.M.O.

469	**148** 75c. multicoloured	30	70

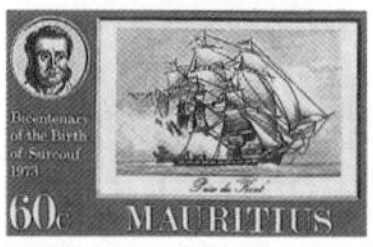

149 Capture of the "Kent" 1800

1973. Birth Bicentenary of Robert Surcouf (privateer).

470	**149** 60c. multicoloured	50	85

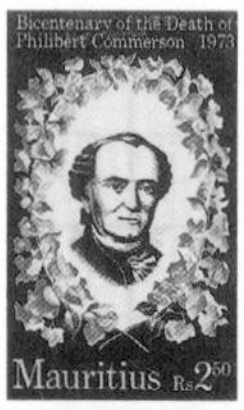

150 P. Commerson

1974. Death Bicentenary (1973) of Philibert Commerson (naturalist).

471	**150** 2r.50 multicoloured	30	40

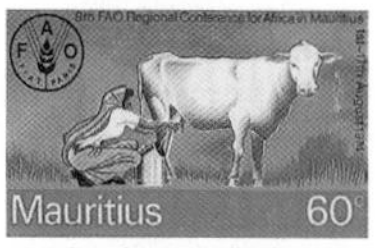

151 Cow being Milked

1974. 8th F.A.O. Regional Conf for Africa, Mauritius.

472	**151** 60c. multicoloured	20	20

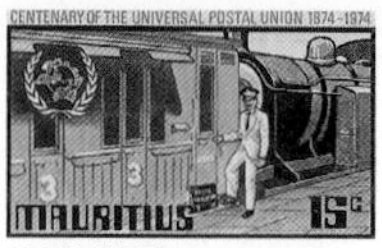

152 Mail Train

1974. Centenary of U.P.U. Multicoloured.

473	15c. Type **152**	40	15
474	1r. New G.P.O., Port Louis	40	20

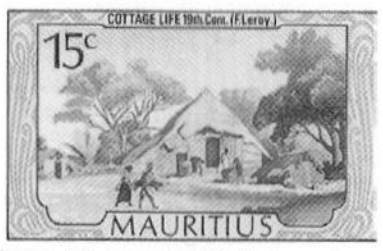

153 "Cottage Life" (F. Leroy)

1975. Aspects of Mauritian Life. Paintings. Mult.

493	15c. Type **153**	20	10
494	60c. "Milk Seller" (A. Richard) (vert)	35	10
495	1r. "Entrance of Port Louis Market" (Thuillier)	35	10
496	2r.50 "Washerwoman" (Max Boullee) (vert)	90	80

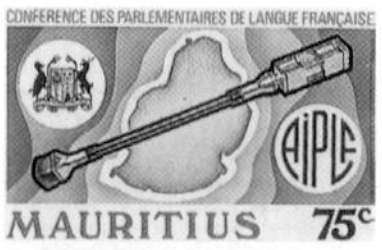

154 Mace across Map

1975. French-speaking Parliamentary Assemblies Conference, Port Louis.

497	**154** 75c. multicoloured	30	1·25

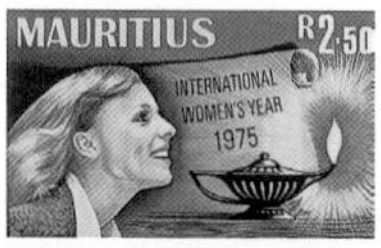

155 Woman with Lamp ("The Light of the World")

1976. International Women's Year.

498	**155** 2r.50 multicoloured	35	2·00

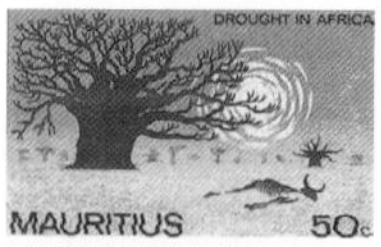

156 Parched Landscape

1976. Drought in Africa. Multicoloured.

499	50c. Type **156**	15	30
500	60c. Map of Africa and carcass (vert)	15	30

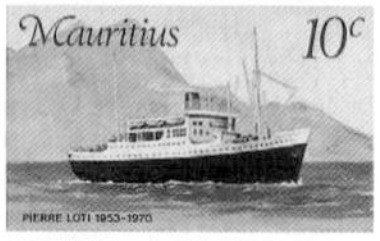

157 "Pierre Loti", 1953–70

1976. Mail Carriers to Mauritius. Multicoloured.

501	10c. Type **157**	70	10
502	15c. "Secunder", 1907	95	10
503	50c. "Hindoostan", 1842	1·60	15
504	60c. "St. Geran", 1740	1·75	15
505	2r.50 "Maen", 1638	4·00	7·50
MS506	115×138 mm. Nos. 501/5	10·00	13·00

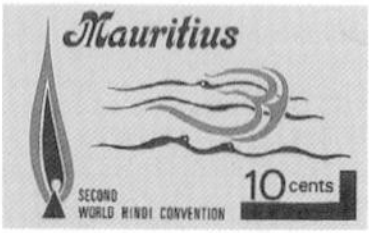

158 "The Flame of Hindi carried across the Seas"

1976. 2nd World Hindi Convention. Multicoloured.

507	10c. Type **158**	10	10
508	75c. Type **158**	10	30
509	1r.20 Hindi script	20	1·25

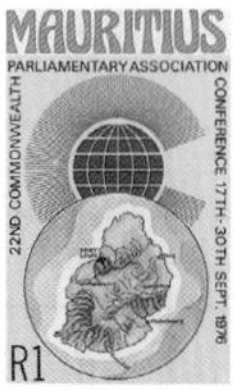

159 Conference Logo and Map of Mauritius

1976. 22nd Commonwealth Parliamentary Association Conference. Multicoloured.

510	1r. Type **159**	40	10
511	2r.50 Conference logo	60	1·75

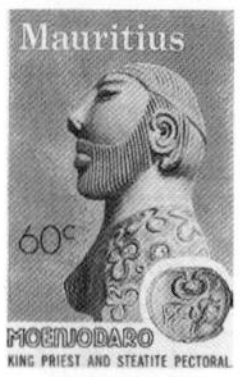

160 King Priest and Breastplate

1976. Moenjodaro Excavations, Pakistan. Mult.

512	60c. Type **160**	50	10
513	1r. House with well and goblet	65	10
514	2r.50 Terracotta figurine and necklace	1·75	1·00

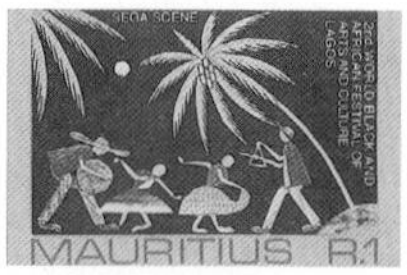

161 Sega Scene

1977. 2nd World Black and African Festival of Arts and Culture, Nigeria.

515	**161** 1r. multicoloured	30	15

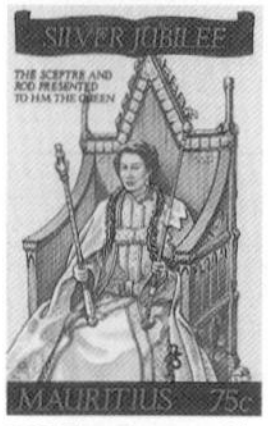

162 The Queen with Sceptre and Rod

1977. Silver Jubilee. Multicoloured.

516	50c. The Queen at Mauritius Legislative Assembly, 1972	15	10
517	75c. Type **162**	20	10
518	5r. Presentation of Sceptre and Rod	55	75

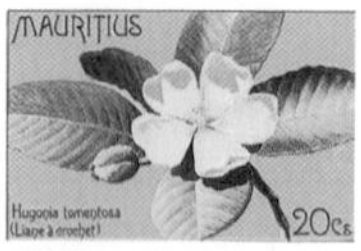

163 "Hugonia tomentosa"

1977. Indigenous Flowers. Multicoloured.

519	20c. Type **163**	25	10
520	1r. "Ochna mauritiana" (vert)	45	10
521	1r.50 "Dombeya acutangula"	60	20
522	5r. "Trochetia blackburniana" (vert)	1·25	1·50
MS523	130×130 mm. Nos. 519/22	4·00	8·00

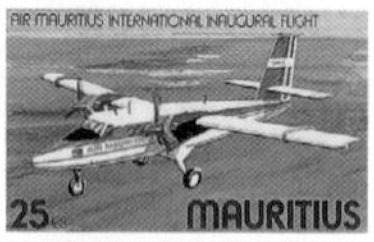

164 De Havilland Twin Otter 200/300

1977. Inaugural International Flight of Air Mauritius. Multicoloured.

524	25c. Type **164**	60	10
525	50c. De Havilland Twin Otter 200/300 and Air Mauritius emblem	80	10
526	75c. Piper Navajo and Boeing 747-100	95	20
527	5r. Boeing 707	3·00	3·75
MS528	110×152 mm. Nos. 524/7	9·00	9·00

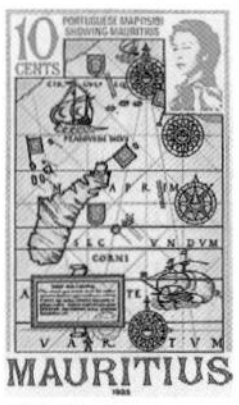

165 Portuguese Map of Mauritius, 1519

1978

529B	**165** 10c. multicoloured	1·00	1·25
530A	- 15c. multicoloured	1·50	2·75

531A	-	20c. multicoloured	80	2·75
532A	-	25c. multicoloured	60	2·00
533B	-	35c. multicoloured	1·00	20
534A	-	50c. multicoloured	50	75
535A	-	60c. multicoloured	60	2·75
536A	-	70c. multicoloured	2·75	4·00
537B	-	75c. multicoloured	1·75	4·00
538A	-	90c. multicoloured	4·00	4·25
539A	-	1r. multicoloured	60	50
540A	-	1r.20 multicoloured	60	50
541B	-	1r.25 multicoloured	1·75	20
542A	-	1r.50 multicoloured	1·00	2·75
543A	-	2r. multicoloured	60	70
544A	-	3r. multicoloured	60	50
545A	-	5r. multicoloured	60	1·75
546A	-	10r. multicoloured	1·50	1·00
547A	-	15r. multicoloured	1·50	3·00
548A	-	25r. green, black & brn	2·50	3·25

DESIGNS—HORIZ: 15c. Dutch Occupation, 1638–1710; 20c. Map by Van Keulen, c. 1700; 50c. Construction of Port Louis, c. 1736; 70c. Map by Bellin, 1763; 90c. Battle of Grand Port, 1810; 1r. Landing of the British, 1810; 1r.20, Government House, c. 1840; 1r.50, Indian immigration, 1835; 2r. Race Course, c. 1870; 3r. Place d'Armes, c. 1880; 5r. Royal Visit postcard, 1901; 10r. Royal College, 1914; 25r. First Mauritian Governor-General and Prime Minister. VERT: 25c. Settlement on Rodriguez, 1691; 35c. French settlers Charter, 1715; 60c. Pierre Poivre, c. 1767; 75c. First coinage, 1794; 1r.25 Lady Gomm's Ball, 1847; 15r. Unfurling of Mauritian flag.

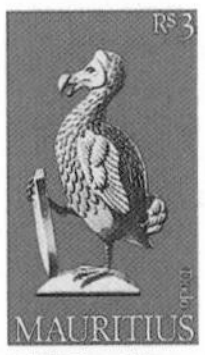

166 Mauritius Dodo

1978. 25th Anniv of Coronation.

549		3r. grey, black and blue	25	45
550		3r. multicoloured	25	45
551	**166**	3r. grey, black and blue	25	45

DESIGNS: No. 549, Antelope of Bohun; No. 550, Queen Elizabeth II.

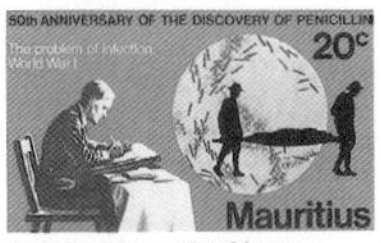

167 Problem of Infection, World War I

1978. 50th Anniv of Discovery of Penicillin.

552	**167**	20c. multicoloured	85	10
553	-	1r. multicoloured	1·75	75
554	-	1r.50 black, brown & grn	2·50	1·40
555	-	5r. multicoloured	3·25	6·00
MS556		150×90 mm. Nos. 552/5	10·00	12·00

DESIGNS: 1r. First mould growth, 1928; 1r.50, "Penicillium chrysogenum" ("notatum"); 5r. Sir Alexander Fleming.

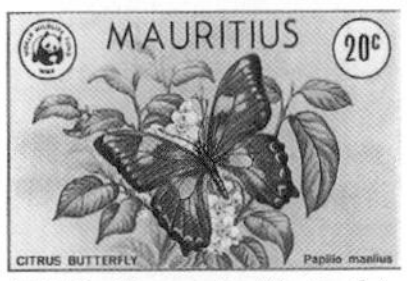

168 "Papilio manlius" (butterfly)

1978. Endangered Species. Multicoloured.

557	20c. Type **168**	2·00	50
558	1r. Geckos	1·00	10
559	1r.50 Greater Mascarene flying fox	1·25	1·00
560	5r. Mauritius kestrel	14·00	9·50
MS561	154×148 mm. Nos. 557/60	50·00	18·00

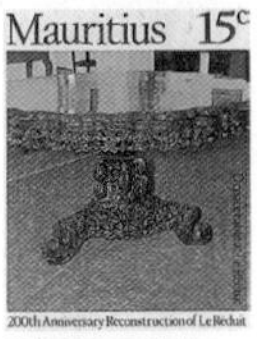

169 Ornate Table

1978. Bicentenary of Reconstruction of Chateau Le Reduit. Multicoloured.

562	15c. Type **169**	10	10
563	75c. Chateau Le Reduit	10	10
564	3r. Le Reduit gardens	40	45

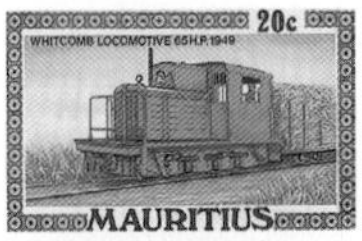

170 Whitcomb Diesel Locomotive 65H.P., 1949

1979. Railway Locomotives. Multicoloured.

565	20c. Type **170**	20	10
566	1r. "Sir William", 1922	40	10
567	1r.50 Kitson type 1930	60	45
568	2r. Garratt type, 1927	75	85
MS569	128×128 mm. Nos. 565/8	3·00	4·50

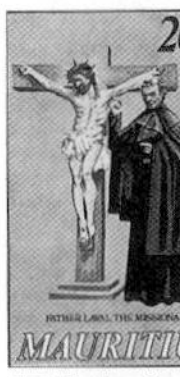

171 Father Laval and Crucifix

1979. Beatification of Father Laval (missionary). Multicoloured.

570	20c. Type **171**	15	10
571	1r.50 Father Laval	40	10
572	5r. Father Laval's tomb (horiz)	85	70
MS573	150×96 mm. Nos. 570/2	2·75	3·50

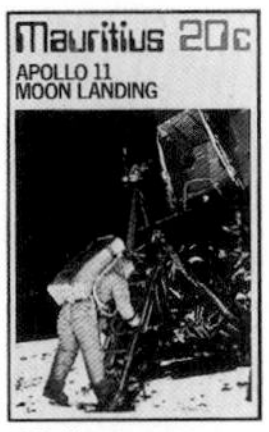

172 Astronaut descending from Lunar Module

1979. 10th Anniv of Moon Landing. Multicoloured. Self-adhesive.

574	20c. Type **172**	40	60
575	3r. Astronaut performing experiment on Moon	70	1·40
576	5r. Astronaut on Moon	4·50	8·00

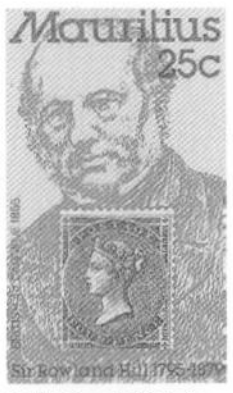

173 Great Britain 1855 4d. Stamp and Sir Rowland Hill

1979. Death Cent of Sir Rowland Hill. Mult.

577	25c. Type **173**	10	10
578	2r. 1954 60c. definitive	70	55
579	5r. 1847 1d. "POST OFFICE"	1·25	1·75
MS580	120×89 mm. 3r. 1847 2d. "POST OFFICE"	1·75	2·00

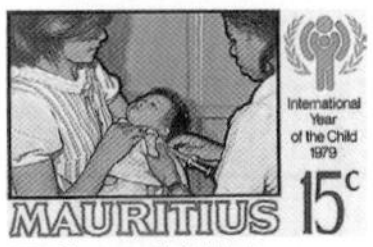

174 Young Child being Vaccinated

1979. International Year of the Child.

581	**174**	15c. multicoloured	10	10
582	-	25c. multicoloured	10	10
583	-	1r. black, blue and light blue	20	10
584	-	1r.50 multicoloured	40	35
585	-	3r. multicoloured	70	1·10

DESIGNS—HORIZ: 25c. Children playing; 1r.50, Girls in chemistry laboratory; 3r. Boy operating lathe. VERT: 1r. I.Y.C. emblem.

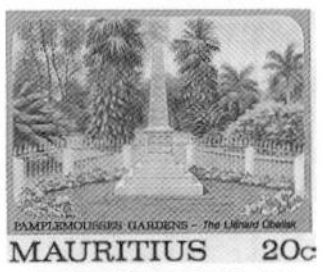

175 The Lienard Obelisk

1980. Pamplemousses Botanical Gardens. Multicoloured.

586	20c. Type **175**	15	10
587	25c. Poivre Avenue	15	10
588	1r. Varieties of Vacoas	30	10
589	2r. Giant water lilies	60	60
590	5r. Mon Plaisir (mansion)	1·00	3·50
MS591	152×105 mm. Nos. 586/90	3·50	5·50

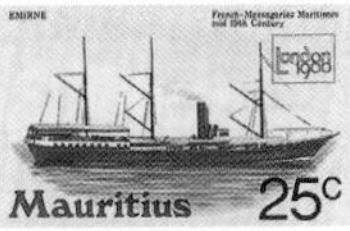

176 "Emirne" (French steam packet)

1980. "London 1980" International Stamp Exhibition. Mail-carrying Ships. Multicoloured.

592	25c. Type **176**	35	10
593	1r. "Boissevain" (cargo liner)	55	10
594	2r. "La Boudeuse" (Bougainville's ship)	75	70
595	5r. "Sea Breeze" (English clipper)	1·00	2·75

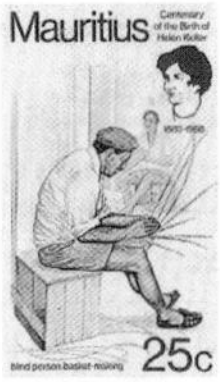

177 Blind Person Basket-making

1980. Birth Centenary of Helen Keller (campaigner for the handicapped). Multicoloured.

596	25c. Type **177**	20	10
597	1r. Deaf child under instruction	45	10
598	2r.50 Helen reading braille	70	35
599	5r. Helen at graduation, 1904	1·25	1·25

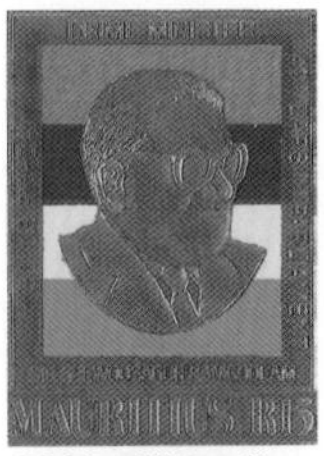

178 Prime Minister Sir Seewoosagur Ramgoolam

1980. 80th Birthday and 40th Year in Parliament of Prime Minister Sir Seewoosagur Ramgoolam.

600	**178**	15r. multicoloured	1·50	2·25

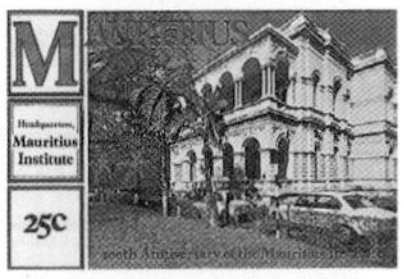

179 Headquarters, Mauritius Institute

1980. Centenary of Mauritius Institute. Mult.

601	25c. Type **179**	15	10
602	2r. Rare copy of Veda	50	20
603	2r.50 Glory of India cone shell	65	25
604	5r. "Le Torrent" (painting by Harpignies)	85	1·50

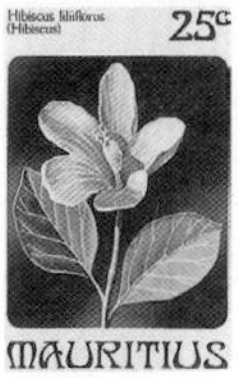

180 "Hibiscus liliiflorus"

1981. Flowers. Multicoloured.

605	25c. Type **180**	20	10
606	2r. "Erythrospermum monticolum"	70	65
607	2r.50 "Chasalia boryana"	75	1·25
608	5r. "Hibiscus columnaris"	1·25	3·25

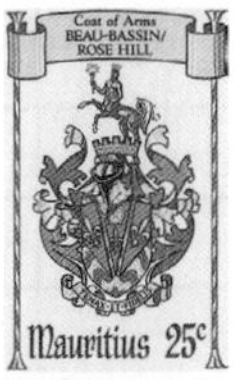

181 Beau-Bassin/ Rose Hill

1981. Coats of Arms of Mauritius Towns. Multicoloured.

609	25c. Type **181**	10	10
610	1r.50 Curepipe	30	25
611	2r. Quatre-Bornes	35	30
612	2r.50 Vacoas/Phoenix	40	50
613	5r. Port Louis	70	1·40
MS614	130×130 mm. Nos. 609/13	2·25	6·50

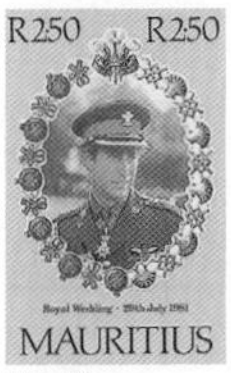

182 Prince Charles as Colonel-in-Chief, Royal Regiment of Wales

1981. Royal Wedding. Multicoloured.

615	25c. Wedding bouquet from Mauritius	10	10
616	2r.50 Type **182**	40	15
617	10r. Prince Charles and Lady Diana Spencer	80	90

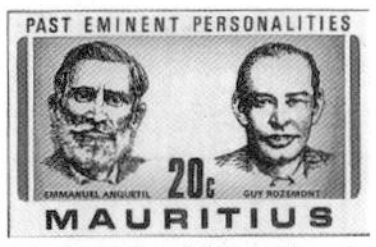

183 Emmanuel Anquetil and Guy Rozemont

1981. Famous Politicians and Physician.

618	**183**	20c. black and red	10	10
619	-	25c. black and yellow	10	10
620	-	1r.25 black and green	30	50
621	-	1r.50 black and red	35	25
622	-	2r. black and blue	45	30
623	-	2r.50 black and brown	50	80
624	-	5r. black and blue	2·00	2·50

DESIGNS: 25c. Remy Ollier and Sookdeo Bissoondoyal; 1r.25, Maurice Cure and Barthelemy Ohsan; 1r.50, Sir Guy Forget and Renganaden Seeneevassen; 2r. Sir Abdul Razak Mohamed and Jules Koenig; 2r.50, Abdoollatiff Mahomed Osman and Dazzi Rama (Pandit Sahadeo); 5r. Sir Thomas Lewis (physician) and electrocardiogram.

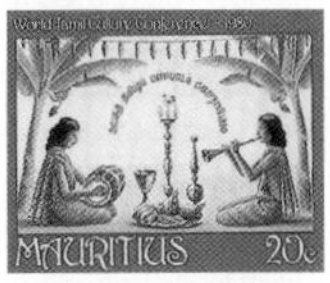

184 Drummer and Piper

1981. Religion and Culture. Multicoloured.

625	20c. Type **184**	10	10
626	2r. Swami Sivananda (vert)	1·25	1·25
627	5r. Chinese Pagoda	1·50	3·75

The 20c. value commemorates the World Tamil Culture Conference (1980).

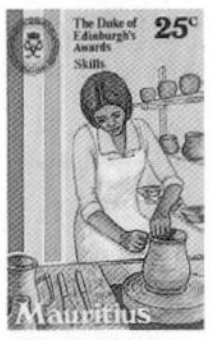

185 "Skills"

1981. 25th Anniv of Duke of Edinburgh Award Scheme. Multicoloured.

628	25c. Type **185**	10	10
629	1r.25 "Service"	10	10
630	5r. "Expeditions"	30	30
631	10r. Duke of Edinburgh	50	70

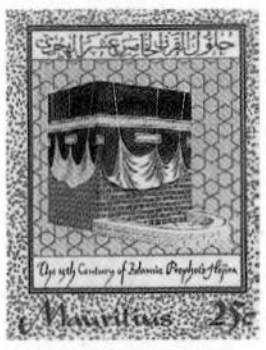

186 Ka'aba (sacred shrine, Great Mosque of Mecca)

1981. Moslem Year 1400 A.H. Commemoration. Multicoloured.

632	25c. Type **186**	30	10
633	2r. Mecca	80	80
634	5r. Mecca and Ka'aba	1·40	2·75

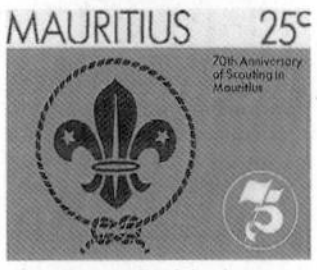

187 Scout Emblem

1982. 75th Anniv of Boy Scout Movement and 70th Anniv of Scouting in Mauritius.

635	**187**	25c. lilac and green	10	10
636	-	2r. brown and ochre	40	30
637	-	5r. green and olive	85	1·00
638	-	10r. green and blue	1·25	2·00

DESIGNS: 2r. Lord Baden-Powell and Baden-Powell House; 5r. Grand Howl; 10r. Ascent of Pieter Both.

188 Charles Darwin

1982. 150th Anniv of Charles Darwin's Voyage. Multicoloured.

639	25c. Type **188**	20	10
640	2r. Darwin's telescope	50	45
641	2r.50 Darwin's elephant ride	1·25	75
642	10r. H.M.S. "Beagle" beached for repairs	1·50	3·00

189 Bride and Groom at Buckingham Palace

1982. 21st Birthday of Princess of Wales. Mult.

643	25c. Mauritius coat of arms	10	10
644	2r.50 Princess Diana in Chesterfield, November 1981	60	45
645	5r. Type **189**	75	1·25
646	10r. Formal portrait	2·75	3·00

190 Prince and Princess of Wales with Prince William

1982. Birth of Prince William of Wales.

647	**190**	2r.50 multicoloured	1·25	65

191 Bois Fandamane Plant

1982. Centenary of Robert Koch's Discovery of Tubercle Bacillus. Multicoloured.

648	25c. Type **191**	30	10
649	1r.25 Central market, Port Louis	60	40
650	2r. Bois Banane plant	70	75
651	5r. Platte de Lezard plant	80	2·50
652	10r. Dr. Robert Koch	1·25	4·00

192 Arms and Flag of Mauritius

1983. Commonwealth Day. Multicoloured.

653	25c. Type **192**	10	10
654	2r.50 Satellite view of Mauritius	20	30
655	5r. Harvesting sugar cane	30	75
656	10r. Port Louis harbour	95	1·50

193 Early Wall-mounted Telephone

1983. World Communications Year. Mult.

657	25c. Type **193**	15	10

658	1r.25 Early telegraph apparatus (horiz)	45	20
659	2r. Earth satellite station	55	50
660	10r. First hot-air balloon in Mauritius, 1784 (horiz)	95	2·75

194 Map of Namibia

1983. Namibia Day. Multicoloured.

661	25c. Type **194**	60	10
662	2r.50 Hand breaking chains	1·50	75
663	5r. Family and settlement	2·00	2·25
664	10r. Diamond mining	5·50	3·75

195 Fish Trap

1983. Fishery Resources. Multicoloured.

665	25c. Type **195**	15	10
666	1r. Fishing boat (horiz)	30	15
667	5r. Game fishing	55	2·50
668	10r. Octopus drying (horiz)	80	4·00

196 Swami Dayananda

1983. Death Centenary of Swami Dayananda. Multicoloured.

669	25c. Type **196**	15	10
670	35c. Last meeting with father	15	10
671	2r. Receiving religious instruction	60	65
672	5r. Swami demonstrating strength	90	2·75
673	10r. At a religious gathering	1·25	4·25

197 Adolf von Plevitz

1983. 125th Anniv of Arrival in Mauritius of Adolf von Plevitz (social reformer). Multicoloured.

674	25c. Type **197**	20	10
675	1r.25 La Laura, Government school	60	30
676	5r. Von Plevitz addressing Commission of Enquiry, 1872	1·40	3·00
677	10r. Von Plevitz with Indian farm workers	2·00	4·50

198 Courtship Chase

1984. The Mauritius Kestrel. Multicoloured.

678	25c. Type **198**	85	30
679	2r. Kestrel in tree (vert)	2·00	1·25
680	2r.50 Young kestrel	2·25	2·25
681	10r. Head (vert)	3·25	8·50

199 Wreck of S.S. "Tayeb"

682	25c. Type **199**	30	10
683	1r. S.S. "Taher"	95	15
684	5r. East Indiaman "Triton"	3·00	3·25
685	10r. M.S. "Astor"	3·50	6·50

1984. 250th Anniv of "Lloyd's List" (newspaper). Multicoloured.

200 Blue Latan Palm

1984. Palm Trees. Multicoloured.

686	25c. Type **200**	10	10
687	50c. "Hyophorbe vaughanii"	20	20
688	2r.50 "Tectiphiala ferox"	1·50	1·75
689	5r. Round Island bottle-palm	2·25	3·50
690	10r. "Hyophorbe amaricaulis"	3·50	7·00

201 Slave Girl

1984. 150th Anniv of Abolition of Slavery and Introduction of Indian Immigrants.

691	**201**	25c. purple, lilac and brown	15	10
692	-	1r. purple, lilac and brown	70	10
693	-	2r. purple and lilac	1·50	1·00
694	-	10r. purple and lilac	7·00	11·00

DESIGNS—VERT: 1r. Slave market. HORIZ: 2r. Indian immigrant family; 10r. Arrival of Indian immigrants.

202 75th Anniversary Production of "Faust" and Leoville L'Homme

1984. Centenary of Alliance Francaise (cultural organization). Multicoloured.

695	25c. Type **202**	20	10
696	1r.25 Prize-giving ceremony and Aunauth Beejadbur	70	50
697	5r. First headquarters and Hector Clarenc	2·00	3·00
698	10r. Lion Mountain and Labourdonnais	2·50	5·50

203 The Queen Mother on Clarence House Balcony, 1980

1985. Life and Times of Queen Elizabeth the Queen Mother. Multicoloured.

699	25c. The Queen Mother in 1926	60	10
700	2r. With Princess Margaret at Trooping the Colour	1·50	45
701	5r. Type **203**	1·60	1·75
702	10r. With Prince Henry at his christening (from photo by Lord Snowdon)	1·90	4·25
MS703	91×73 mm. 15r. Reopening the Stratford Canal, 1964	6·50	5·50

204 High Jumping

1985. 2nd Indian Ocean Islands Games. Multicoloured.

704	25c. Type **204**	40	10

705	50c. Javelin-throwing	70	30
706	1r.25 Cycling	5·00	2·25
707	10r. Wind surfing	8·50	14·00

205 Adult and Fledgling Pink Pigeons

1985. Pink Pigeon. Multicoloured.

708	25c. Type **205**	3·75	50
709	2r. Pink pigeon displaying at nest	9·00	2·00
710	2r.50 On nest	9·50	4·00
711	5r. Pair preening	13·00	16·00

206 Caverne Patates, Rodrigues

1985. 10th Anniv of World Tourism Organization. Multicoloured.

712	25c. Type **206**	50	10
713	35c. Coloured soils, Chamarel	50	40
714	5r. Serpent Island	5·00	5·50
715	10r. Coin de Mire Island	7·00	11·00

207 Old Town Hall, Port Louis

1985. 250th Anniv of Port Louis. Multicoloured.

716	25c. Type **207**	20	10
717	1r. Al-Aqsa Mosque (180th anniv)	1·75	10
718	2r.50 Vase and trees (250th anniv of settlement of Tamil-speaking Indians)	1·50	2·00
719	10r. Port Louis Harbour	7·50	13·00

208 Edmond Halley and Diagram

1986. Appearance of Halley's Comet. Mult.

720	25c. Type **208**	50	10
721	1r.25 Halley's Comet (1682) and Newton's Reflector	1·25	50
722	3r. Halley's Comet passing Earth	1·75	2·25
723	10r. "Giotto" spacecraft	3·75	8·00

1986. 60th Birthday of Queen Elizabeth II. As T 246a of Papua New Guinea. Multicoloured.

724	25c. Princess Elizabeth wearing badge of Grenadier Guards, 1942	15	10
725	75c. Investiture of Prince of Wales, 1969	20	10
726	2r. With Prime Minister of Mauritius, 1972	30	25
727	3r. In Germany, 1978	45	40
728	15r. At Crown Agents Head Office, London, 1983	1·25	2·00

209 Maize (World Food Day)

1986. International Events. Multicoloured.

729	25c. Type **209**	10	10
730	1r. African Regional Industrial Property Organization emblem (10th anniv)	30	10
731	1r.25 International Peace Year emblem	65	50
732	10r. Footballer and Mauritius Football Association emblem (World Cup Football Championship, Mexico)	5·50	10·00

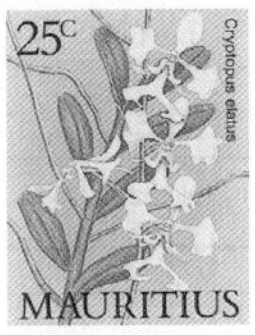

210 "Cryptopus elatus"

1986. Orchids. Multicoloured.

733	25c. Type **210**	50	10
734	2r. "Jumellea recta"	1·25	45
735	2r.50 "Angraecum mauritianum"	1·40	75
736	10r. "Bulbophyllum longiflorum"	2·25	5·50

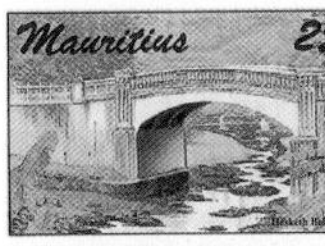

211 Hesketh Bell Bridge

1987. Mauritius Bridges. Multicoloured.

758	25c. Type **211**	35	10
759	50c. Sir Colville Deverell Bridge	50	20
760	2r.50 Cavendish Bridge	90	75
761	5r. Tamarin Bridge	1·10	2·00
762	10r. Grand River North West Bridge	1·25	2·50

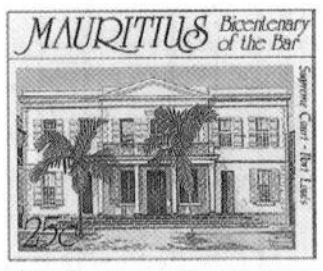

212 Supreme Court, Port Louis

1987. Bicentenary of the Mauritius Bar. Mult.

763	25c. Type **212**	10	10
764	1r. District Court, Flacq	40	10
765	1r.25 Statue of Justice	50	20
766	10r. Barristers of 1787 and 1987	2·00	2·50

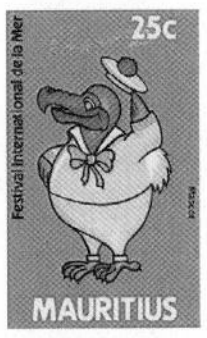

213 Mauritius Dodo Mascot

1987. International Festival of the Sea. Mult.

767	25c. Type **213**	70	20
768	1r.50 Yacht regatta (horiz)	2·25	1·00
769	3r. Water skiing (horiz)	3·25	3·75
770	5r. "Svanen" (barquentine)	3·75	8·00

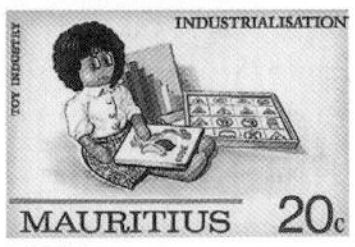

214 Toys

1987. Industrialization. Multicoloured.

771	20c. Type **214**	10	10
772	35c. Spinning factory	10	10
773	50c. Rattan furniture	10	10
774	2r.50 Spectacle factory	85	80
775	10r. Stone carving	2·50	3·00

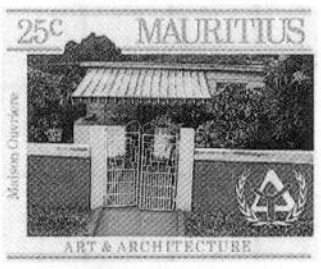

215 Maison Ouvriere (Int Year of Shelter for the Homeless)

1987. Art and Architecture.

776	215	25c. multicoloured	15	10
777	-	1r. black and grey	20	10
778	-	1r.25 multicoloured	45	40
779	-	2r. multicoloured	75	70
780	-	5r. multicoloured	1·50	2·40

DESIGNS: 1r. "Paul et Virginie" (lithograph); 1r.25, Chateau de Rosnay; 2r. "Vieille Ferme" (Boulle); 5r. "Trois Mamelles".

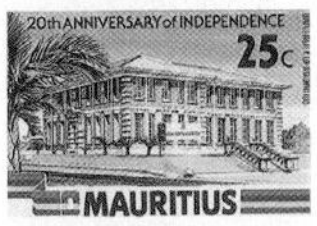

216 University of Mauritius

1988. 20th Anniv of Independence. Mult.

781	25c. Type **216**	10	10
782	75c. Anniversary gymnastic display	20	10
783	2r.50 Hurdlers and aerial view of Sir Maurice Rault Stadium	70	55
784	5r. Air Mauritius aircraft at Sir Seewoosagur Ramgoolam International Airport	1·40	1·60
785	10r. Governor-General Sir Veerasamy Ringadoo and Prime Minister Anerood Jugnauth	2·25	3·00

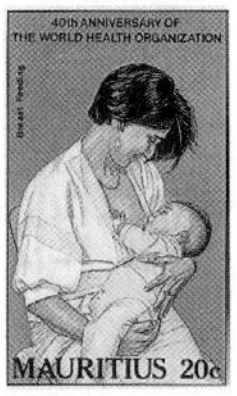

217 Breast Feeding

1988. 40th Anniv of W.H.O. Multicoloured.

786	20c. Type **217**	15	10
787	2r. Baby under vaccination umbrella and germ droplets	1·25	70
788	3r. Nutritious food	1·40	1·25
789	10r. W.H.O. logo	2·75	3·75

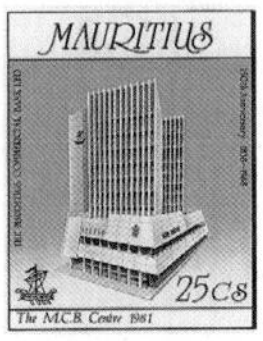

218 Modern Bank Building

1988. 150th Anniv of Mauritius Commercial Bank Ltd.

790	218	25c. black, green and blue	10	10
791	-	1r. black and red	20	10
792	-	1r.25 multicoloured	40	30
793	-	25r. multicoloured	6·50	8·50

DESIGNS—HORIZ: 1r. Mauritius Commercial Bank, 1897; 25r. Fifteen dollar bank note of 1838. VERT: 1r.25, Bank arms.

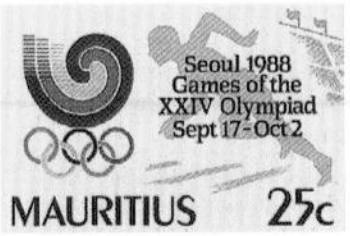

219 Olympic Rings and Athlete

1988. Olympic Games, Seoul. Multicoloured.

794	25c. Type **219**	10	10
795	35c. Wrestling	15	15
796	1r.50 Long distance running	75	60
797	10r. Swimming	2·50	4·25

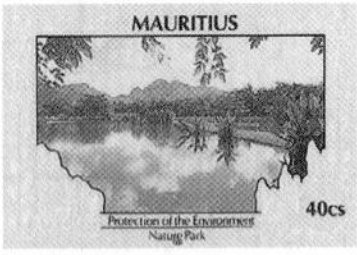

220 Nature Park

1989. Protection of the Environment. Mult.

798B	15c. Underwater view	1·00	1·25
799B	20c. As 15c.	15	1·75
808A	30c. Common greenshank ("Greenshank")	1·50	1·00
801B	40c. Type **220**	20	60
810A	50c. Round Island (vert)	20	60
801cB	60c. As 50c.	20	30
811A	75c. Bassin Blanc	20	60
812A	1r. Mangrove (vert)	20	10
802A	1r.50 Whimbrel	1·00	1·25
813A	2r. Le Morne	20	10
803A	3r. Marine life	30	30
804B	4r. Fern tree (vert)	30	35
814A	5r. Riviere du Poste estuary	20	10
805A	6r. Ecological scenery (vert)	60	50
806B	10r. "Phelsuma ornata" (gecko) on plant (vert)	1·00	1·75
806aB	15r. Benares waves	1·50	3·00
817B	25r. Migratory birds and map (vert)	20	10

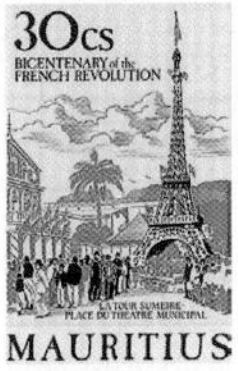

221 La Tour Sumeire, Port Louis

1989. Bicentenary of the French Revolution.

818	221	30c. black, green & yellow	15	10
819	-	1r. black, brown and light brown	35	10
820	-	8r. multicoloured	2·50	2·75
821	-	15r. multicoloured	3·25	4·50

DESIGNS: 1r. Salle de Spectacle du Jardin; 8r. Portrait of Comte de Malartic; 15r. Bicentenary logo.

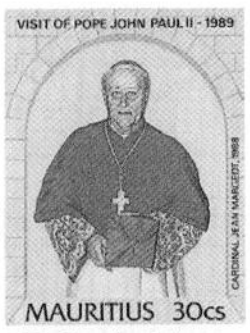

222 Cardinal Jean Margeot

1989. Visit of Pope John Paul II. Multicoloured.

822	30c. Type **222**	30	10
823	40c. Pope John Paul II and Prime Minister Jugnauth, Vatican, 1988	1·50	25
824	3r. Mere Marie Magdeleine de la Croix and Chapelle des Filles de Marie, Port Louis, 1864	1·50	1·25
825	6r. St. Francois d'Assise Church, Pamplemousses, 1756	2·25	2·75
826	10r. Pope John Paul II	8·00	9·00

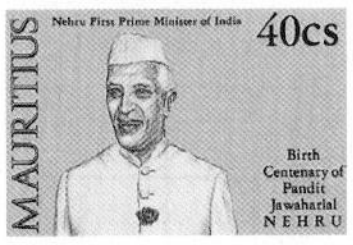

223 Nehru

1989. Birth Centenary of Jawaharlal Nehru (Indian statesman). Multicoloured.

827	40c. Type **223**	1·50	20
828	1r.50 Nehru with daughter, Indira, and grandsons	2·75	85
829	3r. Nehru and Gandhi	5·00	3·00
830	4r. Nehru with Presidents Nasser and Tito	3·50	3·00
831	10r. Nehru with children	6·00	11·00

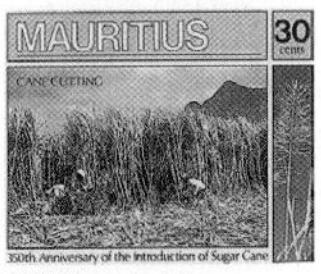

224 Cane Cutting

1990. 350th Anniv of Introduction of Sugar Cane to Mauritius. Multicoloured.

832	30c. Type **224**	15	10
833	40c. Sugar factory, 1867	20	10
834	1r. Mechanical loading of cane	40	10
835	25r. Modern sugar factory	11·00	14·00

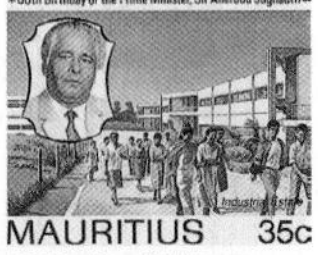

225 Industrial Estate

1990. 60th Birthday of Prime Minister Sir Anerood Jugnauth. Multicoloured.

836	35c. Type **225**	10	10
837	40c. Sir Anerood Jugnauth at desk	10	10
838	1r.50 Mauritius Stock Exchange symbol	40	30
839	4r. Jugnauth with Governor-General Sir Seewoosagur Ramgoolam	1·50	2·25
840	10r. Jugnauth greeting Pope John Paul II	13·50	14·00

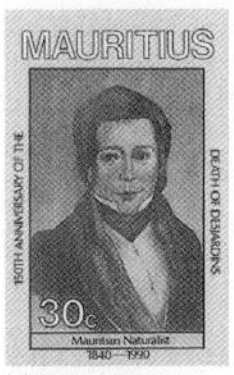

226 Desjardins (naturalist) (150th death anniv)

1990. Anniversaries. Multicoloured.

841	30c. Type **226**	30	10
842	35c. Logo on TV screen (25th anniv of Mauritius Broadcasting Corporation) (horiz)	30	10
843	6r. Line Barracks (now Police Headquarters) (250th anniv)	5·00	5·00
844	8r. Town Hall, Curepipe (centenary of municipality) (horiz)	3·50	6·00

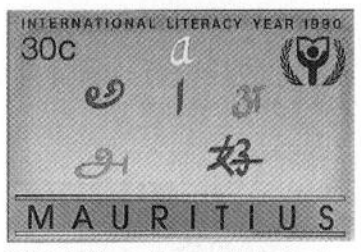

227 Letters from Alphabets

1990. International Literacy Year. Multicoloured.

845	30c. Type **227**	30	10
846	1r. Blind child reading Braille	2·50	15
847	3r. Open book and globe	3·50	2·25
848	10r. Book showing world map with quill pen	13·00	14·00

1991. 65th Birthday of Queen Elizabeth II and 70th Birthday of Prince Philip. As T 120a of Pitcairn Islands. Multicoloured.

849	8r. Queen Elizabeth II	1·75	2·75
850	8r. Prince Philip in Grenadier Guards ceremonial uniform	1·75	2·75

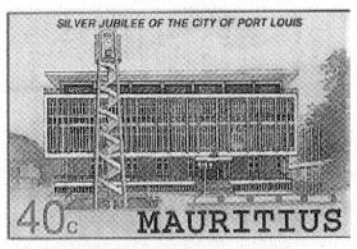

228 City Hall, Port Louis (25th anniv of City status)

1991. Anniversaries and Events. Multicoloured.

851	40c. Type **228**	10	10
852	4r. Colonel Draper (race course founder) (150th death anniv) (vert)	1·75	2·00
853	6r. Joseph Barnard (engraver) and "POST PAID" 2d. stamp (175th birth anniv) (vert)	2·00	2·75
854	10r. Supermarine Spitfire "Mauritius II" (50th anniv of Second World War)	4·50	8·00

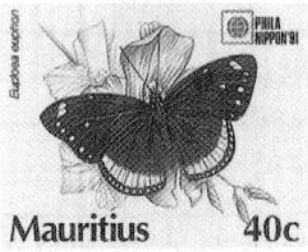

229 "Euploea euphon"

1991. "Phila Nippon '91" International Stamp Exn, Tokyo. Butterflies. Multicoloured.

855	40c. Type **229**	60	20
856	3r. "Hypolimnas misippus" (female)	1·90	1·00
857	8r. "Papilio manlius"	3·50	4·50
858	10r. "Hypolimnas misippus" (male)	3·50	4·75

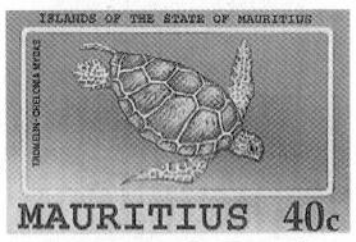

230 Green Turtle, Tromelin

1991. Indian Ocean Islands. Multicoloured.

859	40c. Type **230**	50	20
860	1r. Glossy ibis ("Ibis"), Agalega	1·50	40
861	2r. Takamaka flowers, Chagos Archipelago	1·60	1·10
862	15r. Violet spider conch sea shell, St. Brandon	7·00	11·00

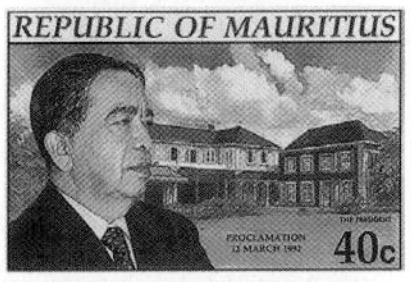

231 Pres. Veerasamy Ringadoo and President's Residence

1992. Proclamation of Republic. Multicoloured.

863	40c. Type **231**	10	10

864	4r. Prime Minister Anerood Jugnauth and Government House	1·00	1·25
865	8r. Children and rainbow	2·25	4·25
866	10r. Presidential flag	9·00	9·00

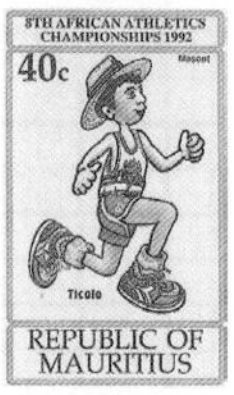

232 Ticolo (mascot)

1992. 8th African Athletics Championships, Port Louis. Multicoloured.

867	40c. Type **232**	10	10
868	4r. Sir Anerood Jugnauth Stadium (horiz)	75	1·25
869	5r. High jumping (horiz)	90	1·40
870	6r. Championships emblem	1·25	1·90

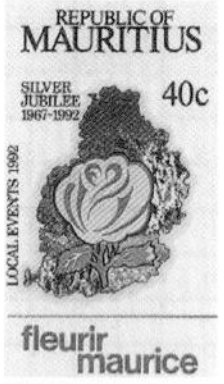

233 Bouquet (25th anniv of Fleurir Maurice)

1992. Local Events and Anniversaries. Mult.

871	40c. Type **233**	15	10
872	1r. Swami Krishnanandji Maharaj (25th anniv of arrival)	60	10
873	2r. Boy with dog (humane education) (horiz)	2·00	75
874	3r. Commission Headquarters (10th anniv of Indian Ocean Commission) (horiz)	1·40	1·00
875	15r. Radio telescope antenna, Bras d'Eau (project inauguration) (horiz)	4·75	9·50

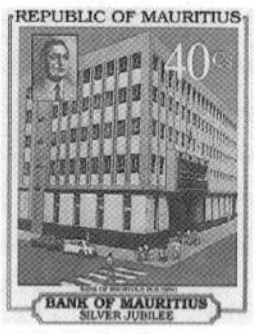

234 Bank of Mauritius Headquarters

1992. 25th Anniv of Bank of Mauritius. Mult.

876	40c. Type **234**	10	10
877	4r. Dodo gold coin (horiz)	2·00	1·10
878	8r. First bank note issue (horiz)	3·00	3·50
879	15r. Graph of foreign exchange reserves, 1967–92 (horiz)	5·00	8·50

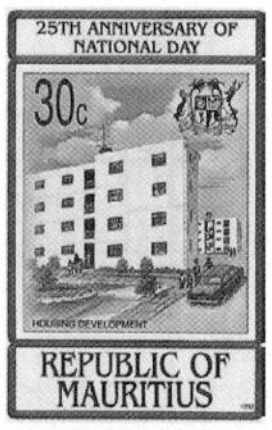

235 Housing Development

1993. 25th Anniv of National Day. Multicoloured.

880	30c. Type **235**	10	10
881	40c. Gross domestic product graph on computer screen	10	10
882	3r. National colours on map of Mauritius	40	60
883	4r. Ballot box	45	75
884	15r. Grand Commander's insignia for Order of Star and Key of the Indian Ocean	2·00	5·00

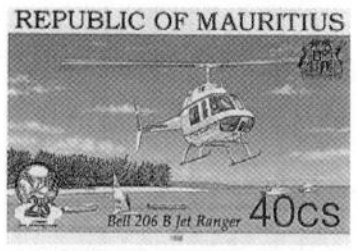

236 Bell 206 B JetRanger Helicopter

1993. 25th Anniv of Air Mauritius Ltd. Mult.

885	40c. Type **236**	1·25	30
886	3r. Boeing 747SP	1·75	1·25
887	4r. Aerospatiale/Aeritalia ATR 42	2·00	1·75
888	10r. Boeing 767-200ER	5·00	7·50
MS889	150×91 mm. Nos. 885/8	1·25	30

1993. No. 811 surch 40cs.

890	40c. on 75c. Bassin Blanc	1·75	1·25

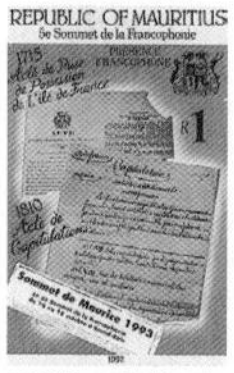

238 French Royal Charter, 1715, and Act of Capitulation, 1810

1993. 5th Summit of French-speaking Nations. Multicoloured.

891	1r. Type **238**	2·00	1·75
892	5r. Road signs	5·00	7·50
893	6r. Code Napoleon	3·00	3·25
894	7r. Early Mauritius newspapers	3·00	3·50

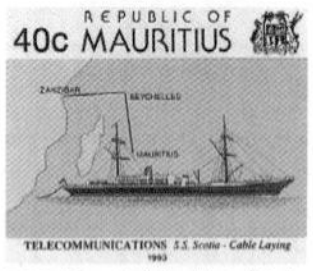

239 "Scotia" (cable ship) and Map of Cable Route

1993. Centenary of Telecommunications. Mult.

895	40c. Type **239**	1·25	30
896	3r. Morse key and code	1·75	1·00
897	4r. Signal Mountain Earth station	2·00	1·75
898	8r. Communications satellite	3·25	6·50

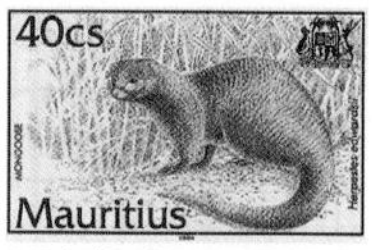

240 Indian Mongoose

1994. Mammals. Multicoloured.

899	40c. Type **240**	40	10
900	2r. Indian black-naped hare	1·25	40
901	8r. Pair of crab-eating macaques	3·25	4·00
902	10r. Adult and infant common tenrec	3·50	4·50

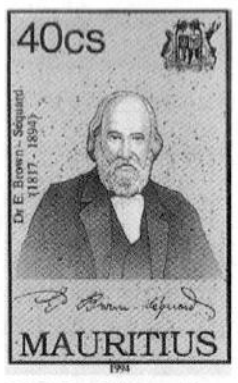

241 Dr Edouard Brown- Sequard (physiologist) (death cent)

1994. Anniversaries and Events. Multicoloured.

903	40c. Type **241**	15	10
904	4r. Family in silhouette (International Year of the Family)	45	55
905	8r. World Cup and map of U.S.A. (World Cup Football Championship, U.S.A.)	1·50	2·25
906	10r. Control tower, SSR International Airport (50th anniv of Civil Aviation Organization)	1·75	2·75

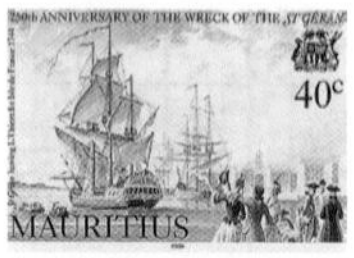

242 "St. Geran" leaving L'Orient for Isle de France, 1744

1994. 250th Anniv of Wreck of "St. Geran" (sailing packet). Multicoloured.

907	40c. Type **242**	40	10
908	5r. In rough seas off Isle de France	1·25	80
909	6r. Bell and main mast	1·25	1·40
910	10r. Artifacts from wreck	2·75	3·50
MS911	119×89 mm. 15r. "St. Geran" leaving L'Orient (vert)	5·00	5·50

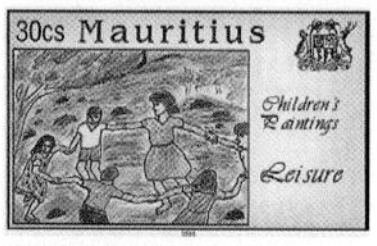

243 Ring-a-ring-a-roses

1994. Children's Games and Pastimes. Children's paintings. Multicoloured.

912	30c. Type **243**	10	10
913	40c. Skipping and ball games	10	10
914	8r. Water sports	1·40	2·25
915	10r. Blind man's buff	1·40	2·25

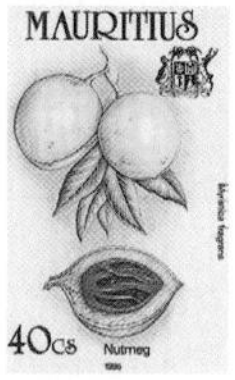

244 Nutmeg

1995. Spices. Multicoloured.

916	40c. Type **244**	15	10
917	4r. Coriander	1·00	75
918	5r. Cloves	1·10	85
919	10r. Cardamom	2·00	3·00

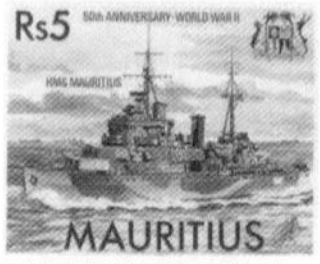

244a H.M.S. "Mauritius" (cruiser)

1995. 50th Anniv of End of Second World War. Multicoloured.

920	5r. Type **244a**	1·75	2·25
921	5r. Mauritian soldiers and map of North Africa	1·75	2·25
922	5r. Consolidated PBY-5 Catalina flying boat, Tombeau Bay	1·75	2·25

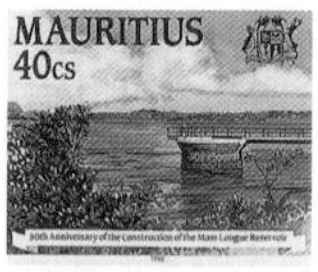

245 Mare Longue Reservoir

1995. Anniversaries. Multicoloured.

923	40c. Type **245** (50th anniv of construction)	15	10
924	4r. Mahebourg to Curepipe road (bicentenary of construction)	1·25	1·40
925	10r. Buildings on fire (centenary of Great Fire of Port Louis)	2·75	4·00

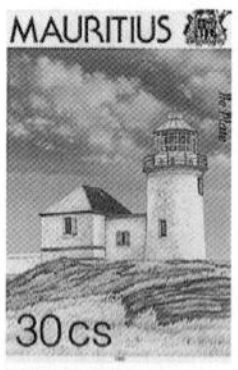

246 Ile Plate Lighthouse

1995. Lighthouses. Multicoloured.

926	30c. Type **246**	85	30
927	40c. Pointe aux Caves	85	30
928	8r. Ile aux Fouquets	3·00	4·00
929	10r. Pointe aux Canonniers	3·50	4·50
MS930	130×100 mm. Nos. 926/9	85	30

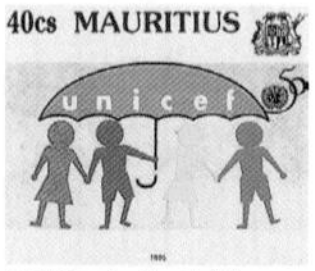

247 Symbolic Children under UNICEF Umbrella

1995. 50th Anniv of United Nations. Multicoloured.

931	40c. Type **247**	85	30
932	4r. Hard hat and building construction (I.L.O.)	3·00	4·00
933	8r. Satellite picture of cyclone (W.M.O.)	3·50	4·50
934	10r. Bread and grain (F.A.O.)	1·50	1·75

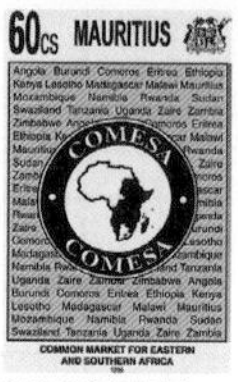

248 C.O.M.E.S.A. Emblem

1995. Inauguration of Common Market for Eastern and Southern Africa.

935	**248**	60c. black and pink	25	10
936	**248**	4r. black and blue	75	60
937	**248**	8r. black and yellow	1·25	1·75
938	**248**	10r. black and green	1·60	2·00

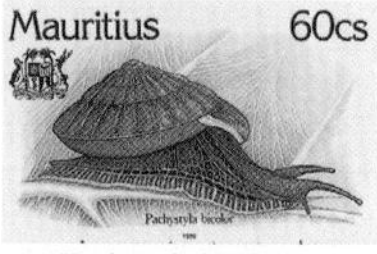

249 "Pachystyla bicolor"

1996. Snails. Multicoloured.

939	60c. Type **249**	20	10
940	4r. "Gonidomus pagodus"	75	65
941	5r. "Harmogenanina implicata"	75	75
942	10r. "Tropidophora eugeniae"	1·25	2·25

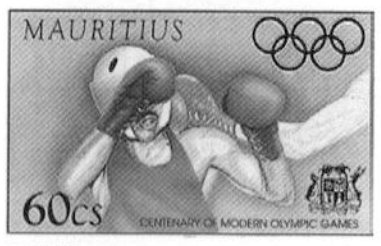

250 Boxing

1996. Centenary of Modern Olympic Games. Mult.

943	60c. Type **250**	10	10
944	4r. Badminton	60	50
945	5r. Basketball	1·25	1·00
946	10r. Table tennis	1·40	2·25

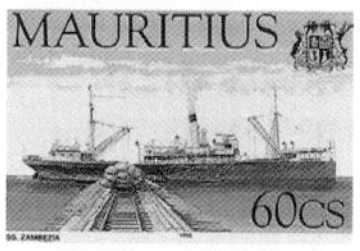

251 "Zambezia" (freighter)

1996. Ships. Multicoloured.

947	60c. Type **251**	30	10
948	4r. "Sir Jules" (coastal freighter)	1·00	70
949	5r. "Mauritius" (cargo liner)	1·25	1·00
950	10r. "Mauritius Pride" (container ship)	1·90	3·00
MS951	125×91 mm. Nos. 947/50	4·00	5·50

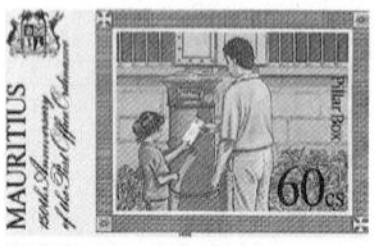

252 Posting a Letter

1996. 150th Anniv of the Post Office Ordinance. Multicoloured.

952	60c. Type **252**	20	10
953	4r. "B53" duplex postmark	60	55
954	5r. Modern mobile post office	85	75
955	10r. Carriole (19th-century horse-drawn postal carriage)	1·75	2·50

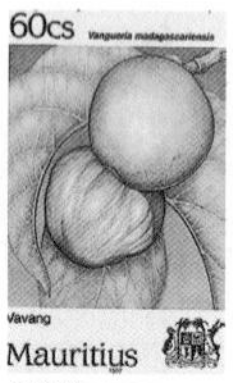

253 Vavang

1997. Fruits. Multicoloured.

956	60c. Type **253**	15	10
957	4r. Pom zako	60	55
958	5r. Zambos	75	70
959	10r. Sapot negro	1·40	2·25

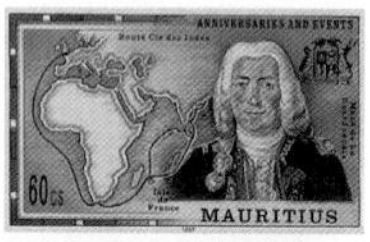

254 Governor Mahe de la Bourdonnais and Map

1997. Aspects of Mauritius History. Multicoloured.

960	60c. Type **254**	90	30

961	1r. La Perouse and map of Pacific	1·40	30
962	4r. Governor Sir William Gomm and Lady Gomm's Ball, 1847	1·50	1·00
963	6r. George Clark discovering skeleton of dodo, 1865	2·00	2·00
964	10r. Professor Brian Abel-Smith and Social Policies report of 1960	1·75	3·50

255 1d. "POST OFFICE" Mauritius

1997. 150th Anniv of "POST OFFICE" Stamps. Multicoloured.

965	60c. Type **255**	55	30
966	4r.2d. "POST OFFICE" Mauritius	1·25	1·00
967	5r. "POST OFFICE" 1d. and 2d. on gold background	1·25	1·00
968	10r. "POST OFFICE" 2d. and 1d. on silver background	2·75	4·25
MS969	127×90 mm. 20r. "POST OFFICE" stamps on cover to Bordeaux	5·00	6·00

256 Wheelwright

1997. Small Businesses. Multicoloured.

970	60c. Type **256**	15	10
971	4r. Laundryman	60	55
972	5r. Shipwright	1·25	90
973	15r. Quarryman	3·75	5·00

257 "Phelsuma guentheri" (gecko)

1998. Geckos. Multicoloured.

974	1r. Type **257**	30	10
975	6r. "Nactus serpensinsula durrelli"	90	75
976	7r. "Nactus coindemirensis"	1·10	1·50
977	8r. "Phelsuma edwardnewtonii"	1·25	1·50

258 Steam Train on Viaduct

1998. Inland Transport. Multicoloured.

978	40c. Type **258**	50	20
979	5r. Early lorry	1·00	70
980	6r. Bus in town street	1·25	1·10
981	10r. Sailing barge at wharf	1·75	3·00

259 President Nelson Mandela

1998. State Visit of President Nelson Mandela of South Africa.

982	**259**	25r. multicoloured	3·00	4·00

260 Count Maurice of Nassau and Dutch Landing

1998. 400th Anniv of Dutch Landing on Mauritius. Multicoloured.

983	50c. Type **260**	55	30
984	1r. Fort Frederik Hendrik and sugar cane	55	30
985	7r. Dutch map of Mauritius (1670)	2·50	2·50
986	8r. Diagram of landing	2·50	2·50

MS987	105×80 mm. 25r. Two Dutch ships	4·50	5·00

261 Cascade Balfour

1998. Waterfalls. Multicoloured.

988	1r. Type **261**	55	10
989	5r. Rochester Falls	1·40	80
990	6r. Cascade G.R.S.E. (vert)	1·60	1·25
991	10r. 500ft. Cascade (vert)	3·00	4·00

262 Plan of Le Reduit

1998. 250th Anniv of Chateau Le Reduit. Multicoloured.

992	1r. Type **262**	30	10
993	4r. "Le Chateau du Reduit, 1814" (P. Thuillier)	75	65
994	5r. "Le Reduit, 1998" (Hassen Edun)	85	80
995	15r. Commemorative monument	2·50	4·00

263 Governor Mahe de la Bourdonnais on 15c. Stamp of 1899

1999. 300th Birth Anniv of Governor Mahe de la Bourdonnais.

996	**263**	7r. blue, black and red	1·60	1·90

264 "Clerodendron laciniatum"

1999. Local Plants. Multicoloured.

997	1r. Type **264**	25	10
998	2r. "Senecio lamarckianus"	40	20
999	5r. "Cylindrocline commersonii"	80	75
1000	9r. "Psiadia pollicina"	1·25	2·50

265 "The Washerwomen" (Herve Masson)

1999. Mauritius through Local Artists' Eyes. Multicoloured.

1001	1r. Type **265**	25	10
1002	3r. "The Casino" (Gaetan de Rosnay)	65	60
1003	4r. "The Four Elements" (Andree Poilly)	75	75
1004	6r. "Going to Mass" (Xavier Le Juge de Segrais)	1·10	1·75

266 Old Chimney, Alma

1999. Old Sugar Mill Chimneys. Multicoloured.

1005	1r. Type **266**	25	10
1006	2r. Antoinette	50	20
1007	5r. Belle Mare	90	90
1008	7r. Grande Rosalie	1·25	2·00
MS1009	132×100 mm. Nos. 1005/8	2·75	3·25

267 Mosquito and Sprayer (Eradication of Malaria)

1999. 20th-century Achievements. Multicoloured.

1010	1r. Type **267**	45	10
1011	2r. Judge's robes, silhouette and airliner (emancipation of women)	1·00	30
1012	5r. Conference room (inter- national conference centre)	1·00	1·00
1013	9r. Spoons full of sugar (devel- opment of sugar industry)	2·00	3·00

268 Crest

2000. 150th Anniv of Mauritius Chamber of Commerce and Industry. Multicoloured.

1014	1r. Type **268**	40	25
1015	2r. Unity, Vision and Service logos	65	40
1016	7r. Francis Channell (First Secretary, 1850–72)	1·50	2·00
1017	15r. Louis Lechelle (First President, 1850)	2·50	5·00

269 "Cratopus striga" (beetle)

2000. Beetles. Multicoloured.

1018	1r. Type **269**	25	10
1019	2r. "Cratopus armatus"	35	15
1020	3r. "Cratopus chrysochlorus"	55	40
1021	15r. "Cratopus nigrogranatus"	2·25	3·00
MS1022	130×100 mm. Nos. 1018/21	3·50	3·75

270 Handball

2000. Olympic Games, Sydney. Multicoloured.

1023	1r. Type **270**	25	10
1024	2r. Archery	50	15
1025	5r. Sailing	85	75
1026	15r. Judo	2·00	3·00

271 Sir Seewoosagur Ramgoolam greeting Mother Teresa, 1984

2000. Birth Centenary of Sir Seewoosagur Ramgoolam (former Prime Minister). Multicoloured.

1027	1r. Type **271**	1·25	30
1028	2r. Election as member of Leg- islative Council, 1948 (vert)	35	15
1029	5r. As a student, 1926 (vert)	80	70
1030	15r. As Prime Minister, 1968 (vert)	2·00	3·25

272 *Scarus ghobban*

2000. Fish. Multicoloured.

1031	50c. Type **272**	20	50
1032	1r. *Cephalopholis sonnerati*	30	10
1033	2r. *Naso brevirostris*	40	15
1034	3r. *Lethrinus nebulosus*	55	15
1035	4r. *Centropyge debelius*	70	20
1036	5r. *Amphiprion chrysogaster*	80	25
1037	6r. *Forcipiger flavissimus*	90	30
1038	7r. *Acanthurus leucosternon*	1·00	40
1039	8r. *Pterois volitans*	1·10	50
1040	10r. *Siderea grisea*	1·25	75
1041	15r. *Carcharhinus wheeleri*	1·60	2·00
1042	25r. *Istiophrous platypterus*	2·25	3·50

MS1043	Three sheets, each 132×102 mm. (a) Nos. 1031/3 and 1042. (b) Nos. 1035 and 1038/40. (c) Nos. 1034, 1036/7 and 1041 Set of 3 sheets	6·50	8·00

273 Affan Tank Wen

2000. Famous Mauritians. Multicoloured.

1044	1r. Type **273**	30	10
1045	5r. Alphonse Ravatoni	75	50
1046	7r. Dr. Idrice Goumany	1·10	1·25
1047	9r. Anjalay Coopen	1·40	1·60

274 Finished Pullover

2001. Textile Industry. Multicoloured.

1048	1r. Type **274**	40	10
1049	3r. Computer-aided machinery	75	50
1050	6r. T-shirt folding	1·40	1·10
1051	10r. Embroidery machine	1·90	2·25

275 African Slave and Indian Indentured Labourer

2001. Anti-slavery and Indentured Labour Campaign Commemoration.

1052	**275**	7r. multicoloured	1·60	2·00

276 *Foetidia mauritiana*

2001. Trees. Multicoloured.

1053	1r. Type **276**	40	10
1054	3r. *Diospyros tessellaria*	85	30
1055	5r. *Sideroxylon puberulum*	1·25	85
1056	15r. *Gastonia mauritiana*	2·75	3·25

277 *Geographe* and *Naturaliste* (French corvettes)

2001. Bicentenary of Baudin's Expedition to New Holland (Australia). Multicoloured.

1057	1r. Type **277**	55	25
1058	4r. Capt. Nicholas Baudin and map of voyage	1·25	55
1059	6r. Mascarene martin (bird)	1·50	1·25
1060	10r. M. F. Peron and title page of book (vert)	1·75	2·50

278 Hotel School

2001. Mauritius Economic Achievements during the 20th Century. Multicoloured.

1061	2r. Type **278**	40	15
1062	3r. Steel bar milling	50	30
1063	6r. Solar energy panels, Agalega	1·00	1·00
1064	10r. Indian Ocean Rim Association for Regional Co-operation	1·75	2·75

279 Gandhi on Mauritius Stamp of 1969

2001. Centenary of Gandhi's Visit to Mauritius.
1065	**279**	15r. multicoloured	2·75	3·25

280 De-husking Coconuts

2001. Coconut Industry. Multicoloured.
1066	1r. Type **280**	35	10
1067	5r. Shelling coconuts (horiz)	90	55
1068	6r. Drying copra (horiz)	1·10	1·00
1069	10r. Extracting coconut oil	2·00	2·75

281 New Container Port

2002. 10th Anniv of Republic. Multicoloured.
1070	1r. Type **281**	60	20
1071	4r. Symbols of Mauritius stock exchange	70	55
1072	5r. New reservoir under construction	90	90
1073	9r. Motorway junction	2·00	2·50

282 Abricta

2002. Cicadas. Multicoloured.
1074	1r. Type **282**	30	15
1075	6r. Fractuosella darwini	85	75
1076	7r. Distantada thomaseti	95	1·10
1077	8r. Dinarobia claudeae	1·10	1·40
MS1078	130×100 mm. Nos. 1074/7	3·25	4·00

283 Map by Alberto Cantino, 1502

2002. 16th-century Maps of the South-west Indian Ocean. Multicoloured.
1079	1r. Type **283**	50	20
1080	3r. Map by Jorge Reinel, 1520	1·00	65
1081	4r. Map by Diogo Ribeiro, 1529	1·25	85
1082	10r. Map by Gerard Mercator, 1569	2·50	2·50

284 Constellation of Orion

2002. Constellations. Multicoloured.
1083	1r. Type **284**	40	15
1084	7r. Sagittarius	1·00	90
1085	8r. Scorpius	1·10	1·25
1086	9r. Southern Cross	1·25	1·75

285 African Growth and Opportunity Act Logo

2003. 2nd United States/Sub-Saharan Africa Trade and Economic Co-operation Forum.
1087	**285**	1r. red, blue and yellow	25	10
1088	**285**	25r. red, ultramarine and blue	2·75	3·50

286 Echo Parakeet Chick

2003. Endangered Species. Echo Parakeet. Multicoloured.
1089	1r. Type **286**	40	15
1090	2r. Fledgling	60	25
1091	5r. Female parakeet	1·00	70
1092	15r. Male parakeet	2·25	2·75

287 Trochetia boutoniana

2003. Trochetias. Multicoloured.
1093	1r. Type **287**	30	10
1094	4r. Trochetia uniflora	75	40
1095	7r. Trochetia triflora	1·25	1·50
1096	9r. Trochetia parviflora	1·50	2·25

288 Dolphin Emblem (Sixth Indian Ocean Games, Mauritius)

2003. Anniversaries and Events. Multicoloured.
1097	2r. Type **288**	50	20
1098	6r. Crop in field and emblem (150th anniv of Mauritius Chamber of Agriculture)	1·00	70
1099	9r. Journal of voyage of Bonne-Esperance (250th anniv of visit of Abbe de la Caille)	1·60	2·00
1100	10r. Sugar cane and emblem (50th anniv of Mauritius Sugar Industry Research Institute)	1·60	2·00

289 Batterie de la Pointe du Diable

2003. Fortifications. Multicoloured.
1101	2r. Type **289**	40	20
1102	5r. Donjon St. Louis	80	60
1103	6r. Martello Tower	1·00	1·00
1104	12r. Fort Adelaide	1·75	2·50

290 Emblem

2004. 20th Anniv of the Indian Ocean Commission.
1105	290	10r. multicoloured	1·60	2·00

291 Le Pouce

2004. Mountains. Multicoloured.
1106	2r. Type **291**	30	15
1107	7r. Corps de Garde	1·00	80
1108	8r. Le Chat et La Souris	1·10	80
1109	25r. Piton du Milieu	3·00	5·00

292 Tinman

2004. Traditional Trades. Multicoloured.
1110	2r. Type **292**	30	15
1111	7r. Shoe maker	90	80
1112	9r. Blacksmith	1·40	1·40
1113	15r. Basket maker	2·00	3·00

293 Work Station, Emblem and SADC Head Quarters

2004. 24th Southern African Development Community Summit. Multicoloured.
1114	2r. Type **293**	30	30
1115	50r. As Type **293** but with "24th SADC Summit" in bright purple banner	4·50	6·00

294 Plaine Corail Airport

2004. Rodrigues Regional Assembly. Multicoloured.
1116	2r. Type **294**	50	20
1117	7r. Eco Tourism	1·25	1·50
1118	8r. Agricultural products	1·25	1·50
1119	10r. Coat-of-Arms	1·40	1·75

295 Anthurium andreanum var acropolis

2004. Anthurium Species. Multicoloured.
1120	2r. Type **295**	30	15
1121	8r. Anthurium andreanum var tropical	1·10	1·00
1122	10r. Anthurium andreanum var paradisio	1·40	1·25
1123	25r. Anthurium andreanum var fantasia	3·00	4·25

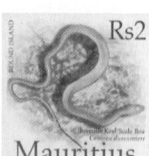

296 Juvenile Keel Scale Boa

2005. Round Island. Multicoloured.
1124	2r. Type **296**	40	15
1125	8r. Hurricane palm	1·10	1·10
1126	9r. Round Island petrel	2·00	1·75
1127	25r. Mazambron	3·25	4·75

297 Counter Services

2005. Postal Services. Multicoloured.
1128	2r. Type **297**	40	10
1129	7r. Mail sorting	1·25	85
1130	8r. Mail distribution	1·40	1·40
1131	10r. Mail transfer	1·60	2·00

298 Vagrant Depot

2005. Stone Buildings. Multicoloured.
1132	2r. Type **298**	25	10
1133	7r. Postal Museum, Port Louis	80	75
1134	16r. Carnegie Library, Curepipe	2·25	3·25

299 100 Gun Ship

2005. Model Ships. Multicoloured.
1135	7r. Type **299**	90	60
1136	8r. Sampan	1·00	85
1137	9r. Roman galley	1·10	1·10
1138	16r. Drakkur	2·25	3·00
MS1139	129×98 mm. 25r. Prow of drakkur with figurehead (horiz)	3·25	4·00

300 The Market

2006. Bicentenary of Mahebourg. Multicoloured.
1140	2r. Type **300**	35	10
1141	7r. Regattas	1·00	75
1142	8r. Le Lavoir	1·25	1·00
1143	25r. Pointe des Regates	2·25	3·25
MS1144	137×87 mm. 16r. Francois Mahe de la Bourdonnais (Governor 1735–46) (vert); 16r. Charles Decaen (Governor, 1803–10) (vert)	4·50	5·50

301 Prof. Basdeo Bissoondoyal

2006. Birth Centenary of Professor Basdeo Bissoondoyal (Indo-Mauritian scholar, writer and social reformer).
1145	301	10r. multicoloured	1·60	2·00

302 Indian Mynah (biological control of locusts), 1763

2006. Ecology. Multicoloured.
1146	2r. Type **302**	50	20
1147	8r. Fish and artificial reef (fish repopulation), 1980	1·00	80
1148	10r. Terraces (erosion control), Rodrigues, 1958	1·50	1·40
1149	25r. Giant tortoises (first captive breeding programme), 1881	3·50	4·25

303 Cardisoma carnifex (tourloulou crab)

2006. Non Marine Crabs. Multicoloured.
1150	2r. Type **303**	30	10
1151	7r. Geograpsus grayi (land crab)	85	75
1152	8r. Varuna litterata (freshwater crab)	90	85
1153	25r. Birgus latro (coconut crab)	2·40	3·00

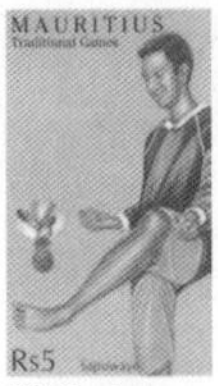

304 Sapsiwaye

2006. Traditional Children's Games. Multicoloured.

1154	5r. Type **304**	60	30
1155	10r. Marbles (horiz)	1·00	85
1156	15r. Hop scotch (horiz)	1·50	1·75
1157	25r. Kite flying	2·40	2·75

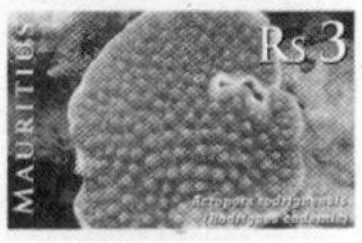

305 *Acropora rodriguensis*

2007. Corals. Multicoloured.

1158	3r. Type **305**	40	25
1159	5r. *Dendronephthya* sp.	50	35
1160	10r. *Ctenella chagius*	90	70
1161	15r. *Porites lobata*	1·40	1·40
1162	22r. *Acropora clathrata*	1·75	2·25
1163	25r. *Tubastrea coccinea*	1·90	2·25

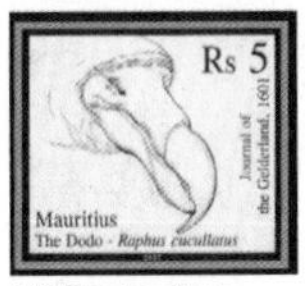

306 Drawing from Journal of the *Gelderland*, 1601

2007. Dodo (Raphus cucullatus). Multicoloured.

1164	5r. Type **306**	60	35
1165	10r. Pen drawing by Adrian Van de Venne, 1626	1·00	70
1166	15r. Painting published by Harrison, 1798	1·40	1·60
1167	25r. Chromolithograph by J. W. Frohawk, 1905	2·00	2·25
MS1168	122×90 mm. 25r. Painting by Julian Pender Hulme, 2001 (28×45 mm)	10·50	11·00

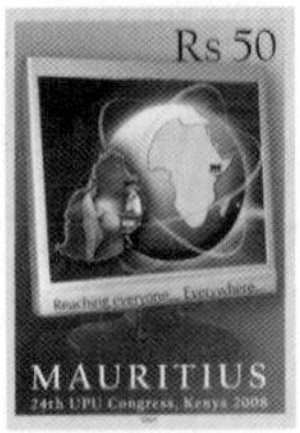

307 Computer Screen showing Globe and Postman

2007. 24th UPU Congress, Nairobi.

1169	**307**	50r. multicoloured	3·25	4·00

308 Ministers and Arms of Colony, 1957

2007. Anniversaries and Events. Multicoloured.

1170	5r. Type **308** (50th anniv of Ministerial System)	50	35
1171	10r. Statue of Manilall Doctor (centenary of arrival) (vert)	90	70
1172	15r. Scout camp and badge (centenary of scouting) (vert)	1·40	1·60
1173	25r. Port Louis Observatory (175th anniv of first meteorological observatory)	1·90	2·25

309 Bernardin de St. Pierre, 1737–1814 (*Paul et Virginie*)

2008. Mauritius in World Literature. Designs showing authors. Multicoloured.

1175	5r. Type **309**	50	30
1176	10r. Alexandre Dumas, 1802–70 (*Georges*)	90	70
1177	15r. Charles Baudelaire, 1821–67 (sonnet *A une Dame Creole*)	1·40	1·40
1178	22r. Mark Twain, 1835–1910 (*Following the Equator*)	2·00	2·25
1179	25r. Joseph Conrad, 1857–1924 (*A Smile of Fortune*)	2·00	2·25

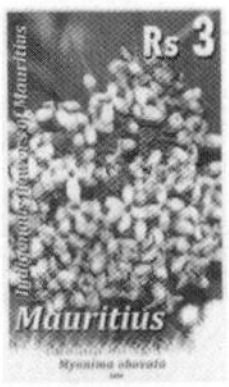

310 *Myonima obovata*

2009. Indigenous Flowers of Mauritius. Multicoloured.

1180	3r. Type **310**	20	10
1181	4r. *Cylindrocline lorencei*	25	15
1182	5r. *Crinum mauritianum*	30	20
1183	6r. *Elaeocarpus bojeri*	35	20
1184	7r. *Bremeria landia*	35	20
1185	8r. *Distephanus populifolius*	45	35
1186	9r. *Gaertnera longifolia* var. *longifolia*	45	35
1187	10r. *Dombeya acutangula* var. *rosea*	65	40
1188	15r. *Aphloia theiformis*	90	60
1189	22r. *Barleria observatrix*	1·40	90
1190	25r. *Roussea simplex*	1·60	1·20
1191	50r. *Hibiscus fragilis*	3·00	2·50

311 *Cylindraspis peltastes*

2009. Extinct Mauritian Giant Tortoises. Multicoloured.

1192	5r. Type **311**	50	30
1193	10r. *Cylindraspis vosmaeri* (vert)	90	70
1194	15r. *Cylindraspis inepta*	1·40	1·50
1195	25r. *Cylindraspis triserrata* (vert)	2·25	2·50
MS1196	117×72 mm. 50r. *Cylindraspis peltastes* grazing. Wmk sideways	3·25	2·75

312 Brand Mauritius Logo

2009. Branding Mauritius. Multicoloured.

1197	7r. Type **312**	50	65
1198	7r. Pieter Both Mountain	50	65

Nos. 1197-1198 were printed together *se-tenant*, in vertical pairs throughout the sheets.

313 Dragons

2009. Anniversaries and Events. Multicoloured.

1199	7r. Type **313** (Centenary (2008) of Chinese Chamber of Commerce, Mauritius)	50	30
1200	14r. Dr. K. Hazareesingh (writer) (birth centenary) (vert)	1·10	85
1201	20r. Document and map of 1809 (bicentenary of capture of Rodrigues Island by the British)	1·75	2·00
1202	21r. T. Callychurn (birth centenary) (vert)	1·75	2·00

313a Player, Football, Mauritius Flag and Zakumi Mascot

2010. Third Joint Issue of Southern Africa Postal Operators Association Members. World Cup Football Championship, South Africa. Multicoloured.

1202a	7r. Type **313a**	45	25
MS1202b	181×160 mm. 7r.×9 Namibia; South Africa; Zimbabwe; Malawi; Swaziland; Botswana; As No. 1202a; Lesotho; Zambia	3·50	3·50

314 Al-Idrissi

2010. Al-Idrissi (geographer and cartographer) Commemoration.

1203	**314**	27r. multicoloured	1·90	2·40

315 Mauritius 1847 2d. Blue

2010. Expo 2010, Shanghai, China.

1204	**315**	30r. deep violet-blue and vermilion	2·00	2·50

316 Battle of Grand Port, 1810

2010. Bicentenary of the Battle of Grand Port. Multicoloured.

1205	14r. Type **316**	1·00	1·00
1206	21r. Map of Ile de la Passe	1·75	2·00

317 Sir Seewoosagur Ramgoolam

2010. Sir Seewoosagur Ramgoolam ('Father of the Nation') Commemoration

1207	**317**	100r. multicoloured	6·75	7·50

The centre of No. 1207 is embossed in 22 carat gold.

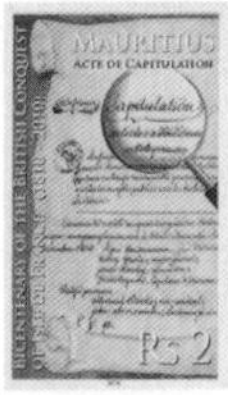

318 'Acte de Capitulation'

2010. Bicentenary of the British Conquest of Isle de France. Multicoloured.

1208	2r. Type **318**	30	20
1209	7r. British troops on road to Port Louis, 1810 (horiz)	70	90

319 The Steps at Aapravasi Ghat

2011. Mauritius in World Heritage. Multicoloured.

1210	7r. Type **319**	60	30
1211	14r. Le Morne (The Mountain) (horiz)	1·10	85
1212	15r. The Monument, Le Morne (horiz)	1·25	1·10
1213	25r. The hospital kitchen, Aapravasi Ghat	2·00	2·50
MS1214	120×100 mm. Nos. 1210/13	4·50	4·50

320 19th-century Census Form

2011. Anniversaries and Events. Multicoloured.

1215	7r. Type **320** (Population Census 2011)	60	30
1216	14r. Sir Moilin Jean Ah Chuen (industrialist) (birth centenary) (vert)	1·10	85
1217	21r. Dr. Maurice Curé (founder of Mauritius Labour Party) (125th birth anniv) (vert)	1·60	1·90
1218	25r. Aerial view of Médine sugar factory (centenary of the Médine sugar estates)	2·00	2·50

321 Map of Rodrigues and Telescope

2011. Commemorative Events. Multicoloured.

1219	11r. Type **321** (250th anniv of the observation of the transit of Venus from Rodrigues)	1·00	1·00
1220	12r. Laboratory (International Year of Chemistry)	1·00	1·00
1221	17r. Forest (International Year of Forests)	1·40	1·60

322 Emblem

2011. HIV/AIDS Awareness. 30th Anniv of Discovery of HIV/AIDS Virus

1222	**322**	7r. multicoloured	1·00	80

323 Post Office, La Criée

2011. 150th Anniv of Post Office in Rodrigues

1223	**323**	21r. multicoloured	1·60	1·90

324 Tea Leaves

2011. Tea Industry. Multicoloured.

1224	7r. Type **324**	60	40
1225	8r. Tea picking (horiz)	80	50
1226	15r. Leaf tea and tea bags (horiz)	1·10	75
1227	25r. Pouring cup of tea	1·75	1·40

EXPRESS DELIVERY STAMPS

1903. No. 136 surch EXPRESS DELIVERY 15c.

E1	**40**	15c. on 15c. blue	14·00	35·00

1903. No. 136 surch EXPRESS DELIVERY (INLAND) 15c.

E3	15c. on 15c. blue	8·50	3·25

1904. T 42 without value in label. (a) Surch (FOREIGN) EXPRESS DELIVERY 18 CENTS.

E5	**42**	18c. green	3·50	30·00

(b) Surch EXPRESS DELIVERY (INLAND) 15c.

E6	15c. green	17·00	6·00

POSTAGE DUE STAMPS

D1

1933

D1	**D1**	2c. black	1·25	50
D2	**D1**	4c. violet	50	65
D3	**D1**	6c. red	60	80
D11	**D1**	10c. green	30	2·00
D5	**D1**	20c. blue	70	2·50
D13	**D1**	50c. purple	75	12·00
D7	**D1**	1r. orange	70	17·00

1982. Nos. 530/1, 535, 540, 542 and 547 surch POSTAGE DUE and value.

D14	10c. on 15c. Dutch Occupation, 1638–1710	20	50
D15	20c. on 20c. Van Keulen's map, c. 1700	30	50
D16	50c. on 60c. Pierre Poivre, c. 1767 (vert)	30	30
D17	1r. on 1r.20 Government House, c. 1840	40	30
D18	1r.50 on 1r.50 Indian immigration, 1835	50	75
D19	5r. on 15r. Unfurling Mauritian flag, 1968	1·00	2·25

Pt. 6

MAYOTTE

One of the Comoro Islands adjacent to Madagascar. In 1974 (when the other islands became an independent state) Mayotte was made an Overseas Department of France, using French stamps. From 1997 it again had its own issues.

100 centimes = 1 franc.

1892. "Tablet" key-type inscr "MAYOTTE".

1	D	1c. black and red on blue	2·20	65
2	D	2c. brown and blue on buff	2·00	2·00
3	D	4c. brown and blue on grey	3·50	2·75
4	D	5c. green and red on green	4·50	4·50
5	D	10c. black and blue on lilac	10·00	10·50
15	D	10c. red and blue	60·00	75·00
6	D	15c. blue and red	23·00	19·00
16	D	15c. grey and red	£130	£130
7	D	20c. red and blue on green	25·00	22·00
8	D	25c. black and red on blue	15·00	13·00
17	D	25c. black and red	14·50	20·00
9	D	30c. brown and blue on drab	30·00	35·00
18	D	35c. black and red on yellow	9·00	4·50
10	D	40c. red and blue on yellow	23·00	26·00
19	D	45c. black on green	26·00	29·00
11	D	50c. red and blue on pink	48·00	43·00
20	D	50c. brown and red on blue	22·00	46·00
12	D	75c. brown & red on orange	30·00	50·00
13	D	1f. green and red	34·00	44·00
14	D	5f. mauve and blue on lilac	£150	£150

1912. Surch in figures.

22A	D	05 on 4c. brown and blue on grey	3·00	5·50
23A	D	05 on 15c. blue and red	2·20	2·75
21A	D	05 on 20c. brown and blue on buff	2·20	8·50
24A	D	05 on 20c. red and blue on green	2·00	5·75
25A	D	05 on 25c. black and red on pink	3·00	4·50
26A	D	05 on 30c. brown and blue on drab	2·40	6·25
27A	D	10 on 40c. red and blue on yellow	2·00	5·75
28A	D	10 on 45c. black and red on green	1·80	1·20
29A	D	10 on 50c. red and blue on pink	5·75	11·50
30A	D	10 on 75c. brown and red on orange	3·75	9·25
31A	D	10 on 1f. green and red	5·75	8·00

1997. Stamps of France optd MAYOTTE. (a) Nos. 2907/10, 2912, 2917, 2924 and 2929/30.

40	1118	10c. brown	85	40
41	1118	20c. green	30	40
42	1118	50c. violet	30	40
43	1118	1f. orange	55	60
44	1118	2f. blue	1·00	1·10
45	1118	2f.70 green	1·50	80
46	1118	3f.80 blue	1·70	70
47	1118	5f.	2·30	2·30
48	1118	10f. violet	4·50	4·25

(b) No. 3121. No value expressed.

49	1118	(–) red	1·50	50

No. 49 was sold at 3f.

6 Ylang-ylang

1997

50	6	2f.70 multicoloured	1·30	1·20

7 Arms

1997

51	7	3f. multicoloured	1·60	1·40

8 Terminal Building and Airplane

1997. Air. Inauguration of New Airport.

52	8	20f. indigo, red and blue	7·75	7·00

9 Le Banga

1997

53	9	3f.80 multicoloured	1·80	1·60

10 Dzen-dze (musical instrument)

1997

54	10	5f.20 multicoloured	2·20	2·40

1997. Stamps of France optd MAYOTTE. (a) On Nos. 3415/20, 3425, 3430 and 3432.

55	1318	10c. brown	30	40
56	1318	20c. green	30	40
57	1318	50c. violet	45	40
58	1318	1f. orange	45	40
59	1318	2f. blue	85	60
60	1318	2f.70 green	1·10	60
62	1318	3f.80 blue	1·70	1·50
66	1318	5f. blue	1·80	1·50
68	1318	10f. violet	3·75	2·30

(b) On No. 3407. No value expressed. Ordinary or self-adhesive gum.

69	1318	(3f.) red	1·10	50

11 Lemur

1997

71	11	3f. brown and red	1·50	1·30

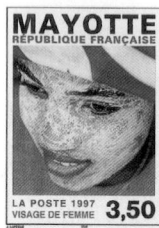
12 Woman's Face

1997

72	12	3f.50 multicoloured	1·60	1·40

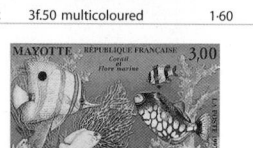
13 Fishes and Corals

1997. Marine Life.

73	13	3f. multicoloured	1·50	1·30

14 Reunion, Maps and Airplane

1997. Air. 20th Anniv of First Mayotte–Reunion Air Flight.

74	14	5f. black, blue and green	2·30	2·20

15 Longoni Port

1998

75	15	2f.70 multicoloured	1·30	1·20

16 Indian Ocean Green Turtle

1998

76	16	3f. multicoloured	1·50	1·30

17 Family on Island

1998. Family Planning.

77	17	1f. multicoloured	55	50

18 Cattle Egret on Zebu's Head

1998. Air.

78	18	30f. multicoloured	11·00	11·00

19 Children in Costume

1998. Children's Carnival.

79	19	3f. multicoloured	1·40	1·20

20 "Salama Djema II" (ferry)

1998. Mamoudzou–Dzaoudzi Ferry.

80	20	3f.80 multicoloured	1·70	1·50

21 Tsingoni Mosque

1998

81	21	3f. multicoloured	1·40	1·40

22 Mariama Salim

1998. 2nd Death Anniv of Mariama Salim (women's rights activist).

82	22	2f.70 multicoloured	1·20	1·10

23 Spreading Nets

1998. Traditional Fishing, Djarifa.

83	23	2f. multicoloured	1·10	1·00

24 Emperor Angelfish

1998

84	24	3f. multicoloured	1·40	1·30

25 Chombos and Workers

1998. The Chombo (agricultural tool).

85	25	3f. multicoloured	1·40	1·30

26 Map of Mayotte

1999

86	26	3f. multicoloured	1·30	1·30

27 Reservoir, Combani

1999

87	27	8f. multicoloured	3·50	3·50

28 Coral Hind

1999. Lagoon Fishes. Multicoloured.

88	2f.70 Type **28**	1·00	80
89	3f. Lionfish (horiz)	1·20	1·00
90	5f.20 Regal angelfish (horiz)	1·90	1·70
91	10f. Powder-blue surgeonfish (horiz)	3·75	3·00

1999. The Euro (European currency). No. 3553 of France optd MAYOTTE.

| 92 | 3f. red and blue | 1·10 | 80 |

29 Genet

1999

| 93 | **29** | 5f.40 orange, black & stone | 2·20 | 2·00 |

30 Baobab Tree

1999

| 94 | **30** | 8f. multicoloured | 3·50 | 3·50 |

1999. "Philexfrance 99" International Stamp Exhibition, Paris. Sheet 150×120 mm.

| MS95 | No. 51 ×4, multicoloured | 6·50 | 6·50 |

31 Prefecture Building

1999. Dzaoudzi Prefecture.

| 96 | **31** | 3f. multicoloured | 1·10 | 80 |

32 Pirogues

1999. Pirogues. Sheet 163×84 mm containing T 32 and similar multicoloured designs.

| MS97 | 5f. Type **32**; 5f. Two pirogues (vert); 5f. Three pirogues | 6·50 | 6·50 |

33 Vanilla

1999

| 98 | **33** | 4f.50 multicoloured | 1·50 | 1·50 |

34 "Le Deba"

1999. Air.

| 99 | **34** | 10f. multicoloured | 3·75 | 3·50 |

35 Map of Mayotte, Arrow and "2000"

1999. Year 2000.

| 100 | **35** | 3f. multicoloured | 1·10 | 80 |

36 Soulou Waterfall

1999

| 101 | **36** | 10f. multicoloured | 3·75 | 3·75 |

37 Sailing Boat

2000. Indian Ocean.

| 102 | **37** | 3f. multicoloured | 1·10 | 80 |

38 Two Whales

2000. Whales.

| 103 | **38** | 5f.20 multicoloured | 2·00 | 1·90 |

39 Emblem

2000. District 920 of Inner Wheel (women's section of Rotary International).

| 104 | **39** | 5f.20 multicoloured | 1·80 | 1·70 |

40 L'île au Lagon

2000

| 105 | **40** | 3f. multicoloured | 1·10 | 80 |

41 Woman wearing Traditional Clothes

2000. Women of Mayotte. Sheet 90×70 mm containing T 41 and similar vert design. Multicoloured.

| MS106 | 3f. Type **41**; 5f.20, Women wearing modern clothes | 3·50 | 3·50 |

42 Tyre Race

2000

| 107 | **42** | 3f. multicoloured | 1·10 | 80 |

43 Sultan Andriantsouli's Tomb

2000

| 108 | **43** | 5f.40 multicoloured | 2·00 | 1·90 |

44 Horned Helmet

2000. Shells. Multicoloured.

109	3f. Type **44**	1·40	1·40
110	3f. Trumpet triton (*Charonia tritonis*)	1·40	1·40
111	3f. Bullmouth helmet (*Cyprae-cassis rufa*)	1·40	1·40
112	3f. Humpback cowrie (*Cyprae mauritiana*) (wrongly inscr "mauritania") and tiger cowrie (*Cyprae tigris*)	1·40	1·40

Nos. 109/12 were issued together, se-tenant, with the backgrounds forming a composite design of a beach.

45 M'Dere

2000. 1st Death Anniv of Zena M'Dere.

| 113 | **45** | 3f. multicoloured | 1·30 | 90 |

46 Distillery

2000. Ylang-ylang Distillery.

| 114 | **46** | 2f.70 multicoloured | 1·30 | 90 |

47 Building

2000. New Hospital.

| 115 | **47** | 10f. multicoloured | 4·50 | 4·25 |

48 Map of Mayotte

2001

| 116 | **48** | 2f.70 black and green | 1·20 | 65 |

2001. No value expressed. As T 48.

| 120 | (3f.) black and red | 1·30 | 75 |

49 Mother breast-feeding

2001. Breast-feeding.

| 130 | **49** | 3f. multicoloured | 1·30 | 1·00 |

50 Pilgrims

2001. Pilgrimage to Mecca.

| 131 | **50** | 2f.70 multicoloured | 1·20 | 1·00 |

51 Bush Taxi

2001

| 132 | **51** | 3f. multicoloured | 1·30 | 1·00 |

52 Children playing Football

2001

| 133 | **52** | 3f. multicoloured | 1·30 | 1·00 |

53 Pyjama Cardinalfish

2001

| 134 | **53** | 10f. multicoloured | 4·50 | 4·25 |

54 Legionnaire, Map and Market Scene

2001. 25th Anniv of Mayotte Foreign Legion Detachment.

| 135 | **54** | 5f.20 multicoloured | 2·20 | 1·90 |

55 Bats in Tree

2001. The Comoro Roussette. Sheet 65×90 mm containing T 55 and similar horiz design. Multicoloured.

| MS136 | 3f. Type **55**; 5f.20, Bat in flight | 4·25 | 4·25 |

56 Airplanes and Club House

2001. Air. Dzaoudzi Flying Club.

| 137 | **56** | 20f. multicoloured | 8·75 | 6·50 |

57 Military Personnel and Building

2001. 1st Anniv of Adapted Military Service Units.

| 138 | **57** | 3f. multicoloured | 1·30 | 90 |

58 Protea sp.

2001. Flower and Fruit. Multicoloured.

| 139 | 3f. Type **58** | 1·30 | 90 |
| 140 | 5f.40 Selection of fruit | 2·50 | 2·00 |

59 Dziani Dzaha Lake

2001

| 141 | **59** | 5f.20 multicoloured | 2·20 | 1·90 |

60 Mayotte Post Office

2001
| 142 | **60** | 10f. multicoloured | 4·50 | 4·25 |

2002. Stamps of France optd MAYOTTE. (a) Nos. 3770/85.
143	**1318**	1c. yellow	35	45
144	**1318**	2c. brown	35	45
145	**1318**	5c. green	35	45
146	**1318**	10c. violet	50	55
147	**1318**	20c. orange	85	80
148	**1318**	41c. green	1·20	70
149	**1318**	50c. blue	1·70	1·40
150	**1318**	53c. green	2·00	90
151	**1318**	58c. blue	2·20	1·60
152	**1318**	64c. orange	2·50	1·60
153	**1318**	67c. blue	2·50	2·10
154	**1318**	69c. mauve	2·50	2·00
155	**1318**	€1 turquoise	3·00	2·75
156	**1318**	€1.02 green	3·00	2·75
157	**1318**	€2 violet	6·25	5·25

(b) No value expressed. No. 3752.
| 166 | | 41e. red | 1·50 | 45 |

No. 166 was sold at the rate for inland letters up to 20 grammes.

61 Arms

2002. Attainment of Department Status within France (11 July 2001).
| 167 | **61** | 46c. multicoloured | 1·50 | 95 |

62 Runners

2002. Athletics.
| 168 | **62** | 41c. multicoloured | 1·40 | 85 |

63 Mangroves, Kaweni Basin

2002
| 169 | **63** | €1.52 multicoloured | 5·25 | 4·50 |

64 Building Facade

2002. 25th Anniv of Mayotte Commune.
| 170 | **64** | 46c. multicoloured | 1·50 | 95 |

65 Women processing Salt

2002. Salt Production at Bandrele.
| 171 | **65** | 79c. multicoloured | 2·75 | 2·10 |

66 House and People

2002. National Census.
| 172 | **66** | 46c. multicoloured | 1·50 | 95 |

67 Sunbird (inscr "Souimanga")

2002. Birds. Sheet 61×141 mm containing T 67 and similar horiz designs. Multicoloured.
| MS173 | | 46c. Type **67**; 46c. Drongo; 46c. Olive white eye (inscr "Oiseau-lunette"); 46c. Red-headed fody (inscr "Foudy") | 6·50 | 6·50 |

68 Processing Machinery

2002. Remains of the Sugar Industry.
| 174 | **68** | 82c. multicoloured | 2·75 | 2·10 |

69 Mount Choungui

2002
| 175 | **69** | 46c. multicoloured | 1·60 | 1·00 |

70 Jack Fruit (inscr "Le Jaquier")

2002
| 176 | **70** | €1.22 multicoloured | 3·75 | 3·50 |

71 Museum Buildings

2003. Vanilla and Ylang Ylang Eco-museum.
| 177 | **71** | 46c. multicoloured | 1·60 | 1·00 |

72 Bananas

2003
| 178 | **72** | 79c. multicoloured | 2·40 | 2·00 |

73 Woman with Painted Face

2003. Festival Masks.
| 179 | **73** | 46c. multicoloured | 1·60 | 1·00 |

74 Sailfish

2003
| 180 | **74** | 79c. multicoloured | 2·40 | 2·00 |

75 Gecko

2003
| 181 | **75** | 50c. multicoloured | 1·60 | 1·20 |

76 Mraha Board and Counters (game)

2003
| 182 | **76** | €1.52 brown and mauve | 4·75 | 3·75 |

77 Mtzamboro College

2003
| 183 | **77** | 45c. multicoloured | 1·60 | 1·20 |

78 Ziyara de Pole

2003
| 184 | **78** | 82c. multicoloured | 2·75 | 2·10 |

79 Players, Ball and Basket

2003. Basketball.
| 185 | **79** | 50c. multicoloured | 1·80 | 1·40 |

80 Dzaoudzi Islet (½-size illustration)

2003
| 186 | **80** | $1.50 multicoloured | 5·25 | 4·25 |

81 Women Dancing ("Le Wadaha")

2004
| 187 | **81** | 50c. multicoloured | 1·80 | 1·40 |

2004. Map. As T 48 but new currency.
188	**48**	1c. yellow and black	20	20
189	**48**	2c. grey and black	20	20
190	**48**	5c. green and black	20	20
191	**48**	10c. mauve and black	30	30
192	**48**	20c. orange and black	60	55
193	**48**	45c. blue green and black	1·30	1·20
194	**48**	50c. ultramarine and black	1·50	1·40
195	**48**	€1 green and black	3·00	3·00
196	**48**	€2 violet and black	6·00	5·75

82 Blue Argus (*Junonia* (*Precis*) *rhadama*)

2004. Butterflies. Sheet 100×80 mm containing T 82 and similar horiz designs. Multicoloured.
| MS200 | | 50c. ×4 Type **82**; Citrus butterfly (*Papilio demodocus*); *Acraea ranavalona*; *Danaus chrysippus* | 6·25 | 6·25 |

83 Sada Bay

2004
| 201 | **83** | 90c. multicoloured | 2·75 | 2·50 |

84 Papaya Tree and Fruit

2004
| 202 | **84** | 50c. multicoloured | 1·80 | 1·40 |

85 Filigree Jewellery

2004
| 203 | **85** | €2.40 ultramarine, black and gold | 7·25 | 7·25 |

86 Bridge over Kwale River

2004
| 204 | **86** | 50c. multicoloured | 1·80 | 1·40 |

87 Maki (monkey) and Young

2004
| 205 | **87** | 75c. multicoloured | 2·50 | 2·10 |

88 Mamas Brochettis (street vendor)

2004
| 206 | **88** | 45c. multicoloured | 1·50 | 1·20 |

89 Playing Dominoes

2004
| 207 | 89 | 75c. multicoloured | 2·50 | 2·10 |

90 Ylang-ylang

2005
| 208 | 90 | 50c. multicoloured | 1·80 | 1·40 |

91 Two Women

2005. Women's Traditional Costume.
| 209 | 91 | 53c. multicoloured | 2·50 | 1·50 |

92 Breadfruit Tree and Fruit

2005
| 210 | 92 | 64c. multicoloured | 2·10 | 1·80 |

93 Baleen Whale

2005. Sea Mammals. Sheet 100×80 mm containing T 93 and similar horiz designs. Multicoloured.
MS211 53c.×4 Type 93; Beaked dolphins; Great sperm whale; Dugongs 6·50 6·50
The stamps and margins of **MS**211 form a composite design.

94 Emblem

2005. Centenary of Rotary International.
| 212 | 94 | 90c. multicoloured | 2·75 | 2·50 |

95 Symbols of Island Life

2005. My Island.
| 213 | 95 | 48c. multicoloured | 1·70 | 1·40 |

96 Mamoudzou

2005
| 214 | 96 | 48c. multicoloured | 1·70 | 1·40 |

97 Fishing from a Pirogue

2005
| 215 | 97 | 75c. multicoloured | 2·40 | 2·10 |

98 Tam Tam Boeuf (festival)

2005
| 216 | 98 | 53c. multicoloured | 1·80 | 1·40 |

98a Blacksmithing

2005
| 216a | 98a | 53c. multicoloured | 1·80 | 1·40 |

99 Woman grating Coconut

2006
| 217 | 99 | 53c. multicoloured | 1·80 | 1·40 |

100 Stall Holders

2006. Bush Market.
| 218 | 100 | 53c. multicoloured | 1·80 | 1·40 |

101 Les Amphidromes (ferry)

2006
| 219 | 101 | €1.07 multicoloured | 3·25 | 2·75 |

102 Moya Beach

2006
| 220 | 102 | 48c. multicoloured | 1·70 | 1·30 |

103 Turtle

2006. Turtle Protection. Sheet 60×110 mm containing T 103 and similar horiz designs showing turtles. Multicoloured.
MS221 53c.×3, Type 103; Laying eggs; Hatchlings 5·25 5·25
The stamps and margins of **MS**221 form a composite design.

104 Aloe mayottensis (inscr 'Aloes mayottensis')

2006
| 222 | 104 | 53c. multicoloured | 1·80 | 1·40 |

105 Frangipani

2006
| 223 | 105 | 53c. multicoloured | 1·80 | 1·40 |

106 Moulidi Dance

2006
| 224 | 106 | 75c. multicoloured | 2·40 | 2·10 |

107 Tropicbird

2006
| 225 | 107 | 54c. multicoloured | 1·80 | 1·40 |

108 Stamps as Map

2007. 10th Anniv of Mayotte Philately.
| 226 | 108 | 54c. multicoloured | 1·80 | 1·40 |

109 Phanelopsis

2007
| 227 | 109 | 54c. multicoloured | 1·80 | 1·40 |

110 Building Facade

2007. Bicentenary of Court of Auditors.
| 228 | 110 | 54c. new blue and vermilion | 1·80 | 1·40 |

111 Phyllostachys edulis

2007. Giant Bamboos.
| 229 | 111 | €1.01 multicoloured | 3·25 | 2·75 |

112 Seahorse

2007. 30th Anniv of General Council.
| 230 | 112 | 54c. multicoloured | 1·90 | 1·60 |

113 Traditional House

2007
| 231 | 113 | 54c. multicoloured | 1·90 | 1·60 |

114 Elk Horn Coral

2007. Coral. Sheet 60×110 mm containing T 114 and similar horiz designs showing coral. Multicoloured.
MS232 54c.×4, Type 114; Gorgon fan; Staghorn coral; Brain coral 6·75 6·75
The stamps and margins of **MS**232 form a composite design.

115 Mango Tree

2007
| 233 | 115 | 54c. multicoloured | 1·90 | 1·60 |

116 Chameleon

2007
| 234 | 116 | 54c. multicoloured | 1·90 | 1·60 |

117 N'Gouja Beach

2007
| 235 | 117 | 54c. multicoloured | 2·00 | 1·70 |

118 'Le voule'

2007
| 236 | 118 | 54c. multicoloured | 2·00 | 1·70 |

119 Coconut Palm

2008
| 237 | 119 | 54c. multicoloured | 2·00 | 1·70 |

120 Zebu

2008
| 238 | 120 | 54c. multicoloured | 2·00 | 1·70 |

121 Cinnamon

2008. Spices. Sheet 100×80 mm containing T **121** and similar horiz designs. Multicoloured.
MS239 55c.×4, Type **121**; Nutmeg;
Circuma; Ginger .... 8·00 8·00

122 *Hibiscus*

2008
| 240 | 122 | 55c. multicoloured | 2·30 | 2·00 |

123 'Le Grand Mariage'

2008
| 241 | 123 | 55c. multicoloured | 2·30 | 2·00 |

124 Younoussa Bamana

2008. Younoussa Bamana (politician and first prefect) Commemoration.
| 242 | 124 | 55c. multicoloured | 2·30 | 2·00 |

125 'Le M'Biwi' (dance)

2008
| 243 | 125 | 55c. multicoloured | 2·30 | 2·00 |

126 Embroidery

2008
| 244 | 126 | 55c. multicoloured | 2·40 | 2·10 |

127 Building Façade

2008. Inauguration of New Town Hall, Mamoudzou.
| 245 | 127 | 55c. multicoloured | 2·50 | 2·30 |

128 'Le Cardinal' (red cardinal fody)

2009
| 246 | 128 | 55c. multicoloured. | 2·50 | 2·30 |

129 Central Electricity Plant, Longini

2009
| 247 | 129 | 55c. multicoloured | 2·50 | 2·30 |

130 'La pêche au pétromax' (night fishing with petromax lantern)

2009
| 248 | 130 | 56c. multicoloured | 2·50 | 2·30 |

131 Tamarind Tree and Fruit

2009
| 249 | 131 | 56c. multicoloured | 2·50 | 2·30 |

132 Oranges

2009. Fruit. Sheet 100×80 mm containing T **132** and similar horiz designs. Multicoloured
MS250 56c.×4, Type **132**; Grapefruit;
Lemon; Combava (kaffir lime) .... 9·00 9·00

133 'Les Quatres Freres'

2009. Les Quatres Freres Islands. Sheet 120×110 mm containing T **133** and similar horiz design. Multicoloured.
MS251 56c.×2, Type **133**; Les Quatres
Freres at sunset .... 4·50 4·50

134 Jasmine

2009
| 252 | 134 | 56c. multicoloured | 2·50 | 2·30 |

135 Le Gaboussi

2009. Musical Instruments.
| 253 | 135 | 56c. multicoloured | 2·50 | 2·30 |

MECKLENBURG-SCHWERIN Pt. 7

In northern Germany. Formerly a Grand Duchy, Mecklenburg-Schwerin joined the North German Confederation in 1868.

48 schilling = 1 thaler.

1   **2**

1856. Imperf.
1	1	¼s. red	£190	£160
1a	1	¾s. red	†	£200
2	2	3s. yellow	£130	70·00
4	2	5s. blue	£300	£350

See note below No. 7.

1864. Roul.
5a	1	¼s. red	†	£2000
6a	1	¼s. red	†	£150
5	1	¾s. red	£3750	£2250
6	1	¾s. red	£550	95·00
11	2	2s. purple	£325	£325
9	2	3s. yellow	£200	£160
7	2	5s. bistre	£200	£325

Nos. 1, 1a, 5, 5a have a dotted background, Nos. 6 and 6a a plain background. Prices for Nos. 1a, 5a and 6a are for quarter stamps; prices for Nos. 1, 5 and 6 are for the complete on cover stamp (four quarters) as illustrated in Type **1**.

MECKLENBURG-STRELITZ Pt. 7

In northern Germany. Formerly a Grand Duchy, Mecklenburg-Strelitz joined the North German Confederation in 1868.

30 silbergroschen = 1 thaler.

1   **2**

1864. Roul. Various frames.
2	1	¼sgr. orange	£225	£3250
3	1	⅓sgr. green	£110	£1800
6	1	1sch. mauve	£350	£4250
7	2	1sgr. red	£190	£250
9	2	2sgr. blue	55·00	£1100
11	2	3sgr. bistre	42·00	£1700

Pt. 7

MEMEL

A seaport and district on the Baltic Sea, formerly part of Germany. Under Allied control after the 1914–18 war, it was captured and absorbed by Lithuania in 1923 and returned to Germany in 1939. From 1945 the area has been part of Lithuania.

1920. 100 pfennig = 1 mark.
1923. 100 centu = 1 litas.

1920. Stamps of France surch MEMEL and pfennig or mark with figure of value.

1	18	5pf. on 5c. green	50	75
2	18	10pf. on 10c. red	30	1·40
3	18	20pf. on 25c. blue	75	75
4	18	30pf. on 30c. orange	55	1·40
19	18	40pf. on 20c. brown	2·10	5·75
5	18	50pf. on 35c. violet	40	75
6	13	60pf. on 40c. red and blue	40	1·40
7	13	80pf. on 45c. green and blue	1·10	2·10
8	13	1m. on 50c. brown and lilac	50	2·10
9	13	1m.25 on 60c. violet & blue	1·70	5·75
10	13	2m. on 1f. red and green	40	95
11	13	3m. on 2f. orange and green	16·00	42·00
12	13	3m. on 5f. blue and buff	25·00	42·00
13	13	4m. on 2f. orange and green	65	85
14	13	10m. on 5f. blue and buff	3·50	9·50
15	13	20m. on 5f. blue and buff	42·00	£130

1920. Stamps of Germany inscr "DEUTSCHES REICH" optd Memel- gebiet or Memelgebiet.

25	10	5pf. green	1·10	4·25
26	10	10pf. red	3·00	11·50
27	10	10pf. orange	30	2·10
28	24	15pf. brown	3·25	10·50
29	10	20pf. blue	1·20	4·50
30	10	30pf. black & orange on buff	2·20	5·00
31	10	30pf. blue	55	2·20
32	10	40pf. black and red	30	2·20
33	10	50pf. black & purple on buff	30	2·20
34	10	60pf. green	1·50	6·00
35	10	75pf. black and green	3·50	13·00
36	10	80pf. blue	1·90	6·50
37	12	1m. red	40	2·20
38	12	1m.25 green	15·00	70·00
39	12	1m.50 brown	5·50	18·00
40	13	2m. blue	2·75	8·75
41	13	2m.50 purple	16·00	42·00

1921. Nos. 2-3, 5, 8, 10, 19 and 49 further surch in large figures.

42	18	15 on 10pf. on 10c. red	55	1·60
43	18	15 on 20pf. on 25c. blue	40	1·80
44	18	15 on 50pf. on 35c. violet	30	1·10
45	18	60 on 40pf. on 20c. brown	55	1·30
46	13	75 on 60pf. on 40c. red and blue (49)	75	1·80
47	13	1,25 on 1m. on 50c. brown and lilac	30	1·10
48	13	5,00 on 2m. on 1f. red and green	1·10	3·50

1921. Surch MEMEL and Pfennig or Mark with figure of value.

60	18	5pf. on 5c. orange	25	85
61	18	10pf. on 10c. red	1·10	5·25
62	18	10pf. on 10c. green	25	85
63	18	15pf. on 10c. green	25	95
64	18	20pf. on 20c. brown	9·50	37·00
65	18	20pf. on 25c. blue	9·50	37·00
66	18	25pf. on 5c. orange	25	95
67	18	30pf. on 30c. red	85	5·00
68	18	35pf. on 35c. violet	20	65
77	13	40pf. on 40c. red and blue	25	85
69	15	50pf. on 50c. blue	20	85
49	13	60pf. on 40c. red and blue	4·25	16·00
71	15	75pf. on 15c. green	20	65
70	18	75pf. on 35c. violet	30	85
78	13	80pf. on 45c. green & blue	30	85
72	18	1m. on 25c. blue	20	65
79	13	1m. on 40c. red and blue	30	85
73	18	1¼m. on 30c. red	20	65
80	13	1m.25 on 60c. violet & bl	55	1·30
81	13	1m.50 on 45c. green & bl	30	85
82	13	2m. on 45c. green and blue	65	2·10
83	13	2m. on 1f. red and green	30	85
84	13	2¼m. on 40c. red and blue	30	65
85	13	2½m. on 60c. violet and blue	50	2·10
74	18	3m. on 5c. orange	40	3·75
86	13	3m. on 60c. violet and blue	1·10	3·75
87	13	4m. on 45c. green and blue	20	75
88	13	5m. on 1f. red and green	30	85
75	15	6m. on 15c. green	55	4·00
89	13	6m. on 60c. violet and blue	20	75
90	13	6m. on 2f. orange & green	30	85
76	18	8m. on 30c. red	85	10·50
91	13	9m. on 1f. red and green	20	75
92	13	9m. on 5f. blue and buff	50	3·75
93	13	10m. on 45c. green & blue	75	4·50
51	13	10m. on 5f. blue and buff	3·25	10·50
94	13	12m. on 40c. red and blue	25	2·10
95	13	20m. on 40c. red and blue	75	4·75
52	13	20m. on 45c. green & blue	8·50	21·00
96	13	20m. on 2f. orange & green	25	2·10
97	13	30m. on 60c. violet & blue	75	4·50
98	13	30m. on 5f. blue and buff	3·75	20·00
99	13	40m. on 1f. red and green	75	6·25
100	13	50m. on 2f. orange & green	10·50	42·00
101	13	80m. on 2f. orange & green	75	6·25
102	13	100m. on 5f. blue and buff	1·10	11·50

1921. Air. Nos. 6/8, 10, 13 and 49/50 optd FLUGPOST in double-lined letters.

53	13	60pf. on 40c. red and blue	37·00	£150
54	13	60pf. on 40c. red and blue (No. 49)	5·25	19·00
55	13	80pf. on 45c. green and blue	4·25	19·00
56	13	1m. on 50c. brown and lilac	4·25	9·50
57	13	2m. on 1f. red and green	4·00	18·00
58	13	3m. on 60c. violet and blue (No. 50)	4·75	19·00
59	13	4m. on 2f. orange and green	5·25	22·00

1922. Air. Nos. 13, 50, 77/81, 83, 86, 88, 90 and 92 further optd Flugpost in script letters.

103	13	40pf. on 40c. red and blue (No. 77)	50	2·75
104	13	80pf. on 45c. green and blue (No. 78)	50	2·75
105	13	1m. on 40c. red and blue (No. 68)	50	2·75
106	13	1m.25 on 60c. violet and blue (No. 80)	1·10	3·50
107	13	1m.50 on 45c. green and blue (No. 81)	1·10	4·00
108	13	2m. on 1f. red and green (No. 83)	1·10	4·00
110	13	3m. on 60c. violet and blue (No. 86)	1·10	4·00
111	13	4m. on 2f. orange and green (No. 13)	1·10	4·00
112	13	5m. on 1f. red and green (No. 88)	1·60	4·00
113	13	6m. on 2f. orange and green (No. 90)	1·60	4·00
114	13	9m. on 5f. blue and buff (No. 92)	1·60	4·00

1922. Air. Surch as in 1921 and optd FLUGPOST in ordinary capitals.

115	13	40pf. on 40c. red and blue	1·60	12·50
116	13	1m. on 40c. red and blue	1·60	12·50
117	13	1m.25 on 60c. violet and blue	1·60	12·50
118	13	1m.50 on 45c. green and blue	1·60	12·50
119	13	2m. on 1f. red and green	1·60	12·50
120	13	3m. on 60c. violet and blue	1·60	12·50
121	13	4m. on 2f. orange & green	1·60	12·50
122	13	5m. on 1f. red and green	1·60	12·50
123	13	6m. on 2f. orange & green	1·60	12·50
124	13	9m. on 5f. blue and buff	1·60	12·50

1922. Nos. 62, 64 and 69 further surch as in 1921 but with additional surch Mark obliterating Pfennig.

125	18	10m. on 10pf. on 10c. green (No. 62)	75	7·50
126	18	20m. on 20pf. on 20c. brown (No. 64)	55	4·00
127	15	50m. on 50pf. on 50c. blue (No. 69)	2·75	12·50

1923. Nos. 77 and 80 with additional surch.

128	13	40m. on 40pf. on 40c. red and blue	1·10	4·25
129	13	80m. on 1m.25 on 60c. violet and blue	1·30	6·75

1923. Nos. 72 and 82 surch with large figures.

130	13	10m. on 2m. on 45c. green and blue	2·75	13·50
131	18	25m. on 1m. on 25c. blue	2·75	13·50

LITHUANIAN OCCUPATION

The port and district of Memel was captured by Lithuanian forces in 1923 and incorporated into Lithuania.

1

1923. (a) Surch KLAIPEDA (MEMEL) and value over curved line and MARKIU.

1	1	10m. on 5c. blue	1·10	4·25
2	1	25m. on 5c. blue	1·10	4·25
3	1	50m. on 25c. red	1·10	4·25
4	1	100m. on 25c. red	1·30	4·75
5	1	400m. on 1l. brown	2·10	9·50

(b) Surch Klaipeda (Memel) and value over two straight lines and Markiu.

6	1	10m. on 5c. blue	1·60	7·50
7	1	25m. on 5c. blue	1·60	7·50
8	1	50m. on 25c. red	1·60	7·50
9	1	100m. on 25c. red	1·60	7·50
10	1	400m. on 1l. brown	2·10	9·50
11	1	500m. on 1l. brown	2·10	9·50

(c) Surch KLAIPEDA (Memel) and value over four stars and MARKIU.

12	1	10m. on 5c. blue	2·10	9·50
13	1	20m. on 5c. blue	2·10	9·50
14	1	25m. on 25c. red	2·10	11·50
15	1	50m. on 25c. red	4·00	11·50
16	1	100m. on 1l. brown	4·25	16·00
17	1	200m. on 1l. brown	5·00	16·00

5

1923

18	5	10m. brown	40	4·75
19	5	20m. yellow	40	4·75
20	5	25m. orange	40	4·75
21	5	40m. violet	40	4·75
22	5	50m. green	1·60	6·25
23	5	100m. red	75	4·75
24	5	300m. green	8·00	£130
25	5	400m. brown	75	5·25
26	5	500m. purple	8·00	£130
27	5	1000m. blue	1·40	8·50

7 Liner, Memel Port

8 Memel Arms

9 Memel Lighthouse

1923. Uniting of Memel with Lithuania and Amalgamation of Memel Harbours.

28	7	40m. green	4·75	30·00
29	7	50m. brown	4·75	30·00
30	7	80m. green	4·75	30·00
31	7	100m. red	4·75	30·00
32	8	200m. blue	4·75	30·00
33	8	300m. brown	4·75	30·00
34	8	400m. purple	4·75	30·00
35	8	500m. orange	4·75	30·00
36	8	600m. green	4·75	30·00
37	9	800m. blue	4·75	30·00
38	9	1000m. purple	4·75	30·00
39	9	2000m. red	4·75	30·00
40	9	3000m. green	4·75	30·00

1923. No. 123 of Memel surch Klaipeda, value and large M between bars, sideways.

41	100m. on 80 on 1m.25 on 60c.	5·00	32·00
42	400m. on 80 on 1m.25 on 60c.	5·25	32·00
43	500m. on 80 on 1m.25 on 60c.	5·00	32·00

1923. Surch in CENTU.

44	5	2c. on 300m. green	8·50	12·50
45	5	3c. on 300m. green	9·50	17·00
46	5	10c. on 25m. orange	9·50	12·50
47	5	15c. on 25m. orange	9·50	12·50
48	5	20c. on 500m. purple	13·00	26·00
49	5	30c. on 500m. purple	10·50	12·50
50	5	50c. on 500m. purple	17·00	32·00

1923. Surch (thin or thick figures) in CENT. or LITAS.

60	5	2c. on 10m. brown	4·25	37·00
51	5	2c. on 20m. yellow	4·25	21·00
52	5	2c. on 50m. green	4·25	17·00
63	5	3c. on 10m. brown	8·50	48·00
53	5	3c. on 40m. violet	6·25	19·00
54	5	3c. on 300m. green	4·25	9·50
55	5	5c. on 100m. red	8·50	9·50
56	5	5c. on 300m. green	5·25	16·00
57	5	10c. on 400m. brown	12·50	26·00
67	5	15c. on 25m. orange	£150	£800
58	5	30c. on 500m. purple	8·50	21·00
68	5	50c. on 1000m. blue	6·25	16·00
69	5	1l. on 1000m. blue	9·50	26·00

1923. Surch in CENT. or LITAS.

70	7	15c. on 40m. green	6·75	32·00
71	7	30c. on 50m. brown	6·75	21·00
72	7	30c. on 80m. green	6·75	42·00
73	7	30c. on 100m. red	6·75	12·50
74	8	50c. on 200m. blue	6·75	32·00
75	8	50c. on 300m. brown	6·75	21·00
76	8	50c. on 400m. purple	6·75	30·00
77	8	50c. on 500m. orange	6·75	26·00
78	8	1l. on 600m. green	8·00	34·00
79	9	1l. on 800m. blue	8·00	34·00
80	9	1l. on 1000m. purple	8·00	34·00
81	9	1l. on 2000m. red	8·00	34·00
82	9	1l. on 3000m. green	8·00	34·00

1923. Surch in large figures and Centu and bars reading upwards.

83	1	10c. on 25m. on 5c. blue (No. 2)	32·00	65·00
84	1	15c. on 100m. on 25c. red (No. 4)	37·00	£275
85	1	30c. on 400m. on 1l. brown (No. 5)	10·50	48·00
86	1	60c. on 50m. on 25c. red (No. 8)	37·00	£375

1923. Surch in large figures and CENT. and bars.

87	7	15c. on 50m. brown	£275	£2750
88	7	25c. on 100m. red	£110	£1600
89	8	30c. on 300m. brown	£200	£1700
90	8	60c. on 500m. orange	£130	£1600

1923. Surch in Centu or Centai (25c.) between bars.

91	5	15c. on 10m. brown	16·00	60·00
92	5	15c. on 20m. yellow	4·25	37·00
93	5	15c. on 25m. orange	5·25	42·00
94	5	15c. on 40m. violet	4·00	37·00
95	5	15c. on 50m. green	3·25	23·00
96	5	15c. on 100m. red	3·25	23·00
97	5	15c. on 400m. brown	2·75	19·00
98	5	15c. on 1000m. blue	85·00	£450
99	5	25c. on 10m. brown	9·50	55·00
100	5	25c. on 20m. yellow	3·75	32·00
101	5	25c. on 25m. orange	5·25	42·00
102	5	25c. on 40m. violet	6·25	55·00
103	5	25c. on 50m. green	3·75	21·00
104	5	25c. on 100m. red	3·50	21·00
105	5	25c. on 400m. brown	3·50	21·00
106	5	25c. on 1000m. blue	85·00	£475
107	5	30c. on 10m. brown	12·50	75·00
108	5	30c. on 20m. yellow	4·75	42·00
109	5	30c. on 25m. orange	6·25	48·00
110	5	30c. on 40m. violet	4·75	26·00
111	5	30c. on 50m. green	3·50	26·00
112	5	30c. on 100m. red	3·50	26·00
113	5	30c. on 400m. brown	3·50	26·00
114	5	30c. on 1000m. blue	85·00	£550

Pt. 15

MEXICO

A republic of Central America. From 1864–67 an Empire under Maximilian of Austria.

8 reales = 100 centavos = 1 peso.

1 Miguel Hidalgo y Costilla

1856. With or without optd district name. Imperf.

1c	1	½r. blue	27·00	27·00
6	1	½r. orange	13·00	16·00
8c	1	½r. black on buff	25·00	37·00
9b	1	1r. black on green	4·25	9·25
7b	1	2r. green	34·00	21·00
10c	1	2r. black on red	2·50	10·00
4b	1	4r. red	85·00	£100
11b	1	4r. black on yellow	39·00	65·00
12a	1	4r. red on yellow	85·00	£110

5c	1	8r. lilac	£140	£140
13a	1	8r. black on brown	85·00	£170
14a	1	8r. green on brown	£110	£140

2

1864. Perf.

15a	2	1r. red	65	
16a	2	2r. blue	65	
17a	2	4r. brown	1·10	
18a	2	1p. black	1·70	

3 Arms of Mexico

1864. Imperf.

19a	3	½r. brown	£110	£100
31	3	½r. purple	49·00	43·00
31c	3	½r. grey	70·00	70·00
32b	3	1r. blue	8·75	5·50
33	3	2r. orange	4·00	2·50
34	3	4r. green	85·00	36·00
35b	3	8r. red	£130	80·00
30	3	3c. brown	£1000	£2250

4 Emperor Maximilian

1864. Imperf.

36c	4	7c. grey	22·00	70·00
40	4	7c. purple	£425	£4750
41	4	13c. blue	8·25	9·25
42	4	25c. orange	7·25	8·50
39c	4	50c. green	12·00	26·00

7 Hidalgo

1868. Imperf or perf.

67	7	6c. black on brown	28·00	19·00
68	7	12c. black on green	26·00	8·50
69	7	25c. blue on pink	15·00	6·50
70b	7	50c. black on yellow	£150	18·00
71	7	100c. black on brown	£225	75·00
76	7	100c. brown on brown	£160	33·00

8 Hidalgo

1872. Imperf or perf.

87	8	6c. green	10·50	10·50
88	8	12c. blue	1·70	1·40
94	8	25c. red	2·20	1·00
90	8	50c. yellow	£120	27·00
91	8	100c. lilac	80·00	41·00

9 Hidalgo

10 Hidalgo

1874. Various frames. Perf.

102a	9	4c. orange	6·50	8·50
97	10	5c. brown	3·00	2·00
98	9	10c. black	1·40	85
105	9	10c. orange	1·40	85
99	10	25c. blue	60	45
107	9	50c. green	8·75	8·75
108	9	100c. red	12·00	10·00

15 Benito Juarez

1879

115	15	1c. brown	2·75	2·75
116	15	2c. violet	2·75	3·00
117	15	5c. orange	1·50	1·00
118	15	10c. blue	2·00	1·70
127a	15	10c. brown	2·00	
128	15	12c. brown	5·00	5·50
129	15	18c. brown	6·00	10·00
130	15	24c. mauve	6·00	7·50
119	15	25c. red	5·50	20·00
132	15	25c. brown	3·75	
120	15	50c. green	10·00	34·00
134	15	50c. yellow	55·00	£225
121	15	85c. violet	13·50	£170
122	15	100c. black	17·00	50·00
137	15	100c. orange	65·00	£275

16

1882

138	16	2c. green	7·50	5·50
139	16	3c. red	7·50	5·50
140	16	6c. blue	4·00	5·75

17 Hidalgo

1884

141	17	1c. green	2·75	50
142	17	2c. green	4·50	1·40
157	17	2c. red	17·00	2·40
143	17	3c. green	8·50	1·40
158	17	3c. brown	13·50	4·00
144	17	4c. green	11·00	1·40
159	17	4c. red	27·00	12·00
145	17	5c. green	12·00	1·00
160	17	5c. blue	17·00	2·40
146	17	6c. green	10·00	1·00
161	17	6c. brown	20·00	4·00
147	17	10c. green	11·00	50
162	17	10c. orange	17·00	1·00
148	17	12c. green	20·00	2·40
163	17	12c. brown	37·00	6·00
149	17	20c. green	60·00	1·70
150	17	25c. green	95·00	3·50
164	17	25c. blue	£140	13·50
151	17	50c. green	40	3·50
152	17	1p. blue	40	7·50
153	17	2p. blue	40	15·00
154	17	5p. blue	£225	£140
155	17	10p. blue	£350	£150

18

1886

196	18	1c. green	50	25
209	18	2c. red	85	70
167	18	3c. lilac	8·00	5·00
189	18	3c. red	70	40
198	18	3c. orange	2·75	1·40
168	18	4c. lilac	12·00	3·50
199	18	4c. orange	2·75	2·00
211	18	4c. red	2·75	2·75
191	18	5c. blue	40	35
170	18	6c. lilac	20·00	5·00
200	18	6c. orange	4·00	1·40
213	18	6c. red	2·50	1·90
171	18	10c. lilac	15·00	75
185a	18	10c. brown	29·00	6·75
193	18	10c. red	35	25
201	18	10c. orange	19·00	1·40
172	18	12c. lilac	17·00	9·50
215	18	12c. red	12·00	12·00
173	18	20c. lilac	£110	70·00
194	18	20c. red	2·40	1·00
202	18	20c. orange	34·00	4·00
174	18	25c. lilac	47·00	12·00
203	18	25c. orange	11·00	3·00
217	18	25c. red	11·00	3·00
206	18	5p. red	£850	£600
207	18	10p. red	£1300	£850

19 Foot Postman

20 Mounted Postman and Pack Mules

21 Statue of Cuauhtemoc

22 Mailcoach

23 Steam Mail Train

1895

253	19	1c. green	2·00	35
219	19	2c. red	2·50	70
220	19	3c. brown	2·50	70
221	20	4c. orange	8·50	1·00
257	21	5c. blue	4·75	25
223	22	10c. purple	3·00	70
224	20	12c. olive	34·00	8·50
225	22	15c. blue	19·00	2·00
226	22	20c. red	22·00	2·00
227	22	50c. mauve	47·00	11·00
228	23	1p. brown	60·00	24·00
229	23	5p. red	£200	£130
230	23	10p. blue	£450	£225

27

28 Juanacatlan Falls

29 Popocatepetl

30 Cathedral, Mexico

1899. Various frames for T 27.

266	27	1c. green	1·20	25
276	27	1c. purple	95	25
267	27	2c. red	2·75	25
277	27	2c. green	1·30	50
268	27	3c. brown	1·90	25
278	27	4c. red	3·00	30
269	27	5c. blue	3·00	25
279	27	5c. orange	75	25
270	27	10c. brown and purple	4·00	25
280	27	10c. orange and blue	3·00	25
271	27	15c. purple and lavender	5·00	25
272	27	20c. blue and red	5·75	25
273a	28	50c. black and purple	27·00	1·50
281	28	50c. black and red	49·00	4·00
274	29	1p. black and blue	50·00	2·40
275	30	5p. black and red	£170	8·00

32 Josefa Ortiz

40 Hidalgo at Dolores

1910. Centenary of First Independence Movement.

282	32	1c. purple	20	25
283	-	2c. green	25	25
284	-	3c. brown	40	25
285	-	4c. red	1·50	30
286	-	5c. orange	25	25
287	-	10c. orange and blue	95	25
288	-	15c. lake and slate	5·00	35
289	-	20c. blue and lake	3·00	25
290	40	50c. black and brown	7·50	1·10
291	-	1p. black and blue	9·00	1·30
292	-	5p. black and red	37·00	10·00

DESIGNS: As Type 32: 2c. L. Vicario; 3c. L. Rayon; 4c. J. Aldama; 5c. M. Hidalgo; 10c. I. Allende; 15c. E. Gonzalez; 20c. M. Abasolo. As Type 40: 1p. Mass on Mt. of Crosses; 5p. Capture of Granaditas.

REVOLUTIONARY PROVISIONALS

For full list of the provisional issues made during the Civil War from 1913 onwards, see the Stanley Gibbons Part 15 (Central America) Catalogue.

CONSTITUTIONALIST GENERAL ISSUES

CT1

1914. "Transitorio".

CT1	CT1	1c. blue	30	30
CT2	CT1	2c. green	40	25
CT3	CT1	4c. blue	7·50	1·70
CT4	CT1	5c. green	7·50	2·00
CT9	CT1	5c. green	70	40
CT5	CT1	10c. red	30	30
CT6	CT1	20c. brown	40	40
CT7	CT1	50c. red	1·70	2·40
CT8	CT1	1p. violet	9·50	11·00

The words of value on No. CT4 are 2×14 mm and on No. CT9 are 2½×16 mm.

1914. Victory of Torreon. Nos. CT1/7 optd Victoria de TORREON ABRIL 2-1914.

CT10	1c. blue	£140	£120
CT11	2c. green	£150	£140
CT12	4c. blue	£170	£200
CT13	5c. green	24·00	34·00
CT14	10c. red	£100	£100
CT15	20c. brown	£1700	£1700
CT16	50c. red	£2250	£2250

CT3

1914. Handstamped with Type CT 3. (a) Nos. D282/6.

CT17	D32	1c. blue	2·40	2·75
CT18	D32	2c. blue	2·40	2·75
CT19	D32	4c. blue	2·40	2·75
CT20	D32	5c. blue	2·40	2·75
CT21	D32	10c. blue	2·40	2·75

(b) Nos. 282/92.

CT22	32	1c. purple	1·00	40
CT23	-	2c. green	2·00	85
CT24	-	3c. brown	2·00	85
CT25	-	4c. red	3·50	1·40
CT26	-	5c. orange	70	25
CT27	-	10c. orange and blue	4·00	1·40
CT28	-	15c. lake and slate	6·75	2·00
CT29	-	20c. blue and lake	13·50	4·00
CT30	40	50c. black and brown	16·00	5·50
CT31	-	1p. black and blue	34·00	6·75
CT32	-	5p. black and red	£120	£100

CT4

1914

CT33	CT4	1c. pink	2·00	27·00
CT34	CT4	2c. green	4·25	24·00
CT35	CT4	3c. orange	6·00	50·00
CT36	CT4	5c. red	3·75	10·00
CT37	CT4	10c. green	6·00	47·00
CT38	CT4	25c. blue	12·00	

CT5

1914. "Denver" issue.

CT39	CT5	1c. blue	25	35
CT40	CT5	2c. green	35	30
CT41	CT5	3c. orange	35	35
CT42	CT5	5c. red	35	25
CT43	CT5	10c. red	45	55
CT44	CT5	15c. mauve	80	1·20
CT45	CT5	50c. yellow	1·40	1·70
CT46	CT5	1p. violet	5·75	8·00

1914. Optd GOBIERNO CONSTITUCIONALISTA. (a) Nos. 279 and 271/2.

CT50	5c. orange	£170	£170
CT51	15c. purple and lavender	£225	£225
CT52	20c. blue and red	£700	£350

(b) Nos. D282/6.

CT53	D32	1c. blue	3·25	3·50
CT54	D32	2c. blue	4·00	3·50
CT55	D32	4c. blue	17·00	18·00
CT56	D32	5c. blue	17·00	18·00
CT57	D32	10c. blue	3·75	3·50

(c) Nos. 282/92.

CT58	32	1c. purple	25	25
CT59	-	2c. green	25	25
CT60	-	3c. brown	25	25
CT61	-	4c. red	35	35
CT62	-	5c. orange	25	25
CT63	-	10c. orange and blue	25	25

CT64	-	15c. lake and slate	45	40
CT65	-	20c. blue and lake	50	45
CT66	40	50c. black and brown	1·20	1·00
CT67	-	1p. black and blue	5·00	3·50
CT68	-	5p. black and red	27·00	20·00

CONVENTIONIST ISSUES

(CV1) Villa–Zapata Monogram

1914. Optd with Type CV 1. (a) Nos. 266/75.

CV1	27	1c. green	£150	
CV2	27	2c. red	£150	
CV3	27	3c. brown	£120	
CV4	27	5c. blue	£140	
CV5	27	10c. brown and purple	£140	
CV6	27	15c. purple and lavender	£325	
CV7	27	20c. blue and red	£425	
CV8	28	50c. black and red	£350	
CV9	29	1p. black and blue	£350	
CV10	30	5p. black and red	£425	

(b) Nos. 276/80.

CV11	27	1c. purple	£150	
CV12	27	2c. green	£300	
CV13	27	4c. red	£150	
CV14	27	5c. orange	31·00	
CV15	27	10c. orange and blue	£200	

(c) Nos. D282/6.

CV16	D32	1c. blue	5·50	6·00
CV17	D32	2c. blue	5·50	6·00
CV18	D32	4c. blue	5·50	6·00
CV19	D32	5c. blue	5·50	6·00
CV20	D32	10c. blue	5·50	6·00

(d) Nos. 282/92.

CV21	32	1c. purple	70	85
CV22	-	2c. green	35	65
CV23	-	3c. brown	50	60
CV24	-	4c. red	3·25	2·50
CV25	-	5c. orange	20	1·60
CV26	-	10c. orange and blue	5·75	3·75
CV27	-	15c. lake and slate	2·50	4·50
CV28	-	20c. blue and lake	4·75	4·75
CV29	40	50c. black and brown	10·50	8·75
CV30	-	1p. black and blue	14·50	14·00
CV31	-	5p. black and red	£100	90·00

CONSTITUTIONALIST PROVISIONAL ISSUES

CT10

1914. Nos. 282/92 handstamped with Type CT 10.

CT69	32	1c. purple	4·50	4·50
CT70	-	2c. green	4·50	4·50
CT71	-	3c. brown	4·50	4·50
CT72	-	4c. red	6·50	5·50
CT73	-	5c. orange	2·00	2·00
CT74	-	10c. orange and blue	6·50	5·50
CT75	-	15c. lake and slate	6·50	5·50
CT76	-	20c. blue and lake	8·00	7·00
CT77	40	50c. black and brown	18·00	18·00
CT78	-	1p. black and blue	32·00	
CT79	-	5p. black and red	£130	

CT11 Carranza Monogram

1915. Optd with Type CT 11. (a) No. 271.

CT80	15c. purple and lavender	85·00	55·00

(b) No. 279.

CT81	5c. orange	20·00	13·50

(c) Nos. D282/6.

CT82	D32	1c. blue	13·50	17·00
CT83	D32	2c. blue	13·50	17·00
CT84	D32	4c. blue	13·50	17·00
CT85	D32	5c. blue	13·50	17·00
CT86	D32	10c. blue	13·50	17·00

(d) Nos. 282/92.

CT87	32	1c. purple	50	60
CT88	-	2c. green	45	40
CT89	-	3c. brown	50	50
CT90	-	4c. red	95	95
CT91	-	5c. orange	20	20
CT92	-	10c. orange and blue	90	90
CT93	-	15c. lake and slate	90	1·00
CT94	-	20c. blue and lake	95	1·10
CT95	40	50c. black and brown	6·00	6·00
CT96	-	1p. black and blue	10·00	9·00
CT97	-	5p. black and red	75·00	65·00

GENERAL ISSUES

43 Coat of Arms

44 Statue of Cuauhtemoc

45 Ignacio Zaragoza

1915. Portraits as T 45. Roul or perf.

293	43	1c. violet	20	15
294	44	2c. green	40	15
304	45	3c. brown	45	25
305	45	4c. red (Morelos)	45	30
306	45	5c. orange (Madero)	65	30
307	45	10c. blue (Juarez)	90	30

46 Map of Mexico

47 Lighthouse, Veracruz

48 Post Office, Mexico City

1915

299	46	40c. grey	65	35
433	46	40c. mauve	1·10	25
300	47	1p. grey and brown	85	50
411	47	1p. grey and blue	42·00	1·30
301	48	5p. blue and lake	8·50	4·25
412	48	5p. grey and green	1·60	10·50

(49)

1916. Silver Currency. Optd with T 49. (a) No. 271.

309	15c. purple and lavender	£400	£375

(b) No. 279.

309a	5c. orange	£110	£120

(c) Nos. 282/92.

310	32	1c. purple	9·00	8·50
311	-	2c. green	50	35
312	-	3c. brown	55	35
313	-	4c. red	5·50	6·75
314	-	5c. orange	25	20
315	-	10c. orange and blue	1·10	1·30
316	-	15c. lake and slate	1·60	2·50
317	-	20c. blue and lake	1·60	2·50
318	40	50c. black and brown	8·00	5·00
319	-	1p. black and blue	14·00	5·75
320	-	5p. black and red	£150	£150

(d) Nos. CT1/3 and CT5/8.

320b	CT1	1c. blue	21·00	
320c	CT1	2c. green	10·50	
320d	CT1	4c. blue	£275	
320e	CT1	10c. red	1·80	
320f	CT1	20c. brown	2·50	
320g	CT1	50c. red	13·00	
320h	CT1	1p. violet	21·00	

(e) Nos. CT39/46.

321	CT5	1c. blue	3·50	13·50
322	CT5	2c. green	3·50	8·00
323	CT5	3c. orange	45	8·00
324	CT5	5c. red	45	8·00
325	CT5	10c. red	45	6·75
326	CT5	15c. mauve	45	8·00
327	CT5	50c. yellow	1·10	10·00
328	CT5	1p. violet	9·75	17·00

(f) Nos. CT58/68.

329	32	1c. purple	2·30	3·50
330	-	2c. green	70	50
331	-	3c. brown	65	60
332	-	4c. red	65	60
333	-	5c. orange	90	30
334	-	10c. orange and blue	70	50
335	-	15c. lake and slate	75	75
336	-	20c. blue and lake	75	75
337	40	50c. black and brown	7·00	5·00
338	-	1p. black and blue	14·00	13·50
339	-	5p. black and red	£140	£120

(g) Nos. CV22/9.

340	32	1c. purple	9·75	13·00
341	-	2c. green	1·30	95
342	-	3c. brown	2·75	4·00
343	-	4c. red	11·50	13·00
344	-	5c. orange	4·00	5·00
345	-	10c. orange and blue	10·50	12·00
346	-	15c. lake and slate	10·50	12·00
347	-	20c. blue and lake	10·50	12·00

(h) Nos. CT87/97.

348	32	1c. purple	4·50	4·25
349	-	2c. green	50	50
350	-	3c. brown	45	50
351	-	4c. red	6·75	7·75
352	-	5c. orange	80	20
353	-	10c. orange and blue	1·30	1·60
354	-	15c. lake and slate	1·10	50
355	-	20c. blue and red	1·10	90
356	40	50c. black and brown	6·75	7·75
357	-	1p. black and blue	10·00	9·75

50 V. Carranza

1916. Carranza's Triumphal Entry into Mexico City.

358	50	10c. brown	12·50	13·00
359	50	10c. blue	1·30	85

(51)

1916. Optd with T 51. (a) Nos. D282/6.

360	D32	5c. on 1c. blue	2·20	2·10
361	D32	10c. on 2c. blue	2·20	2·10
362	D32	20c. on 4c. blue	2·20	2·10
363	D32	25c. on 5c. blue	2·20	2·10
364	D32	60c. on 10c. blue	1·30	1·30
365	D32	1p. on 1c. blue	1·30	1·30
366	D32	1p. on 2c. blue	1·30	1·30
367	D32	1p. on 4c. blue	75	70
368	D32	1p. on 5c. blue	2·20	2·10
369	D32	1p. on 10c. blue	2·20	2·10

(b) Nos. 282, 286 and 283.

370	32	5c. on 1c. purple	45	45
371	32	10c. on 1c. purple	45	45
372	-	20c. on 5c. orange	45	45
373	-	25c. on 5c. orange	45	45
374	-	60c. on 2c. green	22·00	16·00

(c) Nos. CT39/40.

375	CT5	60c. on 1c. blue	2·75	5·00
376	CT5	60c. on 2c. green	2·75	5·00

(d) Nos. CT58, CT62 and CT59.

377	32	5c. on 1c. purple	45	45
378	-	10c. on 1c. purple	85	80
379	-	25c. on 5c. purple	45	45
380	-	60c. on 2c. green	£250	£275

(e) No. CV25.

381	25c. on 5c. orange	20	15

(f) Nos. CT87, CT91 and CT88.

382	32	5c. on 1c. purple	13·00	16·00
383	-	10c. on 1c. purple	4·25	6·25
385	-	25c. on 5c. orange	90	1·30
386	-	60c. on 2c. green	£275	

1916. Nos. D282/6 surch GPM and value.

387	D32	$2.50 on 1c. blue	1·10	1·00
388	D32	$2.50 on 2c. blue	9·25	
389	D32	$2.50 on 4c. blue	9·25	
390	D32	$2.50 on 5c. blue	9·25	
391	D32	$2.50 on 10c. blue	9·25	

52a Arms

1916

392	52a	1c. purple	25	15

53 Zaragoza

1917. Portraits. Roul or perf.

393	53	1c. violet	1·70	80
393a	53	1c. grey	4·25	65
394	-	2c. green (Vazquez)	1·30	45
395	-	3c. brown (Suarez)	1·30	80
396	-	4c. red (Carranza)	2·20	80
397	-	5c. blue (Herrera)	2·20	35
398	-	10c. blue (Madero)	3·50	45
399	-	20c. lake (Dominguez)	34·00	1·70
400	-	30c. purple (Serdan)	80·00	2·50
401	-	30c. black (Serdan)	90·00	3·25

1919. Red Cross Fund. Surch with cross and premium.

413	5c.+3c. blue (No. 397)	16·00	16·00
414	10c.+5c. blue (No. 398)	18·00	16·00

56 Meeting of Iturbide and Guerrero

1921. Centenary of Declaration of Independence.

415	56	10c. brown and blue	23·00	3·00
416	-	10p. black and brown	22·00	36·00

DESIGN: 10p. Entry into Mexico City.

58 Golden Eagle

1922. Air.

454	58	25c. sepia and lake	45	25
455	58	25c. sepia and green	45	25
456	58	50c. red and blue	90	25

59 Morelos Monument

60 Fountain and Aqueduct

61 Pyramid of the Sun, Teotihuacan

62 Castle of Chapultepec

63 Columbus Monument

64 Juarez Colonnade

65 Monument to Dona Josefa Ortiz de Dominguez

66 Cuauhtemoc Monument

68 Ministry of Communications

69 National Theatre and Palace of Fine Arts

74 Benito Juarez

1923. Roul or perf.

436	59	1c. brown	45	25
437	60	2c. red	25	15
438	61	3c. brown	25	15
440	63	4c. green	25	15
429	62	4c. green	1·30	25
441	63	5c. orange	25	15
453	74	8c. orange	25	15
423	64	10c. brown	4·25	15
442	66	10c. lake	25	15

443	65	20c. blue	80	25
426	66	30c. green	49·00	1·60
432	64	30c. green	90	15
434	68	50c. brown	90	25
435	69	1p. blue and lake	90	85

70

72 Sr. Francisco Garcia y Santos

73 Post Office, Mexico City

1926. 2nd Pan-American Postal Congress. Inscr as in T 70/3.

445	70	2c. red	2·20	80
446	-	4c. green	2·75	1·00
447	70	5c. orange	2·20	85
448	-	10c. red	3·50	1·00
449	72	20c. blue	3·50	1·30
450	72	30c. green	6·25	3·25
451	72	40c. mauve	11·00	3·00
452	73	1p. blue and brown	22·00	8·50

DESIGN—As Type **70**: 4c., 10c. Map of North and South America.

1929. Child Welfare. Optd Proteccion a la Infancia.

457	59	1c. brown	45	25

77

1929. Obligatory Tax. Child Welfare.

459	77	1c. violet	25	25
461	77	2c. green	55	25
462	77	5c. brown	55	25

79 Capt. Emilio Carranza

1929. Air. 1st Death Anniv of Carranza (airman).

463	79	5c. sepia and green	1·30	70
464	79	10c. red and sepia	1·40	80
465	79	15c. green and violet	3·25	1·30
466	79	20c. black and sepia	1·30	80
467	79	50c. black and red	6·75	2·75
468	79	1p. sepia and black	13·50	5·00

80

1929. Air. Perf or roul (10, 15, 20, 50c.), roul (5, 25c.), perf (others).

476a	80	5c. blue	25	15
477	80	10c. violet	25	15
478	80	15c. red	30	15
479	80	20c. brown	55	15
480	80	25c. purple	1·10	85
472	80	30c. black	20	15
473	80	35c. blue	35	25
481	80	50c. red	1·10	85
474	80	1p. blue and black	1·30	60
475	80	5p. blue and red	4·00	3·75
476	80	10p. brown and violet	6·25	7·25

81

1929. Air. Aviation Week.

482	81	20c. violet	1·30	1·00
483	81	40c. green	90·00	80·00

1930. 2nd Pan-American Postal Congress issue optd HABILITADO 1930.

484	70	2c. red	4·00	2·20
485	-	4c. green	4·00	2·50
486	70	5c. orange	4·00	1·90
487	-	10c. red	8·00	2·50
488	72	20c. blue	9·75	3·50
489	72	30c. green	9·00	4·00
490	72	40c. mauve	13·50	8·50
491	73	1p. blue and brown	11·50	7·25

1930. Air. National Tourist Congress. Optd Primer Congreso Nacional de Turismo. Mexico. Abril 20-27 de 1930.

492	80	10c. violet (No. 477)	2·20	1·30

1930. Obligatory Tax. Child Welfare. Surch HABILITADO $0.01.

494	77	1c. on 2c. green	2·75	1·30
495	77	1c. on 5c. brown	1·30	80

1930. Air. Optd HABILITADO 1930.

496	79	5c. sepia and green	6·25	5·25
497	79	15c. green and violet	11·00	8·50

1930. Air. Optd HABILITADO Aereo 1930-1931.

498	5c. sepia and green	6·75	6·50
499	10c. red and sepia	3·75	4·00
500	15c. green and violet	7·25	7·00
501	20c. black and sepia	7·50	5·50
502	50c. black and red	13·50	10·50
503	1p. sepia and black	4·00	3·00

1931. Obligatory Tax. Child Welfare. No. CT58 optd PRO INFANCIA.

504	32	1c. purple	45	50

87

1931. Fourth Centenary of Puebla.

505	87	10c. brown and blue	3·25	50

88

1931. Air. Aeronautic Exhibition.

506	88	25c. lake	4·00	4·25

1931. Nos. 446/52 optd HABILITADO 1931.

508	-	4c. green	70·00
509	70	5c. orange	13·50
510	-	10c. red	13·50
511	72	20c. blue	13·50
512	72	30c. green	22·00
513	72	40c. mauve	32·00
514	73	1p. blue and brown	29·00

1931. Air. Surch HABILITADO Quince centavos. Perf or rouletted.

516	80	15c. on 20c. sepia	60	80

1932. Air. Surch in words and figures. Perf. or roul.

517	88	20c. on 25c. lake	70	25
521	80	30c. on 20c. sepia	35	15
519	58	40c. on 25c. sepia and lake	1·00	95
520	58	40c. on 25c. sepia & green	38·00	37·00
522	80	80c. on 25c. (No. 480)	1·60	1·30

1932. Air. 4th Death Anniv of Emilio Carranza. Optd HABILITADO AEREO-1932.

523	79	5c. sepia and green	5·50	3·00
524	79	10c. red and sepia	5·50	3·00
525	79	15c. green and violet	5·50	3·00
526	79	20c. black and sepia	5·50	3·00
527	79	50c. black and red	38·00	36·00

92 Fray Bartolome de las Casas

1933. Roul.

528	92	15c. blue	20	15

93 Mexican Geographical and Statistical Society's Arms

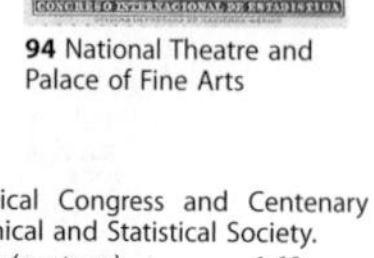
94 National Theatre and Palace of Fine Arts

1933. 21st Int Statistical Congress and Centenary of Mexican Geographical and Statistical Society.

529	93	2c. green (postage)	1·60	60
530	93	5c. brown	1·80	50
531	93	10c. blue	80	15
533	94	20c. violet and red (air)	3·50	1·50
534	94	30c. violet and brown	7·25	6·50
532	93	1p. violet	65·00	55·00
535	94	1p. violet and green	70·00	75·00

95 Mother and Child

98 Nevada de Toluca

1934. National University. Inscr "PRO-UNIVERSIDAD".

543	95	1c. orange (postage)	25	15
544	-	5c. green	2·20	50
545	-	10c. lake	2·75	80
546	-	20c. blue	8·50	5·25
547	-	30c. black	16·00	13·00
548	-	40c. brown	26·00	17·00
549	-	50c. blue	55·00	50·00
550	-	1p. black and red	£100	47·00
551	-	5p. brown and black	£225	£225
552	-	10p. violet and brown	£1100	£950

DESIGNS: 5c. Archer; 10c. Festive headdress; 20c. Woman decorating pot; 30c. Indian and Inca Lily; 40c. Potter; 50c. Sculptor; 1p. Gold craftsman; 5p. Girl offering fruit; 10p. Youth burning incense.

553	98	20c. orange (air)	4·00	3·00
554	-	30c. purple and mauve	8·00	5·75
555	-	50c. brown and green	9·00	9·50
556	-	75c. green and black	9·00	14·50
557	-	1p. blue and green	11·00	10·50
558	-	5p. blue and brown	60·00	85·00
559	-	10p. red and blue	£160	£170
560	-	20p. red and brown	£1300	£1400

DESIGNS—Airplane over: 30c. Pyramids of the Sun and Moon, Teotihuacan; 50c. Mt. Ajusco; 75c. Mts. Ixtaccihuatl and Popocatepetl; 1p. Bridge over R. Papagallo; 5p. Chapultepec Castle entrance; 10p. Orizaba Peak, Mt. Citlaltepetl; 20p. Girl and Aztec calendar stone.

101 Zapoteca Indian Woman

110 Coat of Arms

1934. Pres. Cardenas' Assumption of Office. Designs as Type 101 and 110. Imprint "OFICINA IMPRESORA DE HACIENDA-MEXICO" at foot of stamp. (a) Postage.

561		1c. orange	90	15
562	101	2c. green	90	15
563	-	4c. red	1·30	15
564	-	5c. brown	90	15
565	-	10c. blue	1·10	15
565a	-	10c. violet	1·70	15
566	-	15c. blue	5·50	35
567	-	20c. green	2·75	15
567a	-	20c. blue	2·00	15
568	-	30c. red	1·30	15
653	-	30c. blue	1·30	15
569	-	40c. brown	1·30	15
570	-	50c. black	1·30	15
571	110	1p. red and brown	3·50	15
572	-	5p. violet and orange	11·00	80

DESIGNS: 1c. Yalalteca Indian; 4c. Revolution Monument; 5c. Los Remedios Tower; 10c. Cross of Palenque; 15c. Independence Monument, Mexico City; 20c. Independence Monument, Puebla; 30c. "Heroic Children" Monument, Mexico City; 40c. Sacrificial Stone; 50c. Ruins of Mitla, Oaxaca; 5p. Mexican "Charro" (Horseman).

112 Mictlantecuhtli

120 "Peasant admiration"

(b) Air.

573	112	5c. black	45	15
574	-	10c. brown	1·00	15
575	-	15c. green	1·30	15
576	-	20c. red	3·25	15
577	-	30c. olive	70	15
577a	-	40c. blue	1·30	15
578	-	50c. green	2·75	15
579	-	1p. red and green	3·75	15
580	120	5p. black and red	7·50	70

DESIGNS—HORIZ: 10c. Temple at Quetzalcoatl; 15c. Aeroplane over Citlaltepetl; 20c. Popocatepetl; 30c. Pegasus; 50c. Uruapan pottery; 1p. "Warrior Eagle". VERT: 40c. Aztec idol.

121 Tractor

1935. Industrial Census.

581	121	10c. violet	4·00	50

1935. Air. Amelia Earhart Flight to Mexico. No. 576 optd AMELIA EARHART VUELO DE BUENA VOLUNTAD MEXICO 1935.

581a	20c. red	£3500	£4250

122 Arms of Chiapas

1935. Annexation of Chiapas Centenary.

582	122	10c. blue	55	15

123 E. Zapata

124 Francisco Madero

1935. 25th Anniv of Revolutionary Plans of Ayala and San Luis Potosi.

583	123	10c. violet (postage)	80	15
584	124	20c. red (air)	35	15

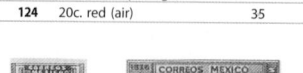

129 Nuevo Laredo Road

131 Rio Corona Bridge

1936. Opening of Nuevo Laredo Highway (Mexico City–U.S.A.).

591	-	5c. red and green (postage)	35	15
592	-	10c. grey	55	15
593	129	20c. green and brown	1·50	1·00

DESIGNS: As Type **129**: 5c. Symbolical Map of Mexico–U.S.A. road; 10c. Matalote Bridge.

594	-	10c. blue (air)	20	15
595	131	20c. orange and violet	35	15
596	-	40c. green and blue	55	50

DESIGNS: As Type **131**: 10c. Tasquillo Bridge over Rio Tula; 40c. Guayalejo Bridge.

1936. 1st Congress of Industrial Medicine and Hygiene. Optd PRIMER CONGRESO NAL. DE HIGIENE Y. MED. DEL TRABAJO.

597	10c. violet (No. 565a)	65	50

1937. As Nos. 561/4, 565a and 576, but smaller. Imprint at foot changed to "TALLERES DE IMP.(RESION) DE EST. (AMPILLAS) Y VALORES-MEXICO".

600	4c. red	1·20	15
601	5c. brown	1·10	15
602	10c. violet	1·00	15
603	20c. red (air)	2·20	15
708	1c. orange (postage)	1·30	15
709	2c. green	1·30	15

134 Blacksmith

1938. Carranza's "Plan of Guadelupe". 25th Anniv. Inscr "CONMEMORATIVO PLAN DE GUADALUPE", etc.

604	134	5c. brown & blk (postage)	90	15
605	-	10c. brown	35	15
606	-	20c. orange and brown	6·75	1·00
607	-	20c. blue and red (air)	55	35
608	-	40c. red and blue	80	35
609	-	1p. blue and yellow	5·50	2·50

DESIGNS—VERT: 10c. Peasant revolutionary; 20c. Preaching revolt. HORIZ: 20c. Horseman; 40c. Biplane; 1p. Mounted horseman.

140 Arch of the Revolution

141 Cathedral and Constitution Square

1938. 16th International Town Planning and Housing Congress, Mexico City. Inscr as in T 140/1.

610	140	5c. brown (postage)	2·30	60
611	-	5c. olive	10·50	2·20
612	-	10c. orange	18·00	11·00
613	-	10c. brown	80	15
614	-	20c. black	23·00	16·00
615	-	20c. lake	4·50	4·25

DESIGNS: As Type **140**: 10c. National Theatre; 20c. Independence Column.

616	141	20c. red (air)	45	25
617	-	20c. violet	18·00	10·50
619	-	40c. green	9·00	5·25
620	-	1p. slate	9·00	5·25
621	-	1p. light blue	9·00	5·25

DESIGNS: As Type **141**: 40c. Chichen Itza Ruins (Yucatan); 1p. Acapulco Beach.

142 Mosquito and Malaria Victim

1939. Obligatory Tax. Anti-malaria Campaign.

622	142	1c. blue	2·00	25

143 Statue of an Indian

144 Statue of Woman Pioneer and Child

1939. Tulsa Philatelic Convention, Oklahoma.

623	143	10c. red (postage)	55	15
624	144	20c. brown (air)	1·10	45
625	144	40c. green	2·75	1·30
626	144	1p. violet	1·80	95

1939. Air. F. Sarabia non-stop Flight to New York. Optd SARABIA Vuelo MEXICO-NUEVA YORK.

626a	146	20c. blue and red	£475	£550

145 Mexican Pavilion, World's Fair

146 Morelos Statue on Mexican Pavilion

1939. New York World's Fair.

627	145	10c. green & blue (postage)	70	15
628	146	20c. green (air)	70	50
629	146	40c. purple	2·20	1·40
630	146	1p. brown and red	1·50	1·00

147 J. de Zumarraga

1939. 400th Anniv of Printing in Mexico.

631	147	2c. black (postage)	1·20	25
632	-	5c. green	1·20	15
633	-	10c. red	35	15
634	-	20c. blue (air)	35	15
635	-	40c. green	1·00	15
636	-	1p. red and brown	1·70	70

DESIGNS: 5c. First printing works in Mexico; 10c. Antonio D. Mendoza; 20c. Book frontispiece; 40c. Title page of first law book printed in America; 1p. Oldest Mexican Colophon.

152 "Building"

154 "Transport"

1939. National Census. Inscr "CENSOS 1939 1940".

637	152	2c. red (postage)	1·30	15
638	-	5c. green	20	15
639	-	10c. brown	20	15
640	154	20c. blue (air)	1·10	15
641	-	40c. orange	80	25
642	-	1p. violet and blue	2·75	80

DESIGNS: As Type **152**: 5c. "Agriculture"; 10c. "Commerce". As Type **154**: 40c. "Industry"; 1p. "Seven Censuses".

155 "Penny Black"

1940. Centenary of First Adhesive Postage Stamps.

643	155	5c. yellow & black (postage)	1·00	50
644	155	10c. purple	25	15
645	155	20c. red and blue	25	15
646	155	1p. red and grey	7·50	4·25
647	155	5p. blue and black	40·00	31·00
648	155	5c. green and black (air)	90	60
649	155	10c. blue and brown	90	25
650	155	20c. violet and red	60	15
651	155	1p. brown and red	7·25	4·75
652	155	5p. brown and green	75·00	60·00

156 Roadside Monument

1940. Opening of Highway from Mexico City to Guadalajara.

654	156	6c. green	80	15

159 Original College at Patzcuaro

1940. 4th Centenary of National College of St. Nicholas de Hidalgo.

655	-	2c. violet (postage)	1·40	50
656	-	5c. red	90	15
657	-	10c. olive	90	35
658	159	20c. green (air)	55	15
659	-	40c. orange	65	35
660	-	1p. violet, brown & orange	1·50	95

DESIGNS—VERT: 2c. V. de Quiroga; 5c. M. Ocampo; 10c. St. Nicholas College Arms; 40c. Former College at Morelia. HORIZ: 1p. Present College at Morelia.

163 Pirate Galleon

1940. 400th Anniv of Campeche. Inscr as in T 163.

661		10c. red & brown (postage)	4·00	1·40
662	163	20c. brown and red (air)	1·50	70
663	-	40c. green and black	2·00	80
664	-	1p. black and blue	6·75	3·00

DESIGNS: 10c. Campeche City Arms; 40c. St. Miguel Castel; 1p. Temple of San Francisco.

165 Helmsman

1940. Inauguration of Pres. Camacho.

665	165	2c. orange & black (postage)	3·25	60
666	165	5c. blue and brown	9·00	3·50
667	165	10c. olive and brown	3·25	85
668	165	20c. grey and orange (air)	2·20	1·00
669	165	40c. brown and green	2·30	1·60
670	165	1p. purple and red	3·25	2·10

166 Miguel Hidalgo y Costilla

1940. Compulsory Tax. Dolores Hidalgo Memorial Fund.

671	166	1c. red	65	25

168 Javelin throwing

1941. National Athletic Meeting.

675	168	10c. green	5·50	50

169 Dark Nebula in Orion

1942. Inauguration of Astro-physical Observatory at Tonanzintla, Puebla.

676	169	2c. blue & violet (postage)	4·75	2·20
677	-	5c. blue	11·50	2·75
678	-	10c. blue and orange	12·50	80
679	-	20c. blue and green (air)	15·00	3·00
680	-	40c. blue and red	12·50	4·25
681	-	1p. black and orange	16·00	4·75

DESIGNS: 5c. Solar Eclipse; 10c. Spiral Galaxy of the "Hunting Dog"; 20c. Extra-Galactic Nebula in Virgo; 40c. Ring Nebula in Lyra; 1p. Russell Diagram.

171 Ruins of Chichen-Itza

172 Merida Nunnery

1942. 400th Anniv of Merida. Inscr as in T 171/2.

682	171	2c. brown (postage)	1·80	80
683	-	5c. red	2·75	60
684	-	10c. violet	2·00	25
685	172	20c. blue (air)	1·80	80
686	-	40c. green	2·75	2·10
687	-	1p. red	3·25	2·10

DESIGNS–VERT: 5c. Mayan sculpture; 10c. Arms of Merida; 40c. Montejo University Gateway. HORIZ: 1p. Campanile of Merida Cathedral.

173 "Mother Earth"

1942. 2nd Inter-American Agricultural Conference.

688	173	2c. brown (postage)	2·20	45
689	-	5c. blue	4·00	1·10
690	-	10c. orange	1·60	60
691	-	20c. green (air)	2·30	70
692	-	40c. brown	2·00	80
693	-	1p. violet	3·25	2·20

DESIGNS: 5c. Sowing wheat; 10c. Western Hemisphere carrying torch; 20c. Corn; 40c. Coffee; 1p. Bananas.

175 Hidalgo Monument

1942. 400th Anniv of Guadalajara.

694	175	2c. brown & blue (postage)	55	35
695	-	5c. red and black	1·80	50
696	-	10c. blue and red	1·80	45
697	-	20c. black and green (air)	2·20	80
698	-	40c. green and olive	2·75	1·00
699	-	1p. violet and brown	2·50	1·40

DESIGNS—VERT: 5c. Government Palace; 10c. Guadalajara. HORIZ: 20c. St. Paul's Church, Zapopan; 40c. Sanctuary of Our Lady of Guadalupe; 1p. Arms of Guadalajara.

186 Saltillo Athenaeum, Coahuila

1942. 75th Anniv of Saltillo Athenaeum.

700	186	10c. black	2·75	80

189 Birthplace of Allende

1943. 400th Anniv of San Miguel de Allende.

701	-	2c. blue (postage)	90	45
702	-	5c. brown	1·10	35
703	-	10c. black	2·75	1·00
704	-	20c. green (air)	1·30	60
705	189	40c. purple	1·80	60
706	-	1p. red	3·50	2·50

DESIGNS—VERT: 2c. Cupola de las Monjas; 5c. Gothic Church; 10c. Gen. de Allende. HORIZ: 20c. San Miguel de Allende; 1p. Church seen through cloisters.

190 "Liberty"

1944

707	190	12c. brown	35	15

192 Dr. de Castorena

1944. 3rd National Book Fair.

732	192	12c. brown (postage)	70	15
733	-	25c. green (air)	75	15

DESIGN: 25c. Microphone, book and camera.

194 "Flight"

1944. Air.

734	194	25c. brown	50	15

195 Hands clasping Globe

1945. Inter-American Conference.

735	**195**	12c. red (postage)	60	15
736	**195**	1p. green	1·10	30
737	**195**	5p. brown	7·25	5·00
738	**195**	10p. black	14·50	8·75
739	**195**	25c. orange (air)	50	20
740	**195**	1p. green	60	35
741	**195**	5p. blue	3·00	2·30
742	**195**	10p. red	8·25	5·50
743	**195**	20p. blue	17·00	14·00

196 La Paz Theatre, San Luis Potosi

1945. Reconstruction of La Paz Theatre, San Luis Potosi.

744	**196**	12c. pur & blk (postage)	40	15
745	**196**	1p. blue and black	70	40
746	**196**	5p. red and black	6·75	5·50
747	**196**	10p. green and black	16·00	13·00
748	**196**	30c. green (air)	40	15
749	**196**	1p. purple and green	50	40
750	**196**	5p. black and green	3·75	2·75
751	**196**	10p. blue and green	7·25	4·75
752	**196**	20p. green and black	16·00	11·00

197 Fountain of Diana the Huntress

1945

753	**197**	3c. violet	55	15

198 Removing Bandage

1945. Literacy Campaign.

754	**198**	2c. blue (postage)	30	20
755	**198**	6c. orange	50	20
756	**198**	12c. blue	50	20
757	**198**	1p. olive	60	30
758	**198**	5p. red and black	3·00	2·40
759	**198**	10p. green and blue	24·00	22·00
760	**198**	30c. green (air)	20	20
761	**198**	1p. red	60	35
762	**198**	5p. blue	4·50	2·75
763	**198**	10p. red	7·25	5·50
764	**198**	20p. brown and green	35·00	26·00

199 Founder of National Post Office

1946. Foundation of Posts in Mexico in 1580.

765	**199**	8c. black	1·60	25

200 O.N.U., Olive Branch and Globe **201** O.N.U. and Flags of United Nations

1946. United Nations.

766	**200**	2c. olive (postage)	30	15
767	**200**	6c. brown	30	20
768	**200**	12c. blue	20	15
769	**200**	1p. green	60	45
770	**200**	5p. red	4·75	5·50
771	**200**	10p. blue	24·00	22·00
772	**201**	3c. brown (air)	20	15
773	**201**	1p. grey	60	30
774	**201**	5p. green and brown	2·40	1·40
775	**201**	10p. brown and sepia	5·75	4·25
776	**201**	20p. red and slate	16·00	10·00

202 Zacatecas City Arms **205** Don Genaro Codina and Zacatecas

1946. 400th Anniv of Zacatecas.

777	**202**	2c. brown (postage)	60	15
778	-	12c. blue	30	15
779	-	1p. mauve	75	20
780	-	5p. red	5·75	3·25
781	-	10p. black and blue	37·00	11·00

DESIGNS: 1p. Statue of Gen. Ortega; 5p. R. L. Velarde (poet); 10p. F. G. Salinas.

782		30c. grey (air)	20	15
783	**205**	1p. green and brown	40	35
784	-	5p. green and red	3·50	3·25
785	-	10p. brown and green	14·50	8·25

PORTRAITS: 30c. Fr. Margil de Jesus; 5p. Gen. Enrique Estrada; 10p. D. Fernando Villalpando.

207 Learning Vowels

1946. Education Plan.

786	**207**	1c. sepia	50	20

208 Postman

1947

787	**208**	15c. blue	30	15

209 Roosevelt and First Mexican Stamp **210** 10c. U.S.A. 1847 and Mexican Eagle

1947. U.S.A. Postage Stamp Centenary.

788	**209**	10c. brown (postage)	2·40	1·10
789	-	15c. green	40	15
790	-	25c. blue (air)	95	55
791	**210**	30c. black	70	25
792	-	1p. blue and red	1·40	45

DESIGNS: 15c. as Type **209** but vert; 25c., 1p. as Type **210** but horiz.

213 Justo Sierra **214** Ministry of Communications

212 Douglas DC-4

1947

793		10p. red and brown (air)	1·90	1·60
794	**212**	20p. red and blue	3·00	3·00
795	**213**	10p. green and brown (postage)	£140	26·00
796	**214**	20p. mauve and green	1·40	2·30

DESIGN—HORIZ: 10p. E. Carranza.

215 Manuel Rincon **217** Vicente Suarez

1947. Battle Centenaries. Portraits of "Child Heroes" etc. Inscr "1er CENTENARIO CHAPULTEPEC ("CHURUBUSCO" or "MOLINO DEL REY") 1847 1947".

797	-	2c. black (postage)	60	15
798	-	5c. red	40	15
799	-	10c. brown	30	15
800	-	15c. green	30	15
801	**215**	30c. olive	50	15
802	-	1p. blue	60	45
803	-	5p. red and blue	2·50	2·00

DESIGNS—VERT: 2c. Francisco Marquez; 5c. Fernando Montes de Oca; 10c. Juan Escutin; 15c. Agustin Melgar; 1p. Lucas Balderas; 5p. Flag of San Blas Battalion.

804	**217**	25c. violet (air)	20	15
805	-	30c. blue	20	15
806	-	50c. green	40	15
807	-	1p. violet	50	15
808	-	5p. brown and blue	2·10	2·20

DESIGNS—HORIZ: 30c. Juan de la Barrera; 50c. Military Academy; 1p. Pedro Maria Anaya; 5p. Antonio de Leon.

218 Puebla Cathedral **221** Dance of the Half Moons, Puebla

1950. (a) Postage. As T 218.

835		3c. blue	50	15
874		5c. brown	40	15
875a		10c. green	1·90	15
876a		15c. green	95	25
877e	**218**	20c. blue	1·90	55
840		30c. red	90	15
879	-	30c. brown	1·20	15
880b	-	40c. orange	95	15
1346b	-	50c. blue	1·20	15
1327b	-	80c. green	1·00	45
843		1p. brown	7·50	15
1011ab	-	1p. grey	1·30	20
1346f	-	1p. green	1·20	15
1327d	-	3p. red	2·10	45
1012a	-	5p. blue and green	6·25	50
1013ab	-	10p. black and blue	6·50	3·75
846		20p. violet and green	9·50	9·25
1014	-	20p. violet and black	11·50	5·00
1327e	-	50p. orange and green	16·00	9·00

DESIGNS: 3 c, 3p. La Purisima Church, Monterrey; 5c. Modern building, Mexico City; 10c. Convent of the Nativity, Tepoztlan; 15 c, 50p. Benito Juarez; 30c., 80c. Indian dancer, Michoacan; 40c. Sculpture, Tehuantepec; 50c. Carved head, Veracruz; 1p. Actopan Convent and carved head; 5p. Galleon, Campeche; 10p. Francisco Madero; 20p. Modern building, Mexico City.

(b) Air. As T 221.

897		5c. blue	40	15
898a		10c. brown	50	15
899a		20c. red	50	15
850		25c. brown	2·20	15
851		30c. olive	90	15
902		35c. violet	1·80	15
1327f	-	40c. blue	70	35
904c		50c. green	85	15
1056	-	80c. red	1·20	45
906a	**221**	1p. grey	2·30	1·30
1327h	-	1p.60 red	3·50	45
1327i	-	1p.90 red	3·50	45
907ab	-	2p. brown	85	45
908	-	2p.25 purple	75	50
1327j	-	4p.30 blue	1·20	25
1017a	-	5p. orange and brown	3·00	75
1327k	-	5p.20 lilac	2·10	35
1327l	-	5p.60 green	4·25	45
895		10p. blue and black	10·00	1·20
859a		20p. blue and red	£700	85·00

DESIGNS: 5c., 1p.90 Bay of Acapulco; 10c., 4p.30, Dance of the Plumes, Oaxaca; 20c. Mayan frescoes, Chiapas; 25c., 2p.25, 5p.60, Masks, Michoacan; 30c. Cuauhtemoc; 35c., 2p., 5p.20, Taxco, Guerrero; 40c. Sculpture, San Luis Potosi; 50c., 1p.60, Ancient carvings, Chiapas; 80c. University City, Mexico City; 5p. Architecture, Queretaro; 10p. Hidalgo; 20p. National Music Conservatoire, Mexico City.

222 Arterial Road

1950. Opening of Mexican Section of Pan-American Highway. Inscr "CARRETERA INTER-NACIONAL 1950".

860		15c. violet (postage)	60	15
861	**222**	20c. blue	40	20
862	-	25c. pink (air)	2·75	25
863	-	35c. green	30	15

DESIGNS—HORIZ: 15c. Bridge; 25c. Pres. M. Aleman, bridge and map; 35c. B. Juarez and map.

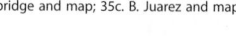

224 Diesel Locomotive and Map

1950. Inauguration of Mexico–Yucatan Railway.

864		15c. purple (postage)	1·30	15
865	**224**	20c. red	50	15
866	-	25c. green (air)	50	25
867	-	35c. blue	40	25

DESIGNS—VERT: 15c. Rail-laying. HORIZ: 25c. Diesel trains crossing Isthmus of Tehuantepac; 35c. M. Aleman and railway bridge at Coatzacoalcos.

227 Hands and Globe

1950. 75th Anniv of U.P.U.

868		50c. violet (postage)	40	15
869		25c. red (air)	40	20
870	**227**	80c. blue	60	30

DESIGNS—HORIZ: 25c. Aztec runner. VERT: 50c. Letters "U.P.U.".

228 Miguel Hidalgo **229**

1953. Birth Bicentenary of Hidalgo.

871	**228**	20c. sepia & blue (postage)	1·60	30
872	-	25c. lake and blue (air)	1·20	20
873	**229**	35c. green	1·20	30

DESIGN: As Type **229**: 25c. Full face portrait.

231 Aztec Athlete **232** View and Mayan Bas-relief

1954. 7th Central American and Caribbean Games.

918	**231**	20c. blue & pink (postage)	1·20	20
919	**232**	25c. brown and green (air)	1·30	35
920	-	35c. turquoise and purple	95	30

DESIGN: 35c. Stadium.

233 **234**

1954. Mexican National Anthem Centenary.

921	**233**	5c. lilac and blue (postage)	75	20
922	**233**	20c. brown and purple	1·10	15
923	**233**	1p. green and red	65	40
924	**234**	25c. blue and lake (air)	60	25
925	**234**	35c. purple and blue	30	15
926	**234**	80c. green and blue	30	25

235 Torchbearer and Stadium

236 Aztec God and Map

1955. 2nd Pan-American Games, Mexico City. Inscr "II JUEGOS DEPORTIVOS PANAMER-ICANOS".

927	**235**	20c. green & brn (postage)	95	20
928	**236**	25c. blue and brown (air)	75	35
929	-	35c. brown and red	75	35

DESIGN: As Type **236**: 35c. Stadium and map.

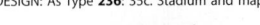

237 Olin Design

1956. Mexican Stamp Centenary.

930	**237**	5c. green & brn (postage)	50	15
931	-	10c. blue and grey	50	15
932	-	30c. purple and red	40	15
933	-	50c. brown and blue	40	15
934	-	1p. black and green	50	15
935	-	5p. sepia and bistre	2·50	2·50
MS936		190×150 mm. Nos. 930/5. Imperf (sold at 15p.)	60·00	55·00

DESIGNS: As Type **237**: 10c. Tohtli bird; 30c. Zochitl flower; 50c. Centli corn; 1p. Mazatl deer; 5p. Teheutli man's head.

238 Feathered Serpent and Mask

937	**238**	5c. black (air)	60	15
938	-	10c. blue	60	15
939	-	50c. purple	40	15
940	-	1p. violet	60	15
941	-	1p.20 mauve	60	20
942	-	5p. turquoise	1·80	1·40
MS943		190×150 mm. Nos. 937/42 (sold at 15p.)	60·00	55·00

DESIGNS: As Type **238**: 10c. Bell tower, coach and Viceroy Enriquez de Almanza; 50c. Morelos and cannon; 1p. Mother, child and mounted horseman; 1p.20, Sombrero and spurs; 5p. Emblems of food and education and pointing hand.

239 Stamp of 1856

1956. Centenary Int Philatelic Exn, Mexico City.

944	**239**	30c. blue and brown	80	30

240 F. Zarco

241 V. Gomez Farias and M. Ocampo

1956. Inscr "CONSTITUYENTE(S) DE 1857".

945	-	25c. brown (postage)	95	35
946	-	45c. blue	40	25
947	-	60c. purple	40	30
1346d	**240**	70c. blue	70	30
1327c	-	2p.30 blue	1·20	35
949	**241**	15c. blue (air)	50	15
1327g	-	60c. green	1·00	35
950	-	1p.20 violet and green	85	30
951	**241**	2p.75 purple	1·20	75

PORTRAITS: As T **240** (postage): 25, 45c., 2p.30, G. Prieto; 60c. P. Arriagan. As T **41** (air): 60c., 1p.20, L. Guzman and I. Ramirez.

242 Paricutin Volcano

1956. Air. 20th International Geological Congress.

952	**242**	50c. violet	60	20

243 Map of Central America and the Caribbean

1956. Air. 4th Inter-American Congress of Caribbean Tourism.

953	**243**	25c. blue and grey	40	20

244 Assembly of 1857

245 Mexican Eagle and Scales

1957. Centenary of 1857 Constitution.

958	-	30c. gold & lake (postage)	60	20
959	**244**	1p. green and sepia	40	30
960	**245**	50c. brown and green (air)	30	20
961	-	1p. lilac and blue	50	30

DESIGNS—VERT: 30c. Emblem of Constitution. HORIZ: 1p. (Air), "Mexico" drafting the Constitution.

246 Globe, Weights and Dials

1957. Air. Centenary of Adoption of Metric System in Mexico.

962	**246**	50c. black and silver	50	20

247 Train Disaster

1957. Air. 50th Anniv of Heroic Death of Jesus Garcia (engine driver) at Nacozari.

963	**247**	50c. purple and red	40	20

248 Oil Derrick

1958. 20th Anniv of Nationalization of Oil Industry.

964	**248**	30c. black & blue (postage)	50	15
965	-	5p. red and blue	5·50	3·75
966	-	50c. green and black (air)	35	15
967	-	1p. black and red	40	15

DESIGNS—HORIZ: 50c. Oil storage tank and "AL SERVICIO DE LA PATRIA" ("At the service of the Fatherland"); 1p. Oil refinery at night. VERT: 5p. Map of Mexico and silhouette of oil refinery.

249 Angel, Independence Monument, Mexico City

1958. Air. 10th Anniv of Declaration of Human Rights.

968	**249**	50c. blue	30	15

250 UNESCO Headquarters, Paris

1959. Inauguration of UNESCO Headquarters Building, Paris.

969	**250**	30c. black and purple	70	15

251 U.N. Headquarters, New York

1959. U.N. Economic and Social Council Meeting, Mexico City.

970	**251**	30c. blue and yellow	70	15

252 President Carranza

1960. "President Carranza Year" (1959) and his Birth Centenary.

971	**252**	30c. pur & grn (postage)	35	15
972	-	50c. violet and salmon (air)	30	15

DESIGN—HORIZ: 50c. Inscription "Plan de Guadalupe Constitucion de 1917" and portrait as Type **252**.

253 Alexander von Humboldt (statue)

1960. Death Centenary of Alexander von Humboldt (naturalist).

973	**253**	40c. green and brown	35	15

254 Alberto Braniff's Voisin "Boxkite" and Bristol Britannia

1960. Air. 50th Anniv of Mexican Aviation.

974	**254**	50c. brown and violet	55	15
975	**254**	1p. brown and green	40	25

255 Francisco I. Madero

1960. Visit to Mexico of Members of Elmhurst Philatelic Society (American Society of Mexican Specialists). Inscr "HOMENAJE AL COLEC-CIONISTA".

976	**255**	10p. sepia, green and purple (postage)	65·00	55·00
977	-	20p. sepia, green and purple (air)	85·00	95·00

DESIGN: As No. 1019a 20p. National Music Conservatoire inscr "MEX. D.F.".

257 Dolores Bell

1960. 150th Anniv of Independence.

978	**257**	30c. red & green (postage)	1·30	15
979	-	1p. sepia and green	40	30
980	-	5p. blue and purple	5·00	4·50
981	-	50c. red and green (air)	40	15
982	-	1p.20 sepia and blue	50	30
983	-	5p. sepia and green	5·75	2·40

DESIGNS—VERT: No. 979, Independence Column; 980, Hidalgo, Dolores Bell and Mexican Eagle. HORIZ: No. 981, Mexican Flag; 982, Eagle breaking chain and bell tolling; 983, Dolores Church.

259 Children at Desk, University and School Buildings

1960. 50th Anniv of Mexican Revolution.

984		10c. multicoloured (postage)	75	20
985		15c. brown and green	2·75	55
986		20c. blue and brown	1·30	20
987		30c. violet and sepia	50	20
988	**259**	1p. slate and purple	70	20
989	-	5p. grey and purple	5·75	3·25
990	-	50c. black and blue (air)	50	20
991	-	1p. green and red	60	30
992	-	1p.20 sepia and green	60	30
993	-	5p. lt blue, blue & mauve	3·75	1·70

DESIGNS: No. 984, Pastoral scene (35½×45½ mm). As Type **259** VERT: No. 985, Worker and hospital buildings; 986, Peasant, soldier and marine; 987, Power lines and pylons; 989, Coins, banknotes and bank entrance. HORIZ: No. 990, Douglas DC-8 airliner; 991, Riggers on oil derrick; 992, Main highway and map; 993, Barrage.

261 Count S. de Revillagigedo

1960. Air. National Census.

994	**261**	60c. black and lake	70	15

262 Railway Tunnel

1961. Opening of Chihuahua State Railway.

995	**262**	40c. black & grn (postage)	50	15
996	-	60c. blue and black (air)	50	20
997	-	70c. black and blue	50	20

DESIGNS—HORIZ: 60c. Railway tracks and map of railway; 70c. Railway viaduct.

263 Mosquito Globe and Instruments

1962. Malaria Eradication.

998	**263**	40c. brown and blue	50	15

264 Pres. Goulart of Brazil

1962. Visit of President of Brazil.

999	**264**	40c. bistre	1·00	30

265 Soldier
and Memorial
Stone

1962. Centenary of Battle of Puebla.

1000	265	40c. sepia and green		
		(postage)	40	15
1001	-	1p. olive and green (air)	70	20

DESIGN—HORIZ: 1p. Statue of Gen. Zaragoza.

266 Draughtsman
and Surveyor

1962. 25th Anniv of National Polytechnic Institute.

1002	266	40c. turquoise and blue		
		(postage)	1·10	20
1003	-	1p. olive and blue (air)	70	20

DESIGN—HORIZ: 1p. Scientist and laboratory assistant.

267 Plumb-line

1962. Mental Health.

1004	267	20c. blue and black	1·50	20

268 Pres. J. F. Kennedy

1962. Air. Visit of U.S. President.

1005	268	80c. blue and red	1·90	45

269 Tower and
Cogwheels

1962. "Century 21" Exn ("World's Fair"), Seattle.

1006	269	40c. black and green	40	15

270 Globe and
O.E.A. Emblem

1962. Inter-American Economic and Social Council.

1007	270	40c. sepia and grey		
		(postage)	40	15
1008	-	1p.20 sepia & violet (air)	70	30

DESIGN—HORIZ: 1p.20, Globe, Scroll and O.E.A. emblem.

271 Pres.
Alessandri of
Chile

1962. Visit of President of Chile.

1009	271	20c. brown	95	20

272 Balloon
over Mexico
City

1962. Air. 1st Mexican Balloon Flight Centenary.

1010	272	80c. black and blue	1·90	65

273 "ALALC" Emblem

1963. Air. 2nd "ALALC" Session.

1023	273	80c. purple and orange	1·30	35

274 Pres.
Betancourt of
Venezuela

1963. Visit of President of Venezuela.

1024	274	20c. blue	95	20

275 Petroleum Refinery

1963. Air. 25th Anniv of Nationalization of Mexican Petroleum Industry.

1025	275	80c. slate and orange	70	20

276 Congress
Emblem

1963. 19th International Chamber of Commerce Congress, Mexico City.

1026	276	40c. brown and black		
		(postage)	70	20
1027	-	80c. black and blue (air)	95	35

DESIGN—HORIZ: 80c. World map and "C.I.C." emblem.

277 Campaign
Emblem

1963. Freedom from Hunger.

1028	277	40c. red and blue	75	20

278 Arms and
Mountain

1963. 4th Centenary of Durango.

1029	278	20c. brown and blue	75	20

279 B.
Dominguez

1963. Birth Centenary of B. Dominguez (revolutionary).

1030	279	20c. olive and green	75	20

280 Exhibition
Stamp of 1956

1963. 77th American Philatelic Society Convention, Mexico City.

1031	280	1p. brown & bl (postage)	1·50	85
1032	-	5p. red (air)	3·00	1·90

DESIGN—HORIZ: 5p. EXMEX "stamp" and "postmark".

281 Pres. Tito

1963. Air. Visit of President of Yugoslavia.

1033	281	2p. green and violet	2·40	75

283 Part of
U.I.A. Building

1963. Air. International Architects' Day.

1034	283	80c. grey and blue	75	30

284 Red Cross
on Tree

1963. Red Cross Centenary.

1035	284	20c. red & grn (postage)	50	20
1036	-	80c. red and green (air)	1·50	35

DESIGN—HORIZ: 80c. Red Cross on dove.

285 Pres.
Estenssoro

1963. Visit of President of Bolivia.

1037	285	40c. purple and brown	75	20

286 Jose
Morelos

1963. 150th Anniv of First Anahuac Congress.

1038	286	40c. bronze and green	70	20

287 Don Quixote as
Skeleton

1963. Air. 50th Death Anniv of Jose Posada (satirical artist).

1039	287	1p.20 black	1·90	55

288 University
Arms

1963. 90th Anniv of Sinaloa University.

1040	288	40c. bistre and green	75	20

289 Diesel-electric Train

1963. 11th Pan-American Railways Congress, Mexico City.

1041	289	20c. brn & blk (postage)	1·20	55
1042	-	1p.20 blue and violet (air)	1·10	45

DESIGN: 1p.20, Steam and diesel-electric loco- motives and horse-drawn tramcar.

290 "F.S.T.S.E."
Emblem

1964. 25th Anniv of Workers' Statute.

1075	290	20c. sepia and orange	50	20

291 Mrs. Roosevelt, Flame
and U.N. Emblem

1964. Air. 15th Anniv of Declaration of Human Rights.

1076	291	80c. blue and orange	95	30

292 Pres. De Gaulle

1964. Air. Visit of President of France.

1077	292	2p. blue and brown	3·00	95

293 Pres. Kennedy and
Pres. A. Lopez Mateos

1964. Air. Ratification of Chamizal Treaty (1963).

1078	293	80c. black and blue	95	30

294 Queen Juliana and
Arms

1964. Air. Visit of Queen Juliana of the Netherlands.

1079	294	20c. bistre and blue	1·40	30

295 Academy
Emblem

1964. Centenary of National Academy of Medicine.
1080 **295** 20c. gold and black 50 20

296 Lieut. Jose Azueto and Cadet Virgillo Uribe

1964. Air. 50th Anniv of Heroic Defence of Veracruz.
1081 **296** 40c. green and brown 60 20

297 Arms and World Map

1964. Air. International Bar Assn Conf, Mexico City.
1082 **297** 40c. blue and brown 75 20

298 Colonel G. Mendez

1964. Centenary of Battle of the Jahuactal Tabasco.
1083 **298** 40c. olive and brown 60 20

299 Dr. Jose Rizal

1964. 400 Years of Mexican–Philippine Friendship. Inscr "1564 AMISTAD MEXICANO–FILIPINA 1964".
1084 **299** 20c. blue & grn (post-age) 70 20
1085 - 40c. blue and violet 75 20
1086 - 80c. blue & lt blue (air) 3·00 45
1087 - 2p.75 black and yellow 3·50 1·20
DESIGNS—As Type **299**: VERT: 40c. Legaspi. HORIZ: 80c. "San Pedro" (16th-century Spanish galleon). LARGER (44×36 mm): 2p.75, Ancient map of Pacific Ocean.

300 Zacatecas

1964. 50th Anniv of Conquest of Zacatecas.
1088 **300** 40c. green and red 70 20

301 Morelos Theatre, Aguascalientes

1965. 50th Anniv of Aguascalientes Convention.
1089 **301** 20c. purple and grey 45 20

302 Andres Manuel del Rio

1965. Andres M. del Rio Commemoration.
1090 **302** 30c. black 50 20

303 Netzahualcoyotl Dam

1965. Air. Inauguration of Netzahualcoyotl Dam.
1091 **303** 80c. slate and purple 70 20

304 J. Morelos (statue)

1965. 150th Anniv (1964) of First Constitution.
1092 **304** 40c. brown and green 50 20

305 Microwave Tower

1965. Air. Centenary of I.T.U.
1093 **305** 80c. blue and indigo 75 30
1094 - 1p.20 green and black 80 30
DESIGN: 1p.20, Radio-electric station.

306 Fir Trees

1965. Forest Conservation.
1095 **306** 20c. green and blue 40 20
The inscription "¡CUIDALOS!" means "CARE FOR THEM!".

307 I.C.Y. Emblem

1965. International Co-operation Year.
1096 **307** 40c. brown and green 40 20

308 Camp Fire and Tent

1965. Air. World Scout Conference, Mexico City.
1097 **308** 30c. ultramarine and blue 85 35

309 King Baudouin and Queen Fabiola

1965. Air. Visit of Belgian King and Queen.
1098 **309** 2p. blue and green 1·40 45

310 Mexican Antiquities and Unisphere

1965. Air. New York World's Fair.
1099 **310** 80c. green and yellow 70 20

311 Dante (after R. Sanzio)

1965. Air. Dante's 700th Birth Anniv.
1100 **311** 2p. red 1·60 85

312 Sling-thrower

1965. Olympic Games (1968) Propaganda (1st series). Museum pieces.
1101 **312** 20c. blue & olive (postage) 1·80 20
1102 - 40c. sepia and red 55 20
1103 - 80c. slate and red (air) 85 30
1104 - 1p.20 indigo and blue 1·10 35
1105 - 2p. brown and blue 75 30
MS1106 140×90 mm. Nos. 1101/4 (sold at 3p.90). Imperf. No gum 3·75 3·75
MS1107 71×90 mm. No. 1105 (sold at 3p.). Imperf. No gum 3·75 3·75
DESIGNS—As Type **312**: VERT: 40c. Batsman. HORIZ: 2p. Ball game. HORIZ (36×20 mm): 80c. Fieldsman. 1p.20, Scoreboard.

313 Jose M. Morelos y Pavon (leader of independence movement)

1965. 150th Anniv of Morelos's Execution.
1108 **313** 20c. black and blue 50 20

314 Agricultural Produce

1966. Centenary of Agrarian Reform Law.
1109 **314** 20c. red 40 15
1110 - 40c. black 50 15
DESIGN: 40c. Emilio Zapata, pioneer of agrarian reform.

315 Ruben Dario

1966. Air. 50th Death Anniv of Ruben Dario (Nicaraguan poet).
1111 **315** 1p.20 sepia 75 45

316 Father Andres de Urdaneta and Compass Rose

1966. Air. 400th Anniv of Father Andres de Urdaneta's Return from the Philippines.
1112 **316** 2p.75 black 1·60 75

317 Flag and Postal Emblem

1966. 9th Postal Union of Americas and Spain Congress (U.P.A.E.), Mexico City.
1113 **317** 20c. blk & grn (postage) 50 30
1114 - 80c. black & mauve (air) 30 30
1115 - 1p.20 black and blue 40 30
DESIGNS—VERT: 80c. Flag and posthorn. HORIZ: 1p.20, U.P.A.E. emblem and flag.

318 Friar B. de Las Casas

1966. 400th Death Anniv of Friar Bartolome de Las Casas ("Apostle of the Indies").
1116 **318** 20c. black on buff 50 30

319 E.S.I.M.E. Emblem and Diagram

1966. 50th Anniv of Higher School of Mechanical and Electrical Engineering.
1117 **319** 20c. green and grey 40 20

320 U Thant and U.N. Emblem

1966. Air. U.N. Secretary-General U Thant's Visit to Mexico.
1118 **320** 80c. black and blue 95 30

321 "1966 Friendship Year"

1966. Air. "Year of Friendship" with Central American States.
1119 **321** 80c. green and red 40 20

322 F.A.O. Emblem

1966. International Rice Year.
1120 **322** 40c. green 40 20

323 Running and Jumping

1966. Olympic Games (1968) Propaganda (2nd series).
1121 **323** 20c. black & bl (postage) 95 30
1122 - 40c. black and lake 60 30
MS1123 100×60 mm. As Nos. 1121/2. Imperf 3·00 3·00
1124 80c. black & brown (air) 60 30
1125 2p.25 black and green 95 45
1126 2p.75 black and violet 2·10 55
MS1127 125×70 mm. As Nos. 1124/6. Imperf (sold at 8p.70) 4·25 4·25
DESIGNS: 40c. Wrestling. LARGER (57×20 mm): 80c. Obstacle race; 2p.25, American football; 2p.75, Lighting Olympic flame.

324 UNESCO Emblem

1966. Air. 20th Anniv of UNESCO.
1128 **324** 80c. multicoloured 60 30

325
Constitution of
1917

1967. 50th Anniv of Mexican Constitution.
1129 **325** 40c. black (postage) 75 30
1130 - 80c. brown & ochre (air) 50 30
DESIGN: 80c. President V. Carranza.

326 Earth and
Satellite

1967. Air. World Meteorological Day.
1131 **326** 80c. blue and black 60 20

327 Oil
Refinery

1967. 7th World Petroleum Congress, Mexico City.
1132 **327** 40c. black and blue 50 20

328 Nayarit
Indian

1967. 50th Anniv of Nayarit State.
1133 **328** 20c. black and green 40 15

329 Degollado Theatre

1967. Cent of Degollado Theatre, Guadalajara.
1134 **329** 40c. brown and mauve 40 20

330 Mexican
Eagle and Crown

1967. Centenary of Triumph over the Empire.
1135 **330** 20c. black and ochre 40 20

331 School
Emblem

1967. Air. 50th Anniv of Military Medical School.
1136 **331** 80c. green and yellow 45 30

332 Capt. H.
Ruiz Gavino

1967. Air. 50th Anniv of 1st Mexican Airmail Flight,
Pachuca–Mexico City.
1137 **332** 80c. brown and black 30 15
1138 - 2p. brown and black 55 30
DESIGN—HORIZ: 2p. De Havilland D.H.6A biplane.

333 Marco
Polo

1967. Air. International Tourist Year.
1139 **333** 80c. red and black 35 20

334 Canoeing

1967. Olympic Games (1968) Propaganda (3rd series).
1140 **334** 20c. black & bl (postage) 60 30
1141 - 40c. black and red 50 30
1142 - 50c. black and green 50 30
1143 - 80c. black and violet 80 30
1144 - 2p. black and orange 1·40 35
MS1145 Two sheets each 130×90 mm.
Nos. 1140/2 (sold at 1p.50) and Nos.
1143/4 (sold at 3p.50). Imperf 15·00 9·00

1146 80c. black & mauve (air) 50 30
1147 1p.20 black and green 50 30
1148 2p. black and lemon 1·40 45
1149 5p. black and yellow 1·70 95
MS1150 Two sheets each 130×90 mm.
Nos. 1146/7 (sold at 2p.50) and Nos.
1148/9 (sold at 9p.). Imperf 13·50 7·50
DESIGNS: 40c. Basketball; 50c. Hockey; 80c. (No. 1143),
Cycling; 80c. (No. 1146), Diving; 1p.20, Running; 2p. (No.
1144), Fencing; 2p. (No. 1148), Weightlifting; 5p. Football.

335 A. del
Valle-Arizpe
(writer)

1967. Centenary of Fuente Athenaeum, Saltillo.
1151 **335** 20c. slate and brown 50 30

336 Hertz and Clark
Maxwell

1967. Air. International Telecommunications Plan
Conference, Mexico City.
1152 **336** 80c. green and black 50 30

337 P. Moreno

1967. 150th Death Anniv of Pedro Moreno
(revolutionary).
1153 **337** 40c. black and blue 50 20

338 Gabino
Berreda
(founder of
Preparatory
School)

1968. Centenary of National Preparatory and Engineering
Schools.
1154 **338** 40c. red and blue 50 20
1155 - 40c. blue and black 50 20
DESIGN: No. 1155, Staircase, Palace of Mining.

339 Exhibition
Emblem

1968. Air. "Efimex '68" International Stamp Exn, Mexico
City.
1156 **339** 80c. green and black 60 30
1157 **339** 2p. red and black 60 30
The emblem reproduces the "Hidalgo" Official stamp
design of 1884.

1968. Olympic Games (1968) Propaganda (4th series).
Designs as T 334, but inscr "1968".
1158 20c. black and olive (postage) 55 15
1159 40c. black and purple 55 15
1160 50c. black and green 55 15
1161 80c. black and mauve 65 25
1162 1p. black and brown 3·00 1·60
1163 2p. black and grey 3·75 2·20
MS1164 Two sheets each 106×70 mm.
Nos. 1158/60 (sold at 1p.50) and
Nos. 1161/3 (sold at 5p.). Imperf 13·50 7·75

1165 80c. black and blue (air) 30 20
1166 1p. black and turquoise 40 20
1167 2p. black and yellow 75 35
1168 5p. black and brown 1·50 1·40
MS1169 Two sheets each 106×70 mm.
Nos. 1165/6 (sold at 2p.50) and Nos.
1167/8 (sold at 9p.). Imperf 10·00 7·00
DESIGNS: 20c. Wrestling; 40c. Various sports; 50c. Water-
polo; 80c. (No. 1161), Gymnastics; 80c. (No. 1165), Yachting; 1p. (No. 1162), Boxing; 1p. (No. 1166), Rowing; 2p.
(No. 1163), Pistol-shooting; 2p. (No. 1167), Volleyball; 5p.
Horse-racing.

340 Dr. Martin
Luther King

1968. Air. Martin Luther King Commemorative.
1170 **340** 80c. black and grey 50 30

341 Olympic
Flame **342** Emblems of Games

1968. Olympic Games, Mexico. (i) Inaug Issue.
1171 **341** 10p. multicoloured 4·75 3·00

(ii) Games Issue. Multicoloured designs as T 341 (20, 40,
50c. postage and 80c., 1, 2p. air) or as T 342 (others).
1172 20c. Dove of Peace on map
(postage) 50 20
1173 40c. Stadium 55 20
1174 50c. Telecommunications Tower,
Mexico City 55 20
1175 2p. Palace of Sport, Mexico City 2·75 50
1176 5p. Cultural symbols of Games 6·25 1·20
MS1177 Two sheets each 110×70 mm.
Nos. 1172/4 (sold at 1p.50) and Nos.
1175/6 (sold at 9p.). Imperf 39·00 34·00

1178 80c. Dove and Olympic rings
(air) 30 20

1179 1p. "The Discus-thrower" 35 20
1180 2p. Olympic medals 95 50
1181 5p. Type **342** 3·00 1·40
1182 10p. Line-pattern based on
"Mexico 68" and rings 3·50 1·90
MS1183 Two sheets each 110×70 mm.
Nos. 1178/80 (sold at 5p.) and Nos.
1181/2 (sold at 20p.). Imperf 32·00 23·00

1968. Air. Efimex 68 International Stamp Exhibition,
Mexico City. Sheet 100×70 mm. Imperf.
MS1184 **339** 5p. ultramarine and black 3·50 2·75

343 Arms of
Vera Cruz

1969. 450th Anniv of Vera Cruz.
1185 **343** 40c. multicoloured 45 20

344 "Father Palou" (M.
Guerrero)

1969. Air. 220th Anniv of Arrival in Mexico of Father
Serra (colonizer of California).
1186 **344** 80c. multicoloured 50 15
It was intended to depict Father Serra in this design,
but the wrong detail of the painting by Guerrero, which
showed both priests, was used.

345 Football and
Spectators

1969. Air. World Cup Football Championship (1st issue).
Multicoloured.
1187 80c. Type **345** 70 30
1188 2p. Foot kicking ball 1·10 30
See also Nos. 1209/10.

346 Underground Train

1969. Inauguration of Mexico City Underground Railway
System.
1189 **346** 40c. multicoloured 45 15

347 Mahatma
Gandhi

1969. Air. Birth Centenary of Mahatma Gandhi.
1190 **347** 80c. multicoloured 40 15

348 Footprint
on Moon

1969. Air. 1st Man on the Moon.
1191 **348** 2p. black 60 30

349 Bee and
Honeycomb

1969. 50th Anniv of I.L.O.
1192 **349** 40c. brown, blue & yell 40 15

350 "Flying" Dancers and Los Nichos Pyramid, El Tajin

1969. Tourism (1st series). Multicoloured.
1193	40c. Type **350** (postage)		60	20
1193a	40c. Puerto Vallarta, Jalisco (vert)		60	20
1194	80c. Acapulco (air)		1·20	25
1195	80c. Pyramid, Teotihuacan		1·20	25
1196	80c. "El Caracol" (Maya ruin), Yucatan		1·20	25

See also Nos. 1200/2 and 1274/7.

351 Red Crosses and Sun

1969. Air. 50th Anniv of League of Red Cross Societies.
1197	**351**	80c. multicoloured	40	20

352 "General Allende" (D. Rivera)

1969. Birth Bicentenary of General Ignacio Allende ("Father of Mexican Independence").
1198	**352**	40c. multicoloured	40	20

353 Dish Aerial

1969. Air. Inauguration of Satellite Communications Station, Tulancingo.
1199	**353**	80c. multicoloured	45	20

1969. Tourism (2nd series). As T **350** but dated "1970". Multicoloured.
1200	40c. Puebla Cathedral		50	20
1201	40c. Anthropological Museum, Mexico City		50	20
1202	40c. Belaunzaran Street, Guanajuato		50	20

354 Question Marks

1970. 9th National and 5th Agricultural Census. Multicoloured.
1204	20c. Type **354**		40	15
1205	40c. Horse's head and agricultural symbols		30	15

355 Diagram of Human Eye

1970. 21st International Ophthalmological Congress, Mexico City.
1206	**355**	40c. multicoloured	40	20

356 Cadet Ceremonial Helmet and Kepi

1970. 50th Anniv of Military College Reorganization.
1207	**356**	40c. multicoloured	30	20

357 Jose Pino Suarez

1970. Birth Centenary (1969) of Jose Maria Pino Suarez (statesman).
1208	**357**	40c. multicoloured	30	20

358 Football and Masks

1970. Air. World Cup Football Championship (2nd issue). Multicoloured.
1209	80c. Type **358**		60	20
1210	2p. Football and Mexican idols		75	35

359 "STORTMEX" Emblem

1970. Air. SPORTMEX Philatelic Exhibition, Mexico City. Miniature sheet 60×50 mm.
MS1211	**359**	2p. carmine and grey	5·75	4·25

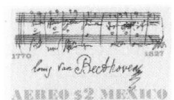

360 Composition by Beethoven

1970. Air. Birth Bicentenary of Beethoven.
1212	**360**	2p. multicoloured	60	30

361 Arms of Celaya

1970. 400th Anniv of Celaya.
1213	**361**	40c. multicoloured	35	20

362 "General Assembly"

1970. Air. 25th Anniv of U.N.O.
1214	**362**	80c. multicoloured	40	20

363 "Eclipse de Sol"

1970. Total Eclipse of the Sun.
1215	**363**	40c. black	30	20

364 "Galileo" (Susterman)

1971. Air. Conquest of Space. Early Astronomers. Multicoloured.
1216	2p. Type **364**		60	30
1217	2p. "Kepler" (unknown artist)		60	30
1218	2p. "Sir Isaac Newton" (Kneller)		60	30

365 "Sister Juana" (M. Cabrera)

1971. Air. Mexican Arts and Sciences (1st series). Paintings. Multicoloured.
1219	80c. Type **365**		40	20
1220	80c. "El Paricutin" (volcano) (G. Murillo)		40	20
1221	80c. "Men of Flames" (J. C. Orozco)		40	20
1222	80c. "Self-portrait" (J. M. Velasco)		40	20
1223	80c. "Mayan Warriors" ("Dresden Codex")		40	20

See also Nos. 1243/7, 1284/8, 1323/7, 1351/5, 1390/4, 1417/21, 1523/7, 1540/4, 1650/4, 1688/92, 1834 and 1845.

366 Stamps from Venezuela, Mexico and Colombia

1971. Air. "Philately for Peace". Latin-American Stamp Exhibitions.
1224	**366**	80c. multicoloured	45	20

367 Lottery Balls

1971. Bicentenary of National Lottery.
1225	**367**	40c. black and green	40	30

368 "Francisco Clavijero" (P. Carlin)

1971. Air. Return of the Remains of Francisco Javier Clavijero (historian) to Mexico (1970).
1226	**368**	2p. brown and green	60	30

369 Vasco de Quiroga and "Utopia" (O'Gorman)

1971. 500th Birth Anniv of Vasco de Quiroga, Archbishop of Michoacan.
1227	**369**	40c. multicoloured	30	20

370 "Amado Nervo" (artist unknown)

1971. Birth Centenary of Amado Nervo (writer).
1228	**370**	80c. multicoloured	30	20

371 I.T.U. Emblem

1971. Air. World Telecommunications Day.
1229	**371**	80c. multicoloured	30	15

372 "Mariano Matamoros" (D. Rivera)

1971. Air. Birth Bicentenary of Mariano Matamoros (patriot).
1230	**372**	2p. multicoloured	60	20

373 "General Guerrero" (O'Gorman)

1971. Air. 150th Anniv of Independence from Spain.
1231	**373**	2p. multicoloured	50	20

374 Loudspeaker and Sound Waves

1971. 50th Anniv of Radio Broadcasting in Mexico.
1232	**374**	40c. black, blue and green	40	20

375 Pres. Cardenas and Banners

1971. 1st Death Anniv of General Lazaro Cardenas.
1233	**375**	40c. black and lilac	40	20

376 Stamps of Venezuela, Mexico, Colombia and Peru

1971. Air. "EXFILIMA 71" Stamp Exhibition Lima, Peru.
1234	**376**	80c. multicoloured	60	20

377 Abstract of Circles

1971. Air. 25th Anniv of UNESCO.
1235	**377**	80c. multicoloured	40	20

378 Piano Keyboard

1971. 1st Death Anniv of Agustin Lara (composer).
1236	**378**	40c. black, blue & yellow	40	15

379 "Mental Patients"

1971. Air. 5th World Psychiatric Congress, Mexico City.
1237 **379** 2p. multicoloured 60 20

380 City Arms of Monterrey

1971. 375th Anniv of Monterrey.
1238 **380** 40c. multicoloured 40 15

381 Durer's Bookplate

1971. Air. 500th Anniv of Albrecht Durer (artist).
1239 **381** 2p. black and brown 85 30

382 Scientific Symbols

1972. Air. 1st Anniv of National Council of Science and Technology.
1240 **382** 2p. multicoloured 50 15

383 Emblem of Mexican Cardiological Institute

1972. World Health Month. Multicoloured.
1241 40c. Type **383** (postage) 35 20
1242 80c. Heart specialists (air) 35 20

1972. Air. Mexican Arts and Sciences (2nd series). Portraits. As T 365.
1243 80c. brown and black 1·50 30
1244 80c. green and black 1·50 30
1245 80c. brown and black 1·50 30
1246 80c. blue and black 1·50 30
1247 80c. red and black 1·50 30
PORTRAITS: Nos. 1243, King Netzahualcoyotl of Texcoco (patron of the arts); No. 1244, J. R. de Alarcon (lawyer); No. 1245, J. J. Fernandez de Lizardi (writer); No. 1246, E. G. Martinez (poet); No. 1247, R. L. Velardo (author).

384 Rotary Emblems

1972. Air. 50th Anniv of Rotary Movement in Mexico.
1248 **384** 80c. multicoloured 30 20

385 Indian Laurel and Fruit

1972. Centenary of Chilpancingo as Capital of Guerrero State.
1249 **385** 40c. black, gold and green 30 20

386 Track of Car Tyre

1972. Air. 74th Assembly of International Tourist Alliance, Mexico City.
1250 **386** 80c. black and grey 30 20

387 First issue of "Gaceta De Mexico"

1972. 250th Anniv of Publication of "Gaceta De Mexico" (1st newspaper to be published in Latin America).
1251 **387** 40c. multicoloured 30 20

388 Emblem of Lions Organization

1972. Lions' Clubs Convention, Mexico City.
1252 **388** 40c. multicoloured 30 20

389 "Zaragoza" (cadet sail corvette)

1972. 75th Anniv of Naval Academy, Veracruz.
1253 **389** 40c. multicoloured 30 20

390 "Margarita Maza de Juarez" (artist unknown)

1972. Death Centenary of Pres. Benito Juarez.
1254 **390** 20c. mult (postage) 50 15
1255 - 40c. multicoloured 50 15
1256 - 80c. black and blue (air) 30 15
1257 - 1p.20 multicoloured 30 15
1258 - 2p. multicoloured 40 15
DESIGNS: 40c. "Benito Juarez" (D. Rivera); 80c. Page of Civil Register with Juarez signature; 1p.20, "Benito Juarez" (P. Clave); 2p. "Benito Juarez" (J. C. Orozco).

391 "Emperor Justinian I" (mosaic)

1972. 50th Anniv of Mexican Bar Association.
1259 **391** 40c. multicoloured 85 20

392 Atomic Emblem

1972. Air. 16th General Conference of Int Atomic Energy Organization, Mexico City.
1260 **392** 2p. black, blue and grey 50 15

393 Caravel on "Stamp"

1972. Stamp Day of the Americas.
1261 **393** 80c. violet and brown 45 15

394 "Sobre las Olas" (sheet-music cover by O'Brandstetter)

1972. Air. 28th International Authors' and Composers' Society Congress, Mexico City.
1262 **394** 80c. brown 40 15

395 "Mother and Child" (G. Galvin)

1972. Air. 25th Anniv of UNICEF.
1263 **395** 80c. multicoloured 95 15

396 "Father Pedro de Gante" (Rodriguez y Arangorti)

1972. Air. 400th Death Anniv of Father Pedro de Gante (founder of first school in Mexico).
1264 **396** 2p. multicoloured 50 20

397 Olympic Emblems

1972. Olympic Games, Munich.
1265 **397** 40c. multicoloured (postage) 60 20
1266 - 80c. multicoloured (air) 40 20
1267 - 2p. black, green and blue 70 20
DESIGNS—HORIZ: 80c. "Football". VERT: 2p. Similar to Type **397**.

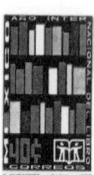

398 Books on Shelves

1972. International Book Year.
1268 **398** 40c. multicoloured 30 20

399 Common Snook ("Pure Water")

1972. Anti-pollution Campaign.
1269 **399** 40c. black & bl (postage) 50 15
1270 - 80c. black and blue (air) 30 15
DESIGN—VERT: 80c. Pigeon on cornice ("Pure Air").

400 "Footprints on the Americas"

1972. Air. Tourist Year of the Americas.
1271 **400** 80c. multicoloured 35 15

401 Stamps of Mexico, Colombia, Venezuela, Peru and Brazil

1973. Air. "EXFILBRA 72" Stamp Exhibition, Rio de Janeiro, Brazil.
1272 **401** 80c. multicoloured 35 15

402 "Metlac Viaduct" (J. M. Velasco)

1973. Centenary of Mexican Railways.
1273 **402** 40c. multicoloured 1·30 20

403 Ocotlan Abbey

1973. Tourism (3rd series). Multicoloured.
1274 40c. Type **403** (postage) 45 20
1275 40c. Indian hunting dance, Sonora (vert) 45 20
1276 80c. Girl in local costume (vert) (air) 50 20
1277 80c. Sport fishing, Lower California 50 20

404 "God of the Winds"

1973. Air. Centenary of W.M.O.
1278 **404** 80c. black, blue & mauve 75 30

405 Copernicus

1973. Air. 500th Birth Anniv of Copernicus (astronomer).
1279 **405** 80c. green 40 15

406 Cadet

1973. 150th Anniv of Military College.
1280 **406** 40c. multicoloured 45 20

407 "Francisco Madero" (D. Rivera)

1973. Birth Centenary of Pres. Francisco Madero.
1281 **407** 40c. multicoloured 30 20

408 Antonio Narro (founder)

1973. 50th Anniv of "Antonio Narro" Agricultural School, Saltillo.
1282 **408** 40c. grey 40 20

409 San Martin Statue

1973. Air. Argentina's Gift of San Martin Statue to Mexico City.
1283 **409** 80c. multicoloured 30 20

1973. Air. "Mexican Arts and Sciences" (3rd series). Astronomers. As T 365 but dated "1973".
1284 80c. green and red 40 15
1285 80c. multicoloured 40 15
1286 80c. multicoloured 40 15
1287 80c. multicoloured 40 15
1288 80c. multicoloured 40 15
DESIGNS: No. 1284, Aztec "Sun" stone; No. 1285, Carlos de Siguenza y Gongora; No. 1286, Francisco Diaz Covarrubias; No. 1287, Joaquin Gallo; No. 1288, Luis Enrique Erro.

410 Caryon Molecules

1973. 25th Anniv of Chemical Engineering School.
1289 **410** 40c. black, yellow and red 30 20

411 Fist with Pointing Finger

1974. Promotion of Exports.
1294 **411** 40c. black and green 30 15

412 "EXMEX 73" Emblem

1974. "EXMEX 73" National Stamp Exhibition, Cuernavaca.
1295 **412** 40c. black (postage) 30 15
1296 - 80c. multicoloured (air) 30 15
DESIGN: 80c. Cortes' Palace, Cuernavaca.

413 Manuel Ponce

1974. 25th Death Anniv (1973) of Manuel M. Ponce (composer).
1297 **413** 40c. multicoloured 30 15

414 Gold Brooch, Mochica Culture

1974. Air. Exhibition of Peruvian Gold Treasures, Mexico City.
1298 **414** 80c. multicoloured 30 20

415 C.E.P.A.L. Emblem and Flags

1974. Air. 25th Anniv of U.N. Economic Commission for Latin America (C.E.P.A.L.).
1299 **415** 80c. multicoloured 30 15

416 Baggage

1974. Air. 16th Confederation of Latin American Tourist Organizations (C.O.T.A.L.) Convention, Acapulco.
1300 **416** 80c. multicoloured 30 15

417 Silver Statuette

1974. 1st International Silver Fair, Mexico City.
1301 **417** 40c. multicoloured 30 15

418 "The Enamelled Saucepan" (Picasso)

1974. Air. 1st Death Anniv of Pablo Picasso (artist).
1302 **418** 80c. multicoloured 40 10

419 "Dancing Dogs" (Indian statuette)

1974. 6th Season of Dog Shows.
1303 **419** 40c. multicoloured 30 15

420 Mariano Azuela

1974. Birth Cent (1973) of Mariano Azuela (writer).
1304 **420** 40c. multicoloured 30 15

421 Tepotzotlan Viaduct

1974. National Engineers' Day.
1305 **421** 40c. black and blue 70 20

422 R. Robles (surgeon)

1974. 25th Anniv of W.H.O.
1306 **422** 40c. brown and green 30 15

423 U.P.U. Emblem

1974. "Exfilmex 74" Inter-American Stamp Exhibition, Mexico City.
1307 **423** 40c. black and green on yellow (postage) 30 15
1308 **423** 80c. black and brown on yellow (air) 30 15

424 Demosthenes

1974. 2nd Spanish-American Reading and Writing Studies Congress, Mexico City.
1309 **424** 20c. green and brown 40 15

425 Lincoln Standard Biplane

1974. Air. 50th Anniv of "Mexicana" (Mexican Airlines). Multicoloured.
1310 80c. Type **425** 30 15
1311 2p. Boeing 727-200 jetliner 30 15

426 Map and Indian Head

1974. 150th Anniv of Union with Chiapas.
1312 **426** 20c. green and brown 30 15

427 "Sonar Waves"

1974. Air. 1st International Electrical and Electronic Communications Congress, Mexico City.
1313 **427** 2p. multicoloured 30 10

428 S. Lerdo de Tejada

1974. Centenary of Restoration of Senate.
1314 **428** 40c. black and blue 30 15

429 Manuscript of Constitution

1974. 150th Anniv of Federal Republic.
1315 **429** 40c. black and green 30 15

430 Ball in Play

1974. Air. 8th World Volleyball Championships, Mexico City.
1316 **430** 2p. black, brown & orge 30 10

431 (image scaled to 47% of original size)

1974. Air. Exfilmex 74 Stamp Exhibition, Mexico City. Sheet 105×70 mm. Imperf.
MS1317 **431** 10p. multicoloured 4·00 1·90

432 F. C. Puerto

1974. Air. Birth Centenary of Felipe Carrillo Puerto (politician and journalist).
1318 **432** 80c. brown and green 30 30

433 Mask, Bat and Catcher's Glove

1974. Air. 50th Anniv of Mexican Baseball League.
1319 **433** 80c. brown and green 30 30

434 U.P.U. Monument

1974. Centenary of U.P.U.

1320	**434**	40c. brown and blue (postage)	30	15
1321	-	80c. multicoloured (air)	30	15
1322	-	2p. brown and green	30	15

DESIGNS: 80c. Man's face as letter-box, Colonial period; 2p. Heinrich von Stephan, founder of U.P.U.

1974. Air. Mexican Arts and Sciences (4th series). Music and Musicians. As T 365 but dated "1974". Multicoloured.

1323	80c. "Musicians" – Mayan painting, Bonampak	30	15
1324	80c. First Mexican-printed score, 1556	30	15
1325	80c. Angela Peralta (soprano and composer)	30	15
1326	80c. "Miguel Lerdo de Tejada" (composer)	30	15
1327	80c. "Silvestre Revueltas" (composer) (bronze by Carlos Bracho)	30	15

435 I.W.Y. Emblem

1975. Air. International Women's Year.

1328	**435**	1p.60 black and red	30	15

436 Economic Charter

1975. Air. U.N. Declaration of Nations' Economic Rights and Duties.

1329	**436**	1p.60 multicoloured	30	20

437 Jose Maria Mora

1975. 150th Anniv of Federal Republic.

1330	**437**	20c. multicoloured	30	20

438 Trans-Atlantic Balsa Raft "Acali"

1975. Air. Trans-Atlantic Voyage of "Acali", Canary Islands to Yucatan (1973).

1331	**438**	80c. multicoloured	30	20

439 Dr. M. Jimenez

1975. Air. 5th World Gastroenterological Congress.

1332	**439**	2p. multicoloured	50	15

440 Aztec Merchants with Goods ("Codex Florentino")

1975. Centenary (1974) of Mexican Chamber of Commerce.

1333	**440**	80c. multicoloured	30	20

441 Miguel de Cervantes Saavedra (Spanish author)

1975. Air. 3rd International Cervantes Festival, Guanajuato.

1334	**441**	1p.60 red and black	30	15

442 4-reales Coin of 1675

1975. Air. International Numismatics Convention "Mexico 74".

1335	**442**	1p.60 bronze and blue	40	20

443 Salvador Novo

1975. Air. 1st Death Anniv of Salvador Novo (poet and writer).

1336	**443**	1p.60 multicoloured	30	20

444 "Self-portrait" (Siqueiros)

1975. Air. 1st Death Anniv of David Alfaro Siqueiros (painter).

1337	**444**	1p.60 multicoloured	30	20

445 General Juan Aldama (detail from mural by Diego Rivera)

1975. Birth Bicentenary (1974) of General Aldama.

1338	**445**	80c. multicoloured	30	20

466 Perforation Gauge

1975. Air. International Women's Year and World Conference.

1339	**446**	1p.60 blue and pink	30	15

447 Eagle and Snake ("Codex Duran")

1975. 650th Anniv of Tenochtitlan (now Mexico City). Multicoloured.

1340	80c. Type **447** (postage)	30	20
1341	1p.60 Arms of Mexico City (air)	30	20

448 Domingo F. Sarmiento (educator and statesman)

1975. Air. 1st International Congress of "Third World" Educators, Acapulco.

1342	**448**	1p.60 green and brown	30	15

449 Teachers' Monument, Mexico City

1975. Air. Mexican–Lebanese Friendship.

1343	**449**	4p.30 green and brown	40	15

450 Games' Emblem

1975. Air. 7th Pan-American Games, Mexico City.

1344	**450**	1p.60 multicoloured	30	15

451 Julian Carrillo (composer)

1975. Birth Centenary of J. Carrillo.

1345	**451**	80c. brown and green	30	20

452 Academy Emblem

1975. Cent of Mexican Languages Academy.

1346	**452**	80c. yellow and brown	30	20

453 University Building

1975. 50th Anniv of Guadalajara University.

1347	**453**	80c. black, brown & pink	30	20

454 Dr. Atl

1975. Air. Atl (Gerardo Murillo, painter and writer). Birth Centenary.

1348	**454**	4p.30 multicoloured	40	20

455 Road Builders

1975. "50 Years of Road Construction" and 15th World Road Congress, Mexico City.

1349	**455**	80c. black & grn (postage)	30	20
1350	-	1p.60 black & blue (air)	30	15

DESIGN: 1p.60, Congress emblem.

1975. Air. Mexican Arts and Sciences (5th series). As T 365, but dated "1975". Multicoloured.

1351	1p.60 Title page, F. Hernandez' "History of New Spain"	30	15
1352	1p.60 A. L. Herrera (naturalist)	30	15
1353	1p.60 Page from "Badiano Codex" (Aztec herbal)	30	15
1354	1p.60 A. Rosenblueth Stearns (neurophysiologist)	30	15
1355	1p.60 A. A. Duges (botanist and zoologist)	30	15

456 Car Engine Parts

1975. Mexican Exports. Multicoloured.

1356	-	5c. blue (postage)	50	15
1471	-	20c. black	50	20
1356b	-	40c. brown	1·00	25
1356c	**456**	50c. blue	1·10	20
1472	**456**	50c. black	30	15
1473	-	80c. red	1·20	25
1474	-	1p. violet and yellow	40	20
1358	-	1p. black and orange	85	45
1475	-	2p. blue and turquoise	55	20
1476	-	3p. brown	75	20
1359ba	-	4p. red and brown	60	30
1359ca	-	5p. brown	65	25
1359d	-	6p. red	50	25
1359e	-	6p. grey	35	25
1359f	-	7p. blue	35	25
1359g	-	8p. brown	30	20
1359h	-	9p. blue	55	30
1360a	-	10p. lt green & green	85	35
1360ac	-	10p. red	30	25
1360ad	-	15p. orange and brown	65	25
1480	-	20p. black	4·25	1·00
1360bc	-	20p. black and red	8·25	1·50
1360be	-	25p. chestnut	6·50	1·50
1360bh	-	35p. chestnut	2·75	90
1360bk	-	40p. yellow and chestnut	80	35
1360bl	-	40p. gold and green	60	25
1360bm	-	40p. black	30	20
1360c	-	50p. multicoloured	6·50	1·50
1360d	-	50p. yellow and blue	3·00	50
1360da	-	50p. red and green	85	25
1360db	-	60p. brown	70	25
1360dc	-	70p. brown	2·10	70
1360de	-	80p. gold and mauve	2·10	55
1360df	-	80p. blue	60	20
1360dg	-	90p. blue and green	60	20
1360e	-	100p. red, green and grey	2·10	80
1360ea	-	100p. brown	85	35
1360f	-	200p. yellow, green and grey	4·50	45
1360fb	-	200p. yellow and green	60	25
1360g	-	300p. blue, red and grey	4·50	2·30
1360gb	-	300p. blue and red	1·00	25
1360h	-	400p. bistre, chestnut and grey	1·20	80
1360ha	-	450p. brown and mauve	60	25
1360i	-	500p. green, orange and grey	90	60
1360ia	-	500p. grey and blue	50	30
1360j	-	600p. multicoloured	4·25	45

1360k	-	700p. black, red and green	8·25	45
1360ka	-	750p. black, red and green	2·30	45
1360l	-	800p. brown & dp brown	4·25	55
1360m	456	900p. black	3·00	45
1360n	-	950p. blue	2·30	45
1481a	-	1000p. black, red and grey	3·50	60
1360p	-	1000p. red and black	2·10	80
1360q	-	1100p. grey	1·60	70
1360r	-	1300p. red, green and grey	2·30	45
1360rb	-	1300p. red and green	2·30	45
1360rc	-	1400p. black	3·00	45
1360s	-	1500p. brown	3·00	55
1360t	-	1600p. orange	2·30	45
1360u	-	1700p. green and deep green	3·00	55
1360w	-	1900p. blue and green	3·00	90
1481b	-	2000p. black and grey	4·00	85
1360x	-	2000p. black	4·25	1·10
1360y	-	2100p. black, orange and grey	3·50	90
1360yb	-	2200p. red	2·50	70
1360z	-	2500p. blue and grey	3·50	1·00
1360zb	-	2800p. black	3·50	70
1481c	-	3000p. green, grey and orange	3·75	1·40
1360zc	456	3600p. black and grey	3·75	90
1360zd	-	3900p. grey and blue	4·75	1·20
1481d	-	4000p. yellow, grey and red	4·00	1·60
1360zf	-	4800p. red, green and grey	5·75	1·20
1481e	-	5000p. grey, green and orange	5·25	2·00
1360zh	-	6000p. green, yellow and grey	7·75	1·30
1360zi	-	7200p. multicoloured	8·75	1·60
1361	-	30c. bronze (air)	20	15
1482	-	50c. green and brown	25	20
1361a	-	80c. blue	30	15
1361b	-	1p.60 black and orange	40	20
1361c	-	1p.90 red and green	40	20
1361d	-	2p. gold and blue	90	25
1485	-	2p.50 red and green	45	25
1486	-	4p. yellow and brown	50	25
1361f	-	4p.30 mauve and green	50	25
1361g	-	5p. blue and yellow	1·80	30
1361h	-	5p.20 black and red	1·00	30
1361i	-	5p.60 green and yellow	50	30
1488	-	10p. green and light green	95	65
1361j	-	20p. black, red and green	1·60	45
1361k	-	50p. multicoloured	3·75	1·60

DESIGNS—POSTAGE. 5c., 6, 1600p. Steel tubes; 20c., 40 (1360bm), 1400, 2800p. Laboratory flasks; 40c., 100p. (1360ea) Cup of coffee; 80c., 10 (1360ac), 2200p. Steer marked with beef cuts; 1, 3000p. Electric cable; 2, 90, 1900p. Abalone shell; 3, 60p. Men's shoes; 4p. Ceramic tiles; 5, 1100p. Chemical formulae; 7, 8, 9, 80 (1360df), 2500p. Textiles; 10 (1360a), 1700p. Tequila; 15p. Honeycomb; 20 (1480), 2000p. Wrought iron; 20 (1360bc), 2100p. Bicycles; 25, 70, 1500p. Hammered copper vase; 35, 40 (1360bl), 50 (1360d), 80p. (1360de) Books; 50 (1360c), 600p. Jewellery; 50 (1360da), 4800p. Tomato; 100 (1360e), 1300p. Strawberries; 200, 6000p. Citrus fruit; 300p. Motor vehicles; 400, 450p. Printed circuit; 500 (1360i), 5000p. Cotton boll; 500 (1360ib), 3900p. Valves (petroleum) industry; 700, 750, 7200p. Film; 800p. Construction materials; 1000p. Farm machinery; 4000p. Bee and honeycomb. AIR. 30c. Hammered copper vase; 50c. Electronic components; 80c. Textiles; 1p.60, Bicycles; 1p.90, Valves (petroleum) industry; 2p. Books; 2p.50, Tomato; 4p. Bee and honeycomb; 4p.30, Strawberry; 5p. Motor vehicles; 5p.20, Farm machinery; 5p.60, Cotton boll; 10p. Citrus fruit; 20p. Film; 50p. Cotton.

457 Aguascalientes Cathedral

1975. 400th Anniv of Aguascalientes.
1362　457　50c. black and green　1·00　15

458 J. T. Bodet

1975. 1st Death Anniv of Jaime T. Bodet (author and late Director-General of UNESCO).
1363　458　80c. brown and blue　30　20

459 "Fresco" (J. C. Orozco)

1975. 150th Anniv of Mexican Supreme Court of Justice.
1364　459　80c. multicoloured　30　20

460 "Death of Cuautemoc" (Chavez Morado)

1975. 450th Death Anniv of Emperor Cuautemoc.
1365　460　80c. multicoloured　30　20

461 Allegory of Irrigation

1976. 50th Anniv of Nat Irrigation Commission.
1366　461　80c. deep blue and blue　30　20

462 City Gateway

1976. 400th Anniv of Leon de los Aldamas, Guanajuato.
1367　462　80c. yellow and purple　30　20

463 Early Telephone

1976. Air. Telephone Centenary.
1368　463　1p.60 black and grey　30　15

464 Gold Coin

1976. Air. 4th Int Numismatics Convention.
1369　464　1p.60 gold, brown & blk　30　15

465 Tlaloc (Aztec god of rain) and Calles Dam

1976. Air. 12th Int Great Dams Congress.
1370　465　1p.60 purple and green　30　15

466 Perforation Gauge

1976. Air. "Interphil '76" International Stamp Exhibition, Philadelphia.
1371　466　1p.60 black, red and blue　30　15

467 Rainbow over Industrial Skyline

1976. Air. U.N. Conf on Human Settlements.
1372　467　1p.60 multicoloured　30　15

470 Liberty Bell

1976. Air. Bicentenary of American War of Independence.
1378　470　1p.60 blue and mauve　30　20

471 Forest Fire

1976. Fire Prevention Campaign.
1379　471　80c. multicoloured　30　20

472 Peace Texts

1976. Air. 30th International Asian and North American Science and Humanities Congress, Mexico City.
1380　472　1p.60 multicoloured　30　15

473 Children on TV Screen

1976. Air. 1st Latin-American Forum on Children's Television.
1381　473　1p.60 multicoloured　30　15

474 Scout's Hat

1976. 50th Anniv of Mexican Boy Scout Movement.
1382　474　80c. olive and brown　30　20

475 Exhibition Emblem

1976. "Mexico Today and Tomorrow" Exhibition.
1383　475　80c. black, red & turq　30　20

476 New Buildings

1976. Inaug of New Military College Buildings.
1384　476　50c. brown and ochre　30　20

477 Dr. R. Vertiz

1976. Centenary of Ophthalmological Hospital of Our Lady of the Light.
1385　477　80c. brown and black　30　20

478 Guadalupe Basilica

1976. Inauguration of Guadalupe Basilica.
1386　478　50c. bistre and black　30　20

479 "40" and Emblem

1976. 40th Anniv of National Polytechnic Institute.
1387　479　80c. black, red and green　30　20

480 Blast Furnace

1976. Inauguration of Lazaro Cardenas Steel Mill, Las Truchas.
1388　480　50c. multicoloured　30　20

481 Natural Elements

1976. Air. World Urbanization Day.
1389　481　1p.60 multicoloured　30　20

1976. Air. Mexican Arts and Sciences (6th series). As T 365 but dated "1976". Multicoloured.
1390　1p.60 black and red　30　15
1391　1p.60 multicoloured　30　15
1392　1p.60 black and yellow　30　15
1393　1p.60 multicoloured　30　15
1394　1p.60 brown and black　30　15
DESIGNS: No. 1390, "The Signal" (Angela Gurria); No. 1391, "The God of Today" (L. Ortiz Monasterio); No. 1392, "The God Coatlicue" (traditional Mexican sculpture); No. 1393, "Tiahuicole" (Manuel Vilar); No. 1394, "The Horseman" (Manuel Tolsa).

482 Score of "El Pesebre"

1977. Air. Birth Centenary of Pablo Casals (cellist).
1395　482　4p.30 blue and brown　50　20

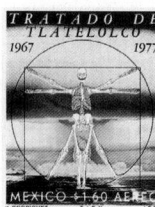

483 "Man's Destruction"

1977. Air. 10th Anniv of Treaty of Tlatelolco.
1396　483　1p.60 multicoloured　30　20

484 Saltillo Cathedral

1977. 400th Anniv of Founding of Saltillo.
1397　484　80c. brown and yellow　30　20

485 Light
Switch, Pylon
and Engineers

1977. 40 Years of Development in Mexico. Federal
Electricity Commission.

1398	**485**	80c. multicoloured	30	20

486 Footballers

1977. Air. 50th Anniv of Mexican Football Federation.

1399	**486**	1p.60 multicoloured	30	15
1400	-	4p.30 yellow, blue & blk	50	15

DESIGN: 4p.30, Football emblem.

487 Hands and Scales

1977. Air. 50th Anniv of Federal Council of Reconciliation
and Arbitration.

1401	**487**	1p.60 orange, brn & blk	30	20

488 Flags of Spain and
Mexico

1977. Resumption of Diplomatic Relations with Spain.

1402	**488**	50c. multicoloured (postage)	30	20
1403	**488**	80c. multicoloured	30	20
1404	-	1p.60 black and grey (air)	30	20
1405	-	1p.90 red, green & lt grn	30	20
1406	-	4p.30 grey, brown & grn	45	20

DESIGNS: 1p.60, Arms of Mexico and Spain; 1p.90, Maps
of Mexico and Spain; 4p.30, President Jose Lopez Portillo
and King Juan Carlos.

489 Tlaloc
(weather god)

1977. Air. Centenary of Central Meterological
Observatory.

1407	**489**	1p.60 multicoloured	30	20

490 Ludwig
van Beethoven

1977. Air. 150th Death Anniv of Beethoven.

1408	**490**	1p.60 green and brown	30	20
1409	**490**	4p.30 red and blue	40	20

491 A. Serdan

1977. Birth Centenary of Aquiles Serdan (revolutionary
martyr).

1410	**491**	80c. black, turq & grn	30	20

492 Mexico City–Guernavaca
Highway

1977. Air. 25th Anniv of First National Highway.

1411	**492**	1p.60 multicoloured	30	20

493 Poinsettia

1977. Christmas.

1412	**493**	50c. multicoloured	30	20

494 Arms of
Campeche

1977. Air. Bicentenary of Naming of Campeche.

1413	**494**	1p.60 multicoloured	30	20

495 Tractor and Dam

1977. Air. U.N. Desertification Conference, Mexico City.

1414	**495**	1p.60 multicoloured	30	20

496 Congress Emblem

1977. Air. 20th World Education, Hygiene and Recreation
Congress.

1415	**496**	1p.60 multicoloured	30	20

497 Freighter "Rio Yaqui"

1977. Air. 60th Anniv of National Merchant Marine.

1416	**497**	1p.60 multicoloured	30	20

498 Mayan
Dancer

1977. Air. Mexican Arts and Sciences (7th series). Pre-
colonial statuettes.

1417	**498**	1p.60 red, black and pink	30	20
1418	-	1p.60 blue, black and light blue	30	20
1419	-	1p.60 grey, black and yellow	30	20
1420	-	1p.60 green, black and turquoise	30	20
1421	-	1p.60 red, black and grey	30	20

DESIGNS: No. 1418, Aztec god of dance; No. 1419, Snake
dance; No. 1420, Dancer, Monte Alban; No. 1421, Dancer,
Totonaca.

499 Hospital Scene

1978. Air. 35th Anniv of Mexican Social Insurance
Institute. Multicoloured.

1422	**499**	1p.60 Type **499**	30	20
1423	**499**	4p.30 Workers drawing benefits	45	20

500 Moorish Fountain

1978. Air. 450th Anniv of Chiapa de Corzo, Chiapas.

1424	**500**	1p.60 multicoloured	30	20

501 Telephones,
1878 and 1978

1978. Centenary of Mexican Telephone.

1425	**501**	80c. red and salmon	30	20

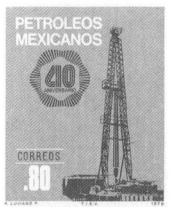

502 Oilwell

1978. 40th Anniv of Nationalization of Oil Resources.

1426	**502**	80c. red and salmon (postage)	30	20
1427	-	1p.60 blue and red (air)	30	20
1428	-	4p.30 black, light blue and blue	40	20

DESIGNS: 1p.60, General I. Cardenas (President, 1938);
4p.30, Oil rig, Gulf of Mexico.

503 Arms of San Cristobal
de las Casas

1978. Air. 450th Anniv of San Cristobal de las Casas,
Chiapas.

1429	**503**	1p.60 purple, pink and black	30	20

504 Fairchild FC-71 Mail
Plane

1978. Air. 50th Anniv of First Mexican Airmail Route.

1430	**504**	1p.60 multicoloured	30	20
1431	**504**	4p.30 multicoloured	40	20

505 Globe and Cogwheel

1978. Air. World Conference on Technical Co- operation
between Underdeveloped Countries. Multicoloured.

1432	**505**	1p.60 Type **505**	30	20
1433	**505**	4p.30 Globe and cogwheel joined by flags	40	20

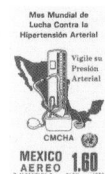

506 Blood
Pressure Gauge
and Map of
Mexico

1978. Air. World Hypertension Month and World Health
Day.

1434	**506**	1p.60 blue and red	30	20
1435	-	4p.30 salmon and blue	40	20

DESIGN: 4p.30, Hand with stethoscope.

507 Kicking Ball

1978. Air. World Cup Football Championship, Argentina.

1436	**507**	1p.60 bl, lt orge & orge	30	20
1437	-	1p.90 blue, brn & orge	30	20
1438	-	4p.30 blue, grn & orge	40	20

DESIGNS: 1p.90, Saving a goal; 4p.30, Footballer.

508 Francisco (Pancho)
Villa

1978. Air. Birth Centenary of Francisco Villa (revolutionary
leader).

1439	**508**	1p.60 multicoloured	30	20

509 Emilio Carranza Stamp
of 1929

1978. Air. 50th Anniv of Mexico–Washington Flight by
Emilio Carranza.

1440	**509**	1p.60 red and brown	30	20

510 Woman
and Calendar
Stone

1978. Air. Miss Universe Contest, Acapulco.

1441	**510**	1p.60 black, brn & red	30	20
1442	**510**	1p.90 black, brn & grn	30	20
1443	**510**	4p.30 black, brn & red	40	20

511 Alvaro Obregon (J.
Romero)

1978. Air. 50th Death Anniv of Alvaro Obregon
(statesman).

1444	**511**	1p.60 multicoloured	30	20

Mexico   **599**

512 Institute Emblem

1978. 50th Anniv of Pan-American Institute for Geography and History.

1445	512	80c. blue and black (postage)	30	20
1446	-	1p.60 green and black (air)	30	20
1447	-	4p.30 brown and black	40	20

DESIGNS: 1p.60, 4p.30, Designs as Type **512**, showing emblem.

513 Sun rising over Ciudad Obregon

1978. Air. 50th Anniv of Ciudad Obregon.

1448	513	1p.60 multicoloured	30	20

514 Mayan Statue, Rook and Pawn

1978. Air. World Youth Team Chess Championship, Mexico City.

1449	514	1p.60 multicoloured	30	20
1450	514	4p.30 multicoloured	40	20

515 Aristotle

1978. Air. 2300th Death Anniv of Aristotle.

1451	515	1p.60 grey, blue and yellow	30	20
1452	-	4p.30 grey, red and yellow	40	20

DESIGN: 4p.30, Statue of Aristotle.

516 Mule Deer

1978. Air. World Youth Team Chess Championship, Mexico City.

1453		1p.60 Type **516**	90	20
1454		1p.60 Ocelot	90	20

See also Nos. 1548/9, 1591/2, 1638/9 and 1683/4.

517 Man's Head and Dove

1978. Air. International Anti-Apartheid Year.

1455	517	1p.60 green, red and black	30	20
1456	-	4p.30 grey, lilac and black	40	20

DESIGN: 4p.30, Woman's head and dove.

518 "Dahlia coccinea". ("Dalia" on stamp)

1978. Mexican Flowers (1st series). Multicoloured.

1457		50c. Type **518**	30	20
1458		80c. "Plumeria rubra"	45	20

See also Nos. 1550/1, 1593/4, 1645/6, 1681/2, 1791/2 and 1913/14.

519 Emblem

1978. Air. 12th World Architects' Congress.

1459	519	1p.60 red, black and orange	30	20

520 Dr. Rafael Lucio

1978. Air. 11th International Leprosy Congress.

1460	520	1p.60 green	30	20

521 Franz Schubert and "Death and the Maiden"

1978. Air. 150th Death Anniv of Franz Schubert (composer).

1461	521	4p.30 brown, black and green	40	20

522 Decorations and Candles

1978. Christmas. Multicoloured.

1462		50c. Type **522** (postage)	30	20
1463		1p.60 Children and decoration (air)	30	20

523 Antonio Vivaldi

1978. Air. 300th Birth Anniv of Antonio Vivaldi (composer).

1464	523	4p.30 red, stone and brown	40	15

524 Wright Flyer III

1978. Air. 75th Anniv of First Powered Flight.

1465	524	1p.60 orange, yell & mve	30	15
1466	-	4p.30 yellow, red & flesh	40	20

DESIGN: 4p.30, Side view of Wright Flyer I.

525 Albert Einstein and Equation

1979. Air. Birth Centenary of Albert Einstein (physicist).

1467	525	1p.60 multicoloured	30	20

526 Arms of Hermosillo

1979. Centenary of Hermosillo, Sonora.

1468	526	80c. multicoloured	30	20

527 Sir Rowland Hill

1979. Air. Death Centenary of Sir Rowland Hill.

1469	527	1p.60 multicoloured	30	20

528 "Children" (Adriana Blas Casas)

1979. Air. International Year of the Child.

1470	528	1p.60 multicoloured	30	20

529 Registered Letter from Mexico to Rome, 1880

1979. Air. "Mepsipex 79", Third International Exhibition of Elmhurst Philatelic Society, Mexico City.

1499	529	1p.60 multicoloured	30	20

530 Football

1979. "Universiada '79", 10th World University Games, Mexico City (1st issue).

1500	530	50c. grey, black and blue (postage)	30	20
1501	-	80c. multicoloured	30	20
1502	-	1p. multicoloured	30	20
MS1503		105×75 mm. 5p. multicoloured. Imperf	2·20	1·90
1504		1p.60 multicoloured (air)	30	25
1505		4p.30 multicoloured	40	25
MS1506		105×75 mm. 10p. multicoloured. Imperf	3·00	2·20

DESIGNS—VERT: 80c. Aztec ball player; 1p. Wall painting of athletes; 1p.60, Games emblem, 4p.30, Flame and dove. HORIZ: 5p. Runners; 10p. Gymnasts.
See also Nos. 1514/**MS**1520.

531 Josefa Ortiz de Dominguez

1979. 150th Death Anniv of Josefa Ortiz de Dominguez (Mayor of Queretaro).

1507	531	80c. pink, black and bright pink	30	20

532 "Allegory of National Culture" (Alfaro Siqueiros)

1979. 50th Anniv of National University's Autonomy. Multicoloured.

1508		80c. Type **532** (postage)	30	20
1509		3p. "The Conquest of Energy" (Chavez Morado)	40	20
1510		1p.60 "The Return of Quetzal-coati" (Chavez Morado) (air)	30	20
1511		4p.30 "Students reaching for Culture" (Alfaro Siqueiros)	40	20

533 Messenger and U.P.U. Emblem

1979. Air. Centenary of Mexico's Admission to U.P.U.

1512	533	1p.60 yellow, black and brown	30	20

534 Emiliano Zapata (after Diego Rivera)

1979. Birth Centenary of Emiliano Zapata (revolutionary).

1513	534	80c. multicoloured	30	20

535 Football

1979. "Universiada '79", 10th World University Games, Mexico City (2nd issue). Multicoloured.

1514		50c. Type **535** (postage)	30	20
1515		80c. Volleyball	30	20
1516		1p. Basketball	30	20
MS1517		105×75 mm. 5p. Fencing. Imperf	1·80	1·60
1518		1p.60 Tennis (air)	30	20
1519		5p.50 Swimming	40	20
MS1520		105×75 mm. 10p. Sports emblems (light green, black and green). Imperf	3·00	2·20

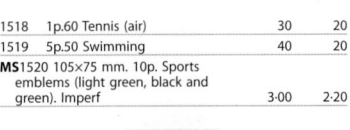

536 Tepoztlan, Morelos

1979. Tourism (1st series). Multicoloured.

1526		80c. Type **536** (postage)	30	20
1527		80c. Mexcaltitan, Nayarit	30	20
1528		1p.60 Agua Azul waterfall, Chipas (air)	30	20
1529		1p.60 King Coliman statue, Colima	30	20

See also Nos. 1631/4 and 1675/8.

537 Congress Emblem

1979. Air. 11th Congress and Assembly of International Industrial Design Council.

1530	537	1p.60 black, mauve and turquoise	30	20

538 Edison Lamp

1979. Air. Centenary of Electric Light.

1531	538	1p.60 multicoloured	30	20

539 Martin de Olivares (postmaster)

1979. 400th Anniv of Royal Proclamation of Mail Services in the New World. Multicoloured.

1532		80c. Type 539 (postage)	30	20
1533		1p.60 Martin Enriquez de Almanza (viceroy of New Spain) (air)	30	20
1534		5p.50 King Philip II of Spain	40	25
MS1535		122×92 mm. 10p. Spanish galleon (horiz). Imperf	3·50	1·60

540 Assembly Emblem

1979. Air. 8th General Assembly of Latin American Universities Union.

1536	540	1p.60 multicoloured	30	20

541 Shepherd

1979. Christmas. Multicoloured.

1537	541	50c. Type 541 (postage)	30	20
1538		1p.60 Girl and Christmas tree (air)	30	20

542 Moon Symbol from Mexican Codex

1979. Air. 10th Anniv of First Man on Moon.

1539	542	2p.50 multicoloured	30	20

543 Church, Yanhuitlan

1980. Air. Mexican Arts and Sciences (8th series). Multicoloured.

1540		1p.60 Type 543	30	20
1541		1p.60 Monastery, Yuriria	30	20
1542		1p.60 Church, Tlayacapan	30	20
1543		1p.60 Church, Actopan	30	20
1544		1p.60 Church, Acolman	30	20

544 Steps and Snake's Head

1980. National Pre-Hispanic Monuments (1st series). Multicoloured.

1545		80c. Type 544 (postage)	20	15
1546		1p.60 Doble Tlaloc (rain god) (air)	30	15
1547		5p.50 Coyolzauhqui (moon goddess)	40	25

See also Nos. 1565/7 and 1605/7.

1980. Mexican Fauna (2nd series). As T 516. Multicoloured.

1548		80c. Common turkey (postage)	55	15
1549		1p.60 Greater flamingo (air)	95	25

1980. Mexican Flowers (2nd series). As T 518. Multicoloured.

1550		80c. "Tajetes erecta" (postage)	25	15
1551		1p.60 "Vanilla planifolia" (air)	30	15

545 Jules Verne

1980. Air. 75th Death Anniv of Jules Verne (author).

1552	545	5p.50 brown and black	40	20

546 Skeleton smoking Cigar (after Guadalupe Posada)

1980. Air. World Health Day. Anti-smoking Campaign.

1553	546	1p.60 purple, blue & red	30	25

547 China Poblana, Puebla

1980. National Costumes (1st series). Multicoloured.

1554		50c. Type 547 (postage)	30	20
1555		80c. Jarocha, Veracruz	30	20
1556		1p.60 Chiapaneca, Chiapas (air)	30	20

See also Nos. 1588/90.

548 Family

1980. 10th Population and Housing Census.

1557	548	3p. black and silver	35	15

549 Cuauhtemoc (last Aztec Emperor)

1980. Pre-Hispanic Personalities (1st series). Multicoloured.

1558		80c. Type 549	25	15
1559		1p.60 Nezahualcoyotl (governor of Tetzcoco)	25	15
1560		5p.50 Eight Deer Tiger's Claw (11th Mixtec king)	50	15

See also Nos. 1642/4 and 1846/8.

550 Xipe (Aztec god of medicine)

1980. 22nd World Biennial Congress of International College of Surgeons, Mexico City.

1561	550	1p.60 multicoloured	30	20

551 Bronze Medal

1980. Olympic Games, Moscow.

1562	551	1p.60 bronze, black and turquoise	30	15
1563	-	3p. silver, black and blue	40	20
1564	-	5p.50 gold, black and red	50	25

DESIGNS: 3p. Silver medal; 5p.50, Gold medal.

1980. National Pre-Hispanic Monuments (2nd series). As T 554. Multicoloured.

1565		80c. Sacred glass	30	15
1566		1p.60 Stone snail	30	15
1567		5p.50 Chac Mool (god)	50	25

552 Sacromonte Sanctuary, Amecameca

1980. Colonial Architecture (1st series).

1568	552	2p.50 grey and black	30	15
1569	-	2p.50 grey and black	30	15
1570	-	3p. grey and black	35	20
1571	-	3p. grey and black	35	20

DESIGNS—HORIZ: No. 1552, St. Catherine's Convent, Patzcuaro; No. 1554, Hermitage, Cuernavaca. VERT: No. 1553, Basilica, Culiapan.
See also Nos. 1617/20, 1660/3, 1695/8 and 1784/7.

553 Quetzalcoatl (god)

1980. World Tourism Conference, Manila, Philippines.

1572	553	2p.50 multicoloured	30	15

554 Arms of Sinaloa

1980. 150th Anniv of Sinaloa State.

1573	554	1p.60 multicoloured	30	15

555 Straw Angel

1980. Christmas. Multicoloured.

1574		50c. Type 555	30	15
1575		1p.60 Poinsettia in a jug	30	15

556 Congress Emblem

1980. 4th International Civil Justice Congress.

1576	556	1p.60 multicoloured	30	15

557 Glass Demijohn and Animals

1980. Mexican Crafts (1st series). Multicoloured.

1577		50c. Type 557	20	10
1578		1p. Poncho	20	10
1579		3p. Wooden mask	45	15

See also Nos. 1624/6.

558 "Simon Bolivar" (after Paulin Guerin)

1980. 150th Death Anniv of Simon Bolivar.

1580	558	4p. multicoloured	50	25

559 Vicente Guerrero

1981. 150th Death Anniv of Vicente Guerrero (liberator).

1581	559	80c. multicoloured	30	15

560 Valentin Gomez Farias

1981. Birth Bicentenary of Valentin Gomez Farias.
1582 **560** 80c. black and green 30 20

561 Table Tennis Balls in Flight

1981. 1st Latin-American Table Tennis Cup.
1583 **561** 4p. multicoloured 50 25

562 Jesus Gonzalez Ortega

1981. Death Centenary of Jesus Gonzalez Ortega.
1584 **562** 80c. light brown & brown 30 20

563 Gabino Barreda

1981. Death Centenary of Gabino Barreda (politician).
1585 **563** 80c. pink, black and green 30 20

564 Benito Juarez

1981. 175th Birth Anniv of Benito Juarez (patriot).
1586 **564** 1p.60 green, brn & lt brn 30 20

565 Foundation Monument

1981. 450th Anniv of Puebla City.
1587 **565** 80c. multicoloured 30 20

1981. National Costumes (2nd series). Vert designs as T 547. Multicoloured.
1588 50c. Purepecha, Michoacan 30 15
1589 80c. Charra, Jalisco 30 15
1590 1p.60 Mestiza, Yucatan 30 15

1981. Mexican Fauna (3rd series). Vert designs as T 516. Multicoloured.
1591 80c. Northern mockingbird 55 15
1592 1p.60 Mexican trogon 90 30

1981. Mexican Flowers (3rd series). Vert designs as T 518. Multicoloured.
1593 80c. Avocado 25 15
1594 1p.60 Cacao 25 15

566 "Martyrs of Cananea" (David A. Siqueiros)

1981. 75th Anniv of Martyrs of Cananea.
1595 **566** 1p.60 multicoloured 30 15

567 Toy Drummer with One Arm

1981. International Year of Disabled People.
1596 **567** 4p. multicoloured 45 25

568 Arms of Queretaro

1981. 450th Anniv of Queretaro City.
1597 **568** 80c. multicoloured 30 20

569 Mexican Stamp of 1856 and Postal Service Emblem

1981. 125th Anniv of First Mexican Stamp.
1598 **569** 4p. multicoloured 40 25

570 Sir Alexander Fleming

1981. Birth Centenary of Sir Alexander Fleming (discoverer of penicillin).
1599 **570** 5p. blue and orange 45 25

571 Union Congress Building and Emblem

1981. Opening of New Union Congress Building.
1600 **571** 1p.60 green and red 30 20

572 St. Francisco Xavier Claver

1981. 250th Birth Anniv of St. Francis Xavier Claver.
1601 **572** 80c. multicoloured 30 15

573 "Desislava" (detail of Bulgarian Fresco)

1981. 1300th Anniv of Bulgarian State. Mult.
1602 1p.60 Type **573** 30 10
1603 4p. Horse-headed cup from Thrace 45 20
1604 7p. Madara Horseman (relief) 60 35

1981. Pre-Hispanic Monuments. As T 544. Multicoloured.
1605 80c. Seated God 30 10
1606 1p.60 Alabaster deer's head 35 15
1607 4p. Jade fish 50 25

574 Pablo Picasso

1981. Birth Centenary of Pablo Picasso (artist).
1608 **574** 5p. deep green and green 50 25

575 Shepherd

1981. Christmas. Multicoloured.
1609 50c. Type **575** 30 15
1610 1p.60 Praying girl 30 15

576 Wheatsheaf

1981. World Food Day.
1611 **576** 4p. multicoloured 35 20

577 Thomas Edison, Lightbulb and Gramophone

1981. 50th Death Anniv of Thomas Edison (inventor).
1612 **577** 4p. stone, brown & green 35 20

578 Co-operation Emblem and Wheat

1981. International Meeting on Co-operation and Development, Cancun.
1613 **578** 4p. blue, grey and black 35 25

579 Globe and Diesel Locomotive

1981. 15th Pan-American Railway Congress.
1614 **579** 1p.60 multicoloured 45 15

580 Film Frame

1981. 50th Anniv of Mexican Sound Movies.
1615 **580** 4p. grey, black and green 35 20

581 Postcode and Bird delivering Letter

1981. Inauguration of Postcodes.
1616 **581** 80c. multicoloured 30 15

1981. Colonial Architecture (2nd series). As T 552. Multicoloured.
1617 4p. Mascarones House 25 15
1618 4p. La Merced Convent 25 15
1619 5p. Chapel of the Third Order, Texcoco 30 20
1620 5p. Father Tembleque Aqueduct, Otumba 30 20

582 "Martyrs of Rio Blanco" (Orozco)

1982. 75th Anniv of Martyrs of Rio Blanco.
1621 **582** 80c. multicoloured 25 15

583 Ignacio Lopez Rayon

1982. 150th Death Anniv of Ignacio Lopez Rayon.
1622 **583** 1p.60 green, red & black 25 15

584 Postal Headquarters

1982. 75th Anniv of Postal Headquarters.
1623 **584** 4p. pink and green 30 25

1982. Mexican Crafts (2nd series). As T 557. Multicoloured.
1624 50c. "God's Eye" (Huichol art) 20 15
1625 1p. Ceramic snail 20 15
1626 3p. Tiger mask 25 15

585 Postcoded Letter and Bird

1982. Postcode Publicity.
1627 **585** 80c. multicoloured 25 15

586 Dr. Robert Koch and Cross of Lorraine

1982. Centenary of Discovery of Tubercle Bacillus.
| 1628 | **586** | 4p. multicoloured | 30 | 20 |

587 Military Academy

1982. 50th Anniv of Military Academy.
| 1629 | **587** | 80c. yellow, black & gold | 25 | 15 |

588 Arms of Oaxaca

1982. 450th Anniv of Oaxaca City.
| 1630 | **588** | 1p.60 multicoloured | 25 | 15 |

1982. Tourism (2nd series). As T 563. Multicoloured.
1631		80c. Basaseachic Falls, Chihuahua	25	15
1632		80c. Natural rock formation, Pueblo Nuevo, Durango	25	15
1633		1p.60 Mayan City of Edzna, Campeche	25	15
1634		1p.60 La Venta (Olmeca sculpture, Tabasco)	25	15

589 Footballers

1982. World Cup Football Championship, Spain. Multicoloured.
1635		1p.60 Type **589**	75	20
1636		4p. Dribbling	90	20
1637		7p. Tackling	1·00	25

590 Hawksbill Turtles

1982. Mexican Fauna. Multicoloured.
| 1638 | | 1p.60 Type **590** | 90 | 20 |
| 1639 | | 4p. Grey Whales | 1·90 | 25 |

591 Vicente Guerrero

1982. Birth Bicentenary of Vicente Guerrero (independence fighter).
| 1640 | **591** | 80c. multicoloured | 30 | 15 |

592 Symbols of Peace and Communication

1982. Second U.N. Conference on the Exploration and Peaceful Uses of Outer Space, Vienna.
| 1641 | **592** | 4p. multicoloured | 30 | 20 |

1982. Pre-Hispanic Personalities (2nd series). As T 549. Multicoloured.
| 1642 | | 80c. Tariacuri | 25 | 15 |

| 1643 | | 1p.60 Acamapichtli | 25 | 15 |
| 1644 | | 4p. Ten Deer Tiger's breastplate | 25 | 15 |

593 Pawpaw ("Carica papaya")

1982. Mexican Flora. Multicoloured.
| 1645 | | 80c. Type **593** | 45 | 10 |
| 1646 | | 1p.60 Maize ("Zea mays") | 45 | 10 |

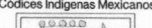

594 Astrologer

1982. Native Mexican Codices. Florentine Codex. Multicoloured.
1647		80c. Type **594**	25	25
1648		1p.60 Arriving at School	25	25
1649		4p. Musicians	30	25

595 Manuel Gamio (anthropologist)

1982. Mexican Arts and Scientists. Multicoloured.
1650		1p.60 Type **595**	25	10
1651		1p.60 Isaac Ochoterena (biologist)	25	10
1652		1p.60 Angel Maria Garibay (philologist)	25	10
1653		1p.60 Manuel Sandoval Vallarta (nuclear physicist)	25	10
1654		1p.60 Guillermo Gonzalez Camarena (electronics engineer)	25	10

596 State Archives Building

1982. Inaug of State Archives Building.
| 1655 | **596** | 1p.60 black and green | 25 | 15 |

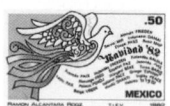

597 Dove and Peace Text

1982. Christmas. Multicoloured.
| 1656 | | 50c. Type **597** | 25 | 15 |
| 1657 | | 1p.60 Dove and Peace text (different) | 25 | 15 |

598 Hands holding Food

1982. Mexican Food System.
| 1658 | **598** | 1p.60 multicoloured | 25 | 15 |

599 "Revolutionary Mexico" Stamp, 1956

1982. Inauguration of Revolution Museum, Chihuahua.
| 1659 | **599** | 1p.60 grey and green | 25 | 15 |

1982. Colonial Architecture (3rd series). As T 552. Multicoloured.
1660		1p.60 College of Sts. Peter and Paul, Mexico City	25	10
1661		8p. Convent of Jesus Maria, Mexico City	30	20
1662		10p. Open Chapel, Tlalmanalco	30	20
1663		14p. Convent, Actopan	45	30

600 Alfonso Garcia Robles and Laurel

1982. Alfonso Garcia Robles (Nobel Peace Prize Winner) Commemoration.
| 1664 | **600** | 1p.60 grey, black & gold | 25 | 15 |
| 1665 | – | 14p. pink, black and gold | 45 | 30 |
DESIGN: 14p. Robles and medal.

601 Jose Vasconcelos

1982. Birth Centenary of Jose Vasconcelos (philosopher).
| 1666 | **601** | 1p.60 black and blue | 25 | 15 |

602 W.C.Y. Emblem and Methods of Communication

1983. World Communications Year.
| 1667 | **602** | 16p. multicoloured | 40 | 20 |

603 Sonora State Civil War Stamp, 1913

1983. "Herfilex 83" Mexican Revolution Stamp Exhibition.
| 1668 | **603** | 6p. brown, black & green | 25 | 15 |

604 "Nauticas Mexico" (container ship), World Map and I.M.O.

1983. 25th Anniv of International Maritime Organization.
| 1669 | **604** | 16p. multicoloured | 50 | 25 |

605 Doctor treating Patient

1983. Constitutional Right to Health Protection.
| 1670 | **605** | 6p. green and red | 25 | 15 |

606 Valentin Gomez Farias (founder) and Arms of Society

1983. 150th Anniv of Mexican Geographical and Statistical Society.
| 1671 | **606** | 6p. multicoloured | 25 | 15 |

607 Football

1983. 2nd World Youth Football Championship, Mexico.
1672	**607**	6p. black and green	25	15
1673	**607**	13p. black and red	40	20
1674	**607**	14p. black and blue	45	20

1983. Tourism. As T 536. Multicoloured.
1675		6p. Federal Palace, Queretaro	25	10
1676		6p. Water tank, San Luis Potosi	25	10
1677		13p. Cable car, Zacatecas	30	20
1678		14p. Carved head of Kohunlich, Quintana Roo	40	20

608 Bolivar on Horseback

1983. Birth Bicentenary of Simon Bolivar.
| 1679 | **608** | 21p. multicoloured | 60 | 25 |

609 Angela Peralta

1983. Death Centenary of Angela Peralta (opera singer).
| 1680 | **609** | 9p. light brown & brown | 35 | 20 |

610 Agave

1983. Mexican Flora and Fauna (5th series). Multicoloured.
1681		9p. Type **610**	40	20
1682		9p. Sapodilla	40	20
1683		9p. Swallowtail	2·10	20
1684		9p. Boa constrictor	2·00	20

611 Two Candles

1983. Christmas. Multicoloured.
1685		9p. Type **611**	30	20
1686		20p. Three candles	40	25

612 S.C.T. Emblem

1983. Integral Communications and Transport System.
1687	**612**	13p. blue and black	35	20

613 Carlos Chavez (musician)

1983. Mexican Arts and Sciences (10th series). Contemporary Artists. Multicoloured.
1688	**613**	9p. brown, light brown and deep brown	35	20
1689	-	9p. brown, light brown and deep brown	35	20
1690	-	9p. deep brown, light brown and brown	35	20
1691	-	9p. light brown, deep brown and brown	35	20
1692	-	9p. deep brown, stone and brown	35	20

DESIGNS: No. 1689, Francisco Goitia (painter); No. 1690, S. Diaz Miron (poet); No. 1691, Carlos Bracho (sculptor); No. 1692, Fanny Anitua (singer).

614 Orozco (self-portrait)

1983. Birth Centenary of Jose Clemente Orozco (artist).
1693	**614**	9p. multicoloured	35	20

615 Human Rights Emblem

1983. 35th Anniv of Human Rights Declaration.
1694	**615**	20p. deep blue, yellow and blue	40	25

1983. Colonial Architecture (4th series). As T 552. Each grey and black.
1695		9p. Convent, Malinalco	35	20
1696		20p. Cathedral, Cuernavaca	45	25
1697		21p. Convent, Tepeji del Rio	45	30
1698		24p. Convent, Atlatlahucan	45	30

616 Antonio Caso and Books

1983. Birth Centenary of Antonio Caso (philospher).
1699	**616**	9p. blue, lilac and red	35	20

617 Joaquin Velazquez

1983. Bicentenary of Royal Legislation on Mining.
1700	**617**	9p. multicoloured	35	20

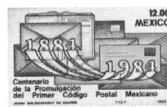

618 Book and Envelopes

1984. Centenary of First Postal Laws.
1701	**618**	12p. multicoloured	40	20

619 Children dancing around Drops of Anti-Polio Serum

1984. World Anti-polio Campaign.
1702	**619**	12p. multicoloured	40	20

620 Muscovy Duck

1984. Mexican Fauna (6th series). Multicoloured.
1703	**620**	12p. Type **620**	60	20
1704		20p. Red-billed whistling duck	60	20

621 Xoloitzcuintle Dog

1984. World Dog Show.
1705	**621**	12p. multicoloured	1·00	20

622 Bank Headquarters

1984. Centenary of National Bank.
1706	**622**	12p. multicoloured	40	20

623 Hands holding Trees

1984. Protection of Forest Resources.
1707	**623**	20p. multicoloured	45	15

624 Putting the Shot

1984. Olympic Games, Los Angeles. Multicoloured.
1708		14p. Type **624**	60	20
1709		20p. Show jumping	60	20
1710		23p. Gymnastics (floor exercise)	60	20
1711		24p. Diving	60	20
1712		25p. Boxing	60	20
1713		26p. Fencing	60	20
MS1714	56x61 mm. 40p. Gymnastics (rings exercise). Imperf		3·00	1·50

625 Mexican and Russian Flags

1984. 60th Anniv of Diplomatic Relations with U.S.S.R.
1715	**625**	23p. multicoloured	60	25

626 Hand holding U.N. emblem

1984. International Population Conference.
1716	**626**	20p. multicoloured	60	20

627 Gen. Mugica

1984. Birth Centenary of General Francisco Mugica (politician).
1717	**627**	14p. brown and black	30	20

628 Emblem and Dates

1984. 50th Anniv of Economic Culture Fund.
1718	**628**	14p. brown, black and red	35	20

629 Airline Emblem

1984. 50th Anniv of Aeromexico (state airline).
1719		14p. multicoloured	40	25
1720	**629**	20p. black and red	40	25

DESIGN—36x44 mm: 14p. "Red Cactus" (sculpture, Sebastian).

630 Palace of Fine Arts

1984. 50th Anniv of Palace of Fine Arts.
1721	**630**	14p. blue, black and brown	30	20

631 Metropolitan Cathedral (detail of facade)

1984. 275th Anniv of Chihuahua City.
1722	**631**	14p. brown and black	30	20

632 Coatzacoalcos Bridge

1984. Inaug of Coatzacoalcos Bridge.
1723	**632**	14p. multicoloured	30	20

633 Dove and Hand holding Flame

1984. World Disarmament Week.
1724	**633**	20p. multicoloured	30	20

634 Christmas Tree and Toy Train

1984. Christmas. Multicoloured.
1725		14p. Type **634**	30	20
1726		20p. Breaking the pinata (balloon filled with gifts) (vert)	30	20

635 Ignacio Manuel Altamirano

1984. 150th Birth Anniv of Ignacio Manuel Altamirano (politician and journalist).
1727	**635**	14p. red and black	30	20

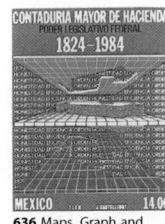

636 Maps, Graph and Text

1984. 160th Anniv of State Audit Office.
1728	**636**	14p. multicoloured	30	20

637 Half a Football and Mexican Colours

1984. Mexico, Site of 1986 World Cup Football Championship. Multicoloured.
1729		20p. Type **637**	1·30	20

1730	24p. Football and Mexican colours	1·60	20

638 Romulo Gallegos

1984. Birth Centenary of Romulo Gallegos.

1731	**638**	20p. black and blue	30	20

639 State Arms and Open Register

1984. 125th Anniv of Mexican Civil Register.

1732	**639**	24p. blue	35	20

640 Mexican Flag

1985. 50th Anniv of National Flag.

1733	**640**	22p. multicoloured	50	25

641 Johann Sebastian Bach

1985. 300th Birth Anniv of Johann Sebastian Bach (composer).

1734	**641**	35p. red and black	40	25

642 I.Y.Y. Emblem

1985. International Youth Year.

1735	**642**	35p. purple, gold and black	35	25

643 Children and Fruit within Book

1985. Child Survival Campaign.

1736	**643**	36p. multicoloured	40	20

644 Commemorative Medallion

1985. 450th Anniv of State Mint.

1737	**644**	35p. gold, mauve & blue	40	20

645 Victor Hugo, Text and Gateway

1985. Death Centenary of Victor Hugo (novelist).

1738	**645**	35p. grey	40	25

646 Hidalgo 8r. Stamp, 1856

1985. "Mexfil 85" Stamp Exhibition.

1739	**646**	22p. grey, black and purple	30	30
1740	-	35p. grey, black and blue	40	30
1741	-	36p. multicoloured	40	30
MS1742		101×80 mm. 90p. multicoloured. Imperf	3·00	1·60

DESIGNS: 35p. Carranza 10c. stamp, 1916; 36p. Juarez 50p. stamp, 1975; 90p. 1881 cover.

647 Rockets, Satellite, Nurse and Computer Operator

1985. Launching of First Morelos Satellite. Mult.

1743	**647**	22p. Type **647**	25	20
1744		36p. Camera, dish aerial, satellite and computers	25	20
1745		90p. Camera, dish aerial, satellite, television and couple telephoning	55	40
MS1746		160×95 mm. 100p. As Nos. 1743/5. Imperf	3·25	2·20

Nos. 1743/5 were printed together, se-tenant, forming a composite design.

648 Conifer

1985. 9th World Forestry Congress, Mexico.

1747	**648**	22p. brown, black and green	30	20
1748	-	35p. brown, black and green	30	20
1749	-	36p. brown, black and green	30	20

DESIGNS: 35p. Silk-cotton trees; 36p. Mahogany tree.

649 Martin Luis Guzman

1985. Mexican Arts and Sciences (11th series). Contemporary Writers.

1750	**649**	22p. grey and blue	25	20
1751	-	22p. grey and blue	25	20
1752	-	22p. grey and blue	25	20
1753	-	22p. grey and blue	25	20
1754	-	22p. grey and blue	25	20

DESIGNS: No. 1751, Augustin Yanez; 1752, Alfonso Reyes; 1753, Jose Ruben Romero; 1754, Artemio de Valle-Arizpe.

650 Miguel Hidalgo

1985. 175th Anniv of Independence Movement. Each green, black and red.

1755	**650**	22p. Type **650**	25	20
1756		35p. Jose Ma. Morelos	25	20
1757		35p. Ignacio Allende	25	20
1758		36p. Leona Vigario	25	20

1759		110p. Vicente Guerrero	70	60
MS1760		157×127 mm. 90p. emblem (48×41 mm). Imperf	2·75	2·10

651 San Ildefonso

1985. 75th Anniv of National University. Mult.

1761		26p. Type **651**	25	20
1762		26p. Emblem	25	20
1763		40p. Modern building	30	20
1764		45p. 1910 crest and Justo Sierra (founder)	30	20
1765		90p. University crest	60	40

652 Rural and Industrial Landscapes

1985. 25th Anniv of Inter-American Development Bank.

1766	**652**	26p. multicoloured	30	20

653 Guns and Doves

1985. United Nations Disarmament Week.

1767	**653**	36p. multicoloured	30	20

654 Hands and Dove

1985. 40th Anniv of U.N.O.

1768	**654**	26p. multicoloured	25	20

655 "Girls Skipping" (Mishinoya K. Maki)

1985. Christmas. Children's Paintings. Mult.

1769		26p. Disabled and able-bodied children playing (Margarita Salazar)	25	20
1770		35p. Type **655**	25	20

656 Soldadera

1985. 75th Anniv of 1910 Revolution. Each red, black and green.

1771		26p. Type **656**	25	20
1772		35p. Pancho Villa	25	20
1773		40p. Emiliano Zapata	25	20
1774		45p. Venustiano Carranza	25	20
1775		110p. Francisco Madero	55	25
MS1776		122×88 mm. 90p. emblem (48×40 mm). Imperf	2·75	1·80

657 "Vigilante" (Federico Silva)

1985. 2nd "Morelos" Telecommunications Satellite Launch.

1777	-	26p. black and blue	25	20
1778	**657**	35p. grey, pink and black	25	20
1779	-	45p. multicoloured	25	20
MS1780		90×60 mm. 100p. multicoloured (46×36 mm). Imperf	2·75	1·80

DESIGNS—VERT: 26p. "Cosmonaut" (sculpture by Sebastian). HORIZ: 45p. "Mexican Astronaut" (painting by Cauduro); 100p. Satellite transmitting to Earth.

658 "Mexico" holding Book

1985. 25th Anniv of Free Textbooks National Commission.

1781	**658**	26p. multicoloured	25	20

659 Olympic Stadium, University City

1985. World Cup Football Championship, Mexico. Each grey and black.

1782		26p. Type **659**	75	20
1783		45p. Azteca Stadium	95	25

1985. Colonial Architecture (5th series). Vert designs as T 552. Each brown and black.

1784		26p. Vizcayan College, Mexico City	30	25
1785		35p. Counts of Heras y Soto Palace, Mexico City	30	25
1786		40p. Counts of Calimaya Palace, Mexico City	30	25
1787		45p. St. Carlos Academy, Mexico City	30	25

661 Luis Enrique Erro Planetarium

1986. 50th Anniv of National Polytechnic Institute. Multicoloured.

1788		40p. Type **661**	25	20
1789		65p. National School of Arts and Crafts	30	20
1790		75p. Founders, emblem and "50"	40	25

1986. Mexican Flowers (6th series). As T 518. Multicoloured.

1791		40p. Calabash	30	20
1792		65p. "Nopalea coccinellifera" (cactus)	45	25

663 Doll

1986. World Health Day.

1793	**663**	65p. multicoloured	30	20

664 Halley and Comet

1986. Appearance of Halley's Comet.

1794	**664**	90p. multicoloured	50	25

665 Emblem

1986. Centenary of Geological Institute.
1795 **665** 40p. multicoloured 35 20

666 "Three Footballers with Berets"

1986. World Cup Football Championship, Mexico (2nd issue). Paintings by Angel Zarraga. Multicoloured.
1796 30p. Type **666** 40 15
1797 40p. "Portrait of Ramon Novaro" 40 20
1798 65p. "Sunday" 50 25
1799 70p. "Portrait of Ernest Charles Gimpel" 55 30
1800 90p. "Three Footballers" 60 40
MS1801 120×90 mm. 110p. Flags and footballing scenes. Imperf 5·75 2·10

667 Ignacio Allende

1986. 175th Death Annivs of Independence Heroes. Multicoloured.
1802 40p. Type **667** 40 20
1803 40p. Miguel Hidalgo (after J. C. Orozco) 40 20
1804 65p. Juan Aldama 50 20
1805 75p. Mariano Jimenez 50 20

668 Mexican Arms over "FTF"

1986. 50th Anniv of Fiscal Tribunal.
1806 **668** 40p. black, blue and grey 40 20

669 Nicolas Bravo

1986. Birth Bicentenary of Nicolas Bravo (independence fighter).
1807 **669** 40p. multicoloured 40 20

670 "Zapata Landscape"

1986. Paintings by Diego Rivera. Multicoloured.
1808 50p. Type **670** 40 25
1809 80p. "Nude with Arum Lilies" 55 25
1810 110p. "Vision of a Sunday Afternoon Walk on Central Avenue" (horiz) 70 35

671 Guadalupe Victoria

1986. Birth Bicentenary of Guadalupe Victoria (first President).
1811 **671** 50p. multicoloured 35 20

672 People depositing Produce

1986. 50th Anniv of National Depositories.
1812 **672** 40p. multicoloured 35 20

673 Pigeon above Hands holding Posthorn

1986. World Post Day.
1813 **673** 120p. multicoloured 50 25

674 Emblem

1986. Foundation of National Commission to Mark 500th Anniv (1992) of Discovery of America.
1814 **674** 50p. black and red 40 20

675 Ministry of Mines

1986. 15th Pan-American Roads Congress.
1815 **675** 80p. grey and black 40 20

676 Liszt

1986. 175th Birth Anniv of Franz Liszt (composer).
1816 **676** 100p. brown and black 50 20

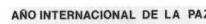

677 U.N. and "Pax Cultura" Emblems

1986. International Peace Year.
1817 **677** 80p. blue, red and black 40 20

678 Jose Maria Pino Suarez (1st Vice-President of Revolutionary Govt.)

1986. Famous Mexicans buried in The Rotunda of Illustrious Men (1st series).
1818 **678** 50p. multicoloured 35 20
See also Nos. 1823/4, 1838 and 1899.

679 King

1986. Christmas. Multicoloured.
1819 50p. Type **679** 35 20
1820 80p. Angel 35 20

680 "Self-portrait"

1986. Birth Centenary of Diego Rivera (artist).
1821 **680** 80p. multicoloured 35 20

681 Baby receiving Vaccination

1987. National Days for Poliomyelitis Vaccination.
1822 **681** 50p. multicoloured 35 20

1987. Famous Mexicans buried in The Rotunda of Illustrious Men (2nd series). As T 678. Mult.
1823 100p. Jose Maria Iglesias 50 30
1824 100p. Pedro Sainz de Baranda 50 30

682 Perez de Leon College

1987. Centenary of Higher Education.
1825 **682** 100p. multicoloured 55 30

683 Kino and Map

1987. 300th Anniv of Father Eusebio Francisco Kino's Mission to Pimeria Alta.
1826 **683** 100p. multicoloured 55 30

684 Baby's Head

1987. Child Immunization Campaign.
1827 **684** 100p. deep blue and blue 55 30

685 Staircase

1987. 50th Anniv of Puebla Independent University.
1828 **685** 200p. grey, pink and black 85 45

686 "5th of May, 1862, and the Siege of Puebla" Exhibition Poster, 1887

1987. 125th Anniv of Battle of Puebla.
1829 **686** 100p. multicoloured 45 20

687 Stylized City

1987. "Metropolis 87" World Association of Large Cities Congress.
1830 **687** 310p. red, black and green 1·20 65

688 Lacquerware Tray, Uruapan, Michoacan

1987. Handicrafts. Multicoloured.
1831 100p. Type **688** 40 20
1832 200p. Woven blanket, Santa Ana Chiautempan, Tlaxcala 75 40
1833 230p. Ceramic jar with lid, Puebla, Puebla 95 50

689 Genaro Estrada (author and pioneer of democracy)

1987. Mexican Arts and Sciences (12th series).
1834 **689** 100p. brown, black and pink 40 20
See also Nos. 1845, 1880 and 1904/5.

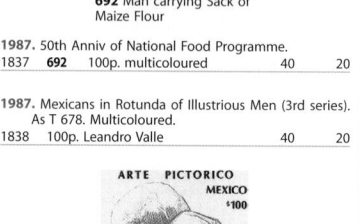

690 "Native Traders" (mural, P. O'Higgins)

1987. 50th Anniv of National Foreign Trade Bank.
1835	**690**	100p. multicoloured	40	20

691 Diagram of Longitudinal Section through Ship's Hull

1987. 400th Anniv of Publication of First Shipbuilding Manual in America, Diego Garcia de Palacio's "Instrucion Nautica".
1836	**691**	100p. green, blue & brn	40	20

692 Man carrying Sack of Maize Flour

1987. 50th Anniv of National Food Programme.
1837	**692**	100p. multicoloured	40	20

1987. Mexicans in Rotunda of Illustrious Men (3rd series). As T 678. Multicoloured.
1838		100p. Leandro Valle	40	20

693 "Self-portrait with Skull"

1987. Paintings by Saturnino Herran.
1839	**693**	100p. brown and black	45	20
1840	-	100p. multicoloured	45	20
1841	-	400p. multicoloured	1·50	95

DESIGNS: No. 1840, "The Offering"; 1841, "Creole with Shawl".

694 Flags of Competing Countries

1987. 10th Pan-American Games, Indianapolis.
1842	**694**	100p. multicoloured	35	20
1843	-	200p. black, red and green	40	20

DESIGN: 200p. Running.

695 Electricity Pylon

1987. 50th Anniv of Federal Electricity Commission.
1844	**695**	200p. multicoloured	50	30

1987. Mexican Arts and Sciences (13th series). As T 689. Multicoloured.
1845		100p. J. E. Hernandez y Davalos (author)	35	20

1987. Pre-Hispanic Personalities (3rd series). As T 549. Multicoloured.
1846		100p. Xolotl (Chichimeca commander)	35	25
1847		200p. Nezahualpilli (leader of Tezcoco tribe)	60	40
1848		400p. Motecuhzoma Ilhuicamina (leader of Tenochtitlan tribe)	1·20	45

696 Stylized Racing Car

1987. Mexico Formula One Grand Prix.
1849	**696**	100p. multicoloured	35	20

697 Mexican Cultural Centre, Mexico City

1987. Mexican Tourism.
1850	**697**	100p. multicoloured	35	20

698 "Santa Maria" and 1922 Mexican Festival Emblem

1987. 500th Anniv of "Meeting of Two Worlds" (discovery of America by Columbus) (1st issue)
1851	**698**	150p. multicoloured	3·00	35

See also Nos. 1902, 1941, 1979, 2038 and 2062/6.

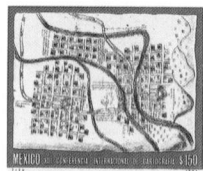

699 16th-century Spanish Map of Mexico City

1987. 13th International Cartography Conference.
1852	**699**	150p. multicoloured	35	20

1987. Mexican Tourism. As T 697. Multicoloured.
1853		150p. Michoacan	30	20
1854		150p. Garcia Caves, Nuevo Leon	30	20
1855		150p. View of Mazatlan, Sinaloa	30	20

700 Pre-Hispanic Wedding Ceremony

1987. Native Codices. Mendocino Codex. Mult.
1856		150p. Type 700	45	20
1857		150p. Moctezuma's council chamber	45	20
1858		150p. Foundation of Tenochtitlan	45	20

701 Dove with Olive Twig

1987. Christmas.
1859	**701**	150p. mauve	30	20
1860	-	150p. blue	30	20

DESIGN: No. 1860, As T 701 but dove facing left.

702 "Royal Ordinance for the Carriage of Maritime Mail" Title Page

1987. World Post Day.
1861	**702**	150p. green and grey	30	20
MS1862		129×102 mm. 600p. yellow and lake. Imperf	2·75	80

DESIGN: 600p. Detail of register of inland mail 29 June, 1857.

703 Circle of Flags

1987. 1st Meeting of Eight Latin-American Presidents, Acapulco. Multicoloured.
1863		250p. Type 703	40	20
1864		500p. Flags and doves	70	45

704 "Dualidad 1964"

1987. Rufino Tamayo (painter). "70 Years of Creativity".
1865	**704**	150p. multicoloured	40	20

705 Train on Metlac Viaduct

1987. 50th Anniv of Railway Nationalization.
1866	**705**	150p. multicoloured	70	20

706 Stradivarius at Work (detail, 19th-century engraving)

1987. 250th Death Anniv of Antonio Stradivarius (violin-maker).
1867	**706**	150p. light violet and violet	40	20

707 Statue of Manuel Crescensio Rejon (promulgator of Yucatan State Constitution)

1988. Constitutional Tribunal, Supreme Court of Justice.
1868	**707**	300p. multicoloured	55	35

708 American Manatee

1988. Animals. Multicoloured.
1869		300p. Type 708	90	35

1870		300p. Mexican mole salamander	90	35

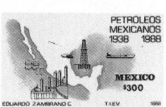

709 Map and Oil Industry Symbols

1988. 50th Anniv of Pemex (Nationalized Petroleum Industry).
1871	**709**	300p. blue and black	40	30
1872	-	300p. multicoloured	40	30
1873	-	500p. multicoloured	55	40

DESIGNS:—36×43 mm: No. 1872, PEMEX emblem. 43×36 mm: No. 1873, "50" and oil exploration platform.

710 "The Vaccination"

1988. World Health Day (1874) and 40th Anniv of W.H.O. (1875). Paintings by Diego Rivera.
1874	**710**	300p. brown and green	50	30
1875	-	300p. multicoloured	50	30

DESIGN:—43×36 mm: No. 1875, "The People demand Health".

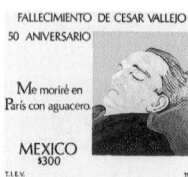

711 "Death Portrait" (Victor Delfin)

1988. 50th Death Anniv of Cesar Vallejo (painter and poet). Multicoloured.
1876		300p. Type 711	50	30
1877		300p. Portrait by Arnold Belkin and "Hoy me palpo ..."	50	30
1878		300p. Portrait as in T 711 but larger (30×35 mm)	50	30
1879		300p. Portrait as in No. 1877 but larger (23×35 mm)	50	30

1988. Mexican Arts and Sciences (14th series). As T 689.
1880		300p. brown, black and violet	50	30

DESIGN: 300p. Carlos Pellicer (poet).

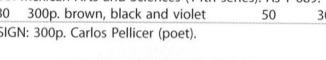

712 Girl and Boy holding Stamp in Tweezers

1988. "Mepsirrey '88" Stamp Exhibition, Monterrey. Multicoloured.
1881		300p. Type 712	50	30
1882		300p. Envelope with "Monterrey" handstamp	50	30
1883		500p. Exhibition emblem	75	50

713 Hernandos Rodriguez Racing Circuit, Mexico City

1988. Mexico Formula One Grand Prix.
1884	**713**	500p. multicoloured	65	40

714 Lopez Verlarde and Rose

1988. Birth Centenary of Ramon Lopez Verlarde (poet). Multicoloured.
1885	300p. Type **714**	40	25
1886	300p. Abstract	40	25

715 Emblem

1988. 50th Anniv of Military Sports.
1887	**715** 300p. multicoloured	40	25

716 Chrysanthemum, Container Ship and Flags

1988. Centenary of Mexico–Japan Friendship, Trade and Navigation Treaty.
1888	**716** 500p. multicoloured	65	35

717 Map

1988. Oceanographical Assembly.
1889	**717** 500p. multicoloured	65	35

718 Runners

1988. Olympic Games, Seoul. Multicoloured.
1890	500p. Type **718**	85	40
MS1891	72×55 mm. 700p. Flame, Seoul emblem and mascot and Barcelona emblem. Imperf	2·20	90

719 Boxer and Flags

1988. 25th Anniv of World Boxing Council.
1892	**719** 500p. multicoloured	65	35

720 Hospital and Emblem

1988. 125th Anniv of Red Cross.
1893	**720** 300p. grey, red and black	40	25

721 Posada

1988. 75th Death Anniv of Jose Guadalupe Posada (painter).
1894	**721** 300p. black and silver	40	25

722 "Danaus plexippus"

1988. Endangered Insects. The Monarch Butterfly. Multicoloured.
1895	300p. Type **722**	2·50	45
1896	300p. Butterflies on wall	2·50	45
1897	300p. Butterflies on leaves	2·50	45
1898	300p. Caterpillar, butterfly and chrysalis	2·50	45

1988. Mexicans in Rotunda of Illustrious Persons (4th series). As T 678. Multicoloured.
1899	300p. Manuel Sandoval Vallarta	40	25

723 Envelopes forming Map

1988. World Post Day.
1900	**723** 500p. black and blue	65	35
MS1901	75×44 mm. 700p. multicoloured	3·00	90

DESIGN: 700p. Envelope, doves and globe.

724 Indian and Monk writing

1988. 500th Anniv of "Meeting of Two Worlds" (2nd issue). Yanhuitian Codex.
1902	**724** 500p. multicoloured	70	40

725 Man watering Plant

1988. World Food Day. "Rural Youth".
1903	**725** 500p. multicoloured	65	35

1988. Mexican Arts and Sciences (15th series). As T 689.
1904	300p. black and grey	40	20
1905	300p. brown, black & yellow	40	20

DESIGNS: No. 1904, Alfonso Caso; 1905, Vito Alessio Robles.

726 Act

1988. 175th Anniv of Promulgation of Act of Independence.
1906	**726** 300p. flesh and brown	40	20

727 "Self-portrait 1925"

1988. 25th Death Anniv of Antonio Ruiz (painter). Multicoloured.
1907	300p. Type **727**	40	20
1908	300p. "La Malinche"	40	20
1909	300p. "March Past"	40	20

728 Children and Kites

1988. Christmas. Multicoloured.
1910	300p. Type **728**	40	20
1911	300p. Food (horiz)	40	20

729 Emblem

1988. 50th Anniv of Municipal Workers Trade Union.
1912	**729** 300p. black and brown	45	25

1988. Mexican Flowers (7th series). As T 518. Multicoloured.
1913	300p. "Mimosa tenuiflora"	40	20
1914	300p. "Ustilago maydis"	40	20

731 "50" and Emblem

1989. 50th Anniv of State Printing Works.
1915	**731** 450p. brown, grey and red	60	35

732 Arms and Score of National Anthem

1989. 145th Anniv of Dominican Independence.
1916	**732** 450p. multicoloured	60	35

733 Emblem

1989. Centenary of International Boundary and Water Commission.
1917	**733** 1100p. multicoloured	1·40	85

734 Emblem

1989. 10th International Book Fair, Mineria.
1918	**734** 450p. multicoloured	60	35

735 Composer at Work

1989. 25th Anniv of Society of Authors and Composers.
1919	**735** 450p. multicoloured	60	35

736 People

1989. Anti-AIDS Campaign.
1920	**736** 450p. multicoloured	60	35

737 Vicario

1989. Birth Bicentenary of Leona Vicario (Independence fighter).
1921	**737** 450p. brown, deep brown and black	60	35

738 Statue of Reyes

1989. Birth Centenary of Alfonso Reyes (writer).
1922	**738** 450p. multicoloured	60	35

739 Speeding Cars

1989. Mexico Formula One Grand Prix.
1923	**739** 450p. multicoloured	60	35

740 Sea and Mountains

1989. 14th Travel Agents' Meeting, Acapulco.
1924	**740** 1100p. multicoloured	1·40	85

741 Huehuetcotl (god)

1989. 14th International Congress on Ageing.
1925	**741** 450p. pink, black and stone	60	35

742 Revolutionary and Battle Site

1989. 75th Death Anniv of Battle of Zacatecas.
1926	**742** 450p. black	60	35

743 Catchers

1989. Baseball Professionals' Hall of Fame. Multicoloured.
1927	550p. Type **743**		1·30	50
1928	550p. Striker		1·30	50

Nos. 1927/8 were printed together, se-tenant, forming a composite design.

744 Bows and Arrows

1989. World Archery Championships, Switzerland. Multicoloured.
1929	650p. Type **744**		1·60	50
1930	650p. Arrows and target		1·60	50

Nos. 1929/30 were printed together, se-tenant, forming a composite design.

745 Arms

1989. Centenary of Tijuana.
1931	**745**	1100p. multicoloured	1·10	75

746 Storming the Bastille

1989. Bicentenary of French Revolution.
1932	**746**	1300p. multicoloured	1·40	85

747 Mina

1989. Birth Bicentenary of Francisco Xavier Mina (independence fighter).
1933	**747**	450p. multicoloured	55	30

748 Cave Paintings

1989. 25th Anniv of National Anthropological Museum, Chapultepec.
1934	**748**	450p. multicoloured	60	35

749 Runners

1989. 7th Mexico City Marathon.
1935	**749**	450p. multicoloured	55	30

750 Printed Page

1989. 450th Anniv of First American and Mexican Printed Work.
1936	**750**	450p. multicoloured	55	30

751 Posthorn and Cancellations

1989. World Post Day.
1937	**751**	1100p. multicoloured	1·00	70

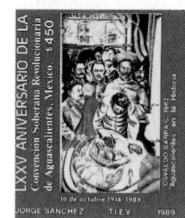

752 "Aguascalientes in History" (Osvaldo Barra)

1989. 75th Anniv of Aguascalientes Revolutionary Convention.
1938	**752**	450p. multicoloured	50	30

753 Patterns

1989. America. Pre-Columbian Culture.
1939	450p. Type **753**		55	30
1940	450p. Traditional writing		55	30

754 Old and New World Symbols

1989. 500th Anniv of "Meeting of Two Worlds" (3rd issue).
1941	**754**	1300p. multicoloured	1·20	80

755 Cross of Lorraine

1989. 50th Anniv of Anti-tuberculosis National Committee.
1942	**755**	450p. multicoloured	50	30

756 Mask of God Murcielago

1989.
1943	**756**	450p. green, black & mve	60	30

757 Bank

1989. 125th Anniv of Serfin Commercial Bank.
1944	**757**	450p. blue, gold and black	50	30

758 Cortines

1989. Birth Centenary of Adolfo Ruiz Cortines (President, 1952–58).
1945	**758**	450p. multicoloured	50	30

759 Man with Sparkler

1989. Christmas. Multicoloured.
1946	450p. Type **759**		45	30
1947	450p. People holding candles (horiz)		45	30

760 Emblem

1989. 50th Anniv of National Institute of Anthropology and History.
1948	**760**	450p. gold, red and black	45	30

761 Steam Locomotive, Diesel Train and Felipe Pescador

1989. 80th Anniv of Nationalization of Railways.
1949	**761**	450p. multicoloured	45	30

762 Bridge

1990. Opening of Tampico Bridge.
1950	**762**	600p. black, gold and red	65	35

763 Smiling Children

1990. Child Vaccination Campaign.
1951	**763**	700p. multicoloured	70	40

764 People in Houses

1990. 11th General Population and Housing Census.
1952	**764**	700p. green, yell & lt grn	70	40

765 Stamp under Magnifying Glass

1990. 10th Anniv of Mexican Philatelic Association.
1953	**765**	700p. multicoloured	60	35

766 Archive

1990. Bicentenary of National Archive.
1954	**766**	700p. blue	60	35

767 Emblem and "90"

1990. 1st International Poster Biennale.
1955	**767**	700p. multicoloured	60	35

768 Messenger, 1790

1990. "Stamp World London 90" International Stamp Exhibition.
1956	**768**	700p. yellow, red & black	70	35

769 Penny Black

1990. 150th Anniv of the Penny Black.
1957	**769**	700p. black, red and gold	60	35

770 National Colours and Pope John Paul II

1990. Papal Visit.
1958	**770**	700p. multicoloured	60	35

771 Church

1990. 15th Travel Agents' Congress.
1959 **771** 700p. multicoloured 70 35

772 Mother and Child

1990. Mother and Child Health Campaign.
1960 **772** 700p. multicoloured 60 35

773 Smoke
Rings forming
Birds

1990. World Anti-Smoking Day.
1961 **773** 700p. multicoloured 60 35

774 Globe as Tree

1990. World Environment Day.
1962 **774** 700p. multicoloured 60 35

775 Racing Car and
Chequered Flag

1990. Mexico Formula One Grand Prix.
1963 **775** 700p. black, red and
green 60 35

776 Aircraft Tailfin

1990. 25th Anniv of Airports and Auxiliary Services.
1964 **776** 700p. multicoloured 60 35

777 Family

1990. United Nations Anti-drugs Decade.
1965 **777** 700p. multicoloured 60 35

778 Tree Trunk

1990. Forest Conservation.
1966 **778** 700p. multicoloured 60 35

779 Emblem

1990. "Solidarity".
1967 **779** 700p. multicoloured 60 35
See also No. 2047.

780 Columns and Native
Decoration

1990. World Heritage Site. Oaxaca.
1968 **780** 700p. multicoloured 60 35

781 Elegant Tern

1990. Conservation of Rasa Island, Gulf of California.
1969 **781** 700p. grey, black and red 1·20 45

782 Institute Activities

1990. 25th Anniv of Mexican Petroleum Institute.
1970 **782** 700p. blue and black 60 35

783 National Colours, City
Monuments and Runners

1990. 18th International Mexico City Marathon.
1971 **783** 700p. black, red & green 60 35

784 Facade

1990. 50th Anniv of Colima University.
1972 **784** 700p. multicoloured 60 35

785 Abstract

1990. Mexico City Consultative Council.
1973 **785** 700p. multicoloured 80 45

786 Electricity Worker

1990. 30th Anniv of Nationalization of Electricity Industry.
1974 **786** 700p. multicoloured 60 35

787 Violin and Bow

1990. 50th Death Anniv of Silvestre Revueltas (violinist).
1975 **787** 700p. multicoloured 60 35

788 Building

1990. 450th Anniv of Campeche.
1976 **788** 700p. multicoloured 60 35

789 Crossed Rifle and Pen

1990. 80th Anniv of San Luis Plan.
1977 **789** 700p. multicoloured 60 35

790 Emblem

1990. 14th World Supreme Councils Conference.
1978 **790** 1500p. multicoloured 1·40 85

791 Spanish Tower and Mexican
Pyramid

1990. 500th Anniv of "Meeting of Two Worlds" (4th issue).
1979 **791** 700p. multicoloured 60 35

792 Glass of
Beer, Ear of
Barley and
Hop

1990. Centenary of Brewing Industry.
1980 **792** 700p. multicoloured 60 35

793 Carving

1990. Bicentenary of Archaeology in Mexico.
1981 **793** 1500p. multicoloured 1·50 85

794 Ball-game Field

1990. 16th Central American and Caribbean Games.
Multicoloured.
1982 750p. Type **794** 1·10 40
1983 750p. Amerindian ball-game
player 1·10 40
1984 750p. Amerindian ball-game
player (different) (horiz) 1·10 40
1985 750p. Yutsil and Balam (mascots) (horiz) 1·10 40

795 Globe and
Poinsettia

1990. Christmas. Multicoloured.
1986 700p. Type **795** 60 40
1987 700p. Fireworks and candles 60 40

796 Dog (statuette)

1990. 50th Anniv of Mexican Canine Federation.
1988 **796** 700p. multicoloured 85 40

797 Microscope, Dolphin
and Hand holding Map

1991. 50th Anniv of Naval Secretariat.
1989 **797** 1000p. gold, black
& blue 85 50

798 Means of Transport

1991. Accident Prevention.
1990 **798** 700p. multicoloured 70 45

799 Products
in Bags

1991. 15th Anniv of National Consumer Institute.
1991 **799** 1000p. multicoloured 1·00 60

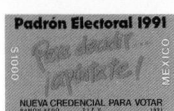

800 "In order to Decide, Register"

1991. Electoral Register.
1992 **800** 1000p. orange, grn & blk 1·00 60

801 Basketball Player

1991. Olympic Games, Barcelona (1992) (1st issue).
1993 **801** 1000p. black and yellow 1·00 60
   See also Nos. 2050, 2057 and 2080/9.

802 Flowers and Caravel

1991. America (1990). Natural World. Mult.
1994 **802** Type **802** 90 40
1995 700p. Right half of caravel, blue and yellow macaw and flowers 90 40
   Nos. 1994/5 were issued together, se-tenant, forming a composite design.

803 Children in Droplet

1991. Children's Month. Vaccination Campaign.
1996 **803** 1000p. multicoloured 1·00 60

804 Map

1991. World Post Day (1990).
1997 **804** 1500p. multicoloured 1·40 85

805 Dove and Children

1991. Children's Days for Peace and Development.
1998 **805** 1000p. multicoloured 1·00 60

806 Dove

1991. Family Health and Unity.
1999 **806** 1000p. multicoloured 1·00 60

807 Mining

1991. 500th Anniv of Mining.
2000 **807** 1000p. multicoloured 1·00 60

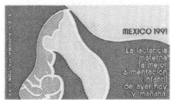

808 Mother feeding Baby

1991. Breastfeeding Campaign.
2001 **808** 1000p. buff, blue & brn 1·00 60

809 Emblem

1991. 16th Tourism Fair, Acapulco.
2002 **809** 1000p. green & dp green 1·10 65

810 Rotary Emblem and Independence Monument, Mexico City

1991. Rotary International Convention. "Let us Preserve the Planet Earth".
2003 **810** 1000p. gold and blue 1·10 65

811 "Communication"

1991. Centenary of Ministry of Transport and Communications (S.C.T.). Multicoloured.
2004 **811** Type **811** 1·20 65
2005 1000p. Boeing 737 landing 1·20 65
2006 1000p. Facsimile machine 1·40 65
2007 1000p. Van 1·40 65
2008 1000p. Satellites and Earth 1·40 65
2009 1000p. Railway freight wagons on bridge 1·40 65
2010 1000p. Telephone users 1·40 65
2011 1000p. Road bridge over road 1·40 65
2012 1000p. Road bridge and cliffs 1·40 65
2013 1000p. Stern of container ship and dockyard 1·40 65
2014 1000p. Television camera and presenter 1·40 65
2015 1000p. Front of truck at toll gate 1·40 65
2016 1000p. Roadbuilding ("Solidarity") 1·40 65
2017 1500p. Boeing 737 and control tower 1·60 80
2018 1500p. Part of fax machine, transmitters and dish aerials on S.C.T. building 1·60 80
2019 1500p. Satellite (horiz) 1·60 80
2020 1500p. Diesel and electric trains 1·60 80
2021 1500p. S.C.T. building 1·60 80
2022 1500p. Road bridge over ravine 1·60 80
2023 1500p. Bow of container ship and dockyard 1·60 80
2024 1500p. Bus at toll gate 1·60 80
2025 1500p. Rear of truck and trailer at toll gate 1·60 80
   Nos. 2005/25 were issued together, se-tenant, each block containing several composite designs.

812 Jaguar

1991. Lacandona Jungle Conservation.
2026 **812** 1000p. black, orge & red 1·50 80

813 Driver and Car

1991. Mexico Formula 1 Grand Prix.
2027 **813** 1000p. multicoloured 1·10 60

814 Emblem and Left-hand Sections of Sun and Earth

1991. Total Eclipse of the Sun. Multicoloured.
2028 1000p. Type **814** 1·70 1·10
2029 1000p. Emblem and right-hand sections of sun and Earth 1·70 1·10
2030 1500p. Emblem and centre of sun and Earth showing north and central America 1·70 1·10
   Nos. 2028/30 were issued together, se-tenant, forming a composite design.

815 "Solidarity" (Rufino Tamayo)

1991. 1st Latin American Presidential Summit, Guadalajara.
2031 **815** 1500p. black, orge & yell 1·40 85

816 Bridge

1991. Solidarity between Nuevo Leon and Texas.
2032 **816** 2000p. multicoloured 2·00 1·30

817 Runners

1991. 9th Mexico City Marathon.
2033 **817** 1000p. multicoloured 1·00 55

818 Cogwheel

1991. 50th Anniv (1990) of National Chambers of Industry and Commerce.
2034 **818** 1500p. multicoloured 1·30 75

819 Emblem

1991. 55th Anniv of Federation Fiscal Tribunal.
2035 **819** 1000p. silver and blue 1·10 65

820 National Colours forming Emblem

1991. "Solidarity—Let us Unite in order to Progress".
2036 **820** 1000p. multicoloured 1·00 55

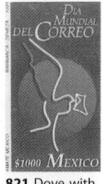

821 Dove with Letter

1991. World Post Day.
2037 **821** 1000p. multicoloured 1·00 55

822 World Map

1991. 500th Anniv of "Meeting of Two Worlds" (5th issue).
2038 **822** 1000p. multicoloured 1·80 80

823 Caravel, Sun and Trees

1991. America. Voyages of Discovery. Mult.
2039 1000p. Type **823** 1·20 65
2040 1000p. Storm cloud, caravel and broken snake 1·20 65

824 Flowers and Pots

1991. Christmas. Multicoloured.
2041 1000p. Type **824** 1·00 55
2042 1000p. Children with decoration 1·00 55

825 Abstract

1991. Carlos Merida (artist) Commemoration.
2043 **825** 1000p. multicoloured 1·10 65

826 Score and Portrait

1991. Death Bicentenary of Wolfgang Amadeus Mozart (composer).
2044 **826** 1000p. multicoloured 1·00 55

827 Kidney Beans and Maize

1991. Self-sufficiency in Kidney Beans and Maize.
2045 **827** 1000p. multicoloured 95 55

828 City Plan

1991. 450th Anniv of Morelia.
2046 **828** 1000p. brown, stone and red 1·00 60

1991. "Solidarity". As No. 1967 but new value.
2047 **779** 1000p. multicoloured 1·00 55

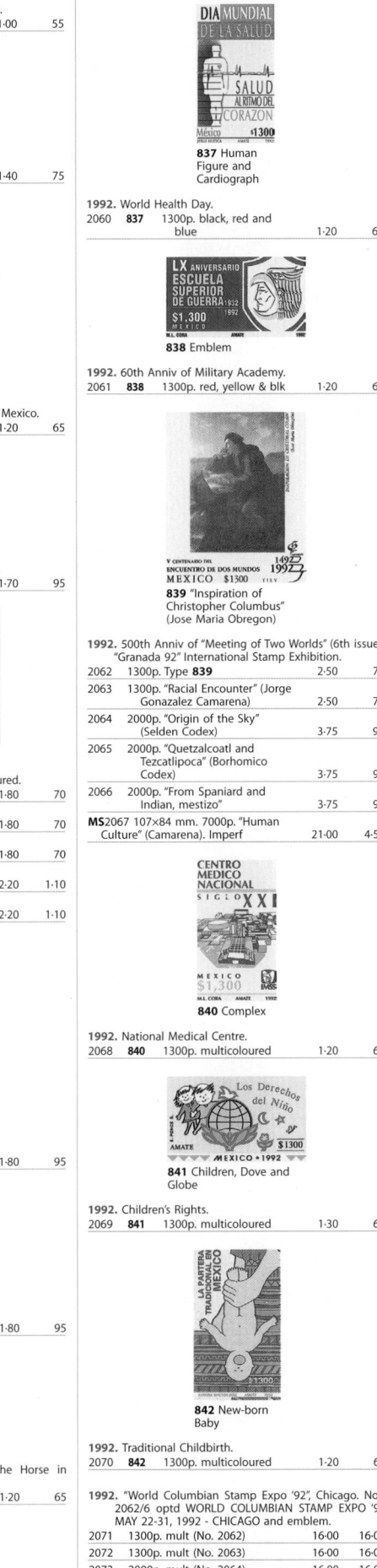

829 Merida

1992. 450th Anniv of Merida.
2048 **829** 1300p. multicoloured 1·40 75

830 Colonnade

1992. Bicentenary of Engineering Training in Mexico.
2049 **830** 1300p. blue and red 1·20 65

831 Horse Rider

1992. Olympic Games, Barcelona (2nd issue).
2050 **831** 2000p. multicoloured 1·70 95

832 City Arms

1992. 450th Anniv of Guadalajara. Multicoloured.
2051 1300p. Type **832** 1·80 70
2052 1300p. "Guadalajara Town Hall" (Jorge Navarro) 1·80 70
2053 1300p. "Guadalajara Cathedral" (Gabriel Flores) 1·80 70
2054 1900p. "Founding of Guadalajara" (Rafael Zamarripa) 2·20 1·10
2055 1900p. Anniversary emblem (Ignacio Vazquez) 2·20 1·10

833 Children and Height Gauge

1992. Child Health Campaign.
2056 **833** 2000p. multicoloured 1·80 95

834 Olympic Torch and Rings

1992. Olympic Games, Barcelona (3rd issue).
2057 **834** 2000p. multicoloured 1·80 95

835 Horse and Racing Car

1992. "500th Anniv of the Wheel and the Horse in America". Mexico Formula 1 Grand Prix.
2058 **835** 2000p. multicoloured 1·20 65

836 Satellite and Map of Americas

1992. "Americas Telecom '92" Telecommunications Exhibition.
2059 **836** 1300p. multicoloured 1·20 65

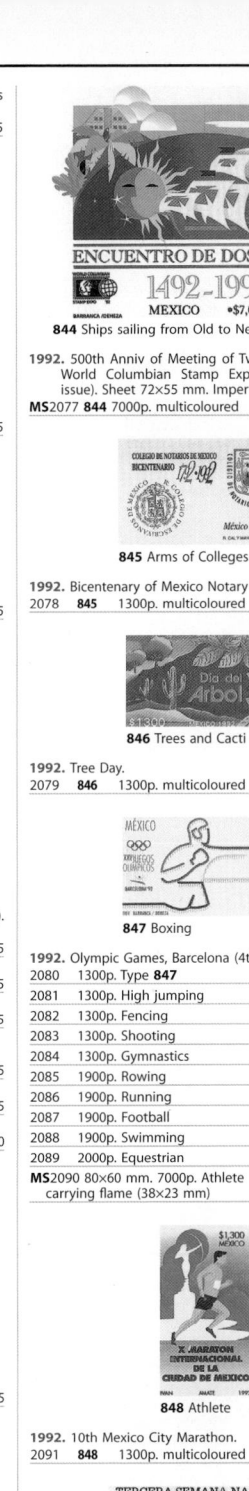

837 Human Figure and Cardiograph

1992. World Health Day.
2060 **837** 1300p. black, red and blue 1·20 65

838 Emblem

1992. 60th Anniv of Military Academy.
2061 **838** 1300p. red, yellow & blk 1·20 65

839 "Inspiration of Christopher Columbus" (Jose Maria Obregon)

1992. 500th Anniv of "Meeting of Two Worlds" (6th issue). "Granada 92" International Stamp Exhibition.
2062 1300p. Type **839** 2·50 75
2063 1300p. "Racial Encounter" (Jorge Gonazalez Camarena) 2·50 75
2064 2000p. "Origin of the Sky" (Selden Codex) 3·75 95
2065 2000p. "Quetzalcoatl and Tezcatlipoca" (Borhomico Codex) 3·75 95
2066 2000p. "From Spaniard and Indian, mestizo" 3·75 95
MS2067 107×84 mm. 7000p. "Human Culture" (Camarena). Imperf 21·00 4·50

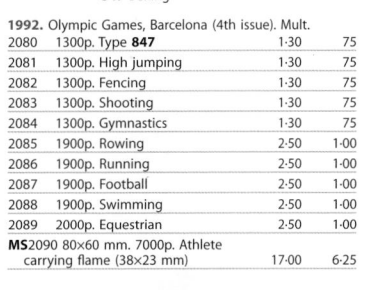

840 Complex

1992. National Medical Centre.
2068 **840** 1300p. multicoloured 1·20 65

841 Children, Dove and Globe

1992. Children's Rights.
2069 **841** 1300p. multicoloured 1·30 65

842 New-born Baby

1992. Traditional Childbirth.
2070 **842** 1300p. multicoloured 1·20 65

1992. "World Columbian Stamp Expo '92", Chicago. Nos. 2062/6 optd WORLD COLUMBIAN STAMP EXPO '92 MAY 22-31, 1992 - CHICAGO and emblem.
2071 1300p. mult (No. 2062) 16·00 16·00
2072 1300p. mult (No. 2063) 16·00 16·00
2073 2000p. mult (No. 2064) 16·00 16·00
2074 2000p. mult (No. 2065) 16·00 16·00
2075 2000p. mult (No. 2066) 16·00 16·00
MS2076 7000p. multicoloured 85·00 85·00

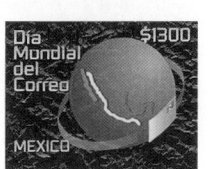

844 Ships sailing from Old to New World

1992. 500th Anniv of Meeting of Two Worlds (7th issue). World Columbian Stamp Expo 92, Chicago (2nd issue). Sheet 72×55 mm. Imperf.
MS2077 **844** 7000p. multicoloured 10·50 4·50

845 Arms of Colleges

1992. Bicentenary of Mexico Notary College.
2078 **845** 1300p. multicoloured 1·20 75

846 Trees and Cacti

1992. Tree Day.
2079 **846** 1300p. multicoloured 1·20 75

847 Boxing

1992. Olympic Games, Barcelona (4th issue). Mult.
2080 1300p. Type **847** 1·30 75
2081 1300p. High jumping 1·30 75
2082 1300p. Fencing 1·30 75
2083 1300p. Shooting 1·30 75
2084 1300p. Gymnastics 1·30 75
2085 1900p. Rowing 2·50 1·00
2086 1900p. Running 2·50 1·00
2087 1900p. Football 2·50 1·00
2088 1900p. Swimming 2·50 1·00
2089 2000p. Equestrian 2·50 1·00
MS2090 80×60 mm. 7000p. Athlete carrying flame (38×23 mm) 17·00 6·25

848 Athlete

1992. 10th Mexico City Marathon.
2091 **848** 1300p. multicoloured 1·20 65

849 Emblem

1992. "Solidarity".
2092 **849** 1300p. multicoloured 1·20 65

850 Stylized Ship and Globe

1992. Genova 92 International Thematic Stamp Exhibition. Sheet 81×60 mm.
MS2093 **850** 7000p. multicoloured 11·50 4·25

851 Television, Map and Radio

1992. 50th Anniv of National Chamber of Television and Radio Industry.
2094 **851** 1300p. multicoloured 1·20 65

852 Letter orbiting Globe

1992. World Post Day.
2095 **852** 1300p. multicoloured 1·20 65

853 Satellite above South and Central America and Flags

1992. American Cadena Communications System.
2096 **853** 2000p. multicoloured 2·30 1·30

854 Gold Compass Rose

1992. America. 500th Anniv of Discovery of America by Columbus. Multicoloured.
2097 2000p. Type **854** 2·30 1·30
2098 2000p. Compass rose (different) and fish 2·30 1·30
Nos. 2097/8 were issued together, se-tenant, forming a composite design.

855 Scroll

1992. 400th Anniv of San Luis Potosi.
2099 **855** 1300p. black and mauve 1·20 65

856 Berrendos Deer

1992. Conservation.
2100 **856** 1300p. multicoloured 1·80 65

857 Schooner, Landing Ship, Emblem and Sailors

1992. Navy Day.
2101 **857** 1300p. multicoloured 1·20 65

858 Christmas Tree, Children and Crib

1992. Christmas. Children's Drawings. Mult.
2102 1300p. Type **858** 1·20 65
2103 2000p. Street celebration (horiz) 2·40 1·00

859 Anniversary Emblem

1993. 50th Anniv of Mexican Social Security Institute (1st issue).

2104	**859**	1p.50 green, gold & blk	1·30	85

See also Nos. 2110 and 2152/3.

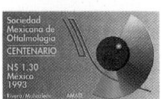

860 Emblem

1993. Centenary of Mexican Ophthalmological Society.

2105	**860**	1p.30 multicoloured	1·10	75

861 Children

1993. Children's Month.

2106	**861**	1p.30 multicoloured	1·10	75

862 Society Arms and Founders

1993. 160th Anniv of Mexican Geographical and Statistical Society.

2107	**862**	1p.30 multicoloured	1·10	75

863 1824 Constitution

1993. 150th Death Anniv of Miguel Ramos Arizpe, "Father of Federalism".

2108	**863**	1p.30 multicoloured	1·10	75

864 Gomez, Children and Hospital

1993. 50th Anniv of Federico Gomez Children's Hospital.

2109	**864**	1p.30 multicoloured	1·10	75

865 Doctor with Child

1993. 50th Anniv of Mexican Social Institute (2nd issue). Medical Services.

2110	**865**	1p.30 multicoloured	1·10	70

866 Mother feeding Baby

1993. "Health begins at Home".

2111	**866**	1p.30 multicoloured	1·10	75

867 Seal and Map

1993. Upper Gulf of California Nature Reserve.

2112	**867**	1p.30 multicoloured	1·10	75

868 Cantinflas

1993. Mexican Film Stars. Mario Moreno (Cantinflas).

2113	**868**	1p.30 black and blue	1·30	75

See also Nos. 2156/60.

869 Campeche

1993. Tourism. Value expressed as "NS". Mult.

2114	90c. Type **869**	1·10	50
2115	1p. Guanajuato	1·30	60
2263	1p.10 As No. 2115	1·40	35
2116	1p.30 Colima	1·50	75
2264	1p.80 As No. 2124	1·70	45
2265	1p.80 As No. 2118	1·20	55
2266	1p.80 As No. 2116	1·40	55
2267	1p.80 As Type **869**	1·50	55
2117	1p.90 Michoacan (vert)	2·40	1·10
2118	2p. Coahuila	2·30	1·10
2269	2p. As No. 2266	1·70	60
2119	2p.20 Queretaro	2·75	1·30
2272	2p.40 As No. 2123	2·20	60
2120	2p.50 Sonora	3·75	1·40
2274	2p.70 As No. 2122	3·50	80
2121	2p.80 Zacatecas (vert)	4·00	1·50
2276	3p. Type **869**	2·75	70
2278	3p.40 As No. 2271	3·75	90
2122	3p.70 Sinaloa	7·00	2·30
2280	3p.80 As No. 2272	2·40	95
2123	4p.40 Yucatan	6·25	2·40
2124	4p.80 Chiapas	6·50	2·50
2125	6p. Mexico City	7·75	3·25
2290	6p.80 As No. 2120	4·50	1·60

See also Nos. 2410/29.

870 Dr. Maximiliano Ruiz Castaneda

1993. 50th Anniv of Health Service. Multicoloured.

2126	1p.30 Type **870**	1·10	75
2127	1p.30 Dr. Bernardo Sepulveda Gutierrez	1·10	75
2128	1p.30 Dr. Ignacio Chavez Sanchez	1·10	75
2129	1p.30 Dr. Mario Salazar Mallen	1·10	75
2130	1p.30 Dr. Gustavo Baz Prada	1·10	75

871 Brazil 30r. "Bull's Eye" Stamp

1993. 150th Anniv of First Brazilian Stamps.

2131	**871**	2p. multicoloured	1·70	1·10

872 Runners

1993. 11th Mexico City Marathon.

2132	**872**	1p.30 multicoloured	1·10	75

873 Emblem

1993. "Solidarity".

2133	**873**	1p.30 multicoloured	1·10	75

874 Open Book and Symbols

1993. 50th Anniv of Monterrey Institute of Technology and Higher Education. Multicoloured.

2134	1p.30 Type **874**	1·10	75
2135	2p. Buildings and mountains	1·60	1·10

Nos. 2134/5 were issued together, se-tenant, forming a composite design.

875 Cogwheels and Emblem

1993. 75th Anniv of Concamin.

2136	**875**	1p.30 multicoloured	1·10	75

876 Torreon

1993. Centenary of Torreon.

2137	**876**	1p.30 multicoloured	1·10	75

877 Emblem

1993. "Europalia 93 Mexico" Festival.

2138	**877**	2p. multicoloured	1·70	1·10

878 Globe in Envelope

1993. World Post Day.

2139	**878**	2p. multicoloured	1·70	1·10

879 Gen. Guadalupe Victoria

1993. 150th Death Anniv of General Manuel Guadalupe Victoria (first President, 1824–28).

2140	**879**	1p.30 multicoloured	1·10	75

880 Emblem

1993. National Civil Protection System and International Day for Reduction of Natural Disasters.

2141	**880**	1p.30 red, black & yell	1·10	75

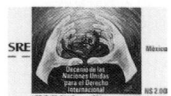

881 Hands protecting Foetus

1993. United Nations Decade of International Law.

2142	**881**	2p. multicoloured	1·70	1·10

882 Torch Carrier

1993. 20th National Wheelchair Games.

2143	**882**	1p.30 multicoloured	1·10	75

883 Peon y Contreras

1993. 150th Birth Anniv of Jose Peon y Contreras (poet, dramatist and founder of National Romantic Theatre).

2144	**883**	1p.30 violet and black	1·10	75

884 Horned Guan

1993. America. Endangered Birds. Multicoloured.

2145	2p. Type **884**	3·00	1·10
2146	2p. Resplendent quetzal on branch (horiz)	3·00	1·10

885 Presents around Trees

1993. Christmas. Multicoloured.

2147	1p.30 Type **885**	1·30	75
2148	1p.30 Three wise men (horiz)	1·30	75

886 Satellites orbiting Earth

1993. "Solidarity".

2149	**886**	1p.30 multicoloured	1·10	75

887 School and Arms

1993. 125th Anniv of National Preparatory School.

2150	**887**	1p.30 multicoloured	1·10	75

888 Emblem on Map

1993. 55th Anniv of Municipal Workers Trade Union.

2151	**888**	1p.30 multicoloured	1·10	75

889 Hands

1993. 50th Anniv of Mexican Social Security Institute (3rd issue). Multicoloured.

2152	1p.30 Type **889** (social security)	1·10	75
2153	1p.30 Ball, building blocks, child's painting and dummy (day nurseries)	1·10	75

890 Mezcala Solidarity
Bridge

1993. Tourism. Multicoloured.
2154	1p.30 Type **890**		1·10	75
2155	1p.30 Mexico City–Acapulco motorway		1·10	75

1993. Mexican Film Stars. As T 868.
2156	1p.30 black and blue		1·10	75
2157	1p.30 black and orange		1·10	75
2158	1p.30 black and green		1·10	75
2159	1p.30 black and violet		1·10	75
2160	1p.30 black and pink		1·10	75

DESIGNS:—No, 2156, Pedro Armendariz in "Juan Charrasqueado"; 2157, Maria Felix in "The Lover"; 2158, Pedro Infante in "Necesito dinero"; 2159, Jorge Negrete in "It is not enough to be a Peasant"; 2160, Dolores del Rio in "Flor Silvestre".

891 Estefania Castaneda
Nunez

1994. 72nd Anniv of Secretariat of Public Education. Educationists. Multicoloured.
2161	1p.30 Type **891**		1·20	75
2162	1p.30 Lauro Aguirre Espinosa		1·20	75
2163	1p.30 Rafael Ramirez Castaneda		1·20	75
2164	1p.30 Moises Saenz Garza		1·20	75
2165	1p.30 Gregorio Torres Quintero		1·20	75
2166	1p.30 Jose Vasconcelos		1·20	75
2167	1p.30 Rosaura Zapato Cano		1·20	75

892 Zapata (after H.
Velarde)

1994. 75th Death Anniv of Emiliano Zapata (revolutionary).
2168	**892**	1p.30 multicoloured	1·30	75

893 Emblem
and Worker

1994. 75th Anniv of I.L.O.
2169	**893**	2p. multicoloured	1·60	1·10

894 Map and Emblem

1994. 50th Anniv of National Schools Building Programme Committee.
2170	**894**	1p.30 multicoloured	1·10	75

895 "Earth and
Communication"
(frieze, detail)

1994. 3rd Death Anniv of Francisco Zuniga (sculptor).
2171	**895**	1p.30 multicoloured	1·20	75

896 Flower and Children

1994. Children's Organization for Peace and Development.
2172	**896**	1p.30 multicoloured	1·30	75

897 Greater Flamingo

1994. DUMAC Nature Protection Organization.
2173	**897**	1p.30 multicoloured	2·20	90

898 Children and
Silhouette of Absentee

1994. Care and Control of Minors.
2174	**898**	1p.30 black and green	1·30	75

899 Man and
Letters

1994. 34th World Advertising Congress, Cancun.
2175	**899**	2p. multicoloured	1·60	1·10

900 Route Map

1994. 50th Anniv of National Association of Importers and Exporters.
2176	**900**	1p.30 multicoloured	1·10	75

901 Head and Emblem

1994. International Telecommunications Day.
2177	**901**	2p. multicoloured	1·60	1·00

902 Animals

1994. Yumka Wildlife Centre, Villahermosa.
2178	**902**	1p.30 multicoloured	1·10	75

903 Town Centre

1994. UNESCO World Heritage Site, Zacatecas.
2179	**903**	1p.30 multicoloured	1·30	75

904 Mother
and Baby

1994. Friendship Hospital. Mother and Child Health Month.
2180	**904**	1p.30 multicoloured	1·30	75

1994. Prevention of Mental Retardation.
2181	**905**	1p.30 multicoloured	1·10	75

905 Foot and
Heart

1994. Nature Conservation. Multicoloured.
2182	1p.30 Type **906**		1·50	90
2183	1p.30 Game birds (silhouettes)		1·50	90
2184	1p.30 Threatened animals (silhouettes)		1·50	90
2185	1p.30 Animals in danger of extinction (silhouettes)		1·50	90
2186	1p.30 Orange-fronted conures		1·50	90
2187	1p.30 Yellow-tailed oriole		1·50	90
2188	1p.30 Pyrrhuloxias		1·50	90
2189	1p.30 Loggerhead shrike		1·50	90
2190	1p.30 Northern mockingbird		1·50	90
2191	1p.30 Common turkey		1·50	90
2192	1p.30 White-winged dove		1·50	90
2193	1p.30 Red-billed whistling duck		1·50	90
2194	1p.30 Snow goose		1·50	90
2195	1p.30 Gambel's quail		1·50	90
2196	1p.30 Peregrine falcon		1·50	90
2197	1p.30 Jaguar		1·50	90
2198	1p.30 Jaguarundi		1·50	90
2199	1p.30 Mantled howler monkey		1·50	90
2200	1p.30 Californian sealions		1·50	90
2201	1p.30 Pronghorn		1·50	90
2202	1p.30 Scarlet macaw		1·50	90
2203	1p.30 Mexican prairie dogs		1·50	90
2204	1p.30 Wolf		1·50	90
2205	1p.30 American manatee		1·50	90

907 Player

1994. World Cup Football Championship, U.S.A. Multicoloured.
2206	2p. Type **907**		1·70	1·10
2207	2p. Goalkeeper		1·70	1·10

Nos. 2206/7 were issued together, se-tenant, forming a composite design.

908 Fish

1994. International Fishing Festival, Veracruz.
2208	**908**	1p.30 multicoloured	1·10	75

909 Stylized
Figure and
Emblem

1994. 25th Anniv of Juvenile Integration Centres.
2209	**909**	1p.30 multicoloured	1·00	70

910 "Butterflies" (Carmen
Parra)

1994. 50th Anniv of Diplomatic Relations with Canada.
2210	**910**	2p. multicoloured	1·90	1·10

911 Emblems

1994. 20th Anniv of National Population Council.
2211	**911**	1p.30 multicoloured	1·00	70

912 Emblem
and Family

1994. International Year of the Family.
2212	**912**	2p. multicoloured	1·90	95

913 Runner
breasting Tape

1994. 12th Mexico City International Marathon.
2213	**913**	1p.30 multicoloured	1·20	70

914 Giant
Panda

1994. Chapultepec Zoo.
2214	**914**	1p.30 multicoloured	1·70	75

915 Tree

1994. Tree Day.
2215	**915**	1p.30 brown and green	1·00	70

916
Anniversary
Emblem

1994. 60th Anniv of Economic Culture Fund.
2216	**916**	1p.30 multicoloured	1·00	70

917 Statue and
Light Rail
Transit Train

1994. 25th Anniv of Mexico City Transport System.
2217	**917**	1p.30 multicoloured	1·00	70

918 Cathedral and
Gardens

1994. 350th Anniv of Salvatierra City, Guanajuato.
2218	**918**	1p.30 purple, grey and black	1·00	70

919 State Flag and National Anthem

1994. National Symbols Week.
2219 **919** 1p.30 multicoloured   1·20   70

920 Building and Anniversary Emblem

1994. 40th Anniv of University City.
2220 **920** 1p.30 multicoloured   1·00   70

921 Figures with Flags

1994. 5th Solidarity Week.
2221 **921** 1p.30 black, red and
green   1·00   70

922 Lopez Mateos

1994. 25th Death Anniv of Adolfo Lopez Mateos (President, 1958–64).
2222 **922** 1p.30 multicoloured   1·00   70

923 Palace Facade

1994. 60th Anniv of Palace of Fine Arts.
2223 **923** 1p.30 black and grey   1·20   70

924 Rings and "100"

1994. Centenary of International Olympic Committee.
2224 **924** 2p. multicoloured   2·40   95

925 Quarter Horse (Juan Rayas)

1994. Horses. Paintings by artists named. Multicoloured.
2225   1p.30 Aztec horse (Heladio
Velarde)   1·50   1·00
2226   1p.30 Type **925**   1·50   1·00
2227   1p.30 Quarter horse (Rayas)
(different)   1·50   1·00
2228   1p.30 Vaquero on horseback
(Velarde)   1·50   1·00
2229   1p.30 Aztec horse (Velarde)   1·50   1·00
2230   1p.30 Rider with lance (Velarde)   1·50   1·00

926 Emblem

1994. Inauguration of 20 November National Medical Centre.
2231 **926** 1p.30 multicoloured   1·00   70

927 Saint-Exupery and The Little Prince (book character)

1994. 50th Death Anniv of Antoine de Saint-Exupery (pilot and writer).
2232 **927** 2p. multicoloured   1·90   95

928 Man writing Letters to Woman

1994. World Post Day.
2233 **928** 2p. multicoloured   1·60   95

929 Urban Postman on Bicycle

1994. America. Postal Transport. Multicoloured.
2234   2p. Type **929**   1·60   1·00
2235   2p. Rural postman on rail
tricycle   1·60   1·00
Nos. 2234/5 were issued together, se-tenant, forming a composite design.

930 Couple (Sofia Bassi)

1994. Ancestors' Day.
2236 **930** 1p.30 multicoloured   1·00   70

931 Water Drop and Hand

1994. National Clean Water Programme.
2237 **931** 1p.30 multicoloured   1·00   70

932 Dr. Mora

1994. Birth Bicentenary of Dr. Jose Maria Luis Mora (journalist and politician).
2238 **932** 1p.30 multicoloured   1·00   70

933 Theatre and Soler (actor)

1994. 15th Anniv of Fernando Soler Theatre, Saltillo, Coahuila.
2239 **933** 1p.30 multicoloured   1·00   70

934 Allegory of Flight

1994. 50th Anniv of I.C.A.O.
2240 **934** 2p. multicoloured   1·60   95

935 Museum's Central Pillar

1994. 30th Anniv of National Anthropological Museum.
2241 **935** 1p.30 multicoloured   1·00   70

936 Theatrical Masks

1994. 60th Anniv of National Association of Actors.
2242 **936** 1p.30 multicoloured   1·00   70

937 Allende

1994. 225th Birth Anniv of Ignacio Allende (independence hero).
2243 **937** 1p.30 multicoloured   1·00   70

938 Chapultepec Castle

1994. 50th Anniv of National History Museum.
2244 **938** 1p.30 multicoloured   1·20   70

939 Dome

1994. Centenary of Coahuila School.
2245 **939** 1p.30 multicoloured   1·00   70

940 Anniversary Emblem

1994. 40th Anniv of Pumas University Football Club.
2246 **940** 1p.30 blue and gold   1·00   70

941 Decorated Tree

1994. Christmas. Multicoloured.
2247   2p. Type **941**   1·50   95
2248   2p. Couple watching shooting
star (horiz)   1·50   95

942 Valley

1994. "Solidarity". Chalco Valley.
2249 **942** 1p.30 multicoloured   1·00   70

943 Ines de la Cruz (after Miguel de Cabrera)

1995. 300th Birth Anniv of Juana Ines de la Cruz (mystic poet).
2250 **943** 1p.80 multicoloured   1·20   60

944 X-Ray of Hand and Rontgen

1995. Centenary of Discovery of X-Rays by Wilhelm Rontgen.
2251 **944** 2p. multicoloured   1·10   70

945 Ignacio Altamirano

1995. Teachers' Day.
2252 **945** 1p.80 black, green & bl   1·00   60

946 Emblem

1995. World Telecommunications Day. "Telecommunications and the Environment".
2253 **946** 2p.70 multicoloured   1·40   85

947 Anniversary Emblem

1995. 40th Anniv of National Institute of Public Administration.
2254 **947** 1p.80 green, mve & lilac   1·00   60

948 Marti

1995. Death Centenary of Jose Marti (Cuban writer and revolutionary).
2255 **948** 2p.70 multicoloured   1·40   85

949 Carranza

1995. 75th Death Anniv of Venustiano Carranza (President 1914–20).
2256 **949** 1p.80 multicoloured   1·00   60

950 Kite

1995. 20th Anniv of National Tourist Organization.
2257	**950**	2p.70 multicoloured	1·50	85

951 Drugs, Skull and Unhappy Face

1995. International Day against Drug Abuse and Trafficking. Multicoloured.
2258	1p.80 Type **951**	1·00	60
2259	1p.80 Drug addict on swing	1·00	60
2260	1p.80 Faces behind bars	1·00	60

952 Cardenas del Rio

1995. Birth Centenary of Gen. Lazaro Cardenas del Rio (President 1934–40).
2261	**952**	1p.80 black	1·00	60

953 Man with White Stick and Hand reading Braille

1995. 125th Anniv of National Blind School. Mult.
2262	**953**	1p.30 brown and black	1·00	50

954 Northern Pintails

1995. Animals. Multicoloured.
2295	2p.70 Type **954**	1·80	1·20
2296	2p.70 Belted kingfisher	1·80	1·20
2297	2p.70 Orange tiger	1·80	1·20
2298	2p.70 Hoary bat	1·80	1·20

955 Runners

1995. 13th International Marathon, Mexico City.
2299	**955**	2p.70 multicoloured	1·40	85

956 Envelopes

1995. 16th Congress of Postal Union of the Americas, Spain and Portugal, Mexico City.
2300	**956**	2p.70 multicoloured	1·30	85

957 Pasteur

1995. Death Centenary of Louis Pasteur (chemist).
2301	**957**	2p.70 blue, black and green	1·30	85

958 Hands holding Envelopes

1995. World Post Day.
2302	**958**	2p.70 multicoloured	1·20	80

959 Basket of Shopping

1995. World Food Day.
2303	**959**	1p.80 multicoloured	1·10	70

960 Anniversary Emblem

1995. 50th Anniv of F.A.O.
2304	**960**	2p.70 multicoloured	1·20	80

961 Elias Calles

1995. 50th Death Anniv of General Plutarco Elias Calles (President 1924–28).
2305	**961**	1p.80 multicoloured	1·10	70

962 Cuauhtemoc

1995. 500th Birth Anniv of Cuauhtemoc (Aztec Emperor of Tenochtitlan).
2306	**962**	1p.80 multicoloured	1·10	70

963 National Flag, National Anthem and Constitution

1995. National Constitution and Patriotic Symbols Day.
2307	**963**	1p.80 multicoloured	1·10	70

964 Flags as Tail of Dove

1995. 50th Anniv of U.N.O.
2308	**964**	2p.70 multicoloured	1·20	80

965 Airplane, Streamlined Train and Motor Vehicle

1995. International Passenger Travel Year.
2309	**965**	2p.70 multicoloured	1·20	85

966 "The Holy Family" (Andres de Concha)

1995. 30th Anniv of Museum of Mexican Art in the Vice-regency Period.
2310	**966**	1p.80 multicoloured	1·10	60

967 Pedro Maria Anaya

1995. Generals in Mexican History. Each black, yellow and gold.
2311	1p.80 Type **967**	90	60
2312	1p.80 Felipe Berriozabal	90	60
2313	1p.80 Santos Degollado	90	60
2314	1p.80 Sostenes Rocha	90	60
2315	1p.80 Leandro Valle	90	60
2316	1p.80 Ignacio Zaragoza	90	60

968 Children playing in Garden (Pablo Osorio Gomez)

1995. Christmas. Children's Drawings. Multicoloured.
2317	1p.80 Type **968**	80	60
2318	2p.70 Adoration of the Wise Men (Oscar Enrique Carrillo)	1·30	85

969 Emblem

1995. 10th Anniv of Mexican Health Foundation.
2319	**969**	1p.80 multicoloured	1·10	70

970 Ocelot

1995. Nature Conservation.
2320	**970**	1p.80 multicoloured	1·70	70

971 Louis Lumiere and Cine-camera

1995. Centenary of Motion Pictures.
2321	**971**	1p.80 black, mauve and blue	1·10	70

972 Library

1995. National Education Library, Mexico City.
2322	**972**	1p.80 green, blue and yellow	1·10	70

973 "Proportions of Man" (Leonardo da Vinci)

1995. 50th Anniv of National Science and Arts Prize.
2323	**973**	1p.80 multicoloured	1·10	70

974 Pedro Vargas

1995. Radio Personalities. Multicoloured.
2324	1p.80 Type **974**	1·30	80
2325	1p.80 Agustin Lara	1·30	80
2326	1p.80 Aguila Sisters	1·30	80
2327	1p.80 Tona "La Negra"	1·30	80
2328	1p.80 F. Gabilondo Soler "Cri-Cri"	1·30	80
2329	1p.80 Emilio Teuro	1·30	80
2330	1p.80 Gonzalo Curiel	1·30	80
2331	1p.80 Lola Beltran	1·30	80

975 Robot Hand holding Optic Fibres

1995. 25th Anniv of Science and Technology Council.
2332	**975**	1p.80 multicoloured	1·10	70

976 Boeing 727 and Standard JR biplane

1996. National Aviation Day. Multicoloured.
2333	1p.80 Type **976**	1·10	70
2334	1p.80 Republic P-47 Thunder-bolt. 201 Squadron, 1945	1·10	70
2335	2p.70 Ley Airport and Boeing 727	1·70	1·00
2336	2p.70 Grumman Gulfstream IV (Type 976)	1·70	1·00

977 Child and Caso

1996. Birth Centenary of Dr. Alfonso Caso (anthropologist).
2337	**977**	1p.80 multicoloured	1·10	70

978 Silverio Perez, Carlos Arruza and Manolo Martinez

1996. 50th Anniv of Plaza Mexico (bullring). Matadors. Multicoloured.
2338	1p.80 Type **978**	1·00	70
2339	2p.70 Roldolfo Gaona, Fermin Espinosa and Lorenzo Garza	1·60	1·00

Nos. 2338/9 were issued together, se-tenant, forming a composite design of the bullring.

979 Bag of Groceries

1996. 20th Anniv of Federal Consumer Council.
2340	**979**	1p.80 multicoloured	1·10	70

980 "Treatment of Fracture" (from Sahagun Codex)

1996. 50th Anniv of Mexican Society of Orthopaedics.
2341 **980** 1p.80 multicoloured ... 1·10 ... 70

981 Rulfo

1996. 10th Death Anniv of Juan Rulfo (writer).
2342 **981** 1p.80 multicoloured ... 1·10 ... 70

982 Anniversary Emblem and Map of Mexico

1996. 60th Anniv of National Polytechnic Institute.
2343 **982** 1p.80 grey, black and red ... 1·00 ... 65

983 Healthy Hand reaching for Sick Hand

1996. United Nations Decade against the Abuse and Illicit Trafficking of Drugs. Multicoloured.
2344 1p.80 Type **983** ... 1·20 ... 80
2345 1p.80 Man helping addict out of dark hole ... 1·20 ... 80
2346 2p.70 Stylized figures ... 1·90 ... 1·20

984 Gymnastics

1996. Olympic Games, Atlanta, U.S.A. Multicoloured.
2347 1p.80 Type **984** ... 1·10 ... 75
2348 1p.80 Hurdling ... 1·10 ... 75
2349 2p.70 Football ... 1·50 ... 95
2350 2p.70 Running ... 1·50 ... 95
2351 2p.70 Show jumping ... 1·50 ... 95

985 Cameraman and Film Frames of Couples

1996. Centenary of Mexican Films. Multicoloured.
2352 1p.80 Type **985** ... 60 ... 40
2353 1p.80 Camera and film frames of individuals ... 60 ... 40

986 Scales

1996. 60th Anniv of Fiscal Tribunal.
2354 **986** 1p.80 multicoloured ... 1·00 ... 60

987 Runners' Feet

1996. 14th Mexico City International Marathon.
2355 **987** 2p.70 multicoloured ... 1·10 ... 65

988 Flask, Open Books, Atomic Model and Microscope

1996. Science.
2356 **988** 1p.80 multicoloured ... 1·10 ... 60

989 "Allegory of Foundation of Zacatecas" (anon)

1996. 450th Anniv of Zacatecas.
2357 **989** 1p.80 multicoloured ... 1·10 ... 60

990 Rural Education

1996. 25th Anniv of National Council for the Improvement of Education.
2358 **990** 1p.80 multicoloured ... 1·10 ... 60

991 "The Foundation of Monterrey" (Crescencio Garza)

1996. 400th Anniv of Monterrey. Sheet 100×72 mm.
MS2359 **991** 7p.40 multicoloured ... 4·50 ... 4·50

992 Emblem

1996. Family Planning Month.
2360 **992** 1p.80 green, mauve and blue ... 1·10 ... 60

993 Flag of the "Three Guarantees", 1821

1996. 175th Anniv of Declaration of Independence.
2361 **993** 1p.80 multicoloured ... 1·10 ... 60

994 Blue Morpho, Monkey, Harpy Eagle and other Birds

1996. Nature Conservation. Multicoloured.
2362 1p.80 Type **994** ... 85 ... 55
2363 1p.80 Turtle dove, yellow grosbeak with chicks in nest, trogon and hummingbird ... 85 ... 55
2364 1p.80 Mountains, monarchs (butterflies) in air and American black bear with cub ... 85 ... 55
2365 1p.80 Fishing buzzard, mule deer, lupins and monarchs (butterflies) on plant ... 85 ... 55
2366 1p.80 Scarlet macaws, monarchs, toucan, peafowl and spider monkey hanging from tree ... 85 ... 55
2367 1p.80 Resplendent quetzal, emerald toucanet, bromeliads and tiger-cat ... 85 ... 55
2368 1p.80 Parrots, white-tailed deer and rabbit by river ... 85 ... 55
2369 1p.80 Snake, wolf, puma and lizard on rock and blue-capped bird ... 85 ... 55
2370 1p.80 Coyote, prairie dogs at burrow, quail on branch, deer, horned viper and caracara on cactus ... 85 ... 55
2371 1p.80 Jaguar, euphonias, long-tailed bird, crested bird and bat ... 85 ... 55

2372 1p.80 "Martucha", peacock, porcupine, butterfly and green snake ... 85 ... 55
2373 1p.80 Blue magpie, green-headed bird, owl, woodpecker and hummingbird by river ... 85 ... 55
2374 1p.80 Cinnamon cuckoo in tree, fox by river and green macaws in tree ... 85 ... 55
2375 1p.80 Wild sheep by rocks, bird on ocotillo plant, bats, owl, lynx and woodpecker on cactus ... 85 ... 55
2376 1p.80 Ant-eater climbing sloping tree, jaguarundi, bat, orchid and ocellated turkey in undergrowth ... 85 ... 55
2377 1p.80 Ocelot, "grison", coral snake, "temazate", paca and otter by river ... 85 ... 55
2378 1p.80 Grey squirrel in tree, salamander, beaver, bird, shrew-mole, mountain hen and racoon by river ... 85 ... 55
2379 1p.80 Butterfly, trogon in red tree, "chachalaca", crested magpie and "tejon" ... 85 ... 55
2380 1p.80 Bat, "tlalcoyote", "rata neotoma", "chichimoco", hare, cardinal (bird), lizard, kangaroo rat and tortoise ... 85 ... 55
2381 1p.80 Beetle on leaf, tapir, tree frog and "tunpache" ... 85 ... 55
2382 1p.80 Crocodile, insect, cup fungus, boa constrictor and butterfly ... 85 ... 55
2383 1p.80 Armadillo, "tlacuache", iguana, turkey and butterfly ... 85 ... 55
2384 1p.80 Turkey, collared peccary, zorilla, lizard, rattlesnake and mouse ... 85 ... 55
2385 1p.80 Cacomistle, "matraca", lark, collared lizard and cacti ... 85 ... 55

Nos. 2362/85 were issued together, se-tenant, forming a composite design of habitats and wildlife under threat.

995 Bird with Letter in Beak

1996. World Post Day.
2386 **995** 2p.70 multicoloured ... 1·30 ... 60

996 Institute

1996. 50th Anniv of Salvador Zubiran National Nutrition Institute.
2387 **996** 1p.80 multicoloured ... 1·20 ... 70

997 Constantino de Tarnava

1996. 75th Anniv of Radio Broadcasting in Mexico.
2388 **997** 1p.80 multicoloured ... 1·20 ... 70

998 "Portrait of a Woman" (Baltasar de Echave Ibia)

1996. Virreinal Art Gallery. Multicoloured.
2389 1p.80 Type **998** ... 1·20 ... 40
2390 1p.80 "Portrait of the Child Joaquin Manuel Fernandez de Santa Cruz" (Nicolas Rodriguez Xuarez) ... 1·20 ... 40
2391 1p.80 "Portrait of Dona Maria Luisa Gonzaga Foncerrada y Labarrieta" (Jose Maria Vazquez) ... 1·20 ... 40
2392 1p.80 "Archangel Michael" (Luis Juarez) ... 1·50 ... 60

2393 2p.70 "Virgin of the Apocalypse" (Miguel Cabrera) ... 1·50 ... 60

999 Isidro Fabela and Genaro Estrada

1996. "Precursors of Foreign Policy".
2394 **999** 1p.80 multicoloured ... 1·20 ... 60

1000 Maize

1996. World Food Day.
2395 **1000** 2p.70 multicoloured ... 1·20 ... 70

1001 Underground Train around Globe

1996. International Metros Conference.
2396 **1001** 2p.70 multicoloured ... 1·10 ... 70

1002 Star (Elias Martin del Campo)

1996. Christmas. Multicoloured.
2397 1p. Type **1002** ... 60 ... 40
2398 1p.80 Man with star-shaped bundles on stick (Ehecatl Cabrera Franco) (vert) ... 1·00 ... 65

1003 Henestrosa

1996. Andres Henestrosa (writer) Commemoration.
2399 **1003** 1p.80 multicoloured ... 1·20 ... 65

1004 Old and New Institute Buildings

1996. 50th Anniv of National Cancer Institute.
2400 **1004** 1p.80 multicoloured ... 1·20 ... 65

1005 Emblem

1996. Paisano Programme.
2401 **1005** 2p.70 multicoloured ... 1·20 ... 70

1006 Painting

1996. Birth Centenary of David Alfaro Siqueiros (painter).
2402 **1006** 1p.80 multicoloured ... 1·20 ... 65

1007 Dr. Jose Maria Barcelo de Villagran

1996. 32nd National Assembly of Surgeons.
2403 **1007** 1p.80 multicoloured ... 1·20 ... 65

1008 Black Bears

1996. Nature Conservation.
2404 **1008** 1p.80 multicoloured 1·70 90

1009 Smiling Sun

1996. 50th Anniv of UNICEF.
2405 **1009** 1p.80 multicoloured 1·20 65

1010 Library

1996. 350th Anniv of Palafoxiana Library, Puebla.
2406 **1010** 1p.80 multicoloured 1·20 65

1011 Sphere and Atomic Symbol

1996. National Institute for Nuclear Research.
2407 **1011** 1p.80 multicoloured 1·20 65

1012 Sun's Rays and Earth

1996. World Day for the Preservation of the Ozone Layer.
2408 **1012** 1p.80 multicoloured 1·20 65

1013 Sculpture

1996. 30 Years of Work by Sebastian (sculptor).
2409 **1013** 1p.80 multicoloured 1·20 65

1997. Tourism. As Nos. 2263 etc but with value expressed as "$".
2409a 50c. Coahuila 50 20
2409b 70c. Yucatan 65 20
2410 1p. Colima 75 20
2411 1p.80 Chiapas 90 20
2412 2p. Colima 90 25
2413 2p. Guanajuato 95 20
2413a 2p. Coahiula 80 25
2414 2p.30 Chiapas 1·10 30
2415 2p.50 Queretaro 1·10 35
2415a 2p.50 Yucatan 1·00 25
2416 2p.60 Colima 1·20 30
2417 2p.70 Mexico City 1·40 35
2418 3p. Type **869** 1·40 40
2418a 3p. Michoacan 1·10 40
2419 3p.10 Coahuila 1·80 35
2420 3p.40 Sinaloa 1·80 50
2421 3p.50 Mexico City 2·20 50
2421a 3p.60 Sonora 1·80 40
2421b 3p.60 Coahuila 1·40 40
2421c 3p.70 Campeche 1·90 40
2422 4p. Michoacan (vert) 2·10 50
2422a 4p.20 Guanajuato 1·90 45
2422b 4p.20 Zacatecas 1·50 45
2423 4p.40 Yucatan 2·10 50
2423a 4p.50 Mexico City 1·90 50

2424 4p.90 Sonora 2·20 55
2425 5p. Queretaro 2·75 70
2426 5p. Colima 2·50 45
2426a 5p.30 Michoacan (vert) 2·20 55
2426b 5p.90 Queretaro 2·50 55
2427 6p. Zacatacas (vert) 3·00 65
2427a 6p. Sinaloa 2·50 30
2427b 6p. Coahuila 2·50 60
2427c 6p.50 Sinaloa 3·50 65
2428 7p. Sonora 4·00 75
2428a 8p. Zacatecas (vert) 3·00 1·10
2428b 8p. Sinaloa 3·25 65
2429 8p.50 Mexico City 4·75 90
2430 8p.50 Zacatecas 3·50 80
2433 10p. Campeche 4·50 1·00
2433a 10p. Chiapas 4·00 1·00

1014 Pellicer (after D. Rivera)

1997. Birth Centenary of Carlos Pellicer (lyricist).
2435 **1014** 2p.30 multicoloured 1·20 70

1015 Eloy Blanco (after Oswaldo)

1997. Birth Centenary (1996) of Andres Eloy Blanco (poet).
2436 **1015** 3p.40 multicoloured 1·50 80

1016 Book, Inkwell and Pencil

1997. Confederation of American Educationalists' International Summit Conference.
2437 **1016** 3p.40 multicoloured 1·40 70

1017 Tree, Globe and Atomic Cloud

1997. 30th Anniv of Tlatelolco Treaty (Latin American and Caribbean treaty banning nuclear weapons).
2438 **1017** 3p.40 multicoloured 1·40 70

1018 Foyer

1997. 90th Anniv of Fifth Main Post Office. Sheet 100×72 mm.
MS2439 **1018** 7p.40 multicoloured 6·00 5·75

1019 Felipe Angeles

1997. Noted Generals. Multicoloured.
2440 2p.30 Type **1019** 95 55
2441 2p.30 Joaquin Amaro Dominguez 95 55
2442 2p.30 Mariano Escobedo 95 55
2443 2p.30 Jacinto Trevino Glez 95 55

2444 2p.30 Candido Aguilar Vargas 95 55
2445 2p.30 Francisco Urquizo 95 55

1020 Woman dancing

1997. International Women's Day.
2446 **1020** 2p.30 multicoloured 90 55

1021 "Grammar" (Juan Correa)

1997. 1st International Spanish Language Congress.
2447 **1021** 3p.40 multicoloured 1·60 1·00

1022 Chavez

1997. Birth Centenary of Dr. Ignacio Chavez.
2448 **1022** 2p.30 multicoloured 90 55

1023 State Emblem and Venustiano Carranza (President 1915–20)

1997. 80th Anniv of 1917 Constitution.
2449 **1023** 2p.30 multicoloured 90 55

1024 Yanez

1997. 50th Anniv of First Edition of "At the Water's Edge" by Agustin Yanez.
2450 **1024** 2p.30 multicoloured 90 55

1025 Mexican Mythological Figures (Luis Nishizawa)

1997. Centenary of Japanese Immigration.
2451 **1025** 3p.40 red, gold and black 1·90 1·00

1026 Rafael Ramirez

1997. Teachers' Day.
2452 **1026** 2p.30 green and black 90 55

1027 University

1997. 40th Anniv of Autonomous University of Lower California.
2453 **1027** 2p.30 multicoloured 90 55

1028 Dove flying Free

1997. International Day against Illegal Use and Illicit Trafficking of Drugs. Multicoloured.
2454 2p.30 Type **1028** 1·20 55
2455 3p.40 Dove imprisoned behind bars 1·60 80
2456 3p.40 Man opening cage 1·60 80
Nos. 2454/6 were issued together, se-tenant, forming a composite design.

1029 Freud

1997. 58th Death Anniv of Sigmund Freud (pioneer of psychoanalysis).
2457 **1029** 2p.30 blue, green and violet 90 50

1030 School Arms

1997. Centenary of Naval School.
2458 **1030** 2p.30 multicoloured 90 50

1031 Emblem

1997. Introduction of New Social Security Law.
2459 **1031** 2p.30 multicoloured 95 50

1032 Globes and Anniversary Emblem

1997. 60th Anniv of National Bank of Foreign Commerce.
2460 **1032** 3p.40 multicoloured 1·30 70

1033 Common Porpoises

1997. Nature Conservation.
2461 **1033** 2p.30 multicoloured 1·70 90

1034 Passenger Airliners, 1947 and 1997

1997. 50th Anniv of Mexican Air Pilots' College.
2462 **1034** 2p.30 multicoloured 90 50

1035 Runners

1997. 15th Mexico City Marathon.
2463 **1035** 3p.40 multicoloured 1·30 70

1036 Hospital Entrance

1997. 150th Anniv of Juarez Hospital.
2464 **1036** 2p.30 multicoloured 90 50

1037 Battle of Padierna

1997. 150th Anniversaries of Battles. Multicoloured.
2465 2p.30 Type **1037** 90 50
2466 2p.30 Battle of Churubusco 90 50
2467 2p.30 Battle of Molino del Rey 90 50
2468 2p.30 Defence of Chapultepec
Fort 90 50

1038 Prieto

1997. Death Centenary of Guillermo Prieto (writer).
2469 **1038** 2p.30 blue 90 50

1039 Commemorative
Cross

1997. 150th Anniv of Mexican St. Patrick's Battalion.
2470 **1039** 3p.40 multicoloured 1·90 1·10

1040 Emblem

1997. Adolescent Reproductive Health Month.
2471 **1040** 2p.30 multicoloured 95 50

1041 Bird
carrying Letter

1997. World Post Day. Multicoloured.
2472 3p.40 Type **1041** 1·30 70
2473 3p.40 Heinrich von Stephan
(founder of U.P.U.) (horiz) 1·30 70

1042 Gomez
Morin

1997. Birth Centenary of Manuel Gomez Morin
(politician).
2474 **1042** 2p.30 multicoloured 95 50

1043 Hospital

1997. 50th Anniv of Dr. Manuel Gea Gonzalez General
Hospital.
2475 **1043** 2p.30 multicoloured 95 50

1044 Emblem

1997. 75th Anniv of Mexican Bar College of Law.
2476 **1044** 2p.30 red and black 95 50

1045 Children celebrating
Christmas (Ana Botello)

1997. Christmas. Children's Paintings. Multicoloured.
2477 2p.30 Type **1045** 95 50
2478 2p.30 Children playing blind-
man's-buff (Adrian Laris) 95 50

1046 Emblem and Hospital
Facade

1997. Centenary of Central University Hospital,
Chihuahua.
2479 **1046** 2p.30 multicoloured 90 50

1047 Molina and Nobel
Medal

1997. Dr. Mario Molina (winner of Nobel Prize for
Chemistry, 1995).
2480 **1047** 3p.40 multicoloured 1·20 65

1048 Products and Storage
Shelves

1997. National Chamber of Baking Industry.
Multicoloured.
2481 2p.30 Type **1048** 90 55
2482 2p.30 Baker putting loaves
in oven 90 55
2483 2p.30 Wedding cake, ingredients and baker 90 55
Nos. 2481/3 were issued together, se-tenant, forming a
composite design.

1049 "Buildings"
(Jose Chavez
Morado)

1997. 25th Cervantes Festival, Guanajuato.
2484 **1049** 2p.30 multicoloured 85 50

1050 Galleon
and Map of
Loreto,
California

1997. 300th Anniv of Loreto.
2485 **1050** 2p.30 multicoloured 85 50

1051 Sword and Rifle

1998. 50th Anniv of Military Academy, Puebla.
2486 **1051** 2p.30 multicoloured 85 50

1052 Hands holding
Children on Heart

1998. International Women's Day.
2487 **1052** 2p.30 multicoloured 85 50

1053 Dancers
(5th of May
Festival)

1998. Festivals.
2488 **1053** 3p.50 multicoloured 1·20 70

1054 Eiffel Tower, Player
and Flag

1998. World Cup Football Championship, France.
Multicoloured.
2489 2p.30 Type **1054** 1·10 55
2490 2p.30 Mascot, Eiffel Tower
and flag 1·10 55
MS2491 118×202 mm. (a) 6p.20, As No.
2490 (23×40 mm); (b) 8p.60, As No.
2489 (23×40 mm) 8·75 7·75

1055 Sierra

1998. 150th Birth Anniv of Justo Sierra (educationist).
2492 **1055** 2p.30 multicoloured 85 50

1056 Zubiran

1998. Birth Centenary of Salvador Zubiran (physician).
2493 **1056** 2p.30 multicoloured 90 50

1057 Emblem

1998. 50th Anniv of Organization of American States.
2494 **1057** 3p.40 multicoloured 1·10 65

1058 University Emblem

1998. 25th Anniv of People's Autonomous University of
Puebla State.
2495 **1058** 2p.30 red, silver and
black 85 50

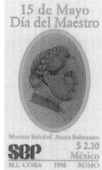

1059 Soledad
Anaya
Solorzano

1998. Teachers' Day.
2496 **1059** 2p.30 bistre, black and
cream 85 50

1060 Crops

1998. 250th Anniv of Tamaulipas (formerly New
Santander) (1st issue).
2497 **1060** 2p.30 multicoloured 85 50
See also Nos. 2548.

1061 Macuilxochitl

1998. 20th Anniv of Sports Lottery.
2498 **1061** 2p.30 multicoloured 85 50

1062 Manila Galleon

1998. Centenary of Philippine Independence.
2499 **1062** 3p.40 multicoloured 1·20 75
MS2500 99×70 mm. 7p.40 Motif as
in Type **1062** but with additional
Philippine flag 5·25 4·50

1063 Garcia Lorca

1998. Birth Centenary of Federico Garcia Lorca (poet).
2501 **1063** 3p.40 multicoloured 1·00 45

1064 Emblems

1998. 50th Anniv of Universal Declaration of Human
Rights.
2502 **1064** 3p.40 green and black 1·00 45

1065 Open
Book and Dove

1998. International Day against the Use and Illegal Trafficking of Drugs.
| 2503 | **1065** | 2p.30 multicoloured | 85 | 45 |

1066 Alfonso Herrera (founder) and Leopard

1998. 75th Anniv of Chapultepec Zoo.
| 2504 | **1066** | 2p.30 multicoloured | 85 | 45 |

1067 Tree

1998. Tree Day.
| 2505 | **1067** | 2p.30 multicoloured | 85 | 45 |

1068 St. Peter and St. Paul's Monastery, Teposcolula

1998. Inauguration of Philatelic Museum, Oaxaca. Multicoloured.
2506		2p.30 Type **1068**	1·30	75
2507		2p.30 Clay pot, San Bartolo Coyotepec	1·30	75
2508		2p.30 "The Road" (painting, Francisco Toledo)	2·10	1·20
2509		2p.30 Gold pectoral from Tomb 7, Monte Alban	2·10	1·20

1069 Juarez

1998. 126th Death Anniv of Benito Juarez (President 1859–64 and 1867–72).
| 2510 | **1069** | 2p.30 stone, black and brown | 85 | 45 |

1070 Cultural Museum

1998. St. Dominic's Cultural Centre, Oaxaca. Multicoloured.
2511		2p.30 Type **1070**	85	45
2512		2p.30 Francisco de Burgoa Library	85	45
2513		2p.30 Historical botanic garden	85	45
2514		3p.40 St. Dominic's Monastery (after Teodoro Velasco)	1·20	65

1071 Frigate Bird, Blue-footed Booby, Whales and Cacti

1998. Marine Life. Multicoloured.
2515		2p.30 Type **1071**	1·20	70
2516		2p.30 Albatross, humpback whale and seagulls	1·20	70
2517		2p.30 Tail of whale and swordfish	1·20	70
2518		2p.30 Fish eagle, flamingo, herons and dolphins	1·20	70
2519		2p.30 Turtles, flamingoes, cormorant and palm tree	1·20	70
2520		2p.30 Oystercatcher, turnstone, elephant seal and sealions	1·20	70
2521		2p.30 Dolphin, turtle, seagulls and swallows	1·20	70
2522		2p.30 Killer whale, dolphins and ray	1·20	70
2523		2p.30 Flamingoes, pelican, kingfishers and spider	1·20	70
2524		2p.30 Crocodile, roseate spoonbill and tiger heron	1·20	70
2525		2p.30 Schools of sardines and anchovies	1·20	70
2526		2p.30 Turtle, squid, gold-finned tunnyfish and shark	1·20	70
2527		2p.30 Jellyfish, dolphins and fishes	1·20	70
2528		2p.30 Dolphin (fish), barracudas and haddock	1·20	70
2529		2p.30 Manatee, fishes, anemone and coral	1·20	70
2530		2p.30 Seaweed, starfish, coral and fishes	1·20	70
2531		2p.30 Hammerhead shark, angelfish, gudgeon, eels and coral	1·20	70
2532		2p.30 Shrimps, ray and other fishes	1·20	70
2533		2p.30 Octopus, bass, crayfish and other fishes	1·20	70
2534		2p.30 Turtle, porcupinefish, coral, angelfish and other fishes	1·20	70
2535		2p.30 Abalone, clams, razor clam, crayfish and anemone	1·20	70
2536		2p.30 Seahorses, angelfishes, coral and shells	1·20	70
2537		2p.30 Octopus, turtle, crab and moray eel	1·20	70
2538		2p.30 Butterflyfishes and other fishes	1·20	70
2539		2p.30 Reef shark, angelfish and corals	1·20	70

Nos. 2515/39 were issued together, se-tenant, forming a composite design.

1072 Runners

1998. 16th International Marathon, Mexico City.
| 2540 | **1072** | 3p.40 multicoloured | 1·10 | 70 |

1073 Aztec Deity

1998. World Tourism Day.
| 2541 | **1073** | 3p.40 multicoloured | 1·10 | 70 |

1074 Lucas Alaman (founder)

1998. 175th Anniv of National Archives.
| 2542 | **1074** | 2p.30 green, red and black | 1·00 | 60 |

1075 Emblem

1998. 75th Anniv of Interpol.
| 2543 | **1075** | 3p.40 multicoloured | 1·10 | 70 |

1076 Stylized Couple

1998. Healthy Pregnancy Month.
| 2544 | **1076** | 2p.30 multicoloured | 70 | 45 |

1077 Painting by Luis Nishizawa

1998
| 2545 | **1077** | 2p.30 multicoloured | 70 | 45 |

1078 Key and Globe

1998. World Post Day.
| 2546 | **1078** | 3p.40 multicoloured | 1·10 | 70 |

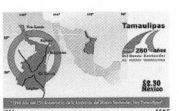

1079 College Campus

1998. 175th Anniv of Military College.
| 2547 | **1079** | 2p.30 multicoloured | 70 | 45 |

1080 Map

1998. 250th Anniv of Tamaulipas (formerly New Santander) (2nd issue).
| 2548 | **1080** | 2p.30 multicoloured | 70 | 45 |

1081 Golden Eagle

1998. Nature Conservation.
| 2549 | **1081** | 2p.30 multicoloured | 1·40 | 90 |

1082 Woman and Potatoes

1998. World Food Day.
| 2550 | **1082** | 3p.30 multicoloured | 1·10 | 70 |

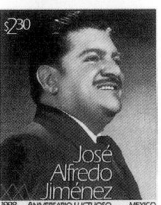

1083 Mexico arrowed on Globe

1998. National Migration Week.
| 2551 | **1083** | 2p.30 multicoloured | 70 | 45 |

1084 Jimenez

1998. 25th Death Anniv of Jose Alfredo Jimenez (writer).
| 2552 | **1084** | 2p.30 multicoloured | 70 | 45 |

1085 Oil Rig and Emblem

1998. 25th Anniv of Mexican Petroleum Engineers' Association.
| 2553 | **1085** | 3p.40 multicoloured | 1·10 | 70 |

1086 Mexican Stone Carving and Eiffel Tower

1998. Mexican–French Economic and Cultural Co-operation.
| 2554 | **1086** | 3p.40 multicoloured | 1·80 | 1·10 |

1087 Franciscan Monastery, Colima

1998. 475th Anniv of Colima.
| 2555 | **1087** | 2p.30 multicoloured | 70 | 45 |

1088 Wise Men approaching Stable

1998. Christmas. Multicoloured. Self-adhesive.
| 2556 | | 2p.30 Type **1088** | 70 | 45 |
| 2557 | | 3p.40 Decorations and pot (vert) | 1·10 | 70 |

1089 Woman with Baby

1998. 50th Anniv of National Institute of Indigenous Peoples.
| 2558 | **1089** | 2p.30 multicoloured | 70 | 45 |

1090 Eagle holding Statute

1998. 60th Anniv of Federation of Civil Servants' Trade Unions.
| 2559 | **1090** | 2p.30 multicoloured | 70 | 45 |

1091 Airplane and Aztec Bird-man

1998. 25th Anniv of Latin-American Civil Aviation Commission.
| 2560 | **1091** | 3p.40 multicoloured | 1·10 | 70 |

1092 University Arms

1998. 125th Anniv of Sinaloa Autonomous University.
| 2561 | **1092** | 2p.30 multicoloured | 70 | 45 |

1093 Pope John Paul II, Madonna and Map of the Americas

1999. Papal Visit. Sheet 101×73 mm.
| MS2562 | **1093** | 10p. multicoloured | 5·50 | 4·75 |

1094 "Satmex 5" and Earth

1999. Launch of "Satmex 5" Satellite.
| 2563 | **1094** | 3p. multicoloured | 95 | 45 |

1095 Maracas Player and Streamers

1999. Veracruz Carnival.
2564	**1095**	3p. multicoloured	95	45

1096 Couple in Hammock

1999. Bicentenary of Acapulco, Guerrero. Mult.
2565		3p. Type **1096**	90	45
2566		4p.20 Diving from cliff	1·20	55

Nos. 2565/6 were issued together, se-tenant, forming a composite design.

1097 Internet Website

1999. International Women's Day.
2567	**1097**	4p.20 multicoloured	1·30	55

1098 "Mexico" (Jorge Gonzalez Camarena)

1999. 40th Anniv of National Commission for Free Textbooks.
2568	**1098**	3p. multicoloured	1·00	45

1099 Family Members

1999. 25th Anniv of National Population Council.
2569	**1099**	3p. multicoloured	1·00	45

1100 Diaz fighting Bull

1999. Death Centenary of Ponciano Diaz (toreador). Sheet 95×240 mm.
MS2570	**1100**	10p. multicoloured	5·50	4·75

1101 Guadalupe Ceniceros de Perez

1999. Teachers' Day.
2571	**1101**	3p. multicoloured	95	45

1102 Pitcher

1999. 75th Anniv of Mexican Baseball League. Each black and grey.
2572		3p. Type **1102**	1·00	90
2573		3p. Catcher	1·00	90
2574		3p. Skeletal pitcher	1·00	90
2575		3p. Pitcher (different)	1·00	90

1103 10p. Banknote

1999. 115th Anniv of National Bank of Mexico. Multicoloured.
2576		3p. Type **1103**	1·00	65
2577		3p. Former and current head-quarters	1·00	65

1104 German Shepherd

1999. World Dog Show. Sheet 98×110 mm containing T 1104 and similar vert designs. Multicoloured.
MS2578		3p. Type **1104**; 3p. Rottweiler; 4p.20 Chihuahua; 4p.20 Xoloitzcuintle	7·25	6·75

1105 Couple holding Hands

1999. International Day against Illegal Use and Illicit Trafficking of Drugs.
2579	**1105**	4p.20 multicoloured	1·40	90

1106 Skyscraper

1999. 65th Anniv of National Financial Institute.
2580	**1106**	3p. multicoloured	1·00	70

1107 Tree

1999. Tree Day.
2581	**1107**	3p. multicoloured	1·00	70

1108 Registration Documents and Fingerprint

1999. 140th Anniv of National Civil Register.
2582	**1108**	3p. multicoloured	1·00	70

1109 Runner's Feet

1999. 17th International Marathon, Mexico City.
2583	**1109**	4p.20 multicoloured	1·90	1·20

1110 Children, Flag and Book on Island ("Conoce nuestra Constitucion")

1999. 40th Anniv of National Commission for Free Textbooks (2nd issue). Multicoloured.
2584		3p. Type **1110**	1·10	75
2585		3p. Children dancing ("Tsuni tsame")	1·10	75
2586		3p. Bird on flower ("Ciencias naturales")	1·10	75

1111 "Self-portrait"

1999. Birth Centenary of Rufino Tamayo (artist).
2587	**1111**	3p. multicoloured	1·00	70

1112 Building

1999. Bicentenary of Toluca City.
2588	**1112**	3p. black and copper	1·00	70

1113 State Arms, Model Figures and Signature

1999. 175th Anniv of State of Mexico.
2589	**1113**	3p. multicoloured	1·10	70

1114 "50" and Map of Americas

1999. 50th Anniv of Union of Universities of Latin America.
2590	**1114**	4p.20 multicoloured	1·40	90

1115 Emblem

1999. 40th Anniv of Institute of Security and Social Services of State Workers (I.S.S.S.T.E.).
2591	**1115**	3p. multicoloured	1·10	75

1116 Map and State Emblem

1999. 25th Anniv of State of Baja California Sur.
2592	**1116**	3p. multicoloured	1·10	75

1117 Emblem, "25" and Map

1999. 25th Anniv of Mexican Family Planning.
2593	**1117**	3p. multicoloured	1·10	75

1118 Harpy Eagle

1999. Nature Conservation.
2594	**1118**	3p. multicoloured	1·10	75

1119 Stone Carving and Arms

1999. 25th Anniv of State of Quintana Roo.
2595	**1119**	3p. multicoloured	1·10	75

1120 U.P.U. Messengers

1999. 125th Anniv of Universal Postal Union.
2596	**1120**	4p.20 multicoloured	1·60	1·00

1121 Globe and Stamps

1999. World Post Day.
2597	**1121**	4p.20 multicoloured	1·60	1·00

1122 Emblem and Monument

1999. 12th General Assembly of International Council on Monuments and Sites.
2598	**1122**	4p.20 silver, blue and black	1·60	1·00

1123 Chavez and Revueltas

1999. Birth Centenaries of Carlos Chavez and Silvestre Revueltas (composers).
2599	**1123**	3p. multicoloured	1·10	75

1124 Emblem

1999. 25th Anniv of Autonomous Metropolitan University.
2600	**1124**	3p. multicoloured	1·10	75

1125 Map, Cave Painting and State Arms

1999. 150th Anniv of State of Guerrero.
2601	**1125**	3p. multicoloured	1·10	75

1126 "Mexico 1999" in Star and Children (Alfredo Carciarreal)

1999. Christmas. Children's Drawings. Multicoloured.
2602	3p. Type **1126**	1·30	55
2603	4p.20 Christmas decorations (Rodrigo Santiago Salazar)	1·80	75

1127 Anniversary Emblem

1999. 20th Anniv of National Commission on Professional Education.
2604	**1127**	3p. green, ultramarine and black	1·10	75

1128 Humboldt (naturalist)

1999. Bicentenary of Alexander von Humboldt's Exploration of South America.
2605	**1128**	3p. multicoloured	1·50	75

1129 National Free University

1999. Education. Sheet 223×135 mm in shape of flag containing T 1129 and similar multicoloured designs.
MS2606 3p. Type **1129**; 3p. National Polytechnic Institute and Metropolitan Free University (79×24 mm); 3p. Justo Sierra and Jose Nasconcelos and SEP emblem; 3p. National Commission for Free Text-books and teachers (General Directorate of Schoolteachers) (79×24 mm); 4p.20 Reading campaign emblem and students working (oval-shaped, 39×49 mm) 7·50 6·50

1130 Emblem and Crowd

2000. Census.
2607	**1130**	3p. multicoloured	1·20	80

1131 Woman ascending Stairs

2000. International Women's Day.
2608	**1131**	4p.20 multicoloured	1·70	1·10

1132 Politicians and Constitution

2000. Democracy. Sheet 227×139 mm in shape of flag containing T 1132 and similar multicoloured designs.
MS2609 3p. Type **1132**; 3p. Politicians and newspaper headlines (38×24 mm); 3p. Horsemen; 3p. Politicians and boy carrying newspapers (38×24 mm); 4p.20 Boy posting voting paper and electoral card (oval-shaped, 39×49 mm) 7·75 6·75

1133 Children using Computers

2000. Millennium Messages. Sheet 101×74 mm.
MS2610 **1133** 10p. multicoloured 5·50 4·75

1134 Totonaca Temple, El Tajin

2000
2611	**1134** 3p. multicoloured	1·20	80

1135 Emblem, Books and Keyboard

2000. 50th Anniv of National Association of Universities and Institutes of Higher Education.
2612	**1135** 3p. multicoloured	1·20	80

1136 Emblem

2000. 25th Tourism Fair, Acapulco.
2613	**1136** 4p.20 multicoloured	1·70	1·10

1137 Men in Canoe and Sailing Ship

2000. 500th Anniv of the Discovery of Brazil.
2614	**1137** 4p.20 multicoloured	1·80	1·10

1138 Luis Alvarez Barret

2000. Teachers' Day.
2615	**1138** 3p. multicoloured	1·20	80

1139 Flying Cars and Boy with Dog (Alejandro Guerra Millan)

2000. "Stampin the Future". Winning Entries in Children's International Painting Competition. Mult.
2616	3p. Type **1139**	1·20	80
2617	4p.20 Houses and space ships (Carlos Hernandez García)	1·70	1·10

1140 Emblem

2000. 4th Asian–Pacific Telecommunications and Information Industry Economic Co-operation Forum.
2618	**1140**	4p.20 multicoloured	1·70	1·10

1141 Young Children

2000. International Anti-drugs Day.
2619	**1141**	4p.20 multicoloured	1·70	1·10

1142 Pre-hispanic Sculpture

2000. Provision for Two Million Homes by the National Institute for Worker's Houses. Sheet 115×170 mm containing T 1142 and similar multicoloured designs.
MS2620 3p. Type **1142**; 3p. Sculpture of temple; 10p. Human figures sitting in circle (sculpture) (oval-shaped, 49×39 mm) 6·75 6·25

1143 Mosaica and Men in Costume

2000. Identity and Culture. Sheet 227×139 mm in shape of a flag containing T 1143 and similar multicoloured designs.
MS2621 3p. Type **1143**; 3p. Film actors (79×25 mm); 3p. Gondolas and horse riding act; 3p. Table of food (79×25 mm); 4p.20 Acrobats and children wearing national costumes (oval-shaped, 39×49 mm) 7·75 7·00

1144 Pictograms

2000. Convive (disabled persons' organization).
2622	**1144**	3p. multicoloured	1·20	80

1145 Globe and Member Flags

2000. 20th Anniv of Association of Latin American Integration.
2623	**1145**	4p.20 multicoloured	1·70	1·10

1146 Emblem

2000. 125th Anniv of Restoration of Senate.
2624	**1146**	3p. multicoloured	1·20	80

1147 Drawings and Skeleton (image scaled to 49% of original size)

2000. EXPO 2000 World's Fair, Hanover, Germany. Sheet 223×222 mm containing T 1147 and similar horiz designs. Multicoloured.
MS2625 1p. Type **1147**; 1p. Musicians, stone devil and child's face; 1p.80 Painting and eye; 1p.80 Drawing and old photographs; 2p. Computer, factory and car assembly line; 2p. Stone carvings, paintings and modern art; 3p. Chameleon, parrots and fish; 3p. Jewellery, fruit and weaving; 3p. Construction site, machinist and combine harvester; 3p.60 Globe and exhibition building, Hanover; 4p.20 Emblem (oval-shaped, 39×49 mm) 12·00 11·00

1148 Building Façade and Bank Note

2000. 75th Anniv of Bank of Mexico. Sheet 100×72 mm.
MS2626 10p. multicoloured 4·75 4·25

1149 Runners crossing Finishing Line

2000. 18th International Marathon, Mexico City.
2627	**1149**	4p.20 multicoloured	1·70	1·10

1150 Athletes and Sydney Opera House

2000. Olympic Games, Sydney.
2628	**1150**	4p.20 multicoloured	1·70	1·10

1151 Emblem and Family

2000. Paisano Programme (support for Mexicans returning home from abroad).
2629	**1151**	4p.20 multicoloured	1·70	1·10

1152 Emblem

2000. 2nd International UNESCO World Conference, Colima.
2630	**1152**	4p.20 multicoloured	1·70	1·10

1153 Profiles

2000. Women's Health Month.
2631	**1153**	3p. multicoloured	1·20	80

1154 Building and Emblem

2000. 250th Anniv of Ciudad Victoria, Tamaulipas.
2632	**1154**	3p. multicoloured	1·20	80

1155 Bird holding Letter

2000. World Post Day.
2633   **1155**   4p.20 multicoloured   1·70   1·10

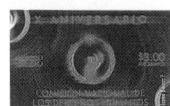
1156 Emblem

2000. 50th Anniv of National Human Rights Commission.
2634   **1156**   3p. silver and blue   1·20   80

1157 Doctors and Ambulance

2000. New Millennium. Sheet 223×135 mm in shape of flag, containing T 1157 and similar multicoloured designs.
MS2635 3p. Type **1157**; 3p. Posters, doctors and globe (79×25 mm); 3p. Children receiving injections; 3p. Poster showing tractor and crowd demonstrating (79×25 mm); 4p.20, Modern medical technology (oval-shaped, 39×49 mm)   8·00   7·25

1158 Clouds and Emblem

2000. 50th Anniv of World Meteorological Organization.
2636   **1158**   3p. multicoloured   1·20   80

1159 Emblem

2000. 50th Anniv of International Diabetes Federation.
2637   **1159**   4p.20 gold and red   1·70   1·10

1160 Contemporary Art with Sculpture

2000. Art. Sheet 223×39 mm in shape of flag, containing T 1160 and similar multicoloured designs.
MS2638 3p. Type **1160**; 3p. Photographs (39×25 mm); 3p. Opera singer and movie actors; 3p. Dancers (39×25 mm); 4p.20 Ballet dancers and musicians (oval-shaped, 39×49 mm)   8·00   7·25

1161 Samuel Morse, Juan de la Granja and Telegraph Apparatus

2000. 150th Anniv of Telegraph in Mexico.
2639   **1161**   3p. multicoloured   1·20   80
   Samuel Morse invented the telegraph and Morse code system and Juan de la Granja introduced the telegraph to Mexico.

1162 Bunuel

2000. Birth Centenary of Luis Bunuel (film director).
2640   **1162**   3p. silver, black and red   1·20   80

1163 Lightning

2000. 25th Anniv of Electric Investigation Institute.
2641   **1163**   3p. multicoloured   1·20   80

1164 Building Customs House, and Bridge

2000. Centenary of Customs.
2642   **1164**   3p. multicoloured   1·20   80

1165 Star and Girl (Maria Carina Lona Martinez)

2000. Christmas. Children's paintings. Multicoloured.
2643   3p. Type **1165**   1·20   80
2644   4p.20 Poinsettia (Daniela Escamilla Rodriguez)   1·70   1·10

1166 Television Set and Emblem

2000. 50th Anniv of Television in Mexico.
2645   **1166**   3p. multicoloured   1·20   80

1167 Adamo Boari (architect)

2000. Centenary of Commencement of Construction of Postal Headquarters, Mexico City. Sheet 92×100 mm, containing T 1167 and similar designs. Multicoloured.
MS2646 3p. multicoloured; 3p. black, brown and red; 3p. multicoloured; 10p. black, brown and red (71×39 mm)   8·00   7·25
DESIGNS: As Type 1167—3p. Building facade; 3p. Gonzalo Garita y Frontera (engineer). 71×39 mm—10p. Completed building.

1168 Coiled Mattress (Manuel Alvarez Bravo)

2000. Photography. Sheet 223×135 mm in shape of flag, containing T 1168 and similar multicoloured designs.
MS2647 3p. Type **1168**; 3p. Various portraits (79×25 mm); 3p. Roses (Tina Modotti); 3p. Various photographs including a lift, a lake, a 1925 car, a helicopter, a ruined building, a street scene, men in costume and boot heels (79×25 mm); 4p.20 Men in gas masks (oval-shaped, 39×49 mm)   8·00   7·25

1169 Pyramid of the Niches

2000. El Tajin.
2648   **1169**   3p. multicoloured   1·20   80

1170 Manatee

2000. Nature Conservation.
2649   **1170**   3p. multicoloured   1·20   80

1171 Sarabia

2000. Birth Centenary of Francisco Sarabia (aviator).
2650   **1171**   3p. multicoloured   1·20   80

1172 Telephone Exchange and Fabric Shops

2000. Industry. Sheet 223×135 mm in shape of flag, containing T 1172 and similar multicoloured designs.
MS2651 3p. Type **1172**; 3p. Tractor and modern farming (39 ×25 mm); 3p. Traditional farming methods and car; 3p. Manufacturing and industrial plant (39×25 mm); 4p.20 Globe and industries (oval-shaped, 39×49 mm)   8·00   7·25

1173 Stamps and Post Collection

2000. Forms of Communication. Sheet 223×135 mm in shape of flag, containing T 1173 and similar multicoloured designs.
MS2652 3p. Type **1173**; 3p. Telephone operators and telegraph clerk (39×25 mm); 3p. Old and modern train and station; 3p. Motorway (39× 25 mm); 4p.20 Globe and satellite and satellite dish (oval-shaped, 39×49 mm)   8·00   7·25

2001. Tourism. As Nos. 2410 etc but with face value changed.
2658   6p.50 Queretaro   2·75   70
2662   11p.50 Queretaro   4·50   1·40
2668   30p Queretaro   10·50   2·75

1174 Chiapas

2001. Tourism.
2670   **1174**   1p.50 multicoloured   1·00   60
2673   **1174**   8p.50 multicoloured   4·00   1·70

1175 Emblem, Book and Building

2001. 50th Anniv of National Autonomous University.
2680   **1175**   3p. multicoloured   1·20   80

1176 Woman

2001. International Women's Day.
2681   **1176**   4p.20 multicoloured   1·70   1·10

1177 Cement Factory

2001. 53rd Anniv of National Cement Chamber.
2682   **1177**   3p. multicoloured   1·20   80

1178 Vasconcelos and Ink Pen

2001. 42nd Death Anniv of Jose Vasconcelos (lawyer).
2683   **1178**   3p. multicoloured   1·20   80

1179 People Running and Flames

2001. 50th Anniv of United Nations High Commissioner for Refugees.
2684   **1179**   4p.20 multicoloured   1·70   1·10

1180 "Self-portrait wearing Jade Necklace"

2001. Frida Kahlo (artist) Commemoration.
2685   **1180**   4p.20 multicoloured   1·70   1·10
   A stamp of similar design was issued by the United States of America.

1181 Stylized Bird

2001. Anti-drugs Campaign.
2686   **1181**   4p.20 multicoloured   1·70   1·10

1182 De la Cueva

2001. Birth Centenary of Mario de la Cueva (university director).
2687   **1182**   3p. blue and gold   1·20   80

1183 Emblem

2001. International Year of Volunteers.
2688   **1183**   4p.20 multicoloured   1·70   1·10

1184 Women and Flowers (painting)

2001. Rodolfo Morales (artist) Commemoration. Sheet 121×60 mm.
MS2689 **1184** 10p. multicoloured   4·50   4·00

1185 Owl

2001. 65th Anniv of Federal Justice Tribunal.
2690   **1185**   3p. multicoloured   1·20   85

1186 Emblems and Building

2001. 450th Anniv of University of Mexico.
2691   **1186**   3p. multicoloured   1·20   85

1187 Adela Formoso

2001. 20th Death Anniv of Adela Formoso de Obregon Santalla (women's rights activist).
2692 **1187** 3p. multicoloured — 1·20 — 85

1188 Daniel Villegas

2001. 25th Death Anniv of Daniel Cosío Villegas (historian).
2693 **1188** 3p. multicoloured — 1·20 — 85

1189 Past and Present Pharmaceutical Drugs

2001
2694 **1189** 3p. multicoloured — 1·20 — 85

1190 Girl with Grandfather

2001. Grandparents Day.
2695 **1190** 3p. multicoloured — 1·20 — 85

1191 Children encircling Globe

2001. United Nations Year of Dialogue among Civilizations.
2696 **1191** 3p. multicoloured — 1·20 — 85

1192 Envelope as Bicycle

2001. Stamp Day.
2697 **1192** 3p. yellow, red and blue — 1·20 — 85

1193 Lily

2001. Women's Health Day.
2698 **1193** 3p. multicoloured — 1·20 — 85

1194 Eye and People

2001. 25th Anniv of Ophthalmic Institute.
2699 **1194** 4p.20 multicoloured — 1·20 — 85

1195 Tufted Jay (*Cyanocorax dickeyi*)

2001. Endangered Species.
2700 **1195** 5p.30 multicoloured — 2·40 — 1·60

1196 Children (Eunice Gonzalez)

2001. Christmas. Children's Paintings. Multicoloured.
2701 3p. Type **1196** — 1·20 — 80
2702 4p.20 Candles (Javier Nunez) — 1·70 — 1·10

1197 Nurse and Children

2001. Educational Scholarship Fund for Indigenous Children. Sheet 101×72 mm. P 14.
MS2703 **1197** 3p. multicoloured — 1·40 — 1·30

1198 Technicians

2001. National Fund for Education. Sheet 101×72 mm.
MS2704 **1198** 3p. multicoloured — 1·40 — 1·30

1199 Boy and Girl

2001. Children's Accident Prevention Campaign.
2705 **1199** 3p. multicoloured — 1·20 — 80

1200 Apple

2001. World Food Day.
2706 **1200** 3p. multicoloured — 1·20 — 80

1201 Wild Sheep

2002. Endangered Species.
2707 **1201** 6p. multicoloured — 2·50 — 1·60

1202 Squash and Snail

2002. Birth Centenary of Manuel Alvarez Bravo (photographer).
2708 **1202** 6p. black — 2·40 — 1·60

1203 Chinese Dragon and Quetzalcoatl

2002. 30th Anniv of China—Mexico Diplomatic Relations.
2709 **1203** 6p. multicoloured — 2·30 — 1·60

1204 Mangroves

2002. Conservation. Multicoloured.
2710 50c. Type **1204** — 15 — 15
2710a 50c. No. 2732 — 15 — 15
2734 50c. Deserts (No. 2732) — 15 — 15
2711 1p. Rivers — 15 — 15
2711a 1p. No. 2728 — 15 — 15
2711b 1p. Lakes and lagoons (No. 2733) — 15 — 15
2712 1p. Forests — 30 — 15
2735 1p. Orchids (No. 2828) — 15 — 15
2713 1p.50 Terrestrial mammals — 40 — 15
2714 2p. Cacti — 55 — 15
2715 2p. Cloud forest — 55 — 15
2716 2p.50 No. 2715 — 50 — 20
2717 2p.50 No. 2713 — 50 — 20
2717a 2p.50 No. 2720 — 50 — 20
2736 2p.50 No. 2720 — 40 — 20
2718 4p.50 Birds — 1·20 — 35
2719 5p. Reptiles — 1·40 — 40
2720 5p. Marine turtles — 1·40 — 40
2720a 5p. No. 2733 — 80 — 35
2720b 5p. Tropical forests (No. 2724) — 80 — 35
2721 6p. Birds of prey — 1·60 — 45
2722 6p. Butterflies — 1·60 — 45
2722a 6p.50 No. 2712 — 1·00 — 40
2722b 6p.50 No. 2725 — 1·00 — 40
2722c 6p.50 No. 2719 — 1·00 — 40
2722d 6p.50 No. 2718 — 1·00 — 40
2722e 6p.50 Rivers (No. 2711) — 1·00 — 40
2738 6p.50 Marine mammals (No. 2725) — 1·00 — 40
2739 6p.50 Birds (No. 2718) — 1·00 — 40
2723 7p. Reefs — 1·90 — 55
2723a 7p. No. 2724 — 1·10 — 50
2740 7p. Seas (No. 2729) — 1·10 — 50
2723b 7p.50 No. 2729 — 1·10 — 50
2723c 7p.50 No. 2713 — 1·10 — 50
2723d 7p.50 No. 2727 — 1·10 — 50
2740a 7p.50 Wild cats (No. 2727) — 1·10 — 50
2724 8p.50 Tropical forests — 2·20 — 65
2741 8p.50 Marine mammals (No. 2725) — 1·20 — 55
2725 10p. Marine mammals — 2·75 — 75
2726 10p. No. 2713 — 2·75 — 75
2727 10p.50 Wild cats — 2·75 — 90
2728 10p.50 Orchids — 2·75 — 90
2728a 10p.50 No. 2723 — 2·75 — 90
2741a 10p.50 Wild cats (No. 2727) — 1·50 — 65
2729 11p.50 Seas — 3·00 — 90
2730 11p.50 Coastal birds — 3·00 — 90
2731 12p. No. 2724 — 3·25 — 90
2731a 13p. No. 2711 — 2·00 — 90
2731b 13p. No. 2710 — 2·00 — 90
2731c 13p. No. 2715 — 2·00 — 90
2731d 14p.50 No. 2730 — 2·20 — 1·00
2731e 14p.50 Marine mammals (No. 2725) — 2·20 — 1·00
2732 30p. Deserts — 8·00 — 2·30
2733 30p. Lakes and lagoons — 8·00 — 2·30
2733a 30p.50 No. 2722 — 4·75 — 1·90
2733b 30p.50 Sea turtles (No. 2720) — 4·75 — 1·90

1205 Emblems

2002. Olympic Games, Salt Lake City, USA.
2760 **1205** 8p.50 multicoloured — 3·25 — 2·10

1206 Stylized Ship

2002. Centenary of Modernization of Veracruz Artificial Port.
2761 **1206** 6p. multicoloured — 2·40 — 1·60

1207 Mayan Head and Korean Symbol

2002. 40th Anniv of Korea—Mexico Diplomatic Relations.
2762 **1207** 8p.50 multicoloured — 2·50 — 1·70

1208 Mexico City Buildings

2002. Consultative Council for the Restoration of Historic Buildings.
2763 **1208** 6p. multicoloured — 2·40 — 1·60

1209 Emblem

2002. International Women's Day. National Women's Institute.
2764 **1209** 8p.50 blue and vermilion — 3·25 — 2·10

1210 "La Despedida del Revolucionario"

2002. 150th Birth Anniv of Jose Guadalupe Posada (artist).
2765 **1210** 6p. black and olive — 2·40 — 1·50

1211 Jose Sierra Mendez

2002. 90th Death Anniv of Jose Sierra Mendez (writer).
2766 **1211** 6p. multicoloured — 2·40 — 1·50

1212 "Esteban and the Striped Cat" (Abel Quezada)

2002. United Nations Special Session for Children.
2767 **1212** 6p. multicoloured — 2·40 — 1·50

1213 Alberto Lhuillier (discoverer), Ruins and Mayan Head

2002. 50th Anniv of Discovery of Tumba de Pakal (Mayan archaeological site).
2768 **1213** 6p. multicoloured — 2·40 — 1·50

1214 Players at Goalmouth

2002. World Cup Football Championship, Japan and South Korea.
2769 **1214** 8p.50 multicoloured   3·25   2·10

1215 Pot with Map of Americas holding People as Tree

2002. International Day against Drug Abuse.
2770 **1215** 6p. multicoloured   2·40   1·50

1216 Stylized Map of Americas

2002. 5th Mexico—Central American Summit.
2771 **1216** 6p. multicoloured   2·40   1·50

1217 Mountain

2002. International Year of Mountains.
2772 **1217** 6p. multicoloured   2·40   1·50

1218 Boy wearing Traditional Costume

2002. International Day of Indigenous Peoples.
2773 **1218** 6p. multicoloured   2·40   1·50

1219 High Tension Power Lines

2002. Federal Commission of Electricity.
2774 **1219** 6p. multicoloured   2·40   1·50

1220 Face enclosed in Blood Droplet

2002. National Blood Donors' Day.
2775 **1220** 6p. multicoloured   2·40   1·50

1221 Apple and Map of Mexico

2002. Administrative Secretariat for Development Control (SECODAM).
2776 **1221** 6p. multicoloured   2·40   1·50

1222 Scales and Code

2002. Code of Practise for Public Administrations.
2777 **1222** 6p. multicoloured   2·40   1·50

1223 Clasped Hands

2002. International Day of Tourism.
2778 **1223** 8p.50 purple, black and lemon   3·25   2·10

1224 Torso, Electrocardiogram Diagram and Watch

2002. National Organ Donation Week.
2779 **1224** 6p. multicoloured   2·40   1·60

1225 Birds and Envelopes

2002. Stamp Day.
2780 **1225** 8p.50 multicoloured   3·25   2·10

1226 Mountains, Whale Tail, Sun and Cactus

2002. 50th Anniv of Baja California Peninsula.
2781 **1226** 6p. multicoloured   2·40   1·50

1227 Stairs

2002. Birth Centenary of Luis Barragan (architect).
2782 **1227** 6p. multicoloured   2·40   1·50

1228 "Man's Conquest of the Air" (detail) (Juan O'Gorman)

2002. 50th Anniv of Mexico City Airport. Details from "Man's Conquest of the Air" by Juan O'Gorman. Multicoloured.
2783   6p. Type **1228**   2·40   1·50
2784   6p. Early aviators, parachutist and man wearing protective suit   2·50   1·70
2785   8p.50 Mexico city and aviators   4·00   3·50
   Nos. 2783/5 were issued together, se-tenant, forming a composite design.

1229 Mexican and Spanish Flags

2002. 25th Anniv of Renewal of Spain—Mexico Diplomatic Relations.
2786 **1229** 8p.50 multicoloured   2·75   1·90

1230 Globe, "e" and Binary Codes

2002. 75th Anniv of the Development of Information Technology in Mexico.
2787 **1230** 6p. violet, vermilion and black   2·00   1·30

1231 Anniversary Emblem

2002. Centenary of Pan American Health Organization.
2788 **1231** 8p.50 multicoloured   2·50   1·90

1232 Nezahualcoyotl

2002. 600th Birth Anniv of Nezahualcoyotl (King of the Texcoco).
2789 **1232** 6p. multicoloured   2·00   1·30

1233 Nativity (Sara Elisa Miranda Alcaraz)

2002. Christmas. Children's Paintings. Multicoloured.
2790   6p. Type **1233**   2·00   1·30
2791   8p.50 Nativity (Alejandro Ruiz Sampedro)   2·75   1·80

1234 Emblem

2002. "Life without Violence" Campaign.
2792 **1234** 8p.50 multicoloured   2·75   1·90

1235 Early Bi-plane

2003. Centenary of Powered Flight. Phosphorescent markings.
2793 **1235** 8p.50 multicoloured   2·50   1·60

1236 Emblem

2003. 60th Anniv of Iberoamericana University, Mexico City.
2794 **1236** 6p. multicoloured   1·80   1·20

1237 Woman

2003. International Woman's Day.
2795 **1237** 8p.50 multicoloured   2·50   1·60

1238 City Arms and Buildings

2003. Centenary of Mexicali City.
2796 **1238** 6p. multicoloured   1·80   1·20

1239 Dam and Crane

2003. 50th Anniv of Industry and Construction (cmic).
2797 **1239** 6p. multicoloured   1·80   1·20

1240 Emblem and Children

2003. 60th Anniv of Frederico Gomez Children's Hospital.
2798 **1240** 6p. multicoloured   1·80   1·20

1241 Miguel Hildago y Costilla

2003. 250th Birth Anniv of Miguel Hildago y Costilla (social reformer and independence pioneer).
2799 **1241** 6p. multicoloured   1·80   1·20

1242 Gregorio Torres Quintero

2003. Teacher's Day. Gregorio Torres Quintero (writer) Commemoration.
2800 **1242** 6p. multicoloured   1·80   1·20

1243 Telescope, Planets and Eclipse

2003. 125th Anniv of National Astronomical Observatory.
2801 **1243** 6p. multicoloured   1·80   1·20

1244 Film, Cigarette and Stop Sign

2003. International No-Smoking Day. Smoking-free Cinemas Campaign.
2802 **1244** 8p.50 multicoloured   2·50   1·60

1245 Map

2003. 1st Satellite Network.
2803 **1245** 6p. multicoloured   1·80   1·20

1246 Hands enclosing Globe

2003. International Day against Drug Abuse.
2804 **1246** 8p.50 multicoloured   2·50   1·60

1247 Baseball and Bat

2003. 30th Anniv of Professional Baseball Hall of Fame.
2805 **1247** 6p. multicoloured 1·80 1·20

1248 Xavier Villaurrutia

2003. Birth Centenary of Xavier Villaurrutia (writer).
2806 **1248** 6p. multicoloured 1·80 1·20

1249 Early Vet and Modern Veterinary Surgery

2003. 150th Anniv of Veterinary Education in Mexico and America.
2807 **1249** 6p. multicoloured 1·80 1·20

1250 University Building

2003. 25th Anniv of National Teachers' University.
2808 **1250** 6p. multicoloured 1·80 1·20

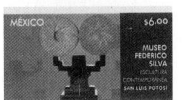

1251 "Tlaloc" (sculpture) (Federico Silva)

2003. Museo Federico Silva (contemporary culture museum), San Luis Potosi.
2809 **1251** 6p. multicoloured 1·80 1·20

1252 Family

2003. National Seminar on Organ Donation.
2810 **1252** 6p. multicoloured 1·80 1·20

1253 Bird carrying Envelope

2003. Stamp Day.
2811 **1253** 8p.50 multicoloured 2·50 1·60

1254 Voting Slip, Ballot Box and Women

2003. 50th Anniv of Vote for Women.
2812 **1254** 6p. multicoloured 1·70 1·20

1255 Secretariat Building

2003. 60th Anniv of Health Secretariat.
2813 **1255** 6p. multicoloured 1·70 1·20

1256 Auditorium

2003. Centenary of Juarez Theatre, Guanajuato City.
2814 **1256** 6p. multicoloured 1·70 1·20

1257 Emblem

2003. 450th Anniv of First Chair of Law in America.
2815 **1257** 8p.50 multicoloured 2·50 1·60

1258 "Development and Impact of the Electricity" (German Reyes Retana)

2003. Centenary of Centralized Light and Power.
2816 **1258** 6p. multicoloured 1·70 1·20

1259 The Nativity (Valeria Baez)

2003. Christmas. Children's Paintings. Multicoloured.
2817 6p. Type **1259** 1·70 1·20
2818 8p.50 Nativity (Octavio Aleman) 2·50 1·60

1260 Laughing Child

2003. Rights of the Child.
2819 **1260** 6p. multicoloured 1·70 1·20

1261 Globe as Heart and Leaves

2003. International Day of Freshwater.
2820 **1261** 8p.50 multicoloured 2·50 1·60

1262 College Facade and Students

2003. 25th Anniv of Professional Technical College (CONALEP).
2821 **1262** 6p. multicoloured 1·70 1·20

1263 John Paul II

2004. 25th Anniv of Pope John Paul II's First Visit to Mexico.
2822 **1263** 6p. multicoloured 1·60 90

1264 Agustin Yanez

2004. Birth Centenary of Agustin Yanez (writer and politician).
2823 **1264** 8p.50 multicoloured 2·10 1·10

1265 Enrique Aguilar Gonzalez

2004. Teachers' Day. Enrique Aguilar Gonzalez Commemoration.
2824 **1265** 8p.50 blue 2·10 1·10

1266 Satellite, Cable and Globe

2004. 50th Anniv of Cable Television.
2825 **1266** 6p. multicoloured 1·60 90

1267 Quartz and Society Emblem

2004. Centenary of Geological Society.
2826 **1267** 8p.50 multicoloured 2·10 1·10

1268 Stylized Figures

2004. International Day against Drug Abuse.
2827 **1268** 8p.50 multicoloured 2·10 1·10

1269 Salvador Novo

2004. Writer's Birth Centenaries. Multicoloured.
2828 7p. Type **1269** 1·80 1·00
2829 7p. Gilberto Owen 1·80 1·00
2830 7p. Celestino Gorostiza 1·80 1·00

1270 Boys and Centenary Emblem

2004. Centenary of FIFA (Federation Internationale de Football).
2831 **1270** 11p.50 multicoloured 2·50 1·30

1271 Borola Tacuche

2004. La Familia Burron (comic created by Gabriel Vargas Bernal).
2832 **1271** 6p. multicoloured 1·60 90

1272 Athena, Columns and Swimmer

2004. Olympic Games, Athens.
2833 **1272** 10p.50 multicoloured 2·75 1·30

1273 Mountain and Town

2004. 450th Anniv of Fresnillo.
2834 **1273** 7p. multicoloured 1·80 1·00

1274 University Building

2004. 50th Anniv of Chihuahua University.
2835 **1274** 7p. multicoloured 1·80 1·00

1275 Building

2004. Economic and Cultural Fund (CFE).
2836 **1275** 8p.50 multicoloured 2·10 1·10

1276 Emblem

2004. 75th Anniv of National Independent University (UNAM).
2837 **1276** 11p.50 multicoloured 2·50 1·30

1277 Building Facade

2004. 70th Anniv of Palace of Arts.
2838 **1277** 7p. multicoloured 1·80 1·00

1278 Fund Workers

2004. 45th Anniv of Official Federal Social Fund (ISSSTE).
2839 **1278** 6p. multicoloured 1·70 1·00

1279 City Symbols and Plaque

2004. 300th Anniv of Completion of Campeche City Walls.
2840 **1279** 6p. multicoloured 1·70 1·00

1280 Francisco Gonzalez Bocanegra (lyricist) and Jaime Nuno (composer)

2004. 150th Anniv of National Anthem.
2841 **1280** 6p.50 multicoloured   1·80   1·10

1281 Dove holding Envelope and Post Box

2004. Stamp Day.
2842 **1281** 6p. magenta   1·70   1·00

1282 Envelope and Seal

2004. 125th Anniv of Universal Postal Union Membership.
2843 **1282** 8p.50 multicoloured   2·10   1·10

1283 Cameraman and Images

2004. 45th Anniv of Once Television Station (Channel 11).
2844 **1283** 8p.50 multicoloured   2·10   1·10

1284 "180"

2004. 180th Anniv of Control Board (ASF).
2845 **1284** 6p.50 multicoloured   1·80   1·00

1285 General Escobedo (statue)

2004. 400th Anniv of General Escobedo Municipality.
2846 **1285** 8p.50 multicoloured   2·20   1·20

1286 Seated Woman

2004. 75th Anniv of Health Secretariat.
2847 **1286** 8p.50 multicoloured   2·20   1·20

1287 Boy listening to Radio

2004. 60th Anniv of Radio Educacion (XEEP).
2848 **1287** 6p.50 multicoloured   1·80   1·00

1288 Building Facade

2004. 50th Anniv of SCT (ministry of transport) National Centre. Multicoloured.
2849   6p.50 Type **1288**   1·80   1·00
MS2850 92×100 mm. 7p.50 As No.
2849 (72×39 mm)   2·10   1·10

1289 Miguel Hidalgo, Benito Juarez and Francisco I. Madero (painting) (David Alfaro Siqueiros)

2004. 45th Anniv of National Free Books Committee.
2851 **1289** 10p.50 multicoloured   2·50   1·30

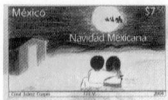

1290 Couple watching Sky (Coral Juarez Cuapio)

2004. Christmas. Children's Paintings. Mult.
2852   7p.50 Type **1290**   2·00   1·10
2853   10p.50 Pinata and presents (Malinalli Ramirez MTZ) (vert)   2·50   1·30

1291 Car, Seat Belt and Roadway

2004. Road Accident Prevention Campaign.
2854 **1291** 8p.50 multicoloured   2·20   1·20

1292 Amethyst

2004. Minerals.
2855 **1292** 8p.50 multicoloured   1·60   70

1293 Building Facade

2005. Centenary of General Hospital.
2856 **1293** 6p.50 multicoloured   1·80   1·00

1294 Faces

2005. International Women's Day.
2857 **1294** 6p.50 multicoloured   1·80   1·00

1295 Face

2005. 50th Anniv of "Pedro Paramo" (novel by Juan Rulfo).
2858 **1295** 6p.50 multicoloured   1·80   1·00

1296 Athletes

2005. Universiada 2005 (games).
2859 **1296** 7p.50 multicoloured   2·00   1·10

1297 Globe, Child and Vaccine Droplets

2005. World without Polio Campaign.
2860 **1297** 10p.50 multicoloured   2·50   1·30

1298 Eulalia Guzman

2005. Teachers' Day. Eulalia Guzman Commem.
2861 **1298** 6p.50 multicoloured   1·80   1·00

1299 Don Quixote

2005. 400th Anniv of Publication of "Don Quixote de la Mancha" (novel by Miguel de Cervantes). Sheet 120×159 mm containing T 1299 and similar horiz designs. Multicoloured.
MS2862 6p.50 Type **1299**; 10p.50 Riding Rocinante; 10p.50 Don Quixote   6·25   5·50

1300 Albert Einstein riding Bicycle

2005. International Year of Physics.
2863 **1300** 7p.50 multicoloured   2·00   1·10

1301 Flower of Hands and Emblem

2005. National Commission for Human Rights.
2864 **1301** 6p.50 multicoloured   1·80   1·00

1302 Building Facade

2005. Centenary of National Association of Architects.
2865 **1302** 6p.50 multicoloured   1·80   1·00

1303 Child and Hands

2005. International Day against Drug Abuse.
2866 **1303** 10p.50 multicoloured   2·50   1·30

1304 Eye and Emblem

2005. Transparency and Access to Information.
2867 **1304** 6p.50 multicoloured   1·80   1·00

1305 Players

2005. Baseball.
2868 **1305** 7p.50 multicoloured   2·10   1·10

1306 Memin Pinguin

2005. "Memin Pinguin" (comic character created by Yolanda Vargas). Multicoloured.
2869   6p.50 Type **1306**   2·40   1·30
2870   6p.50 Holding flower   2·40   1·30
2871   6p.50 Delivering papers   2·40   1·30
2872   6p.50 Wearing evening clothes   2·40   1·30
2873   6p.50 With mother   2·40   1·30

1307 Juan O'Gorman

2005. Birth Centenary of Juan O'Gorman (artist).
2874 **1307** 7p.50 multicoloured   2·00   1·10

1308 Silver

2005. Minerals. Multicoloured.
2875   6p.50 Type **1308**   1·80   1·00
2876   6p.50 Acanthitite   1·80   1·00
2877   6p.50 Marcasite   1·80   1·00
2878   6p.50 Meteorite   1·80   1·00
2879   6p.50 Gold   1·80   1·00
2880   6p.50 Galena   1·80   1·00
2881   6p.50 Pyrites   1·80   1·00
2882   6p.50 Inscr "Yeso" (plaster)   1·80   1·00
2883   6p.50 Mango Calcite   1·80   1·00
2884   6p.50 Baryte   1·80   1·00
2885   6p.50 Stephanite   1·80   1·00
2886   6p.50 Red Calcite   1·80   1·00
2887   6p.50 Calcite   1·80   1·00
2888   6p.50 Asbestos   1·80   1·00
2889   6p.50 Valencianite   1·80   1·00
2890   6p.50 Livingstonite   1·80   1·00
2891   6p.50 Beryl   1·80   1·00
2892   6p.50 Smithsonite   1·80   1·00

2893	6p.50 Flouride	1·80	1·00
2894	6p.50 Amethyst	1·80	1·00
2895	6p.50 Azurite	1·80	1·00
2896	6p.50 Inscr "Leminorfita"	1·80	1·00
2897	6p.50 Apatite	1·80	1·00
2898	6p.50 Pyromorphyte	1·80	1·00
2899	6p.50 Actinolite	1·80	1·00

1309 Miguel Dominguez (independence leader)

2005. Anniversaries. Multicoloured.

2900	6p.50 Type **1309** (175th anniv of National Supreme Court)	1·80	1·00
2901	6p.50 Building (10th anniv of Federal Justice Administration)	1·80	1·00
2902	10p.50 Jose Maria Morelos (independence leader) (190th anniv of Supreme Court)	2·50	1·30
MS2903	140×115 mm. Nos. 2900/2	5·75	5·00

1310 Ignacio Vallarta

2005. 175th Birth Anniv of Ignacio Vallarta (politician).

2904	**1310** 7p.50 multicoloured	2·00	1·10

1311 Plants and Buildings

2005. EXPO 2005, Aichi, Japan.

2905	**1311** 13p. multicoloured	3·00	1·60

1312 Building Facades and Open Book

2005. 150th Anniv of Federal District Supreme Court. Multicoloured.

2906	6p.50 Type **1312**	1·80	1·00
2907	6p.50 Ink well, trees and buildings	1·80	1·00
2908	7p.50 Court building, gavel and ink stand	2·00	1·10

1313 Globe and International Buildings

2005. Stamp Day.

2909	**1313** 10p.50 multicoloured	2·50	1·30

1314 Fundacion Jesus Alvarez del Castillo Building

2005. Centenary of Jalisco Philatelic Organization. Phosphorescent markings.

2910	**1314** 6p.50 multicoloured	1·80	1·00

1315 Statue and Cedar of Lebanon Tree

2005. 125th Anniv of Lebanese Immigration.

2911	**1315** 10p.50 multicoloured	2·50	1·30

1316 Rodolfo Usigli

2005. Birth Centenary of Rodolfo Usigli (writer).

2912	**1316** 7p.50 multicoloured	1·80	1·10

1317 Ships and Fort

2005. San Juan de Ulua, last Spanish Redoubt (battle for independence).

2913	**1317** 7p.50 multicoloured	2·10	1·30

1318 Colonnade and Horseman (statue)

2005. Centenary of Gomez Palace, Durango.

2914	**1318** 6p.50 multicoloured	1·80	1·00

1319 Flag, Dove and Emblem

2005. 60th Anniv of United Nations Membership.

2915	**1319** 10p.50 multicoloured	2·50	1·30

1320 Terracotta Pot

2005. Crafts. Multicoloured.

2916	50c. Type **1320**	20	20
2917	1p. Lacquered chest	25	20
2918	1p.50 Horn comb	40	25
2919	2p. Black jar	55	30
2920	2p.50 Paper bull	70	40
2921	5p. Silk shawl	1·40	80
2922	6p.50 Wooden mask	1·80	1·00
2923	6p.50 Tin cockerel	1·80	1·00
2924	6p.50 Model house and garden	1·80	1·00
2925	6p.50 Glazed and decorated bowl	1·80	1·00
2926	6p.50 Decorated vase	1·80	1·00
2926a	6p.50 Mask	1·30	1·00
2927	7p. Woman wearing traditional dress (statue)	2·00	1·10
2928	7p.50 Copper ridged vase	2·10	1·10
2929	9p. Embroidered tablecloth	2·30	1·20
2930	10p.50 Woven basket	2·50	1·30
2931	13p. Silver pear	3·00	1·60
2932	14p.50 Amber marimba	3·25	1·70
2933	30p.50 Obsidian and opal turtle	6·75	3·25

1321 Jean-Baptiste De La Salle (founder)

2005. Centenary of Christian Brothers (educational organization) in Mexico.

2961	**1321** 6p.50 multicoloured	1·80	1·00

1322 Cactus as Menorah

2005. Centenary of Jewish Community in Mexico.

2962	**1322** 7p.50 multicoloured	2·00	1·10

1323 Decorated Toys

2005. Indigenous Popular Culture.

2963	**1323** 6p.50 multicoloured	1·80	1·00

1324 Pinata and Nativity (Jose R. Angulo)

2005. Christmas. Multicoloured.

2964	6p.50 Type **1324**	1·80	1·00
2965	7p.50 Multicoloured pinata (Jose Bauza Acevedo)	2·00	1·10

1325 Man as Machine

2006. 70th Anniv of National Technical Services. Sheet 100×90 mm.

MS2966	**1325** 10p.50 multicoloured	4·25	3·50

1326 Mozart

2006. 250th Birth Anniv of Wolfgang Amadeus Mozart (composer and musician).

2967	**1326** 7p.50 multicoloured	2·10	1·10

1327 Floodlit Building

2006. 50th Anniv of UNAM Central Library.

2968	**1327** 6p.50 multicoloured	1·80	1·00

1328 Tower

2006. 50th Anniv of Latin American Tower.

2969	**1328** 6p.50 multicoloured	1·80	1·00

1329 Isidro Castillo Perez

2006. Teacher's Day. Isidro Castillo Perez Commemoration.

2970	**1329** 6p.50 multicoloured	1·80	1·00

1330 Book enclosing Building and Shelving

2006. Vasconcelos Library—Cultural Space.

2971	**1330** 6p.50 multicoloured	1·80	1·00

1331 Map and Women

2006. International Women's Day.

2972	**1331** 6p.50 multicoloured	1·80	1·00

1332 Feet and Ball

2006. World Cup Football Championship, Germany.

2973	**1332** 13p. multicoloured	3·75	2·00

1333 Benito Juarez Garcia

2006. Birth Bicentenary of Benito Juarez Garcia (politician). Sheet 100×215 mm.

MS2974	**1333** 13p. multicoloured	3·75	3·75

1334 Statues and Ship

2006. 50th Anniv of Navy School.

2975	**1334** 6p.50 multicoloured	1·80	1·00

1335 El Chavo del Ocho

2006. Television Heroes. Characters created by Roberto Gomez Bolanos (Chespirito). Multicoloured.

2976	6p.50 Type **1335**	1·80	1·00

2977		7p.50 El Chapulin Colorado	2·00	1·10
2978		10p.50 El Chavo del Ocho with leg raised	2·50	1·30
2979		13p. El Chapulin Colorado (different)	3·00	1·60
2980		14p.50 El Chavo del Ocho (different)	3·25	1·70

Nos. 2976/80 were issued together, se-tenant, forming a composite design.

1336 Cacti and Desert

2006. International Year of Deserts and Desertification.

2981	**1336**	6p.50 multicoloured	1·80	1·00

1337 Inscr "Muzzy"

2006. Dinosaurs. Sheet 96×131 mm containing T 1337 and similar multicoloured designs.

MS2982 6p.50 Type **1337**; 7p.50 Inscr "Sabinosaurio" (40×48 mm); 10p.50 Inscr "Monstruo de aramberri" (40×48 mm)   6·25   6·25

The stamps and background of No. **MS**2982 form a composite design.

1338 Students and Engineering Constructions

2006. 50th Anniv of Engineering Institute (UNAM).

2983	**1338**	6p.50 multicoloured	1·80	1·00

1339 Dove carrying Envelope

2006. World Post Day.

2984	**1339**	13p. multicoloured	3·00	1·60

1339a Miguel Hidalgo y Costilla (Agusascalientes)

2006. 150th Anniv of First Stamp. Sheet 195×218 mm containing T 1339a and similar multicoloured designs showing Miguel Gregorio Antonio Ignacio Hidalgo y Costilla Gallaga Mondarte Villaseñor (Roman Catholic priest and revolutionary rebel leader) and district name.

MS2984a 6p.50×7, Type **1339a** (Agusascalientes); Colima; Edo. de Mexico; Michoacan; Nayarit; Quintana Roo; Tamaulipas; 7p.50×7, Baja California; Chiapas; Guanajuato; Morelos; Nuevo Leon; San Luis Potosi; Tlaxcala; 9p.×7, Baja California Sur; Chihuahua; Guerrero; Oaxca; Sinaloa; Veracruz; 10p.50×7, Campeche; Distrito Federal; Hidalgo; Puebla; Sonora; Yucatan; 13p.×7, Coahuila; Durango; Jalisco; Queretaro; Tabasco; Zacatecas; 50p. Miguel Hidalgo y Costilla (72×24 mm)   32·00   32·00

1340 Chabelo (cartoon)

2006. Television Heroes. Characters created by Xavier Lopez. Multicoloured.

2985		6p.50 Type **1340**	1·80	1·00
2986		10p.50 Chabelo (Xavier Lopez)	2·50	1·30

No. 2985/6 were issued together, se-tenant, forming a composite design.

1341 Postman (statue) and Envelopes

2006. 75th Anniv of Postmen's Day.

2987	**1341**	6p.50 multicoloured	1·80	1·00

1342 Building Facade

2006. 50th Anniv of University.

2988	**1342**	10p.50 multicoloured	2·50	1·30

1343 Children

2006. Children—The Future.

2989	**1343**	10p.50 multicoloured	2·50	1·30

1344 Andres Henestrosa

2006. Birth Centenary of Andres Henestrosa (writer).

2990	**1344**	9p. multicoloured	2·30	1·20

1345 Edmundo O'Gorman

2006. Birth Centenary of Edmundo O'Gorman (historian).

2991	**1345**	10p.50 multicoloured	2·50	1·30

1346 Satellite

2006. Centenary of Mexico's Membership of International Telecommunications Union.

2992	**1346**	7p. multicoloured	2·00	1·10

1347 Baubles (Ricardo Salas Pineda)

2006. Children's Drawings. Christmas. Multicoloured.

2993		7p.50 Type **1347**	2·10	1·10
2994		10p.50 Holly and baubles (Maria Jose Gaytia)	2·50	1·30

1348 Newspapers

2006. 90th Anniv of Journalism in Mexico.

2995	**1348**	10p.50 multicoloured	2·50	1·30

1349 Apple and Book

2007. Teachers' Day.

2996	**1349**	7p.50 multicoloured	2·10	1·10

1350 *Autorretrato con Changuito* (self portrait with small monkey)

2007. Birth Centenary of Frida Kahlo (artist).

2997	**1350**	13p. multicoloured	3·00	1·60

1351 Dove

2007. Centenary of Scouting. Multicoloured.

2998		6p.50 Type **1351**	1·80	1·00
2999		10p.50 Emblem	2·50	1·30

No. 2998/9 were issued together, se-tenant, forming a composite design.

1352 Carved Ring (Gran juego de pelota) and Temple of the Jaguars

2007. Archaeology. Chichen Itza. Sheet 161×94 mm containing T 1352 and similar horiz designs. Multicoloured.

MS3000 6p.50 Type **1352**; 6p.50 Thousand columns; 10p.50 El Caracol observatory; 13p. Chac Mool (statue); 13p. Carved head of jaguar and El Castillo   10·00   10·00

The stamps, label and margins of **MS**3000 form a composite design.

1353 Cathedral, Marlin and Map

2007. 150th Anniv of Colima.

3001	**1353**	10p.50 multicoloured	2·50	1·50

1354 Boy writing (fresco)

2007. Centenary of Postal Palace. Sheet 220×196 mm containing T 1354 and similar multicoloured designs.

MS3002 5p.50 Type **1354**; 5p.50 Boy using telegraph machine; 6p.50 Two boys hand stamping; 6p.50 Two boys with hand press and ink; 6p.50 Boy with hammer and cog wheel; 6p.50 Clocks; 6p.50 Early photographs and UPU emblem (statue) (80×24 mm); 9p. Boy as Mercury; 9p. Two boys emptying mail bag; 10p.50 Two boys with letters; 13p. Boy sending carrier pigeon; 13p. Boy reading letter from carrier pigeon; 14p.50 Stairwell (40×48 mm); 14p.50 Glass roof (40×48 mm); 15p.50 Central staircases (80×48 mm); 39p.50 Postal building facade (80×48 mm)   32·00   32·00

The stamps and margins of **MS**3002 form a composite background design.

1355 Steam Locomotive and Museum

2007. Centenary of Torreon, Coahuila. Mult.

3003		5p. Type **1355**	1·40	80
3004		6p.50 Bridge over Nazas river and Our Lady of Guadalupe Parish Church	1·80	1·00
3005		6p.50 Isauro Martinez theatre	1·80	1·00
3006		14p.50 Cristo del Cerro de las Noas	3·00	1·60
3007		14p.50 Dunes and Tower	3·00	1·60

No. 3003/7 were issued together, se-tenant, forming a composite design.

1356 Dove (peace)

2007. Universal Cultural Forum, Monterey. Mult.

3008		7p. Type **1356**	2·00	1·10
3009		7p.50 Child writing and books (knowledge)	2·10	1·10
3010		7p.50 Hand holding fruit, children and wind turbine (sustainability)	2·10	1·10
3011		13p. African woman, traditional costume and calligrapher (cultural diversity)	3·00	1·60
3012		13p. Primitive statue and Thai dolls	3·00	1·60

No. 3008/12 were issued together, se-tenant, forming a composite design.

1357 Olympic Stadium

2007. Cultural Heritage. National Autonomous University of Mexico (Ciudad Universitaria). Multicoloured.

3013		6p.50 Type **1357**	1·80	1·00
3014		9p. Building on pillars with decorated facade	2·30	1·20
3015		13p. Tall building	3·00	1·60

No. 3013/15 were issued together, se-tenant, forming a composite background design.

1358 University Building Facade

2007. 50th Anniv of Universidad Autonoma de Baja California.

3016	**1358**	7p.50 multicoloured	2·10	1·10

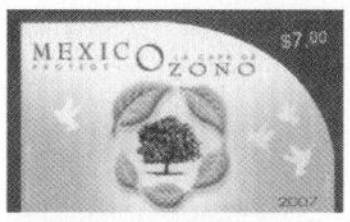

1359 Leaves and Trees

2007. Ozone Layer Protection Campaign. Mult.

3017	7p. Type **1359**	2·00	1·10
3018	14p.50 Hands enclosing Earth	3·00	1·60

Nos. 3017/18 were issued together, se-tenant, forming a composite design.

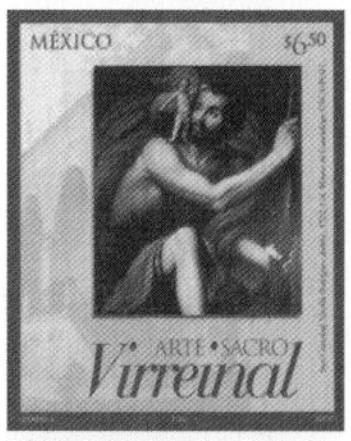

1360 *St Christopher* (Nicolas Rodriguez Juarez)

2007. Sacred Art.

3019	**1360** 6p.50 multicoloured	1·80	1·00

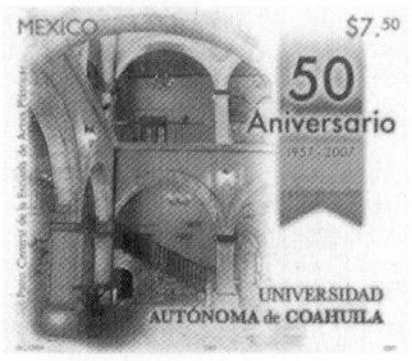

1361 Central Plaza, School of Plastic Arts

2007. 50th Anniv of Universidad Autonoma de Coahuila.

3020	**1361** 7p.50 multicoloured	2·10	1·10

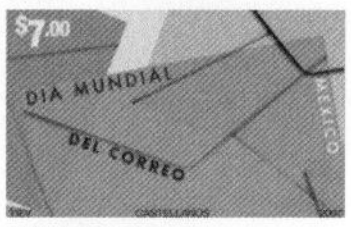

1362 Envelopes

2007. Stamp Day. Multicoloured.

3021	7p. Type **1362**	2·00	1·10
3022	10p.50 Envelopes	2·50	1·30

No. 3021/2 were issued together, se-tenant, forming a composite design.

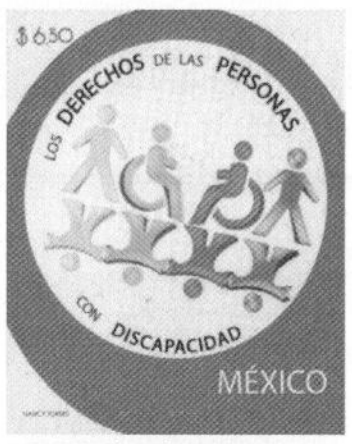

1363 Stylized Figures

2007. Rights for the Disabled.

3023	**1363** 6p.50 multicoloured	1·90	1·10

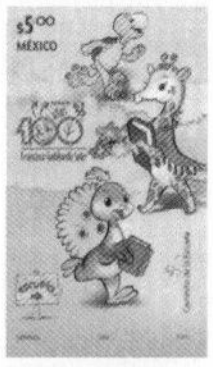

1364 Caminito de la Escuela

2007. Birth Centenary of Francisco Gabiliando Soler (Cri-Cri) (composer and performer of children's songs). Sheet 141×141 mm containing T 1364 and similar vert designs. Multicoloured.

MS3024 5p. Type **1364**; 5p. Caminito de la Escuela (different); 6p.50 la Patita; [6p.50] La Muneca Fea; 6p.50 Gato de Barrio; 6p.50 Bombon I; 6p.50 Cochinitos Domilones; 6.50p. Cochinitos Domilones (different); 6p.50 Di Por Que; 6p.50 El Raton Vaquero; 6p.50 Negrito Sandia; 7p. Cri-Cri (cricket); 7p. Francisco Gabiliando Soler; 7p. Song; 7p.50 El Chorrito 22·00 22·00

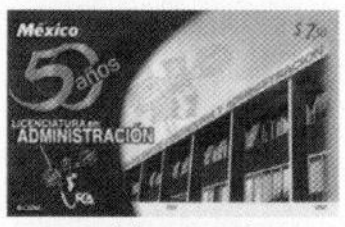

1365 Building Facade

2007. 50th Anniv of Administration Degree.

3025	**1365** 7p.50 multicoloured	2·10	1·10

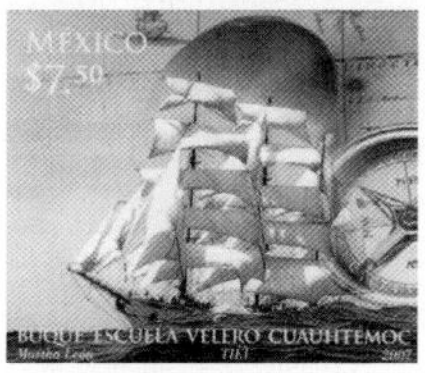

1366 Sail Ship

2007. Ship Sailing School, Cuahtemoc.

3026	**1366** 7p.50 multicoloured		

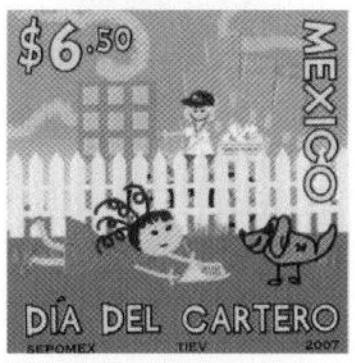

1367 Girl writing Letter

2007. Day of the Postman. Multicoloured.

3027	6p.50 Type **1367**	1·80	1·00
3028	6p.50 Girl posting letter	1·80	1·00
3029	6p.50 Postman riding bicycle	1·80	1·00
3030	6p.50 Boy receiving letter	1·80	1·00
3031	6p.50 Early mail boat	1·80	1·00
3032	6p.50 Postman	1·80	1·00
3033	6p.50 Modern post woman	1·80	1·00
3034	6p.50 Early horse-drawn mail van	1·80	1·00
3035	6p.50 Early post men	1·80	1·00
3036	6p.50 Modern postman riding bicycle	1·80	1·00
3037	6p.50 Early postman riding bicycle	1·80	1·00
3038	6p.50 Post men	1·80	1·00
3039	6p.50 Postman riding motorcycle	1·80	1·00
3040	10p.50 Postman (painting)		

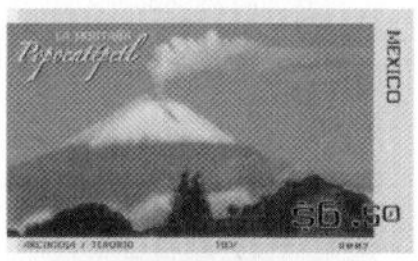

1368 Popocatepetl (Mexico)

2007. Mountains. Multicoloured.

3041	6p.50 Type **1368**	1·80	1·00
3042	6p.50 Mount Gongga (China)	1·80	1·00

Stamps of a similar design were issued by China.

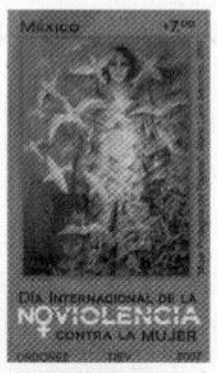

1369 Woman and Doves

2007. International 'No Violence Against Women' Day.

3043	**1369** 7p. multicoloured	2·00	1·10

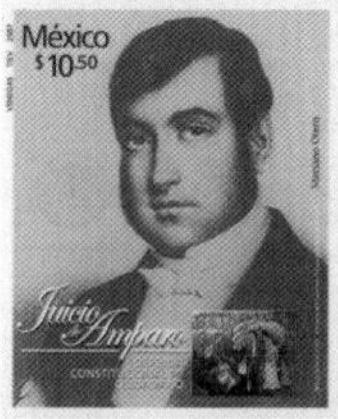

1370 Mariano Otero (politician) and Supreme Court (mural by Alfredo Zake)

2007. Amparo Law, Constitutional Proceeding to Protect Citizen's Rights .

3044	**1370** 10p.50 multicoloured	2·50	1·30

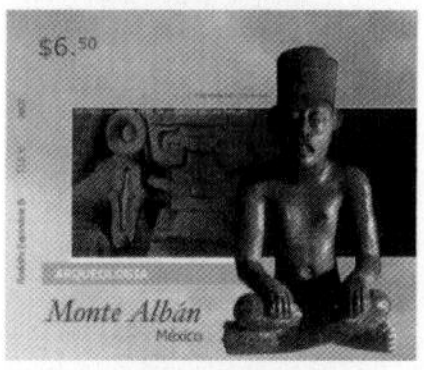

1371 Scribe (statue)

2007. Archaeology. Monte Alban. Sheet containing T 1371 and similar horiz designs. Multicoloured.

MS3045 6p.50 6p.50 Type **1371**; 6p.50 Man wearing jaguar headdress (detail, statue); 10p.50 Urn and platform; 13p. Platform and ruins, Central Plaza; 13p. Obserservatory platform, Central Plaza 12·00 12·00

The stamp, margins and label of **MS**3045 form a composite design of the site.

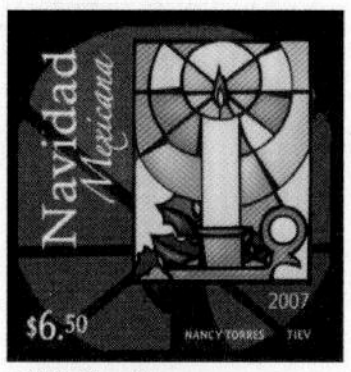

1372 Candle

2007. Christmas. Multicoloured.

3046	6p.50 Type **1372**	1·80	1·00
3047	7p. Bells	2·00	2·10
3048	10p.50 Angel	2·50	1·30
3049	13p.50 Three Kings	3·00	1·60
3050	14p.50 The Nativity	3·25	1·70

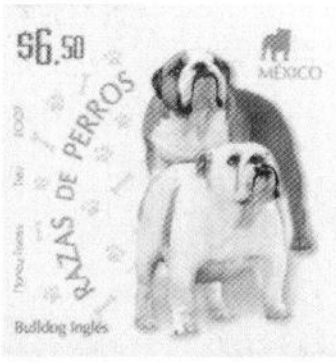

1373 Bulldogs

2007. Dogs. Multicoloured.

3051	6p.50 Type **1373**	1·80	1·00
3052	6p.50 Rotweilers	1·80	1·00
3053	6p.50 Boxers	1·80	1·00
3054	6p.50 Beagles	1·80	1·00
3055	7p. Bulldog (head)	2·00	1·10
3056	7p. Rottweiller (head)	2·00	1·10
3057	7p. Boxer (head)	2·00	1·10
3058	7p. Beagle (head)	2·00	1·10
3059	10p.50 Bulldog	2·50	1·30
3060	10p.50 Rottweiller	2·50	1·30
3061	10p.50 Boxer	2·50	1·30
3062	10p.50 Beagle	2·50	1·30

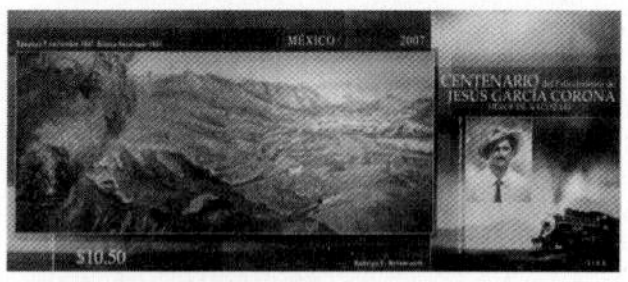

1374 Burning Train

2007. Death Centenary of Jesus Garcia Corona (train explosion hero).

3063	**1374** 10p.50 multicoloured	2·75	1·50

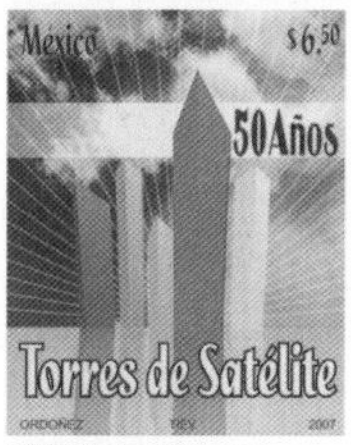

1375 Stylized Towers

2007. 50th Anniv of Torres de Satelite, Naucalpan de Juarez.

3064	**1375** 6p.50 multicoloured	1·80	1·00

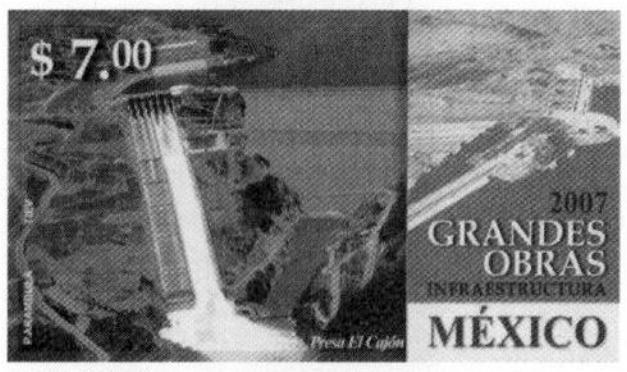

1376 Outflow

2007. Infrastructure. El Cajon Dam. Multicoloured.

3065	7p. Type **1376**	2·00	1·10
3066	13p. Aerial view	3·00	1·60

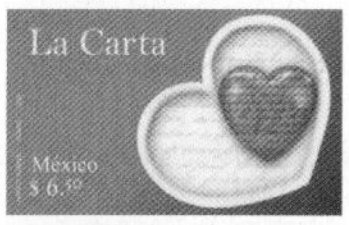

1377 Hearts enclosing Script

2008. The Letter.

3067	**1377** 6p.50 multicoloured	1·90	1·10

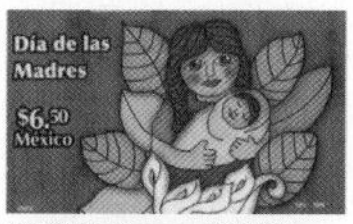

1378 Mother and Child

2008. Mothers' Day.

3068	**1378** 6p.50 multicoloured	1·90	1·10

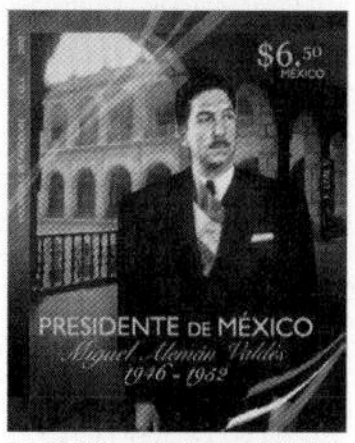

1379 Miguel Aleman Valdes

2008. Miguel Aleman Valdes (president 1946–1952) Commemoration.

3069	**1379** 6p.50 multicoloured	1·90	1·10

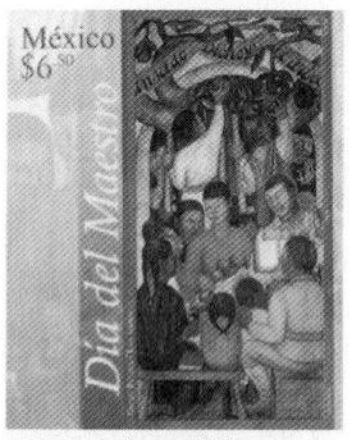

1380 *Los frutos* (Diego Rivera)

2008. Teachers' Day.

3070	**1380** 6p.50 multicoloured	1·90	1·10

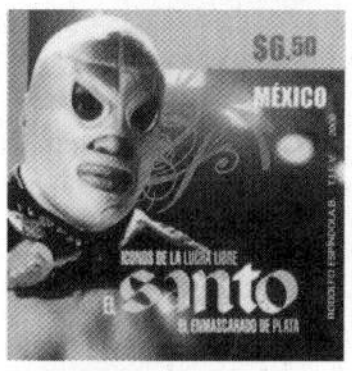

1381 Santo

2008. Wrestling Heroes. Rodolfo Guzman Huerta (Santo, el Enmascarado de Plata (Saint, the Silver Masked Man)) (wrestler) Commemoration. Multicoloured.

MS3071 6p.50×6, Type **1381**; In ring; With hands raised; Head and shoulders, looking up; Flying leap; Head and shoulders, facing front 12·00 12·00

A miniature sheet was on sale on 19 June 2008 at 150p., for the same anniversary.

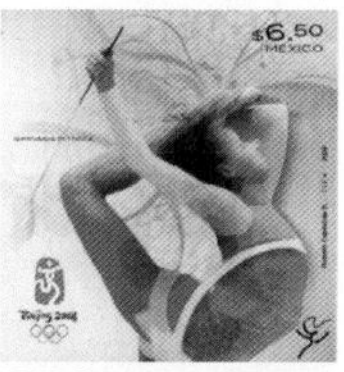

1382 Gymnast

2008. Olympic Games, Beijing. Multicoloured.

3072	6p.50 Type **1382**	1·90	1·10
3073	6p.50 Rower	1·90	1·10
3074	6p.50 Weight lifter	1·90	1·10

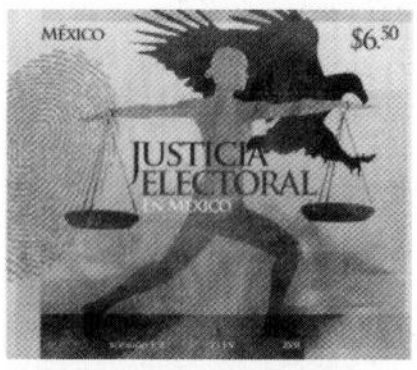

1383 Fingerprint, Justice and Raptor

2008. Electoral Justice.

3075	**1383** 6p.50 multicoloured	1·90	1·10

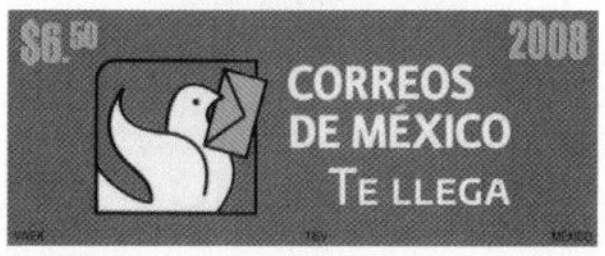

1384 Bird holding Envelope

2008. Mexico Post.
3076	**1384**	6p.50 magenta and green	1·90	1·10

1385 *Ignacio Allende (Ramon Perez)*

2008. Bicentenary of Independence. Multicoloured.
3077		6p.50 Type **1385**	1·90	1·10
3078		6p.50 *Jose Maria Morelos y Pavon (El Mixtequito)*	1·90	1·10
3079		6p.50 *Josefa Ortiz de Dominguez*	1·90	1·10
3080		6p.50 *Batalla del Monte de las Cruces (47×39 mm)*	1·90	1·10
3081		6p.50 *Casa Municipal and Francisco Primo de Verdad y Ramos (71×30 mm)*	1·90	1·10
3082		6p.50 *Meeting of Hidalgo and Morelos (71×30 mm)*	1·90	1·10
3083		6p.50 *Conspiracion de Queretaro (71×30 mm)*	1·90	1·10
3084		6p.50 *Batalla de la Alhondiga de Granaditas (71×30 mm)*	1·90	1·10
MS3085	80×81 mm (a) 10p.50 *Rompiendo Cadenas.* Imperf; (b) 10p.50 *La Almeda de la Ciudad de Mexico en un Domingo Porla Manana.* Imperf		6·00	6·00

1386 *La Historia*

2008. 75th Anniv of Nuevo Leon University. Sheet 157×158 mm containing T 1386 and similar square designs showing stained glass windows by Roberto Montenegro. Multicoloured.
MS3086	6p.50×6, Type **1386**; *La Agricultura; La Ciencia y la Sabiduria; La Historia* lower; *La Agricultura* lower; *La Ciencia y la Sabiduria* lower	12·00 12·00

The stamps of No. **MS**3086 form composite designs of the windows named. The two left hand stamps forming *La Historia*, the centre stamps forming *La Agricultura* and the right hand stamps forming *La Ciencia y la Sabiduria.*

1387 *Origami Dove*

2008. Stamp Day.
3087	**1387**	10p.50 multicoloured	2·75	1·50

1388 *Hylocereus undatus*

2008. Flora. Multicoloured.
3088		6p.50 Type **1388**	1·90	1·10
3089		6p.50 *Curcubita pepo*	1·90	1·10

1389 *Building Facade*

2008. 50th Anniv of Juarez Autonoma de Tabasco University.
3090	**1389**	6p.50 multicoloured	1·90	1·10

1390 *Postman*

2008. Day of the Postman. Multicoloured.
3091		6p.50 Type **1390**	1·90	1·10
3092		6p.50 Postman cycling	1·90	1·10
3093		6p.50 Early post motor cycle	1·90	1·10
3094		6p.50 Modern post motor cycle	1·90	1·10
3095		6p.50 Early post vehicle	1·90	1·10
3096		10p.50 Modern post van	1·90	1·10
3097		6p.50 Postmen loading cycles onto van	1·90	1·10
3098		6p.50 Post woman cycling and post van	1·90	1·10

1391 *Workers*

2008. National Employment Service.
3099	**1391**	6p.50 multicoloured	1·90	1·10

1392 *Jose Maria Pino Suarez*

2008. Centenary (2010) of Revolution. Multicoloured.
3100	6p.50 Type **1392** (revolutionary leader and Vice Pres. 1911–1913)	1·90	1·10
3101	6p.50 Ricardo Flores Magon and *Regeneracion* (anarchist magazine)	1·90	1·10
3102	6p.50 Aquiles Serdan	1·90	1·10
3103	6p.50 *La Junta Revolucionaria de Puebla* (Daniel Guzman) (72×30 mm)	1·90	1·10
3104	6p.50 Steam locomotive (72×30 mm)	1·90	1·10
3105	6p.50 *Del Porfirismo la Revolucion* (David Alfaro Siqueiros) (72×30 mm)	1·90	1·10
3106	6p.50 Mexican Liberal Party watching soldiers beat demonstrators (72×30 mm)	1·90	1·10
MS3107	81×81 mm. 10p.50 Triumphal entry of Francisco I. Madero (revolutionary and Pres. 1911–1913) Imperf	2·75	2·75
MS3108	81×81 mm. 10p.50 *El Feudalismo Portfirista* (Juan O'Gorman). Imperf	2·75	2·75

1393 *Museum Exhibits*

2008. 50th Anniv of La Venta Park Museum.
3109	**1393**	6p.50 multicoloured	1·90	1·10

1394 *Adoracion de los Pastores (Cristobal de Villapando)*

2008. Christmas. Multicoloured.
3110		6p.50 Type **1394**	1·90	1·10
3111		10p.50 *Adoracion de los Reyes* (anonymous Flemish painter)	2·75	1·50

1395 *Gonzalo Aguirre Beltran*

2008. Birth Centenary of Gonzalo Aguirre Beltran (anthropologist).
3112	**1395**	6p.50 multicoloured	1·90	1·10

1397 *Trophy*

2008. 50th Anniv of Entrega del Ariel (cinematography awards).
3114	**1397**	6p.50 multicoloured	1·90	1·10

No. 3113 and Type **1396** have been left for Archaeology, issued on 19 Dec 2008, not yet received.

1398 *Cupid*

2009. Day of Love and Friendship.
3115	**1398**	6p.50 multicoloured	1·90	1·10

1399 *Mask*

2009. Veracruz Carnival.
3116	**1399**	6p.50 multicoloured	1·90	1·10

1400 *Jointed Yoke and Eagle-shaped Ax Head*

2009. Archaeology. El Tajin. Sheet 161×96 mm containing T 1400 and similar horiz designs. Multicoloured.
MS3117	6p.50 Type **1400**; 6p.50 Carved plaque showing ball game; 10p.50 Terracotta ball player and ball game building; 13p. Carved chest defence and temple to the god Tajin; 13p. Pyramid of Niches and parrot-shaped ax head	14·00 14·00

No. **MS**3117 also contains a stamp size label the whole forming a composite design.

1401 *Symbols of Programme Production*

2009. 50th Anniv of Canal Once (television channel).
3118	**1401**	6p.50 multicoloured	2·00	1·20

1402 *Construccion de un Nuevo Mundo—La Maestra (Diego Rivera)*

2009. Day of the Teacher.
3119	**1402**	6p.50 multicoloured	2·00	1·20

1403 *Palacio de los Condes de San Mateo Valparaiso, Mexico City (c. 1800)*

2009. 125th Anniv of National Bank. Sheet 161×96 mm containing T 1403 and similar horiz designs. Multicoloured.
MS3120	6p.50×6, Type **1403**; Principal courtyard, Counts of San Mateo Valparaiso Palace; Details of columns, Palace of Iturbide; Casa Montejo, Fachada, Merida; Casa del Mayorazgo de Canal, San Miguel de Allende; Palacio de los Valle de Suchil, Durango	14·00 14·00

1404 *Sea, Globe and Pre-Columbian Bas Relief*

2009. World Environment Day.
3121	**1404**	10p.50 multicoloured	3·00	1·75

1405 *Central Courtyard*

2009. Aguascalientes University.
3122	**1405**	10p.50 multicoloured	3·00	1·75

1406 *Californian Condor*

2009. Endangered Species. Gymnogyps californianus.
3123	**1406**	10p.50 multicoloured	3·00	1·75

1407 *Indigenous Textiles, Pot and Dance*

2009. International Day of Indigenous Peoples.
3124	**1407**	6p.50 multicoloured	2·00	1·20

1408 *La Patria (Jorge Gonzalez Camarena)*

2009. 50th Anniv of National Commission for Free Text Books.
3125	**1408**	6p.50 multicoloured	2·00	1·20

1409 Popocatepetl and Iztaccihuatl Mountains

2009. Preserve Polar Regions and Glaciers. Multicoloured.
3126	10p.50 Type **1409**	3·00	1·75
3127	13p. Citlaltepetl mountain	3·75	2·20

Nos. 3126/7 were printed, setenant, each pair forming a composite design.

1410 Congress of Chilpancingo, 1813

2009. Bicentenary of Independence. Multicoloured.
3128	6p.50 Type **1410**	2·00	1·20
3129	6p.50 Leona Vicario and Andres Quintana Roo (members of Los Guadalupes (independence society))	2·00	1·20
3130	6p.50 Installation of supreme governing junta	2·00	1·20
3131	6p.50 Execution of Miguel Hidalgo (horiz)	2·00	1·20
3132	6p.50 Execution of Jose María Morelos (horiz)	2·00	1·20
3133	6p.50 Capture of the early leaders (horiz)	2·00	1·20
3134	6p.50 Cuatla, site of battle of War of Independence (72×30 mm)	2·00	1·20
3135	6p.50 Constitution of Apatzingan (72×30 mm)	2·00	1·20
MS3136	81×81 mm. 10p.50 Leaders of the revolution	2·75	2·75
MS3137	81×81 mm. 10p.50 Abolition of slavery	2·75	2·75

1411 Postal Messengers

2009. Americas UNI Post and Logistics Meeting.
3138	**1411** 6p.50 multicoloured	2·00	1·20

1412 Institute Building

2009. 150th Anniv of Literary and Scientific Institute, University of San Luis Potosi.
3139	**1412** 6p.50 multicoloured	2·00	1·20

1413 Envelope as Paper Plane

2009. Stamp Day.
3140	**1413** 10p.50 multicoloured	3·00	1·75

1414 Metropolitan Cathedral of Chihuahua

2009. 300th Anniv of Chihuahua.
3141	**1414** 6p.50 multicoloured	2·00	1·20

1415 Day of the Dead

2009. Traditions. Day of the Dead. Multicoloured.
3142	6p.50 Type **1415**	2·00	1·20
3143	6p.50 Wheel of Fortune	2·00	1·20

1416 Juan Bosch

2009. Birth Centenary of Juan Emilio Bosch Gavino (Juan Bosch) (politician, historian, writer and first freely elected president of Dominican Republic).
3144	**1416** 10p.50 multicoloured	3·00	1·75

1417 El Carmen, Mexico

2009. Wilderness Areas. Multicoloured.
3145	6p.50 Type **1417**	2·00	1·20
3146	10p.50 Nahanni, Canada	3·00	1·75
3147	10p.50 Zion, USA	3·00	1·75
3148	13p. Kronotsky, Russia	3·00	1·75
3149	14p.50 Baviaanskloof, South Africa	3·00	1·75

1418 Postman riding Bicycle

2009. Day of the Postman.
3150	6p.50 black and magenta	2·00	1·20
3151	6p.50 black and apple green	2·00	1·20

DESIGNS: Type **1418**; Postman riding motorcycle

1419 Revolutionaries (fresco)

2009. Threshold of Centenary of Mexican Revolution. Multicoloured.
3152	6p.50 Type **1419**	2·00	1·20
3153	6p.50 Francisco Indalecio Madero Gonzalez (politician, writer, revolutionary and President of Mexico 1911–1913)	2·00	1·20
3154	6p.50 Emiliano Zapata Salazar (revolutionary leader)	2·00	1·20
3155	6p.50 Women revolutionaries (horiz)	2·00	1·20
3156	6p.50 Battle of Zacatecas (horiz)	2·00	1·20
3157	6p.50 The Ten Days, February 1913 (uprising against Pres. Madero) (72×30 mm)	2·00	1·20
3158	6p.50 Revolutionary train (72×30 mm)	2·00	1·20
3159	6p.50 Jose Doroteo Arango Arambula (Francisco Villa or Pancho Villa) (revolutionary leader) (72×30 mm)	2·00	1·20
MS3160	80×80 mm. 10p.50 Revolutionaries	2·75	2·75
MS3161	80×80 mm. 10p.50 Venustiano Carranza de la Garza (revolutionary leader and President of Mexico 1914)	2·75	2·75

1420 Vehicle and Safety Symbols

2009. Road Safety.
3162	**1420** 6p.50 multicoloured	2·00	1·20

1421 Jaime Sabines

2009. 10th Death Anniv of Jaime Sabines Gutierrez (poet).
3163	**1421** 6p.50 multicoloured	2·00	1·20

1422 Audit Office and Notice

2009. 50th Anniv of Federal Tax Audit.
3164	**1422** 6p.50 multicoloured	2·00	1·20

1423 Balthasar (inscr 'Baltazar')

2009. Christmas.
3165	6p.50 Type **1423**	2·00	1·20
3166	6p.50 Melchior (inscr 'Melchor')	2·00	1·20
3167	6p.50 Caspar (inscr 'Gaspar')	2·00	1·20
3168	6p.50 Santa Claus	2·00	1·20

1424 Mother, Children and Symbols of Education and Good Diet

2009. Human Development Programme.
3169	**1424** 6p.50 multicoloured	2·00	1·20

1425 Girl plugging into Sun (Camila Hernandez Sanchez Chavez)

2009. Energy Conservation. Winning Designs in Children's Drawing Competition. Multicoloured.
3170	6p.50 Type **1425**	2·00	1·20
3171	6p.50 Solar powered light bulbs (Luis Javier Alvarez Santoyo)	2·00	1·20
3172	6p.50 Children as light bulbs (Martha Patricia Agundez)	2·00	1·20

Nos. 3170/2 were printed, se-tenant, in horizontal strips of three stamps within the sheet.

1426 Agricultural Workers and City Skyline

2009. Civil Programme.
3173	**1426** 6p.50 multicoloured	2·00	1·20

1427 Venustiano Carranza

2009. 150th Birth Anniv of Venustiano Carranza de la Garza (revolutionary leader).
3174	**1427** 6p.50 multicoloured	2·00	1·20

1428 Voisin Aircraft and Alberto Braniff Ricard (first flight in Mexico)

2010. Centenary of Mexican Aviation
3175	**1428** 7p. multicoloured	2·00	1·20

1429 Surgeons and Hospital Interior

2010. 50th Anniv of ISSSTE (Institute of Security and Social Services for State Employees)
3176	**1429** 7p. multicoloured	2·00	1·20

1430 Balloons, Heart, Star and Envelope

2010. Day of Love and Friendship
3177	**1430** 7p. multicoloured	2·00	1·20

1431 Tiger

2010. Chinese New Year. Year of the Tiger
3178	**1431** 7p. multicoloured	2·00	1·20

1432 Luz Gonzalez Cosio de Lopez (founder)

2010. Centenary of Mexican Red Cross
3179	**1432** 10p.50 black and scarlet-vermilion	2·00	1·20

1433 Emblem and Governor's Palace, Uxmal

2010. BIDCII, 2010 (Inter-American Development Bank Board of Governors' Meeting), Cancun, Mexico
3180	**1433** 11p.50 multicoloured	2·00	1·20

1434 Decorated
Pot with Legs

2010. Popular Crafts. Multicoloured.

3181	50c. Type **1434**		15	10
3182	1p. Lacquered wooden trunk		25	15
3183	1p.50 Decorative horn comb		20	10
3184	2p. Black clay pitcher		25	15
3185	2p.50 Paper bull within cage of paper flags		30	15
3186	5p. Silk shawl		1·10	60
3187	7p. Statuette of woman wearing traditional dress (inscr 'Muñeca de plata pella')		2·00	1·20
3188	7p.50 Copper vase		2·10	1·30
3189	11p.50 Bowl shaped basket		3·00	1·75
3190	13p.50 Silver incised pear		3·25	2·00
3191	15p. Marimba		3·25	2·00

Nos. 3192/210 are left for possible additions to this series.

1435 Jose Luis Sandoval

2010. Baseball in Mexico. Los Diablos Rojos del México. Multicoloured.

MS3211 158×93 mm. 7p.×3, Type **1435**; Miguel Oieda; Roberto Saucedo		5·50	5·50

1436 Gerberas

2010. Mothers' Day

3212	**1436**	7p. multicoloured	2·00	1·20

1437 La Escuela Rural
(detail from mural
Reconstruccion y la fiesta
de la Santa Cruz by
Roberto Montenegro
Nervo)

2010. Teachers' Day

3213	**1437**	7p. multicoloured	2·00	1·20

1438 Mexican Team (for Mexico versus
New Zealand match)

2010. World Cup Football Championships, South Africa. Multicoloured.

3214	7p. Type **1438**		2·00	1·20
3215	7p. Gerardo Torrado (No. 6) and Giovani dos Santos (No. 17)		2·00	1·20
3216	11p.50 Andres Guardado (No. 18) and Guillermo Ochoa (goalkeeper)		3·00	1·75

Nos. 3214/16 were printed, *se-tenant*, froming a composite design.

1439 Profiles and Indigenous
Languages

2010. International Day of Indigenous Languages

3217	**1439**	11p.50 multicoloured	3·00	1·75

1440 Adolfo López Mateos

2010. Birth Centenary of Adolfo López Mateos (politician)

3218	**1440**	7p. multicoloured	2·00	1·20

1441 Flower
containing
Figures

2010. National Commission for Human Rights

3219	**1441**	7p. multicoloured	2·00	1·20

1442 Scouts crossing Forest
Bridge

2010. Scouts, Mexico

3220	**1442**	7p. multicoloured	2·00	1·20

1443 Grandparents and
Grandchild

2010. Grandparents' Day

3221	**1443**	7p. multicoloured	2·00	1·20

1444 Symbols of Petroleum Production

2010. Mexican Institute of Petroleum

3222	**1444**	7p. multicoloured	2·00	

1445 Pedro Moreno

2010. Bicentenary of Independence. Multicoloured.

3223	7p. Type **1445**		2·00	1·20
3224	7p. José Servando Teresa de Mier Noriega y Guerra (Servando Teresa de Mier)		2·00	1·20
3225	7p. Trigarante Army flag		2·00	1·20
3226	7p. Vicente Ramón Guerrero Saldaña (Vicente Guerrero)		2·00	1·20
3227	7p. José Miguel Ramón Adaucto Fernández y Félix (Guadalupe Victoria)		2·00	1·20
3228	7p. Francisco Javier Mina (Xavier Mina)		2·00	1·20
3229	7p. Interview between Agustín de Iturbide and Juan O'Donojú y O'Rian (Juan O'Donojú) (horiz)		2·00	1·20
3230	7p. Ignacio López Rayón (horiz)		2·00	1·20
3231	7p. Cannon at Celaya battle (horiz)		2·00	1·20
3232	7p. José Manuel Rafael Simeón de Mier y Terán (Manuel de Mier y Terán) (horiz)		2·00	1·20

MS3233 80×80 mm. 11p.50 José Miguel Domínguez Alemán and members of the Independence movement. Imperf	2·00 1·20
MS3233a 80×80 mm. 11p.50 Entry of Trigarante Army. Imperf	2·00 1·20

1446 Justo Sierra Méndez
(founder) and Inauguration
of UNAM

2010. Centenary of the National University of Mexico . Multicoloured.

MS3234 7p.×6, Type **1446**; National Preparatory School, stained glass window and San Ildefonso College; San Carlos Academy; National Art Studies School; Campus murals; Philharmonic Orchestra and choreography workshop; University Museum of Contemporary Art	14·00 14·00

1447 The Guide Sign

2010. Guides, Mexico

3235		7p. multicoloured	2·00	1·20

1448 Satellites and ITU Emblem

2010. Plenipotentiary Conference of the International Telecommunication Union

3236	**1448**	11p.50 multicoloured	3·00	1·75

1449 Paper as Hand
holding Pen and Script

2010. Stamp Day

3237	**1449**	11p.50 multicoloured	3·00	1·75

1449a Pyramid of the
Moon, Teotihuacan (Mexico)

2010. Ancient Architecture. Multicoloured.

MS3237a 7p.×2, Type **1449a**; Ateshgah (Temple of fire), Azerbaijan	4·00 4·00

Stamps of a similar design were issued by Azerbaijan.

1450 Dealing with Disaster

2010. 20th Anniv of National Center for Disaster Prevention

3238	**1450**	7p. multicoloured	2·00	1·20

1451 Catrina and
Catrin

2010. Mexican Traditions. Day of the Dead

3239	**1451**	7p. multicoloured	2·00	1·20

1452 The Nativity

2010. Christmas. Multicoloured.

3240	7p. Type **1452**		2·00	1·20
3241	7p. Children playing piñata		2·00	1·20
3242	7p. Three Magi		2·00	1·20

1453 Christmas Tree, Santa
and Children peeking
around Door

2010. Christmas (2nd issue)

3243	**1453**	7p. multicoloured	2·00	1·20

1454 Early Postman and
Mail Van

2010. Day of the Postman. Multicoloured.

3245	7p. Type **1454**		2·00	1·20
3246	11p.50 Modern postman riding motorcycle and mail vans		3·00	1·75

1455 Rodolfo Neri Vela and
Satellites

2010. 25th Anniversary of the First Mexican in Space. Multicoloured.

3247	7p. Type **1455**		2·00	1·20
3248	7p. Rodolfo Neri Vela, flag and shuttle launch		2·00	1·20

1456 Building Façade

2010. Palace of Arts

3249	**1456**	7p. multicoloured	2·00	1·20

1457 Convention of Aguascalientes

2010. Centenary of Mexican Revolution
3250	7p. Type **1457**	2·00	1·20
3251	7p. Revolutionaries fighting at battle of Celaya	2·00	1·20
3252	7p. Crowd (*Constitucion de 1917* (detail) (Jorge Gonzalez Camarena))(vert)	2·00	1·20
3253	7p. Farm Bill and Luis Cabrera (vert)	2·00	1·20
3254	7p. Venustiano Carranza (constitutional president)	2·00	1·20
3255	7p. Venustiano Carranza (*Constitucion de 1917* (detail) (Jorge Gonzalez Camarena)) (vert)	2·00	1·20
3256	7p. Woman and children (*Las Mujeres en la Revolucion Mexicana*) (71×30 mm)	2·00	1·20
3257	7p. Eulalio Gutierrez and Roque Gonzalez Garza (provincila presidents) (71×30 mm)	2·00	1·20
MS3258	80×80mm. 11p.50 Francisco Villa, Emiliano Zapata and Venustiano Carranza on horse back. Imperf	3·00	3·00
MS3259	80×80mm. 11p.50 (*Revolucion de 1910*) (Diego Rivera). Imperf	3·00	3·00

1458 Justice (bronze statue) and Hands

2010. International Day of Eradication of Violence against Women
3260	**1458**	11p.50 multicoloured	3·00	1·75

1458a Clock Tower

2010. Centenary of Monumental Clock of Pachuca Hidalgo
3260a	**1458a**	7p. multicoloured	2·00	1·20

1458b Tree and Butterflies (conference emblem)

2010. Climate Change Conferences. COP16 (Conference of Parties to United Nations Framework Convention on Climate Change) and CMP6 (Conference of Parties to Kyoto Protocol), Cancún
3260b	**1458b**	7p. multicoloured	2·00	1·20

1459 Symbols of Science and Technology

2010. 40th Anniv of National Council of Science and Technology, CONACYT
3261	**1459**	7p. multicoloured	2·00	1·20

1460 Octavio Paz

2010. 20th Anniv of Octavio Paz's Nobel Prize for Literature
3262	**1460**	7p. multicoloured	2·00	1·20

1461 Men and Women at Work

2010. Week of Small and Medium Enterprises
3263	**1461**	7p. multicoloured	2·00	1·20

1462 Amalia Hernandez's Ballet Folklorico de Mexico

2010. Dance. Multicoloured.
MS3264	7p.×2, Type **1462**; Kalibelia Dance, India	4·00	4·00

1462a Great Blue Heron

2010. Fauna of Gulf of Mexico. Great Blue Heron (*Ardea herodias*)
3264a	**1462a**	11p.50 multicoloured	3·00	1·75

1463

2010. Archaeology. Teotihuacan. Multicoloured.
MS3265	7p. Type **1463**; 7p. Sun enclosing skull and Quetzalpapalotl Palace entrance columns; 11p.50 Stone incense burner and decorated vase; 13p.50 Pyramid of the Moon and Pyramid of the Sun; 13p.50 Steps leading up Pyramid of the Moon	10·50	10·50

The stamps, label and margins of **MS**3265 form a composite design.

1464 *Cypripedium irapeanum*

2010. Orchids. Multicoloured.
MS3266	7p.×6, Type **1464**; *Sobralia macrantha*; *Prostnechea ionophlebia*; *Laelia anceps*; *Trichocentrum oerstedii*; *Laelia rubescens*	14·00	14·00

1465 Seedling, Electricity Pylon and Anniversary Emblem

2010. 20th Anniv of FIDE (energy saving trust)
3267	**1465**	7p. multicoloured	2·00	1·20

1466 Flowers and Hearts

2011. Day of Love and Friendship
3268	7p. Type **1466**	2·00	1·20
3269	7p. Large heart and banner enclosed by flowers	2·00	1·20

1467 Anniversary Emblem

2011. Centenary of UPAEP
3270	**1467**	13p.50 multicoloured	3·25	2·00

1468 Mother and Children

2011. Mothers' Day
3271	**1468**	7p. multicoloured	2·00	1·20

1469 Seeds

2011. 50th Anniv of National Control and Seed Certfication. Multicoloured.
3272	7p. Type **1469**	2·00	1·20
3273	7p. Flowering plants and plant assessment	2·00	1·20
3274	7p. Fruit and flowers	2·00	1·20

1470 Building and Decorative Detail

2011. Postal Palace
3275	**1470**	7p. multicoloured	2·00	1·20

1471 Mil Máscaras

2011. Wrestling Heros. Aaron Rodríguez Arellano (Mil Máscaras (A Thousand Masks)). Multicoloured.
MS3276	7p.×3, Type **1471**; With left hand raised; Posing with other wrestlers in background; Seated head and shoulders, facing front	6·00	6·00

1472 *La Mestra Rural* (fresco, Diego Rivera)

2011. Teachers' Day
3277	**1472**	7p. multicoloured	2·00	1·20

1473 Armillita

2011. Birth Centenary of Fermin Espinosa (Armillita) (bull fighter)
3278	**1473**	7p. multicoloured	2·00	1·20

1474 Trophy and Players tackling for Ball

2011. FIFA U-17 World Cup, Mexico. Multicoloured.
3279	7p. Type **1474**	2·00	1·20
3280	11p.50 Player, goalkeeper and ball in net	3·00	1·75
3281	13p.50 Player, wearing green strip, and ball	3·25	2·00

EXPRESS LETTER STAMPS

E55 Express Service Messenger

1919
E445	**E55**	20c. black and red	40	25

E95

1934
E536	**E95**	10c. blue and red	25	50

1934. New President's Assumption of Office. Imprint "OFICINA IMPRESORA DE HACIENDA–MEXICO".
E581	**E121**	10c. violet	1·60	50

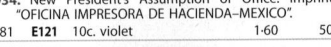

E121 Indian Archer

1938. Imprint "TALLERES DE IMP. DE EST. Y VALORES-MEXICO".
E610	10c. violet	90	25
E731	20c. orange	90	25

1940. Optd 1940.
E665	**E55**	20c. black and red	45	25

E222

1950
E860	**E222**	25c. orange	50	20
E910	-	60c. green	1·20	1·00

DESIGN: 60c. Hands and letter.

E244   **E245**

1956
E954	**E244**	35c. purple	50	20
E1065	**E244**	50c. green	2·40	55
E956	**E 245**	80c. red	50	65
E1066	**E 245**	1p.20 lilac	3·50	1·10
E1346p	**E 244**	2p. orange	3·75	60
E1346q	**E 245**	5p. blue	2·75	1·20

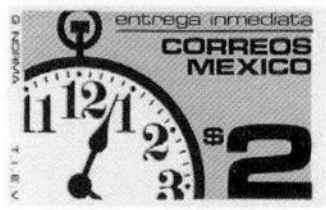

E468 Watch Face

1979

E1373	**E468**	2p. black and orange	30	20

INSURED LETTER STAMPS

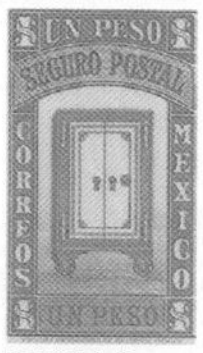

IN125 Safe

1935. Inscr as in Type **IN125**.

IN583	-	10c. red	2·75	95
IN733	-	50c. blue	2·00	70
IN734	**IN 125**	1p. green	1·70	85

DESIGNS: 10c. Bundle of insured letters; 50c. Registered mailbag.

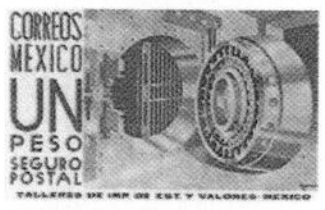

IN222 P.O. Treasury Vault

1950

IN911	**IN 222**	20c. blue	40	20
IN912	**IN 222**	40c. purple	40	20
IN913	**IN 222**	1p. green	50	20
IN914	**IN 222**	5p. green and blue	1·50	1·10
IN915	**IN 222**	10p. blue and red	7·25	2·75

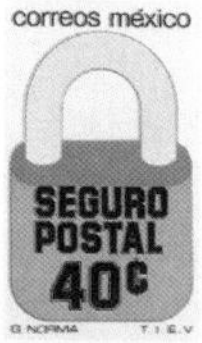

IN469 Padlock

1976

IN1374	**IN469**	40c. black & turq	45	25
IN1522	**IN469**	1p. black & turq	70	35
IN1376	**IN469**	2p. black and blue	40	25
IN1380	**IN469**	5p. black & turq	2·00	50
IN1524	**IN469**	10p. black & turq	3·00	45
IN1525	**IN469**	20p. black & turq	3·00	90
IN1383	**IN469**	50p. black & turq	1·70	70
IN1384	**IN469**	100p. black & turq	2·75	1·60

The 5, 10, 20p. exist with the padlock either 31 or 32½ mm high.

OFFICIAL STAMPS

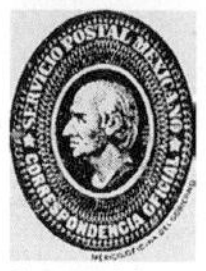

O 18 Hidalgo

1884. No value shown.

O156	**O 18**	Red	95	70
O157	**O 18**	Brown	60	45
O158	**O 18**	Orange	1·70	60
O159	**O 18**	Green	95	55
O160	**O 18**	Blue	2·00	1·90

1894. Stamps of 1895 handstamped OFICIAL.

O231	**19**	1c. green	12·00	4·00
O232	**19**	2c. red	13·50	4·00
O233	**19**	3c. brown	12·00	4·00
O234	**20**	4c. orange	18·00	8·00
O235	**21**	5c. blue	24·00	8·00
O236	**22**	10c. purple	22·00	2·00
O237	**20**	12c. olive	47·00	20·00
O238	**22**	15c. blue	29·00	12·00
O239	**22**	20c. red	29·00	12·00
O240	**22**	50c. mauve	60·00	29·00
O241	**23**	1p. brown	£140	60·00
O242	**23**	5p. red	£325	£170
O243	**23**	10p. blue	£500	£350

1899. Stamps of 1899 handstamped OFICIAL.

O276	**27**	1c. green	25·00	1·70
O286	**27**	1c. purple	12·50	2·00
O277	**27**	2c. red	34·00	2·75
O287	**27**	2c. green	12·50	2·00
O278	**27**	3c. brown	34·00	1·70
O288	**27**	4c. red	22·00	1·50
O279	**27**	5c. blue	34·00	3·00
O289	**27**	5c. orange	22·00	5·00
O280	**27**	10c. brown and purple	44·00	3·75
O290	**27**	10c. orange and blue	24·00	2·00
O281	**27**	15c. purple and lavender	44·00	3·75
O282	**27**	20c. blue and red	50·00	1·70
O283	**28**	50c. black and purple	£100	17·00
O291	**28**	50c. black and red	65·00	9·25
O284	**29**	1p. black and blue	£200	17·00
O285	**30**	5p. black and red	£400	50·00

1911. Independence stamps optd OFICIAL.

O301	**32**	1c. purple	3·50	3·50
O302	-	2c. green	2·50	1·50
O303	-	3c. brown	3·50	1·70
O304	-	4c. red	3·75	1·50
O305	-	5c. orange	8·50	4·75
O306	-	10c. orange and blue	3·75	1·50
O307	-	15c. lake and slate	8·75	5·75
O308	-	20c. blue and lake	6·75	1·70
O309	**40**	50c. black and brown	24·00	10·00
O310	-	1p. black and blue	41·00	17·00
O311	-	5p. black and red	£200	85·00

1915. Stamps of 1915 optd OFICIAL.

O321	**43**	1c. violet	70	1·40
O322	**44**	2c. green	70	1·40
O323	**45**	3c. brown	70	1·40
O324	**45**	4c. red	70	1·40
O325	**45**	5c. orange	70	1·40
O326	**45**	10c. blue	70	1·40

1915. Stamps of 1915 optd OFICIAL.

O318	**46**	40c. grey	5·50	9·75
O455	**46**	40c. mauve	5·00	3·50
O319	**47**	1p. grey and brown	7·25	9·75
O456	**47**	1p. grey and blue	25·00	17·00
O320	**48**	5p. blue and lake	42·00	40·00
O457	**48**	5p. grey and green	£225	£225

1916. Nos. O301/11 optd with T 49.

O358	**32**	1c. purple	4·50	
O359	-	2c. green	90	
O360	-	3c. brown	1·20	
O361	-	4c. red	5·00	
O362	-	5c. orange	1·20	
O363	-	10c. orange and blue	1·20	
O364	-	15c. lake and slate	1·20	
O365	-	20c. blue and lake	1·30	
O366	**40**	50c. black and brown	£140	
O367	-	1p. black and blue	7·50	
O368	-	5p. black and red	£3000	

1918. Stamps of 1917 optd OFICIAL.

O424	**53**	1c. violet	4·25	4·00
O446	**53**	1c. grey	2·10	1·10
O447	-	2c. green	1·30	45
O448	-	3c. brown	55	45
O449	-	4c. red	13·50	1·70
O450	-	5c. blue	70	45
O451	-	10c. blue	70	45
O452	-	20c. lake	3·75	1·70
O454	-	30c. black	7·50	3·50

1923. No. 416 optd OFICIAL.

O485	10p. black and brown	£140	£200

1923. Stamps of 1923 optd OFICIAL.

O471	**59**	1c. brown	45	55
O473	**60**	2c. red	45	70
O475	**61**	3c. brown	1·40	1·00
O461	**62**	4c. green	4·25	3·50
O476	**63**	4c. green	1·10	75
O477	**63**	5c. orange	2·75	1·90
O489	**74**	8c. orange	6·75	4·75
O479	**66**	10c. lake	1·60	1·50
O480	**65**	20c. blue	8·50	6·75
O464	**64**	30c. green	1·10	70
O467	**68**	50c. brown	1·10	1·00
O469	**69**	1p. blue and lake	11·00	10·50

1929. Air. Optd OFICIAL.

O501	**80**	5c. blue (roul)	1·00	1·00
O502	**81**	20c. violet	1·20	1·90
O490	**58**	25c. sepia and green	4·00	4·25
O492	**58**	25c. sepia and lake	11·00	13·00

1929. Air. As 1926 Postal Congress stamp optd HABILITADO Servicio Oficial Aereo.

O493	**70**	2c. black	70·00	80·00
O494	-	4c. black	70·00	80·00
O495	**70**	5c. black	70·00	80·00
O496	-	10c. black	70·00	80·00
O497	**72**	20c. black	70·00	80·00
O498	**72**	30c. black	70·00	80·00
O499	**72**	40c. black	70·00	80·00
O500	**73**	1p. black	£2250	£2000

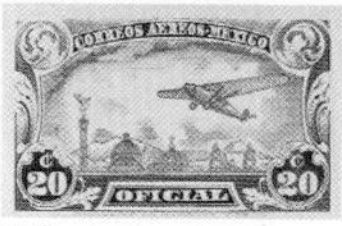

O85

1930. Air.

O503	**O85**	20c. grey	7·25	7·00
O504	**O85**	35c. violet	1·30	2·20
O505	**O85**	40c. blue and brown	1·50	2·10
O506	**O85**	70c. sepia and violet	1·50	2·20

1931. Air. Surch HABILITADO Quince centavos.

O515	15c. on 20c. grey	45	55

1932. Air. Optd SERVICIO OFICIAL in one line.

O532	**80**	10c. violet (perf or roul)	45	60
O533	**80**	15c. red (perf or roul)	1·50	2·10
O534	**80**	20c. sepia (roul)	1·50	2·10
O531	**58**	50c. red and blue	1·50	1·90

1932. Stamps of 1923 optd SERVICIO OFICIAL in two lines.

O535	**59**	1c. brown	45	70
O536	**60**	2c. red	55	60
O537	**61**	3c. brown	2·10	2·00
O538	**63**	4c. green	7·00	5·25
O539	**63**	5c. red	9·50	5·25
O540	**66**	10c. lake	2·40	2·00
O541	**65**	20c. blue	10·50	6·75
O544	**64**	30c. green	5·50	2·00
O545	**46**	40c. mauve	10·50	4·00
O546	**68**	50c. brown	1·80	2·00
O547	**69**	1p. blue and lake	2·00	2·00

1933. Air. Optd SERVICIO OFICIAL in two lines.

O553	**58**	50c. red and blue	1·50	2·10

1933. Air. Optd SERVICIO OFICIAL in two lines.

O548	**80**	5c. blue (No. 476a)	45	60
O549	**80**	10c. violet (No. 477)	45	35
O550	**80**	20c. sepia (No. 479)	80	1·10
O551	**80**	50c. lake (No. 481)	1·50	2·10

1934. Optd OFICIAL.

O565	**92**	15c. blue	70	70

1938. Nos. 561/71 optd OFICIAL.

O622	1c. orange	1·40	2·75
O623	2c. green	85	1·40
O624	4c. red	85	95
O625	10c. violet	85	1·70
O626	20c. blue	1·10	1·70
O627	30c. red	1·40	2·75
O628	40c. brown	1·80	2·75
O629	50c. black	2·00	1·90
O630	1p. red and brown	5·50	8·25

PARCEL POST STAMPS

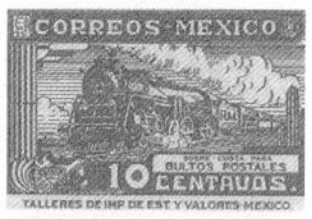

P167 Steam Mail Train

1941

P732	**P 167**	10c. red	2·30	1·30
P733	**P 167**	20c. violet	6·75	3·25

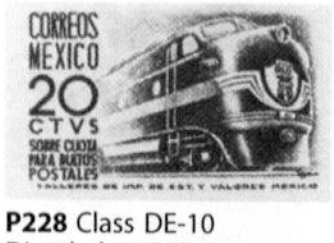

P228 Class DE-10 Diesel-electric Locomotive

1951

P916	**P 228**	10c. pink	2·50	85
P917	**P 228**	20c. violet	2·50	2·00

POSTAGE DUE STAMPS

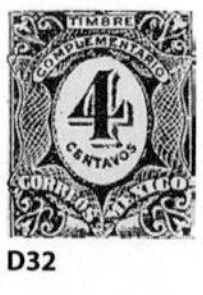

D32

1908

D282	**D 32**	1c. blue	70	1·10
D283	**D 32**	2c. blue	70	1·10
D284	**D 32**	4c. blue	70	1·10
D285	**D 32**	5c. blue	70	1·10
D286	**D 32**	10c. blue	70	1·10

Pt. 22

MICRONESIA

A group of islands in the Pacific, from 1899 to 1914 part of the German Caroline Islands. Occupied by the Japanese in 1914 the islands were from 1920 a Japanese mandated territory, and from 1947 part of the United States Trust Territory of the Pacific Islands, using United States stamps. Micronesia assumed control of its postal services in 1984.

100 cents = 1 dollar.

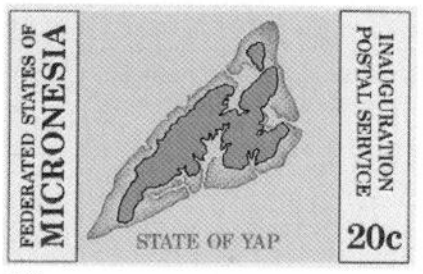

1 Yap

1984. Inauguration of Postal Independence. Maps. Multicoloured.

1	20c. Type **1**	60	55
2	20c. Truk	60	55
3	20c. Pohnpei	60	55
4	20c. Kosrae	60	55

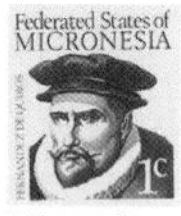

2 Fernandez de Quiros

1984

5	**2**	1c. blue	10	10
6	-	2c. brown	10	10
7	-	3c. blue	10	10
8	-	4c. green	10	10
9	-	5c. brown and olive	10	10
10	-	10c. purple	25	15
11	-	13c. blue	25	15
11a	-	15c. red	35	35
12	-	17c. brown	30	30
13	**2**	19c. purple	35	35
14	-	20c. green	35	35
14a	-	22c. green	55	50
14b	-	25c. orange	60	55
15	-	30c. red	55	50
15a	-	36c. blue	85	80
16	-	37c. violet	90	85
16a	-	45c. green	1·10	1·00
17	-	50c. brown and sepia	1·20	1·10
18	-	$1 olive	1·80	1·70
19	-	$2 blue	3·50	3·50
20	-	$5 brown	8·75	8·50
20a	-	$10 blue	18·00	17·00

DESIGNS: 2, 20c. Louis Duperrey; 3, 30c. Fyodor Lutke; 4, 37c. Jules Dumont d'Urville; 5c. Men's house, Yap; 10, 45c. Sleeping Lady (mountains), Kosrae; 13, 15c. Liduduhriap waterfall, Pohnpei; 17, 25c. Tonachau Peak, Truk; 22, 36c. "Senyavin" (full-rigged sailing ship); 50c. Devil mask, Truk; $1 Sokehs Rock, Pohnpei; $2 Outrigger canoes, Kosrae; $5 Stone money, Yap; $10 Official seal.

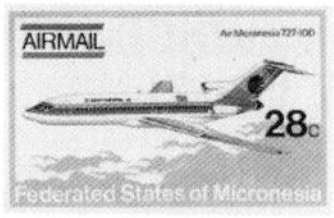

3 Boeing 727-100

1984. Air. Multicoloured.

21	28c. Type **3**	80	70
22	35c. Grumman SA-16 Albatros flying boat	1·10	95
23	40c. Consolidated PBY-5A Catalina amphibian	1·30	1·20

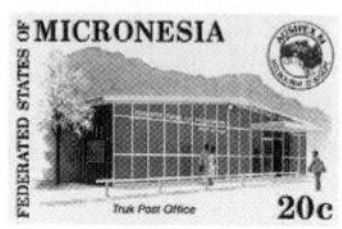

4 Truk Post Office

1984. "Ausipex 84" International Stamp Exhibition, Melbourne. Multicoloured.

24	20c. Type **4** (postage)	55	45
25	28c. German Caroline Islands 1919 3pf. yacht stamp (air)	85	75
26	35c. German 1900 20pf. stamp optd for Caroline Islands	1·10	1·00
27	40c. German Caroline Islands 1915 5m. yacht stamp	1·50	1·30

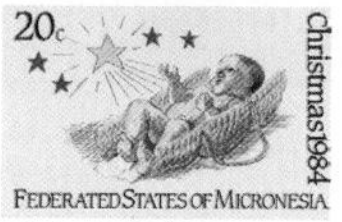

5 Baby in Basket

1984. Christmas. Multicoloured.

28	20c. Type **5** (postage)	1·20	1·10
29	28c. Open book showing Christmas scenes (air)	85	75
30	35c. Palm tree decorated with lights	1·20	1·10
31	40c. Women preparing food	1·50	1·30

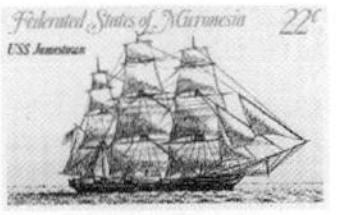

6 U.S.S. "Jamestown" (warship)

1985. Ships.

32	**6**	22c. black & brown (postage)	75	65
33	-	33c. black and lilac (air)	85	75
34	-	39c. black and green	1·10	95
35	-	44c. black and red	1·30	1·20

DESIGNS: 33c. "L'Astrolabe" (D'Urville's ship); 39c. "La Coquille" (Duperrey's ship); 44c. "Shenandoah" (Confederate warship).

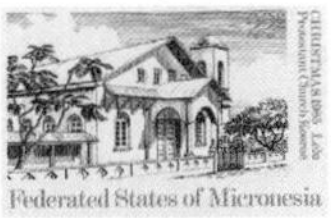

7 Lelu Protestant Church, Kosrae

1985. Christmas.

36	**7**	22c. black and orange (postage)	1·00	90
37	-	33c. black and violet (air)	1·20	1·10
38	-	44c. black and green	1·60	1·50

DESIGNS: 33c. Dublon Protestant Church; 44c. Pohnpei Catholic Church.

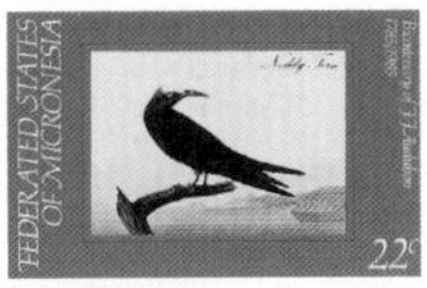

8 "Noddy Tern"

1985. Birth Bicentenary of John J. Audubon (ornithologist). Multicoloured.

39	22c. Type **8** (postage)	80	70
40	22c. "Turnstone"	80	70
41	22c. "Golden Plover"	80	70
42	22c. "Black-bellied Plover"	80	70
43	44c. "Sooty Tern" (air)	1·30	1·20

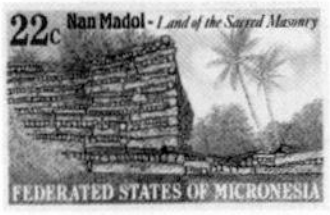

9 Land of Sacred Masonry

1985. Nan Madol, Pohnpei. Multicoloured.

44	22c. Type **9** (postage)	80	70
45	33c. Nan Tauas inner courtyard (air)	90	85
46	39c. Nan Tauas outer wall	1·10	95
47	44c. Nan Tauas burial vault	1·20	1·10

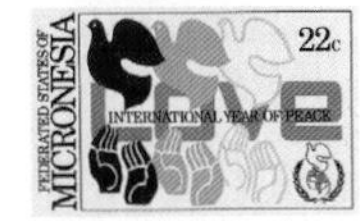

10 Doves, "LOVE" and Hands

1986. Anniversaries and Events. Multicoloured.

48	22c. Type **10** (International Peace Year)	85	75
49	44c. Halley's comet	1·80	1·70
50	44c. "Trienza" (cargo liner) arriving at jetty (40th anniv of return of Nauruans from Truk)	1·80	1·70

1986. Nos. 1/4 surch.

51	22c. on 20c. Type **1**	55	45
52	22c. on 20c. Truk	55	45
53	22c. on 20c. Pohnpei	55	45
54	22c. on 20c. Kosrae	55	45

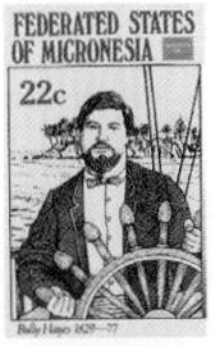

12 Bully Hayes

1986. "Ameripex 86" International Stamp Exhibition, Chicago. Bully Hayes (buccaneer). Multicoloured.

55	22c. Type **12** (postage)	65	60
56	33c. Angelo (crew member) forging Hawaii 5c. blue stamp (air)	75	65
57	39c. "Leonora" sinking off Kosrae	90	85
58	44c. Hayes escaping capture on Kosrae	1·00	90
59	75c. Cover of book "Bully Hayes, Buccaneer" by Louis Becke	2·00	1·80
MS60	128×70 mm. $1 Hayes holding Chief to ransom	4·25	3·75

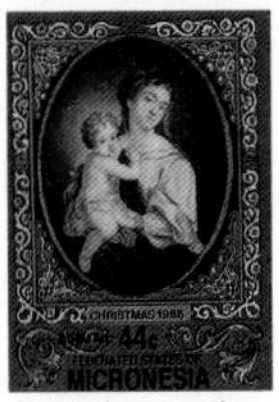

13 "Madonna and Child"

1986. Christmas. "Madonna and Child" Paintings.

61	-	5c. multicoloured (postage)	25	10
62	-	22c. multicoloured	1·00	90
63	-	33c. multicoloured (air)	1·30	1·20
64	**13**	44c. multicoloured	1·80	1·70

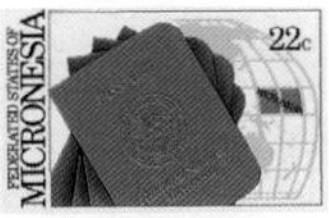

14 Passports on Globe

1986. First Micronesian Passport.

65	**14**	22c. blue, black and yellow	80	70

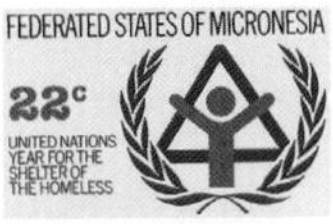

15 Emblem (International Year of Shelter for the Homeless)

1987. Anniversaries and Events.

66	**15**	22c. blue, red and black (postage)	65	60
67	-	33c. green, red and black (air)	80	70
68	-	39c. blue, black and red	1·30	1·20
69	-	44c. blue, red and black	1·50	1·30
MS70		85×550 mm. $1 multicoloured	4·25	3·75

DESIGNS: 33c. Dollar sign (bicentenary of dollar currency); 39c. Space capsule (25th Anniv of First American to orbit Earth); 44c. "200 USA" (bicentenary of U.S.consitiution; $1 Micronesian and Canadian flags ("Capex '87") International Stamp Exhibition, Toronto).

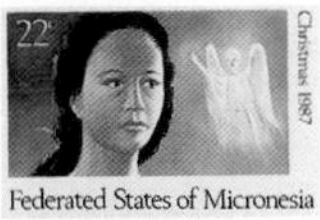

16 Archangel Gabriel appearing to Mary

1987. Christmas. Multicoloured.

71	22c. Type **16** (postage)	80	75
72	33c. Joseph praying and Mary with baby Jesus (air)	1·10	1·00
73	39c. Shepherds with their sheep	1·20	1·10
74	44c. Wise men	1·30	1·20

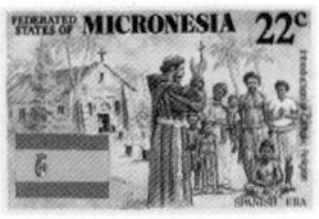

17 Spanish Missionary and Flag

1988. Micronesian History. Multicoloured.

75	22c. Type **17** (postage)	80	75
76	22c. Natives producing copra and German flag	80	75
77	22c. School pupils and Japanese flag	80	75
78	22c. General store and U.S. flag	80	75
79	44c. Traditional boatbuilding and fishing skills (air)	1·30	1·20
80	44c. Welcoming tourists from Douglas DC-10 airliner and divers investigating World War II wreckage	1·30	1·20

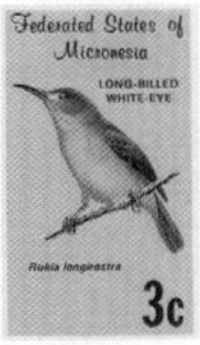

18 Ponape White Eye

1988. Birds. Multicoloured.

81	3c. Type **18** (postage)	15	10
82	14c. Truk monarch	40	35
83	22c. Ponape starling	55	50
84	33c. Truk white eye (air)	75	70
85	44c. Blue-faced parrot finch	90	85
86	$1 Yap monarch	2·30	2·10

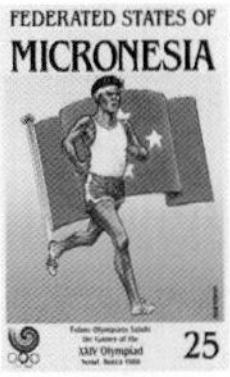

19 Marathon

1988. Olympic Games, Seoul. Multicoloured.

87	25c. Type **19**	65	60
88	25c. Hurdling	65	60
89	45c. Basketball	1·10	1·00
90	45c. Volleyball	1·10	1·00

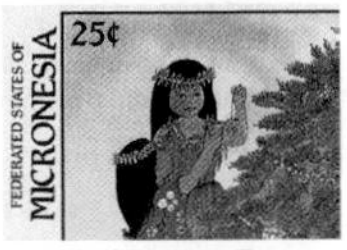

20 Girls decorating Tree

1988. Christmas. Multicoloured.

91	25c. Type **20**	60	55
92	25c. Dove with mistletoe in beak and children holding decorations	60	55
93	25c. Boy in native clothing and girl in floral dress sitting at base of tree	60	55
94	25c. Boy in T-shirt and shorts and girl in native clothing sitting at base of tree	60	55

Nos. 91/4 were printed together in blocks of four, se-tenant, forming a composite design.

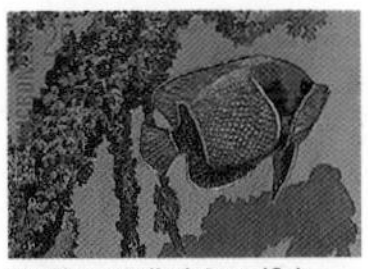

21 Blue-girdled Angelfish

1988. Truk Lagoon, "Micronesia's Living War Memorial". Multicoloured.

95	25c. Type **21**	75	70
96	25c. Jellyfish and shoal of small fishes	75	70
97	25c. Snorkel divers	75	70
98	25c. Two golden trevally (black-striped fishes facing left)	75	70
99	25c. Blackfinned reef shark	75	70
100	25c. Deck railings of wreck and fishes	75	70
101	25c. Soldierfish (red fish) and damselfish	75	70
102	25c. Damselfish, narrow-banded batfish and aircraft cockpit	75	70
103	25c. Three Moorish idols (fishes with long dorsal fins)	75	70
104	25c. Four pickhandle barracuda and shoal	75	70
105	25c. Spot-banded butterflyfish and damselfish (facing alternate directions)	75	70
106	25c. Three-spotted dascyllus and aircraft propeller	75	70
107	25c. Fox-faced rabbitfish and shoal	75	70
108	25c. Lionfish (fish with spines)	75	70
109	25c. Scuba diver and white-tailed damselfish	75	70
110	25c. Tubular corals	75	70
111	25c. White-tailed damselfish, ornate butterflyfish and brain coral	75	70
112	25c. Pink anemonefish, giant clam and sea plants	75	70

Nos. 95/112 were printed together, se-tenant, in sheetlets of 18 stamps, the backgrounds of the stamps forming an overall design of the remains of a Japanese ship and "Zero" fighter plane on the Lagoon bed colonized by marine life.

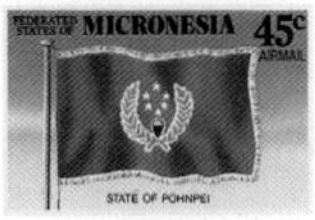

22 Flag of Pohnpei

1989. Air. State Flags. Multicoloured.

113	45c. Type **22**	90	85
114	45c. Truk	90	85
115	45c. Kosrae	90	85
116	45c. Yap	90	85

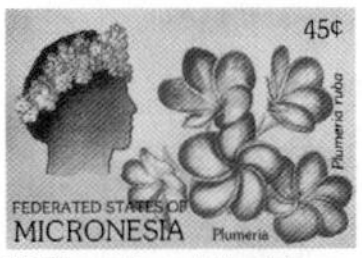

23 Plumeria and Headdress

1989. Mwarmwarms (floral decorations). Multicoloured.

117	45c. Type **23**	90	85
118	45c. Hibiscus and lei	90	85
119	45c. Jasmine and Yap religious mwarmwarm	90	85
120	45c. Bougainvillea and Truk dance mwarmwarm	90	85

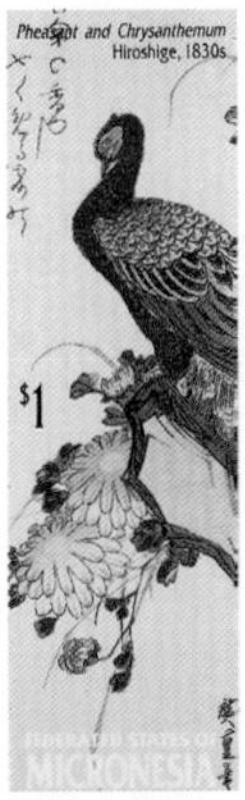

24 Whale Shark

1989. Sharks. Multicoloured.

121	25c. Type **24**	30	30
122	25c. Smooth hammerhead	55	50
123	45c. Tiger shark (vert)	55	50
124	45c. Great white shark (vert)	1·00	90

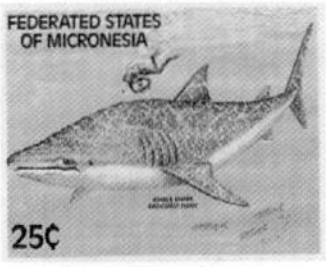

25 "Pheasant and Chrysanthemum" (Ando Hiroshige)

1989. Emperor Hirohito of Japan Commemoration. Sheet 89×1170 mm.

MS125	**25** $1 multicoloured	1·20	1·10

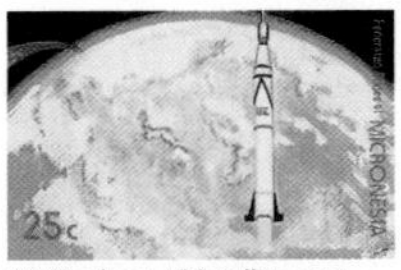

26 "Explorer 1" Satellite over North America

1989. 20th Anniv of First Manned Landing on the Moon. Multicoloured.

126	25c. Bell XS-15 rocket plane	80	75
127	25c. Type **26**	80	75
128	25c. Ed White on space walk during "Gemini 4" mission	80	75
129	25c. "Apollo 18" spacecraft	80	75
130	25c. "Gemini 4" space capsule over South America	80	75
131	25c. Space Shuttle "Challenger"	80	75
132	25c. Italian "San Marco 2" satellite	80	75
133	25c. Russian "Soyuz 19" spacecraft	80	75
134	25c. Neil Armstrong descending ladder to Moon's surface during "Apollo 11" mission	80	75
135	$2.40 Lunar module "Eagle" on Moon (34×46 mm)	6·00	5·50

Nos. 126/34 were printed together in se-tenant sheetlets of nine stamps, the backgrounds of the stamps forming an overall design of Earth as viewed from the Moon.

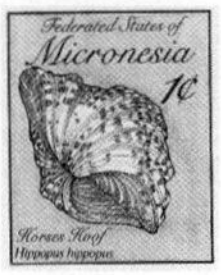

27 Horse's Hoof

1989. Sea Shells. Multicoloured.

136	1c. Type **27**	15	10
137	3c. Rare spotted cowrie	15	10
138	15c. Commercial trochus	25	25
139	20c. General cone	40	35
140	25c. Trumpet triton	55	50
141	30c. Laciniate conch	60	55
142	36c. Red-mouth olive	75	70
143	45c. All-red map cowrie	90	85
144	50c. Textile cone	1·00	90
145	$1 Orange spider conch	2·30	2·10
146	$2 Golden cowrie	4·50	4·25
147	$5 Episcopal mitre	11·00	10·50

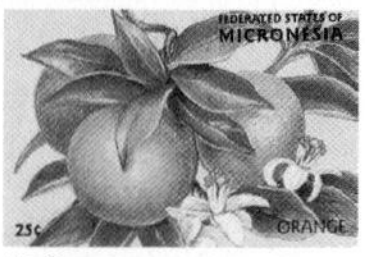

28 Oranges

1989. "World Stamp Expo '89" International Stamp Exhibition, Washington D.C. "Kosrae–The Garden State". Multicoloured.

155	25c. Type **28**	65	60
156	25c. Limes	65	60
157	25c. Tangerines	65	60
158	25c. Mangoes	65	60
159	25c. Coconuts	65	60
160	25c. Breadfruit	65	60
161	25c. Sugar cane	65	60
162	25c. Kosrae house	65	60
163	25c. Bananas	65	60
164	25c. Children with fruit and flowers	65	60
165	25c. Pineapples	65	60
166	25c. Taro	65	60
167	25c. Hibiscus	65	60
168	25c. Ylang ylang	65	60
169	25c. White ginger	65	60
170	25c. Plumeria	65	60
171	25c. Royal poinciana	65	60
172	25c. Yellow allamanda	65	60

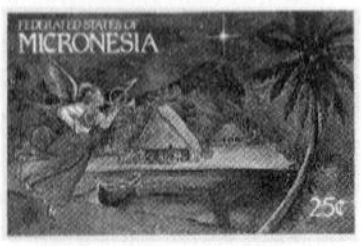

29 Angel over Micronesian Village

1989. Christmas. Multicoloured.

173	25c. Type **29**	65	60
174	45c. Truk children dressed as Three Kings	1·20	1·10

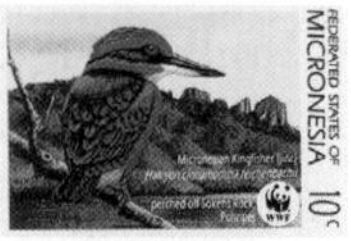

30 Young Kingfisher and Sokehs Rock, Pohnpei

1990. Endangered Species. Micronesian Kingfisher and Micronesian Pigeon.

175	10c. Type **30**	75	70
176	15c. Adult kingfisher and rain forest, Pohnpei	1·10	1·00
177	20c. Pigeon flying over lake at Sleeping Lady, Kosrae	1·50	1·40
178	25c. Pigeon perched on leaf, Tol Island, Truk	2·00	1·80

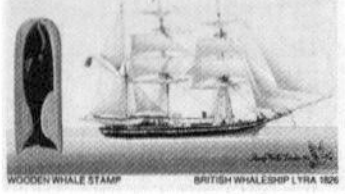

31 Wooden Whale Stamp and "Lyra"

1990. "Stamp World London 90" International Stamp Exhibition. 19th-century British Whaling Ships. Multicoloured.

179	45c. Type **31**	1·10	1·00
180	45c. Harpoon heads and "Prudent"	1·10	1·00
181	45c. Carved whale bone and "Rhone"	1·10	1·00
182	45c. Carved whale tooth and "Sussex"	1·10	1·00
MS183	98×86 mm. $1 Whalers at point of kill (41×28 mm)	2·75	2·50

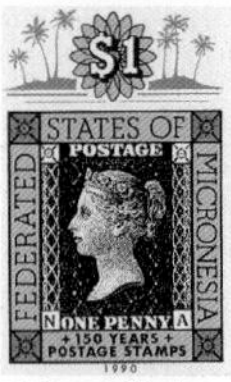

32 Penny Black

1990. 150th Anniv of Penny Black. Sheet 149×86 mm.

MS184	**32** $1 black, yellow and blue	2·75	2·50

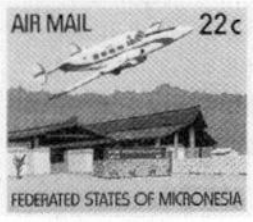

33 Beech 18 over Kosrae Airport

1990. Air. Aircraft. Multicoloured.

185	22c. Type **33**	55	50
186	36c. Boeing 727 landing at Truk	85	80
187	39c. Britten Norman Islander over Pohnpei	1·00	90
188	45c. Beech Queen Air over Yap	1·10	1·00

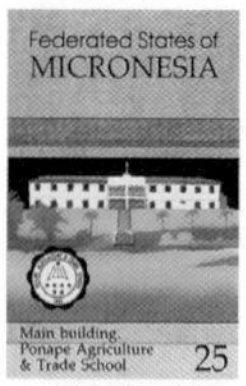

34 School Building

1990. 25th Anniv of Pohnpei Agriculture and Trade School. Multicoloured.

190	25c. Type **34**	65	60
191	25c. Fr. Costigan (founder) and students	65	60
192	25c. Fr. Hugh Costigan	65	60
193	25c. Ispahu Samuel Hadley (Metelanim chief) and Fr. Costigan	65	60
194	25c. Statue of Liberty, New York City Police Department badge and Empire State Building	65	60

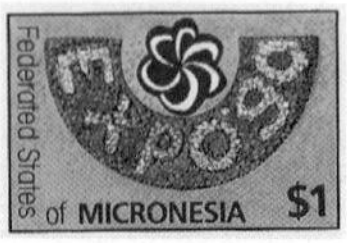

35 Flower Bed spelling EXPO '90

1990. "Expo 90" International Garden and Greenery Exposition, Osaka. Sheet 115×850 mm.

MS195	**35** $1 multicoloured	2·30	2·10

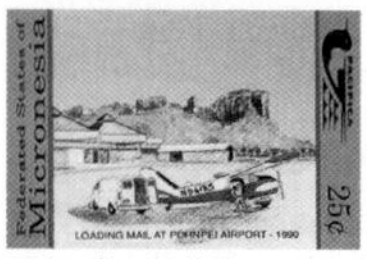

36 Loading Mail Plane at Pohnpei Airport

1990. Pacific Postal Transport. Multicoloured.

196	25c. Type **36**	65	60
197	45c. Launch meeting "Nantaku" (inter-island freighter) in Truk Lagoon to exchange mail, 1940	1·60	1·50

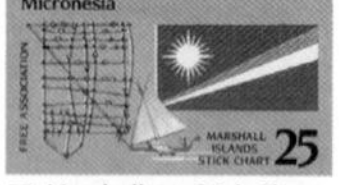

37 Marshallese Stick Chart, Outrigger Canoe and Flag

1990. Fourth Anniv of Ratification of Micronesia and Marshall Islands Compacts of Free Association. Multicoloured.

198	25c. Type **37**	75	70
199	25c. Great frigate bird, U.S.S. "Constitution" (frigate), U.S. flag and American bald eagle	75	70
200	25c. Micronesian outrigger canoe and flag	75	70

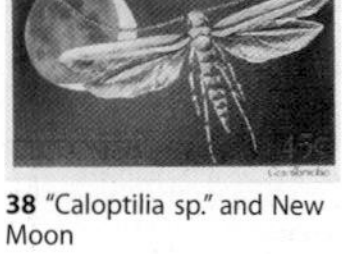

38 "Caloptilia sp." and New Moon

1990. Moths. Multicoloured.

201	45c. Type **38**	1·10	1·00
202	45c. "Anticrates sp." (inscr "Yponomeatidae") and waxing moon	1·10	1·00
203	45c. "Cosmopterigidae" family and full moon	1·10	1·00
204	45c. "Cosmopteridigae" family and waning moon	1·10	1·00

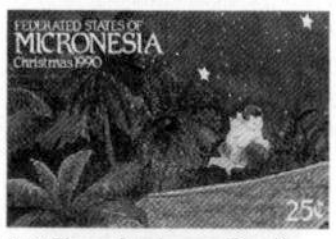

39 Cherub above Roof

1990. Christmas. "Micronesian Holy Night". Multicoloured.

205	25c. Type **39**	65	60
206	25c. Two cherubs and Star of Bethlehem	65	60
207	25c. Cherub blowing horn	65	60
208	25c. Lambs, goat, pig and chickens	65	60
209	25c. Native wise men offering gifts to Child	65	60
210	25c. Children and dog beside lake	65	60
211	25c. Man blowing trumpet triton	65	60
212	25c. Adults and children on path	65	60
213	25c. Man and children carrying gifts	65	60

Nos. 205/13 were printed together, se-tenant, forming a composite design.

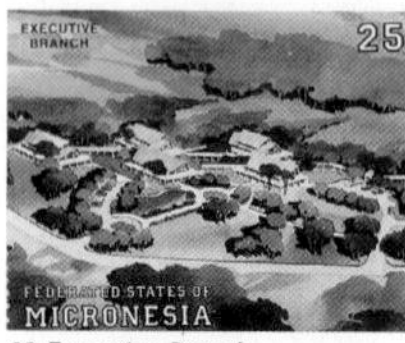

40 Executive Branch

1991. New Capital, Palikir Valley, Pohnpei. Two sheets, each 121×76 mm containing horiz designs as T **40**.

MS214	Two sheets. (a) 25c. Type **40**; 45c. Legislative and Judiciary Branches; (b) $1 New Capitol	4·50	4·25

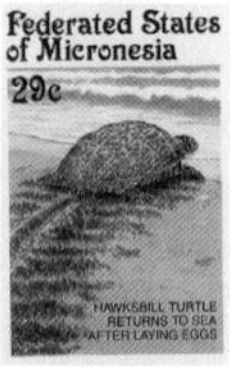

41 Hawksbill Turtle returning to Sea

1991. Sea Turtles. Multicoloured.

215	29c. Type **41**	1·30	1·20
216	29c. Green turtles swimming underwater	1·30	1·20
217	50c. Hawksbill turtle swimming underwater	1·80	1·70
218	50c. Leatherback turtle swimming underwater	1·80	1·70

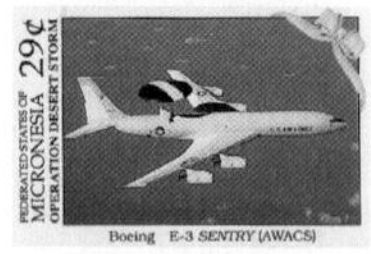

42 Boeing E-3 Sentry

1991. Operations Desert Shield and Desert Storm (liberation of Kuwait). Multicoloured.

219	29c. Type **42**	80	75
220	29c. Grumman F-14 Tomcat fighter	80	75
221	29c. U.S.S. "Missouri" (battleship)	80	75
222	29c. Multiple Launch Rocket System	80	75
223	$2.90 Great frigate bird with yellow ribbon and flag of Micronesia (50×37 mm)	6·50	6·25
MS224	127×96 mm. No. 223	7·25	6·75

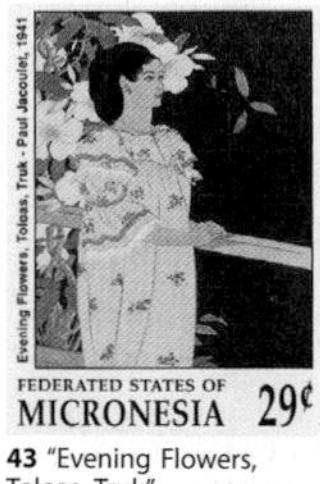

43 "Evening Flowers, Toloas, Truk"

1991. "Phila Nippon '91" International Stamp Exhibition, Tokyo. 90th Birth Anniv (1992) of Paul Jacoulet (artist). Micronesian Ukiyo-e Prints by Jacoulet. Multicoloured.

225	29c. Type **43**	1·00	90
226	29c. "The Chief's Daughter, Mogomog"	1·00	90
227	29c. "Yagourouh and Mio, Yap"	1·00	90
228	50c. "Yap Beauty and Orchids"	1·60	1·50
229	50c. "The Yellow-Eyed Boys, Ohlol"	1·60	1·50
230	50c. "Violet Flowers, Tomil, Yap"	1·60	1·50
MS231	143×790 mm. $1 First Love, Yap	3·25	3·00

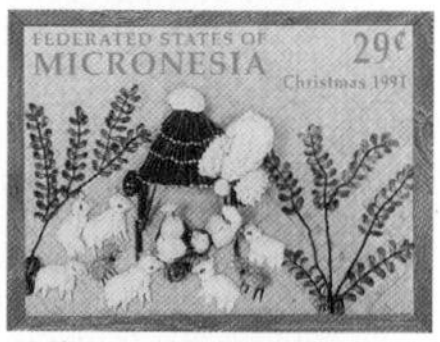

44 Sheep and Holy Family

1991. Christmas. Shell Cribs. Multicoloured.

232	29c. Type **44**	65	60
233	40c. Three Kings arriving at Bethlehem	1·00	90
234	50c. Sheep around manger	1·30	1·20

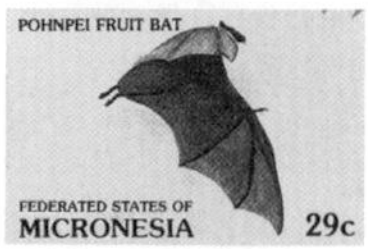

45 Pohnpei Fruit Bat

1991. Pohnpei Rain Forest. Multicoloured.

235	29c. Type **45**	90	85
236	29c. Purple-capped fruit dove	90	85
237	29c. Micronesian kingfisher	90	85
238	29c. Birdnest fern	90	85
239	29c. Caroline swiftlets ("Island Swiftlet")	90	85
240	29c. Ponape white-eye ("Long-billed White-eye")	90	85
241	29c. Common noddy ("Brown Noddy")	90	85
242	29c. Ponape lory ("Pohnpei Lory")	90	85
243	29c. Micronesian flycatcher ("Pohnpei Flycatcher")	90	85
244	29c. Truk Island ground dove ("Caroline Ground-Dove")	90	85
245	29c. White-tailed tropic bird	90	85
246	29c. Cardinal honeyeater ("Micronesian Honeyeater")	90	85
247	29c. Ixora	90	85
248	29c. Rufous fantail ("Pohnpei Fantail")	90	85
249	29c. Grey-brown white-eye ("Grey White-eye")	90	85
250	29c. Blue-faced parrot finch	90	85
251	29c. Common Cicadabird ("Cicadabird")	90	85
252	29c. Green skink	90	85

Nos. 235/52 were issued together, se-tenant, forming a composite design.

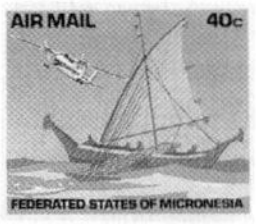

46 Britten Norman Islander and Outrigger Canoe

1992. Air. Multicoloured.

253	40c. Type **46**	90	85
254	50c. Boeing 727-200 airliner and outrigger canoe (different)	1·10	1·00

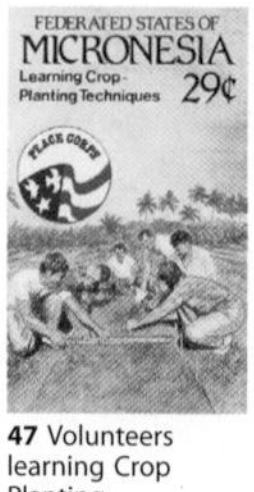

47 Volunteers learning Crop Planting

1992. 25th Anniv of Presence of United States Peace Corps in Micronesia. Multicoloured.

255	29c. Type **47**	65	60
256	29c. Education	65	60
257	29c. Pres. John Kennedy announcing formation of Peace Corps	65	60
258	29c. Public health nurses	65	60
259	29c. Recreation	65	60

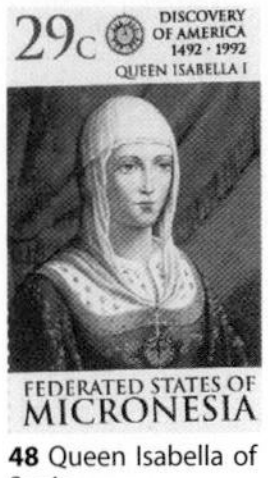

48 Queen Isabella of Spain

1992. 500th Anniv of Discovery of America by Christopher Columbus. Multicoloured.

260	29c. Type **48**	2·00	1·80
261	29c. "Santa Maria"	2·00	1·80
262	29c. Christopher Columbus	2·00	1·80

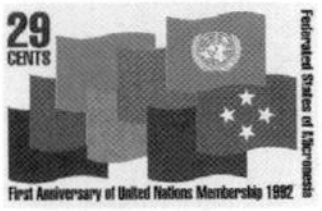

49 Flags

1992. First Anniv of U.N. Membership.

263	**49** 29c. multicoloured	1·80	1·80
264	**49** 50c. multicoloured	2·75	2·50
MS265	114×73 mm. Nos. 263/4	4·50	4·25

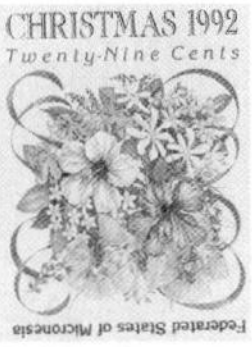

50 Bouquet

1992. Christmas.

266	**50** 29c. multicoloured	2·10	2·00

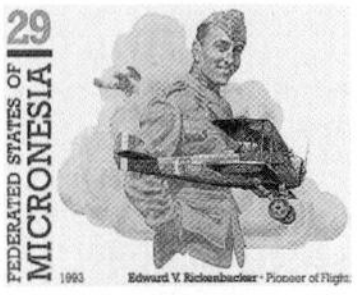

51 Edward Rickenbacker (fighter pilot)

1993. Pioneers of Flight (1st series). Pioneers and aircraft. Multicoloured.

267	29c. Type **51**	80	75
268	29c. Manfred von Richthofen (fighter pilot)	80	75
269	29c. Andrei Tupolev (aeronautical engineer)	80	75
270	29c. John Macready (first non-stop crossing of U.S.A.)	80	75
271	29c. Sir Charles Kingsford-Smith (first trans-Pacific flight)	80	75
272	29c. Igor Sikorsky (aeronautical engineer)	80	75
273	29c. Lord Trenchard ("Father of the Royal Air Force")	80	75
274	29c. Glenn Curtiss (builder of U.S. Navy's first aircraft)	80	75

See also Nos. 322/9, 364/71, 395/402, 418/25, 441/8, 453/60 and 514/21.

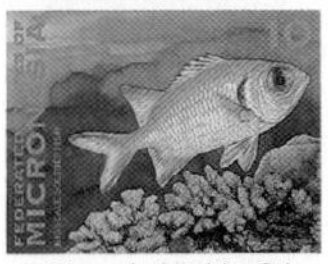

52 Big-scaled Soldierfish

1993. Fish. Multicoloured.

275	10c. Type **52**	25	10
276	19c. Bennett's butterflyfish	45	45
277	20c. Peacock hind ("Peacock Grouper")	45	45
278	22c. Great barracuda	55	50
279	23c. Yellow-finned tuna	60	55
280	25c. Coral hind ("Coral Grouper")	60	55
281	29c. Regal angelfish	75	70
282	30c. Bleeker's parrotfish	75	70
283	32c. Saddle butterflyfish (dated "1995")	85	80
284	35c. Picasso triggerfish ("Picassofish")	85	80
285	40c. Mandarin fish	90	85
286	45c. Clown ("Bluebanded") surgeonfish	1·00	90
287	46c. Red-tailed surgeonfish ("Achilles Tang")	1·30	1·20
288	50c. Undulate ("Orange-striped") triggerfish	1·20	1·10
289	52c. Palette surgeonfish	1·30	1·20
290	55c. Moorish idol	1·50	1·40
291	60c. Skipjack tuna	1·60	1·50
292	75c. Oriental sweetlips	1·80	1·70
293	78c. Square-spotted anthias ("Square-spot Fairy Basslet")	2·00	1·80
294	95c. Blue-striped ("Blue-lined") snapper	2·50	2·30
295	$1 Zebra moray	2·30	2·10
296	$2 Fox-faced rabbitfish	4·50	4·25
297	$2.90 Masked ("Orangespine") unicornfish	7·25	6·75
298	$3 Flame angelfish	8·00	7·25
299	$5 Six-blotched hind ("Cave Grouper")	13·00	12·50

See also Nos. 465/89 and 522/5.

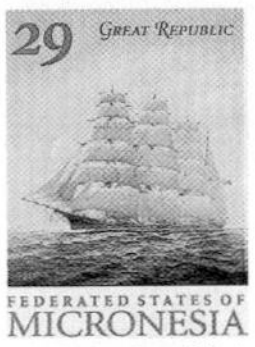

53 "Great Republic"

1993. American Clipper Ships. Multicoloured.

301	29c. Type **53**	1·60	1·50
302	29c. "Benjamin F. Packard"	1·60	1·50
303	29c. "Stag Hound"	1·60	1·50
304	29c. "Herald of the Morning"	1·60	1·50
305	29c. "Rainbow" and junk	1·60	1·50
306	29c. "Flying Cloud"	1·60	1·50
307	29c. "Lightning"	1·60	1·50
308	29c. "Sea Witch"	1·60	1·50
309	29c. "Columbia"	1·60	1·50
310	29c. "New World"	1·60	1·50
311	29c. "Young America"	1·60	1·50
312	29c. "Courier"	1·60	1·50

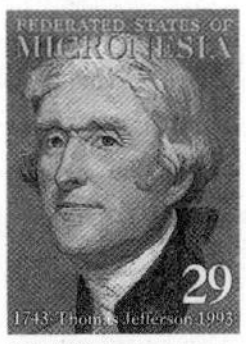

54 Jefferson

1993. 250th Birth Anniv of Thomas Jefferson (U.S. President, 1801–09).

313	**54** 29c. multicoloured	1·10	1·00

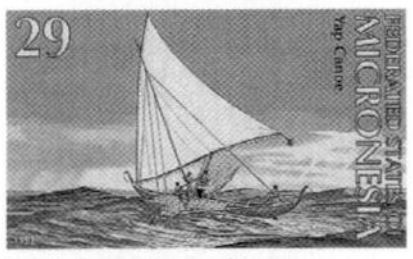

55 Yap Outrigger Canoe

1993. Traditional Canoes. Multicoloured.

314	29c. Type **55**	1·10	1·00
315	29c. Kosrae outrigger canoe	1·10	1·00
316	29c. Pohnpei lagoon outrigger canoe	1·10	1·00
317	29c. Chuuk war canoe	1·10	1·00

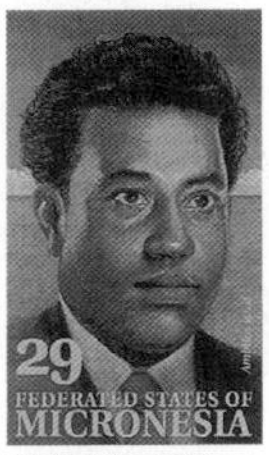

56 Ambilos Iehsi

1993. Local Leaders (1st series). Multicoloured.

318	29c. Type **56** (Pohnpei)	80	75
319	29c. Andrew Roboman (Yap)	80	75
320	29c. Joab Sigrah (Kosrae)	80	75
321	29c. Petrus Mailo (Chuuk)	80	75

See also Nos. 409/12.

1993. Pioneers of Flight (2nd series). As T **51**. Multicoloured.

322	50c. Lawrence Sperry (inventor of the gyro)	1·10	1·00
323	50c. Alberto Santos-Dumont (first powered flight in Europe)	1·10	1·00
324	50c. Hugh Dryden (developer of first guided missile)	1·10	1·00
325	50c. Theodore von Karman (space pioneer)	1·10	1·00
326	50c. Orville Wright (first powered flight)	1·10	1·00
327	50c. Wilbur Wright (second powered flight)	1·10	1·00
328	50c. Otto Lilienthal (first heavier-than-air flight)	1·10	1·00
329	50c. Sir Thomas Sopwith (aircraft designer)	1·10	1·00

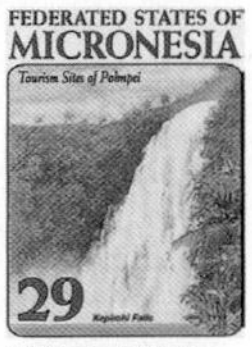

57 Kepirohi Falls

1993. Pohnpei Tourist Sites. Multicoloured.

330	29c. Type **57**	1·00	90
331	50c. Spanish Wall	2·00	1·80
MS332	115×870 mm. $1 Sokehs Rock (79×49 mm)	2·75	2·50

See also Nos. 357/9.

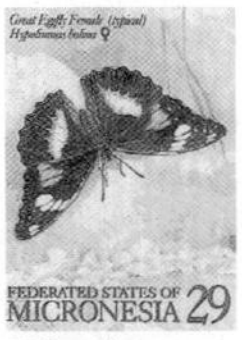

58 Female Common ("Great") Eggfly

1993. Butterflies. Multicoloured.

333	29c. Type **58**	1·00	90
334	29c. Female common ("great") eggfly (variant)	1·00	90
335	50c. Male monarch	2·00	1·80
336	50c. Male common ("great") eggfly	2·00	1·80

See also Nos. 360/3.

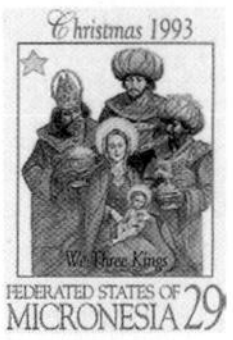

59 "We Three Kings"

1993. Christmas. Carols. Multicoloured.

337	29c. Type **59**	1·00	90
338	50c. "Silent Night, Holy Night"	2·00	1·80

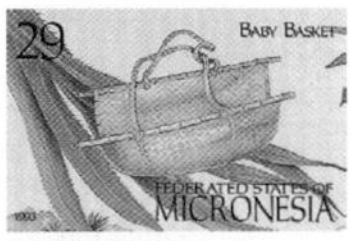

60 Baby Basket

1993. Yap. Multicoloured.

339	29c. Type **60**	90	85
340	29c. Bamboo raft	90	85
341	29c. Basketry	90	85
342	29c. Fruit bat	90	85
343	29c. Forest	90	85
344	29c. Outrigger canoes	90	85
345	29c. Dioscorea yams	90	85
346	29c. Mangroves	90	85
347	29c. Manta ray	90	85
348	29c. "Cyrtosperma taro"	90	85
349	29c. Fish weir	90	85
350	29c. Seagrass, golden rabbitfish and masked rabbitfish	90	85
351	29c. Taro bowl	90	85
352	29c. Thatched house	90	85
353	29c. Coral reef	90	85
354	29c. Lavalava	90	85
355	29c. Dancers	90	85
356	29c. Stone money	90	85

1994. Kosrae Tourist Sites. As T **57** but horiz. Multicoloured.

357	29c. Sleeping Lady (mountains)	75	70
358	40c. Walung	1·00	90
359	50c. Lelu Ruins	1·30	1·20

1994. "Hong Kong '94" International Stamp Exhibition. Designs as Nos. 333/6 but with inscriptions in brown and additionally inscribed "Hong Kong '94 Stamp Exhibition" in English (361/2) or Chinese (others).

360	29c. As No. 333	1·10	1·00
361	29c. As No. 334	1·10	1·00
362	50c. As No. 335	1·70	1·60
363	50c. As No. 336	1·70	1·60

1994. Pioneers of Flight (3rd series). As T **51**. Multicoloured.

364	29c. Octave Chanute (early glider designer)	90	85
365	29c. T. Claude Ryan (founder of first commercial airline)	90	85
366	29c. Edwin (Buzz) Aldrin ("Apollo 11" crew member and second man to step onto moon)	90	85
367	29c. Neil Armstrong (commander of "Apollo 11" and first man on moon)	90	85
368	29c. Frank Whittle (developer of jet engine)	90	85
369	29c. Waldo Waterman (aircraft designer)	90	85
370	29c. Michael Collins ("Apollo 11" crew member)	90	85
371	29c. Wernher von Braun (rocket designer)	90	85

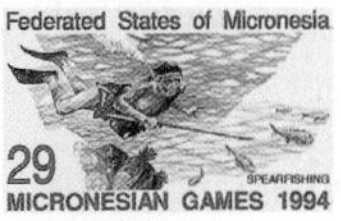

61 Spearfishing

1994. Third Micronesian Games. Multicoloured.

372	29c. Type **61**	90	85
373	29c. Basketball	90	85
374	29c. Coconut husking	90	85
375	29c. Tree climbing	90	85

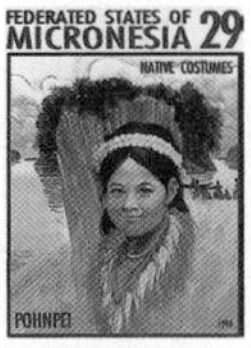

62 Pohnpei

1994. Traditional Costumes. Multicoloured.

376	29c. Type **62**	90	85
377	29c. Kosrae	90	85
378	29c. Chuuk	90	85
379	29c. Yap	90	85

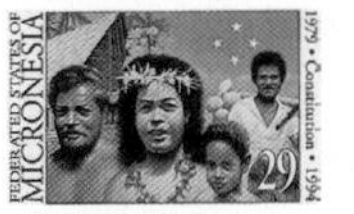

63 People

1994. 15th Anniv of Constitution.

380	**63** 29c. multicoloured	1·70	1·60

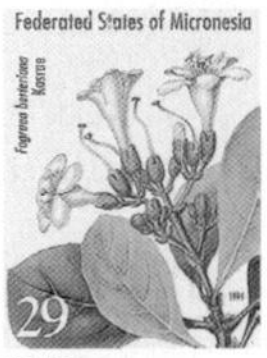

64 "Fagraea berteriana" (Kosrae)

1994. Native Flowers. Multicoloured.

381	29c. Type **64**	90	85
382	29c. "Pangium edule" (Yap)	90	85
383	29c. "Pittosporum ferrugineum" (Chuuk)	90	85
384	29c. "Sonneratia caseolaris" (Pohnpei)	90	85

Nos. 381/4 were issued together, se-tenant, forming a composite design.

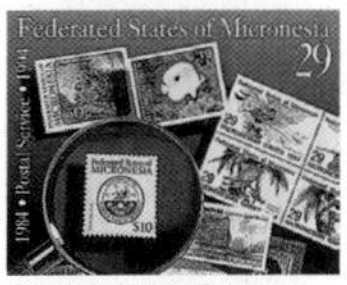

65 1985 $10 Definitive under Magnifying Glass

1994. Tenth Anniv of Postal Independence. Multicoloured.

385	29c. Type **65**	1·60	1·50
386	29c. 1993 traditional canoes block	1·60	1·50
387	29c. 1984 postal independence block	1·60	1·50
388	29c. 1994 native costumes block	1·60	1·50

Nos. 385/8 were issued together, se-tenant, forming a composite design of various Micronesian stamps. Nos. 386/8 are identified by the block in the centre of the design.

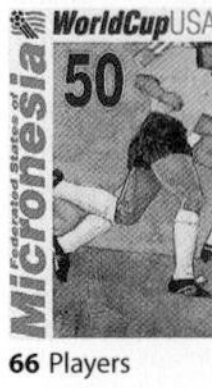

66 Players

1994. World Cup Football Championship, U.S.A. Multicoloured.

| 389 | 50c. Type **66** | 3·00 | 2·75 |
| 390 | 50c. Ball and players | 3·00 | 2·75 |

Nos. 389/90 were issued together, se-tenant, forming a composite design.

67 United States 1969 10c. Stamp

1994. 25th Anniv of First Manned Moon Landing. Sheet 115×870 mm.

| MS391 **67** $2·90 multicoloured | 5·50 | 5·25 |

68 Iguanodons

1994. "Philakorea 1994" International Stamp Exhibition, Seoul. Prehistoric Animals. Multicoloured.

392	29c. Type **68**	2·30	2·10
393	52c. Iguanodons and coelurosaurs	2·30	2·10
394	$1 Camarasaurus	2·30	2·10

Nos. 392/4 were issued together, se-tenant, forming a composite design.

1994. Pioneers of Flight (4th series). As T **51**. Multicoloured.

395	50c. Yuri Gagarin (first man in space)	1·10	1·00
396	50c. Alan Shepard Jr. (first American in space)	1·10	1·00
397	50c. William Bishop (fighter pilot)	1·10	1·00
398	50c. "Atlas" (first U.S. intercontinental ballistic missile) and Karel Bossart (aerospace engineer)	1·10	1·00
399	50c. John Towers (world endurance record, 1912)	1·10	1·00
400	50c. Hermann Oberth (space flight pioneer)	1·10	1·00
401	50c. Marcel Dassault (aircraft producer)	1·10	1·00
402	50c. Geoffrey de Havilland (aircraft designer)	1·10	1·00

69 Oriental Cuckoo

1994. Migratory Birds. Multicoloured.

403	29c. Type **69**	80	75
404	29c. Long-tailed koel ("Long-tailed Cuckoo")	80	75
405	29c. Short-eared owl	80	75
406	29c. Eastern broad-billed roller ("Dollarbird")	80	75

70 Doves

1994. Christmas. Multicoloured.

| 407 | 29c. Type **70** | 80 | 75 |
| 408 | 50c. Angels | 1·30 | 1·20 |

1994. Local Leaders (2nd series). As T **56**. Multicoloured.

409	32c. Anron Ring Buas	85	80
410	32c. Belarmino Hatheylul	85	80
411	32c. Johnny Moses	85	80
412	32c. Paliknoa Sigrah (King John)	85	80

71 Pig

1995. New Year. Year of the Pig. Sheet 115×870 mm.

| MS413 **71** 50c. multicoloured | 1·30 | 1·20 |

72 Diver, Coral, Clown Triggerfish and Black-backed Butterflyfish

1995. Chuuk Lagoon. Multicoloured.

414	32c. Type **72**	85	80
415	32c. Black-backed butterflyfish, lionfish, regal angelfish and damselfishes	85	80
416	32c. Diver, thread-finned butterflyfish and damselfishes	85	80
417	32c. Pink anemonefish and damselfishes amongst anemone tentacles	85	80

Nos. 414/17 were issued together, se-tenant, forming a composite design.

1995. Pioneers of Flight (5th series). As T **51**. Multicoloured.

418	32c. Robert Goddard (first liquid-fuelled rocket)	85	80
419	32c. Leroy Grumman (first fighter with retractable landing gear)	85	80
420	32c. Louis-Charles Breguet (aeronautics engineer)	85	80
421	32c. Juan de la Cierva (inventor of autogyro)	85	80
422	32c. Hugo Junkers (aircraft engineer)	85	80
423	32c. James Lovell Jr. (astronaut)	85	80
424	32c. Donald Douglas (aircraft designer)	85	80
425	32c. Reginald Mitchell (designer of Spitfire fighter)	85	80

73 West Highland White Terrier

1995. Dogs. Multicoloured.

426	32c. Type **73**	85	80
427	32c. Welsh springer spaniel	85	80
428	32c. Irish setter	85	80
429	32c. Old English sheepdog	85	80

74 "Hibiscus tiliaceus"

1995. Hibiscus. Multicoloured.

430	32c. Type **74**	85	80
431	32c. "Hibiscus huegelii"	85	80
432	32c. "Hibiscus trionum"	85	80
433	32c. "Hibiscus splendens"	85	80

Nos. 430/3 were issued together, se-tenant, forming a composite design.

75 U.N. Flag draped over Girder (new Headquarters, 1949)

1995. 50th Anniv of United Nations Organization. Sheet 82×112 mm.

| MS434 **75** $1 multicoloured | 2·75 | 2·50 |

76 "Paphiopedilum" "Henrietta Fujiwara"

1995. "Singapore '95" International Stamp Exhibition. Orchids. Sheet 120×93 mm containing T **76** and similar horiz designs. Multicoloured.

| MS435 32c. Type "76"; 32c. "Thunia alba"; 32c. "Lycaste virginalis"; 32c. "Laeliocattleya" "Prism Palette" | 3·50 | 3·25 |

77 U.S.S. "Portland" (cruiser)

1995. 50th Anniv of End of Second World War. Liberation of Micronesia. Multicoloured.

436	60c. Type **77** (liberation of Chuuk)	1·60	1·50
437	60c. U.S.S. "Tillman" (destroyer) (Yap)	1·60	1·50
438	60c. U.S.S. "Soley" (destroyer) (Kosrae)	1·60	1·50
439	60c. U.S.S. "Hyman" (destroyer) (Pohnpei)	1·60	1·50

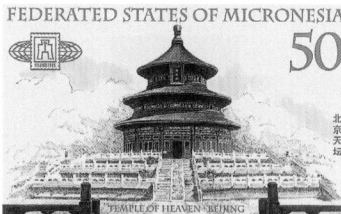

78 Temple of Heaven, Peking

1995. "Beijing 1995" International Stamp and Coin Exhibition. Sheet 110×870 mm.

| MS440 **78** 50c. multicoloured | 1·30 | 1·20 |

1995. Pioneers of Flight (6th series). As T **51**. Multicoloured.

441	60c. Frederick Rohr (developer of mass-production techniques)	1·60	1·50
442	60c. Juan Trippe (founder of Pan-American Airways)	1·60	1·50
443	60c. Konstantin Tsiolkovsky (rocket pioneer)	1·60	1·50
444	60c. Count Ferdinand von Zeppelin (airship inventor)	1·60	1·50
445	60c. Air Chief Marshal Hugh Dowding (commander of R.A.F. Fighter Command, 1940)	1·60	1·50
446	60c. William Mitchell (pioneer of aerial bombing)	1·60	1·50
447	60c. John Northrop (aircraft designer)	1·60	1·50
448	60c. Frederick Handley Page (producer of first twin-engine bomber)	1·60	1·50

79 Poinsettia

1995. Christmas.

| 449 | **79** 32c. multicoloured | 85 | 80 |
| 450 | **79** 60c. multicoloured | 1·60 | 1·50 |

80 Rabin

1995. Yitzhak Rabin (Israeli Prime Minister) Commemoration.

| 451 | **80** 32c. multicoloured | 85 | 80 |

81 Rat

1996. New Year. Year of the Rat. Sheet 110×870 mm.

| MS452 **81** 50c. multicoloured | 1·30 | 1·20 |

1995. Pioneers of Flight (7th series). As T **51**. Multicoloured.

453	32c. James Doolittle (leader of America's Second World War bomb raid on Japan)	85	80
454	32c. Claude Dornier (aircraft designer)	85	80
455	32c. Ira Eaker (leader of air effort against occupied Europe during Second World War)	85	80
456	32c. Jacob Ellehammer (first European manned flight)	85	80
457	32c. Henry Arnold (Commander of U.S. air operations during Second World War)	85	80
458	32c. Louis Bleriot (first flight across the English Channel)	85	80
459	32c. William Boeing (founder of Boeing Corporation)	85	80
460	32c. Sydney Camm (aircraft designer)	85	80

82 Meeting House

1995. Tourism in Yap. Multicoloured.

461	32c. Type **82**	85	80
462	32c. Stone money	85	80
463	32c. Churu dancing	85	80
464	32c. Traditional canoe	85	80

1995. Fish. As Nos. 275/95 but face values changed. Multicoloured.

465	32c. Bennett's butterflyfish	85	80
466	32c. Regal angelfish	85	80
467	32c. Undulate ("Orange-striped") triggerfish	85	80
468	32c. Zebra moray	85	80
469	32c. Great barracuda	85	80
470	32c. Bleeker's parrotfish	85	80
471	32c. Mandarin fish	85	80
472	32c. Clown ("Blue-banded") surgeonfish	85	80
473	32c. Big-scaled soldierfish	85	80
474	32c. Peacock hind ("Peacock Grouper")	85	80
475	32c. Picasso triggerfish ("Picassofish")	85	80
476	32c. Masked ("Orangespine") unicornfish	85	80
477	32c. Red-tailed surgeonfish	85	80
478	32c. Coral hind ("Coral Grouper")	85	80
479	32c. Palette surgeonfish	85	80
480	32c. Oriental sweetlips	85	80

481	32c. Fox-faced rabbitfish	85	80
482	32c. Saddle butterflyfish (dated "1996")	85	80
483	32c. Moorish idol	85	80
484	32c. Square-spotted anthias ("Square-spot Fairy Basslet")	85	80
485	32c. Flame angelfish	85	80
486	32c. Yellow-finned tuna	85	80
487	32c. Skipjack tuna	85	80
488	32c. Blue-striped ("Blue-lined") snapper	85	80
489	32c. Six-blotched hind ("Cave Grouper")	85	80

See also Nos. 522/5.

83 Necklace Sea Star

1996. Starfishes. Multicoloured.

490	55c. Type **83**	1·30	1·20
491	55c. Rhinoceros sea star	1·30	1·20
492	55c. Blue sea star	1·30	1·20
493	55c. Thick-skinned sea star	1·30	1·20

Nos. 490/3 were issued together, se-tenant, forming a composite design.

84 10l. Stamp

1996. Centenary of Modern Olympic Games. Designs reproducing 1896 Greek Olympic Issue. Multicoloured.

494	60c. Type **84**	1·40	1·30
495	60c. 25l. stamp	1·40	1·30
496	60c. 20l. stamp	1·40	1·30
497	60c. 10d. stamp	1·40	1·30

85 "Palikir"

1996. Patrol Boats. Multicoloured.

| 498 | 32c. Type **85** | 75 | 70 |
| 499 | 32c. "Micronesia" | 75 | 70 |

Nos. 498/9 were issued together, se-tenant, forming a composite design.

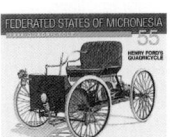

86 Gardens of Suzhou, Chins

1996. "China 96" International Stamp Exhibition, Peking. Sheet 110×870 mm.

| MS500 **86** 50c. multicoloured | 1·20 | 1·10 |

87 1896 Quadricycle

1996. Centenary of Ford Motor Vehicle Production. Multicoloured.

501	55c. Type **87**	1·30	1·20
502	55c. 1917 Model T Truck	1·30	1·20
503	55c. 1928 Model A Tudor Sedan	1·30	1·20
504	55c. 1932 V-8 Sport Roadster	1·30	1·20
505	55c. 1941 Lincoln Continental	1·30	1·20
506	55c. 1953 F-100 Truck	1·30	1·20
507	55c. 1958 Thunderbird convertible	1·30	1·20
508	55c. 1996 Mercury Sable	1·30	1·20

88 Reza

1996. Reza (National Police Drug Enforcement Unit's dog).

| 509 | **88** | 32c. multicoloured | 75 | 70 |

89 Oranges

1996. Citrus Fruits. Multicoloured.

510	50c. Type **89**	1·20	1·10
511	50c. Limes	1·20	1·10
512	50c. Lemons	1·20	1·10
513	50c. Tangerines	1·20	1·10

Nos. 510/13 were issued together, se-tenant, forming a composite design.

1996. Pioneers of Flight (8th series). As T **51**. Multicoloured.

514	60c. Curtis LeMay (commander of Strategic Air Command)	1·80	1·60
515	60c. Grover Loening (first American graduate in aeronautical engineering)	1·80	1·60
516	60c. Gianni Caproni (aircraft producer)	1·80	1·60
517	60c. Henri Farman (founder of Farman Airlines)	1·80	1·60
518	60c. Glenn Martin (aircraft producer)	1·80	1·60
519	60c. Alliot Verdon Roe (aircraft designer)	1·80	1·60
520	60c. Sergei Korolyov (rocket scientist)	1·80	1·60
521	60c. Isaac Laddon (aircraft designer)	1·80	1·60

1996. Tenth Asian International Stamp Exhibition, Taipeh. Fishes. As previous designs but additionally inscr for the exhibition in English (522, 525) or Chinese (523/4).

522	32c. As No. 465	75	70
523	32c. As No. 468	75	70
524	32c. As No. 475	75	70
525	32c. As No. 483	75	70

90 Wise Men following Star

1996. Christmas.

| 526 | **90** | 32c. multicoloured | 75 | 70 |
| 527 | **90** | 60c. multicoloured | 1·50 | 1·40 |

91 Outrigger Canoe and State Flag

1996. Tenth Anniv of Ratification of Compact of Free Association with U.S.A.

| 528 | **91** | $3 multicoloured | 7·00 | 6·50 |

92 Water Buffalo

1997. New Year. Year of the Ox.

| 529 | **92** | 32c. multicoloured | 75 | 70 |
| MS530 76×106 mm. **92** $2 multicoloured | | | 4·75 | 4·25 |

93 Walutahanga, Melanesia

1997. "Pacific 97" International Stamp Exhibition, San Francisco. Sea Goddesses of the Pacific. Multicoloured.

531	32c. Type **93**	75	70
532	32c. Tien-Hou holding lantern, China	75	70
533	32c. Lorop diving in ocean, Micronesia	75	70
534	32c. Oto-Hime with fisherman, Japan	75	70
535	32c. Nomoi holding shell, Micronesia	75	70
536	32c. Junkgowa Sisters in canoe, Australia	75	70

94 Deng Xiaoping

1997. Deng Xiaoping (Chinese statesman) Commemoration. Multicoloured.

537	60c. Type **94**	1·40	1·30
538	60c. Facing left (bare-headed)	1·40	1·30
539	60c. Facing right	1·40	1·30
540	60c. Facing left wearing cap	1·40	1·30
MS541 106×76 mm. $3 facing left		7·00	6·50

95 "Melia azedarach"

1997. Return of Hong Kong to China. Multicoloured.

542	60c. Type **95**	1·40	1·30
543	60c. Victoria Peak	1·40	1·30
544	60c. "Dendrobium chrysotoxum"	1·40	1·30
545	60c. "Bauhinia blakeana"	1·40	1·30
546	60c. "Cassia surattensis"	1·40	1·30
547	60c. Sacred lotus ("Nelumbo nucifera")	1·40	1·30
MS548 Two sheets. (a) 137×950 mm. $2 Central Business District (38½×24½ mm); (b) 63×650 mm. $3 Jade vine ("Strongylodon macrobotrys") and Hong Kong Tower (27½ ×41 mm)		7·00	6·50

96 Tennis

1997. Second National Games. Multicoloured.

549	32c. Type **96**	75	70
550	32c. Throwing the discus	75	70
551	32c. Swimming	75	70
552	32c. Canoeing	75	70

97 Rapids

1997. Birth Bicentenary of Hiroshige Ando (painter). Designs depicting details from "Whirlpools at Naruto in Awa Province" (Nos. 553/5), "Tail of Genji: Viewing the Plum Blossoms" (Nos. 556/8) and "Snow on the Sumida River" (Nos. 559/61). Multicoloured.

553	20c. Type **97**	45	45
554	20c. Whirlpools (rocky island at left)	45	45
555	20c. Whirlpools (rocky island at right)	45	45
556	50c. Woman on stepping stones	1·20	1·10
557	50c. Woman	1·20	1·10
558	50c. Woman on balcony of house	1·20	1·10
559	60c. House and junks	1·40	1·30
560	60c. Two women	1·40	1·30
561	60c. Woman alighting from junk	1·40	1·30
MS562 Two sheets, each 102×130 mm. (a) $2 "Fuji from Satta Point"; (b) $2 "Rapids in Bitchu Province"		9·50	8·75

Nos. 553/5, 556/8 and 559/61 respectively, were issued, se-tenant, forming composite designs of the paintings depicted.

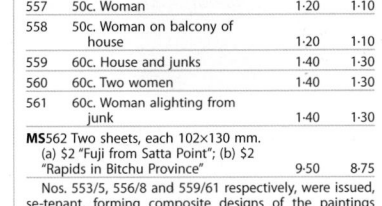

98 Presley from High School Graduation Yearbook

1997. 20th Death Anniv of Elvis Presley (entertainer). Multicoloured.

563	50c. Type **98**	1·20	1·10
564	50c. With hound dog Nipper (R.C.A. Records mascot)	1·20	1·10
565	50c. Wearing red striped shirt in publicity photograph for "Loving You" (film), 1957	1·20	1·10
566	50c. Wearing sailor's cap in scene from "Girls, Girls, Girls!" (film), 1963	1·20	1·10
567	50c. Wearing knitted jacket with collar turned up, 1957	1·20	1·10
568	50c. Wearing stetson in scene from "Flaming Star" (film), 1960	1·20	1·10

99 Simon Lake and his Submarine "Argonaut", 1897

1997. Ocean Exploration: Pioneers of the Deep. Multicoloured.

569	32c. Type **99**	75	70
570	32c. William Beebe and Otis Barton's bathysphere (record depth, 1934)	75	70
571	32c. Auguste Piccard and his bathyscaphe, 1954	75	70
572	32c. Harold Edgerton and his deep sea camera, 1954	75	70
573	32c. Jacques Piccard and U.S. Navy bathyscaphe "Trieste" (designed by Auguste Piccard) (record depth with Don Walsh, 1960)	75	70
574	32c. Edwin Link and diving chamber ("Man-in-Sea" projects, 1962)	75	70
575	32c. Melvin Fisher and diver (discovery of "Atocha" and "Santa Margarita" (Spanish galleons), 1971)	75	70
576	32c. Robert Ballard and submersible "Alvin", 1978	75	70
577	32c. Sylvia Earle and submersible "Deep Rover" (record dive in armoured suit, 1979)	75	70
MS578 Three sheets, each 111×86 mm. (a) $2 Jacques Yves Cousteau (undersea researcher) (vert); (b) $2 Charles Wyville Thomson and deep sea dredge (vert); (c) $2 "Shinkai 6500" (Japanese submersible) on ocean floor (vert)		14·00	13·00

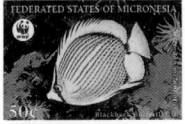

100 Black-backed Butterflyfish

1997. Butterflyfishes. Multicoloured.

579	50c. Type **100**	1·80	1·60
580	50c. Saddle butterflyfish	1·80	1·60
581	50c. Thread-finned butterflyfish	1·80	1·60
582	50c. Bennett's butterflyfish	1·80	1·60

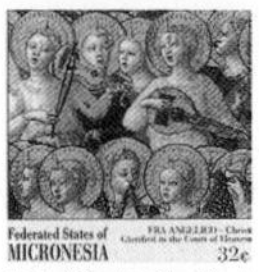

101 "Christ Glorified in the Court of Heaven" (Fra Angelico) (left detail)

1997. Christmas. Multicoloured.

583	32c. Type **101**	75	70
584	32c. "Christ Glorified in the Court of Heaven" (right detail)	75	70
585	60c . "A Choir of Angels" (detail, Simon Marmion)	1·40	1·30
586	60c. "A Choir of Angels" (different detail)	1·40	1·30

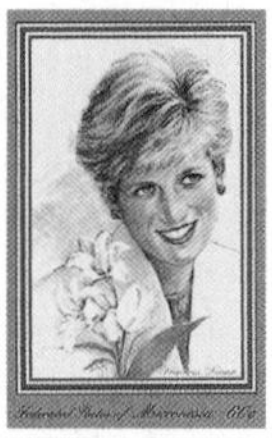

102 Diana, Princess of Wales

1997. Diana, Princess of Wales Commemoration.

587	**102** 60c. multicoloured	1·50	1·40

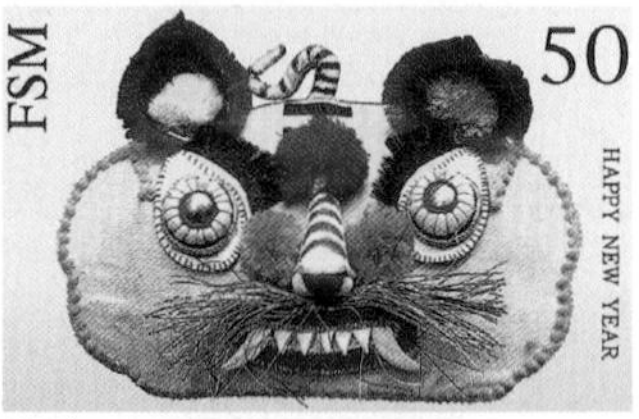

103 Tiger

1998. New Year. Year of the Tiger, Two sheets, each 117×92 mm containing T **103** or similar horiz design.

MS588	Two sheets. (a) 50c. multicoloured (Type **103**); 50c. scarlet, emerald and lemon (paper cut-outs of tigers)	2·40	2·20

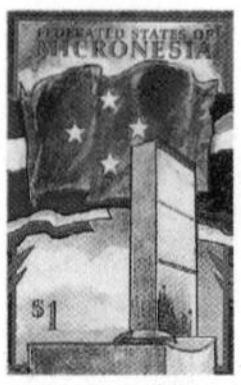

104 U.N. Building, New York, and Flags

1998. Seventh Anniv of Admission to United Nations Organization. Sheet 65×80 mm.

MS589	**104** $1 multicoloured	2·40	2·20

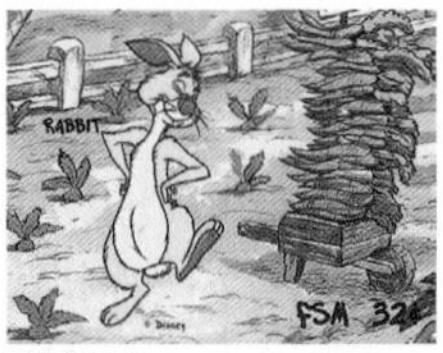

105 Rabbit

1998. Children's Libraries. The Hundred Acre Wood. Featuring characters from the Winnie the Pooh children's books. Multicoloured.

590	32c. Type **105**	75	70
591	32c. Owl	75	70
592	32c. Eeyore	75	70
593	32c. Kanga and Roo	75	70
594	32c. Piglet	75	70
595	32c. Tigger	75	70
596	32c. Pooh	75	70
597	32c. Christopher Robin	75	70
MS598	Two sheets, each 130×106 mm. (a) $2 Tigger pulling Pooh from Rabbit's hole; (b) $2 Rabbit pushing Pooh out of hole	9·50	8·75

Nos. 590/7 were issued together, se-tenant, forming a composite design.

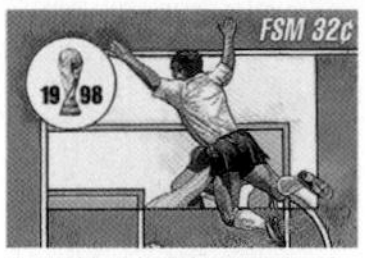

106 Player celebrating Goal

1998. World Cup Football Championship, France. Multicoloured.

599	32c. Type **106**	75	70
600	32c. Player in green shirt kicking ball	75	70
601	32c. Player in yellow shirt tackling another player	75	70
602	32c. Goalkeeper throwing ball	75	70
603	32c. Player in yellow shirt kicking ball overhead	75	70
604	32c. Goalkeeper in red shirt	75	70
605	32c. Player in yellow shirt with ball between legs	75	70
606	32c. Player in red shirt and player on ground	75	70
MS607	Two sheets, each 70×100 mm. (a) $2 Player in green shirt; (b) $2 Player in striped shirt	9·50	8·75

Nos. 599/606 were issued together, se-tenant, forming a composite design of a pitch.

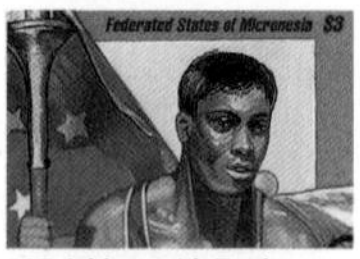

107 Athlete with Torch

1998. Recognition of Micronesia by International Olympic Committee. Sheet 75×100 mm.

MS608	**107** $3 multicoloured	7·00	6·50

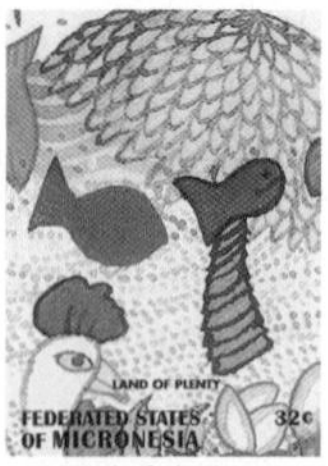

108 Land of Plenty

1998. Old Testament Stories. Multicoloured.

609	32c. Type **108**	75	70
610	32c. Adam and Eve	75	70
611	32c. Serpent of Temptation	75	70
612	40c. Three of Joseph's brothers	1·00	95
613	40c. Joseph and merchants	1·00	95
614	40c. Ishmaelites	1·00	95
615	60c. Rebekah in front of well	1·40	1·30
616	60c. Eliezer, Abraham's servant	1·40	1·30
617	60c. Angel	1·40	1·30
MS618	Three sheets, each 100×1280 mm. (a) $2 Adam and Eve banished from Paradise; (b) $2 Joseph forgiving his brothers; (c) $2 Isaac and Rebekah	14·00	13·00

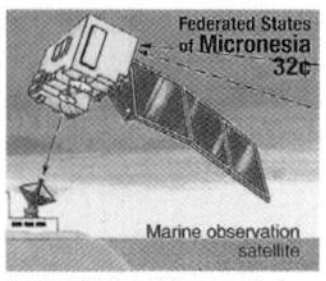

109 Marine Observation Satellite

1998. International Year of the Ocean. Deep Sea Research. Multicoloured.

619	32c. Type **109**	75	70
620	32c. "Natsushima" (support vessel)	75	70
621	32c. "Kaiyo" (research vessel)	75	70
622	32c. Anemone	75	70
623	32c. "Shinkai 2000" (deep-sea research vessel)	75	70
624	32c. Deep-towed research vessel	75	70
625	32c. Tripod fish	75	70
626	32c. Towed deep-survey system	75	70
627	32c. Black smokers	75	70
MS628	Three sheets. (a) 80×110 mm. $2 Weather satellite (vert); (b) 80×110 mm. $2 Ocean observation buoy (vert); (c) 110×80 mm. $2 Communications satellite	14·00	13·00

Nos. 619/27 were issued together, se-tenant, forming a composite design.

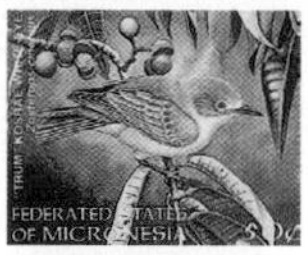

110 Grey-brown White-Eye ("Kosrae White-eye")

1998. Birds. Multicoloured.

629	50c. Type **110**	1·20	1·10
630	50c. Truk monarch ("Chuuk Monarch")	1·20	1·10
631	50c. Yap monarch	1·20	1·10
632	50c. Pohnpei starling	1·20	1·10
MS633	114×950 mm. $3 Pohnpei starling	7·00	6·50

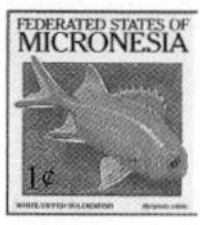

111 Ribbon-striped ("White-tipped") Soldierfish

1998. Fishes. Multicoloured.

634	1c. Type **111**	10	10
635	2c. Red-breasted wrasse	10	10
636	3c. Bicoloured ("Bicolor") angelfish	10	10
637	4c. Falco hawkfish	10	10
638	5c. Convict tang	20	15
639	10c. Square-spotted anthias ("Square-spot Fairy Basslet")	25	20
640	13c. Orange-spotted ("Orange-band") surgeonfish	30	25
641	15c. Multibarred goatfish	35	35
642	17c. Masked rabbitfish	40	40
643	20c. White-spotted surgeonfish	45	45
644	22c. Blue-girdled angelfish	55	50
645	32c. Rectangle triggerfish ("Wedge Picassofish")	75	70
646	33c. Black jack	75	70
647	39c. Red parrotfish	90	80
648	40c. Lemon-peel angelfish	95	85
649	50c. White-cheeked ("Whitecheek") surgeonfish	1·20	1·10
650	55c. Scarlet-finned ("Long-jawed") squirrelfish	1·30	1·20
651	60c. Hump-headed ("Hump-head") wrasse	1·40	1·30
652	77c. Onespot snapper	1·80	1·60
653	78c. Blue ("Sapphire") damselfish	1·80	1·60
654	$1 Blue-finned ("Bluefin") trevally	2·40	2·20
655	$3 Whitespot hawkfish	7·00	6·50
656	$3.20 Tan-faced parrotfish	7·50	6·75
657	$5 Spotted boxfish ("Trunkfish")	12·00	11·00
658	$10.75 Pink-tailed ("Pinktail") triggerfish	25·00	23·00
659	$11.75 Yellow-faced angelfish (48×25 mm)	27·00	25·00

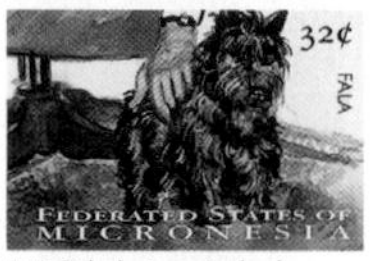

112 Fala being stroked

1998. Fala (Scottish terrier owned by Franklin D. Roosevelt). Multicoloured.

665	32c. Type **112**	75	70
666	32c. Fala and left half of wireless	75	70
667	32c. Fala and right half of wireless	75	70
668	32c. Fala and Roosevelt in car	75	70
669	32c. Fala's seal	75	70
670	32c. Fala	75	70

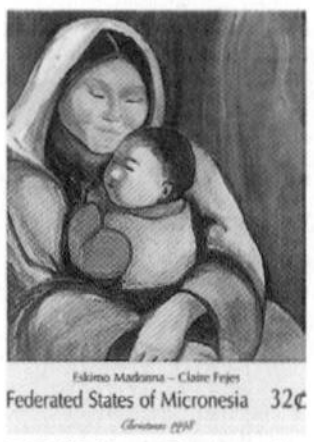

113 "Eskimo Madonna" (Claire Fejes)

1998. Christmas. Works of Art. Multicoloured.

671	32c. Type **113**	75	70
672	32c. "Madonna" (Man Ray)	75	70
673	32c. "Peasant Mother" (David Siquerios)	75	70
674	60c. "Mother and Child" (Pablo Picasso)	1·40	1·30
675	60c. "Gypsy Woman with Baby" (Amedeo Modigliani)	1·40	1·30
676	60c. "Mother and Child" (Jose Orozco)	1·40	1·30
MS677	97×121 mm. $2 "The Family" (Marisol) (horiz)	4·75	4·25

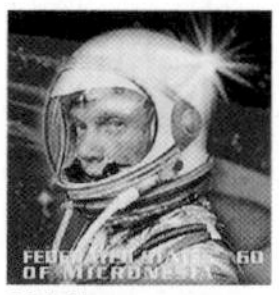

114 Glenn

1998. John Glenn's (first American to orbit Earth) Return to Space. Multicoloured.

678	60c. Type **114**	1·40	1·30
679	60c. Launch of "Friendship 7"	1·40	1·30
680	60c. Glenn (bare-headed and in spacesuit) and United States flag on spaceship	1·40	1·30
681	60c. Glenn (in spacesuit) and "Friendship" space capsule	1·40	1·30
682	60c. Glenn (in spacesuit) and United States flag on pole	1·40	1·30
683	60c. Head and shoulders of Glenn in civilian clothes and stars (dated "1992")	1·40	1·30
684	60c. "Friendship 7"	1·40	1·30
685	60c. John Glenn with President Kennedy	1·40	1·30
686	60c. Glenn in overalls	1·40	1·30
687	60c. Launch of "Discovery" (space shuttle)	1·40	1·30
688	60c. Glenn in cockpit	1·40	1·30
689	60c. Head of Glenn in civilian suit	1·40	1·30
690	60c. Glenn fastening inner helmet	1·40	1·30
691	60c. Glenn with full helmet on	1·40	1·30
692	60c. Model of "Discovery"	1·40	1·30
693	60c. Head of Glenn smiling (bare-headed) in spacesuit	1·40	1·30
MS694	Two sheets, each 110×90 mm. (a) $2 Launch of "Friendship 7" (28×42 mm); (b) $2 John Glenn, 1988 (28×42 mm)	9·50	8·75

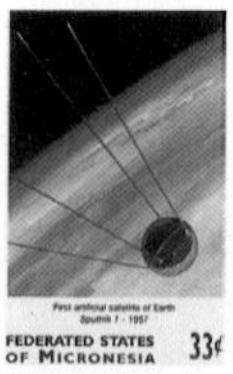

115 "Sputnik 1"

1999. Exploration of the Solar System. Multicoloured. (a) Space Achievements of Russia.

695	33c. Type **115** (first artificial satellite, 1957)	75	70
696	33c. Space dog Laika (first animal in space, 1957) (wrongly inscr "Leika")	75	70
697	33c. "Luna 1", 1959	75	70
698	33c. "Luna 3", 1959	75	70
699	33c. Yuri Gagarin (first man in space, 1961)	75	70
700	33c. "Venera 1" probe, 1961	75	70
701	33c. "Mars 1" probe, 1962	75	70
702	33c. Valentina Tereshkova (first woman in space, 1963)	75	70
703	33c. "Voskhod 1", 1964	75	70
704	33c. Aleksei Leonov and "Voskhod 2" (first space walk, 1965)	75	70
705	33c. "Venera 3" probe, 1966	75	70
706	33c. "Luna 10", 1966	75	70
707	33c. "Luna 9" (first landing on moon, 1966)	75	70
708	33c. "Lunokhod 1" moon-vehicle from "Luna 17" (first roving vehicle on Moon, 1970) (wrongly inscr "First robot mission ... Luna 16")	75	70
709	33c. "Luna 16" on Moon's surface (first robot mission, 1970) (wrongly inscr "First roving vehicle ... Luna 17")	75	70
710	33c. "Mars 3", 1971	75	70
711	33c. Leonid Popov, "Soyuz 35" and Valery Ryumin (first long manned space mission, 1980)	75	70
712	33c. Balloon ("Vega 1" Venus-Halley's Comet probe, 1985–86)	75	70
713	33c. "Vega 1" and Halley's Comet, 1986	75	70
714	33c. "Mir" space station	75	70

(b) Achievements of the United States of America.

715	33c. "Explorer 1", 1958	75	70
716	33c. Space observatory "OSO-1", 1962	75	70

717	33c. "Mariner 2" Venus probe, 1962 (first scientifically successful planetary mission)	75	70
718	33c. "Mariner 2" Venus probe, 1962 (first scientific interplanetary space discovery)	75	70
719	33c. "Apollo 8" above Moon's surface	75	70
720	33c. Astronaut descending ladder on "Apollo 11" mission (first manned Moon landing, 1969)	75	70
721	33c. Astronaut taking Moon samples, 1969	75	70
722	33c. Lunar Rover of "Apollo 15", 1971	75	70
723	33c. "Mariner 9" Mars probe, 1971	75	70
724	33c. "Pioneer 10" passing Jupiter, 1973	75	70
725	33c. "Mariner 10" passing Mercury, 1974	75	70
726	33c. "Viking 1" on Mars, 1976	75	70
727	33c. "Pioneer 11" passing Saturn, 1979	75	70
728	33c. "STS-1" (first re-usable spacecraft, 1981)	75	70
729	33c. "Pioneer 10" (first man-made object to leave solar system, 1983)	75	70
730	33c. Solar Maximum Mission, 1984	75	70
731	33c. "Cometary Explorer", 1985	75	70
732	33c. "Voyager 2" passing Neptune, 1989	75	70
733	33c. "Galileo" space probe, 1992	75	70
734	33c. "Sojourner" (Mars rover), 1997	75	70
MS735	Four sheets, each 116×86 mm. (a) $2 "Soyuz 19" and "Apollo 18" docking (horiz); (b) $2 Astronaut repairing Hubble space telescope, 1993 (horiz); (c) $2 "Mir" space station, 1998; (d) $2 International space station (horiz)	19·00	17·00

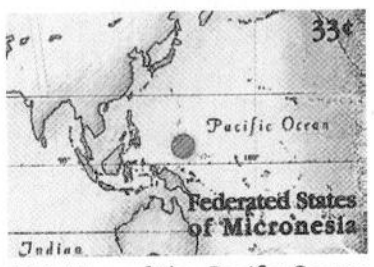

116 Map of the Pacific Ocean

1999. Voyages of the Pacific. Multicoloured.

736	33c. Type **116**	75	70
737	33c. Black-fronted parakeet	75	70
738	33c. Red-tailed tropic bird	75	70
739	33c. Plan of ship's hull	75	70
740	33c. Sketches of winches	75	70
741	33c. Yellow flowers	75	70
742	33c. Full-rigged sailing ship	75	70
743	33c. Three flowers growing from seeds and top of compass rose	75	70
744	33c. Fish (background of ship's planking)	75	70
745	33c. Flag of Yap	75	70
746	33c. Flag of Truk (palm tree)	75	70
747	33c. Flag of Kosrae (four stars) and bottom of compass rose	75	70
748	33c. Sketches of fruit	75	70
749	33c. Three plants and leaves	75	70
750	33c. Fish (leaves at left)	75	70
751	33c. Flag of Pohnpei and equator	75	70
752	33c. Sextant	75	70
753	33c. Red plant	75	70
754	33c. Fish and left side of compass rose	75	70
755	33c. Right side of compass rose and full-rigged sailing ship	75	70

Nos. 736/55 were issued together, se-tenant, forming a composite design.

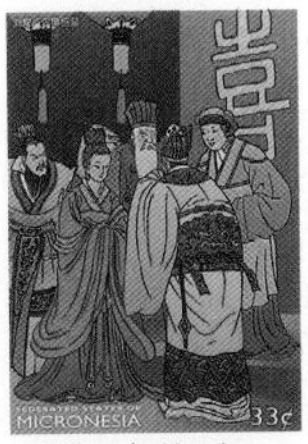

117 Couple Meeting

1999. "Romance of the Three Kingdoms" (Chinese novel by Luo Guanzhong). Multicoloured.

756	33c. Type **117**	75	70
757	33c. Four men (one with lance) in room	75	70
758	33c. Two riders in combat	75	70
759	33c. Four men watching fifth man walking through room	75	70
760	33c. Captives before man on wheeled throne	75	70
761	50c. Riders approaching castle	1·20	1·10
762	50c. Warrior pointing at fire	1·20	1·10
763	50c. Opposing warriors riding through thick smoke	1·20	1·10
764	50c. Couple kneeling before man on dais	1·20	1·10
765	50c. Cauldron on fire	1·20	1·10
MS766	77×110 mm. $2 Archers on boat shooting flaming arrows (51×78 mm)	4·75	4·25

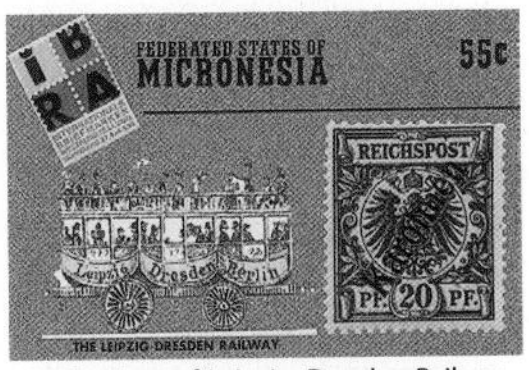

118 Carriage of Leipzig–Dresden Railway and Caroline Islands 1900 20pf. Stamp

1999. "iBRA" International Stamp Fair, Nuremberg, Germany. Multicoloured.

767	55c. Type **118**	1·30	1·20
768	55c. Golsdorf steam railway locomotive and Caroline Islands 1m. "Yacht" stamp	1·30	1·20
MS769	160×106 mm. $2 Caroline Islands 1900 50pf. stamp and exhibition emblem (39×59 mm)	4·75	4·25

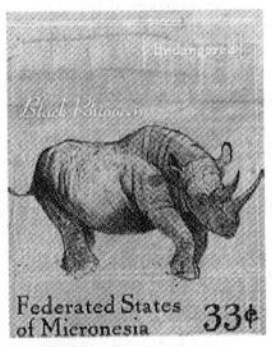

119 Black Rhinoceros

1999. Earth Day. Multicoloured.

770	33c. Type **119**	75	70
771	33c. Cheetah	75	70
772	33c. Jackass penguin	75	70
773	33c. Blue whale	75	70
774	33c. Red-headed woodpecker	75	70
775	33c. African elephant	75	70
776	33c. Aurochs	75	70
777	33c. Dodo	75	70
778	33c. Tasmanian wolf	75	70
779	33c. Giant lemur	75	70
780	33c. Quagga	75	70
781	33c. Steller's sea cow	75	70
782	33c. Pteranodon	75	70
783	33c. Shonisaurus	75	70
784	33c. Stegosaurus	75	70
785	33c. Gallimimus	75	70
786	33c. Tyrannosaurus	75	70
787	33c. Archelon	75	70
788	33c. Brachiosaurus	75	70
789	33c. Triceratops	75	70
MS790	Two sheets, each 86×1050 mm. (a) $2 Moa (37×50 mm); (b) $2 "Suchominus tenerensis" (50×37 mm)	9·50	8·75

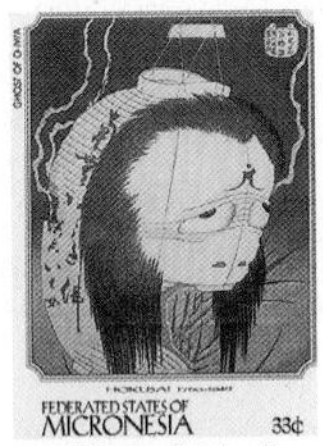

120 "Ghost of O-Iwa"

1999. 150th Death Anniv of Hokusai Katsushika (Japanese artist). Multicoloured.

791	33c. Type **120**	75	70
792	33c. Spotted horse with head lowered	75	70
793	33c. "Abe Nakamaro"	75	70
794	33c. "Ghost of Kasane"	75	70
795	33c. Bay horse with head held up	75	70
796	33c. "The Ghost of Kiku and the Priest Mitazuki"	75	70
797	33c. "Belly Band Float"	75	70
798	33c. Woman washing herself	75	70
799	33c. "Swimmers"	75	70
800	33c. "Eel Climb"	75	70
801	33c. Woman playing lute	75	70
802	33c. "Kimo Ga Imo ni Naru"	75	70
MS803	Two sheets, each 102×72 mm. (a) $2 "Whaling off Goto"; (b) $2 "Fishing by Torchlight"	9·50	8·75

Nos. 792 and 795 are inscribed "Horse Drawings" and No. **MS**803b "Fishing by Torchlight".

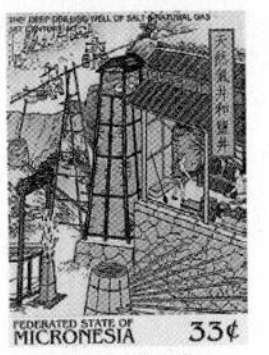

121 Deep-drilling for Brine Salt

1999. New Millennium. Multicoloured. (a) Science and Technology of Ancient China.

804	33c. Type **121**	75	70
805	33c. Chain pump	75	70
806	33c. Magic lantern	75	70
807	33c. Chang Heng's seismograph	75	70
808	33c. Dial and pointer devices	75	70
809	33c. Page of Lui Hui's mathematics treatise (value of Pi)	75	70
810	33c. Porcelain production	75	70
811	33c. Water mill	75	70
812	33c. Relief of horse from tomb of Tang Tai-Tsung (the stirrup)	75	70
813	33c. Page of Lu Yu's tea treatise and detail of Liu Songnian's painting of tea-making	75	70
814	33c. Umbrella	75	70
815	33c. Brandy and whisky production	75	70
816	33c. Page from oldest surviving printed book, woodblock and its print (printing)	75	70
817	33c. Copper plate and its print (paper money)	75	70
818	33c. Woodcut showing gunpowder demonstration	75	70
819	33c. Anji Bridge (segmented arch) (56½×36 mm)	75	70
820	33c. Mercator's star map and star diagram on bronze mirror	75	70

(b) People and Events of the Twelfth Century (1100–1150).

821	20c. Holy Roman Emperor Henry IV (death, 1106)	45	45
822	20c. Chastisement of monks of Enryakuji Temple, Kyoto, 1108	45	45
823	20c. Founding of Knights of the Hospital of St. John, 1113	45	45
824	20c. Invention of nautical compass, 1117	45	45
825	20c. Drowning of Prince William, heir of King Henry I of England, 1120	45	45
826	20c. Pope Callixtus II (Treaty of Worms, 1122, between Papacy and Holy Roman Emperor Henry V)	45	45
827	20c. Death of Omar Khayyam (Persian poet), 1126	45	45
828	20c. Death of Duke Guilhem IX, Count of Poitiers and Duke of Aquitaine (earliest known troubadour, 1127)	45	45
829	20c. Coronation of King Roger II of Sicily, 1130	45	45
830	20c. King Stephen and Queen Matilda (start of English civil war, 1135)	45	45
831	20c. Moses Maimonides (philosopher, birth, 1138)	45	45
832	20c. Abelard and Heloise (Church's censure of Abelard, 1140)	45	45
833	20c. Defeat of French and German crusaders at Damascus, 1148	45	45
834	20c. Fall of Mexican city of Tula, 1150s	45	45
835	20c. Completion of Angkor Vat, Cambodia, 1150	45	45
836	20c. Rise of Kingdom of Chimu, Peru, 1150s (56½×36 mm)	45	45
837	20c. Honen (Buddhist monk) becomes hermit, 1150	45	45

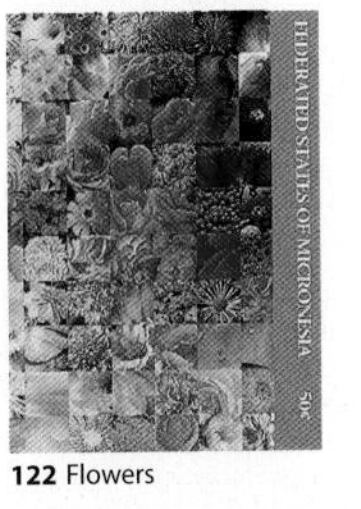

122 Flowers

1999. Faces of the Millennium: Diana, Princess of Wales. Showing collage of miniature flower photographs. Multicoloured, country panel at left (a) or right (b).

838	50c. Deep red shades (a)	1·20	1·10
839	50c. Deep red shades (b)	1·20	1·10
840	50c. Deep red shades with violet shades at bottom left (a)	1·20	1·10
841	50c. Blackish shades in bottom left corner (b)	1·20	1·10
842	50c. Violet shades at left and bottom, pinkish shades at right (a)	1·20	1·10
843	50c. Lemon and pink shades (b)	1·20	1·10
844	50c. Violet shades (a)	1·20	1·10
845	50c. Type **122** (rose in bottom row) (b)	1·20	1·10

Nos. 838/45 were issued together, se-tenant, and when viewed as a whole, form a portrait of Diana, Princess of Wales.

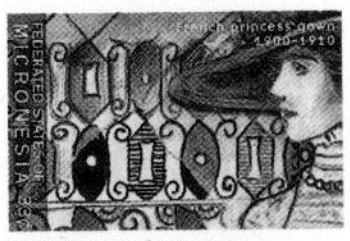

123 Face of Woman

1999. Costumes of the World. Multicoloured.

846	33c. Type **123**	75	70
847	33c. Tools for fabric making	75	70
848	33c. Head of African Masai warrior and textile pattern	75	70
849	33c. Head of woman and textile pattern (inscr "French Renaissance costume")	75	70
850	33c. Head of woman in hat with black feathers ("French princess gown 1900–1910")	75	70
851	33c. Head of Micronesian woman in wedding costume	75	70
852	33c. Body of African Masai warrior and head of woman	75	70
853	33c. Body of woman ("Textile patterns of French Renaissance costume")	75	70
854	33c. Body of woman ("1900–1910 French princess gown")	75	70
855	33c. Body and head of two Micronesian women in wedding costumes	75	70
856	33c. Hem of costume and body of woman ("Details of woman costume from African fabrics")	75	70
857	33c. Lower part of dress and head of woman ("French Renaissance costume")	75	70
858	33c. Hem of dress and furled umbrella	75	70
859	33c. Body and legs of two Micronesian women in wedding costumes	75	70
860	33c. Head of woman in Japanese Kabuki costume	75	70
861	33c. Rulers for tailoring	75	70
862	33c. Scissors	75	70
863	33c. Japanese fabrics	75	70
864	33c. Head and body of two women in Japanese Kabuki costumes	75	70
865	33c. Iron	75	70

Nos. 846/65 were issued together, se-tenant, forming several composite designs.

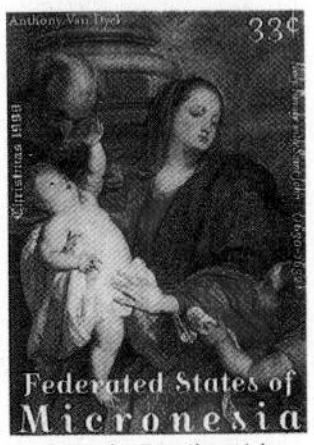

124 "Holy Family with St. John"

1999. Christmas. Paintings by Anthony van Dyck. Multicoloured.

866	33c. Type **124**	85	80
867	60c. "Madonna and Child"	1·50	1·50
868	$2 "Virgin and Child with Two Donors" (detail)	5·00	5·00
MS869	102×127 mm. $2 "Adoration of the Shepherds"	5·00	5·00

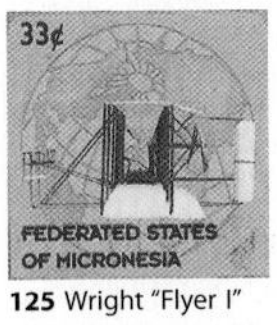

125 Wright "Flyer I"

1999. Man's First Century of Flight. Multicoloured.

870	33c. Type **125**	85	80
871	33c. Bleriot XI and Notre Dame Cathedral, Paris	85	80
872	33c. Fokker D.VII biplane and Brandenburg Gate, Berlin	85	80
873	33c. Dornier Komet I (numbered B 240) and Amsterdam	85	80
874	33c. Charles Lindbergh's Ryan NYP Special "Spirit of St. Louis" and steeple	85	80

875	33c. Mitsubishi A6M Zero-Sen fighter and Mt. Fuji	85	80
876	33c. Boeing B-29 Superfortress bomber and roof of building	85	80
877	33c. Messerschmitt Me 262A jet fighter (swastika on tail)	85	80
878	33c. Chuck Yeager's Bell X-1 rocket plane and Grand Canyon	85	80
879	33c. Mikoyan Gurevich MiG-19 over Russian church	85	80
880	33c. Lockheed U-2 reconnaissance plane over building at night	85	80
881	33c. Boeing 707 jetliner and head of Statue of Liberty, New York	85	80
882	33c. British Aerospace/Aerospatiale Concorde supersonic jetliner and top of Eiffel Tower, Paris	85	80
883	33c. McDonnell Douglas DC-10 jetliner and Sydney Opera House	85	80
884	33c. B-2 Spirit stealth bomber and globe	85	80

MS885 Two sheets, each 108×108 mm. (a) $2 Dornier Do-X flying boat (47×31 mm); (b) $2 P38 (31×47 mm) — 10·00 — 9·75

Nos. 870/84 were issued together, se-tenant, forming a composite design of the globe.

126 *Oncidium obryzatum*

2000. Orchids. Multicoloured.

886	33c. Type **126**	85	80
887	33c. *Oncidium phalaenopsis*	85	80
888	33c. *Oncidium pulvinatum*	85	80
889	33c. *Paphiodedilum armeniacum*	85	80
890	33c. *Paphiopedilum dayanum*	85	80
891	33c. *Paphiopedilum druryi*	85	80
892	33c. *Baptistonia echinata*	85	80
893	33c. *Bulbophyllum lobbii*	85	80
894	33c. *Cattleya bicolor*	85	80
895	33c. *Cischweinfia dasyandra*	85	80
896	33c. *Cochleanthes discolor*	85	80
897	33c. *Dendrobium bellatulum*	85	80
898	33c. *Esmeralda clarkei*	85	80
899	33c. *Gomesa crispa*	85	80
900	33c. *Masdevallia elephanticeps*	85	80
901	33c. *Maxillaria variabilis*	85	80
902	33c. *Mitoniopsis roezlii*	85	80
903	33c. *Oncidium cavendishianum*	85	80

MS904 Two sheets, each 98×70 mm. (a) $1 "Ticoglossum oerstedii" (31×53 mm); (b) $2 "Paphiopedilum hirutissimum" (31×53 mm) — 5·00 — 5·00

127 Martin Luther King (civil rights leader)

2000. Personalities of the Twentieth Century. Multicoloured.

905	33c. Type **127**	85	80
906	33c. Dr. Albert Schweitzer (philosopher and missionary)	85	80
907	33c. Pope John Paul II	85	80
908	33c. Sarvepalli Radhakrishnan (philosopher and Indian statesman)	85	80
909	33c. Toyohiko Kagawa (social reformer)	85	80
910	33c. Mahatma Gandhi (Indian leader)	85	80
911	33c. Mother Teresa (nun and missionary)	85	80
912	33c. Khyentse Rinpoche (poet and philosopher)	85	80
913	33c. Desmond Tutu (religious leader)	85	80
914	33c. Chiara Lubich (founder of Focolare movement)	85	80
915	33c. Dalai Lama (religious leader)	85	80
916	33c. Abraham Heschel (theologian)	85	80

128 Dragon

2000. New Year. Year of the Dragon. 80×6 mm.
MS917 **128** $2 multicoloured — 5·00 — 5·00

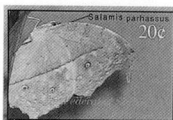

129 Mother-of-Pearl (*Salamis parhassus*)

2000. Butterflies. Multicoloured.

918	20c. Type **129**	50	50
919	20c. Blue morpho (*Morpho rhetenor*)	50	50
920	20c. Monarch (*Danaus plexippus*)	50	50
921	20c. *Phyciodes actinote*	50	50
922	20c. *Idea leuconoe*	50	50
923	20c. *Actinote negra sobrina*	50	50
924	55c. Blue triangle (*Graphium sarpedon*)	1·40	1·40
925	55c. Swallowtail (*Papilio machaon*)	1·40	1·40
926	55c. Cairn's birdwing (*Ornithoptera priamus*)	1·40	1·40
927	55c. *Ornithoptera chimaera*	1·40	1·40
928	55c. Five-bar swallowtail (*Graphium antiphates*)	1·40	1·40
929	55c. *Pachliopta aristolochiae*	1·40	1·40

MS930 Three sheets, each 95×132 mm. (a) $2 King cracker ("Hamadryas amphinome") (vert); (b) $2 Man with butterfly wing (vert); (c) $2 Clouded yellow ("Colias crocea") (wrongly inscr "croceus") (vert) — 15·00 — 14·50

130 Mahatma Gandhi (Indian leader)

2000. New Millennium. Multicoloured.

931	20c. Type **130**	50	50
932	20c. Poster (Dada Art fair, Berlin, 1920)	50	50
933	20c. Women with American flags (female suffrage, 1930)	50	50
934	20c. Nicola Sacco and Bartolomeo Vanzetti (anarchists) (international controversy over murder conviction, 1921)	50	50
935	20c. Hermann Rorschach (psychiatrist and neurologist) (developed inkblot test, 1921)	50	50
936	20c. George W. Watson (incorporation of I.B.M., 1924)	50	50
937	20c. Leica camera (first commercial 35 mm camera, 1925)	50	50
938	20c. Scientists and John Thomas Scopes (brought to trial for teaching Darwin's theory of evolution, 1925)	50	50
939	20c. Charles Lindbergh (aviator) and Ryan NYP Special Spirit of St. Louis (first solo transatlantic flight, 1927)	50	50
940	20c. "Big Bang" (George Henri Lemaître) (astrophysicist and cosmologist) (formulated "Big Bang" theory, 1927)	50	50
941	20c. Chiang Kai-Shek (Chinese nationalist leader)	50	50
942	20c. Werner Heisenberg (theoretical physicist) developed "Uncertainty Principle", 1927	50	50
943	20c. Sir Alexander Fleming (bacteriologist) and microscope (discovery of penicillin, 1928)	50	50
944	20c. Emperor Hirohito of Japan	50	50
945	20c. Car and man (U.S. Stock Market crash causes Great Depression)	50	50
946	20c. Douglas World Cruiser seaplanes and men (round-the-world formation flight, 1924) (59×39 mm)	50	50
947	20c. *All Quiet on the Western Front* (novel by Erich Maria Remarque published 1929)	50	50

131 Mikhail Gorbachev (statesman)

2000. International Relations in the Twentieth Century. Multicoloured.

948	33c. Type **131**	85	80
949	33c. U.S.S.R. and U.S. flags, Gorbachev and Reagan (end of Cold War)	85	80
950	33c. Ronald Reagan (U.S. President, 1980–88)	85	80
951	33c. Le Duc Tho (Vietnamese politician)	85	80
952	33c. Le Duc Tho and Henry Kissinger (resolution to Vietnam conflict)	85	80
953	33c. Henry Kissinger (U.S. Secretary of State)	85	80
954	33c. Linus Pauling (chemist)	85	80
955	33c. Pauling at protest against nuclear weapons	85	80
956	33c. Peter Benenson (founder of Amnesty International, 1961)	85	80
957	33c. Amnesty International emblem and prisoners	85	80
958	33c. Mahatma Gandhi (Indian leader)	85	80
959	33c. Gandhi fasting	85	80
960	33c. John F. Kennedy (U.S. President, 1960–3) making speech initiating Peace Corps	85	80
961	33c. President Kennedy	85	80
962	33c. Dalai Lama (Tibetan religious leader) praying	85	80
963	33c. Dalai Lama	85	80
964	33c. United Nations Headquarters, New York	85	80
965	33c. Cordell Hull (U.S. Secretary of State 1933–44) (active in creation of United Nations)	85	80
966	33c. Frederick Willem de Klerk (South African politician)	85	80
967	33c. De Klerk and Nelson Mandela (end of Apartheid)	85	80
968	33c. Nelson Mandela	85	80
969	33c. Franklin D. Roosevelt (U.S. President)	85	80
970	33c. Winston Churchill, Roosevelt and Josef Stalin (Soviet leader) (Yalta Conference, 1945)	85	80
971	33c. Winston Churchill (British Prime Minister)	85	80

132 Andrew Carnegie (industrialist)

2000. Philanthropists of the Twentieth Century. Multicoloured.

972	33c. Type **132**	85	80
973	33c. John D. Rockefeller (oil magnate)	85	80
974	33c. Henry Ford (motor manufacturer)	85	80
975	33c. C. J. Walker	85	80
976	33c. James B. Duke	85	80
977	33c. Andrew Mellon (financier)	85	80
978	33c. Charles F. Kettering (engineer)	85	80
979	33c. R. W. Woodruff	85	80
980	33c. Brooke Astor	85	80
981	33c. Howard Hughes (businessman and aviator)	85	80
982	33c. Jesse H. Jones	85	80
983	33c. Paul Mellon	85	80
984	33c. Jean Paul Getty (oil executive)	85	80
985	33c. George Soros	85	80
986	33c. Phyllis Wattis	85	80
987	33c. Ted (Robert Edward) Turner (entrepreneur)	85	80

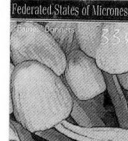

133 Fairies' Bonnets (*Coprinus disseminatus*)

2000. Fungi. Multicoloured.

988	33c. Type **133**	85	80
989	33c. Black Bulgar (*Bulgaria inquinans*)	85	80
990	33c. Amethyst deceiver (*Laccaria amethystina*) (inscr "amethystea")	85	80
991	33c. Common morel (*Morchella esculenta*)	85	80
992	33c. Common bird's nest (*Crucibulum laeve*)	85	80
993	33c. Trumpet agaric (*Clitocybe geotropa*)	85	80
994	33c. Bonnet mycena (*Mycena galericulata*)	85	80
995	33c. Underside of horse mushroom (*Agaricus arvensis*)	85	80
996	33c. Part of *Boletus subtomento*	85	80
997	33c. Oyster mushroom (*Pleurotus ostreatus*)	85	80
998	33c. Fly agaric (*Amanita muscaria*)	85	80
999	33c. Aztec mushroom mandala design	85	80

MS1000 Two sheets, each 100×100 mm. (a) $2 Toad on brown birch bolete; (b) $2 Magpie ink cap — 10·00 — 9·75

134 *Freycinetia arborea*

2000. Flowers. Multicoloured.

1001	33c. Type **134**	85	80
1002	33c. Mount Cook lily (*Ranunculus lyallii*) (inscr "lyalli")	85	80
1003	33c. Sun orchid (*Thelymitra nuda*)	85	80
1004	33c. *Bossiaea ensata*	85	80
1005	33c. Swamp hibiscus (*Hibiscus diversifolius*)	85	80
1006	33c. *Gardenia brighamii*	85	80
1007	33c. Elegant brodiaea (*Brodiaea elegans*)	85	80
1008	33c. Skyrocket (*Ipomopsis aggregata*)	85	80
1009	33c. Hedge bindweed (*Convovulus sepium*)	85	80
1010	33c. Woods' rose (*Rosa woodsii*)	85	80
1011	33c. Swamp rose (*Rosa palustris*)	85	80
1012	33c. Wake robin (*Trillium erectum*)	85	80

MS1013 Two sheets. (a) 95×80 mm. $2 Black-eyed susan (*Tetratheca juncea*). (b) 108×80 mm. $2 Yellow meadow lily (*Lilium canadense*) Set of 2 sheets — 10·00 — 9·75

135 Two Siamese Cats

2000. Cats and Dogs. Multicoloured.

1014	33c. Type **135**	85	80
1015	33c. Red mackerel tabbies	85	80
1016	33c. British shorthair	85	80
1017	33c. Red Persian	85	80
1018	33c. Turkish angora	85	80
1019	33c. Calico	85	80
1020	33c. Afghan hounds	85	80
1021	33c. Yellow labrador retriever	85	80
1022	33c. Greyhound	85	80
1023	33c. German shepherd	85	80
1024	33c. King Charles spaniel	85	80
1025	33c. Jack Russell terrier	85	80

MS1026 Two sheets, each 85×110 mm. (a) $2 Tortoiseshell and white cat watching bird. (b) $2 Setter and trees Set of 2 sheets — 10·00 — 9·75

Nos. 1014/19 (cats) and 1020/5 (dogs) respectively were issued together, se-tenant, each sheetlet forming a composite design.

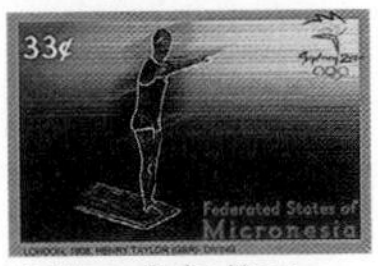

136 Henry Taylor (Great Britain) preparing to Dive, 1908, London

2000. Olympic Games, Sydney. Multicoloured.

1027	33c. Type **136**	85	80
1028	33c. Cyclist	85	80
1029	33c. Munich stadium and flag, West Germany	85	80
1030	33c. Ancient Greek wrestlers	85	80

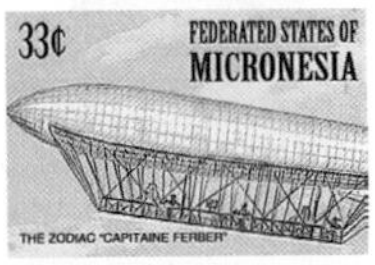

137 Zodiac Airship *Capitaine Ferber*

2000. Centenary of First Zeppelin Flight and Airship Development. Multicoloured.

1031	33c. Type **137**	85	80
1032	33c. Astra airship *Adjutant Reau*	85	80
1033	33c. Airship 1A, Italy	85	80
1034	33c. Astra-Torres No. 14	85	80
1035	33c. Front of Astra-Torres No. 14, Schuttle-Lanz SL3 and front of Siemens-Schukert airship	85	80
1036	33c. Siemens-Schukert airship	85	80

MS1037 Two sheets, each 110×85 mm. (a) $2 LZ-130 *Graf Zeppelin II*. (b) $2 Dupuy de Lome airship Set of 2 sheets 10·00 9·75

Nos. 1031/6 were issued together, *se-tenant*, forming a composite design.

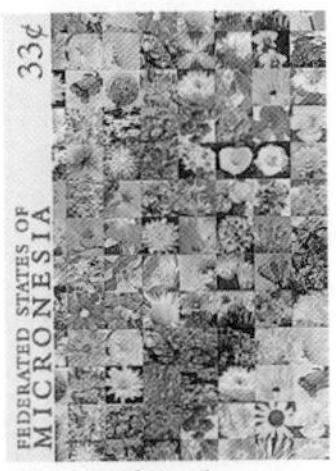

138 Top of Head

2000. 100th Birthday of Queen Elizabeth the Queen Mother. T **138** and similar vert designs showing collage of miniature flower photographs. Multicoloured, country inscription and face value at left (a) or right (b).

1038	33c. Type **138**	85	80
1039	33c. Top of head (b)	85	80
1040	33c. Eye and temple (a)	85	80
1041	33c. Temple (b)	85	80
1042	33c. Cheek (a)	85	80
1043	33c. Cheek (b)	85	80
1044	33c. Chin (a)	85	80
1045	33c. Chin and neck (b)	85	80

Nos. 1038/45 were issued together in *se-tenant* sheetlets of eight with the stamps arranged in two vertical columns separated by a gutter also containing miniature photographs. When viewed as a whole, the sheetlet forms a portrait of Queen Elizabeth the Queen Mother.

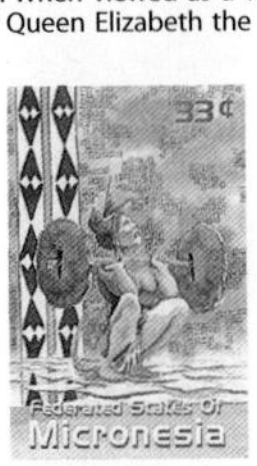

139 Woman Weightlifter and Traditional Cloth

2000. "OLYMPHILEX 2000" International Olympic Stamp Exhibition, Sydney. Sheet 137× 82 mm, containing T **139** and similar vert designs. Multicoloured.

MS1046 33c. Type **139**; 33c. Woman playing basketball; $1 Male weight-lifter 4·50 4·25

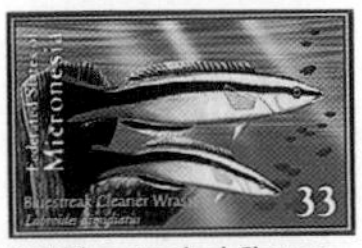

140 Blue-streaked Cleaner Wrasse (*Labroides dimidiatus*)

2000. Coral Reef. Multicoloured.

1047	33c. Type **140**	85	80
1048	33c. Pennant coralfish (*Heniochus acuminatus*)	85	80
1049	33c. Chevron butterflyfish (*Chaetodon trifascialis*)	85	80
1050	33c. Rock beauty (*Holacanthus tricolor*)	85	80
1051	33c. Mandarin fish (*Synchiropus splendidus*)	85	80
1052	33c. Emperor snapper (*Lutjanus sebae*) (wrongly inscr "timorensis")	85	80
1053	33c. Copper-banded butterfly-fish (*rostratus*)	85	80
1054	33c. Chevron butterflyfish (*Chaetodon trifascialis*) (different)	85	80
1055	33c. Lemon-peel angelfish (*Centropyge flavissimus*)	85	80
1056	33c. Lemon-peel angelfish and harlequin tuskfish (*Choerodon fasciatus*)	85	80
1057	33c. Crown triggerfish (*Balistoides conspicillum*)	85	80
1058	33c. Coral hind (*Cephalopholis miniata*)	85	80
1059	33c. Pennant coralfish (*Heniochus acuminatus*) (different)	85	80
1060	33c. Scuba diver and six-blotched hind (*Cephalopholis sexmaculata*)	85	80
1061	33c. Common jellyfish (*Aurelia aurita*)	85	80
1062	33c. Palette surgeonfish (*Paracanthurus hepatus*) and common jellyfish	85	80
1063	33c. Bicoloured angelfish (*Centropyge bicolor*)	85	80
1064	33c. Thread-finned butterflyfish (*Chaetodon auriga*) and clown anemonefish	85	80
1065	33c. Clown anemonefish (*Amphiprion percula*)	85	80
1066	33c. Three-banded damselfish (*Chrysiptera tricincta*)	85	80
1067	33c. Three-banded damselfish and grey reef shark (*Carcharhinus amblyrhynchs*) (inscr "amblyrhynchos")	85	80
1068	33c. Tail of grey reef shark and starfish (*Luidia ciliaris*)	85	80

MS1069 Two sheets, each 98×68 mm. (a) $2 Forceps butterflyfish (*Forcipiger flavissimus*). (b) $2 Emperor angelfish (*Pomacanthus imperator*) Set of 2 sheets 10·00 9·75

Nos. 1051/59 and 1060/8 respectively were issued, se-tenant, forming a composite design.

141 Back of Head

2000. 80th Birthday of Pope John Paul II. T 141 and similar vert designs showing collage of miniature religious photographs. Multicoloured, country Inscription and face value at left (a) or right (b).

1070	50c. Type **141**	1·40	1·30
1071	50c. Forehead (b)	1·40	1·30
1072	50c. Ear (a)	1·40	1·30
1073	50c. Forehead and eye (b)	1·40	1·30
1074	50c. Neck and collar (a)	1·40	1·30
1075	50c. Nose and cheek (b)	1·40	1·30
1076	50c. Shoulder (a)	1·40	1·30
1077	50c. Hands (b)	1·40	1·30

Nos. 1070/7 were issued together in se-tenant sheetlets of eight with the stamps arranged in two vertical columns separated by a gutter also containing miniature photographs. When viewed as a whole, the sheetlet forms a portrait of Pope John Paul II.

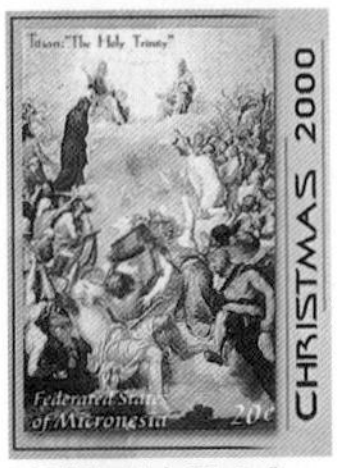

142 "The Holy Trinity" (Titian)

2000. Christmas. Multicoloured.

1078	20c. Type **142**	55	50
1079	33c. "Adoration of the Magi" (Diego de Silva y Velasquez)	90	85
1080	60c. "Holy Nereus" (Peter Paul Rubens)	1·60	1·50
1081	$3.20 "St. Gregory, St. Maurus, St. Papianus and St. Domitilla" (Rubens)	8·50	8·00

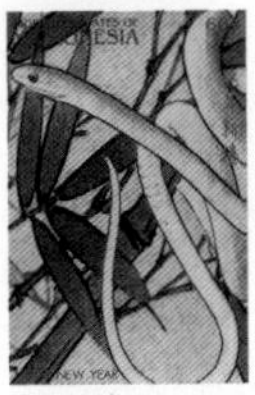
143 Snake

2001. New Year. Year of the Snake. Two sheets, each 72×101 mm, containing horiz design as T **143**. Multicoloured.

MS1082 (a) 60c. Type **143**. (b) 60c. Brown snake 3·25 3·00

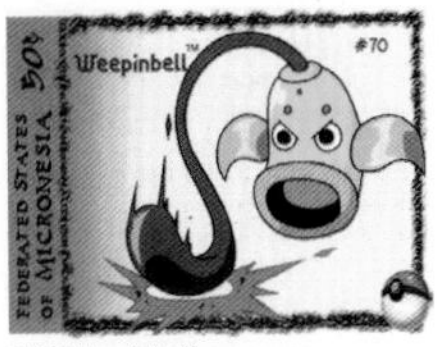

144 Weepinbell

2001. Pokemon (children's computer game). Showing various Pokemon characters. Mult.

1083	50c. Type **144**	1·40	1·30
1084	50c. Snorlax	1·40	1·30
1085	50c. Seel	1·40	1·30
1086	50c. Hitmonchan	1·40	1·30
1087	50c. Jynx	1·40	1·30
1088	50c. Pontya	1·40	1·30

MS1089 74×114 mm. $2 Farfetch'd (37×50 mm) 5·50 5·00

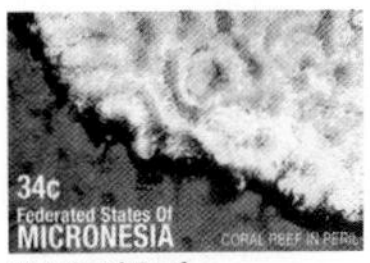

145 Coral Reef

2001. Environmental Protection. Multicoloured.

1090	34c. Type **145**	95	90
1091	34c. Galapagos turtle	95	90
1092	34c. Tasmanian tiger	95	90
1093	34c. Yanomami	95	90
1094	34c. Pelican and Florida Keys	95	90
1095	34c. Bird of prey	95	90
1096	60c. Factory chimneys (Pollution)	1·60	1·50
1097	60c. Desert and tree stump (Deforestation)	1·60	1·50
1098	60c. Forest (Acid rain)	1·60	1·50
1099	60c. Horse, mother and child, tree and Globe (Greenhouse effect)	1·60	1·50

MS1100 Two sheets each 110×77 mm. (a) $2 Sea bird (visit by Jacques Cousteau); (b) $2 Chimpanzee (Jane Goodall Institute) Set of 2 sheets 11·00 10·00

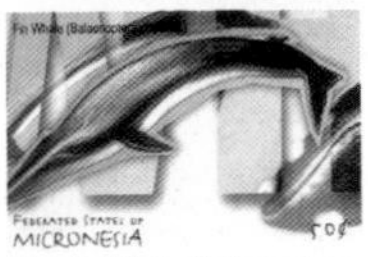

146 Fin Whale (*Balaenoptera physalus*)

2001. Whales of the Pacific. Multicoloured.

1101	50c. Type **146**	1·40	1·30
1102	50c. Right whale (*Balaena galacials*)	1·40	1·30
1103	50c. Pygmy right whale (*Caperea marginata*)	1·40	1·30
1104	50c. Humpback whale (*Megaptera novaeangliae*) (inscr "novaengliae")	1·40	1·30
1105	50c. Blue whale (*Balaenoptera musculus*)	1·40	1·30
1106	50c. Bowhead whale (*Balaena mysticetus*)	1·40	1·30
1107	60c. True's beaked whale (*Mesoplodon mirus*)	1·60	1·50
1108	60c. Cuvier's beaked whale (*Ziphius cavirostris*)	1·60	1·50
1109	60c. Shepherd's beaked whale (*Tasmacetus shepherdi*)	1·60	1·50
1110	60c. Baird's beaked whale (*Berardius bairdii*)	1·60	1·50
1111	60c. Northern bottlenose whale (*Hyperodon ampullatus*)	1·60	1·50
1112	60c. Pygmy sperm whale (*Kogia breviceps*)	1·60	1·50

MS1113 Two sheets each 100×70 mm. (a) $2 Killer whale (*Orcinus orca*); (b) $2 Sperm whale (*Physeter macrocephalus*) Set of 2 sheets 11·00 10·00

Nos. 1101/6 and 1107/12 respectively were issued together, se-tenant, forming a composite design.

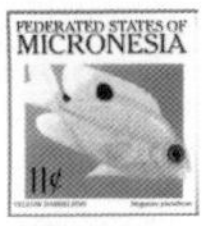

147 Three-spotted ("Yellow") Damselfish (*Stegastes planifrons*)

2001. Fish. Multicoloured.

1114	11c. Type **147**	35	30
1115	34c. Rainbow runner (*Elegatis bipinnulatus*)	95	90
1118	70c. Whitelined grouper (*Anyperodon leucogrammicus*)	1·90	1·80
1119	80c. Purple queen anthias (*Pseudanthias pascalus*)	2·20	2·00
1123	$3.50 Eibl's angelfish (*Centropye eibli*)	8·75	8·25
1127	$12.25 Spotted ("Blue-spotted") boxfish (*Ostracion meleagris*)	34·00	32·00

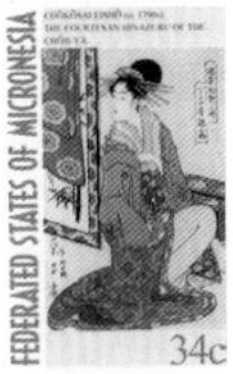

148 "The Courtesan Hinazuru of the Choji-ya" (Chokosai Eisho)

2001. "PHILANIPPON '01" International Stamp Exhibition, Tokyo. Japanese Art. Multicoloured.

1130	34c. Type **148**	95	90
1131	34c. "The Iris Garden" (Torii Kiyonaga)	95	90
1132	34c. "Girl tying her Hair Ribbon" (Tori Kiyomine)	95	90
1133	34c. "The Courtesan of the Mayuzumi of the Daimonji-ya" (Katsukawa Shuncho)	95	90
1134	34c. "Parody of the Allegory of the Sage Chin Kao Riding a Carp" (Suzuki Harunobo)	95	90
1135	34c. "Bath-house Scene" (Utagawa Toyokuni)	95	90
1136	34c. "Dance of Kamisha" (Kitagawa Utamaro)	95	90
1137	34c. "The Courtesan Hinazura at the Keizetsuro" (Kitagawa Utamaro)	95	90
1138	34c. "Toilet Scene" (Kitagawa Utamaro)	95	90
1139	34c. "Applying Lip Rouge" (Kitagawa Utamaro)	95	90
1140	34c. "Beauty reading a Letter" (Kitagawa Utamaro)	95	90
1141	34c. "The Geisha Kamekichi" (Kitagawa Utamaro)	95	90

MS1142 Two sheets each 118×88 mm. (a) $2 "Girl seated by a Brook at Sunset" (Suzuki Harunobu). Imperf; (b) $2 "Allegory of Ariwara No Narihira" (Kikugawa Eizan). Imperf Set of 2 shets 11·00 10·00

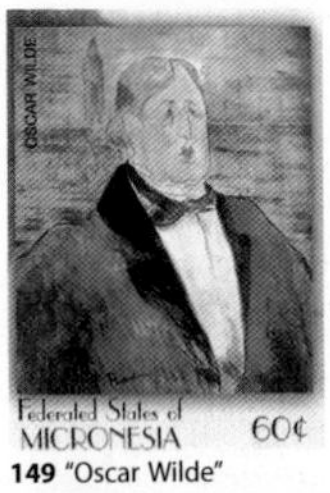

149 "Oscar Wilde"

2001. Death Centenary of Henri de Toulouse-Lautrec (artist). Multicoloured.

1143	60c. Type **149**	1·60	1·50
1144	60c. "Doctor Tapié in a Theatre Corridor"	1·60	1·50
1145	60c. "Monsieur Delaporte"	1·60	1·50

MS1146 54×84 mm. $2 "The Clowness Cha-U-Kao" 5·50 5·00

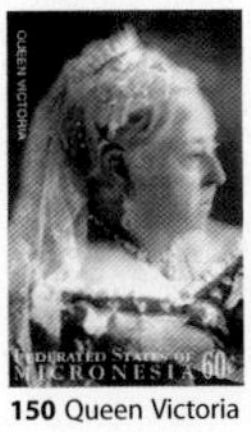

150 Queen Victoria

644 Micronesia

2001. Death Centenary of Queen Victoria. Each black (except **MS**1151 multicoloured).

1147	60c. Type **150**	1·60	1·50
1148	60c. Facing right	1·60	1·50
1149	60c. Facing left wearing black decorated hat	1·60	1·50
1150	60c. Facing forwards	1·60	1·50
1151	60c. Holding baby	1·60	1·50
1152	60c. Facing left wearing lace headdress	1·60	1·50
MS1153	84×110 mm. $2 Queen Victoria (37×50 mm)	5·50	5·00

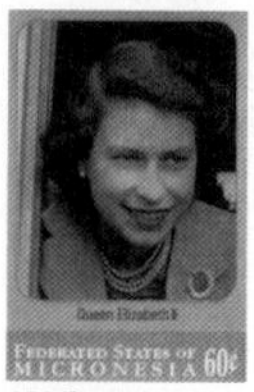
FEDERATED STATES OF MICRONESIA 60¢

151 Queen Elizabeth

2001. 75th Birthday of Queen Elizabeth II. Each black (except No. 1153 and **MS**1158 multicoloured).

1154	60c. Type **151**	1·60	1·50
1155	60c. Wearing blue jacket	1·60	1·50
1156	60c. As young girl	1·60	1·50
1157	60c. As infant	1·60	1·50
1158	60c. With dog	1·60	1·50
1159	60c. In profile	1·60	1·50
MS1160	78×108 mm. $2 Princess Elizabeth	5·50	5·00

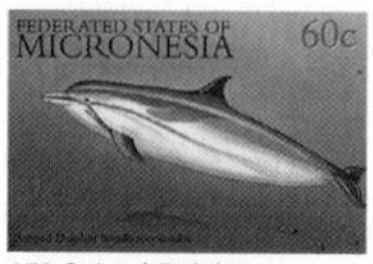
FEDERATED STATES OF MICRONESIA 60¢

152 Striped Dolphin

2001. Marine Life. Four sheets containing T **152** and similar multicoloured designs.

MS1161 (a) 162×153 mm. 60c. ×6, Type **152**; Olive ridley turtle; Goldrim tang; Blue shark; Picasso triggerfish; Polkadot grouper; (b) 152×164 mm. 60c. ×6, Loggerhead turtle; Striped marlin; Bicolor cherub; Clown wrasse (*Coris gaimard*) (inscr "gaimardi"); Clown triggerfish; Japanese tang; (c) 96×68 mm. $2 Harlequin tusk (50×38 mm); (d) 70×100 mm. $2 Emperor angelfish (38×50 mm) 31·00 29·00

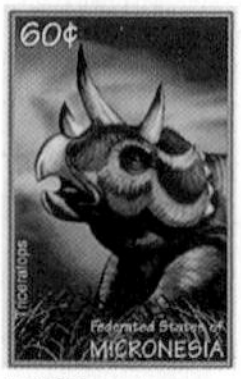
60¢
Federated States of MICRONESIA

153 Triceratops

2001. Dinosaurs. Multicoloured.

1162	60c. Type **153**	1·60	1·50
1163	60c. Psittacosaurus	1·60	1·50
1164	60c. Two Archaeopteryx	1·60	1·50
1165	60c. Head of Allosaurus	1·60	1·50

MS1166 Four sheets (a) 103×124 mm. 60c. ×6, Tyrannosaurus; Pteranodon; Brachiosaurus; Spinosaurus; Deinonychus; Teratosaurus; (b) 104×123 mm. 60c. ×6, Parasaurolophus; Plateosaurus; Archaeopteryx in flight; Allosaurus (different); Torosaurus; Euoplocephalus; (c) 68×98 mm. $2 Tyrannosaurus (different); (d) 68×98 mm. $2 Parasaurolophus (different) (horiz) 31·00 29·00

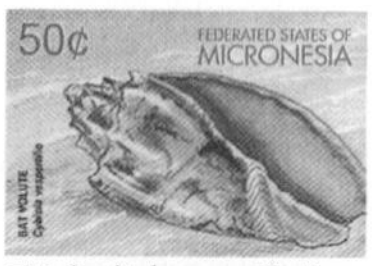
50¢
FEDERATED STATES OF MICRONESIA

154 *Cymbiola vespertilio* (inscr "Cybiola")

2001. Shells. Four sheets containing T **154** and similar multicoloured designs.

MS1167 (a) 152×107 mm. 50c. ×6, Type **154**; *Cassis cornuta*; *Murex troscheli*; *Cymatium lotorium* (incr "lortrium"); *Oliva sericea*; *Phos senticosus*; (b) 111×145 mm. 50c. ×6; *Oblique nutmeg* (vert); *Cymbiola imperialis* (vert); Pontifical mitre (vert); *Conus eburneus Hwass in Bruguiere* (vert); *Heliacus areola* (inscr "variegated gmelin") (vert); *Corculum cardissa* (vert); (c) 76×59 mm. $2 *Eyed auger*; (d) 76×59 mm. $2 Geography cone 27·00 25·00

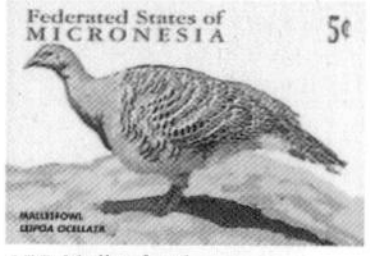
Federated States of MICRONESIA 5¢

155 Malleefowl

2001. Birds. Multicoloured.

1168	5c. Type **155**	15	15
1169	22c. Corncrake	60	55
1170	23c. Hooded merganser	60	55
1171	$2.10 Purple gallinule	5·50	5·00

MS1172 Four sheets. (a) 146×167 mm. 60c. ×6, Fairy wren; Golden crowned kinglet (*Regulus satrapa*) (inscr " Bebrornis rodericanus"); Flame tempered babbler; Golden headed cisticola (*Cisticola exilis*) (inscr " Orthotomus moreauii"); White browed babbler; White throated dipper (inscr "breasted"); (b) 146×167 mm. Logrunner; Common tree creeper (inscr "Eurasian"); Chaffinch (inscr "Goldfinch"); Rufous fantail; Orange bellied flower pecker (inscr "billed"); Goldfinch (inscr "American goldfinch"); (c) 79×109 mm. $2 Emperor bird of paradise; (d) 79×109 mm. $2 Yellow eyed cuckoo shrike (vert) Set of 4 sheets 31·00 29·00

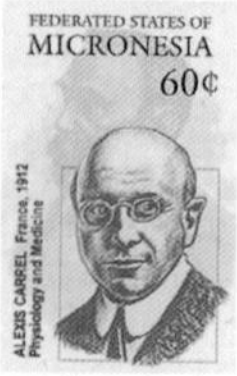
FEDERATED STATES OF MICRONESIA 60¢

156 Alexis Carrel (Physiology and Medicine, 1912)

2001. Centenary of First Nobel Prize. Four sheets containing T **156** and similar vert designs. Multicoloured.

MS1173 (a) 183× 29 mm. 60c. ×6, Type **156**; Max Theiler, 1951 (Physiology and Medicine); Niels Finsen, 1903 (Physiology and Medicine); Philip S. Hench, 1950 (Physiology and Medicine); Sune Bergstrom, 1982 (Physiology and Medicine); JohnVane, 1982 (Physiology and Medicine) (b) 183×129 mm. 60c. ×6, Bengt Samuelsson, 1982 (Physiology and Medicine); Johannes Fibiger, 1926 (Physiology and Medicine); Theodore Richards, 1914 (Chemistry); Tadeus Reichstein, 1950 (Physiology and Medicine); Frederick Soddy, 1921 (Chemistry); Albert Szent-Gyorgi von Nagyrapolt, 1937 (Physiology and Medicine) (c) 106 × 75 mm. Irving Langmuir, 1932 (Chemistry); (d) 106×75 mm. Artturi Ilmari Virtanen, 1945 (Chemistry) 31·00 29·00

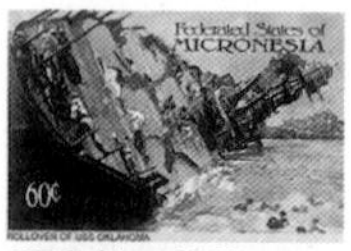
Federated States of MICRONESIA
60¢

157 Sinking of USS *Oklahoma*

2001. 60th Anniv of Attack on Pearl Harbour. Four sheets containing T **157** and similar horiz designs. Multicoloured.

MS1174 (a) 149×161 mm. 60c. ×6, Type **157**; Attack on Wheeler airfield; Japanese bomber; USS *Ward* sinking submarine; Bombing of USS *Arizona*; Attack on EWA marine base (b) 149×161 mm. 60c. ×6, "Remember Pearl Harbour" poster; Hideki Tojo (Japanese prime minister); Rescuing wounded, Bellows Field; Rescuing crew of USS *Arizona*; Isoroku Yamamoto (Japanese admiral); "Remember Pearl Harbour" poster (different) (c) 80×110 mm.; USS *Arizona Memorial*, Hawaii (d) 80×110 mm. President F. D. Roosevelt 31·00 29·00

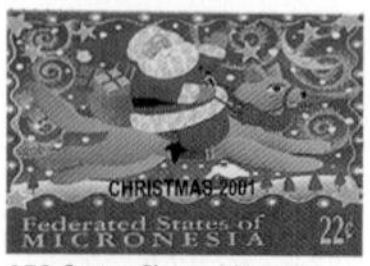
CHRISTMAS 2001
Federated States of MICRONESIA 22¢

158 Santa Claus riding Cat

2001. Christmas. Santa Claus. Multicoloured.

1175	22c. Type **158**	60	55
1176	34c. Between decorated trees	95	90
1177	60c. Flying in sleigh	1·60	1·50
1178	$1 Riding dog	2·75	2·50
MS1179	78×111 mm. $2 Climbing into chimney (vert)	5·50	5·00

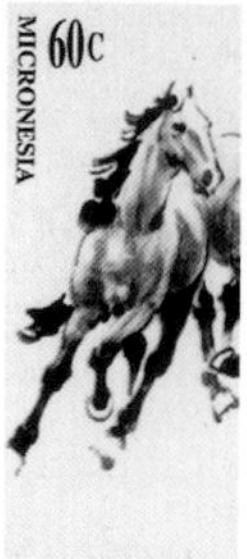
MICRONESIA 60c

159 Horse

2002. Year of the Horse. Sheet containing T **159** and similar vert designs. Each black.

MS1180 60c.×6, Type **159**; Two horses; Two horses (different); Two horses' heads; Galloping horse 8·25 7·75

No. **MS**1180 forms a composite design of a herd of horses.

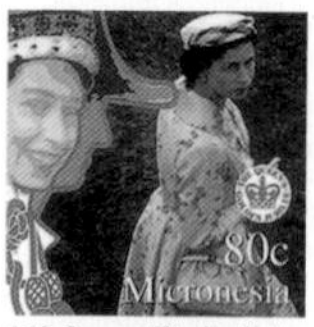
80c
Micronesia

160 Queen Elizabeth II

2002. Golden Jubilee. 50th Anniv of Queen Elizabeth II's Accession to the Throne. Two sheets containing T **160** and similar square designs. Multicoloured.

MS1181 (a) 132×100 mm. 80c.×4, Type **160**; Prince Phillip; Queen Elizabeth wearing white hat; Queen Elizabeth and children; (b) 76×109 mm. $2 Queen Elizabeth wearing headscarf 14·50 13·50

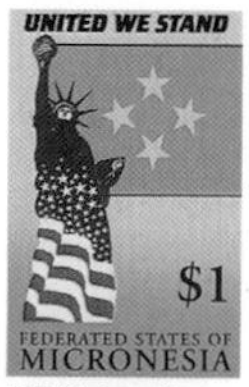
UNITED WE STAND
$1
FEDERATED STATES OF MICRONESIA

161 Statue of Liberty and American Flag

2002. "United We Stand".

1182	**161**	$1 multicoloured	2·75	2·50

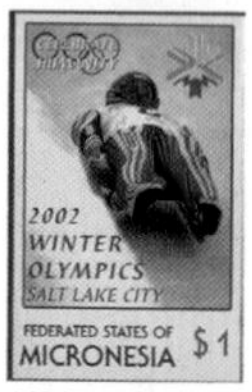
2002
WINTER
OLYMPICS
SALT LAKE CITY
FEDERATED STATES OF MICRONESIA $1

162 Luge Racer

2002. Winter Olympic Games, Salt Lake City (1st issue). Multicoloured.

1183	$1 Type **162**	2·75	2·50
1184	$1 Ice hockey player	2·75	2·50
MS1185	88×119 mm. Nos. 1183/4	5·50	5·00

See also Nos. 1191/**MS**1193.

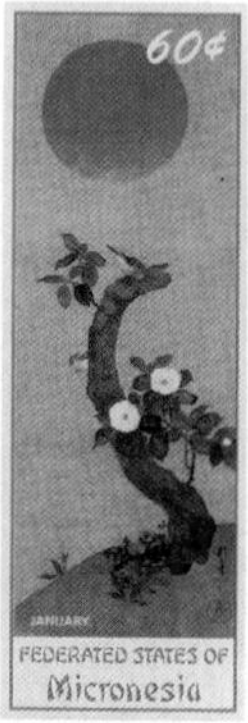
60¢
FEDERATED STATES OF
Micronesia

163 Sun, Bird and Flowering Tree (January)

2002. Japanese Art. "Birds and Flowers of Months of Year" (Nos. **MS**1186a/b). Four sheets containing T **163** and similar vert designs. Multicoloured.

MS1186 Two sheets (a/b), each 135×210 mm. (a) 60c.×6, Type **163**; February; March; April; May; June. (b) 60c.×6, July; August; September; October; November; December. Two sheets (c/d), each 100×69 mm. (c) $2 "Seashells and Plums" (Suzuki Kitsu). Imperf. (d) "Peacock and Peonies" (Nagasawa Rosetsu). Imperf Set of 4 sheets 31·00 29·00

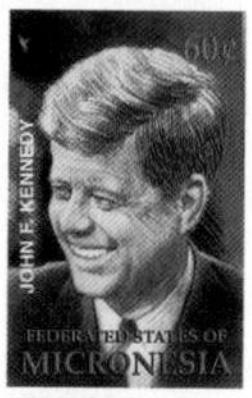
60¢
JOHN F. KENNEDY
FEDERATED STATES OF MICRONESIA

164 John F. Kennedy

2002. 85th Birth Anniv of John Fitzgerald Kennedy (USA president 1961–3) (**MS**1187a/b). Fifth Death Anniv of Diana, Princess of Wales (**MS**1187b/c). Four sheets containing T **164** and similar vert designs. Multicoloured.

MS1187 (a) 132×136 mm. 60c.×4, Type **164**; Facing left; Looking left; Facing front. (b) 80×112 mm. $2 Facing right. (c) 114×133 mm. 60c.×6, Princess Diana as bride; Wearing tiara; Wearing hat; Wearing scarf; Wearing pearl earrings; Wearing tiara facing left. (d) 87×60 mm. $2 Wearing wide-brimmed hat Set of 4 sheets 29·00 27·00

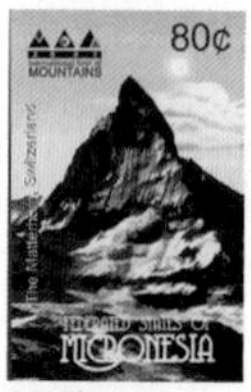
80¢
MICRONESIA

165 The Matterhorn, Switzerland

2002. International Year of Mountains. Two sheets containing T **165** and similar vert designs.

MS1188 (a) 136×95 mm. 80c.×4, Type **165**; Maroon Bells, USA; Wetterhorn, Switzerland; Mount Tasaranoro, Africa (inscr "Tasaranora"). (b) 96×62 mm. $2 Cerro Fitzroy, South America 14·50 13·50

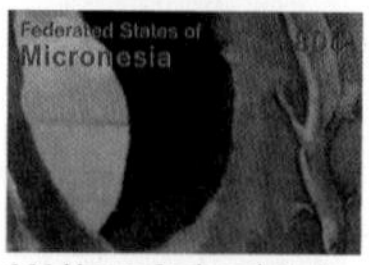
Federated States of Micronesia

166 Money Rock and Gecko

2002. International Year of Eco Tourism. Two sheets containing T **166** and similar horiz designs. Multicoloured.

MS1189 (a) 138×99 mm. 80c.×6, Type **166**; Outrigger canoe; Tribal meeting house; Children wearing ceremonial costumes; Girl wearing lei; Two boys. (b) 85×55 mm. $2 Fishermen 19·00 18·00

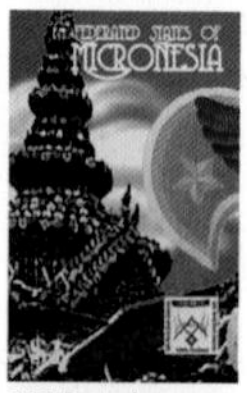
Federated States of MICRONESIA

167 Pagoda

2002. World Scout Jamboree, Thailand. Multicoloured.

MS1190 (a) 161×68 mm. $1×3, Type **167**; American eagle; Scout cap. (b) 97×67 mm. $2 Scout badges 13·50 12·50

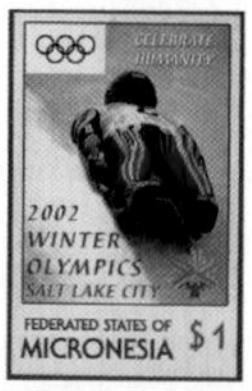
2002
WINTER
OLYMPICS
SALT LAKE CITY
FEDERATED STATES OF MICRONESIA $1

168 Luge Racer

2002. Winter Olympic Games, Salt Lake City (2nd issue). Multicoloured.

1191	$1 Type **168**	2·75	2·50
1192	$1 Ice hockey player	2·75	2·50
MS1193	88×119 mm. Nos. 1191/2	5·50	5·00

Nos. 1191/**MS**1193 differ from the issue of 18 March in the design of the Olympic rings.

169 School Buildings

2002. 50th Anniv of Xavier High School, Sapwuk, Weno Island.

| 1194 | **169** | 37c. multicoloured | 1·00 | 95 |

170 Elizabeth Bowes-Lyon riding Pony

2002. Queen Elizabeth the Queen Mother Commemoration. Two sheets containing T **170** and similar multicoloured designs.
MS1195 (a) 176×126 mm. 80c.×4, Type **170**; Wedding of Duke and Duchess of York; Holding Princess Elizabeth; Coronation of George VI and Queen Elizabeth. (b) 76×106 mm. \$2 Queen Elizabeth the Queen Mother wearing hat with veil (vert) .... 14·50 13·50

171 Teddy Bear dressed as Burglar

2002. Centenary of the Teddy Bear. Sheet 141×145 mm containing T **171** and similar vert designs. Multicoloured.
MS1196 80c.×4, Type **171**; Girl bear holding heart; Blue bear holding flowers; Boy bear holding heart .... 8·75 8·25

172 Elvis Presley

2002. 25th Death Anniv of Elvis Presley (entertainer). Sheet 214×163 mm containing T **172** and similar vert designs. Multicoloured.
MS1197 37c.×6, Type **172**; Kissing guitar; Wearing hat; Wearing checked shirt; With raised arms; Holding microphone .... 6·25 5·75

173 "Madonna and Child" (detail) (Agnolo Bronzino)

2002. Christmas. Multicoloured.
1198	21c. Type **173**	55	50
1199	37c. "Madonna And Child" (Giovanni Bellini)	1·00	95
1200	70c. "Madonna and Child between St. Stephen and St. Ladislaus" (Simone Martini) (horiz)	1·90	1·80
1201	80c. "Holy Family" (Angola Bronzino)	2·20	2·00
1202	\$2 "Holy Family" (Simone Martini)	5·50	5·00
MS1203	102×76 mm. \$2 "Sacred Conversation" (Giovanni Bellini) (inscr "Giovanna")	5·50	5·00

174 *Hyles lineate*

2002. Flora and Fauna. Ten sheets containing T **174** and similar multicoloured designs.
MS1204 Five sheets (a/e), each 127×157 mm. (a) Moths. 37c.×6, Type **174**; *Othreis fullonia*; Inscr "Dysphania cuprina"; *Agarista agricola*; *Actias elene*; Inscr "Rhodogastria crokeri". (b) Fungi. 55c.×6, *Phellinus robustus*; Inscr "Collybia iocephala"; *Leucocoprinus rachodes*; *Boletus edulis*; *Boletus crocipodius*; *Lepiota acutesquamosa*. (c) Butterflies. 60c.×6, *Junonia villida*; *Ornithoptera priamus*; *Danis danis*; *Libythea geoffroyi*; Inscr "Elyminas agondas"; *Eurema brigiitta*. (d) Orchids. 60c.×6, *Eria javanica*; *Cymbidium finlaysonianum*; *Coelogyne asperata*; *Spathoglottis affinis*; *Vanda tricolour*; *Calanthe rosea*. (e) Insects. Inscr "Pseudolucanus capreolus"; Honey bee (*Apis mellifera*); Black widow spider (*Latrodectus mactans*); Mosquito (*Anopheles*); Black ant (*Monomorium minimum*); Cicada (*Tibicen septendecim*). Five sheets (f/j), each 82×113 mm. (f) \$2 *Alcides zodiaca*. (g) \$2 *Lepiota acutesquamosa*. (h) \$2 *Loxura atymnus*. (i) \$2 *Dendrobium phalaenopsis*. (j) \$2 *Anax junius* (horiz) .... 75·00 70·00

The stamps and margins of **MS**1204a/j form composite designs.

175 Greater Flame-backed Woodpecker (*Chrysocolaptes lucidas*)

2002. Birds. Multicoloured.
1204a	2c. Blue-grey gnatcatcher (*Polioptila caerulea*)	15	15
1205	3c. Type **175**	15	15
1206	5c. Red-tailed tropicbird (*Phaethon rubricauda*)	15	15
1206a	10c. Clapper rail (*Rallus longirostris*)	25	25
1207	21c. Hair-crested drongo (*Dicrurus hottentottus*) (inscr "forficatus")	55	50
1208	22c. *Zosterops citronella*	60	55
1209	23c. *Lonchura striata*	60	55
1209a	24c. Slaty-headed parakeet *Psittacula himalayana*	70	65
1210	37c. Yap monarch (*Monarcha godeffroyi*)	1·00	95
1210a	39c. Purple sunbird *Nectarinia asiatica*	1·10	1·00
1211	60c. Eclectus parrot (*Eclectus roratus*)	1·60	1·50
1212	70c. Sulphur-crested cockatoo (*Cacatua galerita*)	1·90	1·80
1212a	75c. Plum-headed parakeet (*Psittacula cyanocephala*)	2·00	1·90
1213	80c. Inscr "Magazosterops palauensis"	2·20	2·00
1214	\$2 Green magpie (*Cissa chinensis*)	5·50	5·00
1215	\$3.85 Eastern broad-billed roller (inscr "Dollarbird") (*Eurystomus orientalis*)	10·50	9·75
1215a	\$4.05 Eurasian collared dove (*Streptopelia decaocto*) (horiz)	11·50	10·50
1216	\$5 Great frigate bird (*Fregata minor*)	13·50	12·50
1217	\$13.65 Micronesian pigeon (*Ducula oceanica*)	38·00	35·00

176 Charles Lindbergh, Donald Hall and *Spirit of St. Louis*

2003. 75th Anniv of First Transatlantic Flight. Sheet 135×118 mm containing T **176** and similar horiz designs. Multicoloured.
MS1218 60c.×6, Type **176**; *Spirit of St. Louis*; *Spirit of St. Louis* on Curtis Field; *Spirit of St. Louis* airborne; Arriving in Paris; Ticker tape parade, New York .... 9·75 9·25

177 Long-haired Goat

2003. New Year. "Year of the Ram" (stamps show goats). Sheet 110×121 mm containing T **177** and similar vert designs. Multicoloured.
MS1219 37c.×6, Type **177**×2; Angora goat×2; Dark-coloured goat×2 .... 6·25 5·75

178 David Brown

2003. Colombia Space Shuttle Disaster, 1 February 2003. Crew Members. Sheet 184×146 mm containing T **178** and similar vert designs. Multicoloured.
MS1220 37c.×7, Type **178**; Rick Husband; Laurel Blair; Kalpana Chawla; Michael Anderson; William McCool; Ilan Ramon .... 7·25 6·75

179 Princess Elizabeth

2003. 50th Anniv (2002) of Coronation of Queen Elizabeth. Two sheets containing T **179** and similar vert designs. Multicoloured.
MS1221 (a) 147×85 mm. \$1×3, Type **179**; Wearing tiara; Wearing robe. (b) 68×98 mm. \$2 Wearing state crown .... 13·50 12·50

180 Boeing B-52 Bomber

2003. Military Operations in Iraq. Two sheets, each 136×136 mm containing T **180** and similar horiz designs. Multicoloured.
MS1222 (a) 37c.×5, Type **180**; General Dynamics F-16 Fighting Falcon; Bell Cobra helicopter; Hughes AH Apache helicopter; T8,000 Tow missile; US M3A2 Bradley tank. (b) 37c.×6, Stealth aircraft; Lockheed AC-130; Sikorsky MH-53j Pave Low II helicopter; General Atomics RQ-1 Predator; Vickers Challenger Two tank; Aegis cruiser .... 12·50 11·50

181 Prince William as Small Boy

2003. 21st Birthday of Prince William. Two sheets containing T **181** and similar vert designs. Multicoloured.
MS1223 (a) 148×78 mm. \$1×3, Type **181**; As schoolboy; As young man. (b) 98×68 mm. \$2 As boy .... 13·50 12·50

182 Greg Lemond (1990)

2003. Centenary of Tour de France Cycle Race. Two sheets containing T **182** and similar vert designs. Multicoloured. Litho.
MS1224 (a) 161×100 mm. 60c.×4, Type **182**; Miguel Indurain (1991); Miguel Indurain (1992); Miguel Indurain (1993). (b) 101×70 mm. \$2 Marco Pantani (1998) .... 12·50 11·50

183 Kosrae Mangroves

2003. International Year of Freshwater. Two sheets containing T **183** and similar vert designs. Multicoloured.
MS1225 (a) 150×88 mm. \$1×3, Type **183**; Chuuk lagoon; Pohnpei waterfalls. (b) 101×70 mm. \$2 Pohnpei lagoon .... 13·50 12·50

184 Concorde

2003. Centenary of Powered Flight. Two sheets containing T **184** and similar horiz designs. Multicoloured.
MS1226 (a) 117×175 mm. 55c.×6, Type **184**; Boeing 757; Junkers F13a; Martin M-130 China Clipper; Handley Page HP 42W; *Wright Flyer II*. (b) 106×76 mm. \$2 Boeing 747 .... 14·50 13·50

185 Glen Little

2003. Centenary of Circus. Two sheets containing T **185** and similar vert designs. Multicoloured.
MS1227 (a) 118×200 mm. Clowns. 80c.×4, Type **185**; Joseph Grimaldi; Beverley Rebo Bergerson; Coco Michael Polakov. (b) 146×219 mm. Performers. 80c.×4, Jane Mandana (animal entertainer); Maxim Papazov (acrobat); Harry Keaton (illusionist); Giraffe .... 17·00 16·00

186 Scout wearing Tartan Scarf

2003. 25th Death Anniv of Norman Rockwell (illustrator). Two sheets containing T **186** and similar vert designs. Multicoloured.
MS1228 (a) 152×190 mm. 80c.×4, Type **186**; Scout carrying child; Scoutmaster. (b) 66×84 mm. \$2 Boys and dog running away ("No Swimming"). Imperf .... 14·00 13·00

187 "Vahine No Te Tiare"

2003. Death Centenary of Paul Gauguin (artist). Two sheets containing T **187** and similar horiz designs. Multicoloured.

MS1229 (a) 140×127 mm. 80c.×4, Type **187**; "Les Amants"; "Trois Tahitiens Conversation"; "Arearea". (b) 79×64 mm. $2 "Ta Matete". Imperf .... 14·00 ... 13·00

188 "Blue and Silver Blue Wave, Biaritz"

2003. Death Centenary of James Whistler (artist). Multicoloured.

1230	37c. Type **188**	1·00	95
1231	55c. "Brown and Silver: Old Battersea Bridge"	1·50	1·40
1232	60c. "Nocturne in Blue and Silver: The Lagoon, Venice"	1·60	1·50
1233	80c. "Crepuscule In Flesh Colour and Green: Valparaiso"	2·20	2·00

MS1234 (a) 193×117 mm. $1×3, "Symphony in White No. 2: The Little White Girl" (38×51 mm); "At the Piano" (76×51 mm); "Symphony in White No. 1: The White Girl" (38×51 mm) . (b) 83×104 mm. $2 "Portrait of Thomas Carlyle" Imperf .... 13·50 ... 12·50

189 "Madonna of the Carnation" (Leonardo da Vinci)

2003. Christmas. Multicoloured.

1235	37c. Type **189**	1·00	95
1236	60c. "Madonna with Yarn Winder"	1·60	1·50
1237	80c. "Litta Madonna"	2·20	2·00
1238	$1 "Madonna of the grand Duke" (Raphael)	2·75	2·50

MS1239 78×103 mm. $2 "The Adoration of the Magi" (Giambattista Tiepolo) .... 5·50 ... 5·00

190 Green-winged Macaw

2003. Birds. Two sheets containing T **190** and similar multicoloured designs.

MS1240 (a) 179×155 mm. 80c.×4, Type **190**; Greater flamingo (inscr "American flamingo"); Blue and gold macaw; Abyssinian ground hornbill. (b) 62×76 mm. $2 Greater flamingo (inscr "American flamingo") (vert) .... 14·00 ... 13·00

191 Leopard gecko

2003. Reptiles. Two sheets containing T **191** and similar horiz designs. Multicoloured.

MS1241 (a) 103×81 mm. 80c.×4, Type **191**; Red-eyed tree frog; Panther chameleon; Green and black poison frog. (b) 96×66 mm. $2 Madagascan chameleon .... 14·00 ... 13·00

192 Australian Shepherd Dog

2003. Dogs and Cats. Four sheets containing T **192** and similar vert designs. Multicoloured.

MS1242 (a) 89×120 mm. 80c.×4, Type **192**; Greyhound; Bulldog; Schnauzer. (b) 96×67 mm. $2 Poodle. (c) 140×164 mm. 80c.×4, Ragdoll; Calico shorthair; Exotic shorthair; Dilute calico. (d) 66×96 mm. $2 Colour point shorthair .... 28·00 ... 26·00

193 "Moonstruck Gibbon" (Gao Qi-Feng)

2004. New Year. Year of the Monkey. Multicoloured.

| 1243 | 50c. Type **193** | 1·40 | 1·30 |

MS1244 70×101 mm. $1 "Moonstruck Gibbon" (detail) (30×40 mm) .... 2·75 ... 2·50

194 Bailey Olter

2004. Bailey Olter (president 1991—1996) Commemoration.

| 1245 | **194** 37c. multicoloured | 1·00 | 95 |

195 Luke Walton

2004. Basketball Players. Multicoloured.

1246	20c. Type **195**	55	50
1247	20c. Dirk Nowitzki	55	50
1248	20c. Vince Carter	55	50

196 "A Young Lady in a Theatrical Costume" (Alexis Grimou)

2004. 300th Anniv of St. Petersburg. Paintings from Hermitage Museum. Multicoloured.

1249	22c. Type **196**	60	55
1250	37c. "Mrs Greer" (George Romney)	1·00	95
1251	80c. "Portrait of Prince Nikolai Yuspov" (Friedrich Heinrich Fuger)	2·20	2·00
1252	$1 "Portrait of Richard Brinsley Sheridan" (John Hoppner)	2·75	2·50

MS1253 64×81 mm. $2 "Conversation Espagnole" (Carle Vanloo). Imperf .... 5·50 ... 5·00

197 "Marie Therese leaning on One Elbow"

2004. 30th Death Anniv (2003) of Pablo Picasso (artist). Multicoloured.

1254- 80c.×4, Type **197**; "Portrait of 1257 Jaime Sabartes"; "Portrait of Emmilie Marguerite Walter"; "Bust of a Woman leaning on One Elbow" .... 8·00 ... 7·25

MS1258 62×78 mm. $2 "Seated Bather". Imperf .... 5·50 ... 5·00

198 Landing Craft

2004. 60th Anniv of D-Day (the Normandy invasion). Multicoloured.

1259- 50c.×6, Type **198**; *Thompson* 1269 (destroyer); Vehicles disembarking; Rhino ferry 2 and Rhino tug 3; HMS *Mauritius*; *Arkansas* (battleship) .... 7·50 ... 7·00

MS1265 97×77 mm. $2 Soldiers seated in landing craft .... 5·50 ... 5·00

199 Pope John Paul II

2004. 25th Anniv of Pontificate of Pope John Paul II (2003). Sheet 95×117 mm containing T **199** and similar horiz designs. Multicoloured.

MS1266 80c.×4, Type **199** (visit to Mexico); With President and Mrs Clinton; Wearing mitre (visit to Ukraine); Praying (visit to Spain) .... 8·75 ... 8·25

200 Lars Olsen

2004. European Football Championships, Portugal. Two sheets containing T **200** and similar multicoloured designs.

MS1267 (a) 148×86 mm. 80c.×4, Type **200**; Jurgen Klinsmann; Peter Schmeichel: Nya Ullevi Stadium, Goteburg. (b) 98×85 mm. Denmark team, 1992 Cup Winners (horiz) .... 8·75 ... 8·25

The stamps and margin of No. **MS**1267a form a composite design.

201 Locomotive RS122

2004. Bicentenary of Steam Locomotives. Multicoloured.

1268- 80c.×4, Type **201**; Diesel 1271 locomotive class 630; Hitachi monorail, Okinawa; Eurostar .... 8·00 ... 7·25

1272- 80c.×4, Locomotive CFL N5520; 1275 inscr "Inter region trains"; Locomotive SW 600; Locomotive WSOR 3801 .... 8·00 ... 7·25

1276- 80c.×4, Locomotive Baldwin 1279 280;: Diesel locomotive F 1011114;: inscr "Okinawa Hitachi trains"; Shinkansen (Japanese high-speed train) .... 8·00 ... 7·25

MS1280 Three sheets. (a) 93×67 mm. $2 Michigan Central locomotive. (b) 93×67 mm. $2 Locomotive 231 065. (c) 66×91 mm. $2 Eurostar (different) .... 16·00 ... 15·00

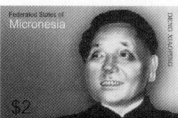

202 Deng Xiaoping

2004. Birth Centenary of Deng Xiaoping (leader of China, 1978—89). Sheet 97×67 mm.

MS1281 **202** $2 multicoloured .... 5·50 ... 5·00

203 Horseman (bronze statue)

2004. Olympic Games, Athens. Multicoloured.

1282	37c. Type **203**	1·00	95
1283	55c. Athlete (Olympic pin, Stockholm, 1912) (vert)	1·50	1·40
1284	80c. Pierre de Coubertin (founder modern Olympic Games) (vert)	2·20	2·00
1285	$1 Olympic poster, Mexico, 1968 (vert)	2·75	2·50

204 *Aeschnanthus*

2004. Flora and Fauna. Eight sheets containing T **204** and similar multicoloured designs.

MS1286 (a) 100×142 mm. Flowers. 55c.×6, Type **204**; *Darwinia collina*; *Rhododendron*; *Rhododendron retusum*; *Eucryphia lucida*; *Microporus xanthopus*. (b) 136×96 mm. Fish and Coral. 55c.×6, Clown triggerfish (*Balistoides conspicillum*); Masked unicornfish (*Naso lituratus*); *Nemateleotris magnifica*; Longnosed hawkfish (*Oxycirrhites typus*); *Annella mollis*; *Dendronephthya*. (c) 96×137 mm. Reptiles and amphibians. 55c.×6, *Maticora bivirgata*; *Ceratobatrachus guentheri*; *Sphenodon punctatus*; *Draco volans*; *Platymantis vitiensis*; *Candoia carinata*. (d) 94×126 mm. Birds. 55c.×6, *Artamus cinereus* (vert); Brown booby (*Sula leucogaster*) (vert); Rainbow lorry (*Trichoglossus haematodus*) (vert); Wandering albatross (*Diomedea exulans*) (vert); Kagu (*Rhynochetos jubatus*) (vert); Great frigate bird (*Fregata minor*) (vert). (e) 67×93 mm. Flowers. $2 Grevillea. (f) 97×67 mm. Fish. Great barracuda (*Sphyrna barracuda*). (g) 68×94 mm. Reptiles. $2 *Caretta caretta*. (h) 64×92 mm. Birds. $2 Golden whistler (*Pachycephala pectoralis*) .... 9·00 ... 8·50

The stamps and margins of **MS**1286a/h, respectively, form composite designs.

205 Nelson Mandela

2004. United Nations International Year of Peace. Multicoloured.

1287- 80c.×3, Type **205**; Dalai Lama; 1289 Pope John Paul II .... 6·00 ... 5·50

206 Elvis Presley

2004. 50th Anniv of "That's alright Mama" (record by Elvis Presley). Showing Elvis Presley. Multicoloured.

1290- 80c.×4, Type **206**; Wearing dark 1293 shirt; Smiling; Facing left .... 8·00 ... 7·25

MS1294 112×148 mm. 80c.×4, Bearded ("Charro") (horiz); Wearing boxing gloves ("Kid Galaghad") (horiz); Wearing Arab headdress ("Harum Scarum") (horiz); Wearing hat .... 9·00 ... 8·50

The stamps and margin of No. **MS**1294 form a composite design.

207 Herman Crespo (Argentina) (image scaled to 56% of original size)

2004. Centenary of FIFA (Federation Internationale de Football Association). Two sheets containing T **207** and similar horiz designs showing players. Multicoloured.
MS1295 (a) 193×97 mm. 80c.×4, Type **207**; Peter Shilton (England); Klaus Augenthaler (Germany); Bryan Robson (England). (b) 108×87 mm. $2 Ruud Gullit (Holland) — 14·50 13·50

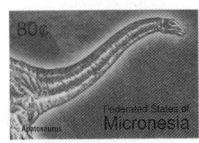

208 Apatosaurus

2004. Prehistoric Animals. Six sheets containing T **208** and similar multicoloured designs.
MS1296 (a) 143×113 mm. 80c.×4, Type **208**; Pachyrinosaurus; Kentosaurus; Saltosaurus. (b) 112×144 mm. 80c.×4, Allosaurus (vert); Tyrannosaurus (vert); Troodon (vert); Carnotaurus (vert). (c) 113×128 mm. 80c.×4, Indricotheres; Hyaenodons; Deinotherium; Chalicotheres. (d) 102×71 mm. $2 Deinonychus. (e) 103×71 mm. $2 Coelophysis. (f) 71×102 mm. $2 Moeritherium — 43·00 40·00

209 "Madonna of the Goldfinch" (Giovanni Battista Tiepolo)

2004. Christmas. Multicoloured.
1297 37c. Type **209** — 1·00 95
1298 60c. "Madonna and Child" (Raphael) — 1·60 1·50
1299 80c. "Madonna and Child" (Jan Gossaert de Mabuse) (inscr "Gossart") — 2·20 2·00
1300 $1 "Madonna and Child with Angels" (Fra Filippo Lippi) — 2·75 2·50
MS1301 76×107 mm. $2 Madonna and child (modern painting) — 5·50 5·00

210 Rooster

2005. New Year. Year of the Rooster.
1302 **210** 50c. multicoloured — 1·40 1·30

211 Ronald Reagan and Prime Minister Margaret Thatcher

2005. Ronald Reagan (USA president) Commemoration. Multicoloured.
1303 55c. Type **211** — 1·50 1·40
1304 $1 Ronald Reagan and Israeli Prime Minister Yitzchak Shamir — 1·50 1·40

212 Elvis Presley

2005. 70th Birth Anniv of Elvis Presley (entertainer). Multicoloured.
1305- 60c.×6, Type **212**; With backing
1310 singers; With arm outstretched; Seated with guitar; Facing right; Facing left — 10·50 10·00
1311 80c. Elvis Presley — 2·20 2·00

213 "Evening of Battle" (W. J. Huggins)

2005. Bicentenary of Battle of Trafalgar. Multicoloured.
1312 37c. Type **213** — 1·00 95
1313 55c. "Destruction of L' Orient" (George Arnauld) — 1·50 1·40
1314 80c. "Surrender of Santissima Trinidad" (painting) — 2·20 2·00
1315 $1 "Captain attacking Spanish Ship" (Sir William Allan) — 2·75 2·50
MS1316 86×122 mm. $2 Death of Nelson (painting) — 5·50 5·00

214 US Soldiers in Ireland

2005. 60th Anniv of End of World War II. Multicoloured.
1317- 60c.×5, Type **214**; British troops,
1321 Italy (1943); Hawker Typhoon, Rhine (1944); Aftermath of Remagen Bridge, Germany attack (1944); Russian and American soldiers, Germany (1945) (VE day—8 May 1945) — 7·25 6·75
1322- 60c.×5, "These Colours won't
1326 Run" (poster); Chula beach; Paul Tibbets and Enola Gay (aircraft); Atomic cloud (Hiroshima); "PEACE" (headline) (VJ day—15 August 1945) — 7·25 6·75

215 Friedrich Von Schiller

2005. Death Bicentenary of Friedrich Von Schiller (writer). Multicoloured.
MS1330 53×76 mm. $2 Facing right margin — 5·50 5·00

216 Air Balloon ("Around the World in Eighty Days")

2005. Death Centenary of Jules Verne (writer). Two sheets containing T **216** and similar multicoloured designs.
MS1331 105×133 mm. $1×3, Type **216**; Phileas (inscr "Phineas") Fogg in India; Phileas (inscr "Phineas") Fogg — 8·25 7·75
MS1332 108×101 mm. $2 *Nautilus* ("20000 Leagues under the Sea") (horiz) — 5·50 5·00

217 Papyrus Boat

2005. Boats. Two sheets containing T **217** and similar horiz designs. Multicoloured.
MS1333 203×173 mm. 37c. Type **217**; 55c. Outrigger canoe; 80c. Papyrus sail boat; $1 Dhow — 7·50 7·00
MS1334 89×101 mm. $2 Nile riverboat — 5·50 5·00

218 Grey Nurse Shark

2005. EXPO 2005, Aichi, Japan. Multicoloured.
1327- $1×3, Type **215**; Friedrich Von
1329 Schiller (statue); With head resting on hand — 7·50 6·75
1335- 80c.×4, Type **218**; Surfer;
1338 Volcano; Coral — 8·00 7·75

219 Pope John Paul II

2005. Pope John Paul II Commemoration.
1339 **219** $1 multicoloured — 2·75 2·50

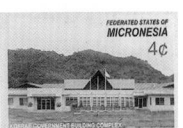

220 Building Entrance

2005. Government Building, Kosrae. Multicoloured.
1340 4c. Type **220** — 15 15
1341 10c. Rear of building — 25 25
1342 22c. Type **220** — 60 55
1343 37c. As No. 1341 — 1·00 95

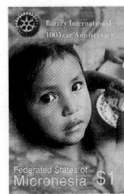

221 Child

2005. Centenary of Rotary International. Two sheets containing T **221** and similar multicoloured designs.
MS1344 139×110 mm. $1×3, Type **221**; Emblem; Glenn Estess (president 2004—5) — 8·25 7·75
MS1345 100×70 mm. $2 Bhicai Rattakul (president 2002—3) (horiz) — 5·50 5·00

222 1939 75c. Vatican City Stamp

2005. Vacant See.
1346 **222** 37c. multicoloured — 1·00 95

223 *Dichrometra flagellata*

2005. Corals. Multicoloured.
1347- 50c.×8, Type **223**; *Alloecocom-
1350 atella polycladia; Oxycomanthus bennetti; Stephanometra echinus* — 5·00 4·75

2005. 50th Death Anniv of Albert Einstein (physicist). Multicoloured.
1351- $1×4 Type **224**; In middle age;
1354 In front of blackboard; As older man — 10·00 9·00

225 Mother feeding Child

2005. Karat Banana. Multicoloured.
1355 4c. Type **225** — 15 15
1356 10c. Different varieties — 25 25
1357 22c. Bunch — 60 55
1358 37c. Growing on plant — 1·00 95

2005. Flowers. Multicoloured.
1365 80c. *Tapeinochilos ananassae* — 2·20 2·00
1366 80c. *Bauhinia monandra* — 2·20 2·00
1367 80c. *Galphima gracilis* — 2·20 2·00
1368 80c. *Hibiscus rosa-sinensis* — 2·20 2·00
MS1369 60×54 mm. $2 *Helianthus annuus* — 5·50 5·00

227 Hans Christian Andersen

2005. Birth Bicentenary of Hans Christian Andersen. Multicoloured.
1370 80c. Type **227** — 2·20 2·00
1371 80c. Statue — 2·20 2·00
1372 80c. Bust — 2·20 2·00
MS1373 70×100 mm. $2 Statue (different) — 5·50 5·00

228 Pope Benedict XVI

2005. Pope Benedict XVI.
1374 **228** 80c. multicoloured — 2·20 2·00

229 "Kanigani Madonna" (Raphael)

2005. Christmas. Multicoloured.
1375 37c. Type **229** — 1·00 95
1376 60c. "Madonna with the Fish" (detail) (Raphael) — 1·60 1·50
1377 80c. "The Holy Family" (Bartolome Esteban Murillo) — 2·20 2·00
1378 $1 "Madonna with the Book" (detail) (Raphael) (inscr "Rapha") — 2·75 2·50
MS1379 66×96 mm. $2 "The Holy Family" (Bartolome Esteban Murillo) (different) — 5·50 5·00

230 "Wolf Dog" (sitting) (Liu Jiyou)

2006. New Year. Year of the Dog. Multicoloured.
1380 50c. Type **230** — 1·40 1·30
MS1381 100×70 mm. $1 "Wolf Dog" (lying down) (Liu Jiyou) (51×37 mm.) — 2·75 2·50

231 Petrus Tun

2006. Petrus Tun (vice-president) Commemoration.

1382	**231**	39c. multicoloured	1·10	1·00

233 "Saskia as Flora"
(detail)

2006. 400th Birth Anniv of Rembrandt Harmenszoon van Rijn. Multicoloured.

1388	$1 Type **233**	2·75	2·50
1389	$1 "Girl with Broom" (detail)	2·75	2·50
1390	$1 "Young Girl at Window" (detail)	2·75	2·50
1391	$1 "Prodigal Son at the Tavern" (detail)	2·75	2·50
MS1392	70×100 mm. $2 "Man in Oriental Costume" (detail). Imperf	5·50	5·00

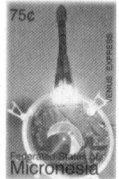

234 Rocket
(Venus Express
mission)

2006. Space Exploration. Multicoloured. (a) Venus Express Mission.

1393	75c. Type **234**	2·00	1·90
1394	75c. Probe in orbit (blue fins)	2·00	1·90
1395	75c. Probe above Venus (red fins)	2·00	1·90
1396	75c. Probe above Venus	2·00	1·90
1397	75c. Probe (soft focus)	2·00	1·90
1398	75c. Probe (vertical)	2·00	1·90

(b) Return of Space Shuttle Discovery.

1399	$1 *Discovery* (horiz)	2·75	2·50
1400	$1 Earth from space (horiz)	2·75	2·50
1401	$1 Shuttle showing solar array (horiz)	2·75	2·50
1402	$1 Shuttle fins (horiz)	2·75	2·50

(c) Project Prometheus.

1403	$1 Spacecraft (Future trip to the Moon) (horiz)	2·75	2·50
1404	$1 Moon and spacecraft (Future trip to the Moon) (horiz)	2·75	2·50
1405	$1 Projectile (Future trip to Mars) (horiz)	2·75	2·50
1406	$1 Spacecraft (Future trip to Mars) (horiz)	2·75	2·50
MS1407	68×98 mm. $2 Space walk (Return of Space Shuttle *Discovery*)	5·50	5·00
MS1408	Two sheets, each 98×68 mm. (a) $2 Mars Reconnaissance Orbiter. (b) $2 *Stardust* Spacecraft	11·00	10·00

Nos. 1405/6 were issued together, se-tenant, forming a composite design.

235 *Papilio euchenor*

2006. Butterflies. Multicoloured.

1409	1c. Type **235**	15	15
1410	2c. *Troides aeacus*	15	15
1411	4c. *Delias henningia*	15	15
1412	5c. *Bassarona duda*	15	15
1413	10c. *Graphium sarpedon*	25	25
1414	19c. *Arhopala cleander*	55	50
1415	20c. *Arhopala argentea*	55	50
1416	22c. *Danaus aspasia*	60	55
1417	75c. *Arhopala aurea*	2·00	1·90
1418	84c. *Caleta mindarus*	2·30	2·20
1419	$1 *Hyplycaena danis*	2·75	2·50
1420	$4.05 *Jacona amrita*	11·00	10·00
1420a	$10 Inscr *Para lascita lacoon*	27·00	25·00

236 Tree

2006. Christmas. Multicoloured.

1421	22c. Type **236**	60	55
1422	24c. Stocking	70	65
1423	39c. Snowman	1·00	95
1424	75c. Candle	2·00	1·90
1425	84c. Bauble	2·30	2·20

237 In Flight

2006. Concorde. Multicoloured.

1426	75c. Type **237**	2·00	1·90
1427	75c. On ground	2·00	1·90

238 Marilyn
Monroe

2007. 80th Birth Anniv of Marilyn Monroe. Multicoloured.

1428	$1 Type **238**	2·75	2·50
1429	$1 Blowing kiss	2·75	2·50
1430	$1 Wearing beret	2·75	2·50
1431	$1 Facing left	2·75	2·50

239 '100'

2007. Centenary of Scouting. Multicoloured.

1432	$1 Type **239**	2·75	2·50
MS1433	80×110 mm. $2 Scouts and flag (37×51 mm)	5·50	5·00

240 Wolfgang
Mozart

2007. 250th Birth Anniv of Wolfgang Amadeus Mozart (composer). Sheet 100×70 mm.

MS1434	$2 multicoloured	5·50	5·00

241 Pig (painting
by Liu Jiyou)

2007. New Year. Year of the Pig.

1435	**241**	75c. multicoloured	2·00	1·90

242 Pope Benedict
XVI

2007. 80th Birth Anniv of Pope Benedict XVI.

1436	**242**	50c. multicloured	1·40	1·30

243 Diana, Princess
of Wales

2007. Diana, Princess of Wales Commemoration. Multicoloured.

1437	90c. Type **243**	2·50	2·30
1438	90c. Wearing blue ruffled dress	2·50	2·30
1439	90c. Wearing gold dress and jacket	2·50	2·30
1440	90c. Wearing tiara and yellow dress	2·50	2·30
MS1441	100×70 mm. $3 Diana, Princess of Wales	5·50	5·00

244 Queen
Elizabeth II and
Prince Philip on
Maundy Thursday

2007. 60th Wedding Anniversary of Queen Elizabeth II and Prince Philip. Multicoloured.

1442	60c. Type **244**	1·60	1·50
1443	60c. At state opening of Parliament	1·60	1·50
1444	60c. As Type **244** (white border)	1·60	1·50
1445	60c. As No. 1443 (white border)	1·60	1·50
1446	60c. As Type **244** (violet border)	1·60	1·50
1447	60c. As No. 1443 (violet border)	1·60	1·50

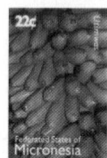

245 Utim was

2007. Bananas. Multicoloured.

1448	22c. Type **245**	60	55
1449	26c. Utin lap	70	65
1450	41c. Mangat	1·10	1·00
1451	58c. Ipali	1·60	1·50
1452	80c. Daiwang	2·30	2·20
1453	90c. Akadhn Weitahta (horiz)	2·50	2·30
1454	$1.14 Peleu	3·00	2·75
1455	$4.60 Utin Kerenis	12·50	11·50

246 Elvis Presley

2007. 30th Death Anniv of Elvis Presley. Multicoloured.

1456	75c. Type **246**	2·00	1·90
1457	75c. Wearing short sleeved shirt	2·00	1·90
1458	75c. Wearing striped jacket	2·00	1·90
1459	75c. Wearing brown shirt	2·00	1·90
1460	75c. Wearing collarless jacket	2·00	1·90
1461	75c. Wearing light grey jacket	2·00	1·90
1462	75c. Wearing check shirt (38×50 mm)	2·00	1·90
1463	75c. Seated with guitar facing left (38×50 mm)	2·00	1·90
1464	75c. Seated with guitar facing right (38×50 mm)	2·00	1·90

1465	75c. As No. 1464 (green) (38×50 mm)	2·00	1·90
1466	75c. As No. 1463 (brown) (38×50 mm)	2·00	1·90
1467	75c. As No. 1462 (lilac) (38×50 mm)	2·00	1·90

247 *Oxycirrhites
typus*

2007. Fish. Two sheets containing T **247** and similar vert designs. Multicoloured.

MS1468	131×108 mm. 90c.×4, Type **247**; *Canthigaster compressa*; *Chaetodon ornatissimus*; *Oxymonacanthus longirostris*	10·00	9·25
MS1469	70×100 mm. $2 *Parupeneus multifasciatus*	5·50	5·00

248 Yap State Peace Corps Emblem

2007. 40th Anniv of Peace Corps in Micronesia. Sheet 108×131 mm containing T **248** and similar horiz designs. Multicoloured.

MS1470	90c.×4, Type **248**; Kosrae State emblem; Volunteer and students, Pohnpei State; Stick fighting, Chuuk State	10·00	9·25

249 African Penguin

2007. International Polar Year. Penguins. Two sheets containing T **249** and similar vert designs showing penguins. Multicoloured.

MS1471	178×126 mm. 75c.×6, Type **249**; Emperor; Galapagos; Humboldt; Magellanic; Rockhopper	12·50	11·50
MS1472	100×70 mm. $3.50 Gentoo	9·50	9·00

250 Gerald Ford

2007. Gerald Ford Commemoration. Sheet 170×100 mm containing T **250** and similar vert designs. Multicoloured.

MS1473	$1×6, Type **250**; Seated reading; As Vice President with Richard Nixon, standing; In conversation with Richard Nixon; With Mrs Betty Ford; Signing Richard Nixon's pardon	16·00	15·00

251 Red Cross Workers

2007. Ninth Anniv of Micronesia Red Cross Society. Sheet 131×108 mm containing T **251** and similar horiz designs. Multicoloured.

MS1474	90c.×4, Type **251**; Women and damaged house; Teaching resuscitation techniques; Distributing aid	10·00	9·25

252 Scottish Fold
Cat

2007. Cats. Multicoloured.

1475	22c. Type **252**	60	55
1476	26c. Inscr 'Munchkin'	70	65
1477	41c. Inscr 'Abyssinian'	1·10	1·00
1478	90c. Somali (horiz)	2·50	2·30
MS1479	70×100 mm. $2 Inscr 'Blue Silver Shaded Tiffanie' (28×43 mm)	5·50	5·00

253 *Plumeria rubra*

2007. Flowers. Two sheets containing T **253** and similar vert designs. Multicoloured.

MS1480	132×98 mm. 90c.×4, Type **253**; *Plumeria rubra; Lilium candidum; Hedychium flavescens*	10·00	9·25
MS1481	100×70 mm. $2 *Bouganvillea glabra*	5·50	5·00

253a Mother
Church, Pohnpei

2007. Churches. Multicoloured.

1481a	22c. Type **253a**	60	55
1481b	26c. St Mary's church, Yap (horiz)	70	65
1481d	90c. Lelu Congregational Church, Kosrae (horiz)	2·50	2·30
1486c	41c. Sapore Bethesda Church, Fefan, Chuuk (horiz)	1·10	1·00

It has been reported that stamps were issued on:
11 January 2007 for Ludwig Durr Commemoraton.
12 June 2008 for Elvis Presley Commemoration.

254 FA 223 Drache Transport
Helicopter

2007. Centenary of First Helicopter Flight. Sheet 100×70 mm.

MS1482	**254** $2.50 multicoloured	6·75	6·25

255 Yacht

2007. Valencia, 32nd Americas Cup. Designs showing yacht sails. Multicoloured, country name panel colour given.

1483	26c. Type **255**	70	65
1484	80c. Sails (vermilion)	2·20	2·00
1485	$1.14 Sails (yellow)	3·00	2·75
1486	$2 Sails (orange)	5·50	5·00

255a 1904 St Louis
World Fair Poster

2008. History of the Olympic Games. St Louis–1904. Sheet 178×102 mm containing T **255a** and similar vert designs. Multicoloured.

MS1486a	50c.×4, Type **255a**; 1904 Olympic Games World Fair poster; Jim Lightbody–track gold medalist; Martin Sheridan–discus gold medalist	5·50	5·00

256 John F.
Kennedy

2008. John F. Kennedy (president, 1961–1963) Commemoration. Multicoloured.

1487	90c. Type **256**	2·50	2·30
1488	90c. Facing front head raised	2·50	2·30
1489	90c. Facing front	2·50	2·30
1490	90c. At microphone facing left	2·50	2·30

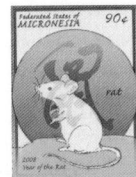

256a Rat

2008. Chinese New Year. Year of the Rat.

1490a	**256a** 90c. multicoloured	2·50	2·30

257 Woman (As
USA Type **2342**)

2008. Breast Cancer Awareness Campaign. Sheet 100×70 mm.

MS1491	**257** $2 multicoloured	5·50	5·00

258 Panavia Tornado

2008. 90th Anniv of Royal Air Force. Sheet 136×110 mm containing T **258** and similar horiz designs. Multicoloured.

MS1492	90c.×4, Type **258**; Hawker Siddley Harrier; Eurofighter EF–2000 Typhoon; British Aerospace Hawk	10·00	9·25

259 Hummer

2008. Hummer H3. Design showing vehicles. Multicoloured.

1493	90c. Type **259**	2·50	2·30
1494	90c. Side view	2·50	2·30
1495	90c. Front grill	2·50	2·30
1496	90c. Rear view	2·50	2·30
MS1497	100×70 mm. $2 On track	5·50	5·00

260 Entrance to the City of David (image scaled to 44% of original size)

2008. World Stamp Championship, Israel. Sheet 110×100 mm.

MS1498	**260** $3 multicoloured	8·25	7·75

260a Amare Stoudemire

2008. Baseball. Phoenix Suns. Designs showing players. Multicoloured.

1498a	42c. Type **260a**	1·00	95
1498b	42c. Boris Diaw	1·00	95
1498c	42c. Brian Skinner	1·00	95
1498d	42c. D. J. Strawberry	1·00	95
1498e	42c. Shaquille O'Neal	1·00	95
1498f	42c. Grant Hill	1·00	95
1498g	42c. Leandro Barbosa	1·00	95
1498h	42c. Raja Bell	1·00	95
1498i	42c. Steve Nash	1·00	95

261 USS *Enterprise*

2008. Star Trek (television series). Multicoloured.

1499	75c. Type **261**	2·00	1·90
1500	75c. Spock (Leonard Nimoy)	2·00	1·90
1501	75c. Captain Kirk (William Shatner)	2·00	1·90
1502	75c. Uhuru (Nichelle Nichols) and Chekov (Walter Koenig)	2·00	1·90
1503	75c. Starbase II	2·00	1·90
1504	75c. Dr. McCoy (DeForest Kelley)	2·00	1·90
MS1505	178×127 mm. Size 37×51 mm. 94c.×4, Scotty (James Doohan); Captain Kirk; Dr. McCoy and Uhuru; Chekov	10·50	9·75

The stamps and margins of No. **MS**1505 form a composite design.

262 Muhammad Ali

2008. Muhammad Ali. Two sheets, each 179×126 mm, containing T **262** and similar multicoloured designs showing Muhammad Ali.

MS1506	75c.×6, Type **262**; Adjusting helmet; Facing right; Facing right, head lowered; Facing left; Bandaging hands	12·50	11·50
MS1507	Size 37×51 mm. 94c.×4, Left hook; Left hook facing opponent; Facing left showing gum shield; Receiving punch to abdomen	10·50	9·75

The stamps of Nos. **MS**1507 share a common background.

263 Pope Benedict XVI
and Papal Arms

2008. Pope Benedict XVI's visit to USA. Sheet 178×127 mm containing T **263** and similar vert designs. Multicoloured.

MS1508	94c.×4, Type **263**; As Type **263**, arms lower left; As Type **263**, arms upper right; As Type **263**, arms upper left	10·50	9·75

The stamps of No. **MS**1508 form a composite design.

264 Ioanis Artui

2008. Leaders of Micronesia. Multicoloured.

1509	94c. Type **264**	2·50	2·40
1510	94c. Eluel K. Pretrick	2·50	2·40

265 Angel

2008. Christmas. Tree decorations. Multicoloured.

1511	22c. Type **265**	60	55
1512	27c. Star	70	65
1513	42c. Cross	1·10	1·00
1514	94c. Mobile	2·50	2·40

266 Barack Obama

2009. Inauguration of Barack Hussein Obama as President of USA. Sheet 178×126 containing T **266** and similar vert designs showing President Obama. Multicoloured.

MS1515	42c. Type **266**; 42c. Facing left; 42c. Smiling facing left; 75c. Smiling facing left; 75c. Facing left; 75c. As Type **266**	5·00	4·50

Nos. 1516/19 and Type **267** are left for Marilyn Monroe issued on 22 January 2009 not yet received.

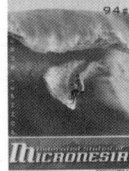

268 Surfer

2009. Surfing. Designs showing surfers. Multicoloured.

1520	94c. Type **268**	2·50	2·40
1521	$1.17 Surfer wearing white t-shirt	3·00	2·75
1522	$4.80 Surfer wearing dark long sleeved t-shirt	13·00	12·00

Nos. 1523/34 are left for additions to this set.

Nos. 1535/6 and Type **269** are left for Year of the Ox issued on 26 January 2009 not received.
Nos. 1537 and Type **270** are left for Paeony issued on 10 April 2009 not yet received.
Nos. 1538/41 and Type **271** are left for China 2009 (1st issue) issued on 10 April 2009 not yet received.

272 Emperor
Taizong

2009. China 2009 International Stamp Exhibition, Luoyang. Emperor Taizong–Second Tang Dynasty. Multicoloured.

1542	59c. Type **272**	1·60	1·50
1543	59c. With wives	1·60	1·50
1544	59c. Calligraphy	1·60	1·50
1545	59c. Emperor Taizong (mural, Dunhuang)	1·60	1·50

273 Elvis Presley

2009. 40th Anniv of *Change of Habit* (film starring Elvis Presley). Four sheets containing vert designs as T **273** showing Elvis Presley. Multicoloured.

MS1546	125×90 mm. $2.50 Type **273**	6·75	6·25
MS1547	91×126 mm. $2.50 Wearing open necked shirt	6·75	6·25
MS1548	90×125 mm. $2.50 As doctor	6·75	6·25
MS1549	125×90 mm. $2.50 Poster for film	6·75	6·25

274 Brown Booby (*Sula leucogaster*)

2009. Birds of the Pacific. Multicoloured.

1550	28c. Type **274**	80	75
1551	44c. Sacred kingfisher (*Todiramphus sanctus*)	1·20	1·10
1552	98c. White faced heron (*Egretta novaehollandiae*)	2·75	2·50
1553	$1.05 Rainbow lorikeet (*Trichoglossus haematodus*)	2·75	2·75
MS1554	100×130 mm. All horiz. 98c.×4, Brandt's cormorant (*Phalacrocorax pencillatus*); Red footed booby (*Sula sula*); Beach thick knee (*Esacus giganteus*); Common (brown) noddy (*Anous stolidus*)	11·00	10·00
MS1555	100×70 mm. All horiz. $1.56×2, Blue footed booby (*Sula nebouxii*); Australian pelican (*Pelecanus conspicillatus*)	8·50	8·00

275 Hawksbill Turtle (*Eretmochelys imbricata*)

2009. Turtles of the Pacific. Multicoloured.

1556	22c. Type **275**	60	55
1557	88c. Australian flat back turtle (*Natator depresus*)	2·50	2·30
1558	95c. Loggerhead turtle (*Caretta caretta*)	2·50	2·40
1559	$2.80 Green sea turtle (*Celonia mydas*)	7·75	7·25
MS1560	100×130 mm. 98c.×4, Kemp's ridley turtle (*Lepidochelys kempi*); Leatherback turtle (*Dermochelys coriacea*); Loggerhead turtle (different); Olive ridley turtle (*Lepidochelys olivacea*)	11·00	10·00
MS1561	100×70 mm. $1.56×2, Green sea turtle (different); Hawksbill turtle (different)	18·50	8·00

276 Pope Benedict XVI and Vaclav Klaus (Czech president)

2009. Visit of Pope Benedict XVI to Czech Republic. Sheet 150×100 mm containing T **276** and similar horiz designs. Multicoloured.

MS1562	98c.×4, Type **276**; Pope Benedict XVI; Pope Benedict XVI and Miroslav Vik (Czech cardinal); Pope Benedict XVI wearing green	11·00	10·00

277 Santa and Stylized Palm Tree

2009. Christmas. Multicoloured.

1563	22c. Type **277**	60	55
1564	44c. Baubles	1·20	1·10
1565	98c. Christmas stockings	2·75	2·50
1566	$4.80 Arms of Micronesia and other baubles on tree	13·50	12·50

APPENDIX

The following stamps have either been issued in excess of postal needs, or have not been available to the public in reasonable quantities at face value. Such stamps may later be given full listings if there is evidence of regular postal use. Miniature sheets and imperforate stamps are excluded from this listing.

2007

Diana, Princess of Wales Commemoration. $8 (gold)

Pt. 6

MIDDLE CONGO

One of three colonies into which Fr. Congo was divided in 1906. Became part of Fr. Equatorial Africa in 1937. Became part of the Congo Republic within the French Community on 28 November 1958.

100 centimes = 1 franc.

1 Leopard in Ambush

2 Bakalois Woman

3 Coconut Palms, Libreville

1907

1	**1**	1c. olive and brown	45	50
2	**1**	2c. violet and brown	1·70	60
3	**1**	4c. blue and brown	1·90	1·00
4	**1**	5c. green and blue	2·75	1·40
21	**1**	5c. yellow and blue	2·50	5·75
5	**1**	10c. red and blue	2·75	85
22	**1**	10c. green and light green	5·50	10·00
6	**1**	15c. purple and pink	2·75	3·75
7	**1**	20c. brown and blue	6·00	9·50
8	**2**	25c. blue and green	4·50	1·20
23	**2**	25c. green and grey	3·50	5·75
9	**2**	30c. pink and green	3·00	5·25
24	**2**	30c. red	2·00	6·00
10	**2**	35c. brown and blue	3·25	3·00
11	**2**	40c. green and brown	3·75	3·75
12	**2**	45c. violet and orange	5·50	6·75
25	**2**	50c. blue and green	2·20	5·75
13	**2**	50c. green and orange	5·00	7·50
14	**2**	75c. brown and blue	7·75	10·00
15	**3**	1f. green and violet	13·00	21·00
16	**3**	2f. violet and green	12·00	17·00
17	**3**	5f. blue and pink	60·00	60·00

1916. Surch 5c and red cross.

20	**1**	10c.+5c. red and blue	1·30	4·25

1924. Surch AFRIQUE EQUATORIALE FRANCAISE and new value.

26	**3**	25c. on 2f. green and violet	1·40	6·50
27	**3**	25c. on 5f. pink and blue	1·40	1·10
28	**3**	65 on 1f. brown and orange	1·30	7·00
29	**3**	85 on 1f. brown and orange	1·70	7·50
30	**2**	90 on 75c. scarlet and red	3·00	3·75
31	**2**	1f.25 on 1f. ultramarine & bl	1·20	2·50
32	**2**	1f.50 on 1f. blue & ultram	2·40	3·00
33	**2**	3f. on 5f. pink and brown	4·50	4·25
34	**2**	10f. on 5f. green and red	10·00	17·00
35	**2**	20f. on 5f. purple and brown	13·00	14·00

1924. Optd AFRIQUE EQUATORIALE FRANCAISE.

36	**1**	1c. olive and brown	45	4·00
37	**1**	2c. violet and brown	45	4·00
38	**1**	4c. blue and brown	1·10	2·30
39	**1**	5c. yellow and blue	1·00	2·50
40	**1**	10c. green and light green	1·40	6·00
41	**1**	10c. red and grey	1·70	2·75
42	**1**	15c. purple and pink	1·50	2·75
43	**1**	20c. brown and blue	90	5·50
44	**1**	20c. green and light green	1·10	4·50
45	**1**	20c. brown and mauve	3·75	5·50
46	**2**	25c. green and grey	1·10	55
47	**2**	30c. red	1·70	5·75
48	**2**	30c. grey and mauve	1·10	1·40
49	**2**	30c. deep green and green	3·25	7·25
50	**2**	35c. brown and blue	1·40	7·00
51	**2**	40c. green and brown	2·00	2·30
52	**2**	45c. violet and orange	1·20	5·25
53	**2**	50c. blue and green	1·90	2·40
54	**2**	50c. yellow and black	1·10	55
55	**2**	65c. brown and blue	4·50	8·50
56	**2**	75c. brown and blue	2·00	3·25
57	**2**	90c. red and pink	6·50	11·50
58	**3**	1f. green and violet	2·50	1·70
59	**3**	1f.10 mauve and brown	5·75	11·50
60	**3**	1f.50 ultramarine and blue	11·50	12·00
61	**3**	2f. violet and green	2·20	2·50
62	**3**	3f. mauve on pink	14·50	13·00
63	**3**	5f. blue and pink	4·50	3·50

1931. "Colonial Exhibition" key-types inscr "MOYEN CONGO".

65	**E**	40c. green and black	6·50	12·00
66	**F**	50c. mauve and black	4·25	4·75
67	**G**	90c. red and black	3·75	7·50
68	**H**	1f.50 blue and black	7·25	6·75

15 Mindouli Viaduct

1933

69	**15**	1c. brown	40	3·50
70	**15**	2c. blue	35	5·50
71	**15**	4c. olive	60	1·50
72	**15**	5c. red	75	3·00
73	**15**	10c. green	2·75	4·50
74	**15**	15c. purple	3·50	6·25
75	**15**	20c. red on rose	14·00	18·00
76	**15**	25c. orange	3·25	3·00
77	**15**	30c. green	4·50	5·50
78	-	40c. brown	3·25	6·25
79	-	45c. black on green	3·25	5·75
80	-	50c. purple	2·30	55
81	-	65c. red on green	3·75	7·75
82	-	75c. black on red	18·00	19·00
83	-	90c. red	4·50	8·00
84	-	1f. red	2·30	1·50
85	-	1f.25 green	4·25	4·25
86	-	1f.50 blue	9·00	7·50
87	-	1f.75 violet	4·50	2·75
88	-	2f. olive	3·25	3·00
89	-	3f. black on red	6·50	5·25
90	-	5f. grey	21·00	37·00
91	-	10f. black	55·00	48·00
92	-	20f. brown	49·00	41·00

DESIGNS: 40c. to 1f.50 Pasteur Institute, Brazzaville; 1f.75 to 20f. Government Building, Brazzaville.

POSTAGE DUE STAMPS

1928. Postage Due type of France optd MOYEN-CONGO A. E. F.

D64	**D11**	5c. blue	35	5·75
D65	**D11**	10c. brown	55	6·25
D66	**D11**	20c. olive	1·10	6·25
D67	**D11**	25c. red	1·10	7·50
D68	**D11**	30c. red	90	6·50
D69	**D11**	45c. green	1·70	6·50
D70	**D11**	50c. purple	1·50	8·00
D71	**D11**	60c. brown on cream	1·70	9·25
D72	**D11**	1f. red on cream	2·40	7·50
D73	**D11**	2f. red	2·50	11·00
D74	**D11**	3f. violet	3·25	20·00

D13 Village

1930

D75	**D13**	5c. olive and blue	1·50	6·00
D76	**D13**	10c. brown and red	1·50	6·25
D77	**D13**	20c. brown and green	3·25	9·50
D78	**D13**	25c. brown and blue	3·50	9·75
D79	**D13**	30c. green and brown	3·75	17·00
D80	**D13**	45c. olive and green	5·00	15·00
D81	**D13**	50c. brown and mauve	5·50	17·00
D82	**D13**	60c. black and violet	6·50	18·00
D83	-	1f. black and brown	19·00	38·00
D84	-	2f. brown and mauve	13·00	45·00
D85	-	3f. brown and red	13·00	45·00

DESIGN: 1 to 3f. "William Guinet" (steamer) on the River Congo.

D17 "Le Djoue"

1933

D93	**D17**	5c. green	55	6·50
D94	**D17**	10c. blue on blue	2·30	6·50
D95	**D17**	20c. red on yellow	3·50	6·75
D96	**D17**	25c. red	3·50	7·00
D97	**D17**	30c. red	3·25	7·50
D98	**D17**	45c. purple	4·50	8·25
D99	**D17**	50c. black	5·25	9·50
D100	**D17**	60c. black on red	6·75	12·50
D101	**D17**	1f. red	6·00	17·00
D102	**D17**	2f. orange	11·50	24·00
D103	**D17**	3f. blue	23·00	27·00

For later issues see **FRENCH EQUATORIAL AFRICA**.

Pt. 8

MODENA

A state in Upper Italy, formerly a duchy and now part of Italy. Used stamps of Sardinia after the cessation of its own issues in 1860. Now uses Italian stamps.

100 centesimi = 1 lira.

1 Arms of Este

1852. Imperf.

9	**1**	5c. black on green	55·00	60·00
3	**1**	10c. black on pink	£600	£110
4	**1**	15c. black on yellow	80·00	38·00
5	**1**	25c. black on buff	£120	55·00
12	**1**	40c. black on blue	65·00	£150
13	**1**	1l. black on white	80·00	£2500

5 Cross of Savoy

1859. Imperf.

18a	**5**	5c. green	£900	£750
19	**5**	15c. brown	£2750	£4000
20	**5**	15c. grey	£375	
21	**5**	20c. black	£2250	£180
22	**5**	20c. lilac	70·00	£1400
23	**5**	40c. red	£225	£1500
24	**5**	80c. brown	£225	£24000

NEWSPAPER STAMPS

1853. As T 1 but in the value tablet inscr "B.G. CEN" and value. Imperf.

N15	**1**	9c. black on mauve	£900	95·00
N16	**1**	10c. black on lilac	90·00	£350

N4

1859. Imperf.

N17	**N4**	10c. black	£1300	£2750

Pt. 6

MOHELI

An island in the Comoro Archipelago adjacent to Madagascar. A separate French dependency until 1914 when the whole archipelago was placed under Madagascar whose stamps were used until 1950. Now part of the Comoro Islands.

100 centimes = 1 franc.

1906. "Tablet" key-type inscr "MOHELI" in blue (2, 4, 10, 20, 30, 40c., 5f.) or red (others).

1	D	1c. black on blue	4·75	2·50
2	D	2c. brown on buff	1·10	2·10
3	D	4c. brown on grey	2·75	4·00
4	D	5c. green	4·00	2·75
5	D	10c. red	3·50	2·75
6	D	20c. red on green	11·00	20·00
7	D	25c. blue	16·00	7·25
8	D	30c. brown on drab	17·00	33·00
9	D	35c. black on yellow	8·00	4·00
10	D	40c. red on yellow	11·50	23·00
11	D	45c. black on green	65·00	85·00
12	D	50c. brown on blue	17·00	18·00
13	D	75c. brown on orange	47·00	60·00
14	D	1f. green	16·00	50·00
15	D	2f. violet on pink	49·00	75·00
16	D	5f. mauve on lilac	£140	£140

1912. Surch in figures.

17A	05 on 4c. brown & bl on grey	3·00	8·00
18A	05 on 20c. red & blue on grn	2·75	12·00
19A	05 on 30c. brn & bl on drab	2·00	9·75
20A	10 on 40c. red & blue on yell	2·40	8·75
21A	10 on 45c. blk & red on grn	1·70	3·00
22A	10 on 50c. brown & red on bl	2·40	8·25

Pt. 10

MOLDOVA

Formerly Moldavia, a constituent republic of the Soviet Union. Moldova declared its sovereignty within the Union in 1990 and became independent in 1991.

1991. 100 kopeks = 1 rouble.
1993. Kupon (temporary currency).
1993. 100 bani = 1 leu.

1 Arms

1991. First Anniv of Declaration of Sovereignty. Multicoloured. Imperf.

1	7k. Type **1**	10	10
2	13k. Type **1**	30	25
3	30k. Flag (35×23 mm)	85	50

2 Codrii Nature Reserve

1992

4	2	25k. multicoloured	45	40

3 Arms

1992

5	3	35k. green	20	10
6	3	50k. red	30	25
7	3	65k. brown	40	35
8	3	1r. purple	45	40
9	3	1r.50 blue	55	50

4 Tupolev Tu-144

1992. Air.

15	4	1r.75 red	35	30
16	4	2r.50 mauve	45	30
17	4	7r.75 violet	60	50
18	4	8r.50 green	1·10	95

See also Nos. 70/3.

5 European Bee Eater

1992. Birds. Multicoloured.

19	50k. Type **5**	45	40
20	65k. Golden oriole	45	40
21	2r.50 Green woodpecker	70	65
22	6r. European roller	1·20	1·00
23	7r.50 Hoopoe	1·40	1·30
24	15r. European cuckoo	3·25	3·00

See also Nos. 63/9.

6 St. Panteleimon's Church

1992. Centenary (1991) of St. Panteleimon's Church, Chisinau.

25	6	1r.50 multicoloured	30	25

7 Wolf suckling Romulus and Remus

1992. Trajan Memorial, Chisinau.

26	7	5r. multicoloured	95	65

1992. Various stamps of Russia surch **MOLDOVA** and value.

27	2r.50 on 4k. red (No. 4672)	30	20
28	6r. on 3k. red (No. 4671)	30	20
29	8r.50 on 4k. red (No. 4672)	45	30
30	10r. on 3k. green (No. 6074)	75	50

9 High Jumping

1992. Olympic Games, Barcelona. Multicoloured.

31	35k. Type **9**	20	15
32	65k. Wrestling	20	15
33	1r. Archery	25	20
34	2r.50 Swimming	45	35
35	10r. Show jumping	2·75	2·50
MS36	147×110 mm. Nos. 31/5 plus label	4·00	3·50

(11)

12 Tudor Casapu (gold medal, weightlifting)

1992. Nos. 4669/71 of Russia surch **MOLDOVA**, new value and bunch of grapes.

37	45k. on 2k. mauve	30	15
38	46k. on 2k. mauve	30	15
39	63k. on 1k. green	30	15
40	63k. on 3k. red	45	40
41	70k. on 1k. green	30	15
42	4r. on 1k. green	45	40

1992. Moldovan Olympic Games Medal Winners. Nos. 33/4 optd with Type **11**.

(a) Nos. 33/4 optd with T **11** or similar

43	1r. Archery (optd **NATALIA VALEEVbronz** and emblem)	65	45
44	2r.50 Swimming (optd **IURIE BASCATOVargint** and emblem)	1·20	85

(b) Miniature sheet 69x69 mm

MS45	**12** 25r. multicoloured	6·50	5·75

13 Moldovan Flag, Statue of Liberty and U.N. Emblem and Building

1992. Admission of Moldova to U.N.O. Multicoloured.

46	1r.30 Type **13**	60	30
47	12r. As Type **13** but with motifs differently arranged	1·20	65

14 Moldovan Flag and Prague Castle

1992. Admission of Moldova to European Security and Co-operation Conference. Multicoloured.

48	2r.50 Type **14**	70	30
49	25r. Helsinki Cathedral and Moldovan flag	2·10	1·10

15 Carpet and Pottery

1992. Folk Art.

50	15	7r.50 multicoloured	1·40	65

16 Galleon

1992. 500th Anniv of Discovery of America by Columbus. Multicoloured.

51	1r. Type **16**	45	20
52	6r. Carrack	2·00	1·00
53	6r. Caravel	2·00	1·00
MS54	89×69 mm. 25r. Christopher Columbus	8·75	8·75

17 Letter Sorter, Diesel Train, State Flag and U.P.U. Emblem

1992. Admission to U.P.U. Multicoloured.

55	5r. Type **17**	1·10	55
56	10r. Douglas DC-10 jetliner, computerized letter sorting equipment, state flag and U.P.U. emblem	1·50	75

18 Aesculapius Snake

1993. Protected Animals. Snakes. Multicoloured.

57	3r. Type **18**	55	35
58	3r. Aesculapius in tree	55	35
59	3r. Aesculapius on path	55	35
60	3r. Aesculapius on rock	55	35
61	15r. Grass snake	1·70	1·10
62	25r. Adder	2·75	2·20

Nos. 57/60 were issued together, *se-tenant*, forming a composite design.

1993. Birds. As Nos. 19/24 but with values changed and additional design. Multicoloured.

63	2r. Type **5**	10	10
64	3r. As No. 20	20	10
65	5r. As No. 21	35	15
66	10r. As No. 22	45	20
67	15r. As No. 23	55	35
68	50r. As No. 24	1·10	75
69	100r. Barn swallow	2·75	1·50

1993. Air.

70	4	25r. red	45	40
71	4	45r. brown	65	55
72	4	50r. green	75	65
73	4	90r. blue	1·70	1·40

19 Arms

20 Arms

1993

74	19	2k. blue	35	15
75	19	3k. purple	35	15
76	19	6k. green	35	15
77	-	10k. violet and green	35	15
78	-	15k. violet and green	35	15
79	-	20k. violet and grey	45	35
80	-	30k. violet and yellow	45	35
81	-	50k. violet and red	55	45
82	20	100k. multicoloured	75	65
83	20	250k. multicoloured	1·90	1·40

DESIGN: 10 to 50k. Similar to Type **19** but with inscription and value at foot differently arranged.

21 Red Admiral

1993. Butterflies and Moths. Multicoloured.

94	6b. Type **21**	55	35
95	10b. Swallowtail	55	35
96	50b. Peacock	1·10	55
97	250b. Emperor moth	4·50	2·75

22 "Tulipa bibersteiniana"

1993. Flowers. Multicoloured.

98	6b. Type **22**	20	10
99	15b. Lily of the valley	40	35
100	25b. Snowdrop	55	45
101	30b. Peony	75	65
102	50b. Snowdrop	1·50	1·10
103	90b. Pasque flower	2·75	2·20
MS104	88×68 mm. 250b. Lady's Slipper (*Cypripedium caleolus*) (44×29 mm)	6·00	6·00

23 Dragos Voda (1352–53)

1993. 14th-century Princes of Moldavia. Multicoloured.

105	6b. Type **23**	20	10
106	25b. Bogdan Voda I (1359–65)	20	10
107	50b. Latcu Voda (1365–75)	35	20
108	100b. Petru I Musat (1375–91)	55	45
109	150b. Roman Voda Musat (1391–94)	70	55
110	200b. Stefan I (1394–99)	2·75	2·20

24 "Story of One Life" (M. Grecu)

1993. Europa. Contemporary Art. Multicoloured.

111	3b. Type **24**	1·10	65
112	150b. "Coming of Spring" (I. Vieru)	2·50	1·50

25 Biathletes

1994. Winter Olympic Games, Lillehammer, Norway. Multicoloured.

| 113 | 3b. Type **25** | 2·20 | 1·10 |
| 114 | 150b. Close-up of biathlete shooting | 3·25 | 1·70 |

1994. No. 4669 of Russia surch **MOLDOVA**, grapes and value.

115	3b. on 1k. green	55	35
116	25b. on 1k. green	55	35
117	50b. on 1k. green	90	55

27 State Arms

1994

118	**27**	1b. multicoloured	15	10
119	**27**	10b. multicoloured	15	10
120	**27**	30b. multicoloured	20	15
121	**27**	38b. multicoloured	30	15
122	**27**	45b. multicoloured	30	15
123	**27**	75b. multicoloured	45	30
124	**27**	1l.50 multicoloured	1·40	1·00
125	**27**	1l.80 multicoloured	1·50	1·10
126	**27**	2l.50 mult (24×29 mm)	1·70	1·30
127	**27**	4l.50 multicoloured	2·50	1·70
128	**27**	5l.40 multicoloured	3·00	1·80
129	**27**	6l.90 multicoloured	3·75	2·20
130	**27**	7l.20 mult (24×29 mm)	4·50	2·50
131	**27**	13l. mult (24×29 mm)	7·50	3·75
132	**27**	24l. mult (24×29 mm)	12·00	7·50

28 Launch of "Titan II" Rocket

1994. Europa. Inventions and Discoveries. 25th Anniv of First Manned Moon Landing. Multicoloured.

136	1b. Type **28**	30	20
137	45b. Ed White (astronaut) on space walk ("Gemini 4" flight, 1965)	2·20	1·70
138	2l.50 Lunar module landing, 1969	5·25	3·75

29 Maria Cibotari (singer)

1994. Entertainers' Death Anniversaries. Multicoloured.

139	3b. Type **29** (45th)	45	20
140	90b. Dumitru Caraciobanu (actor, 14th)	55	35
141	150b. Eugeniu Coca (composer, 40th)	1·30	65
142	250b. Igor Vieru (actor, 11th)	3·25	1·70

30 Preparing Stamp Design

1994. Stamp Day.

143	**30**	10b. black, blue and mauve	45	30
144	-	45b. black, mauve and yellow	65	45
145	-	2l. multicoloured	3·25	1·70

DESIGNS: 45b. Printing stamps; 2l. Checking finished sheets.

31 Pierre de Coubertin (founder)

1994. Centenary of International Olympic Committee. Multicoloured.

| 146 | 60b. Type **31** | 1·10 | 65 |
| 147 | 1l.50 Rings and "Paris 1994" centenary congress emblem | 2·75 | 1·50 |

32 Map

1994. Partnership for Peace Programme (co-operation of N.A.T.O. and Warsaw Pact members).

| 148 | - | 60b. black, ultram and bl | 1·90 | 1·10 |
| 149 | **32** | 2l.50 multicoloured | 5·50 | 4·25 |

DESIGN: 60b. Manfred Worner (Secretary-General of N.A.T.O.) and President Mircea Snegur of Moldova.

34 Map (image scaled to 57% of original size)

1994. Air. Self-adhesive. Roul.

| 152 | **34** | 1l.50 multicoloured | 85 | 55 |
| 153 | **34** | 4l.50 multicoloured | 2·20 | 1·70 |

The individual stamps are peeled directly from the card backing. Each card contains six different designs with the same face value forming the composite design illustrated. Each stamp is a horizontal strip with a label indicating the main class of mail covered by the rate at the left, separated by a vertical line of rouletting. The outer edges of the cards are imperforate.

35 Family

1994. International Year of the Family. Multicoloured.

154	30b. Type **35**	45	35
155	60b. Mother breast-feeding baby	90	55
156	1l.50 Child drawing	2·75	2·20

36 Handshake

1994. Preliminary Rounds of European Football Championship, England (1996). Multicoloured.

157	10b. Type **36**	35	20
158	40b. Players competing for ball	65	45
159	2l.40 Goalkeeper making save	3·25	2·75

MS160 140×105 mm. 1l.10 Moldovan and German pennants; 2l.20, German and Moldovan shields on ball; 2l.40, Players | 7·75 | 7·75 |

37 "Birth of Jesus Christ" (anon)

1994. Christmas. Multicoloured.

| 161 | 20b. Type **37** | 45 | 30 |
| 162 | 3l.60 "Birth of Jesus Christ" (Gherasim) | 4·50 | 3·25 |

38 Cracked Green Russula

1995. Fungi. Multicoloured.

163	4b. Type **38**	45	35
164	10b. Oak mushroom	65	45
165	20b. Chanterelle	2·20	1·10
166	90b. Red-capped scaber stalk	5·50	3·25
167	1l.80 "Leccinum duriusculum"	9·50	6·50

39 Booted Eagle

1995. European Nature Conservation Year. Multicoloured.

168	4b. Type **39**	55	35
169	45b. Roe deer	2·75	2·10
170	90b. Wild boar	5·50	4·25

40 Earthenware Urns and Necklace

1995. National Museum Exhibits. Multicoloured.

171	4b. Type **40**	55	35
172	10b.+2b. Representation and skeleton of "Dinotherium gigantissimum"	1·70	1·10
173	1l.80+30b. Silver coins	7·75	5·50

41 "May 1945" (Igor Vieru)

1995. Europa. Peace and Freedom. Paintings. Multicoloured.

174	10b. Type **41**	40	35
175	40b. "Peace" (Sergiu Cuciuc)	1·70	1·10
176	2l.20 "Spring 1944" (Cuciuc)	5·50	4·50

42 Constantin Stere (writer, 130th birth)

1995. Anniversaries.

177	**42**	9b. brown and grey	55	35
178	-	10b. purple and grey	55	35
179	-	40b. lilac and grey	1·70	1·10
180	-	1l.80 green and grey	6·00	5·50

DESIGNS: 10b. Tamara Ceban (singer, 5th death); 40b. Alexandru Plamadeala (sculptor, 55th death); 1l.80, Lucian Blaga (philosopher, birth centenary).

43 Alexandru cel Bun (1400–32)

1995. 15th and 16th-century Princes of Moldavia. Multicoloured.

| 181 | 10b. Type **43** | 35 | 20 |
| 182 | 10b. Petru Aron (1451–52 and 1454–57) | 35 | 20 |

183	10b. Stefan cel Mare (1457–1504)	35	20
184	45b. Petru Rares (1527–38 and 1541–46)	1·10	90
185	90b. Alexandru Lapusneanu (1552–61 and 1564–68)	2·20	1·70
186	1l.80 Ioan Voda cel Cumplit (1572–74)	9·25	7·75

MS187 83×66 mm. 5l. Stefan del Mare (1457–1504) (24×29 mm) | 2·75 | 2·75 |

44 Soroca Castle

1995. Castles. Multicoloured.

188	10b. Type **44**	35	20
189	20b. Tighina Castle	75	55
190	60b. Alba Castle	1·20	1·00
191	1l.30 Hotin Castle	4·50	3·75

45 Seal in Eye   **46** "50" and Emblem

1995. 50th Anniv of U.N.O. Multicoloured. (a) Ordinary gum. Perf.

192	10b. Type **45**	45	35
193	10b. Airplane in eye	45	35
194	1l.50 Child's face and barbed wire in eye	7·25	6·50

(b) Self-adhesive. Rouletted.

| 195 | 90b. Type **46** | 55 | 45 |
| 196 | 1l.50 Type **46** | 1·10 | 90 |

47 "Last Moon of Autumn"

1995. Centenary of Motion Pictures.

197	**47**	10b. red and black	35	20
198	-	40b. green and black	90	75
199	-	2l.40 blue and black	7·75	7·25

DESIGNS: 40b. "Lautarii"; 2l.40, "Dimitrie Cantemir".

48 Fly Agaric

1996. Fungi. Multicoloured.

200	10b. Type **48**	55	45
201	10b. Satan's mushroom	55	45
202	65b. Death cap	1·70	1·40
203	1l.30 Clustered woodlover	2·20	1·70
204	2l.40 Destroying angel	5·00	4·50

49 Weightlifting

1996. Olympic Games, Atlanta, U.S.A. Multicoloured.

205	10b. Type **49**	35	20
206	20b.+5b. Judo	45	35
207	45b.+10b. Running	90	75
208	2l.40+30b. Canoeing	6·00	5·50

MS209 123×75 mm. 2l.20 Archery (horiz) | 2·75 | 2·75 |

50 Rudi Monastery

1996. Monasteries. Multicoloured.

| 210 | 10b. Type **50** | 20 | 10 |
| 211 | 90b. Japca | 90 | 75 |

212	1l.30 Curchi	1·10	90
213	2l.80 Saharna	2·20	1·90
214	4l.40 Capriana	4·50	3·75

51 Moorhens

1996. Birds. Multicoloured.

215	9b. Type **51**	35	20
216	10b. Greylag geese	35	20
217	2l.20 Turtle doves	2·75	2·20
218	4l.40 Mallard	7·75	7·25
MS219	82×65 mm. 2l.20 Ring-necked pheasant (*Phasianus colchicus*)	2·20	2·20

52 Elena Alistar (president of Women's League)

1996. Europa. Famous Women. Multicoloured.

220	10b. Type **52**	45	35
221	3l.70 Marie Sklodowska-Curie (physicist)	5·00	4·50
MS222	94×104 mm. 2l.20 Iulia Hasdeu (writer)	6·00	6·00

53 Mihail Eminescu (poet) (146th birth anniv)

1996. Birth Anniversaries.

223	53	10b. brown and deep brown	35	20
224	-	10b. sepia and brown	35	20
225	-	2l.20 green and brown	1·70	1·40
226	-	3l.30 green and deep brown	2·75	2·50
227	-	5l.40 brown and deep brown	5·00	4·50
MS228		96×66 mm. 1l.80 brown	2·20	2·20

DESIGNS—HORIZ: 10b. Gavriil Banulescu-Bodoni (Metropolitan of Chisinau, 250th); 2l.20, Ion Creanga (writer, 159th); 3l.30, Vasile Alecsandri (writer, 172nd); 5l.40, Petru Movila and printing press (400th). VERT—1l.80, Mihail Eminesai (different).

54 Town Hall

1996. 560th Anniv of Chisinau. Multicoloured.

229	10b. Type **54**	20	10
230	1l.30 Cultural Palace	90	75
231	2l.40 Mazarache Church	5·00	4·50

55 Carol Singers with Star

1996. Christmas. Multicoloured.

232	10b. Type **55**	20	10
233	2l.20+30b. Mother and child at centre of star	1·80	1·50
234	2l.80+50b. Children decorating Christmas tree	2·40	2·20

1996. Moldovan Olympic Games Medal Winners. No. **MS**209 optd **Nicolae JURAVSCHI Victor RENEISCHI – canoe, argint -, Serghei MUREICO – lupt Greco-romame, bronz.**

MS235	123×75 mm. 2l.20 mult	5·50	5·50

57 Feteasca

1997. Moldovan Wines. Each showing a grape variety and bottle of wine. Multicoloured.

236	10b. Type **57**	35	20
237	45b. Cabernet Sauvignon	90	75
238	65b. Sauvignon	1·10	90
239	3l.70 Rara Neagra	4·50	3·75

58 Franz Schubert

1997. Composers. Each green and grey.

240	10b. Type **58** (birth bicentenary)	35	20
241	10b. Gavriil Musicescu (150th birth anniv)	35	20
242	45b. Sergei Rachmaninov	55	35
243	4l.40 Georges Enesco	5·00	4·50

59 Girl with Eggs

1997. Easter. Multicoloured.

244	10b. Type **59**	35	20
245	3l.30 Easter dish	3·75	3·50
MS246	87×70 mm. 5l. Easter basket with bread and eggs	5·50	5·00

60 White Stork flying over Battlements

1997. Europa. Tales and Legends. Multicoloured.

247	10b. Type **60**	65	55
248	2l.80 Master Manole	7·75	7·50
MS249	90×70 mm. 5l. The Spring Fairy	11·00	11·00

61 Praying Mantis

1997. Insects in the Red Book. Multicoloured.

250	25b. Type **61**	55	45
251	80b. "Ascalaphus macaronius" (owl-fly)	1·10	90
252	1l. Searcher	1·70	1·40
253	2l.20 "Liometopum microcephalum" (ant)	3·25	3·00
MS254	84×67 mm. 5l. *Scolia maculata* (dagger wasp)	6·00	6·00

62 Post Office No. 12, Chisinau

1997. World Post Day.

255	62	10b. green and olive	35	20
256	-	2l.20 green and brown	2·20	2·00
257	-	3l.30 olive and green	4·50	4·25

DESIGNS—HORIZ: 2l.20, District Head Post and Telegraph Office, Chisinau. VERT: 3l.30, Heinrich von Stephan (founder of U.P.U.) (death centenary).

63 Nicolai Zelinski School, Tiraspol

1997. Protection of Buildings.

258	63	7b. black and violet	20	10
259	-	10b. black and purple	35	20
260	-	10b. black and blue	35	20
261	-	90b. black and yellow	90	75
262	-	1l.30 black and blue	1·30	1·10
263	-	3l.30 black and grey	4·50	4·25

DESIGNS: No. 259, Railway station, Tighina; 260, Sts. Constantine and Elena Cathedral, Balti; 261, Church, Causeni; 262, Archangel Michael Cathedral, Cahul; 263, Academy of Art, Chisinau.

64 Noul Neamt Monastery, Chitcani

1997. Christmas. Multicoloured.

264	10b. Type **64**	35	20
265	45b. "Birth of Our Lord Jesus Christ"	45	35
266	5l. "Birth of Jesus Christ" (different)	5·00	4·75

65 Petru Schiopul (1574–77, 1578–79 and 1582–91)

1997. 16th and 17th-century Princes of Moldavia. Multicoloured.

267	10b. Type **65**	35	20
268	10b. Ieremia Movila (1595–1606)	35	20
269	45b. Stefan Tomsa (1611–15 and 1621–23)	55	45
270	1l.80 Radu Mihnea (1616–19 and 1623–26)	2·00	1·80
271	2l.20 Miron Barnovschi Movila (1626–29 and 1633)	2·75	2·50
272	2l.80 Bogdan Orbul (1504–1517)	3·00	2·75
MS273	93×75 mm. 5l. Mihai Viteazul (May–Sept 1600) (25×30 mm)	5·50	5·50

66 Skiing

1998. Winter Olympic Games, Nagano, Japan. Multicoloured.

274	10b. Type **66**	35	20
275	45b. Pairs figure skating	90	75
276	2l.20 Biathlon	2·75	2·50

67 Alexei Mateeici

1998. Anniversaries. Multicoloured.

277	10b. Type **67** (110th birth anniv)	20	10
278	40b. Pantelimon Halippa (115th birth anniv)	55	45
279	60b. Stefan Ciobanu (115th birth anniv)	75	65
280	2l. Constantin Stamati-Ciurea (death centenary)	2·50	2·20
MS281	100×80 mm. 5l. Nicolae Milescu-Spatarul (290th death anniv)	5·50	5·50

68 Statue of Stefan cel Mare (Alexandru Plamadeala), Chisinau

1998. Art. Multicoloured.

282	10b. Type **68**	35	20
283	60b. "The Resurrection of Christ" (icon)	55	45
284	1l. Modern sculpture (Constantin Brancusi), Targu-Jiu	1·10	90
285	2l.60 Trajan's Column, Rome	3·75	3·50

69 Masks and Eye

1998. Europa. National Festivals. Multicoloured.

286	10b. Type **69** (Eugene Ionescu Theatre Festival)	75	65
287	2l.20 Medallion showing potter (Cermanics Fair)	4·50	4·25
MS288	70×58 mm. 5l. Bar of music (Martisor International Music Festival)	7·75	7·75

70 Cherries

1998. Fruits. Multicoloured.

289	7b. Type **70**	20	10
290	10b. Plums	35	20
291	1l. Apples	90	65
292	2l. Pears	2·20	2·00

71 Diana, Princess of Wales

1998. Diana, Princess of Wales Commemoration. Sheet 144×116 mm containing T **71** and similar horiz designs. Multicoloured.

MS293	10d. Type **71**; 90b. Wearing orange jacket; 1l.80, Wearing burgundy jacket; 2l.20 Wearing jacket with white collar; 5l. Wearing jacket with velvet collar	8·75	8·75

72 Chilia

1998. Medieval Towns.

294	72	10b. grey and black	35	20
295	-	60b. brown and black	65	55
296	-	1l. red and black	1·10	90
297	-	2l. blue and black	2·50	2·20

DESIGNS: 60b. Orhei; 1l. Suceava; 2l. Ismail.

73 1858 Moldavia Stamps

1998. 140th Anniv of Stamp Issues for Moldavia. Multicoloured.

298	10b. Type **73**	35	20
299	90b. 1858 Moldavia 54p. and 1928 Rumania 1 and 5l. stamps	55	45
300	2l.20 1858 Moldavia 81p. and Russian stamps	2·75	2·50
301	2l.40 1858 Moldavia 108p. and Moldova 1996 10b. and 1994 45b. stamps	3·25	3·00

74 Northern Eagle Owl

1998. Birds. Multicoloured.

302	25b. Type **74**	45	35
303	2l. Demoiselle crane (horiz)	2·20	2·00

75 Couple from Vara

1998. Regional Costumes. Multicoloured.

304	25b. Type **75**	35	20
305	90b. Couple from Vara (different)	1·10	90
306	1l.80 Couple from Iarna	2·50	2·20
307	2l. Couple from Iarna (different)	2·75	2·50

76 Anniversary Emblem and "Proportions of Man" (Leonardo da Vinci)

1998. 50th Anniv of Universal Declaration of Human Rights.

308	**76**	2l.40 multicoloured	3·25	3·00

77 Conference Members

1998. 80th Anniv of Union of Bessarabia and Rumania.

309	**77**	90b. brown, blue and black	90	65

78 Mail Coach

1999. Anniversaries. Multicoloured.

310	25b. Type **78** (125th anniv of U.P.U.)	55	45
311	2l.20 Map of Europe and Council of Europe emblem (50th anniv)	2·75	2·50

79 Prutul de Jos Park

1999. Europa. Parks and Gardens. Multicoloured.

312	25b. Type **79**	55	45
313	2l.40 Padurea Domneasca Park	3·25	3·25
MS314	84×65 mm. 5l. Codru Park	7·25	7·25

80 Balzac

1999. Birth Bicent of Honore de Balzac (writer).

315	**80**	90b. multicoloured	1·10	90

81 "Aleksandr Pushkin and Constantin Stamati" (B. Lebedev)

1999. Birth Bicentenary of Aleksandr Pushkin (poet).

316	**81**	65b. brown, deep brown and black	90	75

82 Tranta

1999. National Sports.

317	**82**	25b. green and light green	45	35
318	-	1l.80 green and yellow	2·00	1·80

DESIGN: 1l.80, Oina.

83 Neil Armstrong (first man on Moon)

1999. 30th Anniv of First Manned Moon Landing. Multicoloured.

319	25b. Type **83**	45	35
320	25b. Michael Collins (pilot of Command Module)	45	35
321	5l. Edwin Aldrin (pilot of Lunar Module)	5·00	4·75

84 Military Merit

1999. Orders and Medals. Multicoloured.

322	25b. Type **84**	35	20
323	25b. For Valour	35	20
324	25b. Civil Merit	35	20
325	90b. Mihai Eminescu Medal	90	65
326	1l.10 Order of Gloria Muncii	1·10	90
327	2l.40 Order of Stefan al Mare	2·75	2·50
MS328	70×50 mm. 5l. Order of the Republic	5·50	5·50

85 Embroidered Shirt

1999. Crafts. Multicoloured.

329	5b. Inlaid wine flask	20	10
330	25b. Type **85**	35	20
331	95b. Ceramic jugs	90	65
332	1l.80 Wicker table and chairs	2·20	2·00

86 Goethe

1999. 250th Birth Anniv of Johann Wolfgang von Goethe (poet).

333	**86**	1l.10 multicoloured	1·70	1·40

87 Emblem

1999. Tenth Anniv of Adoption of Latin Alphabet.

334	**87**	25b. multicoloured	55	45

88 Metropolitan Varlaam

1999. Patriarchs of the Orthodox Church. Multicoloured.

335	25b. Type **88**	45	35
336	2l.40 Metropolitan Gurie Grosu	3·00	2·75

89 Bogdan II (1449–51)

1999. 15th to 17th-century Princes of Moldavia. Multicoloured.

337	25b. Type **89**	35	20
338	25b. Bogdan IV (1568–72)	35	20
339	25b. Constantin Cantemir (1685–93)	35	20
340	1l.50 Simon Movila (1606–07)	1·10	90
341	3l. Gheorghe III Duca (1665–66, 1668–72 and 1678–84)	2·75	2·50
342	3l.90 Ilias Alexandru (1666–68)	4·50	3·75
MS343	97×78 mm. 5l. Vasile Lupu (1634–53) (25×30 mm)	5·50	5·50

90 European Otter ("Lutra lutra")

1999. Animals in the Red Book. Multicoloured.

344	25b. Type **90**	55	45
345	1l.80 Beluga ("Huso huso")	1·70	1·40
346	3l.60 Greater horseshoe bat ("Rhinolophus ferrumequinum")	3·25	3·00

91 Player and Chessboard

1999. World Women's Chess Championship, Chisinau. Multicoloured.

347	25b. Type **91**	45	35
348	2l.20+30b. Championship venue and emblem	3·00	2·75

92 4th-century B.C. Bronze Helmet and Candle Holder

1999. National History Museum Exhibits. Multicoloured.

349	25b. Type **92**	55	45
350	1l.80 10th-century B.C. ceramic pot	1·70	1·40
351	3l.60 Gospel, 1855	4·50	4·25

93 Raluca Eminovici

2000. 150th Birth Anniv of Mihail Eminescu (poet). Sheet 141×111 mm containing T **93** and similar vert designs. Multicoloured.

MS352	20b. Type **93**; 25b. Gheorghe Eminovici; 1l.50 Iosif Vulcan; 3l. Veronica Micle; 5l. Mihail Eminescu	8·75	8·75

94 Ileana Cosinzeana

2000. Folk Heroes. Multicoloured.

353	25b. Type **94**	55	45
354	1l.50 Fat-Frumos	1·70	1·40
355	1l.80 Harap Alb	2·20	2·00

95 Henri Coanda (aeronautical engineer)

2000. Birth Anniversaries. Each pink and black.

356	25b. Type **95** (114th anniv)	45	35
357	25b. Toma Ciorba (physician, 136th)	45	35
358	2l. Guglielmo Marconi (physicist, 126th)	2·20	2·00
359	3l.60 Norbert Wiener (mathematician, 106th)	4·25	3·75

96 Globe in Palm and Astronaut on Moon

2000. The Twentieth Century. Multicoloured.

360	25b. Type **96** (first manned moon landing, 1969)	35	20
361	1l. Model of nuclear fission and hand (use of nuclear energy)	1·50	1·30
362	3l. Computer and mouse (development of electronic data processing)	3·00	2·75
363	3l.90 P. F. Teoctist (patriarch) and Pope John Paul II (consultation between Eastern and Roman churches) (horiz)	4·25	3·75

97 "Resurrection" (anon)

2000. Easter. Paintings in the National Gallery. Multicoloured.

364	25b. Type **97**	35	20
365	3l. "Resurrection" (anon)	3·75	3·50

98 "Building Europe"

2000. Europa.

366	**98**	3l. multicoloured	3·75	3·50

99 Emblem and Profiles

2000. "EXPO 2000" World's Fair, Hanover, Germany (367) and "WIPA 2000" International Stamp Exhibition, Vienna, Austria (368). Multicoloured.

367	25b. Type **99**	65	45
368	3l.60+30b. Hands holding tweezers and 1994 1b. State Arms stamp	4·50	3·75

100 Monastery, Tipova

2000. Churches and Monasteries. Multicoloured.

369	25b. Type **100**	65	45
370	1l.50 St. Nicolas's Church (vert)	1·40	1·10
371	1l.80 Palanca Church (vert)	1·90	1·70
372	3l. Butucheni Monastery	3·50	3·25

101 Judo

2000. Olympic Games, Sydney. Multicoloured.

373	25b. Type **101**	65	55
374	1l.80 Wrestling	1·90	1·70
375	5l. Weightlifting	5·00	4·75

102 Child and Schoolroom

2000. International Teachers' Day.

376	**102**	25b. grey and green	65	55
377	-	3l.60 blue and lilac	3·75	3·50

DESIGN: 3l.60, Teacher holding book.

103 Adoration of the Shepherds (icon)

2000. Christmas. Multicoloured.

378	**103**	25b. Type **103**	65	55
379		1l.50 The Nativity (icon)	1·40	1·10
MS380 84×66 mm. 5l. Mary and Baby Jesus (icon) (27×32 mm)			5·50	5·50

104 Mother and Child

2001. 50th Anniv of United Nations High Commissioner for Refugees.

381	**104**	3l. multicoloured	2·75	2·50

105 Corncrake

2001. Endangered Species. The Corncrake. Multicoloured.

382	**105**	3l. Type **105**	2·20	2·00
383		3l. Singing	2·20	2·00
384		3l. In reeds	2·20	2·00
385		3l. With chicks	2·20	2·00

Nos. 382/5 were issued together, *se-tenant*, forming a composite design.

106 Yuri Gagarin and *Vostok* (spacecraft)

2001. 40th Anniv of First Manned Space Flight.

386	**106**	1l.80 multicoloured	1·90	1·70

107 Maria Dragan

2001. Anniversaries. Multicoloured.

387		25b. Type **107** (singer, 15th death anniv)	55	45
388		1l. Marlene Dietrich (actress, birth centenary)	1·10	90
389		2l. Ruxandra Lupu (314th death anniv)	2·20	2·00
390		3l. Lidia Lipkovski (opera singer, 43rd death anniv)	2·75	2·50

108 Waterfall

2001. Europa. Water Resources.

391	**108**	3l. multicoloured	2·75	2·50

109 Prunariu

2001. 20th Anniv of Space Flight by Dumitru Prunariu (first Rumanian cosmonaut).

392	**109**	1l.80 multicoloured	1·90	1·70

110 Stylized Humans (Aliona Valeria Samburic)

2001. Winning Entries in Children's Painting Competition. Designs by named artist. Multicoloured.

393		25b. Type **110**	35	20
394		25b. Cars inside house and sun (Ion Sestacovschi)	35	20
395		25b. House, balloons and sun (Cristina Mereacre)	35	20
396		1l.80 Abstract painting (Andrei Sestacovschi)	2·20	1·90

111 1991 7k. Arms Stamp

2001. Tenth Anniv of First Moldovan Stamps. Sheet 100×74 mm, containing T **111** and similar multicoloured designs.

MS397 40b. Type **111**; 2l. 1991 13k. Arms stamp; 3l. 30k. 1991 Flag stamp (42×25 mm)			5·50	5·50

112 Tiger (*Panthera tigris*)

2001. Chisinau Zoo. Multicoloured.

398		40b. Type **112**	45	35
399		1l. Quagga (*Equus quagga*)	1·00	75
400		1l.50 Brown bear (*Ursus arctos*)	1·40	1·10
401		3l.+30b. *Antilopa nilgau*	3·00	2·75
MS402 84×70 mm. 5l. Lion (*Panthera leo*)			5·00	5·00

113 Flag and Buildings

2001. Tenth Anniv of Independence.

403	**113**	1l. multicoloured	1·40	1·10

114 Cimpoi

2001. Musical Instruments. Multicoloured.

404	**114**	40b. Type **114**	65	55
405		1l. Fluier	1·20	1·00
406		1l.80 Nai	1·80	1·40
407		3l. Tar'agot	3·25	3·00

115 Women's Profiles and Space Ship

2001. United Nations Year of Dialogue among Civilizations. Multicoloured.

408		40b. Type **115**	65	55
409		3l.60 Children encircling globe (vert)	3·75	3·50

116 Nicolai Mavrocordat (1711–15)

2001. Rulers. Multicoloured (except **MS**416).

410		40b. Type **116**	65	55
411		40b. Mihai Racovita (1716–26)	65	55
412		40b. Constantin Mavrocordat (1748–49)	65	55
413		40b. Grigore Callimachi (1767–69)	65	55
414		1l. Grigore Alexandru Gnica (1774–77)	1·40	1·10
415		3l. Anton Cantemir (1705–7)	3·50	3·25
MS416 61×88 mm. 5l. Dimitrie Cantemir (1710–11) (black, yellow and red) (horiz)			5·50	5·50

117 St. Treime Basilica, Manastirea Saharna

2001. Christmas. Multicoloured.

417		40b. Type **117**	65	55
418		1l. Adormirea Maicii Domnului Basilica, Manastirea Hancu	1·20	1·00
419		3l. St. Dumitru Basilica, Orhei	2·75	2·50
420		3l.90 Nasterea Domnului Cathedral, Chisinau	4·50	4·25

118 Emblem

2001. Tenth Anniv of Union of Independent States.

421	**118**	1l.50 multicoloured	1·80	1·40

119 Cross Country Skiing

2002. Winter Olympic Games, Salt Lake City. Multicoloured.

422		40b. Type **119**	65	55
423		5l. Biathlon	4·25	3·75

120 Hora

2002. Traditional Dances. Multicoloured.

424		40b. Type **120**	65	55
425		1l.50 Sirba	1·80	1·50

121 "Fetele din Ceadir-lunga" (Mihai Grecu)

2002. Art. Multicoloured.

426		40b. Type **121**	65	55
427		40b. "Meleag Natal" (Eleonora Romanescu)	65	55
428		1l.50 "Fata la Fereastra" (Valentina Rusu-Ciobanu)	2·00	1·70
429		3l. "In Doi" (Igor Vieru)	3·25	3·00

122 Entrance to Kishinev Circus

2002. Europa. Circus.

430	**122**	3l. multicoloured	5·50	5·50

123 Rose

2002. Botanical Gardens, Kishinev. Sheet 130×85 mm containing T **123** and similar vert designs. Multicoloured.

MS431 40b. Type **123**; 40b. Peony; 1l.50 Aster; 3l. Iris			6·50	6·50

124 Portrait of Cecilia Gallerani

2002. 550th Birth Anniv of Leonardo da Vinci (artist). Sheet 129×85 mm containing T **124** and similar vert designs. Multicoloured.

MS432 40b. Type **124**; 1l.50 The Virgin and Child with St. Anne; 3l. Mona Lisa (La Gioconda)			5·50	5·50

125 Ion Neculce (chronicler) (Lady with an Ermine)

2002. Personalities. All sepia.

433		40b. Type **125**	65	55
434		40b. Nicolae Costin (chronicler)	65	55
435		40b. Grigore Ureche (chronicler)	65	55
436		40b. Nicolae Testemiteanu (rector, Faculty of Medicine, Chisnau University)	65	55
437		1l.50 Sergiu Radautan (rector, Technical Faculty, Chisnau University)	2·50	2·20
438		3l.90 Alexandre Dumas (writer)	3·00	2·75

126 Vladimir Horse

2002. Horses. Showing horse breeds. Multicoloured.

439		40b. Type **126**	35	20
440		1l.50 Orlov	1·70	1·40
441		3l. Arab	4·25	3·75

127 Stork, Houses and Man carrying Grapes (Alexandru Catranji)

2002. Children's Paintings. The Post. Multicoloured.

442		40b. Type **127**	65	55
443		1l.50 Birds, flower and globe	1·90	1·70
444		2l. Postman and globe	2·50	2·20

128 Union Emblem,
Member States
Presidents and Flags

2002. Union of Independent States Conference, Chisnau.
Multicoloured.

445	1l.50 Type **128**	1·90	1·70
446	3l.60 Emblem and handshake	3·50	3·25

129 Entrance to Underground
Warehouse

2002. 50th Anniv of Cricova Wine Factory. Multicoloured.

447	40b. Type **129**	55	35
448	40b. Barrels in warehouse	55	35
449	1l.50 Dining hall (vert)	1·80	1·50
450	2l. Interior of warehouse	1·90	1·70
451	3l.60 Glasses and bottles of wine (vert)	3·50	3·25

130 Tissandier Brothers' Airship
(1883)

2003. Airships. Multicoloured.

452	40b. Type **130**	65	55
453	2l. "Uchebny" (Training Craft) (1908)	2·50	2·20
454	5l. LZ 127 "Graf Zeppelin" (1928) (inscr "Count Zeppelin")	6·50	6·00

131 Scarce Swallowtail
(*Iphiclides podalirius*)

2003. Butterflies and Moths. Multicoloured.

455	40b. Type **131**	65	55
456	2l. Jersey tiger moth (*Callimorpha quadripunctaria*)	1·40	1·10
457	3l. Oak hawk moth (*Marumba quercus*)	2·50	2·20
458	5l. Meleager's Blue (*Polyommatus daphnis*)	6·50	6·00
MS459	127×82 mm. Nos. 455/8	9·50	9·50

132 Rural Landscape

2003. Tenth Anniv of Europa Stamps. Sheet 130×85 mm containing T **132** and similar horiz design. Multicoloured.

MS460	1l.50 Type **132**; 5l. Chisinau	5·50	5·50

133 Folk Ensemble
"JOC"

2003. Europa. Poster Art. Multicoloured.

461	3l. Type **133**	2·20	2·00
462	5l. Exhibition poster (Mihai Eminescu, 150th birth anniv (Rumanian writer))	3·25	3·00

134 Emblem and Flag

2003. Red Cross Society of Moldova. Multicoloured.

463	40b. Type **134**	65	55
464	5l. Damaged buildings and Red Cross workers	2·75	2·50

135 Runner

2003. European Youth Olympics Festival, Paris. Multicoloured.

465	40b. Type **135**	65	55
466	3l. Cyclists	1·80	1·50
467	5l. Gymnast	3·75	3·50

136 "Luminari"
(A. Akhlupin)

2003. "World without Terror". Multicoloured.

468	40b. Type **136**	65	55
469	3l.90 "Pax Cultura" (N. Roerich)	3·25	3·00

137 Dimitrie Cantemir

2003. 340th Birth Anniv of Dimitrie Cantemir (linguist and scholar).

470	**137** 3l.60 multicoloured	3·75	3·50

138 Vladimir Voronin
(president of Moldova)

2003. Moldova—Chairman, Council of Europe Committee of Ministers, May–November 2003.

471	**138** 3l. multicoloured	3·50	3·25

139 Nicolae Donici

2003. Personalities. Multicoloured.

472	40b. Type **139** (astronomer)	65	55
473	1l.50 Nicolae Dimo (soil scientist)	1·80	1·50
474	2l. Nicolai Costenco (writer)	1·90	1·80
475	3l.90 Milestone Lewis (Lev Milstein) (film director)	3·00	2·75
476	5l. Vincent van Gogh (artist)	4·50	4·25

140 Mute Swan (*Cygnus olor*)

2003. Birds. Multicoloured.

477	40b. Type **140**	75	65
478	2l. Great egret (*Egretta alba*)	2·20	1·90
479	3l. Tawny eagle (*Aquila rapax*) (vert)	3·25	3·00
480	5l. Little bustard (*Tetrax tetrax*) (vert)	5·50	5·25
MS481	131×86 mm. Nos. 477/80	11·00	11·00

141 Natalie Gheorghiu

2004. Personalities. Multicoloured.

482	40b. Type **141** (doctor)	45	35
483	1l.50 Metropolitan Dosoftei (scholar)	1·70	1·40

142 Archaeological Dig

2004. Europa. Holidays. Multicoloured.

484	40b. Type **142**	75	65
485	4l.40 Winemaking	5·00	4·75

143 Stefan III
holding Sword

2004. 500th Death Anniv of Stefan III (Stefan cel Mare) (Moldavian ruler). Multicoloured.

486	40b. Type **143**	55	45
487	2l. Kneeling holding church	2·20	1·90
MS488	110×92 mm. 4l.40 Head and shoulders of Stefan III	5·50	5·50

144 Goalkeeper
and Ball

2004. Centenary of FIFA (Federation Internationale de Football Association). Multicoloured.

489	2l. Type **144**	2·20	1·90
490	4l.40 Player and ball	4·75	4·50

145 Memorial

2004. 60th Anniv of Iasi-Chisinau Battle. Sheet 81×62 mm.

MS491	2l. multicoloured	2·50	2·20

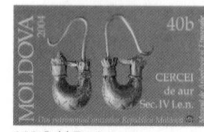

146 Gold Earrings

2004. Ancient Jewellery. Multicoloured.

492	40b. Type **146**	30	20
493	1l. Gold torque	60	50
494	1l.50 Silver earrings	90	75
495	2l. Bronze bracelet	1·30	1·10

147 Boxers

2004. Olympic Games, Athens. Multicoloured.

496	40b. Type **147**	35	30
497	4l.40 Weightlifter	2·50	2·40

148 Ephedra
distachya

2004. Plants. Multicoloured.

498	40b. Type **148**	25	20
499	1l.50 Pyrus elaeagrifolia	80	65
500	2l. Padus avium	1·20	1·00
501	2l. Crataegus pentagyna	1·20	1·00

149 Locomotive ER

2005. Railways. Multicoloured.

502	60b. Type **149**	35	25
503	1l. Locomotive ChME3	55	45
504	1l.50 Diesel locomotive D777-3	80	75
505	4l.40 Locomotive 3TE10M	2·30	2·00

150 Building
Facade

2005. Centenary of St. George's Church, Capriana Monastery.

506	**150**	40b. multicoloured	35	25

151 Memorial
Monument

2005. 60th Anniv of End of World War II.

507	**151**	1l.50 multicoloured	1·00	85

152 Cheese, Bowls, Jug and
Cup

2005. Europa. Gastronomy. Multicoloured.

508	1l.50 Type **152**	95	80
509	4l.40 Pastries, flask and mug	2·40	2·00

153 Pawn and
Championship
Emblem

2005. European Women's Chess Championship, Chisinau.

510	**153**	4l.40 multicoloured	2·40	2·10

154 Serghi Lunchevici

2005. Composers. Multicoloured.

511	40b. Type **154**	20	10
512	1l. Valeriu Cupcea	65	55
513	2l. Anton Rubenstein	1·20	1·00

155 Map and
National Symbols

2005. 50th Anniv of Europa Stamps. Multicoloured.
514	1l.50 Type **155**	65	55
515	15l. First Europa stamp	6·00	5·75
MS516	83×70 mm. Nos. 514/15	6·75	6·75

156 Emblem and
Globe

2005. World Information Society Summit, Tunis.
| 517 | **156** | 4l.40 multicoloured | 1·60 | 1·40 |

157 Passport
Pages

2005. Tenth Anniv of National Passport. Sheet 109×68 mm containing T **157** and similar vert designs. Multicoloured.
| MS518 | 40b. Type **157**; 1l.50 Passport covers; 4l.40 Two passport pages | 2·20 | 2·20 |

158 Emys orbicularis

2005. Reptiles and Amphibians. Multicoloured.
519	40b. Type **158**	25	20
520	1l. *Eremias arguta*	55	40
521	1l.50 *Pelobates fuscus*	80	65
522	2l. *Vipera ursinii* (inscr "ursine")	1·00	80
MS523	114×109 mm. Nos. 519/22	2·30	2·30

159 St. Nicolae
Church (1937)

2005.
| 524 | **159** | 40b. multicoloured | 35 | 25 |

160 St. Nicolae Church, Falesti
(1795)

2005. Christmas. Multicoloured.
| 525 | 40b. Type **160** | 20 | 10 |
| 526 | 1l. Varzharesti monastery (1420) | 2·00 | 1·70 |

161 Newspapers

2006. 15th Anniv of Makler Newspaper.
| 527 | **161** | 60b. emerald and black | 25 | 20 |

162 Luge

2006. Winter Olympic Games, Turin. Multicoloured.
| 528 | 60b. Type **162** | 35 | 20 |
| 529 | 6l.20 Skier | 2·30 | 2·00 |

163 Postal
Building, Balti

2006. Architecture.
530	**163**	22b. ultramarine	10	10
531	-	40b. chocolate	15	10
532	-	53b. blue	20	15
533	-	57b. green	25	15
534	-	60b. green	35	20
535	-	3l.50 claret	1·70	1·40

DESIGNS: 22b. Type **163**; 40b. Monument, Chisinau; 53b. Single storey building, Cahul; 57b. Post and Telegraph building, Soroca; 60b. Biserica Adormirea Maicii Domnului, Copceac; 3l.50 Museum, Chisinau.

164 Lace

2006. Costumes and Textiles. Multicoloured.
536	40b. Type **164**	15	10
537	60b. Woman's costume (vert)	20	15
538	3l. Man's costume (vert)	1·30	1·00
539	4l.50 Embroidery	2·00	1·70

165 Gheorghe Mustea

2006. Gheorghe Mustea (composer and conductor).
| 540 | **165** | 60b. multicoloured | 35 | 25 |

166 Globe as Street of Flags

2006. Europa. Integration. Multicoloured.
| 541 | 60b. Type **166** | 35 | 25 |
| 542 | 4l.50 Artist and musicians (vert) | 2·00 | 1·70 |

167 Chess Board and clocks

2006. 37th Chess Olympiad, Turin.
| 543 | **167** | 4l.50 multicoloured | 2·00 | 1·70 |

168 Trophy and Two Players

2006. World Cup Football Championship, Germany. Multicoloured.
544	2l. Type **168**	1·00	85
545	3l. Goleo VI and Pille (mascots)	1·30	1·10
546	4l.50 Two players and high ball	1·70	1·50

169 Ion Halippa
(historian) (135th
birth anniv)

2006. Personalities. Multicoloured.
547	40b. Type **169**	25	15
548	1l. Eufrosinia (Valentina) Cuza (opera singer) (150th birth anniv)	55	35
549	2l. Petre Stefanuca (ethnographer) (birth centenary)	85	65

| 550 | 4l.50 Wolfgang Amadeus Mozart (composer) (250th birth anniv) | 1·50 | 1·30 |

170 Martes martes

2006. Animals. Multicoloured.
551	60b. Type **170**	35	20
552	1l. *Mustela erminea*	55	35
553	2l. *Mustela lutrola*	85	65
554	3l. *Mustela eversmanni*	1·10	80
MS555	81×67 mm. 6l.20 *Felis silvestris* (vert)	2·30	2·30

171 Flag and
Government
Building

2006. 15th Anniv of Republic.
| 556 | **171** | 2l.60 multicoloured | 1·00 | 75 |

172 German Shepherd

2006. Dogs. Multicoloured.
557	40b. Type **172**	20	15
558	60b. Collie	35	20
559	2l. Poodle	85	65
560	6l.20 Magyar Agar (Hungarian sight-hound)	2·20	1·80

173 Grapes, Glass and
Vineyard

2006. Wine.
| 561 | **173** | 60b. multicoloured | 1·00 | 60 |

No. 565 and Type **175** have been left for 'Surcharge'. not yet received.

174 Landscape (Valerii
Metleaev)

2006. Christmas. Multicoloured.
562	40b. Type **174**	15	10
563	3l. Mummers (Elena Bontea)	1·40	85
564	6l.20 Mummers (Mihail Statnii) (vert)	2·25	1·30

No. 565 and Type **175** have been left for 'Surcharge', not yet received.

176 'Francesco
Petrarca' (Raphael
Morghen)

2007. National Art Museum. Multicoloured.
566	65b. Type **176**	40	20
567	85b. Napoleon Bonaparte	45	25
568	2l. Friedrich von Schiller	90	65
569	4l.50 Johann Wolfgang von Goethe	1·70	1·50

177 Morchella steppicola

2007. Fungi. Multicoloured.
| 570 | 65b. Type **177** | 40 | 20 |

571	85b. *Phylloporus rhodoxantus*	45	25
572	2l. *Amanita solitaria*	90	65
573	6l.20 *Boletus aereus*	2·75	2·50

178 Scouts

2007. Europa. Centenary of Scouting. Multicoloured.
| 574 | 2l.85 Type **178** | 1·30 | 1·10 |
| 575 | 4l.50 Scouts examining flowers and butterfly | 1·70 | 1·50 |

2007. Nos. 85 and No. 75 surch.
| 576 | 25b. on 3k. purple | 20 | 10 |
| 577 | 85b. on 3k. purple | 80 | 60 |

180 Tabby Cat

2007. Cats. Multicoloured.
578	65b. Type **180**	40	20
579	1l. Siamese (vert)	80	60
580	1l.50 Birman (vert)	1·20	90
581	6l.20 Persian	2·75	2·50

181 Otis tarda (great bustard)

2007. Birds. Multicoloured.
582	75b. Type **181**	40	25
583	1l. *Neophron percnopterus* (Egyptian vulture)	80	60
584	2l.50 *Lyrurus tetrix* (black grouse)	3·25	3·00
585	5l. *Gyps fulvus* (griffon vulture)	6·50	6·00
MS586	67×81 mm. 6l.20 *Tetrao urogallus* (capercaillie)	7·00	7·00

No. **MS586** also contains a stamp size label which, with the stamp and margins form a composite design of capercaille cock, hen and chicks.

182 Acipenser gueldenstaedtii

2007. Preservation of Dniestr Fauna. Fish. Multicoloured.
| 587 | 1l. Type **182** | 80 | 60 |
| 588 | 3l. *Zingel zingel* | 2·40 | 1·80 |

183 Ion Luca Caragiale
(Romanian playwright and short
story writer)

2007. Personalities. Multicoloured.
589	75b. Type **183** (155th birth anniv)	35	25
590	1l. Anastasia Dicescu (opera singer) (120th birth anniv)	65	45
591	3l. Mircea Eliade (Romanian historian, writer and philosopher) (birth centenary)	95	65
MS592	80×67 mm. 6l.20 Maria Bieshu (singer) (vert)	2·40	2·40

No. **MS592** also contains a stamp size label which, with the stamp and margins form a composite design.

184 Chess Pieces

2007. Chess Championship, Mexico.
| 593 | **184** | 6l.20 multicoloured | 2·40 | 1·80 |

185 Christmas Tree

2007. Christmas. Multicoloured.

594	1l. Type **185**	80	60
595	4l.50 Santa Claus (46×27 mm)	1·70	1·50

186 Peresecina, Orhei

2008. Wells. Multicoloured.

596	10b. blue	10	10
597	75b. green	40	25
598	1l. purple (vert)	65	45
599	3l. brown (vert)	90	75

DESIGNS: 10b. Type **186**; 75b. Duruitoarea, Riscani; 1l. Ciripcau, Floresti; 3l. Ocnita.

187 Cycling

2008. Olympic Games, Beijing. Multicoloured.

600	1l. Type **187**	80	60
601	6l.20 Boxing	2·75	2·50
602	15l. Weightlifting	12·00	11·00

188 Early Messenger

2008. Europa. The Letter. Multicoloured.

603	3l.50 Type **188**	1·40	1·10
604	4l.50 VDU, '@' and envelopes	1·90	1·70

189 1858 27p. and 54p. Stamps of Moldavia (As Type **1**) and (No. 2)

2008. 150th Anniv of First Moldavian Stamps. Multicoloured.

605	1l. Type **189**	60	40
606	3l. 1858 81p. and 108p. stamps of Moldavia (As No. 3) and (No. 4)	1·00	80

190 Football and Stadium

2008. European Football Championship–Euro 2008.

607	**190**	4l.50 multicoloured	6·00	5·75

191 *Maianthemum bifolium*

2008. Flora. Multicoloured.

608	1l. Type **191**	1·20	1·00
609	3l. *Hepatica nobilis*	3·75	3·50
610	5l. *Nymphaea alba*	10·25	9·75
MS611	160×83 mm. As Nos. 608/10	15·00	15·00

The stamps, margins and labels of **MS**611 form a composite design of a pond.

192 Onisifor Ghibu (politician)

2008. Personalities. Multicoloured.

612	1l.20 Type **192**	55	40

613	1l.50 Ciprian Porumbescu (composer)	70	60
614	3l. Lev Tolstoi (Leo Tolstoy) (writer)	1·50	1·30
615	4l.50 Maria Tanase (singer)	2·25	2·00

193 *Cervus nippon* (sika deer)

2008. Fauna. Multicoloured.

616	3l. Type **193**	1·50	1·30
617	3l. *Cervus elaphus* (red deer)	1·50	1·30

Stamps of the same design were issued by Kazakhstan.

194 Early Town

2008. 600th Anniv of Bender. Sheet 113×81 mm.

MS618	multicoloured	2·00	2·00

195 Antioh Cantemir (Antiochus Kantemir) (diplomat)

2008. Cantemir Dynasty. Each red-brown.

619	1l.20 Type **195**	1·00	80
MS620	81×67 mm. 3l. Dimitri Cantemir (Prince of Moldova)	1·50	1·50

196 Mikhail Grigory Sutu

2008. Princes of Moldova. Multicoloured.

621	85b. Type **196**	35	25
622	1l.20 Grigory Alexandru Ghica	45	35
623	1l.50 Mikhail Sturza	80	60
624	2l. Alexandru Ipsilanti	95	75
625	3l. Ioan Sandu Sturza	1·30	1·10
626	4l.50 Scarlat Callimachi	2·25	2·00
MS627	108×113 mm. 6l.20 Alexandru Ioan Cuza	2·75	2·75

2008. Vyacheslav Gozhan, Boxing Bronze Medalist, Olympic Games, Beijing. No. 601 optd Veaceslav GOJAN Box–Bronz.

628	6l.20 As No. 601	2·75	2·50

198 Emblem and Globe

2008. Moldovan Presidency of Central European Initiative Organization. Sheet 82×68 mm containing T 198 and similar vert design. Multicoloured.

MS629	1l.20 Type **198**; 4l.50 Emblem and globe (different)	9·00	9·00

199 Christmas Goat

2008. Christmas. Multicoloured.

630	1l.20 Type **199**	2·10	2·00
MS631	90×53 mm. 6l.20 Children caroling (46×27 mm)	9·50	9·50

200 Emblem and Open Book

2008. 60th Anniv of Universal Declaration of Human Rights.

632	**200** 4l.50 multicoloured	7·25	7·00

201 Symbols of Moldova

2009. 650th Anniv of State. Multicoloured.

633	1l.20 Type **201**	1·00	90
MS634	69×83 mm. 6l.20 Bogdan Voda (Bogdan I of Moldavia) on horseback	3·00	3·00

202 Weapons (10th–14th century)

2009. Ancient Weapons. Multicoloured.

635	1l.20 Type **202**	75	55
636	4l.50 Weapons (8th–13th century)	2·10	2·00

203 Penguin

2009. Preserve Polar Regions and Glaciers. Multicoloured.

637	1l.20 Type **203**	1·00	90
638	6l.20 Polar bear	2·50	2·20

204 Decorated Eggs

2009. Easter. Multicoloured.

639	1l.20 Type **204**	1·50	1·20
640	3l. Decorated eggs on plate	3·50	3·25

205 Emblems

2009. 60th Anniv of Council of Europe.

641	**205** 4l.50 multicoloured	2·00	1·80

206 Nicolae Donici (astrophysicist)

2009. Europa. Astronomy. Multicoloured.

642	4l.20 Type **206**	1·70	1·50
643	4l.50 Galileo Galilei (astronomer)	1·70	1·50

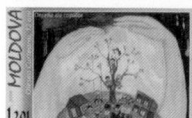

207 Children in Tree (Olesya Curtyanu)

2009. Winning Designs in Children's Drawing Competition 'A Healthy Child'. Multicoloured.

644	1l.20 Type **207**	45	35
645	1l.50 Child sleeping in bird's nest (Yulia Strutsa) (vert)	65	50
646	5l.+20b. Child kneeling in diseased world (Irina Simion) (vert)	2·20	2·00

208 *Viola suavis* (Russian violet)

2009. Flora. Multicoloured.

647	1l.20 Type **208**	45	35
648	1l.50 *Adonis vernalis* (pheasant's eye)	80	60
649	3l. *Campanula persicifolia* (bellflower)	1·70	1·50
MS650	100×65mm. 4l.50 *Papaver rhoeas* (poppy)	1·75	1·75
MS651	134×100 mm. 1l.20 As Type **208**; 1l.50 As No. 648; 3l. As No. 649; 4l.50 Poppy	5·00	5·00

209 *Bombus paradoxus*

2009. Insects. Multicoloured.

652	1l.20 Type **209**	55	45
653	1l.50 *Xylocopa valga*	70	55
654	3l. *Carabus clathratus*	1·40	1·20
655	4l.50 *Coenagrion lindeni*	2·20	2·00

210 Post Horn

2009. Personal Stamps. Multicoloured.

656	1l.20 Type **210**	55	45
657	1l.20 Post Horn (blue frame)	55	45
658	1l.20 Stefan Cel Mare monument	55	45
659	1l.20 Cathedral	55	45
660	1l.20 Bouquet of flowers	55	45
661	1l.20 Wedding bouquet and rings	55	45

211 Walnut

2009. Fruit and Nut. Multicoloured.

662	50b. Type **211**	15	10
663	85b. Mulberry (*Morus nigra*)	35	25
664	1l.20 Pears	45	35
665	5l. Apricots (*Prunus armeniaca*)	2·75	2·50

212 Corjeuti, Briceni

2009. Rural Houses. Houses. Multicoloured.

666	1l.20 Type **212**	45	35
667	4l.50 Chirsova, Comrat	2·20	2·00
668	7l. Batuceni, Orhei	2·75	2·50

213 'Moldova'
Grape

2009
669 **213** 4l.50 multicoloured 2·20 2·00

214 Face and Web

2009. European Day Against Human Trafficking.
670 **214** 4l.50 multicoloured 2·20 2·00

215 Eufrosinia Antonovna
Kersnovskaya (Gulag camp
survivor and memoir writer)

2009. Personalities. Multicoloured.
671 1l.20 Type **215** 45 35
672 1l.20 Eugène Ionesco
(Romanian playwright and
dramatist) 45 35
673 4l.50 Nicolai Gogol (writer) 2·20 2·00
674 7l. Charles Robert Darwin
(naturalist and evolutionary
theorist) 2·75 2·50

216 Capra

2009. Christmas. Showing scenes from Christmas by
Vasily Movilyanu. Multicoloured.
675 1l.20 Type **216** 55 45
676 4l.50 Plugusorul 2·20 2·00

217 Natalia Dadiani
(educationalist) (145th birth
anniv)

2010. Personalities. Multicoloured.
677 1l.20 Type **217** 55 45
678 1l.20 Grigore Vieru (poet and
writer) (85th birth anniv) 55 45
679 5l.40 Ivan Zaikin (wrestler and
aviator) (130th birth anniv) 2·50 2·30
680 7l. Maria Cebotari (soprano and
actress) (birth centenary) 2·75 2·50
MS681 115×165 mm. 4l.50 Mihai Eminescu (poet, novelist and journalist)
(160th birth anniv) (vert) 2·20 2·00

218 Alpine Skiing

2010. Olympic Winter Games. Vancouver
682 1l.20 Type **218** 55 50
683 8l.50 Biathlon (vert) 3·25 3·00

219 Necklace of Shells

2010. National Museum of Archaeology and History.
Multicoloured.
684 1l.20 Type **219** 55 50
685 7l. Circular and perforated
pendants 2·75 2·50

220 Frederic Chopin

2010. Birth Bicentenary of Fryderyk Franciszek Chopin
686 **220** 5l.40 multicoloured 2·00 1·90

221 Lactarius
piperatus

2010. Fungi. Multicoloured.
687 1l.20 Type **221** 40 30
688 2l. Amanita pantherina 85 75
689 5l.40 Russula sanguinea 2·00 1·80
690 7l. Coprinus picaceus 2·75 2·00
MS691 136×67 mm. Nos. 687/90 6·00 5·50

222 Carduelis carduelis
(goldfinch)

2010. Birds. Multicoloured.
692 85b. Type **222** 35 25
693 1l. Passer domesticus (house
sparrow) 45 35
694 1l.20 Strix uralensis Pallas
(Ural owl) 55 25
695 4l.50 Pica pica (pica pica) 2·00 1·80
MS696 101×66 mm. 8l.50 Columba
livia (pigeon) 3·25 3·00

223 Pungata cu Doi Bani

2010. Europa. Childrens' Books. Multicoloured.
697 1l.20 Type **223** 40 30
698 5l.40 Guguta si Prietenii 2·00 1·80

224 Victory
Monument

2010. 65th Anniv of End of World War II
699 **224** 4l.50 multicoloured 1·75 1·50

225 Player and Ball

2010. World Football Championship, South Africa
700 1l.20 Type **225** 50 40
701 8l.50 Goalkeeper making save
(vert) 3·25 3·00

226 Broken Heart and Syringe

2010. AIDS Awareness Campaign
702 **226** 1l.20 multicoloured 1·00 90

227 Flowers (Ion
Tabirta)

2010. Flower Paintings. Multicoloured.
703 1l. Type **227** 20 15
704 1l.20 Bouquet of Poppies (Oleg
Cojocaru) 30 25
705 2l. Flowers (Mikhail Statnii) 1·10 90
706 5l.40 Chrysanthemums (Leonid
Grigorasenko) 2·10 1·90

228 Flood Victims

2010. Support for Flood Victims of July 2010
707 **228** 1l.20 +50b. multicol-
oured 65 55

229 'Moldovenesca'

2010. Traditional Dances. Multicoloured.
708 85b. Type **229** 35 25
709 5l.40 'Calusharii' (vert) 2·50 2·30

230 Feteasca
Grapes

2010. Grapes
710 **230** 4l.50 multicoloured 2·20 2·00

231 Arms of Moldova

2010. State Symbols. Multicoloured.
711 1l.20 Type **231** 40 30
712 4l.50 National flag 1·90 1·75
MS713 135×100 mm. Nos. 711/12,
each×3 7·00 6·50

232 Mammoth

2010. Prehistoric Animals. Multicoloured (grey tone).
714 85b. Type **232** 25 20
715 1l. Ursus spelaeus 35 30
716 1l.20 Panthera leo spelaea 55 50
717 4l.20 Bison 1·60 1·70
MS718 114×108 mm. 1l.20 Pontoceros;
1l.50 Anancus; 5l.40 Stephanorhinus;
8l.50 Homotherium 6·50 6·25

233 Angel carrying
Gift and Child at
Window

2010. Christmas and New Year. Multicoloured.
719 1l.20 Type **233** 1·00 90
MS720 102×203 mm. 5l.40 Cathedral
Church and Bell Tower, Chisinau 2·00 1·80

2011. National Museum of Archaeology and History.
Multicoloured.
721 85b. Anthropomorphic amphora with lid 55 50
722 1l.20 Biconical vessel with
zoomorphic designs 70 65
723 8l.50 Taller biconical vessel with
handles anthropomorphic
designs 2·75 2·50
MS724 136×102 mm. Nos. 721, 722×2
and 723 4·50 4·25
As T **219**

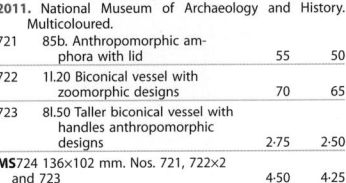

234 Ralli Mansion
(now Museum),
Dolna, Strǎşeni

2011. Architecture
725 10b. red brown 10 10
726 25b. deep ultramarine 10 10
727 85b. deep turquoise-green 30 25
728 1l. deep claret 40 35
729 1l.20 dark steel blue 55 50
730 1l.50 deep green 70 65
DESIGNS: 10b. Type **234**; 25b. Mirzoian Mansion, Hînceşti;
85b. Balioz Mansion, Ivancea; 1l. Secondary School for
Girls, Soroca; 1l.20 Pommer Mansion and Parki, Taul,
Donduşeni; 1l.50 Hasnaş Mansion, Sofia, Drochia.

235 Mǎrţişor
(Ludmila Berezin)

2011. Handicraft Art. Multicoloured.
731 1l.20 Type **235** 55 50
732 4l.20 Portrait (Natalia Cangea) 2·00 1·80
733 7l. Carpet (Ecaterina Popescu) 2·20 2·00

Nos. 734/7 and Type **236** are left for Paintings, issued
on 1 April 2011, not yet received.

237 Yuri Gagarin

2011. 50th Anniversary of First Manned Space Flight.
Multicoloured.
MS738 1l.20 Type **237**; 5l.40 Gherman
Titov; 7l. Virgil I. Grissom; 8l.50 Alan
B. Shepard 9·00 8·50

238 Leaf, Fire, Deer
and Forest

2011. Europa. Forests. Multicoloured.
739 4l.20 Type **238** 2·20 2·00
740 5l.40 Forest, owl and slice
through tree 2·75 2·50
MS741 134×100 mm. Nos. 739/70,
each×3 15·00 15·00

Nos. 742/5 and Type **239** are left for Flowers, issued on
20 May 2011, not yet received.
No. 746 and Type **240** are left for Deportation, issued
on 12 June 2011, not yet received.

241 1991 7c. Stamp
(As Type **1**)

2011. 20th Anniv of First Moldovan Stamp. Multicoloured.
MS747 85b. As Type **1**; 1l.20 As No. 2;
4l.20 As No.3 9·50 9·50

POSTAGE DUE STAMPS

D33 Postal Emblems

1994

D150	**D33**	30b. brown and green	1·10	1·10
D151	**D33**	40b. green and lilac	1·70	1·70

One stamp in the pair was put on insufficiently franked mail, the other stamp on associated documents.

Pt. 6

MONACO

A principality on the S. coast of France including the town of Monte Carlo.

1885. 100 centimes = 1 French franc.
2002. 100 cents = 1 euro.

1 Prince Charles III

1885

1	**1**	1c. olive	28·00	18·00
2	**1**	2c. lilac	65·00	32·00
3	**1**	5c. blue	80·00	41·00
4	**1**	10c. brown on yellow	£100	46·00
5	**1**	15c. red	£425	28·00
6	**1**	25c. green	£750	85·00
7	**1**	40c. blue on red	90·00	50·00
8	**1**	75c. black on red	£300	£140
9	**1**	1f. black on yellow	£1800	£600
10	**1**	5f. red on green	£3500	£2500

2 Prince Albert

1891

11	**2**	1c. green	90	65
12	**2**	2c. purple	90	65
13	**2**	5c. blue	60·00	7·25
22	**2**	5c. green	65	45
14	**2**	10c. brown on yellow	£130	20·00
23	**2**	10c. red	3·25	65
15	**2**	15c. pink	£225	12·00
24	**2**	15c. brown on yellow	4·25	90
25	**2**	15c. green	2·30	2·75
16	**2**	25c. green	£375	37·00
26	**2**	25c. blue	17·00	5·50
17	**2**	40c. black on pink	3·75	3·25
18	**2**	50c. brown on orange	9·25	5·50
23	**2**	75c. brown on buff	32·00	28·00
20	**2**	1f. black on yellow	23·00	11·00
21	**2**	5f. red on green	90·00	£100
28	**2**	5f. mauve	£225	£250
29	**2**	5f. green	37·00	34·00

1914. Surcharged **+5c.**

30	10c.+5c. red	10·00	9·25

4 War Widow and Monaco

1919. War Orphans Fund.

31	**4**	2c.+3c. mauve	41·00	46·00
32	**4**	5c.+5c. green	25·00	25·00
33	**4**	15c.+10c. red	26·00	26·00
34	**4**	25c.+15c. blue	55·00	46·00
35	**4**	50c.+50c. brown on orange	£225	£225
36	**4**	1f.+1f. black on yellow	£425	£450
37	**4**	5f.+5f. red	£1300	£1400

1920. Princess Charlotte's Marriage. Nos. 33/7 optd **20 mars 1920** or surch also.

38	2c.+3c. on 15c.+10c. red	70·00	75·00
39	2c.+3c. on 25c.+15c. blue	70·00	75·00
40	2c.+3c. on 50c.+50c. brown on orange	70·00	75·00
41	5c.+5c. on 1f.+1f. black on yellow	70·00	75·00
42	5c.+5c.on 5f.+5f. red	70·00	75·00
43	15c.+10c. red	32·00	37·00
44	25c.+15c. blue	28·00	12·00
45	50c.+50c. brown on orange	85·00	90·00
46	1f.+1f. black on yellow	£130	£140
47	5f.+5f. red	£9500	£9500

1921. Princess Antoinette's Baptism. Optd **28 DECEMBRE 1920** or surch also.

48	**2**	5c. green	1·00	1·00
49	**2**	75c. brown on buff	7·00	9·00
50	**2**	2f. on 5f. mauve	50·00	60·00

1922. Surch.

51	20c. on 15c. green	1·50	2·00
52	25c. on 10c. red	1·00	1·50
53	50c. on 1f. black on yellow	6·75	9·00

8 Prince Albert I

9 St. Devote Viaduct

1922

54	**8**	25c. brown	7·00	7·50
55	-	30c. green	1·50	2·50
56	-	30c. red	60	70
57	**9**	40c. brown	1·00	1·00
58	-	50c. blue	6·25	6·50
59	-	60c. grey	60	50
60	-	1f. black on yellow	50	30
61	-	2f. red	70	60
62	-	5f. brown	50·00	60·00
63	-	5f. green on blue	14·00	15·00
64	-	10f. red	22·00	25·00

DESIGNS:—As Type **9**: 30, 50c. Oceanographic Museum; 60c., 1, 2f. The Rock; 5, 10f. Prince's Palace, Monaco.

12 Prince Louis

13 Prince Louis and Palace

1923

65	**12**	10c. green	40	50
66	**12**	15c. red	60	1·00
67	**12**	20c. brown	40	50
68	**12**	25c. purple	20	30
69	**13**	50c. blue	40	50

1924. Surch with new value and bars.

70	**2**	45c. on 50c. brown on orange	60	1·00
71	**2**	75c. on 1f. black on yellow	60	1·00
72	**2**	85c. on 5f. green	60	1·00

14

15

16

17 St. Devote Viaduct

1924

73	**14**	1c. grey	10	20
74	**14**	2c. brown	10	20
75	**14**	3c. mauve	3·50	3·00
76	**14**	5c. orange	30	40
77	**14**	10c. blue	20	20
78	**15**	15c. green	20	20
79	**15**	15c. violet	4·00	2·30
80	**15**	20c. mauve	20	20
81	**15**	20c. pink	40	30
82	**15**	25c. pink	20	20
83	**15**	25c. red on yellow	20	20
84	**15**	30c. orange	20	20
85	**15**	40c. brown	20	20
86	**15**	40c. blue on blue	20	30
87	**15**	45c. black	1·30	90
88	**16**	50c. green	20	30
89	**15**	50c. brown on yellow	20	20
90	**16**	60c. brown	20	30
91	**15**	60c. green on green	20	30
92	**15**	75c. green on green	90	50
93	**15**	75c. red on yellow	30	20
94	**15**	75c. black	1·10	70
95	**15**	80c. red on yellow	50	30
96	**15**	90c. red on yellow	2·50	2·00
97	**17**	1f. black on yellow	30	50
98	**17**	1f.05 mauve	50	1·00
99	**17**	1f.10 green	15·00	7·50
100	**15**	1f.25 blue on blue	30	30
101	**15**	1f.50 blue on blue	4·75	3·00
102	-	2f. brown and mauve	2·50	1·50
103	-	3f. lilac and red on yellow	30·00	16·00
104	-	5f. red and green	10·00	8·00
105	-	10f. blue and brown	30·00	22·00

DESIGN—As Type **17**: 2f. to 10f. Monaco.

1926. Surch.

106	**15**	30c. on 25c. pink	35	40
107	**15**	50c. on 60c. green on green	1·80	50
108	**17**	50c. on 1f.05 mauve	1·30	80
109	**17**	50c. on 1f.10 green	16·00	11·00
110	**15**	50c. on 1f.25 blue on blue	1·80	80
111	**15**	1f.25 on 1f. blue on blue	1·00	70
112	-	1f.50 on 2f. brown and mauve (No. 102)	8·00	7·50

20 Prince Charles III, Louis II and Albert I

1928. International Philatelic Exn, Monte Carlo.

113	**20**	50c. red	3·00	6·00
114	**20**	1f.50 blue	3·00	6·00
115	**20**	3f. violet	3·00	6·00

20a

21 Palace Entrance

22 St. Devote's Church

23 Prince Louis II

1933

116	**20a**	1c. plum	20	30
117	**20a**	2c. green	20	30
118	**20a**	3c. purple	20	30
119	**20a**	5c. red	20	30
120	**20a**	10c. blue	20	30
121	**20a**	15c. violet	2·40	2·30
122	**21**	15c. red	1·00	30
123	**21**	20c. brown	1·00	30
124	**A**	25c. sepia	1·20	60
125	**22**	30c. green	1·50	60
126	**23**	40c. sepia	4·00	3·50
127	**B**	45c. brown	4·50	2·50
128	**23**	50c. violet	4·00	2·00
129	**C**	65c. green	4·50	1·40
130	**D**	75c. blue	5·00	2·50
131	**23**	90c. red	12·00	4·50
132	**22**	1f. brown	35·00	10·00
133	**D**	1f.25 red	8·50	6·00
134	**23**	1f.50 blue	50·00	15·00
135	**A**	1f.75 claret	45·00	14·00
136	**A**	1f.75 carmine	31·00	16·00
137	**B**	2f. blue	18·00	6·00
138	**21**	3f. violet	27·00	12·00
139	**A**	3f.50 orange	60·00	50·00
140	**22**	5f. purple	37·00	30·00
141	**A**	10f. blue	£150	£100
142	**C**	20f. black	£200	£180

DESIGNS—HORIZ (as Type **21**): A, The Prince's Residence; B, The Rock of Monaco; C, Palace Gardens; D, Fortifications and Harbour.

For other stamps in Type **20a** see Nos. 249, etc.

1933. Air. Surch with Bleriot XI airplane and 1f50.

143	1f.50 on 5f. red & grn (No. 104)	35·00	35·00

28 Palace Gardens

1937. Charity.

144	**28**	50c.+50c. green	5·00	4·00
145	-	90c.+90c. red	5·00	4·00
146	-	1f.50+1f.50 blue	10·00	8·00
147	-	2f.+2f. violet	15·00	14·00
148	-	5f.+5f. red	£140	£150

DESIGNS—HORIZ: 90c. Exotic gardens; 1f.50, The Bay of Monaco. VERT: 2, 5f. Prince Louis II.

1937. Postage Due stamps optd **POSTES** or surch also.

149	**D18**	5 on 10c. violet	1·50	1·50
150	**D18**	10c. violet	1·50	1·50
151	**D18**	15 on 30c. bistre	1·50	1·50
152	**D18**	20 on 30c. bistre	1·50	1·50
153	**D18**	25 on 60c. red	2·30	2·50
154	**D18**	30c. bistre	3·00	3·50
155	**D18**	40 on 60c. red	2·75	3·00
156	**D18**	50 on 60c. red	3·00	5·00
157	**D18**	65 on 1f. blue	2·75	2·50
158	**D18**	85 on 1f. blue	6·50	6·25
159	**D18**	1f. blue	10·50	10·00
160	**D18**	2f.15 on 2f. red	10·50	15·00
161	**D18**	2f.25 on 2f. red	25·00	26·00
162	**D18**	2f.50 on 2f. red	35·00	35·00

30a Prince Louis II

1938. National Fete Day. Sheet 100×120 mm.

MS163 **30a**	10f. purple	£100	£130

31

1938

164	**31**	55c. brown	8·50	3·50
165	**31**	65c. violet	33·00	30·00
166	**31**	70c. brown	30	40
167	**31**	90c. violet	40	50
168	**31**	1f. red	20·00	12·50
169	**31**	1f.25 red	40	50
170	**31**	1f.75 blue	20·00	12·00
171	**31**	2f.25 blue	40	50

33 Monaco Hospital

1938. Anti-cancer Fund. 40th Anniv of Discovery of Radium.

172	-	65c.+25c. green	15·00	15·00
173	**33**	1f.75+50c. blue	17·00	20·00

DESIGN—VERT: 65c. Pierre and Marie Curie.

34 The Cathedral

38 Monaco Harbour

1939

174	**34**	20c. mauve	20	50
175	-	25c. brown	70	50
176	-	30c. green	60	50
177	-	40c. red	1·20	70
178	-	45c. purple	90	70
179	-	50c. green	60	50
180	-	60c. red	70	50
181	-	60c. green	2·00	1·20
182	**38**	70c. lilac	60	50
183	**38**	75c. green	60	50
184	-	1f. black	60	50
185	-	1f.30 brown	60	50
186	-	2f. purple	70	50
187	-	2f.50 red	30·00	30·00
188	-	2f.50 blue	2·50	2·10
189	**38**	3f. red	70	50
190	**34**	5f. blue	6·50	5·00
191	-	10f. green	1·80	2·00
192	-	20f. blue	1·80	2·00

DESIGNS—VERT: 25, 40c., 2f. Place St. Nicholas; 30, 60c., 20f. Palace Gateway; 50c., 1f., 1f.30, Palace of Monaco. HORIZ: 45c., 2f.50, 10f. Aerial view of Monaco.

40 Louis II Stadium

1939. Inauguration of Louis II Stadium, Monaco.

198	**40**	10f. green	£150	£150

41 Lucien

1939. National Relief. 16th–18th-century portrait designs and view.

199	**41**	5c.+5c. black	3·00	3·00
200	-	10c.+10c. purple	3·00	3·00
201	-	45c.+15c. green	9·00	9·00
202	-	70c.+30c. mauve	14·00	15·00
203	-	90c.+35c. violet	14·00	15·00
204	-	1f.+1f. blue	30·00	32·00
205	-	2f.+2f. red	39·00	35·00
206	-	2f.25+1f.25 blue	50·00	45·00
207	-	3f.+3f. red	55·00	65·00
208	-	5f.+5f. red	£100	£130

DESIGNS—VERT: 10c. Honore II; 45c. Louis I; 70c. Charlotte de Gramont; 90c. Antoine I; 1f. Marie de Lorraine; 2f. Jacques I; 2f.25, Louise-Hippolyte; 3f. Honore III. HORIZ: 5f. The Rock of Monaco.

1939. Eighth International University Games. As T **40** but inscr "VIIIeme JEUX UNIVERSITAIRES INTERNATIONAUX 1939".

209	40c. green	1·50	1·50
210	70c. brown	3·75	2·00
211	90c. violet	2·75	2·75
212	1f.25 red	4·00	4·50
213	2f.25 blue	5·50	6·00

1940. Red Cross Ambulance Fund. As Nos. 174/92 in new colours surch with Red Cross and premium.

214	**34**	20c.+1f. violet	4·50	5·00
215	-	25c.+1f. green	4·50	5·00
216	-	30c.+1f. red	4·50	5·00
217	-	40c.+1f. blue	4·50	5·00
218	-	45c.+1f. red	4·50	5·00
219	-	50c.+1f. brown	4·50	5·00
220	-	60c.+1f. green	5·00	6·00
221	**38**	75c.+1f. black	5·00	6·00
222	-	1f.+1f. red	5·50	7·00
223	-	2f.+1f. slate	5·50	7·00
224	-	2f.50+1f. green	17·00	17·00
225	**38**	3f.+1f. blue	17·00	17·00
226	**34**	5f.+1f. black	25·00	25·00
227	-	10f.+5f. blue	40·00	45·00
228	-	20f.+5f. purple	40·00	45·00

44 Prince Louis II

1941

229	**44**	40c. red	50	70
230	**44**	80c. green	50	70
231	**44**	1f. violet	20	30
232	**44**	1f.20 green	20	30
233	**44**	1f.50 red	20	30
234	**44**	1f.50 violet	20	30
235	**44**	2f. green	80	60
236	**44**	2f.40 red	25	30
237	**44**	2f.50 blue	70	1·20
238	**44**	4f. blue	20	30

45

46

1941. National Relief Fund.

239	**45**	25c.+25c. purple	2·20	2·20
240	**46**	50c.+25c. brown	2·20	2·20
241	**46**	75c.+50c. purple	3·25	3·25
242	**45**	1f.+1f. blue	3·25	3·25
243	**46**	1f.50+1f.50 red	4·50	4·50
244	**45**	2f.+2f. green	4·50	4·50
245	**46**	2f.50+2f. blue	6·50	6·50
246	**45**	3f.+3f. brown	7·50	7·50
247	**46**	5f.+5f. green	10·00	10·00
248	**45**	10f.+8f. sepia	16·00	16·00

1941. New values and colours.

249	**20a**	10c. black	20	30
250	-	30c. red (as No. 176)	50	30
251	**20a**	30c. green	20	30
252	**20a**	40c. red	20	30
253	**20a**	50c. violet	20	30
362	**34**	50c. brown	40	30
254	**20a**	60c. blue	20	30
363	-	60c. pink (as No. 175)	40	30
255	**20a**	70c. brown	20	30
256	**34**	80c. green	20	30
257	-	1f. brown (as Nos. 178)	20	30
258	**38**	1f.20 blue	60	40
259	-	1f.50 blue (as Nos. 175)	80	35
260	**38**	2f. blue	20	30
261	-	2f. green (as No. 179)	90	40
262	-	3f. black (as No. 175)	30	30
364	-	3f. purple (as No. 176)	1·40	30
391	-	3f. green (as No. 175)	4·00	1·00
263	**34**	4f. purple	3·00	1·00
365	-	4f. green (as No. 175)	1·30	30
264	-	4f.50 violet (as No. 179)	20	30
265	-	5f. green (as No. 176)	20	30
392	-	5f. green (as No. 178)	1·00	50
393	-	5f. red (as No. 176)	1·50	1·50
266	-	6f. violet (as No. 179)	2·00	1·00
368	-	8f. brown (as No. 179)	3·50	1·60
267	**34**	10f. blue	40	50
370	-	10f. brown (as No. 179)	5·50	2·30
394	**38**	10f. yellow	2·00	80
268	**38**	15f. red	40	50
269	-	20f. brown (as No. 178)	40	50
373	-	20f. red (as No. 178)	2·00	80
270	**38**	25f. green	3·50	1·80
374	**38**	25f. black	36·00	20·00
397	-	25f. blue (as No. 176)	60·00	20·00
398	-	25f. red (as No. 179)	5·00	1·00
399	-	30f. blue (as No. 176)	13·00	5·00
400	-	35f. blue (as No. 179)	12·50	7·00
401	**34**	40f. red	10·50	7·50
402	**34**	50f. violet	6·50	1·50
403	-	65f. violet (as No. 178)	15·00	11·00
404	**34**	70f. yellow	12·00	10·00
405	-	75f. green (as No. 175)	30·00	12·00
406	-	85f. red (as No. 175)	20·00	10·00
407	-	100f. turquoise (as No. 178)	20·00	10·00

47 Caudron C-530 Rafale over Monaco

48 Propeller and Palace

49 Arms, Airplane and Globe

1942. Air.

271	**47**	5f. green	10	40
272	**47**	10f. blue	20	40
273	**48**	15f. brown	50	90
274	-	20f. brown	70	1·30
275	-	50f. purple	3·50	5·00
276	**49**	100f. red and purple	4·00	5·00

DESIGNS—VERT: 20f. Pegasus. HORIZ: 50f. Mew gull over Bay of Monaco.

50 Charles II

1942. National Relief Fund. Royal Personages.

277	-	2c.+3c. blue	30	50
278	**50**	5c.+5c. red	30	50
279	-	10c.+5c. black	30	50
280	-	20c.+10c. green	30	50
281	-	30c.+30c. purple	30	50
282	-	40c.+40c. red	30	50
283	-	50c.+50c. violet	30	50
284	-	75c.+75c. purple	30	50
285	-	1f.+1f. green	30	50
286	-	1f.50+1f. red	30	50
287	-	2f.50+2f.50 violet	3·50	6·00
288	-	3f.+3f. blue	3·50	6·00
289	-	5f.+5f. sepia	4·00	8·00
290	-	10f.+5f. purple	4·50	9·00
291	-	20f.+5f. blue	5·50	10·00

PORTRAITS: 2c. Rainier Grimaldi; 10c. Jeanne Grimaldi; 20c. Charles Auguste, Goyon de Matignon; 30c. Jacques I; 40c. Louise-Hippolyte; 50c. Charlotte Grimaldi; 75c. Marie Charles Grimaldi; 1f. Honore III; 1f.50, Honore IV; 2f.50, Honore V; 3f. Florestan I; 5f. Charles III; 10f. Albert I; 20f. Princess Marie-Victoire.

52 Prince Louis II

1943

292	**52**	50f. violet	1·10	1·60

53 St. Devote

54 Blessing the Sea

55 Arrival of St. Devote at Monaco

1944. Charity. Festival of St. Devote.

293	**53**	50c.+50c. brown	10	30
294	-	70c.+80c. blue	10	30
295	-	80c.+70c. green	10	30
296	-	1f.+1f. purple	10	30
297	-	1f.50+1f.50 red	50	50
298	**54**	2f.+2f. purple	80	80
299	-	5f.+2f. violet	80	80
300	-	10f.+40f. blue	80	80
301	**55**	20f.+60f. blue	4·00	6·00

DESIGNS—VERT: 70c., 1f. Various processional scenes; 1f.50, Burning the boat; 10f. Trial scene. HORIZ: 80c. Procession; 5f. St. Devote's Church.

1945. Air. For War Dead and Deported Workers. As Nos. 272/6 (colours changed) surch.

302	1f.+4f. on 10f. red	80	60
303	1f.+4f. on 15f. brown	80	60
304	1f.+4f. on 20f. brown	80	60
305	1f.+4f. on 50f. blue	80	60
306	1f.+4f. on 100f. purple	80	60

57 Prince Louis II

58 Prince Louis II

1946

361	**57**	30c. black	20	30
389	**57**	50c. olive	20	20
390	**57**	1f. violet	20	20
307	**57**	2f.50 green	80	40
308	**57**	3f. mauve	60	40
366	**57**	5f. brown	50	40
309	**57**	6f. red	60	40
367	**57**	6f. purple	5·75	3·25
310	**57**	10f. blue	60	40
369	**57**	10f. orange	50	30
371	**57**	12f. red	6·75	4·00
395	**57**	12f. slate	9·50	8·50
396	**57**	15f. lake	9·50	7·50
372	**57**	18f. blue	11·00	9·00
311	**58**	50f. grey	4·50	3·00
312	**58**	100f. red	6·25	4·00

59 Child Praying

1946. Child Welfare Fund.

313	**59**	1f.+3f. green	40	40
314	**59**	2f.+4f. red	40	40
315	**59**	4f.+6f. blue	40	40
316	**59**	5f.+40f. mauve	1·50	1·20
317	**59**	10f.+60f. red	1·50	1·20
318	**59**	15f.+100f. blue	2·10	1·70

60 Nurse and Baby

1946. Anti-tuberculosis Fund.

319	**60**	2f.+8f. blue	90	90

1946. Air. Optd **POSTE AERIENNE** over Sud Ouest SO.95 Corse II airplane.

320	**58**	50f. grey	6·00	5·50
321	**58**	100f. red	6·00	5·50

62 Steamship and Chart

1946. Stamp Day.

322	**62**	3f.+2f. blue	60	60

63

1946. Air.

323	**63**	40f. red	1·50	1·30
324	**63**	50f. brown	2·50	2·30
325	**63**	100f. green	3·75	3·00
326	**63**	200f. violet	4·25	5·00
326a	**63**	300f. blue and ultramarine	95·00	95·00
326b	**63**	500f. green and deep green	60·00	60·00
326c	**63**	1000f. violet and brown	£100	90·00

64 Pres. Roosevelt and Palace of Monaco

66 Pres. Roosevelt

1946. President Roosevelt Commemoration.

327	**66**	10c. mauve (postage)	60	50
328	-	30c. blue	60	50
329	**64**	60c. green	60	50
330	-	1f. sepia	1·50	1·50
331	-	2f.+3f. green	1·10	1·10
332	-	3f. violet	2·50	2·00
333	-	5f. red (air)	90	90
334	-	10f. black	1·10	90
335	**66**	15f.+10f. orange	3·00	2·20

DESIGNS—HORIZ: 30c., 5f. Rock of Monaco; 2f. Viaduct and St. Devote. VERT: 1, 3, 10f. Map of Monaco.

67 Prince Louis II

1947. Participation in the Centenary International Philatelic Exhibition, New York. (a) Postage.

336	**67**	10f. blue	5·00	5·00

68 Pres. Roosevelt as a Philatelist

69 Statue of Liberty, New York Harbour and Sud Ouest SO.95 Corse II

(b) Air. Dated "1847 1947".

337	**68**	50c. violet	1·50	1·50
338	-	1f.50 mauve	50	70
339	-	3f. orange	50	70
340	-	10f. blue	5·00	5·00
341	**69**	15f. red	9·50	9·50

DESIGNS—HORIZ: As Type **68**: 1f.50, G.P.O., New York; 3f. Oceanographic Museum, Monte Carlo. As Type **69**: 10f. Bay of Monaco and Sud Ouest SO.95 Corse II.

1947. Twenty-fifth Year of Reign of Prince Louis II. Sheet 85×98 mm.

MS341a 200f.+300f. brown	50·00	35·00

70 Prince Charles III

1948. Stamp Day.

342	**70**	6f.+4f. green on blue	50	50

71 Diving

72 Tennis

1948. Olympic Games, Wembley. Inscr "JEUX OLYMPIQUES 1948".

343	-	50c. green (postage)	20	30
344	-	1f. red	30	40
345	-	2f. blue	1·50	1·00
346	-	2f.50 red	4·50	3·25
347	**71**	4f. slate	5·00	4·00
348	-	5f.+5f. brown (air)	15·00	13·00
349	-	6f.+9f. violet	20·00	18·00
350	**72**	10f.+15f. red	30·00	25·00
351	-	15f.+25f. blue	40·00	35·00

DESIGNS—HORIZ: 50c. Hurdling; 15f. Yachting. VERT: 1f. Running; 2f. Throwing the discus; 2f.50, Basketball; 5f. Rowing; 6f. Skiing.

75 The Salmacis Nymph

77 F. J. Bosio (wrongly inscr "J. F.")

1948. Death Centenary of Francois Joseph Bosio (sculptor).

352	**75**	50c. green (postage)	80	50
353	-	1f. red	90	50
354	-	2f. blue	2·30	1·50
355	-	2f.50 violet	5·50	3·00
356	**77**	4f. mauve	4·50	3·00
357	-	5f.+5f. blue (air)	28·00	24·00
358	-	6f.+9f. green	28·00	24·00
359	-	10f.+15f. red	28·00	24·00
360	-	15f.+25f. brown	33·00	28·00

DESIGNS—VERT: 1, 5f. Hercules struggling with Achelous; 2, 6f. Aristaeus (Garden God); 15f. The Salmacis Nymph (36×48 mm). HORIZ: 2f.50, 10f. Hyacinthus awaiting his turn to throw a quoit.

79 Exotic Gardens

80 *Princess Alice II*

1949. Birth Centenary of Prince Albert I.

375		2f. blue (postage)	20	30
376	**79**	3f. green	20	20
377	-	4f. brown and blue	30	20
378	**80**	5f. red	1·00	1·00
379	-	6f. violet	1·20	1·00
380	-	10f. sepia	1·50	1·50
381	-	12f. pink	3·50	2·75
382	-	18f. orange and brown	5·00	4·25
383	-	20f. brown (air)	1·00	1·20
384	-	25f. blue	1·00	1·20
385	-	40f. green	2·30	2·30
386	-	50f. green, brown and black	3·25	3·25
387	-	100f. red	12·00	8·00
388	-	200f. orange	20·00	15·00

DESIGNS—HORIZ: 2f. Yacht *Hirondelle I* (1870); 4f. Oceanographic Museum, Monaco; 10f. *Hirondelle II* (1914); 12f. Albert harpooning whale; 18f. Buffalo (Palaeolithic mural); 20f. Constitution Day, 1911; 25f. Paris Institute of Palaeontology; 200f. Coin with effigy of Albert. VERT: 6f. Statue of Albert at tiller; 40f. Anthropological Museum; 50f. Prince Albert I; 100f. Oceanographic Institute, Paris.

82a Princess Charlotte

1949. Red Cross Fund. Sheet 150×172½ mm, containing vert portraits as T **82a**.

MS408 10f.+5f. brown and red; 40f.+5f. green and red; 15f.+5f. red and 25f.+5f. blue and red. Each ×4	£500	£600
MS409 As **MS**408 but imperf	£500	£600

DESIGNS: 10, 40f. T **82a**; 15, 25f, Prince Rainier.

83 Palace of Monaco and Globe

1949. 75th Anniv of U.P.U.

410	**83**	5f. green (postage)	60	80
411	**83**	10f. orange	8·75	7·00
412	**83**	15f. red	80	70
413	**83**	25f. blue (air)	90	80
414	**83**	40f. sepia and brown	3·50	3·25
415	**83**	50f. blue and green	4·50	4·75
416	**83**	100f. blue and red	8·00	7·50

84 Prince Rainier III and Monaco Palace

1950. Accession of Prince Rainier III.

417	**84**	10c. purple & red (postage)	10	20
418	**84**	50c. brown, lt brn & orge	10	20
419	**84**	1f. violet	50	30
420	**84**	5f. deep green and green	4·25	2·50
421	**84**	15f. carmine and red	7·00	6·00
422	**84**	25f. blue, green & ultram	7·00	6·00
423	**84**	50f. brown and black (air)	10·00	8·00
424	**84**	100f. blue, dp brn & brn	15·00	13·00

85 Prince Rainier III

1950

425	**85**	50c. violet	20	20
426	**85**	1f. brown	20	20
434	**85**	5f. green	16·00	6·00
427	**85**	6f. green	2·50	1·00
428	**85**	8f. green	11·00	3·00
429	**85**	8f. orange	2·50	1·00
435	**85**	10f. orange	27·00	10·50
430	**85**	12f. blue	3·00	50
431	**85**	15f. red	5·00	80
432	**85**	15f. blue	3·00	50
433	**85**	18f. red	10·00	4·00

86 Prince Albert I

1951. Unveiling of Prince Albert Statue.

436	**86**	15f. blue	14·00	8·00

87 Edmond and Jules de Goncourt

1951. 50th Anniv of Goncourt Academy.

437	**87**	15f. purple	14·00	8·00

88 St. Vincent de Paul

89 Judgement of St. Devote

90 St. Peter's Keys and Papal Bull

1951. Holy Year.

438	**88**	10c. blue, ultramarine & red	20	30
439	-	50c. violet and red	20	30
440	**89**	1f. green and brown	20	30
441	**90**	2f. red and purple	30	50
442	-	5f. green	40	50
443	-	12f. violet	60	70
444	-	15f. red	6·75	6·50
445	-	20f. brown	10·50	9·00
446	-	25f. blue	13·00	12·00
447	-	40f. violet and mauve	15·00	14·00
448	-	50f. brown and olive	18·00	15·00
449	-	100f. brown	40·00	35·00

DESIGNS—TRIANGULAR: 50c. Pope Pius XII. HORIZ (as Type **90**): 5f. Mosaic. VERT (as Type **90**): 12f. Prince Rainier III in St. Peter's; 15f. St. Nicholas of Patara; 20f. St. Romain; 25f. St. Charles Borromeo; 40f. Coliseum; 50f. Chapel of St. Devote. VERT (as Type **89**): 100f. Rainier of Westphalia.

93 Wireless Mast and Monaco

1951. Monte Carlo Radio Station.

450	**93**	1f. orange, red and blue	1·00	60
451	**93**	15f. purple, red and violet	5·00	2·00
452	**93**	30f. brown and blue	30·00	10·00

94 Seal of Prince Rainier III

1951

453	**94**	1f. violet	1·00	70
454	**94**	5f. black	5·00	3·25
512	**94**	5f. violet	5·00	2·00
513	**94**	6f. red	9·00	3·50
455	**94**	8f. red	10·00	5·25
514	**94**	8f. brown	9·50	5·00
456	**94**	15f. green	20·00	10·00
515	**94**	15f. blue	22·00	8·50
457	**94**	30f. blue	30·00	25·00
516	**94**	30f. green	35·00	25·00

1951. Nos. **MS**408/9 surch **1f. on 10f.+5f., 3f. on 15f.+5f., 5f. on 25f. + 5f., 6f. on 40f.+5f.**

MS458 As above	£550	£600
MS459 As above imperf	£550	£600

95 Gallery of Hercules

1952. Monaco Postal Museum.

460	**95**	5f. chestnut and brown	2·50	90
461	**95**	15f. violet and purple	3·25	1·00
462	**95**	30f. indigo and blue	4·50	1·40

96 Football

1953. 15th Olympic Games, Helsinki. Inscr "HELSINKI 1952".

463	-	1f. mauve & violet (postage)	20	30
464	**96**	2f. blue and green	20	30
465	-	3f. pale and deep blue	20	30
466	-	5f. green and brown	1·20	50
467	-	8f. red and lake	3·00	2·00
468	-	15f. brown, green and blue	1·50	1·20
469	-	40f. black (air)	15·00	13·00
470	-	50f. violet	20·00	13·00
471	-	100f. green	25·00	20·00
472	-	200f. red	35·00	25·00

DESIGNS: 1f. Basketball; 3f. Sailing; 5f. Cycling; 8f. Gymnastics; 15f. Louis II Stadium, Monaco; 40f. Running; 50f. Fencing; 100f. Rifle target and Arms of Monaco; 200f. Olympic torch.

97 "Journal Inedit"

1953. Centenary of Publication of Journal by E. and J. de Goncourt.

473	**97**	5f. green	1·00	50
474	**97**	15f. brown	5·00	1·30

98 Physalia, Yacht *Princess Alice*, Prince Albert, Richet and Portier

1953. 50th Anniv of Discovery of Anaphylaxis.

475	**98**	2f. violet, green and brown	40	10
476	**98**	5f. red, lake and green	1·20	70
477	**98**	15f. lilac, blue and green	4·50	3·00

99 F. Ozanam

1954. Death Centenary of Ozanam (founder of St. Vincent de Paul Conferences).

478	**99**	1f. red	30	30
479	-	5f. blue	70	70
480	**99**	15f. black	2·50	2·50

DESIGN: 5f. Outline drawing of Sister of Charity.

100 St. Jean-Baptiste de la Salle

1954. St. J.-B. de la Salle (educationist).

481	**100**	1f. red	30	30
482	-	5f. sepia	70	70
483	**100**	15f. blue	2·50	2·50

DESIGN: 5f. Outline drawing of De la Salle and two children.

101 **102** **103**

1954. Arms.

484	-	50c. red, black and mauve	10	20
485	-	70c. red, black and blue	10	20
486	**101**	80c. red, black and green	10	20
487	-	1f. red, black and blue	20	20
488	**102**	2f. red, black and orange	20	20
489	-	3f. red, black and green	20	20
490	**103**	5f. multicoloured	50	50

DESIGNS—HORIZ: 50c. as Type **101**. VERT: 70c., 1, 3f. as Type **102**.

104 Seal of Prince Rainier III

1954. Precancelled.

491	**104**	4f. red	2·00	1·00
492	**104**	5f. blue	50	40
493	**104**	8f. green	2·00	1·10
494	**104**	8f. purple	1·00	70
495	**104**	10f. green	50	40
496	**104**	12f. violet	7·00	2·75
497	**104**	15f. orange	1·50	1·00
498	**104**	20f. green	2·00	1·30
499	**104**	24f. brown	12·00	6·50
500	**104**	30f. blue	2·00	1·50
501	**104**	40f. brown	4·00	2·50
502	**104**	45f. red	3·00	2·30
503	**104**	55f. blue	9·00	4·50

See also Nos. 680/3.

105 Lambarene **106** Dr. Albert Schweitzer

1955. 80th Birthday of Dr. Schweitzer (humanitarian).

504	**105**	2f. grn, turq & bl (postage)	50	40
505	**106**	5f. blue and green	1·70	1·70
506	-	15f. purple, black and green	4·50	3·50
507	-	200f. slate, grn & bl (air)	60·00	45·00

DESIGNS—As Type **106**: 15f. Lambarene Hospital. HORIZ (48×27 mm): 200f. Schweitzer and jungle scene.

107 Great Cormorants

1955. Air.

508		100f. indigo and blue	35·00	17·00
509		200f. black and blue	36·00	18·00
510		500f. grey and green	60·00	40·00
511a	**107**	1,000f. black, turq & grn	£130	85·00

DESIGNS—As Type **107**: 100f. Roseate tern; 200f. Herring gull; 500f. Wandering albatrosses.

108 Eight Starting Points

1955. 25th Monte Carlo Car Rally.

517	**108**	100f. red and brown	£110	80·00

109 Prince Rainier III

1955

518	**109**	6f. purple and green	1·00	50
519	**109**	8f. violet and red	1·00	50
520	**109**	12f. green and red	1·00	50
521	**109**	15f. blue and purple	1·90	50
522	**109**	18f. blue and orange	7·00	90
523	**109**	20f. turquoise	3·75	1·00
524	**109**	25f. black and orange	1·50	80
525	**109**	30f. black and blue	21·00	9·00
526	**109**	30f. violet	6·50	3·00
527	**109**	35f. brown	6·00	3·75
528	**109**	50f. lake and green	9·00	4·00

See also Nos. 627/41.

110 "La Maison a Vapeur" **111** "The 500 Millions of the Begum"

113 U.S.S. *Nautilus*

112 "Round the World in Eighty Days"

1955. 50th Death Anniv of Jules Verne (author). Designs illustrating his works.

529	-	1f. blue & brown (postage)	10	20
530	-	2f. sepia, indigo and blue	10	20
531	**110**	3f. blue, black and brown	10	20
532	-	5f. sepia and red	20	30
533	**111**	6f. grey and sepia	60	50
534	-	8f. turquoise and olive	60	60
535	-	10f. sepia, turquoise & ind	1·60	1·20
536	**112**	15f. red and brown	1·20	1·00
537	-	25f. black and green	3·25	2·20
538	**113**	30f. black, purple & turq	8·00	7·00
539	-	200f. indigo and blue (air)	40·00	35·00

DESIGNS—VERT (as Type **111**): 1f. "Five Weeks in a Balloon". HORIZ (as Type **110**): 2f. "A Floating Island"; 10f. "Journey to the Centre of the Earth"; 25f. "20,000 Leagues under the Sea"; 200f. "From the Earth to the Moon". (as Type **111**): 5f. "Michael Strogoff"; 8f. "Le Superbe Orenoque".

114 "The Immaculate Virgin" (F. Brea)

1955. Marian Year.

540	**114**	5f. green, grey and brown	20	30
541	-	10f. green, grey and brown	30	40
542	-	15f. brown and sepia	1·00	1·00

DESIGNS—As Type **114**: 10f. "Madonna" (L. Brea). As Type **113**: 15f. Bienheureux Rainier.

115 Rotary Emblem

1955. 50th Anniv of Rotary International.

543	**115**	30f. blue and yellow	2·00	2·00

116 George Washington **118** President Eisenhower

117 Abraham Lincoln

1956. Fifth International Stamp Exhibition, New York.

544	**116**	1f. violet and lilac	10	20
545	-	2f. lilac and purple	10	20
546	**117**	3f. blue and violet	10	20
547	**118**	5f. red	20	30
548	-	15f. brown and chocolate	1·00	80
549	-	30f. black, indigo and blue	5·25	4·00
550	-	40f. brown	7·75	5·00
551	-	50f. red	7·75	5·00
552	-	100f. green	7·75	5·00

DESIGNS—As Type **117**: 2f. F. D. Roosevelt. HORIZ (as Type **116**): 15f. Monaco Palace in the 18th century; 30f. Landing of Columbus. (48×36 mm): 50f. Aerial view of Monaco Palace in the 18th century; 100f. Louisiana landscape in 18th century. VERT (as Type **118**): 40f. Prince Rainier III.

120

1956. Seventh Winter Olympic Games, Cortina d'Ampezzo and 16th Olympic Games, Melbourne.

553		15f. brown, green & pur	1·50	1·00
554	**120**	30f. red	3·50	2·20

DESIGN: 15f. "Italia" ski-jump.

1956. Nos. D482/95 with "TIMBRE TAXE" barred out and some surch also. (a) Postage.

555	2f. on 4f. slate and brown	60	60
556	2f. on 4f. brown and slate	60	60
557	3f. lake and green	60	60
558	3f. green and lake	60	60
559	5f. on 4f. slate and brown	1·00	1·00
560	5f. on 4f. brown and slate	1·00	1·00
561	10f. on 4f. slate and brown	1·80	1·80
562	10f. on 4f. brown and slate	1·80	1·80
563	15f. on 5f. violet and blue	2·50	2·50
564	15f. on 5f. blue and violet	2·50	2·50
565	20f. violet and blue	4·00	4·00
566	20f. blue and violet	4·00	4·00
567	25f. on 20f. violet and blue	6·50	6·50
568	25f. on 20f. blue and violet	6·50	6·50
569	30f. on 10f. indigo and blue	12·00	12·00
570	30f. on 10f. blue and indigo	12·00	12·00
571	40f. on 50f. brown and red	15·00	15·00
572	40f. on 50f. red and brown	15·00	15·00
573	50f. on 100f. green and purple	20·00	20·00
574	50f. on 100f. purple and green	20·00	20·00

(b) Air. Optd **POSTE AERIENNE** also.

575	100f. on 20f. violet and blue	14·00	14·00
576	100f. on 20f. blue and violet	14·00	14·00

121 Route Map from Glasgow

1956. 26th Monte Carlo Car Rally.

577	**121**	100f. brown and red	35·00	32·00

122 Princess Grace and Prince Rainier III

1956. Royal Wedding.

578	**122**	1f. black & grn (postage)	10	20
579	**122**	2f. black and red	25	30
580	**122**	3f. black and blue	45	50
581	**122**	5f. black and green	1·10	1·00
582	**122**	15f. black and brown	2·00	1·50
583	**122**	100f. brown & purple (air)	1·50	1·50
584	**122**	200f. brown and red	2·50	2·50
585	**122**	500f. brown and grey	5·00	5·00

123 Princess Grace

1957. Birth of Princess Caroline.

586	**123**	1f. grey	10	20
587	**123**	2f. olive	10	20
588	**123**	3f. brown	10	20
589	**123**	5f. red	30	30
590	**123**	15f. pink	30	30
591	**123**	25f. blue	1·20	1·00
592	**123**	30f. violet	1·30	1·00
593	**123**	50f. red	2·50	1·20
594	**123**	75f. orange	4·00	3·25

124 Princess Grace with Princess Caroline

1958. Birth of Prince Albert.
| 595 | 124 | 100f. black | 12·00 | 8·00 |

125 Order of St. Charles

1958. Centenary of Creation of National Order of St. Charles.
| 596 | 125 | 100f. multicoloured | 4·00 | 3·00 |

126 Route Map from Munich

1958. 27th Monte Carlo Rally.
| 597 | 126 | 100f. multicoloured | 10·00 | 10·00 |

127 Statue of the Holy Virgin and Popes Pius IX and Pius XII

1958. Centenary of Apparition of Virgin Mary at Lourdes.
598	127	1f. grey & brown (postage)	10	20
599	-	2f. violet and blue	10	20
600	-	3f. sepia and green	10	20
601	-	5f. blue and sepia	10	20
602	-	8f. multicoloured	30	20
603	-	10f. multicoloured	30	30
604	-	12f. multicoloured	50	40
605	-	20f. myrtle and purple	60	50
606	-	35f. myrtle, bistre and brown	70	60
607	-	50f. blue, green and lake	1·20	1·00
608	-	65f. turquoise and blue	1·60	1·50
609	-	100f. grey, myrtle and blue (air)	2·50	2·00
610	-	200f. brown and chestnut	3·50	3·00

DESIGNS—VERT (26½×36 mm): 2f. St. Bernadette; 3f. St. Bernadette at Bartres; 5f. The Miracle of Bourriette; 20f. St. Bernadette at prayer; 35f. St. Bernadette's canonization. (22×36 mm): 8f. Stained-glass window. As Type **127**: 50f. St. Bernadette, Pope Pius XI, Mgr. Laurence and Abbe Peyramale. HORIZ (48×36 mm): 10f. Lourdes grotto; 12f. Interior of Lourdes grotto. (36×26½ mm): 65f. Shrine of St. Bernadette; (48×27 mm): 100f. Lourdes Basilica; 200f. Pope Pius X and subterranean interior of Basilica.

128 Princess Grace and Clinic

1959. Opening of new Hospital Block in "Princess Grace" Clinic, Monaco.
| 611 | 128 | 100f. grey, brown & green | 6·25 | 3·50 |

129 UNESCO Headquarters, Paris, and Cultural Emblems

1959. Inaug of UNESCO Headquarters Building.
| 612 | 129 | 25f. multicoloured | 25 | 30 |
| 613 | - | 50f. turquoise, black & ol | 40 | 50 |

DESIGN: 50f. As Type **129** but with heads of children and letters of various alphabets in place of the emblems.

130 Route Map from Athens

1959. 28th Monte Carlo Rally.
| 614 | 130 | 100f. blue, red & grn on bl | 10·00 | 8·00 |

131 Prince Rainier and Princess Grace

1959. Air.
| 615 | 131 | 300f. violet | 22·00 | 14·00 |
| 616 | 131 | 500f. blue | 30·00 | 25·00 |

See also Nos. 642/3.

132 "Princess Caroline" Carnation

1959. Flowers.
617	132	5f. mauve, green & brown	20	10
618	-	10f. on 3f. pink, green and brown	50	25
619	-	15f. on 1f. yellow & green	50	40
620	-	20f. purple and green	1·00	80
621	-	25f. on 6f. red, yellow and green	1·50	1·30
622	-	35f. pink and green	3·25	2·50
623	-	50f. green and sepia	4·75	3·25
624	-	85f. on 65f. lavender, bronze and green	5·00	4·00
625	-	100f. red and green	7·50	6·50

FLOWERS—As Type **132**: 10f. "Princess Grace" carnation; 100f. "Grace of Monaco" rose. VERT (22×36 mm): 15f. Mimosa; 25f. Geranium. HORIZ (36×22 mm): 20f. Bougainvillea; 35f. "Laurier" rose; 50f. Jasmine; 85f. Lavender.

133 "Uprooted Tree"

1960. World Refugee Year.
| 626 | 133 | 25c. green, blue and black | 40 | 30 |

1960. Prince Rainier types with values in new currency.
627	109	25c. blk & orge (postage)	80	20
628	109	30c. violet	80	20
629	109	40c. red and brown	1·00	40
630	109	45c. brown and grey	1·00	40
631	109	50c. red and green	3·75	60
632	109	50c. red and brown	1·00	60
633	109	60c. brown and green	2·50	1·10
634	109	60c. brown and purple	3·50	2·00
635	109	65c. blue and brown	22·00	7·00
636	109	70c. blue and plum	2·00	1·00
637	109	85c. green and violet	3·00	2·20
638	109	95c. blue	1·00	1·20
639	109	1f.10 blue and brown	4·00	3·00
640	109	1f.30 brown and red	3·00	2·50
641	109	2f.30 purple and orange	4·00	1·70
642	131	3f. violet (air)	60·00	27·00
643	131	5f. blue	60·00	35·00

134 Oceanographic Museum

1960
644	-	5c. green, black and blue	10	20
645	134	10c. brown and blue	70	40
646	-	10c. blue, violet and green	70	30
647	-	40c. purple, grn & dp grn	1·00	50
648	-	45c. brown, green and blue	9·00	1·10
649	-	70c. brown, red and green	1·00	70
650	-	80c. red, green and blue	2·50	1·00
651	-	85c. black, brown and grey	13·50	4·50
652	-	90c. red, blue and black	4·00	2·00
653	-	1f. multicoloured	2·00	60
654	-	1f.15 black, red and blue	4·00	2·75
655	-	1f.30 brown, green & blue	1·50	1·00
656	-	1f.40 orange, green & vio	4·50	3·50

DESIGNS—HORIZ: 5c. Palace of Monaco; 10c. (No. 646), Aquatic Stadium; 40, 45, 80c., 1f.40, Aerial view of Palace; 70, 85, 90c., 1f.15, 1f.30, Court of Honour, Monaco Palace; 1f. Palace floodlit.

134a St. Devote

1960. Air.
668	134a	2f. violet, blue and green	2·00	1·50
669	134a	3f. brown, green and blue	3·00	2·00
670	134a	5f. red	5·50	4·00
671	134a	10f. brown, grey and green	9·00	6·00

135 Long-snouted Seahorse

1960. Marine Life and Plants. (a) Marine Life.
672	-	1c. red and turquoise	20	20
673	-	12c. brown and blue	30	20
674	135	15c. green and red	70	50
675	-	20c. multicoloured	90	50

DESIGNS—HORIZ: 1c. "Macrocheira kampferi" (crab); 20c. Lionfish. VERT: 12c. Trapezium horse conch.

(b) Plants.
676	-	2c. multicoloured	20	20
677	-	15c. orange, brown and olive	70	50
678	-	18c. multicoloured	70	30
679	-	20c. red, olive and brown	90	50

PLANTS—VERT: 2c. "Selenicereus sp."; 15c. "Cereus sp."; 18c. "Aloe ciliaris"; 20c. "Nopalea dejecta".

1960. Prince Rainier Seal type with values in new currency. Precancelled.
680	104	8c. purple	2·00	1·40
681	104	20c. green	3·00	2·00
682	104	40c. brown	4·50	2·50
683	104	55c. blue	8·50	4·00

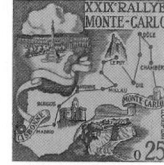

136 Route Map from Lisbon

1960. 29th Monte Carlo Rally.
| 684 | 136 | 25c. black, red & bl on bl | 4·00 | 3·00 |

137 Stamps of Monaco 1885, France and Sardinia, 1860

1960. 75th Anniv of First Monaco Stamp.
| 685 | 137 | 25c. bistre, blue and violet | 1·10 | 80 |

138 Aquarium

1960. 50th Anniv of Oceanographic Museum, Monaco.
686	-	5c. black, blue and purple	70	40
687	138	10c. grey, brown and green	80	45
688	-	15c. black, bistre and blue	80	50
689	-	20c. black, blue and mauve	1·50	80
690	-	25c. turquoise	3·00	2·00
691	-	50c. brown and blue	3·75	2·00

DESIGNS—VERT: 5c. Oceanographic Museum (similar to Type **134**). HORIZ: 15c. Conference Hall; 20c. Hauling-in catch; 25c. Museum, aquarium and underwater research equipment; 50c. Prince Albert, "Hirondelle I" (schooner) and "Princess Alice" (steam yacht).

139 Horse-jumping

1960. Olympic Games.
692	139	5c. brown, red and green	20	20
693	-	10c. brown, blue and green	30	30
694	-	15c. red, brown and purple	50	50
695	-	20c. black, blue and green	4·00	4·00
696	-	25c. purple, turq & grn	1·00	1·00
697	-	50c. purple, blue & turq	1·50	1·50

DESIGNS: 10c. Swimming; 15c. Long-jumping; 20c. Throwing the javelin; 25c. Free-skating; 50c. Skiing.

140 Rally Badge, Old and Modern Cars

1961. 50th Anniv of Monte Carlo Rally.
| 698 | 140 | 1f. violet, red and brown | 2·50 | 2·50 |

141 Route Map from Stockholm

1961. 30th Monte Carlo Rally.

699	**141**	1f. multicoloured	2·00	2·00

142 Marine Life

1961. World Aquariological Congress. Orange network background.

700	**142**	25c. red, sepia and violet	30	30

143 Leper in Town of Middle Ages

1961. Sovereign Order of Malta.

701	**143**	25c. black, red and brown	30	30

144 Semi-submerged Sphinx of Ouadi-es-Saboua

1961. UNESCO Campaign for Preservation of Nubian Monuments.

702	**144**	50c. purple, blue & brown	1·40	1·20

145 Insect within Protective Hand

1962. Nature Preservation.

703	**145**	25c. mauve and purple	50	40

146 Chevrolet, 1912

1961. Veteran Motor Cars.

704	**146**	1c. brown, green and chestnut	10	20
705	-	2c. blue, purple and red	10	20
706	-	3c. purple, black and mauve	10	20
707	-	4c. blue, brown and violet	10	20
708	-	5c. green, red and olive	10	20
709	-	10c. brown, red and blue	10	20
710	-	15c. green and turquoise	20	30
711	-	20c. brown, red and violet	30	50
712	-	25c. violet, red and brown	50	50
713	-	30c. lilac and green	1·70	1·50
714	-	45c. green, purple and brown	3·00	3·00
715	-	50c. blue, red and brown	3·50	3·50
716	-	65c. brown, red and grey	4·50	4·00
717	-	1f. blue, red and violet	6·00	5·00

MOTOR CARS: 2c. Peugeot, 1898; 3c. Fiat, 1901; 4c. Mercedes, 1901; 5c. Rolls Royce, 1903;. 10c. Panhard-Lavassor, 1899; 15c. Renault, 1898; 20c. Ford "N", 1906 (wrongly inscr "FORD-S-1908"); 25c. Rochet-Schneider, 1894; 30c. FN-Herstal, 1901; 45c. De Dion Bouton, 1900; 50c. Buick, 1910; 65c. Delahaye, 1901; 1f. Cadillac, 1906.

147 Racing Car and Race Route

1962. 20th Monaco Motor Grand Prix.

718	**147**	1f. purple	2·50	2·20

148 Route Map from Oslo

1962. 31st Monte Carlo Rally.

719	**148**	1f. multicoloured	1·80	1·80

149 Louis XII and Lucien Grimaldi

1962. 450th Anniv of Recognition of Monegasque Sovereignty by Louis XII.

720	**149**	25c. black, red and blue	30	30
721	-	50c. brown, lake and blue	70	60
722	-	1f. red, green and brown	1·00	80

DESIGNS: 50c. Parchment bearing declaration of sovereignty; 1f. Seals of two Sovereigns.

150 Mosquito and Swamp

1962. Malaria Eradication.

723	**150**	1f. green and olive	70	70

151 Sun, Bouquet and "Hope Chest"

1962. National Multiple Sclerosis Society, New York.

724	**151**	20c. multicoloured	30	30

152 Harvest Scene

1962. Europa.

725	**152**	25c. brown, green and blue (postage)	1·00	50
726	**152**	50c. olive and turquoise	1·00	60
727	**152**	1f. olive and purple	1·50	1·00
728	-	2f. slate, brown & green (air)	2·00	2·00

DESIGN: 2f. Mercury in flight over Europe.

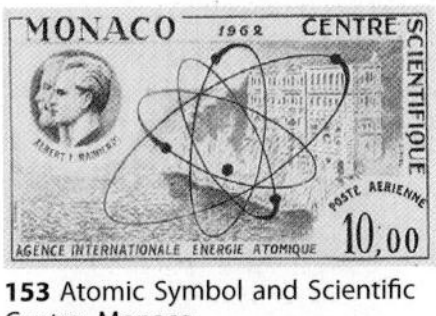

153 Atomic Symbol and Scientific Centre, Monaco

1962. Air. Scientific Centre, Monaco.

729	**153**	10f. violet, brown and blue	6·50	6·00

154 Yellow Wagtails

1962. Protection of Birds useful to Agriculture.

730	**154**	5c. yellow, brown & green	20	25
731	-	10c. red, bistre and purple	20	25
732	-	15c. multicoloured	30	30
733	-	20c. sepia, green & mauve	50	60
734	-	25c. multicoloured	80	80
735	-	30c. brown, blue & myrtle	1·10	90
736	-	45c. brown and violet	2·00	1·60
737	-	50c. black, olive & turq	3·00	2·20
738	-	85c. multicoloured	4·00	2·50
739	-	1f. sepia, red and green	4·50	3·25

BIRDS: 10c. European robins; 15c. Eurasian goldfinches; 20c. Blackcaps; 25c. Greater spotted woodpeckers; 30c. Nightingale; 45c. Barn owls; 50c. Common starlings; 85c. Red crossbills; 1f. White storks.

155 Galeazzi's Diving Turret

1962. Underwater Exploration.

740		5c. black, violet and blue	10	10
741	**155**	10c. blue, violet and brown	20	20
742	-	25c. bistre, green and blue	30	30
743	-	45c. black, blue and green	50	50
744	-	50c. green, bistre and blue	70	70
745	-	85c. blue and turquoise	1·50	1·40
746	-	1f. brown, green and blue	2·50	1·70

DESIGNS—HORIZ: 5c. Divers; 25c. Williamson's photosphere (1914) and bathyscaphe "Trieste"; 45c. Klingert's diving-suit (1797) and modern diving-suit; 50c. Diving saucer; 85c. Fulton's "Nautilus" (1800) and modern submarine; 1f. Alexander the Great's diving bell and Beebe's bathysphere.

156 Donor's Arm and Globe

1962. 3rd Int Blood Donors' Congress Monaco.

747	**156**	1f. red, sepia and orange	1·00	1·00

157 "Ring-a-ring o' Roses"

158 Feeding Chicks in Nest

1963. U.N. Children's Charter.

748	**157**	5c. red, blue and ochre	20	20
749	**158**	10c. green, sepia and blue	20	20
750	-	15c. blue, red and green	20	30
751	-	20c. multicoloured	20	30
752	-	25c. blue, purple & brown	30	30
753	-	50c. multicoloured	80	60
754	-	95c. multicoloured	2·00	1·00
755	-	1f. purple, red & turquoise	2·50	2·00

DESIGNS—As Type **157**: 1f. Prince Albert and Princess Caroline; Children's paintings as Type **158**: HORIZ: 15c. Children on scales; 50c. House and child. VERT: 20c. Sun's rays and children of three races; 25c. Mother and child; 95c. Negress and child.

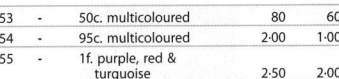

159 Ship's Figurehead

1963. International Red Cross Centenary.

756	**159**	50c. red, brown & turquoise	50	60
757	-	1f. multicoloured	1·00	1·00

DESIGN—HORIZ: 1f. Moynier, Dunant and Dufour.

160 Racing Cars

1963. European Motor Grand Prix.

758	**160**	50c. multicoloured	80	70

161 Emblem and Charter

1963. Founding of Lions Club of Monaco.

759	**161**	50c. blue, bistre and violet	80	80

162 Hotel des Postes and U.P.U. Monument, Berne

1963. Paris Postal Conference Centenary.

760	**162**	50c. lake, green and yellow	60	60

163 "Telstar" Satellite and Globe

1963. First Link Trans-Atlantic T.V. Satellite.

761	**163**	50c. brown, green & purple	80	80

164 Route Map from Warsaw

1963. 32nd Monte Carlo Rally.

762	**164**	1f. multicoloured	1·50	1·50

165 Feeding Chicks

1963. Freedom from Hunger.

763	**165**	1f. multicoloured	80	80

166 Allegory

1963. Second Ecumenical Council, Vatican City.

764	**166**	1f. turquoise, green and red	80	80

167 Henry Ford and Ford "A" Car of 1903

1963. Birth Centenary of Henry Ford (motor pioneer).

765	**167**	20c. green and purple	40	40

168 H. Garin (winner of 1903 race) cycling through Village

1963. 50th "Tour de France" Cycle Race.

766	**168**	25c. green, brown and blue	50	50
767	-	50c. sepia, green and blue	70	70

DESIGN: 50c. Cyclist passing Desgrange Monument, Col du Galibier, 1963.

169 P. de Coubertin and Discus-thrower

1963. Birth Centenary of Pierre de Coubertin (reviver of Olympic Games).

768	**169**	1f. brown, red and lake	1·00	1·00

170 Roland Garros and Morane Saulnier Type I

1963. Air. 50th Anniv of First Aerial Crossing of Mediterranean Sea.

769	**170**	2f. sepia and blue	1·50	1·00

171 Route Map from Paris

1963. 33rd Monte Carlo Rally.

770	**171**	1f. red, turquoise and blue	1·50	1·50

172 Children with Stamp Album

1963. "Scolatex" International Stamp Exn, Monaco.

771	**172**	50c. blue, violet and red	40	40

173 "Europa"

1963. Europa.

772	**173**	25c. brown, red and green	1·00	50
773	**173**	50c. sepia, red and blue	1·80	1·00

174 Wembley Stadium

1963. Cent of (English) Football Association.

774	**174**	1c. violet, green and red	10	10
775	-	2c. red, black and green	10	10
776	-	3c. orange, olive and red	10	10
777	-	4c. multicoloured	10	10

Multicoloured horiz designs depicting (a) "Football through the Centuries".

778	10c. "Calcio", Florence (16th cent)	10	10
779	15c. "Soule", Brittany (19th cent)	10	10
780	20c. English military college (after Cruickshank, 1827)	20	20
781	25c. English game (after Overend, 1890)	20	20

(b) "Modern Football".

782	30c. Tackling	40	40
783	50c. Saving goal	80	80
784	95c. Heading ball	1·40	1·40
785	1f. Corner kick	1·90	1·70

DESIGNS—As Type **174**: 4c. Louis II Stadium, Monaco. This stamp is optd in commemoration of the Association Sportive de Monaco football teams in the French Championships and in the Coupe de France, 1962–63. HORIZ (36×22 mm): 2c. Footballer making return kick; 3c. Goalkeeper saving ball.

Nos. 778/81 and 782/5 were respectively issued together in sheets and arranged in blocks of 4 with a football in the centre of each block.

175 Communications in Ancient Egypt, and Rocket

1964. PHILATEC 1964 Int Stamp Exn, Paris.

786	**175**	1f. brown, indigo and blue	70	70

176 Reproduction of Rally Postcard Design and Deperdussin Monocoque Racer

1964. 50th Anniv of First Aerial Rally, Monte Carlo.

787	**176**	1c. olive, blue & grn (postage)	10	20
788	-	2c. bistre, brown and blue	10	20
789	-	3c. brown, blue and green	10	20
790	-	4c. red, turquoise and blue	10	20
791	-	5c. brown, red and violet	10	20
792	-	10c. violet, brown and blue	20	20
793	-	15c. orange, brown and blue	30	30
794	-	20c. sepia, green and blue	35	35
795	-	25c. brown, blue and red	40	40
796	-	30c. myrtle, purple and blue	60	60
797	-	45c. sepia, turquoise and brown	1·00	90
798	-	50c. ochre, olive and violet	1·10	1·00
799	-	65c. red, slate and turquoise	2·00	1·50
800	-	95c. turquoise, red and bistre	2·50	2·20
801	-	1f. brown, blue and turquoise	3·50	2·75
802	-	5f. sepia, blue and brown (air)	5·00	7·00

DESIGNS: 48×27 mm—Rally planes: 2c. Renaux's Farman M.F.7 floatplane; 3c. Espanet's Nieuport 4 seaplane; 4c. Moineau's Breguet HU-3 seaplane; 5c. Roland Garros' Morane Saulnier Type I seaplane; 10c. Hirth's WDD Albatros seaplane; 15c. Prevost's Deperdussin Monocoque Racer. Famous planes and flights: 20c. Vickers-Vimy G-EAOU (Ross Smith: London–Port Darwin, 1919); 25c. Douglas World Cruiser seaplane (U.S. World Flight, 1924); 30c. Savoia Marchetti S-55M flying boat "Santa Maria" (De Pinedo's World Flight, 1925); 45c. Fokker F. VIIa/3m "Josephine Ford" (Flight over North Pole, Byrd and Bennett, 1925); 50c. Ryan NYP Special "Spirit of St. Louis" (1st solo crossing of N. Atlantic, Lindbergh, 1927); 65c. Breguet 19 Super Bidon TR "Point d'Interrogation" (Paris–New York, Coste and Bellonte, 1930); 95c. Latecoere 28-3 seaplane F-AJNQ "Comte de la Vaulx" (Dakar–Natal, first S. Atlantic airmail flight, Mermoz, 1930); 1f. Dornier Do-X flying boat (Germany–Rio de Janeiro, Christiansen, 1930); 5f. Convair B-58 Hustler (New York–Paris in 3 hours, 19′41′ Major Payne, U.S.A.F., 1961).

177 Aquatic Stadium

1964. Precancelled.

803	**177**	10c. multicoloured	2·50	2·00
803a	**177**	15c. multicoloured	1·00	1·00
804	**177**	25c. turquoise, blue & blk	1·00	1·00
805	**177**	50c. violet, turq & blk	2·00	2·00

The "1962" date has been obliterated with two bars. See also Nos. 949/51a and 1227/30.

178 Europa "Flower"

1964. Europa.

806	**178**	25c. red, green and blue	1·00	50
807	**178**	50c. brown, bistre and blue	2·00	1·50

179 Weightlifting

1964. Olympic Games, Tokyo and Innsbruck.

808	**179**	1c. red, brown and blue (postage)	10	10
809	-	2c. red, green and olive	10	10
810	-	3c. blue, brown and red	10	10
811	-	4c. green, olive and red	10	10
812	-	5f. red, brown and blue (air)	3·00	3·00

DESIGNS: 2c. Judo; 3c. Pole vaulting; 4c. Archery; 5f. Bobsleighing.

180 Pres. Kennedy and Space Capsule

1964. Pres. Kennedy Commemoration.

813	**180**	50c. indigo and blue	70	70

181 Monaco and Television Set

1964. Fifth Int Television Festival, Monte Carlo.

814	**181**	50c. brown, blue and red	60	60

182 F. Mistral and Statue

1964. 50th Death Anniv of Frederic Mistral (poet).

815	**182**	1f. brown and olive	70	70

183 Scales of Justice

1964. 15th Anniv of Declaration of Human Rights.

816	**183**	1f. green and brown	70	70

184 Route Map from Minsk

1964. 34th Monte Carlo Rally.

817	**184**	1f. brown, turq & ochre	1·70	1·70

185 FIFA Emblem

1964. 60th Anniv of Federation Internationale de Football Association (FIFA).

818	**185**	1f. bistre, blue and red	1·20	1·20

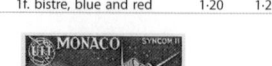

186 "Syncom 2" and Globe

1965. Centenary of I.T.U.

819	**186**	5c. grn & ultram (postage)	10	20
820	-	10c. chestnut, brown & bl	10	20
821	-	12c. purple, red and grey	10	20
822	-	18c. blue, red and purple	20	20
823	-	25c. violet, bistre & purple	30	30
824	-	30c. bistre, brown & sepia	35	35
825	-	50c. blue and green	40	40
826	-	60c. blue and brown	1·20	1·00
827	-	70c. sepia, orange and blue	1·30	1·10
828	-	95c. black, indigo and blue	1·60	1·30
829	-	1f. brown and blue	2·30	2·00
830	-	10f. green, bl & brn (air)	6·00	5·00

DESIGNS—HORIZ (as Type **186**): 10c. "Echo 2"; 18c. "Lunik 3"; 30c. A. G. Bell and telephone; 50c. S. Morse and telegraph; 60c. E. Belin and "belinograph". (48½×27 mm): 25c. "Telstar" and Pleumeur-Bodou Station; 70c. Roman beacon and Chappe's telegraph; 95c. Cable ships "Great Eastern" and "Alsace"; 1f. E. Branly, G. Marconi and English Channel. VERT (as Type **186**): 12c. "Relay"; 10f. Monte Carlo television transmitter.

187 Europa "Sprig"

1965. Europa.

831	**187**	30c. brown and green	2·50	1·00
832	**187**	60c. violet and red	3·50	1·50

188 Monaco Palace (18th cent)

1966. 750th Anniv of Monaco Palace.

833	**188**	10c. violet, green and blue	10	20
834	-	12c. bistre, blue and black	10	20

835	-	18c. green, black and blue	20	30
836	-	30c. brown, black and blue	30	30
837	-	60c. green, blue and bistre	1·00	1·00
838	-	1f.30 brown and green	2·00	1·90

DESIGNS (Different views of Palace): 12c. 17th century; 18c. 18th century; 30c. 19th century; 60c. 19th century; 1f.30, 20th century.

189 Dante

1966. 700th Anniv of Dante's Birth.

839	189	30c. green, deep green and red	40	40
840	-	60c. blue, turquoise & grn	70	70
841	-	70c. black, green and red	80	80
842	-	95c. blue, violet and purple	1·00	1·00
843	-	1f. turquoise, blue & dp bl	1·30	1·30

DESIGNS (Scenes from Dante's works): 60c. Dante harassed by the panther (envy); 70c. Crossing the 5th circle; 95c. Punishment of the arrogant; 1f. Invocation of St. Bernard.

190 "The Nativity"

1966. World Association of Children's Friends (A.M.A.D.E.).

844	190	30c. brown	35	35

191 Route Map from London

1966. 35th Monte Carlo Rally.

845	191	1f. blue, purple and red	1·70	1·70

192 Princess Grace with Children

1966. Air. Princess Stephanie's 1st Birthday.

846	192	3f. brown, blue and violet	2·75	2·20

193 Casino in 19th Century

1966. Centenary of Monte Carlo.

847	-	12c. black, red and blue (postage)	10	10
848	193	25c. multicoloured	15	20
849	-	30c. multicoloured	20	20
850	-	40c. multicoloured	20	35
851	-	60c. multicoloured	55	55
852	-	70c. blue and lake	55	55
853	-	95c. black and purple	1·50	1·50
854	-	1f.30 purple, brown and chestnut	1·70	1·70
855	-	5f. lake, ochre and blue (air)	3·25	3·25

DESIGNS—VERT: 12c. Prince Charles III. HORIZ (as Type 143): 40c. Charles III Monument; 95c. Massenet and Saint-Saens; 1f.30, Faure and Ravel. (48×27 mm): 30c. F. Blanc, originator of Monte Carlo, and view of 1860; 60c. Prince Rainier III and projected esplanade; 70c. Rene Blum and Diaghilev, ballet character from "Petrouchka". (36×36 mm): 5f. Interior of Opera House, 1879.

194 Europa "Ship"

1966. Europa.

856	194	30c. orange	1·10	55
857	194	60c. green	2·20	1·70

195 Prince Rainier and Princess Grace

1966. Air.

858	195	2f. slate and red	1·70	1·10
859	195	3f. slate and green	3·25	2·00
860	195	5f. slate and blue	4·50	2·40
860a	195	10f. slate and bistre	7·75	4·50
860b	195	20f. brown and orange	70·00	50·00

196 Prince Albert I and Yachts "Hirondelle I" and "Princess Alice"

1966. 1st International Oceanographic History Congress, Monaco.

861	196	1f. lilac and blue	1·10	1·10

197 "Learning to Write"

1966. 20th Anniv of UNESCO.

862	197	30c. purple and mauve	20	20
863	197	60c. brown and blue	45	45

198 T.V. Screen, Cross and Monaco Harbour

1966. 10th Meeting of International Catholic Television Association (U.N.D.A.), Monaco.

864	198	60c. red, purple & crimson	45	35

199 "Precontinent III"

1966. 1st Anniv of Underwater Research Craft "Precontinent III".

865	199	1f. yellow, brown and blue	75	55

200 W.H.O. Building

1966. Inaug of W.H.O. Headquarters, Geneva.

866	200	30c. brown, green and blue	20	20

867	200	60c. brown, red and green	45	45

201 Bugatti, 1931

1967. 25th Motor Grand Prix, Monaco. Multicoloured. (a) Postage.

868		1c. Type **201**	10	20
869		2c. Alfa-Romeo, 1932	10	20
870		5c. Mercedes, 1936	10	20
871		10c. Maserati, 1948	10	20
872		18c. Ferrari, 1955	90	55
873		20c. Alfa-Romeo, 1950	20	20
874		25c. Maserati, 1957	35	35
875		30c. Cooper-Climax, 1958	55	35
876		40c. Lotus-Climax, 1960	90	65
877		50c. Lotus-Climax, 1961	1·10	90
878		60c. Cooper-Climax, 1962	1·70	1·20
879		70c. B.R.M., 1963–6	2·20	1·90
880		1f. Walter Christie, 1907	2·75	2·20
881		2f.30 Peugeot, 1910	4·50	3·50

(b) Air. Diamond. 50×50 mm.

882		3f. black and blue	3·75	3·75

DESIGN: 3f. Panhard-Phenix, 1895.

202 Dog (Egyptian bronze)

1967. Int Cynological Federation Congress, Monaco.

883	202	30c. black, purple & green	55	55

203 View of Monte Carlo

1967. International Tourist Year.

884	203	30c. brown, green and blue	55	55

204 Pieces on Chessboard

1967. Int Chess Grand Prix, Monaco.

885	204	60c. black, plum and blue	1·10	1·10

205 Melvin Jones (founder), Lions Emblem and Monte Carlo

1967. 50th Anniv of Lions International.

886	205	60c. blue, ultramarine and brown	75	75

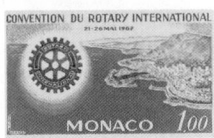

206 Rotary Emblem and Monte Carlo

1967. Rotary International Convention.

887	206	1f. bistre, blue and green	1·10	1·10

207 Fair Buildings

1967. World Fair, Montreal.

888	207	1f. red, slate and blue	75	75

208 Squiggle on Map of Europe

1967. European Migration Committee (C.I.M.E.).

889	208	1f. brown, bistre and blue	75	75

209 Cogwheels

1967. Europa.

890	209	30c. violet, purple and red	1·10	55
891	209	60c. green, turq & emer	2·20	1·10

210 Dredger and Coastal Chart

1967. 9th Int Hydrographic Congress, Monaco.

892	210	1f. brown, blue and green	75	75

211 Marie Curie and Scientific Equipment

1967. Birth Centenary of Marie Curie.

893	211	1f. blue, olive and brown	75	75

212 Skiing

1967. Winter Olympic Games, Grenoble.

894	212	2f.30 brown, blue & slate	2·10	1·70

213 "Prince Rainier I" (E. Charpentier)

1967. Paintings. "Princes and Princesses of Monaco". Multicoloured.

895		1f. Type **213**	90	90
896		1f. "Lucien Grimaldi" (A. di Predis)	90	90

See also Nos. 932/3, 958/9, 1005/6, 1023/4, 1070/1, 1108/9, 1213/14, 1271/2, 1325, 1380/1, 1405/6, 1460/1 and 1531/2.

214 Putting the Shot

1968. Olympic Games, Mexico.

897	214	20c. blue, brown and green (postage)	20	20
898	-	30c. brown, blue and plum	35	35
899	-	60c. blue, purple and red	45	45
900	-	70c. red, blue and ochre	55	55
901	-	1f. blue, brown and orange	90	90
902	-	2f.30 olive, blue and lake	2·30	2·30
903	-	3f. violet, blue & grn (air)	1·70	1·70

DESIGNS: 30c. High-jumping; 60c. Gymnastics; 70c. Water-polo; 1f. Greco-Roman wrestling; 2f.30, Gymnastics (different); 3f. Hockey.

215 "St. Martin"

1968. 20th Anniv of Monaco Red Cross.

904	215	2f.30 blue and brown	1·70	1·40

216 "Anemones" (after Raoul Dufy)

1968. Monte Carlo Floral Exhibitions.

905	216	1f. multicoloured	1·30	1·10

217 Insignia of Prince Charles III and Pope Pius IX

1968. Centenary of "Nullius Diocesis" Abbey.

906	217	10c. brown and red	10	20
907	-	20c. red, green and brown	20	20
908	-	30c. brown and blue	35	35
909	-	60c. brown, blue and green	45	45
910	-	1f. indigo, bistre and blue	75	75

DESIGNS—VERT: 20c. "St. Nicholas" (after Louis Brea); 30c. "St. Benedict" (after Simone Martini); 60c. Subiaco Abbey. HORIZ: 1f. Old St. Nicholas' Church (on site of present cathedral).

218 Europa "Key"

1968. Europa.

911	218	30c. red and orange	1·70	1·10
912	218	60c. blue and red	2·75	1·70
913	218	1f. brown and green	3·75	2·75

219 First Locomotive on Monaco Line, 1868

1968. Centenary of Nice–Monaco Railway.

914	219	20c. black, blue and purple	90	55
915	-	30c. black, blue and olive	1·10	90
916	-	60c. black, blue and ochre	1·90	1·70
917	-	70c. black, violet & brown	3·25	2·40
918	-	1f. black, blue and red	5·00	3·75
919	-	2f.30 blue, black and red	7·25	5·50

DESIGNS: 30c. Class 220-C steam locomotive, 1898; 60c. Class 230-C steam locomotive, 1910; 70c. Class 231-F steam locomotive, 1925; 1f. Class 241-A steam locomotive, 1932; 2f.30, Class BB 25200 electric locomotive, 1968.

220 Chateaubriand and Combourg Castle

1968. Birth Centenary of Chateaubriand (novelist).

920	220	10c. plum, green & myrtle	10	10
921	-	20c. violet, purple and blue	10	10
922	-	25c. brown, violet and blue	20	20
923	-	30c. violet, choc & brn	30	35
924	-	60c. brown, green and red	50	55
925	-	2f.30 brown, mauve & bl	2·10	1·90

Scenes from Chateaubriand's novels: 20c. "Le Genie du Christianisme"; 25c. "Rene"; 30c. "Le Dernier Abencerage"; 60c. "Les Martyrs"; 2f.30, "Atala".

221 Law Courts, Paris, and statues–"La France et la Fidelite"

1968. Birth Centenary of J. F. Bosio (Monegasque sculptor).

926	221	20c. brown and purple	20	20
927	-	25c. brown and red	35	30
928	-	30c. blue and green	35	35
929	-	60c. green and myrtle	75	55
930	-	2f.30 black and slate	1·70	1·10

DESIGNS—VERT (26×36 mm): 25c. "Henry IV as a Child"; 30c. "J. F. Bosio (lithograph)"; 60c. "Louis XIV". HORIZ (as Type 221): 2f.30, "Napoleon I, Louis XVIII and Charles X".

222 W.H.O. Emblem

1968. 20th Anniv of W.H.O.

931	222	60c. multicoloured	35	35

1968. Paintings. "Princes and Princesses of Monaco". As T 213. Multicoloured.

932		1f. "Prince Charles II" (Mimault)	1·00	90
933		2f.30 "Princess Jeanne Grimaldi" (Mimault)	1·90	1·80

223 The Hungarian March

1969. Death Centenary of Hector Berlioz (composer).

934	223	10c. brown, violet and green (postage)	10	20
935	-	20c. brown, olive & mauve	10	20
936	-	25c. brown, blue & mauve	20	20
937	-	30c. black, green and blue	30	35
938	-	40c. red, black and slate	35	35
939	-	50c. brown, slate & purple	45	45
940	-	70c. brown, slate and green	50	50
941	-	1f. black, mauve & brown	55	55
942	-	1f.15 black, blue & turq	1·10	90
943	-	2f. black, blue & grn (air)	1·70	1·70

DESIGNS—HORIZ: 20c. Mephistopheles appears to Faust; 25c. Auerbach's tavern; 30c. Sylphs' ballet; 40c. Minuet of the goblins; 50c. Marguerite's bedroom; 70c. "Forests and caverns"; 1f. The journey to Hell; 1f.15, Heaven; All scenes from Berlioz's "The Damnation of Faust". VERT: 2f. Bust of Berlioz.

224 "St. Elisabeth of Hungary"

1969. Monaco Red Cross.

944	224	3f. blue, brown and red	2·20	2·20

225 "Napoleon I" (P. Delaroche)

1969. Birth Bicentenary of Napoleon Bonaparte.

945	225	3f. multicoloured	2·20	2·20

226 Colonnade

1969. Europa.

946	226	40c. red and purple	1·70	1·10
947	226	70c. blue, brown and black	3·25	2·20
948	226	1f. ochre, brown and blue	5·50	3·25

1969. Precancelled. As T 177. No date.

949		22c. brown, blue and black	55	55
949a		26c. violet, blue and black	55	55
949b		30c. multicoloured	55	55
950		35c. multicoloured	55	55
950a		45c. multicoloured	1·10	1·10
951		70c. black and blue	1·10	1·10
951a		90c. green, blue and black	2·20	2·20

227 "Head of Woman" (Da Vinci)

1969. 450th Death Anniv of Leonardo da Vinci.

952	227	30c. brown	35	35
953	-	40c. red and brown	45	35
954	-	70c. green	50	35
955	-	80c. sepia	55	55
956	-	1f.15 brown	1·20	90
957	-	3f. brown	2·75	2·30

DRAWINGS: 40c. Self-portrait; 70c. "Head of an Old Man"; 80c. "Head of St. Madeleine"; 1f.15, "Man's Head"; 3f. "The Condottiere".

1969. Paintings. "Princes and Princesses of Monaco". As T 213. Multicoloured.

958		1f. "Prince Honore II" (Champaigne)	1·10	90
959		3f. "Princess Louise-Hippolyte" (Champaigne)	2·00	1·80

228 Marine Fauna, King Alfonso XIII of Spain and Prince Albert I of Monaco

1969. 50th Anniv of Int Commission for Scientific Exploration of the Mediterranean, Madrid.

960	228	40c. blue and black	55	55

229 I.L.O. Emblem

1969. 50th Anniv of I.L.O.

961	229	40c. multicoloured	55	55

230 Aerial View of Monaco and T.V. Camera

1969. 10th International Television Festival.

962	230	40c. purple, lake and blue	55	55

231 J.C.C. Emblem

1969. 25th Anniv of Junior Chamber of Commerce.

963	231	40c. violet, bistre and blue	55	55

232 Alphonse Daudet and Scenes from "Lettres"

1969. Centenary of Daudet's "Lettres de Mon Moulin".

964	232	30c. lake, violet and green	20	35
965	-	40c. green, brown and green	35	45
966	-	70c. multicoloured	75	55
967	-	80c. violet, brown & green	90	65
968	-	1f.15 brown, orange & bl	1·10	1·10

DESIGNS (Scenes from the book): 40c. "Installation" (Daudet writing); 70c. "Mule, Goat and Wolf"; 80c. "Gaucher's Elixir" and "The Three Low Masses"; 1f.15, Daudet drinking, "The Old Man" and "The Country Sub-Prefect".

233 Conference Building, Albert I and Rainier III

1970. Interparliamentary Union's Spring Meeting, Monaco.

969	233	40c. black, red and purple	35	35

234 Baby Common Seal

1970. Protection of Baby Seals.

970	234	40c. drab, blue and purple	1·10	1·10

235 Japanese Print

1970. Expo 70.

971	**235**	20c. brown, green and red	20	20
972	–	30c. brown, buff and green	30	30
973	–	40c. bistre and violet	35	35
974	–	70c. grey and red	90	90
975	–	1f.15 red, green & purple	1·10	1·10

DESIGNS—VERT: 30c. Manchurian Cranes (birds); 40c. Shinto temple gateway. HORIZ: 70c. Cherry blossom; 1f.15, Monaco Palace and Osaka Castle.

236 Dobermann

1970. International Dog Show, Monte Carlo.

976	**236**	40c. black and brown	2·00	1·40

237 Apollo

1970. 20th Anniv of World Federation for Protection of Animals.

977	**237**	30c. black, red and blue	45	55
978	–	40c. brown, blue and green	90	65
979	–	50c. brown, ochre and blue	1·20	75
980	–	80c. brown, blue and green	2·75	2·20
981	–	1f. brown, bistre and slate	3·25	3·50
982	–	1f.15 brown, green & blue	4·50	3·75

DESIGNS—HORIZ: 40c. Basque ponies; 50c. Common seal. VERT: 80c. Chamois; 1f. White-tailed sea eagles; 1f.15, European otter.

238 "St. Louis" (King of France)

1970. Monaco Red Cross.

983	**238**	3f. green, brown and slate	2·20	2·75

See also Nos. 1022, 1041, 1114, 1189 and 1270.

239 "Roses and Anemones" (Van Gogh)

1970. Monte Carlo Flower Show.

984	**239**	3f. multicoloured	3·25	3·50

See also Nos. 1042 and 1073.

240 Moon Plaque, Presidents Kennedy and Nixon

1970. 1st Man on the Moon (1969). Multicoloured.

985		40c. Type **240**	65	75
986		80c. Astronauts on Moon	1·10	1·10

241 New U.P.U. Building and Monument

1970. New U.P.U. Headquarters Building.

987	**241**	40c. brown, black & green	35	35

242 "Flaming Sun"

1970. Europa.

988	**242**	40c. purple	1·70	1·10
989	**242**	80c. green	3·25	2·20
990	**242**	1f. blue	5·50	3·25

243 Camargue Horse

1970. Horses.

991	**243**	10c. slate, olive and blue (postage)	20	20
992	–	20c. brown, olive and blue	20	35
993	–	30c. brown, green and blue	75	90
994	–	40c. grey, brown and slate	1·90	1·30
995	–	50c. brown, olive and blue	2·75	1·70
996	–	70c. brown, orange & grn	4·25	3·25
997	–	85c. blue, green and olive	4·50	3·50
998	–	1f.15 black, green & blue	4·50	3·50
999	–	3f. multicoloured (air)	2·75	2·75

HORSES—HORIZ: 20c. Anglo-Arab; 30c. French saddle-horse; 40c. Lippizaner; 50c. Trotter; 70c. English thorough-bred; 85c. Arab; 1f.15, Barbary. DIAMOND (50×50 mm): 3f. Rock-drawings of horses in Lascaux grotto.

244 Dumas, D'Artagnan and the Three Musketeers

1970. Death Centenary of Alexandre Dumas (pere) (author).

1000	**244**	30c. slate, brown and blue	35	20

245 Henri Rougier and Voisin "Boxkite"

1970. 60th Anniv of First Mediterranean Flight.

1001	**245**	40c. brown, blue and slate	40	20

246 De Lamartine and scene from "Meditations Poetiques"

1970. 150th Anniv of "Meditations Poetiques" by Alphonse de Lamartine (writer).

1002	**246**	80c. brown, blue & turq	45	55

247 Beethoven

1970. Birth Bicentenary of Beethoven.

1003	**247**	1f.30 brown and red	3·25	2·20

1970. 50th Death Anniv of Modigliani. Vert Painting as T 213. Multicoloured.

1004		3f. "Portrait of Dedie"	4·50	3·25

1970. Paintings. "Princes and Princesses of Monaco". As T 213.

1005		1f. red and black	90	90
1006		3f. multicoloured	2·20	2·20

PORTRAITS: 1f. "Prince Louis I" (F. de Troy); 3f. "Princess Charlotte de Gramont" (S. Bourdon).

248 Cocker Spaniel

1971. International Dog Show, Monte Carlo.

1007	**248**	50c. multicoloured	3·75	3·00

See also Nos. 1036, 1082, 1119, 1218 and 1239.

249 Razorbill

1971. Campaign Against Pollution of the Sea.

1008	**249**	50c. indigo and blue	75	75

250 Hand holding Emblem

1971. 7th Int Blood Donors Federation Congress.

1009	**250**	80c. red, violet and grey	55	55

251 Sextant, Scroll and Underwater Scene

1971. 50th Anniv of Int Hydrographic Bureau.

1010	**251**	80c. brown, green & slate	75	75

252 Detail of Michelangelo Painting ("The Arts")

1971. 25th Anniv of UNESCO.

1011	**252**	30c. brown, blue & violet	20	35
1012	–	50c. blue and brown	20	35
1013	–	80c. brown and green	35	45
1014	–	1f.30 green	1·10	75

DESIGNS—VERT: 50c. Alchemist and dish aerial ("Sciences"); 1f.30, Prince Pierre of Monaco (National UNESCO Commission). HORIZ: 80c. Ancient scribe, book and T.V. screen ("Culture").

253 Europa Chain

1971. Europa.

1015	**253**	50c. red	2·20	1·70
1016	**253**	80c. blue	3·75	2·20
1017	**253**	1f.30 green	7·25	3·75

254 Old Bridge, Sospel

1971. Protection of Historic Monuments.

1018	**254**	50c. brown, blue & green	35	40
1019	–	80c. brown, green & grey	55	45
1020	–	1f.30 red, green & brown	90	90
1021	–	3f. slate, blue and olive	2·20	1·70

DESIGNS—HORIZ: 80c. Roquebrune Chateau; 1f.30, Grimaldi Chateau, Cagnes-sur-Mer. VERT: 3f. Roman "Trophy of the Alps", La Turbie.

1971. Monaco Red Cross. As T 238.

1022		3f. brown, olive and green	2·20	2·30

DESIGN: 3f. St. Vincent de Paul.

1972. Paintings. "Princes and Princesses of Monaco". As T 213. Multicoloured.

1023		1f. "Prince Antoine I" (Rigaud)	90	90
1024		3f. "Princess Marie de Lorraine" (18th-century French School)	1·80	2·20

255 La Fontaine and Animal Fables (350th)

1972. Birth Anniversaries (1971).

1025	**255**	50c. brown, emer & grn	90	55
1026	–	1f.30 purple, black & red	1·30	1·10

DESIGN: 1f.30, Baudelaire, nudes and cats (150th).

256 Saint-Saens and scene from Opera, "Samson and Delilah"

1972. 50th Death Anniv (1971) of Camile Saint-Saens.

1027	**256**	90c. brown and sepia	75	65

257 Battle Scene

1972. 400th Anniv (1971) of Battle of Lepanto.

1028	**257**	1f. blue, brown and red	65	55

258 "Christ before Pilate" (engraving by Durer)

1972. 500th Birth Anniv (1971) of Albrecht Durer.

1029	**258**	2f. black and brown	2·20	2·00

259 "The Cradle" (B. Morisot)

1972. 25th Anniv (1971) of UNICEF.
1030 **259** 2f. multicoloured   2·30   1·80

260 "Gilles" (Watteau)

1972. 250th Death Anniv (1971) of Watteau.
1031 **260** 3f. multicoloured   3·75   2·75

261 Santa Claus

1972. Christmas (1971).
1032 **261** 30c. red, blue and brown   20   35
1033 **261** 50c. red, green & orange   20   35
1034 **261** 90c. red, blue and brown   65   65

262 Class 743 Steam Locomotive, Italy, and TGV 001 Turbotrain, France

1972. 50th Anniv of International Railway Union.
1035 **262** 50c. purple, lilac and red 1·40   1·10

1972. Int Dog Show, Monte Carlo. As T 248.
1036   60c. multicoloured   3·75   2·75
DESIGN: 60c. Great Dane.

263 "Pollution Kills"

1972. Anti-pollution Campaign.
1037 **263** 90c. brown, green & black   1·00   65

264 Ski-jumping

1972. Winter Olympic Games, Sapporo, Japan.
1038 **264** 90c. black, red and green   1·00   75

1972. Europa.
1039 **265** 50c. blue and orange   3·75   1·70
1040 **265** 90c. blue and green   5·00   3·75

265 "Communications"

1972. Monaco Red Cross. As T 238.
1041   3f. brown and purple   2·00   2·20
DESIGN: 3f. St. Francis of Assisi.

1972. Monte Carlo Flower Show. As T 239.
1042   3f. multicoloured   6·00   4·50
DESIGN: 3f. "Vase of Flowers" (Cezanne).

266 "SS. Giovanni e Paolo" (detail, Canaletto)

1972. UNESCO "Save Venice" Campaign.
1043 **266** 30c. red   35   35
1044   60c. violet   65   65
1045   2f. blue   1·80   1·90
DESIGNS—27×48 mm: 60c. "S. Pietro di Castello" (F. Guradi). As Type **266**: 2f. "Piazetta S. Marco" (B. Bellotto).

267 Dressage

1972. Olympic Games, Munich. Equestrian Events.
1046 **267** 60c. brown, blue and lake 1·10   1·10
1047   90c. lake, brown and blue   1·40   1·40
1048   1f.10 blue, lake & brown   2·20   2·20
1049   1f.40 brown, lake & blue   3·50   3·50
DESIGNS: 90c. Cross country; 1f.10, Show jumping (wall); 1f.40, Show jumping (parallel bars).

268 Escoffier and Birthplace

1972. 125th Birth Anniv of Auguste Escoffier (master chef).
1050 **268** 45c. black and brown   45   55

269 Drug Addiction

1972. Campaign Against Drugs.
1051 **269** 50c. red, brown & orange 65   55
1052 **269** 90c. green, brown & blue 90   75
See also Nos. 1088/91 and 1280/1.

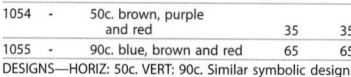

270 Globe, Birds and Animals

1972. 17th Int Congress of Zoology, Monaco.
1053 **270** 30c. green, brown and red 20   20

1054   50c. brown, purple and red 35   35
1055   90c. blue, brown and red   65   65
DESIGNS—HORIZ: 50c. VERT: 90c. Similar symbolic design.

271 Bouquet

1972. Monte Carlo Flower Show, 1973 (1st issue). Multicoloured.
1056   30c. Lilies in vase   1·10   55
1057   50c. Type **271**   1·40   1·10
1058   90c. Flowers in vase   2·75   2·00
See also Nos. 1073, 1105/7, 1143/4, 1225/6, 1244, 1282/3 and 1316/17.

272 "The Nativity" and Child's face

1972. Christmas.
1059 **272** 30c. grey, blue and purple 20   20
1060 **272** 50c. red, purple & brown   30   20
1061 **272** 90c. violet, plum & pur   65   65

273 Louis Bleriot and Bleriot XI (Birth cent)

1972. Birth Anniversaries.
1062 **273** 30c. blue and brown   20   35
1063   50c. blue, turq & new blue   1·40   1·20
1064   90c. brown and buff   1·10   1·10
DESIGNS AND ANNIVERSARIES: 50c. Amundsen and polar scene (birth centenary); 90c. Pasteur and laboratory scene (150th birth anniv).

274 "Gethsemane"

1972. Protection of Historical Monuments. Frescoes by J. Canavesio, Chapel of Notre-Dame des Fontaines, La Brigue.
1065 **274** 30c. red   20   20
1066   50c. grey   40   40
1067   90c. green   55   55
1068   1f.40 red   1·00   1·00
1069   2f. purple   1·70   1·70
DESIGNS: 50c. "Christ Outraged"; 90c. "Ascent to Calvary"; 1f.40, "The Resurrection"; 2f. "The Crucifixion".

1972. Paintings. "Princes and Princesses of Monaco". As T 213. Multicoloured.
1070   1f. "Prince Jacques 1" (N. Largilliere) 90   90
1071   3f. "Princess Louise-Hippolyte" (J. B. Vanloo) 2·00   2·20

275 "St. Devote" (triptych by Louis Brea)

1973. 25th Anniv of Monaco Red Cross. Sheet 100×130 mm.
MS1072 **275** 5f. red   23·00 23·00

1973. Monte Carlo Flower Show (2nd issue). As T 239.
1073   3f.50 multicoloured   7·75   6·00

DESIGN: 3f.50, "Bouquet of Flowers".

276 Europa "Posthorn"

1973. Europa.
1074 **276** 50c. orange   5·50   3·75
1075 **276** 90c. green   8·25   6·50

277 Moliere and Characters from "Le Malade Imaginaire"

1973. 300th Death Anniv of Moliere.
1076 **277** 20c. red, brown and blue 50   55

278 Colette, Cat and Books

1973. Birth Anniversaries.
1077 **278** 30c. black, blue and red 1·10   90
1078   45c. multicoloured   2·75   2·40
1079   50c. lilac, purple and blue 45   45
1080   90c. multicoloured   65   65
DESIGNS AND ANNIVERSARIES—HORIZ: 30c, Type **278** (nature writer, birth cent); 45c. J.-H. Fabre and insects (entomologists, 150th birth anniv); 90c. Sir George Cayley and his "convertiplane" (aviation pioneer, birth bicent). VERT: 50c. Blaise Pascal (philosopher and writer, 350th birth anniv).

279 E. Ducretet, "Les Invalides" and Eiffel Tower

1973. 75th Anniv of Eugene Ducretet's First Hertzian Radio Link.
1081 **279** 30c. purple and brown   35   35

1973. International Dog Show, Monte Carlo. As T 248. Inscr "1973". Multicoloured.
1082   45c. Alsatian   15·00 10·50

280 C. Peguy and Chartres Cathedral

1973. Birth Bicentenary of Charles Peguy (writer).
1083 **280** 50c. brown, mauve & grey 35   35

281 Telecommunications Equipment

1973. 5th World Telecommunications Day.
1084 **281** 60c. violet, blue & brown 45   45

282 Stage Characters

1973. 5th World Amateur Theatre Festival.

1085	**282**	60c. lilac, blue and red	55	55

283 Ellis and Rugby Tackle

1973. 150th Anniv of Founding of Rugby Football by William Webb Ellis.

1086	**283**	90c. red, lake and brown	65	75

284 St. Theresa

1973. Birth Centenary of St. Theresa of Lisieux.

1087	**284**	1f.40 multicoloured	75	90

285 Drug Addiction

1973. Campaign Against Drugs.

1088	**285**	50c. red, green and blue	35	35
1089	-	50c. multicoloured	35	35
1090	**285**	90c. violet, green and red	75	75
1091	-	90c. multicoloured	75	75

DESIGN: Nos. 1089, 1091, Children, syringes and addicts.

286 "Institution of the Creche" (Giotto)

1973. 750th Anniv of St. Francis of Assisi Creche.

1092	**286**	30c. purple (postage)	50	55
1093	-	45c. red	90	90
1094	-	50c. brown	1·30	1·10
1095	-	1f. green	2·40	1·80
1096	-	2f. brown	5·00	5·00
1097	-	3f. blue (air)	3·25	3·25

DESIGN—HORIZ: 45c. "The Nativity" (School of F. Lippi); 50c. "The Birth of Jesus Christ" (Giotto). VERT: 1f. "The Nativity" (15th-century miniature); 2f. "The Birth of Jesus" (Fra Angelico); 3f. "The Nativity" (Flemish school).

287 Country Picnic

1973. 50th Anniv of National Committee for Monegasque Traditions.

1098	**287**	10c. blue, green & brown	10	15
1099	-	20c. violet, blue and green	20	20
1100	-	30c. sepia, brown & green	35	35
1101	-	45c. red, violet and purple	75	75
1102	-	50c. black, red and brown	1·00	1·00
1103	-	60c. red, violet and blue	1·10	1·10
1104	-	1f. violet, blue and brown	2·00	2·00

DESIGNS—VERT: 20c. Maypole dance. HORIZ: 30c. "U Bradi" (local dance); 45c. St. Jean fire-dance; 50c. Blessing the Christmas loaf; 60c. Blessing the sea, Festival of St. Devote; 1f. Corpus Christi procession.

1973. Monte Carlo Flower Show, 1974. As T 271. Multicoloured.

1105	45c. Roses and Strelitzia	2·20	1·40
1106	60c. Mimosa and myosotis	2·75	1·90
1107	1f. "Vase of Flowers" (Odilon Redon)	5·50	3·25

1973. Paintings. "Princes and Princesses of Monaco". As T 213. Multicoloured.

1108	2f. "Charlotte Grimaldi" (in day dress, P. Gobert)	2·75	2·30
1109	2f. "Charlotte Grimaldi" (in evening dress, P. Gobert)	2·75	2·30

288 Prince Rainier

1974. 25th Anniv of Prince Rainer's Accession. Sheet 100×130 mm.

MS1110 **288**	10f. black	11·00	11·00

289 U.P.U. Emblem and Symbolic Heads

1974. Centenary of Universal Postal Union.

1111	**289**	50c. purple and brown	35	35
1112	-	70c. multicoloured	55	55
1113	-	1f.10 multicoloured	1·10	1·10

DESIGNS: 70c. Hands holding letters; 1f.10, "Countries of the World" (famous buildings).

1974. Monaco Red Cross. As T 238.

1114	3f. blue, green and purple	2·20	1·90

DESIGN: 3f. St. Bernard of Menthon.

290 Farman, Farman F.60 Goliath and Farman H.F.III

1974. Birth Centenary of Henry Farman (aviation pioneer).

1115	**290**	30c. brown, purple & blue	35	35

291 Marconi, Circuit Plan and Destroyer

1974. Birth Centenary of Guglielmo Marconi (radio pioneer).

1116	**291**	40c. red, deep blue & blue	55	35

292 Duchesne and "Penicillium glaucum"

1974. Birth Centenary of Ernest Duchesne (microbiologist).

1117	**292**	45c. black, blue & purple	55	55

293 Forest and Engine

1974. 60th Death Anniv of Fernand Forest (motor engineer and inventor).

1118	**293**	50c. purple, red and black	55	35

1974. International Dog Show, Monte Carlo. As T 248, inscr "1974".

1119	60c. multicoloured	7·25	5·00

DESIGN: 60c. Schnauzer.

294 Ronsard and Characters from "Sonnet to Helene"

1974. 450th Birth Anniv of Pierre de Ronsard (poet).

1120	**294**	70c. brown and red	55	65

295 Sir Winston Churchill (after bust by O. Nemon)

1974. Birth Centenary of Sir Winston Churchill.

1121	**295**	1f. brown and grey	65	65

296 Interpol Emblem, and Views of Monaco and Vienna

1974. 60th Anniv of 1st International Police Judiciary Congress and 50th Anniv of International Criminal Police Organization (Interpol).

1122	**296**	2f. blue, brown and green	1·40	1·30

297 "The King of Rome" (Bosio)

1974. Europa. Sculptures by J. F. Bosio.

1123	**297**	45c. green and brown	2·20	1·80
1124	-	1f.10 bistre and brown	3·75	3·00
MS1125		170×140 mm. Nos. 1123/5 ×5	55·00	55·00

DESIGN: 1f.10, "Madame Elizabeth".

298 "The Box" (A. Renoir)

1974. "The Impressionists". Multicoloured.

1126	1f. Type **298**	2·75	2·75
1127	1f. "The Dance Class" (E. Degas)	2·75	2·75
1128	2f. "Impression-Sunrise" (C. Monet) (horiz)	6·00	6·00
1129	2f. "Entrance to Voisins Village" (C. Pissarro) (horiz)	6·00	6·00
1130	2f. "The Hanged Man's House" (P. Cezanne) (horiz)	6·00	6·00
1131	2f. "Floods at Port Marly" (A. Sisley) (horiz)	6·50	6·00

299 Tigers and Trainer

1974. 1st International Circus Festival, Monaco.

1132	**299**	2c. brown, green and blue	10	15
1133	-	3c. brown and purple	10	15
1134	-	5c. blue, brown and red	20	20
1135	-	45c. brown, black and red	65	75
1136	-	70c. multicoloured	1·20	1·00
1137	-	1f.10 brown, green and red	2·00	2·00
1138	-	5f. green, blue and brown	8·75	6·50

DESIGNS—VERT: 3c. Performing horse; 45c. Equestrian act; 1f.10, Acrobats; 5f. Trapeze act. HORIZ: 5c. Performing elephants; 70c. Clowns.

300 Honore II on Medal

1974. 350th Anniv of Monegasque Numismatic Art.

1139	**300**	60c. green and red	45	55

301 Marine Flora and Fauna

1974. 24th Congress of the International Commission for the Scientific Exploration of the Mediterranean. Multicoloured.

1140	45c. Type **301**	1·70	1·40
1141	70c. Sea-bed flora and fauna	2·75	1·90
1142	1f.10 Sea-bed flora and fauna (different)	3·75	3·25

Nos. 1141/2 are larger, size 52×31 mm.

1974. Monte Carlo Flower Show. As T 271. Multicoloured.

1143	70c. Honeysuckle and violets	1·70	1·10
1144	1f.10 Iris and chrysanthemums	2·75	1·80

302 Prince Rainier III (F. Messina)

303

1974

1145	**302**	60c. green (postage)	1·90	90
1146	**302**	80c. red	2·00	1·70
1147	**302**	80c. green	65	45
1148	**302**	1f. brown	3·75	1·90
1149	**302**	1f. red	1·00	65
1149a	**302**	1f. green	65	55
1149b	**302**	1f.10 green	1·00	75
1150	**302**	1f.20 violet	11·50	4·50
1150a	**302**	1f.20 red	1·00	65
1150b	**302**	1f.20 green	1·10	75
1151	**302**	1f.25 blue	2·40	1·30
1151a	**302**	1f.30 red	1·10	90
1152	**302**	1f.40 red	1·20	90
1152a	**302**	1f.50 black	1·30	90
1153	**302**	1f.60 grey	1·70	1·10
1153a	**302**	1f.70 blue	1·50	1·00
1153b	**302**	1f.80 blue	2·75	2·50
1154	**302**	2f. mauve	4·50	3·75
1154a	**302**	2f.10 brown	2·20	1·70
1155	**302**	2f.30 violet	3·75	2·30
1156	**302**	2f.50 black	3·50	2·75
1157	**302**	9f. violet	9·25	6·00
1158	**303**	10f. violet (air)	10·00	7·75
1159	**303**	15f. red	13·00	10·00
1160	**303**	20f. blue	19·00	13·00

304 Coastline, Monte Carlo

1974

1161	**304**	25c. blue, green & brown	3·75	1·10
1162	-	25c. brown, green & blue	35	45
1163	-	50c. brown and blue	3·75	1·70
1164	**304**	65c. blue, brown & green	45	55
1165	-	70c. multicoloured	90	75
1166	**304**	1f.10 brown, green & bl	3·25	2·20
1167	-	1f.10 black, brown & bl	1·10	90
1168	-	1f.30 brown, green & bl	1·20	75
1169	-	1f.40 green, grey & brn	3·75	2·20
1170	-	1f.50 green, blue & black	2·20	1·70
1171	-	1f.70 brown, green & bl	6·50	3·75
1172	-	1f.80 brown, green & bl	2·30	1·70
1173	-	2f.30 brown, grey & blue	3·75	2·20

1174	-	3f. brown, grey and green	9·25	6·50
1175	-	5f.50 brown, green & blue	15·00	13·00
1176	-	6f.50 brown, blue & grn	6·00	4·50

DESIGNS—VERT: 50c. Palace clock tower; 70c. Botanical gardens; 1f.30, Monaco Cathedral; 1f.40, 1f.50, Prince Albert I statue and Museum; 3f. Fort Antoine. HORIZ: 25c. (1162), 1f.70, "All Saints" Tower; 1f.10 (1167), Palais de Justice; 1f.80, 5f.50, La Condamine; 2f.30, North Galleries of Palace; 6f.50, Aerial view of hotels and harbour.

305 "Haagocereus chosicensis"

1975. Plants. Multicoloured.

1180		10c. Type **305**	20	20
1181		20c. "Matucana madisoniarum"	20	35
1182		30c. "Parodia scopaioides"	65	55
1183		85c. "Mediolobivia arachnacantha"	3·75	2·50
1184		1f.90 "Matucana yanganucensis"	6·00	4·50
1185		4f. "Echinocereus marksianus"	8·75	8·25

306 "Portrait of a Sailor" (P. Florence)

1975. Europa.

1186	**306**	80c. purple	3·25	2·20
1187	-	1f.20 blue	4·50	3·25
MS1188		170×130 mm. Nos. 1186/7 ×5	55·00	55·00

DESIGN: 1f.20, "St. Devote" (Ludovic Brea).

307 "St. Bernardin de Sienne"

1975. Monaco Red Cross.

1189	**307**	4f. blue and purple	3·25	2·75

308 "Prologue"

1975. Centenary of "Carmen" (opera by Georges Bizet).

1190	**308**	30c. violet, brown & blk	20	20
1191	-	60c. grey, green and red	35	45
1192	-	80c. green, brown & blk	90	75
1193	-	1f.40 purple, brn & ochre	1·10	1·30

DESIGNS—HORIZ: 60c. Lilla Pastia's tavern; 80c. "The Smuggler's Den"; 1f.40, "Confrontation at Seville".

309 Saint-Simon

1975. 300th Birth Anniv of Louis de Saint-Simon (writer).

1194	**309**	40c. blue	35	20

310 Dr. Albert Schweitzer

1975. Birth Centenary of Dr. Schweitzer (Nobel Peace Prize Winner).

1195	**310**	60c. red and brown	75	65

311 "Stamp" and Calligraphy

1975. "Arphila 75" International Stamp Exhibition, Paris.

1196	**311**	80c. brown and orange	90	65

312 Seagull and Sunrise

1975. International Exposition, Okinawa.

1197	**312**	85c. blue, green & orange	1·10	90

313 Pike smashing Crab

1975. Anti-cancer Campaign.

1198	**313**	1f. multicoloured	1·10	75

314 Christ with Crown of Thorns

1975. Holy Year.

1199	**314**	1f.15 black, brn & pur	1·10	90

315 Villa Sauber, Monte Carlo

1975. European Architectural Heritage Year.

1200	**315**	1f.20 green, brown & bl	1·10	1·10

316 Woman's Head and Globe

1975. International Women's Year.

1201	**316**	1f.20 multicoloured	1·10	90

317 Rolls-Royce "Silver Ghost" (1907)

1975. History of the Motor Car.

1202	**317**	5c. blue, green and brown	10	10
1203	-	10c. indigo and blue	15	15
1204	-	20c. blue, ultram & black	20	20
1205	-	30c. purple and mauve	35	35
1206	-	50c. blue, purple & mauve	1·10	1·10
1207	-	60c. red and green	1·70	1·70
1208	-	80c. indigo and blue	2·75	2·20
1209	-	85c. brown, orange & grn	3·75	3·25
1210	-	1f.20 blue, red and green	4·50	4·50
1211	-	1f.40 green and blue	6·50	4·75
1212	-	5f.50 blue, emerald and green	22·00	17·00

DESIGNS: 10c. Hispano-Suiza "H.6B" (1926); 20c. Isotta Fraschini "8A" (1928); 30c. Cord "L.29"; 50c. Voisin "V12" (1930); 60c. Duesenberg "SJ" (1933); 80c. Bugatti "57 C" (1938); 85c. Delahaye "135 M" (1940); 1f.20, Cisitalia "Pininfarina" (1945); 1f.40, Mercedes-Benz "300 SL" (1955); 5f.50, Lamborghini "Countach" (1974).

1975. Paintings. "Princes and Princesses of Monaco". As T 213. Multicoloured.

1213		2f. "Prince Honore III"	2·75	2·20
1214		4f. "Princess Catherine de Brignole"	5·00	3·75

318 Dog behind Bars

1975. 125th Birth Anniv of Gen. J. P. Delmas de Grammont (author of Animal Protection Code).

1215	**318**	60c. black and brown	1·70	1·10
1216	-	80c. black and brown	2·75	1·70
1217	-	1f.20 green and purple	3·75	3·25

DESIGNS—VERT: 80c. Cat chased up tree. HORIZ: 1f.20, Horse being ill-treated.

1975. International Dog Show, Monte Carlo. As T 248, but inscr "1975". Multicoloured.

1218		60c. black and purple	7·25	5·00

DESIGN: 60c. French poodle.

319 Maurice Ravel

1975. Birth Centenaries of Musicians.

1219	**319**	60c. brown and purple	1·10	65
1220	-	1f.20 black and purple	3·25	2·30

DESIGN: 1f.20, Johann Strauss (the younger).

320 Circus Clown

1975. 2nd International Circus Festival.

1221	**320**	80c. multicoloured	1·70	1·30

321 Monaco Florin Coin, 1640

1975. Monaco Numismatics.

1222	**321**	80c. brown and blue	90	75

See also Nos. 1275, 1320 and 1448.

322 Andre Ampere with Electrical Meter

1975. Birth Centenary of Andre Ampere (physicist).

1223	**322**	85c. indigo and blue	1·10	90

323 "Lamentations for the Dead Christ"

1975. 500th Birth Anniv of Michelangelo.

1224	**323**	1f.40 olive and black	1·70	1·30

1975. Monte Carlo Flower Show (1976). As T 271. Multicoloured.

1225		60c. Bouquet of wild flowers	1·70	1·20
1226		80c. Ikebana flower arrangement	2·20	1·70

1975. Precancelled. Surch.

1227		42c. on 26c. violet, blue and black (No. 949a)	3·50	2·75
1228		48c. on 30c. multicoloured (No. 949b)	4·50	3·25
1229		70c. on 45c. multicoloured (No. 950a)	5·75	4·50
1230		1f.35 on 90c. green, blue and black (No. 951a)	7·25	6·00

325 Prince Pierre de Monaco

1976. 25th Anniv of Literary Council of Monaco.

1231	**325**	10c. black	20	20
1232	-	20c. blue and red	30	35
1233	-	25c. blue and red	35	45
1234	-	30c. brown	65	55
1235	-	50c. blue, red and purple	65	55
1236	-	60c. brown, grn & lt brn	90	55
1237	-	80c. purple and blue	1·70	1·10
1238	-	1f.20 violet, blue & mve	3·25	2·20

COUNCIL MEMBERS—HORIZ: 20c. A. Maurois and Colette; 25c. Jean and Jerome Tharaud; 30c. E. Henriot, M. Pagnol and G. Duhamel; 50c. Ph. Heriat, J. Supervielle and L. Pierard; 60c. R. Dorgeles, M. Achard and G. Bauer; 80c. F. Hellens, A. Billy and Mgr. Grente; 1f.20, J. Giono, L. Pasteur Vallery-Radot and M. Garcon.

326 Dachshunds

1976. International Dog Show, Monte Carlo.

1239	**326**	60c. multicoloured	10·00	6·50

327 Bridge Table and Monte Carlo Coast

1976. 5th Bridge Olympiad, Monte Carlo.

1240	**327**	60c. brown, green and red	65	65

328 Alexander Graham Bell and Early Telephone

1976. Telephone Centenary.

1241	**328**	80c. brown, light brown and grey	65	65

329 Federation Emblem on Globe

1976. 50th Anniv of International Philatelic Federation.

1242	**329**	1f.20 red, blue and green	90	75

330 U.S.A. 2c. Stamp, 1926

1976. Bicent of American Revolution.

1243	**330**	1f.70 black and purple	1·10	1·10

331 "The Fritillaries" (Van Gogh)

1976. Monte Carlo Flower Show.
1244 **331** 3f. multicoloured 17·00 11·00

332 Diving

1976. Olympic Games, Montreal.
1245 **332** 60c. brown and blue 45 55
1246 - 80c. blue, brown & green 55 65
1247 - 85c. blue, green & brown 65 75
1248 - 1f.20 brown, green & bl 1·10 90
1249 - 1f.70 brown, blue & grn 1·70 1·30
MS1250 150×145 mm. Nos. 1245/9 6·50 6·50
DESIGNS—VERT: 80c. Gymnastics; 85c. Hammer-throwing.
HORIZ: 1f.20, Rowing; 1f.70, Boxing.

333 Decorative Plate

1976. Europa. Monegasque Ceramics. Multicoloured.
1251 80c. Type **333** 2·20 1·70
1252 1f.20 Grape-harvester (statuette) 3·75 2·75
MS1253 170×140 mm. Nos. 1251/2 ×5 55·00 55·00

334 Palace Clock Tower

1976. Precancelled.
1254 **334** 50c. red 65 65
1255 **334** 52c. orange 65 65
1256 **334** 54c. green 65 65
1257 **334** 60c. green 65 65
1258 **334** 62c. mauve 65 65
1259 **334** 68c. yellow 65 65
1260 **334** 90c. violet 1·70 1·70
1261 **334** 95c. red 1·70 1·70
1262 **334** 1f.05 brown 1·70 1·70
1263 **334** 1f.60 blue 2·50 2·50
1264 **334** 1f.70 turquoise 2·50 2·50
1265 **334** 1f.85 brown 2·50 2·50

335 "St. Louise de Marillac" (altar painting)

1976. Monaco Red Cross.
1270 **335** 4f. black, purple & green 3·25 3·25

1976. Paintings. "Princes and Princesses of Monaco". As T 213.
1271 2f. purple 3·25 2·75
1272 4f. multicoloured 6·00 4·50
DESIGNS: 2f. "Prince Honore IV"; 4f. "Princess Louise d'Aumont-Mazarin".

336 St. Vincent-de-Paul

1976. Centenary of St. Vincent-de-Paul Conference, Monaco.
1273 **336** 60c. black, brown & blue 55 45

337 Marie de Rabutin Chantal

1976. 350th Birth Anniv of Marquise de Sevigne (writer).
1274 **337** 80c. black, violet and red 65 65

338 Monaco 2g. "Honore II" Coin, 1640

1976. Monaco Numismatics.
1275 **338** 80c. blue and green 65 65

339 Richard Byrd, "Josephine Ford", Airship "Norge" and Roald Amundsen

1976. 50th Anniv of First Flights over North Pole.
1276 **339** 85c. black, blue and green 2·75 1·90

340 Gulliver and Lilliputians

1976. 250th Anniv of Jonathan Swift's "Gulliver's Travels".
1277 **340** 1f.20 multicoloured 1·30 75

341 Girl's Head and Christmas Decorations

1976. Christmas.
1278 **341** 60c. multicoloured 55 45
1279 **341** 1f.20 green, orge & pur 1·30 90

342 "Drug" Dagger piercing Man and Woman

1976. Campaign against Drug Abuse.
1280 **342** 80c. blue, orge & bronze 80 55
1281 **342** 1f.20 lilac, purple & brn 1·30 90

1976. Monte Carlo Flower Show (1977). As T 271. Multicoloured.
1282 80c. Flower arrangement 2·75 1·70
1283 1f. Bouquet of flowers 4·00 2·75

343 Circus Clown

1976. 3rd International Circus Festival, Monte Carlo.
1284 **343** 1f. multicoloured 3·25 1·90

344 Schooner "Hirondelle I"

1977. 75th Anniv of Publication of "Career of a Navigator" by Prince Albert I (1st issue). Illustrations by L. Tinayre.
1285 **344** 10c. brown, blue & turq 15 10
1286 - 20c. black, brown & lake 25 20
1287 - 30c. green, blue & orange 55 45
1288 - 80c. black, blue and red 80 65
1289 - 1f. black and brown 1·30 1·10
1290 - 1f.25 olive, green & violet 1·70 1·40
1291 - 1f.40 brown, olive & grn 2·75 2·20
1292 - 1f.90 blue, lt blue & red 5·25 3·25
1293 - 2f.50 brown, blue and turquoise 7·25 4·50
DESIGNS—VERT: 20c. Prince Albert I; 1f. Helmsman; 1f.90, Bringing in the trawl. HORIZ: 30c. Crew-members; 80c. "Hirondelle" in a gale; 1f.25, Securing the lifeboat; 1f.40, Shrimp fishing; 2f.50, Capture of an oceanic sunfish.
See also Nos. 1305/13.

345 Pyrenean Sheep and Mountain Dogs

1977. International Dog Show, Monte Carlo.
1294 **345** 80c. multicoloured 11·50 6·50

346 "Maternity" (M. Cassatt)

1977. World Association of the "Friends of Children".
1295 **346** 80c. deep brown, brown and black 2·00 1·70

347 Archers

1977. 10th International Archery Championships.
1296 **347** 1f.10 black, brown & bl 1·30 75

348 Charles Lindbergh and Ryan NYP "Spirit of St. Louis"

1977. 50th Anniv of Lindbergh's Transatlantic Flight.
1297 **348** 1f.90 light blue, blue and brown 2·75 1·90

349 "Harbour, Deauville"

1977. Birth Centenary of Raoul Dufy (painter).
1298 **349** 2f. multicoloured 8·00 5·00

350 "Portrait of a Young Girl"

1977. 400th Birth Anniv of Peter Paul Rubens (painter).
1299 **350** 80c. orange, brown & blk 1·30 1·10
1300 - 1f. red 1·70 1·40
1301 - 1f.40 orange and red 3·00 2·40
DESIGNS: 1f. "Duke of Buckingham"; 1f.40, "Portrait of a Child".

351 "L'Oreillon" Tower

1977. Europa. Views.
1302 **351** 1f. brown and blue 2·75 1·10
1303 - 1f.40 blue, brown and bistre 4·00 2·20
MS1304 169×130 mm. Nos. 1302/3 ×5 55·00 55·00
DESIGN: 1f.40, St. Michael's Church, Menton.

1977. 75th Anniv of Publication of "Career of a Navigator" by Prince Albert I (2nd issue). Illustrations by L. Tinayre. As T 344.
1305 10c. black and blue 15 20
1306 20c. blue 25 35
1307 30c. blue, light blue and green 40 45
1308 80c. brown, black and green 95 75
1309 1f. grey and green 1·20 1·10
1310 1f.25 black, brown and lilac 1·70 1·70
1311 1f.40 purple, blue and brown 3·00 2·75
1312 1f.90 black, blue and light blue 5·50 3·25
1313 3f. blue, brown and green 6·75 5·00
DESIGNS—HORIZ: 10c. "Princess Alice" (steam yacht) at Kiel; 20c. Ship's laboratory; 30c. "Princess Alice" in ice floes; 1f. Polar scene; 1f.25, Bridge of "Princess Alice" during snowstorm; 1f.40, Arctic camp; 1f.90, Ship's steam launch in floating ice; 3f. "Princess Alice" passing iceberg. VERT: 80c. Crewmen in Arctic dress.

352 Santa Claus and Sledge

1977. Christmas.
1314 **352** 80c. red, green and blue 95 55
1315 **352** 1f.40 multicoloured 1·30 90

1977. Monte Carlo Flower Show. As T 271. Mult.
1316 80c. Snapdragons and campanula 2·10 1·30
1317 1f. Ikebana 3·25 1·70

353 Face, Poppy and Syringe

1977. Campaign Against Drug Abuse.
1318 **353** 1f. black, red and violet 1·10 90

354 Clown and Flags

1977. 4th International Festival of Circus, Monaco.
1319 **354** 1f. multicoloured 3·25 2·20

355 Gold Coin of Honore II

1977. Monaco Numismatics.

1320	**355**	80c. brown and red	1·10	65

356 Mediterranean divided by Industry

1977. Protection of the Mediterranean Environment.

1321	**356**	1f. black, green and blue	1·10	90

357 Dr. Guglielminetti and Road Tarrers

1977. 75th Anniv of First Experiments at Road Tarring in Monaco.

1322	**357**	1f.10 black, bistre and brown	1·20	65

358 F.M.L.T. Badge and Monte Carlo

1977. 50th Anniv of Monaco Lawn Tennis Federation.

1323	**358**	1f. blue, red and brown	2·00	1·70

359 Wimbledon and First Championships

1977. Centenary of Wimbledon Lawn Tennis Championships.

1324	**359**	1f.40 grey, green & brown	2·75	2·20

1977. Paintings. "Princes and Princesses of Monaco". As T 213. Multicoloured.

1325	6f. "Prince Honore V"	6·75	5·50

360 St. Jean Bosco

1977. Monaco Red Cross. Monegasque Art.

1326	**360**	4f. green, brown and blue	4·00	2·75

1978. Precancelled. Surch.

1327	**334**	58c. on 54c. green	80	75
1328	**334**	73c. on 68c. yellow	1·20	1·20
1329	**334**	1f.15 on 1f.05 brown	2·75	2·40
1330	**334**	2f. on 1f.85 brown	3·00	2·75

362 Aerial Shipwreck from "L'Ile Mysterieuse"

1978. 150th Birth Anniv of Jules Verne.

1331	**362**	5c. brown, red and olive	15	20
1332	-	25c. turquoise, blue & red	20	20
1333	-	30c. blue, brown & lt blue	25	35
1334	-	80c. black, green & orge	65	65
1335	-	1f. brown, lake and blue	1·20	90
1336	-	1f.40 bistre, brown and green	1·30	1·10
1337	-	1f.70 brown, light blue and blue	2·50	1·70
1338	-	5f.50 violet and blue	7·00	4·50

DESIGNS: 25c. The abandoned ship from "L'Ile Mysterieuse"; 30c. The secret of the island from "L'Ile Mysterieuse"; 80c. "Robur the Conqueror"; 1f. "Master Zacharius"; 1f.40, "The Castle in the Carpathians"; 1f.70, "The Children of Captain Grant"; 5f.50, Jules Verne and allegories.

363 Aerial View of Congress Centre

1978. Inauguration of Monaco Congress Centre.

1339	**363**	1f. brown, blue and green	65	55
1340	-	1f.40 blue, brown & grn	1·00	90

DESIGN: 1f.40, View of Congress Centre from sea.

364 Footballers and Globe

1978. World Cup Football Championship, Argentina.

1341	**364**	1f. blue, slate and green	75	75

365 Antonio Vivaldi

1978. 300th Birth Anniv of Antonio Vivaldi (composer).

1342	**365**	1f. brown and red	1·00	1·00

366 "Ramoge" (research vessel) and Grimaldi Palace

1978. Environment Protection. "RAMOGE" Agreement.

1343	**366**	80c. multicoloured	65	65
1344	-	1f. red, blue and green	65	65

DESIGN—HORIZ (48×27 mm): 1f. Map of coastline between St. Raphael and Genes.

367 Monaco Cathedral

1978. Europa. Monaco Views.

1345	**367**	1f. green, brown and blue	1·90	1·10
1346	-	1f.40 brown, green & bl	2·50	2·20
MS1347		170×143 mm. Nos. 1345/6 ×5	50·00	50·00

DESIGN: 1f.40, View of Monaco from the east.

368 Monaco Congress Centre

1978. Precancelled.

1348	**368**	61c. orange	65	55
1349	**368**	64c. green	65	55
1350	**368**	68c. blue	65	55
1351	**368**	78c. purple	65	55
1352	**368**	83c. violet	65	55
1353	**368**	88c. orange	65	55
1354	**368**	1f.25 brown	1·50	1·30
1355	**368**	1f.30 red	1·50	1·30
1356	**368**	1f.40 green	1·50	1·30
1357	**368**	2f.10 blue	2·20	1·90
1358	**368**	2f.25 orange	2·20	1·90
1359	**368**	2f.35 mauve	2·20	1·90

369 "Cinderella"

1978. 350th Birth Anniv of Charles Perrault (writer).

1360	**369**	5c. red, olive and violet	25	20
1361	-	25c. black, brown & mve	25	20
1362	-	30c. green, lake & brown	25	20
1363	-	80c. multicoloured	75	65
1364	-	1f. red, brown and olive	1·00	90
1365	-	1f.40 mauve, ultramarine and blue	1·30	1·10
1366	-	1f.70 green, blue & grey	1·90	1·70
1367	-	1f.90 multicoloured	2·50	2·20
1368	-	2f.50 blue, orange & grn	3·75	3·25

DESIGNS: 25c. "Puss in Boots"; 30c. "The Sleeping Beauty"; 80c. "Donkey's Skin"; 1f. "Little Red Riding Hood"; 1f.40, "Bluebeard"; 1f.70, "Tom Thumb"; 1f.90, "Riquet with a Tuft"; 2f.50, "The Fairies".

370 "The Sunflowers" (Van Gogh)

1978. Monte Carlo Flower Show (1979) and 125th Birth Anniv of Vincent Van Gogh. Multicoloured.

1369	1f. Type **370**	5·75	3·25
1370	1f.70 "The Iris" (Van Gogh)	7·75	4·50

371 Afghan Hound

1978. International Dog Show, Monte Carlo. Multicoloured.

1371	1f. Type **371**	5·75	3·25
1372	1f.20 Borzoi	7·75	5·00

372 Girl with Letter

1978. Christmas.

1373	**372**	1f. brown, blue and red	90	75

373 Catherine and William Booth

1978. Centenary of Salvation Army.

1374	**373**	1f.70 multicoloured	1·80	1·50

374 Juggling Seals

1978. 5th International Circus Festival, Monaco.

1375	**374**	80c. orange, black & blue	75	65
1376	-	1f. multicoloured	1·30	1·10
1377	-	1f.40 brown, mauve and bistre	2·10	1·80
1378	-	1f.90 blue, lilac and mauve	2·50	2·75
1379	-	2f.40 multicoloured	4·50	3·25

DESIGNS—HORIZ: 1f.40, Horseback acrobatics; 1f.90, Musical monkeys; 2f.40, Trapeze. VERT: 1f. Lion tamer.

1978. Paintings. "Princes and Princesses of Monaco". As T 213. Multicoloured.

1380	2f. "Prince Florestan I" (G. Dauphin)	3·75	2·75
1381	4f. "Princess Caroline Gilbert de la Metz" (Marie Verroust)	6·50	5·00

375

1978. 150th Anniv of Henri Dunant (founder of Red Cross). Sheet 100×130 mm.

MS1382	**375**	5f. chocolate, crimson and red	7·00	7·25

376

1979. 21st Birthday of Prince Albert. Sheet 80×105 mm.

MS1383	**376**	10f. green and brown	11·50	11·50

377 "Jongleur de Notre-Dame" (Massenet)

1979. Centenary of "Salle Garnier" (Opera House) (1st issue).

1384	**377**	1f. blue, orange & mauve	75	65
1385	-	1f.20 violet, black & turq	1·30	1·10
1386	-	1f.50 maroon, grn & turq	1·90	1·70
1387	-	1f.70 multicoloured	2·10	1·80
1388	-	2f.10 turquoise and violet	3·25	2·75
1389	-	3f. multicoloured	3·75	3·25

DESIGNS—HORIZ: 1f.20, "Hans the Flute Player" (L. Ganne); 1f.50, "Don Quixote" (J. Massenet); 2f.10, "The Child and the Sorcerer" (M. Ravel); 3f. Charles Garnier (architect) and south facade of Opera House. VERT: 1f.70, "L'Aiglon" (A. Honegger and J. Ibert).

See also Nos. 1399/1404.

378 Flower, Bird and Butterfly

1979. International Year of the Child. Children's Paintings.

1390	**378**	50c. pink, green and black	25	35
1391	-	1f. slate, green and orange	75	65
1392	-	1f.20 slate, orange & mve	1·30	1·10
1393	-	1f.50 yellow, brown & bl	2·20	1·90
1394	-	1f.70 multicoloured	2·75	2·30

DESIGNS: 1f. Horse and Child; 1f.20, "The Gift of Love"; 1f.50, "Peace in the World"; 1f.70, "Down with Pollution".

379 Armed Foot Messenger

1979. Europa.

1395	**379**	1f.20 brown, green & bl	1·30	1·10
1396	-	1f.50 brown, turq & bl	1·90	1·70
1397	-	1f.70 brown, green & bl	2·50	2·20
MS1398		129×149 mm. Nos. 1395/7, each ×2	32·00	32·00

DESIGNS: 1f.50, 18th-cent felucca; 1f.70, Arrival of first train at Monaco.

380 "Instrumental Music" (G. Boulanger) (detail of Opera House interior)

1979. Centenary of "Salle Garnier" (Opera House) (2nd issue).

1399		1f. brown, orange & turq	90	75
1400		1f.20 multicoloured	1·30	1·10
1401		1f.50 multicoloured	1·70	1·40
1402		1f.70 blue, brown and red	2·30	2·00
1403		2f.10 red, violet & black	2·75	2·40
1404	**380**	3f. green, brown and light green	3·75	3·25

DESIGNS (as Type 377)—HORIZ: 1f. "Les Biches" (F. Poulenc); 1f.20, "The Sailors" (G. Auric); 1f.70, "Gaiete Parisienne" (J. Offenbach). VERT: 1f.50, "La Spectre de la Rose" (C. M. Weber) (after poster by Jean Cocteau); 2f.10, "Salome" (R. Strauss).

1979. Paintings. "Princes and Princesses of Monaco". As T 213. Multicoloured.

1405		3f. "Prince Charles III" (B. Biard)	3·25	2·75
1406		4f. "Antoinette de Merode"	3·75	3·25

381 St. Pierre Claver

1979. Monaco Red Cross.

1407	**381**	5f. multicoloured	3·25	2·75

382 "Princess Grace" Orchid

1979. Monte Carlo Flora 1980.

1408	**382**	1f. multicoloured	3·25	2·75

383 "Princess Grace" Rose

1979. Monte Carlo Flower Show.

1409	**383**	1f.20 multicoloured	3·75	2·75

384 Clown balancing on Ball

1979. 6th International Circus Festival.

1410	**384**	1f.20 multicoloured	2·50	1·90

385 Sir Rowland Hill and Penny Black

1979. Death Centenary of Sir Rowland Hill.

1411	**385**	1f.70 brown, blue & blk	1·00	90

386 Albert Einstein

1979. Birth Centenary of Albert Einstein (physicist).

1412	**386**	1f.70 brown, grey and red	1·00	90

387 St. Patrick's Cathedral

1979. Centenary of St. Patrick's Cathedral, New York.

1413	**387**	2f.10 black, blue & brn	1·40	1·10

388 Nativity Scene

1979. Christmas.

1414	**388**	1f.20 blue, orange & mve	90	75

389 Early Racing Cars

1979. 50th Anniv of Grand Prix Motor Racing.

1415	**389**	1f. multicoloured	1·40	1·20

390 Arms of Charles V and Monaco

1979. 450th Anniv of Visit of Emperor Charles V.

1416	**390**	1f.50 brown, blue & blk	90	75

391 Setter and Pointer

1979. International Dog Show, Monte Carlo.

1417	**391**	1f.20 multicoloured	6·50	5·50

392 Spring

1980. Precancels. The Seasons.

1418	**392**	76c. brown and green	65	55
1419	**392**	88c. olive, emerald & grn	70	60
1420	-	99c. green and brown	90	75
1421	-	1f.14 green, emer & brn	95	85
1422	-	1f.60 brown, grey and deep brown	1·30	1·10
1423	-	1f.84 lake, grey & brown	1·40	1·20
1424	-	2f.65 brown, lt blue & bl	2·50	2·20
1425	-	3f.05 brown, bl & slate	2·75	2·30

DESIGNS: 99c., 1f.14, Summer; 1f.60, 1f.84, Autumn; 2f.65, 3f.05, Winter.

394 Paul P. Harris (founder) and View of Chicago

1980. 75th Anniv of Rotary International.

1434	**394**	1f.80 olive, blue & turq	1·00	90

395 Gymnastics

1980. Olympic Games, Moscow and Lake Placid.

1435	**395**	1f.10 blue, brown & grey	40	35
1436	-	1f.30 red, brown & blue	65	55
1437	-	1f.60 red, blue & brown	75	65
1438	-	1f.80 brown, bis & grn	1·00	90
1439	-	2f.30 grey, violet & mve	1·30	1·10
1440	-	4f. green, blue and brown	2·20	1·90

DESIGNS: 1f.30, Handball; 1f.60, Pistol-shooting; 1f.80, Volleyball; 2f.30, Ice hockey; 4f. Skiing.

396 Colette (novelist)

1980. Europa. Each black, green and red.

1441	**396**	1f.30 Type 396	1·30	55
1442		1f.80 Marcel Pagnol (writer)	1·90	1·10
MS1443	171×143 mm. Nos. 1441/2, each ×5		19·00	17·00

397 "La Source"

1980. Birth Bicentenary of Jean Ingres (artist).

1444	**397**	4f. multicoloured	11·50	10·00

398 Montaigne

1980. 400th Anniv of Publication of Montaigne's "Essays".

1445	**398**	1f.30 black, red and blue	90	75

399 Guillaume Apollinaire (after G. Pieret)

1980. Birth Centenary of Guillaume Apollinaire (poet).

1446	**399**	1f.10 brown	75	65

400 Congress Centre

1980. Kiwanis International European Convention.

1447	**400**	1f.30 black, blue and red	90	75

401 Honore II Silver Ecu, 1649

1980. Numismatics.

1448	**401**	1f.50 black and blue	1·30	1·10

402 Lhassa Apso and Shih Tzu

1980. International Dog Show, Monte Carlo.

1449	**402**	1f.30 multicoloured	7·00	5·50

403 "The Princess and the Pea"

1980. 175th Birth Anniv of Hans Christian Andersen.

1450	**403**	70c. sepia, red and brown	40	35
1451	-	1f.30 blue, turq & red	90	75
1452	-	1f.50 black, blue & turq	1·30	1·10
1453	-	1f.60 red, black & brown	1·50	1·30
1454	-	1f.80 yellow, brn & turq	1·90	1·70
1455	-	2f.30 brown, pur & vio	2·30	2·00

DESIGNS: 1f.30, "The Little Mermaid"; 1f.50, "The Chimneysweep and Shepherdess"; 1f.60, "The Brave Little Lead Soldier"; 1f.80, "The Little Match Girl"; 2f.30, "The Nightingale".

404 "The Road" (M. Vlaminck)

1980. 75th Anniv of 1905 Autumn Art Exhibition. Multicoloured.

1456		2f. Type **404**	3·75	2·75
1457		3f. "Woman at Balustrade" (Van Dongen)	5·25	4·00
1458		4f. "The Reader" (Henri Matisse)	6·75	5·50
1459		5f. "Three Figures in a Meadow" (A. Derain)	7·75	6·00

1980. Paintings. "Princes and Princesses of Monaco". As T 213. Multicoloured.

1460		4f. "Prince Albert I" (L. Bonnat)	3·75	3·25
1461		4f. "Princess Marie Alice Heine" (L. Maeterlinck)	3·75	3·25

405 "Sunbirds"

1980. Monaco Red Cross.

1462	**405**	6f. red, bistre and brown	5·25	3·75

406 "MONACO" balanced on Tightrope

1980. 7th International Circus Festival, Monaco.

1463	**406**	1f.30 red, turquoise & blue	2·40	1·70

407 Children and Nativity

1980. Christmas.

1464	**407**	1f.10 blue, carmine and red	65	55

| 1465 | **407** | 2f.30 violet, orange and pink | 1·30 | 1·10 |

1980. Monte Carlo Flower Show, 1981. As T 383. Multicoloured.

| 1466 | | 1f.30 "Princess Stephanie" rose | 1·50 | 90 |
| 1467 | | 1f.80 Ikebana | 2·30 | 1·70 |

408 "Alcyonium"

1980. Marine Fauna. Multicoloured.

1468		5c. "Spirographis spallanzanli"	15	20
1469		10c. "Anemonia sulcata"	15	20
1470		15c. "Leptopsammia pruvoti"	15	20
1471		20c. "Pteroides"	25	35
1472		30c. "Paramuricea clavata" (horiz)	25	35
1473		40c. Type **408**	40	45
1474		50c. "Corallium rubrum"	65	55
1475		60c. Trunculus murex ("Calliactis parasitica") (horiz)	1·30	1·10
1476		70c. "Cerianthus membranaceus" (horiz)	1·50	1·30
1477		1f. "Actinia equina" (horiz)	1·90	1·40
1478		2f. "Protula" (horiz)	3·75	2·20

409 Fish with Hand for Tail

1981. "Respect the Sea".

| 1479 | **409** | 1f.20 multicoloured | 1·30 | 1·10 |

410 Prince Rainier and Princess Grace

1981. Royal Silver Wedding.

1480	**410**	1f.20 black and green	1·90	1·70
1481	**410**	1f.40 black and red	2·50	2·20
1482	**410**	1f.70 black and green	3·25	2·75
1483	**410**	1f.80 black and brown	3·75	3·25
1484	**410**	2f. black and blue	5·25	3·25

411 Mozart (after Lorenz Vogel)

1981. 225th Birth Anniv of Wolfgang Amadeus Mozart (composer).

1485	**411**	2f. brown, dp brown & bl	2·30	2·00
1486	-	2f.50 blue, brn & dp brn	3·25	2·75
1487	-	3f.50 dp brown, bl & brn	3·25	3·25

DESIGNS—HORIZ: 2f.50, "Mozart at 7 with his Father and Sister" (engraving by Delafoose after drawing by Carmontelle); 3f.50 "Mozart directing Requiem two Days before his Death" (painting by Baude).

412 Palm Cross

1981. Europa. Multicoloured.

1488	**412**	1f.40 green, brown & red	1·90	1·10
1489	-	2f. multicoloured	2·50	1·70
MS1490		171×143 mm. Nos. 1488/9, each ×5	24·00	17·00

DESIGN: 2f. Children carrying palm crosses.

413 Paris Football Stadium, Cup and Footballer

1981. 25th Anniv of European Football Cup.

| 1491 | **413** | 2f. black and blue | 1·50 | 1·30 |

414 I.Y.D.P. Emblem and Girl in Wheelchair

1981. International Year of Disabled Persons.

| 1492 | **414** | 1f.40 blue and green | 1·30 | 1·10 |

415 Palace flying Old Flag, National Flag and Monte Carlo

1981. Centenary of National Flag.

| 1493 | **415** | 2f. red, blue and brown | 1·50 | 1·30 |

416 Oceanographic Institute, Paris and Oceanographic Museum, Monaco

1981. 75th Anniv of Oceanographic Institute.

| 1494 | **416** | 1f.20 blue, black & brn | 1·00 | 90 |

417 Bureau Building and "Faddey Bellingshausen" (hydrographic research ship)

1981. 50th Anniv of Int Hydrographic Bureau.

| 1495 | **417** | 2f.50 sepia, brown and light brown | 1·90 | 1·70 |

418 Rough Collies and Shetland Sheepdogs

1981. International Dog Show, Monte Carlo.

| 1496 | **418** | 1f.40 multicoloured | 7·75 | 5·50 |

419 Rainier III and Prince Albert

1981. (a) 23×28 mm.

1497	**419**	1f.40 green (postage)	1·30	65
1498	**419**	1f.60 red	1·90	75
1499	**419**	1f.60 green	1·30	75
1500	**419**	1f.70 green	1·30	90
1501	**419**	1f.80 red	1·50	1·00
1502	**419**	1f.80 green	1·50	1·10
1503	**419**	1f.90 green	2·50	2·00
1504	**419**	2f. red	1·90	90
1505	**419**	2f. green	1·30	90
1506	**419**	2f.10 red	1·90	1·10
1507	**419**	2f.20 red	1·80	1·20
1508	**419**	2f.30 blue	5·75	3·75
1509	**419**	2f.50 brown	2·50	1·30
1510	**419**	2f.60 blue	3·75	2·75
1511	**419**	2f.80 blue	3·75	2·20

1512	**419**	3f. blue	3·75	2·40
1513	**419**	3f.20 blue	3·75	2·40
1514	**419**	3f.40 blue	5·75	3·00
1515	**419**	3f.60 blue	3·75	2·75
1516	**419**	4f. brown	3·25	2·20
1517	**419**	5f.50 black	3·75	2·75
1518	**419**	10f. purple	5·25	2·75
1519	**419**	15f. green	12·00	5·00
1520	**419**	20f. blue	13·00	5·50

(b) 36×27 mm.

1521		5f. violet (air)	2·50	1·10
1522		10f. red	6·50	2·75
1523		15f. green	7·75	3·25
1524		20f. blue	11·50	4·50
1525		30f. brown	15·00	8·75

DESIGN: Nos. 1521/5, Double portrait and monograms.

421 Arctic Scene and Map

1981. 1st International Congress on Discovery and History of Northern Polar Regions, Rome.

| 1530 | **421** | 1f.50 multicoloured | 1·90 | 1·70 |

1981. Paintings. "Princes and Princesses of Monaco". Vert designs as T 213. Multicoloured.

| 1531 | | 3f. "Prince Louis II" (P.-A. de Laszlo) | 3·75 | 2·75 |
| 1532 | | 5f. "Princess Charlotte" (P.-A. de Laszlo) | 5·25 | 3·25 |

422 Hercules fighting the Nemean Lion

1981. Monaco Red Cross. The Twelve Labours of Hercules (1st series).

| 1533 | **422** | 2f.50+50c. green, brown and red | 1·90 | 1·70 |
| 1534 | - | 3f.50+50c. blue, green and red | 2·50 | 2·20 |

DESIGN: 3f.50, Slaying the Hydra of Lerna.
See also Nos. 1584/5, 1631/2, 1699/1700, 1761/2 and 1794/5.

423 Ettore Bugatti (racing car designer) (Cent)

1981. Birth Anniversaries.

1535	**423**	1f. indigo, blue and red	1·30	1·10
1536	-	2f. black, blue and brown	1·90	1·70
1537	-	2f.50 brown, black and red	2·50	2·20
1538	-	4f. multicoloured	4·50	3·75
1539	-	4f. multicoloured	4·50	3·75

DESIGNS: No. 1536, George Bernard Shaw (dramatist, 125th anniv); 1537, Fernand Leger (painter, centenary). LARGER: (37×48 mm): 1538, Pablo Picasso (self-portrait) (centenary); 1539, Rembrandt (self-portrait) (375th anniv).

424 Eglantines and Morning Glory

1981. Monte Carlo Flower Show (1982). Mult.

| 1540 | **424** | 1f.40 Type **424** | 2·50 | 1·70 |
| 1541 | | 2f. "Ikebana" (painting by Ikenobo) | 3·75 | 2·20 |

425 "Catherine Deneuve"

1981. 1st International Rose Show, Monte Carlo.

| 1542 | **425** | 1f.80 multicoloured | 5·25 | 3·75 |

426 Tiger, Clown, Acrobat and Elephants

1981. 8th International Circus Festival, Monaco.

| 1543 | **426** | 1f.40 violet, mauve & blk | 3·75 | 2·20 |

427 Praying Children and Nativity

1981. Christmas.

| 1544 | **427** | 1f.20 blue, mauve & brn | 90 | 75 |

428 "Lancia-Stratos" Rally Car

1981. 50th Monte Carlo Rally (1982).

| 1545 | **428** | 1f. blue, red & turquoise | 2·50 | 1·30 |

429 Spring

1981. Seasons of the Persimmon Tree. Sheet 143×100 mm containing T 429 and similar horiz designs.

| **MS**1546 | | 1f. green, yellow and blue (T 429); 2f. green and blue (Summer); 3f. red, brown and yellow (Autumn); 4f. brown and red (Winter) | 11·00 | 9·25 |

430 "Hoya bella"

1981. Plants in Exotic Garden. Multicoloured.

1547	**430**	1f.40 Type **430**	3·75	2·20
1548		1f.60 "Bolivicereus samaipatanus"	3·75	1·70
1549		1f.80 "Trichocereus grandiflorus" (horiz)	3·75	1·70
1550		2f. "Argyroderma roseum"	2·20	1·10
1551		2f.30 "Euphorbia milii"	4·25	2·75
1552		2f.60 "Echinocereus fitchii" (horiz)	4·25	3·25
1553		2f.90 "Rebutia heliosa" (horiz)	3·75	3·25
1554		4f.10 "Echinopsis multiplex cristata" (horiz)	5·25	4·50

431 Spring

1982. Precancels. The Seasons of the Peach Tree.

1555	**431**	97c. mauve and green	65	55
1556	-	1f.25 green, orge & mve	90	75
1557	-	2f.03 brown	1·40	1·20
1558	-	3f.36 brown and blue	2·50	2·20

DESIGNS: 1f.25, Summer; 2f.03, Autumn; 3f.36, Winter.

432 Common Nutcracker

1982. Birds from Mercantour National Park.
1559	**432**	60c. black, brown & grn	1·70	90
1560	-	70c. black and mauve	1·90	1·30
1561	-	80c. red, black & orange	2·10	1·40
1562	-	90c. black, red and blue	3·25	1·70
1563	-	1f.40 brown, black & red	3·50	2·75
1564	-	1f.60 brown, black & blue	4·50	3·25

DESIGNS:—VERT: 70c. Black grouse; 80c. Rock partridge; 1f.60, Golden eagle. HORIZ: 90c. Wallcreeper; 1f.40, Rock ptarmigan.

433 Capture of Monaco Fortress, 1297

1982. Europa.
1565	**433**	1f.60 blue, brown and red	1·50	90
1566	-	2f.30 blue, brown and red	1·90	1·10
MS1567	173×143 mm. Nos. 1565/6, each ×5		26·00	22·00

DESIGN: 2f.30, Signing the Treaty of Peronne, 1641.

434 Old Quarter

1982. Fontvieille.
1568	**434**	1f.40 blue, brown & grn	1·30	90
1569	-	1f.60 light brown, brown and red	1·50	65
1570	-	2f.30 purple	1·90	1·10

DESIGNS: 1f.60, Land reclamation; 2f.30, Urban development.

435 Stadium

1982. Fontvieille Sports Stadium (1st series).
| 1571 | **435** | 2f.30 green, brown & blue | 1·90 | 1·10 |

See also No. 1616.

436 Arms of Paris

1982. "Philexfrance" International Stamp Exhibition, Paris.
| 1572 | **436** | 1f.40 red, grey and deep red | 1·20 | 1·00 |

437 Old English Sheepdog

1982. International Dog Show, Monte Carlo. Multicoloured.
| 1573 | 60c. Type **437** | 3·75 | 2·75 |
| 1574 | 1f. Briard | 5·25 | 3·25 |

438 Monaco Cathedral and Arms

1982. Creation of Archbishopric of Monaco (1981).
| 1575 | **438** | 1f.60 black, blue and red | 1·20 | 1·00 |

439 St. Francis of Assisi

1982. 800th Birth Anniv of St. Francis of Assisi.
| 1576 | **439** | 1f.40 grey and light grey | 1·00 | 90 |

440 Dr. Robert Koch

1982. Centenary of Discovery of Tubercle Bacillus.
| 1577 | **440** | 1f.40 purple and lilac | 1·50 | 1·30 |

441 Lord Baden-Powell

1982. 125th Birth Anniv of Lord Baden-Powell (founder of Boy Scout Movement).
| 1578 | **441** | 1f.60 brown and black | 1·50 | 1·30 |

442 Running for Ball

1982. World Cup Football Championship, Spain. Sheet 143×120 mm containing T 442 and similar square designs, each brown, blue and green.
| MS1579 | 1f. Type **442**; 2f. Kicking ball; 3f. Heading ball; 4f. Goalkeeper | 11·00 | 10·00 |

443 St. Hubert (18th-century medallion)

1982. 29th Meeting of International Hunting Council, Monte Carlo.
| 1580 | **443** | 1f.60 multicoloured | 1·40 | 1·20 |

444 Books, Reader and Globe

1982. International Bibliophile Association General Assembly, Monte Carlo.
| 1581 | **444** | 1f.60 blue, purple & red | 1·20 | 1·00 |

445 "Casino, 1870"

1982. Monaco in the "Belle Epoque" (1st series). Paintings by Hubert Clerissi. Multicoloured.
| 1582 | 3f. Type **445** | 3·25 | 2·20 |
| 1583 | 5f. "Porte d'Honneur, Royal Palace, 1893" | 4·75 | 2·75 |

See also Nos. 1629/30, 1701/2, 1763/4, 1801/2, 1851/2, 1889/90 and 1965/6.

1982. Monaco Red Cross. The Twelve Labours of Hercules (2nd series). As T 422.
| 1584 | 2f.50+50c. green, red and bright red | 1·90 | 1·70 |
| 1585 | 3f.50+50c. brown, blue and red | 2·50 | 2·20 |

DESIGNS: 2f.50, Capturing the Erymanthine Boar; 3f.50, Shooting the Stymphalian Birds.

446 Nicolo Paganini (violinist and composer, bicent)

1982. Birth Anniversaries.
1586	**446**	1f.60 brown and purple	1·50	1·30
1587	-	1f.80 red, mauve & brn	2·30	1·70
1588	-	2f.60 green and red	3·00	2·75
1589	-	4f. multicoloured	5·25	4·50
1590	-	4f. multicoloured	5·25	4·50

DESIGNS:—VERT: No. 1587, Anna Pavlova (ballerina, centenary); 1588, Igor Stravinsky (composer, centenary). HORIZ (47×36 mm): 1589, "In a Boat" (Edouard Manet, 150th anniv); 1590, "The Black Fish" (Georges Braque, centenary).

447 Vase of Flowers

1982. Monte Carlo Flower Show (1983). Mult.
| 1591 | 1f.60 Type **447** | 2·50 | 1·70 |
| 1592 | 2f.60 Ikebana arrangement | 3·25 | 2·20 |

448 Bowl of Flowers

1982
| 1593 | **448** | 1f.60 multicoloured | 2·50 | 1·70 |

449 The Three Kings

1982. Christmas.
1594	**449**	1f.60 green, blue & orge	1·00	45
1595	-	1f.80 green, blue & orge	1·20	55
1596	-	2f.60 green, blue & orge	2·10	90
MS1597	143×105 mm. Nos. 1594/6	4·50	4·50

DESIGNS: 1f.80, The Holy Family; 2f.60, Shepherds and angels.

450 Prince Albert I and Polar Scene

1982. Centenary of First International Polar Year.
| 1598 | **450** | 1f.60 brown, green & bl | 3·25 | 2·20 |

451 Viking Longships off Greenland

1982. Millenary of Discovery of Greenland by Erik the Red.
| 1599 | **451** | 1f.60 blue, brown & blk | 3·25 | 2·20 |

452 Julius Caesar in the Port of Monaco ("Aeneid", Book VI)

1982. 2000th Death Anniv of Virgil (poet).
| 1600 | **452** | 1f.80 deep blue, blue and brown | 3·25 | 2·20 |

453 Spring

1983. Precancels. The Seasons of the Apple Tree.
1601	**453**	1f.05 purple, green and yellow	1·00	90
1602	-	1f.35 light green, deep green and turquoise	1·20	1·00
1603	-	2f.19 red, brown & grey	2·10	1·80
1604	-	3f.63 yellow and brown	1·90	2·40

DESIGNS: 1f.35, Summer; 2f.19, Autumn; 3f.63, Winter.

454 Tourism

1983. 50th Anniv of Exotic Garden. Mult.
1605	1f.80 Type **454**	1·90	1·70
1606	2f. Cactus plants (botanical collections)	2·40	1·90
1607	2f.30 Cactus plants (international flower shows)	2·75	2·20
1608	2f.60 Observatory grotto (horiz)	3·25	2·40
1609	3f.30 Museum of Prehistoric Anthropology (horiz)	3·75	2·75

455 Alaskan Malamute

1983. International Dog Show, Monte Carlo.
| 1610 | **455** | 1f.80 multicoloured | 9·75 | 5·50 |

456 Princess Grace

1983. Princess Grace Commemoration. Sheet 105×143 mm.
| MS1611 | **456** 10f. black | 13·00 | 13·00 |

457 St. Charles Borromee and Church

1983. Centenary of St. Charles Church, Monte Carlo.
| 1612 | **457** | 2f.60 deep blue, blue and green | 1·30 | 1·10 |

458 Montgolfier Balloon, 1783

1983. Europa.
| 1613 | **458** | 1f.80 blue, brown & grey | 1·90 | 75 |
| 1614 | - | 2f.60 grey, blue & brown | 1·90 | 1·10 |

MS1615 170×143 mm. Nos. 1613/14, each ×5		32·00	28·00

DESIGN: 2f.60, Space shuttle.

459 Franciscan College

1983. Centenary of Franciscan College, Monte Carlo.

1616	**459**	2f. grey, brown and red	1·30	1·10

460 Stadium

1983. Fontvieille Sports Stadium (2nd series).

1617	**460**	2f. green, blue and brown	1·30	1·10

461 Early and Modern Cars

1983. Centenary of Petrol-driven Motor Car.

1618	**461**	2f.90 blue, brown & green	3·75	2·75

462 Blue Whale

1983. International Commission for the Protection of Whales.

1619	**462**	3f.30 blue, light blue and grey	4·50	4·00

463 Dish Aerial, Pigeon, W.C.Y. Emblem and Satellite

1983. World Communications Year.

1620	**463**	4f. lilac and mauve	1·90	1·70

464 Smoking Moor

1983. Nineteenth Century Automata from the Galea Collection. Multicoloured.

1621	50c. Type **464**	40	35
1622	60c. Clown with diabolo	40	35
1623	70c. Smoking monkey	40	35
1624	80c. Peasant with pig	50	45
1625	90c. Buffalo Bill smoking	65	55
1626	1f. Snake charmer	75	65
1627	1f.50 Pianist	1·50	1·00
1628	2f. Young girl powdering herself	1·90	1·10

1983. Monaco in the "Belle Epoque" (2nd series). As T 445. Multicoloured.

1629	3f. "The Beach, 1902"	4·00	3·25
1630	5f. "Cafe de Paris, 1905"	5·25	4·50

1983. Monaco Red Cross. The Twelve Labours of Hercules (3rd series). As T 422.

1631	2f.50+50c. brn, bl & red	2·00	1·70
1632	3f.50+50c. violet, mve & red	2·75	2·20

DESIGNS: 2f.50, Capturing the Hind of Ceryneia; 3f.50, Cleaning the Augean stables.

465 Johannes Brahms (composer)

1983. Birth Anniversaries.

1633	**465**	3f. deep brown, brown and green	2·00	1·70
1634	-	3f. black, brown and red	2·00	1·70
1635	-	4f. multicoloured	4·00	2·75
1636	-	4f. multicoloured	4·00	2·75

DESIGNS—HORIZ: No. 1633, Type **465** (150th anniv); 1634, Giacomo Puccini (composer) and scene from "Madame Butterfly" (125th anniv). VERT (37×48 mm): 1635, "Portrait of a Young Man" (Raphael (artist), 500th anniv); 1636, "Cottin Passage" (Utrillo (artist), centenary).

466 Circus Performers

1983. 9th International Circus Festival, Monaco.

1637	**466**	2f. blue, red and green	2·00	1·70

467 Bouquet

1983. Monte Carlo Flower Show (1984). Mult.

1638	1f.60 Type **467**	1·90	1·10
1639	2f.60 Arrangement of poppies	3·00	2·40

468 Provencale Creche

1983. Christmas.

1640	**468**	2f. multicoloured	2·00	1·10

469 Nobel Literature Prize Medal

1983. 150th Birth Anniv of Alfred Nobel (inventor of dynamite and founder of Nobel Prizes).

1641	**469**	2f. black, grey and red	1·30	1·10

470 O. F. Ozanam (founder) and Paris Headquarters

1983. 150th Anniv of Society of St. Vincent de Paul.

1642	**470**	1f.80 violet and purple	1·30	1·10

471 "Tazerka" (oil rig)

1983. Oil Industry.

1643	**471**	5f. blue, brown & turq	3·00	1·70

472 Spring

1983. Seasons of the Fig. Sheet 143×100 mm containing T 472 and similar horiz designs.

MS1644 1f. green (Type **472**); 2f. green, yellow and red (Summer); 3f. green and (Autumn); 4f. green and red (Winter)	12·00	12·00

473 Gymnast with Ball

1984. Olympic Games, Los Angeles. Sheet 161×143 mm containing T 473 and similar vert designs, each brown, slate and red.

MS1645 2f. Type **473**; 3f. Gymnast with clubs; 4f. Gymnast with ribbon; 5f. Gymnast with hoop	11·00	11·00

474 Skater and Stadium

1984. Winter Olympic Games, Sarajevo.

1646	**474**	2f. blue, green and turquoise	1·30	1·10
1647	-	4f. blue, violet and purple	2·40	2·00

DESIGN: 4f. Skater and snowflake.

475 Bridge

1984. Europa. 25th Anniv of European Post and Telecommunications Conference.

1648	**475**	2f. blue	2·00	1·70
1649	**475**	3f. green	2·75	2·20
MS1650 143×170 mm. Nos. 1648/9, each ×4			33·00	28·00

476 Balkan Fritillary

1984. Butterflies and Moths in Mercantour National Park. Multicoloured.

1651	1f.60 Type **476**	2·75	1·70
1652	2f. "Zygaena vesubiana"	3·50	1·90
1653	2f.80 False mnestra ringlet	4·25	2·40
1654	3f. Small apollo (horiz)	4·75	2·75
1655	3f.60 Southern swallowtail (horiz)	5·25	3·25

477 Auvergne Pointer

1984. International Dog Show, Monte Carlo.

1656	**477**	1f.60 multicoloured	5·25	3·25

478 Sanctuary and Statue of Virgin

1984. Our Lady of Laghet Sanctuary.

1657	**478**	2f. blue, brown and green	1·30	55

479 Piccard's Stratosphere Balloon "F.N.R.S."

1984. Birth Centenary of Auguste Piccard (physicist).

1658	**479**	2f.80 black, green & blue	1·30	90
1659	-	4f. blue, green & turq	2·00	1·10

DESIGN: 4f. Bathyscaphe.

480 Concert

1984. 25th Anniv of Palace Concerts.

1660	**480**	3f.60 blue and deep blue	2·00	1·10

481 Place de la Visitation

1984. Bygone Monaco (1st series). Paintings by Hubert Clerissi.

1661	**481**	5c. brown	15	20
1662	-	10c. red	15	20
1663	-	15c. violet	25	20
1664	-	20c. blue	15	20
1665	-	30c. blue	25	20
1666	-	40c. green	1·10	35
1667	-	50c. red	25	10
1668	-	60c. blue	25	15
1669	-	70c. orange	65	45
1670	-	80c. green	65	35
1671	-	90c. mauve	65	35
1672	-	1f. blue	65	20
1673	-	2f. black	1·30	50
1674	-	3f. red	3·25	1·50
1675	-	4f. blue	2·00	1·10
1676	-	5f. green	2·75	1·50
1677	-	6f. green	4·00	2·20

DESIGNS: 10c. Town Hall; 15c. Rue Basse; 20c. Place Saint-Nicolas; 30c. Quai du Commerce; 40c. Rue des Iris; 50c. Ships in harbour; 60c. St. Charles's Church; 70c. Religious procession; 80c. Olive tree overlooking harbour; 90c. Quayside; 1f. Palace Square; 2f. Fishing boats in harbour; 3f. Bandstand; 4f. Railway station; 5f. Mail coach; 6f. Monte Carlo Opera House.

See also Nos. 2015/27.

482 Spring

1984. Precancels. The Seasons of the Quince.

1678	**482**	1f.14 red and green	80	80
1679	-	1f.47 deep green & green	85	90
1680	-	2f.38 olive, turquoise and green	1·60	1·50
1681	-	3f.95 green	2·10	2·00

DESIGNS: 1f.47, Summer; 2f.38, Autumn; 3f.95, Winter.

483 Shepherd

1984. Christmas. Crib Figures from Provence. Multicoloured.

1682	70c. Type **483**	65	45
1683	1f. Blind man	80	55
1684	1f.70 Happy man	1·60	1·10
1685	2f. Spinner	2·00	1·40
1686	2f.10 Angel playing trumpet	2·10	1·50
1687	2f.40 Garlic seller	2·30	1·60
1688	3f. Drummer	2·75	1·80
1689	3f.70 Knife grinder	3·25	2·30
1690	4f. Elderly couple	4·00	2·75

484 Gargantua and Cattle

1984. 450th Anniv of First Edition of "Gargantua" by Francois Rabelais.

1691	**484**	2f. black, red and brown	2·00	1·40
1692	-	2f. black, red and blue	2·00	1·40
1693	-	4f. green	3·25	2·30

DESIGNS—As T **484**: No. 1692, Panurge's sheep. 36×48 mm: 1693, Francois Rabelais.

485 Bowl of Mixed Flowers

1984. Monte Carlo Flower Show (1985). Mult.

1694		2f.10 Type **485**	2·00	1·40
1695		3f. Ikebana arrangement	3·25	2·30

486 Television Lights and Emblem

1984. 25th Int Television Festival, Monte Carlo.

1696	**486**	2f.10 blue, grey and mauve	1·30	90
1697	-	3f. grey, blue and red	2·10	1·50

DESIGN: 3f. "Golden Nymph" (Grand Prix).

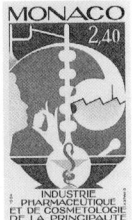

487 Chemical Equipment

1984. Pharmaceutical and Cosmetics Industry.

1698	**487**	2f.40 blue, deep blue and green	1·30	90

1984. Monaco Red Cross. The Twelve Labours of Hercules (4th series). As T 422.

1699	3f.+50c. brown, light brown and red	2·00	1·80
1700	4f.+50c. green, brown and red	2·75	2·30

DESIGNS: 3f. Killing the Cretan bull; 4f. Capturing the Mares of Diomedes.

1984. Monaco in the "Belle Epoque" (3rd series). Paintings by Hubert Clerissi. As T 445. Mult.

1701	4f. "Grimaldi Street, 1908" (vert)	4·75	3·75
1702	5f. "Railway Station, 1910" (vert)	6·75	5·25

488 Clown

1984. Tenth International Circus Festival, Monaco. Sheet 88 x 72 mm.

MS1703	**488** 5f. multicoloured	8·00	7·50

489 "Woman with Chinese Vase"

1984. 150th Birth Anniv of Edgar Degas (artist).

1704	**489**	6f. multicoloured	6·75	4·75

490 Spring

1985. Precancels. Seasons of the Cherry.

1705	**490**	1f.22 olive, green and blue	1·10	85
1706	-	1f.57 red, green and yellow	1·20	95
1707	-	2f.55 orange and brown	1·50	1·70
1708	-	4f.23 purple, green and blue	2·10	2·30

DESIGNS: 1f.57, Summer; 2f.55, Autumn; 4f.23, Winter.

491 First Stamp

1985. Centenary of First Monaco Stamps.

1709	**491**	1f.70 green	95	75
1710	**491**	2f.10 red	1·20	95
1711	**491**	3f. blue	1·90	1·50

493 "Berardia subacaulis"

1985. Flowers in Mercantour National Park. Mult.

1724	1f.70 Type **493**	1·30	90
1725	2f.10 "Saxifraga florulenta" (vert)	1·60	1·10
1726	2f.40 "Fritillaria moggridgei" (vert)	1·90	1·30
1727	3f. "Sempervivum allionii" (vert)	2·40	1·70
1728	3f.60 "Silene cordifolia" (vert)	3·00	2·00
1729	4f. "Primula allionii"	3·25	2·30

494 Spring

1985. Seasons of the Japanese Medlar. Sheet 144×100 mm containing T 494 and similar horiz designs.

MS1730	1f. olive and deep olive (Type **494**); 2f. olive, yellow and deep olive (Summer); 3f. olive and deep olive (Autumn); 4f. orange, yellow and olive (Winter)	9·50	8·25

495 Nadia Boulanger (composer)

1985. 25th Anniv of First Musical Composition Competition.

1731	**495**	1f.70 brown	1·20	85
1732	-	2f.10 blue	1·70	1·20

DESIGN: 2f.10, Georges Auric (composer).

496 Stadium and Runners

1985. Inauguration of Louis II Stadium, Fontvieille, and Athletics and Swimming Championships.

1733	**496**	1f.70 brown, red and violet	1·20	85
1734	-	2f.10 blue, brown and green	1·70	1·20

DESIGN: 2f.10, Stadium and swimmers.

497 Prince Antoine I

1985. Europa.

1735	**497**	2f.10 blue	2·00	1·40
1736	-	3f. red	2·75	1·80

MS1737 170×143 mm. Nos. 1735/6, each ×5   40·00   37·00

DESIGN: 3f. John-Baptiste Lully (composer).

498 Museum, "Hirondelle I" (schooner) and "Denise" (midget submarine)

1985. 75th Anniv of Oceanographic Museum.

1738	**498**	2f.10 black, green and blue	1·40	1·00

499 Boxer

1985. International Dog Show, Monte Carlo.

1739	**499**	2f.10 multicoloured	3·00	2·30

500 Scientific Motifs

1985. 25th Anniv of Scientific Centre.

1740	**500**	3f. blue, black and violet	1·90	1·10

501 Children and Hands holding Seedling and Emblem

1985. International Youth Year.

1741	**501**	3f. brown, green and light brown	1·90	1·10

502 Regal Angelfish

1985. Fishes in Oceanographic Museum Aquarium (1st series). Multicoloured.

1742	1f.80 Type **502**	2·00	1·50
1743	1f.90 Type **502**	3·00	1·80
1744	2f.20 Powder blue surgeonfish	2·10	1·60
1745	3f.20 Red-tailed butterflyfish	2·75	2·00
1746	3f.40 As No. 1745	4·75	2·75
1747	3f.90 Clown triggerfish	3·25	2·40
1748	7f. Fishes in aquarium (36×48 mm)	5·00	3·75

See also Nos. 1857/62.

503 Catamaran

1985. Monaco–New York Sailing Race. Sheet 143×105 mm containing T 503 and similar vert designs. Each black, blue and turquoise.

MS1749	4f. Type **503**; 4f. Single hull yacht; 4f. Trimaran	7·50	7·50

504 Rome Buildings and Emblem

1985. "Italia '85" International Stamp Exhibition, Rome.

1750	**504**	4f. black, green and red	2·00	1·50

505 Clown

1985. 11th International Circus Festival, Monaco.

1751	**505**	1f.80 multicoloured	1·90	1·40

506 Decorations

1985. Christmas.

1752	**506**	2f.20 multicoloured	1·50	1·10

507 Ship and Marine Life

1985. Fish Processing Industry.

1753	**507**	2f.20 blue, turquoise and brown	1·10	85

508 Arrangement of Roses, Tulips and Jonquil

1985. Monte Carlo Flower Show (1986). Mult.

1754		2f.20 Type **508**	1·90	1·40
1755		3f.20 Arrangement of chrysanthemums and heather	2·75	2·00

509 Globe and Satellite

1985. European Telecommunications Satellite Organization.

1756	**509**	3f. black, blue and violet	1·90	1·40

510 Sacha Guitry (actor, centenary)

1985. Birth Anniversaries.

1757	**510**	3f. orange and brown	1·90	1·40
1758	-	4f. blue, brown and mauve	2·50	1·80
1759	-	5f. turquoise, blue and grey	3·00	2·30

| 1760 | - | 6f. blue, brown and black | 3·75 | 2·75 |

DESIGNS: 4f. Wilhelm and Jacob Grimm (folklorists, bicentenaries); 5f. Frederic Chopin and Robert Schumann (composers, 175th annivs); 6f. Johann Sebastian Bach and Georg Friedrich Handel (composers, 300th annivs).

1985. Monaco Red Cross. The Twelve Labours of Hercules (5th series). As T 422.

| 1761 | | 3f.+70c. green, deep red and red | 1·90 | 1·40 |
| 1762 | | 4f.+80c. brown, blue & red | 2·10 | 1·60 |

DESIGNS: 3f. The Cattle of Geryon; 4f. The Girdle of Hippolyte.

1985. Monaco in the "Belle Epoque" (4th series). As T 445, showing paintings by Hubert Clerissi. Multicoloured.

| 1763 | | 4f. "Port of Monaco, 1912" | 3·75 | 2·75 |
| 1764 | | 6f. "Avenue de la Gare 1920" | 5·00 | 3·75 |

511 Prince Charles III

1985. Centenary of First Monaco Stamps (2nd issue). Sheet 142×71 mm containing T 511 and similar vert designs. Each blue and black.

| MS1765 | 5f. Type 511; 5f. Prince Albert I; 5f. Prince Louis II; 5f. Prince Rainier III | | 10·00 | 10·00 |

512 Spring

1986. Precancels. Seasons of the Hazel Tree.

1766	512	1f.28 brown, green & bl	75	75
1767	-	1f.65 green, brown & yell	80	85
1768	-	2f.67 grey, brown and deep brown	1·50	1·50
1769	-	4f.44 green and brown	2·00	2·00

DESIGNS: 1f.65, Summer; 2f.67, Autumn; 4f.44, Winter.

513 Ancient Monaco

1986. 10th Anniv of "Annales Monegasques" (historical review).

| 1770 | 513 | 2f.20 grey, blue and brown | 1·20 | 90 |

514 Scotch Terriers

1986. International Dog Show, Monte Carlo.

| 1771 | 514 | 1f.80 multicoloured | 6·25 | 4·25 |

515 Mouflon

1986. Mammals in Mercantour National Park. Multicoloured.

1772	2f.20 Type 515		1·40	1·00
1773	2f.50 Ibex		1·90	1·40
1774	3f.20 Chamois		2·50	1·80
1775	3f.90 Alpine marmot (vert)		3·00	2·30
1776	5f. Arctic hare (vert)		3·75	2·75
1777	7f.20 Stoat (vert)		5·00	3·75

516 Research Vessel "Ramoge"

1986. Europa. Each green, blue and red.

| 1778 | 2f.20 Type 516 | | 2·50 | 1·20 |

| 1779 | 3f.20 Underwater nature reserve, Larvotto beach | 3·00 | 1·60 |

| MS1780 | 171×144 mm. Nos. 1778/79, each ×5 | 37·00 | 32·00 |

517 Prince Albert I and National Council Building

1986. Anniversaries and Events.

1781	517	2f.50 brown and green	1·20	90
1782	-	3f.20 brown, red and black	2·20	1·70
1783	-	3f.90 purple and red	3·00	2·30
1784	-	5f. green, red and blue	3·75	1·40

DESIGNS—HORIZ: 2f.50, Type 517 (75th anniv of First Constitution); 3f.20, Serge Diaghilev and dancers (creation of new Monte Carlo ballet company); 3f.90, Henri Rougier and Turcat-Mery car (75th Anniv of first Monte Carlo Rally). VERT: 5f. Flags and Statue of Liberty (centenary).

518 Chicago and Flags

1986. "Ameripex '86" International Stamp Exhibition, Chicago.

| 1785 | 518 | 5f. black, red and blue | 2·50 | 1·80 |

519 Player and Mayan Figure

1986. World Cup Football Championship, Mexico. Sheet 100×143 mm containing T 519 and similar vert design. Each black, red and blue.

| MS1786 | 5f. Type 519; 7f. Goalkeeper and Mayan figures | 8·75 | 8·25 |

520 Comet, Telescopes and 1532 Chart by Apian

1986. Appearance of Halley's Comet.

| 1787 | 520 | 10f. blue, brown & green | 5·00 | 3·25 |

521 Monte Carlo and Congress Centre

1986. 30th International Insurance Congress.

| 1788 | 521 | 3f.20 blue, brown & grn | 1·70 | 1·30 |

522 Christmas Tree Branch and Holly

1986. Christmas. Multicoloured.

| 1789 | 1f.80 Type 522 | | 1·00 | 45 |
| 1790 | 2f.50 Christmas tree branch and poinsettia | | 1·50 | 75 |

523 Clown's Face and Elephant on Ball

1986. 12th International Circus Festival, Monaco.

| 1791 | 523 | 2f.20 multicoloured | 2·20 | 1·70 |

524 Posy of Roses and Acidanthera

1986. Monte Carlo Flower Show (1987). Mult.

| 1792 | 2f.20 Type 524 | | 2·00 | 1·30 |
| 1793 | 3f.90 Lilies and beech in vase | | 3·00 | 2·00 |

1986. Monaco Red Cross. The Twelve Labours of Hercules (6th series). As T 422.

| 1794 | 3f.+70c. green, yell & red | | 1·90 | 1·40 |
| 1795 | 4f.+80c. blue, brown & red | | 2·50 | 1·80 |

DESIGNS: 3f. The Golden Apples of the Hesperides; 4f. Capturing Cerberus.

525 Making Plastic Mouldings for Car Bodies

1986. Plastics Industry.

| 1796 | 525 | 3f.90 turquoise, red and grey | 2·00 | 1·50 |

526 Scenes from "Le Cid" (Pierre Corneille)

1986. Anniversaries.

| 1797 | 526 | 4f. deep brown & brown | 2·00 | 1·50 |
| 1798 | - | 5f. brown and blue | 2·50 | 1·80 |

DESIGNS: 4f. Type 526 (350th anniv of first performance); 5f. Franz Liszt (composer) and bible (175th birth anniv).

527 Horace de Saussure, Mont Blanc and Climbers

1986. Bicentenary of First Ascent of Mont Blanc by Dr. Paccard and Jacques Balmat.

| 1799 | 527 | 5f.80 blue, red and black | 3·00 | 2·20 |

528 "The Olympic Diver" (Emma de Sigaldi)

1986. 25th Anniv of Unveiling of "The Olympic Diver" (statue).

| 1800 | 528 | 6f. multicoloured | 3·00 | 2·30 |

1986. Monaco in the "Belle Epoque" (5th series). Paintings by Hubert Clerissi. As T 445. Mult.

| 1801 | 6f. "Bandstand and Casino, 1920" (vert) | | 5·00 | 3·75 |
| 1802 | 7f. "Avenue du Beau Rivage, 1925" (vert) | | 6·25 | 4·50 |

1986. Seasons of the Strawberry Tree. Sheet 143×100 mm containing T 529 and similar horiz designs.

| MS1803 | 3f. red and olive (T 529); 4f. olive, lake and red (Summer); 5f. lake, olive and brown-red (Autumn); 6f. olive and red (Winter) | 12·50 | 12·00 |

530 Spring

1987. Precancels. Seasons of the Chestnut.

1804	530	1f.31 green, yellow & brn	75	75
1805	-	1f.69 green and brown	80	85
1806	-	2f.74 brown, yellow & bl	1·20	1·50
1807	-	4f.56 brown, grn & grey	1·90	2·00

DESIGNS: 1f.69, Summer; 2f.74, Autumn; 4f.56, Winter.

531 Golden Hunter

1987. Insects in Mercantour National Park. Multicoloured.

1808	1f. Type 531		60	55
1809	1f.90 Golden wasp (vert)		1·20	90
1810	2f. Green tiger beetle		1·40	1·00
1811	2f.20 Brown aeshna (vert)		1·60	1·20
1812	3f. Leaf beetle		3·00	1·80
1813	3f.40 Grasshopper (vert)		4·00	2·75

532 St. Devote Church

1987. Centenary of St. Devote Parish Church.

| 1814 | 532 | 1f.90 brown | 1·00 | 75 |

533 Dogs

1987. International Dog Show, Monte Carlo.

| 1815 | 533 | 1f.90 grey, black & brn | 2·50 | 1·80 |
| 1816 | - | 2f.70 black and green | 4·00 | 2·75 |

DESIGN: 2f.70, Poodle.

534 Stamp Album

1987. Stamp Day.

| 1817 | 534 | 2f.20 red, purple and mauve | 1·20 | 65 |

535 Louis II Stadium, Fontvieille

1987. Europa. Each blue, green and red.

| 1818 | 2f.20 Type 535 | | 2·50 | 1·40 |
| 1819 | 3f.40 Crown Prince Albert Olympic swimming pool | | 3·00 | 1·80 |

| MS1820 | 143×71 mm. Nos. 1818/19, each ×5 | 37·00 | 32·00 |

536 Cathedral

1987. Centenary of Monaco Diocese.

| 1821 | 536 | 2f.50 green | 1·50 | 90 |

537 Spring

1987. Seasons of the Vine. Sheet 142×100 mm containing T 537 and similar horiz designs.
MS1822 3f. green and brown (Type
537); 4f. green and brown (Summer);
5f. violet, brown and green (Autumn); 6f. orange-brown (Winter)   19·00   17·00

538 Lawn Tennis

1987. 2nd European Small States Games, Monaco.
1823 **538** 3f. black, red and purple   2·75   2·00
1824 - 5f. blue and black   3·50   2·50
DESIGN: 5f. Sailing dinghies and windsurfer.

539 "Red Curly Tail" (Alexander Calder)

1987. "Monte Carlo Sculpture 1987" Exhibition.
1825 **539** 3f.70 multicoloured   2·00   1·50

540 Prince Rainier III

1987. 50th Anniv of Monaco Stamp Issuing Office.
1826 **540** 4f. blue   2·20   2·30
1827 - 4f. red   2·20   2·30
1828 - 8f. black   4·50   3·75
DESIGNS: No. 1827, Prince Louis II. (47×37 mm): 1828, Villa Miraflores.

541 Swallowtail on Stamp

1987. International Stamp Exhibition.
1829 **541** 1f.90 deep green and green   85   65
1830 **541** 2f.20 purple and red   1·20   90
1831 **541** 2f.50 purple and mauve   1·40   1·00
1832 **541** 3f.40 deep blue and blue   2·00   1·50

542 Festival Poster (J. Ramel)

1987. 13th International Circus Festival, Monaco (1988).
1833 **542** 2f.20 multicoloured   2·50   1·80

543 Christmas Scenes

1987. Christmas.
1834 **543** 2f.20 red   1·20   90

544 Strawberry Plants and Campanulas in Bowl

1987. Monte Carlo Flower Show (1988). Mult.
1835 2f.20 Type **544**   1·90   1·20
1836 3f.40 Ikebana arrangement of water lilies and dog roses (horiz)   2·10   1·60

545 Obverse and Reverse of Honore V 5f. Silver Coin

1987. 150th Anniv of Revival of Monaco Coinage.
1837 **545** 2f.50 black and red   1·20   90

546 Graph, Factory, Electron Microscope and Printed Circuit

1987. Electro-Mechanical Industry.
1838 **546** 2f.50 blue, green and red   1·20   90

547 St. Devote

1987. Monaco Red Cross. St. Devote, Patron Saint of Monaco (1st series). Multicoloured.
1839 4f. Type **547**   2·20   1·40
1840 5f. St. Devote and her nurse   2·75   2·00
See also Nos. 1898/9, 1956/7, 1980/1, 2062/3 and 2101/2.

1987. 50th Anniv of Monaco Stamp Issuing Office (2nd issue). Sheet 140×70 mm containing T 540 and other designs. Each purple.
MS1841 4f. Type **540**; 4f. As No. 1827; 8f. As No. 1828   8·75   8·25

548 Oceanographic Museum and I.A.E.A. Headquarters, Vienna

1987. 25th Anniv of International Marine Radioactivity Laboratory, Monaco.
1842 **548** 5f. black, brown and blue   2·50   1·80

549 Jouvet

1987. Birth Centenary of Louis Jouvet (actor).
1843 **549** 3f. black   1·50   1·10

550 River Crossing

1987. Bicentenary of First Edition of "Paul and Virginia" by Bernardin de Saint-Pierre.
1844 **550** 3f. green, orange and blue   1·50   1·10

551 Marc Chagall (painter)

1987. Anniversaries.
1845 **551** 4f. black and red   2·10   1·60
1846 - 4f. purple, red and brown   2·10   1·60
1847 - 4f. red, blue and brown   2·10   1·60
1848 - 4f. green, brown & purple   2·10   1·60
1849 - 5f. blue, brown and green   3·00   2·30
1850 - 5f. brown, green and blue   3·00   2·30
DESIGNS: No. 1845, Type **551** (birth centenary); 1846, Chapel of Ronchamp and Charles Edouard Jeanneret (Le Corbusier) (architect, birth centenary); 1847, Sir Isaac Newton (mathematician) and diagram (300th anniv of publication of "Principia Mathematica"); 1848, Key and Samuel Morse (inventor, 150th Anniv of Morse telegraph); 1849, Wolfgang Amadeus Mozart and scene from "Don Juan" (opera, bicentenary of composition); 1850, Hector Berlioz (composer) and scene from "Mass for the Dead" (150th anniv of composition).

1987. Monaco in the "Belle Epoque" (6th series). As T 445 showing paintings by Hubert Clerissi. Multicoloured.
1851 6f. "Main Ramp to Palace Square, 1925" (vert)   5·00   3·75
1852 7f. "Monte Carlo Railway Station, 1925" (vert)   5·50   4·25

552 Coat of Arms

1987
1853 **552** 2f. multicoloured   1·10   85
1854 **552** 2f.20 multicoloured   1·00   75

553 Spanish Hogfish

1988. Fishes in Oceanographic Museum Aquarium (2nd series). Multicoloured.
1857 2f. Type **553**   1·20   90
1858 2f.20 Copper-banded butterflyfish   1·50   1·10
1859 2f.50 Harlequin filefish   2·00   1·50
1860 3f. Blue boxfish   2·20   1·70
1861 3f.70 Lionfish   3·00   2·30
1862 7f. Moon wrasse (horiz)   5·00   3·75

554 Spring

1988. Precancels. Seasons of the Pear Tree. Multicoloured.
1863 1f.36 Type **554**   75   75
1864 1f.75 Summer   80   85
1865 2f.83 Autumn   1·20   1·50
1866 4f.72 Winter   1·90   2·00
See also Nos. 1952/5.

555 Cross-country Skiing

1988. Winter Olympic Games, Calgary. Sheet 143×93 mm containing T 555 and similar horiz design. Each black, lilac and blue.
MS1867 4f. Type **555**; 6f. Shooting   25·00   18·00

556 Dachshunds

1988. European Dachshunds Show, Monte Carlo.
1868 **556** 3f. multicoloured   3·00   2·30

557 Children of different Races around Globe

1988. 25th Anniv of World Association of Friends of Children.
1869 **557** 5f. green, brown and blue   3·00   2·30

558 Satellite Camera above Man with World as Brain

1988. Europa. Transport and Communications. Each black, brown and red.
1870 2f.20 Type **558**   2·50   1·80
1871 3f.60 Atlantique high speed mail train and aircraft propeller   3·75   2·75
MS1872 170×143 mm. Nos. 1870/1, each ×5   37·00   32·00

559 Coxless Four

1988. Centenary of Monaco Nautical Society (formerly Regatta Society).
1873 **559** 2f. blue, green and red   1·50   1·10

560 Jean Monnet (statesman)

1988. Birth Centenaries.
1874 **560** 2f. black, brown and blue   3·75   2·75
1875 - 2f. black and blue   3·75   2·75
DESIGN: No. 1875, Maurice Chevalier (entertainer).

561 "Leccinum rotundifoliae"

1988. Fungi in Mercantour National Park. Multicoloured.
1876 2f. Type **561**   1·50   1·10
1877 2f.20 Crimson wax cap   1·90   1·40
1878 2f.50 "Pholiota flammans"   2·20   1·70
1879 2f.70 "Lactarius lignyotus"   2·75   2·00
1880 3f. Goaty smell (vert)   3·00   2·30
1881 7f. "Russula olivacea" (vert)   5·25   3·75

562 Nansen

1988. Centenary of First Crossing of Greenland by Fridtjof Nansen (Norwegian explorer).
1882 **562** 4f. violet   3·00   2·20

563 Church and "Miraculous Virgin"

1988. Restoration of Sanctuary of Our Lady of Laghet.
| 1883 | **563** | 5f. multicoloured | 2·50 | 1·80 |

564 Anniversary Emblem

1988. 40th Anniv of W.H.O.
| 1884 | **564** | 6f. red and blue | 3·25 | 2·40 |

565 Anniversary Emblem

1988. 125th Anniv of Red Cross.
| 1885 | **565** | 6f. red, grey and black | 3·25 | 2·40 |

566 Congress Centre

1988. 10th Anniv of Monte Carlo Congress Centre.
| 1886 | **566** | 2f. green | 1·20 | 90 |
| 1887 | - | 3f. red | 1·50 | 1·10 |
DESIGN: 3f. Auditorium.

567 Tennis

1988. Olympic Games, Seoul. New Women's Disciplines. Sheet 143×100 mm containing T 567 and similar horiz designs. Each brown, black and blue.
| MS1888 | 2f. Type **567**; 3f. Table tennis; 5f. "470" dinghy; 7f. Cycling | 12·50 | 12·00 |

1988. Monaco in the "Belle Epoque" (7th series). Paintings by Hubert Clerissi. As T 445. Mult.
| 1889 | | 6f. "Steam packet in Monte Carlo Harbour, 1910" | 5·00 | 3·25 |
| 1890 | | 7f. "Place de la Gare, 1910" | 6·25 | 4·25 |

568 Festival Poster (J. Ramel)

1988. 14th International Circus Festival, Monaco (1989).
| 1891 | **568** | 2f. multicoloured | 1·90 | 1·40 |

569 Star Decoration

1988. Christmas.
| 1892 | **569** | 2f. multicoloured | 1·40 | 1·00 |

570 Arrangement of Fuchsias, Irises, Roses and Petunias

1988. Monte Carlo Flower Show (1989).
| 1893 | **570** | 3f. multicoloured | 2·20 | 1·70 |

571 Models

1988. Ready-to-Wear Clothing Industry.
| 1894 | **571** | 3f. green, orange & black | 1·90 | 1·40 |

572 Lord Byron (bicentenary)

1988. Writers' Birth Anniversaries.
| 1895 | **572** | 3f. black, brown and blue | 1·90 | 1·40 |
| 1896 | - | 3f. purple and blue | 1·90 | 1·40 |
DESIGN: No. 1896, Pierre de Marivaux (300th anniv).

573 Spring

1988. Seasons of the Olive Tree. Sheet 143×100 mm containing T 573 and similar horiz designs.
| MS1897 | 3f. deep olive, yellow and olive (Type **573**); 4f. deep olive and olive (Summer); 5f. deep olive and olive (Autumn); 6f. deep olive and olive (Winter) | 17·00 | 17·00 |

1988. Monaco Red Cross. St. Devote, Patron Saint of Monaco (2nd series). As T 547. Multicoloured.
| 1898 | | 4f. Roman governor Barbarus arriving at Corsica | 2·40 | 1·70 |
| 1899 | | 5f. St. Devote at the Roman senator Eutychius's house | 3·00 | 2·30 |

574 "Le Nain and his Brothers" (Antoine Le Nain)

1988. Artists' Birth Anniversaries.
| 1900 | **574** | 5f. brown, olive and red | 3·50 | 2·50 |
| 1901 | - | 5f. black, green and blue | 3·50 | 2·50 |
DESIGNS: No. 1900, Type **574** (400th anniv); 1901, "The Great Archaeologists" (bronze statue, Giorgio de Chirico) (centenary).

575 Sorcerer

1989. Rock Carvings in Mercantour National Park. Multicoloured.
1902		2f. Type **575**	1·20	90
1903		2f.20 Oxen in yoke	1·20	90
1904		3f. Hunting implements	1·90	1·40
1905		3f.60 Tribal chief	2·50	1·80

| 1906 | | 4f. Puppet (vert) | 3·00 | 2·30 |
| 1907 | | 5f. Jesus Christ (vert) | 3·75 | 2·75 |

576 Rue des Spelugues

1989. Old Monaco (1st series). Multicoloured.
| 1908 | | 2f. Type **576** | 1·10 | 85 |
| 1909 | | 2f.20 Place Saint Nicolas | 1·40 | 1·00 |
See also Nos. 1969/70 and 2090/1.

577 Prince Rainier

1989
1910	**577**	2f. blue and azure	1·00	65
1911	**577**	2f.10 blue and azure	1·10	45
1912	**577**	2f.20 brown and pink	1·20	75
1913	**577**	2f.20 blue and azure	1·20	65
1914	**577**	2f.30 brown and pink	1·20	65
1915	**577**	2f.40 blue and azure	1·20	65
1916	**577**	2f.50 brown and pink	1·20	90
1917	**577**	2f.70 blue	1·00	55
1918	**577**	2f.80 brown and pink	1·50	75
1919	**577**	3f. brown and pink	1·10	85
1920	**577**	3f.20 blue and cobalt	1·90	1·40
1922	**577**	3f.40 blue and cobalt	2·00	1·50
1923	**577**	3f.60 blue and cobalt	2·10	1·60
1924	**577**	3f.70 blue and cobalt	2·50	1·00
1925	**577**	3f.80 purple and lilac	2·50	1·80
1926	**577**	3f.80 blue and cobalt	1·40	90
1927	**577**	4f. purple and lilac	2·50	1·80
1930	**577**	5f. brown and pink	2·50	1·70
1932	**577**	10f. deep green and green	4·00	2·30
1934	**577**	15f. blue and grey	7·50	5·00
1936	**577**	20f. red and pink	8·00	5·00
1938	**577**	25f. black and grey	10·00	6·50
1940	**577**	40f. brown and pink	15·00	9·25
See also Nos. 2388/90.

578 Yorkshire Terrier

1989. International Dog Show, Monte Carlo.
| 1941 | **578** | 2f.20 multicoloured | 1·90 | 1·30 |

579 Magician, Dove and Cards

1989. 5th Grand Prix of Magic, Monte Carlo.
| 1942 | **579** | 2f.20 black, blue and red | 1·50 | 1·10 |

580 Nuns and Monks around "Our Lady of Misericorde"

1989. 350th Anniv of Archiconfrerie de la Misericorde.
| 1943 | **580** | 3f. brown, black and red | 1·70 | 1·30 |

581 Charlie Chaplin (actor) and Film Scenes

1989. Birth Centenaries.
| 1944 | | 3f. green, blue and mauve | 1·70 | 1·30 |
| 1945 | **581** | 4f. purple, green and red | 2·50 | 1·80 |
DESIGN: 3f. Jean Cocteau (writer and painter), scene from "The Double-headed Eagle" and frescoes in Villefrance-sur-Mer chapel.

582 Spring

1989. Seasons of the Pomegranate. Sheet 144×100 mm containing T 582 and similar horiz designs.
| MS1946 | 3f. red, green and (Type **582**); 4f. brown, green and red (Summer); 5f. green, red and brown (Autumn); 6f. brown and green (Winter) | 12·00 | 12·00 |

583 Boys playing Marbles

1989. Europa. Children's Games. Each mauve, brown and grey.
1947		2f.20 Type **583**	1·90	1·40
1948		3f.60 Girls skipping	3·00	2·30
MS1949	171×143 mm. Nos. 1947/8, each ×5	31·00	31·00

584 Prince Rainier

1989. 40th Anniv of Reign of Prince Rainier. Sheet 100×130 mm.
| MS1950 | **584** | 20f. lilac | 12·50 | 12·00 |

585 "Lliberty"

1989. "Philexfrance 89" International Stamp Exhibition, Paris. Sheet 143×105 mm containing T 585 and similar vert designs.
| MS1951 | 5f. blue (Type **585**); 5f. black ("Equality"); 5f. red ("Fraternity") | 8·25 | 8·25 |

1989. Precancels. As Nos. 1863/6 but values changed. Multicoloured.
1952		1f.39 Type **554**	75	75
1953		1f.79 Summer	80	85
1954		2f.90 Autumn	1·20	1·50
1955		4f.84 Winter	1·90	2·00

1989. Monaco Red Cross. St. Devote, Patron Saint of Monaco (3rd series). As T 547. Multicoloured.
| 1956 | | 4f. St. Devote beside the dying Eutychius | 2·10 | 1·60 |
| 1957 | | 5f. Barbarus condemns St. Devote to torture for refusing to make a sacrifice to the gods | 3·00 | 2·30 |

586 "Artist's Mother" (Philibert Florence)

1989. Artists' 150th Birth Anniversaries.
| 1958 | **586** | 4f. brown | 3·00 | 2·30 |
| 1959 | - | 6f. multicoloured | 3·75 | 2·75 |

1960	-	8f. multicoloured	5·00	3·75

DESIGNS—HORIZ: 6f. "Molesey Regatta" (Alfred Sisley).
VERT: 8f. "Farmyard at Auvers" (Paul Cezanne).

587 Poinsettia,
Christmas Roses
and Holly

1989. Christmas.

1961	**587**	2f. multicoloured	2·75	2·00

588 Map and Emblem

1989. Centenary of Interparliamentary Union.

1962	**588**	4f. black, green and red	2·50	1·80

589 Princess Grace
(founder)

1989. 25th Anniv of Princess Grace Foundation. Sheet
133×104 mm containing T 589 and similar vert
design. Each blue.

MS1963	5f. Type **589**; 5f. Princess Caroline (Foundation president)	10·00	10·00

590 Monaco Palace, White House,
Washington, and Emblem

1989. 20th U.P.U. Congress, Washington D.C.

1964	**590**	6f. blue, brown and black	3·00	2·30

1989. Monaco in the "Belle Epoque" (8th series). Paintings
by Hubert Clerissi. As T 445. Mult.

1965	7f. "Barque in Monte Carlo Harbour, 1915" (vert)	4·25	3·00
1966	8f. "Gaming Tables, Casino, 1915" (vert)	5·25	3·75

591 World Map

1989. 10th Anniv of Monaco Aide et Presence (welfare
organization).

1967	**591**	2f.20 brown and red	3·00	2·30

592 Clown and
Horses

1989. 15th International Circus Festival, Monte Carlo.

1968	**592**	2f.20 multicoloured	3·75	2·75

1990. Old Monaco (2nd series). Paintings by Claude
Rosticher. As T 576. Multicoloured.

1969	2f.10 La Rampe Major	1·00	75
1970	2f.30 Town Hall Courtyard	1·10	85

593 Phalaenopsis
"Princess Grace"

1990. International Garden and Greenery Exposition,
Osaka, Japan. Multicoloured.

1971	2f. Type **593**	1·20	90
1972	3f. Iris "Grace Patricia"	1·90	1·40
1973	3f. "Paphiopedilum" "Prince Rainier III"	1·90	1·40
1974	4f. "Cattleya" "Principessa Grace"	2·50	1·80
1975	5f. Rose "Caroline of Monaco"	3·50	2·30

594 Bearded Collie

1990. International Dog Show, Monte Carlo.

1976	**594**	2f.30 multicoloured	2·30	1·70

595 Noghes and Racing Car

1990. Birth Centenary of Antony Noghes (founder of
Monaco Grand Prix and Monte Carlo Rally).

1977	**595**	3f. red, lilac and black	1·70	1·20

596 Cyclist and
Lancia Rally Car

1990. Centenary of Automobile Club of Monaco
(founded as Cycling Racing Club).

1978	**596**	4f. blue, brown & purple	2·30	1·70

597 Telephone, Satellite and Dish
Aerial

1990. 125th Anniv of I.T.U.

1979	**597**	4f. lilac, mauve and blue	2·30	1·70

1990. Monaco Red Cross. St. Devote, Patron Saint of
Monaco (4th series). As T 547. Multicoloured.

1980	4f. St. Devote being flogged	2·30	1·70
1981	5f. Placing body of St. Devote in fishing boat	3·00	2·20

598 Sir Rowland Hill and Penny
Black

1990. 150th Anniv of Penny Black.

1982	**598**	5f. blue and black	3·25	2·30

599 "Post Office,
Place de la Mairie"

1990. Europa. Post Office Buildings. Paintings by Hubert
Clerissi. Multicoloured.

1983	2f.30 Type **599**	1·90	1·40
1984	3f.70 "Post Office, Avenue d'Ostende"	3·25	2·30
MS1985	170×145 mm. Nos. 1983/4, each ×4	39·00	32·00

600 Ball, Player and Trophy

1990. World Cup Football Championship, Italy. Sheet
142×100 mm containing T 600 and similar horiz
designs.

MS1986	5f. green, black and red; (Type **600**); 5f. black, red and green (Players); 5f. black and green (Pitch, ball and map of Italy); 5f. red, green and black (Pitch, players and stadium)	17·00	17·00

601 Anatase

1990. Minerals in Mercantour National Park. Mult.

1987	2f.10 Type **601**	1·30	90
1988	2f.30 Albite	1·40	1·00
1989	3f.20 Rutile	1·90	1·40
1990	3f.80 Chlorite	2·50	1·80
1991	4f. Brookite (vert)	2·75	2·00
1992	6f. Quartz (vert)	4·50	3·25

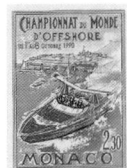

602 Powerboat

1990. World Offshore Powerboat Racing Championship.

1993	**602**	2f.30 brown, red & blue	1·50	1·10

603 Pierrot writing
(mechanical toy)

1990. Philatelic Round Table.

1994	**603**	3f. blue	1·80	1·30

604 Christian Samuel Hahnemann
(founding of homeopathy)

1990. Bicentenaries.

1995	**604**	3f. purple, green & black	1·80	1·30
1996	-	5f. chestnut, brown & bl	2·75	2·00

DESIGN: 5f. Jean-Francois Champollion (Egypt-ologist)
and hieroglyphics (birth bicentenary).

605 Bell 206B Jet-Ranger III
Helicopters at Monaco
Heliport, Fontvieille

1990. 30th International Civil Airports Association
Congress, Monte Carlo.

1997	**605**	3f. black, red and brown	1·90	1·40
1998	-	5f. black, blue and brown	3·25	1·80

DESIGN: 5f. Aerospatiale AS-350 Ecureuil helicopters over
Monte Carlo Congress Centre.

606 Petanque
Player

1990. 26th World Petanque Championship.

1999	**606**	6f. blue, brown & orange	3·75	2·75

607 Spring

1990. Precancels. Seasons of the Plum Tree.
Multicoloured.

2000	1f.46 Type **607**	75	75
2001	1f.89 Summer	85	85
2002	3f.06 Autumn	1·30	1·50
2003	5f.10 Winter	1·90	2·00

608 Miller on
Donkey

1990. Christmas. Crib figures from Provence.
Multicoloured.

2004	2f.30 Type **608**	1·30	90
2005	3f.20 Woman carrying faggots	1·90	1·40
2006	3f.80 Baker	2·50	1·80

See also Nos. 2052/4, 2097/9, 2146/8 and 2191/3.

609 Spring

1990. Seasons of the Lemon Tree. Sheet 143×100
mm containing T 609 and similar horiz designs.
Multicoloured.

MS2007	3f. Type **609**; 4f. Summer; 5f. Autumn; 6f. Winter	13·00	12·00

610 Pyotr Ilich
Tchaikovsky
(composer)

1990. 150th Birth Anniversaries.

2008	**610**	5f. blue and green	2·75	2·00
2009	-	5f. bistre and blue	2·75	2·00
2010	-	7f. multicoloured	6·50	5·50

DESIGNS—As T **610**: No. 2009, "Cathedral" (Auguste Rodin, sculptor). 48×37 mm: "The Magpie" (Claude Monet,
painter).

611 Clown playing
Concertina

1991. 16th International Circus Festival, Monte Carlo.

2011	**611**	2f.30 multicoloured	1·90	1·30

See also No. 2069.

1991. Bygone Monaco (2nd series). Paintings by Hubert
Clerissi. As T 481.

2015	20c. purple	25	20
2017	40c. green	25	20
2018	50c. red	25	20
2019	60c. blue	25	20
2020	70c. green	40	30
2021	80c. blue	40	30
2022	90c. lilac	40	30

2023	1f. blue	55	35
2024	2f. red	80	55
2025	3f. black	1·30	90
2027	7f. grey and black	3·25	2·30

DESIGNS: 20c. Rock of Monaco and Fontvieille; 40c. Place du Casino; 50c. Place de la Cremaillere and railway station; 60c. National Council building; 70c. Palace and Rampe Major; 80c. Avenue du Beau Rivage; 90c. Fishing boats, Fontvieille; 1f. Place d'Armes; 2f. Marche de la Condamine; 3f. Yacht; 7f. Oceanographic Museum.

612 Abdim's Stork

1991. International Symposium on Bird Migration. Multicoloured.
2029	2f. Type **612**	1·30	90
2030	3f. Broad-tailed hummingbirds	2·00	1·40
2031	4f. Garganeys	2·75	1·80
2032	5f. Eastern broad-billed roller	3·25	2·30
2033	6f. European bee eaters	4·00	2·75

613 Phytoplankton

1991. Oceanographic Museum (1st series).
| 2034 | **613** | 2f.10 multicoloured | 1·60 | 1·10 |

See also Nos. 2095/6.

614 Schnauzer

1991. International Dog Show, Monte Carlo.
| 2035 | **614** | 2f.50 multicoloured | 2·75 | 1·80 |

615 Cyclamen, Lily-of-the-Valley and Pine Twig in Fir-cone

1991. Monte Carlo Flower Show.
| 2036 | **615** | 3f. multicoloured | 1·90 | 1·30 |

616 Corals

1991. "Joys of the Sea" Exhibition. Multicoloured.
| 2037 | 2f.20 Type **616** | 1·30 | 90 |
| 2038 | 2f.40 Coral necklace | 2·00 | 1·40 |

617 Control Room, "Eutelsat" Satellite and Globe

1991. Europa. Europe in Space. Each blue, black and green.
2039	2f.30 Type **617**	2·75	1·80
2040	3f.20 Computer terminal, "Inmarsat" satellite, research ship transmitting signal and man with receiving equipment	4·00	2·75
MS2041	143×171 mm. Nos. 2039/40, each ×5	37·00	32·00

618 Cross-country Skiers and Statue of Skiers by Emma de Sigaldi

1991. 1992 Olympic Games. (a) Winter Olympics, Albertville.
| 2042 | **618** | 3f. green, blue and olive | 1·90 | 1·30 |
| 2043 | - | 4f. green, blue and olive | 2·40 | 1·70 |

(b) Olympic Games, Barcelona.
| 2044 | 3f. green, lt brown & brown | | 1·30 |
| 2045 | 5f. black, brown and green | 3·25 | 2·20 |

DESIGNS: No. 2043, Right-hand part of statue and cross-country skiers; 2044, Track, relay runners and left part of statue of relay runners by Emma de Sigaldi; 2045, Right part of statue, view of Barcelona and track.

619 Head of "David" (Michelangelo), Computer Image and Artist at Work

1991. 25th International Contemporary Art Prize.
| 2046 | **619** | 4f. green, dp green & lilac | 2·75 | 1·80 |

620 Prince Pierre, Open Book and Lyre

1991. 25th Anniv of Prince Pierre Foundation.
| 2047 | **620** | 5f. black, blue and brown | 3·25 | 2·30 |

621 Tortoises

1991. Endangered Species. Hermann's Tortoise. Multicoloured.
2048	1f.25 Type **621**	1·60	1·10
2049	1f.25 Head of tortoise	1·60	1·10
2050	1f.25 Tortoise in grass	1·60	1·10
2051	1f.25 Tortoise emerging from among plants	1·60	1·10

1991. Christmas. As T 608 showing crib figures from Provence. Multicoloured.
2052	2f.50 Consul	1·70	1·20
2053	3f.50 Arlesian woman	2·75	1·80
2054	4f. Mayor	3·00	2·00

622 Norway Spruce

1991. Conifers in Mercantour National Park. Multicoloured.
2055	2f.50 Type **622**	1·30	90
2056	3f.50 Silver fir	2·00	1·40
2057	4f. "Pinus uncinata"	2·30	1·60
2058	5f. Scots pine (vert)	2·75	1·80
2059	6f. Arolla pine	3·25	2·30
2060	7f. European larch (vert)	4·00	2·75

623 Spring

1991. Seasons of the Orange Tree. Sheet 142×101 mm containing T 623 and similar horiz designs.
| MS2061 | 3f. orange, green and brown (Type **623**); 4d. green and brown (Summer); 5f. green, orange and brown (Autumn); 6f. green and olive-brown (Winter) | 13·50 | 13·00 |

1991. Monaco Red Cross. St. Devote, Patron Saint of Monaco (5th series). As T 547. Multicoloured.
| 2062 | 4f.50 Fishing boat carrying body caught in storm | 2·75 | 1·80 |
| 2063 | 5f.50 Dove guiding boatman to port of Monaco | 3·00 | 2·00 |

624 "Portrait of Claude Monet"

1991. 150th Birth Anniv of Auguste Renoir (painter).
| 2064 | **624** | 5f. multicoloured | 3·25 | 2·30 |

625 Prince Honore II of Monaco

1991. 350th Anniv of Treaty of Peronne (giving French recognition of sovereignty of Monaco). Paintings by Philippe de Champaigne. Mult.
| 2065 | 6f. Type **625** | 4·00 | 2·75 |
| 2066 | 7f. King Louis XIII of France | 5·25 | 3·75 |

626 Princess Grace (after R. Samini)

1991. 10th Anniv of Princess Grace Theatre.
| 2067 | **626** | 8f. multicoloured | 5·50 | 3·75 |

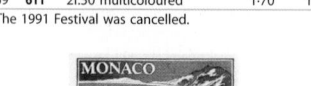

627 1891 Stamp Design

1991. Centenary of Prince Albert Stamps. Sheet 114×72 mm.
| MS2068 | **627** | 10f. red; 10f. green; 10f. lilac | 17·00 | 18·00 |

1992. 16th International Circus Festival, Monte Carlo. As No. 2011 but value and dates changed.
| 2069 | **611** | 2f.50 multicoloured | 1·70 | 1·20 |

The 1991 Festival was cancelled.

628 Two-man Bobsleighs

1992. Winter Olympic Games, Albertville (7f.), and Summer Games, Barcelona (8f.).
| 2070 | 7f. blue, turquoise & blk | 4·00 | 2·75 |
| 2071 | - | 8f. purple, blue and green | 4·25 | 3·00 |

DESIGN: 8f. Football.

629 Spring

1992. Exotic Gardens. Seasons of the Prickly Pear. Sheet 142×100 mm containing T 629 and similar horiz designs. Multicoloured.
| MS2072 | 3f. Type **629**; 4f. Summer; 5f. Autumn; 6f. Winter | 13·50 | 12·00 |

630 Spring

1992. Precancels. Seasons of the Walnut Tree. Mult.
2073	1f.60 Type **630**	80	85
2074	2f.08 Summer	85	90
2075	2f.98 Autumn	1·30	1·50
2076	5f.28 Winter	2·00	2·00

631 Golden Labrador

1992. International Dog Show, Monte Carlo.
| 2077 | **631** | 2f.20 multicoloured | 3·00 | 1·50 |

632 Racing along Seafront

1992. 50th Monaco Grand Prix.
| 2078 | **632** | 2f.50 black, purple & bl | 1·60 | 1·10 |

633 Mixed Bouquet

1992. 25th Monte Carlo Flower Show.
| 2079 | **633** | 3f.40 multicoloured | 2·75 | 1·80 |

634 Ford Sierra Rally Car

1992. 60th Monte Carlo Car Rally.
| 2080 | **634** | 4f. black, green and red | 3·00 | 2·00 |

635 Rough-toothed Dolphin (Steno bredanensis)

1992. Mediterranean Dolphins. Sheet 142×100 mm containing T 635 and similar horiz designs. Multicoloured.
| MS2081 | 4f. Type **635** 5f. Common dolphin (Delphinus delphis); 6f. Bottle-nosed dolphin (Tursiops truncates); 7f. Striped dolphin (Stenella coeruleoalba) | 16·00 | 16·00 |

636 "Pinta" off Palos

1992. Europa. 500th Anniv of Discovery of America by Columbus. Multicoloured.
| 2082 | 2f.50 Type **636** | 2·00 | 1·40 |
| 2083 | 3f.40 "Santa Maria" in the Antilles | 3·25 | 2·30 |

2084 4f. "Nina" off Lisbon 4·25 3·00

MS2085 140×170 mm. Nos. 2082/4, each ×2 33·00 28·00

637 Produce

1992. "Ameriflora" Horticultural Show, Columbus, Ohio. Multicoloured.

2086 4f. Type **637** 2·75 1·80

2087 5f. Vase of mixed flowers 3·25 2·30

638 Prince Rainier I and Fleet (detail of fresco by E. Charpentier, Spinola Palace, Genoa)

1992. Columbus Exhibition, Genoa (6f.), and "Expo '92" World's Fair, Seville (7f.).

2088 **638** 6f. brown, red and blue 3·25 2·30

2089 - 7f. brown, red and blue 4·00 2·75

DESIGN: 7f. Monaco pavilion.

1992. Old Monaco (3rd series). Paintings by Claude Rosticher. As T 576. Multicoloured.

2090 2f.20 La Porte Neuve (horiz) 1·30 90

2091 2f.50 La Placette Bosio (horiz) 1·30 90

639 "Christopher Columbus"

1992. "Genova '92" International Thematic Stamp Exhibition. Roses. Multicoloured.

2092 3f. Type **639** 2·40 1·70

2093 4f. "Prince of Monaco" 3·00 2·00

640 Lammergeier

1992

2094 **640** 2f.20 orange, blk & grn 2·00 1·40

1992. Oceanographic Museum (2nd series). As T 613. Multicoloured.

2095 2f.20 "Ceratium ranipes" 2·00 1·40

2096 2f.50 "Ceratium hexacanthum" 2·00 1·40

1992. Christmas. As T 608 showing crib figures from Provence. Multicoloured.

2097 2f.50 Basket-maker 2·00 1·40

2098 3f.40 Fishwife 2·40 1·70

2099 5f. Rural constable 3·00 2·00

641 "Seabus" (projected tourist submarine)

1992

2100 **641** 4f. blue, red and brown 2·40 1·70

642 Burning Boat Ceremony, St. Devote's Eve

1992. Monaco Red Cross. St. Devote, Patron Saint of Monaco (6th series).

2101 **642** 6f. red, blue and brown 3·25 2·30

2102 - 8f. purple, orange and red 4·00 2·75

DESIGN: 8f. Procession of reliquary, St. Devote's Day.

643 Athletes, Sorbonne University and Coubertin

1992. Centenary of Pierre de Coubertin's Proposal for Revival of Olympic Games.

2103 **643** 10f. blue 5·50 3·75

644 Baux de Provence and St. Catherine's Chapel

1992. Titles of Princes of Monaco. Marquis of Baux de Provence.

2104 **644** 15f. multicoloured 7·25 5·00

645 1856 40c. Sardinian Stamp

1992. Stamp Museum. Sheet 115×72 mm containing T 645 and similar vert design.

MS2105 10f. red and black (Type **645**); 10f. green and black (1860 1c. French stamp) 12·00 12·00

646 Clown and Tiger

1993. 17th Int Circus Festival, Monte Carlo.

2106 **646** 2f.50 multicoloured 1·60 1·10

647 Short-toed Eagles

1993. Birds of Prey in Mercantour National Park.

2107 **647** 2f. chestnut, brown and orange 1·30 90

2108 - 3f. indigo, orange & blue 2·00 1·40

2109 - 4f. brown, ochre and blue 2·75 1·80

2110 - 5f. brown, chestnut and green 3·00 2·00

2111 - 6f. brown, mauve & grn 4·00 2·75

DESIGNS—HORIZ: 3f. Peregrine falcon. VERT: 4f. Eagle owl; 5f. Western honey buzzard; 6f. Tengmalm's owl.

648 Fin Wale (*Balaenoptera physalus*)

1993. Mediterranean Whales. Sheet 143×100 mm containing T 648 and similar horiz designs. Multicoloured.

MS2112 4f. Type **648**; 5f. Minke whale (*Balaenoptera acutorostrata*); 6f. Sperm whale (Physeter catodon); 7f. Cuvier's beaked whale (Ziphius cavirostris) 16·00 18·00

649 Spring

1993. Seasons of the Almond. Sheet 142×100 mm containing T 649 and similar horiz designs. Multicoloured.

MS2113 5f. Type **649**; 5f. Summer; 5f. Autumn; 5f. Winter 13·50 13·00

650 Mixed Bouquet

1993. Monte Carlo Flower Show.

2114 **650** 3f.40 multicoloured 1·90 1·30

651 Pennants, Auditorium and Masks

1993. 10th International Amateur Theatre Festival.

2115 **651** 4f.20 multicoloured 2·40 1·70

652 Fire Fighting and Rescue

1993. World Civil Protection Day.

2116 **652** 6f. black, red and green 4·00 2·75

653 Newfoundland

1993. International Dog Show, Monte Carlo.

2117 **653** 2f.20 multicoloured 1·70 1·20

654 Golfer

1993. 10th Monte Carlo Open Golf Tournament.

2118 **654** 2f.20 multicoloured 1·30 90

655 Princess Grace

1993. 10th Death Anniv (1992) of Princess Grace.

2119 **655** 5f. blue 2·30 1·60

656 Mirror and Candelabra

1993. 10th Antiques Biennale.

2120 **656** 7f. multicoloured 3·50 2·40

657 "Echinopsis multiplex"

1993. Cacti.

2121 **657** 2f.50 green, purple & yell 1·20 85

2122 - 2f.50 green and purple 1·20 85

2123 - 2f.50 green, purple & yell 1·20 85

2124 - 2f.50 green and yellow 1·20 85

DESIGNS: No. 2122, "Zygocactus truncatus"; 2123, "Echinocereus procumbens"; 2124, "Euphorbia virosa".

See also Nos. 2154/66.

658 Monte Carlo Ballets

1993. Europa. Contemporary Art.

2125 **658** 2f.50 black, brn & pink 2·00 1·40

2126 - 4f.20 grey and brown 2·75 1·80

MS2127 143×172 mm. Nos. 2125/6, each ×3 14·50 14·50

DESIGN: 4f.20, "Evolution" (sculpture, Emma de Sigaldi).

659

1993. Admission to United Nations Organization. Sheet 115×72 mm.

MS2128 10f. blue (T **659**); 10f. brown (T **577**); 10f. red and brown (State Arms) 16·00 14·50

660 State Arms and Olympic Rings

1993. 110th International Olympic Committee Session, Monaco.

2129 **660** 2f.80 red, brown & blue 1·10 90

2130 - 2f.80 blue, lt blue & red 1·10 90

2131 - 2f.80 brown, blue & red 1·10 90

2132 - 2f.80 blue, lt blue & red 1·10 90

2133 - 2f.80 brown, blue & red 1·10 90

2134 - 2f.80 blue, lt blue & red 1·10 90

2135 - 2f.80 brown, blue & red 1·10 90

2136 **660** 2f.80 blue, lt blue & red 1·10 90

2137 - 4f.50 multicoloured 2·00 1·40

2138 - 4f.50 black, yellow & bl 2·00 1·60

2139 - 4f.50 red, yellow & blue 2·00 1·60

2140 - 4f.50 black, yellow & bl 2·00 1·60

2141 - 4f.50 red, yellow & blue 2·00 1·60

2142 - 4f.50 black, yellow & bl 2·00 1·60

2143 - 4f.50 red, yellow & blue 2·00 1·60

2144 - 4f.50 red, yellow & blue 2·00 1·60

DESIGNS: 2130, Bobsleighing; 2131, Skiing; 2132, Yachting; 2133, Rowing; 2134, Swimming; 2135, Cycling; 2136, 2144, Commemorative inscription; 2138, Gymnastics (rings exercise); 2139, Judo; 2140, Fencing; 2141, Hurdling; 2142, Archery; 2143, Weightlifting.

661 Examining 1891 1c. Stamp

1993. Centenary of Monaco Philatelic Union.

2145 **661** 2f.40 multicoloured 1·30 90

1993. Christmas. Crib figures from Provence. As T 608. Multicoloured.

2146 2f.80 Donkey 1·30 90

2147 3f.70 Shepherd holding lamb 2·00 1·40

2148 4f.40 Ox lying down in barn 2·40 1·70

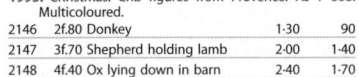

662 Grieg, Music and Trolls

1993. 150th Birth Anniv of Edvard Grieg (composer).
2149 **662** 4f. blue   3·25   2·30

663 Abstract Lithograph

1993. Birth Centenary of Joan Miro (painter and sculptor).
2150 **663** 5f. multicoloured   3·25   2·30

664 Monaco Red Cross Emblem

1993. Monaco Red Cross.
2151 **664** 5f. red, yellow and black   2·75   1·80
2152 –   6f. red and black   3·00   2·00
DESIGN: 6f. Crosses inscribed with fundamental principles of the International Red Cross.

665 "St. Joseph the Carpenter"

1993. 400th Birth Anniv of Georges de la Tour (painter).
2153 **665** 6f. multicoloured   3·25   2·30

1994. Cacti. As Nos. 2121/4 but values changed and additional designs.
2153a   10c. green, orange and red   15   20
2154 **657** 20c. green, purple and yellow   25   20
2155 –   30c. green and purple   25   20
2156 –   40c. green and yellow   25   20
2157 –   50c. green, red and olive   25   20
2158 –   60c. green, red and yellow   35   25
2159 –   70c. green, red and blue   40   30
2160 –   80c. green, orange and red   40   30
2161 –   1f. green, brown and yellow   40   30
2162 –   2f. green, red and yellow   80   55
2163 –   2f.70 green, red and yellow   1·10   75
2164 –   4f. green, purple and yellow   1·50   1·00
2165 –   4f. green, red and yellow   2·00   1·40
2166 –   5f. green, mauve and brown   2·10   1·50
2167 –   6f. brown, green and red   2·40   1·70
2167a –   7f. green, brown and red   2·75   1·80
DESIGNS: 10c. "Bromelia brevifolia"; 30c. "Zygocactus truncatus"; 40c. "Euphorbia virosa"; 50c. "Selenicereus grandiflorus"; 60c. "Opuntia basilaris"; 70c. "Aloe plicatilis"; 80c. "Opuntia hybride"; 1f. "Stapelia flavirostris"; 2f. "Aporocactus flagelliformis"; 2f.70, "Opuntia dejecta"; 4f. (2164), "Echinocereus procumbens"; 4f. (2165), "Echinocereus blanckii"; 5f. "Cereus peruvianus"; 6f. "Euphorbia milii"; 7f. "Stapelia variegata".

666 Festival Poster

1994. 18th Int Circus Festival, Monte Carlo.
2168 **666** 2f.80 multicoloured   1·60   1·10

667 Artist/Poet

1994. Mechanical Toys.
2169 **667** 2f.80 blue   1·20   95
2170 –   2f.80 red   1·20   95
2171 –   2f.80 purple   1·20   95
2172 –   2f.80 green   1·20   95
DESIGNS: No. 2170, Bust of Japanese woman; 2171, Shepherdess with sheep; 2172, Young Parisienne.

1994. Mediterranean Whales and Dolphins. Sheet 143×100 mm containing horiz designs as T 648. Multicoloured.
MS2173 4f. Killer whale (*Orcimus orca*); 5f. Risso's dolphin (*Grampus griseus*); 6f. False killer whale (*Pseudorca crassidens*); 7f. Long-finned pilot whale (*Globicephala melas*)   16·00   16·00

668

1994. Winter Olympic Games, Lillehammer, Norway. Sheet 123×80 mm containing T 668 and similar horiz design. Each blue and red.
MS2174 10f. Type 668; 10f. Bobsleighing   12·00   12·00

669 King Charles Spaniels

1994. International Dog Show, Monte Carlo.
2175 **669** 2f.40 multicoloured   1·90   1·30

670 Couple, Leaves and Pollution

1994. Monaco Committee of Anti-tuberculosis and Respiratory Diseases Campaign.
2176 **670** 2f.40+60c. mult   1·60   1·10

671 Iris

1994. Monte Carlo Flower Show.
2177 **671** 4f.40 multicoloured   2·75   1·80

672 Levitation Trick

1994. 10th Monte Carlo Magic Grand Prix.
2178 **672** 5f. blue, black and red   2·75   1·80

673 Ingredients and Dining Table overlooking Harbour

1994. 35th Anniv of Brotherhood of Cordon d'Or French Chefs.
2179 **673** 6f. multicoloured   3·25   2·30

674 Isfjord, Prince Albert I, Map of Spitzbergen and "Princess Alice II"

1994. Europa. Discoveries made by Prince Albert I. Each black, blue and red.
2180   2f.80 Type 674   2·00   1·40
2181   4f.50 Oceanographic Museum, Grimaldi's spookfish and "Eryoneicus alberti" (crustacean)   2·75   1·80
MS2182 155×130 mm. Nos. 2180/1, each ×3   16·00   14·50

675 Olympic Flag and Sorbonne University

1994. Centenary of International Olympic Committee.
2183 **675** 3f. multicoloured   1·60   1·10

676 Dolphins through Porthole

1994. Economic Institute of the Rights of the Sea Conference, Monaco.
2184 **676** 6f. multicoloured   3·25   2·30

677 Family around Tree of Hearts

1994. International Year of the Family.
2185 **677** 7f. green, orange and blue   3·50   2·40

678 Footballer's Legs and Ball

1994. World Cup Football Championship, U.S.A.
2186 **678** 8f. red and black   4·00   2·75

679 Athletes and Villa Miraflores

1994. Inauguration of New Seat of International Amateur Athletics Federation.
2187 **679** 8f. blue, purple and bistre   4·00   2·75

680 De Dion Bouton, 1903

1994. Vintage Car Collection of Prince Rainier III.
2188 **680** 2f.80 black, brown and mauve   1·60   1·10

681 Emblem and Monte Carlo

1994. 1st Association of Postage Stamp Catalogue Editors and Philatelic Publications Grand Prix.
2189 **681** 3f. multicoloured   1·70   1·20

682 Emblem and Korean Scene

1994. 21st Universal Postal Union Congress, Seoul.
2190 **682** 4f.40 black, blue and red   3·00   2·00

1994. Christmas. As T 608 showing crib figures from Provence. Multicoloured.
2191   2f.80 Virgin Mary   1·50   1·00
2192   4f.50 Baby Jesus   2·30   1·60
2193   6f. Joseph   3·00   2·00

683 Prince Albert I

1994. Inaug of Stamp and Coin Museum (1st issue). Coins.
2194 **683** 3f. stone, brown and red   1·30   90
2195 –   4f. grey, brown and red   2·00   1·40
2196 –   7f. stone, brown and red   4·00   2·75
MS2197 115×73 mm. 10f. ×3, As Nos. 2194/6   17·00   17·00
DESIGNS: 4f. Arms of House of Grimaldi; 7f. Prince Rainier III.
See also Nos. MS2225; 2265/7 and 2283/MS6.

684 Three Ages of Voltaire (writer, 300th anniv)

1994. Birth Anniversaries.
2198 **684** 5f. green   2·75   1·80
2199 –   6f. brown and purple   3·25   2·30
DESIGN—HORIZ: 6f. Sarah Bernhardt (actress, 150th anniv).

685 Heliport and Bell 206 Helicopter

1994. 50th Anniv of International Civil Aviation Organization.
2200	685	5f. green, black and blue	2·75	1·80
2201	-	7f. brown, black and red	3·50	2·40

DESIGN: 7f. Harbour and Eurocopter AS365 Dauphin 2 helicopter.

686 Spring

1994. 1st European Stamp Salon, Flower Gardens, Paris. Seasons of the Apricot. Sheet 142×100 mm containing T 686 and similar horiz designs. Multicoloured.
MS2202	6f. Type 686; 7f. Summer; 8f. Autumn; 9f. Winter	17·00	17·00

687 Blood Vessels on Woman (anti-cancer)

1994. Monaco Red Cross. Health Campaigns.
2203	687	6f. blue, black and red	2·75	1·80
2204	-	8f. green, black and red	4·00	2·75

DESIGN: 8f. Tree and woman (anti-AIDS).

688 Robinson Crusoe and Friday

1994. Anniversaries. Multicoloured.
2205	7f. Type 688 (275th anniv of publication of "Robinson Crusoe" by Daniel Defoe)	4·00	2·75
2206	9f. "The Snake Charmer" (150th birth anniv of Henri Rousseau, painter)	4·75	3·25

689 Clown playing Trombone

1995. 19th Int Circus Festival, Monte Carlo.
2207	689	2f.80 multicoloured	1·60	1·10

690 Crown Prince Albert

1995. 35th Television Festival, Monte Carlo.
2208	690	8f. brown	4·00	2·75

691 Fontvieille

1995. European Nature Conservation Year.
2209	691	2f.40 multicoloured	1·50	1·00

692 American Cocker Spaniel

1995. International Dog Show, Monte Carlo.
2210	692	4f. multicoloured	2·10	1·40

693 Parrot Tulips

1995. Monte Carlo Flower Show.
2211	693	5f. multicoloured	2·50	1·70

694 "Acer palmatum"

1995. European Bonsai Congress.
2212	694	6f. multicoloured	3·00	2·00

695 Alfred Nobel (founder of Nobel Prizes) and Dove

1995. Europa. Peace and Freedom. Multicoloured.
2213	2f.80 Type 695	2·75	1·80
2214	5f. Roses, broken chain and watchtower	3·50	2·30

696 Emblem of Monagasque Disabled Children Association

1995. Int Special Olympics, New Haven, U.S.A.
2215	696	3f. multicoloured	1·20	85

697 Emblem

1995. Rotary International Convention, Nice.
2216	697	4f. blue	1·90	1·30

699 Jean Giono

1995. Writers' Birth Centenaries.
2218	699	5f. lilac, brown and green	2·50	1·70
2219	-	6f. brown, violet and green	3·00	2·00

DESIGN: 6f. Marcel Pagnol.

700 Saint Hubert (patron saint of hunting)

1995. General Assembly of International Council for Hunting and Conservation of Game.
2220	700	6f. blue	3·00	2·00

701 Princess Caroline (President)

1995. World Association of Friends of Children General Assembly, Monaco.
2221	701	7f. blue	3·50	2·40

702 Athletes and Medal

1995. International Amateur Athletics Federation Grand Prix, Monaco.
2222	702	7f. mauve, purple and grey	3·50	2·40

703 "Trophee des Alpes" (Hubert Clerissi)

1995. 2000th Anniv of Emperor Augustus Monument, La Turbie.
2223	703	8f. multicoloured	4·25	2·75

704 Prince Pierre (after Philip Laszlo de Lombos)

1995. Birth Centenary of Prince Pierre of Monaco.
2224	704	10f. purple	5·00	3·25

705 1974 60c. Honore II Stamp

1995. Inauguration of Stamp and Coin Museum (2nd issue). Sheet 135×89 mm containing T 705 and similar designs.
MS2225	10f. red, brown and blue (T 706); 10f. blue and brown (entrance of museum) (vert); 10f. blue (1051 30f. first museum stamp)	15·00	16·00

706 St. Antony (wooden statue)

1995. 800th Birth Anniv of St. Antony of Padua.
2226	706	2f.80 multicoloured	1·10	75

707 United Nations Charter and Peacekeeping Soldiers

1995. 50th Anniv of U.N.O.
2227	707	2f.50 multicoloured	1·40	90
2228	-	2f.50 multicoloured	1·40	90
2229	-	2f.50 multicoloured	1·40	90
2230	-	2f.50 blue, black and brown	1·40	90
2231	-	3f. black, brown and blue	1·70	1·10
2232	-	3f. multicoloured	1·70	1·10
2233	-	3f. multicoloured	1·70	1·10
2234	-	3f. multicoloured	1·70	1·10

MS2235 112×151 mm. 3f. As No. 2227; 3f. As No. 2228; 3f. As No. 2229; 3f. As No. 2230; 4f.50 As No. 2231; 4f.50, As No. 2232; 4f.50, As No. 2233; 4f.50, As No. 2234   17·00   17·00

DESIGNS: No. 2228, Wheat ears, boy and arid ground; 2229, Children from different nationalities; 2230, Head of Colossus, Abu Simbel Temple; 2231, United Nations meeting; 2232, Growing crops and hand holding seeds; 2233, Figures and alphabetic characters; 2234, Lute and UNESCO head-quarters, Paris.

Nos. 2228 and 2232 commemorate the F.A.O., Nos. 2229 and 2233 International Year of Tolerance, Nos. 2230 and 2234 UNESCO.

708 Rose "Grace de Monaco"

1995. Flowers. Multicoloured.
2236	3f. Type 708		1·50	1·00
2237	3f. Fuchsia "Lakeland Princess"		1·50	1·00
2238	3f. Carnation "Centenaire de Monte-Carlo"		1·50	1·00
2239	3f. Fuchsia "Grace"		1·50	1·00
2240	3f. Rose "Princesse de Monaco"		1·50	1·00
2241	3f. Alstroemeria "Gracia"		1·50	1·00
2242	3f. Lily "Princess Gracia"		1·50	1·00
2243	3f. Carnation "Princesse Caroline"		1·50	1·00
2244	3f. Rose "Stephanie de Monaco"		1·50	1·00
2245	3f. Carnation "Prince Albert"		1·50	1·00
2246	3f. Sweet pea "Grace de Monaco"		1·50	1·00
2247	3f. Gerbera "Gracia"		1·50	1·00

709 Balthazar

1995. Christmas. Crib Figures from Provence of the Three Wise Men. Multicoloured.
2248	3f. Type 709	1·20	75
2249	5f. Gaspard	2·10	1·30
2250	6f. Melchior	2·75	1·70

710 Tree, Bird, Seahorse and Association Emblem

1995. 20th Anniv of Monaco Association for Nature Protection.
2251	710	4f. green, black and red	2·10	1·30

711 Rontgen and X-Ray of Hand

1995. Centenary of Discovery of X-Rays by Wilhelm Rontgen.

| 2252 | **711** | 6f. black, yellow and green | 3·25 | 2·00 |

712 First Screening to Paying Public, Paris, December 1895

1995. Centenary of Motion Pictures.

| 2253 | **712** | 7f. blue | 3·75 | 2·40 |

713 Allegory of Anti-leprosy Campaign

1995. Monaco Red Cross. Multicoloured.

| 2254 | | 7f. Type **713** | 3·75 | 2·30 |
| 2255 | | 8f. Doctors Prakash and Mandakini Amte (anti-leprosy campaign in India) | 4·50 | 2·75 |

714 First Car with Tyres

1995. Centenary of Invention of Inflatable Tyres.

| 2256 | **714** | 8f. purple and claret | 4·50 | 2·75 |

715 "Spring"

1995. 550th Birth Anniv of Sandro Botticelli (artist).

| 2257 | **715** | 15f. blue | 10·50 | 7·75 |

716 Poster

1996. 20th International Circus Festival, Monte Carlo.

| 2258 | **716** | 2f.40 multicoloured | 1·50 | 90 |

717 Illusion

1996. Magic Festival, Monte Carlo.

| 2259 | **717** | 2f.80 black | 1·60 | 1·00 |

718 Rhododendron

1996. Monte Carlo Flower Show.

| 2260 | **718** | 3f. multicoloured | 1·80 | 1·10 |

719 Wire-haired Fox Terrier

1996. International Dog Show, Monte Carlo.

| 2261 | **719** | 4f. multicoloured | 2·30 | 1·50 |

720 "Chapel" (Hubert Clerissi)

1996. 300th Anniv of Chapel of Our Lady of Mercy.

| 2262 | **720** | 6f. multicoloured | 3·25 | 2·00 |

721 Prince Albert I of Monaco

1996. Centenary of Oceanographic Expeditions. Multicoloured.

| 2263 | | 3f. Type **721** | 1·80 | 1·10 |
| 2264 | | 4f.50 King Carlos I of Portugal | 2·75 | 1·70 |

722 Prince Rainier III (after F. Messina)

1996. Inauguration of Stamp and Coin Museum (2nd issue). 1974 Prince Rainier design.

2265	**722**	10f. violet	4·50	3·00
2266	**722**	15f. brown	6·50	4·50
2267	**722**	20f. blue	8·75	6·00

723 Princess Grace

1996. Europa. Famous Women.

| 2268 | **723** | 3f. brown and red | 4·50 | 2·50 |

724 Fishes, Sea and Coastline

1996. 20th Anniv of Ramoge Agreement on Environmental Protection of Mediterranean.

| 2269 | **724** | 3f. multicoloured | 1·80 | 1·20 |

725 Saint Nicolas (detail of altarpiece by Louis Brea)

1996. 20th Anniv of Annales Monegasques (historical review). Sheet 180×100 mm containing T 725. and similar vert designs. Each brown.

MS2270 3f. Type **725**; 3f. hector Berlioz (composer); 4f. Guillaume Apollinaire (poet and art critic); 4f. Niccolo Machiavelli (statesman); 5f. Jean-Baptiste Bosio (painter); 5f. Sidonie Colette (writer); 6f. Francois-Joseph Bosio (sculptor); 6f. Michel Eyquém de Montaigne (writer and philosopher)   26·00   25·00

726 Chinese Acrobatics Group in Monaco

1996. Monaco–Chinese Diplomatic Relations. Sheet 100×60 mm containing T 726 and similar horiz design. Multicoloured.

MS2271 5f. Type **726**; 5f. Fuling Tomg, Peking   6·00   6·00

727 Code and Monaco

1996. Introduction of International Dialling Code "377".

| 2272 | **727** | 3f. blue | 1·80 | 1·20 |
| 2273 | **727** | 3f.80 red | 2·10 | 1·40 |

728 Throwing the Javelin

1996. Olympic Games, Atlanta. Multicoloured.

2274		3f. Type **728**	1·60	1·20
2275		3f. Baseball	1·60	1·20
2276		4f.50 Running	2·50	1·90
2277		4f.50 Cycling	2·50	1·90

729 Children of Different Races with Balloon

1996. 50th Anniv of UNICEF.

| 2278 | **729** | 3f. brown, blue and lilac | 1·60 | 1·20 |

730 Angel and Star

1996. Christmas. Multicoloured.

| 2279 | | 3f. Type **730** | 1·50 | 1·10 |
| 2280 | | 6f. Angels heralding | 3·25 | 2·40 |

731 Planet and Neptune, God of the Sea (after Roman mosaic, Sousse)

1996. Anniversaries.

| 2281 | **731** | 4f. red, blue and black | 2·10 | 1·50 |
| 2282 | - | 5f. blue and red | 2·75 | 2·00 |

DESIGNS—4f. Type **731** (150th anniv of discovery of planet Neptune by Johann Galle); 5f. Rene Descartes (after Franz Hals) (philosopher and scientist, 400th birth anniv).

732 Coins and Press

1996. Inauguaration of Stamp and Coin Museum (3rd issue).

2283	**732**	5f. brown and blue	2·75	2·00
2284	-	5f. brown and purple	2·75	2·00
2285	-	10f. blue and brown	5·25	3·75
MS2286		130×80 mm. Nos. 2283/5	10·50	11·00

DESIGNS—As T **733**: 5f. Stamp press and engraver. 48×37 mm: 10f. Museum entrance.

733 Camille Corot (bicentenary)

1996. Artists' Birth Anniversaries. Self-portraits. Multicoloured.

| 2287 | | 6f. Type **733** | 3·25 | 2·40 |
| 2288 | | 7f. Francisco Goya (250th anniv) | 3·75 | 2·75 |

734 Allegory

1996. Monaco Red Cross. Anti-tuberculosis Campaign. Multicoloured.

| 2289 | | 7f. Type **734** | 3·75 | 2·75 |
| 2290 | | 8f. Camille Guerin and Albert Calmette (developers of vaccine) | 4·50 | 3·25 |

735 Spring

1996. Seasons of the Blackberry. Sheet 143×100 mm containing T 735 and similar horiz designs. Multicoloured.

MS2291 4f. Type **735**; 5f. Summer; 6f. Autumn; 7f. Winter   13·00   13·00

736 "Gloria" (cadet barque), Club, Motorboat and "Tuiga" (royal yacht)

1996. Monaco Yacht Club.

| 2292 | **736** | 3f. multicoloured | 1·80 | 1·30 |

737 Seal of Prince Rainier III

1996. 700th Anniv of Grimaldi Dynasty (1st issue).

| 2293 | **737** | 2f.70 red, brown and blue | 1·50 | 1·10 |

See also Nos. 2302/14 and 2326/38.

738 Clown

1996. 21st International Circus Festival, Monte Carlo (1997).

| 2294 | **738** | 3f. multicoloured | 1·60 | 1·20 |

739 Old and New Racing and Rally Cars

1996. Motor Sport.
2295	**739**	3f. multicoloured	1·90	1·40

740 Pictures, Engraving Tools and "Stamps"

1996. 60th Anniv of Stamp Issuing Office (2296) and "Monaco 97" International Stamp Exhibition, Monte Carlo (2297). Each brown, mauve and blue.
2296	3f. Type **740**		3·00	2·20
2297	3f. Stamp, magnifying glass and letters		3·00	2·20

Nos. 2296/7 were issued together, *se-tenant*, forming a composite design featuring the Grand Staircase of the Prince's Palace.

741 Double Red Camellia

1996. Monte Carlo Flower Show (1997).
2298	**741**	3f.80 multicoloured	2·20	1·70

742 Afghan Hound

1996. International Dog Show, Monte Carlo.
2299	**742**	4f.40 multicoloured	3·50	2·75

743 Award

1996. 37th Television Festival, Monte Carlo (1997).
2300	**743**	4f.90 multicoloured	2·75	2·00

744 Giant Bellflower and Carob Pods and Leaves

1996
2301	**744**	5f. multicoloured	2·75	2·00

745 Rainier I, Battle of Zerikzee, Arms of his wife Andriola Grillo and Chateau de Cagnes

1997. 700th Anniv of Grimaldi Dynasty (2nd issue). The Seigneurs. Multicoloured.
2302	1f. Type **745**		45	35
2303	1f. Seal of Charles I, Battle of Crecy, Chateau de Roquebrune and Rocher fortifications		45	35

2304	1f. Siege of Rocher by Boccanegra, seal of Rainier II, arms of his two wives Ilaria del Caretto and Isabelle Asinari, Vatican and Papal Palace, Avignon		45	35
2305	2f. Defeat of combined fleets of Venice and Florence and Jean I on horseback and with his wife Pomelline Fregoso		1·00	75
2306	2f. Claudine, acclamation by crowd of her husband Lambert, seals of Lambert and his father Nicolas and strengthening of Monaco Castle		1·00	75
2307	7f. Statue of Francois Grimaldi disguised as Franciscan monk and clashes between Ghibellines and Guelphs at Genoa		3·75	2·75
2308	7f. Honore I flanked by Pope Paul III and Duke of Savoy and Battle of Lepanto		3·75	2·75
2309	7f. Charles II, flags of Genoa and Savoy and attack on Rocher by Capt. Cartier		3·75	2·75
2310	7f. Hercule I, flags of Savoy, Nice and Provence, assassination of Hercule and acclamation of his infant son Honore II		3·75	2·75
2311	9f. Catalan aiding Doge of Venice in war against Aragon, exercising "Right of the Sea" and entrusting education of his heiress Claudine to his wife Pomelline		4·75	3·50
2312	9f. Jean II with his wife Antoinette of Savoy, retable in Chapel of St. Nicholas and assassination of Jean by his brother Lucien		4·75	3·50
2313	9f. Lucien and siege of Monaco by Genoa		4·75	3·50
2314	9f. Seal of Augustin, Treaty of Tordesillas, visit by King Charles V and Augustin as bishop with his nephew and heir Honore		4·75	3·50
MS2315 **737** 150×80 mm. 2 ×2f.70 red; 2 ×2f.70 brown; 2 ×2f.70 blue; 2 ×2f.70 red, brown and blue			13·00	13·00

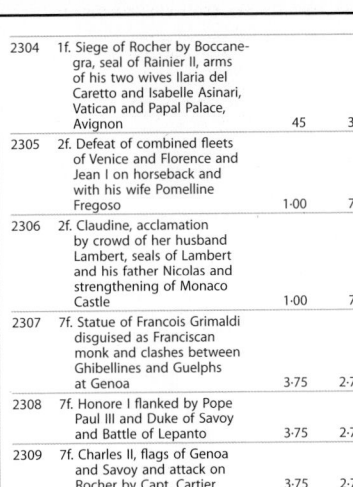

746 Tennis Match and Players

1997. Centenary of Monaco Tennis Championships.
2316	**746**	4f.60 multicoloured	2·75	2·00

747 Prince Rainier, Trophy and Stamp and Coin Museum

1997. Award to Prince Rainier of International Philately Grand Prix (made to "Person who has Contributed Most to Philately") by Association of Catalogue Editors.
2317	**747**	4f.60 multicoloured	2·75	2·00

748 Images of St.Devote (patron saint)

1997. Europa. Tales and Legends.
2318	**748**	3f. orange and brown	3·00	2·20
2319	-	3f. blue	3·00	2·20

DESIGN: No. 2319, Hercules.

749 Syringe and Drug Addicts

1997. Monaco Red Cross. Anti-drugs Campaign.
2320	**749**	7f. black, blue and red	3·75	2·75

750 First Stamps of United States and Monaco 1996
1f. Stamp

1997. "Pacific 97" International Stamp Exhibiton, San Francisco. 150th Anniv of First United States Stamps.
2321	**750**	4f.90 multicoloured	2·75	2·00

751 Winter and Summer Uniforms, 1997

1997. The Palace Guard. Multicoloured.
2322	3f. Type **751**		1·80	1·30
2323	3f.50 Uniforms of 1750, 1815, 1818, 1830 and 1853		2·20	1·70
2324	5f.20 Uniforms of 1865, 1870, 1904, 1916 and 1935		2·75	2·00

1997. Victory of Marcelo M. Rios at Monaco Tennis Championships. No. 2316 optd M. RIOS.
2325	**746**	4f.60 multicoloured	2·75	2·00

1997. 700th Anniv of Grimaldi Dynasty (3rd issue). The Princes. As T 745. Multicoloured.
2326	1f. Honore II		45	35
2327	1f. Louis I		45	35
2328	1f. Antoine I		45	35
2329	2f. Jacques I		1·00	75
2330	7f. Charles III		3·25	2·40
2331	7f. Albert I		3·25	2·40
2332	7f. Louis II		3·25	2·40
2333	7f. Rainier III		3·25	2·40
2334	9f. Louise-Hippolyte		4·50	3·25
2335	9f. Honore IV (wrongly inscr "Honore III")		4·50	3·25
2336	9f. Honore III (wrongly inscr "Honore IV")		4·50	3·25
2337	9f. Honore V		4·50	3·25
2338	9f. Florestan I		4·50	3·25

753 Club Badge, Ball as Globe and Stadium

1997. Monaco, Football Champion of France, 1996–97.
2339	**753**	3f. multicoloured	1·30	1·00

754 Magic Wand, Hands and Stars

1997. 13th Magic Grand Prix, Monte Carlo.
2340	**754**	4f.40 black and gold	1·90	1·40

755 "Francois Grimaldi" (Ernando Venanzi)

1997. Paintings. Multicoloured.
2341	8f. Type **755**		3·50	2·75
2342	9f. "St. Peter and St. Paul" (Peter Paul Rubens)		3·75	2·75

756 Monaco in 13th Century and 1861

1997. 700th Anniv of Grimaldi Dynasty (4th issue). Geographical Evolution of Monaco. Sheet 120×145 mm containing T 756 and similar vert designs. Multicoloured.
MS2343 5f. Type **756**; 5f. Monaco from 15th–19th centuries; 5f. Left half of Monaco; 5f. Right half of Monaco	8·75	8·75

The bottom two stamps of the miniature sheet form a composite design of present-day Monaco with a map showing dates at which the territory was expanded.

757 Map of Europe and Blue Whales

1997. 49th Session of International Whaling Commission, Monaco.
2344	**757**	6f.70 multicoloured	3·00	2·20

1997. Election of 1995 Botticelli Stamp as Most Beautiful Stamp in the World. Sheet 115×100 mm.
MS2345 **715** 15f. blue	7·25	7·25

758 Princess Charlotte

1997. 20th Death Anniv of Princess Charlotte.
2346	**758**	3f.80 brown	1·60	1·20

759 Dancer of Russian Ballet and Kremlin, Moscow

1997. "Moskva 97" International Stamp Exhbition, Moscow.
2347	**759**	5f. multicoloured	2·20	1·70

760 Trees in Monaco

1997. 10th Anniv of Marcel Korenlein Arboretum.
2348	**760**	9f. multicoloured	3·75	2·75

761 Diamond-Man (Ribeiro)

1997. Winning Entries in Schoolchildren's Drawing Competition.
2349	**761**	4f. multicoloured	1·80	1·30
2350	-	4f.50 blue, ultramarine and red	1·90	1·40

DESIGN—HORIZ: 4f.50, Flying diamonds (Testa).

762 Four-man Bobsleighing, Speed and Figure Skating and Ice Hockey

1997. Winter Olympic Games, Nagano, Japan (1998). Multicoloured.
2351   4f.90 Type **762**   2·20   1·70
2352   4f.90 Alpine skiing, biathlon, two-man bobsleighing and ski-jumping   2·20   1·70
Nos. 2351/2 were issued together, *se-tenant*, forming a composite design.

763 Albert I (statue)

1997. 150th Birth Anniv of Prince Albert I (1st issue).
2353   **763**   8f. multicoloured   3·50   2·75
See also No. 2368.

764 Clown and Horse

1997. 22nd International Circus Festival, Monte Carlo (1998).
2354   **764**   3f. multicoloured   1·30   1·10

765 Pink Campanula and Carob Plant

1997. Monte Carlo Flower Show (1998).
2355   **765**   4f.40 multicoloured   1·90   1·60

766 "The Departure of Marcus Attilius Regulus for Carthage"

1997. 250th Birth Anniv of Louis David (painter).
2356   **766**   5f.20 green and red   2·20   1·80

767 Pope Innocent IV

1997. 750th Anniv of Creation of Parish of Monaco by Papal Bull.
2357   **767**   7f.50 brown and blue   3·25   2·50

768 Baseball Hat, Television Controller, Ballet Shoe and Football Boot

1998. 38th Television Festival.
2358   **768**   4f.50 multicoloured   1·90   1·60

769 Past and Present Presidents

1998. 50th Anniv of Monaco Red Cross.
2359   **769**   5f. brown and red   2·20   1·80

770 Boxer and Dobermann

1998. International Dog Show, Monte Carlo.
2360   **770**   2f.70 multicoloured   1·20   95

771 White Doves and Laurel Wreath

1998. 30th Meeting of Academy of Peace and International Security.
2361   **771**   3f. green and blue   1·30   1·10

772 Ballet Dancer, Piano Keys, Music Score and Violin

1998. 15th Spring Arts Festival.
2362   **772**   4f. multicoloured   1·80   1·40

773 Pierre and Marie Curie

1998. Centenary of Discovery of Radium.
2363   **773**   6f. blue and mauve   2·75   2·10

774 Caravel and Globe

1998. "Expo '98" World's Fair, Lisbon. International Year of the Ocean.
2364   **774**   2f.70 multicoloured   1·20   95

775 St. Devote (stained glass window, Palace Chapel)

1998. Europa (1st issue). National Festivals.
2365   **775**   3f. multicoloured   2·20   1·80
See also No. 2372.

776 Monte Carlo

1998. Junior Chamber of Commerce European Conference, Monte Carlo.
2366   **776**   3f. multicoloured   1·30   1·10

777 Kessel

1998. Birth Centenary of Joseph Kessel (writer).
2367   **777**   3f.90 multicoloured   1·60   1·30

778 Prince Albert I at different Ages

1998. 150th Birth Anniv of Prince Albert I (2nd issue).
2368   **778**   7f. brown   3·00   2·40

779 Garnier and Monte Carlo Casino

1998. Death Centenary of Charles Garnier (architect).
2369   **779**   10f. multicoloured   4·50   3·50

780 Trophy and Monte Carlo

1998. 10th World Music Awards, Monte Carlo.
2370   **780**   10f. multicoloured   4·50   3·50

781 Racing Cars

1998. 1st Formula 3000 Grand Prix, Monte Carlo.
2371   **781**   3f. red and black   1·30   1·10

782x Prince Rainier III, Prince Albert and Royal Palace

1998. Europa (2nd issue). National Festivals.
2372   **782**   3f. multicoloured   2·20   1·80

783 Porcelain Teapot and Figure of Francois Grimaldi

1998. Fine Arts. Multicoloured.
2373   8f. Type **783**   3·50   2·75
2374   9f. Fine-bound books and illustration   3·75   3·00

784 Player on Map of France

1998. World Cup Football Championship, France.
2375   **784**   15f. multicoloured   6·50   5·25

785 Modern and Old Motor Cars and Ferrari

1998. Birth Centenary of Enzo Ferrari (motor manufacturer).
2376   **785**   7f. multicoloured   3·00   2·40

786 Gershwin, Trumpeter, Dancers and Opening Bars of "Rhapsody in Blue"

1998. Birth Cent of George Gershwin (composer).
2377   **786**   7f.50 ultramarine, blue and black   3·25   2·50

787 Int Marine Pollution College and Marine Environment Laboratory

1998. Int Marine Pollution Conference, Monaco.
2378   **787**   4f.50 multicoloured   1·90   1·60

788 Venue

1998. Post Europ (successor to C.E.P.T.) Plenary Assembly, Monaco.
2379   **788**   5f. multicoloured   2·20   1·80

789 Belem Tower, Lisbon, and Palace, Monaco

1998. "Expo '98" World's Fair and Stamp Exhibition, Lisbon.
2380   **789**   6f.70 multicoloured   3·00   2·40

790 Sportsmen

1998. 30th Anniv of International Association against Violence in Sport.
2381   **790**   4f.20 multicoloured   1·80   1·40

791 Magician

1998. "Magic Stars" Magic Festival, Monte Carlo.
2382 **791** 3f.50 gold and red 1·50 1·20

792 Statue and Vatican Colonnade

1998. 400th Birth Anniv of Giovanni Lorenzo Bernini (architect and sculptor).
2383 **792** 11f.50 blue and brown 5·25 4·25

793 Milan Cathedral

1998. "Italia 98" Int Stamp Exhibition, Milan.
2384 **793** 4f.90 green and red 2·20 1·80

794 Christmas Tree Decoration

1998. Christmas. Multicoloured.
2385 3f. Type **794** 1·30 1·10
2386 6f.70 "The Nativity" (detail of icon) (horiz) 3·00 2·40
MS2387 86×95 mm. 15f. "Virgin and Child" (detail of icon) (36×49 mm) 6·50 6·50

1998. As Nos. 1910 etc but no value expressed.
2388 **577** (2f.70) turquoise & blue 1·20 25
2389 **577** (3f.) red and pink 1·30 35
2390 **577** (3f.80) blue and cobalt 1·60 70

795 Lion

1998. 23rd International Circus Festival, Monte Carlo (1999).
2391 **795** 2f.70 multicoloured 1·20 95

796 Map and Elevation of Seamounts

1998. Grimaldi Seamounts.
2392 **796** 10f. multicoloured 4·50 3·50

797 Prince's Arms and Monogram

1998. 50th Anniv (1999) of Accession of Prince Rainier III (1st issue). Sheet 100×130 mm.
MS2393 **797** 25f. gold and red 14·50 14·50
See also No. MS2417.

798 1860 Cover and Stamp and Coin Museum

1999. "Monaco 99" International Stamp Exhibition.
2394 **798** 3f. multicoloured 1·30 1·00
MS2395 160×111 mm. No. 2394 ×4 6·00 6·00

799 Festival Poster

1999. 39th Television Festival.
2396 **799** 3f.80 multicoloured 2·20 1·40

800 Cocker Spaniel and American Cocker

1999. International Dog Show, Fontvieille.
2397 **800** 4f. multicoloured 2·20 1·40

801 World Map

1999. 50th Anniv of Geneva Conventions.
2398 **801** 4f.40 red, brown and black 2·20 1·40

802 Arrangement of Flowers named after Grimaldi Family Members

1999. Monte Carlo Flower Show.
2399 **802** 4f.50 multicoloured 2·20 1·40

803 Children and Heart

1999. 20th Anniv of Monaco Aid and Presence.
2400 **803** 6f.70 multicoloured 4·50 2·75
No. 2400 is also denominated in euros.

804 Palace and Centre

1999. 20th Anniv of Congress Centre Auditorium.
2401 **804** 2f.70 multicoloured 1·50 90

DENOMINATION. From No. 2402 Monaco stamps are denominated both in francs and in euros. As no cash for the latter was in circulation until 2002, the catalogue continues to use the franc value.

805 Globe and Piano Keys

1999. 10th Piano Masters, Monte Carlo.
2402 **805** 4f.60 multicoloured 2·20 1·40

806 Rose "Jubile du Prince de Monaco"

1999. Flowers. Multicoloured.
2403 4f.90 Type **806** 2·40 1·40
2404 6f. Rose "Prince de Monaco", rose "Grimaldi" and orchid "Prince Rainier III" 3·25 1·80

807 Williams's Bugatti (winner of first race) and Michael Schumacher's Car (winner of 1999 race)

1999. 70th Anniv of Monaco Motor Racing Grand Prix.
2405 **807** 3f. multicoloured 1·60 90

808 Olympic Rings and Trophy

1999. 3rd Association of Postage Stamp Catalogue Editors and Philatelic Publications Grand Prix.
2406 **808** 4f.40 multicoloured 2·40 1·40

809 Riders jumping over Monte Carlo

1999. 5th International Show Jumping Competition, Monte Carlo.
2407 **809** 5f.20 red, black and blue 3·00 1·70

810 Footballer, Runner and Palace

1999. 75th Anniv of Monaco Sports Association. Multicoloured.
2408 7f. Type **810** 3·25 1·80
2409 7f. Boxer, footballer, harbour, runner and handballer 3·25 1·80

811 Architect's Drawing of Forum

1999. Construction of Grimaldi Forum (congress and exhibition centre).
2410 **811** 3f. multicoloured 1·60 90

812 Facade and Construction

1999. Centenary of Laying of First Stone of Oceanographic Museum.
2411 **812** 5f. multicoloured 3·00 1·70

813 Eiffel Tower on Map of France, 1849 20c. "Ceres" Stamp and Emblem

1999. "Philexfrance 99" International Stamp Exhibition, Paris (1st issue). 150th Anniv of First French Stamps.
2412 **813** 2f.70 multicoloured 1·60 90
See also No. 2423.

814 Casino and Rock

1999. Europa. Parks and Gardens. Multicoloured.
2413 3f. Type **814** 1·90 1·10
2414 3f. Fontvieille (48×27 mm) 1·90 1·10

815x Fontvieille in 1949, Line Graph and Underground Station in 1999

1999. 50 Years of the Economy. Multicoloured.
2415 5f. Type **815** (second sector) 2·40 1·70
2416 5f. Le Larvotto in 1949, line graph and Grimaldi Forum in 1999 (third sector) 2·40 1·70

816 Definitive Stamps, 1950–89

1999. 50th Anniv of Accession of Prince Rainier III (2nd issue). Two sheets, 100×130 mm (a) or 119×145 mm (b).
MS2417 Two sheets. (a) 20f. blue and gold (as Type **584** but with monogram superimposed); (b) 30f. multicoloured (Type **816**) .... 24·00 24·00

817 Honore de Balzac

1999. Writers' Birth Bicentenaries.
2418 **817** 4f.50 blue and scarlet .... 2·40 1·70
2419 – 5f.20 brown, blue and red .... 3·00 2·20
DESIGN: 5f.20, Sophie Rostopchine, Comtesse de Segur.

818 Emblem and Chinese Drawing

1999. 125th Anniv of Universal Postal Union.
2420 **818** 3f. blue, red and yellow .... 1·60 1·20

819 Iris "Rainier III" and Rose "Rainier III"

1999. Flowers.
2421 **819** 4f. multicoloured .... 2·10 1·50

820 Anniversary Emblem

1999. 50th Anniv of Monaco's Admission to United Nations Educational, Scientific and Educational Organization.
2422 **820** 4f.20 multicoloured .... 2·20 1·70

821 Emblem and Monaco 1885 and French 1878 Stamps

1999. "Philexfrance 99" International Stamp Exhibition, Paris (2nd issue).
2423 **821** 7f. black, blue and mauve .... 3·25 2·40

822 Athletes

1999. 10th Sportel (sport and television) Congress, Fontvieille.
2424 **822** 10f. multicoloured .... 5·25 3·75

823 Maltese Cross, Knights and Valletta

1999. 900th Anniv of Sovereign Military Order of Malta and 25th Anniv of National Association of the Order.
2425 **823** 11f.50 red, brown and blue .... 5·75 4·50

824 1999 Postcard of Monaco, 1989 Definitive Design and Obverse of Jubilee Coin

1999. Postcard, Coin and Stamp Exhibition, Fontvieille (1st issue).
2426 **824** 3f. multicoloured .... 1·50 1·10
See also No. 2429.

1999. "Magic Stars" Magic Festival, Monte Carlo. As No. 2382 but face value and date changed.
2427 **791** 4f.50 gold and red .... 2·20 1·70

825 Fontvieille Project, Stage 2

1999. Achievements and Projects. Sheet 150×100 mm containing T 825 and similar multicoloured designs.
MS2428 4f. Type **825**; 9f. New harbour mole; 9f. Grimaldi Forum (congress centre); 19f. Underground train, harbour and station (76×36 mm) .... 20·00 20·00

826 1949 Postcard of Monaco, Reverse of Jubilee Coin and 1950 Definitive

1999. Postcard, Coin and Stamp Exhibition, Fontvieille (2nd issue).
2429 **826** 6f.50 multicoloured .... 3·25 2·40

827 Pierrot juggling "2000"

1999. 24th International Circus Festival, Monte Carlo (2000).
2430 **827** 2f.70 multicoloured .... 1·80 1·30

828 "Madonna and Child" (Simone Cantarini)

1999. Christmas.
2431 **828** 3f. multicoloured .... 1·60 1·20

829 Blessing and Holy Door, St. Peter's Cathedral, Rome

1999. Holy Year 2000.
2432 **829** 3f.50 multicoloured .... 1·90 1·40

830 Mixed Arrangement

1999. 33rd Monte Carlo Flower Show.
2433 **830** 4f.50 multicoloured .... 2·30 1·80

831 Emblem

1999. "Monaco 2000" International Stamp Exhibitions.
2434 **831** 3f. multicoloured .... 1·60 1·20

832 Bust of Napoleon (Antonio Canova)

2000. 30th Anniv of Napoleonic Museum.
2435 **832** 4f.20 multicoloured .... 2·30 1·80

833 Festival Emblem

2000. 40th Television Festival, Monte Carlo.
2436 **833** 4f.90 multicoloured .... 2·75 2·10

834 St. Peter and St. James the Major

2000. The Twelve Apostles. Multicoloured.
2437 **834** 4f. blue, orange and gold .... 1·60 1·20
2438 – 5f. red and gold .... 2·30 1·80
2439 – 6f. violet and gold .... 3·00 2·40
2440 – 7f. brown and gold .... 4·00 3·00
2441 – 8f. green and gold .... 4·75 3·50
2442 – 9f. red, orange and gold .... 5·50 4·25
DESIGNS: 5f. St. John and St. Andrew; 6f. St. Philip and St. Bartholomew; 7f. St. Matthew and St. Thomas; 8f. St. James the Minor and St. Jude; 9f. St. Simon and St. Mathias.

835 Golden Labrador and Golden Retriever

2000. International Dog Show, Monte Carlo.
2443 **835** 6f.50 multicoloured .... 3·50 2·50

836 Man's Head, Drawings and Key (Adami)

2000. Monaco and the Sea. Multicoloured.
2444 6f.55 Type **836** .... 3·50 2·50
2445 6f.55 "Monaco" above sea (Arman) .... 3·50 2·50
2446 6f.55 Abstract designs (Cane) .... 3·50 2·50
2447 6f.55 Hand touching sun in sky (Folon) .... 3·50 2·50
2448 6f.55 Angel sleeping and boats (Fuchs) .... 3·50 2·50
2449 6f.55 Harbour (E. de Sigaldi) .... 3·50 2·50
2450 6f.55 Views of harbour on silhouettes of yachts (Sosno) .... 3·50 2·50
2451 6f.55 Waves and floating ball (Verkade) .... 3·50 2·50

837 Olympic Rings on Globe and Flags

2000. Olympic Games, Sydney, Australia.
2452 **837** 7f. multicoloured .... 3·50 2·50

838 "Building Europe"

2000. Europa. Multicoloured.
2453 3f. Type **838** .... 3·00 2·40
2454 3f. Map of Europe and Post Europ member countries' flags (56×37 mm) .... 3·00 2·40

839 Racing Cars

2000. 2nd Historic Vehicles Grand Prix.
2455 **839** 4f.40 multicoloured .... 2·30 1·80

840 Monaco Pavilion and Emblem

2000. "EXPO 2000" World's Fair, Hanover.
2456 **840** 5f. multicoloured .... 2·75 2·10

841 Sts. Mark, Matthew, John and Luke

2000. The Four Evangelists.
2457 **841** 20f. black, flesh and green .... 11·00 11·00

842 St. Stephen and Emblem

2000. "WIPA 2000" International Stamp Exhibition, Vienna.
2458 **842** 4f.50 black, blue and red .... 2·30 1·80

843 Golfer

2000. Pro-celebrity Golf Tournament, Monte Carlo.
2459 **843** 4f.40 multicoloured 2·30 1·80

844 Fencing

2000. Olympic Games, Sydney. Multicoloured.
2460 2f.70 Type **844** 1·60 1·20
2461 4f.50 Rowing 2·30 1·80

845 Humber Beeston and Woman with Parasol, 1911

2000. Motor Cars and Fashion. Motor cars from the Royal Collection. Multicoloured.
2462 3f. Type **845** 2·30 1·80
2463 6f.70 Jaguar 4-cylinder and woman, 1947 4·00 3·00
2464 10f. Rolls Royce Silver Cloud and woman wearing swing coat, 1956 5·50 4·25
2465 15f. Lamborghini Countach and woman wearing large hat, 1986 8·50 6·50

846 Entrance to Museum

2000. Philatelic Rarities Exhibition (1999), Stamp and Coin Museum, Monte Carlo.
2466 **846** 3f.50 multicoloured 2·00 1·60

847 Open Hands and Emblem

2000. Monaco Red Cross.
2467 **847** 10f. multicoloured 5·50 4·25

848 Magnifying Glass, Stamps and Exhibition Hall

2000. "WORLD STAMP USA" International Exhibition, Anaheim, California.
2468 **848** 4f.40 multicoloured 2·30 1·80

849 Magician

2000. "Magic Stars" Magic Festival, Monte Carlo.
2469 **849** 4f.60 multicoloured 2·30 1·80

850 Da Vinci's "Man" and Mathematical Symbols

2000. World Mathematics Year.
2470 **850** 6f.50 brown 3·50 2·50

851 Right-hand Section of Screen

2000. Holy Year. Restoration of Altar Screen, Monaco Cathedral. Sheet 120×100 mm containing T 851 and similar design.
MS2471 10f. Type **851**; 20f. Left-hand and central sections (53×52 mm) 16·00 16·00

852 Shark and Museum Facade

2000. Opening of New Aquarium, Oceanographical Museum.
2472 **852** 3f. multicoloured 1·60 1·20

853 Cathedral and Statue of Bear

2000. "ESPANA 2000" International Stamp Exhibition, Madrid.
2473 **853** 3f.80 multicoloured 2·30 1·80

854 Fishes and Corals

2000. 5th International Congress on Aquaria (5f.) and 25th Anniv of Monaco Nature Protection Association (9f.). Multicoloured.
2474 5f. Type **854** 2·75 2·10
2475 9f. Starfish, water plant and fish 4·75 3·50

855 Museum Facade and Plants

2000. 50th Anniv of Observatory Cave and 40th Anniv of Anthropological Museum.
2476 **855** 5f.20 purple, green and brown 3·00 2·40

856x Fresco, Oceanography Museum

2000. International Aquariological Congress.
2477 **856** 7f. multicoloured 3·50 2·50

857 18th-century Crib

2000. Christmas.
2478 **857** 3f. multicoloured 1·60 1·20

2000. Motor Cars and Fashion. Motor cars from the Royal Collection. As T 845. Multicoloured.
2479 5f. Ferrari Formula 1 racing car and woman in racing clothes, 1989 3·00 2·40
2480 6f. Fiat 600 "Jolly" and woman wearing swimming costume, 1955 4·00 3·00
2481 8f. Citroen C4F "Autochenille" and woman wearing coat and hat, 1929 4·75 3·50

858 Princess Stephanie (President)

2000. Association for Help and Protection of Disabled Children (A.M.A.P.E.I.).
2482 **858** 11f.50 blue and red 6·25 4·75

859 Exhibition Poster

2000. "Monaco 2000" Stamp Exhibition, Sheet 150×90 mm containing two examples of T 859.
MS2483 20f. ×2 multicoloured 23·00 24·00

860 Warrior kneeling

2000. Terracotta Warrior Exhibition, Grimaldi Forum (2001).
2484 **860** 2f.70 black and red 1·60 1·20

861 Museum Building

2000. 50th Anniv of Postal Museum.
2485 **861** 3f. multicoloured 1·70 1·30

862 Arms

2000. Self-adhesive.
2486 **862** (3f.) black and red 1·70 1·30

863 Iris "Princess Caroline of Monaco"

2000. 34th Monte Carlo Flower Show.
2487 **863** 3f.80 multicoloured 2·00 1·60

864 Sardinian 1851 5c., 20c. and 40c. Stamps

2000. 150th Anniv (2001) of First Sardinian Stamp.
2488 **864** 6f.50 blue, red and black 3·50 2·50

865 Seahorse, Marine Life and Life Belt

2000. 25th Anniv (2001) of the Ramoge Agreement on Environmental Protection of Mediterranean.
2489 **865** 6f.70 multicoloured 3·50 2·50

866 Breitling Orbiter and 1984 2f.80 Stamp

2000. 1st Non-Stop Balloon Circumnavigation of Globe (1999). Award to Bertrand Picard of International Philately Grand Prix by Association of Catalogue Editors.
2490 **866** 9f. multicoloured 4·75 3·50

867 Clown with Seal balancing Ball

2000. 25th International Circus Festival, Monte Carlo (2001). Different poster designs by artist named. Multicoloured (except no. 2492).
2491 2f.70 Type **867** 1·90 1·40
2492 6f. Clown playing guitar (Hodge) (black, red and blue) 3·00 2·40
2493 6f. Clown resting head (Knie) 3·00 2·40
2494 6f. Tiger and circus tent (P. Merot) 3·00 2·40
2495 6f. Lions, horses and trapeze artists (Poulet) 3·00 2·40
2496 6f. Monkey and circus tents (T. Mordant) 3·00 2·40

868 Player kicking Ball

2000. Monaco, Football Champion of France, 1999–2000.
2497 **868** 4f.50 multicoloured 2·30 1·80

869 Sea Mammals and Mediterranean Sea

2000. Mediterranean Sea Marine Mammals Sanctuary.
2498 **869** 5f.20 multicoloured   3·00   2·40

870 Nativity Scene

2000. Christmas.
2499 **870** 10f. multicoloured   5·50   4·25

871 Poster

2001. 41st Television Festival, Monte Carlo.
2500 **871** 3f.50 multicoloured   1·90   1·40

872 Leonberger and
Newfoundland Dogs

2001. International Dog Show, Monte Carlo.
2501 **872** 6f.50 multicoloured   3·50   2·50

873 Flower
Arrangement

2001. Flower Show, Genoa.
2502 **873** 6f.70 multicoloured   3·50   2·50

874 Monaco
Palace

2001. Europa. Water Resources. Multicoloured.
2503   3f. Type **874**   2·75   2·10
2504   3f. Undercover washing area   2·75   2·10

875 Princess
Caroline and
Portrait of Prince
Pierre of Monaco
(founder)

2001. 50th Anniv of Literary Council of Monaco.
2505 **875** 2f.70 black, brown and
green   1·60   1·20

876 Malraux

2001. Birth Centenary of Andre Malraux (writer).
2506 **876** 10f. black and red   5·50   4·25

877 Town Hall

2001. "BELGICA 2001" International Stamp Exhibition, Brussels.
2507 **877** 4f. blue and red   2·30   1·80

878 Coins, Stamp
and Book

2001. Postcard, Coin and Stamp Exhibition, Fontvielle.
2508 **878** 2f.70 multicoloured   1·60   1·20

879 Princess Grace
and Ballet Dancer

2001. 25th Anniv of Princess Grace Dance Academy.
2509 **879** 4f.40 multicoloured   2·30   1·80

880 Model

2001. Naval Museum, Fontvielle.
2510 **880** 4f.50 multicoloured   2·30   1·80

881 Petanque Balls

2001. World Petanque Championships.
2511 **881** 5f. multicoloured   2·75   2·10

882 Fireplace, Throne Room

2001. Royal Palace (1st series). Multicoloured.
2512   3f. Type **882**   1·60   1·20
2513   4f.50 Blue Room   2·30   1·80
2514   6f.70 York Chamber   4·00   3·00
2515   15f. Throne room ceiling fresco   7·75   6·00
See also Nos. 2541/3.

883 Littre and Diderot

2001. 250th Anniv of Encyclopaedia or Critical Dictionary of Sciences, Arts and Trades (Denis Diderot) and Birth Bicentenary of Emile Littre (compiler of Dictionary of the French Language).
2516 **883** 4f.20 black, blue and
green   2·30   1·80

884 Medal and Steam
Yacht

2001. 30th Anniv of Prince Albert Oceanography Prize.
2517 **884** 9f. blue   4·75   3·50

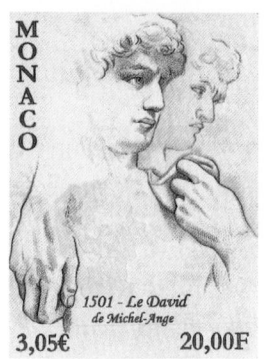
885 Drawings

2001. 500th Anniv of David (sculpture, Michaelangelo).
2518 **885** 20f. multicoloured   11·00   9·50

886 Alfred Nobel
(prize fund
founder)

2001. Centenary of the Nobel Prize. Multicoloured.
2519   5f. Type **886**   3·00   2·40
2520   8f. Henri Dunant (founder of
Red Cross and winner of
Peace Prize, 1901)   4·75   3·50
2521   11f.50 Enrico Fermi (physicist
and winner of Physics Prize,
1938)   6·25   4·75

887 Prince Rainier, Prince Albert,
Map, Satellite, Ship, and
Submarine

2001. 36th International Commission for Scientific Exploration of the Mediterranean Meeting.
2522 **887** 3f. multicoloured   1·90   1·40

888 Virgin and
Child

2001. Christmas.
2523 **888** 3f. multicoloured   1·90   1·40

889 Garden Tiger
Moth (*Artica caja*)

2002. Flora and Fauna.
2524 **889** 1c. black, red and sepia   15   10
2525   -   2c. multicoloured   15   10
2526   -   5c. multicoloured   25   20
2527   -   10c. black, green and
yellow   30   25
2528   -   20c. red, yellow and
black   60   50
2529   -   41c. multicoloured   1·20   95
2530   -   50c. multicoloured   1·70   1·10
2531   -   €1 multicoloured   3·00   1·80
2532   -   €2 multicoloured   6·25   3·00
2533   -   €5 brown, green and
black   16·00   7·25
2534   -   €10 green, red and black   31·00   12·00

DESIGNS—-VERT: 5c. Blue trumpet vine (*Thunbergia grandiflora*); 41c. *Helix aspera*; 50c. Foxy charaxes (*Charaxes jasius*); €2 Red thorn apple (*Datura sanguinea*); €5 Crested tit (*Parus crisatus*). HORIZ: 2c. *Luria lurida*; 10c. Great tit (*Parus major*); 20c. Common barberfish (*Anthias anthias*); €1 Zoned mitre (*Mitra zonata*); €10 Common snipefish (*Macroramphosus scolopax*).

890 Lion and
Ringmaster

2002. 26th International Circus Festival, Monte Carlo.
2540 **890** 41c. multicoloured   1·40   95

891 Crystal
Gallery

2002. Royal Palace (2nd series). Multicoloured.
2541   41c. Type **891**   1·20   95
2542   46c. Throne room (horiz)   1·60   1·20
2543   58c. Landscape painting in
Crystal Gallery (horiz)   1·90   1·40

892 Rocking Horse of
Flowers

2002. 35th Monte Carlo Flower Show.
2544 **892** 53c. multicoloured   1·70   1·30

893 Old and
Modern Rally Cars

2002. Motoring Events in Monaco. Sheet 124×95 mm, containing T **893** and similar vert design. Multicoloured.
MS2545 €1.07, Type **893** (70th Monte Carlo car rally); €1.22, Old racing car (Historic Vehicles third Grand Prix) and modern Formula 1 racing car (60th Monaco Grand Prix)   7·25   7·25

894 Skiers, Ice Skater and
Ice Hockey Player

2002. Winter Olympic Games, Salt Lake City, U.S.A. Multicoloured.
2546 **894** 23c. Type **894**   80   60
2547   23c. Bobsleigh, luge and skiers
(face value, emblem and
country inscription at right)   80   60
Nos. 2446/7 were issued together, se-tenant, forming a composite design.

895 Exhibition Cases and
Prince Albert I

2002. Anniversaries. Multicoloured.
2548 **895** 64c. Type **895** (centenary of
Prehistoric Anthropology
Museum)   2·00   1·40
2549   67c. Title page, Prince Albert
I and ship (centenary of
publication of "La Carriere
d'un Navigateur" (memoirs)
by Prince Albert I)   2·20   1·50

896 Mazarin (painting, Phillippe de Champaigne)

2002. 400th Birth Anniv of Jules Mazarin (cardinal to Louis XIV).

2550	**896**	69c. multicoloured	2·20	1·50

897 Bust of Napoleon Bonaparte and Medal

2002. Bicentenary of Legion d'Honneur.

2551	**897**	70c. multicoloured	2·20	1·50

898 Whales and Dolphins

2002. 1st Meeting of Signatories to Agreement on the Conservation of Cetaceans of the Black Sea, Mediterranean Sea and Contiguous Atlantic Area (ACCOBAMS), Monaco.

2552	**898**	75c. multicoloured	2·30	1·70

899 Da Vinci

2002. 550th Birth Anniv of Leonardo da Vinci (artist).

2553	**899**	76c. multicoloured	2·30	1·70

900 St. Bernard and Bouvier

2002. International Dog Show, Monte Carlo.

2554	**900**	99c. multicoloured	3·00	2·20

901 Police Officers and Badge

2002. Centenary of Police Force.

2555	**901**	53c. multicoloured	1·70	1·20

902 Map of Europe and Flag

2002. 25th Anniv of European Academy of Postal Studies.

2556	**902**	58c. multicoloured	1·90	1·30

903 Circus and Globe

2002. Europa. Circus. Multicoloured.

2557	46c. Type **903**	2·00	1·40
2558	46c. "JOURS DE CIRQUE" and performers	2·00	1·40

904 Emblem

2002. 20th International Swimming Competition.

2559	**904**	64c. multicoloured	2·00	1·40

905 Tarmac Roads

2002. Centenary of First Tarmac Roads.

2560	**905**	41c. red, black and brown	1·40	1·00

906 Exhibition Hall and Displays

2002. "Monacophil 2002" International Stamp Exhibition.

2561	**906**	46c. green, violet and red	1·60	1·10

907 Emblem

2002. 42nd Television Festival, Monte Carlo.

2562	**907**	70c. multicoloured	2·20	1·50

908 Footballers and Globe

2002. World Cup Football Championship, Japan and South Korea.

2563	**908**	75c. green, blue and red	2·30	1·70

909 Obverse of 1, 2 and 5 cent Coins and Reverse

2002. Coins.

2564	**909**	46c. copper, red and black	1·60	1·10
2565	-	46c. gold, red and black	1·60	1·10
2566	-	€1.50 multicoloured	4·75	3·25
2567	-	€1.50 multicoloured	4·75	3·25

DESIGNS: Type **909**; 46c. Obverse of 10, 20 and 50 cent coins and reverse; €1.50, Obverse and reverse of 1 euro coin; €1.50, Obverse and reverse of 2 euro coin.

910 Debussy, Pelleas and Melisande

2002. Centenary of First Performance of Claude Debussy's Opera "Pelleas and Melisande".

2568	**910**	69c. green, blue and red	2·20	1·50

911 Saint Devote, Boat and Dove

2002. Monaco Red Cross.

2569	**911**	€1.02 red, greenish blue and black	3·00	2·20

912 Aerial View of Monaco

2002. International Year of Mountains.

2570	**912**	€1.37 multicoloured	4·25	3·00

913 Hugo

2002. Birth Bicentenary of Victor Hugo (writer). Each blue, brown and red.

2571	50c. Type **913**	1·60	1·10
2572	57c. Scenes from his books	1·90	1·30

Nos. 2571/2 were issued together, se-tenant, forming a composite design.

914 Dumas

2002. Birth Bicentenary of Alexandre Dumas (writer). Multicoloured.

2573	61c. Type **914**	2·00	1·40
2574	61c. Scenes from his books	2·00	1·40

Nos. 2573/4 were issued together, se-tenant, forming a composite design.

915 Princess Grace

2002. 26th Publication of "Annales Monegasques" (archives).

2575	**915**	€1.75 multicoloured	5·50	3·75

916 Star-shaped Flower

2002. Christmas.

2576	**916**	50c. multicoloured	1·60	1·10

917 Frame from Film and Melies

2002. Centenary of "Le Voyage dans la Lune" (film by Georges Melies).

2577	**917**	76c. multicoloured	2·30	1·70

918 Magician

2002. "Magic Stars" Magic Festival, Monte Carlo.

2578	**918**	€1.52 multicoloured	4·75	3·25

919 1949 Mercedes 220A Cabriolet

2002. Motor Cars from the Royal Collection. Multicoloured.

2579	46c. Type **919**	1·40	1·00
2580	69c. 1956 Rolls Royce Silver Cloud	2·20	1·50
2581	€1.40 1974 Citroen DS 21	4·25	3·00

920 Spring

2002. Royal Palace (3rd series). Frescoes. Sheet 120×100 mm containing T 920 and similar horiz designs showing the Four Seasons. Multicoloured.

MS2582	50c. Type **920**; €1 Summer; €1.50, Autumn; €2 Winter	16·00	16·00

921 Footballer and Golden Ball

2002. Award of International Philatelic Grand Prix to Luis Figo (footballer and 2001 Golden Ball winner). Centenary of Real Madrid Football Club.

2583	**921**	91c. multicoloured	2·75	2·00

922 Exhibition Poster

2002. "MonacoPhil 2002" Stamp Exhibition (2nd issue). Sheet 120×82 mm, containing T 922 and similar vert design. Multicoloured. Imperf.

MS2584	€3 Type **922**; €3 Exhibition emblem	19·00	19·00

923 Flower Arrangement

2002. 36th Monte Carlo Flower Show.

2585	**923**	67c. multicoloured	2·20	1·50

924 Princesses Caroline and Stephanie (presidents)

2002. 40th Anniv of "Association Mondiale des Amis de l'Enfance" (children's society).

2586	**924**	€1.25 multicoloured	4·00	2·75

925 St. George
(statue)

2002. 1700th Anniv of St. George's Martyrdom.
2587 **925** 53c. multicoloured   1·70   1·20

926 Prince Louis II,
Flag, Arch and
Building

2002. Bicentenary of Saint-Cyr Imperial Military School.
2588 **926** 61c. multicoloured   1·90   1·30

927 Clown

2003. 27th International Circus Festival, Monte Carlo.
2589 **927** 59c. multicoloured   1·90   1·30

928 Crossed
Pennants and Part
of Yacht and Crew

2003. 50th Anniv of Monaco Yacht Club.
2590 **928** 46c. multicoloured   1·60   1·10

929 Children

2003. 15th Premiere Rampe (children's circus) Festival.
2591 **929** €2.82 multicoloured   9·00   6·50

930 Team Members
pushing Bobsleigh

2003. 10th World Bobsleigh Pushing Championship.
2592 **930** 80c. multicoloured   2·50   1·80

931 Dove, Globe
and Prince Albert I

2003. Centenary of Monaco International Peace Institute.
2593 **931** €1.19 multicoloured   3·75   2·75

932 Leaves,
Spectator, Tennis
Court and Player

2003. Tennis Masters Championship, Monte Carlo.
2594 **932** €1.30 multicoloured   4·00   2·75

933 Rough Collie

2003. International Dog Show, Monte Carlo.
2595 **933** 79c. multicoloured   2·75   2·00

934 Anniversary Emblem

2003. 40th Anniv of Monaco Junior Chamber of
Commerce.
2596 **934** 41c. multicoloured   1·20   90

935 Club Grounds

2003. 75th Anniv of Monte Carlo Country Club.
2597 **935** 46c. multicoloured   1·40   1·00

936 Prince Albert I, Sextant, Maps and Emblem

2003. Centenary of First General Bathymetric Chart of the
Oceans. Multicoloured.
2598   €1.25 Type **936**   4·00   2·75
2599   €1.25, Buildings and maps   4·00   2·75
   Nos. 2598/9 were issued together, se-tenant, forming a
composite design.

937 Girl on Diving
Board (Jean-Gabriel
Domergue)

2003. Europa. Poster Art. Multicoloured.
2600   50c. Type **937**   2·00   1·40
2601   50c. Monte-Carlo (Alphonse
     Mucha)   2·00   1·40

938 Castle, Coin
and Ship

2003. Postcard Coin and Stamp Exhibition, Fontvielle.
2602 **938** 45c. multicoloured   1·60   1·10

939 Face

2003. 43rd International Television Festival.
2603 **939** 90c. multicoloured   2·75   2·00

940 Bronze
Statuette

2003. 15th Biannual Antique Dealers Meeting.
2604 **940** €1.80 multicoloured   5·50   4·00

941 Roald Amundsen and
Polar Scene

2003. Centenaries. Multicoloured.
2605   90c. Type **941** (1st crossing of
     North Pole)   2·75   2·00
2606   €1.80 Wright brothers and
     Flyer 1   5·50   4·00

942 Hector Berlioz

2003. Composers Birth Anniversaries.
2607 **942** 75c. black and red   2·30   1·70
2608   -   €1.60 blue, sepia and red   5·00   3·50
DESIGNS—VERT: Type **942** (bicentenary). HORIZ: €1.60
Aram Khatchaturian (centenary).

943 Woman's Head
(Francois Boucher) (300th
anniv)

2003. Artists' Birth Anniversaries.
2609 **943** €1.30 multicoloured   4·00   2·75
2610   -   €3 mauve and black   9·25   6·50
2611   -   €3.60 brown and black   11·00   7·75
DESIGNS: €1.30, Type **943**; €3 Vincent Van Gogh (150th
anniv); €3.60, Girolamo Francesco Maria Mazzola (Le Par-
migianino) (500th anniv).

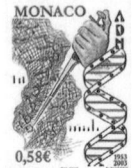

944 Hand holding
Pipette and DNA
Double Helix (50th
anniv of discovery)

2003. Scientific Anniversaries.
2612 **944** 58c. black, blue and red   1·90   1·30
2613   -   €1.11 chestnut, blue
     and red   3·50   2·40
DESIGNS: Type **944**; Alexander Fleming (75th anniv of
discovery of penicillin).

945 Nostradamus

2003. 500th Birth Anniv of Michel de Nostre-Dame
(Nostradamus) (astrologer).
2614 **945** 70c. multicoloured   2·20   1·50

946 Magician

2003. "Magic Stars" Magic Festival, Monte Carlo.
2615 **946** 75c. multicoloured   2·30   1·70

947 Marie and Pierre Curie

2003. Centenary of Award of Nobel Prize for Physics to
Antoine Henri Becquerel and Pierre and Marie Curie.
2616 **947** €1.20 multicoloured   3·75   2·75

948 St. Devote
kneeling before
Cross

2003. 1700th (2004) Anniv of Arrival of St. Devote
(patron saint) in Monaco (1st series). Each blue,
black and red.
2617   45c. Type **948**   1·40   1·00
2618   45c. St. Devote facing Barbarus   1·40   1·00
2619   45c. Boat carrying St. Devote's
     body   1·40   1·00
2620   45c. St. Devote (statue)   1·40   1·00
   See also No. 2626/30.

949 Edmund Hilary and
Mount Everest

2003. 50th Anniv of First Ascent of Mount Everest.
2621 **949** €1 multicoloured   3·25   2·20

950 Star-shaped
Flower

2003. Christmas.
2622 **950** 50c. multicoloured   1·60   1·10

951 Lion and Lion
Tamer

2003. MonacoPhil 2004 Stamp Exhibition (December
2004).
2623 **951** 50c. multicoloured   1·60   1·10

952 Exhibition Poster

2003. 28th International Circus Festival (January 2004), Monte Carlo.
2624 **952** 70c. multicoloured — 2·20 1·50

953 Tram and Buildings

2004. Centenary of Beausoleil Municipality.
2625 **953** 75c. multicoloured — 2·40 1·70

954 St. Devote kneeling before Alta

2004. 1700th Anniv of St. Devote's Arrival (2nd series).
2626 **954** 50c. red and brown — 1·60 1·10
2627 — 75c. orange and brown (horiz) — 2·40 1·70
2628 — 90c. brown and deep brown (horiz) — 3·00 2·00
2629 — €1 brown and deep brown — 3·25 2·20
2630 — €4 purple and brown (horiz) — 13·00 8·75

DESIGNS: 75c. Before Barbarus; 90c. Martyrdom; €1 Boat carrying St. Devote's body; €4 Arrival in Monaco.

955 Princesses Grace and Caroline

2004. 40th Anniv of Princess Grace Foundation.
2640 **955** 50c. multicoloured — 1·60 1·10

956 Hyla meridionalis

2004. Amphibians.
2641 **956** 75c. green, yellow and black — 2·40 1·70
2642 — €4.50 green, blue and black — 14·50 10·00

DESIGN: Type **956**; €4.50, Lacerte viridis.

957 Princess Grace and Shamrock Leaf

2004. 20th Anniv of Princess Grace Irish Library.
2643 **957** €1.11 green and brown — 3·50 2·40

958 Hands

2004. 6th Biennial Oncological Meeting.
2644 **958** €1.11 multicoloured — 3·50 2·40

959 Princess Grace (statue) (Daphne du Barry)

2004
2645 **959** €1.45 multicoloured — 4·75 3·25

960 Garden

2004. 20th Anniv of Princess Grace Rose Garden.
2646 **960** €1.90 multicoloured — 6·25 4·25

961 Mask, Musical Instruments, Dancer and Actor

2004. Spring Arts Festival.
2647 **961** €1 brown, scarlet and green — 3·25 2·20

962 Cathedral Facade, Choirboy and Emblem

2004. Centenary of Cathedral Choir.
2648 **962** 45c. multicoloured — 1·50 1·00

963 Flower Arrangement

2004. 37th Monte Carlo Flower Show.
2649 **963** 58c. multicoloured — 2·00 1·30

964 Cavalier King Charles Spaniels

2004. International Dog Show, Monte Carlo.
2650 **964** 90c. multicoloured — 3·00 2·00

965 Antony Noghes, King Louis II and Bugatti 35B Race Car driven by William Grover-Williams

2004. 75th Anniv of First Monaco Motor Racing Grand Prix.
2651 **965** €1.20 multicoloured — 4·00 2·75

966 Hands enclosing Children

2004. Monaco International School.
2652 **966** 50c. multicoloured — 1·70 1·10

967 Athens Stadium (1896) and Modern Runners

2004. Olympic Games, Athens. Multicoloured.
2653 45c. Type **967** — 1·40 1·00
2654 45c. Classical Greek runners and Athens stadium (2004) — 1·40 1·00

Nos. 2653/4 were issued together, se-tenant, forming a composite design.

968 Women wearing Swimsuits ("What Joy to Live the Summer in Monte Carlo") (poster, 1948)

2004. Europa. Holidays. Multicoloured.
2655 50c. Type **968** — 1·60 1·10
2656 50c. Frontier sign ("The border of your dreams") (poster, 1951) — 1·60 1·10

969 Medal

2004. 50th Anniv of Order of Grimaldi (medal).
2657 **969** 90c. multicoloured — 2·75 2·00

970 Napoleon, Crown Prince Honore-Gabriel and Prince Joseph (officers in Napoleon's army)

2004. Bicentenary of Coronation of Emperor Napoleon I. Multicoloured.
2658 58c. Type **970** — 1·90 1·30
2659 75c. Eagle and bees (imperial insignia) (horiz) — 2·30 1·70
2660 €1.90 Stephanie de Beauharnais (Napoleon's niece and adopted daughter) — 6·00 4·25
2661 €2.40 Napoleon I wearing coronation robes — 7·75 5·50

971 George Balanchine (choreographer) and Serge Diaghilev (ballet impresario)

2004. First Production of Russian Ballet in Monaco.
2662 **971** €1.60 multicoloured — 5·25 3·50

972 Eye enclosing Globe

2004. 44th International Television Festival.
2663 **972** €1.80 multicoloured — 6·00 4·00

973 Frederic Mistral

2004. Centenary of Frederic Mistral's Nobel Prize for Literature.
2664 **973** 45c. vermilion, brown and green — 1·50 1·00

974 Bird holding Envelope and Globe

2004. 23rd UPU Conference, Bucharest.
2665 **974** 50c. multicoloured — 1·70 1·10

975 Chinese Landscape and Marco Polo

2004. 750th Birth Anniv of Marco Polo (traveller).
2666 **975** 50c. multicoloured — 1·70 1·10

976 Stamps and Park

2004. Salon de Timbre International Stamp Exhibition, Paris.
2667 **976** 75c. brown, green and vermilion — 2·50 1·70

977 Scenes from the Stories

2004. 300th Anniv of French Translation of "One Thousand and One Nights" (collection of stories).
2668 **977** €1 indigo — 3·25 2·20

978 Hotel Complex

2004. 75th Anniv of Monte Carlo Beach Hotel.
2669 **978** 45c. multicoloured — 1·50 1·00

979 Anniversary Emblem

2004. Centenary of FIFA (Federation Internationale de Football Association).
2670 **979** €1.60 multicoloured — 5·25 3·50

698   Monaco

980 Female Magician

2004. "Magic Stars" Magic Festival.
2671 980   45c. multicoloured   1·50   1·00

981 Cacti and Presents

2004. Christmas.
2672 981   50c. multicoloured   1·70   1·10

982 Princess Grace

2004. 75th Birth Anniv of Princess Grace (MS2673a).
MonacoPhil 2004 (MS2673b). Two sheets, each
141×75 mm containing T 982 and similar vert
designs. Each ultramarine and green.
MS2673 (a) 75c. Type 982; €1.75 Wearing tiara; €3.50 Wearing earrings. (b)
As No. MS2673a but with colours
reversed. Imperf Set of 2 sheets   20·00 20·00

983 Monte Carlo and Emblem

2004. Monaco's Accession to the Council of Europe.
2674 983   50c. blue and vermilion   1·70   1·10

984 Equestrian Performer

2004. 29th International Circus Festival (January 2005),
Monte Carlo.
2675 984   70c. multicoloured   1·50   1·00

985 Stadium Building, Pool and Court

2004. 20th Anniv of Louis II Stadium, Monte Carlo.
2676 985   50c. ultramarine, brown
            and vermilion   1·70   1·10

986 Prince Rainier III

2004. Monaco Prince's Palace. Each salmon, deep green
and green.
2677 50c. Type 986   1·70   1·10
2678 50c. Palace facade (60×27 mm)   1·70   1·10
2679 50c. Prince Albert   1·70   1·10
   Nos. 2677/9 were issued together, se-tenant, forming a
composite design.

987 Entrance

2004. 70th Anniv of Foundation of Monaco Hall of
Residence, Cité University, Paris.
2680 987   58c. brown, black and
            vermilion   2·00   1·30

988 Building Facade

2004. 75th Anniv of Law Courts.
2681 988   75c. multicoloured   2·50   1·70

989 Artistic and Cultural Symbols

2004. 25th Anniv of "Alliance Francaise" (French language
and culture promotion organization).
2682 989   75c. multicoloured   2·50   1·70

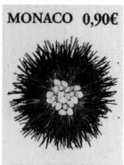
990 Flower Arrangement

2004. 38th Monte Carlo Flower Show (2005).
2683 990   90c. multicoloured   3·00   2·00

991 Luigi Valentino Brugnatelli (inventor)

2004. Bicentenary of Electroplating.
2684 991   €1 brown and black   3·25   2·20

992 Goalkeeper's Hands holding Ball

2004. 75th Anniv of First Football World Cup
Championship. Multicoloured.
2685 €1 Type 992   3·25   2·20
2686 €1 Players' legs and ball   3·25   2·20

993 Jean-Paul Sartre

2004. Birth Centenary of Jean-Paul Sartre (writer).
2687 993   €1.11 multicoloured   3·75   2·40

994 Johan Edvard Lundstrom (Swedish inventor)

2004. 150th Anniv of Safety Matches.
2688 994   €1.20 multicoloured   4·00   2·75

995 Don Quixote and Sancho Panza

2004. 400th Anniv of "Don Quixote de la Mancha" (novel
by Miguel de Cervantes Saavedra).
2689 995   €1.20 black, brown and
            vermilion   4·00   2·75

996 Leo Ferre

2004. Leo Ferre (songwriter, singer and poet)
Commemoration.
2690 996   €1.40 multicoloured   4·50   3·00

997 Hand holding Hypodermic

2004. 150th Anniv of Invention of Hypodermic Syringe
by Alexander Wood.
2691 997   €1.60 purple, black and
            vermilion   5·25   3·50

998 Frank Libby

2004. 25th Death Anniv of Frank Willard Libby (inventor
of Carbon 14 dating and winner of Nobel Prize for
Chemistry, 1960).
2692 998   €1.80 multicoloured   6·00   4·00

999 Emblem and Founder Members (Rotary Club, Chicago)

2005. Centenary of Rotary International (charitable
organization). Multicoloured.
2693 55c. Type 999   1·80   1·20
2694 70c. Emblem and "100 ans"
      (vert)   2·30   1·50

1000 Artist and Castle

2005. 50th Anniv of Fine Arts Committee Exhibition.
2695 1000 48c. multicoloured   1·70   1·10

1001 Albert Einstein

2005. Centenary of Publication of Five Papers by Albert
Einstein.
2696 1001 53c. multicoloured   1·80   1·20

1002 Emblem

2005. Granting of University Diploma to Bosio Pavilion
Fine Arts School.
2697 1002 64c. vermilion and black 2·10   1·40

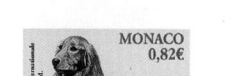
1003 Dachshund

2005. International Dog Show, Monte Carlo.
2698 1003 82c. multicoloured   2·75   1·90

1004 Centenary Emblem and Race Cars

2005. Centenary of FIA (Federation Internationale de
L'Automobile).
2699 1004 55c. multicoloured   1·80   1·20

1005 Venturi Fetish

2005. 21st Electric Car Congress (EVS 21), Monaco.
Multicoloured.
2700 75c. Type 1005   2·50   1·70
2701 €1.30 Car enclosing exhibition
      centre   4·25   2·75

1006 Show Jumper

2005. 10th International Show Jumping Competition,
Monaco.
2702 1006 90c. green and vermilion 3·00   2·00

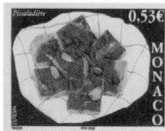
1007 Pissaladiere (pizza)

2005. Europa. Gastronomy. Multicoloured.
2703 53c. Type 1007   1·80   1·20
2704 53c. Barbagiuans   1·80   1·20
2705 55c. Pastries   1·80   1·20
2706 55c. Chard pie   1·80   1·20

1008 Louis II Stadium and Emblem

2005. 25th Anniv of Monaco Special Olympics.
2707 1008 €1.20 multicoloured   4·00   2·75

1009 Poster

2005. Centenary of First Industries. Advertising posters. Multicoloured.

2708		77c. Type **1009** (tourism)	2·75	1·80
2709		€2.50 Woman and bath (sanitary ware)	8·25	5·50
2710		€3.10 Harlequin and biscuits (biscuit making)	10·00	6·75

1010 Yachts in Berth

2005. Yacht Show.

2711	**1010**	82c. multicoloured	2·75	1·90

1011 Edmond Halley (predicted the continuing return of Halley's comet)

2005. Astronomers.

2712	**1011**	€1.22 violet, vermilion and green	4·25	2·75
2713	-	€1.98 deep green, vermilion and green	6·50	4·50
2714	-	€3.80 brown, vermilion and green	12·50	8·25

DESIGNS: €1.22 Type **1011**; €1.98 Gerald Kuiper (discovered Kuiper's belt) (birth centenary); €3.80 Clyde Tombaugh (75th anniv of discovery of Pluto).

1012 Emblem

2005. 50th Anniv of Universal Postal Union Membership.

2715	**1012**	€3.03 ultramarine, purple and vermilion	10·00	6·50

1013 Arms

2005. Self-adhesive.

2716	**1013**	(48c.) emerald, black and vermilion	1·70	1·10

No. 2716 was for use on mail up to 20 grammes within Monaco and France.

1014 Emblem

2005. 10th "Journee du Patrimoine" (culture day).

2717	**1014**	48c. multicoloured	1·70	1·10

1015 Emblem

2005. "Magic Stars" Magic Festival.

2718	**1015**	€1.45 scarlet and gold	5·00	3·25

1016 Virgin and Child

2005. Christmas.

2719	**1016**	53c. black and vermilion	1·80	1·20

1017 Monte-Carlo Bay Hotel

2005

2720	**1017**	55c. multicoloured	1·80	1·20

1018 Nadia and Lili Boulanger

2005. 25th Anniv of Nadia and Lili Boulanger Music Competition.

2721	**1018**	90c. indigo, vermilion and green	2·75	2·00

1019 Singer (Le Chant)

2005. 180th Birth Anniv of Charles Garnier (architect).

2722	**1019**	82c. claret and vermilion	2·50	1·80
2723	-	82c. claret and vermilion	2·50	1·80
2724	-	82c. claret and vermilion	2·50	1·80
2725	-	82c. claret and vermilion	2·50	1·80
2726	-	82c. green and vermilion	2·50	1·80
2727	-	82c. claret and vermilion	2·50	1·80

DESIGNS: 82c.×6, Type **1019**; Casino (Salle Garnier); Three figures (La Comedie); Two figures (La Danse); Charles Garnier; Musicians (La Musique).

1020 Prince Albert II

2005. No value expressed.

2728	**1020**	(48c.) green	1·60	1·10
2729	**1020**	(53c.) carmine	1·70	1·20
2730	**1020**	(75c.) blue	2·30	1·70

1021 Monte Carlo

2005. National Day. Multicoloured.

2731		€1.01 Type **1021**	3·00	2·20
2732		€1.01 Palace facade (60×32 mm)	3·00	2·20
2733		€1.01 Fontvielle	3·00	2·20

Nos. 2731/3 were issued together, se-tenant, forming a composite design.

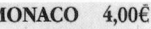 

1022 Prince Rainier III

2005. Prince Rainier III Commemoration. Sheet 101×130 mm.

MS2734	**1022**	€4 black	12·50	12·50

1023 Stamp Museum

2005. MonacoPhil 2006 International Stamp Exhibition.

2735	**1023**	55c. multicoloured	1·70	1·20

1024 Clown

2005. 30th International Circus Festival (January 2006), Monte Carlo. Multicoloured.

2736		64c. Type **1024**	2·00	1·40
2737		75c. Charlie Rivel — Clown d'Or 1974	2·30	1·70
2738		75c. Fredy Knie — Clown d'Or 1977	2·30	1·70
2739		75c. Alexis Gruss Senior — Clown d'Or 1975	2·30	1·70
2740		75c. Clown d'Or statue	2·30	1·70
2741		75c. Georges Carl — Clown d'Or 19791	2·30	1·70

1025 Neve (mascot)

2006. Winter Olympic Games, Turin. Multicoloured.

2742		55c. Type **1025**	1·70	1·20
2743		55c. Gliz	1·70	1·20
2744		82c. Bobsleigh and skier (40×30 mm)	2·75	1·90

Nos. 2742/3 were issued together, se-tenant, forming a composite design.

1026 Stamps, Coins and Printing Press

2006. Centenary of Stamp and Coin Museum.

2745	**1026**	53c. black, vermilion and brown	1·70	1·20

1027 Book as Clapperboard

2006. Cinema and Literature Forum.

2746	**1027**	82c. multicoloured	2·75	1·90

1028 Leopold Senghor

2006. Birth Centenary of Leopold Sedar Senghor (writer and politician). Organisation Internationale de la Francophonie.

2747	**1028**	€1.45 multicoloured	4·50	3·25

1029 Player and Emblem

2006. Centenary of Masters Tennis Tournament.

2748	**1029**	55c. multicoloured	1·80	1·20

1030 Grimaldi Arms

2006. Self-adhesive.

2749	**1030**	A (55c.) black and vermilion	1·80	1·20

1031 Conductors and Musical Instruments

2006. 150th Anniv of Philharmonic Orchestra.

2750	**1031**	64c. multicoloured	2·10	1·40

1032 Map and Ship

2006. Centenary of Prince Albert I's Arctic Expeditions.

2751	**1032**	€1.60 multicoloured	5·00	3·50

1033 Schnauzer

2006. International Dog Show, Monte Carlo.

2752	**1033**	64c. multicoloured	2·00	1·40

1034 Blooms

2006. 39th Monte Carlo Flower Show.

2753	**1034**	77c. multicoloured	2·50	1·80

1035x 1035 Trophy and Stadium

2006. World Cup Football Championship, Germany. Multicoloured.
2754	90c. Type **1035**		2·75	2·00
2755	90c. Stadium and emblem		2·75	2·00

1036 Boxes enclosing Shapes

2006. Europa. Integration. Multicoloured.
2756	53c. Type **1036**		1·70	1·20
2757	55c. Globe containing face, and microchip (horiz)		1·70	1·20

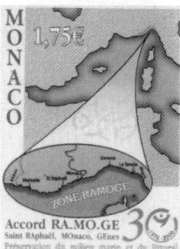

1037 Mediterranean Coastline

2006. 30th Anniv of RAMOGE (Monaco, France and Italy accord to combat coastal and maritime pollution).
2758	**1037**	€1.75 multicoloured	5·50	3·75

1038 Capitol

2006. Washington 2006 International Stamp Exhibition.
2759	**1038**	90c. ultramarine and vermilion	2·75	2·00

1039 John Huston

2006. Birth Centenary of John Huston (actor and director).
2760	**1039**	90c. slate and red	5·50	4·00

1040 Prince Albert and Fencers

2006. 20th Prince Albert Challenge Fencing Competition.
2761	**1040**	48c. multicoloured	1·60	1·10

1041 Pierre Corneille

2006. 400th Birth Anniv of Pierre Corneille (dramatist).
2762	**1041**	53c. multicoloured	1·70	1·20

1042 Hand and TV Screen

2006. 46th International Television Festival.
2763	**1042**	82c. multicoloured	2·75	1·90

1043 Mozart and Scenes from his Operas

2006. 250th Birth Anniv of Wolfgang Amadeus Mozart.
2764	**1043**	€1.22 blue and vermilion	4·00	2·75

1044 Prince Pierre and Cultural Symbols

2006. 40th Anniv of Prince Pierre Foundation (art and culture).
2765	**1044**	€2.50 lilac, blue and vermilion	7·75	5·50

1045 Dino Buzzati

2006. Birth Centenary of Dino Buzzati (writer).
2766	**1045**	55c. multicoloured	1·70	1·20

1046 Cetaceans

2006. 10th Anniv of ACCOBAMS.
2767		90c. multicoloured	2·75	2·00

1047 Luchino Visconti

2006. Birth Centenary of Luchino Visconti (film director).
2768	**1047**	€1.75 Indian red	5·50	3·75

1048 Rolls Royce Motor Car

2006. Centenary of Rolls Royce (car manufacturer).
2769	**1048**	64c. multicoloured	2·00	1·40

1049 Hand and Cards

2006. "Magic Stars" Magic Festival.
2770	**1049**	77c. multicoloured	2·50	1·80

1050 Heads

2006. Red Cross.
2771	**1050**	48c. multicoloured	1·60	1·10

1051 Virgin and Child

2006. Christmas.
2772	**1051**	53c. multicoloured	1·70	1·20

1052 Josephine Baker

2006. Birth Centenary of Josephine Baker (entertainer). 25th Anniv of Princess Grace Theatre.
2773	**1052**	49c. multicoloured	1·60	1·10

1053 Emblems

2006. 10th Anniv of AIDS Awareness Campaign.
2774	**1053**	49c. multicoloured	1·60	1·10

1054 Prince Albert II

2006. No value expressed.
2775	**1054**	(49c.) green	1·60	1·10
2776	**1054**	(54c.) scarlet	1·70	1·20
2777	**1054**	(85c.) blue	2·75	1·90

1055 Emblems, Envelopes and Stamps

2006. 70th Anniv of Stamp Issuing Office. 20th Anniv of Consultative Committee to the Prince of Monaco's Philatelic Collection.
2778	**1055**	54c. multicoloured	1·70	1·20

1056 Clown and Elephant

2006. 31st International Circus Festival (January 2007), Monte Carlo. Multicoloured.
2779	60c. Type **1056**		1·90	1·30
2780	84c. Poster		2·75	1·90

1057 Prince Albert II

2006. Official Photographic Portrait.
2781	**1057**	60c. multicoloured	1·90	1·30

1058 Formula 1 Race Car

2006. 65th Anniv of Monte Carlo Formula 1 Grand Prix (2782). 75th Anniv of Monte Carlo Rally (2783). Multicoloured.
2782	60c. Type **1058**		1·90	1·30
2783	60c. Rally race car		1·90	1·30

1059 Face

2006. 10th Anniv of Les Enfants de Frankie (children's charitable association).
2784	**1059**	70c. multicoloured	2·20	1·50

1060 Albert Camus

2006. 50th Anniv of Albert Camus's Nobel Prize for Literature.
2785	**1060**	84c. black, blue and vermilion	2·75	1·90

1061 Auguste Escoffier

2006. 160th Birth Anniv of Auguste Escoffier (chef).
2786	**1061**	85c. chestnut, vermilion and ultramarine	2·75	1·90

1062 Daniel Bovet and Alfred Nobel

2006. Red Cross. Birth Centenary (2007) of Daniel Bovet—Winner of 1957 Nobel Prize for Medicine.
2787	**1062**	86c. lilac and vermilion	2·75	1·90

1063 Blue and Pink Bouquet

2006. 40th Anniv of International Flower Competition. Multicoloured.

2788	€1.30 Type **1063**		4·00	2·75
2789	€1.30 Two orange flowers and thin leaves		4·00	2·75
2790	€1.30 Tall arrangement		4·00	2·75
2791	€1.30 Gerberas		4·00	2·75

1064 Cardio-Thoracic Centre Building

2006. 20th Anniv of Cardio Thoracic Centre (2792). Opening of Institute of Medicine and Sports Surgery (2793).

2792	**1064**	€1.15 ultramarine, vermilion and black	3·50	2·50
2793	-	€1.70 vermilion, black and cinnamon	5·00	3·75

DESIGNS: €1.15 Type **1064**; €1.70 Institute building.

1065 Frontispiece and Rudyard Kipling

2006. Centenary of Rudyard Kipling's Nobel Prize for Literature.

2794	**1065**	€1.57 green, vermilion and black	4·75	3·50

1066 Prince Albert II and Pope Benedict XVI

2006. Prince Albert II's Official Visit to the Vatican.

2795	**1066**	€1.70 multicoloured	5·00	3·75

1067 "Sunrise"

2006. Grimaldi Forum. Paintings by Nall. Multicoloured.

2796	€1.70 Type **1067**		5·00	3·75
2797	€1.70 "Sunset"		5·00	3·75

1068 Paul-Emile Victor and dog

2006. Birth Centenary of Paul-Emile Victor (explorer).

2798	**1068**	€2.11 blue, black and vermilion	6·25	4·50

1069 Flags as Map of Europe

2006. 30th Anniv of European Academy of Philately.

2799	**1069**	€2.30 multicoloured	6·75	5·00

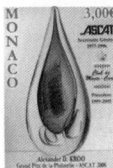

1070 Trophy

2006. Alexander Kroo—ASCAT 2006 Philatelic Grand Prix Winner.

2800	**1070**	€3 multicoloured	8·75	6·50

1071 Prince Albert II

2006. MonacoPhil (2006). Sheet 101×126 mm.

MS2801	**1071**	€6 multicoloured	16·00	16·00

1072 *Stenella coeruleoalba*

2007. Pre-cancelled. No value expressed.

2802	**1072**	(36c.) multicoloured	1·30	90

No. 2802 was for mass mailing within France weighing less than 35g.

1073 Guiseppe Garibaldi

2007. Birth Bicentenary of Guiseppe Garibaldi (soldier).

2803	**1073**	€1.40 sepia and vermilion	4·50	3·00

1074 Carlo Goldoni

2007. 300th Birth Anniv of Carlo Goldoni (playwright).

2804	**1074**	€4.54 multicoloured	12·50	10·00

1075 Albert Gautier-Vignal and Committee Emblem

2007. Centenary of Monaco Olympic Committee.

2805	**1075**	60c. multicoloured	1·90	1·30

1076 Dalmatian

2007. International Dog Show, Monte Carlo.

2806	**1076**	70c. multicoloured	2·20	1·50

1077 Members' Flags and Emblem

2007. Small European States' Games.

2807	**1077**	86c. multicoloured	2·75	2·00

1078 Grace Kelly

2007. 25th Death Anniv of Princess Grace. "The Grace Kelly Years" Exhibition, Grimaldi Forum.

2808	**1078**	85c. black and vermilion	2·75	1·90

1079 Leger and Modern Helicopter

2007. Centenary of First Flight of Leger Helicopter (created by Maurice Stanislas Leger).

2809	**1079**	€1.15 violet, ultramarine and vermilion	3·75	2·75

1080 Scouts and Campfire

2007. Europa. Centenary of Scouting. Multicoloured.

2810	60c. Type **1080**		1·90	1·40
2811	60c. Robert Baden Powell (founder)		1·90	1·40

Nos. 2810/11 were issued together, *se-tenant*, forming a composite design.

1081 Lights

2007. 47th International Television Festival.

2812	**1081**	€2.90 multicoloured	8·75	7·00

1082 Postcard, Coin and Stamp

2007. Postcard Coin and Stamp Exhibition.

2813	**1082**	49c. multicoloured	1·80	1·30

1083 Magician

2007. 'Magic Stars' Magic Festival.

2814	**1083**	€1.30 vermilion and black	4·25	3·00

1084 Virgin Mary

2007. Christmas (Visions of Virgin Mary by Bernadette Soubirous at Lourdes, 1858).

2815	**1084**	54c. multicoloured	1·90	1·40

1085 Bay

2007. SEPAC (small European mail services).

2816	**1085**	85c. brown, blue and red	3·00	2·20

1086 Ringmaster

2007. 32nd International Circus Festival (January 2008), Monte Carlo.

2817	**1086**	60c. multicoloured	2·10	1·50

1087 Giacomo Puccini

2007. 140th Birth Anniv of Giacomo Puccini (composer).

2818	**1087**	€1.40 blue and vermilion	5·00	3·50

1088 Church Building

2008. 50th Anniv of Reformed Church.

2819	**1088**	49c. brown and blue	1·90	1·40

1089 Flower Arrangement

2008. 41st International Flower Competition.

2820	**1089**	49c. multicoloured	1·90	1·40

1090 Church Building

2008. 125th Anniv of Consecration of St Charles Church.

2821	**1090**	54c. slate and vermilion	2·00	1·50

1091 Quadriga and Arc de Triomphe du Carrousel

2008. Bicentenary of Francois Bosio's Quadriga (statue of chariot drawn by four horses).

2822	**1091**	54c. brown, vermilion and carmine	2·00	1·50

1092 Andrea Palladio

2008. 500th Birth Anniv of Andrea Palladio (architect).

2823	**1092**	60c. multicoloured	2·20	1·70

1093 Monte Carlo Country Club

2008. Posters of 1932 by Raymond Gid. Multicoloured.
2824	**1093**	70c. Type **1093**	2·50	1·90
2825		85c. Monte Carlo Beach Hotel	3·00	2·30
2826		€1.15 Monte Carlo Golf Club	4·25	3·25

1094 Hands enclosing Emblem

2008. 10th Special Session of United Nations Environment Programme Forum.
2827	**1094**	85c. multicoloured	3·00	2·30

1095 Johannes Brahms

2008. 175th Birth Anniv of Johannes Brahms (composer and pianist).
2828	**1095**	€1.15 green and vermilion	4·25	3·25

1096 Comet and Castle

2008. 250th Anniv of First Recorded Appearance of Halley's Comet.
2829	**1096**	€1.57 multicoloured	5·75	4·50

1097 Leaves and Cones

2008. 20th Anniv of Marcel Kronenlein's Arboretum.
2830	**1097**	€2.11 olive, ultramarine and vermilion	7·25	5·75

1098 'Monte Carlo, Pole d'Attraction' (1948)

2008. Poster by Louis Rue.
2831	**1098**	€2.90 multicoloured	10·00	8·00

1099 Andre Massena

2008. 250th Birth Anniv of Andre Massena (Marshal of France).
2832	**1099**	86c. green and brown	3·00	2·30

1100 Bernadette Soubirous

2008. 150th Anniv of Apparition at Lourdes.
2833	**1100**	€1.30 ultramarine and blue	4·75	3·50

1101 Henry Ford and Model 'T' Ford Car

2008. Anniversaries.
2834	**1101**	€1.70 brown, green and vermilion	6·25	4·75
2835	-	€2.30 indigo, vermilion and ultramarine	8·50	6·25
2836	-	€4 brown and red	14·00	11·00

DESIGNS: €1.70 Type **1101** (centenary); €2.30 *Apollo*, *Atlantis* and *Mercury* spacecraft (50th anniv of NASA); €4 Alfred Nobel and nitroglycerine (175th birth anniv).

1102 Van Gogh (greyhound)

2008. International Dog Show, Monte Carlo.
2837	**1102**	88c. multicoloured	3·25	2·50

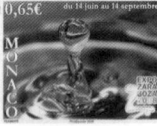

1103 Water Droplet

2008. Zaragoza 2008 International Water and Sustainable Development Exhibition.
2838	**1103**	65c. multicoloured	2·50	2·00

1104 Arms and Map

2008. Centenary of Cap d'Ail.
2839	**1104**	55c. black, brown and vermilion	2·10	1·60

1105 Heart enclosing Children and Flowers

2008. Mothers' Day.
2840	**1105**	55c. multicoloured	2·10	1·60

1106 Pagoda and Stylized Athletes

2008. Olympic Games, Beijing. Each vermilion and black.
2841	**1106**	55c. Type **1106**	2·10	1·60
2842		85c. Athletes and games emblem	3·25	2·40

1107 Stendhal and Scenes from his Novels

2008. 225th Birth Anniv of Henri Beyle (Stendhal) (writer).
2843	**1107**	€1.33 blue, lilac and vermilion	5·25	3·75

1108 Boris Pasternak and Scene from *Dr. Zhivago*

2008. 50th Anniv of Boris Pasternak's Nobel Prize for Literature.
2844	**1108**	€2.18 vermilion and green	8·50	6·25

1109 Plants and Monaco

2008. 75th Anniv of Jardin Exotique (garden created by Prince Albert I).
2845	**1109**	50c. olive, purple and vermilion	2·00	1·40

1110 Globe circled by Mail

2008. Europa. The Letter.
2846		55c. brown, orange and vermilion	2·20	1·60
2847		65c. light brown, brown and vermilion	2·50	1·80

DESIGNS: 55c. Type **1110**; 65c. Symbols of transport.

1111 Magician

2008. Magic Stars Festival, Monte-Carlo.
2848	**1111**	72c. multicoloured	3·00	2·10

1112 Skater

2008. International Skating Union Congress.
2849	**1112**	50c. multicoloured	2·00	1·40

1113 *Gypaetus barbatus* (bearded vulture), Emblem and *Hieraaectus fasciatus* (Bonelli's eagle)

2008. Prince Albert II Foundation.
2850	**1113**	88c. multicoloured	3·50	2·50

1114 Face, Hand and Colours

2008. 48th International Television Festival.
2851	**1114**	€2.80 multicoloured	10·50	7·75

1115 School Children

2008. International Co-operation.
2852		65c. black and vermilion	2·50	1·80
2853		€1 agate and vermilion	4·00	2·75
2854		€1.25 blue and vermilion	5·00	3·50
2855		€1.70 green and vermilion	6·75	4·75

DESIGNS: 65c. Type **1115** (campaign for education); €1 Health worker (health—Monegasque Red Cross); €1.25 Women (campaign against poverty); €1.70 Oasis and desert dwellers (campaign against desertification).

1116 Honore II Pistole (1648) and Monegasque Euro

2008. Monaco Numismatique 2008 Exhibition.
2856	**1116**	65c. multicoloured	2·75	2·00

1117 Franc 'Germinal', 1837

2008. Coins. Multicoloured.
2857		50c. Type **1117**	2·10	1·60
2858		55c. Franc, 1943	2·30	1·70
2859		72c. Franc 'Rainier III', 1950	3·00	2·30
2860		€1.25 Franc 'Rainier III', 1960	5·25	4·00
2861		€1.64 Euro coins, 1999	6·75	5·25
2862		€1.72 Euro coins, 2006	7·00	5·25

1118 Schonbrunn Palace

2008. WIPA 2008 International Stamp Exhibition, Vienna.
2863	**1118**	65c. multicoloured	2·75	2·00

1119 Order

2008. 150th Anniv of Order of St Charles
2864	**1119**	€1.50 multicoloured	6·25	4·75

1120 Sleigh and Globe

2008. Christmas.
2865	**1120**	55c. multicoloured	2·30	1·70

1121 Symbols of Festival

2008. 33rd International Circus Festival.
2866 **1121** 85c. multicoloured 4·00 3·00

1122 Prince Albert I

2008. International Polar Year. Multicoloured.
2867 85c. Type **1122** 4·00 3·00
2868 85c. Flag of Monaco (41×41 mm) 4·00 3·00
2869 85c. Prince Albert II 4·00 3·00

1123 Robert Peary

2008. Centenary of Robert Peary's Expedition to North Pole. Multicoloured.
2870 87c. Type **1123** 4·25 3·25
2871 87c. USA flag and North Pole (41×41 mm) 4·25 3·25
2872 87c. Matthew Henson and *Theodore Roosevelt* (expedition ship) 4·25 3·25

1124 Railway and Road Emergency Vehicle

2009. Centenary of Monaco Firefighters. Multicoloured.
2873 50c. Type **1124** 2·30 1·70
2874 72c. Emergency vehicle, 1909 3·50 2·50
2875 87c. Long ladder emergency vehicle 4·25 3·25

1125 Rose Garden

2009. 25th Anniv of Princess Grace Rose Garden.
2876 **1125** €1.25 multicoloured 5·50 4·25

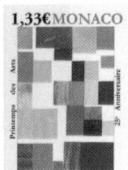

1126 Abstract

2009. 25th Anniv of Spring Arts Festival.
2877 **1126** €1.33 multicoloured 6·00 4·75

1127 Louis Bleriot and *Bleriot XI*

2009. Centenary of First Flight over English Channel.
2878 **1127** 87c. multicoloured 4·00 3·25

1128 Felix Mendelssohn

2009. Birth Bicentenary of Jakob Ludwig Felix Mendelssohn Bartholdy (composer).
2879 **1128** €1.50 indigo and olive 6·75 5·25

1129 Joan of Arc

2009. Centenary of Beatification of Joan of Arc.
2880 **1129** €2.22 scarlet, black and green 9·75 7·75

1130 Stamps and Building

2009. MonacoPhil 2009 International Stamp Exhibition.
2881 **1130** 56c. multicoloured 2·50 2·10

1131 Chihuahua and Cavalier King Charles Spaniel

2009. International Dog Show, Monte Carlo.
2882 **1131** 72c. multicoloured 3·50 2·50

1132 Blue-point Birman

2009. 2nd International Cat Show.
2883 **1132** 88c. multicoloured 4·25 3·25

1133 Palms and Map

2009. World Conference of Order of Academic Palms Association Members.
2884 **1133** 88c. violet, brown and scarlet 4·25 3·25

1134 Barbie

2009. 50th Anniv of Barbie Doll.
2885 **1134** 88c. multicoloured 4·25 3·25

1135 Flowers

2009. 42nd International Flower Exhibition.
2886 **1135** 89c. multicoloured 4·25 3·25

1136 Fencer and Arms

2009. Centenary of Monaco Fencing and Handgun Club.
2887 **1136** 55c. black, scarlet and lemon 3·00 2·00

1137 Race Winner and Map of Italy

2009. Centenary of Tour of Italy (Giro) Cycle Race.
2888 **1137** 70c. multicoloured 3·75 2·50

1138 Arthur Conan Doyle and Outline of Sherlock Holmes (character)

2009. 150th Birth Anniv of Arthur Conan Doyle (writer).
2889 **1138** 85c. purple, scarlet and vermilion 4·50 3·00

1139 Edgar Allen Poe and Death

2009. Birth Bicentenary of Edgar Allen Poe (writer).
2890 **1139** €1.70 green and scarlet 9·00 6·25

1140 Arms

2009. Booklet Stamp. Self-adhesive.
2891 **1140** (70c.) multicoloured 3·00 2·40
No. 2891 was issued in single sided booklets of ten stamps for use on mail up to 20g. within Zone 1 (EU and Switzerland).

1141 Louis Notari and Script

2009. Centenary of Louis Notari Library.
2892 **1141** 51c. scarlet vermilion and bright violet 2·40 1·90

1142 Early and Modern Race Cars

2009. Centenary of First Formula I Grand Prix.
2893 **1142** 70c. multicoloured 3·00 2·40

1143 Flags of Members

2009. 60th Anniv of Monaco's Membership of UNESCO.
2894 **1143** €1.70 multicoloured 7·75 7·75

1144 Louis Braille

2009. Birth Bicentenary of Louis Braille (inventor of Braille writing for the blind).
2895 **1144** €3.80 indigo, scarlet and bistre 16·00 13·00

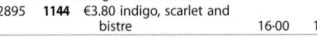

1145 Orchestra

2009. 50th Anniv of Prince's Palace Summer Concerts.
2896 **1145** 51c. bright violet and black 2·40 1·00

1146 Francesco Maria Grimaldi

2009. Europa. Astronomy.
2897 56c. deep brown, deep blue and scarlet 2·50 1·90
2898 70c. deep brown, turquoise blue and scarlet 3·00 2·40
DESIGNS: 56c. Type **1146**; 70c. Galileo.

1147 Dancer

2009. Ballet. Multicoloured.
2899 73c. Type **1147** (Ballet de Monte-Carlo) 3·25 2·50
2900 89c. Early dancers and audience (centenary of Ballets Russe) 4·00 3·25
2901 €1.35 Modern dancers (centenary of Ballets Russe) 6·00 4·75

1148 Georges Seurat

2009. 150th Birth Anniv of Georges Seurat (artist)
2902 **1148** 73c. multicoloured 3·25 2·50

1149 Pope Innocent III and Francis of Assisi

2009. 800th Anniv of Franciscan Order.
2903 **1149** 90c. new blue and black 4·00 3·25

1150 John Calvin

2009. 500th Birth Anniv of John Calvin (religious reformer).
2904 **1150** €1.67 black, scarlet and pale orange 7·25 5·75

1151 'Waves'

2009. 49th International Television Festival.
2905 **1151** €1.60 multicoloured 7·25 5·50

1152 Niccolo Machiavelli

2009. 30th Anniv of Dante Alighieri Society (for the promulgation of Italian language and culture).
2906 70c. slate grey, scarlet and orange-brown 3·00 2·40
2907 85c. orange, scarlet and yellow-brown 3·75 3·00
2908 €1.30 new blue, scarlet and bright orange-brown 5·75 4·50
DESIGNS: 70c. Type **1152**; 85c. Giovanni Boccaccio; €1.30 Francesco Petrarca.

1153 Cornucopia

2009. Postcard, Coin and Stamp Exhibition.
2909 **1153** 51c. multicoloured 2·20 1·70

1154 Emblem and Young People

2009. Centenary of Youth Hostels.
2910 **1154** 90c. multicoloured 4·00 3·25

1155 Tuiga

2009. Centenary of Tuiga (racing yacht).
2911 **1155** 70c. multicoloured 3·00 2·40

1156 Cyclist

2009. Start of Tour de France Cycle Race in Monaco.
2912 **1156** 56c. multicoloured 2·50 2·25

1157 Pig as Magician

2009. Magic Stars Festival.
2913 **1157** 73c. multicoloured 3·00 2·40

1158 Place de la Marie

2009. SEPAC (small European mail services).
2914 **1158** 85c. multicoloured 3·25 4·75

1159 Big Ben

2009. 150th Anniv of Big Ben Clock, Palace of Westminster.
2915 **1159** €1 black, lemon and scarlet-vermilion 4·50 4·00

1160 Symbols of Christmas

2009. Christmas.
2916 **1160** 56c. new blue, light green and scarlet-vermilion 2·50 2·25

1161 Inscr 'Bengal' (name– Junglewhisper Elia)

2009. International Cat Show, 2010, Rainer III Auditorium.
2917 **1161** 56c. multicoloured 5·75 4·50

1162 Ayrton Senna

2009. 50th Birth Anniv of Ayrton Senna da Silva (racing driver).
2918 **1162** 73c. purple-brown, green and scarlet-vermilion 5·00 2·40

No. 2919 and Type **1163** are left for Birth Centenary of Jean Anouilth, issued on 4 December 2009, not yet received.

1164 Auguste Rodin and Le Baiser (sculpture)

2009. 170th (2010) Birth Anniv of Auguste Rodin (sculptor).
2920 **1164** 85c. blue-black and scarlet-vermilion 3·75 3·00

1165 Grace Kelly receiving Oscar for Best Actress, 1955

2009. 80th Birth Anniv of Grace Kelly (actress and Princess Grace of Monaco).
2921 **1165** 89c. black and scarlet-vermilion 4·00 3·25

1166 Gustav Mahler

2009. 150th (2010) Birth Anniv of Gustav Mahler (composer).
2922 **1166** 90c. deep dull purple and new blue 4·00 3·25

1167 Skier

2009. Winter Olympic Games, Vancouver.
2923 90c. turquoise-green, scarlet-vermilion and deep blue 4·00 3·25
2924 90c. deep blue, scarlet-vermilion and dull orange 4·00 3·25
DESIGNS: Type **1167**; 2924 Snowboarder.

1168 Monte Carlo vu de Roquebrune

2009. 170th (2010) Birth Anniv of Oscar Claude Monet (Claude Monet) (artist).
2925 **1168** €1.30 multicoloured 5·75 4·50

1169 USA 1868 1c. (Z grill) Stamp and Association Emblem

2009. 2009 ASCAT Grand Prix to William H. Gross (for complete 19th-century USA collection).
2926 **1169** €1.35 multicoloured 6·00 4·75

1170 La Naissance de Venus (William Bouguereau)

2009. Art.
2927 **1170** €1.60 multicoloured 7·25 5·75

1171 Anton Chekov and Scenes from Three Sisters, The Cherry Orchard and The Seagull

2009. 150th (2010) Birth Anniv of Anton Pavlovich Chekhov (dramatist).
2928 **1171** €1.67 indigo, brown-olive and scarlet-vermilion 7·50 6·00

1172 Rally Race Car

2009. 120th Anniv of Automobile Club de Monaco. Sheet 123×94 mm containing T **1172** and similar horiz design. Multicoloured.
MS2929 €1.30 Type **1172**; €1.70 Formula I race car 14·00 14·00

1173 Prince Albert II

2009. MonacoPhil 2009 International Stamp Exhibition. Sheet 120×100 mm.
MS2930 **1173** €4 black and scarlet-vermilion 21·00 21·00
The margins of No. **MS**2930 were printed in multicoloured offset.

1174 Big Top and Performers

2009. 34th International Circus Festival.
2931 **1174** 70c. multicoloured 3·00 2·40

1175 Crystal Blue Velvet (Australian shepherd dog)

2010. International Dog Show, Monte Carlo
2952 **1175** 51c. multicoloured 2·50 2·25

1176 Scenes from Seven Samurai

2010. Birth Centenary of Akira Kurosawa (film director, producer, screenwriter and editor)
2933　**1176**　51c. blackish purple and greenish yellow　2·50　2·25

1177 Players

2010. Centenary of First Five Nations Rugby Championship
2934　**1177**　70c. multicoloured　3·00　2·40

1178 Firebird

2010. 43rd International Flower Exhibition
2935　**1178**　70c. multicoloured　3·00　2·40

1179 Centre Court

2010. Monte-Carlo Rolex Masters Tennis Tournament
2936　**1179**　85c. multicoloured　3·75　2·75

1180 Albert II

2010. Expo 2010, Shanghai. Sheet 114×95 mm
MS2937 **1180** €1 multicoloured　5·25　5·25

1181 Player and Ball

2010. World Cup Football Championships, South Africa. Multicoloured.
2938　89c. Type **1181**　3·75　3·00
2939　89c. Player wearing red　3·75　3·00
　Nos. 2938/9 were printed, *se-tenant*, each pair forming a composite design of the South African flag, stadium, two players and ball.

1182 Prince Albert I

2010. Centenary of Oceanographic Museum. Multicoloured.
MS2940 51c. Type **1182**; 56c. *Ursus maritimus* (polar bear); 73c. *Pterapogon kauderni* (Banggai cardinalfish) (horiz); 90c. Hands and starfish (horiz)　12·00　12·00

1183 Comte de Thann

2010. Former Grimaldi Family Fiefdoms. Multicoloured.
MS2941 €1×4, Type **1183**; Barony of Altkirch; Comte de Rosemont; Comte de Ferrette　21·00　21·00

1184 *Pinna nobilis*

2010. Larvotto Submarine Reserve
2942　**1184**　2c. multicoloured　1·00　60

1185 Mother Teresa carrying Child

2010. Birth Centenary of Mother Teresa (founder of Missionaries of Charity)
2943　**1185**　multicoloured　3·75　3·00

1186 Lilium martagon (inscr 'Lis martagon')

2010. Mercantour National Park
2944　**1186**　€2 multicoloured　12·00　12·00

1187 Children and Books

2010. Europa. Multicoloured.
2945　56c. Type **1187**　2·00　1·50
2946　70c. Boy reading, open book and pages　3·00　2·40

1188 Anniversary Emblem

2010. 15th Anniv of United Nations AIDS Programme
2947　**1188**　89c. multicoloured　3·75　3·00

1189 Tower Bridge

2010. London 2010 Festival of Stamps. London 2010 International Stamp Exhibition
2948　**1189**　€1.30 scarlet vermilion and indigo　5·25　2·75

1190 Emblem

2010. 50th International Television Festival
2949　**1190**　€2.80 multicoloured　11·00　6·50

1191 Abbe Breuil, Prince Albert I, Institute Building and Grimaldi Caves

2010. Centenary of Institute of Human Paleontology, Paris
2950　56c. multcoloured　2·25　1·40

1192 Forum Building Façade

2010. Tenth Anniv of Grimaldi Forum
2951　**1192**　75c. multicoloured　3·25　2·00

1193 Singapore Skyline and Athletes

2010. Youth Olympic Games, Singapore
2952　**1193**　87c. multicoloured　3·75　2·25

1194 *Vigilante* (police launch)

2010. 50th Anniv of Maritime and Airport Police Division
2953　**1194**　53c. multicoloured　2·25　1·40

1195 Nicolas Appert

2010. Bicentenary of Canning. Nicolas Appert (French chef and discoverer of method of conserving food by enclosing in hermetically sealed containers) Commemoration
2954　**1195**　95c. brownish maroon and scarlet-vermilion　3·50　2·10

1196 Jean-Joseph Etienne Lenoir

2010. 150th Anniv of First Gas Engine. Jean-Joseph Etienne Lenoir (first to successfully develop an engine functioning in accordance with principle of internal combustion) Commemoration
2955　**1196**　€1.75 brown-olive, brownish black and scarlet-vermilion　7·00　4·25

1198 MC30E LSA

2010. First International Electrically Propelled Mail Flight
2957　**1198**　95c. multicoloured　4·00　2·40

1199 *Stylophora pistillata*

2010. 50th Anniv of Monaco Scientific Centre
2958　**1199**　58c. multicoloured　2·50　1·50

1200 Train in Station

2010. TER Monaco
2959　**1200**　€1.35 black, scarlet-vermilion and ochre　5·75　3·50

1201 Anniversary Poster

2010. 25th Anniv of 'Magic Stars' Magic Festival
2960　**1201**　€1.40 multicoloured　6·00　3·50

1202 Santa riding Reindeer

2010. Christmas
2961　**1202**　58c. multicoloured　2·75　1·70

1203 Building Façade

2010. Centenary of Albert I Lycee
2962　**1203**　75c. multicoloured　3·25　2·00

1204 2011 Poster

2010. 35th International Circus Festival
2963　**1204**　75c. multicoloured　3·35　2·00

1205 Monaco Castle and Constitution

2011. Centenary of Constitution
2964　**1205**　53c. multicoloured　2·40　1·50

2010. 'Little Africa' Garden
2956　**1197**　€2.30 multicoloured　9·75　5·75

1206 Egyptian Mau

2011. International Cat Show

2965	**1206**	87c. multicoloured	3·75	2·25

No. 2966 and Type **1207** are left for Birth Centenary of Fangio, issued on 12 January 2011, not yet received

No. 2967 and Type **1208** are left for Indianapolis, issued on 12 January 2011, not yet received

No. 2968 and Type **1209** are left for Centenary of Monte Carlo Rally, issued on 12 January 2011, not yet received.

1210 Sea Floor

2011. 50th Anniv of Monaco in International Atomic Energy Agency (IAEA). 50th Anniv of AIEA's Marine Environment Laboratory

2969	**1210**	87c. multicoloured	3·75	2·25

1211 Symbols of Solar, Wind, Geothermal, Hydro and Biomass Power

2011. Renewable Energy

2970	**1211**	€1.80 multicoloured	7·50	4·50

1212 Children and 'MISSION enfance 20 ans!'

2011. 20th Anniv of Mission Enfance Association (educational aid and assistance to children in need)

2971	**1212**	53c. multicoloured	2·25	1·40

1213 Labrador Retriever

2011. International Dog Show, Monte Carlo

2972	**1213**	53c. multicoloured	2·75	1·70

1214 Émile Antoine Bourdelle

2011. 150th Birth Anniversaries. Sculptors

2973	75c. black and scarlet-vermilion	3·25	2·00
2974	75c. chocolate and scarlet-vermilion	3·25	3·00
2975	95c. indigo and scarlet-vermilion	4·00	2·40
2976	95c. deep lilac and scarlet-vermilion	4·00	2·40

Designs: 75c. Type **1214**; 75c. Horse for 'Alvear' Monument (detail); 95c. Aristide Maillol; 95c. *La Nuit*

1215 Irish Coast and Arms of Monaco and Ireland

2011. Visit of Prince Albert II to Ireland

2977	**1215**	€1.40 multicoloured	6·00	3·50

1216 Match on Court

2011. Monte-Carlo Rolex Masters Tennis Tournament

2978	**1216**	75c. multicoloured	3·25	2·00

1217 Napoleon II as Child and as Young Man

2011. Birth Bicentenary of Napoléon François Joseph Charles Bonaparte (Napoléon II)

2979	**1217**	€1 deep blue and brown	4·50	2·75

1218 Ocean Currents Class Bouquet

2011. 44th International Flower Exhibition

2980	**1218**	95c. multicoloured	4·25	2·50

1219 Big Ben, Houses of Parliament and GB Flag

2011. Royal Horticultural Society Chelsea Flower Show, London

2981	**1219**	€1.75 multicoloured	7·50	4·50

1220 Japanese Garden

2011. Japanese Garden of Monaco (designed by Yasuo Beppu, based on the principals of Zen)

2982	**1220**	€2.35 multicoloured	10·00	7·50

1221 Cathedral Façade

2011. Centenary of Consecration of Cathedral of Our Lady of the Immaculate Conception (Saint Nicholas Cathedral) (Monaco Cathedral)

2983	**1221**	58c. black and scarlet-vermilion	2·75	2·10

1222 Lions International Emblem

2011. 50th Anniv of Lions Club de Monaco

2984	**1222**	75c. multicoloured	3·50	2·75

1223 Saint-Rémy-de-Provence

2011. Former Grimaldi Family Fiefdoms. Multicoloured.

MS2985	€1.75 Type **1223**; €1.80 Les Baux-de-Provence	15·00	15·00

1224 *Aqulegia bertolonii*

2011. Mercantour National Park. Columbine

2986	**1224**	3c. multicoloured	1·00	75

1225 *Tarentola mauritanica*

2011. Wall Gecko (*Tarentola mauritanica*)

2987	**1225**	€2.30 multicoloured	10·00	7·50

1226 Alpine Forest

2011. Europa. Forests. Multicoloured.

2988	58c. Type **1226**	2·00	1·40
2989	75c. Mediterranean forest	3·75	2·75

1227 Stop Pollution (Anaïs Aziadjonou)

2011. Children's Drawing Competition. Environment and Ecology in Monaco

2990	**1227**	53c. multicoloured	1·00	75

1228 Prince Albert II and Miss Charlene Wittstock

2011. Royal Wedding of Prince Albert II to Miss Charlene Wittstock

2991	**1228**	55c. black and light green	2·00	1·40
2992	**1228**	60c. black, vermilion and carmine-red	2·20	1·70
2993	**1228**	77c. black, reddish violet and bright violet	3·25	2·50
2994	**1228**	89c. black, new blue and bright ultramarine	3·75	2·75
2995	**1228**	€4.10 agate, carmine-red and gold	10·00	7·50

1229 Prince Albert II and Miss Charlene Wittstock

2011. Royal Wedding of Prince Albert II to Miss Charlene Wittstock. Sheet 110×120 mm

MS2996	**1229**	€5 multicoloured	21·00	21·00

POSTAGE DUE STAMPS

D3

1906

D29a	**D3**	1c. green	45	55
D30	**D3**	5c. green	65	90
D31	**D3**	10c. red	65	90
D32	**D3**	10c. brown	£475	£150
D33	**D3**	15c. purple on cream	3·25	1·80
D113	**D3**	20c. bistre on buff	50	40
D34	**D3**	30c. blue	65	90
D114	**D3**	40c. mauve	50	40
D35	**D3**	50c. brown on buff	6·00	5·25
D115	**D3**	50c. green	50	40
D116	**D3**	60c. black	50	70
D117	**D3**	60c. mauve	26·00	35·00
D118	**D3**	1f. purple on cream	70	50
D119	**D3**	2f. red	1·50	1·80
D120	**D3**	3f. red	1·50	1·80
D121	**D3**	5f. blue	1·80	2·00

D4

1910

D36	**D4**	1c. olive	30	45
D37	**D4**	10c. lilac	65	90
D38	**D4**	30c. bistre	£225	£225

1919. Surch.

D39	20c. on 10c. lilac	4·50	9·25
D40	40c. on 30c. bistre	5·50	11·00

D18

1925

D106	**D18**	1c. olive	40	60
D107	**D18**	10c. violet	40	60
D108	**D18**	30c. bistre	60	1·00
D109	**D18**	60c. red	60	1·30
D110	**D18**	1f. blue	£110	£120
D111	**D18**	2f. red	£140	£150

1925. Surch 1 franc a percevoir.

D112	**D3**	1f. on 50c. brown on buff	1·00	1·20

D64

D65

1946

D327	**D64**	10c. black	10	20
D328	**D64**	30c. violet	10	20
D329	**D64**	50c. blue	10	20
D330	**D64**	1f. green	10	30
D331	**D64**	2f. brown	10	30
D332	**D64**	3f. mauve	10	30
D333	**D64**	4f. red	50	70
D334	**D65**	5f. brown	50	70
D335	**D65**	10f. blue	70	70
D336	**D65**	20f. turquoise	1·00	1·20
D337	**D65**	50f. red and mauve	60·00	65·00
D338	**D65**	100f. red and green	15·00	15·00

D99 Buddicom Locomotive, 1843

1953

D478	-	1f. red and green	10	20
D479	-	1f. green and red	10	20
D480	-	2f. turquoise and blue	10	20
D481	-	2f. blue and turquoise	10	20
D482	**D 99**	3f. lake and green	10	30
D483	-	3f. green and lake	10	30
D484	-	4f. slate and brown	10	30
D485	-	4f. brown and slate	10	30
D486	-	5f. violet and blue	60	70
D487	-	5f. blue and violet	60	70
D488	-	10f. indigo and blue	10·00	10·00
D489	-	10f. blue and indigo	10·00	10·00

Column 1

D490	-	20f. violet and blue	7·00	7·00
D491	-	20f. blue and violet	7·00	7·00
D492	-	50f. brown and red	15·00	15·00
D493	-	50f. red and brown	15·00	15·00
D494	-	100f. green and purple	24·00	24·00
D495	-	100f. purple and green	24·00	24·00

TRIANGULAR DESIGNS: Nos. D478, Pigeons released from mobile loft; D479, Sikorsky S-51 helicopter; D480, Brig; D481, "United States" (liner); D483, Streamlined steam locomotive; D484, Santos-Dumont's monoplane No. 20 "Demoiselle"; D485, De Havilland Comet 1 airliner; D486, Old motor car; D487, "Sabre" racing-car; D488, Leonardo da Vinci's drawing of "flying machine"; D489, Postal rocket; D490, Mail balloon, Paris, 1870; D491, Airship LZ-127 "Graf Zeppelin"; D492, Postilion; D493, Motor cycle messenger; D494, Mail coach; D495, Railway mail van.

D140 18th-century Felucca

1960

D698	D140	1c. brown, green & bl	10	20
D699	-	2c. sepia, blue & grn	10	20
D700	-	5c. purple, blk & turq	10	25
D701	-	10c. black, green & bl	20	40
D702	-	20c. purple, grn & bl	1·20	1·20
D703	-	30c. brown, bl & grn	2·00	2·00
D704	-	50c. blue, brn & myrtle	2·50	2·50
D705	-	1f. brown, myrtle & bl	3·00	3·00

DESIGNS: 2c. Paddle-steamer "La Palmaria"; 5c. Arrival of first railway train at Monaco; 10c. 15th–16th-century armed messenger; 20c. 18th-century postman; 30c. "Charles III" (paddle-steamer); 50c. 17th-century courier; 1f. Mail coach (19th-century).

D393 Prince's Seal

1980

D1426	D393	5c. red and brown	15	20
D1427	D393	10c. orange and red	15	20
D1428	D393	15c. violet and red	15	20
D1429	D393	20c. green and red	15	30
D1430	D393	30c. blue and red	15	35
D1431	D393	40c. bistre and red	30	35
D1432	D393	50c. violet and red	40	45
D1433	D393	1f. grey and blue	75	75
D1434	D393	2f. brown and black	1·00	1·20
D1435	D393	3f. red and green	2·30	2·30
D1436	D393	4f. green and red	3·25	3·00
D1437	D393	5f. brown and mauve	3·50	3·25

D492 Coat of Arms

1985

D1712	D492	5c. multicoloured	15	20
D1713	D492	10c. multicoloured	15	20
D1714	D492	15c. multicoloured	15	20
D1715	D492	20c. multicoloured	15	20
D1716	D492	30c. multicoloured	15	20
D1717	D492	40c. multicoloured	15	25
D1718	D492	50c. multicoloured	15	25
D1719	D492	1f. multicoloured	55	55
D1720	D492	2f. multicoloured	1·10	95
D1721	D492	3f. multicoloured	2·00	1·70
D1722	D492	4f. multicoloured	2·40	2·00
D1723	D492	5f. multicoloured	2·75	2·75

Pt. 10

MONGOLIA

A republic in Central Asia between China and Russia, independent since 1921.

1924. 100 cents = 1 dollar (Chinese).
1926. 100 mung = 1 tugrik.

1 Eldev-Otchir Symbol

Column 2

1924. Inscr in black.

1A	1	1c. brown, pink and grey on bistre	12·50	13·00
2B	1	2c. brown, blue and red on brown	10·50	6·00
3A	1	5c. grey, red and yellow	41·00	26·00
4A	1	10c. blue and brown on blue	21·00	17·00
5B	1	20c. grey, blue and white on blue	29·00	19·00
6A	1	50c. red and orange on pink	41·00	26·00
7A	1	$1 bistre, red and white on yellow	60·00	43·00

Stamps vary in size according to the face value.

2 Soyombo Symbol

1926. Fiscal stamps as T **2** optd POSTAGE in frame in English and Mongolian.

8A	2	1c. blue	12·50	13·00
9A	2	2c. buff	16·00	11·00
10A	2	5c. purple	16·00	10·50
11A	2	10c. green	16·00	17·00
12A	2	20c. brown	25·00	21·00
13A	2	50c. brown and yellow	£160	£150
14B	2	$1 brown and pink	£600	£350
15A	2	$5 red and olive	£600	

Stamps vary in size according to the face value.

4 State Emblem: Soyombo Symbol

1926. New Currency.

16	4	5m. black and lilac	12·50	13·00
17	4	20m. black and blue	21·00	26·00

5 State Emblem: Soyombo Symbol

1926

18	5	1m. black and yellow	3·25	3·50
19	5	2m. black and brown	4·00	3·50
20	5	5m. black and lilac (A)	5·00	4·25
28	5	5m. black and lilac (B)	18·00	13·50
21	5	10m. black and blue	4·00	2·10
30	5	20m. black and blue	29·00	30·00
22	5	25m. black and green	8·25	4·25
23	5	40m. black and yellow	11·50	5·25
24	5	50m. black and brown	16·00	6·75
25	5	1t. black, green and brown	33·00	13·00
26	5	3t. black, yellow and red	75·00	50·00
27	5	5t. black, red and purple	£100	65·00

In (A) the Mongolian numerals are in the upper and in (B) in the lower value tablets.
These stamps vary in size according to the face value.

(6)

1930. Surch as T **6.**

32		10m. on 1m. black & yellow	33·00	34·00
33		20m. on 2m. black & brown	45·00	43·00
34		25m. on 40m. black & yellow	55·00	50·00

Column 3

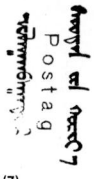

(7)

1931. Optd with T **7**

35A	2	1c. blue	25·00	13·00
36A	2	2c. buff	29·00	10·50
37A	2	5c. purple	37·00	10·50
38A	2	10c. green	33·00	10·50
39A	2	20c. brown	49·00	13·00
40A	2	50c. brown and yellow	£130	
41A	2	$1 brown and pink	£200	

1931. Surch Postage and value in menge.

43	5m. on 5c. purple	41·00	17·00
44	10m. on 10c. green	60·00	30·00
45	20m. on 20c. brown	65·00	39·00

9 Govt Building, Ulan Bator    **11** Sukhe Bator

12 Lake and Mountain Scenery

1932

46	-	1m. brown	3·25	1·70
47	-	2m. red	3·25	1·70
48	-	5m. blue	2·10	85
49	9	10m. green	2·10	85
50	-	15m. brown	2·10	85
51	-	20m. red	2·10	85
52	-	25m. violet	2·50	85
53	11	40m. black	2·50	1·30
54	-	50m. blue	2·10	85
55	12	1t. green	3·00	1·30
56	-	3t. violet	5·75	2·10
57	-	5t. brown	20·00	13·00
58	-	10t. blue	41·00	21·00

DESIGNS.—Type **9**: 1m. Weavers; 5m. Machinist. As Type **11**: 2m. Telegraphist; 15m. Revolutionary soldier carrying flag; 20m. Mongols learning Latin alphabet; 25m. Soldier; 50m. Sukhe Bator's monument. As Type **12**: 3t. Sheep-shearing; 5t. Camel caravan; 10t. Lassoing wild horses (after painting by Sampilon).

13 Mongol Man   **14** Camel Caravan

1943. Network background in similar colour to stamps.

59	13	5m. green	8·25	6·00
60	-	10m. blue	12·50	6·50
61	-	15m. red	14·00	8·50
62	14	20m. brown	21·00	15·00
63	-	25m. brown	21·00	19·00
64	-	30m. red	25·00	21·00
65	-	45m. purple	33·00	30·00
66	-	60m. green	60·00	50·00

DESIGNS—VERT: 10m. Mongol woman; 15m. Soldier; 30m. Arms of the Republic; 45m. Portrait of Sukhe Bator, dated 1894–1923. HORIZ: 25m. Secondary school; 60m. Pastoral scene.

15 Marshal Kharloin Choibalsan

1945. 50th Birthday of Choibalsan.

67	15	1t. black	65·00	75·00

Column 4

16 Choibalsan and Sukhe Bator   **17** Victory Medal

1946. 25th Anniv of Independence. Surch as T **16/17**

68	-	30m. bistre	6·25	6·50
69	16	50m. purple	7·50	7·75
70	-	60m. brown	8·25	8·50
71	-	60m. black	15·00	15·00
72	17	80m. brown	14·00	14·50
73	-	1t. blue	16·00	17·00
74	-	2t. brown	25·00	26·00

DESIGNS—VERT: (21½×32 mm): 30m. Choibalsan, aged four. As Type **17**: 60m. (No. 71), Choibalsan when young man; 1t. 25th Anniversary Medal; 2t. Sukhe Bator. HORIZ: As Type **16**: 60m. (No. 70), Choibalsan University.

17a Flags of Communist Bloc

1951. Struggle for Peace.

75	17a	1t. multicoloured	12·50	13·00

17b Lenin (after P. Vasilev)

1951. Honouring Lenin.

76	17b	3t. multicoloured	25·00	26·00

18 State Shop   **19** Sukhe Bator

1951. 30th Anniv of Independence.

77	-	15m. green on azure	5·00	5·25
78	18	20m. orange	5·00	5·25
79	-	20m. multicoloured	5·75	6·00
80	-	25m. blue on azure	5·75	6·00
81	-	30m. multicoloured	6·50	6·75
82	-	40m. violet on pink	7·50	7·75
83	-	50m. brown on azure	14·00	14·50
84	-	60m. black on pink	13·00	13·50
85	19	1t. brown	25·00	26·00

DESIGNS—HORIZ: (As Type **18**): 15m. Alti Hotel; 40m. State Theatre, Ulan Bator; 50m. Pedagogical Institute. 55½×26 mm: 25m. Choibalsan University. VERT: (As Type **19**): 20m. (No. 79); 30m. Arms and flag; 60m. Sukhe Bator Monument.

20 Schoolchildren

1952. Culture.

86	-	5m. brown on pink	5·00	5·25
87	20	10m. blue on pink	5·25	5·50

DESIGN: 5m. New houses.

21 Choibalsan in National Costume   **22** Choibalsan and Farm Worker

1953. First Death Anniv of Marshal Choibalsan. As T **21/22**.

88	**21**	15m. blue	4·00	3·50
89	**22**	15m. green	4·00	3·50
90	**21**	20m. green	8·25	7·75
91	**22**	20m. sepia	4·00	3·50
92	-	20m. blue	4·00	3·50
93	-	30m. sepia	6·25	5·25
94	-	50m. brown	6·25	5·25
95	-	1t. red	6·50	6·00
96	-	1t. purple	6·50	6·00
97	-	2t. red	9·75	8·50
98	-	3t. purple	15·00	13·00
99	-	5t. red	29·00	26·00

DESIGNS: As Type **21**: 1t. (96); 2t. Choibalsan in uniform. 33×48 mm: 3, 5t. Busts of Choibalsan and Sukhe Bator. 33×46 mm: 50m., 1t. (95), Choibalsan and young pioneer. 48×33 mm: 20m. (92); 30m. Choibalsan and factory hand.

23 Arms of the Republic

1954

100	**23**	10m. red	8·25	5·25
101	**23**	20m. red	16·00	6·75
102	**23**	30m. red	8·25	6·00
103	**23**	40m. red	9·75	10·50
104	**23**	60m. red	8·25	8·50

23a Lenin

1955. 85th Birth Anniv of Lenin.

105	**23a**	2t. blue	6·50	3·00

23b Flags of the Communist Bloc

1955. Struggle for Peace.

106	**23b**	60m. multicoloured	2·10	1·30

24 Sukhe Bator and Choibalsan

1955

107	**24**	30m. green	80	85
108	-	30m. blue	1·20	1·30
109	-	30m. red	80	85
110	-	40m. purple	2·50	3·50
111	-	50m. brown	2·50	3·50
112	-	1t. multicoloured	5·00	5·25

DESIGNS—HORIZ: 30m. blue, Lake Khobsogol; 50m. Choibalsan University. VERT: 30m. red, Lenin Statue, Ulan Bator; 40m. Sukhe Bator and dog; 1t. Arms and flag of the Republic.

24a Steam Train linking Ulan Bator and Moscow

1956. Mongol–Soviet Friendship. Multicoloured.

113		1t. Type **24a**	29·00	17·00
114		2t. Flags of Mongolia and Russia	6·25	4·25

25 Arms of the Republic

1956

115	**25**	20m. brown	80	85
116	**25**	30m. brown	1·00	1·00
117	**25**	40m. blue	1·30	1·40
118	**25**	60m. green	1·60	1·70
119	**25**	1t. red	2·75	2·75

26 Hunter and Golden Eagle

27 Arms

27a Wrestlers

1956. 35th Anniv of Independence.

120	**26**	30m. brown	41·00	21·00
121	**27**	30m. blue	6·25	5·25
122	**27a**	60m. green	21·00	21·00
123	-	60m. orange	21·00	21·00

DESIGN: As Type **26**: 60m. (No. 123), Children. Also inscr "xxxv".

28

1958. With or without gum.

124	**28**	20m. red	2·50	1·70

29

1958. 13th Mongol People's Revolutionary Party Congress. With or without gum.

125	**29**	30m. red and salmon	4·00	3·50

1958. As T **27a** but without "xxxv". With or without gum.

126		50m. brown on pink	7·50	6·75

30 Dove and Globe

1958. Fourth Congress of International Women's Federation, Vienna. With or without gum.

127	**30**	60m. blue	5·00	3·75

31 Ibex

32 Yak

1958. Mongolian Animals. As T **31/2**.

128	-	30m. pale blue	16·00	3·50
129	-	30m. turquoise	16·00	3·50
130	**31**	30m. green	4·00	2·50
131	**31**	30m. turquoise	4·00	2·50
132	**32**	60m. bistre	4·00	2·50
133	**32**	60m. orange	4·00	1·70
134	-	1t. blue	6·25	3·75
135	-	1t. light blue	5·00	2·50
136	-	1t. red	6·25	4·25
137	-	1t. red	5·00	2·50

DESIGNS—VERT: 30m. (Nos. 128/9), Dalmatian pelicans. HORIZ: 1t. (Nos. 134/5), Yak, facing right; 1t. (Nos. 136/7), Bactrian camels.

33 Goat

1958. Mongolian Animals.

138	**33**	5m. sepia and yellow	15	10
139	-	10m. sepia and green	15	10
140	-	15m. sepia and lilac	35	10
141	-	20m. sepia and blue	35	10
142	-	25m. sepia and red	40	10
143	-	30m. purple and mauve	50	10
144	**33**	40m. green	50	15
145	-	50m. brown and salmon	60	25
146	-	60m. blue	1·00	25
147	-	1t. bistre and yellow	1·80	50

ANIMALS: 10, 30m. Ram; 15, 60m. Stallion; 20, 50m. Bull; 25m., 1t. Bactrian camel.

34 "Tulaga"

1959

148	**34**	1t. multicoloured	5·00	3·75

35 Taming a Wild Horse

1959. Mongolian Sports. Centres and inscriptions multicoloured: frame colours given below.

149	**35**	5m. yellow and orange	15	10
150	-	10m. purple	15	10
151	-	15m. yellow and green	15	10
152	-	20m. lake and red	25	10
153	-	25m. blue	40	15
154	-	30m. yellow, green & turq	60	15
155	-	70m. red and yellow	75	25
156	-	80m. purple	1·20	60

DESIGNS: 10m. Wrestlers; 15m. Introducing young rider; 20m. Archer; 25m. Galloping horseman; 30m. Archery contest; 70m. Hunting a wild horse; 80m. Proclaiming a champion.

36 Child Musician

1959. Mongolian Youth Festival (1st issue).

157	**36**	5m. purple and blue	20	10
158	-	10m. brown and green	25	10
159	-	20m. green and purple	25	10
160	-	25m. blue and green	45	15
161	-	40m. violet and myrtle	1·30	60

DESIGNS—VERT: 10m. Young wrestlers; 20m. Youth on horse; 25m. Artists in national costume. HORIZ: 40m. Festival parade.

37 Festival Badge

1959. Mongolian Youth Festival (2nd issue).

162	**37**	30m. purple and blue	45	25

38 Kalmuck Script

1959. Mongolists' Congress. Designs as T **38** incorporating "MONGOL" in various scripts.

163	-	30m. multicoloured	6·75	6·50
164	-	40m. red, blue and yellow	6·75	6·50
165	**38**	50m. multicoloured	9·00	8·50
166	-	60m. red, blue and yellow	14·00	13·50
167	-	1t. yellow, turquoise & orge	18·00	17·00

SCRIPTS (29½×42½ mm): 30m. Stylized Ulghur; 40m. Soyombo; 60m. Square (Pagspa). (21½×31 mm): 1t. Cyrillic.

39 Military Monument

1959. 20th Anniv of Battle of Khalka River.

168		40m. red, brown and yellow	60	15
169	**39**	50m. multicoloured	60	15

DESIGN: 40m. Mounted horseman with flag (emblem), inscr "AUGUST 1959 HALHIN GOL".

40 Herdswoman and Lamb

1959. Second Meeting of Rural Economy Co-operatives.

170	**40**	30m. green	4·50	4·25

41 Sable

1959. Mongolian Fauna.

171	**41**	5m. purple, yellow and blue	20	10
172	-	10m. multicoloured	90	10
173	-	15m. black, green and red	45	10
174	-	20m. purple, blue and red	45	10
175	-	30m. myrtle, purple & grn	55	15
176	-	50m. black, blue and green	1·20	35
177	-	1t. black, green and red	1·80	45

ANIMALS—HORIZ: (58×21 mm): 10m. Common pheasants; 20m. European otter; 50m. Saiga; 1t. Siberian musk deer. As Type **41**: 15m. Muskrat; 30m. Argali.

42 "Lunik 3" in Flight

1959. Launching of "Lunik 3" Rocket.

178	**42**	30m. yellow and violet	90	85
179	-	50m. red, green and blue	1·40	1·40

DESIGN—HORIZ: 50m. Trajectory of "Lunik 3" around the Moon.

43 Motherhood Badge

44 "Flower" Emblem

1960. International Women's Day.

180	**43**	40m. bistre and blue	80	15
181	**44**	50m. yellow, green and blue	1·20	45

45 Lenin

1960. 90th Birth Anniv of Lenin.

182	45	40m. red	60	15
183	45	50m. violet	90	35

46 Larkspur

1960. Flowers.

184	46	5m. blue, green and bistre	10	10
185	-	10m. red, green and orange	10	10
186	-	15m. violet, green and bistre	10	10
187	-	20m. yellow, green and olive	20	10
188	-	30m. violet, green & emer	35	15
189	-	40m. orange, green & violet	60	15
190	-	50m. violet, green and blue	90	35
191	-	1t. mauve, green & lt green	1·20	85

FLOWERS: 10m. Tulip; 15m. Jacob's ladder; 20m. Asiatic globe flower; 30m. Clustered bellflower; 40m. Grass of Parnassus; 50m. Meadow cranesbill; 1t. "Begonia vansiana".

47 Horse-jumping

1960. Olympic Games. Inscr "ROMA 1960" or "ROMA MCMLX". Centres in greenish grey.

192	47	5m. red, black & turquoise	10	10
193	-	10m. violet and yellow	10	10
194	-	15m. turquoise, black & red	20	10
195	-	20m. red and blue	25	10
196	-	30m. ochre, black and green	45	15
197	-	50m. blue and turquoise	55	25
198	-	70m. green, black and violet	70	35
199	-	1t. mauve and green	1·10	45

DESIGNS—DIAMOND SHAPED: 10m. Running; 20m. Wrestling; 50m. Gymnastics; 1t. Throwing the discus. As Type 47: 15m. Diving; 30m. Hurdling; 70m. High-jumping.

48

1960. Red Cross.

200	48	20m. red, yellow and blue	90	45

49 Newspapers

1960. 40th Anniv of Mongolian Newspaper "Unen" ("Truth").

201	49	20m. buff, green and red	25	15
202	49	30m. red, yellow and green	35	10

50 Hoopoe

1961. Mongolian Songbirds.

203	-	5m. mauve, black and green	70	15
204	50	10m. red, black and green	80	15
205	-	15m. yellow, black & green	1·00	25
206	-	20m. green, black and bistre	1·20	25
207	-	50m. blue, black and red	1·80	50
208	-	70m. yellow, black & mauve	2·20	70
209	-	1t. mauve, orange and black	2·75	95

BIRDS: As Type 50: 15m. Golden oriole; 20m. Black-billed capercaillie. Inverted triangulars: 5m. Rose-coloured starling; 50m. Eastern broad-billed roller; 70m. Tibetan sandgrouse; 1t. Mandarin.

51 Foundry Worker

1961. 15th Anniv of World Federation of Trade Unions.

210	51	30m. red and black	25	15
211	-	50m. red and violet	35	25

DESIGN—HORIZ: 50m. Hemispheres.

52 Patrice Lumumba

1961. Patrice Lumumba (Congolese politician) Commemoration.

212	52	30m. brown	2·20	1·30
213	52	50m. purple	2·75	1·70

53 Bridge

1961. 40th Anniv of Independence (1st issue). Mongolian Modernization.

214	53	5m. green	10	10
215	-	10m. blue	10	10
216	-	15m. red	20	10
217	-	20m. brown	20	10
218	-	30m. blue	25	15
219	-	50m. green	35	25
220	-	1t. violet	60	35

DESIGNS: 10m. Shoe-maker; 15m. Store at Ulan Bator; 30m. Government Building, Ulan Bator; 50m. Machinist; 1t. Ancient and modern houses. (59×20½ mm): 20m. Choibalsan University.

See also Nos. 225/MS32a, 233/MS241c, MS241d, 242/8 and 249/56.

54 Yuri Gagarin with Capsule

1961. World's First Manned Space Flight. Multicoloured

221	54	20m. Type 54	45	15
222	-	30m. Gagarin and globe (horiz)	70	35
223	-	50m. Gagarin in capsule making parachute descent	90	50
224	-	1t. Globe and Gagarin (horiz)	1·30	70

55 Postman with Reindeer

1961. 40th Anniv of Independence (2nd issue). Mongolian Postal Service.

225	55	5m. red, brown and blue (postage)	20	10
226	-	15m. violet, brown & bistre	30	10
227	-	20m. blue, black and green	30	10
228	-	25m. violet, bistre and green	30	20
229	-	30m. green, black & lav	4·75	90

MS229a 115×90 mm. 5, 10, 15 and 50m. in designs of Nos. 226/9 but new colours — 6·75 5·00

230	-	10m. orange, black and green (air)	40	10
231	-	50m. black, pink and green	75	20
232	-	1t. multicoloured	1·40	35

MS232a 115×90 mm. 20, 25, 30m., 1t. in designs of Nos. 225, 230/2 but new colours — 3·75 3·75

DESIGNS: Postman with—10m. Horses; 15m. Camels; 20m. Yaks; 25m. "Sukhe Bator" (lake steamer); 30m. Diesel mail train; 50m. Ilyushin Il-14M mail plane over map; 1t. Postal emblem.

56 Rams

1961. 40th Anniv of Independence (3rd issue). Animal Husbandry.

233	56	5m. black, red and blue	10	10
234	-	10m. black, green & purple	20	10
235	-	15m. black, red and green	20	10
236	-	20m. sepia, blue and brown	30	10
237	-	25m. black, yellow & green	30	20
238	-	30m. black, red and violet	30	20
239	-	40m. black, green and red	40	20
240	-	50m. black, brown and blue	50	30
241	-	1t. black, violet and olive	65	65

MS241a 105×150 mm. 5, 15 and 40m. in designs of Nos. 241, 237 and 234 but new colours — 1·40 1·40

MS241b 105×150 mm. 25, 50m. and 1t. in designs of Nos. 236, 239 and 240, but new colours — 1·90 1·90

MS241c 105×150 mm. 25, 50m. and 1t. in designs of Nos. 235, 239 and 233 but new colours — 2·40 2·30

DESIGNS: 10m. Oxen; 15m. Camels; 20m. Pigs and poultry; 25m. Angora goats; 30m. Mongolian horses; 40m. Ewes; 50m. Cows; 1t. Combine-harvester.

56a

1961. 40th Anniv of Independence (4th issue). Sheet 118×128 mm. Imperf.

MS241d 2t. gold, red and blue (pair separated by label) — 7·75 7·50

57 Children Wrestling

1961. 40th Anniv of Independence (5th issue). Mongolian Sports.

242	57	5m. multicoloured	20	10

243	-	10m. sepia, red and green	20	10
244	-	15m. purple blue and yellow	20	10
245	-	20m. red, black and green	95	30
246	-	30m. purple, green & lav	40	35
247	-	50m. indigo, orange & blue	50	35
248	-	1t. purple, blue and grey	75	75

DESIGNS: 10m. Horse-riding; 15m. Children on camel and pony; 20m. Falconry; 30m. Skiing; 50m. Archery; 1t. Dancing.

58 Young Mongol

1961. 40th Anniv of Independence (6th issue). Mongolian Culture.

249	58	5m. purple and green	10	10
250	-	10m. blue and red	10	10
251	-	15m. brown and blue	20	10
252	-	20m. green and violet	20	10
253	-	30m. red and blue	30	20
254	-	50m. violet and bistre	60	20
255	-	70m. green and mauve	65	35
256	-	1t. red and blue	1·20	90

DESIGNS—HORIZ: 10m. Mongol chief; 70m. Orchestra; 1t. Gymnast. VERT: 15m. Sukhe Bator Monument; 20m. Young singer; 30m. Young dancer; 50m. Dombra-player.

59 Mongol Arms

1961. Arms multicoloured; inscr in blue; background colours given.

257	59	5m. salmon	20	10
258	59	10m. lilac	20	10
259	59	15m. brown	20	10
260	59	20m. turquoise	20	10
261	59	30m. ochre	30	20
262	59	50m. mauve	40	30
263	59	70m. olive	50	35
264	59	1t. orange	60	45

60 Congress Emblem

1961. Fifth World Federation of Trade Unions Congress, Moscow.

265	60	30m. red, yellow and blue	30	20
266	60	50m. red, yellow and sepia	40	30

61 Dove, Map and Globe

1962. Admission of Mongolia to U.N.O.

267	61	10m. multicoloured	10	10
268	-	30m. multicoloured	30	20
269	-	50m. multicoloured	60	35
270	-	60m. multicoloured	65	35
271	-	70m. multicoloured	75	45

DESIGNS: 30m. U.N. Emblem and Mongol Arms; 50m. U.N. and Mongol flags; 60m. U.N. Headquarters and Mongolian Parliament building; 70m. U.N. and Mongol flags, and Assembly.

62 Football, Globe and Flags

1962. World Cup Football Championship, Chile. Multicoloured.

272	10m. Type **62**		10	10
273	30m. Footballers, globe and ball		30	20
274	50m. Footballers playing in stadium		40	30
275	60m. Goalkeeper saving goal		50	35
276	70m. Stadium		65	35

63 D. Natsagdorj

1962. Third Congress of Mongolian Writers.

277	**63**	30m. brown	30	20
278	**63**	50m. green	40	20

64 Torch and Handclasp

1962. Afro-Asian People's Solidarity.

279	**64**	20m. multicoloured	20	20
280	**64**	30m. multicoloured	30	20

65 Flags of Mongolia and U.S.S.R.

1962. Mongol–Soviet Friendship.

281	**65**	30m. multicoloured	30	20
282	**65**	50m. multicoloured	50	30

1962. Malaria Eradication. Nos. 184/91 optd with Campaign emblem and LUTTE CONTRE LE PALUDISME.

283	**46**	5m.	30	20
284	-	10m.	30	20
285	-	15m.	30	20
286	-	20m.	30	20
287	-	30m.	40	30
288	-	40m.	50	35
289	-	50m.	60	45
290	-	1t.	95	75

67 Victory Banner

1962. 800th Birth Anniv of Genghis Khan.

291	**67**	20m. multicoloured	7·75	7·50
292	-	30m. multicoloured	14·50	14·00
293	-	50m. black, brown and red	9·50	9·25
294	-	60m. buff, blue and brown	19·00	19·00

DESIGNS: 30m. Engraved lacquer tablets; 50m. Obelisk; 60m. Genghis Khan.

68 Eurasian Perch

1962. Fish. Multicoloured.

295	5m. Type **68**		20	10
296	10m. Burbot		20	10
297	15m. Arctic grayling		30	10
298	20m. Short-spined seascorpion		50	20
299	30m. Estuarine zander		65	30
300	50m. Siberian sturgeon		95	35
301	70m. Waleck's dace		1·40	65
302	1t.50 Yellow-winged bullhead		2·50	1·00

69 Sukhe Bator

1963. 70th Birth Anniv of Sukhe Bator.

303	**69**	30m. blue	20	10
304	**69**	60m. lake	50	30

70 Dog "Laika" and "Sputnik 2"

1963. Space Flights. Multicoloured.

305	5m. Type **70**		10	10
306	15m. Rocket blasting off		20	10
307	25m. "Lunik 2" (1959)		40	20
308	70m. Nikolaev and Popovich		75	35
309	1t. Rocket "Mars" (1962)		95	55

SIZES: As Type **70**: 70m., 1t. VERT: (21×70 mm): 15m., 25m.

71 Children packing Red Cross Parcels

1963. Red Cross Centenary Multicoloured.

310	20m. Type **71**		20	10
311	30m. Blood transfusion		30	20
312	50m. Doctor treating child		50	30
313	60m. Ambulance at street accident		60	35
314	1t.30 Centenary emblem		85	45

72 Karl Marx

1963. 145th Birth Anniv of Karl Marx.

315	**72**	30m. blue	30	20
316	**72**	60m. lake	40	30

73 Woman

1963. Fifth World Congress of Democratic Women, Moscow.

317	**73**	30m. multicoloured	30	20

74 Peacock

1963. Mongolian Butterflies. Multicoloured.

318	5m. Type **74**		40	10
319	10m. Brimstone		50	10
320	15m. Small tortoiseshell		65	20
321	20m. Apollo		75	30
322	30m. Swallowtail		1·20	30
323	60m. Damon blue		1·80	65
324	1t. Poplar admiral		2·50	85

75 Globe and Scales of Justice

1963. 15th Anniv of Declaration of Human Rights.

325	**75**	30m. red, blue and brown	30	20
326	**75**	60m. black, blue and yellow	40	30

76 Shaggy Ink Cap

1964. Fungi. Multicoloured.

327	5m. Type **76**		40	20
328	10m. Woolly milk cap		60	30
329	15m. Field mushroom		65	35
330	20m. Milk-white russula		75	35
331	30m. Granulated boletus		1·20	55
332	50m. "Lactarius scrobiculatus"		1·40	75
333	70m. Saffron milk cap		2·10	90
334	1t. Variegated boletus		3·25	1·40

77 Lenin when a Young Man

1964. 60th Anniv of London Bolshevik (Communist) Party.

335	**77**	30m. red and brown	60	30
336	**77**	50m. ultramarine and blue	75	45

77a Cross-country Skier

1964. Ninth Winter Olympic Games, Innsbruck. Sheet 86×72 mm.

MS336a	**77a**	4t. black	3·00	2·75

78 Gymnastics

1964. Olympic Games, Tokyo. Multicoloured.

337	5m. Type **78**		10	10
338	10m. Throwing the javelin		20	10
339	15m. Wrestling		30	10
340	20m. Running		30	10
341	30m. Horse-jumping		40	20
342	50m. High-diving		60	30
343	60m. Cycling		75	35
344	1t. Emblem of Tokyo Games		95	65

MS344a 87×77 mm. 4t. black, green and red (Wrestlers–Horiz 38×28 mm) 3·25 3·25

79 Congress Emblem

1964. Fourth Mongolian Women's Congress.

345	**79**	30m. multicoloured	30	20

80 "Lunik 1"

1964. Space Research. Multicoloured.

346	5m. Type **80**		10	10
347	10m. "Vostoks 1 and 2"		20	10
348	15m. "Tiros" (vert)		20	10
349	20m. "Cosmos" (vert)		20	10
350	30m. "Mars Probe" (vert)		30	10
351	60m. "Luna 4" (vert)		40	20
352	80m. "Echo 2"		50	40
353	1t. Radio telescope		60	60

81 Horseman and Flag

1964. 40th Anniv of Mongolian Constitution.

354	**81**	25m. multicoloured	30	20
355	**81**	50m. multicoloured	40	30

81a Austrian and Mongolian stamps encircling Globe

1965. "WPIA" Stamp Exhibition, Vienna. Sheet 90×130 mm.

MS355a	**81a**	4t. red	3·25	3·25

82 Marine Exploration

1965. International Quiet Sun Year. Multicoloured.

356	5m. Type **82** (postage)		20	10
357	10m. Weather balloon		20	10
358	60m. Northern Lights		85	30
359	80m. Geomagnetic emblems		1·10	35
360	1t. Globe and I.Q.S.Y. emblem		1·60	65
361	15m. Weather satellite (air)		60	10
362	20m. Antarctic exploration		3·25	65
363	30m. Space exploration		75	20

83 Horses Grazing

1965. Mongolian Horses. Multicoloured.

364	5m. Type **83**		20	10
365	10m. Hunting with golden eagles		1·40	20
366	15m. Breaking-in wild horse		30	20
367	20m. Horses racing		30	20
368	30m. Horses jumping		40	20

369		60m. Hunting wolves	50	30
370		80m. Milking a mare	60	35
371		1t. Mare and colt	1·30	45

84 Farm Girl with Lambs

1965. 40th Anniv of Mongolian Youth Movement.

372	84	5m. orange, bistre and green	10	10
373	-	10m. bistre, blue and red	20	10
374	-	20m. ochre, red and violet	30	20
375	-	30m. lilac, brown and green	40	30
376	-	50m. orange, buff and blue	65	45

DESIGNS: 10m. Young drummers; 20m. Children around campfire; 30m. Young wrestlers; 50m. Emblem.

85 Chinese Perch

1965. Mongolian Fish. Multicoloured.

377	5m. Type 85	30	10
378	10m. Lenok	30	10
379	15m. Siberian sturgeon	30	20
380	20m. Taimen	50	20
381	30m. Banded catfish	75	30
382	60m. Amur catfish	1·20	30
383	80m. Northern pike	1·70	55
384	1t. Eurasian perch	1·90	85

86 Marx and Lenin

1965. Organization of Socialist Countries' Postal Administrations Conference, Peking.

385	86	10m. black and red	20	10

87 I.T.U. Emblem and Symbols

1965. Air. I.T.U. Centenary.

386	87	30m. blue and bistre	30	20
387	87	50m. red, bistre and blue	50	30

MS387a 86×130 mm. 4t. blue, black and gold (Communications satellite, 38×51 mm) 4·75 4·50

88 Sable

1966. Mongolian Fur Industry.

388	88	5m. purple, black & yellow	20	10
389	-	10m. brown, black and grey	20	10
390	-	15m. brown, black and blue	30	10
391	-	20m. multicoloured	30	10
392	-	30m. brown, black & mauve	40	20
393	-	60m. brown, black & green	60	30
394	-	80m. multicoloured	75	35
395	-	1t. blue, black and olive	1·40	65

DESIGNS (Fur animals): HORIZ: 10m. Red fox; 30m. Pallas's cat; 60m. Beech marten. VERT: 15m. European otter; 20m. Cheetah; 80m. Stoat; 1t. Woman in fur coat.

89 W.H.O. Building

1966. Inauguration of W.H.O. Headquarters, Geneva.

396	89	30m. blue, gold and green	30	20
397	89	50m. blue, gold and red	50	30

90 Footballers

91

1966. World Cup Football Championship. Multicoloured.

398	10m. Type 90	10	10
399	30m. Footballers (different)	30	20
400	60m. Goalkeeper saving goal	65	30
401	80m. Footballers (different)	85	55
402	1t. World Cup flag	95	65
MS403	91 4t. brown and grey	4·75	4·50

92 Sukhe Bator and Parliament Buildings, Ulan Bator

1966. 15th Mongolian Communist Party Congress.

404	92	30m. multicoloured	30	10

93 Wrestling

1966. World Wrestling Championships, Toledo (Spain). Similar wrestling designs.

405	93	10m. black, mauve & purple	10	10
406		30m. black, mauve and grey	30	10
407		60m. black, mauve & brown	50	20
408		80m. black, mauve and lilac	60	30
409	-	1t. black, mauve & turq	75	35

94 "Luna 10", Globe and Moon

1966. Air. "Luna 10" Commemoration. Sheet 84×130 mm.

MS410 94 4t. multicoloured 3·25 3·25

95 State Emblem

1966. 45th Anniv of Independence. Multicoloured

411	30m. Type 95	1·40	75
412	50m. Sukhe Bator, emblems of agriculture and industry (horiz)	3·00	90

96 "Physochlaena physaloides"

1966. Flowers. Multicoloured.

413	5m. Type 96	10	10
414	10m. Onion	20	10
415	15m. Red lily	30	10
416	20m. "Thermopsis lanceolata"	40	10
417	30m. "Amygdalus mongolica"	60	30
418	60m. Bluebeard	75	35
419	80m. "Piptanthus mongolicus"	95	55
420	1t. "Iris bungei"	1·20	75

1966. 60th Birth Anniv of D. Natsagdorj. Nos. 277/8 optd 1906 1966.

420a	63	30m. brown	7·75	7·50
420b	63	50m. green	9·50	9·25

97 Child with Dove

1966. Children's Day. Multicoloured.

421	10m. Type 97	20	10
422	15m. Children with reindeer (horiz)	30	10
423	20m. Boys wrestling	30	10
424	30m. Boy riding horse (horiz)	40	20
425	60m. Children on camel	60	30
426	80m. Shepherd boy with sheep (horiz)	75	35
427	1t. Boy archer	95	45

98 "Proton 1"

1966. Space Satellites. Multicoloured.

428	5m. "Vostok 2" (vert)	10	10
429	10m. Type 98	10	10
430	15m. "Telstar 1" (vert)	20	10
431	20m. "Molniya 1" (vert)	30	10
432	30m. "Syncom 3" (vert)	40	20
433	60m. "Luna 9" (vert)	50	30
434	80m. "Luna 12" (vert)	60	35
435	1t. Mars and photographs taken by "Mariner 4"	75	45

99 Tarbosaurus

1966. Prehistoric Animals. Multicoloured.

436	5m. Type 99	40	10
437	10m. Talararus	50	10
438	15m. Protoceratops	60	20
439	20m. Indricotherium	60	20
440	30m. Saurolophus	85	30
441	60m. Mastodon	1·70	35
442	80m. Mongolotherium	1·90	65
443	1t. Mammuthus	2·10	90

100 Congress Emblem

1967. Ninth International Students' Union Congress.

444	100	30m. ultramarine and blue	30	20
445	100	50m. blue and pink	50	30

101 Sukhe Bator and Mongolian and Soviet Soldiers

1967. 50th Anniv of October Revolution.

446	101	40m. multicoloured	40	30
447	101	60m. multicoloured	60	35

DESIGN: 60m. Lenin, and soldiers with sword.

102 Vietnamese Mother and Child

1967. Help for Vietnam.

448	102	30m.+20m. brown, red and blue	40	30
449	102	50m.+30m. brown, blue and red	65	45

103 Figure Skating

1967. Winter Olympic Games, Grenoble. Multicoloured

450	5m. Type 103	10	10
451	10m. Speed skating	20	10
452	15m. Ice hockey	30	10
453	20m. Skijumping	40	20
454	30m. Bob sleighing	60	30
455	60m. Figure skating (pairs)	75	35
456	80m. Downhill skiing	95	55
MS457	92×92 mm. 4t. Figure skating (different)	3·25	3·25

104 Bactrian Camel and Calf

1968. Young Animals. Multicoloured.

458	5m. Type 104	10	10
459	10m. Yak	20	10
460	15m. Lamb	20	10
461	20m. Foal	30	10

462	30m. Calf	30	10
463	60m. Bison	40	20
464	80m. Roe deer	60	35
465	1t. Reindeer	85	55

105 Prickly Rose

1968. Mongolian Berries.

466	**105**	5m. ultramarine on blue	10	10
467	-	10m. brown on buff	20	10
468	-	15m. emerald on green	30	10
469	-	20m. red on cream	30	10
470	-	30m. red on pink	40	10
471	-	60m. brown on orange	50	30
472	-	80m. turquoise on blue	75	35
473	-	1t. red on cream	95	55

DESIGNS: 10m. Blackcurrant; 15m. Gooseberry; 20m. Crab-apple; 30m. Strawberry; 60m. Redcurrant; 80m. Cowberry; 1t. Sea buckthorn.

ДЭХБ
20 ЖИЛ
W HO
(106)

1968. 20th Anniv of World Health Organization. Nos. 396/7 optd with T **106**.

| 474 | **89** | 30m. blue, gold and green | 3·75 | 3·75 |
| 475 | **89** | 50m. blue, gold and red | 3·75 | 3·75 |

107 Human Rights Emblem

1968. Human Rights Year.

| 476 | **107** | 30m. green and blue | 30 | 20 |

108 "Das Kapital"

1968. 150th Birth Anniv of Karl Marx. Multicoloured.

| 477 | | 30m. Type **108** | 30 | 20 |
| 478 | | 50m. Karl Marx | 50 | 30 |

109 "Portrait of Artist Sharab" (A. Sangatzohyo)

1968. Mongolian Paintings. Multicoloured.

479		5m. Type **109**	20	10
480		10m. "On Remote Roads" (A. Sangatzohyo)	30	10
481		15m. "Camel Calf" (B. Avarzad)	30	10
482		20m. "The Milk" (B. Avarzad)	50	30
483		30m. "The Bowman" (B. Gombosuren)	65	35
484		80m. "Girl Sitting on a Yak" (A. Sangatzohyo)	1·30	65
485		1t.40 "Cagan Dara Ekke" (Janaivajara)	2·50	1·20
MS486		120×86 mm. 4t. "Meeting" (A. Sangatzohyo) (horiz)	5·75	5·50

110 Volleyball

1968. Olympic Games, Mexico. Multicoloured.

487	5m. Type **110**	10	10
488	10m. Wrestling	10	10
489	15m. Cycling	10	10
490	20m. Throwing the javelin	20	10
491	30m. Football	30	20
492	60m. Running	40	30
493	80m. Gymnastics	60	35
494	1t. Weightlifting	75	45
MS495	92×92 mm. 4t. Horse-jumping	3·00	2·75

111 Hammer and Spade

1968. Seventh Anniv of Darkhan Town.

| 496 | **111** | 50m. orange and blue | 30 | 10 |

112 Gorky

1968. Birth Centenary of Maksim Gorky (writer).

| 497 | **112** | 60m. ochre and blue | 30 | 20 |

113 "Madonna and Child" (Boltraffio)

1968. 20th Anniv (1966) of UNESCO. Paintings by European Masters in National Gallery, Budapest. Multicoloured.

498	5m. Type **113**	20	10
499	10m. "St. Roch healed by an angel" (Moretto of Brescia)	30	10
500	15m. "Madonna and Child with St. Anne" (Macchietti)	40	20
501	20m. "St. John on Patmos" (Cano)	50	30
502	30m. "Young lady with viola da gamba" (Kupetzky)	60	30
503	80m. "Study of a head" (Amerling)	1·20	45
504	1t.40 "The death of Adonis" (Furini)	1·70	85
MS505	80×120 mm. 4t. "Portrait of a Lady" (Renoir)	5·75	5·50

114 Paavo Nurmi (running)

1969. Olympic Games' Gold-medal Winners. Multicoloured.

506	5m. Type **114**	10	10
507	10m. Jesse Owens (running)	10	10
508	15m. F. Blankers-Koen (hurdling)	10	10
509	20m. Laszlo Papp (boxing)	20	10
510	30m. Wilma Rudolph (running)	30	20
511	60m. Boris Sahlin (gymnastics)	50	30
512	80m. D. Schollander (swimming)	65	45
513	1t. A. Nakayama (ring exercises)	95	55
MS514	118×80 mm. 4t. J. Munhbat (wrestling)	4·75	4·50

115 Bayit Costume (woman)

1969. Mongolian Costumes. Multicoloured.

515	5m. Type **115**	20	10
516	10m. Torgut (man)	20	10
517	15m. Sakhchin (woman)	30	10
518	20m. Khalka (woman)	50	10
519	30m. Daringanga (woman)	50	20
520	60m. Mingat (woman)	65	20
521	80m. Khalka (man)	95	30
522	1t. Barga (woman)	1·50	55

116 Emblem and Helicopter Rescue

1969. 30th Anniv of Mongolian Red Cross.

| 523 | **116** | 30m. red and blue | 95 | 20 |
| 524 | - | 50m. red and violet | 75 | 30 |

DESIGN: 50m. Shepherd and ambulance.

117 Yellow Lion's-foot

1969. Landscapes and Flowers. Multicoloured.

525	5m. Type **117**	20	10
526	10m. Variegated pink	20	10
527	15m. Superb pink	30	10
528	20m. Meadow cranesbill	30	10
529	30m. Mongolian pink	60	20
530	60m. Asiatic globe flower	65	30
531	80m. Long-lipped larkspur	95	45
532	1t. Saxaul	1·40	55

118 "Bullfight" (O. Tsewegdjaw)

1969. Tenth Anniv of Co-operative Movement. Paintings in National Gallery, Ulan Bator. Multicoloured.

533	5m. Type **118**	10	10
534	10m. "Colts Fighting" (O. Tsewegdjaw)	10	10
535	15m. "Horse-herd" (A. Sengetsohyo)	10	10
536	20m. "Camel Caravan" (D. Damdinsuren)	20	10
537	30m. "On the Steppe" (N. Tsultem)	30	20
538	60m. "Milking Mares" (O. Tsewegdjaw)	60	30
539	80m. "Off to School" (B. Avarzad)	75	45
540	1t. "After Work" (G. Odon)	1·20	55
MS541	121×85 mm. 4t. "Horse-herd" (D. Damdinsuren) (60×40 mm)	3·75	3·75

119 Astronaut and Module on Moon

1969. Air. First Man on the Moon. Sheet 86×121 mm.

| **MS**542 | **119** | 4t. multicoloured | 4·25 | 4·25 |

120 Army Crest

1969. 30th Anniv of Battle of Khalka River.

| 543 | **120** | 50m. multicoloured | 40 | 20 |

БНМАУ-ыг
тунхагласны
45
жилийн ой
1969—XI—26
(121)

1969. 45th Anniv of Mongolian People's Republic. Nos. 411/12 optd with T **121**.

| 544 | **95** | 30m. multicoloured | 5·75 | 5·50 |
| 545 | - | 50m. multicoloured | 7·75 | 7·50 |

122 "Sputnik 3"

1969. Exploration of Space. Multicoloured.

546	5m. Type **122**	10	10
547	10m. "Vostok 1"	10	10
548	15m. "Mercury 7"	20	10
549	20m. Space-walk from "Voskhod 2"	30	10
550	30m. "Apollo 8" in Moon orbit	30	20
551	60m. Space-walk from "Soyuz 5"	60	35
552	80m. "Apollo 12" and Moon landing	75	45
MS553	108×77 mm. 4t. "Apollo 12"	2·40	2·30

123 Wolf

1970. Wild Animals. Multicoloured.

554	5m. Type **123**	20	10
555	10m. Brown bear	30	10
556	15m. Lynx	40	10
557	20m. Wild boar	60	10
558	30m. Elk	65	20
559	60m. Bobak marmot	75	35
560	80m. Argali	1·20	55
561	1t. "Hun Hunter and Hound" (tapestry)	1·70	75

124 "Lenin Centenary" (silk panel, Cerenhuu)

1970. Birth Centenary of Lenin. Multicoloured.

562	20m. Type **124**	20	10
563	50m. "Mongolians meeting Lenin" (Sangatzohyo) (horiz)	40	20
564	1t. "Lenin" (Mazhig)	60	30

125 "Fairy Tale" Pavilion

1970. "EXPO 70" World Trade Fair, Osaka, Japan. Multicoloured.

| 565 | 1t.50 Type **125** | 75 | 55 |
| **MS**566 | 111×81 mm. 4t. Matsushita Pavilion and "Time Capsule" (51×38 mm) | 5·25 | 5·00 |

126 Footballers

1970. World Cup Football Championship, Mexico.

567	**126**	10m. multicoloured	20	10
568	-	20m. multicoloured	20	10
569	-	30m. multicoloured	30	10
570	-	50m. multicoloured	50	20
571	-	60m. multicoloured	60	20
572	-	1t. multicoloured	95	20
573	-	1t.30 multicoloured	1·20	45

MS574 122×95 mm 4t. multicoloured (50×37 mm) — 3·25 / 3·25

DESIGNS: Nos. 568/**MS**574, Different football scenes.

127 Common Buzzard

1970. Birds of Prey. Multicoloured.

575	10m. Type **127**	85	10
576	20m. Tawny owls	1·20	20
577	30m. Northern goshawk	1·30	20
578	50m. White-tailed sea eagle	1·40	30
579	60m. Peregrine falcon	1·90	55
580	1t. Common kestrels	2·40	55
581	1t.30 Black kite	2·75	75

128 Soviet Memorial, Berlin-Treptow

1970. 25th Anniv of Victory in Second World War.

582	**128**	60m. multicoloured	50	30

129 Mongol Archery

1970. Mongolian Traditional Life. Multicoloured.

583	10m. Type **129**	40	20
584	20m. Bodg-gegeen's Palace, Ulan Bator	40	20
585	30m. Mongol horsemen	40	20
586	40m. "The White Goddess-Mother"	40	30
587	50m. Girl in National costume	85	65
588	60m. "Lion's Head" (statue)	95	75
589	70m. Dancer's mask	1·20	85
590	80m. Gateway, Bogd-gegeen's Palace	1·30	1·10

130 Frogmen boarding "Apollo 13"

1970. Safe Return of "Apollo 13" Spacecraft. Sheet 110×80 mm.

MS591	**130**	4t. multicoloured	5·75	5·75

131 I.E.Y. and U.N. Emblems with Flag

1970. International Education Year.

592	**131**	60m. multicoloured	60	30

132 Horseman, "50" and Sunrise

1970. 50th Anniv of National Press.

593	**132**	30m. multicoloured	50	30

133 "Vostok 3" and "4"

1971. Space Research. Multicoloured.

594	10m. Type **133**	10	10
595	20m. Space-walk from "Voskhod 2"	10	10
596	30m. "Gemini 6" and "7"	20	10
597	50m. Docking of "Soyuz 4" and "5"	30	20
598	60m. "Soyuz 6", "7" and "8"	40	30
599	80m. "Apollo 11" and lunar module	50	30
600	1t. "Apollo 13" damaged	60	35
601	1t.30 "Luna 16"	75	45

MS602 120×90 mm. 4t. Satellite communications station, Ulan Bator — 3·25 / 3·25

No. 594 is incorrectly inscribed "Vostok 2-3". The date refers to flight of "Vostoks 3" and "4".

134 Sukhe Bator addressing Meeting

1971. 50th Anniv of Revolutionary Party. Multicoloured.

603	30m. Type **134**	20	10
604	60m. Horseman with flag	30	10
605	90m. Sukhe Bator with Lenin	40	20
606	1t.20 Mongolians with banner	60	35

135 "Lunokhod 1"

1971. Exploration of the Moon. Sheet 114×95 mm containing T **135** and similar vert design. Multicoloured.

MS607 2t. ×2 (a) Type **135**; (b) "Apollo 14" module on Moon — 3·25 / 3·25

136 Tsam Mask

1971. Mongol Tsam Masks.

608	**136**	10m. multicoloured	20	10
609	-	20m. multicoloured	30	10
610	-	30m. multicoloured	50	10
611	-	50m. multicoloured	50	20
612	-	60m. multicoloured	60	20
613	-	1t. multicoloured	1·10	45
614	-	1t.30 multicoloured	1·20	65

DESIGNS: Nos. 609/14, Different dance masks.

137 Banner and Party Emblems

1971. 16th Revolutionary Party Congress.

615	**137**	60m. multicoloured	30	20

138 Steam Locomotive

1971. "50 Years of Transport Development". Multicoloured.

616	20m. Type **138**	75	20
617	30m. Diesel locomotive	85	20
618	40m. Russian "Urals" lorry	85	20
619	50m. Russian "Moskovich 412" car	95	20
620	60m. Polikarpov Po-2 biplane	1·20	30
621	80m. Antonov An-24B airliner	1·30	45
622	1t. Lake steamer "Sukhe Bator"	2·40	90

139 Soldier

1971. 50th Anniv of People's Army and Police. Multicoloured.

623	60m. Type **139**	40	10
624	1t.50 Policeman and child	60	30

140 Emblem and Red Flag

1971. 50th Anniv of Revolutionary Youth Organization.

625	**140**	60m. multicoloured	30	20

141 Mongolian Flag and Year Emblem

1971. Racial Equality Year.

626	**141**	60m. multicoloured	30	20

142 "The Old Man and the Tiger"

1971. Mongolian Folk Tales. Multicoloured.

627	10m. Type **142**	20	10
628	20m. "The Boy Giant-killer"	20	10
629	30m. Cat and mice	30	10
630	50m. Mongolians riding on eagle	40	20
631	60m. Girl on horseback ("The Wise Bride")	60	20
632	80m. King and courtiers with donkey	75	30
633	1t. Couple kneeling before empty throne ("Story of the Throne")	1·10	35
634	1t.30 "The Wise Bird"	1·30	55

143 Yaks

1971. Livestock Breeding. Multicoloured.

635	20m. Type **143**	20	10
636	30m. Bactrian camels	20	10
637	40m. Sheep	30	20
638	50m. Goats	50	20
639	60m. Cattle	65	35
640	80m. Horses	75	35
641	1t. Pony	1·20	55

144 Cross-country Skiing

1972. Winter Olympic Games, Sapporo, Japan. Multicoloured.

642	10m. Type **144**	20	10
643	20m. Bobsleighing	20	10
644	30m. Figure skating	30	10
645	50m. Slalom skiing	40	20
646	60m. Speed skating	50	20
647	80m. Downhill skiing	60	20
648	1t. Ice hockey	75	30
649	1t.30 Pairs figure skating	95	35

MS650 110×90 mm. 4t. Ski jumping (50×38 mm) — 2·40 / 2·30

145 "Horse-breaking" (A. Sengatzohyo)

1972. Paintings by Contemporary Artists from the National Gallery, Ulan Bator. Multicoloured.

651	10m. Type **145**	20	10
652	20m. "Black Camel" (A. Sengatzohyo)	20	10
653	30m. "Jousting" (A. Sengatzohyo)	30	10
654	50m. "Wrestling Match" (A. Sengatzohyo)	40	20
655	60m. "Waterfall" (A. Sengatzohyo)	50	20
656	80m. "Old Musician" (U. Yadamsuren)	75	35
657	1t. "Young Musician" (U. Yadamsuren)	85	35
658	1t.30 "Ancient Prophet" (B. Avarzad)	1·20	45

146 "Apollo 16"

1972. Air. "Co-operation in Space Exploration". Sheet 111×90 mm.

MS659	**146**	4t. multicoloured	4·25	4·25

147 "Calosoma fischeri"
(ground beetle)

1972. Beetles. Multicoloured.

660	10m. Type **147**	20	10
661	20m. "Mylabris mongolica" (blister beetle)	30	10
662	30m. "Sternoplax zichyi" (meal-worm beetle)	40	10
663	50m. "Rhaebus komarovi" (snout weevil)	50	20
664	60m. "Meloe centripubens" (oil beetle)	65	20
665	80m. "Eodorcadion mongoli-cum" (longhorn beetle)	1·10	30
666	1t. "Platyope maongolica" (mealworm beetle)	1·20	45
667	1t.30 "Lixus nigrolineatus" (weevil)	1·90	65

148 Przewalski's Wild Horse

1972. Air. Centenary of Discovery of Wild Horse Species by Nikolai Przewalski. Sheet 115×90 mm.

MS668	**148** 4t. multicoloured	10·50	9·25

149 Satellite and Dish Aerial ("Telecommunications")

1972. Air. National Achievements. Multicoloured.

669	20m. Type **149**	20	10
670	30m. Horse-herd ("Livestock Breeding")	30	10
671	40m. Diesel train and Tupolev Tu-144 jetliner ("Transport")	1·20	20
672	50m. Corncob and farm ("Agriculture")	40	20
673	60m. Ambulance and hospital ("Public Health")	60	30
674	80m. Actors ("Culture")	75	35
675	1t. Factory ("Industry")	95	45

150 Globe, Flag and Dish Aerial

1972. Air. World Telecommunications Day.

676	**150** 60m. multicoloured	50	30

151 Running

1972. Olympic Games, Munich. Multicoloured.

677	10m. Type **151**	10	10
678	15m. Boxing	20	10
679	20m. Judo	20	10
680	25m. High jumping	20	10
681	30m. Rifle-shooting	30	10
682	60m. Wrestling	40	30
683	80m. Weightlifting	50	35
684	1t. Mongolian flag and Olympic emblems	60	55
MS685	90×110 mm. 4t. Archery (vert)	3·00	3·00

152 E.C.A.F.E. Emblem

1972. 25th Anniv of E.C.A.F.E.

686	**152** 60m. blue, gold and red	40	20

153 Mongolian Racerunner

1972. Reptiles. Multicoloured.

687	10m. Type **153**	20	10
688	15m. Radde's toad	30	10
689	20m. Halys viper	30	10
690	25m. Toad-headed agama	50	10
691	30m. Asiatic grass frog	60	20
692	60m. Plate-tailed geckol	75	35
693	80m. Steppe ribbon snake	1·20	55
694	1t. Mongolian agama	1·90	65

154 "Technical Knowledge"

1972. 30th Anniv of Mongolian State University. Multicoloured.

695	50m. Type **154**	40	10
696	60m. University building	50	20

155 "Madonna and Child with St. John the Baptist and a Holy Woman" (Bellini)

1972. Air. UNESCO "Save Venice" Campaign. Paintings. Multicoloured.

697	10m. Type **155**	20	10
698	20m. "The Transfiguration" (Bellini) (vert)	20	10
699	30m. "Blessed Virgin with the Child" (Bellini) (vert)	30	20
700	50m. "Presentation of the Christ in the Temple" (Bellini) (vert)	50	20
701	60m. "St. George" (Bellini) (vert)	65	20
702	80m. "Departure of Ursula" (detail, Carpaccio) (vert)	75	35
703	1t. "Departure of Ursula" (different detail, Carpaccio)	1·10	65
MS704	90×111 mm. 3t.+1t. As No. 703	4·75	4·75

156 Manlay-Bator Damdinsuren

1972. National Heroes. Multicoloured.

705	10m. Type **156**	20	10
706	20m. Ard Ayus in chains (horiz)	30	10
707	50m. Hatan-Bator Magsarzhav	40	20
708	60m. Has-Bator on the march (horiz)	50	30
709	1t. Sukhe Bator	95	35

157 Spassky Tower, Moscow Kremlin

1972. 50th Anniv of U.S.S.R.

710	**157** 60m. multicoloured	50	20

158 Snake and "Mars 1"

1972. Air. Animal Signs of the Mongolian Calendar and Progress in Space Exploration. Multicoloured.

711	60m. Type **158**	85	35
712	60m. Horse and "Apollo 8" (square)	85	35
713	60m. Sheep and "Electron 2" (square)	85	35
714	60m. Monkey and "Explorer 6"	85	35
715	60m. Dragon and "Mariner 2"	85	35
716	60m. Pig and "Cosmos 110" (square)	85	35
717	60m. Dog and "Ariel 2" (square)	85	35
718	60m. Cockerel and "Venus 1"	85	35
719	60m. Hare and "Soyuz 5"	85	35
720	60m. Tiger and "Gemini 7" (square)	85	35
721	60m. Ox and "Venus 4" (square)	85	35
722	60m. Rat and "Apollo 15" lunar rover	85	35

The square designs are size 40×40 mm.

159 Swimming Gold Medal (Mark Spitz, U.S.A.)

1972. Gold Medal Winners, Munich Olympic Games. Multicoloured.

723	5m. Type **159**	10	10
724	10m. High jumping (Ulrike Meyfarth, West Germany)	20	10
725	20m. Gymnastics (Savao Kato, Japan)	30	10
726	30m. Show jumping (Andras Balczo, Hungary)	30	20
727	60m. Running (Lasse Viren, Finland)	50	20
728	80m. Swimming (Shane Gould, Australia)	65	30
729	1t. Putting the shot (Anatoli Bondarchuk, U.S.S.R.)	85	35
MS730	111×91 mm. 4t. Wrestling silver medal (Khorloo Baianmunk, Mongolia)	3·00	3·00

160 Monkey on Cycle

1973. Mongolian Circus (1st series). Multicoloured

731	5m. Type **160**	10	10
732	10m. Seal with ball	20	10
733	15m. Bear on mono-wheel	30	10
734	20m. Acrobat on camel	40	10
735	30m. Acrobat on horse	50	20
736	50m. Clown playing flute	60	20
737	60m. Contortionist	75	35
738	1t. New Circus Hall, Ulan Bator	1·10	65

See also Nos. 824/30.

161 Mounted Postman

1973

739	**161**	50m. brown (postage)	75	10
740	-	60m. green	3·00	30
741	-	1t. purple	1·40	35
742	-	1t.50 blue (air)	2·40	45

DESIGNS: 60m. Diesel train; 1t. Mail truck; 1t.50, Antonov An-24 airliner.

162 Sukhe Bator receiving Traditional Gifts

1973. 80th Birth Anniv of Sukhe Bator. Multicoloured

743	10m. Type **162**	10	10
744	20m. Holding reception	20	10
745	50m. Leading army	40	20
746	60m. Addressing council	50	20
747	1t. Giving audience (horiz)	75	30

163 W.M.O. Emblem and Meteorological Symbols

1973. Air. Centenary of World Meteorological Organization.

748	**163** 60m. multicoloured	50	30

164 "Copernicus" (anon)

1973. 500th Birth Anniv of Nicholas Copernicus (astronomer). Multicoloured.

749	50m. Type **164**	40	20
750	60m. "Copernicus in his Observatory" (J. Matejko) (55×35 mm)	50	30
751	1t. "Copernicus" (Jan Matejko)	85	35
MS752	151×115 mm. As Nos. 749/51 but face values 1, 2 and 1t. respectively	3·25	3·50

165 "Tulaga" Stamp of 1959

1973. "IBRA 73" International Stamp Exhibition, Munich. Sheet 81×116 mm.

MS753	**165** 4t. multicoloured	3·75	3·75

Нэгдлийн Холбооны IV Их
Хурал 1973–6–11
(166)

1973. Fourth Agricultural Co-operative Congress, Ulan Bator. No. 538 optd with T **166**.
754   60m. multicoloured

167 Marx and Lenin

1973. Ninth Organization of Socialist States Postal Ministers Congress, Ulan Bator.
755   **167**   60m. multicoloured   50   20

168 Russian Stamp and Emblems

1973. Air. Council for Mutual Economic Aid Posts and Telecommunications Conference, Ulan Bator. Multicoloured.
756   30m. Type **168**   75   30
757   30m. Mongolia   75   30
758   30m. Bulgaria   75   30
759   30m. Hungary   75   30
760   30m. Czechoslovakia   75   30
761   30m. German Democratic Republic   75   30
762   30m. Cuba   75   30
763   30m. Rumania   75   30
764   30m. Poland   75   30

169 Common Shelduck

1973. Aquatic Birds. Multicoloured.
765   5m. Type **169**   60   20
766   10m. Black-throated diver   75   20
767   15m. Bar-headed geese   1·20   20
768   30m. Great crested grebe   1·50   30
769   50m. Mallard   2·10   45
770   60m. Mute swan   2·50   55
771   1t. Greater scaups   3·00   75

170 Siberian Weasel

1973. Small Fur Animals. Multicoloured.
772   5m. Type **170**   20   10
773   10m. Siberian chipmunk   20   10
774   15m. Siberian flying squirrel   30   10
775   20m. Eurasian badger   40   10
776   30m. Eurasian red squirrel   60   20
777   60m. Wolverine   95   35
778   80m. American mink   1·20   55
779   1t. Arctic hare   1·70   75

171 Launching "Soyuz" Spacecraft

1973. Air. "Apollo" and "Soyuz" Space Programmes. Multicoloured.
780   5m. Type **171**   10   10
781   10m. "Apollo 8"   10   10
782   15m. "Soyuz 4" and "5" linked   10   10
783   20m. "Apollo 11" module on Moon   20   10
784   30m. "Apollo 14" after splash-down   30   20
785   50m. Triple flight by "Soyuz 6", "7" and "8"   40   20
786   60m. "Apollo 16" lunar rover   50   30
787   1t. "Lunokhod 1"   60   35
MS788 110×91 mm. 4t. Proposed "Soyuz" and "Apollo" link-up   2·40   2·30

172 Global Emblem

1973. 15th Anniv of Review "Problems of Peace and Socialism".
789   **172**   60m. red, gold and blue   40   20

173 Alpine Aster

1973. Mongolian Flowers. Multicoloured.
790   5m. Type **173**   20   10
791   10m. Mongolian catchfly   30   10
792   15m. "Rosa davurica"   40   10
793   20m. Mongolian dandelion   50   10
794   30m. "Rhododendron dahuricum"   60   10
795   50m. "Clematis tangutica"   75   35
796   60m. Siberian primrose   95   75
797   1t. Pasque flower   1·20   85

174 Poplar Admiral

1974. Butterflies and Moths. Multicoloured.
798   5m. Type **174**   40   10
799   10m. Hebe tiger moth   50   10
800   15m. Purple tiger moth   50   10
801   20m. Rosy underwing   65   10
802   30m. "Isoceras kaszabi" (moth)   95   20
803   50m. Spurge hawk moth   1·30   35
804   60m. Garden tiger moth   1·50   45
805   1t. Clouded buff   1·90   65

175 "Hebe Namshil" (L. Merdorsh)

1974. Mongolian Opera and Drama. Multicoloured.
806   15m. Type **175**   20   10
807   20m. "Sive Hiagt" (D. Luvsansharav) (horiz)   30   10
808   25m. "Edre" (D. Namdag)   40   10
809   30m. "The Three Khans of Saragol" (horiz)   50   20
810   60m. "Amarsana" (B. Damdinsuren)   60   20
811   80m. "Edre" (different scene)   75   30
812   1t. "Edre" (different scene)   95   75

176 Comecon Headquarters, Moscow

1974. Air. 25th Anniv of Communist Council for Mutual Economic Aid ("Comecon").
813   **176**   60m. multicoloured   50   30

177 Government Building and Sukhe Bator Monument, Ulan Bator

1974. 50th Anniv of Renaming of Capital as Ulan Bator.
814   **177**   60m. multicoloured   50   30

178 Mongolian 10c. Stamp of 1924

1974. Air. 50th Anniv of First Mongolian Stamps. Sheet 130×85 mm.
MS815 **178** 4t. multicoloured   4·75   4·50

179 Mounted Courier

1974. Air. Centenary of U.P.U (1st issue). Multicoloured.
816   50m. Type **179**   1·70   45
817   50m. Reindeer mail sledge   1·70   45
818   50m. Mail coach   1·70   45
819   50m. Balloon post   1·90   45
820   50m. Lake steamer "Sukhe Bator" and Polikarpov Po-2 biplane   2·40   45
821   50m. Diesel train and P.O. truck   2·40   45
822   50m. Rocket in orbit   1·90   45
MS823 100×90 mm. 4t. "UPU" over globe (24×45 mm)   21·00   20·00
See also 883/**MS**890.

180 Performing Horses

1974. Mongolian Circus (2nd series). Multicoloured.
824   10m. Type **180** (postage)   20   10
825   20m. Juggler (vert)   40   10
826   30m. Elephant on ball (vert)   50   20
827   40m. Performing yak   75   30
828   60m. Acrobats (vert)   95   30
829   80m. Trick cyclist (vert)   1·10   65
830   1t. Contortionist (vert) (air)   1·90   85

181 "Training a Young Horse"

1974. International Children's Day. Drawings by Lhamsurem. Multicoloured.
831   10m. Type **181**   10   10
832   20m. "Boy with Calf"   20   10
833   30m. "Riding untamed Horse"   30   10
834   40m. "Boy with Foal"   40   10
835   60m. "Girl dancing with Doves"   60   20
836   80m. "Wrestling"   75   35
837   1t. "Hobby-horse Dance"   95   55

182 Archer on Foot

1974. "Nadam" Sports Festival. Multicoloured.
838   10m. Type **182**   10   10
839   20m. "Kazlodanie" (Kazakh mounted game)   20   10
840   30m. Mounted archer   30   10
841   40m. Horse-racing   40   20
842   60m. Bucking horse-riding   60   20
843   80m. Capturing wild horse   75   35
844   1t. Wrestling   95   55

183 Giant Panda

1974. Bears. Multicoloured.
845   10m. Brown bear   20   10
846   20m. Type **183**   30   10
847   30m. Giant Panda   60   20
848   40m. Brown bear   60   30
849   60m. Sloth bear   95   35
850   80m. Asiatic black bear   1·10   65
851   1t. Brown bear   1·90   85

184 Red Deer

1974. Games Reserves. Fauna. Multicoloured.
852   10m. Type **184**   20   10
853   20m. Eurasian beaver   40   10
854   30m. Leopard   60   20
855   40m. Herring gull   1·50   35
856   60m. Roe deer   1·20   35
857   80m. Argali   1·30   55
858   1t. Siberian musk deer   1·50   65

185 Detail of Buddhist Temple, Palace of Bogdo Gegen

1974. Mongolian Architecture. Multicoloured.
859   10m. Type **185**   20   10
860   15m. Buddhist temple (now museum)   20   10

861	30m. "Charity" Temple, Ulan Bator	30	20
862	50m. Yurt (tent)	50	30
863	80m. Arbour in court-yard	75	35

186 Spassky Tower, Moscow, and Sukhe Bator Statue, Ulan Bator

1974. Brezhnev's Visit to Mongolia.

864	**186**	60m. multicoloured	50	20

187 Proclamation of the Republic

1974. 50th Anniv of Mongolian People's Republic. Multicoloured.

865	60m. Type **187**	50	20
866	60m. "First Constitution" (embroidery)	50	20
867	60m. Mongolian flag	50	20

188 Gold Decanter

1974. Goldsmiths' Treasures of the 19th Century. Multicoloured.

868	10m. Type **188**	20	10
869	20m. Silver jug	30	10
870	30m. Night lamp	40	10
871	40m. Tea jug	50	20
872	60m. Candelabra	60	20
873	80m. Teapot	75	35
874	1t. Silver bowl on stand	95	55

189 Northern Lapwing

1974. Protection of Water and Nature Conservation. Multicoloured.

875	10m. Type **189** (postage)	50	10
876	20m. Lenok (fish)	60	10
877	30m. Marsh marigolds	65	20
878	40m. Dalmatian pelican	95	20
879	60m. Eurasian perch	95	35
880	80m. Sable	1·20	45
881	1t. Hydrologist with jar of water (air)	1·40	65
MS882	83×117 mm. 4t. Wild roses (60×60 mm)	4·75	4·50

190 U.S. Mail Coach

1974. Centenary of U.P.U. Multicoloured.

883	10m. Type **190**	20	10
884	20m. French postal cart	30	10

885	30m. Changing horses, Russian mail and passenger carriage	40	20
886	40m. Swedish postal coach with caterpillar tracks	50	30
887	75m. First Hungarian mail van	75	35
888	60m. German Daimler-Benz mail van and trailer	95	45
889	1t. Mongolian postal courier	1·20	75
MS890	111×90 mm. 4t. UPU emblem	7·75	7·75

191 Red Flag

1975. 30th Anniv of Victory.

891	**191**	60m. multicoloured	50	30

192 "Zygophyllum xanthoxylon" (image scaled to 57% of original size)

1975. 12th International Botanical Conference. Rare Medicinal Plants. Multicoloured.

892	10m. Type **192**	20	10
893	20m. "Incarvillea potaninii"	40	10
894	30m. "Lancea tibetica"	60	20
895	40m. "Jurinea mongolica"	65	20
896	50m. "Saussurea involucrata"	75	30
897	60m. "Allium mongolicum"	95	35
898	1t. "Adonis mongolica"	1·70	65

193 Mongolian Woman

1975. International Women's Year.

899	**193**	60m. multicoloured	50	30

194 "Soyuz" on Launch-pad

1975. Air. Joint Soviet–American Space Project. Multicoloured.

900	10m. Type **194**	10	10
901	20m. Launch of "Apollo"	20	10
902	30m. "Apollo" and "Soyuz" spacecraft	30	20
903	40m. Docking manoeuvre	50	30
904	50m. Spacecraft docked together	65	35
905	60m. "Soyuz" in orbit	85	35
906	1t. "Apollo" and "Soyuz" spacecraft and communications satellite	1·20	75
MS907	102×83 mm. 4t. "Soyuz" and "Apollo" crewmen	4·25	4·25

195 Child and Lamb

1975. International Children's Day. Multicoloured.

908	10m. Type **195**	10	10
909	20m. Child riding horse	20	10
910	30m. Child with calf	30	20
911	40m. Child and "orphan camel"	50	20
912	50m. "The Obedient Yak"	60	30
913	60m. Child riding on swan	65	35
914	1t. Two children singing	1·10	55

See also Nos. 979/85.

196 Pioneers tending Tree

1975. 50th Anniv of Mongolian Pioneer Organization. Multicoloured.

915	50m. Type **196**	40	20
916	60m. Children's study circle	50	20
917	1t. New emblem of Mongolian pioneers	65	35

Тээвэр—50
1975—7—15.
(197)

1975. 50th Anniv of Public Transport. Nos. 616/22 optd with T **197**.

918	**138**	20m. multicoloured	3·25	3·25
919	-	30m. multicoloured	3·25	3·25
920	-	40m. multicoloured	2·40	2·30
921	-	50m. multicoloured	2·40	2·30
922	-	60m. multicoloured	3·25	3·25
923	-	80m. multicoloured	4·25	4·25
924	-	1t. multicoloured	5·75	5·50

198 Argali

1975. Air. South Asia Tourist Year.

925	**198**	1t.50 multicoloured	1·30	55

199 Golden Eagle attacking Red Fox

1975. Hunting Scenes. Multicoloured.

926	10m. Type **199**	60	10
927	20m. Lynx-hunting (vert)	65	20
928	30m. Hunter stalking bobak marmots	75	20
929	40m. Hunter riding on reindeer (vert)	85	30
930	50m. Shooting wild boar	95	35
931	60m. Wolf in trap (vert)	1·10	45
932	1t. Hunters with brown bear	1·30	75

200 Haite`s Bullhead

1975. Fish. Multicoloured.

933	10m. Type **200**	20	10
934	20m. Flat-headed asp	40	10
935	30m. Altai osman	60	20
936	40m. Tench	75	30
937	50m. Hump-backed whitefish	95	35
938	60m. Mongolian redfin	1·20	45
939	1t. Goldfish	1·90	75

201 "Morin Hur" (musical instrument)

1975. Mongolian Handicrafts. Multicoloured.

940	10m. Type **201**	10	10
941	20m. Saddle	20	10
942	30m. Headdress	30	20
943	40m. Boots	40	20
944	50m. Cap	50	30
945	60m. Pipe and tobacco pouch	60	30
946	1t. Fur hat	95	55

202 Revolutionary with Banner

1975. 70th Anniv of 1905 Russian Revolution.

947	**202**	60m. multicoloured	40	20

203 "Taming a Wild Horse"

1975. Mongolian Paintings. Multicoloured.

948	10m. Type **203**	10	10
949	20m. "Camel Caravan" (horiz)	30	10
950	30m. "Man playing Lute"	40	20
951	40m. "Woman adjusting Head-dress" (horiz)	50	20
952	50m. "Woman in ceremonial Costume"	60	30
953	60m. "Woman fetching Water"	65	30
954	1t. "Woman playing Yaga" (musical instrument)	1·20	55
MS955	110×90 mm. 4t. "Warrior on horse-back"	4·25	3·75

204 Ski Jumping

1975. Winter Olympic Games, Innsbruck. Multicoloured.

956	10m. Type **204**	10	10
957	20m. Ice hockey	20	10
958	30m. Slalom skiing	30	20
959	40m. Bobsleighing	40	20
960	50m. Rifle shooting (biathlon)	50	30
961	60m. Speed skating	60	30
962	1t. Figure skating	95	35
MS963	110×70 mm. 4t. Skier carrying torch	3·00	3·00

205 "House of Young Technicians"

1975. Public Buildings.

964	**205**	50m. blue	50	10
965	-	60m. green	60	20
966	-	1t. brown	95	35

DESIGNS: 60m. Hotel, Ulan Bator; 1t. "Museum of the Revolution".

206 "Molniya" Satellite

1976. Air. 40th Anniv of Mongolian Meteorological Office.

967	**206**	60m. blue and yellow	60	30

207 Mongolian Girl

1976. Air. 30th Anniv of United Nations Educational, Scientific and Cultural Organization. Sheet 100× 86 mm.
MS968 **207** 4t. multicoloured   4·75   4·25

208 "The Wise Musician" (Sharav)

1976. Air "Interphil 76" International Stamp Exhibition, Philadelphia. Sheet 97×70 mm.
MS969 **208** 4t. multicoloured   4·25   3·75

209 "National Economy" Star

1976. 17th Mongolian People's Revolutionary Party Congress, Ulan Bator.
970 **209** 60m. multicoloured   50   20

210 Archery

1976. Olympic Games, Montreal. Multicoloured.
971	10m. Type **210**	10	10
972	20m. Judo	20	10
973	30m. Boxing	30	15
974	40m. Gymnastics	50	20
975	60m. Weightlifting	65	30
976	80m. High jumping	95	35
977	1t. Rifle shooting	1·20	55
MS978 105×78 mm. 4t. Wrestling		2·40	2·40

1976. Int Children's Day. As T 195. Mult.
979	10m. Gobi Desert landscape	20	10
980	20m. Horse-taming	30	10
981	30m. Horse-riding	40	15
982	40m. Pioneers' camp	50	20
983	60m. Young musician	60	25
984	80m. Children's party	85	35
985	1t. Mongolian wrestling	1·10	55

211 Cavalry Charge

1976. 55th Anniv of Revolution. Multicoloured.
986	60m. Type **211** (postage)	60	30
987	60m. Man and emblem (vert)	60	30
988	60m. "Industry and Agriculture" (air)	60	30

212 "Sukhe Bator" Star

1976. Mongolian Orders and Awards. Sheet 116× 77 mm.
MS989 **212** 4t. multicoloured   2·40   2·40

213 Osprey

1976. Protected Birds. Multicoloured.
990	10m. Type **213**	75	20
991	20m. Griffon vulture	1·20	20
992	30m. Lammergeier	1·40	30
993	40m. Marsh harrier	1·70	35
994	60m. Cinerous vulture	2·10	45
995	80m. Golden eagle	2·40	65
996	1t. Tawny eagle	3·00	75

214 "Rider on Wild Horse"

1976. Paintings by O. Tsewegdjaw. Multicoloured.
997	10m. Type **214**	20	10
998	20m. "The First Nadam" (game on horse-back) (horiz)	30	10
999	30m. "Harbour on Khobsogol Lake" (horiz)	40	15
1000	40m. "Awakening the Steppe" (horiz)	50	20
1001	80m. "Wrestling" (horiz)	85	35
1002	1t. "The Descent" (yak hauling timber)	1·60	85

215 "Industrial Development"

1976. Mongolian–Soviet Friendship.
1003 **215** 60m. multicoloured   1·90   30

216 John Naber of U.S.A. (Swimming)

1976. Olympic Games, Montreal. Gold Medal Winners. Multicoloured.
1004	10m. Type **216** (postage)	10	10
1005	20m. Nadia Comaneci of Rumania (gymnastics)	10	10
1006	30m. Kornelia Ender of East Germany (swimming)	20	15
1007	40m. Mitsuo Tsukahara of Japan (gymnastics)	30	20
1008	60m. Gregor Braun of West Germany (cycling)	50	30
1009	80m. Lasse Viren of Finland (running)	65	35
1010	1t. Nikolai Andrianov of U.S.S.R. (gymnastics)	85	55
MS1011 103×78 mm. 4t. Zeveg Oidov of Mongolia (wrestling) (air)		2·40	2·40

217 Tablet on Tortoise

1976. Archaeology.
1012	**217**	50m. brown and blue	80	15
1013	-	60m. black and green	1·00	25

DESIGN: 60m. 6th-century stele.

218 R-1 Biplane

1976. Aircraft. Multicoloured.
1014	10m. Type **218**	20	10
1015	20m. Polikarpov R-5 biplane	30	10
1016	30m. Kalinin K-5 monoplane	40	10
1017	40m. Polikarpov Po-2 biplane	50	15
1018	60m. Polikarpov I-16 jet fighter	70	25
1019	80m. Yakovlev Ya-6 Air 6 monoplane	90	35
1020	1t. Junkers F-13 monoplane	1·10	50

219 Dancers in Folk Costume

1977. Mongolian Folk Dances. Multicoloured.
1021	10m. Type **219**	30	10
1022	20m. Dancing girls in 13th-century costume	40	10
1023	30m. West Mongolian dance	60	15
1024	40m. "Ekachi" dance	80	20
1025	60m. "Bielge" ("Trunk") dance	1·10	25
1026	80m. "Hodak" dance	1·30	35
1027	1t. "Dojarka" dance	1·50	50

220 Gravitational Effects on "Pioneer"

1977. 250th Death Anniv of Sir Isaac Newton (mathematician). Multicoloured.
1028	60m. Type **220** (postage)	40	20
1029	60m. Apple tree (25×32 mm)	40	20
1030	60m. Planetary motion and sextant	40	20
1031	60m. Sir Isaac Newton (25×32 mm)	40	20
1032	60m. Spectrum of light	40	20
1033	60m. Attraction of Earth	40	20
1034	60m. Laws of motion of celestial bodies (25×32 mm)	40	20
1035	60m. Space-walking (air)	40	20
1036	60m. "Pioneer 10" and Jupiter	40	20

221 Natsagdorj, Mongolian Scenes and Extract from poem "Mother"

1977. Natsagdorj (poet) Commemoration. Multicoloured
1037	60m. Type **221**	60	30
1038	60m. Border stone, landscape and extract from poem "My Homeland"	60	30

222 Horse Race

1977. Horses. Multicoloured.
1039	10m. Type **222**	30	10
1040	20m. Girl on white horse	40	10
1041	30m. Rangeman on brown horse	50	15
1042	40m. Tethered horses	60	20
1043	60m. White mare with foal	80	25
1044	80m. Brown horse with shepherd	1·10	35
1045	1t. White horse	1·30	55

223 "Mongolemys elegans"

1977. Prehistoric Animals. Multicoloured.
1046	10m. Type **223**	40	10
1047	20m. "Embolotherium ergiliense"	60	15
1048	30m. "Psittacosaurus mongoliensis"	70	20
1049	40m. Enthelodon	90	25
1050	60m. "Spirocerus kiakhtensis"	1·40	35
1051	80m. Hipparion	2·00	45
1052	1t. "Bos primigenius"	2·30	60

224 Netherlands 5c. Stamp, 1852, and Mongolian $1 Fiscal Stamp, 1926

1977. "Amphilx 77" International Stamp Exhibition, Amsterdam. Sheet 100×76 mm.
MS1053 **224** 4t. multicoloured   2·50   2·50

225 Child feeding Lambs

1977. Children's Day and First Balloon Flight in Mongolia. Multicoloured.
1054	10m.+5m. Type **225** (postage)	20	10
1055	20m.+5m. Boy playing flute and girl dancing	40	15
1056	30m.+5m. Girl chasing butterflies	50	20
1057	40m.+5m. Girl with ribbon	70	25
1058	60m.+5m. Girl with flowers	1·00	35
1059	80m.+5m. Girl with bucket	1·30	45
1060	1t.+5m. Boy going to school	1·70	60
MS1061 83×72 mm. 4t.+50m. Children in balloon (air)		7·75	6·75

226 Industrial Plant and Transport

1977. Erdenet (New Town).
1062 **226** 60m. multicoloured   1·50   25

227 Trade Unions Emblem

1977. Air. 11th Mongolian Trade Unions Congress.

1063	**227**	60m. multicoloured	1·20	25

228 Mounting Bell-shaped Gear on Rocket

1977. Air. 11th Anniv of "Intercosmos" Co-operation. Multicoloured.

1064	10m. Type **228**	10	10
1065	20m. Launch of "Intercosmos 3"	20	15
1066	30m. Research ship "Kosmonavt Yury Gargarin"	30	20
1067	40m. Observation of lunar eclipse	40	25
1068	60m. Earth station's multiple antennae	60	35
1069	80m. Magnetosphere examination, Van Allen Zone	80	45
1070	1t. Meteorological satellites	1·00	55
MS1071	126×90 mm. 4t. Satellite linked to "Intercosmos" countries on globe (58×36 mm)	2·50	2·50

229 Fire-fighters' Bucket Chain

1977. Mongolian Fire-fighting Services. Multicoloured.

1072	10m. Type **229**	10	10
1073	20m. Horse-drawn hand pump	20	15
1074	30m. Horse-drawn steam pump	30	20
1075	40m. Fighting forest fire	40	20
1076	60m. Mobile foam extinguisher	50	25
1077	80m. Modern fire engine	60	35
1078	1t. Mil Mi-8 helicopter spraying fire	80	45

230 "Molniya" Satellite and Dish Aerial on TV Screen

1977. 40th Anniv of Technical Institute.

1079	**230**	60m. blue, black and grey	50	25

231 Black-veined White

1977. Butterflies and Moths. Multicoloured.

1080	10m. Type **231**	30	10
1081	20m. Lappet moth	60	15
1082	30m. Lesser clouded yellow	80	20
1083	40m. Dark tussock moth	1·20	25
1084	60m. Lackey moth	1·60	30
1085	80m. Clouded buff	2·10	45
1086	1t. Scarce copper	2·50	60

232 Lenin Museum

1977. Inauguration of Lenin Museum, Ulan Bator.

1087	**232**	60m. multicoloured	60	25

233 Cruiser "Aurora" and Soviet Flag

1977. 60th Anniv of Russian Revolution. Multicoloured

1088	50m. Type **233**	70	20
1089	60m. Dove and globe (horiz)	80	25
1090	1t.50 Freedom banner around the globe (horiz)	1·30	55

234 Giant Pandas

1977. Giant Pandas. Multicoloured.

1091	10m. Eating bamboo shoot (vert)	20	10
1092	20m. Type **234**	40	15
1093	30m. Female and cub in washtub (vert)	60	20
1094	40m. Male and cub with bamboo shoot	80	25
1095	60m. Female and cub (vert)	1·20	35
1096	80m. Family (horiz)	2·10	60
1097	1t. Male on hind legs (vert)	2·50	80

235 "Helene Fourment and her Chiildren"

1977. 400th Birth Anniv of Peter Paul Rubens (artist). Sheet 78×104 mm.

MS1098	**235** 4t. multicoloured	5·25	5·25

236 Montgolfier Brothers' Balloon

1977. Air. Airships and Balloons. Multicoloured.

1099	20m. Type **236**	20	10
1100	30m. Airship "Graf Zeppelin" over North Pole	25	15
1101	40m. Airship "Osoaviakhim" over the Arctic	30	20
1102	50m. Soviet Airship "Sever"	40	25
1103	60m. Aereon 340 airship	60	35
1104	80m. Nestrenko's planned airship	80	45
1105	1t.20 "Flying Crane" airship	1·20	55
MS1106	104×75 mm. 4t. Russian Zeppelin stamp of 1931 and statue of Sukhe Bator (46×31 mm)	3·00	3·00

237 Ferrari "312-T2"

1978. Racing Cars. Multicoloured.

1107	20m. Type **237**	30	10
1108	30m. Ford McLaren "M-23"	40	15
1109	40m. Soviet experimental car	50	20
1110	50m. Japanese Mazda	70	25
1111	60m. Porsche "936-Turbo"	80	30
1112	80m. Model of Soviet car	1·00	35
1113	1t.20 American rocket car "Blue Flame"	1·30	45

238 Variegated Boletus (image scaled to 59% of original size)

1978. Mushrooms. Multicoloured.

1114	20m. Type **238**	50	20
1115	30m. The charcoal burner	80	25
1116	40m. Red cap	1·10	30
1117	50m. Brown birch bolete	1·40	35
1118	60m. Yellow swamp russula	1·90	45
1119	80m. "Lactarius resimus"	2·50	55
1120	1t.20 "Flammula spumosa"	3·50	80

239 Aleksandr Mozhaisky and his Monoplane, 1884

1978. Air. History of Aviation. Multicoloured.

1121	20m. Type **239**	20	10
1122	30m. Henri Farman and Farman H.F.III biplane	30	15
1123	40m. Geoffrey de Havilland and De Havilland FE-1 biplane	40	20
1124	50m. Charles Lindbergh and "Spirit of St. Louis"	50	25
1125	60m. Shagdarsuren, Demberel, biplane and glider	60	30
1126	80m. Chkalov, Baidukov, Belyakov and Tupolev ANT-25 airliner	80	35
1127	1t.20 A. N. Tupolev and Tupolev Tu-154 jetliner	1·20	55
MS1128	110×75 mm. 4t. Wright Brothers and Wright Flyer III	3·50	3·50

240 Footballers and View of Rio de Janeiro

1978. World Cup Football Championship, Argentina. Multicoloured.

1129	20m. Type **240** (postage)	20	10
1130	30m. Footballers and Old Town Tower, Berne	30	15
1131	40m. Footballers and Stockholm Town Hall	40	20
1132	50m. Footballers and University of Chile	50	25
1133	60m. Footballers, Houses of Parliament and Tower of London	60	30
1134	80m. Footballers and Theatre Degolladeo of Guadalajara, Mexico	80	35
1135	1t.20 Footballers and Munich Town Hall	1·20	55
MS1136	105×70 mm. 4t. Footballers (44×38 mm) (air)	4·00	4·00

241 Mongolian Youth and Girl

1978. Mongolian Youth Congress, Ulan Bator.

1137	**241**	60m. multicoloured	60	25

242 Eurasian Beaver and 1954 Canadian Beaver Stamp

1978. "CAPEX '78". International Stamp Exhibition, Toronto. Multicoloured.

1138	20m. Type **242** (postage)	30	10
1139	30m. Tibetan sandgrouse and Canada S.G. 620	50	20
1140	40m. Black-throated diver and Canada S.G. 495	70	25
1141	50m. Argali and Canada S.G. 449	1·00	35
1142	60m. Brown bear and Canada S.G. 447	1·20	45
1143	80m. Elk and Canada S.G. 448	1·30	55
1144	1t.20 Herring gull and Canada S.G. 474	2·10	80
MS1145	100×80 mm. 4t. Mongolian 1969 stamp and Canadian 1971 stamp depicting paintings (58×36 mm) (air)	5·25	5·25

243 Marx, Engels and Lenin

1978. 20th Anniv of Review "Problems of Peace and Socialism".

1146	**243**	60m. red, gold and black	60	25

244 Map of Cuba, Liner, Tupolev Tu-134 Jetliner and Emblem

1978. Air. 11th World Youth Festival, Havana.

1147	**244**	1t. multicoloured	1·40	35

245 "Open-air Repose"

1978. 20th Anniv of Philatelic Co-operation between Mongolia and Hungary. Paintings by P. Angalan. Multicoloured.

1148	1t.50 Type **245**	1·00	1·00
1149	1t.50 "Winter Night"	1·00	1·00
1150	1t.50 "Saddling"	1·00	1·00

246 A. Gubarev, V. Remek and Exhibition Emblem

1978. Air. "PRAGA 1978" International Stamp Exhibition, Prague. Sheet 103×88 mm.

MS1151	**246** 4t. multicoloured	3·00	3·00

247 Butterfly Dog

1978. Dogs. Multicoloured.

1152	10m. Type **247**	30	10
1153	20m. Black Mongolian sheepdog	35	15
1154	30m. Puli (Hungarian sheepdog)	50	20
1155	40m. St. Bernard	60	25
1156	50m. German shepherd dog	80	30
1157	60m. Mongolian watchdog	90	35
1158	70m. Semoyedic spitz	1·00	45
1159	80m. Laika (space dog)	1·20	50
1160	1t.20 Black and white poodles and cocker spaniel	1·50	70

248 Open Book showing Scenes from Mongolian Literary Works

1978. 50th Anniv of Mongolian Writers' Association.

1161	**248**	60m. blue and red	50	25

249 "Dressed Maja" (Goya, 150th death anniv)

1978. Painters' Anniversaries.

1162	**249**	1t.50 multicoloured	1·70	1·70
1163	-	1t.50 multicoloured	1·70	1·70

1164	-	1t.50 multicoloured	1·70	1·70
MS1165	105×132 mm. 4t. black and stone		5·25	5·25

DESIGNS: As T **249**—No. 1163, "Ta Matete" (Gauguin, 75th death Anniv); 1164, "Bridge at Arles" (Van Gogh, 125th birth anniv). 49×49 mm—4t. "Melancoly" (Durer, 450th death anniv).

250 Young Bactrian Camel

1978. Bactrian Camels. Multicoloured.

1166	20m. Camel with Foal	30	20
1167	30m. Type **250**	40	20
1168	40m. Two camels	60	25
1169	50m. Woman leading loaded camel	80	30
1170	60m. Camel in winter coat	1·00	35
1171	80m. Camel-drawn water waggon	1·30	55
1172	1t.20 Camel racing	1·90	70

251 Flags of COMECON Countries

1979. 30th Anniv of Council of Mutual Economic Assistance.

1173	**251**	60m. multicoloured	50	25

252 Children riding Camel

1979. International Year of the Child. Multicoloured.

1174	10m.+5m. Type **252**	30	10
1175	30m.+5m. Children feeding chickens	40	20
1176	50m.+5m. Children with deer	50	25
1177	60m.+5m. Children picking flowers	70	35
1178	70m.+5m. Children watering tree	90	40
1179	80m.+5m. Young scientists	1·00	45
1180	1t.+5m. Making music and dancing	1·20	55
MS1181	78×99 mm. 4t.+50m. Girl on horse	5·75	5·00

See also No. **MS**1449.

253 Silver Tabby

1978. Domestic Cats. Multicoloured.

1182	10m. Type **253**	30	10
1183	30m. White Persian	50	20
1184	60m. Red Persian	70	20
1185	60m. Blue-cream Persian	1·00	25
1186	70m. Siamese	1·20	35
1187	80m. Smoke Persian	1·30	45
1188	1t. Birman	1·50	60

254 "Potaninia mongolica"

1979. Flowers. Multicoloured.

1189	10m. Type **254**	30	10
1190	30m. "Sophora alopecuroides"	50	15
1191	50m. "Halimodendron halodendron"	60	20
1192	60m. "Myosotis asiatica"	70	25
1193	70m. "Scabiosa comosa"	80	35
1194	80m. "Leucanthemum sibiricum"	90	45
1195	1t. "Leontopodium ochroleucum"	1·00	60

255 Finland v. Czechoslovakia

1979. World Ice Hockey Championships, Moscow. Multicoloured.

1196	10m. Type **255**	10	10
1197	30m. West Germany v. Sweden	20	15
1198	50m. U.S.A. v. Canada	30	20
1199	60m. Russia v. Sweden	40	25
1200	70m. Canada v. Russia	50	30
1201	80m. Swedish goalkeeper	60	35
1202	1t. Czechoslovakia v. Russia	80	45

256 Lambs (Sanzhid)

1979. Agriculture Paintings. Multicoloured.

1203	10m. Type **256**	10	10
1204	30m. "Milking camels" (Budbazar)	30	15
1205	50m. "Aircraft bringing help" (Radnabazar)	50	20
1206	60m. "Herdsmen" (Budbazar)	60	25
1207	70m. "Milkmaids" "Nanzadsguren" (vert)	70	35
1208	80m. "Summer Evening" (Sanzhid)	1·00	45
1209	1t. "Country Landscape" (Tserendondog)	1·30	55
MS1210	86×70 mm. 4t. "After Rain" (Khaidav)	5·25	5·25

257 First Mongolian and Bulgarian Stamps

1979. Death Centenary of Sir Rowland Hill, and "Philaserdica 79" International Stamp Exhibition, Sofia. Each black, grey and brown.

1211	1t. Type **257**	2·10	1·20
1212	1t. American mail coach	2·10	1·20
1213	1t. Travelling post office, London–Birmingham railway	2·10	1·20
1214	1t. Paddle-steamer "Hindoostan"	2·10	1·20

258 Stephenson's "Rocket"

1979. Development of Railways. Multicoloured.

1215	10m. Type **258**	20	10
1216	20m. Locomotive "Adler", 1835, Germany	40	10
1217	30m. Steam locomotive, 1860, U.S.A.	60	15
1218	40m. Class KB4 steam locomotive, 1931, Mongolia	70	20

1219	50m. Class Er steam locomotive, 1936, Mongolia	80	25
1220	60m. Diesel train, 1970, Mongolia	90	35
1221	70m. "Hikari" express train, 1963, Japan	1·20	40
1222	80m. Monorail aerotrain "Orleans", France	1·30	55
1223	1t.20 Experimental jet train "Rapidity", Russia	1·40	70

259 Flags of Mongolia and Russia

1979. 40th Anniv of Battle of Khalka River.

1224	**259**	60m. gold, red and yellow	60	35
1225	-	60m. red, yellow and blue	60	35

DESIGN: No. 1225, Ribbons, badge and military scene.

260 Pallas's Cat

1979. Wild Cats. Multicoloured.

1226	10m. Type **260**	20	10
1227	30m. Lynx	50	20
1228	50m. Tiger	80	25
1229	60m. Snow leopard	90	30
1230	70m. Leopard	1·10	35
1231	80m. Cheetah	1·20	45
1232	1t. Lion	1·90	60

262 East German Flag, Berlin Buildings and "Soyuz 31"

1979. 30th Anniv of German Democratic Republic (East Germany).

1234	**262**	60m. multicoloured	60	25

263 Demoiselle Crane

1979. Air. Protected Birds. Multicoloured.

1235	10m. Type **263**	40	20
1236	30m. Barred warbler	60	20
1237	50m. Ruddy shelduck	80	25
1238	60m. Azure-winged magpie	1·00	30
1239	70m. Goldfinch	1·20	35
1240	80m. Great tit	1·40	40
1241	1t. Golden oriole	1·60	45

264 "Venus 5" and "6"

1979. Air. Space Research. Multicoloured.

1242	10m. Type **264**	10	10
1243	30m. "Mariner 5"	20	15
1244	50m. "Mars 3"	30	20
1245	60m. "Viking 1" and "2"	40	20
1246	70m. "Luna 1", "2" and "3"	50	25
1247	80m. "Lunokhod 2"	60	35
1248	1t. "Apollo 15" Moon-rover	70	40

MS1249	83×77 mm. 4t. Armstrong and Aldrin on Moon	2·50	2·20

265 Cross-country Skiing

1980. Winter Olympic Games, Lake Placid. Multicoloured.

1250	20m. Type **265**	10	10
1251	30m. Biathlon	20	15
1252	40m. Ice hockey	30	20
1253	50m. Ski jumping	40	20
1254	60m. Slalom	50	25
1255	80m. Speed skating	60	35
1256	1t.20 Four-man bobsleigh	70	45
MS1257	90×105 mm. 4t. Ice skating	2·50	2·50

266 "Andrena scita" (mining bee)

1980. Air. Wasps and Bees. Multicoloured.

1258	20m. Type **266**	20	10
1259	30m. "Paravespula germanica" (wasp)	30	20
1260	40m. "Perilampus ruficornis" (parasitic wasp)	40	25
1261	50m. Buff-tailed bumble bee	50	30
1262	60m. Honey bee	60	35
1263	80m. "Stilbum cyanurum" (cuckoo wasp)	80	45
1264	1t.20 "Parnopes grandior" (cuckoo wasp)	1·20	55

1980. "London 1980" International Stamp Exhibition. Sheet 95×64 mm.

MS1265	117 4t. multicoloured	2·50	2·50

267 Weightlifting

1980. Olympic Games, Moscow. Multicoloured.

1266	20m. Type **267**	10	10
1267	30m. Archery	20	15
1268	40m. Gymnastics	30	20
1269	50m. Running	40	20
1270	60m. Boxing	50	25
1271	80m. Judo	60	30
1272	1t.20 Cycling	70	45
MS1273	91×84 mm. 4t. Wrestling	2·50	2·50

268 Zlin Z-526 AFs Akrobat Special

1980. Air. World Acrobatic Championship, Oshkosh, Wisconsin. Multicoloured.

1274	20m. Type **268**	10	10
1275	30m. Socata RF-6B Sportsman (inscr "RS-180")	20	15
1276	40m. Grumman A-1 Yankee	30	20
1277	50m. MJ-2 Tempete	40	20
1278	60m. Pitts S-2A biplane (inscr "Pits")	50	25
1279	80m. Hirth Acrostar	60	35
1280	1t.20 Yakovlev Yak-50	90	45
MS1281	89×68 mm. 4t. Yakolev Yak-52 (49×42 mm)	3·00	3·00

269 Swimming

1980. Olympic Medal Winners. Multicoloured.

1282	20m. Type **269** (postage)		10	10
1283	30m. Fencing		20	15
1284	50m. Judo		30	20
1285	80m. Athletics		40	25
1286	80m. Boxing		50	30
1287	1t. Weightlifting		70	35
1288	1t.20 Kayak-canoe		90	45

MS1289 112×95 mm. 4t. Wrestling (silver medal, J. Davaazhav of Mongolia) (air)   2·50   2·50

270 Sukhe Bator

1980. Mongolian Politicians.

1290	**270**	60m. brown	30	20
1291	-	60m. blue	30	20
1292	-	60m. turquoise	30	20
1293	-	60m. bronze	30	20
1294	-	60m. green	30	20
1295	-	60m. red	30	20
1296	-	60m. brown	30	20

DESIGNS—VERT: No. 1291, Marshal Choibalsan; 1292, Yu. Tsedenbal aged 13; 1293, Tsedenbal as soldier, 1941; 1294, Pres. Tsedenbal in 1979; 1295, Tsedenbal with children. HORIZ: No. 1296, Tsedenbal and President Brezhnev of Russia.

See also **MS**1522.

271 Gubarev

1980. "Intercosmos" Space Programme. Multicoloured.

1297	40m. Type **271**	30	15
1298	40m. Czechoslovak stamp showing Gubarev and Remek	30	15
1299	40m. P. Klimuk	30	15
1300	40m. Polish stamp showing M. Hermaszewski	30	15
1301	40m. V. Bykovsky	30	15
1302	40m. East German stamp showing S. Jahn	30	15
1303	40m. N. Rukavishnikov	30	15
1304	40m. Bulgarian stamp showing G. Ivanov	30	15
1305	40m. V. Kubasov	30	15
1306	40m. Hungarian stamp showing Kubasov and B. Farkas	30	15

272 Benz, 1885

1980. Classic Cars. Multicoloured.

1307	20m. Type **272**	30	10
1308	30m. "President" Czechoslovakia, 1897	35	15
1309	40m. Armstrong Siddeley, 1904	50	20
1310	50m. Russo-Balt, 1909	60	25
1311	60m. Packard, 1909	70	35
1312	80m. Lancia, 1911	1·00	45
1313	1t.60 "Marne" taxi, 1914	2·30	80

MS1314 70×90 mm. 4t. "NAMI-1", Russia, 1927   6·25   6·25

273 Adelie Penguin

1980. Antarctic Exploration. Multicoloured.

1315	20m. Type **273**	80	20
1316	30m. Blue whales	1·20	25
1317	40m. Wandering albatross and Jacques Cousteau's ship "Calypso" and bathysphere	1·50	35
1318	50m. Weddell seals and mobile research station	1·90	40
1319	60m. Emperor penguins	2·30	45
1320	70m. Great skuas	2·50	60
1321	80m. Killer whales	3·00	70
1322	1t.20 Adelie penguins, research station, Ilyushin Il-18B airplane and tracked vehicle	4·00	1·10

MS1323 90×120 mm. 4t. Map of Antarctica during carbon age (*circular*, 43 mm diameter)   10·50   9·00

274 Kepler

1980. Air. 350th Death Anniv of Johannes Kepler (astronomer). Sheet 98×78 mm.

MS1324 **274** 4t. black and yellow   2·50   2·50

275 "Yurta Picture"

1980. 50th Anniv of Gombosuren (painter). Sheet 80×98 mm containing T **275** and similar horiz design. Multicoloured.

MS1325 2t. Type **275**; 2t. "Old-time Market"   2·50   2·50

276 "The Shepherd speaking the Truth"

1980. Nursery Tales. Multicoloured.

1326	20m. Type **276**	10	10
1327	30m. Children under umbrella and rainbow ("Above them the Sky is always clear")	20	15
1328	40m. Children on sledge and skis ("Winter's Joys")	30	20
1329	50m. Girl watching boy playing flute ("Little Musicians")	40	25
1330	60m. Boys giving girl leaves ("Happy Birthday")	50	30
1331	80m. Children with flowers and briefcase ("First Schoolday")	60	35
1332	1t.20 Girls dancing ("May Day")	70	45

MS1333 79×89 mm. Children and squirrels ("The Wonder-working Squirrels")   2·50   2·50

277 Soldier

1981. 60th Anniv of Mongolian People's Army.

1334	**277**	60m. multicoloured	60	25

278 Economy Emblems within Party Initials

1981. 60th Anniv of Mongolian Revolutionary People's Party.

1335	**278**	60m. gold, red and black	60	25

279 Motocross

1981. Motor Cycle Sports. Multicoloured.

1336	10m. Type **279**	10	10
1337	20m. Tour racing	20	10
1338	30m. Ice racing	30	10
1339	40m. Road racing	35	10
1340	50m. Motocross (different)	40	15
1341	60m. Road racing (different)	45	15
1342	70m. Speedway	50	15
1343	80m. Sidecar racing	60	20
1344	1t.20 Road racing (different)	65	25

280 Cosmonauts entering Space Capsule

1981. Soviet–Mongolian Space Flight. Multicoloured.

1345	20m. Type **280**	20	10
1346	30m. Rocket and designer S. P. Korolev	30	15
1347	40m. "Vostok 1" and Yuri Gagarin	35	20
1348	50m. "Soyuz"–"Salyut" space station	40	30
1349	60m. Spectral photography	45	35
1350	80m. Crystal and space station	60	40
1351	1t.20 Space complex, Moscow Kremlin and Sukhe Bator statue, Ulan Bator	80	55

MS1352 70×80 mm. 4t. Cosmonauts Dzhanibekov and Gurragchaa (31×42 mm)   2·50   2·50

281 Ulan Bator Buildings and 1961 Mongolian Stamp

1981. Stamp Exhibitions.

1353	**281**	1t. multicoloured	3·00	1·10
1354	-	1t. multicoloured	3·00	1·10
1355	-	1t. black, blue and magenta	3·00	1·10
1356	-	1t. multicoloured	3·00	1·10

DESIGNS: No. 1353, Type **281** (Mongolian stamp exhibition); 1354, Wurttemberg stamps of 1947 and 1949 and view of Old Stuttgart ("Naposta '81" exhibition); 1355, Parliament building and sculpture, Vienna, and Austrian stamp of 1933 ("WIPA 1981" exhibition); 1356, Japanese stamp of 1964, cherry blossom and girls in Japanese costume ("Japex '81" exhibition, Tokyo).

282 Star and Industrial and Agricultural Scenes

1981. 18th Mongolian Revolutionary People's Party Congress.

1357	**282**	60m. multicoloured	50	25

283 Sukhe Bator Statue, Ulan Bator

1981. 60th Anniv of Mongolian Revolutionary People's Party (2nd issue). Sheet 70×90 mm.

MS1358 **283** 4t. multicoloured   2·50   2·50

284 Sheep Farming

1981. "Results of the People's Economy". Multicoloured.

1359	20m. Type **284**	20	10
1360	30m. Transport	30	15
1361	40m. Telecommunications	40	20
1362	50m. Public health service	50	25
1363	60m. Agriculture	60	30
1364	80m. Electrical industry	80	35
1365	1t.20 Housing	1·20	55

285 UN Emblem

1981. 20th Anniv of United Nations Membership. Sheet 70×90 mm.

MS1366 **285** 4t. multicoloured   2·50   2·50

286 Pharaonic Ship (15th century B.C.)

1981. Sailing Ships. Multicoloured.

1367	10m. Type **286**	20	10
1368	20m. Mediterranean sailing ship (9th century)	30	15
1369	40m. Hanse kogge (12th century) (vert)	40	25
1370	50m. Venetian felucca (13th century) (vert)	60	30
1371	60m. Columbus's "Santa Maria" (vert)	70	35
1372	80m. Cook's H.M.S. "Endeavour" (vert)	80	40
1373	1t. "Poltava" (Russian ship of the line) (vert)	1·00	45
1374	1t.20 American schooner (19th century) (vert)	1·20	55

287 Arms of Mongolia and Russia

1981. Soviet–Mongolian Friendship Pact.

1375	**287**	60m. red, blue and gold	60	25

288 "Hendrickje in Bed"

1981. 375th Birth Anniv of Rembrandt (artist). Multicoloured.

1376	20m. "Flora"	20	10
1377	30m. Type **288**	30	20
1378	40m. "Young Woman with Earrings"	50	25
1379	50m. "Young girl in the Window"	60	35
1380	60m. "Hendrickje like Flora"	80	40
1381	80m. "Saskia with Red Flower"	1·10	45
1382	1t.20 "The Holy Family with Drape" (detail)	1·50	55
MS1383	68×85 mm. 4t. "Self-portrait with Saskia"	5·25	5·25

289 Billy Goat (pawn)

1981. Mongolian Chess Pieces. Multicoloured.

1384	20m. Type **289**	30	10
1385	40m. Horse-drawn cart (rook)	60	20
1386	50m. Camel (bishop)	70	25
1387	60m. Horse (knight)	80	35
1388	80m. Lion (queen)	1·10	45
1389	1t.20 Man with dog (king)	1·50	70
MS1390	90×70 mm. 4t. Chess game (illustration of Mongolian folk tale)	5·25	5·25

290 White-tailed Sea Eagle and German 1m. "Zeppelin" Stamp

1981. Air. 50th Anniv of "Graf Zeppelin" Polar Flight. Multicoloured.

1391	20m. Type **290**	40	20
1392	30m. Arctic fox and German 2m. "Zeppelin" stamp	50	20
1393	40m. Walrus and German 4m. "Zeppelin" stamp	60	25
1394	50m. Polar bear and Russian 30k. "Zeppelin" stamp	70	30
1395	60m. Snowy owl and Russian 35k. "Zeppelin" stamp	1·10	35
1396	80m. Atlantic puffin and Russian 1r. "Zeppelin" stamp	1·30	55
1397	1t.20 Northern sealion and Russian 2r. "Zeppelin" stamp	1·50	60
MS1398	93×77 mm. 4t. *Graf Zeppelin* and Russian ice-breaker *Malygin* (36×51 mm)	5·25	5·25

291 Circus Camel and Circus Building, Ulan Bator

1981. Mongolian Sport and Art. Multicoloured.

1399	10m. Type **291**	10	10
1400	20m. Horsemen and stadium (National holiday cavalcade)	20	20
1401	40m. Wrestling and Ulan Bator stadium	40	25
1402	50m. Archers and stadium	50	30
1403	60m. Folk singer-dancer and House of Culture	60	35
1404	80m. Girl playing jatga (folk instrument) and Ulan Bator Drama Theatre	80	40
1405	1t. Ballet dancers and Opera House	1·10	55
1406	1t.20 Exhibition Hall and statue of man on bucking horse	1·30	60

292 Mozart and scene from "The Magic Flute"

1981. Composers. Multicoloured.

1407	20m. Type **292**	30	10
1408	30m. Beethoven and scene from "Fidelio"	35	15
1409	40m. Bartok and scene from "The Miraculous Mandarin"	40	20
1410	50m. Verdi and scene from "Aida"	50	25
1411	60m. Tchaikovsky and scene from "The Sleeping Beauty"	60	30
1412	80m. Dvorak and score of "New World" symphony	80	35
1413	1t.20 Chopin, piano, score and quill pens	1·20	55

293 "Mongolian Women in Everyday Life" (detail, Davaakhuu)

1981. International Decade for Women. Multicoloured

1414	20m. Type **293**	30	10
1415	30m. "Mongolian Women in Everyday Life" (different detail)	40	20
1416	40m. "National Day" (detail, Khishigbaiar)	50	25
1417	50m. "National Day" (detail) (different)	60	30
1418	60m. "National Day" (detail) (different)	70	45
1419	80m. "Ribbon Weaver" (Ts. Baidi)	1·00	55
1420	1t.20 "Expectant Mother" (Senghesokhio)	1·50	90

294 Gorbatko

1981. "Intercosmos" Space Programme. Multicoloured.

1422	50m. Type **294**	40	20
1423	50m. Vietnam stamp showing Gorbatko and Pham Tuan	40	20
1424	50m. Romanenko	40	20
1425	50m. Cuban stamp showing Tamayo	40	20
1426	50m. Dzhanibekov	40	20
1427	50m. Mongolian stamp showing Dzhanibekov and Gurrugchaa	40	20
1428	50m. Popov	40	20
1429	50m. Rumanian stamp showing "Salyut" space station and "Soyuz" space ship	40	20

295 Karl von Drais Bicycle, 1816

1982. History of the Bicycle. Multicoloured.

1430	10m. Type **295**	10	10
1431	20m. Macmillan bicycle, 1838	20	10
1432	40m. First American pedal bicycle by Pierre Lallament, 1866	30	15
1433	50m. First European pedal bicycle by Ernest Michaux	40	20
1434	60m. "Kangaroo" bicycle, 1877	50	25
1435	80m. Coventry Rotary Tandem, 1870s	60	30
1436	1t. Chain-driven bicycle, 1878	70	35
1437	1t.20 Modern bicycle	80	40
MS1438	95×90 mm. 4t. Modern road racers (43×43 mm)	3·00	3·00

296 Footballers (Brazil, 1950)

1982. World Cup Football Championship, Spain. Multicoloured.

1439	10m. Type **296** (postage)	10	10
1440	20m. Switzerland, 1954	20	10
1441	40m. Sweden, 1958	30	15
1442	50m. Chile, 1962	40	20
1443	60m. England, 1966	50	25
1444	80m. Mexico, 1970	60	30
1445	1t. West Germany, 1974	70	35
1446	1t.20 Argentina, 1978	80	40
MS1447	90×70 mm. 4t. Spain, 1982 (44×44 mm) (air)	3·00	3·00

297 Trade Union Emblem and Economic Symbols

1982. 12th Mongolian Trade Unions Congress.

1448	**297** 60m. multicoloured	1·50	45

298 Children with Deer

1982. "Philefrance 82" International Stamp Exhibition, Paris. Sheet 105×68 mm.

MS1449	**298** 4t. multicoloured	3·00	3·00

For 50m.+5m. as Type **298** but larger, see No. 1176.

299 Dimitrov

1982. Birth Centenary of Georgi Dimitrov (Bulgarian statesman).

1450	**299** 60m. black, grey and gold	60	25

300 Chicks

1982. Young Animals. Multicoloured.

1451	10m. Type **300**	10	10
1452	20m. Colt	20	10
1453	30m. Lamb	20	10
1454	40m. Roe deer fawn	30	10
1455	50m. Bactrian camel	40	15
1456	60m. Kid	50	20
1457	70m. Calf	60	20
1458	1t.20 Wild piglet	70	25

301 Coal-fired Industry

1982. Coal Mining.

1459	**301** 60m. multicoloured	60	25

302 Emblem

1982. 18th Revsomol Youth Congress.

1460	**302** 60m. multicoloured	60	25

303 Siberian Pine

1982. Trees. Multicoloured.

1461	20m. Type **303**	10	10
1462	30m. Siberian fir	20	10
1463	40m. Poplar	30	15
1464	50m. Siberian larch	40	20
1465	60m. Scots pine	50	25
1466	80m. Birch	60	30
1467	1t.20 Spruce	90	35

304 Revsomol Emblem within "Flower"

1982. 60th Anniv of Revsomol Youth Organization.

1468	**304** 60m. multicoloured	60	25

305 World Map and Satellite

1982. Air. I.T.U. Delegates' Conference, Nairobi.

1469	**305** 60m. multicoloured	70	35

306 Japanese "Iseki-6500" Tractor

1982. Tractors. Multicoloured.

1470	10m. Type **306**	10	10
1471	20m. West German "Deutz-DX230"	20	10
1472	40m. British "Bonser"	30	10
1473	50m. American "Interna-tional-884"	40	20
1474	60m. French Renault "TX 145-14"	50	20
1475	80m. Russian "Belarus-611"	60	25
1476	1t. Russian "K-7100"	70	30
1477	1t.20 Russian "DT-75"	80	35

307 Hump-backed Whitefish and
Lake Hevsgel

1982. Landscapes and Animals. Multicoloured.
1478	20m. Type **307**	20	10
1479	30m. Zavkhan Highlands and sheep	25	15
1480	40m. Lake Hovd and Eurasian beaver	30	20
1481	50m. Lake Uvs and horses	40	30
1482	60m. Bajankhongor Steppe and goitred gazelle	50	35
1483	80m. Bajan-Elgii Highlands and rider with golden eagle	3·00	40
1484	1t.20 Gobi Desert and bactrian camels	1·50	45

308 "Sputnik 1"

1982. Air. Second U.N. Conference on the Exploration and Peaceful Uses of Outer Space. Multicoloured.
1485	60m. Type **308**	40	20
1486	60m. "Sputnik 2" and Laika (first dog in space)	40	20
1487	60m. "Vostok 1" and Yuri Gagarin (first man in space)	40	20
1488	60m. "Venera 8"	40	20
1489	60m. "Vostok 6" and V. Tereshkova (first woman in space)	40	20
1490	60m. Aleksei Leonov and space walker	40	20
1491	60m. Neil Armstrong and astronaut on Moon's surface	40	20
1492	60m. V. Dzhanibekov, Jean-Loup Chretien and "Soyuz T-6"	40	20
MS1493	88×70 mm. 4t. "Soyuz" and "Salyut" coupling (49×33 mm)	3·00	3·00

309 Montgolfier
Brothers' Balloon, 1783

1982. Air. Bicentenary of Manned Flight. Multicoloured.
1494	20m. Type **309**	10	10
1495	30m. Jean-Pierre Blanchard and John Jeffries crossing the channel, 1785	20	10
1496	40m. Charles Green's flight to Germany in balloon "Royal Vauxhall", 1836	30	15
1497	50m. Salomon Andree's North Pole flight in balloon "Ornen", 1897	40	20
1498	60m. First Gordon Bennett balloon race, Paris, 1906	50	25
1499	80m. First stratosphere flight by Auguste Piccard in balloon "F.N.R.S.", Switzerland, 1931	60	30
1500	1t.20 Stratosphere balloon USSR-VR-62 flight, 1933	1·00	35
MS1501	78×98 mm. 4t. First Mongolian balloon flight, 1977	3·00	3·00

310 Sorcerer tells Mickey Mouse
to clean up Quarters

1983. Drawings from "The Sorcerer's Apprentice" (section of Walt Disney's film "Fantasia"). Multicoloured
1502	25m. Type **310**	20	10
1503	35m. Mickey notices Sorcerer has left his cap behind	30	20
1504	45m. Mickey puts cap on and commands broom to fetch water	40	25

1505	55m. Broom carrying water	50	30
1506	65m. Mickey sleeps while broom continues to fetch water, flooding the room	60	35
1507	75m. Mickey uses axe on broom to try to stop it	70	45
1508	85m. Each splinter becomes a broom which continues to fetch water	90	50
1509	1t.40 Mickey, clinging to Sorcerer's Book of Spells, caught in whirlpool	1·40	60
1510	2t. Mickey handing cap back to Sorcerer	2·10	90
MS1511	127×102 mm. 7t. Mickey dreaming himself to be Master of the Universe	7·75	6·75

311 Foal with Mother

1983. "The Foal and the Hare" (folk tale). Multicoloured
1512	10m. Type **311**	10	10
1513	20m. Foal wanders off alone	20	15
1514	30m. Foal finds sack	30	20
1515	40m. Foal unties sack	40	25
1516	50m. Wolf jumps out of sack	50	30
1517	60m. Hare appears as wolf is about to eat foal	60	35
1518	70m. Hare tricks wolf into re-entering sack	80	40
1519	80m. Hare ties up sack with wolf inside	90	45
1520	1t.20 Hare and foal look for foal's mother	1·20	55
MS1521	121×94 mm. 7t. Boy with foal (58×58 mm). Imperf	7·75	6·75

311a Tank Monument, Ulan Bator

1983. Air. 40th Anniv of Formation of "Revolutionary Mongolia" Tank Regiment of Soviet Army. Sheet 110×75 mm.
MS1522	311a 4t. multicoloured	3·00	3·00

1983. 90th Birth Anniv of Sukhe Bator. Sheet 65×72 mm containing designs as T **270** but smaller, 25×32 mm.
MS1523	270 4t. purple	3·00	3·00

312 Antonov An-24B Aircraft

1983. Tourism. Multicoloured.
1524	20m. Type **312**	20	10
1525	30m. Skin tent	30	15
1526	40m. Roe deer	40	20
1527	50m. Argali	50	25
1528	60m. Imperial eagle	2·10	45
1529	80m. Khan Museum, Ulan Bator	90	35
1530	1t.20 Sukhe Bator statue, Ulan Bator	1·20	45

313 Rose

1983. Flowers. Multicoloured.
1531	20m. Type **313**	20	10
1532	30m. Dahlia	25	10
1533	40m. Marigold	30	15
1534	50m. Narcissus	40	20
1535	60m. Viola	50	25
1536	80m. Tulip	60	30
1537	1t.20 Sunflower	70	35

314 Border Guard

1983. 50th Anniv of Border Guards.
1538	**314** 60m. multicoloured	60	25

315 Boy riding Buffalo (image scaled to 38% of original size)

1983. "Brasiliana 83" International Stamp Exhibition, Rio de Janeiro. Sheet 135×88 mm.
MS1539	**325** 4t. multicoloured	2·50	2·50

316 Karl Marx

1983. Death Centenary of Karl Marx.
1540	**316** 60m. red, gold and blue	60	25

317 Agriculture

1983. 18th Communist Party Congress Five Year Plan. Multicoloured.
1541	10m. Type **317**	15	10
1542	20m. Power industry	20	15
1543	30m. Textile industry	30	20
1544	40m. Science in industry and agriculture	40	25
1545	60m. Improvement of living standards	60	30
1546	80m. Communications	2·50	55
1547	1t. Children (education)	1·00	45

318 Young Inventors

1983. Children's Year. Multicoloured.
1548	10m. Type **318**	20	10
1549	20m. In school	30	15
1550	30m. Archery	40	20
1551	40m. Shepherdess playing flute	70	25
1552	50m. Girl with deer	1·00	35
1553	70m. Collecting rocks and mushrooms	2·75	55
1554	1t.20 Girl playing lute and boy singing	1·90	70

319 Skating

1555	20m. Type **319**	20	10

320 Pallas's Pika

1983. Tenth Anniv of Children's Fund. Multicoloured
1555	20m. Type **319**	20	10
1556	30m. Shepherds	30	15
1557	40m. Tree-planting	40	20
1558	50m. Playing by the sea	45	25
1559	60m. Carrying water	50	30
1560	80m. Folk dancing	60	35
1561	1t.20 Ballet	1·00	40
MS1562	93×110 mm. 4t. Christmas	3·00	3·00

1983. Small Mammals. Multicoloured.
1563	20m. Type **320**	40	15
1564	30m. Long-eared jerboa	60	25
1565	40m. Eurasian red squirrel	80	35
1566	50m. Daurian hedgehog	1·00	45
1567	60m. Harvest mouse	1·20	50
1568	80m. Eurasian water shrew	1·60	75
1569	1t.20 Siberian chipmunk	2·10	1·10

321 "Sistine Madonna"

1983. 500th Birth Anniv of Raphael (artist). Sheet 102×138 mm.
MS1570	**321** 4t. multicoloured	5·25	5·25

322 Bobsleighing

1984. Winter Olympic Games, Sarajevo. Multicoloured
1571	20m. Type **322**	15	10
1572	30m. Cross-country skiing	20	10
1573	40m. Ice hockey	25	15
1574	50m. Speed skating	30	20
1575	60m. Ski jumping	40	25
1576	80m. Ice dancing	50	30
1577	1t.20 Biathlon (horiz)	60	35
MS1578	133×105 mm. 4t. Ski jumping (horiz)	2·50	2·50

323 Mail Van

1984. World Communications Year. Multicoloured.
1579	10m. Type **323**	20	10
1580	20m. Earth receiving station	30	15
1581	40m. Airliner	40	25
1582	50m. Central Post Office, Ulan Bator	50	35
1583	1t. Transmitter	1·10	45
1584	1t.20 Diesel train	3·50	1·30
MS1585	90×110 mm. 4t. Aerials (41×22 mm)	3·00	3·00

324 "Ausipex 84" Emblem and Tupolev Tu-154

1984. "Espana 84", Madrid and "Ausipex 84", Melbourne, International Stamp Exhibitions. Sheet 104×90 mm.
MS1586	**324** 4t. multicoloured	4·00	4·00

325 Cycling

1984. Olympic Games, Los Angeles. Multicoloured.

1587	20m. Gymnastics (horiz)		15	10
1588	30m. Type **325**		20	10
1589	40m. Weightlifting		30	15
1590	50m. Judo		35	20
1591	60m. Archery		40	25
1592	80m. Boxing		45	30
1593	1t.20 High jumping (horiz)		50	35
MS1594 105×85 mm. 4t. Wrestling (horiz)			2·50	2·50

326 Flag, Rocket and Coastal Scene

1984. 25th Anniv of Cuban Revolution.

1595	**326**	60m. multicoloured	60	25

327 1924 1c. Stamp

1984. 60th Anniv of Mongolian Stamps. Sheet 90×110 mm.

MS1596	**327**	4t. multicoloured	3·00	3·00

328 Douglas DC-10

1984. Air. Civil Aviation. Multicoloured.

1597	20m. Type **328**		20	10
1598	30m. Airbus Industrie A300B2		30	15
1599	40m. Concorde supersonic jetliner		40	25
1600	50m. Boeing 747-200		50	35
1601	60m. Ilyushin Il-62M		60	40
1602	80m. Tupolev Tu-154		80	45
1603	1t.20 Ilyushin Il-86		1·20	50
MS1604 110×90 mm. 4t. Yakovlev Yak-42			4·00	4·00

329 Speaker, Radio and Transmitter

1984. 50th Anniv of Mongolian Broadcasting.

1605	**329**	60m. multicoloured	80	35

330 Silver and Gold Coins

1984. 60th Anniv of State Bank.

1606	**330**	60m. multicoloured	50	25

331 Donshy Mask

1984. Traditional Masks. Multicoloured.

1607	20m. Type **331**		30	10
1608	30m. Zamandi		40	15
1609	40m. Ulaan-Yadam		50	25
1610	50m. Lkham		60	35
1611	60m. Damdinchoizhoo		70	40
1612	80m. Ochirvaan		90	45
1613	1t.40 Namsrai		1·40	45
MS1614 90×110 mm. 4t. Ulaanzham-sran			5·25	5·25

332 Golden Harp

1984. Scenes from Walt Disney's "Mickey and the Beanstalk" (cartoon film). Multicoloured.

1615	25m. Type **332**		30	10
1616	35m. Mickey holding box of magic beans		40	15
1617	45m. Mickey about to eat bean		60	25
1618	55m. Mickey looking for magic bean		70	30
1619	65m. Goofy, Mickey and Donald at top of beanstalk		80	35
1620	75m. Giant holding Mickey		1·00	45
1621	85m. Giant threatening Mickey		1·10	50
1622	140m. Goofy, Mickey and Donald cutting down beanstalk		1·60	70
1623	2t. Goofy and Donald rescuing golden harp		2·50	85
MS1624 126×101 mm. 7t. Mickey, Goofy, Donald and giant plants (50×37 mm)			8·75	7·25

333 Sukhe Bator Statue

1984. 60th Anniv of Ulan Bator City.

1625	**333**	60m. multicoloured	80	35

334 Arms, Flag and Landscape

1984. 60th Anniv of Mongolian People's Republic.

1626	**334**	60m. multicoloured	80	35

335 Rider carrying Flag

1984. 60th Anniv of Mongolian People's Revolutionary Party.

1627	**335**	60m. multicoloured	60	25

336 Collie

1984. Dogs. Multicoloured.

1628	20m. Type **336**		20	10
1629	30m. German shepherd		30	15
1630	40m. Papillon		40	25
1631	50m. Cocker spaniel		55	30
1632	60m. Terrier puppy (diamond-shaped)		65	35
1633	80m. Dalmatians (diamond-shaped)		80	40
1634	1t.20 Mongolian shepherd		1·30	50

337 Gaetan Boucher (speed skating)

1984. Winter Olympic Gold Medal Winners. Multicoloured.

1635	20m. Type **337**		20	10
1636	30m. Eirik Kvalfoss (biathlon)		30	15
1637	40m. Marja-Liisa Hamalainen (cross-country skiing)		40	25
1638	50m. Max Julen (slalom)		50	35
1639	60m. Jens Weissflog (ski jumping) (vert)		60	40
1640	80m. W. Hoppe and D. Schauerhammer (two-man bobsleigh) (vert)		70	45
1641	1t.20 J. Valova and O. Vassiliev (pairs figure skating) (vert)		80	50
MS1642 110×90 mm. 4t. Russia (ice hockey)			3·00	3·00

338 Four Animals and Tree

1984. "The Four Friendly Animals" (fairy tale). Multicoloured.

1643	10m. Type **338**		10	10
1644	20m. Animals discussing who was the oldest		25	10
1645	30m. Monkey and elephant beside tree		30	15
1646	40m. Elephant as calf and young tree		40	20
1647	50m. Monkey and young tree		50	25
1648	60m. Hare and young tree		60	30
1649	70m. Dove and sapling		70	35
1650	80m. Animals around mature tree		90	45
1651	1t.20 Animals supporting each other so that dove could reach fruit		1·30	60
MS1652 103×84 mm. 4t. Dove passing fruit to other animals (vert)			5·75	5·75

339 Fawn

1984. Red Deer. Multicoloured.

1653	50m. Type **339**		60	35

1654	50m. Stag		60	35
1655	50m. Adults and fawn by river		60	35
1656	50m. Doe in woodland		60	35

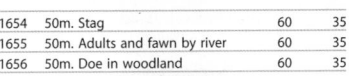

340 Flag and Pioneers

1985. 60th Anniv of Mongolian Pioneer Organization.

1657	**340**	60m. multicoloured	60	25

341 Shar Tarlan

1985. Cattle. Multicoloured.

1658	20m. Type **341**		20	10
1659	30m. Bor khalium		40	15
1660	40m. Sarlag		50	20
1661	50m. Dornod talin bukh		60	25
1662	60m. Char tarlan		70	30
1663	80m. Nutgiin uulderiin unee		80	35
1664	1t.20 Tsagaan tolgoit		1·00	35
MS1665 90×110 mm. 4t. Girl with calf (vert)			5·25	5·25

342 Black Stork

1985. Birds. Multicoloured.

1666	20m. Type **342**		20	10
1667	30m. White-tailed sea eagle		30	15
1668	40m. Great white crane		50	25
1669	50m. Heude's parrotbill		60	30
1670	60m. Hooded crane		80	35
1671	80m. Japanese white-naped crane		1·00	45
1672	1t.20 Rough-legged buzzard		1·60	50
MS1673 125×70 mm. 4t. Brandt's cormorant (*Phalacrocorax penicillatus*) (47×39 mm)			6·25	6·25

343 Footballers

1985. World Junior Football Championship, U.S.S.R.

1674	**343**	20m. multicoloured	10	10
1675	-	30m. multicoloured	15	10
1676	-	40m. multicoloured	20	10
1677	-	50m. multicoloured	30	15
1678	-	60m. multicoloured	40	15
1679	-	80m. multicoloured	50	20
1680	-	1t.20 multicoloured	60	25
MS1681 110×90 mm. 4t. multicoloured (horiz)			2·50	2·50

DESIGNS: 30m. to 4t., Different footballing scenes.

344 Monument

1985. 40th Anniv of Victory in Europe.

1682	**344**	60m. multicoloured	60	25

345 Snow Leopards

1985. The Snow Leopard. Multicoloured.

1683	50m. Type **345**	60	35
1684	50m. Leopard	60	35
1685	50m. Leopard on cliff ledge	60	35
1686	50m. Mother and cubs	60	35

346 Moscow Kremlin and Girls of Different Races

1985. 12th World Youth and Students' Festival, Moscow.

1687	**346**	60m. multicoloured	60	25

347 Monument

1985. 40th Anniv of Victory in Asia.

1688	**347**	60m. multicoloured	70	30

348 "Rosa dahurica"

1985. Plants. Multicoloured.

1689	20m. Type **348**	20	10
1690	30m. False chamomile	30	15
1691	40m. Dandelion	50	20
1692	50m. "Saxzitraga nirculus"	60	25
1693	60m. Cowberry	70	30
1694	80m. "Sanguisorba officinalis"	90	35
1695	1t.20 "Plantago major"	1·30	45
MS1696	90×110 mm. 4t. Sea buckthorn (*Hippophae rhamnoides*) (wrongly inscr "Hippopae thamnoides")	5·25	5·25

See also Nos. 1719/25.

349 Camel

1985. The Bactrian Camel. Multicoloured.

1697	50m. Type **349**	1·20	50
1698	50m. Adults and calf	1·20	50
1699	50m. Calf	1·20	50
1700	50m. Adult	1·20	50

350 "Soyuz" Spacecraft

1985. Space. Multicoloured.

1701	20m. Type **350**	10	10
1702	30m. "Kosmos" satellite	20	10
1703	40m. "Venera-9" satellite	30	15
1704	50m. "Salyut" space station	40	20
1705	60m. "Luna-9" landing vehicle	50	25

1706	80m. "Soyuz" rocket on transporter	1·50	60
1707	1t.20 Dish aerial receiving transmission from "Soyuz"	1·00	25
MS1708	110×90 mm. 4t. Cosmonauts on space walk	2·50	2·50

351 Horseman

1985. "Italia '85" International Stamp Exhibition, Rome. Sheet 110×90 mm.

MS1709	**351**	4t. multicoloured	2·50	2·50

352 U.N. and Mongolian Flags and U.N. Headquarters, New York

1985. 40th Anniv of U.N.O.

1710	**352**	60m. multicoloured	60	25

353 "Tricholoma mongolica"

1985. Fungi. Multicoloured.

1711	20m. Type **353**	30	10
1712	30m. Chanterelle	50	15
1713	40m. Honey fungus	60	20
1714	50m. Caesar's mushroom	70	25
1715	70m. Chestnut mushroom	90	35
1716	80m. Red-staining mushroom	1·20	40
1717	1t.20 Cep	1·90	45

354 Congress Emblem

1986. 19th Mongolian Revolutionary People's Party Congress.

1718	**354**	60m. multicoloured	60	25

1986. Plants. As T **348**. Multicoloured.

1719	20m. "Valeriana officinalis"	30	10
1720	30m. "Hyoscymus niger"	40	10
1721	40m. "Ephedra sinica"	50	15
1722	50m. "Thymus gobica"	60	20
1723	60m. "Paeonia anomalia"	80	25
1724	80m. "Achilea millefolium"	1·00	35
1725	1t.20 "Rhododendron adamsii"	1·40	45

355 Scene from Play

1986. 80th Birth Anniv of D. Natsagdorj (writer).

1726	**355**	60m. multicoloured	70	30

356 Thalmann

1986. Birth Centenary of Ernst Thalmann (German politician).

1727	**356**	60m. multicoloured	60	25

357 Man wearing Patterned Robe

1986. Costumes. Multicoloured.

1728	60m. Type **357**	50	15
1729	60m. Man in blue robe and fur-lined hat with ear flaps	50	15
1730	60m. Woman in black and yellow dress and bolero	50	15
1731	60m. Woman in pink dress patterned with stars	50	15
1732	60m. Man in cream robe with fur cuffs	50	15
1733	60m. Man in brown robe and mauve and yellow tunic	50	15
1734	60m. Woman in blue dress with black, yellow and red overtunic	50	15

358 Footballers

1986. World Cup Football Championship, Mexico.

1735	**358**	20m. multicoloured	15	10
1736	-	30m. multicoloured	20	15
1737	-	40m. multicoloured	30	15
1738	-	50m. multicoloured	40	20
1739	-	60m. multicoloured	50	25
1740	-	80m. multicoloured	60	25
1741	-	1t.20 multicoloured	1·00	35
MS1742	110×90 mm. 4t. multicoloured (horiz)		4·00	4·00

DESIGNS: 30m. to 4t., Different footballing scenes.

359 Mink

1986. Mink. Multicoloured.

1743	60m. Type **359**	60	25
1744	60m. Mink on rock	60	25
1745	60m. Mink on snow-covered branch	60	25
1746	60m. Two mink	60	25

See also Nos. 1771/4, 1800/3, 1804/7, 1840/3 and 1844/7.

360 "Neptis coenobita"

1986. Butterflies and Moths. Multicoloured.

1747	20m. Type **360**	20	10
1748	30m. "Colias tycha"	30	15
1749	40m. "Leptidea amurensis"	40	20
1750	50m. "Oeneis tarpenledevi"	50	25

1751	60m. "Mesoacidalia charlotta"	60	30
1752	80m. Eyed hawk moth	80	35
1753	1t.20 Large tiger moth	1·20	45

361 Sukhe Bator Statue

1986. 65th Anniv of Independence.

1754	**361**	60m. multicoloured	60	25

362 Yak and Goats Act

1986. Circus. Multicoloured.

1755	20m. Type **362**	20	10
1756	30m. Acrobat	30	10
1757	40m. Yak act	40	15
1758	50m. Acrobats (vert)	50	20
1759	60m. High wire act (vert)	60	25
1760	80m. Fire juggler on camel (vert)	70	30
1761	1t.20 Acrobats on camel-drawn cart (vert)	1·10	35

363 Morin Khuur

1986. Musical Instruments. Multicoloured.

1762	20m. Type **363**	20	10
1763	30m. Bishguur (wind instrument)	30	15
1764	40m. Ever buree (wind)	50	20
1765	50m. Shudarga (string)	60	25
1766	60m. Khiil (string)	70	30
1767	80m. Janchir (string) (horiz)	90	35
1768	1t.20 Jatga (string) (horiz)	1·30	40

364 Flag and Emblem

1986. International Peace Year.

1770	**364**	10m. multicoloured	70	30

1986. Przewalski's Horse. As T **359**. Mult.

1771	50m. Horses grazing on sparsely grassed plain	70	25
1772	50m. Horses grazing on grassy plain	70	25
1773	50m. Adults with foal	70	25
1774	50m. Horses in snow	70	25

365 Temple

1986. Ancient Buildings. Multicoloured.

1775	60m. Type **365**	90	45
1776	60m. Temple with light green roof and white doors	90	45
1777	60m. Temple with porch	90	45
1778	60m. White building with three porches	90	45

366 Redhead ("Aythya americana")

1986. Birds. Multicoloured.

1779	60m. Type **366**	1·00	35
1780	60m. Ruffed grouse ("Bonasa umbellus")	1·00	35
1781	60m. Tundra swan ("Olor columbianus")	1·00	35
1782	60m. Water pipit ("Anthus spinoletta")	1·00	35

367 Alfa Romeo "RL Sport", 1922

1986. Cars. Multicoloured.

1783	20m. Type **367**	10	10
1784	30m. Stutz "Bearcat", 1912	20	10
1785	40m. Mercedes "Simplex", 1902	30	15
1786	50m. Tatra "11", 1923	40	20
1787	60m. Ford Model "T", 1908	50	25
1788	80m. Vauxhall, 1905	70	35
1789	1t.20 Russo-Balt "K", 1913	1·00	45
MS1790	110×90 mm. 4t. As No. 1789	3·00	3·00

368 Wilhelm Steinitz and Curt von Bardeleben Game, 1895

1986. World Chess Champions. Multicoloured.

1791	20m. Type **368**	20	10
1792	30m. Emanuel Lasker and Harry Pilsberi game, 1895	25	10
1793	40m. Alexander Alekhine and Richard Retti game, 1925	30	15
1794	50m. Mikhail Botvinnik and Capablanca game, 1938	40	20
1795	60m. Anatoly Karpov and Wolfgang Untsiker game, 1975	50	25
1796	80m. Nona Gaprindashvili and Lasarevich game, 1961	60	30
1797	1t.20 Maia Chirburdanidze and Irina Levitina game, 1984	1·00	35
MS1798	110×100 mm. 4t. Players around International Chess Federation emblem	4·00	4·00

369 "Vega 2" Spacecraft and Comet

1986. Appearance of Halley's Comet. Sheet 110×90 mm.

MS1799	**369** 4t. multicoloured	2·50	2·50

1986. Saiga Antelope. As T 359. Multicoloured.

1800	60m. Male	70	25
1801	60m. Female with calf	70	25
1802	60m. Male and female	70	25
1803	60m. Male and female in snow	70	25

1986. Pelicans. As T 359. Multicoloured.

1804	60m. Dalmatian pelican ("Pelecanus crispus")	1·00	40
1805	60m. Dalmatian pelican preening	1·00	40
1806	60m. Eastern white pelican ("Pelecanus onocrotalus")	1·00	40
1807	60m. Eastern white pelicans in flight	1·00	40

370 Siamese Fighting Fish

1987. Aquarium Fishes. Multicoloured.

1808	20m. Type **370**	20	10
1809	30m. Goldfish	30	10
1810	40m. Glowlight rasbora	40	15
1811	50m. Acara	50	20
1812	60m. Platy	60	25
1813	80m. Green swordtail	70	30
1814	1t.20 Freshwater angelfish (vert)	80	35
MS1815	111×91 mm. 4t. Sail-finned tetra (*Crenuchus spilurus*) (53×32 mm)	5·25	5·25

371 Lassoing Horse

1987. Traditional Equestrian Sports. Multicoloured.

1816	20m. Type **371**	20	10
1817	30m. Breaking horse	30	10
1818	40m. Mounted archer	30	15
1819	50m. Race	40	20
1820	60m. Horseman snatching flag from ground	45	25
1821	80m. Tug of war	50	30
1822	1t.20 Racing wolf	70	35

372 Grey-headed Woodpecker

1987. Woodpeckers. Multicoloured.

1823	20m. Type **372**	10	10
1824	30m. Wryneck	20	10
1825	40m. Great spotted woodpecker	30	15
1826	50m. White-backed woodpecker	40	20
1827	60m. Lesser spotted woodpecker	60	25
1828	80m. Black woodpecker	80	35
1829	1t.20 Three-toed woodpecker	1·20	45
MS1830	85×105 mm. 4t. Pryer's woodpecker (*Saphopipo noguchi*)	4·50	4·50

373 Butterfly Hunting

1987. Children's Activities. Multicoloured.

1831	20m. Type **373**	10	10
1832	30m. Feeding calves	20	10
1833	40m. Drawing on ground in chalk	30	15
1834	50m. Football	40	20
1835	60m. Go-carting	45	25
1836	80m. Growing vegetables	50	30
1837	1t.20 Playing string instrument	70	35

374 Industry and Agriculture

1987. 13th Congress and 60th Anniv of Mongolian Trade Union.

1838	**374** 60m. multicoloured	1·50	40

375 Women in Traditional Costume

1987. 40th Anniv of Mongol–Soviet Friendship.

1839	**375** 60m. multicoloured	60	25

1987. Argali. As T 359. Multicoloured.

1840	60m. On grassy rock (full face)	60	25
1841	60m. On rock (three-quarter face)	60	25
1842	60m. Family	60	25
1843	60m. Close-up of head and upper body	60	25

1987. Swans. As T 359. Multicoloured.

1844	60m. Mute Swan ("Cygnus olor") in water	70	25
1845	60m. Mute swan on land	70	25
1846	60m. Tundra swan ("Cygnus bewickii")	70	25
1847	60m. Tundra swan, ("Cygnus gunus") and mute swan	70	25

376 Flags of Member Countries

1987. 25th Anniv of Membership of Council for Mutual Economic Aid.

1848	**376** 60m. multicoloured	60	25

377 Sea Buckthorn

1987. Fruits. Multicoloured.

1849	20m. Type **377**	20	10
1850	30m. Blackcurrants	30	10
1851	40m. Redcurrants	40	15
1852	50m. Redcurrants	45	20
1853	60m. Raspberries	50	25
1854	80m. "Padus asiatica"	60	30
1855	1t.20 Strawberries	70	30
MS1856	90×110 mm. 4t. Child with apple (29×51 mm)	3·50	3·50

378 Couple in Traditional Costume

1987. Folk Art. Multicoloured.

1857	20m. Type **378**	10	10
1858	30m. Gold-inlaid baton and pouch	20	10
1859	40m. Gold and jewelled ornaments	30	15
1860	50m. Bag and dish	40	20
1861	60m. Earrings	50	25
1862	80m. Pipe, pouch and bottle	60	30
1863	1t.20 Decorative headdress	70	30

379 Dancer

1987. Dances.

1864	**379** 20m. multicoloured	10	10
1865	- 30m. multicoloured	20	10
1866	- 40m. multicoloured	30	15
1867	- 50m. multicoloured	40	20
1868	- 60m. multicoloured	50	25
1869	- 80m. multicoloured	60	30
1870	- 1t.20 multicoloured	70	30

DESIGNS: 30m. to 1t.20, Different dances.

380 Lute Player

1987. Hafnia 87 International Stamp Exhibition, Copenhagen. Sheet 90×114 mm.

MS1871	**380** 4t. multicoloured	3·25	3·25

381 Scottish Fold

1987. Cats. Multicoloured.

1872	20m. Type **381**	10	10
1873	30m. Grey	20	15
1874	40m. Oriental	30	20
1875	50m. Abyssinian (horiz)	40	25
1876	60m. Manx (horiz)	50	30
1877	80m. Black shorthair (horiz)	70	30
1878	1t.20 Spotted (horiz)	80	35
MS1879	91×111 mm. 4t. Tabby shorthair	3·25	3·25

382 Mil Mi-V12

1987. Helicopters. Multicoloured.

1880	20m. Type **382**	10	10
1881	30m. Westland WG-30	20	15
1882	40m. Bell 206L LongRanger II	30	20
1883	50m. Kawasaki-Hughes 369HS	40	25
1884	60m. Kamov Ka-32	50	30
1885	80m. Mil Mi-17	70	30
1886	1t.20 Mil Mi-10K	80	35

383 City Scene

1987. 19th Mongolian People's Revolutionary Party Congress. Multicoloured.

1887	60m. Type **383**	40	15
1888	60m. Clothing and mining industries	40	15
1889	60m. Agriculture	40	15
1890	60m. Family	40	15
1891	60m. Workers, factories and fields	40	15
1892	60m. Building construction	40	15
1893	60m. Scientist	40	15

384 Kremlin, Lenin and Revolutionaries

1987. 70th Anniv of Russian October Revolution.

1894	**384**	60m. multicoloured	60	25

385 Seven with One Blow

1987. Walt Disney Cartoons. Multicoloured (a) "The Brave Little Tailor" (Grimm Brothers).

1895	25m. Type **385**		20	10
1896	35m. Brought before the King		30	10
1897	45m. Rewards for bravery		40	15
1898	55m. Fight between Mickey and the giant		50	20
1899	2t. Happy ending		1·20	70
MS1900	126×102 mm. 7t. Mickey victorious		5·00	5·00

(b) "The Celebrated Jumping Frog of Calaveras County" (Mark Twain).

1901	65m. "He'd bet on anything"		60	25
1902	75m. "He never done nothing but … learn that frog to jump"		70	30
1903	85m. "What might it be that you've got in that box?"		80	30
1904	1t. "40 He got the frog out and filled him full of quail shot"		90	50
MS1905	12×102 mm. 7t. "He set the frog down and took after that feller"		5·00	5·00

386 Head

1987. The Red Fox. Multicoloured.

1906	60m. Type **386**		60	25
1907	60m. Vixen and cubs		60	25
1908	60m. Stalking		60	25
1909	60m. In the snow		60	25

387 "Mir" Space Station

1987. Intercosmos XX. Sheet 118×97 mm.

MS1910	**387** 4t. multicoloured		2·50	2·50

388 Bobsleighing

1988. Air. Winter Olympic Games, Calgary. Multicoloured

1911	20m. Type **388**		10	10
1912	30m. Ski jumping		20	10
1913	40m. Skiing		30	15
1914	50m. Biathlon		40	20
1915	60m. Speed skating		50	25
1916	80m. Figure skating		60	30
1917	1t.20 Ice hockey		70	35
MS1918	91×110 mm. 4t. Cross-country skiing		2·50	2·50

389 Sukhe Bator

1988. 95th Birth Anniv of Sukhe Bator.

1919	**389**	60m. multicoloured	60	25

390 "Invitation"

1988. Roses. Multicoloured.

1920	20m. Type **390**		10	10
1921	30m. "Meilland"		20	10
1922	40m. "Pascali"		30	15
1923	50m. "Tropicana"		45	20
1924	60m. "Wendy Cussons"		55	25
1925	80m. "Rosa sp." (wrongly inscr "Blue Moon")		65	30
1926	1t.20 "Diorama"		75	35
MS1927	97×117 mm. 4t. Red rose		2·50	2·50

391 "Ukhaant Ekhner"

1988. Puppets. Multicoloured.

1928	20m. Type **391**		10	10
1929	30m. "Altan Everte Mungun Turuut"		20	10
1930	40m. "Aduuchyn Khuu"		30	15
1931	50m. "Suulenkhuu"		45	20
1932	60m. "Khonchyn Khuu"		55	25
1933	80m. "Argat Byatskhan Baatar"		65	30
1934	1t.20 "Botgochyn Khuu"		75	35

392 "Tatra 11" Car, 1923

1988. "Praga 88" International Stamp Exhibition, Prague. Sheet 110×90 mm.

MS1935	**392** 4t. multicoloured		2·50	2·50

393 Judo

1988. Olympic Games, Seoul. Multicoloured.

1936	20m. Type **393**		10	10
1937	30m. Archery		20	10
1938	40m. Weightlifting		30	15
1939	50m. Gymnastics		45	20
1940	60m. Cycling		55	25
1941	80m. Running		65	30
1942	1t.20 Wrestling		75	35
MS1943	90×110 mm. 4t. Boxing		2·50	2·50

394 Marx

1988. 170th Birth Anniv of Karl Marx.

1944	**394**	60m. multicoloured	85	35

395 Couple and Congress Banner

1988. 19th Revsomol Youth Congress.

1945	**395**	60m. multicoloured	1·30	45

396 "Kosmos"

1988. Spacecraft and Satellites. Multicoloured.

1946	20m. Type **396**		10	10
1947	30m. "Meteor"		15	10
1948	40m. "Salyut"–"Soyuz" space complex		25	10
1949	50m. "Prognoz-6"		30	10
1950	60m. "Molniya-1"		40	15
1951	80m. "Soyuz"		50	20
1952	1t.20 "Vostok"		65	25
MS1953	96×115 mm. 4t. Satellite scanning areas of Earth		4·25	4·25

397 Buddha

1988. Religious Sculptures.

1954	**397**	20m. multicoloured	10	10
1955	-	30m. multicoloured	20	10
1956	-	40m. multicoloured	30	15
1957	-	50m. multicoloured	45	20
1958	-	60m. multicoloured	55	25
1959	-	70m. multicoloured	65	30
1960	-	80m. multicoloured	75	40
1961	-	1t.20 multicoloured	85	45

DESIGNS: 30m. to 1t.20, Different Buddhas.

398 Emblem

1988. 30th Anniv of Problems of "Peace and Socialism" (magazine).

1962	**398**	60m. multicoloured	85	35

399 Eagle

1988. White-tailed Sea Eagle. Multicoloured.

1963	60m. Type **399**		75	30
1964	60m. Eagle on fallen branch and eagle landing		75	30
1965	60m. Eagle on rock		75	30
1966	60m. Eagle (horiz)		75	30

400 Ass

1988. Asiatic Wild Ass. Multicoloured.

1967	60m. Type **400**		75	25
1968	60m. Head of ass		75	25
1969	60m. Two adults		75	25
1970	60m. Mare and foal		75	25

401 Athlete

1988. Traditional Sports. Multicoloured.

1971	10m. Type **401**		10	10
1972	20m. Horseman		20	10
1973	30m. Archery		30	15
1974	40m. Wrestling		45	20
1975	50m. Archery (different)		55	25
1976	70m. Horsemen (national holiday cavalcade)		75	30
1977	1t.20 Horsemen, wrestlers and archers		1·10	50

402 "Mongolian Camp" (H. Jargalsuren)

1988. Childrens' Fund. Sheet 115×95 mm.

MS1978	**402** 4t. multicoloured		2·50	2·50

403 U.S.S.R. (ice hockey)

1988. Winter Olympic Games Gold Medal Winners. Multicoloured.

1979	1t.50 Type **403**		65	25
1980	1t.50 Bonnie Blair (speed skating)		65	25
1981	1t.50 Alberto Tomba (slalom)		65	25
1982	1t.50 Matti Nykanen (ski jumping) (horiz)		65	25
MS1983	110×87 mm. 4t. Katarina Witt (figure skating) (horiz)		2·50	2·50

404 Brown Goat

1988. Goats. Multicoloured.
1984	20m. Type **404**		10	10
1985	30m. Black goat		20	10
1986	40m. White long-haired goats		30	15
1987	50m. Black long-haired goat		45	20
1988	60m. White goat		55	25
1989	80m. Black short-haired goat		65	30
1990	1t.20 Nanny and kid		75	40
MS1991 95×116 mm. 4t. Head of goat (vert)			2·50	2·50

405 Emblem

1989. 60th Anniv of Mongolian Writers' Association.
1992	**405**	60m. multicoloured	65	25

406 Beaver gnawing Trees

1989. Eurasian Beaver. Multicoloured.
1993	60m. Type **406**		65	25
1994	60m. Beaver with young		65	25
1995	60m. Beavers beside tree stump and in water		65	25
1996	60m. Beaver rolling log		65	25

407 Dancers

1989. Ballet.
1997	**407**	20m. multicoloured	10	10
1998	-	30m. multicoloured	20	10
1999	-	40m. multicoloured (vert)	30	15
2000	-	50m. multicoloured	45	20
2001	-	60m. multicoloured	55	25
2002	-	80m. multicoloured (vert)	65	30
2003	-	1t.20 multicoloured (vert)	75	40

DESIGNS: 30m. to 1t.20, Different dancing scenes.

408 "Ursus pruinosis"

1989. Bears. Multicoloured.
2004	20m. Type **408**		20	10
2005	30m. Brown bear		30	15
2006	40m. Asiatic black bear		45	20
2007	50m. Polar bear		65	25
2008	60m. Brown bear		85	35
2009	80m. Giant panda		1·10	45
2010	1t.20 Brown bear		1·30	50
MS2011 110×90 mm. 4t. Giant panda (different)			5·25	5·25

409 "Soyuz" Spacecraft

1989. Space. Multicoloured.
2012	20m. Type **409**		20	10
2013	30m. "Apollo"–"Soyuz" link		30	15
2014	40m. "Columbia" space shuttle (vert)		45	20
2015	50m. "Hermes" spacecraft		55	25
2016	60m. "Nippon" spacecraft (vert)		65	30
2017	80m. "Energy" rocket (vert)		85	35

2018	1t.20 "Buran" space shuttle (vert)		1·30	50
MS2019 110×88 mm. 4t. German "Sanger" project			3·50	3·50

410 Tupolev Tu-154

1989. "Philexfrance 89", Paris (1st issue). and "Bulgaria '89", Sofia, International Stamp Exhibitions. Sheet 90×110 mm.
MS2020 **410** 4t. multicoloured			3·00	3·00

See also **MS**2034.

411 Nehru

1989. Birth Centenary of Jawaharial Nehru (Indian statesman).
2021	**411**	10m. multicoloured	85	45

412 "Opuntia microdasys"

1989. Cacti. Multicoloured.
2022	20m. Type **412**		10	10
2023	30m. "Echinopsis multipiex"		20	10
2024	40m. "Rebutia tephracanthus"		30	15
2025	45m. "Brasilicactus haselbergii"		45	20
2026	60m. "Gymnocalycium mih-anovichii"		55	25
2027	80m. "C. strausii"		65	30
2028	1t.20 "Horridocactus tuberis-vicatus"		75	35
MS2029 90×110 mm. 4t. Astrophytum ornatum			2·50	2·50

1989. 800th Anniv of Coronation of Genghis Khan. Nos. 291/4 optd CHINGGIS KHAN CROWNATION 1189.
2030	**67**	20m. multicoloured	4·25	4·25
2031	-	30m. multicoloured	7·50	7·75
2032	-	50m. black, brown and red	10·50	10·50
2033	-	60m. buff, blue and brown	16·00	16·00

414 Concorde

1989. "Philexfrance 89" International Stamp Exhibition, Paris (2nd issue). Sheet 130×55 mm containing T **414** and similar horiz designs. Multicoloured.
MS2034 20m. Type **414**; 60m. French TGV express train; 1t.20, Sukhe Bator statue
	6·00	6·00

415 Citroen "BX"

1989. Motor Cars. Multicoloured.
2035	20m. Type **415**		10	10
2036	30m. Volvo "760 GLF"		20	10
2037	40m. Honda "Civic"		30	15
2038	50m. Volga		45	20

2039	60m. Ford "Granada"		55	25
2040	80m. Baz "21099"		75	30
2041	1t.20 Mercedes "190"		1·30	35
MS2042 110×90 mm. 4t. As No. 2038			2·50	2·50

416 Monument

1989. 50th Anniv of Battle of Khalka River.
2043	**416**	60m. multicoloured	85	45

417 Florence Griffith-Joyner (running)

1989. Olympic Games Medal Winners. Multicoloured
2044	60m. Type **417** (wrongly inscr "Joyner-Griffith")		65	25
2045	60m. Stefano Cerioni (fencing)		65	25
2046	60m. Gintautas Umaras (cycling)		65	25
2047	60m. Kristin Otto (swimming)		65	25
MS2048 90×110 mm. 4t. N. Enkhbat (boxing)			2·20	2·20

418 "Malchin Zaluus" (N. Sandagsuren)

1989. 30th Anniv of Co-operative Movement. Paintings. Multicoloured.
2049	20m. Type **418**		20	10
2050	30m. "Tsaatny Tukhai Dursam-kh" (N. Sandagsuren) (vert)		30	15
2051	40m. "Uul Shig Tushigtei" (D. Amgalan)		55	25
2052	50m. "Goviin Egshig" (D. Amgalan)		65	35
2053	60m. "Tsagaan Sar" (Ts. Dagvanyam)		75	45
2054	80m. "Tumen Aduuny Bayar" (M. Butemkh) (vert)		95	50
2055	1t.20 "Bilcheer Deer" (N. Tsultem)		1·50	60
MS2056 110×90 mm. 4t. "Naadam" (detail, Ts. Dagvanyam)			5·25	5·25

419 Four-man Bobsleighing

1989. Ice Sports. Multicoloured.
2057	20m. Type **419**		10	10
2058	30m. Luge		20	10
2059	40m. Figure skating		30	15
2060	50m. Two-man bobsleighing		45	20
2061	60m. Ice dancing		55	25
2062	80m. Speed skating		65	30
2063	1t.20 Ice speedway		75	35
MS2064 90×110 mm. 4t. Ice hockey			2·50	2·50

420 Victory Medal

1989. Orders. Designs showing different badges and medals. Multicoloured, background colour given.
2065	**420**	60m. blue	65	25
2066	-	60m. orange	65	25
2067	-	60m. mauve	65	25
2068	-	60m. violet	65	25
2069	-	60m. green	65	25
2070	-	60m. blue	65	25
2071	-	60m. red	65	25

1989. "World Stamp Expo 89" International Stamp Exhibition, Washington D.C. No. **MS**2034 optd WORLD STAMP EXPO'89, WASHINGTON DC, WASHINGTON DC and logo on the margin.
MS2072 130× 55 mm. 20m. multicol-oured; 60m. multicoloured; 1t.20, multicoloured
	6·00	6·00

422 Chu Lha

1989. Buddhas. Multicoloured.
2073	20m. Damdin Sandub		20	10
2074	30m. Pagwa Lama		30	15
2075	40m. Type **422**		45	25
2076	50m. Agwanglobsan		65	35
2077	60m. Dorje Dags Dan		75	40
2078	80m. Wangchikdorje		95	45
2079	1t.20 Buddha		1·40	65
MS2080 74×89 mm. 4t. Migjid Jang-Rasek			5·25	5·25

423 Sukhe Bator Statue

1990. New Year.
2081	**423**	10m. multicoloured	1·10	50

424 Newspapers and City

1990. 70th Anniv of "Khuvisgalt Khevlel" (newspaper).
2082	**424**	60m. multicoloured	95	45

425 Emblem

1990. 20th Mongolian People's Revolutionary Party Congress.
2083	**425**	60m. multicoloured	75	35

426 Male Character

1990. "Mandukhai the Wise" (film).

2084	**426**	20m. multicoloured	30	15
2085	-	30m. multicoloured	45	25
2086	-	40m. multicoloured	65	35
2087	-	50m. multicoloured	85	45
2088	-	60m. multicoloured	1·10	50
2089	-	80m. multicoloured	1·40	70
2090	-	1t.20 multicoloured	1·90	1·00

MS2091 83×105 mm. 4t. multicoloured
(vert)   5·25   5·25

DESIGNS: 30m. to 4t., Different characters from the film.

427 Trophy and Players

1990. World Cup Football Championship, Italy.

2092	**427**	20m. multicoloured	10	10
2093	-	30m. multicoloured	15	10
2094	-	40m. multicoloured	20	10
2095	-	50m. multicoloured	25	10
2096	-	60m. multicoloured	30	15
2097	-	80m. multicoloured	45	20
2098	-	1t.20 multicoloured	55	25

MS2099 89×110 mm. 4t. multicoloured
(Trophy) (vert)   2·50   2·50

DESIGNS: 30m. to 4t., Trophy and different players.

428 Lenin

1990. 120th Birth Anniv of Lenin.

2100	**428**	60m. black, red and gold	95	50

429 Mother with Fawn

1990. Siberian Musk Deer. Multicoloured.

2101	60m. Type **429**		95	50
2102	60m. Deer in wood		95	50
2103	60m. Deer on river bank		95	50
2104	60m. Deer in winter landscape		95	50

430 Clock Tower,
Houses of
Parliament, London

1990. "Stamp World London '90" International Stamp
Exhibition (1st issue) Sheet 91×105 mm.

MS2105 **430** 4t. multicoloured   3·50   3·50

See also Nos. **MS**2107 and 2191/**MS**2200.

431 Genghis Khan

1990. 800th Anniv (1989) of Coronation of Genghis Khan
(2nd issue). Sheet 116×142 mm.

MS2106 **431** 7t. multicoloured   4·25   4·25

1990. "Stamp World London '90" International Stamp
Exhibition (2nd issue). No. **MS**2106 optd with Penny
Black and Stamp World London 90 in margin.

MS2107 **431** 7t. multicoloured   4·25   4·25

433 Russian Victory
Medal

1990. 45th Anniv of End of Second World War.

2108	**433**	60m. multicoloured	95	50

434 Crane

1990. The Japanese White-naped Crane. Multicoloured

2109	60m. Type **434**		95	45
2110	60m. Crane feeding (horiz)		95	45
2111	60m. Cranes flying (horiz)		95	45
2112	60m. Crane on river bank		95	45

435 Fin Whale

1990. Marine Mammals. Multicoloured.

2113	20m. Type **435**		20	10
2114	30m. Humpback whale		45	15
2115	40m. Narwhal		65	25
2116	50m. Risso's dolphin		85	35
2117	60m. Bottle-nosed dolphin		1·10	45
2118	80m. Atlantic white-sided
dolphin		1·30	50
2119	1t.20 Bowhead whale		1·50	60

MS2120 90×110 mm. 4t. Dall's porpoise (vert)   4·75   4·75

436 Weapons and Black
Standard

1990. 750th Anniv of "Secret History of the Mongols"
(book). Multicoloured.

2121	10m. Type **436**		10	10
2122	10m. Weapons and white
standard		10	10
2123	40m. Brazier (17½×22 mm)		55	15
2124	60m. Genghis Khan (17½×22
mm)		75	25
2125	60m. Horses galloping		75	25
2126	60m. Tartar camp		75	25
2127	80m. Men kneeling to ruler		1·10	45
2128	80m. Court		1·10	45

437 Panda

1990. The Giant Panda. Multicoloured.

2129	10m. Type **437**		30	10
2130	20m. Panda eating bamboo		45	15
2131	30m. Adult eating bamboo,
and cub		55	25
2132	40m. Panda on tree branch
(horiz)		65	35
2133	50m. Adult and cub resting
(horiz)		85	45
2134	60m. Panda and mountains
(horiz)		95	50
2135	80m. Adult and cub playing
(horiz)		1·30	70
2136	1t.20 Panda on snow-covered
river bank (horiz)		1·90	1·00

MS2137 94×114 mm. 4t. Panda holding bamboo shoots (vert)   5·75   5·75

438 Chasmosaurus

1990. Prehistoric Animals. Multicoloured.

2138	20m. Type **438**		20	10
2139	30m. Stegosaurus		45	15
2140	40m. Probactrosaurus		65	25
2141	50m. Opisthocoelicaudia		85	35
2142	60m. Iguanodon (vert)		1·10	45
2143	80m. Tarbosaurus		1·30	60
2144	1t.20 Mamenchisaurus (after
Mark Hallett) (60×22 mm)		1·90	80

MS2145 110×90 mm. 4t. Allosaurus attacking herd of Brachiosaurus (after
John Gurche)   4·75   4·75

439 Lighthouse,
Alexandria, Egypt

1990. Seven Wonders of the World. Multicoloured

2146	20m. Type **439**		20	10
2147	30m. Pyramids of Egypt (horiz)		30	15
2148	40m. Statue of Zeus, Olympia		55	25
2149	50m. Colossus of Rhodes		65	30
2150	60m. Mausoleum, Halicarnassus		75	45
2151	80m. Temple of Artemis, Ephe-
sus (horiz)		1·10	55
2152	1t.20 Hanging Gardens of
Babylon		1·60	70

MS2153 89×110 mm. 4t. Map and
pyramids   5·25   5·25

440 Kea

1990. Parrots. Multicoloured.

2154	20m. Type **440**		20	10
2155	30m. Hyacinth macaw		30	15
2156	40m. Australian king parrot		45	25
2157	50m. Grey parrot		65	35
2158	60m. Kakapo		75	45
2159	80m. Alexandrine parakeet		95	50
2160	1t.20 Scarlet macaw		1·50	60

MS2161 84×104 mm. 4t. Electus parrot   4·25   4·25

441 Purple Tiger Moth

1990. Moths and Butterflies. Multicoloured.

2162	20m. Type **441**		30	10
2163	30m. Viennese emperor moth		45	15
2164	40m. Comma		65	25
2165	50m. Magpie moth		85	35
2166	60m. Chequered moth		95	45
2167	80m. Swallowtail		1·20	55
2168	1t.20 Orange-tip		1·60	80

MS2169 90×110 mm. 4t. Striped hawk
moth (vert). Perf or imperf   4·25   4·25

442 Jetsons in Flying
Saucer

1991. The Jetsons (cartoon characters). Multicoloured

2170	20m. Type **442**		10	10
2171	25m. Family walking on planet,
and dragon (horiz)		20	15
2172	30m. Jane, George, Elroy and
dog Astro		30	20
2173	40m. George, Judy, Elroy and
Astro crossing river		45	25
2174	50m. Flying in saucer (horiz)		50	30
2175	60m. Jetsons and Cosmo
Spacely (horiz)		55	35
2176	70m. George and Elroy flying
with jetpacks		60	40
2177	80m. Elroy (horiz)		75	45
2178	1t.20 Judy and Astro watching
Elroy doing acrobatics
on tree		1·20	50

MS2179 Two sheets, each 102×127
mm. (a) 7t. Elroy with hands in
pocket; (b) 7t. Elroy jumping   9·50   9·50

443 Dino and Bam-Bam meeting
Mongolian Boy with Camel

1991. The Flintstones (cartoon characters). Multicoloured.

2180	25m. Type **443**		20	10
2181	35m. Bam-Bam and Dino pos-
ing with boy (vert)		25	15
2182	45m. Mongolian mother
greeting Betty Rubble, Wilma
Flintstone and children		30	20
2183	55m. Barney Rubble and Fred
riding dinosaurs		45	25
2184	65m. Flintstones and Rubbles
by river		55	30
2185	75m. Bam-Bam and Dino racing
boy on camel		60	35
2186	85m. Fred, Barney and Bam-
Bam with Mongolian boy		65	40
2187	1t.40 Flintstones and Rubbles
in car		1·30	50
2188	2t. Fred and Barney taking
refreshments with Mongolian		1·70	85

MS2189 Two sheets, each 126×101
mm. (a) 7t. Wilma, Betty and Bam-
Bam; (b) 7t. Bam-Bam and Pebbles
riding Dino   9·50   9·50

444 Party Emblem

1991. 70th Anniv of Mongolian People's Revolutionary
Party.

2190	**444**	60m. multicoloured	85	35

445
Black-capped
Chickadee

1991. "Stamp World London 90" International Stamp Exhibition. Multicoloured.

2191	25m. Type **445**	20	10
2192	35m. Common cardinal	25	10
2193	45m. Crested shelduck	30	15
2194	55m. Mountain bluebird	45	20
2195	65m. Northern oriole	55	25
2196	75m. Bluethroat (horiz)	65	35
2197	85m. Eastern bluebird	75	45
2198	1t.40 Great reed warbler	1·20	50
2199	2t. Golden eagle	1·60	60

MS2200 Two sheets. (a) 94×76 mm. 7t. Ring-necked pheasant (horiz); (b) 76 x 94 mm. 7t. Great scaup — 9·50 9·50

446 Black Grouse

1991. Birds. Multicoloured.

2201	20m. Type **446**	30	10
2202	30m. Common shelduck	55	20
2203	40m. Common pheasant	65	30
2204	50m. Long-tailed duck	85	35
2205	60m. Hazel grouse	1·10	45
2206	80m. Red-breasted merganser	1·60	50
2207	1t.20 Goldeneye	1·90	80

MS2208 96×115 mm. 4t. Green-winged teal (*Anas crecca*) (vert) — 5·25 5·25

447 Emblem

1991. 70th Anniv of Mongolian People's Army.

2209	**447**	60m. multicoloured	85	35

448 Superb Pink

1991. Flowers. Multicoloured.

2210	20m. Type **448**	20	10
2211	30m. "Gentiana pneumonanthe" (wrongly inscr "puenmonan-the")	45	15
2212	40m. Dandelion	65	25
2213	50m. Siberian iris	85	35
2214	60m. Turk's-cap lily	90	45
2215	80m. "Aster amellus"	1·20	55
2216	1t.20 Thistle	1·70	70

MS2217 95×115 mm. 4t. Bellflower (*Campanula persicifolia*) — 4·75 4·75

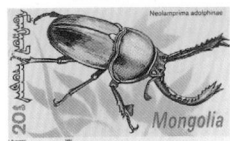

449 Stag Beetle

1991. Beetles. Multicoloured.

2218	20m. Type **449**	30	10
2219	30m. "Chelorrhina polyphemus"	45	15
2220	40m. "Coptolabrus coelestis"	65	25
2221	50m. "Epepeotes togatus"	85	35
2222	60m. Tiger beetle	95	45
2223	80m. "Macrodontia cervicornis"	1·20	60
2224	1t.20 Hercules beetle	1·60	70

MS2225 95×115 mm. 4t. *Cercopis sanguinolenta* (vert) — 4·75 4·75

450 Defend

1991. Buddhas. Multicoloured.

2226	20m. Type **450**	20	10
2227	30m. Badmasanhava	30	15
2228	40m. Avalokitecvara	55	25
2229	50m. Buddha	75	35
2230	60m. Mintugwa	85	45
2231	80m. Shyamatara	1·20	50
2232	1t.20 Samvara	1·30	70

MS2233 95×116 mm. 4t. Lamidhatara — 4·00 4·00

451 Zebras

1991. African Wildlife. Multicoloured.

2234	20m. Type **451**	30	10
2235	30m. Cheetah (wrongly inscr "Cheetan")	45	15
2236	40m. Black rhinoceros	65	25
2237	50m. Giraffe (vert)	85	35
2238	60m. Gorilla	95	45
2239	80m. Elephants	1·20	50
2240	1t.20 Lion (vert)	1·60	70

MS2241 95×116 mm. 4t. Gazelle (vert) — 4·75 4·75

452 Communications

1991. Meiso Mizuhara Stamp Exhibition, Ulan Bator.

2242	**452**	1t.20 multicoloured	3·25	85

453 Scotch Bonnet

1991. Fungi. Multicoloured.

2243	20m. Type **453**	30	15
2244	30m. Oak mushroom	45	20
2245	40m. "Hygrophorus marzuelus"	65	25
2246	50m. Chanterelle	75	30
2247	60m. Field mushroom	85	35
2248	80m. Bronze boletus	1·10	45
2249	1t.20 Caesar's mushroom	1·60	70
2250	2t. "Tricholoma terreum"	2·40	1·10

MS2251 95×80 mm. 4t. *Mitrophora hybrida* (31×39 mm) — 5·75 5·75

454 Emblem

1991. 70th Anniv of Revolution. Sheet 84×109 mm.

MS2252 **454**	4t. multicoloured	2·20	2·20

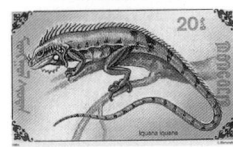

455 Green Iguana

1991. Reptiles. Multicoloured.

2253	20m. Type **455**	20	10
2254	30m. Flying gecko	45	15
2255	40m. Frilled lizard	65	25
2256	50m. Common cape lizard	85	35
2257	60m. Common basilisk	1·10	45
2258	80m. Common tegu	1·30	50
2259	1t.20 Marine iguana	1·90	60

MS2260 75×96 mm. 4t. Bengal monitor lizard (Varanus bengalensis) (32×54 mm) — 4·75 4·75

456 Warrior

1991. Masked Costumes. Multicoloured.

2261	35m. Type **456**	30	15
2262	45m. Mask with fangs	45	25
2263	55m. Bull mask	50	30
2264	65m. Dragon mask	55	35
2265	85m. Mask with beak	85	50
2266	1t.40 Old man	1·40	85
2267	2t. Gold mask with earrings	1·90	1·00

MS2268 90×110 mm. 4t. Lion mask — 5·25 5·25

457 German Shepherd

1991. Dogs. Multicoloured.

2269	20m. Type **457**	20	10
2270	30m. Dachshund (vert)	45	15
2271	40m. Yorkshire terrier (vert)	65	25
2272	50m. Standard poodle	85	35
2273	60m. Springer spaniel	1·10	45
2274	80m. Norfolk terrier	1·30	60
2275	1t.20 Keeshund	1·90	85

MS2276 110×90 mm. 4t. Herding dog (54×32 mm) — 4·75 4·75

458 Siamese

1991. Cats. Multicoloured.

2277	20m. Type **458**	20	10
2278	30m. Black and white long-haired (vert)	45	15
2279	40m. Ginger red	65	25
2280	50m. Tabby (vert)	85	35
2281	60m. Red and white (vert)	1·10	45
2282	80m. Maine coon (vert)	1·30	50
2283	1t.20 Blue-eyed white persian (vert)	1·90	80

MS2284 101×91 mm. 4t. Tortoiseshell and white — 4·75 4·75

459 Pagoda

1991. "Phila Nippon '91" International Stamp Exhibition, Tokyo. Multicoloured.

2285	1t. Type **459**	55	25
2286	2t. Japanese woman	85	50
2287	3t. Mongolian woman	1·30	70
2288	4t. Temple	2·10	1·10

(b) No. MS2233 optd PHILA NIPPON'91 and logos in the margin.

MS2288a 95×115 mm. 4t. multicoloured — 3·25 2·20

460 "Zegris fausti"

1991. Butterflies and Flowers. Multicoloured.

2289	20m. Type **460**	20	10
2290	25m. Yellow roses	25	10
2291	30m. Apollo	30	15
2292	40m. Purple tiger moth	45	20
2293	50m. "Pseudochazara regeli"	55	25
2294	60m. "Colotis fausta"	60	30
2295	70m. Red rose	65	35
2296	80m. Margueritas	75	40
2297	1t.20 Lily	1·10	45

1991. "Expo '90" International Garden and Greenery Exhibition, Osaka. Nos. 2289/97 optd EXPO '90 and symbol.

2298	20m. multicoloured	20	10
2299	25m. multicoloured	25	10
2300	30m. multicoloured	30	15
2301	40m. multicoloured	45	20
2302	50m. multicoloured	55	25
2303	60m. multicoloured	60	30
2304	70m. multicoloured	65	35
2305	80m. multicoloured	75	40
2306	1t.20 multicoloured	1·10	45

(b) Two sheets, each 94×77 mm, containing horiz design as T **460**. Multicoloured.

MS2307 Two sheets. (a) 7t. Cactus; (b) 7t. Butterfly — 12·00 12·00

462 Poster for 1985 Digital Stereo Re-issue

1991. 50th Anniv (1990) of Original Release of Walt Disney's "Fantasia" (cartoon film). Mult.

2308	1t.70 Type **462**	20	10
2309	2t. 1940 poster for original release	45	15
2310	2t.30 Poster for 1982 digital re-issue	50	25
2311	2t.60 Poster for 1981 stereo re-issue	55	30
2312	4t.20 Poster for 1969 "Psych-edelic Sixties" release	65	45
2313	10t. 1941 poster for original release	1·60	70
2314	15t. Mlle. Upanova (sketch by Campbell Grant)	2·50	1·10
2315	16t. Mickey as the Sorcerer's Apprentice (original sketch)	2·75	1·30

MS2316 Four sheets, each 127×102 mm. (a) 30t. "Russian Dance" (50×37 mm); (b) 30t. Stravinsky's "Rite of Spring" (48×35 mm); (c) 30t. "The Sorcerer's Apprentice"; (d) 30t. "Chinese Dance" (50×36 mm) — 21·00 21·00

463 Speed Skating

1992. Winter Olympic Games, Albertville. Multicoloured

2317	60m. Type **463**	10	10
2318	80m. Ski jumping	20	10
2319	1t. Ice hockey	25	10
2320	1t.20 Ice skating	30	10
2321	1t.50 Biathlon (horiz)	40	15
2322	2t. Skiing (horiz)	45	20
2323	2t.40 Two-man bobsleigh (horiz)	55	25

MS2324 90×110 mm. 8t. Four-man bobsleigh (32×54 mm) — 2·20 2·20

464 Zeppelin

1992. 75th Death Anniv of Count Ferdinand von Zeppelin (airship pioneer). Sheet 78×102 mm.

MS2325	**464** 16t. multicoloured	3·25	3·25

465 Elk

1992. The Elk. Multicoloured.

2326	3t. Type **465**	1·10	45
2327	3t. Female with young (horiz)	1·10	45
2328	3t. Adult male (horiz)	1·10	45
2329	3t. Female	1·10	45

466 Steam Locomotive, Darjeeling–Himalaya Railway, India

1992. Multicoloured. (a) Railways of the World.

2330	3t. Type **466**	75	35
2331	3t. The "Royal Scot", Great Britain	75	35
2332	6t. Steam train on bridge over River Kwai, Burma–Siam Railway	1·70	80
2333	6t. Baltic steam locomotive No. 767, Burma	1·70	80
2334	8t. Baldwin steam locomotive, Thailand	2·30	1·00
2335	8t. Western Railways steam locomotive, Pakistan	2·30	1·00
2336	16t. Class P36 locomotive, Russia	4·75	2·20
2337	16t. Shanghai–Peking express, China	4·75	2·20
MS2338	Two sheets, each 112×83 mm. (a) 30t. "Hikari" express train, Japan (56×41 mm); (b) 30t. TGV express train, France (56×41 mm)	11·50	11·50

(b) "Orient Express". Black and gold (MS2347a) or multicoloured (others).

2339	3t. 1931 advertising poster	75	35
2340	3t. 1928 advertising poster	75	35
2341	6t. Dawn departure	1·70	80
2342	6t. The "Golden Arrow" leaving Victoria Station, London	1·70	80
2343	8t. Standing in station, Yugoslavia	2·30	1·00
2344	8t. Train passing through mountainous landcape, early 1900s	2·30	1·00
2345	16t. "Fleche d'Or" approaching Etaples	4·75	2·20
2346	16t. Arrival in Istanbul	4·75	2·20
MS2347	Two sheets, each 113×84 mm. (a) 30t. Crowded railway platform; (b) 30t. Pullman Car Company arms; 30t. Compagnie Internationale des Wogons-Lits et des Grands Express Europeens arms	14·00	14·00

467 Columbus

1992. 500th Anniv of Discovery of America by Columbus (1st issue). World Columbian Stamp "Expo '92", Chicago and "Genova '92" International Thematic Stamp Exhibition. Sheet 100 x 70 mm containing T **467** and similar vert design. Multicoloured.

MS2348	30t. Type **467**; 30t. *Santa Maria*	8·50	8·50

See also Nos. 2370/**MS**2377.

468 Black-billed Magpie

1992. Multicoloured. (a) Birds.

2349	3t. Type **468**	55	35
2350	3t. Northern eagle owl	55	35
2351	6t. Relict gull (horiz)	1·10	80
2352	6t. Redstart (horiz)	1·10	80
2353	8t. Demoiselle crane	1·60	1·00
2354	8t. Black stork (horiz)	1·60	1·00
2355	16t. Rough-legged buzzard	3·25	2·20
2356	16t. Golden eagle (horiz)	3·25	2·20
MS2357	Two sheets, each 115×90 mm. (a) 30t. Mallards swimming and in flight (50×37); (b) 30t. Red-breasted goose (50×37 mm)	10·50	10·50

(b) Butterflies and Moths.

2358	3t. Scarce swallowtail (horiz)	45	25
2359	3t. Small tortoiseshell	45	25
2360	6t. "Thyria jacobaeae" (value at right) (horiz)	95	70
2361	6t. Peacock (value at left) (horiz)	95	70
2362	8t. Camberwell beauty (value at left) (horiz)	1·30	85
2363	8t. Red admiral (value at right) (horiz)	1·30	85
2364	16t. "Hyporhaia audica" (horiz)	2·75	1·90
2365	16t. Large tortoiseshell (flying over river) (horiz)	2·75	1·90
MS2366	Two sheets. (a) 114×90 mm. 30t. Swallowtail (50×37 mm); (b) 113×90 mm. 30t. Purple tiger moth (50×37 mm)	10·50	10·50

469 Bugler

1992. Celebrities and Events. Five sheets containing T **469** and similar horiz designs. Multicoloured.

MS2367	Five sheets (a) 120×80 mm. 30t. Mother Teresa of Calcutta (winner of Nobel Peace Prize, 1979); (b) 120×80 mm. 30t. Pope John Paul II celebrating Mass; (c) 115×89 mm. 30t. President Punsalmaagiyn Ochirbat of Mongolia and President George Bush of U.S.A.; (d) 120 ×80 mm. 30t. Type **469** (17th World Scout Jamboree, Korea (1991)); (e) 120×80 mm. 30t. Type **469** (18th World Scout Jamboree, Netherlands (1995))	27·00	27·00

470 Genghis Khan

1992. 830th Birth Anniv of Genghis Khan. Sheet 100×120 mm.

MS2368	**470** 16t. multicoloured	8·00	8·00

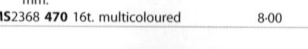

471 Gold Medal

1992. Olympic Games, Barcelona (1st issue), "Granada '92" International Thematic Stamp Exhibition and "Expo '92" World's Fair, Seville. Sheet 100×70 mm containing T **471** and similar vert' design. Multicoloured.

MS2369	30t. Type **471**; 30t. Olympic torch	13·00	13·00

See also Nos. 2379/**MS**2388.

472 Fleet

1992. 500th Anniv of Discovery of America by Columbus (2nd issue). Multicoloured.

2370	3t. Type **472**	20	10
2371	7t. Amerindians' canoe approaching "Santa Maria"	30	15
2372	10t. "Pinta"	55	25
2373	16t. "Santa Maria" in open sea (vert)	85	35
2374	30t. "Santa Maria" passing coastline	1·70	85
2375	40t. Dolphins and "Santa Maria"	2·40	1·60
2376	50t. "Nina"	2·75	1·90
MS2377	Two sheets, each 94×115 mm. (a) 80t. Christopher Columbus (37×49 mm); (b) 80t. *Santa Maria* (37×49 mm)	9·75	9·75

1992. Mongolian Stamp Exhibition, Taiwan. No. **MS**1449 optd MONGOLIAN STAMP EXHIBITION 1992 – TAIWAN in margin.

MS2378	105×68 mm. **298** 4t. multicoloured	5·25	5·25

474 Long Jumping

1992. Olympic Games, Barcelona. Multicoloured.

2379	3t. Type **474**	10	10
2380	6t. Gymnastics (pommel exercise)	20	10
2381	8t. Boxing	45	15
2382	16t. Wrestling	55	20
2383	20t. Archery (vert)	65	25
2384	30t. Cycling	75	30
2385	40t. Show jumping	85	35
2386	50t. High jumping	1·10	40
2387	60t. Weightlifting	1·30	45
MS2388	Two sheets, each 100×82 mm. (a) 80t. Throwing the javelin (38×26 mm); (b) 80t. Judo (38×26 mm)	7·50	7·50

1993. Birth Centenary of Sukhe Bator. No. **MS**1523 optd 1893 – 1993 in the margin.

MS2389	65×72 mm. **270** 4t. purple	5·25	5·25

Eight designs, each 200t. and embossed on both gold and silver foil and accompanied by matching miniature sheets, were issued in 1993 in limited printings, depicting animals, sports or transport.

476 Black Grouse

1993. Birds. Multicoloured.

2390	3t. Type **476**	10	10
2391	8t. Moorhen	45	25
2392	10t. Golden-crowned kinglet	55	35
2393	16t. River kingfisher	85	60
2394	30t. Red-throated diver	1·60	1·20
2395	40t. Grey heron	2·10	1·60
2396	50t. Hoopoe	2·75	2·20
2397	60t. Blue-throated niltava	3·25	2·40
MS2398	Two sheets, each 115×90 mm. (a) 80t. Great crested grebe (*Podiceps cristatus*) (45×35 mm); (b) 80t. Griffon vulture (*Gyps fulvus*) (48×35 mm)	8·50	8·50

477 Orange-tip

1993. Butterflies and Moths. Multicoloured.

2399	3t. Type **477**	10	10
2400	8t. Peacock	45	25
2401	10t. High brown fritillary	55	35
2402	16t. "Limenitis reducta"	85	60
2403	30t. Common burnet	1·60	1·20
2404	40t. Common blue	2·10	1·60
2405	50t. Apollo	2·75	2·20
2406	60t. Great peacock	3·25	2·40
MS2407	Two sheets, each 115×90 mm. (a) 80t. Poplar admiral (*Limenitis populi*) (49×37 mm); (b) 80t. Scarce copper (Heodes virgaureae) (49×37 mm)	7·50	7·50

1993. No. 1221 surch XXX 15Ter.

2408	15t. on 70m. multicoloured	4·75	2·20

479 Nicolas Copernicus (astronomer)

1993. "Polska'93" International Stamp Exhibition, Poznan. Multicoloured.

2409	30t. Type **479** (520th birth anniv)	2·50	1·30
2410	30t. Frederic Chopin (composer)	2·50	1·30
2411	30t. Pope John Paul II	2·50	1·30
MS2412	Two sheets, each 98×122 mm. (a) 80t. Type **479**; (b) 80t. As No. 2411	16·00	16·00

1993. No. 263 surch 8-Ter.

2413	8t. on 70m. multicoloured	85	35

481 Sun Yat-sen (Chinese statesman)

1993. "Taipei '93" International Stamp Exhibition. Two sheets each containing vert design as T **481**. Multicoloured.

MS2414	Two sheets, each 100×124 mm. (a) 80t. Type **481**; (b) 80t. Genghis Khan (portrait as in Type **431**)	4·25	4·25

482 Hologram of Airship

1993. Airship Flight over Ulan Bator.

2415	**482** 80t. multicoloured	3·25	2·50

483 Buddha

1993. "Bangkok 1993" International Stamp Exhibition. Multicoloured.

2416	50t. Buddha on throne	60	25
2417	100t. Buddha (different)	1·20	55
2418	150t. Type **483**	1·70	85
2419	200t. Multi-armed Buddha	2·30	1·20
MS2420	90×125 mm. 300t. Buddha with right hand raised	3·25	3·25

484 Clouds, Mountains and Dog

1994. New Year. Year of the Dog. Multicoloured.

2421	60t. Type **484**	1·60	70
2422	60t. Dog reclining between mountains and waves (horiz)	1·60	70

485 Uruguay (1930, 1950)

1994. World Cup Football Championship, U.S.A. Previous Winners. Multicoloured.

2423	150t. Type **485**	75	25
2424	150t. Italy (1934)	75	25
2425	150t. German Federal Republic (1954)	75	25
2426	150t. Brazil (1958)	75	25
2427	150t. Argentina (1978, 1986)	75	25
2428	200t. Italy (1938)	1·10	45
2429	200t. Brazil (1962)	1·10	45
2430	200t. German Federal Republic (1974)	1·10	45
2431	250t. Brazil (1970)	1·30	60
2432	250t. Italy (1982)	1·30	60
2433	250t. German Federal Republic (1990)	1·30	60
MS2434	Five sheets. (a) 167×120 mm. Nos. 2427 and 2431/3; (b) 118×93 mm. Nos. 2423 and 2427; (c) 118×93 mm. Nos. 2424, 2428 and 2432; (d) 118×93 mm. Nos. 2425, 2430 and 2433; (e) 118×93 mm. Nos. 2426, 2429 and 2431	20·00	20·00

486 Boeing 727

1994. Air. "Hong Kong '94" International Stamp Exhibition. Sheet 96×69 mm.

MS2435	**486** 600t. multicoloured	3·75	3·75

487 Pres. Punsalmaagin Ochirbat

1994. First Direct Presidential Election. Sheet 86×91 mm.

MS2436	**487** 150t. multicoloured	2·10	2·10

488 Biathlon

1994. Winter Olympic Games, Lillehammer, Norway. Multicoloured.

2437	50t. Type **488**	40	20
2438	60t. Two-man bobsleigh	45	25
2439	80t. Skiing	65	45
2440	100t. Ski jumping	75	50
2441	120t. Ice skating	85	60
2442	200t. Speed skating	1·30	95
MS2443	100×125 mm. 400t. Ice hockey	4·75	4·75

489 Dalai Lama

1994. Award of Nobel Peace Prize to Dalai Lama. Sheet 85×104 mm.

MS2444	**489** 400t. multicoloured	6·00	6·00

490 Lammergeier

1994. Wildlife. Multicoloured.

2445	60t. Type **490**	65	35

2446	60t. Grey-headed woodpecker on tree trunk	65	35
2447	60t. Japanese white-naped cranes	65	35
2448	60t. Western marsh harrier	65	35
2449	60t. Golden oriole on branch	65	35
2450	60t. Bank swallows	65	35
2451	60t. Montagu's harrier perched on rock	65	35
2452	60t. Pallid harriers in flight	65	35
2453	60t. Squirrel on branch	65	35
2454	60t. Dragonfly	65	35
2455	60t. Black stork	65	35
2456	60t. Northern pintail	65	35
2457	60t. Spotted nutcracker standing on rock	65	35
2458	60t. Marmot	65	35
2459	60t. Ladybird on flower	65	35
2460	60t. Clutch of eggs in ground nest	65	35
2461	60t. Grasshopper	65	35
2462	60t. Butterfly	65	35

Nos. 2445/62 were issued together, *se-tenant*, forming a composite design.

491 Command Module

1994. 25th Anniv of First Manned Moon Landing. Multicoloured.

2463	200t. Type **491**	85	50
2464	200t. Earth, astronaut in chair and shuttle wing	85	50
2465	200t. Shuttle approaching Earth	85	50
2466	200t. Astronaut on Moon	85	50
MS2467	105×130 mm. Nos. 2463/6	4·25	3·25

492 Flowers

1994

2468	**492**	10t. green and black	55	15
2469	-	18t. purple and black	55	15
2470	-	22t. blue and black	55	25
2471	-	44t. purple and black	65	25

DESIGNS: 18, 44t. Argali; 22t. Airplane.

493 Korean Empire 1884 5m. Stamp

1994. "Philakorea 1994" International Stamp Exhibition, Seoul. Multicoloured.

2472	600t. Type **493**	2·75	1·30
2473	600t. Mongolia 1924 1c. stamp	2·75	1·30
2474	600t. Mongolia 1966 Children's Day 15 m. stamp (47×34 mm)	2·75	1·30
2475	600t. South Korea 1993 New Year 110 w. stamp (47×34 mm)	2·75	1·30
MS2476	94×76 mm. 600t. Korean man in traditional dress (34×47 mm)	4·25	4·25

494 Butterfly

1994. "Singpex '94" National Stamp Exhibtion, Singapore. Year of the Dog. Multicoloured.

2477	300t. Type **494**	1·60	85
MS2478	105×78 mm. 400t. Dog	4·50	4·50

495 1924 20c. Stamp

1994. 70th Anniv of First Mongolian Stamp. Sheet 91×111 mm.

MS2479	**495** 400t. multicoloured	4·50	4·50

496 Mammoth

1994. Prehistoric Animals. Multicoloured.

2480	60t. Type **496**	45	25
2481	80t. Stegosaurus	55	35
2482	100t. Talararus (horiz)	85	45
2483	120t. Gorythosaurus (horiz)	1·10	60
2484	200t. Tyrannosaurus (horiz)	1·70	95
MS2485	124×99 mm. 400t. Triceratops (horiz)	4·25	3·00

497 National Flags

1994. Mongolia–Japan Friendship and Co-operation.

2486	**497** 20t. multicoloured	30	15

498 Boar and Mountains

1995. New Year. Year of the Pig. Multicoloured.

2487	200t. Type **498**	75	45
2488	200t. Boar reclining amongst clouds (vert)	75	45

499 Dancer

1995. Tsam Religious Mask Dance.

2489	**499** 20t. multicoloured	20	10
2490	- 50t. multicoloured	30	15
2491	- 60t. multicoloured	45	25
2492	- 100t. multicoloured	55	35
2493	- 120t. multicoloured	75	35
2494	- 150t. multicoloured	95	45
2495	- 200t. multicoloured	1·10	50
MS2496	92×133 mm. 400t. multicoloured	4·25	4·25

DESIGNS: 50t. to 400t. Different masked characters.

500 Saiga

1995. The Saiga. Multicoloured.

2497	40t. Type **500**	40	20
2498	50t. Male and female	50	25
2499	70t. Male running	60	35
2500	200t. Head and neck of male	1·70	90

501 Garden Tiger Moth

1995. "Hong Kong '95" Stamp and Collecting Fair. Sheet 104×100 mm containing T **501** and similar square design plus two labels. Multicoloured.

MS2501	200t. Type **501**; 200t. Dandelion and anemone	5·50	5·50

502 Yellow Oranda

1995. Goldfish. Multicoloured.

2502	20t. Type **502**	20	10
2503	50t. Red and white veil-tailed wen-yu	45	20
2504	60t. Brown oranda red-head	55	25
2505	100t. Pearl-scaled	90	45
2506	120t. Red lion-head	1·10	55
2507	150t. Brown oranda	1·60	65
2508	200t. Red and white oranda with narial	2·10	90
MS2509	136×110 mm. 400t. Red and white goldfish (49×37 mm)	4·50	4·50

See also No. MS2510.

1995. "Singapore '95" International Stamp Exhibition. As No. MS2509 but with exhibition emblem in the margin.

MS2510	136×110 mm. 400t. multicoloured	4·50	4·50

503 Bishop

1995. X-Men (comic strip). Designs showing characters. Multicoloured.

2511	30t. Type **503**	10	10
2512	50t. Beast	20	15
2513	60t. Rogue	30	20
2514	70t. Gambit	35	25
2515	80t. Cyclops	45	30
2516	100t. Storm	80	35
2517	200t. Professor X	1·10	80
2518	250t. Wolverine	1·40	1·00
MS2519	168×171 mm. 250t. Wolverine (horiz); 250t. Magneto (horiz)	5·00	5·00

504 Trygve Lie (1946—52)

1995. 50th Anniv of United Nations Organization. Sheet 125×115 mm containing T **504** and similar vert designs showing Secretaries-General and various views of the New York Headquarters complex. Multicoloured.

MS2520	60t. Type **504**; 60t. Dag Hammarskjold (1953–61); 60t. U. Thant (1961–71); 60t. Kurt Waldheim (1972–81); 60t. Javier Perez de Cuellar (1982–91); 60t. Boutros Boutros Ghali (from 1992)	5·00	5·00

505 Presley

1995. 60th Birth Anniv of Elvis Presley (entertainer). Multicoloured.

2521	60t. Type **505**	35	20

2522	80t. Wearing cap	45	25
2523	100t. Holding microphone	55	35
2524	120t. Wearing blue and white striped T-shirt	65	45
2525	150t. With guitar and micro-phone	80	55
2526	200t. On motor bike with girl	1·10	80
2527	250t. On surfboard	1·30	1·00
2528	300t. Pointing with left hand	1·70	1·30
2529	350t. Playing guitar and girl clapping	2·00	1·50

MS2530 Two sheets. (a) 139×91 mm.
400t. Playing guitar; (b) 139×94 mm.
400t. Wearing army uniform with
Priscilla Presley ... 13·50 13·50

Nos. 2521/9 were issued together, *se-tenant*, forming a composite design.
See also No. **MS**2543.

506 Monroe smiling

1995. 70th Birth Anniv (1996) of Marilyn Monroe (actress). Multicoloured.

2531	60t. Type **506**	35	20
2532	80t. Wearing white dress	45	25
2533	100t. Pouting	55	35
2534	120t. With naval officer and cello player	65	45
2535	150t. Wearing off-the-shoulder blouse	80	55
2536	200t. Using telephone and wearing magenta dress	1·10	80
2537	250t. Man kissing Monroe's shoulder	1·30	1·00
2538	300t. With white fur collar	1·70	1·30
2539	350t. With Clark Gable	2·00	1·50

MS2540 Two sheets. (a) 139×90 mm.
300t. Wearing black lace dress; (b)
137×106 mm. 300t. Lying on tiger
skin rug ... 11·00 11·00

Nos. 2531/9 were issued together, *se-tenant*, forming a composite design.
Seel also No. **MS**2544.

507 Rat sitting between Mountains

1996. New Year. Year of the Rat. Multicoloured.

2541	150t. Type **507**	90	55
2542	200t. Rat crouching between mountains and waves (horiz)	1·30	70

1996. 70th Birth Anniv of Marilyn Monroe (actress) (2nd issue). Two sheets containing vert designs as T **506**.
MS2544 Two sheets. (a) 100×136 mm. 200t. Close-up of Monroe; (b) 146×112 mm. 300t. Close-up of Monroe and in scene from *Niagara* ... 11·00 11·00

1996. Mongolian–Chinese Friendship. Sheet 97×133 mm containing T **508** and similar vert designs. Multicoloured.
MS2545 65t. Type **508**; 65t. Temple of Heaven, Peking; 65t. Migjed Jang-Rasek; 65t. The Great Wall of China ... 8·75 8·75

1996. China '96 International Stamp Exhibition, Peking. As No. **MS**2545 but with each stamp additionally bearing either the exhibition emblem or a mascot holding the emblem.
MS2546 65t. ×4 multicoloured ... 8·75 8·75

509 Mongolian 1924 2c. Stamp

1996. Capex '96 International Stamp Exhibition, Toronto. Sheet 116×90 mm containing T **509** and similar design. Multicoloured.
MS2547 350t. Type **509**; 400t. Canadian 1851 3d. stamp (36×26 mm) ... 10·50 10·50

510 Cycling

1996. Olympic Games, Atlanta, U.S.A. Multicoloured

2548	30t. Type **510**	10	10
2549	60t. Shooting	15	10
2550	80t. Weightlifting	20	15
2551	100t. Boxing	35	20
2552	120t. Archery (vert)	40	25
2553	150t. Rhythmic gymnastics (vert)	45	25
2554	200t. Hurdling (vert)	55	35
2555	350t. Show jumping	1·10	80
2556	400t. Wrestling	1·20	90

MS2557 Two sheets, each 130×93 mm.
(a) 500t. Basketball (37×53 mm); (b)
600t. Judo (51×39 *mm*) ... 7·75 7·75
MS2558 Two sheets. As No. **MS**2557 but additionally inscr in top margin " Centenary International Olympic Games 1896—1996" ... 7·75 7·75

511 Genghis Khan

1996. Genghis Khan Commemoration. Self-adhesive gum.
2559 **511** 10000t. gold ... 65·00 55·00

PHILA SEOUL
(512a)

1996. Phila Seoul '96 International Stamp Exhibition. Nos. 2472/5 optd with T **512a** for the exhibition.

2560	600t. 1884 Korean Empire 5m. Stamp	2·20	1·60
2561	600t. 1924 Mongolia 1c. stamp	2·20	1·60
2562	600t. 1966 Mongolia Children's Day stamp (47×34 mm)	2·20	1·60
2563	600t. 1993 South Korea New Year stamp (47×34 mm)	2·20	1·60

MS2564 95×77 mm. 600t. Korean man wearing traditional dress ... 2·30 2·30

513 Emblems

1996. Seventh Anniv of Democratic Union Coalition.
2565 **513** 100t. multicoloured ... 45 35

514 Pagoda

1996. TAIPEI '96. Sheet 73×67 mm.
MS2566 **514** 750t. multicoloured ... 3·25 3·25

515 Girl and Mongolian Flag

1996. 50th Anniv of United Nations Children's Fund. Multicoloured.

2566a	250t. Type **515**	80	55
2566b	250t. Dutch girl	80	55
2566c	250t. Japanese girl	80	55
2566d	250t. German girl in traditional dress	80	55
2566e	250t. Chinese girls dancing	80	55
2566f	250t. Two American girls	80	55

MS2567 107×83 mm. 700t. Mongolian boy ... 4·50 2·75

250Ŧ
(516)

1996. No. 543 surch as T **516**.
2568 **516** 250t. on 50m. multicol-oured ... 2·40 1·90

518 Ox

1997. New Year. Year of the Ox. Multicoloured.

2570	300t. Type **518**	1·20	95
2571	350t. Ox (horiz)	1·50	1·10

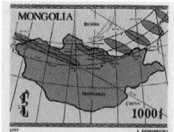

519 Map showing Path of Eclipse

1997. Total Eclipse of the Sun, 9 March 1997. Sheet 83×115 mm.
MS2572 **519** 1000t. multicoloured ... 5·50 5·50

520 Deng Xiaoping (Chinese leader) and Queen Elizabeth

1997. Return of Hong Kong to China. Multicoloured.

2573	200t. Type **520**	1·20	95
2574	250t. Tung Chee-hwa (head of government) and Jiang Zemin (Chinese president)	1·50	1·10

521 Painting and Oil Lamp

1997. Memorial for Victims of Political Oppression.
2575 **521** 150t. black ... 95 75

522 Adelie Penguin

1997. 25th Anniv of Greenpeace (ecological organization). Multicoloured.

2576	200t. Type **522**	85	65
2577	400t. Six Adelie penguins	1·60	1·20
2578	500t. Two Adelie penguins	1·90	1·50
2579	800t. Colony of Emperor penguins	3·25	2·40

MS2580 Two sheets. (a) 120×85 mm. 1000t. *Greenpeace* (ship) amongst icebergs. (b) 183×116 mm. Nos. 2576/9 and **MS**2580a ... 14·50 14·50

523 Dharma Wheel

1997. Religious Symbols. Multicoloured.

2581	200t. Type **523**	1·10	85
2582	200t. Precious Jewels	1·10	85
2583	200t. Precious Minister	1·10	85
2584	200t. Precious Queen	1·10	85
2585	200t. Precious Elephant	1·10	85
2586	200t. Precious Horse	1·10	85
2587	200t. Precious General	1·10	85

524 1961 15m. Stamp (Damdiny Sukhbaatar Monument)

1997. MOCKBA '97 International Stamp Exhibition. Sheet 115×80 mm.
MS2588 **524** 1000t. multicoloured ... 5·25 5·25

525 Electric Locomotive LV-80

1997. Trains. Multicoloured.

2589	20t. Type **525**	10	10
2590	40t. Japanese high-speed electric train	15	15
2591	120t. Diesel locomotive BL-80	25	20
2592	200t. Steam locomotive	35	30
2593	300t. FDP steam locomo-tive *Lass*	60	45
2594	350t. 0-6-0 tank locomotive *Arima*	70	55
2595	400t. Diesel locomotive 216	85	65
2596	500t. Diesel locomotive T6-106	95	75
2597	600t. Monorail *Europa*	1·20	95

MS2598 Two sheets. (a) 133×112 mm.
800t. Eurostar locomotive (57×44
mm). (b) 137×112 mm. 800t. R. and
G. Stephenson's locomotive *Rocket*
(57×44 mm) ... 7·75 7·75

526 *Dendrobium cunninghamii* and Adonis blue

1997. Orchids and Butterflies. Multicoloured.

2599	100t. Type **526**	20	10
2600	150t. Brown hairstreak and *Oncidium ampliatum*	25	20
2601	200t. *Maxillaria triloris* and large skipper	35	30
2602	250t. *Calypso bulbosa* and orange tip	50	40
2603	300t. Painted lady and *Catase-tum pileatum*	60	45
2604	350t. Purple hairstreak and *Epidedrum fimbratum*	65	50
2605	400t. Red admiral and *Celeistes rosea*	70	55
2606	450t. Small copper and *Pontheiva maculate*	85	65
2607	500t. Small tortoiseshell and *Cypripeium calceolus*	95	75

MS2608 Two sheets, each 150×113
mm. (a) 800t. Red admiral and
Macranthum. (b) Adonis blue and
Guttatum ... 7·75 7·75

527 Princess Diana as Child

1997. Diana, Princess of Wales Commemoration. Six sheets containing T **527** and similar vert designs. Multicoloured.

MS2609	Six sheets. (a) 149×193 mm. 50t. Type **527**; 100t. Wearing high-necked blouse; 150t. As teenager; 200t. Wearing drop earrings and evening gown; 250t. Wearing tiara; 300t. Wearing pink outfit and pearl necklace; 350t. Wearing white outfit with gold frogging; 400t. Wearing black sweater; 450t. Wearing halter-necked dress. (b) 149×193 mm. 50t. As young girl; 100t. Wearing checked coat; 150t. As bride; 200t. With Princes William and Harry; 250t. Wearing red dress and tiara; 300t. Wearing black high-necked blouse; 350t. Wearing white blouse; 400t. Wearing pearl necklace and earrings; 450t. Wearing black outfit and pearl necklace. (c) 125×90 mm. 1000t. Wearing pink outfit. (d) 125×90 mm. 1000t. Wearing white dress. (e) 125×90 mm. 1000t. Holding baby Prince Harry. (f) 125×90 mm. 1000t. Wearing tiara Set of 6 sheets	34·00	34·00

528 Soldier

1997. Soldiers of Chingis Khan. Multicoloured.

2610	100t. Type **528**	60	30
2611	150t. Riding galloping horse	1·10	45
2612	200t. Wearing winged helmet, armour and sword	1·50	55
2613	250t. Riding horse and holding flag	1·90	75
2614	300t. Wearing armour and holding two swords	2·20	95
2615	350t. Archer	2·40	1·00
2616	400t. Wearing mailed visor and carrying spear and shield	2·75	1·20
2617	600t. Riding horse and leading cheetah	3·50	1·80
MS2618	175×110 mm. 600t. Three riders; 600t. Two foot soldiers with cheetahs; 1000t. Riders carrying standards (65×60 mm)	8·50	8·50

529 Chingis Khan

1997. Khans of the Mongolian Empire. Multicoloured.

2619	1000t. Type **529**	3·75	2·75
2620	1000t. Ogodei	3·75	2·75
2621	1000t. Guyuk	3·75	2·75
2622	1000t. Mongke	3·75	2·75
2623	1000t. Kubilai (Hubilai)	3·75	2·75
MS2624	Four sheets, each 95×131 mm. (a) As Type **529** (22×32 mm). (b) As No. 2620 (22×32 mm). (c) As Nos. 2621/2 (22×32 mm). (d) As No. 2623 (22×32 mm). Set of 4 sheets	19·00	19·00

530 National Emblem

1998. National Symbols. Multicoloured.

2625	300t. Type **530**	1·20	95
2626	300t. Flag (horiz)	1·20	95

531 Crouching Tiger

1998. New Year. "Year of the Tiger". Multicoloured.

2627	150t. Type **531**	85	65
2628	200t. Tiger facing right	1·20	95
2629	300t. Two tigers (triangle inverted)	1·80	1·40

532 Speed Skating

1998. Winter Olympic Games, Nagano. Multicoloured.

2630	150t.+15t. Type **532**	70	45
2631	200t.+20t. Ski jump	85	55
2632	300t.+30t. Skateboard	1·50	95
2633	600t.+60t. Skiing	2·40	1·90

533 Three Yaks

1998. The Mongolian Yak. Multicoloured.

2634	20t. Type **533**	10	10
2635	30t. White yak	20	15
2636	50t. Yurt, cart and black yak	25	20
2637	100t. White-faced yak with horns	60	45
2638	150t. Mother and calf	85	65
2639	200t. Tethered yak and milking buckets	1·20	95
2640	300t. Large grey yak with horns (53×39 mm)	1·70	1·30
2641	400t. Brown yak with raised tail (53×39 mm)	2·30	1·80
MS2642	95×126 mm. 800t. Yak carrying children and furniture (60×47 mm)	7·25	7·25

534 Players and Competition Emblem

1998. World Cup Football Championship, France. Sheet 121×88 mm.

MS2643	**534** 1000t. multicoloured	6·75	6·75

535 Natsagyn Bagabandi

1998. President Natsagyn Bagabandi. Sheet 70×107 mm.

MS2644	**535** 1000t. multicoloured	6·00	6·00

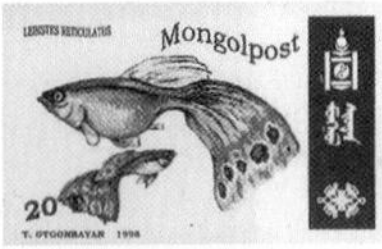

536 *Lebistes reticulates*

1998. Fish. Multicoloured.

2645	20t. Type **536**	10	10
2646	30t. Inscr "Goldfish"	20	15
2647	50t. *Balistes conspcillum*	25	20
2648	100t. Inscr "Goldfish"	35	30
2649	150t. *Synchirops splendidus*	60	45
2650	200t. Inscr "C. auratus"	70	55
2651	300t. *Xiphophorus helleri*	1·20	95
2652	400t. *Pygoplites diacanthus*	1·60	1·20
2653	600t. *Chaetodon auriga*	2·30	1·80
MS2654	Two sheets, each 141×86 mm. (a) 800t. Fish (105×49 mm). (b) 800t. Fish (different) (105×49 mm). Set of 2 sheets	10·50	10·50

537 Bear

1998. Gobi Bear (*Ursus arctos gobiensis*). Multicoloured.

2655	100t. Type **537**	60	45
2656	150t. Facing left	95	75
2657	200t. Two bears	1·30	1·00
2658	250t. Mother and cubs	1·70	1·30
MS2659	Two sheets, each 111×70 mm. (a) 100t. Type **537**; 200t. No. 2657. (b) 150t. No. 2656; 250t. No. 2658	10·50	10·50

538 Brown Cat (inscr "Red Persian")

1998. Cats. Multicoloured.

2660	50t. Type **538**	25	20
2661	100t. Blue shorthair (inscr "Man Cat")	60	45
2662	150t. Smoke Persian	85	65
2663	200t. Cream Persian (inscr "Long hairedwhite Persian")	1·20	95
2664	250t. Two silver tabbies	1·50	1·10
2665	300t. Two Siamese	1·70	1·30
MS2666	106×73 mm. 1000t. Two kittens and basket	5·50	5·50

539 Jerry Garcia

1998. American Musicians. Multicoloured.

2667	100t. Type **539**	60	45
2668	200t. Jerry Garcia wearing grey T-shirt	1·10	85
2669	200t. Bob Marley	1·10	85
2670	200t. Carlos Santana	1·10	85
MS2671	Five sheets (a) 127×165 mm *Grateful Dead*. 50t. Bear as cyclist; 100t. Bear as footballer; 150t. Bear as basketball player; 200t. Bear as golfer; 250t. Bear as baseball player; 300t. Bear as skater; 350t. Bear as ice hockey player; 400t. Bear as American footballer; 450t. Bear as skier. (b) 127×165 mm. *Jerry Garcia*. 50t. Wearing blue T-shirt; 100t. Wearing jacket; 150t. Wearing dark T-shirt, shorter hair; 200t. Microphone, wearing black T-shirt; 250t. Wearing brown T-shirt; 300t. Wearing dark T-shirt; 350t. Wearing grey T-shirt; 400t. Wearing orange T-shirt; 450t. Wearing black T-shirt. (c) 152×102 mm. Jerry Garcia wearing blue T-shirt (51×77 mm). (d) 102×152 mm. 1000t. Jerry Garcia wearing orange T-shirt (51×77 mm). (e) 152×102 mm. 1000t. Bob Marley (51×77 mm). Set of 5 sheets	30·00	30·00

540 Building

1998. Communications and Transport. Multicoloured background colour given.

2672	100t. Type **540** (brown)	50	40
2673	100t. Computer screen (ultramarine)	50	40
2674	100t. Car (green)	50	40
2675	100t. Locomotive (mauve)	50	40
2676	100t. Airplane (violet)	50	40
2677	200t. As No. 2672 (ultramarine)	1·10	85
2678	200t. As No. 2673 (green)	1·10	85
2679	200t. As No. 2674 (mauve)	1·10	85
2680	200t. As No. 2675 (violet)	1·10	85
2681	200t. As No. 2676 (brown)	1·10	85
2682	200t. As No. 2672 (green)	1·10	85
2683	200t. As No. 2673 (mauve)	1·10	85
2684	200t. As No. 2674 (violet)	1·10	85
2685	200t. As No. 2675 (brown)	1·10	85
2686	200t. As No. 2676 (ultramarine)	1·10	85
2687	400t. As No. 2672 (mauve)	2·10	1·60
2688	400t. As No. 2673 (violet)	2·10	1·60
2689	400t. As No. 2674 (brown)	2·10	1·60
2690	400t. As No. 2675 (ultramarine)	2·10	1·60
2691	400t. As No. 2676 (green)	2·10	1·60
2692	400t. As No. 2672 (violet)	2·10	1·60
2693	400t. As No. 2673 (brown)	2·10	1·60
2694	400t. As No. 2674 (ultramarine)	2·10	1·60
2695	400t. As No. 2675 (green)	2·10	1·60
2696	400t. As No. 2676 (mauve)	2·10	1·60

541 Three Stooges

1998. "The Three Stooges" (comedy series starring Moe Howard, Larry Fine and Curly Howard). T **541** and similar multicoloured designs.

MS2697	Six sheets (a) 177×143 mm. 50t. Type **541**; 100t. With mandolin, saw and guitar; 150t. Curly with head in trouser press; 200t. Curly using shower head as microphone; 250t. Curly with head in wooden vice; 300t. Curly having dental treatment with percussion drill; 350t. Curly having dental treatment with pliers; 400t. Stuffing turkey; 450t. Curly with head in door jamb. (b) 177×143 mm. 50t. With pistols and cigars; 100t. Wearing pith helmets; 150t. Curly holding dynamite; 200t. As golfers; 250t. With right hands above heads; 300t. Curly holding bird; 350t. Holding bouquets; 400t. Pulling Moe's ears; 450t. Dressing Curly. (c) 176×130 mm. 50t. Wearing civil war uniforms; 100t. As foreign legionnaires; 150t. With two women; 200t. With horse; 250t. Wearing military uniforms, Curly holding candle; 300t. With anti-aircraft gun; 350t. With laughing general; 400t. With British soldier; 450t. Curly with straw beard. (d) 140×89 mm. 800t. Curly with head in trouser press (42×60 mm). (e) 90×137 mm. 800t. Wearing pith helmets (51×42 mm). (f) 101×127 mm. 800t. Playing football (60×51 mm). Set of 6 sheets	38·00	38·00

542 T. Namnansuren

1998. Prime Ministers. Multicoloured.

2698-2715	200t. ×18, Type **542**; Badamdorj; D. Chagdarjav; D. Bodoo; S. Damdinbazar; B. Tserendorj; A. Amar; Ts. Jigjidjav; P. Genden; Kh. Ghoibalsan; Yu. Tsedenbal; J. Batmunkh; D. Sodnom; Sh. Gungaadorj; D. Byambasuren; P. Jasrai; M. Enkhsaikhan; Ts. Elbegdorj	18·00	14·00

543 Conch Shell

1998. Buddhist Symbols. Multicoloured.

2716	200t. Type **543**	1·10	85
2717	200t. Precious umbrella	1·10	85
2718	200t. Victory banner	1·10	85
2719	200t. Golden fish	1·10	85
2720	200t. Dharma wheel	1·10	85
2721	200t. Auspicious drawing	1·10	85
2722	200t. Lotus flower	1·10	85
2723	200t. Treasure vase	1·10	85

544 People of Many Races and Rainbow

1998. 50th Anniv of Declaration of Human Rights.

2724	**544**	450t. multicoloured	2·20	1·70

545 D. Damien

1998. National Wrestling Champions. Sheet 170×120 mm containing T **545** and similar diamond shaped designs. Multicoloured.
MS2725 200t. ×7, Type **545**; B. Batsuury; J. Munkhbat; H. Bakanmunkh; B. Tubdendorj; D. Tserentogtokh; B. Bat-Erdre ... 8·50 ... 8·50

The stamps and margin of No. **MS**2725 form a composite design of bird and animals.

546 *Mercury 6* Space Capsule and Earth

1998. John Glenn's Return to Space. Two sheets, each 125×170 mm containing T **546** and similar vert designs. Multicoloured.
MS2726 (a) 50t. Type **546**; 100t. NASA emblem and earth; 150t. *Friendship-7* mission emblem and earth; 150t. Rocket lift off; 200t. John Glenn as young man; 250t. Capsule floating in sea; 250t. Capsule; 450t. Moon; 450t. Nebula and star. (b) 50t. NASA emblem and earth; 100t. John Glenn wearing space suit; 150t. *Discovery-7* mission emblem and earth; 150t. Shuttle space craft; 200t. John Glenn as older man; 250t. *Discovery-7* landing; 250t. Space craft, shuttle and moon's surface; 450t. Super nova and moon's surface; 450t. NASA 40th anniversary emblem and moon's surface ... 20·00 ... 20·00

547 Rabbit

1999. New Year. "Year of the Rabbit". Multicoloured.
2727 250t. Type **547** ... 1·20 ... 95
2728 300t. Rabbit facing right (horiz) ... 1·50 ... 1·10

548 Eastern Red-footed Falcon (*Falco amurensis*)

1999. Raptors. Sheet 140×140 mm containing T **548** and similar vert designs. Multicoloured.
MS2729 30t. Type **548**; 50t. Saker falcon (*Falco cherrug*); 100t. Western red-footed falcon (*Falco vespertinus*); 150t. Merlin (*Falco columbarius*); 170t. Peregrine falcon (*Falco peregrinus*); 200t. Common kestrel (*Falco tinnunculus*); 250t. Lesser kestrel (*Falco naumanni*); 300t. Northern hobby (*Falco subbuteo*); 350t. Barbary falcon (*Falco pelegrinoides*); 400t. Barbary falcon with wings spread; 600t. Gyr falcon (*Falco rusticolus*) in flight; 800t. Gyr falcon on nest ... 13·50 ... 13·50

549 Chief Thunderthud

1999. "Howdy Doody" (children's television programme). Four sheets containing T **549** and similar multicoloured designs.
MS2730 131×176 mm. 50t. Type **549**; 100t. Princess Summerfall Winterspring; 150t. Howdy Doody wearing Mexican dress; 150t. Buffalo Bob and Howdy Doody facing each other; 250t. Howdy Doody sitting on Buffalo Bob's lap; 250t. Buffalo Bob and Howdy Doody rubbing noses; 250t. Clarabell the clown; 450t. Howdy Doody as Mountie; 450t. Howdy Doody ... 9·75 ... 9·75

MS2731 Two sheets, each 140×90 mm. (a) 800t. Howdy Doody. (b) 800t. Buffalo Bob and Howdy Doody (horiz) ... 9·25 ... 9·25
MS2732 90×140 mm. 800t. Howdy Doody and Buffalo Bob (48×61 mm) ... 4·75 ... 4·75

550 Gandan Monastery

1999. Migjid Janraisig (Buddha) (statue). Multicoloured.
2733 200t. Type **550** ... 1·20 ... 65
2734 400t. Buddha ... 2·20 ... 1·40
MS2735 Two sheets, each 97×145 mm. (a) 1000t. Buddha and building (49×105 mm). (b) 1000t. Buddha and script (49×105 mm) ... 8·50 ... 8·50

551 Man chasing Demons

1999. Folktales. Multicoloured.
2736 50t. Type **551** ... 25 ... 20
2737 150t. Chess match ... 70 ... 55
2738 200t. Man leading lion carrying wood ... 95 ... 75
2739 250t. Flying horse ... 1·20 ... 95
2740 300t. Archer ... 1·50 ... 1·10
2741 450t. Birds attacking mare and foal ... 2·20 ... 1·70
MS2742 110×70 mm. 1000t. Camel on bird's back ... 6·75 ... 6·75

552 Lucy and Ethel

1999. "I Love Lucy" (television programme). Three sheets containing T **552** and similar vert designs. Multicoloured.
MS2743 137×182 mm. 50t. Type **552**; 100t. Desi, Ethel, Fred and Lucy wrapped in blanket; 150t. Lucy talking; 150t. Lucy pushing buggy through doorway; 200t. Lucy behind window; 250t.Lucy carrying packages; 250t. Desi serenading Ethel; 450t. Lucy and Ethel seated; 450t. Desi, Lucy behind window and Ethel ... 9·75 ... 9·75
MS2744 89×120 mm. 800t. Lucy behind window and Ethel (detail) (38×51 mm) ... 4·75 ... 4·75
MS2745 93×144 mm. 800t. Lucy talking (detail) (38×51 mm) ... 4·75 ... 4·75

553 Betty Boop

1999. Betty Boop (cartoon character). Three sheets containing T **553** and similar multicoloured designs.
MS2746 138×182 mm. 50t. Type **553**; 100t. Wearing torn off shorts and walking boots; 150t. Standing on scales; 150t. Wearing short blue skirt and sandals; 200t. Wearing cap, leggings and leg warmers; 250t. Wearing blue jeans and high heeled shoes; 250t. Wearing striped jersey; 450t. Wearing beach outfit; 450t. Wearing scarf, dress and long white socks ... 9·75 ... 9·75

MS2747 Two sheets, each 125×93 mm. (a) 800t. Dog's eyes containing Betty (51×48 mm). (b) 800t. Betty Boop (51×48 mm) ... 9·75 ... 9·75

(554)

1999. 800th Anniv of Temujin as Chinggis Khan. No. 294 surch as T **554**.
2748 810t. on 60m. buff, ultramarine and brown ... 6·00 ... 6·00

555 Argali Sheep

1999. China 99 International Stamp Exhibition, Beijing.
2749 555 250t. multicoloured ... 1·20 ... 75
2750 555 450t. multicoloured ... 2·10 ... 1·30

556 Zanabazar (city founder)

1999. 360th Anniv of Ulaanbaatar (1st issue). Multicoloured.
2751 300t.+30t. Type **556** ... 95 ... 65
2752 300t.+30t. City arms ... 95 ... 65
2753 300t.+30t. City and country flags ... 95 ... 65
See also MS2762.

(557) **(557a)**

1999. 60th Anniv of Kalkha River Battle. No. 543 surch as T **557** and No. 2043 as T **557a**.
2754 250t. on 50m. multicoloured ... 2·40 ... 1·90
2755 250t. on 60m. multicoloured ... 3·50 ... 2·75

558 Genghis Khan

1999. Genghis Khan Commemoration. Self-adhesive gum.
2756 558 15000t. gold and silver ... 85·00 ... 85·00

559 Early Document and Rider with Two Horses

1999. 125th Anniv of Universal Postal Union. Multicoloured.
2757 250t. Type **559** ... 95 ... 75
2758 250t. Early postal cover and rider ... 95 ... 75
2759 250t. Modern envelope, train and truck ... 95 ... 75
2760 250t. Computer and airplane ... 95 ... 75
MS2761 80×115 mm. 800t. Ogodei Khan (founder of postal relay) (32×41 mm) ... 4·75 ... 4·75

560 Summer Palace

1999. 360th Anniv of Ulaanbaatar (2nd issue). Sheet 155×103 mm containing T **560** and similar horiz designs. Multicoloured.
MS2762 200t.+20t.×9, Type **560**; Parliament building and Sukhbaatar Square; Summer Palace entrance; City Bank; Urga (circa 1900); Opera House; Apartment block; Memorial stone; Aerial view of city ... 9·00 ... 9·00

561 T. Damdinsuren

1999. World Education Day.
2763 561 250t. black and ultramarine ... 85 ... 55
2764 - 250t. black and green ... 85 ... 55
2765 - 450t. black and claret ... 1·30 ... 95
2766 - 450t. black and lake ... 1·30 ... 95
2767 - 600t. multicoloured (56×37 mm) ... 1·70 ... 1·10
DESIGNS: 250t. Type **561**; 250t. B. Rinchin; 450t. No. 2763; 450t. No. 2764; 600t. Teacher and pupils in Ger.

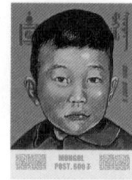

562 Sanjassurengiin Zorig as Child

1999. First Death Anniv of Sanjassurengiin Zorig (politician). Sheet 150×118 mm containing T **562** and similar multicoloured designs.
MS2768 600t. Type **562**; 600t. As adult; 1000t. At political rally (60×40 mm) ... 9·00 ... 9·00

563 Inscribed Stele

1999. Cultural Heritage. Stone Carvings. Multicoloured
2769 50t. Type **563** ... 25 ... 20
2770 150t. 13th century turtle (horiz) ... 60 ... 45
2771 200t. Kul Tegin's burial site ... 70 ... 55
2772 250t. 8th-century carving of Kul Tegin ... 95 ... 75
2773 300t. 8th—9th century dragon (horiz) ... 1·20 ... 95
2774 450t. 5th—7th century figure ... 1·70 ... 1·30

564 Wolves

1999. Wolves. Multicoloured.
2775 150t. Type **564** ... 50 ... 40
2776 250t. Wolves feeding ... 95 ... 75
2777 300t. Mother and cubs ... 1·20 ... 95
2778 450t. Snarling wolf ... 1·70 ... 1·30
MS2779 90×60 mm. 800t. Wolves howling (50×30 mm) ... 4·75 ... 4·75

565 Sunbar Lambs

1999. Mongolian Sheep Breeds. Multicoloured.
2780 50t. Type **565** ... 25 ... 20
2781 100t. Orkhon ... 35 ... 30
2782 150t. Baidrag ... 50 ... 40
2783 250t. Barga ... 70 ... 55
2784 400t. Uzemchin ... 1·50 ... 1·10
2785 450t. Bayad ... 1·70 ... 1·30
MS2786 110×75 mm. 800t. Govi-Altai ... 4·75 ... 4·75

566 "A Day in the Life of Mongolia"

1999. 130th Birth Anniv of Balduugiin Sharav (artist). Sheet 202×159 mm containing T **566** and similar horiz designs showing parts of the painting "A Day in the Life of Mongolia". Multicoloured.

MS2787 50t. Type **566**; 100t. Ger, horsemen and trees; 150t. People seated around fire and workers in fields; 200t. Loaded camels at rest and wrestlers; 250t. Shaman, horse and wrestlers; 300t. Horsemen; 350t. Camels; 450t. Caravan of camels; 600t. Loaded camels and outdoor meal — 11·00 — 11·00

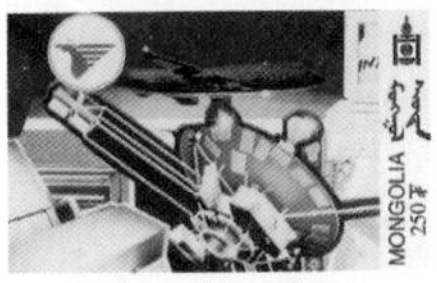

567 Satellite and Aeroplane

1999. 20th Anniv of World Intellectual Property Organization. Sheet 172×112 mm containing T **567** and similar horiz designs. Multicoloured.

MS2788 250t. Type **567**; 250t. Bronze bowl, toy and train; 250t. Printer, stamps and statue; 250t. Racquet, car, bottles and buildings; 250t. Car bonnet, decorated bottles and mobile phones; 250t. Cigarette packet, stereo and boots; 450t. Television, headdress and statue; 450t. Camera, ger and couple; 450t. Perfume bottles — 14·00 — 14·00

568 Prehistoric Ger

1999. Development of the Ger (dwelling). Multicoloured

2789	50t. Type **568**	25	20
2790	100t. Woman, child, dog, horses and early ger	50	40
2791	150t. Woman with elaborate headdress, child, dog and ger	70	55
2792	250t. Windmill, ger and motorbike	1·20	95
2793	450t. Constructing ger	2·20	1·70

MS2794 Two sheets, each 115×80 mm. (a) 800t. Cart carrying ger. (b) 800t. Men seated inside ger — 9·75 — 9·75

569 Dragon

2000. New Year. Year of the Dragon. Multicoloured.

2795	250t. Type **569**	1·10	65
2796	450t. Dragon (vert)	1·90	1·30

570 Wrestler

2000. Mongolia—Japan Friendship. Sheet 149×115 mm containing T **570** and similar vert design. Multicoloured.

MS2797 450t.×2, Type **570**; Emblem — 4·75 — 4·75

1000₮
(571)

2000. Nos. 739/42 surch as T **571**.

2798	1000t. on 50m. brown (post-age)	8·50	3·25
2799	2000t. on 60m. green	12·00	4·75
2800	5000t. on 1t. purple	18·00	6·50
2801	10000t. on 1t.50 blue (air)	28·00	9·50

572 Jerry Garcia

2000. Jerry Garcia (musician) Commemoration. Multicoloured.

2802	50t. Type **572**	25	20
2803	50t. With longer grey hair and sunglasses facing left	25	20
2804	100t. With shorter grey hair facing left	35	30
2805	100t. With shorter grey hair wearing pale t-shirt	35	30
2806	100t. With dark hair and blue guitar	35	30
2807	100t. With longer grey hair facing left	35	30
2808	150t. With dark hair facing left	60	45
2809	150t. With longer grey hair wearing red-tinted glasses	60	45
2810	150t. With dark hair, blue guitar and microphone	60	45
2811	150t. With shorter grey hair, sunglasses and lowered head	60	45
2812	150t. With dark hair and pink and yellow guitar	60	45
2813	150t. With dark hair and pale green guitar	60	45
2814	150t. With shorter grey hair facing left	60	45
2815	150t. With shorter grey hair facing right	60	45
2816	200t. With dark hair wearing green t-shirt	70	55
2817	200t. With longer grey hair and guitar raised	70	55
2818	200t. With dark hair and purple t-shirt facing left	70	55
2819	200t. With dark hair, red t-shirt and yellow guitar	70	55
2820	200t. With shorter grey hair and sunglasses facing left	70	55
2821	200t. With shorter grey hair leaning left	70	55
2822	250t. With dark hair and red and yellow guitar facing right	95	75
2823	250t. With dark hair, purple shirt and pale green guitar facing right	95	75
2824	250t. With shorter grey hair and raised head facing left	95	75
2825	250t. With shorter grey hair tinged with blue	95	75
2826	250t. With shorter grey hair, blue t-shirt facing right	95	75
2827	250t. With longer grey hair and closed eyes facing right	95	75
2828	300t. With shorter grey hair and green t-shirt	1·10	85
2829	300t. With longer grey hair facing left	1·10	85
2830	350t. With shorter grey hair and purple t-shirt facing left	1·30	1·00
2831	350t. With longer grey hair and sunglasses facing left	1·30	1·00

573 Charles Darwin

2000. New Millennium. Sheet 160×230 mm containing T **573** and similar multicoloured designs.

MS2832 100t. Type **573**; 100t. Clematis; 100t. Down House; 100t. Chimpanzee; 200t. Shell (inscr "Mollusk"); 200t. Orchid; 200t. Insect (inscr "Reduviid bug"); 300t. HMS *Beagle*; 300t. Giant tortoise; 300t. Larus relictus (inscr "Duck"); 300t. Turkey; 400t. Peacock; 400t. Dinosaur; 400t. Vormela peregusna (inscr "peregugna"); 550t. Man and woman; 550t. *Equus hemionus*; 600t Ram (59×48 mm) — 18·00 — 18·00

574 High Speed Locomotive (France)

2000. Trains (1st issue). Eight sheets containing T **574** and similar horiz designs. Multicoloured.

MS2833 Two sheets, each 150×113 mm. (a) 200t. Type **574**; 200t. C38 class Pacific (USA); 200t. Inscr "Bo-Bo Electric locomotive" (New Zealand); 300t. Inscr "ALG Bo-Bo electric locomotive" (Britain); 300t. Inscr "E-10 Bo-Bo electric locomotive" (Germany); 300t. 46 Class electric locomotive (USA); 400t. 2-10-0 *Austerity* (Britain); 400t. Diesel-electric locomotive (Australia); 400t. Inscr "Bo-Bo electric locomotive" (Netherlands). (b) 200t. Stephenson 2-2-2 (Russia); 200t. 2-2-2 Walt locomotive (USA); 200t. Ross Winans mud digger (USA); 300t. Italian carriage (1840); 300t. *The General* (USA); 300t. Inscr "4-4-0 Ramopo" (USA); 400t. Carriage (Bodmin & Wadebridge railway); 400t. 4-4-0 Washington (USA); 400t. Braithwaite 0-4-0 — 19·00 — 19·00

MS2834 Two sheets, each 169×120 mm. (a) 350t.×6, As **MS**3833a. (b) 350t.×6, As **MS**2833b — 4·75 — 4·75

MS2835 Two sheets, each 97×71 mm. (a) 800t. Electric Deltic locomotive (Britain). (b) 800t. Inscr "The Ring-master locomotive" (USA) — 9·75 — 9·75

MS2836 Two sheets, each 110×86 mm. (a) 2000t. As **MS**2835a. (b) 2000t. As **MS**2835b — 19·00 — 19·00

See also Nos. **MS**2923/**MS**2924.

575 Emblem

2000. Tenth Anniv of Production and Service Cooperatives.

2837	**575**	300t. indigo	1·50	1·10
2838	**575**	450t. green	2·20	1·70

576 Man's Costume

2000. Traditional Costumes. Multicoloured.

2839	550t. Type **576**	1·70	1·00
2840	550t. Man, closed black top, gold skirt and extended sleeves	1·70	1·00
2841	550t. Man, necklace, gold robe with turned cuffs	1·70	1·00
2842	550t. Man, side fastening, red and gold robe with turned cuffs	1·70	1·00
2843	550t. Man, gold robe, fur cuffs and fur hat with feather	1·70	1·00
2844	550t. Man, crossed white robe under short sleeved gold robe and metal headdress	1·70	1·00
2845	550t. Woman, tall headdress, pink under robe and gold over robe	1·70	1·00
2846	550t. Woman, elaborate furred headdress and blue robe	1·70	1·00

577 Yamantaka

2000. Aspects of Buddha. Multicoloured.

2847	550t. Type **577**	1·70	1·00
2848	550t. Mahakala	1·70	1·00
2849	550t. Inscr "Esura"	1·70	1·00
2850	550t. Begze	1·70	1·00
2851	550t. Shridevi	1·70	1·00
2852	550t. Vajrapani	1·70	1·00
2853	550t. Kubera	1·70	1·00
2854	550t. Siti Mahakala	1·70	1·00
2855	550t. Yama	1·70	1·00
2856	550t. Inscr "Sritzaturtuka"	1·70	1·00

578 Two Horses Grazing

2000. Przewalski Horse (*Equus przewalskii*). Multicoloured.

(a) 51×36 mm.

2857	50t. Two colts	50	40
2858	100t. Mare and foal	95	75
2859	200t. Two horses grazing	1·80	1·40
2860	250t. Two horses galloping	2·40	1·90

(b) 42×28 mm.

2861	100t. Type **578**	95	75
2862	150t. Two horses	85	65
2863	200t. Two colts	1·80	1·40
2864	300t. Mare and foal	2·75	2·10

579 Ferrari 312 T (1975)

2000. Ferrari Race Cars. Multicoloured.

2865-2870	300t.×6, Type **579**; 156 F1 (1961); 312 T4 (1979); 158 F1 (1964); 126 CK (1981); 312 B3 (1974)	8·00	5·25
2871-2876	350t.×6, As Nos. 2865/70	9·25	6·00

580 Boxing

2000. Olympic Games, Sydney. Multicoloured.

2877	100t. Type **580**	60	30
2878	200t. Wrestling	95	55
2879	300t. Judo	1·30	85
2880	400t. Shooting	1·70	1·10

581 Lucy (Lucille Ball) and Ethel Mertz (Vivian Vance)

2000. "I Love Lucy" (television comedy series). Four sheets containing T **581** and similar multicoloured designs.

MS2881 133×172 mm. 100t. Type **581**; 100t. Lucy with chin on hands; 100t. Lucy and Ethel with arms raised; 200t. Lucy serving Fred Mertz (William Fawley); 200t. Lucy holding telephone; 300t. Lucy laughing; 300t. Lucy and Ethel; 400t. Ethel and Lucy reading letter; 550t. Lucy holding bowl and Ethel — 11·00 — 11·00

MS2882 Two sheets, each 96×121 mm. (a) 800t. Lucy wearing glasses and Ethel (horiz) (b) 800t. Lucy wearing checked shirt and Ethel (horiz) — 12·00 — 12·00

582 Moe and Larry

2000. "The Three Stooges" (comedy series starring Moe Howard, Larry Fine and Shemp Howard). Three sheets containing T **582** and similar multicoloured designs.

MS2884 172×134 mm. 100t. Type **582**; 100t. Dentist, Shemp, Moe and Larry; 100t. Larry and Shemp fighting with spoons; 200t. Three Stooges as musicians; 200t. Cooking; 300t. Moe spraying Shemp's mouth, Larry holding Shemp's arm; 300t. Heads together; 400t. Behind bars; 550t. Moe, Shemp and Larry holding spanner — 11·00 — 11·00

MS2885 Two sheets, each 122×96 mm. (a) 800t. Shemp and Larry as soldiers (vert). (b) 800t. Moe and Shemp as musicians — 12·00 — 12·00

583 Bogd Khaan
(Independence)
(1911)

2000. 20th-Century Events. Multicoloured.
2886-	300t.×10, Type **583**; National		
2895	revolution (1921); Declaration of MPR (1924); Political repression (1937); War years (1939–45); Voting for Independence (1945); Agricultural reform (1959); UN membership (1961); Space flight (1981); Democratic revolution (1990)	11·50	7·75

584 Marmot

2000. Marmots (*Marmota sibirica* (inscr "sidisica")). Multicoloured.
2896	100t. Type **584**	50	40
2897	200t. Three marmots	95	75
2898	300t. Two marmots	1·50	1·10
2899	400t. Three marmots, two fighting	2·20	1·70
MS2900	90×60 mm. 800t. Marmot head (horiz)	6·00	6·00

585 Albert
Einstein

2000. Albert Einstein (physicist) Commemoration. Sheet 115×153 mm containing T **585** and similar vert designs. Multicoloured.
MS2901	100t. Type **585**; 100t. As young man reading; 100t. As older man seated holding pen; 200t. As older man with clasped hands; 200t. Holding violin; 300t. Wearing hat and coat; 300t. Holding clock; 400t. Receiving award; 550t. Head and shoulders	11·00	11·00

586 Traditional Design

2000. Traditional Designs. Multicoloured.
2902	50t. Type **586**	25	20
2903	200t. Blue background, central oval design (vert)	85	65
2904	250t. Red background, green border	95	75
2905	300t. Red background, central vase shape and corner decoration (vert)	1·20	95
2906	400t. Soyombo (national symbol) (vert)	1·70	1·30
2907	550t. Violet background, blue vertical border and diamond shaped central design	2·30	1·80

587 John
Fitzgerald Kennedy
Jr.

2000. First Death Anniv of John Fitzgerald Kennedy Junior.
2908	**587**	300t. multicoloured	1·20	95

588 Precious Umbrella

2000. National Symbols. Multicoloured.
2909	300t. Type **588**	95	75
2910	300t. Bishguur (trumpet)	95	75
2911	300t. Bow, arrows and quiver	95	75
2912	300t. Treasure vase	95	75
2913	300t. Flaming swords	95	75
2914	300t. Saddle	95	75
2915	300t. Belt	95	75
2916	300t. Seated Khan	95	75
2917	300t. Throne	95	75

589 Queen Oulen

2000. Queens. Multicoloured.
2918	300t. Type **589**	95	75
2919	300t. Queen Borteujin	95	75
2920	300t. Queen Turakana	95	75
2921	300t. Queen Caymish	95	75
2922	300t. Queen Chinbay	95	75

2000. Trains (2nd issue). Four sheets containing multicoloured designs as T **573**.
MS2923	Two sheets, each 158×121 mm. (a) 100t. Class GS-4 4-8-4 (USA); 100t. Class G85 2-6-2 (Italy); 100t. Class 3700 (Netherlands); 200t. Class 18 4-6-2 (Germany); 200t. Class SY 2-8-2 (China); 200t. Class 231C 4-6-2 (France); 300t. Class 25 4-8-4 (South Africa); 300t. Class HP (India); 300t. LNRA3 Pacific (Britain). (b) 100t. X200 (Sweden); 100t. Deltic (Britain); 100t. GM F7 Warbonnet (USA); 200t. TGV (France); 200t. ICE (Germany); 200t. Class E444 (Italy); 300t. Regio runner (inscr "Holland"); 300t. Type M**1200** (Burma); 300t. G class (Australia)	13·50	13·50
MS2924	Two sheets, each 85×110 mm. (a) 800t. Inscr "Rocket 0-2-2" (Britain) (57×43 mm). (b) 800t. Eurostar (France/Britain) (43×57 mm)	12·00	12·00

590 *Scarabaeus typhoon*

2000. Endangered Species. Sheet 215×115 mm containing T **590** and similar multicoloured designs.
MS2925	100t. Type **590** 100t. *Phrynosephalus helioscopus*; 200t. *Coliber spinalus*; 200t. *Euchoreutes paso* (40×40 mm); 300t. *Camelus bactrianus ferus* (40×40 mm); 300t. *Saiga mongolica* (40×40 mm); 300t. *Chlamydotis undulate* (40×40 mm); 400t. *Ursus arctos gobiensis* (40×40 mm); 550t. *Ovis ammon* (40×40 mm); 550t. *Unicia unicia* (40×40 mm)	14·50	14·50

591 Elephant, Monkey,
Rabbit and Bird

2001. New Millennium. Sheet 120×140 mm.
MS2926	**591**	5000t. multicoloured	24·00	24·00

592 Snake

2001. New Year. Year of the Snake. Multicoloured.
2927	300t. Type **592**	95	75
2928	400t. Snake (vert)	1·50	1·10

593 World War I
(1914)

2001. 20th Century. Multicoloured.
2929	300t. Type **593**	1·10	65
2930	300t. Lenin (October Revolution) (1917)	1·10	65
2931	300t. Adolf Hitler (rise of Fascism) (1933)	1·10	65
2932	300t. Russian, American and British leaders (World War II) (1939)	1·10	65
2933	300t. Albert Einstein (Nuclear weapons) (1945)	1·10	65
2934	300t. Emblem and members flags (United Nations) (1945)	1·10	65
2935	300t. Hand holding torch (end of colonialism) (1940)	1·10	65
2936	300t. Astronaut (space exploration) (1961)	1·10	65
2937	300t. Mikhael Gorbachev (end of socialism) (1989)	1·10	65
2938	300t. Horses and yurts (New Mongolia) (1911)	1·10	65

594 Soldier
(statue)

2001. 80th Anniv of Armed Forces. Multicoloured.
2939	300t. Type **594**	1·30	65
2940	300t. Soldier with scabbard	1·30	65
2941	300t. Mounted soldier	1·30	65

595 Mountaineer

2001. Mongolian Mountaineers. Sheet 115×80 mm containing T **595** and similar vert design. Multicoloured.
MS2942	400t.×2, Type **595**; Everest	6·00	6·00

596 Lucy and Desi

2001. "I Love Lucy" (television comedy series). Three sheets containing T **596** and similar multicoloured designs.
MS2943	172×140 mm. 100t. Type **596**; 100t. Lucy smearing woman with chocolate; 100t. Woman smearing Lucy with chocolate; 200t. Cake making; 200t Lucy and Ethel; 300t. Receiving instruction in cake making; 300t. Lucy with arms raised; 400t. Desi and Fred; 550t. Desi holding stocking and Fred	11·00	11·00
MS2944	Two sheets, each 127×102 mm. (a) 800t. Lucy (vert). (b) 800t. Fred and Desi (vert)	12·00	12·00

597 Larry

2001. "The Three Stooges" (comedy series starring Moe Howard, Larry Fine and Shemp Howard). Three sheets containing T **597** and similar multicoloured designs.
MS2945	172×140 mm. 100t. Type **597**; 100t. Moe; 100t. Mo, Larry and Shemp; 200t. Moe, Larry and Shemp using telephones; 200t. Mo with mallet and man using telephone; 300t. Moe and Shemp surprised; 300t. Three Stooges as chefs; 400t. Larry and Shemp as dentists; 550t. Moe, Shemp and Larry and woman	11·00	11·00
MS2946	128×102 mm. 800t. Shemp and Larry	6·00	6·00
MS2947	102×128 mm. 800t. Shemp as angel (vert)	6·00	6·00

598 Hong Kong 2001 Emblem and
"Nomading" (T. S. Minjuur)

2001. International Stamp Exhibitions. Sheet 175×132 mm containing T **598** and similar horiz designs showing painting "Nomading" by T. S. Minjuur and exhibition emblem.
MS2948	400t.×4, Type **598**; Hafnia 01, Denmark; PhilaNippon '01; Belgica 2001	6·75	6·75

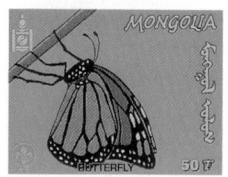

599 Roses

2001. Japan EXPO 2001, Kitakyushu. Sheet 120×180 mm containing T **599** and similar multicoloured designs. Self-adhesive.
MS2949	500t.×5, Type **599**; Woman (32×42 mm); Tarbosaurus (48×25 mm); Iguanodon (25×48 mm); Triceratops (48×25 mm)	13·00	13·00

600 Butterfly

2001. Scouting and Nature. Three sheets containing T **600** and similar multicoloured designs.
MS2950	Two sheets, each 172×95 mm. (a) 50t. Type **600**; 100t. Bat; 200t. Butterfly (different); 300t. Fungi; 400t. Dinosaur; 450t. Puffin. (b) 100t. *Salpingotus*; 200t. *Unica unica*; 300t. *Haliaeetus* (inscr "Haleaeetus") *albicilla*; 400t. *Pandion haliaetus* (inscr "haliatus"); 450t. *Phasianus* (inscr "Panciawus") *colchicus*	14·50	14·50
MS2951	134×172 mm. Size 38×51 mm. 50t. Penguins; 100t. Frog; 150t. Seashell; 200t. Elephant; 250t. Butterfly; 300t. Owl; 350t. Whale; 400t. Orchid; 450t. Sea turtle	11·00	11·00

601 Zeppelin Airship

2001. Transport. Sheet 172×134 mm containing T **601** and similar horiz designs. Multicoloured.
MS2952	50t. Type **601**; 100t. Air balloon; 150t. *Apollo* command module; 200t. *Apollo II* lunar module; 250t. Concorde; 300t. Steam locomotive; 350t. Motorcycle; 400t. Race car; 450t. Yacht	11·00	11·00

602 Flag

2001. 40th Anniv of United Nations Membership. Multicoloured.
2953	400t. Type **602**	1·80	1·40
2954	400t. Dove	1·80	1·40

Nos. 2953/4 were issued together, *se-tenant*, forming a composite design.

603 World Trade Centre and Statue of Liberty

2001. Unite against Terror.

2955	**603**	300t.+50t. multicoloured	1·60	1·20
2956	**603**	400t.+50t. multicoloured	2·10	1·60

604 Children encircling Globe

2001. United Nations Year of Dialogue among Civilizations.

2957	**604**	300t. multicoloured	1·60	95

605 Symbols of Italy

2001. History. Sheet 260×186 mm containing T **605** and similar horiz designs. Multicoloured.

MS2958 200t.×10, Type **605**; Roman senators and centurion; Statue and dancers; Mosque, decoration and mounted soldier; Celtic warrior and decoration; "Mona Lisa" and European art; Polynesian mask, stone heads and musician; Astronomy; Symbols of French revolution; Symbols of space exploration; 300t.×10, Greek statue, Parthenon and vase; Temple, Angkor Wat and statue; Mongolian statue, fountain and masked dancer; Chingis Khan; Yurt; Russian church and icons; Globe and Christopher Columbus; Symbols of America; Early printing press and Albrecht Durer; Symbols of United Kingdom 19·00 19·00

606 *Gazella subgutturosa*

2001. Endangered Species. Sheet 219×116 mm containing T **606** and similar multicoloured designs.

MS2959 100t.×2, Type **606**; *Rana chensinensis*; 200t.×2, *Podoces hendersoni*; *Papilio machaon*; 300t.×3, *Vespertilio superans* (40×40 mm); *Capra sibirica* (40×40 mm); *Equus hemionus hemionus* (40×40 mm); 400t. *Equus przewalskii* (40×40 mm); 550t.×2, *Erinaceus dauricus*; *Vormela peregusna* 14·50 14·50

The stamps and margins of **MS**2959 form a composite design.

607 Horse

2002. New Year. Year of the Horse. Multicoloured.

2960	300t. Type **607**	1·20	95
2961	400t. Galloping horse (horiz)	1·70	1·30

400 ₮

(608)

2002. 20th Anniv of Mongolia—USSR Space Flight. No. **MS**1352 surch as T **608**.

MS2962 400t. on 4t. multicoloured 5·75 5·75

609 *Gyps himalayensis*

2002. Vultures. Multicoloured.

2963	100t. Type **609**	50	40
2964	150t. *Gyps fulvus*	60	45
2965	300t. *Neophron percnopterus*	1·20	95
2966	400t. *Aegypius monachus*	1·70	1·30
2967	550t. *Gypaetus barbatus*	2·40	1·90

610 Horse Rider

2002. 30th Anniv of Mongolia—Japan Diplomatic Relations. Two sheets, each 110×85 mm, containing T **610** and similar multicoloured designs.

MS2968 (a) 550t.×2, Type **610**; Girl's face. (b) 550t.×2, Camel (40×30 mm); Ass (40×30 mm) 10·50 10·50

The stamps and margins of **MS**2968a form a composite design.

611 Dog

2002. The Mongolian Dog. Multicoloured.

2969	100t. Type **611**	50	40
2970	200t. With cattle	95	75
2971	300t. Two puppies	1·50	1·10
2972	400t. With camels	1·90	1·50

MS2973 105×70 mm. 800t. Dog facing right 3·75 3·75

612 Seoul Stadium

2002. World Cup Football Championship. Sheet 120×95 mm containing T **612** and similar horiz designs. Multicoloured.

MS2974 300t.×2, Type **612**; Yokohama stadium; 400t.×2, French team (1998); English team (1966) 5·75 5·75

613 Ikeguchi Ekan

2002. Mongolia—Japan Diplomatic Relations. Two sheets containing T **613** and similar vert designs. Multicoloured.

MS2975 150×90 mm. 150t. Type **613** 60 60

MS2976 110×90 mm. 1500t. Tomoyoshi Wada 4·75 4·75

614 *Thermopsis*

2002. Medicinal Plants. Multicoloured.

2977	100t. Type **614**	50	40
2978	150t. *Chelidonium*	70	55
2979	150t. *Hypericum*	70	55
2980	200t. *Plantago*	95	75
2981	250t. *Saussurea*	1·20	95
2982	300t. *Rosa acicularis*	1·50	1·10
2983	450t. *Lilium*	2·30	1·80

615 Horse-drawn Vehicle

2002. Rock Drawings. Multicoloured.

2984	50t. Type **615**	30	25
2985	100t. Deer	60	45
2986	150t. Horseman	90	70
2987	200t. Horseman (different)	1·20	95
2988	300t. Chariot	1·80	1·40
2989	400t. Camel	2·40	1·90

MS2990 97×77 mm. 800t. Stag's head 4·75 4·75

616 Children on Horseback

2002. Children and Sport. Multicoloured.

2991	500t. Boy cycling	2·40	1·90
2992	500t. Boy holding baseball bat	2·40	1·90
2993	500t. Boy playing chess	2·40	1·90

MS2994 134×172 mm. 100t. Type **616**; 150t. Two girls playing football; 200t. Four horses' heads and two riders; 250t. Boys playing golf; 300t. Girl rider and prayer flags; 350t. Ice hockey player; 400t. Horse's head and three riders; 450t. Girl playing football; 500t. Three horses' heads, one rider and flag 12·00 12·00

617 Ram

2003. New Year. Year of the Sheep (Goat). Multicoloured.

2995	300t. Type **617**	1·50	1·10
2996	400t. Ram, laying down (horiz)	1·90	1·50

618 *Russula aeruginosa* and *Coccothraustes coccothraustes*

2003. Birds and Fungi. Multicoloured.

2997	50t. Type **618**	25	20
2998	100t. *Boletus edulis* and *Loxia curvirostra*	50	40
2999	150t. *Boletus badius* and *Carpodacus erythrinus*	70	55
3000	200t. *Agaricus campester* and *Garrulus glandarius*	95	75
3001	250t. *Marasmius oreades* and *Luscinia megarhyachos*	1·20	95
3002	300t. *Cantharellus cibarius* and *Locustella certhiola*	1·50	1·10
3003	400t. *Amanita phalloides* and *Ardea cinerea*	1·90	1·50
3004	550t. *Suillus granulatus* and *Accipiter gentilis*	2·75	2·10

MS3005 Two sheets, each 105×70 mm. (a) 800t. *Tricholoma pertentosum* and *Lanius collurio* (60×40 mm). (b) 800t. *Lactarius tormmosus* and *Aeqithalos caudatus* (60×40 mm) 7·25 7·25

619 Damdin Sukhbaatur (statue)

2003. Tourism. Two sheets, each 151×80 mm containing T **619** and similar horiz designs. Multicoloured.

MS3006 (a) 100t. Type **619**; 200t. Kharakhorum Monastery; 300t. Turtle rock, Terelj; 400t. Yurts. (b) 100t. Camels; 200t. Yaks; 300t. Falconer; 400t. Snow leopard 9·75 9·75

620 Takumi Ueda

2003. Mongolia—Japan Diplomatic Relations. Sheet 110×90 mm.

MS3007 **620** 300t. multicoloured 2·20 2·20

2003. Endangered Species. Sheet 222×121 mm containing multicoloured designs as T **606**.

MS3008 100t.×2, *Moschus moschiferus* (40×40 mm); *Castor fiber birula* (40×30 mm); 200t.×2, *Dryomys nitedula* (40×30 mm); *Lutra lutra* (40×30 mm); 300t.×3, *Rangifer tarandus* (40×40 mm); *Pandion haliaetus* (40×30 mm); *Sus scrofa nigripes* (40×40 mm); 400t. *Alces alces cameloides* (40×40 mm); 550t.×2, *Alces alces pfizenmayen* (40×40 mm); *Phasianus colchicus* (40×30 mm) 12·00 12·00

The stamps and margins of **MS**3008 form a composite design.

621 Common Bush Tanager

2003. Flora and Fauna. Eight sheets, containing T **621** and similar multicoloured designs.

MS3009 138×98 mm. Birds. 800t.×4, Type **621**; Black-headed hemispingus; Scarlet-rumped tanager; Band-tailed seedeater 9·75 9·75

MS3010 Three sheets, each 139×118 mm. (a) Fungi. 800t.×4, *Hypholoma fasciculare*; *Marasmiellus ramealis*; *Collybia fusipes*; *Kuchneromyces mutabilis*. (b) Orchids. 800t.×4, *Vanda Rothchildiana*; *Paphiopedilum parishii*; *Dendrobium nobile*; *Cattleya loddigesii*. (c) Butterflies. 800t.×4, *Thecla teresina*; *Theritas cypria*; *Theritas coronata*; *Thecla phaleros* 29·00 29·00

MS3011 Four sheets, each 99×69 mm. (a) Birds. 2500t. Andean hillstar. (b) Fungi. 2500t. *Psathyrella multipedata* (vert). (c) Orchids. 2500t. *Barkeria skinneri* (inscr "skinnerii"). (d) Butterflies. 2500t. *Thecla pedusa*. 34·00 34·00

622 Yang Liwei

2003. First Chinese Astronaut. Sheet 80×61 mm.

MS3012 **622** 800t. multicoloured 4·75 4·75

623 Monkey

2004. New Year. Year of the Monkey. Multicoloured.

3013	300t. Type **623**	1·20	95
3014	400t. Monkey facing right	1·60	1·20

624 Heaven

2004. Peace Mandala (patchwork quilt). Two sheets containing T **624** and similar multicoloured designs showing life of Buddha. Self-adhesive.

MS3015 200×290 mm. 50t. Type **624**;
100t. Journey on elephant to birth mother; 150t. Birth from mother's armpit; 200t. Life as prince; 250t. Shaving his hair; 300t. Seated fighting devil; 400t. Seated with hand raised; 550t. Attaining Nirvana; 5000t. Life of Buddha (135×185 mm)   24·00   24·00

MS3016 81×105 mm. 5000t. Seated Buddha (62×78 mm)   19·00   19·00

625 Equus przewalskii

2004. Animals. Value expressed as letter. Multicoloured.

3017	(A) Type **625**	95	75
3018	(?) Ovis ammon	1·50	1·10
3019	(B) Camelus bactrianus ferus	2·40	1·90
3020	(?) Capra sibirica	3·00	2·30

626 Chinggis Khan

2004. 840th Birth Anniv of Chinggis Khan (leader). 800th Anniv of Mongolian State. Multicoloured.

3021	200t. Type **626**	70	55
3022	300t. Facing right (horiz)	1·10	85
3023	350t. Statue	1·30	1·00
3024	550t. On horseback	2·10	1·60

627 Judo

2004. Olympic Games, Athens. Multicoloured.

3025	100t. Type **627**	35	30
3026	200t. Wrestling (horiz)	70	55
3027	300t. Boxing	1·10	85
3028	400t. Shooting (horiz)	1·50	1·10

628 Emblem

2004. 130th Anniv of Universal Postal Union (UPU).

3029	**628** 300t. multicoloured	1·10	85

629 Early Team Members

2004. Juventus Football Club. Multicoloured.

3030	50t. Type **629**	25	20
3031	50t. Team members (different)	25	20
3032	100t. Player and ball	35	30
3033	100t. Goalkeeper	35	30
3034	150t. Player heading ball into goal	50	40
3035	150t. Three players	50	40
3036	200t. Players tackling	70	55
3037	200t. Juventus player preparing to kick ball	70	55

630 1924 $1 Stamp (1st Mongolian stamp)

2004. 80th Anniv of First Mongolian Stamp. Sheet 80×60 mm.

MS3038 **630** 800t. multicoloured   4·75   4·75

631 Lytta caragana (inscr "caraganae")

2004. Insects and Flowers. Two sheets, each 120×80 mm containing T **631** and similar horiz designs. Multicoloured.

MS3039 (a) 100t.×2, Type **631**; Rosa acicularis; 200t.×2, Aquilegia sibirica; Tabanus bivinus; 300t.×2, Corizus hyoscyami; Lilium pumilum. (b) 100t.×2, Mantis religiosa; Aster alpinus; 200t.×2, Echinops bumilis; Apis mellifera; 300t.×2, Angaracris barabensis; Nymphaea candida   11·00   11·00

632 Woman's Headdress, Kazakhstan

2004. Women's Headdresses. Multicoloured.

3040	550t. Type **632**	1·90	1·50
3041	550t. Mongolian headdress	1·90	1·50

Stamps of the same design were issued by Kazakhstan.

633 Rooster

2005. New Year. Year of the Rooster. Mult.

3042	300t. Type **633**	1·10	85
3043	400t. Rooster facing right (vert)	1·30	1·00

634 Butterfly

2005. EXPO 2005, Aichi, Japan. Sheet 161×91 mm containing T **634** and similar vert designs. Multicoloured.

MS3044 100t. Type **634**; 150t. Flower; 200t.; Puppy; 550t. Kitten   6·00   6·00

The stamps and margins of MS3044 form a composite design.

635 Two Children

2005. World Vision (charitable organization) (1st issue).

3045	**635** 550t. multicoloured	1·90	1·50

See also No. 3058.

636 Woman's Costume

2005. Traditional Costumes. Multicoloured, background colour given.

3046	200t. Type **636**	70	55
3047	200t. Man's costume (pink)	70	55
3048	200t. Woman's costume (green)	70	55
3049	200t. Man's costume (green)	70	55
3050	200t. Woman's costume (blue)	70	55
3051	200t. Man's costume (blue)	70	55

637 Guardian

2005. Buddhist Guardians. Multicoloured.

3052	400t. Type **637**	1·30	1·00
3053	400t. Guardian holding sword	1·30	1·00
3054	400t. Guardian holding snake	1·30	1·00
3055	400t. Guardian holding pig and umbrella	1·30	1·00

638 Asashoryu

2005. Asashoryu—Mongolian Sumo Wrestler. Sheet 135×106 mm containing T **638** and similar multicoloured designs.

MS3056 600t. Type **638**; 700t. Asashoryu on horseback (vert); 800t. Asashoryu wearing fight costume (vert)   6·00   6·00

2005. TAIPEI 2005. Sheet 73×67 mm.

MS3057 750t. As No. MS2566   6·00   6·00

No. MS3057 was overprinted in the margin for the exhibition.

640 Child riding Camel

2005. World Vision (charitable organization) (2nd issue).

3058	**640** 550t. multicoloured	1·90	1·50

641 Woman's Headdress

2005. Traditional Headdresses. Multicoloured.

3059	50t. Type **641**	25	20
3060	100t. Woman's with conical centre and train	35	30
3061	150t. Man's with central feather	50	40
3062	200t. Man's with fur rim and tassel	70	55
3063	250t. Woman's with fur trim	85	65
3064	300t. Man's with conical centre and long tassel	1·10	85

MS3065 100×120 mm. 800t. Fur hat with conical centre and streamers (40×60 mm)   4·75   4·75

642 Astronauts in Flight

2005. Shenzhou VI Manned Space Flight. Two sheets, each 100×100 mm containing T **642** and similar horiz design. Multicoloured.

MS3066 (a) 800t. Type **642**. (b) 800t. Astronauts waving   7·50   7·50

643 Gold Coin

2006. 800th Anniv of Mongolia. Ancient coins. Multicoloured.

3067-	550t.×3, Type **643**; Silver coin;		
3069	Copper coin	6·00	4·75

644 Dog

2006. New Year. Year of the Dog. Multicoloured.

3070	300t. Type **644**	1·10	85
3071	400t. Dog (different)	1·30	1·00

645 Archer

2006. 50th Anniv of Europa Stamps. Multicoloured.

3072- 200t.×12, Type **645**; Camels and
3083   dunes; Shepherds and flocks; Horse; Turtle rock; Mosque; Dinosaur skeleton; Gymnasts; Yurt; Wrestlers; Aircraft; Yak   9·00   6·75

MS3084 Six sheets, each 104×50 mm. (a) As Nos. 3072/3. (b) As Nos. 3074/5. (c) As Nos. 3076/7. (d) As Nos. 3078/9. (e) As Nos. 3080/1. (f) As Nos. 3082/3 Set of 6 sheets   9·75   9·75

646 Horse-head Violin

2006. National Symbols. Morin Khuur. Sheet 83×116 mm.

MS3085 **646** 550t. multicoloured   2·40   2·40

647 President Enkhbayar

2006. Nambaryn Enkhbayar, President of Mongolia. Sheet 91×120 mm.

MS3086 **647** 800t. multicoloured   3·25   3·25

648 Two Stylized Players and Goalkeeper

2006. World Cup Football Championship, Germany. Sheet 130×80 mm containing T **648** and similar horiz designs. Multicoloured.

MS3087 200t. Type **648**; 250t. One player; 300t. Two players; 400t. Three players   4·25   4·25

649 Presidents George Bush and Nambaryn Enkhbayar

2006. First Official visit of USA President to Mongolia. Sheet 100×60 mm Multicoloured.

MS3088 **649** 600t. multicoloured   3·00   3·00

650 Armoured Man and Cheetah

2006. 800th Anniv of Mongolia. Sheet 185×80 mm containing T **650** and similar multicoloured designs.
MS3089 50t. Type **650**; 100t. Woman with falcon and cheetah; 300t. Genghis Khan; 400t. Couple with two cheetahs 500t. Army (80×56 mm) 5·50 5·50

651 Early 20th-century Bronze Replica of Equestrian Deity Rao Dev from Bastar, Madhya Pradesh

2006. Art. Sheet 110×60 mm containing T **651** and similar horiz design. Multicoloured.
MS3090 300t. Type **651**; 400t. Ancient bronze horse statue, from Murun city, Mongolia 3·75 3·75
The stamps of MS3090 form a composite background design. Stamps in similar designs were issued by India.

652 Children riding Ox

2006. World Vision. Multicoloured.
3091 550t. Type **652** 1·90 1·50
3092 550t. Boy riding horse 1·90 1·50

653 Genghis Khan

2006. Sheet 100×80 mm. Multicoloured. Silk paper.
MS3093 653 3800t. multicoloured 11·50 11·50

654 Building

2006. Mongolia—China Philatelic Exhibition. Sheet 151×58 mm containing T **654** and similar horiz design. Multicoloured.
MS3094 150t. Type **654**; 200t. Waterfall; 250t. Street at night 3·75 3·75

655 Taimen

2006. Hucho Taimen (Taimen). Multicoloured.
3095 100t. Type **655** 35 30
3096 200t. Facing left 70 55
3097 300t. Facing right 1·10 85
3098 400t. Head facing left and two smaller fish 1·30 1·00
Nos. 3095/6 and 3097/8, respectively, were printed together, se-tenant, forming a composite design.

656 Pig

2006. New Year. Year of the Pig. Multicoloured.
3099 300t. Type **656** 1·10 85
3100 400t. Facing left with lowered head 1·30 1·00

657 Prince Willem-Alexander

2007. State Visit of Prince Willem-Alexander and Princess Maxima of the Netherlands. Multicoloured.
3101 700t. Type **657** 2·40 1·90
3102 700t. Prince Willem-Alexander and Princess Maxima 2·40 1·90
3103 700t. Princess Maxima 2·40 1·90

658 Betty Boop

2007. Betty Boop. Two sheets containing T **658** and similar vert designs. Multicoloured.
MS3104 127×178 mm. 700t.×6, Type **658**; With arms and knee raised; With hands clasped; With left arm raised; With leg raised; With left arm raised and right leg bent 15·00 14·00
MS3105 100×70 mm. 1500t.×2, Wearing red dress; Wearing red dress with additional partial heart on left 12·00 11·50
Nos. MS3104 and MS3105 each form a composite background design.

659 Pope John Paul II

2007. Pope John Paul II.
3106 **659** 880t. multicoloured 3·00 2·30

660 Marilyn Monroe

2007. Marilyn Monroe. Sheet 130×108 mm containing T **660** and similar vert designs. Multicoloured.
MS3107 1050t.×4, Type **660**; Looking over left shoulder; Head only; Wearing red dress 10·50 9·75
The stamps of No. MS3107 share a composite background design.

661 Elvis Presley

2007. 30th Death Anniv of Elvis Presley. Multicoloured.
3108 1050t. Type **661** 3·75 3·00
3109 1050t. With right arm raised 3·75 3·00
3110 1050t. Wearing decorative belt 3·75 3·00
3111 1050t. With longer hair 3·75 3·00

662 Lama Tsongkhapa

2007. 650th Death Anniv of Lama Tsongkhapa (Buddhist teacher and reformer).
3112 **662** 100t. multicoloured 35 30

663 Genghis Khan (statue)

2007. 20th Anniv of Mongolia—USA Diplomatic Relations. Sheet 120×80 mm containing T **663** and similar square design. Multicoloured.
MS3113 400t. Type **663**; 550t. Abraham Lincoln (statue) 4·75 4·25
The stamps and margins of No. MS3113 form a composite background design.

664 Mount Fuji, Japan

2007. 35th Anniv of Mongolia—Japan Diplomatic Relations. Sheet 120×60 mm containing T **664** and similar horiz design. Multicoloured.
MS3114 550t. Type **664**; 700t. Mount Otgontenger, Mongolia 5·50 5·00
The stamps and margins of No. MS3114 form a composite background design.

2007. Irkutsk 2007 Philatelic Exhibition. No. MS2588 inscr 'MOCKBA '97' and '??????? 2007' on sheet margin. Sheet 115×80 mm.
MS3115 1000t. multicoloured 4·00 3·75

665 'Light of Wisdom'

2007. Mongolian Calligraphy. Multicoloured.
3116 50t. Type **665** 20 10
3117 100t. 'Butterfly' 35 30
3118 150t. 'Flower' 50 35
3119 200t. 'Horse' 70 55
3120 250t. 'Spring' 90 70
3121 300t. 'Leaves' 1·10 85
3122 400t. 'Wow' 1·30 1·00
3123 550t. 'Wild Camel' 1·70 1·50
MS3124 96×121 mm. 800t. 'Sky' 6·00 4·75

666 Woman as Waterfall (Ts. Tsegmid)

2007. Modern Art. Five sheets containing T **666** and similar multicoloured designs.
MS3125 Three sheets 62×78 mm. (a) 400t. Type **666**. (b) 400t. Mountain with face (S. Sarantsatsralt). (c) 400t. Woman enclosed in man's outline (Ts. Enkhjin). Two sheets 78×62 mm. (d) 400t. Mare and foal (Sh. Chimeddorj). (e) 400t. Abstract (Do. Bold) 6·50 6·25

667 Naotoshi Yamada (Olympic cheerleader) and Wrestler

2007. 35th Anniv of Mongolia—Japan Friendship. Sheet 171×228 mm containing T **667** and similar horiz designs. Self-adhesive gum.
MS3126 6 stamps (500t.×2, 600t.×2, 700t.×2) showing Naotoshi Yamada and Sumo wrestlers 15·00 14·50

668 Ghengis Khan

2007. 780th Death Anniv of Ghengis Khan.
3127 **668** 230t. multicoloured 75 60
3128 **668** 400t. multicoloured 1·30 1·00
3129 **668** 650t. multicoloured 2·10 1·60
3130 **668** 800t. multicoloured 2·75 2·20
3131 **668** 1000t. multicoloured 3·75 3·00

669 Rat

2008. New Year. Year of the Rat. Multicoloured.
3132 800t. Type **669** 2·75 2·20
3134 800t. Rat looking up 2·75 2·20
No. 3132/3 were issued together, se-tenant, forming a composite design.

2008. No. 1559 surch 1000t.
3135 1000t. on 60m. multicoloured 3·75 3·00
No. 3134 has been left for stamp not yet received.

2008. Taipei 2008 International Stamp Exhibition. No. 2228 surch TAIPEI 2008 250tabd emblem.
3136 250t. on 40m. multicoloured 2·75 2·20

672 Ribbon

2008. AIDS Awareness Campaign.
3137 **672** 500t. multicoloured 1·50 1·30

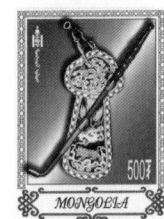

673 Pipe and Pouch

2008. Decorative Arts. Multicoloured.
3138 500t. Type **673** 1·50 1·30
3139 500t. Stone bottle 1·50 1·30
3140 500t. Sword and accoutrements 1·50 1·30
3141 500t. Saddle 1·50 1·30
3142 500t. Decorative metal bowls 1·50 1·30

674 Canoeing

2008. Olympic Games, Beijing. Multicoloured.
3143 600t. Type **674** 2·10 1·90
3144 600t. Fencing 2·10 1·90
3145 600t. Handball 2·10 1·90
3146 600t. Modern Pentathlon 2·10 1·90

675 Boar

2008. Wild Boar. Multicoloured.
3147 800t. Type **675** 2·75 2·20
3148 800t. Mother and piglets 2·75 2·20
3149 800t. Boar facing right 2·75 2·20
3150 800t. Two boar 2·75 2·20
Nos. 3147/50 were issued in together, se-tenant, forming a composite design.

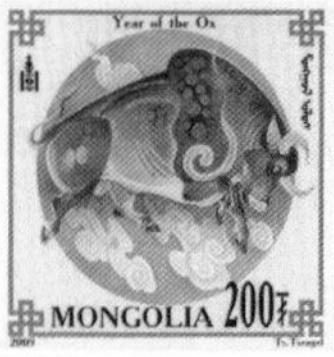

676 Ox

2009. Chinese New Year. Year of the Ox. Multicoloured.

3151	200t. Type **676**	1·40	1·20
3152	300t. Ox (different)	2·75	2·20

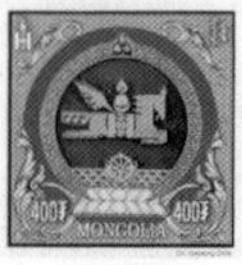

677 State Arms

2009. State Symbols. Multicoloured.

3153	400t. Type **677**	1·30	1·10
3154	500t. Flame of prosperity	1·50	1·30
3155	800t. State flag	2·75	2·20
3156	1000t. Soyonbo	3·75	3·00

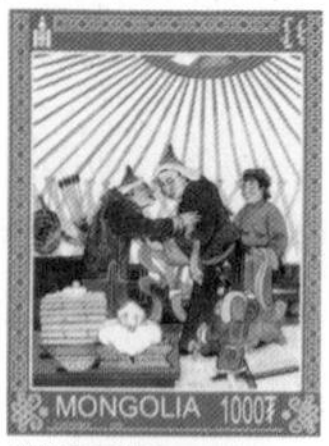

678 Greeting

2009. Hospitality.

3157	**678**	1000t. multicoloured	4·00	3·25

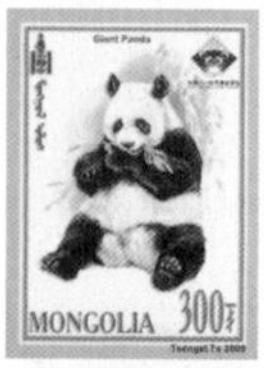

679 Giant Panda

2009. China 2009–International Stamp Exhibition, Luoyang. Multicoloured.

3158	300t. Type **679**	1·40	1·20
3159	300t. *Ursus arctos gobiensis* (Gobi bear)		

800₮
(680)

2009. Nos. 1524/5 surch as T 680.

3160	800t. on 30m. multicoloured (Skin tent)	3·00	2·40
3161	1000t. on 20m. multicoloured (Antonov An-24B)	4·00	3·25

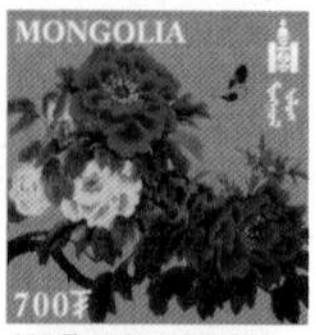

681 Tree Peonies

2009

3162	**681**	700t. multicoloured	2·50	2·00

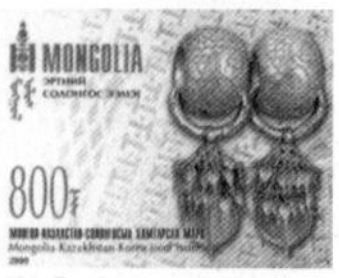

682 Earrings

2009. Jewellery.

3163	**683**	800t. multicoloured	3·00	2·40

APPENDIX

The following stamps have either been issued in excess of postal needs, or have not been available to the public in reasonable quantities at face value. Such stamps may later be given full listings if there is evidence of regular postal use. Miniature sheets and imperforate stamps are excluded from this listing.

2007

Diana, Princess of Wales Commemoration. 1150t.×4 a. Sheetlet of 4

60th Wedding Anniv of Queen Elizabeth II and Prince Philip. 400t.×2 a. Pair

Helicopters. 1150t.×4, a. Sheetlet of 4

Muhammad Ali. 1150×4 a. Sheetlet of 4, 1150t.×4 a. Sheetlet of 4

Pt. 17

MONG-TSEU (MENGTSZ)

An Indo-Chinese P.O. in Yunnan province, China, closed in 1922.

1903. 100 centimes = 1 franc. 1919 100 cents = 1 piastre.

Stamps of Indo-China surcharged.

1903. "Tablet" key-type surch MONGTZE and value in Chinese.

1	D	1c. black and red on buff	10·50	22·00
2	D	2c. brown and blue on buff	6·00	13·50
3	D	4c. brown and blue on grey	10·00	11·50
4	D	5c. green and red	5·50	6·00
5	D	10c. red and blue	8·00	11·50
6	D	15c. grey and red	11·00	10·00
7	D	20c. red and blue on green	17·00	30·00
8	D	25c. blue and red	13·00	11·00
9	D	25c. black and red on pink	£700	£650
10	D	30c. brown & blue on drab	14·00	29·00
11	D	40c. red and blue on yellow	90·00	£100
12	D	50c. red and blue on pink	£325	£325
13	D	50c. brown and red on blue	£130	£130
14	D	75c. brown and red on orge	£140	£140
15	D	1f. green and red	£140	£130
16	D	5f. mauve and blue on lilac	£150	£140

1906. Surch Mong-Tseu and value in Chinese.

17	8	1c. green	1·00	3·50
18	8	2c. purple on yellow	90	8·75
19	8	4c. mauve on blue	90	3·50
20	8	5c. green	3·00	9·75
21	8	10c. pink	2·00	12·00
22	8	15c. brown on blue	1·80	13·00
23	8	20c. red on green	6·00	11·00
24	8	25c. blue	12·00	16·00
25	8	30c. brown on cream	8·00	28·00
26	8	35c. black on yellow	6·50	19·00
27	8	40c. black on grey	8·75	20·00
28	8	50c. brown	15·00	44·00
29	D	75c. brown & red on orange	75·00	75·00
30	8	1f. green	36·00	40·00
31	8	2f. brown on yellow	65·00	80·00
32	D	5f. mauve and blue on lilac	£130	£130
34	8	10f. red on green	£130	£130

1908. Surch MONGTSEU and value in Chinese.

35	10	1c. black and brown	1·10	1·00
36	10	2c. black and brown	1·40	1·10
37	10	4c. black and blue	2·00	1·90
38	10	5c. black and green	1·70	80
39	10	10c. black and red	2·00	2·50
40	10	15c. black and violet	3·75	4·00
41	11	20c. black and violet	6·00	9·75
42	11	25c. black and blue	15·00	16·00
43	11	30c. black and brown	6·25	11·50
44	11	35c. black and green	7·50	9·25
45	11	40c. black and brown	5·50	10·50
46	11	50c. black and red	6·00	13·50
47	12	75c. black and orange	16·00	32·00
48	-	1f. black and red	24·00	38·00
49	-	2f. black and green	38·00	50·00
50	-	5f. black and blue	£130	£130
51	-	10f. black and violet	£140	£140

1919. Nos. 35/51 further surch in figures and words.

52	10	⅖c. on 1c. black and brown	1·50	4·50
53	10	⅘c. on 2c. black and brown	1·30	7·50
54	10	1⅗c. on 4c. black and blue	1·60	3·50
55	10	2c. on 5c. black and green	2·00	3·50
56	10	4c. on 10c. black and red	6·25	3·50
57	10	6c. on 15c. black and violet	3·00	3·50
58	11	8c. on 20c. black and violet	8·00	10·00
59	11	10c. on 25c. black and blue	7·00	7·00
60	11	12c. on 30c. black & brown	4·00	7·50
61	11	14c. on 35c. black & green	4·00	4·50
62	11	16c. on 40c. black & brown	3·00	6·25
63	11	20c. on 50c. black and red	4·50	4·75
64	12	30c. on 75c. black & orange	5·75	12·00
65	-	40c. on 1f. black and red	12·50	16·00
66	-	80c. on 2f. black and green	10·00	10·50
67	-	2p. on 5f. black and blue	£140	£140
68	-	4p. on 10f. black and violet	30·00	60·00

Pt. 3

MONTENEGRO

Formerly a monarchy on the Adriatic Sea, part of Yugoslavia 1918-2006. In Italian and German occupation during 1939–45 war. An independent state since May 2006.

1874. 100 novcic = 1 florin.
1902. 100 heller = 1 krone.
1907. 100 para = 1 krone (1910 = 1 perper).
2003. 100 cents = 1 euro.

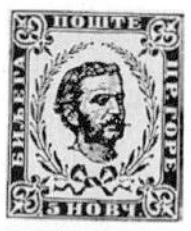

1 Prince Nicholas

1874

45C	1	1n. blue	55	80
38A	1	2n. yellow	4·50	4·25
51A	1	2n. green	55	55
39A	1	3n. green	1·10	1·10
52A	1	3n. red	55	55
40A	1	5n. red	1·10	1·10
53B	1	5n. orange	1·30	75
19	1	7n. mauve	90·00	65·00
41A	1	7n. pink	1·10	1·10
54A	1	7n. grey	65	1·10
42A	1	10n. blue	1·10	1·10
55A	1	10n. purple	80	1·10
56A	1	15n. brown	55	75
46C	1	20n. brown	55	80
7	1	25n. purple	£400	£275
44B	1	25n. brown	1·20	6·50
57A	1	25n. blue	55	75
47C	1	30n. brown	55	80
48A	1	50n. blue	80	80
49B	1	1f. green	2·20	5·50
50B	1	2f. red	2·20	16·00

Прослава
1493 1893
Штампарије
(2)

1893. 400th Anniv of Introduction of Printing into Montenegro. Optd with T 2.

81A	2n. yellow	43·00	3·75
82A	3n. green	4·50	2·75
83A	5n. red	3·25	2·20
84A	7n. pink	4·50	2·75
85A	10n. blue	5·50	4·25
87A	15n. bistre	6·25	4·25
88A	25n. brown	5·50	3·25

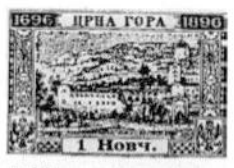

3 Monastery near Cetinje, Royal Mausoleum

1896. Bicentenary of Petrovich Niegush Dynasty.

90A	3	1n. brown and blue	55	1·60
91A	3	2n. yellow and purple	55	1·60
92A	3	3n. green and brown	55	1·60
93A	3	5n. brown and green	55	1·60
94A	3	10n. blue and yellow	55	1·60
95A	3	15n. green and blue	55	1·60
96A	3	20n. blue and green	65	1·80
97A	3	25n. yellow and blue	65	1·80
98A	3	30n. brown and purple	80	1·80
99A	3	50n. blue and red	80	1·80
100	3	1f. blue and pink	1·30	2·20
101	3	2f. black and brown	1·90	2·75

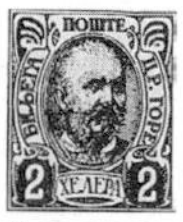

4

1902

102	4	1h. blue	55	55
103	4	2h. mauve	55	55
104	4	5h. green	55	55
105	4	10h. red	55	55
106	4	25h. blue	1·10	1·30
107	4	50h. green	1·10	1·30
108	4	1k. brown	1·10	1·10
109	4	2k. brown	1·10	1·30
110	4	5k. brown	1·30	3·25

УСТАВ
Constitution Никољдан
1905
(5)

1905. Granting of Constitution. Optd with T **5**.

111	1h. blue	55	55
112	2h. mauve	55	55
113	5h. green	1·10	1·10
114	10h. red	1·70	1·30
124a	25h. blue	80	75
125a	50h. green	80	75
126a	1k. brown	80	75
127a	2k. brown	1·10	1·10
119	5k. orange	1·70	1·60

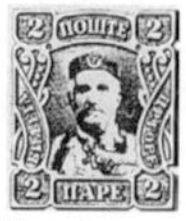

7

1907. New Currency.

129	7	1pa. yellow	45	30
130	7	2pa. black	45	30
131	7	5pa. green	1·90	20
132	7	10pa. red	3·25	20
133	7	15pa. blue	55	55
134	7	20pa. orange	55	55
135	7	25pa. blue	55	55
136	7	35pa. brown	80	55
137	7	50pa. lilac	80	75
138	7	1k. red	80	75
139	7	2k. green	80	75
140	7	5k. red	1·70	1·30

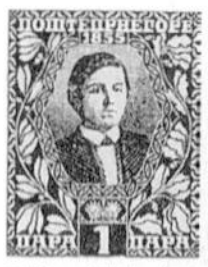
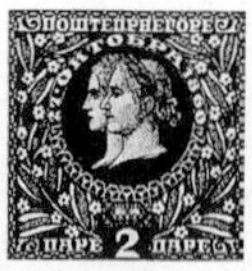
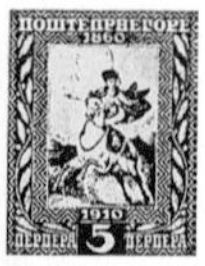

9 King Nicholas when a Youth **10** King Nicholas and Queen Milena **11** Prince Nicholas

1910. Proclamation of Kingdom and 50th Anniv of Reign of Prince Nicholas.

141	9	1pa. black	90	55
142	10	2pa. purple	90	55
143	-	5pa. green	90	55
144	-	10pa. red	90	55
145	-	15pa. blue	90	55
146	10	20pa. olive	1·10	75
147	-	25pa. blue	1·10	75
148	-	35pa. brown	1·70	1·10
149	-	50pa. violet	1·70	1·10
150	-	1per. lake	1·70	1·10
151	-	2per. green	2·00	1·30
152	11	5per. blue	2·20	1·60

DESIGNS: As Type **9**: 5, 10, 25, 35pa. Nicholas I in 1910; 15pa. Nicholas I in 1878; 50pa., 1, 2per. Nicholas I in 1890.

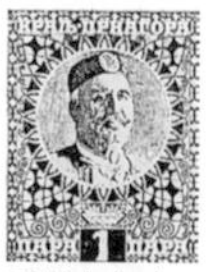

12 Nicholas I

1913

153	12	1pa. orange	55	75
154	12	2pa. purple	55	75
155	12	5pa. green	60	75
156	12	10pa. red	60	75
157	12	15pa. blue	65	75
158	12	20pa. brown	65	75
159	12	25pa. blue	1·10	1·10
160	12	35pa. red	80	75
161	12	50pa. blue	55	1·10
162	12	1per. brown	1·10	1·60
163	12	2per. purple	1·10	1·60
164	12	5per. green	1·10	1·60

These issues were only for sale within Montenegro.

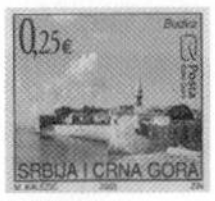

M14 Quay, Budva, Montenegro

2003. Tourism. Multicoloured.

M170	25c. Type M **14**	90	85
M171	40c. Durmitor national park (vert)	1·30	1·30

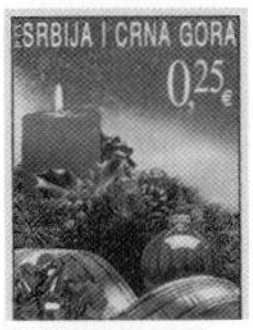

M15 Candle and Baubles

2003. Christmas.

M172	**M15** 25c. multicoloured	90	85

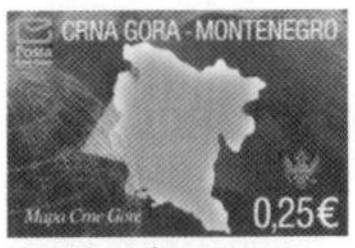

M16 Map of Montenegro

2005. State Symbols. Multicoloured.

M173	25c. Type M **16**	90	85
M174	40c. First Houses of Parliament	1·30	1·30
M175	50c. State emblem	1·70	1·60
M176	60c. State flag	2·75	2·75

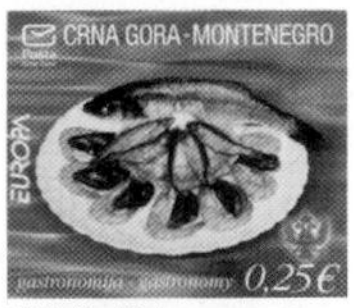

M17 Shellfish

2005. Europa. Gastronomy. Multicoloured.

M177	25c. Type M **17**	3·25	3·25
M178	50c. Smoked ham and olives	6·75	6·50
MSM179	110×50 mm. 25c. Bee and honey; 50c. Wine and grapes	22·00	22·00

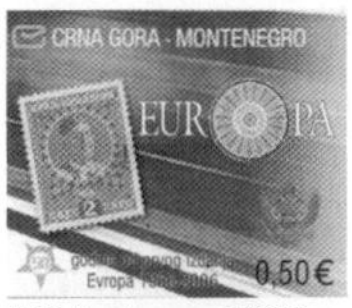

M18 Montenegro 1913 2pa. Stamp (No. 154) and Emblem

2006. 50th Anniv of Europa Stamps. Multicoloured.

M180	50c. Type M **18**	1·10	1·10
M181	€1 Montenegro 1913 5pa. Stamp (No. 155) and doves	2·20	2·20
M182	€2 Montenegro 1913 10pa. Stamp (No. 156) and bee	4·50	4·25
M183	€2 Montenegro 1913 25pa. Stamp (No. 159) and Europa emblem	4·50	4·25
MSM184	107×92 mm. Nos. M180/3	22·00	22·00
MSM185	103×76 mm. €5.50 Map of Europe highlighting Montenegro. Imperf	22·00	22·00

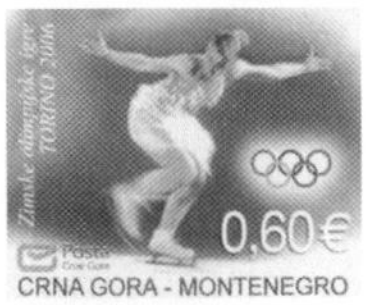

M19 Figure Skater

2006. Winter Olympic Games, Turin. Multicoloured.

M186	60c. Type M **19**	1·30	1·30
M187	90c. Ski jumper	2·00	1·90

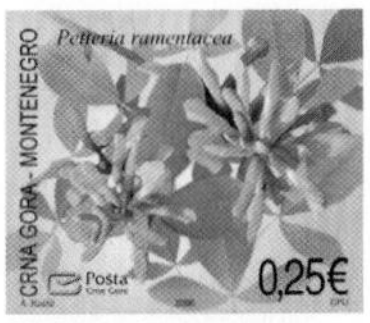

M20 *Petteria ramentacea*

2006. Flora. Multicoloured.

M188	25c. Type M **20**	55	55
M189	50c. *Viola nikolai*	1·10	1·10

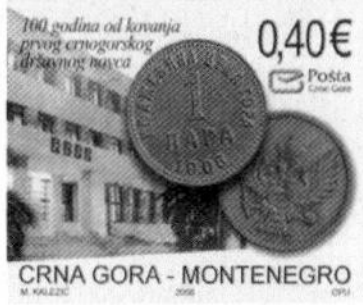

M21 1 para Coin and Central Bank

2006. Coins. Multicoloured.

M190	40c. Type M **21**	90	85
M191	50c. 20 para coin and bank	1·10	1·10

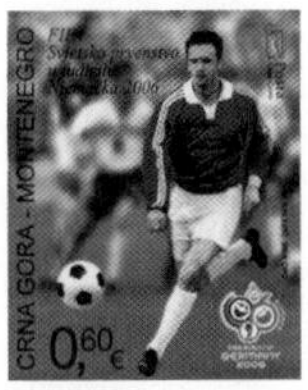

M22 Player

2006. World Cup Football Championship, Germany. Multicoloured.

M192	60c. Type M **22**	1·30	1·30
M193	90c. Player wearing short-sleeved jersey	2·00	1·90
MSM194	100×72 mm. 60c. Player leaning right; 90c. Player facing left	3·25	3·25

The stamps and margins of **MS**M194 form a composite design.

Montenegro declared independence from Serbia on 3 June 2006; from this date all stamps were issued as Montenegro.

Nos. M195/6 and Type M **23** have been left for Tourism, issued on 5 July 2006, not yet received.

No. M197 and Type M **24** have been left for Independence, issued on 13 July 2006, not yet received.

Nos. M198/9 have been left for single stamps not yet received.

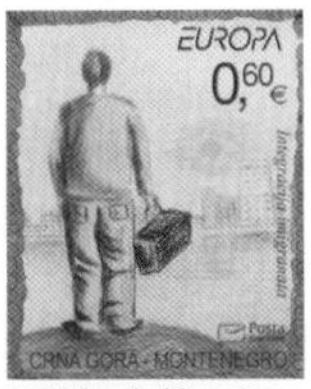

M 25 Boy holding Case

2006. Europa. Integration. Multicoloured.

MSM200	100×72 mm. 60c. Type M **25**; 90c. Young people of different nations	1·60	1·60

No. M201 and Type M **26** have been left for Sailing Ship, issued on 5 September 2006, not yet received.

No. M202 and Type M **27** have been left for Philatelic Accessories, issued on 2 October 2006, not yet received.

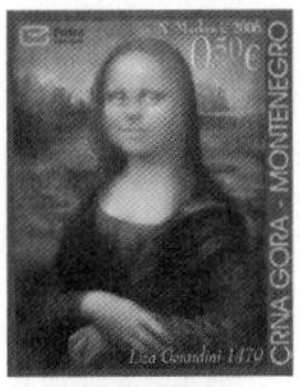

M 28 Mona Lisa as Child

2006. Joy in Europe Meeting. Children's Day.

M203	**M 28** 50c. multicoloured	1·40	1·40

Nos. M204/5 and Type M **29** have been left for Cultural Heritage, issued on 3 November 2006, not yet received.

No. M206 and Type M **30** have been left for Nature Protection, issued on 15 November 2006, not yet received.

No. M207 and Type M **31** have been left for 425th Anniv of Gregorian Calendar, issued on 4 January 2007, not yet received.

No. M208 and Type M **32** have been left for Pelican, issued on 7 February 2007, not yet received.

Nos. M209/10 have been left for single stamps not yet received.

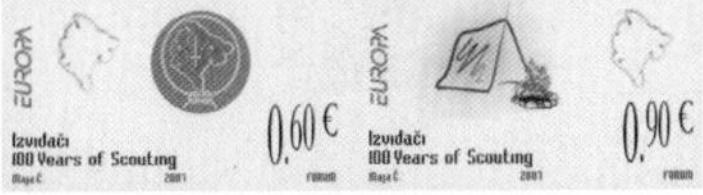

M 33 Emblem (image scaled to 58% of original size)

2007. Europa. Centenary of Scouting. Multicoloured.

MSM211	109×63 mm. 60c.+90c. Type M **33**	1·60	1·60

Nos. M212/13 and Type M **34** have been left for Birds, issued on 11 May 2007, not yet received.

No. M214 and Type M **35** have been left for Church, issued on 6 June 2007, not yet received.

No. M215 and Type M **36** have been left for Postal History, issued on 3 July 2007, not yet received.

No. M216 and Type M **37** have been left for Heritage, issued on 3 July 2007, not yet received.

No. M217 and Type M **38** have been left for Europe, issued on 3 July 2007, not yet received.

No. M218 and Type M **39** have been left for Tourism, issued on 3 July 2007, not yet received.

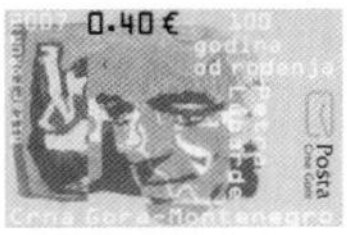

M 40 Petar Lubarda

2007. Birth Centenary of Petar Lubarda (artist).

M219	**M 40** 40c. multicoloured	1·10	1·10

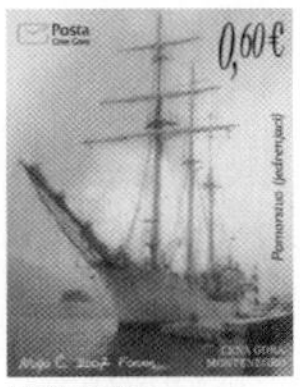

M 41 *Jadran*

2007. Sailing Ships.

M220	**M 41** 60c. multicoloured	1·60	1·60

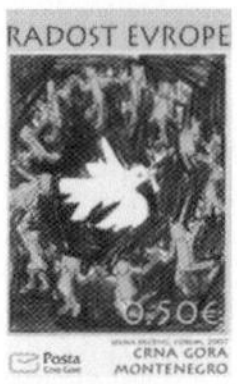

M 42 Children enclosing Dove

2007. Joy in Europe Meeting. Children's Day.

M221	**M 42** 50c. multicoloured	1·40	1·40

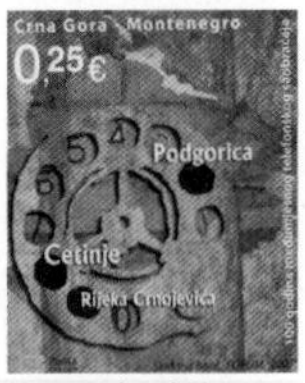

M 43 Dial and Map

2007. Centenary of Interregional Telephone. Multicoloured.

M222	25c. Type M **43**	70	70
M223	50c. Dial and map (different)	1·40	1·40

No. M224/7 and Type M **44** have been left for New Year, issued on 5 December 2007, not yet received.

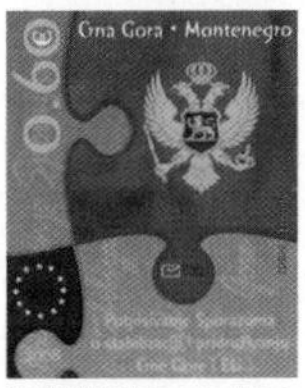

M 45 Montenegro Arms as Jigsaw

2008. Montenegro–European Union Stabilization and Association Aggreement. Multicoloured.

M228	60c. Type M **45**	1·60	1·60
MSM229	90×71 mm. 40c. Arms of Montenegro (different); 50c. Arms of EU	1·75	1·75

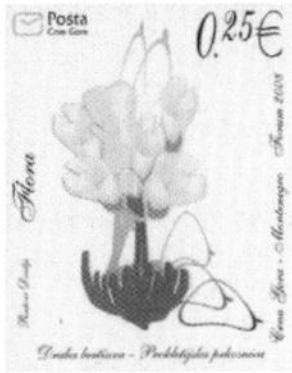

M 46 *Draba bertiscea*

2008. Flora. Multicoloured.

M230	25c. Type M **46**	1·10	1·10
M231	40c. *Edraianthus wettsteinii*	1·20	1·20
M232	50c. *Protoedriantus tarae*	1·30	1·30
M233	60c. *Dianthus nitidus*	1·50	1·50

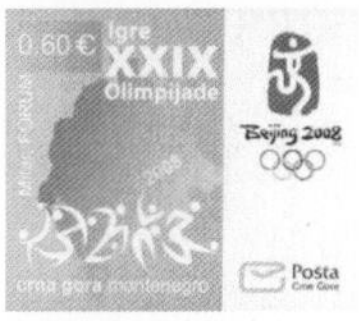

M 47 Stylized Athletes

2008. Olympic Games, Beijing. Multicoloured.

M234	60c. Type M **47**	2·00	2·00
M235	90c. Arms	2·50	2·50

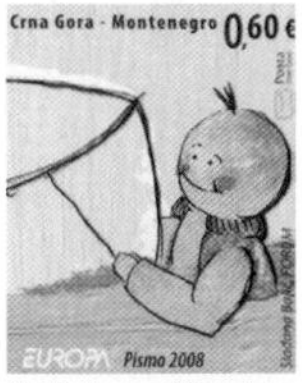

M 48 Boy and Envelope

2008. Europa. The Letter. Multicoloured.

MSM238	109×63 mm. 60c. Type M **48**; 90c. Girl holding envelope	4·50	4·50

Nos. M236/7 have been left for single stamps not yet received.

The stamps and margins of No. **MS**M238 form a composite design.

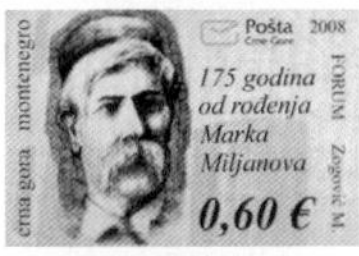

M 49 Marko Miljanov

2008. 175th Birth Anniv of Marko Miljanov Popovic Kuc (writer and Kuci clan leader).

M239	**M 49** 60c. multicoloured	1·75	1·75

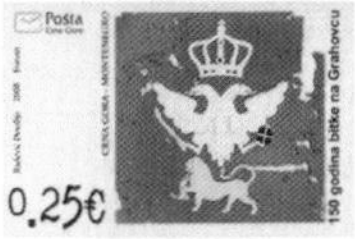

M 50 Arms

2008. 150th Anniv of Battle of Grahovac.

M240	**M 50** 25c. multicoloured	1·10	1·10

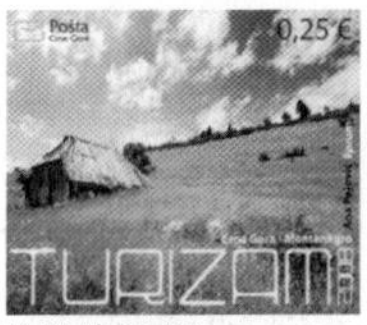

M 51 Alpine Hut

2008. Tourism. Sheet 104×90 mm containing Type M 51 and similar horiz designs. Multicoloured.

MSM241	25c. Type M **51**; 40c. River; 50c. Beach; 60c. Lake	3·50	3·50

Nos. M242/248 are left for stamps not yet received.

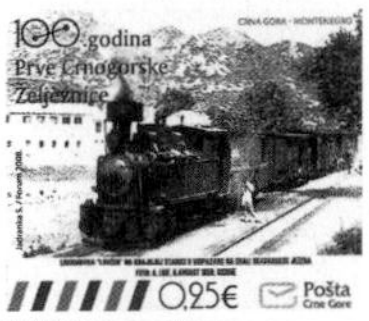

M57 Lovcen Steam Locomotive

2008. Centenary of Montenegrin Railways. Multicoloured.

M249	25c. Type M **57**	1·10	1·10
M250	25c. First locomotive and crowd	1·10	1·10
M251	25c. Lovcen steam locomotive at Virpazar station	1·10	1·10
M252	25c. Departure of steam locomotive for Virpazar	1·10	1·10
M253	25c. Rail track	1·10	1·10
M254	25c. Port railway, 1910	1·10	1·10

Nos. M255/287 are left for stamps not yet received.

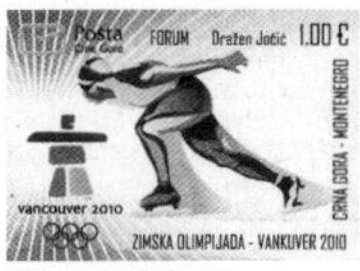

M76 Speed Skater

2010. Winter Olympic Games, Vancouver. Multicoloured.

M288	€1 Type M**76**	4·50	4·50
M289	€1.50 Snow boarder	7·50	7·50

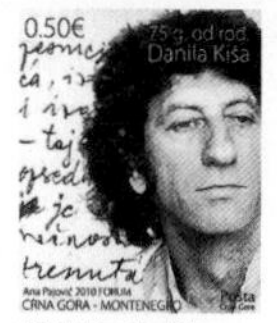

M77 Danilo Kis

2010. 75th Birth Anniv of Danilo Kis (writer and poet)

M290	**M77**	50c. multicoloured	2·50	2·50

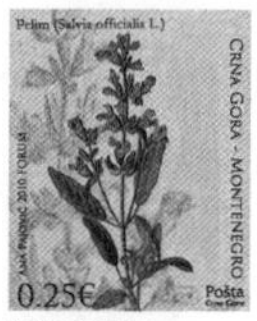

M78 *Salvia officinalis* (sage)

2010. Flowering Plants. Multicoloured.

M291	25c. Type M **78**	1·20	1·20
M292	50c. *Satureja subspicata*	2·50	2·50
M293	60c. *Tilia tomentosa* (lime tree)	3·00	3·00
M294	€1 *Epilobium angustifolium* (fireweed)	4·74	4·75

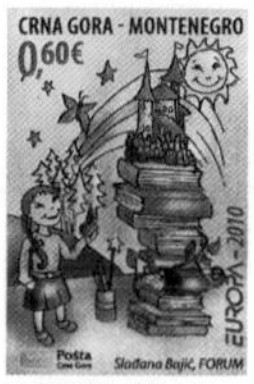

M79 Girl, Pile of Books and Symbols of Stories

2010. Europa. Multicoloured.

M295	60c. Type M**79**	3·50	3·50
M296	90c. Boy standing on pile of books surrounded by symbols of stories	3·75	3·75

MSM297 78×62 mm. 60c. Crown, fairy and dress on bridge of books; 90c. Sword, dragon's tail and ship on bridge of books 7·25 7·25

ITALIAN OCCUPATION

Montenegro
Црна Гора
17-IV-41-XIX

(1)

1941. Stamps of Yugoslavia optd with T 1. (a) Postage. On Nos. 414, etc.

1	**99**	25p. black	1·10	1·80
2	**99**	1d. green	1·10	1·80
3	**99**	1d.50 red	1·10	1·80
4	**99**	2d. mauve	1·10	1·80
5	**99**	3d. brown	1·10	1·80
6	**99**	4d. blue	1·10	1·80
7	**99**	5d. blue	4·50	5·50
8	**99**	5d.50 violet	4·50	5·50
9	**99**	6d. blue	4·50	5·50
10	**99**	8d. brown	4·50	6·50
11	**99**	12d. violet	4·50	5·50
12	**99**	16d. purple	4·50	5·50
13	**99**	20d. blue	£275	£325
14	**99**	30d. pink	£110	£130

(b) Air. On Nos. 360/7.

15	**80**	50p. brown	11·00	11·00
16	-	1d. green	8·50	11·00
17	-	2d. blue	8·50	11·00
18	-	2d.50 red	11·00	11·00
19	**80**	5d. violet	65·00	80·00
20	-	10d. red	65·00	80·00
21	-	20d. green	£140	£150
22	-	30d. blue	80·00	80·00

ЦРНА ГОРА

(2)

1941. Stamps of Italy optd with T 2. (a) On Postage stamps of 1929.

28	**98**	5c. brown	90	1·30
29	-	10c. brown	90	1·30
30	-	15c. green	90	1·30
31	**99**	20c. red	90	1·30
32	-	25c. green	90	1·30
33	**103**	30c. brown	90	1·30
34	**103**	50c. violet	90	1·30
35	-	75c. red	90	1·30
36	-	1l.25 blue	90	1·30

(b) On Air stamp of 1930.

37	**110**	50c. brown	90	1·30

1942. Nos. 416 etc of Yugoslavia optd Governatorato del Montenegro Valore LIRE.

43	**99**	1d. green	2·75	3·75
44	**99**	1d.50 red	£130	85·00
45	**99**	3d. brown	2·75	3·75
46	**99**	4d. blue	2·75	3·75
47	**99**	5d.50 violet	2·75	3·75
48	**99**	6d. blue	2·75	3·75
49	**99**	8d. brown	2·75	3·75
50	**99**	12d. violet	2·75	3·75
51	**99**	16d. purple	2·75	3·75

1942. Air. Nos. 360/7 of Yugoslavia optd Governatorato del Montenegro Valore in Lire.

52	**80**	0.50l. brown	7·75	8·75
53	-	1l. green	7·75	8·75
54	-	2l. blue	7·75	8·75
55	-	2.50l. red	7·75	8·75
56	**80**	5l. violet	7·75	8·75
57	-	10l. brown	7·75	8·75
58	-	20l. green	£225	£250
59	-	30l. blue	60·00	70·00

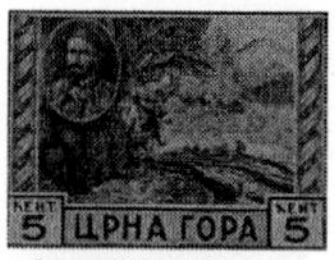

4 Prince Bishop Peter Njegos and View

1943. National Poem Commemoratives. Each stamp has fragment of poetry inscr at back.

60	**4**	5c. violet	3·25	5·50
61	-	10c. green	3·25	5·50
62	-	15c. brown	3·25	5·50
63	-	20c. orange	3·25	5·50
64	-	25c. green	3·25	5·50
65	-	50c. mauve	3·25	5·50
66	-	1l.25 blue	3·25	5·50
67	-	2l. green	5·00	8·00
68	-	5l. red on buff	11·00	14·00
69	-	20l. purple on grey	22·00	30·00

DESIGNS—HORIZ: 10c. Meadow near Mt. Lovcen; 15c. Country Chapel; 20c. Chiefs Meeting; 25, 50c. Folk Dancing; 1l.25, Taking the Oath; 2l. Moslem wedding procession; 5l. Watch over wounded standard-bearer. VERT: 20l. Portrait of Prince Bishop Peter Njegos.

1943. Air. With Junkers G31 airplane (2, 20l.) or Fokker F.VIIa/3m airplane (others).

70	**5**	50c. brown	1·70	3·50
71	-	1l. blue	1·70	3·50
72	-	2l. mauve	2·20	3·50
73	-	5l. green	2·75	4·25
74	-	10l. purple on buff	14·50	20·00
75	-	20l. blue on pink	34·00	43·00

DESIGNS—HORIZ: 1l. Coastline; 2l. Budva; 5l. Mt. Lovcen; 10l. Lake of Scutari. VERT: 20l. Mt. Durmitor.

GERMAN OCCUPATION

1943. Nos. 419/20 of Yugoslavia surch Deutsche Militaer-Verwaltung Montenegro and new value in lire.

76	**99**	50c. on 3d. brown	3·25	37·00
77	**99**	1l. on 3d. brown	3·25	37·00
78	**99**	1l.50 on 3d. brown	3·25	37·00
79	**99**	2l. on 3d. brown	10·50	75·00
80	**99**	4l. on 3d. brown	10·50	75·00
81	**99**	5l. on 4d. blue	10·50	75·00
82	**99**	8l. on 4d. blue	26·00	£150
83	**99**	10l. on 4d. blue	34·00	£225
84	**99**	20l. on 4d. blue	75·00	£550

1943. Appointment of National Administrative Committee. Optd Nationaler Verwaltungsausschuss 10.XI.1943. (a) Postage. On Nos. 64/8.

85	25c. green	21·00	£250
86	50c. mauve	21·00	£250
87	1l.25 blue	21·00	£250
88	2l. green	21·00	£250
89	5l. red on buff	£275	£3250

(b) Air. On Nos. 70/4.

90	**5**	50c. brown	21·00	£250
91	**5**	1l. blue	21·00	£250
92	**5**	2l. mauve	21·00	£250
93	**5**	5l. green	21·00	£250
94	**5**	10l. purple on buff	£2750	£27000

1944. Refugees Fund. Surch Fluchtlingshilfe Montenegro and new value in German currency. (a) On Nos. 419/20 of Yugoslavia.

95	**99**	0.15+0.85Rm. on 3d.	18·00	£275
96	**99**	0.15+0.85Rm. on 4d.	18·00	£275

(b) On Nos. 46/9.

97	0.15+0.85Rm. on 25c.	18·00	£275
98	0.15+1.35Rm. on 50c.	18·00	£275
99	0.25+1.75Rm. on 1l.25	18·00	£275
100	0.25+1.75Rm. on 2l.	18·00	£275

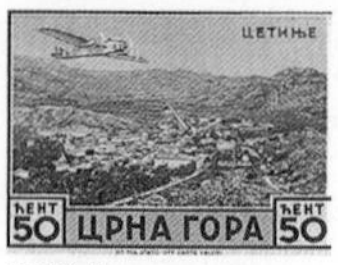

5 Cetinje

(c) Air. On Nos. A52/4.

101	**5**	0.15+0.85Rm. on 50c.	18·00	£275
102	-	0.25+1.25Rm. on 1l.	18·00	£275
103	-	0.50+1.50Rm. on 2l.	18·00	£275

1944. Red Cross. Surch +Crveni krst Montenegro and new value in German currency. (a) On Nos. 419/20 of Yugoslavia.

104	**99**	0.50+2.50Rm. on 3d.	15·00	£225
105	**99**	0.50+2.50Rm. on 4d.	15·00	£225

(b) On Nos. 64/5.

106	0.15+0.85Rm. on 25c.	15·00	£225
107	0.15+1.35Rm. on 50c.	15·00	£225

(c) Air. On Nos. 70/2.

108	**5**	0.25+1.75Rm. on 50c.	15·00	£225
109	-	0.25+2.75Rm. on 1l.	15·00	£225
110	-	0.50+2Rm. on 2l.	15·00	£225

ACKNOWLEDGEMENT OF RECEIPT STAMPS

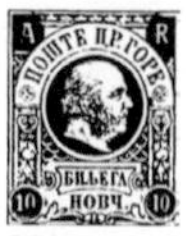

A3

1895

A90	**A3**	10n. blue and red	1·30	1·30

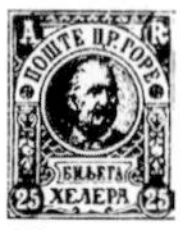

A4

1902

A111	**A4**	25h. orange and red	1·30	1·30

1905. Optd with T 5.

A120	25h. orange and red	1·30	1·30

1907. As T 7, but letters "A" and "R" in top corners.

A141	**7**	25p. olive	1·10	1·60

1913. As T 12, but letters "A" and "R" in top corners.

A169	**12**	25p. olive	1·10	4·00

POSTAGE DUE STAMPS

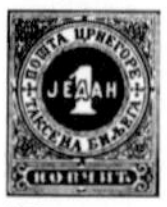

D3

1894

D90	**D3**	1n. red	4·50	4·25
D91	**D3**	2n. green	1·70	1·60
D92	**D3**	3n. orange	1·10	1·10
D93	**D3**	5n. green	80	75
D94	**D3**	10n. purple	80	75
D95	**D3**	20n. blue	80	75
D96	**D3**	30n. green	80	75
D97	**D3**	50n. pale green	80	75

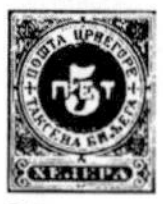

D4

1902

D111	**D4**	5h. orange	55	75
D112	**D4**	10h. green	55	75
D113	**D4**	25h. purple	55	75
D114	**D4**	50h. green	55	75
D115	**D4**	1k. grey	1·10	1·80

1905. Optd with T 5.

D120	5h. orange	80	1·60
D121	10h. olive	1·10	3·25
D122	25h. purple	80	1·60
D123	50h. green	80	1·60
D124	1k. pale green	1·10	2·20

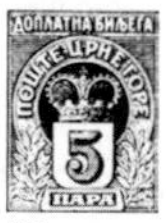

D8

1907

D141	**D8**	5p. brown	55	1·60
D142	**D8**	10p. violet	55	1·60
D143	**D8**	25p. red	55	1·60
D144	**D8**	50p. green	55	1·60

1913. As T 12 but inscr "НОРТОМАРКА" at top.

D165	5p. grey	1·70	2·20
D166	10p. lilac	1·10	1·60
D167	25p. blue	1·10	1·60
D168	50p. red	1·70	2·20

ITALIAN OCCUPATION

1941. Postage Due stamps of Yugoslavia optd Montenegro Upha 17-IV-41-XIX.

D23	**D56**	50p. violet	1·90	2·75
D24	**D56**	1d. mauve	1·90	2·75
D25	**D56**	2d. blue	1·90	2·75
D26	**D56**	5d. orange	£130	£140
D27	**D56**	10d. brown	11·00	14·00

1942. Postage Due stamps of Italy optd UPHATOPA.

D38	**D141**	10c. blue	2·20	3·25
D39	**D141**	20c. red	2·20	3·25
D40	**D141**	30c. orange	2·20	3·25
D41	**D141**	50c. violet	2·20	3·25
D42	**D141**	1l. orange	2·20	3·25

Pt. 1

MONTSERRAT

One of the Leeward Is., Br. W. Indies. Used general issues for Leeward Is. concurrently with Montserrat stamps until 1 July 1956, when Leeward Is. stamps were withdrawn.

1876. 12 pence = 1 shilling; 20 shillings = 1 pound.
1951. 100 cents = 1 West Indian dollar.

1876. Stamps of Antigua as T 1 optd MONTSERRAT.

8c	1d. red	26·00	13·00
2	6d. green	70·00	45·00

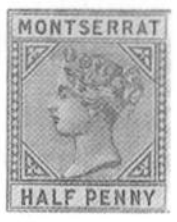

3

1880

7	**3**	½d. green	1·00	11·00
9	**3**	2½d. brown	£275	65·00
10	**3**	2½d. blue	26·00	21·00
12	**3**	4d. mauve	5·50	3·00
5	**3**	4d. blue	£150	40·00

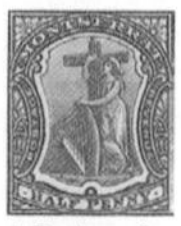

4 Device of the Colony

1903

24a	**4**	½d. green	1·00	1·25
15	**4**	1d. grey and red	75	40
26a	**4**	2d. grey and brown	2·25	1·25
17	**4**	2½d. grey and blue	1·50	1·75
28a	**4**	3d. orange and purple	10·00	2·50
29a	**4**	6d. purple and olive	12·00	5·50
30	**4**	1s. green and purple	12·00	7·00
21	**4**	2s. green and orange	35·00	22·00
22	**4**	2s.6d. green and black	25·00	50·00
33	**5**	5s. black and red	£150	£160

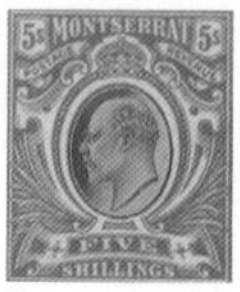

5

1908

36	**4**	1d. red	1·40	30
38	**4**	2d. grey	1·75	20·00
39	**4**	2½d. blue	2·25	3·50
40	**4**	3d. purple on yellow	1·00	18·00
43	**4**	6d. purple	10·00	55·00
44	**4**	1s. black on green	8·50	45·00
45	**4**	2s. purple and blue on blue	48·00	55·00
46	**4**	2s.6d. black and red on blue	35·00	75·00
47	**5**	5s. red and green on yellow	65·00	75·00

1914. As T **5**, but portrait of King George V.

48	5s. red and green on yellow	85·00	£140

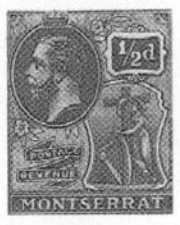

8

1916

63	8	¼d. brown	15	5·50
64	8	½d. green	30	30
50	8	1d. red	1·75	75
65	8	1d. violet	30	60
67	8	1½d. yellow	1·75	9·50
68	8	1½d. red	45	5·50
69	8	1½d. brown	3·00	50
70	8	2d. grey	50	2·00
71a	8	2½d. blue	70	90
72	8	2½d. yellow	1·25	19·00
73	8	3d. blue	75	16·00
74	8	3d. purple on yellow	1·10	5·00
75	8	4d. black and red on yellow	75	13·00
76	8	5d. purple and olive	4·00	10·00
77	8	6d. purple	3·00	7·50
78	8	1s. black on green	3·00	7·00
79	8	2s. purple and blue on blue	7·00	18·00
80	8	2s.6d. black and red on blue	12·00	60·00
81	8	3s. green and violet	12·00	19·00
82	8	4s. black and red	15·00	42·00
83	8	5s. green and red on yellow	32·00	60·00

1917. Optd WAR STAMP.

60	8	½d. green	10	1·50
62	8	1½d. black and orange	10	30

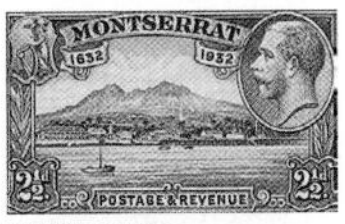

10 Plymouth

1932. 300th Anniv of Settlement of Montserrat.

84	10	½d. green	75	13·00
85	10	1d. red	75	5·50
86	10	1½d. brown	1·25	2·50
87	10	2d. grey	1·50	21·00
88	10	2½d. blue	1·25	18·00
89	10	3d. orange	1·50	21·00
90	10	6d. violet	2·25	38·00
91	10	1s. olive	12·00	50·00
92	10	2s.6d. purple	48·00	80·00
93	10	5s. brown	£110	£180

1935. Silver Jubilee. As T **50a** of Mauritius.

94	1d. blue and red	85	3·25
95	1½d. blue and grey	2·25	3·50
96	2½d. brown and blue	2·25	4·50
97	1s. grey and purple	4·00	17·00

1937. Coronation. As T **50b** of Mauritius.

98	1d. red	35	1·50
99	1½d. brown	1·00	40
100	2½d. blue	60	1·50

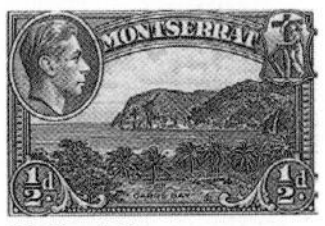

11 Carr's Bay

1938. King George VI.

101a	11	½d. green	15	20
102a	-	1d. red	1·25	30
103a	-	1½d. purple	1·00	50
104a	-	2d. orange	1·50	70
105a	-	2½d. blue	50	30
106a	11	3d. brown	2·25	40
107a	-	6d. violet	3·50	60
108a	11	1s. red	2·25	30
109a	-	2s.6d. blue	24·00	3·00
110a	11	5s. red	29·00	3·00
111	-	10s. blue	19·00	22·00
112	11	£1 black	24·00	40·00

DESIGNS: 1d., 1½d., 2½d. Sea Island cotton; 2d., 6d., 2s.6d., 10s. Botanic station.

1946. Victory. As T **8a** of Pitcairn Islands.

113	1½d. purple	15	15
114	3d. brown	15	15

1949. Silver Wedding. As T **8b/c** of Pitcairn Islands.

115	2½d. blue	10	10
116	5s. red	4·75	13·00

1949. U.P.U. As T **8d/g** of Pitcairn Islands.

117	2½d. blue	15	1·25
118	3d. brown	1·75	1·25
119	6d. purple	30	1·25
120	1s. purple	30	1·25

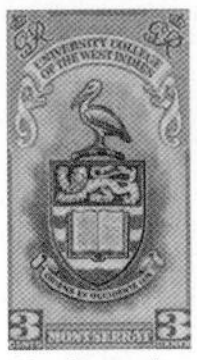

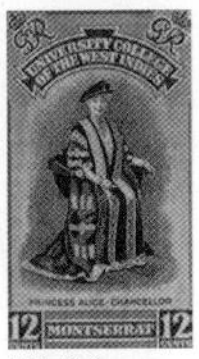

13a Arms of University

13b Princess Alice

1951. Inauguration of B.W.I. University College.

121	13a	3c. black and purple	20	1·25
122	13b	12c. black and violet	20	1·25

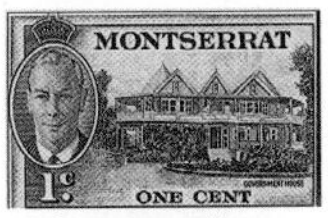

14 Government House

1951

123	14	1c. black	10	2·75
124	-	2c. green	15	1·00
125	-	3c. brown	40	70
126	-	4c. red	30	2·75
127	-	5c. violet	30	1·00
128	-	6c. brown	30	30
129	-	8c. blue	2·75	20
130	-	12c. blue and brown	1·00	30
131	-	24c. red and green	1·25	30
132	-	60c. black and red	9·00	5·00
133	-	$1.20 green and blue	7·00	7·50
134	-	$2.40 black and green	16·00	21·00
135	-	$4.80 black and purple	30·00	30·00

DESIGNS: 2c., $1.20, Sea Island cotton: cultivation; 3c. Map; 4c., 24c. Picking tomatoes; 5c., 12c. St. Anthony's Church; 6c., $4.80, Badge; 8c., 60c. Sea Island cotton: ginning; $2.40, Government House (portrait on right).

1953. Coronation. As T **8i** of Pitcairn Islands.

136	2c. black and green	60	40

1953. As 1951 but portrait of Queen Elizabeth II.

136a	½c. violet (As 3c.) (I)	50	10
136b	½c. violet (II)	80	10
137	1c. black	10	10
138	2c. green	15	10
139	3c. brown (I)	50	10
139a	3c. brown (II)	80	2·00
140	4c. red	30	20
141	5c. violet	30	1·00
142	6c. brown (I)	30	10
142a	6c. brown (II)	55	15
143	8c. blue	1·00	10
144	12c. blue and brown	1·50	10
145	24c. red and green	1·50	20
145a	48c. olive and purple (As 2c.)	13·00	5·00
146	60c. black and red	9·00	2·25
147	$1.20 green and blue	18·00	11·00
148	$2.40 black and green	18·00	22·00
149	$4.80 black and purple (I)	5·00	10·00
149a	$4.80 black and purple (II)	25·00	10·00

I. Inscr "Presidency". II. Inscr "Colony".

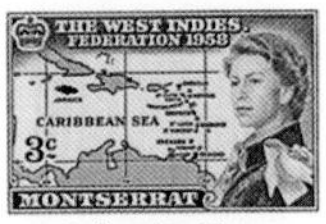

18a Federation Map

1958. Inauguration of British Caribbean Federation.

150	18a	3c. green	60	20
151	18a	6c. blue	80	75
152	18a	12c. red	1·00	15

1963. Freedom from Hunger. As T **20a** of Pitcairn Islands.

153	12c. violet	30	15

1963. Cent of Red Cross. As T **20b** of Pitcairn Islands.

154	4c. red and black	15	20
155	12c. red and blue	35	50

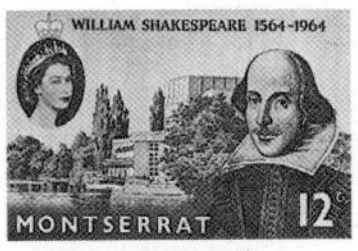

20 Shakespeare and Memorial Theatre, Stratford-upon-Avon

1964. 400th Birth Anniv of Shakespeare.

156	20	12c. blue	35	10

1965. Cent of I.T.U. As T **24a** of Pitcairn Islands.

158	4c. red and violet	15	10
159	48c. green and red	30	20

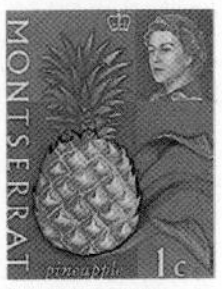

21 Pineapple

1965. Multicoloured

160	1c. Type **21**	10	10
161	2c. Avocado	10	10
162	3c. Soursop	10	10
163	4c. Pepper	10	10
164	5c. Mango	10	10
165	6c. Tomato	10	10
166	8c. Guava	10	10
167	10c. Ochro	10	10
168	12c. Lime	50	40
169	20c. Orange	30	10
170	24c. Banana	20	10
171	42c. Onion	75	60
172	48c. Cabbage	2·00	75
173	60c. Pawpaw	3·00	1·10
174	$1.20 Pumpkin	2·00	5·00
175	$2.40 Sweet potato	7·50	8·50
176	$4.80 Egg plant	7·50	11·00

1965. I.C.Y. As T **24b** of Pitcairn Islands.

177	2c. purple and turquoise	10	20
178	12c. green and lavender	25	10

1966. Churchill Commemoration. As T **24c** of Pitcairn Islands.

179	1c. blue	10	2·00
180	2c. green	25	20
181	24c. brown	80	10
182	42c. violet	90	1·00

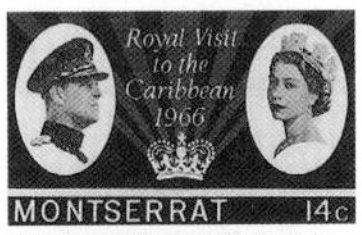

23 Queen Elizabeth II and Duke of Edinburgh

1966. Royal Visit.

183	23	14c. black and blue	1·00	15
184	23	24c. black and mauve	1·50	15

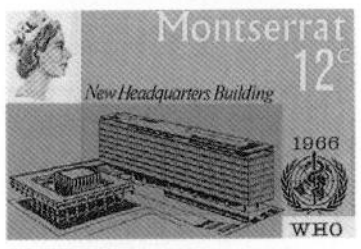

24 W.H.O. Building

1966. Inauguration of W.H.O. Headquarters, Geneva.

185	24	12c. black, green and blue	20	25
186	24	60c. black, pur & ochre	55	75

1966. 20th Anniv of UNESCO. As T **25b/d** of Pitcairn Islands.

187	4c. multicoloured	10	10
188	60c. yellow, violet and olive	55	20
189	$1.80 black, purple and orange	1·75	85

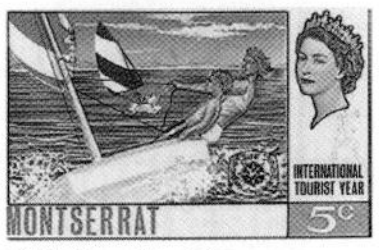

25 Sailing Dinghies

1967. International Tourist Year. Multicoloured.

190	5c. Type **25**	10	10
191	15c. Waterfall near Chance Mountain (vert)	15	10
192	16c. Fishing, skin diving and swimming	20	70
193	24c. Playing golf	1·25	45

1968. Nos. 168, 170, 172, 174/6 surch.

194	15c. on 12c. Lime	20	15
195	25c. on 24c. Banana	25	15
196	50c. on 48c. Cabbage	45	15
197	$1 on $1.20 Pumpkin	1·10	40
198	$2.50 on $2.40 Sweet potato	1·10	4·25
199	$5 on $4.80 Egg plant	1·10	4·25

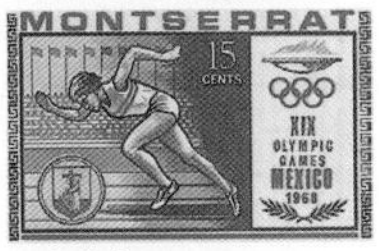

27 Sprinting

1968. Olympic Games, Mexico.

200	27	15c. mauve, green and gold	10	10
201	-	25c. blue, orange and gold	15	10
202	-	50c. green, red and gold	25	15
203	-	$1 multicoloured	35	30

DESIGNS—HORIZ: 25c. Weightlifting; 50c. Gymnastics. VERT: $1 Sprinting and Aztec pillars.

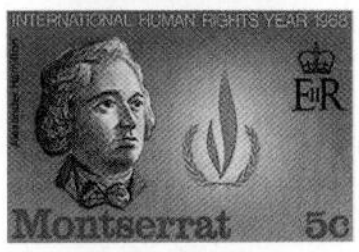

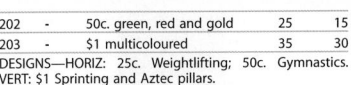

31 Alexander Hamilton

1968. Human Rights Year. Multicoloured.

204	5c. Type **31**	10	10
205	15c. Albert T. Marryshow	10	10
206	25c. William Wilberforce	10	10
207	50c. Dag Hammarskjold	10	15
208	$1 Dr. Martin Luther King	25	30

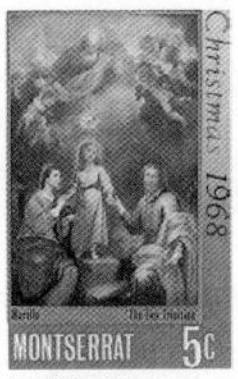

32 "The Two Trinities" (Murillo)

1968. Christmas.

209	32	5c. multicoloured	10	10
210	-	15c. multicoloured	10	10
211	32	25c. multicoloured	10	10
212	-	50c. multicoloured	25	25

DESIGN: 15, 50c. "The Adoration of the Kings" (detail, Botticelli).

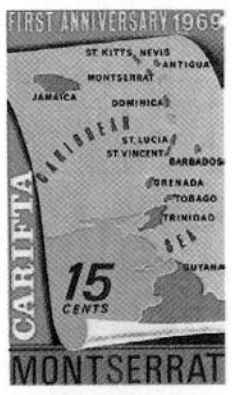

34 Map showing CARIFTA Countries

1969. First Anniv of CARIFTA (Caribbean Free Trade Area). Multicoloured.

223	15c. Type **34**	10	10
224	20c. Type **34**	10	10
225	35c. "Strength in Unity" (horiz)	10	20
226	50c. As 35c. (horiz)	15	20

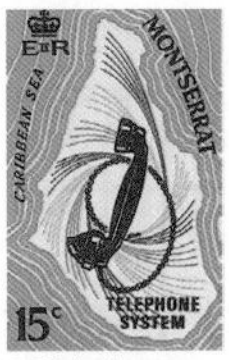

36 Telephone Receiver and Map of Montserrat

1969. Development Projects. Multicoloured.

227	15c. Type **36**	10	10
228	25c. School symbols and map	10	10
229	50c. Hawker Siddeley H.S.748 aircraft and map	15	20
230	$1 Electricity pylon and map	25	75

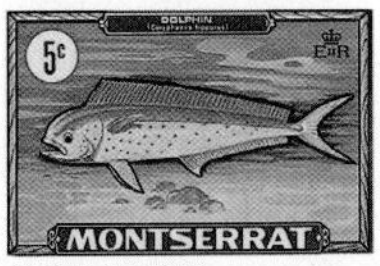

40 Dolphin (fish)

1969. Game Fish. Multicoloured.

231	5c. Type **40**	35	10
232	15c. Atlantic sailfish	50	10
233	25c. Blackfin tuna	60	10
234	40c. Spanish mackerel	80	55

41 King Caspar
before the Virgin
and Child (detail)
(Norman
16th-cent stained
glass window)

1969. Christmas. Paintings. Multicoloured, frame colours given.

235	**41**	15c. black, gold and violet	10	10
236	**41**	25c. black and red	10	10
237	-	50c. black, blue and orange	15	15

DESIGN—HORIZ: 50c. "Nativity" (Leonard Limosin).

43 "Red Cross Sale"

1970. Centenary of British Red Cross. Multicoloured

238		3c. Type **43**	15	25
239		4c. School for deaf children	15	25
240		15c. Transport services for disabled	20	20
241		20c. Workshop	20	60

44 Red-footed Booby

1970. Birds. Multicoloured.

242		1c. Type **44**	10	10
243		2c. American kestrel (vert)	15	15
244		3c. Magnificent frigate bird (vert)	15	15
245		4c. Great egret (vert)	2·00	15
299a		5c. Brown pelican (vert)	75	55
247		10c. Bananaquit (vert)	40	10
248		15c. Smooth-billed ani	30	15
249		20c. Red-billed tropic bird	35	15
250		25c. Montserrat oriole	50	50
251		50c. Green-throated carib (vert)	5·50	1·50
252		$1 Antillean crested hummingbird	10·00	1·00
253		$2.50 Little blue heron (vert)	5·50	12·00
254		$5 Purple-throated carib	7·50	19·00
254c		$10 Forest thrush	18·00	20·00

45 "Madonna and
Child with
Animals"
(Brueghel the Elder,
after Durer)

1970. Christmas. Multicoloured.

255		5c. Type **45**	10	10
256		15c. "The Adoration of the Shepherds" (Domenichino)	10	10
257		20c. Type **45**	10	10
258		$1 As 15c.	35	1·50

46 War Memorial

1970. Tourism. Multicoloured.

259		5c. Type **46**	10	10
260		15c. Plymouth from Fort St. George	10	10
261		25c. Carr's Bay	15	15
262		50c. Golf Fairway	1·00	2·25
MS263		135×109 mm. Nos. 259/62	2·50	2·25

47 Girl Guide and
Badge

1970. Diamond Jubilee of Montserrat Girl Guides. Multicoloured.

264		10c. Type **47**	10	10
265		15c. Brownie and badge	10	10
266		25c. As 15c.	15	15
267		40c. Type **47**	20	80

48 "Descent from
the Cross" (Van
Hemessen)

1971. Easter. Multicoloured.

268		5c. Type **48**	10	10
269		15c. "Noli me tangere" (Orcagna)	10	10
270		20c. Type **48**	10	10
271		40c. As 15c.	15	85

49 D.F.C. and D.F.M.
in Searchlights

1971. Golden Jubilee of Commonwealth Ex-Services League. Multicoloured.

272		10c. Type **49**	15	10
273		20c. M.C., M.M. and jungle patrol	20	10
274		40c. D.S.C., D.S.M. and submarine action	20	15
275		$1 V.C. and soldier attacking bunker	30	80

50 "The Nativity
with Saints"
(Romanino)

1971. Christmas. Multicoloured.

276		5c. Type **50**	10	10
277		15c. "Choir of Angels" (Simon Marmion)	10	10
278		20c. Type **50**	10	10
279		$1 As 15c.	35	40

51 Piper Apache

1971. 14th Anniv of Inauguration of L.I.A.T. (Leeward Islands Air Transport). Multicoloured.

280		5c. Type **51**	10	10
281		10c. Beech 50 Twin Bonanza	15	15
282		15c. De Havilland Heron	30	15
283		20c. Britten Norman Islander	35	15
284		40c. De Havilland Twin Otter 100	50	45
285		75c. Hawker Siddeley H.S.748	1·40	2·25
MS286		203×102 mm. Nos. 280/5	7·00	13·00

52 "Chapel of Christ in
Gethsemane", Coventry Cathedral

1972. Easter. Multicoloured.

287		5c. Type **52**	10	10
288		10c. "The Agony in the Garden" (Bellini)	10	10
289		20c. Type **52**	10	10
290		75c. As 10c.	35	1·25

53 Lizard

1972. Reptiles. Multicoloured.

291		15c. Type **53**	15	10
292		20c. Mountain chicken (frog)	20	10
293		40c. Iguana (horiz)	35	20
294		$1 Tortoise (horiz)	1·00	1·00

54 "Madonna of the
Chair" (Raphael)

1972. Christmas. Multicoloured.

303		10c. Type **54**	10	10
304		35c. "Virgin and Child with Cherub" (Fungai)	15	10
305		50c. "Madonna of the Magnificat" (Botticelli)	20	30
306		$1 "Virgin and Child with St. John and an Angel" (Botticelli)	30	65

55 Lime, Tomatoes and Pawpaw

1972. Royal Silver Wedding. Multicoloured, background colour given.

307	**55**	35c. pink	10	10
308	**55**	$1 blue	20	20

56 "Passiflora
herbertiana"

1973. Easter. Passion Flowers. Multicoloured.

309		20c. Type **56**	20	10
310		35c. "P. vitifolia"	25	10
311		75c. "P. amabilis"	35	75
312		$1 "P. alata-caerulea"	50	80

57 Montserrat Monastery, Spain

1973. 480th Anniv of Columbus's Discovery of Montserrat. Multicoloured.

313		10c. Type **57**	15	10
314		35c. Columbus sighting Montserrat	30	15
315		60c. "Santa Maria" off Montserrat	70	60
316		$1 Island badge and map of voyage	80	70
MS317		126×134 mm. Nos. 313/16	9·00	13·00

58 "Virgin and
Child" (School of
Gerard David)

1973. Christmas. Multicoloured.

318		20c. Type **58**	15	10
319		35c. "The Holy Family with St. John" (Jordaens)	20	10
320		50c. "Virgin and Child" (Bellini)	25	30
321		90c. "Virgin and Child with Flowers" (Dolci)	50	70

58a Princess Anne
and Captain Mark
Phillips

1973. Royal Wedding. Multicoloured, background colour given.

322	**58a**	35c. green	10	10
323	**58a**	$1 blue	20	20

59 Steel Band

1974. 25th Anniv of University of West Indies. Multicoloured.

324		20c. Type **59**	15	10
325		35c. Masqueraders (vert)	15	10
326		60c. Student weaving (vert)	25	45
327		$1 University Centre, Montserrat	30	55
MS328		130×89 mm. Nos. 324/7	1·75	6·00

60 Hands with Letters

1974. Centenary of U.P.U.

329	**60**	1c. multicoloured	10	10
330	-	2c. red, orange and black	10	10
331	**60**	3c. multicoloured	10	10
332	-	5c. orange, red and black	10	10
333	**60**	50c. multicoloured	20	20
334	-	$1 blue, green and black	40	65

DESIGN: 2, 5c., $1 Figures from U.P.U. Monument.

1974. Various stamps surch.

335		2c. on $1 mult (No. 252)	1·00	2·75
336		5c. on 50c. mult (No. 333)	30	60
337		10c. on 60c. mult (No. 326)	65	1·75
338		20c. on $1 mult (No. 252)	30	2·50
339		35c. on $1 blue, green and black (No. 334)	40	1·25

62 Churchill and
Houses of
Parliament

1974. Birth Centenary of Sir Winston Churchill. Multicoloured

340		35c. Type **62**	15	10
341		70c. Churchill and Blenheim Palace	20	20
MS342		81×85 mm. Nos. 340/1	50	70

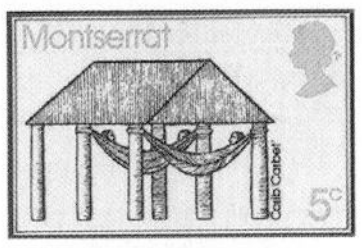

63 Carib "Carbet"

1975. Carib Artefacts. Self-adhesive or ordinary gum.

343	**63**	5c. brown, yellow and black	10	10
344	-	20c. black, brown & yellow	10	10
345	-	35c. black, yellow & brown	15	10
346	-	70c. yellow, brown & black	45	40

DESIGNS: 20c. "Caracoli"; 35c. Club or mace; 70c. Carib canoe.

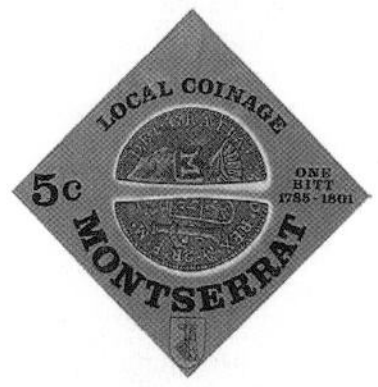

64 One-Bitt Coin

1975. Local Coinage, 1785–1801.

351	**64**	5c. black, blue and silver	10	10
352	-	10c. black, pink and silver	15	10
353	-	35c. black, green and silver	20	15
354	-	$2 black, red and silver	70	1·50
MS355		142×142 mm. Nos. 351/4	1·25	2·75

DESIGNS: 10c. Eighth dollar; 35c. Quarter dollar; $2 One dollar.

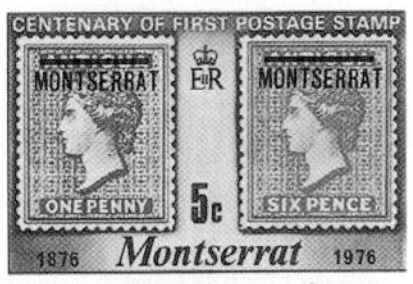

65 1d. and 6d. Stamps of 1876

1976. Centenary of First Montserrat Postage Stamp.

356	**65**	5c. red, green and black	15	10
357	-	10c. yellow, red and black	20	10
358	-	40c. multicoloured	40	40
359	-	55c. mauve, green and black	50	50
360	-	70c. multicoloured	60	70
361	-	$1.10 green, blue and black	80	1·00
MS362		170×159 mm. Nos. 356/61	2·50	5·50

DESIGNS: 10c. G.P.O. and bisected 1d. stamp; 40c. Bisects on cover; 55c. G.B. 6d. used in Montserrat and local 6d. of 1876; 70c. Stamps for 2½d. rate, 1876; $1.10, Packet boat "Antelope" and 6d. stamp.

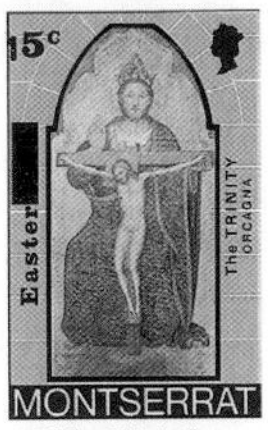

66 "The Trinity"

1976. Easter. Paintings by Orcagna. Multicoloured.

363	15c. Type **66**	10	10
364	40c. "The Resurrection"	20	15
365	55c. "The Ascension"	20	15
366	$1.10 "Pentecost"	35	40
MS367	160×142 mm. Nos. 363/6	1·50	2·25

1976. Nos. 244, 246 and 247 surch.

368	2c. on 5c. multicoloured	10	1·25
369	30c. on 10c. multicoloured	30	30
370	45c. on 3c. multicoloured	40	50

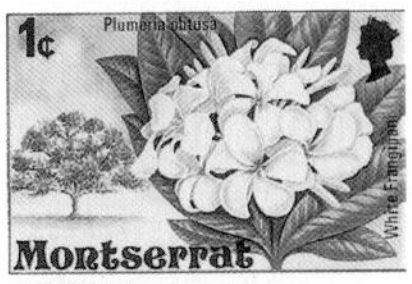

68 White Frangipani

1976. Flowering Trees. Multicoloured.

371	1c. Type **68**	10	10
372	2c. Cannon-ball tree	10	10
373	3c. Lignum vitae	10	10
374	5c. Malay apple	15	10
375	10c. Jacaranda	30	10
376	15c. Orchid tree	50	10
377	20c. Manjak	30	10
378	25c. Tamarind	60	75
379	40c. Flame of the forest	30	30
380	55c. Pink cassia	40	40
381	70c. Long john	40	30
382	$1 Saman	50	80
383	$2.50 Immortelle	75	1·50
384	$5 Yellow poui	1·10	2·25
385	$10 Flamboyant	1·50	4·25

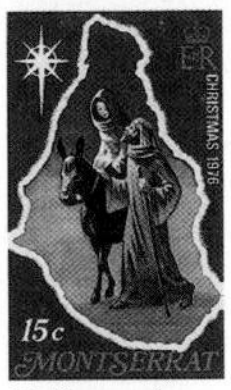

69 Mary and Joseph

1976. Christmas. Multicoloured.

386	5c. Type **69**	10	15
387	20c. The Shepherds	10	15
388	55c. Mary and Jesus	15	15
389	$1.10 The Magi	30	70
MS390	95×135 mm. Nos. 386/9	60	2·25

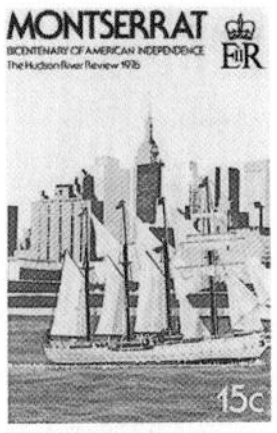

70 Hudson River Review, 1976

1976. Bicentenary of American Revolution. Multicoloured

391	15c. Type **70**	65	50
392	40c. "Raleigh" (American frigate), 1777*	80	70
393	75c. H.M.S. "Druid" (frigate), 1777*	80	70
394	$1.25 Hudson River Review (different detail)	1·00	90
MS395	95×145 mm. Nos. 391/4	2·50	2·75

*The date is wrongly given on the stamps as "1776".
Nos. 391 and 394 and 392/3 respectively were issued in *se-tenant* pairs, each pair forming a composite design.

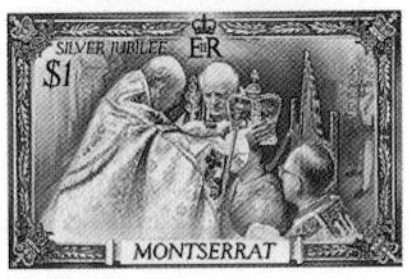

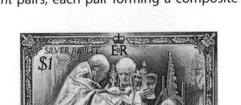

71 The Crowning

1977. Silver Jubilee. Multicoloured.

396	30c. Royal Visit, 1966	10	10
397	45c. Cannons firing salute	15	10
398	$1 Type **71**	25	50

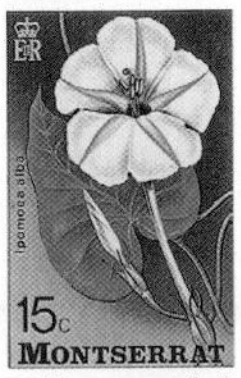

72 "Ipomoea alba"

1977. Flowers of the Night. Multicoloured.

399	15c. Type **72**	15	10
400	40c. "Epiphyllum hookeri" (horiz)	25	30
401	55c. "Cereus hexagonus" (horiz)	25	30
402	$1.50 "Cestrum nocturnum"	60	1·40
MS403	126×130 mm. Nos. 399/402	1·25	3·50

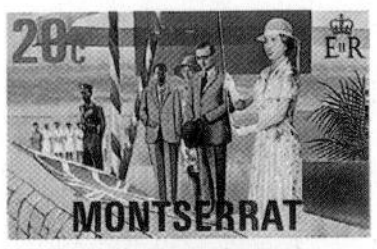

73 Princess Anne laying Foundation Stone of Glendon Hospital

1977. Development. Multicoloured.

404	20c. Type **73**	30	10
405	40c. "Statesman" (freighter) in Plymouth Port	35	15
406	55c. Glendon Hospital	35	20
407	$1.50 Jetty at Plymouth Port	1·00	1·50
MS408	146×105 mm. Nos. 404/7	1·75	3·00

1977. Royal Visit. Nos. 380/1 and 383 surch $1.00 SILVER JUBILEE 1977 ROYAL VISIT TO THE CARIBBEAN.

409	$1 on 55c. Pink cassia	25	45
410	$1 on 70c. Long john	25	45
411	$1 on $2.50 Immortelle	25	45

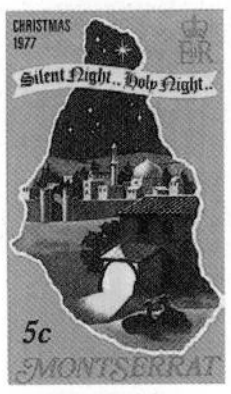

75 The Stable at Bethlehem

1977. Christmas. Multicoloured.

412	5c. Type **75**	10	10
413	40c. The Three Kings	10	10
414	55c. Three Ships	15	10
415	$2 Three Angels	40	2·00
MS416	119×115 mm. Nos. 412/15	1·00	2·25

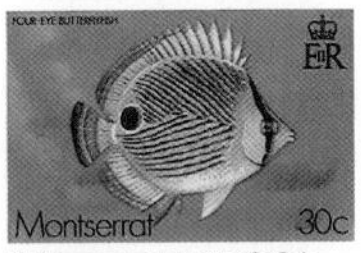

76 Four-eyed Butterflyfish

1978. Fish. Multicoloured.

417	30c. Type **76**	45	10
418	40c. French angelfish	50	15
419	55c. Blue tang	60	15
420	$1.50 Queen triggerfish	90	1·25
MS421	152×102 mm. Nos. 417/20	3·00	3·00

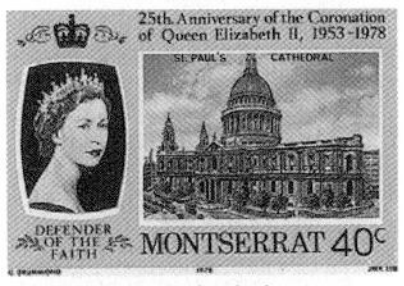

77 St. Paul's Cathedral

1978. 25th Anniv of Coronation. Multicoloured.

422	40c. Type **77**	10	10
423	55c. Chichester Cathedral	10	10
424	$1 Lincoln Cathedral	20	25
425	$2.50 Llandaff Cathedral	40	50
MS426	130×102 mm. Nos. 422/5	70	1·25

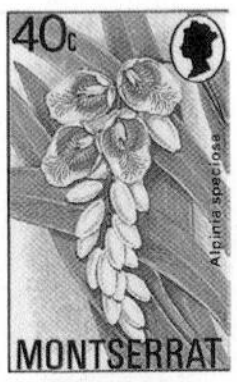

78 "Alpinia speciosa"

1978. Flowers. Multicoloured.

427	40c. Type **78**	20	10
428	55c. "Allamanda cathartica"	20	15
429	$1 "Petrea volubilis"	35	45
430	$2 "Hippeastrum puniceum"	55	80

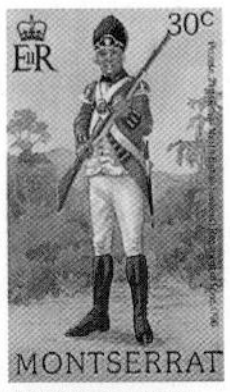

79 Private, 21st (Royal North British Fusiliers), 1786

1978. Military Uniforms (1st series). British Infantry Regiments. Multicoloured.

431	30c. Type **79**	15	15
432	40c. Corporal, 86th (Royal County Down), 1831	20	15
433	55c. Sergeant, 14th (Buckinghamshire), 1837	25	15
434	$1.50 Officer, 55th (Westmorland), 1784	50	80
MS435	140×89 mm. Nos. 431/4	1·50	2·75

See also Nos. 441/5.

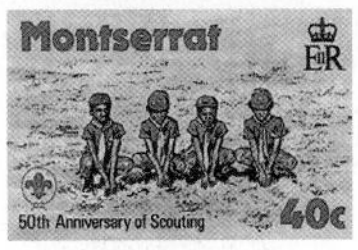

80 Cub Scouts

1979. 50th Anniv of Boy Scout Movement on Montserrat. Multicoloured.

436	40c. Type **80**	20	10
437	55c. Scouts with signalling equipment	20	15
438	$1.25 Camp fire (vert)	35	60
439	$2 Oath ceremony (vert)	45	1·00
MS440	120×110 mm. Nos. 436/9	1·25	2·25

1979. Military Uniforms (2nd series). As T **79**. Multicoloured.

441	30c. Private, 60th (Royal American), 1783	15	15
442	40c. Private, 1st West India, 1819	20	15
443	55c. Officer, 5th (Northumberland), 1819	20	15
444	$2.50 Officer, 93rd (Sutherland Highlanders), 1830	60	1·25
MS445	139×89 mm. Nos. 441/4	1·25	2·50

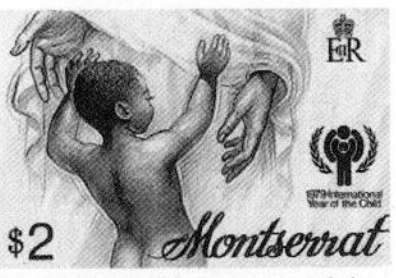

81 Child reaching out to Adult

1979. International Year of the Child.

446	**81**	$2 black, brown and flesh	50	55
MS447		85×99 mm. No. 446	50	1·10

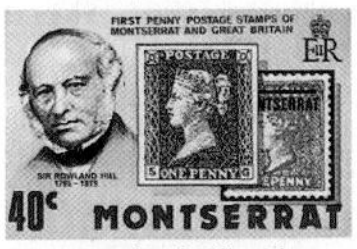

82 Sir Rowland Hill with Penny Black and Montserrat 1876 1d. Stamp

1979. Death Cent of Sir Rowland Hill and Cent of U.P.U. Membership. Multicoloured.

448	40c. Type **82**	20	10
449	55c. U.P.U. emblem and notice announcing Leeward Islands entry into Union	20	15
450	$1 1883 letter following U.P.U. membership	30	50
451	$2 Great Britain Post Office Regulations Notice and Sir Rowland Hill	40	1·50
MS452	135×154 mm. Nos. 448/51	1·00	2·25

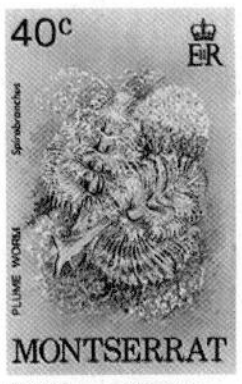

83 Plume Worm

1979. Marine Life. Multicoloured.

453	40c. Type **83**	30	15
454	55c. Sea fans	40	20
455	$2 Sponge and coral	1·00	2·50

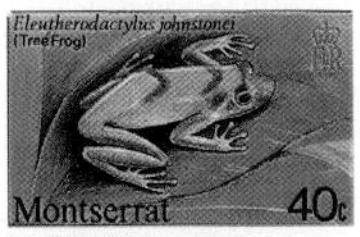

84 Tree Frog

1980. Reptiles and Amphibians. Multicoloured

456	40c. Type **84**	15	15
457	55c. Tree lizard	15	15
458	$1 Crapaud	30	50
459	$2 Wood slave	50	1·00

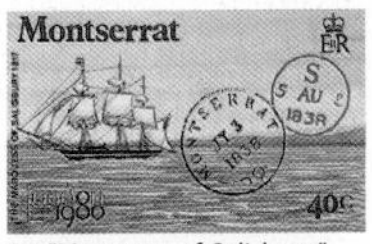

85 "Marquess of Salisbury" and 1838 Handstamps

1980. "London 1980" Int Stamp Exhibition. Multicoloured

460	40c. Type **85**	20	15
461	55c. Hawker Siddeley H.S.748 aircraft and 1976 55c. definitive	25	25

462	$1.20 "La Plata" (liner) and 1903 5s. stamp	30	55
463	$1.20 "Lady Hawkins" (packet steamer) and 1932 Tercentenary 5s. commemorative	30	55
464	$1.20 "Avon I" (paddle-steamer) and Penny Red stamp with "A 08" postmark	30	55
465	$1.20 Aeronca Champion 17 airplane and 1953 $1.20 definitive	30	55
MS466	115×110 mm. Nos. 460/5	1·25	2·25

1980. 75th Anniv of Rotary International. No. 383 optd 75th Anniversary of Rotary International.

467	$2.50 Immortelle	55	85

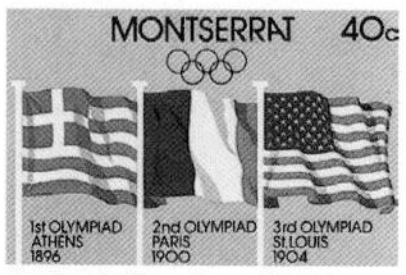

87 Greek, French and U.S.A. Flags

1980. Olympic Games, Moscow. Multicoloured.

468	40c. Type **87**	20	60
469	55c. Union, Swedish and Belgian flags	20	60
470	70c. French, Dutch and U.S.A. flags	25	75
471	$1 German, Union and Finnish flags	30	75
472	$1.50 Australian, Italian and Japanese flags	35	1·00
473	$2 Mexican, West German and Canadian flags	40	1·00
474	$2.50 "The Discus Thrower" (sculpture, Miron)	40	1·10
MS475	150×100 mm. Nos. 468/74	1·50	3·50

1980. Nos. 371, 373, 376 and 379 surch.

476	5c. on 3c. Lignum vitae	10	10
477	35c. on 1c. Type **68**	15	15
478	35c. on 3c. Lignum vitae	15	15
479	35c. on 15c. Orchid tree	15	15
480	35c. on 40c. Flame of the forest	15	15
481	$5 on 40c. Flame of the forest	60	2·00

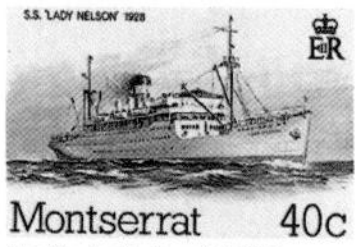

89 "Lady Nelson", 1928

1980. Mail Packet Boats (1st series). Multicoloured.

482	40c. Type **89**	30	15
483	55c. "Chignecto", 1913	30	15
484	$1 "Solent II", 1878	50	65
485	$2 "Dee", 1841	70	1·25

See also Nos. 615/19.

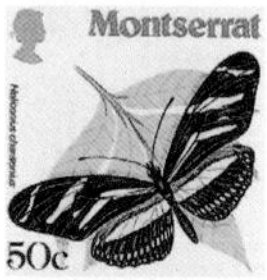

90 "Heliconius charithonia"

1981. Butterflies. Multicoloured.

486	50c. Type **90**	50	40
487	65c. "Pyrgus oileus"	60	45
488	$1.50 "Phoebis agarithe"	70	1·00
489	$2.50 "Danaus plexippus"	1·00	1·50

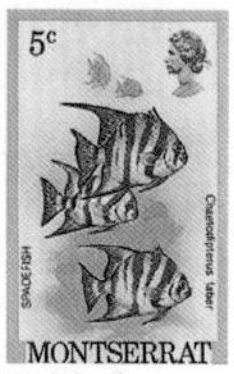

91 Atlantic Spadefish

1981. Fish. Multicoloured.

555	5c. Type **91**	20	10
556	10c. Hogfish and neon goby	25	10
492	15c. Creole wrasse	80	30
493	20c. Three-spotted damselfish	1·00	30
559	25c. Sergeant major	35	20
560	35c. Fin-spot wrasse	45	30
496	45c. Schoolmaster	80	40
497	55c. Striped parrotfish	1·10	45
498	65c. Bigeye	80	60
564	75c. French grunt	75	55
565	$1 Rock beauty	85	65
501	$2 Blue chromis	1·50	1·10
502	$3 Royal gramma ("Fairy basslet") and blueheads	1·50	1·75
503	$5 Cherub angelfish	1·50	2·75
504	$7.50 Long-jawed squirrelfish	2·00	4·75
570	$10 Caribbean long-nosed butterflyfish	2·00	6·00

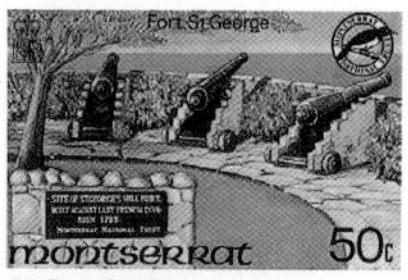

92 Fort St. George

1981. Montserrat National Trust. Multicoloured.

506	50c. Type **92**	2·00	6·50
507	65c. Bird sanctuary, Fox's Bay	45	35
508	$1.50 Museum	50	65
509	$2.50 Bransby Point Battery, c. 1780	60	1·10

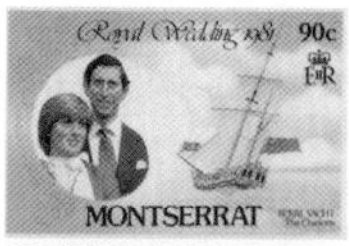

92a "Charlotte"

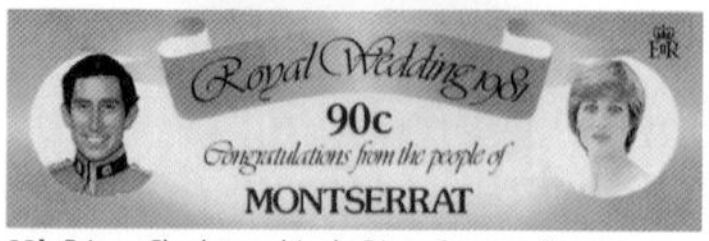

92b Prince Charles and Lady Diana Spencer (image scaled to 59% of original size)

1981. Royal Wedding. Royal Yachts. Multicoloured.

510	90c. Type **92a**	25	25
511	90c. Type **92b**	85	85
512	$3 "Portsmouth"	60	60
513	$3 As No. 511	1·50	1·50
514	$4 "Britannia"	75	75
515	$4 As No. 511	1·75	1·75
MS516	120×109 mm. $5 As No. 511	1·00	1·00

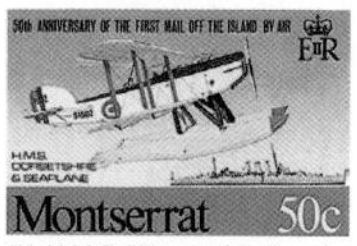

93 H.M.S. "Dorsetshire" and Fairey Firefly Seaplane

1981. 50th Anniv of Montserrat Airmail Service. Multicoloured.

519	50c. Type **93**	30	30
520	65c. Beech 50 Twin Bonanza	40	30
521	$1.50 De Havilland Dragon Rapide "Lord Shaftesbury"	60	1·75
522	$2.50 Hawker Siddeley H.S.748 and maps of Montserrat and Antigua	80	3·00

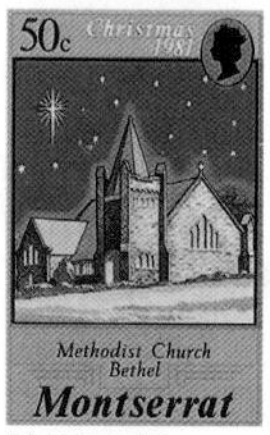

94 Methodist Church, Bethel

1981. Christmas. Churches. Multicoloured.

523	50c. Type **94**	15	15
524	65c. St. George's Anglican Church, Harris	15	15
525	$1.50 St. Peter's Anglican Church, St. Peter's	30	60
526	$2.50 St. Patrick's R.C. Church, Plymouth	50	1·00
MS527	176×120 mm. Nos. 523/6	1·40	3·00

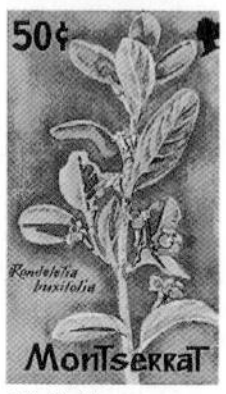

95 Rubiaceae ("Rondeletia buxifolia")

1982. Plant Life. Multicoloured.

528	50c. Type **95**	20	30
529	65c. Boraginaceae ("Heliotropium ternatum") (horiz)	20	40
530	$1.50 Simarubaceae ("Picramnia pentandra")	40	85
531	$2.50 Ebenaceae ("Diospyrus revoluta") (horiz)	55	1·25

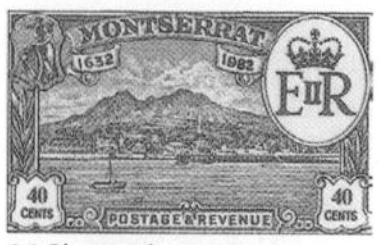

96 Plymouth

1982. 350th Anniv of Settlement of Montserrat by Sir Thomas Warner.

532	**96**	40c. green	20	30
533	**96**	55c. red	20	35
534	**96**	65c. brown	20	50
535	**96**	75c. grey	20	60
536	**96**	85c. blue	20	75
537	**96**	95c. orange	20	80
538	**96**	$1 violet	20	80
539	**96**	$1.50 olive	25	1·25
540	**96**	$2 claret	30	1·50
541	**96**	$2.50 brown	35	1·50

The design of Nos. 532/41 is based on the 1932 Tercentenary set.

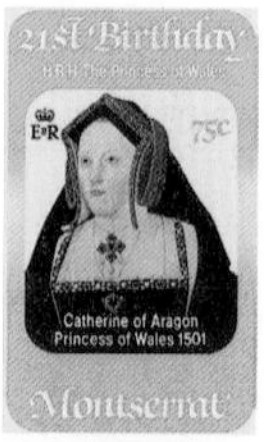

97 Catherine of Aragon, Princess of Wales, 1501

1982. 21st Birthday of Princess of Wales. Multicoloured

542	75c. Type **97**	15	15
543	$1 Coat of Arms of Catherine of Aragon	15	15
544	$5 Diana, Princess of Wales	80	1·25

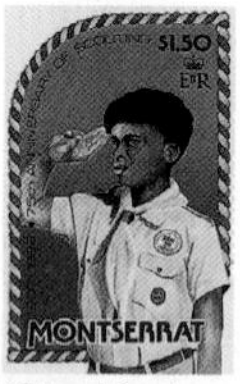

98 Local Scout

1982. 75th Anniv of Boy Scout Movement. Multicoloured

545	$1.50 Type **98**	50	50
546	$2.20 Lord Baden-Powell	60	75

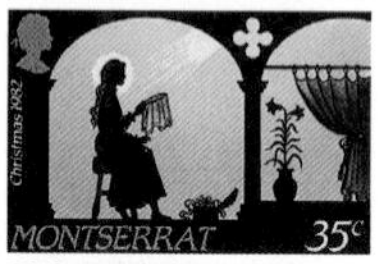

99 Annunciation

1982. Christmas. Multicoloured.

547	35c. Type **99**	15	15
548	75c. Shepherds' Vision	25	35
549	$1.50 The Stable	45	85
550	$2.50 Flight into Egypt	55	1·10

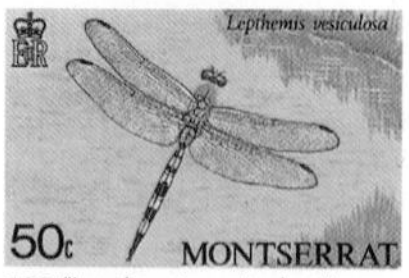

100 "Lepthemis vesiculosa"

1983. Dragonflies. Multicoloured.

551	50c. Type **100**	65	20
552	65c. "Orthemis ferruginea"	75	25
553	$1.50 "Triacanthagyna trifida"	1·40	1·75
554	$2.50 "Erythrodiplax umbrata"	1·90	3·25

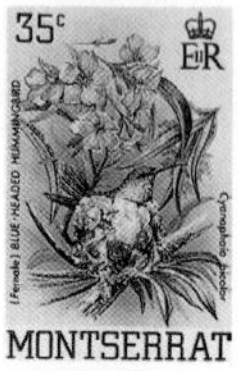

101 Blue-headed Hummingbird

1983. Hummingbirds. Multicoloured.

571	35c. Type **101**	1·50	35
572	75c. Green-throated carib	1·75	85
573	$2 Antilean crested hummingbird	2·75	2·75
574	$3 Purple-throated carib	3·00	3·75

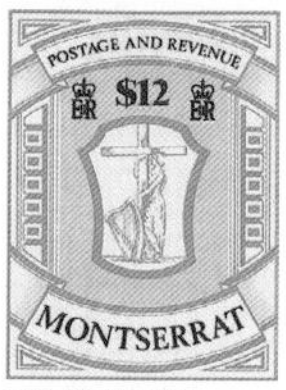

102 Montserrat Emblem

1983

575	**102**	$12 blue and red	2·50	5·00
576	**102**	$30 red and blue	5·50	12·00

1983. Various stamps surch. (a) Nos. 491, 494, 498/9 and 501.

577	40c. on 25c. Sergeant major (No. 494)	30	35
578	70c. on 10c. Hogfish and neon goby (No. 491)	45	50
579	90c. on 65c. Bigeye (No. 498)	55	70
580	$1.15 on 75c. French grunt (No. 499)	65	80
581	$1.50 on $2 Blue chromis (No. 501)	85	1·00

(b) Nos. 512/15.

582	70c. on $3 "Portsmouth"	50	1·00
583	70c. on $3 Prince Charles and Lady Diana Spencer	1·50	2·75
584	$1.15 on $4 "Britannia"	65	1·50
585	$1.15 on $4 As No. 583	1·75	3·25

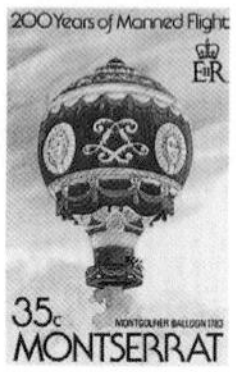

104 Montgolfier Balloon, 1783

1983. Bicentenary of Manned Flight. Multicoloured

586	35c. Type **104**	15	15
587	75c. De Havilland Twin Otter 200/300 (horiz)	25	30
588	$1.50 Lockheed Vega V (horiz)	40	75
589	$2 Beardmore airship R.34 (horiz)	60	1·25
MS590	109×145 mm. Nos. 586/9	1·25	2·75

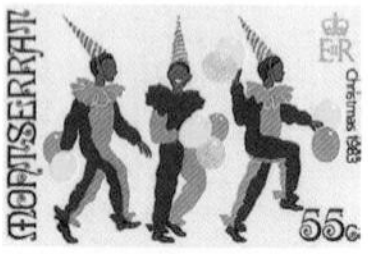

105 Boys dressed as Clowns

1983. Christmas. Carnival. Multicoloured.

591	55c. Type **105**	10	10
592	90c. Girls dressed as silver star bursts	15	20
593	$1.15 Flower girls	20	35
594	$2 Masqueraders	35	1·25

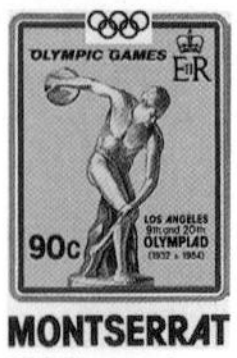

106 Statue of Discus Thrower

1984. Olympic Games, Los Angeles. Multicoloured

595	90c. Type **106**	30	35
596	$1 Olympic torch	35	45
597	$1.25 Los Angeles Olympic stadium	40	50
598	$2.50 Olympic and American flags	65	1·00
MS599	110×110 mm. Nos. 595/8	1·50	2·25

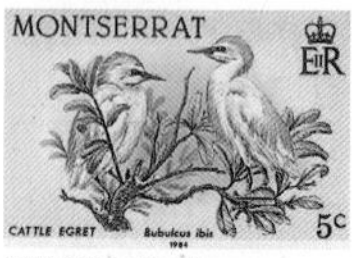

107 Cattle Egret

1984. Birds of Montserrat. Multicoloured.

600	5c. Type **107**	30	50
601	10c. Carib grackle	30	50

602	15c. Moorhen ("Common Gallinule")	30	50
603	20c. Brown booby	40	50
604	25c. Black-whiskered vireo	40	50
605	40c. Scaly-breasted thrasher	60	60
606	55c. Laughing gull	75	40
607	70c. Glossy ibis	90	45
608	90c. Green-backed heron ("Green Heron")	1·00	60
609	$1 Belted kingfisher (vert)	1·25	70
610	$1.15 Bananaquit (vert)	1·50	1·40
611	$3 American kestrel ("Sparrow Hawk") (vert)	3·25	5·50
612	$5 Forest thrush (vert)	4·50	7·50
613	$7.50 Black-crowned night heron (vert)	5·00	13·00
614	$10 Bridled quail dove (vert)	5·50	13·00

1984. Mail Packet Boats (2nd series). As T **89**. Multicoloured.

615	55c. "Tagus II", 1907	20	40
616	90c. "Cobequid", 1913	30	50
617	$1.15 "Lady Drake", 1942	40	70
618	$2 "Factor", 1948	60	1·75
MS619	152×100 mm. Nos. 615/18	1·50	5·00

No. **MS**619 also commemorates the 250th anniversary of "Lloyd's List" (newspaper).

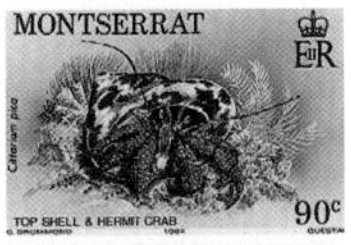

108 Hermit Crab and West Indian Top Shell

1984. Marine Life. Multicoloured.

620	90c. Type **108**	1·50	1·00
621	$1.15 Rough file shell	1·75	1·40
622	$1.50 True tulip	2·50	3·25
623	$2.50 Queen or pink conch	3·25	5·00

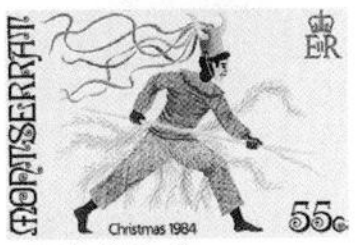

109 "Bull Man"

1984. Christmas. Carnival Costumes. Mult.

624	55c. Type **109**	50	25
625	$1.15 Masquerader Captain	1·50	1·25
626	$1.50 "Fantasy" Carnival Queen	1·75	2·50
627	$2.30 "Ebony and Ivory" Carnival Queen	2·50	4·25

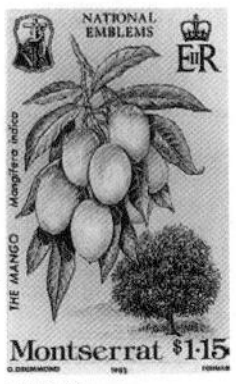

110 Mango

1985. National Emblems. Multicoloured.

628	$1.15 Type **110**	30	60
629	$1.50 Lobster claw	40	1·00
630	$3 Montserrat oriole	60	3·75

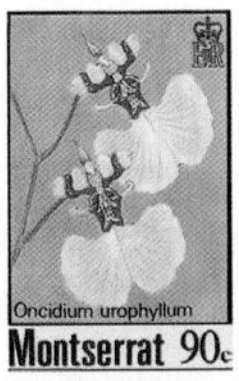

111 "Oncidium urophyllum"

1985. Orchids of Montserrat. Multicoloured.

631	90c. Type **111**	40	55
632	$1.15 "Epidendrum difforme"	40	80
633	$1.50 "Epidendrum ciliare"	45	1·25
634	$2.50 "Brassavola cucullata"	55	2·75
MS635	120×140 mm. Nos. 631/4	3·75	7·00

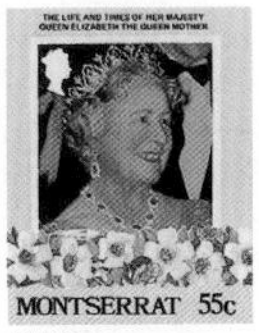

112 Queen Elizabeth the Queen Mother

1985. Life and Times of Queen Elizabeth the Queen Mother. Various vertical portraits.

636	**112**	55c. multicoloured	25	45
637	-	55c. multicoloured	25	45
638	-	90c. multicoloured	25	55
639	-	90c. multicoloured	25	55
640	-	$1.15 multicoloured	25	60
641	-	$1.15 multicoloured	25	60
642	-	$1.50 multicoloured	30	70
643	-	$1.50 multicoloured	30	70
MS644		85×113 mm. $2 multicoloured; $2 multicoloured	65	1·90

Each value was issued in pairs showing a floral pattern across the bottom of the portraits which stops short of the left-hand edge on the first stamp and of the right-hand edge on the second.

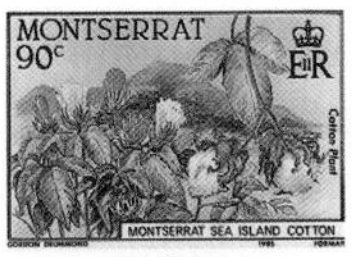

113 Cotton Plants

1985. Montserrat Sea Island Cotton Industry. Multicoloured.

645	90c. Type **113**	25	45
646	$1 Operator at carding machine	25	50
647	$1.15 Threading loom	25	65
648	$2.50 Weaving with hand loom	50	2·75
MS649	148×103 mm. Nos. 645/8	3·00	3·75

1985. Royal Visit. Nos. 514/15, 543, 587/8 and 640/1 optd CARIBBEAN ROYAL VISIT 1985 or surch also.

650	75c. multicoloured (No. 587)	3·00	2·50
651	$1 multicoloured (No. 543)	4·50	3·50
652	$1.15 multicoloured (No. 640)	4·25	6·50
653	$1.15 multicoloured (No. 641)	4·25	6·50
654	$1.50 multicoloured (No. 588)	7·00	7·00
655	$1.60 on $4 mult (No. 514)	2·00	4·25
656	$1.60 on $4 mult (No. 515)	20·00	25·00

No. 656 shows a new face value only, "CARIBBEAN ROYAL VISIT 1985" being omitted from the surcharge.

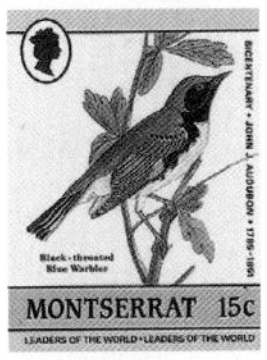

115 Black-throated Blue Warbler

1985. Leaders of the World. Birth Bicentenary of John J. Audubon (ornithologist). Designs showing original paintings. Multicoloured.

657	15c. Type **115**	15	40
658	15c. Palm warbler	15	40
659	30c. Bobolink	15	40
660	30c. Lark sparrow	15	40
661	55c. Chipping sparrow	20	40
662	55c. Northern oriole	20	40
663	$2.50 American goldfinch	40	1·40
664	$2.50 Blue grosbeak	40	1·40

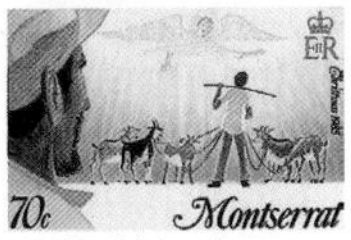

116 Herald Angel appearing to Goatherds

1985. Christmas. Designs showing Caribbean Nativity. Multicoloured.

665	70c. Type **116**	20	15
666	$1.15 Three Wise Men following Star	30	40
667	$1.50 Carol singing around War Memorial, Plymouth	40	85
668	$2.30 Praying to "Our Lady of Montserrat", Church of Our Lady, St. Patrick's Village	50	2·00

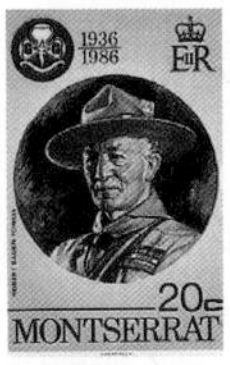

117 Lord Baden-Powell

1986. 50th Anniv of Montserrat Girl Guide Movement. Multicoloured.

669	20c. Type **117**	15	60
670	20c. Girl Guide saluting	15	60
671	75c. Lady Baden-Powell	25	75
672	75c. Guide assisting in old people's home	25	75
673	90c. Lord and Lady Baden-Powell	30	75
674	90c. Guides serving meal in old people's home	30	75
675	$1.15 Girl Guides of 1936	40	80
676	$1.15 Two guides saluting	40	80

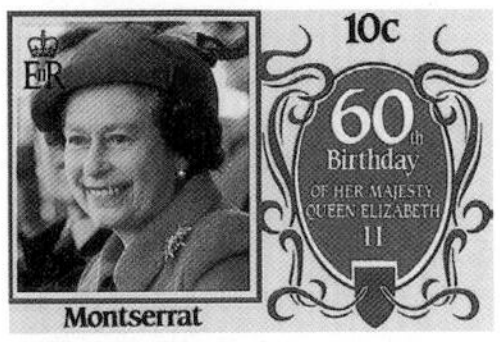

117a Queen Elizabeth II

1986. 60th Birthday of Queen Elizabeth II. Multicoloured.

677	10c. Type **117a**	10	10
678	$1.50 Princess Elizabeth in 1928	25	50
679	$3 In Antigua, 1977	40	1·25
680	$6 In Canberra, 1982 (vert)	65	2·25
MS681	85×115 mm. $8 Queen with bouquet	3·25	5·50

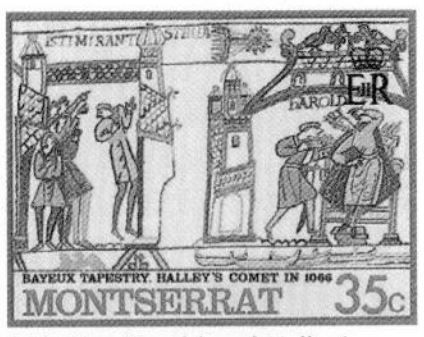

118 King Harold and Halley's Comet, 1066 (from Bayeux Tapestry)

1986. Appearance of Halley's Comet. Multicoloured

682	35c. Type **118**	20	25
683	50c. Comet of 1301 (from Giotto's "Adoration of the Magi")	25	30
684	70c. Edmond Halley and Comet of 1531	25	40
685	$1 Comets of 1066 and 1910	25	40
686	$1.15 Comet of 1910	30	50
687	$1.50 E.S.A. "Giotto" spacecraft and Comet	30	80
688	$2.30 U.S. space telescope and Comet	40	1·75
689	$4 Computer reconstruction of 1910 Comet	50	3·25
MS690	Two sheets, each 140×115 mm. (a) 40c. Type **118**; $1.75, As No. 683; $2 As No. 684; $3 As No. 685. (b) 55c. As No. 686; 60c. As No. 687; 80c. As No. 688; $5 As No. 689 Set of 2 sheets	3·00	9·00

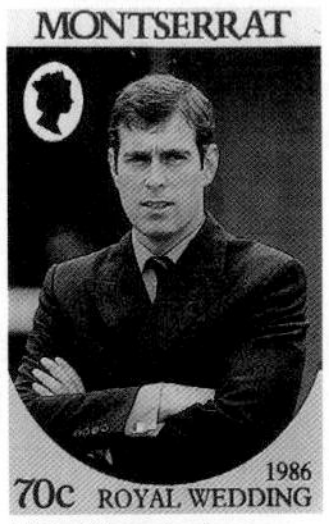

118a Prince Andrew

1986. Royal Wedding (1st issue). Multicoloured.

691	70c. Type **118a**	25	40
692	70c. Miss Sarah Ferguson	25	40
693	$2 Prince Andrew wearing stetson (horiz)	40	90
694	$2 Miss Sarah Ferguson on skiing holiday (horiz)	40	90
MS695	115×85 mm. $10 Duke and Duchess of York on Palace balcony after wedding (horiz)	3·25	6·00

See also Nos. 705/8.

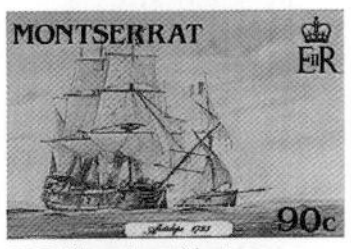

119 "Antelope" being attacked by "L'Atalante"

1986. Mail Packet Sailing Ships. Multicoloured

696	90c. Type **119**	2·00	1·50
697	$1.15 "Montagu" (1810)	2·25	2·00
698	$1.50 "Little Catherine" being pursued by "L'Etoile" (1813)	2·75	2·75
699	$2.30 "Hinchingbrook I" (1813)	3·50	5·00
MS700	165×123 mm. Nos. 696/9	10·00	11·00

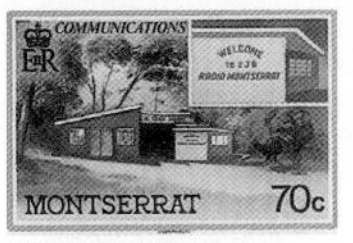

120 Radio Montserrat Building, Dagenham

1986. Communications. Multicoloured.

701	70c. Type **120**	1·00	70
702	$1.15 Radio Gem dish aerial, Plymouth	1·00	1·50
703	$1.50 Radio Antilles studio, O'Garro's	1·75	2·25
704	$2.30 Cable and Wireless building, Plymouth	2·25	4·25

1986. Royal Wedding (2nd issue). Nos. 691/4 optd Congratulations to T.R.H. The Duke & Duchess of York.

705	70c. Prince Andrew	90	1·50
706	70c. Miss Sarah Ferguson	90	1·50
707	$2 Prince Andrew wearing stetson (horiz)	1·25	2·00
708	$2 Miss Sarah Ferguson on skiing holiday (horiz)	1·25	2·00

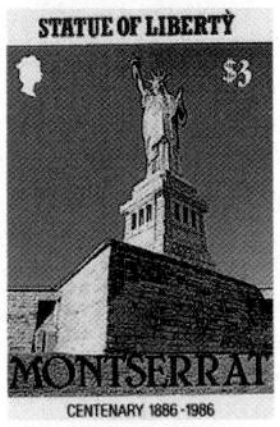

121a Statue of Liberty

1986. Centenary of Statue of Liberty. Vert views of Statue as T **121a** in separate miniature sheets. Multicoloured.

MS709	Three sheets, each 85×115 mm. $3; $4.50; $5 Set of 3 sheets	3·75	9·00

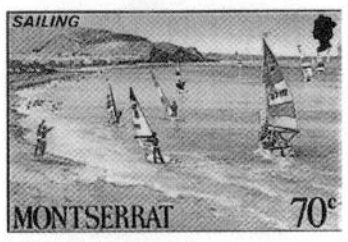

122 Sailing and Windsurfing

1986. Tourism. Multicoloured.

710	70c. Type **122**	40	70
711	$1.15 Golf	70	1·50
712	$1.50 Plymouth market	70	2·00
713	$2.30 Air Recording Studios	80	3·00

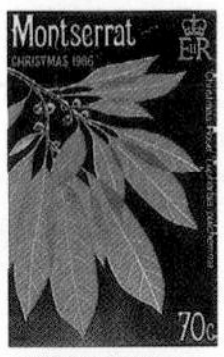

123 Christmas Rose

1986. Christmas. Flowering Shrubs. Multicoloured

714	70c. Type **123**	70	40
715	$1.15 Candle flower	95	85
716	$1.50 Christmas tree kalanchoe	1·50	1·50
717	$2.30 Snow on the mountain	2·00	4·50
MS718	150×110 mm. Nos. 714/17	8·00	9·00

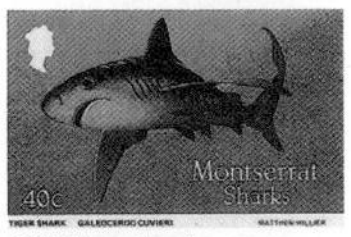

124 Tiger Shark

1987. Sharks. Multicoloured.

719	40c. Type **124**	1·50	55
720	90c. Lemon shark	2·50	1·50
721	$1.15 Great white shark	2·75	2·00
722	$3.50 Whale shark	5·50	8·00
MS723	150×102 mm. Nos. 719/22	13·00	15·00

1987. Nos. 601, 603, 607/8 and 611 surch.

724	5c. on 70c. Glossy ibis	60	3·25
725	$1 on 20c. Brown booby	2·00	1·50
726	$1.15 on 10c. Carib grackle	2·25	1·50
727	$1.50 on 90c. Green-backed heron	2·50	2·75
728	$2.30 on $3 American kestrel (vert)	3·50	9·00

1987. "Capex '87" International Stamp Exhibition, Toronto. No. **MS**690 optd with CAPEX 87 logo.

MS729	Two sheets. As No. **MS**690 Set of 2 sheets	4·00	10·00

No. **MS**729 also carries an overprint commemorating the exhibition on the lower sheet margins.

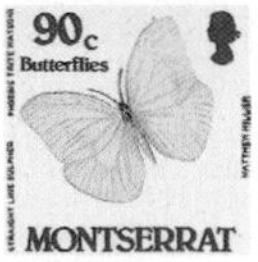

127 "Phoebis trite"

1987. Butterflies. Multicoloured.

730	90c. Type **127**	2·00	1·10
731	$1.15 "Biblis hyperia"	2·50	1·60
732	$1.50 "Polygonus leo"	3·00	2·50
733	$2.50 "Hypolimnas misippus"	4·50	6·50

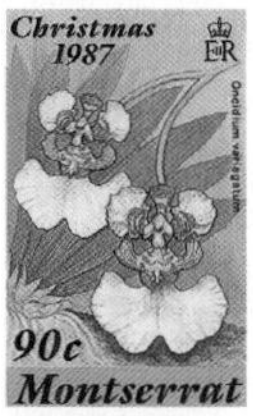

128 "Oncidium variegatum"

1987. Christmas. Orchids. Multicoloured.

734	90c. Type **128**	60	45
735	$1.15 "Vanilla planifolia" (horiz)	85	55
736	$1.50 "Gongora quinquenervis"	1·10	1·10
737	$3.50 "Brassavola nodosa" (horiz)	2·00	5·00
MS738	100×75 mm. $5 "Oncidium lanceanum" (horiz)	12·00	14·00

1987. Royal Ruby Wedding. Nos. 601, 604/5 and 608 surch 40th Wedding Anniversary HM Queen Elizabeth II HRH Duke of Edinburgh. November 1987. and value.

739B	5c. on 90c. Green-backed heron	30	1·00
740B	$1.15 on 10c. Carib grackle	1·00	1·00
741B	$2.30 on 25c. Black-whiskered vireo	1·75	2·25
742B	$5 on 40c. Scaly-breasted thrasher	3·50	5·50

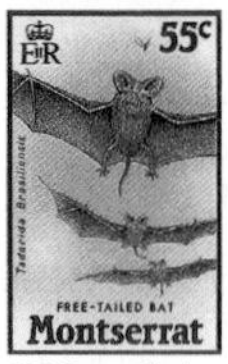

130 Free-tailed Bat

1988. Bats. Multicoloured.

743	55c. Type **130**	80	40
744	90c. "Chiroderma improvisum" (fruit bat)	1·25	90
745	$1.15 Fisherman bat	1·60	1·50
746	$2.30 "Brachyphylla cavernarum" (fruit bat)	3·00	5·50
MS747	133×110 mm. $2.50 Funnel-eared bat	6·50	8·00

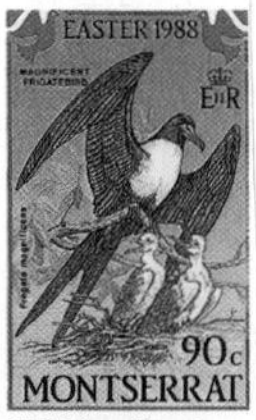

131 Magnificent Frigate Bird

1988. Easter. Birds. Multicoloured.

748	90c. Type **131**	60	45
749	$1.15 Caribbean elaenia	80	75
750	$1.50 Glossy ibis	1·00	1·50
751	$3.50 Purple-throated carib	2·00	4·00
MS752	100×75 mm. $5 Brown pelican	2·50	3·50

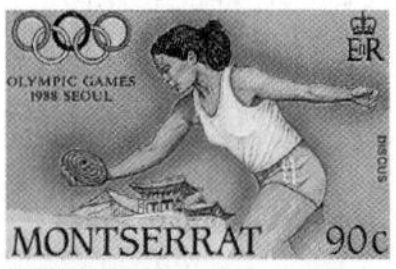

132 Discus throwing

1988. Olympic Games, Seoul. Multicoloured.

753	90c. Type **132**	80	50
754	$1.15 High jumping	90	55
755	$3.50 Athletics	2·25	3·25
MS756	103×77 mm. $5 Rowing	3·00	3·00

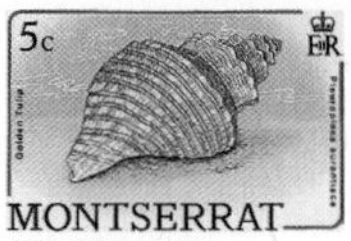

133 Golden Tulip

1988. Sea Shells. Multicoloured.

757	5c. Type **133**	45	75
758	10c. Little knobbed scallop	60	75
759	15c. Sozoni's cone	60	75
760	20c. Globular coral shell	70	40
761	25c. American or common sundial	70	50
762	40c. King helmet	85	50
763	55c. Channelled turban	1·00	50
764	70c. True tulip	1·25	75
765	90c. Music volute	1·50	75
766	$1 Flame auger	1·60	80
767	$1.15 Rooster-tail conch	1·75	90
768	$1.50 Queen or pink conch	1·75	1·40
769	$3 Teramachi's slit shell	2·75	4·50
770	$5 Common or Florida crown conch	3·50	7·00
771	$7.50 Beau's murex	4·25	12·00
772	$10 Atlantic trumpet triton	4·50	12·00

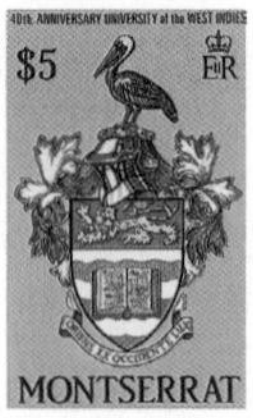

134 University Crest

1988. 40th Anniv of University of West Indies.

773	**134**	$5 multicoloured	2·75	3·50

1988. Princess Alexandra's Visit. Nos. 763, 766 and 769/70 surch HRH PRINCESS ALEXANDRA'S VISIT NOVEMBER 1988 and new value.

774	40c. on 55c. Channelled turban	75	45
775	90c. on $1 Flame auger	1·25	80
776	$1.15 on $3 Teramachi's slit shell	1·50	95
777	$1.50 on $5 Common or Florida crown conch	1·75	1·75

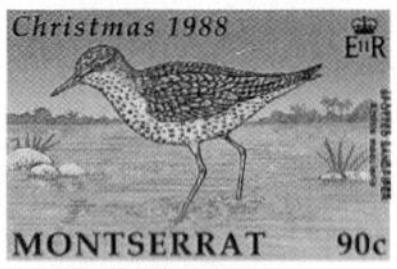

136 Spotted Sandpiper

1988. Christmas. Sea Birds. Multicoloured.

778	90c. Type **136**	70	55
779	$1.15 Ruddy turnstone	85	70
780	$3.50 Red-footed booby	2·00	3·75
MS781	105×79 mm. $5 Audubon's shearwater	2·75	4·00

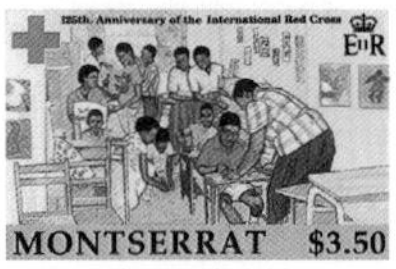

137 Handicapped Children in Classroom

1988. 125th Anniv of International Red Cross.

782	**137**	$3.50 multicoloured	1·50	2·25

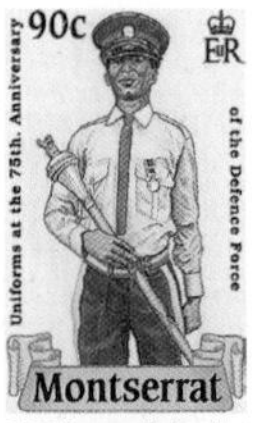

138 Drum Major in Ceremonial Uniform

1989. 75th Anniv (1986) of Montserrat Defence Force. Uniforms. Multicoloured.

783	90c. Type **138**	90	50
784	$1.15 Field training uniform	1·00	75
785	$1.50 Cadet in ceremonial uniform	1·50	2·00
786	$3.50 Gazetted Police Officer in ceremonial uniform	4·00	4·50
MS787	102×76 mm. $5 Island Girl Guide Commissioner and brownie	3·50	4·25

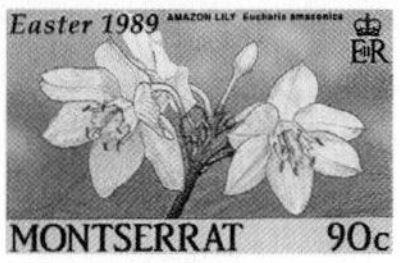

139 Amazon Lily

1989. Easter. Lilies. Multicoloured.

788	90c. Type **139**	50	50
789	$1.15 Salmon blood lily (vert)	70	70
790	$1.50 Amaryllis (vert)	85	1·25
791	$3.50 Amaryllis (vert)	1·90	3·00
MS792	103×77 mm. $5 Resurrection lily (vert)	4·75	7·00

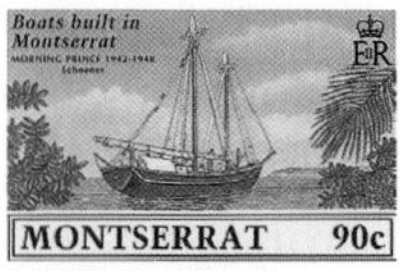

140 "Morning Prince" (schooner), 1942

1989. Shipbuilding in Montserrat. Multicoloured

793	90c. Type **140**	1·40	60
794	$1.15 "Western Sun" (inter-island freighter)	1·90	1·10
795	$1.50 "Kim G" (inter-island freighter) under construction	2·25	2·25
796	$3.50 "Romaris" (inter-island ferry), c. 1942	3·50	5·50

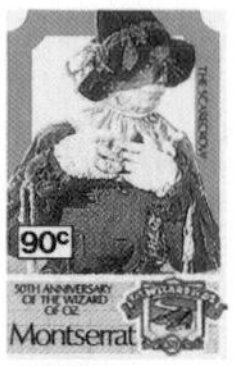

141 The Scarecrow

1989. 50th Anniv of "The Wizard of Oz" (film). Multicoloured.

797	90c. Type **141**	40	45
798	$1.15 The Lion	55	60
799	$1.50 The Tin Man	70	85
800	$3.50 Dorothy	1·60	2·50
MS801	113×84 mm. $5 Characters from film (horiz)	2·40	3·75

1989. Hurricane Hugo Relief Fund. Nos. 795/6 surch Hurricane Hugo Relief Surcharge $2.50.

802	$1.50+$2.50 "Kim G" (inter-island freighter under construction)	2·25	4·00
803	$3.50+$2.50 "Romaris" (inter-island ferry), c. 1942	2·50	5·00

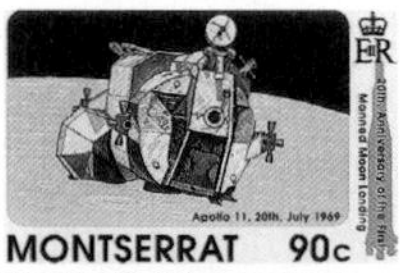

143 "Apollo 11" above Lunar Surface

1989. 20th Anniv of First Manned Landing on Moon. Multicoloured.

804	90c. Type **143**	45	40
805	$1.15 Astronaut alighting from lunar module "Eagle"	55	50
806	$1.50 "Eagle" and astronaut conducting experiment	75	80
807	$3.50 Opening "Apollo 11" hatch after splashdown	1·60	2·50
MS808	101×76 mm. $5 Astronaut on Moon	5·00	6·00

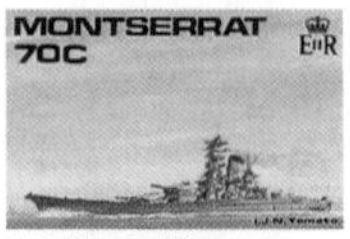

144 "Yamato" (Japanese battleship)

1990. World War II Capital Ships. Multicoloured.

809	70c. Type **144**	3·25	70
810	$1.15 U.S.S."Arizona" at Pearl Harbor	3·75	95
811	$1.50 "Bismarck" (German battleship) in action	4·75	2·75
812	$3.50 H.M.S. "Hood" (battle cruiser)	7·00	10·00
MS813	118×90 mm. $5 "Bismarck" and map of North Atlantic	15·00	15·00

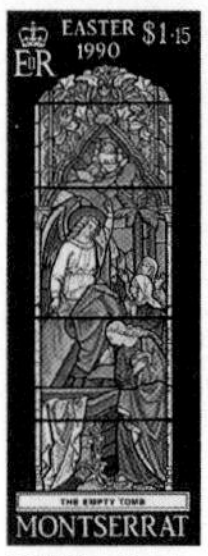

145 The Empty Tomb

1990. Easter. Stained glass windows from St. Michael's Parish Church, Bray, Berkshire. Multicoloured.

814	$1.15 Type **145**	2·25	2·50
815	$1.50 The Ascension	2·25	2·50
816	$3.50 The Risen Christ with Disciples	2·75	3·25
MS817	65×103 mm. $5 The Crucifixion	5·00	6·50

1990. "Stamp World London '90" International Stamp Exhibition. Nos. 460/4 surch Stamp World London 90, emblem and value.

818	70c. on 40c. Type **85**	80	80
819	90c. on 55c. Hawker Siddeley H.S.748 aircraft and 1976 55c. definitive	1·00	1·00
820	$1 on $1.20 "La Plata" (liner) and 1903 5s. stamp	1·25	1·40
821	$1.15 on $1.20 "Lady Hawkins" (packet steamer) and 1932 Tercentenary 5s. commemorative	1·40	1·50
822	$1.50 on $1.20 "Avon I" (paddle-steamer) and Penny Red stamp with "A 08" postmark	1·75	2·00

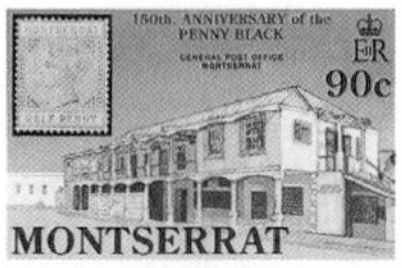

147 General Office, Montserrat and 1884 ½d. Stamp

1990. 150th Anniv of the Penny Black. Multicoloured

823	90c. Type **147**	65	65
824	$1.15 Sorting letters and Montserrat 1d. stamp of 1876 (vert)	85	90
825	$1.50 Posting letters and Penny Black (vert)	1·25	1·75
826	$3.50 Postman delivering letters and 1840 Twopence Blue	3·00	4·50
MS827	102×75 mm. $5 Montserrat soldier's letter of 1836 and Penny Black	8·50	10·00

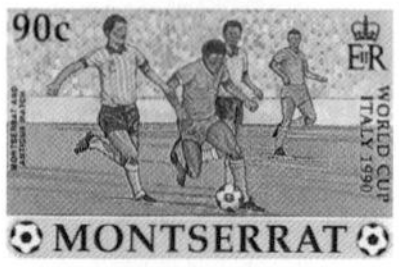

148 Montserrat v. Antigua Match

1990. World Cup Football Championship, Italy. Multicoloured.

828	90c. Type **148**	65	55
829	$1.15 U.S.A. v. Trinidad match	85	75
830	$1.50 Montserrat team	1·25	1·50
831	$3.50 West Germany v. Wales match	2·25	3·50
MS832	77×101 mm. $5 World Cup trophy (vert)	6·00	7·50

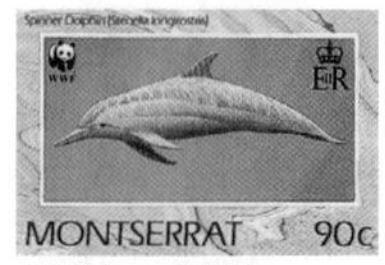

149 Spinner Dolphin

1990. Dolphins. Multicoloured.

833	90c. Type **149**	1·50	85
834	$1.15 Common dolphin	1·75	1·25
835	$1.50 Striped dolphin	2·50	2·50
836	$3.50 Atlantic spotted dolphin	3·75	5·00
MS837	103×76 mm. $5 Atlantic white-sided dolphin	8·50	9·50

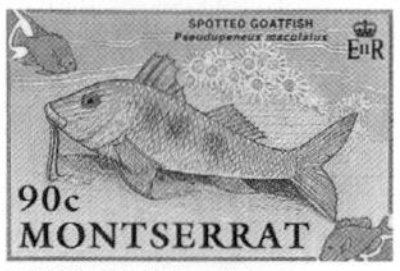

150 Spotted Goatfish

1991. Tropical Fish. Multicoloured.

838	90c. Type **150**	1·50	95

839	$1.15 Cushion star	1·75	1·25
840	$1.50 Rock beauty	2·50	2·75
841	$3.50 French grunt	3·75	5·50
MS842	103×76 mm. $5 Buffalo trunkfish	6·50	8·00

1991. Nos. 760/1, 768 and 771 surch.

843	5c. on 20c. Globular coral shell	65	2·25
844	5c. on 25c. American or common sundial	65	2·25
845	$1.15 on $1.50 Queen or pink conch	2·75	3·25
846	$1.15 on $7.50 Beau's murex	2·75	3·25

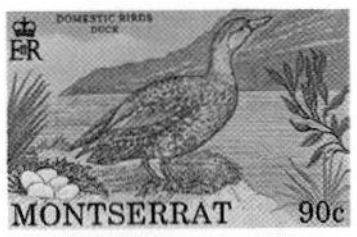

152 Duck

1991. Domestic Birds. Multicoloured.

847	90c. Type **152**	60	60
848	$1.15 Hen and chicks	80	90
849	$1.50 Red junglefowl ("Rooster")	1·10	1·50
850	$3.50 Helmeted guineafowl	2·40	3·50

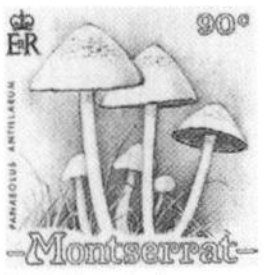

153 "Panaeolus antillarum"

1991. Fungi.

851	**153**	90c. grey	1·50	1·00
852	-	$1.15 red	1·75	1·25
853	-	$1.50 brown	2·50	2·25
854	-	$2 purple	2·75	3·50
855	-	$3.50 blue	4·00	6·00

DESIGNS: $1.15, "Cantharellus cinnabarinus"; $1.50, "Gymnopilus chrysopellus"; $2 "Psilocybe cubensis"; $3.50, "Leptonia caeruleocapitata".

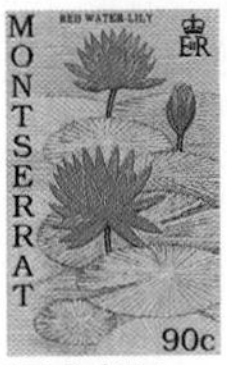

154 Red Water Lily

1991. Lilies. Multicoloured.

856	90c. Type **154**	65	65
857	$1.15 Shell ginger	75	85
858	$1.50 Early day lily	1·00	1·60
859	$3.50 Anthurium	2·50	3·75

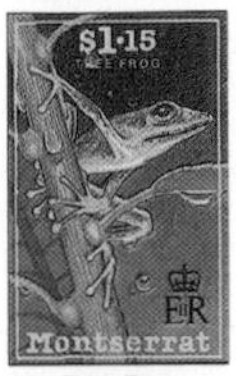

155 Tree Frog

1991. Frogs and Toad. Multicoloured.

860	$1.15 Type **155**	3·75	1·25
861	$2 Crapaud toad	5·00	5·00
862	$3.50 Mountain chicken (frog)	8·50	9·50
MS863	110×110 mm. $5 Tree frog, crapaud toad and mountain chicken (76½×44 mm)	13·00	14·00

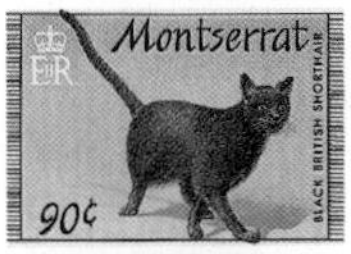

156 Black British Shorthair Cat

1991. Cats. Multicoloured.

864	90c. Type **156**	2·00	90
865	$1.15 Seal point Siamese	2·25	1·10
866	$1.50 Silver tabby Persian	2·75	2·25
867	$2.50 Birman temple cat	3·50	4·50
868	$3.50 Egyptian mau	5·00	7·00

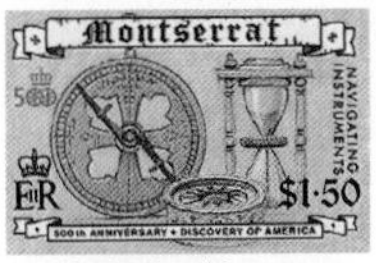

157 Navigational Instruments

1992. 500th Anniv of Discovery of America by Columbus. Multicoloured.

869	$1.50 Type **157**	1·75	1·90
870	$1.50 Columbus and coat of arms	1·75	1·90
871	$1.50 Landfall on the Bahamas	1·75	1·90
872	$1.50 Petitioning Queen Isabella	1·75	1·90
873	$1.50 Tropical birds	1·75	1·90
874	$1.50 Tropical fruits	1·75	1·90
875	$3 Ships of Columbus (81×26 mm)	2·00	2·25

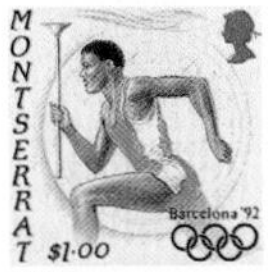

158 Runner with Olympic Flame

1992. Olympic Games, Barcelona. Multicoloured.

876	$1 Type **158**	1·00	60
877	$1.15 Montserrat, Olympic and Spanish flags	2·25	1·00
878	$2.30 Olympic flame on map of Montserrat	3·25	3·50
879	$3.60 Olympic events	3·25	5·50

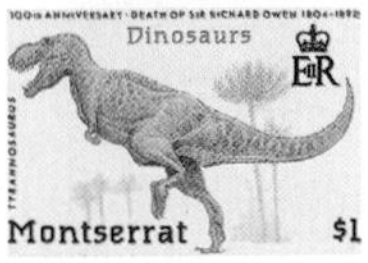

159 Tyrannosaurus

1992. Death Centenary of Sir Richard Owen (zoologist). Multicoloured.

880	$1 Type **159**	2·00	1·25
881	$1.15 Diplodocus	2·25	1·40
882	$1.50 Apatosaurus	2·75	2·75
883	$3.45 Dimetrodon	5·50	8·00
MS884	114×84 mm. $4.60, Sir Richard Owen and dinosaur bone (vert)	8·50	10·00

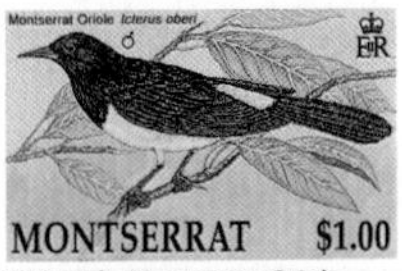

160 Male Montserrat Oriole

1992. Montserrat Oriole. Multicoloured.

885	$1 Type **160**	1·10	1·10
886	$1.15 Male and female orioles	1·40	1·40
887	$1.50 Female oriole with chicks	1·75	2·00
888	$3.60 Map of Montserrat and male oriole	3·50	5·00

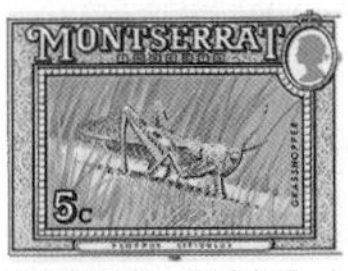

161 "Psophus stridulus" (grasshopper)

1992. Insects. Multicoloured.

889	5c. Type **161**	40	70
890	10c. "Gryllus campestris" (field cricket)	50	70
891	15c. "Lepthemis vesiculosa" (dragonfly)	60	70
892	20c. "Orthemis ferruginea" (red skimmer)	65	75
893	25c. "Gerris lacustris" (pond skater)	65	75
894	40c. "Byctiscus betulae" (leaf weevil)	80	75
895	55c. "Atta texana" (leaf-cutter ants)	85	40
896	70c. "Polistes fuscatus" (paper wasp)	1·00	60
897	90c. "Sparmopolius fulvus" (bee fly)	1·25	60
898	$1 "Chrysopa carnea" (lace wing)	1·75	65
899	$1.15 "Phoebis philea" (butterfly)	2·25	90
900	$1.50 "Cynthia cardui" (butterfly)	2·50	1·75
901	$3 "Utetheisa bella" (moth)	3·25	4·50
902	$5 "Alucita pentadactyla" (moth)	4·50	6·50
903	$7.50 "Anartia jatropha" (butterfly)	6·50	9·50
904	$10 "Heliconius melpomene" (butterfly)	6·50	9·50

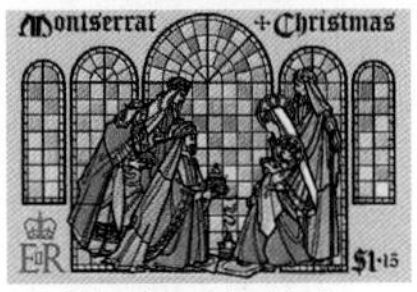

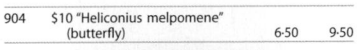

162 Adoration of the Magi

1992. Christmas. Multicoloured.

905	$1.15 Type **162**	2·00	75
906	$4.60 Appearance of angel to shepherds	4·50	6·50

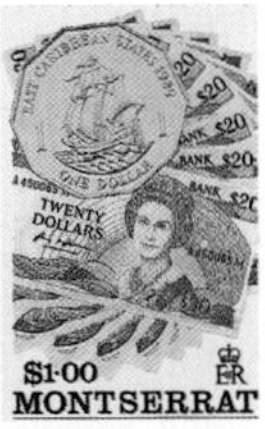

163 $1 Coin and $20 Banknote

1993. East Caribbean Currency. Multicoloured.

907	$1 Type **163**	90	70
908	$1.15 10c. and 25c. coins with $10 banknote	1·25	85
909	$1.50 5c. coin and $5 banknote	1·75	2·00
910	$3.60 1c. and 2c. coins with $1 banknote	4·00	6·00

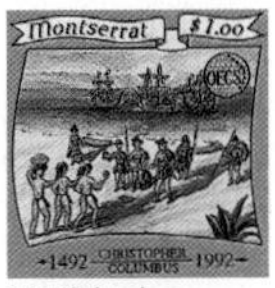

164 Columbus meeting Amerindians

1993. Organization of East Caribbean States. 500th Anniv of Discovery of America by Columbus. Multicoloured.

911	$1 Type **164**	1·25	1·00
912	$2 Ships approaching island	2·25	3·00

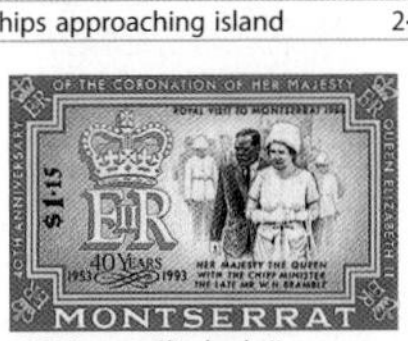

165 Queen Elizabeth II on Montserrat with Chief Minister W. H. Bramble, 1966

1993. 40th Anniv of Coronation. Multicoloured.

913	$1.15 Type **165**	1·50	75
914	$4.60 Queen Elizabeth II in State Coach, 1953	4·50	5·50

1993. 500th Anniv of Discovery of Montserrat. As Nos. 869/75, some with new values, each showing "500th ANNIVERSARY DISCOVERY OF MONTSERRAT" at foot and with additional historical inscr across the centre.

915	$1.15 mult (As Type **157**)	2·25	2·50
916	$1.15 multicoloured (As No. 870)	2·25	2·50
917	$1.15 multicoloured (As No. 871)	2·25	2·50
918	$1.50 multicoloured (As No. 872)	2·50	2·75
919	$1.50 multicoloured (As No. 873)	2·50	2·75
920	$1.50 multicoloured (As No. 874)	2·50	2·75
921	$3.45 multicoloured (As No. 875)	3·75	4·25

Additional inscriptions: No. 915, "PRE-COLUMBUS CARIB NAME OF ISLAND ALLIOUGANA"; 916, "COLUMBUS NAMED ISLAND SANTA MARIA DE MONTSERRATE"; 917, "COLUMBUS SAILED ALONG COASTLINE 11th NOV. 1493"; 918, "ISLAND OCCUPIED BY FRENCH BRIEFLY IN 1667"; 919, "ISLAND DECLARED ENGLISH BY TREATY OF BREDA 1667"; 920, "AFRICAN SLAVES BROUGHT IN DURING 1600's"; 921, "IRISH CATHOLICS FROM ST. KITTS AND VIRGINIA SETTLED ON ISLAND BETWEEN 1628–1634".

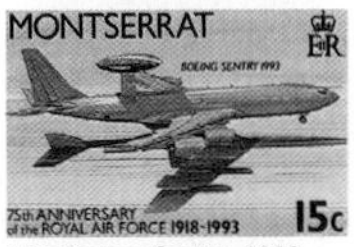

166 Boeing Sentry, 1993

1993. 75th Anniv of Royal Air Force. Multicoloured

922	15c. Type **166**	45	20
923	55c. Vickers Valiant B Mk 1, 1962	65	40
924	$1.15 Handley Page Hastings C Mk 2, 1958	1·25	75
925	$3 Lockheed Ventura, 1943	2·50	4·25
MS926	117×78 mm. $1.50 Felixstowe F5, 1921; $1.50 Armstrong Whitworth Atlas, 1934; $1.50 Fairey Gordon, 1935; $1.50 Boulton & Paul Overstrand, 1936	4·50	6·00

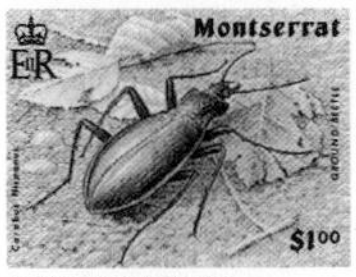

167 Ground Beetle

1994. Beetles. Multicoloured.

927	$1 Type **167**	65	65
928	$1.15 Click beetle	80	80
929	$1.50 Harlequin beetle	1·25	1·50
930	$3.45 Leaf beetle	3·00	4·50
MS931	68×85 mm. $4.50 Scarab beetle	3·50	4·00

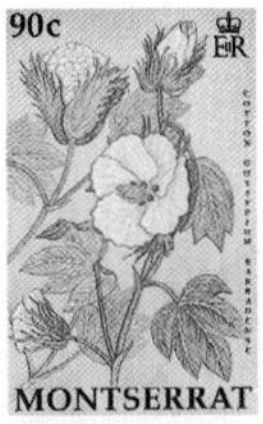

168 "Gossypium barbadense"

1994. Flowers. Multicoloured.

932	90c. Type **168**	1·25	80
933	$1.15 "Hibiscus sabdariffa"	1·50	1·00
934	$1.50 "Hibiscus esculentus"	1·75	1·75
935	$3.50 "Hibiscus rosa-sinensis"	3·75	6·00

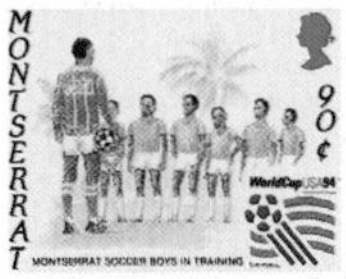

169 Coaching Young Players and Logo

1994. World Cup Football Championship, U.S.A. Multicoloured.

936	90c. Type **169**	1·90	2·25
937	$1 United States scoring against England, 1950	1·90	2·25
938	$1.15 Rose Bowl stadium, Los Angeles, and trophy	1·90	2·25
939	$3.45 German players celebrating with trophy, 1990	3·00	3·50
MS940	114×85 mm. $2 Jules Rimet (founder) and Jules Rimet Trophy; $2 Bobby Moore (England) holding trophy, 1966; $2 Lew Jaschin (U.S.S.R.); $2 Sepp Herberger (Germany) and German players celebrating, 1990	7·00	9·00

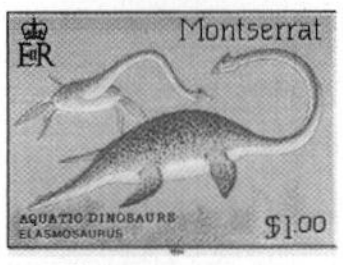

170 Elasmosaurus

1994. Aquatic Dinosaurs. Multicoloured.

941	$1 Type **170**	2·25	2·25
942	$1.15 Plesiosaurus	2·25	2·25
943	$1.50 Nothosaurus	2·75	2·75
944	$3.45 Mosasaurus	3·50	4·25

1994. Space Anniversaries. Nos. 804/7 variously surch or optd, each including Space Anniversaries. Multicoloured.

945	40c. on 90c. Type **143**	1·75	80
946	$1.15 Astronaut alighting from lunar module "Eagle"	2·50	1·50
947	$1.50 "Eagle" and astronaut conducting experiment	3·00	3·00
948	$2.30 on $3.50 Opening "Apollo 11" hatch after splashdown	4·75	7·00

Surcharges and overprints: No. 945, **Juri Gagarin First man in space April 12, 1961**; 946, **First Joint US Soviet Mission July 15, 1975**; 947 **25th Anniversary First Moon Landing Apollo XI – July 20, 1994**; 948, **Columbia First Space Shuttle April 12, 1981.**

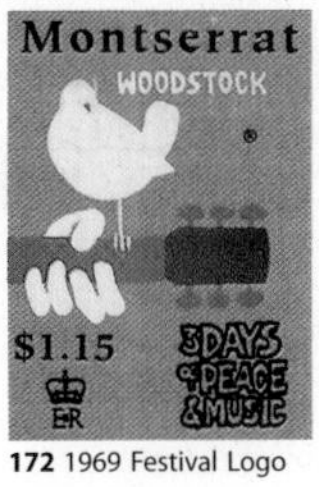

172 1969 Festival Logo

1994. 25th Anniv of Woodstock Music Festival. Multicoloured.

949	$1.15 Type **172**	1·00	1·00
950	$1.50 1994 anniversary festival logo	1·25	1·25

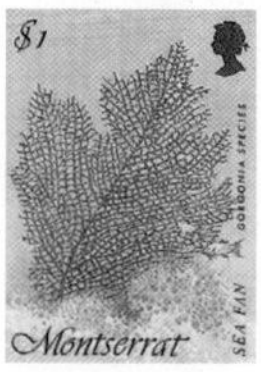

173 Sea Fan

1995. Marine Life. Multicoloured.

951	$1 Type **173**	60	50
952	$1.15 Sea lily	70	60
953	$1.50 Sea pen	90	1·00
954	$3.45 Sea fern	2·00	3·00
MS955	88×96 mm. $4.50 Sea rose	3·00	4·00

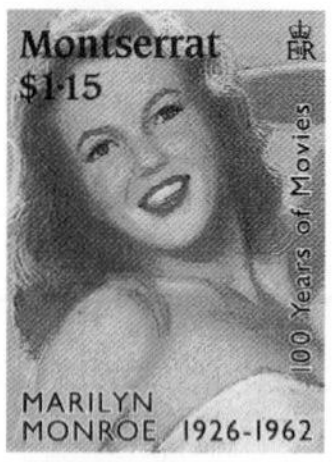

174 Marilyn Monroe

1995. Centenary of Cinema. Portraits of Marilyn Monroe (film star). Multicoloured.

956	$1.15 Type **174**	60	85
957	$1.15 Puckering lips	60	85
958	$1.15 Laughing in brown evening dress and earrings	60	85
959	$1.15 Wearing red earrings	60	85
960	$1.15 In brown dress without earrings	60	85
961	$1.15 With white boa	60	85
962	$1.15 In red dress	60	85
963	$1.15 Wearing white jumper	60	85
964	$1.15 Looking over left shoulder	60	85
MS965	102×132 mm. $6 With Elvis Presley (50×56 mm)	3·75	5·00

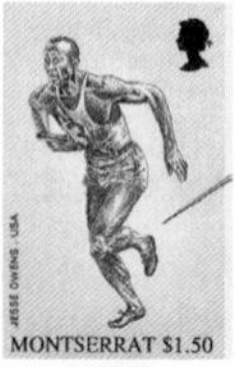

175 Jesse Owens (U.S.A.)

1995. Fifth International Amateur Athletic Federation Games, Göteborg. Sheet 181×103 mm, containing T 175 and similar vert designs.

MS966	$1.50 black and pink (Type **175**); $1.50 black and orange (Eric Lemming (Sweden)); $1.50 black and yellow (Rudolf Harbig (Germany)); $1.50 black and green (young Montserrat athletes)	4·50	6·00

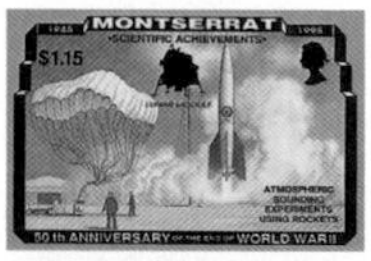

176 Atmospheric Sounding Experiments using V2 Rockets

1995. 50th Anniv of End of Second World War. Scientific Achievements. Multicoloured.

967	$1.15 Type **176**	1·00	1·25
968	$1.15 American space shuttle "Challenger"	1·00	1·25
969	$1.15 Nuclear experiment, Chicago, 1942	1·00	1·25
970	$1.15 Calder Hall Atomic Power Station, 1956	1·00	1·25
971	$1.50 Radar-equipped Ju 88G 7a nightfighter	1·90	2·00
972	$1.50 Boeing E6 A.W.A.C.S. aircraft	1·90	2·00
973	$1.50 Gloster G.41 Meteor Mk III jet fighter	1·90	2·00
974	$1.50 Concorde (airliner)	1·90	2·00

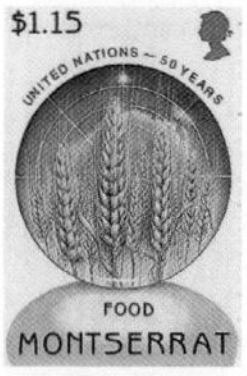

177 Ears of Wheat ("Food")

1995. 50th Anniv of United Nations. Multicoloured.

975	$1.15 Type **177**	90	75
976	$1.50 Open book ("Education")	1·25	1·00
977	$2.30 P.T. class ("Health")	1·75	2·25
978	$3 Dove ("Peace")	2·25	3·50
MS979	105×75 mm. $6 Scales ("Justice")	3·75	6·00

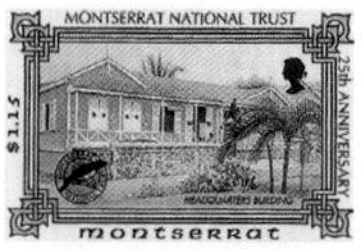

178 Headquarters Building

1995. 25th Anniv of Montserrat National Trust. Multicoloured.

980	$1.15 Type **178**	80	75
981	$1.50 17th-century cannon, Bransby Point	1·25	1·00
982	$2.30 Impression of Galways Sugar Mill (vert)	2·25	2·50
983	$3 Great Alps Falls (vert)	5·00	6·00

1995. 25th Anniv of Air Recording Studios. No. 713 surch air 25TH ANNIVERSARY 1970 - 1995.

984	$2.30+$5 Air Recording Studios	3·50	5·50

The $5 premium on No. 984 was for relief following a volcanic eruption.

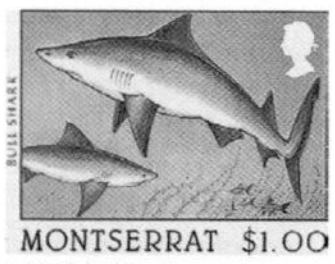

180 Bull Shark

1996. Scavengers of the Sea. Multicoloured.

985	$1 Type **180**	80	70
986	$1.15 Sea mouse	90	80
987	$1.50 Bristleworm	1·25	1·50
988	$3.45 Prawn "Xiphocaris"	2·50	3·50
MS989	69×95 mm. $4.50 Man of war fish	3·00	4·00

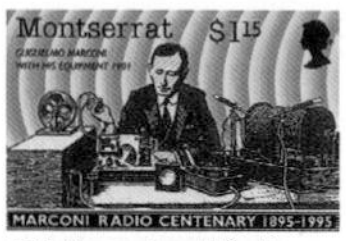

181 Marconi and Radio Equipment, 1901

1996. Centenary of Radio. Multicoloured.

990	$1.15 Type **181**	90	80
991	$1.50 Marconi's steam yacht "Elettra"	1·25	1·00
992	$2.30 Receiving first Trans-atlantic radio message, Newfoundland, 1901	1·75	2·25
993	$3 Imperial Airways airplane at Croydon Airport, 1920	2·25	3·50
MS994	74×105 mm. $4.50 Radio telescope, Jodrell Bank	3·00	4·00

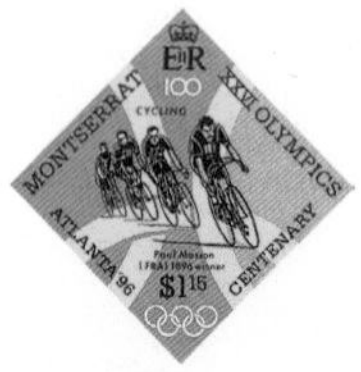

182 Paul Masson (France) (Cycling)

1996. Olympic Games, Atlanta. Gold Medal Winners of 1896. Multicoloured.

995	$1.15 Type **182**	1·25	80
996	$1.50 Robert Garrett (U.S.A.) (Discus)	1·25	1·00
997	$2.30 Spyridon Louis (Greece) (Marathon)	1·50	1·75
998	$3 John Boland (Great Britain) (Tennis)	2·00	3·25

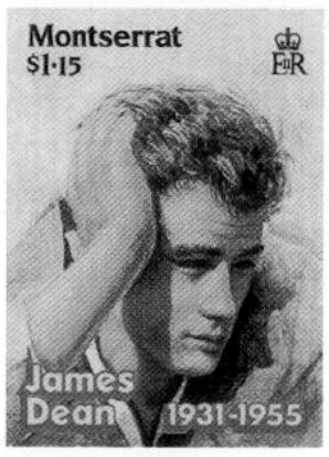

183 James Dean

1996. James Dean (film star) Commemoration. Multicoloured.

999	$1.15 Type **183**	60	80
1000	$1.15 Wearing stetson facing right	60	80
1001	$1.15 Wearing blue sweater	60	80
1002	$1.15 Wearing black sweater	60	80
1003	$1.15 Full face portrait wearing stetson	60	80
1004	$1.15 Wearing fawn jacket	60	80
1005	$1.15 Wearing red wind-cheater	60	80
1006	$1.15 Smoking a cigarette	60	80
1007	$1.15 In open-necked shirt and green jumper	60	80
MS1008	169×133 mm. $6 As No. 1000 (51×57 mm)	4·00	6·00

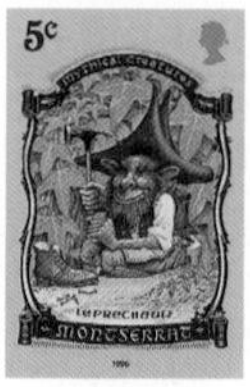

184 Leprechaun

1996. Mythical Creatures. Multicoloured.

1009	5c. Type **184**	10	30
1010	10c. Pegasus	10	30
1011	15c. Griffin	15	30
1012	20c. Unicorn	20	30
1013	25c. Gnomes	25	30
1014	40c. Mermaid	40	40
1015	55c. Cockatrice	50	30
1016	70c. Fairy	65	40
1017	90c. Goblin	80	50
1018	$1 Faun	90	55
1019	$1.15 Dragon	1·00	65
1020	$1.50 Giant	1·25	85
1021	$3 Elves	2·00	2·50
1022	$5 Centaur	3·25	3·75
1023	$7.50 Phoenix	4·75	6·00
1024	$10 Erin	5·50	6·50

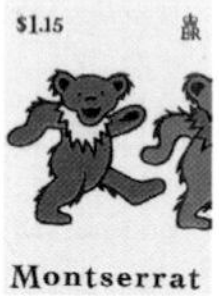

185 Blue and Green Teddybears

1996. Jerry Garcia of the Grateful Dead (rock group) Commemoration. Multicoloured.

1025	$1.15 Type **185**	1·00	1·00
1026	$1.15 Green and yellow teddybears	1·00	1·00
1027	$1.15 Brown and pink teddybears	1·00	1·00
1028	$6 Jerry Garcia (37×50 mm)	5·50	5·50

Nos. 1025/7 were printed together, *se-tenant*, forming a composite design.

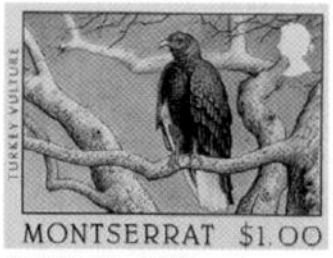

186 Turkey Vulture

1997. Scavengers of the Sky. Multicoloured.

1029	$1 Type **186**	85	70
1030	$1.15 American crow	1·00	70
1031	$1.50 Great skua	1·50	1·50
1032	$3.45 Black-legged kittiwake ("Kittiwake")	2·50	4·00
MS1033	74×95 mm. $4.50 King vulture	3·50	4·50

1997. "HONG KONG '97" International Stamp Exhibition. Nos. 1025/7 optd HONG KONG '97.

1034	$1.15 Type **185**	70	1·00
1035	$1.15 Green and yellow teddybears	70	1·00
1036	$1.15 Brown and pink teddybears	70	1·00

1997. "PACIFIC '97" International Stamp Exhibition, San Francisco. Nos. 999/1007 optd PACIFIC 97 World Philatelic Exhibition San Francisco, California 29 May - 8 June.

1037	$1.15 Type **183**	60	80
1038	$1.15 Wearing stetson facing right	60	80
1039	$1.15 Wearing blue sweater	60	80
1040	$1.15 Wearing black sweater	60	80
1041	$1.15 Full-face portrait wearing stetson	60	80
1042	$1.15 Wearing fawn jacket	60	80
1043	$1.15 Wearing red wind-cheater	60	80
1044	$1.15 Smoking a cigarette	60	80
1045	$1.15 In open-necked shirt and green jumper	60	80

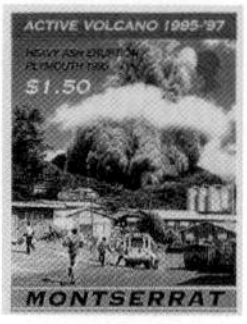

189 Heavy Ash Eruption over Plymouth, 1995

1997. Eruption of Soufriere Volcano. Multicoloured

1046	$1.50 Type **189**	1·40	1·60
1047	$1.50 Burning rock flow entering sea	1·40	1·60
1048	$1.50 Double venting at Castle Peak	1·40	1·60
1049	$1.50 Mangrove cuckoo	1·40	1·60
1050	$1.50 Lava flow at night, 1996	1·40	1·60
1051	$1.50 Antillean crested hummingbird	1·40	1·60
1052	$1.50 Ash cloud over Plymouth	1·40	1·60
1053	$1.50 Lava spine, 1996	1·40	1·60
1054	$1.50 Burning rock flows forming new land	1·40	1·60

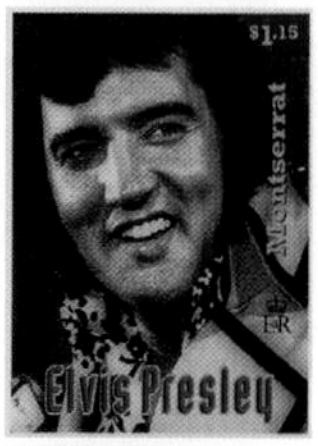

190 Elvis Presley

1997. Rock Legends. Multicoloured.

1055	$1.15 Type **190**	1·75	1·40
1056	$1.15 Jimi Hendrix	1·75	1·40
1057	$1.15 Jerry Garcia	1·75	1·40
1058	$1.15 Janis Joplin	1·75	1·40

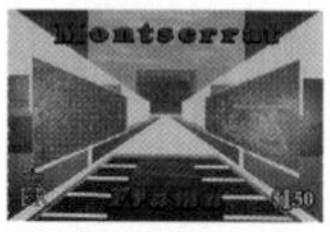

191 Untitled Painting by Frama

1997. Frama Exhibition at Guggenheim Museum, New York.

1059	**191** $1.50 multicoloured	1·00	1·25

1997. No. 1028 surch $1.50.

1060	$1.50 on $6 Jerry Garcia (37×50 mm)	2·25	2·50

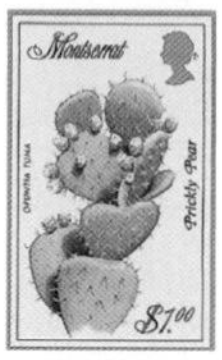

193 Prickly Pear

1998. Medicinal Plants. Multicoloured.

1061	$1 Type **193**	65	50
1062	$1.15 Pomme coolie	70	55
1063	$1.50 Aloe	85	90
1064	$3.45 Bird pepper	1·75	2·50

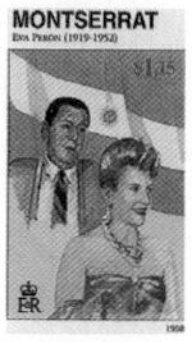

194 Eva and Juan Peron (Argentine politicians)

1998. Famous People of the 20th Century. Multicoloured

1065	$1.15 Type **194**	1·50	1·50
1066	$1.15 Pablo Picasso (painter)	1·50	1·50
1067	$1.15 Wernher von Braun (space scientist)	1·50	1·50
1068	$1.15 David Ben Gurion (Israeli statesman)	1·50	1·50
1069	$1.15 Jean Henri Dunant (founder of Red Cross)	1·50	1·50
1070	$1.15 Dwight Eisenhower (President of U.S.A.)	1·50	1·50
1071	$1.15 Mahatma Gandhi (leader of Indian Independence movement)	1·50	1·50
1072	$1.15 King Leopold III and Queen Astrid of Belgium	1·50	1·50
1073	$1.15 Grand Duchess Charlotte and Prince Felix of Luxembourg	1·50	1·50
1074	$1.50 Charles Augustus Lindbergh (pioneer aviator)	1·50	1·50
1075	$1.50 Mao Tse-tung (Chinese communist leader)	1·50	1·50
1076	$1.50 Earl Mountbatten (last Viceroy of India)	1·50	1·50
1077	$1.50 Konrad Adenauer (German statesman)	1·50	1·50
1078	$1.50 Anne Frank (Holocaust victim)	1·50	1·50
1079	$1.50 Queen Wilhelmina of the Netherlands	1·50	1·50
1080	$1.50 King George VI of Great Britain	1·50	1·50
1081	$1.50 King Christian X of Denmark	1·50	1·50
1082	$1.50 King Haakon VII and Crown Prince Olav of Norway	1·50	1·50
1083	$1.50 King Alfonso XIII of Spain	1·50	1·50
1084	$1.50 King Gustavus V of Sweden	1·50	1·50
MS1085	115×63 mm. $3 John F. Kennedy (Resident of U.S.A.) (50×32 mm)	2·00	2·75

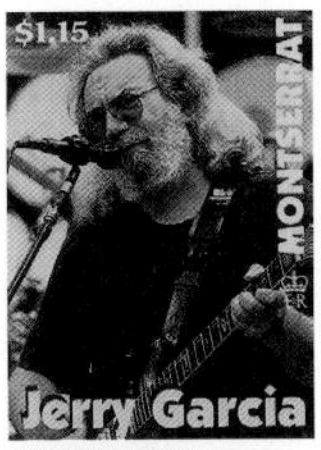

195 Jerry Garcia

1998. Rock Music Legends. Multicoloured. (a) Jerry Garcia.

1086	$1.15 In long-sleeved blue shirt	1·10	1·25
1087	$1.15 With drum kit in background	1·10	1·25
1088	$1.15 Type **195**	1·10	1·25
1089	$1.15 Wearing long-sleeved black t-shirt	1·10	1·25
1090	$1.15 Close-up with left hand in foreground	1·10	1·25
1091	$1.15 With purple and black background	1·10	1·25
1092	$1.15 Holding microphone	1·10	1·25
1093	$1.15 In short-sleeved blue t-shirt	1·10	1·25
1094	$1.15 In sunglasses with cymbal in background	1·10	1·25

(b) Bob Marley. Predominant colour for each design given.

1095	$1.15 Pointing (green)	1·10	1·25
1096	$1.15 Wearing neck chain (green)	1·10	1·25
1097	$1.15 Singing into microphone (green)	1·10	1·25
1098	$1.15 Singing with eyes closed (yellow)	1·10	1·25
1099	$1.15 Facing audience (yellow)	1·10	1·25
1100	$1.15 In striped t-shirt with fingers on chin (red)	1·10	1·25
1101	$1.15 In Rastafarian hat (red)	1·10	1·25
1102	$1.15 In striped t-shirt with hand closed (red)	1·10	1·25
MS1103	152×101 mm. $5 Jerry Garcia (50×75 mm)	3·00	3·75

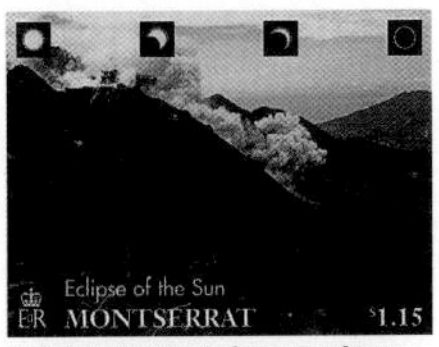

196 Ash Eruption from Soufriere Hills Volcano

1998. Total Eclipse of the Sun. Multicoloured.

1104	$1.15 Type **196**	2·00	1·50
1105	$1.15 Volcano emitting black cloud	2·00	1·50
1106	$1.15 Village below volcano	2·00	1·50
1107	$1.15 Lava flow and wrecked house	2·00	1·50
MS1108	152×102 mm. $6 Solar eclipse (vert)	8·00	8·50

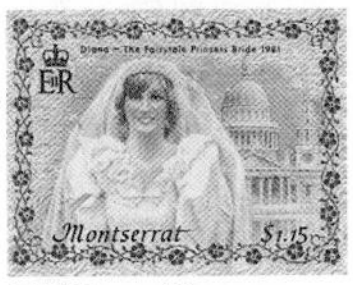

197 Princess Diana on Wedding Day, 1981

1998. Diana, Princess of Wales Commemoration. Multicoloured.

1109	$1.15 Type **197**	1·50	70
1110	$1.50 Accepting bouquet from children	1·75	1·10
1111	$3 At Royal Ascot	3·00	4·00
MS1112	133×100 mm. $6 Diana and "Princess of Wales" rose (50×37 mm)	5·50	5·50

1998. 19th World Scout Jamboree, Chile. Nos. 669/72 optd 19th WORLD JAMBOREE MONDIAL CHILE 1999 and emblem.

1113	20c. Type **117**	30	40
1114	20c. Girl Guide saluting	30	40
1115	75c. Lady Baden-Powell	70	1·00
1116	75c. Guide assisting in old people's home	70	1·00

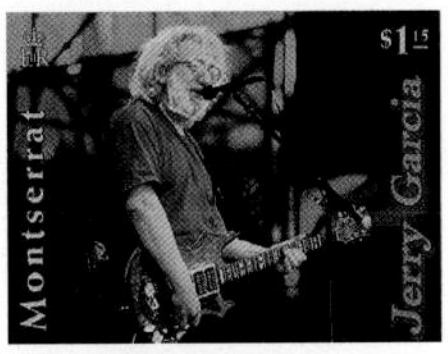

199 Jerry Garcia

1999. Jerry Garcia (rock musician) Commemoration. Multicoloured

1117	$1.15 Type **199**	90	1·00
1118	$1.15 In front of drum kit (violet background)	90	1·00
1119	$1.15 Singing into microphone	90	1·00
1120	$1.15 Playing guitar, facing right (vert)	90	1·00
1121	$1.15 Singing with eyes closed (vert)	90	1·00
1122	$1.15 Singing in white spotlight (vert)	90	1·00
1123	$1.15 In front of drum kit (green background)	90	1·00
1124	$1.15 In long-sleeved black shirt	90	1·00
1125	$1.15 In red shirt	90	1·00
1126	$1.15 In short-sleeved black t-shirt (without frame) (vert)	90	1·00
1127	$1.15 In blue t-shirt (oval frame) (vert)	90	1·00
1128	$1.15 In short-sleeved black t-shirt (oval frame) (vert)	90	1·00
MS1129	Two sheets. (a) 115×153 mm. $6 Jerry Garcia in concert (50×75 mm). (b) 153×115 mm. $6 Singing into microphone (75×50 mm) Set of 2 sheets	8·00	10·00

1999. "iBRA '99" International Stamp Exhibition, Nuremberg. Nos. 975/6 optd iBRA INTERNATIONALE BRIEFMARKEN WELTAUSSTELLUNG NURNBERG 27.4.-4.5.99.

1130	$1.15 Type **177**	2·25	1·75
1131	$1.50 Open book ("Education")	2·25	2·50

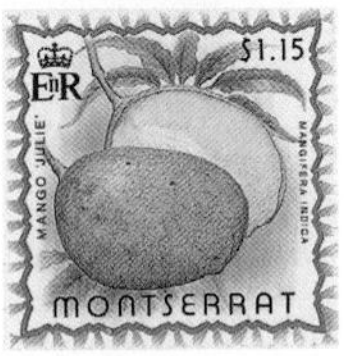

201 Mango

1999. Tropical Caribbean Fruits. Multicoloured.

1132	$1.15 Type **201**	85	70
1133	$1.50 Breadfruit	1·00	85
1134	$2.30 Papaya	1·60	1·60
1135	$3 Lime	2·00	2·50
1136	$6 Akee	3·75	6·00
MS1137	134×95 mm. Nos. 1132/6	10·00	12·00

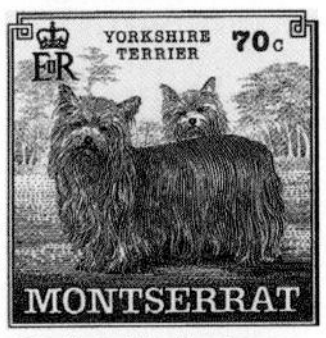

202 Yorkshire Terrier

1999. Dogs. Each black.

1138	70c. Type **202**	1·75	80
1139	$1 Welsh corgi	2·00	90
1140	$1.15 King Charles spaniel	2·25	90
1141	$1.50 Poodle	2·50	1·50
1142	$3 Beagle	4·50	7·00
MS1143	133×95 mm. Nos. 1138/42	11·50	12·00

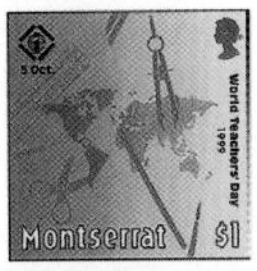

203 Pupil's Equipment and World Map

1999. World Teachers' Day. Multicoloured.

1144	$1 Type **203**	2·00	90
1145	$1.15 Teacher and class	2·00	90
1146	$1.50 Emblems of vocational training	2·25	1·50
1147	$5 Scientific equipment	6·50	8·50

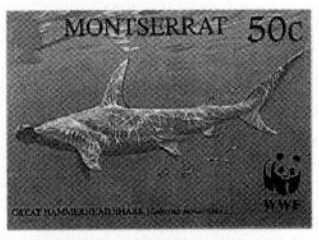

204 Great Hammerhead Shark

1999. Endangered Species. Great Hammerhead Shark. Multicoloured.

1148	50c. Type **204**	85	90
1149	50c. Two hammerhead sharks among fish	85	90
1150	50c. Two hammerhead sharks on sea-bed	85	90
1151	50c. Three hammerhead sharks	85	90

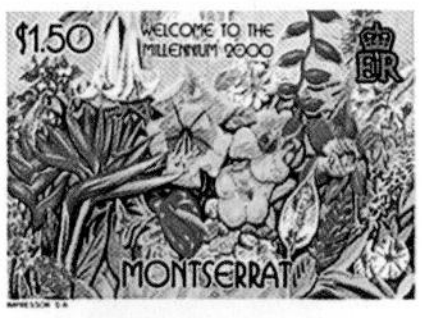

205 Flowers

2000. New Millennium.

1152	**205** $1.50 multicoloured	2·75	2·75

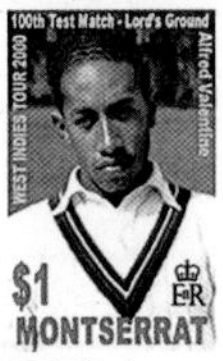

206 Alfred Valentine

2000. West Indies Cricket Tour and 100th Test Match at Lord's. Multicoloured.

1153	$1 Type **206**	2·50	1·00
1154	$5 George Headley batting	5·50	6·50
MS1155	119×101 mm. $6 Lord's Cricket Ground (horiz)	8·00	9·00

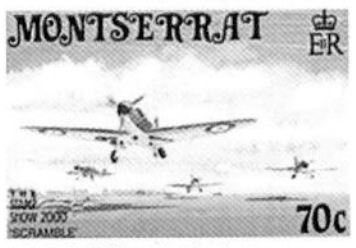

207 Spitfire Squadron taking-off

2000. "The Stamp Show 2000" International Stamp Exhibition, London. 60th Anniv of Battle of Britain. Multicoloured.

1156	70c. Type **207**	1·00	50
1157	$1.15 Overhauling Hurricane Mk I	1·25	65
1158	$1.50 Hurricane MK I attacking	1·50	1·25
1159	$5 Flt. Lt. Frank Howell's Spitfire Mk IA	3·50	5·50
MS1160	110×87 mm. $6 Hawker Hurricane	4·50	5·50

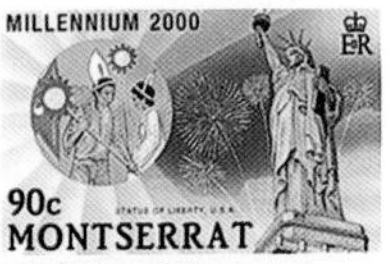

208 Statue of Liberty and Carnival Scene

2000. New Millennium. Landmarks. Each including carnival scene. Multicoloured.

1161	90c. Type **208**	75	50
1162	$1.15 Great Wall of China	95	60
1163	$1.50 Eiffel Tower	1·25	1·25
1164	$3.50 Millennium Dome	2·50	4·00

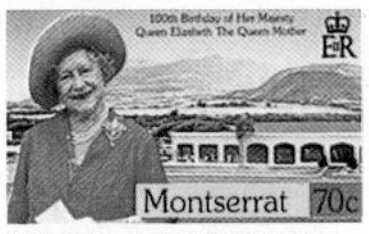

209 Queen Elizabeth the Queen Mother and W.H. Bramble Airport

2000. Queen Elizabeth the Queen Mother's 100th Birthday. Each showing different portrait. Multicoloured

1165	70c. Type **209**	85	40
1166	$1.15 Government House	1·25	65
1167	$3 Court House	2·50	3·00
1168	$6 War Memorial Clock Tower	4·50	6·00
MS1169	120×75 mm. Nos. 1165/8	8·00	9·50

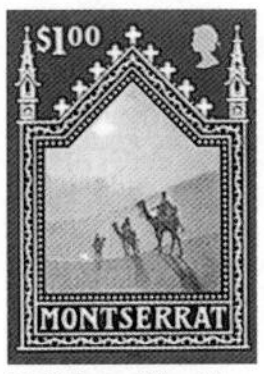

210 Three Wise Men following Star

2000. Christmas. Multicoloured.

1170	$1 Type **210**	1·00	55
1171	$1.15 Cavalla Hill Methodist Church	1·10	65
1172	$1.50 Shepherds with flocks	1·25	85
1173	$3 Mary and Joseph arriving at Bethlehem	2·25	3·75
MS1174	105×75 mm. $6 As $3	4·50	6·00

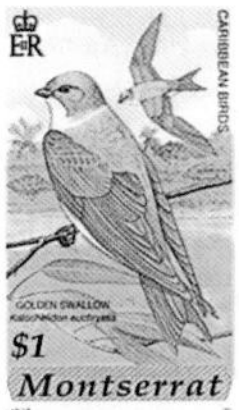

211 Golden Swallow

2001. Caribbean Birds. Multicoloured.

1175	$1 Type **211**	1·25	65
1176	$1.15 Crested quail dove (horiz)	1·40	75
1177	$1.50 Red-legged thrush (horiz)	1·50	1·10
1178	$5 Fernandina's flicker	4·25	6·00
MS1179	95×68 mm. $8 St. Vincent amazon (horiz)	9·00	9·50

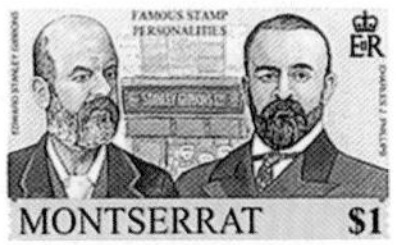

212 Edward Stanley Gibbons, Charles J. Phillips and 391 Strand Shop

2001. Famous Stamp Personalities. Multicoloured.

1180	$1 Type **212**	1·40	75
1181	$1.15 John Lister and Montserrat stamps	1·50	75
1182	$1.50 Theodore Champion and French postilion	1·60	1·25
1183	$3 Thomas De La Rue and De La Rue's stand at Great Exhibition, 1851	3·00	4·50
MS1184	95×68 mm. $8 Sir Rowland Hill and Bruce Castle	6·50	8·50

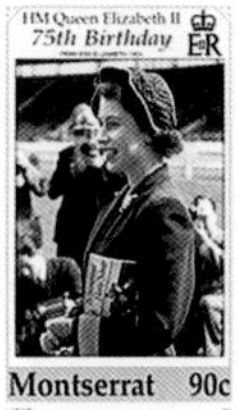

213 Princess Elizabeth at International Horse Show, 1950

2001. Queen Elizabeth II's 75th Birthday. Multicoloured.

1185	90c. Type **213**	1·25	60
1186	$1.15 Queen Elizabeth II, 1986	1·40	75
1187	$1.50 Queen Elizabeth II, 1967	1·60	1·40
1188	$5 Queen Elizabeth, 1976	4·75	5·50
MS1189	90×68 mm. $6 Queen Elizabeth, 2000	7·00	8·00

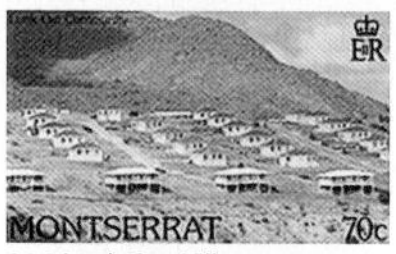

214 Look Out Village

2001. Reconstruction. Multicoloured.

1190	70c. Type **214**	80	60
1191	$1 St. John's Hospital	1·00	65
1192	$1.15 Tropical Mansions Suites Hotel	1·10	70
1193	$1.50 Montserrat Secondary School	1·40	1·25
1194	$3 Golden Years Care Home	3·00	4·50

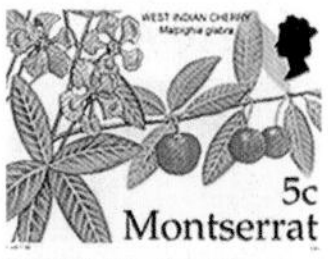

215 West Indian Cherry

2001. Caribbean Fruits. Multicoloured.

1195	5c. Type **215**	40	70
1196	10c. Mammee apple	40	70
1197	15c. Lime	45	70
1198	20c. Grapefruit	45	70
1199	25c. Orange	45	70
1200	40c. Passion fruit	60	50
1201	55c. Banana	70	40
1202	70c. Pawpaw	90	50
1203	90c. Pomegranate	1·00	70
1204	$1 Guava	1·10	75
1205	$1.15 Mango	1·25	75
1206	$1.50 Sugar apple	1·50	1·10
1207	$3 Cashew	2·75	3·00
1208	$5 Soursop	4·50	5·50
1209	$7.50 Watermelon	7·00	9·00
1210	$10 Pineapple	8·00	9·50

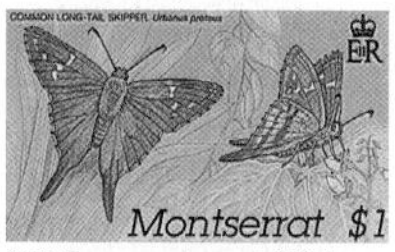

216 Common Long-tail Skipper (butterfly)

2001. Caribbean Butterflies. Multicoloured.

1211	$1 Type **216**	1·10	60
1212	$1.15 Straight-line sulphur	1·25	70
1213	$1.50 Giant hairstreak	1·50	1·25
1214	$3 Monarch	2·50	4·00
MS1215	115×115 mm. $10 Painted Lady	8·50	11·00

The overall design of No. **MS**1215 is butterfly-shaped.

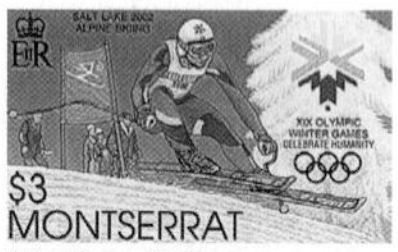

217 Alpine Skiing

2002. Winter Olympic Games, Salt Lake City. Multicoloured

1216	$3 Type **217**	2·25	2·75
1217	$5 Four man bobsleigh	3·25	4·25

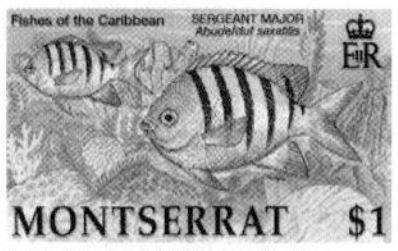

218 Sergeant Major (fish)

2002. Fishes of the Caribbean. Multicoloured.

1218	$1 Type **218**	1·25	60
1219	$1.15 Mutton snapper	1·40	70
1220	$1.50 Lantern bass	1·75	1·25
1221	$5 Shy Hamlet	6·00	7·50
MS1222	102×70 mm. $8 Queen angelfish	9·00	10·00

2002. Queen Elizabeth the Queen Mother Commemoration. Nos. 1165/8 optd Life and Death of Her Majesty Queen Elizabeth The Queen Mother 1900 2002.

1223	70c. Type **209**	70	55
1224	$1.15 Government House	1·00	70
1225	$3 Court House	2·75	3·00
1226	$6 War Memorial Clock Tower	4·75	6·00

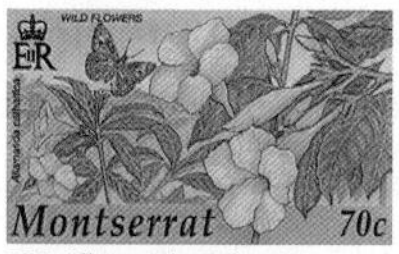

220 *Allamanda cathartica*

2002. Wild Flowers. Multicoloured.

1227	70c. Type **220**	85	55
1228	$1.15 *Lantana camara*	1·25	70
1229	$1.50 *Leonotis nepetifolia*	1·50	1·25
1230	$5 *Plumeria rubra*	5·00	6·50
MS1231	105×75 mm. $8 *Alpinia purpurata*	8·00	9·50

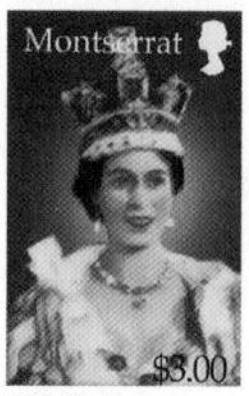

221 Queen Elizabeth II wearing Imperial State

2003. 50th Anniv of Coronation. Two sheets containing vert designs as T **221**. Multicoloured.

MS1232	153×85 mm. $3 Type **221**; $3 St. Edward's Crown; $3 Queen wearing diadem and blue sash	7·00	8·00
MS1233	105×75 mm. $6 Queen wearing Imperial State Crown and Coronation robes	4·50	5·00

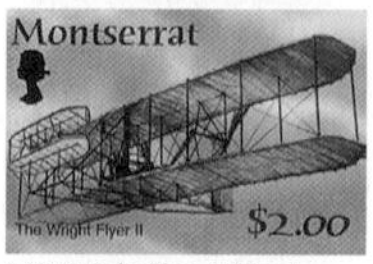

222 *Wright Flyer II* (blue)

2003. Centenary of Powered Flight. Multicoloured.

MS1234	116×125 mm. $2 Type **222**; $2 Wright *Flyer II* (brown); $2 Orville and Wilbur Wright; $2 Wright *Flyer I*	5·50	6·00
MS1235	106×76 mm. $6 Wright *Flyer II*	5·50	6·00

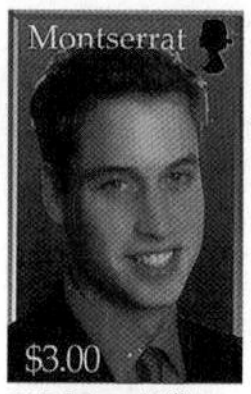

223 Prince William Crown and Coronation Robes

2003. 21st Birthday of Prince William of Wales. Different portraits. Multicoloured.

MS1236	155×85 mm. $3 Type **223**; $3 Prince William (frame incomplete at bottom left); $3 Prince William (frame complete at bottom left)	7·00	8·00
MS1237	106×76 mm. $6 Prince William	4·75	5·50

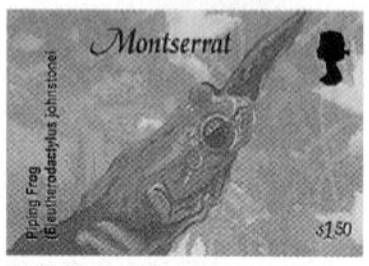

224 Piping Frog

2003. Animals of the Caribbean. Multicoloured.

MS1238	145×90 mm. $1.50 Type **224**; $1.50 Land hermit crab; $1.50 Spix's pinche; $1.50 Dwarf Ggecko; $1.50 Green sea turtle; $1.50 Small Indian mongoose	7·00	8·00
MS1239	92×66 mm. $6 Sally lightfoot crab	6·00	6·00

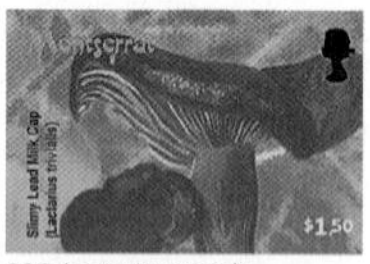

225 *Lactarius trivialis*

2003. Mushrooms of the World. Multicoloured.

MS1240	145×90 mm. $1.50 Type **225**; $1.50 *Gomphidius roseus*; $1.50 *Lycoperdon pyriforme*; $1.50 *Hygrophorus coccineus*; $1.50 *Russula xerampelina*; $1.50 *Gomphus floccosus*	8·00	9·00
MS1241	92×66 mm. $6 *Amanita muscaria*	5·50	6·00

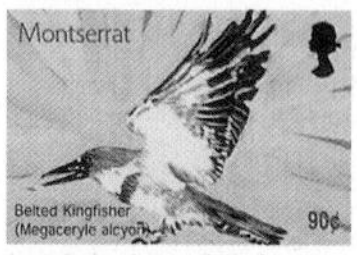

226 Belted Kingfisher

2003. Birds of the Caribbean. Multicoloured.

1242	90c. Type **226**	1·40	75
1243	$1.15 Yellow warbler	1·60	95
1244	$1.50 Hooded warbler	1·90	1·50
1245	$5 Cedar waxwing	7·00	8·50
MS1246	145×90 mm. $1.50 Roseate spoonbill; $1.50 Laughing gull; $1.50 White-tailed tropic bird; $1.50 Bare-eyed thrush; $1.50 Glittering-throated emerald; $1.50 Carib grackle ("Lesser Antillean Grackle")	8·00	9·00
MS1247	92×68 mm. $6 Bananaquit	6·50	6·50

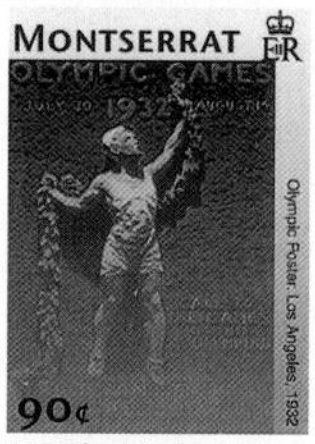

227 Olympic Poster, Los Angeles, 1932

2004. Olympic Games, Athens. Multicoloured.

1248	90c. Type **227**	1·25	70
1249	$1.15 Olympic pin, Munich, 1972	1·50	80
1250	$1.50 Olympic poster, Montreal, 1976	1·75	1·50
1251	$5 Greek art depicting Pankration (horiz)	4·00	6·00

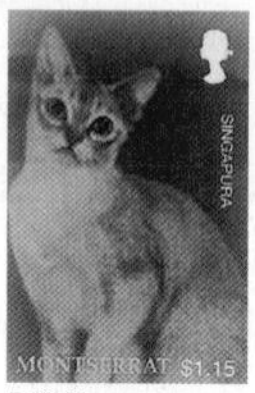

228 Singapura

2004. Cats. Multicoloured.

1252	$1.15 Type **228**	1·50	90
1253	$1.50 Burmese	1·75	1·25
1254	$2 Abyssinian	2·25	2·00
1255	$5 Norwegian	5·50	7·00
MS1256	92×68 mm. $6 Russian blue	6·50	7·50

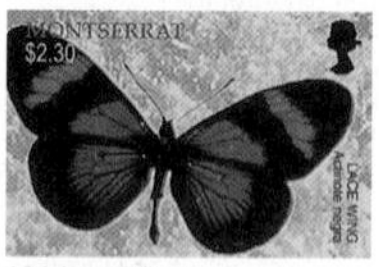

229 Lace Wing

2004. Butterflies. Multicoloured.

MS1257	125×88 mm. $2.30 Type **229**; $2.30 Swallowtail; $2.30 Shoemaker; $2.30 White peacock	7·00	7·50
MS1258	70×96 mm. $6 Flashing astraptes	5·00	5·50

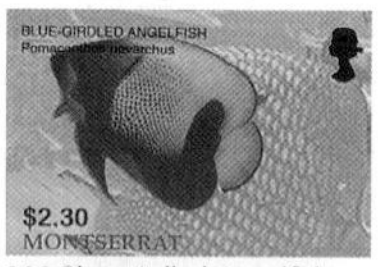

230 Blue-girdled Angelfish

2004. Fish. Multicoloured.

MS1259	122×93 mm. $2.30 Type **230**; $2.30 Regal angelfish; $2.30 Emperor angelfish; $2.30 Blotch-eye soldierfish	7·00	7·50
MS1260	70×96 mm. $6 Banded butterflyfish	5·00	5·50

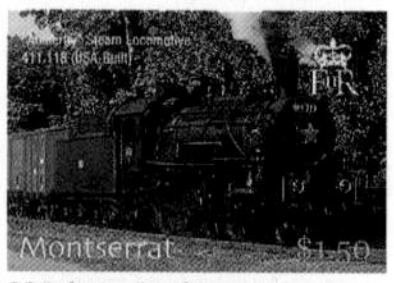

231 Austerity Steam Locomotive

2004. Bicentenary of Steam Locomotives. Multicoloured.

MS1261	159×120 mm. $1.50 Type **231**; $1.50 Deli Vasut No. 109.109; $1.50 Class 424 No. 424.247/287; $1.50 L1646; $1.50 No. 324.1564; $1.50 Class 204	7·00	7·50
MS1262	119×159 mm. $2 375.562 Old Class TV; $2 Class Va 7111; $2 Class 424 No. 424.009; $2 Class III No. 269	6·00	6·50
MS1263	92×106 mm. $6 Class QR1 No. 3038	5·00	5·50

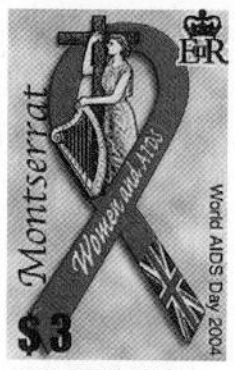

232 AIDS Ribbon

2004. World AIDS Day. Sheet 123×95 mm.

MS1264	$3 **232**×4 multicoloured	8·00	10·00

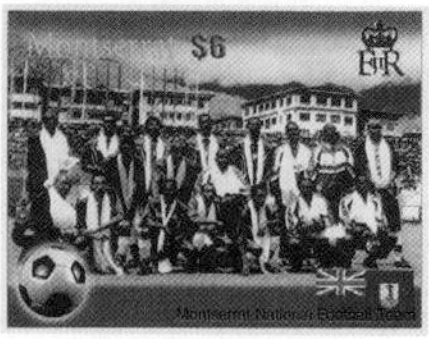

233 National Football Team

2004. Centenary of FIFA (Federation Internationale de Football Association).

1265	**233** $6 multicoloured	5·00	6·50

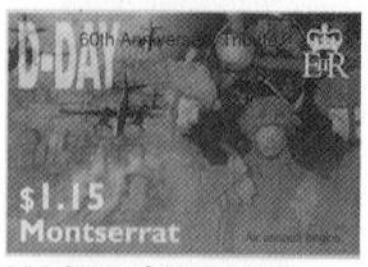

234 Start of Air Assault

2004. 60th Anniv of D-Day Landings. Multicoloured.

1266	$1.15 Type **234**	1·75	1·00
1267	$1.50 Soldiers landing on Normandy beaches	2·25	1·50
1268	$2 Field Marshall Montgomery	2·75	2·75
1269	$5 HMS *Belfast*	7·00	8·50

2005. Royal Visit. Nos. 1190/4 optd THE VISIT OF HRH PRINCESS ROYAL FEBRUARY 2005.

1270	70c. Look Out Village	1·25	85
1271	$1 St John's Hospital	1·75	1·25
1272	$1.15 Tropical Mansions Suites Hotel	1·75	1·25
1273	$1.50 Montserrat Secondary School	2·25	1·75
1274	$3 Golden Years Care Home	4·00	5·50

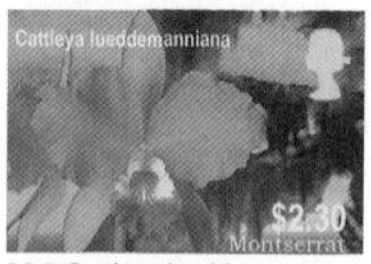

236 *Cattleya lueddemanniana*

2005. Orchids. Multicoloured.

MS1275	140×105 mm. $2.30×4, Type **236**; *Cattleya luteola*; *Cattleya trianaei*; *Cattleya mossiae*	7·50	8·00
MS1276	100×70 mm. $6 *Cattleya mendelii*	5·50	6·00

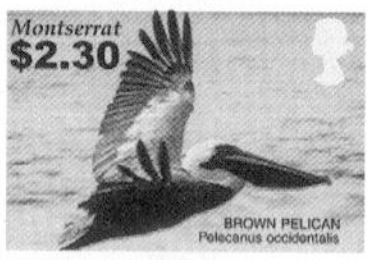

237 Brown Pelican

2005. Seabirds. Multicoloured.

MS1277	140×105 mm. $2.30×4, Type **237**; Red-billed tropic bird; Galapagos Island cormorant; Waved albatross	7·50	8·00
MS1278	100×70 mm. $6 Common tern	6·50	7·00

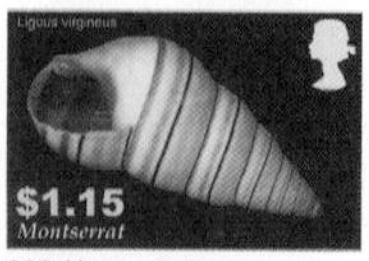

238 *Liguus virgineus*

2005. Molluscs. Multicoloured.

1279	$1.15 Type **238**	1·75	1·00
1280	$1.50 *Liguus fasciatus testudineus*	2·25	1·50
1281	$2 *Liguus fasciatus*	2·75	2·75
1282	$5 *Cerion striatella*	7·00	8·50
MS1283	70×100 mm. $6 *Liguus fasciatus* (vert)	8·00	9·00

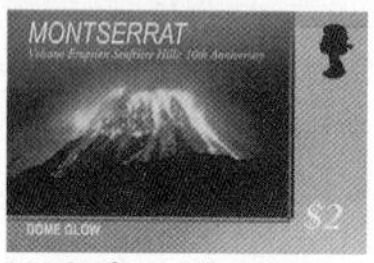

239 Soufriere Hills Volcano

2005. Tenth Anniv of the Eruption of Soufrière Hills Volcano. Sheet, 146×116 mm, containing T 239 and similar horiz designs. Multicoloured.

MS1284	$2×9, Type **239**; Explosion; Tar River Delta; Belham River; Montserrat Volcano Observatory building; Pyroclastic flow; Blackburne airport, destroyed in 1997; Maintenance and monitoring helicopter; Instruments used for monitoring volcano	19·00	22·00

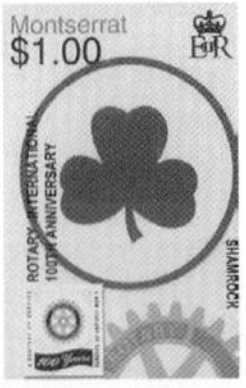

240 Shamrock

2005. Centenary of Rotary International. Multicoloured designs.

1285	$1 Type **240**	1·50	90
1286	$1.15 *Heliconia* (national flower)	1·75	1·00
1287	$1.50 The lady and the harp	2·25	2·00
1288	$5 Map of Montserrat	6·50	8·00
MS1289	100×70 mm. $6 Immunising children (horiz)	6·50	8·50

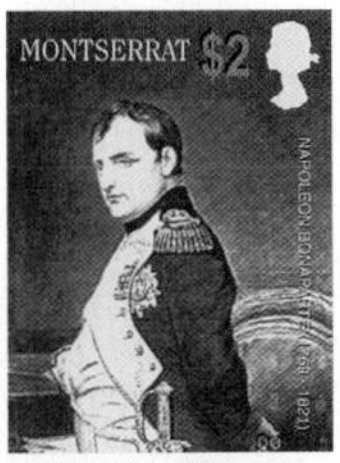

241 Napoleon Bonaparte

2005. Bicentenary of the Battle of Trafalgar. Multicoloured.

1290	$2 Type **241**	3·50	3·50
1291	$2 Admiral Lord Nelson (seated)	3·50	3·50
1292	$2 Battle of the Nile, 1798	3·50	3·50
1293	$2 Battle of Trafalgar, 1805	3·50	3·50
MS1294	109×70 mm. $6 Admiral Lord Nelson	11·00	12·00

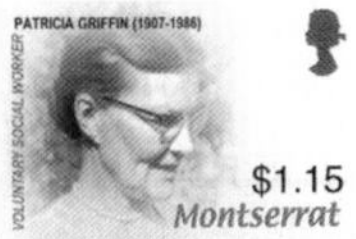

242 Patricia Griffin (voluntary social worker)

2005. Local Personalities. Multicoloured.

1295	$1.15 Type **242**	1·25	1·50
1296	$1.15 Michael Simmons Osborne (merchant/parliamentarian)	1·25	1·50
1297	$1.15 Lilian Cadogan (nurse)	1·25	1·50
1298	$1.15 Samuel Aymer (folk musician)	1·25	1·50
1299	$1.15 William Henry Bramble (first Chief Minister)	1·25	1·50
1300	$1.15 Robert William Griffith (trade union pioneer)	1·25	1·50
MS1301	100×115 mm. Nos. 1295/1300	6·75	8·00

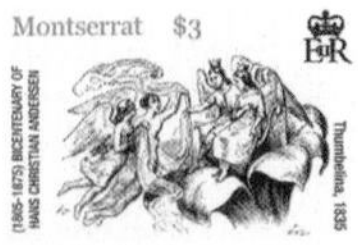

243 *Thumbelina*

2005. Birth Bicentenary of Hans Christian Andersen (writer). Multicoloured.

1302	$3 Type **243**	2·75	3·50
1303	$3 *The Flying Trunk*	2·75	3·50
1304	$3 *The Buckwheat*	2·75	3·50
MS1305	100×70 mm. $6 *The Little Mermaid* (49×38 mm)	6·00	7·00

2006. 30th Anniv of the Philatelic Bureau. Nos. 1175, 1212/13, 1227 and 1230 optd 30th ANNIVERSARY OF THE PHILATELIC BUREAU 1976–2006.

1306	70c. Type **220**	75	55
1307	$1 Type **211**	1·00	85
1308	$1.15 Straight-line sulphur	1·25	90
1309	$1.50 Giant hairstreak	1·50	1·50
1310	$5 *Plumeria rubra*	5·00	6·50

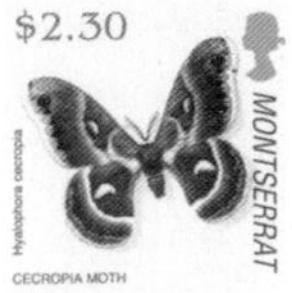

245 Cecropia Moth

2006. Moths and Butterflies of the World. Multicoloured.

1311	$2.30 Type **245**	3·75	4·00
1312	$2.30 Madagascan sunset moth	3·75	4·00
1313	$2.30 Peacock butterfly	3·75	4·00
1314	$2.30 Zodiac moth	3·75	4·00
MS1315	96×76 mm. $6 White-lined sphinx moth	7·00	8·00

No. 1313 is wrongly inscr "GREAT PEACOCK MOTH *Saturnia pyri*".

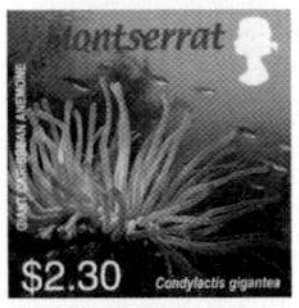

246 Giant Caribbean Anemone

2006. Caribbean "Sea Flowers". Multicoloured.

1316	$2.30 Type **246**	2·75	3·50
1317	$2.30 Beadlet anemone	2·75	3·50
1318	$2.30 Golden crinoid	2·75	3·50
1319	$2.30 Oval cup coral	2·75	3·50
MS1320	96×78 mm. $6 Tube-dwelling anemone	6·50	8·00

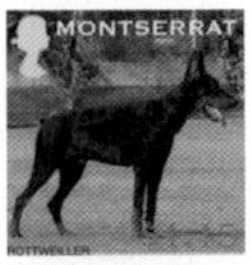

247 Doberman (inscr Rottweiller)

2006. Dogs. Multicoloured.

1321	$1.15 Type **247**	2·00	1·00
1322	$1.50 Boxer	2·25	1·50
1323	$2 Corgi	3·00	2·75
1324	$5 Great Dane	6·00	7·00
MS1325	96×78 mm. $6 St. Bernard	7·50	8·50

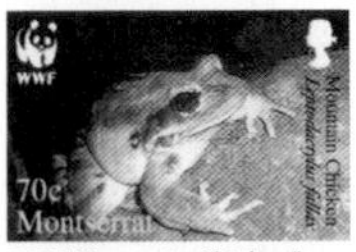

248 "Mountain Chicken"

2006. Endangered Species. "Mountain Chicken" (frog, *Leptodactylus fallax*). Multicoloured.

1326	70c. Type **248**	55	75
1327	$1 In close-up	80	1·00
1328	$1.15 Back view	95	1·25
1329	$1.50 Facing left	1·25	1·40
MS1330	102×152 mm. Nos. 1326/9, each ×2	6·50	8·00

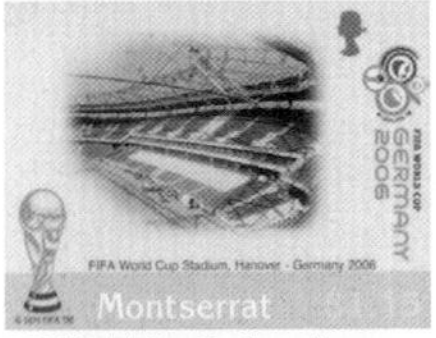

249 World Cup Stadium, Hanover, Germany, 2006

2006. World Cup Football Championship, Germany. Sheet 127×102 mm containing T **249** and similar horiz designs. Multicoloured.

MS1331	$1.15 Type **249**; $1.50 Sir Stanley Matthews; $2 Sir William Ralph "Dixie" Dean; $3 Bobby Moore	8·50	9·50

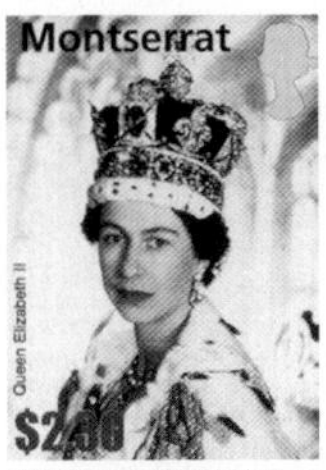

250 Queen Elizabeth II at Coronation, 1953

2006. 80th Birthday of Queen Elizabeth II. Multicoloured.

1332	$2.30 Type **250**	1·75	2·00
1333	$2.30 Queen Elizabeth wearing crown, c. 1977	1·75	2·00
1334	$2.30 Wearing tiara, c. 1980	1·75	2·00
1335	$2.30 Wearing tiara, c. 2002	1·75	2·00
MS1336	120×120 mm. $8 Wearing tiara and pearl drop earrings, c. 2002	6·00	7·50

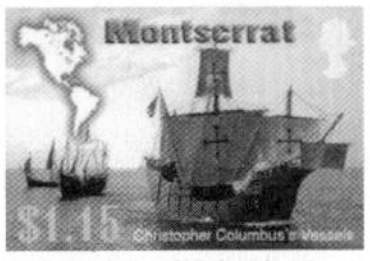

251 Replica of Columbus's Fleet

2006. 500th Death Anniv of Christopher Columbus. Multicoloured.

1337	$1.15 Type **251**	1·75	1·00
1338	$1.50 Columbus and map showing voyage to New World	2·50	1·50
1339	$2 Sailing ships, globe and Columbus	3·00	2·75
1340	$5 Christopher Columbus (vert)	6·00	7·50
MS1341	100×70 mm. $6 Columbus and his crew in New World (vert)	6·50	7·50

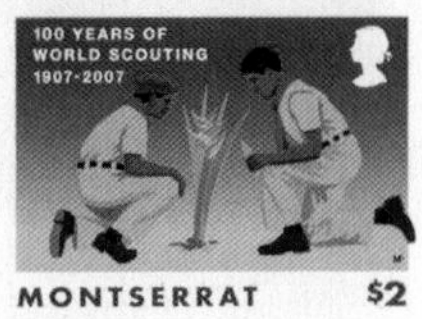

252 Boy Scouts and Bird of Paradise Flower

2007. Centenary of Scouting. Multicoloured.

1342	$2 Type **252**	2·25	2·25
1343	$2 Scouts working in damaged building	2·25	2·25
1344	$2 Scouts sailing dinghy	2·25	2·25
1345	$2 Scout bottle-feeding kid	2·25	2·25
1346	$2 Scout gathering firewood	2·25	2·25
1347	$2 Scouts putting up bird nestbox	2·25	2·25
MS1348	100×70 mm. $6 Lord Baden-Powell (founder) (vert)	6·00	7·00

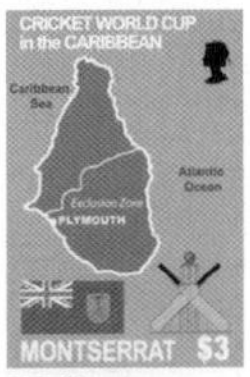

253 Montserrat Flag and Outline Map

2007. World Cup Cricket, West Indies. Multicoloured.

1349	$3 Type **253**	4·00	3·75
1350	$5 Cricket team (horiz)	7·00	7·50
MS1351	117×90 mm. $8 World Cup Cricket emblem	11·00	11·00

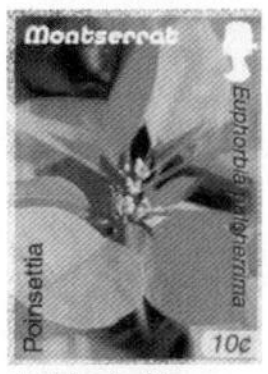

254 *Euphorbia pulcherrima* (poinsettia)

2007. Flowers. Multicoloured.

1352	10c. Type **254**	20	25
1353	30c. *Catharanthus roseus* (periwinkle)	45	50
1354	35c. *Bougainvillea glabra*	50	50
1355	50c. *Ixora macrothyrsa*	70	50
1356	70c. *Heliconia humilis*	90	65
1357	80c. *Ipomoea learii* (morning glory)	1·00	70
1358	90c. *Delonix regia* (poinciana)	1·00	75
1359	$1 *Solandra nitida* (cup of gold)	1·10	85
1360	$1.10 *Acalypha hispida* (chenille plant)	1·25	90
1361	$1.50 *Nerium oleander*	1·75	1·40
1362	$2.25 *Hibiscus rosa-sinensis*	2·25	2·25
1363	$2.50 *Plumeria acuminata* (frangipani)	2·50	2·75
1364	$2.75 *Strelitzia reginae* (bird of paradise flower)	2·75	3·00
1365	$5 *Stephanotis floribunda* (Madagascar jasmine)	4·50	4·75
1366	$10 *Tabebuia serratifolia* (yellow poui)	8·00	9·00
1367	$20 Rosa 'Bucbi'	14·00	16·00

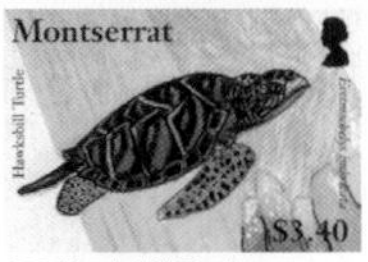

255 Hawksbill Turtle

2007. Turtles of Montserrat. Multicoloured.

MS1368	130×100 mm. $3.40×4 Type **255**; Green turtle; Leatherback turtle; Loggerhead turtle	10·50	10·50
MS1369	100×70 mm. $7 Kemp's Ridley sea turtle	6·50	7·50

The stamps and margins of No. **MS**1368 form a composite design.

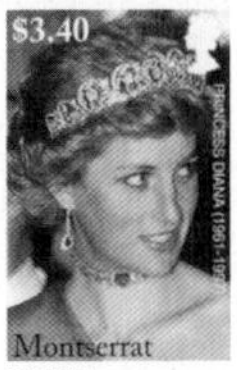

256 Diana, Princess of Wales

2007. Tenth Death Anniv of Diana, Princess of Wales. Multicoloured.

1370	$3.40 Type **256**	3·75	3·75
1371	$3.40 Wearing black dress	3·75	3·75
1372	$3.40 Wearing white dress	3·75	3·75
1373	$3.40 Wearing white jacket with stand-up collar	3·75	3·75
MS1374	100×70 mm. $7 Black/white photograph	7·00	8·00

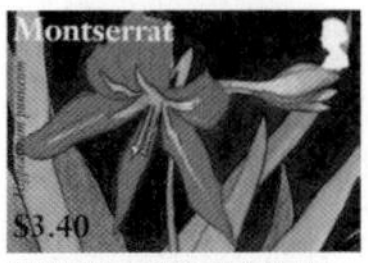

257 *Hippeastrum puniceum*

2007. Lilies of Montserrat. Multicoloured.

MS1375	130×100 mm. $3.40×4 Type **257**; *Hymenocallis caribaea*; *Zephyranthespuertoricensis*; *Belamcanda chinensis*	10·00	11·00
MS1376	100×70 mm. $7 *Crinum erubescens* (vert)	8·00	8·50

The stamps and margins of No. **MS**1375 form a composite background design of lily foliage.

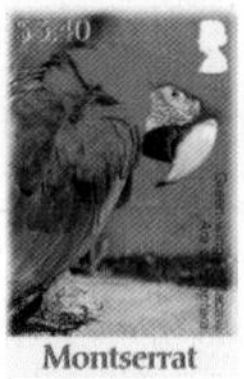

258 Green-winged Macaw

2007. Parrots of the Caribbean. Multicoloured.

1377	$3.40 Type **258**	3·75	3·75
1378	$3.40 Mitred conure	3·75	3·75
1379	$3.40 Sun conure	3·75	3·75
1380	$3.40 Blue-and-yellow macaw	3·75	3·75
MS1381	100×70 mm. $7 Hyacinth macaw	8·00	9·00

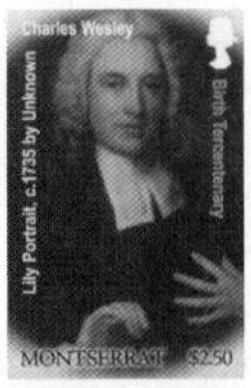

259 Charles Wesley

2007. 300th Birth Anniv of Charles Wesley (founder of Methodism). Multicoloured.

1382	$2.50 Type **259**	2·50	2·75
1383	$2.50 Charles Wesley (hands at left)	2·50	2·75
1384	$2.50 Charles Wesley with Bible	2·50	2·75
1385	$2.50 Bethany Methodist Church	2·50	2·75

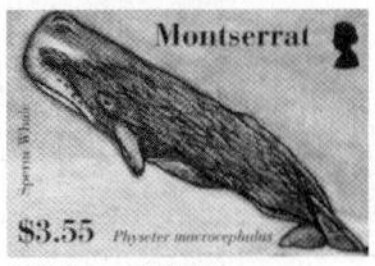

260 Sperm Whale

2008. Whales of the World. Multicoloured.

MS1386	130×100 mm. $3.55×4 Type **260**; Minke whale; Cuvier's beaked whale; Humpback whale	12·00	12·00
MS1387	100×70 mm. $7 Blue whale	7·50	7·50

The stamps and margins of No. **MS**1386 form a composite background design.

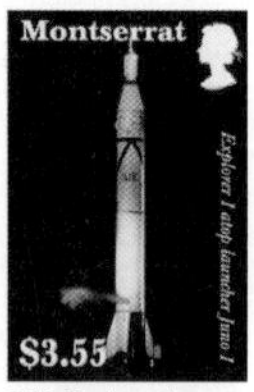

261 *Explorer I* atop Launcher *Juno I*, 1958

2008. 50 Years of Space Exploration and Satellites. Multicoloured.

1388	$3.55 Type **261**	3·50	3·75
1389	$3.55 Dr. James Van Allen and *Explorer I*	3·50	3·75
1390	$3.55 *Explorer I*	3·50	3·75
1391	$3.55 Drs. William Pickering, James Van Allen and Wernher von Braun with *Explorer I* model	3·50	3·75
MS1392	100×70 mm. $7 *Explorer I* (horiz)	7·00	8·00

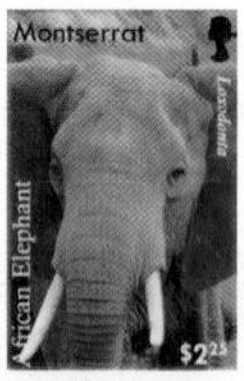

262 African Elephant

2008. Endangered Animals of the World. Multicoloured.

1393	$2.25 Type **262**	3·00	3·00
1394	$2.25 Bald eagle	3·00	3·00
1395	$2.25 Sumatran tiger	3·00	3·00
1396	$2.25 Hawksbill turtle	3·00	3·00
1397	$2.25 Indian rhinoceros	3·00	3·00
1398	$2.25 Western gorilla	3·00	3·00
MS1399	100×70 mm. $7 Rock iguana (horiz)	7·00	8·00

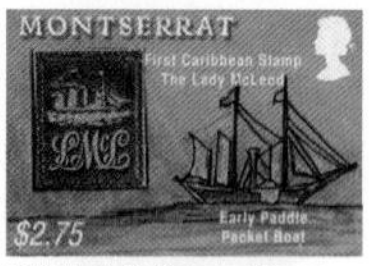

263 First Caribbean Stamp and *Lady McLeod* (early packet ship)

2008. Early Postal History. Multicoloured.

1400	$2.75 Type **263**	3·25	3·25
1401	$2.75 Early Montserrat postcard	3·25	3·25
1402	$2.75 Great Britain Mulready envelopes	3·25	3·25
1403	$2.75 Great Britain Penny Black and Sir Rowland Hill	3·25	3·25
1404	$2.75 Antigua 1d. red and 6d. green stamps overprinted Montserrat, 1876	3·25	3·25
1405	$2.75 Montserrat fleuron and crowned circle handstamps and 'A08' cancellation	3·25	3·25

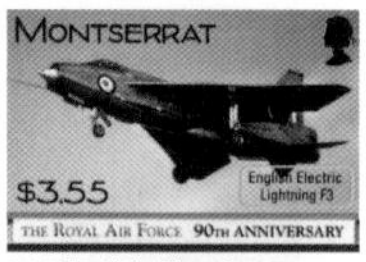

264 English Electric Lightning F3

2008. 90th Anniv of the Royal Air Force. Multicoloured.

1406	$3.55 Type **264**	4·50	4·50
1407	$3.55 Hurricane IIC	4·50	4·50
1408	$3.55 Jet Provost T3A	4·50	4·50
1409	$3.55 Jaguar TR3A	4·50	4·50
1410	$3.55 Westland Sea King HAR.3 helicopter	4·50	4·50
1411	$3.55 Gloster Javelin FAW9	4·50	4·50
1412	$3.55 P-66 Pembroke C1	4·50	4·50
1413	$3.55 Chinook HC2 helicopter	4·50	4·50

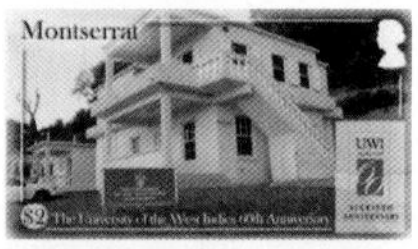

265 University of the West Indies Centre, Montserrat

2008. 60th Anniv of the University of the West Indies. Multicoloured.

1414	$2 Type **265**	3·50	3·00
1415	$5 Scroll	6·50	7·50

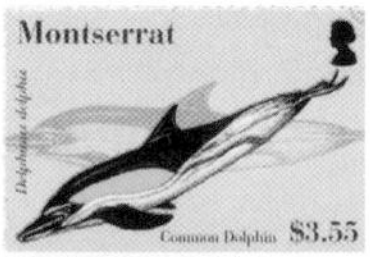

266 Common Dolphin

2008. Dolphins of the World. Multicoloured.

1416	$3.55 Type **266**	5·00	5·00
1417	$3.55 Bottlenose dolphin	5·00	5·00
1418	$3.55 Pantropical spotted dolphin	5·00	5·00
1419	$3.55 Long-snouted spinner dolphin	5·00	5·00
MS1420	100×70 mm. $7 Risso's dolphin	8·50	9·00

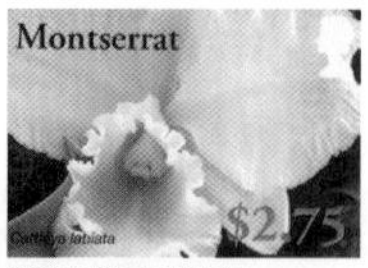

267 *Cattleya labiata*

2008. Orchids of the Caribbean. Multicoloured.

1421	$2.75 Type **267**	3·75	3·75
1422	$2.75 *Phalaenopsis* cultivar	3·75	3·75
1423	$2.75 *Cymbidium annabelle*	3·75	3·75
1424	$2.75 *Phalaenopsis taisuco*	3·75	3·75
1424a	$2.75 *Phalaenopsis amabilis*	3·75	3·75
1424b	$2.75 *Cattleya aurantiaca*	3·75	3·75
1424c	$2.75 *Phalaenopsis* cultivar	3·75	3·75
1424d	$2.75 *Dendrobium nobile*	3·75	3·75

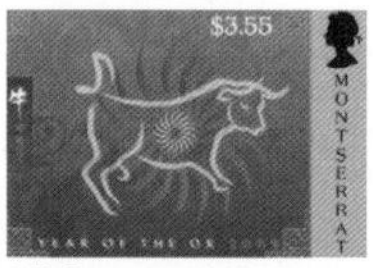

268 Ox

2009. Chinese New Year. Year of the Ox. Multicoloured, outline colours given.

MS1425	Type **268**; Ox (black) (facing left); Ox (purple-brown); Ox (white) (facing left)	15·00	16·00

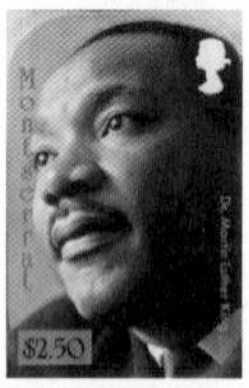

269 Martin Luther King

2009. 80th Birth Anniv of Dr. Martin Luther King (civil rights leader). Two sheets, 130×100 mm, containing T **269** and similar multicoloured designs.

MS1426	Type **269**; Sitting in chair; Wearing hat; Mrs. Coretta Scott King	9·00	10·00
MS1427	Crowd of marchers ('March on Washington for Jobs and Freedom'); Martin Luther King meeting Malcolm X, 1964; With Pres. John F. Kennedy and Civil Rights leaders; Waving to crowd ('March on Washington for Jobs and Freedom') (all horiz)	9·00	10·00

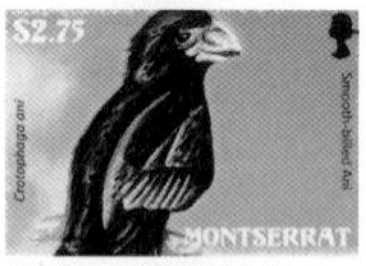

270 Smooth-billed Ani (*Crotophaga ani*)

2009. Birds of Montserrat. Multicoloured.

MS1428	100×130 mm. $2.75×4 Type **270**; American kestrel (*Falco sparverius*); Common moorhen (*Gallinula chloropus*); Cattle egret (*Bubulcus ibis*)	17·00	18·00
MS1429	70×100 mm. $7 Male Montserrat oriole (*Icterus oberi*)	9·00	9·50

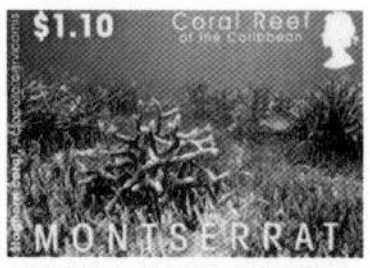

271 Staghorn Coral (*Actopora cervicornis*)

2009. Coral Reef of the Caribbean. Multicoloured.

1430	$1.10 Type **271**	1·75	1·25
1431	$2.25 Zoanthid coral (*Palythoa caesia*)	2·50	2·50
1432	$2.50 Blade fire coral (*Millepora complanata*)	2·75	3·00
1433	$2.75 Brain coral (*Diploria strigosa*)	3·00	3·75
MS1434	100×70 mm. $7 Orange tube coral (*Tubastrea aurea*)	8·00	8·50

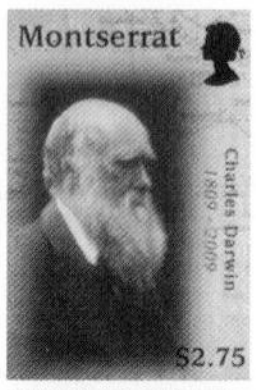

272 Charles Darwin

2009. Birth Bicentenary of Charles Darwin (evolutionary theorist). Multicoloured.

MS1435	$2.75x4Type **272**; Soldier crab (*Coenobita clypeatus*); Tree lizard (*Anolis lividus*); Endemic orchid (*Epidendrum montserratense*)	15·00	16·00
MS1436	70×100 mm. $7 Charles Darwin and Montserrat Centre Hills Project emblem (horiz)	9·00	9·50

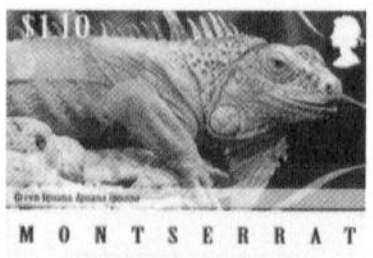

273 Green Iguana (*Iguana iguana*)

2009. Rain Forest Animals of Montserrat. Multicoloured.

MS1437	100×80 mm. $1.10 Type **273**; $2.25 Galliwasp (*Diploglossus montisserrati*); $2.50 Black snake (*Alsophisantillensis manselli*); $2.75 Common agouti (*Dasyprocta leporina*)	12·00	13·00
MS1438	100×70 mm. $5 Yellow-shouldered bat (*Sturnira thomasi vulcanensis*)	6·50	7·00

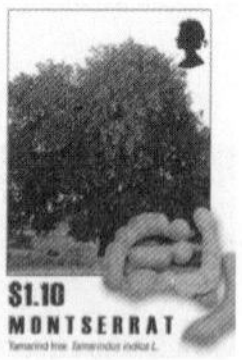

274 Tamarind Tree (*Tamarindus indica*)

2009. Tropical Trees. Multicoloured.

1439	$1.10 Type **274**	1·75	1·25
1440	$2.25 Dwarf coconut tree (*Cocos nucifera*)	2·50	2·00
1441	$2.50 Breadfruit tree (*Artocarpus altilis*)	2·75	2·50
1442	$2.75 Calabash tree (*Crescentia cujete*)	3·00	3·00
1443	$5 Geiger tree (*Cordia sebestena*)	5·00	6·00

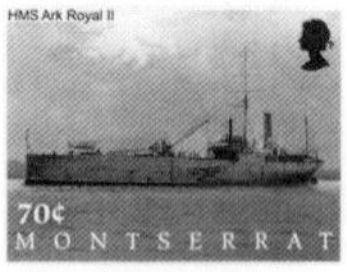

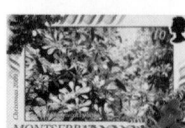

275 HMS *Ark Royal II*

2009. Centenary of Naval Aviation. Aircraft Carriers. Sheet 160×134 mm containing T **275** and similar horiz designs. Multicoloured.

MS1444	70c. Type **275**; $1.10 HMS *Furious*; $2.25 HMS *Argus*; $2.50 HMS *Illustrious*; $2.75 HMS *Ark Royal IV*; $5 HMS *Invincible*	16·00	16·00

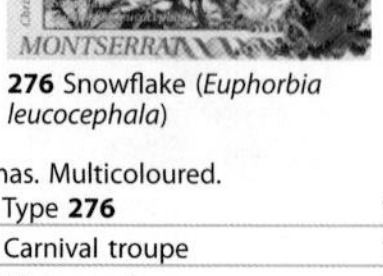

276 Snowflake (*Euphorbia leucocephala*)

2009. Christmas. Multicoloured.

1445	$1.10 Type **276**	1·25	70
1446	$2.25 Carnival troupe	1·75	1·25
1447	$2.50 Masquerade	2·00	1·75
1448	$2.75 St. Patrick's Roman Catholic Church	2·25	3·00
MS1449	100×70 mm. $6 Nativity (vert)	5·00	6·00

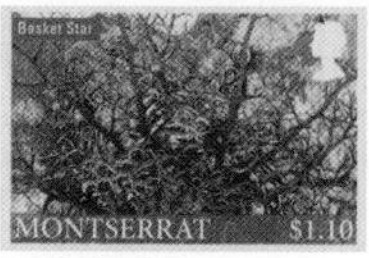

277 Basket Star

2010. Marine Life. Multicoloured.

1450	$1.10 Type **277**	1·75	1·25
1451	$2.25 Spiny lobster	2·50	2·00
1452	$2.50 Spotted drum	2·75	2·50
1453	$2.75 Sea anemone (vert)	3·00	3·00
1454	$5 Batwing coral crab	5·00	6·00

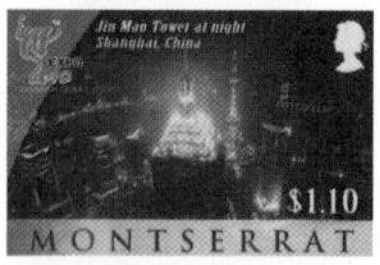

278 Jin Mao Tower at Night, Shanghai, China

2010. Expo 2010, Shanghai, China. Multicoloured.

MS1455	$1.10 Type **278**; $2.25 Montserrat Cultural Centre, Little Bay; $2.50 Assumption Cathedral, Kremlin, Russia; $2.75 Brooklyn Bridge, New York	9·00	10·00
MS1456	$1.10 Fishing village in Shanghai, Hong Kong Island, China; $2.25 Camelot Villa, Montserrat; $2.50 Zaanse Schans Windmill, Zaandam, Holland; $2.75 Reichstag German Parliament, Berlin, Germany	9·00	10·00

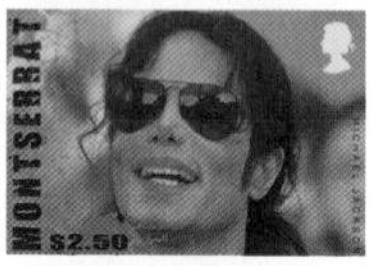

279 Michael Jackson

2010. Michael Jackson Commemoration. Multicoloured.

MS1457	$2.50×4 Type **279**; Wearing red jacket and white T shirt; In close-up, singing, wearing silver jacket; In profile, facing left, wearing red and gold jacket	10·00	11·00
MS1458	$2.50×4 Wearing white jacket and black shirt, in profile facing right; Wearing black jacket, holding microphone, facing left; Wearing white T shirt and black leather jacket; Wearing black shirt and white jacket, facing forwards	10·00	11·00

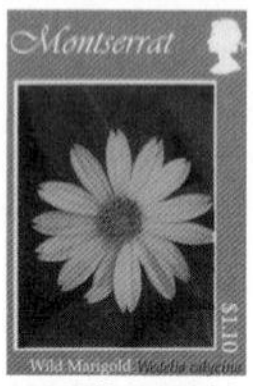

280 Wild Marigold (Wedelia calycina)

2010. Wild Flowers of Montserrat. Multicoloured.

1459	$1.10 Type **280**	1·00	1·00
1460	$2.25 Shrubby toothedthread (*Odontonema nitidum*)	2·10	2·10
1461	$2.50 Wild sweet pea (*Crotalaria retusa*)	2·40	2·40
1462	$2.75 Rosy periwinkle (*Catharanthus roseus*)	3·00	3·00
1463	$5 Measle bush (*Lantana camara*)	6·00	6·00
MS1464	100×70 mm. $7 Pribby (*Rondeletia buxifolia*)	8·00	9·00

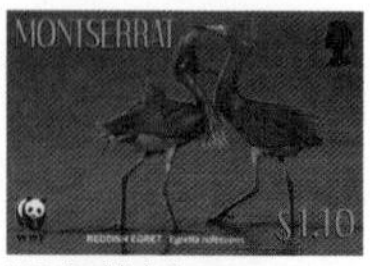

281 Reddish Egret

2010. Endangered Species. Reddish Egret (*Egretta rufescens*). Multicoloured.

1465	$1.10 Type **281**	2·25	2·25
1466	$2.25 White phase and dark phase egrets in flight	2·75	2·75
1467	$2.50 Reddish egret (dark phase) preening	2·75	2·75
1468	$2.75 White phase egret taking off from wetland	3·00	3·00
MS1469	100×139 mm. Nos. 1465/8, each ×2	16·00	16·00

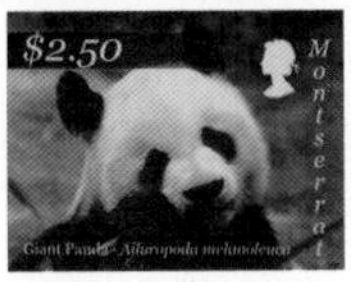

282 Giant Panda

2010. Beijing 2010 International Stamp and Coin Exhibition. Giant Panda (*Ailuropoda melanoleuca*). Multicoloured.

MS1470	160×95 mm. $2.50×4 Type **282**; Panda laying between rock and tree trunk; Panda eating bamboo; Panda looking down (side view of head, shoulders and foreleg)	9·50	9·50
MS1471	90×62 mm. $7 Panda looking down (side view of head and shoulders)	7·00	7·50

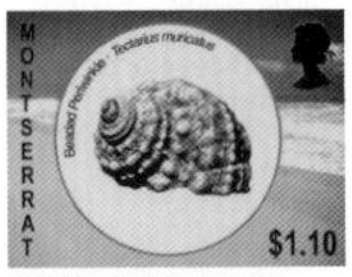

283 Beaded Periwinkle (*Tectarius muricatus*)

2011. Seashells. Multicoloured.

1472	$1.10 Type **283**	1·75	1·25
1473	$2.25 Green star shell (*Astraea tuber*)	2·75	2·25
1474	$2.50 Smooth Scotch bonnet (*Phalium cicatricosum*)	3·00	2·75
1475	$2.75 Calico scallop (*Aequipecten gibbus*)	3·50	3·50
1476	$5 Hawk wing conch (*Strombus raninus*)	5·00	6·00
MS1477	100×80 mm. $7 Atlantic partridge tun (*Tonna maculosa*) (vert)	8·00	8·50

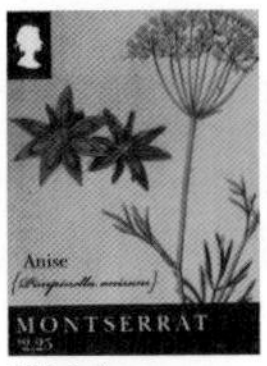

284 Anise (*Pimpinella anisum*)

2011. Medicinal Plants. Multicoloured.

MS1478	$2.25×6 Type **284**; Lemon grass (*Cymbopogon citratus*); Vervain (*Stachytarpheta jamaicensis*); Ram goat bush (*Eryngium foetidum*); Rosemary (*Rosmarinus officinalis*); Inflammation bush (*Peperomia pellucida*)	16·00	16·00

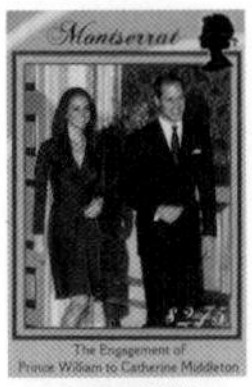

285 Prince William and Miss Catherine Middleton

2011. Royal Engagement. Multicoloured.

MS1479	100×130 mm. $2.75×4 Type **285**; Miss Catherine Middleton waring black hat with white curled feather; Prince William; Prince William and Miss Catherine Middleton (gold framed painting in background)	12·00	12·00
MS1480	80×110 mm. $5 Miss Catherine Middleton; $5 Prince William	10·00	10·00

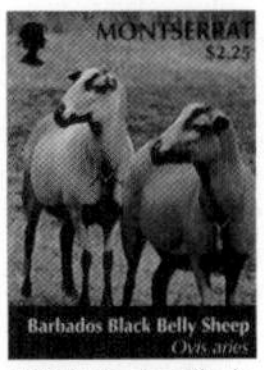

286 Barbados Black Belly Sheep (*Ovis aries*)

2011. Animals of Montserrat. Multicoloured.

1481	$2.25 Type **286**	2·75	2·25
1482	$2.50 Boer goat (*Capra aegagrus hircus*)	3·00	2·75
1483	$2.75 Black donkey (*Equus africanus asinus*)	3·50	3·50
1484	$5 Red cattle (*Bos primigenius*)	5·00	6·00
MS1485	100×100 mm. $7 Arabian horse (*Equus caballus*)	8·00	8·00

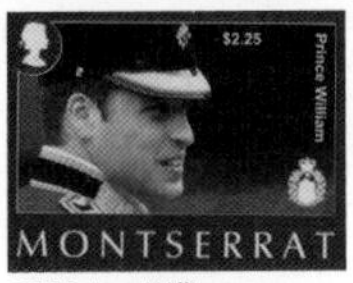

287 Prince William

2011. Royal Wedding. Multicoloured.

MS1486	$2.25×6 Type **287**; Leaving Westminster Abbey after wedding; Duchess of Cambridge; Prince William (no cap); Duke and Duchess of Cambridge in carriage; Duchess of Cambridge (facing right)	16·00	16·00
MS1487	100×70 mm. $7 Duke and Duchess of Cambridge kissing on Buckingham Palace balcony	8·00	8·50

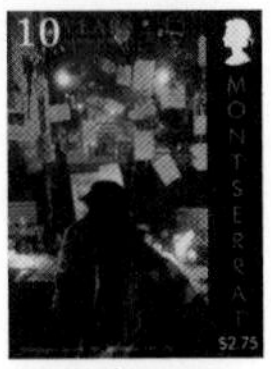

288 Washington Square, New York, 14 September 2001

2011. Tenth Anniv of Attack on World Trade Centre, New York. Multicoloured.

MS1488	100×130 mm. $2.75×4 Type **288**; US flag and 'God Bless the Memory of those Lost' banner; 'Love' and 'No War Peace' messages, Union Square, New York, 13 September 2001; US flag and memorial cross, Stoneycreek township, Pennsylvania	12·00	12·00
MS1489	100×70 mm. $6 Keithroy Maynard, 1971-2001 (Montserrat born New York firefighter)	5·50	6·50

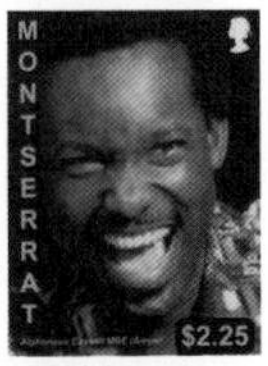

289 Alphonsus Cassell

2011. Alphonsus Cassell 'Mighty Arrow' (soca musician) Commemoration. Multicoloured.

1490	$2.25 Type **289**	2·75	2·25
1491	$2.50 Alphonsus Cassell (wearing red and black jacket)	3·00	2·75
MS1492	130×100 mm. $2.75×4 Alphonsus Cassell (wearing white jacket); Wearing headphones; Wearing tasselled sleeveless top; Wearing patterned V-neck top (all horiz)	12·00	12·00

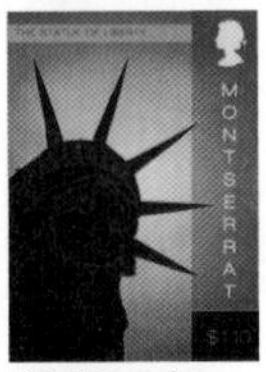

290 Statue of Liberty

2011. 125th Anniv of Statue of Liberty. Multicoloured.

MS1493	100×131 mm. $1.10 Type **290**; $1.10 Torch; $2.25 Head of Statue of Liberty; $2.25 Book; $2.50 Statue of Liberty; $2.50 Back of Statue's head and book	5·00	4·00
MS1494	70×100 mm. $6 Statue of Liberty and base (30×80 mm)	5·00	6·00

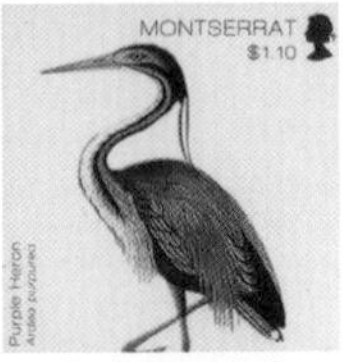

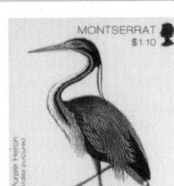

291 Purple Heron (*Ardea purpurea*)

2011. China 2011 27th Asian International Stamp Exhibition, Wuxi. Fauna and Flora of China. Multicoloured.

MS1495	$1.10 Type **291**; $2.25 Indian elephant (*Elephas maximus indicus*); $2.50 Snub-nosed monkey (*Rhinopithecus roxellana*); $2.75 Royal Bengal tiger (*Panthera tigris tigris*)	10·00	8·75
MS1496	$1.10 Chinese plum (*Prunus mume*); $2.25 Opium poppy (*Papaver somniferum*); $2.50 Japanese camellia (*Camellia japonica*); $2.75 Pomegranate (*Punica granatum*)	10·00	8·75

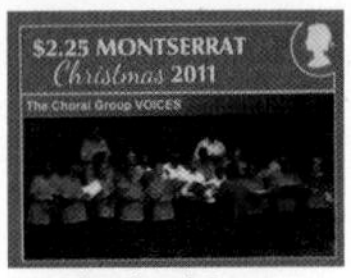

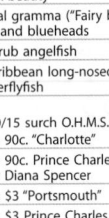

292 The Choral Group Voices

2011. Christmas. Multicoloured.

1497	$2.25 Type **292**	2·50	2·00
1498	$2.50 Emerald Community Singers	2·75	2·50
1499	$2.75 Volpanics Steel Band	3·00	3·00
1500	$5 New Ebenezer SDA Church	5·00	6·00

OFFICIAL STAMPS

1976. Various stamps, some already surch, optd O.H.M.S.

O1	5c. multicoloured (No. 246)		70
O2	10c. multicoloured (No. 247)		1·00
O3	30c. on 10c. mult (No. 369)		1·50
O4	45c. on 3c. mult (No. 370)		2·00
O5	$5 multicoloured (No. 254)		£110
O6	$10 multicoloured (No. 254a)		£650

These stamps were issued for use on mail from the Montserrat Philatelic Bureau. They were not sold to the public, either unused or used.

1976. Nos. 372, 374/82, 384/5 and 476 optd O.H.M.S. or surch also.

O17	5c. Malay apple		10
O28	5c. on 3c. Lignum vitae		20
O18	10c. Jacaranda		10
O19	15c. Orchid tree		10
O20	20c. Manjak		10
O21	25c. Tamarind		15
O33	30c. on 15c. Orchid tree		30
O34	35c. on 2c. Cannon-ball tree		30
O35	40c. Flame of the forest		40
O22	55c. Pink cassia		35
O23	70c. Long john		45
O24	$1 Saman		60
O39	$2.50 on 40c. Flame of the forest		2·00
O25	$5 Yellow poui		1·50
O16	$10 Flamboyant		3·75

1981. Nos. 490/4, 496, 498, 500, 502/3 and 505 optd O.H.M.S.

O42	5c. Type **91**	10	10
O43	10c. Hogfish and neon goby	10	10
O44	15c. Creole wrasse	10	10
O45	20c. Three-spotted damselfish	15	15
O46	25c. Sergeant major	15	15
O47	45c. Schoolmaster	25	20
O48	65c. Bigeye	35	30
O49	$1 Rock beauty	65	65
O50	$3 Royal gramma ("Fairy basslet") and blueheads	1·50	1·75
O51	$5 Cherub angelfish	2·00	2·25
O52	$10 Caribbean long-nosed butterflyfish	3·00	2·25

1983. Nos. 510/15 surch O.H.M.S. and value.

O53	45c. on 90c. "Charlotte"	20	30
O54	45c. on 90c. Prince Charles and Lady Diana Spencer	60	1·00
O55	75c. on $3 "Portsmouth"	25	35
O56	75c. on $3 Prince Charles and Lady Diana Spencer	90	1·40
O57	$1 on $4 "Britannia"	35	50
O58	$1 on $4 Prince Charles and Lady Diana Spencer	1·00	1·50

1983. Nos. 542/4 surch O.H.M.S.

O59	70c. on 75c. Type **97**	60	40
O60	$1 Coat of Arms of Catherine of Aragon	70	50
O61	$1.50 on $5 Diana, Princess of Wales	1·00	80

1985. Nos. 600/12 and 614 optd O H M S.

O62	5c. Type **107**	1·25	1·25
O63	10c. Carib grackle	1·25	1·00
O64	15c. Moorhen	1·50	1·00
O65	20c. Brown booby	1·50	1·00
O66	25c. Black-whiskered vireo	1·50	1·00
O67	40c. Scaly-breasted thrasher	2·00	70
O68	55c. Laughing gull	2·25	70
O69	70c. Glossy ibis	2·50	90
O70	90c. Green-backed heron	2·75	90
O71	$1 Belted kingfisher	2·75	70
O72	$1.15 Bananaquit	3·00	1·00
O73	$3 American kestrel	4·50	2·50
O74	$5 Forest thrush	5·50	2·50
O75	$10 Bridled quail dove	7·00	2·50

1989. Nos. 757/70 and 772 optd O H M S.

O76	5c. Type **133**	40	75
O77	10c. Little knobbed scallop	40	75
O78	15c. Sozoni's cone	50	1·00
O79	20c. Globular coral shell	55	1·00
O80	25c. American or common sundial	55	50
O81	40c. King helmet	60	55
O82	55c. Channelled turban	70	70
O83	70c. True tulip shell	90	1·25
O84	90c. Music volute	1·00	90
O85	$1 Flame auger	1·00	80
O86	$1.15 Rooster-tail conch	1·25	1·00
O87	$1.50 Queen or pink conch	1·40	1·60
O88	$3 Teramachi's slit shell	2·00	2·50
O89	$5 Common or Florida crown conch	3·25	3·25
O90	$10 Atlantic trumpet triton	5·50	5·50

1989. Nos. 578 and 580/1 surch OHMS.

O91	70c. on 10c. Hogfish and neon goby	2·25	1·75
O92	$1.15 on 75c. French grunt	3·00	1·75
O93	$1.50 on $2 Blue chromis	3·00	3·00

1992. Nos. 838/41, 847/50, 856/9 surch or optd OHMS.

O94	70c. on 90c. Type **150**	1·40	1·40
O95	70c. on 90c. Type **152**	1·40	1·40
O96	70c. on 90c. Type **154**	1·40	1·40
O97	70c. on $3.50 French grunt	1·40	1·40
O98	$1 on $3.50 Helmeted guineafowl	1·50	1·50
O99	$1 on $3.50 Anthurium	1·50	1·50
O100	$1.15 Cushion star	1·50	1·75
O101	$1.15 Hen and chicks	1·50	1·75
O102	$1.15 Shell ginger	1·50	1·75
O103	$1.50 Rock beauty	1·60	2·00
O104	$1.50 Red junglefowl	1·60	2·00
O105	$1.50 Early day lily	1·60	2·00

1993. Nos. 889/902 and 904 optd OHMS.

O106	5c. Type **161**	70	1·25
O107	10c. "Gryllus campestris" (field cricket)	70	1·25
O108	15c. "Lepthemis vesiculosa" (dragonfly)	80	1·25
O109	20c. "Orthemis ferruginea" (red skimmer)	80	1·25
O110	25c. "Gerris lacustris" (pond skater)	80	1·25
O111	40c. "Byctiscus betulae" (leaf weevil)	1·25	60
O112	55c. "Atta texana" (leaf-cutter ants)	1·40	60
O113	70c. "Polistes fuscatus" (paper wasp)	1·60	1·25
O114	90c. "Sparmopolius fulvus" (bee fly)	1·75	1·00
O115	$1 "Chrysopa carnea" (lace wing)	1·75	1·00
O116	$1.15 "Phoebis philea" (butterfly)	2·25	1·75
O117	$1.50 "Cynthia cardui" (butterfly)	2·75	2·50
O118	$3 "Utetheisa bella" (moth)	4·00	4·50
O119	$5 "Alucita pentadactyla" (moth)	5·50	6·00
O120	$10 "Heliconius melpomene" (butterfly)	8·00	9·00

1997. Nos. 1009/22 and 1024 optd O.H.M.S.

O121	5c. Type **184**	15	70
O122	10c. Pegasus	25	70
O123	15c. Griffin	35	1·00
O124	20c. Unicorn	35	1·00
O125	25c. Gnomes	15	50
O126	40c. Mermaid	50	70
O127	55c. Cockatrice	60	70
O128	70c. Fairy	70	70
O129	90c. Goblin	90	1·00
O130	$1 Faun	1·00	70
O131	$1.15 Dragon	1·25	70
O132	$1.50 Giant	1·40	1·00
O133	$3 Elves	2·50	2·75
O134	$5 Centaur	4·00	5·50
O135	$10 Erin	6·00	8·50

2002. Nos. 1195/1208 and 1210 optd OHMS.

O137	5c. Type **215**	30	1·00
O138	10c. Mammee apple	35	80
O139	15c. Lime	50	1·00
O140	20c. Grapefruit	55	1·00
O141	25c. Orange	55	1·00
O142	40c. Passion fruit	75	45
O143	55c. Banana	90	65
O144	70c. Pawpaw	1·25	1·00
O145	90c. Pomegranate	1·50	1·00
O146	$1 Guava	1·50	75
O147	$1.15 Mango	1·75	1·00
O148	$1.50 Sugar apple	2·00	1·25
O149	$3 Cashew	3·50	3·50
O150	$5 Soursop	5·00	6·00
O151	$10 Pineapple	7·50	8·50

2008. Nos. 1352/65 and 1367 optd OHMS.

O152	10c. Type **254**	20	30
O153	30c. *Catharanthus roseus* (periwinkle)	45	50
O154	35c. *Bougainvillea glabra*	50	50
O155	50c. *Ixora macrothyrsa*	70	50
O156	70c. *Heliconia humilis*	90	65
O157	80c. *Ipomoea learii* (morning glory)	1·00	1·00
O158	90c. *Delonix regia* (poinciana)	1·00	1·00

O159	$1 *Solandra nitida* (cup of gold)	1·10	85
O160	$1.10 *Acalypha hispida* (chenille plant)	1·25	90
O161	$1.50 *Nerium oleander*	1·75	1·40
O162	$2.25 *Hibiscus rosa-sinensis*	2·25	2·25
O163	$2.50 *Plumeria acuminata*	2·50	2·75
O164	$2.75 *Strelitzia reginae* (bird of paradise flower)	2·75	3·00
O165	$5 *Stephanotis floribunda*	4·50	4·75
O166	$20 Rosa 'Buchi'	14·00	16·00

Pt. 13

MOROCCO

An independent kingdom, established in 1956, comprising the former French and Spanish International Zones.

A. Northern Zone.
100 centimes = 1 peseta.

B. Southern Zone.
100 centimes = 1 franc.

C. Issues for the Whole of Morocco.
1958. 100 centimes = 1 franc.
1962. 100 francs = 1 dirham.

A. NORTHERN ZONE

1 Sultan of Morocco

2 Polytechnic

1956

1	1	10c. brown	30	25
2	-	15c. brown	30	25
3	2	25c. violet	10	10
4	-	50c. green	45	45
5	1	80c. green	1·10	1·10
6	-	2p. lilac	9·50	9·00
7	2	3p. blue	19·00	19·00
8	-	10p. green	42·00	42·00

DESIGNS—HORIZ: 15c., 2p. Villa Sanjurjo harbour. VERT: 50c., 10p. Cultural Delegation building, Tetuan.

3 Lockheed Super Constellation over Lau Dam

1956. Air.

9	3	25c. purple	45	45
10	-	1p.40 mauve	1·10	1·10
11	3	3p.40 red	2·40	2·40
12	-	4p.80 purple	4·25	4·25

DESIGN: 1p.40, 4p.80, Lockheed Super Constellation over Rio Nekor Bridge.

1957. First Anniv of Independence. As T **7** but with Spanish inscriptions and currency.

13	80c. green	95	90
14	1p.50 olive	2·40	2·30
15	3p. red	5·25	5·00

1957. As T **5** but with Spanish inscriptions and currency.

16	30c. indigo and blue	30	10
17	70c. purple and brown	45	10
18	80c. purple	1·90	45
19	1p.50 lake and green	65	35
20	3p. green	95	80
21	7p. red	6·50	1·80

1957. Investiture of Prince Moulay el Hassan. As T **9** but with Spanish inscriptions and currency.

22	80c. blue	75	45
23	1p.50 green	1·90	1·40
24	3p. red	5·75	4·00

1957. Nos. 17 and 19 surch.

25	15c. on 70c. purple and brown	95	95
26	1p.20 on 1p.50 lake and green	1·60	1·60

1957. 30th Anniv of Coronation of Sultan Sidi Mohammed ben Yusuf. As T **10** but with Spanish inscription and currency.

27	1p.20 green and black	75	65
28	1p.80 red and black	1·10	90
29	3p. violet and black	2·10	1·80

B. SOUTHERN ZONE

5 Sultan of Morocco

1956

30	5	5f. indigo and blue	45	10
31	5	10f. sepia and brown	35	10
32	5	15f. lake and green	45	10
33	5	25f. purple	1·50	25
34	5	30f. green	3·00	25
35	5	50f. red	3·75	25
36	5	70f. brown and sepia	5·50	85

6 Classroom

1956. Education Campaign.

37	-	10f. violet and purple	2·20	1·40
38	-	15f. lake and red	3·00	1·80
39	6	20f. green and turquoise	3·50	2·75
40	-	30f. red and lake	6·00	3·50
41	-	50f. blue and indigo	9·25	6·00

DESIGNS: 10f. Peasants reading book; 15f. Two girls reading; 30f. Child reading to old man; 50f. Child teaching parents the alphabet.

7 Sultan of Morocco

1957. First Anniv of Independence.

42	7	15f. green	2·00	1·40
43	7	25f. olive	2·50	1·40
44	7	30f. red	4·75	2·10

8 Emblem over Casablanca

1957. Air. International Fair, Casablanca.

45	8	15f. green and red	1·70	1·20
46	8	25f. turquoise	2·50	1·50
47	8	30f. brown	3·50	1·90

9 Crown Prince Moulay el Hassan

1957. Investiture of Crown Prince Moulay el Hassan.

48	9	15f. blue	1·80	1·10
49	9	25f. green	2·00	1·50
50	9	30f. red	3·50	1·90

10 King Mohammed V

1957. 30th Anniv of Coronation of King Mohammed V.

51	10	15f. green and black	1·00	80
52	10	25f. red and black	1·80	1·10
53	10	30f. violet and black	2·10	1·40

C. ISSUES FOR THE WHOLE OF MOROCCO

11 Moroccan Pavilion

1958. Brussels International Exhibition.

54	11	15f. turquoise	45	25
55	11	25f. red	45	30
56	11	30f. blue	75	55

12 King Mohammed V and UNESCO Headquarters, Paris

1958. Inauguration of UNESCO Headquarters Building, Paris.

57	12	15f. green	45	25
58	12	25f. lake	45	30
59	12	30f. blue	75	55

13 Ben-Smine Sanatorium

1959. "National Aid".

60	13	50f. bistre, green and red	95	55

14 King Mohammed V on Horseback

1959. King Mohammed V's 50th Birthday.

61	14	15f. lake	75	45
62	14	25f. blue	1·00	50
63	14	45f. green	1·20	80

15 Princess Lalla Amina

1959. Children's Week.

64	15	15f. blue	45	25
65	15	25f. green	50	30
66	15	45f. purple	75	55

16

1960. Meeting of U.N. African Economic Commission, Tangier.

67	16	45f. green, brown and violet	1·20	70

+10f

اعانة ضحايا
الزيوت المسممة
اكتوبر 1959

(17)

1960. Adulterated Cooking Oil Victims Relief Fund. Surch as T **17**.

68	5	5f.+10f. indigo and blue	55	45
69	5	10f.+10f. sepia and brown	95	75
70	5	15f.+10f. lake and green	1·50	1·00
71	5	25f.+15f. purple	1·80	1·30
72	5	30f.+20f. green	2·75	2·40

18 Arab Refugees

1960. World Refugee Year.

73	18	15f. black, green and ochre	45	25
74	-	45f. green and black	75	50

DESIGNS: 45f. "Uprooted tree" and Arab refugees.

19 Marrakesh

1960. 900th Anniv of Marrakesh.

75	19	100f. green, brown and blue	1·50	1·10

20 Lantern

1960. 1100th Anniv of Karaouiyne University.

76	20	15f. purple	75	55
77	-	25f. blue	75	75
78	-	30f. brown	1·50	90
79	-	35f. black	2·00	1·10
80	-	45f. green	2·50	1·70

DESIGNS: 25f. Fountain; 30f. Minaret; 35f. Frescoes; 45f. Courtyard.

21 Arab League Centre and King Mohammed V

1960. Inauguration of Arab League Centre, Cairo.

81	21	15f. black and green	45	25

اسبوعا التضامن +5f
1380
1960

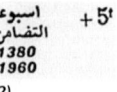

(22)

1960. Solidarity Fund. Nos. 458/9 (Mahakma, Casablanca) of French Morocco surch as T 22.

82	106	15f.+3f. on 18f. myrtle	95	95
83	106	+5f. on 20f. lake	1·30	1·30

23 Wrestling

1960. Olympic Games.

84	23	5f. purple, green and violet	10	10
85	-	10f. chocolate, blue & brown	30	25
86	-	15f. brown, blue and green	45	25
87	-	20f. purple, blue and bistre	50	40
88	-	30f. brown, violet and red	55	45
89	-	40f. brown, blue and violet	95	45
90	-	45f. blue, green and purple	1·20	70
91	-	70f. black, blue and brown	1·80	80

DESIGNS: 10f. Gymnastics; 15f. Cycling; 20f. Weightlifting; 30f. Running; 40f. Boxing; 45f. Sailing; 70f. Fencing.

24 Runner

1961. Third Pan-Arab Games, Casablanca.

92	24	20f. green	45	25
93	24	30f. lake	75	40
94	24	50f. blue	80	70

25 Post Office and Letters

1961. African Postal and Telecommunications Conference, Tangier.

95	25	20f. purple and mauve	45	40
96	-	30f. turquoise and green	75	45
97	-	90f. ultramarine and blue	1·20	80

DESIGNS—VERT: 30f. Telephone operator. HORIZ: 90f. Sud Aviation Caravelle mail plane over Tangier.

26 King Mohammed V and African Map

1962. First Anniv of African Charter of Casablanca.

98	26	20f. purple and buff	35	10
99	26	30f. indigo and blue	65	25

27 Lumumba and Congo Map

1962. Patrice Lumumba Commemoration.

100	27	20f. black and bistre	30	10
101	27	30f. black and brown	50	45

28 King Hassan II

1962. Air.

102	28	90f. black	85	10
103	28	1d. red	1·30	25
104	28	2d. blue	1·50	70
105	28	3d. green	2·75	1·30
106	28	5d. violet	5·25	1·90

29 "Pupils of the Nation"

1962. Children's Education.

107	29	20f. blue, red and green	55	30
108	29	30f. sepia, brown and green	60	45
109	29	90f. blue, purple and green	1·10	70

1962. Arab League Week. As T 76 of Libya.

110		20f. brown	30	25

30 King Hassan II

1962

111	30	1f. olive	10	10
112	30	2f. violet	10	10
113	30	5f. sepia	10	10
114	30	10f. brown	10	10
115	30	15f. turquoise	30	10
116	30	20f. purple (18×22 mm)	45	10
116a	30	20f. purple (17½×23½ mm)	3·00	10
116b	30	25f. red	45	10
117	30	30f. green	55	10
117a	30	35f. slate	70	10
117b	30	40f. blue	70	10
118	30	50f. purple	95	10
118a	30	60f. purple	1·40	25
119	30	70f. blue	1·50	40
120	30	80f. lake	2·40	40

31 Scout with Banner

1962. Fifth Arab Scout Jamboree, Rabat.

121	31	20f. purple and blue	45	25

32 Campaign Emblem and Swamp

1962. Malaria Eradication Campaign.

122	32	20f. blue and green	45	10
123	-	50f. lake and green	75	45

DESIGN—VERT: 50f. Sword piercing mosquito.

33 Aquarium, Brown Trout and Fish

1962. Casablanca Aquarium. Multicoloured.

124		20f. Type 33	75	40
125		30f. Aquarium and Mediterranean moray	75	40

34 Mounted Postman and 1912 Sherifian Stamp

1962. First National Philatelic Exhibition, Rabat, and Stamp Day.

126	34	20f. green and brown	70	35
127	-	30f. black and red	95	35
128	-	50f. bistre and blue	1·60	70

DESIGNS: 30f. Postman and circular postmark; 50f. Sultan Hassan I and octagonal postmark (both stamps commemorate 70th anniv of Sherifian post).

فيضانات
1
9
6
3
20 + 5

(35)

1963. Flood Relief Fund. Surch as T 35.

129	5	20+5f. on 5f. indigo & bl	95	95
130	5	30+10f. on 50f. red	1·30	95

36 King Moulay Ismail

1963. 300th Anniv of Meknes.

131	36	20f. sepia	75	30

37 Ibn Batota (voyager)

1963. "Famous Men of Maghreb".

132	37	20f. purple	65	40
133	-	20f. black	65	40
134	-	20f. myrtle	65	40
134a	37	40f. blue	60	40

PORTRAITS: No. 133, Ibn Khaldoun (historian); 134, Al Idrissi (geographer).

38 Sugar Beet and Refinery

1963. Freedom from Hunger.

135	38	20f. black, brown and green	75	35
136	-	50f. black, brown and blue	95	45

DESIGN—VERT: 50f. Fisherman and tuna.

39 Isis (bas relief)

1963. Nubian Monuments Preservation.

137		20f. black and grey	50	40
138	39	30f. violet	60	40
139	-	50f. purple	1·00	55

DESIGNS—HORIZ: 20f. Heads of Colossi, Abu Simbel; 50f. Philae Temple.

40 Agadir before Earthquake

1963. Reconstruction of Agadir.

140	40	20f. red and blue	75	35
141	40	30f. red and blue	95	55
142	-	50f. red and blue	1·20	70

DESIGNS: 30f. is optd with large red cross and date of earthquake, 29th February, 1960; 50f. Reconstructed Agadir.

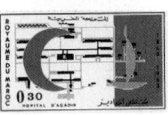

41 Plan of new Agadir Hospital

1963. Centenary of International Red Cross.

143	41	30f. multicoloured	55	40

42 Emblems of Morocco and Rabat

1963. Opening of Parliament.

144	42	20f. multicoloured	55	40

43 Hands breaking Chain

1963. 15th Anniv of Declaration of Human Rights.

145	43	20f. brown, sepia and green	55	40

44 National Flag

1963. Evacuation of Foreign Troops from Morocco.

146	44	20f. red, green and black	65	25

45 "Moulay Abdurrahman" (after Delacroix)

1964. Third Anniv of King Hassan's Coronation.

147	45	1d. multicoloured	3·25	2·10

46 Map, Chart and W.M.O. Emblem

1964. World Meteorological Day. Multicoloured.

148		20f. African weather map (vert) (postage)	50	25
149		30f. Type 46	75	45
150		90f. Globe and weather vane (vert) (air)	1·00	75

47 Fair Entrance

1964. Air. 20th Anniv of Casablanca Int Fair.

151	47	1d. red, drab and blue	1·20	80

48 Moroccan Pavilion at Fair

1964. Air. New York World's Fair.

152	48	1d. multicoloured	1·30	80

49 Children Playing in the Sun

1964. Postal Employees' Holiday Settlements.

153	49	20f. multicoloured	45	25
154	-	30f. multicoloured	75	45

DESIGN: 30f. Boy, girl and holiday settlement.

50 Olympic Torch

1964. Olympic Games, Tokyo.

155	50	20f. green, violet and red	55	40
156	50	30f. purple, blue and green	75	40
157	50	50f. red, blue and green	95	65

51 Lighthouse and Sultan Mohamed ben Abdurrahman (founder)

1964. Centenary of Cape Spartel Lighthouse.
| 158 | **51** | 25f. multicoloured | 75 | 40 |

52 Tangier Iris

1965. Flowers. Multicoloured.
159		25f. Type **52**	1·20	75
160		40f. Gladiolus (vert)	1·50	85
161		60f. Caper (horiz)	2·50	1·60

53 Return of King Mohammed

1965. Tenth Anniv of Return of King Mohammed V from Exile.
| 162 | **53** | 25f. green | 55 | 40 |

54 Early Telegraph Receiver

1965. Centenary of I.T.U. Multicoloured.
| 163 | | 25f. Type **54** | 45 | 35 |
| 164 | | 40f. "TIROS" weather satellite | 75 | 55 |

55 I.C.Y. Emblem

1965. International Co-operation Year.
| 165 | **55** | 25f. black and green | 40 | 25 |
| 166 | **55** | 60f. lake | 55 | 30 |

1965. Sea Shells. As T **52**. Mult, background colours given.
167		25f. violet	1·10	50
168		25f. blue	1·10	50
169		25f. yellow	1·10	50
SEASHELLS: No. 167, Knobbed triton ("Charonia nodifera"); 168, Smooth callista ("Pitaria chione"); 169, "Cymbium tritonis".

1965. Shellfish. As T **52**. Multicoloured.
170		25f. Helmet crab	1·10	55
171		40f. Mantis shrimp	2·00	1·10
172		1d. Royal prawn (horiz)	2·75	1·60

1965. Orchids. As T **52**. Multicoloured.
173		25f. "Ophrys speculum" (vert)	80	55
174		40f. "Ophrys fusca" (vert)	1·20	55
175		60f. "Ophrys tenthredinifera" (horiz)	2·20	1·40

59 Corn

1966. Agricultural Products (1st issue).
| 176 | **59** | 25f. black and ochre | 45 | 25 |

See also Nos. 188/9 and 211.

60 Flag, Map and Dove

1966. Tenth Anniv of Independence.
| 177 | **60** | 25f. red and green | 45 | 25 |

61 King Hassan II and Crown

1966. Fifth Anniv of King Hassan's Coronation.
| 178 | **61** | 25f. blue, green and red | 45 | 20 |

62 Cross-country Runner

1966. 53rd "Cross des Nations" (Cross-country Race).
| 179 | **62** | 25f. green | 55 | 25 |

63 W.H.O. Building

1966. Inauguration of W.H.O. Headquarters, Geneva.
| 180 | **63** | 25f. black and purple | 40 | 25 |
| 181 | - | 40f. black and blue | 55 | 25 |
DESIGN: 40f. W.H.O. Building (different view).

64 King Hassan and Parachutist

1966. Tenth Anniv of Royal Armed Forces.
| 182 | **64** | 25f. black and gold | 75 | 40 |
| 183 | - | 40f. black and gold | 70 | 40 |
DESIGN: 40f. Crown Prince Hassan kissing hand of King Mohammed.

1966. Palestine Week. As No. 110 but inscr "SEMAINE DE LA PALESTINE" at foot and dated "1966".
| 184 | | 25f. blue | 45 | 10 |

65 Brooch

1966. Red Cross Seminar. Moroccan Jewellery. Multicoloured.
| 185 | | 25f.+5f. Type **65** | 1·20 | 70 |
| 186 | | 40f.+10f. Pendant | 1·50 | 90 |
See also Nos. 203/4, 246/7, 274/5, 287/8, 303/4, 324/5, 370/1, 397/8, 414/15, 450/1 and 493.

66 Rameses II, Abu Simbel

1966. Air. 20th Anniv of UNESCO.
| 187 | **66** | 1d. red and yellow | 1·50 | 85 |

1966. Agricultural Products (2nd and 3rd issue). As T **59**.
| 188 | | 40f. multicoloured | 60 | 30 |
| 189 | | 60f. multicoloured | 70 | 30 |
DESIGNS—VERT: 40f. Citrus fruits. HORIZ: 60f. Olives.

67 Class XDd Diesel Train

1966. Moroccan Transport. Multicoloured.
190		25f. Type **67** (postage)	1·10	45
191		40f. Liner "Maroc"	1·00	45
192		1d. Tourist coach	1·20	70
193		3d. Sud Aviation Caravelle of Royal Air Maroc (48×27½ mm) (air)	5·00	2·10

68 Twaite Shad

1967. Fish. Multicoloured.
194		25f. Type **68**	1·00	45
195		40f. Plain bonito	1·20	55
196		1d. Bluefish	2·40	1·50

69 Hilton Hotel, Ancient Ruin and Map

1967. Opening of Hilton Hotel, Rabat.
| 197 | **69** | 25f. black and blue | 45 | 40 |
| 198 | **69** | 1d. purple and blue | 1·00 | 40 |

70 Ait Aadel Dam

1967. Inauguration of Ait Aadel Dam.
| 199 | **70** | 25f. grey, blue and green | 55 | 45 |
| 200 | **70** | 40f. bistre and blue | 95 | 45 |

71 Moroccan Scene and Lions Emblem

1967. 50th Anniv of Lions International.
| 201 | **71** | 40f. blue and gold | 55 | 35 |
| 202 | **71** | 1d. green and gold | 1·30 | 55 |

1967. Moroccan Red Cross. As T **65**. Mult.
| 203 | | 60f.+5f. Necklace | 1·20 | 1·20 |
| 204 | | 1d.+10f. Two bracelets | 2·30 | 2·20 |

72 Three Hands and Pickaxe

1967. Communal Development Campaign.
| 205 | **72** | 25f. green | 45 | 15 |

73 I.T.Y. Emblem

1967. International Tourist Year.
| 206 | **73** | 1d. blue and cobalt | 1·00 | 55 |

74 Arrow and Map

1967. Mediterranean Games, Tunis.
| 207 | **74** | 25f. multicoloured | 45 | 25 |
| 208 | **74** | 40f. multicoloured | 60 | 25 |

75 Horse-jumping

1967. International Horse Show.
| 209 | **75** | 40f. multicoloured | 55 | 30 |
| 210 | **75** | 1d. multicoloured | 95 | 55 |

1967. Agricultural Products (4th issue). As T **59**.
| 211 | | 40f. mult (Cotton plant) | 75 | 40 |

76 Human Rights Emblem

1968. Human Rights Year.
| 212 | **76** | 25f. slate | 45 | 25 |
| 213 | **76** | 1d. lake | 55 | 40 |

77 Msouffa Woman

1968. Moroccan Costumes. Multicoloured.
214		10f. Ait Moussa or Ali	75	25
215		15f. Ait Mouhad	95	40
216		25f. Barquemaster of Rabat-Sale	95	55
217		25f. Townsman	1·20	55
218		40f. Townswoman	1·20	70
219		60f. Royal Mokhazni	2·00	90
220		1d. Type **77**	2·00	1·10
221		1d. Riff	1·90	1·10
222		1d. Zemmour woman	2·75	1·30
223		1d. Meknassa	2·50	80

78 King Hassan

1968
224	**78**	1f. multicoloured	10	10
225	**78**	2f. multicoloured	10	10
226	**78**	5f. multicoloured	10	10
227	**78**	10f. multicoloured	30	10
228	**78**	15f. multicoloured	30	10
229	**78**	20f. multicoloured	30	10
230	**78**	25f. multicoloured	30	10
231	**78**	30f. multicoloured	45	10
232	**78**	35f. multicoloured	55	25
233	**78**	40f. multicoloured	55	10
234	**78**	50f. multicoloured	75	10
235	**78**	60f. multicoloured	95	25
236	**78**	70f. multicoloured	4·50	90
237	**78**	75f. multicoloured	1·20	25
238	**78**	80f. multicoloured	1·20	25
239	-	90f. multicoloured	1·80	45
240	-	1d. multicoloured	2·20	25
241	-	2d. multicoloured	3·00	55
242	-	3d. multicoloured	6·00	1·10
243	-	5d. multicoloured	10·00	2·75
Nos. 239/43 bear a similar portrait of King Hassan, but are larger, 26½×40½ mm.

79 Red Crescent Nurse and Child

1968. 20th Anniv of W.H.O.
244	**79**	25f. brown, red and blue	40	10
245	**79**	40f. brown, red and slate	55	20

1968. Red Crescent. Moroccan Jewellery. As T 65. Multicoloured.
246		25f. Pendant brooch	1·00	55
247		40f. Bracelet	1·50	70

80 Rotary Emblem, Conference Building and Map

1968. Rotary Int District Conf, Casablanca.
248	**80**	40f. gold, blue and green	75	25
249	**80**	1d. gold, ultramarine and blue	1·10	45

81 Belt Pattern

1968. "The Belts of Fez". Designs showing ornamental patterns.
250	**81**	25f. multicoloured	2·30	95
251	-	40f. multicoloured	2·75	1·40
252	-	60f. multicoloured	4·00	2·10
253	-	1d. multicoloured	7·50	4·25

82 Princess Lalla Meryem

1968. World Children's Day. Multicoloured.
254		25f. Type **82**	50	25
255		40f. Princess Lalla Asmaa	75	40
256		1d. Crown Prince Sidi Moham-med	1·50	90

83 Wrestling

1968. Olympic Games, Mexico. Multicoloured.
257		15f. Type **83**	40	25
258		20f. Basketball	45	40
259		25f. Cycling	70	40
260		40f. Boxing	95	45
261		60f. Running	1·50	55
262		1d. Football	1·90	70

84 Silver Crown

1968. Ancient Moroccan Coins.
263	**84**	20f. silver and purple	75	45
264	-	25f. gold and purple	95	55
265	-	40f. silver and green	1·70	80
266	-	60f. gold and red	2·00	90

COINS: 25f. Gold dinar; 40f. Silver dirham; 60f. Gold piece. See also Nos. 270/1.

85 Costumes of Zagora, South Morocco

1969. Traditional Women's Costumes. Mult.
267		15f. Type **85** (postage)	1·70	90
268		25f. Ait Adidou costumes	2·40	1·10
269		1d. Ait Ouaouzguit costumes (air)	3·25	1·40

1969. Eighth Anniv of Coronation of Hassan II. As T **84** (silver coins).
270		1d. silver and blue	5·25	1·80
271		5d. silver and violet	11·50	6·75

COINS: 1d. One dirham coin of King Mohammed V; 5d. One dirham coin of King Hassan II.

86 Hands "reading" Braille on Map

1969. Protection of the Blind Week.
272	**86**	25f.+10f. multicoloured	55	25

87 "Actor"

1969. World Theatre Day.
273	**87**	1d. multicoloured	60	40

1969. 50th Anniv of League of Red Cross Societies. Moroccan Jewellery as T 65. Mult.
274		25f.+5f. Bracelets	1·30	70
275		40f.+10f. Pendant	2·00	90

89 King Hassan II

1969. King Hassan's 40th Birthday.
276	**89**	1d. multicoloured	1·50	60

MS277 75×105 mm. **89** 1d. multicoloured (sold at 2d.50) — 80·00 | 65·00

مؤتمر القمة الاسلامى
الرباط ١٠ رجب ١٣٨٩

(90)

1969. Islamic Summit Conf, Rabat (1st issue). No. 240 optd with T **90**.
278		1d. multicoloured	5·50	4·00

91 Mahatma Gandhi

1969. Birth Centenary of Mahatma Gandhi.
279	**91**	40f. brown and lavender	95	45

92 I.L.O. Emblem

1969. 50th Anniv of I.L.O.
280	**92**	50f. multicoloured	55	40

93 King Hassan on Horseback

1969. Islamic Summit Conference, Rabat (2nd issue).
281	**93**	1d. multicoloured	1·50	60

94 "Spahi Horseman" (Haram al Glaoui)

1970. Moroccan Art.
282	**94**	1d. multicoloured	1·40	60

1970. Flood Victims Relief Fund. Nos. 227/8 surch.
283	**78**	10f.+25f. multicoloured	4·50	4·50
284	**78**	15f.+25f. multicoloured	4·25	4·25

96 Drainage System, Fez

1970. 50th Congress of Public and Municipal Health Officials, Rabat.
285	**96**	60f. multicoloured	55	25

97 "Dance of the Guedra" (P. Beaubrun)

1970. Folklore Festival, Marrakesh.
286	**97**	40f. multicoloured	95	20

1970. Red Crescent. Moroccan Jewellery as T **65**. Multicoloured.
287		25f.+5f. Necklace	1·20	95
288		50f.+10t. Pendant	2·00	1·60

1970. Opening of Moroccan Postal Museum, Rabat. Sheet 244×120 mm containing Nos. 214/23 in se-tenant block of 10. Multicoloured.
MS289 Sold at 10d — 25·00 | 25·00

1970. Population Census. No. 189 surch 1970 0,25 and Arabic inscr.
290		25f. on 60f. multicoloured	55	40

99 Dish Aerial, Souk el Arba des Sehoul Communications Station

1970. 17th Anniv of Revolution.
291	**99**	1d. multicoloured	95	55

100 Ruddy Shelduck

1970. Nature Protection. Wild Birds. Multicoloured.
292		25f. Type **100**	1·20	50
293		40f. Houbara bustard	1·80	70

101 I.E.Y. Emblem and Moroccan with Book

1970. International Education Year.
294	**101**	60f. multicoloured	95	45

102 Symbols of U.N.

1970. 25th Anniv of U.N.O.
295	**102**	50f. multicoloured	75	40

103 League Emblem, Map and Laurel

1970. 25th Anniv of Arab League.
296	**103**	50f. multicoloured	55	40

104 Olive Grove and Extraction Plant

1970. World Olive-oil Production Year.
297	**104**	50f. black, brown & green	95	45

105 Es Sounna Mosque

1971. Restoration of Es Sounna Mosque, Rabat.
298	**105**	60f. multicoloured	75	40

106 "Heart" within Horse

1971. European and North African Heart Week.
299	**106**	50f. multicoloured	55	25

107 King Hassan II and Dam

1971. Tenth Anniv of King Hassan's Accession.
300	**107**	25f. multicoloured	55	25

MS301 115×100 mm. No. 300×4 (sold at 2d.50) — 3·50 | 3·50

108 Palestine on Globe

1971. Palestine Week.
302 **108** 25f.+10f. multicoloured   55   25

1971. Red Crescent, Moroccan Jewellery. As T **65**. Multicoloured.
303 25f.+5f. "Arrow-head" brooch   1·50   90
304 40f.+10f. Square pendant   2·00   1·10

109 Hands holding Peace Dove

1971. Racial Equality Year.
305 **109** 50f. multicoloured   95   35

110 Musical Instrument

1971. Protection of the Blind Week.
306 **110** 40f.+10f. multicoloured   80   40

111 Children at Play

1971. International Children's Day.
307 **111** 40f. multicoloured   55   25

112 Shah Mohammed Reza Pahlavi of Iran

1971. 2,500th Anniv of Persian Empire.
308 **112** 1d. multicoloured   95   55

113 Aerial View of Mausoleum

1971. Mausoleum of Mohammed V. Multicoloured.
309 25f. Type **113**   40   25
310 50f. Tomb of Mohammed V   55   40
311 1d. Interior of Mausoleum (vert)   1·30   70

114 Football and Emblem

1971. Mediterranean Games, Izmir, Turkey. Multicoloured.
312 40f. Type **114**   75   45
313 60f. Athlete and emblem   95   45

115 A.P.U. Emblem

1971. 25th Anniv of Founding of Arab Postal Union at Sofar Conference.
314 **115** 25f. red, blue & light blue   45   25

116 Sun and Landscape

1971. 50th Anniv of Sherifian Phosphates Office.
315 **116** 70f. multicoloured   75   40

117 Torch and Book Year Emblem

1972. International Book Year.
316 **117** 1d. multicoloured   1·20   35

118 Lottery Symbol

1972. Creation of National Lottery.
317 **118** 25f. gold, black and brown   30   10

119 Bridge of Sighs

1972. UNESCO "Save Venice" Campaign. Multicoloured.
318 25f. Type **119**   25   20
319 50f. St. Mark's Basilica (horiz)   45   25
320 1d. Lion of St. Marks (horiz)   1·00   50

120 Mizmar (double-horned flute)

1972. Protection of the Blind Week.
321 **120** 25f.+10f. multicoloured   75   75

121 Bridge and Motorway

1972. Second African Highways Conference, Rabat.
322 **121** 75f. multicoloured   95   45

122 Moroccan Stamp of 1969, and Postmark

1972. Stamp Day.
323 **122** 1d. multicoloured   75   40

1972. Red Crescent. Moroccan Jewellery. As T **65**. Multicoloured.
324 25f.+5f. Jewelled bangles   1·20   1·20
325 70f.+10f. Filigree pendant   1·70   1·40

123 "Betrothal of Imilchil" (Tayeb Lahlou)

1972. Folklore Festival, Marrakesh.
326 **123** 60f. multicoloured   1·00   55

124 Dove on African Map

1972. Ninth Organization of African Unity Summit Conference, Rabat.
327 **124** 25f. multicoloured   45   15

125 Polluted Beach

1972. U.N. Environmental Conservation Conference, Stockholm.
328 **125** 50f. multicoloured   55   25

126 Running

1972. Olympic Games, Munich.
329 **126** 25f. red, pink and black   30   25
330 - 50f. violet, lilac and black   45   25
331 - 75f. green, yellow & black   75   40
332 - 1d. blue, lt blue & black   1·00   65
DESIGNS: 50f. Wrestling; 75f. Football; 1d. Cycling.

127 "Sonchus pinnatifidus"

1972. Moroccan Flowers (1st series). Multicoloured.
333 25f. Type **127**   65   15
334 40f. "Amberboa crupinoides"   1·00   40
   See also Nos. 375/6.

128 Sand Gazelle

1972. Nature Protection. Fauna. Multicoloured.
335 25f. Type **128**   1·50   70
336 40f. Barbary sheep   2·50   90

129 Rabat Carpet

1972. Moroccan Carpets (1st series). Multicoloured
337 50f. Type **129**   1·20   55
338 75f. Rabat carpet with "star-shaped" centre   1·80   80
   See also Nos. 380/1, 406/7, 433/4 and 513.

130 Mother and Child with U.N. Emblem

1972. International Children's Day.
339 **130** 75f. blue, yellow and green   55   25

131 "Postman" and "Stamp"

1973. Stamp Day.
340 **131** 25f. multicoloured   45   25

132 Global Weather Map

1973. Centenary of W.M.O.
341 **132** 70f. multicoloured   95   45

133 King Hassan and Arms

1973
342 **133** 1f. multicoloured   10   10
343 **133** 2f. multicoloured   10   10
344 **133** 5f. multicoloured   10   10
345 **133** 10f. multicoloured   10   10
346 **133** 15f. multicoloured   10   10
347 **133** 20f. multicoloured   30   10
348 **133** 25f. multicoloured   30   10
349 **133** 30f. multicoloured   30   10
350 **133** 35f. multicoloured   45   25
351 **133** 40f. multicoloured   6·00   80
352 **133** 50f. multicoloured   55   10
353 **133** 60f. multicoloured   75   10
354 **133** 70f. multicoloured   55   10
355 **133** 75f. multicoloured   70   25
356 **133** 80f. multicoloured   75   55
357 **133** 90f. multicoloured   95   25
358 **133** 1d. multicoloured   2·50   25
359 **133** 2d. multicoloured   5·50   80
360 **133** 3d. multicoloured   7·25   1·40
361 **133** 5d. multicoloured (brown background)   5·25   1·40
361a **133** 5d. multicoloured (pink background)   5·25   1·40

مناظرة السياحة 1973

(134)

1973. Nat Tourist Conference. Nos. 324/5 surch with T **134**.
362 **65** 25f. on 5f. multicoloured   3·00   3·00
363 **65** 70f. on 10f. multicoloured   3·00   3·00
   On No. 363 the Arabic text is arranged in one line.

135 Tambours

1973. Protection of the Blind Week.
364   **135**   70f.+10f. multicoloured   95   70

136 Kaaba, Mecca, and Mosque, Rabat

1973. Prophet Mohammed's Birthday.
365   **136**   25f. multicoloured   45   10

137 Roses and M'Gouna

1973. M'Gouna Rose Festival.
366   **137**   25f. multicoloured   75   25

138 Handclasp and Torch

1973. Tenth Anniv of Organization of African Unity.
367   **138**   70f. multicoloured   55   25

139 Folk-dancers

1973. Folklore Festival, Marrakesh. Multicoloured.
368   50f. Type **139**   65   25
369   1d. Folk-musicians   1·00   45

1973. Red Crescent. Moroccan Jewellery. As T **65**. Multicoloured.
370   25f.+5f. Locket   1·60   90
371   70f.+10f. Bracelet inlaid with pearls   1·90   1·10

140 Solar System

1973. 500th Birth Anniv of Nicholas Copernicus.
372   **140**   70f. multicoloured   95   40

141 Microscope

1973. 25th Anniv of W.H.O.
373   **141**   70f. multicoloured   75   25

142 Interpol Emblem and Fingerprint

1973. 50th Anniv of International Criminal Police Organization (Interpol).
374   **142**   70f. multicoloured   55   25

1973. Moroccan Flowers (2nd series). As T **127**. Multicoloured.
375   25f. "Chrysanthemum carinatum" (horiz)   1·10   45
376   1d. "Amberboa muricata"   1·70   70

143 Striped Hyena

1973. Nature Protection. Multicoloured.
377   25f. Type **143**   1·70   45
378   50f. Eleonora's falcon (vert)   4·00   1·10

144 Map and Arrows

1973. Meeting of Maghreb Committee for Co-ordination of Posts and Telecommunications, Tunis.
379   **144**   25f. multicoloured   55   25

1973. Moroccan Carpets (2nd series). As T **129**. Multicoloured.
380   25f. Carpet from the High Atlas   1·20   45
381   70f. Tazenakht carpet   1·80   70

145 Golf Club and Ball

1974. International "Hassan II Trophy" Golf Grand Prix, Rabat.
382   **145**   70f. multicoloured   1·50   70

المؤتمر الاسلامي - لاهور
١٣٩٤

(146)

1974. Islamic Summit Conference, Lahore, Pakistan. No. 281 optd with T **146**.
383   1d. multicoloured   4·00   2·10

147 Human Rights Emblem

1974. 25th Anniv (1973) of Declaration of Human Rights.
384   **147**   70f. multicoloured   55   25

148 Vanadinite

1974. Moroccan Mineral Sources. Multicoloured.
385   25f. Type **148**   2·75   90
386   70f. Erythrine   4·25   1·40

149 Marrakesh Minaret

1974. 173rd District of Rotary International Annual Conference, Marrakesh.
387   **149**   70f. multicoloured   95   45

150 U.P.U. Emblem and Congress Dates

1974. Centenary of U.P.U.
388   **150**   25f. black, red and green   45   25
389   -   1d. multicoloured   95   45
DESIGN—HORIZ: 1d. Commemorative scroll.

151 Drummers and Dancers

1974. 15th Folklore Festival, Marrakesh. Multicoloured
390   25f. Type **151**   75   25
391   70f. Juggler with woman   1·50   65

152 Environmental Emblem and Scenes

1974. World Environmental Day.
392   **152**   25f. multicoloured   45   15

154 Flintlock Pistol

1974. Red Crescent. Moroccan Firearms. Multicoloured
397   25f.+5f. Type **154**   95   90
398   70f.+10f. Gunpowder box   1·50   1·50

155 Stamps, Postmark and Magnifying Glass

1974. Stamp Day.
399   **155**   70f. multicoloured   75   25

الاحصاء الفلاحى

1,00

(156)

1974. No. D393 surch with T **156**.
400   1d. on 5f. orange, green & blk   2·30   1·50

157 World Cup Trophy

1974. World Cup Football Championship, West Germany.
401   **157**   1d. multicoloured   1·50   80

158 Erbab (two-string fiddle)

1974. Blind Week.
402   **158**   70f.+10f. multicoloured   1·50   70
See also No. 423.

1974. 8th International Blood Donors' Organization Federation Congress. No. MS289 optd 8 CONGRES DE LA F.I.O.D.S.
MS403   244×120 mm. (Sold at 20d.)   35·00   35·00

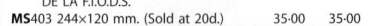

160 Double-spurred Francolin

1974. Moroccan Animals. Multicoloured.
404   25f. Type **160**   75   35
405   70f. Leopard (horiz)   1·20   55

1974. Moroccan Carpets (3rd series). As T **129**. Multicoloured.
406   25f. Zemmour carpet   75   25
407   1d. Beni M'Guild carpet   1·50   65

162 Jasmine

1975. Flowers (1st series). Multicoloured.
408   25f. Type **162**   70   25
409   35f. Orange lilies   1·00   40
410   70f. Poppies   1·50   55
411   90f. Carnations   2·00   80
See also Nos. 417/20.

163 Aragonite

1975. Minerals. Multicoloured.
412   50f. Type **163**   2·10   70
413   1d. Agate   3·75   1·10
See also Nos. 543 and 563/4.

1975. Red Crescent. Moroccan Jewellery. As T **65**. Multicoloured.
414   25f.+5f. Pendant   95   90
415   70f.+10f. Earring   1·50   1·20

165 "The Water-carrier" (Feu Taieb-Lalou)

1975. "Moroccan Painters".
416   **165**   1d. multicoloured   1·40   50

1975. Flowers (2nd series). As T **162**. Mult.
417   10f. Daisies   30   25
418   50f. Pelargoniums   75   25
419   60f. Orange blossom   1·20   60
420   1d. Pansies   1·50   90

166 Collector with Stamp Album

1975. Stamp Day.
421	**166**	40f. multicoloured	45	10

167 Dancer with Rifle

1975. 16th Nat Folklore Festival, Marrakesh.
422	**167**	1d. multicoloured	1·20	45

1975. Blind Week. As T 158. Multicoloured.
423	1d. Mandolin	45	10

168 "Animals in Forest" (child's drawing)

1975. Children's Week.
424	**168**	25f. multicoloured	50	20

169 Games Emblem and Athletes

1975. 7th Mediterranean Games, Algiers.
425	**169**	40f. multicoloured	55	25

170 Waldrapp

1975. Fauna. Multicoloured.
426	40f. Type **170**	2·40	55
427	1d. Caracal (vert)	2·40	85

See also Nos. 470/1.

1975. "Green March" (1st issue). Nos. 370/1 optd 1975 and Arabic inscr.
428	25f. (+ 5f.) multicoloured	3·00	2·75
429	70f. (+ 10f.) multicoloured	3·00	2·75

The premiums on the stamps are obliterated.

172 King Mohammed V greeting Crowd

1975. 20th Anniv of Independence. Mult.
430	40f. Type **172**	55	25
431	1d. King Hassan (vert)	95	55
432	1d. King Hassan V wearing fez (vert)	90	55
MS432a	188×96 mm. Nos. 430/2	22·00	22·00

1975. Moroccan Carpets (4th series). As T 129. Multicoloured.
433	25f. Ouled Besseba carpet	1·00	55
434	1d. Ait Ouaouzguid carpet	1·80	75

See also Nos. 485/7 and 513.

173 Marchers crossing Desert

1975. "Green March" (2nd issue).
435	**173**	40f. multicoloured	45	25

174 Fez Coin of 1883/4

1976. Moroccan Coins (1st series). Multicoloured.
436	5f. Type **174**	45	40
437	15f. Rabat silver coin 1774/5	65	25
438	35f. Sabta coin, 13/14th centuries	1·40	55
439	40f. Type **174**	55	25
440	50f. As No. 437	95	45
441	65f. As No. 438	95	55
442	1d. Sabta coin, 12/13th centuries	1·30	70

See also Nos. 458/67a.
For Nos. 439/40 in smaller size, see Nos. 520/b.

175 Interior of Mosque

1976. Millennium of Ibn Zaidoun Mosque. Mult.
443	40f. Type **175**	45	10
444	65f. Interior archways (vert)	75	40

176 Moroccan Family

1976. Family Planning.
445	**176**	40f. multicoloured	45	25

177 Bou Anania College, Fez

1976. Moroccan Architecture.
446	**177**	1d. multicoloured	95	45

178 Temple Sculpture

1976. Borobudur Temple Preservation Campaign. Multicoloured.
447	40f. Type **178**	70	25
448	1d. View of Temple	1·80	35

179 Dome of the Rock, Jerusalem

1976. 6th Anniv of Islamic Conference.
449	**179**	1d. multicoloured	95	25

1976. Red Crescent. Moroccan Jewellery. As T 65. Multicoloured.
450	40f. Jewelled purse	95	70
451	1d. Jewelled pectoral	1·50	90

180 George Washington, King Hassan I, Statue of Liberty and Mausoleum of Mohammed V

1976. Bicentenary of American Revolution. Mult.
452	40f. Flags of U.S.A. and Morocco (horiz)	75	55
453	1d. Type **180**	1·50	80

181 Wrestling

1976. Olympic Games, Montreal. Multicoloured.
454	35f. Type **181**	45	10
455	40f. Cycling	65	35
456	50f. Boxing	1·10	60
457	1d. Running	1·60	90

1976. Moroccan Coins (2nd series). As T 174. Multicoloured.
458	5f. Medieval silver mohur	45	10
459	10f. Gold mohur	40	10
460	15f. Gold coin	45	10
461	20f. Gold coin (different)	60	35
461a	25f. As No. 437	5·25	90
462	30f. As No. 459	60	35
463	35f. Silver dinar	1·00	45
464	60f. As No. 458	75	25
465	70f. Copper coin	1·60	75
466	75f. As No. 463	95	30
466a	80f. As No. 460	9·00	1·80
467	2d. As No. 465	2·50	70
467a	3d. As No. 461	14·00	2·30

182 Early and Modern Telephones with Dish Aerial

1976. Telephone Centenary.
468	**182**	1d. multicoloured	95	25

183 Gold Medallion

1976. Blind Week.
469	**183**	50f. multicoloured	55	25

1976. Birds. As T 170. Multicoloured.
470	40f. Dark chanting goshawk (vert)	2·50	90
471	1d. Purple swamphen (vert)	3·75	1·40

185 King Hassan, Emblems and Map

1976. 1st Anniv of "Green March".
472	**185**	40f. multicoloured	95	45

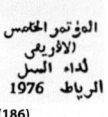

(**186**)

1976. Fifth African Tuberculosis Conference. Nos. 414/15 optd with T 186.
473	25f. multicoloured	2·50	2·40
474	70f. multicoloured	3·00	2·75

187 Globe and Peace Dove

1976. Conference of Non-Aligned Countries, Colombo.
475	**187**	1d. red, black and blue	55	25

188 African Nations Cup

1976. African Nations Football Championship.
476	**188**	1d. multicoloured	75	40

189 Letters encircling Globe

1977. Stamp Day.
477	**189**	40f. multicoloured	45	10

190 "Aeonium arboreum"

1977. Flowers. Multicoloured.
478	40f. Type **190**	75	45
479	50f. "Malope trifida" (24×38 mm)	2·75	90
480	1d. "Hesperolaburnum platyclarpum"	1·50	70

191 Ornamental Candle Lamps

1977. Procession of the Candles, Sale.
481	**191**	40f. multicoloured	55	25

(**192**)

1977. Cherry Festival. No. D394 surch with T 192.
482	40f. on 10f. Cherries	95	45

193 Map and Emblem

1977. 5th Congress. Organization of Arab Towns.
483	**193**	50f. multicoloured	45	10

194 A.P.U. Emblem

1977. 25th Anniv of Arab Postal Union.
484	**194**	1d. multicoloured	75	25

1977. Moroccan Carpets (5th series). As T 129. Multicoloured.
485		35f. Marmoucha carpet	45	25
486		40f. Ait Haddou carpet	75	25
487		1d. Henbel rug, Sale	1·20	55

195 Zither

1977. Blind Week.
488	**195**	1d. multicoloured	1·50	45

196 Mohammed Ali Jinnah

1977. Birth Centenary of Mohammed Ali Jinnah.
489	**196**	70f. multicoloured	55	25

197 Marcher with Flag

1977. 2nd Anniv of "Green March".
490	**197**	1d. multicoloured	75	25

198 Assembly Hall

1977. Opening of House of Representatives.
491	**198**	1d. multicoloured	75	25
MS492		121×86 mm. No. 491 (sold at 3d.)	3·75	3·75

199 Silver Brooch

1977. Red Crescent.
493	**199**	1d. multicoloured	2·75	90

200 Bowl with Funnel

1978. Moroccan Copperware. Multicoloured.
494		40f. Type **200**	45	25
495		1d. Bowl with cover	1·20	55

201 Development Emblem

1978. Sahara Development. Multicoloured.
496		40f. Type **201**	45	25

497		1d. Fishes in net and camels at oasis (horiz)	1·00	40

202 Decorative Pot with Lid

1978. Blind Week. Multicoloured.
498		1d. Type **202**	95	40
499		1d. Decorative jar	1·00	40

203 Map and Red Cross within Red Crescent

1978. 10th Conference of Arab Red Crescent and Red Cross Societies.
500	**203**	1d. red and black	75	40

204 View of Fez

1978. Rotary International Meeting, Fez.
501	**204**	1d. multicoloured	75	40

205 Dome of the Rock

1978. Palestine Welfare.
502	**205**	5f. multicoloured	30	10
503	**205**	10f. multicoloured	30	10

206 Flautist and Folk Dancers

1978. National Folklore Festival, Marrakesh.
504	**206**	1d. multicoloured	2·00	70

207 Sugar Field and Crushing Plant

1978. Sugar Industry.
505	**207**	40f. multicoloured	45	25

208 Yacht

1978. World Sailing Championships.
506	**208**	1d. multicoloured	95	45

209 Tree, Tent and Scout Emblem

1978. Pan-Arab Scout Festival, Rabat.
507	**209**	40f. multicoloured	45	25

210 Moulay Idriss

1978. Moulay Idriss Great Festival.
508	**210**	40f. multicoloured	45	25

211 Human Rights Emblem

1978. 30th Anniv of Declaration of Human Rights.
509	**211**	1d. multicoloured	75	25

212 Houses in Agadir

1979. Southern Moroccan Architecture (1st series). Multicoloured.
510		40f. Type **212**	45	25
511		1d. Old fort at Marrakesh	1·00	25

See also Nos. 536 and 562.

213 Player, Football and Cup

1979. Mohammed V Football Cup.
512	**213**	40f. multicoloured	45	25

1979. Moroccan Carpets (6th series). As T 129. Multicoloured.
513		40f. Marmoucha carpet	75	25

214 Decorated Pot

1979. Blind Week.
514	**214**	1d. multicoloured	1·50	70

215 "Procession from a Mosque"

1979. Paintings by Mohamed Ben Ali Rbati. Mult.
515		40f. Type **215**	45	25
516		1d. "Religious Ceremony in a Mosque" (horiz)	1·00	40

216 Coffee Pot and Heater

1979. Red Cresent. Brassware. Multicoloured.
517		40f. Engraved circular boxes	45	25
518		1d. Type **216**	1·50	55

217 Costumed Girls

1979. National Folklore Festival, Marrakesh.
519	**217**	40f. multicoloured	45	25

1979. Moroccan Coins. As T 174, but smaller, 17½×22½ mm.
520		40f. multicoloured	50	10
520b		50f. multicoloured	60	10

218 Curved Dagger in Jewelled Sheath

1979. Ancient Weapons.
521	**218**	1d. black and yellow	95	25

219 King Hassan II

1979. King Hassan's 50th Birthday.
522	**219**	1d. multicoloured	95	25

220 Festival Emblem

1979. 4th Arab Youth Festival, Rabat.
523	**220**	1d. multicoloured	95	25

221 King Hassan II

1979. "25th Anniv of Revolution of King and People".
524	**221**	1d. multicoloured	55	25

222 World Map superimposed on Open Book

1979. 50th Anniv of Int Bureau of Education.
525	**222**	1d. brown and yellow	75	25

223 Pilgrims in Wuquf, Arafat

1979. Pilgrimage to Mecca.
526	**223**	1d. multicoloured	95	45

استرجاع اقليم وادى الذهب
14–8–1979

(224)

1979. Recovery of Oued Eddahab Province. Design as No. 497, with face value amended (40f.), optd with T 224.
527		40f. multicoloured	45	10
528		1d. multicoloured	1·00	45

225 Centaurium

1979. Flowers. Multicoloured.
529		40f. Type **225**	45	10
530		1d. "Leucanthemum catanance"	1·40	25

226 Children around Globe

1979. International Year of the Child.
531	**226**	40f. multicoloured	1·00	40

227 European Otter

1979. Wildlife. Multicoloured.
532		40f. Type **227**	1·30	55
533		1d. Moussier's redstart	2·50	55

228 Traffic Signs

1980. Road Safety. Multicoloured.
534		40f. Type **228**	30	10
535		1d. Children at crossing	65	25

229 Fortress

1980. South Moroccan Architecture (2nd series).
536	**229**	1d. multicoloured	75	25

230 Copper Bowl with Lid

1980. Red Crescent. Multicoloured.
537		50f. Type **230**	95	45
538		70f. Copper kettle and brazier	1·50	45

231 Pot

1980. Blind Week.
539	**231**	40f. multicoloured	40	10

232 Mechanized Sorting Office, Rabat

1980. Stamp Day.
540	**232**	40f. multicoloured	45	10

233 World Map and Rotary Emblem

1980. 75th Anniv of Rotary International.
541	**233**	1d. multicoloured	75	25

234 Leather Bag and Cloth

1980. 4th Textile and Leather Exhibition, Casablanca.
542	**234**	1d. multicoloured	75	25

1980. Minerals (2nd series). As T 163. Mult.
543		40f. Gypsum	1·90	70

235 Peregrine Falcon

1980. Hunting with Falcon.
544	**235**	40f. multicoloured	1·90	70

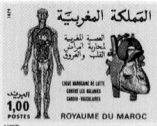

236 Diagram of Blood Circulation and Heart

1980. Campaign against Cardiovascular Diseases.
545	**236**	1d. multicoloured	95	35

237 Decade Emblem and Human Figures

1980. Decade for Women.
546	**237**	40f. mauve and blue	45	10
547	-	1d. multicoloured	1·00	35

DESIGN: 1d. Decade and United Nations emblems.

238 Harnessed Horse

1980. Ornamental Harnesses. Multicoloured.
548		40f. Harnessed horse (different)	45	25
549		1d. Type **238**	1·00	40

239 Satellite orbiting Earth and Dish Aerial

1980. World Meteorological Day.
550	**239**	40f. multicoloured	45	10

240 Light Bulb and Fuel Can

1980. Energy Conservation. Multicoloured.
551		40f. Type **240**	30	10
552		1d. Hand holding petrol pump	1·20	25

241 Conference Emblem

1980. World Tourism Conference, Manila.
553	**241**	40f. multicoloured	30	10

242 Tree bridging Straits of Gibraltar

1980. European–African Liaison over the Straits of Gibraltar.
554	**242**	1d. multicoloured	95	45

243 Flame and Marchers

1980. 5th Anniv of "The Green March".
555	**243**	1d. multicoloured	95	35

244 Holy Kaaba, Mecca

1980. 1400th Anniv of Hegira. Multicoloured.
556		40f. Type **244**	30	10
557		1d. Mosque, Mecca	75	25
MS557a	137×91 mm. Nos. 555/6		2·50	2·50

245 "Senecio antheuphorbium"

1980. Flowers. Multicoloured.
558		40f. Type **245**	1·30	35
559		1d. "Periploca laevigata"	2·50	65

246 Painting by Aherdan

1980. Paintings.
560	-	40f. bistre and brown	30	10
561	**246**	1d. multicoloured	95	25

DESIGN: 40f. Composition of bird and feathers.

247 Nejjarine Fountain, Fez

1981. Moroccan Architecture (3rd series).
562	**247**	40f. multicoloured	30	10

1981. Minerals (3rd series). Vert designs as T 163. Multicoloured.
563		40f. Onyx	1·80	45
564		1d. Malachite-azurite	2·50	1·10

248 King Hassan II

1981. 25th Anniv of Independence. Mult.
565		60f. Type **248**	75	25
566		60f. Map, flags, broken chains and "25"	75	25
567		60f. King Mohammed V.	75	25

249 King Hassan II

1981. 20th Anniv of King Hassan's Coronation.
568	**249**	1d.30 multicoloured	95	45

250 "Source" (Jillali Gharbaoul)

1981. Moroccan Painting.
569	**250**	1d.30 multicoloured	95	40

251 "Anagalis monelli"

1981. Flowers. Multicoloured.
570	40f. Type **251**	60	10
571	70f. "Bubonium intricatum"	1·30	45

252 King Hassan
as Major General

1981. 25th Anniv of Moroccan Armed Forces.
572	**252**	60f. lilac, gold and green	45	25
573	-	60f. multicoloured	45	25
574	-	60f. lilac, gold and green	45	25

DESIGNS: No. 573, Army badge; 574, King Mohammed V (founder).

253 Caduceus
(Telecommunications
and Health)

1981. World Telecommunications Day.
575	**253**	1d.30 multicoloured	95	45

254 Plate with
Pattern

1981. Blind Week. Multicoloured.
576	50f. Type **254**	45	10
577	1d.30 Plate with ship pattern	75	40

255 Musicians and
Dancers

1981. 22nd National Folklore Festival, Marrakesh.
578	**255**	1d.30 multicoloured	1·20	40

256 "Seboula"
Dagger

1981. Ancient Weapons.
579	**256**	1d.30 multicoloured	95	40

257 Pestle and
Mortar

1981. Red Crescent. Moroccan Copperware. Mult.
580	60f. Type **257**	45	25
581	1d.30 Tripod brazier	1·00	40

258 Hands holding
I.Y.D.P. Emblem

1981. International Year of Disabled People.
582	**258**	60f. multicoloured	45	15

259 "Iphiclides
feisthamelii Lotteri"

1981. Butterflies (1st series). Multicoloured.
583	60f. Type **259**	1·90	60
584	1d.30 "Zerynthina rumina africana"	3·75	1·30

See also Nos. 609/10.

260 King Hassan and
Marchers

1981. 6th Anniv of "Green March".
585	**260**	1d.30 multicoloured	95	45

261 Town Buildings and
Congress Emblem

1981. 10th International Twinned Towns Congress, Casablanca.
586	**261**	1d.30 multicoloured	95	50

262 Dome of the
Rock

1981. Palestinian Solidarity Day.
587	**262**	60f. multicoloured	45	10

1981. 12th Arab Summit Conference, Fez. Nos. 502/3 surch 1981 0,40.
588	**205**	40f. on 5f. multicoloured	6·50	5·00
588a	**205**	40f. on 10f. multicoloured	4·75	3·50

264 Terminal
Building and
Runway

1981. 1st Anniv of Mohammed V Airport.
589	**264**	1d.30 multicoloured	95	45

265 Al Massira Dam

1981. Al Massira Dam.
590	**265**	60f. multicoloured	45	20

266 King
Hassan II

1981
591	266	5f. red, blue and gold	10	10
592	266	10f. red, yellow and gold	10	10
593	266	15f. red, green and gold	10	10
594	266	20f. red, pink and gold	10	10
595	266	25f. red, lilac and gold	10	10
596	266	30f. blue, lt blue & gold	10	10
597	266	35f. blue, yellow and gold	10	10
598	266	40f. blue, green and gold	10	10
599	266	50f. blue, pink and gold	30	10
600	266	60f. blue, lilac and gold	30	10
601	266	65f. blue, lilac and gold	30	10
602	266	70f. violet, yellow and gold	30	10
603	266	75f. violet, green and gold	30	15
604	266	80f. violet, pink and gold	30	15
605	266	90f. violet, lilac and gold	45	15
605a	266	1d.25 red, mauve & gold	45	15
605b	266	4d. brown, yell & gold	1·30	55

See also Nos. 624/9, 718/22, 759/61, 866, 895/6, 930 and 940a.

267 Horse Jumping

1981. Equestrian Sports.
606	**267**	1d.30 multicoloured	1·80	45

268 Ait Quaquzguit

1982. Carpets (1st series). Multicoloured.
607	50f. Type **268**	30	10
608	1d.30 Ouled Besseba	95	40

See also Nos. 653/4.

1982. Butterflies and Moths (2nd series). As T 259. Multicoloured.
609	60f. "Celerio oken lineata"	1·70	55
610	1d.30 "Mesoacidalia aglaja lyauteyi"	3·25	1·10

269 Tree and
Emblem

1982. World Forestry Day.
611	**269**	40f. multicoloured	30	10

270 Jug

1982. Blind Week.
612	**270**	1d. multicoloured	55	25

271 Dancers

1982. Popular Art.
613	**271**	1d.40 multicoloured	75	25

272 Candlestick

1982. Red Crescent.
614	**272**	1d.40 multicoloured	95	35

273 Painting by M.
Mezian

1982. Moroccan Painting.
615	**273**	1d.40 multicoloured	95	45

274 Buildings and People
on Graph

1982. Population and Housing Census.
616	**274**	60f. multicoloured	45	25

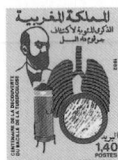

275 Dr. Koch,
Lungs and
Apparatus

1982. Centenary of Discovery of Tubercle Bacillus.
617	**275**	1d.40 multicoloured	1·20	55

276 I.T.U. Emblem

1982. I.T.U. Delegates' Conference, Nairobi.
618	**276**	1d.40 multicoloured	75	25

277 Wheat, Globe,
Sea and F.A.O.
Emblem

1982. World Food Day.
619	**277**	60f. multicoloured	45	15

278 Class XDd Diesel
Locomotive (1956) and
Route Map

1982. Unity Railway.
620 **278** 1d.40 multicoloured 1·20 40

279 A.P.U. Emblem

1982. 30th Anniv of Arab Postal Union.
621 **279** 1d.40 multicoloured 75 25

280 Dome of the
Rock and Map of
Palestine

1982. Palestinian Solidarity.
622 **280** 1d.40 multicoloured 75 25

281 Red Coral

1982. Red Coral of Al Hoceima.
623 **281** 1d.40 multicoloured 1·60 55

1983. Size 25×32 mm but inscribed "1982".
624 **266** 1d. red, blue and gold 45 10
625 **266** 1d.40 brown, lt brown
& gold 45 10
626 **266** 2d. red, green and gold 75 25
627 **266** 3d. brown, yellow and
gold 1·10 30
628 **266** 5d. brown, green and
gold 1·80 70
629 **266** 10d. brown, orange
and gold 3·50 1·30

282 Moroccan
Stamps

1983. Stamp Day.
630 **282** 1d.40 multicoloured 75 25

283 King Hassan
II

1983
631 **283** 1d.40 multicoloured 55 15
632 **283** 2d. multicoloured 75 25
633 **283** 3d. multicoloured 1·00 40
634 **283** 5d. multicoloured 1·70 70
635 **283** 10d. multicoloured 3·50 1·30

284 Decorated Pot

1983. Blind Week.
636 **284** 1d.40 multicoloured 95 35

285 Musicians

1983. Popular Arts.
637 **285** 1d.40 multicoloured 95 45

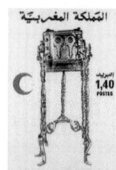

286 Ornamental
Stand

1983. Red Crescent.
638 **286** 1d.40 multicoloured 95 45

287 Commission Emblem

1983. 25th Anniv of Economic Commission for Africa.
639 **287** 1d.40 multicoloured 75 25

288 "Tecoma sp."

1983. Flowers. Multicoloured.
640 60c. Type **288** 70 25
641 1d.40 "Strelitzia sp." 1·80 45

289 King Hassan II, Map and
Sultan of Morocco

1983. 30th Anniv of Revolution.
642 **289** 80c. multicoloured 45 25

290 Games
Emblem and
Stylized Sports

1983. 9th Mediterranean Games, Casablanca.
644 **290** 80c. blue, silver and gold 45 30
645 - 1d. multicoloured 55 35
646 - 2d. multicoloured 1·10 65
MS647 92×151 mm. Nos. 644/6. Imperf.
(sold at 5d) 3·50 3·50
DESIGNS—VERT: 1d. Games emblem. HORIZ: 2d. Stylized
runner.

291 Ploughing

1983. Touiza.
648 **291** 80c. multicoloured 45 25

292 Symbol of "Green
March"

1983. 8th Anniv of "Green March".
649 **292** 80f. multicoloured 45 25

293 Palestinian
formed from Map
and Globe

1983. Palestinian Welfare.
650 **293** 80f. multicoloured 45 20

294 Ouzoud
Waterfall

1983. Ouzoud Waterfall.
651 **294** 80f. multicoloured 45 25

295 Children's
Emblem

1983. Children's Day. Multicoloured.
652 **295** 2d. multicoloured 95 25

1983. Carpets (2nd series). As T 268. Mult.
653 60f. Zemmouri 30 10
654 1d.40 Zemmouri (different) 95 35

296 Transport and W.C.Y.
Emblem

1983. World Communications Year.
655 **296** 2d. multicoloured 1·20 45

297 Views of Jerusalem
and Fez

1984. Twinned Towns.
656 **297** 2d. multicoloured 1·20 40

298 Fennec Fox

1984. Animals. Multicoloured.
657 80f. Type **298** 80 30

658 2d. Lesser Egyptian jerboa 1·80 65

299 Map of League
Members and Emblem

1984. 39th Anniv of League of Arab States.
659 **299** 2d. multicoloured 95 25

(300)

1984. 25th National Folklore Festival, Marrakesh. No. 578
optd with T 300.
660 **255** 1d.30 multicoloured 95 45

301 "Metha viridis"

1984. Flowers. Multicoloured.
661 80f. Type **301** 45 15
662 2d. Aloe 1·20 50

302 Decorated Bowl

1984. Blind Week.
663 **302** 80f. multicoloured 45 25

303 Lidded
Container

1984. Red Crescent.
664 **303** 2d. multicoloured 95 45

304 Sports
Pictograms

1984. Olympic Games, Los Angeles.
665 **304** 2d. multicoloured 95 45

305 Dove carrying
Children

1984. International Child Victims' Day.
666 **305** 2d. multicoloured 95 25

306 U.P.U. Emblem
and Ribbons

1984. Universal Postal Union Day.
667 **306** 2d. multicoloured 75 40

307 Hands holding Ears of Wheat

1984. World Food Day.
668 **307** 80f. multicoloured 70 25

308 Stylized Bird, Airplane and Emblem

1984. 40th Anniv of I.C.A.O.
669 **308** 2d. multicoloured 75 25

309 Inscribed Scroll

1984. 9th Anniv of "Green March".
670 **309** 80f. multicoloured 45 10

311 Flag and Dome of the Rock

1984. Palestinian Welfare.
672 **311** 2d. multicoloured 95 35

312 Emblem and People

1984. 36th Anniv of Human Rights Declaration.
673 **312** 2d. multicoloured 75 25

313 Aidi

1984. Dogs. Multicoloured.
674 80f. Type **313** 1·20 35
675 2d. Sloughi 2·10 75

1984. King Hassan II. Vert design as T 266 inscr '1984'. Size 27×34 mm.
675a 1d.70 lake-brown, azure and gold 60 60

314 Weighing Baby

1985. Infant Survival Campaign.
676 **314** 80f. multicoloured 45 25

315 Children playing in Garden

1985. 1st Moroccan S.O.S. Children's Village.
677 **315** 2d. multicoloured 75 25

316 Sherifian Mail Postal Cancellation, 1892

1985. Stamp Day.
678 **316** 2d. grey, pink and black 95 25
MS679 148×98 mm. **316** 80c.×6, grey, black and (a) emerald; (b) yellow; (c) blue; (d) vermilion; (e) violet; (f) brown (sold at 5d.) 5·00 5·00
   See also Nos. 698/9, 715/16, 757/8, 778/9, 796/7, 818/19, 841/2, 877/8, 910/11 and 924/5.

317 Emblem, Birds, Landscape and Fish

1985. World Environment Day.
680 **317** 80f. multicoloured 45 10

318 Musicians

1985. National Folklore Festival, Marrakesh.
681 **318** 2d. multicoloured 1·20 45

319 Decorated Plate

1985. Blind Week.
682 **319** 80f. multicoloured 45 25

320 Bougainvillea

1985. Flowers. Multicoloured.
683 80f. Type **320** 1·20 55
684 2d. "Hibiscus rosasinensis" 2·50 80

321 Woman in Headdress

1985. Red Crescent.
685 **321** 2d. multicoloured 3·00 90

322 Musicians and Dancers

1985. National Folklore Festival, Marrakesh.
686 **322** 2d. multicoloured 1·50 45

323 Map and Emblem

1985. 6th Pan-Arab Games.
687 **323** 2d. multicoloured 90 25

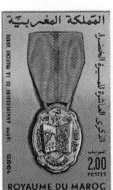

324 Emblem on Globe

1985. 40th Anniv of U.N.O.
688 **324** 2d. multicoloured 1·50 35

325 Emblem

1986. International Youth Year.
689 **325** 2d. multicoloured 1·50 35

326 Medal

1985. 10th Anniv of "Green March".
690 **326** 2d. multicoloured 1·20 35

327 Clasped Hands around Flag

1985. Palestinian Welfare.
691 **327** 2d. multicoloured 95 25

328 "Euphydryas desfontainii"

1985. Butterflies (1st series). Multicoloured.
692 80f. Type **328** 1·40 60
693 2d. "Colotis evagore" 3·25 1·40
   See also Nos. 713/14.

329 Arms

1986. 25th Anniv of King Hassan's Coronation. Multicoloured.
694 80f. Type **329** 55 10
695 2d. King Hassan II (horiz) 1·10 25
MS696 105×90 mm. Nos. 694/5. Imperf 1·50 1·50

330 Emblem

1986. 26th International Military Medicine Congress.
697 **330** 2d. multicoloured 95 25

1986. Stamp Day. As T 316.
698 80f. orange and black 45 10
699 2d. green and black 1·20 25
DESIGNS: 80f. Sherifian postal seal of Maghzen-Safi; 2d. Sherifian postal seal of Maghzen-Safi (different).

331 Vase

1986. Blind Week.
700 **331** 1d. multicoloured 95 25

332 Footballer and Emblem

1986. World Cup Football Championship, Mexico. Multicoloured.
701 1d. Type **332** 95 25
702 2d. Cup, pictogram of footballer and emblem 1·50 65

333 Copper Coffee Pot

1986. Red Crescent.
703 **333** 2d. multicoloured 2·00 70

334 "Warionia saharae"

1986. Flowers. Multicoloured.

704	**334**	1d. Type **334**	1·50	45
705		2d. "Mandragora autumnalis"	3·50	90

335 Emblem

1986. 18th Parachute Championships.

706	**335**	2d. multicoloured	1·50	45

336 Dove and Olive Branch

1986. International Peace Year.

707	**336**	2d. multicoloured	95	45

337 Horsemen

1986. Horse Week.

708	**337**	1d. light brown, pink and brown	1·40	40

338 Book

1986. 11th Anniv of "Green March".

709	**338**	1d. multicoloured	45	10

339 Stylized People and Wheat

1986. Fight against Hunger.

710	**339**	2d. multicoloured	75	25

340 Marrakesh

1986. Aga Khan Architecture Prize.

711	**340**	2d. multicoloured	2·00	45

341 Hands holding Wheat

1986. "1,000,000 Hectares of Grain".

712	**341**	1d. multicoloured	45	10

1986. Butterflies (2nd series). As T 328. Mult.

713		1d. "Elphinstonia charlonia"	1·30	50
714		2d. "Anthocharis belia"	3·25	1·20

1987. Stamp Day. As T 316.

715		1d. blue and black	45	10
716		2d. red and black	75	25

DESIGNS: 1d. Circular postal cancellation of Tetouan; 2d. Octagonal postal cancellation of Tetouan.

الملتقى العالمى الاول لخطباء الجمعة

(342)

1987. Air. 1st World Reunion of Friday Preachers. Optd with T 342.

717	**283**	2d. multicoloured	1·00	70

1987. Size 25×32 mm but inscr "1986".

718	**266**	1d.60 red, brown and gold	50	25
719	**266**	2d.50 red, grey and gold	80	40
720	**266**	6d.50 red, brown and gold	2·10	95
721	**266**	7d. red, brown and gold	2·30	1·00
722	**266**	8d.50 red, lilac and gold	2·75	1·30

343 Sidi Muhammad ben Yusuf addressing Crowd

1987. 40th Anniv of Tangier Conference. Each blue, silver and black.

723	**343**	1d. Type **343**	45	25
724		1d. King Hassan II making speech	45	25
MS725		150×100 mm. Nos. 723/4 (sold at 3d.)	1·50	1·50

344 Copper Lamp

1987. Red Crescent.

726	**344**	2d. multicoloured	95	40

345 Woman with Baby and Packet of Salt being emptied into Beaker

1987. UNICEF Child Survival Campaign.

727	**345**	1d. multicoloured	45	10

346 Decorated Pottery Jug

1987. Blind Week.

728	**346**	1d. multicoloured	45	10

347 "Zygophyllum fontanesii"

1987. Flowers. Multicoloured.

729	**347**	1d. Type **347**	60	10
730		2d. "Otanthus maritimus"	95	25

348 Arabesque from Door, Dar Batha Palace, Fez

1987. Bicentenary of Diplomatic Relations with United States of America.

731	**348**	1d. blue, red and black	45	10

349 Map and King Hassan giving Blood

1987. Blood Transfusion Service.

732	**349**	2d. multicoloured	1·20	45

350 Woman from Melhfa

1987. Sahara Costumes. Multicoloured.

733	**350**	1d. Type **350**	65	25
734		2d. Man from Derraa	1·30	40

351 Emblem and Irrigated Field

1987. 13th International Irrigation and Drainage Congress.

735	**351**	1d. multicoloured	45	25

352 Baby on Hand and Syringe

1987. United Nations Children's Fund Child Survival Campaign.

736	**352**	1d. multicoloured	45	10

353 Azurite

1987. Mineral Industries Congress, Marrakesh. Multicoloured.

737	**353**	1d. Type **353**	1·50	45
738		2d. Wulfenite	2·75	90

354 "12" on Scroll

1987. 12th Anniv of "Green March".

739	**354**	1d. multicoloured	45	25

355 Activities

1987. Armed Forces Social Services Month.

740	**355**	1d. multicoloured	50	10

356 Desert Sparrow

1987. Birds. Multicoloured.

741	**356**	1d. Type **356**	1·20	55
742		2d. Barbary partridge	2·50	80

357 1912 25m. Stamp and Postmark

1987. 75th Anniv of Moroccan Stamps.

743	**357**	3d. mauve, black and green	1·30	55

358 "Cetiosaurus mogrebiensis"

1988. Dinosaur of Tilougguite.

744	**358**	2d. multicoloured	3·25	90

359 King Mohammed V

1988. International Conf on King Mohammed V, Rabat.

745	**359**	2d. multicoloured	95	25

360 Map and Player in Arabesque Frame

1988. 16th African Nations Cup Football Competition.

746	**360**	3d. multicoloured	1·20	45

361 Boy with Horse

1988. Horse Week.

747	**361**	3d. multicoloured	2·20	70

362 Pottery Flask

1988. Blind Week.
748 **362** 3d. multicoloured 1·20 45

363 Anniversary Emblem

1988. 125th Anniv of Red Cross.
749 **363** 3d. black, red and pink 1·50 55

364 "Citrullus colocynthis"

1988. Flowers. Multicoloured.
750 3d.60 Type **364** 1·90 75
751 3d.60 "Calotropis procera" 1·90 75

365 Breastfeeding Baby

1988. UNICEF Child Survival Campaign.
752 **365** 3d. multicoloured 1·90 45

366 Olympic Medals and Rings

1988. Olympic Games, Seoul.
753 **366** 2d. multicoloured 75 25

367 Greater Bustard

1988. Birds. Multicoloured.
754 3d.60 Type **367** 2·40 90
755 3d.60 Greater flamingo 2·40 90

368 "13" on Scroll

1988. 13th Anniv of "Green March".
756 **368** 2d. multicoloured 95 25

1988. Stamp Day. As T 316.
757 3d. brown and black 1·20 45
758 3d. violet and black 1·20 45

DESIGNS: No. 757, Octagonal postal cancellation of Maghzen el Jadida; 758, Circular postal cancel-lation of Maghzen el Jadida.

1988. Size 25×32 mm but inscr "1988".
759 **266** 1d.20 blue, lilac and gold 45 10
760 **266** 3d.60 red and gold 1·20 25
761 **266** 5d.20 brown, bis & gold 1·80 45

369 Housing of the Ksours and Csbaha

1989. Architecture.
762 **369** 2d. multicoloured 75 25

اتحاد المغرب العربي

مراكش-فبراير 89

(370)

1989. Union of Arab Maghreb. No. 631 optd with T 370.
763 **283** 1d.40 multicoloured 55 45

371 King and Bishop with Chess Symbols

1989. 25th Anniv of Royal Moroccan Chess Federation.
764 **371** 2d. multicoloured 1·20 40

372 Copper Vase

1989. Red Crescent.
765 **372** 2d. multicoloured 1·50 35

373 Ceramic Vase

1989. Blind Week.
766 **373** 2d. multicoloured 95 25

374 King Hassan

1989. 60th Birthday of King Hassan II. Mult.
767 2d. Type **374** 95 45
768 2d. King Hassan in robes 1·00 45
MS769 140×105 mm. Nos. 767/8. Imperf. (sold at 5d.) 10·50 10·50

375 "Cerinthe major"

1989. Flowers. Multicoloured.
770 2d. Type **375** 1·20 45
771 2d. "Narcissus papyraceus" 1·20 45

376 Telephone Handset linking Landmarks

1989. World Telecommunications Day.
772 **376** 2d. multicoloured 75 25

377 Gender Symbols forming Globe, Woman and Eggs

1989. 1st World Fertility and Sterility Congress.
773 **377** 2d. multicoloured 95 45

378 Desert Wheatear

1989. Birds. Multicoloured.
774 2d. Type **378** 1·20 45
775 3d. Shore lark 1·50 90

379 House of Representatives

1989. Centenary of Interparliamentary Union.
776 **379** 2d. multicoloured 75 25

380 Scroll

1989. 14th Anniv of "Green March".
777 **380** 3d. multicoloured 1·20 45

1990. Stamp Day. As T 316.
778 2d. orange and black 95 45
779 3d. green and black 1·30 45

DESIGNS: 2d. Round postal cancellation of Casablanca; 3d. Octagonal postal cancellation of Casablanca.

381 Flags forming Map

1990. 1st Anniv of Union of Arab Maghreb.
780 **381** 2d. multicoloured 80 25
MS781 120×85 mm. No. 780 (sold 3d.) 1·60 1·60

382 Oil Press

1990. 3rd World Olive Year. Multicoloured.
782 2d. Type **382** 80 45
783 3d. King Hassan and olives 1·20 55

383 Decorated Pot

1990. Blind Week.
784 **383** 2d. multicoloured 80 30

384 Silver Teapot

1990. Red Crescent.
785 **384** 2d. multicoloured 80 30

385 Arabic Script and Open Book

1990. International Literacy Year.
786 **385** 3d. green, yellow and black 1·20 50

386 Turtle Dove

1990. Birds. Multicoloured.
787 2d. Type **386** 1·10 45
788 3d. Hoopoe (horiz) 1·70 70

387 "15" on Scroll

1990. 15th Anniv of "Green March".
789 **387** 3d. multicoloured 1·20 40

388 "35", Sun's Rays and Flag

1990. 35th Anniv of Independence.
790 **388** 3d. multicoloured 1·00 40

389 Dam

1990
791 **389** 3d. multicoloured 1·20 40

390 Emblem

1990. 10th Anniv of Royal Academy of Morocco.
792 **390** 3d. multicoloured 1·00 40

391 Morse Code Apparatus

1990. 20th Anniv of National Postal Museum. Multicoloured.

793	2d. Type **391**		80	45
794	3d. Horse-drawn mail wagon, 1913		1·30	55
MS795 164×94 mm. Nos. 793/4. Imperf. (sold at 6d.)			3·00	3·00

1991. Stamp Day. As T 316.

796	2d. red and black		80	45
797	3d. blue and black		80	45

DESIGNS: 2d. Round postal cancellation of Rabat; 3d. Octagonal postal cancellation of Rabat.

392 Projects and Emblem

1991. 40th Anniv of United Nations Development Programme.

798	**392**	3d. turquoise, yellow & blk	1·00	40

393 King Hassan

1991. 30th Anniv of Enthronement of King Hassan II. Multicoloured.

799	3d. Type **393**		1·90	70
800	3d. King Hassan in robes		1·90	70
MS801 164×101 mm. Nos. 799/80 (sold at 10d.)			4·25	4·25

394 Mining

1991. 70th Anniv of Mineral Exploitation by Sherifian Phosphates Office.

802	**394**	3d. multicoloured	1·00	45

395 Kettle on Stand

1991. Blind Week.

803	**395**	3d. multicoloured	1·00	55

396 Lantern

1991. Red Crescent.

804	**396**	3d. multicoloured	1·20	55

397 "Cynara humilis"

1991. Flowers. Multicoloured.

805	3d. Type **397**		1·20	55
806	3d. "Pyrus mamorensis"		1·30	55

398 Man

1991. Ouarzazate Costumes. Multicoloured.

807	3d. Type **398**		1·30	45
808	3d. Woman		1·30	45

1991. Inscribed "1991".

809	**266**	1d.35 red, green and gold	45	10

399 Road

1991. 19th World Roads Congress, Marrakesh.

810	**399**	3d. multicoloured	1·00	40

400 Members' Flags and Map

1991. 4th Ordinary Session of Arab Maghreb Union Presidential Council, Casablanca.

811	**400**	3d. multicoloured	1·20	45

401 "16" on Scroll

1991. 16th Anniv of "Green March".

812	**401**	3d. multicoloured	1·20	40

402 White Stork

1991. Birds. Multicoloured.

813	3d. Type **402**		1·90	60
814	3d. European bee eater		1·90	60

403 Figures and Blood Splash

1991. World AIDS Day.

815	**403**	3d. multicoloured	1·00	40

404 Emblem

1991. 20th Anniv of Islamic Conf Organization.

816	**404**	3d. multicoloured	1·00	40

405 Zebra and Map of Africa

1991. African Tourism Year.

817	**405**	3d. multicoloured	1·20	40

1992. Stamp Day. As T 316.

818	3d. green and black		1·30	45
819	3d. violet and black		1·30	45

DESIGNS: No. 818, Circular postal cancellation of Essaouira; No. 819, Octagonal postal cancellation of Essaouira.

406 Satellites around Earth

1992. International Space Year.

820	**406**	3d. multicoloured	1·20	55

407 Bottle

1992. Blind Week.

821	**407**	3d. multicoloured	1·20	55

408 Brass Jug

1992. Red Crescent.

822	**408**	3d. multicoloured	1·20	55

409 Quartz

1992. Minerals. Multicoloured.

823	1d.35 Type **409**		80	45
824	3d.40 Calcite		1·80	90

410 Woman

1992. Tata Costumes. Multicoloured.

825	1d.35 Type **410**		80	25
826	3d.40 Man		1·80	80

411 "Campanula afra"

1992. Flowers. Multicoloured.

827	1d.35 Type **411**		80	25
828	3d.40 "Thymus broussonetii"		1·60	80

412 Olympic Rings and Torch

1992. Olympic Games, Barcelona.

829	**412**	3d.40 multicoloured	1·40	45

413 Map of Africa and Methods of Transport and Communication

1992. Decade of Transport and Communications in Africa.

830	**413**	3d.40 multicoloured	1·60	55

414 La Koutoubia, La Giralda (cathedral bell-tower) and Exhibition Emblem

1992. "Expo '92" World's Fair, Seville.

831	**414**	3d.40 multicoloured	1·40	55

415 Columbus's Fleet and Route Map

1992. 500th Anniv of Discovery of America by Columbus.

832	**415**	3d.40 multicoloured	1·80	65

416 Pin-tailed Sandgrouse

1992. Birds. Multicoloured.

833	3d. Type **416**		1·40	65
834	3d. Griffon vulture ("Gyps fulvus") (vert)		1·40	65

417 "17" on Scroll

1992. 17th Anniv of "Green March".

835	**417**	3d.40 multicoloured	1·60	55

418 Postal Messenger, Route Map and Cancellations

1992. Centenary of Sherifian Post. Multicoloured.
836   1d.35 Type **418**   80   25
837   3d.40 Postal cancellation, "100" on scroll and Sultan Mulay al-Hassan   1·60   65
MS838 165×105 mm. 5d. Postal cancellations, "100" on scroll and Sultan Moulay al-Hassan   2·50   2·50

419 Conference Emblem

1992. International Nutrition Conference, Rome.
839   **419**   3d.40 multicoloured   1·40   75

420 Douglas DC-9 Airliners on Runway

1992. Al Massira Airport, Agadir.
840   **420**   3d.40 multicoloured   1·60   65

1993. Stamp Day. As T 316.
841   1d.70 green and black   80   30
842   3d.80 orange and black   1·60   80
DESIGNS: 1d.70, Round postal cancellation of Tangier; 3d.80, Octagonal postal cancellation of Tangier.

421 Dishes

1993. Blind Week.
843   **421**   4d.40 multicoloured   1·60   40

422 Satellite orbiting Earth

1993. World Meteorological Day.
844   **422**   4d.40 multicoloured   1·90   55

423 Kettle on Stand

1993. Red Crescent.
845   **423**   4d.40 multicoloured   1·60   40

424 Emblem

1993. World Telecommunications Day.
846   **424**   4d.40 multicoloured   1·60   40

425 Woman extracting Argan Oil

1993. Argan Oil. Multicoloured.
847   1d.70 Type **425**   80   25
848   4d.80 Branch and fruit of argan tree   1·80   65

426 Prince Sidi Mohammed

1993. 30th Birthday of Prince Sidi Mohammed.
849   **426**   4d.80 multicoloured   1·60   35

427 King Hassan and Mosque

1993. Inauguration of King Hassan II Mosque.
850   **427**   4d.80 multicoloured   1·60   40

428 Canopy, Sceptres, Flag and "40" on Sun

1993. 40th Anniv of Revolution.
851   **428**   4d.80 multicoloured   1·60   40

429 Post Box and Globe

1993. World Post Day.
852   **429**   4d.80 multicoloured   1·60   40

430 Emblem

1993. Islamic Summer University.
853   **430**   4d.80 multicoloured   1·60   40

431 "18" on Scroll

1993. 18th Anniv of "Green March".
854   **431**   4d.80 multicoloured   1·90   55

432 Marbled Teal

1993. Waterfowl. Multicoloured.
855   1d.70 Type **432**   95   25
856   4d.80 Red-knobbed coot   2·50   65

433 Flags, Scroll and "50"

1994. 50th Anniv of Istaqlal (Independence) Party.
857   **433**   4d.80 multicoloured   2·10   45

434 House

1994. Signing of Uruguay Round Final Act of General Agreement on Tariffs and Trade, Marrakesh.
858   **434**   1d.70 multicoloured   75   30
859   -   4d.80 multicoloured   2·10   95
MS860 165×105 mm. purple, black and yellow (as Nos. 858/9) (sold at 10d.)   4·75   4·75
DESIGN: 4d.80, Mosque.

435 Decorated Vase

1994. Blind Week.
861   **435**   4d.80 multicoloured   3·75   70

436 Copper Vessel

1994. Red Crescent.
862   **436**   4d.80 multicoloured   2·50   55

437 Couple

1994. National Congress on Children's Rights. Children's Drawings. Multicoloured.
863   1d.70 Type **437**   80   25
864   4d.80 Couple under sun   1·80   65

438 Ball, Moroccan and U.S.A. Flags, Pictogram and Trophy

1994. World Cup Football Championship, U.S.A.
865   **438**   4d.80 multicoloured   1·90   55

1994. Size 25×32 mm but inscr "1994".
866   **266**   1d.70 red, blue and gold   1·10   10

439 King Hassan II and Arms

1994. 65th Birthday of King Hassan II. Mult.
867   1d.70 Type **439**   75   25
868   4d.80 King Hassan II (vert)   2·10   65

440 "100" and Rings

1994. Centenary of International Olympic Committee.
869   **440**   4d.80 multicoloured   1·80   55

441 Saint-Exupery, Route Map and Biplane

1994. 50th Death Anniv of Antoine de Saint-Exupery (writer and pilot).
870   **441**   4d.80 multicoloured   2·30   55

442 "Chamaeleon gummifer"

1994. Flowers. Multicoloured.
871   1d.70 Type **442**   75   25
872   4d.80 "Pancratium maritimum" (vert)   2·10   80

443 Slender-billed Curlew

1994. Birds. Multicoloured.
873   1d.70 Type **443**   1·70   25
874   4d.80 Audouin's gull   4·00   80

444 Scroll and March

1994. 19th Anniv of "Green March". Mult.
875   1d.70 Type **444**   65   25
876   4d.80 Marchers and Moroccan coastline   1·90   65

1994. Stamp Day. As T 316.
877   1d.70 blue and black   65   25
878   4d.80 red and black   1·80   80
DESIGNS: 1d.70, Round postal cancellation of Marrakesh; 4d.80, Octagonal postal cancellation of Marrakesh.

445 Decorated Vase

1995. Blind Week.
879   **445**   4d.80 multicoloured   1·90   55

446 Anniversary
Emblem

1995. 50th Anniv of League of Arab States.
880   **446**   4d.80 multicoloured   1·60   40

447 Copper Vessel

1995. Red Crescent.
881   **447**   4d.80 multicoloured   1·70   55

448 "Malva
hispanica"

1995. Flowers. Multicoloured.
882   2d. Type **448**   75   25
883   4d.80 "Phlomis crinita"   2·10   65

449 European
Roller

1995. Birds. Multicoloured.
884   1d.70 Type **449**   50   25
885   4d.80 Eurasian goldfinch   1·80   80

450 Anniversary Emblem,
Building and Map

1995. 50th Anniv of F.A.O.
886   **450**   4d.80 multicoloured   1·50   45

451 "50" and Flags

1995. 50th Anniv of U.N.O. Multicoloured.
887   1d.70 Type **451**   95   25
888   4d.80 U.N. emblem, doves
       and map   2·75   55

452 "20" on Scroll

1995. 20th Anniv of "Green March". Mult.
889   1d.70 Type **452**   50   25
890   4d.80 National flag, book and
       medal   1·60   40

453 "40", National
Flag and Crown

1995. 40th Anniv of Independence. Multicoloured.
891   4d.80 Type **453**   1·50   45
MS892 120×90 mm. 10d. Sultan
       Mohammed V and King Hassan
       II. Imperf   3·25 3·25

1995. Stamp Day. As T 316.
893   1d.70 bistre and black   50   25
894   4d.80 lilac and black   1·60   40
DESIGNS: 1d.70, Round postal cancellation of Meknes;
4d.80, Octagonal cancellation of Meknes.

1996. Size 25×32 mm but inscr "1996".
895   **266**   5d.50 brown, red and
                gold   1·60   45
896   **266**   20d. brown, blue and
                gold   6·25 1·80

454 National Arms

1996. 35th Anniv of Enthronement of King Hassan II.
Multicoloured.
897   2d. Type **454**   60   25
898   5d.50 King Hassan II   1·80   65
MS899 142×93 mm. 10d. King Hassan
       II. Imperf   3·75 3·75

455 Decorated
Vase

1996
900   **455**   5d.50 multicoloured   1·90   45

456 Leather Flask

1996
901   **456**   5d.50 multicoloured   1·90   45

457 "Cleonia
lusitanica"

1996. Flowers. Multicoloured.
902   2d. Type **457**   80   25
903   5d.50 "Tulipa sylvestris"   2·00   80

458 King Hassan II
wearing Military
Uniform

1996. 40th Anniv of Royal Armed Forces. Mult.
904   2d. Type **458**   60   25
905   5d.50 King Hassan II and globe   1·80   65

459 Emblem and
Runners

1996. Centenary of Modern Olympic Games. Olympic
Games, Atlanta, U.S.A.
906   **459**   5d.50 multicoloured   2·10   90

460 Osprey

1996. Birds. Multicoloured.
907   2d. Type **460**   1·00   35
908   5d.50 Little egret   2·75   80

461 "21" on Scroll

1996. 21st Anniv of "Green March".
909   **461**   5d.50 multicoloured   1·90   35

1996. Stamp Day. As T 316.
910   2d. orange and black   60   25
911   5d.50 green and black   1·80   65
DESIGNS: 2d. Round postal cancellation of Maghzen-Fes;
5d.50, Octagonal postal cancellation of Maghzen-Fes.

462 Rainbow and Emblem

1996. 50th Anniv of UNICEF.
912   **462**   5d.50 multicoloured   1·90   55

463 Terracotta Vessel

1997
913   **463**   5d.50 multicoloured   1·90   45

464 Lupin

1997. Flowers. Multicoloured.
914   2d. Type **464**   80   25
915   5d.50 Milk thistle   2·00   80

465 King
Mohammed V

1997. 50th Anniv of Tangier Talks (determining future
status of Tangier).
916   2d. Type **465**   80   25
917   2d. King Hassan II   80   25

466 Map in Open
Book and Quill

1997. World Book Day.
918   **466**   5d.50 multicoloured   2·00   45

467 Ibn Battuta and Globe

1997. International Conference on Ibn Battuta (explorer).
919   **467**   5d.50 multicoloured   1·90   45

468 Copper Door
Knocker

1997
920   **468**   5d.50 multicoloured   2·00   45

469 Demoiselle
Crane

1997. Birds. Multicoloured.
921   2d. Type **469**   80   35
922   5d.50 Blue tit   2·00   80

470 "22" on Scroll

1997. 22nd Anniv of "Green March".
923   **470**   5d.50 multicoloured   2·00   35

1997. Stamp Day. As T 316.
924   2d. blue and black   60   25
925   5d.50 red and black   1·80   65
DESIGNS: 2d. Round postal cancellation of Maghzen-
Larache; 5d.50, Octagonal postal cancellation of
Maghzen-Larache.

471 Flask

1998. Moroccan Pottery.
926   **471**   6d. multicoloured   1·90   45

472 "Rhus
pentaphylla"

1998. Plants. Multicoloured.
927   2d.30 Type **472**   80   25
928   6d. "Orchis papilionacea"   2·00   80

473 Route Map and Emblem

1998. 26th International Road Haulage Union Congress, Marrakesh.
929	**473**	6d. multicoloured	2·10	45

1998. Size 25×32 mm but inscr "1998".
930	**266**	2d.30 red, green and gold	80	20

474 Sconce

1998. Moroccan Copperware.
931	**474**	6d. multicoloured	1·90	45

475 Players and Ball

1998. World Cup Football Championship, France.
932	**475**	6d. multicoloured	2·10	55

476 Emblem, Rainbow, World Map and Hands

1998. International Year of the Ocean.
933	**476**	6d. multicoloured	2·10	45

477 King Mohammed V and King Hassan II

1998. 45th Anniv of Revolution.
934	**477**	6d. multicoloured	1·90	35

478 Globe and Letter

1998. World Stamp Day.
935	**478**	6d. multicoloured	1·90	45

479 Nightingale

1998. Birds. Multicoloured.
936	2d.30 Type **479**		80	35
937	6d. Ostrich		2·00	80

480 Scroll

1998. 23rd Anniv of "Green March".
938	**480**	6d. multicoloured	1·90	35

481 Arabic Script

1998. 40th Anniv of Code of Civil Liberties.
939	**481**	6d. multicoloured	1·90	35

482 Anniversary Emblem

1998. 50th Anniv of Universal Declaration of Human Rights.
940	**482**	6d. multicoloured	2·10	45

1998. King Hassen II. Size 27×35 mm.
940a	**266**	6d. blue and gold	2·10	45

483 Mask and Globe

1999. World Theatre Day.
941	**483**	6d. multicoloured	2·10	45

484 Eryngium triquetrum

1999. Flowers. Multicoloured.
942	2d.30 Type **484**		80	25
943	6d. Mistletoe		2·00	80

485 Bab Mansour Laalej

1999.
944	**485**	6d. multicoloured	1·90	45

486 King Hassan II on Throne

1999. 70th Birthday of King Hassan II. Mult.
945	2d.30 Type **486**		80	35
946	6d. King Hassan wearing robes		1·80	80
MS947	125×95 mm. Nos. 945/6. Imperf. (sold at 10d)		3·75	3·50

487 Necklace

1999. Moroccan Jewellery.
948	**487**	6d. multicoloured	1·90	45

488 Hands holding Globe and Water falling on Tree

1999. World Environment Day.
949	**488**	6d. multicoloured	2·10	45

489 Emblem

1999. 125th Anniv of Universal Postal Union.
950	**489**	6d. multicoloured	2·10	45

490 Obverse and Reverse of Medal

1999. F.A.O. Agriculture Medal.
951	**490**	6d. multicoloured	2·30	45

491 Stylized People

1999. Solidarity Week.
952	**491**	6d. blue, yellow and black	1·90	35

492 "24" on Scroll

1999. 24th Anniv of "Green March".
953	**492**	6d. multicoloured	1·90	35

493 Zebra Seabream

1999. Fishes. Multicoloured.
954	2d.30 Type **493**		80	35
955	6d. Opah		2·20	45

494 Stork on Nest (A. Slaoui)

1999. "Year of Morocco in France". Paintings. Multicoloured.
956	6d. Type **494**		1·90	70
957	6d. Women sitting on mat (Afif Bennani)		1·90	70
958	6d. Guitar (Abdelkader Rhorbal)		1·90	70
959	6d. View of harbour (A. Slaoui)		1·90	70

1999. King Hassan II. Vert designs as T 266 inscr '1999'.
959a	70f. violet, flesh and gold (24×28 mm)		30	30
959b	80f. violet, pale yellow and gold (24×28 mm)		35	35
959c	2d.30 lake, pale green and gold (27×34 mm)		45	45
959d	2d.50 lake-brown, brownish grey and gold (27×34 mm)		50	50
959e	5d.50 lake-brown, pink and gold (27×34 mm)		1·00	1·00
959f	6d. ultramarine, pale turquoise blue and gold (27×34 mm)		1·10	1·10
959g	6d.50 lake-brown, pale orange and gold (27×34 mm)		1·10	1·10
959h	10d. lake-brown, pale orange-red and gold (27×34 mm)		1·80	1·80

495 Players and Globe

2000. African Nations' Cup Football Championship.
960	**495**	6d. multicoloured	2·10	55

496 Globe and "2000"

2000. New Year.
961	**496**	6d. multicoloured	2·10	55

497 Beach and Calendar

2000. 40th Anniv of the Reconstruction of Agadir.
962	**497**	6d.50 multicoloured	2·10	55

498 Emblem and Building

2000. 25th Anniv of Islamic Development Bank.
963	**498**	6d.50 multicoloured	2·10	55

499 Stylized People

2000. National Disabled Persons Day.
964   **499**   6d.50 multicoloured   2·10   70

500 *Jasione montana*

2000. Flowers. Multicoloured.
965   2d.50 Type **500**   80   35
966   6d.60 *Pistorica breviflora*   2·30   80

501 Emblem

2000. 50th Anniv of World Meteorological Organization.
967   **501**   6d.50 multicoloured   2·10   70

502 People dancing

2000. National Festival of Popular Arts, Marrakesh.
968   **502**   6d.50 multicoloured   2·10   70

503 Open Book and White Dove

2000. International Year of Culture and Peace.
969   **503**   6d.50 multicoloured   2·10   70

6,50
(504)

2000. Air. International Conference on Hassan II. No. 631 optd with T 504.
970   6d.50 on 1d.40 multicoloured   2·10   70

505 King Mohammed VI

2000. 1st Anniv of Enthronement of King Mohammed VI. Multicoloured.
971   2d.50 Type **505**   80   35
972   6d.50 King Mohammed VI   2·00   80
MS973 120×91 mm. Nos. 971/2. Imperf. (sold at 10d.)   3·00   3·00

506 Ruins, Volubis and Performers

2000. Mediterranean Song and Dance Festival.
974   **506**   6d.50 multicoloured   2·10   45

507 Emblem and Olympic Torch

2000. Olympic Games, Sydney.
975   **507**   6d.50 multicoloured   2·10   55

508 Emblem, House and Children

2000. 50th Anniv of S.O.S. Children's Villages.
976   **508**   6d.50 multicoloured   2·10   55

509 Quill, Globe and Emblem

2000. International Teachers' Day.
977   **509**   6d.50 multicoloured   2·10   45

510 Emblem

2000. King Mohammed VI Solidarity Foundation.
978   **510**   6d.50 blue, yellow and black   2·10   70

511 "25" on Scroll

2000. 25th Anniv of "Green March". Mult.
979   2d.50 Type **511**   80   25
980   6d.50 "25" and text   2·00   55

512 St. Exupery and Plane

2000. Birth Centenary of Antonie de Saint.-Exupery (author).
981   **512**   6d.50 multicoloured   2·30   55

513 "45" and National Flag

2000. 45th Anniv of Independence.
982   **513**   6d.50 multicoloured   2·10   45

514 Mediterranean Cardinalfish (*Apogon imberbis*)

2000. Fishes. Multicoloured.
983   2d.50 Type **514**   80   35
984   6d.50 Cadenat's rockfish (*Scorpaena loppei*)   2·00   80

515 El Bab el Gharbi

2001
985   **515**   6d.50 multicoloured   2·10   70

516 Hands holding Globe

2001. International Water Day.
986   **516**   6d.50 multicoloured   2·10   70

517 King Mohammed VI enclosed in Droplet of Water

2001. 45th Anniv of Armed Forces. Multicoloured.
987   2d.50 Type **517**   80   25
988   6d.50 King Mohammed VI (different)   2·00   45

518 Spurge (*Euphorbia rigida*)

2001. Flowers. Multicoloured.
989   2d.50 Type **518**   80   35
990   6d.50 Horned poppy (*Glaucium flavum*)   2·00   80

519 Koekelberg Basilica, Brussels

2001. Religious Buildings.
991   2d.50 Type **519**   80   45
992   6d.50 Hassan II Mosque, Casablanca   2·00   90
Stamps of a similar design were issued by Belgium.

520 Globe and Dove

2001. National Diplomacy Day.
993   **520**   6d.50 multicoloured   1·50   35

521 King Mohammed VI

2001. Second Anniv of Enthronement of King Mohammed VI
994   2d.50 Type **521**   55   10
995   6d. Smiling facing left   1·40   35
996   6d.50 Wearing decorated tie (crown upper left)   1·50   40
997   10d. King Mohammed VI (horiz)   2·40   65

522 Black-bellied Angler

2001. Marine Life. Multicoloured.
998   2d.50 Type **522**   55   25
999   6d.50 Monk seal (*Monachus monachus*) (horiz)   1·50   75

523 Postal Seal, Kasir el Kabir (*Lophus budegassa*)

2001. Stamp Day.
1000   **523**   2d.50 bistre and black   55   25
1001   –   6d.50 lilac and black   1·50   75
DESIGN: 6d.50 Octagonal seal.

524 Hands holding Globe

2001. 7th Conference Session of Signatory States to United Nations Framework Convention on Climatic Change, Marrakech.
1002   **524**   6d.50 multicoloured   1·50   35

525 Palm Trees

2001. World Day to Combat Desertification.
1003 **525** 6d.50 multicoloured 1·50 35

526 Flags and Marchers

2001. 26th Anniv of "Green March".
1004 **526** 6d.50 multicoloured 1·60 45

527 King Mohammed VI and Children

2001. King Mohammed VI Solidarity Foundation.
1005 **527** 6d.50 multicoloured 1·60 55
1006 - 6d.50 ultramarine, lemon and black (28×28 mm) 1·60 55
DESIGN: As No. 978 but inscr "2001".

528 Wallace Fountain, Paris

2001. Moroccan—French Cultural Heritage. Fountains. Multicoloured.
1007 2d.50 Type **528** 60 25
1008 6d.50 Nejjarine fountain, Fez 1·60 75
Stamps of the same design were issued by France.

529 Hands holding Globe

2001. United Nations Year of Dialogue among Civilizations.
1009 **529** 6d.50 multicoloured 1·60 45

530 Bab Chellah, Rabat

2002
1010 **530** 6d.50 multicoloured 1·60 45

531 Globe and Woman

2002. International Women's Day.
1011 **531** 6d.50 multicoloured 1·60 75

532 Cedar Tree

2002
1012 **532** 6d.50 multicoloured 1·60 75

533 Baby and Elderly Couple

2002. Second World Assembly on Aging.
1013 **533** 6d.50 multicoloured 1·60 45

534 Emblem

2002. United Nations Special Session for Children (September 2001).
1014 **534** 6d.50 multicoloured 1·60 45

535 Linaria bipartite

2002. Flowers. Multicoloured.
1015 2d.50 Type **535** 60 25
1016 6d.50 Verbascum pseudocreticum 1·60 75

2002. Third Anniv of Enthronement of King Mohammed VI
1016a 2d.50 As Type **521** 55 25
1016b 6d. As No. 955 1·30 25
1016c 6d.50 As No. 995 1·60 45
1016d 10d. As No. 997 (horiz) 2·10 85

536 Emblem and Map

2002. International Union of Telecommunications Conference, Marrakech. Multicoloured.
1017 6d.50 Type **536** 1·60 45
MS1018 120×90 mm. 10d. As No. 1017 but with design enlarged. Imperf 2·50 2·50

537 Mohamed Dorra, Father and Protestors

2002. Al Aqsa Intifada.
1019 **537** 6d.50 multicoloured 1·60 75

538 Oasis

2002. International Year of EcoTourism.
1020 **538** 6d.50 multicoloured 1·60 45

539 Map and Marchers

2002. 27th Anniv of "Green March".
1021 **539** 6d.50 multicoloured 1·60 45

540 King Mohammed VI

2002. King Mohammed VI Solidarity Foundation.
1022 **540** 6d.50 multicoloured 1·60 55
1023 - 6d.50 lemon and ultramarine (28×28 mm) 1·60 55
Design: No. 1023 As No. 978 but inscr '2002'.

541 Sultan Moulay Hassan and City

2002. 110th Anniv of Maghzen Post. Multicoloured.
1024 2d.50 Type **541** 60 25
1025 6d.50 Sultan Moulay Hassan and tall building 1·60 75

542 Fortresses, Dune and Coastline

2002. International Year of Cultural Heritage.
1026 **542** 6d.50 nmulticoloured 1·60 45

543 Allis Shad (Alosa alosa)

2002. Fish. Multicoloured.
1027 2d.50 Type **543** 60 25
1028 6d.50 Epinephelus marginatus 1·60 75

545 Bab El Okla, Tetouan

2003
1032 **545** 6d.50 multicoloured 1·60 45

546 Le Sapin Forest

2003
1033 **546** 6d.50 multicoloured 1·60 75

547 Child and Fountain

2003. International Year of Freshwater.
1034 **547** 6d.50 multicoloured 1·60 55

548 Limonium sinuatum

2003. Flora. Multicoloured.
1035 2d.50 Type **548** 60 25
1036 6d.50 Echinops spinosus 1·60 75

549 King Mohammed VI

2003
1037 **549** 70f. multicoloured 20 10
1038 **549** 80f. multicoloured 20 10
1039 **549** 5d. multicoloured 1·20 25
1039a **549** 13d. multicoloured 3·00 55
1040 **549** 20d. multicoloured 4·75 1·20

550 Courtyard

2003. Millenary of Grand Mosque, Sale.
1060 **550** 6d.50 multicoloured 1·60 45

551 Stylized Figures and Globe

2003. World Youth Congress, Morocco.
1061 **551** 6d.50 multicoloured 1·60 45

552 Kings Mohammed V, Hassan II and Mohammed VI

2003. 50th Anniv of Revolution of King and People.
1062 **552** 6d.50 multicoloured 1·60 55

553 King Mohammed VI

2003. 40th Birthday of King Mohammed VI. Multicoloured.
1063 2d.50 Type **553** 60 25
1064 6d.50 Wearing traditional dress 1·60 75
MS1065 121×90 mm. Nos. 1063/4 2·50 2·50

2003. As T 521. Self-adhesive.
1066 2d.50 As No. 994 60 25
1067 6d.50 As No. 1008 1·60 75

554 *Sparisoma cretense*

2003. Fish. Multicoloured.
1068		2d.50 Type **554**	60	25
1069		6d. *Anthias anthias*	1·60	75

555 Satellites circling Globe

2003. World Post Day.
1070	**555**	6d.50 multicoloured	1·60	35

556 King Mohammed VI and Sick Child

2003. King Mohammed VI Solidarity Foundation.
1071	**556**	6d.50 multicoloured	1·60	55
1072	-	6d.50 lemon and ultramarine (28×28 mm)	1·60	55

Design: No. 1072 As No. 978 but inscr '2003'.

557 "28" and Marchers

2003. 28th Anniv of "Green March".
1073	**557**	6d.50 multicoloured	1·60	35

558 City and Cultural Symbols

2003. Rabat—Arab Cultural Capital, 2003.
1074	**558**	6d.50 multicoloured	1·60	35

559 School Children examining Stamps

2003. Philately in Schools.
1075	**559**	6d.50 multicoloured	1·60	35

560 Sun, Child writing and Clouds

2003. United Nations Decade for Literacy.
1076	**560**	6d.50 multicoloured	1·60	35

561 Chinese and Moroccan Flags as Clasped Hands

2003. 45th Anniv of Morocco—China Diplomatic Relations.
1077	**561**	6d.50 multicoloured	1·60	35

562 Ship and D'Ibn Battutah

2004. 700th Birth Anniv of D'Ibn Battutah (traveller).
1078	**562**	6d.50 multicoloured	1·60	75

563 Bab Agnaou, Marrakech

2004.
1079	**563**	6d.50 multicoloured	1·60	55

564 *Linaria gharbensis*

2004. Flowers. Multicoloured.
1080		2d.50 Type **564**	60	25
1081		6d.50 *Nigella damascene*	1·60	75

565 Equestrian, Globe and Emblem

2004. 16th World Military Equestrian Championship, Temara, Morocco.
1082	**565**	6d.50 multicoloured	1·60	75

566 Trophy

2004. 20th Anniv of Hassan II Tennis Grand Prix.
1083	**566**	6d.50 multicoloured	1·60	75

567 Festival Emblem

2004. 10th World Festival of Sacred Music.
1084	**567**	6d.50 multicoloured	1·60	45

568 Woman wearing Kaftan

2004. Traditional Costume.
1085	**568**	6d.50 multicoloured	1·60	45

569 Tazoudasaurus Naimi

2004. Tazoudasaurus Naimi (dinosaur, newly discovered at Tazouda).
1086	**569**	6d.50 multicoloured	1·60	75

570 Emblem

2004. 30th International Military History Congress, Rabat.
1087	**570**	6d.50 multicoloured	1·60	55

571 King Mohammed VI

2004. 5th Anniv of Enthronement of King Mohammed VI.
1088		2d.50 Type **571**	95	10
1089		6d. Seated	95	10

572 Dove holding Olive Branch and Globe

2004. International Peace Day.
1090	**572**	6d. multicoloured	1·50	35

573 King Mohammed VI and Sick Woman

2004. King Mohammed VI Solidarity Foundation.
1091	**573**	6d.50 multicoloured	1·60	55
1092	-	6d.50 lemon and deep ultramarine (28×28 mm)	1·60	55

Design: No. 1092 As No. 978 but inscr '2004'.

574 "29" and Marchers

2004. 29th Anniv of "Green March".
1093	**574**	6d. multicoloured	1·50	35

575 Swordfish (*Xiphias gladius*)

2004. Marine Fauna. Multicoloured.
1094		2d.50 Type **575**	60	25
1095		6d.50 Octopus (*Octopus vulgaris*)	1·60	75

576 Child Holding Globe and Dove

2004. International Day of the Child.
1096	**576**	6d.50 multicoloured	1·60	45

578 Great Bustard (As No. 754)

2005. Birds. Self-adhesive. Multicoloured.
1099		2d.50 Type **578**	55	10
1100		2d.50 As No. 470	55	10
1101		2d.50 As No. 908	55	10
1102		2d.50 As No. 907	55	10
1103		2d.50 As No. 742	55	10
1104		2d.50 As No. 471	55	10
1105		2d.50 As No. 885	55	10
1106		2d.50 As No. 874	55	10
1107		2d.50 As No. 292	55	10
1108		2d.50 As No. 378	55	10

579 Costumes Zagora, South Morocco (As No. 267)

2005. Costumes. Self-adhesive Multicoloured.
1109		6d. Type **579**	1·30	25
1110		6d. As No. 215	1·30	25
1111		6d. As No. 734	1·30	25
1112		6d. As No. 268	1·30	25
1113		6d. As No. 216	1·30	25
1114		6d. As No. 733	1·30	25
1115		6d. As No. 825	1·30	25
1116		6d. As No. 826	1·30	25
1117		6d. As No. 223	1·30	25
1118		6d. As No. 219	1·30	25

580 Arch, Emblem, Globe and Dove

2005. Centenary of Rotary International.
1119	**580**	6d.50 multicoloured	1·50	25

581 Emblem, Flags and Map of Arab Nations

2005. 60th Anniv of Arab League.
1120	**581**	6d.50 multicoloured	1·50	25

582 Bab Boujloud, Fes

2005.
1121	**582**	6d.50 multicoloured	1·50	25

583 Dove in Chains and Candle encased in Barbed Wire

2005. Amnesty International.
1122	**583**	6d.50 multicoloured	1·50	25

584 Erodium sebaceum

2005. Flowers. Multicoloured.
1123		2d.50 Type **584**	70	10
1124		6d.50 Linaria ventricosa	1·30	25

585 Horse (rock carving)

2005. Cultural Heritage.
1125	**585**	6d.50 multicoloured	1·50	25

586 Head and Globe

2005. World Neurosurgery Congress, Marrakesh.
1126	**586**	6d.50 multicoloured	1·50	25

587 Combine Harvester and Ears of Corn

2005. 85th Anniv of OCP Group (Groupe Office Cherifien des Phosphates).
1127	**587**	6d.50 multicoloured	1·50	25

588 Emblem

2005. 60th Anniv of United Nations.
1128	**588**	6d. multicoloured	1·40	25

589 "30", Procession with Flags and Marchers

2005. 30th Anniv of "Green March". Multicoloured.
1129		2d.50 Type **589**	55	10
1130		6d. "30", dunes and marchers	1·30	25

590 King Mohammed VI giving to Woman

2005. King Mohammed VI Solidarity Foundation.
1131	**590**	6d.50 multicoloured	1·40	25
1132	–	6d.50 lemon and ultramarine (28×28 mm)	1·40	25

Designs: No. 1131, Type **590**; No. 1132, As No. 978 but inscr '2005'.

591 Symbols of Morocco and Netherlands

2005. 400th Anniv of Morocco—Netherlands Diplomatic Relations. Multicoloured.
1133		6d.50 Type **591**	1·40	25
1134		6d.50 Moroccan arch enclosing Dutch canal (vert)	1·40	25

592 Couple, Symbols of Information Dissemination and Globe

2005. World Information Society Summit, Tunis.
1135	**592**	6d. multicoloured	1·80	35

593 King Mohammed V

2005. 50th Anniv of the Return of King Mohammed V. Multicoloured.
1136		6d.50 Type **593**	1·50	25

MS1137 120×90 mm. 6d.50×2, No. 1136; As 1136 but with colours of inscriptions reversed — 3·25, 3·25

594 Children in Circle (Kaoutar Azizi Alaoui)

2005. Children's Paintings. Multicoloured.
1138		2d.50 Type **594**	55	10
1139		2d.50 Dove and girls crying (Sara Bourquiba)	55	10
1140		2d.50 House (Mohcine Kahyouchat)	55	10
1141		2d.50 Hill, sea, sunset and palm tree (Anise Anico)	55	10

595 Emblem

2005. International Year of Microcredit.
1142	**595**	6d.50 multicoloured	1·50	25

596 Sparus aurata

2005. Marine Fauna. Multicoloured.
1143		2d.50 Type **596**	55	10
1144		6d. Sepia officinalis	1·30	25

597 Dove, Traffic, Emblem and Traffic Control Lights

2006. National Road Safety Day.
1145	**597**	6d.50 multicoloured	1·50	25

598 Ship and Oil Rigs

2006. 30th Anniv of OPEC International Development Fund.
1146	**598**	6d.50 multicoloured	1·50	25

599 Bab Marshan, Tanger

2006
1147	**599**	6d.50 multicoloured	1·50	25

600 World Map and Crowd

2006. 50th Anniv of Ministry of Foreign Affairs.
1148	**600**	6d. multicoloured	1·40	25

601 Narcissus cantabricus

2006. Flora. Multicoloured.
1149		2d.50 Type **601**	55	10
1150		6d.50 Paeonia mascula	1·50	30

602 King Mohammed VI and Tanks

2006. 50th Anniv of Royal Armed Forces. Multicoloured.
1151		2d.50 Type **602**	55	10
1152		6d.50 King Mohamed VI and ships	1·50	30

MS1153 120×90 mm. Nos. 1151/2 — 2·30, 2·30

2006. King Mohammed VI.
1154		3d.25 As Type **521**	75	15

603 King Mohammed VI

2006. King Mohammed VI.
1155	**603**	7d.80 multicoloured	1·80	35

604 Barbary Macaque

2006. Fauna. Multicoloured.
1156		3d.25 Type **604**	85	20
1157		7d.80 Barbary lion	2·00	40

605 King Mohammed VI

2006. 31st Anniv of "Green March". Multicoloured.
1158		7d.80 Type **605**	1·80	35
1159		7d.80 Mohammed VI a Boujdour Mosque	2·00	40

606 Emblem

2006. King Mohammed VI Solidarity Foundation.
1160	**606**	7d.80 ultramarine, lemon and black	2·00	40

607 Globe

2006. Stamp Day.
1161	**607**	7d.80 multicoloured	2·00	40

608 Emblem, Flag and Assembly

2006. 50th Anniv of Membership of United Nations.
1162	**608**	7d.80 multicoloured	2·00	40

609 Virus and Bleeding Finger

2006. International AIDS Awareness Day.
1163	**609**	7d.80 multicoloured	2·00	40

610 Dove and Flags

2006. 50th Anniv of Morocco—Japan Diplomatic Relations. Multicoloured.
1164		3d.25 Type **610**	95	25
1165		7d.80 Symbols of Morocco and Japan	2·00	40

611 Thunnus thynnus

2006. Fish. Multicoloured.
1166		3d.25 Type **611**	95	25
1167		7d.80 *Sardina pilchardus*	2·00	40

1999. King Hassan II. Vert designs as T 266 inscr '1999'.
959a	70f. violet, flesh and gold (24×28 mm)	30	30
959b	80f. violet, pale yellow and gold (24×28 mm)	35	35
959c	2d.30 lake, pale green and gold (27×34 mm)	45	45
959d	2d.50 lake-brown, brownish grey and gold (27×34 mm)	50	50
959e	5d.50 lake-brown, pink and gold (27×34 mm)	1·00	1·00
959f	6d. ultramarine, pale turquoise blue and gold (27×34 mm)	1·10	1·10
959g	6d.50 lake-brown, pale orange and gold (27×34 mm)	1·10	1·10
959h	10d. lake-brown, pale orange-red and gold (27×34 mm)	1·80	1·80

612 Emblem

2007. 50th Anniv of Confederation of African Football.
1168	**612**	7d.80 multicoloured	2·00	40

613 Emblem

2007. 50th Anniv of Mohammed V University, Agdal, Rabat.
1169	**613**	3d.25 multicoloured	95	25

614 Ibn Khaldun

2007. 600th Death Anniv of Ibn Khaldun (historian, sociologist and philosopher).
1170	**614**	7d.80 multicoloured	2·00	40

615 Palm

2007. International Agricultural Exhibition, Meknès. Sheet 140×110 mm containing T 615 and similar multicoloured designs.
MS1171	3d.25 Type **615**; 3d.25 Argan tree; 7d.80 Cattle (horiz); 7d.80 Olives (horiz)	3·00	3·00

616 Couscous

2007. Moroccan Cuisine.
1172	**616**	7d.80 multicoloured	1·10	1·10

617 Musicians

2007. Music of Andalusia.
1173	**617**	7d.80 multicoloured	1·10	1·10

618 *Fulgurance* (M. Qotbi)

2007. Art. Sheet 125×135 mm containing T 618 and similar multicoloured designs.
MS1174	3d.25×4, Type **618**; Horsemen (H. Glaoui) (horiz); *Symphonie d'Ete* (M. Qotbi) (horiz); Horses (H. Glaoui) (horiz)	1·90	1·90

619 Scouts

2007. Centenary of Scouting.
1175	**619**	7d.80 multicoloured	1·10	1·10

620 Castelo de Silves, Portugal

2007. Architecture. Multicoloured.
1176		3d.25 Type **620**	1·00	1·00
1177		7d.80 Keep (El Kamara) Tower, Arzila	1·10	1·10

Stamps of a similar design were issued by Portugal.

621 Stamp Outline enclosing UPU Emblem

2007. Stamp Day.
1178	**621**	3d.25 multicoloured	1·00	1·00

622 City Skyline

2007. Fes–Islamic Capital of Culture–2007.
1179	**622**	7d.80 multicoloured	1·10	1·10

623 Marchers

2007. 32nd Anniv of 'Green March'.
1180	**623**	7d.80 multicoloured	1·10	1·10

2007. King Mohammed VI Solidarity Foundation.
1181		7d.80 lemon and ultramarine (28×28 mm)	1·10	1·10

Design: No. 1072 As No. 1160, but inscr '2003'.

625 Medallion

2007. National Quality Week.
1182	**625**	7d.80 multicoloured	1·10	1·10

626 Child

2007. Children's Day.
1183	**626**	7d.80 multicoloured	1·10	1·10

627 Court Building

2007. 50th Anniv of Supreme Court.
1184	**627**	3d.25 multicoloured	1·00	1·00

628 Bab Lamrissa, Sale

2007
1185	**628**	7d.80 multicoloured	1·10	1·10

629 Mohammed V, Hassan II, Mohammed VI and Aircraft

2007. 50th Anniv of Royal Air Maroc.
1186	**629**	7d.80 multicoloured	1·10	1·10

630 Symbols of Sport

2007. 50th Anniv of Moroccan Sport.
1187	**630**	7d.80 multicoloured	1·10	1·10

631 Symbols of Tourism

2008. International Tourism Exhibition, Marrakech.
1188	**631**	7d.80 multicoloured	1·10	1·10

632 Map of Africa and Football

2008. African Nations Cup.
1189	**632**	7d.80 multicoloured	1·10	1·10

633 Export Trophy

2008
1190	**633**	3d.25 multicoloured	1·00	1·00

634 Emblem

2008. 1200th Anniv of Fez (1st issue).
1191	**634**	3d.25 multicoloured	1·00	1·00

See also No. 1202.

635 *Calendula stellata*

2008. Flora. Multicoloured.
1192		3d.25 Type **635**	1·00	1·00
1193		7d.80 *Convolvulus tricolor*	1·00	1·00

636 Falak Ol Aflak Castle, Iran and Script

2008. Morocco—Iran Issue. Multicoloured.
1194		3d.25 Type **636**	1·00	1·00
1195		3d.25 Flags of Morocco and Iran	1·00	1·00
1196		7d.80 La Kasbah des Oudayas, Morocco and script (different)	1·10	1·10

637 Globe (Narjiss Lasfar) (communications)

2008. Children's Drawings. Multicoloured.
1197		3d.25 Type **637**	1·00	1·00
1198		3d.25 House and trees (Chaimae Abbaich) (my childhood)	1·00	1·00
1199		3d.25 Globe enclosing habitats (our environment) (vert)	1·00	1·00
1200		3d.25 House and sunshine (daily life) (vert)	1·00	1·00

638 Damaged and Healthy Environments

2008. International Day of the Environment.
1201	**638**	7d.80 multicoloured	1·10	1·10

639 City

2008. 1200th Anniv of Fez (2nd issue).
1202	**639**	7d.80 multicoloured	1·10	1·10

640 Symbols of Development

2008. Transport. Agency for Development of Bouregreg Valley. Multicoloured.
1203		3d.25 Type **640**	1·10	1·10
1204		7d.80 Gate, walls and modern locomotive	1·20	1·20

641 Runners

2008. Olympic Games, Beijing. Multicoloured.

1205	3d.25 Type **641**		1·10	1·10
1206	3d.25 Hurdlers		1·10	1·10
1207	3d.25 Boxers		1·10	1·10
1208	3d.25 Runner		1·10	1·10

642 Pigeon

2008. Arab Post Day. Sheet 180×51 mm containing T 642 and similar horiz design. Multicoloured.

MS1209	7d.80 Type **642**; 7d.80 Camels	1·20	1·20

643 *Isurus oxyrinchus* (shortfin mako)

2008. Marine Fauna. Multicoloured.

1210	3d.25 Type **643**		1·10	1·10
1211	7d.80 *Haliotis tuberculata*		1·20	1·20

644 Musicians (La musique)

2008. Art and Culture. Sheet 143×106 mm containing T 644 and similar vert designs.

MS1212	3d.25×4, Type **644**; Zellij, hand cut polychrome tiles (Ezzellij); Woman (El haik); Scholar (l'École Coranique)	4·50	4·50

645 Ceramics

2008. 50th Anniv of Morocco–China Diplomatic Relations. Multicoloured.

1213	3d.25 Type **645**		1·10	1·10
1214	7d.80 Moroccan gateway and Great Wall of China (vert)		1·20	1·20
1215	7d.80 Conjoined Chinese and Moroccan symbols		1·20	1·20
MS1215a	170×110 mm. Nos. 1213/15		3·50	3·50

646 '33'

2008. 33rd Anniv of 'Green March'.

1216	**646**	3d.25 multicoloured	1·10	1·10

2008. King Mohammed VI Solidarity Foundation.

1217	7d.80 ultramarine, lemon and black (28×28 mm)		1·20	1·20

Design: As No. 1160, but inscr '2008'.

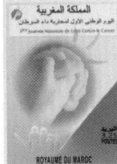

647 Clasped Hands

2008. National Cancer Awareness Day.

1218	**647**	3d.25 multicoloured	1·10	1·10

648 Emblem and Scales

2008. 60th Anniv of Declaration of Human Rights.

1219	**648**	7d.80 multicoloured	1·20	1·20

649 Bab Al Marsa, Essaquira

2008

1220	**649**	7d.80 multicoloured	1·20	1·20

2008. King Mohammed VI.

1221	3d.25 As Type **521**		1·10	1·10

650 Carpet, Hénbale de Salé

2008. Carpets. Multicoloured. Self-adhesive.

1222	7d.80 Type **650**		1·20	1·20
1223	7d.80 Marmoucha		1·20	1·20
1224	7d.80 Ouled Besseba		1·20	1·20
1225	7d.80 Haut Atlas		1·20	1·20
1226	7d.80 Haddou		1·20	1·20
1227	7d.80 Tazenakht		1·20	1·20
1228	7d.80 Marmoucha (different)		1·20	1·20
1229	7d.80 Rabat		1·20	1·20
1230	7d.80 Ouaouzguid		1·20	1·20
1231	7d.80 Rabat (different)		1·20	1·20

651 Louis Braille, Braille Letters and Hands reading

2009. Birth Bicentenary of Louis Braille (inventor of Braille writing for the blind).

1232	**651**	7d.80 multicoloured	1·20	1·20

652 Emblems and Craftsmen

2009. Insurance for Independent Workers and Craftsmen.

1233	**652**	3d.25 multicoloured	1·10	1·10

653 Player

2009. 25th Grand Prix Hassan II Tennis Tournament, Casablanca.

1234	**653**	3d.25 multicoloured	1·10	1·10

654 Emblem

2009. 30th Anniv of Cadi Ayyad University, Marrakesh.

1235	**654**	3d.25 multicoloured	1·10	1·10

655 Sugar Cane

2009. 80th Anniv of Sugar Industry.

1236	**655**	3d.25 multicoloured	1·10	1·10

656 Mask and Script

2009. National Theatre Day.

1237	**656**	3d.25 multicoloured	1·10	1·10

657 Galileo Galilei, Telescope, Satellite and Receiver

2009. International Year of Astronomy.

1238	**657**	7d.80 multicoloured	1·20	1·20

658 Children, PC and Child's Hand holding Adult's Hand

2009. Protection for Children whilst using Internet.

1239	**658**	7d.80 multicoloured	1·20	1·20

659 Stylized Building

2009. 50th Anniv of Al-Maghrib Bank.

1240	**659**	3d.25 chrome yellow, greenish yellow and black	1·10	1·10

660 Mohammed VI

2009. Tenth Anniv of Enthronement of Mohammed VI. Multicoloured. (a) Ordinary gum.

1241	3d.25 Type **660**		1·10	1·10
1242	7d.80 Mohammed VI seated		1·20	1·20
MS1243	144×198 mm. Nos. 1241/2		2·50	2·50

(b) Self-adhesive gum.

1244	15d. Mohammed VI, Hassan II and Mohammed V		3·75	3·75

661 Emblem

2009. al-Quds—2009 Capital of Arab Culture.

1245	**661**	3d.25 multicoloured	1·10	1·10

663 Woman holding Globe

2009. National Women's Day.

1247	**663**	3d.25 multicoloured	1·10	1·10

664 Building Façade

2009. 50th Anniv of Mohammedia School of Engineers.

1248	**664**	3d.25 multicoloured	1·10	1·10

665 Gateway, Mehdia

2009

1249	**665**	7d.80 multicoloured	1·20	1·20

666 Marchers

2009. 34th Anniv of Green March.

1250	**666**	3d.25 multicoloured	1·10	1·10

2009. King Mohammed VI Solidarity Foundation.

1251	7d.80 ultramarine, lemon and black (28×28 mm)		1·20	1·20

Design: As No. 1160, but inscr '2007'.

667 Oil Rigs, Ship and Symbols of Motion

2009. Morocco in Motion. Tanger-Med Port. Multicoloured.

1252	3d.25 Type **667**		1·10	1·10
1253	7d.80 Port, ship and symbols of motion (different)		1·20	1·20

668 '50'

2009. 50th Anniv of Caisse de Depot et de Gestion (financial institution).

1254	**668**	7d.80 ultramarine and gold	1·20	1·20

669 *Sarda sarda*

2009. Fish. Multicoloured.

1255	7d.80 Type **669**		1·20	1·20
1256	7d.80 *Oblada melanura*		1·20	1·20

670 Horses (Ayoub Elaidi)

2009. Children's Drawings. Multicoloured.

1257	3d.25 Type **670**	1·10	1·10
1258	3d.25 Trees (Yahya Elmhayi)	1·10	1·10
1259	3d.25 Mountain and water (Achraf Moussai)	1·10	1·10
1260	3d.25 Building and chimneys (Mohammed Chater)	1·10	1·10

680 Marchers with Flags

2010. 35th Anniv of Green March. Multicoloured.

MS1274	7d.80×2, Type **680**; Flag and dune	1·30	1·30

681 *Sciaena umbra*

2010. Fish

1275	**681**	7d.80 multicoloured	1·30	1·30

2010. King Mohammed VI Solidarity Foundation.

1276	7d.80 ultramarine, lemon and black (28×28 mm)	1·30	1·30

Design: As No. 1160, but inscr '2010'.

682 Symbols of Digital Communication

2010. Maroc Numeric 2013 (strategy for internet access and e-government)

1277	**682**	7d.80 multicoloured	1·30	1·30

683 '10' and Festival Emblem enclosed in Film Strip

2010. Tenth Anniv of Marrakech International Film Festival

1278	**683**	7d.80 multicoloured	1·30	1·30

684 ONCF Electric Locomotive

2010. Transport. Trains

1279	**684**	3d.25 multicoloured	1·00	40

685 'Bonheur'

2010. Greetings. Multicoloured.

1280	3d.25 Type **685**	1·00	40
1281	3d.25 'Santé'	1·00	40
1282	3d.25 'Prospéritié'	1·00	40

POSTAGE DUE STAMPS

D53

1965

D162	**D 53**	5f. green	24·00	9·00
D163	**D 53**	10f. brown	95	45
D164	**D 53**	20f. red	95	45
D165	**D 53**	30f. sepia	2·75	90

D153 Peaches

1974

D393	-	5f. orange, grn & blk	30	25
D394	-	10f. green, red & blk	45	25
D395	-	20f. green and black	70	40
D396	**D 153**	30f. orge, grn & blk	1·00	40
D397	-	40f. green and black	95	20
D398	-	60f. orge, grn & blk	1·30	35
D399	-	80f. orge, grn & blk	1·60	35
D399a	-	1d. multicoloured	95	45
D400	-	1d.20 multicoloured	95	70
D401	-	1d.60 multicoloured	45	35
D402	-	2d. multicoloured	45	55
D403	-	5d. multicoloured	2·10	1·40

DESIGNS: 60f., 1d.60, Peaches. VERT: 5f. Oranges; 10f., 1d.20, Cherries; 20f. Raisins; 40f. Grapes; 80f. Oranges; 1, 5d. Apples; 2d. Strawberries.

D544 Strawberries

2003. Multicoloured.. Multicoloured..

D1029	1d.50 Type D **544**	55	45
D1030	2d. Cherries	75	55
D1031	5d. Apples	2·00	1·50

D577 Peaches

2005. Postage Due.

D1097	**D577**	60f. multicoloured	55	45

2005. Postage Due. As D397. Multicoloured.

D1098	2d. Grapes	75	55

D 662 Bananas

2009. Self-adhesive.

D1246	**D 662**	3d.25 multicoloured	1·10	1·10

Pt. 1

MOROCCO AGENCIES

Stamps used at British postal agencies in Morocco, N. Africa, the last of which closed on 30 April 1957.

I. GIBRALTAR ISSUES OVERPRINTED

For use at all British Post Offices in Morocco.

All British P.O.s in Morocco were under the control of the Gibraltar P.O. until 1907 when control was assumed by H.M. Postmaster-General.

1898. Stamps of Gibraltar (Queen Victoria) optd Morocco Agencies.

9	**7**	5c. green	3·50	2·00
10	**7**	10c. red	5·00	2·00
3	**7**	20c. olive and brown	20·00	3·00
11	**7**	20c. olive	14·00	1·50
4	**7**	25c. blue	7·00	2·00
5	**7**	40c. brown	6·00	3·50
14	**7**	50c. lilac	14·00	4·50
7	**7**	1p. brown and blue	20·00	27·00
8	**7**	2p. black and red	30·00	27·00

1903. Stamps of Gibraltar (King Edward VII) optd Morocco Agencies.

24	**8**	5c. light green and green	18·00	7·50
18	**8**	10c. purple on red	9·00	40
26	**8**	20c. green and red	8·00	32·00
20	**8**	25c. purple and black on blue	8·00	30
28	**8**	50c. purple and violet	9·00	65·00
29	**8**	1p. black and red	42·00	85·00
30	**8**	2p. black and blue	23·00	35·00

II. BRITISH CURRENCY

On sale at British P.O.s throughout Morocco, including Tangier, until 1937.

PRICES. Our prices for used stamps with these overprints are for examples used in Morocco. These stamps could also be used in the United Kingdom, with official sanction, from the summer of 1950 onwards, and with U.K. postmarks are worth about 50 per cent less.

Stamps of Great Britain optd **MOROCCO AGENCIES**

1907. King Edward VII.

31	**83**	½d. green	2·25	9·00
32	**83**	1d. red	9·50	5·50
33	-	2d. green and red	10·00	6·00
34	-	4d. green and brown	3·75	4·25
35a	-	4d. orange	10·00	14·00
36	-	6d. purple	15·00	26·00
37	-	1s. green and red	26·00	17·00
38	-	2s.6d. purple	95·00	£140

1914. King George V.

55	**105**	½d. green	2·50	50
43	**104**	1d. red	1·25	20
44	**105**	1½d. brown	6·50	14·00
45	**106**	2d. orange	4·25	60
58	**104**	2½d. blue	5·00	2·50
46	**106**	3d. violet	1·25	35
47	**106**	4d. green	6·50	1·50
60b	**107**	6d. purple	1·00	60
49	**108**	1s. brown	11·00	1·50
53	**109**	2s.6d. brown	42·00	25·00
74	**109**	5s. red	27·00	£130

1935. Silver Jubilee.

62	**123**	½d. green	1·50	6·50
63	**123**	1d. red	1·50	8·00
64	**123**	1½d. brown	4·50	18·00
65	**123**	2½d. blue	5·50	2·50

1935. King George V.

66	**119**	1d. red	3·25	20·00
67	**118**	1½d. brown	3·25	23·00
68	**120**	2d. orange	1·25	13·00
69	**119**	2½d. blue	1·75	4·25
70	**120**	3d. violet	50	30
71	**120**	4d. green	50	30
72	**122**	1s. brown	80	6·50

1936. King Edward VIII.

75	**124**	1d. red	10	40
76	**124**	2½d. blue	10	15

In 1937 unoverprinted Great Britain stamps replaced overprinted **MOROCCO AGENCIES** issues as stocks became exhausted. In 1949 overprinted issues reappeared and were in use at Tetuan (Spanish Zone), the only remaining British P.O. apart from that at Tangier.

1949. King George VI.

77	**128**	½d. green	1·75	7·00
94	**128**	½d. orange	2·00	1·00
78	**128**	1d. red	2·75	9·00
95	**128**	1d. blue	2·00	1·40
79	**128**	1½d. brown	2·75	8·50
96	**128**	1½d. green	2·00	6·00
80	**128**	2d. orange	3·00	9·00
97	**128**	2d. brown	2·25	4·25
81	**128**	2½d. blue	3·25	10·00
98	**128**	2½d. red	2·00	4·25
82	**128**	3d. violet	1·50	2·00
83	**129**	4d. green	50	1·25
84	**129**	5d. brown	3·00	15·00
85	**129**	6d. purple	1·50	1·75
86	**130**	7d. green	50	16·00
87	**130**	8d. red	3·00	6·50
88	**130**	9d. olive	50	11·00
89	**130**	10d. blue	50	8·00
90	**130**	11d. plum	70	9·00
91	**130**	1s. brown	2·75	6·50
92	**131**	2s.6d. green	21·00	45·00
93	**131**	5s. red	40·00	75·00

1951. Pictorials.

99	**147**	2s.6d. green	13·00	21·00
100	-	5s. red (No. 510)	13·00	23·00

1952. Queen Elizabeth II.

101	**154**	½d. orange	10	10
102	**154**	1d. blue	15	1·75
103	**154**	1½d. green	15	20
104	**154**	2d. brown	20	2·00
105	**155**	2½d. red	15	1·25
106	**155**	4d. blue	2·00	3·75
107	**156**	5d. brown	60	60
108	**156**	6d. purple	1·00	3·50
109	**158**	8d. mauve	60	70
110	**159**	1s. bistre	60	60

III. SPANISH CURRENCY

Stamps surcharged in Spanish currency were sold at British P.O.s throughout Morocco until the establishment of the French Zone and the Tangier International Zone, when their use was confined to the Spanish Zone.

Stamps of Great Britain surch **MOROCCO AGENCIES** and value in Spanish currency.

1907. King Edward VII.

112	**83**	5c. on ½d. green	14·00	20
113	**83**	10c. on 1d. red	19·00	10
114a	-	15c. on 1½d. purple and green	6·50	20
115	-	20c. on 2d. green and red	5·50	1·50
116a	**83**	25c. on 2½d. blue	1·75	20
117	-	40c. on 4d. green & brown	2·75	4·50
118a	-	40c. on 4d. orange	1·25	1·25
119a	-	50c. on 5d. purple and blue	6·50	6·00
120a	-	1p. on 10d. purple and red	23·00	18·00
121	-	3p. on 2s.6d. purple	22·00	29·00
122	-	6p. on 5s. red	35·00	45·00
123	-	12p. on 10s. blue	80·00	80·00

1912. King George V.

126	**101**	5c. on ½d. green	3·50	20
127	**102**	10c. on 1d. red	1·25	10

1914. King George V.

128	**105**	3c. on ½d. green	1·75	8·50
129	**105**	5c. on ½d. green	1·00	10
130	**104**	10c. on 1d. red	3·00	10
131	**105**	15c. on 1½d. brown	1·00	10
132	**106**	20c. on 2d. orange	1·00	25
133	**104**	25c. on 2½d. blue	1·75	25
148	**106**	40c. on 4d. green	5·00	2·50
135	**108**	1p. on 10d. blue	6·00	12·00
142	**109**	3p. on 2s.6d. brown	25·00	75·00
136	**109**	6p. on 5s. red	32·00	50·00
138	**109**	12p. on 10s. blue	£100	£180

1935. Silver Jubilee.

149	**123**	5c. on ½d. green	1·00	1·25
150	**123**	10c. on 1d. red	2·75	2·50
151	**123**	15c. on 1½d. brown	5·50	20·00
152	**123**	25c. on 2½d. blue	3·50	2·25

1935. King George V.

153	**118**	5c. on ½d. green	1·00	21·00
154	**119**	10c. on 1d. red	2·50	17·00
155	**118**	15c. on 1½d. brown	8·50	3·25
156	**120**	20c. on 2d. orange	50	35
157	**119**	25c. on 2½d. blue	1·25	8·50
158	**120**	40c. on 4d. green	50	5·50
159	**122**	1p. on 10d. blue	6·00	1·50

1936. King Edward VIII.

160	**124**	5c. on ½d. green	10	10
161	**124**	10c. on 1d. red	50	2·00
162	**124**	15c. on 1½d. brown	10	15
163	**124**	25c. on 2½d. blue	10	10

1937. Coronation.

164	**126**	15c. on 1½d. brown	1·00	70

1937. King George VI.

165	**128**	5c. on ½d. green	1·25	30
182	**128**	5c. on ½d. orange	2·00	7·00
166	**128**	10c. on 1d. red	1·00	10
183	**128**	10c. on 1d. blue	3·25	10·00
167	**128**	15c. on 1½d. brown	2·50	25
184	**128**	15c. on 1½d. green	1·75	25·00
168	**128**	25c. on 2½d. blue	2·00	1·25
185	**128**	25c. on 2½d. red	1·75	18·00
169	**129**	40c. on 4d. green	38·00	15·00
186	**129**	40c. on 4d. blue	1·00	13·00
170	**130**	70c. on 7d. green	2·00	18·00
171	**130**	1p. on 10d. blue	2·25	7·00

1940. Stamp Centenary.

172	**134**	5c. on ½d. green	30	2·75
173	**134**	10c. on 1d. red	3·75	3·75
174	**134**	15c. on 1½d. brown	70	5·50
175	**134**	25c. on 2½d. blue	80	3·75

1948. Silver Wedding.

176	**137**	25c. on 2½d. blue	1·25	1·00
177	**138**	45p. on £1 blue	17·00	22·00

1948. Olympic Games.

178	**139**	25c. on 2½d. blue	50	1·50
179	**140**	30c. on 3d. violet	50	1·50
180	-	60c. on 6d. purple	50	1·50
181	-	1p.20 on 1s. brown	60	1·50

1954. Queen Elizabeth II.

189	**154**	5c. on ½d. orange	15	4·00
188	**154**	10c. on 1d. blue	50	1·75
190	**155**	40c. on 4d. blue	70	2·50

IV. FRENCH CURRENCY

Stamps surch in French currency were sold at British P.O.s in the French Zone.

Stamps of Great Britain surch **MOROCCO AGENCIES** and value in French currency.

1917. King George V.

191	**105**	3c. on ½d. green	1·75	2·50
192	**105**	5c. on ½d. green	60	20
203	**104**	10c. on 1d. red	30	2·00
194	**105**	15c. on 1½d. brown	3·00	20
205	**104**	25c. on 2½d. blue	2·75	50
206	**106**	40c. on 4d. green	75	80
207	**107**	50c. on 5d. brown	1·50	10
198	**108**	75c. on 9d. green	1·00	75
209	**108**	90c. on 9d. green	22·00	7·50
210	**108**	1f. on 10d. blue	1·25	10
211	**108**	1f.50 on 1s. brown	13·00	2·25
200	**109**	3f. on 2s.6d. brown	5·00	1·50
226	**109**	6f. on 5s. red	7·50	21·00

1935. Silver Jubilee.

212	**123**	5c. on ½d. green	15	20
213	**123**	10c. on 1d. red	3·75	70
214	**123**	15c. on 1½d. brown	50	1·60
215	**123**	25c. on 2½d. blue	30	25

1935. King George V.

216	**118**	5c. on ½d. green	50	5·00
217	**119**	10c. on 1d. red	35	30
218	**118**	15c. on 1½d. brown	6·50	5·50
219	**119**	25c. on 2½d. blue	30	15
220	**120**	40c. on 4d. green	30	15
221	**121**	50c. on 5d. brown	30	15
222	**122**	90c. on 9d. olive	35	1·75
223	**122**	1f. on 10d. blue	30	30
224	**122**	1f.50 on 1s. brown	75	3·50

1936. King Edward VIII.

227	**124**	5c. on ½d. green	10	15
228	**124**	15c. on 1½d. brown	10	15

1937. Coronation.

229	**126**	15c. on 1½d. brown	40	20

1937. King George VI.

230	**128**	5c. on ½d. green	4·25	3·00

V. TANGIER INTERNATIONAL ZONE.

This Zone was established in 1924 and the first specially overprinted stamps issued in 1927.

PRICES. Our note re U.K. usage (at beginning of Section II) also applies to **TANGIER** optd stamps.

Stamps of Great Britain optd TANGIER.

1927. King George V.

231	**105**	½d. green	4·75	20
232	**104**	1d. red	6·50	25
233	**105**	1½d. brown	7·50	6·00
234	**106**	2d. orange	3·25	20

1934. King George V.

235	**118**	½d. green	1·25	1·60
236	**119**	1d. red	9·00	2·75
237	**118**	1½d. brown	75	20

1935. Silver Jubilee optd TANGIER TANGIER.

238	**123**	½d. green	1·50	8·00
239	**123**	1d. red	19·00	20·00
240	**123**	1½d. brown	1·25	2·25

1936. King Edward VIII.

241	**124**	½d. green	10	20
242	**124**	1d. red	10	10
243	**124**	1½d. brown	15	10

1937. Coronation optd TANGIER TANGIER.

244	**126**	1½d. brown	1·00	50

1937. King George VI.

245	**128**	½d. green	5·50	1·75
280	**128**	½d. orange	1·00	1·50
246	**128**	1d. red	21·00	1·75
281	**128**	1d. blue	1·25	3·00
247	**128**	1½d. brown	2·75	40
282	**128**	1½d. green	1·25	19·00
261	**128**	2d. orange	8·50	9·00
283	**128**	2d. brown	1·25	4·50
262	**128**	2½d. blue	5·00	6·50
284	**128**	2½d. red	1·25	8·00
263	**128**	3d. violet	70	1·25
264	**129**	4d. green	11·00	14·00
265	**129**	5d. brown	5·00	28·00
285	**129**	4d. blue	4·25	3·00
266	**129**	6d. purple	1·50	30
267	**130**	7d. green	2·00	17·00
268	**130**	8d. red	4·75	15·00
269	**130**	9d. olive	2·25	14·00
270	**130**	10d. blue	2·00	13·00
271	**130**	11d. plum	4·50	20·00
272	**130**	1s. brown	1·50	2·75
273	**131**	2s.6d. green	7·00	23·00
274	**131**	5s. red	16·00	45·00
275	-	10s. blue (No. 478a)	50·00	£140

1940. Stamp Centenary.

248	**134**	½d. green	30	8·00
249	**134**	1d. red	45	85
250	**134**	1½d. brown	2·00	9·50

1946. Victory.

253	**135**	2½d. blue	1·25	65
254	-	3d. violet	1·25	2·00

1948. Silver Wedding.

255	**137**	2½d. blue	50	15
256	**138**	£1 blue	20·00	25·00

1948. Olympic Games.

257	**139**	2½d. blue	1·00	2·00
258	**140**	3d. violet	1·00	2·25
259	-	6d. purple	1·00	2·25
260	-	1s. brown	1·00	2·25

1949. U.P.U.

276	**143**	2½d. blue	70	2·75
277	**144**	3d. violet	70	4·75
278	-	6d. purple	70	1·25
279	-	1s. brown	70	3·25

1951. Pictorial stamps.

286	**147**	2s.6d. green	10·00	5·00
287	-	5s. red (No. 510)	17·00	17·00
288	-	10s. blue (No. 511)	24·00	17·00

1952. Queen Elizabeth II.

313	**154**	½d. orange	10	40
314	**154**	1d. blue	20	50
291	**154**	1½d. green	10	30
292	**154**	2d. brown	20	1·25
293	**155**	2½d. red	10	1·00
294	**155**	3d. lilac	20	1·25
320	**155**	4d. blue	65	2·00
296	**157**	5d. brown	60	1·00
297	**157**	6d. purple	45	15
298	**157**	7d. green	80	3·00
299	**158**	8d. mauve	60	1·50
300	**158**	9d. olive	1·40	1·50
301	**158**	10d. blue	1·40	2·75
302	**158**	11d. purple	1·40	3·25
303	**159**	1s. brown	50	70
304	**159**	1s.3d. green	65	7·00
305	**159**	1s.6d. blue	1·00	2·25

1953. Coronation.

306	**161**	2½d. red	40	50
307	-	4d. blue	1·00	50
308	**163**	1s.3d. green	1·00	1·25
309	-	1s.6d. blue	1·00	1·50

1955. Pictorials.

310	**166**	2s.6d. brown	3·50	10·00
311	-	5s. red	4·50	22·00
312	-	10s. blue	16·00	27·00

1957. Cent of British Post Office in Tangier. Queen Elizabeth II stamps optd 1857-1957 TANGIER.

323	**154**	½d. orange	10	15
324	**154**	1d. blue	10	15
325	**154**	1½d. green	10	15
326	**154**	2d. brown	10	15
327	**155**	2½d. red	15	1·25
328	**155**	3d. lilac	15	40
329	**155**	4d. blue	30	30
330	**157**	5d. brown	30	35
331	**157**	6d. purple	30	35
332	**157**	7d. green	30	35
333	**158**	8d. mauve	30	1·00
334	**158**	9d. olive	30	30
335	**158**	10d. blue	30	30
336	**158**	11d. plum	30	30
337	**159**	1s. bistre	30	30
338	**159**	1s.3d. green	45	5·00
339	**159**	1s.6d. blue	50	1·60
340	**166**	2s.6d. brown	2·00	5·00
341	-	5s. red (No. 596a)	2·75	10·00
342	-	10s. blue (No. 597a)	3·75	11·00

Pt. 1

MORVI

A state of India, Bombay district. Now uses Indian stamps.

12 pies = 1 anna.

1 Maharaja Lakhdirji

1931

8	**1**	3p. red	5·00	18·00
9b	**1**	6p. green	6·50	18·00
5	**1**	½a. blue	7·00	25·00
6	**1**	1a. brown	3·25	38·00
10	**1**	1a. blue	6·00	18·00
7	**1**	2a. brown	4·00	48·00
11	**1**	2a. violet	13·00	50·00

3 Maharaja Lakhdirji

1934

16	**3**	3p. red	2·25	6·00
17	**3**	6p. green	3·75	5·50
14	**3**	1a. brown	3·25	18·00
19	**3**	2a. violet	2·50	23·00

Pt. 1

MOSUL

Stamps used by Indian forces in Mesopotamia (now Iraq) at the close of the 1914–18 war.

12 pies = 1 anna; 16 annas = 1 rupee.

1919. Turkish Fiscal stamps surch POSTAGE I.E.F. 'D' and value in annas.

1	½a. on 1pi. green and red	2·25	1·90
2	1a. on 20pa. black on red	1·40	1·75
4	2½a. on 1pi. mauve and yellow	1·50	1·50
5	3a. on 20pa. green	1·60	4·00
6	3a. on 20pa. green and orange	80·00	£100
7	4a. on 1pi. violet	3·00	3·50
8	8a. on 10pa. red	4·00	5·00

Pt. 9, Pt. 13, Pt. 1

MOZAMBIQUE

Former Overseas Province of Portugal in East Africa, granted independence in 1975. The Republic of Mozambique joined the Commonwealth on 12 November 1995.

1876. 1000 reis = 1 milreis.
1913. 100 centavos = 1 escudo.
1980. 100 centavos = 1 metical.

1876. "Crown" key-type inscr "MOCAMBIQUE".

1	**P**	5r. black	2·30	1·40
11	**P**	10r. yellow	13·00	6·50
19	**P**	10r. green	1·90	1·30
3	**P**	20r. bistre	2·20	1·20
20	**P**	20r. red	£1600	£950
4a	**P**	25r. red	1·20	85
21	**P**	25r. lilac	6·25	2·50
14	**P**	40r. blue	40·00	18·00
22	**P**	40r. buff	5·50	5·00
6	**P**	50r. green	£325	£160
23	**P**	50r. blue	1·40	1·20
7	**P**	100r. lilac	2·20	1·30
8	**P**	200r. orange	8·50	6·75
9	**P**	300r. brown	5·25	3·25

1886. "Embossed" key-type inscr "PROVINCIA DE MOCAMBIQUE".

30	**Q**	5r. black	2·20	1·40
32	**Q**	10r. green	2·20	1·40
34	**Q**	20r. red	2·20	1·40
48	**Q**	25r. lilac	20·00	9·25
37	**Q**	40r. brown	3·25	2·10
38	**Q**	50r. blue	3·75	1·40
40	**Q**	100r. brown	3·75	1·40
42	**Q**	200r. violet	7·00	4·25
43	**Q**	300r. orange	9·00	5·75

1893. No. 37 surch PROVISORIO 5 5.

53	5 on 40r. brown	£300	£160

1894. "Figures" key-type inscr "MOCAMBIQUE".

56	**R**	5r. orange	1·00	80
57	**R**	10r. mauve	1·00	80
58	**R**	15r. brown	1·50	1·00
59	**R**	20r. lilac	1·50	1·30
65	**R**	25r. green	1·00	60
60	**R**	50r. blue	6·50	1·80
67	**R**	75r. pink	3·00	2·30
61	**R**	80r. green	6·50	3·00
62	**R**	100r. brown on buff	3·25	2·50
68	**R**	150r. red on pink	23·00	8·25
64	**R**	200r. blue on blue	7·00	5·75
69	**R**	300r. blue on brown	11·50	6·50

1895. "Embossed" key-type of Mozambique optd 1195 CENTENARIO ANTONINO 1895.

71	**Q**	5r. black	14·00	10·50
72	**Q**	10r. green	19·00	13·00
73	**Q**	20r. red	22·00	14·00
74	**Q**	25r. purple	22·00	14·00
75	**Q**	40r. brown	23·00	18·00
76	**Q**	50r. blue	23·00	18·00
77	**Q**	100r. brown	23·00	18·00
78	**Q**	200r. lilac	45·00	32·00
79	**Q**	300r. orange	55·00	35·00

1897. No. 69 surch 50 reis.

82	**R**	50r. on 300r. blue on brown	£425	£275

1898. Nos. 34 and 37 surch MOCAMBIQUE and value.

84	**Q**	2½r. on 20r. red	38·00	31·00
85	**Q**	5r. on 40r. brown	50·00	38·00

1898. "King Carlos" key type inscr "MOCAMBIQUE". Name and value in red (500r.) or black (others).

100	**S**	700r. mauve on yellow	30·00	13·50
86	**S**	2½r. grey	65	30
87	**S**	5r. red	65	35
88	**S**	10r. green	65	35
89	**S**	15r. brown	6·25	3·75
138	**S**	15r. green	2·20	1·70
90	**S**	20r. lilac	1·70	90
91	**S**	25r. green	1·80	90
139	**S**	25r. red	2·20	1·70
92	**S**	50r. blue	2·10	1·10
140	**S**	50r. brown	4·50	3·25
141	**S**	65r. blue	14·00	10·50
93	**S**	75r. pink	8·00	3·75
142	**S**	75r. purple	4·50	3·25
94	**S**	80r. mauve	8·00	3·75
95	**S**	100r. blue on blue	4·25	2·75
143	**S**	115r. brown on pink	14·00	8·00
144	**S**	130r. brown on yellow	14·00	8·50
96	**S**	150r. brown on yellow	4·25	4·50
97	**S**	200r. purple on pink	4·00	2·75
98	**S**	300r. blue on pink	8·75	4·50
145	**S**	400r. blue on cream	20·00	16·00
99	**S**	500r. black on blue	18·00	9·50

1902. Various types surch.

146	**S**	50r. on 65r. blue	5·75	4·75
101	**R**	65r. on 10r. mauve	4·50	4·25
102	**R**	65r. on 15r. brown	4·50	4·25
105	**Q**	65r. on 20r. red	6·00	3·25
106	**R**	65r. on 20r. lilac	4·50	4·25
108	**Q**	65r. on 40r. brown	7·00	3·50
110	**Q**	65r. on 200r. violet	6·00	3·25
111	**V**	115r. on 2½r. brown	4·50	4·25
113	**Q**	115r. on 5r. black	2·50	2·10
114	**R**	115r. on 5r. orange	4·50	4·25
115	**R**	115r. on 25r. green	4·50	4·25
117	**Q**	115r. on 50r. blue	2·75	2·10
120	**Q**	130r. on 25r. mauve	3·50	2·10
121	**R**	130r. on 75r. red	4·50	4·25
122	**R**	130r. on 100r. brn on buff	10·00	9·25
123	**R**	130r. on 150r. red on pink	4·50	4·25
124	**R**	130r. on 200r. blue on bl	9·00	8·50
126	**Q**	130r. on 300r. orange	4·00	2·50
128	**Q**	400r. on 10r. green	7·50	6·50
129	**R**	400r. on 50r. blue	2·75	2·10
130	**R**	400r. on 80r. green	2·75	1·80
132	**Q**	400r. on 100r. brown	60·00	42·00
133	**R**	400r. on 300r. bl on brn	2·75	2·10

1902. "King Carlos" key-type of Mozambique optd PROVISORIO.

134	**S**	15r. brown	3·50	1·80
135	**S**	25r. green	3·50	1·80
136	**S**	50r. blue	7·00	4·00
137	**S**	75r. pink	10·00	5·25

1911. "King Carlos" key-type of Mozambique optd REPUBLICA.

147	**S**	2½r. grey	55	35
148	**S**	5r. orange	55	35
149	**S**	10r. green	1·80	1·10
150	**S**	15r. green	45	30
151	**S**	20r. lilac	1·80	45
152	**S**	25r. red	35	30
153	**S**	50r. brown	65	45
154	**S**	75r. purple	1·20	1·10
155	**S**	100r. blue on blue	1·20	1·10
156	**S**	115r. brown on pink	1·80	1·10
157	**S**	130r. brown on yellow	1·80	1·10
158	**S**	200r. purple on pink	3·75	1·80
159	**S**	400r. blue on yellow	3·75	1·80
160	**S**	500r. black on blue	3·75	2·30
161	**S**	700r. mauve on yellow	3·75	2·30

1912. "King Manoel" key-type inscr "MOCAMBIQUE" with opt REPUBLICA.

162	**T**	2½r. lilac	50	30
163	**T**	5r. black	50	35
164	**T**	10r. green	50	35
165	**T**	20r. red	1·30	90
166	**T**	25r. brown	50	35
167	**T**	50r. blue	1·10	65
168	**T**	75r. brown	1·10	65
169	**T**	100r. brown on green	1·10	65
170	**T**	200r. green on orange	3·25	1·50
171	**T**	300r. black on blue	2·00	1·50
172	**T**	500r. brown and green	6·50	3·25

1913. Surch REPUBLICA MOCAMBIQUE and value on "Vasco da Gama" issues. (a) Portuguese Colonies.

173	¼c. on 2½r. green	1·70	1·20
174	½c. on 5r. red	1·70	1·20
175	1c. on 10r. purple	1·70	1·20
176	2½c. on 25r. green	1·70	1·20
177	5c. on 50r. blue	1·80	1·30
178	7½c. on 75r. brown	3·00	2·20
179	10c. on 100r. brown	2·20	1·70
180	15c. on 150r. brown	2·20	1·90

(b) Macao.

181	¼c. on ½a. green	2·30	1·90
182	½c. on 1a. red	2·30	1·90
183	1c. on 2a. purple	2·30	1·90
184	2½c. on 4a. green	2·30	1·90
185	5c. on 8a. blue	6·50	4·50
186	7½c. on 12a. brown	3·50	3·25
187	10c. on 16a. brown	2·50	1·90
188	15c. on 24a. brown	2·50	1·90

(c) Timor.

189	¼c. on ½a. green	2·50	2·00
190	½c. on 1a. red	2·50	2·00
191	1c. on 2a. purple	2·50	2·00
192	2½c. on 4a. green	2·50	2·00
193	5c. on 8a. blue	3·75	2·75
194	7½c. on 12a. brown	3·75	2·75
195	10c. on 16a. brown	2·30	1·50
196	15c. on 24a. brown	2·30	1·50

1914. "Ceres" key-type inscr "MOCAMBIQUE".

264	U	1e. pink	1·90	1·20
197	U	¼c. green	45	30
198	U	½c. black	45	30
199	U	1c. green	45	30
200	U	1½c. brown	45	30
201	U	2c. red	50	30
270	U	2c. grey	35	35
202	U	2½c. violet	50	30
255	U	3c. orange	35	25
256	U	4c. pink	35	25
257	U	4½c. grey	35	25
203	U	5c. blue	50	30
275	U	6c. mauve	35	35
259	U	7c. blue	35	25
260	U	7½c. brown	35	25
278	U	8c. grey	35	25
279	U	10c. red	35	25
280	U	12c. brown	35	35
281	U	12c. green	35	35
283	U	15c. purple	35	25
284	U	20c. green	70	65
285	U	24c. blue	45	35
286	U	25c. brown	55	45
209	U	30c. brown on green	3·50	2·20
287	U	30c. green	50	35
295	U	30c. lilac on pink	2·20	1·80
210	U	40c. brown on pink	3·75	2·30
288	U	40c. turquoise	1·20	45
211	U	50c. orange on orange	6·50	4·75
289	U	50c. mauve	65	45
290	U	60c. blue	1·30	70
291	U	60c. pink	1·90	1·20
297	U	60c. brown on pink	2·30	1·80
293	U	80c. red	1·60	70
298	U	80c. brown on blue	2·00	1·50
299	U	1e. green on blue	4·25	2·50
301	U	1e. blue	1·90	1·40
300	U	2e. mauve on pink	3·00	1·50
302	U	2e. purple	1·60	90
303	U	5e. brown	10·50	6·50
304	U	10e. pink	15·00	7·50
305	U	20e. green	48·00	21·00

1915. Provisional issues of 1902 optd REPUBLICA.

226	S	50r. blue (No. 136)	1·40	1·20
227	S	50r. on 65r. blue	1·40	1·20
213	S	75r. pink (No. 137)	3·25	1·80
228	V	115r. on 2½r. brown	1·40	1·20
216	Q	115r. on 5r. black	75·00	60·00
229	R	115r. on 5r. orange	1·40	1·20
230	R	115r. on 25r. green	1·40	1·20
231	R	130r. on 75r. red	1·40	1·20
220	R	130r. on 100r. brown on buff	2·20	1·80
232	R	130r. on 150r. red on pink	1·40	1·20
233	R	130r. on 200r. blue on bl	1·40	1·20
223	R	400r. on 50r. blue	2·75	2·10
224	R	400r. on 80r. green	2·75	2·10
225	R	400r. on 300r. blue on brn	2·75	2·10

1918. Charity Tax stamp surch 2½ CENTAVOS. Roul or perf.

248	C 16	2½c. on 5c. red	1·40	1·20

1920. Charity Tax stamps surch. (a) CORREIOS and value in figures.

306	C15	1c. on 1c. green	1·30	1·00
307	C16	1½c. on 5c. red	1·30	1·00

(b) SEIS CENTAVOS.

308	6c. on 5c. red	1·40	1·20

1921. "Ceres" stamps of 1913 surch.

309	U	10c. on ½c. black	2·75	1·70
310	U	30c. on 1½c. brown	2·75	1·70
316	U	50c. on 4c. pink	2·20	1·10
311	U	60c. on 2½c. violet	4·00	2·20
328	U	70c. on 2e. purple	1·30	70
329	U	1e.40 on 2e. purple	1·60	70

1922. "Ceres" key-type of Lourenco Marques surch.

312	U	10c. on ½c. black	2·75	1·80
314	U	30c. on 1½c. brown	2·75	1·80

1922. Charity Tax stamp surch 2$00.

315	C16	$2 on 5c. red	2·30	1·10

1924. 4th Death Centenary of Vasco da Gama. "Ceres" key-type of Mozambique optd Vasco da Gama 1924.

317	U	80c. pink	2·20	1·10

1925. Nos. 129 and 130 surch Republica 40 C.

318	R	40c. on 400r. on 50r.	1·50	85
319	R	40c. on 400r. on 80r.	1·50	85

1929. "Due" key-type inscr "MOCAMBIQUE" optd CORREIOS.

320	W	50c. lilac	1·90	1·50

23 Mousinho de Albuquerque

1930. Albuquerque's Victories Commemorative. Vignette in grey.

321	23	50c. lake and red (Macontene)	10·50	10·50
322	23	50c. orge & red (Mujenga)	10·50	10·50
323	23	50c. mve & brn (Coolela)	10·50	10·50
324	23	50c. grey and green (Chaimite)	10·50	10·50
325	23	50c. bl & ind (Ibrahimo)	10·50	10·50
326	23	50c. blue and black (Mucuto-muno)	10·50	10·50
327	23	50c. vio & lilac (Naguema)	10·50	10·50

The above were for compulsory use throughout Mozambique in place of ordinary postage stamps on certain days in 1930 and 1931. They are not listed among the Charity Tax stamps as the revenue was not applied to any charitable fund.

25 "Portugal" and Camoens' "The Lusiads"

1938. Value in red (1, 15c., 1e.40) or black (others).

330	25	1c. brown	20	15
331	25	5c. brown	25	20
332	25	10c. purple	25	20
333	25	15c. black	25	20
334	25	20c. grey	25	20
335	25	30c. green	25	20
336	25	35c. green	9·75	3·75
337	25	40c. red	25	20
338	25	45c. blue	45	35
339	25	50c. brown	45	20
340	25	60c. green	65	30
341	25	70c. brown	65	30
342	25	80c. green	65	30
343	25	85c. red	1·70	1·00
344	25	1e. purple	1·20	30
345	25	1e.40 blue	13·50	3·50
346	25	1e.75 blue	8·75	3·25
347	25	2e. lilac	3·00	1·30
348	25	5e. green	4·75	1·30
349	25	10e. brown	11·00	2·75
350	25	20e. orange	55·00	7·25

1938. As 1938 issue of Macao. Name and value in black.

351	54	1c. green (postage)	25	25
352	54	5c. brown	25	25
353	54	10c. red	25	25
354	54	15c. purple	25	25
355	54	20c. grey	25	25
356	-	30c. purple	25	25
357	-	35c. green	50	25
358	-	40c. brown	50	25
359	-	50c. mauve	50	25
360	-	60c. black	50	25
361	-	70c. violet	50	25
362	-	80c. orange	50	25
363	-	1e. red	1·10	50
364	-	1e.75 blue	4·00	85
365	-	2e. red	4·00	1·00
366	-	5e. green	7·50	1·50
367	-	10e. blue	16·00	2·10
368	-	20e. brown	37·00	4·25
369	56	10c. red (air)	65	60
370	56	20c. violet	65	60
371	56	50c. orange	75	65
372	56	1e. blue	75	65
373	56	2e. red	1·30	65
374	56	3e. green	2·75	65
375	56	5e. brown	4·50	95
376	56	9e. red	8·25	1·70
377	56	10e. mauve	14·00	3·25

DESIGNS: 30 to 50c. Mousinho de Albuquerque; 60c. to 1e. Dam; 1e.75 to 5e. Henry the Navigator; 10, 20e. Afonso de Albuquerque.

1938. No. 338 surch 40 centavos.

378	25	40c. on 45c. blue	6·50	4·25

26a Route of President's Tour

1938. President Carmona's 2nd Colonial Tour.

379	26a	80c. violet on mauve	4·75	3·25
380	26a	1e.75 blue on blue	16·00	6·75
381	26a	3e. green on green	28·00	10·50
382	26a	20e. brown on cream	£140	60·00

27 New Cathedral, Lourenco Marques

1944. 400th Anniv of Lourenco Marques.

383	27	50c. brown	2·20	80
384	-	50c. green	2·20	80
385	-	1e.75 blue	9·75	2·75
386a	-	20e. black	27·00	2·75

DESIGNS—HORIZ: 1e.75, Lourenco Marques Central Railway Station; 20e. Town Hall, Lourenco Marques.
See also No. 405.

1946. Nos. 354, 364 and 375 surch.

387	10c. on 15c. purple (postage)	1·30	75
388	60c. on 1e.75 blue	2·20	85
389	3e. on 5e. brown (air)	18·00	17·00

1947. No. 386a surch.

390	2e. on 20e. black	3·50	1·30

30 Lockheed L.18 Lodestar

1946. Air. Values in black.

391	30	1e.20 red	3·25	1·70
392	30	1e.60 blue	3·25	1·80
393	30	1e.70 purple	6·00	2·50
394	30	2e.90 brown	9·50	5·00
395	30	3e. green	10·50	5·00

1947. Air. Optd Taxe percue. Values in red (50c.) or black (others).

397	50c. black	1·50	95
398	1e. pink	1·50	95
399	3e. green	2·75	1·10
400	4e.50 green	4·50	2·00
401	5e. red	6·50	2·20
402	10e. blue	18·00	5·75
403	20e. violet	47·00	16·00
404	50e. orange	95·00	40·00

1948. As T **27** but without commemorative inscr.

405	4e.50 red	4·25	1·10

31 Antonio Enes

1948. Birth Centenary of Antonio Enes.

406	31	50c. black and cream	1·60	75
407	31	5e. purple and cream	3·75	2·30

33 Lourenco Marques

1948

408	-	5c. brown	45	25
409	-	10c. purple	45	25
410	-	20c. brown	45	25
411	-	30c. purple	45	25
412	-	40c. green	55	25
413	33	50c. grey	55	25
414	-	60c. purple	55	25
415	33	80c. violet	55	25
416	-	1e. red	85	45
417	-	1e.20 grey	95	45
418	-	1e.50 violet	1·30	50
419	-	1e.75 blue	1·90	65
420	-	2e. brown	1·70	50
421	-	2e.50 blue	5·75	45
422	-	3e. green	2·75	45
423	-	3e.50 green	3·75	45
424	-	5e. green	3·75	45
425	-	10e. brown	9·00	60
426	-	15e. red	22·00	3·25
427	-	20e. orange	43·00	5·25

DESIGNS—VERT: 5, 30c. Gogogo Peak; 20, 40c. Zumbo River; 60c., 3e.50, Nhanhangare Waterfall. HORIZ: 10c., 1e.20, Railway bridge over River Zambesi at Sena; 1, 5e. Gathering coconuts; 1e.50, 2e. River Pungue at Beira; 1e.75, 3e. Polana beach, Lourenco Marques; 2e.50, 10e. Bird's eye view of Lourenco Marques; 15, 20e. Malema River.

1949. Honouring the Statue of Our Lady of Fatima. As T **62** of Macao.

428	50c. blue	3·75	1·70
429	1e.20 mauve	8·25	3·50
430	4e.50 green	32·00	10·50
431	20e. brown	60·00	16·00

35 Aircraft and Globe

1949. Air.

432	35	50c. brown	75	30
433	35	1e.20 violet	1·50	70
434	35	4e.50 blue	3·50	1·10
435	35	5e. green	6·00	1·40
436	35	20e. brown	17·00	7·00

1949. 75th Anniv of U.P.U. As T **64** of Macao.

437	4e.50 blue	4·50	1·80

1950. Holy Year. As Nos. 425/6 of Macao.

438	1e.50 orange	1·20	65
439	3e. blue	1·70	95

36 Clown Triggerfish

1951. Fish. Multicoloured.

440	5c. Type **36**	35	15
441	10c. Thread-finned butterflyfish	20	15
442	15c. Racoon butterflyfish	90	45
443	20c. Lionfish	30	15
444	30c. Pearl puffer	25	15
445	40c. Golden filefish	20	15
446	50c. Spot-cheeked surgeonfish	20	15
447	1e. Pennant coralfish (vert)	30	15
448	1e.50 Seagrass wrasse	30	15
449	2e. Sombre sweetlips	30	15
450	2e.50 Blue-striped snapper	1·00	20
451	3e. Convict tang	1·00	20
452	3e.50 Starry triggerfish	1·20	15
453	4e. Cornetfish	1·80	35
454	4e.50 Vagabond butterflyfish	2·75	35
455	5e. Sail-backed mailcheek	2·75	15
456	6e. Dusky batfish (vert)	2·75	15
457	8e. Moorish idol (vert)	4·50	60
458	9e. Triangulate boxfish	4·50	45
459	10e. Eastern flying gurnard	11·00	2·30
460	15e. Red-toothed triggerfish	65·00	19·00
461	20e. Picasso triggerfish	34·00	7·00
462	30e. Long-horned cowfish	41·00	9·50
463	50e. Spotted cowfish	50·00	18·00

1951. Termination of Holy Year. As T **69** of Macao.

464	5e. red and orange	2·75	1·50

37 Victor Cordon (colonist)

1951. Birth Centenary of Cordon.

465	37	1e. brown and light brown	2·75	65
466	37	5e. black and blue	14·00	1·70

1952. First Tropical Medicine Congress, Lisbon. As T 71 of Macao.

467	3e. orange and blue	1·80	75

DESIGN: 3e. Miguela Bombarda Hospital.

39 Liner and Lockheed Constellation Airliner

1952. Fourth African Tourist Congress.

468	**39**	1e.50 multicoloured	1·00	70

40 Missionary

1953. Missionary Art Exhibition.

469	**40**	10c. red and lilac	20	15
470	**40**	1e. red and green	1·10	30
471	**40**	5e. black and blue	2·75	90

41 Citrus Butterfly

1953. Butterflies and Moths. Multicoloured.

472	10c. Type **41**	15	15
473	15c. "Amphicallia thelwalli"	15	15
474	20c. Forest queen	15	15
475	30c. Western scarlet	15	15
476	40c. Black-barred red-tip	15	15
477	50c. Mocker swallowtail	15	15
478	80c. "Nudaurelia hersilia dido"	20	15
479	1e. African moon moth	20	15
480	1e.50 Large striped swallowtail	25	15
481	2e. "Athletes ethica"	6·50	60
482	2e.30 African monarch	5·25	60
483	2e.50 Green swallowtail	11·50	60
484	3e. "Arniocera ericata"	2·10	20
485	4e. Apollo moth	75	15
486	4e.50 Peach moth	95	15
487	5e. "Metarctica lateritia"	95	15
488	6e. "Xanthospilopteryx mozambica"	1·10	30
489	7e.50 White bear	6·50	60
490	10e. Flame-coloured charaxes	10·50	1·90
491	20e. Fervid tiger moth	18·00	1·90

42 Stamps

1953. Philatelic Exhibition, Lourenco Marques.

492	**42**	1e. multicoloured	1·50	55
493	**42**	3e. multicoloured	5·75	1·40

1953. Portuguese Postage Stamp Centenary. As T 75 of Macao.

494	50c. multicoloured	1·20	75

1954. Fourth Centenary of Sao Paulo. As T **76** of Macao.

495	3e.50 multicoloured	60	30

43 Map of Mozambique

1954. Multicoloured map; Mozambique territory in colours given.

496	**43**	10c. lilac	20	15
497	**43**	20c. yellow	20	15
498	**43**	50c. blue	20	15
499	**43**	1e. yellow	25	15
500	**43**	2e.30 white	85	65
501	**43**	4e. orange	95	50
502	**43**	10e. green	2·50	30
503	**43**	20e. brown	4·25	65

44 Arms of Beira

1954. First Philatelic Exhibition, Manica and Sofala.

504	**44**	1e.50 multicoloured	60	30
505	**44**	3e.50 multicoloured	1·40	60

45 Mousinho de Albuquerque

1955. Birth Centenary of M. de Albuquerque.

506	**45**	2e. brown and grey	85	50
507	-	2e.50 multicoloured	1·70	85

DESIGN: 2e.50, Equestrian statue of Albuquerque.

46 Arms and Inhabitants

1956. Visit of President to Mozambique. Multicoloured. Background in colours given.

508	**46**	1e. cream	60	20
509	**46**	2e.50 blue	1·20	60

47 Beira

1957. 50th Anniv of Beira.

510	**47**	2e.50 multicoloured	1·20	60

1958. Sixth International Congress of Tropical Medicine. As T **79** of Macao.

511	1e.50 multicoloured	3·25	1·40

DESIGN: 1e.50, "Strophanthus grandiflorus" (plant).

1958. Brussels International Exn. As T 78 of Macao.

512	3e.50 multicoloured	50	30

48 Caravel

1960. 500th Death Anniv of Prince Henry the Navigator.

513	**48**	5e. multicoloured	1·00	30

49 "Arts and Crafts"

1960. Tenth Anniv of African Technical Co-operation Commission.

514	**49**	3e. multicoloured	80	50

50 Arms of Lourenco Marques

1961. Arms. Multicoloured.

515	5c. Type **50**	20	15
516	15c. Chibuto	20	15
517	20c. Nampula	20	15
518	30c. Inhambane	20	15
519	50c. Mozambique (city)	20	15
520	1e. Matola	35	15
521	1e.50 Quelimane	35	15
522	2e. Mocuba	65	15
523	2e.50 Antonio Enes	2·00	20
524	3e. Cabral	75	20
525	4e. Manica	75	20
526	4e.50 Pery	75	20
527	5e. St. Tiago de Tete	75	20
528	7e.50 Porto Amelia	1·60	55
529	10e. Chinde	2·40	60
530	20e. Joao Belo	5·25	95
531	50e. Beira	10·50	2·20

1962. Sports. As T 82 of Macao. Multicoloured.

532	50c. Water-skiing	20	15
533	1e. Wrestling	1·30	30
534	1e.50 Gymnastics	60	25
535	2e.50 Hockey	50	25
536	4e.50 Netball	1·40	65
537	15e. Outboard speedboat racing	2·75	1·50

1962. Malaria Eradication. Mosquito design as T 83 of Macao. Multicoloured.

538	2e.50 "Anopheles funestus"	1·90	55

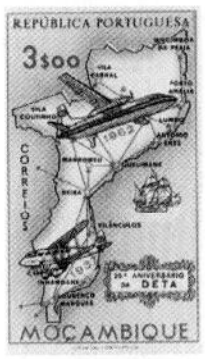

51 Fokker F.27 Friendship and de Havilland DH.89 Dragon Rapide over Route Map

1962. 25th Anniv of D.E.T.A. (Mozambique Airline).

539	**51**	3e. multicoloured	95	30

52 Lourenco Marques in 1887 and 1962

1962. 75th Anniv of Lourenco Marques.

540	**52**	1e. multicoloured	65	30

53 Oil Refinery, Sonarep

1962. Air. Multicoloured.

541	1e.50 Type **53**	85	30
542	2e. Salazar Academy	75	20
543	3e.50 Aerial view of Lourenco Marques Port	75	20
544	4e.50 Salazar Barrage	75	20
545	5e. Trigo de Morais Bridge and Dam	75	20
546	20e. Marcelo Caetano Bridge and Dam	2·75	95

Each design includes an airplane in flight.

54 Arms of Mozambique and Statue of Vasco da Gama

1963. Bicentenary of City of Mozambique.

547	**54**	3e. multicoloured	65	30

1963. 10th Anniv of T.A.P. Airline. As T 52 of Portuguese Guinea.

548	2e.50 multicoloured	60	25

55 Nef, 1430

1963. Evolution of Sailing Ships. Multicoloured.

549	10c. Type **55**	20	15
550	20c. Caravel, 1436 (vert)	20	15
551	30c. Lateen-rigged caravel, 1460 (vert)	20	15
552	50c. Vasco da Gama's ship "Sao Gabriel", 1497 (vert)	20	15
553	1e. Don Manuel's nau, 1498 (vert)	60	15
554	1e.50 Galleon, 1530 (vert)	60	15
555	2e. Nau "Flor de la Mar", 1511 (vert)	60	15
556	2e.50 Caravel "Redonda", 1519	60	15
557	3e.50 Nau, 1520 (vert)	75	20
558	4e. Portuguese Indies galley, 1521	85	25
559	4e.50 Galleon "Santa Tereza", 1639 (vert)	85	25
560	5e. Nau "N. Senhora da Conceicao", 1716 (vert)	17·00	45
561	6e. Warship "N. Senhora do Bom Sucesso", 1764	1·20	45
562	7e.50 Bomb launch, 1788	1·60	55
563	8e. Naval brigantine "Lebre", 1793	1·60	55
564	10e. Corvette "Andorinha", 1799	1·60	55
565	12e.50 Naval schooner "Maria Teresa", 1820	1·80	95
566	15e. Warship "Vasco da Gama", 1841	2·50	95
567	20e. Sail frigate "Don Fernando II e Gloria", 1843 (vert)	3·25	1·20
568	30e. Cadet barque "Sagres I", 1924 (vert)	5·50	2·10

1964. Centenary of National Overseas Bank. As T 84 of Macao but view of Bank building, Lourenco Marques.

569	1e.50 multicoloured	60	20

56 Pres. Tomas

1964. Presidential Visit.

570	**56**	2e.50 multicoloured	60	20

57 State Barge of Joao V, 1728

1964. Portuguese Marine, 18th and 19th Centuries. Multicoloured.

571	15c. Type **57**	20	15
572	35c. State barge of Jose I, 1753	20	15
573	1e. Barge of Alfandega, 1768	55	20
574	1e.50 Oarsman of 1780 (vert)	65	25
575	2e.50 State barge "Pinto da Fonseca", 1780	35	15
576	5e. State barge of Carlota Joaquina, 1790	65	30
577	9e. Don Miguel's state barge, 1831	1·60	95

1965. I.T.U. Centenary. As T 85 of Macao.

578	1e. multicoloured	60	30

1966. 40th Anniv of Portuguese National Revolution. As T 86 of Macao, but showing different building. Multicoloured.

579	1e. Beira railway station and Antonio Enes Academy	55	30

58 Arquebusier, 1560

1967. Portuguese Military Uniforms. Multicoloured.

580	20c. Type **58**	20	15
581	30c. Arquebusier, 1640	20	15
582	40c. Infantryman, 1777	20	15
583	50c. Infantry officer, 1777	20	15
584	80c. Drummer, 1777	60	25
585	1e. Infantry sergeant, 1777	60	20
586	2e. Infantry major, 1784	65	20
587	2e.50 Colonial officer, 1788	70	25
588	3e. Infantryman, 1789	70	25
589	5e. Colonial bugler, 1801	1·40	45
590	10e. Colonial officer, 1807	1·50	65
591	15e. Infantryman, 1817	2·75	1·70

1967. Centenary of Military Naval Association. As T 88 of Macao. Multicoloured.

592	3e. A. Coutinho and paddle-gunboat "Tete"	45	20
593	10e. J. Roby and paddle-gunboat "Granada"	1·40	65

1967. 50th Anniv of Fatima Apparitions. As T 89 of Macao.

594		50c. "Golden Crown"	30	20

1968. 500th Birth Anniv of Pedro Cabral (explorer). As T 90 of Macao.
595	1e. Erecting the Cross at Porto Seguro (horiz)	20	15
596	1e.50 First mission service in Brazil (horiz)	50	15
597	3e. Church of Grace, Santarem	95	50

1969. Birth Centenary of Admiral Gago Coutinho. As T 91 of Macao.
| 598 | 70c. Admiral Gago Coutinho Airport, Lourenco Marques (horiz) | 35 | 20 |

59 Luis de Camoens (poet)

1969. 400th Anniv of Camoens' Visit to Mozambique. Multicoloured.
599	15c. Type **59**	20	15
600	50c. Nau of 1553 (horiz)	25	15
601	1e.50 Map of Mozambique, 1554	35	20
602	2e.50 Chapel of Our Lady of Baluarte (horiz)	50	25
603	5e. Part of the "Lusiad" (poem)	70	55

1969. 500th Birth Anniv of Vasco da Gama (explorer). As T 92 of Macao. Multicoloured.
| 604 | 1e. Route map of Da Gama's Voyage to India (horiz) | 30 | 20 |

1969. Centenary of Overseas Administrative Reforms. As T 93 of Macao.
| 605 | 1e.50 multicoloured | 35 | 20 |

1969. 500th Birth Anniv of King Manoel I. As T 95 of Macao. Multicoloured.
| 606 | 80c. Illuminated arms (horiz) | 30 | 20 |

1970. Birth Centenary of Marshal Carmona. As T 96 of Macao. Multicoloured.
| 607 | 5e. Portrait in ceremonial dress | 55 | 30 |

60 Fossilized Fern

1971. Rocks, Minerals and Fossils. Mult.
608	15c. Type **60**	30	15
609	50c. "Lytodiscoides conduciensis " (fossilized snail)	30	15
610	1e. Stibnite	45	20
611	1e.50 Pink beryl	65	20
612	2e. Endothiodon and fossil skeleton	75	20
613	3e. Tantalocolumbite	1·20	20
614	3e.50 Verdelite	1·60	30
615	4e. Zircon	2·10	45
616	10e. Petrified tree-stump	3·75	1·20

1972. 400th Anniv of Camoens' "The Lusiads" (epic poem). As T 98 of Macao. Multicoloured.
| 617 | 4e. Mozambique Island in 16th century | 60 | 30 |

1972. Olympic Games, Munich. As T 99 of Macao. Multicoloured.
| 618 | 3e. Hurdling and swimming | 45 | 30 |

1972. 50th Anniv of 1st Flight, Lisbon–Rio de Janeiro. As T 100 of Macao. Multicoloured.
| 619 | 1e. Fairey IIID seaplane "Santa Cruz" at Recife | 30 | 20 |

61 Racing Dinghies

1973. World Championships for "Vauriens" Class Yachts, Lourenco Marques.
620	**61**	1e. multicoloured	20	15
621	-	1e.50 multicoloured	30	15
622	-	3e. multicoloured	60	30
DESIGNS: Nos. 621/2 similar to Type **61**.

1973. Centenary of I.M.O./W.M.O. As T 102 of Macao.
| 623 | 2e. multicoloured | 50 | 30 |

62 Dish Aerials

1974. Inauguration of Satellite Communications Station Network.
| 624 | **62** | 50c. multicoloured | 30 | 20 |

63 Bird with "Flag" Wings

1975. Implementation of Lusaka Agreement.
625	**63**	1e. multicoloured	20	15
626	**63**	1e.50 multicoloured	25	15
627	**63**	2e. multicoloured	30	20
628	**63**	3e.50 multicoloured	55	45
629	**63**	6e. multicoloured	1·20	50
MS630	150×75 mm. Nos. 625/9. Imperf	7·00	7·00

1975. Independence. Optd INDEPENDENCIA 25 JUN 75.
631	43	10c. multicoloured (postage)	50	50
632	-	40c. mult (No. 476)	10	10
633	62	50c. mult	20	15
634	61	1e. multicoloured	30	25
635	-	1e.50 mult (No. 621)	85	75
636	-	2e. multicoloured (No. 623)	2·40	2·40
637	-	2e.50 mult (No. 535)	35	30
638	-	3e. multicoloured (No. 618)	40	35
639	-	3e. multicoloured (No. 622)	45	40
640	-	3e.50 mult (No. 614)	2·40	2·40
641	-	4e.50 mult (No. 536)	2·75	1·50
642	-	7e.50 mult (No. 489)	80	30
643	-	10e. mult (No. 616)	1·40	35
644	-	15e. mult (No. 537)	1·75	1·50
645	43	20e. multicoloured	4·75	4·25
646	-	3e.50 multicoloured (No. 543) (air)	35	25
647	-	4e.50 mult (No. 544)	40	25
648	-	5e. multicoloured (No. 545)	1·25	50
649	-	20e. mult (No. 546)	2·00	4·25

66 Workers, Farmers and Children

1975. "Vigilance, Unity, Work". Multicoloured.
650	20c. Type **66**	10	10
651	30c. Type **66**	10	10
652	50c. Type **66**	10	10
653	2e.50 Type **66**	15	10
654	4e.50 Armed family, workers and dancers	25	15
655	5e. As No. 654	35	15
656	10e. As No. 654	95	30
657	50e. As No. 654	4·25	2·10
MS658	132×179 mm. Nos. 650/7 (sold for 75e.)	6·25	3·00

67 Farm Worker

1976. Women's Day.
659	**67**	1e. black and green	10	10
660	-	1e.50 black and brown	10	10
661	-	2e.50 black and blue	15	10
662	-	10e. black and red	90	40
DESIGNS: 1e.50, Teaching; 2e.50, Nurse; 10e. Mother.

1976. Pres. Kaunda's First Visit to Mozambique. Optd PRESIDENTE KENNETH KAUNDA PREMEIRA VISITA 20/4/1976.
663	63	2e. multicoloured	15	10
664	-	3e.50 multicoloured	25	15
665	-	6e. multicoloured	50	30

69 Arrival of President Machel

1976. 1st Anniv of Independence. Mult.
666	50c. Type **69**	10	10
667	1e. Proclamation ceremony	10	10
668	2e.50 Signing ceremony	15	10
669	7e.50 Soldiers on parade	40	20
670	20e. Independence flame	1·50	1·10

70 Mozambique Stamp of 1876 and Emblem

1976. Stamp Centenary.
| 671 | **70** | 1e.50 multicoloured | 10 | 10 |
| 672 | **70** | 6e. multicoloured | 30 | 20 |

1976. "FACIM" Industrial Fair. Optd FACIM 1976.
| 673 | 66 | 2e.50 multicoloured | 30 | 15 |

72 Weapons and Flag

1976. Army Day.
| 674 | **72** | 3e. multicoloured | 20 | 10 |

73 Thick-tailed Bush baby

1977. Animals. Multicoloured.
675	50c. Type **73**	15	10
676	1e. Ratel (horiz)	15	10
677	1e.50 Temminck's ground pangolin	20	10
678	2e. Steenbok (horiz)	20	10
679	2e.50 Diademed monkey	25	10
680	3e. Hunting dog (horiz)	25	10
681	4e. Cheetah (horiz)	35	10
682	5e. Spotted hyena	50	15
683	7e.50 Warthog (horiz)	1·00	25
684	8e. Hippopotamus (horiz)	1·10	25
685	10e. White rhinoceros (horiz)	1·10	30
686	15e. Sable antelope	1·60	65

74 Congress Emblem

1977. 3rd Frelimo Congress, Maputo. Mult.
687	3e. Type **74**	15	10
688	3e.50 Macheje Monument (site of 2nd Congress) (34×24 mm)	20	10
689	20e. Maputo Monument (23×34 mm)	1·40	50

75 "Women" (child's drawing)

1977. Mozambique Women's Day.
| 690 | 75 | 5e. multicoloured | 25 | 10 |
| 691 | 75 | 15e. multicoloured | 65 | 25 |

76 Labourer and Farmer

1977. Labour Day.
| 692 | 76 | 5e. multicoloured | 25 | 10 |

77 Crowd with Arms and Crops

1977. 2nd Anniv of Independence.
693	77	50c. multicoloured	10	10
694	77	1e.50 multicoloured	10	10
695	77	3e. multicoloured	15	10
696	77	15e. multicoloured	60	25

78 "Encepharlartos ferox"

1978. Stamp Day. Nature Protection. Mult.
| 697 | 1e. Type **78** | 10 | 10 |
| 698 | 10e. Nyala | 50 | 20 |

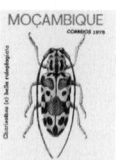
79 "Chariesthes bella"

1978. Beetles. Multicoloured.
699	50c. Type **79**	10	10
700	1e. "Tragocephalus variegata"	10	10
701	1e.50 "Monochamus leuconotus"	10	10
702	3e. "Prosopocera lactator"	25	10
703	5e. "Dinocephalus ornatus"	40	10
704	10e. "Tragiscoschema nigroscriptus"	60	20

80 Violet-crested Turaco

1978. Birds. Multicoloured.
705	50c. Type **80**	35	15
706	1e. Lilac-breasted roller	45	15
707	1e.50 Red-headed weaver	45	15
708	2e.50 Violet starling	50	25
709	3e. Peters's twin-spot	1·00	35
710	15e. European bee eater	2·50	70

81 Mother and Child

1978. Global Eradication of Smallpox.
| 711 | 81 | 15e. multicoloured | 45 | 25 |

82 "Crinum delagoense"

1978. Flowers. Multicoloured.
712	50c. Type **82**		10	10
713	1e. "Gloriosa superba"		10	10
714	1e.50 "Eulophia speciosa"		10	10
715	3e. "Erithrina humeana"		15	10
716	5e. "Astripomoea malvacea"		80	15
717	10e. "Kigelia africana"		1·00	60

83 First Stamps of Mozambique and Canada

1978. "CAPEX '78" International Stamp Exhibition, Toronto.
718	**83**	15e. multicoloured	45	25

84 Mozambique Flag

1978. 3rd Anniv of Independence. Multicoloured.
719	1e. Type **84**		10	10
720	1e.50 Coat of Arms		10	10
721	7e.50 People and Constitution		25	15
722	10e. Band and National Anthem		30	20
MS723	130×100 mm. Nos. 719/22 (sold at 30e.)		75	55

85 Boy with Books

1978. 11th World Youth Festival, Havana. Mult.
724	2e.50 Type **85**		10	10
725	3e. Soldiers		15	10
726	7e.50 Harvesting wheat		25	20

86 Czechoslovakian 50h. Stamp, 1919

1978. "PRAGA '78" International Stamp Exhibition.
727	**86**	15e. blue, ochre and red	45	30
MS728	135×109 mm. No. 727 (sold at 30e.)		45	30

87 Football

1978. Stamp Day. Sports. Multicoloured.
729	50c. Type **87**		10	10
730	1e.50 Putting the shot		10	10
731	3e. Hurdling		15	10
732	7e.50 Basketball		35	20
733	12e.50 Swimming		45	35
734	25e. Roller-skate hockey		1·25	60

88 U.P.U. Emblem and Dove

1979. Membership of U.P.U.
735	**88**	20e. multicoloured	1·00	45

89 Eduardo Mondlane

1979. 10th Death Anniv of Eduardo Mondlane (founder of FRELIMO). Multicoloured.
736	1e. Soldier handing gourd to woman		10	10
737	3e. FRELIMO soldiers		15	10
738	7e.50 Children learning to write		30	20
739	12e.50 Type **89**		40	30

90 Shaded Silver

1979. Domestic Cats. Multicoloured.
740	50c. Type **90**		10	10
741	1e.50 Manx cat		10	10
742	2e.50 British blue		15	10
743	3e. Turkish cat		20	10
744	12e.50 Long-haired tabby		85	55
745	20e. African wild cat		1·50	90

91 I.Y.C. Emblem

1979. Obligatory Tax. International Year of the Child.
746	**91**	50c. red	15	10

92 Wrestling

1979. Olympic Games, Moscow (1980). Mult.
747	1e. Type **92**		10	10
748	2e. Running		10	10
749	3e. Horse jumping		15	10
750	5e. Canoeing		15	10
751	10e. High jump		30	20
752	15e. Archery		50	40
MS753	100×81 mm. 30e. Discus		95	75

93 Flowers

1979. International Year of the Child. Mult.
754	50c. Type **93**		10	10
755	1e.50 Dancers		10	10
756	3e. In the city		15	10
757	5e. Working in the country		15	10
758	7e.50 Houses		25	15
759	12e.50 Transport		1·50	50

94 Flight from Colonialism

1979. 4th Anniv of Independence. Multicoloured.
760	50c. Type **94**		10	10
761	2e. Eduardo Mondlane (founder of FRELIMO)		10	10
762	3e. Armed struggle, death of Mondlane		15	10
763	7e.50 Final fight for liberation		25	15
764	15e. President Samora Machel proclaims victory		45	35
MS765	92×60 mm. 30e. Liberation		90	65

95 Golden Scorpionfish

1979. Tropical Fish. Multicoloured.
766	50c. Type **95**		10	10
767	1e.50 Golden trevally		15	10
768	2e.50 Brick goby		20	10
769	3e. Clown surgeonfish		25	15
770	10e. Lace goby		60	25
771	12e.50 Yellow-edged lyretail		95	40

96 Quartz

1979. Minerals. Multicoloured.
772	1e. Type **96**		10	10
773	1e.50 Beryl		10	10
774	2e.50 Magnetite		15	10
775	5e. Tourmaline		30	10
776	10e. Euxenite		60	20
777	20e. Fluorite		1·40	45

97 Soldier handing out Guns

1979. 15th Anniv of Fight for Independence.
778	**97**	5e. multicoloured	25	15

98 Locomotive No. 1, 1914

1979. Early Locomotives. Multicoloured.
779	50c. Type **98**		15	10
780	1e.50 Gaza Railway locomotive No. 1, 1898		20	10
781	3e. Cape Government Railway 1st Class locomotive, 1878		45	10
782	7e.50 Delagoa Bay Railway locomotive No. 9, 1892		75	20
783	12e.50 Locomotive No. 41, 1896		1·25	30
784	15e. Trans Zambesia Railway Class D steam locomotive		1·40	35

99 Dalmatian

1979. Dogs. Multicoloured.
785	50c. Basenji (vert)		10	10
786	1e.50 Type **99**		15	10
787	3e. Boxer		15	10
788	7e.50 Blue gascon pointer		35	15

789	12e.50 English cocker spaniel		85	25
790	15e. Pointer		1·25	30

100 "Papilio nireus"

1979. Stamp Day. Butterflies. Multicoloured.
791	1e. Type **100**		10	10
792	1e.50 "Amauris ochlea"		10	10
793	2e.50 "Pinacopteryx eriphia"		15	10
794	5e. "Junonia hierta"		35	10
795	10e. "Nephronia argia"		1·00	20
796	20e. "Catacroptera cloanthe"		2·10	90

101 "Dermacentor circumguttatus cunhasilvai" and African Elephant

1980. Ticks. Multicoloured.
797	50c. Type **101**		20	10
798	1e.50 "Dermacentor rhinocerinos" and black rhinoceros		30	10
799	2e.50 "Amblyomma hebraeum" and giraffe		40	15
800	3e. "Amblyomma pomposum" and eland		50	15
801	5e. "Amblyomma theilerae" and cow		60	15
802	7e.50 "Amblyomma eburneum" and African buffalo		85	30

102 Ford "Hercules" Bus, 1950

1980. Road Transport. Multicoloured.
803	50c. Type **102**		10	10
804	1e.50 Scania "Marco-Polo" bus, 1978		10	10
805	3e. Bussing Nag Bus, 1936		15	10
806	5e. Ikarus articulated bus, 1978		20	10
807	7e.50 Ford Taxi, 1929		40	15
808	12e.50 Fiat "131" Taxi, 1978		80	20

103 Soldier and Map of Southern Africa

1980. Zimbabwe Independence.
809	**103**	10e. blue and brown	40	15

104 Marx, Engels and Lenin

1980. International Workers' Day.
810	**104**	10e. multicoloured	40	15

105 "Market" (Moises Simbine)

1980. "London 1980" International Stamp Exhibition. Multicoloured.
811	50c. "Heads" (Malangatana)		10	10
812	1e.50 Type **105**		10	10

813		3e. "Heads with Helmets" (Malangatana)	15	10
814		5e. "Women with Goods" (Machiana)	20	10
815		7e.50 "Crowd with Masks" (Malangatana)	25	15
816		12e.50 "Man and Woman with Spear" (Mankeu)	50	25

106 Telephone

1980. World Telecommunications Day.

| 817 | **106** | 15e. multicoloured | 60 | 25 |

107 Mueda Massacre

1980. 20th Anniv of Mueda Massacre.

| 818 | **107** | 15e. green, brown and red | 60 | 25 |

108 Crowd waving Tools

1980. 5th Anniv of Independence.

819	-	1e. black and red	10	10
820	**108**	2e. multicoloured	10	10
821	-	3e. multicoloured	15	10
822	-	4e. multicoloured	20	10
823	-	5e. black, yellow and red	20	10
824	-	10e. multicoloured	40	15
MS825	140×100 mm. 30e. black, ultramarine and emerald		1·10	45

DESIGNS:—As T **108**: 1e. Crowd, doctor tending patient, soldier and workers tilling land; 3e. Crowd with flags and tools; 4e. Stylized figures raising right hand; 5e. Hand grasping flags, book and plants; 10e. Figures carrying banners each with year date. 55×37 mm: 30e. Soldiers.

109 Gymnastics

1980. Olympic Games, Moscow. Multicoloured.

826	50c. Type **109**		10	10
827	1e.50 Football		10	10
828	2e.50 Running		10	10
829	3e. Volleyball		20	10
830	10e. Cycling		40	15
831	12e.50 Boxing		45	20

110 Narina's Trogon

1980. Birds. Multicoloured.

832	1m. Type **110**		35	10
833	1m.50 South African crowned crane		40	10
834	2m.50 Red-necked spurfowl		45	10
835	5m. Ostrich		85	20
836	7m.50 Spur-winged goose		1·00	25
837	12m.50 African fish eagle		1·40	35

111 Family and Census Officer

1980. First General Census.

| 838 | **111** | 3m.50 multicoloured | 25 | 10 |

112 Animals fleeing from Fire

1980. Campaign against Bush Fires.

| 839 | **112** | 3m.50 multicoloured | 25 | 10 |

113 Common Harp

1980. Stamp Day. Shells. Multicoloured.

840	1m. Type **113**		10	10
841	1m.50 Arthritic spider conch		15	10
842	2m.50 Venus comb murex		20	10
843	5m. Clear sundial		40	15
844	7m.50 Ramose murex		50	20
845	12m.50 Diana conch		1·10	35

114 Pres. Machel, Electricity Pylons, Aircraft and Lorry

1981. "Decade for Victory over Underdevelopment".

846	**114**	3m.50 blue and red	2·00	75
847	-	7m.50 brown and green	25	15
848	-	12m.50 mauve and blue	50	30

DESIGNS: 7m.50, Pres. Machel and armed forces on parade; 12m.50, Pres. Machel and classroom scenes.

115 Footballer and *Athletic de Bilbao* Stadium

1981. World Cup Football Championship, Spain (1982). Multicoloured.

849	1m. Type **115**		10	10
850	1m.50 Valencia, C.F.		10	10
851	2m.50 Oviedo C.F.		10	10
852	5m. R. Betis Balompie		20	10
853	7m.50 Real Zaragoza		25	15
854	12m.50 R.C.D. Espanol		50	25
MS855	Three sheets (a) 125×155 mm. Nos. 849/54; (b) 140×110 mm. 20m. F.C. Barcelona; (c) 105×85 mm. 20m. Atletico de Madrid Set of 3 sheets		2·75	1·60

116 Giraffe

1981. Protected Animals. Multicoloured.

856	50c. Type **116**		10	10
857	1m.50 Topi		10	10
858	2m.50 Aardvark		10	10
859	3m. African python		10	10
860	5m. Loggerhead turtle		20	15
861	10m. Marabou stork		1·10	45
862	12m.50 Saddle-bill stork		1·40	55
863	15m. Kori bustard		1·90	65

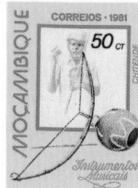

117 Chitende

1981. Musical Instruments. Multicoloured.

864	50c. Type **117**		10	10
865	2m. Pankwe (horiz)		10	10
866	2m.50 Kanyembe		10	10
867	7m. Nyanga (horiz)		30	20
868	10m. Likuti and M'Petheni (horiz)		70	25

118 Disabled Persons making Baskets

1981. International Year of Disabled People.

| 869 | **118** | 5m. multicoloured | 25 | 15 |

119 De Havilland Dragon Rapide

1981. Air. Mozambique Aviation History. Mult.

870	50c. Type **119**		10	10
871	1m.50 Junkers Ju 52/3m		10	10
872	3m. Lockheed Super Electra		20	15
873	7m.50 De Havilland Dove		35	30
874	10m. Douglas DC-3		50	35
875	12m.50 Fokker Friendship		75	50

120 Controlled Killing, Marromeu

1981. World Hunting Exhibition, Plovdiv. Mult.

876	2m. Type **120**		30	15
877	5m. Traditional hunting Cheringoma		20	15
878	6m. Tourist hunting, Save		40	30
879	7m.60 Marksmanship, Gorongosa		40	20
880	12m.50 African elephants, Gorongosa		1·50	60
881	20m. Trap, Cabo Delgado		80	50
MS882	155×100 mm. Nos. 876/81		3·75	2·00

121 50 Centavos Coin

1981. 1st Anniv of New Currency. Mult.

883	50c. Type **121**		10	10
884	1m. One metical coin		10	10
885	2m.50 Two meticals 50 coin		10	10
886	5m. Five meticals coin		20	15
887	10m. Ten meticals coin		50	25
888	20m. Twenty meticals coin		1·40	50
MS889	121×121 mm. Nos. 883/8		2·40	1·25

122 Sunflower

1981. Agricultural Resources.

| 890 | **122** | 50c. orange and red | 10 | 10 |
| 891 | - | 1m. black and red | 10 | 10 |

892	-	1m.50 blue and red	10	10
893	-	2m.50 yellow and red	10	10
894	-	3m.50 green and red	15	10
895	-	4m.50 grey and red	15	10
896	-	10m. blue and red	40	15
897	-	12m.50 brown and red	50	20
898	-	15m. brown and red	60	25
899	-	25m. green and red	1·40	40
900	-	40m. orange and red	2·00	60
901	-	60m. brown and red	2·75	1·00

DESIGNS: 1m. Cotton; 1m.50, Sisal; 2m.50, Cashew; 3m.50, Tea; 4m.50, Sugar cane; 10m. Castor oil; 12m.50, Coconut; 15m. Tobacco; 25m. Rice; 40m. Maize; 60m. Groundnut.

123 Archaeological Excavation, Manyikeni

1981. Archaeological Excavation. Mult.

902	1m. Type **123**		10	10
903	1m.50 Hand-axe (Massingir Dam)		10	10
904	2m.50 Ninth century bowl (Chibuene)		10	10
905	7m.50 Ninth century pot (Chibuene)		30	20
906	12m.50 Gold beads (Manyikeni)		50	30
907	20m. Gong (Manyikeni)		80	50

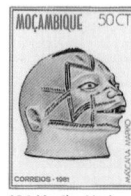

124 Mapiko Mask

1981. Sculptures. Multicoloured.

908	50c. Type **124**		10	10
909	1m. Woman who suffers		10	10
910	2m.50 Woman with a child		10	10
911	3m.50 The man who makes fire		15	10
912	5m. Chietane		20	15
913	12m.50 Chietane (different)		70	30

125 Broken Loaf on Globe

1981. World Food Day.

| 914 | **125** | 10m. multicoloured | 45 | 25 |

126 Tanker "Matchedje"

1981. Mozambique Ships. Multicoloured.

915	50c. Type **126**		15	15
916	1m.50 Tug "Macuti"		15	15
917	3m. Trawler "Vega 7"		25	15
918	5m. Freighter "Linde"		35	25
919	7m.50 Freighter "Pemba"		55	30
920	12m.50 Dredger "Rovuma"		95	55

127 "Portunus pelagicus"

1981. Crustaceans. Multicoloured.

921	50c. Type **127**		10	10
922	1m.50 "Scylla serrata"		10	10
923	3m. "Penacus indicus"		15	10
924	7m.50 "Palinurus delagoae"		35	20
925	12m.50 "Lysiosquilla maculata"		55	35
926	15m. "Panulirus ornatus"		80	45

128 "Hypoxis multiceps"

1981. Flowers. Multicoloured.
927	1m. Type **128**	10	10
928	1m.50 "Pelargonium luridun"	10	10
929	2m.50 "Caralluma melanathera"	10	10
930	7m.50 "Ansellia gigantea"	35	20
931	12m.50 "Stapelia leendertsiae"	60	35
932	25m. "Adenium multiflorum"	1·50	70

129 Telex Tape, Telephone and Globe

1982. 1st Anniv of Mozambique Post and Telecommunications. Multicoloured.
933	6m. Type **129**	35	20
934	15m. Winged envelope and envelope forming railway wagon	3·00	1·50

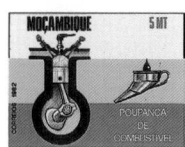

130 Diagram of Petrol Engine

1982. Fuel Saving. Multicoloured.
935	5m. Type **130**	30	15
936	7m.50 Speeding car	45	25
937	10m. Loaded truck	60	35

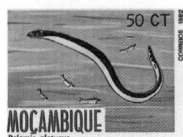

131 Sea-snake

1982. Reptiles. Multicoloured.
938	50c. Type **131**	20	10
939	1m.50 "Naja mossambica mossambica"	10	10
940	3m. "Thelotornis capensis mossambica"	20	15
941	6m. "Dendroaspis polylepis polylepis"	35	25
942	15m. "Dispholidus typus"	80	50
943	20m. "Bitis arietans arietans"	1·50	75

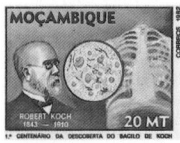

132 Dr. Robert Koch, Bacillus and X-Ray

1982. Centenary of Discovery of Tubercle Bacillus.
944	**132** 20m. multicoloured	1·75	1·00

133 Telephone Line

1982. International Telecommunications Union. Plenipotentiary Conference.
945	**133** 20m. multicoloured	1·00	75

134 Player with Ball

1982. World Cup Football Championship, Spain. Multicoloured.
946	1m.50 Type **134**	10	10
947	3m.50 Player heading ball	25	15
948	7m. Two players fighting for ball	40	20
949	10m. Player receiving ball	60	30
950	20m. Goalkeeper	1·25	1·00
MS951	84×69 mm. 50m. Footballer. Imperf	3·00	1·50

135 Tahitian Woman (detail from painting by Gauguin)

1982. Philexfrance 82 International Stamp Exhibition, Paris. Sheet 98×92 mm.
MS952	**135** 35m. multicoloured	1·90	1·50

136 Political Rally

1982. 25th Anniv of FRELIMO. Multicoloured.
953	4m. Type **136**	25	15
954	8m. Agriculture	45	25
955	12m. Marching workers	70	35

137 "Vangueria infausta"

1982. Fruits. Multicoloured.
956	1m. Type **137**	10	10
957	2m. "Mimusops caffra"	10	10
958	4m. "Sclerocarya caffra"	25	15
959	8m. "Strychnos spinosa"	45	25
960	12m. "Salacia kraussi"	70	40
961	32m. "Trichilia emetica"	1·90	85

138 "Sputnik I"

1982. 25th Anniv of First Artificial Satellite. Multicoloured.
962	1m. Type **138**	10	10
963	2m. First manned space flight	10	10
964	4m. First walk in space	25	15
965	8m. First manned flight to the Moon	45	25
966	16m. "Soyuz"–"Apollo" mission	1·25	70
967	20m. "Intercosmos" rocket	1·50	70

139 Vigilantes

1982. People's Surveillance Day.
968	**139** 4m. multicoloured	25	15

140 Caique

1982. Traditional Boats. Multicoloured.
969	1m. Type **140**	10	10
970	2m. Machua	15	10
971	4m. Calaua (horiz)	30	15
972	8m. Chitatarro (horiz)	60	25
973	12m. Cangaia (horiz)	80	35
974	16m. Chata (horiz)	1·75	60

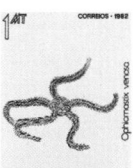

141 "Ophiomostix venosa"

1982. Starfishes and Sea Urchins. Multicoloured.
975	1m. Type **141**	10	10
976	2m. "Protoreaster lincki"	10	10
977	4m. "Tropiometra carinata"	15	10
978	8m. "Holothuria scabra"	35	20
979	12m. "Prionocidaris baculosa"	60	35
980	16m. "Colobocentrotus atnatus"	80	40

142 Soldiers defending Mozambique

1983. 4th Frelimo Party Congress. Multicoloured.
981	4m. Type **142**	15	10
982	8m. Crowd waving voting papers	30	20
983	16m. Agriculture, industry and education	65	40

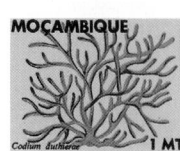

143 "Codium duthierae"

1983. Seaweeds. Multicoloured.
984	1m. Type **143**	10	10
985	2m. "Halimeda cunata"	10	10
986	4m. "Dictyota liturata"	15	10
987	8m. "Endorachne binghamiae"	40	20
988	12m. "Laurencia flexuosa"	60	30
989	20m. "Acrosorium sp."	1·25	55

144 Diving and Swimming

1983. Olympic Games, Los Angeles (1st issue). Multicoloured.
990	1m. Type **144**	10	10
991	2m. Boxing	10	10
992	4m. Basketball	20	10
993	8m. Handball	35	20
994	12m. Volleyball	55	30
995	16m. Running	65	40
996	20m. Yachting	1·25	65
MS997	120×100 mm. 50m. Discus. Imperf	2·50	1·40

See also Nos. 1029/34.

145 Mallet Type Locomotive

1983. Steam Locomotives. Multicoloured.
998	1m. Type **145**	10	10
999	2m. Baldwin, 1915–45	20	10
1000	4m. Class 141-148, 1950	40	15
1001	8m. Baldwin, 1926	75	25
1002	16m. Henschel Garratt type, 1956	1·40	50
1003	32m. Natal Government Class H, 1899–1903	3·00	1·00

146 O.A.U. Emblem

1983. 20th Anniv of Organization of African Unity.
1004	**146** 4m. multicoloured	20	15

147 Four-toed Elephant-shrew

1983. Mozambique Mammals. Multicoloured.
1005	1m. Type **147**	10	10
1006	2m. Four-striped grass mouse	15	10
1007	4m. Vincent's bush squirrel	25	15
1008	8m. Hottentot mole-rat	50	25
1009	12m. Natal red hare	75	40
1010	16m. Straw-coloured fruit bat	1·25	75

148 Aiding Flood Victims

1983. 2nd Anniv of Mozambique Red Cross. Multicoloured.
1011	4m. Type **148**	20	10
1012	8m. Red Cross lorry	40	20
1013	16m. First aid demonstration	75	40
1014	32m. Agricultural worker performing first aid	1·90	75

149 Musician

1983. Brasiliana 83 International Stamp Exhibition, Rio de Janeiro. Sheet 102×73 mm.
MS1015	**149** 30m. multicoloured	1·90	1·50

150 "Communications"

1983. World Communications Year.
1016	**150** 8m. multicoloured	1·50	75

151 Line Fishing

1983. Fishery Resources. Multicoloured.

1017	50c. Type **151**	10	10
1018	2m. Chifonho (basket trap)	10	10
1019	4m. Spear fishing	25	15
1020	8m. Gamboa (fence trap)	40	25
1021	16m. Mono (basket trap)	1·50	40
1022	20m. Lema (basket trap)	1·60	55

152 Kudu Horn

1983. Stamp Day. Multicoloured.

1023	50c. Type **152**	10	10
1024	1m. Drum communication	10	10
1025	4m. Postal runners	20	15
1026	8m. Mail canoe	40	40
1027	16m. Mail van	75	40
1028	20m. Steam mail train	3·25	1·50

153 Swimming

1984. Olympic Games, Los Angeles (2nd issue). Multicoloured.

1029	50c. Type **153**	10	10
1030	4m. Football	20	10
1031	8m. Hurdling	35	20
1032	16m. Basketball	90	50
1033	32m. Handball	1·90	80
1034	60m. Boxing	3·00	1·75

154 "Trichilia emetica"

1984. Indigenous Trees. Multicoloured.

1035	50c. Type **154**	10	10
1036	2m. "Brachystegia spiciformis"	10	10
1037	4m. "Androstachys johnsonii"	20	10
1038	8m. "Pterocarpus angolensis"	35	20
1039	16m. "Milletia stuhlmannii"	80	40
1040	50m. "Dalbergia melanoxylon"	2·75	1·75

155 Dove with Olive Sprig

1984. Nkomati South Africa–Mozambique Non-aggression Pact.

1041	**155** 4m. multicoloured	25	10

156 State Arms

1984. Emblems of the Republic. Multicoloured.

1042	4m. Type **156**	20	10
1043	8m. State Flag	40	20

157 Makway Dance

1984. "Lubrapex '84" Portuguese–Brazilian Stamp Exhibition, Lisbon. Traditional Mozambican dances. Multicoloured.

1044	4m. Type **157**	20	10
1045	8m. Mapiko dance	40	20
1046	16m. Wadjaba dance	1·40	50

158 Nampula Museum and Statuette of Woman with Water Jug

1984. Museums. Multicoloured.

1047	50c. Type **158**	10	10
1048	4m. Natural History Museum and secretary bird	35	10
1049	8m. Revolution Museum and soldier carrying wounded comrade	35	20
1050	16m. Colonial History Museum and cannon	65	40
1051	20m. National Numismatic Museum and coins	1·25	65
1052	30m. St. Paul's Palace and antique chair	1·50	95

159 Imber's Tetra

1984. Fishes. Multicoloured.

1053	50c. Type **159**	10	10
1054	4m. Purple labeo	25	10
1055	12m. Brown squeaker	75	35
1056	16m. Blue-finned notho	95	55
1057	40m. Slender serrate barb	2·50	1·40
1058	60m. Barred minnow	3·75	1·90

160 Badge and Laurels

1984. International Fair, Maputo.

1059	**160** 16m. multicoloured	70	50

161 Rural Landscape and Emblem

1984. 20th Anniv of African Development Bank.

1060	**161** 4m. multicoloured	30	10

162 Knife and Club

1984. Traditional Weapons. Multicoloured.

1061	50c. Type **162**	10	10
1062	4m. Axes	20	10
1063	8m. Spear and shield	35	15
1064	16m. Bow and arrow	75	35
1065	32m. Rifle	1·90	95
1066	50m. Assegai and arrow	2·75	1·90

163 Workers and Emblem

1984. 1st Anniv of Organization of Mozambican Workers.

1067	**163** 4m. multicoloured	20	10

164 Barue 1902 Postmark

1984. Stamp Day. Postmarks. Multicoloured.

1068	4m. Type **164**	15	10
1069	8m. Zumbo postmark and King Carlos 15r. Mozambique "key type" stamp	35	20
1070	12m. Mozambique Company postmark and 1935 airmail stamp	55	30
1071	16m. Macequece postmark and 1937 2e. Mozambique Company stamp	70	40

165 Keeper and Hive

1985. Bee-keeping. Multicoloured.

1072	4m. Type **165**	15	10
1073	8m. Worker bee	45	20
1074	16m. Drone	1·25	40
1075	20m. Queen bee	1·75	60

166 Shot-putter and Emblem

1985. "Olymphilex 85" Olympic Stamps Exhibition, Lausanne.

1076	**166** 16m. blue, black and red	75	35

167 Forecasting Equipment and Desert

1985. World Meteorology Day.

1077	**167** 4m. multicoloured	35	10

168 Map

1985. 5th Anniv of Southern African Development Co-ordination Conference. Multicoloured.

1078	4m. Type **168**	15	10
1079	8m. Map and pylon	45	20
1080	16m. Industry and transport	2·50	1·25
1081	32m. Member states' flags	1·90	95

169 Battle of Mujenga, 1896

1985. 10th Anniv of Independence. Mult.

1082	1m. Type **169**	10	10
1083	4m. Attack on Barue by Macombe, 1917	25	10
1084	8m. Attack on Massangano, 1868	55	20
1085	16m. Battle of Marracuene, 1895, and Gungunhana	1·50	50

170 U.N. Building, New York and Flag

1985. 40th Anniv of U.N.O.

1086	**170** 16m. multicoloured	80	50

171 Mathacuzana

1985. Traditional Games and Sports. Multicoloured.

1087	50c. Type **171**	10	10
1088	4m. Mudzobo	20	10
1089	8m. Muravarava (board game)	40	20
1090	16m. N'tshuwa	90	50

172 "Rana angolensis"

1985. Frogs and Toads. Multicoloured.

1091	50c. Type **172**	10	10
1092	1m. "Hyperolius pictus"	10	10
1093	4m. "Ptychadena porosissima"	15	10
1094	8m. "Afrixalus formasinii"	50	20
1095	16m. "Bufo regularis"	95	50
1096	32m. "Hyperolius marmoratus"	2·40	95
MS1097	89×85 mm. 30m. "Ptychadena porosissima" (different). Imperf	2·25	90

173 "Romulus, Remus and Wolf" (detail)

1985. Italia 85 International Stamp Exhibition, Rome. Sheet 90×85 mm. Imperf.

MS1098	**173** 60m. multicoloured	4·00	2·00

174 "Aloe ferox"

1985. Medicinal Plants. Multicoloured.

1099	50c. Type **174**	10	10
1100	1m. "Boophone disticha"	10	10
1101	3m.50 "Gloriosa superba"	15	10
1102	4m. "Cotyledon orbiculata"	15	10
1103	8m. "Homeria breyniana"	55	20
1104	50m. "Haemanthus coccineus"	3·75	1·90

175 Mozambique Company 1918 10c. Stamp

1985. Stamp Day. Multicoloured.

1105	1m. Type **175**	1·25	75
1106	4m. Nyassa Co. 1911 25r. stamp	15	10
1107	8m. Mozambique Co. 1918 ½c. stamp	50	20
1108	16m. Nyassa Co. 1924 1c. Postage Due stamp	1·25	50

176 Comet and "Giotto" Space Probe

1986. Appearance of Halley's Comet.
1109	176	4m. blue and light blue	20	10
1110	-	8m. violet and light violet	50	20
1111	-	16m. multicoloured	95	50
1112	-	30m. multicoloured	2·00	95

DESIGNS: 8m. Comet orbits; 16m. Small and large telescopes, comet and space probe; 30m. Comet, stars and globe.

177 Vicente

1986. World Cup Football Championship, Mexico. Multicoloured.
1113		3m. Type 177	15	10
1114		4m. Coluna	20	10
1115		8m. Costa Pereira	40	20
1116		12m. Hilario	65	35
1117		16m. Matateu	95	50
1118		50m. Eusebio	3·25	1·90

178 Dove and Emblem

1986. International Peace Year.
1119	178	16m. multicoloured	85	45

179 "Amanita muscaria"

1986. Fungi. Multicoloured.
1120		4m. Type 179	50	20
1121		8m. "Lactarius deliciosus"	95	30
1122		16m. "Amanita phaloides"	2·00	65
1123		30m. "Tricholoma nudum"	4·25	1·25

180 Head and Arm of Statue

1986. Ameripex 86 International Stamp Exhibition, Chicago. Centenary of Statue of Liberty. Sheet 77×105 mm. Imperf.
MS1124	180	100m. multicoloured	7·50	4·75

181 Spiky Style

1986. Women's Hairstyles. Multicoloured.
1125		1m. Type 181	10	10
1126		4m. Beaded plaits	25	10
1127		8m. Plaited tightly to head	50	20
1128		16m. Plaited tightly to head with ponytail	1·25	55

182 Dugong

1986. Marine Mammals. Multicoloured.
1129		1m. Type 182	10	10
1130		8m. Common dolphin	35	20
1131		16m. "Neobalena marginata"	1·25	85
1132		50f. Fin whale	4·25	2·75

183 Children Studying

1986. 1st Anniv of Continuadores Youth Organization.
1133	183	4m. multicoloured	30	15

184 50m. Notes

1986. Savings. Multicoloured.
1134		4m. Type 184	25	10
1135		8m. 100m. notes	50	20
1136		16m. 500m. notes	1·40	50
1137		30m. 1000m. notes	2·75	1·25

185 Quelimane Post Office

1986. Stamp Day. Post Offices. Multicoloured.
1138		3m. Type 185	20	10
1139		4m. Maputo	30	10
1140		8m. Beira	65	20
1141		16m. Nampula	1·40	50

186 Pyrite

1987. Minerals. Multicoloured.
1142		4m. Type 186	30	10
1143		8m. Emerald	60	20
1144		12m. Agate	85	40
1145		16m. Malachite	1·40	50
1146		30m. Garnet	2·50	1·25
1147		50m. Amethyst	4·25	2·00

187 Crowd beneath Flag

1987. 10th Anniv of Mozambique Liberation Front.
1148	187	4m. multicoloured	30	15

188 Little Libombos Dam

1987
1149	188	16m. multicoloured	1·40	60

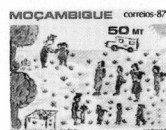

189 Children being Vaccinated

1987. World Health Day. Vaccination Campaign.
1150	189	50m. multicoloured	1·90	1·50

190 Common Grenadier

1987. Birds. Multicoloured.
1151		3m. Type 190	25	15
1152		4m. Woodland kingfisher	30	20
1153		8m. White-fronted bee eater	65	40
1154		12m. Lesser seedcracker	1·10	60
1155		16m. African broad-billed roller	1·25	90
1156		30m. Neergaard's sunbird	2·50	1·60

191 Football

1987. Olympic Games, Seoul (1988) (1st issue). Multicoloured.
1157		12m.50 Type 191	10	10
1158		25m. Running	20	10
1159		50m. Handball	40	20
1160		75m. Chess	1·25	30
1161		100m. Basketball	1·25	35
1162		200m. Swimming	2·00	65

See also Nos. 1176/81.

192 Tower and Canadian Flag

1987. Capex 87 International Stamp Exhibition, Toronto. Sheet 70×100 mm. Imperf.
MS1163	192	200m. multicoloured	2·00	65

193 Work on Loom

1987. Weaving. Multicoloured.
1164		20m. Type 193	15	10
1165		40m. Triangle and diamond design	40	10
1166		80m. "Eye" design	70	20
1167		200m. Red carpet	2·00	60

194 Piper "Navajo"

1987. Air. History of Aviation in Mozambique. Multicoloured.
1168		20m. Type 194	15	10
1169		40m. De Havilland Hornet moth	25	10
1170		80m. Boeing 737	50	20
1171		120m. Beechcraft King Air	75	20
1172		160m. Piper Aztec	1·00	35
1173		320m. Douglas DC-10	2·00	75

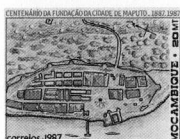

195 Early Plan

1987. Centenary of Maputo as City.
1174	195	20m. multicoloured	20	15

1987. No. 895 surch 4,00 MT.
1175		4m. on 4m.50 grey and red	15	10

197 Javelin throwing

1988. Olympic Games, Seoul (2nd issue). Mult.
1176		10m. Type 197	10	10
1177		20m. Baseball	10	10
1178		40m. Boxing	10	10
1179		80m. Hockey	40	10
1180		100m. Gymnastics	50	15
1181		400m. Cycling	1·50	75

198 "Boophane disticha"

1988. Flowers. Multicoloured.
1182		10m. "Heamanthus nelsonii"	10	10
1183		20m. "Crinum polyphyllum"	15	10
1184		40m. Type 198	15	10
1185		80m. "Cyrtanthus contractus"	35	10
1186		100m. "Nerine angustifolia"	50	15
1187		400m. "Cyrtanthus galpinnii"	2·00	75

199 Man refusing Cigarette

1988. 40th Anniv of W.H.O. Anti-smoking Campaign.
1188	199	20m. multicoloured	20	10

200 Helsinki Cathedral

1988. Finlandia 88 International Stamp Exhibition, Helsinki. Sheet 70×85 mm. Imperf.
MS1189	200	500m. multicoloured	1·90	1·40

201 Mat

1988. Basketry. Multicoloured.
1190		20m. Type 201	10	10
1191		25m. Basket with lid	10	10
1192		80m. Basket with handle	20	10
1193		100m. Fan	30	10
1194		400m. Dish	1·50	1·00
1195		500m. Conical basket	1·90	1·40

202 Cathedral
Spire

1988. Visit of Pope John Paul II. Sheet 83×103 mm.
MS1196 **202** 500m. blue, red and black   1·90   1·40

203 Percheron

1988. Horses. Multicoloured.
1197	20m. Type **203**	15	10
1198	40m. Arab	20	10
1199	80m. Pure blood	40	10
1200	100m. Pony	50	15

204 Machel

1988. 2nd Death Anniv of Samora Machel (President 1975–86).
1201	**204** 20m. multicoloured	15	10

205 Inhambane

1988. Ports. Multicoloured.
1202	20m. Type **205**	15	10
1203	50m. Quelimane (vert)	40	10
1204	75m. Pemba	50	10
1205	100m. Beira	55	20
1206	250m. Nacali (vert)	1·10	50
1207	500m. Maputo	2·75	1·25

206 Mobile Post Office

1988. Stamp Day. Multicoloured.
1208	20m. Type **206**	10	10
1209	40m. Posting box (vert)	15	10

207 Maize

1989. 5th FRELIMO Congress. Multicoloured.
1210	25m. Type **207**	10	10
1211	50m. Hoe	10	10
1212	75m. Abstract	10	10
1213	100m. Cogwheels	20	10
1214	250m. Right-half of cogwheel	50	25

Nos. 1210/14 were printed together, se-tenant, forming a composite design.

208 Mondlane

1989. 20th Anniv of Assassination of Pres. Mondlane.
1215	**208** 25m. black, gold and red	15	10

209 "Storming the Bastille" (Thevenin)

1989. Bicentenary of French Revolution. Mult.
1216	100m. Type **209**	25	10
1217	250m. "Liberty guiding the People" (Delacroix)	60	35

MS1218 78×106 mm. 500m. "Declaration of Rights of Man" (detail, Blanchard)   1·20   1·20

No. MS1218 also commemorates Philexfrance 89 International Stamp Exhibition.

210 "Pandinus sp."

1989. Venomous Animals. Multicoloured.
1219	25m. Type **210**	10	10
1220	50m. Egyptian cobra	10	10
1221	75m. "Bombus sp." (bee)	15	10
1222	100m. "Paraphysa sp." (spider)	25	10
1223	250m. Marble cone	90	40
1224	500m. Lionfish	1·90	70

211 "Acropora pulchra"

1989. Corals. Multicoloured.
1225	25m. Type **211**	10	10
1226	50m. "Eunicella papilosa"	15	10
1227	100m. "Dendrophyla migrantus"	30	10
1228	250m. "Favia fragum"	50	35

212 Footballers

1989. World Cup Football Championship, Italy (1990). Designs showing various footballing scenes.
1229	**212** 30m. multicoloured	10	10
1230	– 60m. multicoloured	15	10
1231	– 125m. multicoloured	30	10
1232	– 200m. multicoloured	50	25
1233	– 250m. multicoloured	65	35
1234	– 500m. multicoloured	1·50	70

213 Macuti Lighthouse

1989. Lighthouses. Multicoloured.
1235	30m. Type **213**	15	10
1236	60m. Pinda	15	10
1237	125m. Cape Delgado	30	10
1238	200m. Goa Island	60	25
1239	250m. Caldeira Point	80	35
1240	500m. Vilhena	1·50	70

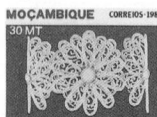

214 Bracelet

1989. Silver Filigree Work.
1241	**214** 30m. grey, red and black	10	10
1242	– 60m. grey, blue and black	15	10
1243	– 125m. grey, red and black	25	10
1244	– 200m. grey, blue & black	40	25
1245	– 250m. grey, purple & blk	55	35

1246	– 500m. grey, green & blk	1·25	70

DESIGNS: 60m. Flower belt; 125m. Necklace; 200m. Casket; 250m. Spoons; 500m. Butterfly.

215 Flag and Soldiers

1989. 25th Anniv of Fight for Independence.
1247	**215** 30m. multicoloured	15	10

216 Rain Gauge

1989. Meteorological Instruments. Multicoloured.
1248	30m. Type **216**	10	10
1249	60m. Radar graph	15	10
1250	125m. Sheltered measuring instruments	30	10
1251	200m. Computer terminal	55	25

217 Washington Monument

1989. World Stamp Expo 89 International Stamp Exhibition, Washington D.C. Sheet 78×104 mm.
MS1252 **217** 500m. multicoloured   1·20   1·20

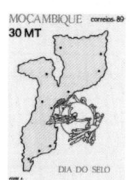

218 Map and U.P.U. Emblem

1989. Stamp Day.
1253	**218** 30m. multicoloured	15	10
1254	– 60m. black, green and red	15	10

DESIGN: 60m. Map and Mozambique postal emblem.

219 Railway Map

1990. 10th Anniv of Southern Africa Development Co-ordination Conference.
1255	**219** 35m. multicoloured	1·00	50

220 Cloth and Woman wearing Dress

1990. Traditional Dresses. Designs showing women wearing different dresses and details of cloth used.
1256	**220** 42m. multicoloured	10	10
1257	– 90m. multicoloured	15	10
1258	– 150m. multicoloured	20	10
1259	– 200m. multicoloured	25	15
1260	– 400m. multicoloured	55	40
1261	– 500m. multicoloured	65	50

221 Sena Fortress, Sofala

1990. Fortresses.
1262	**221** 45m. blue and black	10	10

1263	– 90m. blue and black	15	10
1264	– 150m. multicoloured	20	10
1265	– 200m. multicoloured	30	15
1266	– 400m. red and black	55	40
1267	– 500m. red and black	70	40

DESIGNS: 90m. Sto. Antonio, Ibo Island; 150m. S. Sebastiao, Mozambique Island; 200m. S. Caetano, Sofala; 400m. Our Lady of Conception, Maputo; 500m. S. Luis, Tete.

222 GB Unissued "VR" Penny Black and Mozambique 1876 5r. Stamp

1990. Stamp World London 90 International Stamp Exhibition. 150th Anniv of the Penny Black. Sheet 70×100 mm.
MS1268 **222** 1000m. black, blue and red   1·40   1·40

223 Obverse and Reverse of 50m. Coin

1990. 15th Anniv of Bank of Mozambique.
1269	**223** 100m. multicoloured	20	10

224 Statue of Eduardo Mondlane (founder of FRELIMO)

1990. 15th Anniv of Independence. Mult.
1270	42m.50 Type **224**	10	10
1271	150m. Statue of Samora Machel (President, 1975–86)	25	15

225 White Rhinoceros

1990. Endangered Animals. Multicoloured.
1272	42m.50 Type **225**	15	10
1273	100m. Dugong	20	10
1274	150m. African elephant	35	15
1275	200m. Cheetah	40	15
1276	400m. Spotted-necked otter	70	40
1277	500m. Hawksbill turtle	85	50

226 "Dichrostachys cinerea"

1990. Environmental Protection. Plants. Mult.
1278	42m.50 Type **226**	10	10
1279	100m. Forest fire	20	10
1280	150m. Horsetail tree	25	10
1281	200m. Mangrove	30	15
1282	400m. "Estrato herbaceo" (grass)	65	40
1283	500m. Pod mahogany	80	50

227 Pillar Box waving to Kurika

1990. Kurika (post mascot) at Work. Mult.

1284	42m.50 Type **227**	15	10
1285	42m.50 Hand cancelling envelopes	15	10
1286	42m.50 Leaping across hurdles	15	10
1287	42m.50 Delivering post to chicken	15	10

228 "10" and Posts Emblem

1991. 10th Anniv of National Posts and Telecommunications Enterprises, Mozambique.

1288	**228**	50m. blue, red and black	15	10
1289	-	50m. brown, green & black	15	10

DESIGN: No. 1289, "10" and telecommunications emblem.

229 Bird-of-Paradise Flower

1991. Flowers. Multicoloured.

1290	50m. Type **229**	15	10
1291	125m. Flamingo lily	25	15
1292	250m. Calla lily	50	30
1293	300m. Canna lily	55	35

230 Two Hartebeest

1991. Lichtenstein's Hartebeest. Multicoloured.

1294	50m. Type **230**	15	10
1295	100m. Alert hartebeest	20	10
1296	250m. Hartebeest grazing	1·50	70
1297	500m. Mother feeding young	2·10	1·40

231 Mpompine

1991. Maputo Drinking Fountains. Mult.

1298	50m. Type **231**	10	10
1299	125m. Chinhambanine	15	10
1300	250m. S. Pedro-Zaza	25	10
1301	300m. Xipamanine	35	15

232 Painting by Samate

1991. Paintings by Mozambican Artists. Mult.

1302	180m. Type **232**	15	10
1303	250m. Malangatana Ngwenya	20	15
1304	560m. Malangatana Ngwenya (different)	40	30

233 Diving

1991. Olympic Games, Barcelona (1992). Mult.

1305	10m. Type **233**	10	10
1306	50m. Roller hockey	15	10
1307	100m. Tennis	20	10
1308	200m. Table tennis	30	10
1309	500m. Running	50	20
1310	1000m. Badminton	1·10	40

234 Proposed Boundaries in 1890 Treaty

1991. Centenary of Settling of Mozambique Borders. Multicoloured.

1311	600m. Type **234**	50	25
1312	800m. Frontiers settled in English–Portuguese 1891 treaty	75	35

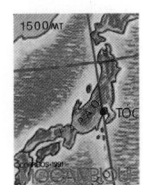

235 Map of Japan

1991. Phila Nippon 91 International Stamp Exhibition, Tokyo. Sheet 102×71 mm.

MS1313	**235**	1500m. multicoloured	1·40	1·40

236 Skipping

1991. Stamp Day. Children's Games. Mult.

1314	40m. Type **236**	10	10
1315	150m. Spinning top	10	10
1316	400m. Marbles	20	10
1317	900m. Hopscotch	45	20

237 "Christ"

1992. Stained Glass Windows. Multicoloured.

1318	40m. Type **237**	10	10
1319	150m. "Faith"	10	10
1320	400m. "IC XC"	20	10
1321	900m. Window in three sections	45	20

238 "Rhisophora mucronata"

1992. Marine Flowers. Multicoloured.

1322	300m. Type **238**	15	10
1323	600m. "Cymodocea ciliata"	30	15
1324	1000m. "Sophora inhambanensis"	85	25

239 Spears

1992. "Lubrapex 92" Brazilian–Portuguese Stamp Exhibition, Lisbon. Weapons. Multicoloured.

1325	100m. Type **239**	10	10

1326	300m. Tridents	15	10
1327	500m. Axe	25	10
1328	1000m. Dagger	85	25

240 Amethyst Sunbird

1992. Birds. Multicoloured.

1329	150m. Type **240**	30	30
1330	200m. Mosque swallow	30	30
1331	300m. Red-capped robin chat	45	30
1332	400m. Lesser blue-eared glossy starling	60	30
1333	500m. Grey-headed bush shrike	1·50	30
1334	800m. African golden oriole	2·25	70

241 Emblem

1992. 30th Anniv of Eduardo Mondlane University.

1335	**241**	150m. green and brown	10	10

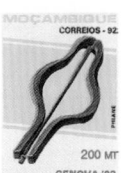

242 Phiane

1992. "Genova '92" International Thematic Stamp Exn. Musical Instruments. Multicoloured.

1336	200m. Type **242**	10	10
1337	300m. Xirupe (rattle)	15	10
1338	500m. Ngulula (drum)	25	10
1339	1500m. Malimba (drum)	75	35
MS1340	130×100 mm. Nos. 1336/9	1·25	1·25

243 Children Eating

1992. International Nutrition Conference, Rome.

1341	**243**	450m. multicoloured	20	10

244 Parachutist

1992. Parachuting. Multicoloured.

1342	50m. Type **244**	10	10
1343	400m. Parachutist and buildings	20	10
1344	500m. Airplane dropping parachutists	25	10
1345	1500m. Parachutist (different)	1·10	1·10

1992. No. 890 surch 50MT.

1346	**122**	50m. on 50c. orge & red	10	10

246 Order of Peace and Friendship

1993. Mozambique Decorations. Multicoloured.

1347	400m. Type **246**	20	10
1348	800m. Bagamoyo Medal	40	20

1349	1000m. Order of Eduardo Mondlane	50	25
1350	1500m. Veteran of the Struggle for National Liberation Medal	70	35

247 Tree Stumps and Girl carrying Wood

1993. Pollution. Multicoloured.

1351	200m. Type **247**	10	10
1352	750m. Chimneys smoking	35	15
1353	1000m. Tanker sinking	50	25
1354	1500m. Car exhaust fumes	70	35

248 Lion (Gorongosa Park, Sofala)

1993. National Parks. Multicoloured.

1355	200m. Type **248**	10	10
1356	800m. Giraffes (Banhine Park, Gaza)	40	20
1357	1000m. Dugongs (Bazoruto Park, Inhambane)	50	25
1358	1500m. Ostriches (Zinave Park, Inhambane)	1·75	75

249 Heroes Monument, Maputo

1993. "Brasiliana 93" International Stamp Exhibition, Rio de Janeiro.

1359	**249**	1500m. multicoloured	55	25

250 Conference Emblem

1993. National Culture Conference, Maputo.

1360	**250**	200m. multicoloured	10	10

251 "Cycas cercinalis"

1993. Forest Plants. Multicoloured.

1361	200m. Type **251**	10	10
1362	250m. "Cycas revoluta"	10	10
1363	900m. "Encephalartos ferox"	25	10
1364	2000m. "Equisetum ramosissimum"	50	25

252 "Anacardium occidentale"

1994. Medicinal Plants. Multicoloured.

1365	200m. Type **252**	10	10
1366	250m. "Sclerocarya caffra"	10	10
1367	900m. "Annona senegalensis"	25	10
1368	2000m. "Crinum delagoense"	50	25

1994. Various stamps surch.

1369	50m. on 7m.50 mult (No. 905)	10	10
1370	50m. on 7m.50 mult (No. 924)	10	10
1371	50m. on 7m.50 mult (No. 930)	10	10
1372	100m. on 10m. blue and red (No. 896)	10	10

1373	100m. on 12m.50 mult (No. 931)	10	10
1374	200m. on 12m.50 brown and red (No. 897)	10	10
1375	250m. on 12m.50 mult (No. 925)	10	10

254 Mozambique Rough-scaled Sand Lizard

1994. "Philakorea 1994" International Stamp Exhibition, Seoul. Reptiles. Multicoloured.

1376	300m. Type **254**	10	10
1377	500m. Olive loggerhead turtle	10	10
1378	2000m. Northern coppery snake	40	20
1379	3500m. Marshall's chameleon	75	35
MS1380	79×70 mm. 4000m. Snake swallowing prey	80	80

255 Crop-spraying

1994. 50th Anniv of I.C.A.O. Multicoloured.

1381	300m. Type **255**	10	10
1382	500m. Airport	10	10
1383	2000m. Air transport	40	20
1384	3500m. Aircraft maintenance	75	35

256 Bean Plant

1994. "Lubrapex'94" Portuguese–Brazilian Stamp Exhibition. World Food Day.

1385	**256** 2000m. multicoloured	40	20

257 Queue of Voters

1994. 1st Multiparty Elections.

1386	**257** 900m. multicoloured	20	10

258 Document and Handshake

1994. 20th Anniv of Lusaka Accord (establishing independence).

1387	**258** 1500m. multicoloured	30	15

259 Couple using Drugs

1994. Anti-drugs Campaign. Multicoloured.

1388	500m. Type **259**	10	10
1389	1000m. Couple, syringe, cigarette and skeleton	20	10
1390	2000m. Addict	40	20
1391	5000m. Sniffer dog capturing man with drugs	1·00	50

260 Basket

1995. Baskets and Bags. Multicoloured.

1392	250m. Type **260**	10	10
1393	300m. Bag with two handles	10	10
1394	1200m. Circular bag with one handle	20	10
1395	5000m. Bag with flap	85	40

261 Dress and Cloak

1995. Women's Costumes. Multicoloured.

1396	250m. Type **261**	10	10
1397	300m. Blouse and calf-length skirt	10	10
1398	1200m. Blouse and ankle-length skirt	20	10
1399	5000m. Strapless top and skirt	85	40

9-12-1994. Investidur
262 State Arms

1995. Investiture (1994) of President Joaquim Chissano. Multicoloured.

1400	900m. Type **262**	15	10
1401	2500m. National flag	45	20
1402	5000m. Pres. Chissano	85	40

Nos. 1400/2 were issued together, se-tenant, the commemorative inscription at the foot extending across the strip.

263 Bushbaby

1995. Mammals. Multicoloured.

1403	500m. Type **263**	10	10
1404	2000m. Greater kudu (horiz)	25	10
1405	3000m. Bush pig (horiz)	40	20
1406	5000m. Bushbuck	65	30

1995. Various stamps surch.

1407	250m. on 12m.50 multicoloured (No. 931)	10	10
1408	300m. on 10m. blue and red (No. 896)	10	10
1409	500m. on 12m.50 multicoloured (No. 925)	10	10
1410	900m. on 12e.50 multicoloured (No. 771)	10	10
1411	1000m. on 12m.50 multicoloured (No. 837)	15	10
1412	1500m. on 16m. multicoloured (No. 1064)	20	10
1413	2000m. on 16m. multicoloured (No. 995)	25	10
1414	2500m. on 12m. multicoloured (No. 880)	35	15

265 Family carrying Foodstuffs

1995. 50th Anniv of F.A.O.

1415	**265** 5000m. multicoloured	65	30

266 Emblem

1995. 50th Anniv of United Nations Organization.

1416	**266** 5000m. blue and black	65	30

1975-1995
267 Child wearing Blue Cloak

1995. 20th Anniv of UNICEF in Mozambique.

1417	**267** 5000m. multicoloured	1·00	1·00

268 Player scoring Goal

1996. Football. Multicoloured.

1418	1000m. Type **268**	35	35
1419	2000m. Goalkeeper holding ball	60	60
1420	4000m. Referee admonishing players	80	80
1421	6000m. Two players tackling for ball	1·10	1·10

269 Mask

1996. Local Masks.

1422	**269** 1000m. multicoloured	35	35
1423	– 2000m. multicoloured	60	60
1424	– 4000m. multicoloured	80	80
1425	– 6000m. multicoloured	1·10	1·10

DESIGNS: 2000 to 6000m. Different masks.

270 "Mae Africa" (De Malangatana)

1996. 15th Anniv of Mozambique Red Cross.

1426	**270** 5000m. multicoloured	1·00	1·00

271 African Elephant

1996. Wild Animals. Multicoloured.

1427	1000m. Type **271**	75	40
1428	2000m. White rhinoceros	1·00	75
1429	4000m. Leopard	1·25	1·00
1430	6000m. Pel's fishing owl	2·00	1·50

272 Mine Field

1996. Land Mine Clearance Campaign. Mult.

1431	2000m. Type **272**	50	35
1432	6000m. Warning sign	1·25	65

1433	8000m. Soldier with mine detector	1·50	1·00
1434	10000m. Soldier lifting mine	2·25	1·50

273 City Street

1996. "Keeping the City Clean".

1435	**273** 2000m. multicoloured	50	25

274 5r. Stamp of 1876 and Magnifying Glass

1996. 120th Anniv of Mozambique Stamps.

1436	**274** 2000m. multicoloured	50	25

275 Mitumbui

1997. Local Boats. Multicoloured.

1437	2000m. Type **275**	40	25
1438	6000m. Muterere	1·25	65
1439	8000m. Lancha	1·50	1·00
1440	10000m. Dhow	2·25	2·00

275a Anhinga

1997. 1st AICEP (Association of Post Office and Telecommunications Operators of Portuguese Speaking Territories) Philatelic Conference, Sao Tome. Sheet 70×91 mm.

MS1440a	5000m. multicoloured	12·00	12·00

276 Village Scene

1997. International Children's Day.

1441	**276** 2000m. multicoloured	50	25

277 "Enaretta conitera"

1997. Beetles. Multicoloured.

1442	2000m. Type **277**	50	25
1443	6000m. "Zographus hieroglyphicus"	1·50	75
1444	8000m. "Tragiscoschema bertolonii"	2·00	1·00
1445	10000m. "Tragocephala ducalis"	2·75	1·50
MS1446	97×105 mm. Nos. 1442/5	6·00	6·00

No. **MS**1446 also commemorates the "LUBRAPEX 97" International Stamp Exhibition, Brazil.

278 Yellow-billed Stork

1997. Aquatic Birds. Multicoloured.

1447	2000m. Type **278**	50	25
1448	4000m. Black-winged stilt	1·50	75

1449	8000m. Long-toed stint (horiz)	2·00	1·00
1450	10000m. Eastern white pelican	2·75	1·50

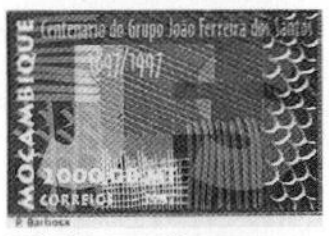

279 Abstract Patterns

1997. Centenary of Joao Ferreira dos Santos Group.

1451	**279**	2000m. multicoloured	1·00	5·00

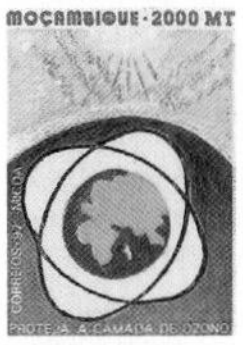

280 Sun and Globe

1997. Protection of Ozone Layer.

1452	**280**	2000m. multicoloured	30	25

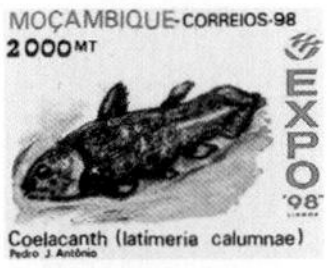

284 Coelacanth

1998. "EXPO '98" International Stamp Exhibition, Lisbon.

1463	**284**	2000m. multicoloured	1·00	50

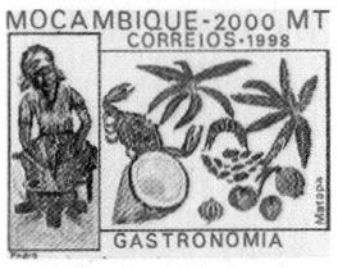

285 Woman with Food Products

1998. Food Production.

1464	**285**	2000m. multicoloured	60	30

1998. No. 1143 surch 12 500 MT.

1465	12500m. on 8m. emerald	4·00	4·00

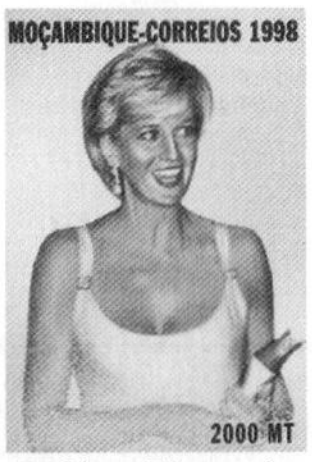

287 Diana, Princess of Wales

1998. Diana, Princess of Wales Commemoration (1st issue). T 287 and similar vert designs. Multicoloured.

MS1473 135×189 mm. 2000m. Type **287**; 2000m. Wearing tiara and white dress; 2000m. Wearing black V-neck dress; 2000m. Wearing blue sleeveless dress and choker; 2000m. With Indian woman and baby; 2000m. Wearing black halter-neck dress; 2000m. In RNLI uniform; 2000m. Wearing red dress; 2000m. Wearing Red Cross badge and protective vest 85 90

MS1474 135×189 mm. 5000m. Wearing red and white hat and pearl necklace; 5000m.Wearing pink check hat and dress; 5000m. Wearing red hat and red patterned dress; 5000m. Wearing blue hat and white jacket with blue edging; 5000m. Wearing red and black hat and red and white check jacket; 5000m. Wearing dark blue and white hat and white jacket with dark blue edging; 5000m. Wearing white and grey hat and white dress; 5000m. Turquoise and white hat and dress; 5000m. Wearing blue hat and blue jacket with flower brooch 2·20 2·30

MS1475 135×190 mm. 8000m. Wearing cream embroidered dress and bolero; 8000m. Wearing black dress and choker; 8000m. Wearing red dress; 8000m. Wearing red dress (different); 8000m. Wearing beige embroidered dress and bolero; 8000m. Wearing white dress and choker; 8000m. Wearing pale blue dress and pearl necklace; 8000m. Wearing dark blue dress; 8000m. Wearing white lace dress and carrying clutch bag 3·25 3·50

MS1476 Two sheets, each 130×100 mm. (a) 30000m. Wearing mauve dress (41×59 mm). (b) 30000m. With African child (41×59 mm). Set of 2 sheets 3·00 3·25

See also Nos. **MS**1506, **MS**1507, **MS**1593 and **MS**1594.

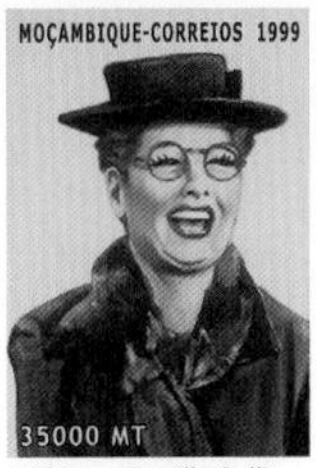

296 Lucy (Lucille Ball) wearing Dark Brown Hat and Coat

1999. Scenes from I Love Lucy (American TV comedy series). Two sheets containing T 296 and similar multicoloured design.

MS1505 (a) 88×121 mm. 35000m. Type **296**; (b) 121×88 mm. 35000m. Lucy as ballet dancer 3·50 3·75

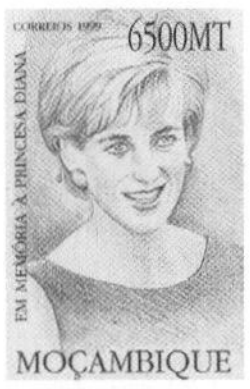

297 Diana, Princess of Wales

1999. Diana, Princess of Wales Commemoration (2nd issue). T 297 and similar vert designs. Stamp colours shown.

MS1506 165×170 mm. 6500m. Type **297** (violet and black); 6500m. In profile, looking left (brown and black); 6500m. Wearing jacket and pearl necklace (chestnut and black); 6500m. Wearing round-collared dress (olive and black); 6500m. Wearing hat with feathers (lilac and black); 6500m. Wearing white blouse with pointed collar, looking to left (brown and black) 1·80 1·90

MS1507 165×170 mm. 6500m. Wearing large white collar (lilac and black); 6500m. Wearing hat (lilac and black); 6500m. Wearing white (brown and black); 6500m. Wearing dress with narrow straps (brown and black); 6500m. Wearing patterned blouse (violet and black); 6500m. In profile, with bouquet of flowers (olive and black) 1·50 1·60

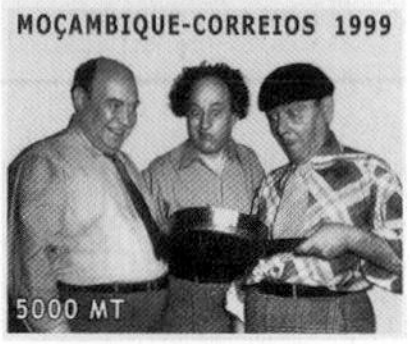

298 Joe Besser, Larry and Moe with Frying Pan

1999. Scenes from "The Three Stooges" (American TV comedy series). T 298 and similar horiz designs. Multicoloured.

MS1508 174×140 mm. 5000m. Type **298**; 5000m. Shemp wearing trilby; 5000m. Moe and Larry putting pan on Joe Besser's head; 5000m. Moe with pipe; 5000m. Larry and Moe pouring drinks on Curly's head; 5000m. Larry wearing straw hat; 5000m. Joe Besser and Larry pulling Moe's tooth; 5000m. Curly wearing mauve shirt; 5000m. Shemp, Larry and Moe behind green sofa 2·20 2·30

MS1509 Two sheets, each 140×89 mm. (a) 35000m. Larry wearing pink shirt. (b) 35000m. Larry holding shovel 3·50 3·75

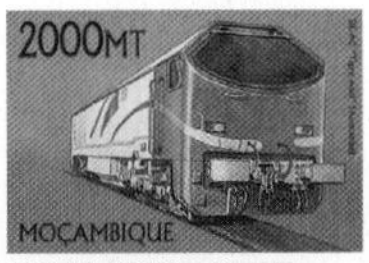

299 AE-AC "Blue Tiger", Germany

1999. Trains. Multicoloured.

1510	2000m. Type **299**	10	15
1511	2500m. DB 218 locomotive, Germany	15	20
1512	3000m. Mt. Pilatus incline railway car, Switzerland	1·20	1·30
1513	3500m. Berlin underground railway train, Germany	1·80	1·90

MS1514 162×219 mm. 2500m. DB V200 locomotive, Germany; 2500m. Union Pacific locomotive, USA; 2500m. Class 613 locomotive, Germany; 2500m. Canadian Pacific 4242 locomotive, Canada; 2500m. *Duchess of Hamilton* steam locomotive, Great Britain; 2500m. Pacific Delhi locomotive, India; 2500m. ISA locomotive, South Africa; 2500m. DR VT 18-16-07 locomotive, Germany; 2500m. DB-DE locomotive, Australia 1·20 1·30

MS1515 162×219 mm. 3000m. DB 218 locomotive, Germany; 3000m. QJ Class 2-10-2 steam locomotive, China; 3000m. 232 232.9 locomotive, Germany; 3000m. *Flying Scotsman* steam locomotive, Great Britain; 3000m. WR 360 CH locomotive, Germany; 3000m. Henschel 2-8-2 steam locomotive; 3000m. Santa Fe 39C locomotive (EUA); 3000m. Steam locomotive heading "Balkan Express", Greece; 3000m. DB 218 locomotive, Germany 1·20 1·30

MS1516 Two sheets, each 81×106 mm. (a) 25000m. German 2-8-2 steam locomotive. (b) 25000m. German DMU Talento Talbot Alamao locomotive 2·50 2·60

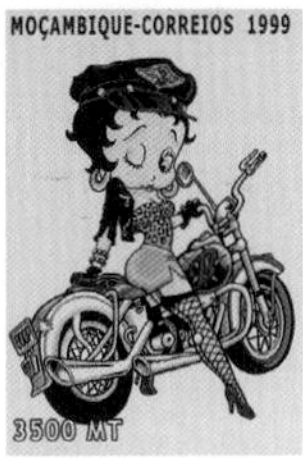

300 Betty Boop astride Motorcycle

1999. Betty Boop (cartoon character). T 300 and similar vert designs. Multicoloured.

MS1517 132×178 mm. 3500m. Type **300**; 3500m. Riding motorcycle, wearing purple top; 3500m. Wearing cap and light brown patterned top; 3500m. Astride motorcycle, wearing cap and jeans; 3500m. Looking through handlebars, wearing blue jacket and cap; 3500m. Riding motorcycle, wearing "Biker Betty" top; 3500m. With gasoline can, hitching lift; 3500m. Astride motorcycle, wearing bandana; 3500m. Astride motorcycle, wearing red jacket 1·80 1·90

MS1518 Two sheets, each 140×89 mm. (a) 35000m. Astride motorcycle, wearing red jacket. (b) 35000m. Sat beside motorcycle, with gasoline can 1·80 1·90

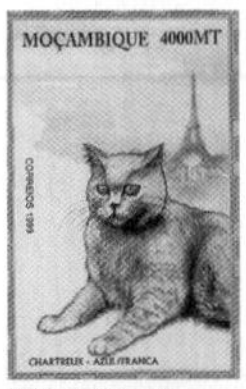

301 Chartreux

2000. Cats and Dogs of the World. T 301 and similar vert designs. Multicoloured.

MS1519 148×186 mm. 4000m. Type **301**; 4000m. Australian Mist; 4000m. Egyptian Mau; 4000m. Scottish fold; 4000m. Cornish Rex; 4000m. Abyssinian 1·20 1·30

MS1520 127×164 mm. 4000m. Himalayan; 4000m. Balinese; 4000m. Persian; 4000m. Turkish van; 4000m. Norwegian forest cat; 4000m. Maine coon 1·20 1·30

MS1521 155×222 mm. 4500m. Shetland sheepdog; 4500m. Basenji; 4500m. Poodle; 4500m. St. Bernard; 4500m. Shar Pei; 4500m. Spinone 1·50 1·60

MS1522 153×218 mm. 4500m. Jack Russell terrier; 4500m. Schweizer laufhound; 4500m. Japanese spitz; 4500m. Australian shepherd dog; 4500m. Saluki; 4500m. Siberian husky 1·50 1·60

MS1523 Four sheets. (a) 75×105 mm. 25000m. Ragdoll. (b) 75×105 mm. 25000m. Siamese. (c) 70×100 mm. 25000m. Chow Chow (horiz). (d) 70×100 mm. 25000m. Border collie (horiz). Set of 4 sheets 6·00 6·00

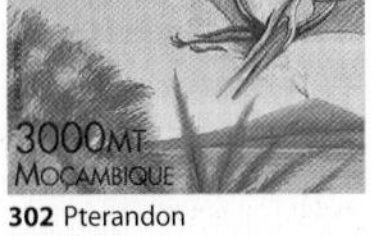

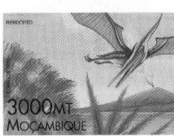

302 Pterandon

2000. Dinosaurs. T **302** and similar horiz designs. Multicoloured.

MS1524 139×116 mm. 3000m. Type **302**; 3000m. Bothriospondylus; 3000m. Iguanodon (head); 3000m. Stegosaurus; 3000m. Nodosaurus; 3000m. Elaphrosaurus and Iguanodon (body); 3000m. Petrolacosaurus; 3000m. Procompsognathus; 3000m. Dimetrodon 1·40 1·50

MS1525 139×116 mm. 3000m. Plesiosaurus; 3000m. Ceresiosaurus; 3000m. Cryptoclidus; 3000m. Placochelys; 3000m. Plotosaurus; 3000m. Ictiosaurus; 3000m. Platecarpus; 3000m. Archelon; 3000m. Mosasaur 1·40 1·50

MS1526 Two sheets, each 110×85 mm. (a) 20000m. Tyrannosaurus rex. (b) 20000m. Honodus. Set of 2 sheets 2·00 2·10

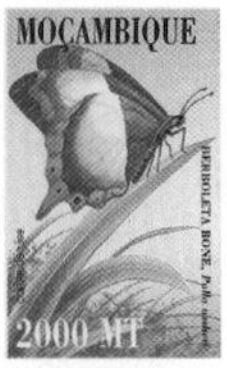

303 *Palla usher*

2000. Butterflies of the World. Multicoloured.

1527	2000m. Type **303**	10	10
1528	2500m. *Euschemon rafflesia*	15	20
1529	3000m. *Buttus philenor*	20	25
1530	3000m. *Hypolimnas bolina*	20	25
1531	3500m. *Lycorea cleobaea*	20	25
1532	4000m. *Dynastor napoleon*	20	25
1533	4500m. *Callimorpha dominula*	25	30
1534	5000m. *Pereute leucodrosime*	25	30

MS1535 95×100 mm. 4500m. *Tisiphone abeone*; 4500m. *Pseudacraea boisduvali*; 4500m. *Mylothris chloris*; 4500m. *Papilio glaucus*; 4500m. *Mimacraea marshalli*; 4500m. *Goneptery Cleopatra* 1·20 1·30

MS1536 95×100 mm. 4500m. *Palla ussheri*; 4500m. *Hypolimnas salmacis*; 4500m. *Pereute leucodrosime*; 4500m. *Anteos clorinde*; 4500m. *Colias eurytheme*; 4500m. *Hebomoia glaucippe* 1·20 1·30

MS1537 95×100 mm. 4500m. *Thauria aliris*; 4500m. *Catocala ilia*; 4500m. *Colotis danae*; 4500m. *Agrias Claudia*; 4500m. *Euploe core*; 4500m. *Scoptes alphaeus* (all horiz) 1·20 1·30

MS1538 95×100 mm. 4500m. *Phoebis philea*; 4500m. *Anteos clorinde*; 4500m. *Arhopala amantes*; 4500m. *Mesene phareus*; 4500m. *Euploea mulciber*; 4500m. *Heliconius ricini* (all horiz) 1·20 1·30

MS1539 141×112 mm. 4500m. *Euphaedra neophorn*; 4500m. *Catopsilia florella*; 4500m. *Charaxes bohemani*; 4500m. *Junonia orithya*; 4500m. *Colotis danae*; 4500m. *Eurytela dryope* 1·20 1·30

MS1540 141×112 mm. 4500m. *Papilio demodocus*; 4500m. *Kallimoides rumia*; 4500m. *Danaus chrysippus*; 4500m. *Palla ussheri*; 4500m. *Hypolimnas salmacis*; 4500m. *Zinina otis* 1·20 1·30

MS1541 Six sheets. (a) 85×110 mm. 20000m. *Papilio glaucus*. (b) 85×110 mm. 20000m. *Delias mysis* (horiz). (c) 85×110 mm. 20000m. *Mylothris cloris* (horiz). (d) 20000m. *Loxura atymnus* (horiz). (e) 70×100 mm. 20000m. *Hemiolaus coeculus* (horiz). (f) 73×103 mm. 20000m. *Euxanthe wakefieldii* (horiz). Set of 6 sheets 6·00 6·25

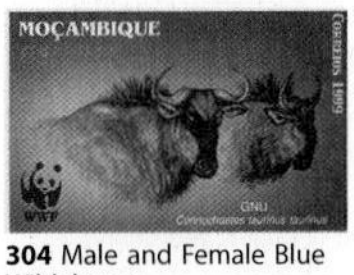

304 Male and Female Blue Wildebeest

2000. Endangered Species. Blue Wildebeest. Multicoloured.

1542	6500m. Type **304**	30	35
1543	6500m. Female and calf	30	35
1544	6500m. Lion catching blue wildebeest	30	35
1545	6500m. Blue wildebeest	30	35

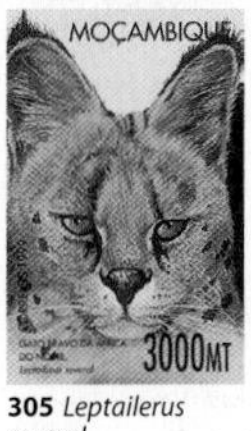

305 *Leptailerus several*

2000. Wild Cats of the World. T 305 and similar multicoloured designs.

MS1546 134×200 mm. 3000m. Type **305**; 3000m. *Panthera onca*; 3000m. *Panthera tigris corbetti*; 3000m. *Puma concolor*; 3000m. *Panthera leo persica*; 3000m. *Felis pardina*; 3000m. *Lepardus pardalia*; 3000m. *Acinonyx jubatus*; 3000m. *Felis wrangeli* 1·30 1·40

MS1547 134×200 mm. 3000m. *Felis silvestris grampia*; 3000m. *Felis ourata*; 3000m. *Panthera tigris tigris*; 3000m. *Panthera uncial*; 3000m. *Felis caracal*; 3000m. *Panthera pardus*; 3000m. *Panthera tigris amoyensis*; 3000m. *Panthera once*; 3000m. *Neofelis nabuluso* 1·30 1·40

MS1548 Two sheets. (a) 25000m.85×110 mm. *Panthera tigris altaica*. (b) 110×85 mm. 25000m. *Panthera tigris* (horiz). Set of 2 sheets 2·50 2·60

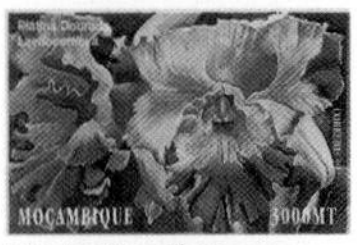

306 *Laetiocottleya*

2000. Exotic Flowers. Multicoloured.

MS1549 137×105 mm. 3000m. Type **306**; 3000m. *Papaver orientale* and *Nomada* (wasp); 3000m. *Anemone blanda*; 3000m. *Ipoema alba* and hawkmoth; 3000m. *Phalaenopsis luma* and *Delta unguiculata* (wasp); 3000m. *Iris ensata* and Colorado beetle; 3000m. *Bomarea caldasil* and *Coenagrion puella* (dragonfly); 3000m. Rosa "Raubritter" and *Bombus hortorum* (bumble bee); 3000m. Iris x daylily hybrid and fly 1·20 1·30

MS1550 137×105 mm. 3000m. *Lilium auratum* and *Tragocephala variegate* (beetle); 3000m. *Oncidim macianthum* and beetle; 3000m. *Dendrobium* and *Agelia petali* (beetle); 3000m. *Cobaea scandens*; 3000m. *Paphiopedium gilda* and *Cotalpa linegera scarabaedae*; 3000m. *Papaver nudicaule* and *Delta unduiculate* (wasp); 3000m. *Colocasia esculenta*; 3000m. *Carinatum tricolor* and butterfly; 3000m. *Phalaenopsis* and locust 1·20 1·30

MS1551 125×103 mm. 3500m. *Euanthe sanderiana* and *Teirataenia surinama* (grasshopper); 3500m. *Torenia fourleri*; 3500m. Pansies and *Papilio polyxenes* caterpillar; 3500m. *Gladiolus* "Preludio"; 3500m. *Dendrobium primulinum* and beetle; 3500m. *Clematis* "Lasurstern" and carrion beetle; 3500m. *Helianthus annuus* and beetle; 3500m. *Jacinto Grana* (all vert) 1·60 1·70

MS1552 Four sheets, each 100×70 mm. (a) 20000m. *Viola×wittrockiana* (pansies). (b) 20000m. *Nelimbo nucifera*. (c) 20000m. *Gerbera jamesoni*. (d) 20000m. Daffodils and anemones. Set of 4 sheets 4·00 4·25

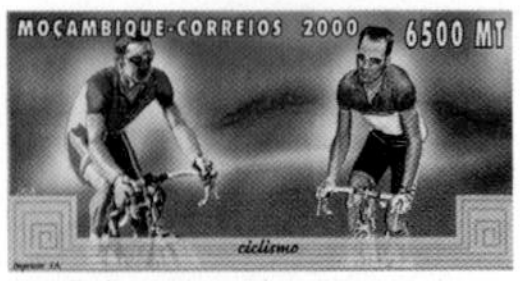

311 Cycling

2000. Sports and Chess. T 311 and similar horiz designs. Multicoloured.

MS1562 140×115 mm. 6500m. Type **311**; 6500m. Volleyball; 6500m. Boxing; 6500m. Weightlifting; 6500m. Fencing; 6500m. Judo 1·80 1·90

MS1563 140×115 mm. 9000m. Six chess pieces, including red queen and elephant carrying palanquin; 9000m. Six pieces, including ivory bishop and grey bishop; 9000m. Five knights; 9000m. Six rooks, including red elephant and sailing ship; 9000m. Six pawns; 9000m. Six pawns, including soldiers, flute player and spearholder 2·75 2·75

MS1564 140×115 mm. 9500m. Paul Morphy; 9500m. Mikhail Botvinnik; 9500m. Emanuel Lasker; 9500m. Wilhelm Steinitz; 9500m. Jose Raul Capablanca; 9500m. Howard Staunton 2·75 2·75

MS1565 140×115 mm. 12500m. Cricket (batsmen and bowler); 12500m. Cricket (four batsmen and fielder); 12500m. Polo players on horseback and elephant polo; 12500m. Four galloping polo players; 12500m. Golf (two men); 12500m. Man and woman playing golf 3·50 3·75

MS1566 140×115 mm. 14000m. Two tennis players (woman with headband serving at right); 14000m. Table tennis (two men); 14000m. Table tennis (man with pink shirt and woman); 14000m. Three tennis players (two men at left); 14000m. Tennis players (man with cap at left); 14000m. Table tennis (man with red shirt and woman) 3·50 3·75

MS1567 Two sheets, each 110×87 mm. (a) 35000m. Garry Kasparov (chess champion) (50×35 mm). (b) 35000m. Table tennis (50×35 mm). Set of 2 sheets 3·75 4·00

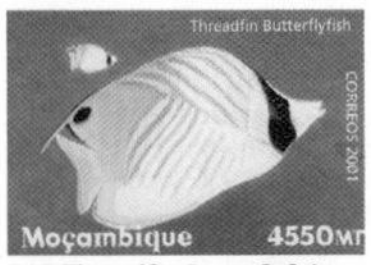

312 Threadfin Butterflyfish

2001. Marine Life. T 312 and similar horiz designs. Multicoloured.

MS1568 162×177 mm. 4550m. Type **312**; 4550m. Common clownfish; 4550m. Regal tang; 4550m. Regal angelfish; 4550m. Copperbanded butterflyfish; 4550m. Blue-girdled angelfish; 4550m. Sharpnosed pufferfish; 4550m. Humbug damselfish; 4550m. Tailbar lionfish; 4550m. Forcepsfish; 4550m. Powder blue surgeonfish; 4550m. Moorish idol 2·00 2·10

MS1569 155×117 mm. 9500m. Oceanic whitetip shark; 9500m. Grey reef shark; 9500m. Tiger shark; 9500m. Silky shark; 9500m. Basking shark; 9500m. Epaulette shark 2·75 3·00

MS1570 117×131 mm. 9500m. Sperm whale; 9500m. Giant squid; 9500m. Killer whale; 9500m. Great hite shark; 9500m. Manta ray; 9500m. Octopus 2·75 3·00

MS1571 117×131 mm. 9500m. Blue whale; 9500m. Dolphinfish; 9500m. Hammerhead shark; 9500m. Whale shark; 9500m. Leatherback turtle; 9500m. Porkfish 2·75 3·00

MS1572 Five sheets, each 85×57 mm. (a) 35000m. Wimple fish. (b) 35000m. Queen angelfish. (c) 35000m. *Phryniehthys wedli*. (d) 35000m. Bull shark. (e) 35000m. Spotted trunkfish. Set of 5 sheets 9·00 9·25

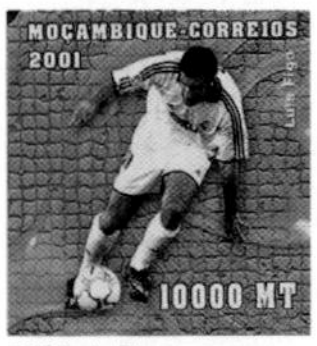

313 Luis Figo

2001. European Football Championship, Belgium and The Netherlands (2000). T 313 and similar square designs. Multicoloured.

MS1573 131×99 mm. 10000m. Type **313**; 10000m. Fernando Couto; 10000m. Luis Figo diving at ball; 10000m. Sergio Conceicao; 10000m. Nuno Gomes; 10000m. Rui Costa 3·00 3·25

MS1574 131×99 mm. 17000m. Nicolas Anelka; 17000m. Didier Deschamps; 17000m. Emmanuel Petit; 17000m. Thierry Henry; 17000m. Marcel Desailly; 17000m. Zinedine Zidane 5·25 5·50

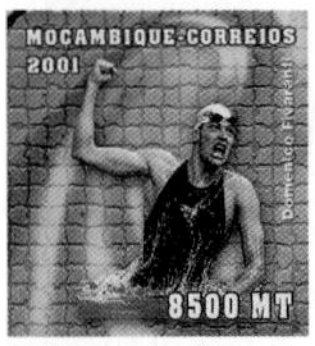

314 Domenico Fivaranti (swimming)

2001. Olympic Games, Sydney (2000). T 314 and similar square designs. Multicoloured.

MS1575 131×135 mm. 8500m. Type **314**; 8500m. Stacy Dragila (pole vault); 8500m. Pieter van den Hoogenband (swimming); 8500m. David O'Connor (three day eventing); 8500m. Venus Williams (tennis); 8500m. Maurice Greene (athletics); 8500m. Joy Fawcett (football); 8500m. Marion Jones (athletics); 8500m. Patricio Ormazabal and Jeff Agoos (football) 3·75 4·00

MS1576 131×135 mm. 10000m. Agnes Kovacs (swimming); 10000m. Youlia Rasksina (gymnastics); 10000m. Kong Linghui and Lui Guoliang (table tennis); 10000m. Nicolas Gill; 10000m. Anky van Grunsven (dressage); 10000m. Brian Olsen; 10000m. Wang Nan (table tennis); 10000m. Megan Quann (swimming); 10000m. Venus Williams (tennis) 6·25 6·50

MS1577 131×99 mm. 17000m. Vince Carter (basketball); 17000m. Blaine Wilson (gymnastics); 17000m. Steve Keir (handball); 17000m. Wen Xiao Wang and Chris Xu (table tennis); 17000m. Venus and Serena Williams (tennis); 17000m. Gu Jun and Ge Fei (table tennis) 5·25 5·50

MS1578 131×99 mm. 20000m. Clara Hughes (cycling); 20000m. Martina Hingis (tennis); 20000m. Otilla Badescu (table tennis); 20000m. Isabel Fernandez (judo); 20000m. Coralie Simmons (water polo). 20000m. Mia Hamm (football) 6·00 6·25

MS1579 131×99 mm. 28000m. Patrick Rafter (tennis); 28000m. Tadahiro Nomura (judo); 28000m. Seiko Iseki (table tennis); 28000m. Michael Dodge (cycling); 28000m. Ann Dow (water polo); 28000m. David Beckham (football) 8·25 8·50

MS1580 Six sheets, each 95×98 mm. (a) 50000m. Andre Agassi (tennis). (b) 50000m.Chang Jun Gao and Michelle Do (table tennis). (c) 50000m. Kong Linghui (table tennis). (d) 50000m. Michelle Do (table tennis); (e) 100000m. Michelle Do. (f) 100000m. Serena Williams (tennis). (g) 100000m. Christophe Legout and Damien Eldi (table tennis). Set of 6 sheets 12·00 12·50

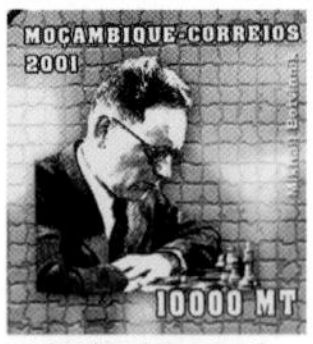

315 Mikhail Botvinnik

2001. Chess Players. Multicoloured.

MS1581 131×135 mm. 10000m. Type **315**; 10000m. Garry Kasparov; 10000m. Wilhelm Steinitz; 10000m. Emanuel Lasker; 10000m. Paul Morphy; 10000m. Anatoly Karpov; 10000m. Tigran Petrossian; 10000m. Mikhail Tal; 10000m. Jose Raul Capablanca 4·00 4·25

MS1582 131×135 mm. 10000m. Judith Polgar (wearing maroon jumper); 10000m. Xie Jun; 10000m. Zsuza Polgar; 10000m. Nana Ioseliani; 10000m. Alisa Galliamova; 10000m. Judith Polgar (with head in hands); 10000m. Judith Polgar (wearing blouse); 10000m. Monica Calzetta; 10000m. Anjelina Belakovskaia 4·00 4·25

MS1583 Two sheets, each 96×100 mm. (a) 100000m. Garry Kasparov. (b) 100000m. Judith Polgar 5·00 5·25

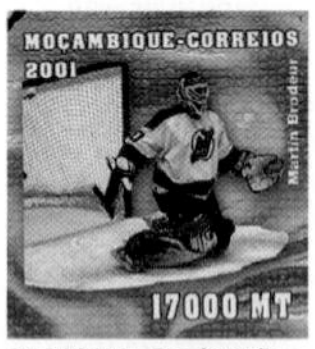

316 Martin Brodeur (ice hockey goalkeeper)

2001. Winter Olympic Games, Salt Lake City (2002) (1st issue). T 316 and similar square designs. Multicoloured.

MS1584 131×99 mm. 17000m. Type **316**; 17000m. Svetlana Vysokova (speed skating); 17000m. Ray Bourque and Patrik Elias (ice hockey); 17000m. Rachel Belliveau (cross-country skiing); 17000m. Scott Gomez and Janne Laukkanen (ice hockey); 17000m. Sonja Nef (skiing) 5·00 5·25

MS1585 131×99 mm. 20000m. Rusty Smith (speed skating); 20000m. Sandra Schmirler (curling); Totmianina and Marinin (ice skating); 20000m. Brigitte Obermoser (skiing); 20000m. Roman Turek (ice hockey); 20000m. Jennifer Heil (skiing) 5·00 5·25

MS1586 131×99 mm. 28000m. Kovarikova and Novotny (skating); 28000m. Li Song (speed skating); 28000m. Armin Zoeggeler (bobsleigh); 28000m. Michael von Grueningen (skiing); 28000m. Tami Bradley (skiing); 28000m. Chris Drury, Turner Stevenson and Greg de Vries (ice hockey) 8·00 8·25

MS1587 Three sheets, each 95×98 mm. (a) 50000m. Armin Zoggeler (toboggan). (b) 75000m. Tommy Salo. (c) 100000m. Jayne Torvill and Christopher Dean (ice dancing) Set of 3 sheets 10·00 10·50

See also 1588/9.

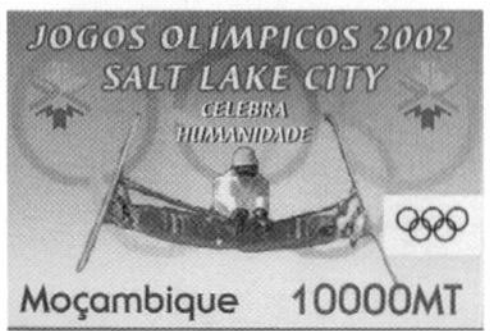

317 Skier

2002. Winter Olympic Games, Salt Lake City, U.S.A. (2nd issue). Multicoloured.

1588 10000m. Type **317** 50 55

1589 17000m. Skier upside down (vert) 85 90

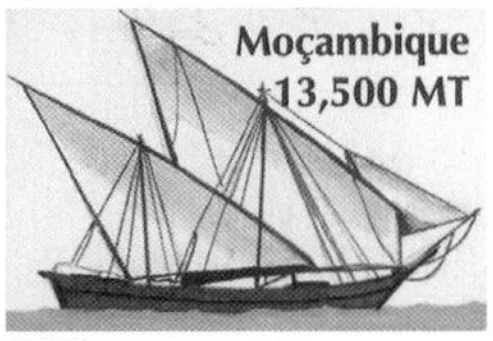

318 Dhow

2002. Ships. Multicoloured.

MS1590 147×105 mm. 13500m. Type **318**; 13500m. Junk; 13500m. Galleon; 13500m. Schooner; 13500m. Full-rigged ship; 13500m. Barque 4·00 4·25

MS1591 147×105 mm. 13500m. Viking Longboat; 13500m. Canoe; 13500m. Gondola; 13500m. Fishing boat; 13500m. Light boat; 13500m. Tug 4·00 4·25

MS1592 Two sheets. (a) 79×60 mm. 40000m. Aircraft carrier; (b) 60×80 mm. 40000m. Figurehead (vert). Set of 2 sheets 4·00 4·25

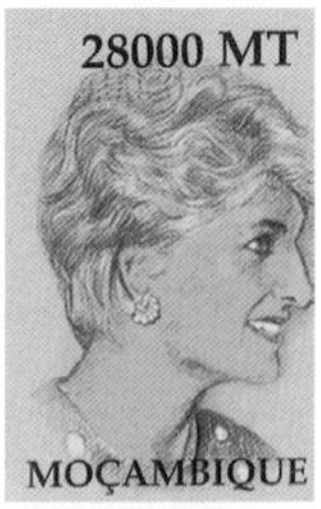

319 Princess Diana

2002. Diana, Princess of Wales Commemoration (3rd issue). T 319 and similar vert designs. Multicoloured.

MS1593 Three sheets each 132×135 mm. (a) 28000m. Type **319**; 28000m. Wearing feathered hat; 28000m. Wearing pearl necklace; 28000m. Wearing wide brimmed hat. (b) 28000m. Wearing blue top; 28000m. Wearing white top; 28000m. Looking right; 28000m. Holding bouquet. (c) 28000m. Wearing pink outfit; 28000m. Wearing black with drop earrings; 28000m. Looking straight ahead; 28000m. Wearing black and white outfit. Set of 3 sheets 12·00 12·50

MS1594 Three sheets each 81×112 mm. (a) 50000m. Wearing hat and wrap. (b) 50000m. With hand on chin; (c) 50000m. Wearing large stud earrings. Set of 3 sheets 7·50 8·00

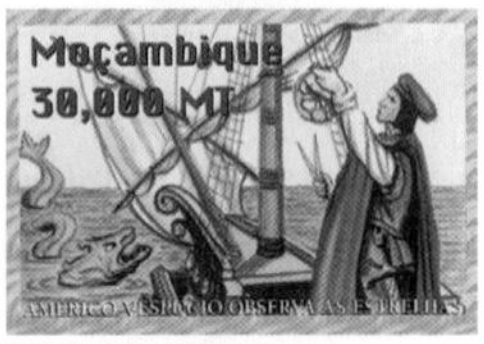

320 Americo Vespucio

2002. 500th Anniv (2001) of Amerigo Vespucci's Third Voyage. T 320 and similar multicoloured designs.

MS1595 157×117 mm. 30000m. Type **320**; 30000m. Green parrot; 30000m. Homes on stilts and ship 4·50 4·75

MS1596 55×76 mm. 50000m. Outline of Brazil and ship's course 2·50 2·75

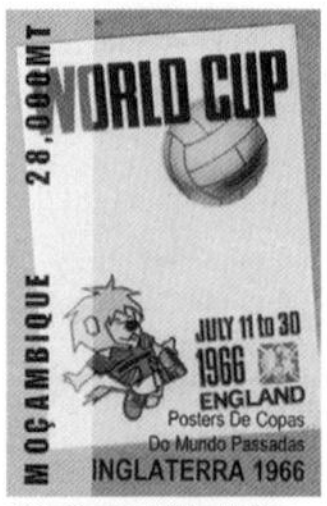

321 England World Cup Poster

2002. World Cup Football Championship, Japan and South Korea. T 321 and similar multicoloured designs.

MS1597 Two sheets each 153×175 mm. (a) 28000m. Type **321**; 28000m. Italian player; 28000m. Danish player (red strip); 28000m. Colombian player; 28000m. Munhak stadium (55×41 mm). (b) 28000m. Brazilian player; 28000m. Swedish poster; 28000m. Nigerian player; 28000m. Danish player (white strip); 28000m. Gwangju stadium (55×41 mm). Set of 2 sheets 12·00 12·50

MS1598 Two sheets. (a) 53×73 mm. 50000m. Pele (Brazilian player). (b) 73×53 mm. 50000m. Max Morlock (German player). Set of 2 sheets 5·00 5·25

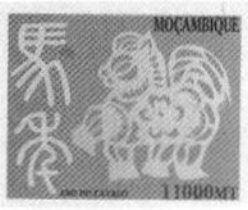

322 Horse

2002. Chinese New Year ("Year of the Horse"). T 322 and similar multicoloured designs.

MS1599 68×58 mm. 11000m. Type **322**; 11000m. Purple and red horse; 11000m. Purple horse; 11000m. Orange and red horse 2·20 2·30

MS1600 100×70 mm. 11000m. Horse cantering (27×41 mm) 55 60

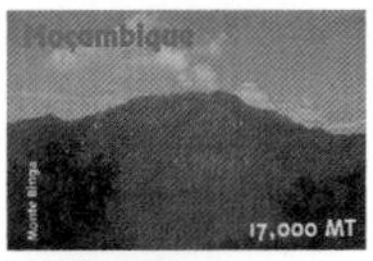

323 Mount Binga, Mozambique

2002. International Year of Mountains. T 323 and similar horiz designs. Multicoloured.

1601	17000m. Type **323**	85	90
1602	17000m. Mount Namuli, Mozambique	85	90

MS1603 160×98 mm. 17000m. Mount Kenya, Kenya; 17000m. Mount Cook, New Zealand; 17000m. Mount Ararat, Turkey; 17000m. Mount Paine, Chile; 17000m. Mount Everest, Nepal; 17000m. Mount Kilimanjaro, Tanzania 5·00 5·25

MS1604 72×51 mm. 50000m. Mount Zugspitze, Germany 2·50 3·00

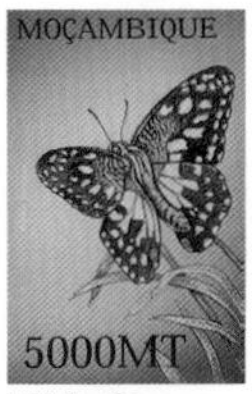

324 *Papilio demoleus*

2002. Butterflies. Multicoloured.

1605	5000m. Type **324**	25	30
1606	10000m. *Euschemon rafflesia*	50	55
1607	17000m. *Liphyra brassolis*	85	90
1608	28000m. *Mimacraea marshalli*	1·40	1·50

MS1609 Two sheets each 112×155 mm. (a) 10000m. *Parides coon*; 10000m. *Delias mysis*; 10000m. *Troides brookiana*; 10000m. *Syrmatia dorilas*; 10000m. *Danis danis*; 10000m. *Lycaena dispar*; 10000m. *Mesene phareus*; 10000m. *Kallima inachus*; 10000m. *Morpho rhetenor*. (b) 10000m. *Eurema brigitta*; 10000m. *Loxura atymunus*; 10000m. *Arhopala amantes*; 10000m. *Junonia coenia*; 10000m. *Eurides isabella*; 10000m. *Heliconius ricini*; 10000m. *Zipaetis xcylax* (scylax); 10000m. *Cepheuptychia cephus*; 10000m. *Philaethria dido*. Set of 2 sheets 9·00 9·25

MS1610 Two sheets each 106×81 mm. (a) 50000m. *Papilio cresphontes*. (b) 50000m. *Ornithoptera alexandrae*. Set of 2 sheets 5·00 5·25

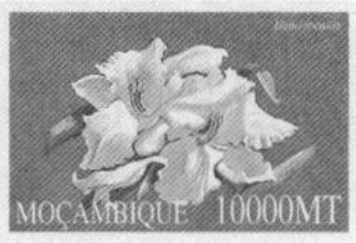

325 *Hemerocallis*

2002. Flowers. T 325 and similar multicoloured designs.

MS1611 Three sheets. (a) 150×117 mm. 10000m. Type **325**; 10000m. *Nazcissys* (Narcissus); 10000m. Hybrid tea; 10000m. Cayenne capers; 10000m. *Araceae*; 10000m. *Hymenocallis narcissiflora*; 10000m. *Hymenocallis*; 10000m. *Tulipa*; 10000m. *Lachenalia aloides* and *meconopsis poppies*. (b) 150×117 mm. 10000m. Narcissus; 10000m. L. *Bulbiferum var croceum*; 10000m. *Iris purpureobractea* and butterfly; 10000m. *Neomarica caerulea*; 10000m. *Peonia lactiflora*, *Primula chungensis* and *Viola cornuta*; 10000m. *Cayenne caper* and beetle; 10000m. *Iris purpureobractea*; 10000m. *Tuberous begonia cultivar*; 10000m. Oriental hybrid lily. (c) 108×160 mm. 10000m. *Viola jeannie*; 10000m. Sunflower; 10000m. *Momo botan*; 10000m. *Scho,buzgkia* orchid; 10000m. Dahlia hybrid; 10000m. *Sparaxis elegans harlequin*; 10000m. Dianthus; 10000m. *Tulipa saxatilis* and *camassia leichtlinii*; 10000m. Hybrid ("Hibrid"). Set of 3 sheets 13·00 13·50

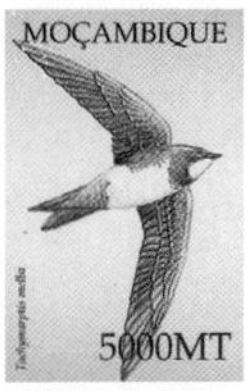

326 *Tachymarptis melba*

2002. Birds. Multicoloured.

1612	5000m. Type **326**	25	30
1613	5000m. *Falco tinnunculus*	25	30
1614	10000m. *Ardea cinerea*	50	55
1615	10000m. *Pitta angolensis*	50	55
1616	17000m. *Corythaeola cristata*	85	90
1617	28000m. *Butastur rufipennis*	1·40	1·50

MS1618 Two sheets each 116×116 mm. (a) 17000m. *Coracias garrulous*; 17000m. *Estrilda astrild*; 17000m. *Upupa epops*; 17000m. *Merops apiaster*; 17000m. *Ploceus Cucullatus*; 17000m. *Clamator glandarius*. (b) 17000m. *Psittacus erithacus*; 17000m. *Ficedula hypoleuca*; 17000m. *Tchagra senegala*; 17000m. *Oriolus oriolus*; 17000m. *Luscinia megarhynchos*; 17000m. *Halcyon malimbica* . Set of 12 sheets 10·00 10·50

MS1619 Four sheets. (a) 83×108 mm. 50000m. *Sitrix varia*. (b) 83×108 mm. 50000m. *Falco subbuteo*. (c) 83×108 mm. 50000m. *Butorides striatus*. (d) 108×83 mm 50000m. *Actophilornis Africana* (*africanus*) (horiz). Set of 4 sheets 10·00 10·50

The stamps in No. **MS**1618a/b were printed together, se-tenant, with the backgrounds forming composite designs.

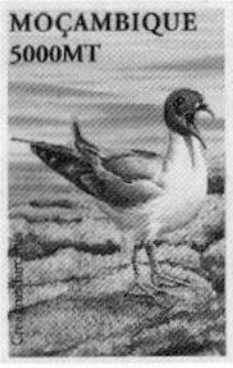

327 *Creagrus furcatus*

2002. Sea Birds. Multicoloured.

1620	5000m. Type **327**	25	30
1621	10000m. *Larosterna inca*	50	55
1622	17000m. *Pelecanus crispus*	85	90
1623	28000m. *Morus bassanus*	1·20	1·50

MS1624 110×162 mm. 10000m. *Phaethon aethereus*; 10000m. *Catharacta Maccormicki*; 10000m. *Diomedea bulleri*; 10000m. *Puffinus iherminieri*; 10000m. *Oceanities oceanicus*; 10000m. *Pterodroma hasitata*; 10000m. *Fregata magnificens*; 10000m. *Sula nebouxii*; 10000m. *Uria aagle* 4·50 4·75

MS1625 Two sheets. (a) 98×68 mm. 50000m. *Spheniscus demersus*. (b) 97×68 mm. 50000m. *Rynchops niger* (horiz). Set of 2 sheets 5·00 5·25

The stamps in No. **MS**1624 were printed together, se-tenant, with the background forming a composite design.

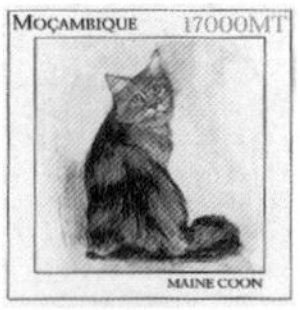

328 Maine Coon Cat

2002. Cats. Multicoloured.

MS1626 118×91 mm. 17000m. Type **328**; 17000m. Cornish Rex; 17000m. La Perm (Red Tabby); 17000m. Sphynx; 17000m. Siamese; 17000m. Persian 4·25 4·25

MS1627 66×96 mm. 50000m. Chestnut (Oriental Longhair) 2·50 2·75

2002. Dogs. As T 328. Multicoloured.

MS1628 118×91 mm. 17000m. Labrador; 17000m. Bulldog; 17000m. Cocker spaniel; 17000m. Golden retriever; 17000m. Boxer; 17000m. Bloodhound 5·00 5·25

MS1629 66×96 mm. 40000m. Basset hound 2·00 2·10

2002. Horses. As T 328. Multicoloured.

MS1630 118×91 mm. 17000m. Hanoverian; 17000m. Haflinger; 17000m. Nonius; 17000m. Belgian Heavy Draughts; 17000m. Australian-bred Arab; 17000m. Thoroughbred 5·00 5·25

MS1631 96×66 mm. 50000m. Two Don horses 2·50 2·75

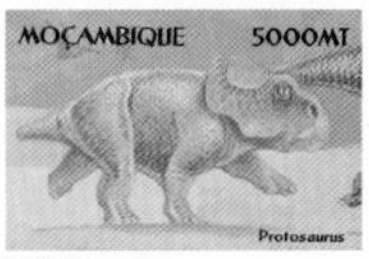

329 Protosaurus

2002. Prehistoric Animals. Multicoloured.

1632	5000m. Type **329**	25	30
1633	10000m. Psittacosaurus	50	55
1634	17000m. Torosaurus	85	90
1635	28000m. Triceratops	1·40	1·50

MS1636 Two sheets each 180×135 mm. (a) 10000m. Diplodocus; 10000m. Pterosaurs; 10000m. Young diplodocus; 10000m. Afrovenator; 10000m. Parasarolophus; 10000m. Ramphorincus; 10000m. Lambeosaur; 10000m. Euoplocephalus; 10000m. Cynodont. (b) 10000m. Brachiosaur; 10000m. Monoclonius; 10000m. Homalocephale; 10000m. Pterodactyl; 10000m. Deinonychus; 10000m. Archaeopteryx; 10000m. Cretaceous landscape; 10000m. Hypsilophodon; 10000m. Lystrosaur. Set of 2 sheets 9·00 9·25

MS1637 Two sheets. (a) 100×68 mm. 50000m. Baryonyx. (b) 100×70 mm. 50000m. Styracosaurus (vert). Set of 2 sheets 5·00 5·25

The stamps in No. **MS**1636a/b were each printed together, se-tenant, plus labels, with the backgrounds forming composite designs.

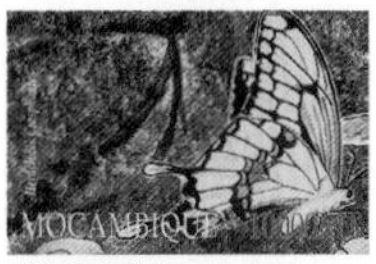

330 *Heraclides cresphontes*

2002. Woodland Fauna and Flora. Multicoloured.

MS1638 Two sheets each 153×115 mm. (a) 10000m. Type **330**; 10000m. *Tyto alba*; 10000m. *Drocopus pileatus*; 10000m. *Archilochus colobris* (colubris) (Ruby-throated Hummingbird) and *Cypripedium parviflorum*; 10000m. *Vulpes vulpes*; 10000m. *Odocoileus virginianus*; 10000m. *Enallagma* sp.; 10000m. *Amanita muscaria*; 10000m. *Tamiasciurus hudsonicus*. (b) 10000m. *Pandion haliaetus*; 10000m. Flying squirrel; 10000m. Fox squirrel; 10000m. *Agelaius phoeniceus*; 10000m. *Papilio polyxenes*; 10000m. *Didelphus virginiana*; 10000m. *Hyla crucifer*; 10000m. Two *Odocoileus virginianus*; 10000m. *Procyon lotor* Set of 2 sheets 9·00 9·25

The stamps in No. **MS**1638a/b were each printed together, se-tenant, with the backgrounds forming composite designs.

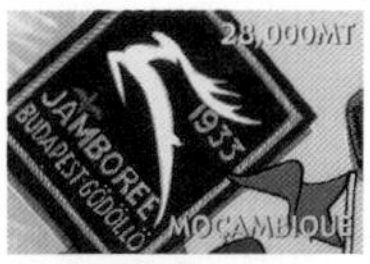

331 Scout Badge

2002. World Scout Congress. T 331 and similar multicoloured designs.

MS1639 109×99 mm. 28000m. Type **331**; 28000m. 19th Jamboree badge; 28000m. Tiger mascot; 28000m. 20th Jamboree logo 5·50 5·75

MS1640 111×82 mm. 28000m. Scout (vert) 1·40 1·50

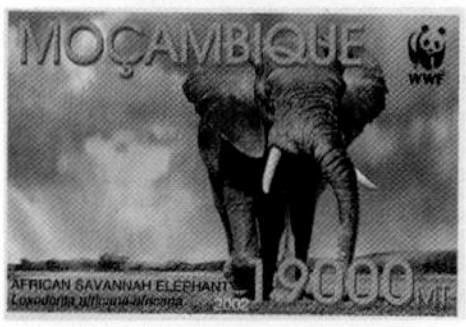

332 African Elephant

2002. Endangered Animals. African Elephant. Multicoloured.

1641	1900m. Type **332**	10	10
1642	1900m. Elephants at waterhole	10	10
1643	1900m. Elephant in swamp	10	10
1644	1900m. Elephant with calf	10	10

MS1645 145×170 mm. Nos. 1641/4 plus four stamp-sized labels, each picturing Prince Bernhard or elephants 45 45

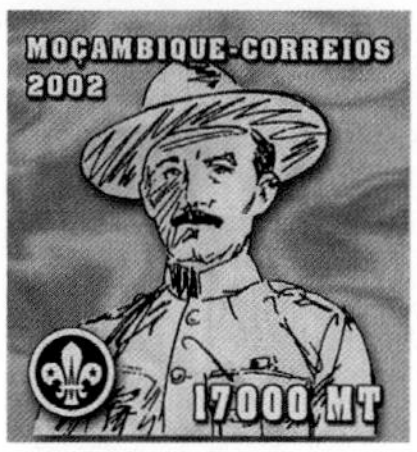

333 Lord Baden Powell

2002. World Scout Jamboree (2003). T 333 and similar vert designs showing Lord Baden Powell and plants or butterflies. Multicoloured.

MS1646 Two sheets each 133×101 mm. (a) 17000m. Type **333**; 17000m. *Morpho Aega*; 17000m. *Prepona meander*; 17000m. *Charaxes bernardus*; 17000m. *Hypolimnas salmacis*; 17000m. *Morpho rhetenor*. (b) 17000m. Four mushrooms; 17000m. Two pink and white flowers; 17000m. Three orange mushrooms; 17000m. Five purple and red flowers; 17000m. Three brownish white mushrooms; 17000m. Two striped-petal flowers 10·00 10·50

MS1647 98×100 mm. 88000m. Lord Baden Powell with arms crossed 4·25 4·50

2002. Aviation. Sheet 96×100 mm containing vert designs as T 333. Multicoloured.

MS1648 22000m. Antoine de Saint-Exupery; 22000m. Charles Lindberg and *Spirit of St. Louis*; 22000m. Charles Lindberg and light aircraft; 22000m. Concorde 2·30 2·40

2002. Cinematic Personalities. Sheet 97×101 mm containing vert designs as T 333. Multicoloured.

MS1649 25000m. Charlie Chaplin; 25000m. Frank Sinatra; 25000m. Alfred Hitchcock; 25000m. Walt Disney 2·50 2·60

2002. John Audubon (ornithologist) Commemoration. Vert designs as T 333. Multicoloured.

MS1650 97×101 mm. 33000m. John Audubon; 33000m. *Aix sponsa*; 33000m. *Toxostoma rufum* ("Toxastoma montanum") and *Ixoreus naevius*; 33000m. *Loxia Leucoptera* 3·25 3·50

MS1651 Two sheets each 97×101 mm. (a) 11000m. *Quiscalus quiscula*. (b) 11000m. *Columba leucocephala* ("Patagioenas leucocephala"). Set of 2 sheets 60 65

2002. 40th Death Anniv of Marilyn Monroe. Vert designs as T 333.

MS1652 Two sheets each 133×101 mm. (a) 17000m. Looking at camera; 17000m.Wearing drop earrings; 17000m. Laughing; 17000m. Wearing choker; 17000m. Looking over shoulder; 17000m. Looking surprised. (b) 17000m. Wearing sleeveless top; 17000m. Looking over shoulder (different); 17000m. Beckoning with finger; 17000m. Wearing fur stole and drop earrings; 17000m. With arms folded; 17000m. Smiling with long hair. Set of 2 sheets 10·00 10·50

MS1653 Two sheets each 97×100 mm. (a) 88000m. Wearing crochet top. (b) 88000m. Wearing red top with pearls. Set of 2 sheets 4·50 4·75

2002. Visits of Pope John Paul II. Vert designs as T 333. Multicoloured.

MS1654 133×100 mm. 15000m. Pope John Paul II waving; 15000m. Wearing red robe; 15000m. Carrying Pastoral staff; 15000m. Wearing mitre; 15000m. Sitting in chair; 15000m. Looking left 4·75 5·00

MS1655 97×100 mm. 20000m. Princess Diana wearing poppy; 20000m. Princess Diana carrying bouquet; 20000m. The Pope looking down; 20000m. The Pope looking up 4·00 4·25

MS1656 Two sheets each 97×100 mm. (a) 88000m. Pope John Paul II. (b) 110000m. Mother Teresa. Set of 2 sheets 5·00 5·25

2002. Egyptian Pharaohs. Vert designs as T 333. Multicoloured.

MS1657 Two sheets each 133×100 mm. (a) 15000m. Seti I; 15000m. Djedefre; 15000m. Smenkhkare; 15000m. Seti II; 15000m. Senusret III; 15000m. Tutankhamun. (b) 17000m. Netjenkhet Djoser; 17000m. Death mask of Tutankhamun (front); 17000m. Neferefre; 17000m. Amenhotep III; 17000m. Pepi I; 17000m. Amenmesses. Set of 2 sheets 7·25 7·50

MS1658 Three sheets each 98×100 mm. (a) 20000m. Amenhotep II; 20000m. Merenptah; 20000m. Amenophis IV; 20000m. Tuthmosis (stone). (b) 20000m. Nefertiti (profile); 20000m. Cleopatra VII; 20000m. Nefertari (facing left); 20000m. Nefertiti (front). (c) 20000m. Nefertari (facing right); 20000m. Death mask of Tutankhamun (from angle); 20000m. Tuthmosis (black and gold); Nefertiti (from angle). Set of 3 sheets 11·00 11·50

MS1659 Two sheets each 97×101 mm. (a) 110000m. Nefertiti. (b) 110000m. Tutankhamun. Set of 3 sheets 1·00 1·50

2002. Nobel Prize Winners. Vert designs as T 333. Multicoloured.

MS1660 Two sheets each 133×100 mm. (a) 15000m. Henri ("Hemri") Dunant; 15000m. Theodore Roosevelt; 15000m. Albert Einstein; 15000m. Ernest Hemingway; 15000m. Thomas Nast; 15000m. Albert Camus. (b) 17000m. Albert Einstein with hands clasped; 17000m. Dalai Lama; 17000m. Winston Churchill; 17000m. Hideki Yukawa; 17000m. Albert Schweitzer; 17000m. Linus Pauling 8·25 8·25

Although included in the set, Thomas Nast was not the recipient of a Nobel Prize.

2002. Robert Stephenson Commemoration. Vert designs as T 333. Multicoloured.

MS1661 97×100 mm. 25000m. Robert Stephenson (black); 25000m. Early U.S steam locomotive; 25000m. Great Western Railway steam locomotive; 25000m. Early steam locomotive 5·00 5·50

MS1662 Two sheets each 97×101 mm. (a) 110000m. Robert Stephenson (sepia). (b) 110000m. Robert Stephenson (green). Set of 2 stamps 2·75 2·50

2002. Explorers. Vert designs as T 333. Multicoloured.

MS1663 97×101 mm. 22000m. Vasco de Gama; 22000m. Ferdinand Magellan; 22000m. Christopher Columbus; 22000m. Amerigo Vespucci 1·10 1·20

MS1664 97×101 mm. 110000m. Vasco de Gama 5·50 5·75

2002. Charles Darwin and Alexander Fleming Commemorations. Sheet 97×100 mm containing vert designs as T 333. Multicoloured.

MS1665 33000m. Charles Darwin and Byronosaurus; 33000m. Alexander Fleming and *Tricholoma terreum*; 33000m. Alexander Fleming and *Boletus edulis*; 33000m. Charles Darwin and Irratator 6·00 6·25

2002. Composers. Vert designs as T 333. Multicoloured.

MS1666 97×101 mm. 5000m. Antonio Vivaldi; 5000m. Franz Liszt; 5000m. Ludwig van Beethoven; 5000m. Wolfgang Mozart 1·00 1·00

MS1667 97×101 mm. 88000m. Wolfgang Mozart at piano 2·20 2·30

2002. 25th Death Anniv of Elvis Presley (entertainer). Vert designs as T 333. Multicoloured.

MS1668 133×101 mm. 15000m. Wearing jacket and tie; 15000m. Looking down in cable-knit sweater; 15000m. Wearing white shirt; 15000m. Wearing square checked shirt; 15000m. Reclining in cable-knit sweater; 15000m. Wearing hat 4·50 4·75

MS1669 97×100 mm. 110000m. Wearing blue jacket 5·50 5·75

2002. Personalities. Vert designs as T 333. Multicoloured.

MS1670 Three sheets each 97×100 mm. (a) 20000m. Che Guevara; 20000m. Pope John Paul II; 20000m. Martin Luther King; 20000m. Mao Zedung. (b) 22000m. Dalai Lama; 22000m. Mother Teresa; 22000m. Pope John Paul II waving; 22000m. Mahatma Gandhi. (c) 33000m. Albert Schweitzer; 33000m. Claude Bernard; 33000m. Henri Dunant; 33000m. Raoul Follerau. Set of 3 sheets 10·00 10·50

2002. Formula 1 Motor Sport. Sheet 97×100 mm containing vert designs as T 333. Multicoloured.

MS1671 20000m. Ayrton Senna; 20000m. Modern Formula 1 racing car; 20000m. Early Formula 1 racing car; 20000m. Juan Manuel Fangio 4·00 4·25

2002. Birth Centenary of Victor Hugo (author). Sheet 97×101 mm containing vert design as T 333. Multicoloured.

MS1672 88000m. Victor Hugo 4·25 4·50

2002. John F. Kennedy (President. of U.S.A. 1961–3) Commemoration. Sheet 97×101 mm. Vert design as T 333. Multicoloured.

MS1673 88000m. John F. Kennedy 4·25 4·50

2002. Political Leaders. Sheet 97×100 mm containing vert designs as T 333. Multicoloured.

MS1674 25000m. Winston Churchill; 25000m. John F. Kennedy; 25000m. Konrad Adenauer; 25000m. Charles de Gaulle 5·00 5·25

2002. Haroun Tazieff (French vulcanologist and geologist) Commemoration. Sheet 97×100 mm containing vert designs as T 333. Multicoloured.

MS1675 25000m. Scipionyx and erupting volcano; 25000m. Beipiaosaurus and erupting volcano; 25000m. Haroun Tazieff wearing radiation suit and vanadinite rock; 25000m. Haroun Tazieff and adamite rock 5·00 5·25

2002. Astronauts and Concorde. Vert designs as T 333. Multicoloured.

MS1676 133×101 mm. 17000m. Michael Collins; 17000m. Concorde taking off to right;17000m. John Glenn ("Genn"); 17000m. Concorde flying left; 17000m. Neil Armstrong; 17000m. Concorde taking off to left 4·75 5·00

MS1677 97×101 mm. 88000m. John Glenn 4·25 4·50

2002. 180th Birth Anniv of Louis Pasteur (French Chemist). Sheet 97×101 mm containing vert designs as T 333, each showing Louis Pasteur with a different breed of dog. Multicoloured.

MS1678 25000m. Husky; 25000m. Weimaraner; 25000m. Wolfhound; 25000m. Springer spaniel 5·00 5·25

2002. 5th Death Anniv of Diana, Princess of Wales. Vert designs as T 333. Multicoloured.

MS1679 133×100 mm. 15000m. Diana and Pope John Paul II; 15000m. Wearing white halter-neck top; 15000m. Wearing red hat and spotted top; 15000m. Holding award; 15000m. Wearing deep purple dress; 15000m. Wearing blue dress and choker 4·75 5·00

MS1680 97×101 mm. 88000m. Wearing tiara 4·25 4·50

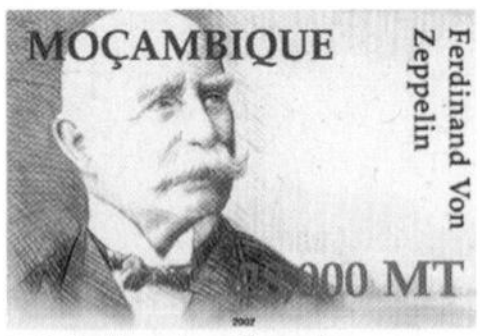

334 Ferdinand von Zeppelin

2002. Ferdinand von Zeppelin (inventor) Commemoration. Multicoloured.

MS1681 Two sheets each 173×120 mm. (a) 28000m. Type **334**; 28000m. LZ 2 airship (1905); 28000m. LZ 10 airship (1911); 28000m. LZ 1 airship (1900). (b) 28000m. LZ 1 airship over water; 28000m. LZ 2 airship over water; 28000m. LZ 10 airship over field of sheep; 28000m. Ferdinand von Zeppelin holding binoculars. Set of 2 sheets 10·00 10·50

MS1682 Two sheets. (a) 106×70 mm. 50000m. Ferdinand von Zeppelin wearing shirt and tie (vert). (b) 70×106 mm. 50000m. Ferdinand von Zeppelin wearing army uniform (vert). Set of 2 sheets 5·00 5·25

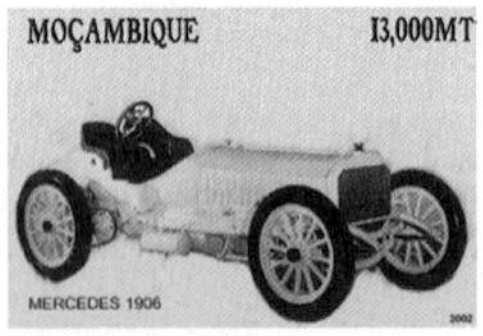

335 Mercedes (1906)

2002. Vintage Cars (1st series). Racing Cars. Multicoloured.

MS1683 Two sheets each 172×146 mm. (a) 13000m. Type **335**; 13000m. Morgan (1951); 13000m. Sunbeam (1912); 13000m. Sunbeam (1922); 13000m. Sunbeam Tiger (1925); 13000m. Austin 100 HP (1908). (b) 13000m. Bentley (1912); 13000m. Delage Grand Prix (1914); 13000m. Healey Silverstone (1949); 13000m. Duesenberg (1922); 13000m. Delage 1500cc Grand Prix; 13000m. Ferrari 375 F1 (1951). Set of 2 sheets 8·25 8·50

MS1684 Two sheets. (a) 100×70 mm. 40000m. Marmon Wasp (1911). (b) 70×100 mm. 40000m. Alfa Romeo (1931). Set of 2 sheets 8·00 8·25

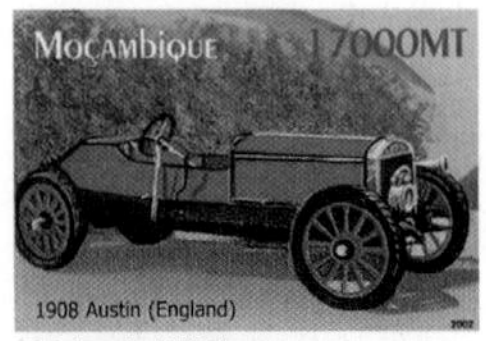

336 Austin (1908)

2002. Vintage Cars (2nd series). Multicoloured.

MS1685 Two sheets each 165×102 mm. (a) 17000m. Type 336; 17000m. Studebaker Coupe (1937): 17000m. Type 40GP Bugatti (1930); 17000m. FordModel A Roadster (1931); 17000m. Alfa Romeo 2900B (1937); 17000m. Cord 812 (1937). (b) 17000m. Type 57 Bugatti Alalanta Coupe (1937); 17000m. Tucker Torpedo (1948); 17000m. Honda S 800M (1966); 17000m. Cisitalia 202 GT (1946): 17000m. Chevy Impala (1958); 17000m. Cadillac LaSalle Convertible (1934). Set of 2 sheets 10·00 10·50

MS1686 Two sheets each 92×60 mm. (a) 50000m. Mercedes Benz SSK (1928). (b) 50000m. Plymouth Fury (1957) Set of 2 sheets 4·75 5·00

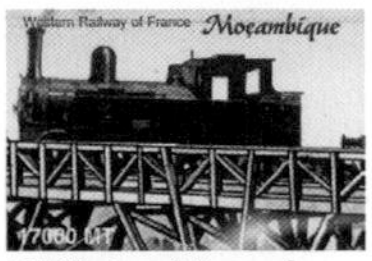

337 Western Railway of France

2002. Trains. Multicoloured.

MS1687 Three sheets each 161×114 mm. (a) 17000m. Type **337**; 17000m. Netherlands State Railway (bridge); 17000m. Great Indian Peninsula Railway; 17000m. Paris Orleans Railway; 17000m. Madras and Southern Mahratta Railway of India; 17000m. Netherlands State Railway. (b) 17000m. Great Southern Railway of Spain; 17000m. Shantung Railway of China; 17000m. Shanghai—Nanking Railway of China; 17000m. Austrian State Railway; 17000m. Victorian Government Railways of Australia; 17000m. London and Northwestern Railways. (c) 17000m. London, Midland and Scottish Railway; 17000m. Great Northern Railway of Ireland; 17000m. Southern Railway of England; 17000m. Great Northern Railway of USA; 17000m. Chicago, Milwaukee, St. Paul and Pacific Railroad; 17000m. London and North-eastern Railway. Set of 3 sheets 12·00 12·50

MS1688 Two sheets each 98×67 mm. (a) 50000m. New York Central Lines (vert). (b) 50000m. London, Brighton and South Coast Railway (vert). Set of 2 sheets 4·75 5·00

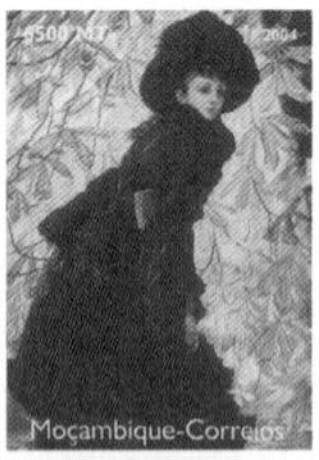

338 "October" (James Jacques Tissot)

2004. Paintings. Multicoloured.

1689-1694 6500m.x6, Type **338**; "Seaside" (James Jacques Tissot); "The Bunch of Lilacs" (James Jacques Tissot); "The Traveller" (James Jacques Tissot); "Young Lady holding Japanese Objects" (James Jacques Tissot); "Young Lady in a Boat" (James Jacques Tissot) 1·80 1·90

1695-1700 6500m.x6, "Portrait of Madame de Senonnes" (Jean Auguste Ingres); "The Virgin of the Host" (Jean Auguste Ingres); "Portrait of Countess D'Haussonville" (Jean Auguste Ingres); "Paolo and Francesca" (Jean Auguste Ingres); "Portrait of Baroness James de Rothschild" (Jean Auguste Ingres); "Portrait of Madame Moitessier Sitting" (Jean Auguste Ingres) 1·80 1·90

1701-1706 10000m.x6, "The Promenade" (Pierre Auguste Renoir); "Alfred Sisley and His Wife" (Pierre Auguste Renoir); "Little Miss Romaine Lacaux" (Pierre Auguste Renoir); "In the Summer" (Pierre Auguste Renoir); "The Dancer" (Pierre Auguste Renoir); "Bouquet of Chrysanthemums" (Pierre Auguste Renoir) 3·00 3·25

1707-1712 17000m.x6, "Miss La La at the Circus Fernando" (Edgar Degas); "Portrait of Madame Dietz-Monnin" (Edgar Degas); "Woman Ironing" (Edgar Degas); "The Star" (Edgar Degas); "Cafe Concert Singer" (Edgar Degas); "The Dance Examination" (Edgar Degas) 3·00 3·25

MS1713 Three sheets, each 87×133 mm. (a) 6500m. As No. 1693. (b) 35000m. "Madame Monet in Japanese Costume" (Claude Monet). (c) 35000m. "Charlotte Dubourg" (Henri Fantin-Latour) 3·50 3·75

CHARITY TAX STAMPS

The notes under this heading in Portugal also apply here.

C15 Arms of Portugal and Mozambique and Allegorical Figures

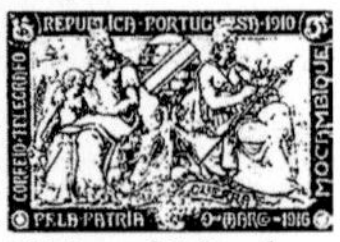

C16 Prow of Galley of Discoveries and Symbols of Declaration of War

1916. War Tax Fund. Imperf, roul or perf.

C234	**C15**	1c. green	95	50
C235	**C16**	5c. red	95	50

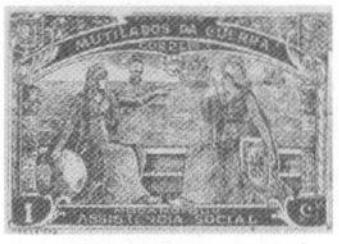

C18 "Charity"

1920. 280th Anniv of Restoration of Portugal. Wounded Soldiers and Social Assistance Funds.

C309	**C 18**	¼c. green	1·60	1·60
C310	**C 18**	½c. black	1·60	1·60
C311	**C 18**	1c. brown	1·60	1·60
C312	**C 18**	2c. brown	1·60	1·60
C313	**C 18**	3c. lilac	1·70	1·70
C314	**C 18**	4c. green	1·70	1·70
C315	-	5c. green	2·00	1·80
C316	-	6c. blue	2·00	1·80
C317	-	7½c. brown	2·00	1·80
C318	-	8c. yellow	2·00	1·80
C319	-	10c. lilac	2·00	1·80
C320	-	12c. pink	2·00	1·80
C321	-	18c. red	2·00	1·80
C322	-	24c. brown	2·75	2·10
C323	-	30c. green	2·75	2·10
C324	-	40c. red	2·75	2·10
C325	-	50c. yellow	2·75	2·10
C326	-	1e. blue	2·75	2·10

DESIGNS: 5c. to 12c. Wounded soldier and nurse; 18c. to 1e. Family scene.

1925. Marquis de Pombal stamps of Portugal, but inscr "MOCAMBIQUE".

C327	**C73**	15c. brown	40	25
C328	-	15c. brown	40	30
C329	**C75**	15c. brown	40	25

1925. Red Cross. Surch 50 CENTAVOS.

C330	**C22**	50c. yellow and grey	95	80

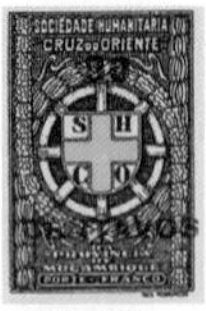

C22 Society's Emblem

1926. Surch CORREIOS and value.

C337	5c. yellow and red	1·30	1·20
C338	10c. yellow and green	1·30	1·20
C339	20c. yellow and grey	1·50	1·40
C340	30c. yellow and blue	1·50	1·40
C331	40c. yellow and grey	2·10	1·50
C341	40c. yellow and violet	1·50	1·40
C332	50c. yellow and grey	2·10	1·50
C342	50c. yellow and red	1·80	1·60
C333	60c. yellow and grey	2·10	1·50
C343	60c. yellow and brown	1·80	1·60
C334	80c. yellow and grey	2·10	1·50
C344	80c. yellow and blue	1·80	1·60
C335	1e. yellow and grey	2·10	1·50
C345	1e. yellow and green	1·80	1·60
C336	2e. yellow and grey	2·20	2·10
C346	2e. yellow and brown	2·20	2·00

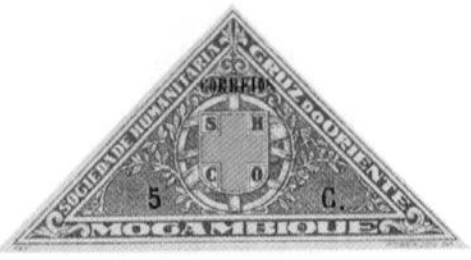

C25

1928. Surch CORREIOS and value in black, as in Type C 25.

C347	**C25**	5c. yellow and green	2·50	2·40
C348	**C25**	10c. yellow and blue	2·50	2·40
C349	**C25**	20c. yellow and black	2·50	2·40
C350	**C25**	30c. yellow and red	2·50	2·40
C351	**C25**	40c. yellow and purple	2·50	2·40
C352	**C25**	50c. yellow and red	2·50	2·40
C353	**C25**	60c. yellow and brown	2·50	2·40
C354	**C25**	80c. yellow and brown	2·50	2·40
C355	**C25**	1e. yellow and grey	2·50	2·40
C356	**C25**	2e. yellow and red	2·50	2·40

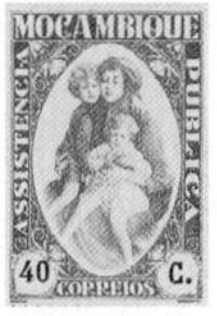
C27

1929. Value in black.

C357	**C27**	40c. purple and blue	2·75	2·50
C358	**C27**	40c. violet and red	2·75	2·50
C359	**C27**	40c. violet and green	2·75	2·50
C360	**C27**	40c. red and brown	2·75	2·50
C361	**C27**	(No value) red & green	2·75	2·50
C362	**C27**	40c. blue and orange	4·25	4·00
C363	**C27**	40c. blue and brown	2·75	2·50
C364	**C27**	40c. purple and green	2·75	2·50
C365	**C27**	40c. black and yellow	4·25	4·00
C366	**C27**	40c. black and brown	4·25	4·00

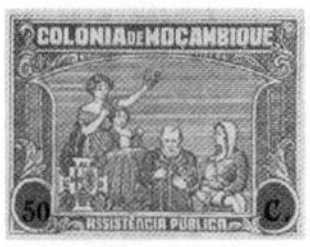
C28 "Charity"

1942

C383	**C28**	50c. pink and black	8·75	2·30

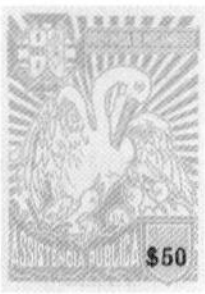
C29 Pelican

1943. Inscr "Colonia de Mocambique". Value in black.

C386	**C29**	50c. violet	9·75	1·30
C387	**C29**	50c. brown	9·75	1·30
C389	**C29**	50c. blue	9·75	1·30
C390	**C29**	50c. red	9·75	1·30
C393	**C29**	50c. green	6·25	1·30

1952. Inscr "Provincia de Mocambique". Value in black.

C469	50c. green	90	65
C470	50c. brown	90	65
C514	30c. yellow	85	65
C515	50c. orange	85	65

1957. No. C470 surch $30.

C511	30c. on 50c. brown	65	35

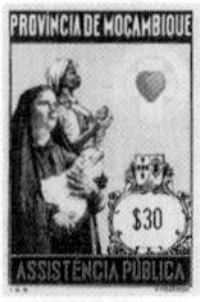
C56 Women and Children

1963

C569	**C56**	30c. black, green & red	35	25
C570	**C56**	50c. black, bistre & red	35	25
C571	**C56**	50c. black, pink & red	35	25
C572	**C56**	50c. black, green & red	35	25
C573	**C56**	50c. black, blue & red	35	25
C574	**C56**	50c. black, buff & red	35	25
C575	**C56**	50c. black, grey & red	35	25
C576	**C56**	50c. black, yell & red	25	15
C577	**C56**	1e. grey, black and red	1·10	45
C578	**C56**	1e. black, buff and red	30	20
C578a	**C56**	1e. black, mauve & red	30	20

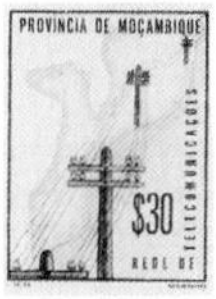
C58 Telegraph Poles and Map

1965. Mozambique Telecommunications Improvement.

C579	**C58**	30c. black, pink & vio	20	15
C580	-	50c. black, brown & blue	20	15
C581	-	1e. black, orange & green	25	20

DESIGN—19½×36 mm: 50c., 1e. Telegraph linesman.

A 2e.50 in Type C **58** was also issued for compulsory use on telegrams.

NEWSPAPER STAMPS

1893. "Embossed" key-type of Mozambique surch. (a) JORNAES 2½ 2½.

N53	**Q**	2½r. on 40r. brown	42·00	23·00

(b) JORNAES 2½ REIS.

N54	2½r. on 40r. brown	£170	£120
N57	5r. on 40r. brown	85·00	50·00

1893. "Newspaper" key-type inscribed "MOCAMBIQUE".

N58	**V**	2½r. brown	60	45

POSTAGE DUE STAMPS

1904. "Due" key-type inscr "MOCAMBIQUE".

D146	**W**	5r. green	25	25
D147	**W**	10r. grey	25	25
D148	**W**	20r. brown	35	35
D149	**W**	30r. orange	75	45
D150	**W**	50r. brown	75	45
D151	**W**	60r. brown	2·75	1·70
D152	**W**	100r. mauve	2·75	1·70
D153	**W**	130r. blue	1·70	1·30
D154	**W**	200r. red	2·30	1·30
D155	**W**	500r. violet	3·00	1·50

1911. "Due" key-type of Mozambique optd REPUBLICA.

D162	5r. green	25	20
D163	10r. grey	45	20
D164	20r. brown	45	20
D165	30r. orange	45	20
D166	50r. brown	50	30
D167	60r. brown	70	35
D168	100r. mauve	90	50
D169	130r. blue	1·00	70
D170	200r. red	1·30	1·10
D171	500r. lilac	1·80	1·30

1917. "Due" key-type of Mozambique, but currency changed.

D246	½c. green	35	30
D247	1c. grey	35	30
D248	2c. brown	35	30
D249	3c. orange	35	30
D250	5c. brown	35	30
D251	6c. brown	35	30
D252	10c. mauve	35	30
D253	13c. blue	70	55
D254	20c. red	70	55
D255	50c. lilac	70	55

1918. Charity Tax stamps optd PORTEADO.

D256	**C15**	1c. green	1·20	90
D257	**C16**	5c. red	1·20	90

1922. "Ceres" key-type of Lourenco Marques (½, 1½c.) and of Mozambique (1, 2½, 4c.) surch PORTEADO and value and bar.

D316	**U**	5c. on ½c. black	1·20	85
D318	**U**	6c. on 1c. green	1·20	85
D317	**U**	10c. on 1½c. brown	1·20	85
D319	**U**	20c. on 2½c. violet	1·20	85
D320	**U**	50c. on 4c. pink	1·20	85

1924. "Ceres" key-type of Mozambique surch Porteado and value.

D321	20c. on 30c. green	75	55
D323	50c. on 60c. blue	1·20	90

1925. Marquis de Pombal charity tax designs as Nos. C327/9, optd MULTA.

D327	**C73**	30c. brown	30	30
D328	-	30c. brown	30	30
D329	**C 75**	30c. brown	30	30

1952. As Type D 70 of Macao, but inscr "MOCAMBIQUE".

D468	10c. multicoloured	15	15
D469	30c. multicoloured	15	15
D470	50c. multicoloured	20	15
D471	1e. multicoloured	25	20
D472	2e. multicoloured	25	20
D473	5e. multicoloured	65	40

APPENDIX

The following issues for Mozambique have either been issued in excess of postal needs, or have not been made available to the public in reasonable quantities at face value. Such stamps mat later be given full listing if there is evidence of regular postal use. Miniature sheets, imperforate stamps etc are excluded from this section.

1999

Birds and Butterflies. 6000m.×6, 7500m.×6
Minerals. 12500m.×6
Dinosaurs. 9000m.×6
Animals. 6500×6
Mushrooms. 9500m.×6

2000

Formula 1 Drivers. 6500m.×6

2001

Artists. 5000m.×6. 10000m.×87, 12000m.×48, 15000m.×6, 17000m.×6, 28000m.×6
Painters. 28000m.×6
World Cup Football (2002). 5000m.×33, 8500m.×18, 12000m.×6, 17000m.×6, 20000m.×6, 28000m.×6

2002

Nelson Mandela. 20000m.×4
World of the Sea. 5000m.×6, 17000m.×146, 20000m.×6, 33000×6

Pt. 9

MOZAMBIQUE COMPANY

The Mozambique Company was responsible from 1891 until 1942 for the administration of Manica and Sofala territory in Portuguese East Africa. Now part of Mozambique.

1899. 1000 reis = 1 milreis.
1913. 100 centavos = 1 escudo.

1892. "Embossed" key-type inscr "PROVINCA DE MOCAMBIQUE" optd COMPA. DE MOCAMBIQUE.

10	**Q**	5r. black	1·30	75
2	**Q**	10r. green	1·40	1·10
3	**Q**	20r. red	1·80	1·10
4	**Q**	25r. mauve	1·40	1·10
5	**Q**	40r. brown	1·40	1·10
6	**Q**	50r. blue	1·90	1·30
7	**Q**	100r. brown	1·90	1·30
8	**Q**	200r. violet	2·30	1·80
9	**Q**	300r. orange	3·25	1·90

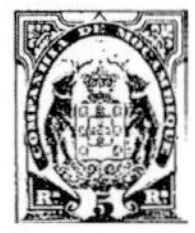
2

1895. Value in black or red (500, 1000r.).

112	**2**	400r. black on blue	3·00	2·30
33	**2**	2½r. yellow	55	50
114	**2**	2½r. grey	1·90	1·10
17	**2**	5r. orange	55	50
36	**2**	10r. mauve	80	55
115	**2**	10r. green	1·40	1·10
39	**2**	15r. brown	80	55
116	**2**	15r. green	1·90	1·10
20	**2**	20r. lilac	60	50
45	**2**	25r. green	70	65
117	**2**	25r. red	1·90	1·10
46	**2**	50r. blue	80	55
118	**2**	50r. brown	1·90	1·40
109	**2**	65r. blue	1·10	85
48	**2**	75r. red	80	55
119	**2**	75r. mauve	3·75	2·10
50	**2**	80r. green	80	55
120	**2**	100r. blue on blue	3·75	2·75
52	**2**	100r. brown on buff	2·20	1·30
110	**2**	115r. pink on pink	3·00	2·30
121	**2**	115r. brown on pink	5·00	3·50
111	**2**	130r. green on pink	3·00	2·30
122	**2**	130r. brown on yellow	5·25	3·50
54	**2**	150r. orange on pink	2·20	1·30
55	**2**	200r. blue on blue	1·80	1·60
123	**2**	200r. lilac on pink	5·25	3·50
56	**2**	300r. blue on brown	2·10	1·60
124	**2**	400r. blue on yellow	7·00	5·75
58	**2**	500r. black	1·80	1·30
125	**2**	500r. black on blue	7·00	5·75
126	**2**	700r. mauve on buff	7·00	6·50
59	**2**	1000r. mauve	2·30	1·60

1895. Surch PROVISORIO 25.

77	25 on 80r. green	38·00	29·00

1895. No. 6 optd PROVISORIO.

78	**Q**	50r. blue	7·50	6·50

1898. Vasco da Gama. Optd 1498 Centenario da India 1898.

80	**2**	2½r. yellow	2·20	1·80
81	**2**	5r. orange	3·00	2·10
82	**2**	10r. mauve	3·00	2·00
84	**2**	15r. brown	3·75	3·25
86	**2**	20r. lilac	5·25	3·50
87	**2**	25r. green	5·75	3·50
99	**2**	50r. blue	3·75	3·25
89	**2**	75r. red	10·00	6·50
91	**2**	80r. green	7·00	5·00
101	**2**	100r. brown on buff	7·50	6·50
102	**2**	150r. orange on pink	7·50	6·50
94	**2**	200r. blue on blue	11·50	7·50
104	**2**	300r. blue on brown	14·00	9·25

1899. Surch 25 PROVISORIO.

105	25 on 75r. red	6·00	5·00

1900. Surch 25 Reis and bar.

106	25r. on 5r. orange	4·75	2·75

1900. Perforated through centre and surch 50 REIS.

108	50r. on half of 20r. lilac	2·20	1·80

1911. Optd REPUBLICA.

145	2½r. grey	70	65
147	5r. orange	70	65
148	10r. green	70	65
150	15r. green	45	35
151	20r. lilac	70	65
153	25r. red	70	65
155	50r. brown	70	65
156	75r. mauve	70	65
157	100r. blue on blue	70	65
159	115r. brown on pink	1·40	95
160	130r. brown on yellow	1·40	95
161	200r. lilac on pink	1·40	95
162	400r. blue on yellow	1·40	95
163	500r. black on blue	1·40	95
164	700r. mauve on yellow	2·10	1·30

1916. Surch REPUBLICA and value in figures.

166	¼c. on 2½r. grey	45	35
168	½c. on 5r. orange	45	35
170	1c. on 10r. green	70	55
173	1½c. on 15r. green	60	55
175	2c. on 20r. lilac	70	55
178	2½c. on 25r. red	60	55
180	5c. on 50r. brown	60	55
181	7½c. on 75r. mauve	1·10	80
182	10c. on 100r. blue on blue	1·10	60
183	11½c. on 115r. brown on pink	2·50	1·20
184	13c. on 130r. brown on yell	2·50	1·20
185	20c. on 200r. lilac on pink	2·75	1·10
186	40c. on 400r. blue on yellow	2·75	1·10
187	50c. on 500r. black on blue	3·00	1·40
188	70c. on 700r. mauve on yell	3·00	1·70

1917. Red Cross Fund. Stamps of 1911 (optd REPUBLICA) optd with red cross and 31.7.17.

189	2½r. grey	10·00	8·00
190	10r. green	10·00	8·00
191	20r. lilac	12·00	10·00
192	50r. brown	40·00	32·00
193	75r. mauve	90·00	85·00
194	100r. blue on blue	£100	£100
195	700r. mauve on yellow	£250	£250

1918. Stamps of 1911 (optd REPUBLICA) surch with new value.

196	½c. on 700r. mauve on yellow	3·25	2·50
197	2½c. on 500r. black on blue	3·25	2·50
198	5c. on 400r. blue on yellow	3·25	2·50

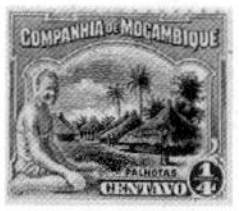
14 Native Village

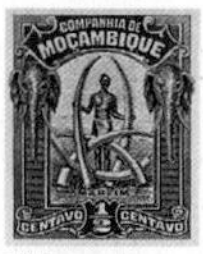
15 Ivory

1918

199A	**14**	¼c. green and brown	55	35
233	**14**	¼c. black and green	45	35
200A	**15**	½c. black	55	35
201A	-	1c. black and green	55	35
202A	-	1½c. green and black	55	35
203A	-	2c. black and red	55	35
235	-	2c. black and grey	45	45
204A	-	2½c. black and lilac	55	35
236	-	3c. black and orange	55	50
205A	-	4c. brown and green	55	35
237	-	4c. black and red	55	50
227A	**14**	4½c. black and grey	55	35
206A	-	5c. black and blue	55	55
207A	-	6c. blue and purple	55	35
238	-	6c. black and mauve	65	50
228A	-	7c. black and blue	55	35
208A	-	7½c. green and orange	1·40	70
239	-	8c. black and lilac	1·30	1·00
210A	-	10c. black and red	1·40	95
229A	-	12c. black and brown	1·90	1·40
241	-	12c. black and green	1·10	75
242	-	15c. black and red	1·10	95
212A	-	20c. black and green	1·40	55
213A	-	30c. black and brown	1·40	95
244	-	30c. black and green	1·30	1·10
214A	-	40c. black and green	1·40	95
246	-	40c. black and blue	1·70	1·30
215A	-	50c. black and orange	1·40	95
247	-	50c. black and mauve	2·10	1·70
230A	-	60c. brown and red	2·20	1·50
231A	-	80c. brown and blue	2·20	1·50
248	-	80c. black and red	2·10	1·70
216A	-	1e. black and green	2·75	2·10
249	-	1e. black and blue	2·10	1·70
232A	-	2e. violet and red	3·25	2·50
250	-	2e. black and lilac	3·75	2·20

DESIGNS—HORIZ: 1, 3c. Maize field; 2c. Sugar factory; 5c., 2e. Beira; 20c. Law Court; 40c. Mangrove swamp. VERT: 1½c. India-rubber; 2½c. River Buzi; 4c. Tobacco bushes; 6c. Coffee bushes; 7, 15c. Steam train, Amatongas Forest; 7½c. Orange tree; 8, 12c. Cotton plants; 10, 80c. Sisal plantation; 30c. Coconut palm; 50, 60c. Cattle breeding; 1e. Mozambique Co's Arms.

1920. Pictorial issue surch in words.

217	½c. on 30c. (No. 213)	6·50	5·75
218	½c. on 1e. (No. 216)	6·50	5·75
219	1½c. on 2½c. (No. 204)	4·75	2·75
220	1½c. on 5c. (No. 206)	4·75	2·75
221	2c. on 2½c. (No. 204)	4·75	2·75
222	4c. on 20c. (No. 212)	5·25	4·00
223	4c. on 40c. (No. 214)	5·25	4·00
224	6c. on 8c. (No. 239)	6·75	4·00
225	6c. on 50c. (No. 215)	6·75	4·00

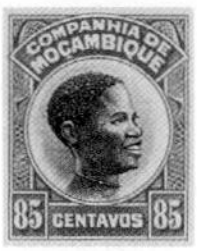
33

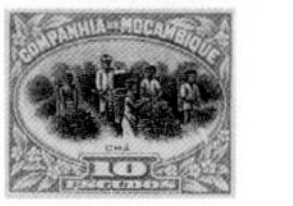
36 Tea

1925

251	33	24c. black and blue	2·75	2·00
252	-	25c. blue and brown	2·75	2·00
253	33	85c. black and red	2·10	1·50
254	-	1e.40 black and blue	2·10	1·50
255	-	5e. blue and brown	3·25	1·30
256	36	10e. black and red	5·75	1·70
257	-	20e. black and green	7·00	2·50

DESIGNS—VERT: 25c., 1e.40, Beira; 5e. Tapping rubber. HORIZ: 20e. River Zambesi.

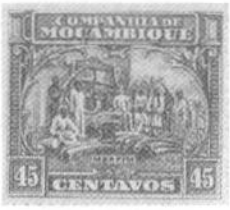
38 Ivory

1931

258	38	45c. blue	4·25	2·40
259	-	70c. brown	2·10	1·50

DESIGN—VERT: 70c. Gold mining.

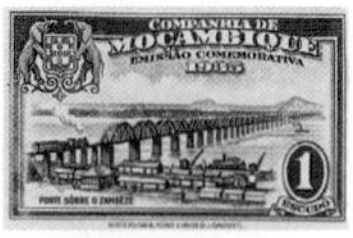
40 Zambesi Bridge

1935. Opening of River Zambesi Railway Bridge at Sena.

260	40	1e. black and blue	6·50	3·25

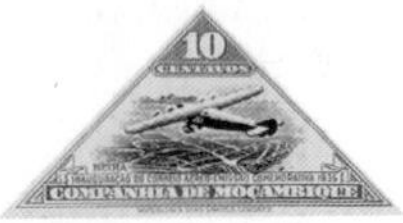
41 Armstrong-Whitworth Atalanta Airliner over Beira

1935. Inauguration of Blantyre–Beira–Salisbury Air Route.

261	41	5c. black and blue	1·30	85
262	41	10c. black and red	1·30	85
263	41	15c. black and red	1·30	85
264	41	20c. black and green	1·30	85
265	41	30c. black and green	1·30	85
266	41	40c. black and blue	1·70	1·10
267	41	45c. black and blue	1·70	1·10
268	41	50c. black and purple	1·70	1·10
269	41	60c. brown and red	2·75	1·70
270	41	80c. black and red	2·75	1·70

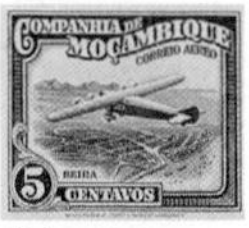
42 Armstrong-Whitworth Atalanta Airliner over Beira

1935. Air.

271	42	5c. black and blue	35	30
272	42	10c. black and red	35	30
273	42	15c. black and red	35	30
274	42	20c. black and green	35	30
275	42	30c. black and green	35	30
276	42	40c. black and green	35	30
277	42	45c. black and blue	35	30
278	42	50c. black and purple	35	30
279	42	60c. brown and red	35	30
280	42	80c. black and red	35	30
281	42	1e. black and blue	35	30
282	42	2e. black and lilac	85	75
283	42	5e. blue and brown	1·40	1·20
284	42	10e. black and red	1·90	1·40
285	42	20e. black and green	3·75	1·80

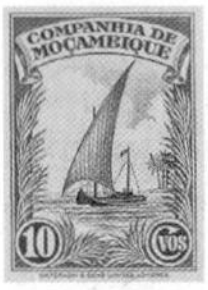
43 Coastal Dhow

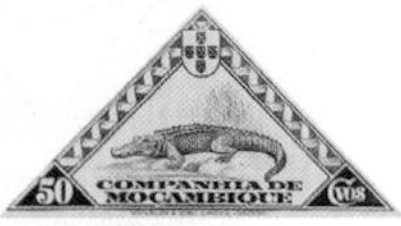
45 Crocodile

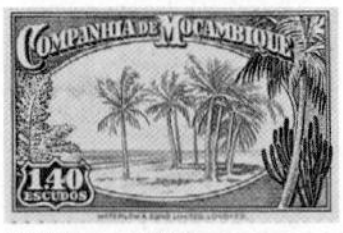
46 Palms at Beira

1937

286	-	1c. lilac and green	35	30
287	-	5c. green and blue	35	30
288	43	10c. blue and red	35	30
289	-	15c. black and red	45	30
290	-	20c. blue and green	45	30
291	-	30c. blue and green	45	30
292	-	40c. black and blue	45	30
293	-	45c. brown and blue	45	30
294	45	50c. green and violet	45	30
295	-	60c. blue and red	45	30
296	-	70c. green and brown	45	30
297	-	80c. green and red	55	45
298	-	85c. black and red	65	50
299	-	1e. black and blue	65	50
300	46	1e.40 green and blue	1·30	50
301	-	2e. brown and lilac	2·10	60
302	-	5e. blue and brown	1·30	60
303	-	10e. black and red	2·10	1·00
304	-	20e. purple and green	3·25	1·90

DESIGNS—VERT: 21×29 mm—1c. Giraffe; 20c. Common zebra; 70c. Native woman. 23×31 mm—10e. Old Portuguese gate, Sena; 20e. Arms. HORIZ: 29×21 mm—5c. Native huts; 15c. S. Caetano fortress, Sofala; 60c. Leopard; 80c. Hippopotami. 37×22 mm—5e. Railway bridge over River Zambesi. TRIANGULAR: 30c. Python; 40c. White rhinoceros; 45c. Lion; 85c. Vasco da Gama's flagship "Sao Gabriel"; 1e. Native in dugout canoe; 2e. Greater kudu.

1939. President Carmona's Colonial Tour. Optd 28-VII-1939 Visita Presidencial.

305		30c. (No. 291)	1·90	1·50
306		40c. (No. 292)	1·90	1·50
307		45c. (No. 293)	1·90	1·50
308	45	50c. green and violet	1·90	1·50
309	-	85c. (No. 298)	1·90	1·50
310	-	1e. (No. 299)	3·50	1·80
311	-	2e. (No. 301)	4·25	3·25

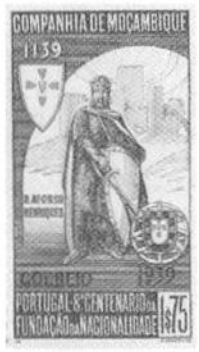
49 King Afonso Henriques

1940. 800th Anniv of Portuguese Independence.

312	49	1e.75 light blue and blue	3·25	1·50

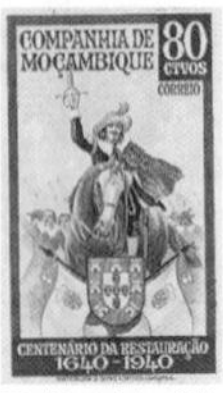
51 "Don John IV" after Alberto de Souza

1940. Tercentenary of Restoration of Independence.

313	51	40c. black and blue	85	65
314	51	50c. green and violet	85	65
315	51	60c. blue and red	85	65
316	51	70c. green and brown	85	65
317	51	80c. green and red	85	65
318	51	1e. black and blue	85	65

CHARITY TAX STAMPS

The notes under this heading in Portugal also apply here.

1932. No. 236 surch Assistencia Publica 2 Ctvos. 2.

C260	2c. on 3c. black and orange	1·50	1·10

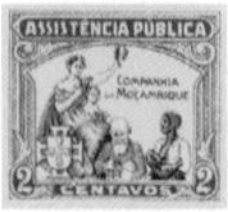
C41 "Charity"

1934

C261	C41	2c. black and mauve	1·60	1·10

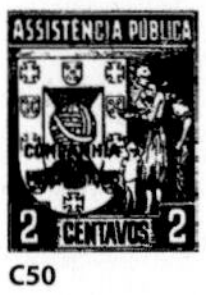
C50

1940

C313	C50	2c. blue and black	8·00	5·25

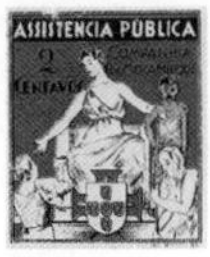
C52

1941

C319	C52	2c. red and black	8·00	5·25

NEWSPAPER STAMPS

1894. "Newspaper" key-type inscr "MOCAMBIQUE" optd COMPA. DE MOCAMBIQUE.

N15	V	2½r. brown	75	60

POSTAGE DUE STAMPS

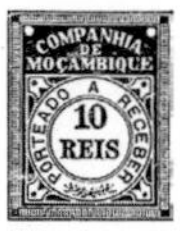
D9

1906

D114	D9	5r. green	50	40
D115	D9	10r. grey	50	40
D116	D9	20r. brown	50	40
D117	D9	30r. orange	80	60
D118	D9	50r. brown	80	60
D119	D9	60r. brown	3·50	3·50
D120	D9	100r. mauve	1·10	1·00
D121	D9	130r. blue	7·00	3·75
D122	D9	200r. red	1·80	1·30
D123	D9	500r. lilac	3·00	2·40

1911. Optd REPUBLICA.

D166	5r. green	25	25
D167	10r. grey	30	30
D168	20r. brown	30	30
D169	30r. orange	30	30
D170	50r. brown	30	30
D171	60r. brown	60	45
D172	100r. mauve	60	45
D173	130r. blue	1·30	1·20
D174	200r. red	1·60	1·30
D175	500r. lilac	1·90	1·60

1916. Currency changed.

D189	D 9	½c. green	25	25
D190	D 9	1c. grey	25	25
D191	D 9	2c. brown	25	25
D192	D 9	3c. orange	25	25
D193	D 9	5c. brown	25	25
D194	D 9	6c. brown	40	40
D195	D 9	10c. mauve	70	70
D196	D 9	13c. blue	1·30	1·30
D197	D 9	20c. red	1·30	1·30
D198	D 9	50c. lilac	2·00	2·00

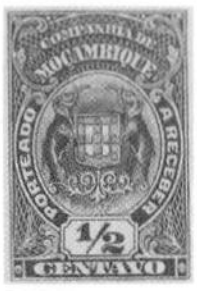
D32

1919

D217	D32	½c. green	10	10
D218	D32	1c. black	10	10
D219	D32	2c. brown	10	10
D220	D32	3c. orange	10	10
D221	D32	5c. brown	15	10
D222	D32	6c. brown	20	20
D223	D32	10c. red	20	20
D224	D32	13c. blue	25	25
D225	D32	20c. red	25	20
D226	D32	50c. grey	30	30

Pt. 1

MUSCAT

Independent Sultanate of Eastern Arabia with Indian and, subsequently, British postal administration.

12 pies = 1 anna; 16 annas = 1 rupee

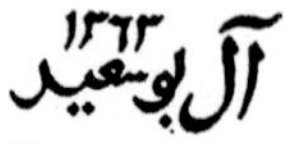
(2)

1944. Bicentenary of Al-Busaid Dynasty. Stamps of India (King George VI) optd as T 2.

1	100a	3p. slate	40	8·50
2	100a	½a. mauve	40	8·50
3	100a	9p. green	40	8·50
4	100a	1a. red	40	8·50
5	101	1½a. plum	40	8·50
6	101	2a. red	50	8·50
7	101	3a. violet	1·00	8·50
8	101	3½a. blue	1·00	8·50
9	102	4a. brown	1·25	8·50
10	102	6a. green	1·25	8·50
11	102	8a. violet	1·50	8·50
12	102	12a. red	1·50	8·50
13	-	14a. purple (No. 277)	4·00	14·00
14	93	1r. slate and brown	4·00	13·00
15	93	2r. purple and brown	10·00	22·00

OFFICIAL STAMPS

1944. Bicentenary of Al-Busaid Dynasty. Official stamps of India optd as T 2.

O1	O20	3p. slate	60	16·00
O2	O20	½a. purple	1·50	16·00
O3	O20	9p. green	1·00	16·00
O4	O20	1a. red	1·00	16·00
O5	O20	1½a. violet	1·50	16·00
O6	O20	2a. orange	1·50	16·00
O7	O20	2½a. violet	7·50	16·00
O8	O20	4a. brown	2·75	16·00
O9	O20	8a. violet	4·50	18·00
O10	93	1r. slate and brown (No. O138)	8·50	30·00

For later issues see **BRITISH POSTAL AGENCIES IN EASTERN ARABIA**.

Pt. 19

MUSCAT AND OMAN

Independent Sultanate in Eastern Arabia. The title of the Sultanate was changed in 1971 to Oman.

1966. 64 baizas = 1 rupee.
1970. 1000 baizas = 1 rial saidi.

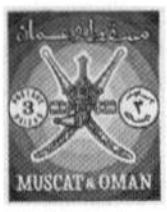
12 Sultan's Crest

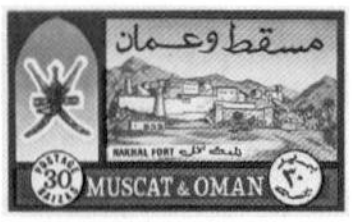
14 Nakhal Fort

1966

94	12	3b. purple	20	20
95	12	5b. brown	20	20
96	12	10b. brown	20	20
97	A	15b. black and violet	1·00	20
98	A	20b. black and blue	1·50	20
99	A	25b. black and orange	2·10	65
100	14	30b. mauve and blue	2·75	65
101	B	50b. green and brown	3·25	1·70
102	C	1r. blue and orange	6·75	1·70
103	D	2r. brown and green	12·50	5·00
104	E	5r. violet and red	28·00	17·00
105	F	10r. red and violet	55·00	36·00

DESIGNS—VERT: 21½×25½ mm: A, Crest and Muscat harbour. HORIZ (as Type **14**): B, Samail Fort; C, Sohar Fort; D, Nizwa Fort; E, Matrah Fort; F, Mirani Fort.

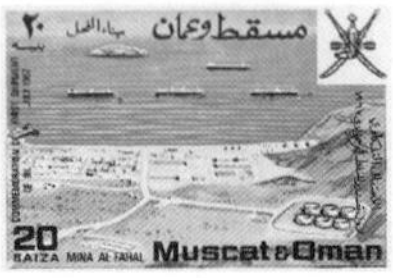
15 Mina el Fahal

1969. 1st Oil Shipment (July 1967). Multicoloured.

106	20b. Type **15**	4·75	1·00
107	25b. Storage tanks	6·75	1·50
108	40b. Desert oil-rig	9·50	2·20
109	1r. Aerial view from "Gemini 4"	25·00	6·75

1970. Designs as issue of 1966, but inscribed in new currency.

110	12	5b. purple	1·00	20
111	12	10b. brown	1·80	45
112	12	20b. brown	2·10	50
113	A	25b. black and violet	3·75	55
114	A	30b. black and blue	4·25	1·00
115	A	40b. black and orange	5·25	1·20
116	14	50b. mauve and blue	7·75	1·50
117	B	75b. green and brown	8·25	2·00
118	C	100b. blue and orange	10·00	2·20
119	D	¼r. brown and green	28·00	6·75
120	E	½r. violet and red	50·00	19·00
121	F	1r. red and violet	90·00	32·00

For later issues see **OMAN**.

MYANMAR

Formerly known as Burma.

100 pyas = 1 kyat.

81 Fountain, National Assembly Park (image scaled to 60% of original size)

1990. State Law and Order Restoration Council.
312	**81**	1k. multicoloured	1·10	70

1990. As Nos. 258/61 of Burma but inscr "UNION OF MYANMAR".
313	15p. deep green and green	15	15
314	20p. black, brown and blue	20	15
315	50p. violet and brown	50	25
316	1k. violet, mauve and black	1·00	70

82 Map and Emblem

1990. 40th Anniv of United Nations Development Programme.
322	**82**	2k. blue, yellow and black	2·20	1·40

83 Nawata Ruby

1991. Gem Emporium.
323	**83**	50p. multicoloured	1·00	70

84 "Grandfather giving Sword to Grandson" (statuette, Nan Win)

1992. 44th Anniv of Independence. Multicoloured.
324		50p. Warrior defending personification of Myanmar and map (poster, Khin Thein)	50	45
325		2k. Type **84**	2·30	1·70

85 Emblem

1992. National Sports Festival.
326	**85**	50p. multicoloured	60	45

86 Campaign Emblem

1992. Anti-AIDS Campaign.
327	**86**	50p. red	50	45

87 Fish, Water Droplet and Leaf

1992. International Nutrition Conference, Rome.
328	**87**	50p. multicoloured	35	15
329	**87**	1k. multicoloured	60	45
330	**87**	3k. multicoloured	1·70	1·30
331	**87**	5k. multicoloured	3·00	2·20

88 Statue

1993. National Convention for Drafting of New Constitution.
332	**88**	50p. multicoloured	25	15
333	**88**	3k. multicoloured	1·70	1·30

89 Hintha (legendary bird)

1993. Statuettes. Multicoloured.
334		5k. Type **89**	2·75	2·30
335		10k. Lawkanat	5·75	4·75

90 Horseman aiming Spear at Target

1993. Festival of Traditional Equestrian Sports, Sittwe.
336	**90**	3k. multicoloured	1·70	1·30

91 Tree, Globe and Figures

1994. World Environment Day.
337	**91**	4k. multicoloured	2·30	1·70

92 Association Emblem

1994. 1st Anniv of Union Solidarity and Development Association.
338	**92**	3k. multicoloured	1·50	1·10

93 City and Emblem

1995. 50th Anniv of Armed Forces Day.
339	**93**	50p. multicoloured	45	45

94 Cross through Poppy Head

1995. International Day against Drug Abuse.
340	**94**	2k. multicoloured	1·60	1·20

95 Camera and Film

1995. 60th Anniv of Myanmar Film Industry.
341	**95**	50p. multicoloured	45	45

96 Figures around Emblem

1995. 50th Anniv of United Nations Organization.
342	**96**	4k. multicoloured	3·00	3·00

97 Convocation Hall

1995. 60th Anniv of Yangon University.
343	**97**	50p. multicoloured	45	45
344	**97**	2k. multicoloured	1·50	1·50

98 Punt

1996. Visit Myanmar Year. Multicoloured.
345		50p. Type **98**	35	35
346		4k. Karaweik Hall	2·75	2·75
347		5k. Mandalay Palace	3·50	3·50

99 Four-man Canoe

1996. International Letter Writing Week. "Unity equals Success". Multicoloured.
348		2k. Type **99**	1·40	1·40
349		5k. Human pyramid holding flag aloft (vert)	3·50	3·50

100 Breastfeeding

1996. 50th Anniv of UNICEF. Multicoloured.
350		1k. Type **100**	70	70
351		2k. Nurse inoculating child	1·40	1·40
352		4k. Children outside school	2·75	2·75

101 Emblem and Map of Myanmar

1997. 30th Anniv of Association of South-East Asian Nations.
353	**101**	1k. multicoloured	85	85
354	**101**	2k. multicoloured	1·70	1·70

102 Throne

1998. 50th Anniv of Independence.
355	**102**	2k. multicoloured	1·60	1·60

103 Xylophone

1998. Musical Instruments. Multicoloured.
356		5k. Type **103**	
357		10k. Mon brass gongs	
358		20k. Rakhine auspicious drum	
359		30k. Myanmar harp	
360		50k. Shan pot drum	
361		100k. Kachin brass gong	

104 Emblem

1999. Asian and Pacific Decade of Disabled Persons. Seventh Far East and South Pacific Region Disabled Games.
365	**104**	2k. multicoloured	1·70	1·70
366	**104**	5k. multicoloured	3·50	3·50

105 Dove and U.P.U. Emblem

1999. 125th Anniv of Universal Postal Union.
367	**105**	2k. multicoloured	1·50	1·50
368	**105**	5k. multicoloured	3·25	3·25

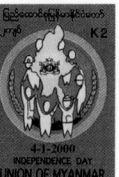

106 People linking Hands around Map of Myanmar

2000. 52nd Anniv of Independence.
369	**106**	2k. multicoloured	1·50	1·50

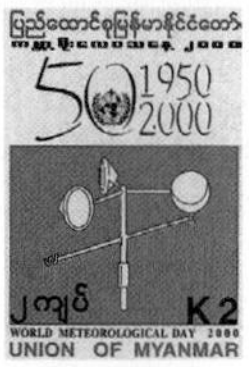

107 Weathervane

2000. World Meteorological Day. 50th Anniv of World Meteorological Organization.

370	**107**	2k. black and blue	1·70	1·70
371	-	5k. multicoloured	4·00	4·00
372	-	10k. multicoloured	7·50	7·50

DESIGNS—HORIZ: 5k. Emblem and globe; 10k. Emblem and symbols for rain and sunshine.

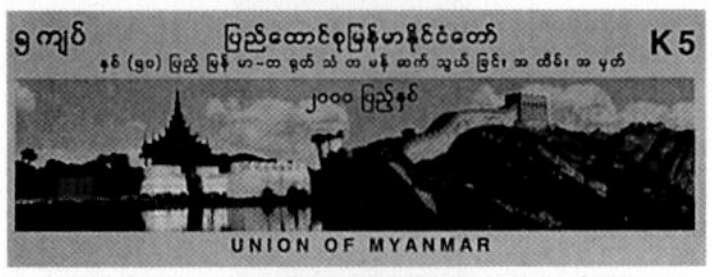

108 Royal Palace Gate, Burma and Great Wall of China (image scaled to 58% of original size)

2000. 50th Anniv of Burma–China Relations.

373	**108**	5k. multicoloured	4·00	4·00

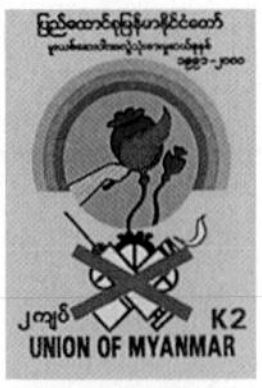

109 Burning Poppy Heads and Needles

2000. Anti-drugs Campaign.

374	**109**	2k. multicoloured	1·50	1·50

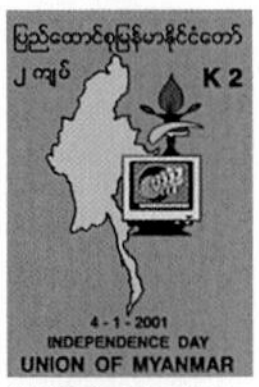

110 Television Set and Map of Myanmar

2001. 53rd Anniv of Independence.

375	**110**	2k. multicoloured	1·50	1·50

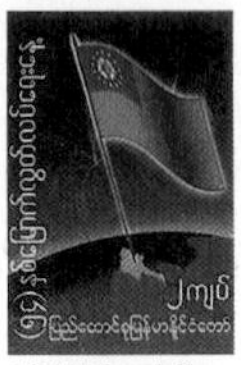
111 National Flag and Globe

2002. 54th Anniv of Independence. Multicoloured.

376	2k. Type **111**	50	50
377	30k. As No. 376 but inscriptions and face value in English	8·25	8·25

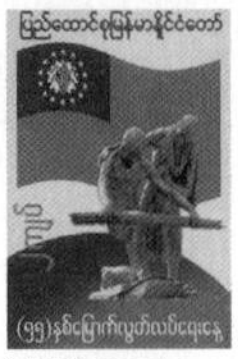
112 Flag and Statue

2003. 55th Anniv of Independence. Multicoloured.

378	2k. Type **112**	50	50
379	30k. As No. 378 but inscriptions and face value in English	8·25	8·25

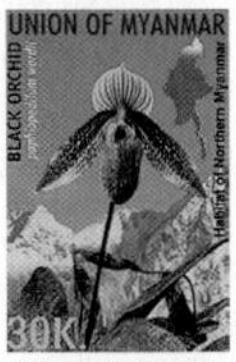

113 Black Orchid

2004. Flora. Multicoloured.

380	30k. Type **113**	5·25	5·25
381	30k. Mango	5·25	5·25

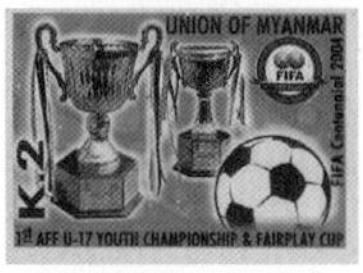

114 Trophies and Football

2004. Centenary of FIFA (Federation Internationale de Football Association).

382	**114**	2k. multicoloured	35	35

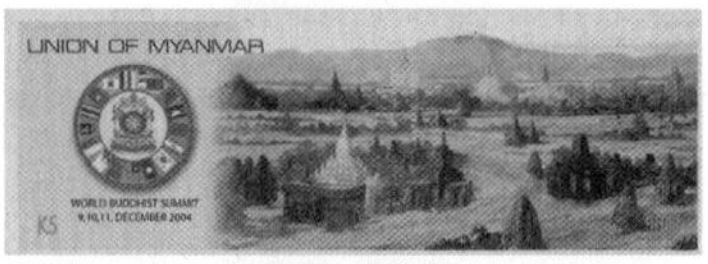

115 Stupas (image scaled to 58% of original size)

2004. World Buddhist Summit, Yangon, Myanmar. Multicoloured.

383	5k. Type **115**	90	90
384	30k. Stupas (different)	5·25	5·25

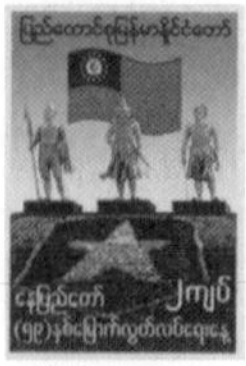
116 Flag and Statues

2007. 59th Independence Day. Multicoloured.

385	(2k.) Type **116**	40	40
386	5k. Map and statues	1·00	1·00

Nos. 387/9 and Type **117** have been left for 'National Convention', issued on 13 August 2007, not yet received.

Stamps of a similar design were issued by all member countries.

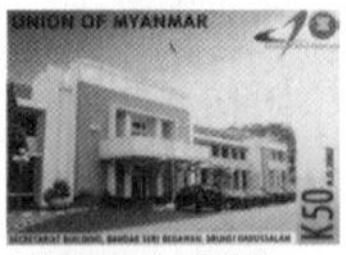

118 Secretariat Building, Bandar Seri Begawan, Brunei Darussalam

2007. Architecture. 40th Anniv of ASEAN (Association of South-East Asian Nations). Multicoloured.

390	50k. Type **118**	4·75	4·25
391	50k. National Museum, Cambodia	4·75	4·25
392	50k. Fatahillah Museum, Jakarta	4·75	4·25
393	50k. Traditional house, Laos	4·75	4·25
394	50k. Railway Headquarters Building, Malaysia	4·75	4·25
395	50k. Yangon Post Office, Union of Myanmar	4·75	4·25
396	50k. Malacanang Palace, Manila	4·75	4·25
397	50k. National Museum, Singapore	4·75	4·25
398	50k. Vimanmek Mansion, Bangkok, Thailand	4·75	4·25
399	50k. Presidential Palace, Hanoi, Vietnam	4·75	4·25

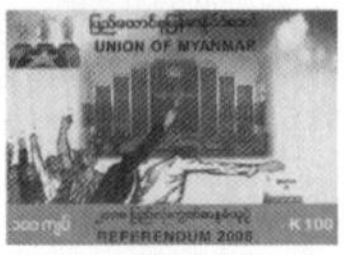

119 Assembly and Crowd

2008. Referendum. Multicoloured.

400	100k. Type **119**	3·25	2·75
401	100k. Assembly	3·25	2·75
402	200k. Assembly, warriors, map and ballot box (*vert*)	6·25	5·50

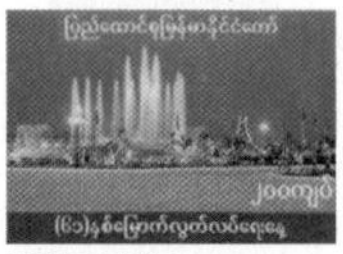
120 Fountains

2009. 61st Anniv of Independence Day. Multicoloured.

403	200k. Type **120**	4·75	4·25
404	300k. Symbols of Myanmar	7·25	6·25

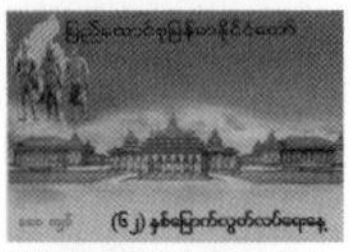
121 Parliament, Map and Figures

2010. 62nd Anniv of Independence Day. Multicoloured.

405	100k. Type **121**	2·40	2·10
406	200k. Parliament, map and figures (different)	4·75	4·25

Pt. 1

NABHA

A "Convention" state in the Punjab, India.

12 pies = 1 anna; 16 annas = 1 rupee.

Stamps of India optd NABHA STATE.

1885. Queen Victoria. Vert opt.

1	**23**	½a. turquoise	6·50	8·50
2	-	1a. purple	70·00	£275
3	-	2a. blue	32·00	85·00
4	-	4a. green (No. 96)	£110	£350
5	-	8a. mauve	£425	
6	-	1r. grey (No. 79)	£475	

1885. Queen Victoria. Horiz opt.

36	**40**	3p. red	30	20
14	**23**	½a. turquoise	75	10
15	-	9p. red	2·50	4·75
16	-	1a. purple	4·50	1·00
18	-	1a.6p. brown	2·75	5·50
11	-	2a. blue	3·50	3·75
22	-	3a. orange	6·50	2·75
12		4a. green (No. 69)	60·00	£325
24	-	4a. green (No. 96)	8·50	3·75
26	-	6a. brown (No. 80)	4·25	6·00
27	-	8a. mauve	5·50	5·50
28	-	12a. purple on red	6·00	7·50
29	-	1r. grey (No. 101)	20·00	80·00
30	**37**	1r. green and red	22·00	13·00
31	**38**	2r. red and orange	£170	£375
32	**38**	3r. brown and green	£170	£475
33	**38**	5r. blue and violet	£180	£700

1903. King Edward VII.

37	**38**	3p. grey	75	15
38	**38**	½a. green (No. 122)	1·10	70
39	**38**	1a. red (No. 123)	2·50	2·00
40a	**38**	2a. lilac	4·50	35
40b	**38**	2½a. blue	19·00	£100
41	**38**	3a. orange	1·75	40
42	**38**	4a. olive	6·50	2·00
43	**38**	6a. bistre	7·00	28·00
44	**38**	8a. mauve	10·00	35·00
45	**38**	12a. purple on red	6·50	35·00
46	**38**	1r. green and red	10·00	24·00

1907. As last, but inscr "INDIA POSTAGE & REVENUE".

47	½a. green (No. 149)	1·50	1·75
48	1a. red (No. 150)	1·75	70

1913. King George V. Optd in two lines.

49a	**55**	3p. grey	50	30
50	**56**	½a. green	80	90
51	**57**	1a. red	1·10	10
59	**57**	1a. brown	10·00	5·50
52	**59**	2a. lilac	1·50	2·25
53	**62**	3a. orange	1·00	60
54	**63**	4a. olive	1·25	3·00
55	**64**	6a. bistre	2·50	7·50
56a	**65**	8a. mauve	10·00	7·50
57	**66**	12a. red	5·50	30·00
58	**67**	1r. brown and green	14·00	13·00

1928. King George V. Optd in one line.

60	**55**	3p. grey	1·75	15
61	**56**	½a. green	1·40	30
73	**79**	½a. green	75	50
61b	**80**	9p. green	4·00	1·10
62	**57**	1a. brown	1·75	15
74	**81**	1a. brown	75	40
63	**82**	1¼a. mauve	3·75	7·50
64	**70**	2a. lilac	2·50	35
65	**61**	2½a. orange	2·00	13·00
66	**62**	3a. blue	4·50	1·50
75	**57**	3a. red	4·00	21·00
67	**71**	4a. green	6·50	3·25
76	**63**	4a. olive	8·50	5·00
71	**67**	2r. red and orange	42·00	£180
72	**67**	5r. blue and purple	95·00	£500

1938. King George VI. Nos. 247/63.

77	**91**	3p. slate	12·00	2·50
78	**91**	½a. brown	7·00	2·00
79	**91**	9p. green	18·00	5·50
80	**91**	1a. red	4·00	2·00
81	**92**	2a. red	1·50	11·00
82	-	2a.6p. violet	2·00	16·00
83	-	3a. green	1·50	8·50
84	-	3a.6p. blue	4·00	35·00
85	-	4a. brown	8·50	7·00
86	-	6a. green	3·50	38·00
87	-	8a. violet	2·50	32·00
88	-	12a. red	2·50	30·00
89	**93**	1r. slate and brown	15·00	45·00
90	**93**	2r. purple and brown	38·00	£160
91	**93**	5r. green and blue	45·00	£300
92	**93**	10r. purple and red	60·00	£500
93	**93**	15r. brown and green	£250	£1100
94	**93**	25r. slate and purple	£160	£1100

1942. King George VI. Optd NABHA only.

95	**91**	3p. slate	48·00	8·00
105	**100a**	3p. slate	1·25	1·25
96	**91**	½a. brown	90·00	8·50
106	**100a**	½a. mauve	3·00	2·50
97	**91**	9p. green	11·00	17·00
107	**100a**	9p. green	2·50	2·75
98	**91**	1a. red	14·00	5·50
108	**100a**	1a. red	1·00	5·00
109	**101**	1a.3p. brown	1·00	4·50
110	**101**	1½a. violet	2·50	3·25
111	**101**	2a. red	2·00	4·50
112	**101**	3a. violet	6·50	7·50
113	**101**	3½a. blue	18·00	85·00
114	**102**	4a. brown	2·25	1·00
115	**102**	6a. green	18·00	65·00
116	**102**	8a. violet	17·00	55·00
117	**102**	12a. purple	16·00	85·00

OFFICIAL STAMPS

Stamps of Nabha optd SERVICE.

1885. Nos. 1-3 (Queen Victoria).

O1	½a. turquoise	9·00	2·25
O2	1a. purple	70	20
O3	2a. blue	£110	£225

1885. Nos. 14/30 (Queen Victoria).

O6	½a. turquoise	40	10
O7	1a. purple	2·75	60
O5	2a. blue	1·75	55
O11	3a. orange	28·00	£120
O13	4a. green (No. 4)	4·75	2·00
O15	6a. brown	26·00	45·00
O17	8a. mauve	4·25	2·75
O18	12a. purple on red	6·50	26·00
O19	1r. grey	55·00	£450
O20	1r. green and red	38·00	£110

1903. Nos. 37/46 (King Edward VII).

O25	3p. grey	4·50	26·00
O26	½a. green	80	50
O27	1a. red	80	10
O29	2a. lilac	4·50	40
O30	4a. olive	2·25	50
O32	8a. mauve	2·25	1·50
O34	1r. green and red	2·25	2·75

1907. Nos. 47/8 (King Edward VII inscr "INDIA POSTAGE & REVENUE").

O35	½a. green	2·00	50
O36	1a. red	1·00	30

1913. Nos. 54 and 58 (King George V).

O37	**63**	4a. olive	10·00	75·00
O38	**67**	1r. brown and green	65·00	£550

1913. Official stamps of India (King George V) optd NABHA STATE.

O39a	**55**	3p. grey	1·75	11·00
O40	**56**	½a. green	70	30
O41	**57**	1a. red	1·00	10
O42	**59**	2a. purple	1·75	1·25
O43	**63**	4a. olive	1·25	75
O44	**65**	8a. mauve	2·25	2·00
O46	**67**	1r. brown and green	7·00	6·00

1932. Stamps of India (King George V) optd NABHA STATE SERVICE.

O47	**55**	3p. grey	10	15
O48	**81**	1a. brown	25	15
O49	**63**	4a. olive	27·00	2·50
O50	**65**	8a. mauve	1·00	2·75

1938. Stamps of India (King George VI) optd NABHA STATE SERVICE.

O53	**91**	9p. green	8·00	4·00
O54	**91**	1a. red	18·00	1·10

1943. Stamps of India (King George VI) optd NABHA.

O55	**O20**	3p. slate	1·25	3·00
O56	**O20**	½a. brown	1·10	30
O57	**O20**	½a. purple	7·00	2·50
O58	**O20**	9p. green	1·25	40
O59	**O20**	1a. red	1·50	20
O61	**O20**	1½a. violet	70	40
O62	**O20**	2a. orange	2·25	1·50
O64	**O20**	4a. brown	3·50	4·25
O65	**O20**	8a. violet	5·50	27·00

1943. Stamps of India (King George VI) optd NABHA SERVICE.

O66	**93**	1r. slate and brown	9·00	50·00
O67	**93**	2r. purple and brown	40·00	£275
O68	**93**	5r. green and blue	£250	£750

Pt. 10

NAGORNO-KARABAKH

The mountainous area of Nagorno-Karabakh, mainly populated by Armenians, was declared an Autonomous Region within the Azerbaijan Soviet Socialist Republic in 1923.

Following agitation for union with Armenia in 1998 Nagorno-Karabakh was placed under U.S.S.R. rule in 1989. On 2 September 1991 the Regional Societ declared its independence and this was confirmed by popular vote on 10 December. By 1993 fighting between Azerbaijan forces and those of Nagorno-Karabakh, supported by Armenia, led to the occupation of all Azerbaijan territory separating Nagorno-Karabakh from the border with Armenia. A ceasefire under Russian auspices was signed on 18 February 1994.

1993. 100 kopeks = 1 rouble.
1995. 100 louma = 1 dram

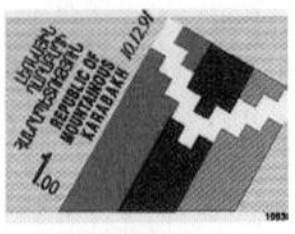

1 National Flag

1993. Inscr "REPUBLIC OF MOUNTAINOUS KARABAKH".

1	**1**	1r. multicoloured	95	95
2	-	3r. blue, purple and brown	2·75	2·75
3	-	15r. red and blue	13·50	13·50
MS4		80×80 mm. 20r. brown, ultramarine and red	4·25	4·25
MS5		60×80 mm. 20r. brown, ultramarine and red (imperf)	4·25	4·25

DESIGNS: 3r. President Arthur Mkrtchian; 15r. "We are Our Mountains" (sculpture of man and woman); 20r. Gandzasar Monastery.

Ա Ր Գ
2 "A" **2a** "P" **2b** "K"

1995. Nos. 1 and 3 surch in Armenian script as T 2/2b.

6	**2**	(50d.) on 1r. multicoloured	4·25	4·25
7	**2a**	(100d.) on 15r. red and blue	8·50	8·50
8	**2b**	(200d.) on 15r. red and blue	17·00	17·00

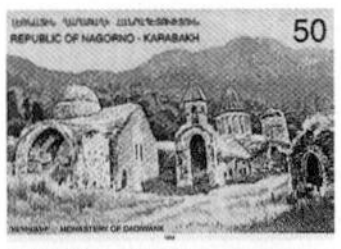

3 Dadiwank Monastery

1996. 5th Anniv of Independence. Multicoloured.

9	50d. Type **3**	45	45
10	100d. Parliament Building, Stepanakert	85	85
11	200d. "We are Our Mountains" (sculpture of man and woman)	1·30	1·30
MS12	110×82 mm. 50d. Map and flag; 100d. As No. 10; 200d. As No. 11; 500d. Republic coat-of-arms (colours of national flag extend diagonally across the miniature sheet from bottom left to top right with the order incorrectly shown as orange, blue and red)	4·25	4·25

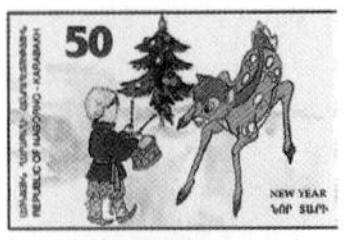

4 Boy playing Drum and Fawn (Erna Arshakyan)

1997. Festivals. Multicoloured.

13	50d. Type **4** (New Year)	45	45
14	200d. Madonna and Child with angels (Mihran Akopyan) (Christmas) (vert)	85	85

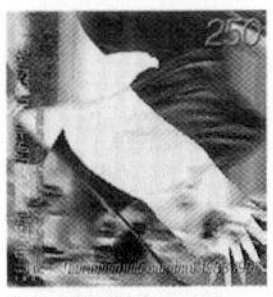

5 Eagle and Demonstrator with Flag

1998. 10th Anniv of Karabakh Movement.

15	**5**	250d. multicoloured	2·10	2·10

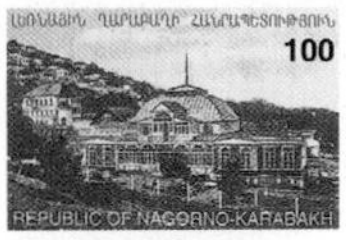

6 Parliament Summer Palace

1998. 5th Anniv of Liberation of Shushi. Mult.

16	100d. Type **6**	85	85
17	250d. Church of the Saviour (vert)	1·30	1·30
MS18	124×92 mm. 750d. Type **6**	4·25	4·25

Pt. 10

NAKHICHEVAN

An autonomous province of Azerbaijan, separated from the remainder of the republic by Armenian territory. Nos. 1 and 2 were issued during a period when the administration of Nakhichevan was in dispute with the central government.

100 qopik = 1 manat.

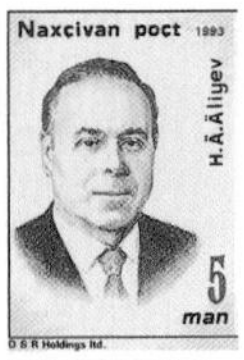

1 President Aliev

1993. 70th Birthday of President H. Aliev of Nakhichevan.

1	**1**	5m. black and red	6·50	6·50
2	-	5m. multicoloured	6·50	6·50
MS3		110×90 mm. Nos. 1/2	£120	£120

DESIGN: No. 2, Map of Nakhichevan.

Pt. 1

NAMIBIA

Formerly South West Africa, which became independent on 21 March 1990.

1990. 100 cents = 1 rand.
1993. 100 cents = 1 Namibia dollar.

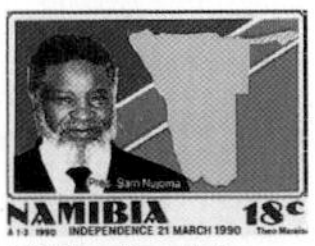

141 Pres. Sam Nujoma, Map of Namibia and National Flag

1990. Independence. Multicoloured.

538	18c. Type **141**	20	15
539	45c. Hands releasing dove and map of Namibia (vert)	50	75
540	60c. National flag and map of Africa	1·00	1·50

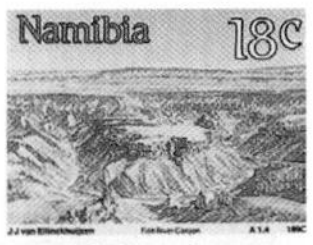

142 Fish River Canyon

1990. Namibia Landscapes. Multicoloured.

541	18c. Type **142**	25	20
542	35c. Quiver-tree forest, Keetmanshoop	50	35
543	45c. Tsaris Mountains	60	55
544	60c. Dolerite boulders, Keetmanshoop	70	65

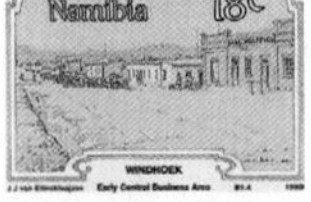

143 Stores on Kaiser Street, c. 1899

1990. Centenary of Windhoek. Multicoloured.

545	18c. Type **143**	20	20
546	35c. Kaiser Street, 1990	30	35
547	45c. City Hall, 1914	40	65
548	60c. City Hall, 1990	50	1·00

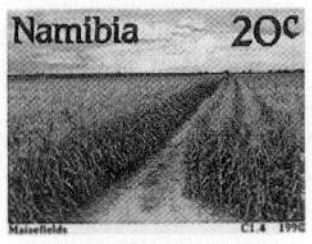

144 Maizefields

1990. Farming. Multicoloured.

549	20c. Type **144**	15	20
550	35c. Sanga bull	30	35
551	50c. Damara ram	40	45
552	65c. Irrigation in Okavango	50	60

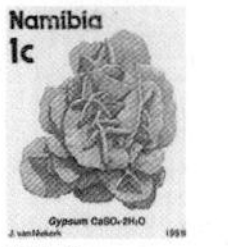

145 Gypsum

1991. Minerals. As Nos. 519/21 and 523/33 of South West Africa, some with values changed and new design (5r.), inscr "Namibia" as T 145. Multicoloured.

553	1c. Type **145**	15	30
554	2c. Fluorite	25	30
555	5c. Mimetite	35	30
556	10c. Azurite	50	30
557	20c. Dioptase	65	10
558	25c. Type **139**	1·00	20
559	30c. Tsumeb lead and copper complex	85	20
560	35c. Rosh Pinah zinc mine	85	20
561	40c. Diamonds	1·50	25
562	50c. Uis tin mine	1·00	25
563	65c. Boltwoodite	90	35
564	1r. Rossing uranium mine	1·25	50
565	1r.50 Wulfenite	1·40	70
566	2r. Gold	2·00	1·10
567	5r. Willemite (vert as T **145**)	3·00	2·75

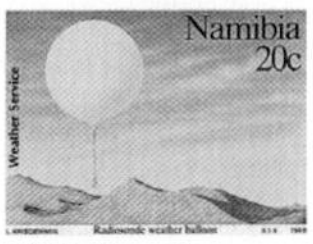

146 Radiosonde Weather Balloon

1991. Centenary of Weather Service. Mult.

568	20c. Type **146**	20	20
569	35c. Sunshine recorder	35	30
570	50c. Measuring equipment	45	50
571	65c. Meteorological station, Gobabeb	50	60

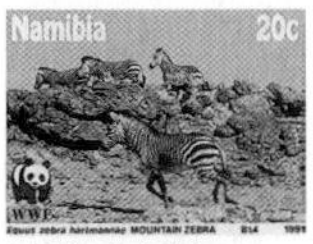

147 Herd of Zebras

1991. Endangered Species. Mountain Zebra. Mult.

572	20c. Type **147**	1·00	60
573	25c. Mare and foal	1·10	70
574	45c. Zebras and foal	1·50	1·75
575	60c. Two zebras	1·75	3·00

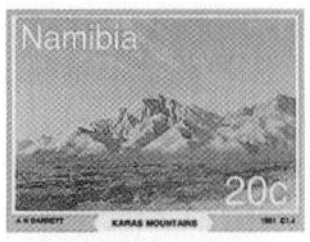

148 Karas Mountains

1991. Mountains of Namibia. Multicoloured.

576	20c. Type **148**	20	20
577	25c. Gamsberg Mountains	30	30
578	45c. Mount Brukkaros	45	70
579	60c. Erongo Mountains	65	1·00

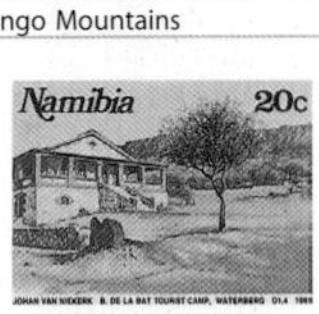

149 Bernabe de la Bat Camp

1991. Tourist Camps. Multicoloured.

580	20c. Type **149**	45	30
581	25c. Von Bach Dam Recreation Resort	55	45
582	45c. Gross Barmen Hot Springs	85	65
583	60c. Namutoni Rest Camp	1·00	1·00

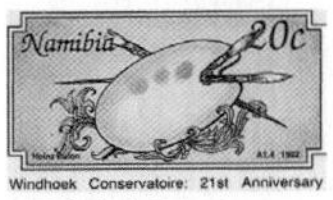

150 Artist's Pallet

1992. 21st Anniv of Windhoek Conservatoire. Multicoloured.

584	20c. Type **150**	20	15
585	25c. French horn and cello	25	20
586	45c. Theatrical masks	50	60
587	60c. Ballet dancers	65	1·00

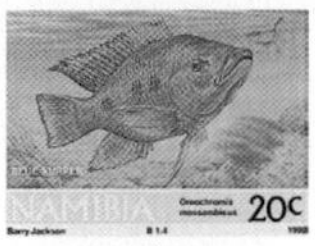

151 Mozambique Mouthbrooder

1992. Freshwater Angling. Multicoloured.

588	20c. Type **151**	40	20
589	25c. Large-mouthed yellowfish	45	20
590	45c. Common carp	85	50
591	60c. Sharp-toothed catfish	95	65

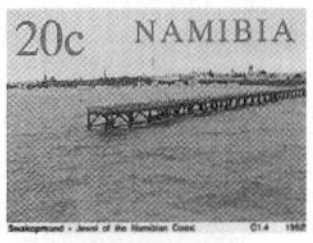

152 Old Jetty

1992. Centenary of Swakopmund. Mult.

592	20c. Type **152**	25	25
593	25c. Recreation centre	25	25
594	45c. State House and lighthouse	80	60
595	60c. Sea front	85	75
MS596	118×93 mm. Nos. 592/5	3·25	3·75

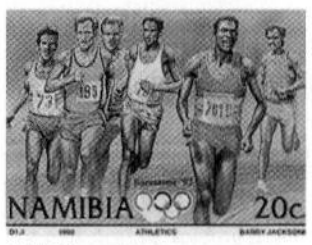

153 Running

1992. Olympic Games, Barcelona. Mult.

597	20c. Type **153**	25	20
598	25c. Map of Namibia, Namibian flag and Olympic rings	30	20
599	45c. Swimming	50	40
600	60c. Olympic Stadium, Barcelona	65	55
MS601	115×75 mm. Nos. 597/600 (sold at 2r.)	2·25	3·00

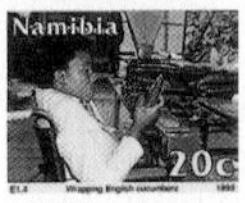

154 Wrapping English Cucumbers

1992. Integration of the Disabled. Mult.

602	20c. Type **154**	20	15
603	25c. Weaving mats	20	15
604	45c. Spinning thread	40	30
605	60c. Preparing pot plants	55	50

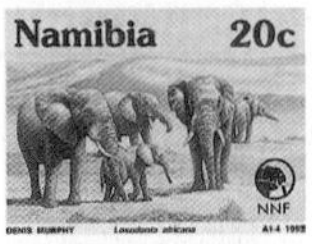

155 Elephants in Desert

1993. Namibia Nature Foundation. Rare and Endangered Species. Multicoloured.

606	20c. Type **155**	60	20
607	25c. Sitatunga in swamp	30	20
608	45c. Black rhinoceros	90	50
609	60c. Hunting dogs	65	60
MS610	217×59 mm. Nos. 606/9 (sold at 2r.50)	3·75	3·50

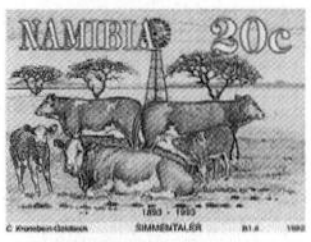

156 Herd of Simmentaler Cattle

1993. Centenary of Simmentalar Cattle in Namibia. Multicoloured.

611	20c. Type **156**	30	10
612	25c. Cow and calf	30	15
613	45c. Bull	60	40
614	60c. Cattle on barge	85	75

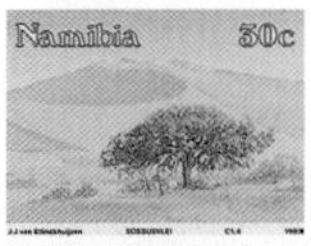

157 Sand Dunes, Sossusvlei

1993. Namib Desert Scenery. Multicoloured.

615	30c. Type **157**	25	20
616	40c. Blutkuppe	25	20
617	65c. River Kuiseb, Homeb	40	45
618	85c. Desert landscape	60	65

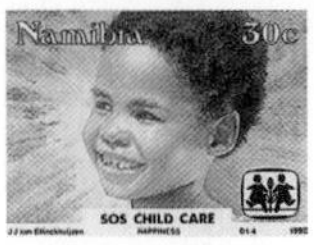

158 Smiling Child

1993. S.O.S. Child Care in Namibia. Mult.

619	30c. Type **158**	20	20
620	40c. Family	25	20
621	65c. Modern house	45	55
622	85c. Young artist with mural	65	80

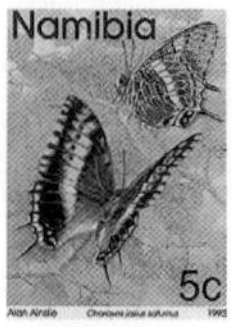

159 "Charaxes jasius"

1993. Butterflies. Multicoloured.

623	5c. Type **159**	20	40
624	10c. "Acraea anemosa"	20	40
625	20c. "Papilio nireus"	30	30
626	30c. "Junonia octavia"	30	10
627	40c. "Hypolimnus misippus"	30	10
628	50c. "Physcaeneura panda"	40	20
629	65c. "Charaxes candiope"	40	30
630	85c. "Junonia hierta"	50	40
631	90c. "Colotis cellmene"	50	40
632	$1 "Cacyreus dicksoni"	55	35
633	$2 "Charaxes bohemani"	80	80
634	$2.50 "Stugeta bowkeri"	1·00	1·10
635	$5 "Byblia anvatara"	1·50	1·75

See also No. 648.

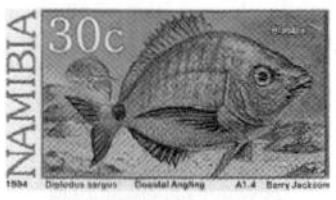

160 White Seabream

1994. Coastal Angling. Multicoloured.

636	30c. Type **160**	25	25
637	40c. Kob	25	25
638	65c. West coast steenbras	40	40
639	85c. Galjoen	60	60
MS640	134×89 mm. Nos. 636/9 (sold at $2.50)	2·00	2·50

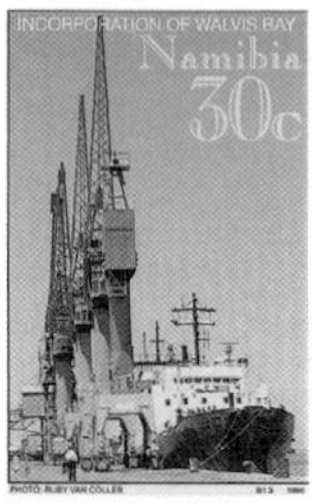

161 Container Ship at Wharf

1994. Incorporation of Walvis Bay Territory into Namibia. Multicoloured.

641	30c. Type **161**	40	30
642	65c. Aerial view of Walvis Bay	60	90
643	85c. Map of Namibia	95	1·40

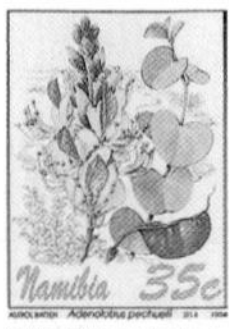

162 "Adenolobus pechuelii"

1994. Flowers. Multicoloured.

644	35c. Type **162**	25	25
645	40c. "Hibiscus elliottiae"	25	25
646	65c. "Pelargonium cortusifolium"	40	40
647	85c. "Hoodia macrantha"	50	60

1994. Butterflies. As T 159, but inscr "STANDARDISED MAIL". Multicoloured.

648	(–) "Graphium antheus"	40	20

No. 648 was initially sold at 35c., but this was subsequently increased to reflect changes in postal rates.

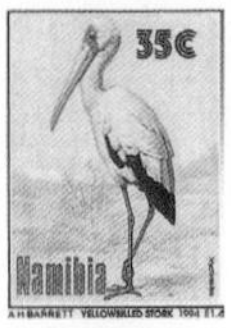

163 Yellow-billed Stork

1994. Storks. Multicoloured.

649	35c. Type **163**	60	30
650	40c. Abdim's stork	60	40
651	80c. African open-bill stork	80	80
652	$1.10 White stork	1·00	1·25

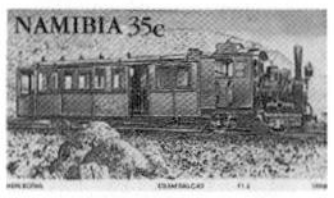

164 Steam Railcar, 1908

1994. Steam Locomotives. Multicoloured.

653	35c. Type **164**	45	30
654	70c. Krauss side-tank locomotive No. 106, 1904	70	50
655	80c. Class 24 locomotive, 1948	75	55
656	$1.10 Class 7C locomotive, 1914	1·10	80

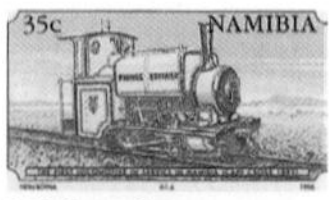

165 Cape Cross Locomotive No. 84 "Prince Edward", 1895

1995. Cent of Railways in Namibia. Mult.

657	35c. Type **165**	45	25
658	70c. Steam locomotive, German South West Africa	70	35
659	80c. South African Railways Class 8 steam locomotive	75	40
660	$1.10 Trans-Namib Class 33-400 diesel-electric locomotive	1·10	55
MS661	101×94 mm. Nos. 657/60	2·75	2·50

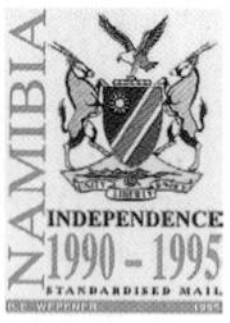

166 National Arms

1995. 5th Anniv of Independence.

662	**166**	(–) multicoloured	45	30

No. 662 is inscribed "STANDARDISED MAIL" and was initially sold for 35c., but this was subsequently increased to reflect changes in postal rates.

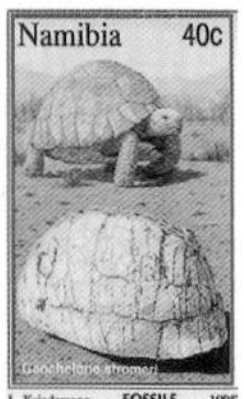

167 Living Tortoise and "Geochelone stromeri" (fossil)

1995. Fossils. Multicoloured.

663	40c. Type **167**	65	25
664	80c. Ward's diamond bird and "Diamantornis wardi" (fossil eggs)	1·00	70
665	90c. Hyraxes and "Prohyrax hendeyi" skull	1·10	1·00
666	$1.20 Crocodiles and "Crocodylus lloydi" skull	1·40	2·00

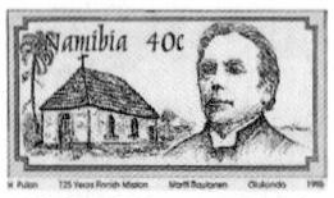

168 Martii Rautanen and Church

1995. 125th Anniv of Finnish Missionaries in Namibia. Multicoloured.

667	40c. Type **168**	25	20
668	80c. Albin Savola and hand printing press	50	50
669	90c. Karl Weikkolin and wagon	60	65
670	$1.20 Dr. Selma Rainio and Onandjokwe Hospital	85	95

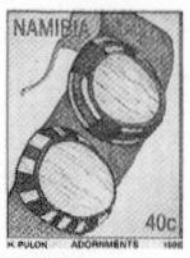

169 Ivory Buttons

1995. Personal Ornaments. Multicoloured.

671	40c. Type **169**	20	20
672	80c. Conus shell pendant	45	45
673	90c. Cowrie shell headdress	55	55
674	$1.20 Shell button pendant	85	95

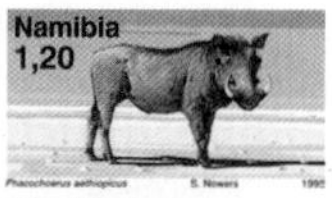

169a Warthog

1995. "Singapore '95" International Stamp Exhibition. Sheet 110×52 mm, containing design as No. 359b of South West Africa.

MS675	**169a** $1.20 multicoloured	1·10	1·40

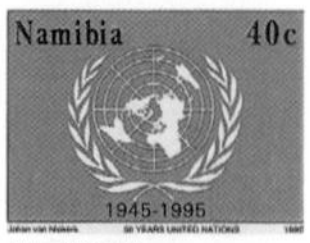

170 U.N. Flag

1995. 50th Anniv of the United Nations.

676	**170**	40c. blue and black	25	30

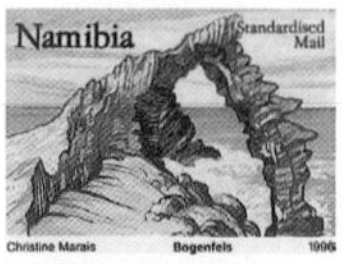

171 Bogenfels Arch

1996. Tourism. Multicoloured.

677	(–) Type **171**	15	15
678	90c. Ruacana Falls	30	30
679	$1 Epupa Falls	30	30
680	$1.30 Herd of wild horses	35	50

No. 677 is inscribed "Standardised Mail" and was initially sold at 45c.

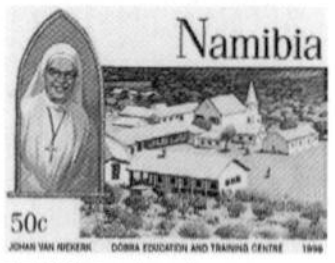

172 Sister Leoni Kreitmeier and Dobra Education and Training Centre

1996. Centenary of Catholic Missions in Namibia. Multicoloured.

681	50c. Type **172**	20	20
682	95c. Father Johann Malinowski and Heirachabis Mission	30	40
683	$1 St. Mary's Cathedral, Windhoek	30	40
684	$1.30 Archbishop Joseph Gotthardt and early church, Ovamboland	35	80

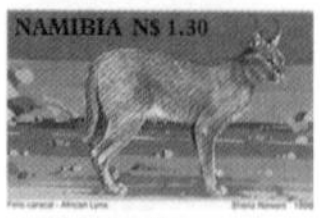

172a Caracal

1996. "CAPEX '96" International Stamp Exhibition, Toronto. Sheet 105×45 mm, containing design as No. 358c of South West Africa.

MS685	**172a** $1.30 multicoloured	1·00	1·40

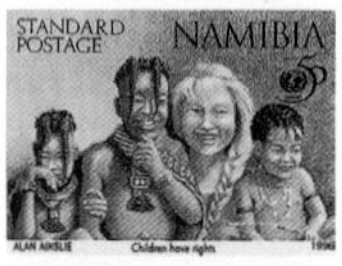

173 Children and UNICEF Volunteer

1996. 50th Anniv of UNICEF. Multicoloured.

686	(–) Type **173**	15	15
687	$1.30 Girls in school	60	60

No. 686 is inscribed "STANDARD POSTAGE" and was initially sold at 50c.

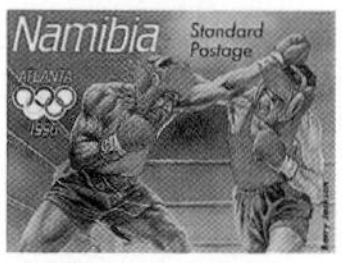

174 Boxing

1996. Centennial Olympic Games, Atlanta. Mult.

688	(–) Type **174**	15	15
689	90c. Cycling	50	40
690	$1 Swimming	30	40
691	$1.30 Running	30	55

No. 688 is inscribed "Standard Postage" and was initially sold at 50c.

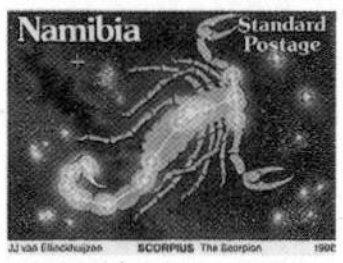

175 Scorpius

1996. Stars in the Namibian Sky. Multicoloured.

692	(–) Type **175**	15	15
693	90c. Sagittarius	25	30
694	$1 Southern Cross	30	30
695	$1.30 Orion	40	50
MS696	100×80 mm. No. 694	1·50	1·75

No. 692 is inscribed "Standard Postage" and was initially sold at 50c.

See also No. **MS**706.

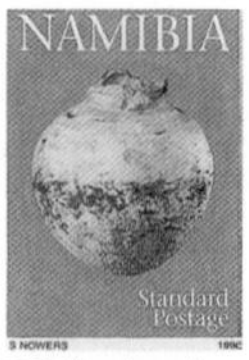

176 Urn-shaped Pot

1996. Early Pottery. Multicoloured.

697	(–) Type **176**	15	15
698	90c. Decorated storage pot	30	40
699	$1 Reconstructed cooking pot	30	40
700	$1.30 Storage pot	35	70

No. 697 is inscribed "Standard Postage" and was initially sold at 50c.

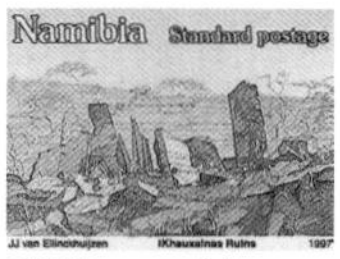

177 Khauxanas Ruins

1997. Khaux!nas Ruins.

701	**177**	(–) multicoloured	35	20
702	-	$1 multicoloured	75	55
703	-	$1.10 multicoloured	85	75
704	-	$1.50 multicoloured	1·40	2·00

DESIGNS: $1 to $1.50, Different views.

No. 701 is inscribed "Standard postage" and was initially sold at 50c.

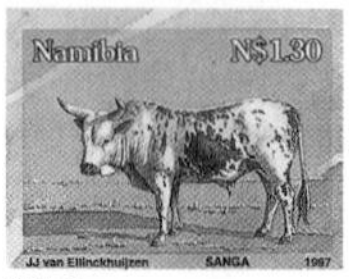

178 Ox

1997. "HONG KONG '97" International Stamp Exhibition and Chinese New Year ("Year of the Ox"). Sheet 103×67 mm.

MS705	**178** $1.30 multicoloured	1·10	1·40

1997. Support for Organised Philately. No. MS696 with margin additionally inscr "Reprint February 17 1997. Sold in aid of organised philately N$3.50".

MS706	$1 Southern Cross (sold at $3.50)	2·00	2·25

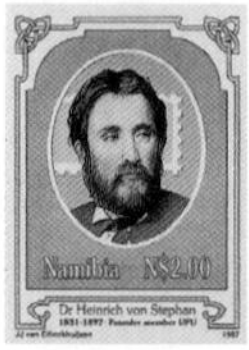

179 Heinrich von Stephan

1997. Death Centenary of Heinrich von Stephan (founder of U.P.U.).

709	**179**	$2 multicoloured	1·25	1·40

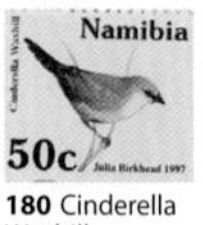

180 Cinderella Waxbill

1997. Waxbills. Multicoloured.

710	50c. Type **180**	25	30
711	60c. Black-cheeked waxbill	25	30

181 Helmeted Guineafowl

1997. Greetings Stamp.
712	**181**	$1.20 multicoloured	1·00	1·00

For similar designs see Nos. 743/6.

182 Jackass Penguins Calling

1997. Endangered Species. Jackass Penguin. Mult.
713	(–)	Type **182**	35	30
714		$1 Incubating egg	55	40
715		$1.10 Adult with chick	60	50
716		$1.50 Penguins swimming	75	60

MS717 101×92 mm. As Nos. 713/16, but without WWF symbol (sold at $5) 1·90 1·50

No. 713 is inscribed "STANDARD POSTAGE" and was initially sold at 50c.

183 Caracal

1997. Wildcats. Multicoloured.
718	(–)	Type **183**	20	20
719		$1 "Felis lybic"	40	30
720		$1.10 Serval	50	40
721		$1.50 Black-footed cat	60	55

MS722 100×80 mm. $5 As No. 721 2·00 2·25

No. MS722 was sold in aid of organised philately in Southern Africa.
No. 718 is inscribed "STANDARD POSTAGE" and was initially sold at 50c.

184 "Catophractes alexandri"

1997. Greeting Stamps. Flowers and Helmeted Guineafowl. Multicoloured.
723	(–)	Type **184**	30	30
724	(–)	"Crinum paludosum"	30	30
725	(–)	"Gloriosa superba"	30	30
726	(–)	"Tribulus zeyheri"	30	30
727	(–)	"Aptosimum pubescens"	30	30
728		50c. Helmeted guineafowl raising hat	30	30
729		50c. Holding bouquet	30	30
730		50c. Ill in bed	30	30
731		$1 With heart round neck	50	60
732		$1 With suitcase and backpack	50	60

Nos. 723/7 are inscribed "Standard Postage" and were initially sold at 50c. each.

185 Collecting Bag

1997. Basket Work. Multicoloured.
733		50c. Type **185**	20	20
734		90c. Powder basket	30	30
735		$1.20 Fruit basket	35	35
736		$2 Grain basket	70	75

186 Veterinary Association Coat of Arms

1997. 50th Anniv of Namibian Veterinary Association.
737	**186**	$1.50 multicoloured	50	50

187 Head of Triceratops

1997. Youth Philately. Dinosaurs. Sheet 82×56 mm.
MS738 **187** $5 multicoloured 1·50 1·75

188 German South West Africa Postman

1997. World Post Day.
739	**188**	(–) multicoloured	30	30

No. 739 is inscribed "STANDARD POSTAGE" and was initially sold at 50c.

189 False Mopane

1997. Trees. Multicoloured.
740	(–)	Type **189**	15	20
741		$1 Ana tree	30	40
742		$1.10 Shepherd's tree	35	55
743		$1.50 Kiaat	50	70

No. 740 is inscribed "STANDARD POSTAGE" and was initially sold at 50c.

1997. Christmas. As T 181, showing Helmeted Guineafowl, each with festive frame. Mult.
744	(–)	Guineafowl facing right	20	20
745		$1 Guineafowl in grass	35	30
746		$1.10 Guineafowl on rock	35	40
747		$1.50 Guineafowl in desert	50	55

MS748 110×80 mm. $5 Helmeted guineafowl (vert) 3·00 3·25

No. 744 is inscribed "standard postage" and was initially sold at 50c.

190 Flame Lily

1997. Flora and Fauna. Multicoloured.
749		5c. Type **190**	10	50
750		10c. Bushman poison	10	50
751		20c. Camel's foot	10	50
752		30c. Western rhigozum	50	50
753		40c. Blue-cheeked bee-eater	50	50
754		50c. Laughing dove	50	20
755a		(–) Peach-faced lovebird ("Roseyfaced Lovebird")	25	25
756		60c. Lappet-faced vulture	60	25
757		90c. Southern yellow-billed hornbill ("Yellow-billed Hornbill")	60	25
758		$1 Lilac-breasted roller	60	30
759		$1.10 Hippopotamus	1·00	40
760		$1.20 Giraffe	1·00	40
761a		(–) Leopard	35	35
762		$1.50 Elephant	1·25	45
763		$2 Lion	75	45
764		$4 Buffalo	1·25	85
765		$5 Black rhinoceros	2·00	1·25
766		$10 Cheetah	2·50	2·25

No. 755a is inscribed "standard postage" and was initially sold at 50c.; No. 761a is inscribed "postcard rate" and was initially sold at $1.20.
Nos. 755, 758 and 761 exist with ordinary or self-adhesive gum.

191 John Muafangejo

1997. 10th Death Anniv of John Muafangejo (artist).
770	**191**	(50c.) multicoloured	60	50

No. 770 is inscribed "STANDARD POSTAGE" and was initially sold at 50c.

192 Gabriel B. Taapopi

1998. Gabriel B. Taapopi (writer) Commemoration.
771	**192**	(–) silver and brown	40	40

No. 771 is inscribed "STANDARD POSTAGE" and was initially sold at 50c.

193 Year of the Tiger

1998. International Stamp and Coin Exhibition, 1997, Shanghai. Sheets 165×125 mm or 97×85 mm, containing multicoloured designs as T 193. (a) Lunar New Year.
MS772 165×125 mm. $2.50×6. Type **193**; Light green tiger and circular symbol; Yellow tiger and head symbol; Blue tiger and square symbol; Emerald tiger and square symbol; Mauve tiger and triangular symbol (61×29 mm) 2·50 3·25
MS773 97×85 mm. $6 Symbolic tiger designs (71×40 mm) 1·25 1·40

(b) Chinese Calendar.
MS774 165×125 mm. $2.50×6. Various calendar symbols (24×80 mm) 2·50 3·25
MS775 97×85 mm. $6 Soft toy tigers (71×36 mm) 1·25 1·40

(c) 25th Anniv of Shanghai Communique.
MS776 165×125 mm. $3.50×4. Pres. Nixon's visit to China, 1972; Vice Premier Deng Xiaoping's visit to U.S.A., 1979; Pres. Reagan's visit to China, 1984; Pres. Bush's visit to China, 1989 (61×32 mm) 2·00 3·00
MS777 97×85 mm. $6 China–U.S.A. Communique, 1972 (69×36 mm) 1·25 1·40

(d) Pres. Deng Xiaoping's Project for Unification of China.
MS778 165×125 mm. $3.50×4. Beijing as national capital; Return of Hong Kong; Return of Macao; Links with Taiwan (37×65 mm) 2·00 3·00
MS779 97×85 mm. $6 Reunified China (71×41 mm) 1·25 1·40

(e) Return of Macao to China, 1999.
MS780 Two sheets, each 165×120 mm. (a) $4.50×3 Carnival dragon and modern Macao (44×33 mm). (b) $4.50×3 Ruins of St. Paul's Church, Macao (62×29 mm) Set of 2 sheets 3·00 5·50
MS781 Two sheets, each 97×85 mm. (a) $6 Carnival dragon and modern Macao (62×32 mm). (b) $6 Deng Xiaoping and ruins of St. Paul's Church, Macao (71×36 mm) Set of 2 sheets 1·75 2·50

194 Leopard

1998. Large Wild Cats. Multicoloured.
782		$1.20 Type **194**	60	25
783		$1.90 Lioness and cub	80	65
784		$2 Lion	80	1·00
785		$2.50 Cheetah	95	1·40

MS786 112×98 mm. Nos. 782/5 3·50 3·50

195 Narra Plant

1998. Narra Cultivation.
787	**195**	$2.40 multicoloured	55	65

196 Collecting Rain Water

1998. World Water Day.
788	**196**	(–) multicoloured	50	40

No. 788 is inscribed "STANDARD POSTAGE" and was initially sold at 50c. On 1 April 1998 the standard postage rate was increased to 55c.

1998. Diana, Princess of Wales Commemoration. Sheet 145×70 mm, containing vert designs as T 91 of Kiribati. Multicoloured.
MS789 $1 Princess Diana wearing protective mask; $1 Wearing Red Cross badge; $1 Wearing white shirt; $1 Comforting crippled child 1·60 1·75

197 White-faced Scops Owl ("Whitefaced Owl")

1998. Owls of Namibia. Multicoloured.
790		55c. Black-tailed tree rat (20×24 mm)	40	40
791		$1.50 Type **197**	90	95
792		$1.50 African barred owl ("Barred Owl")	90	95
793		$1.90 Spotted eagle owl	1·00	1·25
794		$1.90 Barn owl (61×24 mm)	1·00	1·25

See also No. MS850.

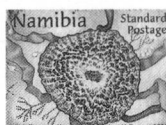
198 "Patella ganatina" (Limpet)

1998. Shells. Multicoloured.
795	(–)	Type **198**	30	10
796		$1.10 "Cymatium cutaceum africanum" ("Triton")	65	30
797		$1.50 "Conus mozambicus" ("Cone")	85	65
798		$6 "Venus verrucosa" (Venus clam)	2·75	3·75

MS799 109×84 mm. Nos. 795/8 4·50 5·50

No. 795 is inscribed "Standard Postage" and was initially sold at 55c.

199 Underwater Diamond Excavator

1998. Marine Technology. Sheet 70×90 mm.
MS800 **199** $2.50 multicoloured 2·50 2·50

200 "Chinga" (cheetah)

1998. Wildlife Conservation. "Racing for Survival" (Olympic sprinter Frank Frederiks v cheetah). Sheet 108×80 mm.
MS801 **200** $5 multicoloured 1·75 2·25

201 Namibian Beach

1998. World Environment Day. Multicoloured.

802	(–) Type **201**	20	10
803	$1.10 Okavango sunset	40	30
804	$1.50 Sossusvlei	55	60
805	$1.90 African Moringo tree	80	1·00

No. 802 is inscribed "STANDARD POSTAGE" and was initially sold at 55c.

202 Two
Footballers

1998. World Cup Football Championship, France. Sheet 80×56 mm.

MS806 **202** $5 multicoloured	1·25	1·75

203 Chacma
Baboon

1998. Animals with their Young. Sheet 176×60 mm, containing T 203 and similar vert designs.

MS807 $1.50, Type **203**; $1.50, Blue Wildebeest; $1.50, Meercat (suricate); $1.50, African Elephant; $1.50, Burchell's Zebra	1·75	2·50

204 Carmine Bee Eater

1998. Wildlife of the Caprivi Strip. Multicoloured.

808	60c. Type **204**	75	75
809	60c. Sable antelope (40×40 mm)	75	75
810	60c. Lechwe (40×40 mm)	75	75
811	60c. Woodland waterberry	75	75
812	60c. Nile monitor (40×40 mm)	75	75
813	60c. African jacana	75	75
814	60c. African fish eagle	75	75
815	60c. Woodland kingfisher	75	75
816	60c. Nile crocodile (55×30 mm)	75	75
817	60c. Black mamba (32×30 mm)	75	75

Nos. 808/17 were printed together, se-tenant, with the backgrounds forming a composite design.

205 Black Rhinoceros and
Calf

1998. "ILSAPEX '98" International Stamp Exhibition, Johannesburg. Sheet 103×68 mm.

MS818 **205** $5 multicoloured	1·75	2·25

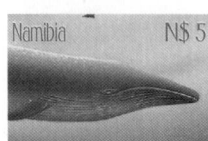

206 Blue Whale

1998. Whales of the Southern Oceans (joint issue with Norfolk Island and South Africa). Sheet 103×70 mm.

MS819 **206** $5 multicoloured	1·75	2·25

207 Damara
Dik-dik

1999. "Fun Stamps for Children". Animals. Mult.

820	$1.80 Type **207**	2·00	1·50
821	$2.65 Striped tree squirrel (26×36 mm)	3·50	3·00

208 Yoka
perplexed

1999. "Yoka the Snake" (cartoon). Multicoloured. Self-adhesive.

822	$1.60 Type **208**	35	40
823	$1.60 Yoka under attack (33×27 mm)	35	40
824	$1.60 Yoka caught on branch	35	40
825	$1.60 Yoka and wasps (33×27 mm)	35	40
826	$1.60 Yoka and footprint	35	40
827	$1.60 Yoka and tail of red and white snake	35	40
828	$1.60 Mouse hunt (33×27 mm)	35	40
829	$1.60 Snakes entwined	35	40
830	$1.60 Red and white snake singing	35	40
831	$1.60 Yoka sulking (33×27 mm)	35	40

209 "Windhuk" (liner)

1999. "Windhuk" (liner) Commemoration. Sheet 110×90 mm.

MS832 **209** $5.50 multicoloured	1·50	2·00

210 Zogling Glider, 1928

1999. Gliding in Namibia. Multicoloured.

833	$1.60 Type **210**	40	50
834	$1.80 Schleicher glider, 1998	60	75

211 Yoka the Snake with Toy
Zebra

1999. "iBRA '99" International Stamp Exhibition, Nuremberg. Sheet 110×84 mm.

MS835 **211** $5.50 multicoloured	1·25	1·75

212 Greater Kestrel

1999. Birds of Prey. Multicoloured.

836	60c. Type **212**	60	35
837	$1.60 Common kestrel ("Rock Kestrel")	1·10	80
838	$1.80 Red-headed falcon ("Red-necked Falcon")	1·10	90
839	$2.65 Lanner falcon	1·75	2·50

213 Wattled Crane

1999. Wetland Birds. Multicoloured.

840	$1.60 Type **213**	1·00	65
841	$1.80 Variegated sandgrouse ("Burchell's Sandgrouse")	1·10	85
842	$1.90 White-collared pratincole ("Rock Pratincole")	1·10	85
843	$2.65 Eastern white pelican	1·75	2·25

214 "Termitomyces
schimperi" (fungus)

1999. "PhilexFrance '99" International Stamp Exhibition, Paris. Sheet 79×54 mm.

MS844 **214** $5.50 multicoloured	1·75	2·25

215 "Eulophia hereroensis"
(orchid)

1999. "China '99" International Philatelic Exhibition, Beijing. Orchids. Multicoloured.

845	$1.60 Type **215**	80	65
846	$1.80 "Ansellia africana"	90	75
847	$2.65 "Eulophia leachii"	1·40	1·50
848	$3.90 "Eulophia speciosa"	2·00	2·25
MS849 72×72 mm. $5.50 "Eulophia walleri"		2·00	2·50

1999. Winning entry in 5th Stamp World Cup, France. Sheet 120×67 mm, design as No. 794, but with changed face value. Multicoloured.

MS850 $11 Barn owl (61×24 mm)	7·00	7·00

216 Johanna
Gertze

1999. Johanna Gertze Commemoration.

851	**216** $20 red, pink and blue	4·00	5·00

217 Sunset over Namibia

1999. New Millennium. Multicoloured.

852	$2.20 Type **217**	90	1·00
853	$2.40 Sunrise over Namibia	1·00	1·25
MS854 77×54 mm. $9 Globe (hologram) (37×44 mm)		3·00	3·50

218 South African
Shelduck

2000. Ducks of Namibia. Multicoloured.

855	$2 Type **218**	90	60
856	$2.40 White-faced whistling duck	1·10	75
857	$3 Comb duck ("Knobbilled duck")	1·40	1·25
858	$7 Cape shoveler	3·00	4·00

No. 858 is inscribed "Cape shoveller" in error.

2000. Nos. 749/52 surch with standard postage (859) or new values (others).

859	(–) on 5c. Type **190**	40	15
860	$1.80 on 30c. Western rhigozum	75	40
861	$3 on 10c. Bushman poison	1·00	1·00
862	$6 on 20c. Camel's foot	1·75	2·25

No. 859 was initially sold at 65c. The other surcharges show face values.

220 Namibian Children

2000. 10th Anniv of Independence. Multicoloured.

863	65c. Type **220**	50	15
864	$3 Namibian flag	1·75	1·75

221 Actor playing Jesus
wearing Crown of Thorns

2000. Easter Passion Play. Multicoloured.

865	$2.10 Type **221**	70	70
866	$2.40 On the way to Calvary	80	80

222 Tenebrionid
Beetle

2000. "The Stamp Show 2000" International Stamp Exhibition, London. Wildlife of Namibian Dunes. Sheet 165×73 mm, containing T 222 and similar multicoloured designs.

MS867 $2 Type **222**; $2 Namib golden mole; $2 Brown hyena; $2 Shovel-snouted lizard (49×30 mm); $2 Dune lark (25×36 mm); $6 Namib side-winding adder (25×36 mm)	7·00	7·50

223 *Welwitschia
mirabilis*

2000. Welwitschia mirabilis (prehistoric plant). Multicoloured.

868	(–) Type **223**	40	20
869	$2.20 *Welwitschia mirabilis* from above	1·00	60
870	$3 Seed pods	1·40	1·40
871	$4 Flats covered by *Welwitschia mirabilis*	1·50	2·00

No. 868 is inscribed "Standard inland mail" and was originally sold for 65c.

224 High Energy
Stereoscopic System
Telescopes

2000. High Energy Stereoscopic System Telescopes Project. Namibian Khomas Highlands. Sheet 100×70 mm.

MS872 **224** $11 multicoloured	5·00	6·00

225 Jackal-berry Tree

2000. Trees with Nutritional Value. Multicoloured.

873	(–) Type **225**	45	25
874	$2 Sycamore fig	1·00	80
875	$2.20 Bird plum	1·10	85
876	$7 Marula	3·25	4·00

No. 873 is inscribed "Standard inland mail" and was originally sold for 65c.

226 Yoka and Nero the
Elephant

2000. "Yoka the Snake" (cartoon) (2nd series). Sheet 103×68 mm.

MS877 **226** $11 multicoloured	4·50	5·50

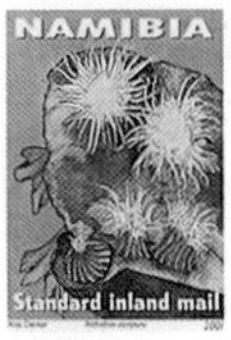

227 Striped Anemone

2001. Sea Anemone. Multicoloured.

878	(–) Type **227**	45	15
879	$2.45 Violet-spotted anemone	1·00	70
880	$3.50 Knobbly anemone	1·40	1·40
881	$6.60 False plum anemone	2·50	3·00

No. 878 is inscribed "Standard inland mail" and was originally sold for 70c.

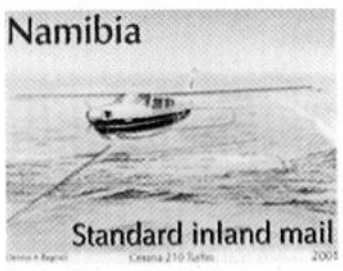

228 Cessna 210 Turbo Aircraft

2001. Civil Aviation. Multicoloured.

882	(–) Type **228**	70	25
883	$2.20 Douglas DC-6B airliner	1·50	70
884	$2.50 Pitts S2A bi-plane	1·50	80
885	$13.20 Bell 407 helicopter	5·75	6·50

No. 882 is inscribed "Standard inland mail" and was originally sold for 70c.

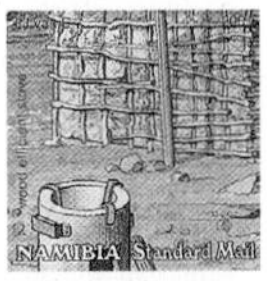

229 Wood-burning Stove

2001. Renewable Energy Sources. Multicoloured.

886	(–) Type **229**	70	70
887	(–) Biogas digester	70	70
888	(–) Solar cooker	70	70
889	(–) Re-cycled tyre	70	70
890	(–) Solar water pump	70	70
891	$3.50 Solar panel above traditional hut	1·10	1·40
892	$3.50 Solar street light	1·10	1·40
893	$3.50 Solar panels on hospital building	1·10	1·40
894	$3.50 Solar telephone	1·10	1·40
895	$3.50 Wind pump	1·10	1·40

Nos. 886/95 were printed together, se-tenant, with the backgrounds forming a composite design.

Nos. 886/90 are inscribed "Standard Mail" and were originally sold for $1 each.

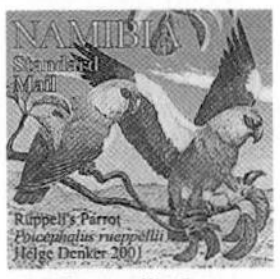

230 Ruppell's Parrot

2001. Flora and Fauna from the Central Highlands. Multicoloured.

896	(–) Type **230**	90	90
897	(–) Flap-necked chameleon (40×30 mm)	90	90
898	(–) Klipspringer (40×30 mm)	90	90
899	(–) Rockrunner (40×30 mm)	90	90
900	(–) Pangolin (40×40 mm)	90	90
901	$3.50 Camel thorn (55×30 mm)	1·25	1·50
902	$3.50 Berg aloe (40×30 mm)	1·25	1·50
903	$3.50 Kudu (40×40 mm)	1·25	1·50
904	$3.50 Rock agama (40×40 mm)	1·25	1·50
905	$3.50 Armoured ground cricket (40×30 mm)	1·25	1·50

Nos. 896/905 were printed together, se-tenant, with the backgrounds forming a composite design.

Nos. 896/900 are inscribed "Standard Mail" and were originally sold for $1 each.

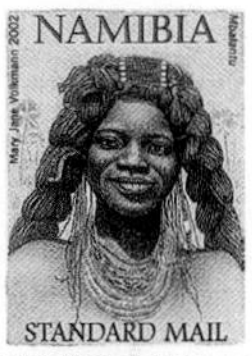

231 Plaited Hair, Mbalantu

2002. Traditional Women's Hairstyles and Headdresses. Multicoloured.

906	(–) Type **231**	55	65
907	(–) Cloth headdress, Damara	55	65
908	(–) Beaded hair ornaments, San	55	65
909	(–) Leather ekori headdress, Herero	55	65
910	(–) Bonnet, Baster	55	65
911	(–) Seed necklaces, Mafue	55	65
912	(–) Thihukeka hairstyle, Mbukushu	55	65
913	(–) Triangular cloth headdress, Herero	55	65
914	(–) Goat-skin headdress, Himba	55	65
915	(–) Horned headdress, Kwanyama	55	65
916	(–) Headscarf, Nama	55	65
917	(–) Plaits and oshikoma, Ngandjera/Kwaluudhi	55	65

Nos. 906/17 are inscribed "STANDARD MAIL" and were originally sold for $1 each.

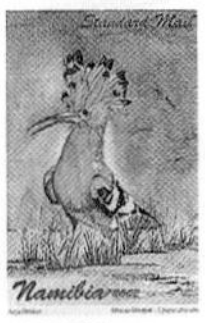

232 African Hoopoe

2002. Birds. Multicoloured.

918	(–) Type **232**	1·00	55
919	$2.20 Paradise flycatcher	1·50	75
920	$2.60 Swallowtailed bee eater	1·75	1·50
921	$2.80 Malachite kingfisher	1·90	2·00

No. 918 is inscribed "Standard Mail" and was originally sold for $1.

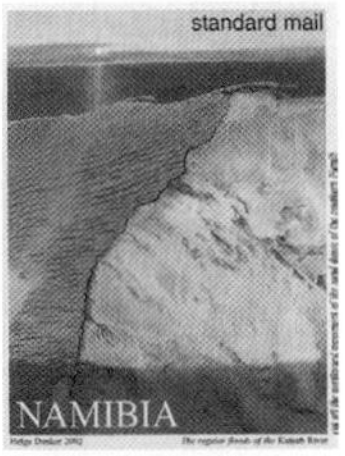

233 The Regular Floods of Kuiseb River

2002. Ephemeral Rivers. Multicoloured.

922	$1.30 Type **233**	70	25
923	$2.20 Tsauchab River after heavy rainfall (39×31 mm)	1·10	50
924	$2.60 Elephants in the sandbed of the Hoarusib River (89×24 mm)	1·75	1·25
925	$2.80 Nossob River after heavy rainfall (39×32 mm)	1·40	1·40
926	$3.50 Fish River and birds (23×57 mm)	2·25	3·00

No. 922 is inscribed "Standard Mail" and was initially sold for $1.30.

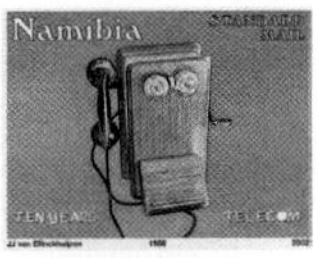

234 Wall Mounted Telephone, 1958

2002. 10th Anniv of Nampost and Telecommunication. Multicoloured.

MS927	102×171 mm. ($1.30) Type **234**; ($1.30) Courier van; ($1.30) Black wall mounted phone; ($1.30) Pillar box and envelope; ($1.30) Black desk top phone; ($1.30) Computer; ($1.30) Unplugged phone; ($1.30) Dolphin carrying envelope; ($1.30) Modern multi-function phone; ($1.30) Plane and envelopes	5·00	6·00
MS928	102×171 mm. ($1.30) Type **234** ×2; ($1.30) Black wall mounted phone ; ($1.30) Black desk top phone ×2; ($1.30) Unplugged phone ×2; ($1.30) Modern multi-function phone ×2	5·00	6·00
MS929	102×171 mm. ($1.30) Courier van ×2; ($1.30) Pillar box and envelope ×2; ($1.30) Computer ×2; ($1.30) Dolphin carrying envelope ×2; ($1.30) Plane and envelopes ×2	5·00	6·00

The stamps in Nos. **MS**927/9 were all inscribed "Standard Mail" and were initially sold for $1.30.

2002. Nos. 749/50 optd standard postage.

930	($1.30) Type 190	65	40
931	($1.30) Bushman poison	65	40

Nos. 930/1 are inscribed "standard postage" and were initially sold for $1.30.

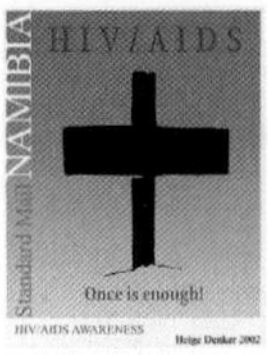

235 Black Cross

2002. Health Care. AIDS Awareness. Multicoloured.

932	($1.30) Type **235**	45	25
933	$2.45 Blood cell	85	45
934	$2.85 Hand reaching to seated man	90	65
935	$11.50 Three test tubes	4·50	6·00

No. 932 was inscribed "Standard Mail" was initially sold for $1.30.

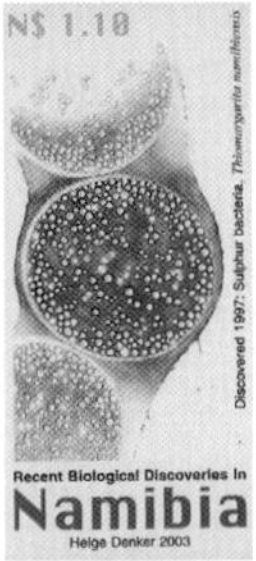

236 Sulphur Bacteria

2003. New Discoveries in Namibia. Multicoloured.

936	$1.10 Type **236**	40	20
937	$2.45 *Whiteheadia etesionamibensis*	80	45
938	$2.85 Cunene Flathead (horiz)	90	65
939	$3.85 Zebra Racer (horiz)	1·25	1·00
940	$20 Gladiator	6·00	7·50

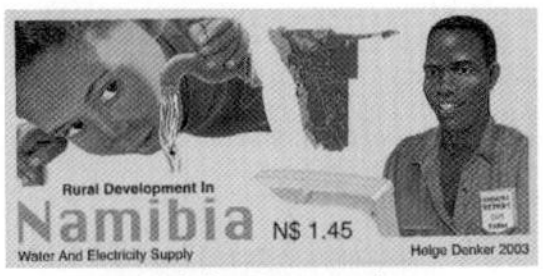

237 Water and electricity supply

2003. Rural Development. Multicoloured.

941	$1.45 Type **237**	50	30
942	($2.85) Conservancy formation and land use diversification	70	50
943	$4.40 Education and health services	1·75	1·40
944	($11.50) Communication and road infrastructure	4·50	5·50

Nos. 942 and 944 were inscribed "Postcard Rate" (942) "Registered Mail" (944) were initially sold at $2.75 and $11.50 respectively.

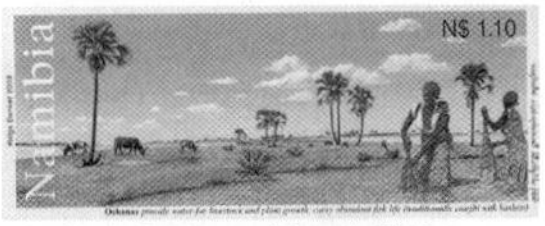

238 Cattle Grazing and People Fishing at an Oshana

2003. Cuvelai Drainage System. Multicoloured.

945	$1.10 Type **238**	50	25
946	$2.85 Omadhiya Lakes	1·40	1·00
947	($3.85) Aerial view of Oshanas	2·00	2·50

No. 947 was inscribed "Non Standard Mail" and initially sold for $3.85.

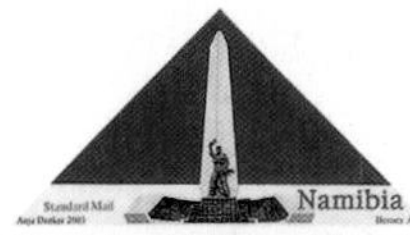

239 Statue of Soldier and Obelisk

2003. National Monuments, Heroes Acre, Windhoek. Multicoloured.

948	($1.45) Type **239**	75	75
949	($2.75) Statue of woman	1·40	1·50
950	($3.85) Stone monument	1·75	2·25

No. 948 was inscribed "Standard Mail" and sold for $1.45. No. 949 was inscribed "Postcard Rate" and sold for $2.75. No. 950 was inscribed "Non Standard Mail" and sold for $3.85.

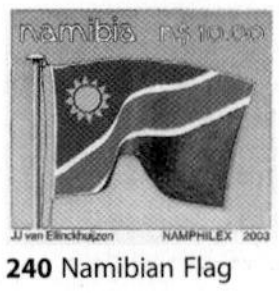

240 Namibian Flag

2003. 25th Anniv of the Windhoek Philatelic Society. Sheet 67×57 mm.

MS951	$10 multicoloured	6·00	7·00

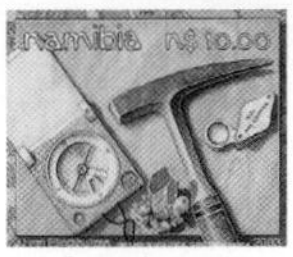

241 Surveying Equipment

2003. Centenary of Geological Survey. Sheet 67×57 mm.

MS952	$10 multicoloured	6·50	7·00

2003. Winning Stamp of the Eighth Stamp World Cup. Sheet 140×80 mm. Multicoloured.

MS953	$3.15 As No. 924	3·00	3·50

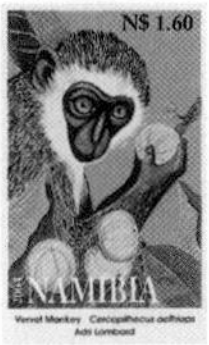

242 Vervet Monkey

2004. Vervet Monkeys. Multicoloured.

954	$1.60 Type **242**	60	30
955	$3.15 Two monkeys in tree	1·10	90
956	$3.40 Adult monkey with offspring	1·25	90
957	($14.25) Monkey chewing twig	5·00	6·50
MS958	80×60 mm. $4.85 As No. 957	2·50	2·75

No. 957 was inscribed "Inland Registered Mail Paid" and was initially sold for $14.25.

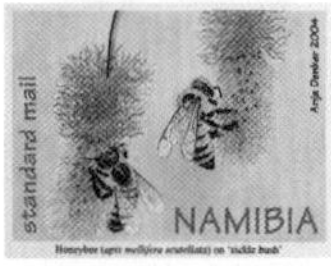

243 Honey Bees on Sickle Bush

2004. Honey Bees. Multicoloured.

959	($1.60) Type **243**	60	30
960	($2.70) Bee on daisy	90	75
961	($3.05) Bee on aloe	95	80
962	($3.15) Bee on cats claw	1·00	85
963	($14.25) Bees on edging senecio	4·50	6·00
MS964	75×55 mm. $4.85 Bee on pretty lady (flower)	2·50	2·75

Nos. 959, 961 and 963 were each inscribed "standard mail" (959), "postcard rate" (961) "inland registered mail paid" (963) and were initially sold for $1.60, $3.05 and $14.25 respectively.

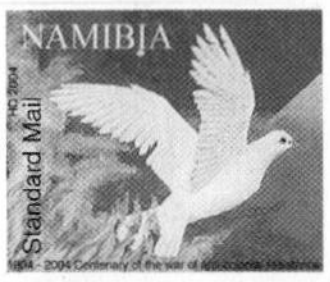

244 Dove

2004. Centenary of the War of Anti-Colonial Resistance.

965	($1.60) Type **244**	1·00	60
MS966	105×70 mm. $5 As No. 965	2·25	2·75

No. 965 was inscribed "Standard Mail" and sold for $1.60 initially.

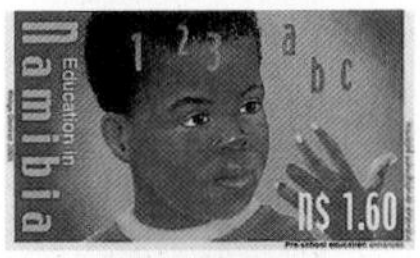

245 Boy and Pre-school Lessons

2004. Education. Multicoloured.

967	Type **245**	60	30
968	$2.75 Teacher and primary and secondary school lessons	90	75
969	$4.40 Teacher and vocational lessons	1·25	1·25
970	($12.65) Teacher and life skill lessons	4·00	5·50

No. 970 was inscribed "Registered Mail" and sold for $12.65.

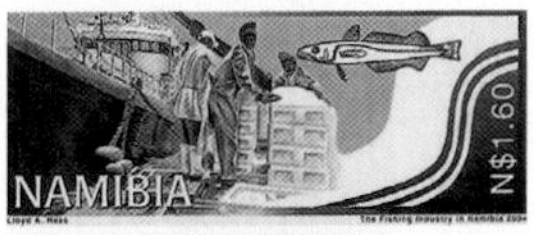

246 Loading Fish on Dockside

2004. Fishing Industry. Multicoloured.

971	$1.60 Type **246**	1·00	35
972	$2.75 Ship at dockside	1·60	90
973	$4.85 Preparing fish	2·50	3·25

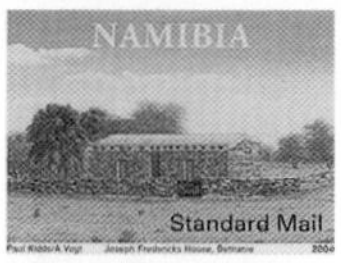

247 Joseph Fredericks House

2004. Historical Buildings of Bethanie. Multicoloured.

974	($1.60) Type **247**	60	30
975	($3.05) Schmelen House	90	75
976	($4.40) Rhenish Mission Church	1·10	1·10
977	($12.65) Stone Church	4·00	5·50

No. 974 was inscribed "Standard Mail" and sold for $1.60. No. 975 was inscribed "Postcard Rate" and sold for $3.05. No. 976 was inscribed "Non Standard Mail" and sold for $4.40. No 977 was inscribed "Registered Mail" and sold for $12.65.

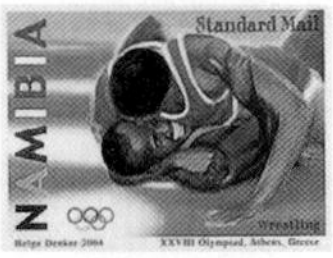

248 Wrestling

2004. Olympic Games, Athens. Multicoloured.

978	($1.60) Type **248**	60	30
979	$2.90 Boxing (vert)	1·10	90
980	$3.40 Shooting	1·40	1·40
981	$3.70 Mountain biking (vert)	1·50	1·75

No. 978 was inscribed "Standard Mail" and sold for $1.60.

No. 981 was also issued incorrectly inscribed "XVIII Olympiad".

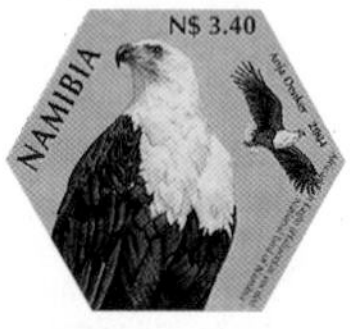

248a African Fish Eagle (Namibia)

2004. 1st Joint Issue of Southern Africa Postal Operators Association Members. Sheet 170×95 mm containing T 248a and similar hexagonal designs showing national birds of Association members. Multicoloured.

MS982	$3.40 Type **248a**; $3.40 Two African fish eagles perched (Zimbabwe); $3.40 Peregrine falcon (Angola); $3.40 Cattle egret (Botswana); $3.40 Purple-crested turaco ("Lourie") (Swaziland); $3.40 Stanley ("Blue") Crane (South Africa); $3.40 Bar-tailed trogon (Malawi) (inscribed "apaloderma vittatum"); $3.40 Two African fish eagles in flight (Zambia)	13·00	14·00

The stamp depicting the Bar-tailed trogon is not inscribed with the country of which the bird is a national symbol.

Miniature sheets of similar designs were also issued by Zimbabwe, Angola, Botswana, Swaziland, South Africa, Malawi and Zambia.

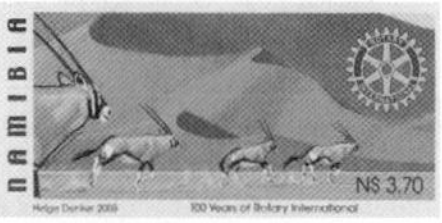

249 Gemsbok

2005. Centenary of Rotary International.

983	**249**	$3.70 multicoloured	2·00	2·00

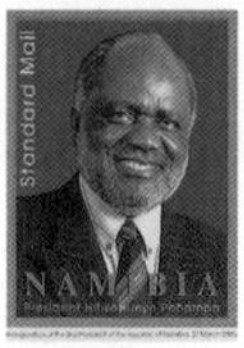

250 President Hifikepunye Pohamba

2005. Inauguration of Pres. Hifikepunye Pohamba.

984	**250**	($1.70) multicoloured	1·00	45

No. 984 was inscribed "Standard mail" and initially sold for $1.70.

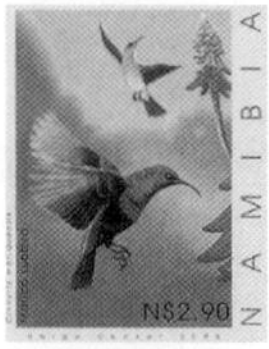

251 Mariqua ("Marico") Sunbird

2005. Sunbirds. Multicoloured.

985	$2.90 Type **251**	1·25	70
986	$3.40 Dusky sunbird	1·40	80
987	($4.80) White-breasted ("bellied") sunbird	1·60	1·50
988	($15.40) Scarlet-chested sunbird	5·50	6·50
MS989	100×70 mm. $10 Amethyst sunbird	3·75	4·00

No. 987 was inscribed "Non Standard Mail" and No. 988 "Registered Inland Postage Paid" and sold for $4.80 and $15.40 respectively.

2005. Nos. 750/1, 754, 757/8, 762 and 764/6 surch.

990	(–) on 10c. Bushman poison flower (surch **Standard Mail 10c.**)	£140	50·00
991	(–) on 20c. Camel's foot (flower) (surch **Standard Mail 20c.**)	60	30
993	(–) on 50c. Laughing dove (surch **Standard Mail 50c.**)	75	30
994	(–) on 90c. Yellow-billed hornbill (surch **Standard Mail 90c.**)	75	30
995	(–) on $1 Lilac-breasted roller (surch **Standard Mail 90c.**)	75	30
996	$2.90 on 20c. Camel's foot (surch **$2.90 on 20c.**)	30·00	6·00
997	$2.90 on 20c. Camel's foot (surch **$2.90 on 20c.**)	2·50	75
998	$2.90 on 90c. Yellow-billed hornbill (surch **$2.90 on 90c.**)	2·50	1·00
999	(–) on $1.50 Elephant as T **253** (surch in two lines **Standard Mail 90c.**)	1·75	90
1000	(–) on $4 Buffalo (surch **Standard Mail 50c.**)	1·50	1·25
1001	$5.20 on 20c. Camel's foot (surch **$2.90 on 20c.**)	2·50	1·50
1002	$5.20 on 90c. Yellow-billed hornbill (surch **$2.90 on 20c.**)	2·75	1·50
1003	(–) on $4 Buffalo (surch **Registered Standard Mail**)	3·25	2·50
1004	(–) on $10 Cheetah (surch **Registered Standard Mail**)	4·50	4·00
1005	$25 on $5 Black rhinoceros (surch **$2.90 on 20c.**)	9·50	5·00
1006	$50 on $10 Cheetah (surch **$50 on $10**)	14·00	7·00

Nos. 990/5 are inscribed "Standard Mail" and were originally sold for $1.70. Nos. 999/1000 are inscribed "Non Standard Mail" and was originally sold for $4.80. No. 1003 is inscribed "Registered Standard Mail" and was originally sold for $15.40. No. 1004 is inscribed "Registered Non Standard Mail" and was originally sold for $18.50.

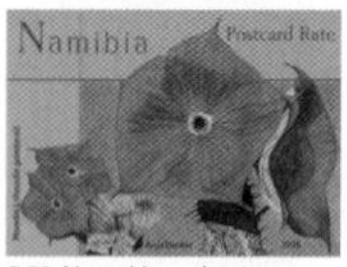

261 Nara (*Acanthosicyos horridus*)

2005. Plants with Medicinal Value. Multicoloured.

1013	(–) Type **261**	65	30
1014	$2.90 Devil's claw	1·10	80
1015	(–) *Hoodia gordonii*	1·25	85
1016	(–) *Tsamma*	1·75	2·25

No. 1013 is inscribed "Standard Mail", 1015 "Postcard Rate" and 1016 "Non Standard Mail" and they were originally sold for $1.70, $3.10 and $4.80 respectively.

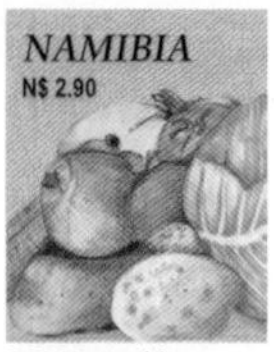

262 Vegetables

2005. Crop Production in Namibia. Multicoloured.

1017	$2.90 Type **262**	1·10	60
1018	$3.40 Pearl millet	1·25	70
1019	(–) Maize	5·00	6·00

No. 1019 is inscribed "Registered Mail" and was originally sold for $13.70.

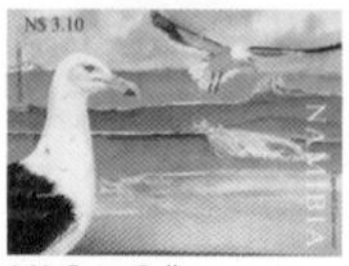

263 Cape Gull

2006. Seagulls of Namibia. Multicoloured.

1020	$3.10 Type **263**	1·40	65
1021	$4 Hartlaub's gull	1·50	1·00
1022	$5.50 Sabine's gull	1·75	1·40
1023	(–) Grey-headed gull	5·50	6·50

No. 1023 is inscribed "Inland Registered Mail Paid" and was originally sold for $16.20.

2006. 933, 960 and 972 surch.

1024	$3.10 on $2.45 Blood cell	1·75	1·00
1025	$3.10 on $2.70 Bee on daisy	1·75	1·00
1026	$3.10 on $2.75 Ship at dockside	1·75	1·00

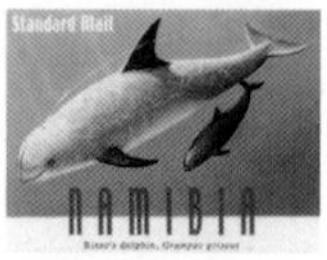

267 Risso's Dolphin

2006. Dolphins. Multicoloured.

1027	($1.80) Type **267**	65	20
1028	$3.10 Southern right-whale dolphin	1·25	65
1029	$3.70 Benguela dolphin	1·40	1·25
1030	$4 Common dolphin	1·50	1·60
1031	$5.50 Bottlenose dolphin	2·00	2·50

No. 1027 is inscribed "Standard Mail" and was originally sold for $1.80.

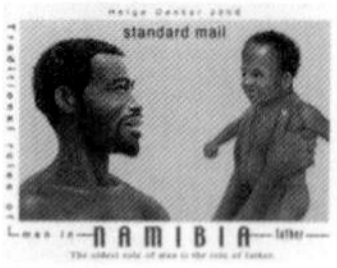

268 Father with Young Child

2006. Traditional Role of Men in Namibia. Multicoloured.

1032	($1.80) Type **268**	50	50
1033	($1.80) Musicians	50	50
1034	($1.80) Wood carver	50	50
1035	($1.80) Shaman and rock painting	50	50
1036	($1.80) Planter with ox-drawn plough	50	50
1037	($1.80) Hunter with bow and arrow	50	50
1038	($1.80) Leader speaking	50	50
1039	($1.80) Blacksmith	50	50
1040	($1.80) Warrior guarding houses ("protector")	50	50
1041	($1.80) Pastoralist and cattle	50	50
1042	($1.80) Trader	50	50
1043	($1.80) Storyteller	50	50

Nos. 1032/43 are all inscribed "standard mail" and were originally sold for $1.80 each.

2006. Nos. 758 and 760 surch.

1044	($3.30) on $1 Lilac-breasted roller	2·50	1·25
1045	($3.30) on $1.20 Giraffe	2·50	1·25

Nos. 1044/5 are surch "Postcard Rate" and were sold for $3.30 each.

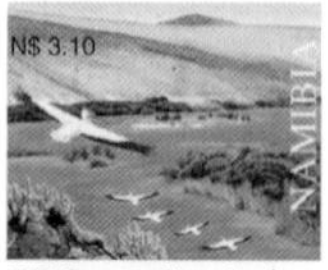

270 Orange River in the Southern Namib

2006. Perennial Rivers of Namibia. Multicoloured.

1046	$3.10 Type **270**	1·50	60
1047	$5.50 Kunene River, northern Namib (24×58 mm)	2·00	1·50
1048	($19.90) Zambezi River and African fish eagle (90×25 mm)	6·50	8·00

No. 1048 is inscribed "Registered Non Standard Mail" and sold for $19.90 each.

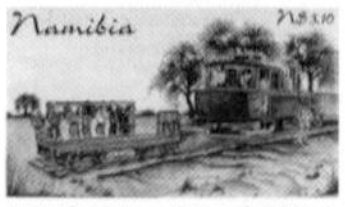

271 Construction of OMEG Railway Line

2006. Centenary of OMEG Railway Line. Multicoloured.

1049	$3.10 Type **271**	1·50	60
1050	$3.70 Henschel Class NG15 locomotive No. 41	1·75	90
1051	$5.50 Narrow gauge Class Jung tank locomotive No. 9 pulling iron ore train	2·50	3·25

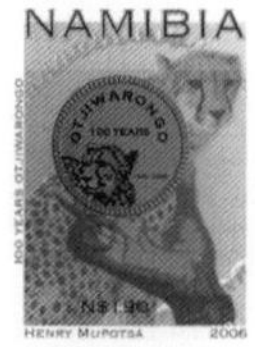

272 Centenary Emblem and Cheetah

2006. Centenary of Otjiwarongo.

1052	**272**	$1.90 multicoloured	1·00	1·00

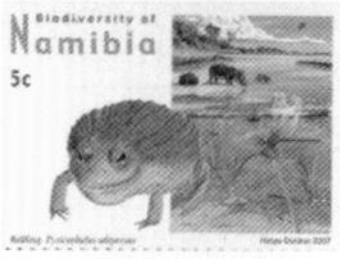

273 Bullfrog (*Pyxicephalus adspersus*) and River

2007. Biodiversity. Multicoloured.

1053	5c. Type **273**	10	10
1054	10c. Mesemb (*Namibia cinerea*) and desert landscape	10	10
1055	30c. Solifuge (*Ceroma inerme*) and seashore with shell, plover and seal	10	10
1056	40c. Jewel beetle (*Julodis egho*) and antelopes in desert	15	10
1057	60c. Compass jellyfish (*Chrysaora hysoscella*), turtle and seabirds	20	10
1058	($1.90) Web-footed gecko (*Palmatogecko rangei*) and sand dunes	60	20
1059	$2 Otjikoto tilapia (*Tilapia guinasana*)	70	30
1059a	$4.10 Thimble grass (*Fingerhuthia africana*)	1·00	45
1059b	$4.60 Bronze whaler shark (*Carchahinus brachyurus*)	1·10	50
1059c	$5.30 Deep sea red crab (*Chaceon maritae*)	1·50	1·10
1060	($6) Milkbush (*Euphorbia damarana*) and zebras in desert	1·75	70
1061	$6 African Hawk-eagle with prey and landscape with trees	1·75	70
1062	$10 Black-faced impala and sandy river-bed	2·50	1·50
1062a	$18.20 False ink cap (*Podxis Pistillaris*)	1·80	1·90
1063	$25 Lichens (*Santessonia* and *Xanthoreasp.*) on seashore rocks	5·50	4·50
1064	$50 Baobab, elephant and antelopes in bushveldt	9·00	9·00

No. 1058 is inscr "Standard Mail" and sold for $1.90.

No. 1061 is inscr "Non-Standard Mail" and sold for $6.

No. 1062a was inscr "Registered Mail" and originally sold for $18.20.

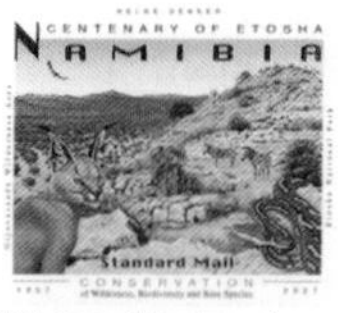

274 Caracal, Snake and Zebras, Otjovasandu Wilderness Area ("Conservation")

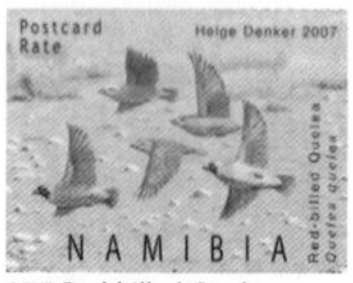

275 Red-billed Quelea

2007. Centenary of Etosha National Park. Multicoloured.

(a) As T 274.

1065	($1.90) Type **274**	1·00	35
1066	$3.40 Lions, elephants and gemsbok, Okaukuejo Waterhole and Resort ("Tourism")	1·75	90
1067	($17.20) Researcher and elephant herd ("Anthrax Research")	7·00	8·00

(b) As T 275. Multicoloured.

MS1068	172×112 mm. ($2.25)×10 Gabar goshawk (29×29 mm); *Acacia tortillis* (umbrella thorn) (49×29 mm); Type **275**; Burchell's zebra; Elephant; Blue Wildebeest; *Salvadora persica* (mustard tree); *Anax tristis* (black emperor dragonfly) (39×40 mm); Springbok (39×40 mm); *Agama aculeata* (ground agama) (39×40 mm)	9·50	11·00

No. 1065 is inscr "Standard Mail" and sold for $1.90.

No. 1067 is inscr "Inland Registered Mail Paid" and sold for $17.20.

The stamps within **MS**1068 are all inscr "Postcard Rate", and the miniature sheet sold for $22.50.

The stamps and margins of **MS**1068 form a composite design showing wildlife at the Salvadora Waterhole.

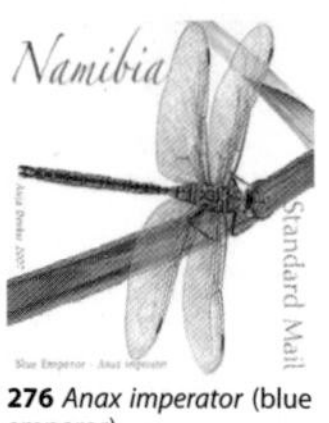

276 *Anax imperator* (blue emperor)

2007. Dragonflies of Namibia. Multicoloured.

1069	($1.90) Type **276**	75	20
1070	$3.90 *Trithemis kirbyi ardens* (rock dropwing)	1·50	70
1071	$4.40 *Trithemis arteriosa* (red-veined dropwing)	1·60	2·00
1072	($6) *Trithemis stictica* (jaunty dropwing)	2·00	2·25
MS1073	75×54 mm. $6 *Urothemis edwardsii* (blue basker)	2·00	2·50

No. 1069 is inscr "Standard Mail" and sold for $1.90.
No. 1072 is inscr "Non Standard Mail Paid" and sold for $6.

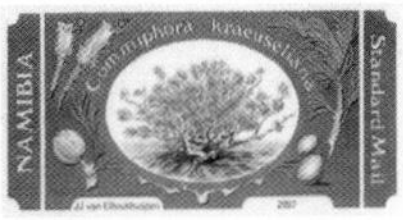

277 *Commiphora kraeuseliana*

2007. Commiphora (corkwood) Trees of Namibia. Multicoloured.

1074	($1.90) Type **277**	70	20
1075	$3.40 *Commiphora wildii*	1·25	60
1076	$3.90 *Commiphora glaucescens*	1·50	90
1077	($6) *Commiphora dinteri*	2·50	3·00

No. 1074 is inscr 'Standard Mail' and sold for $1.90.
No. 1077 is inscr 'Non-standard Mail' and sold for $6.

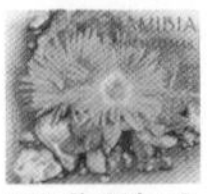
278 *Cheiridopsis caroli-schmidtii*

2007. Indigenous Flowers of Namibia. Multicoloured.

1078	($1.90) Type **278**	70	20
1079	($6) *Namibia ponderosa*	2·25	2·25
1080	($17.20) *Fenestraria rhopalophylla*	6·50	7·50

No. 1078 is inscr 'STANDARD MAIL' and sold for $1.90. No. 1079 is inscr 'NON-STANDARD MAIL' and sold for $6. No. 1080 is inscr 'INLAND REGISTERED MAIL PAID' and sold for $17.20.

2007. Nos. 757, 760, 762 and 764 surch.

1081	($2) on 90c. Yellow-billed hornbill	1·25	50
1082	($2) on $1.20 Giraffe	1·25	50
1083	($2) on $1.50 Elephant	1·25	50
1084	($2) on $4 Buffalo	1·25	50
1085	$3.70 on $1.20 Giraffe	1·75	1·00
1086	$4.20 on $1.20 Giraffe	2·25	1·75
1087	$4.85 on $1.20 Giraffe	2·25	1·75
1088	($6.50) on $1.20 Giraffe	2·75	2·50
1089	($16.45) on $1.20 Giraffe	7·00	8·00

Nos. 1081/4 are surch 'Standard Mail' and sold for $2, No. 1088 is surch 'Non Standard Mail' and sold for $6.50 and No. 1089 is surch 'Registered Mail' and sold for $16.45.

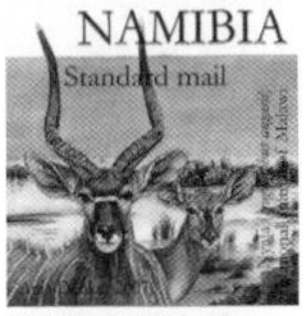

285 Nyala (Malawi)

2007. 2nd Joint Issue of Southern Africa Postal Operators Association Members. Sheet 135×170 mm containing T 285 and similar square designs showing national mammals of Association members. Multicoloured.

MS1090	($2) Type **285**; ($2) Nyala (Zimbabwe); ($2) Burchell's zebra (Botswana); ($2) Oryx (Namibia); ($2) Buffalo (Zambia)	3·00	3·25

The stamps within **MS**1090 are all inscr 'Standard mail'. Miniature sheets of similar designs were also issued by Botswana, Malawi, Zambia and Zimbabwe. Botswana and Zambia also issued sheet stamps.

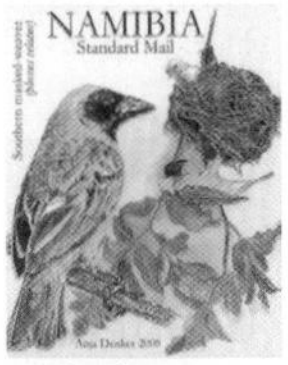

286 Southern Masked-weaver (*Ploceus velatus*)

2008. Weaver Birds of Namibia. Multicoloured.

1091	($2) Type **286**	60	20
1092	$3.70 Red-headed weaver (*Anaplectes rubriceps*)	1·00	35
1093	($3.90) White-browed sparrow-weaver (*Plocepasser mahali*)	1·00	35
1094	$4.20 Sociable weaver (*Philetarius socius*)	1·25	1·00
1095	($18.45) Thick-billed weaver (*Amblyospiza albifrons*)	6·00	7·50

No. 1091 is inscr 'Standard Mail' and sold for $2, No. 1093 is inscr 'Postcard Rate' and sold for $3.90 and No. 1095 is inscr 'Inland Registered Mail Paid' and sold for $18.45.

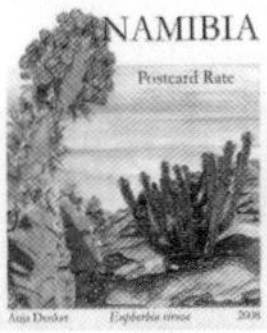

287 *Euphorbia virosa*

2008. Euphorbias of Namibia. Multicoloured.

1096	($3.90) Type **287**	1·00	25
1097	$6.45 *Euphorbia dregeana*	1·75	1·75
1098	($22.95) *Euphorbia damarana*	5·00	6·50

No. 1096 is inscr 'Postcard Rate' and sold for $3.90 and No. 1098 is inscr 'Registered Non Standard Mail' and sold for $22.95.

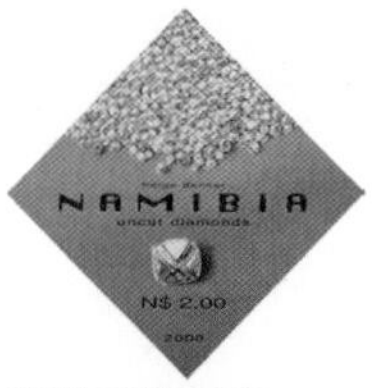

288 Uncut Diamonds

2008. Centenary of the Discovery of Diamonds in Namibia. Sheet 128×91 mm containing T 288 and similar diamond-shaped designs. Multicoloured.

MS1099	Type **288**; Land mining; Marine mining; Diamond jewellery	3·00	3·00

No. **MS**1099 is an irregular diamond-shape with the top point missing. The stamps are printed in a block of four within the sheet, with the land mining and marine mining designs oriented with the top of the stamp facing left (land) or right (marine) within the block.

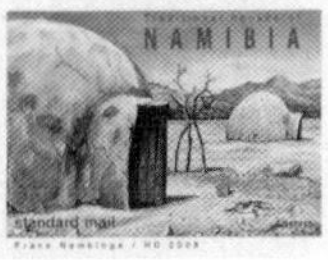

289 Herero

2008. Traditional Houses of Namibia. Multicoloured.

1100	($2) Type **289**	55	55
1101	($2) Kavango	55	55
1102	($2) Owambo	55	55
1103	($2) Nama	55	55
1104	($2) Caprivi	55	55
1105	($2) San	55	55

Nos. 1100/5 are all inscr 'standard mail' and sold for $2 each.

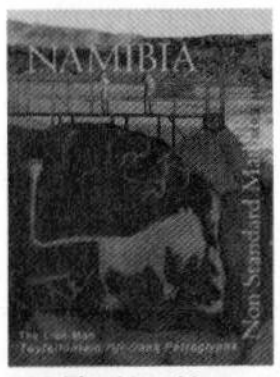

290 The Lion-Man

2008. Petroglyphs at Twyfelfontein World Heritage Site. Multicoloured.

1106	($6.50) Type **290**	2·00	2·00
1107	($6.50) The Giraffe and the Dancing Kudu	2·00	2·00
1108	($6.50) The Elephant	2·00	2·00
MS1109	105×70 mm. (2r.)×3 As Nos. 1106/8	2·00	2·00

Nos. 1106/8 were inscr 'Non Standard Mail' and sold for $6.50.
The stamps within **MS**1109 were inscr 'Standard Mail' and were valid for 2r. each.

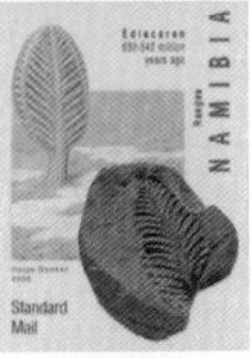

291 Rangea

2008. Ediacaran Fossils. Multicoloured.

1110	($2) Type **291**	55	55
1111	($3.90) Swartpuntia	1·00	30
1112	($18.45) Pteridinium	5·25	5·50
1113	($22.95) Ernietta	6·25	5·75

No. 1110 is inscr 'Standard Mail' and sold for $2, 1111 is inscr 'Postcard Rate' and sold for $3.90, 1112 is inscr 'Registered Non-Standard Mail' and sold for $18.45, and 1113 is inscr 'Registered Inland Mail Paid' and sold for $22.95.

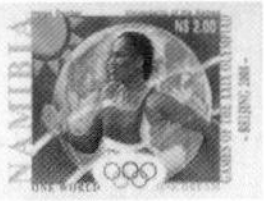

292 Athlete and Globe

2008. Olympic Games, Beijing. Multicoloured.

1114	$2 Type **292**	55	55
1115	$3.70 Athlete with fist raised and bronze medal	1·00	30
1116	$3.90 Athlete with arms raised in triumph and gold medal	1·00	30
1117	$4.20 Athlete and silver medal	1·60	2·00

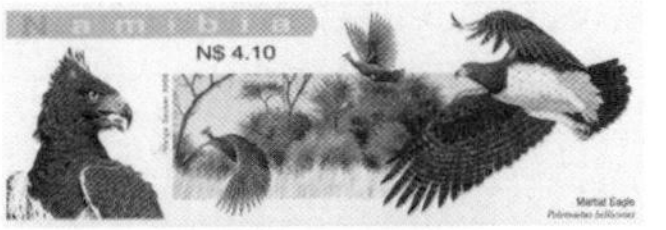

293 Martial Eagle (*Polemaetus bellicosus*)

2009. Eagles of Namibia. Multicoloured.

1118	$4.10 Type **293**	1·40	75
1119	($4.30) Bateleur (*Terathopius ecaudatus*)	1·40	85
1120	$4.60 Verreaux's eagle (*Aquila verreauxii*)	1·50	95
1121	($25.40) Tawny eagle (*Aquila rapax*)	6·50	8·00

No. 1119 was inscr 'Postcard Rate' and sold for $4.30.
No. 1121 was inscr 'Registered Non-Standard Mail' and sold for $25.40.

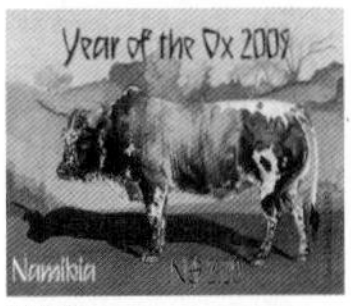

294 Ox

2009. Chinese New Year. Year of the Ox.

1122	**294**	$2.20 multicoloured	1·00	55

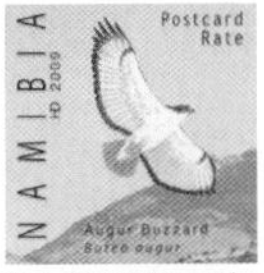

295 Augur Buzzard (*Buteo augur*)

2009. The Brandberg. Sheet 172×112 mm containing T 295 and similar multicoloured designs.

MS1123	(4r.30)×10 Type **295**; Numasfels peak (49×29 mm); Quiver tree (*Aloe dichotoma*) (39×29 mm); CMR beetle (*Mylabrisoculata*) (39×29 mm); Leopard (*Panthera pardus*) (39×29 mm); Kobas tree (*Cyphostemma curiorii*) (39×29 mm); Bokmakiri (*Telophorus zeylonus*) (39×29 mm); Jameson's red rock rabbit (*Pronolagus randensis*) (39×39 mm); Brandberg halfmens (*Euphorbia monteiri* ssp. *brandbergensis*) (39×39 mm); Jordan's girdled lizard (*Cordylus jordani*) (39×39 mm)	3·75	4·25

The stamps within **MS**1123 are all inscr 'Postcard Rate', and the miniature sheet sold for $43.
The stamps and margins of **MS**1123 form a composite design showing wildlife in a view towards Wasserfallfläche and Numasfels.

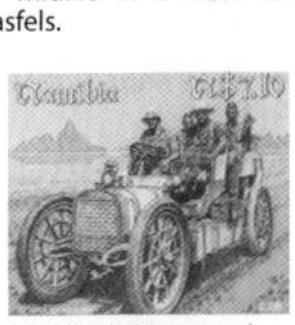

296 Paul Graetz and his Team in their Special Vehicle, 1909

2009. Centenary of First Africa Crossing (from Dar es Salaam to Swakopmund) by Car. Sheet 67×56 mm.

MS1124	Type **296**; multicoloured	1·75	2·00

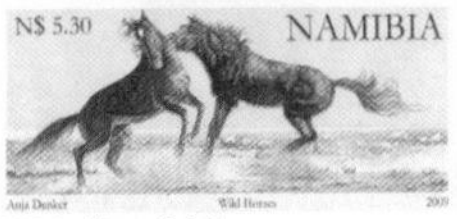

297 Stallions fighting

2009. Wild Horses of Namibia. Multicoloured.

1124a	(4r.60)	1·00	50
1125	$5.30 Type **297**	1·25	50
1126	$8 Bay horses in a rocky landscape	1·75	1·00
1127	($20.40) Chestnut stallion and mares with foal grazing	5·00	6·00

No. 1124a was inscr 'Postcard Rate' and originally sold for 4r.60.
No. 1127 was inscr 'Inland Registered Mail Paid' and initially sold for $20.40. The rate increased to $22.20 from 1 October 2009.

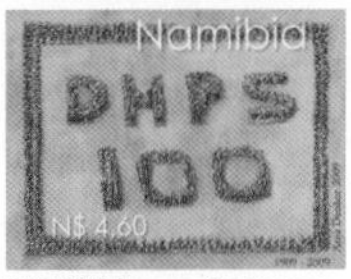

298 Children as Centenary Emblem

2009. Centenary of DHPS (Deutsche Höhere Privatschule), Windhoek. Sheet 75×55 mm.

MS1128	Type **298**; multicoloured	2·00	2·25

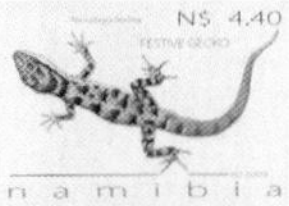

299 Festive Gecko (*Narudasia festiva*)

2009. Geckos. Multicoloured.

1129	$4.40 Type **299**	1·10	1·10
1130	$5 Koch's barking gecko (*Ptenopus kochi*)	1·25	1·25
1131	$6 Giant ground gecko (*Chondrodactylus angulifer namibensis*)	1·50	1·50
1132	$7.70 Velvety thick-toed gecko (*Pachydactylus bicolor*)	1·90	1·90
1133	($20.40) Bradfield's namib day gecko (*Rhoptropus bradfieldi*)	5·25	5·25

No. 1133 was inscr 'Registered Mail' and originally sold for $20.40.

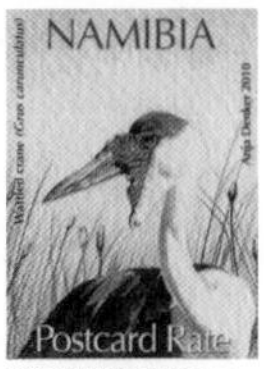

300 Wattled Crane (*Grus carunculatus*)

2010. Endangered Species. Multicoloured.

1134	($4.60) Type **300**	2·50	2·50
1135	($4.60) *Gazania thermalis*	2·50	2·50
1136	($4.60) Leatherback turtle (*Dermochelys coriacea*) and jellyfish	2·50	2·50
1137	($4.60) Giant quiver tree (*Aloe pillansii*)	2·50	2·50
1138	($4.60) Cape vulture (*Gyps coprotheres*)	2·50	2·50
1139	($4.60) White Namib toktokkie (*Cauricara eburnea*)	2·50	2·50
1140	($4.60) Two cheetahs (*Acinonyx jubatus*)	2·50	2·50
1141	($4.60) Hook-lipped rhinoceros (*Diceros bicornis*)	2·50	2·50
1142	($4.60) Wild dog (*Lycaon pictus*)	2·50	2·50
1143	($4.60) Nama-padloper tortoise (*Homopus solus*)	2·50	2·50

Nos. 1134/43 were inscr 'Postcard Rate' and were initially valid for $4.60.

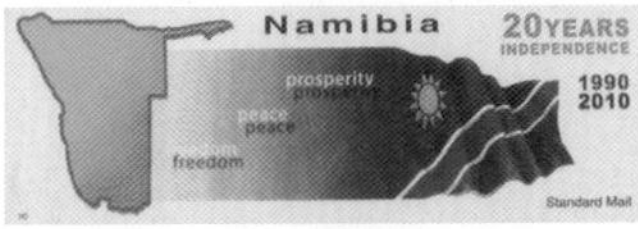

301 Map and Flag of Namiibia

2010. 20th Anniv of Independence

1144	**301**	($2.50) multicoloured	1·00	85

No. 1144 was inscr 'Standard Mail' and originally sold for $2.50.

2010. Third Joint Issue of Southern Africa Postal Operators Association Members. World Cup Football Championship, South Africa. Multicoloured.

MS1145	(4r.60)×9 Namibia; South Africa; Zimbabwe; Malawi; Swaziland; Botswana, Mauritius; Lesotho; Zambia	14·00	14·00

The stamps within **MS**1145 were each inscr 'postcard rate' and were originally valid for $4.60 each.
Similar designs were issued by Botswana, Lesotho, Malawi, Mauritius, South Africa, Swaziland, Zambia and Zimbabwe.

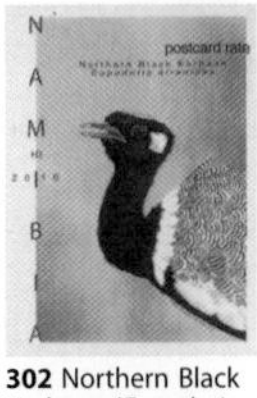

302 Northern Black Korhaan (*Eupodotis afraoides*)

2010. Bustards and Korhaans. Multicoloured.

1146	($4.60) Type **302**	2·50	2·50
1147	($4.60) Red-crested korhaan (*Eupodotis ruficrista*)	2·50	2·50

1148	($4.60) Black-bellied bustard (*Eupodotis melanogaster*)	2·50	2·50
1149	($4.60) Rüppell's korhaan (*Eupodotis rueppellii*)	2·50	2·50
1150	($4.60) Ludwig's bustard (*Neotis ludwigii*)	2·50	2·50
1151	($4.60) Kori bustard (*Ardeotis kori*)	2·50	2·50

Nos. 1146/51 were all inscr 'postcard rate' and originally sold for $4.60 each.

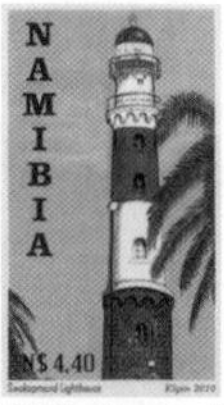

303 Swakopmund Lighthouse

2010. Lighthouses. Multicoloured.

1152	$4.40 Type **303**	2·00	1·25
1153	($9.50) Diaz Point Lighthouse, Lüderitzbucht	4·00	4·00
1154	($18.20) Pelican Point Lighthouse, Walvis Bay	7·00	8·00

No. 1153 was inscr 'Non Standard Mail' and originally sold for $9.50.

No. 1154 was inscr 'Registered Mail' and originally sold for $18.20.

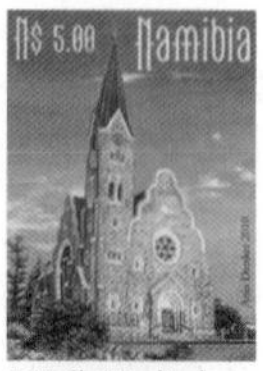

304 Christuskirche, Windhoek

2010. Centenary of the Christuskirche, Windhoek. Sheet 76×56 mm

MS1155	**304** $5 multicoloured	2·00	2·50

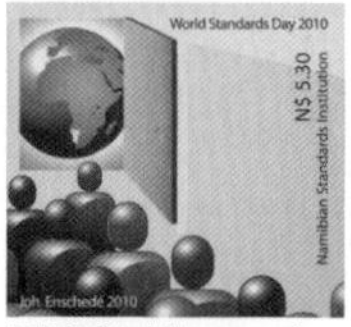

305 Stylized Figures and Globe

2010. World Standards Day. Sheet 75×55 mm

MS1156	**305** $5.30 multicoloured	2·00	2·50

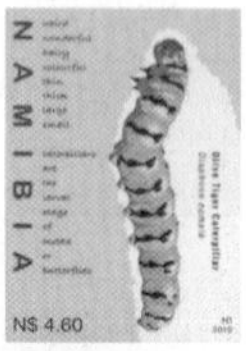

306 Olive Tiger Caterpillar (*Diaphone eumela*)

2010. Caterpillars. Multicoloured.

1157	$4.60 Type **306**	2·00	1·75
1158	$5.30 African armyworms (*Spodoptera exempta*)	2·50	2·50
1159	$6.40 Wild Silk Caterpillar (*Gonometa postica*)	2·75	2·75
1160	($29.40) Mopane caterpillar (*Imbrasia belina*)	10·00	12·00

No. 1160 was inscr 'Registered Non-Standard Mail' and originally sold for $29.40.

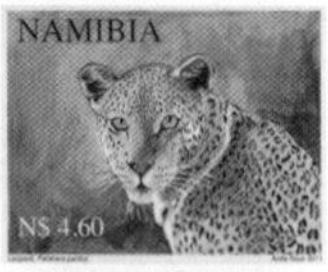

307 Leopard (*Panthera pardus*)

2011. The Big Five (animals). Multicoloured.

1161	$4.60 Type **307**	1·50	1·75
1162	($5) African elephant (*Loxodonta africana*) (vert)	2·25	2·25
1163	$5.30 Black rhino (*Diceros bicornis*)	2·25	2·25
1164	$6.40 African buffalo (*Syncerus caffer*)	2·25	2·50
1165	($8.50) Lion (*Panthera leo*) (vert)	2·50	2·75

No. 1162 was inscr 'Postcard Rate' and originally sold for $5.

No. 1165 was inscr 'Non Standard Mail' and originally sold for $8.50.

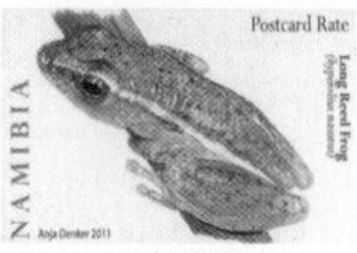

308 Long Reed Frog (*Hyperolius nasutus*)

2011. Frogs. Multicoloured.

MS1166	($5)×4 Type **308**; Bubbling kassina (*Kassina senegalensis*); Tandy's sand frog (*Tomopterna tandyi*); Angolan reed frog (*Hyperolius parallelus*)	7·75	7·75

The stamps within **MS**1166 were all inscr 'Postcard Rate' and were originally valid for $5.

No. **MS**1166 was cut around in the shape of a giant bullfrog.

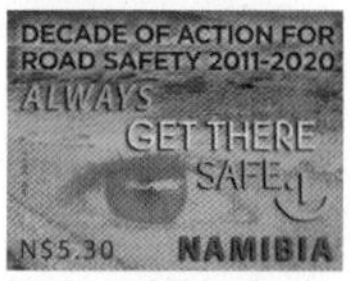

309 Eye and Desert Road

2011. Decade of Action for Road Safety 20112020. Sheet 75×55 mm

MS1167	**309** $5.30 multicoloured	10·75	10·75

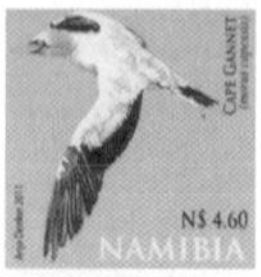

310 Cape Gannet (*Morus capensis*)

2011. Endangered Marine Life. Multicoloured.

MS1168	$4.60×8 Type **310**; Atlantic yellow-nosed albatross (*Thalassarche chlororhynchos*) (50×30 mm); African penguin (*Spheniscus demersus*) (40×30 mm); Southern right whale (*Eubalaena australis*) (40×30 mm); Bank cormorant (*Phalacrocorax neglectus*) (40×30 mm); Westcoast steenbras (fish) (*Lithognathus aureti*) (40×30 mm); Split-fan kelp (*Laminaria pallida*) (40×40 mm); Cape rock lobster (*Jasus lalandii*) (40×40 mm)	12·00	12·00

The stamps and margins of **MS**1168 form a composite design showing rocks and ocean.

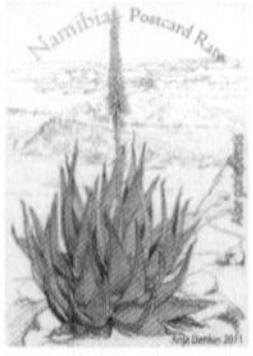
311 *Aloe gariepensis*

2011. Aloes. Multicoloured.

1169	($5) Type **311**	2·00	1·90
1170	($8.50) *Aloe variegata*	3·00	2·75
1171	($20.90) *Aloe striata* sp. *Karasbergensis*	6·00	7·00

No. 1169 was inscr 'Postcard Rate' and originally sold for $5.

No. 1170 was inscr 'Non Standard Mail' and originally sold for $8.50.

No. 1171 was inscr 'Registered Mail' and originally sold for $20.90.

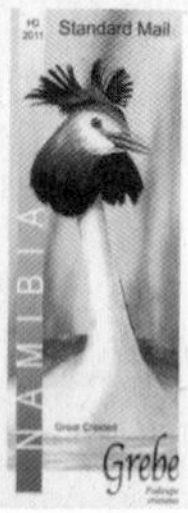

312 Great Crested Grebe (*Podiceps cristatus*)

2011. Grebes of Namibia. Multicoloured.

1172	($2.70) Type **312**	1·00	85
1173	($2.70) Little grebe (*Tachybaptus ruficollis*)	1·00	85
1174	($20.90) Black-necked grebe (*Podiceps nigricollis*) (horiz)	6·00	7·00

Nos. 1172/3 were each inscr 'Standard Mail' and originally sold for $2.70.

No. 1174 was inscr 'Inland Registered Mail' and initially sold for $20.90.

Pt. 1

NANDGAON

A state of central India. Now uses Indian stamps.

12 pies = 1 anna; 16 annas = 1 rupee.

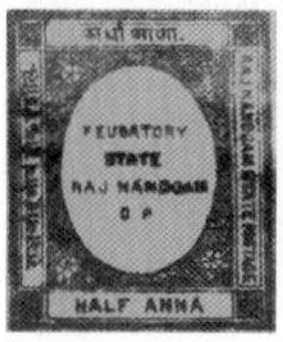

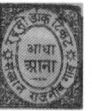

1

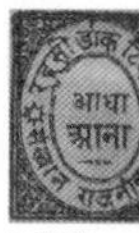
2 (½a.)

1891. Imperf.

1	1	½a. blue	9·00	£200
2	1	2a. pink	32·00	£650

1893. Imperf.

5	2	½a. green	32·00	85·00
6	2	1a. red	75·00	£130
4	2	2a. red	16·00	£120

OFFICIAL STAMPS

1893. Optd M.B.D. in oval.

O1	1	½a. blue	£475	
O4	2	½a. green	7·50	16·00
O5	2	1a. red	15·00	48·00
O6	2	2a. red	11·00	32·00

Pt. 8

NAPLES

A state on the S.W. coast of Central Italy, formerly part of the Kingdom of Sicily, but now part of Italy.

200 tornesi = 100 grano = 1 ducato.

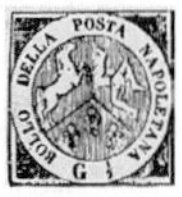
1 Arms under Bourbon Dynasty

1858. The frames differ in each value. Imperf.

8	1	½t. blue	£203000	£13000
1A	1	½g. red	£2250	£375
2	1	1g. red	£600	60·00
3	1	2g. red	£425	20·00
4A	1	5g. red	£3000	80·00
5A	1	10g. red	£7000	£325
6A	1	20g. red	£6000	£1500
7A	1	50g. red	£12000	£3500

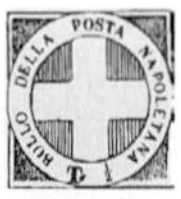
4 Cross of Savoy

1860. Imperf.

9	4	½t. blue	£45000	£4250

Pt. 1

NATAL

On the east coast of S. Africa. Formerly a British Colony, later a province of the Union of S. Africa.

12 pence = 1 shilling; 20 shillings = 1 pound.

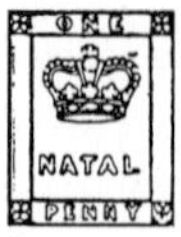

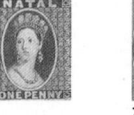

1

1857. Embossed stamps. Various designs.

1	1	1d. blue		£1200
2	1	1d. red		£1900
3	1	1d. buff		£1200
4	-	3d. red		£400
5	-	6d. green		£1100
6	-	9d. blue		£7000
7	-	1s. buff		£5500

The 3d., 6d., 9d. and 1s. are larger. Beware of reprints.

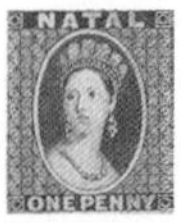

6

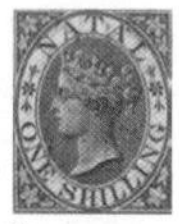

7

1859

19	6	1d. red	£110	27·00
12	6	3d. blue	£150	40·00
13	6	6d. grey	£250	70·00
24	6	6d. violet	75·00	35·00

1867

25	7	1s. green	£250	45·00

1869. Variously optd POSTAGE or Postage.

50	6	1d. red	£130	50·00
82	6	1d. yellow	85·00	85·00
53	6	3d. blue	£200	50·00
83	6	6d. violet	80·00	8·00
84	7	1s. green	£120	7·50

1870. Optd POSTAGE in a curve.

59	1s. green	£130	10·00
108	1s. orange	8·50	1·75

1870. Optd POSTAGE twice, reading up and down.

60	6	1d. red	£100	13·00
61	6	3d. blue	£110	13·00
62	6	6d. violet	£200	38·00

1873. Optd POSTAGE once, reading up.

63	7	1s. brown	£350	27·00

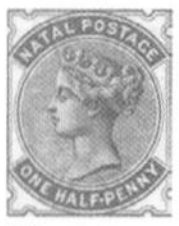

23

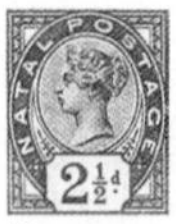

28

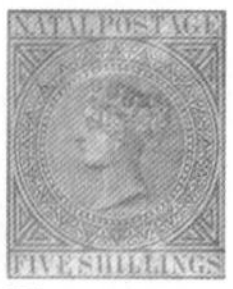

16

1874. Queen Victoria. Various frames.

97a	23	½d. green	4·75	1·25
99	-	1d. red	5·50	25
107	-	2d. olive	5·50	1·40
113	28	2½d. blue	9·50	1·50
100	-	3d. blue	£140	17·00
101	-	3d. grey	8·00	4·50
102	-	4d. brown	12·00	1·75
103	-	6d. lilac	9·00	2·50
73	16	5s. red	£100	38·00

1877. No. 99 surch ½ HALF.

85	16	½d. on 1d. red	40·00	75·00

POSTAGE

Half-penny

(21)

1877. Surch as T 21.

91	6	½d. on 1d. yellow	10·00	21·00
92	6	1d. on 6d. violet	70·00	11·00
93	6	1d. on 6d. red	£130	55·00

1885. Surch in words.

104	½d. on 1d. red (No. 99)	20·00	11·00
105	2d. on 3d. grey (No. 101)	28·00	5·50
109	2½d. on 4d. brown (No. 102)	16·00	15·00

POSTAGE.

Half-Penny

(29)

1895. No. 23 surch with T 29.

114	½d. on 6d. violet	2·50	8·50

1895. No. 99 surch HALF.

125	HALF on 1d. red	3·00	2·25

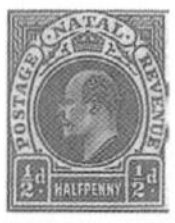

31

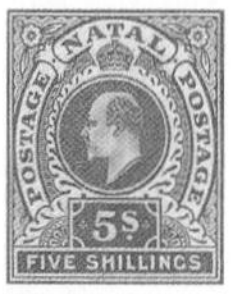

32

1902

127	31	½d. green	5·00	50
147	31	1d. red	9·50	15
129	31	1½d. green and black	4·00	4·75
130	31	2d. red and olive	4·50	40
131	31	2½d. blue	1·75	5·50
132	31	3d. purple and grey	1·25	2·50
152	31	4d. red and brown	2·75	1·25
134	31	5d. black and orange	3·50	3·75
135	31	6d. green and purple	3·50	4·50
136	31	1s. red and blue	4·50	4·75
137	31	2s. green and violet	50·00	9·00
138	31	2s.6d. purple	40·00	12·00
139	31	4s. red and yellow	80·00	80·00
140	32	5s. blue and red	50·00	12·00
141	32	10s. red and purple	£100	35·00

142	**32**	£1 black and blue	£300	70·00
143	**32**	£1.10s. green and violet	£500	£120
162	**32**	£1.10s. orange and purple	£1600	£3000
144	**32**	£5 mauve and black	£4500	£1200
145	**32**	£10 green and orange	£10000	£5000
145b	**32**	£20 red and green	£22000	£14000

1908. As T 31/2 but inscr "POSTAGE POSTAGE".

165	**31**	6d. purple	4·50	3·00
166	**31**	1s. black on green	6·00	3·00
167	**31**	2s. purple and blue on blue	15·00	3·00
168	**31**	2s.6d. black and red on blue	25·00	3·00
169	**32**	5s. green and red on yellow	26·00	40·00
170	**32**	10s. green and red on green	£110	£110
171	**32**	£1 purple and black on red	£375	£325

OFFICIAL STAMPS

1904. Optd OFFICIAL.

O1	**31**	½d. green	3·00	35
O2	**31**	1d. red	10·00	1·00
O3	**31**	2d. red and olive	38·00	19·00
O4	**31**	3d. purple and grey	22·00	4·75
O5	**31**	6d. green and purple	75·00	70·00
O6	**31**	1s. red and blue	£200	£225

Pt. 1

NAURU

An island in the W. Pacific Ocean, formerly a German possession and then administered by Australia under trusteeship. Became a republic on 31 January 1968.

1916. 12 pence = 1 shilling; 20 shillings = 1 pound.
1966. 100 cents = 1 Australian dollar.

1916. Stamps of Gt. Britain (King George V) optd NAURU.

1	**105**	½d. green	2·25	10·00
2	**104**	1d. red	2·00	11·00
4	**106**	2d. orange	2·00	13·00
6	**104**	2½d. blue	2·75	7·00
7	**106**	3d. violet	2·00	5·50
8	**106**	4d. green	2·00	8·50
9	**107**	5d. brown	2·25	10·00
10	**107**	6d. purple	7·50	10·00
11	**108**	9d. black	8·50	23·00
12	**108**	1s. brown	7·00	19·00
15	**105**	1½d. brown	27·00	50·00
20	**109**	2s.6d. brown	70·00	£110
22	**109**	5s. red	£100	£140
23	**109**	10s. blue	£250	£325

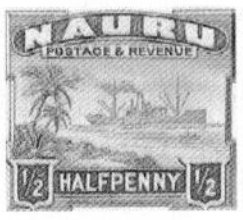

4

1924

26A	**4**	½d. brown	1·75	2·75
27B	**4**	1d. green	2·50	3·00
28B	**4**	1½d. red	1·00	1·50
29B	**4**	2d. orange	3·50	8·00
30B	**4**	2½d. blue	3·25	4·00
31A	**4**	3d. blue	4·00	13·00
32B	**4**	4d. green	4·25	13·00
33B	**4**	5d. brown	9·00	4·00
34B	**4**	6d. violet	9·00	5·00
35A	**4**	9d. olive	9·50	19·00
36B	**4**	1s. red	9·50	2·75
37B	**4**	2s.6d. green	32·00	35·00
38B	**4**	5s. purple	38·00	50·00
39B	**4**	10s. yellow	85·00	£100

1935. Silver Jubilee. Optd HIS MAJESTY'S JUBILEE. 1910-1935.

40	1½d. red	75	80
41	2d. orange	1·50	4·25
42	2½d. blue	1·50	1·50
43	1s. red	6·25	3·50

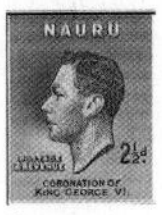

6

1937. Coronation.

44	**6**	1½d. red	45	1·75
45	**6**	2d. orange	45	2·75
46	**6**	2½d. blue	45	1·75
47	**6**	1s. purple	65	2·00

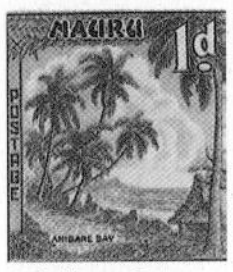

8 Anibare Bay

1954

48a	-	½d. violet	20	80
49a	**8**	1d. green	20	40
50	-	3½d. red	1·75	75
51	-	4d. blue	2·00	1·75
52	-	6d. orange	70	20
53	-	9d. red	60	20
54	-	1s. purple	30	30
55	-	2s.6d. green	2·50	1·00
56	-	5s. mauve	8·00	2·25

DESIGNS—HORIZ: ½d. Nauruan netting fish; 3½d. Loading phosphate from cantilever; 4d. Great frigate bird; 6d. Canoe; 9d. Domaneab (meeting house); 2s.6d. Buada Lagoon. VERT: 1s. Palm trees; 5s. Map of Nauru.

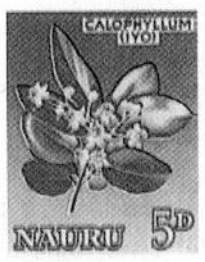

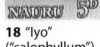

18 "Iyo" ("calophyllum")

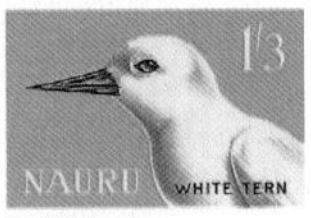

21 White Tern

1963

57		2d. multicoloured	75	2·25
58		3d. multicoloured	40	35
59	**18**	5d. multicoloured	40	75
60	-	8d. black and green	1·75	80
61	-	10d. black	40	30
62	**21**	1s.3d. blue, black and green	1·00	4·75
63	-	2s.3d. blue	2·00	55
64	-	3s.3d. multicoloured	1·00	3·75

DESIGNS—VERT (As Type **21**): 2d. Micronesian pigeon. (26×29 mm): 10d. Capparis (flower). HORIZ (As Type **18**): 3d. Poison nut (flower); 8d. Black lizard; 2s.3d. Coral pinnacles; 3s.3d. Nightingale reed warbler ("Red Warbler").

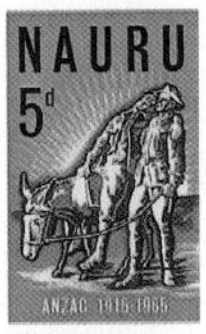

22 "Simpson and his Donkey"

1965. 50th Anniv of Gallipoli Landing.

65	**22**	5d. sepia, black and green	15	10

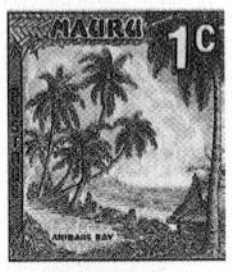

24 Anibare Bay

1966. Decimal Currency. As earlier issues but with values in cents and dollars as in T 24. Some colours changed.

66	**24**	1c. blue	15	10
67	-	2c. purple (as No. 48)	15	50
68	-	3c. green (as No. 50)	30	2·00
69	-	4c. multicoloured (as T **18**)	20	10
70	-	5c. blue (as No. 54)	25	60
71	-	7c. black & brn (as No. 60)	30	10
72	-	8c. green (as No. 61)	20	10
73	-	10c. red (as No. 51)	40	10
74	-	15c. bl, blk and grn (as T **21**)	60	2·75
75	-	25c. brown (as No. 63)	30	1·25
76	-	30c. mult (as No. 58)	45	30
77	-	35c. mult (as No. 64)	75	35
78	-	50c. mult (as No. 57)	1·50	80
79	-	$1 mauve (as No. 56)	75	1·00

The 25c. is as No. 63 but larger, 27½×25 mm.

1968. Nos. 66/79 optd REPUBLIC OF NAURU.

80	**24**	1c. blue	10	30
81	-	2c. purple	10	10
82	-	3c. green	15	10
83	-	4c. multicoloured	15	10
84	-	5c. blue	10	10
85	-	7c. black and brown	25	10
86	-	8c. green	15	10
87	-	10c. red	60	15
88	-	15c. blue, black and green	1·25	2·75
89	-	25c. brown	20	15
90	-	30c. multicoloured	55	15
91	-	35c. multicoloured	1·25	30
92	-	50c. multicoloured	1·25	35
93	-	$1 purple	75	50

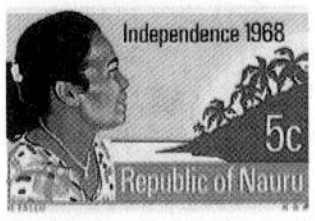

27 "Towards the Sunrise"

1968. Independence.

94	**27**	5c. multicoloured	10	10
95	-	10c. black, green and blue	10	10

DESIGN: 10c. Planting seedling, and map.

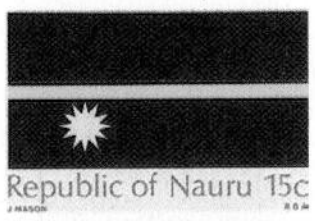

29 Flag of Independent Nauru

1969

96	**29**	15c. yellow, orange and blue	50	15

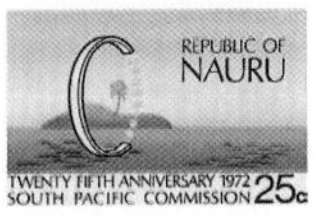

30 Island, "C" and Stars

1972. 25th Anniv of South Pacific Commission.

97	**30**	25c. multicoloured	30	30

1973. 5th Anniv of Independence. No. 96 optd Independence 1968-1973.

98	**29**	15c. yellow, orange and blue	20	30

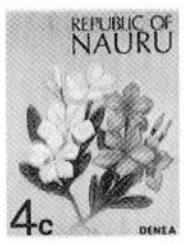

32 Denea

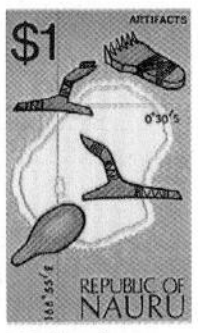

33 Artefacts and Map

1973. Multicoloured.

99	1c. Ekwenababae	40	20
100	2c. Kauwe iud	45	20
101	3c. Rimone	45	20
102	4c. Type **32**	45	40
103	5c. Erekogo	45	40
104	7c. Racoon butterflyfish ("Ikimago") (horiz)	50	80
105	8c. Catching flying fish (horiz)	30	20
106	10c. Itsibweb (ball game) (horiz)	30	20
107	15c. Nauruan wrestling	35	20
108	20c. Snaring great frigate birds ("Frigate Birds")	70	70
109	25c. Nauruan girl	40	30
110	30c. Catching common noddy birds ("Noddy Birds") (horiz)	60	40
111	50c. Great frigate birds ("Frigate Birds") (horiz)	80	75
112	$1 Type **33**	80	75

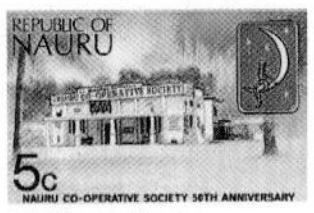

34 Co-op Store

1973. 50th Anniv of Nauru Co-operative Society. Multicoloured.

113	5c. Type **34**	20	30
114	25c. Timothy Detudamo (founder)	20	15
115	50c. N.C.S. trademark (vert)	45	55

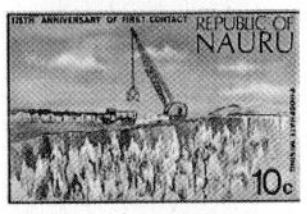

35 Phosphate Mining

1974. 175th Anniv of First Contact with the Outside World. Multicoloured.

116	7c. M.V. "Eigamoiya" (bulk carrier)	65	90
117	10c. Type **35**	50	25
118	15c. Fokker Fellowship "Nauru Chief"	65	30
119	25c. Nauruan chief in early times	50	35
120	35c. Capt. Fearn and 18th-century frigate (70×22 mm)	2·25	2·50
121	50c. 18th-century frigate off Nauru (70×22 mm)	1·25	1·40

The ship on the 35c. and 50c. is wrongly identified as the "Hunter" (snow).

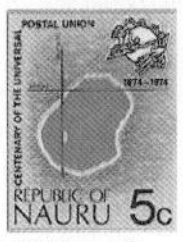

36 Map of Nauru

1974. Centenary of U.P.U. Multicoloured.

122	5c. Type **36**	15	20
123	8c. Nauru Post Office	15	20
124	20c. Nauruan postman	15	10
125	$1 U.P.U. Building and Nauruan flag	40	60
MS126	157×105 mm. Nos. 122/5. Imperf	2·00	5·50

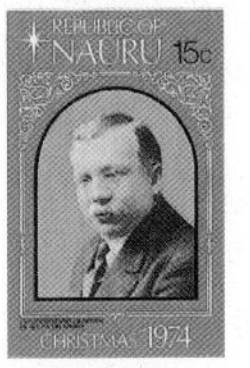

37 Rev. P. A. Delaporte

1974. Christmas and 75th Anniv of Rev. Delaporte's Arrival.

127	**37**	15c. multicoloured	20	20
128	**37**	20c. multicoloured	30	30

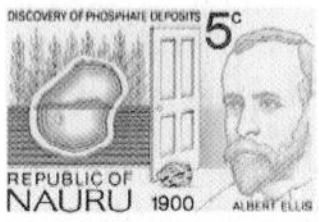

38 Map of Nauru, Lump of Phosphate Rock and Albert Ellis

1975. Phosphate Mining Anniversaries. Mult.

129	5c. Type **38**	25	40
130	7c. Coolies and mine	35	40
131	15c. Electric phosphate train, barges and ship	1·00	1·40
132	25c. Modern ore extraction	1·25	1·50

ANNIVERSARIES: 5c. 75th anniv of discovery; 7c. 70th anniv of Mining Agreement; 15c. 55th anniv of British Phosphate Commissioners; 25c. 5th anniv of Nauru Phosphate Corporation.

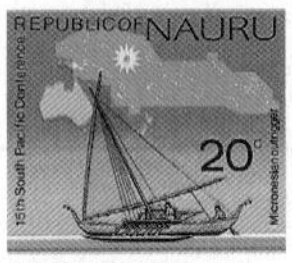

39 Micronesian Outrigger

1975. South Pacific Commission Conf, Nauru (1st issue). Multicoloured.

133	20c. Type **39**	75	75
134	20c. Polynesian double-hull	75	75
135	20c. Melanesian outrigger	75	75
136	20c. Polynesian outrigger	75	75

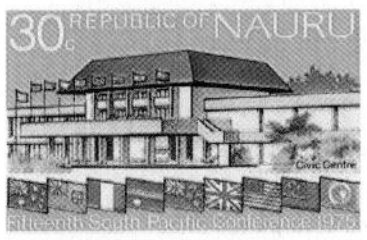

40 New Civic Centre

1975. South Pacific Commission Conf, Nauru (2nd issue). Multicoloured.

137	30c. Type **40**	15	15
138	50c. Domaneab (meeting-house)	30	30

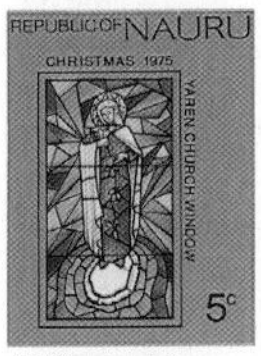

41 "Our Lady" (Yaren Church)

1975. Christmas. Stained-glass Windows. Mult.

139	5c. Type **41**	15	30
140	7c. "Suffer little children" (Orro Church)	15	30
141	15c. As 7c.	20	60
142	25c. Type **41**	25	80

42 Flowers floating towards Nauru

1976. 30th Anniv of Islanders' Return from Truk. Multicoloured.

143	10c. Type **42**	10	15
144	14c. Nauru encircled by garland	15	20
145	25c. Nightingale reed warbler and maps	85	30
146	40c. Return of the islanders	45	45

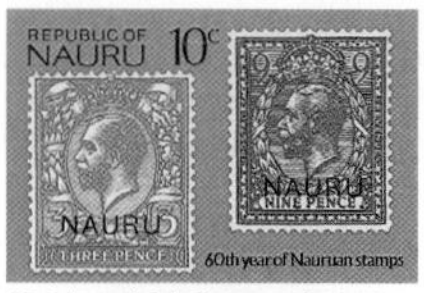

43 3d. and 9d. Stamps of 1916

1976. 60th Anniv of Nauruan Stamps. Mult.

147	10c. Type **43**	15	15
148	15c. 6d. and 1s. stamps	15	15
149	25c. 2s.6d. stamp	20	25
150	50c. 5s. "Specimen" stamp	25	35

44 "Pandanus mei" and "Enna G" (cargo liner)

1976. South Pacific Forum, Nauru. Mult.

151	10c. Type **44**	25	25
152	20c. "Tournefortia argentea" with Boeing 737 and Fokker Fellowship aircraft	40	40
153	30c. "Thespesia populnea" and Nauru Tracking Station	40	40
154	40c. "Cordia subcordata" and produce	40	40

45 Nauruan Choir

1976. Christmas. Multicoloured.

155	15c. Type **45**	10	10
156	15c. Nauruan choir	10	10
157	20c. Angel in white dress	15	15
158	20c. Angel in red dress	15	15

46 Nauru House and Coral Pinnacles

1977. Opening of Nauru House, Melbourne. Mult.

159	15c. Type **46**	15	15
160	30c. Nauru House and Melbourne skyline	25	25

47 Cable Ship "Anglia"

1977. 75th Anniv of First Trans-Pacific Cable and 20th Anniv of First Artificial Earth Satellite.

161	**47**	7c. multicoloured	20	10
162	-	15c. blue, grey and black	30	15
163	-	20c. blue, grey and black	30	20
164	-	25c. multicoloured	30	20

DESIGNS: 15c. Tracking station, Nauru; 20c. Stern of "Anglia"; 25c. Dish aerial.

48 Father Kayser and First Catholic Church

1977. Christmas. Multicoloured.

165	15c. Type **48**	10	10
166	25c. Congregational Church, Orro	15	15
167	30c. Catholic Church, Arubo	15	15

49 Arms of Nauru

1978. 10th Anniv of Independence.

168	**49**	15c. multicoloured	20	15
169	**49**	60c. multicoloured	35	30

1978. Nos. 159/60 surch.

170	**46**	4c. on 15c. multicoloured	45	1·50
171	**46**	5c. on 15c. multicoloured	45	1·50
172	-	8c. on 30c. multicoloured	45	1·50
173	-	10c. on 30c. multicoloured	45	1·50

51 Collecting Shellfish

1978

174	**51**	1c. multicoloured	50	30
175	-	2c. multicoloured	50	30
176	-	3c. multicoloured	2·00	1·00
177	-	4c. brown, blue and black	50	30
178	-	5c. multicoloured	2·25	1·00
179	-	7c. multicoloured	30	1·50
180	-	10c. multicoloured	30	20
181	-	15c. multicoloured	40	30
182	-	20c. grey, black and blue	30	30
183	-	25c. multicoloured	30	30
184	-	30c. multicoloured	1·75	45
185	-	32c. multicoloured	2·75	1·25
186	-	40c. multicoloured	1·75	2·25
187	-	50c. multicoloured	1·50	1·25
188	-	$1 multicoloured	55	1·00
189	-	$2 multicoloured	60	1·10
190	-	$5 grey, black and blue	1·10	2·25

DESIGNS: 2c. Coral outcrop; 3c. Reef scene; 4c. Girl with fish; 5c. Reef heron; 7c. Catching fish, Buada Lagoon; 10c. Ijuw Lagoon; 15c. Girl framed by coral; 20c. Pinnacles, Anibare Bay reef; 25c. Pinnacle at Meneng; 30c. Head of great frigate bird; 32c. White-capped noddy birds in coconut palm; 40c. Wandering tattler; 50c. Great frigate birds on perch; $1 Old coral pinnacles at Topside; $2 New pinnacles at Topside; $5 Blackened pinnacles at Topside.

52 A.P.U. Emblem

1978. 14th General Assembly of Asian Parliamentarians' Union. Nauru.

191	**52**	15c. multicoloured	20	25
192	-	20c. black, blue and gold	20	25

DESIGN: 20c. As Type **52**, but with different background.

53 Virgin and Child

1978. Christmas. Multicoloured.

193	7c. Type **53**	10	10
194	15c. Angel in sunrise scene (horiz)	10	10
195	20c. As 15c.	15	15
196	30c. Type **53**	20	20

54 Baden-Powell and Cub Scout

1978. 70th Anniv of Boy Scout Movement. Mult.

197	20c. Type **54**	20	15
198	30c. Scout	25	20
199	50c. Rover Scout	35	30

55 Wright Flyer I over Nauru

1979. Flight Anniversaries. Multicoloured.

200	10c. Type **55**	25	15
201	15c. Fokker F.VIIa/3m "Southern Cross" superimposed on nose of Boeing 737	35	20
202	15c. "Southern Cross" and Boeing 737 (front view)	35	20
203	30c. Wright Flyer I over Nauru airfield	60	30

ANNIVERSARIES: Nos. 200, 203, 75th anniv of powered flight; 201/2, 50th anniv of Kingsford-Smith's Pacific flight.

56 Sir Rowland Hill and Marshall Islands 10pf. stamp of 1901

1979. Death Cent of Sir Rowland Hill. Mult.

204	5c. Type **56**	15	10
205	15c. Sir Rowland Hill and "Nauru" opt on G.B. 10s. "Seahorse" stamp of 1916–23	25	20
206	60c. Sir Rowland Hill and Nauru 60c. 10th anniv of Independence stamp, 1978	55	40
MS207	159×101 mm. Nos. 204/6	85	1·25

57 Dish Antenna, Transmitting Station and Radio Mast

1979. 50th Anniv of International Consultative Radio Committee. Multicoloured.

208	7c. Type **57**	15	10
209	32c. Telex operator	35	25
210	40c. Radio operator	40	25

58 Smiling Child

1979. International Year of the Child.

211	**58**	8c. multicoloured	10	10
212	-	15c. multicoloured	15	15
213	-	25c. multicoloured	20	20
214	-	32c. multicoloured	20	20
215	-	50c. multicoloured	25	25

DESIGNS: 15c. to 50c. Smiling children.

59 Ekwenababae (flower), Scroll inscribed "Peace on Earth" and Star

1979. Christmas. Multicoloured.

216	7c. Type **59**	10	10
217	15c. "Thespia populnea" (flower), scroll inscribed "Goodwill towards Men" and star	10	10
218	20c. Denea (flower), scroll inscribed "Peace on Earth" and star	10	10
219	30c. Erekogo (flower), scroll inscribed "Goodwill toward Men" and star	20	20

60 Dassault Bregeut Mystere Falcon 50 over Melbourne

1980. 10th Anniv of Air Nauru. Multicoloured.

220	15c. Type **60**	40	15
221	20c. Fokker F.28 Fellowship over Tarawa	45	15
222	25c. Boeing 727-100 over Hong Kong	45	15
223	30c. Boeing 737 over Auckland	45	15

61 Steam Locomotive

1980. 10th Anniv of Nauru Phosphate Corporation. Multicoloured.

224	8c. Type **61**	10	10
225	32c. Electric locomotive	20	20
226	60c. Diesel-hydraulic locomotive	35	35
MS227	168×118 mm. Nos. 224/6	1·00	2·50

No. **MS**227 also commemorates the "London 1980" International Stamp Exhibition.

62 Verse 10 from Luke, Chapter 2 in English

1980. Christmas. Verses from Luke, Chapter 2. Multicoloured.

228	20c. Type **62**	10	10
229	20c. Verse 10 in Nauruan	10	10
230	30c. Verse 14 in English	15	15
231	30c. Verse 14 in Nauruan	15	15

See also Nos. 248/51.

63 Nauruan, Australia, Union and New Zealand Flags on Aerial View of Nauru

1980. 20th Anniv of U.N. Declaration on the Granting of Independence to Colonial Countries and Peoples. Multicoloured.

232	25c. Type **63**	15	15
233	50c. U.N. Trusteeship Council (72×23 mm)	15	15
234	50c. Nauru independence ceremony, 1968 (72×23 mm)	25	25

64 Timothy Detudamo

1981. 30th Anniv of Nauru Local Government Council. Head Chiefs. Multicoloured.

235	20c. Type **64**	15	15
236	30c. Raymond Gadabu	15	15
237	50c. Hammer DeRoburt	25	25

65 Casting Net by Hand

1981. Fishing. Multicoloured.

238	8c. Type **65**	15	10
239	20c. Outrigger canoe	25	15
240	32c. Outboard motor boat	35	20
241	40c. Trawler	35	25
MS242	167×116 mm. No. 241×4	2·25	2·00

No. **MS**242 was issued to commemorate the "WIPA 1981" International Stamp Exhibition, Vienna.

66 Bank of Nauru Emblem and Building

1981. 5th Anniv of Bank of Nauru.

243	**66** $1 multicoloured	60	60

67 Inaugural Speech

1981. U.N. Day. E.S.C.A.P. (United Nations Economic and Social Commission for Asia and the Pacific) Events. Multicoloured.

244	15c. Type **67**	15	15
245	20c. Presenting credentials	15	15
246	25c. Unveiling plaque	20	20
247	30c. Raising U.N. flag	25	25

1981. Christmas. Bible Verses. Designs as T 62. Multicoloured.

248	20c. Matthew 1, 23 in English	15	15
249	20c. Matthew 1, 23 in Nauruan	15	15
250	30c. Luke 2, 11 in English	20	20
251	30c. Luke 2, 11 in Nauruan	20	20

68 Earth Satellite Station

1981. 10th Anniv of South Pacific Forum. Mult.

252	10c. Type **68**	20	15
253	20c. "Enna G" (cargo liner)	25	20
254	30c. Boeing 737 airliner	25	25
255	40c. Local produce	25	30

69 Nauru Scouts leaving for 1935 Frankston Scout Jamboree

1982. 75th Anniv of Boy Scout Movement. Mult.

256	7c. Type **69**	15	15
257	8c. Two Nauru scouts on "Nauru Chief", 1935 (vert)	15	15
258	15c. Nauru scouts making pottery, 1935 (vert)	15	20
259	20c. Lord Huntingfield addressing Nauru scouts, Frankston Jamboree, 1935	20	25
260	25c. Nauru cub and scout, 1982	20	30
261	40c. Nauru cubs, scouts and scouters, 1982	30	45
MS262	152×114 mm. Nos. 256/61. Imperf	1·25	2·25

No. **MS**262 also commemorates Nauru's participation in the "Stampex" National Stamp Exhibition, London.

70 100 kw Electricity Generating Plant under Construction (left side)

1982. Ocean Thermal Energy Conversion. Mult.

263	25c. Type **70**	60	30
264	25c. 100 kw Electricity Generating Plant under construction (right side)	60	30
265	40c. Completed plant (left)	80	40
266	40c. Completed plant (right)	80	40

Nos. 263/4 and 265/6 were each issued as horizontal se-tenant pairs, forming composite designs.

71 S.S. "Fido"

1982. 75th Anniv of Phosphate Shipments. Mult.

267	5c. Type **71**	40	10
268	10c. Steam locomotive "Nellie"	50	20
269	30c. Class "Clyde" diesel locomotive	60	50
270	60c. M.V. "Eigamoiya" (bulk carrier)	65	80
MS271	165×107 mm. $1 "Eigamoiya", "Rosie-D" and "Kolle-D" (bulk carriers) (67×27 mm)	1·50	2·25

No. **MS**271 was issued to commemorate "ANPEX 82" National Stamp Exhibition, Brisbane.

72 Queen Elizabeth II on Horseback

1982. Royal Visit. Multicoloured.

272	20c. Type **72**	30	20
273	50c. Prince Philip, Duke of Edinburgh	40	45
274	$1 Queen Elizabeth II and Prince Philip (horiz)	45	1·00

73 Father Bernard Lahn

1982. Christmas. Multicoloured.

275	10c. Type **73**	20	35
276	30c. Reverend Itubwa Amram	20	50
277	40c. Pastor James Aingimen	25	80
278	50c. Bishop Paul Mea	30	1·10

74 Speaker of the Nauruan Parliament

75 Nauru Satellite Earth Station

1983. 15th Anniv of Independence. Mult.

279	15c. Type **74**	20	20
280	20c. Family Court in session	25	25
281	30c. Law Courts building (horiz)	25	25
282	50c. Parliamentary chamber (horiz)	40	40

1983. World Communications Year. Mult.

283	5c. Type **75**	20	10
284	10c. Omni-directional range installation	20	15
285	20c. Emergency short-wave radio	25	25
286	25c. Radio Nauru control room	40	30
287	40c. Unloading air mail	90	45

76 Return of Exiles from Truk on M.V. "Trienza", 1946

1983. Angam Day. Multicoloured.

288	15c. Type **76**	20	25
289	20c. Mrs. Elsie Agio (exile community leader) (vert) (25×41 mm)	20	25
290	30c. Child on scales (vert) (25×41 mm)	35	40
291	40c. Nauruan children (vert) (25×41 mm)	45	50

77 "The Holy Virgin, Holy Child and St. John" (School of Raphael)

1983. Christmas. Multicoloured.

292	5c. Type **77**	10	10
293	15c. "Madonna on the Throne, surrounded by Angels" (School of Sevilla)	20	15
294	50c. "The Mystical Betrothal of St. Catherine with Jesus" (School of Veronese) (horiz)	60	40

78 S.S. "Ocean Queen"

1984. 250th Anniv of "Lloyd's List" (newspaper). Multicoloured.

295	20c. Type **78**	30	20
296	25c. M.V "Enna G"	35	25
297	30c. M.V "Baron Minto"	40	30
298	40c. Sinking of M.V. "Triadic", 1940	50	45

79 1974 U.P.U. $1 Stamp

1984. Universal Postal Union Congress, Hamburg.

299	**79** $1 multicoloured	70	1·25

80 "Hypolimnas bolina" (female)

1984. Butterflies. Multicoloured.

300	25c. Type **80**	35	40
301	30c. "Hypolimnas bolina" (male)	35	55
302	50c. "Danaus plexippus"	40	85

81 Coastal Scene

1984. Life in Nauru. Multicoloured.

303	1c. Type **81**	10	40
304	3c. Nauruan woman (vert)	15	40
305	5c. Modern trawler	40	50
306	10c. Golfer on the links	90	50
307	15c. Excavating phosphate (vert)	90	65
308	20c. Surveyor (vert)	65	55
309	25c. Air Nauru Boeing 727 airliner	80	55
310	30c. Elderly Nauruan (vert)	50	50
311	40c. Loading hospital patient onto Boeing 727 aircraft	90	55
312	50c. Skin-diver with fish (vert)	1·00	80
313	$1 Tennis player (vert)	2·50	3·25
314	$2 Anabar Lagoon	2·50	3·75

82 Buada Chapel

1984. Christmas. Multicoloured.

315	30c. Type **82**	40	50
316	40c. Detudamo Memorial Church	50	65
317	50c. Candle-light service, Kayser College (horiz)	60	70

83 Air Nauru Boeing 737 Jet on Tarmac

1985. 15th Anniv of Air Nauru. Multicoloured.

318	20c. Type **83**	50	35
319	30c. Stewardesses on Boeing 737 aircraft steps (vert)	60	60
320	40c. Fokker F.28 Fellowship over Nauru	75	75
321	50c. Freight being loaded onto Boeing 727 (vert)	85	85

84 Open Cut Mining

1985. 15th Anniv of Nauru Phosphate Corporation. Multicoloured.

322	20c. Type **84**	1·00	60
323	25c. Diesel locomotive hauling crushed ore	2·00	1·00
324	30c. Phosphate drying plant	1·75	1·00
325	50c. Early steam locomotive	2·50	1·75

85 Mother and Baby on Beach

1985. Christmas. Multicoloured.

326	50c. Beach scene	1·50	2·25
327	50c. Type **85**	1·50	2·25

Nos. 326/7 were printed together, se-tenant, forming a composite design.

86 Adult Common Noddy with Juvenile

1985. Birth Bicentenary of John J. Audubon (ornithologist). Common ("Brown") Noddy. Mult.

328	10c. Type **86**	35	35
329	20c. Adult and immature birds in flight	50	70
330	30c. Adults in flight	65	85
331	50c. "Brown Noddy" (John J. Audubon)	80	1·10

87 Douglas Motor Cycle

1986. Early Transport on Nauru. Multicoloured.

332	15c. Type **87**	80	70
333	20c. Primitive lorry	95	95
334	30c. German-built steam locomotive, 1910	1·50	1·50
335	40c. "Baby" Austin car	1·75	1·75

88 Island and Bank of Nauru

1986. 10th Anniv of Bank of Nauru. Children's Paintings. Multicoloured.

336	20c. Type **88**	20	30
337	25c. Borrower with notes and coins	25	35
338	30c. Savers	30	40
339	40c. Customers at bank counter	35	55

89 "Plumeria rubra"

1986. Flowers. Multicoloured.

340	20c. Type **89**	30	70
341	25c. "Tristellateia australis"	40	85
342	30c. "Bougainvillea cultivar"	50	1·00
343	40c. "Delonix regia"	60	1·25

90 Carol Singers

1986. Christmas. Multicoloured.
344	20c. Type **90**	40	30
345	$1 Carol singers and hospital patient	1·60	3·50

91 Young Girls Dancing

1987. Nauruan Dancers. Multicoloured.
346	20c. Type **91**	80	80
347	30c. Stick dance	1·00	1·25
348	50c. Boy doing war dance (vert)	1·75	2·50

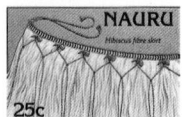
92 Hibiscus Fibre Skirt

1987. Personal Artefacts. Multicoloured.
349	25c. Type **92**	75	75
350	30c. Headband and necklets	85	85
351	45c. Decorative necklets	1·10	1·10
352	60c. Pandanus leaf fan	1·60	1·60

93 U.P.U. Emblem and Air Mail Label

1987. World Post Day.
353	**93** 40c. multicoloured	1·50	1·25

MS354 122×82 mm. $1 U.P.U. emblem and map of Pacific showing mail routes (114×74 mm)   3·25   4·00

94 Open Bible

1987. Centenary of Nauru Congregational Church.
355	**94** 40c. multicoloured	1·50	1·75

95 Nauruan Children's Party

1987. Christmas. Multicoloured.
356	20c. Type **95**	75	50
357	$1 Nauruan Christmas dinner	2·75	3·25

96 Loading Phosphate on Ship

1988. 20th Anniv of Independence. Mult.
358	25c. Type **96**	1·00	1·00
359	40c. Tomano flower (vert)	1·50	1·50
360	55c. Great frigate bird (vert)	2·25	2·25
361	$1 Arms of Republic (35×35 mm)	2·50	3·50

97 Map of German Marshall Is. and 1901 5m. Yacht Definitive

1988. 80th Anniv of Nauru Post Office. Mult.
362	30c. Type **97**	75	75
363	50c. Letter and post office of 1908	1·00	1·25
364	70c. Nauru Post Office and airmail letter	1·25	1·50

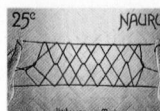
98 "Itubwer" (mat)

1988. String Figures. Multicoloured.
365	25c. Type **98**	35	35
366	40c. "Etegerer – the Pursuer"	50	60
367	55c. "Holding up the Sky"	65	70
368	80c. "Manujie's Sword"	1·00	1·75

99 U.P.U. Emblem and National Flag

1988. Cent of Nauru's Membership of U.P.U.
369	**99** $1 multicoloured	1·25	1·25

100 "Hark the Herald Angels"

1988. Christmas. Designs showing words and music from "Hark the Herald Angels Sing".
370	**100** 20c. black, red and yellow	60	30
371	– 60c. black, red and mauve	1·40	1·25
372	– $1 black, red and green	2·25	2·25

101 Logo (15th anniv of Nauru Insurance Corporation)

1989. Anniversaries and Events. Multicoloured.
373	15c. Type **101**	30	30
374	50c. Logos (World Telecommunications Day and 10th anniv of Asian-Pacific Telecommunity)	75	85
375	$1 Photograph of island scene (150 years of photography)	1·75	2·00
376	$2 Capitol and U.P.U. emblem (20th U.P.U. Congress, Washington)	2·75	4·50

102 Mother and Baby

1989. Christmas. Multicoloured.
377	20c. Type **102**	50	30
378	$1 Children opening presents	2·25	3·25

103 Eigigu working while Sisters play

1989. 20th Anniv of First Manned Landing on Moon. Legend of "Eigigu, the Girl in the Moon". Multicoloured.
379	25c. Type **103**	3·00	2·75
380	30c. Eigigu climbing tree	3·25	3·00
381	50c. Eigigu stealing toddy from blind woman	6·00	5·50
382	$1 Eigigu on Moon	8·00	7·50

104 Early Mining by Hand

1990. 20th Anniv of Nauru Phosphate Corporation. Multicoloured.
383	50c. Type **104**	1·00	1·00
384	$1 Modern mining by excavator	1·50	2·00

105 Sunday School Class

1990. Christmas. Multicoloured.
385	25c. Type **105**	90	1·25
386	25c. Teacher telling Christmas story	90	1·25

Nos. 385/6 were printed together, se-tenant, forming a composite design.

106 Eoiyepiang laying Baby on Mat

1990. Legend of "Eoiyepiang, the Daughter of Thunder and Lightning". Multicoloured.
387	25c. Type **106**	1·50	60
388	30c. Eoiyepiang making floral decoration	1·75	70
389	50c. Eoiyepiang left on snow-covered mountain	2·25	2·00
390	$1 Eoiyepiang and warrior	3·25	3·50

107 Oleander

1991. Flowers. Multicoloured.
391	15c. Type **107**	15	30
392	20c. Lily	15	30
393	25c. Passion flower	20	35
394	30c. Lily (different)	25	40
395	35c. Caesalpinia	30	45
396	40c. Clerodendron	35	50
397	45c. "Baubina pinnata"	40	50
398	50c. Hibiscus (vert)	40	50
399	75c. Apocymaceae	65	70
400	$1 Bindweed (vert)	85	90
401	$2 Tristellateia (vert)	1·75	2·00
402	$3 Impala lily (vert)	2·50	3·25

108 Jesus Christ and Children (stained glass window)

1991. Christmas. Sheet 124×82 mm.
MS403 **108** $2 multicoloured   4·25   5·00

109 Star and Symbol of Asian Development Bank

1992. 25th Annual Meeting of Asian Development Bank.
404	**109** $1.50 multicoloured	2·00	2·50

110 Gifts under Christmas Tree

1992. Christmas. Children's Paintings. Mult.
405	45c. Type **110**	75	75
406	60c. Father Christmas in sleigh	1·00	1·50

111 Hammer DeRoburt

1993. 25th Anniv of Independence and Hammer DeRoburt (former President) Commemoration.
407	**111** $1 multicoloured	2·50	3·00

112 Running, Constitution Day Sports

1993. 15th Anniv of Constitution Day. Mult.
408	70c. Type **112**	1·40	1·40
409	80c. Part of Independence Proclamation	1·40	1·40

113 Great Frigate Birds, Flying Fish and Island

1993. 24th South Pacific Forum Meeting, Nauru. Multicoloured.
410	60c. Type **113**	1·40	1·50
411	60c. Red-tailed tropic bird, great frigate bird, dolphin and island	1·40	1·50
412	60c. Racoon butterflyfish ("Ikimago"), coral and sea urchins	1·40	1·50
413	60c. Three different types of fish with corals	1·40	1·50

MS414 140×130 mm. Nos. 410/13   7·00   8·00

Nos. 410/13 were printed together, se-tenant, forming a composite design.

114 "Peace on Earth, Goodwill to Men" and Star

1993. Christmas. Multicoloured.
415	55c. Type **114**	85	85
416	65c. "Hark the Herald Angels Sing" and star	90	90

115 Girls with Dogs

1994. "Hong Kong '94" International Stamp Exhibition. Chinese New Year ("Year of the Dog"). Multicoloured.
417	$1 Type **115**	1·50	2·00
418	$1 Boys with dogs	1·50	2·00

MS419 100×75 mm. Nos. 417/18   3·50   4·25

1994. "Singpex '94" National Stamp Exhibition, Singapore. No. MS419 optd "SINGPEX '94" and emblem in gold on sheet margin.

MS420	100×75 mm. Nos. 417/18		3·00	3·75

116 Weightlifting

1994. 15th Commonwealth Games, Victoria, Canada.

421	**116**	$1.50 multicoloured	1·40	2·00

117 Peace Dove and Star over Island

1994. Christmas. Multicoloured.

422	65c. Type **117**	90	90
423	75c. Star over Bethlehem	1·00	1·00

118 Air Nauru Airliner and Emblems

1994. 50th Anniv of I.C.A.O. Multicoloured.

424	55c. Type **118**	50	55
425	65c. Control tower, Nauru International Airport	60	65
426	80c. D.V.O.R. equipment	70	1·00
427	$1 Crash tenders	90	1·10
MS428	165×127 mm. Nos. 424/7	4·00	4·50

119 Emblem and Olympic Rings

1994. Nauru's Entry into Int Olympic Committee.

429	**119**	50c. multicoloured	50	50

120 Nauruan Flag

1995. 50th Anniv of United Nations (1st issue). Multicoloured.

430	75c. Type **120**	1·40	1·40
431	75c. Arms of Nauru	1·40	1·40
432	75c. Outrigger canoe on coastline	1·40	1·40
433	75c. Airliner over phosphate freighter	1·40	1·40
MS434	110×85 mm. Nos. 430/3	5·50	6·50

Nos. 430/3 were printed together, se-tenant, forming a composite design.
See also Nos. 444/5.

121 Signing Phosphate Agreement, 1967

1995. 25th Anniv of Nauru Phosphate Corporation. Multicoloured.

435	60c. Type **121**	80	1·00
436	60c. Pres. Bernard Dowiyogo and Prime Minister Keating of Australia shaking hands	80	1·00
MS437	120×80 mm. $2 Excavating phosphate	2·75	3·25

1995. International Stamp Exhibitions. No. 309 surch.

438	50c. on 25c. multicoloured (surch **at Beijing**)	1·40	1·40
439	$1 on 25c. multicoloured (surch **at Jakarta**)	1·40	1·75
440	$1 on 25c. multicoloured (surch **at Singapore**)	1·40	1·75

123 Sea Birds (face value at top right)

1995. Olympic Games, Atlanta. Sheet 140×121 mm, containing T **123** and similar vert designs. Multicoloured.

MS441	60c.+15c. Type **123**; 60c.+15c. Sea brids (face value at top left); 60c.+15c. Four dolphins; 60c.+15c. Pair of dolphins	4·50	5·50

The premiums on No. **MS**441 were for Nauru sport development.

124 Children playing on Gun

1995. 50th Anniv of Peace. Multicoloured.

442	75c. Type **124**	1·75	2·00
443	$1.50 Children making floral garlands	1·75	2·00

125 Nauru Crest, Coastline and U.N. Anniversary Emblem

1995. 50th Anniv of United Nations (2nd issue). Multicoloured.

444	75c. Type **125**	90	1·00
445	$1.50 Aerial view of Nauru and U.N. Headquarters, New York	1·60	2·00

126 Young Girl praying

1995. Christmas. Multicoloured.

446	60c. Type **126**	90	1·00
447	70c. Man praying	90	1·00

127 Returning Refugees and Head Chief Timothy Detudamo

1996. 50th Anniv of Nauruans' Return from Truk.

448	127	75c. multicoloured	90	1·00
449	127	$1.25 multicoloured	1·60	2·00
MS450		120×80 mm. Nos. 448/9	3·50	4·25

128 Nanjing Stone Lion

1996. "CHINA '96" 9th Asian International Stamp Exhibition, Peking. Sheet 130×110 mm.

MS451	**128**	45c. multicoloured	1·00	1·25

129 Symbolic Athlete

1996. Centenary of Modern Olympic Games. Mult.

452	40c. Type **129**	1·00	80
453	50c. Symbolic weightlifter	1·25	1·00
454	60c. Weightlifter (horiz)	1·25	1·10
455	$1 Athlete (horiz)	1·75	2·25

130 The Nativity and Angel

1996. Christmas. Multicoloured.

456	50c. Type **130**	60	60
457	70c. Angel, world map and wild animals	80	1·00

131 Dolphin (fish)

1997. Endangered Species. Fish. Multicoloured.

458	20c. Type **131**	1·10	1·10
459	30c. Wahoo	1·25	1·25
460	40c. Sailfish	1·40	1·40
461	50c. Yellow-finned tuna	1·50	1·50

132 Statue of Worshipper with Offering

1997. "HONG KONG '97" International Stamp Exhibition. Statues of different worshippers (1c. to 15c.) or Giant Buddha of Hong Kong (25c.).

462	**132**	1c. multicoloured	20	30
463	-	2c. multicoloured	20	30
464	-	5c. multicoloured	25	35
465	-	10c. multicoloured	30	40
466	-	12c. multicoloured	30	40
467	-	15c. multicoloured	30	40
468	-	25c. multicoloured	40	45

133 Princess Elizabeth and Lieut. Philip Mountbatten, 1947

1997. Golden Wedding of Queen Elizabeth and Prince Philip.

469	**133**	80c. black and gold	90	1·00
470	-	$1.20 multicoloured	1·40	1·60
MS471		150×110 mm. Nos. 469/70 (sold at $3)	3·00	3·75

DESIGN: $1.20, Queen Elizabeth and Prince Philip, 1997.

134 Conference Building

1997. 28th Parliamentary Conference of Presiding Officers and Clerks. Sheet 150×100 mm.

MS472	**134**	$2 multicoloured	1·75	2·25

135 Commemorative Pillar

1997. Christmas. 110th Anniv of Nauru Congregational Church. Multicoloured.

473	60c. Type **135**	60	55
474	80c. Congregational Church	80	90

136 Weightlifter

1998. Commonwealth, Oceania and South Pacific Weightlifting Championships, Nauru. Sheet 180×100 mm, containing T **136** and similar vert designs showing weightlifters.

MS475	40c., 60c., 80c., $1.20 multicoloured	2·25	2·75

137 Juan Antonio Samaranch and Aerial View

1998. Visit of International Olympic Committee President.

476	**137**	$2 multicoloured	1·75	2·25

138 Diana, Princess of Wales

1998. Diana, Princess of Wales Commemoration. Multicoloured.

477	70c. Type **138**	55	60
478	70c. Wearing white shirt	55	60
479	70c. With tiara	55	60
480	70c. In white jacket	55	60
481	70c. Wearing pink hat	55	60
482	70c. In white suit	55	60

139 Gymnastics

1998. 16th Commonwealth Games, Kuala Lumpur, Malaysia. Multicoloured.

483	40c. Type **139**	40	40
484	60c. Athletics	55	60
485	70c. Sprinting	65	70
486	80c. Weightlifting	70	80
MS487	153×130 mm. Nos. 483/6	1·90	2·40

140 Sqn. Ldr. Hicks (Composer of Nauru's National Anthem) conducting

1998. 30th Anniv of Independence. Multicoloured.

488	$1 Type **140**	85	80
489	$2 Sqn. Ldr. Hicks and score	1·75	2·25
MS490	175×110 mm. Nos. 488/9	2·50	3·25

141 Palm Trees, Fish, Festive Candle and Flower

1998. Christmas. Multicoloured.

491	85c. Type **141**	80	1·00
492	95c. Flower, present, fruit and island scene	85	1·00

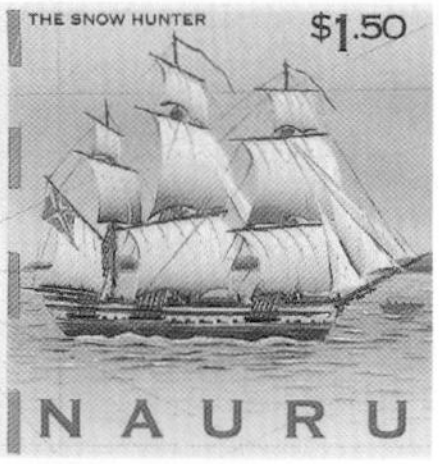

142 18th-century Frigate

1998. Bicentenary of First Contact with the Outside World. Multicoloured.

493	$1.50 Type **142**	1·50	1·75
494	$1.50 Capt. John Fearn	1·50	1·75
MS495	173×131 mm. Nos. 493/4	3·00	3·50

No. 493 is wrongly identified as "Hunter" (snow).

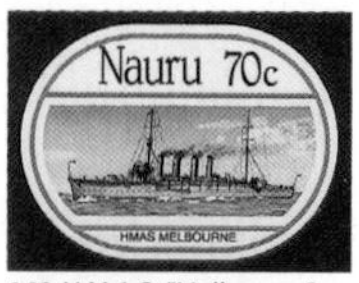

143 H.M.A.S. "Melbourne" (cruiser)

1999. "Australia '99" World Stamp Exhibition, Melbourne. Ships. Sheet 101×120 mm, containing T 143 and similar multicoloured designs.

MS496	70c. Type **143**; 80c. H.M.A.S. "D'Amantina" (frigate); 90c. "Alcyone" (experimental ship); $1 "Rosie-D" (bulk carrier); $1.10 Outrigger canoe (80×30 mm)	4·25	4·75

1999. 30th Anniv of First Manned Landing on Moon. As T 98a of Kiribati. Multicoloured.

497	70c. Neil Armstrong (astronaut)	65	70
498	80c. Service and lunar module on way to Moon	70	80
499	90c. Aldrin and "Apollo 11" on Moon's surface	85	1·00
500	$1 Command module entering Earth's atmosphere	90	1·25
MS501	90×80 mm. $2 Earth as seen from Moon (circular, 40 mm diam)	1·90	2·40

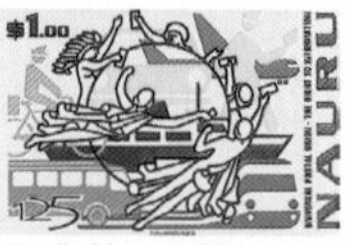

144 Emblem and Forms of Transport

1999. 125th Anniv of Universal Postal Union.

502	**144**	$1 multicoloured	1·00	1·25

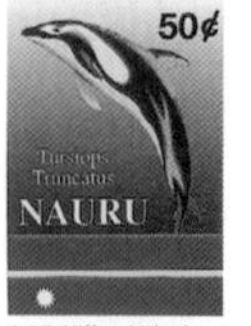

145 Killer Whale

1999. "China '99" International Philatelic Exhibition, Beijing. Sheet 185×85 mm, containing T 145 and similar vert design. Multicoloured.

MS503	50c. Type **145**; 50c. Swordfish	1·50	1·75

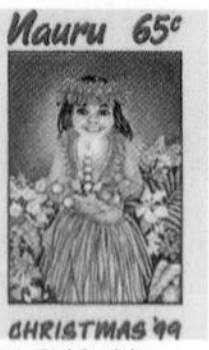

146 Girl holding Candle

1999. Christmas. Multicoloured.

504	65c. Type **146**	70	75
505	70c. Candle and Christmas tree	80	85

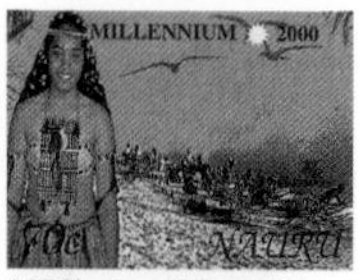

147 Nauruan Woman in Traditional Dress and Canoes

2000. New Millennium. Multicoloured.

506	70c. Type **147**	1·50	1·50
507	$1.10 Aspects of modern Nauru	2·25	2·25
508	$1.20 Woman holding globe and man at computer	2·25	2·25
MS509	149×88 mm. Nos. 506/8	5·50	6·00

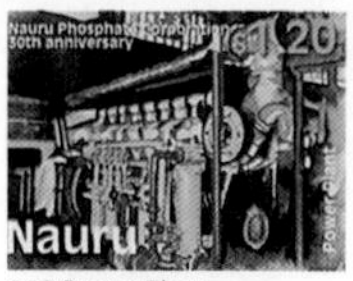

148 Power Plant

2000. Centenary of Phosphate Discovery. Mult.

510	$1.20 Type **148**	1·25	1·25
511	$1.80 Phosphate train	2·00	2·00
512	$2 Albert Ellis and phosphate sample	2·00	2·25
MS513	79×131 mm. Nos. 510/12	4·50	5·50

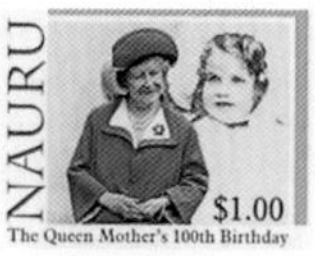

149 Queen Mother in Royal Blue Hat and Coat

2000. 100th Birthday of Queen Elizabeth the Queen Mother. Sheet 150×106 mm, containing T 149 and similar horiz designs, each including photograph of Queen Mother as a child. Multicoloured.

MS514	150×106 mm. $1 Type **149**; $1.10 In lilac hat and coat; $1.20 In turquoise hat and coat; $1.40 In greenish blue hat and coat with maple leaf brooch	4·50	5·50

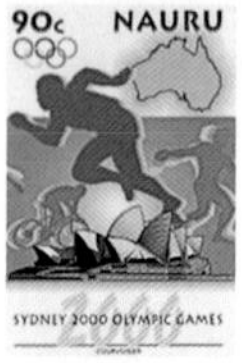

150 Running and Sydney Opera House

2000. Olympic Games, Sydney. Multicoloured.

515	90c. Type **150**	1·75	1·25
516	$l Basketball	1·75	1·40
517	$1.10 Weightlifting and cycling	1·75	1·75
518	$1.20 Running and Olympic Torch	1·75	2·00

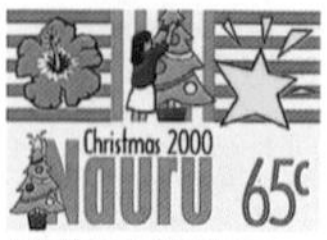

151 Flower, Christmas Tree and Star

2000. Christmas. Multicoloured.

519	65c. Type **151**	1·00	1·10
520	75c. Decorations, toy engine and palm tree	1·25	1·40
MS521	134×95 mm. Nos. 519/20	2·50	2·75

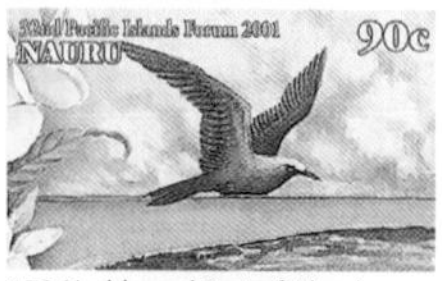

152 Noddy and Part of Island

2001. 32nd Pacific Islands Forum, Nauru. Multicoloured.

522	90c. Type **152**	2·25	2·25
523	$1 Frigate bird in flight and part of island	2·40	2·40
524	$1.10 Two frigate birds and part of island	2·40	2·40
525	$2 Frigate bird and Nauru airport	3·00	3·00
MS526	145×130 mm. Nos. 522/5	9·00	9·50

Nos. 522/5 were printed together, se-tenant, forming a composite view of Nauru.

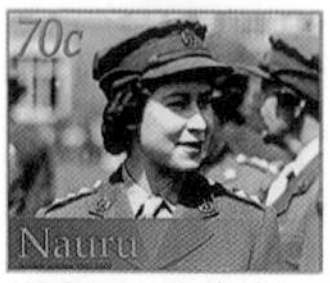

153 Princess Elizabeth in A.T.S. Uniform, 1946

2002. Golden Jubilee.

527	**153**	70c. black, mauve and gold	1·75	1·75
528	-	80c. multicoloured	1·75	1·75
529	-	90c. black, mauve and gold	1·75	1·75
530	-	$1 multicoloured	1·90	1·90
MS531		162×95 mm. Nos. 527/30 and $4 multicoloured	8·00	8·50

DESIGNS—HORIZ: 80c. Queen Elizabeth in multicoloured hat; 90c. Princess Elizabeth at Cheltenham Races, 1951; $1 Queen Elizabeth in evening dress, 1997. VERT (38 x 51 mm)—$4 Queen Elizabeth after Annigoni.

Designs as Nos. 527/30 in No. **MS**531 omit the gold frame around each stamp and the "Golden Jubilee 1952–2002" inscription.

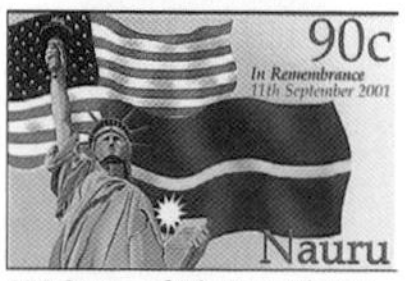

154 Statue of Liberty with U.S. and Nauru Flags

2002. In Remembrance. Victims of Terrorist Attacks on U.S.A. (11 September 2001).

532	**154**	90c. multicoloured	1·40	1·40
533	**154**	$1 multicoloured	1·50	1·50
534	**154**	$1.10 multicoloured	1·60	1·60
535	**154**	$2 multicoloured	2·25	2·25

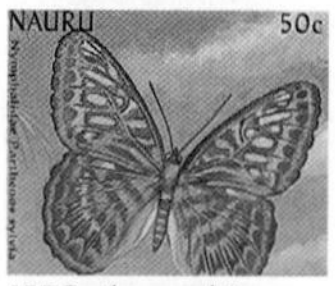

155 *Parthenos sylvia*

2002. Butterflies of the Pacific. Multicoloured.

536	50c. Type **155**	1·00	1·00
537	50c. *Delias madetes*	1·00	1·00
538	50c. *Danaus philene*	1·00	1·00
539	50c. *Arhopala hercules*	1·00	1·00
540	50c. *Paipilio canopus*	1·00	1·00
541	50c. *Danaus schenkii*	1·00	1·00
542	50c. *Pairthenos tigrina*	1·00	1·00
543	50c. *Mycalesis phidon*	1·00	1·00
544	50c. *Vindula sapor*	1·00	1·00
MS545	85×60 mm. $2 *Graphium agamemnon*	3·25	3·75

Nos. 536/44 were printed together, se-tenant, forming a composite design.

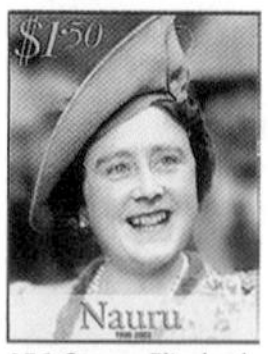

156 Queen Elizabeth in London, 1940

2002. Queen Elizabeth the Queen Mother Commemoration.

546	**156**	$1.50 black, gold and purple	3·25	3·25
547	-	$1.50 multicoloured	3·25	3·25
MS548		145×70 mm. Nos. 546/7	6·50	7·00

DESIGNS: No. 547, Queen Mother in Norwich, 1990.

Designs as Nos. 546/7 in No. **MS**548 omit the "1900–2002" inscription and the coloured frame.

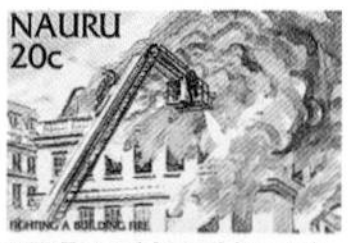

157 Turntable Ladder and Burning Building

2002. International Firefighters. Multicoloured.

549	20c. Type **157**	65	55
550	50c. Firefighting tug and burning ship	1·25	75
551	90c. Fighting a forest fire	1·60	1·25
552	$1 Old and new helmets	1·60	1·25
553	$1.10 Steam-driven pump and modern fire engine	1·75	1·40
554	$2 19th-century and present day hose teams	3·25	4·50
MS555	110×90 mm. $5 Airport fire engine	11·00	11·00

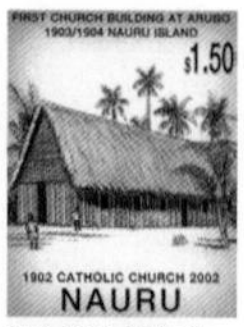

158 First Catholic Church, Arubo

2002. Centenary of Catholic Church on Nauru.

556	**158**	$1.50 brown and black	2·25	2·25
557	-	$1.50 violet and black	2·25	2·25
558	-	$1.50 blue and black	2·25	2·25
559	-	$1.50 green and black	2·25	2·25
560	-	$1.50 blue and black	2·25	2·25
561	-	$1.50 red and black	2·25	2·25

DESIGNS: No. 557, Father Friedrich Gründl (first missionary); 558, Sister Stanisla; 559, Second Catholic church, Ibwenape; 560, Brother Kalixtus Bader (lay brother); 561, Father Alois Kayser (missionary).

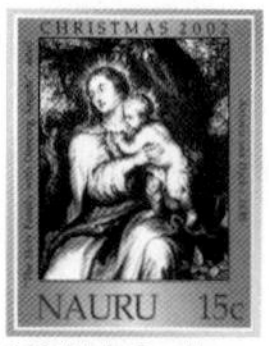

159 "Holy Family with dancing Angels" (Van Dyck)

2002. Christmas. Religious Art. Multicoloured.

562	15c. Type **159**	60	45
563	$1 "Holy Virgin with Child" (Cornelis Bloemaert after Lucas Cangiasius)	2·00	1·10
564	$1.20 "Holy Family with Cat" (Rembrandt)	2·25	1·40
565	$3 "Holy Family with St. John" (Pierre Brebiette after Raphael)	5·00	6·50

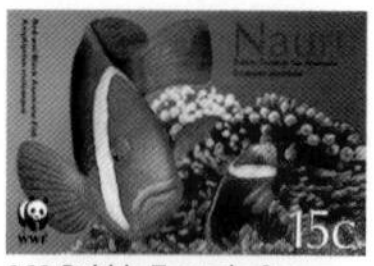

160 Bubble Tentacle Sea Anemone and Fire Anemonefish ("Red-and-Black Anemone Fish")

2003. Endangered Species. Sea Anemones and Anemonefish. Multicoloured.

566	15c. Type **160**	75	80
567	$1 Leathery sea anemone and orange-finned anemonefish	1·75	1·75
568	$1.20 Magnificent sea anemone and pink anemonefish	2·00	2·00
569	$3 Merten's sea anemone and yellow-tailed anemonefish ("Clark's Anemone Fish")	4·00	5·00

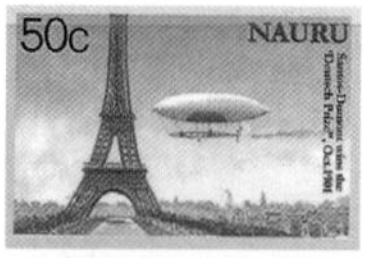

161 Santos-Dumont's *Ballon No. 6* flying around Eiffel Tower, 1901

2003. Centenary of Powered Flight. Airships. Multicoloured.

570	50c. Type **161**	1·10	1·10
571	50c. USS *Shenandoah*	1·10	1·10
572	50c. Airship R101, 1929	1·10	1·10
573	50c. British Beardmore Airship R34, 1919 (first double crossing of North Atlantic)	1·10	1·10
574	50c. Zeppelin LZ-1 (first flight, 1900)	1·10	1·10
575	50c. Airship USS *Los Angeles* moored to airship tender USS *Patoka*	1·10	1·10
576	50c. Goodyear C-71 airship	1·10	1·10
577	50c. LZ-130 *Graf Zeppelin II*	1·10	1·10
578	50c. Zeppelin airship over Alps	1·10	1·10
MS579	150×100 mm. $2 LZ-127 *Graf Zeppelin* over Mount Fuji; $2 LZ-127 *Graf Zeppelin* over San Francisco; $2 LZ-127 *Graf Zeppelin* exchanging mail with Soviet ice breaker over Franz Josef Land	11·00	12·00

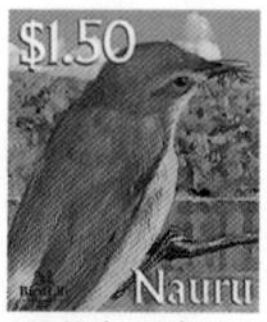

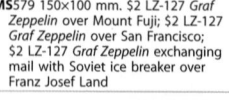

162 Nightingale Reed Warbler

2003. Bird Life International. Nightingale Reed Warbler ("Nauru Reed Warbler"). Multicoloured.

580	$1.50 Type **162**	3·75	3·75
581	$1.50 Nightingale reed warbler on reeds (horiz)	3·75	3·75
MS582	175×80 mm. $1.50 Head (horiz); Type **162**; $1.50 Singing; $1.50 No. 581; $1.50 Adult and nestlings (horiz)	12·00	12·00

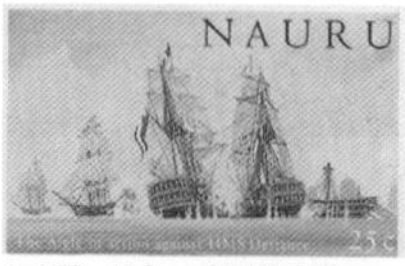

163 *The Aigle* and HMS *Defiance*

2005. Bicentenary of the Battle of Trafalgar (1st issue). Multicoloured.

583	25c. Type **163**	90	70
584	50c. French *Eprouvette*	1·10	90
585	75c. *The Santissima Trinidad* and HMS *Africa*	1·50	1·40
586	$1 Emperor Napoleon Bonaparte (vert)	1·60	1·60
587	$1.50 HMS *Victory*	3·00	3·25
588	$2.50 Vice-Admiral Sir Horatio Nelson (vert)	4·00	4·50
MS589	120×79 mm. $2.50 Admiral Villeneuve (vert); $2.50 *Formidable* (vert)	8·00	8·50

No. 587 contains traces of powdered wood from HMS *Victory*.

See also Nos. 603/5.

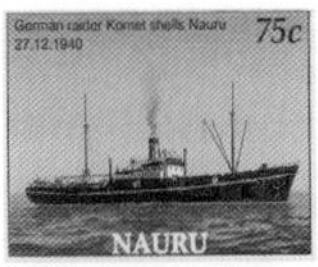

164 *Komet* (German raider)

2005. 60th Anniv of the End of World War II. Pacific Explorer World Stamp Exhibition (MS600). Multicoloured.

590	75c. Type **164**	1·25	1·25
591	75c. *Le Triomphant* (French warship)	1·25	1·25
592	75c. Type 97 Te-Ke (Japanese tank)	1·25	1·25
593	75c. USAF B-24 Liberator aircraft	1·25	1·25
594	75c. USS *Paddle* (US submarine)	1·25	1·25
595	75c. *Coral Princess* (B-25G Mitchell aircraft)	1·25	1·25
596	75c. Spitfires	1·25	1·25
597	75c. HMAS *Diamantina* (River Class Frigate)	1·25	1·25
598	75c. D-Day Landings	1·25	1·25
599	75c. Crowds gathered and Union Jack flag	1·25	1·25
MS600	90×60 mm. $5 HMAS *Manoora* (Australian troop ship)	8·00	8·50

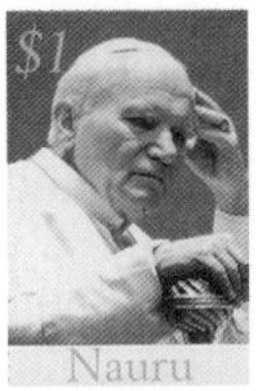

165 Pope John Paul II

2005. Commemoration of Pope John Paul II.

601	**165**	$1 multicoloured	1·60	1·60

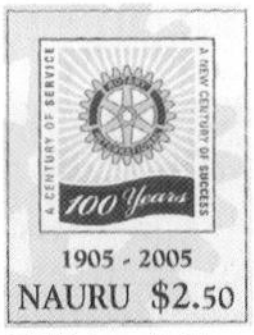

166 Rotary Emblem

2005. Centenary of Rotary International.

602	**166**	$2.50 multicoloured	3·25	3·50

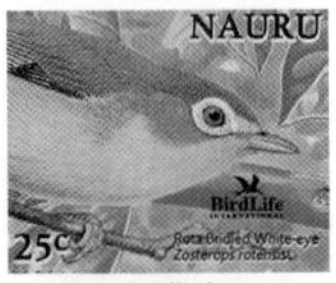

167 Rota Bridled White-Eye

2005. Birdlife International. Multicoloured.

MS603 Three sheets each 170×85 mm. (a) 25c.×6, Type **167**; Truk ("Faichuk") White-eye; Savaii ("Samoan") White-eye; Bridled white-eye; Ponape ("Long-billed") White-eye; Golden white-eye. (b) 50c.×6, Kuhl's ("Lorikeet") Lory; Masked shining parrot; Kandavu ("Crimson") shining parrot; Tahitian lorikeet ("Blue Lory"); Stephen's lory ("Henderson Lorikeet"); Ultramarine ("Lorikeet") lory. (c) $1×6, Atoll fruit dove; Henderson Island fruit dove; Rarotongan ("Cook Islands") fruit dove; Rapa Island fruit dove; Whistling dove; Mariana fruit dove 19·00 22·00

The backgrounds of Nos. **MS**603a/c form composite designs.

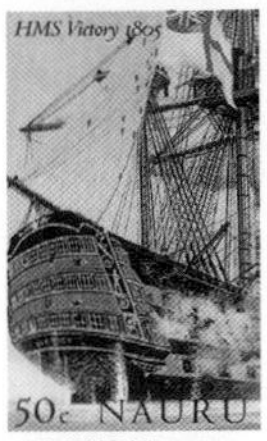

168 HMS *Victory*

2005. Bicentenary of the Battle of Trafalgar (2nd issue). Multicoloured.

604	50c. Type **168**	1·50	85
605	$1 Ships engaged in battle (horiz)	2·00	1·60
606	$5 Admiral Lord Nelson	7·00	8·00

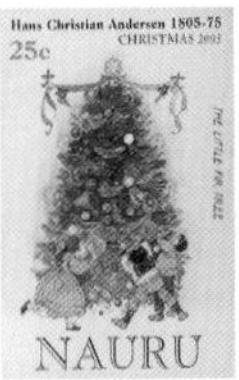

169 *The Little Fir Tree*

2005. Christmas and Birth Bicentenary of Hans Christian Andersen (writer). Multicoloured.

607	25c. Type **169**	40	30
608	50c. *The Wild Swans*	70	60
609	75c. *The Farmyard Cock and the Weather Cock*	1·00	1·00
610	$1 *The Storks*	1·25	1·25
611	$2.50 *The Toad*	3·00	3·50
612	$5 *The Ice Maiden*	5·00	6·50

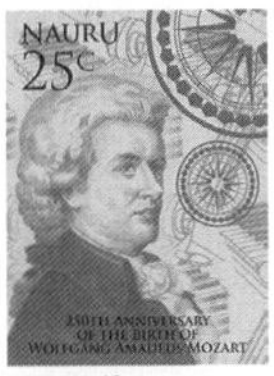

170 Wolfgang Amadeus Mozart (composer, 250th birth anniv)

2006. Exploration and Innovation. Anniversaries. Multicoloured.

613	25c. Type **170**	1·25	1·25
614	25c. Violin heads and piano keyboards	1·25	1·25
615	50c. Isambard Kingdom Brunel (engineer, birth bicentenary)	1·25	1·25
616	50c. Cogwheels	1·25	1·25
617	75c. Edmund Halley (astronomer, 350th birth anniv)	1·40	1·40
618	75c. Halley's quadrant	1·40	1·40
619	$1 Charles Darwin (originator of "Theory of Evolution", 175th anniv of voyage on *Beagle*)	1·50	1·50
620	$1 Early microscope	1·50	1·50
621	$1.25 Thomas Edison (inventor and physicist, 75th death anniv)	1·50	1·50
622	$1.25 Edison's lightbulb	1·50	1·50
623	$1.50 Christopher Columbus (discoverer of New World, 500th death anniv)	2·00	2·00
624	$1.50 Astrolabe	2·00	2·00

Nos. 613/14, 615/16, 617/18, 619/20, 621/2 and 623/4 were each printed together, se-tenant, each pair forming a composite background design.

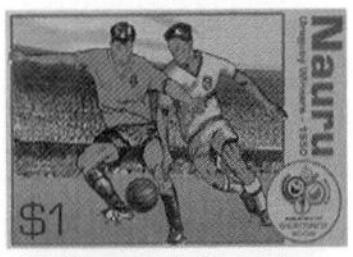

171 Uruguay (winners) v. Brazil, 1950

2006. World Cup Football Championship, Germany. showing scenes from previous World Cup finals. Multicoloured.

625	$1 Type **171**	1·50	1·50
626	$1.50 Argentina (winners) v. Netherlands, 1978	2·50	2·75
627	$2 Italy (winners) v. West Germany, 1982	3·00	3·25
628	$3 Brazil (winners) v. Germany, 2002	4·00	4·50

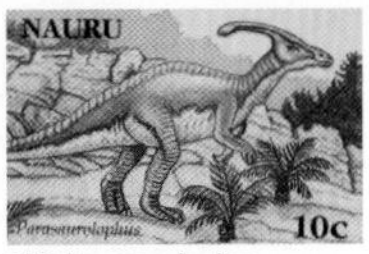

172 Parasaurolophus

2006. Dinosaurs. Multicoloured.

629	10c. Type **172**	40	50
630	25c. Quetzalcoatlus	70	60
631	50c. Spinosaurus	1·00	85
632	75c. Triceratops	1·25	1·25
633	$1 Tyrannosaurus rex	1·50	1·50
634	$1.50 Euoplocephalus	2·50	2·75
635	$2 Velociraptor	3·00	3·25
636	$2.50 Protoceratops	3·00	3·75

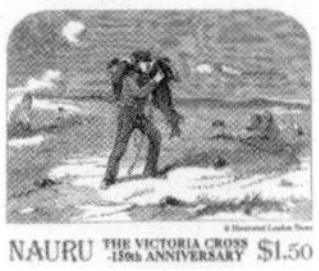

173 Lieut. Gerald Graham bringing in Wounded Man

2006. 150th Anniv of the Victoria Cross. Designs showing Victoria Cross recipients of Crimean War. Multicoloured.

637	$1.50 Type **173**	2·50	2·50
638	$1.50 Private MacGregor driving Russians from rifle pits	2·50	2·50
639	$1.50 Private Alexander Wright repelling a sortie	2·50	2·50
640	$1.50 Corporal John Ross ascertaining the evacuation of the Redan	2·50	2·50
641	$1.50 Sgt McWheeney digging cover with bayonet for wounded Corporal Courtney	2·50	2·50
642	$1.50 Brevet Major G. L. Goodlake surprising the enemy's picket at Windmill Ravine	2·50	2·50

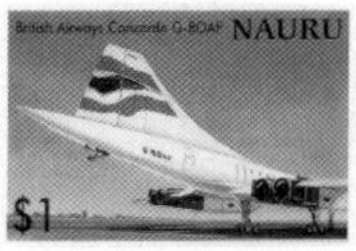

174 British Airways Concorde G-BOAF

2006. 30th Anniv of Inaugural Flight of Concorde. Multicoloured.

643	$1 Type **174**	2·00	2·00
644	$1 First flight of Concorde 002, 9 April 1969	2·00	2·00
645	$1 Concorde at take-off	2·00	2·00
646	$1 Concorde and Red Arrows in Golden Jubilee Flypast, 4 June 2002	2·00	2·00
647	$1 Concorde and Spitfire, Battle of Britain 50th anniversary, 6 June 1990	2·00	2·00
648	$1 Concorde at 60000 feet at Mach 2	2·00	2·00
649	$1 Extreme condition testing	2·00	2·00
650	$1 Concorde on runway	2·00	2·00
651	$1 First commercial flight, 21 January 1976	2·00	2·00
652	$1 Concorde above Earth	2·00	2·00
653	$1 British Airways Concorde G-BOAF at take-off	2·00	2·00
654	$1 Two Concordes on ground	2·00	2·00

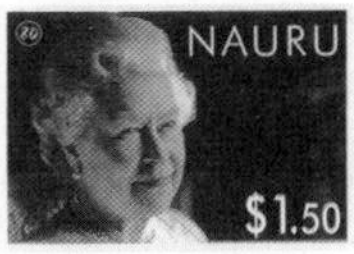

175 Queen Elizabeth II

2006. 50th Anniv of the Year of Three Kings. Multicoloured.

655	**175**	$1.50 multicoloured	2·50	2·50
656	-	$1.50 black and grey	2·50	2·50
657	-	$1.50 black and grey	2·50	2·50
658	-	$1.50 black and grey	2·50	2·50

DESIGNS: No. 656, King George V and Princess Elizabeth; 657, King Edward VIII and Princess Elizabeth; 658, King George VI and Princess Elizabeth.

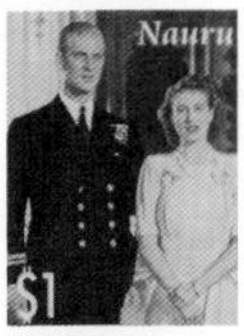

176 Princess Elizabeth and Lt. Philip Mountbatten, 1947

2007. Diamond Wedding of Queen Elizabeth II and Prince Philip. Multicoloured.

659	$1 Type **176**	1·50	1·50
660	$1.50 Princess Elizabeth and Prince Philip on wedding day	2·50	2·50
661	$2 Wedding ceremony	3·00	3·25
662	$3 Princess Elizabeth and Prince Philip walking in the countryside, c. 1947	4·00	4·50
MS663	125×85 mm. $5 Wedding portrait of Princess Elizabeth (42×56 mm)	7·00	7·50

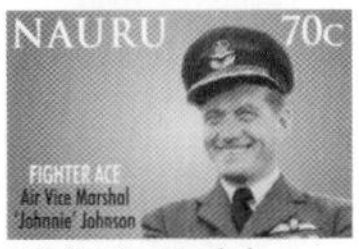

177 Air Vice Marshal 'Johnnie' Johnson (fighter ace)

2008. 90th Anniv of the Royal Air Force. Multicoloured.

664	70c. Type **177**	1·40	1·40
665	70c. R. J. Mitchell (Spitfire designer)	1·40	1·40
666	70c. Sir Sydney Camm (Hawker Hurricane designer)	1·40	1·40
667	70c. Sir Frank Whittle (inventor of the jet engine)	1·40	1·40
668	70c. Sir Douglas Bader ('flying legend')	1·40	1·40
MS669	110×70 mm. $3 Avro Vulcan	5·50	6·00

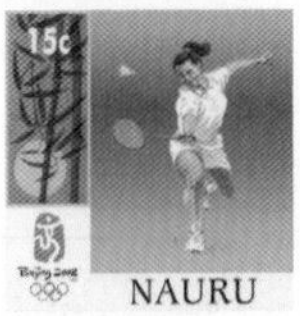

178 Badminton

2008. Olympic Games, Beijing. Multicoloured.

670	15c. Type **178**	50	50
671	25c. Archery	70	70
672	75c. Weightlifting	1·25	1·25
673	$1 Diving	1·50	1·50

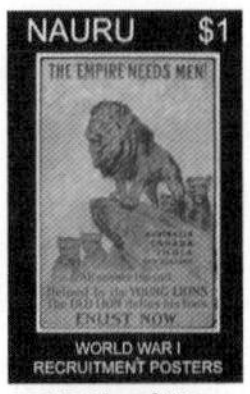

179 Pride of Lions ('THE EMPIRE NEEDS MEN!')

2008. 90th Anniv of the End of World War I. Designs showing recruitment posters. Multicoloured.

674	$1 Type **179**	1·75	1·75
675	$1 Column of soldiers marching into sunrise ('VICTORY JOIN NOW')	1·75	1·75
676	$1 Officer beckoning ('AN APPEAL TO YOU')	1·75	1·75
677	$1 Proud soldier with old man ('YOUR KING & COUNTRY NEED YOU')	1·75	1·75
678	$1 Officer calling ('SOUTH AUSTRALIANS COME AND HELP')	1·75	1·75
679	$1 Lord Kitchener pointing ('BRITONS JOIN YOUR COUNTRY'S ARMY')	1·75	1·75
MS680	110×70 mm. $2 The Queen's Wreath of Remembrance	3·25	3·50

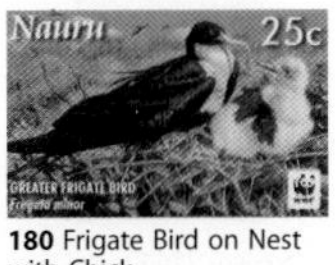

180 Frigate Bird on Nest with Chick

2008. Endangered Species. Greater Frigate Bird (*Fregata minor*). Multicoloured.

681	25c. Type **180**	70	65
682	75c. Two frigate birds in flight	1·60	1·40
683	$1 Frigate bird landing on branch	1·75	1·75
684	$2 Male frigate bird displaying red pouch in flight	3·00	3·25

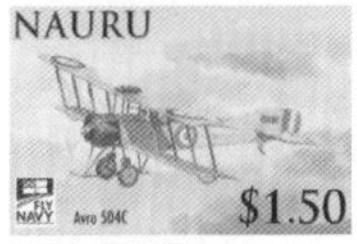

181 Avro 504C

2009. Centenary of Naval Aviation. Multicoloured.

685	$1.50 Type **181**	2·75	2·75

686	$1.50 Fairey Flycatcher	2·75	2·75
687	$1.50 de Havilland Sea Vixen	2·75	2·75
688	$1.50 Short Folder seaplane	2·75	2·75
MS689	110×70 mm. $3 Grumman Avenger, Operation Meridian, 1945	4·25	4·25

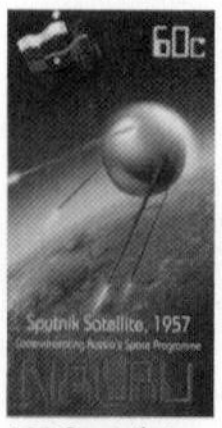

182 Sputnik 1 Satellite, 1957

2011. Russia's Space Programme. Multicoloured.

690	60c. Type **182**	1·25	1·25
691	60c. Cosmonaut Yuri Gagarin (first man in space, 12 April 1961)	1·25	1·25
692	$1.20 Nauru Island seen from space	2·50	2·50
693	$2.25 Launch of Vostok 1, 12 April 1961	4·75	4·75
694	$3 International Space Station	5·75	9·75

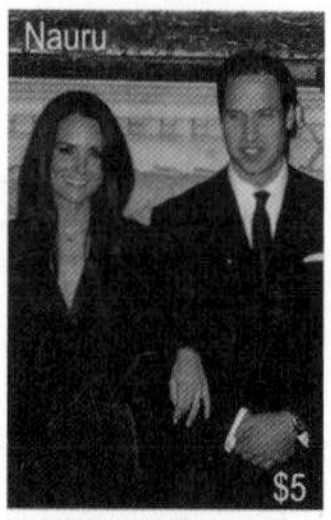

183 Prince William and Miss Catherine Middleton

2011. Royal Wedding. Sheet 118×90 mm. Multicoloured.

MS695	**183** $5 multicoloured	11·50	11·50

Pt. 1

NAWANAGAR

A state of India, Bombay District. Now uses Indian stamps.

6 docra = 1 anna.

1 (1 docra)

1877. Imperf or perf.

1	1	1doc. blue	75	27·00

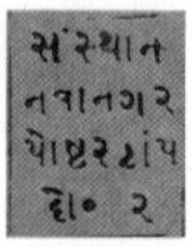

2 (2 docra)

1880. Imperf.

6ab	2	1doc. lilac	4·75	14·00
8c	2	2doc. green	4·75	15·00
9b	2	3doc. yellow	6·00	13·00

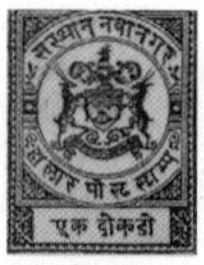

4 (1 docra)

1893. Imperf or perf.

13	4	1doc. black	1·75	7·00
14	4	2doc. green	3·25	12·00
15b	4	3doc. yellow	3·25	16·00

Pt. 8

NEAPOLITAN PROVINCES

Temporary issues for Naples and other parts of S. Italy which adhered to the new Kingdom of Italy in 1860.

200 tornesi = 100 grano = 1 ducato.

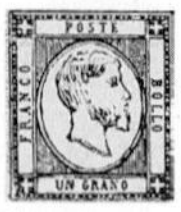

1

1861. Embossed. Imperf.

2	1	½t. green	19·00	£275
5	1	½g. brown	£200	£275
9	1	1g. black	£425	40·00
10	1	2g. blue	£130	17·00
15	1	5g. red	£150	90·00
18	1	10g. orange	£130	£190
19	1	20g. yellow	£600	£2500
23	1	50g. slate	75·00	£9000

Pt. 1

NEGRI SEMBILAN

A state of the Federation of Malaya, incorporated in Malaysia in 1963.

100 cents = 1 dollar (Straits or Malayan).

1891. Stamp of Straits Settlements optd Negri Sembilan.

1	5	2c. red	3·00	9·00

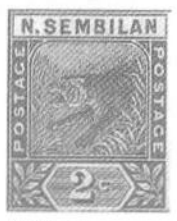

2 Tiger

1891

2	2	1c. green	3·25	1·00
3	2	2c. red	3·25	13·00
4	2	5c. blue	30·00	48·00

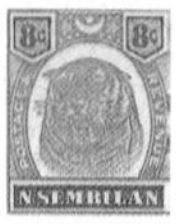

3

1896

5	3	1c. purple and green	22·00	9·50
6	3	2c. purple and brown	35·00	£120
7	3	3c. purple and red	17·00	2·25
8	3	5c. purple and yellow	10·00	14·00
9	3	8c. purple and blue	29·00	21·00
10	3	10c. purple and orange	27·00	14·00
11	3	15c. green and violet	50·00	85·00
12	3	20c. green and olive	70·00	40·00
13	3	25c. green and red	75·00	95·00
14	3	50c. green and black	90·00	70·00

1898. Surch in words and bar.

15		1c. on 15c. green and violet	£110	£300
16	2	4c. on 1c. green	3·50	22·00
17	3	4c. on 3c. purple and red	4·50	24·00
18	2	4c. on 5c. blue	1·50	15·00

1898. Surch in words only.

19	3	4c. on 8c. purple and blue	10·00	4·25

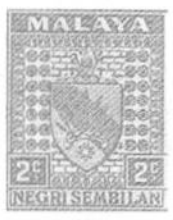

6 Arms of Negri Sembilan

1935

21	6	1c. black	1·00	20
22	6	2c. green	1·00	20
23	6	2c. orange	4·25	75·00
24a	6	3c. green	8·00	16·00
25	6	4c. orange	2·00	10
26	6	5c. brown	2·00	10
27	6	6c. red	18·00	3·00
28	6	6c. grey	4·75	£130
29	6	8c. grey	2·00	10
30	6	10c. purple	1·25	10
31	6	12c. blue	3·25	50
32	6	15c. blue	11·00	60·00
33	6	25c. purple and red	1·50	70
34	6	30c. purple and orange	3·50	2·00
35	6	40c. red and purple	3·50	2·00
36	6	50c. black on green	6·50	2·25
37	6	$1 black and red on blue	5·00	5·50
38	6	$2 green and red	55·00	18·00
39	6	$5 green and red on green	32·00	£110

1948. Silver Wedding. As T 8b/c of Pitcairn Islands.

40	10c. violet	40	50
41	$5 green	23·00	32·00

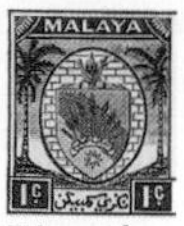

7 Arms of Negri Sembilan

1949

42	7	1c. black	1·25	10
43	7	2c. orange	1·25	10
44	7	3c. green	60	30
45	7	4c. brown	30	10
46a	7	5c. purple	1·50	45
47	7	6c. grey	2·50	10
48	7	8c. red	1·00	75
49	7	8c. green	7·00	1·60
50	7	10c. mauve	40	10
51	7	12c. red	7·00	2·75
52	7	15c. blue	4·75	10
53	7	20c. black and green	3·25	2·50
54	7	20c. blue	3·25	10
55	7	25c. purple and orange	1·25	10
56	7	30c. red and purple	1·25	2·50
57	7	35c. red and purple	5·50	1·00
58	7	40c. red and purple	6·50	4·75
59	7	50c. black and blue	6·50	20
60	7	$1 blue and purple	7·50	2·25
61	7	$2 green and red	23·00	38·00
62	7	$5 green and brown	55·00	85·00

1949. U.P.U. As T 8d/g of Pitcairn Islands.

63	10c. purple	20	20
64	15c. blue	1·40	3·50
65	25c. orange	30	3·00
66	50c. black	60	3·25

1953. Coronation. As T 8h of Pitcairn Islands.

67	10c. black and purple	1·25	50

1957. As Nos. 92/102 of Kedah but inset Arms of Negri Sembilan.

68	1c. black	10	10
69	2c. red	10	10
70	4c. sepia	10	10
71	5c. lake	10	10
72	8c. green	2·25	1·40
73	10c. sepia	2·00	10
74	10c. purple	12·00	10
75	20c. blue	1·00	10
76a	50c. black and blue	75	10
77	$1 blue and purple	6·50	2·00
78	$2 green and red	15·00	16·00
79	$5 brown and green	18·00	25·00

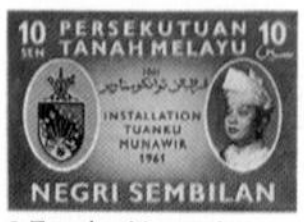

8 Tuanku Munawir

1961. Installation of Tuanku Munawir as Yang di-Pertuan Besar of Negri Sembilan.

80	8	10c. multicoloured	30	70

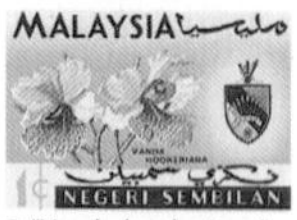

9 "Vanda hookeriana"

1965. As Nos. 115/21 of Kedah but with Arms of Negri Sembilan inset and inscr "NEGERI SEMBILAN" as in T 6.

81	9	1c. multicoloured	10	1·60
82	-	2c. multicoloured	10	1·60
83	-	5c. multicoloured	50	10
84	-	6c. multicoloured	40	60
85	-	10c. multicoloured	50	10
86	-	15c. multicoloured	80	10
87	-	20c. multicoloured	1·75	1·00

The higher values used in Negri Sembilan were Nos. 20/7 of Malaysia (National Issues).

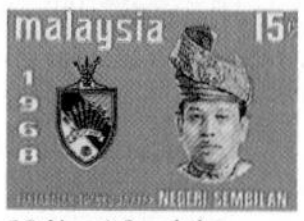

10 Negri Sembilan Crest and Tuanku Ja'afar

1968. Installation of Tuanku Ja'afar as Yang di-Pertuan Besar of Negri Sembilan.

88	10	15c. multicoloured	15	70
89	10	50c. multicoloured	30	1·40

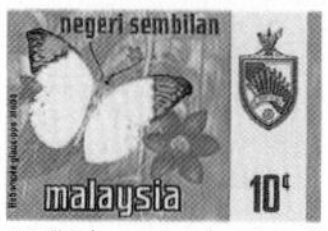

11 "Hebomoia glaucippe"

1971. Butterflies. As Nos. 124/30 of Kedah but with Arms of Negri Sembilan inset as T 11 and inscr "negeri sembilan".

91	-	1c. multicoloured	40	2·00
92	-	2c. multicoloured	70	2·00
93	-	5c. multicoloured	1·00	20
94	-	6c. multicoloured	1·00	2·00
95	11	10c. multicoloured	1·00	10
96	-	15c. multicoloured	1·40	10
97	-	20c. multicoloured	1·40	50

The higher values in use with this issue were Nos. 64/71 of Malaysia (National Issues).

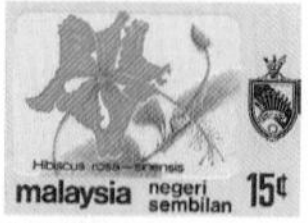

12 "Hibiscus rosa-sinensis"

1979. Flowers. As Nos. 135/41 of Kedah but with Arms of Negri Sembilan and inscr "negeri sembilan" as in T 12.

103	1c. "Rafflesia hasseltii"	10	1·25
104	2c. "Pterocarpus indicus"	10	1·25
105	5c. "Lagerstroemia speciosa"	15	40
106	10c. "Durio zibethinus"	20	10
107	15c. Type **12**	20	10
108	20c. "Rhododendron scortechinii"	25	10
109	25c. "Etlingera elatior" (inscr "Phaeomeria speciosa")	45	25

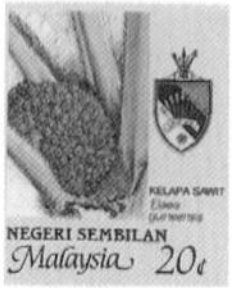

13 Oil Palm

1986. As Nos. 152/8 of Kedah but with Arms of Negri Sembilan and inscr "NEGERI SEMBILAN" as T 13.

117	1c. Coffee	10	30
118	2c. Coconuts	10	30
119	5c. Cocoa	15	10
120	10c. Black pepper	15	10
121	15c. Rubber	25	10
122	20c. Type **13**	25	10
123	30c. Rice	30	10

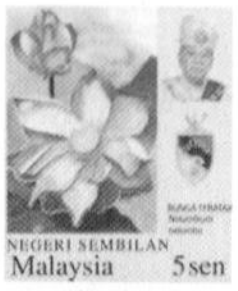

14 *Nelumbium nelumbo* (sacred lotus)

2007. Garden Flowers. As Nos. 210/15 of Johore, but with portrait of Sultan Tuanku Ja'afar and Arms of Negri Sembilan as in T 14. Multicoloured.

124	5s. Type **14**	10	10
125	10s. *Hydrangea macrophylla*	15	10
126	20s. *Hippeastrum reticulatum*	25	15
127	30s. *Bougainvillea*	40	20
128	40s. *Ipomoea indica*	50	30
129	50s. *Hibiscus rosa-sinensis*	65	35

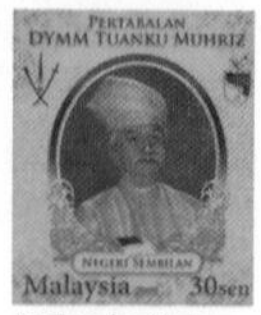

15 Tuanku Muhriz Ibni Almarhum

2009. Coronation of Tuanku Muhriz Ibni Almarhum. Multicoloured.

130	30s. Type **15**	40	40
131	50s. Tuanku Muhriz Ibni Almarhum (wearing black hat)	65	75
132	1r. Tuanku Muhriz Ibni Almarhun and Tuanku Aishah Rohani (58×34 mm)	1·40	1·75

2009. Garden Flowers. Sheet 100x85mm.

MS134	5s. *Nelumbium nelumbo* (sacred lotus); 10s. *Hydrangea macrophylla*; 20s. *Hippeastrum reticulatum*; 30s. *Bougainvillea*; 40s. *Ipomoea indica*; 50s. *Hibiscus rosa-sinensis*	2·25	2·75

Pt. 21

NEPAL

An independent kingdom in the Himalayas N. of India.

1861. 16 annas = 1 rupee.
1907. 64 pice = 1 rupee.
1954. 100 paisa = 1 rupee.

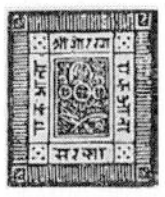
1 (1a.) Crown and Kukris

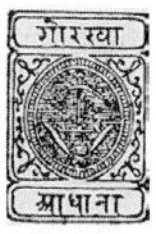
2 (½a.) Bow and Arrow and Kukris

1881. Imperf or pin-perf.

34	**2**	½a. black	2·75	1·80
35	**2**	½a. orange	£375	£190
14	**1**	1a. green	48·00	48·00
42	**1**	1a. blue	6·75	2·00
16c	**1**	2a. violet	37·00	37·00
40	**1**	2a. brown	11·00	4·50
41	**1**	4a. green	7·50	7·50

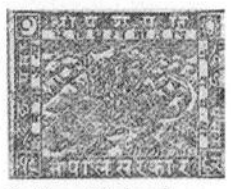
3 Siva Mahadeva (2p.)

1907. Various sizes.

57	**3**	2p. brown	35	35
58	**3**	4p. green	1·10	75
59	**3**	8p. red	75	50
60	**3**	16p. purple	11·00	2·75
61	**3**	24p. orange	11·00	1·80
62	**3**	32p. blue	15·00	2·20
63	**3**	1r. red	30·00	18·00
50	**3**	5r. black and brown	26·00	12·00

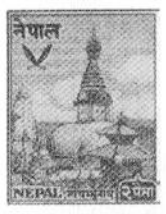
5 Swayambhunath Temple, Katmandu

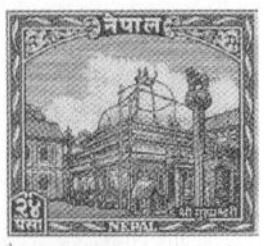
7 Guheswari Temple, Patan

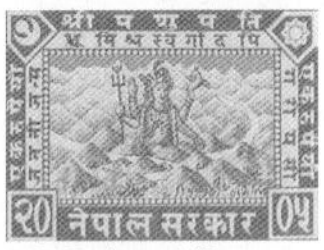
8 Sri Pashupati (Siva Mahadeva)

1949

64	**5**	2p. brown	90	75
65	-	4p. green	90	75
66	-	6p. pink	1·80	75
67	-	8p. red	1·80	1·10
68	-	16p. purple	1·80	1·10
69	-	20p. blue	3·75	1·80
70	**7**	24p. red	3·00	1·10
71	-	32p. blue	5·50	1·80
72	**8**	1r. orange	30·00	18·00

DESIGNS—As Type **5**: 4p. Pashupatinath Temple, Katmandu; 6p. Tri-Chundra College; 8p. Mahabuddha Temple. 26×30 mm: 16p. Krishna Mandir Temple, Patan. As Type **7**: 20p. View of Katmandu; 32p. The twenty-two fountains, Balaju.

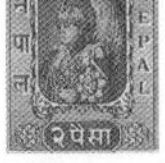
9 King Tribhuvana

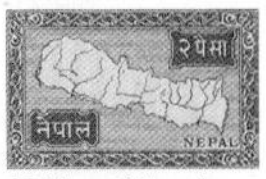
10 Map of Nepal

1954. (a) Size 18×22 mm.

73	**9**	2p. brown	1·80	35
74	**9**	4p. green	6·00	1·10
75	**9**	6p. red	1·50	35
76	**9**	8p. lilac	1·10	35
77	**9**	12p. orange	11·00	1·80

(b) Size 25½×29½ mm.

78	16p. brown	1·50	35
79	20p. red	3·00	1·10
80	24p. purple	2·50	1·10
81	32p. blue	3·75	1·10
82	50p. mauve	30·00	5·50
83	1r. red	44·00	8·75
84	2r. orange	37·00	7·50

(c) Size 30×18 mm.

85	**10**	2p. brown	1·50	75
86	**10**	4p. green	6·00	1·10
87	**10**	6p. red	15·00	1·80
88	**10**	8p. lilac	1·10	75
89	**10**	12p. orange	15·00	1·80

(d) Size 38×21½ mm.

90	16p. brown	1·80	75
91	20p. red	3·00	75
92	24p. purple	2·20	75
93	32p. blue	5·50	1·50
94	50p. mauve	30·00	5·50
95	1r. red	48·00	7·50
96	2r. orange	37·00	7·50

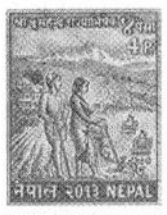
11 Mechanization of Agriculture

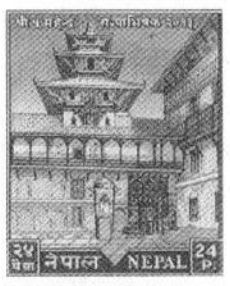
13 Hanuman Dhoka, Katmandu

1956. Coronation.

97	**11**	4p. green	6·00	6·00
98	-	6p. red and yellow	3·75	3·00
99	-	8p. violet	3·00	1·50
100	**13**	24p. red	6·00	6·00
101	-	1r. red	£110	95·00

DESIGNS—As Type **11**: 8p. Processional elephant. As Type **13**: 6p. Throne; 1r. King and Queen and mountains.

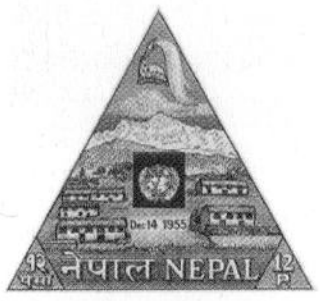
15 U.N. Emblem and Nepalese Landscape

1956. 1st Anniv of Admission into U.N.O.

102	**15**	12p. blue and brown	7·50	6·00

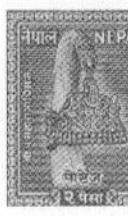
16 Nepalese Crown

1957. (a) Size 18×22 mm.

103	**16**	2p. brown	75	75
104	**16**	4p. green	1·10	75
105	**16**	6p. red	75	75
106	**16**	8p. violet	75	75
107	**16**	12p. red	4·00	1·10

(b) Size 25½×29½ mm.

108	16p. brown	5·50	1·80
109	20p. red	8·75	2·50
110	24p. mauve	5·50	2·20
111	32p. blue	7·50	2·50
112	50p. pink	15·00	5·50
113	1r. salmon	37·00	11·00
114	2r. orange	22·00	7·50

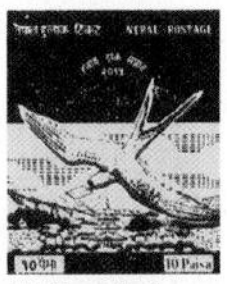
17 Gaunthali carrying Letter

1958. Air. Inauguration of Nepalese Internal Airmail Service.

115	**17**	10p. blue	1·90	1·90

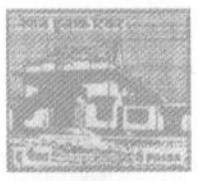
18 Temple of Lumbini

1958. Human Rights Day.

116	**18**	6p. yellow	1·50	1·50

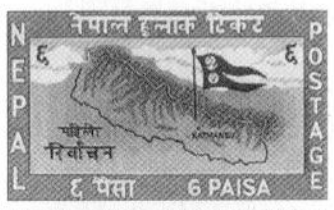

19 Nepalese Map and Flag

1959. 1st Nepalese Elections.

117	**19**	6p. red and green	50	45

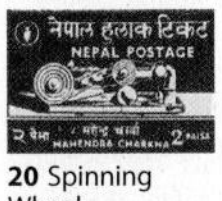

20 Spinning Wheel

1959. Cottage Industries.

118	**20**	2p. brown	45	45

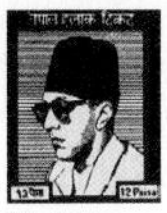
21 King Mahendra

1959. Admission of Nepal to U.P.U.

119	**21**	12p. blue	50	45

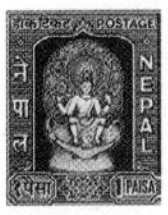
22 Vishnu

23 Nyatopol Temple, Bhaktapur

1959

120	**22**	1p. brown	15	15
121	-	2p. violet	15	15
122	-	4p. blue	50	35
123	-	6p. pink	50	15
124	-	8p. brown	35	15
125	-	12p. grey	50	15
126	**23**	16p. violet and brown	50	15
127	**23**	20p. red and blue	1·80	75
128	**23**	24p. red and green	1·80	75
129	**23**	32p. blue and lilac	1·10	75
130	**23**	50p. green and red	1·80	75
131	-	1r. blue and brown	16·00	6·00
132	-	2r. blue and purple	15·00	6·25
133	-	5r. red and violet	60·00	55·00

DESIGNS—As Type **22**. HORIZ: 2p. Krishna; 8p. Siberian musk deer; 12p. Indian rhinoceros. VERT: 4p. Himalayas; 6p. Gateway, Bhaktapur Palace. As Type **23**. VERT: 1r., 2r. Himalayan monal pheasant; 5r. Satyr tragopan.

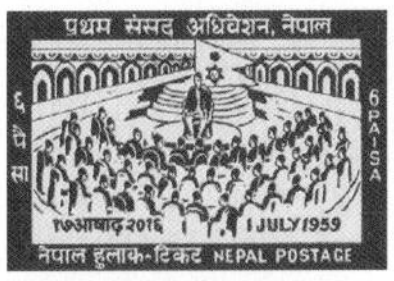

24 King Mahendra opening Parliament

1959. Opening of 1st Nepalese Parliament.

134	**24**	6p. red	1·10	1·10

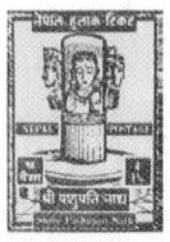
25 Sri Pashupatinath

1959. Renovation of Sri Pashupatinath Temple, Katmandu.

135	**25**	4p. green (18×25 mm)	75	75
136	**25**	8p. red (21×28½ mm)	1·50	75
137	**25**	1r. blue (24½×33½ mm)	8·75	6·00

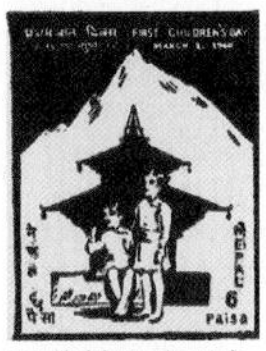
26 Children, Pagoda and Mt. Everest

1960. Children's Day.

137a	**26**	6p. blue	15·00	11·00

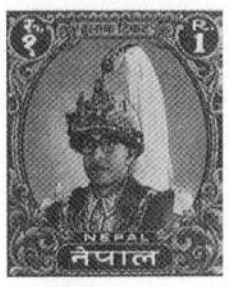
27 King Mahendra

1960. King Mahendra's 41st Birthday.

138	**27**	1r. purple	1·60	1·10

See also Nos. 163/4a.

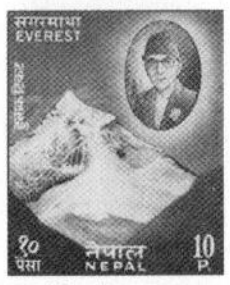

28 Mt. Everest

1960. Mountain Views.

139	-	5p. brown and purple	35	15
140	**28**	10p. purple and blue	50	20
141	-	40p. brown and violet	1·30	80

DESIGNS: 5p. Machha Puchhre; 40p. Manaslu (wrongly inscr "MANSALU").

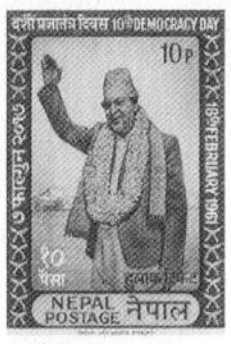

29 King Tribhuvana

1961. 10th Democracy Day.

142	**29**	10p. orange and brown	15	15

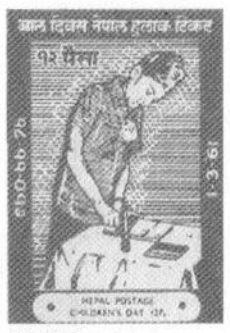
30 Prince Gyanendra cancelling Children's Day Stamps of 1960

1961. Children's Day.

143	**30**	12p. orange	37·00	37·00

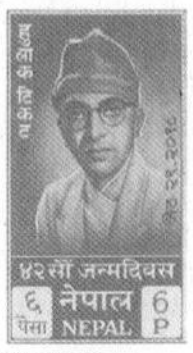

31 King Mahendra

1961. King Mahendra's 42nd Birthday.

144	**31**	6p. green	35	35
145	**31**	12p. blue	50	50
146	**31**	50p. red	1·10	1·10
147	**31**	1r. brown	1·80	1·80

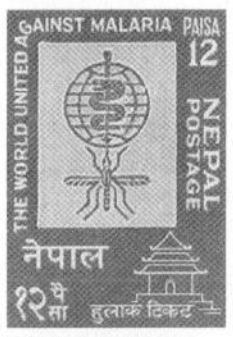

32 Campaign Emblem and House

1962. Malaria Eradication.

148	**32**	12p. blue	35	35
149	-	1r. orange and red	1·10	1·10

DESIGN: 1r. Emblem and Nepalese flag.

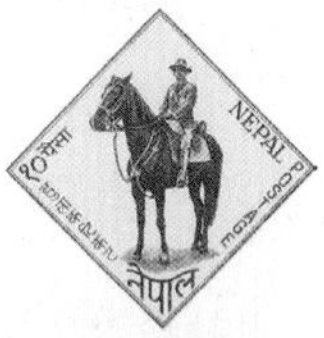

33 King Mahendra on Horseback

1962. King Mahendra's 43rd Birthday.

150	**33**	10p. blue	20	20
151	**33**	15p. brown	35	35
152	**33**	45p. brown	75	75
153	**33**	1r. grey	1·10	1·10

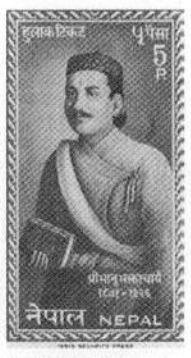

34 Bhana Bhakta Acharya

1962. Nepalese Poets.

154	**34**	5p. brown	35	35
155	-	10p. turquoise	35	35
156	-	40p. green	50	50

PORTRAITS: 10p. Moti Ram Bhakta; 40p. Sambhu Prasad.

35 King
Mahendra

36 King
Mahendra

1962

157	35	1p. red	15	10
158	35	2p. blue	15	10
158a	35	3p. grey	50	35
159	35	5p. brown	15	10
160	36	10p. purple	15	15
161	36	40p. brown	35	35
162	36	75p. green	11·00	11·00
162a	35	75p. green	1·50	75
163	27	2r. red	1·50	1·50
164	27	5r. green	3·00	3·00
164a	27	10r. violet	11·00	8·75

No. 162a is smaller, 17½×20 mm.

37 Emblems of Learning

1963. UNESCO "Education for All" Campaign.

165	37	10p. black	35	15
166	37	15p. brown	50	35
167	37	50p. blue	90	75

38 Hands holding
Lamps

1963. National Day.

168	38	5p. blue	15	15
169	38	10p. brown	15	15
170	38	50p. purple	75	50
171	38	1r. green	1·50	75

39 Campaign
Symbols

1963. Freedom from Hunger.

172	39	10p. orange	35	15
173	39	15p. blue	50	35
174	39	50p. green	1·10	75
175	39	1r. brown	1·50	1·30

40 Map of Nepal and
Open Hand

1963. Rastruya Panchayat.

176	40	10p. green	15	15
177	40	15p. purple	35	35
178	40	50p. grey	95	50
179	40	1r. blue	1·50	90

41 King
Mahendra

1963. King Mahendra's 44th Birthday.

180	41	5p. violet	15	15
181	41	10p. brown	35	15
182	41	15p. green	50	35

42 King Mahendra and
Highway Map

1964. Inauguration of East–West Highway.

183	42	10p. orange and blue	15	15
184	42	15p. orange and blue	35	20
185	42	50p. brown and green	60	35

43 King
Mahendra at
Microphone

1964. King Mahendra's 45th Birthday.

186	43	1p. brown	15	15
187	43	2p. grey	20	20
188	43	2r. brown	1·10	1·10

44 Crown
Prince
Birendra

1964. Crown Prince's 19th Birthday.

189	44	10p. green	90	75
190	44	15p. brown	90	75

45 Flag, Kukris, Rings
and Torch

1964. Olympic Games, Tokyo.

191	45	10p. blue, red and pink	95	75

46 Nepalese
Family

1965. Land Reform.

192	-	2p. black and green	35	35
193	-	5p. brown and green	35	35
194	-	10p. purple and grey	35	35
195	46	15p. brown and yellow	50	35

DESIGNS: 2p. Farmer ploughing; 5p. Ears of wheat; 10p.
Grain elevator.

47 Globe and Letters

1965. Introduction of International Insured and Parcel
Service.

196	47	15p. violet	35	35

48 King
Mahendra

1965. King Mahendra's 46th Birthday.

197	48	50p. purple	90	75

49 Four Martyrs

1965. "Nepalese Martyrs".

198	49	15p. green	20	15

50 I.T.U. Emblem

1965. I.T.U. Centenary.

199	50	15p. black and purple	50	35

51 I.C.Y. Emblem

1965. International Co-operation Year.

200	51	1r. multicoloured	1·10	90

52 Devkota
(poet)

1965. Devkota Commemoration.

201	52	15p. brown	35	30

54 Flag and King
Mahendra

1966. Democracy Day.

202	54	15p. red and blue	75	50

55 Siva Parvati
and Pashuvati
Temple

1966. Maha Siva-Ratri Festival.

203	55	15p. violet	45	35

56 "Stamp" Emblem

1966. Nepalese Philatelic Exhibition, Katmandu.

204	56	15p. orange and green	50	35

57 King Mahendra

1966. King Mahendra's 47th Birthday.

205	57	15p. brown and yellow	45	30

58 Queen
Mother

1966. Queen Mother's 60th Birthday.

206	58	15p. brown	35	35

59 Queen Ratna

1966. Children's Day.

207	59	15p. brown and yellow	45	35

60 Flute-player
and Dancer

1966. Krishna Anniv.

208	60	15p. violet and yellow	45	35

61 "To render service..."

1966. 1st Anniv of Nepalese Red Cross.

209	61	50p. red and green	4·50	1·50

62 W.H.O. Building
on Flag

1966. Inaug. of W.H.O. Headquarters, Geneva.

210	62	1r. violet	2·20	1·50

63 Paudyal

1966. Leknath Paudyal (poet) Commemoration.

211	63	15p. blue	45	35

64 Rama and
Sita

1967. Rama Navami, 2024, birthday of Rama.

212	64	15p. brown and yellow	45	35

65 Buddha

1967. Buddha Jayanti, birthday of Buddha.

213	65	75p. purple and orange	35	35

66 King Mahendra addressing
Nepalese

1967. King Mahendra's 48th Birthday.

214	66	15p. brown and blue	45	35

67 Queen Ratna and Children

1967. Children's Day.
215 **67** 15p. brown and cream 45 35

68 Ama Dablam (mountain)

1967. International Tourist Year.
216 **68** 5p. violet (postage) 35 35
217 - 65p. brown 75 75
218 - 1r.80 red and blue (air) 1·80 1·50
DESIGNS—38×20 mm: 65p. Bhaktapur Durbar Square. 35½×25½ mm: 1r.80, Plane over Katmandu.

69 Open-air Class

1967. Constitution Day. "Go to the Village" Educational Campaign.
219 **69** 15p. multicoloured 45 35

70 Crown Prince Birendra, Campfire and Scout Emblem

1967. Diamond Jubilee of World Scouting.
220 **70** 15p. blue 75 50

71 Prithvi Narayan Shah (founder of Kingdom)

1968. Bicentenary of the Kingdom.
221 **71** 15p. blue and red 75 50

72 Arms of Nepal

1968. National Day.
222 **72** 15p. blue and red 75 50

73 W.H.O. Emblem and Nepalese Flag

1968. 20th Anniv of W.H.O.
223 **73** 1r.20 blue, red and yellow 3·00 2·20

74 Sita and Janaki Temple

1968. Sita Jayanti.
224 **74** 15p. brown and violet 50 35

75 King Mahendra, Mountains and Himalayan Monal Pheasant

1968. King Mahendra's 49th Birthday.
225 **75** 15p. multicoloured 65 35

76 Garuda and Airline Emblem

1968. Air. 10th Anniv of Royal Nepalese Airlines.
226 **76** 15p. brown and blue 35 35
227 - 65p. blue 75 75
228 - 2r.50 blue and orange 2·50 2·20
DESIGNS—DIAMOND (25½×25½ mm): 65p. Route-map. As Type **76**: 2r.50, Convair Metropolitan airliner over Mount Dhaulagiri.

77 Flag, Queen Ratna and Children

1968. Children's Day and Queen Ratna's 41st Birthday.
229 **77** 5p. red, yellow and green 35 30

78 Human Rights Emblem and Buddha

1968. Human Rights Year.
230 **78** 1r. red and green 3·00 2·20

79 Crown Prince Birendra and Dancers

1968. Crown Prince Birendra's 24th Birthday, and National Youth Festival.
231 **79** 25p. blue 75 50

80 King Mahendra, Flags and U.N. Building, New York

1969. Nepal's Election to U.N. Security Council.
232 **80** 1r. multicoloured 1·10 90

81 Amsu Varma (7th-century ruler)

1969. Famous Nepalese.
233 **81** 15p. violet and green 50 1·50
234 - 25p. turquoise 75 75
235 - 50p. brown 95 95
236 - 1r. purple and brown 1·10 90
DESIGNS—VERT: 25p. Ram Shah (17th-century King of Gurkha); 50p. Bhimsen Thapa (19th-century Prime Minister). HORIZ: 1r. Bal Bhadra Kunwar (19th-century warrior).

82 I.L.O. Emblem

1969. 50th Anniv of I.L.O.
237 **82** 1r. brown and mauve 5·50 3·75

83 King Mahendra

1969. King Mahendra's 50th Birthday.
238 **83** 25p. multicoloured 45 45

84 King Tribhuvana and Queens

1969. 64th Birth Anniv of King Tribhuvana.
239 **84** 25p. brown and yellow 45 45

1969. National Children's Day.
240 **85** 25p. mauve and brown 45 45

86 Rhododendron

1969. Flowers. Multicoloured.
241 25p. Type **86** 60 50
242 25p. Narcissus 60 50
243 25p. Marigold 60 50
244 25p. Poinsettia 60 50

87 Durga, Goddess of Victory

1969. Durga Pooja Festival.
245 **87** 15p. black and orange 35 35
246 **87** 50p. violet and brown 80 80

88 Crown Prince Birendra and Princess Aishwarya

1970. Royal Wedding.
247 **88** 25p. multicoloured 45 20

89 Produce, Cow and Landscape

1970. Agricultural Year.
248 **89** 25p. multicoloured 45 35

90 King Mahendra, Mt. Everest and Nepalese Crown

1970. King Mahendra's 51st Birthday.
249 **90** 50p. multicoloured 75 50

91 Lake Gosainkunda

1970. Nepalese Lakes. Multicoloured.
250 5p. Type **91** 35 35
251 25p. Lake Phewa Tal 50 50
252 1r. Lake Rara Daha 90 90

92 A.P.Y. Emblem

1970. Asian Productivity Year.
253 **92** 1r. blue 90 75

93 Queen Ratna and Children's Palace, Taulihawa

1970. National Children's Day.
254 **93** 25p. grey and brown 45 35

94 New Headquarters Building

1970. New U.P.U. Headquarters, Berne.
255 **94** 2r.50 grey and brown 1·80 80

95 U.N. Flag

1970. 25th Anniv of United Nations.
256 **95** 25p. blue and purple 45 35

96 Durbar Square, Patan

1970. Tourism. Multicoloured.
257 15p. Type **96** 35 15
258 25p. Boudhanath Stupa (temple) (vert) 50 35
259 1r. Mt. Gauri Shankar 90 75

97 Statue of Harihar, Valmiki Ashram

1971. Nepalese Religious Art.
260 **97** 25p. black and brown 45 30

98 Torch within Spiral

1971. Racial Equality Year.
261 **98** 1r. red and blue 1·10 80

99 King Mahendra taking Salute

1971. King Mahendra's 52nd Birthday.
262 **99** 15p. purple and blue 45 30

100 Sweta Bhairab

1971. Bhairab Statues of Shiva.
263 **100** 15p. brown and chestnut 35 35
264 - 25p. brown and green 35 35
265 - 50p. brown and blue 75 75

DESIGNS: 25p. Mahankal Bhairab; 50p. Kal Bhairab.

101 Child presenting
Queen Ratna with
Garland

1971. National Children's Day.
266 **101** 25p. multicoloured 45 30

102 Iranian and Nepalese
Flags on Map of Iran

1971. 2,500th Anniv of Persian Empire.
267 **102** 1r. multicoloured 1·10 75

103 Mother and Child

1971. 25th Anniv of UNICEF.
268 **103** 1r. blue 1·10 75

104 Mt. Everest

1971. Tourism. Himalayan Peaks.
269 **104** 25p. dp brown, brn
and bl 35 15
270 - 1r. black, brown and
blue 75 50
271 - 1r.80 green, brown
& blue 1·30 95
DESIGNS: 1r. Mt. Kanchenjunga; 1r.80, Mt. Annapurna I.

105 Royal
Standard

1972. National Day.
272 **105** 25p. black and red 45 30

106 Araniko and
White Dagoba,
Peking

1972. Araniko (13th-century architect) Commem.
273 **106** 15p. brown and blue 20 20

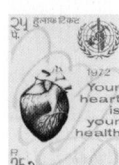

107 Open Book

1972. International Book Year.
274 **107** 2p. brown and buff 15 15
275 **107** 5p. black and brown 15 15
276 **107** 1r. black and blue 90 75

108 Human Heart

1972. World Heart Month.
277 **108** 25p. red and green 45 35

109 King Mahendra

1972. 1st Death Anniv of King Mahendra.
278 **109** 25p. brown and black 45 30

110 King Birendra

1972. King Birendra's 28th Birthday.
279 **110** 50p. purple and brown 50 45

111 Northern Border
Costumes

1973. National Costumes. Multicoloured.
280 25p. Type **111** 35 15
281 50p. Hill-dwellers 45 35
282 75p. Katmandu Valley 60 45
283 1r. Inner Terai 90 60

112 Sri Baburam
Acharya

**1973. 85th Birth Anniv of Sri Baburam Acharya
(historian).**
284 **112** 25p. grey and red 15 10

113 Nepalese Family

1973. 25th Anniv of W.H.O.
285 **113** 1r. blue and orange 90 75

114 Birthplace of Buddha, Lumbini

1973. Tourism. Multicoloured.
286 25p. Type **114** 35 15
287 75p. Mt. Makalu 50 35
288 1r. Castle, Gurkha 75 75

115 Transplanting Rice

1973. 10th Anniv of World Food Programme.
289 **115** 10p. brown and violet 15 15

116 Interpol H.Q., Paris

**1973. 50th Anniv of International Criminal Police
Organization (Interpol).**
290 **116** 25p. blue and brown 35 20

117 Shri Shom
Nath Sigdyal

**1973. 1st Death Anniv of Shri Shom Nath Sigdyal
(scholar).**
291 **117** 1r.25 violet 90 75

118 Cow

1973. Domestic Animals. Multicoloured.
292 2p. Type **118** 15 15
293 3r.25 Yak 1·60 1·10

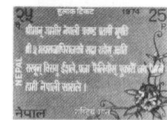

119 King Birendra

1974. King Birendra's 29th Birthday.
294 **119** 5p. brown and black 15 15
295 **119** 15p. brown and black 20 15
296 **119** 1r. brown and black 75 50

120 Text of National
Anthem

1974. National Day.
297 **120** 25p. purple 35 15
298 - 1r. green 50 45
DESIGN: 1r. Anthem musical score.

121 King Janak
seated on
Throne

1974. King Janak Commemoration.
299 **121** 2r.50 multicoloured 1·80 1·50

122 Emblem and Village

1974. 25th Anniv of SOS Children's Village International.
300 **122** 25p. blue and red 35 35

123 Football

1974. Nepalese Games. Multicoloured.
301 2p. Type **123** 15 15
302 2r.75 Baghchal (diagram) 1·10 90

124 W.P.Y.
Emblem

1974. World Population Year.
303 **124** 5p. blue and brown 20 15

125 U.P.U.
Monument, Berne

1974. Centenary of U.P.U.
304 **125** 1r. black and green 75 50

126 Red Lacewing

1974. Nepalese Butterflies. Multicoloured.
305 10p. Type **126** 15 15
306 15p. Leaf buttefly 45 20
307 1r.25 Leaf butterfly (underside) 1·10 75
308 1r.75 Red-breasted jezebel 1·30 1·10

127 King
Birendra

1974. King Birendra's 30th Birthday.
309 **127** 25p. black and green 20 20

128 Muktinath

1974. "Visit Nepal" Tourism. Multicoloured.
310 25p. Type **128** 35 15
311 1r. Peacock window, Bhaktapur
(horiz) 75 45

129 Guheswari
Temple

1975. Coronation of King Birendra. Multicoloured.
312 25p. Type **129** 35 15
313 50p. Lake Rara (37×30 mm) 35 15
314 1r. Throne and sceptre (46×26
mm) 50 35
315 1r.25 Royal Palace, Katmandu
(46×26 mm) 1·10 50
316 1r.75 Pashupatinath Temple
(25×31 mm) 75 75
317 2r.75 King Birendra and Queen
Aishwarya (46×25 mm) 1·10 90
MS318 143×105 mm. Nos. 314/15 and
317. Imperf 4·00 4·00

130 Tourism Year
Emblem

1975. South Asia Tourism Year. Multicoloured.
319 2p. Type **130** 15 15
320 25p. Temple stupa (vert) 35 35

131 Tiger

1975. Wildlife Conservation. Multicoloured.
321 2p. Type **131** 35 35
322 5p. Swamp deer (vert) 35 35
323 1r. Lesser panda 75 75

132 Queen Aishwarya and I.W.Y.
Emblem

1975. International Women's Year.
324 **132** 1r. multicoloured 50 35

133 Rupse Falls

1975. Tourism. Multicoloured.
325		2p. Mt. Ganesh Himal (horiz)	15	15
326		25p. Type **133**	15	15
327		50p. Kumari ("Living Goddess")	50	35

134 King Birendra

1975. King Birendra's 31st Birthday.
328	**134**	25p. violet and mauve	20	15

136 Flag and Map

1976. Silver Jubilee of National Democracy Day.
330	**136**	2r.50 red and blue	90	75

137 Transplanting Rice

1976. Agriculture Year.
331	**137**	25p. multicoloured	20	15

138 Flags of Nepal and Colombo Plan

1976. 25th Anniv of Colombo Plan.
332	**138**	1r. multicoloured	50	45

139 Running

1976. Olympic Games, Montreal.
333	**139**	3r.25 black and blue	1·50	1·10

140 "Dove of Peace"

1976. 5th Non-aligned Countries' Summit Conf.
334	**140**	5r. blue, yellow and black	1·90	1·30

141 Lakhe Dance

1976. Nepalese Dances. Multicoloured.
335		10p. Type **141**	15	15
336		15p. Maruni dance	15	15
337		30p. Jhangad dance	35	20
338		1r. Sebru dance	50	35

142 Nepalese Lily

1976. Flowers. Multicoloured.
339		30p. Type **142**	50	15
340		30p. "Meconopsis grandis"	50	15
341		30p. "Cardiocrinum giganteum" (horiz)	50	15
342		30p. "Megacodon stylophorus" (horiz)	50	15

143 King Birendra

1976. King Birendra's 32nd Birthday.
343	**143**	5p. green	15	10
344	**143**	30p. dp brown, brn & yell	20	15

144 Liberty Bell

1976. Bicentenary of American Revolution.
345	**144**	10r. multicoloured	2·75	2·40

145 Kaji Amarsingh Thapa

1977. Kaji Amarsingh Thapa (19th-century warrior) Commemoration.
346	**145**	10p. green and brown	15	15

146 Terracotta Figurine and Kapilavastu

1977. Tourism.
347	**146**	30p. violet	15	15
348	-	5r. green and brown	1·50	1·10

DESIGN: 5r. Ashokan pillar, Lumbini.

147 Great Indian Hornbill

1977. Birds. Multicoloured.
349		5p. Type **147**	45	20
350		15p. Cheer pheasant (horiz)	80	20
351		1r. Green magpie (horiz)	1·30	50
352		2r.30 Spiny babbler	2·40	75

148 Tukuche Himal and Police Flag

1977. 1st Anniv of Ascent of Tukuche Himal by Police Team.
353	**148**	1r.25 multicoloured	20	15

149 Map of Nepal and Scout Emblem

1977. 25th Anniv of Scouting in Nepal.
354	**149**	3r.50 multicoloured	45	30

150 Dhanwantari, the Health-giver

1977. Health Day.
355	**150**	30p. green	20	15

151 Map of Nepal and Flags

1977. 26th Consultative Committee Meeting of Colombo Plan, Katmandu.
356	**151**	1r. multicoloured	35	20

152 King Birendra

1977. King Birendra's 33rd Birthday.
357	**152**	5p. brown	15	15
358	**152**	1r. brown	35	35

153 General Post Office, Katmandu, and Seal

1978. Centenary of Nepalese Post Office.
359	**153**	25p. brown and agate	15	15
360		75p. brown and agate	35	35

DESIGN: 75p. General Post Office, Katmandu, and early postmark.

154 South-west Face of Mt. Everest

1978. 25th Anniv of First Ascent of Mt. Everest.
361	**154**	2r.30 grey and brown	90	50
362	-	4r. blue and green	1·30	1·10

DESIGN: 4r. South face of Mt. Everest.

155 Sun, Ankh and Landscape

1978. World Environment Day.
363	**155**	1r. green and orange	35	20

156 Queen Mother Ratna

1978. Queen Mother's 50th Birthday.
364	**156**	2r.30 green	75	50

157 Rapids, Tripsuli River

1978. Tourism. Multicoloured.
365		10p. Type **157**	15	10
366		50p. Window, Nara Devi, Katmandu	20	15
367		1r. Mahakali dance (vert)	45	35

158 Lapsi ("Choerospondias axillaris")

1978. Fruits. Multicoloured.
368		5p. Type **158**	20	10
369		1r. Katus (vert)	50	35
370		1r.25 Rudrakshya	75	45

159 Lamp and U.N. Emblem

1978. 30th Anniv of Human Rights Declaration.
371	**159**	25p. brown and red	15	10
372	**159**	1r. blue and red	35	20

160 Wright Flyer I and Boeing 727-100

1978. Air. 75th Anniv of First Powered Flight.
373	**160**	2r.30 blue and brown	90	75

161 King Birendra

1978. King Birendra's 34th Birthday.
374	**161**	30p. blue and brown	15	10
375	**161**	2r. brown and violet	60	45

162 Red Machchhindranath and Kamroop and Patan Temples

1979. Red Machchhindranath (guardian deity) Festival.
376	**162**	75p. brown and green	35	20

163 "Buddha's Birth" (carving, Maya Devi Temple)

1979. Lumbini Year.
377	**163**	1r. yellow and brown	35	20

164 Planting a Sapling

1979. Tree Planting Festival.
378	**164**	2r.30 brown, green & yellow	90	75

165 Chariot of Red Machchhindranath

1979. Bhoto Jatra (Vest Exhibition) Festival.
| 379 | **165** | 1r.25 multicoloured | 45 | 35 |

166 Nepalese Scouts and Guides

1979. International Year of the Child.
| 380 | **166** | 1r. brown | 45 | 35 |

167 Mount Pabil

1979. Tourism.
381	**167**	30p. green	15	15
382	–	50p. red and blue	15	15
383	–	1r.25 multicoloured	45	45

DESIGNS: 50p. Yajnashala, Swargadwari. 1r.25, Shiva-Parbati (wood carving, Gaddi Baithak Temple).

168 Great Grey Shrike

1979. International World Pheasant Association Symposium, Katmandu. Multicoloured.
384	10p. Type **168** (postage)		20	15
385	–	10r. Fire-tailed sunbird	5·50	3·50
386	3r.50 Himalayan monal pheasant (horiz) (air)		1·90	1·60

169 Lichchhavi Coin (obverse)

1979. Coins.
387	**169**	5p. orange and brown	15	15
388	–	5p. orange and brown	15	15
389	–	15p. blue and indigo	15	15
390	–	15p. blue and indigo	15	15
391	–	1r. blue and deep blue	45	45
392	–	1r. blue and deep blue	45	45

DESIGNS: No. 388, Lichchhavi coin (reverse); 389, Malla coin (obverse); 390, Malla coin (reverse); 391, Prithvi Narayan Shah coin (obverse); 392, Prithvi Narayan Shah coin (reverse).

170 King Birendra

1979. King Birendra's 35th Birthday. Mult.
| 393 | 25p. Type **170** | | 15 | 10 |
| 394 | 2r.30 Reservoir | | 75 | 50 |

171 Samyak Pooja Festival

1980. Samyak Pooja Festival, Katmandu.
| 395 | **171** | 30p. brown, grey & purple | 15 | 15 |

172 Sacred Basil

1980. Herbs. Multicoloured.
396	5p. Type **172**		15	10
397	30p. Valerian		20	10
398	1r. Nepalese pepper		35	20
399	2r.30 Himalayan rhubarb		75	50

173 Gyandil Das

1980. Nepalese Writers.
400	**173**	5p. lilac and brown	10	10
401	–	30p. purple and brown	15	10
402	–	1r. green and blue	30	20
403	–	2r.30 blue and green	60	50

DESIGNS: 30p. Siddhidas Amatya; 1r. Pahalman Singh Swanr; 2r.30, Jay Prithvi Bahadur Singh.

174 Everlasting Flame and Temple, Shirsasthan

1980. Tourism. Multicoloured.
404	10p. Type **174**		10	10
405	1r. Godavari Pond		35	20
406	5r. Mount Dhaulagiri		1·20	90

175 Bhairab Dancer

1980. World Tourism Conf, Manila, Philippines.
| 407 | **175** | 25r. multicoloured | 5·25 | 4·00 |

176 King Birendra

1980. King Birendra's 36th Birthday.
| 408 | **176** | 1r. multicoloured | 35 | 20 |

177 I.Y.D.P. Emblem and Nepalese Flag

1981. International Year of Disabled Persons.
| 409 | **177** | 5r. multicoloured | 1·50 | 1·10 |

178 Nepal Rastra Bank

1981. 25th Anniv of Nepal Rastra Bank.
| 410 | **178** | 1r.75 multicoloured | 45 | 35 |

179 One Anna Stamp of 1881

1981. Nepalese Postage Stamp Centenary.
411	**179**	10p. blue, brown and black	15	10
412	–	40p. purple, brown & blk	15	10
413	–	3r.40 green, brown & blk	90	75
MS414	117×77 mm. Nos. 411/13 (sold at 5r.)		2·20	2·20

DESIGNS: 40p. 2a. stamp of 1881; 3r.40, 4a. stamp of 1881.

180 Nepalese Flag and Association Emblem

1981. 70th Council Meeting of International Hotel Association, Katmandu.
| 415 | **180** | 1r.75 multicoloured | 45 | 35 |

181 Hand holding Stamp

1981. "Nepal 81" Stamp Exhibition, Katmandu.
| 416 | **181** | 40p. multicoloured | 15 | 10 |

182 King Birendra

1981. King Birendra's 37th Birthday.
| 417 | **182** | 1r. multicoloured | 30 | 20 |

183 Image of Hrishikesh, Ridi

1981. Tourism. Multicoloured.
418	5p. Type **183**		10	10
419	25p. Tripura Sundari Temple, Baitadi		10	10
420	2r. Mt. Langtang Lirung		45	20

184 Academy Building

1982. 25th Anniv of Royal Nepal Academy.
| 421 | **184** | 40p. multicoloured | 15 | 15 |

185 Balakrishna Sama

1982. 1st Death Anniv of Balakrishna Sama (writer).
| 422 | **185** | 1r. multicoloured | 20 | 20 |

186 "Intelsat V" and Dish Aerial

1982. Sagarmatha Satellite Earth Station, Balambu.
| 423 | **186** | 5r. multicoloured | 1·30 | 75 |

187 Mount Nuptse

1982. 50th Anniv of Union of International Alpinist Associations. Multicoloured.
424	25p. Type **187**		15	15
425	2r. Mount Lhotse (31×31 mm)		50	35
426	3r. Mount Everest (39×31 mm)		1·10	50

Nos. 424/6 were issued together, se-tenant, forming a composite design.

188 Games Emblem and Weights

1982. 9th Asian Games, New Delhi.
| 427 | **188** | 3r.40 multicoloured | 90 | 75 |

189 Indra Sarobar Lake

1982. Kulekhani Hydro-electric Project.
| 428 | **189** | 2r. multicoloured | 50 | 35 |

190 King Birendra

1982. King Birendra's 38th Birthday.
| 429 | **190** | 5p. multicoloured | 15 | 15 |

191 N.I.D.C. Emblem

1983. 25th Anniv (1984) of Nepal Industrial Development Corporation.
| 430 | **191** | 50p. multicoloured | 15 | 15 |

192 Boeing 727 over Himalayas

1983. 25th Anniv of Royal Nepal Airlines.
| 431 | **192** | 1r. multicoloured | 45 | 20 |

193 W.C.Y. Emblem and Nepalese Flag

1983. World Communications Year.
| 432 | **193** | 10p. multicoloured | 15 | 15 |

194 Sarangi

1983. Musical Instruments. Multicoloured.

433		5p. Type **194**	10	10
434		10p. Kwota (drum)	10	10
435		50p. Narashinga (horn)	20	20
436		1r. Murchunga	35	35

195 Chakrapani Chalise

1983. Birth Centenary of Chakrapani Chalise (poet).

437	**195**	4r.50 multicoloured	45	35

196 King Birendra and Doves

1983. King Birendra's 39th Birthday.

438	**196**	5r. multicoloured	50	30

197 Barahkshetra Temple and Image of Barah

1983. Tourism. Multicoloured.

439		1r. Type **197**	10	10
440		2r.20 Temple, Triveni	20	15
441		6r. Mount Cho-oyu	50	35

198 Auditing Accounts

1984. 25th Anniv of Auditor General.

442	**198**	25p. multicoloured	50	45

199 Antenna and Emblem

1984. 20th Anniv of Asia-Pacific Broadcasting Union.

443	**199**	5r. multicoloured	1·30	1·10

200 University Emblem

1984. 25th Anniv of Tribhuvan University.

444	**200**	50p. multicoloured	20	15

201 Boxing

1984. Olympic Games, Los Angeles.

445	**201**	10r. multicoloured	2·20	1·50

202 Family and Emblem

1984. 25th Anniv of Nepal Family Planning Association.

446	**202**	1r. multicoloured	20	15

203 National Flag and Emblem

1984. Social Service Day.

447	**203**	5p. multicoloured	15	15

204 Gharial

1984. Wildlife. Multicoloured.

448		10p. Type **204**	15	15
449		25p. Snow leopard	20	20
450		50p. Blackbuck	35	35

205 "Vishnu as Giant" (stone carving)

1984. Tourism. Multicoloured.

451		10p. Type **205**	10	10
452		1r. Temple of Chhinna Masta Bhagavati and sculpture (horiz)	20	15
453		5r. Mount Api	1·30	80

206 King Birendra

1984. King Birendra's 40th Birthday.

454	**206**	1r. multicoloured	20	15

207 Animals and Mountains

1985. Sagarmatha (Mt. Everest) National Park.

455	**207**	10r. multicoloured	4·00	1·50

208 Shiva

1985. Traditional Paintings. Details of cover of "Shiva Dharma Purana". Multicoloured.

456		50p. Type **208**	20	20
457		50p. Multi-headed Shiva talking to woman	20	20
458		50p. Brahma and Vishnu making offering (15×22 mm)	20	20
459		50p. Shiva in single- and multi-headed forms	20	20
460		50p. Shiva talking to woman	20	20

Nos. 456/60 were printed together, se-tenant, forming a composite design.

209 U.N. Flag

1985. 40th Anniv of U.N.O.

461	**209**	5r. multicoloured	1·10	75

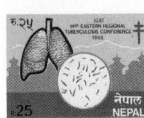

210 Lungs and Bacilli

1985. 14th Eastern Regional Tuberculosis Conf, Katmandu.

462	**210**	25r. multicoloured	5·25	3·75

211 Flags of Member Countries

1985. 1st South Asian Association for Regional Co-operation Summit.

463	**211**	5r. multicoloured	1·10	75

212 Jaleshwar Temple

1985. Tourism. Multicoloured.

464		10p. Type **212**	10	10
465		1r. Temple of Goddess Shaileshwari, Silgadi	20	15
466		2r. Phoksundo Lake	45	20

213 I.Y.Y. Emblem

1985. International Youth Year.

467	**213**	1r. multicoloured	20	15

214 King Birendra

1985. King Birendra's 41st Birthday.

468	**214**	50p. multicoloured	15	15

215 Devi Ghat Hydro-electric Project

1985

469	**215**	2r. multicoloured	50	35

216 Emblem

1986. 25th Anniv of Panchayat System (partyless government).

470	**216**	4r. multicoloured	90	75

217 Royal Crown

1986

471	**217**	5p. brown and deep brown	10	10
472	-	10p. blue	15	15
473	-	50p. blue	15	15
474	-	1r. brown and ochre	20	20

DESIGNS: 10p. Mayadevi Temple of Lumbini (Buddha's birthplace); 50p. Pashupati Temple; 1r. Royal Crown.

218 Pharping Hydro-electric Station

1986. 75th Anniv of Pharping Hydro-electric Power Station.

480	**218**	15p. multicoloured	15	15

219 Emblem and Map

1986. 25th Anniv of Asian Productivity Organization.

481	**219**	1r. multicoloured	20	15

220 Mt. Pumori, Himalayas (35×22 mm)

1986. Tourism. Multicoloured.

482		60p. Type **220**	15	10
483		8r. "Budhanilkantha" (sculpture of reclining Vishnu), Katmandu Valley	1·50	1·10

221 King Birendra

1986. King Birendra's 42nd Birthday.

484	**221**	1r. multicoloured	20	15

222 I.P.Y. Emblem

1986. International Peace Year.

485	**222**	10r. multicoloured	1·60	1·30

223 National Flag and Council Emblem

1987. 10th Anniv of National Social Service Co-ordination Council.

486	**223**	1r. multicoloured	20	15

224 Emblem and Forest

1987. 1st Nepal Scout Jamboree, Katmandu.

487	**224**	1r. brown, orange and blue	45	15

225 Ashokan Pillar and Maya Devi

1987. Lumbini (Buddha's Birthplace) Development Project.

488	**225**	4r. multicoloured	75	50

226 Emblem

1987. 3rd South Asian Association for Regional Co-operation Summit, Katmandu.

489 **226** 60p. gold and red   15 15

227 Emblem

1987. 25th Anniv of Rastriya Samachar Samiti (news service).

490 **227** 4r. purple, blue and red   75 50

228 Kashthamandap, Katmandu

1987

491 **228** 25p. multicoloured   15 15

229 Gyawali

1987. 89th Birth Anniv of Surya Bikram Gyawali.

492 **229** 60p. multicoloured   15 15

230 Emblem

1987. International Year of Shelter for the Homeless.

493 **230** 5r. multicoloured   90 75

231 King Birendra

1987. King Birendra's 43rd Birthday.

494 **231** 25p. multicoloured   15 15

232 Mt. Kanjiroba

1987

495 **232** 10r. multicoloured   1·60 1·10

233 Crown Prince Dipendra

1988. Crown Prince Dipendra's 17th Birthday.

496 **233** 1r. multicoloured   20 15

234 Baby in Incubator

1988. 25th Anniv of Kanti Children's Hospital, Katmandu.

497 **234** 60p. multicoloured   15 15

235 Swamp Deer

1988. 12th Anniv of Royal Shukla Phanta Wildlife Reserve.

498 **235** 60p. multicoloured   35 15

236 Laxmi, Goddess of Wealth

1988. 50th Anniv of Nepal Bank Ltd.

499 **236** 2r. multicoloured   35 20

237 Queen Mother

1988. 60th Birthday of Queen Mother.

500 **237** 5r. multicoloured   90 75

238 Hands protecting Blood Droplet

1988. 25th Anniv of Nepal Red Cross Society.

501 **238** 1r. red and brown   20 15

239 Temple and Statue

1988. Temple of Goddess Bindhyabasini, Pokhara.

502 **239** 15p. multicoloured   15 15

240 King Birendra

1988. King Birendra's 44th Birthday.

503 **240** 4r. multicoloured   75 45

241 Temple

1989. Pashupati Area Development Trust.

504 **241** 1r. multicoloured   20 15

242 Emblem

1989. 10th Anniv of Asia-Pacific Telecommunity.

505 **242** 4r. green, black and violet   45 30

243 S.A.A.R.C. Emblem

1989. South Asian Association for Regional Co-operation Year against Drug Abuse and Trafficking.

506 **243** 60p. multicoloured   15 15

244 King Birendra

1989. King Birendra's 45th Birthday.

507 **244** 2r. multicoloured   35 15

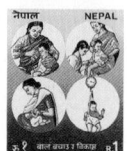

245 Child Survival Measures

1989. Child Survival Campaign.

508 **245** 1r. multicoloured   15 15

246 Lake Rara

1989. Rara National Park.

509 **246** 4r. multicoloured   45 30

247 Mt. Amadablam

1989

510 **247** 5r. multicoloured   75 35

248 Crown Prince Dipendra

1989. Crown Prince Dipendra's Coming-of-Age.

511 **248** 1r. multicoloured   15 15

249 Temple of Manakamana, Gorkha

1990

512 **249** 60p. black and violet   15 15

250 Emblem and Children

1990. 25th Anniv of Nepal Children's Organization.

513 **250** 1r. multicoloured   15 15

251 Emblem

1990. Centenary of Bir Hospital.

514 **251** 60p. red, blue and yellow   15 15

252 Emblem

1990. 20th Anniv of Asian–Pacific Postal Training Centre, Bangkok.

515 **252** 4r. multicoloured   50 30

253 Goddess and Bageshwori Temple, Nepalgunj

1990. Tourism. Multicoloured.

516   1r. Type **253**   15 15
517   5r. Mt. Saipal (36×27 mm)   60 35

254 Leisure Activities

1990. South Asian Association for Regional Co-operation Girls' Year.

518 **254** 4r.60 multicoloured   25 15

255 King Birendra

1990. King Birendra's 46th Birthday.

519 **255** 2r. multicoloured   20 15

256 Koirala

1990. 76th Birth Anniv of Bisweswar Prasad Koirala (Prime Minister, 1959–60).

520 **256** 60p. black, orange and red   10 10

257 Indian Rhinoceros and Lake

1991. Royal Chitwan National Park.

521 **257** 4r. multicoloured   75 35

258 Flower
and Crowd

1991. 1st Anniv of Abrogation of Ban on Political Parties.
522 **258** 1r. multicoloured 15 15

259 Official and
Villagers

1991. National Population Census.
523 **259** 60p. multicoloured 15 15

260 Federation
and Jubilee
Emblems

1991. 25th Anniv of Federation of Nepalese Chambers of
Commerce and Industry.
524 **260** 3r. multicoloured 35 20

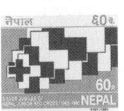

261 Crosses

1991. 25th Anniv (1990) of Nepal Junior Red Cross.
525 **261** 60p. red and grey 10 10

262 Delegates

1991. 1st Session of Revived Parliament.
526 **262** 1r. multicoloured 15 15

263 King Birendra making
Speech

1991. Constitution Day.
527 **263** 50p. multicoloured 10 10

264 Rama and
Janaki (statues)
and Vivaha
Mandap

1991. 5th Anniv of Rebuilt Vivaha Mandap Pavilion,
Janaki Temple.
528 **264** 1r. multicoloured 15 15

265 Mt. Kumbhakarna

1991. Tourism.
529 **265** 4r.60 multicoloured 50 30

266 King Birendra

1991. King Birendra's 47th Birthday.
530 **266** 8r. multicoloured 90 50

267 Houses

1991. South Asian Association for Regional Co-operation
Year of Shelter.
531 **267** 9r. multicoloured 90 60

268 Glass
magnifying Society
Emblem

1992. 25th Anniv (1991) of Nepal Philatelic Society.
532 **268** 4r. multicoloured 45 30

269 Rainbow over River
and Trees

1992. Environmental Protection.
533 **269** 60p. multicoloured 15 15

270 Nutrition,
Education and Health
Care

1992. Rights of the Child.
534 **270** 1r. multicoloured 15 15

271 Thakurdwara
Temple, Bardiya

1992. Temples. Multicoloured.
535 75p. Type **271** (postage) 10 10
536 1r. Namo Buddha Temple, Kavre 10 10
537 2r. Narijhowa Temple, Mustang 15 10
538 11r. Dantakali Temple, Bijayapur
(air) 1·00 65

272 Bank
Emblem

1992. 25th Anniv of Agricultural Development Bank.
539 **272** 40p. brown and green 15 15

273 Pin-tailed Green
Pigeon

1992. Birds. Multicoloured.
540 1r. Type **273** 10 10
541 3r. Bohemian waxwing 30 15
542 25r. Rufous-tailed desert (inscr
"Finch") lark 2·20 1·50

274 King Birendra
exchanging Swords with
Goddess Sree Bhadrakali

1992. King Birendra's 48th Birthday.
543 **274** 7r. multicoloured 60 35

275 Pandit
Kulchandra
Gautam

1992. Poets. Multicoloured, frame colour given in
brackets.
544 1r. Type **275** 15 10
545 1r. Chittadhar Hridaya (drab) 15 10
546 1r. Vidyapati (stone) 15 10
547 1r. Teongsi Sirijunga (grey) 15 10

276 Shooting
and Marathon

1992. Olympic Games, Barcelona.
548 **276** 25r. multicoloured 2·20 1·50

277 Golden Mahseer

1993. Fish. Multicoloured.
549 25p. Type **277** 10 10
550 1r. Marinka 10 10
551 5r. Indian eel 20 10
552 10r. False loach 35 20
MS553 90×70 mm. Nos. 549/52 1·80 1·80

278 Antibodies
attacking Globe

1993. World AIDS Day.
554 **278** 1r. multicoloured 15 15

279 Tanka
Prasad Acharya
(Prime Minister,
1956–57)

1993. Death Anniversaries. Multicoloured.
555 25p. Type **279** (1st anniv) 10 10
556 1r. Sundare Sherpa (mountaineer) (4th anniv) 10 10
557 7r. Siddhi Charan Shrestha
(poet) (1st anniv) 50 30
558 15r. Falgunanda (religious
leader) (44th anniv) 1·10 75

280 Bagh Bairab Temple,
Kirtipur

1993. Holy Places. Multicoloured.
559 1r.50 Type **280** 10 10
560 5r. Devghat (gods' bathing
place), Tanahun 35 20
561 8r. Halesi Mahadev Cave (hiding
place of Shiva), Khotang 60 35

281 Tushahiti Fountain,
Sundari Chowk, Patan

1993. Tourism. Multicoloured.
562 5r. Type **281** 35 20
563 8r. White-water rafting 60 35

282 King Birendra

1993. King Birendra's 49th Birthday.
564 **282** 10r. multicoloured 75 45

283 **284** Mt. Everest
Monument

1994.
565 **283** 20p. brown 10 10
566 – 25p. red 10 10
567 – 30p. green 10 10
568 **284** 1r. multicoloured 15 15
569 – 5r. multicoloured 35 20
DESIGNS—20×22 mm: 25p. State arms. 22×20 mm: 30p.
Lumbini. 25×15 mm: 5r. Map of Nepal, crown and state
arms and flag.

285 Pasang Sherpa

1994. 1st Death Anniv of Pasang Sherpa (mountaineer).
570 **285** 10r. multicoloured 75 45

286 Cigarette, Lungs
and Crab's Claws

1994. Anti-smoking Campaign.
571 **286** 1r. multicoloured 15 15

287 Postal
Delivery

1994.
572 **287** 1r.50 multicoloured 15 15

288 Khuda

1994. Weapons. Multicoloured.
573 5r. Kukris (three swords and
two scabbards) 35 20
574 5r. Type **288** 35 20
575 5r. Dhaal (swords and shield) 35 20
576 5r. Katari (two daggers) 35 20

289 Workers and Emblem

1994. 75th Anniv of I.L.O.
| 577 | **289** | 15r. gold, blue & ultram | 1·10 | 75 |

290 Landscape

1994. World Food Day.
| 578 | **290** | 25r. multicoloured | 1·80 | 1·20 |

291 "Dendrobium densiflorum"

1994. Orchids. Multicoloured.
579	**291**	10r. Type **291**	75	45
580		10r. "Coelogyne flaccida"	75	45
581		10r. "Cymbidium devonianum"	75	45
582		10r. "Coelogyne corymbosa"	75	45

292 Family

1994. International Year of the Family.
| 583 | **292** | 9r. emerald, green and red | 65 | 45 |

293 Emblem and Airplane

1994. 50th Anniv of I.C.A.O.
| 584 | **293** | 11r. blue, gold and deep blue | 80 | 50 |

294 "Russula nepalensis"

1994. Fungi. Multicoloured.
585	**294**	7r. Type **294**	50	30
586		7r. Morels ("Morchella conica")	50	30
587		7r. Caesar's mushroom ("Amanita caesarea")	50	30
588		7r. "Cordyceps sinensis"	50	30

295 Dharanidhar Koirala (poet)

1994. Celebrities. Multicoloured.
589	**295**	1r. Type **295**	10	10
590		2r. Narayan Gopal Guruwacharya (singer)	15	10
591		6r. Bahadur Shah (vert)	45	30
592		7r. Balaguru Shadananda	50	30

296 King Birendra, Flag, Map and Crown

1994. King Birendra's 50th Birthday (1st issue).
| 593 | **296** | 9r. multicoloured | 65 | 45 |

See also No. 621.

297 Lake Tilicho, Manang

1994. Tourism. Multicoloured.
| 594 | **297** | 9r. Type **297** | 65 | 45 |
| 595 | | 11r. Taleju Temple, Katmandu (vert) | 80 | 50 |

298 Health Care

1994. Children's Activities. Multicoloured.
596	**298**	1r. Type **298**	10	10
597		1r. Classroom	10	10
598		1r. Playground equipment	10	10
599		1r. Stamp collecting	10	10

299 Singhaduarbar

1995
| 600 | **299** | 10p. green | 10 | 10 |
| 601 | - | 50p. blue | 10 | 10 |

DESIGN—VERT: 50p. Pashupati.

300 Crab on Lungs

1995. Anti-cancer Campaign.
| 602 | **300** | 2r. multicoloured | 15 | 15 |

301 Chandra Man Singh Maskey (artist)

1995. Celebrities. Multicoloured.
603	**301**	3r. Type **301**	20	15
604		3r. Parijat (writer)	20	15
605		3r. Bhim Nidhi Tiwari (writer)	20	15
606		3r. Yuddha Prasad Mishra (writer)	20	15

302 Bhakti Thapa (soldier)

1995. Celebrities. Multicoloured.
607	**302**	15p. Type **302**	10	10
608		1r. Madan Bhandari (politician)	10	10
609		4r. Prakash Raj Kaphley (human rights activist)	10	15

303 Gaur ("Bos gaurus")

1995. "Singapore '95" International Stamp Exhibition. Mammals. Multicoloured.
610	**303**	10r. Type **303**	75	45
611		10r. Lynx ("Felis lynx")	75	45
612		10r. Assam macaque ("Macaca assamensis")	75	45
613		10r. Striped hyena ("Hyaena hyaena")	75	45

304 Anniversary Emblem

1995. 50th Anniv of F.A.O.
| 614 | **304** | 7r. multicoloured | 50 | 30 |

305 Figures around Emblem

1995. 50th Anniv of U.N.O.
| 615 | **305** | 50r. multicoloured | 3·75 | 2·40 |

306 Bhimeswor Temple, Dolakha

1995. Tourism. Multicoloured.
616	**306**	1r. Type **306**	10	10
617		5r. Ugra Tara Temple, Dadeldhura (horiz)	35	20
618		7r. Mt. Nampa (horiz)	50	30
619		18r. Nrity Aswora (traditional Pauba painting) (27×39 mm)	1·30	90
620		20r. Lumbini (Buddha's birthplace) (28×28 mm)	1·50	95

307 King Birendra

1995. King Birendra's 50th Birthday (1994) (2nd issue).
| 621 | **307** | 1r. multicoloured | 15 | 15 |

308 Anniversary Emblem

1995. 10th Anniv of South Asian Association for Regional Co-operation.
| 622 | **308** | 10r. multicoloured | 75 | 45 |

309 King Birendra

1995. King Birendra's 51st Birthday.
| 623 | **309** | 12r. multicoloured | 90 | 60 |

310 Karnali Bridge

1996
| 624 | **310** | 7r. multicoloured | 50 | 30 |

311 State Arms

1996
| 625 | **311** | 25p. red | 15 | 15 |

312 Kaji Kalu Pande (soldier and royal adviser)

1996. Political Figures. Multicoloured.
626	**312**	75p. Type **312**	10	10
627		1r. Pushpa Lal Shrestha (Nepal Communist Party General-Secretary)	10	10
628		5r. Suvarna Shamsher Rana (founder of Nepal Democratic Congress Party)	35	20

313 Hem Raj Sharma (grammarian)

1996. Writers. Multicoloured.
629	**313**	1r. Type **313**	10	10
630		3r. Padma Prasad Bhattarai (Sanskrit scholar)	20	15
631		5r. Bhawani Bhikshu (novelist)	35	20

314 Runner and Track

1996. Olympic Games, Atlanta.
| 632 | **314** | 7r. multicoloured | 50 | 30 |

315 Kasthamandap, Katmandu

1996. Temples.
633	**315**	10p. red and black	10	10
634	**315**	50p. black and red	10	10
635	-	1r. red and blue	10	10

DESIGN—VERT: 1r. Nyata Pola temple, Bhaktapur.

316 Hindu Temple, Arjundhara

1996. Tourism. Multicoloured.
636	**316**	1r. Type **316**	10	10
637		2r. Durbar, Nuwakot	15	10
638		8r. Gaijatra Festival, Bhaktapur	65	45
639		10r. Lake Beganas, Kaski	90	60

317 Krishna Peacock

1996. Butterflies and Birds. Multicoloured.

640	5r. Type **317**		45	30
641	5r. Great barbet ("Great Himalayan Barbet")		45	30
642	5r. Sarus crane		45	30
643	5r. Northern jungle queen		45	30

Nos. 640/3 were issued together, se-tenant, forming a composite design.

318 Ashoka Pillar

1996. Centenary of Rediscovery of Ashoka Pillar, Lumbini (birthplace of Buddha).

644	**318**	12r. multicoloured	1·00	65

319 King Birendra

1996. King Birendra's 52nd Birthday.

645	**319**	10r. multicoloured	60	60

320 Mt. Annapurna South and Mt. Annapurna I

1996. The Himalayas. Multicoloured.

646	18r. Type **320**		1·10	75
647	18r. Mt. Machhapuchhre and Mt. Annapurna III		1·10	75
648	18r. Mt. Annapurna IV and Mt. Annapurna II		1·10	75

Nos. 646/8 were issued together, *se-tenant*, forming a composite design.

321 King Birendra before Throne

1997. Silver Jubilee of King Birendra's Accession.

649	**321**	2r. multicoloured	15	15

322 Mountains and National Flags

1997. 40th Anniv of Nepal–Japan Diplomatic Relations.

650	**322**	18r. multicoloured	1·30	90

323 Postal Emblem

1997

651	**323**	2r. red and brown	15	15

324 Campaign Emblem

1997. National Tourism Year.

652	**324**	2r. red and blue	15	10
653	-	10r. multicoloured	75	45
654	-	18r. multicoloured	1·30	90
655	-	20r. multicoloured	1·50	95

DESIGNS—HORIZ: 10r. Upper Mustang mountain peak; 18r. Rafting, River Sunkoshi. VERT: 20r. Changunarayan.

325 Chepang Couple

1997. Ethnic Groups. Multicoloured.

656	5r. Type **325**		35	20
657	5r. Gurung couple		35	20
658	5r. Rana Tharu couple		35	20

326 National Flags and Handshake

1997. 50th Anniv of Nepal United States Diplomatic Relations.

659	**326**	20r. multicoloured	1·50	95

327 Riddhi Bahadur Malla (writer)

1997. Celebrities. Multicoloured.

660	2r. Type **327**		15	10
661	2r. Dr. K. I. Singh (politician)		15	10

328 "Jasminum gracile"

1997. Flowers. Multicoloured.

662	40p. Type **328**		10	10
663	1r. China aster		10	10
664	2r. "Manglietia insignis"		15	10
665	15r. "Luculia gratissima"		1·20	75

329 Dhiki (corn crusher)

1997. Traditional Technology. Multicoloured.

666	5r. Type **329**		35	2·20
667	5r. Janto (mill stone)		35	2·20
668	5r. Kol (oil mill) (vert)		35	2·20
669	5r. Okhal (implement for pounding rice) (vert)		35	2·20

330 King Birendra

1997. King Birendra's 53rd Birthday.

670	**330**	10r. multicoloured	75	45

331 Sunrise, Shree Antudanda, Ilam

1998. Tourism. Multicoloured. VERT.

671	2r. Type **331**		15	10

672	10r. Maitidevi Temple, Katmandu		75	45
673	18r. Great Renunciation Gate, Kapilavastu	1·30		90
674	20r. Mt. Cholatse, Solukhumbu (vert)		1·50	95

332 Ram Prasad Rai (nationalist)

1998. Personalities.

675	**332**	75p. black and brown	10	10
676	-	1r. black and mauve	15	15
677	-	2r. black and green	20	15
678	-	2r. black and blue	20	15
679	-	5r.40 black and red	35	20

DESIGNS: No. 676, Imansing Chemjong (Kiranti language specialist); 677, Tulsi Meher Shrestha (social worker); 678, Maha Pundit Dadhi Ram Marasini (poet); 679, Mahananda Sapkota (educationalist and writer).

333 Match Scenes

1998. World Cup Football Championship, France.

680	**333**	12r. multicoloured	90	60

334 Ganesh Man Singh

1998. 1st Death Anniv of Ganesh Man Singh (politician).

681	**334**	5r. multicoloured	35	20

335 World Map and Nepalese Soldiers

1998. 40 Years of Nepalese Army Involvement in United Nations Peace Keeping Missions.

682	**335**	10r. multicoloured	75	45

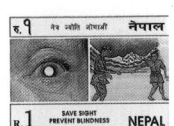

336 Cataract and Guiding of Blind Man

1998. Cataract Awareness Campaign.

683	**336**	1r. multicoloured	15	15

337 King Cobra

1998. Snakes. Multicoloured.

684	1r.70 Type **337**		10	10
685	2r. Golden tree snake		15	10
686	5r. Asiatic rock python		35	20
687	10r. Karan's pit viper		75	45

338 Dove and Profile

1998. 50th Anniv of Universal Declaration of Human Rights.

688	**338**	10r. multicoloured	75	45

339 Disabled Persons

1998. Asian and Pacific Decade of Disabled Persons.

689	**339**	10r. multicoloured	75	45

340 King Birendra

1998. King Birendra's 54th Birthday.

690	**340**	2r. multicoloured	15	15

341 Dam and Power House

1998. River Marsyangdi Hydro-electric Power Station.

691	**341**	12r. multicoloured	90	60

342 Hospital and Emblem

1999. 25th Anniv of Nepal Eye Hospital.

692	**342**	2r. multicoloured	15	15

343 Kalika Bhagawati Temple, Baglung

1999. Tourism. Multicoloured.

693	2r. Type **343**		15	10
694	2r. Chandan Nath Temple, Jumla (vert)		15	75
695	12r. Bajrayogini Temple, Sankhu (vert)		1·10	75
696	15r. Mt. Everest		1·30	90
697	15r. Ashokan Pillar, Lumbini, and English translation of its inscription (39×27 mm)		1·30	90

344 Four-horned Antelope

1999. Mammals. Multicoloured.

698	10r. Type **344**		90	60
699	10r. Argali (Ovis ammon)		90	60

345 Him Kanchha (mascot) and Games Emblem

1999. 8th South Asian Sports Federation Games, Katmandu.

700	**345**	10r. multicoloured	90	60

346 U.P.U. Emblem and Cockerel

1999. 125th Anniv of Universal Postal Union.
701 **346** 15r. multicoloured 1·30 15

347 Ramnarayan Mishra (revolutionary, 1922–67)

1999. Personalities.
702 **347** 1r. green and black 10 10
703 – 1r. brown and black 10 10
704 – 1r. blue and black 10 10
705 – 2r. red and black 15 10
706 – 2r. blue and black 15 10
707 – 2r. buff and black 15 10

DESIGNS: No. 703, Master Mitrasen (writer, 1895–1946); 704, Bhupi Sherchan (poet, 1935–89); 705, Rudraraj Pandey (writer, 1901–87); 706, Gopalprasad Rimal (writer, 1917–73); 707, Mangaladevi Singh (revolutionary, 1924–96).

348 Sorathi Dance

1999. Local Dances. Multicoloured.
708 **348** 5r. Type 348 45 30
709 5r. Bhairav dance 45 30
710 5r. Jhijhiya dance 45 30

349 Children working and writing

1999. Nepal's involvement in International Programme on the Elimination of Child Labour.
711 **349** 12r. multicoloured 1·10 75

350 King Birendra

1999. King Birendra's 55th Birthday.
712 **350** 5r. multicoloured 45 30

351 Headquarters

2000. 60th Anniv of Radio Nepal.
713 **351** 2r. multicoloured 15 15

352 Queen Aishwarya

2000. Queen Aishwarya's 50th Birthday.
714 **352** 15r. multicoloured 1·30 1·30

353 Front Page of Newspaper and Emblem

2000. Centenary of Gorkhapatra (newspaper).
715 **353** 10r. multicoloured 80 80

354 Tchorolpa Glacial Lake, Dolakha

2000. Tourist Sights. Multicoloured.
716 12r. Type 354 1·00 1·00
717 15r. Dakshinkali Temple, Kathmandu 1·30 1·30
718 18r. Mount Annapurna (50th anniv of first ascent) 1·50 1·50

355 Ranipokhari Pagoda, Kathmandu

2000
719 **355** 50p. black and orange 10 10
720 **355** 1r. black and blue 10 10
721 **355** 2r. black and brown 15 15

356 Soldier and Child

2000. 50th Anniv of Geneva Convention.
725 **356** 5r. multicoloured 45 45

357 Runners

2000. Olympic Games, Sydney.
726 **357** 25r. multicoloured 2·20 2·20

358 Hridayachandra Singh Pradhan (writer)

2000. Personalities.
727 **358** 2r. black and yellow 15 15
728 – 2r. black and brown 15 15
729 – 5r. black and blue 45 45
730 – 5r. black and red 45 45

DESIGNS: No. 728, Thir Barn Malla (revolutionary); 729, Krishna Prasad Koirala (social reformer); 730, Manamohan Adhikari (politician).

359 Indian Rhinoceros (male)

2000. Wildlife. Multicoloured.
731 10r. Type 359 90 90
732 10r. Indian rhinoceros (Rhinoceros unicornis) (female) 90 90
733 10r. Lesser adjutant stork (Leptoptilos javanicus) 90 90
734 10r. Bengal florican (Houbaropsis bengalensis) 90 90

360 Orchid (Dactylorhiza hatagirea)

2000. Flowers. Multicoloured.
735 5r. Type 360 45 45
736 5r. Mahonia napaulensis (horiz) 45 45
737 5r. Talauma hodgsonii (horiz) 45 45

361 King Birendra

2000. King Birendra's 56th Birthday.
738 **361** 5r. multicoloured 45 45

362 King Tribhuvana and Crowd

2001. 50th Anniv of Constitutional Monarchy.
739 **362** 5r. multicoloured 45 45

363 Crowd and Emblem

2001. Population Census.
740 **363** 2r. multicoloured 15 15

364 Khaptad Baba (religious leader)

2001. Personalities.
741 **364** 2r. pink and black 15 15
742 – 2r. mauve and black 15 15
743 – 2r. magenta and black 15 15
744 – 2r. red and black 15 15
745 – 2r. blue and black 15 15

DESIGNS: No. 742, Bhikkhu Pragyananda Mahathera (Buddhist writer and teacher); 743, Guru Prasad Mainali (author); 744, Tulsi Lal Amatya Politician); 745, Madan Lal Agrawal (industrialist).

365 Asiatic Coinwort (Centella asiatica)

2001. Plants. Multicoloured.
746 5r. Type 365 45 45
747 15r. Bergenia ciliata 1·50 1·50
748 30r. Himalayan yew (Taxus baccata wallichania) 3·00 3·00

366 Pipal Tree (Ficus religiosa)

2001
749 **366** 10r. multicoloured 90 90

367 Tents

2001. 50th Anniv of United Nations High Commissioner for Refugees.
750 **367** 20r. multicoloured 1·80 1·80

368 National Flag

2001
751 **368** 10p. red and blue 15 15

369 Amargadi Fort

2001. Tourism. Multicoloured.
752 2r. Type 369 15 15
753 5r. Hiranyavarna Mahavihar (Golden Temple) (vert) 45 45
754 15r. Jugal mountain range 1·30 1·30

370 King Birendra

2001. 57th Birth Anniv of King Birendra.
755 **370** 15r. multicoloured 1·30 1·30

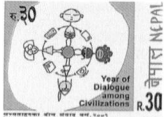

371 Children encircling Globe

2001. United Nations Year of Dialogue among Civilizations.
756 **371** 30r. multicoloured 2·50 2·50

372 Scout Emblem

2002. 50th Anniv of Nepalese Scouts.
757 **372** 2r. chestnut and olive 20 20

373 World Cup Emblem and Footballer

2002. World Cup Football Championships, Japan and South Korea.
758 **373** 15r. multicoloured 1·30 1·30

374 King Gyanendra

2002. 1st Anniv of Accession of King Gyanendra.
759 **374** 5r. multicoloured 45 45

375 King Birendra and Queen Aishwarya

2002. King Birendra and Queen Aishwarya Commemoration.
760 **375** 10r. multicoloured 45 45

376 "Aryabalokiteshwor"

2002. Paintings. Multicoloured.
761 **376** 5r. Type **376** 45 45
762 5r. "Moti (pearl)" (King Birendra) (horiz) 45 45

377 Family encircled by Barbed Wire (Siddhimuni Shakya)

2002. Social Awareness.
763 **377** 1r. black and brown 10 10
764 - 2r. black and lilac 15 15
DESIGNS: Type **377** (integration of untouchables); 2r. Children leaving for school (treatment of girls).

378 Leaf Beetle

2002. Insects. Multicoloured.
765 **378** 3r. Type **378** 30 30
766 5r. Short horn grasshopper 45 45

379 Valley and Mountains

2002. International Year of Mountains.
767 **379** 5r. multicoloured 45 45

380 Pathibhara Devisthan, Taplejung

2002. Tourism. Multicoloured.
768 **380** 5r. Type **380** 45 45
769 5r. Galeshwor Mahadevsthan, Myagdi 45 45
770 5r. Ramgram Stupa, Nawalparasi 45 45
771 5r. Mt. Nilgiri, Mustang 45 45

381 Dayabor Singh Kansakar (philanthropist)

2002. Personalities. Multicoloured.
772 2r. Type **381** 15 15
773 25r. Ekai Kawaguchi (first Japanese to visit Nepal) 2·20 2·20

382 Members Flags and Organization Emblem

2002. South Asian Association for Regional Co-operation (SAARC) Charter Day.
774 **382** 15r. multicoloured 1·30 1·30

383 Anniversary Emblem

2003. 50th Anniv of Chamber of Commerce.
775 **383** 5r. multicoloured 10 10

384 FNCCI Emblem

2003. Industry and Commerce Day.
776 **384** 5r. multicoloured 10 10

385 Mt. Everest

2003. 50th Anniv of the First Ascent of Mount Everest.
777 **385** 25r. multicoloured 40 20

386 Babu Chiri Sherpa

2003. Babu Chiri Sherpa (mountaineer) Commemoration.
778 **386** 5r. multicoloured 10 10

387 King Gyanendra

2003. 57th Birth Anniv of King Gyanendra.
779 **387** 5r. multicoloured 10 10

388 Tea Garden

2003. Eastern Nepal Tea Gardens.
780 **388** 25r. multicoloured 40 20

389 Dilli Raman Regmi

2003. 2nd Death Anniv of Dilli Raman Regmi (politician and historian).
781 **389** 5r. brown and black 10 10

390 Gopal Das Shrestha

2003. 5th Death Anniv of Gopal Das Shrestha (journalist).
782 **390** 5r. green and black 10 10

391 Container, Crane and Emblem

2003. Export Year.
783 **391** 25r. multicoloured 40 20

392 Sankhadhar Sakhwaa (statue) and Celebrating Crowd

2003. Sankhadhar Sakhwaa (founder of Nepal calender).
784 **392** 5r. multicoloured 10 10

393 Ganesh (statue), Kageshwar

2003. Tourist Sights. Multicoloured.
785 5r. Type **393** 10 10
786 5r. Hydroelectric dam on Kali Gandaki river (horiz) 10 10
787 30r. Buddha (statue), Swayambhu (horiz) 50 25

394 Lotus

2003. Flowers. Multicoloured.
788 10r. Type **394** 20 10
789 10r. Picrorhiza 20 10
790 10r. Himalayan rhubarb 20 10
791 10r. Jasmine 20 10

395 Emblem and Symbols of Social Work

2004. 50th Anniv of Social Services of United Mission to Nepal.
792 **395** 5r. multicoloured 10 10

396 NNJS Emblem

2004. 25th Anniv of Nepal Netra Jyoti Sangh (NNJS) (eye care organization).
793 **396** 5r. multicoloured 10 10

397 Society Emblem

2004. 50th Anniv of Marwadi Sewa Samiti, Nepal (charitable organization).
794 **397** 5r. multicoloured 10 10

398 King Gyanendra

2004. 58th Birth Anniv of King Gyanendra.
795 **398** 5r. multicoloured 10 10

399 APT Emblem

2004. 25th Anniv of Asia—Pacific Tele-Community (APT).
796 **399** 5r. multicoloured 10 10

400 Anniversary Emblem

2004. 50th Anniv of Management Education.
797 **400** 5r. multicoloured 10 10

401 Anniversary Emblem

2004. Centenary of FIFA (Fédération Internationale de Football Association).
798 **401** 20r. multicoloured 30 15

402 Mt. Lhotse

2004. 50th Anniv of Assent Mt Cho Oyu. Multicoloured.
799 10r. Type **402** 20 10
800 10r. Makalu 20 10
801 10r. Manasalu 20 10
802 10r. Annapurna 20 10
803 10r. Everest 20 10
804 10r. Kanchenjunga main peak 20 10
805 10r. Cho Oyu 20 10
806 10r. Dhaulagiri 20 10

403 Narahari Nath

2004. Personalities. Multicoloured.
807 5r. Type **403** (religious scholar) 10 10
808 5r. Nayaraj Panta (historian) 10 10

404 Sasia ochracea Hodgson (inscr "Rufous piculet" woodpecker)

2004. Biodiversity. Multicoloured.
809 10r. Type **404** 20 10
810 10r. Atlas moth (Attacus atlas) 20 10
811 10r. Swertia multicaulis 20 10
812 10r. High altitude rice (Oryza sativa) 20 10

405 Mayadevi Temple, Lumbini

2004. Tourism. Multicoloured.
813 10r. Type **405** 20 10
814 10r. Gadhimai, Bara 20 10

406 Writer and Emblem

2004. 50th Anniv of Madan Puraskar (language and literature prize).
815 **406** 5r. multicoloured 10 10

407 Jayavarma

2004. Sculpture. Multicoloured.
816 10r. Type **407** (National museum, Kathmandu) 20 10
817 10r. Umamaheswar (Kathmandu) 20 10
818 10r. Vishwarupa (Bhaktapur) 20 10
819 10r. Krishna playing flute (Makawanpur) 20 10

408 Building Facade

2005. 50th Anniv of Nepal Rasta Bank.
820 **408** 2r. multicoloured 10 10

409 Mt. Makalu

2005. 50th Anniv of First Ascent of Mt. Makalu.
821 **409** 10r. multicoloured 20 10

410 Mt. Kanchanjunga

2005. 50th Anniv of First Ascent of Mt. Kanchanjunga.
822 **410** 12r. multicoloured 20 10

411 King Gyanendra

2005. 59th Birth Anniv of King Gyanendra.
823 **411** 5r. multicoloured 10 10

412 Birth of Buddha

2005. Buddha. Showing the life of Buddha. Multicoloured border given.
824 10r. Type **412** 20 10
825 10r. Enlightenment 20 10
826 10r. First sermon 20 10
827 10r. Mahaparinirvana 20 10
828 10r. Type **412** (green) 20 10
829 10r. As No. 825 (green) 20 10
830 10r. As No. 826 (green) 20 10
831 10r. As No. 827 (green) 20 10
832 10r. Type **412** (vermilion) 20 10
833 10r. As No. 825 (vermilion) 20 10
834 10r. As No. 826 (vermilion) 20 10

835 10r. As No. 827 (vermilion) 20 10
836 10r. Type **412** (violet) 20 10
837 10r. As No. 825 (violet) 20 10
838 10r. As No. 826 (violet) 20 10
839 10r. As No. 827 (violet) 20 10

413 *Phyllanthus emblica*

2005. Fruit. Multicoloured.
840 10r. Type **413** 20 10
841 10r. *Juglans regia* 20 10
842 10r. *Aegle marmelos* 20 10
843 10r. *Rubus ellipticus* 20 10

414 Queen Mother Ratna Rajya Laxmi Devi Shah

2005. 77th Birth Anniv of Queen Mother Ratna Rajya Laxmi Devi Shah.
844 **414** 20r. multicoloured 30 15

415 Asian Elephant

2005. Endangered Species. Mammals. Multicoloured border colour given.
845 10r. Type **415** 20 10
846 10r. Clouded leopard 20 10
847 10r. Gangetic dolphin 20 10
848 10r. Indian pangolin 20 10
849 10r. Type **415** (green) 20 10
850 10r. As No. 846 (green) 20 10
851 10r. As No. 847 (green) 20 10
852 10r. As No. 848 (green) 20 10
853 10r. Type **415** (vermilion) 20 10
854 10r. As No. 846 (vermilion) 20 10
855 10r. As No. 847 (vermilion) 20 10
856 10r. As No. 848 (vermilion) 20 10
857 10r. Type **415** (violet) 20 10
858 10r. As No. 846 (violet) 20 10
859 10r. As No. 847 (violet) 20 10
860 10r. As No. 848 (violet) 20 10

416 Bhupalmansingh Karki

2005. Bhupalmansingh Karki (politician) Commemoration.
861 **416** 2r. multicoloured 10 10

417 Kalinchok Bhagawati, Dolakha

2005. Tourism. Multicoloured.
862 5r. Type **417** 10 10
863 5r. Panauti City, Kabhrepalanchok 10 10
864 5r. Ghodaghodi Lake, Kailali 10 10
865 5r. Budhasubba, Sunasari 10 10

418 Sherpa Jewellery

2005. Tribal Jewellery. Multicoloured.
866 25r. Type **418** 40 20
867 25r. Newar 40 20
868 25r. Tharu 40 20

869 25r. Limbu 40 20

419 Stupa and Chinese and Nepalese Flags

2005. 50th Anniv of Nepal–China Diplomatic Relations.
870 **419** 30r. multicoloured 50 25

420 Flags

2005. 50th Anniv of United Nations Membership.
871 **420** 50r. multicoloured 80 40

421 King Tribhuvan

2006. King Tribhuvan Bir Bikram Shah Dev Commemoration. 55th National Democracy Day.
872 **421** 5r. multicoloured 10 10

422 Queen Komal Rajya Laxmi Devi Shah

2006. Queen Komal Rajya Laxmi Devi Shah. 30th Anniv (2005) of International Women's Day.
873 **422** 5r. multicoloured 10 10

423 Emblem

2006. 25th Anniv of World Hindu Federation.
874 **423** 2r. multicoloured 10 10

424 Mt. Lohtse

2006. 50th Anniv of Mountain Ascents. Multicoloured.
875 25r. Type **424** 40 20
876 25r. Mt. Manaslu 40 20

425 Court Building

2006. 50th Anniv of Supreme Court.
877 **425** 5r. multicoloured 10 10

426 *Primula sharmae*

2006. Flora and Fauna. Multicoloured.
878 10r. Type **426** 20 10
879 10r. *Amolops formosus* 20 10
880 10r. *Dicranocephalus wallichi* 20 10

881 10r. *Russula kathmanduensis* 20 10
882 10r. *Teinopalpus imperialis* 20 10

427 Sandal Buddha, Burytiya, Russia and Swayambohunath, Kathmandu

2006. 50th Anniv of Nepal—Russia Diplomatic Relations.
883 **427** 30r. multicoloured 45 20

428 Nyatapole Temple, Bhaktapur, Nepal

2006. 50th Anniv of Nepal—Japan Diplomatic Relations.
884 **428** 30r. multicoloured 45 20

429 Changtse and Everest and Horyuji Temple, Nara, Japan

2006. Mount Everest. Multicoloured.
885 1r. Type **429** 10 10
886 5r. Changtse and Everest (32×27 mm) 10 10

430 *Dorcus giraffe*

2006
887 **430** 2r. multicoloured 10 10

431 Envelope with 1881 1 anna Stamp (Type **1**)

2006. 125th Anniv of First Stamp. Showing first stamps issued by Nepal. Multicoloured.
888 5r. Type **431** 10 10
889 20r. Envelope with 2 anna stamp 30 15
890 100r. Envelope with 3 anna stamp 1·50 75
MS891 91×75 mm. 125r. First stamps and technical details. Imperf 2·00 2·00
No. **MS**891 has perforations surrounding the three stamp images.

432 Emblems

2006. 50th Anniv of UPU Membership.
892 **432** 15r. multicoloured 25 10

433 Buddha descending

2006. 2550th Anniv of Buddha.
893 **433** 30r. multicoloured 45 20

434 Dentistry and Examinations

2007. 50th Anniv of Chhatrapati Free Clinic.
894 **434** 2r. multicoloured 10 10

435 Mount Everest

2007
895 **435** 5r. multicoloured 10 10

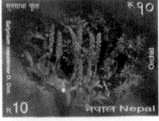

436 Satyrium nepalense

2007. Orchids. Multicoloured.
896 10r. Type **436** 20 10
897 10r. Dendrobium heterocarpum 20 10
898 10r. Pelatantheria insectifera 20 10
899 10r. Coelogyne ovalis 20 10
900 10r. Coelogyne cristata 20 10
901 10r. Dendrobium chrysanthum 20 10
902 10r. Phaleneopsis mannii 20 10
903 10r. Dendrobium densiflorum 20 10
904 10r. Esmeralda clarkei 20 10
905 10r. Acampe rigida 20 10
906 10r. Bulbophyllum leopardinum 20 10
907 10r. Dendrobium fimbriatum 20 10
908 10r. Arundina graminifolia 20 10
909 10r. Dendrobium moschatum 20 10
910 10r. Rhynchostylis retusa 20 10
911 10r. Cymbidium devonianum 20 10

437 Competitors

2007. Taekwondo.
912 **437** 5r. multicoloured 10 10

438 Batsman and Fielders

2007. Cricket.
913 **438** 5r. multicoloured 10 10

439 Setu BK

2007. Democratic Movement (Jana Aandolan) Martyrs. Multicoloured.
914 2r. Type **439** 10 10
915 2r. Tulasi Chhetri 10 10
916 2r. Anil Lama 10 10
917 2r. Umesh Chandra Thapa 10 10
918 2r. Chakraraj Joshi 10 10
919 2r. Chandra Bayalkoti 10 10
920 2r. Devilal Poudel 10 10
921 2r. Govindanath Sharma 10 10
922 2r. Hari Raj Adhikari 10 10
923 2r. Horilal Rana Tharu 10 10
924 2r. Lai Bahadur Bista 10 10
925 2r. Mohamad Jahangir 10 10
926 2r. Pradhumna Khadka 10 10
927 2r. Rajan Giri 10 10
928 2r. Suraj Bishwas 10 10
929 2r. Sagun Tamrakar 10 10
930 2r. Bhimsen Dahal 10 10
931 2r. Shivahari Kunwar 10 10
932 2r. Basudev Ghimire 10 10
933 2r. Bishnu Prasad Panday 10 10
934 2r. Yamlal Lamichhane 10 10
935 2r. Deepak Kami 10 10

936 2r. Darshanlal Yadab 10 10
937 2r. Tahir Hussain Ansari 10 10
938 2r. Hiralal Gautam 10 10

440 Symbols of Nepal and Sri Lanka

2007. 50th Anniv of Nepal–Sri Lanka Diplomatic Relations.
939 **440** 5r. multicoloured 15 15

441 Symbols of Nepal and Egypt

2007. 50th Anniv of Nepal–Egypt Diplomatic Relations.
940 **441** 5r. multicoloured 15 15

441a Robert Baden Powell (founder) and Baden Powell Scout Peak (Urkema mountain)

2007. Centenary of Scouting.
941 **441a** 2r. multicoloured 10 10

442 Emblem

2007. 25th Anniv of Cancer Relief Society.
942 **442** 1r. multicoloured 10 10

443 House of Parliament

2007. Re-instatement of Parliament. Multicoloured.
943 1r. Type **443** 10 10
944 1r. Building and document 'Interim Constitution of Nepal' 10 10
945 1r. As Type **443** but inscr 'The re-instatement of The House of Representatives' 10 10
946 1r. As No. 944 but different document inscr 'The Proclamation of The House of Representatives' 10 10

444 Chaya Devi Parajuli

2007. Chaya Devi Parajuli (activist) Commem.
947 **444** 2r. multicoloured 10 10

445 Mount Abi

2007. Tourism. Multicoloured.
948 5r. Type **445** 15 15
949 5r. Shree Bhageshwor, Dadeldhura 15 15
950 5r. Shree Shaillya Malikarjun, Darchula 15 15
951 5r. Shiddhakali, Bhojpur 15 15
952 5r. Buddha (victory over the mali of Siddhartha Gautam) 15 15

446 Shree Govindananda Bharati (Shivapuri Baba) (Hindi saint)

2007. Personalities. Multicoloured.
953 5r. Type **446** 15 15
954 5r. Mahesh Chandra Regmi (historian) 15 15
955 5r. Bhrikuti Devi (first wife of Songtsan Gampo (emperor of Tibet)) (statue) 15 15
956 5r. Pt. Udayananda Arijyal (writer) 15 15
957 5r. Ganesh Lal Shrestha (musician) 15 15
958 5r. Tara Devi (singer) 15 15

447 Dattatreya Temple, Bhaktapur, Nepal and Cologne Cathedral, Germany

2008. 50th Anniv of Nepal–Germany Diplomatic Relations.
959 **447** 25r. multicoloured 75 75

448 Buddha's Birth at Lumbini

2008
960 **448** 2r. multicoloured 15 15

449 National Arms

2008
961 **449** 1r. multicoloured 15 15

450 Athletes and Emblem

2008. Olympic Games, Beijing.
962 **450** 15r. multicoloured 40 40

451 Script

2008. National Anthem.
963 **451** 1r. multicoloured 15 15

452 Interior

2008. Centenary of Kaiser Library.
964 **452** 5r. multicoloured 20 20

453 Harka Gurung and Mountain

2008. Renaming of Mt. Nagdi Chuli to Mt. Harka Gurung Chuli.
965 **453** 5r. multicoloured 20 20

454 Rauvolfia serpentina

2008. Bio-Diversity. Multicoloured.
966 5r. Type **454** 20 20
967 5r. Demonax bicincta 20 20
968 5r. Russula chloroides 20 20
969 5r. Varanus flavescens 20 20

455 Mustang Village

2008. Tourism. Multicoloured.
970 5r. Type **455** 20 20
971 5r. Syarpu Lake 20 20
972 5r. Jal Jala Hill 20 20
973 5r. Pindeshwor Babadham Shrine 20 20
974 5r. Shree Kumari Chariot Festival 20 20

456 Emblems

2009. 50th Anniv of National Family Planning Association.
975 **456** 1r. multicoloured 20 20

457 Emblem and University Building

2009. 50th Anniv of Tribhuvan University.
976 **457** 5r. multicoloured 25 25

458 Emblem and Book of Records

2009. 50th Anniv of Auditor General's Office.
977 **458** 5r. multicoloured 25 25

459 Marker Stone and Nativity Sculpture

2009. World Heritage Site. Buddha's Birthplace, Lumbini. Multicoloured.
978 10r. Type **459** 45 45
979 10r. Puskarini (holy pond) 45 45
980 10r. Ashokan Pillar 45 45
981 10r. Ruins of stupas and viharas 45 45
982 10r. Mayadevi Temple 45 45

460 Map of Nepal containing Flag and Arms

2009. Federal Democratic Republic.
| 983 | 460 | 2r. multicoloured | 20 | 20 |

461 *Parnassius hardwickei*

2009. Butterflies. Multicoloured.
984	10r. Type **461**		45	45
985	10r. *Euploea mulciber*		45	45
986	10r. *Papilio machaon*		45	45
987	10r. *Polyura athamus*		45	45
988	10r. *Aulocera swaha* (inscr 'Aulocera padma')		45	45
989	10r. *Pieris brassicae nepalensis*		45	45
990	10r. *Danaus genutia*		45	45
991	10r. *Gonepteryx rhammni*		45	45
992	10r. *Ixias pyrene*		45	45
993	10r. *Graphium cloanthus* (inscr 'Idaides cloanthus')		45	45
994	10r. *Parnassius acdestis*		45	45
995	10r. *Kaniska canace*		45	45
996	10r. *Papilio demoleus*		45	45
997	10r. *Menelaides helenus*		45	45
998	10r. *Pathysa nomius* (inscr 'Deoris nomius')		45	45
999	10r. *Heliophorus androcles*		45	45

462 Govinda Biyogi

2009. 80th Birth Anniv of Govinda Biyogi (journalist).
| 1000 | 462 | 5r. multicoloured | 25 | 25 |

463 Guru Mangal Das

2009. Guru Mangal Das (religious philanthropist and writer) Commemoration.
| 1001 | 463 | 5r. multicoloured | 25 | 25 |

464 Tej Bahadur Chitrakar

2009. Tej Bahadur Chitrakar (artist) Commemoration.
| 1002 | | 5r. Type **464** | 25 | 25 |
| 1003 | | 5r. *Tribute to Forefathers* | | |

465 Rameshwor Sharma Chalise

2009. Rameshwor Sharma Chalise (Ramesh Vikal) (writer) Commemoration.
| 1004 | 465 | 2r. multicoloured | 20 | 20 |

466 Krishna Sen

2009. Krishna Sen (Ichhuk) (writer) Commemoration.
| 1006 | 466 | 5r. multicoloured | 25 | 25 |

467 L. P. Devkota

2009. Birth Centenary of Laxmi Prasad Devkota (writer)
| 1006 | 467 | 1r. multicoloured | 10 | 10 |

468 Lahurya Folk Dance

2009. Cultural Heritage. Multicoloured.
| 1007 | | 5r. Type **468** | 25 | 25 |
| 1008 | | 5r. Chhath Festival | 25 | 25 |

469 Mountain Biking

2009. Sport. Multicoloured.
| 1009 | | 10r. Type **469** | 45 | 45 |
| 1010 | | 10r. Kayaking | 45 | 45 |

470 Stupa

2010. 25th Anniv of Television Broadcasting
| 1011 | 470 | 2r. multicoloured | 15 | 15 |

471 Tiger

2010. Chinese New Year
| 1012 | 471 | 5r. multicoloured | 25 | 25 |

472 Pemba Doma Sherpa

2010. 40th Birth Anniv of Pemba Doma Sherpa (mountaineer)
| 1013 | 472 | 25r. multicoloured | 1·10 | 1·10 |

473 Mountain Peak

2010. 50th Anniv of First Ascent of Mt. Dhaulagiri
| 1014 | 473 | 25r. multicoloured | 1·10 | 1·10 |

474

2010. Maru Ganesh Shrine, Kathmandu
| 1015 | 474 | 2r. multicoloured | 15 | 15 |

475 Kankalini Mai and Temple Building

2010. Kankalini Mai Temple of Bhardah, Saptari
| 1016 | 475 | 2r. multicoloured | 15 | 15 |

476 Bhairav Aryal

2010. Bhairav Aryal (writer) Commemoration
| 1017 | 476 | 5r. multicoloured | 25 | 25 |

477 Nati Kaji Shrestha

2010. Nati Kaji Shrestha (musician and singer) Commemoration. Mohan Rana.
| 1018 | 477 | 5r. multicoloured | 25 | 25 |

478 Jibraj Ashrit

2010. Jibraj Ashrit (politician) Commemoration
| 1019 | 478 | 5r. multicoloured | 25 | 25 |

479 Bhikkchu Amritananda

2010. 20th Death Anniv of Bhikkchu Amritananda (Buddhist monk)
| 1020 | 479 | 5r. multicoloured | 25 | 25 |

480 Bhagat Sarbjit Bishwakarma (inscr 'Bhagat Sarbajit Biswokarma')

2010. Bhagat Sarbjit Bishwakarma (social reformer) Commemoration
| 1021 | 480 | 5r. multicoloured | 25 | 25 |

481 Sadhana Adhikari

2010. Sadhana Adhikari (politician) Commemoration
| 1022 | 481 | 5r. multicoloured | 25 | 25 |

482 Mai Pokhari

2010. Mai Pokhari, Illam (ponds and place of pilgrimage)
| 1023 | 482 | 2r. multicoloured | 25 | 25 |

483 Washing Hands

2010. Hand Washing and Health Campaign
| 1024 | 483 | 2r. multicoloured | 15 | 15 |

484 'NEPAL TOURISM YEAR' and '2011'

2010. 2011–Nepal Tourism Year
| 1025 | 484 | 5r. multicoloured | 25 | 25 |

OFFICIAL STAMPS

O25 Nepalese Arms and Soldiers

1960. (a) Size 30×18 mm.
O135	**O25**	2p. brown	10	10
O136	**O25**	4p. green	15	10
O137	**O25**	6p. red	15	10
O138	**O25**	8p. violet	15	15
O139	**O25**	12p. orange	20	20

(b) Size 38×27 mm.
O140	16p. brown	35	30
O141	24p. red	50	45
O142	32p. purple	60	60
O143	50p. blue	1·10	1·00
O144	1r. red	2·20	1·90
O145	2r. orange	4·50	4·00

फौज सरकारी

(O28)

1960. Optd as Type O 28.
| O146 | 27 | 1r. purple | 90 | |

1961. Optd with Type O 28.
O148	35	1p. red	15	15
O149	35	2p. blue	15	15
O150	35	5p. brown	20	20
O151	36	10p. purple	10	10
O152	36	40p. brown	15	15
O153	36	75p. green	20	20
O154	27	2r. red	60	60
O155	27	5r. green	1·60	1·60

Pt. 4

NETHERLANDS

A kingdom in the N.W. of Europe on the North Sea.

1852. 100 cents = 1 gulden (florin).
2002. 100 cents = 1 euro.

1

1852. Imperf.
1	1	5c. blue	£550	50·00
2	1	10c. red	£600	39·00
3b	1	15c. orange	£1100	£190

3 King William III

1864. Perf.
8	3	5c. blue	£425	22·00
9	3	10c. red	£600	11·00
10	3	15c. orange	£1500	£130

4

1867
| 17b | 4 | 5c. blue | £130 | 4·00 |

18c	4	10c. red	£250	4·50
19c	4	15c. brown	£950	45·00
20	4	20c. green	£900	33·00
15	4	25c. purple	£3000	£140
16	4	50c. gold	£3750	£225

5

1869

58	5	½c. brown	33·00	4·50
53	5	1c. black	£300	£100
59	5	1c. green	22·00	3·25
55a	5	1½c. red	£225	£110
56	5	2c. yellow	85·00	20·00
62	5	2½c. mauve	£650	£100

6

1872

80	6	5c. blue	20·00	1·80
81	6	7½c. brown	50·00	25·00
100	6	10c. red	85·00	2·20
83	6	12½c. grey	90·00	3·25
102	6	15c. brown	£500	11·00
85	6	20c. green	£600	7·75
86	6	22½c. green	£110	60·00
87	6	25c. lilac	£750	5·50
97	6	50c. bistre	£950	17·00
90	6	1g. violet	£700	55·00
75	-	2g.50 blue and red	£1200	£150

No. 75 is similar to Type **6** but larger and with value and country scrolls transposed.

8

1876

133	8	½c. red	4·50	35
134	8	1c. green	15·00	45
137	8	2c. yellow	45·00	4·00
139	8	2½c. mauve	20·00	45

9 Queen Wilhelmina

1891

147a	9	3c. orange	11·00	3·25
148a	9	5c. blue	5·50	35
149b	9	7½c. brown	22·00	11·00
150b	9	10c. red	33·00	2·20
151b	9	12½c. grey	33·00	2·20
152a	9	15c. brown	80·00	7·25
153b	9	20c. green	90·00	4·50
154a	9	22½c. green	45·00	20·00
155	9	25c. mauve	£160	8·50
156a	9	50c. bistre	£800	28·00
159	-	50c. brown and green	£120	22·00
157	9	1g. violet	£900	£110
160	-	1g. green and brown	£275	33·00
161	-	2g.50 blue and red	£600	£200
165	-	5g. red and green	£1100	£650

Nos. 159, 160, 161 and 165 are as Type **9** but larger and with value and country scrolls transposed.

11

12

13

1898. Nos. 174 and 176 also exist imperf.

167	12	½c. lilac	65	35
168	12	1c. red	1·30	15
170	12	1½c. blue	4·00	45
171	12	2c. brown	5·50	35
172	12	2½c. green	4·50	35
173	13	3c. orange	25·00	5·00
174	13	3c. green	1·70	35
175	13	4c. purple	2·20	1·70
176	13	4½c. mauve	5·00	5·00
177	13	5c. red	2·20	35
178	13	7½c. brown	1·10	35
179	13	10c. grey	9·00	3·25
180	13	12½c. blue	5·00	45
181	13	15c. brown	£160	5·00
182	13	15c. red and blue	9·00	35
183	13	17½c. mauve	75·00	18·00
184	13	17½c. brown and blue	22·00	1·30
185	13	20c. green	£225	1·10
186	13	20c. grey and green	15·00	80
187	13	22½c. green and brown	14·00	90
188	13	25c. blue and pink	14·00	65
189	13	30c. purple and mauve	36·00	80
190	13	40c. orange and green	50·00	1·70
191	13	50c. red and green	£170	1·70
192	13	50c. violet and grey	90·00	1·70
193	13	60c. green and olive	50·00	1·70
194b	11	1g. green	75·00	1·10
195c	11	2½g. lilac	£130	4·00
196b	11	5g. red	£300	9·00
197	11	10g. red	£1200	£1000

14

1906. Society for the Prevention of Tuberculosis.

208	14	1c. (+1c.) red	28·00	17·00
209	14	3c. (+3c.) green	45·00	39·00
210	14	5c. (+5c.) violet	45·00	22·00

15 Admiral M. A. de Ruyter

1907. Birth Tercentenary of Admiral de Ruyter.

211	15	½c. blue	2·75	1·70
212	15	1c. red	4·50	3·25
213	15	2½c. red	9·00	3·25

16 William I

1913. Independence Centenary.

214	16	2½c. green on green	1·70	1·10
215	-	3c. yellow on cream	2·75	2·20
216	-	5c. red on buff	2·20	1·10
217	-	10c. grey	5·50	4·00
218	16	12½c. blue on blue	4·50	3·25
219	-	20c. brown	17·00	17·00
220	-	25c. blue	22·00	11·00
221	-	50c. green	45·00	45·00
222	16	1g. red	90·00	28·00
223	-	2½g. lilac	£170	60·00
224	-	5g. yellow on cream	£325	50·00
225	-	10g. orange	£1200	£1100

DESIGNS: 3c., 20c., 2½g. William II; 5c., 25c., 5g. William III; 10c., 50c., 10g. Queen Wilhelmina.

1919. Surch Veertig Cent (40c.) or Zestig Cent (60c.).

234	13	40c. on 30c. purple & mve	39·00	7·75
235	13	60c. on 30c. purple & mve	39·00	7·75

1920. Surch in figures.

236	11	2.50 on 10g. red	£225	£170
237	-	2.50 on 10g. red (No. 225)	£225	£170
238	13	4c. on 4½c. mauve	5·50	2·20

23

1921. Air.

239	23	10c. red	2·20	1·70
240	23	15c. green	9·00	2·75
241	23	60c. blue	28·00	55

24

1921

242	24	5c. green	17·00	35
243	24	12½c. red	28·00	2·75
244	24	20c. blue	39·00	35

25 Lion in Dutch Garden and Orange Tree (emblematic of Netherlands)

26

27

1923

248	25	1c. violet	80	80
249	25	2c. orange	7·50	35
250	26	2½c. green	2·20	90
251	27	4c. blue	1·80	80

1923. Surch.

252	12	2c. on 1c. red	70	35
253	12	2c. on 1½c. blue	70	45
254	13	10c. on 3c. green	6·50	35
255	13	10c. on 5c. red	12·50	80
256	13	10c. on 12½c. blue	10·50	1·20
257a	13	10c. on 17½c. brown & blue	4·25	4·75
258a	13	10c. on 22½c. olive & brown	4·25	4·75

30

31

1923. 25th Anniv of Queen's Accession.

259b	31	2c. green	30	35
260a	30	5c. green	60	45
261b	31	7½c. red	85	45
262b	31	10c. red	60	35
263	31	20c. blue	5·75	1·50
264a	31	25c. yellow	11·50	2·30
265	31	35c. orange	8·25	4·75
266a	31	50c. black	23·00	1·70
267	30	1g. red	35·00	7·25
268	30	2½g. black	£325	£350
269	30	5g. blue	£300	£300

1923. Surch DIENST ZEGEL PORTEN AAN TEEKEN RECHT and value.

270	13	10c. on 3c. green	1·70	1·70
271	13	1g. on 17½c. brown & blue	£100	29·00

33

1923. Culture Fund.

272	33	2c. (+5c.) blue on pink	26·00	26·00
273	-	10c. (+5c.) red on pink	26·00	26·00

DESIGN: 10c. Two women.

35 Carrier Pigeon

36 Queen Wilhelmina

1924

304C	35	½c. grey	60	60
305A	35	1c. red	35	10
306C	35	1½c. mauve	60	60
424a	35	1½c. grey	35	10
425	35	2c. orange	35	10
426a	35	2½c. green	1·20	60
427	35	3c. green	35	10
427a	35	4c. blue	35	10
428	36	5c. green	35	25
429	36	6c. brown	35	10
279A	36	7½c. yellow	60	10
313A	36	7½c. violet	4·75	10
314A	36	7½c. red	45	10
279cA	36	9c. red and black	2·30	1·70
281A	36	10c. red	2·30	10
317A	36	10c. blue	4·00	10
282A	36	12½c. red	2·30	60
319A	36	12½c. blue	60	10
320A	36	15c. blue	10·50	35
321C	36	15c. yellow	1·20	95
322C	36	20c. blue	7·50	4·00
434	36	21c. brown	35·00	1·20
324B	36	22½c. brown	9·25	3·50
434a	36	22½c. orange	23·00	26·00
435	36	25c. green	5·75	35
326A	36	27½c. grey	5·75	1·20
286cA	36	35c. brown	50·00	14·00
437	36	30c. violet	8·25	60
437a	36	40c. brown	17·00	35
330A	36	50c. green	8·25	35
289A	36	60c. violet	46·00	1·20
331A	36	60c. black	41·00	1·50
301	36	1g. blue (23×29 mm)	11·50	1·20
302	36	2½g. red (23×29 mm)	£140	8·25
303	36	5g. black (23×29 mm)	£275	4·00

For further stamps in Type **35**, see Nos. 546/57.

1924. International Philatelic Exn, The Hague.

290	10c. green	60·00	60·00
291	15c. black	70·00	70·00
292	35c. red	60·00	60·00

37

38

1924. Dutch Lifeboat Centenary.

293	37	2c. brown	5·25	3·75
294	38	10c. brown on yellow	9·25	3·25

39

1924. Child Welfare.

295	39	2c. (+2c.) green	3·00	3·00
296	39	7½c. (+3½c.) brown	10·50	13·00
297	39	10c. (+2½c.) red	6·50	3·00

40 Arms of South Holland

1925. Child Welfare. Arms as T 40.

298A	-	2c. (+2c.) green and yellow	1·20	1·20
299A	-	7½c. (+3½c.) violet and blue	6·50	7·00
300A	40	10c. (+2½c.) red and yellow	4·75	60

ARMS: 2c. North Brabant; 7½c. Gelderland.
See also Nos. 350/3A and 359/62A.

1926. Child Welfare. Arms as T 40.

350A	2c. (+2c.) red and silver	1·20	60
351A	5c. (+3c.) green and blue	2·30	2·30
352A	10c. (+3c.) red and green	3·50	60
353A	15c. (+3c.) yellow and blue	10·50	9·25

ARMS: 2c. Utrecht; 5c. Zeeland; 10c. North Holland; 15c. Friesland.

46 Queen Wilhelmina

47 Red Cross Allegory

1927. 60th Anniv of Dutch Red Cross Society.

354	46	2c. (+2c.) red	5·75	5·25
355	-	3c. (+2c.) green	11·50	14·00
356	-	5c. (+3c.) blue	2·30	2·30
357	-	7½c. (+3½c.) blue	7·50	3·00
358	47	15c. (+5c.) red and blue	16·00	16·00

PORTRAITS: 2c. King William III; 3c. Queen Emma; 5c. Henry, Prince Consort.

1927. Child Welfare. Arms as T 40.

359A	2c. (+2c.) red and lilac	1·20	1·20
360A	5c. (+3c.) green and yellow	2·30	2·30
361A	7½c. (+3½c.) red and black	5·75	60
362A	15c. (+3c.) blue and brown	8·25	7·50

ARMS: 2c. Drente; 5c. Groningen; 7½c. Limburg; 15c. Overyssel.

48 Sculler

49 Footballer

1928. Olympic Games, Amsterdam.

363	48	1½c.+1c. green	4·75	4·75
364	-	2c.+1c. purple	4·75	5·75
365	49	3c.+1c. green	7·00	7·00
366	-	5c.+1c. blue	5·75	3·50
367	-	7½c.+2½c. orange	5·75	3·50

368	-	10c.+2c. red	10·50	8·25
369	-	15c.+2c. blue	14·00	8·25
370	-	30c.+3c. sepia	28·00	29·00

DESIGNS—HORIZ: 2c. Fencing. VERT: 5c. Sailing; 7½c. Putting the shot; 10c. Running; 15c. Show-jumping; 30c. Boxing.

50 Lieut. Koppen

1928. Air.

| 371 | 50 | 40c. red | 85 | 70 |
| 372 | - | 75c. green | 85 | 70 |

DESIGN: 75c. Van der Hoop.

52 J. P. Minckelers

1928. Child Welfare.

373	52	1½c.+1½c. violet	80	70
374	-	5c.+3c. green	2·75	1·20
375a	-	7½c.+2½c. red	5·25	45
376a	-	12½c.+3½c. blue	14·50	13·00

PORTRAITS: 5c. Boerhaave; 7½c. H. A. Lorentz; 12½c. G. Huygens.

53 Mercury

1929. Air.

377	53	1½g. black	3·50	2·30
378	53	4½g. red	3·50	7·00
379	53	7½g. green	39·00	7·00

1929. Surch 21.

| 380 | 36 | 21c. on 22½c. brown | 29·00 | 2·30 |

55 "Friendship and Security"

1929. Child Welfare.

381A	55	1½c. (+1½c.) grey	3·25	80
382A	55	5c. (+3c.) green	5·25	1·30
383A	55	6c. (+4c.) red	3·25	60
384A	55	12½c. (+3½c.) blue	17·00	18·00

56 Rembrandt and "De Staalmeesters"

1930. Rembrandt Society.

385	56	5c. (+5c.) green	10·50	10·50
386	56	6c. (+5c.) black	8·25	8·25
387	56	12½c. (+5c.) blue	16·00	16·00

57 Spring

1930. Child Welfare.

388A	57	1½c. (+1½c.) red	2·30	80
389A	-	5c. (+3c.) green	3·50	1·20
390A	-	6c. (+4c.) purple	3·00	95
391A	-	12½c. (+3½c.) blue	23·00	17·00

DESIGNS (allegorical): 5c. Summer; 6c. Autumn; 12½c. Winter.

58

1931. Gouda Church Restoration Fund.

| 392 | 58 | 1½c.+1½c. green | 27·00 | 26·00 |
| 393 | - | 6c.+4c. red | 31·00 | 29·00 |

DESIGN: No. 393, Church facade.

59 Queen Wilhelmina and Fokker F.XII Monoplanes

1931

394	59	36c. red and blue (air)	20·00	1·20
395	-	70c. blue and red (postage)	44·00	1·20
395b	-	80c. green and red	£160	4·75

DESIGNS: 70c. Portrait and factory; 80c. Portrait and shipyard.

61 Mentally Deficient Child

1931. Child Welfare.

396A	-	1½c. (+1½c.) red and blue	2·30	2·30
397A	61	5c. (+3c.) green and purple	8·25	2·30
398A	-	6c. (+4c.) purple and green	9·25	2·30
399D	-	12½c. (+3½c.) blue and red	41·00	29·00

DESIGNS: 1½c. Deaf mute; 6c. Blind girl; 12½c. Sick child.

62 Windmill and Dykes, Kinderdijk

1932. Tourist Propaganda.

400	62	2½c.+1½c. green and black	11·50	9·25
401	-	6c.+4c. grey and black	16·00	9·25
402	-	7½c.+3½c. red and black	45·00	26·00
403	-	12½c.+2½c. blue and black	49·00	31·00

DESIGNS: 6c. Aerial view of Town Hall, Zierikzee; 7½c. Bridges at Schipluiden and Moerdijk; 12½c. Tulips.

63 Gorse (Spring)

1932. Child Welfare.

404A	63	1½c. (+1½c.) brown & yell	3·25	80
405A	-	5c. (+3c.) blue and red	4·25	1·40
406A	-	6c. (+4c.) green and orange	3·25	70
407A	-	12½c. (+3½c.) blue & orange	42·00	35·00

DESIGNS: Child and: 5c. Cornflower (Summer); 6c. Sunflower (Autumn); 12½c. Christmas rose (Winter).

64 Arms of House of Orange   **65** Portrait by Goltzius

1933. 4th Birth Centenary of William I of Orange. T 64 and portraits of William I inscr "1533", as T 65.

408	64	1½c. black	80	60
409	65	5c. green	2·75	60
410	-	6c. purple	4·00	60
411	-	12½c. blue	24·00	5·25

DESIGNS: 6c. Portrait by Key; 12½c. Portrait attributed to Moro.

68 Dove of Peace

1933. Peace Propaganda.

| 412 | 68 | 12½c. blue | 13·50 | 60 |

69 Projected Monument at Den Helder    **70** "De Hoop" (hospital ship)

1933. Seamen's Fund.

413	69	1½c. (+1½c.) red	5·75	5·25
414	70	5c. (+3c.) green and red	17·00	8·75
415	-	6c. (+4c.) green	26·00	6·50
416	-	12½c. (+3½c.) blue	38·00	32·00

DESIGNS: 6c. Lifeboat; 12½c. Seaman and Seamen's Home.

73 Pander S.4 Postjager

1933. Air. Special Flights.

| 417 | 73 | 30c. green | 1·20 | 1·20 |

74 Child and Star of Epiphany

1933. Child Welfare.

418A	74	1½c. (+1½c.) orange and grey	2·30	95
419A	74	5c. (+3c.) yellow and brown	3·25	1·00
420A	74	6c. (+4c.) gold and green	3·75	95
421A	74	12½c. (+3½c.) silver and blue	37·00	32·00

75 Princess Juliana

1934. Crisis stamps.

| 438 | - | 5c. (+4c.) purple | 19·00 | 5·25 |
| 439 | 75 | 6c. (+5c.) blue | 16·00 | 6·50 |

DESIGN: 5c. Queen Wilhelmina.

76 Dutch Warship

1934. Tercentenary of Curacao.

| 440 | - | 6c. black | 5·25 | 30 |
| 441 | 76 | 12½c. blue | 31·00 | 4·25 |

DESIGN: 6c. Willemstad Harbour.

77 Dowager Queen Emma

1934. Anti-T.B. Fund.

| 442 | 77 | 6c. (+2c.) blue | 19·00 | 2·30 |

78 Destitute child

1934. Child Welfare.

443	78	1½c. (+1½c.) brown	2·30	1·20
444	78	5c. (+3c.) red	4·00	5·25
445	78	6c. (+4c.) green	4·00	60
446	78	12½c. (+3½c.) blue	36·00	26·00

79 H. D. Guyot

1935. Cultural and Social Relief Fund.

447	79	1½c. (+1½c.) red	3·00	3·00
448	-	5c. (+3c.) brown	7·00	7·50
449	-	6c. (+4c.) green	8·25	1·20
450	-	12½c. (+3½c.) blue	40·00	11·50

PORTRAITS: 5c. A. J. M. Diepenbrock; 6c. F. C. Donders; 12½c. J. P. Sweelinck.
See also Nos. 456/9, 469/72, 478/82 and 492/6.

80 Aerial Map of Netherlands

1935. Air Fund.

| 451 | 80 | 6c. (+4c.) brown | 42·00 | 15·00 |

81 Child picking Fruit

1935. Child Welfare.

452	81	1½c. (+1½c.) red	85	60
453	81	5c. (+3c.) green	2·30	1·70
454	81	6c. (+4c.) brown	4·00	60
455	81	12½c. (+3½c.) blue	33·00	14·50

1936. Cultural and Social Relief Fund. As T 79.

456	-	1½c. (+1½c.) sepia	1·20	1·20
457	-	5c. (+3c.) green	7·00	5·25
458	-	6c. (+4c.) red	5·75	1·20
459	-	12½c. (+3½c.) blue	21·00	4·00

PORTRAITS: 1½c. H. Kamerlingh Onnes; 5c. Dr. A. S. Talma; 6c. Mgr. Dr. H. J. A. M. Schaepman; 12½c. Desiderius Erasmus.

83 Pallas Athene

1936. Tercentenary of Utrecht University Foundation.

| 460 | 83 | 6c. red | 2·30 | 60 |
| 461 | - | 12½c. blue | 8·25 | 7·50 |

DESIGN: 12½c. Gisbertus Voetius.

84 Child Herald

1936. Child Welfare.

462	84	1½c. (+1½c.) slate	60	60
463	84	5c. (+3c.) green	3·50	1·20
464	84	6c. (+4c.) brown	3·00	60
465	84	12½c. (+3½c.) blue	22·00	7·00

85 Scout Movement

1937. Scout Jamboree.

466	-	1½c. black and green	60	35
467	85	6c. brown and black	1·70	35
468	-	12½c. black and blue	5·75	2·20

DESIGNS: 1½c. Scout Tenderfoot Badge; 12½c. Hermes.

1937. Cultural and Social Relief Fund. Portraits as T 79.

469	-	1½c.+1½c. sepia	60	60
470	-	5c.+3c. green	6·50	5·25
471	-	6c.+4c. purple	1·70	60
472	-	12½c.+3½c. blue	11·50	3·50

PORTRAITS: 1½c. Jacob Maris; 5c. F. de la B. Sylvius; 6c. J. van den Vondel; 12½c. A. van Leeuwenhoek.

86 "Laughing Child" by Frans Hals

1937. Child Welfare.

473	**86**	1½c. (+1½c.) black	30	30
474	**86**	3c. (+2c.) green	2·30	1·70
475	**86**	4c. (+2c.) red	95	60
476	**86**	5c. (+3c.) green	80	30
477	**86**	12½c. (+3½c.) blue	10·00	3·00

1938. Cultural and Social Relief Fund. As T 79.

478	1½c.+1½c. sepia	50	85
479	3c.+2c. green	95	60
480	4c.+2c. red	3·00	3·25
481	5c.+3c. green	3·75	60
482	12½c.+3½c. blue	13·00	1·70

PORTRAITS: 1½c. M. van St. Aldegonde; 3c. O. G. Heldring; 4c. Maria Tesselschade; 5c. Rembrandt; 12½c. H. Boerhaave.

87 Queen Wilhelmina

1938. 40th Anniv of Coronation.

483	**87**	1½c. black	30	30
484	**87**	5c. red	40	30
485	**87**	12½c. blue	5·00	2·30

88 Carrion Crow

1938. Air. Special Flights.

486	**88**	12½c. blue and grey	80	60
790a	**88**	25c. blue and grey	4·75	2·30

89 Boy with Flute

1938. Child Welfare.

487	**89**	1½c.+1½c. black	30	30
488	**89**	3c.+2c. brown	70	60
489	**89**	4c.+2c. green	1·40	1·20
490	**89**	5c.+3c. red	50	30
491	**89**	12½c.+3½c. blue	13·00	3·00

1939. Cultural and Social Relief Fund. As T 79.

492	1½c.+1½c. brown	1·20	60
493	2½c.+2½c. green	5·25	3·50
494	3c.+3c. red	1·20	1·70
495	5c.+3c. green	4·00	60
496	12½c.+3½c. blue	9·25	1·70

PORTRAITS: 1½c. M. Maris; 2½c. Anton Mauve; 3c. Gerardus van Swieten; 5c. Nicolas Beets; 12½c. Pieter Stuyvesant.

91 St. Willibrord's landing in the Netherlands

1939. 12th Death Centenary of St. Willibrord.

497	**91**	5c. green	85	30
498	-	12½c. blue	7·75	4·00

DESIGN: 12½c. St. Willibrord as Bishop of Utrecht.

92 Replica of Locomotive "De Arend"

1939. Centenary of Netherlands Railway.

499	**92**	5c. green	1·20	30
500	-	12½c. blue	11·50	5·75

DESIGN: 12½c. Electric railcar.

93 Child and Cornucopia

1939. Child Welfare.

501	**93**	1½c.+1½c. black	35	60
502	**93**	2½c.+2½c. green	7·00	3·50
503	**93**	3c.+3c. red	80	60
504	**93**	5c.+3c. green	1·70	60
505	**93**	12½c.+3½c. blue	5·75	2·30

94 Queen Wilhelmina

1940

506	**94**	5c. green	40	10
506a	**94**	6c. brown	80	30
507	**94**	7½c. red	40	10
508	**94**	10c. purple	40	10
509	**94**	12½c. blue	40	30
510	**94**	15c. blue	40	30
510a	**94**	17½c. blue	1·90	1·20
511	**94**	20c. violet	95	30
512	**94**	22½c. olive	3·25	3·00
513	**94**	25c. red	70	30
514	**94**	30c. ochre	1·60	60
515	**94**	40c. green	3·00	1·20
515a	**94**	50c. orange	12·00	1·20
515b	**94**	60c. purple	12·00	3·75

95 Vincent Van Gogh

1940. Cultural and Social Relief Fund.

516	**95**	1½c.+1½c. brown	3·50	80
517	-	2½c.+2½c. green	5·75	1·60
518	-	3c.+3c. red	3·50	1·60
519	-	5c.+3c. green	8·75	70
520	-	12½c.+3½c. blue	7·00	2·75

PORTRAITS: 1½c. E. J. Potgieter; 3c. Petrus Camper; 5c. Jan Steen; 12½c. Joseph Scaliger.

See also Nos. 558/62 and 656/60.

1940. As No. 519, colour changed. Surch.

521	7½c.+2½c. on 5c.+3c. red	60	60

1940. Surch with large figures and network.

522	**35**	2½ on 3c. red	7·00	35
523	**35**	5 on 3c. green	35	35
524	**35**	7½ on 3c. red	35	10
525	**35**	10 on 3c. green	35	35
526	**35**	12½ on 3c. blue	60	60
527	**35**	17½ on 3c. green	1·70	60
528	**35**	20 on 3c. green	1·20	35
529	**35**	22½ on 3c. green	5·75	7·00
530	**35**	25 on 3c. green	2·10	60
531	**35**	30 on 3c. green	1·70	70
532	**35**	40 on 3c. green	4·75	3·25
533	**35**	50 on 3c. green	2·10	95
534	**35**	60 on 3c. green	3·50	1·90
535	**35**	70 on 3c. green	15·00	5·75
536	**35**	80 on 3c. green	19·00	9·25
537	**35**	100 on 3c. green	55·00	50·00
538	**35**	250 on 3c. green	65·00	65·00
539	**35**	500 on 3c. green	60·00	60·00

98 Girl with Dandelion

1940. Child Welfare.

540	**98**	1½c.+1½c. violet	1·40	35
541	**98**	2½c.+2½c. olive	4·75	1·40
542	**98**	4c.+3c. blue	5·75	1·40
543	**98**	5c.+3c. green	6·00	35
544	**98**	7½c.+3½c. red	1·70	35

1941

546	**35**	5c. green	10	10
547	**35**	7½c. red	10	10
548	**35**	10c. violet	1·50	35
549	**35**	12½c. blue	60	45
550	**35**	15c. blue	1·50	60
551	**35**	17½c. red	35	35
552	**35**	20c. violet	1·50	35
553	**35**	22½c. olive	35	60
554	**35**	25c. lake	60	45
555	**35**	30c. brown	5·25	45
556	**35**	40c. green	35	45
557	**35**	50c. brown	35	35

1941. Cultural and Social Relief Fund. As T 95 but inscr "ZOMERZEGEL 31.12.46".

558	1½c.+1½c. brown	1·40	45
559	2½c.+2½c. green	1·40	45
560	4c.+3c. red	1·40	45
561	5c.+3c. green	1·40	45
562	7½c.+3½c. purple	1·40	45

PORTRAITS: 1½c. Dr. A. Mathijsen; 2½c. J. Ingenhousz; 4c. Aagje Deken; 5c. Johan Bosboom; 7½c. A. C. W. Staring.

100 "Titus Rembrandt"

1941. Child Welfare.

563	**100**	1½c.+1½c. black	70	45
564	**100**	2½c.+2½c. olive	70	45
565	**100**	4c.+3c. blue	70	45
566	**100**	5c.+3c. green	70	45
567	**100**	7½c.+3½c. red	70	45

101 Legionary

1942. Netherlands Legion Fund.

568	**101**	7½c.+2½c. red	1·70	1·00
569	-	12½c.+87½c. blue	13·50	13·00

MS569a 155×110 mm. No. 568 (block of ten) £190 £130

MS569b 96×97 mm. No. 569 (block of ten) £150 £150

DESIGN—HORIZ: 12½c. Legionary with similar inscription.

1943. 1st European Postal Congress. As T 26 but larger (21×27½ mm) surch EUROPEESCHE P T T VEREENIGING 19 OCTOBER 1942 10 CENT.

570	**26**	10c. on 2½c. yellow	1·00	45

103 Seahorse

1943. Old Germanic Symbols.

571	**103**	1c. black	10	10
572	-	1½c. red	10	10
573	-	2c. blue	10	10
574	-	2½c. green	10	10
575	-	3c. red	10	10
576	-	4c. brown	10	10
577	-	5c. olive	10	10

DESIGNS—VERT: 1½c. Triple crowned tree; 2½c. Birds in ornamental tree; 4c. Horse and rider. HORIZ: 2c. Swans; 3c. Trees and serpentine roots; 5c. Prancing horses.

104 Michiel A. de Ruyter

1943. Dutch Naval Heroes.

578	**104**	7½c. red	15	10
579	-	10c. green	15	10
580	-	12½c. blue	15	15
581	-	15c. violet	35	15
582	-	17½c. grey	15	15
583	-	20c. brown	15	15
584	-	22½c. red	15	15
585	-	25c. purple	70	80
586	-	30c. blue	15	35
587	-	40c. grey	15	45

PORTRAITS: 10c. Johan Evertsen; 12½c. Maarten H. Tromp; 15c. Piet Hein; 17½c. Wilhelm Joseph van Gent; 20c. Witte de With; 22½c. Cornelis Evertsen; 25c. Tjerk Hiddes de Fries; 30c. Cornelis Tromp; 40c. Cornelis Evertsen the younger.

105 Mail Cart

1943. Stamp Day.

589	**105**	7½c.+7½c. red	25	35

106 Child and Doll's House

1944. Child Welfare and Winter Help Funds. Inscr "WINTERHULP" (1½c. and 7½c.) or "VOLKSDIENST" (others).

590	**106**	1½c.+3½c. black	35	45
591	-	4c.+3½c. brown	35	45
592	-	5c.+5c. green	35	45
593	-	7½c.+7½c. red	35	45
594	-	10c.+40c. blue	35	45

DESIGNS: 4c. Mother and child; 5c., 10c. Mother and children; 7½c. Child and wheatsheaf.

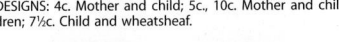

107 Infantryman

111 Queen Wilhelmina

1944

595	**107**	1½c. black	15	10
596	-	2½c. green	15	10
597	-	3c. brown	15	10
598	-	5c. blue	15	10
599	**111**	7½c. red	15	10
600	**111**	10c. orange	15	10
601	**111**	12½c. blue	15	10
602	**111**	15c. red	2·30	2·30
603	**111**	17½c. green	1·60	1·60
604	**111**	20c. violet	70	45
605	**111**	22½c. red	1·70	1·70
606	**111**	25c. brown	2·75	2·10
607	**111**	30c. green	45	45
608	**111**	40c. purple	3·50	3·50
609	**111**	50c. mauve	2·40	1·60

The above set was originally for use on Netherlands warships serving with the Allied Fleet, and was used after liberation in the Netherlands.

112 Lion and Dragon

1945. Liberation.

610	**112**	7½c. orange	25	15

113

1945. Child Welfare.

611	**113**	1½c.+2½c. grey	45	45
612	**113**	2½c.+3½c. green	45	45
613	**113**	5c.+5c. brown	45	45
614	**113**	7½c.+4½c. red	45	45
615	**113**	12½c.+5½c. blue	45	45

114 Queen Wilhelmina

1946

616	**114**	1g. blue	4·75	1·50
617	**114**	2½g. red	£225	23·00
618	**114**	5g. green	£225	50·00
619	**114**	10g. violet	£225	50·00

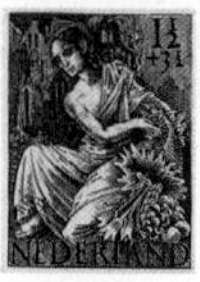

115 Emblem of Abundance

1946. War Victims' Relief Fund.

620	**115**	1½c.+3½c. black	70	45
621	**115**	2½c.+5c. green	80	80
622	**115**	5c.+10c. violet	80	80
623	**115**	7½c.+15c. red	70	45
624	**115**	12½c.+37½c. blue	1·40	95

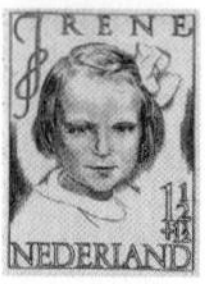

116 Princess Irene

1946. Child Welfare.

625	**116**	1½c.+1½c. brown	80	80
626	-	2½c.+1½c. green	80	80
627	**116**	4c.+2c. red	1·00	80
628	-	5c.+2c. brown	1·00	80
629	-	7½c.+2½c. red	80	35
630	-	12½c.+7½c. blue	80	1·20

PORTRAITS: 2½c., 5c. Princess Margriet; 7½c., 12½c. Princess Beatrix.

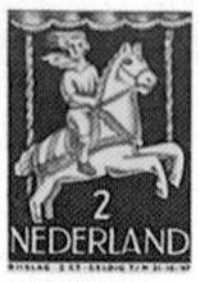

117 Boy on Roundabout

1946. Child Welfare.

631	**117**	2c.+2c. violet	80	70
632	**117**	4c.+2c. green	80	70
633	**117**	7½c.+2½c. red	80	70
634	**117**	10c.+5c. purple	1·00	35
635	**117**	20c.+5c. blue	1·40	95

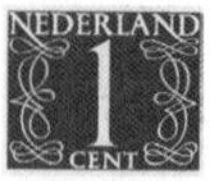

118 Numeral

1946

636	**118**	1c. red	10	10
637	**118**	2c. blue	10	10
638	**118**	2½c. orange	7·75	2·30
638a	**118**	3c. brown	10	10
639	**118**	4c. green	45	10
639a	**118**	5c. orange	10	10
639c	**118**	6c. grey	60	35
639d	**118**	7c. red	35	10
639f	**118**	8c. mauve	35	10

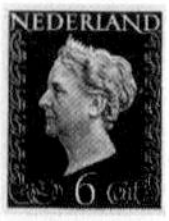

119 Queen Wilhelmina

1947

640	**119**	5c. green	1·60	10
641	**119**	6c. black	45	10
642	**119**	6c. blue	80	10
643	**119**	7½c. red	60	10
644	**119**	10c. purple	1·20	10
645	**119**	12½c. red	1·20	60
646	**119**	15c. violet	13·50	10
647	**119**	20c. blue	14·50	10
648	**119**	22½c. green	1·20	1·20
649	**119**	25c. blue	27·00	10
650	**119**	30c. orange	27·00	45
651	**119**	35c. blue	26·00	80
652	**119**	40c. brown	30·00	80
653	-	45c. blue	33·00	17·00
654	-	50c. brown	21·00	60
655	-	60c. red	27·00	3·50

Nos. 653/5 are as Type **119** but have the inscriptions in colour on white ground.

1947. Cultural and Social Relief Fund. As T 95 but inscr "ZOMERZEGEL ... 13.12.48".

656	2c.+2c. red	1·40	70
657	4c.+2c. green	1·90	95
658	7½c.+2½c. violet	3·00	1·20
659	10c.+5c. brown	2·75	60
660	20c.+5c. blue	2·20	95

PORTRAITS: 2c. H. van Deventer; 4c. P. C. Hooft; 7½c. Johan de Witt; 10c. J. F. van Royen; 20c. Hugo Grotius.

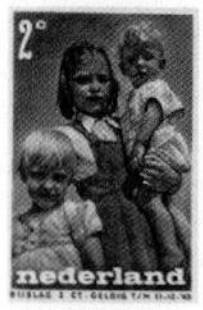

122 Children

1947. Child Welfare.

661	**122**	2c.+2c. brown	35	35
662	-	4c.+2c. green	1·60	1·00
663	-	7½c.+2½c. brown	1·60	1·30
664	-	10c.+5c. lake	1·90	35
665	**122**	20c.+5c. blue	2·10	1·60

DESIGN: 4c. to 10c. Baby.

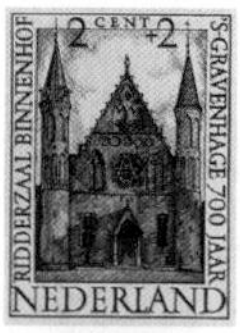

124 Ridderzaal, The Hague

1948. Cultural and Social Relief Fund.

666	**124**	2c.+2c. brown	2·75	95
667	-	6c.+4c. green	3·00	95
668	-	10c.+5c. red	2·10	60
669	-	20c.+5c. blue	3·00	1·60

BUILDINGS: 6c. Palace on the Dam; 10c. Kneuterdijk Palace; 20c. Nieuwe Kerk, Amsterdam.

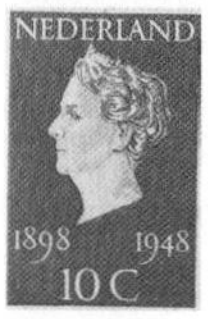

125 Queen Wilhelmina

1948. Queen Wilhelmina's Golden Jubilee.

670	**125**	10c. red	35	25
671	**125**	20c. blue	3·25	2·75

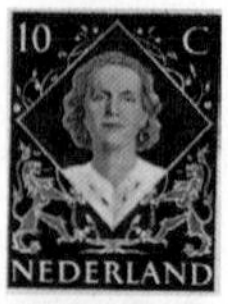

126 Queen Juliana

1948. Coronation.

672	**126**	10c. brown	2·50	25
673	**126**	20c. blue	3·25	70

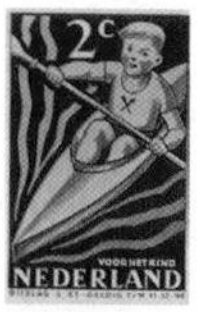

127 Boy in Canoe

1948. Child Welfare.

674	**127**	2c.+2c. green	35	25
675	-	5c.+3c. green	3·50	1·00
676	-	6c.+4c. grey	1·90	45
677	-	10c.+5c. red	70	25
678	-	20c.+8c. blue	3·50	1·90

DESIGNS: 5c. Girl swimming; 6c. Boy on toboggan; 10c. Girl on swing; 20c. Boy skating.

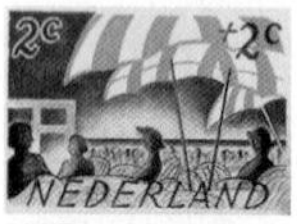

128 Terrace near Beach

1949. Cultural and Social Relief Fund.

679	**128**	2c.+2c. yellow and blue	3·00	25
680	-	5c.+3c. yellow and blue	5·25	3·00
681	-	6c.+4c. green	4·25	70
682	-	10c.+5c. yellow and blue	5·00	25
683	-	20c.+5c. blue	5·25	3·00

DESIGNS: 5c. Hikers in cornfield; 6c. Campers by fire; 10c. Gathering wheat; 20c. Yachts.

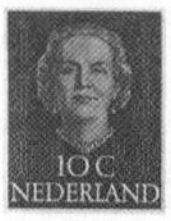

129 Queen Juliana

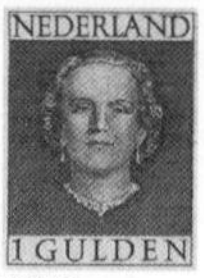

130 Queen Juliana

1949

684	**129**	5c. green	1·20	10
685	**129**	6c. blue	60	10
686	**129**	10c. orange	60	10
687	**129**	12c. red	3·50	4·75
688	**129**	15c. green	7·00	10
689	**129**	20c. blue	5·75	10
690	**129**	25c. brown	21·00	10
691	**129**	30c. violet	14·50	10
692	**129**	35c. blue	39·00	35
693	**129**	40c. purple	65·00	45
694	**129**	45c. orange	3·00	1·40
695	**129**	45c. violet	80·00	80
696	**129**	50c. green	19·00	45
697	**129**	60c. brown	29·00	45
697a	**129**	75c. red	£120	3·00
698	**130**	1g. red	5·75	60
699	**130**	2½g. brown	£325	5·75
700a	**130**	5g. brown	£700	8·25
701	**130**	10g. violet	£475	26·00

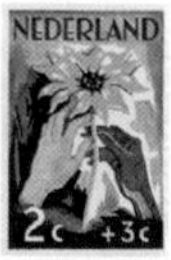

131 Hands reaching for Sunflower

1949. Red Cross and Indonesian Relief Fund.

702	**131**	2c.+3c. yellow and grey	1·70	45
703	**131**	6c.+4c. yellow and red	3·00	60
704	**131**	10c.+5c. yellow and blue	5·75	35
705	**131**	30c.+10c. yellow & brn	14·00	5·00

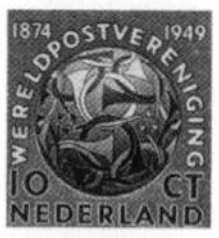

132 Posthorns and Globe

1949. 75th Anniv of U.P.U.

706	**132**	10c. lake	1·20	10
707	**132**	20c. blue	13·00	3·75

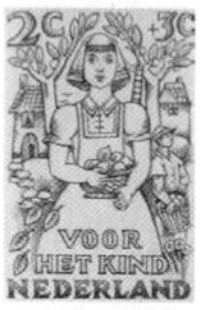

133 "Autumn"

1949. Child Welfare Fund. Inscr "VOOR HET KIND".

708	**133**	2c.+3c. brown	60	25
709	-	5c.+3c. red	11·50	3·00
710	-	6c.+4c. green	7·00	60
711	-	10c.+5c. grey	60	25
712	-	20c.+7c. blue	10·50	3·00

DESIGNS: 5c. "Summer"; 6c. "Spring"; 10c. "Winter"; 20c. "New Year".

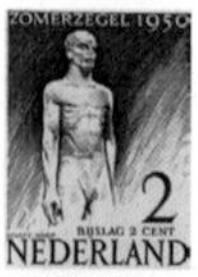

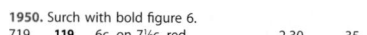

134 Resistance Monument

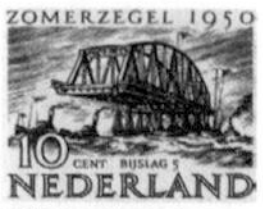

135 Section of Moerdijk Bridge

1950. Cultural and Social Relief Fund. Inscr "ZOMERZEGEL 1950".

713	**134**	2c.+2c. brown	4·75	1·70
714	-	4c.+2c. green	19·00	17·00
715	-	5c.+3c. grey	15·00	8·25
716	-	6c.+4c. violet	8·25	1·20
717	**135**	10c.+5c. slate	9·25	60
718	-	20c.+5c. blue	24·00	23·00

DESIGNS—VERT: 4c. Sealing dykes; 5c. Rotterdam skyscraper. HORIZ: 6c. Harvesting; 20c. "Overijssel" (canal freighter).

1950. Surch with bold figure 6.

719	**119**	6c. on 7½c. red	2·30	35

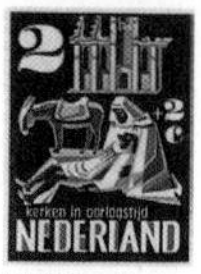

137 Good Samaritan and Bombed Church

1950. Bombed Churches Rebuilding Fund.

720	**137**	2c.+2c. olive	15·00	4·75
721	**137**	5c.+3c. brown	20·00	17·00
722	**137**	6c.+4c. green	13·00	7·00
723	**137**	10c.+5c. red	37·00	1·20
724	**137**	20c.+5c. blue	49·00	42·00

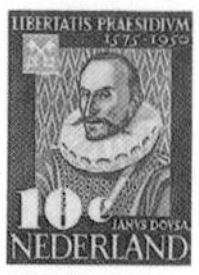

138 Janus Dousa

1950. 375th Anniv of Leyden University.

725	**138**	10c. olive	7·00	35
726	-	20c. blue	7·00	2·30

PORTRAIT: 20c. Jan van Hout.

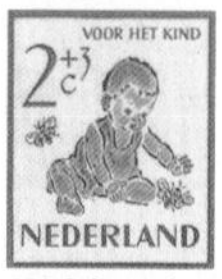

139 Baby and Bees

1950. Child Welfare. Inscr "VOOR HET KIND".

727	**139**	2c.+3c. red	60	35
728	-	5c.+3c. olive	19·00	8·75
729	-	6c.+4c. green	5·75	1·00
730	-	10c.+5c. purple	60	35
731	-	20c.+7c. blue	19·00	13·00

DESIGNS: 5c. Boy and fowl; 6c. Girl and birds; 10c. Boy and fish; 20c. Girl, butterfly and frog.

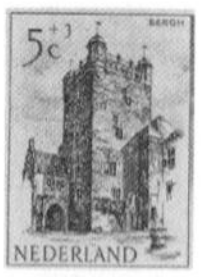

140 Bergh Castle

1951. Cultural and Social Relief Fund. Castles.

732		2c.+2c. violet	5·75	1·90
733	**140**	5c.+3c. red	16·00	11·50
734	-	6c.+4c. sepia	7·00	1·70
735	-	10c.+5c. green	10·50	45
736	-	20c.+5c. blue	16·00	12·00

DESIGNS—HORIZ: 2c. Hillenraad; 6c. Hernen. VERT: 10c. Rechteren; 20c. Moermond.

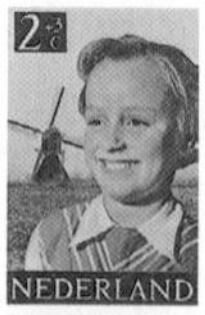

141 Girl and Windmill

1951. Child Welfare.

737	**141**	2c.+3c. green	1·20	35
738	-	5c.+3c. blue	13·00	6·50
739	-	6c.+4c. brown	8·25	1·00
740	-	10c.+5c. lake	60	35
741	-	20c.+7c. blue	13·00	11·50

DESIGNS: Each shows boy or girl: 5c. Crane; 6c. Fishing nets; 10c. Factory chimneys; 20c. Flats.

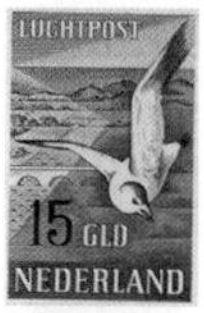

142 Gull

1951. Air.

742	**142**	15g. brown	£400	£170
743	**142**	25g. black	£400	£170

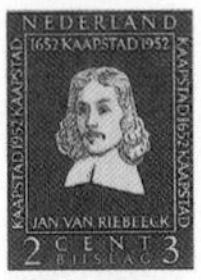

143 Jan van Riebeeck

1952. Tercentenary of Landing in South Africa and Van Riebeeck Monument Fund.

744	**143**	2c.+3c. violet	7·50	5·75
745	**143**	6c.+4c. green	9·25	7·00
746	**143**	10c.+5c. red	10·50	5·75
747	**143**	20c.+5c. blue	7·50	7·00

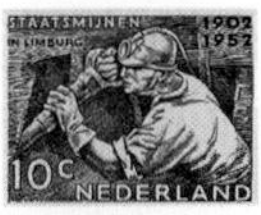

144 Miner

1952. 50th Anniv of State Mines, Limburg.

748	**144**	10c. blue	3·00	25

145 Wild Rose

1952. Cultural and Social Relief Fund. Floral designs inscr "ZOMERZEGEL 1952".

749	**145**	2c.+2c. green and red	1·40	80
750	-	5c.+3c. yellow and green	6·75	5·75
751	-	6c.+4c. green and red	3·50	1·60
752	-	10c.+5c. green & orange	3·00	45
753	-	20c.+5c. green and blue	16·00	11·50

FLOWERS: 5c. Marsh marigold; 6c. Tulip; 10c. Marguerite; 20c. Cornflower.

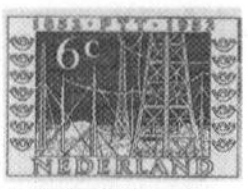

146 Radio Masts

1952. Netherlands Stamp Centenary and Centenary of Telegraph Service.

754		2c. violet	70	10
755	**146**	6c. red	80	25
756	-	10c. green	80	10
757	-	20c. slate	11·50	2·75

DESIGNS: 2c. Telegraph poles and steam train; 10c. Postman delivering letters, 1852; 20c. Postman delivering letters, 1952.

1952. International Postage Stamp Exn, Utrecht ("ITEP"). Nos. 754/7 but colours changed.

757a		2c. brown	37·00	20·00
757b	**146**	6c. blue	37·00	20·00
757c	-	10c. lake	37·00	20·00
757d	-	20c. blue	37·00	20·00

Nos. 757a/d were sold only in sets at the Exhibition at face plus 1g. entrance fee.

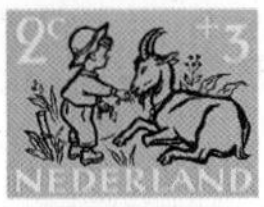

147 Boy feeding Goat

1952. Child Welfare.

758	**147**	2c.+3c. black and olive	25	35
759	-	5c.+3c. black and pink	4·75	2·75
760	-	6c.+4c. black and green	3·75	70
761	-	10c.+5c. black & orange	25	35
762	-	20c.+7c. black and blue	11·00	8·75

DESIGNS: 5c. Girl riding donkey; 6c. Girl playing with dog; 10c. Boy and cat; 20c. Boy and rabbit.

1953. Flood Relief Fund. Surch 19 53 10c +10 WATERSNOOD.

763	**129**	10c.+10c. orange	95	15

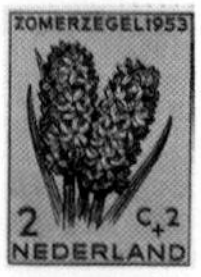

149 Hyacinth

1953. Cultural and Social Relief Fund.

764	**149**	2c.+2c. green and violet	1·20	60
765	-	5c.+3c. green & orange	7·00	6·50
766	-	6c.+4c. yellow and green	3·50	1·20
767	-	10c.+5c. green and red	5·75	60
768	-	20c.+5c. green and blue	21·00	17·00

FLOWERS: 5c. African marigold; 6c. Daffodil; 10c. Anemone; 20c. Dutch iris.

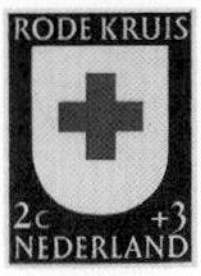

150 Red Cross

1953. Red Cross Fund. Inscr "RODE KRUIS".

769	**150**	2c.+3c. red and sepia	1·50	80
770	-	6c.+4c. red and brown	7·50	5·25
771	-	7c.+5c. red and olive	1·70	80
772	-	10c.+5c. red	1·20	35
773	-	25c.+8c. red and blue	12·50	8·00

DESIGNS: 6c. Man with lamp; 7c. Rescue worker in flooded area; 10c. Nurse giving blood transfusion; 25c. Red Cross flags.

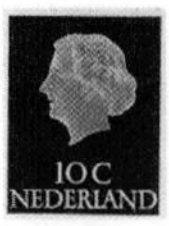

151 Queen Juliana

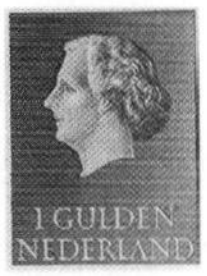

152 Queen Juliana

1953

775	**151**	10c. brown	15	10
776	**151**	12c. turquoise	15	10
777	**151**	15c. red	15	10
777b	**151**	18c. turquoise	15	10
778	**151**	20c. purple	15	10
778b	**151**	24c. olive	45	25
779	**151**	25c. blue	1·90	10
780	**151**	30c. orange	60	10
781	**151**	35c. brown	1·20	10
781a	**151**	37c. turquoise	60	25
782	**151**	40c. slate	60	10
783	**151**	45c. red	45	10
784	**151**	50c. green	95	10
785	**151**	60c. brown	1·20	10
785a	**151**	62c. red	3·50	3·50
785b	**151**	70c. blue	1·40	10
786	**151**	75c. purple	1·40	10
786a	**151**	80c. violet	1·40	10
786b	**151**	85c. green	1·90	10
786c	**151**	95c. brown	1·90	45
787	**152**	1g. red	3·00	10
788	**152**	2½g. green	13·50	25
789	**152**	5g. black	5·25	45
790	**152**	10g. blue	25·00	2·75

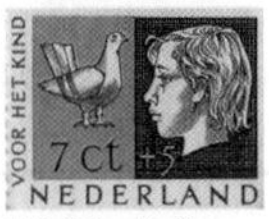

153 Girl with Pigeon

1953. Child Welfare. Inscr "VOOR HET KIND".

791	-	2c.+3c. blue and yellow	35	35
792	-	5c.+3c. lake and green	8·25	5·75
793	**153**	7c.+5c. brown and blue	5·00	1·60
794	-	10c.+5c. lilac and bistre	35	35
795	-	25c.+8c. turq & pink	16·00	14·00

DESIGNS: 2c. Girl, bucket and spade; 5c. Boy and apple; 10c. Boy and tjalk (sailing boat); 25c. Girl and tulip.

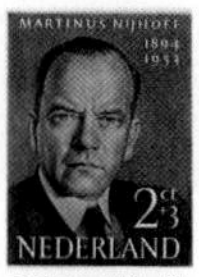

154 M. Nijhoff (poet)

1954. Cultural and Social Relief Fund.

796	**154**	2c.+3c. blue	3·50	2·75
797	-	5c.+3c. brown	7·00	7·00
798	-	7c.+5c. red	7·00	2·10
799	-	10c.+5c. green	11·50	1·00
800	-	25c.+8c. purple	17·00	16·00

PORTRAITS: 5c. W. Pijper (composer); 7c. H. P. Berlage (architect); 10c. J. Huizinga (historian); 25c. Vincent van Gogh (painter).

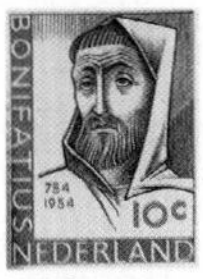

155 St. Boniface

1954. 1200th Anniv of Martyrdom of St. Boniface.

801	**155**	10c. blue	3·00	35

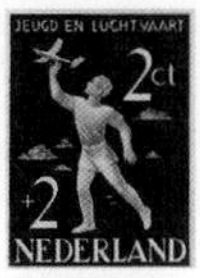

156 Boy and Model Glider

1954. National Aviation Fund.

802	**156**	2c.+2c. green	1·70	1·20
803	-	10c.+4c. blue	4·00	1·20

PORTRAIT: 10c. Dr. A. Plesman (aeronautical pioneer).

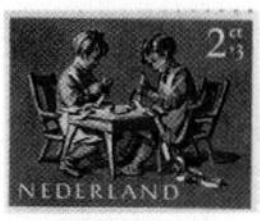

157 Making Paperchains

1954. Child Welfare.

804	**157**	2c.+3c. brown	25	25
805	-	5c.+3c. olive	6·50	6·25
806	-	7c.+5c. blue	3·00	80
807	-	10c.+5c. red	35	25
808	-	25c.+8c. blue	14·50	9·25

DESIGNS—VERT: 5c. Girl brushing her teeth; 7c. Boy and toy boat; 10c. Nurse and child. HORIZ: 25c. Invalid boy drawing in bed.

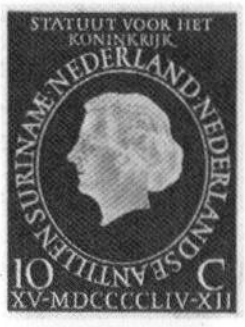

158 Queen Juliana

1954. Ratification of Statute for the Kingdom.

809	**158**	10c. red	1·20	25

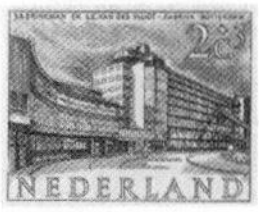

159 Factory, Rotterdam

1955. Cultural and Social Relief Fund.

810	**159**	2c.+3c. brown	2·30	1·90
811	-	5c.+3c. green	5·25	4·75
812	-	7c.+5c. red	2·30	1·60
813	-	10c.+5c. blue	4·00	35
814	-	25c.+8c. brown	19·00	14·50

DESIGNS—HORIZ: 5c. Post Office, The Hague; 10c. Town Hall, Hilversum; 25c. Office Building, The Hague. VERT: 7c. Stock Exchange, Amsterdam.

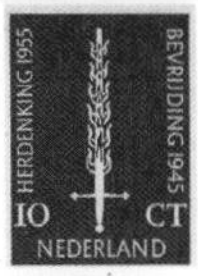

160 "The Victory of Peace"

1955. 10th Anniv of Liberation.

815	**160**	10c. red	1·70	35

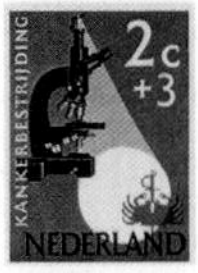

161 Microscope and Emblem of Cancer

1955. Queen Wilhelmina Anti-cancer Fund.

816	**161**	2c.+3c. black and red	1·40	80
817	**161**	5c.+3c. green and red	4·75	3·50
818	**161**	7c.+5c. purple and red	2·75	1·00
819	**161**	10c.+5c. blue and red	2·10	35
820	**161**	25c.+8c. olive and red	10·00	8·25

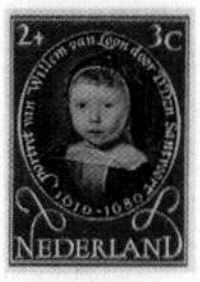

162 "Willem van Loon" (D. Dircks)

1955. Child Welfare Fund.

821	**162**	2c.+3c. green	60	35
822	-	5c.+3c. red	5·75	4·00
823	-	7c.+5c. brown	5·75	1·20
824	-	10c.+5c. blue	60	35
825	-	25c.+8c. lilac	14·00	12·50

PORTRAITS: 5c. "Portrait of a Boy" (J. A. Backer); 7c. "Portrait of a Girl" (unknown); 10c. "Philips Huygens" (A. Hanneman); 25c. "Constantin Huygens" (A. Hanneman).

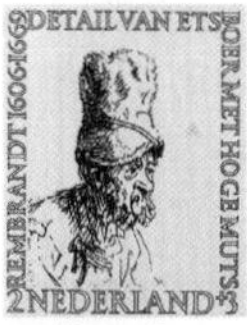

163 "Farmer"

1956. Cultural and Social Relief Fund and 350th Birth Anniv of Rembrandt. Details from Rembrandt's paintings.

826	**163**	2c.+3c. slate	4·75	4·00
827	-	5c.+3c. olive	4·75	4·00
828	-	7c.+5c. brown	7·00	7·00
829	-	10c.+5c. green	17·00	60
830	-	25c.+8c. brown	24·00	22·00

PAINTINGS: 5c. "Young Tobias with Angel"; 7c. "Persian wearing Fur Cap"; 10c. "Old Blind Tobias"; 25c. Self-portrait, 1639.

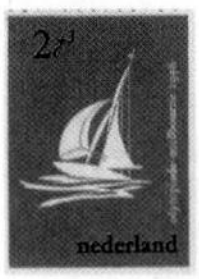

164 Yacht

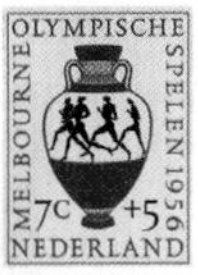

165 Amphora

1956. 16th Olympic Games, Melbourne.

831	**164**	2c.+3c. black and blue	1·40	1·30
832	-	5c.+3c. black and yellow	2·10	2·00
833	**165**	7c.+5c. black and brown	2·30	2·00
834	-	10c.+5c. black and grey	3·50	1·00
835	-	25c.+8c. black and green	7·00	7·00

DESIGNS: As Type **164**: 5c. Runner; 10c. Hockey player; 25c. Water polo player.

1956. Europa. As T 110 of Luxembourg.

836	10c. black and lake	5·75	35
837	25c. black and blue	70·00	2·30

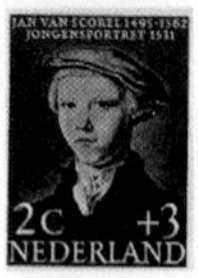

167 "Portrait of a Boy" (Van Scorel)

1956. Child Welfare Fund. 16th-century Dutch Paintings.

838	**167**	2c.+3c. grey and cream	60	35
839	-	5c.+3c. olive and cream	1·90	1·70
840	-	7c.+5c. purple & cream	5·25	2·30
841	-	10c.+5c. red and cream	45	35
842	-	25c.+8c. blue and cream	9·25	6·75

PAINTINGS: 5c. "Portrait of a Boy"; 7c. "Portrait of a Girl"; 10c. "Portrait of a Girl"; 25c. "Portrait of Eechie Pieters".

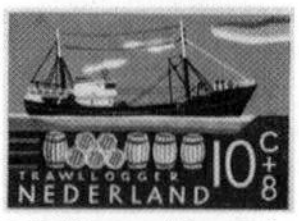

168 "Curacao" (trawler) and Fish Barrels

1957. Cultural and Social Relief Fund. Ships.

843		4c.+3c. blue	2·10	1·70
844		6c.+4c. lilac	5·50	5·25
845		7c.+5c. red	3·25	2·10
846	**168**	10c.+8c. green	6·00	60
847	-	30c.+8c. brown	7·75	6·50

DESIGNS: 4c. "Gaasterland" (freighter); 6c. Coaster; 7c. "Willem Barendsz" (whale factory ship) and whale; 30c. "Nieuw Amsterdam" (liner).

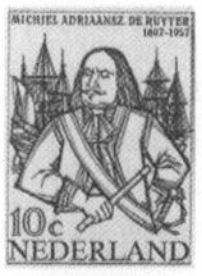

169 Admiral M. A. de Ruyter

1957. 350th Birth Anniv of M. A. de Ruyter.

848	**169**	10c. orange	1·00	35
849	-	30c. blue	6·00	1·70

DESIGN: 30c. De Ruyter's flagship, "De Zeven Provincien".

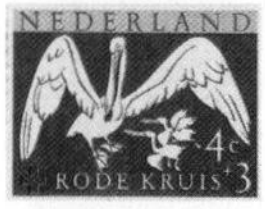

170 Blood Donors' Emblem

1957. 90th Anniv of Netherlands Red Cross Society and Red Cross Fund.

850	170	4c.+3c. blue and red	1·60	1·60
851	-	6c.+4c. green and red	2·10	1·90
852	-	7c.+5c. red and green	2·10	1·90
853	-	10c.+8c. red and ochre	1·90	35
854	-	30c.+8c. red and blue	4·00	3·50

DESIGNS: 6c. "J. Henry Dunant" (hospital ship); 7c. Red Cross; 10c. Red Cross emblem; 30c. Red Cross on globe.

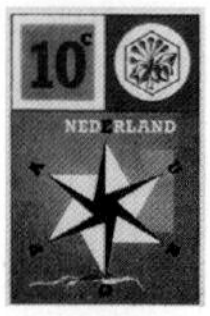

171 "Europa" Star

1957. Europa.

855	171	10c. black and blue	2·30	35
856	171	30c. green and blue	9·25	2·30

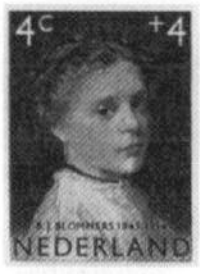

172 Portrait by B. J. Blommers

1957. Child Fund Welfare. 19th- and 20th-Century Paintings by Dutch Masters.

857	172	4c.+4c. red	60	35
858	-	6c.+4c. green	5·50	5·25
859	-	8c.+4c. sepia	5·00	3·00
860	-	12c.+9c. purple	45	35
861	-	30c.+9c. blue	11·50	9·25

PORTRAITS: Child paintings by: W. B. Tholen (6c.); J. Sluyters (8c.); M. Maris (12c.); C. Kruseman (30c.).

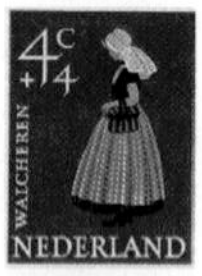

173 Walcheren Costume

1958. Cultural and Social Relief Fund. Provincial Costumes.

862	173	4c.+4c. blue	2·30	80
863	-	6c.+4c. ochre	5·25	4·00
864	-	8c.+4c. red	8·25	2·75
865	-	12c.+9c. brown	3·50	35
866	-	30c.+9c. lilac	13·00	10·50

COSTUMES: 6c. Marken; 8c. Scheveningen; 12c. Friesland; 30c. Volendam.

1958. Surch 12 C.

867	151	12c. on 10c. brown	1·60	10

1958. Europa. As T 119a of Luxembourg.

868	12c. blue and red	60	35
869	30c. red and blue	2·30	1·00

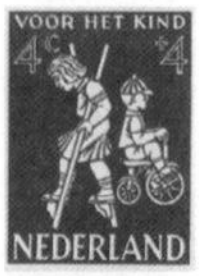

176 Girl on Stilts and Boy on Tricycle

1958. Child Welfare Fund. Children's Games.

870	176	4c.+4c. blue	35	35
871	-	6c.+4c. red	4·75	4·00
872	-	8c.+4c. green	3·00	1·60
873	-	12c.+9c. red	25	35
874	-	30c.+9c. blue	9·25	7·00

DESIGNS: 6c. Boy and girl on scooter; 8c. Boys playing leap-frog; 12c. Boys on roller-skates; 30c. Girl skipping and boy in toy car.

1959. 10th Anniv of N.A.T.O. As T 123 of Luxembourg (N.A.T.O. emblem).

875	12c. blue and yellow	35	35
876	30c. blue and red	1·40	80

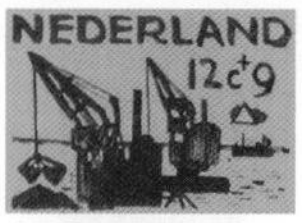

177 Cranes

1959. Cultural and Social Relief Fund. Prevention of Sea Encroachment.

877	-	4c.+4c. blue on green	2·30	2·10
878	-	6c.+4c. brown on grey	3·50	3·00
879	-	8c.+4c. violet on blue	3·50	2·30
880	177	12c.+9c. green on yell	5·75	35
881	-	30c.+9c. black on red	9·25	8·50

DESIGNS: 4c. Tugs and caisson; 6c. Dredger; 8c. Labourers making fascine mattresses; 30c. Sand-spouter and scoop.

1959. Europa. As T 123a of Luxembourg.

882	12c. red	1·70	35
883	30c. green	5·75	2·30

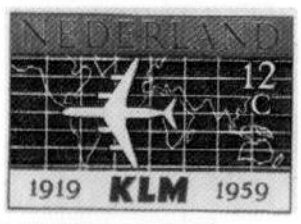

178 Silhouette of Douglas DC-8 Airliner and World Map

1959. 40th Anniv of K.L.M. (Royal Dutch Airlines).

884	178	12c. blue and red	35	35
885	-	30c. blue and green	2·30	1·70

DESIGN: 30c. Silhouette of Douglas DC-8 airliner.

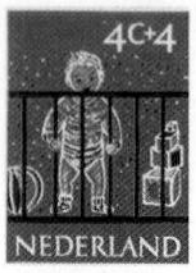

179 Child in Play-pen

1959. Child Welfare Fund.

886	179	4c.+4c. blue and brown	35	35
887	-	6c.+4c. brown and green	2·75	2·10
888	-	8c.+4c. blue and red	4·25	2·75
889	-	12c.+9c. red, black and blue	35	35
890	-	30c.+9c. turquoise and yellow	6·50	6·50

DESIGNS: 6c. Boy as "Red Indian" with bow and arrow; 8c. Boy feeding geese; 12c. Traffic warden escorting children; 30c. Girl doing homework.

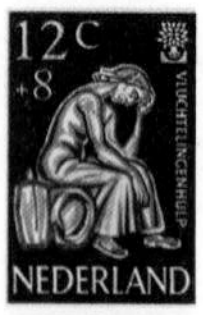

180 Refugee Woman

1960. World Refugee Year.

891	180	12c.+8c. purple	60	35
892	180	30c.+10c. green	5·25	3·50

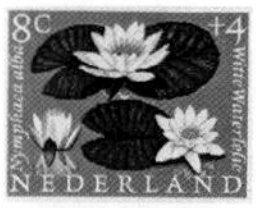

181 White Water-lily

1960. Cultural and Social Relief Fund. Flowers.

893	-	4c.+4c. red, green and grey	2·30	95
894	-	6c.+4c. yellow, green and salmon	3·50	3·50
895	181	8c.+4c. multicoloured	5·75	3·50
896	-	12c.+8c. red, green and buff	4·75	35
897	-	30c.+10c. blue, green and yellow	9·25	7·00

FLOWERS—VERT: 4c. "The Princess" tulip; 6c. Gorse; 12c. Poppy; 30c. Blue sea-holly.

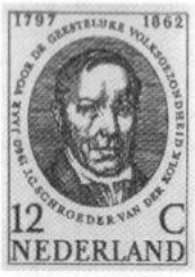

182 J. van der Kolk

1960. World Mental Health Year.

898	182	12c. red	1·20	35
899	-	30c. blue (J. Wier)	8·25	2·30

1960. Europa. As T 113a of Norway.

900	12c. yellow and red	60	35
901	30c. yellow and blue	4·75	2·30

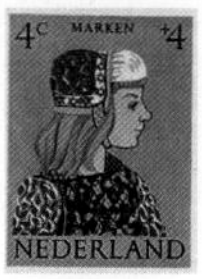

183 Marken Costume

1960. Child Welfare Fund. Costumes. Mult portraits.

902	183	4c.+4c. slate	60	35
903	-	6c.+4c. ochre	4·75	3·25
904	-	8c.+4c. turquoise	8·25	3·25
905	-	12c.+9c. violet	60	35
906	-	30c.+9c. grey	9·25	8·00

DESIGNS: Costumes of: 6c. Volendam; 8c. Bunschoten; 12c. Hindeloopen; 30c. Huizen.

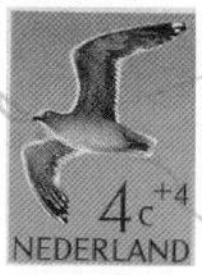

184 Herring Gull

1961. Cultural and Social Relief Fund. Beach and Meadow Birds.

907	184	4c.+4c. slate and yellow	2·10	1·90
908	-	6c.+4c. sepia and brown	3·25	3·00
909	-	8c.+4c. brown and olive	1·90	1·60
910	-	12c.+8c. black and blue	3·75	60
911	-	30c.+10c. black & green	4·25	4·25

BIRDS—HORIZ: 6c. Oystercatcher; 12c. Pied avocet. VERT: 8c. Curlew; 30c. Northern lapwing.

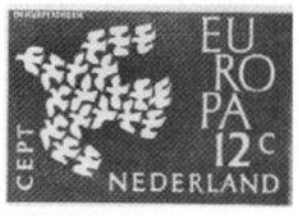

185 Doves

1961. Europa.

912	185	12c. brown	25	25
913	185	30c. turquoise	35	35

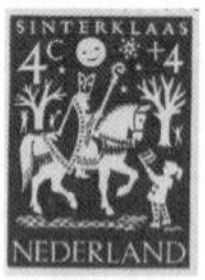

186 St. Nicholas

1961. Child Welfare.

914	186	4c.+4c. red	35	35
915	-	6c.+4c. blue	1·90	1·30
916	-	8c.+4c. bistre	1·60	1·50
917	-	12c.+9c. green	35	35
918	-	30c.+9c. orange	5·00	4·75

DESIGNS: 6c. Epiphany; 8c. Palm Sunday; 12c. Whitsuntide; 30c. Martinmas.

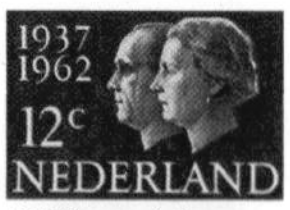

187 Queen Juliana and Prince Bernhard

1962. Silver Wedding.

919	187	12c. red	35	35
920	187	30c. green	2·00	1·20

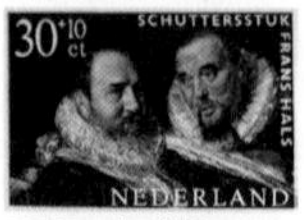

188 Detail of "The Repast of the Officers of the St. Jorisdoelen" after Frans Hals

1962. Cultural, Health and Social Welfare Funds.

921	-	4c.+4c. green	1·90	1·40
922	-	6c.+4c. black	1·60	1·40
923	-	8c.+4c. purple	2·30	2·10
924	-	12c.+8c. bistre	2·30	60
925	188	30c.+10c. blue	2·30	2·30

DESIGNS—HORIZ: 4c. Roman cat (sculpture). VERT: 6c. "Pleuroceras spinatus" (ammonite); 8c. Pendulum clock (after principle of Huygens); 12c. Ship's figurehead.

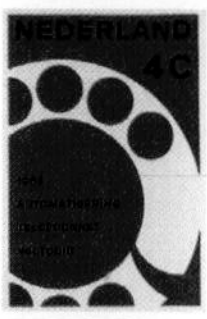

189 Telephone Dial

1962. Completion of Netherlands Automatic Telephone System. Inscr "1962".

926	189	4c. red and black	35	35
927	-	12c. drab and black	1·20	35
928	-	30c. ochre, blue and black	3·25	2·20

DESIGNS—VERT: 12c. Diagram of telephone network. HORIZ: 30c. Arch and telephone dial.

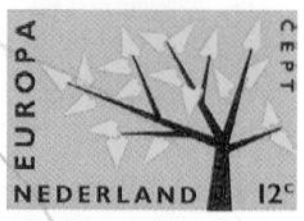

190 Europa "Tree"

1962. Europa.

929	190	12c. black, yellow & bistre	45	25
930	190	30c. black, yellow and blue	1·90	1·00

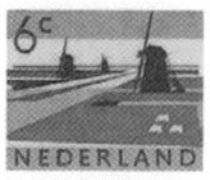

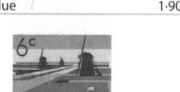

191 "Polder" Landscape (reclaimed area)

1962

935	-	4c. deep blue and blue	10	10
937	191	6c. deep green and green	45	10
938	-	10c. deep purple and purple	10	10

DESIGNS: 4c. Cooling towers, State mines, Limburg; 10c. Delta excavation works.

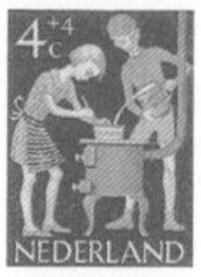

192 Children cooking Meal

1962. Child Welfare.

940	192	4c.+4c. red	35	35
941	-	6c.+4c. bistre	1·50	80
942	-	8c.+4c. blue	2·30	2·10
943	-	12c.+9c. green	35	35
944	-	30c.+9c. lake	4·25	4·00

DESIGNS—Children: 6c. Cycling; 8c. Watering flowers; 12c. Feeding poultry; 30c. Making music.

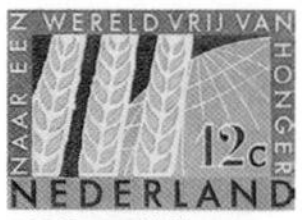

193 Ears of Wheat

1963. Freedom from Hunger.

945	193	12c. ochre and blue	35	35
946	193	30c. ochre and red	1·60	1·60

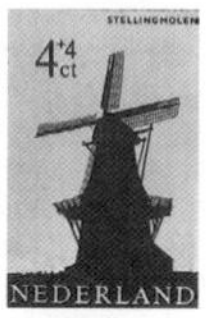

194 "Gallery" Windmill

1963. Cultural, Health and Social Welfare Funds. Windmill types.

947	194	4c.+4c. blue	1·90	1·60
948	-	6c.+4c. violet	1·90	1·60
949	-	8c.+4c. green	2·30	2·10
950	-	12c.+8c. brown	2·30	45
951	-	30c.+10c. red	3·25	3·25

WINDMILLS—VERT: 6c. North Holland polder; 12c. "Post"; 30c. "Wip". HORIZ: 8c. South Holland polder.

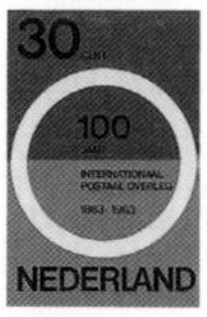

195

1963. Paris Postal Conference Centenary.

952	**195**	30c. blue, green & blk	2·10	1·90

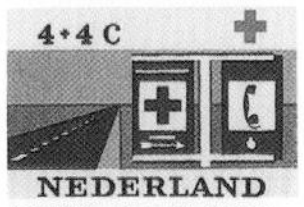

196 Wayside First Aid Post

1963. Red Cross Fund and Centenary (8c.).

953	**196**	4c.+4c. blue and red	60	60
954	-	6c.+4c. violet and red	95	95
955	-	8c.+4c. red and black	1·60	1·20
956	-	12c.+9c. brown and red	35	35
957	-	30c.+9c. green and red	2·30	2·30

DESIGNS: 6c. "Books" collection-box; 8c. Crosses; 12c. "International Aid" (Negro children at meal); 30c. First aid party tending casualty.

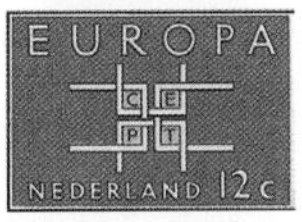

197 "Co-operation"

1963. Europa.

958	**197**	12c. orange and brown	60	35
959	**197**	30c. orange and green	2·30	1·40

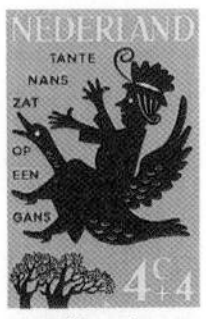

198 "Auntie Luce sat on a goose ..."

1963. Child Welfare.

960	**198**	4c.+4c. ultramarine & bl	25	35
961	-	6c.+4c. green and red	1·70	1·20
962	-	8c.+4c. brown & green	2·30	95
963	-	12c.+9c. violet & yellow	25	35
964	-	30c.+8c. blue and pink	2·40	2·30

DESIGNS (Nursery rhymes): 6c. "In the Hague there lives a count ..."; 8c. "One day I passed a puppet's fair ..."; 12c. "Storky, storky, Billy Spoon ..."; 30c. "Ride on a little pram ..."

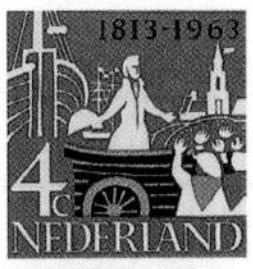

199 William, Prince of Orange, landing at Scheveningen

1963. 150th Anniv of Kingdom of the Netherlands.

965	**199**	4c. black, bistre and blue	25	10
966	**199**	5c. black, red and green	25	10
967	-	12c. bistre, blue and black	25	10
968	-	30c. red and black	1·00	1·00

DESIGNS: 12c. Triumvirate: Van Hogendorp, Van Limburg, and Van der Duyn van Maasdam; 30c. William I taking oath of allegiance.

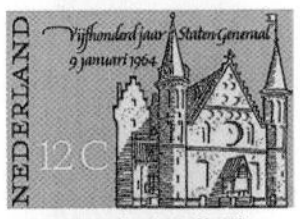

200 Knights' Hall, The Hague

1964. 500th Anniv of 1st States-General Meeting.

969	**200**	12c. black and olive	35	10

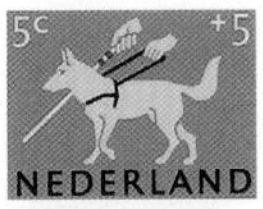

201 Guide Dog for the Blind

1964. Cultural, Health and Social Welfare Funds. Animals.

970	**201**	5c.+5c. red, black and olive	80	70
971	-	8c.+5c. brown, black and red	60	45
972	-	12c.+9c. black, grey and bistre	80	35
973	-	30c.+9c. multicoloured	1·00	95

DESIGNS: 8c. Three red deer; 12c. Three kittens; 30c. European bison and calf.

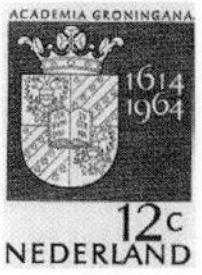

202 University Arms

1964. 350th Anniv of Groningen University.

974	**202**	12c. slate	35	25
975	-	30c. brown	45	45

DESIGN: 30c. "AG" monogram.

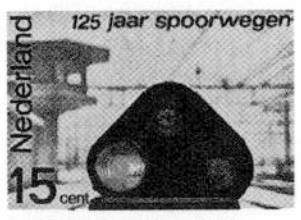

203 Signal No. 144, Amersfoort Station

1964. 125th Anniv of Netherlands Railways.

976	**203**	15c. black and green	35	25
977	-	40c. black and yellow	1·20	1·20

DESIGN: 40c. Class ELD-4 electric train.

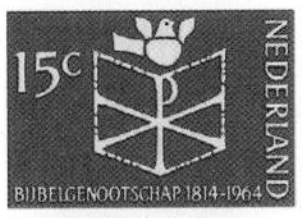

204 Bible and Dove

1964. 150th Anniv of Netherlands Bible Society.

978	**204**	15c. brown	35	25

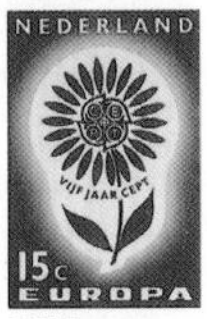

205 Europa "Flower"

1964. Europa.

979	**205**	15c. green	45	25
980	**205**	20c. brown	1·30	60

1964. 20th Anniv of "BENELUX". As T 150a of Luxembourg, but smaller 35×22 mm.

981		15c. violet and flesh	35	25

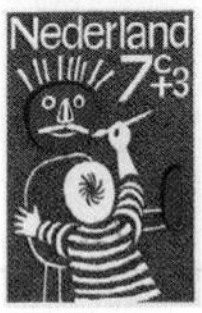

206 Young Artist

1964. Child Welfare.

982	**206**	7c.+3c. blue and green	70	60
983	-	10c.+5c. red, pink and green	60	60
984	-	15c.+10c. yellow, black and bistre	35	35
985	-	20c.+10c. red, sepia and mauve	1·20	80
986	-	40c.+15c. green & blue	1·50	1·20

DESIGNS: 10c. Ballet-dancing; 15c. Playing the recorder; 20c. Masquerading; 40c. Toy-making.

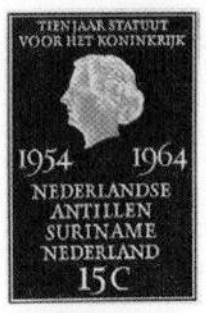

207 Queen Juliana

1964. 10th Anniv of Statute for the Kingdom.

987	**207**	15c. green	35	25

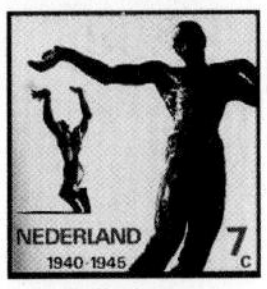

208 "Killed in Action" (Waalwijk) and "Destroyed Town" (Rotterdam) (monuments)

1965. "Resistance" Commemoration.

988	**208**	7c. black and red	35	35
989	-	15c. black and olive	35	35
990	-	40c. black and red	1·40	1·30

MONUMENTS: 15c. "Docker" (Amsterdam) and "Killed in Action" (Waalwijk); 40c. "Destroyed Town" (Rotterdam) and "Docker" (Amsterdam).

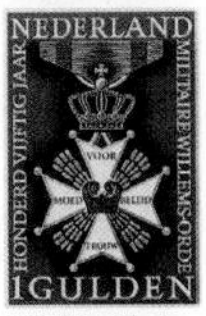

209 Medal of Knight (Class IV)

1965. 150th Anniv of Military William Order.

991	**209**	1g. grey	1·90	1·80

210 I.T.U. Emblem and "Lines of Communication"

1965. Centenary of I.T.U.

992	**210**	20c. blue and drab	25	25
993	**210**	40c. brown and blue	65	55

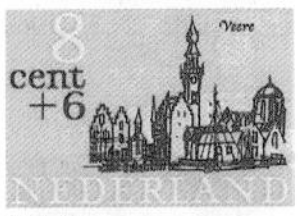

211 Veere

1965. Cultural, Health and Social Welfare Funds.

994	**211**	8c.+6c. black and yellow	35	25
995	-	10c.+6c. black & turq	55	45
996	-	18c.+12c. black & brn	45	25
997	-	20c.+10c. black & blue	55	45
998	-	40c.+10c. black & green	65	55

DESIGNS: (Dutch towns): 10c. Thorn; 18c. Dordrecht; 20c. Staveren; 40c. Medemblik.

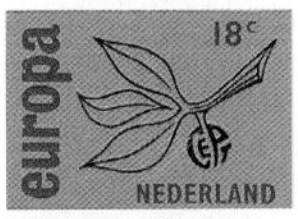

212 Europa "Sprig"

1965. Europa.

999	**212**	18c. black, red and brown	25	20
1000	**212**	20c. black, red and blue	45	35

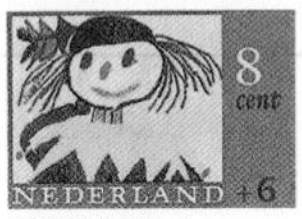

213 Girl's Head

1965. Child Welfare. Multicoloured.

1001		8c.+6c. Type **213**	25	25
1002		10c.+6c. Ship	1·00	70
1003		18c.+12c. Boy (vert)	20	25
1004		20c.+10c. Duck-pond	1·30	70
1005		40c.+10c. Tractor	1·70	1·10
MS1006		143×124 mm. Nos. 1001 (5) and 1003 (6)	31·00	29·00

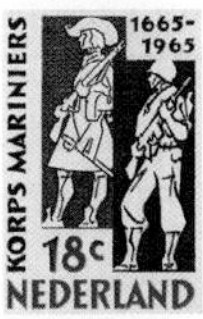

214 Marines of 1665 and 1965

1965. Tercentenary of Marine Corps.

1007	**214**	18c. blue and red	25	20

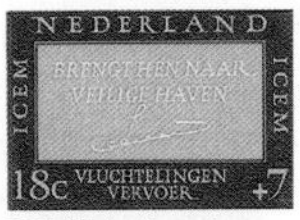

215 "Help them to a safe Haven" (Queen Juliana)

1966. Intergovernmental Committee for European Migration (I.C.E.M.) Fund.

1008	**215**	10c.+7c. yellow & blk	65	35
1009	**215**	40c.+20c. red & black	35	25
MS1010		117×44 mm. Nos. 1008 and 1009 (2)	3·25	1·30

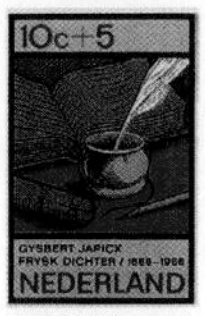

216 Writing Materials

1966. Cultural, Health and Social Welfare Funds. Gysbert Japicx Commem and 200th Anniv of Netherlands Literary Society. Multicoloured.

1011	10c.+5c. Type **216**	45	45
1012	12c.+8c. Part of MS, Japicx's poem "Wobbelke"	45	45
1013	20c.+10c. Part of miniature, "Knight Walewein"	65	45
1014	25c.+10c. Initial "D" and part of MS, novel, "Ferguut"	80	65
1015	40c.+20c. 16th-century printery (woodcut)	65	65

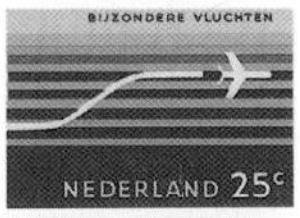

217 Aircraft in Flight

1966. Air (Special Flights).

1016	**217**	25c. multicoloured	20	45

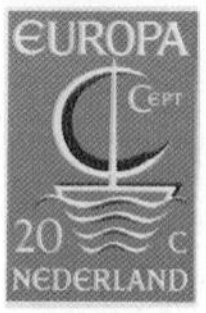

218 Europa "Ship"

1966. Europa.

1017	**218**	20c. green and yellow	25	20
1018	**218**	40c. deep blue and blue	1·10	25

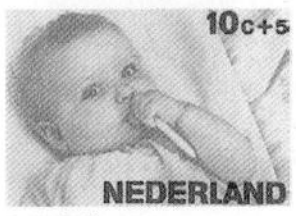

219 Infant

1966. Child Welfare.

1019	**219**	10c.+5c. red and blue	25	25
1020	-	12c.+8c. green and red	25	25
1021	-	20c.+10c. blue and red	25	25
1022	-	25c.+10c. purple & bl	1·00	1·00
1023	-	40c.+20c. red & green	90	90
MS1024		132×125 mm. Nos. 1019×4, 1020 ×5, 1021 ×3	3·25	3·25

DESIGNS: 12c. Young girl; 20c. Boy in water; 25c. Girl with moped; 40c. Young man with horse.

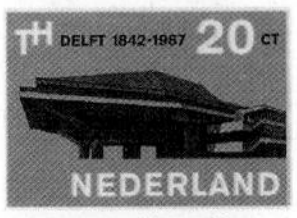

220 Assembly Hall

1967. 125th Anniv of Delft Technological University.

1025	**220**	20c. sepia and yellow	25	20

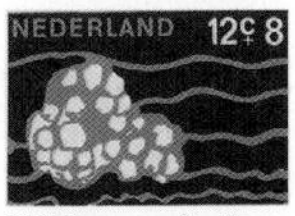

221 Common Northern Whelk Eggs

1967. Cultural, Health and Social Welfare Funds. Marine Fauna.

1026	**221**	12c.+8c. brown & grn	35	35
1027	-	15c.+10c. blue, light blue and deep blue	35	35
1028	-	20c.+10c. mult	35	25
1029	-	25c.+10c. brown, purple and bistre	65	65
1030	-	45c.+20c. mult	90	70

DESIGNS: 15c. Common northern whelk; 20c. Common blue mussel; 25c. Jellyfish; 45c. Crab.

222 Cogwheels

1967. Europa.

1031	**222**	20c. blue and light blue	70	25

1032	222	45c. purple & light purple	1·50	90

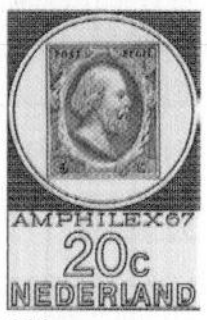

223
Netherlands 5c.
Stamp of 1852

1967. "Amphilex 67" Stamp Exn, Amsterdam.

1035	223	20c. blue and black	3·50	2·75
1036	-	25c. red and black	3·50	2·75
1037	-	75c. green and black	3·50	2·75

DESIGNS: 25c. Netherlands 10c. stamp of 1864; 75c. Netherlands 20c. stamp of 1867.

Nos. 1035/7 were sold at the exhibition and at post offices at 3g.70, which included entrance fee to the exhibition.

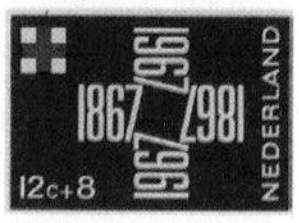

224 "1867–1967"

1967. Centenary of Dutch Red Cross.

1038		12c.+8c. blue and red	35	30
1039		15c.+10c. red	45	45
1040		20c.+10c. olive and red	35	25
1041		25c.+10c. green and red	55	55
1042		45c.+20c. grey and red	80	80

DESIGNS: 12c. Type **224**; 15c. Red crosses; 20c. "NRK" ("Nederlandsche Rood Kruis") in the form of a cross; 25c. Maltese cross and "red" crosses; 45c. "100" in the form of a cross.

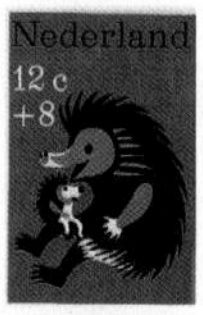

225 "Porcupine Lullaby"

1967. Child Welfare. Multicoloured.

1043		12c.+8c. Type **225**	25	25
1044		15c.+10c. "The Whistling Kettle"	25	25
1045		20c.+10c. "Dikkertje Dap" (giraffe)	25	25
1046		25c.+10c. "The Flower-seller"	1·50	90
1047		45c.+20c. "Pippeloentje" (bear)	1·50	1·00
MS1048		150×108 mm. Nos. 1043 (3), 1044 (4), 1045 (3)	6·25	6·25

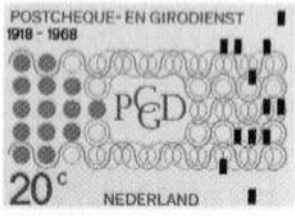

226 "Financial Automation"

1968. 50th Anniv of Netherlands Postal Cheque and Clearing Service.

1049	226	20c. red, black and yellow	25	20

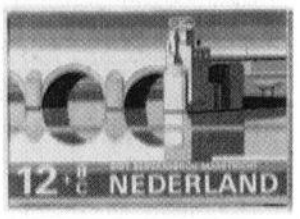

227 St. Servatius' Bridge, Maastricht

1968. Cultural, Health and Social Welfare Funds. Dutch Bridges.

1050	227	12c.+8c. green	65	65
1051	-	15c.+10c. brown	80	80
1052	-	20c.+10c. red	55	25
1053	-	25c.+10c. blue	65	65
1054	-	45c.+20c. blue	1·00	1·00

BRIDGES: 15c. Magere ("Narrow"), Amsterdam; 20c. Railway, Culemborg; 25c. Van Brienenoord, Rotterdam; 45c. Oosterschelde, Zeeland.

228 Europa "Key"

1968. Europa.

1055	228	20c. blue	65	65
1056	228	45c. red	1·30	90

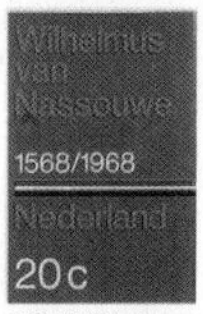

229 "Wilhelmus van Nassouwe"

1968. 400th Anniv of Dutch National Anthem, "Wilhelmus".

1057	229	20c. multicoloured	25	20

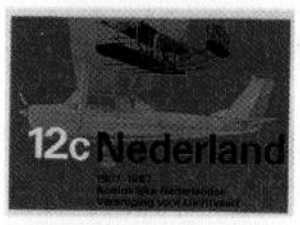

230 Wright Type A and Cessna 150F

1968. Dutch Aviation Anniversaries.

1058		12c. black, red and mauve	25	20
1059		20c. black, emerald and green	25	20
1060		45c. black, blue and green	1·40	1·30

DESIGNS AND EVENTS: 12c. T **230** (60th anniv (1967) of Royal Netherlands Aeronautical Assn); 20c. Fokker F.II H-NABC and Fokker F.28 Fellowship aircraft (50th anniv (1969) of Royal Netherlands Aircraft Factories "Fokker"); 45c. Airco de Havilland D.H.9B biplane H-NABE and Douglas DC-9 airliner (50th anniv (1969) of Royal Dutch Airlines "KLM").

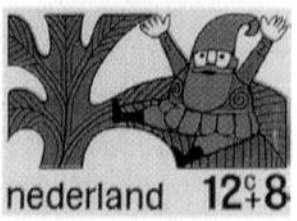

231 "Goblin"

1968. Child Welfare.

1061	231	12c.+8c. pink, black and green	25	25
1062	-	15c.+10c. pink, blue and black	25	25
1063	-	20c.+10c. blue, green and black	25	25
1064	-	25c.+10c. red, yellow and black	2·20	1·90
1065	-	45c.+20c. yellow, orange and black	2·20	1·90
MS1066		106½×151 mm. Nos. 1061 (3), 1062 (2), 1063 (3)	8·50	8·50

DESIGNS: 15c. "Giant"; 20c. "Witch"; 25c. "Dragon"; 45c. "Sorcerer".

232 "I A O" (Internationale Arbeidsorganisatie)

1969. 50th Anniv of I.L.O.

1067	232	25c. red and black	65	20
1068	232	45c. blue and black	1·20	1·00

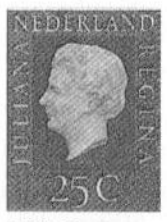

233 Queen Juliana

1969. (a) Type 233.

1069	233	25c. red	55	10
1069b	233	30c. brown	25	10
1070	233	35c. blue	25	10
1071	233	40c. red	35	10
1072	233	45c. blue	35	10
1073	233	50c. purple	45	10
1073bc	233	55c. red	20	10
1074a	233	60c. blue	55	20
1075	233	70c. brown	65	10
1076	233	75c. green	65	10
1077	233	80c. red	70	10
1077a	233	90c. grey	70	10

(b) Size 22×33 mm.

1078		1g. green	80	10
1079		1g.25 lake	1·00	10
1080		1g.50 brown	1·30	10
1081		2g. mauve	1·60	20
1082		2g.50 blue	2·10	20
1083		5g. grey	4·00	20
1084		10g. blue	8·00	90

DESIGN: 1g.to 10g. similar to Type **233**.

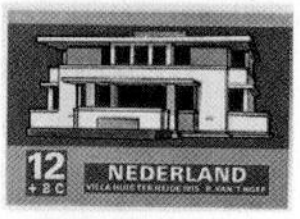

234 Villa, Huis ter Heide (1915)

1969. Cultural, Health and Social Welfare Funds. 20th-century Dutch Architecture.

1085	234	12c.+8c. black & brn	90	90
1086	-	15c.+10c. black, red and blue	90	90
1087	-	20c.+10c. black & vio	90	90
1088	-	25c.+10c. brown & grn	90	35
1089	-	45c.+20c. black, blue and yellow	90	90

DESIGNS: 15c. Private House, Utrecht (1924); 20c. Open-air School, Amsterdam (1930); 25c. Orphanage, Amsterdam (1960); 45c. Congress Building, The Hague (1969).

235 Colonnade

1969. Europa.

1090	235	25c. blue	45	20
1091	235	45c. red	1·80	1·30

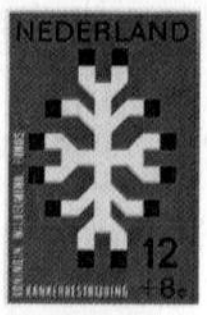

236 Stylized "Crab" (of Cancer)

1969. 20th Anniv of Queen Wilhelmina Cancer Fund.

1092	236	12c.+8c. violet	70	70
1093	236	25c.+10c. orange	1·10	45
1094	236	45c.+20c. green	1·80	1·80

1969. 25th Anniv of "BENELUX" Customs Union. As T 186 of Luxembourg.

1095		25c. multicoloured	30	10

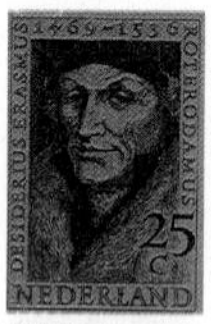

238 Erasmus

1969. 500th Birth Anniv of Desiderius Erasmus.

1096	238	25c. purple on green	25	10

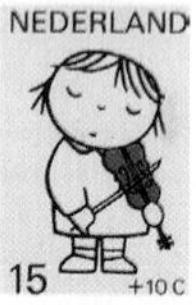

239 Child with Violin

1969. Child Welfare.

1097	-	12c.+8c. black, yellow and blue	25	25
1098	239	15c.+10c. black and red	25	25
1099	-	20c.+10c. black, yellow and red	2·75	2·30
1100	-	25c.+10c. black, red and yellow	25	25
1101	-	45c.+20c. black, red and green	2·75	2·40
MS1102		150×99 mm. Nos. 1097 (4), 1098 (4), 1100 (2)	9·75	9·75

DESIGNS—VERT: 12c. Child with recorder; 20c. Child with drum. HORIZ: 25c. Three choristers; 45c. Two dancers.

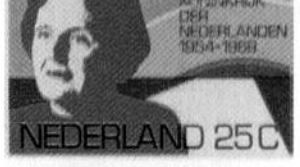

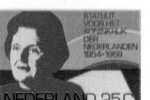

240 Queen Juliana and "Sunlit Road"

1969. 25th Anniv of Statute for the Kingdom.

1103	240	25c. multicoloured	25	10

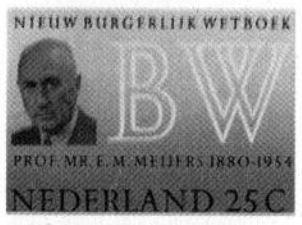

241 Prof. E. M. Meijers (author of "Burgerlijk Wetboek")

1970. Introduction of New Netherlands Civil Code ("Burgerlijk Wetboek").

1104	241	25c. ultramarine, green and blue	35	10

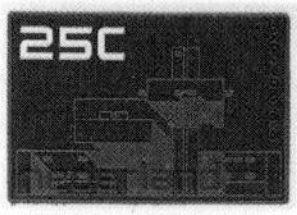

242 Netherlands Pavilion

1970. Expo 70 World Fair, Osaka, Japan.

1105	242	25c. grey, blue and red	35	10

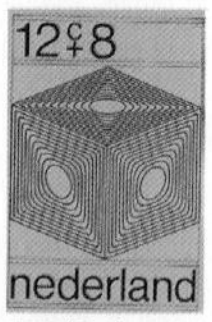

243 "Circle to Square"

1970. Cultural, Health and Social Welfare Funds.

1106	243	12c.+8c. black on yell	1·30	1·30
1107	-	15c.+10c. black on silver	1·30	1·30
1108	-	20c.+10c. black	1·30	1·30
1109	-	25c.+10c. black on bl	1·30	70
1110	-	45c.+20c. white on grey	1·30	1·30

DESIGNS: 15c. Parallel planes in cube; 20c. Overlapping scales; 25c. Concentric circles in transition; 45c. Spirals.

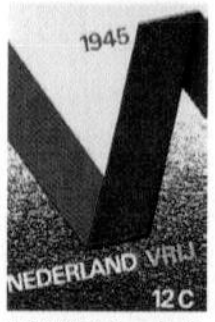

244 "V" Symbol

1970. 25th Anniv of Liberation.

1111	244	12c. red, blue and brown	35	10

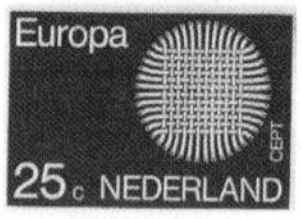

245 "Flaming Sun"

1970. Europa.

1112	245	25c. red	70	20
1113	245	45c. blue	1·50	1·30

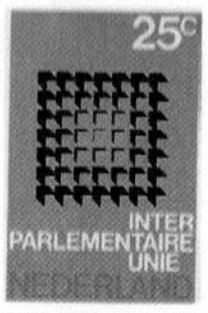

246 "Work and Co-operation"

1970. Inter-Parliamentary Union Conference.

1114	246	25c. green, black and grey	65	10

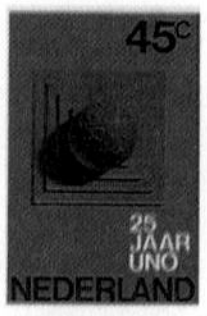

247 Globe on Plinth

1970. 25th Anniv of United Nations.

1115	247	45c. black, violet & blue	1·20	1·00

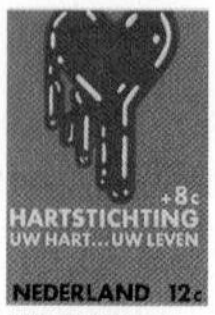

248 Human Heart

1970. Netherlands Heart Foundation.

1116	248	12c.+8c. red, black and yellow	80	80
1117	248	25c.+10c. red, black and mauve	80	65
1118	248	45c.+20c. red, black and green	80	80

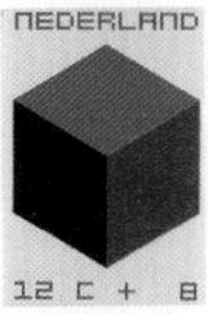

249 Toy Block

1970. Child Welfare. "The Child and the Cube".

1119	**249**	12c.+8c. blue, violet and green	20	15
1120	-	15c.+10c. green, blue and yellow	1·90	1·50
1121	**249**	20c.+10c. mauve, red and violet	1·90	1·50
1122	-	25c.+10c. red, yellow and mauve	25	25
1123	**249**	45c.+20c. grey, cream and black	2·20	1·80
MS1124		126×145 mm. Nos. 1119 (9), 1122 (2)	18·00	16·00

DESIGN: 15c., 25c. As Type **249**, but showing underside of block.

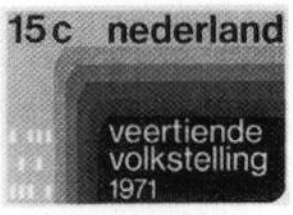

250 "Fourteenth Census 1971"

1971. 14th Netherlands Census.

1125	**250**	15c. purple	25	10

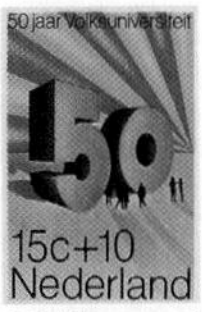

251 "50 years of Adult University Education"

1971. Cultural, Health and Social Welfare Funds. Other designs show 15th-century wooden statues by unknown artists.

1126	**251**	15c.+10c. black, red and yellow	1·40	1·30
1127	-	20c.+10c. black and green on green	1·40	1·30
1128	-	25c.+10c. black and orange on orange	1·40	55
1129	-	30c.+15c. black and blue on blue	1·40	1·30
1130	-	45c.+20c. black and red on pink	1·40	1·30

STATUES: 20c. "Apostle Paul"; 25c. "Joachim and Ann"; 30c. "John the Baptist and Scribes"; 45c. "Ann, Mary and Christ-Child" (detail).

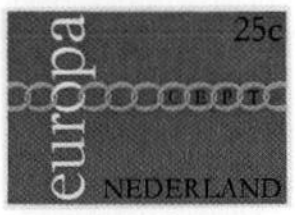

252 Europa Chain

1971. Europa.

1131	**252**	25c. yellow, red and black	70	20
1132	**252**	45c. yellow, blue & black	1·80	1·30

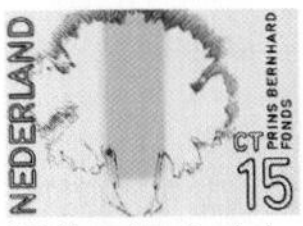

253 Carnation Symbol of Prince Bernhard Fund

1971. Prince Bernhard's 60th Birthday.

1133	**253**	15c. yellow, grey & black	25	20
1134	-	20c. multicoloured	90	35
1135	-	25c. multicoloured	35	20
1136	-	45c.+20c. black, purple and yellow	2·50	2·50

DESIGNS—HORIZ: 20c. Panda symbol of World Wildlife Fund. VERT: 25c. Prince Bernhard, Boeing 747 and Fokker F.27 Friendship; 45c. Statue, Borobudur Temple, Indonesia.

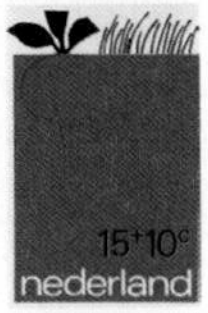

254 "The Good Earth"

1971. Child Welfare.

1137	**254**	15c.+10c. red, purple and black	25	25
1138	-	20c.+10c. mult	45	45
1139	-	25c.+10c. mult	25	25
1140	-	30c.+15c. blue, violet and black	1·30	80
1141	-	45c.+20c. blue, green and black	2·10	1·80
MS1142		100×145 mm. Nos. 1137 (6), 1138 and 1139 (2)	11·50	11·00

DESIGNS—VERT: 20c. Butterfly; 45c. Reflecting water. HORIZ: 25c. Sun waving; 30c. Moon winking.

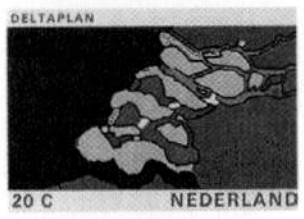

255 Delta Map

1972. Delta Sea-Defences Plan.

1143	**255**	20c. multicoloured	25	10

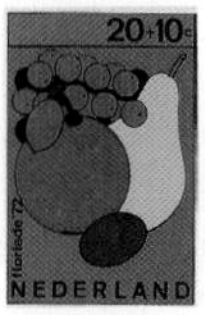

256 "Fruits"

1972. Cultural, Health and Social Welfare Funds. "Floriade Flower Show" (20c., 25c.) and "Holland Arts Festival" (30c., 45c.). Multicoloured.

1144	20c.+10c. Type **256**	1·30	1·20
1145	25c.+10c. "Flower"	1·30	1·20
1146	30c.+15c. "Sunlit Landscape"	1·30	70
1147	45c.+25c. "Music"	1·30	1·20

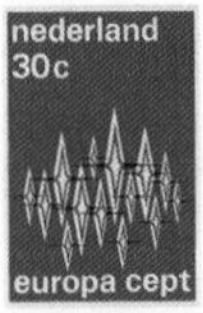

257 "Communications"

1972. Europa.

1148	**257**	30c. brown and blue	90	20
1149	**257**	45c. brown and orange	1·30	1·20

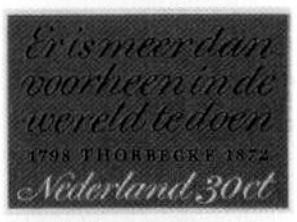

258 "There is more to be done in the world than ever before" (Thorbecke)

1972. Death Centenary of J. R. Thorbecke (statesman).

1150	**258**	30c. black and blue	90	25

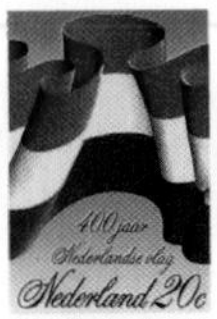

259 Netherlands Flag

1972. 400th Anniv of Netherlands Flag.

1151	**259**	20c. multicoloured	55	20
1152	**259**	25c. multicoloured	1·30	20

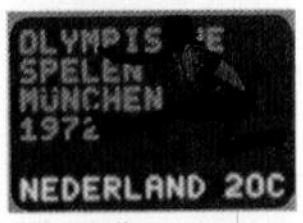

260 Hurdling

1972. Olympic Games, Munich. Multicoloured.

1153	20c. Type **260**	35	25
1154	30c. Diving	35	25
1155	45c. Cycling	1·10	1·10

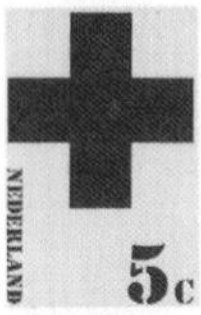

261 Red Cross

1972. Netherlands Red Cross.

1156	**261**	5c. red	40	30
1157	-	20c.+10c. red and pink	65	65
1158	-	25c.+10c. red & orange	1·10	1·20
1159	-	30c.+15c. red & black	80	55
1160	-	45c.+25c. red and blue	1·20	1·10

DESIGNS: 20c. Accident services; 25c. Blood transfusion; 30c. Refugee relief; 45c. Child care.

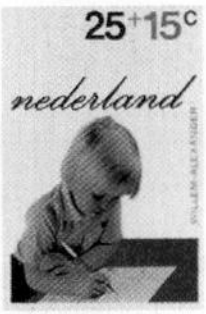

262 Prince Willem-Alexander

1972. Child Welfare. Multicoloured.

1161	25c.+15c. Type **262**	25	25
1162	30c.+10c. Prince Johan Friso (horiz)	1·00	80
1163	35c.+15c. Prince Constantin (horiz)	1·00	25
1164	50c.+20c. The Three Princes (horiz)	3·00	2·50
MS1165	126×109 mm. Nos. 1161 ×4 and 1163 ×3	9·00	9·00

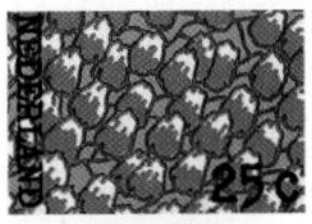

263 Tulips in Bloom

1973. Tulip Exports.

1166	**263**	25c. multicoloured	70	10

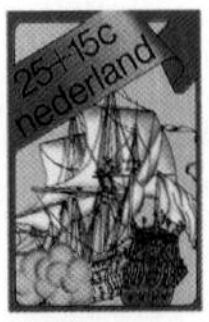

264 "De Zeven Provincien" (De Ruyter's flagship)

1973. Cultural, Health and Social Welfare Funds. Dutch Ships. Multicoloured.

1167	25c.+15c. Type **264**	1·10	1·10
1168	30c.+10c. "W.A. Scholten" (steamship) (horiz)	1·10	1·10
1169	35c.+15c. "Veendam" (liner) (horiz)	1·30	80
1170	50c.+20c. Fishing boat (from etching by R. Nooms)	1·30	1·30

265 Europa "Posthorn"

1973. Europa.

1171	**265**	35c. light blue and blue	90	20
1172	**265**	50c. blue and violet	1·80	90

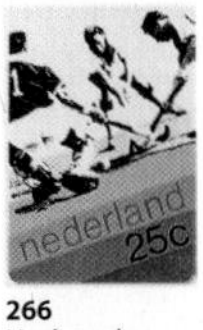

266 Hockey-players

1973. Events and Anniversaries. Multicoloured.

1173	25c. Type **266**	65	20
1174	30c. Gymnastics	1·30	70
1175	35c. Dish aerial (vert)	90	25
1176	50c. Rainbow	1·30	90

EVENTS—VERT: 25c. 75th anniv of Royal Netherlands Hockey Association; 30c. World Gymnastics Championships, Rotterdam. HORIZ: 35c. Opening of Satellite Station, Burum; 50c. Centenary of World Meteorological Organization.

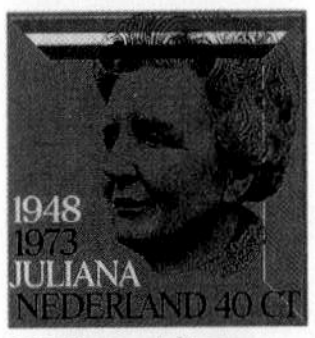

267 Queen Juliana

1973. Silver Jubilee of Queen Juliana's Accession.

1177	**267**	40c. multicoloured	55	25

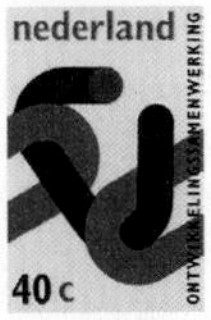

268 "Co-operation"

1973. International Development Co-operation.

1178	**268**	40c. multicoloured	70	25

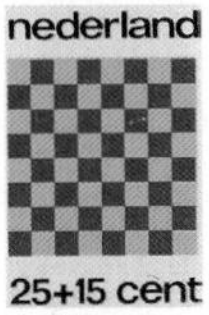

269 "Chess"

1973. Child Welfare.

1179	**269**	25c.+15c. red, yellow and black	35	25
1180	-	30c.+10c. green, mauve and black	90	70
1181	-	40c.+20c. yellow, green and black	35	25
1182	-	50c.+20c. blue, yellow and black	2·75	2·30
MS1183		74×144 mm. Nos. 1179 ×2, 1180 and 1181 ×3	10·50	10·50

DESIGNS: 30c. "Noughts and crosses"; 40c. "Maze"; 50c. "Dominoes".

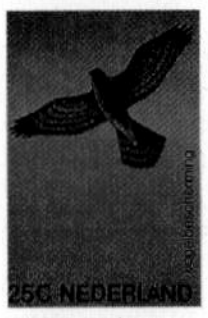

270 Northern Goshawk

1974. "Nature and Environment". Multicoloured.

1184	25c. Type **270**	90	45
1185	25c. Tree	90	45
1186	25c. Fisherman and frog	90	45

Nos. 1184/6 were issued together, se-tenant, forming a composite design.

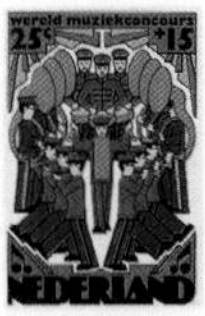

271 Bandsmen (World Band Contest, Kerkrade)

1974. Cultural, Health and Social Welfare Funds.

1187	**271**	25c.+15c. mult	1·10	1·10
1188	-	30c.+10c. mult	1·10	1·10
1189	-	40c.+20c. brown, black and red	1·20	80
1190	-	50c.+20c. purple, black and red	1·20	1·10

DESIGNS: 30c. Dancers and traffic-lights ("Modern Ballet"); 40c. Herman Heijermans; 50c. "Kniertje" (character from Heijermans' play "Op hoop van zegen"). The 40c. and 50c. commemorate the 50th death anniv of the playwright.

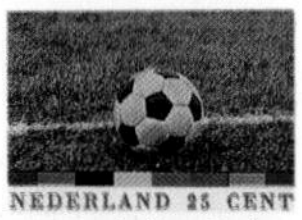

272 Football on Pitch

1974. Sporting Events.

1191	**272**	25c. multicoloured	80	25
1192	-	40c. yellow, red & mauve	80	25

DESIGNS AND EVENTS—HORIZ: 25c. (World Cup Football Championship, West Germany). VERT: 40c. Hand holding tennis ball (75th anniv of Royal Dutch Lawn Tennis Association).

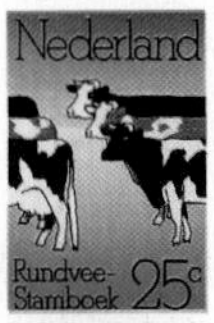

273 Netherlands Cattle

1974. Anniversaries. Multicoloured.

1193	25c. Type **273**	9·75	2·20
1194	25c. "Cancer"	1·80	25
1195	40c. "Suzanna" (lifeboat) seen through binoculars	1·80	25

EVENTS AND ANNIVERSARIES: No. 1193, Cent of Netherlands Cattle Herdbook Society; 1194, 25th anniv of Queen Wilhelmina Cancer Research Fund; 1195, 150th anniv of Dutch Lifeboat Service.

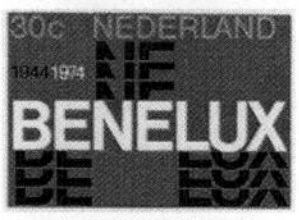

274 "BENELUX" (30th Anniv of Benelux (Customs Union))

1974. International Anniversaries.

1196	**274**	30c. green, turquoise & blue	90	25
1197	-	45c. deep blue, silver & blue	90	25
1198	-	45c. yellow, blue & black	90	25

DESIGNS—VERT: No. 1197, NATO emblem (25th anniv); 1198, Council of Europe emblem (25th anniv).

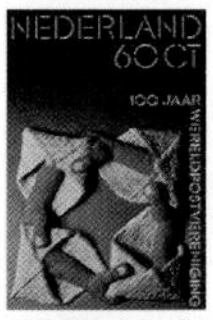

275 Hands with Letters

1974. Centenary of Universal Postal Union.

1199	**275**	60c. multicoloured	70	35

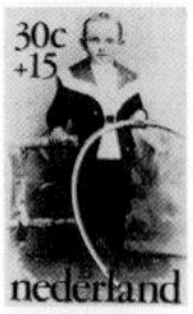

276 Boy with Hoop

1974. 50th Anniv of Child Welfare Issues. Early Photographs.

1200	**276**	30c.+15c. brown & blk	35	25
1201	-	35c.+20c. brown	90	65
1202	-	45c.+20c. black	90	25
1203	-	60c.+20c. black	2·10	1·70
MS1204 75×145 mm. Nos. 1200 ×4 and 1201/2			4·75	4·50

DESIGNS: 35c. Child and baby; 45c. Two young girls; 60c. Girl sitting on balustrade.

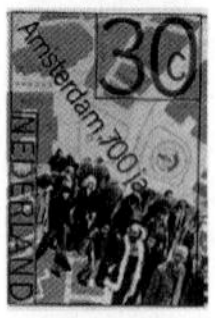

277 Amsterdam

1975. Anniversaries. Multicoloured.

1205	30c. Type **277**	45	25
1206	30c. Synagogue and map	45	35
1207	35c. Type **277**	45	25
1208	45c. "Window" in human brain	55	25

ANNIVERSARIES: Nos. 1205, 1207, Amsterdam (700th anniv); 1206, Portuguese-Israelite Synagogue, Amsterdam (300th anniv); 1208, Leyden University and university education (400th anniv).

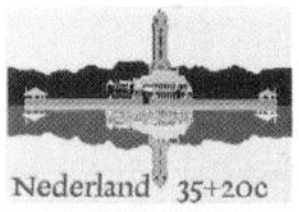

278 St. Hubertus Hunting Lodge, De Hoge Veluwe National Park

1975. Cultural, Health and Social Welfare Funds. National Monument Year. Preserved Monuments. Multicoloured.

1209	35c.+20c. Type **278**	65	65
1210	40c.+15c. Bergijnhof (Beguinage), Amsterdam (vert)	65	65
1211	50c.+20c. "Kuipersport" (Cooper's gate), Middelburg (vert)	80	65
1212	60c.+20c. Orvelte village, Drenthe	1·10	1·10

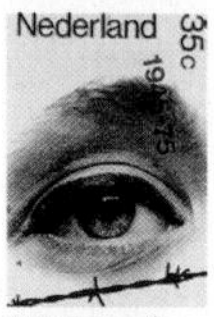

279 Eye and Barbed Wire

1975. 30th Anniv of Liberation.

1213	**279**	35c. black and red	45	25

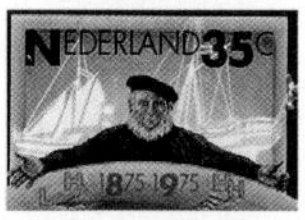

280 Company Emblem and "Stad Middelburg" (schooner)

1975. Centenary of Zeeland Shipping Company.

1214	**280**	35c. multicoloured	55	25

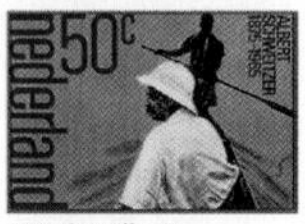

281 Dr. Albert Schweitzer crossing Lambarene River

1975. Birth Centenary of Dr. Schweitzer (medical missionary).

1215	**281**	50c. multicoloured	55	25

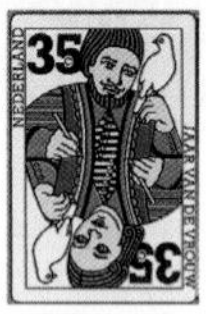

282 Man and Woman on "Playing-card"

1975. International Events. Multicoloured.

1216	35c. Type **282** (Int Women's Year)	55	25
1217	50c. Metric scale (Metre Convention cent) (horiz)	55	25

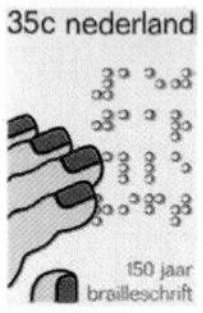

283 Braille Reading

1975. 150th Anniv of Invention of Braille.

1218	**283**	35c. multicoloured	55	25

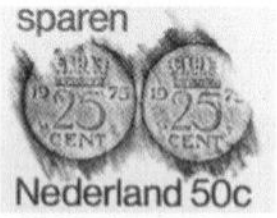

284 Dutch 25c. Coins

1975. Savings Campaign.

1219	**284**	50c. grey, green and blue	55	25

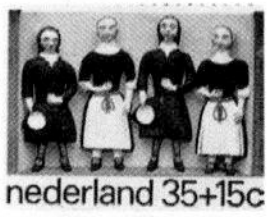

285 "Four Orphans" (C. Simons), Torenstraat Orphanage, Medemblik

1975. Child Welfare. Historic Ornamental Stones. Multicoloured.

1220	35c.+15c. Type **285**	25	25
1221	40c.+15c. "Milkmaid" Kooltuin Alkmaar	90	55
1222	50c.+25c. "Four Sons of Aymon seated on Beyaert", Herengracht	45	25
1223	60c.+25c. "Life at the Orphanage", Molenstraat Orphanage, Gorinchem	1·30	1·00
MS1224 145×75 mm. Nos. 1220 ×3 and 1222 ×2		3·50	3·50

286 18th-century Lottery Ticket

1976. 250th Anniv of National Lottery.

1225	**286**	35c. multicoloured	35	25

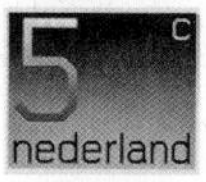

287 Numeral

1976. (a) Ordinary gum.

1226	**287**	5c. grey	10	10
1227	**287**	10c. blue	20	10
1228	**287**	25c. violet	25	10
1229	**287**	40c. brown	45	10
1230	**287**	45c. blue	45	10
1231	**287**	50c. mauve	55	10
1232	**287**	55c. green	70	10
1233	**287**	60c. yellow	80	10
1234	**287**	65c. brown	1·30	10
1235	**287**	70c. violet	1·30	10
1236	**287**	80c. mauve	1·80	20

(b) Self-adhesive gum.

1237	5c. grey	20	10
1238	10c. blue	25	10
1239	25c. violet	35	10

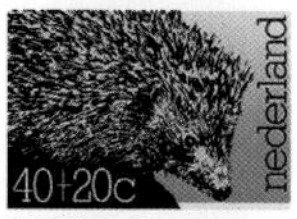

288 West European Hedgehog

1976. Cultural, Health and Social Welfare Funds. Nature Protection (40, 75c.) and Anniversaries. Multicoloured.

1241	40c.+20c. Type **288**	90	65
1242	45c.+20c. Open book (vert)	80	65
1243	55c.+20c. People and organization initials	80	25
1244	75c.+25c. Frog and spawn (vert)	1·10	90

ANNIVERSARIES: No. 1242, 175th anniv of Primary education and centenary of Agricultural education; 1243, 75th anniv of Social Security Bank and legislation.

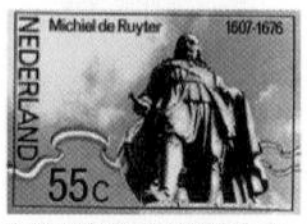

289 Admiral Michiel de Ruyter (statue)

1976. 300th Death Anniv of Admiral Michiel de Ruyter.

1245	**289**	55c. multicoloured	45	15

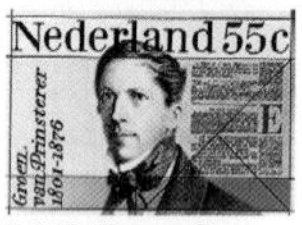

290 Guillaume Groen van Prinsterer

1976. Death Centenary of Guillaume Groen van Prinsterer (statesman).

1246	**290**	55c. multicoloured	45	15

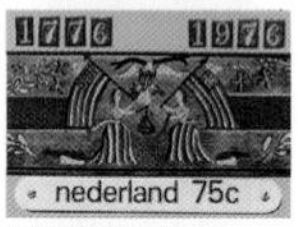

291 Detail of 18th-century Calendar

1976. Bicentenary of American Revolution.

1247	**291**	75c. multicoloured	65	35

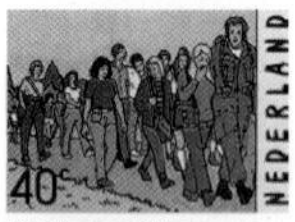

292 Long-distance Marchers

1976. Sport and Recreation Anniversaries. Mult.

1248	40c. Type **292**	45	25
1249	55c. Runners "photo-finish"	90	25

ANNIVERSARIES: 40c. 60th Nijmegen Long-distance March; 55c. Royal Dutch Athletics Society (75th anniv).

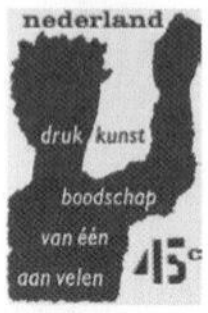

293 The Art of Printing

1976. Anniversaries.

1250	**293**	45c. red and blue	65	25
1251	-	55c.+25c. mult	70	55

DESIGNS AND EVENTS: 45c. Type **293** (75th anniv of Netherlands Printers' organization); 55c. Rheumatic patient "Within Care" (50th anniv of Dutch Anti-Rheumatism Association).

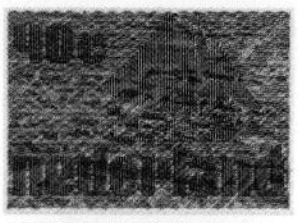

294 Dutch Tjalk and Reclaimed Land

1976. Zuider Zee Project—Reclamation and Urbanization. Multicoloured.

1252	**294**	40c. blue, olive and red	65	25
1253	-	75c. yellow, red and blue	90	55

DESIGN: 75c. Duck flying over reclaimed land.

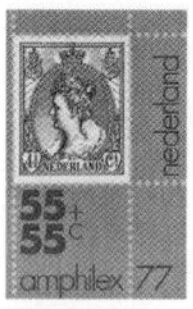

295 Queen Wilhelmina 4½c. Stamp, 1919

1976. "Amphilex '77" International Stamp Exhibition, Amsterdam (1977) (1st series). Stamp Portraits of Queen Wilhelmina. Multicoloured.

1254		55c.+55c. blue, deep grey and grey	1·00	90
1255	**295**	55c.+55c. purple, deep grey and grey	1·00	90
1256	-	55c.+55c. brown, deep grey and grey	1·00	90
1257	-	75c.+75c. turquoise, deep grey and grey	1·00	90
1258	-	75c.+75c. blue, deep grey and grey	1·00	90

DESIGNS: No. 1254, 5c. stamp, 1891; 1256, 25c. stamp, 1924; 1257, 15c. stamp, 1940; 1258, 25c. stamp, 1947.

See also Nos. 1273/6.

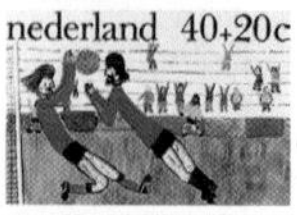

296 "Football" (J. Raats)

1976. Child Welfare. Children's Paintings. Mult.

1259	40c.+20c. Type **296**	45	25
1260	45c.+20c. "Boat" (L. Jacobs)	55	25
1261	55c.+20c. "Elephant" (M. Lugtenburg)	65	25
1262	75c.+25c. "Caravan" (A. Seeleman)	2·00	90
MS1263 145×75 mm. Nos. 1259/61 ×2		3·50	2·20

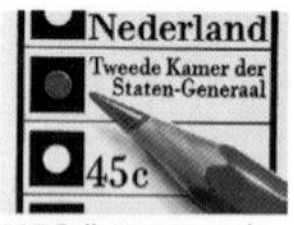

297 Ballot-paper and Pencil

1977. National Events. Multicoloured.

1264	40c. "Energy" (vert)	45	25
1265	45c. Type **297**	45	25

EVENTS: 40c. "Be wise with energy" campaign; 45c. Elections to Lower House of States-General.

See also No. 1268.

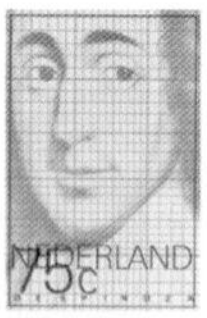

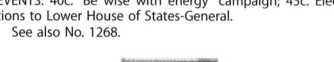

298 Spinoza

1977. 300th Death Anniv of Barach (Benedictus) de Spinoza (philosopher).

1266	**298**	75c. multicoloured	80	35

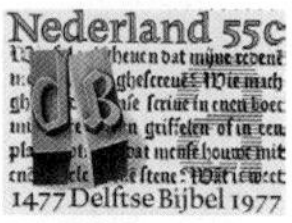

299 Early Type Faces and "a" on Bible Script

1977. 500th Anniv of Printing of "Delft Bible".

1267	**299**	55c. multicoloured	55	45

1977. Elections to Lower House of States-General. As T 297 but also inscribed "25 MEI '77".

1268	45c. multicoloured	45	25

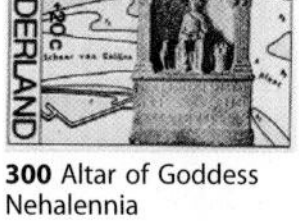

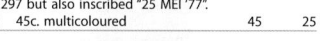

300 Altar of Goddess Nehalennia

1977. Cultural, Health and Social Welfare Funds. Roman Archaeological Discoveries.

1269	-	40c.+20c. mult	65	35
1270	**300**	45c.+20c. black, stone and green	70	35
1271	-	55c.+20c. black, blue and red	70	35
1272	-	75c.+25c. black, grey and yellow	90	65

DESIGNS: 40c. Baths, Heerlen; 55c. Remains of Zwammerdam ship; 75c. Parade helmet.

1977. "Amphilex 1977" International Stamp Exhibition, Amsterdam (2nd series). As T 295.

1273	55c.+45c. grn, brn & grey	95	45
1274	55c.+45c. blue, brn & grey	95	70
1275	55c.+45c. blue, brn & grey	95	70
1276	55c.+45c. red, brn & grey	95	45
MS1277 100×72 mm. Nos. 1273 and 1276		2·20	1·20

DESIGNS: No. 1273, Queen Wilhelmina 1g. stamp, 1898; 1274, Queen Wilhelmina 20c. stamp, 1923; 1275, Queen Wilhelmina 12½c. stamp, 1938; 1276, Queen Wilhelmina 10c. stamp, 1948.

301 "Kaleidoscope"

1977. Bicentenary of Netherlands Society for Industry and Commerce.

1278	**301**	55c. multicoloured	70	10

302 Man in Wheelchair and Maze of Steps

1977. Anniversaries.

1279	**302**	40c. brown, green & blue	60	35
1280	-	45c. multicoloured	60	35
1281	-	55c. multicoloured	60	35

DESIGNS—HORIZ: 40c. Type **302** (50th anniv of A.V.O. Nederland); 45c. Diagram of water current (50th anniv of Delft Hydraulic Laboratory). VERT: 55c. Teeth (centenary of dentists' training in Netherlands).

303 Risk of Drowning

1977. Child Welfare. Dangers to Children. Mult.

1282	40c.+20c. Type **303**	60	35
1283	45c.+20c. Medicine cabinet (poisons)	70	35
1284	55c.+20c. Balls in road (traffic)	70	35
1285	75c.+25c. Matches (fire)	1·70	95
MS1286 75×144 mm. Nos. 1282/4 ×2		4·75	3·00

304 "Postcode"

1978. Introduction of Postcodes.

1287	**304**	40c. red and blue	60	10
1288	**304**	45c. red and blue	70	10

305 Makkum Dish

1978. Cultural, Health and Social Welfare Funds. Multicoloured.

1289	40c.+20c. Anna Maria van Schurman (writer)	70	45
1290	45c.+20c. Passage from letter by Belle de Zuylen (Mme. de Charriere)	80	45
1291	55c.+20c. Delft dish	95	45
1292	75c.+25c. Type **305**	1·00	70

306 "Human Rights" Treaty

1978. European Series.

1293	**306**	45c. grey, black and blue	60	35
1294	-	55c. black, stone and orange	60	35

DESIGN: 55c. Haarlem Town Hall (Europa).

307 Chess

1978. Sports.

1295	**307**	40c. multicoloured	60	35
1296	-	45c. red and blue	70	35

DESIGN: 45c. The word "Korfbal".

308 Kidney Donor

1978. Health Care. Multicoloured.

1297	**308**	40c. black, blue and red	60	35
1298	-	45c. multicoloured	70	35
1299	-	55c.+25c. red, grey and black	70	45
MS1300 144×50 mm. No. 1299 ×3			2·30	2·10

DESIGNS—VERT: 45c. Heart and torch. HORIZ: 55c. Red crosses on world map.

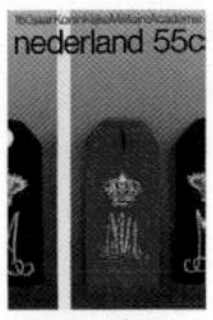

309 Epaulettes

1978. 150th Anniv of Royal Military Academy, Breda.

1301	**309**	55c. multicoloured	60	35

310 Verkade as Hamlet

1978. Birth Centenary of Eduard Rutger Verkade (actor and producer).

1302	**310**	45c. multicoloured	60	35

311 Boy ringing Doorbell

1978. Child Welfare. Multicoloured.

1303	40c.+20c. Type **311**	60	35
1304	45c.+20c. Child reading	70	35
1305	55c.+20c. Boy writing (vert)	70	35
1306	75c.+25c. Girl and blackboard	1·60	95
MS1307 144×75 mm. Nos. 1303/5 ×2		4·75	3·00

312 Clasped Hands and Arrows

1979. 400th Anniv of Treaty of Utrecht.

1308	**312**	55c. blue	70	35

313 Names of European Community Members

1979. First Direct Elections to European Assembly.

1309	**313**	45c. red, blue and black	60	35

314 Queen Juliana

1979. Queen Juliana's 70th Birthday.

1310	**314**	55c. multicoloured	70	35

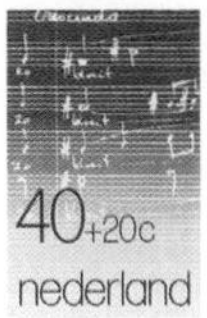

315 Fragment of "Psalmen Trilogie" (J. Andriessen)

1979. Cultural, Health and Social Welfare Funds.

1311	**315**	40c.+20c. grey and red	70	45
1312	-	45c.+20c. grey and red	80	45
1313	-	55c.+20c. mult	95	35
1314	-	75c.+25c. mult	1·00	70

DESIGNS AND EVENTS: 150th anniv of Musical Society; 45c. Choir. Restoration of St. John's Church, Gouda (stained glass windows); 55c. Mary (detail, "Birth of Christ"); 75c. William of Orange (detail, "Relief of Leyden").

316 Netherlands Stamps and Magnifying Glass

1979. Europa and 75th Anniv of Scheveningen Radio. Multicoloured.

1315	55c. Type **316**	60	15
1316	75c. Liner and Morse Key	95	45

317 Map of Chambers of Commerce

1979. 175th Anniv of First Dutch Chamber of Commerce, Maastricht.

1317	**317**	45c. multicoloured	60	35

318 Action Shot of Football Match

1979. Anniversaries. Multicoloured.

1318	45c. Type **318** (centenary of organized football)	60	20
1319	55c. Women's suffrage meeting (60th anniv of Women's suffrage) (vert)	70	20

319 Porch of Old Amsterdam Theatre

1979. 300th Death Annivs of Joost van den Vondel (poet) and Jan Steen (painter). Multicoloured.

1320	40c. Type **319**	60	25
1321	45c. "Gay Company" (detail) (Jan Steen)	60	25

320 Hindustani Girl on Father's Shoulder (The Right to Love)

1979. Child Welfare. International Year of the Child.

1322	**320**	40c.+20c. grey, red and yellow	60	35
1323	-	45c.+20c. grey, red and black	70	35
1324	-	55c.+20c. grey, black and yellow	70	35
1325	-	75c.+25c. black, blue and red	1·50	70
MS1326 144×75 mm. Nos. 1322/4, each ×2			4·75	3·00

DESIGNS—HORIZ: 45c. Chilean child from refugee camp (The Right to Medical Care). VERT: 55c. Senegalese boy from Sahel area (The Right to Food); 75c. Class from Albert Cuyp School, Amsterdam (The Right to Education).

321 A. F. de Savornin Lohman

1980. Dutch Politicians. Multicoloured.

1327	45c. Type **321** (Christian Historical Union)	60	20
1328	50c. P. J. Troelstra (Socialist Party)	70	20
1329	60c. P. J. Oud (Liberal Party)	80	20

322 Dunes

1980. Cultural, Health and Social Welfare Funds. Multicoloured.

1330	45c.+20c. Type **322**	95	45
1331	50c.+20c. Country estate (vert)	95	45
1332	60c.+25c. Lake District	1·00	45
1333	80c.+35c. Moorland	1·30	70

323 Avro Type 683 Lancaster dropping Food Parcels

1980. 35th Anniv of Liberation. Multicoloured.

1334	45c. Type **323**	80	25
1335	60c. Anne Frank (horiz)	95	25

324 Queen Beatrix and New Church, Amsterdam

1980. Installation of Queen Beatrix.

1336	**324**	60c. blue, red and yellow	70	10
1337	**324**	65c. blue, red and yellow	80	10

325 Young Stamp Collectors

1980. "Jupostex 1980" Stamp Exhibition, Eindhoven, and Dutch Society of Stamp Dealers Show, The Hague.

1338	**325**	50c. multicoloured	60	35

326 "Flight"

1980. Air. (Special Flights).

1339	**326**	1g. blue and black	1·20	1·20

327 Bridge Players and Cards

1980. Sports Events. Multicoloured.

1340	50c. Type **327** (Bridge Olympiad, Valkenburg)	70	20
1341	60c.+25c. Sportswoman in wheelchair (Olympics for the Disabled, Arnhem and Veenendaal)	95	45

328 Road Haulage

1980. Transport.

1342	**328**	50c. multicoloured	60	25
1343	-	60c. blue, brown & black	70	25
1344	-	80c. multicoloured	95	35

DESIGNS: 60c. Rail transport; 80c. Motorized canal barge.

329 Queen Wilhelmina

1980. Europa.

1345	**329**	60c. black, red and blue	80	10
1346	-	80c. black, red and blue	1·00	35

DESIGN: 80c. Sir Winston Churchill.

330 Abraham Kuyper (first rector) and University Seal

1980. Centenary of Amsterdam Free University.

1347	**330**	50c. multicoloured	60	20

331 "Pop-up" Book

1980. Child Welfare. Multicoloured.

1348	45c.+20c. Type **331**	60	35
1349	50c.+20c. Child flying on a book (vert)	1·30	45
1350	60c.+30c. Boy reading "Kikkerkoning" (vert)	80	35
1351	80c.+30c. Dreaming in a book	1·50	95
MS1352	144×75 mm. Nos. 1348 ×2 and 1350 ×3	5·00	2·75

332 Saltmarsh

1981. Cultural, Health and Social Welfare Funds. Multicoloured.

1353	45c.+20c. Type **332**	70	35
1354	55c.+25c. Dyke	80	35
1355	60c.+25c. Drain	95	35
1356	65c.+30c. Cultivated land	1·00	35

333 Parcel (Parcel Post)

1981. P.T.T. Centenaries. Multicoloured.

1357	45c. Type **333**	60	15
1358	55c. Telephone, dish aerial and telephone directory page (public telephone service)	70	15
1359	65c. Savings bank books, deposit transfer card and savings bank stamps (National Savings Bank)	80	15
MS1360	145×75 mm. Nos. 1357/9	1·70	1·40

334 Huis ten Bosch Royal Palace, The Hague

1981

1361	**334**	55c. multicoloured	70	35

335 Carillon

1981. Europa. Multicoloured.

1362	45c. Type **335**	70	25
1363	65c. Barrel organ	1·00	25

336 Council of State Emblem and Maps of 1531 and 1981

1981. 450th Anniv of Council of State.

1364	**336**	65c. orange, deep orange and red	80	10

337 Marshalling Yard, Excavator and Ship's Screw

1981. Industrial and Agricultural Exports. Mult.

1365	45c. Type **337**	60	25
1366	55c. Inner port, cast-iron component and weighing machine	70	25
1367	60c. Airport, tomato and lettuce	80	45
1368	65c. Motorway interchange, egg and cheese	95	25

338 "Integration in Society"

1981. Child Welfare. Integration of Handicapped Children. Multicoloured.

1369	45c.+25c. Type **338**	60	25
1370	55c.+20c. "Integration in the Family" (vert)	70	60
1371	60c.+25c. Child vaccinated against polio (Upper Volta project) (vert)	80	60
1372	65c.+30c. "Integration among Friends"	95	25
MS1373	144×76 mm. Nos. 1369 ×3 and 1372 ×2	4·00	2·30

339 Queen Beatrix

1981

1374	**339**	65c. brown and black	80	10
1375	**339**	70c. lilac and black	1·00	10
1376	**339**	75c. pink and black	1·00	10
1377	**339**	90c. green and black	1·00	10
1378	**339**	1g. lilac and black	1·70	20
1379	**339**	1g.20 bistre and black	1·70	25
1380	**339**	1g.40 green and black	1·70	35
1381	**339**	1g.50 lilac and black	1·60	35
1382	**339**	2g. bistre and black	2·10	15
1383	**339**	2g.50 orange and black	2·75	35
1384	**339**	3g. blue and black	3·25	35
1385	**339**	4g. green and black	4·25	35
1386	**339**	5g. blue and black	5·25	35
1387	**339**	6g.50 lilac and black	7·00	45
1388	**339**	7g. blue and black	8·25	60
1389	**339**	7g.50 green and black	11·50	3·00

For this design but on uncoloured background see Nos. 1594/1605.

340 Agnieten Chapel and Banners

1982. 350th Anniv of University of Amsterdam.

1395	**340**	65c. multicoloured	70	10

341 Skater

1982. Centenary of Royal Dutch Skating Association.

1396	**341**	45c. multicoloured	60	25

342 Apple Blossom

1982. Cultural, Health and Social Welfare Funds. Multicoloured.

1397	50c.+20c. Type **342**	1·20	45
1398	60c.+25c. Anemones	1·20	45
1399	65c.+25c. Roses	1·20	45
1400	70c.+30c. African violets	1·20	70

343 Stripes in National Colours

1982. Bicentenary of Netherlands–United States Diplomatic Relations.

1401	**343**	50c. red, blue and black	60	25
1402	**343**	65c. red, blue and black	80	25

344 Sandwich Tern and Eider

1982. Waddenzee. Multicoloured.

1403	50c. Type **344**	70	25
1404	70c. Barnacle Geese	95	25

345 Zebra Crossing

1982. 50th Anniv of Dutch Road Safety Organization.

1405	**345**	60c. multicoloured	60	25

346 Ground Plan of Enkhuizen Fortifications

1982. Europa. Multicoloured.

1406	50c. Type **346**	70	25
1407	70c. Part of ground plan of Coevorden fortifications	95	25

347 Aerial view of Palace and Liberation Monument

1982. Royal Palace, Dam Square, Amsterdam. Mult.

1408	50c. Facade, ground plan and cross-section of palace	60	25
1409	60c. Type **347**	70	25

348 Great Tits and Child

1982. Child Welfare. Child and Animal. Mult.

1410	50c.+30c. Type **348**	60	35
1411	60c.+20c. Child arm-in-arm with cat	80	35
1412	65c.+20c. Child with drawing of rabbit	1·30	95
1413	70c.+30c. Child with palm cockatoo	1·50	95
MS1414	75×144 mm. Nos. 1410 ×4 and 1411	4·00	2·50

349 Touring Club Activities

1983. Centenary of Royal Dutch Touring Club.

1415	**349**	70c. multicoloured	80	25

350 Johan van Oldenbarnevelt (statesman) (after J. Houbraken)

1983. Cultural, Health and Social Welfare Funds.

1416	**350**	50c.+20c. pink, blue and black	95	60
1417	-	60c.+25c. mult	95	60
1418	-	65c.+25c. mult	95	80
1419	-	70c.+30c. grey, black and gold	95	80

DESIGNS: 60c. Willem Jansz Blaeu (cartographer) (after Thomas de Keijser); 65c. Hugo de Groot (statesman) (after J. van Ravesteyn); 70c. "Saskia van Uylenburch" (portrait of his wife by Rembrandt).

351 Newspaper

1983. Europa. Multicoloured.

1420	50c. Type **351** (75th anniv of Netherlands Newspaper Publishers Association)	60	25
1421	70c. European Communications Satellite and European Telecommunication Satellites Organization members' flags	80	25

352 "Composition 1922" (P. Mondriaan)

1983. De Stijl Art Movement. Multicoloured.

1422	50c. Type **352**	60	25
1423	65c. Contra construction from "Maison Particuliere" (C. van Eesteren and T. van Doesburg)	80	35

353 "Geneva Conventions"

1983. Red Cross.

1424	**353**	50c.+25c. mult	95	60
1425	-	60c.+20c. mult	95	70
1426	-	65c.+25c. mult	95	70
1427	-	70c.+30c. grey, black and red	95	70

DESIGNS: 60c. Red Cross and text "charity, independence, impartiality"; 65c. "Socio-medical work"; 70c. Red Cross and text "For Peace".

354 Luther's Signature

1983. 500th Birth Anniv of Martin Luther (Protestant Reformer).

| 1428 | **354** | 70c. multicoloured | 80 | 10 |

355 Child looking at Donkey and Ox through Window

1983. Child Welfare. Child and Christmas. Mult.

1429		50c.+10c. Type **355**	1·20	70
1430		50c.+25c. Child riding flying snowman	70	35
1431		60c.+30c. Child in bed and star	1·30	95
1432		70c.+30c. Children dressed as the three kings	1·00	35
MS1433	144×75 mm. Nos. 1430 ×4 and 1432 ×2		5·00	4·50

356 Parliament

1984. Second Elections to European Parliament.

| 1434 | **356** | 70c. multicoloured | 80 | 10 |

357 Northern Lapwings

1984. Cultural, Health and Social Welfare Funds. Pasture Birds. Multicoloured.

1435		50c.+20c. Type **357**	45	35
1436		60c.+25c. Ruffs	1·30	45
1437		65c.+25c. Redshanks (vert)	1·30	70
1438		70c.+30c. Black-tailed godwits (vert)	1·30	70

358 St. Servaas

1984. 1600th Death Anniv of St. Servaas (Bishop of Tongeren and Maastricht).

| 1439 | **358** | 60c. multicoloured | 70 | 15 |

359 Bridge

1984. Europa. 25th Anniv of European Post and Telecommunications Conference.

| 1440 | **359** | 50c. deep blue and blue | 60 | 25 |
| 1441 | **359** | 70c. green and light green | 80 | 25 |

360 Eye and Magnifying Glass

1984. Centenary of Organized Philately in the Netherlands and "Filacento" International Stamp Exhibition, The Hague. Multicoloured.

1442		50c.+20c. Type **360**	1·00	80
1443		60c.+25c. 1909 cover	1·20	95
1444		70c.+30c. Stamp club meeting, 1949	1·30	1·20
MS1445	144×50 mm. Nos. 1442/4		4·25	3·25

361 William of Orange (after Adriaen Thomaszoon Key)

1984. 400th Death Anniv of William of Orange.

| 1446 | **361** | 70c. multicoloured | 80 | 15 |

362 Giant Pandas and Globe

1984. World Wildlife Fund.

| 1447 | **362** | 70c. multicoloured | 1·20 | 20 |

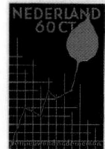

363 Graph and Leaf

1984. 11th International Small Business Congress, Amsterdam.

| 1448 | **363** | 60c. multicoloured | 70 | 20 |

364 Violin Lesson

1984. Child Welfare. Strip Cartoons. Mult.

1449		50c.+25c. Type **364**	60	35
1450		60c.+20c. At the dentist	1·50	80
1451		65c.+20c. The plumber	1·60	1·00
1452		70c.+30c. The king and money chest	95	35
MS1453	75×144 mm. Nos. 1449 ×4 and 1452 ×2		4·75	4·00

365 Sunny, First Dutch Guide-Dog

1985. 50th Anniv of Royal Dutch Guide-Dog Fund.

| 1454 | **365** | 60c. black, ochre and red | 70 | 20 |

366 Plates and Cutlery on Place-mat

1985. Tourism. Multicoloured.

| 1455 | | 50c. Type **366** (centenary of Travel and Holidays Association) | 60 | 20 |
| 1456 | | 70c. Kroller-Muller museum emblem, antlers and landscape (50th anniv of De Hoge Veluwe National Park) | 80 | 20 |

367 Saint Martin's Church, Zaltbommel

1985. Cultural, Health and Social Welfare Funds. Religious Buildings. Multicoloured.

1457a		50c.+20c. Type **367**	45	25
1458		60c.+25c. Winterswijk synagogue and Holy Ark (horiz)	1·40	80
1459		65c.+25c. Bolsward Baptist church	1·40	80
1460		70c.+30c. Saint John's Cathedral, 's-Hertogen-bosch (horiz)	1·40	60

368 Star of David, Illegal Newspapers and Rifle Practice (Resistance Movement)

1985. 40th Anniv of Liberation.

1461	**368**	50c. black, stone and red	60	25
1462	-	60c. black, stone and blue	70	25
1463	-	65c. black, stone & orge	80	60
1464	-	70c. black, stone & green	95	25

DESIGNS: 60c. Fighters over houses, "De Vliegende Hollander" (newspaper) and soldier (Allied Forces); 65c. Soldiers and civilians, "Parool" (newspaper) and American war cemetery, Margraten (Liberation); 70c. Women prisoners, prison money and Burma Railway (Dutch East Indies).

369 Piano Keyboard

1985. Europa. Music Year. Multicoloured.

| 1465 | **369** | 50c. Type **369** | 60 | 25 |
| 1466 | | 70c. Organ | 80 | 35 |

370 National Museum, Amsterdam (centenary)

1985. Anniversaries and Events. Multicoloured.

1467	**370**	50c. Type **370**	60	25
1468		60c. Teacher with students (bicentenary of Amsterdam Nautical College)	60	25
1469		70c. Ship's mast and rigging ("Sail '85", Amsterdam)	80	25

371 Porpoise and Graph

1985. Endangered Animals.

| 1470 | **371** | 50c. black, blue and red | 70 | 35 |
| 1471 | - | 70c. black, blue and red | 95 | 35 |

DESIGN: 70c. Seal and PCB molecule structure.

372 Ignition Key and Framed Photograph ("Think of Me")

1985. Child Welfare. Road Safety. Multicoloured.

1472		50c.+25c. Type **372**	60	35
1473		60c.+20c. Child holding target showing speeds	1·50	1·00
1474		65c.+20c. Girl holding red warning triangle	1·50	1·20
1475		70c.+30c. Boy holding "Children Crossing" sign	1·00	35
MS1476	132×80 mm. Nos. 1472 ×4 and 1475 ×2		5·00	4·25

373 Penal Code Extract

1986. Centenary of Penal Code.

| 1477 | **373** | 50c. black, yellow & purple | 60 | 35 |

374 Surveyor with Pole and N.A.P. Water Gauge

1986. 300th Anniv of Height Gauging Marks at Amsterdam.

| 1478 | **374** | 60c. multicoloured | 70 | 25 |

375 Windmill, Graph and Cloudy Sky

1986. Inaug of Windmill Test Station, Sexbierum.

| 1479 | **375** | 70c. multicoloured | 80 | 10 |

376 Scales

1986. Cultural, Health and Social Welfare Funds. Antique Measuring Instruments. Multicoloured.

1480a		50c.+20c. Type **376**	45	35
1481		60c.+25c. Clock (vert)	1·30	45
1482		65c.+25c. Barometer (vert)	1·30	95
1483		70c.+30c. Jacob's staff	1·30	95

377 Het Loo Palace Garden, Apeldoorn

1986. Europa. Multicoloured.

| 1484 | **377** | 50c. Type **377** | 60 | 35 |
| 1485 | | 70c. Tree with discoloured crown | 80 | 25 |

378 Cathedral

1986. Utrecht Events.

1486	**378**	50c. multicoloured	95	35
1487	-	60c. blue, pink and black	1·00	35
1488	-	70c. multicoloured	1·20	35

DESIGNS—VERT: 50c. Type **378** (completion of interior restoration); 60c. German House (75th anniv of Heemschut Conservation Society). HORIZ: 70c. Extract from foundation document (350th anniv of Utrecht University).

379 Drees at Binnenhof, 1947

1986. Birth Centenary of Dr. Willem Drees (politician).

| 1489 | **379** | 55c. multicoloured | 60 | 20 |

380 Draughts as Biscuits in Saucer

1986. 75th Anniversary of Royal Dutch Draughts Association (1490) and Royal Dutch Billiards Association (1491). Multicoloured.
| 1490 | 75c. Type 380 | 95 | 25 |
| 1491 | 75c. Player in ball preparing to play | 95 | 35 |

381 Map of Flood Barrier

1986. Delta Project Completion. Multicoloured.
| 1492 | 65c. Type 381 | 80 | 35 |
| 1493 | 75c. Flood barrier | 95 | 25 |

382 Children listening to Music (experiencing)

1986. Child Welfare. Child and Culture.
1494	55c.+25c. Type 382	1·50	95
1495	65c.+35c. Boy drawing (achieving)	1·30	45
1496	75c.+35c. Children at theatre (understanding)	1·30	35
MS1497	150×72 mm. Nos. 1494, 1495 ×2 and 1496 ×2	5·75	3·75

383 Engagement Picture

1987. Golden Wedding of Princess Juliana and Prince Bernhard.
| 1498 | **383** | 75c. orange, black and gold | 1·00 | 20 |

384 Block of Flats and Hut

1987. International Year of Shelter for the Homeless (65c.) and Centenary of Netherlands Salvation Army (75c.). Multicoloured.
| 1499 | 65c. Type 384 | 80 | 35 |
| 1500 | 75c. Army officer, meeting and tramp | 95 | 25 |

385 Eduard Douwes Dekker (Multatuli) and De Harmonie Club

1987. Writers' Death Anniv. Multicoloured.
| 1501 | 55c. Type 385 (centenary) | 80 | 25 |
| 1502 | 75c. Constantijn Huygens and Scheveningseweg, The Hague (300th anniv) | 95 | 25 |

386 Steam Pumping Station, Nijerk

1987. Cultural Health and Social Welfare Funds. Industrial Buildings.
1503a	**386**	55c.+30c. red, grey and black	45	35
1504	-	65c.+35c. grey, black and blue	1·40	1·20
1505	-	75c.+35c. grey, yellow and black	1·50	95
DESIGNS: 65c. Water tower, Deventer; 75c. Brass foundry, Joure.

387 Dance Theatre, Scheveningen (Rem Koolhaas)

1987. Europa. Architecture. Multicoloured.
| 1506 | 55c. Type 387 | 60 | 25 |
| 1507 | 75c. Montessori School, Amsterdam (Herman Hertzberger) | 80 | 25 |

388 Auction at Broek op Langedijk

1987. Centenary of Auction Sales (55, 75c.) and 150th Anniv of Groningen Agricultural Society (65c.). Multicoloured.
1508	55c. Type 388	60	25
1509	65c. Groningen landscape and founders' signatures	70	25
1510	75c. Auction sale and clock	80	25

389 Telephone Care Circles

1987. Dutch Red Cross. Multicoloured.
1511a	55c.+30c. Type 389	45	35
1512	65c.+35c. Red cross and hands (Welfare work)	1·40	1·00
1513	75c.+35c. Red cross and drip (Blood transfusion)	1·50	70

390 Map of Holland

1987. 75th Anniv of Netherlands Municipalities Union.
| 1514 | **390** | 75c. multicoloured | 95 | 20 |

391 Noordeinde Palace, The Hague

1987
| 1515 | **391** | 65c. multicoloured | 80 | 10 |

392 Woodcutter

1987. Child Welfare. Child and Profession. Mult.
1516	55c.+25c. Type 392	1·20	60
1517	65c.+35c. Woman sailor	1·20	45
1518	75c.+35c. Woman pilot	1·20	25
MS1519	150×72 mm. Nos. 1516, 1517 ×2 and 1518 ×2	5·75	4·25

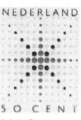

393 Star

1987. Christmas.
1520	393	50c. red, blue and green	80	35
1521	393	50c. yellow, red and blue	80	35
1522	393	50c. red, blue and yellow	80	35
1523	393	50c. yellow, red and green	80	35
1524	393	50c. blue, green and red	80	35
The first colour described is that of the St. George's Cross.

394 "Narcissus cyclamineus" "Peeping Tom" and Extract from "I Call You Flowers" (Jan Hanlo)

1988. "Filacept" European Stamp Exhibition, The Hague (1st issue). Flowers. Multicoloured.
| 1525 | 55c.+55c. Type 394 | 1·40 | 1·20 |

| 1526 | 75c.+70c. "Rosa gallica" "Versicolor" and "Roses" (Daan van Golden) | 1·40 | 1·20 |
| 1527 | 75c.+70c. Sea holly and 1270 map of The Hague | 1·40 | 1·20 |
See also No. **MS**1542.

395 Quagga

1988. Cultural, Health and Social Welfare Funds. 150th Anniv of Natura Artis Magistra Zoological Society. Multicoloured.
1528a	55c.+30c. Type 395	45	35
1529	65c.+35c. American manatee	1·70	1·20
1530	75c.+35c. Orang-utan (vert)	1·70	95

396 Man's Shoulder

1988. 75th Anniv of Netherlands Cancer Institute.
| 1531 | **396** | 75c. multicoloured | 95 | 20 |

397 Traffic Scene with Lead Symbol crossed Through

1988. Europa. Transport. Multicoloured.
| 1532 | 55c. Type 397 (lead-free petrol) | 80 | 35 |
| 1533 | 75c. Cyclists reflected in car wing mirror (horiz) | 1·00 | 25 |

398 Pendulum, Prism and Saturn

1988. 300th Anniv of England's Glorious Revolution. Multicoloured.
| 1534 | 65c. Type 398 | 85 | 25 |
| 1535 | 75c. Queen Mary, King William III and 17th-century warship | 95 | 25 |

399 "Cobra Cat" (Appel)

1988. 40th Anniv of Founding of Cobra Painters Group. Multicoloured.
1536	55c. Type 399	1·30	95
1537	65c. "Kite" (Corneille)	1·30	95
1538	75c. "Stumbling Horse" (Constant)	1·30	50

400 Sailing Ship and Map of Australia

1988. Bicentenary of Australian Settlement.
| 1539 | **400** | 75c. multicoloured | 1·10 | 20 |

401 Statue of Erasmus, Rotterdam

1988. 75th Anniv of Erasmus University, Rotterdam (1540) and Centenary of Concertgebouw Concert Hall and Orchestra (1541).
| 1540 | **401** | 75c. deep green and green | 1·10 | 20 |
| 1541 | - | 75c. violet | 1·10 | 20 |

DESIGN: No. 1541, Violin and Concertgebouw concert hall.

1988. "Filacept" European Stamp Exhibition, The Hague (2nd issue). Flowers. Sheet 144×62 mm.
| **MS**1542 | Nos. 1525/7 | 5·00 | 4·75 |

402 "Rain"

1988. Child Welfare. Centenary of Royal Netherlands Swimming Federation. Children's drawings. Multicoloured.
1543	55c.+25c. Type 402	1·60	85
1544	65c.+35c. "Getting Ready for the Race"	1·30	70
1545	75c.+35c. "Swimming Test"	1·30	35
MS1546	150×72 mm. Nos. 1543, 1544 ×2 and 1545 ×2	7·50	5·50

403 Stars

1988. Christmas.
| 1547 | **403** | 50c. multicoloured | 60 | 10 |

404 Postal and Telecommunications Services

1989. Privatization of Netherlands PTT.
| 1548 | **404** | 75c. multicoloured | 1·10 | 25 |

405 "Solidarity"

1989. Trade Unions. Multicoloured.
| 1549 | 55c. Type 405 | 70 | 35 |
| 1550 | 75c. Talking mouths on hands | 95 | 20 |

406 Members' Flags

1989. 40th Anniv of NATO.
| 1551 | **406** | 75c. multicoloured | 95 | 25 |

407 Boier

1989. Cultural, Health and Social Welfare Funds. Old Sailing Vessels.
1552a	**407**	55c.+30c. green & blk	1·20	85
1553	-	65c.+35c. blue & black	1·70	1·10
1554	-	75c.+35c. brown & blk	1·70	1·10
DESIGNS: 65c. Fishing smack; 75c. Clipper.

408 Boy with Homemade Telephone

1989. Europa. Children's Games. Multicoloured.
| 1555 | 55c. Type 408 | 60 | 20 |
| 1556 | 75c. Girl with homemade telephone | 85 | 20 |

409 Wheel on Rail

1989. 150th Anniv of Netherlands' Railways. Mult.
| 1557 | 55c. Type 409 | 70 | 25 |

| 1558 | | 65c. Steam, electric and diesel locomotives | 85 | 25 |
| 1559 | | 75c. Diesel train, station clock and "The Kiss" (sculpture by Rodin) | 1·10 | 25 |

410 Boy with Ball and Diagram of Goal Scored in European Championship

1989. Centenary of Royal Dutch Football Assn.

| 1560 | **410** | 75c. multicoloured | 85 | 20 |

411 Map

1989. 150th Anniv of Division of Limburg between Netherlands and Belgium.

| 1561 | **411** | 75c. multicoloured | 85 | 20 |

412 Right to Housing

1989. Child Welfare. 30th Anniv of Declaration of Rights of the Child. Multicoloured.

1562		55c.+25c. Type **412**	1·20	95
1563		65c.+35c. Right to food	1·20	60
1564		75c.+35c. Right to education	1·20	50
MS1565	150×72 mm. Nos. 1562, 1563 ×2 and 1564 ×2		6·00	4·75

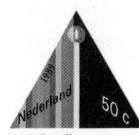

413 Candle

1989. Christmas.

| 1566 | **413** | 50c. multicoloured | 60 | 10 |

414 "Arms of Leiden" (tulip) and Plan of Gardens in 1601

1990. 400th Anniv of Hortus Botanicus (botanical gardens), Leiden.

| 1567 | **414** | 65c. multicoloured | 85 | 25 |

415 Pointer on Graduated Scale

1990. Centenary of Labour Inspectorate.

| 1568 | **415** | 75c. multicoloured | 95 | 25 |

416 "Self-portrait" (detail)

1990. Death Centenary of Vincent van Gogh (painter). Multicoloured.

| 1569 | | 55c. Type **416** | 85 | 20 |
| 1570 | | 75c. "Green Vineyard" (detail) | 1·10 | 20 |

417 Summer's Day

1990. Cultural, Health and Social Welfare Funds. The Weather. Multicoloured.

1571a		55c.+30c. Type **417**	1·20	85
1572		65c.+35c. Clouds and isobars (vert)	1·70	1·10
1573a		75c.+35c. Satellite weather picture (vert)	1·20	85

418 Zuiderkerk Ruins

1990. 50th Anniv of German Bombing of Rotterdam.

1574	**418**	55c. deep brown, brown and black	70	25
1575	-	65c. multicoloured	85	25
1576	-	75c. multicoloured	95	25

DESIGNS: 65c. City plan as stage; 75c. Girder and plans for future construction.

419 Postal Headquarters, Groningen, and Veere Post Office

1990. Europa. Post Office Buildings.

| 1577 | | 55c. grey, mauve & brn | 70 | 25 |
| 1578 | **419** | 75c. blue, green and grey | 95 | 25 |

DESIGN: 55c. As Type **419** but inscr "Postkantoor Veere".

420 Construction of Indiaman and Wreck of "Amsterdam"

1990. 3rd Anniv of Dutch East India Company Ships Association (replica ship project) (1579) and "Sail 90", Amsterdam (1580). Multicoloured.

| 1579 | | 65c. Type **420** | 85 | 25 |
| 1580 | | 75c. Crew manning yards on sailing ship | 95 | 25 |

421 Queens Emma, Wilhelmina, Juliana and Beatrix

1990. Netherlands Queens of the House of Orange.

| 1581 | **421** | 150c. multicoloured | 2·20 | 1·10 |

422 Flames, Telephone Handset and Number

1990. Introduction of National Emergency Number.

| 1582 | **422** | 65c. multicoloured | 85 | 25 |

423 Girl riding Horse

1990. Child Welfare. Hobbies. Multicoloured.

1583		55c.+25c. Type **423**	1·60	85
1584		65c.+35c. Girl at computer	1·30	60
1585		75c.+35c. Young philatelist	1·40	35

| **MS**1586 | 150×71 mm. Nos. 1583, 1584 ×2 and 1585 ×2 | | 7·75 | 5·50 |

424 Falling Snow

1990. Christmas.

| 1587 | **424** | 50c. multicoloured | 60 | 10 |

425 Industrial Chimneys, Exhaust Pipes and Aerosol Can (Air Pollution)

1991. Environmental Protection. Multicoloured.

1588		55c. Type **425**	70	25
1589		65c. Outfall pipes and chemicals (sea pollution)	85	25
1590		75c. Agricultural chemicals, leaking drums and household landfill waste (soil pollution)	95	25

426 German Raid on Amsterdam Jewish Quarter and Open Hand

1991. 50th Anniv of Amsterdam General Strike.

| 1591 | **426** | 75c. multicoloured | 95 | 25 |

427 Princess Beatrix and Prince Claus on Wedding Day

1991. Royal Silver Wedding Anniversary. Mult.

| 1592 | | 75c. Type **427** | 1·10 | 35 |
| 1593 | | 75c. Queen Beatrix and Prince Claus on horseback | 1·10 | 35 |

428 Queen Beatrix

1991. (a) Ordinary gum.

1594	**428**	75c. deep green & green	1·20	25
1595	**428**	80c. brown & lt brown	1·20	10
1597	**428**	90c. blue	2·40	1·80
1598	**428**	1g. violet	2·40	60
1599	**428**	1g.10 blue	3·50	3·50
1600	**428**	1g.30 blue and violet	1·80	35
1601	**428**	1g.40 green and olive	1·80	35
1601a	**428**	1g.50 green	3·50	2·40
1602	**428**	1g.60 purple and mauve	2·40	25
1603	**428**	2g. brown	3·50	60
1603a	**428**	2g.50 purple	4·75	2·40
1604	**428**	3g. blue	3·50	1·80
1605	**428**	5g. red	6·00	1·80
1706	**428**	7g.50 violet	14·50	6·00
1708	**428**	10g. green	7·25	1·20

(b) Self-adhesive gum.

1606		1g. violet	1·80	1·20
1607		1g.10 blue	2·10	2·10
1608		1g.45 green	2·20	2·20
1609		2g.50 purple	4·25	3·50
1609a		5g. red	8·50	6·75

429 "Meadow" Farm, Wartena, Friesland

1991. Cultural, Health and Social Welfare Funds. Traditional Farmhouses. Multicoloured.

1611		65c.+35c. "T-house" farm, Kesteren, Gelderland	1·60	1·10
1613		75c.+30c. Type **429**	85	35
1614		75c.+35c. "Courtyard" farm, Nuth, Limburg	85	35

430 Gerard Philips's Experiments with Carbon Filaments

1991. 75th Anniv of Netherlands Standards Institute (65c.) and Centenary of Philips Organization (others). Multicoloured.

1615		55c. Type **430**	70	50
1616		65c. Wiring to Standard NEN 1010 (horiz)	85	20
1617		75c. Laser beams reading video disc	95	20

431 Man raising Hat to Space

1991. Europa. Europe in Space. Multicoloured.

| 1618 | | 55c. Type **431** | 85 | 35 |
| 1619 | | 75c. Ladders stretching into space | 1·10 | 25 |

432 Sticking Plaster over Medal

1991. 75th Anniv of Nijmegen International Four Day Marches.

| 1620 | **432** | 80c. multicoloured | 95 | 20 |

433 Jacobus Hendericus van't Hoff

1991. Dutch Nobel Prize Winners (1st series). Multicoloured.

1621		70c. Type **433** (chemistry, 1901)	70	25
1622		70c. Pieter Zeeman (physics, 1902)	85	25
1623		80c. Tobias Michael Carel Asser (peace, 1911)	95	25

See also Nos. 1690/2 and 1773/5.

434 Children and Open Book

1991. Centenary (1992) of Public Libraries in the Netherlands.

| 1624 | **434** | 70c. drab, black & mauve | 95 | 25 |
| 1625 | - | 80c. multicoloured | 1·10 | 25 |

DESIGN: 80c. Books on shelf.

435 Girls with Doll and Robot

1991. Child Welfare. Outdoor Play. Multicoloured.

1626		60c.+30c. Type **435**	1·10	35
1627		70c.+35c. Bicycle race	1·80	1·30
1628		80c.+40c. Hide and seek	1·40	1·70
MS1629	144×75 mm. Nos. 1626 ×4 and 1638 ×2		8·50	6·75

436 "Greetings Cards keep People in Touch"

1991. Christmas.

| 1630 | **436** | 55c. multicoloured | 60 | 10 |

437 Artificial Lightning, Microchip and Oscilloscope

1992. 150th Anniv of Delft University of Technology.
1631	**437**	60c. multicoloured	85	25

438 Extract from Code

1992. Implementation of Property Provisions of New Civil Code.
1632	**438**	80c. multicoloured	1·10	25

439 Volleyball

1992. Winter Olympic Games, Albertville and Summer Games, Barcelona. Sheet 125×72 mm containing T 439 and similar vert designs. Multicoloured.
MS1633	80c. Type **439**; 80c. Putting the shot and rowing; 80c. Speed skating and rowing; 80c. Hockey	4·75	4·00

440 Tulips ("Mondrian does not like Green")

1992. "Expo '92" World's Fair, Seville. Mult.
1634		70c. Type **440**	95	25
1635		80c. "Netherland Expo '92"	1·10	25

441 Tasman's Map of Staete Landt (New Zealand)

1992. 350th Anniv of Discovery of Tasmania and New Zealand by Abel Tasman.
1636	**441**	70c. multicoloured	95	25

442 Yellow and Purple Flowers

1992. Cultural, Health and Social Welfare Funds. "Floriade" Flower Show, Zoetermeer. Mult.
1639		80c.+40c. Type **442**	1·40	1·20
1640		60c.+30c. Water lilies	85	50
1641		70c.+35c. Orange and purple flowers	95	85

443 Geometric Planes

1992. 150th Anniv of Royal Association of Netherlands Architects (60c.) and Inauguration of New States General Lower House (80c.). Mult.
1643	**443**	60c. Type **443**	85	35
1644		80c. Atrium and blue sky (symbolizing sending of information into society)	95	35

444 Globe and Columbus

1992. Europa. 500th Anniv of Discovery of America by Columbus.
1645	**444**	60c. multicoloured	85	35
1646	-	80c. black, mauve & yellow	1·20	35

DESIGN—VERT: 80c. Galleon.

445 Moneta (Goddess of Money)

1992. Centenary of Royal Netherlands Numismatics Society.
1647	**445**	70c. multicoloured	95	25

446 Teddy Bear wearing Stethoscope

1992. Centenary of Netherlands Paediatrics Society.
1648	**446**	80c. multicoloured	1·20	25

447 List of Relatives and Friends

1992. 50th Anniv of Departure of First Deportation Train from Westerbork Concentration Camp.
1649	**447**	70c. multicoloured	95	25

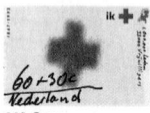

448 Cross

1992. 125th Anniv of Netherlands Red Cross. Multicoloured.
1652		80c.+40c. Red cross on dirty bandage	1·40	1·20
1653		60c.+30c. Type **448**	85	50
1654		70c.+35c. Supporting injured person	95	85

449 "United Europe" and European Community Flag

1992. European Single Market.
1656	**449**	80c. multicoloured	95	25

450 Queen Beatrix on Official Birthday, 1992, and at Investiture

1992. 12½ Years since Accession to the Throne of Queen Beatrix.
1657	**450**	80c. multicoloured	95	25

451 Saxophone Player

1992. Child Welfare. Child and Music. Mult.
1658		60c.+30c. Type **451**	1·10	50
1659		70c.+35c. Piano player	1·30	70
1660		80c.+40c. Double bass player	1·80	1·10
MS1661	144×75 mm. Nos. 1658 ×3, 1659 ×2 and 1660		7·75	6·00

452 Poinsettia

1992. Christmas.
1662	**452**	55c. multicoloured (centre of flower silver)	70	10
1663	**452**	55c. multicoloured (centre red)	70	10

453 Cycling

1993. Centenary of Netherlands Cycle and Motor Industry Association.
1664	**453**	70c. multicoloured	1·10	25
1665	-	80c. brown, grey & yell	1·20	25

DESIGN: 80c. Car.

454 Collages

1993. Greetings Stamps. Multicoloured.
1666		70c. Type **454**	85	25
1667		70c. Collages (different)	85	25

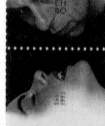

455 Mouth to Mouth Resuscitation

1993. Anniversaries. Multicoloured.
1668		70c. Type **455** (centenary of Royal Netherlands First Aid Association)	95	25
1669		80c. Pests on leaf (75th anniv of Wageningen University of Agriculture)	95	25
1670		80c. Lead driver and horses (bicentenary of Royal Horse Artillery)	95	25

456 Emblems

1993. 150th Anniv of Royal Dutch Notaries Association. Each red and violet.
1671		80c. Type **456** ("150 Jaar" reading up)	1·20	25
1672		80c. As Type **456** but emblems inverted and "150 Jaar" reading down	1·20	25

Nos. 1671/2 were issued together in horizontal tete-beche pairs, each pair forming a composite design.

457 Large White

1993. Butterflies. Multicoloured.
1673		70c. Pearl-bordered fritillary	1·20	60
1674		80c. Large tortoiseshell	1·20	35
1675		90c. Type **457**	1·20	1·20

MS1676	104×71 mm. 160c. Common blue	3·50	3·25

458 Elderly Couple

1993. Cultural, Health and Social Welfare Funds. Senior Citizens' Independence.
1677		70c.+35c. Type **458**	1·40	1·30
1681		70c.+35c. Elderly man	1·10	85
1682		80c.+40c. Elderly woman with dog	95	70

459 Broadcaster

1993. Radio Orange (Dutch broadcasts from London during Second World War). Mult.
1683		80c. Type **459**	1·20	25
1684		80c. Man listening to radio in secret	1·20	25

460 Sports Pictograms

1993. 2nd European Youth Olympic Days. Mult.
1685		70c. Type **460**	85	25
1686		80c. Sports pictograms (different)	95	25

461 "The Embodiment of Unity" (Wessel Couzijn)

1993. Europa. Contemporary Art. Multicoloured.
1687		70c. Type **461**	1·20	50
1688		80c. Architectonic sculpture (Per Kirkeby)	1·20	35
1689		160c. Sculpture (Naum Gabo) (vert)	2·40	2·20

462 Johannes Diderik van der Waals (Physics, 1910)

1993. Dutch Nobel Prize Winners (2nd series).
1690	**462**	70c. blue, black and red	85	50
1691	-	80c. mauve, black & red	95	35
1692	-	90c. multicoloured	1·10	1·40

DESIGNS: 80c. Willem Einthoven (medicine, 1924); 90c. Christiaan Eijkman (medicine, 1929).

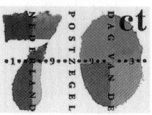

463 Pen and Pencils

1993. Letter Writing Campaign. Multicoloured.
1693		80c. Type **463**	95	25
1694		80c. Envelope	95	25

464 "70"

1993. Stamp Day (70c.) and Netherlands PTT (80c.). Multicoloured.
1695		70c. Type **464**	85	25
1696		80c. Dish aerial and dove carrying letter	95	25

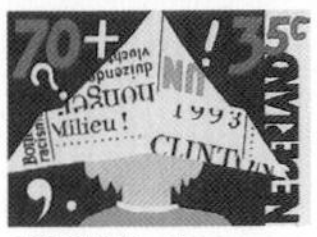

465 Child in Newspaper Hat

1993. Child Welfare. Child and the Media. Mult.

1697	70c.+35c. Type **465**	1·20	60
1698	70c.+35c. Elephant using headphones	1·20	60
1699	80c.+40c. Television	1·20	60
MS1700	143×75 mm. Nos. 1697/99, each ×2	7·75	6·75

466 Candle

1993. Christmas. Multicoloured.

1711	55c. Type **466**	60	25
1712	55c. Fireworks	60	25

Both designs have a number of punched holes.

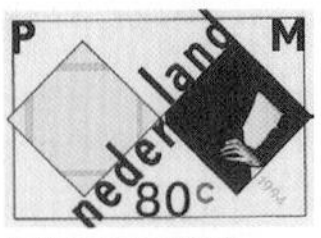

467 "Composition"

1994. 50th Death Anniv of Piet Mondriaan (artist). Multicoloured.

1713	70c. "The Red Mill" (detail)	95	50
1714	80c. Type **467**	1·10	35
1715	90c. "Broadway Boogie Woogie" (detail)	1·20	1·20

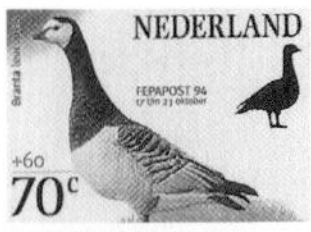

468 Barnacle Goose

1994. "Fepapost 94" European Stamp Exhibition, The Hague. Multicoloured.

1716	70c.+60c. Type **468**	1·80	1·40
1717	80c.+70c. Bluethroat	1·80	1·40
1718	90c.+80c. Garganey	1·80	1·40

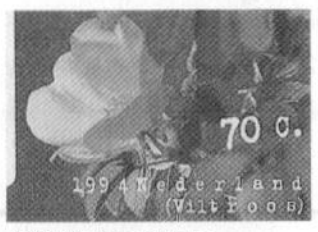

469 Downy Rose

1994. Wild Flowers. Multicoloured.

1719	70c. Type **469**	95	50
1720	80c. Daisies	1·10	35
1721	90c. Wood forgetmenot	1·20	1·40
MS1722	71×50 mm. 160c. Orange lily	3·50	3·50

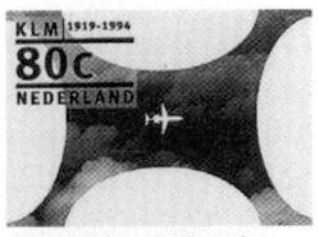

470 Fokker F.28 Airliner

1994. 75th Aircraft Industry Anniversaries.

1723 **470**	80c. blue and black	1·10	25
1724 -	80c. grey, red and black	1·10	25
1725 -	80c. multicoloured	1·10	25

DESIGNS: No. 1723, Type **470** (KLM (Royal Dutch Airlines)); 1724, Plan and outline of aircraft and clouds (Royal Netherlands Fokker Aircraft Industries); 1725, Airplane and clouds (National Aerospace Laboratory).

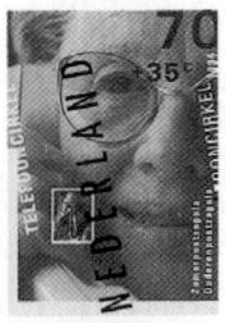

471 Woman using Telephone

1994. Cultural, Health and Social Welfare Funds. Senior Citizens' Security. Multicoloured.

1727	80c.+40c. Man using telephone	1·10	85
1728	90c.+35c. Man using telephone (different)	1·40	1·40
1729	70c.+35c. Type **471**	95	85

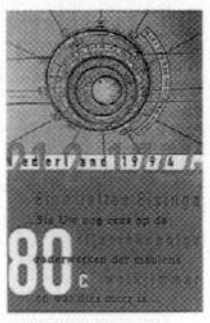

472 Eisinga's Planetarium

1994. Anniversaries. Multicoloured.

1732	80c. Type **472** (250th birth anniv of Eise Eisinga)	95	25
1733	90c. Astronaut and boot print on Moon surface (25th anniv of first manned Moon landing)	1·20	95

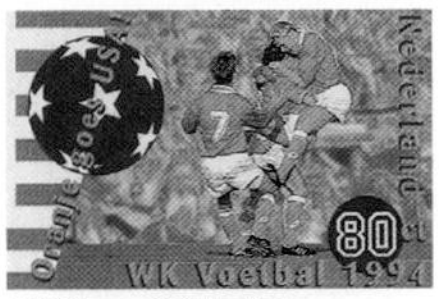

473 Players Celebrating

1994. World Cup Football Championship, U.S.A.

1734 **473**	80c. multicoloured	1·20	70

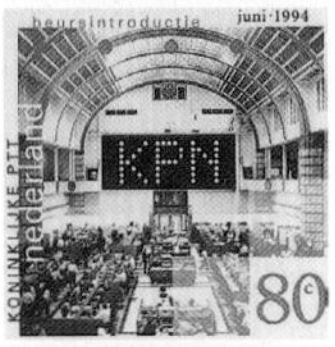

474 Stock Exchange

1994. Quotation of Netherlands PTT (KPN) on Stock Exchange.

1735 **474**	80c. multicoloured	1·10	25

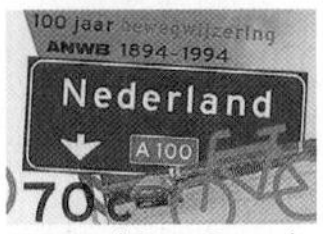

475 Road Sign, Car and Bicycle

1994. Anniversaries and Events. Multicoloured.

1736	70c. Type **475** (centenary of provision of road signs by Netherlands Motoring Association)	1·10	25
1737	80c. Equestrian sports (World Equestrian Games, The Hague)	1·20	25

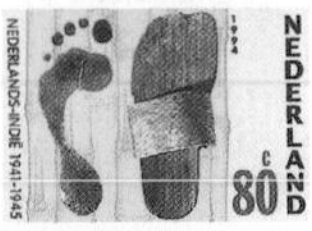

476 Footprint and Sandal

1994. Second World War. Multicoloured.

1738	80c. Type **476** (war in Netherlands Indies, 1941–45)	95	25
1739	90c. Soldier, children and Douglas C-47 dropping paratroops (50th anniv of Operation Market Garden (Battle of Arnhem)) (vert)	1·20	1·20

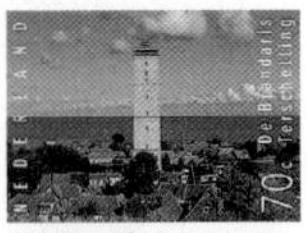

477 Brandaris Lighthouse, Terschelling

1994. Lighthouses. Multicoloured.

1740	70c. Type **477**	1·70	60
1741	80c. Ameland (vert)	1·70	25
1742	90c. Vlieland (vert)	1·70	1·40

1994. "Fepapost '94" European Stamp Exhibition, The Hague (2nd issue). Sheet 144×62 mm.

MS1743	Nos. 1716/18 plus 3 labels	7·25	6·00

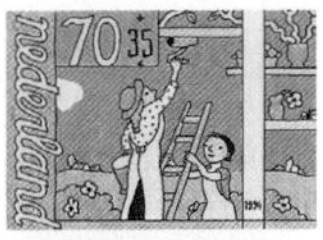

478 Decorating

1994. Child Welfare. "Together". Multicoloured.

1744	70c.+35c. Type **478**	1·20	60
1745	80c.+40c. Girl on swing knocking fruit off tree (vert)	1·20	60
1746	90c.+35c. Girl helping boy onto playhouse roof (vert)	1·20	1·80

MS1747	144×75 mm. No. 1744×2, 1745×3 and 1746	8·25	7·25

479 Star and Christmas Tree

1994. Christmas. Multicoloured.

1748	55c. Type **479**	60	10
1749	55c. Candle and star	60	10

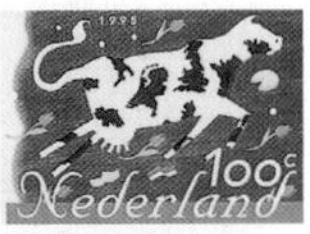

480 Flying Cow

1995

1750 **480**	100c. multicoloured	2·20	35

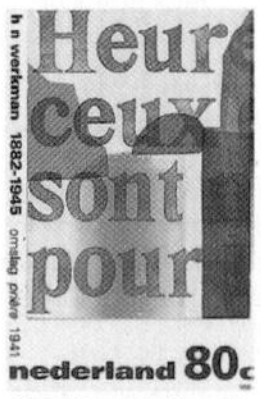

481 "Prayer" (detail)

1995. Anniversary and Events.

1751 **481**	80c. multicoloured	1·20	50
1752 -	80c. multicoloured	1·20	50
1753 -	80c. black and red	1·20	50

DESIGNS—VERT: No. 1751, Type **481** (50th death anniv of Hendrik Werkman (graphic designer); 1752, "Mesdag Panorama" (detail) (re-opening of Mesdag Museum). HORIZ: No. 1753, Mauritius 1847 2d. "POST OFFICE" stamp (purchase of remaining mint example in private hands by PTT Museum).

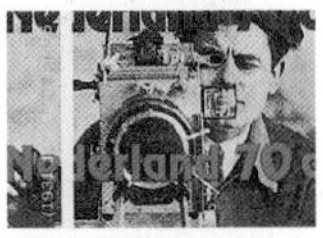

482 Joriz Ivens (documentary maker)

1995. Year of the Film (centenary of motion pictures). Multicoloured.

1754	70c. Type **482**	1·10	25
1755	80c. Scene from "Turkish Delight"	1·20	25

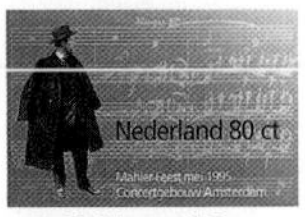

483 Mahler and Score of 7th Symphony

1995. Mahler Festival, Amsterdam.

1756 **483**	80c. black and blue	1·10	25

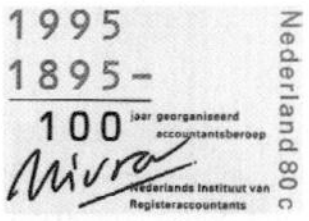

484 Dates and Acronym

1995. Centenaries. Multicoloured.

1757	80c. Type **484** (Netherlands Institute of Chartered Accountants)	1·30	40
1758	80c. Builders, bricklayer's trowel and saw (Netherlands Association of Building Contractors)	1·30	40

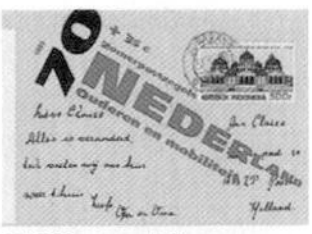

485 Postcard from Indonesia

1995. Cultural, Health and Social Welfare Funds. Mobility of the Elderly. Multicoloured.

1759	70c.+35c. Type **485**	1·50	1·90
1760	80c.+40c. Couple reflected in mirror	1·60	65
1761	100c.+45c. Couple with granddaughter at zoo	1·90	1·90
MS1762	144×75 mm. Nos. 1759 ×2, 1760 ×3 and 1761	10·50	9·00

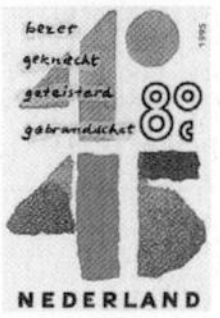

486 "40 45"

1995. 50th Anniversaries. Multicoloured.

1763	80c. Type **486** (end of Second World War)	1·30	40
1764	80c. "45 95" (liberation)	1·30	40
1765	80c. "50" (U.N.O.)	1·30	40

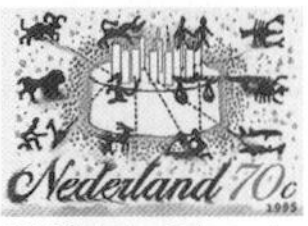

487 Birthday Cake and Signs of the Zodiac

1995. Birthday Greetings.

1766 **487**	70c. multicoloured	1·30	40

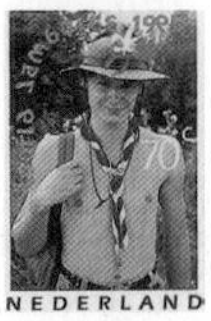

488 Scout

1995. Events. Multicoloured.

1767	70c. Type **488** (World Scout Jamboree, Dronten)	1·30	50
1768	80c. Amsterdam harbour ("Sail '95" and finish of Tall Ships Race) (horiz)	1·30	40

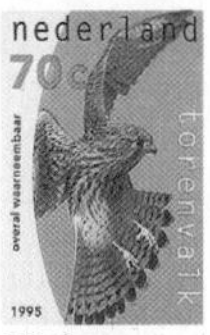

489 Common Kestrel

1995. Birds of Prey. Multicoloured.

1769	70c. Type **489**	1·30	40
1770	80c. Face of hen harrier (horiz)	1·30	25
1771	100c. Red kite (horiz)	1·90	1·90
MS1772	72×50 mm. 160c. Honey buzzard	3·75	3·75

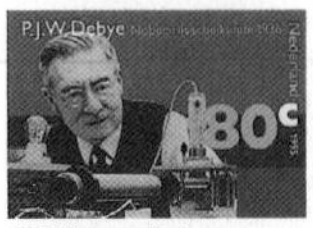

490 Petrus Debye (Chemistry, 1936)

1995. Dutch Nobel Prize Winners (3rd series). Multicoloured.

1773	80c. Type **490**	1·30	40
1774	80c. Frederik Zernike (Physics, 1953)	1·30	40
1775	80c. Jan Tinbergen (Economics, 1969)	1·30	40

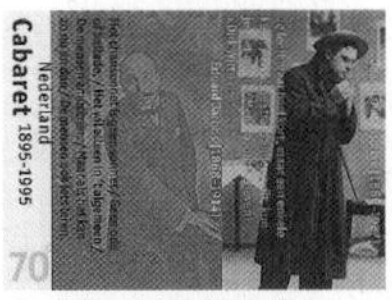

491 Eduard Jacobs and Jean-Louis Pisuisse

1995. Centenary of Dutch Cabaret. Multicoloured.

1776	70c. Type **491**	90	40
1777	80c. Wim Kan and Freek de Jonge	1·00	40

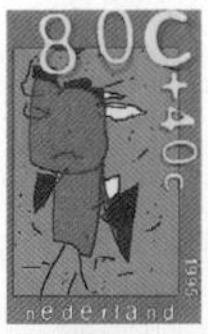

492 "The Schoolteacher" (Leonie Ensing)

1995. Child Welfare. "Children and Fantasy". Children's Computer Drawings. Multicoloured.

1778	70c.+35c. "Dino" (Sjoerd Stegeman) (horiz)	1·30	65

1779 80c.+40c. Type **492** 1·30 65
1780 100c.+50c. "Children and Colours" (Marcel Jansen) (horiz) 2·50 1·90
MS1781 144×74 mm. Nos. 1778 ×2, 1779 ×3 and 1780 9·00 8·50

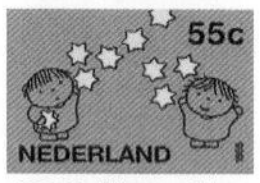

493 Children with Stars

1995. Christmas. Self-adhesive.
1782 **493** 55c. red, yellow and black 90 15
1783 - 55c. blue, yellow and black 90 15
DESIGN: No. 1783, Children looking at star through window.

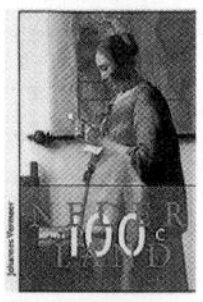

494 "Woman in Blue reading a Letter"

1996. Johannes Vermeer Exhibition, Washington and The Hague. Details of his Paintings. Mult.
1784 70c. "Lady writing a Letter with her Maid" 1·50 65
1785 80c. "The Love Letter" 1·60 40
1786 100c. Type **494** 1·90 1·80
MS1787 144×75 mm. Nos. 1784/6 5·75 5·00

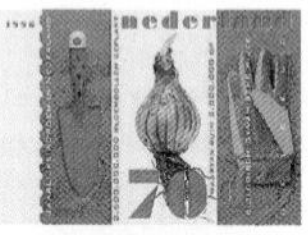

495 Trowel, Daffodil Bulb and Glove

1996. Spring Flowers. Multicoloured.
1788 70c. Type **495** 1·50 50
1789 80c. Tulips "kissing" woman 1·60 40
1790 100c. Snake's-head fritillary (detail of painting, Charles Mackintosh) 1·90 1·80
MS1791 72×50 mm. 160c. Crocuses 3·75 3·75

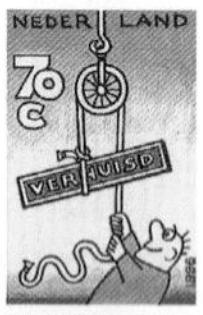

496 Putting up "MOVED" sign

1996. Change of Address Stamp.
1792 **496** 70c. multicoloured 90 50
For 80c. self-adhesive version of this design see No. 1826.

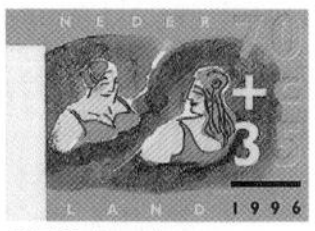

497 Swimming

1996. Cultural, Health and Social Welfare Funds. The Elderly in the Community. Multicoloured.
1793 70c.+35c. Type **497** 1·30 90
1794 80c.+40c. Grandad bottle-feeding baby 1·30 90
1795 100c.+50c. Playing piano 2·50 2·00
MS1796 144×75 mm. Nos. 1793 ×2, 1794 ×3 and 1795 10·00 10·00

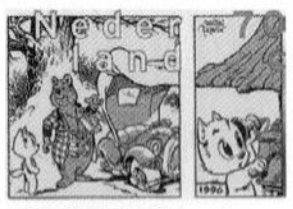

498 Beside Car

1996. Heer Bommel (cartoon character). Sheet 108×50 mm containing T 498 and similar horiz design. Multicoloured.
MS1797 70c. Type **498**; 80c. Reading letter 3·75 3·75

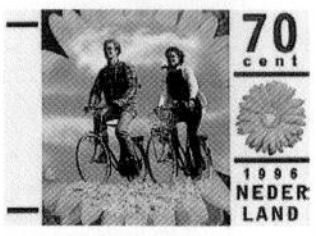

499 Cycling

1996. Tourism. Multicoloured.
1798 70c. Type **499** 1·40 40

1799 70c. Paddling in sea 1·50 65
1800 80c. Traditional architecture, Amsterdam 1·50 40
1801 100c. Windmills, Zaanse Schand Open-Air Museum 1·50 65

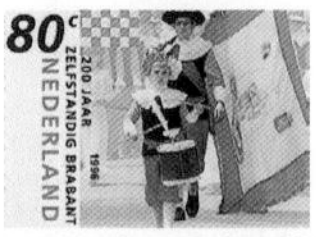

500 Parade in Traditional Costumes

1996. Bicentenary of Province of North Brabant.
1802 **500** 80c. multicoloured 1·10 40

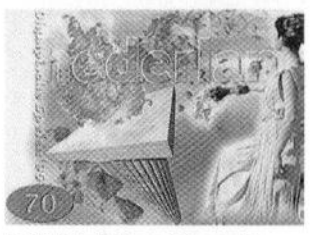

501 Lighting Olympic Torch

1996. Sporting Events. Multicoloured.
1803 70c. Type **501** (Olympic Games, Atlanta) 1·30 50
1804 80c. Flag and cyclists (Tour de France cycling championship) 1·30 40
1805 100c. Player, ball and Wembley Stadium (European Football Championship, England) 1·50 1·40
1806 160c. Olympic rings and athlete on starting block (Olympic Games, Atlanta) 2·30 1·50

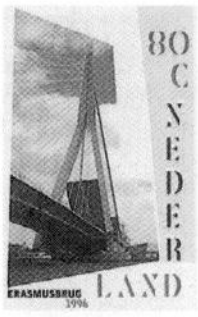

502 Erasmus Bridge

1996. Bridges and Tunnels. Multicoloured.
1807 80c. Type **502** 1·30 40
1808 80c. Wijker Tunnel (horiz) 1·30 40
1809 80c. Martinus Nijhoff Bridge (horiz) 1·30 40

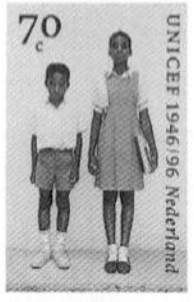

503 Children in School Uniforms

1996. 50th Anniv of UNICEF. Multicoloured.
1810 70c. Type **503** 1·10 25
1811 80c. Girl carrying platter on head 1·10 25

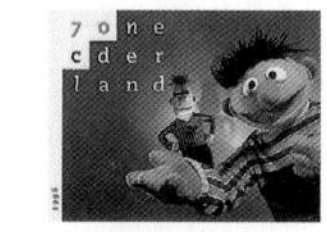

504 Bert and Ernie

1996. Sesame Street (children's television programme). Multicoloured.
1812 70c. Type **504** 1·10 40
1813 80c. Bears holding Big Bird's foot 1·00 40

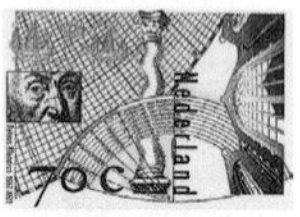

505 Petrus Plancius

1996. 16th-century Voyages of Discovery.
1814 **505** 70c. black, yellow and red 1·40 50
1815 - 80c. multicoloured 1·40 40
1816 - 80c. multicoloured 1·40 40
1817 - 100c. multicoloured 2·10 1·50
DESIGNS: No. 1815, Cornelis de Houtman; 1816, Willem Barentsz; 1817, Mahu en De Cordes.

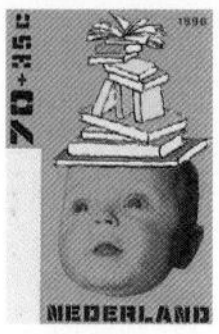

506 Books and Baby

1996. Child Welfare. Multicoloured.
1818 70c.+35c. Type **506** 1·30 65
1819 80c.+40c. Animals and boy 1·30 65
1820 80c.+40c. Tools and girl 1·30 65
MS1821 75×144 mm. Nos. 1818/20, each ×2 8·25 8·25

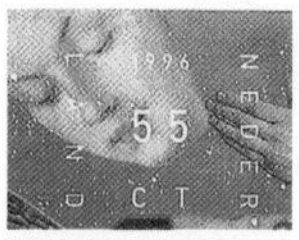

507 Woman's Face and Hand

1996. Christmas. Multicoloured. Self-adhesive.
1822 55c. Type **507** 65 25
1823 55c. Woman's eyes and man shouting 65 25
1824 55c. Bird's wing, hands and detail of man's face 65 25
1825 55c. Men's faces and bird's wing 65 25
Nos. 1822/5 were issued together, se-tenant, forming a composite design.

1997. Change of Address Stamp. Self-adhesive.
1826 **496** 80c. multicoloured 1·00 65
No. 1826 was intended for use by people moving house.

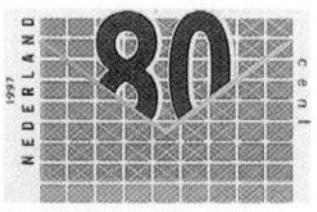

508 Numeral on Envelope with Top Flap

1997. Business Stamps. Multicoloured. Self-adhesive.
1827 80c. Type **508** 90 20
1828 160c. Numeral on envelope with side flap 1·80 20

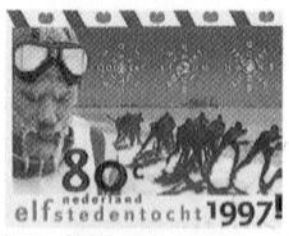

509 Skaters

1997. 15th Eleven Cities Skating Race.
1829 **509** 80c. multicoloured 1·10 40

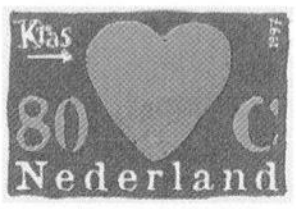

510 Heart

1997. Greetings Stamps.
1830 **510** 80c. multicoloured 90 65
The price quoted for No. 1830 is for an example with the heart intact. The heart can be scratched away to reveal different messages.

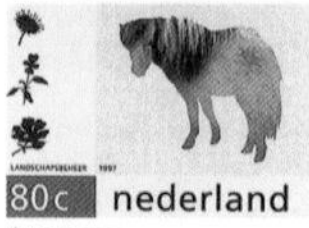

511 Pony

1997. Nature and the Environment. Multicoloured.
1831 80c. Type **511** 1·40 40
1832 100c. Cow 1·80 1·40
MS1833 72×50 mm. 160c. Sheep 3·75 3·75

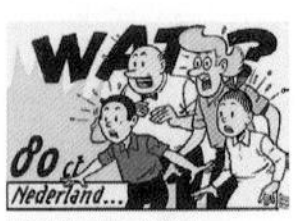

512 Suske, Wiske, Lambik and Aunt Sidonia

1997. Suske and Wiske (cartoon by Willy Vandersteen). Multicoloured.
1834 80c. Type **512** 1·00 25
MS1835 108×50 mm. 80c. Wilbur; 80c. Type **512** 5·00 4·50

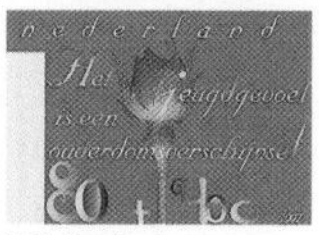

513 Rosebud

1997. Cultural, Health and Social Welfare Funds. The Elderly and their Image. Multicoloured.
1836 80c.+40c. Type **513** 1·50 1·50
1837 80c.+40c. Rose stem 1·50 1·50
1838 80c.+40c. Rose 1·50 1·50
MS1839 144×75 mm. Nos. 1836/8, each ×2 9·00 9·00

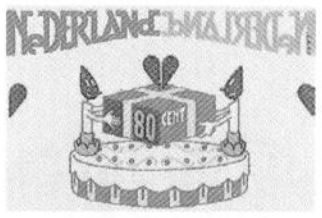

514 Birthday Cake

1997. Greetings Stamps. Multicoloured.
1840 80c. Type **514** 1·00 25
1841 80c. Cup of coffee, glasses of wine, candles, writing letter, and amaryllis 1·00 25
See also No. 1959.

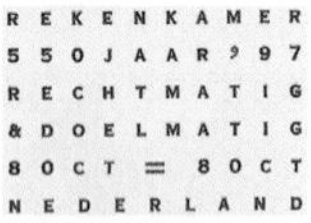

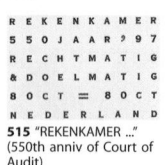

515 "REKENKAMER ..." (550th anniv of Court of Audit)

1997. Anniversaries.
1842 **515** 80c. multicoloured 1·40 40
1843 - 80c. red, yellow and black 1·40 40
1844 - 80c. red, black and blue 1·40 40
DESIGNS—50th anniv of Marshall Plan (post-war American aid for Europe): No. 1843, Map of Europe; 1844, Star and stripes.

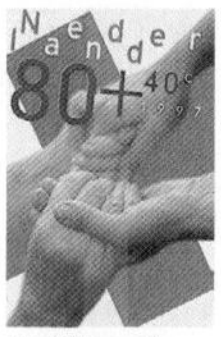

516 Clasped Hands over Red Cross

1997. Red Cross.
1845 **516** 80c.+40c. mult 1·70 1·40

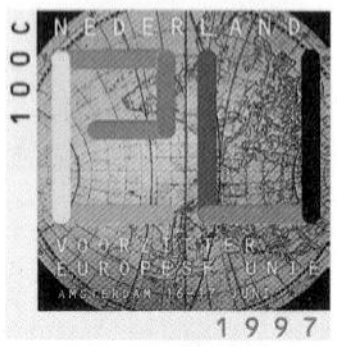

517 "eu" and Globe

1997. European Council of Ministers' Summit, Amsterdam.
1846 **517** 100c. multicoloured 1·60 1·10

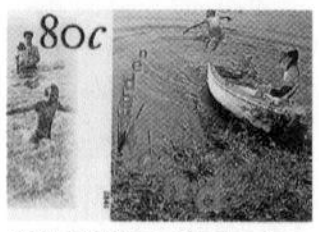

518 Children playing in Boat

1997. Water Activities. Multicoloured.
1847 80c. Type **518** 1·10 40
1848 1g. Skutsje (sailing barges) race, Friesland 1·50 1·00

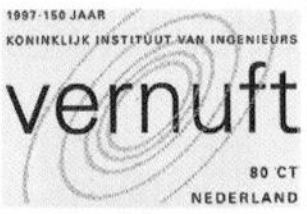

519 "vernuft"

1997. Anniversaries. Multicoloured.
1849 **519** 80c. ultramarine and blue 1·30 45
1850 - 80c. ultramarine and blue 1·30 45
1851 - 80c. multicoloured 1·30 45
1852 - 80c. multicoloured 1·30 45
DESIGNS: No. 1849, Type **519** (150th anniv of Royal Institute of Engineers); 1850, "adem" (centenary of Netherlands Asthma Centre, Davos, Switzerland); 1851, Flower (centenary of Florens College (horticultural college) and 125th anniv of Royal Botanical and Horticultural Society); 1852, Pianist accompanying singer (birth bicentenary of Franz Schubert (composer)).

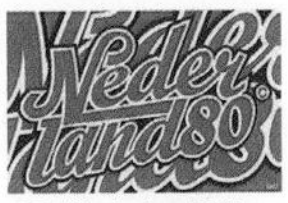
520 "Nederland80"

1997. Youth. Multicoloured.

1853	520	80c. red and blue	1·00	40
1854	-	80c. multicoloured	1·00	40

DESIGN: No. 1854, "NEDERLAND80" in style of computer games giving appearance of three-dimensional block on race track.

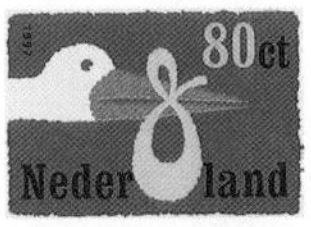

521 Stork with Bundle

1997. New Baby Stamp. Self-adhesive gum.

1855	521	80c. multicoloured	1·10	30

See also Nos. 1960, 2120 amd 2189.

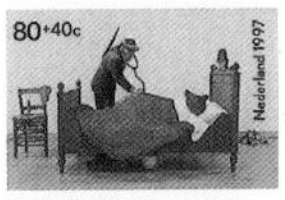

522 "Little Red Riding Hood"

1997. Child Welfare. Fairy Tales. Multicoloured.

1856	80c.+40c. Type **522**	1·50	65
1857	80c.+40c. Man laying loaves on ground ("Tom Thumb")	1·50	65
1858	80c.+40c. Woodman with bottle ("Genie in the Bottle")	1·50	65
MS1859	144×75 mm. Nos. 1856/8, each ×2	9·25	9·00

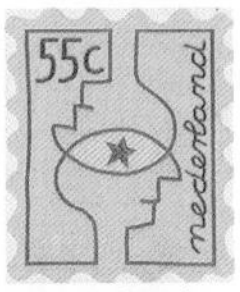

523 Heads and Star

1997. Christmas. Multicoloured, colour of background given.

1860	523	55c. yellow	75	25
1861	523	55c. blue	75	25
1862	-	55c. orange	75	25
1863	-	55c. red	75	25
1864	-	55c. green	75	25
1865	523	55c. green	75	25

DESIGN: Nos. 1862/4, Heads and heart.

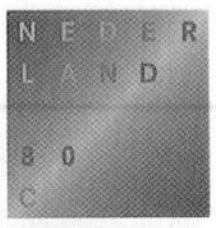

524 Light across Darkness

1998. Bereavement Stamp.

1866	524	80c. blue	1·10	25

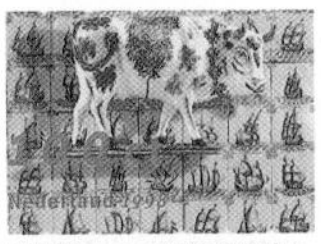
525 Cow and "Ship" Tiles

1998. Delft Faience.

1867	525	100c. multicoloured	1·30	65
1868	-	160c. blue	2·00	1·30

DESIGN: 160c. Ceramic tile showing boy standing on head.

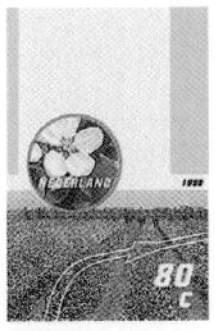

526 Strawberries in Bloom (Spring)

1998. The Four Seasons. Multicoloured.

1869	80c. Type **526**	1·30	1·30
1870	80c. Strawberry, flan and straw-berry plants (Summer)	1·30	1·30
1871	80c. Bare trees and pruning diagram (Winter)	1·30	1·30
1872	80c. Orchard and apple (Autumn)	1·30	1·30

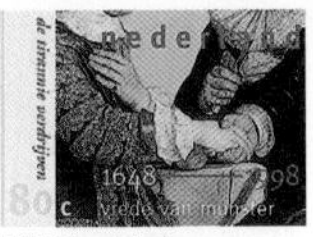
527 Handshake

1998. Anniversaries. Multicoloured.

1873	80c. Type **527** (350th anniv of Treaty of Munster)	1·00	45
1874	80c. Statue of Johan Thorbecke (politician) (150th anniv of Constitution)	1·00	45
1875	80c. Child on swing (50th anniv of Declaration of Human Rights)	1·00	45

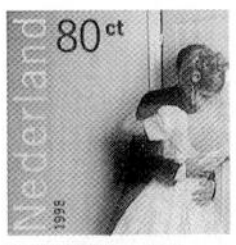

528 Bride and Groom

1998. Wedding Stamp. Self-adhesive gum.

1876	528	80c. multicoloured	1·10	25

See also No. 1961.

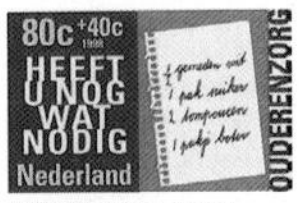

529 Shopping List

1998. Cultural, Health and Social Welfare Funds. Care and the Elderly.

1877	80c.+40c. Type **529**	1·50	1·40
1878	80c.+40c. Sweet	1·50	1·40
1879	80c.+40c. Training shoe	1·50	1·40
MS1880	144×75 mm. Nos. 1877/9, each ×2	9·00	9·00

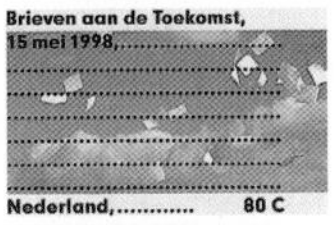

530 Letters blowing in Wind

1998. Letters to the Future.

1881	530	80c. multicoloured	1·10	35

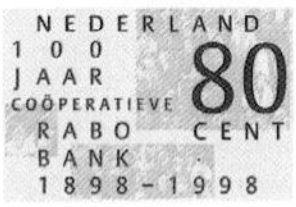

531 Customers

1998. Centenary of Rabobank.

1882	531	80c. yellow, green and blue	1·10	35

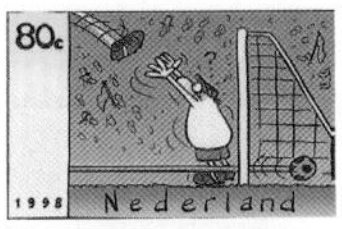

532 Goalkeeper catching Boot

1998. Sport. Multicoloured.

1883	80c. Type **532** (World Cup Foot-ball Championship, France)	1·10	35
1884	80c. Family hockey team (cen-tenary of Royal Netherlands Hockey Federation) (35×24 mm)	1·10	35

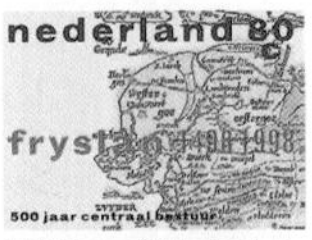

533 Map of Friesland, c. 1600

1998. 500th Anniv of Central Administration of Friesland.

1885	533	80c. multicoloured	1·10	35

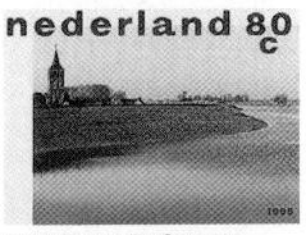

534 River Defences

1998. Bicentenary of Directorate-General of Public Works and Water Management. Multicoloured.

1886	80c. Type **534**	1·00	35
1887	1g. Sea defences	1·30	95

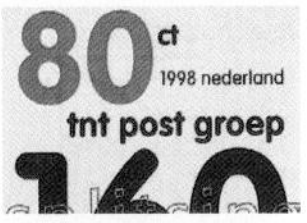

535 "tnt post groep"

1998. Separation of Royal Netherlands PTT into TNT Post Groep and KPN NV (telecommunications).

1888	535	80c. black, blue and red	1·00	55
1889	-	80c. black, blue and green	1·00	55

DESIGN: No. 1889, "kpn nv".

Nos. 1888/9 were issued together, se-tenant, forming a composite design of the complete "160".

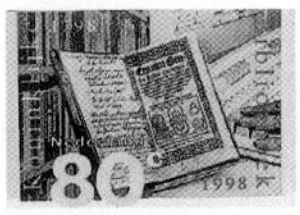

536 Books and Keyboard

1998. Cultural Anniversaries. Multicoloured.

1890	80c. Type **536** (bicentenary of National Library)	1·10	40
1891	80c. Maurits Escher (graphic artist, birth centenary) look-ing at his mural "Metamor-phose" in The Hague Post Office (vert)	1·10	50
1892	80c. Simon Vestdijk (writer, birth centenary) and page from "Fantoches" (vert)	1·10	50

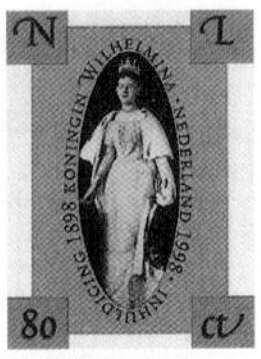

537 Queen Wilhelmina

1998. Royal Centenaries. Sheet 144×75 mm containing T 537 and similar vert design. Multicoloured.

MS1893	80c. Type **537** (coronation); 80c. Gilded Coach	4·50	3·75

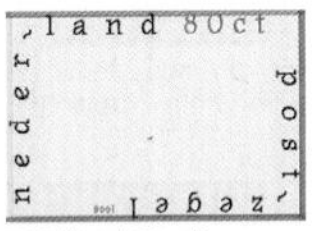

538 "land 80 ct"

1998. Greetings Stamps. Multicoloured. Self-adhesive.

1894	80c. Type **538** (top of frame red)	1·30	65
1895	80c. "80 ct post" (top of frame mauve)	1·30	65
1896	80c. Type **538** (top of frame orange)	1·30	65
1897	80c. "80 ct post" (top of frame orange)	1·30	65
1898	80c. Type **538** (top of frame yellow)	1·30	65

The part of the frame used for identification purposes is above the face value.

Nos. 1894/8 were only available in sheetlets of ten stamps and 20 labels (five stamps and ten labels on each side of the card). It was intended that the sender should insert the appropriate greetings label into the rectangular space on each stamp before use.

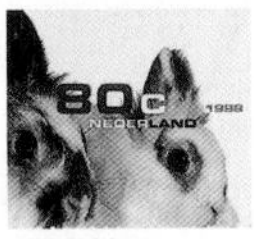

539 Rabbits

1998. Domestic Pets. Multicoloured.

1899	80c. Type **539**	1·30	50
1900	80c. Drent partridge dog	1·30	50
1901	80c. Kittens	1·30	50

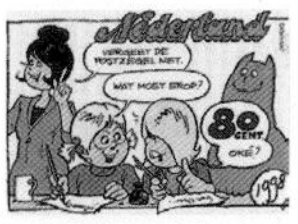

540 Cathy and Jeremy writing a Letter

1998. 25th Anniv of Jack, Jacky and the Juniors (comic strip characters).

1902	80c. Type **540**	1·10	40
MS1903	108×50 mm. 80c. Type **540**; 80c. Posting letter	4·50	3·75

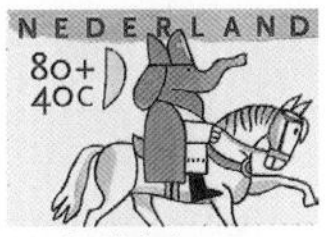

541 St. Nicholas on Horseback

1998. Child Welfare. Celebrations. Multicoloured.

1904	80c.+40c. Type **541**	1·90	65
1905	80c.+40c. Making birthday cake	1·90	65
1906	80c.+40c. Carnival parade	1·90	65
MS1907	144×75 mm. Nos. 1904/6, each ×2	11·50	9·50

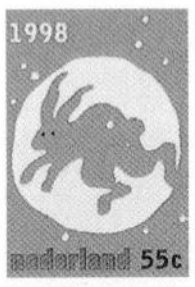

542 Hare and Snowball

1998. Christmas. Self-adhesive.

1908	542	55c. blue, red and black	75	40
1909	-	55c. multicoloured	75	40
1910	-	55c. blue, red and black	75	40
1911	-	55c. multicoloured	75	40
1912	-	55c. blue, red and black	75	40
1913	-	55c. green, blue and red	75	40
1914	-	55c. green, blue and red	75	40
1915	-	55c. green, blue and red	75	40
1916	-	55c. green, blue and red	75	40
1917	-	55c. green, blue and red	75	40
1918	-	55c. blue, green and red	75	40
1919	-	55c. red, green and black	75	40
1920	-	55c. blue, green and red	75	40
1921	-	55c. green, red and black	75	40
1922	-	55c. blue, green and red	75	40
1923	-	55c. blue, green and red	75	40
1924	-	55c. blue, green and red	75	40
1925	-	55c. blue, green and red	75	40
1926	-	55c. blue, green and red	75	40
1927	-	55c. blue, green and red	75	40

DESIGNS: No. 1909, House and snowball; 1910, Dove and snowball; 1911, Christmas tree and snowball; 1912, Reindeer and snowball; 1913, Hare; 1914, House; 1915, Dove; 1916, Christmas tree; 1917, Reindeer; 1918, House and hare; 1919, House and heart; 1920, Dove and house; 1921, Christmas tree and house; 1922, House and rein-deer; 1923, Christmas tree and hare; 1924, Christmas tree and house; 1925, Christmas tree and dove; 1926, Christ-mas tree and heart; 1927, Christmas tree and reindeer.

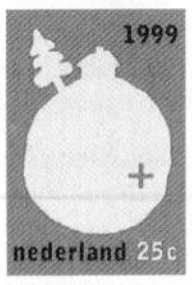

543 House and Tree on Snowball

1999. Make-up Rate Stamp.

1928	543	25c. red and black	40	25

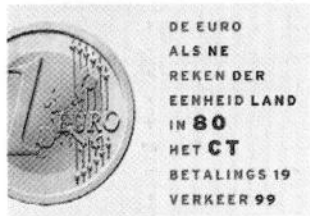

544 Euro Coin

1999. Introduction of the Euro (European currency).

1929	544	80c. multicoloured	1·10	80

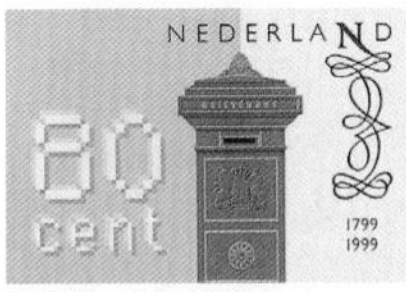

545 Pillar Box, 1850

1999. Bicentenary of Netherlands Postal Service.

1930	545	80c. multicoloured	1·30	1·00

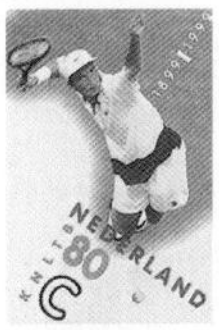

546 Richard Krajicek serving

1999. Centenary of Royal Dutch Lawn Tennis Federation.

1931	546	80c. multicoloured	1·00	40

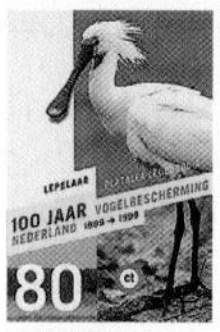

547 White Spoonbill

1999. Protection of Bird and Migrating Waterfowl. Multicoloured.

1932	80c. Type **547** (centenary of Dutch Bird Protection Society)	1·00	40
1933	80c. Section of globe and arctic terns (African–Eurasian Waterbird Agreement)	1·00	40

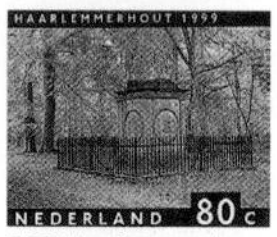

548 Haarlemmerhout in Autumn

1999. Parks during the Seasons. Multicoloured.

1934	80c. Type **548**	1·30	1·40
1935	80c. Sonsbeek in winter	1·30	1·40
1936	80c. Weerribben in summer	1·30	1·40
1937	80c. Keukenhof in spring	1·30	1·40

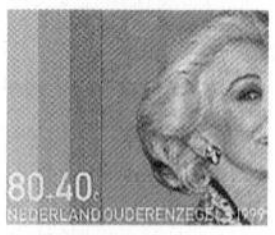

549 Woman

1999. Cultural, Health and Social Welfare Funds. International Year of the Elderly. Multicoloured.

1938	80c.+40c. Type **549**	1·90	1·90
1939	80c.+40c. Man (green background)	1·90	1·90
1940	80c.+40c. Man (blue background)	1·90	1·90
MS1941	144×75 mm. Nos. 1938/40, each ×2	11·50	11·50

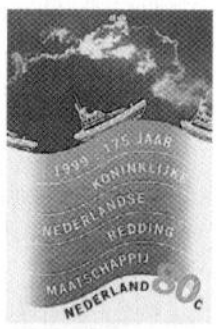

550 Lifeboats on Rough Sea

1999. Water Anniversaries. Multicoloured.

1942	80c. Type **550** (175th Anniv of Royal Netherlands Lifeboat Association)	1·00	40
1943	80c. Freighters in canal (150th Anniv of Royal Association of Ships' Masters "Schuttevaer")	1·00	40

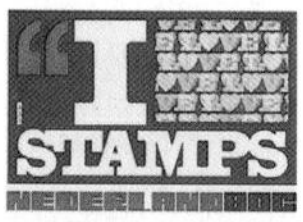

551 "I Love Stamps"

1999

1944	**551**	80c. blue and red	1·00	25
1945	-	80c. red and blue	1·50	1·30

DESIGN: No. 1945, "Stamps love Me".

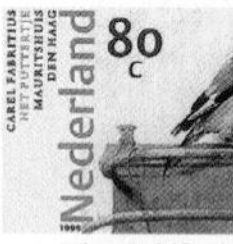

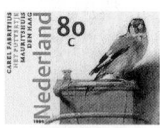

552 "The Goldfinch" (Carel Fabritius)

1999. 17th-century Dutch Art. Multicoloured. Self-adhesive gum (1g.).

1946	80c. Type **552**	1·30	1·20
1947	80c. "Self-portrait" (Rembrandt)	1·30	1·20
1948	80c. "Self-portrait" (Judith Leyster)	1·30	1·20
1949	80c. "St. Sebastian" (Hendrick ter Brugghen)	1·30	1·20
1950	80c. "Beware of Luxury" (Jan Steen)	1·30	1·20
1951	80c. "The Sick Child" (Gabriel Metsu)	1·30	1·20
1952	80c. "Gooseberries" (Adriaen Coorte)	1·30	1·20
1953	80c. "View of Haarlem" (Jacob van Ruisdael)	1·30	1·20
1954	80c. "Mariaplaats, Utrecht" (Pieter Saenredam)	1·30	1·20
1955	80c. "Danae" (Rembrandt)	1·30	1·20
1956	1g. "The Jewish Bride" (Rembrandt)	1·30	1·20

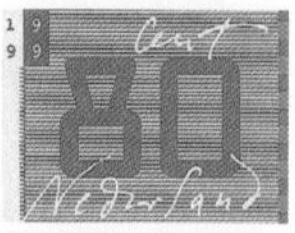

553 "80" on Computer Screen

1999. Ordinary or self-adhesive gum.

1957	**553**	80c. multicoloured	1·10	30

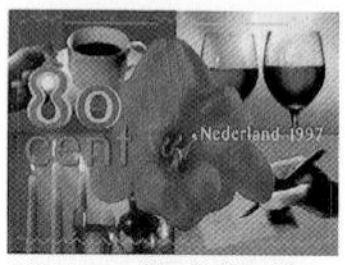

554 Amaryllis, Coffee Cup, Candles, Letter Writing and Wine Glasses

1999. Greetings Stamp. Self-adhesive.

1959	**554**	80c. multicoloured	1·10	30

1999. New Baby Stamp. As No. 1855 but ordinary gum.

1960	**521**	80c. multicoloured	1·30	40

1999. Wedding Stamp. As No. 1876 but ordinary gum.

1961	**528**	80c. multicoloured	1·30	40

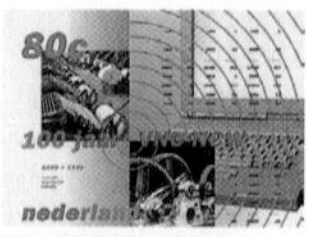

555 Victorian Heavy Machinery and Modern Computer

1999. Centenary of Confederation of Netherlands Industry and Employers.

1962	**555**	80c. multicoloured	1·10	35

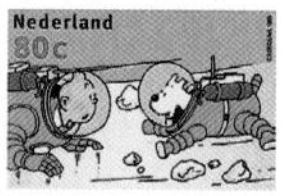

556 Tintin and Snowy wearing Space Suits

1999. 70th Anniv of Tintin (comic strip character by Herge). Scenes from "Explorers on the Moon". Multicoloured.

1963	80c. Type **556**	1·30	30
MS1964	108×50 mm. 80c. Tintin, Snowy and Captain Haddock in moon buggy; 80c. Type **556**	5·25	5·00

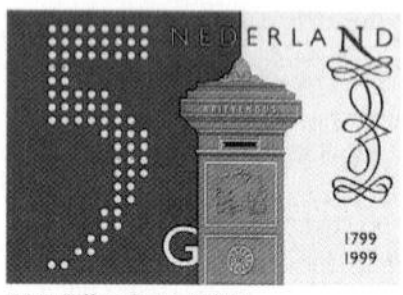

557 Pillar Box, 1850

1999. Bicentenary of Netherlands Postal Service (2nd issue). Sheet 144×75 mm.

MS1965	**557** 5g. red, black and blue	6·50	6·50

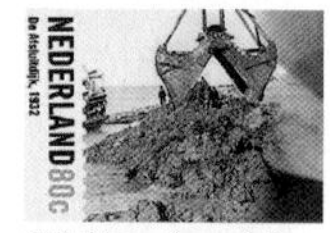

558 Digger (completion of Afsluitdijk, 1932)

1999. The Twentieth Century. Multicoloured.

1966	80c. Type **558**	1·70	1·40
1967	80c. Space satellite	1·70	1·40
1968	80c. Berlage Commodity Exchange, Amsterdam (inauguration, 1903)	1·70	1·40
1969	80c. Empty motorway (car-free Sundays during oil crisis, 1973–74)	1·70	1·40
1970	80c. Old man (Old Age Pensions Act, 1947)	1·70	1·40
1971	80c. Delta Flood Project, 1953–97	1·70	1·40
1972	80c. Players celebrating (victory of Netherlands in European Cup Football Championship, 1998)	1·70	1·40
1973	80c. Four riders on one motor cycle (liberation and end of Second World War, 1945)	1·70	1·40
1974	80c. Woman posting vote (Women's Franchise, 1919)	1·70	1·40
1975	80c. Ice skaters (eleven cities race)	1·70	1·40

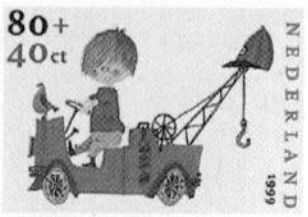

559 Pluk van de Pettevlet on Fire Engine

1999. Child Welfare. Characters created by Fiep Westendorp. Multicoloured.

1976	80c.+40c. Type **559**	1·90	75
1977	80c.+40c. Otje drinking through straw	1·90	75
1978	80c.+40c. Jip and Janneke with cat	1·90	75
MS1979	144×75 mm. Nos. 1976/8, each ×2	11·50	9·50

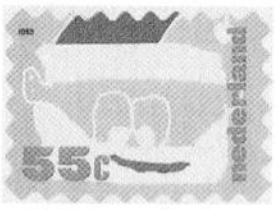

560 Father Christmas (Robin Knegt)

1999. Christmas. Winning entries in design competition. Multicoloured.

1980	55c. Type **560**	75	30
1981	55c. Angel singing (Davinia Bovenlander) (vert)	75	30
1982	55c. Dutch doughnuts in box (Henk Drenth)	75	30
1983	55c. Moon wearing Christmas hat (Lizet van den Berg) (vert)	75	30
1984	55c. Father Christmas carrying sacks (Noortje Kruse)	75	30
1985	55c. Clock striking midnight (Hucky de Haas) (vert)	75	30
1986	55c. Ice skater (Marleen Bos)	75	30
1987	55c. Human Christmas tree (Mariette Strik) (vert)	75	30
1988	55c. Woman wearing Christmas tree earrings (Saskia van Oversteeg)	75	30
1989	55c. Woman vacuuming pine needles (Frans Koenis) (vert)	75	30
1990	55c. Angel with harp and music score (Evelyn de Zeeuw)	75	30
1991	55c. Hand balancing candle, star, hot drink, hat and Christmas tree on fingers (Aafke van Ewijk) (vert)	75	30
1992	55c. Christmas tree (Daan Roepman) (vert)	75	30
1993	55c. Cat wearing crown (Sjoerd van der Zee) (vert)	75	30
1994	55c. Bird flying over house (Barbara Vollers)	75	30
1995	55c. Baby with angel wings (Rosmarijn Schmink) (vert)	75	30
1996	55c. Dog wearing Christmas hat (Casper Heijstek and Mirjam Cnosser)	75	30
1997	55c. Angel flying (Patricia van der Neut) (vert)	75	30
1998	55c. Nativity (Marco Cockx)	75	30
1999	55c. Christmas tree with decorations (Matthias Meiling) (vert)	75	30

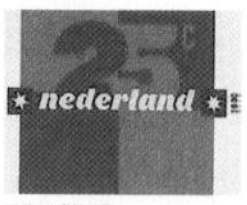

561 "25"

2000. Make-up Rate Stamp.

2000	**561**	25c. red, blue and yellow	30	25

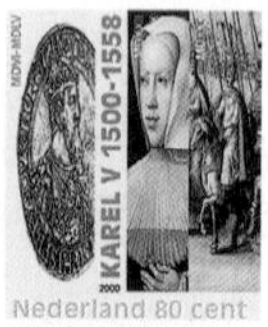

562 1 Guilder Coin, Margaret of Austria (Regent of Netherlands) (after Bernard van Orley) and "Coronation of Charles V" (Juan de la Coate)

2000. 500th Birth Anniv of Charles V, Holy Roman Emperor. Multicoloured.

2001	80c. Type **562**	1·40	1·20
2002	80c. Map of the Seventeen Provinces, "Charles V after the Battle of Muehlberg" (Titian) and Margaret of Parma (Regent of Netherlands) (after Antonius Mohr)	1·40	1·20

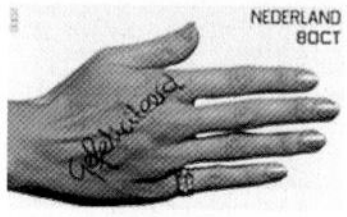

563 "Gefeliciteerd" ("Congratulations")

2000. Greetings stamps. Showing greetings messages on hands. Multicoloured.

2003	80c. Type **563**	1·20	1·10
2004	80c. "Succes met je nieuwe baan" ("Good luck with your new job")	1·20	1·10
2005	80c. "gefeliciteerd met je huis" ("Congratulations on your new home")	1·20	1·10
2006	80c. "PROFICIAT" ("Congratulations")	1·20	1·10
2007	80c. "Succes" ("Hope you have success")	1·20	1·10
2008	80c. "Veel geluk samen" ("Good luck together")	1·20	1·10
2009	80c. "Proficiat met je diploma" ("Congratulations on passing your exam")	1·20	1·10
2010	80c. "Geluk" ("Good luck")	1·20	1·10
2011	80c. "Van Harte" ("Cordially")	1·20	1·10
2012	80c. "GEFELICITEERD MET JE RUBEWIUS!" ("Congratulations on passing your driving test!")	1·20	1·10

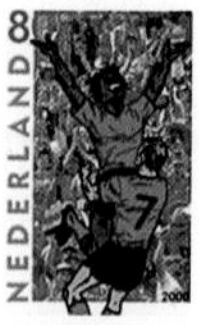

564 Players celebrating

2000. European Football Championship, Netherlands and Belgium. Multicoloured.

2013	80c. Type **564**	95	40
2014	80c. Football	1·20	95

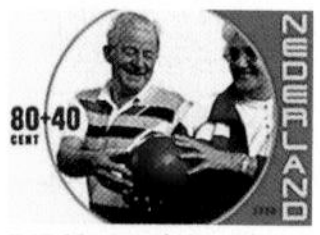

565 Man and Woman passing Ball

2000. Cultural, Health and Social Welfare Funds. Senior Citizens. Multicoloured.

2015	80c.+40c. Type **565**	1·90	1·60
2016	80c.+40c. Woman picking apples	1·90	1·60
2017	80c.+40c. Woman wearing swimming costume	1·90	1·60
MS2018	144×74 mm. Nos. 2015/17, each ×2	11·50	9·50

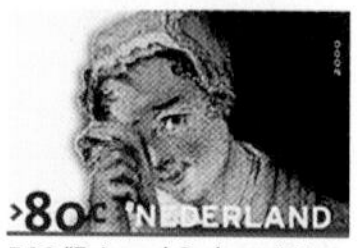

566 "Feigned Sadness" (C. Troost)

2000. Bicentenary of the Rijksmuseum, Amsterdam. Multicoloured. (a) Ordinary gum.

2019	80c. Type **566**	1·40	1·30
2020	80c. "Harlequin and Columbine" (porcelain figurine) (J. J. Kandler)	1·40	1·30
2021	80c. "Ichikawa Ebizo IV" (woodcut) (T. Sharaku)	1·40	1·30
2022	80c. "Heavenly Beauty" (sandstone sculpture)	1·40	1·30
2023	80c. "St. Vitus" (wood sculpture)	1·40	1·30
2024	80c. "Woman in Turkish Costume" (J. E. Liotard)	1·40	1·30
2025	80c. "J. van Speyk" (J. Schoemaker Doyer)	1·40	1·30
2026	80c. "King Saul" (engraving) (L. van Leyden)	1·40	1·30
2027	80c. "L'Amour Menacant" (marble sculpture) (E. M. Falconet)	1·40	1·30
2028	80c. "Sunday" (photograph) (C. Ariens)	1·40	1·30

(b) Self-adhesive.

2029	100c. "The Nightwatch" (Rembrandt)	1·70	1·30

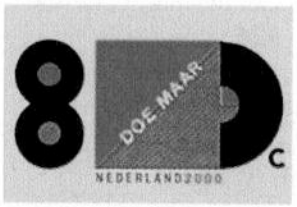

567 "80" and "Doe Maar" Record Cover

2000. Doe Maar (Dutch pop group). Multicoloured.

2030	80c. Type **567**	1·00	40
2031	80c. "80" and song titles	1·50	1·30

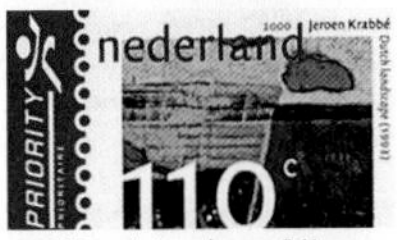

568 "Dutch Landscape" (Jeroen Krabb)

2000. Priority Mail. Contemporary Art. Self-adhesive.

2033	**568**	110c. multicoloured	1·90	1·60

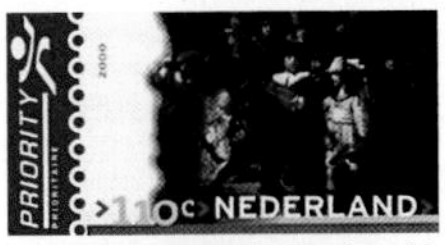

569 "The Nightwatch" (Rembrandt)

2000. Priority Mail. Self-adhesive.

2034	**569**	110c. multicoloured	1·90	1·60

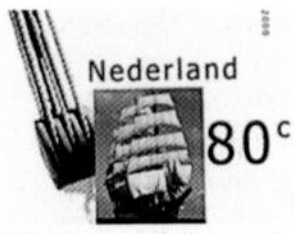

570 *Libertad* (full-rigged cadet ship)

2000. "Sail Amsterdam 2000". Sailing Ships. Multicoloured.

2036	80c. Type **570**	1·40	1·30
2037	80c. *Amerigo Vespucci* (cadet ship) and figurehead	1·40	1·30
2038	80c. *Dar Mlodziezy* (full-rigged cadet ship) and sail	1·40	1·30
2039	80c. *Europa* (cadet ship) and wheel	1·40	1·30
2040	80c. *Kruzenshtern* (cadet barque) and bell	1·40	1·30
2041	80c. *Sagres II* (cadet barque) and sail	1·40	1·30
2042	80c. *Alexander von Humboldt* (barque) and sail	1·40	1·30
2043	80c. *Sedov* (cadet barque) and sailors dropping sail	1·40	1·30
2044	80c. *Mir* (square-rigged training ship)	1·40	1·30
2045	80c. *Oosterschelde* (schooner) and rope	1·40	1·30

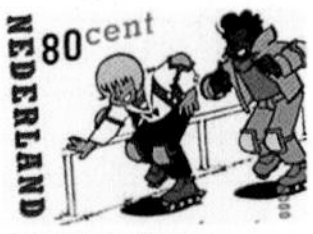

571 Roller Skating

2000. Sjors and Sjimmie (comic strip characters by Frans Piet). Multicoloured.

2046	80c. Type **571**	1·40	1·10
2047	80c. In car	1·40	1·10
MS2048	108×50 mm. 80c. As No. 2049; 80c. As No. 2047	4·50	3·75
2049	80c. Listening to radio	1·40	1·10
2050	80c. Swinging on rope	1·40	1·10

2000. Bereavement Stamp. As No. 1866 but self-adhesive.

2051	**524**	80c. blue	1·30	65

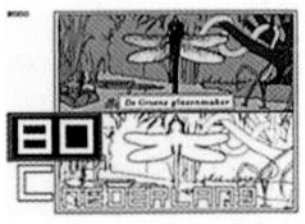

572 Green Dragonfly

2000. Endangered Species. Multicoloured.

2052	80c. Type **572**	1·10	30
2053	80c. Weather loach	1·30	95

573 Canal Boat

2000. 150th Anniv (2002) of Netherlands Stamps (1st issue). Sheet 108×50 mm containing T 573 and similar horiz design. Multicoloured.

MS2054	80c. Type **573**; 80c. Mail carriage	3·25	2·50

See also Nos. **MS**2138 and **MS**2250.

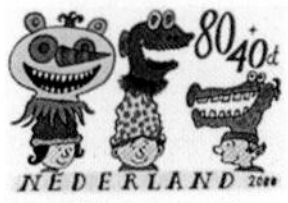

574 Children wearing Monster Hats

2000. Child Welfare. Multicoloured. (a) Self-adhesive gum.

2055	80c.+40c. Type **574**	2·20	2·20
2056	80c.+40c. Boy sailing bath-tub	2·20	2·20
2057	80c.+40c. Children brewing magical stew	2·20	2·20

(b) Ordinary gum.

MS2058	80c.+40c. Type **574**; 80c.+40c. Ghostly games; 80c.+40c. Girl riding crocodile; 80c.+40c. As No. 2056; 80c.+40c. As No. 2057; 80c.+40c. Children playing dragon	9·75	8·75

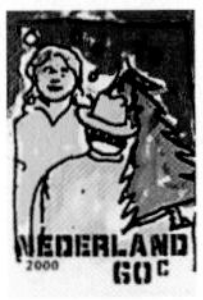

575 Couple with Christmas Tree

2000. Christmas. Multicoloured.

2059	60c. Type **575**	95	30
2060	60c. Children making snow balls	95	30
2061	60c. Couple dancing	95	30
2062	60c. Man playing French horn	95	30
2063	60c. Man carrying Christmas tree	95	30
2064	60c. Man carrying young child	95	30
2065	60c. Woman reading book	95	30
2066	60c. Couple kissing	95	30
2067	60c. Man playing piano	95	30
2068	60c. Woman watching from window	95	30
2069	60c. Woman sitting in chair	95	30
2070	60c. Man sitting beside fire	95	30
2071	60c. Snowman flying	95	30
2072	60c. Couple in street	95	30
2073	60c. Child playing violin	95	30
2074	60c. Children on sledge	95	30
2075	60c. Man writing letter	95	30
2076	60c. Woman carrying plate of food	95	30
2077	60c. Family	95	30
2078	60c. Woman sleeping	95	30

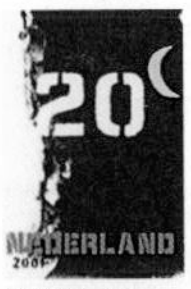

576 Moon

2001. Make-up Rate Stamp.

2079	**576**	20c. multicoloured	30	25

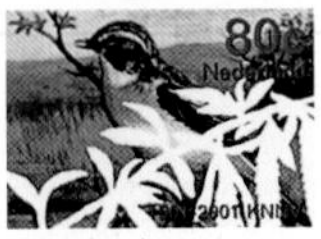

577 Whinchat

2001. Centenary of Royal Dutch Nature Society. Multicoloured.

2080	80c. Type **577**	1·20	1·10
2081	80c. Family in rowing boat	1·60	1·10
2082	80c. Fox	1·20	1·10
2083	80c. Couple bird watching	1·60	1·10
2084	80c. Flowers	1·20	1·10

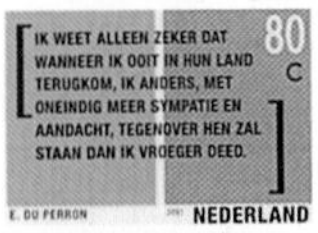

578 Poem (by E. du Perron)

2001. "Between Two Cultures". National Book Week. Multicoloured.

2085	80c. Type **578**	1·20	1·20
2086	80c. Men in street	1·20	1·20
2087	80c. Poem (by Hafid Bouazza)	1·20	1·20
2088	80c. Woman and young men	1·20	1·20
2089	80c. Poem (by Adriaan van Dis)	1·20	1·20
2090	80c. Profiles of two women	1·20	1·20
2091	80c. Poem (by Kader Abdolah)	1·20	1·20
2092	80c. Two young girls	1·20	1·20
2093	80c. Poem (by Ellen Ombre)	1·20	1·20
2094	80c. Boy carrying map	1·20	1·20

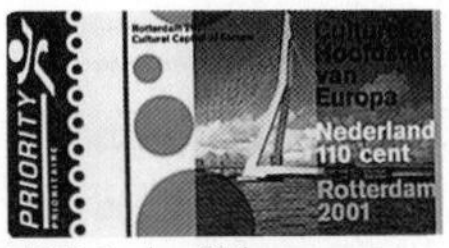

579 Rotterdam Bridge

2001. Priority Mail. Rotterdam, European City of Culture. Self-adhesive gum.

2095	**579**	110c. multicoloured	1·80	1·30

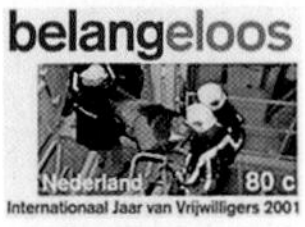

580 Emergency Rescuers

2001. International Year of Volunteers. Sheet 108×50 mm. containing Type 580 and similar horiz design. Multicoloured.

MS2096	80c. Type 508, 80c. Animal rescuers	3·25	3·25

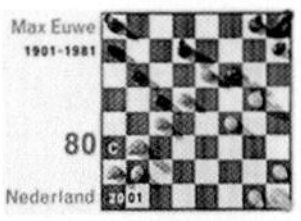

581 Chess Board

2001. Birth Centenary of Machgielis "Professor Max" Euwe (chess player). Sheet 108×50 mm containing T 581 and similar horiz design. Multicoloured.

MS2097	80c. Type **581**; 80c. Euwe and chess pieces	3·25	3·25

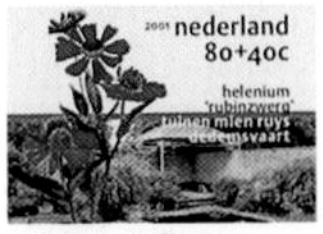

582 Helen's Flower (*Helenium rubinzwerg*)

2001. Flowers. Multicoloured. (a) Self-adhesive gum.

2098	80c.+40c. Type **582**	2·75	2·75
2099	80c.+40c. Russian hollyhock (*Alcea rugosa*)	2·75	2·75
2100	80c.+40c. Persian cornflower (*Centaurea dealbata*)	2·75	2·75

(b) Ordinary gum.

MS2101	144×75 mm. 80c.+40c. *Caryopteris* "Heavenly Blue"; 80c.+40c. Type **582**; 80c.+40c. As No. 2099; 80c.+40c. Spurge (*Euphorbia schillingii*); 80c.+40c. As No. 2100; 80c.+40c. Hooker inula (*Inula hookeri*)	11·50	9·50

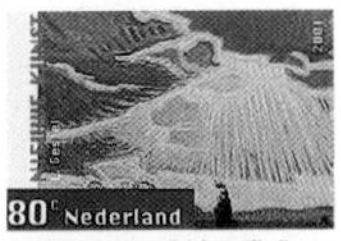

583 "Autumn" (detail) (L. Gestel)

2001. Art Nouveau. Multicoloured.

2102	80c. Type **583**	1·30	1·30
2103	80c. Book cover by C. Lebeau for *De Stille Kracht*	1·30	1·30
2104	80c. Burcht Federal Council Hall, Amsterdam (R. N. Roland Holst and H. P. Berlage)	1·30	1·30
2105	80c. "O Grave Where is Thy Victory" (painting) (J. Throop)	1·30	1·30
2106	80c. Vases by C. J. van der Hoef from Amphora factory	1·30	1·30
2107	80c. Capital from staircase of Utrecht building (J. Mendes da Costa)	1·30	1·30
2108	80c. Illustration of common peafowl from *The Happy Owls* (T. van Hoytema)	1·30	1·30
2109	80c. "The Bride" (detail) (painting) (J. Thorn Prikker)	1·30	1·30
2110	80c. Factory-printed cotton fabric (M. Duco Crop)	1·30	1·30
2111	80c. Dentz van Schaik room (L. Zyl)	1·30	1·30

2001. As T 428 but with face value expressed in euros and cents. Self-adhesive gum.

2112	85c. blue	1·40	25

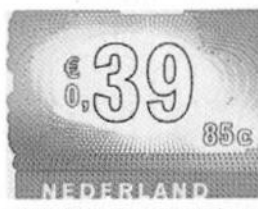

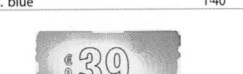

584 Sky and Landscape

2001. Self-adhesive gum.

2113	**584**	85c. multicoloured	1·40	45

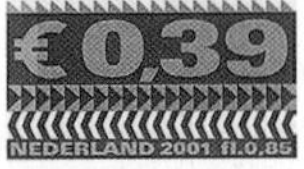

585 Arrows

2001. Business Coil Stamp. Self-adhesive gum.

2114	**585**	85c. purple and silver	1·10	25

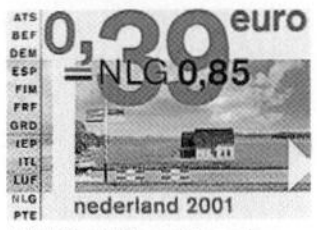

586 Reclaimed Land

2001. Multicoloured. Self-adhesive gum.

2115	85c. Type **586** (postage)	1·40	40
2116	1g.20 Beach (priority mail)	1·90	1·40
2117	1g.65 Town and canal	2·50	2·10

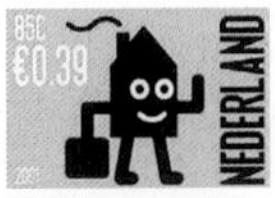

587 House carrying Suitcase

2001. Greetings Stamps. Self-adhesive gum.

2118	**587**	85c. black and yellow	1·30	1·10
2119	-	85c. red, yellow and gold	1·30	95
2120	-	85c. multicoloured	1·40	1·10
2121	-	85c. multicoloured	2·10	1·30

DESIGNS: No. 2118, Type **587** (change of address stamp); 2119, Couple (wedding stamp); 2120, As Type **521** (new baby); 2121, As Type **524** (bereavement stamp).

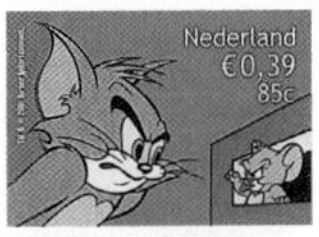

588 Tom and Jerry

2001. Cartoon Characters. Multicoloured.

2122	85c. Type **588**	1·30	1·30
2123	85c. Fred Flintstone and Barney Rubble	1·30	1·30
2124	85c. Johnny Bravo	1·30	1·30
2125	85c. Dexter posting letter	1·30	1·30
2126	85c. Powerpuff Girls	1·30	1·30

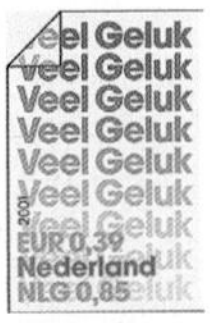

589 "Veel Geluk" ("Good Luck")

2001. Greetings Stamps. Multicoloured. Self-adhesive gum.

2127	85c. Type **589**	1·40	1·30
2128	85c. "Gefeliciteerd!" ("Congratulations!")	1·40	1·30
2129	85c. "Veel Geluk" with envelope flap (horiz)	1·40	1·30
2130	85c. "Gefeliciteerd!" with envelope flap (horiz)	1·40	1·30
2131	85c. "Proficiat" ("Congratulations")	1·40	1·30
2132	85c. "Succes !" ("Success")	1·40	1·30
2133	85c. "Van Harte ..." ("Cordially ...")	1·40	1·30
2134	85c. "Proficiat" with envelope flap (horiz)	1·40	1·30
2135	85c. "Succes !" with envelope flap (horiz)	1·40	1·30
2136	85c. "Van Harte ..." with envelope flap (horiz)	1·40	1·30

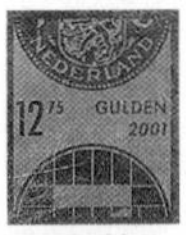

590 Guilder Coins

2001. Replacement of the Guilder. Self-adhesive.

2137	**590**	12g.75 silver	18·00	14·50

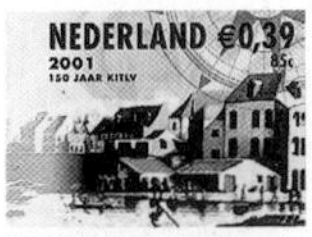

591 Waaigat Canal and Williamstad, Curacao (J. E. Heemskerk after G. C. W. Voorduin)

2001. 150th Annivs of Netherlands Stamps (2002) (2nd issue) and of Royal Institute foe Linguistics and Anthropology. Sheet 108×50 mm containing T 591 and similar horiz design. Multicoloured.

MS2138	39c. Type **591**; 39c. Pangka sugar refinery, Java (J.C. Grieve after A. Salm)	3·25	2·50

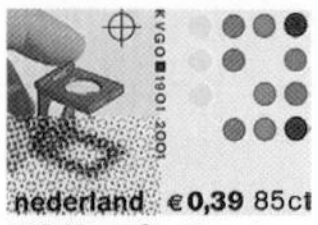

592 Magnifier, Target Mark and Dots

2001. Centenary of Royal Dutch Printers' Association. Sheet 108×50 mm containing T 592 and similar horiz design. Multicoloured.

MS2139 39c. Type **592**; 39c. Magnifier, computer zoom symbol and colour palette	3·25	2·50

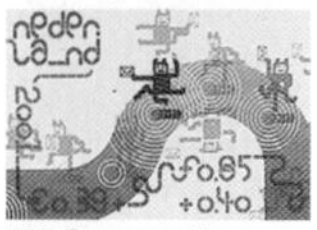

593 Computer Figure and River

2001. Child Welfare. Multicoloured. (a) Self-adhesive gum.

2140	85c.+40c. Type **593**	3·25	2·75

(b) Ordinary gum.

MS2141 146×76 mm. 85c.+40c. Figure and printer; 85c.+40c. Road, car and figure; 85c.+40c. Post box, blocks and droplets; 85c.+40c. Post box, figure and stairs; 85c.+40c. Type **593**; 85c.+40c. Figure swinging on rope and log in river	11·50	9·50

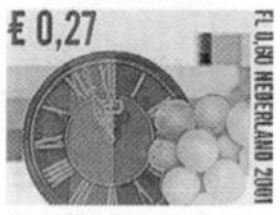

594 Clock and Grapes

2001. Christmas. Multicoloured. Self-adhesive gum.

2142	27c. Type **594**	75	25
2143	27c. Stars and bun	75	25
2144	27c. Steeple and buns	75	25
2145	27c. Cherub and coins	75	25
2146	27c. Champagne bottle	75	25
2147	27c. Wreath around chimney	75	25
2148	27c. Tower	75	25
2149	27c. Christmas tree bauble	75	25
2150	27c. Playing card with Christmas tree as sign	75	25
2151	27c. Cake seen through window	75	25
2152	27c. Decorated Christmas tree	75	25
2153	27c. Father Christmas	75	25
2154	27c. Sign displaying hot drink	75	25
2155	27c. Candles seen through window	75	25
2156	27c. Illuminated roof-tops	75	25
2157	27c. Reindeer	75	25
2158	27c. Snowman	75	25
2159	27c. Parcel	75	25
2160	27c. Bonfire	75	25
2161	27c. Children on toboggan	75	25

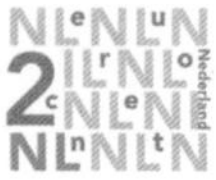

595 "12"

2002. Make-up Rate Stamp. (a) Self-adhesive gum.

2162	**595**	2c. red	5·00	15
2166	**595**	12c. green	40	25

(b) Ordinary gum.

2169	2c. red	15	15
2170	3c. agate	15	15
2171	5c. mauve	15	15
2172	10c. blue	15	15

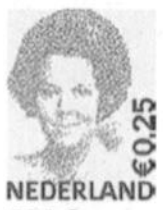

596 Queen Beatrix

2002. Queen Beatrix. Self-adhesive gum

2175	**596**	25c. brown and green	65	30
2176	**596**	39c. blue and pink	1·10	25
2177	**596**	40c. blue and brown	1·10	65
2177b	**596**	44c. rose and olive	1·10	75
2178	**596**	50c. pink and green	1·30	65
2179	**596**	55c. mauve and brown	2·50	1·40
2180	**596**	57c. blue and purple	2·50	1·90
2180b	**596**	61c. violet and brown	2·75	1·90
2181	**596**	65c. green and violet	2·75	1·40
2181b	**596**	67c. rose and olive	2·75	2·20
2181b	**596**	88c. violet and green	2·10	1·30
2182	**596**	70c. deep green and green	2·75	2·10
2183	**596**	72c. ochre and blue	3·00	2·20
2183a	**596**	76c. ochre and green	16·00	90
2184	**596**	78c. blue and brown	1·90	30
2184a	**596**	80c. blue and purple	10·00	40
2185	**596**	€1 green and blue	2·50	65
2187	**596**	€3 mauve and green	7·50	1·30

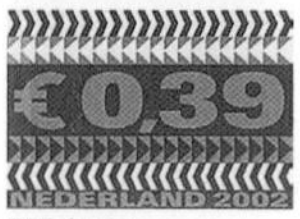

597 Arrows

2002. Business Coil Stamps. Self-adhesive gum.

2195	**597**	39c. purple and silver	95	25
2196	**597**	78c. blue and gold	1·90	45

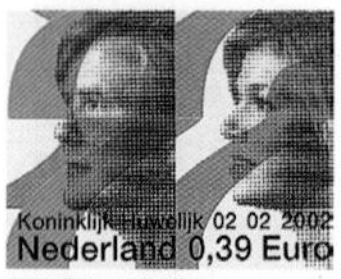

598 Prince Willem-Alexander and Máxima Zorreguieta

2002. Marriage of Prince Willem-Alexander and Maxima Zorreguieta. Sheet 145×75 mm, containing T 598 and similar horiz design.

MS2197 **598** 39c. black, silver and orange; 39c. multicoloured	3·25	3·25

DESIGN: 39c. "Willem-Alexander Maxima" and "222".

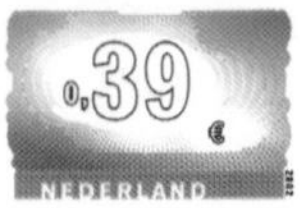

599 Sky and Landscape

2002. Self-adhesive gum.

2198	**599**	39c. multicoloured	95	25

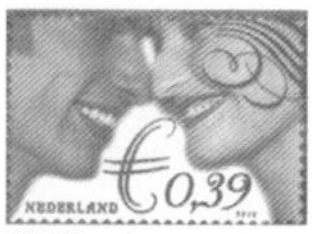

600 Couple

2002. Greetings Stamps. Face values in euros. Self-adhesive gum.

2199	-	39c. black and yellow	1·10	30
2200	**600**	39c. red, yelow and gold	1·00	30
2201	-	39c. multicoloured	1·00	30
2202	-	39c. blue	1·00	30

DESIGNS: No. 2199, As Type **587** (change of address stamp); 2200, Type **600** (wedding stamp); 2201, As Type **521** (new baby); 2202, As Type **524** (bereavement stamp).

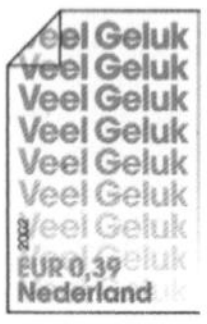

601 "Veel Geluk" ("Good Luck")

2001. Greetings Stamps. Face values in euros. Multicoloured. Self-adhesive gum.

2203	39c. Type **601**	1·30	95
2204	39c. "Gefeliciteerd!" ("Congratulations!")	1·30	95
2205	39c. "Veel Geluk" ("Good Luck") (horiz)	1·30	95
2206	39c. "Gefeliciteerd!" with envelope flap (horiz)	1·30	95
2207	39c. "Proficiat" ("Congratulations")	1·30	95
2208	39c. "Succes !" ("Success")	1·30	95
2209	39c. "Van Harte..." ("Cordially ...")	1·30	95
2210	39c. "Proficiat" with envelope flap (horiz)	1·30	95
2211	39c. "Succes !" with envelope flap (horiz)	1·30	95
2212	39c. "Van Harte..." with envelope flap (horiz)	1·30	95

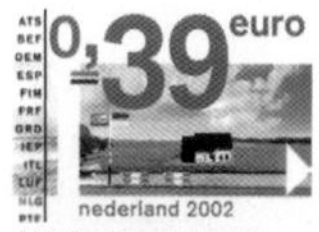

602 Reclaimed Land

2002. Landscapes. Face values in euros. Multicoloured. Self-adhesive gum.

2213	39c. Type **603** (postage)	95	25
2214	54c. Beach (priority mail)	1·40	90
2215	75c. Town and canal	1·80	1·30

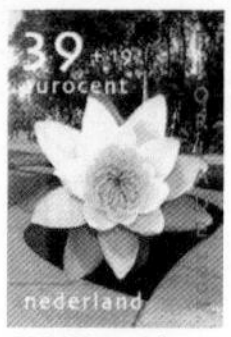

603 Water Lily

2002. "Floriade 2002" International Horticultural Exhibition, Harlemmermeer. Flowers. Multicoloured.

2216	39c. + 19c. Type **603**	1·40	1·10
2217	39c. + 19c. Dahlia	1·40	1·10
2218	39c. + 19c. Japanese cherry blossom	1·40	1·10
2219	39c. + 19c. Rose	1·40	1·10
2220	39c. + 19c. Orchid	1·40	1·10
2221	39c. + 19c. Tulip	1·40	1·10

Nos. 2216/21 were printed on paper impregnated with perfume which was released when the stamps were scratched.

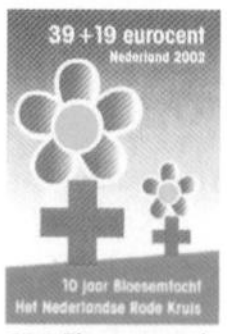

604 Flowers and Red Crosses

2002. Red Cross. 10th Annual Blossom Walk.

2222	**604**	39c. + 19c. multicoloured	1·50	1·40

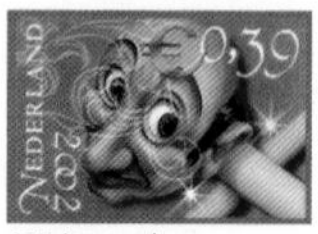

605 Langnek

2002. 50th Anniv of Efteling Theme Park. Multicoloured. Self-adhesive gum.

2223	39c. Type **605**	1·10	55
2224	39c. Pardoes de Tovernar	1·10	55
2225	39c. Droomvlucht Elfje	1·10	55
2226	39c. Kleine Boodschap	1·10	55
2227	39c. Holle Bolle Gijs	1·10	55

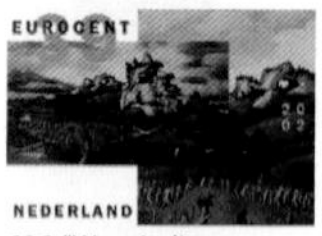

606 "West Indies Landscape" (Jan Mostaert)

2002. Landscape Paintings. Showing paintings and enlarged detail in foreground. Multicoloured.

2228	39c. Type **606**	1·10	1·00
2229	39c. "Riverbank with Cows" (Aelbert Cuyp)	1·10	1·00
2230	39c. "Cornfield" (Jacob van Ruisdael)	1·10	1·00
2231	39c. "Avenue at Middelharnis" (Meindert Hobbema)	1·10	1·00
2232	39c. "Italian Landscape with Umbrella Pines" (Hendrik Voogd)	1·10	1·00
2233	39c. "Landscape in Normandy" (Andreas Schelfhout)	1·10	1·00
2234	39c. "Landscape with Waterway" (Jan Toorop)	1·10	1·00
2235	39c. "Landscape" (Jan Sluijters)	1·10	1·00
2236	39c. "Kismet" (Michael Raedecker)	1·10	1·00
2237	39c. "Untitled" (Robert Zandvliet)	1·10	1·00

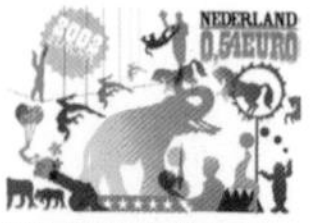

607 Circus Performers

2002. Priority Mail. Europa. Circus. Multicoloured.

2238	54c. Type **607**	1·90	1·30
2239	54c. Lions and Big Top	1·90	1·30

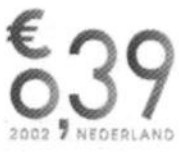

608 Circles

2002. Business Coil Stamp. Self-adhesive gum.

2240	**608**	39c. deep blue, blue and red	1·00	25
2241	**608**	78c. green, light green and red	2·00	25

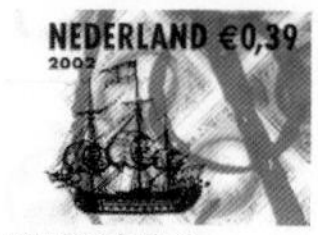

609 Dutch East Indiaman and 1852 Stamps

2002. 150th Anniv of Netherlands Stamps. 400th Anniv of Dutch East India Company (V. O. C.). Sheet 108×50 mm, containing T 609 and similar horiz design. Multicoloured.

MS2250 39c. Type **609**; 39c. Two Dutch East Indiamen and and stamps of 1852	3·25	3·25

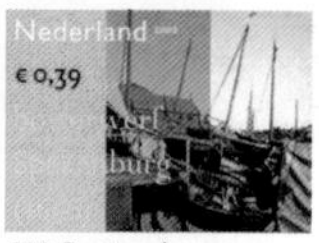

610 Boatyard, Spakenburg

2002. Industrial Heritage. Multicoloured.

2251	39c. Type **610**	1·10	1·10
2252	39c. Limekiln, Dedemsvaart	1·10	1·10
2253	39c. Steam-driven pumping station, Cruquius	1·10	1·10
2254	39c. Mine-shaft winding gear, Heerlen	1·10	1·10
2255	39c. Salt drilling tower, Hengelo	1·10	1·10
2256	39c. Windmill, Weidum	1·10	1·10
2257	39c. Brick-works, Zevenaar	1·10	1·10
2258	39c. "Drie Hoefijzers" brewery, Breda	1·10	1·10
2259	39c. Water-treatment plant, Tilburg	1·10	1·10
2260	39c. "Nodding-donkey" oil pump, Schoonebeck	1·10	1·10

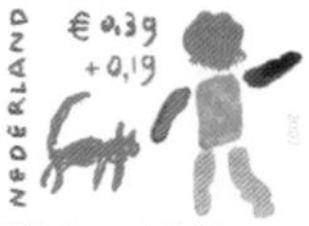

611 Cat and Child

2002. Child Welfare. Sheet 147×76 mm, containing T 611 and similar horiz designs. Multicoloured.

MS2261 Type **611**, 39c.+19c. Blue figure and upper part of child with green head; 39c.+19c. Child and ball; 39c.+19c. Child with yellow head and raised arms; 39c.+19c. Child with brown head and left arm raised; 39c.+19c. Dog and child	10·00	8·75

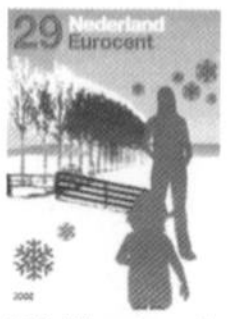

612 Woman and Child

2002. Christmas. Multicoloured. Self-adhesive gum.

2262	29c. Type **612**	75	55
2263	29c. Seated man facing left	75	55
2264	29c. Profile with raised collar	75	55
2265	29c. Stream and figure wearing scarf	75	55
2266	29c. Woman, tree and snowflakes	75	55
2267	29c. Snowflakes and man wearing knee-length coat beside grasses	75	55
2268	29c. Snowflakes, man, and gate and stream	75	55
2269	29c. Snowflakes, windmill, stream and woman	75	55
2270	29c. Seated man facing right	75	55
2271	29c. Willow tree and profile of child facing left	75	55
2272	29c. Man leaning against tree	75	55
2273	29c. Man with hands in pockets	75	55
2274	29c. Seated couple	75	55
2275	29c. Fir tree and man's profile facing left	75	55
2276	29c. Man carrying child on shoulders	75	55
2277	29c. Profile of boy facing right	75	55
2278	29c. Standing child facing left	75	55
2279	29c. Snowflakes, sea and upper part of man with raised collar	75	55
2280	29c. Sea behind man wearing hat and glasses	75	55
2281	29c. Figure with out-stretched arms	75	55

Nos. 2262/81 were issued together, se-tenant, the stamps arranged in strips of five, each strip forming a composite design.

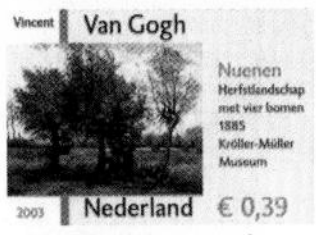

613 "Landscape with Four Trees"

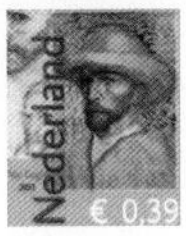

614 "Self-portrait with Straw Hat"

2003. 150th Birth Anniv of Vincent Van Gogh (artist). Multicoloured. (a) Ordinary gum.

2282	39c. Type **613**	1·20	1·10
2283	39c. "The Potato Eaters"	1·20	1·10
2284	39c. "Four Cut Sunflowers"	1·20	1·10
2285	39c. "Self-portrait with Grey Felt Hat"	1·20	1·10
2286	39c. "The Zouave"	1·20	1·10
2287	39c. "Place Du Forum Cafe Terrace by Night, Arles"	1·20	1·10
2288	39c. "Tree Trunks in Long Grass"	1·20	1·10
2289	39c. "Almond Blossom"	1·20	1·10
2290	39c. "Auvers-sur-Oise"	1·20	1·10
2291	39c. "Wheatfield with Crows, Auvers-sur-Oise"	1·20	1·10

(b) Self-adhesive gum.

2292	39c. Type **614**	1·10	75
2293	59c. "Vase with Sunflowers"	1·40	1·10
2294	75c. "The Sower"	2·10	1·60

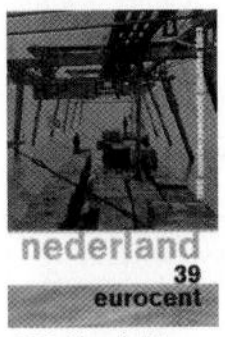

615 North Pier, Ijmuiden

2003. 50th Anniv of Floods in Zeeland, North Brabant and South Holland. Designs showing photographs from national archives. Each grey and black.

2295	39c. Type **615**	1·10	1·10
2296	39c. Hansweert Lock	1·10	1·10
2297	39c. Building dam, Wieringermeer	1·10	1·10
2298	39c. Ijsselmeer Dam	1·10	1·10
2299	39c. Breached dyke, Willemstad	1·10	1·10
2300	39c. Repairing dyke, Stavenisse	1·10	1·10
2301	39c. Building dam, Zandkreek	1·10	1·10
2302	39c. Building dam, Grevelingen	1·10	1·10
2303	39c. Flood barrier, Oosterschelde	1·10	1·10
2304	39c. Floods, Roermond	1·10	1·10

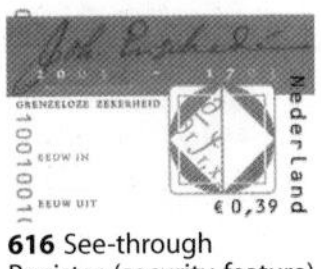

616 See-through Register (security feature)

2003. 300th Anniv of Joh. Enschede (printers). Multicoloured.

2305	39c. Type **616**	1·00	70
2306	39c. Fleischman's musical notation	1·00	70

No. 2305 has the remaining symbols of the see-through register printed on the back over the gum. This forms a complete design when held up to the light.

No. 2305 was embossed with a notional barcode and No. 2306 with a security device.

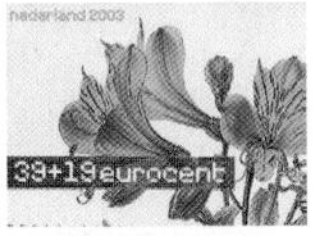

617 Alstroemeria

2003. Flower Paintings. Multicoloured.

2307	39c.+19c. Type **617**	1·20	95
2308	39c.+19c. Sweet pea	1·20	95
2309	39c.+19c. Pansies	1·20	95
2310	39c.+19c. Trumpet vine	1·20	95
2311	39c.+19c. Lychnis	1·20	95
2312	39c.+19c. Irises	1·20	95

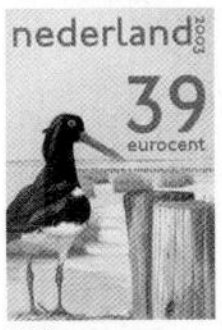

618 Oystercatcher

2003. Fauna of the Dutch Shallows. Winning Entry in Stamp Design Competition. Multicoloured.

MS2313	Two sheets, each 140×82 mm. (a) 39c. ×4, Type **618**; Spoonbill (horiz); Eider duck: Grey seal (horiz) (b) 59c. ×4, Herring gull; Curlew (horiz); Seals and gull; Crab (horiz)	4·75	4·75

MS2313 (b) were issued with "PRIORITY/Prioritaire" label attached at either upper or lower edge.

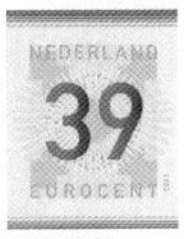

619 "39"

2003. Greetings Stamps. Two sheets, each 122×170 mm, containing T 619 and similar vert designs. Multicoloured.

MS2314	(a) 39c. ×10, Type **619** (blue) (green) (purple) (pink) (orange) (yellow) (olive) (turquoise) (red) (brown); (b) 39c. ×10, Flowers; Flag; Present; Champagne glass; Medal; Guitar; Balloons; Cut-out figures; Slice of cake; Garland	6·00	6·00

Nos. **MS**2314a/b were each issued with a se-tenant label attached at left showing either Marjolein Bastin (artist); Paint tubes and splashes (painting, Marjolein Bastin); Humberto Tan (television presenter); Figures symbolising Red Cross; Daphne Deckers (presenter and actress); Fanmail; Prime Minister Jan Balkenende; Palm top computer; Sien Diels (Sesame Street presenter); Tommie (character from Sesame Street) (**MS**2314a) or a girl (**MS**2314b). The labels could be personalised by the addition of a photograph for an inclusive fee of €12 for the first sheet and €5.95 for subsequent sheets bearing the same design.

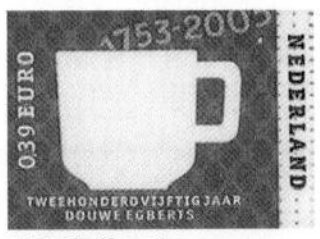

620 Coffee Cup

2003. 250th Anniv of Douwe Egberts (coffee and tea retailers). Multicoloured.

2315	39c. Type **620**	95	35
2316	39c. As No. 2315 but with colours reversed	95	35

Nos. 2315/16 were impregnated with the scent of coffee which was released when the stamps were rubbed.

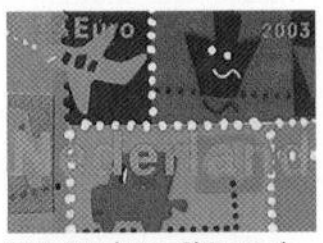

621 Airplane, Ship and Trucks

2003. Land, Air and Water. Winning Entry in Stamp Design Competition. Multicoloured.

2317	39c. Type **621**	95	35
2318	39c. Cat, bird, fish and envelope	95	35

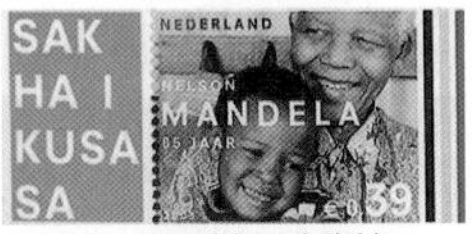

622 Nelson Mandela and Child

2003. 85th Birth Anniv of Nelson Mandela (President of South Africa). Multicoloured.

2319	39c. Type **622**	95	35
2320	39c. Children (Nelson Mandela's Children's Fund)	95	35

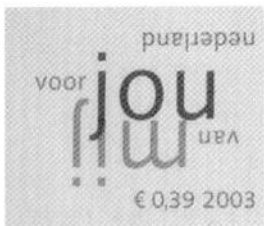

623 "For You from Me"

2003. Self-adhesive gum.

2321	**623** 39c. multicoloured	95	35

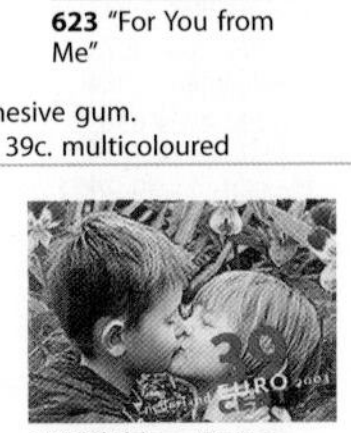

624 Children Kissing

2003. Winning Entries in Stamp Design Competition. Sheet 108×151 mm containing T 624 and similar horiz designs. Multicoloured.

MS2322	39c. ×10, Type **624**; Traditional costume; Cat; Puppies; Child; Bride and groom; 2CV cars; Motorcycle; Peacock butterfly; Flowers	13·50	12·00

625 "39"

2003. Company Stamp. Self-adhesive.

2323	**625** 39c. multicoloured	1·20	1·20

626 Coloured Squares

2003. Stamp Day. 75th Anniv of Netherlands Association of Stamp Dealers (NVPH).

2324	**626** 39c. multicoloured	95	60

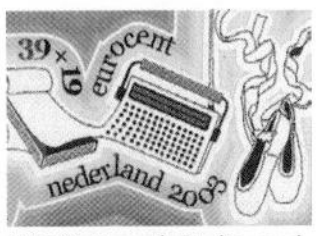

627 Notepad, Radio and Ballet Shoes

2003. Child Welfare. Sheet 147×76 mm containing T 627 and similar horiz designs. Multicoloured.

MS2325	39c.+19c. ×6, Type **627**; Masks and open book; Microphone, music notation and paint brush; Violin, pencil, football and television; Drum and light bulbs; Trumpet, light bulbs, hat and earphones	8·50	8·50

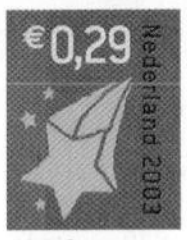

628 Star

2003. Greetings Stamp.

2326	**628** 29c. multicoloured	75	65

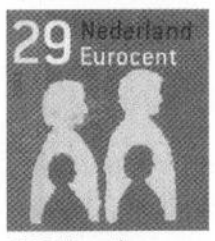

629 Family

2003. Christmas. Multicoloured. Self-adhesive.

2327	29c. Type **629**	75	40
2328	29c. Parcel	75	40
2329	29c. Cat and dog	75	40
2330	29c. Tree	75	40
2331	29c. Hands holding glasses	75	40
2332	29c. Bell	75	40
2333	29c. Hand holding pen	75	40
2334	29c. Stag's head	75	40
2335	29c. Hand holding toy windmill	75	40
2336	29c. Holly leaf	75	40
2337	29c. Candle flame	75	40
2338	29c. Star	75	40
2339	29c. Couple	75	40
2340	29c. Snowman	75	40
2341	29c. Fireplace and fire	75	40
2342	29c. Angel	75	40
2343	29c. Couple dancing	75	40
2344	29c. Round bauble	75	40
2345	29c. Mother and child	75	40
2346	29c. Pointed bauble	75	40

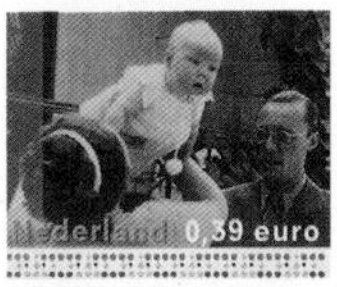

630 Queen Beatrix as Baby

2003. The Royal Family. Queen Beatrix. Sheet 123×168 mm containing T 630 and similar horiz designs. Multicoloured.

MS2347	39c.×10, Type **630**; Sitting on swing as small child; As young girl leading pony; Reading magazine; With Claus von Amsberg on their engagement; Holding baby Prince Willem-Alexander; Royal family when young; Queen Beatrix and Prince Claus dancing; Prince Willem-Alexander, Prince Johan Friso, Prince Claus, Queen Beatrix and Prince Constantijn, Queen Beatrix viewing painting in art gallery	9·00	9·00

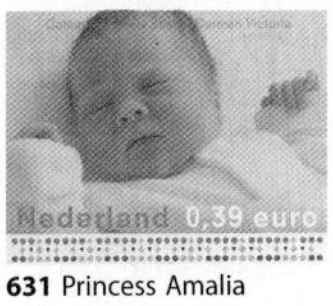

631 Princess Amalia

2003. Birth of Princess Amalia of Netherlands. Sheet 104×71 mm.

MS2348	39c. multicoloured	90	90

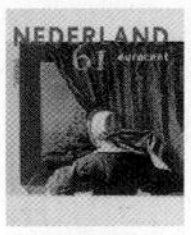

632 "Woman Reading a Letter" (Gabriel Metsu) (detail)

2004. Art. Multicoloured. Self-adhesive.

2349	61c. Type **632**	1·50	55
2350	77c. "The Love Letter" (Jan Vermeer) (detail)	1·80	1·00

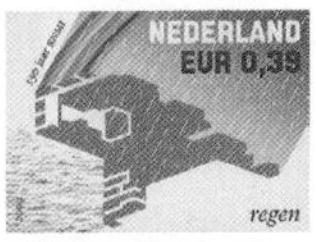

633 Water, Buildings and Rainbow

2004. 150th Anniv of Royal Netherlands Meteorological Institute (KNMI). Multicoloured.

2351	39c. Type **633**	90	55
2352	39c. Water, buildings and rainbow (different)	90	55

Nos. 2351/2 were issued together, se-tenant, forming a composite design.

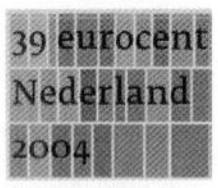

634 Patchwork

2004. Business Stamp. Self-adhesive.

2353	**634** 39c. multicoloured	1·00	25
2354	**634** 78c. multicoloured	2·00	40

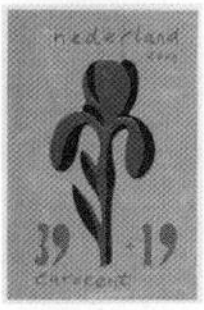

635 Iris

2004. Flower Paintings. Multicoloured.

2355	39c.+19c. Type **635**	1·30	90
2356	39c.+19c. Lily	1·30	90
2357	39c.+19c. Poppy	1·30	90
2358	39c.+19c. Tulips	1·30	90
2359	39c.+19c. Orange flower	1·30	90
2360	39c.+19c. Thistle	1·30	90

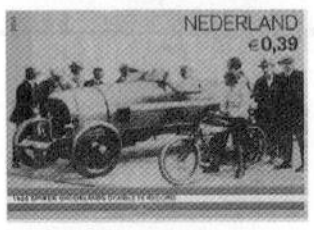

636 Spiker C4 (1922)

2004. 50th Anniv of Dutch Youth Philately Association.

2361	**636** 39c. multicoloured	1·00	75
2362	- 39c. orange and black	1·00	75

DESIGNS: No. 2361, Type **636**; 2362, Spiker C8 Double12 R (2003).

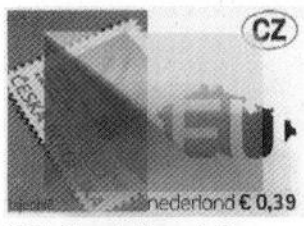

637 Czech Republic Flag, Stamp, Map and Country Identification Code

2004. Enlargement of European Union. Sheet 108×150 mm containing T 637 and similar horiz designs showing the flag, stamp, map and country identification code of the new member states. Multicoloured.

MS2363	39c. ×10, Type **637**; Lithuania; Estonia; Poland; Malta; Hungary. Latvia; Slovakia; Cyprus; Slovenia	10·00	10·00

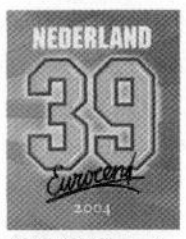

638 "39" and Rays

2004. Greetings Stamp.

2364	**638** 39c. multicoloured	1·00	90

2004. Company Stamp. Self-adhesive.

2365	**625** 39c. multicoloured	1·50	1·50

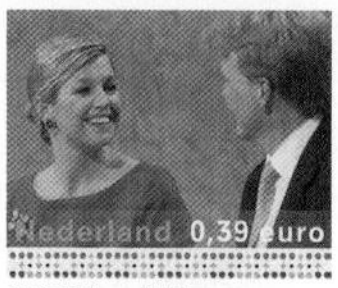

639 Prince Willem-Alexander and Máxima Zorreguieta on their Engagement

2004. The Royal Family. Prince Willem-Alexander. Sheet 123×168 mm containing T 639 and similar horiz designs. Multicoloured.

MS2366	39c. ×10, Type **639**; Máxima Zorreguieta showing engagement ring; Facing each other on their wedding day; Facing left; Kissing; Princess Maxima leaning towards Prince Willem-Alexander; Royal couple with Princess Amalia; With Princess Amalia and reading book; Princess Maxima holding Princess Amalia at christening font; At font Princess Amalia looking upwards	9·25	9·25

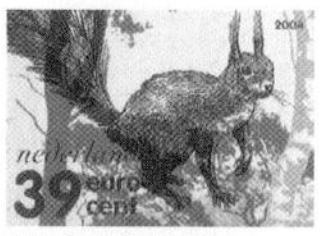

640 Red Squirrel

2004. Veluwe Nature Reserve. Two sheets, each 144×81 mm containing T 640 and similar horiz designs. Multicoloured.

MS2367	(a) 39c. ×4, Type **640**; Hoopoe; Deer; Wild boar (b) 61c. ×4, Fox; Woodpecker; Stag and hind; Mouflon sheep	13·00	13·00

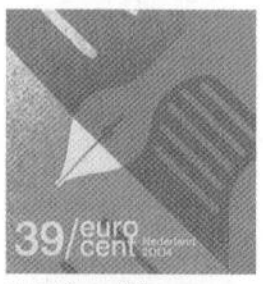

641 Pen Nib

2004. Greetings Stamps. Sheet 144×75 mm containing T 641 and similar square designs.

MS2368	39c. light orange and orange; 39c. multicoloured; 39c. blue and red	3·00	3·00

DESIGNS: 39c.Type **641**; 39c. Hand; 39c. Profiles.

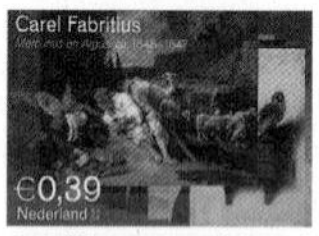

642 "Mercury and Argus"

2004. 350th Death Anniv of Carel Fabritius (artist). Paintings. Multicoloured.

2369	39c. Type **642**	1·00	90
2370	39c. "Self Portrait" (wearing large hat)	1·00	90
2371	39c. "Mercury and Aglauros"	1·00	90
2372	39c. "Abraham de Potter"	1·00	90
2373	39c. "Hagar and the Angel"	1·00	90
2374	39c. "The Sentry"	1·00	90
2375	78c. "Hera"	1·60	1·40
2376	78c. "Self Portrait" (wearing small-brimmed hat)	1·60	1·40
2377	78c. "Self Portrait" (hatless)	1·60	1·40
2378	78c. "The Goldfinch"	1·60	1·40

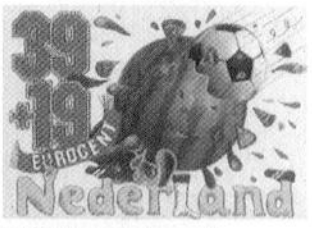

643 Pumpkin and Football

2004. Child Welfare. 80th Anniv of Foundation for Children's Welfare Stamps. Sheet 144×75 mm containing T 643 and similar horiz designs. Multicoloured.

MS2379	39c.+19c.×6, Type **643**; Lemon skipping; Orange cycling; Pear skateboarding; Banana doing sit-ups; Strawberry weightlifting	8·25	8·25

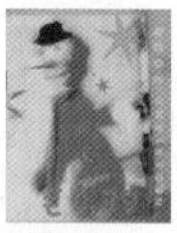

644 Snowman

2004. Greetings Stamp.

2380	**644** 29c. multicoloured	90	70

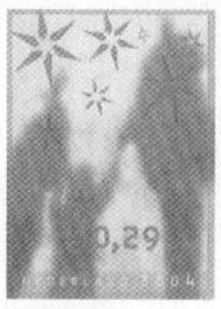

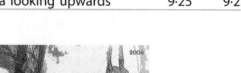

645 Family as Shadows

2004. Christmas. Multicoloured.

2381	29c. Type **645**	90	70
2382	29c. Girls holding parcels	90	70
2383	29c. Girl and dog	90	70
2384	29c. Two children	90	70
2385	29c. Sheep	90	70
2386	29c. Two polar bears	90	70
2387	29c. Children making snowman	90	70
2388	29c. Couple pulling tree	90	70
2389	29c. Couple swimming	90	70
2390	29c. Three people wearing fur hats	90	70

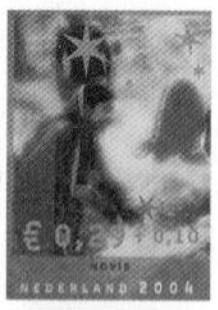

646 Woman (NOVIB)

2004. Christmas. Charity Stamps. Multicoloured. Self-adhesive.

2401	29c.+10c. Type **646**	1·30	1·10
2402	29c.+10c. Children (Stop AIDS Now)	1·30	1·10
2403	29c.+10c. Deer (Natuurmonumenten)	1·30	1·10
2404	29c.+10c. Two boys (KWF Kankerbestrijding)	1·30	1·10
2405	29c.+10c. Girl holding baby (UNICEF)	1·30	1·10
2406	29c.+10c. Two boys writing (Plan Nederland)	1·30	1·10
2407	29c.+10c. Bauble containing mother and child (Tros Helpt)	1·30	1·10
2408	29c.+10c. Canoeist and snow covered mountains (Greenpeace)	1·30	1·10
2409	29c.+10c. Woman and child (Artsen Zonder Grenzen)	1·30	1·10
2410	29c.+10c. Girl feeding toddler (World Food Programme)	1·30	1·10

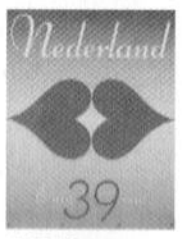

647 Two Hearts

2005. Greetings Stamp. Self-adhesive.

2411	**647** 39c. multicoloured	1·10	90

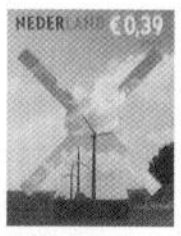

648 Traditional and Modern Windmills

2005. Dutch Buildings. Multicoloured. Self-adhesive gum.

2412	39c. Type **648**	1·10	90
2413	65c. Canal-side house and modern housing	1·70	1·50
2414	81c. Farmhouse and greenhouse	2·10	1·80

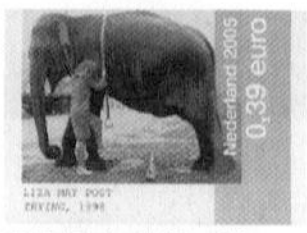

651 "Trying" (Liza May Post)

2005. Art. Multicoloured.

2415	39c. Type **651**	1·00	85
2416	39c. "Emilie" (Sidi el Karchi)	1·00	85
2417	39c. "ZT" (Koen Vermeule)	1·00	85
2418	39c. "Het Bedrijf" (Atelier van Lieshout)	1·00	85
2419	39c. "Me kissing Vinoodh" (Inez van Lamsweerde)	1·00	85
2420	39c. "Lena" (Carla van de Puttelaar)	1·00	85
2421	39c. "NR. 13" (Tom Claassen)	1·00	85
2422	39c. "Zonder Titel" (Pieter Kusters)	1·00	85
2423	39c. "Witte Roos" (Ed van der Kooy)	1·00	85
2424	39c. "Portrait of a Boy" (Tiong Ang)	1·00	85

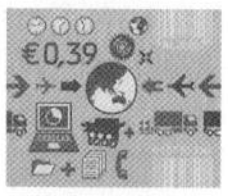

652 Symbols of Industry

2005. Business Stamps. Entrepreneur Week. Self-adhesive.

2425	**652** 39c. multicoloured	1·50	1·30

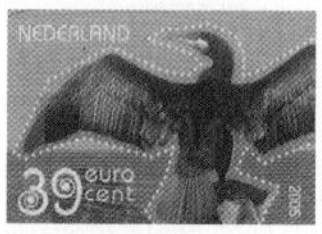

653 Cormorant

2005. Centenary of Vereniging Natuurmonumenten (Nature preservation society). Multicoloured.

2426	39c. Type **653**	1·90	1·60
2427	39c. Pike	1·90	1·60
2428	39c. Blue-tailed damsel fly	1·90	1·60
2429	39c. Water lily	1·90	1·60
2430	65c. Hawfinch	3·00	2·50
2431	65c. Sconebeeker sheep	3·00	2·50
2432	65c. Sand lizard	3·00	2·50
2433	65c. Common blue butterfly	3·00	2·50
MS2434	Two sheets, each 144×81 mm. (a) 39c.×4, As Nos. 2426/9 (b) 65c.×4, As Nos. 2430/3	11·00	11·00

Nos. 2430/3 and the stamps of **MS**2434b, each have a Priority label attached at left.

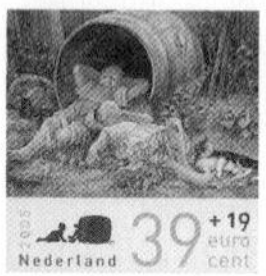

654 "Who is the Wisest"

2005. Birth Centenary of Cornelis Jetses (children's reading book illustrator). Showing illustrations from "Ot en Sien". Multicoloured.

2435	39c.+19c. Type **654**	1·50	1·30
2436	39c.+19c. "Two old chums"	1·50	1·30
2437	39c.+19c. "His own fault"	1·50	1·30
2438	39c.+19c. "What does Puss think?"	1·50	1·30
2439	39c.+19c. "Nothing forgotten"	1·50	1·30
2440	39c.+19c. "Two bright things"	1·50	1·30

Nos. 2435/7 and 2438/40, each had a se-tenant label at head and foot, the upper inscribed with text from the book, the lower showing a modern photograph on the same theme.

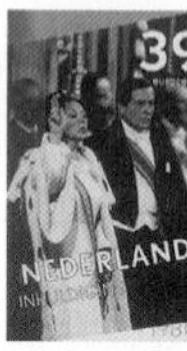

655 Queen Beatrix and Prince Claus (Coronation, 1980)

2005. 25th Anniv of Coronation of Queen Beatrix. Multicoloured.

2441	39c. Type **655**	1·00	85
2442	78c. Seated (Queen's speech, 1991)	2·10	1·70
2443	117c. With Nelson Mandela (state visit, 1999)	3·00	2·50
2444	156c. Wearing glasses (visit to Netherlands Antilles, 1999)	4·00	3·50
2445	225c. Wearing hat (speech to European Parliament, 2004)	5·75	5·00
MS2446	144×75 mm. 39c. Type **655**; 78c. As No. 2442; 117c. As No. 2443; 156c. As No. 2444; 225c. As No. 2445	16·00	16·00

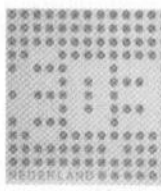

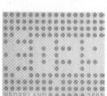

656 Circles

2005. Business Coil Stamps.

2447	**656** 39c. copper	1·00	85
2448	**656** 78c. silver	2·10	1·70

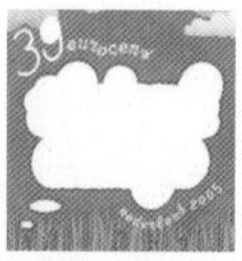

657 Thought Bubble

2005. Greetings Stamps. Sheet 144×75 mm containing T 657 and similar square designs. Two phosphor bands. Multicoloured background colour given.

MS2451	39c.×3, Type **657**; Thought bubble (yellow); Thought bubble (blue)	3·00	3·00

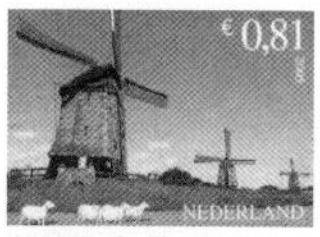

658 Windmill, Netherlands

2005. Waterwheels and Windmills. Multicoloured.

2452	81c. Type **658**	2·10	1·70
2453	81c. Waterwheel, China	2·10	1·70

Stamps of the same design were issued by China.

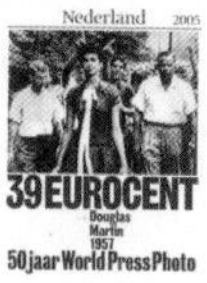

659 Dorothy Counts (black student) (Douglas Martin, 1957)

2005. 50th Anniv of World Press Photo (photojournalism competition). Multicoloured.

2454	39c. Type **659**	1·00	85
2455	39c. Chaplin Luis Padillo with wounded soldier (Hector Rondon Lovera, 1962)	1·00	85
2456	39c. Tank commander, Vietnam (Co Rentmeester, 1967)	1·00	85
2457	39c. Catholic graffiti (Hans-Jorg Anders, 1969)	1·00	85
2458	39c. Niger drought victims (Ovie Cartor, 1974)	1·00	85
2459	39c. Cambodian famine victim (Devid Burnett, 1979)	1·00	85
2460	39c. South Korea soldiers and mother (Anthony Suau, 1987)	1·00	85
2461	39c. Mourners at deathbed of Elshani Nashim (Georges Merillon, 1990)	1·00	85
2462	39c. Wounded man, Kukes (Claus Bjorn Larsen, 1999)	1·00	85
2463	39c. Woman mourns tsunami victims (Arko Datta, 2004)	1·00	85

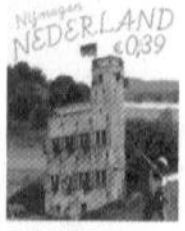

660 Nijmegen

2005. Tourism. Multicoloured.

2464	39c. Type **660**	1·00	85
2465	39c. Rotterdam	1·00	85
2466	39c. Amsterdam	1·00	85
2467	39c. Roermond	1·00	85
2468	39c. Goer	1·00	85
2469	39c. Boalsert	1·00	85
2470	39c. Monnickendam	1·00	85
2471	39c. Netherland	1·00	85
2472	39c. Weesp	1·00	85
2473	39c. Papendrecht	1·00	85

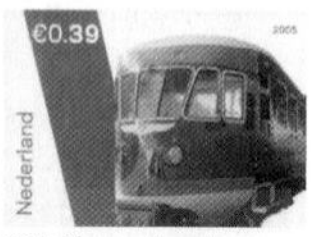

661 *Blauwe Engel*

2005. Trains. Multicoloured.

2474	39c. Type **661**	1·10	90
2475	39c. Steam locomotive 3737	1·10	90
2476	39c. Intercity Express (ICE)	1·60	1·30
2477	39c. *Koploper*	1·60	1·30

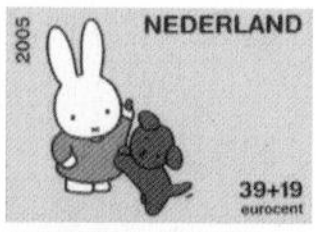

662 Miffy and Snuffy

2005. Child Welfare. Miffy created by Dick Bruna. Sheet 144×75 mm containing T 662 and similar horiz designs. Multicoloured.

MS2478	39c.+19c.×6, Type **662**; Miffy and friends; Miffy and bear; Miffy writing; Miffy and Nina; Miffy at school	9·50	9·50

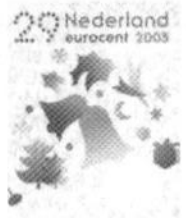

663 Bells

2005. Personal Stamps.

2479	**663**	29c. multicoloured	1·00	80

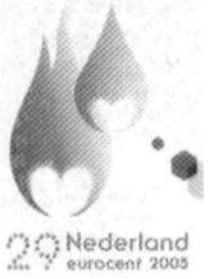

664 Flames

2005. Christmas. Multicoloured. Self-adhesive.

2480	29c. Type **664**	1·00	80
2481	29c. Parcel	1·00	80
2482	29c. Stars	1·00	80
2483	29c. Bells	1·00	80
2484	29c. Doves	1·00	80
2485	29c. Snowmen hugging	1·00	80
2486	29c. Balloons	1·00	80
2487	29c. Ice skates	1·00	80
2488	29c. Trees	1·00	80
2489	29c. Glasses	1·00	80

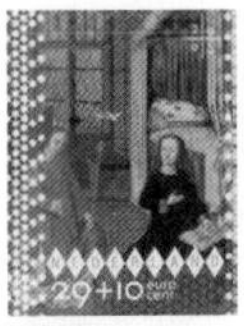

665 The Annunciation

2005. Christmas. Charity Stamps. Multicoloured. Self-adhesive.

2490	29c.+10c. Type **665**	1·10	95
2491	29c.+10c. Mary and Jesus	1·10	95
2492	29c.+10c. Adoration of the shepherds	1·10	95
2493	29c.+10c. Adoration of the Magi	1·10	95
2494	29c.+10c. Journey to Bethlehem	1·10	95
2495	29c.+10c. The Annunciation (different)	1·10	95
2496	29c.+10c. Mary and Jesus (different)	1·10	95
2497	29c.+10c. Adoration of the shepherds (different)	1·10	95
2498	29c.+10c. Adoration of the Magi (different)	1·10	95
2499	29c.+10c. Journey to Bethlehem (different)	1·10	95

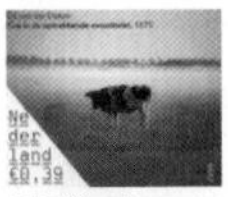

666 "Koe in optrekkende avondmist" (Ed van der Elsken)

2006. Contemporary Art. Multicoloured. Self-adhesive.

2500	39c. Type **666**	1·10	95
2501	39c. "Double Dutch" (Berend Strik)	1·10	95
2502	39c. "Hollandese Velden" (Hans van der Meer)	1·10	95
2503	39c. "Tomorrow" (Marijke van Warmerdam)	1·10	95
2504	39c. "A Day in Holland/Holland in a Day" (Barbara Visser)	1·10	95
2505	39c. "Compositie met rode ruit" (Daan van Golden)	1·10	95
2506	39c. "Untitled" (JCJ Vanderheyden)	1·10	95
2507	39c. "De Goene Kathedraal" (Marinus Boezem)	1·10	95
2508	39c. "Hollandpan" (John Kormeling)	1·10	95
2509	39c. "Drijftbeeld" (Atelier Van Lieshout)	1·10	95
2510	69c. "Study for the horizon" (Sigurdur Gudmundsson)	2·00	1·60
2511	69c. "Lost luggage depot" (Jeff Wall)	2·00	1·60
2512	69c. "11000 Tulips" (Daniel Buren)	2·00	1·60
2513	69c. "Fiets & Stal" (FAT)	2·00	1·60
2514	69c. "Double sunset" (Olafur Eliasson)	2·00	1·60
2515	85c. "Untitled" (Dustin Larson)	2·40	2·00
2516	85c. "Working Progress" (Tadshi Kawamata)	2·40	2·00
2517	85c. "Boerderligezichten" (Sean Snyder)	2·40	2·00
2518	85c. "Toc Toc" (Amalie Pica)	2·40	2·00
2519	85c. "Freude" (Rosemarie Trockel)	2·40	2·00

Nos. 2500/9 were for use on mail within Netherlands, Nos. 2510/14 were for use within Europe and Nos. 2515/19 were for use worldwide.

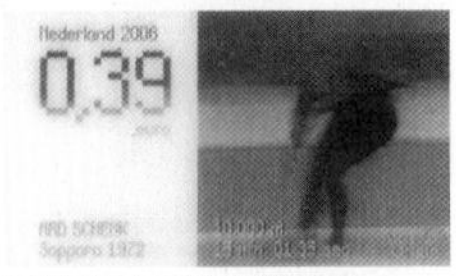

667 Ard Schenk (10000 metres, Sapporo (1972))

2006. Winter Olympic Gold Medal Winners. Sheet 141×102 mm containing T 667 and similar horiz design. Multicoloured.

MS2520	39c.×2, Type **667**; Yvonne van Gennip (3000 metres, Calgary (1988))	5·75	5·75

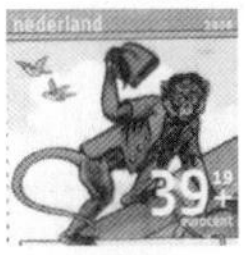

668 Monkey

2006. Summer Charity Stamps. Designs showing traditional reading boards. Multicoloured.

2521	39c.+19c. Type **668**	1·70	1·40
2522	39c.+19c. Nut	1·70	1·40
2523	39c.+19c. Cat	1·70	1·40
2524	39c.+19c. Boy and puzzle	1·70	1·40
2525	39c.+19c. Toddler	1·70	1·40
2526	39c.+19c. Girl and doll	1·70	1·40

The premium was for the benefit of Nationaal Fonds Ouderenhulp (for the assistance of vulnerable seniors).

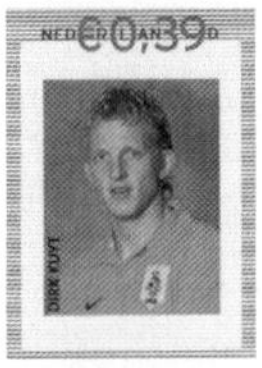

669 Dirk Kuyt

2006. Personal Stamp.

2527	**669**	39c. multicoloured	1·10	95

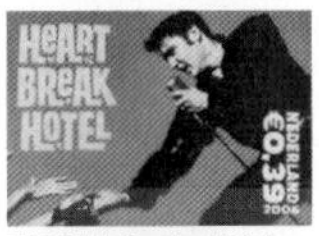

670 Elvis Presley (50th anniv of "Heartbreak Hotel" (record))

2006. The Dutch Choice. Winning Designs in Stamp of your Choice Competition. Multicoloured.

2528	39c. Type **670**	1·10	95
2529	39c. Square and compass (250th anniv of Masons in Netherlands)	1·10	95
2530	39c. Purk and Pino (30th anniv of "Sesame Street" (children's TV programme))	1·10	95
2531	39c. Sampler (regional languages)	1·10	95
2532	39c. Multatuli (creator of Max Havelaar (Dutch fictional character))	1·10	95

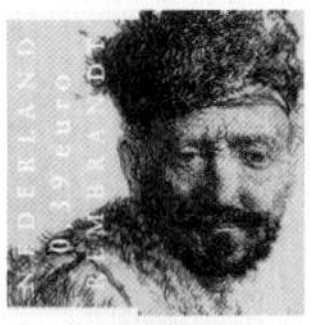

671 "Bearded Man in Oriental Cap"

2006. 400th Birth Anniv of Rembrandt Harmenszoon van Rijn (artist). Multicoloured.

2533	39c. Type **671**	1·10	95
2534	39c. "Old Woman seated at a Table"	1·10	95
2535	39c. "Saskia"	1·10	95
2536	39c. "Titus"	1·10	95
2537	39c. "Woman at Window"	1·10	95
MS2538	104×71 mm. €6.45 "Self-portrait with Saskia"	17·00	17·00

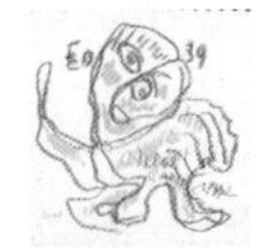

672 Figure

2006. Greetings Stamp.

2539	**672**	39c. multicoloured	1·10	95

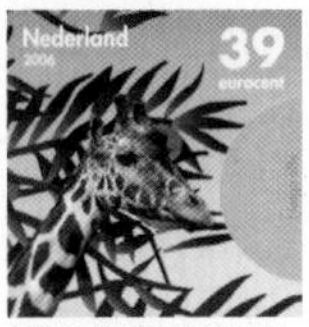

673 Reticulated Giraffe

2006. World Animal Day. Endangered Species. Sheet 135×170 mm containing T 673 and similar square designs. Multicoloured.

MS2540	39c×12, Type **673**; Tropical butterfly; Manchurian crane; Francois's leaf monkey; Blue poison dart frog; Red panda; Lowland gorilla; Sumatran tiger; Asiatic lion; Indian rhinoceros; Asian elephant; Pygmy hippopotamus	13·00	13·00

The stamps and margins of No. **MS**2540 form a composite design of a forest.

2006. Tourism. As T 660. Multicoloured.

2541	39c. Sittard	1·10	95
2542	39c. Leiden	1·10	95
2543	39c. Woudrichem	1·10	95
2544	39c. Vlieland	1·10	95
2545	39c. Enkhuizen	1·10	95
2546	39c. Zutphen	1·10	95
2547	39c. Schoonhoven	1·10	95
2548	39c. Deventer	1·10	95
2549	39c. Zwolle	1·10	95
2550	39c. Kampen	1·10	95

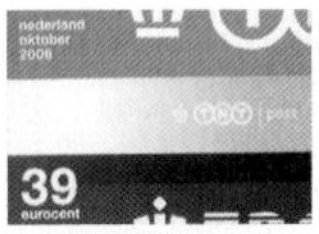

674 Bands

2006. Change of Postal Service Name from TPG Post to Royal TNT Post.

2551	**674**	39c. multicoloured	1·10	95

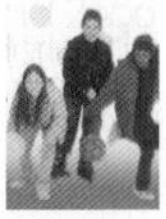

675 Children

2006. Child Welfare. Sheet 144×75 mm containing T 675 and similar horiz designs. Multicoloured.

MS2552	39c.+19c.×6, Type **675**; Children, boy wearing green jumper looking up; Children, boy riding bicycle facing right; Children, boy wearing orange jumper with football; Children, girl wearing purple jumper nursing baby; Children, girl seated holding teddy bear	10·00	10·00

The stamps of No. **MS**2552 were laid in two strips of three, each strip forming a composite design.

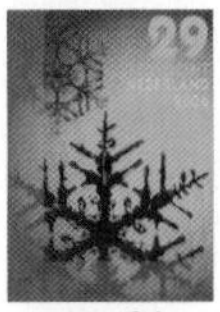

676 Snowflakes

2006. Christmas. Sheet 143×80 mm containing T 676 and similar vert designs showing snowflakes, colours given. Multicoloured. Self-adhesive.

MS2553	29c.×10, Type **676**; Small orange and large magenta; Large brown and small orange; Large blue and small orange; Large brown and small blue; Large orange and small blue; Large blue and brown; Small blue and large magenta; Small brown and large orange; Large blue and small magenta	8·50	8·50

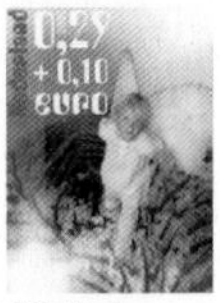

677 Boy as Angel

2006. Christmas. Charity Stamps. Designs showing children as angels. Multicoloured. Self-adhesive.

2554	29c.+10c. Type **677**	11·50	95
2555	29c.+10c. Girl with dark hair	1·10	95
2556	29c.+10c. Girl lying	1·10	95
2557	29c.+10c. Boy with blonde hair standing	1·10	95
2558	29c.+10c. Boy with blonde hair facing right	1·10	95
2559	29c.+10c. Child with brown hair facing left	1·10	95
2560	29c.+10c. Girl with long hair seated	1·10	95
2561	29c.+10c. Boy with curly hair facing left	1·10	95
2562	29c.+10c. Angel wearing blue	1·10	95
2563	29c.+10c. Girl with blonde hair standing	1·10	95

2006. Greetings Stamps. As T 521, 524 and 647. Self-adhesive gum.

2564	44c. multicoloured	1·50	1·20
2565	44c. multicoloured	1·50	1·20
2566	44c. multicoloured	1·50	1·20

DESIGNS: 2564, As Type **521** (new baby); 2565 As Type **524** (bereavement stamp); 2566 As Type **647** (Valentine's Day).

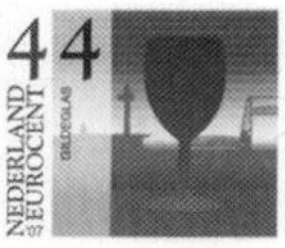

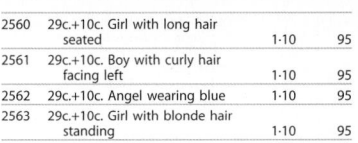

678 Glass ('Glidglas')

2006. Dutch Manufacture. Multicoloured. Self-adhesive.

2567	44c. Type **678**	1·50	1·20
2568	44c. Chair ('Revolt Stoel')	1·50	1·20
2569	44c. Beer bottle ('Heineken Longneck')	1·50	1·20
2570	44c. Child's buggy ('Bugaboo')	1·50	1·20
2571	44c. Kettle ('Fluitketel')	1·50	1·20
2572	44c. Lamp ('Flessenlamp')	1·50	1·20
2573	44c. Cargo bicycle ('Bakfiets')	1·50	1·20
2574	44c. Light bulb ('Spaarlamp')	1·50	1·20
2575	44c. Sausage ('Unox Rookworst')	1·50	1·20
2576	44c. Tulip ('Tulp')	1·50	1·20
2577	72c. Ice skate ('Klapschaats')	2·50	1·90
2578	89c. Cheese slice ('Kaasschaaf')	3·00	2·30

2006. Business Stamps. Self-adhesive.

2579	**634**	44c. multicoloured	1·50	1·20
2580	**634**	88c. multicoloured	3·00	2·30

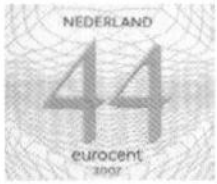

679 '44'

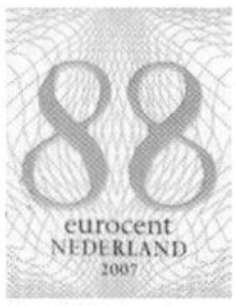

680 '88'

2006. Business Stamps.

2581	**679**	44c. multicoloured	1·50	1·20
2582	**680**	88c. multicoloured	3·00	2·30

2007. As Type 679. Self-adhesive gum.

2583	**679**	44c. multicoloured	1·50	1·20

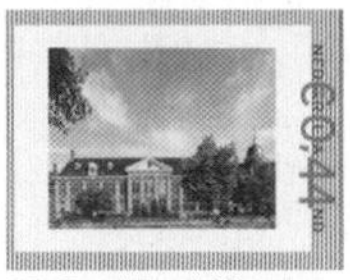

681 Royal Dutch Mint, Utrecht

2007. Personal Stamp. Bicentenary of Royal Dutch Mint.

2584	**681**	44c. multicoloured	1·50	1·20

2007. Tourism. As T 660. Multicoloured.

2585	44c. Groningen	1·50	1·20
2586	44c. Gouda	1·50	1·20

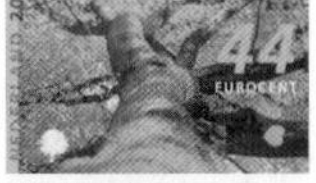

682 Lime Tree

2007. Trees (1st issue). Spring. 50th Anniv of National Tree Planting Committee. Multicoloured. Self-adhesive.

2587	44c. Type **682**	1·50	1·20
2588	44c. Chestnut flower bud	1·50	1·20

See also Nos. 2594/5, 2607/8 and 2611/12.

2007. Tourism. As T 660. Multicoloured.

2589	44c. Hoorn	1·50	1·20
2590	44c. Vissingen	1·50	1·20

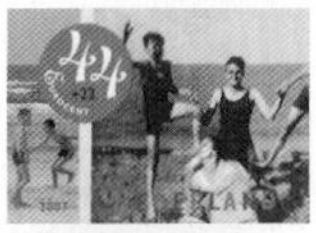

683 Children (c. 2000) playing and Group (c. 1920)

2007. Summer Charity Stamps. Two sheets, each 145×76 mm containing T 683 and similar horiz designs showing beach holiday photographs. Multicoloured.

MS2591	(a) 44c.+22c. Type **683**; 44c.+22c. Three women in cane seat; 44c.+22c. Sand yacht. (b) 44c.+22c. Woman wearing traditional dress paddling; 44c.+22c. Woman (c. 1910) in sea and children (c. 1950) riding donkeys; 44c.+22c. Children riding donkeys and children (c. 2000) playing	9·25	9·25

The stamps and margins of **MS**2591a/b each form a composite design. The premium was for the benefit of Nationaal Fonds Ouderenhulp (for the assistance of vulnerable seniors).

Nos. 2592 has been left for 'Tourism. Schone (as T **660**), issued on 13 April 2007, respectively, not yet received.

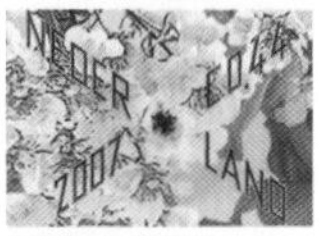

684 Snapdragons

2007. Flowers. Sheet 107×150 mm containing T 684 and similar horiz designs. Multicoloured.

MS2593	44c.×8, Type **684**; Blue lobelia; Snapdragons and red dianthus; White petunias; Arabis; Red and white petunias; Arabis and sweet peas; Pink flox and red and white petunias; 88c.×2, Red and white dianthus and sweet peas; Pink flox	15·00	15·00

The stamps of **MS**2593 form a composite design and each contain a small amount of seeds placed centrally.

2007. Trees. Summer. 50th Anniv of National Tree Planting Committee (2nd issue). As T 682. Multicoloured.

2594	44c. Plane tree bark (detail)	1·50	1·20
2595	44c. Oak	1·50	1·20

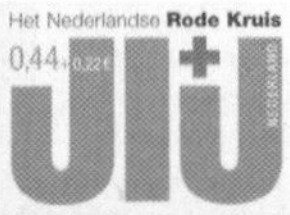

685 'JIJ' (you)

2007. 140th Anniv of Dutch Red Cross.

2596	**685** 44c.+22c. multicoloured	2·20	1·70

2007. Tourism. As T 660. Multicoloured.

2597	44c. Den Helder	1·50	1·20

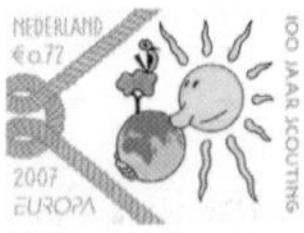

686 Knot, Globe and Sun

2007. Centenary of Scouting. Multicoloured.

2598	72c. Type **686**	2·00	1·60
2599	72c. Moon, globe and knot	2·00	1·60

2007. Tourism. As T 660. Multicoloured.

2600	44c. Lelystad	1·50	1·20
2601	44c. The Hague	1·50	1·20

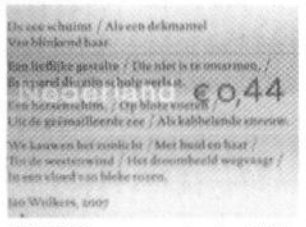

687 'De zee schuimt/Al seen?' and *Snow* (detail, paintings) (Jan Wolkers)

2007. Greetings Stamp.

2602	**687** 44c. multicoloured	1·50	1·20

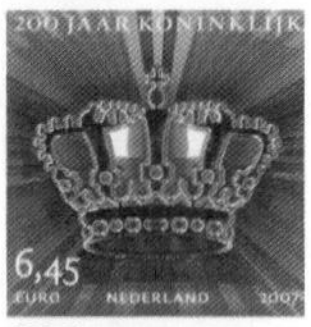

688 Crown

2007. Bicentenary of Dutch Monarchy and Royal Designation of Products. Sheet 104×71 mm.

MS2603	**688** €6.45 multicoloured	17·00	17·00

The stamp and margins of **MS**2603 form a composite design.

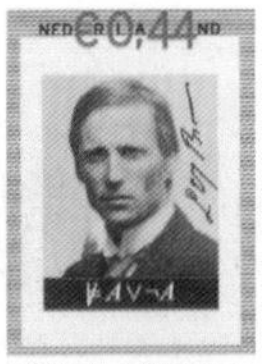

689 L. E. J. Brouwer

2007. Personal Stamp. Centenary of Publication of Mathematic Dissertation by L. E. J. Brouwer. Self-adhesive.

2604	**689** 44c. multicoloured	1·50	1·20

2007. Trees. Autumn. 50th Anniv of National Tree Planting Committee (3rd issue). As T 682. Multicoloured.

2605	44c. Norway maple seeds	1·50	1·20
2606	44c. Purple beech trunk and branches	1·50	1·20

2007. Tourism. As T 660. Multicoloured.

2607	44c. Utrecht	1·50	1·20
2608	44c. Edam	1·50	1·20

2007. Tourism. Two sheets each 144×75 mm containing vert designs as T 660 Multicoloured.

MS2609	(a) 44c.×5, Den Helder; Lelystad; Hoorn; The Hague; Vissingen. (b) 44c.×5, Gouda; Edam; Leerdam; Groningen; Utrecht	10·00	10·00

The stamps and margins of **MS**2609a/b, respectively, each form a composite design.

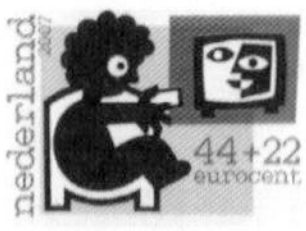

690 Child watching Television

2007. Child Welfare. Sheet 144×75 mm containing T 690 and similar horiz designs. Multicoloured.

MS2610	44c.+22c.×6, Type **690**; Girl looking through window at tall building; Child in bed playing with flashlight; Girl using computer; Boy holding cat; Girl reading	10·00	10·00

The stamps of No. **MS**2610 share a common background.

2007. Trees. Winter. 50th Anniv of National Tree Planting Committee (4th issue). As T 682. Multicoloured.

2611	44c. Black alder	1·50	1·20
2612	44c. Willows in water	1·50	1·20

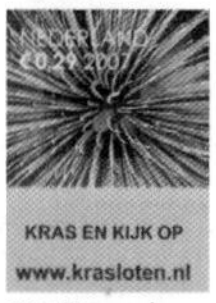

691 Firework

2007. December Lottery Stamps (scratch stamps). Sheet 141×79 mm containing T 691 and similar vert designs showing fireworks, colours given. Multicoloured. Self-adhesive.

2613	29c. Type **691**	1·00	80
2614	29c. Pink with green edges	1·00	80
2615	29c. Green with pink tips	1·00	80
2616	29c. Orange with pale centre	1·00	80
2617	29c. Pink with multicoloured centre	1·00	80
2618	29c. Orange with lavender centre	1·00	80
2619	29c. Green with pink and yellow centre	1·00	80
2620	29c. Purplish blue with multicoloured centre	1·00	80
2621	29c. Blue with pink centre	1·00	80
2622	29c. Large pink with dark centre	1·00	80

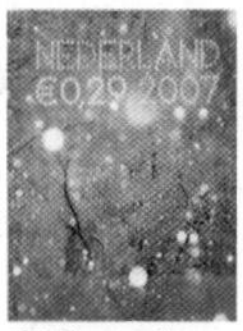

692 Tree and Snow

2007. Christmas. Sheet 143×79 mm containing T 692 and similar vert designs showing trees in snow. Multicoloured. Self-adhesive.

2623	29c. Type **692**	1·00	80
2624	29c. Branches to left and falling snow	1·00	80
2625	29c. Outline of snow covered tree	1·00	80
2626	29c. Large central snow flake and falling snow	1·00	80
2627	29c. Falling snow and outline of buildings	1·00	80
2628	29c. Falling snow	1·00	80
2629	29c. Trunk, branches and falling snow	1·00	80
2630	29c. Conifer	1·00	80
2631	29c. Copse	1·00	80
2632	29c. Snow covered trunk and branches	1·00	80

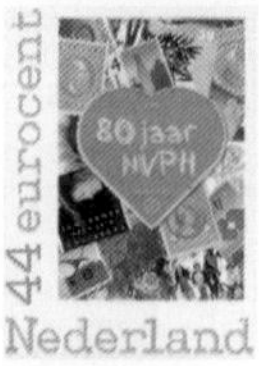

693 Heart, '80' and Stamps

2008. Personal Stamps. Multicoloured.

2633	44c. Type **693** (80th anniv of NVPH (Netherlands Association of Stamp Dealers))	1·50	1·20
2634	44c. Pigeons in flight (centenary of NBFV (Netherlands Federation of Philatelic Associations))	1·50	1·20

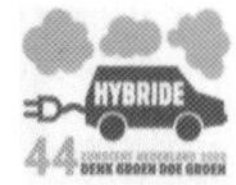

694 Hybrid Fuel Car

2008. Think Green, Act Green. Multicoloured. Self-adhesive.

2635	44c. Type **694**	1·50	1·20
2636	44c. House and sun (solar power)	1·50	1·20
2637	44c. Cow (methane—bio-fuel)	1·50	1·20
2638	44c. Wind turbines	1·50	1·20
2639	44c. Trees (CO^2 offsetting)	1·50	1·20
2640	44c. Car sharing	1·50	1·20
2641	44c. Plug with leaves (green energy)	1·50	1·20
2642	44c. Lorry with soot filter (pollution control)	1·50	1·20
2643	44c. Envelope (greener postal service)	1·50	1·20
2644	44c. House enclosed (home insulation)	1·50	1·20
2645	75c. Cycle with globes as wheels (25×30 mm)	2·50	1·90
2646	92c. Globe as heart (25×30 mm)	3·25	2·50

Nos. 2645/6 each include a label inscribed 'PRIORITY' attached at top.

Nos. 2635/44 were for use on domestic mail.

No. 2645 was for use on mail within Europe, No. 2646 was for use on mail for rest of the world.

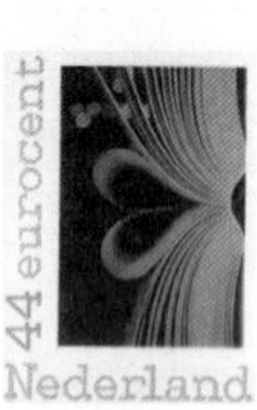

695 Book Pages as Heart (Bart Kuipers)

2008. Winning Designs in Design a Stamp Competition. Multicoloured.

2647	44c. Type **695**	1·50	1·20
2648	44c. Man, woman and 'heart' tree (Ramona)	1·50	1·20
2649	44c. Love	1·50	1·20
2650	44c. Stylized red heart (Palle van der Lijke)	1·50	1·20
2651	44c. Heart in checkerboard (Jasper)	1·50	1·20

2008. Tourism. As T 660. Multicoloured.

2652	44c. Cow, rowing boat and Coevorden Castle enclosed in goose silhouette (Coevorden)	1·50	1·20
2653	44c. Skûsje boat, Water Gate and peppermints enclosed in silhouette of Pieter Gerbrandy (prime minister during WW II) (Sneek)	1·50	1·20

696 Stylized Forget-me-not

2008. Summer Charity Stamps. Two sheets, each 144×75 mm containing T 696 and similar horiz designs. Multicoloured.

MS2654	(a) 44c.+22c.×3, Type **696**; Blue flower (crane's bill); Pink flower (larkspur). (b) 44c.+22c.×3, Japanese anemone; Globe thistle; Stylized forget-me-not (different)	10·00	10·00

The stamps and margins of **MS**2654a/b each form a composite design and, if the sheets are laid horizontally together, they also form a continuous composite design.

The premium was for the benefit of Nationaal Fonds Ouderenhulp (for the assistance of vulnerable seniors).

2008. Tourism. As T 660. Multicoloured.

2655	44c. Heiligenbergbeek, blue butterfly, Amersfoort boulder and Tower of Our Lady enclosed in silhouette of Piet Mondriaan (artist) (Amersfoort)	1·50	1·20
2656	44c. Windmill, St George and dragon enclosed in silhouette of Gisbertus Voetius (theologian) (Heusden)	1·50	1·20

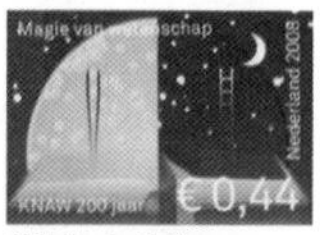

697 Book, Cells, Tweezers, Moon and Ladder

2008. Anniversaries. Multicoloured.

2657	44c. Type **697** (bicentenary of KNAW (Royal Netherlands Academy of Arts and Science))	1·50	1·20
2658	44c. Bridge, map, currency symbols and De Nederlandsche Bank building (tenth anniv of European Central Bank)	1·50	1·20
2659	44c. Amsterdam skyline, Beurs van Berlage tower, share price graph, trader and market (25th anniv of AEX (Amsterdam Exchanges))	1·50	1·20
2660	44c. Girl reading, book piles, bookshelves and elderly man reading (140th anniv of Bruna (bookshop))	1·50	1·20
2661	44c. Tent and symbols of tourism (125th anniv of ANWB (Royal Dutch Tourist Board))	1·50	1·20

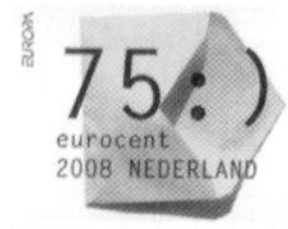

698 Envelope and Smiley

2008. Europa. The Letter.

2662	**698** 75c. multicoloured	2·50	1·90

No. 2657 was issued with a se-tenant label inscribed 'PRIORITY'.

2008. Tourism. As T 660. Multicoloured.

2663	44c. De Nieuwe Polder pumping station, Old Church, snow boarder and snow crystal enclosed in silhouette of Dappere Dirk (Zoetermeer)	1·50	1·20

2008. Tourism. Sheet 144×75 mm containing vert designs as T 660. Multicoloured.

MS2664	44c.×5, Sneek; Zoetermeer; Heusden; Amersfoort; Coevorden	6·50	6·50

The stamps and margins of **MS**2664 form a composite design.

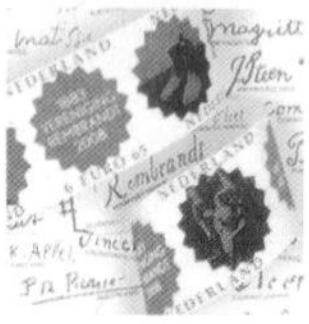

699 Artists' Signatures and Coils

2008. 125th Anniv of Vereniging Rembrandt (Rembrandt Association). Sheet 104×71 mm.

MS2665	**699** €6.65 multicoloured	17·00	17·00

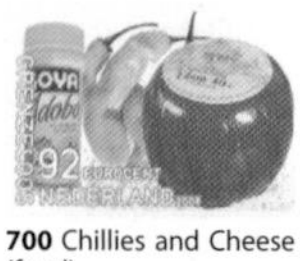

700 Chillies and Cheese (food)

2008. Netherlands and Beyond. Sheet 145×75 mm containing T 700 and similar multicoloured.

MS2666	92c.×3, Type **700**; Peas, condensed milk and papaya (vert); Ham, plantain and Ponche Pistachio (vert)	6·50	6·50

No. **MS**2666 also includes Netherlands Antilles 5c. stamp (Houses (architecture)) and Aruba 240c. stamp (Script (poem by Frederico Oduber)).

The 'foreign' stamps could only be used in their country of origin.

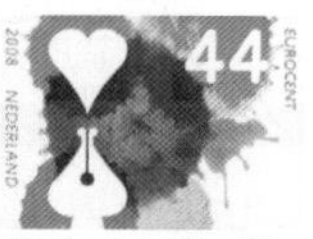

701 Heart and Pen Nib

2008. Greetings Stamp.

2667	**701** 44c. multicoloured	1·50	1·20

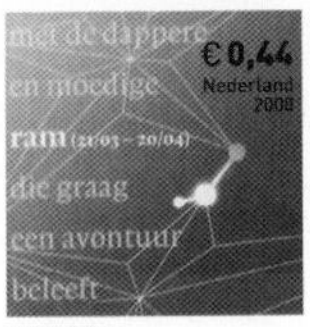

702 Aries

2008. Constellations. Signs of the Zodiac. Multicoloured.

2668	44c. Type **702**	1·50	1·20
2669	44c. Taurus	1·50	1·20
2670	44c. Gemini	1·50	1·20
2671	44c. Cancer	1·50	1·20
2672	44c. Leo	1·50	1·20
2673	44c. Virgo	1·50	1·20
2674	44c. Libra	1·50	1·20
2675	44c. Scorpio	1·50	1·20
2676	44c. Sagittarius	1·50	1·20
2677	44c. Capricorn	1·50	1·20
2678	44c. Pisces	1·50	1·20
2679	44c. Aquarius	1·50	1·20

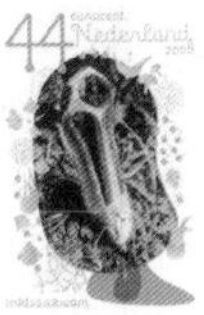
703 Squid-shaped Fungi

2008. Centenary of Mycological Society. Showing fungi. Multicoloured.

2680	44c. Type **703**	1·50	1·20
2681	44c. Star-shaped	1·50	1·20
2682	44c. Fly agaric	1·50	1·20
2683	44c. Nest-shaped	1·50	1·20
2684	44c. Ink cap	1·50	1·20
2685	44c. Squid-shaped decaying	1·50	1·20
2686	44c. Star-shaped decaying	1·50	1·20
2687	44c. Fly agaric (different)	1·50	1·20
2688	44c. Nest-shaped decaying	1·50	1·20
2689	44c. Ink cap decaying	1·50	1·20

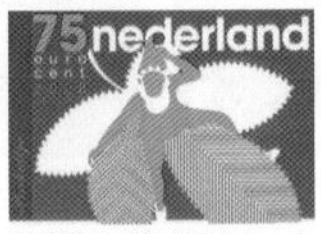

704 Pinkeltje (Dick Laan)

2008. Gnomes from Dutch Literature. Multicoloured.

2690	75c. blue, orange and bright violet	2·20	1·70
2691	75c. bistre, new blue and blue	2·20	1·70
2692	75c. orange, blue and new blue	2·20	1·70
2693	75c. blue, violet and bistre	2·20	1·70
2694	75c. violet, bistre and orange	2·20	1·70

DESIGNS: 2690 Type **704**; 2691 Wipneus en Pim (Leonardus van der Made); 2692 Piggelmee (L. C. Steenhuizen); 2693 Paulus de boskabouter (Jean Dulieu); 2694 de Kabouter (Rien Poorlvliet).

Nos. 2690/4 were issued each with a label inscribed 'Priority' attached at left.

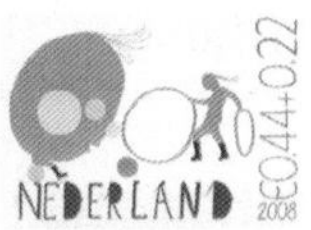

705 'O'

2008. Child Welfare. Sheet 144×75 mm containing T 705 and similar horiz designs. Multicoloured.

MS2695 44c.+22c.×6,Type **705**; 'N' and 'D'; 'E' and 'R'; 'W'; 'I' and 'J'; 'S' 11·50 11·50

The stamps of **MS**2695 share a common background, and spell out 'ONDERWIJS' (education).

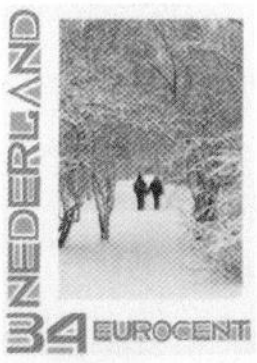

706 Walkers in Snowy Landscape

2008. Personal Stamp. Self-adhesive.

2696 **706** 34c. multicoloured 1·20 90

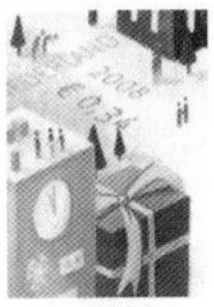
707 Clock Tower and Present

2008. Christmas. Sheet 144×75 mm containing vert designs as T 707. Multicoloured. Self-adhesive.

MS2697 34c.×10, Type **707**; Envelopes and Christmas tree in glass box; Christmas tree in glass box and rockets; Bell, Christmas tree and three-storied building; Three-storied building and pile of presents; Christmas tree and three-storied building with narrow windows; Three-storied building with narrow windows and candle; Snow-covered house; Envelope and left-side of fireplace; Fireplace as building 12·00 12·00

The stamps and margins of **MS**2697 form a composite design of a stylized townscape.

2009. Think Green, Act Green. As T 694. Self-adhesive gum.

2698	77c. Cycle with globes as wheels (As No. 2645) (25×30 mm)	2·75	2·10
2699	95c. Globe as heart (As No. 2646) (25×30 mm)	3·25	2·50

Nos. 2698/9 each include a label inscribed 'PRIORITY' attached at top.

Designs as Nos. 2635/44 were re-issued on the same date.

No. 2698 was for use on mail within Europe, No. 2699 was for use on mail for rest of the world.

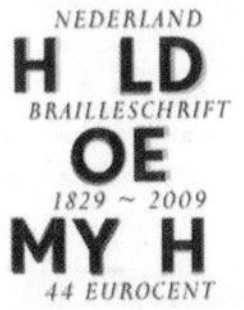

708 'H LD OE MY H

2009. Birth Bicentenary of Louis Braille (inventor of Braille writing for the blind). Sheet 135×170 mm containing T 708 and similar vert designs. Multicoloured.

MS2700 44c.×12, Type **708**; 'DR K MS T UI'; 'NI K Z LF AN'; 'S PE O R AD U'; 'EV G DW S N IE'; 'M D XTR KA S'; ' EG N M RG XA T'; ' FI N B AF K S'; 'GE U W S RAV'; 'F BE CR O L FS'; 'Q A I N TS PHE'; 'RI F VU G H RT' 17·00 17·00

The letters missing from the front of the stamps of No. **MS**2700 are printed on the back.

The stamps are also embossed with Braille letters.

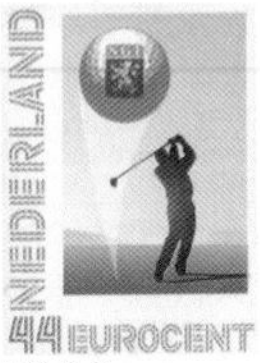

709 Golfer

2009. Personal Stamps. 125th Anniv of NVPV (philatelic society) (2702). Multicoloured. Self-adhesive.

2701	44c. Type **709**	1·50	1·20
2702	44c. Young stamp collector	1·50	1·20

2009. Tourism. As T 660. Multicoloured.

2703	44c. Spinner, ferris wheel and buildings (Tilburg)	1·50	1·20
2704	44c. Barje (character created by Anne de Vries) (statue), Pedal cars and motorcycles (Assen)	1·50	1·20

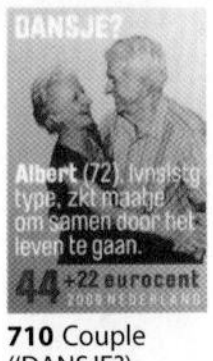

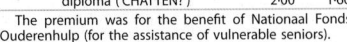

710 Couple ('DANSJE?)

2009. Summer Charity Stamps. Multicoloured.

2705	44c.+22c. Type **710**	2·00	1·60
2706	44c.+22c. Woman ('ER-OP-UIT!')	2·00	1·60
2707	44c.+22c. Ballet dancer ('JONG GELLEERD OUD GEDAN')	2·00	1·60
2708	44c.+22c. Woman and dog ('VERGEET ME NIET')	2·00	1·60
2709	44c.+22c. Trumpeter ('LET'S TWIST AGAIN!')	2·00	1·60
2710	44c.+22c. Woman holding diploma ('CHATTEN?')	2·00	1·60

The premium was for the benefit of Nationaal Fonds Ouderenhulp (for the assistance of vulnerable seniors).

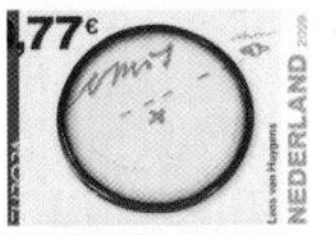

711 Christian Huygens' Lens and Sketch of Saturn and Titan

2009. Europa. Astronomy. Multicoloured.

2711	77c. Type **711**	2·50	1·90
2712	77c. Locations of LOFAR (Low frequency Array) radio telescope antennae	2·50	1·90

Nos. 2711/12, respectively, have a label inscribed 'PRIORITY' attached at left, with the face value of the stamps leaching into the label.

2009. Tourism. As T 660. Multicoloured.

2713	44c. Pheasant, locomotive and stylized roses (Roosendaal)	1·50	1·20
2714	44c. Antenna, entertainers and St. Driehoek Church (Ousterhout)	1·50	1·20

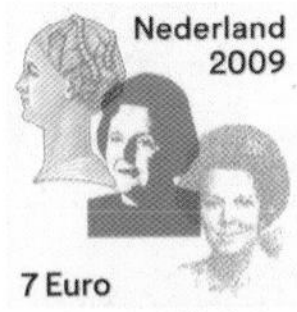

712 Queens Wilhelmina Heleana Pauline Maria, Juliana Louise Emma Marie Wilhelmina and Beatrix Wilhelmina Armgard

2009. Three Queens. Sheet 104×71 mm.

MS2715 **712** €7 multicoloured 20·00 20·00

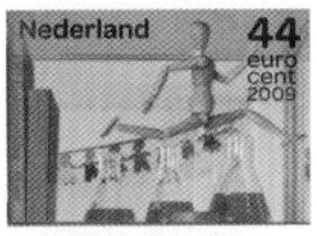

713 Books, Wooden Figure and Bottles

2009. Charities' Anniversaries. Multicoloured.

2716	44c. Type **713** (60th anniv of Cancer Support Fund)	1·50	1·20
2717	44c. Swallow, binoculars and egg (110th anniv of Bird Protection League)	1·50	1·20
2718	44c. Figures sheltered by book (95th anniv of Cordaid–People in need charity)	1·50	1·20
2719	44c. Pouring coffee (60th anniv of The Sunflower Care Association)	1·50	1·20
2720	44c. Children's building blocks as house (60th anniv of SOS Childrens' Villages)	1·50	1·20

2009. Tourism. As T 660. Multicoloured.

2721	44c. Sail ship, Maigret and container ship (Delfzijl)	1·50	1·20

MS2722 144×75 mm. As Nos. 2703/4; 2713/14; 2721 7·50 7·50

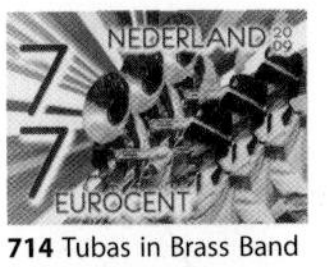

714 Tubas in Brass Band

2009. Music. World Music and Europa Cantat 2009 Competitions, Netherlands. Multicoloured.

2723	77c. Type **714**	2·50	1·90
2724	77c. WHEN YOU SING YOU BEGIN WITH DO RE MI	2·50	1·90
2725	77c. Drum majorettes	2·50	1·90
2726	77c. JAUCHZET FROH-LOCKET	2·50	1·90
2727	77c. Tubas in military band	2·50	1·90
2728	77c. para bailar la bamba	2·50	1·90

Nos. 2723/4×2, 2725/6×2 and 2727/8 were printed, each stamp having a label inscribed 'PRIORITY', attached at left or right.

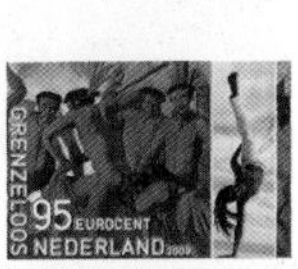

715 Aboriginal Dancers (detail of painting by Albert Eckhout)

2009. Netherlands and Beyond. Netherlands and Brazil. Sheet 108×150 mm containing T 715 and similar horiz designs. Multicoloured.

MS2729 95c.×6, Type **915**; Capoeira dancers and aboriginal warrior; Passion fruit (extract from *Historia Naturalis Brasiliae*); Cashew nut (extract from *Historia Naturalis Brasiliae*); Farmer and sugar plantation (detail of painting by Frans Post); Church ruins, Olinda (detail of painting by Frans Post) 9·50 9·50

The stamps of **MS**2729 were laid in pairs within the sheet, each stamp having a label inscribed 'PRIORITY', attached at either left or right.

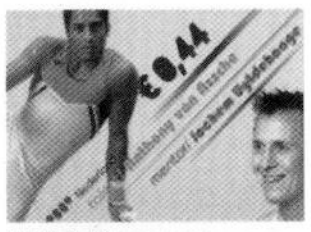

716 Anthony van Assiche (gymnast) and Jochem Uyldehaage (mentor)

2009. Sport. Stichting Sporttop–Mentoring for Olympic Athletes. Multicoloured.

2730	44c. Type **716**	1·50	1·20
2731	44c. Leon Commandeur (cyclist) and Johan Kenkhuis (mentor)	1·50	1·20
2732	44c. Mike Marissen (swimmer) and Bas van de Goor (mentor)	1·50	1·20
2733	44c. Maureen Groefsema (judo) and Lobke Berkhout (mentor)	1·50	1·20
2734	44c. Aniek van Koot (wheelchair tennis player) and Marko Koers (mentor)	1·50	1·20

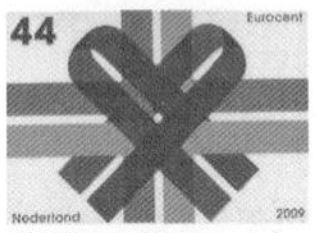

717 Parcel Ribbon and Bow

2009. Greetings Stamp.

2735 **717** 44c. multicoloured 1·50 1·20

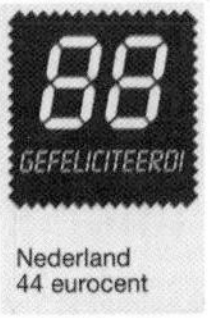

718 '88' and 'GEFELICITEERD!'

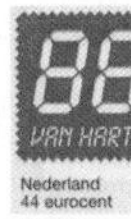

719 '88' and 'VAN HARTE!'

2009. Greetings Stamps. Birthdays. (a) Ordinary gum.

2736	44c. bright ultramarine and black	1·50	1·20
2737	44c. bright scarlet and black	1·50	1·20
2738	44c. bright emerald and black	1·50	1·20
2739	44c. bright ultramarine and black	1·50	1·20
2740	44c. bright scarlet and black	1·50	1·20

(b) Size 21×26 mm. Self-adhesive.

2741	44c. bright scarlet and black	1·50	1·20
2742	44c. bright emerald and black	1·50	1·20
2743	44c. bright ultramarine and black	1·50	1·20
2744	44c. bright ultramarine and black	1·50	1·20
2745	44c. bright scarlet and black	1·50	1·20

DESIGNS: 2736 Type **718**; 2737 '88' and 'HOERA!'; 2738 '88' and 'PROFICIAT!'; 2739 '88' and 'NOG VELE JAREN!'; 2740 '88' and 'VAN HARTE!'; 2741 Type **719**; 2742 As No. 2737; 2743 As No. 2738; 2744 As No. 2739; 2745 As Type **718**.

The phosphor bands were laid at right-angles along the left and bottom edge of the stamps.

The numerals on the stamps could be altered with a ballpoint pen to show the age of the recipient.

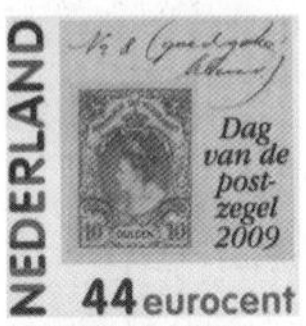

720 1905 10g. Stamp (As Type **11**)

2009. Stamp Day. Personal Stamp.

2746 **720** 44c. multicoloured 1·50 1·20

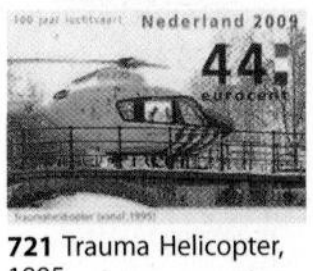

721 Trauma Helicopter, 1995

2009. Centenary of Powered Flight in the Netherlands. Sheet 108×150 mm containing T 721 and similar horiz designs. Multicoloured.

MS2747 44c.×10, Type **721**; Boeing 747, 1971; Apache helicopter, 1998; Schipol airport (opened 1967); Fokker F-27 Friendship, 1955; Lockheed Super Constellation, 1953; Fokker F-18 Pelican and crew (flew Christmas post to Jakarta in record time of four days); Douglas DC-2 Univer (handicap class winner and second overall in London to Melbourne air race, 1934); Wright Flyer, 1909; Anthony Fokker piloting *Spin*, 1911 — 15·00 15·00

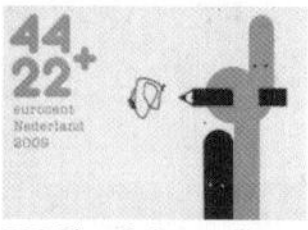

722 Blue Stripe as Figure holding Pencil

2009. Child Welfare. Sheet 145×75 mm containing T 722 and similar horiz designs showing stripes as figures. Multicoloured.

MS2748 44c.+22c.×6,Type **722**; Turquoise stripe holding magnifying glass; Six stripe figures watching falling star;Blue stripe curved around red stripe; Eight stripe figures reading; Three stripe figures leaning to right watching pegasus figure — 12·00 12·00

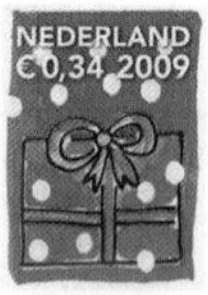

723 Parcel

2009. Christmas. Christmas rate stamps. Multicoloured. Self-adhesive.

2749	34c. Type **723**	90	80
2750	34c. Candlestick in window	90	80
2751	34c. Christmas tree on parcel (green background)	90	80
2752	34c. Pink parcel	90	80
2753	34c. Woman holding glass in window	90	80
2754	34c. Man holding glass in window	90	80
2755	34c. Christmas tree on parcel (pink background)	90	80
2756	34c. Tall magenta parcel	90	80
2757	34c. Christmas tree on parcel (blue background)	90	80
2758	34c. Blue parcel with white ribbon and Christmas tree	90	80

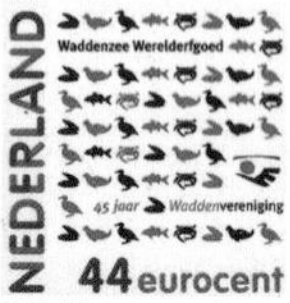

724 Silhouettes of Wildlife

2010. Personal Stamp

2759	**724**	44c. rosine, blue-black and indigo	1·50	1·20

2010. Tourism. Multicoloured.

2760	44c. Silhouette of Vleeshal, Frans Hals, De Adriaan windmill, St. Bavo church, Toneelschuur and city seal (Haarlem)		
2761	44c. City Hall, Abbey, Veerse-poort district building and Hans Lipperhey (Middelburg)	1·50	1·20

Vert designs as T **660**.

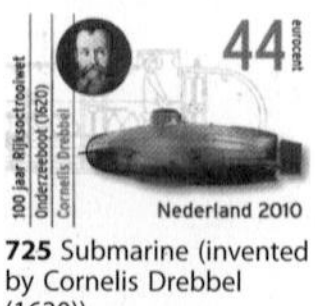

725 Submarine (invented by Cornelis Drebbel (1620))

2010. Centenary of Patents Act. Multicoloured.

MS2762 44c.×10, Type **725**; LED light (Philips (2007)); Artificial kidney (Willem Kolff (1943)); Wine bottle vacuum valve (Bernd Schneider (1987)); Milking machine robot (Van der Lely (1987)); Bicycle chain casing (Wilhelmine J. van der Woerd (1974)); TNT Post's automated handwriting recognition (1980); Solar vehicle (Solar Team Twente (University of Twente and Saxion University of Applied Sciences, Twente) (2009)); Dyneema fibre, world's strongest fibre (DSM (1979); Telescope (Hans Lipperhey (1608)) — 15·00 15·00

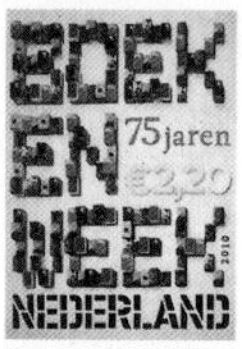

726 'BOEKENWEEK'

2010. 75th Anniv of Book Week

2763	**726**	€2.20 multicoloured	6·50	5·25

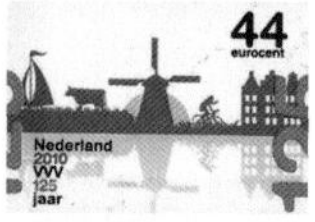

727 VVV (Tourist Information Office of the Netherlands (125th anniv))

2010. Tourism and Environmental Anniversaries. Multicoloured.

2764	44c. Type **727**	1·50	1·20
2765	44c. Silhouettes of Africa (Royal Tropical Institute (centenary))	1·50	1·20
2766	44c. Duinrell, Wassenaar (holiday and amusement park) (75th anniv)	1·50	1·20
2767	44c. Euromast Tower, Rotterdam (50th anniv)	1·50	1·20
2768	44c. Pyramids of Giza, Sphinx and camels (Djoser (tour organization) (25th anniv))	1·50	1·20

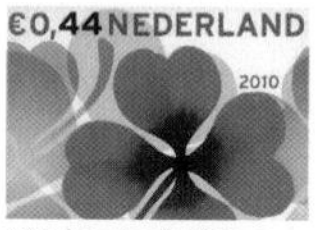

728 Four-leafed Clover

2010. Greetings Stamp

2769	**728**	44c. multicoloured	1·50	1·20

2010. Tourism. Multicoloured.

2770	44c. Basilica of Saint Servatius, Helspoort gate, St Servatius Bridge, Church of St John, Bonnefanten Museum, fool's cap (reference to the Carnival festivities held annually in Maastricht) and André Rieu playing violin (Maastricht)	1·50	1·20
2771	44c. St Eusebius Church tower, City Hall, John Frost Bridge, the Rhine, ArtEZ Institute of Arts, sculpture by French artist François Pompon, Le grand cerf (big deer), Sonsbeek Park and Dutch singer-songwriter Ilse DeLange (Arnhem)	1·50	1·20

Vert designs as T **660**.

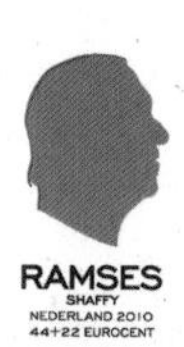

729 Ramses Shaffy

2010. 75th Anniv of Summer Stamps

MS2772 44c.+22c.×6, olive-bistre and black; orange and black; reddish purple and black; grey-blue and black; deep yellow-brown and black; dull yellow-green and black — 14·00 14·00

Designs-: Type **729** (songwriter); Fanny Blankers-Koen (female athlete); Mies Bouwman (children's author and TV personality); Willy Alberti (singer); Dick Bruna (children's author); Annie M. G. Schmidt (children's author)

The premium was for the benefit of Nationaal Ouderenfonds (senior aid foundation).

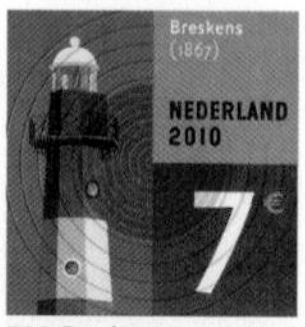

730 Breskens Lighthouse

2010. Lighthouses

MS2773 **730** €7 multicoloured — 10·50 10·50

No. **MS**2773 was for use on domestic registered mail.

2010. Tourism. Multicoloured.

2774	44c. Oldehove Tower, the Chancellery, Church of St Boniface, Achmea Tower, Harmonie Municipal Theatre, golden skate (reference to Elfstedentocht) and Jan Jacob Slauerhoff (poet) (Leeuwarden)	1·50	1·20

Vert designs as T **660**

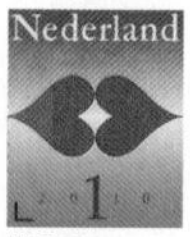

731 Two Hearts

2010. Greetings Stamp

2775	**731**	1 (46c.) multicoloured	1·60	1·30

See also No. 2411.

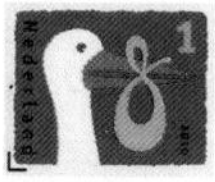

732 Stork carrying Bundle

2010. Greetings Stamp

2776	**732**	1 (46c.) multicoloured	1·60	1·30

See also No. 1855.

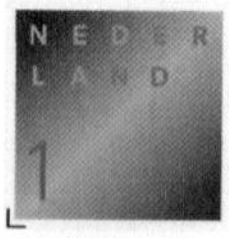

733 Light across Darkness

2010. Beareavement Stamp

2777	**733**	1 (46c.) deep turquoise	1·60	1·30

See also No. 1866.

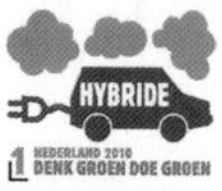

734 Hybrid Car

2010. Think Green, Act Green. Multicoloured.

2778	1 (46c.) Type **734**	1·60	1·30
2779	1 (46c.) House and sun (solar power)	1·60	1·30
2780	1 (46c.) Cow (methane—bio-fuel)	1·60	1·30
2781	1 (46c.) Wind turbines	1·60	1·30
2782	1 (46c.) Trees (CO^2 offsetting)	1·60	1·30
2783	1 (46c.) Car sharing	1·60	1·30
2784	1 (46c.) Plug with leaves (green energy)	1·60	1·30
2785	1 (46c.) Lorry with soot filter (pollution control)	1·60	1·30
2786	1 (46c.) Envelope (greener postal service)	1·60	1·30
2787	1 (46c.) House enclosed (home insulation)	1·60	1·30
2788	1 EUROPA (79c.) Cycle with globes as wheels (25×30 mm)	2·50	1·90
2789	1 WERELD (95c.) Globe as heart (25×30 mm)	3·25	2·50

Nos. 2788/9 each include a label inscribed 'PRIORITY' attached at top, separated from the design by a line of rouletting.

See also Nos. 2635/46.

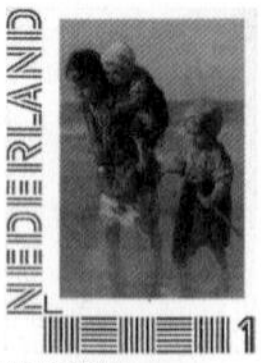

735 Children (painting)

2010. Personal Stamp

2790	**735**	1 (46c.) multicoloured	1·60	1·30

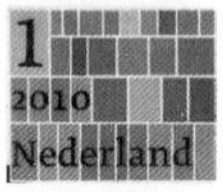

736 Patchwork

2010. Business Stamp

2791	**736**	1 (46c.) multicoloured	1·60	1·30

See also Nos. 2353/4.

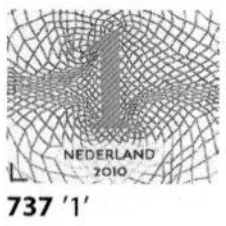

737 '1'

2010. Business Stamps

2792	1 (46c.) Type **737**	1·60	1·30
2793	2 (92c.) As Type **737**	3·25	2·50

See also Nos. 2581/2.

2010. Horiz design as Type **737**

2794	1 (46c.) multicoloured	1·60	1·30

See also No. 2583.

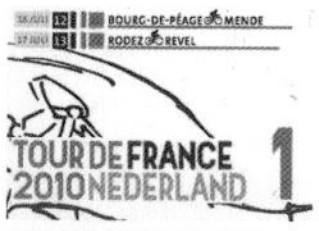

738 'GRAND DEPART ROTTERDAM'

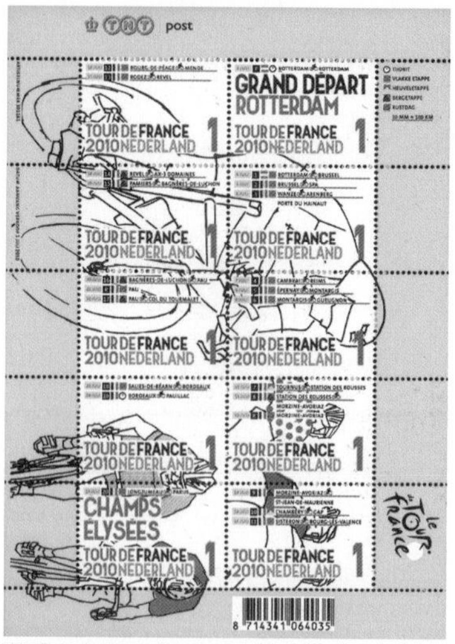

739 Tour de France (image scaled to 45% of original size)

2010. Tour de France. Multicoloured.

MS2795 1 (46c.)×10, Type **738**; Stages 1-3; Stages 4-6; Stages 7-R; Stages 9-11; Stages 12-13; Stages 14-15; Stages 16-17; 18-19; Stage 20, 'CHAMPS ELYSEES' — 17·00 17·00

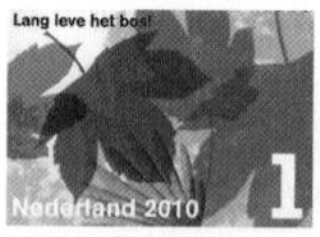

740 Maple Leaves

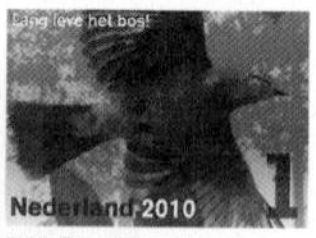

741 Forests

2010. Centenary of Royal Dutch Forestry Association. Multicoloured.

MS2796 1 (46c.)×10, Type **740**; Maple leaf (different); Jay; Pine trees; Rose hips; Rose leaves; Rose hips and fern; Ferns and logs; Tree roots; Fungi — 16·00 16·00

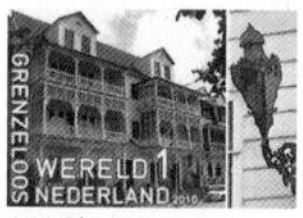

742 Plantation House and Lamp

2010. Netherlands and Beyond. Multicoloured.

MS2797 1 WERELD (95c.) ×6, Type **742**; Handrail and building; Surinam and Dutch costume; Surinam and Dutch caps; Coloured feathers; Fruit — 3·25 2·50

The stamps of **MS**2797 have a label inscribed 'PRIORITY', attached at either left or right.

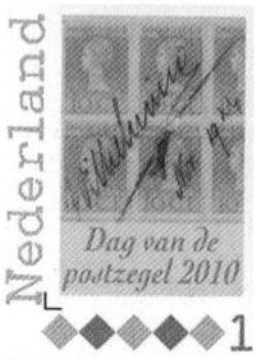

743 1923 10c. Stamp

2010. Stamp Day

2798	**743**	1 (46c.) multicoloured	1·60	1·30

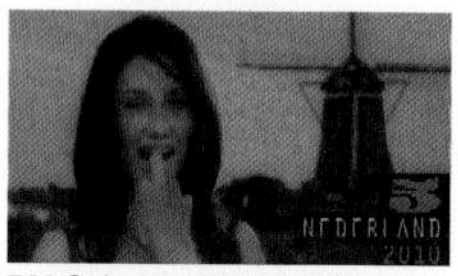

744 Carice van Houten and Windmill (scene from *Kleinste Kortste Film* (Tiniest, shortest film) directed by Anton Corbijn)

2010. 30th Anniv of Netherlands Film Festival

2799	**744**	5 (€2.30) muluticoloured	8·00	6·50

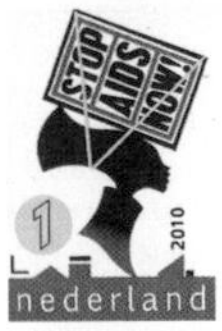

745 Poster on Woman's Head

2010. AIDS Awareness Campaign. Each scarlet, black and bright lemon.

2800	1 (46c.) Type **745**	1·60	1·30
2801	1 (46c.) AIDS emblem as woman's skirt	1·60	1·30
2802	1 (46c.) Hand holding pill	1·60	1·30
2803	1 (46c.) Woman wearing sari teaching	1·60	1·30
2804	1 (46c.) Mother and child	1·60	1·30
2805	1 (46c.) Woman with eyes downcast	1·60	1·30

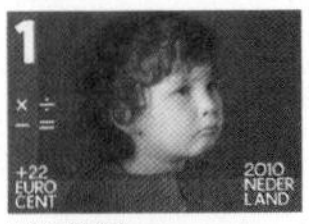

746 Child

2010. Child Welfare. Multicoloured.

MS2806	1 (46c.)+22c.×6, Type **746**; Boy with hand to his head; Boy with dark curly hair; Girl looking up, facing right; Child with hands behind head; Child with left hand raised	13·00	13·00

Nos. 2807/8 are vacant.

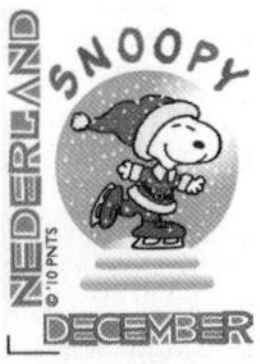

747 Snoopy

2010. 60th Anniv of *Peanuts* (comic strip)

2809	**747**	'DECEMBER' (32c.) multi-coloured	1·20	95

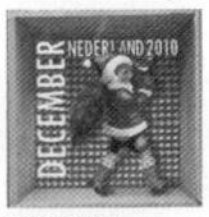

748 Child carrying Christmas Tree

2010. Christmas. Multicoloured.

2810	'DECEMBER' (32c.) Type **748**	1·20	95
2811	'DECEMBER' (32c.) Bell	1·20	95
2812	'DECEMBER' (32c.) Rocking horse	1·20	95
2813	'DECEMBER' (32c.) Embroidered heart-shaped cushion	1·20	95
2814	'DECEMBER' (32c.) Candle	1·20	95
2815	'DECEMBER' (32c.) Deer wearing ribbon	1·20	95
2816	'DECEMBER' (32c.) Santa enclosed in roundel	1·20	95
2817	'DECEMBER' (32c.) Clasped hands and roses (old-style Christmas card)	1·20	95
2818	'DECEMBER' (32c.) Angel kneeling	1·20	95

MARINE INSURANCE STAMPS

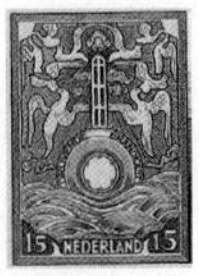

M22

1921

M238	**M22**	15c. green	17·00	£110
M239	**M22**	60c. red	22·00	£110
M240	**M22**	75c. brown	28·00	£110
M241	-	1g.50 blue	£100	£950
M242	-	2g.25 brown	£160	£1300
M243	-	4½g. black	£250	£1600
M244	-	7½g. red	£375	£2250

DESIGNS (inscr "DRIJVENDE BRANDKAST"): 1g.50, 2g.25, "Explosion"; 4½g., 7½g. Lifebelt.

OFFICIAL STAMPS

1913. Stamps of 1898 optd ARMENWET.

O214	**12**	1c. red	5·00	4·00
O215	**12**	1½c. blue	1·10	3·25
O216	**12**	2c. brown	9·00	10·00
O217	**12**	2½c. green	22·00	18·00
O218	**13**	3c. green	5·00	2·20
O219	**13**	5c. red	5·00	7·25
O220	**13**	10c. grey	50·00	55·00

POSTAGE DUE STAMPS

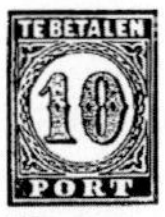

D8

1870

D76	**D8**	5c. brown on yellow	£100	17·00
D77	**D8**	10c. purple on blue	£225	22·00

For same stamps in other colours, see Netherlands Indies, Nos. D1/5.

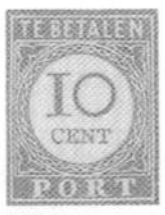

D9

1881

D174	**D9**	½c. black and blue	55	55
D175	**D9**	1c. black and blue	1·70	55
D176	**D9**	1½c. black and blue	1·10	55
D177	**D9**	2½c. black and blue	2·20	1·10
D178	**D9**	3c. black and blue	2·20	1·70
D179	**D9**	4c. black and blue	2·20	2·20
D180	**D9**	5c. black and blue	14·00	55
D181	**D9**	6½c. black and blue	45·00	46·00
D182	**D9**	7½c. black and blue	2·75	85
D183	**D9**	10c. black and blue	39·00	85
D184	**D9**	12½c. black and blue	33·00	1·70
D185	**D9**	15c. black and blue	39·00	1·10
D186	**D9**	20c. black and blue	22·00	9·00
D187	**D9**	25c. black and blue	47·00	55
D173b	**D9**	1g. red and blue	£120	33·00

No. D188 is inscribed "EEN GULDEN".

1906. Surch.

D213b	3c. on 1g. red and blue	39·00	39·00
D215	4 on 6½c. black and blue	5·50	7·75
D216	6½ on 20c. black & blue	5·50	6·75
D214b	50c. on 1g. red & blue	£180	£180

1907. De Ruyter Commemoration. PORTZEGEL and value.

			stamps	surch
D217A	**15**	½c. on 1c. red	1·70	2·20
D218A	**15**	1c. on 1c. red	1·10	1·10
D219A	**15**	1½c. on 1c. red	1·10	1·10
D220A	**15**	2½c. on 1c. red	3·25	3·25
D221A	**15**	5c. on 2½c. red	2·20	1·10
D222A	**15**	6½c. on 2½c. red	4·00	4·50
D223A	**15**	7½c. on ½c. blue	2·75	2·20
D224A	**15**	10c. on ½c. blue	2·75	1·70
D225A	**15**	12½c. on ½c. blue	5·50	6·25
D226A	**15**	15c. on 2½c. red	9·00	5·50
D227A	**15**	25c. on ½c. blue	11·00	10·00
D228A	**15**	50c. on ½c. blue	65·00	55·00
D229A	**15**	1g. on ½c. blue	90·00	75·00

1912. Re-issue of Type D 9 in one colour.

D230	**D 9**	½c. blue	55	55
D231	**D 9**	1c. blue	55	55
D232	**D 9**	1½c. blue	2·75	2·20
D233	**D 9**	2½c. blue	90	55
D234	**D 9**	3c. blue	1·70	1·10
D235	**D 9**	4c. blue	90	90
D236	**D 9**	4½c. blue	7·25	7·25
D237	**D 9**	5c. blue	55	55
D238	**D 9**	5½c. blue	7·75	6·75
D239	**D 9**	7c. blue	3·25	3·25
D240	**D 9**	7½c. blue	4·50	2·20
D241	**D 9**	10c. blue	90	90
D242	**D 9**	12½c. blue	90	90
D453	**D 9**	15c. blue	95	95
D244	**D 9**	20c. blue	90	55
D245	**D 9**	25c. blue	£100	1·10
D246	**D 9**	50c. blue	90	55

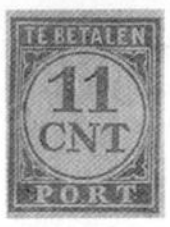

D25

1921

D442	**D25**	3c. blue	45	45
D445	**D25**	6c. blue	45	45
D446	**D25**	7c. blue	95	95
D447	**D25**	7½c. blue	95	95
D448	**D25**	8c. blue	95	95
D449	**D25**	9c. blue	1·00	95
D247	**D25**	11c. blue	14·00	4·50
D451	**D25**	12c. blue	95	60
D455	**D25**	25c. blue	95	60
D456	**D25**	30c. blue	95	60
D458	**D25**	1g. red	1·20	60

1923. Surch in white figures in black circle.

D272	**D9**	1c. on 3c. blue	1·20	1·00
D273	**D9**	2½c. on 7c. blue	1·70	95
D274	**D9**	25c. on 1½c. blue	11·50	1·00
D275	**D9**	25c. on 7½c. blue	14·50	95

1924. Stamps of 1898 surch TE BETALEN PORT and value in white figures in black circle.

D295	**13**	4c. on 3c. green	2·30	1·60
D296	**12**	5c. on 1c. red	1·20	60
D297	**12**	10c. on 1½c. blue	1·70	95
D298	**13**	12½c. on 5c. red	1·70	95

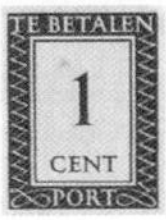

D121

1947

D656	**D121**	1c. blue	30	30
D657	**D121**	3c. blue	30	40
D658	**D121**	4c. blue	14·50	1·30
D659	**D121**	5c. blue	30	30
D660	**D121**	6c. blue	50	50
D661	**D121**	7c. blue	40	40
D662	**D121**	8c. blue	40	40
D663	**D121**	10c. blue	40	30
D664	**D121**	11c. blue	70	70
D665	**D121**	12c. blue	1·30	1·30
D666	**D121**	14c. blue	1·30	1·00
D667	**D121**	15c. blue	50	30
D668	**D121**	16c. blue	1·20	1·30
D669	**D121**	20c. blue	50	40
D670	**D121**	24c. blue	1·60	1·90
D671	**D121**	25c. blue	50	40
D672	**D121**	26c. blue	2·30	3·50
D673	**D121**	30c. blue	80	30
D674	**D121**	35c. blue	1·00	30
D675	**D121**	40c. blue	1·00	30
D676	**D121**	50c. blue	1·30	40
D677	**D121**	60c. blue	1·50	70
D678	**D121**	85c. blue	23·00	80
D679	**D121**	90c. blue	4·00	1·00
D680	**D121**	95c. blue	4·00	95
D681	**D121**	1g. red	3·25	30
D682	**D121**	1g.75 red	8·00	50

For stamps as Types D **121**, but in violet, see under Surinam.

INTERNATIONAL COURT OF JUSTICE

Stamps specially issued for use by the Headquarters of the Court of International Justice.

1934. Optd COUR PER- MANENTE DE JUSTICE INTERNATIONALE.

J1	**35**	1½c. mauve		2·30
J2	**35**	2½c. green		2·30
J3	**36**	7½c. red		3·50
J4	**68**	12½c. blue		41·00
J7	**36**	12½c. blue		23·00
J5	**36**	15c. yellow		3·00
J6	**36**	30c. purple		5·75
J8		30c. purple		3·50

1940. Optd COUR PER- MANANTE DE JUSTICE INTERNATIONALE.

J9	**94**	7½c. red		13·00
J10	**94**	12½c. blue		13·00
J11	**94**	15c. blue		13·00
J12	**94**	30c. bistre		13·00

1947. Optd COUR INTERNATIONALE DE JUSTICE.

J13	7½c. red		1·60
J14	10c. purple		1·60
J15	12½c. blue		1·60
J16	20c. violet		1·60
J17	25c. red		1·60

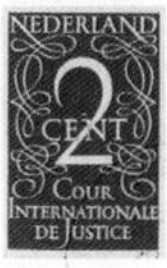

J3

1950

J18	**J3**	2c. blue		11·50
J19	**J3**	4c. green		11·50

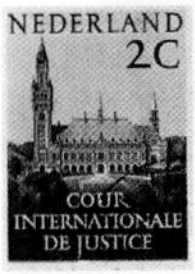

J4 Peace Palace, The Hague

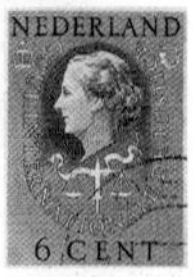

J5 Queen Juliana

1951

J20	**J4**	2c. lake		95
J21	**J4**	3c. blue		95
J22	**J4**	4c. green		95
J23	**J4**	5c. brown		95
J24	**J5**	6c. mauve		3·50
J25	**J4**	6c. green	1·30	1·30
J26	**J4**	7c. red	1·30	1·30
J27	**J5**	10c. green		35
J28	**J5**	12c. red		2·75
J29	**J5**	15c. red		60
J30	**J5**	20c. blue		60
J31	**J5**	25c. brown		60
J32	**J5**	30c. purple		60
J33	**J4**	40c. blue		60
J34	**J4**	45c. red		60
J35	**J4**	50c. mauve		85
J36	**J5**	1g. grey		1·20

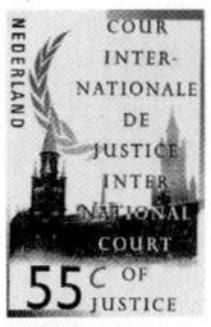

J6 Olive Branch and Peace Palace, The Hague

1989

J37	**J 6**	5c. black and yellow	30	30
J38	**J 6**	10c. black and blue	30	30
J39	**J 6**	25c. black and red	35	35
J41	**J 6**	50c. black and green	60	60
J42	**J 6**	55c. black and mauve	60	60
J43	**J 6**	60c. black and bistre	60	60
J44	**J 6**	65c. black and green	60	60
J45	**J 6**	70c. black and blue	65	65
J46	**J 6**	75c. black and yellow	60	60
J47	**J 6**	80c. black and green	75	75
J49	**J 6**	1g. black and orange	90	90
J50	**J 6**	1g.50 black and blue	1·20	1·20
J51	**J 6**	1g.60 black and brown	3·00	3·00
J54	-	5g. multicoloured	5·00	5·00
J56	-	7g. multicoloured	6·75	6·50

DESIGNS: 5, 7g. Olive branch and column.

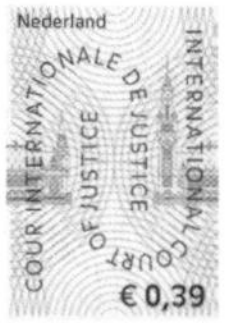

J7 Peace Palace, The Haag

2004

J57	**J7**	39c. blue, green and black	90	95
J58	-	61c. blue, azure and black	1·30	1·40

DESIGNS: 39c. Type J **7**; 61c. Seal.

PROVINCIAL STAMPS

The following stamps, although valid for postage throughout Netherlands, were only available from Post Offices within the province depicted and from the Philatelic Bureau.

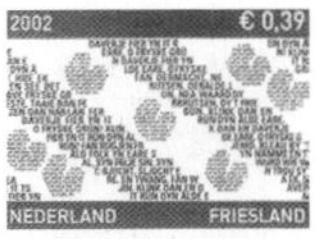

V1 Freisland

2002. Multicoloured.

V1	39c. Type V **1**	90	50
V2	39c. Drenthe	90	50
V3	39c. North Holland	90	50
V4	39c. Gelderland	90	50
V5	39c. North Brabant	90	50
V6	39c. Groningen	90	50
V7	39c. South Holland	90	50
V8	39c. Utrecht	90	50
V9	39c. Limburg	90	50
V10	39c. Zeeland	90	50
V11	39c. Flevoland	90	50
V12	39c. Overijssel	90	50

The following stamps, although valid for postage throughout Netherlands, were only available from Post Offices within the province depicted and from the Philatelic Bureau.

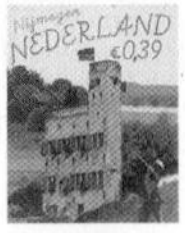

V2 Nijmegen

2005. Multicoloured.

V13	39c. Type V **2**	65	55
V14	39c. Nederland, Overijssel	65	55
V15	39c. Rotterdam	65	55
V16	39c. Weesp	65	55
V17	39c. Monnickendam	65	55
V18	39c. Goes	65	55

Pt. 4

NETHERLANDS ANTILLES

Curacao and other Netherlands islands in the Caribbean Sea. In December 1954 these were placed on an equal footing with Netherlands under the Crown.

100 cents = 1 gulden.

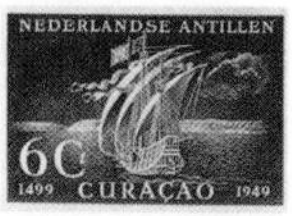
48 Spanish Galleon

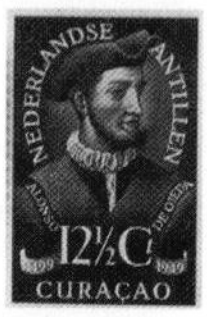
49 Alonso de Ojeda

1949. 450th Anniv of Discovery of Curacao.

306	**48**	6c. green	6·50	4·00
307	**49**	12½c. red	7·00	5·25
308	**48**	15c. blue	7·50	5·75

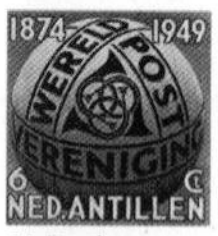
50 Posthorns and Globe

1949. 75th Anniv of U.P.U.

309	**50**	6c. red	7·00	4·75
310	**50**	25c. blue	7·00	2·30

1950. As numeral and portrait types of Netherlands but inscr "NED. ANTILLEN".

325	**118**	1c. brown	35	10
326	**118**	1½c. blue	35	10
327	**118**	2c. orange	35	10
328	**118**	2½c. green	1·70	35
329	**118**	3c. violet	45	10
329a	**118**	4c. green	1·40	60
310a	**129**	5c. yellow	35	35
330	**118**	5c. red	35	10
311	**129**	6c. purple	2·30	10
311a	**129**	7½c. brown	8·25	10
312a	**129**	10c. red	2·50	2·30
313	**129**	12½c. green	4·00	25
314a	**129**	15c. blue	35	35
315a	**129**	20c. orange	35	35
316	**129**	21c. black	5·75	3·50
316a	**129**	22½c. green	9·25	25
317a	**129**	25c. violet	35	35
318	**129**	27½c. brown	12·00	3·00
319a	**129**	30c. sepia	1·70	1·70
319b	**129**	40c. blue	60	60
320	**129**	50c. olive	19·00	25
321	**130**	1½g. green	60·00	60
322	**130**	2½g. brown	60·00	3·00
323	**130**	5g. red	85·00	26·00
324	**130**	10g. purple	£300	£100

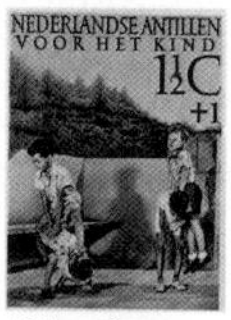
51 Leap-frog

1951. Child Welfare.

331	**51**	1½c.+1c. violet	17·00	8·25
332	-	5c.+2½c. brown	17·00	8·25
333	-	6c.+2½c. blue	17·00	8·25
334	-	12½c.+5c. red	17·00	8·25
335	-	25c.+10c. turquoise	17·00	8·25

DESIGNS: 5c. Kite-flying; 6c. Girl on swing; 12½c. Girls playing "Oranges and Lemons"; 25c. Bowling hoops.

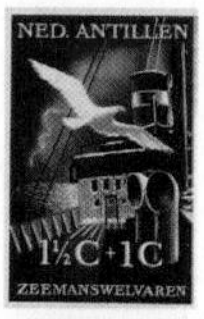
52 Gull over Ship

1952. Seamen's Welfare Fund. Inscr "ZEEMANSWELVAREN".

336	**52**	1½c.+1c. green	13·00	3·00
337	-	6c.+4c. brown	22·00	6·50
338	-	12½c.+7c. mauve	16·00	6·50
339	-	15c.+10c. blue	19·00	7·50
340	-	25c.+15c. red	17·00	5·75

DESIGNS: 6c. Sailor and lighthouse; 12½c. Sailor on ship's prow; 15c. Tanker in harbour; 25c. Anchor and compass.

1953. Netherlands Flood Relief Fund. No. 321 surch 22½ Ct. +7½ Ct. WATERSNOOD NEDERLAND 1953.

341	**130**	22½c.+7½c. on 1½g. green	3·00	2·30

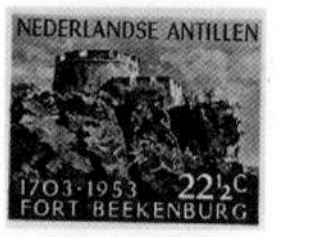
54 Fort Beekenburg

1953. 250th Anniv of Fort Beekenburg.

342	**54**	22½c. brown	11·50	1·20

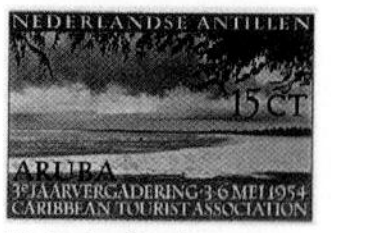
55 Aruba Beach

1954. Third Caribbean Tourist Assn Meeting.

343	**55**	15c. blue and buff	9·25	4·75

1954. Ratification of Statute of the Kingdom. As No. 809 of Netherlands.

344	**158**	7½c. green	2·30	1·70

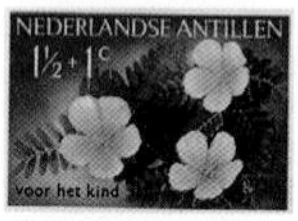
56 "Anglo" Flower

1955. Child Welfare.

345	**56**	1½c.+1c. bl, yell & turq	5·25	1·70
346	-	7½c.+5c. red, yellow & vio	7·00	3·50
347	-	15c.+5c. red, grn & olive	7·00	4·00
348	-	22½c.+7½c. red, yell & bl	7·00	3·50
349	-	25c.+10c. red, yell & grey	7·00	3·50

FLOWERS: 7½c. White Cayenne; 15c. "French" flower; 22½c. Cactus; 25c. Red Cayenne.

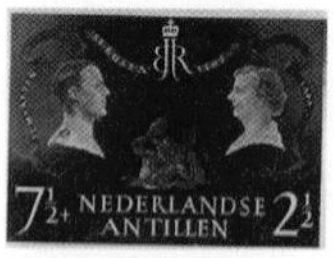
57 Prince Bernhard and Queen Juliana

1955. Royal Visit.

350	**57**	7½c.+2½c. red	60	60
351	**57**	22½c.+7½c. blue	1·70	1·70

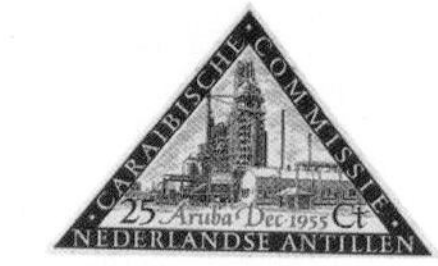
59 Oil Refinery

1955. 21st Meeting of Caribbean Commission.

352	-	15c. blue, green and brown	5·75	4·00
353	**59**	25c. blue, green and brown	7·00	4·75

DESIGN (rectangle, 36×25 mm): 15c. Aruba Beach.

60 St. Anne Bay

1956. Tenth Anniv of Caribbean Commission.

354	**60**	15c. blue, red and black	60	60

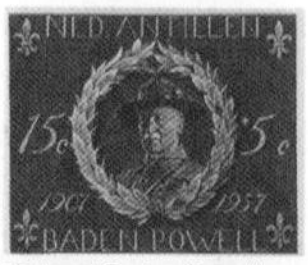
61 Lord Baden-Powell

1957. 50th Anniv of Boy Scout Movement.

355	**61**	6c.+1½c. yellow	1·40	80
356	**61**	7½c.+2½c. green	1·40	80
357	**61**	15c.+5c. red	1·40	80

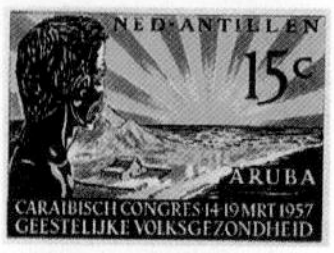
62 "Dawn of Health"

1957. First Caribbean Mental Health Congress, Aruba.

358	**62**	15c. black and yellow	60	60

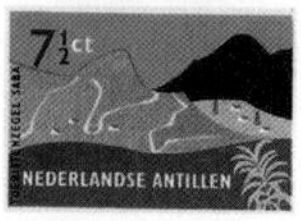
63 Saba

1957. Tourist Publicity. Multicoloured.

359	7½c. Type **63**	1·20	70
360	15c. St. Maarten	1·20	70
361	25c. St. Eustatius	1·20	70

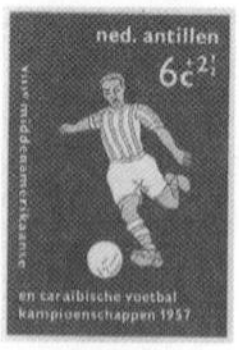
64 Footballer

1957. Eighth Central American and Caribbean Football Championships.

362	**64**	6c.+2½c. orange	3·00	1·20
363	-	7½c.+5c. red	3·00	1·70
364	-	15c.+5c. green	3·00	1·70
365	-	22½c.+7½c. blue	3·00	1·70

DESIGNS—HORIZ: 7½c. Caribbean map. VERT: 15c. Goalkeeper saving ball; 22½c. Footballers with ball.

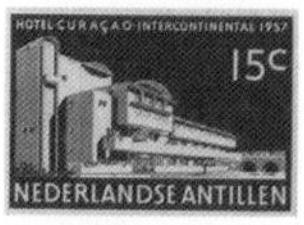
65 Curacao Intercontinental Hotel

1957. Opening of Curacao Intercontinental Hotel.

366	**65**	15c. blue	60	60

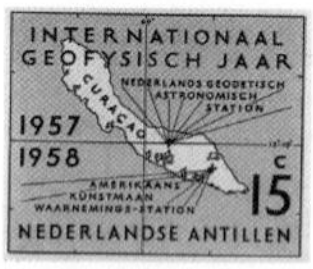
66 Map of Curacao

1957. International Geophysical Year.

367	**66**	15c. deep blue and blue	1·20	1·00

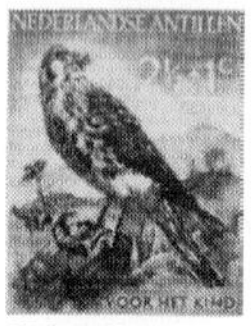
67 American Kestrel

1958. Child Welfare. Bird design inscr "VOOR HET KIND". Multicoloured.

368	2½c.+1c. Type **67**	2·30	1·70
369	7½c.+1½c. Yellow oriole	2·30	1·70
370	15c.+2½c. Scaly-breasted ground doves	2·30	1·70
371	22½c.+2½c. Brown-throated conure	2·30	1·70

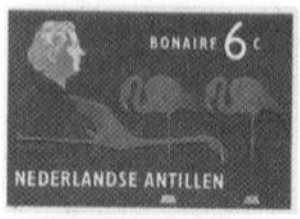
68 Greater Flamingoes (Bonaire)

1958. Size 33½×22 mm.

372	**68**	6c. pink and green	3·50	15
373	**A**	7½c. yellow and brown	35	15
374	**A**	8c. yellow and blue	35	15
375	**B**	10c. yellow and grey	35	15
376	**C**	12c. grey and green	35	15
377	**D**	15c. blue and green	35	15
377a	**D**	15c. lilac and green	35	15
378	**E**	20c. grey and red	35	15
379	**A**	25c. green and blue	45	15
380	**D**	30c. green and brown	45	15
381	**E**	35c. pink and grey	60	15
382	**C**	40c. green and mauve	70	15
383	**B**	45c. blue and violet	70	15
384	**68**	50c. pink and brown	70	15
385	**E**	55c. green and red	80	35
386	**68**	65c. pink and green	1·20	45
387	**D**	70c. orange and purple	2·00	80
388	**68**	75c. pink and violet	1·00	80
389	**B**	85c. green and brown	1·20	1·00
390	**E**	90c. orange and blue	1·40	1·30
391	**C**	95c. yellow and orange	1·60	1·40
392	**D**	1g. grey and red	1·50	15
393	**A**	1½g. brown and violet	2·10	20
394	**C**	2½g. yellow and blue	4·00	60
395	**B**	5g. mauve and brown	7·75	1·00
396	**68**	10g. pink and blue	13·50	7·50

DESIGNS: A. Dutch Colonial houses (Curacao); B. Mountain and palms (Saba); C. Town Hall (St. Maarten); D. Church tower (Aruba); E. Memorial obelisk (St. Eustatius).

For larger versions of some values see Nos. 653/6.

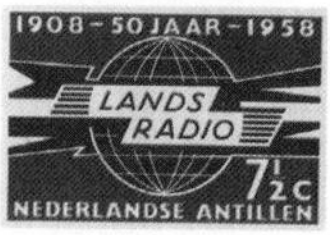
69

1958. 50th Anniv of Netherlands Antilles Radio and Telegraph Administration.

397	**69**	7½c. lake and blue	35	35
398	**69**	15c. blue and red	60	60

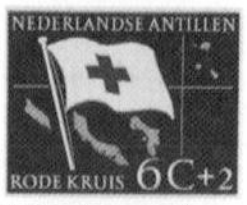
70 Red Cross Flag and Antilles Map

1958. Neth. Antilles Red Cross Fund. Cross in red.

399	**70**	6c.+2c. brown	1·40	95
400	**70**	7½c.+2½c. green	1·40	95
401	**70**	15c.+5c. yellow	1·40	95
402	**70**	22½c.+7½c. blue	1·40	95

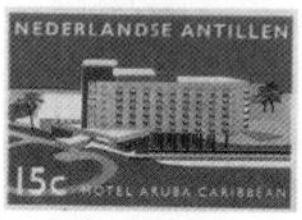
71 Aruba Caribbean Hotel

1959. Opening of Aruba Caribbean Hotel.

403	**71**	15c. multicoloured	60	60

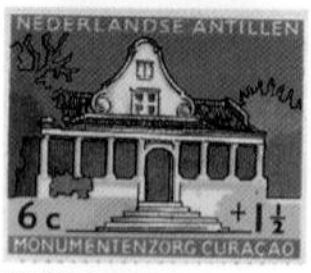
72 Zeeland

1959. Curacao Monuments Preservation Fund. Multicoloured.

404	6c.+1½c. Type **72**	2·30	1·70
405	7½c.+2½c. Saba Island	2·30	1·70
406	15c.+5c. Molenplein (vert)	2·30	1·70
407	22½c.+7½c. Scharloobrug	2·30	1·70
408	25c.+7½c. Brievengat	2·30	1·70

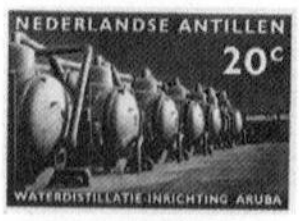
73 Water-distillation Plant

1959. Inauguration of Aruba Water-distillation Plant.

409	**73**	20c. light blue and blue	70	70

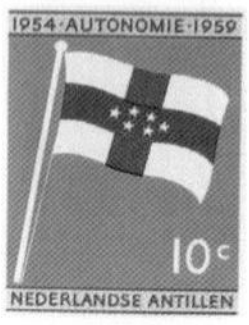
74 Antilles Flag

1959. Fifth Anniv of Ratification of Statute of the Kingdom.

410	**74**	10c. red, blue and light blue	70	60
411	**74**	20c. red, blue and yellow	70	60
412	**74**	25c. red, blue and green	70	60

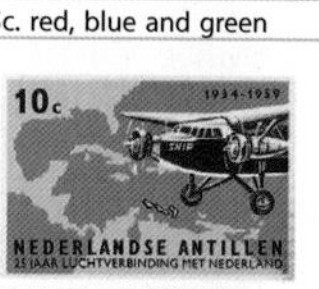
75 Fokker F.XVIII "De Snip" over Caribbean

1959. 25th Anniv of K.L.M. Netherlands–Curacao Air Service. Each yellow, deep blue and blue.
413 10c. Type **75** — 1·20 60
414 20c. Fokker F.XVIII "De Snip" over globe — 1·20 60
415 25c. Douglas DC-7C "Seven Seas" over Handelskade (bridge), Willemstad — 1·20 35
416 35c. Douglas DC-8 at Aruba Airport — 1·20 80

76 Mgr. Niewindt

1960. Death Centenary of Mgr. M. J. Niewindt.
417 **76** 10c. purple — 1·40 70
418 **76** 20c. violet — 1·40 80
419 **76** 25c. olive — 1·40 80

77 Flag and Oil-worker

1960. Labour Day.
420 **77** 20c. multicoloured — 70 70

78 Frogman

1960. Princess Wilhelmina Cancer Relief Fund. Inscr "KANKERBESTRIJDING".
421 **78** 10c.+2c. blue — 2·50 1·70
422 - 20c.+3c. multicoloured — 2·50 2·30
423 - 25c.+5c. red, blue & blk — 2·50 2·30
DESIGNS—HORIZ: 20c. Queen angelfish; 25c. Big-scaled soldierfish.

79 Child on Bed

1961. Child Welfare. Inscr "voor het kind".
424 6c.+2c. black and green — 80 45
425 10c.+3c. black and red — 80 45
426 20c.+6c. black and yellow — 80 45
427 25c.+8c. black and orange — 80 45
DESIGNS: 6c. Type **79**; 10c. Girl with doll; 20c. Boy with bucket; 25c. Children in classroom.

80 Governor's Salute to the American Naval Brig "Andrew Doria" at St. Eustatius.

1961. 185th Anniv of 1st Salute to the American Flag.
428 **80** 20c. multicoloured — 1·20 95

1962. Royal Silver Wedding. As T 187 of Netherlands.
429 10c. orange — 70 45
430 25c. blue — 70 45

81 Jaja (nursemaid) and Child

1962. Cultural Series.
431 - 6c. brown and yellow — 60 60
432 - 10c. multicoloured — 60 60
433 - 20c. multicoloured — 60 60
434 **81** 25c. brown, green and black — 60 60

MS435 108×134 mm. Nos. 431/4 — 3·50 3·50
DESIGNS: 6c. Corn-masher; 10c. Benta player; 20c. Petji kerchief.

82 Knight and World Map

1962. Fifth International Candidates Chess Tournament, Curacao.
436 **82** 10c.+5c. green — 1·70 1·20
437 **82** 20c.+10c. red — 95 70
438 **82** 25c.+10c. blue — 95 70

1963. Freedom from Hunger. No. 378 surch TEGEN DE HONGER wheat sprig and +10c.
439 20c.+10c. grey and red — 80 80

84 Family Group

1963. Fourth Caribbean Mental Health Congress, Curacao.
440 **84** 20c. buff and blue — 60 60
441 - 25c. red and blue — 60 60
DESIGN: 25c. Egyptian Cross emblem.

85 "Freedom"

1963. Centenary of Abolition of Slavery in Dutch West Indies.
442 **85** 25c. brown and yellow — 60 45

86 Hotel Bonaire

1963. Opening of Hotel Bonaire.
443 **86** 20c. brown — 60 45

87 Child and Flowers

1963. Child Welfare. Child Art. Multicoloured.
444 5c.+2c. Type **87** — 60 45
445 6c.+3c. Children and flowers (horiz) — 60 45
446 10c.+5c. Girl with ball (horiz) — 60 45
447 20c.+10c. Men with flags (horiz) — 60 45
448 25c.+12c. Schoolboy — 60 45

1963. 150th Anniv of Kingdom of the Netherlands. As No. 968 of Netherlands, but smaller, 26×27 mm.
449 25c. green, red and black — 60 45

88 Test-tube and Flask

1963. Chemical Industry, Aruba.
450 **88** 20c. red, light green and green — 70 70

89 Winged Letter

1964. 35th Anniv of 1st U.S.–Curacao Flight. Multicoloured.
451 20c. Type **89** — 60 60
452 25c. Route map, Sikorsky S-38 flying boat and Boeing 707 — 60 60

90 Trinitaria

1964. Child Welfare. Multicoloured.
453 6c.+3c. Type **90** — 60 45
454 10c.+5c. Magdalena — 60 45
455 20c.+10c. Yellow keiki — 60 45
456 25c.+11c. Bellisima — 60 45

91 Caribbean Map

1964. Fifth Caribbean Council Assembly.
457 **91** 20c. yellow, red and blue — 60 45

92 "Six Islands"

1964. Tenth Anniv of Statute for the Kingdom.
458 **92** 25c. multicoloured — 60 45

93 Princess Beatrix

1965. Visit of Princess Beatrix.
459 **93** 25c. red — 60 60

94 I.T.U. Emblem and Symbols

1965. Centenary of I.T.U.
460 **94** 10c. deep blue and blue — 35 35

95 "Asperalla" (tanker) at Curacao

1965. 50th Anniv of Curacao's Oil Industry. Multicoloured.
461 10c. Catalytic cracking plant (vert) — 60 45
462 20c. Type **95** — 60 45
463 25c. Super fractionating plant (vert) — 60 45

96 Flag and Fruit Market, Curacao

1965
464 **96** 1c. blue, red and green — 35 10
465 - 2c. blue, red and yellow — 35 10
466 - 3c. blue, red and cobalt — 35 10
467 - 4c. blue, red and orange — 35 10
468 - 5c. blue, red and blue — 35 10
469 - 6c. blue, red and pink — 35 10
DESIGNS (Flag and): 2c. Divi-divi tree; 3c. Lace; 4c. Greater flamingoes; 5c. Church; 6c. Lobster.
Each is inscr with a different place-name.

97 Cup Sponges

1965. Child Welfare. Marine Life. Multicoloured.
470 6c.+3c. Type **97** — 45 35
471 10c.+5c. Cup sponges (diff) — 45 35
472 20c.+10c. Sea anemones on star coral — 60 35
473 25c.+11c. Basket sponge, blue chromis and "Brain" coral — 60 45

98 Marine and Seascape

1965. Tercentenary of Marine Corps.
474 **98** 25c. multicoloured — 35 35

1966. Intergovernmental Committee for European Migration (I.C.E.M.) Fund. As T 215 of Netherlands.
475 35c.+15c. bistre and brown — 45 45

99 Budgerigars and Wedding Rings

1966. Marriage of Crown Princess Beatrix and Herr Claus von Amsberg.
476 **99** 25c. multicoloured — 60 35

100 Admiral de Ruyter and Map

1966. 300th Anniv of Admiral de Ruyter's Visit to St. Eustatius.
477 **100** 25c. ochre, violet and blue — 45 35

101 "Grammar"

1966. 25 Years of Secondary Education.
478 **101** 6c. black, blue and yellow — 35 35
479 - 10c. black, red and green — 35 35
480 - 20c. black, blue and yellow — 45 35
481 - 25c. black, red and green — 45 35
DESIGNS: The "Free Arts", figures representing: 10c. "Rhetoric" and "Dialect"; 20c. "Arithmetic" and "Geometry"; 25c. "Astronomy" and "Music".

102 Cooking

1966. Child Welfare. Multicoloured.
482 6c.+3c. Type **102** — 45 35
483 10c.+5c. Nursing — 45 35
484 20c.+10c. Metal-work fitting — 45 35
485 25c.+11c. Ironing — 45 35

103 "Gelderland" (cruiser)

1967. 60th Anniv of Royal Netherlands Navy League.
486 **103** 6c. bronze and green — 45 35
487 - 10c. ochre and yellow — 45 35
488 - 20c. brown and sepia — 45 35
489 - 25c. blue and indigo — 45 35
SHIPS: 10c. "Pioneer" (schooner); 20c. "Oscilla" (tanker); 25c. "Santa Rosa" (liner).

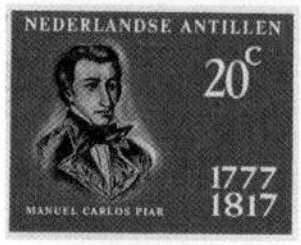

104 M. C. Piar

1967. 150th Death Anniv of Manuel Piar (patriot).

490	**104**	20c. brown and red	45	35

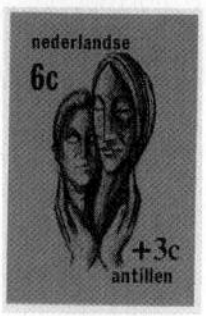

105 "Heads in Hands"

1967. Cultural and Social Relief Funds.

491	**105**	6c.+3c. black and blue	45	35
492	**105**	10c.+5c. black & mauve	45	35
493	**105**	20c.+10c. purple	45	35
494	**105**	25c.+11c. blue	45	35

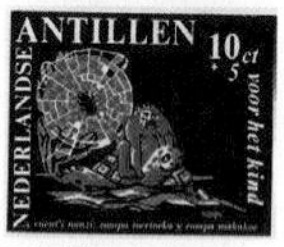

106 "The Turtle and the Monkey"

1967. Child Welfare. "Nanzi" Fairy Tales. Mult.

495	6c.+3c. "Princess Long Nose" (vert)	35	35
496	10c.+5c. Type **106**	35	35
497	20c.+10c. "Nanzi (spider) and the Tiger"	45	35
498	25c.+11c. "Shon Arey's Balloon" (vert)	45	35

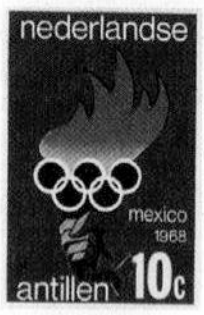

107 Olympic Flame and Rings

1968. Olympic Games, Mexico. Multicoloured.

499	10c. Type **107**	60	45
500	20c. "Throwing the discus" (statue)	60	45
501	25c. Stadium and doves	60	45

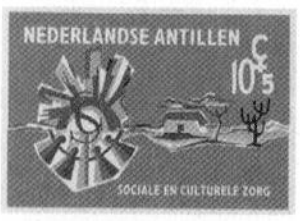

108 "Dance of the Ribbons"

1968. Cultural and Social Relief Funds.

502	**108**	10c.+5c. multicoloured	45	35
503	**108**	15c.+5c. multicoloured	45	35
504	**108**	20c.+10c. multicoloured	45	35
505	**108**	25c.+10c. multicoloured	45	35

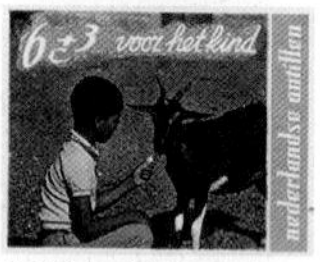

109 Boy with Goat

1968. Child Welfare Fund. Multicoloured.

506	6c.+3c. Type **109**	45	35
507	10c.+5c. Girl with dog	45	35
508	20c.+10c. Boy with cat	45	35
509	25c.+11c. Girl with duck	45	35

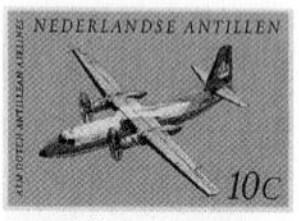

110 Fokker Friendship 500

1968. Dutch Antillean Airlines.

510	**110**	10c. blue, black and yellow	60	45
511	-	20c. blue, black and brown	60	45
512	-	25c. blue, black and pink	60	45

DESIGNS: 20c. Douglas DC-9; 25c. Fokker Friendship 500 in flight and Douglas DC-9 on ground.

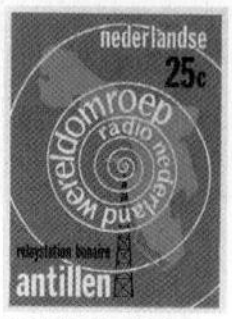

111 Radio Pylon, "Waves" and Map

1969. Opening of Broadcast Relay Station, Bonaire.

513	**111**	25c. green, dp blue & blue	45	45

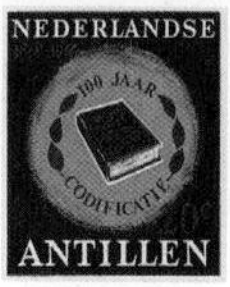

112 "Code of Laws"

1969. Centenary of Netherlands Antilles Court of Justice.

514	**112**	20c. green, gold & lt green	45	45
515	-	25c. multicoloured	45	45

DESIGN: 25c. "Scales of Justice".

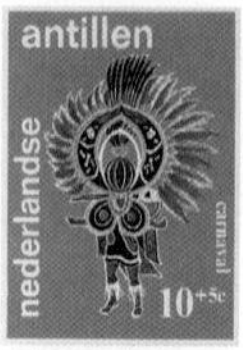

113 "Carnival"

1969. Cultural and Social Relief Funds. Antilles' Festivals. Multicoloured.

516	10c.+5c. Type **113**	60	60
517	15c.+5c. "Harvest Festival"	60	60
518	20c.+10c. "San Juan Day"	60	60
519	25c.+10c. "New Years' Day"	60	60

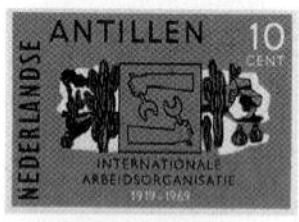

114 I.L.O. Emblem, "Koenoekoe" House and Cacti

1969. 50th Anniv of I.L.O.

520	**114**	10c. black and blue	45	35
521	**114**	25c. black and red	45	35

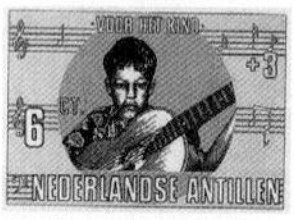

115 Boy playing Guitar

1969. Child Welfare.

522	**115**	6c.+3c. violet & orange	60	60
523	-	10c.+5c. green & yellow	60	60
524	-	20c.+10c. red and blue	60	60
525	-	25c.+11c. brown & pink	60	60

DESIGNS: 10c. Girl playing recorder; 20c. Boy playing "marimula"; 25c. Girl playing piano.

1969. 15th Anniv of Statute of the Kingdom. As T 240 of the Netherlands, but inscr "NEDER-LANDSE ANTILLEN".

526	25c. multicoloured	60	45

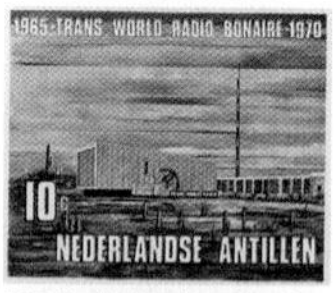

117 Radio Station, Bonaire

1970. Fifth Anniv of Trans-World Religious Radio Station, Bonaire. Multicoloured.

527	10c. Type **117**	35	35
528	15c. Trans-World Radio emblem	35	35

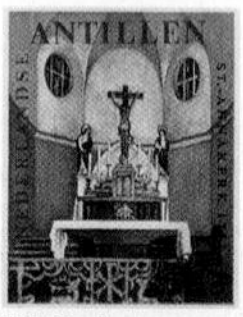

118 St. Anna Church, Otrabanda, Curacao

1970. Churches of the Netherlands Antilles. Mult.

529	10c. Type **118**	60	45
530	20c. "Mikve Israel-Emanuel" Synagogue, Punda, Curacao (horiz)	60	45
531	25c. Pulpit Fort Church Curacao	60	45

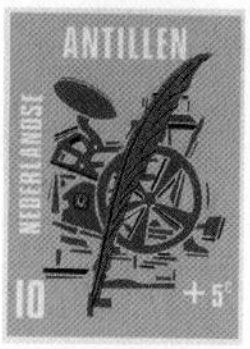

119 "The Press"

1970. Cultural and Social Relief Funds. "Mass-media". Multicoloured.

532	10c.+5c. Type **119**	70	70
533	15c.+5c. "Films"	70	70
534	20c.+10c. "Radio"	70	70
535	25c.+10c. "Television"	70	70

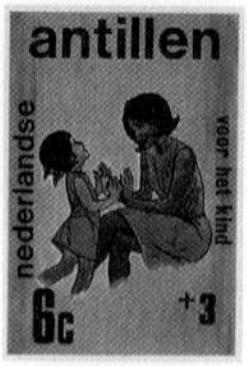

120 Mother and Child

1970. Child Welfare. Multicoloured.

536	6c.+3c. Type **120**	70	70
537	10c.+5c. Child with piggy-bank	70	70
538	20c.+10c. Children's Judo	70	70
539	25c.+11c. "Pick-a-back"	70	70

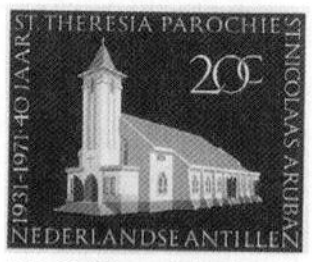

121 St. Theresia's Church, St. Nicolaas, Aruba

1971. 40th Anniv of St. Theresia Parish, Aruba.

540	**121**	20c. multicoloured	45	45

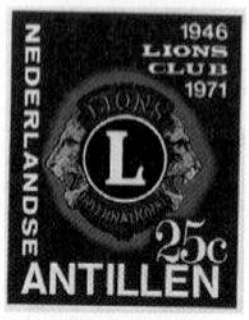

122 Lions Emblem

1971. 25th Anniv of Curacao Lions Club.

541	**122**	25c. multicoloured	60	60

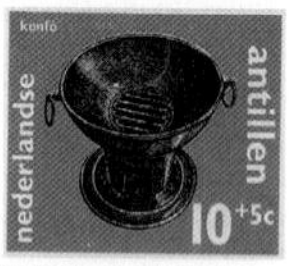

123 Charcoal Stove

1971. Cultural and Social Relief Funds. Household Utensils. Multicoloured.

542	10c.+5c. Type **123**	80	80
543	15c.+5c. Earthenware water vessel	80	80
544	20c.+10c. Baking oven	80	80
545	25c.+10c. Kitchen implements	80	80

1971. Prince Bernhard's 60th Birthday. Design as No. 1135 of Netherlands.

546	45c. multicoloured	1·20	95

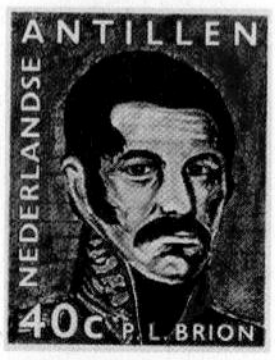

125 Admiral Brion

1971. 150th Death Anniv of Admiral Pedro Luis Brion.

547	**125**	40c. multicoloured	60	60

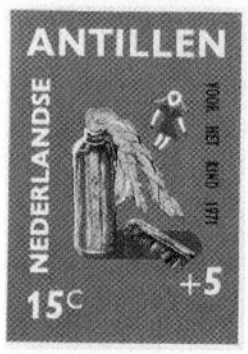

126 Bottle Doll

1971. Child Welfare. Home-made Toys. Mult.

548	15c.+5c. Type **126**	95	95
549	20c.+10c. Simple cart	95	95
550	30c.+15c. Spinning-tops	95	95

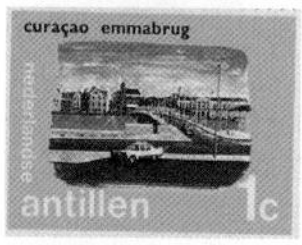

127 Queen Emma Bridge, Curacao

1971. Views of the Islands. Multicoloured.

551	1c. Type **127**	35	10
552	2c. The Bottom, Saba	35	10
553	3c. Greater flamingoes, Bonaire	35	10
554	4c. Distillation plant, Aruba	35	10
555	5c. Fort Amsterdam, St. Maarten	35	10
556	6c. Fort Oranje, St. Eustatius	35	10

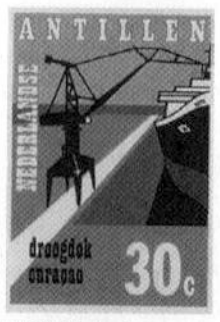

128 Ship in Dock

1972. Inauguration of New Dry Dock Complex, Willemstad, Curacao.

557	**128**	30c. multicoloured	60	60

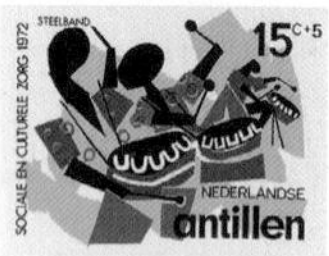

129 Steel Band

1972. Cultural and Social Relief Funds. Folklore. Multicoloured.

558	15c.+5c. Type **129**	1·20	1·20
559	20c.+10c. "Seu" festival	1·20	1·20
560	30c.+15c. "Tambu" dance	1·20	1·20

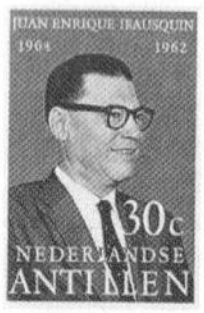

130 J. E. Irausquin

1972. Tenth Death Anniv of Juan Enrique Irausquin (Antilles statesman).

561	**130**	30c. red	60	60

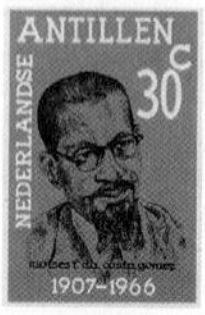

131 Dr. M. F. da Costa Gomez

1972. 65th Birth Anniv of Moises F. da Costa Gomez (statesman).

562	**131**	30c. black and green	60	60

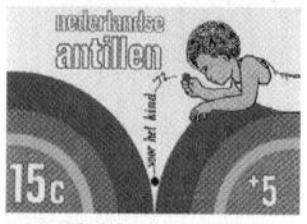

132 Child playing with Earth

1972. Child Welfare. Multicoloured.

563	15c.+5c. Type **132**	1·00	1·00
564	20c.+10c. Child playing in water	1·00	1·00
565	30c.+15c. Child throwing ball into the air	1·00	1·00

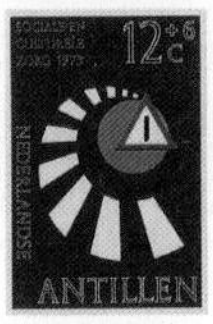

133 Pedestrian Crossing

1973. Cultural and Social Relief Funds. Road Safety.

566	**133**	12c.+6c. multicoloured	1·20	1·20
567	-	15c.+7c. grn, orge & red	1·20	1·20
568	-	40c.+20c. multicoloured	1·20	1·20

DESIGNS: 15c. Road-crossing patrol; 40c. Traffic lights.

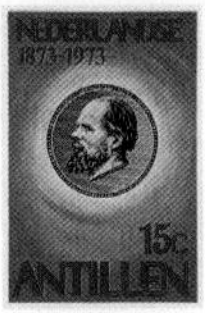

134 William III (portrait from stamp of 1873)

1973. Stamp Centenary.

569	**134**	15c. violet, mauve and gold	60	45
570	-	20c. multicoloured	70	60
571	-	30c. multicoloured	70	60

DESIGNS: 20c. Antilles postman; 30c. Postal Service emblem.

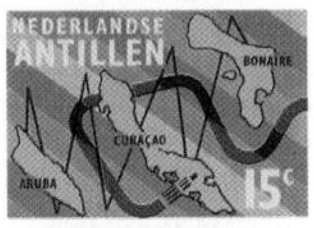

135 Map of Aruba, Curacao and Bonaire

1973. Inauguration of Submarine Cable and Microwave Telecommunications Link. Multicoloured.

572	15c. Type **135**	70	70
573	30c. Six stars ("The Antilles")	70	70
574	45c. Map of Saba, St. Maarten and St. Eustatius	70	70
MS575	145×50 mm. Nos. 572/4	4·75	4·00

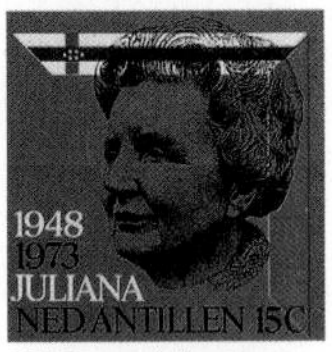

136 Queen Juliana

1973. Silver Jubilee of Queen Juliana's Reign.

576	**136**	15c. multicoloured	80	80

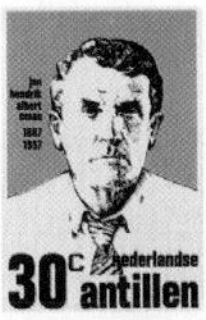

137 Jan Eman

1973. 16th Death Anniv of Jan Eman (Aruba statesman).

577	**137**	30c. black and green	60	60

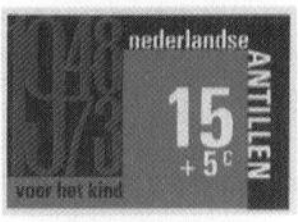

138 "1948–1973"

1973. Child Welfare Fund. 25th Anniv of 1st Child Welfare Stamps.

578	**138**	15c.+5c. light green, green and blue	1·20	1·20
579	-	20c.+10c. brown, green and blue	1·20	1·20
580	-	30c.+15c. violet, blue and light blue	1·20	1·20
MS581		108×75 mm. Nos. 578 ×2, 579 ×2	5·75	5·25

DESIGNS: No. 579, Three Children; 580, Mother and child.

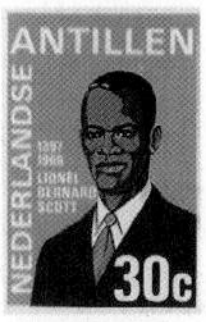

139 L. B. Scott

1974. Eighth Death Anniv of Lionel B. Scott (St. Maarten statesman).

582	**139**	30c. multicoloured	60	60

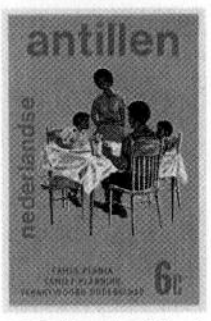

140 Family Meal

1974. Family Planning Campaign. Multicoloured.

583	6c. Type **140**	60	45
584	12c. Family at home	60	45
585	15c. Family in garden	60	45

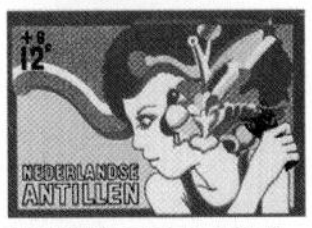

141 Girl combing Hair

1974. Cultural and Social Relief Funds. "The Younger Generation". Multicoloured.

586	12c.+6c. Type **141**	1·50	1·30
587	15c.+7c. "Pop dancers"	1·50	1·30
588	40c.+20c. Group drummer	1·50	1·30

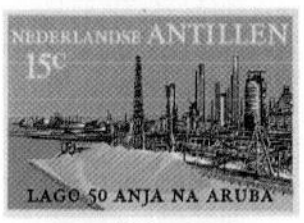

142 Desulphurisation Plant

1974. 50th Anniv of Lago Oil Co, Aruba. Mult.

589	15c. Type **142**	45	45
590	30c. Fractionating towers	60	60
591	45c. Lago refinery at night	80	80

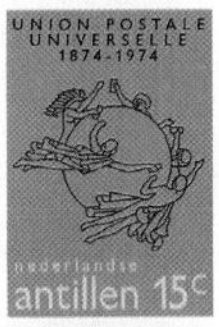

143 U.P.U. Emblem

1974. Centenary of Universal Postal Union.

592	**143**	15c. gold, green and black	70	70
593	**143**	30c. gold, blue and black	70	70

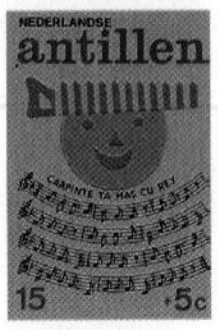

144 "A Carpenter outranks a King"

1974. Child Welfare. Children's Songs. Mult.

594	15c.+5c. Type **144**	1·20	1·20
595	20c.+10c. Footprints ("Let's Do a Ring-dance")	1·20	1·20
596	30c.+15c. "Moon and Sun"	1·20	1·20

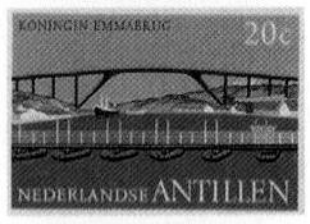

145 Queen Emma Bridge

1975. Antillean Bridges. Multicoloured.

597	20c. Type **145**	70	70
598	30c. Queen Juliana Bridge	70	70
599	40c. Queen Wilhelmina Bridge	80	80

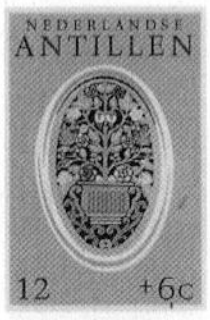

146 Ornamental Ventilation Grid

1975. Cultural and Social Welfare Funds.

600	**146**	12c.+6c. multicoloured	1·30	1·20
601	-	15c.+7c. brown & stone	1·30	1·20
602	-	40c.+20c. multicoloured	1·30	1·20

DESIGNS: 15c. Knight accompanied by buglers (tombstone detail); 40c. Foundation stone.

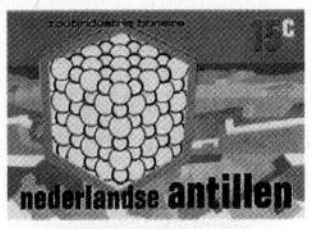

147 Sodium Chloride Molecules

1975. Bonaire Salt Industry. Multicoloured.

603	15c. Type **147**	80	60
604	20c. Salt incrustation and blocks	80	70
605	40c. Map of salt area (vert)	95	70

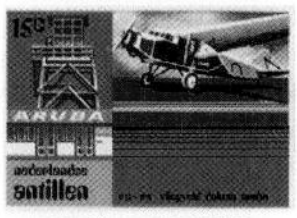

148 Fokker F.XVIII "De Snip" and Old Control Tower

1975. 40th Anniv of Aruba Airport. Mult.

606	15c. Type **148**	70	60
607	30c. Douglas DC-9-30 and modern control tower	70	60
608	40c. Tail of Boeing 727-200 and "Princess Beatrix" Airport buildings	70	70

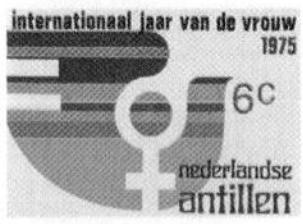

149 I.W.Y. Emblem

1975. International Women's Year. Multicoloured.

609	6c. Type **149**	45	35
610	12c. "Social Development"	60	45
611	20c. "Equality of Sexes"	70	60

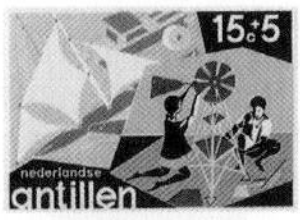

150 Children making Windmill

1975. Child Welfare. Multicoloured.

612	15c.+5c. Type **150**	1·20	1·90
613	20c.+10c. Child modelling clay	1·20	1·20
614	30c.+15c. Children drawing pictures	1·20	1·20

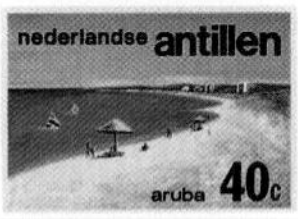

151 Beach, Aruba

1976. Tourism. Multicoloured.

615	40c. Type **151**	80	80
616	40c. Fish Kiosk, Bonaire	80	80
617	40c. "Table Mountain", Curacao	80	80

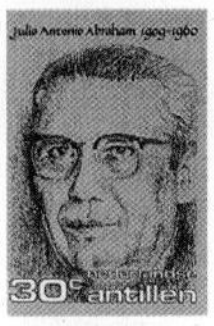

152 J. A. Abraham (statesman)

1976. Abraham Commemoration.

618	**152**	30c. purple on brown	95	70

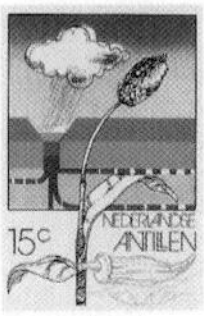

153 Dyke Produce

1976. Agriculture, Animal Husbandry and Fisheries. Multicoloured.

619	15c. Type **153**	70	60
620	35c. Cattle	80	70
621	45c. Fishes	80	80

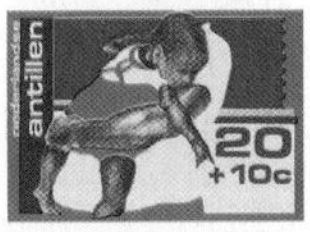

154 Arm holding Child

1976. Child Welfare. "Carrying the Child".

622	**154**	20c.+10c. multicoloured	1·20	1·20
623	-	25c.+12c. multicoloured	1·20	1·20
624	-	40c.+18c. multicoloured	1·20	1·20

DESIGNS—HORIZ: 25c. VERT: 40c. Both similar to Type **154** showing arm holding child.

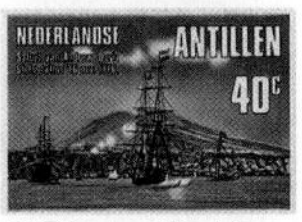

155 "Andrew Doria" (naval brig) receiving Salute

1976. Bicentenary of American Revolution. Multicoloured.

625	25c. Flags and plaque, Fort Oranje	1·20	70
626	40c. Type **155**	1·20	70
627	55c. Johannes de Graaff, Governor of St. Eustatius	1·20	1·00

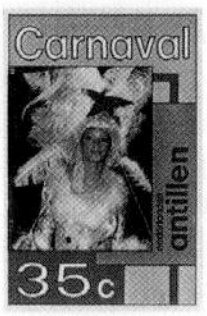

156 Carnival Costume

1977. Carnival.

628	-	25c. multicoloured	95	70
629	**156**	35c. multicoloured	95	70
630	-	40c. multicoloured	95	70

DESIGNS: 25c., 40c. Women in Carnival costumes.

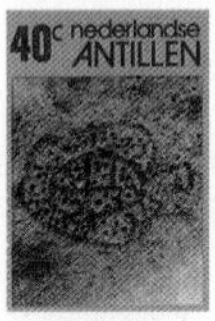

157 Tortoise (Bonaire)

1977. Rock Paintings. Multicoloured.

631	25c. Bird (Aruba)	95	70
632	35c. Abstract (Curaca)	95	70
633	40c. Type **157**	95	70

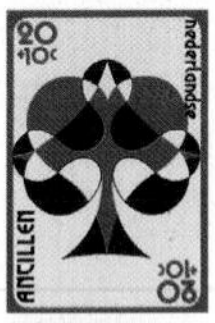

158 "Ace" Playing Card

1977. Sixth Central American and Caribbean Bridge Championships. Multicoloured.

634	**158**	20c.+10c. red and black	80	70
635	-	25c.+12c. multicoloured	80	80
636	-	40c.+18c. multicoloured	1·00	1·00
MS637		75×108 mm. Nos. 634/5 ×2	3·50	3·00

DESIGNS—VERT: 25c. "King" playing card. HORIZ: 40c. Bridge hand.

1977. "Amphilex 77" International Stamp Exhibition, Amsterdam. Sheet 175×105 mm.

MS638	Nos. 634/6 but with green backgrounds	5·75	5·75

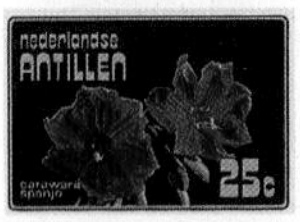

159 "Cordia sebestena"

1977. Flowers. Multicoloured.

639	25c. Type **159**	80	70
640	40c. "Albizzia lebbeck" (vert)	95	70
641	55c. "Tamarindus indica"	1·00	95

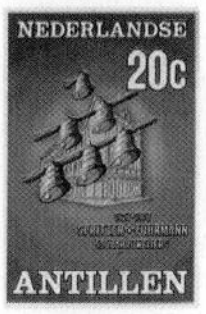

160 Bells outside Main Store

1977. 50th Anniv of Spritzer and Fuhrmann (jewellers). Multicoloured.

642	20c. Type **160**	80	70
643	40c. Globe basking in sun	95	70

644   55c. Antillean flag and diamond ring   1·00   95

161 Children with Toy Animal

1977. Child Welfare. Multicoloured.
645   15c.+15c. Type **161**   70   60
646   20c.+10c. Children with toy rabbit   80   70
647   25c.+12c. Children with toy cat   95   80
648   40c.+18c. Children with toy beetle   1·00   80
MS649   108×75 mm. Nos. 646 ×2, 648 ×2   2·40   2·10

162 "The Unspoiled Queen" (Saba)

1977. Tourism. Multicoloured.
650   25c. Type **162**   45   35
651   35c. "The Golden Rock" (St. Eustatius)   60   45
652   40c. "The Friendly Island" (St. Maarten)   60   60

1977. As Nos. 378, 381/2 and 385, but larger, (39×22 mm).
653   E   20c. grey and red   2·30   2·30
654   E   35c. pink and brown   6·25   4·75
655   C   40c. green and mauve   80   80
656   E   55c. green and red   1·20   1·20

163 19th-century Chest

1978. 150th Anniv of Netherlands Antilles' Bank. Multicoloured.
657   **163**   15c. blue and light blue   45   35
658   -   20c. orange and gold   45   35
659   -   40c. green and deep green   45   35
DESIGNS: 20c. Bank emblem; 40c. Strong-room door.

164 Water-skiing

1978. Sports Funds. Multicoloured.
660   15c.+5c. Type **164**   60   35
661   20c.+10c. Yachting   60   35
662   25c.+12c. Football   60   35
663   40c.+18c. Baseball   60   35

165 "Erythrina velutina"

1978. Flora of Netherlands Antilles. Multicoloured.
664   15c. "Delconix regia"   60   45
665   25c. Type **165**   60   45
666   50c. "Gualacum officinale" (horiz)   70   60
667   55c. "Gilricidia sepium" (horiz)   95   80

166 "Polythysana rubrescens"

1978. Butterflies. Multicoloured.
668   15c. Type **166**   70   45
669   25c. "Caligo sp."   70   45
670   35c. "Prepona praeneste"   70   60

671   40c. "Morpho sp."   80   70

167 "Conserve Energy" (English)

1978. Energy Conservation.
672   **167**   15c. orange and black   45   45
673   -   20c. green and black   60   45
674   -   40c. red and black   70   60
DESIGNS: As No. 672 but text in Dutch (20c.) or in Papiamento (40c.).

168 Red Cross

1978. 150th Birth Anniv of Henri Dunant (founder of Red Cross).
675   **168**   55c.+25c. red and blue   60   60
MS676   144×50 mm. No. 675 ×3   3·50   3·50

169 Curacao from Sea, and Punched Tape

1978. 70th Anniv of Antilles Telecommunications Corporation (Landsradio). Multicoloured.
677   20c. Type **169**   60   45
678   40c. Ship's bridge, punched tape and radio mast   70   60
679   55c. Satellite and aerial (vert)   80   80

170 Boy Rollerskating

1978. Child Welfare. Multicoloured.
680   15c.+5c. Type **170**   70   70
681   20c.+10c. Boy and girl flying kite   80   70
682   25c.+12c. Boy and girl playing marbles   80   80
683   40c.+18c. Girl riding bicycle   95   80
MS684   75×108 mm. Nos. 680/1 ×2   3·50   3·00

171 Ca'i Awa (pumping station)

1978. 80th Death Anniv of Leonard Burlington Smith (entrepreneur and U.S. Consul).
685   **171**   25c. multicoloured   45   35
686   -   35c. black, greenish yellow and yellow   60   45
687   -   40c. multicoloured   70   60
DESIGNS—VERT: 35c. Leonard Burlington Smith. HORIZ: 40c. Opening ceremony of Queen Emma Bridge, 1888.

172 Aruba Coat of Arms (float)

1979. 25th Aruba Carnival. Multicoloured.
688   40c.+10c. Float representing heraldic fantasy   80   70
689   75c.+20c. Type **172**   1·20   1·00

173 Goat and P.A.H.O. Emblem

1979. 12th Inter-American Ministerial Meeting on Foot and Mouth Disease and Zoonosis Control, Curacao. Multicoloured.
690   50c. Type **173**   70   60
691   75c. Horse and conference emblem   95   80
692   150c. Cows, flag and Pan-American Health Organization (P.A.H.O.) and W.H.O. emblems   1·50   1·50
MS693   143×50 mm. As Nos. 690/2 but background colours changed   4·00   3·50

174 Yacht and Sun

1979. 12th International Sailing Regatta, Bonaire. Multicoloured.
694   15c.+5c. Type **174**   45   35
695   35c.+25c. Yachts   60   60
696   40c.+15c. Yacht and globe (horiz)   80   70
697   55c.+25c. Yacht, sun and flamingo   95   80
MS698   124×72 mm. Nos. 694/7   3·00   3·00

175 Corps Members

1979. 50th Anniv of Curacao Volunteer Corps.
699   **175**   15c.+10c. blue, red and ultramarine   60   60
700   -   40c.+20c. blue, violet and gold   80   80
701   -   1g. multicoloured   1·00   95
DESIGNS: 40c. Sentry in battle dress and emblem; 1g. Corps emblem, flag and soldier in ceremonial uniform.

176 "Melochia tomentosa"

1979. Flowers. Multicoloured.
702   25c. "Casearia tremula"   70   45
703   40c. "Cordia cylindrostachya"   95   70
704   1g.50 Type **176**   1·90   1·60

177 Girls reading Book

1979. International Year of the Child.
705   **177**   20c.+10c. multicoloured   60   60
706   -   25c.+12c. multicoloured   70   60
707   -   35c.+15c. violet, brown and black   95   70
708   -   50c.+20c. multicoloured   1·00   1·00
MS709   75×108 mm. Nos. 705 and 707, each ×2   3·50   3·00
DESIGNS: 25c. Toddler and cat; 35c. Girls carrying basket; 50c. Boy and girl dressing-up.

178 Dove and Netherlands Flag

1979. 25th Anniv of Statute of the Kingdom. Multicoloured.
710   65c. Type **178**   95   80
711   1g.50 Dove and Netherlands Antilles flag   1·70   1·70

179 Map of Aruba and Foundation Emblem

1979. 30th Anniv of Aruba Cultural Centre Foundation. Multicoloured.
712   95c. Type **179**   1·20   1·20
713   1g. Foundation headquarters   1·40   1·40

180 Brass Chandelier

1980. 210th Anniv of Fort Church, Curacao.
714   **180**   20c.+10c. yellow, black and brown   60   60
715   -   50c.+25c. multicoloured   80   80
716   -   100c. multicoloured   1·40   1·20
DESIGNS: 50c. Pipe organ; 100c. Cupola tower, 1910.

181 Rotary Emblem and Cogwheel

1980. 75th Anniv of Rotary International. Multicoloured.
717   45c. Rotary emblem   70   50
718   50c. Globe and cogwheels   70   50
719   85c. Type **181**   95   95
MS720   120×75 mm. Nos. 717/19   3·00   3·00

182 Savings Box

1980. 75th Anniv of Post Office Savings Bank. Multicoloured.
721   25c. Type **182**   60   60
722   150c. Savings box (different)   1·70   1·70

183 Queen Juliana Accession Stamp

1980. Accession of Queen Beatrix.
723   **183**   25c. red, green and gold   45   45
724   -   60c. green, red and gold   70   70
DESIGN: 60c. 1965 Royal Visit stamp.

184 Sir Rowland Hill

1980. "London 1980" International Stamp Exhibition.
725   **184**   45c. black and green   70   70
726   -   60c. black and red   80   80
727   -   1g. red, black and blue   1·40   1·40
MS728   160×90 mm. 45c. black and red; 60c. black and blue; 1g. red, black and green   3·50   3·50
DESIGNS: 60c. "London 1980" logo; 1g. Airmail label.

185 Gymnastics (beam exercise)

1980. Sports Funds.
729   **185**   25c.+10c. red and black   60   60
730   -   30c.+15c. yellow & blk   70   70
731   -   45c.+20c. light green, green and black   95   80
732   -   60c.+25c. pink, orange and black   1·00   95
MS733   75×144 mm. Nos. 729 and 732, each ×3   5·25   4·75
DESIGNS: 30c. Gymnastics (horse vaulting); 45c. Volleyball; 60c. Basketball.

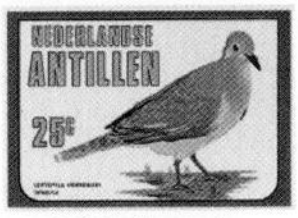

186 White-fronted Dove

1980. Birds. Multicoloured.

734	25c. Type **186**	1·20	45
735	60c. Tropical mockingbird	1·40	80
736	85c. Bananaquit	1·70	1·00

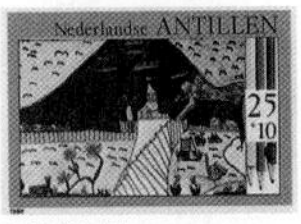

187 "St. Maarten Landscape"

1980. Child Welfare. Children's Drawings. Multicoloured.

737	25c.+10c. Type **187**	70	45
738	30c.+15c. "Bonaire House"	80	80
739	40c.+20c. "Child writing on Board"	95	95
740	60c.+25c. "Dancing Couple" (vert)	1·00	95
MS741	149×108 mm. Nos. 737 and 740, each ×3 plus four labels	3·00	2·73

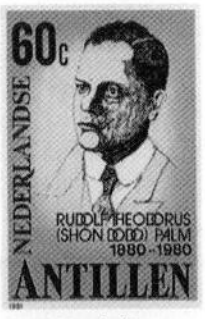

188 Rudolf Theodorus Palm

1981. Birth Centenary (1980) of Rudolf Theodorus Palm (musician).

742	**188**	60c. brown and yellow	95	95
743	-	1g. buff and blue	1·50	1·40

DESIGN: 1g. Musical score and hands playing piano.

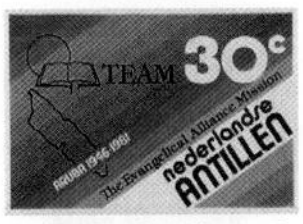

189 Map of Aruba and TEAM Emblem

1981. 50th Anniv of Evangelical Alliance Mission (TEAM) in Antilles. Multicoloured.

744	30c. Type **189**	60	60
745	50c. Map of Curacao and emblem	95	70
746	1g. Map of Bonaire and emblem	1·50	1·40

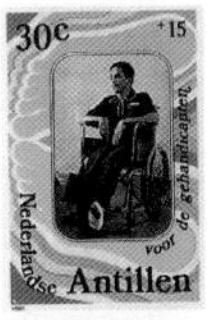

190 Boy in Wheelchair

1981. International Year of Disabled Persons. Multicoloured.

747	25c.+10c. Blind woman	70	70
748	30c.+15c. Type **190**	80	80
749	45c.+20c. Child in walking frame	1·00	1·00
750	60c.+25c. Deaf girl	1·20	1·20

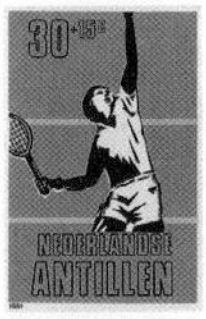

191 Tennis

1981. Sports Funds. Multicoloured.

751	30c.+15c. Type **191**	95	80
752	50c.+20c. Swimming	1·20	1·00
753	70c.+25c. Boxing	1·50	1·40
MS754	100×72 mm. Nos. 751/3	4·00	4·00

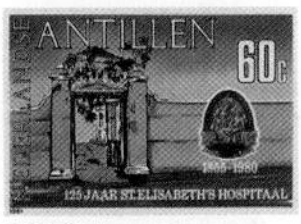

192 Gateway

1981. 125th Anniv of St. Elisabeth's Hospital. Multicoloured.

755	60c. Type **192**	80	80
756	1g.50 St. Elisabeth's Hospital	2·00	2·00

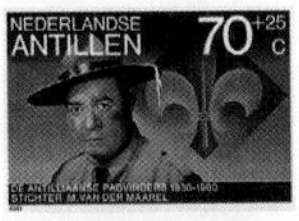

193 Marinus van der Maarel (promoter)

1981. 50th Anniv (1980) of Antillean Boy Scouts Association. Multicoloured.

757	45c.+20c. Wolf Cub and leader	1·40	1·40
758	70c.+25c. Type **193**	1·70	1·70
759	1g.+50c. Headquarters, Ronde Klip	2·40	2·40
MS760	144×50 mm. Nos. 757/9	5·75	5·75

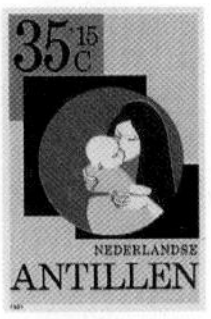

194 Mother and Child

1981. Child Welfare. Multicoloured.

761	35c.+15c. Type **194**	80	80
762	45c.+20c. Boy and girl	95	95
763	55c.+25c. Child with cat	1·20	1·20
764	85c.+40c. Girl with teddy bear	1·70	1·70
MS765	75×108 mm. Nos. 761 and 763, each ×2	4·00	4·00

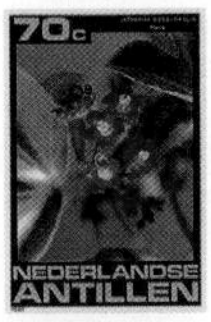

195 "Jatropha gossypifolia"

1981. Flowers. Multicoloured.

766	45c. "Cordia globosa"	70	70
767	70c. Type **195**	1·20	1·20
768	100c. "Croton flavens"	1·40	1·40

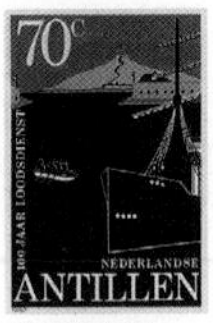

196 Pilot Gig approaching Ship

1982. Centenary of Pilotage Service. Mult.

769	70c. Type **196**	1·50	1·40
770	85c. Modern liner and map of Antilles	1·60	1·50
771	1g. Pilot boarding ship	1·70	1·60

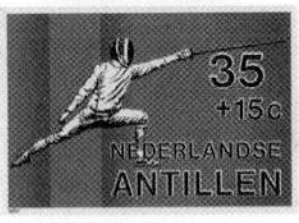

197 Fencing

1982. Sports Funds.

772	**197**	35c.+15c. mauve and violet	1·20	95
773	-	45c.+20c. blue and deep blue	1·50	1·20
774	-	70c.+35c. multicoloured	2·00	1·90
775	-	85c.+40c. brown and deep brown	2·30	2·10
MS776		144×50 mm. No. 774 ×2 plus label	5·25	4·75

DESIGNS: 45c. Judo; 70c. Football; 85c. Cycling.

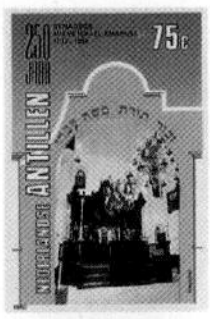

198 Holy Ark

1982. 250th Anniv of Dedication of Mikve Israel-Emanuel Synagogue, Curacao. Mult.

777	75c. Type **198**	1·50	1·20
778	85c. Synagogue facade	1·60	1·20
779	150c. Tebah (raised platform)	2·30	2·00

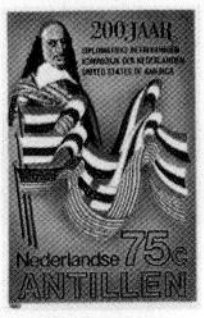

199 Peter Stuyvesant (Governor) and Flags of Netherlands, Netherlands Antilles and United States

1982. Bicentenary of Netherlands–United States Diplomatic Relations.

780	**199**	75c. multicoloured	1·70	1·40
MS781		101×70 mm. No. 780	2·30	2·10

See also No. **MS**996.

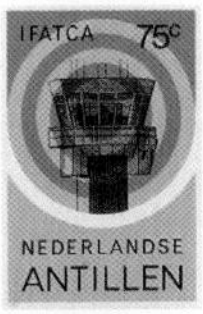

200 Airport Control Tower

1982. International Federation of Air Traffic Controllers.

782	-	35c. black, ultramarine and blue	95	60
783	**200**	75c. black, green and light green	1·50	1·20
784	-	150c. black, orange and salmon	2·20	2·00

DESIGNS: 35c. Radar plot trace; 150c. Radar aerials.

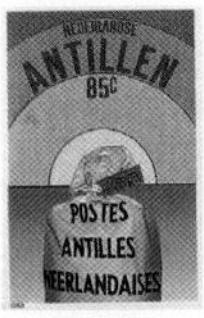

201 Mail Bag

1982. "Philexfrance 82" International Stamp Exhibition, Paris. Multicoloured.

785	45c. Exhibition emblem	1·00	80
786	85c. Type **201**	1·50	1·30
787	150c. Netherlands Antilles and French flags	2·40	2·10
MS788	125×64 mm. Nos. 785/7	5·25	4·75

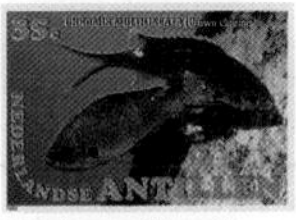

202 Brown Chromis

1982. Fishes. Multicoloured.

789	35c. Type **202**	1·40	80
790	75c. Spotted trunkfish	1·90	1·40
791	85c. Blue tang	2·10	1·60
792	100c. French angelfish	2·30	1·70

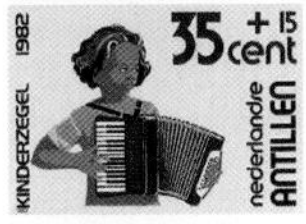

203 Girl playing Accordion

1982. Child Welfare. Multicoloured.

793	35c.+15c. Type **203**	1·30	95
794	75c.+35c. Boy playing guitar	2·10	1·90
795	85c.+40c. Boy playing violin	2·40	2·10
MS796	144×50 mm. Nos. 793/5	6·50	5·75

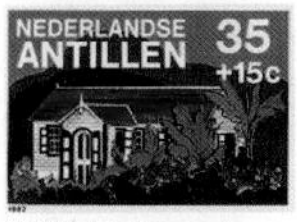

204 Saba House

1982. Cultural and Social Relief Funds. Local Houses. Multicoloured.

797	35c.+15c. Type **204**	1·50	1·20
798	75c.+35c. Aruba House	2·30	1·90
799	85c.+40c. Curacao House	2·50	2·10
MS800	72×100 mm. Nos. 797/9	7·00	5·75

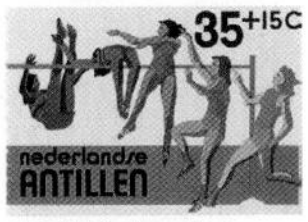

205 High Jumping

1983. Sports Funds. Multicoloured.

801	35c.+15c. Type **205**	1·20	1·00
802	45c.+20c. Weightlifting	1·60	1·40
803	85c.+40c. Wind-surfing	2·40	2·20

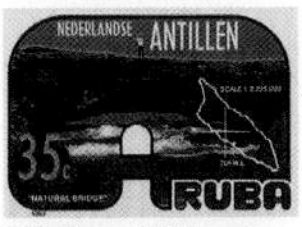

206 Natural Bridge, Aruba

1983. Tourism. Multicoloured.

804	35c. Type **206**	95	80
805	45c. Lac Bay, Bonaire	1·00	95
806	100c. Willemstad, Curacao	2·00	1·90

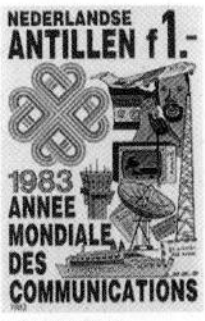

207 W.C.Y. Emblem and Means of Communication

1983. World Communications Year.

807	**207**	1g. multicoloured	2·00	1·90
MS808		100×72 mm. No. 807	2·30	2·30

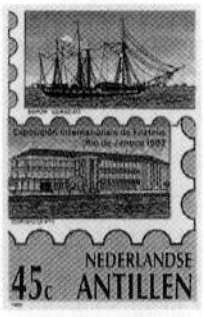

208 "Curacao" (paddle-steamer) and Post Office Building

1983. "Brasiliana 83" International Stamp Exhibition, Rio de Janeiro. Multicoloured.

809	45c. Type **208**	1·40	1·20
810	55c. Brazil flag, exhibition emblem and Netherlands Antilles flag and postal service emblem	1·50	1·30
811	100c. Governor's Palace, Netherlands Antilles, and Sugarloaf Mountain, Rio de Janeiro	2·20	2·00
MS812	100×72 mm. Nos. 809/11	5·25	4·75

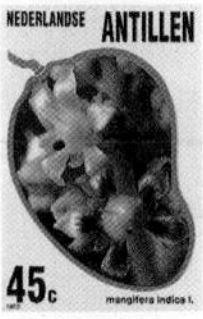

209 Mango ("Mangifera indica")

1983. Flowers. Multicoloured.

813	45c. Type **209**	1·40	1·20
814	55c. "Malpighia punicifolia"	1·50	1·30
815	100c. "Citrus aurantifolia"	2·30	2·10

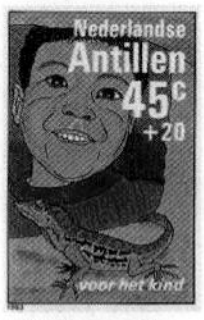

210 Boy and Lizard

1983. Child Welfare. Multicoloured.

816	45c.+20c. Type **210**	1·60	1·40
817	55c.+25c. Girl watching ants	1·90	1·60
818	100c.+50c. Girl feeding donkey	3·00	2·75
MS819	100×72 mm. Nos. 816/18	7·00	6·50

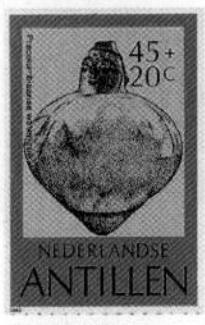

211 Aruba Water Jar

1983. Cultural and Social Relief Funds. Pre-Columbian Pottery.

820	**211**	45c.+20c. light blue, blue and black	1·70	1·60

821	-	55c.+25c. pink, red and black	2·00	1·70
822	-	85c.+40c. stone, green and black	2·40	2·10
823	-	100c.+50c. light brown, brown and black	3·25	3·00

DESIGNS: 55c. Aruba decorated bowl; 85c. Curacao human figurine; 100c. Fragment of Curacao female figurine.

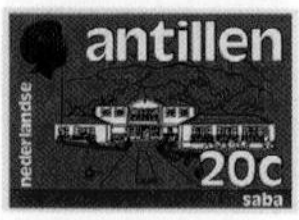

212 Saba

1983. Local Government Buildings. Multicoloured.

824	20c. Type **212**	45	35
825	25c. St. Eustatius	45	35
826	30c. St. Maarten	60	60
827	35c. Aruba	3·50	70
828	45c. Bonaire	80	80
829	55c. Curacao	1·20	95
830	60c. Type **212**	95	95
831	65c. As No. 825	1·00	1·00
832	70c. Type **212**	1·40	70
833	75c. As No. 826	1·40	1·40
834	85c. As No. 827	4·25	1·60
835	85c. As No. 828	1·60	80
836	90c. As No. 828	1·60	1·60
837	95c. As No. 829	1·70	1·70
838	1g. Type **212**	2·00	1·60
839	1g.50 As No. 825	2·40	2·10
841	2g.50 As No. 826	4·00	3·00
842	5g. As No. 828	8·25	5·25
843	10g. As No. 829	14·00	8·75
844	15g. Type **212**	21·00	14·00

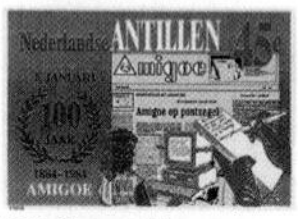

213 Note-taking, Typesetting and Front Page of "Amigoe"

1984. Centenary of "Amigoe de Curacao" (newspaper). Multicoloured.

845	45c. Type **213**	1·20	1·00
846	55c. Printing press and newspapers	1·30	1·20
847	85c. Reading newspaper	2·00	1·50

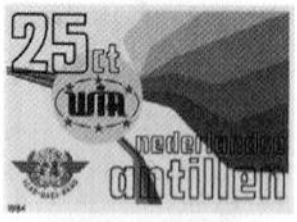

214 W.I.A. and I.C.A.O. Emblems

1984. 40th Anniv of I.C.A.O.

848	**214**	25c. multicoloured	95	60
849	-	45c. violet, blue and black	1·40	1·00
850	-	55c. multicoloured	1·50	1·20
851	-	100c. multicoloured	2·30	1·90

DESIGNS: 45c. I.C.A.O. anniversary emblem; 55c. A.L.M. and I.C.A.O. emblems; 100c. Fokker F.XIII airplane "De Snip".

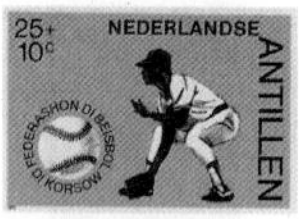

215 Fielder

1984. Sports Funds. 50th Anniv of Curacao Baseball Federation. Multicoloured.

852	25c.+10c. Type **215**	1·40	95
853	45c.+20c. Batter	2·00	1·60
854	55c.+25c. Pitcher	2·40	2·00
855	85c.+40c. Running for base	2·75	2·40
MS856	144×50 mm. Nos. 852/5	9·25	7·50

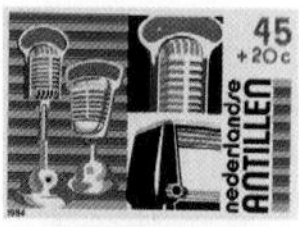

216 Microphones and Radio

1984. Cultural and Social Relief Funds. Radio and Gramophone. Multicoloured.

857	45c.+20c. Type **216**	2·20	1·60
858	55c.+25c. Gramophones and record	2·75	2·10
859	100c.+50c. Gramophone with horn	3·25	2·75

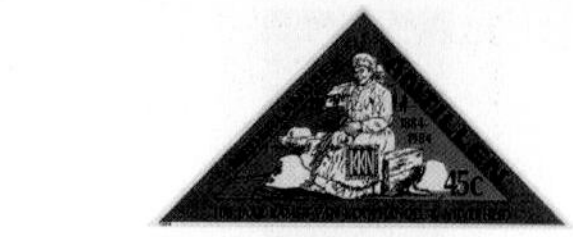

217 Bonnet-maker

1984. Centenary of Curacao Chamber of Commerce and Industry. Multicoloured.

860	45c. Type **217**	1·70	1·40
861	55c. Chamber emblem	1·90	1·40
862	1g. "Southward" (liner) passing under bridge	2·50	2·00

No. 861 is an inverted triangle.

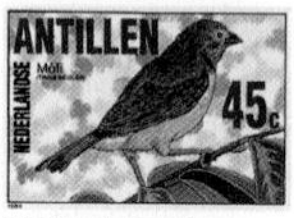

218 Black-faced Grassquit

1984. Birds. Multicoloured.

863	45c. Type **218**	1·70	1·40
864	55c. Rufous-collared sparrow	2·10	1·70
865	150c. Blue-tailed emerald	3·75	3·50

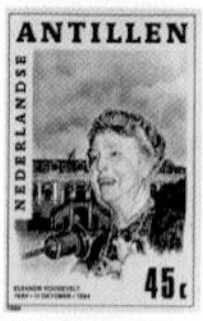

219 Eleanor Roosevelt and Val-Kill, Hyde Park, New York

1984. Birth Centenary of Eleanor Roosevelt.

866	**219**	45c. multicoloured	1·20	95
867	-	85c. black, gold and bistre	1·90	1·60
868	-	100c. black, yellow and red	2·00	1·70

DESIGNS: 85c. Portrait in oval frame; 100c. Eleanor Roosevelt with children.

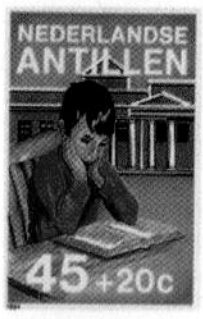

220 Child Reading

1984. Child Welfare. Multicoloured.

869	45c.+20c. Type **220**	1·60	1·60
870	55c.+25c. Family reading	2·10	2·10
871	100c.+50c. Family in church	2·75	2·75
MS872	100×72 mm. Nos. 869/71	6·75	6·50

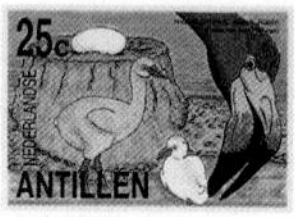

221 Adult Flamingo and Chicks

1985. Greater Flamingoes. Multicoloured.

873	25c. Type **221**	1·20	95
874	45c. Young flamingoes	1·70	1·20
875	55c. Adult flamingoes	1·70	1·40
876	100c. Flamingoes in various flight positions	2·75	2·10

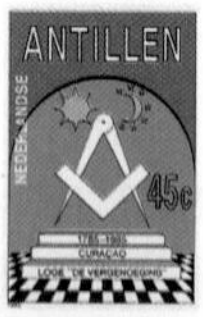

222 Symbols of Entered Apprentice

1985. Bicentenary of De Vergenoeging Masonic Lodge, Curacao. Multicoloured.

877	45c. Type **222**	2·30	1·20
878	55c. Symbols of the Fellow Craft	2·30	1·50
879	100c. Symbols of the Master Mason	3·00	2·40

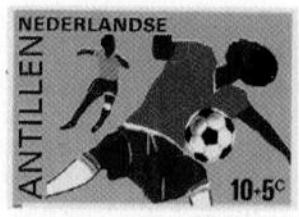

223 Players with Ball

1985. Sports Funds. Football. Multicoloured.

880	10c.+5c. Type **223**	80	60
881	15c.+5c. Dribbling ball	95	70
882	45c.+20c. Running with ball	1·60	1·50
883	55c.+25c. Tackling	2·00	1·90
884	85c.+40c. Marking player with ball	2·75	2·75

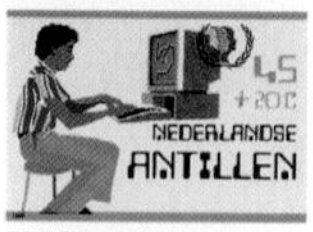

224 Boy using Computer

1985. Cultural and Social Welfare Funds. International Youth Year. Multicoloured.

885	45c.+20c. Type **224**	1·70	1·60
886	55c.+25c. Girl listening to records	2·30	2·10
887	100c.+50c. Boy break-dancing	3·25	3·00

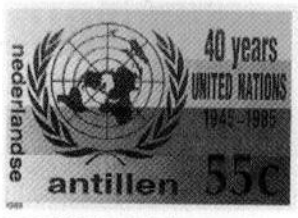

225 U.N. Emblem

1985. 40th Anniv of U.N.O.

888	**225**	55c. multicoloured	1·50	1·30
889	**225**	1g. multicoloured	2·30	2·10

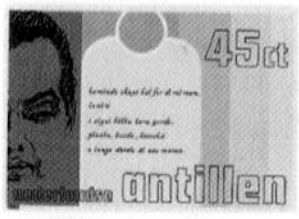

226 Pierre Lauffer and Poem

1985. Papiamentu (Creole language). Multicoloured.

890	45c. Type **226**	95	95
891	55c. Wave inscribed "Papiamentu"	1·20	1·20

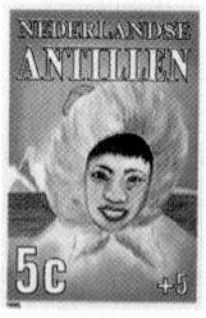

227 Eskimo

1985. Child Welfare. Multicoloured.

892	5c.+5c. Type **227**	60	35
893	10c.+5c. African child	70	45
894	25c.+10c. Chinese girl	1·00	80
895	45c.+20c. Dutch girl	1·90	1·40
896	55c.+25c. Red Indian girl	1·90	1·70
MS897	100×72 mm. Nos. 894/6	5·25	4·00

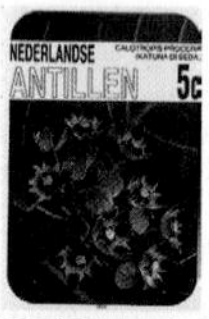

228 "Calotropis procera"

1985. Flowers. Multicoloured.

898	5c. Type **228**	70	35
899	10c. "Capparis flexuosa"	70	35
900	20c. "Mimosa distachya"	1·00	60
901	45c. "Ipomoea nil"	1·50	95
902	55c. "Heliotropium ternatum"	1·70	1·00
903	150c. "Ipomoea incarnata"	3·00	2·30

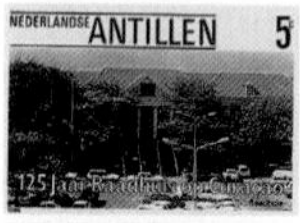

229 Courthouse

1986. 125th Anniv of Curacao Courthouse. Multicoloured.

904	5c. Type **229**	45	35
905	15c. States room (vert)	60	35
906	25c. Court room	80	60
907	55c. Entrance (vert)	1·40	1·00

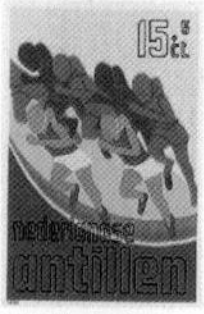

230 Sprinting

1986. Sports Funds. Multicoloured.

908	15c.+5c. Type **230**	1·40	80
909	25c.+10c. Horse racing	1·60	1·20
910	45c.+20c. Motor racing	2·10	1·50
911	55c.+25c. Football	2·40	1·90

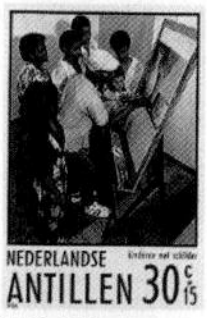

231 Girls watching Artist at work

1986. Curacao Youth Care Foundation. Multicoloured.

912	30c.+15c. Type **231**	1·40	1·00
913	45c.+20c. Children watching sculptor at work	1·60	1·20
914	55c.+25c. Children watching potter at work	2·00	1·60

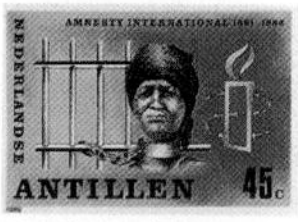

232 Chained Man

1986. 25th Anniv of Amnesty International.

915	45c. Type **232**	1·30	95
916	55c. Dove behind bars	1·40	1·00
917	100c. Man behind bars	2·00	1·60

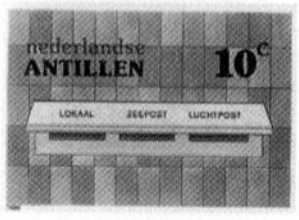

233 Post Office Mail Box

1986. Mail Boxes. Multicoloured.

918	10c. Type **233**	35	35
919	25c. Street mail box on pole	60	35
920	45c. Street mail box in brick column	95	80
921	55c. Street mail box	1·20	95

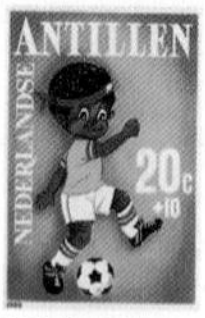

234 Boy playing Football

1986. Child Welfare. Multicoloured.

922	20c.+10c. Type **234**	95	70
923	25c.+15c. Girl playing tennis	1·20	80
924	45c.+20c. Boy practising judo	1·40	1·20
925	55c.+25c. Boy playing baseball	1·60	1·50
MS926	75×72 mm. Nos. 924/5	3·50	3·00

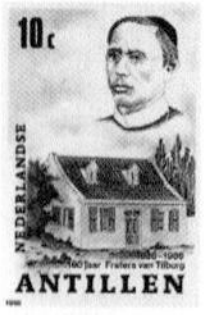

235 Brothers' First House and Mauritius Vliegendehond

1986. Centenary of Friars of Tilburg Mission. Multicoloured.

927	10c. Type **235**	45	20
928	45c. St. Thomas College and Mgr. Ferdinand E. C. Kieckens	1·00	80
929	55c. St. Thomas College courtyard and Fr. F.S. de Beer	1·30	1·00

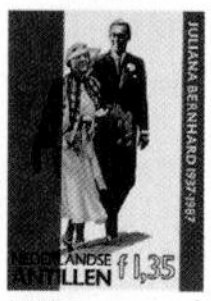

236 Engagement Picture

1987. Golden Wedding of Princess Juliana and Prince Bernhard.

930	**236**	1g.35 orange, blk & gold	3·25	2·30
MS931		50×72 mm. No. 930	5·25	4·00

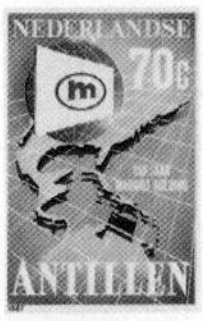

237 Map

1987. 150th Anniv of Maduro Holding Inc. Multicoloured.

932	70c. Type **237**	1·20	95
933	85c. Group activities	1·40	1·20
934	1g.55 Saloman Elias Levy Maduro (founder)	2·40	2·30

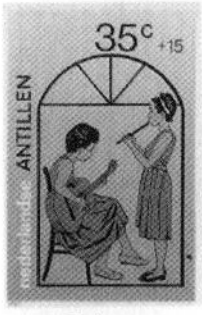

238 Girls playing Instruments

1987. Cultural and Social Relief Funds.

935	**238**	35c.+15c. multicoloured	1·00	95
936	-	45c.+25c. light green, green and blue	1·60	1·20
937	-	85c.+40c. multicoloured	2·10	1·90

DESIGNS: 45c. Woman pushing man in wheelchair. 85c. Bandstand.

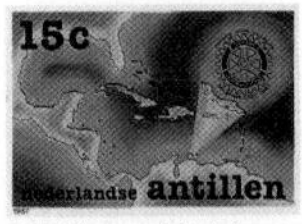

239 Map and Emblem

1987. 50th Anniv of Curacao Rotary Club. Multicoloured.

938	15c. Type **239**	60	35
939	50c. Zeelandia country house (meeting venue)	1·20	95
940	65c. Emblem on map of Curacao	1·50	1·00

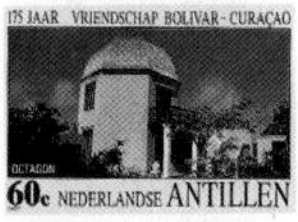

240 Octagon (house where Bolivar's sisters lived)

1987. 175th Anniv of Simon Bolivar's Exile on Curacao (60, 80c.) and 50th Anniv of Bolivarian Society (70, 90c.). Multicoloured.

941	60c. Type **240**	1·00	95
942	70c. Society headquarters, Willemstad, Curacao	1·20	1·00
943	80c. Room in Octagon	1·50	1·40
944	90c. Portraits of Manuel Carlos Piar, Simon Bolivar and Pedro Luis Brion	1·60	1·50

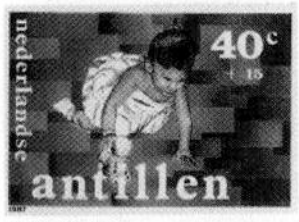

241 Baby

1987. Child Welfare. Multicoloured.

945	40c.+15c. Type **241**	1·50	1·20
946	55c.+25c. Child	1·90	1·50
947	115c.+50c. Youth	2·50	2·10
MS948	144× 50 mm. Nos. 945/7	6·25	5·00

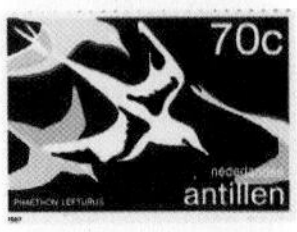

242 White-tailed Tropic Birds

1987. 25th Anniv of Netherlands Antilles National Parks Foundation. Multicoloured.

949	70c. Type **242**	1·20	95
950	85c. White-tailed deer	1·40	1·20
951	155c. Iguana	2·40	2·30

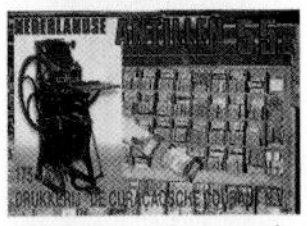

243 Printing Press and Type

1987. 175th Anniv of "De Curacaosche Courant" (periodical and printing shop). Multicoloured.

952	55c. Type **243**	1·00	95
953	70c. Keyboard and modern printing press	1·20	1·00

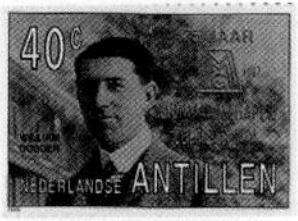

244 William Godden (founder)

1988. 75th Anniv of Curacao Mining Company. Multicoloured.

954	40c. Type **244**	95	70
955	105c. Phosphate processing plant	1·70	1·50
956	155c. Tafelberg (source of phosphate)	2·40	2·10

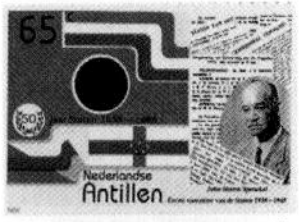

245 Flags, Minutes and John Horris Sprockel (first President)

1988. 50th Anniv of Netherlands Antilles Staten (legislative body). Multicoloured.

957	65c. Type **245**	1·20	1·00
958	70c. Ballot paper and schematic representation of extension of voting rights	1·40	1·00
959	155c. Antilles and Netherlands flags and birds representing five Antilles islands and Aruba	2·40	2·10

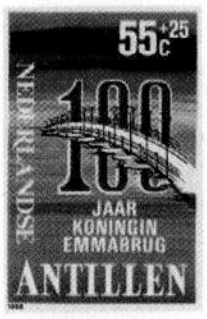

246 Bridge through "100"

1988. Cultural and Social Relief Funds. Centenary of Queen Emma Bridge, Curacao. Mult.

960	55c.+25c. Type **246**	1·60	1·00
961	115c.+55c. Willemstad harbour (horiz)	2·50	2·00
962	190c.+60c. Leonard B. Smith (engineer) and flags (horiz)	4·00	3·75

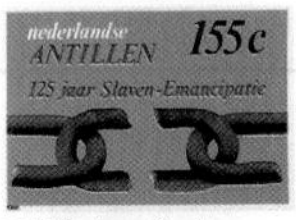

247 Broken Chain

1988. 125th Anniv of Abolition of Slavery. Mult.

963	155c. Type **247**	2·10	1·90
964	190c. Breach in slave wall	2·50	2·20

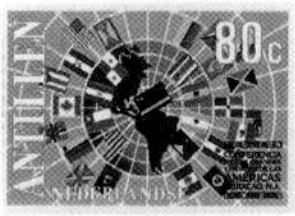

248 Flags and Map

1988. Third Inter-American Foundation of Cities "Let us Build Bridges" Conference, Curacao. Multicoloured.

965	80c. Type **248**	1·40	1·00
966	155c. Bridge and globe	2·10	1·90

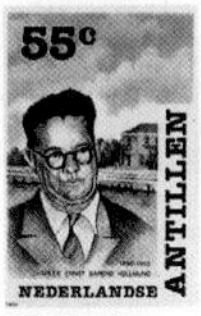

249 Charles Hellmund (Bonaire councillor)

1988. Celebrities. Multicoloured.

967	55c. Type **249**	95	70
968	65c. Atthelo Maud Edwards-Jackson (founder of Saba Electric Company)	1·00	80
969	90c. Nicolaas Debrot (Governor of Antilles, 1962–69)	1·60	1·30
970	120c. William Charles de la Try Ellis (lawyer and politician)	1·70	1·50

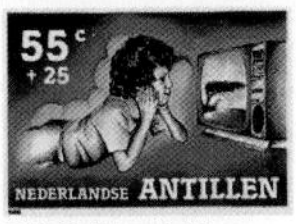

250 Child watching Television

1988. Child Welfare. Multicoloured.

971	55c.+25c. Type **250**	1·50	1·20
972	65c.+30c. Boy with radio	1·60	1·40
973	115c.+55c. Girl using computer	2·30	2·10
MS974	118×67 mm. Nos. 971/3	7·50	5·00

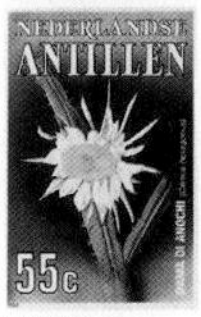

251 "Cereus hexagonus"

1988. Cacti. Multicoloured.

975	55c. Type **251**	1·20	80
976	115c. Melocactus	1·90	1·30
977	125c. "Opuntia wentiana"	2·20	1·30

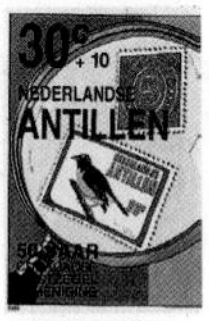

252 Magnifying Glass over 1936 and 1980 Stamps

1989. Cultural and Social Relief Funds. 50th Anniv of Curacao Stamp Association. Multicoloured.

978	30c.+10c. Type **252**	1·70	95
979	55c.+20c. Picking up stamp with tweezers (winning design by X. Rico in drawing competition)	1·70	1·50
980	80c.+30c. Barn owl and stamp album	1·70	1·70

Nos. 978/80 were printed together, se-tenant, forming a composite design.

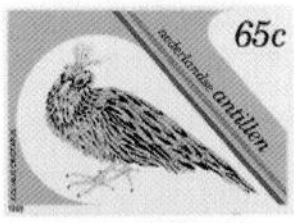

253 Crested Bobwhite

1989. 40th Anniv of Curacao Foundation for Prevention of Cruelty to Animals. Multicoloured.

981	65c. Type **253**	1·70	1·00
982	115c. Dogs and cats	2·00	1·60

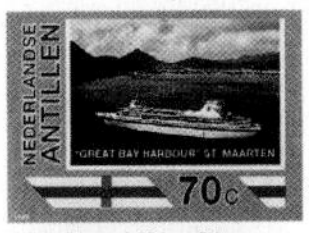

254 "Sun Viking" in Great Bay Harbour, St. Maarten

1989. Tourism. Cruise Liners. Multicoloured.

983	70c. Type **254**	1·40	1·00
984	155c. "Eugenio C" entering harbour, St. Annabay, Curacao	2·40	2·10

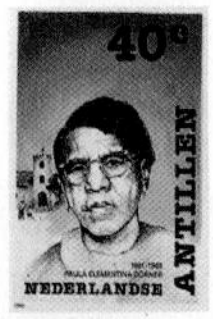

255 Paula Clementina Dorner (teacher)

1989. Celebrities. Multicoloured.

985	40c. Type **255**	95	70
986	55c. John Aniseto de Jongh (pharmacist and politician)	1·00	80
987	90c. Jacobo Jesus Maria Palm (musician)	1·50	1·20
988	120c. Abraham Mendes Chumaceiro (lawyer and social campaigner)	1·90	1·60

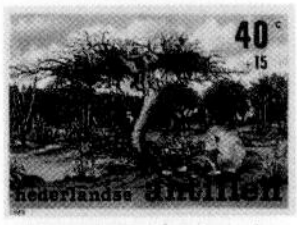

256 Boy and Girl under Tree

1989. Child Welfare. Multicoloured.

989	40c.+15c. Type **256**	1·40	95
990	65c.+30c. Two children playing on shore	1·60	1·30
991	115c.+35c. Adult carrying child	2·40	2·10
MS992	92×62 mm. 155c.+75c. Children playing on shore	5·25	3·50

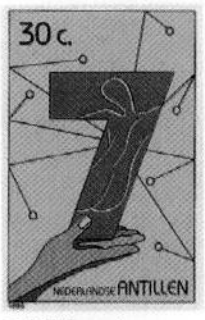

257 Hand holding "7"

1989. 40th Anniv of Queen Wilhelmina Foundation for Cancer Care. Multicoloured.

993	30c. Type **257**	80	70
994	60c. Seated figure and figure receiving radiation treatment	1·30	1·00
995	80c. Figure exercising and Foundation emblem	1·50	1·00

1989. "World Stamp Expo '89" International Stamp Exhibition, Washington, D.C. Sheet 112×65 mm containing multicoloured designs as previous issues but with changed values.

MS996	70c. As No. 625; 155c. Type **199**; 250c. Type **80**	8·25	7·50

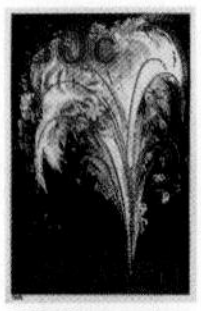

258 Fireworks

1989. Christmas. Multicoloured.

997	30c. Type **258**	80	60
998	100c. Christmas tree decorations	1·70	1·40

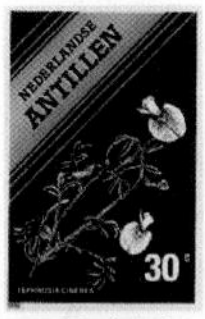

259 "Tephrosia cinerea"

1990. Flowers. Multicoloured.

999	30c. Type **259**	60	50
1000	55c. "Erithalis fruticosa"	1·00	80
1001	65c. "Evolvulus antillanus"	1·20	95
1002	70c. "Jacquinia arborea"	1·30	1·00
1003	125c. "Tournefortia onaphalodes"	2·30	2·00
1004	155c. "Sesuvium portulacastrum"	3·00	2·40

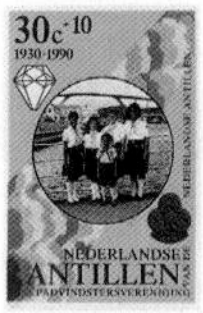

260 Girl Guides

1990. Cultural and Social Relief Funds. Mult.

1005	30c.+10c. Type **260** (60th anniv)	1·00	75
1006	40c.+15c. Totolika (care of mentally handicapped organization) (17th anniv)	1·30	1·00
1007	155c.+65c. Boy scout (60th anniv)	3·75	3·75

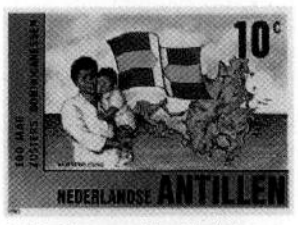

261 Nun with Child, Flag and Map

1990. Centenary of Arrival of Dominican Nuns in Netherlands Antilles. Multicoloured.

1008	10c. Type **261**	30	20
1009	55c. St. Rose Hospital and St. Martin's Home, St. Maarten	95	75
1010	60c. St. Joseph School, St. Maarten	1·00	95

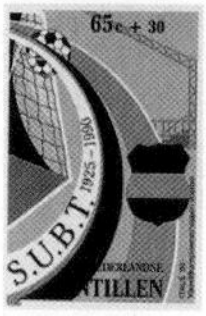

262 Goal Net, Ball and Shield

1990. Multicoloured.

1011	65c.+30c. Type **262** (65th anniv of Sport Unie Brion Trappers football club)	1·60	1·50
1012	115c.+55c. Guiding addict from darkness towards sun (anti-drugs campaign)	2·50	2·50

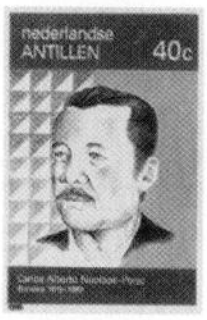

263 Carlos Nicolaas-Perez (philologist and poet)

1990. Meritorious Antilleans. Multicoloured.

1013	40c. Type **263**	70	50
1014	60c. Evert Kruythoff (writer)	1·00	95
1015	80c. John de Pool (writer)	1·30	1·20
1016	150c. Joseph Sickman Corsen (poet and composer)	2·50	2·40

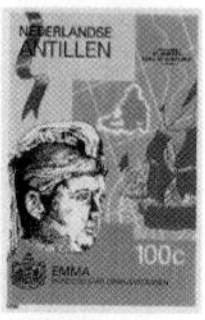

264 Queen Emma

1990. Dutch Queens of the House of Orange. Multicoloured.

1017	100c. Type **264**	2·00	1·60
1018	100c. Queen Wilhelmina	2·00	1·60
1019	100c. Queen Juliana	2·00	1·60
1020	100c. Queen Beatrix	2·00	1·60
MS1021	77×64 mm. 250c. Queens Emma, Wilhelmina, Juliana and Beatrix (35×24 mm)	9·75	8·25

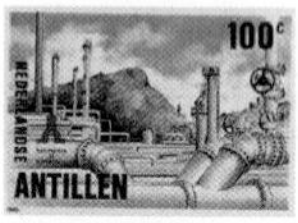

265 Isla Refinery

1990. 75th Anniv of Oil Refining on Curacao.

1022	**265**	100c. multicoloured	1·90	1·70

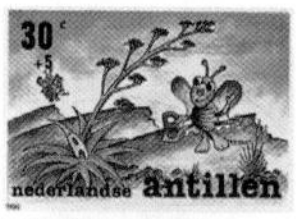

266 Flower and Bees

1990. Child Welfare. International Literacy Year. Designs illustrating letters of alphabet. Multicoloured.

1023	30c.+5c. Type **266**	95	65
1024	55c.+10c. Dolphins and sun	1·50	1·00
1025	65c.+15c. Donkey with bicycle	1·60	1·30
1026	100c.+20c. Goat dreaming of house	2·40	2·10
1027	115c.+25c. Rabbit carrying food on yoke	2·75	2·20
1028	155c.+55c. Lizard, moon and cactus	4·25	3·75

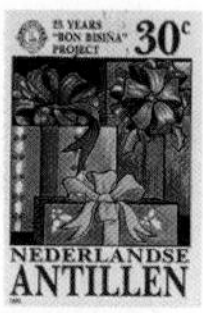

267 Parcels

1990. Christmas. Multicoloured.

1029	30c. Type **267** (25th anniv of Curacao Lions Club's Good Neighbour project)	80	50
1030	100c. Mother and child	2·10	1·60

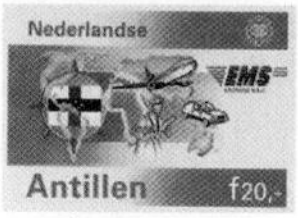

268 Flag, Map and Distribution of Mail

1991. Sixth Anniv of Express Mail Service.

1031	**268**	20g. multicoloured	35·00	33·00

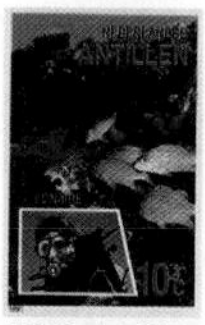

269 Scuba Diver and French Grunt

1991. Fish. Multicoloured.

1032	10c. Type **269**	60	20
1033	40c. Spotted trunkfish	1·00	70
1034	55c. Copper sweepers	1·30	1·00
1035	75c. Skindiver and yellow goatfishes	1·60	1·40
1036	100c. Black-barred soldier-fishes	2·40	1·70

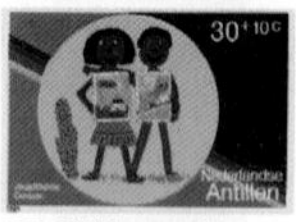

270 Children and Stamps

1991. Cultural and Social Relief Funds. Mult.

1037	30c.+10c. Type **270** (12th anniv of Philatelic Club of Curacao)	1·20	95
1038	65c.+25c. St. Vincentius Brass Band (50th anniv)	1·90	1·60
1039	155c.+55c. Games and leisure pursuits (30th anniv of FESEBAKO) (Curacao community centres)	4·00	3·75

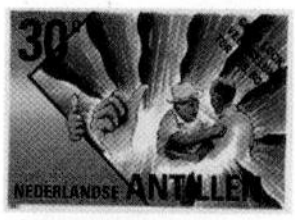

271 "Good Luck"

1991. Greetings Stamps. Multicoloured.

1040	30c. Type **271**	60	60
1041	30c. "Thank You"	60	60
1042	30c. Couple and family ("Love You")	60	60
1043	30c. Song birds ("Happy Day")	60	60
1044	30c. Greater flamingo and medicines ("Get Well Soon")	60	60
1045	30c. Flowers and balloons ("Happy Birthday")	60	60

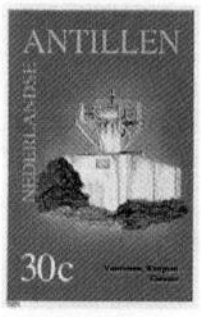

272 Westpoint Lighthouse, Curacao

1991. Lighthouses. Multicoloured.

1046	30c. Type **272**	3·00	1·70
1047	70c. Willems Toren, Bonaire	3·00	1·70
1048	115c. Klein Curacao lighthouse	3·00	1·70

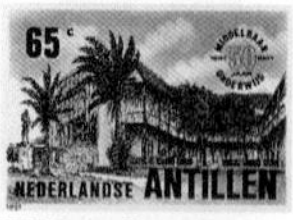

273 Peter Stuyvesant College

1991. 50th Anniv of Secondary Education in Netherlands Antilles (65c.) and "Espamer '91" Spain–Latin America Stamp Exhibition, Buenos Aires (125c.). Multicoloured.

1049	65c. Type **273**	1·20	1·20
1050	125c. Dancers of Netherlands Antilles, Argentina and Portugal (vert)	2·30	2·30

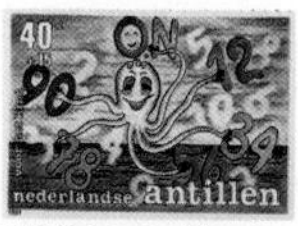

274 Octopus with Letters and Numbers

1991. Child Welfare. Multicoloured.

1051	40c.+15c. Type **274**	1·50	1·00
1052	65c.+30c. Parents teaching arithmetic	2·00	1·70
1053	155c.+65c. Bird and tortoise with clock	3·75	3·75
MS1054	118×67 mm. 55c.+25c. Owl with letters and national flag; 100c.+35c. Books and bookworms; 115c.+50c. Dragon, ice-cream cone and icicles. Imperf	8·75	7·00

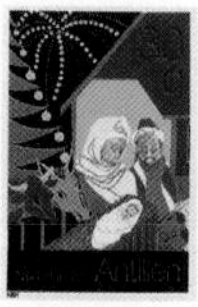

275 Nativity

1991. Christmas. Multicoloured.

1055	30c. Type **275**	50	50
1056	100c. Angel appearing to shepherds	1·70	1·70

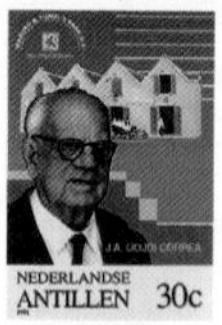

276 Joseph Alvarez Correa (founder) and Headquarters of S.E.L. Maduro and Sons

1991. 75th Anniv of Maduro and Curiel's Bank. Multicoloured.

1057	30c. Type **276**	1·20	70
1058	70c. Lion rampant (bank's emblem) and "75"	1·90	1·40
1059	155c. Isaac Haim Capriles (Managing Director, 1954–74) and Scharloo bank branch	2·75	2·50

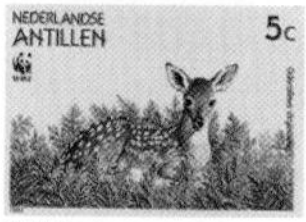

277 Fawn

1992. The White-tailed Deer. Multicoloured.

1060	5c. Type **277** (postage)	1·30	1·20
1061	10c. Young adults	1·30	1·20
1062	30c. Stag	1·30	1·20
1063	40c. Stag and hind in water	1·30	1·20
1064	200c. Stag drinking (air)	4·00	3·75
1065	355c. Stag calling	6·50	6·50

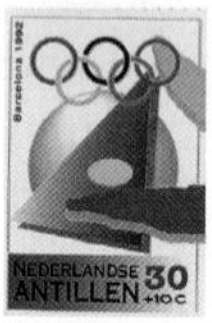

278 Windsurfer

1992. Cultural and Social Relief Funds. Olympic Games, Barcelona. Multicoloured.

1066	30c.+10c. Type **278** (award of silver medal to Jan Boersma, 1988 Games)	1·20	80
1067	55c.+25c. Globe, national flag and Olympic rings	1·60	1·30
1068	115c.+55c. Emblem of National Olympic Committee (60th anniv)	3·25	3·00

Nos. 1066/8 were issued together, se-tenant, forming a composite design.

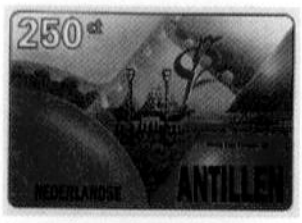

279 The Alhambra, Grenada

1992. "Granada '92" International Stamp Exhibition (250c.) and "Expo '92" World's Fair, Seville (500c.). Sheet 92×52 mm containing T 279 and similar horiz design. Multicoloured.

MS1069	250c. Type **279**; 500c. Carthusian Monastery, Seville, and Columbus	15·00	14·00

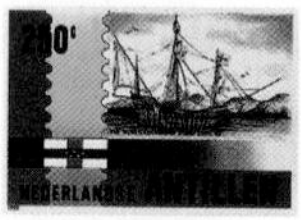

280 "Santa Maria"

1992. "World Columbian Stamp Expo '92", Chicago. Multicoloured.

1070	250c. Type **280**	4·75	4·00
1071	500c. Chart and Columbus	9·25	8·25

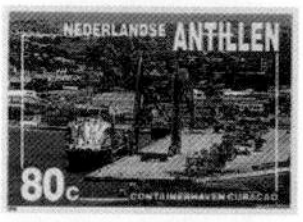

281 View of Dock and Town

1992. Curacao Port Container Terminal. Mult.

1072	80c. Type **281**	1·50	1·40
1073	125c. Crane and ship	2·20	2·10

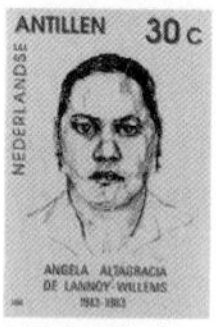

282 Angela de Lannoy-Willems

1992. Celebrities.

1074	**282**	30c. black, brown & grn	70	60
1075	-	40c. black, brown & blue	95	70
1076	-	55c. black, brown & orge	1·20	95
1077	-	70c. black, brown and red	1·30	1·00
1078	-	100c. black, brown & blue	1·70	1·70

DESIGNS: 30c. Type **282** (first woman Member of Parliament); 40c. Lodewijk Daniel Gerharts (entrepreneur on Bonaire); 55c. Cyrus Wilberforce Wathey (entrepreneur on St. Maarten); 70c. Christian Winkel (Deputy Governor of Antilles); 100c. Mother Joseph (founder of Roosendaal Congregation (Franciscan welfare sisterhood)).

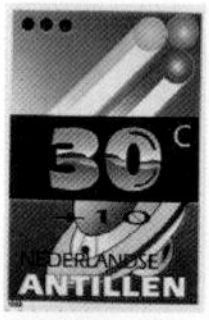

283 Spaceship

1992. Child Welfare. Multicoloured.

1079	30c.+10c. Type **283**	95	70
1080	70c.+30c. Robot	1·60	1·60
1081	100c.+40c. Extra-terrestrial being	2·40	2·30
MS1082	94×54 mm. 155c.+70c. Martian	5·25	4·75

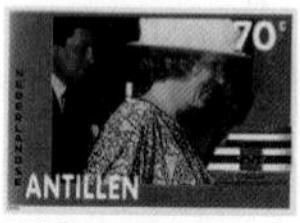

284 Queen Beatrix and Prince Claus

1992. 12½ Years since Accession to the Throne of Queen Beatrix (100c.) and Royal Visit to Netherlands Antilles (others). Designs showing photos of previous visits to the Antilles. Mult.

1083	70c. Type **284**	1·30	1·20
1084	100c. Queen Beatrix signing book	1·70	1·60
1085	175c. Queen Beatrix and Prince Claus with girl	3·00	2·75

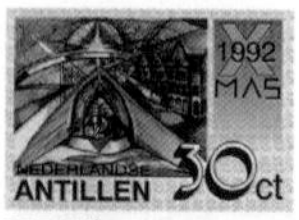

285 Crib

1992. Christmas. Multicoloured.

1086	30c. Type **285**	70	60
1087	100c. Mary and Joseph searching for lodgings (vert)	2·00	1·60

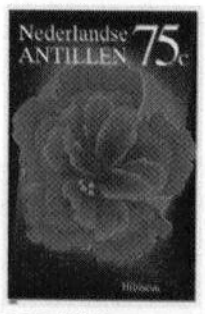

286 Hibiscus

1993. Flowers. Multicoloured.

1088	75c. Type **286**	1·40	1·20
1089	90c. Sunflower	1·60	1·50
1090	175c. Ixora	3·00	2·75
1091	195c. Rose	3·25	3·25

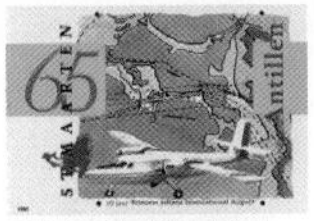

287 De Havilland Twin Otter and Flight Paths

1993. Anniversaries. Multicoloured.

1092	65c. Type **287** (50th anniv of Princess Juliana International Airport, St. Maarten)	1·20	1·00
1093	75c. Laboratory worker and National Health Laboratory (75th anniv)	1·30	1·20
1094	90c. De Havilland Twin Otter on runway at Princess Juliana International Airport	1·50	1·50
1095	175c. White and yellow cross (50th anniv of Princess Margriet White and Yellow Cross Foundation for District Nursing)	2·75	2·75

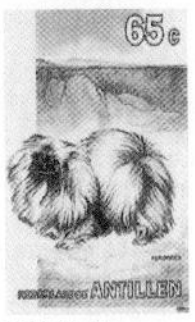

288 Pekingese

1993. Dogs. Multicoloured.

1096	65c. Type **288**	1·30	1·00
1097	90c. Standard poodle	1·70	1·50
1098	100c. Pomeranian	2·10	1·60
1099	175c. Papillon	3·25	2·75

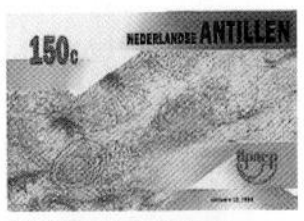

289 Cave Painting, Bonaire

1993. "Brasiliana '93" International Stamp Exhibition, Rio de Janeiro, and Admittance of Antilles to Postal Union of the Americas, Spain and Portugal. Multicoloured.

1100	150c. Type **289**	3·50	2·50
1101	200c. Exhibition emblem and Antilles flag	4·00	3·25
1102	250c. Globe and hand signing U.P.A.E.P. agreement	4·75	4·00

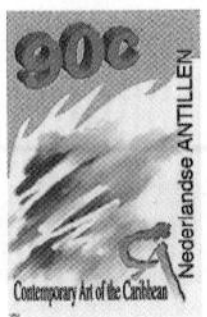

290 "Sun and Sea"

1993. "Carib-Art" Exhibition, Curacao. Multicoloured.

1103	90c. Type **290**	1·50	1·50
1104	150c. "Heaven and Earth"	2·40	2·40

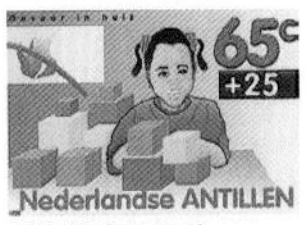

291 "Safety in the Home"

1993. Child Welfare. Child and Danger. Mult.

1105	65c.+25c. Type **291**	1·70	1·50
1106	90c.+35c. Child using seat belt ("Safety in the Car") (vert)	2·10	2·00
1107	175c.+75c. Child wearing armbands ("Safety in the Water")	4·00	4·00
MS1108	168×79 mm. 35c.+15c.×5, Child writing in exercise book ("Danger of Failing at School")	8·25	8·25

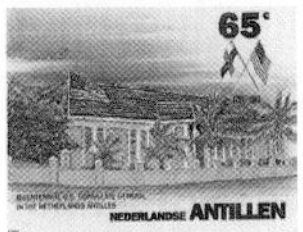

292 Consulate, Curacao

1993. Bicentenary of United States Consul General to the Antilles. Multicoloured.

1109	65c. Type **292**	1·20	1·00
1110	90c. Arms of Netherlands Antilles and U.S.A	1·70	1·50
1111	175c. American bald eagle	3·00	2·75

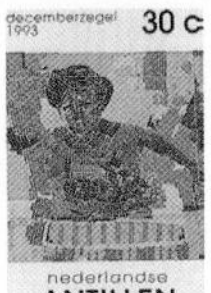

293 "Mother and Child" (mosaic)

1993. Christmas. Works by Lucila Engels-Boskaljon. Multicoloured.

1112	30c. Type **293**	70	45
1113	115c. "Madonna and Christ" (painting)	2·00	1·90

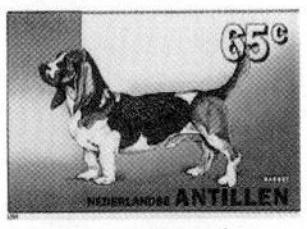

294 Basset Hound

1994. Dogs. Multicoloured.

1114	65c. Type **294**	1·50	1·20
1115	75c. Pit bull terrier	1·70	1·30
1116	90c. Cocker spaniel	2·10	1·50
1117	175c. Chow-chow	3·50	2·75

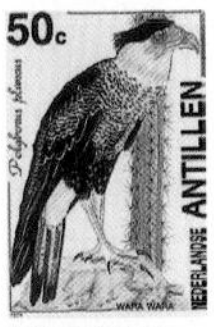

295 Common Caracara

1994. Birds. Multicoloured.

1118	50c. Type **295**	2·30	95
1119	95c. Green peafowl	2·40	1·70
1120	100c. Scarlet macaw	2·40	2·00
1121	125c. Troupial	3·00	2·40

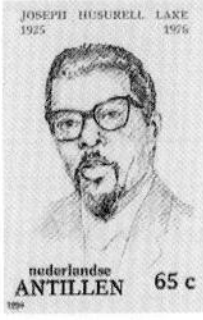

296 Joseph Husurell Lake

1994. Celebrities. Multicoloured.

1122	65c. Type **296** (founder of United People's Liberation Front)	1·20	1·20
1123	75c. Efrain Jonckheer (politician and diplomat)	1·30	1·30
1124	100c. Michiel Martinus Romer (teacher)	1·70	1·60
1125	175c. Carel Nicolaus Winkel (social reformer)	3·00	2·75

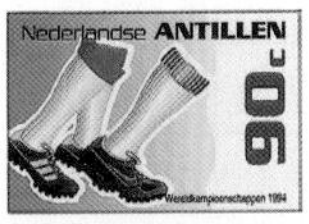

297 Players' Legs

1994. World Cup Football Championship, U.S.A. Multicoloured.

1126	90c. Type **297**	1·70	1·50
1127	150c. Foot and ball	2·75	2·40
1128	175c. Referee's whistle and cards	3·00	3·00

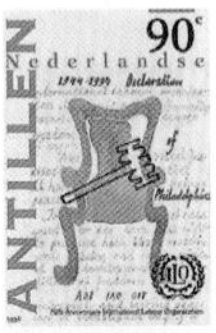

298 Chair and Hammer

1994. 75th Anniv of International Labour Organization. Multicoloured.

1129	90c. Type **298**	1·70	1·60
1130	110c. Heart and "75"	2·00	1·90
1131	200c. Tree	3·75	3·75

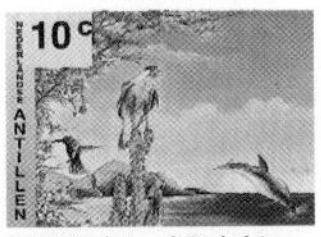

299 Birds and Dolphin

1994. Nature Protection. Multicoloured.

1132	10c. Type **299**	95	45
1133	35c. Dolphin, magnificent frigate bird, brown pelican and troupial	95	70
1134	50c. Coral, iguana, lobster and fish	1·00	95
1135	125c. Fish, turtle, queen conch, greater flamingoes and American wigeons	2·30	2·30
MS1136	84×70 mm. Nos. 1132/5	7·00	5·75

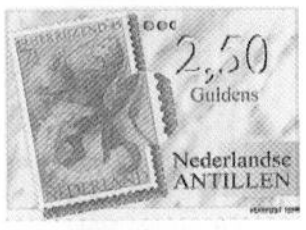

300 1945 7½c. Netherlands Stamp

1994. "Fepapost '94" European Stamp Exhibition, The Hague. Multicoloured.

1137	2g.50 Type **300**	4·00	4·00
1138	5g. Curacao 1933 6c. stamp	8·25	8·00
MS1139	96×55 mm. Nos. 1137/8	14·00	12·00

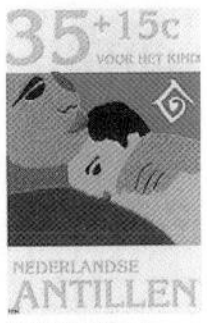

301 Mother and Child

1994. Child Welfare. International Year of the Family. Multicoloured.

1140	35c.+15c. Type **301**	95	80
1141	65c.+25c. Father and daughter reading together	1·70	1·60
1142	90c.+35c. Grandparents	3·25	3·00
MS1143	86×51 mm. 175c.+75c. I.Y.F. emblem	5·25	4·75

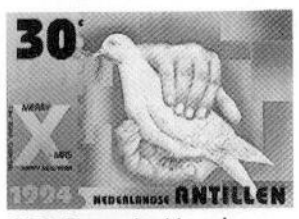

302 Dove in Hands

1994. Christmas. Multicoloured.

1144	30c. Type **302**	1·20	60
1145	115c. Globe and planets in hands	2·30	1·90

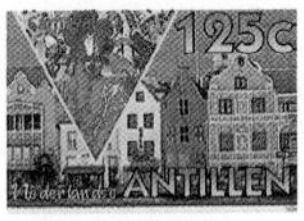

303 Carnival and Houses

1995. Carnival. Multicoloured.

1146	125c. Type **303**	2·30	2·10
1147	175c. Carnival and harbour	3·25	2·75
1148	250c. Carnival and rural house	4·50	4·00

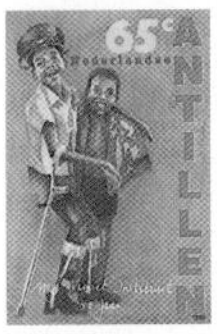

304 Handicapped and Able-bodied Children

1995. 50th Anniv of Mgr. Verriet Institute (for the physically handicapped). Multicoloured.

1149	65c. Type **304**	1·20	1·00
1150	90c. Cedric Virginie (wheelchair-bound bookbinder)	1·60	1·50

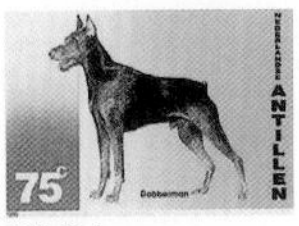

305 Dobermann

1995. Dogs. Multicoloured.

1151	75c. Type **305**	1·70	1·30
1152	85c. German shepherd	2·10	1·50
1153	100c. Bouvier	2·30	1·60
1154	175c. St. Bernard	3·75	2·75

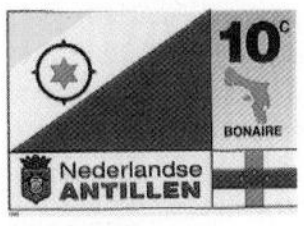

306 Bonaire

1995. Flags and Arms of the Constituent Islands of the Netherlands Antilles. Multicoloured.

1155	10c. Type **306**	35	35
1156	35c. Curacao	80	60
1157	50c. St. Maarten	1·00	80
1158	65c. Saba	1·30	1·00
1159	75c. St. Eustatius (also state flag and arms)	1·50	1·20
1160	90c. Island flags and state arms	1·70	1·50

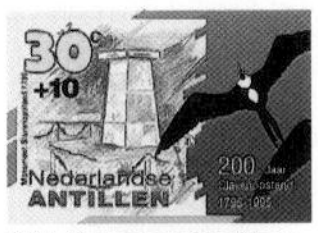

307 Monument to Slave Revolt of 1795

1995. Cultural and Social Relief Funds. Bicentenary of Abolition of Slavery in the Antilles (1161/2) and Children's Drawings on Philately (1163/4). Multicoloured.

1161	30c.+10c. Type **307**	1·20	95
1162	45c.+15c. Magnificent frigate bird and slave bell	1·70	1·40
1163	65c.+25c. "Stamps" from Curacao and Bonaire (Nicole Wever and Sabine Anthonio)	2·00	1·50
1164	75c.+35c. "Stamps" from St. Maarten, St. Eustatius and Saba (Chad Jacobs, Martha Hassell and Dion Humphreys)	2·10	1·70

1995. Hurricane Relief Fund. Nos. 831, 833 and 838 surch ORKAAN LUIS and premium.

1165	65c.+65c. multicoloured	2·50	2·30
1166	75c.+75c. multicoloured	2·75	2·50
1167	1g.+1g. multicoloured	3·50	3·25

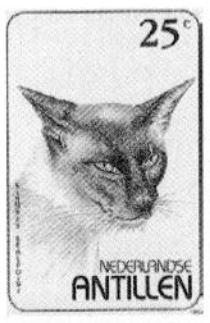

309 Sealpoint Siamese

1995. Cats. Multicoloured.

1168	25c. Type **309**	1·20	45
1169	60c. Maine coon	1·70	95
1170	65c. Silver Egyptian mau	1·90	1·00
1171	90c. Angora	2·30	1·50
1172	150c. Blue smoke Persian	3·50	2·40

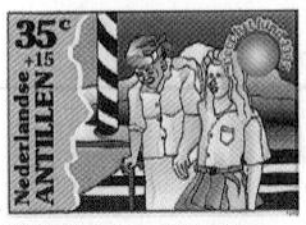

310 Helping Elderly Woman across Road

1995. Child Welfare. Children and Good Deeds. Multicoloured.

1173	35c.+15c. Type **310**	95	80
1174	65c.+25c. Reading newspaper to blind person	1·60	1·50
1175	90c.+35c. Helping younger brother	2·10	2·00
1176	175c.+75c. Giving flowers to the sick	4·00	4·00

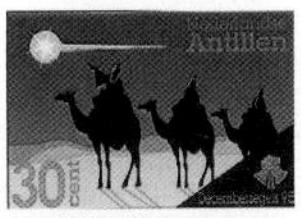

311 Wise Men on Camels

1995. Christmas. Multicoloured.

1177	30c. Type **311**	80	60
1178	115c. Fireworks over houses	2·20	1·90

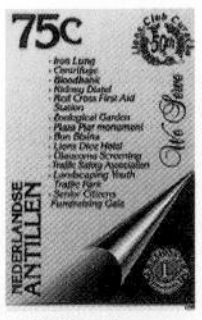

312 Serving the Community

1996. 50th Anniv of Curacao Lions Club. Multicoloured.

1179	75c. Type **312**	1·70	1·20
1180	105c. Anniversary emblem	2·10	1·70
1181	250c. Handshake	4·75	4·00

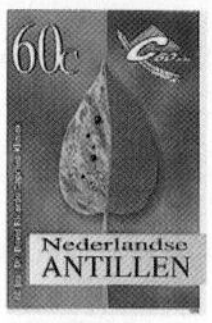

313 Disease on Half of Leaf

1996. 60th Anniv of Capriles Psychiatric Clinic, Otrabanda on Rif. Multicoloured.

1182	60c. Type **313**	1·20	95
1183	75c. Tornado and sun over house	1·70	1·20

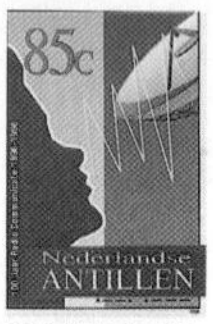

314 Dish Aerial and Face

1996. Centenary of Guglielmo Marconi's Patented Wireless Telegraph. Multicoloured.

1184	85c. Type **314**	1·60	1·50
1185	175c. Dish aerial and morse transmitter	3·00	2·75

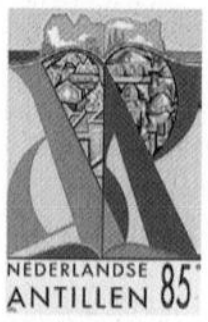

315 Letters and Buildings

1996. Translation of Bible into Papiamentu (Creole language). Multicoloured.

1186	85c. Type **315**	1·60	1·50
1187	225c. Bible and alphabets	4·00	3·50

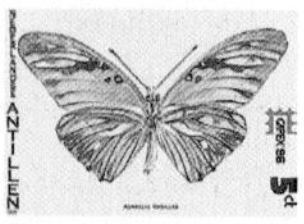

316 Gulf Fritillary

1996. "Capex '96" International Stamp Exhibition, Toronto, Canada. Butterflies. Multicoloured.

1188	5c. Type **316**	1·20	35
1189	110c. "Callithea philotima"	2·30	1·90
1190	300c. Clipper	5·75	4·75
1191	750c. "Euphaedra francina"	13·50	12·00
MS1192	132×75 mm. Nos. 1189/90	9·75	7·00

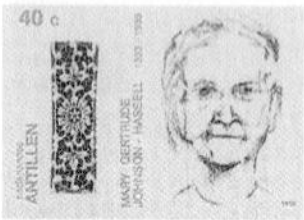

317 Mary Johnson-Hassell (introducer of drawn-thread work to Saba, 57th death)

1996. Anniversaries.

1193	**317**	40c. orange and black on grey	95	70
1194	-	50c. green and black on grey	1·00	80
1195	-	75c. red and black on grey	1·50	1·20
1196	-	80c. blue and black on grey	1·60	1·50

DESIGNS: 40c. Type **317** (introducer of drawn-thread work to Saba); 50c. Cornelius Marten (Papa Cornes) (pastor to Bonaire); 75c. Phelippi Chakutoe (union leader); 85c. Chris Engels (physician, artist, author and fencing champion).

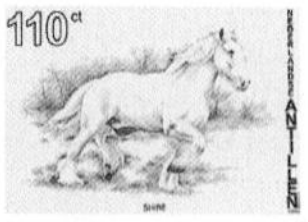

318 Shire

1996. Horses. Multicoloured.

1197	110c. Type **318**	2·40	1·90
1198	225c. Shetland ponies	4·50	3·75
1199	275c. British thoroughbred	5·25	4·50
1200	350c. Przewalski mare and foal	7·00	5·75

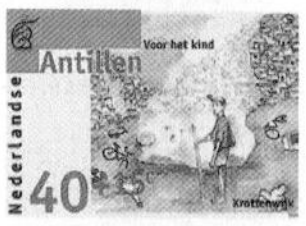

319 Street Child and Shanty Town

1996. Child Welfare. 50th Anniv of UNICEF. Multicoloured.

1201	40c.+15c. Type **319**	1·00	95
1202	75c.+25c. Asian child weaver	1·90	1·70
1203	110c.+45c. Child in war zone of former Yugoslavia (vert)	2·75	2·75
1204	225c.+100c. Impoverished Caribbean mother and child (vert)	5·50	5·25

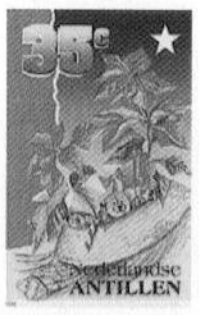

320 Straw Hat with Poinsettias and Gifts

1996. Christmas. Multicoloured. Self-adhesive.

1205	35c. Type **320**	1·20	60
1206	150c. Father Christmas	3·00	2·30

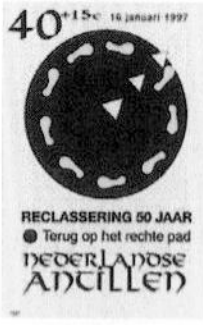

321 Emblem

1997. Cultural and Social Relief Funds.

1207	**321**	40c.+15c. black and yellow	1·30	95
1208	-	75c.+30c. blue, mauve and black	1·90	1·70
1209	-	85c.+40c. red and black	2·30	2·20
1210	-	110c.+50c. black, green and red	2·75	2·75

DESIGNS: 40c. Type **321** (50th anniv of Curacao Foundation for Care and Resettlement of Ex-prisoners); 75c. Emblem (60th anniv (1996) of General Union of Public Servants (ABVO)); 85c. Flag of Red Cross (65th anniv of Curacao division); 110c. National Red Cross emblem (65th anniv of Curacao division).

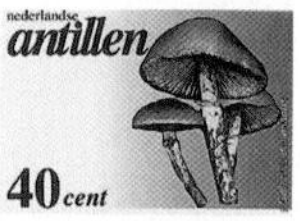

322 Deadly Galerina

1997. Fungi. Multicoloured.

1211	40c. Type **322**	1·20	70
1212	50c. Destroying angel	1·40	80
1213	75c. Cep	2·10	1·20
1214	175c. Fly agaric	3·50	3·00

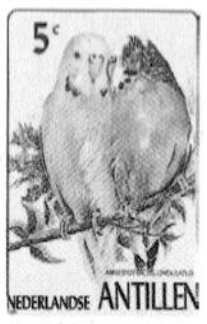

323 Budgerigars

1997. Birds. Multicoloured.

1215	5c. Type **323**	1·40	45
1216	25c. Sulphur-crested cockatoo	1·70	45
1217	50c. Yellow-shouldered Amazon	2·10	80
1218	75c. Purple heron	2·50	1·20
1219	85c. Ruby topaz hummingbird	2·75	1·40
1220	100c. South African crowned crane	3·00	1·70
1221	110c. Vermilion flycatcher	3·25	1·70
1222	125c. Greater flamingo	3·25	2·10
1223	200c. Osprey	4·25	3·25
1224	225c. Keel-billed toucan	5·00	3·75

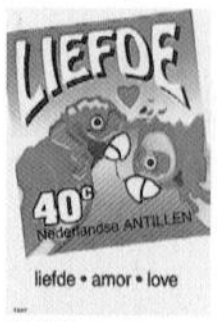

324 Parrots ("Love")

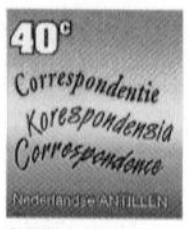

325 "Correspondence"

1997. Greetings Stamps. Multicoloured. (a) As T 324.

1225	40c. Type **324**	80	70
1226	75c. Waterfall ("Positivism")	1·40	1·20
1227	85c. Roses ("Mothers' Day")	1·60	1·50
1228	100c. Quill pen ("Correspondence")	1·70	1·60
1229	110c. Leaves, rainbow and heart ("Success")	2·00	1·90
1230	225c. Ant on flower ("Congratulations")	4·00	3·75

(b) As T 325.

1231	40c. Motif as in Type **324**	1·20	1·20
1232	40c. Type **325**	1·20	1·20
1233	75c. Petals and moon ("Positivism")	1·70	1·70
1234	75c. Motif as No. 1226	1·70	1·70
1235	75c. Sun and moon ("Success")	1·70	1·70
1236	85c. Motif as No. 1227	1·70	1·70
1237	100c. Motif as No. 1228	2·30	2·30
1238	110c. Motif as No. 1229	2·30	2·30
1239	110c. Heart between couple ("Love")	2·30	2·30
1240	225c. Motif as No. 1230	4·75	4·75

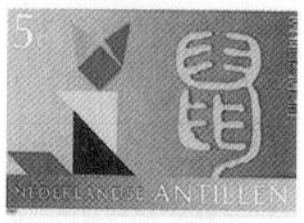

326 Rat

1997. "Pacific '97" International Stamp Exhibition, San Francisco. Chinese Zodiac. Designs showing Tangram (puzzle) representations and Chinese symbols for each animal. Multicoloured.

1241	5c. Type **326**	35	35
1242	5c. Ox	35	35
1243	5c. Tiger	35	35
1244	40c. Rabbit	95	70
1245	40c. Dragon	95	70
1246	40c. Snake	95	70
1247	75c. Horse	1·50	1·20
1248	75c. Goat	1·50	1·20
1249	75c. Monkey	1·50	1·20
1250	100c. Rooster	1·90	1·60
1251	100c. Dog	1·90	1·60
1252	100c. Pig	1·90	1·60
MS1253	145×150 mm. Nos. 1241/52	15·00	15·00

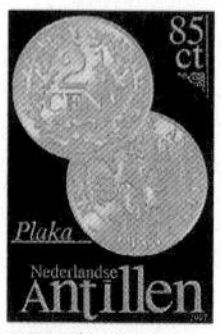

327 2½ Cent Coin (Plaka)

1997. Coins. Obverse and reverse of coins. Multicoloured.

1254	85c. Type **327**	1·70	1·50
1255	175c. 5 cent (Stuiver)	3·50	3·00
1256	225c. 2½ gulden (Fuerte)	4·75	3·75

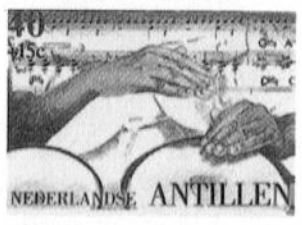

328 Score of "Atras de Nos" and Salsa Drummer

1997. Child Welfare. The Child and Music. Multicoloured.

1257	40c.+15c. Type **328**	1·20	95
1258	75c.+25c. Score of "For Elise" and pianist	1·70	1·60
1259	110c.+45c. Score of "Blues for Alice" and flautist	3·00	2·50
1260	225c.+100c. Score of "Yesterday" and guitarist	4·00	3·75

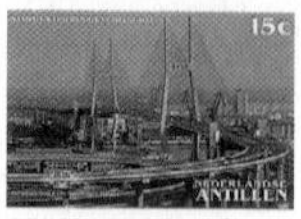

329 Nampu Grand Bridge, Shanghai

1997. "Shanghai 1997" International Stamp and Coin Exhibition, China. Multicoloured.

1261	15c. Type **329**	1·20	60
1262	40c. Giant panda	1·70	1·20
1263	75c. Tiger (New Year) (vert)	2·30	1·70
MS1264	108×78 mm. 90c. The Bund, Shanghai	4·00	3·50

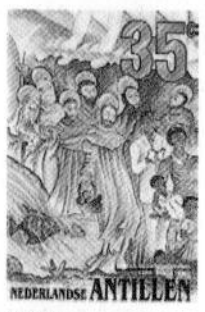

330 Worshippers (detail of mural by Marcolino Maas in Church of the Holy Family, Willemstad, Curacao)

1997. Christmas and New Year. Multicoloured.

1265	35c. Type **330**	1·20	60
1266	150c. Popping champagne cork and calendar (New Year)	3·00	2·40

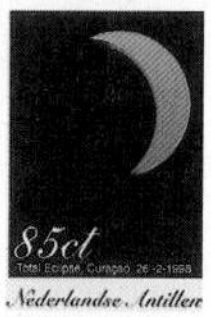

331 Partial Eclipse

1998. Total Solar Eclipse, Curacao. Multicoloured.

1267	85c. Type **331**	2·00	1·60
1268	110c. Close-up of sun in total eclipse	2·75	1·90
1269	225c. Total eclipse	4·75	4·00
MS1270	85×52 mm. 750c. Hologram of stages of the eclipse	17·00	17·00

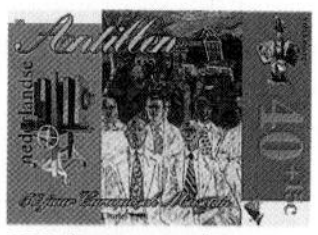

332 Camera and Painting

1998. Cultural and Social Relief Funds. Mult.

1271	40c.+15c. Type **332** (50th anniv of Curacao Museum)	1·20	95
1272	40c.+15c. Desalination plant and drinking water (70 years of seawater desalination)	1·20	95
1273	75c.+25c. Mangrove roots and shells (Lac Cai wetlands, Bonaire) (vert)	2·00	1·70
1274	85c.+40c. Lake and underwater marine life (Little Bonaire wetlands) (vert)	2·75	2·40

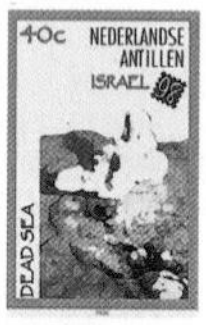

333 Salt Deposit, Dead Sea

1998. "Israel 98" International Stamp Exhibition, Tel Aviv. Multicoloured.

1275	40c. Type **333**	1·20	80
1276	75c. Zion Gate, Jerusalem	1·40	1·20
1277	110c. Masada	2·10	1·70
MS1278	58×91 mm. 225c. Mikve Israel-Emanuel Synagogue, Curacao	5·25	4·75

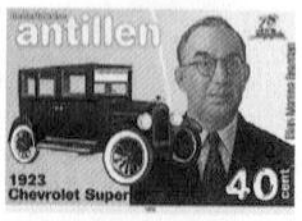

334 Superior, 1923, and Elias Moreno Brandao

1998. 75th Anniv of E. Moreno Brandao and Sons (car dealers). Chevrolet Motor Cars. Multicoloured.

1279	40c. Type **334**	1·50	70
1280	55c. Roadster, 1934	1·60	1·20
1281	75c. Styleline deluxe sedan, 1949	2·00	1·20
1282	110c. Bel Air convertible, 1957	2·75	1·70
1283	225c. Corvette Stingray coupe, 1963	3·75	3·75
1284	500c. Chevelle SS-454 2-door hardtop, 1970	10·00	8·25

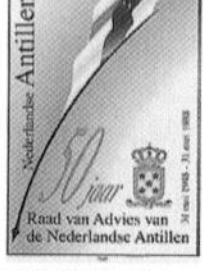

335 State Flag and Arms

1998. 50th Anniv of Netherlands Antilles Advisory Council. Multicoloured.

1285	75c. Type **335**	1·40	1·20
1286	85c. Gavel	1·60	1·40

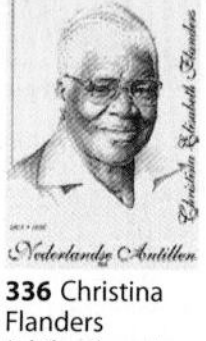

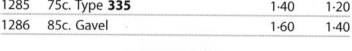

336 Christina Flanders (philanthropic worker)

1998. Death Anniversaries. Multicoloured.

1287	40c. Type **336** (second anniv)	80	70
1288	75c. Abraham Jesurun (writer and first president of Curacao Chamber of Commerce, 80th anniv)	1·40	1·20
1289	85c. Capt. Gerrit Newton (seaman and shipyard manager, 50th anniv (1999))	1·50	1·40
1290	110c. Eduardo Adriana (sportsman, first anniv)	2·10	1·70

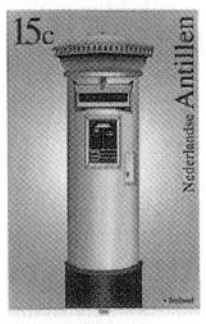

337 Ireland Pillar Box

1998. Postboxes (1st series). Multicoloured.

1291	15c. Type **337**	45	35
1292	40c. Nepal postbox	95	70
1293	75c. Uruguay postbox	1·50	1·20
1294	85c. Curacao postbox	1·60	1·50

See also Nos. 1413/16.

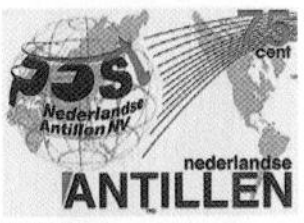

338 Globe and New Post Emblem

1998. Privatization of Postal Services.

1295	**338**	75c. black, blue and red	1·40	1·20
1296	-	110c. multicoloured	2·10	1·70
1297	-	225c. multicoloured	3·75	3·50

DESIGNS—VERT: 110c. Tree and binary code. HORIZ: 225c. 1949 25c. U.P.U. stamp, reproduction of No. 1296 and binary code.

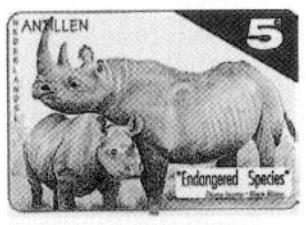

339 Black Rhinoceros

1998. Endangered Species. Multicoloured.

1298	5c. Type **339**	1·70	1·20
1299	75c. White-tailed hawk (vert)	2·30	1·70
1300	125c. White-tailed deer	2·30	2·30
1301	250c. Tiger ("Tigris") (vert)	5·25	4·00

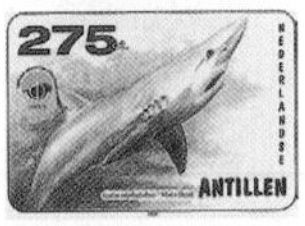

340 Short-finned Mako ("Mako Shark")

1998. Fish. Multicoloured.

1302	275c. Type **340**	7·00	4·75
1303	350c. Manta ray	8·25	5·75

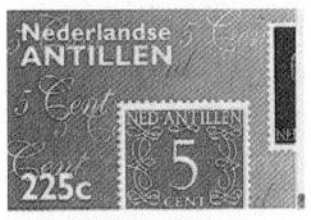

341 1950 5c. Stamp

1998. "70th Anniv of Dutch Stamp Dealers Club" Stamp Exhibition, The Hague. Multicoloured.

1304	225c. Type **341**	4·00	4·00
1305	500c. 1950 Queen Juliana 15c. stamp	8·25	8·25
MS1306	72×50 mm. 500c. Curacao 1922 12½c. stamp	9·25	8·75

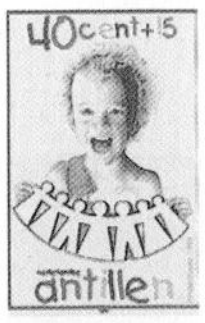

342 Child with Family Paper Chain

1998. Child Welfare. Universal Rights of the Child. Multicoloured.

1307	40c.+15c. Type **342** (right to name and nationality)	1·20	95
1308	75c.+25c. Children eating water melons (right to health care)	1·70	1·60
1309	110c.+45c. Children painting (right of handicapped children to special care)	2·75	2·50
1310	225c.+100c. Children playing with can telephones (right to freedom of expression)	5·50	5·25

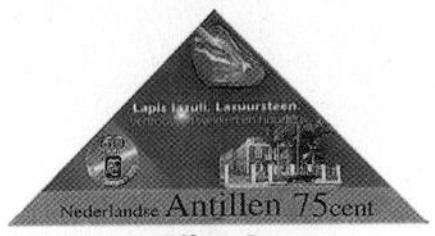

343 Former Office, Curacao

1998. 60th Anniv of PriceWaterhouseCoopers (accountancy firm). Multicoloured.

1311	75c. Type **343**	2·50	2·30
1312	225c. Modern office, Curacao	4·50	4·75

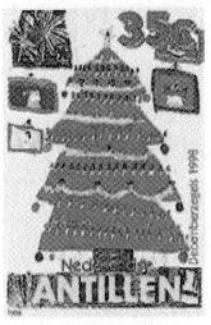

344 "Christmas Tree" (Theodora van Ierland)

1998. Christmas. Children's Paintings. Multicoloured.

1313	35c. Type **344**	80	80
1314	150c. "Post in mail box" (Anna Sordam)	3·25	2·40

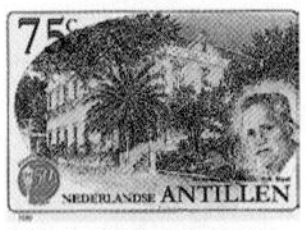

345 Avila Beach Hotel and Dr. Pieter Maal (founder)

1999. 50th Anniv of Avila Beach Hotel. Mult.

1315	75c. Type **345**	1·50	1·20
1316	110c. Beach and flamboyant tree	2·30	1·70
1317	225c. Mesquite tree	4·00	3·50

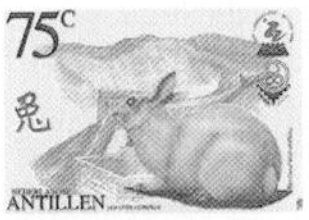

346 Rabbit and Great Wall of China

1999. "China 1999" International Stamp Exhibition, Peking. Year of the Rabbit. Multicoloured.

1318	75c. Type **346**	2·10	1·20
1319	225c. Rabbit and Jade Pagoda (vert)	5·00	3·50
MS1320	88×53 mm. 225c. Rabbit (vert)	5·75	4·75

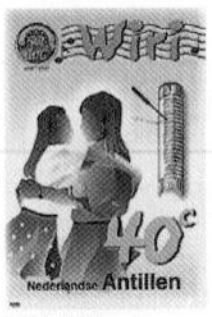

347 Girls hugging and Wiri

1999. 50th Anniv of Government Correctional Institute. Musical instruments. Multicoloured.

1321	40c. Type **347**	95	70
1322	75c. Institute building and bamba	1·50	1·20
1323	85c. Boy at lathe and triangle (horiz)	1·70	1·40

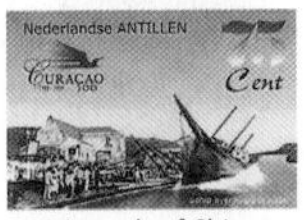

348 Launch of Ship

1999. 500th Anniv of First Written Record (by Amerigo Vespucci) of Curacao. Multicoloured.

1324	75c. Type **348**	1·70	1·20
1325	110c. Otrobanda, 1906	2·30	1·70
1326	175c. Nos. 1324/5 and anniversary emblem	3·25	3·00
1327	225c. Fort Beeckenburg, Caracasbaai	4·25	3·50
1328	500c. 1949 12½c. stamp and sailing ship	8·25	8·25

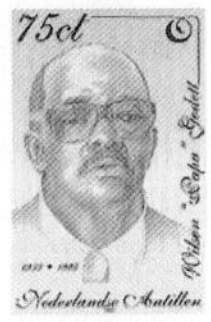

349 Godett

1999. Fourth Death Anniv of Wilson Godett (politician).

1329	**349**	75c. multicoloured	1·60	1·20

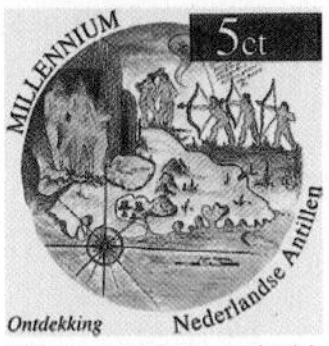

350 Amerindians and Old Map

1999. The Millennium. Multicoloured. (a) Size 35½×35½ mm. Ordinary gum.

1330	5c. Type **350** (arrival of Alonso de Ojeda, Amerigo Vespucci and Juan de la Cosa, 1499)	60	60
1331	10c. Dutch ship, indian and soldier on horseback (Dutch conquest, 1634)	60	60
1332	40c. Flags of constituent islands of Netherlands Antilles, Autonomy Monument in Curacao and document granting autonomy, 1954	1·20	95
1333	75c. Telephone and Curacao 1873 25c. King William III stamp (installation of telephones on Curacao, 1892)	1·70	1·50
1334	85c. Fokker F.XVIII airplane "De Snip" (first Amsterdam–Curacao flight, 1934)	1·70	1·70
1335	100c. Oil refinery, Curacao (inauguration, 1915)	1·70	1·70
1336	110c. Dish aerial, undersea fibre optic cable and dolphins (telecommunications)	2·30	2·10
1337	125c. Curacao harbour, bridge and bow of cruise liner (tourism)	3·00	2·75
1338	225c. Ka'i orgel (musical instrument) and couple in folk costume (culture)	4·00	4·00
1339	350c. Brown-throated conure, common caracara, yellow-shouldered amazon and greater flamingoes (nature)	6·50	6·50

(b) Size 29×29 mm. Self-adhesive.

1340	5c. Type **350**	60	60
1341	10c. As No. 1331	60	60
1342	40c. As No. 1332	1·20	95
1343	75c. As No. 1333	1·70	1·50
1344	85c. As No. 1334	1·70	1·70
1345	100c. As No. 1335	1·70	1·70
1346	110c. As No. 1336	2·30	2·10
1347	125c. As No. 1337	3·00	2·75
1348	225c. As No. 1338	4·00	4·00
1349	350c. As No. 1339	6·50	6·50

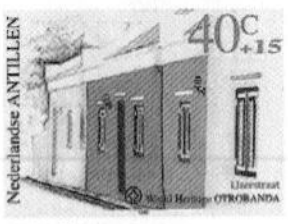

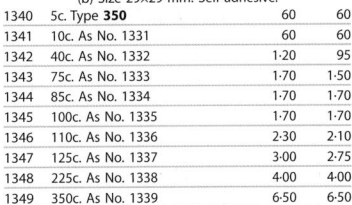

351 Ijzerstraat, Otrobanda

1999. Cultural and Social Relief Funds. Willemstad, World Heritage Site. Multicoloured.

1350	40c.+15c. Type **351**	1·00	95
1351	75c.+30c. Oldest house in Punda (now Postal Museum) (vert)	2·00	1·70
1352	110c.+50c. "The Bridal Cake" (now Central National Archives), Scharloo	3·00	2·50

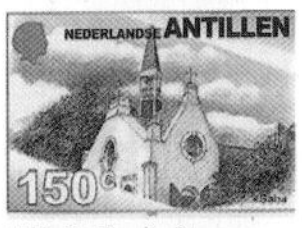

352 St. Paul's Roman Catholic Church, Saba

1999. Tourist Attractions. Multicoloured.

1357	150c. Type **352**	4·00	2·30
1359	250c. Greater flamingoes, Bonaire	5·25	4·00
1361	500c. Courthouse, St. Maarten	9·25	8·25

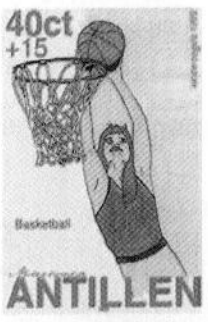

353 Basketball

1999. Child Welfare. Sports. Multicoloured.

1370	40c.+15c. Type **353**	1·70	1·00
1371	75c.+25c. Golf	2·30	1·70
1372	110c.+45c. Fencing	3·50	2·50
1373	225c.+100c. Tennis	6·50	5·25

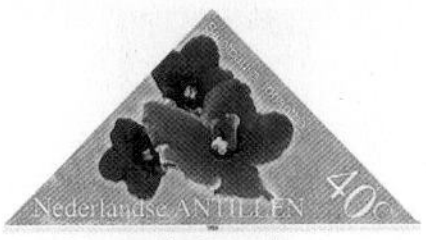

354 *Saintpaulia ionantha*

1999. Flowers. Multicoloured.

1374	40c. Type **354**	1·60	1·20
1375	40c. *Gardenia jasminioides*	1·60	1·20
1376	40c. Allamanda	1·60	1·20
1377	40c. Bougainvillea	1·60	1·20
1378	75c. Strelitzia	1·90	1·70
1379	75c. Cymbidium	1·90	1·70
1380	75c. Phalaenopsis	1·90	1·70
1381	75c. *Cassia fistula*	1·90	1·70
1382	110c. Doritaenopsis	3·00	2·30
1383	110c. Guzmania	3·00	2·30
1384	225c. *Catharanthus roseus*	4·75	4·00
1385	225c. *Caralluma hexagona*	4·75	4·00

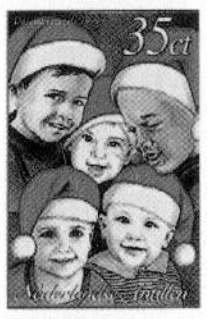

355 Children wearing Hats

1999. Christmas. Multicoloured.

1386	35c. Type **355**	1·20	60
1387	150c. Clock face and islands	3·00	2·40

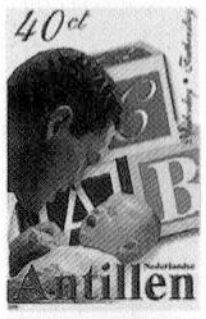

356 Man, Baby and Building Blocks (Fathers' Day)

2000. Greetings Stamps. Multicoloured.

1388	40c. Type **356**	80	70
1389	40c. Women and globe (Mothers' Day)	80	70
1390	40c. Hearts and flowers (Valentine's Day)	80	70
1391	75c. Puppy and present ("Thank You")	1·40	1·30
1392	110c. Butterfly and vase of flowers (Special Occasions)	2·30	1·70
1393	150c. As No. 1389	3·25	3·25
1394	150c. As No. 1390	3·25	3·25
1395	225c. Hands and wedding rings (Anniversary)	4·25	4·25

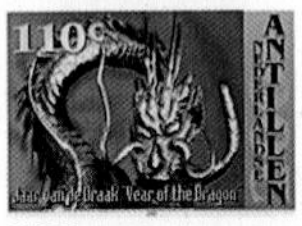

357 Dragon

2000. Chinese Year of the Dragon. Multicoloured.

1396	110c. Type **357**	3·00	2·30
MS1397	50×85 mm. 225c. Chinese dragons	5·75	4·75

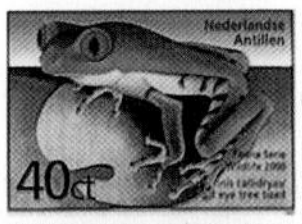

358 Red Eyed Tree Frog

2000. Endangered Animals. Multicoloured.

1398	40c. Type **358**	2·30	1·70
1399	75c. King penguin (vert)	3·00	2·30
1400	85c. Killer whale (vert)	3·00	2·30
1401	100c. African elephant (vert)	3·00	2·30
1402	110c. Chimpanzee (vert)	3·00	2·30
1403	225c. Tiger	4·75	4·75

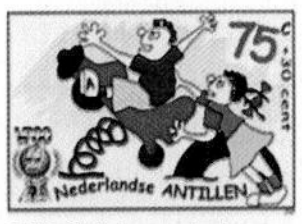

359 Children playing

2000. Cultural and Social Relief Funds. Mult.

1404	75c.+30c. Type **359**	1·70	1·50
1405	110c.+50c. Schoolchildren performing science experiments	3·50	3·25
1406	225c.+100c. Teacher giving lesson (vert)	5·75	5·25

360 Space
Shuttle Launch

2000. "World Stamp Expo 2000", Anaheim, California. Space Exploration. Multicoloured.
1407	75c. Type **360**	3·00	1·70
1408	225c. Astronaut, Moon and space station	5·25	4·75
MS1409	100×70 mm. 225c. Futuristic space station	5·75	5·75

361 Cycling

2000. Olympic Games, Sydney. Multicoloured.
1410	75c. Type **361**	2·30	1·70
1411	225c. Athletics	5·25	4·75
MS1412	50×72 mm. 225c. Swimming	5·75	5·75

2000. Postboxes (2nd series). As T 337. Multicoloured.
1413	110c. Mexico postbox	2·10	2·10
1414	175c. Dubai postbox	3·25	3·25
1415	350c. Great Britain postbox	6·25	6·25
1416	500c. United States of America postbox	8·75	8·75

362 People

2000. Social Insurance Bank. Multicoloured.
1417	75c. Type **362**	1·70	1·70
1418	110c. Adult holding child's hand (horiz)	2·30	2·30
1419	225c. Anniversary emblem	4·75	4·75

363 Child
reaching
towards Night
Sky

2000. Child Welfare. Multicoloured.
1420	40c.+15c. Type **363**	1·50	1·50
1421	75c.+25c. Children using Internet (horiz)	2·40	2·40
1422	110c.+45c. Children playing with toy boat (horiz)	3·50	3·50
1423	225c.+100c. Children consulting map	5·75	5·75

364 Angels and
Score of *Jingle
Bells* (carol)

2000. Christmas. Multicoloured.
1424	40c. Type **364**	1·20	1·20
1425	150c. Seasonal messages in different languages (horiz)	3·50	3·50

365 Red King Snake

2001. Chinese Year of the Snake. Multicoloured.
1426	110c. Type **365**	3·00	2·30
MS1427	87×53 mm. 225c. Indian cobra (*Naja naja*) (vert)	6·50	6·50

366 Forest

2001. "HONG KONG 2001" World Stamp Exhibition. Landscapes. Multicoloured.
1428	25c. Type **366**	1·00	80
1429	40c. Palm trees and waterfall	1·30	1·20
1430	110c. Spinner dolphins (*Stenella longirostris*)	3·00	1·90

367 Persian
Shaded Golden
Cat

2001. Cats and Dogs. Multicoloured.
1431	55c. Type **367**	2·30	1·50
1432	75c. Burmese bluepoint cat and kittens	3·00	2·10
1433	110c. American wirehair	3·00	2·50
1434	175c. Golden retriever dog	4·00	3·25
1435	225c. German shepherd dog	5·25	4·50
1436	750c. British shorthair silver tabby	13·50	13·00

368 *Mars*
(Dutch ship of
the line)

2001. Ships. Multicoloured.
1437	110c. Type **368**	3·00	2·30
1438	275c. *Alphen* (frigate)	5·75	5·00
1439	350c. *Curacao* (paddle-steamer) (horiz)	7·50	6·50
1440	500c. *Pioneer* (schooner) (horiz)	11·00	9·25

369 Pen and
Emblem

2001. Fifth Anniv of Caribbean Postal Union. Multicoloured.
1441	75c.+25c. Type **369**	2·30	2·00
1442	110c.+45c. Emblem	3·50	3·25
1443	225c. + 100c. Silhouettes encircling globe	7·00	6·50

370 Fedjai riding
Bicycle

2001. Fedjai (cartoon postman) (1st series). Multicoloured.
1444	5c. Type **370**	1·20	30
1445	40c. Fedjai and children	1·20	80
1446	75c. Fedjai and post box containing bird's nest and chicks	1·70	1·50
1447	85c. Fedjai and elderly woman	2·30	1·60
1448	100c. Barking dog and Fedjai sitting on postbox	2·30	2·00
1449	110c. Fedjai and boy reading comic	3·00	2·30

See also Nos. 1487/90.

371 Cave Entrance and
Area Map

2001. Kueba Boza (Muzzle Cave). Multicoloured.
1450	85c. Type **371**	2·10	1·60

1451	110c. *Leptonycteris nivalis cursoae* (bat)	2·40	2·30
1452	225c. *Glosophaga elongata* (bat)	5·00	4·75

372
Streamertail
(*Trochilus
polytmus*)

2001. Birds. Multicoloured.
1453	10c. Type **372**	95	60
1454	85c. Eastern white pelican (*Pelecanus onocrotalus*)	2·75	1·90
1455	110c. Gouldian finch (*Erythrura gouldiae*)	3·00	2·30
1456	175c. Painted bunting (*Passerina ciris*)	4·00	3·50
1457	250c. Atlantic puffin (*Fratercula artica*)	5·25	5·00
1458	350c. American darter (*Anhinga anhinga*)	8·25	7·50

373 Chapel Facade and
Map of St. Maarten
Island

2001. 150th Anniv of Philipsburg Methodist Chapel. Multicoloured.
1459	75c. Type **373**	1·70	1·50
1460	110c. Rainbow, open Bible and map of St. Maarten	2·75	2·20

374 Boy feeding Toddler

2001. Child Welfare. Youth Volunteers. Multicoloured.
1461	40c.+15c. Type **374**	2·00	1·30
1462	75c.+25c. Girls dancing (vert)	2·30	2·10
1463	110c.+45c. Boy and elderly woman (vert)	3·75	3·25

375 Children of
Different Nations

2001. Christmas. Multicoloured.
1464	40c. Type **375**	1·20	80
1465	150c. Children and Infant Jesus (vert)	3·50	3·00

376 Prince
Willem-
Alexander

2002. Wedding of Crown Prince Willem-Alexander to Maxima Zorreguieta. Multicoloured.
1466	75c. Type **376**	1·70	1·50
1467	110c. Princess Maxima	2·75	2·30
MS1468	75×72 mm. 2g.25, Prince Willem-Alexander facing left; 2g.75, Princess Maxima facing left	11·50	10·50

377 Horse

2002. Chinese New Year. Year of the Horse. Multicoloured.
1469	25c. Type **377**	1·40	1·20
MS1470	52×86 mm. 95c. Horse's head	3·50	3·00

378 Blue-tailed
Emerald
(*Chlorostilbon
mellisugus*) and
Passion Flower
(*Passiflora
foetida*)

2002. Flora and Fauna. Multicoloured.
1471	50c. Type **378**	1·20	1·00
1472	95c. Lineated anole (*Anolis lineatus*) and *Cordia sebestena* (flower) (horiz)	2·20	2·00
1473	120c. Dragonfly (*Odonata*) (horiz)	2·75	2·40
1474	145c. Hermit crab (*Coenobita clypeatus*) (horiz)	3·25	3·00
1475	285c. Paper wasp (*Polistes versicolor*)	5·75	5·50

379 Flambeau
(*Dryas julia*)

2002. Butterflies. Multicoloured.
1480	25c. Type **379**	1·20	60
1481	145c. Monarch (*Danaus plexippus*) (horiz)	3·50	2·75
1482	400c. *Mechanitis polymnia* (horiz)	8·75	8·25
1483	500c. *Pyrrhopygopsis socrates* (wrongly inscr "Pyrhapygopsis socrates") (horiz)	10·50	10·00

380 Flags as
Football

2002. World Cup Football Championship, Japan and South Korea. Multicoloured.
1484	95c.+35c. Type **380**	3·00	2·50
1485	145c.+55c. Player and globe as football	4·25	4·00
1486	240c.+110c. Player and ball	7·50	6·75

381 Fedjai skipping

2002. Fedjai (cartoon postman) (2nd series). Multicoloured.
1487	10c. Type **381**	1·20	45
1488	55c. Fedjai and dog in rubbish bin (vert)	1·70	1·30
1489	95c. Fedjai presenting envelope on tray (vert)	2·30	2·10
1490	240c. Fedjai helping elderly woman across road (vert)	5·25	5·00

382 Man

2002. "The Potato Eaters" (Vincent Van Gogh). Amphilex 2002 International Stamp Exhibition, Amsterdam. Designs showing parts of painting. Multicoloured.
1491	70c. Type **382**	1·70	1·50
1492	95c. Man (different)	2·30	2·10
1493	145c. Woman facing front	3·50	3·00
1494	240c. Woman facing left	5·25	5·00
MS1495	98×75 mm. 550c. As No. 1494 but design enlarged (horiz)	11·50	11·50

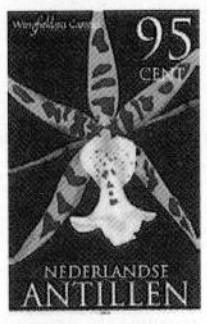

383 *Wingfieldara casseta*

2002. Orchids. Multicoloured.

1496	95c. Type **383**	2·30	2·00
1497	285c. *Cymbidium Magna Charta*	5·75	5·75
1498	380c. *Brassolaeliocattleya*	8·25	7·75
1499	750c. *Miltonia spectabilis*	15·00	15·00

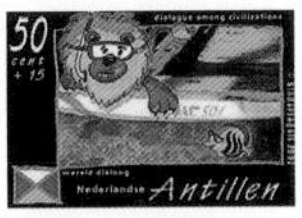

384 Lion wearing Snorkel

2001. Child Welfare. Multicoloured.

1500	50c.+15c. Type **384**	1·50	1·40
1501	95c.+35c. Kangaroo	3·00	2·75
1502	145c.+55c. Goat and penguin	4·50	4·00
1503	240c.+100c. Lizard and toucan	7·50	7·25

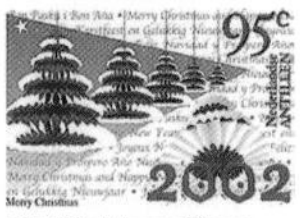

385 Christmas Trees

2002. Christmas. Multicoloured.

1504	95c. Type **385**	2·10	2·00
1505	240c. Lanterns	5·25	5·00

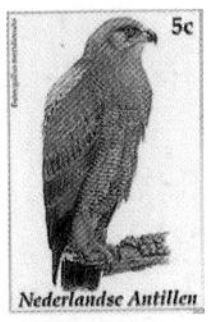

386 Savanna Hawk (*Buteogallus meridionalis*)

2002. Birds. Multicoloured.

1506	5c. Type **386**	60	45
1507	20c. Black-spotted barbet (*Capito niger*)	70	60
1508	30c. Scarlet macaw (*Ara macao*)	80	70
1509	35c. Great jacamar (*Jacamerops aurea*)	95	80
1510	70c. White-necked jacobin (*Florisuga mellivora*)	1·50	1·40
1511	85c. Crimson fruit-crow (*Haematoderis militaris*) (inscr "Heamatoderus")	1·70	1·60
1512	90c. Peach-fronted conure (*Aratinga aurea*)	1·90	1·70
1513	95c. Green oropendula (*Psarocolius viridis*)	2·00	1·90
1514	100c. Eastern meadowlark (*Stumella magna*) (horiz)	2·10	2·00
1515	145c. Sun conure (*Aratinga solstitalis*) (horiz)	3·00	2·75
1516	240c. White-tailed toucan (*Trogon virdis*)	5·00	4·75
1517	285c. Red-billed toucan (*Ramphastos tucanus*)	5·75	5·75

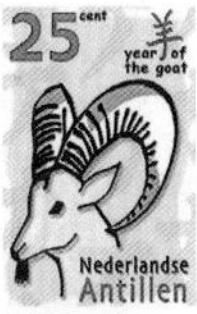

387 Goat's Head

2003. New Year. Year of the Goat.

1518	**387** 25c. multicoloured	1·40	1·20
MS1519	86×52 mm. 96c. black, red and grey	3·00	3·00

DESIGN: 95c. Rearing goat.

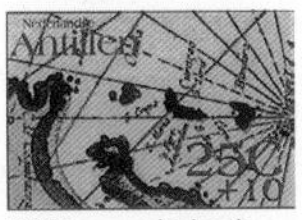

388 Leeward Islands

2003. Cultural and Social Relief Funds. Sheet 150× 61 mm containing T 388 and similar multicoloured designs showing maps.

MS1520	25c.+10c. Type **388**; 30c.+15c. Windward Islands (vert); 55c.+25c. Curacao and Bonaire; 85c.+35c. St. Marten, Saba and St. Eustatius (vert); 95c +40c. Caribbean	9·25	9·25

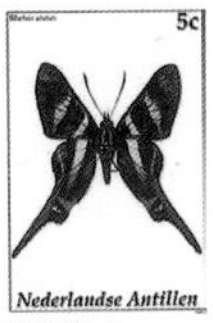

389 *Rhetus arcius*

2003. Butterflies. Multicoloured.

1521	5c. Type **389**	45	35
1522	10c. *Evenus teresina* (horiz)	60	45
1523	25c. *Bhutanitis thaidina* (horiz)	70	60
1524	30c. *Semomesia capanea* (horiz)	80	70
1525	45c. *Papilio machaon* (horiz)	95	80
1526	55c. *Papilio multicaudata*	1·30	1·20
1527	65c. *Graphium weiskei*	1·50	1·40
1528	95c. *Aneyluris formosissima venahalis*	2·00	1·90
1529	100c. *Euphaedra neophron* (horiz)	2·10	2·00
1530	145c. *Ornithoptera goliath Samson* (horiz)	3·00	2·75
1531	275c. *Aneyluris colubra*	5·50	5·25
1532	350c. *Papilio lorquinianus*	7·00	6·75

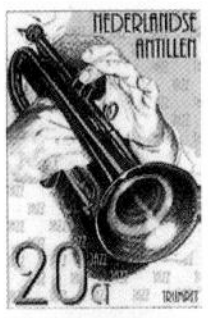

390 Trumpet

2003. Musical Instruments. Sheet 125×61 mm containing T 390 and similar vert designs. Multicoloured.

MS1533	20c. Type **390**; 75c. Drums; 145c. Tenor saxophone; 285c. Double bass	10·50	10·50

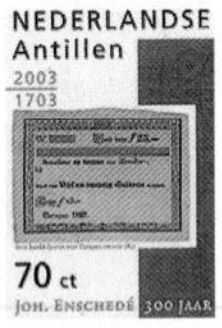

391 Early Banknote

2003. 300th Anniv of Joh. Enschede (printers). Two sheets containing T 391 and similar vert designs. Multicoloured.

MS1534	(a) 120×61 mm. 70c. Type **391**; 95c. 1873 stamp; 145c. Revenue stamp; 240c. 1967 banknote (b) 85×52 mm. 550c. Johan Enschede building, Haarlem	21·00	21·00

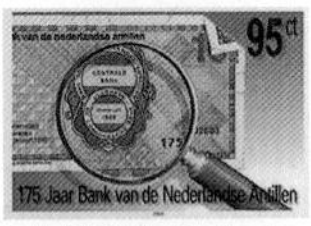

392 10 Gilder Banknote

2003. 175th Anniv of Central Bank. Multicoloured.

1535	95c. Type **392**	2·00	1·90
1536	145c. Street map and bank building	3·00	2·75
1537	285c. "First Instructions of the Bank of Curacao" (vert)	5·00	4·75

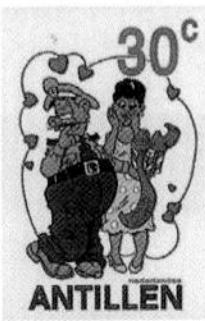

393 Fedjai proposing to Angelina

2003. Fedjai (cartoon postman) (3rd series). Sheet 120×61 mm containing T 393 and similar multicoloured designs.

MS1538	30c. Type **393**; 95c. Married couple; 145c. Taking Angelina to maternity hospital (horiz); 240c. With baby in post bag	10·50	10·50

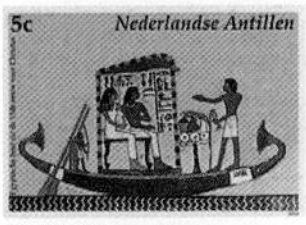

394 15th-century Egyptian Boat

2003. Watercraft.

1539	**394** 5c. multicoloured	70	55
1540	- 5c. multicoloured	70	55
1541	- 35c. reddish orange and black	95	80
1542	- 35c. multicoloured	95	80
1543	- 40c. multicoloured	1·00	90
1544	- 40c. multicoloured	1·00	90
1545	- 60c. multicoloured	1·20	1·00
1546	- 60c. orange and black	1·20	1·00
1547	- 75c. multicoloured	1·40	1·20
1548	- 75c. multicoloured	1·40	1·20
1549	- 85c. multicoloured (horiz)	1·60	1·50
1550	- 85c. multicoloured (horiz)	1·60	1·50

DESIGNS: 5c. Type **394**; 5c. Model boat from Tutankhamen's tomb; 35c. Ulysseus and the Sirens (vase decoration); 35c .Egyptian river craft; 40c. Greek dromon (galley); 40c. Illustration from *Vergilius Aenes* (15th-century book); 60c. Javanese fusta (galley); 60c. Greek trading ship; 75c. 16th-century Venetian; 75c. Mora (Bayeux tapestry); 85c. Captain Cook's *Earl of Pembroke*; 85c. *Savannah* (transatlantic steamship).

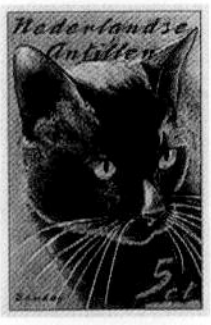

395 Bombay Cat

2003. Cats. Multicoloured.

1551	5c. Type **395**	45	35
1552	20c. Persian seal point	60	45
1553	25c. British shorthair	65	55
1554	50c. British blue	1·20	1·00
1555	65c. Persian chinchilla	1·30	1·10
1556	75c. Tonkinese red point	1·40	1·20
1557	85c. Balinese lilac tabby point	1·50	1·30
1558	95c. Persian shaded cameo	1·70	1·60
1559	100c. Burmilla	1·90	1·70
1560	145c. Chocolate tortie shaded silver eastern shorthair	2·50	2·30
1561	150c. Devon rex	2·75	2·50
1562	285c. Persian black tabby	5·00	4·75

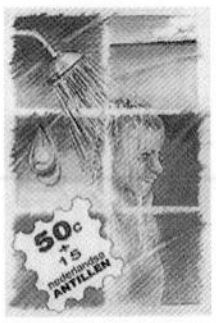

396 Child under Shower

2003. Child Welfare. Sheet 125×61 mm containing T 396 and similar vert designs. Multicoloured.

MS1563	50c.+15c. Type **396**; 95c.+35c. Girl holding umbrella; 145c.+55c. Boy watering plants; 240c.+110c. Hands under water tap	13·00	13·00

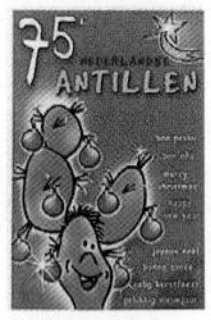

397 Cacti hung with Baubles

2003. Christmas. Multicoloured.

1564	75c. Type **397**	1·40	1·30
1565	240c. Cacti as figures holding fairy lights and clock	3·50	3·25

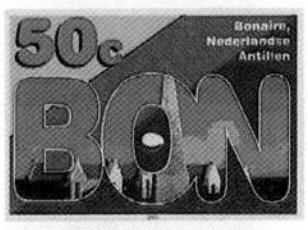

398 "BON" (Bonaire)

2003. Tourism. Multicoloured.

1566	50c. Type **398**	80	80
1567	75c. "CUR" (Curaçao)	1·30	1·20
1568	95c. "SAB" (Saba)	1·50	1·50
1569	120c. "EUX" (St. Eustatius)	1·90	1·80
1570	145c. "SXM" (Saint Martin)	2·10	2·00
1571	240c. "CUR" (Curaçao)	3·50	3·25
1572	285c. "SXM" (Saint Martin)	4·00	4·00
1573	380c. Emblem	5·25	5·00

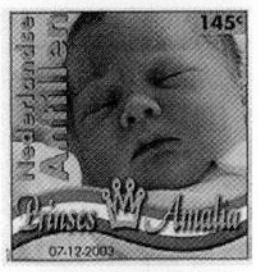

399 Princess Amalia

2004. Birth of Princess Amalia of Netherlands. Two sheets containing T 399 and similar square design. Multicoloured.

MS1574	(a) 120×61 mm. 145c. Type **399**; 380c. Crown Prince Willem Alexander holding Princess Amalia (b) 90×120 mm. No. **MS**1574×2	24·00	24·00

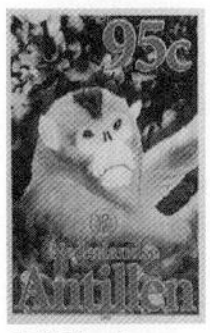

400 Monkey

2004. New Year. Year of the Monkey. Multicoloured.

1575	95c. Type **400**	2·20	2·00
MS1576	100×72 mm. 145c. Monkey and fan	3·00	3·00

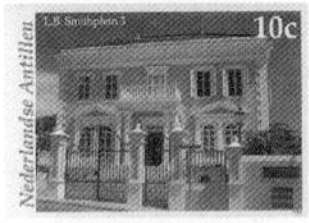

401 Belevedere (inscr "L.B. Smithplein 3)

2004. Houses. Multicoloured.

1577	10c. Type **401**	60	55
1578	25c. Hoogstraat 27	85	80
1579	35c. Landhuis, Brievengat	1·10	1·00
1580	65c. Scharlooweg 102	1·40	1·30
1581	95c. Hoogstrat 21–25	1·60	1·50
1582	145c. Villa Maria	2·20	2·00
1583	275c. Werfstraat 6	4·25	4·00
1584	350c. Landhuis, Ronde Klip	5·50	5·00

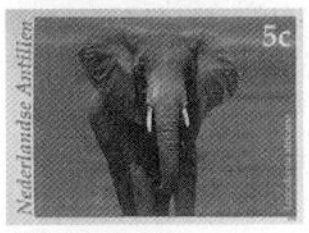

402 Elephant

2004. Fauna. Multicoloured.

1585	5c. Type **402**	20	15
1586	10c. Elephant facing left	35	35
1587	25c. Elephant amongst trees	65	60
1588	35c. Chimpanzee	80	75
1589	45c. Chimpanzee holding stick	90	85
1590	55c. Head of chimpanzee	1·00	95
1591	65c. Polar bear and cub	1·10	1·10
1592	95c. Polar bear facing left	1·40	1·30
1593	100c. Polar bear and cub (different)	1·60	1·50
1594	145c. Lion facing right	2·20	2·00
1595	275c. Lion facing left	4·25	4·00
1596	350c. Head of lion	4·75	4·50

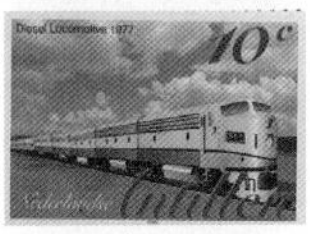

403 Diesel Locomotive (1977)

2004. Transport. Multicoloured.

1597	10c. Type **403**	35	20
1598	55c. Water-carrier (1900)	1·20	1·10
1599	75c. Ford Model A (1903)	1·60	1·50
1600	85c. Tanker (2004)	1·70	1·60
1601	95c. Wright Flyer (1903)	1·90	1·80
1602	145c. Penny Farthing bicycle (1871)	2·40	2·20

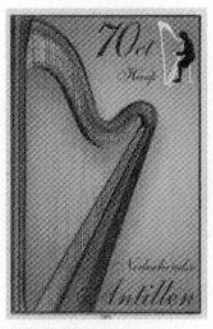

404 Harp

2004. Musical Instruments. Multicoloured.

1603	70c. Type **404**	1·20	1·10
1604	95c. Lute	1·70	1·60
1605	145c. Violin (horiz)	2·40	2·20
1606	240c. Zither (horiz)	4·00	3·75

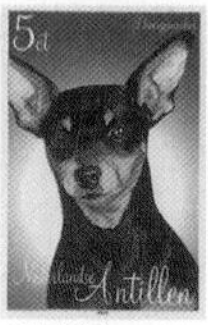

405 Miniature Pinscher

2004. Dogs. Multicoloured.

1607	5c. Type **405**	35	20
1608	5c. Pomeranian	35	20
1609	35c. Longhaired Teckel (dachshund)	85	80
1610	35c. Shih Tzu	85	80
1611	40c. Boxer puppy	95	90
1612	40c. Jack Russell terrier	95	90
1613	60c. Basset hound	1·30	1·20
1614	60c. Braque de l'Ariege	1·30	1·20
1615	75c. Afghan hound	1·60	1·50
1616	75c. Old English sheepdog	1·60	1·50
1617	85c. Entlebucher Sennen	1·70	1·60
1618	85c. Mastiff	1·70	1·60

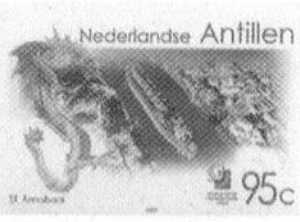

406 Dragon and Curacao Harbour

2004. International Stamp Exhibition, Singapore. Multicoloured.

1619	95c. Type **406**	1·70	1·60
1620	95c. Merlion and flags	1·70	1·60
1621	145c. Dragon and Brion Plaza, Otrobanda	2·40	2·20
1622	145c. Dr. A. C. Wathey Cruise and Cargo Facility, St. Maarten	2·40	2·20
MS1623	106×72 mm. 500c. As No. 1620	7·75	7·75

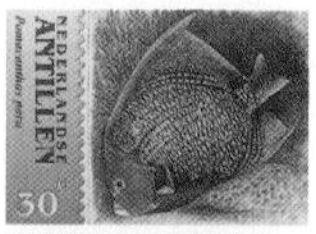

407 *Pomacanthus paru*

2004. Fish and Ducks. Multicoloured.

1624	30c. Type **407**	50	45
1625	65c. *Epinephelus guttatus*	85	80
1626	70c. *Mycteroperca interstitialis*	1·10	1·10
1627	75c. *Holacanthus isabelita*	1·20	1·10
1628	85c. *Epinephelus itajara*	1·30	1·20
1629	95c. *Holacanthus ciliaris*	1·40	1·30
1630	100c. American widgeon (*Anas Americana*) and *Sphyraena barracuda* (inscr "Sphyreana")	1·60	1·50
1631	145c. Blue-winged teal (*Anas discors*)	2·30	2·10
1632	250c. Bahama pintail (*Anas bahamensis*)	4·00	3·75
1633	285c. Lesser scaup (*Aythya affinis*)	4·50	4·25

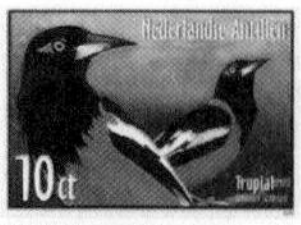

408 *Icterus icterus* (troupial)

2004. Birds. Multicoloured.

1634	10c. Type **408**	10	10
1635	95c. *Coereba flaveola* (bananaquit)	80	65
1636	100c. *Zonotrichia capensis* (rufous-collared sparrow)	80	65
1637	145c. *Sterna hirundo* (common tern)	1·10	85
1638	250c. *Phoenicopterus ruber* (greater flamingo)	1·90	1·70
1639	500c. *Buteo albicaudatus* (white-tailed hawk)	3·75	3·50

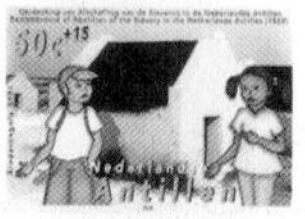

409 Lulu, Basje and Slave Huts, Bonaire

2004. Child Welfare. Designs showing Lulu and Basje. Multicoloured.

1640	50c.+15c. Type **409**	50	35
1641	95c.+35c. Lulu and Autonomy Monument	1·00	85
1642	95c.+35c. Visiting slave houses on Curçao	1·00	85
1643	145c.+55c. Visiting Kenepa plantation house	1·50	1·30
1644	145c.+55c. Basje and part of Constitution document	1·50	1·30

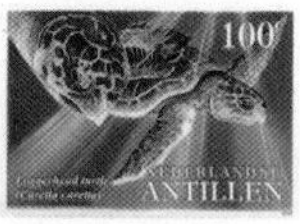

410 *Caretta caretta* (loggerhead turtle)

2004. Turtles. Multicoloured.

1645	100c. Type **410**	75	60
1646	145c. *Lepidochelys kempii* (Kemps's Ridley)	1·10	95
1647	240c. *Chelonia mydas* (green)	1·90	1·70
1648	285c. *Lepidochelys olivacea* (Olive Ridley)	2·20	1·90
1649	380c. *Eretmochelys imbricata* (hawksbill)	2·75	2·50
1650	500c. *Dermochelys coriacea* (leatherback)	3·75	3·50

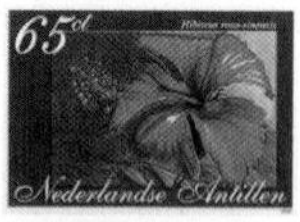

413 *Hibiscus rosa-sinensis*

2005. Flowers. Multicoloured.

1658	65c. Type **413**	50	35
1659	76c. *Plumbago auriculata*	60	45
1660	97c. *Tecoma stans*	75	55
1661	100c. *Ixora coccinea*	75	60
1662	122c. *Catharanthus roseus*	95	80
1663	148c. *Lantana camara*	1·20	95
1664	240c. *Tradescantia pallida*	1·90	1·70
1665	270c. *Nerium oleander*	2·10	1·90
1666	285c. *Plumeria obtusa*	2·20	1·90
1667	350c. *Bougainvillea spectabilis*	2·75	2·50

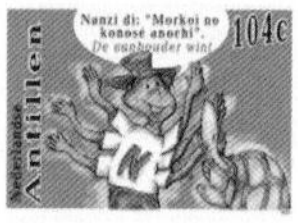

443 Nanzi and Turtle

2007. Cartoons. Nanzi. Multicoloured.

1824	104c. Type **443**	1·90	1·70
1825	104c. Nanzi and shark	1·90	1·70
1826	104c. Nanzi and bird	1·90	1·70
1827	104c. Nanzi and cow	1·90	1·70
1828	104c. Nanzi and dog	1·90	1·70
1829	104c. Nanzi and goat	1·90	1·70
1830	104c. Nanzi and chicken	1·90	1·70
1831	104c. Nanzi and donkey	1·90	1·70

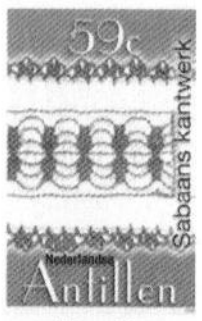

444 'Double Bee' (Wilda Johnson)

2007. Saba Lacework. Designs showing lacework crafted by women of Saba Island. Multicoloured.

1832	59c. Type **444**	1·00	90
1833	80c. The Cross	1·40	1·30
1834	95c. The Leaf	1·70	1·60
1835	104c. The Cross	1·90	1·70
1836	155c. Wallamina	2·75	2·50
1837	159c. The Ada	2·75	2·50

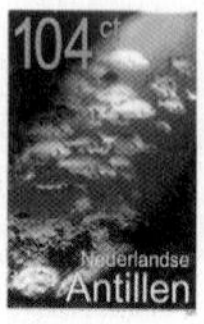

445 School of Fish

2007. Marine Fauna. Multicoloured.

1838	104c. Type **445**	1·60	1·40
1839	155c. Jellyfish	2·30	2·10
1840	195c. Coral reef	2·75	2·50
1841	335c. Turtle	4·75	4·50
1842	405c. Pink coral	5·75	5·25
1843	525c. Three fish	7·50	6·75

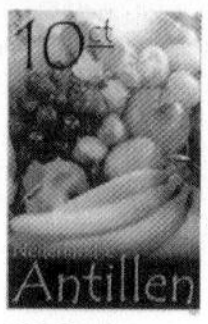

446 Grapes, Tomatoes, Bananas, Sprouts and Peppers

2007. Fruit and Vegetables. Multicoloured.

1844	10c. Type **446**	30	25
1845	25c. Pumpkin	45	40
1846	35c. Cucumber, tomato, leek and sweetcorn	55	50
1847	65c. Pear, pineapple, strawberry and orange	1·00	90
1848	95c. Avocado (*horiz*)	1·40	1·30
1849	145c. Lemon (*horiz*)	2·10	1·90
1850	275c. Peppers, mushrooms, potato, sweetcorn and tomato (*horiz*)	4·00	3·75
1851	350c. Mangoes (*horiz*)	5·00	4·50

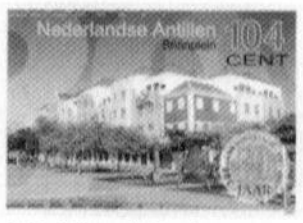

447 Brionplein Square, Willemstad

2007. 300th Anniv Otrobanda (3rd issue). Multicoloured.

1852	104c. Type **447**	1·60	1·40
1853	155c. Jopi building and Hotel Otrobanda	2·30	2·10
1854	285c. Kura Hulanda Hotel	4·25	4·00
1855	380c. Luna Blou Theatre	5·75	5·25

Stamps were issued in both 2005 and 2006 for this celebration.

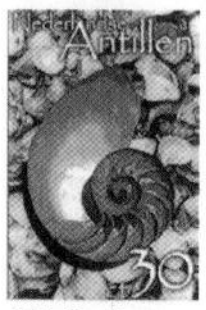

448 Shell

2007. Natural World. Multicoloured.

1856	30c. Type **448**	45	40
1857	65c. Young turtles crossing beach	1·00	90
1858	70c. Cricket	1·10	95
1859	75c. Cacti in flower	1·10	1·00
1860	85c. River edge	1·30	1·20
1861	95c. Woodpecker on cacti	1·40	1·30
1862	104c. Waves breaking against rocks	1·60	1·40
1863	145c. Shoreline	2·10	1·90
1864	250c. Rainforest	3·50	3·25
1865	285c. Sunset	4·25	3·75

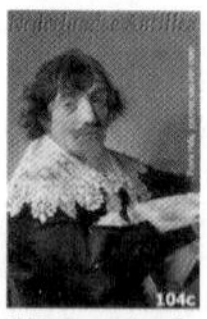

449 *Portrait of a Man*

2007. Art. Paintings by Frans Hals. Multicoloured.

1866	104c. Type **449**	1·60	1·40
1867	104c. *Marriage*	1·60	1·40
1868	155c. *The Merry Drinker*	2·30	2·10
1869	155c. *Judith Leyster, The Serenade*	2·30	2·10
MS1870	130×65 mm. 550c. *De Magere Compagnie* (detail) (*horiz*)	7·75	7·75

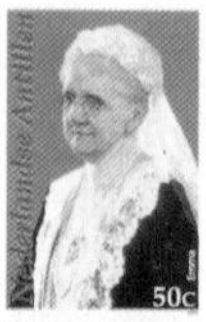

450 Emma (second wife of Willem III)

2007. Women of the Royal Family. Multicoloured.

1871	50c. Type **450**	70	65
1872	104c. Queen Wilhelmina (1890–1948 (abdicated))	1·60	1·40
1873	155c. Queen Juliana (1840–1980 (abdicated))	2·30	2·10
1874	285c. Queen Beatrix	4·25	3·75
1875	380c. Princess Maxima (wife of Crown Prince Willem Alexander)	5·50	5·00
1876	550c. Princess Amalia (daughter of Crown Prince Willem Alexander)	7·75	7·00

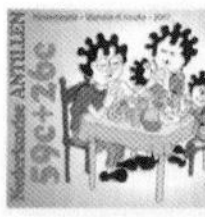

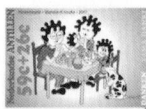

451 Family saying Grace at Table (giving thanks)

2007. Child Welfare. Multicoloured.

1877	59c.+26c. Type **451**	1·30	1·20
1878	104c.+46c. Raising flag (respect)	2·10	1·90
1879	155c.+65c. Baseball team members (Team spirit)	3·25	2·75
1880	285c.+125c. Teacher and pupils (education)	5·75	5·25

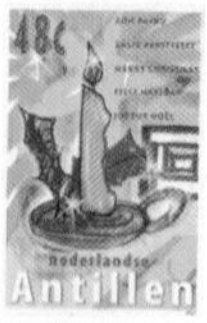

452 Candle and 'Merry Christmas'

2007. December Stamps. Multicoloured.

1881	48c. Type **452**	70	65
1882	104c. Tree, presents and 'Merry Christmas'	1·60	1·40
1883	155c. Notes of song and 'Happy New Year' (*horiz*)	2·30	2·10
1884	215c. 2008–2007	3·25	2·75

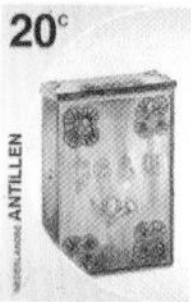

453 Early Mailbox

2007. Mailboxes. Multicoloured.

1885	20c. Type **453**	45	40
1886	104c. Modern mailbox	1·60	1·40
1887	240c. Mailbox with postal emblem	3·50	3·00
1888	285c. Early box with postal emblem	4·25	3·75
1889	380c. Tall decorative mailbox	5·50	5·00
1890	500c. Decorative mailbox on stand	7·25	6·50

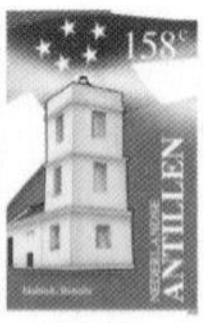

454 Malmok Lighthouse, Bonaire

2008. Lighthouses. Designs showing lighthouses. Multicoloured.

1891	158c. Type **454**	2·30	2·10
1892	158c. Fort Oranje, Bonaire	2·30	2·10
1893	158c. Klein, Curacao	2·30	2·10
1894	158c. Noordpunt, Curacao	2·30	2·10
1895	158c. Bullenbaai, Curacao	2·30	2·10
1896	158c. Willemstoren, Bonaire	2·30	2·10

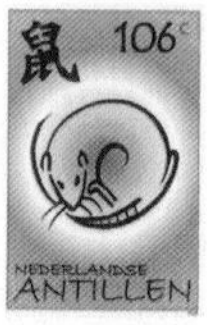

455 Stylized Rat

2008. Chinese New Year. Year of the Rat. Multicoloured.

1897	106c. Type **455**	1·60	1·40
1898	158c. White rat	2·30	2·10
MS1899	44×70 mm. 500c. Rat on twig (horiz)	7·25	7·25

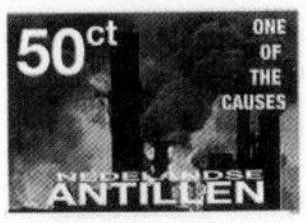

456 Pollution ('One of the Causes')

2008. Global Warming. Multicoloured.

1900	50c. Type **456**	70	65
1901	75c. Polar bear ('One of the Victims')	1·10	1·00
1902	125c. Wind farm ('One of the Solutions')	1·90	1·70
1903	250c. Beach ('One of the Hopes')	3·50	3·25

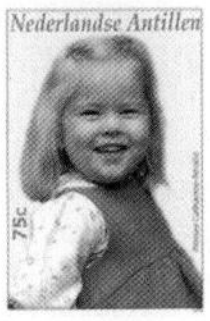

457 Princess Catharina Amelia

2008. Heirs to the Throne of the Netherlands. Multicoloured.

1904	75c. Type **457**	1·10	1·00
1905	100c. Princess Catharina Amelia wearing white	1·40	1·30
1906	125c. Prince Willem Alexander	1·90	1·70
1907	250c. Prince Willem Alexander, head and shoulders	3·50	3·25
1908	375c. Queen Beatrix wearing court dress	5·50	5·00
1909	500c. Queen Beatrix wearing evening coat	7·25	6·50

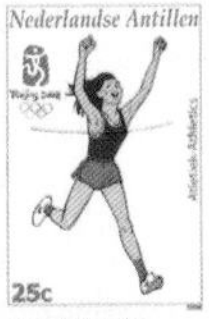

458 Athletics

2008. Olympic Games, Beijing. Multicoloured.

1910	25c. Type **458**	45	40
1911	35c. Gymnastics	55	50
1912	75c. Swimming	1·10	1·00
1913	215c. Cycling	3·25	2·75

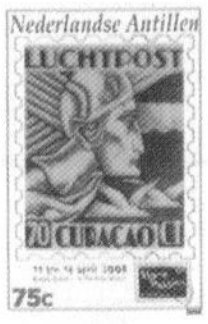

459 Curacao 1931 70c. Stamp (No. 132)

2008. Stamp Passion 2008 Exhibition. Designs showing early stamps. Multicoloured.

1914	75c. Type **459**	1·10	1·00
1915	100c. Netherlands 1901 12½c. stamp optd 'Curacao' (No. 51 of Curacao)	1·40	1·30
1916	125c. Curaçao 1944 40c.+50c. Red Cross stamp (No. 230)	1·90	1·70
1917	250c. Netherlands 1951 7c. International Court of Justice stamp (No. J26)	3·50	3·25
1918	375c. Netherland 1923 5g. stamp (No. 269)	5·50	5·00
1919	500c. Curacao 1946 10g. stamp (No. 261)	7·25	6·50

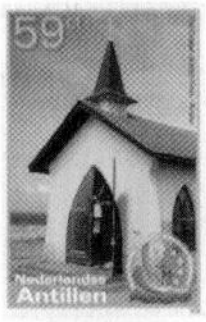

460 Alto Vista Chapel, Aruba

2008. 50th Anniv of Diocese of Aruba and Netherlands Antilles. Multicoloured.

1920	59c. Type **460**	85	80
1921	106c. Cross, Seru Larga, Bonaire	1·60	1·40
1922	158c. St. Ana Basilica, Curacao	2·30	2·10
1923	240c. Sacred Heart Church, Saba	3·50	3·00
1924	285c. Roman Catholic Church, Oranjestad, St. Eustatius	4·25	3·75
1925	335c. May Star of the Sea Church, St. Maarten	4·75	4·50

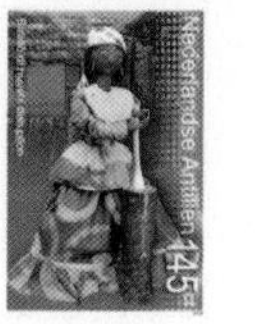

461 Pounding Corn

2008. Women's Work. Designs showing dolls as women working. Multicoloured.

1926	145c. Type **461**	2·10	1·90
1927	145c. Fishmonger	2·10	1·90
1928	145c. Frying mackerel	2·10	1·90
1929	145c. Grinding coffee	2·10	1·90
1930	155c. Laundress washing clothes	2·30	2·10
1931	155c. Ironing clothes	2·30	2·10
1932	155c. Grinding corn	2·30	2·10
1933	155c. Weaving straw hat	2·30	2·10

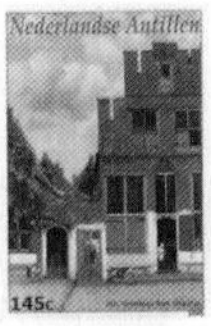

462 *Little Street*

2008. Art. Paintings by Johannes (Jan) Vermeer. Two sheets containing T 462 and similar vert designs. Multicoloured.

MS1934	105×103 mm. 145c. Type **462**; 145c. *Girl with a Pearl Earring*; 155c. *Woman in Blue reading Letter*; 155c. *The Love Letter*	8·75	8·75
MS1935	65×123 mm. 500c. *The Milk-maid* (detail)	7·25	7·25

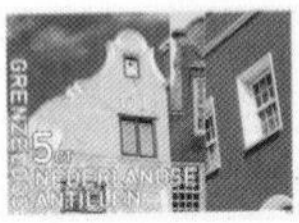

463 Houses (architecture)

2008. Netherlands and Beyond. Sheet 145×75 mm containing T 463 and similar multicoloured designs.

MS1936	5c. Type **463**; 106c. White and blue building (vert); 285c. Roofs (vert)	6·75	6·75

No. **MS**1936 also includes Netherlands 90c. stamps (Chillies and cheese (food)) and Aruba 240c. stamp (Script (poem by Frederico Oduber)).

The 'foreign' stamps could only be used in their country of origin.

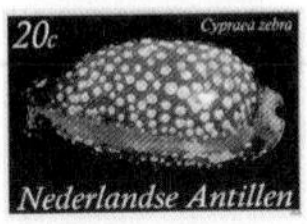

464 *Cypraea zebra*

2008. Shells. Multicoloured.

1937	20c. Type **464**	30	25
1938	40c. *Charonia varigata Lamarck*	55	50
1939	65c. *Callistoma armillata*	1·00	90
1940	106c. *Strombus gigas Linne*	1·60	1·40
1941	158c. *Pina carnea*	2·30	2·10
1942	285c. *Olivia sayana Ravenel*	4·25	3·75
1943	335c. *Natica canrena Linne*	4·75	4·50
1944	405c. *Voluta musica*	5·75	5·25

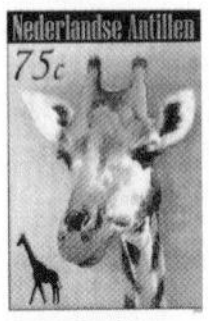

465 Giraffe

2008. African Fauna. Multicoloured.

1945	75c. Type **465**	1·10	1·00
1946	150c. Elephants (horiz)	2·10	1·90
1947	175c. Cheetah (horiz)	2·50	2·30
1948	250c. Zebra (horiz)	3·50	3·25
MS1949	90×62 mm. 250c. Impala	3·75	3·75

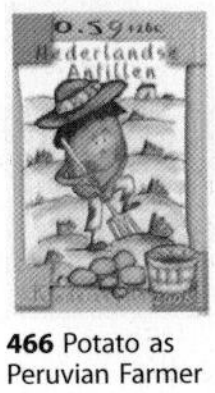

466 Potato as Peruvian Farmer

2008. Child Welfare. International Year of the Potato. Multicoloured.

1950	59c.+26c. Type **466**	1·30	1·20
1951	106c.+46c. Potato preparing potatoes	2·10	1·90
1952	158c.+65c. Potato as Belgian girl eating chips	3·25	2·75
1953	285c.+125c. Potatoes as Irish family	5·75	5·25

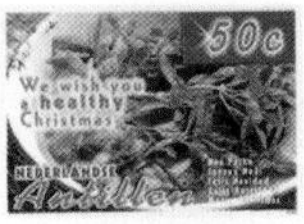

467 Leaves and 'We wish you a healthy Christmas'

2008. December Stamps. Multicoloured.

1954	50c. Type **467**	70	65
1955	106c. Ponsettias and 'We wish you a merry Christmas'	1·60	1·40
1956	158c. Boat and 'We wish you a prosperous New Year'	2·30	2·10
1957	215c. Dock and 'We wish you a peaceful New Year'	3·25	2·75

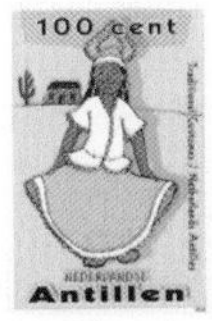

468 Girl wearing Seu Festival Clothes, Papiamentu

2008. Traditional Costumes. Multicoloured.

1958	100c. Type **468**	1·40	1·30
1959	104c. Boy wearing Dutch costume	1·60	1·40
1960	155c. Girl wearing kimono	2·30	2·10

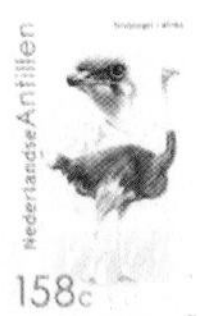

469 Ostrich

2008. Birds. Multicoloured.

1961	158c. Type **469**	2·30	2·10
1962	158c. Wild turkey	2·30	2·10
1963	158c. Mandarin duck (horiz)	2·30	2·10
1964	158c. Green heron (horiz)	2·30	2·10
1965	158c. Cassowary	2·30	2·10
1966	158c. Penguin	2·30	2·10
1967	158c. Cormorant (horiz)	2·30	2·10
1968	158c. Goldfinch (horiz)	2·30	2·10

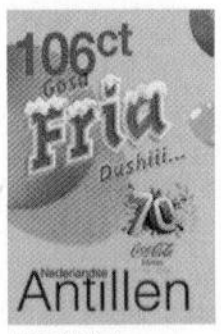

470 'Fria'

2008. 70th Anniv of Coca Cola in Curaçao. Three sheets, each 170×130 mm containing T 470 and similar multicoloured designs.

MS1969	106c.×8, Type **470**; Fria bottle, bronze contents; Fria bottle, purple contents; Fria bottle, yellow contents; Fria bottle, orange-yellow contents; Fria bottle, pink contents; Fria bottle, pale pink contents; Fria bottle, pale green contents	13·00	13·00
MS1970	106c. Coca Cola bottle, 1899; 106c. Coca Cola bottle, 1900; 158c. Coca Cola bottle, 1905; 158c. Coca Cola bottle, 1913; 158c. Coca Cola bottle, 1915; 285c. Girl with striped umbrella; 285c. Girl with yellow umbrella; 285c. Coca Cola bottle, 1923	18·00	18·00
MS1971	158c.×8, 'WELCOME TO CURACAO' (horiz); Early Coca Cola advertising promotion (horiz); Coca Cola building (horiz); Early advertising hoarding; Two men holding Coca cola bottles (horiz); 1950's bar serving Coca Cola (horiz); Man smoking cigar holding advertising poster (horiz); Early delivery lorry (horiz)	13·00	13·00

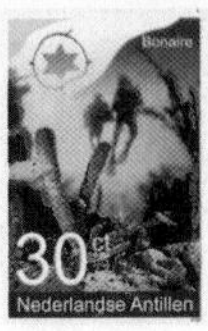

471 Divers, Bonaire

2009. Islands. Multicoloured.

1972	30c. Type **471** (As Type **442**)	45	40
1973	59c. Oil storage tanks, Statia (As No. 1822)	85	80
1974	110c. Flowers, Curacao (As No. 1815) (vert)	1·60	1·40
1975	164c. Cruise ship and pier (As No. 1818) (vert)	1·70	1·60
1976	168c. Flamingoes, Bonaire (As No. 1819)	2·40	2·20
1977	285c. Houses, Saba (As No. 1821)	4·00	3·75

Nos. 1972/7 are as the 'Island' stamps of 2007, not yet been received, but for which numbers are left.

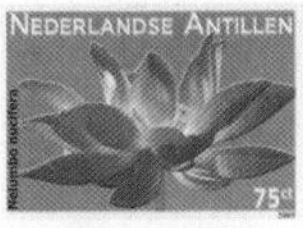

472 *Nelumbo nucifera*

2009. Flowers. Multicoloured.

1978	75c. Type **472**	1·00	90
1979	150c. *Chrysanthemum leucanthemum*	1·60	1·40
1980	200c. *Hepatica nobilis*	2·30	2·10
1981	225c. *Cistus incanus*	3·00	2·75
1982	350c. Alamanda flower	5·00	4·50
1983	500c. Rose 'Wise portia'	7·25	6·50

Nos. 1978-1983 were printed *se-tenant*, in blocks of six stamps within the sheet.

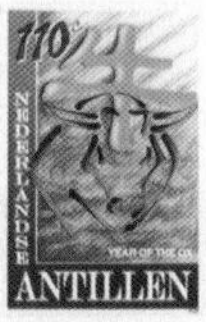

473 Symbol

2009. Year of Ox. Multicoloured.

1984	110c. Type **473**	1·60	1·40
1985	168c. Ox (horiz)	2·40	2·20

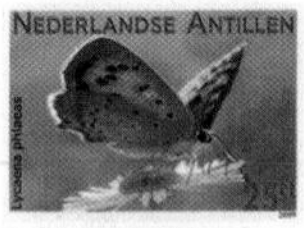

474 *Lycaena Phlaeas*

2009. Butterflies. Multicoloured.

1986	25c. Type **474**	55	50
1987	35c. *Danus plexippus*	70	65
1988	50c. *Nymphalis antiopa*	85	80
1989	105c. *Carterocephalus palaemon*	1·60	1·40
1990	115c. *Inachis io*	1·70	1·60
1991	115c. *Phyciodes tharos*	2·10	1·90
1992	185c. *Papilio glaucus*	2·50	2·30
1993	240c. *Dryas julia*	3·50	3·00
1994	315c. *Libytheana carinenta*	4·50	4·00
1995	375c. *Melanis pixe*	5·25	4·75
1996	400c. *Astrocampa celtis*	5·50	5·00
1997	1000c. *Historis acheronta*	14·00	12·50

Nos. 1986-1997 x2 were printed *se-tenant*, in blocks of 12 stamps within the sheet.

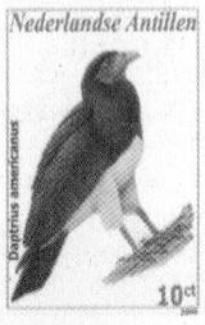

475 *Daptrius americanus* (red-throated caracara)

2009. Birds. Multicoloured.

1998	10c. Type **475**	30	25
1999	45c. *Amazona amazonica* (orange-winged Amazon)	1·10	65
2000	80c. *Querula purpurata* (purple-throated fruitcrow)	1·10	1·00
2001	145c. *Aratinga leucophthalmus* (white-eyed parakeet)	2·10	1·90
2002	190c. *Xipholena punicea* (pompadour cotinga)	2·75	2·50
2003	235c. *Celeus torquatus* (ringed woodpecker)	3·50	3·00

2004	285c. *Lamprospiza melanoleuca* (red-billed pied tanager)	4·00	3·75
2005	300c. *Selenidera culik* (guianan toucanet)	4·25	4·00
2006	335c. *Amazila viridigaster* (green-bellied hummingbird)	4·75	4·25
2007	425c. *Tangara gyrola* (bay-headed tanager)	6·00	5·50
2008	450c. *Nyctibius grandis* (great potoo)	6·25	5·50
2009	500c. *Galbula leucogastra* (bronzy jacamar)	6·75	6·25

Nos. 1998-2009 x2 were printed *se-tenant*, in blocks of 12 stamps within the sheet.

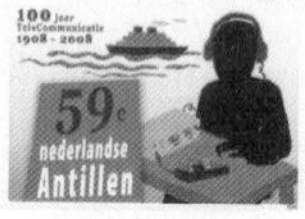

476 Telegraph Operator

2009. Centenary of Post and Telecommunications. Multicoloured.

2010	59c. Type **476**	85	80
2011	110c. Telephone user and living room	1·60	1·40
2012	164c. Laptop user and symbols of modern communications	2·40	2·10

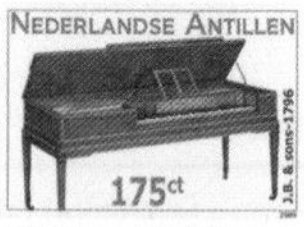

477 Piano, J.B. & Sons, 1796

2009. 300th Anniv of Pianos. Multicoloured designs showing pianos, maker given.

2013	175c. Type **477**	2·50	2·30
2014	225c. J. Schantz, 1818 (vert)	3·25	3·00
2015	250c. Steinway-Welt, 1927 (vert)	3·50	3·25
2016	350c. Yamaha, 2007	5·00	4·50

Nos. 2017/18 and Type **478** are left for Birds issued on 20 July 2009, not yet received.

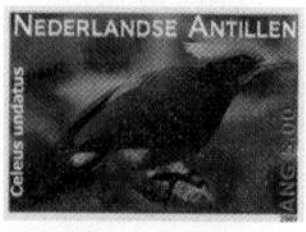

478 Celeus elegans (chestnut woodpecker)

2009. Birds. Multicoloured.

MS2018	5g. Type **478**; 10g. *Iodopleura fusca* (dusky purpletuft)	7·00	6·50

No. 2017 is vacant.

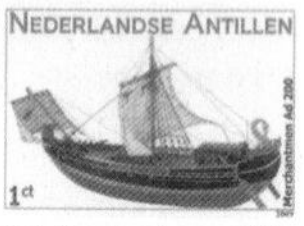

479 Merchantman, 200 AD

2009. Ships. Multicoloured.

2019	1c. Type **479**	15	15
2020	2c. Caravel, 1490	30	25
2021	3c. Inscr 'Naos, 1492'	45	40
2022	4c. *Constant*, 1605	55	50
2023	5c. Merchant ship, 1620	70	65
2024	80c. *Vasa*, 1628	1·10	1·00
2025	220c. Hoy, 1730	3·25	2·75
2026	275c. Bark, 1750	4·00	3·50
2027	385c. Schooner, 1838	5·50	5·00
2028	475c. Sailing rig, 1884	6·75	6·25
2029	500c. Inscr 'Fifie, 1903'	7·25	6·50
2030	750c. Junk, 1938	10·50	9·75

Nos. 2019-2030 were printed, *se-tenant* in blocks of 12 stamps within the sheet.

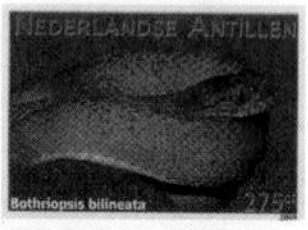
480 *Bothriopsis bilineata*

2009. Snakes. Multicoloured.

2031	275c. Type **480**	4·00	3·50
2032	325c. *Bothriechis schlegelii*	4·50	4·00
2033	340c. *Agkistrodon piscivorus* (inscr 'Agkistrodeon piscivorus')	5·50	5·00
2034	390c. *Erythrolamprus aesculapii*	5·50	5·00
2035	420c. *Atropoides mexicanus*	6·00	5·50
2036	450c. *Bothriechis nigroviridis*	6·00	5·50

Nos. 2031-2036 were printed, *se-tenant*, in blocks of six stamps within the sheet.

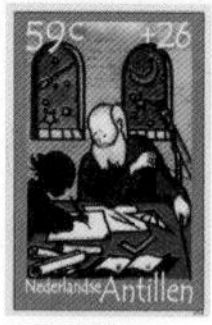
481 Galileo Galilei

2009. Child Welfare. Multicoloured.

2037	59c.+26c. Type **481**	1·20	1·10
2038	110c.+45c. Family and telescope	2·40	2·10
2039	168c.+75c. Children and Space Shuttle	3·50	3·00
2040	285c.+125c. Astronaut walking on moon	6·00	5·50

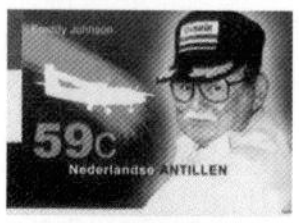
482 Walter Frederick Martinus (Freddy) Johnson

2009. Aviation Pioneers. Multicoloured.

2041	59c. Type **482**	1·20	1·10
2042	110c. Norman Chester Wathey	1·70	1·50
2043	164c. José (Pipe) Domoy	1·80	1·70

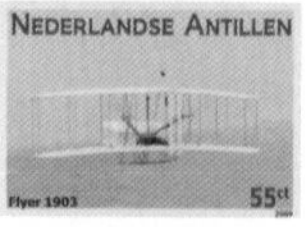

483 Wright Flyer I, 1903

2009. Aircraft. Multicoloured.

2044	55c. Type **483**	90	85
2045	100c. Douglas DC 3 (inscr 'DST Skysleeper'), 1935	1·60	1·50
2046	205c. Cesna 170, 1948	2·30	2·20
2047	395c. Lockheed Constellation, 1943	5·50	5·00
2048	645c. de Havilland Comet I (inscr 'Havilland Comet'), 1949	9·25	9·00
2049	800c. Vickers (insc 'BAC') Super VC10, 1962	12·00	11·00

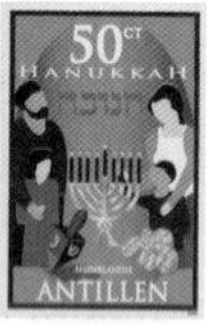
484 Family and Menorah (Hanukkah)

2009. December Stamps. Multicoloured.

2050	50c. Type **484**	1·10	1·00
2051	110c. Family and decorated tree (Christmas)	1·70	1·60
2052	168c. Family wearing traditional dress and candles (Kwanza)	2·50	2·40
2053	215c. Analogue clock, digital clock and fireworks (New Year)	2·75	2·50

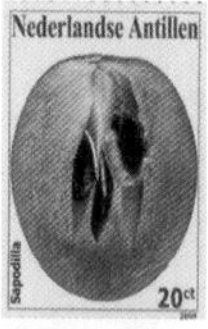

485 Sapodilla

2009. Fruit. Multicoloured.

2054	20c. Type **485**	40	35
2055	45c. Pineapple	1·10	1·00
2056	125c. Mamey sapote	2·10	2·00
2057	145c. Avocado	2·20	2·10
2058	160c. Mangosteen	2·40	2·30
2059	210c. Rambutan	2·75	2·50
2060	295c. Pomelo	4·00	3·75
2061	1000c. Watermelon	13·00	12·00

Nos. 2062/71 and Type **486** are left for stamps not yet received.

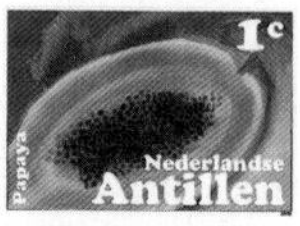

487 Papaya

2010. Fruits. Multicoloured.

2072	1c. Type **487**	15	10
2073	5c. Pomegranate	20	15
2074	30c. Mango	40	35
2075	59c. Bananas	85	80
2076	79c. Cashews	1·00	1·10
2077	111c. Soursop	1·60	1·50
2078	164c. Tamarind	2·10	2·00
2079	170c. Watermelon	2·10	2·00
2080	199c. Gennip	2·50	2·40
2081	285c. Seagrape	4·00	3·75

Nos. 2072/81 are as those issued in 2005, with new face values.

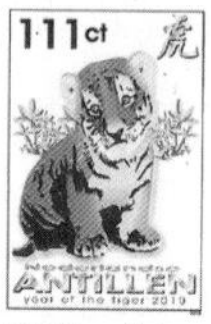

488 Tiger Cub

2010. Chinese New Year. Multicoloured.

2082	111c. Type **488**	1·60	1·50
2083	164c. Mother and cub	2·40	2·30
2084	170c. White tiger	2·75	2·50

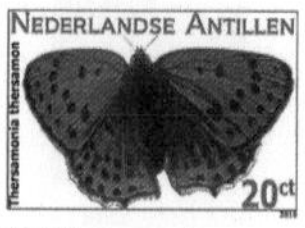

489 *Thersamonia thersamon*

2010. Butterflies. Multicoloured.

2085	20c. Type **489**	35	30
2086	50c. *Acrea natalica*	65	60
2087	80c. *Vanessa carye*	1·10	1·00
2088	100c. *Apodemia mormo*	1·60	1·50
2089	125c. *Siproeta stelenes meridionalis*	1·80	1·70
2090	175c. *Anartia amathea*	2·40	2·30
2091	200c. *Doxocopa laure*	2·60	2·75
2092	250c. *Euphaedra uganda*		
2093	350c. *Precis westermanni* (inscr 'Precis westermannii')	2·75	2·60
2094	450c. *Precis octavia*	6·00	5·75
2095	500c. *Euphaedra neophron*	7·00	6·75
2096	700c. *Vanessa cardui*	8·50	8·25

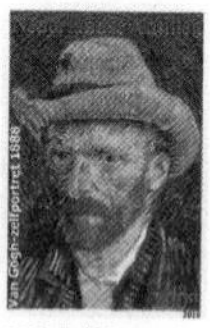
490 *Self-Portrait*

2010. Paintings by Vincent van Gogh. Multicoloured.

2097	200c. Type **490**	3·00	2·75
2098	400c. *Agostina Segatori*	5·25	5·00
2099	500c. *L'Arlesienne Woman*	6·75	6·50
2100	700c. *Emperor Moth*	7·75	7·50

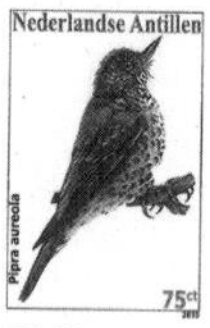

491 *Pipra aureola* (crimson-hooded manakin)

2010. Birds. Multicoloured.

2101	75c. Type **491**	1·00	90
2102	150c. *Neopelma chrysocephalum* (saffron-crested tyrant-manakin)	1·60	1·40
2103	200c. *Pipra aureola* (crimson-hooded manakin) (inscr '*Oxyruncus cristatus*' (sharpbill))	3·25	3·00
2104	225c. *Automolus rufipileatus* (chestnut-crowned foliage-gleaner)	3·25	3·00
2105	350c. *Empidonomus varius* (variegated flycatcher)	5·00	4·75
2106	500c. *Venilornis sanquineus* (blood-coloured woodpecker)	7·25	7·00

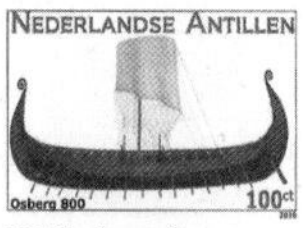

492 Oseberg (inscr 'Osberg'), 800

2010. Ships. Multicoloured.

2107	100c. Type **492**	1·60	1·50
2108	125c. *Dromon*, 910	1·80	1·70
2109	175c. *Cocca*, 1500	2·10	2·00
2110	200c. *Mary*, 1661	2·40	2·30
2111	250c. *Houtport*, 1700	2·50	2·30
2112	300c. *Santissima Trinidad*, 1769	2·75	2·50
2113	350c. Cargo ship (inscr 'Vrachtschip'), 1800	3·00	2·75
2114	400c *Amistad*, 1839	4·50	4·25
2115	450c. Two masted warship (inscr 'Oorlogsschip'), 1840	5·50	5·25
2116	650c. Inscr 'Netherlands schip', 1850	9·25	9·00

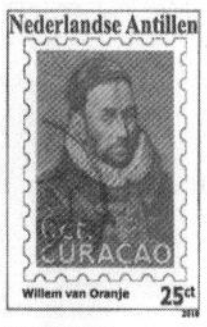

493 1933 Curacao 6c. Stamp (As Type 24a)

2010. Stamp on Stamp. Multicoloured.

2117	25c. Type **493**	45	40
2118	50c. 1933 Curaçao 30c. Stamp (As No. 168)	1·00	95
2119	100c. 1923 Curaçao 6c. Stamp (As No. 100)	1·30	1·20
2120	250c. 1938 Curaçao 1½c. Stamp (As Type **29**)	2·50	2·30
2121	275c. Netherlands Antilles 25c. Stamp (As Type **93**)	2·50	2·30
2122	300c. 1923 Curaçao 5c. Stamp (As Type **17**)	2·75	2·50
2123	400c. 1947 Curaçao 15c. AIR Stamp (As No. 265)	4·00	4·25
2124	600c. 1948 Curaçao 6c. Stamp (As No. 297)	8·00	7·75
MS2125	75×72mm. 700c. 1949 Curaçao 12½c. Stamp (As Type **49**) 800c. 1936 Curaçao 50c. Stamp (As No. 169)	8·50	8·50

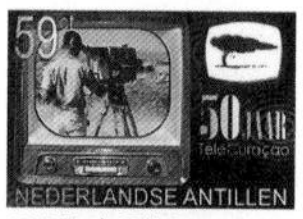

494 Early TV Set

2010. 50th Anniv of TeleCuraçao. Multicoloured.

2126	59c. Type **494**	1·00	95
2127	111c. TV set showing transmitter	1·30	1·20
2128	164c. Modern TV showing anniversary emblem	2·10	2·00

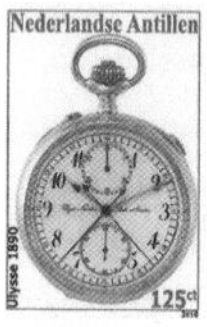

495 Ulysse, 1890

2010. Pocket Watches. Multicoloured.

2129	125c. Type **495**	1·70	1·70
2130	175c. Hampden, 1910	2·10	2·00
2131	250c. Elgin, 1924	2·50	2·30
2132	300c. Illinois, 1928	2·75	2·50
2133	350c. Vacheron, 1955	3·00	2·75

POSTAGE DUE STAMPS

1952. As Type D 121 of Netherlands but inscr "NEDERLANDSE ANTILLEN".

D336	1c. green	35	14
D337	2½c. green	95	95
D338	5c. green	35	35
D339	6c. green	1·20	1·20
D340	7c. green	1·20	1·20
D341	8c. green	1·20	1·20
D342	9c. green	1·20	1·20
D343	10c. green	50	35
D344	12½c. green	45	35
D345	15c. green	1·20	1·20
D346	20c. green	1·20	1·20
D347	25c. green	95	35
D348	30c. green	2·30	2·30
D349	35c. green	2·30	2·30
D350	40c. green	2·30	2·30
D351	45c. green	2·30	2·30
D352	50c. green	2·30	2·30

Pt. 4

NETHERLANDS INDIES

A former Dutch colony, consisting of numerous settlements in the East Indies, of which the islands of Java and Sumatra and parts of Borneo and New Guinea are the most important. Renamed Indonesia in 1948, Independence was granted during 1949. Netherlands New Guinea remained a Dutch possession until 1962 when it was placed under U.N. control, being incorporated with Indonesia in 1963.

100 cents = 1 gulden.

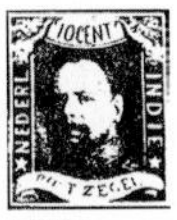

1 King William III

1864. Imperf.

1	1	10c. red	£450	£140

1868. Perf.

2		10c. red	£1700	£250

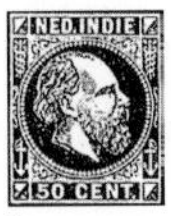

2

1870. Perf.

27	2	1c. green	8·25	5·50
28	2	2c. purple	£140	£140
29	2	2c. brown	11·00	6·75
30	2	2½c. buff	65·00	33·00
12	2	5c. green	95·00	10·00
32	2	10c. brown	33·00	1·70
40	2	12½c. drab	8·25	3·25
34	2	15c. brown	33·00	3·25
5	2	20c. blue	£150	5·50
36	2	25c. purple	33·00	2·20
44	2	30c. green	65·00	6·75
17	2	50c. red	39·00	4·50
38	2	2g.50 green and purple	£130	29·00

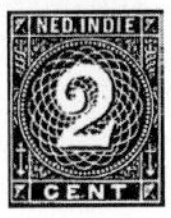

5

1883

87	5	1c. green	1·70	55
88	5	2c. brown	1·70	55
89	5	2½c. buff	1·70	1·10
90	5	3c. purple	2·75	55
86	5	5c. green	65·00	36·00
91	5	5c. blue	20·00	55

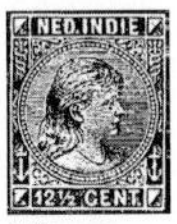

6 Queen Wilhelmina

1892

94	6	10c. brown	11·00	55
95	6	12½c. grey	17·00	45·00
96	6	15c. brown	28·00	3·25
97	6	20c. blue	55·00	2·20
98	6	25c. purple	50·00	2·75
99	6	30c. green	65·00	5·00
100	6	50c. red	50·00	2·75
101	6	2g.50 blue and brown	£200	60·00

1900. Netherlands stamps of 1898 surch NED.-INDIE and value.

111	13	10c. on 10c. lilac	5·50	55
112	13	12½c. on 12½c. blue	5·50	85
113	13	15c. on 15c. brown	5·50	85
114	13	20c. on 20c. green	28·00	85
115	13	25c. on 25c. blue and pink	22·00	85
116	13	50c. on 50c. red and green	45·00	1·70
117	11	2½g. on 2½g. lilac	85·00	28·00

1902. Surch.

118	5	½ on 2c. brown	65	55
119	5	2½ on 3c. purple	80	65

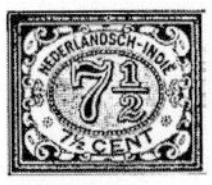

11

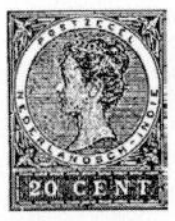

12

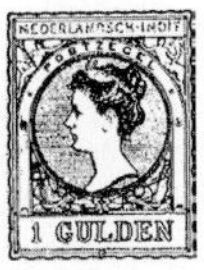

13

1902

120	11	½c. lilac	1·10	55
121	11	1c. olive	1·10	55
122	11	2c. brown	5·50	55
123	11	2½c. green	3·25	55
124	11	3c. orange	5·50	1·70
125	11	4c. blue	20·00	11·50
126	11	5c. red	8·25	55
127	11	7½c. grey	5·50	55
128	12	10c. slate	5·50	55
129	12	12½c. blue	2·75	55
130	12	15c. brown	14·00	2·75
131	12	17½c. bistre	5·50	55
132	12	20c. grey	2·75	2·20
133	12	20c. olive	39·00	1·10
134	12	22½c. olive and brown	5·50	55
135	12	25c. mauve	17·00	55
136	12	30c. brown	45·00	55
137	12	50c. red	39·00	55
138	13	1g. lilac	90·00	55
206	13	1g. lilac on blue	85·00	11·00
139	13	2½g. grey	£110	2·75
207	13	2½g. grey on blue	£170	55·00

1902. No. 130 optd with horiz bars.

140		15c. brown	2·75	1·10

1905. No. 132 surch 10 cent.

141		10c. on 20c. grey	4·00	1·70

1908. Stamps of 1902 optd JAVA.

142		½c. lilac	55	55
143		1c. olive	85	55
144		2c. brown	3·25	3·50
145		2½c. green	2·20	35
146		3c. orange	1·70	1·30
147		5c. red	3·25	35
148		7½c. grey	2·75	2·50
149		10c. slate	2·00	35
150		12½c. blue	2·75	1·10
151		15c. brown	5·00	5·00
152		17½c. bistre	2·75	1·10
153		20c. olive	14·00	1·10
154		22½c. olive and brown	7·25	4·00
155		25c. mauve	7·25	55
156		30c. brown	39·00	4·00
157		50c. red	28·00	1·10
158		1g. lilac	65·00	4·50
159		2½g. grey	£100	85·00

1908. Stamps of 1902 optd BUITEN BEZIT.

160		½c. lilac	85	55
161		1c. olive	85	55
162		2c. brown	2·75	4·25
163		2½c. green	1·70	55
164		3c. orange	1·70	1·70
165		5c. red	4·50	55
166		7½c. grey	4·25	4·25
167		10c. slate	1·70	20
168		12½c. blue	14·00	3·25
169		15c. brown	9·00	5·50
170		17½c. bistre	3·00	2·75
171		20c. olive	14·00	3·25
172		22½c. olive and brown	11·00	9·50
173		25c. mauve	11·00	55
174		30c. brown	22·00	3·00
175		50c. red	11·00	1·10
176		1g. lilac	85·00	8·25
177		2½g. grey	£140	90·00

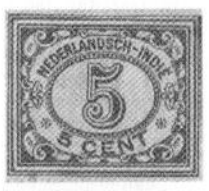

19

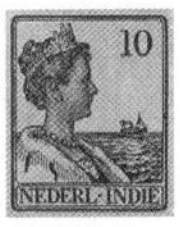

20

1912

208	19	½c. lilac	35	35
209	19	1c. green	30	35
210	19	2c. brown	85	35
264	19	2c. grey	85	35
211	19	2½c. green	2·00	35
265	19	2½c. pink	1·10	35
212	19	3c. brown	85	35
266	19	3c. green	1·70	35
213	19	4c. blue	1·70	35
267	19	4c. green	1·70	35
268	19	4c. bistre	11·00	6·75
214	19	5c. pink	1·70	35
269	19	5c. green	1·70	35
270	19	5c. blue	1·10	35
215	19	7½c. brown	1·10	35
271	19	7½c. bistre	1·10	35
216	20	10c. red	1·70	35
272	19	10c. lilac	2·75	35
217	20	12½c. blue	1·70	35
273	20	12½c. red	1·70	55
274	20	15c. blue	11·00	35
218	20	17½c. brown	1·70	35
219	20	20c. green	2·75	35
275	20	20c. blue	2·75	35
276	20	20c. orange	20·00	35
220	20	22½c. orange	2·75	1·10
221	20	25c. mauve	2·75	35
222	20	30c. grey	2·75	35
277	20	32½c. violet and orange	2·75	35
278	20	35c. brown	10·00	80
279	20	40c. green	5·50	35

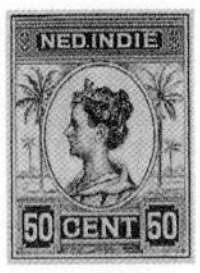

21

1913

223	21	50c. green	8·25	35
280	21	60c. blue	8·25	35
281	21	80c. orange	8·25	55
224	21	1g. brown	8·25	35
283	21	1g.75 lilac	28·00	2·30
225	21	2½g. pink	22·00	55

1915. Red Cross. Stamps of 1912 surch +5 cts. and red cross.

243		1c.+5c. green	8·25	8·25
244		5c.+5c. pink	8·25	8·25
245		10c.+5c. red	11·00	11·00

1917. Stamps of 1902, 1912 and 1913 surch.

246		½c. on 2½c. (No. 211)	55	55
247		1c. on 4c. (No. 213)	55	85
250		12½c. on 17½c. (No. 218)	55	35
251		12½c. on 22½c. (No. 220)	55	35
248		17½c. on 22½c. (No. 134)	2·75	1·10
252		20c. on 22½c. (No. 220)	55	55
249		30c. on 1g. (No. 138)	9·00	2·50
253		32½c. on 50c. (No. 223)	1·70	35
254		40c. on 50c. (No. 223)	5·00	55
255		60c. on 1g. (No. 224)	8·25	55
256		80c. on 1g. (No. 224)	10·00	1·10

1922. Bandoeng Industrial Fair. Stamps of 1912 and 1917 optd 3de N. I. JAARBEURS BANDOENG 1922.

285		1c. green	11·00	11·00
286		2c. brown	11·00	11·00
287		2½c. pink	80·00	90·00
288		3c. yellow	11·00	11·00
289		4c. blue	45·00	55·00
290		5c. green	17·00	11·00
291		7½c. brown	11·00	11·00
292		10c. lilac	90·00	£130
293		12½c. on 22½c. orge (No. 251)	11·00	11·00
294		17½c. brown	11·00	11·00
295		20c. blue	11·00	11·00

Nos. 285/95 were sold at a premium for 3, 4, 5, 6, 8, 9, 10, 12½, 15, 20 and 22c. respectively.

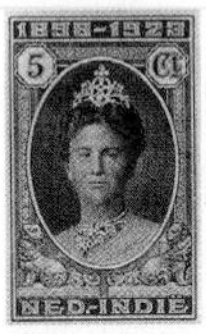

33

1923. Queen's Silver Jubilee.

296	33	5c. green	55	55
297	33	12½c. red	55	55
298	33	20c. blue	1·10	55
299	33	50c. orange	2·75	1·10
300	33	1g. purple	6·25	1·10
301	33	2½g. grey	55·00	55·00
302	33	5g. brown	£170	£190

1928. Air. Stamps of 1912 and 1913 surch LUCHTPOST, Fokker F.VII airplane and value.

303		10c. on 12½c. red	1·70	1·70
304		20c. on 25c. mauve	4·00	4·00
305		40c. on 80c. orange	4·00	4·00
306		75c. on 1g. sepia	1·70	1·70
307		1½g. on 2½g. red	11·00	11·00

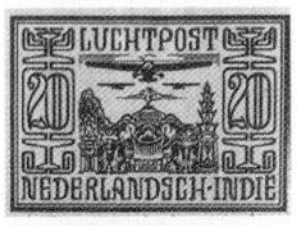

36 Fokker F.VIIa

1928. Air.

308	36	10c. purple	55	55
309	36	20c. brown	1·40	1·10
310	36	40c. red	1·70	1·10
311	36	75c. green	3·25	55
312	36	1g.50 orange	7·00	1·10

1930. Air. Surch 30 between bars.

313		30c. on 40c. red	1·70	55

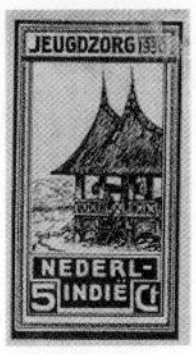

38 Watch-tower

1930. Child Welfare. Centres in brown.

315	-	2c. (+1c.) mauve	1·70	1·70
316	38	5c. (+2½c.) green	6·75	5·00
317	-	12½c. (+2½c.) red	4·50	1·10
318	-	15c. (+5c.) blue	6·75	9·00

DESIGNS—VERT: 2c. Bali Temple. HORIZ: 12½c. Minangkabau Compound; 15c. Buddhist Temple, Borobudur.

1930. No. 275 surch 12½.

319		12½c. on 20c. blue	1·20	35

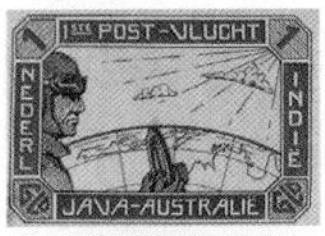

40 M. P. Pattist in Flight

1931. Air. 1st Java–Australia Mail.

320	40	1g. brown and blue	23·00	23·00

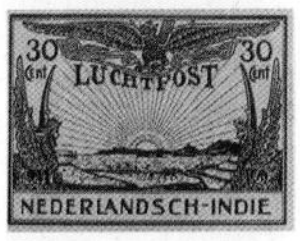

41

1931. Air.

321	41	30c. red	4·75	60
322	41	4½g. blue	13·00	4·75
323	41	7½g. green	17·00	6·50

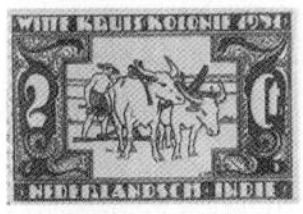

42 Ploughing

1931. Lepers' Colony.

324	42	2c. (+1c.) brown	4·00	3·00
325	-	5c. (+2½c.) green	5·75	5·75
326	-	12½c. (+2½c.) red	4·75	1·20
327	-	15c. (+5c.) blue	11·50	11·50

DESIGNS: 5c. Fishing; 12½c. Native actors; 15c. Native musicians.

1932. Air. Surch 50 on Fokker F.VIIa/3m airplane.

328	36	50c. on 1g.50 orange	4·75	85

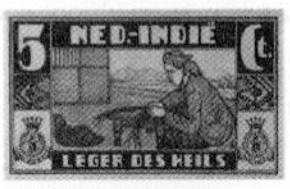

44 Plaiting Rattan

1932. Salvation Army. Centres in brown.

329	-	2c. (+1c.) purple	85	85
330	44	5c. (+2½c.) green	4·75	3·50
331	-	12½c. (+2½c.) red	1·50	60
332	-	15c. (+5c.) blue	6·50	5·50

DESIGNS: 2c. Weaving; 12½c. Textile worker; 15c. Metal worker.

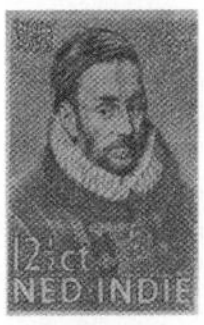

45 William of Orange

1933. 400th Birth Anniv of William I of Orange.

333	45	12½c. red	2·30	60

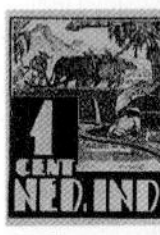

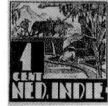

46 Rice Cultivation

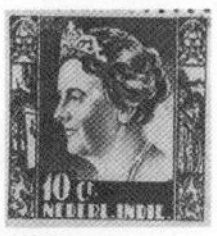

47 Queen Wilhelmina

1933

335	46	1c. violet	35	35
397	46	2c. purple	60	60
337	46	2½c. bistre	35	35
338	46	3c. green	35	35
339	46	3½c. grey	35	35
340	46	4c. green	1·40	35
401	46	5c. blue	60	60

342	**46**	7½c. violet	1·40	35
343	**46**	10c. red	2·75	35
403	**47**	10c. red	30	60
334	**47**	12½c. brown	11·50	60
345	**47**	12½c. red	85	35
404	**47**	15c. blue	30	60
405	**47**	20c. purple	60	60
348	**47**	25c. green	3·25	35
349	**47**	30c. blue	5·25	35
350	**47**	32½c. bistre	11·50	11·50
408	**47**	35c. violet	8·25	2·30
352	**47**	40c. green	4·00	35
353	**47**	42½c. yellow	4·00	1·70
354	**47**	50c. blue	8·75	60
355	**47**	60c. blue	8·75	1·20
356	**47**	80c. red	11·50	1·70
357	**47**	1g. violet	11·50	60
358	**47**	1g.75 green	29·00	19·00
414	**47**	2g. green	38·00	20·00
359	**47**	2g.50 purple	29·00	3·00
415	**47**	5g. bistre	35·00	20·00

The 50c. to 5g. are larger, 30×30 mm.

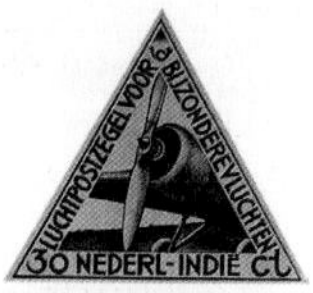

48 Pander S.4 Postjager

1933. Air. Special Flights.

360	**48**	30c. blue	2·30	2·30

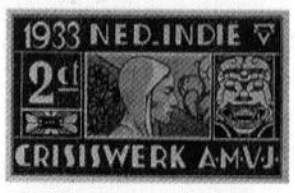

49 Woman and Lotus Blossom

1933. Y.M.C.A. Charity.

361	**49**	2c. (+1c.) brown & purple	1·20	60
362	-	5c. (+2½c.) brown and green	3·50	3·00
363	-	12½c. (+2½c.) brown & orge	3·50	35
364	-	15c. (+5c.) brown and blue	4·75	3·75

DESIGNS: 5c. Symbolizing the sea of life; 12½c. Y.M.C.A. emblem; 15c. Unemployed man.

1934. Surch.

365	**36**	2c. on 10c. purple	60	60
366	**36**	2c. on 20c. brown	60	60
367	**41**	2c. on 30c. red	60	1·20
368	**36**	42½c. on 75c. green	7·00	60
369	**36**	42½c. on 1g.50 orange	7·00	60

1934. Anti-tuberculosis Fund. As T 77 of Netherlands.

370	12½c. (+2½c.) brown	2·50	85

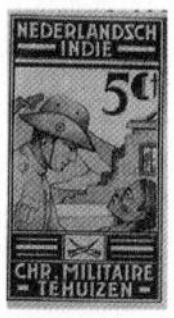

53 Cavalryman and Wounded Soldier

1935. Christian Military Home.

371	-	2c. (+1c.) brown and purple	3·00	2·30
372	**53**	5c. (+2½c.) brown and green	5·25	5·25
373	-	12½c. (+2½c.) brown & orge	5·25	60
374	-	15c. (+5c.) brown and blue	7·50	7·50

DESIGNS: 2c. Engineer chopping wood; 12½c. Artilleryman and volcano victim; 15c. Infantry bugler.

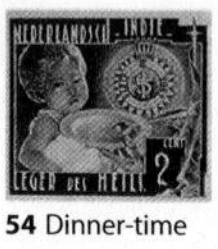

54 Dinner-time

1936. Salvation Army.

375	**54**	2c. (+1c.) purple	1·90	1·20
376	**54**	5c. (+2½c.) blue	2·20	1·70
377	**54**	7½c. (+2½c.) violet	2·20	2·30
378	**54**	12½c. (+2½c.) orange	2·20	60
379	**54**	15c. (+5c.) blue	4·75	3·50

Nos. 376/9 are larger, 30×27 mm.

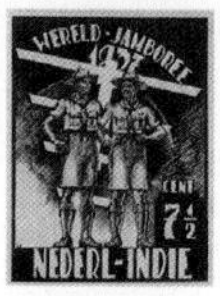

55 Boy Scouts

1937. Scouts' Jamboree.

380	**55**	7½c. (+2½c.) green	1·50	1·40
381	**55**	12½c. (+2½c.) red	1·50	1·20

1937. Nos. 222 and 277 surch in figures.

382	10c. on 30c. slate	4·00	60
383	10c. on 32½c. violet and orange	4·00	60

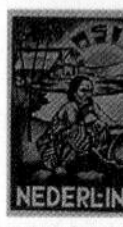

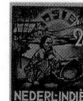

59 Sifting Rice

1937. Relief Fund. Inscr "A.S.I.B.".

385	**59**	2c. (+1c.) sepia and orange	2·00	1·20
386	-	3½c. (+1½c.) grey	2·00	1·40
387	-	7½c. (+2½c.) green & orange	2·30	1·70
388	-	10c. (+2½c.) red and orange	2·30	45
389	-	20c. (+5c.) blue	2·00	2·00

DESIGNS: 3½c. Mother and children; 7½c. Ox-team ploughing rice-field; 10c. Ox-team and cart; 20c. Man and woman.

1938. 40th Anniv of Coronation. As T 87 of Netherlands.

390	2c. violet	25	25
391	10c. red	35	35
392	15c. blue	1·60	1·70
393	20c. red	80	60

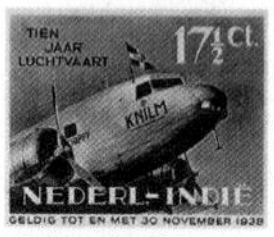

62 Douglas DC-2 Airliner

1938. Air Service Fund. 10th Anniv of Royal Netherlands Indies Air Lines.

394	**62**	17½c. (+5c.) brown	1·40	1·40
395	-	20c. (+5c.) slate	1·40	1·20

DESIGN: 20c. As Type **62**, but reverse side of airliner.

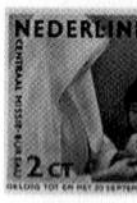

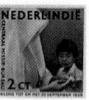

63 Nurse and Child

1938. Child Welfare. Inscr "CENTRAAL MISSIE-BUREAU".

416	**63**	2c. (+1c.) violet	1·20	80
417	-	3½c. (+1½c.) green	1·70	1·70
418	-	7½c. (+2½c.) red	1·50	1·20
419	-	10c. (+2½c.) red	1·50	60
420	-	20c. (+5c.) blue	1·70	1·50

DESIGNS—(23×23 mm): Nurse with child suffering from injuries to eye (3½c.), arm (7½c.), head (20c.) and nurse bathing a baby (10c.).

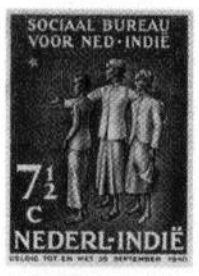

63a Group of Natives

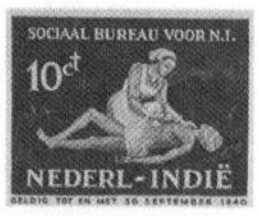

64 European Nurse and Patient

1939. Netherlands Indies Social Bureau and Protestant Church Funds.

421		2c. (+1c.) violet	45	45
422		3½c. (+1½c.) green	60	45
423	**63a**	7½c. (+2½c.) brown	45	45
424	-	10c. (+2½c.) red	2·50	1·40
425	**64**	10c. (+2½c.) red	2·30	1·40
426	-	20c. (+5c.) blue	1·00	80

DESIGNS—VERT: 2c. as Type **63a** but group in European clothes. HORIZ: 3½c., 10c. (No. 424) as Type **64**, but Native nurse and patient.

1940. Red Cross Fund. No. 345 surch 10+5 ct and cross.

428	**47**	10c.+5c. on 12½c. red	5·25	80

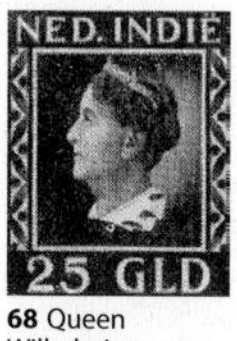

68 Queen Wilhelmina

1941. As T 94 of Netherlands but inscr "NED. INDIE" and T 68.

429	-	10c. red	1·20	60
430	-	15c. blue	4·75	4·75
431	-	17½c. orange	2·30	2·30
432	-	20c. mauve	50·00	70·00
433	-	25c. green	65·00	85·00
434	-	30c. brown	8·25	3·50
435	-	35c. purple	£225	£600
436	-	40c. green	23·00	17·00
437	-	50c. red	7·00	2·30
438	-	60c. blue	5·75	2·30
439	-	80c. red	5·75	2·30
440	-	1g. violet	5·75	1·20
441	-	2g. green	23·00	3·50
442	-	5g. bistre	£475	£1500
443	-	10g. green	60·00	35·00
444	**68**	25g. orange	£375	£225

Nos 429/36 measure 18×23 mm, Nos. 431/43 20½×26 mm.

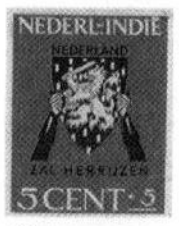

69 Netherlands Coat of Arms

1941. Prince Bernhard Fund for Dutch Forces.

453	**69**	5c.+5c. blue and orange	1·70	60
454	**69**	10c.+10c. blue and red	1·70	60
455	**69**	1g.+1g. blue and grey	23·00	23·00

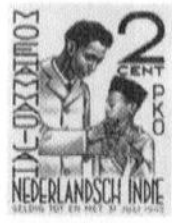

70 Doctor and Child

1941. Indigent Mohammedans' Relief Fund.

456	**70**	2c. (+1c.) green	1·60	1·60
457	-	3½c. (+1½c.) brown	7·75	7·75
458	-	7½c. (+2½c.) violet	6·50	6·50
459	-	10c. (+2½c.) red	2·50	60
460	-	15c. (+5c.) blue	19·00	19·00

DESIGNS: 3½c. Native eating rice; 7½c. Nurse and patient; 10c. Nurse and children; 15c. Basket-weaver.

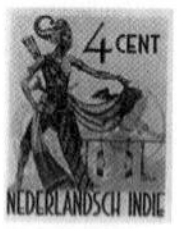

71 Wayangwong Dancer

1941

461		2c. red	60	35
462		2½c. purple	80	1·20
463		3c. green	80	1·20
464	**71**	4c. green	70	1·20
465	-	5c. blue	35	35
466	-	7½c. violet	80	45

DESIGNS (dancers): 2c. Menari; 2½c. Nias; 3c. Legon; 5c. Padjoge; 7½c. Dyak.

See also Nos. 514/16.

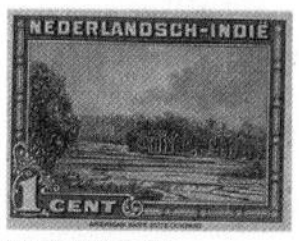

72 Paddyfield

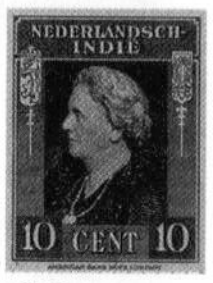

73 Queen Wilhelmina

1945

467	**72**	1c. green	80	35
468	-	2c. mauve	80	45
469	-	2½c. purple	80	35
470	-	5c. blue	55	35
471	-	7½c. olive	1·10	35
472	**73**	10c. brown	55	35
473	**73**	15c. blue	55	35
474	**73**	17½c. red	55	35
475	**73**	20c. purple	55	35
476	**73**	30c. grey	55	35
477	-	60c. grey	1·10	35
478	-	1g. green	1·70	35
479	-	2½g. orange	5·00	1·00

DESIGNS: As Type **72**: 2c. Lake in W. Java; 2½c. Medical School, Batavia; 5c. Seashore; 7½c. Douglas DC-2 airplane over Bromo Volcano. (30×30 mm): 60c. to 2½g. Portrait as Type **73** but different frame.

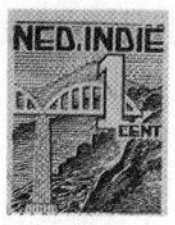

76 Railway Viaduct near Soekaboemi

1946

484	**76**	1c. green	45	35
485	-	2c. brown	45	34
486	-	2½c. red	45	35
487	-	5c. blue	45	35
488	-	7½c. blue	45	35

DESIGNS: 2c. Power station; 3c. Minangkabau house; 5c. Tondano scene (Celebes); 7½c. Buddhist Stupas, Java.

1947. Surch in figures.

502		3c. on 2½c. red (No. 486)	45	35
503		3c. on 7½c. blue (No. 488)	45	35
504	**76**	4c. on 1c. green	45	35
505	-	45c. on 60c. blue (No. 355)	2·00	1·30

No. 505 has three bars.

1947. Optd 1947.

506	**47**	12½c. red	55	35
507	**47**	25c. green	55	35
508	-	40c. green (No. 436)	1·10	35·00
509	**47**	50c. blue	1·10	45
510	**47**	80c. red	1·70	1·70
511	-	2g. green (No. 441)	5·50	2·00
512	-	5g. brown (No. 442)	15·00	13·50

1948. Relief for Victims of the Terror. Surch PELITA 15+10 Ct. and lamp.

513	**47**	15c.+10c. on 10c. red	45	45

1948. Dancers. As T 71.

514	3c. red (Menari)	55	35
515	4c. green (Legon)	55	35
516	7½c. brown (Dyak)	1·10	90

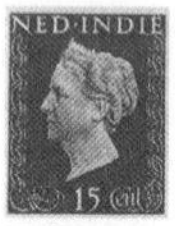

81 Queen Wilhelmina

1948

517	**81**	15c. orange	1·10	2·75
518	**81**	20c. blue	55	55
519	**81**	25c. green	55	55
520	**81**	40c. green	55	55
521	**81**	45c. mauve	80	1·10
522	**81**	50c. lake	65	55
523	**81**	80c. red	80	80
524	**81**	1g. violet	55	55
525	**81**	10g. green	45·00	22·00
526	**81**	25g. orange	85·00	85·00

Nos. 524-526 are larger, 21×26 mm.

1948. Queen Wilhelmina's Golden Jubilee. As T 81 but inscr "1898 1948".

528	15c. orange	55	55
529	20c. blue	55	40

1948. As T 126 of Netherlands.

530	15c. red	65	55
531	20c. blue	65	55

MARINE INSURANCE STAMPS

1921. As Type M 22 of the Netherlands, but inscribed "NED. INDIE".

M257	15c. green	14·00	55·00
M258	60c. red	14·00	85·00
M259	75c. brown	14·00	£110
M260	1g.50 blue	42·00	£325
M261	2g.25 brown	50·00	£275
M262	4½g. black	90·00	£750
M263	7½g. red	£110	£850

OFFICIAL STAMPS

1911. Stamps of 1892 optd D in white on a black circle.

O178	**6**	10c. brown	3·25	2·20
O179	**6**	12½c. grey	5·50	11·00
O180	**6**	15c. bistre	5·50	5·50
O181	**6**	20c. blue	5·50	3·25
O182	**6**	25c. mauve	19·00	14·00
O183	**6**	50c. red	5·50	2·75
O184	**6**	2g.50 blue and brown	85·00	85·00

1911. Stamps of 1902 (except No. O185) optd DIENST.

O186	½c. lilac	55	1·10
O187	1c. olive	55	55
O188	2c. brown	55	55
O185	2½c. yellow (No. 91)	1·30	2·75
O189	2½c. green	2·75	2·75
O190	3c. orange	90	90
O191	4c. blue	55	55
O192	5c. red	1·70	1·30

O193	7½c. grey	4·00	4·00
O194	10c. slate	55	55
O195	12½c. blue	4·00	4·00
O196	15c. brown	1·50	1·30
O197	15c. brown (No. 140)	55·00	
O198	17½c. bistre	5·50	4·00
O199	20c. olive	1·30	90
O200	22½c. olive and brown	5·50	5·50
O201	25c. mauve	3·25	2·75
O202	30c. brown	1·70	1·10
O203	50c. red	22·00	14·00
O204	1g. lilac	5·50	2·75
O205	2½g. grey	47·00	49·00

POSTAGE DUE STAMPS

1874. As Postage Due stamps of Netherlands. Colours changed.

D56	**D8**	5c. yellow	£425	£400
D57	**D8**	10c. green on yellow	£170	£140
D59	**D8**	15c. orange on yellow	28·00	28·00
D60	**D8**	20c. green on blue	55·00	28·00

1882. As Type D 10 of Netherlands.

D63b	2½c. black and red	1·10	1·70
D64b	5c. black and red	1·10	1·70
D65b	10c. black and red	5·50	5·50
D70c	15c. black and red	5·50	4·50
D71c	20c. black and red	£140	1·10
D76b	30c. black and red	5·00	6·25
D72	40c. black and red	3·25	4·50
D73b	50c. black and pink	1·70	2·20
D67a	75c. black and red	1·70	2·20

1892. As Type D 9 of Netherlands.

D102	2½c. black and pink	1·70	45
D103	5c. black and pink	5·50	35
D104	10c. black and pink	2·20	55
D105	15c. black and pink	22·00	4·00
D106b	20c. black and pink	5·50	35
D107	30c. black and pink	33·00	14·00
D108	40c. black and pink	31·00	4·50
D109	50c. black and pink	14·00	2·20
D110	75c. black and pink	42·00	7·25

1913. As Type D 9 of Netherlands.

D226	1c. orange	35	2·75
D489	1c. violet	1·10	1·70
D227	2½c. orange	35	35
D527	2½c. brown	1·70	2·75
D228	3½c. orange	35	4·00
D491	3½c. blue	1·10	1·70
D229	5c. orange	35	2·20
D230	7½c. orange	35	35
D493	7½c. green	1·10	1·70
D231	10c. orange	35	35
D494	10c. mauve	1·10	1·70
D232	12½c. orange	4·00	55
D448	15c. orange	3·00	2·30
D234	20c. orange	35	35
D495	20c. blue	1·10	1·70
D235	25c. orange	35	35
D496	25c. yellow	1·10	1·70
D236	30c. orange	35	35
D497	30c. brown	1·70	2·20
D237	37½c. orange	25·00	28·00
D238	40c. orange	35	35
D498	40c. green	1·70	2·20
D239	50c. orange	2·75	35
D499	50c. yellow	2·20	2·20
D240	75c. orange	4·00	35
D500	75c. blue	2·20	2·20
D501	100c. green	2·20	2·20
D241	1g. orange	7·25	11·00
D452	1g. blue	2·30	2·30

1937. Surch 20.

D384	**D5**	20c. on 37½c. red	1·20	60

1946. Optd TE BETALEN PORT or surch also.

D480	2½c. on 10c. red (No. 429)	1·70	1·70
D481	10c. red (No. 429)	2·75	2·75
D482	20c. mauve (No. 432)	8·25	8·25
D483	40c. green (No. 436)	65·00	65·00

For later issues see **INDONESIA**.

Pt. 4

NETHERLANDS NEW GUINEA

The Western half of the island of New Guinea was governed by the Netherlands until 1962, when control was transferred to the U.N. (see West New Guinea). The territory later became part of Indonesia as West Irian (q.v.).

100 cents = 1 gulden.

1950. As numeral and portrait types of Netherlands but inscr "NIEUW GUINEA".

1	**118**	1c. grey	45	35
2	**118**	2c. orange	45	35
3	**118**	2½c. olive	70	35
4	**118**	3c. mauve	3·00	2·30
5	**118**	4c. green	3·00	1·90
6	**118**	5c. blue	5·00	20
7	**118**	7½c. brown	80	35
8	**118**	10c. violet	1·50	35
9	**118**	12½c. red	2·75	2·40
10	**129**	15c. brown	4·00	1·20
11	**129**	20c. blue	1·70	35
12	**129**	25c. red	1·70	35
13	**129**	30c. blue	18·00	60
14	**129**	40c. green	3·00	35
15	**129**	45c. brown	8·75	1·20
16	**129**	50c. orange	2·30	35
17	**129**	55c. grey	17·00	80
18	**129**	80c. purple	19·00	3·25
19	**130**	1g. red	20·00	4·75
20	**130**	2g. brown	17·00	2·10
21	**130**	5g. green	23·00	2·00

1953. Netherlands Flood Relief Fund. Nos. 6, 10 and 12 surch hulp nederland 1953 and premium.

22	**118**	5c.+5c. blue	17·00	17·00
23	**129**	15c.+10c. brown	17·00	17·00
24	**129**	25c.+10c. red	17·00	17·00

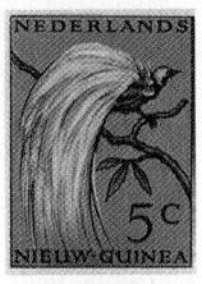

5 Lesser Bird of Paradise

1954

25	**5**	1c. yellow and red	35	35
26	**5**	5c. yellow and brown	60	35
27	-	10c. brown and blue	60	35
28	-	15c. brown and yellow	60	35
29	-	20c. brown and green	1·70	95

DESIGN: 10, 15, 20c. Greater bird of paradise.

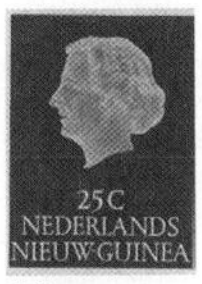

6 Queen Juliana

1954

30	**6**	25c. red	60	35
31	**6**	30c. blue	80	45
32	**6**	40c. orange	3·75	3·50
33	**6**	45c. green	1·70	2·10
34	**6**	55c. turquoise	1·20	35
35	**6**	80c. grey	2·30	60
36	**6**	85c. brown	3·00	80
37	**6**	1g. purple	7·75	3·50

1955. Red Cross. Nos. 26/8 surch with cross and premium.

38	**5**	5c.+5c. yellow and sepia	2·50	2·50
39	-	10c.+10c. brown and blue	2·50	2·50
40	-	15c.+10c. brown and lemon	2·50	2·50

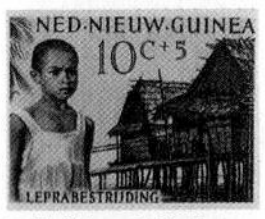

8 Child and Native Hut

1956. Anti-leprosy Fund.

41		5c.+5c. green	1·70	1·70
42	**8**	10c.+5c. purple	1·70	1·70
43	-	25c.+10c. blue	1·70	1·70
44	**8**	30c.+10c. buff	1·70	1·70

DESIGN: 5c., 25c. Palm-trees and native hut.

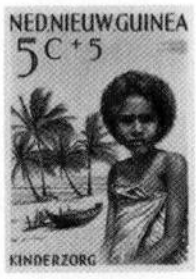

10 Papuan Girl and Beach Scene

1957. Child Welfare Fund.

51	**10**	5c.+5c. lake	1·70	1·70
52	-	10c.+5c. green	1·70	1·70
53	**10**	25c.+10c. brown	1·70	1·70
54	-	30c.+10c. blue	1·70	1·70

DESIGN: 10c., 30c. Papuan child and native hut.

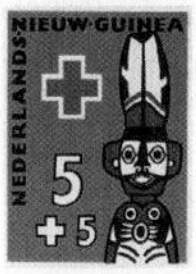

11 Red Cross and Idol

1958. Red Cross Fund.

55	**11**	5c.+5c. multicoloured	1·70	1·70
56	-	10c.+5c. multicoloured	1·70	1·70
57	**11**	25c.+10c. multicoloured	1·70	1·70
58	-	30c.+10c. multicoloured	1·70	1·70

DESIGN: 10c., 30c. Red Cross and Asman-Papuan bowl in form of human figure.

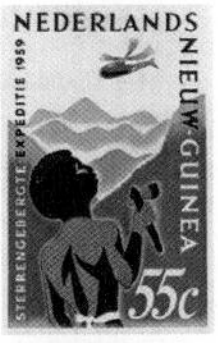

12 Papuan and Helicopter

1959. Stars Mountains Expedition, 1959.

59	**12**	55c. brown and blue	2·10	1·40

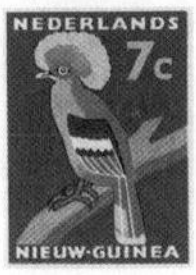

13 Blue-crowned Pigeon

1959

60	**13**	7c. purple, blue and brown	80	50
61	**13**	12c. purple, blue and green	80	50
62	**13**	17c. purple and blue	80	40

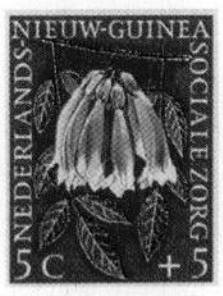

14 "Tecomanthe dendrophila"

1959. Social Welfare. Inscr "SOCIALE ZORG".

63	**14**	5c.+5c. red and green	1·20	1·20
64	-	10c.+5c. purple, yellow and olive	1·20	1·20
65	-	25c.+10c. yellow, green and red	1·20	1·20
66	-	30c.+10c. green and violet	1·20	1·20

DESIGNS: 10c. "Dendrobium attenuatum Lindley"; 25c. "Rhododendron zoelleri Warburg"; 30c. "Boea cf. urvillei".

1960. World Refugee Year. As T 180 of Netherlands.

67	25c. blue	95	95
68	30c. ochre	95	95

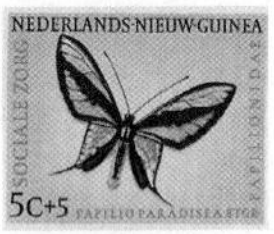

16 Paradise Birdwing

1960. Social Welfare Funds. Butterflies.

69	**16**	5c.+5c. multicoloured	1·70	90
70	-	10c.+5c. bl, blk & salmon	1·70	1·70
71	-	25c.+10c. red, sepia & yell	1·70	1·70
72	-	30c.+10c. multicoloured	1·70	1·70

BUTTERFLIES: 10c. Large green-banded blue; 25c. Red lacewing; 30c. Catops owl butterfly.

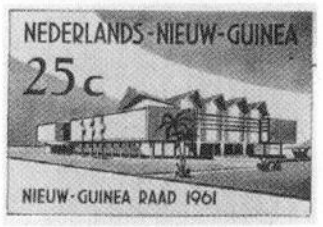

17 Council Building, Hollandia

1961. Opening of Netherlands New Guinea Council.

73	**17**	25c. turquoise	45	60
74	**17**	30c. red	45	60

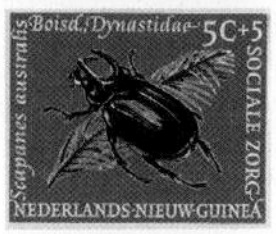

18 "Scapanes australis"

1961. Social Welfare Funds. Beetles.

75	**18**	5c.+5c. multicoloured	1·20	1·20
76	-	10c.+5c. multicoloured	1·20	1·20
77	-	25c.+10c. multicoloured	1·20	1·20
78	-	30c.+10c. multicoloured	1·20	1·20

BEETLES: 10c. Brenthid weevil; 25c. "Neolamprima adolphinae" (stag beetle); 30c. "Aspidomorpha aurata" (leaf beetle).

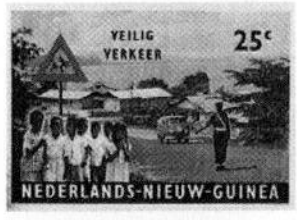

19 Children's Road Crossing

1962. Road Safety Campaign. Triangle in red.

79	**19**	25c. blue	60	60
80	-	30c. green (Adults at road crossing)	60	60

1962. Silver Wedding of Queen Juliana and Prince Bernhard. As T 187 of Netherlands.

81	55c. brown	60	70

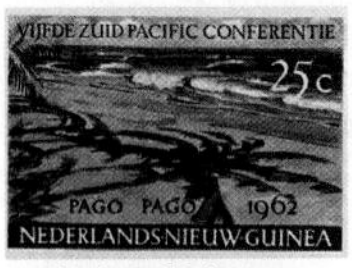

21 Shadow of Palm on Beach

1962. 5th South Pacific Conference, Pago Pago. Multicoloured.

82	25c. Type **21**	45	60
83	30c. Palms on beach	45	60

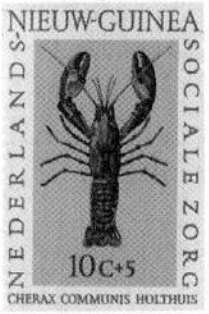

22 Lobster

1962. Social Welfare Funds. Shellfish. Multicoloured.

84	5c.+5c. Crab (horiz)	45	45
85	10c.+5c. Type **22**	45	45
86	25c.+10c. Spiny lobster	45	45
87	30c.+10c. Shrimp (horiz)	45	45

POSTAGE DUE STAMPS

1957. As Type D 121 of Netherlands but inscr "NEDERLANDS NIEUW GUINEA".

D45	1c. red	70	70
D46	5c. red	2·10	2·10
D47	10c. red	4·25	4·25
D48	25c. red	5·00	5·00
D49	40c. red	5·00	5·00
D50	1g. blue	7·50	7·50

For later issues see **WEST NEW GUINEA** and **WEST IRIAN**.

Pt. 1

NEVIS

One of the Leeward Islands, Br. W. Indies. Used stamps of St. Kitts-Nevis from 1903 until June 1980 when Nevis, although remaining part of St. Kitts-Nevis, had a separate postal administration.

1861. 12 pence = 1 shilling; 20 shillings = 1 pound.
1980. 100 cents = 1 dollar.

(The design on the stamps refers to a medicinal spring on the Island).

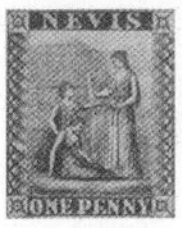

1

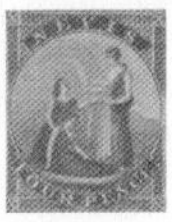
2

1862. Various frames.

15	**1**	1d. red	28·00	21·00
6	**2**	4d. red	£150	70·00
12	**2**	4d. orange	£140	23·00
7	-	6d. lilac	£150	60·00
20	-	1s. green	90·00	£110

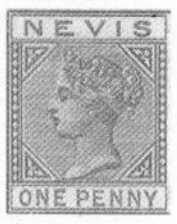

5

1879

25	**5**	½d. green	11·00	22·00
23	**5**	1d. mauve	80·00	50·00
27a	**5**	1d. red	17·00	17·00
28	**5**	2½d. brown	£120	50·00
29	**5**	2½d. blue	20·00	24·00
30	**5**	4d. blue	£350	50·00
31	**5**	4d. grey	22·00	8·00
32	**5**	6d. green	£450	£350
33	**5**	6d. brown	24·00	65·00
34	**5**	1s. violet	£110	£200

1883. Half of No. 23 surch NEVIS. ½d.

35	½d. on half 1d. mauve	£900	55·00

1980. Nos. 394/406 of St. Christopher, Nevis and Anguilla with "St. Christopher" and "Anguilla" obliterated.

37	5c. Radio and T.V. station	10	10
38	10c. Technical college	10	10
39	12c. T.V. assembly plant	10	30
40	15c. Sugar cane harvesting	10	10
41	25c. Crafthouse (craft centre)	10	10
42	30c. "Europa" (liner)	20	15
43	40c. Lobster and sea crab	20	40
44	45c. Royal St. Kitts Hotel and golf course	80	70
45	50c. Pinney's Beach, Nevis	20	30
46	55c. New runway at Golden Rock	40	15
47	$1 Picking cotton	15	30
48	$5 Brewery	30	75
49	$10 Pineapples and peanuts	40	1·00

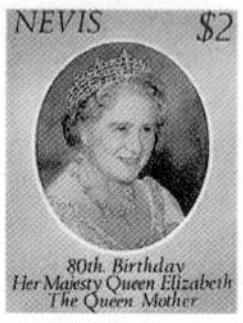

7a Queen Elizabeth the Queen Mother

1980. 80th Birthday of Queen Elizabeth the Queen Mother.

50	**7a**	$2 multicoloured	20	30

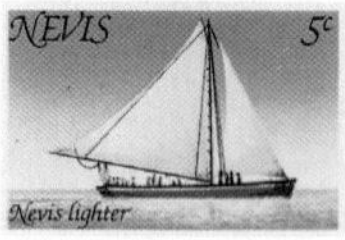

8 Nevis Lighter

1980. Boats. Multicoloured.

51	5c. Type **8**	10	10
52	30c. Local fishing boat	15	10
53	55c. "Caona" (catamaran)	15	10
54	$3 "Polynesia" (cruise schooner) (39×53 mm)	40	40

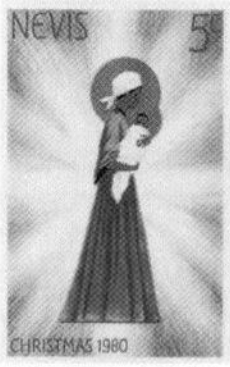

9 Virgin and Child

1980. Christmas. Multicoloured.

55	5c. Type **9**	10	10
56	30c. Angel	10	10
57	$2.50 The Wise Men	20	30

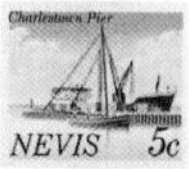

10 Charlestown Pier

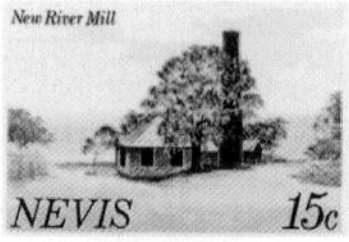

11 New River Mill

1981. Multicoloured.

58A	5c. Type **10**	10	10
59A	10c. Court House and Library	10	10
60A	15c. Type **11**	10	10
61A	20c. Nelson Museum	10	10
62A	25c. St. James' Parish Church	15	15
63A	30c. Nevis Lane	15	15
64A	40c. Zetland Plantation	20	20
65A	45c. Nisbet Plantation	20	25
66A	50c. Pinney's Beach	25	25
67A	55c. Eva Wilkin's Studio	25	30
68A	$1 Nevis at dawn	30	45
69A	$2.50 Ruins of Fort Charles	35	80
70A	$5 Old Bath House	40	1·00
71A	$10 Beach at Nisbet's	50	1·50

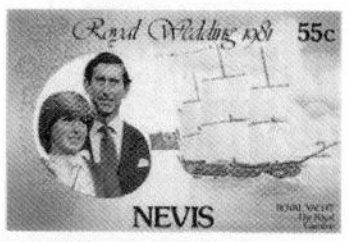

11a "Royal Caroline"

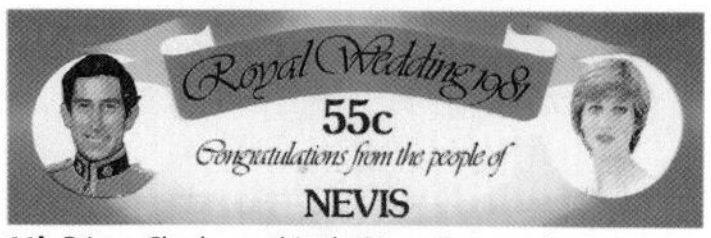

11b Prince Charles and Lady Diana Spencer (image scaled to 59% of original size)

1981. Royal Wedding. Royal Yachts. Multicoloured.

72	55c. Type **11a**	15	15
73	55c. Type **11b**	40	40
74	$2 "Royal Sovereign"	30	30
75	$2 As No. 73	80	1·25
76	$5 "Britannia"	45	80
77	$5 As No. 73	1·00	2·00
MS78	120×109 mm. $4.50 As No. 73	1·10	1·25

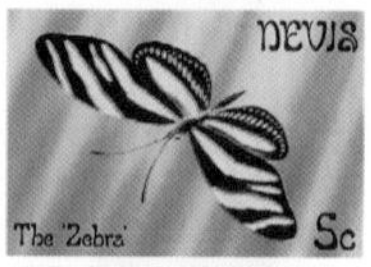

12 "Heliconius charithonia"

1982. Butterflies (1st series). Multicoloured.

81	5c. Type **12**	10	10
82	30c. "Siproeta stelenes"	20	10
83	55c. "Marpesia petreus"	25	15
84	$2 "Phoebis agarithe"	60	80

See also Nos. 105/8.

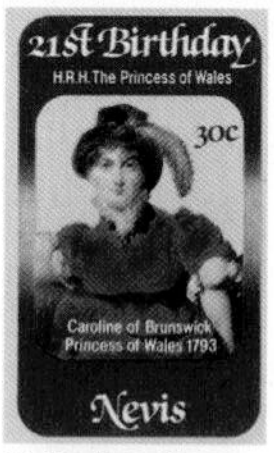

13 Caroline of Brunswick, Princess of Wales, 1793

1982. 21st Birthday of Princess of Wales. Mult.

85	30c. Type **13**	10	10
86	55c. Coat of arms of Caroline of Brunswick	15	15
87	$5 Diana, Princess of Wales	60	1·00

1982. Birth of Prince William of Wales. Nos. 85/7 optd ROYAL BABY.

88	30c. As Type **13**	10	10
89	55c. Coat of arms of Caroline of Brunswick	15	15
90	$5 Diana, Princess of Wales	60	1·00

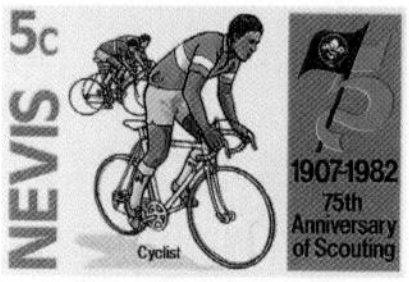

14 Cyclist

1982. 75th Anniv of Boy Scout Movement. Multicoloured.

91	5c. Type **14**	20	10
92	30c. Athlete	25	10
93	$2.50 Camp cook	50	65

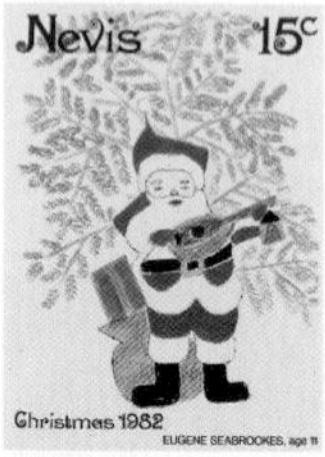

15 Santa Claus

1982. Christmas. Children's Paintings. Mult.

94	15c. Type **15**	10	10
95	30c. Carollers	10	10
96	$1.50 Decorated house and local band (horiz)	15	25
97	$2.50 Adoration of the Shepherds (horiz)	25	40

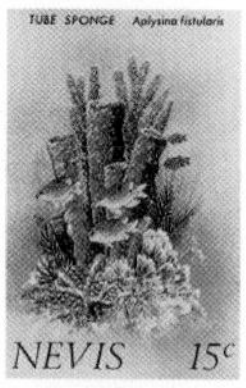

16 Tube Sponge

1983. Corals (1st series). Multicoloured.

98	15c. Type **16**	10	10
99	30c. Stinging coral	15	10
100	55c. Flower coral	15	10
101	$3 Sea rod and red fire sponge	50	90
MS102	82×115 mm. Nos. 98/101	1·60	3·00

See also Nos. 423/6.

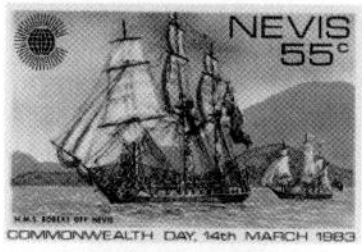

17 H.M.S. "Boreas" off Nevis

1983. Commonwealth Day. Multicoloured.

103	55c. Type **17**	15	10
104	$2 Capt. Horatio Nelson and H.M.S. "Boreas" at anchor	45	60

1983. Butterflies (2nd series). As T 12. Mult.

105	30c. "Pyrgus oileus"	25	10
106	55c. "Junonia evarete" (vert)	25	10
107	$1.10 "Urbanus proteus" (vert)	40	40
108	$2 "Hypolimnas misippus"	50	75

1983. Nos. 58 and 60/71 optd INDEPENDENCE 1983.

109B	5c. Type **10**	10	10
110B	15c. Type **11**	10	10
111B	20c. Nelson Museum	10	10
112B	25c. St. James' Parish Church	10	15
113B	30c. Nevis Lane	15	15
114B	40c. Zetland Plantation	15	20
115B	45c. Nisbet Plantation	15	25
116B	50c. Pinney's Beach	15	25
117B	55c. Eva Wilkin's Studio	15	30
118B	$1 Nevis at dawn	15	20
119B	$2.50 Ruins of Fort Charles	15	25
120B	$5 Old Bath House	15	25
121B	$10 Beach at Nisbet's	15	30

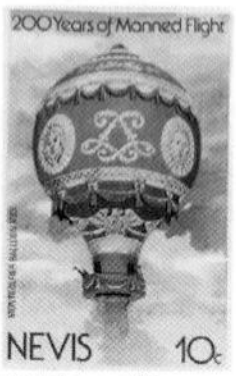

19 Montgolfier Balloon, 1783

1983. Bicentenary of Manned Flight. Mult.

122	10c. Type **19**	10	10
123	45c. Sikorsky S-38 flying boat (horiz)	25	10
124	50c. Beech 50 Twin Bonanza (horiz)	25	10
125	$2.50 Hawker Siddeley Sea Harrier (horiz)	55	1·25
MS126	118×145 mm. Nos. 122/5	75	1·25

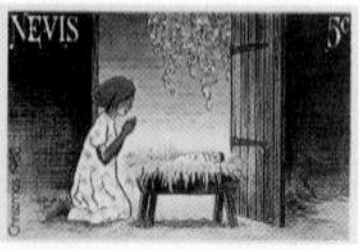

20 Mary praying over Holy Child

1983. Christmas. Multicoloured.

127	5c. Type **20**	10	10
128	30c. Shepherds with flock	10	10
129	55c. Three Angels	10	10
130	$3 Boy with two girls	30	60
MS131	135×149 mm. Nos. 127/30	85	2·00

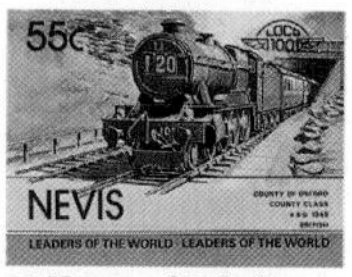

21 "County of Oxford" (1945)

1983. Leaders of the World. Railway Locomotives (1st series). The first in each pair shows technical drawings and the second the locomotive at work.

132	**21**	55c. multicoloured	10	20
133	-	55c. multicoloured	10	20
134	-	$1 red, blue and black	10	20
135	-	$1 multicoloured	10	20
136	-	$1 purple, blue and black	10	20
137	-	$1 multicoloured	10	20
138	-	$1 red, black and yellow	10	20
139	-	$1 multicoloured	10	20
140	-	$1 multicoloured	10	20
141	-	$1 multicoloured	10	20
142	-	$1 yellow, black and blue	10	20
143	-	$1 multicoloured	10	20
144	-	$1 yellow, black and purple	10	20
145	-	$1 multicoloured	10	20
146	-	$1 multicoloured	10	20
147	-	$1 multicoloured	10	20

DESIGNS: Nos. 132/3, "County of Oxford", Great Britain (1945); 134/5, "Evening Star", Great Britain (1960); 136/7, Stanier Class 5 No. 44806, Great Britain (1934); 138/9, "Pendennis Castle", Great Britain (1924); 140/1, "Winston Churchill", Great Britain (1946); 142/3, "Mallard", Great Britain (1938) (inscr "1935" in error); 144/5, "Britannia", Great Britain (1951); 146/7, "King George V", Great Britain.

See also Nos. 219/26, 277/84, 297/308, 352/9 and 427/42.

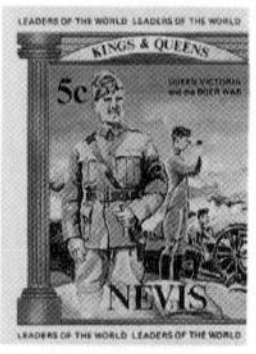

22 Boer War

1984. Leaders of the World. British Monarchs (1st series). Multicoloured.

148	5c. Type **22**	10	10
149	5c. Queen Victoria	10	10
150	50c. Queen Victoria at Osborne House	10	30
151	50c. Osborne House	10	30
152	60c. Battle of Dettingen	10	30
153	60c. George II	10	30
154	75c. George II at the Bank of England	10	30
155	75c. Bank of England	10	30
156	$1 Coat of Arms of George II	10	30
157	$1 George II (different)	10	30
158	$3 Coat of Arms of Queen Victoria	20	50
159	$3 Queen Victoria (different)	20	50

See also Nos. 231/6.

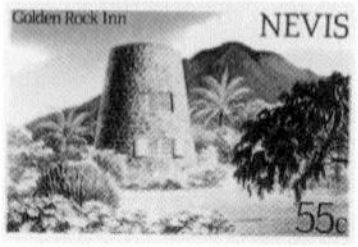

23 Golden Rock Inn

1984. Tourism (1st series). Multicoloured.

160	55c. Type **23**	25	20
161	55c. Rest Haven Inn	25	20
162	55c. Cliffdwellers Hotel	25	20
163	55c. Pinney's Beach Hotel	25	20

See also Nos. 245/8.

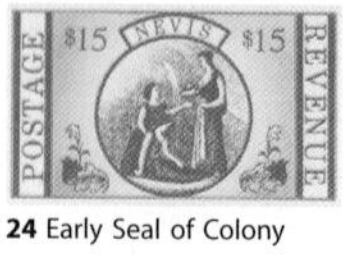

24 Early Seal of Colony

1984

164	**24**	$15 red	1·10	4·00

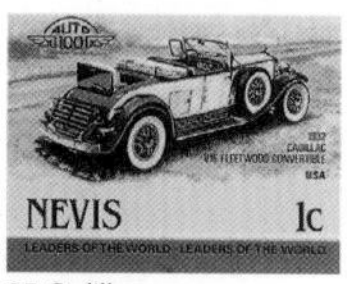

25 Cadillac

1984. Leaders of the World Automobiles (1st series). As T 25. The first design in each pair shows technical drawings and the second paintings.

165	1c. yellow, black and mauve	10	10
166	1c. multicoloured	10	10
167	5c. blue, mauve and black	10	10
168	5c. multicoloured	10	10
169	15c. multicoloured	10	15
170	15c. multicoloured	10	15
171	35c. mauve, yellow and black	10	25
172	35c. multicoloured	10	25
173	45c. blue, mauve and black	10	25

174	45c. multicoloured	10	25
175	55c. multicoloured	10	25
176	55c. multicoloured	10	25
177	$2.50 mauve, black and yellow	20	40
178	$2.50 multicoloured	20	40
179	$3 blue, yellow and black	20	40
180	$3 multicoloured	20	40

DESIGNS: No. 165/6, Cadillac "V16 Fleetwood Convertible" (1932); 167/8, Packard "Twin Six Touring Car" (1916); 169/70, Daimler "2 Cylinder" (1886); 171/2, Porsche "911 S Targa" (1970); 173/4, Benz "Three Wheeler" (1885); 175/6, M.G. "TC" (1947); 177/8, Cobra "Roadster 289" (1966); 179/80, Aston Martin "DB6 Hardtop" (1966).

See also Nos. 203/10, 249/64, 326/37, 360/371 and 411/22.

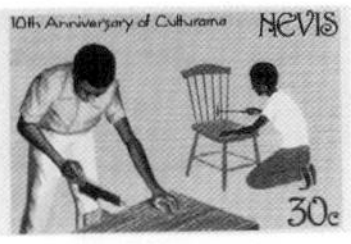

26 Carpentry

1984. 10th Anniv of Culturama Celebrations. Multicoloured.

181	30c. Type **26**	10	10
182	55c. Grass mat and basket making	10	10
183	$1 Pottery firing	15	25
184	$3 Culturama Queen and dancers	40	55

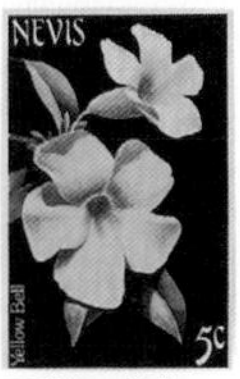

27 Yellow Bell

1984. Flowers. Multicoloured.

185A	5c. Type **27**	10	10
186A	10c. Plumbago	10	10
187A	15c. Flamboyant	10	10
188B	20c. Eyelash orchid	60	30
189A	30c. Bougainvillea	10	15
190B	40c. Hibiscus	30	30
191A	50c. Night-blooming cereus	15	20
192A	55c. Yellow mahoe	15	25
193A	60c. Spider-lily	15	25
194A	75c. Scarlet cordia	20	30
195A	$1 Shell-ginger	20	40
196A	$3 Blue petrea	30	1·10
197A	$5 Coral hibiscus	50	2·00
198A	$10 Passion flower	80	3·50

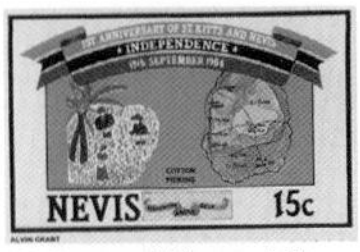

28 Cotton-picking and Map

1984. 1st Anniv of Independence of St. Kitts–Nevis. Multicoloured.

199	15c. Type **28**	10	10
200	55c. Alexander Hamilton's birthplace	10	10
201	$1.10 Local agricultural produce	20	40
202	$3 Nevis Peak and Pinney's Beach	50	1·00

1984. Leaders of the World. Automobiles (2nd series). As T 25. The first in each pair shows technical drawings and the second the paintings.

203	5c. black, blue and brown	10	10
204	5c. multicoloured	10	10
205	30c. black, turquoise and brown	15	15
206	30c. multicoloured	15	15
207	50c. black, drab and brown	15	15
208	50c. multicoloured	15	15
209	$3 black, brown and green	30	45
210	$3 multicoloured	30	45

DESIGNS: Nos. 203/4, Lagonda "Speed Model" touring car (1929); 205/6, Jaguar "E-Type" 4.2 litre (1967); 207/8, Volkswagen "Beetle" (1947); 209/10, Pierce Arrow "V12" (1932).

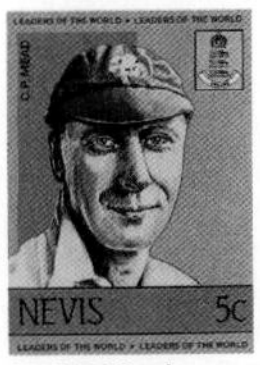

29 C. P. Mead

1984. Leaders of the World. Cricketers (1st series). As T 29. The first in each pair shows a head portrait and the second the cricketer in action. Multicoloured.

211	5c. Type **29**	10	10
212	5c. C. P. Mead	10	10
213	25c. J. B. Statham	20	30
214	25c. J. B. Statham	20	30
215	55c. Sir Learie Constantine	30	40
216	55c. Sir Learie Constantine	30	40
217	$2.50 Sir Leonard Hutton	50	1·25
218	$2.50 Sir Leonard Hutton	50	1·25

See also Nos. 237/4.

1984. Leaders of the World. Railway Locomotives (2nd series). As T 21. The first in each pair shows technical drawings and the second the locomotive at work.

219	5c. multicoloured	10	10
220	5c. multicoloured	10	10
221	10c. multicoloured	10	10
222	10c. multicoloured	10	10
223	60c. multicoloured	15	25
224	60c. multicoloured	15	25
225	$2.50 multicoloured	50	70
226	$2.50 multicoloured	50	70

DESIGNS: Nos. 219/20, Class EF81 electric locomotive, Japan (1968); 221/22, Class 5500 electric locomotive, France (1927); 223/4, Class 240P, France (1940); 225/6, "Hikari" express train, Japan (1964).

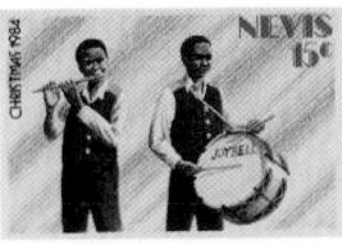

30 Fifer and Drummer from Honeybees Band

1984. Christmas. Local Music. Multicoloured.

227	15c. Type **30**	15	10
228	40c. Guitar and "barhow" players from Canary Birds Band	25	10
229	60c. Shell All Stars steel band	30	10
230	$3 Organ and choir, St. John's Church, Fig Tree	1·25	1·00

1984. Leaders of the World. British Monarchs (2nd series). As T 22. Multicoloured.

231	5c. King John and Magna Carta	10	10
232	5c. Barons and King John	10	10
233	55c. King John	10	15
234	55c. Newark Castle	10	15
235	$2 Coat of arms	25	40
236	$2 King John (different)	25	40

1984. Leaders of the World. Cricketers (2nd series). As T 29. The first in each pair listed shows a head portrait and the second the cricketer in action. Multicoloured.

237	5c. J. D. Love	10	10
238	5c. J. D. Love	10	10
239	15c. S. J. Dennis	10	15
240	15c. S. J. Dennis	10	15
241	55c. B. W. Luckhurst	15	20
242	55c. B. W. Luckhurst	15	20
243	$2.50 B. L. D'Oliveira	40	60
244	$2.50 B. L. D'Oliveira	40	60

1984. Tourism (2nd series). As T 23. Multicoloured.

245	$1.20 Croney's Old Manor Hotel	15	25
246	$1.20 Montpelier Plantation Inn	15	25
247	$1.20 Nisbet's Plantation Inn	15	25
248	$1.20 Zetland Plantation Inn	15	25

1985. Leaders of the World. Automobiles (3rd series). As T 25. The first in each pair shows technical drawings and the second the paintings.

249	1c. black, green and light green	10	10
250	1c. multicoloured	10	10
251	5c. black, blue and light blue	10	10
252	5c. multicoloured	10	10
253	10c. black, green and light green	10	10
254	10c. multicoloured	10	10
255	50c. black, green and brown	10	10
256	50c. multicoloured	10	10
257	60c. black, green and blue	10	10
258	60c. multicoloured	10	10
259	75c. black, red and orange	10	10
260	75c. multicoloured	10	10
261	$2.50 black, green and blue	20	30
262	$2.50 multicoloured	20	30
263	$3 black, green and light green	20	30
264	$3 multicoloured	20	30

DESIGNS: Nos. 249/50, Delahaye "Type 35 Cabriolet" (1935); 251/2, Ferrari "Testa Rossa" (1958); 253/4, Voisin "Aerodyne" (1934); 255/6, Buick "Riviera" (1963); 257/8, Cooper "Climax" (1960); 259/60, Ford "999" (1904); 261/2, MG "M-Type Midget" (1930); 263/4, Rolls- Royce "Corniche" (1971).

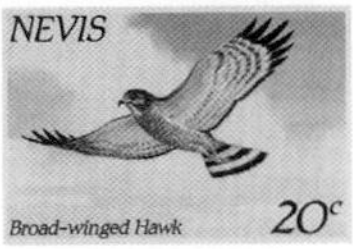

31 Broad-winged Hawk

1985. Local Hawks and Herons. Multicoloured.

265	20c. Type **31**	1·25	20
266	40c. Red-tailed hawk	1·40	30
267	60c. Little blue heron	1·40	40
268	$3 Great blue heron (white phase)	2·75	1·90

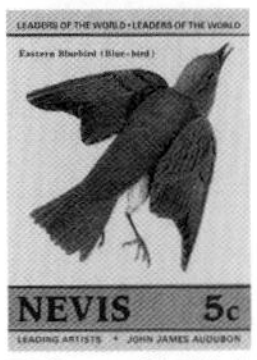

32 Eastern Bluebird

1985. Leaders of the World. Birth Bicentenary of John J. Audubon (ornithologist) (1st issue). Multicoloured.

269	5c. Type **32**	10	10
270	5c. Common cardinal	10	10
271	55c. Belted kingfisher	20	55
272	55c. Mangrove cuckoo	20	55
273	60c. Yellow warbler	20	55
274	60c. Cerulean warbler	20	55
275	$2 Burrowing owl	60	1·25
276	$2 Long-eared owl	60	1·25

See also Nos. 285/92.

1985. Leaders of the World. Railway Locomotives (3rd series). As T 21. The first in each pair showing technical drawings and the second the locomotive at work.

277	1c. multicoloured	10	10
278	1c. multicoloured	10	10
279	60c. multicoloured	20	20
280	60c. multicoloured	20	20
281	90c. multicoloured	25	25
282	90c. multicoloured	25	25
283	$2 multicoloured	40	60
284	$2 multicoloured	40	60

DESIGNS: Nos. 277/8, Class "Wee Bogie", Great Britain (1882); 279/80, "Comet", Great Britain (1851); 281/2, Class 8H No. 6173, Great Britain (1908); 283/4, Class A No. 23, Great Britain (1866).

1985. Leaders of the World. Birth Bicentenary of John J. Audubon (ornithologist) (2nd issue). As T 32. Multicoloured.

285	1c. Painted bunting	10	10
286	1c. Golden-crowned kinglet	10	10
287	40c. Common flicker	25	40
288	40c. Western tanager	25	40
289	60c. Varied thrush	25	45
290	60c. Evening grosbeak	25	45
291	$2.50 Blackburnian warbler	50	80
292	$2.50 Northern oriole	50	80

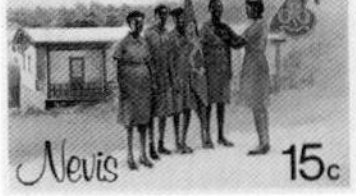

33 Guides and Guide Headquarters

1985. 75th Anniv of Girl Guide Movement. Multicoloured.

293	15c. Type **33**	10	10
294	60c. Girl Guide uniforms of 1910 and 1985 (vert)	15	25
295	$1 Lord and Lady Baden-Powell (vert)	20	40
296	$3 Princess Margaret in Guide uniform (vert)	50	1·25

1985. Leaders of the World. Railway Locomotives (4th series). As T 21. The first in each pair shows technical drawings and the second the locomotive at work.

297	5c. multicoloured	10	10
298	5c. multicoloured	10	10
299	30c. multicoloured	10	15
300	30c. multicoloured	10	15
301	60c. multicoloured	10	20
302	60c. multicoloured	10	20
303	75c. multicoloured	10	25
304	75c. multicoloured	10	25
305	$1 multicoloured	10	25
306	$1 multicoloured	10	25
307	$2.50 multicoloured	20	60
308	$2.50 multicoloured	20	60

DESIGNS: Nos. 297/8, "Snowdon Ranger" (1878); 299/300, Large Belpaire locomotive, Great Britain (1904); 301/2, Class "County" No. 3821, Great Britain (1904); 303/4, "L'Outrance", France (1877); 305/6, Class PB-15, Australia (1899); 307/8, Class 64, Germany (1928).

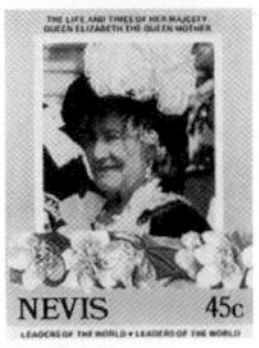

34 The Queen Mother at Garter Ceremony

1985. Leaders of the World. Life and Times of Queen Elizabeth the Queen Mother. Various vertical portraits.

309	34	45c. multicoloured	10	15
310	-	45c. multicoloured	10	15
311	-	75c. multicoloured	10	20
312	-	75c. multicoloured	10	20
313	-	$1.20 multicoloured	15	35
314	-	$1.20 multicoloured	15	35
315	-	$1.50 multicoloured	20	40
316	-	$1.50 multicoloured	20	40

MS317 85×114 mm. $2 multicoloured; $2 multicoloured 50 1·40

Each value was issued in pairs showing a floral pattern across the bottom of the portraits which stops short of the left-hand edge on the first stamp and of the right-hand edge on the second.

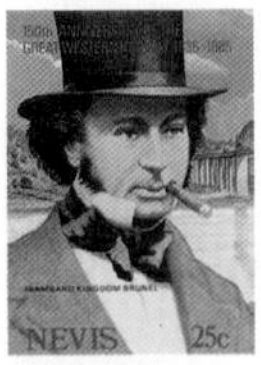

35 Isambard Kingdom Brunel

1985. 150th Anniv of Great Western Railway. Designs showing railway engineers and their achievements. Multicoloured.

318	25c. Type **35**	15	35
319	25c. Royal Albert Bridge, 1859	15	35
320	50c. William Dean	20	45
321	50c. Locomotive "Lord of the Isles", 1895	20	45
322	$1 Locomotive "Lode Star", 1907	25	65
323	$1 G. J. Churchward	25	65
324	$2.50 Locomotive "Pendennis Castle", 1924	35	80
325	$2.50 C. B. Collett	35	80

Nos. 318/19, 320/1, 322/3 and 324/5 were printed together se-tenant, each pair forming a composite design.

1985. Leaders of the World. Automobiles (4th series). As T 25. The first in each pair shows technical drawings and the second paintings.

326	10c. black, blue and red	10	10
327	10c. multicoloured	10	10
328	35c. black, turquoise and blue	10	25
329	35c. multicoloured	10	25
330	75c. black, green and brown	10	40
331	75c. multicoloured	10	40
332	$1.15 black, brown and green	15	45
333	$1.15 multicoloured	15	45
334	$1.50 black, blue and red	15	50
335	$1.50 multicoloured	15	50
336	$2 black, lilac and violet	20	60
337	$2 multicoloured	20	60

DESIGNS: Nos. 326/7, Sunbeam "Coupe de l'Auto" (1912); 328/9, Cisitalia "Pininfarina Coupe" (1948); 330/1, Porsche "928S" (1980); 332/3, MG "K3 Magnette" (1933); 334/5, Lincoln "Zephyr" (1937); 336/7, Pontiac 2 Door (1926).

1985. Royal Visit. Nos. 76/7, 83, 86, 92/3, 98/9 and 309/10 optd CARIBBEAN ROYAL VISIT 1985 or surch also.

338	16	15c. multicoloured	75	1·25
339	-	30c. multicoloured (No. 92)	1·75	1·75
340	-	30c. multicoloured (No. 99)	75	1·25
341	-	40c. on 55c. mult (No. 86)	1·75	2·00
342	34	45c. multicoloured	1·50	3·25
343	-	45c. multicoloured (No. 310)	1·50	3·25
344	-	55c. multicoloured (No. 83)	1·50	1·25
345	-	$1.50 on $5 multicoloured (No. 76)	2·25	3·00
346	-	$1.50 on $5 multicoloured (No. 77)	13·00	17·00
347	-	$2.50 mult (No. 93)	2·25	3·50

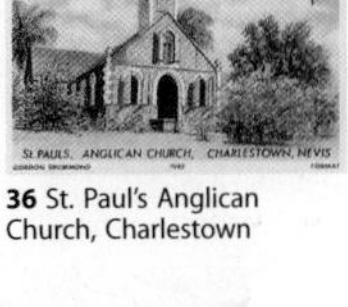

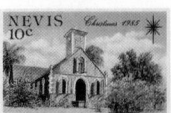

36 St. Paul's Anglican Church, Charlestown

1985. Christmas. Churches of Nevis (1st series). Multicoloured.

348	10c. Type **36**	15	10
349	40c. St. Theresa Catholic Church, Charlestown	35	30
350	60c. Methodist Church, Gingerland	40	50
351	$3 St. Thomas Anglican Church, Lowland	80	2·75

See also Nos. 462/5.

1986. Leaders of the World. Railway Locomotives (5th series). As T 21. The first in each pair shows technical drawings and the second the locomotive at work.

352	30c. multicoloured	15	25
353	30c. multicoloured	15	25
354	75c. multicoloured	25	50
355	75c. multicoloured	25	50
356	$1.50 multicoloured	40	70
357	$1.50 multicoloured	40	70
358	$2 multicoloured	50	80
359	$2 multicoloured	50	80

DESIGNS: Nos. 352/3, "Stourbridge Lion", U.S.A. (1829); 354/5, EP-2 Bi-Polar electric locomotive, U.S.A. (1919); 356/7, Gas turbine No. 59, U.S.A. (1953); 358/9 Class FL9 diesel locomotive No. 2039, U.S.A. (1955).

1986. Leaders of the World. Automobiles (5th series). As T 25. The first in each pair showing technical drawings and the second paintings.

360	10c. black, brown and green	10	10
361	10c. multicoloured	10	10
362	60c. black, orange and red	15	25
363	60c. multicoloured	15	25
364	75c. black, light brown and brown	15	25
365	75c. multicoloured	15	25
366	$1 black, light grey and grey	15	30
367	$1 multicoloured	15	30
368	$1.50 black, yellow and green	20	35
369	$1.50 multicoloured	20	35
370	$3 black, light blue and blue	30	65
371	$3 multicoloured	30	65

DESIGNS: Nos. 360/1, Adler "Trumpf" (1936); 362/3, Maserati "Tipo 250F" (1957); 364/5, Oldsmobile "Limited" (1910); 366/7, Jaguar "C-Type" (1951); 368/9, ERA "1.5L B Type" (1937); 370/1, Chevrolet "Corvette" (1953).

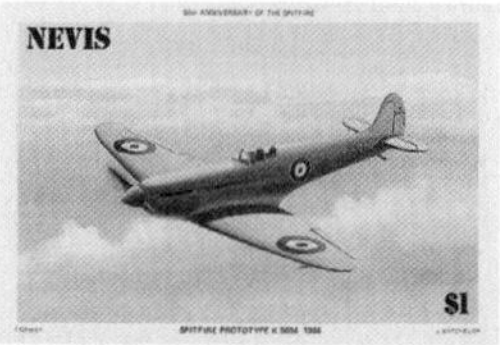

37 Supermarine Spitfire Prototype, 1936

1986. 50th Anniv of Spitfire (fighter aircraft). Multicoloured.

372	$1 Type **37**	20	50
373	$2.50 Supermarine Spitfire Mk 1A in Battle of Britain, 1940	30	75
374	$3 Supermarine Spitfire Mk XII over convoy, 1944	30	75
375	$4 Supermarine Spitfire Mk XXIV, 1948	30	1·25
MS376	114×86 mm. $6 Supermarine Seafire Mk III on escort carrier H.M.S. "Hunter"	1·10	3·75

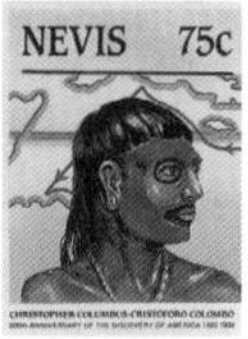

38 Head of Amerindian

1986. 500th Anniv (1992) of Discovery of America by Columbus (1st issue). Multicoloured.

377	85c. Type **38**	85	1·00
378	85c. Exchanging gifts for food from Amerindians	85	1·00
379	$1.75 Columbus's coat of arms	1·40	2·00
380	$1.75 Breadfruit plant	1·40	2·00
381	$2.50 Columbus's fleet	1·40	2·25
382	$2.50 Christopher Columbus	1·40	2·25
MS383	95×84 mm. $6 Christopher Columbus (different)	6·00	9·50

The two designs of each value were printed together, se-tenant, each pair forming a composite design showing charts of Columbus's route in the background.

See also Nos. 546/54, 592/600, 678/84 and 685/6.

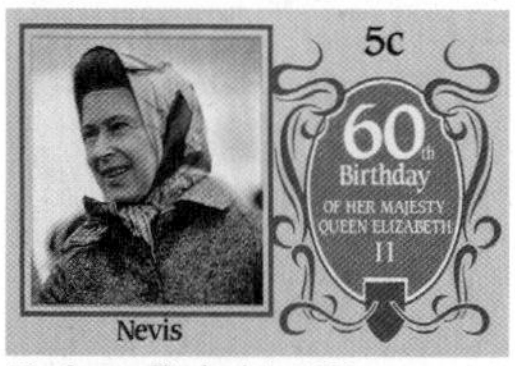

38a Queen Elizabeth in 1976

1986. 60th Birthday of Queen Elizabeth II. Multicoloured.

384	5c. Type **38a**	10	10
385	75c. Queen Elizabeth in 1953	15	25
386	$2 In Australia	20	60
387	$8 In Canberra, 1982 (vert)	75	2·00
MS388	85×115 mm. $10 Queen Elizabeth II	4·50	7·50

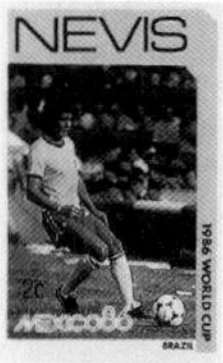

39 Brazilian Player

1986. World Cup Football Championship, Mexico. Multicoloured.

389	1c. Official World Cup mascot (horiz)	10	10
390	2c. Type **39**	10	10
391	5c. Danish player	10	10
392	10c. Brazilian player (different)	10	10
393	20c. Denmark v Spain	20	20
394	30c. Paraguay v Chile	30	30
395	60c. Italy v West Germany	40	55
396	75c. Danish team (56×36 mm)	40	65
397	$1 Paraguayan team (56×36 mm)	50	70
398	$1.75 Brazilian team (56×36 mm)	60	1·25
399	$3 Italy v England	75	1·90
400	$6 Italian team (56×36 mm)	1·10	3·00
MS401	Five sheets, each 85×115 mm. (a) $1.50 As No. 398. (b) $2 As No. 393. (c) $2 As No. 400. (d) $2.50 As No. 395. (e) $4 As No. 394 Set of 5 sheets	12·00	15·00

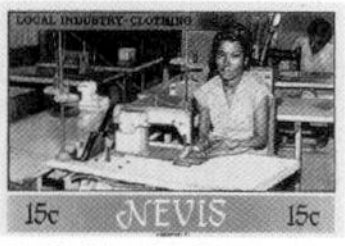

40 Clothing Machinist

1986. Local Industries. Multicoloured.

402	15c. Type **40**	20	15
403	40c. Carpentry/joinery workshop	45	30
404	$1.20 Agricultural produce market	1·25	1·50
405	$3 Fishing boats landing catch	2·50	3·25

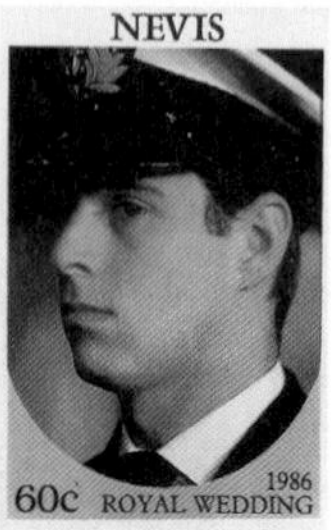

40a Prince Andrew in Midshipman's Uniform

1986. Royal Wedding. Multicoloured.

406	60c. Type **40a**	15	25
407	60c. Miss Sarah Ferguson	15	25
408	$2 Prince Andrew on safari in Africa (horiz)	40	60
409	$2 Prince Andrew at the races (horiz)	40	60
MS410	115×85 mm. $10 Duke and Duchess of York on Palace balcony after wedding (horiz)	2·50	5·00

See also Nos. 454/7.

1986. Automobiles (6th series). As T 25. The first in each pair showing technical drawings and the second paintings.

411	15c. multicoloured	10	10
412	15c. multicoloured	10	10
413	45c. black, light blue and blue	20	25
414	45c. multicoloured	20	25
415	60c. multicoloured	20	30
416	60c. multicoloured	20	30
417	$1 black, light green and green	25	40
418	$1 multicoloured	25	40
419	$1.75 black, lilac and deep lilac	30	50
420	$1.75 multicoloured	30	50
421	$3 multicoloured	50	90
422	$3 multicoloured	50	90

DESIGNS: Nos. 411/12, Riley "Brooklands Nine" (1930); 413/14, Alfa Romeo "GTA" (1966); 415/16, Pierce Arrow "Type 66" (1913); 417/18, Willys-Knight "66A" (1928); 419/20, Studebaker "Starliner" (1953); 421/2, Cunningham "V-8" (1919).

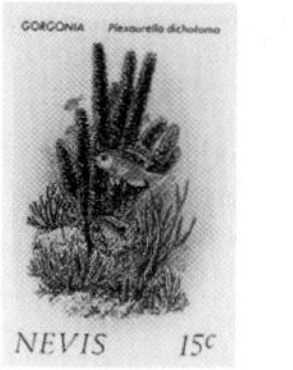

41 Gorgonia

1986. Corals (2nd series). Multicoloured.

423	15c. Type **41**	25	15
424	60c. Fire coral	55	55
425	$2 Elkhorn coral	90	2·00
426	$3 Vase sponge and feather star	1·10	2·50

1986. Railway Locomotives (6th series). As T 21. The first in each pair showing technical drawings and the second the locomotive at work.

427	15c. multicoloured	10	10
428	15c. multicoloured	10	10
429	45c. multicoloured	15	25
430	45c. multicoloured	15	25
431	60c. multicoloured	20	30
432	60c. multicoloured	20	30
433	75c. multicoloured	20	40
434	75c. multicoloured	20	40
435	$1 multicoloured	20	50
436	$1 multicoloured	20	50
437	$1.50 multicoloured	25	60
438	$1.50 multicoloured	25	60
439	$2 multicoloured	30	65
440	$2 multicoloured	30	65
441	$3 multicoloured	35	80
442	$3 multicoloured	35	80

DESIGNS: Nos. 427/8, Connor Single Class, Great Britain (1859); 429/30, Class P2 "Cock o' the North", Great Britain (1934); 431/2, Class 7000 electric locomotive, Japan (1926); 433/4, Class P3, Germany (1897); 435/6, "Dorchester", Canada (1836); 436/7, Class "Centennial" diesel locomotive, U.S.A. (1969); 439/40, "Lafayette", U.S.A. (1837); 441/2, Class C-16 No. 222, U.S.A. (1882).

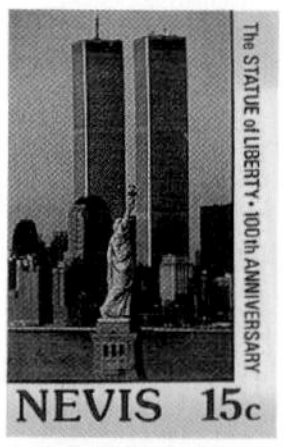

41a Statue of Liberty and World Trade Centre, Manhattan

1986. Centenary of Statue of Liberty. Multicoloured.

443	15c. Type **41a**	20	15
444	25c. Sailing ship passing statue	30	20
445	40c. Statue in scaffolding	30	25
446	60c. Statue (side view) and scaffolding	30	30
447	75c. Statue and regatta	40	40
448	$1 Tall Ships parade passing statue (horiz)	40	45
449	$1.50 Head and arm of statue above scaffolding	40	60
450	$2 Ships with souvenir flags (horiz)	55	80
451	$2.50 Statue and New York waterfront	60	90
452	$3 Restoring statue	80	1·25
MS453	Four sheets, each 85×115 mm. (a) $3.50 Statue at dusk. (b) $4 Head of Statue. (c) $4.50 Statue and lightning. (d) $5 Head and torch at sunset Set of 4 sheets	3·50	11·00

1986. Royal Wedding (2nd issue). Nos. 406/9 optd Congratulations to T.R.H. The Duke & Duchess of York.

454	60c. Prince Andrew in midshipman's uniform	15	40
455	60c. Miss Sarah Ferguson	15	40
456	$2 Prince Andrew on safari in Africa (horiz)	40	1·00
457	$2 Prince Andrew at the races (horiz)	40	1·00

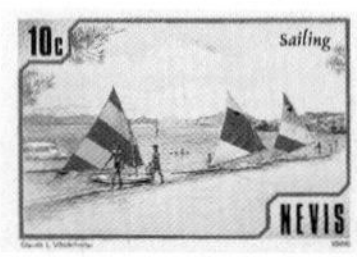

42 Dinghy sailing

1986. Sports. Multicoloured.

458	10c. Type **42**	20	10
459	25c. Netball	35	15
460	$2 Cricket	3·00	2·50
461	$3 Basketball	3·75	3·00

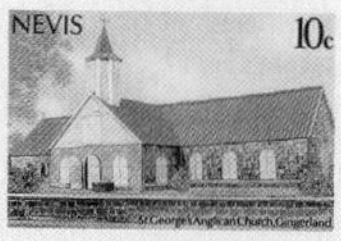

43 St. George's Anglican Church, Gingerland

1986. Christmas. Churches of Nevis (2nd series). Multicoloured.

462	10c. Type **43**	15	10
463	40c. Trinity Methodist Church, Fountain	30	25
464	$1 Charlestown Methodist Church	60	65
465	$5 Wesleyan Holiness Church, Brown Hill	2·75	4·00

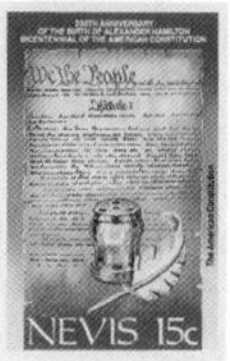

44 Constitution Document, Quill and Inkwell

1987. Bicentenary of U.S. Constitution and 230th Birth Anniv of Alexander Hamilton (U.S. statesman). Multicoloured.

466	15c. Type **44**	10	10
467	40c. Alexander Hamilton and Hamilton House	20	25
468	60c. Alexander Hamilton	25	35
469	$2 Washington and his Cabinet	90	1·40
MS470	70×82 mm. $5 Model ship "Hamilton" on float, 1788	6·50	7·50

1987. Victory of "Stars and Stripes" in America's Cup Yachting Championship. No. 54 optd America's Cup 1987 Winners 'Stars & Stripes'.

471	$3 Windjammer S.V. "Polynesia"	1·10	1·60

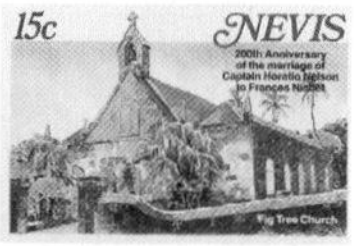

46 Fig Tree Church

1987. Bicentenary of Marriage of Horatio Nelson and Frances Nisbet. Multicoloured.

472	15c. Type **46**	20	10
473	60c. Frances Nisbet	50	30
474	$1 H.M.S. "Boreas" (frigate)	1·50	1·25
475	$3 Captain Horatio Nelson	3·00	3·75
MS476	102×82 mm. $3 As No. 473; $3 No. 475	5·00	6·50

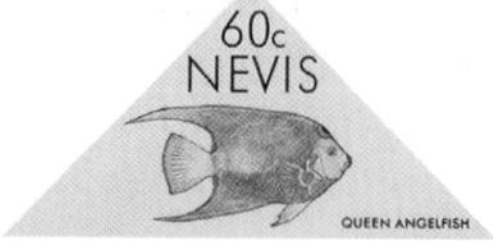

47 Queen Angelfish

1987. Coral Reef Fishes. Multicoloured.

477	60c. Type **47**	35	60
478	60c. Blue angelfish	35	60
479	$1 Stoplight parrotfish (male)	40	80
480	$1 Stoplight parrotfish (female)	40	80
481	$1.50 Red hind	45	90
482	$1.50 Rock hind	45	90
483	$2.50 Coney (bicoloured phase)	50	1·50
484	$2.50 Coney (red-brown phase)	50	1·50

Nos. 478, 480, 482 and 484 are inverted triangles.

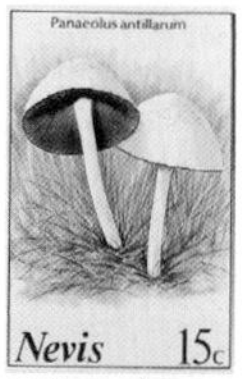

48 "Panaeolus antillarum"

1987. Fungi (1st series). Multicoloured.

485	15c. Type **48**	80	30
486	50c. "Pycnoporus sanguineus"	1·50	80
487	$2 "Gymnopilus chrysopellus"	2·75	3·25
488	$3 "Cantharellus cinnabarinus"	3·25	4·50

See also Nos. 646/53.

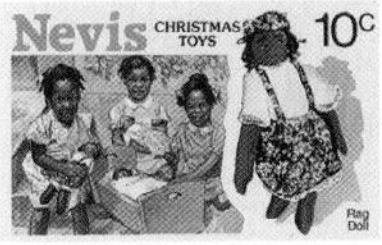

49 Rag Doll

1987. Christmas. Toys. Multicoloured.

489	10c. Type **49**	10	10
490	40c. Coconut boat	20	25
491	$1.20 Sandbox cart	55	60
492	$5 Two-wheeled cart	1·75	4·00

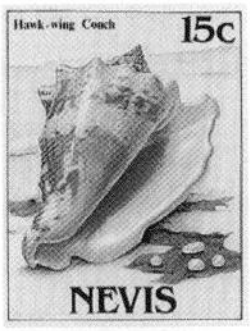

50 Hawk-wing Conch

1988. Sea Shells and Pearls. Multicoloured.

493	15c. Type **50**	20	15
494	40c. Rooster-tail conch	30	20
495	60c. Emperor helmet	50	40
496	$2 Queen or pink conch	1·60	2·00
497	$3 King helmet	1·75	2·25

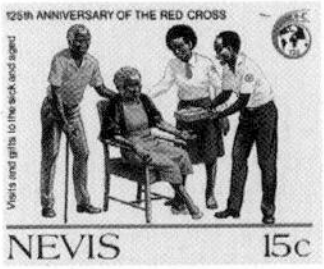

51 Visiting Pensioners at Christmas

1988. 125th Anniv of International Red Cross. Multicoloured.

498	15c. Type **51**	10	10
499	40c. Teaching children first aid	15	20
500	60c. Providing wheelchairs for the disabled	25	35
501	$5 Helping cyclone victim	2·10	3·50

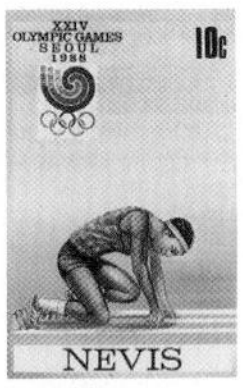

52 Athlete on Starting Blocks

1988. Olympic Games, Seoul. Multicoloured.

502	10c. Type **52**	10	35
503	$1.20 At start	50	85
504	$2 During race	85	1·25
505	$3 At finish	1·25	1·50
MS506	137×80 mm. As Nos. 502/5, but each size 24×36 mm	2·75	3·75

Nos. 502/5 were printed together, se-tenant, each strip forming a composite design showing an athlete from start to finish of race.

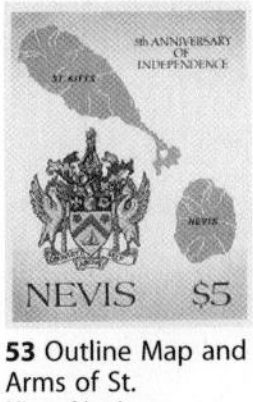

53 Outline Map and Arms of St. Kitts–Nevis

1988. 5th Anniv of Independence.

507	**53**	$5 multicoloured	2·10	3·00

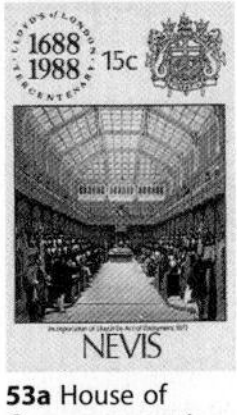

53a House of Commons passing Lloyd's Bill, 1871

1988. 300th Anniv of Lloyd's of London. Multicoloured.

508	15c. Type **53a**	25	10
509	60c. "Cunard Countess" (liner) (horiz)	1·60	65
510	$2.50 Space shuttle deploying satellite (horiz)	2·75	3·00
511	$3 "Viking Princess" (cargo liner) on fire, 1966	3·25	3·00

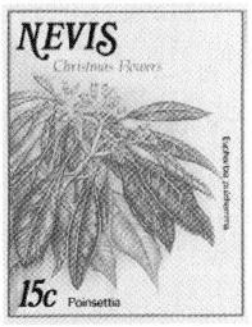

54 Poinsettia

1988. Christmas. Flowers. Multicoloured.

512	15c. Type **54**	10	10
513	40c. Tiger claws	15	20
514	60c. Sorrel flower	25	30
515	$1 Christmas candle	40	60
516	$5 Snow bush	1·60	3·75

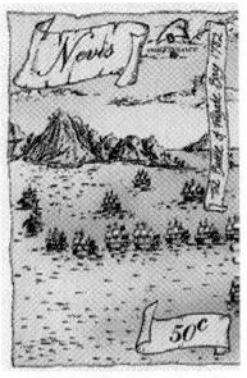

55 British Fleet off St. Kitts

1989. "Philexfrance 89" International Stamp Exhibition, Paris. Battle of Frigate Bay, 1782. Multicoloured.

517	50c. Type **55**	1·40	1·50
518	$1.20 Battle off Nevis	1·60	1·90
519	$2 British and French fleets exchanging broadsides	2·00	2·25
520	$3 French map of Nevis, 1764	2·50	2·75

Nos. 517/19 were printed together, se-tenant, forming a composite design.

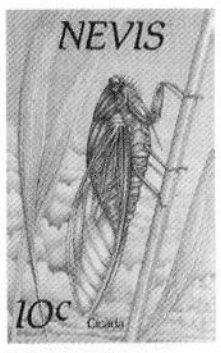

56 Cicada

1989. "Sounds of the Night". Multicoloured.

521	10c. Type **56**	20	15
522	40c. Grasshopper	40	35
523	60c. Cricket	55	50
524	$5 Tree frog	3·75	5·50
MS525	135×81 mm. Nos. 521/4	5·50	7·00

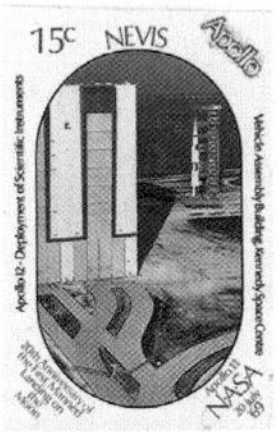

56a Vehicle Assembly Building, Kennedy Space Centre

1989. 20th Anniv of First Manned Landing on Moon. Multicoloured.

526	15c. Type **56a**	15	10
527	40c. Crew of "Apollo 12" (30×30 mm)	20	20
528	$2 "Apollo 12" emblem (30×30 mm)	1·00	1·75
529	$3 "Apollo 12" astronaut on Moon	1·40	2·00
MS530	100×83 mm. $6 Aldrin undertaking lunar seismic experiment	2·50	3·50

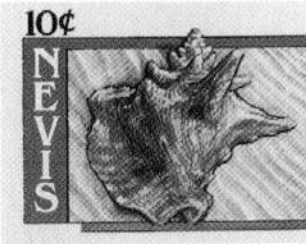

57 Queen or Pink Conch feeding

1990. Queen or Pink Conch. Multicoloured.

531	10c. Type **57**	60	30
532	40c. Queen or pink conch from front	90	40
533	60c. Side view of shell	1·25	90
534	$1 Black and flare	1·60	2·00
MS535	72×103 mm. $5 Underwater habitat	3·50	4·50

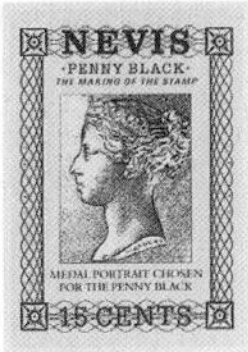

58 Wyon Medal Portrait

1990. 150th Anniv of the Penny Black.

536	**58**	15c. black and brown	15	10
537	-	40c. black and green	30	25
538	-	60c. black	45	55
539	-	$4 black and blue	2·50	3·25
MS540		114×84 mm. $5 black, red and brown	4·00	5·00

DESIGNS: 40c. Engine-turned background; 60c. Heath's engraving of portrait; $4 Essay with inscriptions; $5 Penny Black.

No. **MS**540 also commemorates "Stamp World London 90" International Stamp Exhibition.

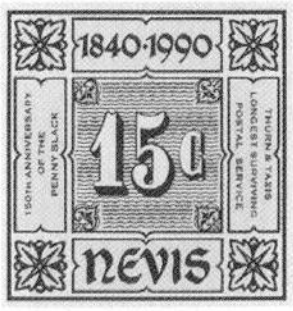

59

1990. 500th Anniv of Regular European Postal Services.

541	**59**	15c. brown	20	15
542	-	40c. green	35	25
543	-	60c. violet	55	65
544	-	$4 blue	2·75	3·75
MS545		110×82 mm. $5 red, brown and grey	4·00	5·00

Nos. 541/5 commemorate the Thurn and Taxis postal service and the designs are loosely based on those of the initial 1852–58 series.

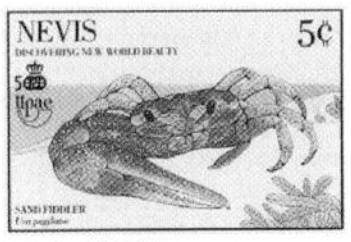

60 Sand Fiddler

1990. 500th Anniv (1992) of Discovery of America by Columbus (2nd issue). New World Natural History—Crabs. Multicoloured.

546	5c. Type **60**	10	10
547	15c. Great land crab	15	15
548	20c. Blue crab	15	15
549	40c. Stone crab	30	30
550	60c. Mountain crab	45	45
551	$2 Sargassum crab	1·40	1·75
552	$3 Yellow box crab	1·75	2·25
553	$4 Spiny spider crab	2·25	3·00
MS554	Two sheets, each 101×70 mm. (a) $5 Sally Lightfoot. (b) $5 Wharf crab Set of 2 sheets	9·00	10·00

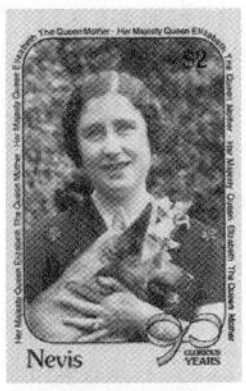

60a Duchess of York with Corgi

1990. 90th Birthday of Queen Elizabeth the Queen Mother.

555	**60a**	$2 black, mauve and buff	1·40	1·60
556	-	$2 black, mauve and buff	1·40	1·60
557	-	$2 black, mauve and buff	1·40	1·60
MS558		90×75 mm. $6 brown, mauve and black	3·50	4·25

DESIGNS: No. 556, Queen Elizabeth in Coronation robes, 1937; 557, Duchess of York in garden; **MS**558, Queen Elizabeth in Coronation robes, 1937 (different).

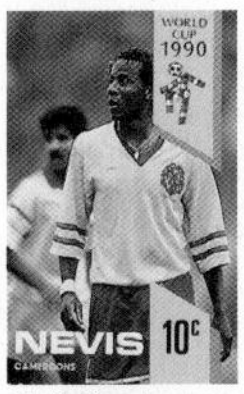

61 MaKanaky, Cameroons

1990. World Cup Football Championship, Italy. Star Players. Multicoloured.

559	10c. Type **61**	40	10
560	25c. Chovanec, Czechoslovakia	45	15
561	$2.50 Robson, England	2·75	3·25
562	$5 Voller, West Germany	3·75	5·50
MS563	Two sheets, each 90×75 mm. (a) $5 Maradona, Argentina. (b) $5 Gordillo, Spain Set of 2 sheets	6·75	8·00

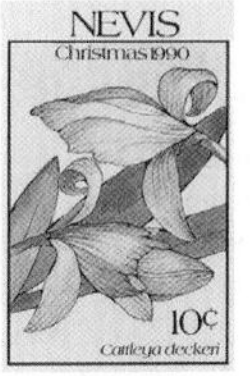

62 "Cattleya deckeri"

1990. Christmas. Native Orchids. Mult.

564	10c. Type **62**	55	20
565	15c. "Epidendrum ciliare"	55	20
566	20c. "Epidendrum fragrans"	65	20
567	40c. "Epidendrum ibaguense"	85	25
568	60c. "Epidendrum latifolium"	1·10	50
569	$1.20 "Maxillaria conferta"	1·40	1·75
570	$2 "Epidendrum strobiliferum"	1·75	2·75
571	$3 "Brassavola cucullata"	2·00	3·00
MS572	102×71 mm. $5 "Rodriguezia lanceolata"	7·00	8·00

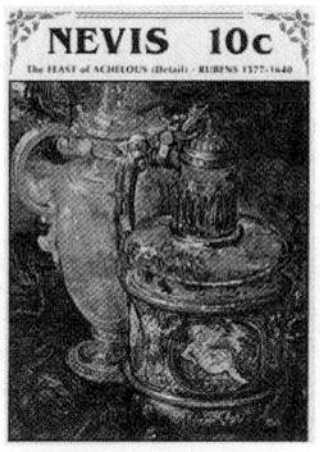

62a Two Jugs

1991. 350th Death Anniv of Rubens. Details from "The Feast of Achelous". Multicoloured.

573	10c. Type **62a**	55	15
574	40c. Woman at table	1·00	30
575	60c. Two servants with fruit	1·25	45
576	$4 Achelous	3·25	5·50
MS577	101×71 mm. $5 "The Feast of Achelous"	4·50	5·50

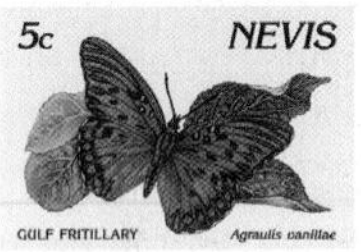

63 "Agraulis vanillae"

1991. Butterflies. Multicoloured.

578B	5c. Type **63**	40	60
579A	10c. "Historis odius"	40	50
580B	15c. "Marpesia corinna"	50	20
581B	20c. "Anartia amathea"	30	30
582B	25c. "Junonia evarete"	60	30
583B	40c. "Heliconius charithonia"	70	30
584B	50c. "Marpesia petreus"	70	35
585A	60c. "Dione juno"	75	50
586B	75c. "Heliconius doris"	80	60
586cB	80c. As 60c.	80	60
587A	$1 "Hypolimnas misippus"	90	80
588A	$3 "Danaus plexippus"	2·00	2·75
589A	$5 "Heliconius sara"	2·75	4·00
590A	$10 "Tithorea harmonia"	5·00	8·00
591A	$20 "Dryas julia"	9·50	13·00

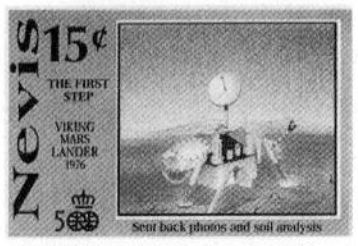

64 "Viking Mars Lander", 1976

1991. 500th Anniv of Discovery of America by Columbus (1992) (3rd issue). History of Exploration. Multicoloured.

592	15c. Type **64**	20	20
593	40c. "Apollo 11", 1969	30	25
594	60c. "Skylab", 1973	45	45
595	75c. "Salyut 6", 1977	55	55
596	$1 "Voyager 1", 1977	65	65
597	$2 "Venera 7", 1970	1·25	1·60
598	$4 "Gemini 4", 1965	2·50	3·25
599	$5 "Luna 3", 1959	2·75	3·25
MS600	Two sheets, each 105×76 mm. (a) $6 Bow of "Santa Maria" (vert). (b) $6 Christopher Columbus (vert) Set of 2 sheets	8·00	9·00

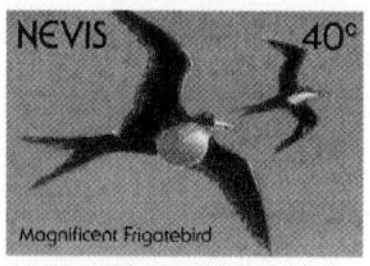

65 Magnificent Frigate Bird

1991. Island Birds. Multicoloured.

601	40c. Type **65**	85	65
602	40c. Roseate tern	85	65
603	40c. Red-tailed hawk	85	65
604	40c. Zenaida dove	85	65
605	40c. Bananaquit	85	65
606	40c. American kestrel	85	65
607	40c. Grey kingbird	85	65
608	40c. Prothonotary warbler	85	65
609	40c. Blue-hooded euphonia	85	65
610	40c. Antillean crested hummingbird	85	65
611	40c. White-tailed tropic bird	85	65
612	40c. Yellow-bellied sapsucker	85	65
613	40c. Green-throated carib	85	65
614	40c. Purple-throated carib	85	65
615	40c. Red-billed whistling duck ("Black-bellied tree-duck")	85	65
616	40c. Ringed kingfisher	85	65
617	40c. Burrowing owl	85	65
618	40c. Ruddy turnstone	85	65
619	40c. Great blue heron	85	65
620	40c. Yellow-crowned night-heron	85	65
MS621	76×59 mm. $6 Great egret	10·00	11·00

Nos. 601/20 were printed together, se-tenant, forming a composite design.

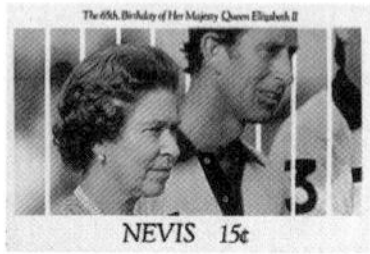

65a Queen Elizabeth at Polo Match with Prince Charles

1991. 65th Birthday of Queen Elizabeth II. Multicoloured.

622	15c. Type **65a**	40	20
623	40c. Queen and Prince Philip on Buckingham Palace balcony	50	35
624	$2 In carriage at Ascot, 1986	1·75	1·75
625	$4 Queen Elizabeth II at Windsor polo match, 1989	3·00	3·75
MS626	68×90 mm. $5 Queen Elizabeth and Prince Philip	4·25	5·00

1991. 10th Wedding Anniv of Prince and Princess of Wales. As T 65a. Multicoloured.

627	10c. Prince Charles and Princess Diana	85	20
628	50c. Prince of Wales and family	90	30
629	$1 Prince William and Prince Harry	1·40	1·00
630	$5 Prince and Princess of Wales	4·50	4·00
MS631	68×90 mm. $5 Prince and Princess of Wales in Hungary, and young princes at Christmas	6·00	6·00

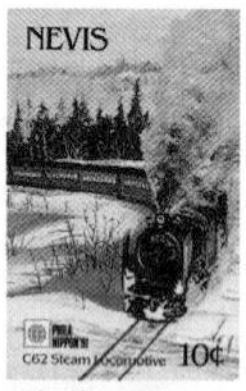

65b Class C62 Steam Locomotive

1991. "Phila Nippon '91" International Stamp Exhibition, Tokyo. Japanese Railway Locomotives. Multicoloured.

632	10c. Type **65b**	90	30
633	15c. Class C56 steam locomotive (horiz)	1·00	30
634	40c. Class C55 streamlined steam locomotive (horiz)	1·50	50
635	60c. Class 1400 steam locomotive (horiz)	1·60	80
636	$1 Class 485 diesel rail car	1·90	1·00
637	$2 Class C61 steam locomotive	3·00	2·50
638	$3 Class 485 diesel train (horiz)	3·25	3·00
639	$4 Class 7000 electric train (horiz)	3·50	3·75
MS640	Two sheets, each 108×72 mm. (a) $5 Class D51 steam locomotive (horiz). (b) $5 "Hikari" express train (horiz) Set of 2 sheets	8·50	9·00

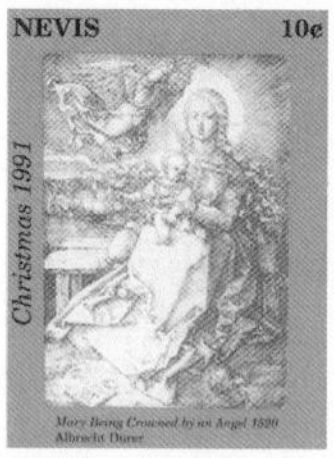

65c "Mary being Crownd by an Angel"

1991. Christmas. Drawings by Albrecht Durer.

641	**65c**	10c. black and green	15	10
642	-	40c. black and orange	30	25
643	-	60c. black and blue	35	30
644	-	$3 black and mauve	1·40	2·75
MS645		Two sheets, each 96×124 mm. (a) $6 black. (b) $6 black Set of 2 sheets	5·50	6·25

DESIGNS: 40c. "Mary with the Pear"; 60c. "Mary in a Halo"; $3 "Mary with Crown of Stars and Sceptre"; $6 (**MS**645a) "The Holy Family" (detail); $6 (**MS**645b) "Mary at the Yard Gate" (detail).

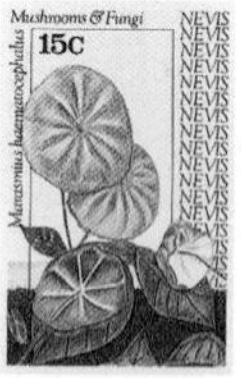

66 "Marasmius haemtocephalus"

1991. Fungi (2nd series). Multicoloured.

646	15c. Type **66**	30	20
647	40c. "Psilocybe cubensis"	40	30
648	60c. "Hygrocybe acutoconica"	50	40
649	75c. "Hygrocybe occidentalis"	60	60
650	$1 "Boletellus cubensis"	70	70
651	$2 "Gymnopilus chrysopellus"	1·25	1·50
652	$4 "Cantharellus cinnabarinus"	2·25	2·75
653	$5 "Chlorophyllum molybdites"	2·25	2·75
MS654	Two sheets, each 70×58 mm. (a) $6 "Psilocybe cubensis", "Hygrocybe acutoconica" and "Boletellus cubensis" (horiz). (b) $6 "Hygrocybe occidentalis", "Marasmius haematocephalus" and "Gymnopilus chrysopellus" (horiz) Set of 2 sheets	9·00	9·50

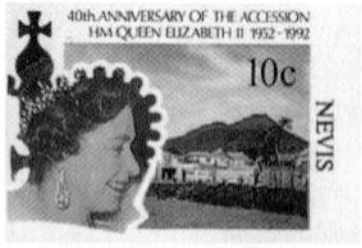

66a Charlestown from the Sea

1992. 40th Anniv of Queen Elizabeth II's Accession. Multicoloured.

655	10c. Type **66a**	50	10
656	40c. Charlestown square	70	25
657	$1 Mountain scenery	1·25	60
658	$5 Early cottage	3·25	3·75
MS659	Two sheets, each 74×97 mm. (a) $6 Queen or pink conch on beach. (b) $6 Nevis sunset Set of 2 sheets	8·50	9·00

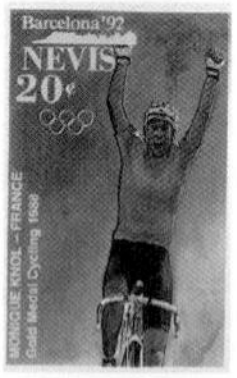

67 Monique Knol (cycling), Netherlands

1992. Olympic Games, Barcelona. Gold Medal Winners of 1988. Multicoloured.

660	20c. Type **67**	1·25	50
661	25c. Roger Kingdom (hurdles), U.S.A.	60	40
662	50c. Yugoslavia (men's waterpolo)	1·00	50
663	80c. Anja Fichtel (foil), West Germany	1·10	70
664	$1 Said Aouita (mid-distance running), Morocco	1·25	80
665	$1.50 Yuri Sedykh (hammer throw), U.S.S.R.	1·40	1·60
666	$3 Shushunova (women's gymnastics), U.S.S.R.	2·50	3·00
667	$5 Valimir Artemov (men's gymnastics), U.S.S.R.	2·75	3·50
MS668	Two sheets, each 103×73 mm. (a) $6 Niam Suleymanoglu (weight-lifting), Turkey. (b) $6 Florence Griffith-Joyner (women's 100 metres), U.S.A. Set of 2 sheets	5·50	7·00

No. 660 is inscribed "France" in error.

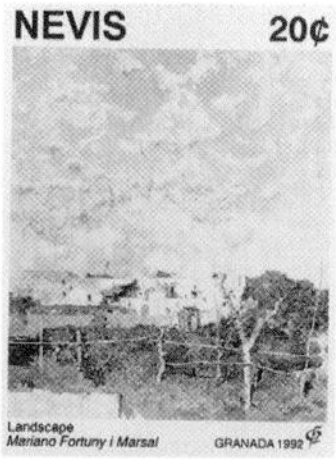

68 "Landscape" (Mariano Fortuny i Marsal)

1992. "Granada '92" International Stamp Exhibition, Spain. Spanish Paintings. Multicoloured.

669	20c. Type **68**	40	30
670	25c. "Dona Juana la Loca" (Francisco Pradilla Ortiz) (horiz)	40	30
671	50c. "Idyll" (Fortuny i Marsal)	60	50
672	80c. "Old Man Naked in the Sun" (Fortuny i Marsal)	80	70
673	$1 "The Painter's Children in the Japanese Salon" (detail) (Fortuny i Marsal)	90	80
674	$2 "The Painter's Children in the Japanese Salon" (different detail) (Fortuny i Marsal)	1·40	1·40
675	$3 "Still Life: Sea Bream and Oranges" (Luis Eugenio Melendez) (horiz)	2·25	2·75
676	$5 "Still Life: Box of Sweets, Pastry and Other Objects" (Melendez)	2·75	3·50
MS677	Two sheets, each 121×95 mm. (a) $6 "Bullfight" (Fortuny i Marsal) (111×86 mm). (b) $6 "Moroccans" (Fortuny i Marsal) (111×86 mm). Imperf Set of 2 sheets	5·50	6·50

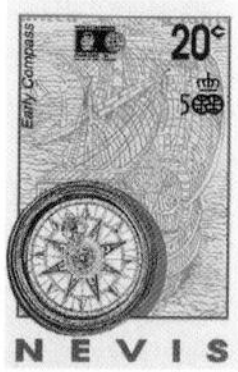

69 Early Compass and Ship

1992. 500th Anniv of Discovery of America by Columbus (4th issue) and "World Columbian Stamp Expo '92", Chicago. Multicoloured.

678	20c. Type **69**	75	25
679	50c. Manatee and fleet	1·25	50
680	80c. Green turtle and "Santa Maria"	1·50	80
681	$1.50 "Santa Maria" and arms	2·25	1·75
682	$3 Queen Isabella of Spain and commission	2·50	3·25
683	$5 Pineapple and colonists	3·00	4·50
MS684	Two sheets, each 101×70 mm. (a) $6 British storm petrel and town (horiz). (b) $6 Peppers and carib canoe (horiz) Set of 2 sheets	10·00	12·00

1992. 500th Anniv of Discovery of America by Columbus (5th issue). Organization of East Caribbean States. As Nos. 911/12 of Montserrat. Multicoloured.

685	$1 Columbus meeting Amerindians	50	50
686	$2 Ships approaching island	1·25	1·40

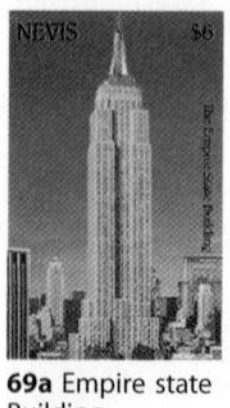

69a Empire state Building

1992. Postage Stamp Mega Event, New York. Sheet 100×70 mm.

MS687	$6 multicolured	4·50	5·00

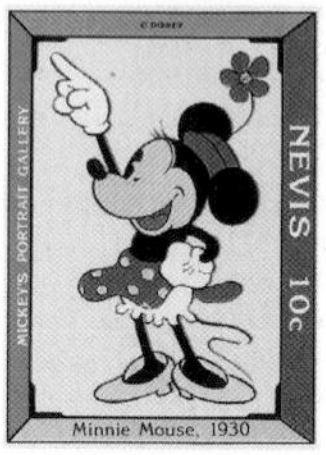

70 Minnie Mouse

1992. Mickey's Portrait Gallery. Mult.

688	10c. Type **70**	50	20
689	15c. Mickey Mouse	50	20
690	40c. Donald Duck	70	30
691	80c. Mickey Mouse, 1930	90	70
692	$1 Daisy Duck	1·00	80
693	$2 Pluto	1·75	1·50
694	$4 Goofy	2·75	3·00
695	$5 Goofy, 1932	2·75	3·00
MS696	Two sheets. (a) 102×128 mm. $6 Mickey in armchair (horiz). (b) 128×102 mm. $6 Mickey and Minnie in airplane (horiz) Set of 2 sheets	10·00	11·00

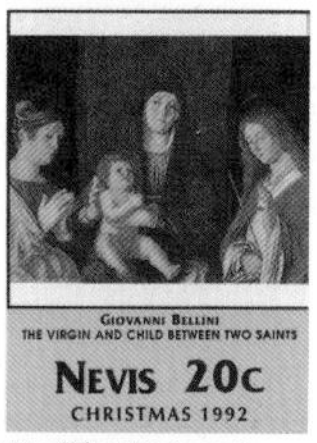

70a "The Virgin and Child between Two Saints" (Giovanni Bellini)

1992. Christmas. Religious Paintings. Mult.

697	20c. Type **70a**	50	15
698	40c. "The Virgin and Child surrounded by Four Angels" (Master of the Castello Nativity)	60	25
699	50c. "Virgin and Child surrounded by Angels with St. Frediano and St. Augustine" (detail) (Filippo Lippi)	70	30
700	80c. "The Virgin and Child between St. Peter and St. Sebastian" (Bellini)	95	70
701	$1 "The Virgin and Child with St. Julian and St. Nicholas of Myra" (Lorenzo di Credi)	1·25	80
702	$2 "St. Bernadino and a Female Saint presenting a Donor to Virgin and Child" (Francesco Bissolo)	2·00	1·50
703	$4 "Madonna and Child with Four Cherubs" (ascr Barthel Bruyn)	3·00	3·75
704	$5 "The Virgin and Child" (Quentin Metsys)	3·25	3·75
MS705	Two sheets, each 76×102 mm. (a) $6 "Virgin and Child surrounded by Two Angels" (detail) (Perugino). (b) $6 "Madonna and Child with the Infant, St. John and Archangel Gabriel" (Sandro Botticelli) Set of 2 sheets	7·00	8·00

No. 699 is inscribed "Fillipo Lippi" in error.

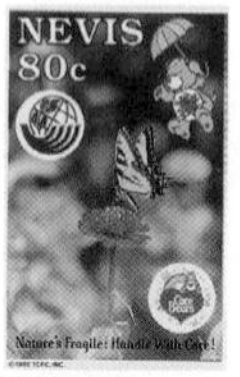

71 Care Bear and Butterfly

1993. Ecology. Multicoloured.

706	80c. Type **71**	60	60
MS707	71×101 mm. $2 Care Bear on beach	2·25	3·50

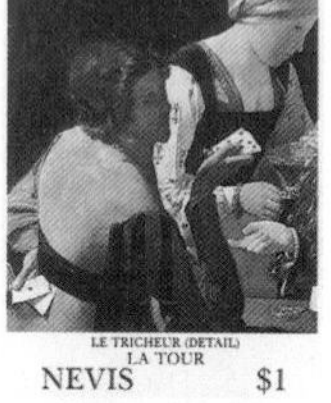

71a "The Card Cheat" (left detail) (La Tour)

1993. Bicentenary of the Louvre, Paris. Multicoloured.

708	$1 Type **71a**	85	85
709	$1 "The Card Cheat" (centre detail) (La Tour)	85	85
710	$1 "The Card Cheat" (right detail) (La Tour)	85	85
711	$1 "St. Joseph, the Carpenter" (La Tour)	85	85
712	$1 "St. Thomas" (La Tour)	85	85
713	$1 "Adoration of the Shepherds" (left detail) (La Tour)	85	85
714	$1 "Adoration of the Shepherds" (right detail) (La Tour)	85	85
715	$1 "Mary Magdalene with a Candle" (La Tour)	85	85

MS716 70×100 mm. $6 "Archangel Raphael leaving the Family of Tobius" (Rembrandt) (52×85 mm) 4·25 4·75

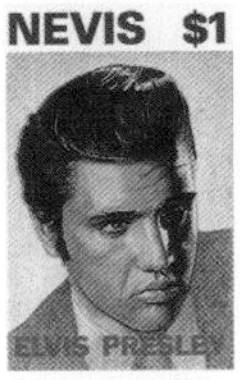

71b Elvis Presley

1993. 15th Death Anniv of Elvis Presley (singer). Multicoloured.

717	$1 Type **71b**	1·40	1·00
718	$1 Elvis with guitar	1·40	1·00
719	$1 Elvis with microphone	1·40	1·00

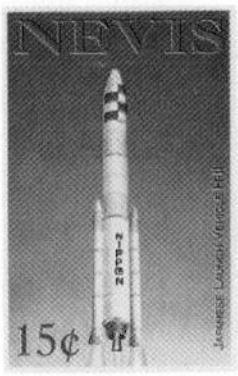

72 Japanese Launch Vehicle H-11

1993. Anniversaries and Events. Mult.

720	15c. Type **72**	60	30
721	50c. Airship "Hindenburg" on fire, 1937 (horiz)	1·00	65
722	75c. Konrad Adenauer and Charles de Gaulle (horiz)	65	65
723	80c. Red Cross emblem and map of Nevis (horiz)	1·25	80
724	80c. "Resolute" (yacht), 1920	1·25	80
725	80c. Nelson Museum and map of Nevis (horiz)	1·25	80
726	80c. St. Thomas's Church (horiz)	70	80
727	$1 Blue whale (horiz)	2·00	1·25
728	$3 Mozart	3·00	2·75
729	$3 Graph and U.N. emblems (horiz)	1·75	2·25
730	$3 Lions Club emblem	1·75	2·25
731	$5 Soviet "Energia" launch vehicle SL-17	3·25	3·75
732	$5 Lebaudy-Juillot airship No. 1 "La Jaune" (horiz)	3·25	3·75
733	$5 Adenauer and Pres. Kennedy (horiz)	3·25	3·75

MS734 Five sheets. (a) 104×71 mm. $6 Astronaut. (b) 104×71 mm. $6 Zeppelin LZ-5, 1909 (horiz). (c) 100×70 mm. $6 Konrad Adenauer (horiz). (d) 75×103 mm. $6 "America 3" (yacht), 1992 (horiz). (e) 98×66 mm. $6 Masked reveller from "Don Giovanni" (horiz) Set of 5 sheets 18·00 19·00

ANNIVERSARIES AND EVENTS—Nos. 720, 731, **MS**734a, International Space Year; 721, 732, **MS**734b, 75th death anniv of Count Ferdinand von Zeppelin (airship pioneer); 722, 733, **MS**734c, 25th death anniv of Konrad Adenauer (German statesman); 723, 50th anniv of St. Kitts-Nevis Red Cross; 724, **MS**734d, Americas Cup Yachting Championship; 725, Opening of Nelson Museum; 726, 150th anniv of Anglican Diocese of North-eastern Caribbean and Aruba; 727, Earth Summit '92, Rio; 728, **MS**734e, Death bicent of Mozart; 729, International Conference on Nutrition, Rome; 730, 75th anniv of International Association of Lions Clubs.

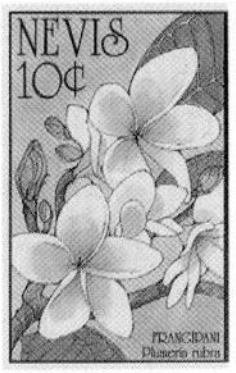

73 "Plumeria rubra"

1993. West Indian Flowers. Multicoloured.

735	10c. Type **73**	75	30
736	25c. "Bougainvillea"	90	30
737	50c. "Allamanda cathartica"	1·10	50
738	80c. "Anthurium andraeanum"	1·50	70
739	$1 "Ixora coccinea"	1·75	75
740	$2 "Hibiscus rosa-sinensis"	2·75	2·25
741	$4 "Justicia brandegeeana"	4·00	4·75
742	$5 "Antigonon leptopus"	4·00	4·75

MS743 Two sheets, each 100×70 mm. (a) $6 "Lantana camara". (b) $6 "Petrea volubilis" Set of 2 sheets 7·50 8·50

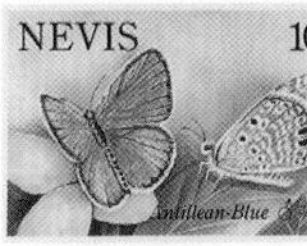

74 Antillean Blue (male)

1993. Butterflies. Multicoloured.

744	10c. Type **74**	60	40
745	25c. Cuban crescentspot (female)	75	40
746	50c. Ruddy daggerwing	1·00	50
747	80c. Little yellow (male)	1·25	75
748	$1 Atala	1·25	90
749	$1.50 Orange-barred giant sulphur	2·00	2·25
750	$4 Tropic queen (male)	3·25	4·50
751	$5 Malachite	3·25	4·50

MS752 Two sheets, each 76×105 mm. (a) $6 Polydamus swallowtail (male). (b) $6 West Indian buckeye Set of 2 sheets 10·00 11·00

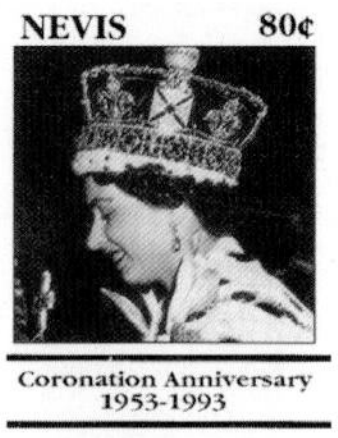

74a 10c. Queen Elizabeth II at Coronation (photograph by Cecil Beaton)

1993. 40th Anniv of Coronation.

753	**74a** 10c. multicoloured	15	20
754	- 80c. brown and black	45	55
755	- $2 multicoloured	1·10	1·40
756	- $4 multicoloured	2·00	2·25

MS757 71×101 mm. $6 multicoloured 3·00 3·50

DESIGNS—38×47 mm: 80c. Queen wearing Imperial State Crown; $2 Crowning of Queen Elizabeth II; $4 Queen and Prince Charles at polo match. 28½×42½ mm: $6 "Queen Elizabeth II, 1977" (detail) (Susan Crawford).

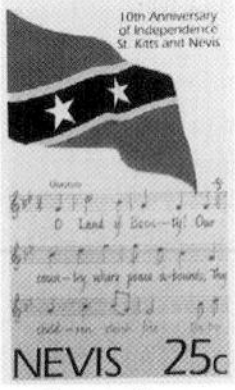

75 Flag and National Anthem

1993. 10th Anniv of Independence of St. Kitts–Nevis. Multicoloured.

758	25c. Type **75**	1·40	35
759	80c. Brown pelican and map of St. Kitts–Nevis	1·60	1·25

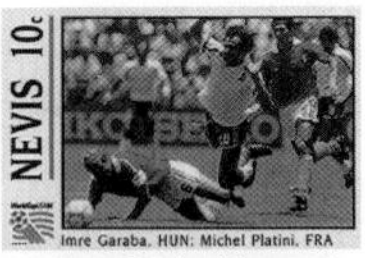

75a Imre Garaba (Hungary) and Michel Platini (France) (horiz)

1993. World Cup Football Championship 1994, U.S.A. Multicoloured.

760	10c. Type **75a**	70	30
761	25c. Diego Maradona (Argentina) and Giuseppe Bergomi (Italy)	85	30
762	50c. Luis Fernandez (France) and Vasily Rats (Russia)	1·10	45
763	80c. Victor Munez (Spain)	1·50	65
764	$1 Preben Elkjaer (Denmark) and Andoni Goicoechea (Spain)	1·75	85
765	$2 Elzo Coelho (Brazil) and Jean Tigana (France)	2·75	2·25
766	$3 Pedro Troglio (Argentina) and Sergei Alejnikov (Russia)	3·00	3·25
767	$5 Jan Karas (Poland) and Antonio Luiz Costa (Brazil)	3·75	4·75

MS768 Two sheets. (a) 100×70 mm. $5 Belloumi (Algeria) (horiz). (b) 70×100 mm. $5 Trevor Steven (England) Set of 2 sheets 11·00 11·00

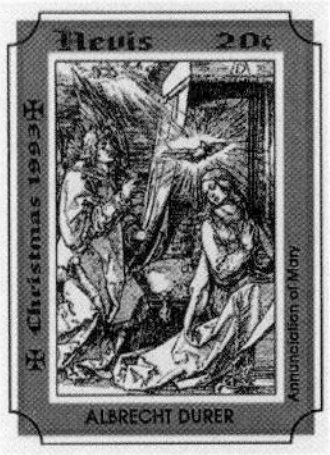

76 "Annunciation of Mary"

1993. Christmas. Religious Paintings by Durer. Black, yellow and red (Nos. 769/73 and 776) or multicoloured (others).

769	20c. Type **76**	50	15
770	40c. "The Nativity" (drawing)	70	30
771	50c. "Holy Family on a Grassy Bank"	80	30
772	80c. "The Presentation of Christ in the Temple"	1·00	55
773	$1 "Virgin in Glory on the Crescent"	1·25	70
774	$1.60 "The Nativity" (painting)	2·00	2·25
775	$3 "Madonna and Child"	2·50	3·25
776	$5 "The Presentation of Christ in the Temple" (detail)	3·25	4·75

MS777 Two sheets, each 105×130 mm. (a) $6 "Mary, Child and the Long-tailed Monkey" (detail) (Durer). (b) $6 "The Rest on the Flight into Egypt" (detail) (Jean-Honure Fragonard) (horiz) Set of 2 sheets 8·50 9·50

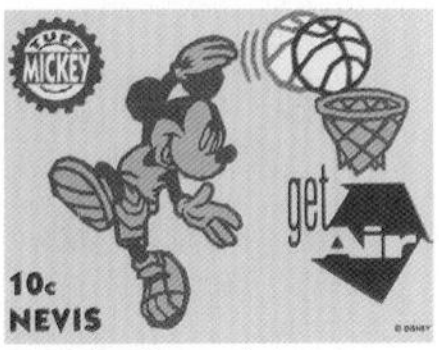

77 Mickey Mouse playing Basketball

1994. Sports and Pastimes. Walt Disney cartoon characters. Multicoloured (except No. MS786a).

778	10c. Type **77**	40	30
779	25c. Minnie Mouse sunbathing (vert)	50	20
780	50c. Mickey playing volleyball	70	40
781	80c. Minnie dancing (vert)	80	60
782	$1 Mickey playing football	1·00	70
783	$1.50 Minnie hula hooping (vert)	1·75	2·00
784	$4 Minnie skipping (vert)	2·75	3·50
785	$5 Mickey wrestling Big Pete	2·75	3·50

MS786 Two sheets. (a) 127×102 mm. $6 Mickey, Donald Duck and Goofy in tug of war (black, red and green). (b) 102×127 mm. $6 Mickey using Test your Strength machine Set of 2 sheets 9·00 10·00

1994. "Hong Kong '94" International Stamp Exhibition. No. MS752 optd with "HONG KONG '94" logo on sheet margins.

MS787 Two sheets, each 76×105 mm. (a) $6 Polydamas swallowtail (male). (b) $6 West Indian buckeye Set of 2 sheets 7·50 8·00

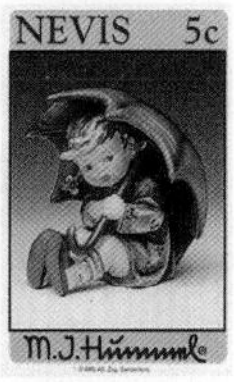

77a Girl with Umbrella

1994. Hummel Figurines. Multicoloured.

788	5c. Type **77a**	15	40
789	25c. Boy holding beer mug and parsnips	45	15
790	50c. Girl sitting in tree	65	35
791	80c. Boy in hat and scarf	85	60
792	$1 Boy with umbrella	1·00	70
793	$1.60 Girl with bird	1·75	1·75
794	$2 Boy on sledge	2·00	2·00
795	$5 Boy sitting in apple tree	2·75	3·75

MS796 Two sheets, each 94×125 mm. (a) Nos. 788 and 792/4. (b) Nos. 789/91 and 795 Set of 2 sheets 6·50 7·50

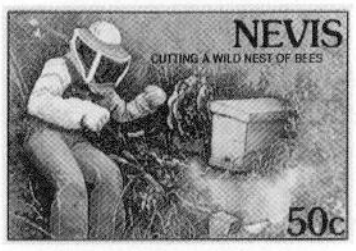

79 Beekeeper collecting Wild Nest

1994. Beekeeping. Multicoloured.

797	50c. Type **79**	65	30
798	80c. Beekeeping club	90	40
799	$1.60 Extracting honey from frames	1·75	1·75
800	$3 Keepers placing queen in hive	2·75	3·75

MS801 100×70 mm. $6 Queen and workers in hive and mechanical honey extractor 5·00 5·50

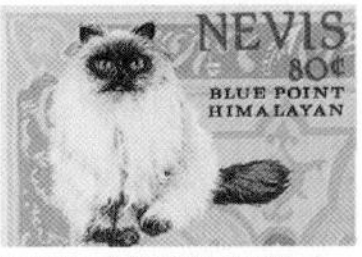

80 Blue Point Himalayan

1994. Persian Cats. Multicoloured.

802	80c. Type **80**	1·10	90
803	80c. Black and white Persian	1·10	90
804	80c. Cream Persian	1·10	90
805	80c. Red Persian	1·10	90
806	80c. Persian	1·10	90
807	80c. Persian black smoke	1·10	90
808	80c. Chocolate smoke Persian	1·10	90
809	80c. Black Persian	1·10	90

MS810 Two sheets, each 100×70 mm. (a) $6 Silver tabby Persian. (B) $6 Brown tabby Persian Set of 2 sheets 10·00 11·00

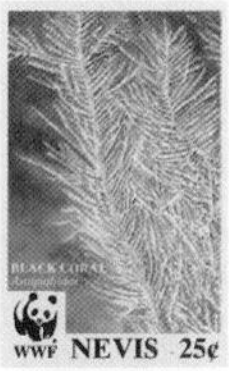

81 Black Coral

1994. Endangered Species. Black Coral.

811	**81** 25c. multicoloured	60	75
812	- 40c. multicoloured	70	80
813	- 50c. multicoloured	70	80
814	- 80c. multicoloured	80	90

DESIGNS: 40c. to 80c. Different forms of coral.

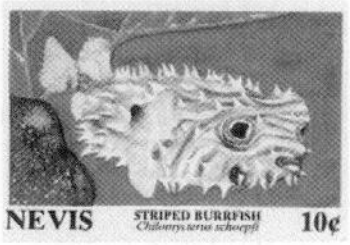

82 Striped Burrfish

1994. Fishes. Multicoloured.

815	10c. Type **82**	50	50
816	50c. Flame-backed angelfish	55	55
817	50c. Reef bass	55	55
818	50c. Long-finned damselfish ("Honey Gregory")	55	55
819	50c. Saddle squirrelfish	55	55
820	50c. Cobalt chromis	55	55
821	50c. Genie's neon goby	55	55
822	50c. Slender-tailed cardinalfish	55	55
823	50c. Royal gramma	55	55
824	$1 Blue-striped grunt	75	75
825	$1.60 Blue angelfish	1·00	1·25
826	$3 Cocoa damselfish	1·50	1·75

MS827 Two sheets, each 100×70 mm. (a) $6 Blue marlin. (b) $6 Sailfish (vert) Set of 2 sheets 8·00 8·50

Nos. 816/23 were printed together, se-tenant, forming a composite design.

No. 824 is inscribed "BLUESRIPED GRUNT" in error.

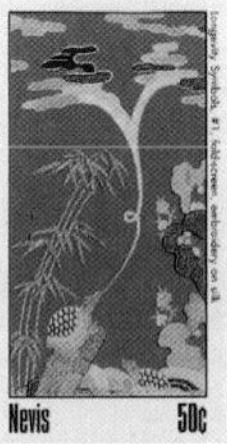

83 Symbol 1. Turtles and Cloud

1994. "Philakorea '94" International Stamp Exhibition, Seoul. Longevity symbols. Multicoloured.

828	50c. Type **83**	45	50
829	50c. Symbol 2. Manchurian cranes and bamboo	45	50
830	50c. Symbol 3. Deer and bamboo	45	50
831	50c. Symbol 4. Turtles and Sun	45	50
832	50c. Symbol 5. Manchurian cranes under tree	45	50
833	50c. Symbol 6. Deer and tree	45	50
834	50c. Symbol 7. Turtles and rock	45	50

835	50c. Symbol 8. Manchurian cranes above tree	45	50

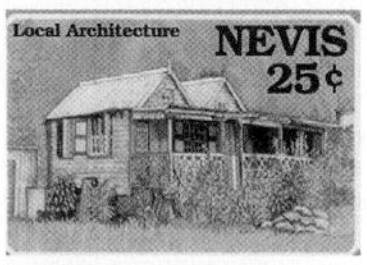

84 Twin-roofed House with Veranda

1994. Island Architecture. Multicoloured.

836	25c. Type **84**	70	20
837	50c. Two-storey house with outside staircase	95	30
838	$1 Government Treasury	1·40	1·10
839	$5 Two-storey house with red roof	4·00	6·00
MS840	102×72 mm. $6 Raised bungalow with veranda	3·75	5·00

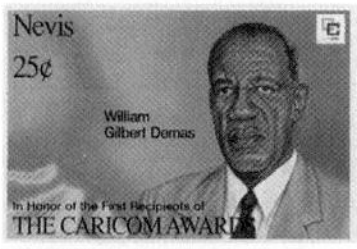

85 William Demas

1994. First Recipients of Order of Caribbean Community. Multicoloured.

841	25c. Type **85**	30	10
842	50c. Sir Shridath Ramphal	50	45
843	$1 Derek Walcott	2·25	1·25

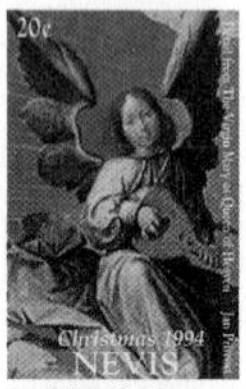

86 "The Virgin Mary as Queen of Heaven" (detail) (Jan Provost)

1994. Christmas. Religious Paintings. Multicoloured.

844	20c. Type **86**	20	10
845	40c. "The Virgin Mary as Queen of Heaven" (different detail) (Provost)	35	25
846	50c. "The Virgin Mary as Queen of Heaven" (different detail) (Provost)	40	30
847	80c. "Adoration of the Magi" (detail) (Circle of Van der Goes)	60	40
848	$1 "Adoration of the Magi" (different detail) (Circle of Van der Goes)	70	50
849	$1.60 "Adoration of the Magi" (different detail) (Circle of Van der Goes)	1·25	1·50
850	$3 "Adoration of the Magi" (different detail) (Circle of Van der Goes)	2·00	2·50
851	$5 "The Virgin Mary as Queen of Heaven" (different detail) (Provost)	3·00	3·75
MS852	Two sheets, each 96×117 mm. (a) $5 "The Virgin Mary as Queen of Heaven" (different detail) (Provost). (b) $6 "Adoration of the Magi" (different detail) (Circle of Van der Goes) Set of 2 sheets	8·25	8·50

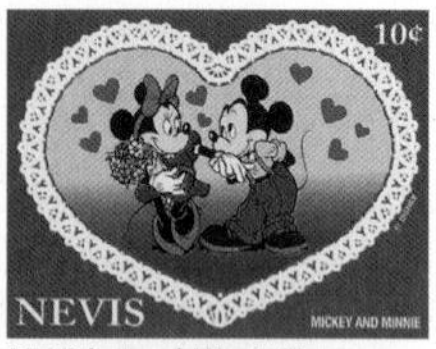

87 Mickey and Minnie Mouse

1995. Disney Sweethearts (1st series). Walt Disney Cartoon Characters. Multicoloured.

853	10c. Type **87**	20	20
854	25c. Donald and Daisy Duck	35	20
855	50c. Pluto and Fifi	50	35
856	80c. Clarabelle Cow and Horace Horsecollar	70	50
857	$1 Pluto and Figaro	85	65
858	$1.50 Polly and Peter Penguin	1·25	1·50
859	$4 Prunella Pullet and Hick Rooster	2·50	3·25
860	$5 Jenny Wren and Cock Robin	2·50	3·25
MS861	Two sheets, each 133×107 mm. (a) $6 Daisy Duck (vert). (b) $6 Minnie Mouse (vert) Set of 2 sheets	8·50	9·00

See also Nos. 998/1007.

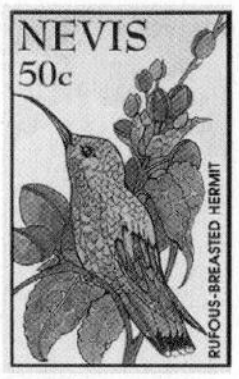

88 Rufous-breasted Hermit

1995. Birds. Multicoloured.

862	50c. Type **88**	50	50
863	50c. Purple-throated carib	50	50
864	50c. Green mango	50	50
865	50c. Bahama woodstar	50	50
866	50c. Hispaniolan emerald	50	50
867	50c. Antillean crested hummingbird	50	50
868	50c. Green-throated carib	50	50
869	50c. Antillean mango	50	50
870	50c. Vervain hummingbird	50	50
871	50c. Jamaican mango	50	50
872	50c. Cuban emerald	50	50
873	50c. Blue-headed hummingbird	50	50
874	50c. Hooded merganser	50	50
875	80c. Green-backed heron	75	50
876	$2 Double-crested cormorant	1·25	1·40
877	$3 Ruddy duck	1·50	1·75
MS878	Two sheets, each 100×70 mm. (a) $6 Black skimmer. (b) $6 Snowy plover Set of 2 sheets	8·00	8·50

No. 870 is inscribed "VERVIAN" in error.

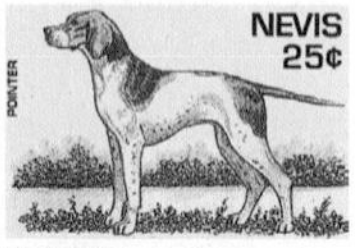

89 Pointer

1995. Dogs. Multicoloured.

879	25c. Type **89**	30	20
880	50c. Old Danish pointer	50	50
881	80c. Irish setter	65	65
882	80c. Weimaraner	65	65
883	80c. Gordon setter	65	65
884	80c. Brittany spaniel	65	65
885	80c. American cocker spaniel	65	65
886	80c. English cocker spaniel	65	65
887	80c. Labrador retriever	65	65
888	80c. Golden retriever	65	65
889	80c. Flat-coated retriever	65	65
890	$1 German short-haired pointer	75	75
891	$2 English setter	1·40	1·40
MS892	Two sheets, each 72×58 mm. (a) $6 German shepherds. (b) $6 Bloodhounds Set of 2 sheets	8·00	8·50

"POINTER" is omitted from the inscription on No. 890. No. **MS**892a is incorrectly inscribed "SHEPHARD".

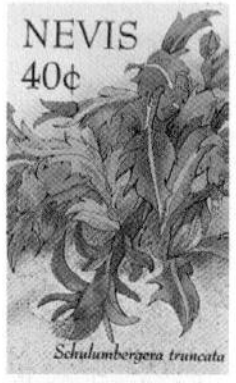

90 "Schulumbergera truncata"

1995. Cacti. Multicoloured.

893	40c. Type **90**	30	20
894	50c. "Echinocereus pectinatus"	40	25
895	80c. "Mammillaria zeilmanniana alba"	65	40
896	$1.60 "Lobivia hertriehiana"	1·10	1·25
897	$2 "Hammatocactus setispinus"	1·40	1·50
898	$3 "Astrophytum myriostigma"	1·60	2·00
MS899	Two sheets, each 106×76 mm. (a) $6 "Opuntia robusta". (b) $6 "Rhipsalidopsis gaertneri" Set of 2 sheets	7·00	7·50

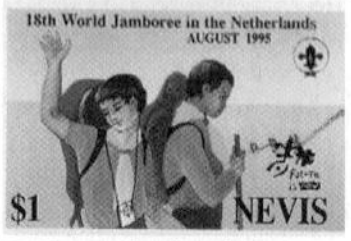

91 Scouts backpacking

1995. 18th World Scout Jamboree, Netherlands. Multicoloured.

900	$1 Type **91**	1·00	1·10
901	$2 Scouts building aerial rope way	1·50	1·75
902	$4 Scout map reading	2·00	2·25
MS903	101×71 mm. $6 Scout in canoe (vert)	4·00	4·50

Nos. 900/2 were printed together, se-tenant, forming a composite design.

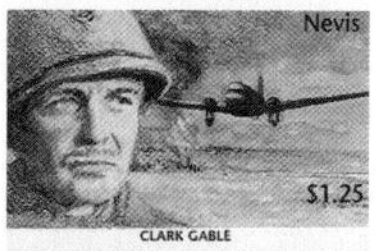

91a Clark Gable and Aircraft

1995. 50th Anniv of End of Second World War in Europe. Multicoloured.

904	$1.25 Type **91a**	1·00	1·00
905	$1.25 Audie Murphy and machine-gunner	1·00	1·00
906	$1.25 Glenn Miller playing trombone	1·00	1·00
907	$1.25 Joe Louis and infantry	1·00	1·00
908	$1.25 Jimmy Doolittle and U.S.S. "Hornet" (aircraft carrier)	1·00	1·00
909	$1.25 John Hersey and jungle patrol	1·00	1·00
910	$1.25 John F. Kennedy in patrol boat	1·00	1·00
911	$1.25 James Stewart and bombers	1·00	1·00
MS912	101×71 mm. $6 Jimmy Doolittle (vert)	4·00	4·50

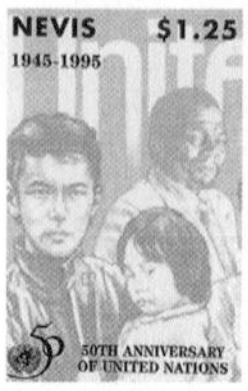

92 Oriental and African People

1995. 50th Anniv of United Nations. Each lilac and black.

913	$1.25 Type **92**	55	80
914	$1.60 Asian people	75	1·10
915	$3 American and European people	1·40	1·60
MS916	105×75 mm. $6 Pres. Nelson Mandela of South Africa	3·00	3·50

Nos. 913/15 were printed together, se-tenant, forming a composite design.

1995. 50th Anniv of F.A.O. As T 92. Multicoloured.

917	40c. Woman wearing yellow headdress	15	60
918	$2 Babies and emblem	85	1·25
919	$3 Woman wearing blue headdress	1·25	1·60
MS920	105×80 mm. $6 Man carrying hoe	2·75	3·75

Nos. 917/19 were printed together, se-tenant, forming a composite design.

No. **MS**920 is inscribed "1945–1955" in error.

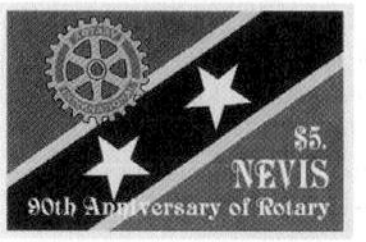

93 Rotary Emblem on Nevis Flag

1995. 90th Anniv of Rotary International. Multicoloured.

921	$5 Type **93**	2·50	3·25
MS922	95×66 mm. $6 Rotary emblem and beach	3·00	3·75

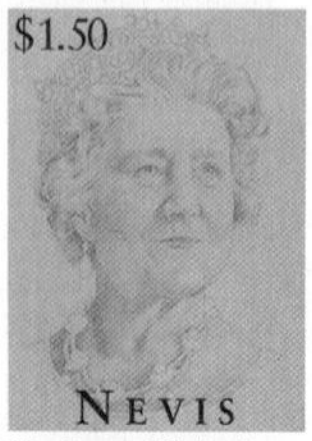

93a Queen Elizabeth the Queen Mother (pastel drawing)

1995. 95th Birthday of Queen Elizabeth the Queen Mother.

923	**93a**	$1.50 brown, light brown and black	2·25	1·75
924	-	$1.50 multicoloured	2·25	1·75
925	-	$1.50 multicoloured	2·25	1·75
926	-	$1.50 multicoloured	2·25	1·75
MS927		102×127 mm. $6 multicoloured	6·00	6·00

DESIGNS: No. 924, Wearing pink hat; 925, At desk (oil painting); 926, Wearing blue hat; **MS**927, Wearing tiara.

No. **MS**927 was also issued additionally inscribed "IN MEMORIAM 1900–2002" on margin.

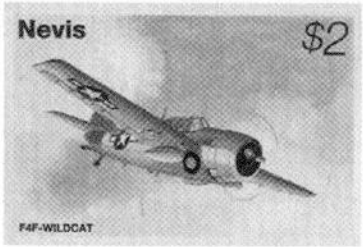

93b Grumman F4F Wildcat

1995. 50th Anniv of End of Second World War in the Pacific. United States Aircraft. Multicoloured.

928	$2 Type **93a**	1·40	1·40
929	$2 Chance Vought F4U-1A Corsair	1·40	1·40
930	$2 Vought SB2U Vindicator	1·40	1·40
931	$2 Grumman F6F Hellcat	1·40	1·40
932	$2 Douglas SDB Dauntless	1·40	1·40
933	$2 Grumman TBF-1 Avenger	1·40	1·40
MS934	108×76 mm. $6 Chance Vought F4U-1A Corsair on carrier flight deck	5·50	6·50

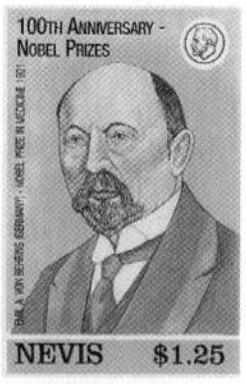

94 Emil von Behring (1901 Medicine)

1995. Centenary of Nobel Trust Fund. Past Prize Winners. Multicoloured.

935	$1.25 Type **94**	75	85
936	$1.25 Wilhelm Rontgen (1901 Physics)	75	85
937	$1.25 Paul Heyse (1910 Literature)	75	85
938	$1.25 Le Duc Tho (1973 Peace)	75	85
939	$1.25 Yasunari Kawabata (1968 Literature)	75	85
940	$1.25 Tsung-dao Lee (1957 Physics)	75	85
941	$1.25 Werner Heisenberg (1932 Physics)	75	85
942	$1.25 Johannes Stark (1919 Physics)	75	85
943	$1.25 Wilhelm Wien (1911 Physics)	75	85
MS944	101×71 mm. $6 Kenzaburo Oe (1994 Literature)	3·25	3·75

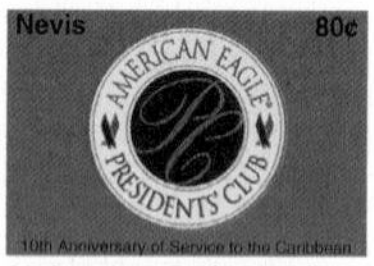

95 American Eagle Presidents' Club Logo

1995. 10th Anniv of American Eagle Air Services to the Caribbean. Sheet 70×100 mm, containing T 95 and similar horiz design. Multicoloured.

MS945	80c. Type **95**; $3 Aircraft over Nevis beach	2·40	2·50

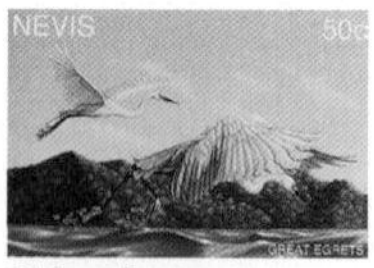

96 Great Egrets

1995. Marine Life. Multicoloured.

946	50c. Type **96**	55	55
947	50c. 17th-century galleon	55	55
948	50c. Galleon and marlin	55	55
949	50c. Herring gulls	55	55
950	50c. Nassau groupers	55	55
951	50c. Spotted eagleray	55	55
952	50c. Leopard shark and hammerhead	55	55
953	50c. Hourglass dolphins	55	55
954	50c. Spanish hogfish	55	55
955	50c. Jellyfish and seahorses	55	55
956	50c. Angelfish and buried treasure	55	55
957	50c. Hawksbill turtle	55	55
958	50c. Common octopus	55	55
959	50c. Moray eel	55	55
960	50c. Queen angelfish and butterflyfish	55	55
961	50c. Ghost crab and sea star	55	55
MS962	Two sheets. (a) 106×76 mm. $5 Nassau grouper. (b) 76×106 mm. $5 Queen angelfish (vert) Set of 2 sheets	7·00	7·00

No. **MS**962 also commemorates the "Singapore '95" International Stamp Exhibition.

Nos. 946/61 were printed together, se-tenant, forming a composite design.

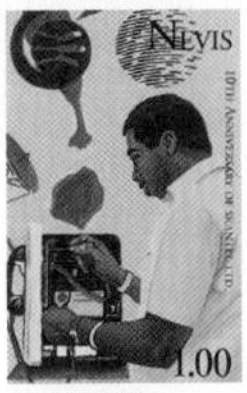

97 SKANTEL Engineer

1995. 10th Anniv of SKANTEL (telecommunications company). Multicoloured.

963	$1 Type **97**	60	50
964	$1.50 SKANTEL sign outside Nevis office	80	1·25
MS965	76×106 mm. $5 St. Kitts SKANTEL office (horiz)	3·00	3·50

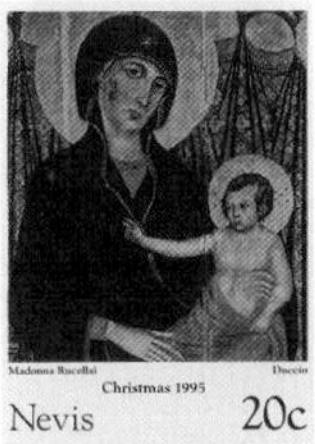

98 "Rucellai Madonna and Child" (detail) (Duccio)

1995. Christmas. Religious Paintings by Duccio di Buoninsegna. Multicoloured.

966	20c. Type **98**	20	15
967	50c. "Angel form the Rucellai Madonna" (detail)	40	25
968	80c. "Madonna and Child" (different)	60	40
969	$1 "Angel from the Annunciation" (detail)	75	60
970	$1.60 "Madonna and Child" (different)	1·25	1·50
971	$3 "Angel from the Rucellai Madonna" (different)	1·90	2·75
MS972	Two sheets, each 102×127 mm. (a) $5 "Nativity with the Prophets Isaiah and Ezekiel" (detail). (b) $6 "The Crevole Madonna" (detail) Set of 2 sheets	6·50	7·50

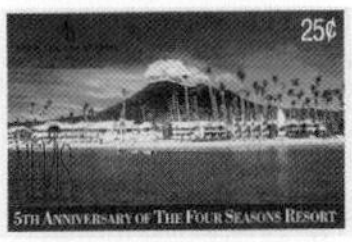

99 View of Nevis Four Seasons Resort

1996. 5th Anniv of Four Seasons Resort, Nevis. Multicoloured.

973	25c. Type **99**	15	20
974	50c. Catamarans, Pinney's Beach	25	30
975	80c. Robert Trent Jones II Golf Course	40	45
976	$2 Prime Minister Simeon Daniel laying foundation stone	1·00	1·40
MS977	76×106 mm. $6 Sunset over resort	3·00	3·50

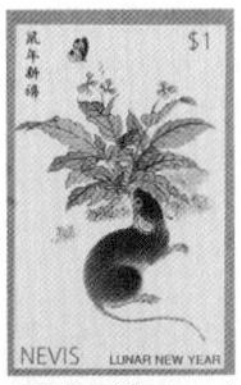

100 Rat, Plant and Butterfly

1996. Chinese New Year ("Year of the Rat"). Multicoloured.

978	$1 Type **100**	50	60
979	$1 Rat with prickly plant	50	60
980	$1 Rat and bee	50	60
981	$1 Rat and dragonfly	50	60
MS982	74×104 mm. Nos. 978/81	2·25	2·50
MS983	74×104 mm. $3 Rat eating	2·00	2·25

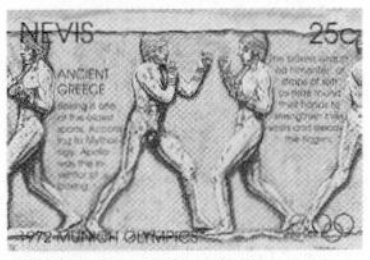

101 Ancient Greek Boxers

1996. Olympic Games, Atlanta. Previous Medal Winners. Multicoloured.

984	25c. Type **101**	25	20
985	50c. Mark Spitz (U.S.A.) (Gold – swimming, 1972)	35	30
986	80c. Siegbert Horn (East Germany) (Gold – single kayak slalom, 1972)	50	45
987	$1 Jim Thorpe on medal (U.S.A.), 1912 (vert)	60	70
988	$1 Glenn Morris on medal (U.S.A.), 1936 (vert)	60	70
989	$1 Bob Mathias on medal (U.S.A.), 1948 and 1952 (vert)	60	70
990	$1 Rafer Johnson on medal (U.S.A.), 1960 (vert)	60	70
991	$1 Bill Toomey (U.S.A.), 1968 (vert)	60	70
992	$1 Nikolay Avilov (Russia), 1972 (vert)	60	70
993	$1 Bruce Jenner (U.S.A.), 1976 (vert)	60	70
994	$1 Daley Thompson (Great Britain), 1980 and 1984 (vert)	60	70
995	$1 Christian Schenk (East Germany), 1988 (vert)	60	70
996	$3 Olympic Stadium and Siegestor Arch, Munich (vert)	1·60	2·00
MS997	Two sheets, each 105×75 mm. (a) $5 Willi Holdorf (West Germany) (Gold – decathlon, 1964) (vert). (b) $5 Hans-Joachim Walde (West Germany) (Silver – decathlon, 1968) (vert) Set of 2 sheets	6·50	7·00

1996. Disney Sweethearts (2nd series). As T 87. Walt Disney Cartoon Characters. Multicoloured.

998	$2 Pocahontas and John Smith	2·00	1·50
999	$2 Mowgli and the Girl	2·00	1·50
1000	$2 Belle and the Beast	2·00	1·50
1001	$2 Cinderella and Prince Charming	2·00	1·50
1002	$2 Pinocchio and the Dutch Girl	2·00	1·50
1003	$2 Grace Martin and Henry Coy	2·00	1·50
1004	$2 Snow White and the Prince	2·00	1·50
1005	$2 Aladdin and Jasmine	2·00	1·50
1006	$2 Pecos Bill and Slue Foot Sue	2·00	1·50
MS1007	Two sheets, each 110×130 mm. (a) $6 Sleeping Beauty and Prince Phillip (vert). (b) $6 Ariel and Eric Set of 2 sheets	10·00	11·00

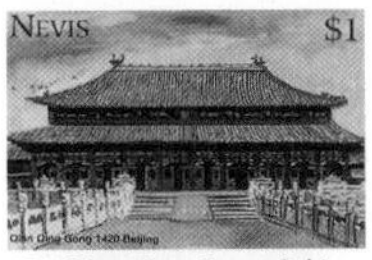

102 Qian Qing Gong, Peking

1996. "CHINA '96" 9th Asian International Stamp Exhibition, Peking. Peking Pagodas. Multicoloured.

1008	$1 Type **102**	50	60
1009	$1 Temple of Heaven	50	60
1010	$1 Zhongnanhai	50	60
1011	$1 Da Zing Hall, Shehyang Palace	50	60
1012	$1 Temple of the Sleeping Buddha	50	60
1013	$1 Huang Qiong Yu, Altar of Heaven	50	60
1014	$1 The Grand Bell Temple	50	60
1015	$1 Imperial Palace	50	60
1016	$1 Pu Tuo Temple	50	60
MS1017	104×74 mm. $6 Summer Palace of Emperor Wan Yan-liang (vert)	3·00	3·50

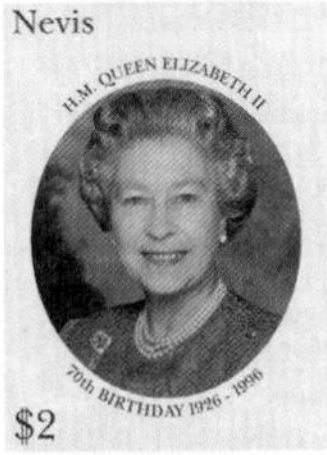

102a Queen Elizabeth II

1996. 70th Birthday of Queen Elizabeth II. Multicoloured.

1018	$2 Type **102a**	1·25	1·40
1019	$2 Wearing evening dress	1·25	1·40
1020	$2 In purple hat and coat	1·25	1·40
MS1021	125×103 mm. $6 Taking the salute at Tropping the Colour	4·00	4·25

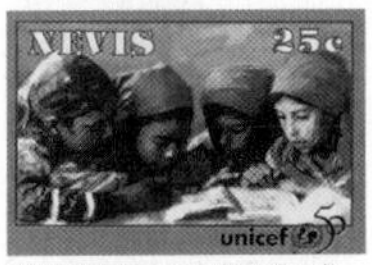

103 Children reading Book

1996. 50th Anniv of UNICEF. Multicoloured.

1022	25c. Type **103**	30	20
1023	50c. Doctor and child	60	30
1024	$4 Children	2·75	3·50
MS1025	75×105 mm. $6 Young girl (vert)	3·00	3·50

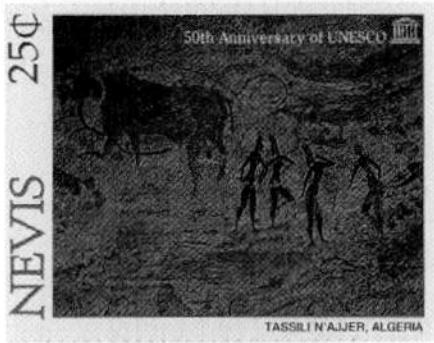

104 Cave Paintings, Tassili n'Ajjer, Algeria

1996. 50th Anniv of UNESCO. Multicoloured.

1026	25c. Type **104**	80	25
1027	$2 Temple, Tikai National Park, Guatemala (vert)	1·50	1·60
1028	$3 Temple of Hera, Samos, Greece	1·90	2·50
MS1029	106×76 mm. $6 Pueblo, Taos, U.S.A.	3·00	3·50

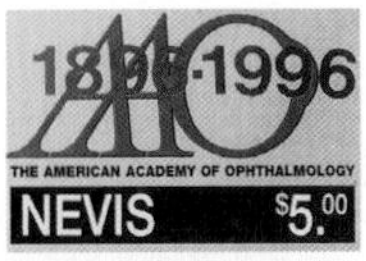

105 American Academy of Ophthalmology Logo

1996. Centenary of American Academy of Ophthalmology.

1030	**105** $5 multicoloured	3·25	3·50

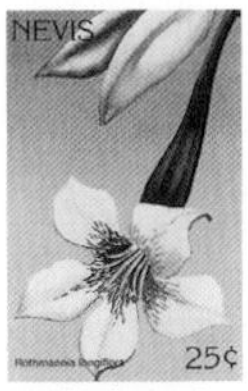

106 "Rothmannia longiflora"

1996. Flowers. Multicoloured.

1031	25c. Type **106**	25	20
1032	50c. "Gloriosa simplex"	35	30
1033	$1 "Monodora myristica"	60	70
1034	$1 Giraffe	60	70
1035	$1 "Adansonia digitata"	60	70
1036	$1 "Ansellia gigantea"	60	70
1037	$1 "Geissorhiza rochensis"	60	70
1038	$1 "Arctotis venusta"	60	70
1039	$1 "Gladiotus cardinalis"	60	70
1040	$1 "Eucomis bicolor"	60	70
1041	$1 "Protea obtusifolia"	60	70
1042	$2 "Catharanthus roseus"	1·10	1·25
1043	$3 "Plumbago auriculata"	1·60	1·90
MS1044	75×105 mm. $5 "Strelitzia reginae"	2·50	3·00

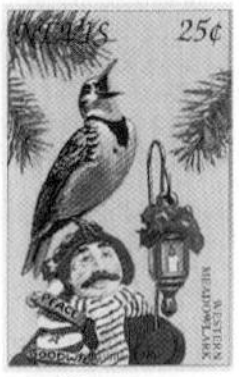

107 Western Meadowlark on Decoration

1996. Christmas. Birds. Multicoloured.

1045	25c. Type **107**	30	20
1046	50c. Bird (incorrectly inscr as "American goldfinch") with decorations (horiz)	45	30
1047	80c. Santa Claus, sleigh and reindeer (horiz)	60	45
1048	$1 American goldfinch on stocking	70	55
1049	$1.60 Northern mockingbird ("Mockingbird") with snowman decoration	1·00	1·10
1050	$5 Yellow-rumped cacique and bauble	2·75	3·50
MS1051	Two sheets. (a) 106×76 mm. $6 Blue and yellow macaw ("Macaw") (horiz). (b) 76×106 mm. $6 Vermilion flycatcher (horiz) Set of 2 sheets	7·00	7·50

No. 1048 is inscribed "WESTERN MEADOWLARK" and No. 1050 "YELLOW-RUMPED CAIEQUE", both in error.

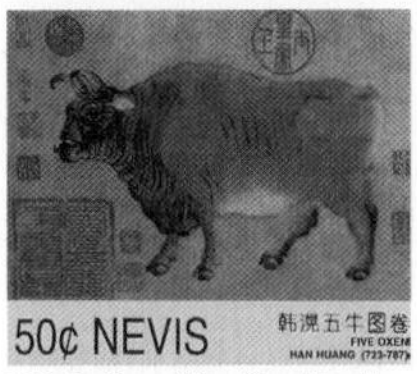

108 Ox (from "Five Oxen" by Han Huang)

1997. Chinese New Year ("Year of the Ox"). T 108 and similar oxen from the painting by Han Huang. Sheet 230×93 mm.

MS1052	50c., 80c., $1.60, $2 multicoloured	3·50	3·75

The fifth ox appears on a small central label.

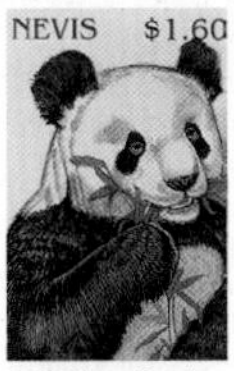

109 Giant Panda eating Bamboo Shoots

1997. "HONG KONG '97" International Stamp Exhibition. Giant Pandas. Multicoloured.

1053	$1.60 Type **109**	1·25	1·25
1054	$1.60 Head of panda	1·25	1·25
1055	$1.60 Panda with new-born cub	1·25	1·25
1056	$1.60 Panda hanging from branch	1·25	1·25
1057	$1.60 Panda asleep on tree	1·25	1·25
1058	$1.60 Panda climbing trunk	1·25	1·25
MS1059	73×103 mm. $5 Panda with cub	2·50	3·00

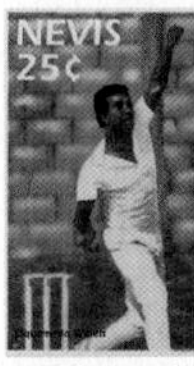

110 Elquemedo Willett

1997. Nevis Cricketers. Multicoloured.

1060	25c. Type **110**	30	25
1061	80c. Stuart Williams	70	50
1062	$2 Keith Arthurton	1·25	1·50
MS1063	Two sheets, each 106×76 mm. (a) $5 Willett, Arthurton and Williams as part of the 1990 Nevis team (horiz). (b) $5 Williams and Arthurton as part of the 1994 West Indies team Set of 2 sheets	6·00	6·50

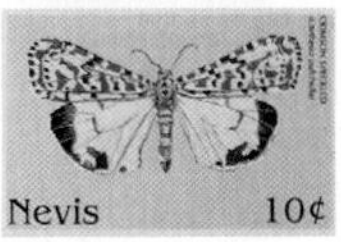

111 Crimson-speckled Moth

1997. Butterflies and Moths. Multicoloured.

1064	10c. Type **111**	20	30
1065	25c. Purple emperor	35	20
1066	50c. Regent skipper	45	30
1067	80c. Provence burnet moth	70	45
1068	$1 Common wall butterfly	70	80
1069	$1 Red-lined geometrid	70	80
1070	$1 Boisduval's autumnal moth	70	80
1071	$1 Blue pansy	70	80
1072	$1 Common clubtail	70	80
1073	$1 Tufted jungle king	70	80
1074	$1 Lesser marbled fritillary	70	80
1075	$1 Peacock royal	70	80
1076	$1 Emperor gum moth	70	80
1077	$1 Orange swallow-tailed moth	70	80
1078	$4 Cruiser butterfly	2·25	2·75
MS1079	Two sheets. (a) 103×73 mm. $5 Great purple. (b) 73×103 mm. $5 Jersey tiger moth Set of 2 sheets	5·50	6·50

No. 1073 is inscribed "TUFTED JUNGLE QUEEN" in error.

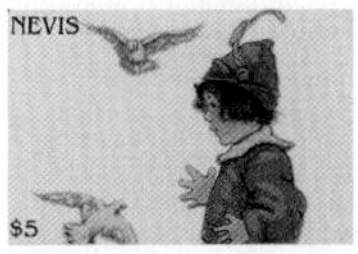

112 Boy with Two Pigeons

1997. 300th Anniv of Mother Goose Nursery Rhymes. Sheet 72×102 mm.

MS1080	**112** $5 multicoloured	2·75	3·50

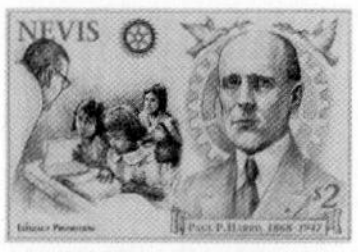

113 Paul Harris and Literacy Class

1997. 50th Death Anniv of Paul Harris (founder of Rotary International). Multicoloured.

1081	$2 Type **113**	1·00	1·25
MS1082	78×108 mm. $5 Football coaching session, Chile	2·50	3·00

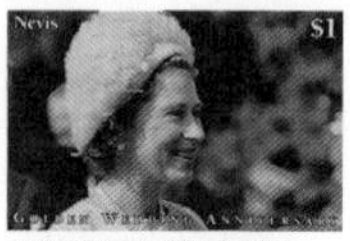

113a Queen Elizabeth II

1997. Golden Wedding of Queen Elizabeth and Prince Philip. Multicoloured.

1083	$1 Type **113a**	95	95
1084	$1 Royal Coat of Arms	95	95
1085	$1 Queen Elizabeth wearing red hat and coat with Prince Philip	95	95
1086	$1 Queen Elizabeth in blue coat and Prince Philip	95	95
1087	$1 Caernarvon Castle	95	95
1088	$1 Prince Philip in R.A.F. uniform	95	95
MS1089	100×70 mm. $5 Queen Elizabeth at Coronation	3·00	3·50

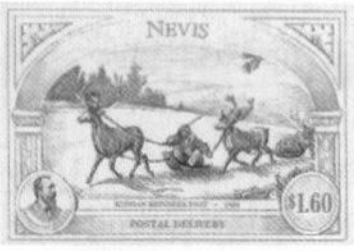

113b Russian reindeer post, 1859

1997. "Pacific '97" International Stamp Exhibition, San Francisco. Death Centenary of Heinrich von Stephan.

1090	**113b**	$1.60 green	90	1·10
1091	-	$1.60 brown	90	1·10
1092	-	$1.60 blue	90	1·10
MS1093		82×118 mm. $5 sepia	2·50	3·00

DESIGNS: No. 1091, Von Stephan and Mercury; 1092, "City of Cairo" (paddle-steamer), Mississippi, 1800s; **MS**1093, Von Stephan and Bavarian postal messenger, 1640.

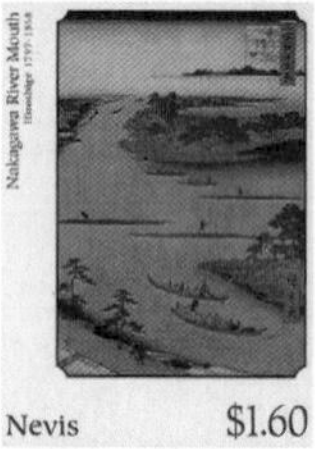

113c "Scattered Pines, Tone River"

1997. Birth Bicentenary of Hiroshige (Japanese painter). "One Hundred Famous Views of Edo". Multicoloured.

1094	$1.60 Type **113c**	1·25	1·25
1095	$1.60 "Mouth of Nakagawa River"	1·25	1·25
1096	$1.60 "Niijuku Ferry"	1·25	1·25
1097	$1.60 "Horie and Nekozane"	1·25	1·25
1098	$1.60 "Konodai and the Tone River"	1·25	1·25
1099	$1.60 "Maple Trees, Tekona Shrine and Bridge, Mama"	1·25	1·25
MS1100	Two sheets, each 102×127 mm. (a) $6 "Mitsumata Wakarenofuchi". (b) $6 "Moto-Hachiman Shrine, Sunamura" Set of 2 sheets	7·00	7·50

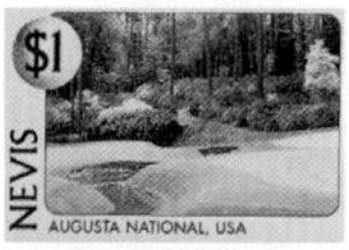

114 Augusta National Course, U.S.A.

1997. Golf Courses of the World. Multicoloured.

1101	$1 Type **114**	80	80
1102	$1 Cabo del Sol, Mexico	80	80
1103	$1 Cypress Point, U.S.A.	80	80
1104	$1 Lost City, South Africa	80	80
1105	$1 Moscow Country Club, Russia	80	80
1106	$1 New South Wales, Australia	80	80
1107	$1 Royal Montreal, Canada	80	80
1108	$1 St. Andrews, Scotland	80	80
1109	$1 Four Seasons Resort, Nevis	80	80

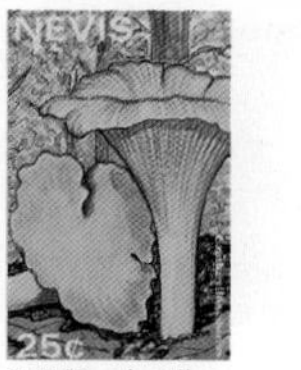

115 "Cantharellus cibarius"

1997. Fungi. Multicoloured.

1110	25c. Type **115**	30	20
1111	50c. "Stropharia aeruginosa"	40	30
1112	80c. "Suillus hiteus"	60	65
1113	80c. "Amanita muscaria"	60	65
1114	80c. "Lactarius rufus"	60	65
1115	80c. "Amanita rubescens"	60	65
1116	80c. "Armillaria mellea"	60	65
1117	80c. "Russula sardonia"	60	65
1118	$1 "Boletus edulis"	65	70
1119	$1 "Pholiota lenta"	65	70
1120	$1 "Cortinarius bolaris"	65	70
1121	$1 "Coprinus picaceus"	65	70
1122	$1 "Amanita phalloides"	65	70
1123	$1 "Cystolepiota aspera"	65	70
1124	$3 "Lactarius turpis"	1·75	2·00
1125	$4 "Entoloma clypeatum"	2·25	2·50
MS1126	Two sheets, each 98×68 mm. (a) $5 "Galerina mutabilis". (b) $5 "Gymnopilus junonius" Set of 2 sheets	6·00	6·50

Nos. 1112/17 and 1118/23 respectively were printed together, se-tenant, with the backgrounds forming composite designs.

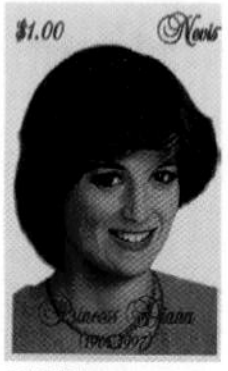

116 Diana, Princess of Wales

1997. Diana, Princess of Wales Commemoration. Multicoloured.

1127	$1 Type **116**	1·00	90
1128	$1 Wearing white blouse	1·00	90
1129	$1 In wedding dress, 1981	1·00	90
1130	$1 Wearing turquoise blouse	1·00	90
1131	$1 Wearing tiara	1·00	90
1132	$1 Wearing blue blouse	1·00	90
1133	$1 Wearing pearl necklace	1·00	90
1134	$1 Wearing diamond drop earrings	1·00	90
1135	$1 Wearing sapphire necklace and earrings	1·00	90

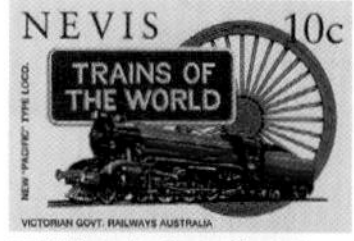

117 Victoria Govt Class S Pacific Locomotive, Australia

1997. Trains of the World. Multicoloured.

1136	10c. Type **117**	35	20
1137	50c. Express steam locomotive, Japan	55	30
1138	80c. L.M.S. steam-turbine locomotive, Great Britain	75	45
1139	$1 Electric locomotive, Switzerland	90	55
1140	$1.50 "Mikado" steam locomotive, Sudan	1·25	1·40
1141	$1.50 "Mohammed Ali el Kebir" steam locomotive, Egypt	1·25	1·40
1142	$1.50 Southern Region steam locomotive "Leatherhead"	1·25	1·40
1143	$1.50 Great Southern Railway Drumm battery-powered railcar, Ireland	1·25	1·40
1144	$1.50 Pacific locomotive, Germany	1·25	1·40
1145	$1.50 Canton–Hankow Railway Pacific locomotive, China	1·25	1·40
1146	$2 L.M.S. high-pressure locomotive, Great Britain	1·60	1·75
1147	$3 Great Northern Railway "Kestrel", Ireland	2·00	2·25
MS1148	Two sheets, each 71×48 mm. (a) $5 L.M.S. high-pressure locomotive. (b) $5 G.W.R. "King George V" Set of 2 sheets	7·00	7·50

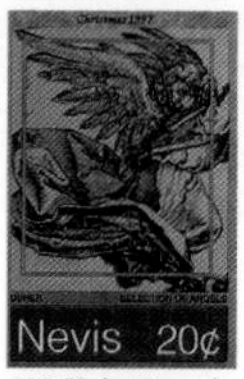

118 "Selection of Angels" (detail) (Durer)

1997. Christmas. Paintings. Multicoloured.

1149	20c. Type **118**	30	15
1150	25c. "Selection of Angels" (different detail) (Durer)	35	20
1151	50c. "Andromeda and Perseus" (Rubens)	55	30
1152	80c. "Harmony" (detail) (Raphael)	75	45
1153	$1.60 "Harmony" (different detail) (Raphael)	1·40	1·50
1154	$5 "Holy Trinity" (Raphael)	3·50	4·50
MS1155	Two sheets, each 114×104 mm. (a) $5 "Study Muse" (Raphael) (horiz). (b) $5 "Ezekiel's Vision" (Raphael) (horiz) Set of 2 sheets	6·50	7·00

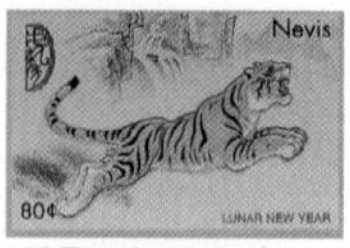

119 Tiger (semi-circular character at top left)

1998. Chinese New Year ("Year of the Tiger"). Multicoloured.

1156	80c. Type **119**	60	60
1157	80c. Oblong character at bottom right	60	60
1158	80c. Circular character at top left	60	60
1159	80c. Square character at bottom right	60	60
MS1160	67×97 mm. $2 Tiger (vert)	1·40	1·60

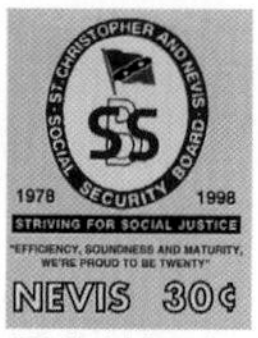

120 Social Security Board Emblem

1998. 20th Anniv of Social Security Board. Multicoloured.

1161	30c. Type **120**	20	15
1162	$1.20 Opening of Social Security building, Charlestown (horiz)	80	1·00
MS1163	100×70 mm. $6 Social Security staff (59×39 mm)	3·50	4·00

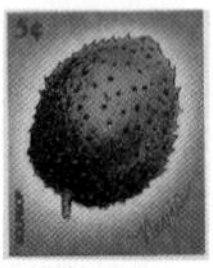

121 Soursop

1998. Fruits. Multicoloured.

1164A	5c. Type **121**	10	30
1165B	10c. Carambola	10	10
1166A	25c. Guava	25	15
1167B	30c. Papaya	15	20
1168A	50c. Mango	35	25
1169A	60c. Golden apple	40	30
1170A	80c. Pineapple	50	35
1171A	90c. Watermelon	60	40
1172A	$1 Bananas	70	50
1173B	$1.80 Orange	90	95
1174A	$3 Honeydew	1·75	1·75
1175B	$5 Canteloupe	2·50	2·75
1176B	$10 Pomegranate	5·00	5·25
1177A	$20 Cashew	9·50	11·00

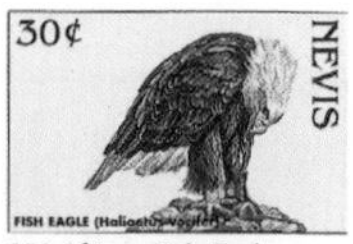

122 African Fish Eagle ("Fish Eagle")

1998. Endangered Species. Multicoloured.

1178	30c. Type **122**	40	25
1179	80c. Summer tanager at nest	60	35
1180	90c. Orang-Utan and young	65	40
1181	$1 Young chimpanzee	70	80
1182	$1 Keel-billed toucan	70	80
1183	$1 Chaco peccary	70	80
1184	$1 Spadefoot toad and insect	70	80
1185	$1 Howler monkey	70	80
1186	$1 Alaskan brown bear	70	80
1187	$1 Koala bears	70	80
1188	$1 Brown pelican	70	80
1189	$1 Iguana	70	80
1190	$1.20 Tiger cub	80	80
1191	$2 Cape pangolin	1·40	1·50
1192	$3 Hoatzin	1·75	1·90
MS1193	Two sheets, each 69×99 mm. (a) $5 Young mandrill. (b) $5 Polar bear cub Set of 2 sheets	6·50	7·00

No. 1185 is inscribed "MOWLER MONKEY" and No. 1192 "MOATZIN", both in error.

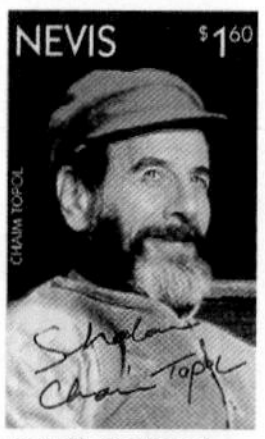

123 Chaim Topol (Israeli actor)

1998. "Israel 98" International Stamp Exn, Tel-Aviv.

1194	**123**	$1.60 multicoloured	1·60	1·60

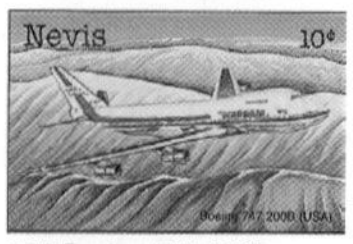

124 Boeing 747 200B (U.S.A.)

1998. Aircraft. Multicoloured.

1195	10c. Type **124**	30	30
1196	90c. Cessna 185 Skywagon (U.S.A.)	65	40
1197	$1 Northrop B-2 A (U.S.A.)	70	80
1198	$1 Lockheed SR-71A (U.S.A.)	70	80
1199	$1 Beechcraft T-44A (U.S.A.)	70	80
1200	$1 Sukhoi Su-27UB (U.S.S.R.)	70	80
1201	$1 Hawker Siddeley Harrier GR. Mk1 (Great Britain)	70	80
1202	$1 Boeing E-3A Sentry (U.S.A.)	70	80
1203	$1 Convair B-36H (U.S.A.)	70	80
1204	$1 IAI KFIR C2 (Israel)	70	80
1205	$1.80 McDonnell Douglas DC-9 SO (U.S.A.)	1·40	1·40
1206	$5 Airbus A-300 B4 (U.S.A.)	3·50	4·00
MS1207	Two sheets, each 76×106 mm. (a) $5 Lockheed F-117A (U.S.A.) (56×42 mm). (b) $5 Concorde (Great Britain) (56×42 mm) Set of 2 sheets	7·50	7·50

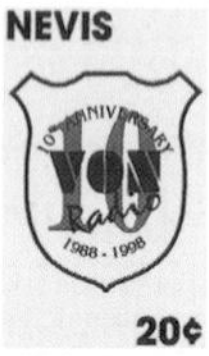

125 Anniversary Logo

1998. 10th Anniv of "Voice of Nevis" Radio.

1208	**125**	20c. vio, lt vio & blk	30	25
1209	-	30c. multicoloured	30	25
1210	-	$1.20 multicoloured	1·00	1·25
MS1211		110×85 mm. $5 multicoloured	3·25	3·50

DESIGNS: 30c. Evered Herbert (Station Manager); $1.20, V.O.N. studio; $5 Merritt Herbert (Managing Director).

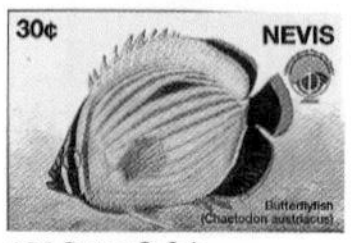

126 Butterflyfish

1998. International Year of the Ocean. Multicoloured.

1212	30c. Type **126**	30	15
1213	80c. Bicolor cherub	65	35
1214	90c. Copperbanded butterflyfish (vert)	70	80
1215	90c. Forcepsfish (vert)	70	80
1216	90c. Double-saddled butterflyfish (vert)	70	80
1217	90c. Blue surgeonfish (vert)	70	80
1218	90c. Orbiculate batfish (vert)	70	80
1219	90c. Undulated triggerfish (vert)	70	80
1220	90c. Rock beauty (vert)	70	80
1221	90c. Flamefish (vert)	70	80
1222	90c. Queen angelfish (vert)	70	80
1223	$1 Pyjama cardinal fish	70	80
1224	$1 Wimplefish	70	80
1225	$1 Long-nosed filefish	70	80
1226	$1 Oriental sweetlips	70	80

1227	$1 Blue-spotted boxfish	70	80
1228	$1 Blue-stripe angelfish	70	80
1229	$1 Goldrim tang	70	80
1230	$1 Blue chromis	70	80
1231	$1 Common clownfish	70	80
1232	$1.20 Silver badgerfish	80	80
1233	$2 Asfur angelfish	1·40	1·50
MS1234	Two sheets. (a) 76×106 mm. $5 Red-faced batfish (vert). (b) 106×76 mm. $5 Longhorned cowfish (vert) Set of 2 sheets	7·00	7·50

Nos. 1214/22 and 1223/31 respectively were printed together, se-tenant, with the backgrounds forming composite designs.

No. 1223 is inscribed "Pygama" in error.

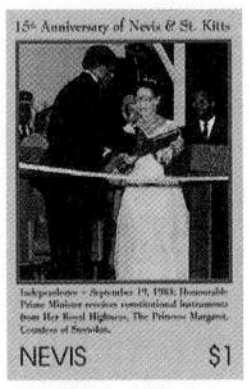

127 Prime Minister Kennedy Simmonds receiving Constitutional Instruments from Princess Margaret, 1983

1998. 15th Anniv of Independence.

1235	**127**	$1 multicoloured	70	70

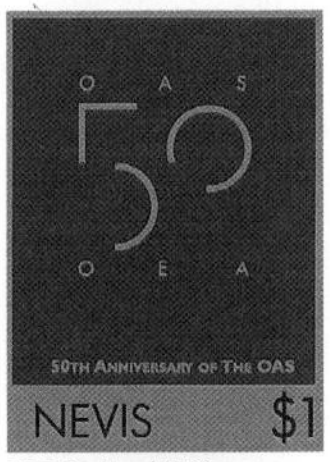

128 Stylized "50"

1998. 50th Anniv of Organization of American States.

1236	**128**	$1 blue, light blue and black	70	70

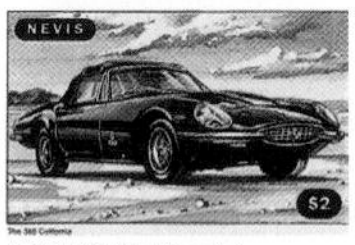

129 365 "California"

1998. Birth Centenary of Enzo Ferrari (car manufacturer). Multicoloured.

1237	$2 Type **129**	1·60	1·60
1238	$2 Pininfarina's P6	1·60	1·60
1239	$2 250 LM	1·60	1·60
MS1240	104×70 mm. $5 212 "Export Spyder" (91×34 mm)	4·50	4·75

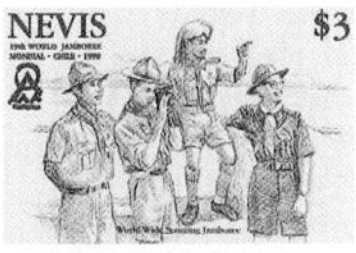

130 Scouts of Different Nationalities

1998. 19th World Scout Jamboree, Chile. Multicoloured.

1241	$3 Type **130**	2·00	2·25
1242	$3 Scout and Gettysburg veterans, 1913	2·00	2·25
1243	$3 First black scout troop, Virginia, 1928	2·00	2·25

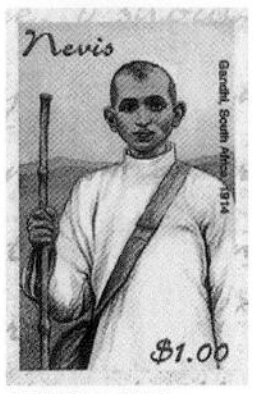

131 Gandhi in South Africa, 1914

1998. 50th Death Anniv of Mahatma Gandhi. Multicoloured.

1244	$1 Type **131**	80	80
1245	$1 Gandhi in Downing Street, London	80	80

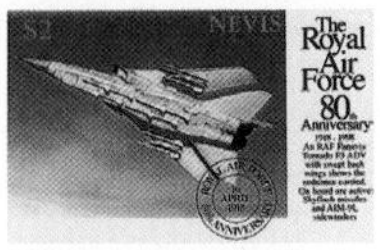

132 Panavia Tornado F3

1998. 80th Anniv of Royal Air Force. Multicoloured.

1246	$2 Type **132**	1·50	1·60
1247	$2 Panavia Tornado F3 firing Skyflash missile	1·50	1·60
1248	$2 Tristar Mk1 Tanker refuelling Tornado GR1	1·50	1·60
1249	$2 Panavia Tornado GR1 firing AIM-9L missile	1·50	1·60
MS1250	Two sheets, each 91×68 mm. (a) $5 Bristol F2B Fighter and two peregrine falcons (birds). (b) $5 Wessex helicopter and EF-2000 Eurofighter Set of 2 sheets	8·00	8·00

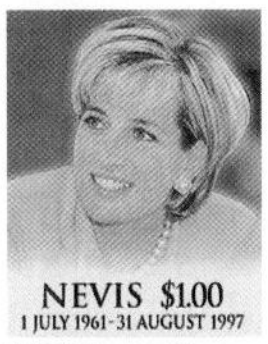

133 Princess Diana

1998. 1st Death Anniv of Diana, Princess of Wales.

1251	**133**	$1 multicoloured	75	75

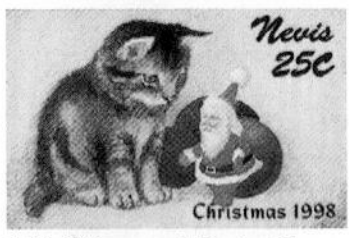

134 Kitten and Santa Claus Decoration

1998. Christmas. Multicoloured.

1252	25c. Type **134**	25	15
1253	60c. Kitten playing with bauble	40	30
1254	80c. Kitten in Christmas stocking (vert)	50	35
1255	90c. Fox Terrier puppy and presents	60	40
1256	$1 Angel with swallows	70	45
1257	$3 Boy wearing Santa hat (vert)	2·00	2·50
MS1258	Two sheets. (a) 71×102 mm. $5 Two dogs. (b) 102×71 mm. $5 Family with dog (vert) Set of 2 sheets	7·00	7·50

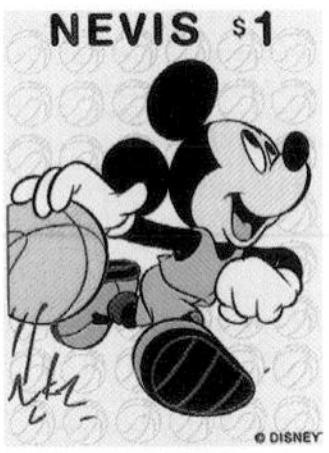

135 Mickey Mouse

1998. 70th Birthday of Mickey Mouse. Walt Disney cartoon characters playing basketball. Mult.

1259	$1 Type **135**	95	85
1260	$1 Donald Duck bouncing ball	95	85
1261	$1 Minnie Mouse in green kit	95	85
1262	$1 Goofy wearing purple	95	85
1263	$1 Huey in green baseball cap	95	85
1264	$1 Goofy and Mickey	95	85
1265	$1 Mickey bouncing ball	95	85
1266	$1 Huey, Dewey and Louie	95	85
1267	$1 Mickey, in purple, shooting ball	95	85
1268	$1 Goofy in yellow shorts and vest	95	85
1269	$1 Minnie in purple	95	85
1270	$1 Mickey in yellow vest and blue shorts	95	85
1271	$1 Minnie in yellow	95	85
1272	$1 Donald spinning ball on finger	95	85
1273	$1 Donald and Mickey	95	85
1274	$1 Dewey shooting for goal	95	85
MS1275	Four sheets. (a) 127×105 mm. $5 Minnie wearing purple bow (horiz). (b) 105×127 mm. $5 Minnie wearing green bow (horiz). (c) 105×127 mm. $6 Mickey in yellow vest (horiz). (d) 105×127 mm. $6 Mickey in purple vest (horiz) Set of 4 sheets	15·00	15·00

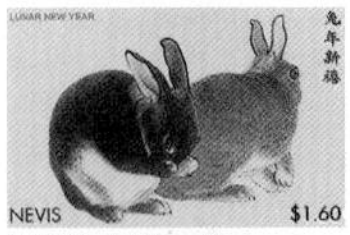

136 Black Silver Fox Rabbits

1999. Chinese New Year ("Year of the Rabbit"). Multicoloured.

1276	$1.60 Type **136**	1·25	1·25
1277	$1.60 Dutch rabbits (brown with white "collar")	1·25	1·25
1278	$1.60 Dwarf rabbits (brown)	1·25	1·25
1279	$1.60 Netherlands Dwarf rabbits (white with brown markings)	1·25	1·25
MS1280	106×76 mm. $5 Dwarf albino rabbit and young (57×46 mm)	3·25	3·50

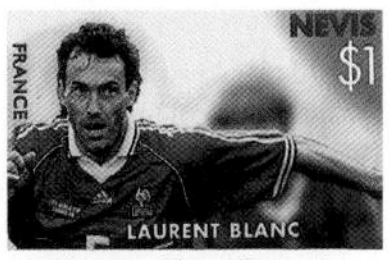

137 Laurent Blanc (France)

1999. Leading Players of 1998 World Cup Football Championship, France. Multicoloured.

1281	$1 Type **137**	75	75
1282	$1 Dennis Bergkamp (Holland)	75	75
1283	$1 Davor Sukor (Croatia)	75	75
1284	$1 Ronaldo (Brazil)	75	75
1285	$1 Didier Deschamps (France)	75	75
1286	$1 Patrick Kluivert (Holland)	75	75
1287	$1 Rivaldo (Brazil)	75	75
1288	$1 Zinedine Zidane (France)	75	75
MS1289	121×96 mm. $5 Zinedine Zidane (France)	3·25	3·50

Nos. 1281/8 were printed together, se-tenant, with the backgrounds forming a composite design.

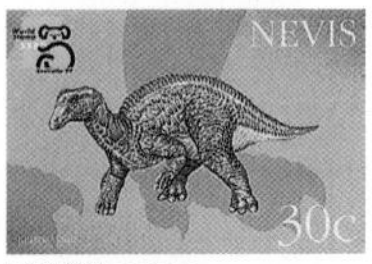

138 Kritosaurus

1999. "Australia '99" World Stamp Exhibition, Melbourne. Prehistoric Animals. Multicoloured.

1290	30c. Type **138**	40	20
1291	60c. Oviraptor	50	30
1292	80c. Eustreptospondylus	60	35
1293	$1.20 Tenontosaurus	80	85
1294	$1.20 Edmontosaurus	80	85
1295	$1.20 Avimimus	80	85
1296	$1.20 Minmi	80	85
1297	$1.20 Segnosaurus	80	85
1298	$1.20 Kentrosaurus	80	85
1299	$1.20 Deinonychus	80	85
1300	$1.20 Saltasaurus	80	85
1301	$1.20 Compsoganthus	80	85
1302	$1.20 Hadrosaurus	80	85
1303	$1.20 Tuojiangosaurus	80	85
1304	$1.20 Euoplocephalus	80	85
1305	$1.20 Anchisaurus	80	85
1306	$2 Ouranosaurus	1·40	1·50
1307	$3 Muttaburrasaurus	1·90	1·25
MS1308	Two sheets, each 110×85 mm. (a) $5 Triceratops. (b) $5 Stegosaurus Set of 2 sheets	7·00	7·50

Nos. 1294/9 and 1300/5 respectively were printed together, se-tenant, with the backgrounds forming composite designs.

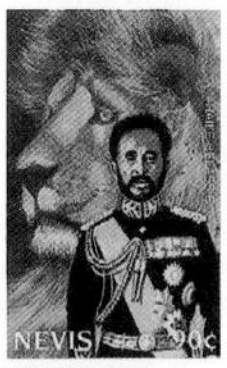

139 Emperor Haile Selassie of Ethiopia

1999. Millennium Series. Famous People of the Twentieth Century. World Leaders. Multicoloured.

1309	90c. Type **139**	80	70
1310	90c. Haile Selassie and Ethiopian warriors (56×41 mm)	80	70
1311	90c. David Ben-Gurion, woman soldier and ancient Jewish prophet (56×41 mm)	80	70
1312	90c. David Ben-Gurion (Prime Minister of Israel)	80	70
1313	90c. President Franklin D. Roosevelt of U.S.A. and Mrs. Roosevelt	80	70
1314	90c. Franklin and Eleanor Roosevelt campaigning (56×41 mm)	80	70
1315	90c. Mao Tse-tung and the Long March, 1934 (56×41 mm)	80	70
1316	90c. Poster of Mao Tse-tung (founder of People's Republic of China)	80	70
MS1317	Two sheets. (a) 76×105 mm. $5 President Nelson Mandela of South Africa. (b) 105×76 mm. $5 Mahatma Gandhi (leader of Indian Independence movement) Set of 2 sheets	7·00	7·50

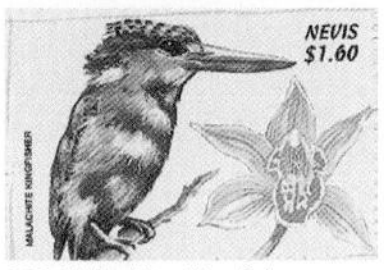

140 Malachite Kingfisher

1999. Birds. Multicoloured.

1318	$1.60 Type **140**	1·00	1·10
1319	$1.60 Lilac-breasted roller	1·00	1·10
1320	$1.60 Swallow-tailed bee eater	1·00	1·10
1321	$1.60 Jay ("Eurasian Jay")	1·00	1·10
1322	$1.60 Black-collared apalis	1·00	1·10
1323	$1.60 Grey-backed camaroptera	1·00	1·10
1324	$1.60 Yellow warbler	1·00	1·10
1325	$1.60 Common yellowthroat	1·00	1·10
1326	$1.60 Painted bunting	1·00	1·10
1327	$1.60 Belted kingfisher	1·00	1·10
1328	$1.60 American kestrel	1·00	1·10
1329	$1.60 Northern oriole	1·00	1·10
MS1330	Two sheets, each 76×106 mm. (a) $5 Bananaquit. (b) $5 Ground-scraper thrush (vert) Set of 2 sheets	7·00	7·50

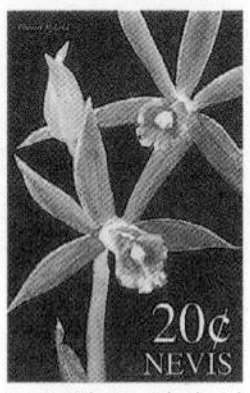

141 "Phaius" hybrid

1999. Orchids. Multicoloured.

1331	20c. Type **141**	30	20
1332	25c. "Cuitlauzina pendula"	30	20
1333	50c. "Bletilla striata"	45	25
1334	80c. "Cymbidium" "Showgirl"	60	35
1335	$1 "Cattleya intermedia"	70	75
1336	$1 "Cattleya" "Sophia Martin"	70	75
1337	$1 "Phalaenopsis" "Little Hal"	70	75
1338	$1 "Laeliocattleya alisal" "Rodeo"	70	75
1339	$1 "Laelia lucasiana fournieri"	70	75
1340	$1 "Cymbidium" "Red Beauty"	70	75
1341	$1 "Sobralia" sp.	70	75
1342	$1 "Promenaea xanthina"	70	75
1343	$1 "Cattleya pumpernickel"	70	75
1344	$1 "Odontocidium artur elle"	70	75
1345	$1 "Neostylis lou sneary"	70	75
1346	$1 "Phalaenopsis aphrodite"	70	75
1347	$1 "Arkundina graminieolia"	70	75
1348	$1 "Cymbidium" "Hunter's Point"	70	75
1349	$1 "Rhynchostylis coelestis"	70	75
1350	$1 "Cymbidium" "Elf's Castle"	70	75
1351	$1.60 "Zygopetalum crinitium" (horiz)	1·00	1·00
1352	$3 "Dendrobium nobile" (horiz)	1·90	2·25
MS1353	Two sheets, each 106×81 mm. (a) $5 "Spathoglottis plicata" (horiz). (b) $5 "Arethusa bulbosa" Set of 2 sheets	7·00	7·50

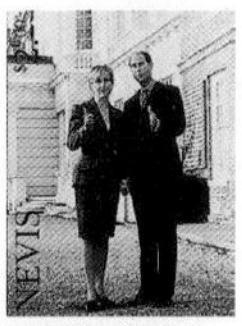

142 Miss Sophie Rhys-Jones and Prince Edward

1999. Royal Wedding. Multicoloured.

1354	$2 Type **142**	1·40	1·40
1355	$2 Miss Sophie Rhys-Jones at Ascot	1·40	1·40
1356	$2 Miss Sophie Rhys-Jones smiling	1·40	1·40
1357	$2 Prince Edward smiling	1·40	1·40
1358	$2 Miss Sophie Rhys-Jones wearing black and white checked jacket	1·40	1·40
1359	$2 Prince Edward and Miss Sophie Rhys-Jones wearing sunglasses	1·40	1·40
1360	$2 Miss Sophie Rhys-Jones wearing black hat and jacket	1·40	1·40
1361	$2 Prince Edward wearing red-striped tie	1·40	1·40
MS1362	Two sheets, each 83×66 mm. (a) $5 Prince Edward and Miss Sophie Rhys-Jones smiling (horiz). (b) $5 Prince Edward kissing Miss Sophie Rhys-Jones (horiz) Set of 2 sheets	7·00	7·50

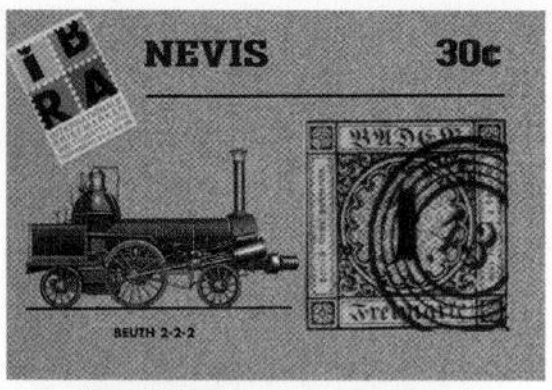

142a "Beuth" (railway locomotive) and Baden 1851 1k. stamp

1999. "iBRA '99" International Stamp Exhibition, Nuremberg. Multicoloured.

1363	30c. Type **142a**	30	25
1364	80c. "Beuth" and Brunswick 1852 1sgr. stamp	50	45
1365	90c. "Kruzenshtern" (cadet barque) and Bergedorf 1861 ½s. and 1s. stamps	60	50
1366	$1 "Kruzenshtern" and Bremen 1855 3gr. stamp	70	70
MS1367	134×90 mm. $5 1912 First Bavarian air flight label	3·25	3·50

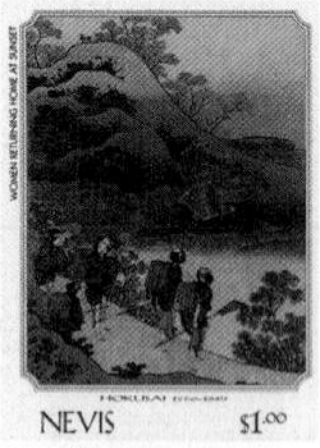

142b "Women returning Home at Sunset" (women by lake)

1999. 150th Death Anniv of Katsushika Hokusai (Japanese artist). Multicoloured.

1368	$1 Type 142a	70	80
1369	$1 "Blind Man" (without beard)	70	80
1370	$1 "Women returning Home at Sunset" (women descending hill)	70	80
1371	$1 "Young Man on a White Horse"	70	80
1372	$1 "Blind Man" (with beard)	70	80
1373	$1 "Peasant crossing a Bridge"	70	80
1374	$1.60 "Poppies" (one flower)	1·00	1·10
1375	$1.60 "Blind Man" (with beard)	1·00	1·10
1376	$1.60 "Poppies" (two flowers)	1·00	1·10
1377	$1.60 "Abe No Nakamaro gazing at the Moon from a Terrace"	1·00	1·10
1378	$1.60 "Blind Man" (without beard)	1·00	1·10
1379	$1.60 "Cranes on a Snowy Pine"	1·00	1·10
MS1380	Two sheets, each 74×103 mm. (a) $5 "Carp in a Waterfall". (b) $5 "Rider in the Snow" Set of 2 sheets	7·00	7·50

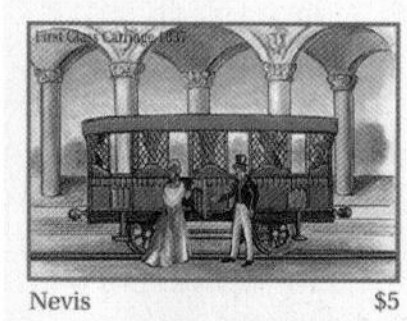

142c First Class carriage, 1837.

1999. "PhilexFrance '99" International Stamp Exhibition, Paris. Two sheets, each 106×81 mm, containing horiz designs. Multicoloured.

MS1381	(a) $5 Type 142c. (b) $5 "141.R" Mixed Traffic steam locomotive Set of 2 sheets	7·00	7·50

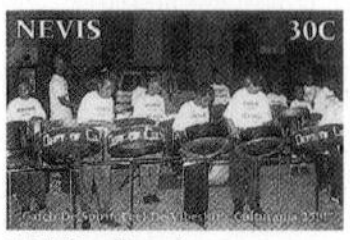

143 Steelband

1999. 25th Culturama Festival. Multicoloured.

1382	30c. Type **143**	30	15
1383	80c. Clowns	60	35
1384	$1.80 Masqueraders with band	1·40	1·10
1385	$5 Local string band	3·25	3·50
MS1386	91×105 mm. $5 Carnival dancers (50×37 mm)	3·25	3·50

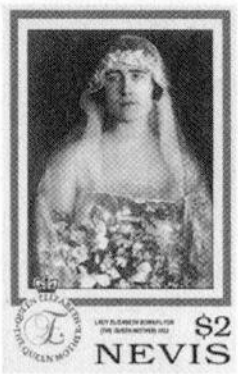

143a Lady Elizabeth Bowes-Lyon on Wedding Day, 1923

1999. "Queen Elizabeth the Queen Mother's Century".

1387	**143a**	$2 black and gold	1·50	1·50
1388	-	$2 multicoloured	1·50	1·50
1389	-	$2 black and gold	1·50	1·50
1390	-	$2 multicoloured	1·50	1·50
MS1391		153×157 mm. $6 multicoloured	3·75	4·00

DESIGNS: No. 1388, Duchess of York with Princess Elizabeth, 1926; 1389, King George VI and Queen Elizabeth during Second World War; 1390, Queen Mother in 1983. 37×49 mm: No. **MS**1391, Queen Mother in 1957.

No. **MS**1391 was also issued with the embossed gold coat of arms at bottom left replaced by the inscription "Good Health and Happiness to Her Majesty the Queen Mother on her 101st Birthday".

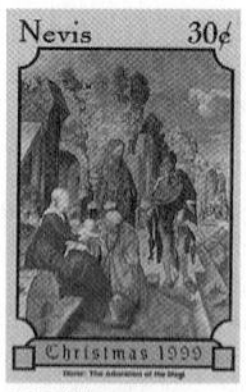

144 "The Adoration of the Magi" (Durer)

1999. Christmas. Religious Paintings. Multicoloured.

1392	30c. Type **144**	25	15
1393	90c. "Canigiani Holy Family" (Raphael)	55	40
1394	$1.20 "The Nativity" (Durer)	95	55
1395	$1.80 "Madonna and Child surrounded by Angels" (Rubens)	1·25	1·10
1396	$3 "Madonna and Child surrounded by Saints" (Rubens)	1·90	2·25
MS1397	76×106 mm. $5 "Madonna and Child by a Window" (Durer) (horiz)	3·00	3·50

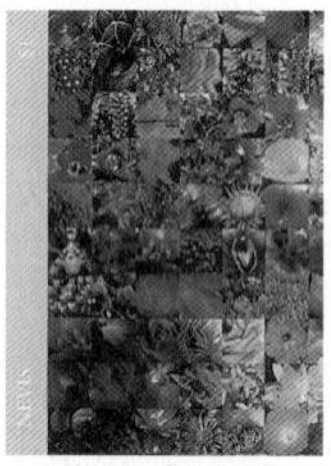

145 Flowers forming Top of Head

1999. Faces of the Millennium: Diana, Princess of Wales. Showing collage of miniature flower photographs. Multicoloured.

1398	$1 Type **145** (face value at left)	75	75
1399	$1 Top of head (face value at right)	75	75
1400	$1 Ear (face value at left)	75	75
1401	$1 Eye and temple (face value at right)	75	75
1402	$1 Cheek (face value at left)	75	75
1403	$1 Cheek (face value at right)	75	75
1404	$1 Blue background (face value at left)	75	75
1405	$1 Chin (face value at right)	75	75

Nos. 1398/1405 were printed together, se-tenant, and when viewed as a sheetlet, forms a portrait of Diana, Princess of Wales.

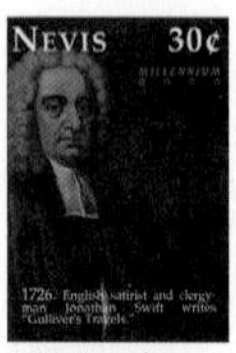

145a Jonathan Swift ("Gulliver's Travels", 1726)

2000. New Millennium. People and Events of Eighteenth Century (1700–49). Multicoloured.

1406	30c. Type **145a**	35	30
1407	30c. Emperor Kangxi of China	35	30
1408	30c. Bartolommeo Cristofori (invention of piano, 1709)	35	30
1409	30c. Captain William Kidd hanging on gibbet, 1701	35	30
1410	30c. William Herschel (astronomer)	35	30
1411	30c. King George I of Great Britain, 1714	35	30
1412	30c. Peter the Great of Russia (trade treaty with China, 1720)	35	30
1413	30c. "Death" (bubonic plague in Austria and Germany, 1711)	35	30
1414	30c. "Standing Woman" (Kaigetsudo Dohan (Japanese artist))	35	30
1415	30c. Queen Anne of England, 1707	35	30
1416	30c. Anders Celcius (invention of centigrade thermometer, 1742)	35	30
1417	30c. Vitus Bering (discovery of Alaska and Aleutian Islands, 1741)	35	30
1418	30c. Edmund Halley (calculation of Halley's Comet, 1705)	35	30
1419	30c. John Wesley (founder of Methodist Church, 1729)	35	30
1420	30c. Sir Isaac Newton (publication of "Optick Treatise", 1704)	35	30
1421	30c. Queen Anne (Act of Union between England and Scotland, 1707) (59×39 mm)	35	30
1422	30c. Johann Sebastian Bach (composition of "The Well-tempered Klavier", 1722)	35	30

No. 1418 is inscribed "cometis" in error.

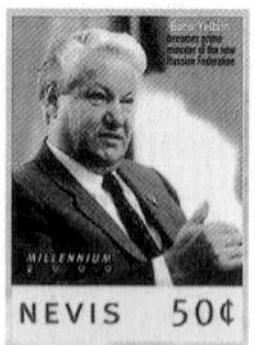

146 Boris Yeltsin (President of Russian Federation, 1991)

2000. New Millennium. People and Events of Twentieth Century (1990–99). Multicoloured.

1423	50c. Type **146**	45	40
1424	50c. American soldiers and burning oil wells (Gulf War, 1991)	45	40
1425	50c. Soldiers (Bosnian Civil War, 1992)	45	40
1426	50c. Pres. Clinton, Yitzchak Rabin and Yasser Arafat (Oslo Accords, 1993)	45	40
1427	50c. Prime Ministers John Major and Albert Reynolds (Joint Declaration on Northern Ireland, 1993)	45	40
1428	50c. Frederik de Klerk and Nelson Mandela (end of Apartheid, South Africa, 1994)	45	40
1429	50c. Cal Ripkin (record number of consecutive baseball games, 1995)	45	40
1430	50c. Kobe from air (earthquake, 1995)	45	40
1431	50c. Mummified Inca girl preserved in ice, 1995	45	40
1432	50c. NASA's "Sojourner" on Mars, 1997	45	40
1433	50c. Dr. Ian Wilmat and cloned sheep, 1997	45	40
1434	50c. Death of Princess Diana, 1997	45	40
1435	50c. Fireworks over Hong Kong on its return to China, 1997	45	40
1436	50c. Mother with septuplets, 1998	45	40
1437	50c. Guggenheim Museum, Bilbao, 1998	45	40
1438	50c. "2000" and solar eclipse, 1999 (59×39 mm)	45	40
1439	50c. Pres. Clinton (impeachment in 1999)	45	40

No. 1423 incorrectly identifies his office as "Prime Minister".

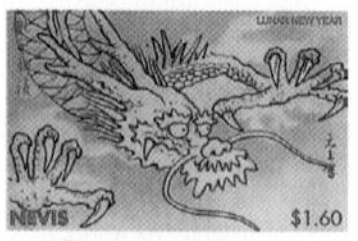

147 Dragon

2000. Chinese New Year ("Year of the Dragon"). Multicoloured.

1440	$1.60 Type **147**	1·10	1·10
1441	$1.60 Dragon with open claws (face value bottom left)	1·10	1·10
1442	$1.60 Dragon holding sphere (face value bottom right)	1·10	1·10
1443	$1.60 Dragon looking up (face value bottom left)	1·10	1·10
MS1444	76×106 mm. $5 Dragon (37×50 mm)	3·50	3·75

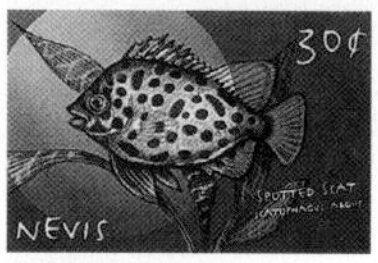

148 Spotted Scat

2000. Tropical Fish. Showing fish in spotlight. Multicoloured.

1445	30c. Type **148**	30	15
1446	80c. Delta topsail platy ("Platy Variatus")	55	35
1447	90c. Emerald betta	65	40
1448	$1 Sail-finned tang	75	80
1449	$1 Black-capped basslet ("Black-capped Gramma")	75	80
1450	$1 Sail-finned snapper ("Majestic Snapper")	75	80
1451	$1 Purple fire goby	75	80
1452	$1 Clown triggerfish	75	80
1453	$1 Forceps butterflyfish ("Yellow Long-nose")	75	80
1454	$1 Clown wrasse	75	80
1455	$1 Yellow-headed jawfish	75	80
1456	$1 Oriental sweetlips	75	80
1457	$1 Royal gramma	75	80
1458	$1 Thread-finned butterflyfish	75	80
1459	$1 Yellow tang	75	80
1460	$1 Bicoloured angelfish	75	80
1461	$1 Catalina goby	75	80
1462	$1 Striped mimic blenny ("False Cleanerfish")	75	80
1463	$1 Powder-blue surgeonfish	75	80
1464	$4 Long-horned cowfish	2·75	3·00
MS1465	Two sheets, each 97×68 mm. (a) $5 Clown killifish. (b) $5 Twin-spotted wrasse ("Clown Coris") Set of 2 sheets	7·00	7·50

Nos. 1448/55 and 1456/63 were each printed together, se-tenant, the backgrounds forming composite designs.

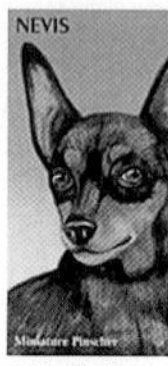

149 Miniature Pinscher

2000. Dogs of the World. Multicoloured.

1466	10c. Type **149**	20	30
1467	20c. Pyrenean mountain dog	25	30
1468	30c. Welsh springer spaniel	30	20
1469	80c. Alaskan malamute	65	40
1470	90c. Beagle (horiz)	75	80
1471	90c. Bassett hound (horiz)	75	80
1472	90c. St. Bernard (horiz)	75	80
1473	90c. Rough collie (horiz)	75	80
1474	90c. Shih tzu (horiz)	75	80
1475	90c. American bulldog (horiz)	75	80
1476	$1 Irish red and white setter (horiz)	75	80
1477	$1 Dalmatian (horiz)	75	80
1478	$1 Pomeranian (horiz)	75	80
1479	$1 Chihuahua (horiz)	75	80
1480	$1 English sheepdog (horiz)	75	80
1481	$1 Samoyed (horiz)	75	80
1482	$2 Bearded collie	1·40	1·50
1483	$3 American cocker spaniel	1·90	2·25
MS1484	Two sheets. (a) 76×106 mm. $5 Leonberger dog. (b) 106×76 mm. $5 Longhaired miniature dachshund (horiz) Set of 2 sheets	7·00	7·50

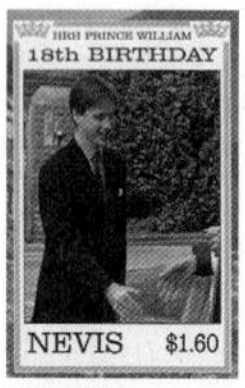

149a Prince William shaking hands

2000. 18th Birthday of Prince William. Mult.

1485	$1.60 Type **149a**	1·10	1·10
1486	$1.60 Wearing ski outfit	1·10	1·10
1487	$1.60 At airport	1·10	1·10
1488	$1.60 Wearing blue shirt and jumper	1·10	1·10
MS1489	100×80 mm. $5 At official engagement (38×50 mm)	3·50	3·75

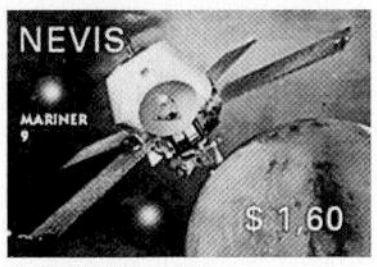

150 "Mariner 9"

2000. "EXPO 2000" World Stamp Exhibition, Anaheim, U.S.A. Exploration of Mars. Multicoloured.

1490	$1.60 Type **150**	1·10	1·10
1491	$1.60 "Mars 3"	1·10	1·10
1492	$1.60 "Mariner 4"	1·10	1·10
1493	$1.60 "Planet B"	1·10	1·10
1494	$1.60 "Mars Express Lander"	1·10	1·10
1495	$1.60 "Mars Express"	1·10	1·10
1496	$1.60 "Mars 4"	1·10	1·10
1497	$1.60 "Mars Water"	1·10	1·10
1498	$1.60 "Mars 1"	1·10	1·10
1499	$1.60 "Viking"	1·10	1·10
1500	$1.60 "Mariner 7"	1·10	1·10
1501	$1.60 "Mars Surveyor"	1·10	1·10
MS1502	Two sheets, each 106×76 mm. (a) $5 "Mars Observer" (horiz). (b) $5 "Mars Climate Orbiter" Set of 2 sheets	7·00	7·50

Nos. 1490/5 and 1496/1501 were each printed together, se-tenant, with the backgrounds forming composite designs.

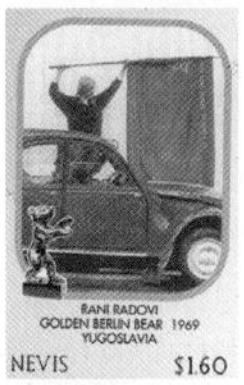

150b "Rani Radovi", 1969

2000. 50th Anniv of Berlin Film Festival. Showing actors, directors and film scenes with awards. Multicoloured.

1503	$1.60 Type **150b**	1·10	1·10
1504	$1.60 Salvatore Giuliano (director), 1962	1·10	1·10
1505	$1.60 "Schonzeit fur Fuches", 1966	1·10	1·10
1506	$1.60 Shirley Maclaine (actress), 1971	1·10	1·10
1507	$1.60 Simone Signoret (actress), 1971	1·10	1·10
1508	$1.60 Tabejad Bijad (director), 1974	1·10	1·10
MS1509	97×103 mm. $5 "Komissar", 1988	3·50	3·75

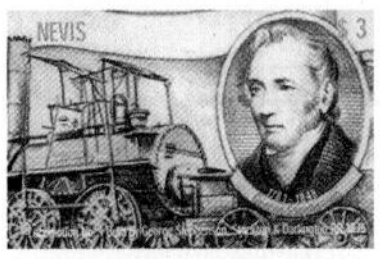

150c Locomotion No. 1, 1875, and George Stephenson

2000. 175th Anniv of Stockton and Darlington Line (first public railway). Multicoloured.

1510	$3 Type**150b**	2·25	2·25
1511	$3 Original drawing of Richard Trevithick's locomotive, 1804	2·25	2·25

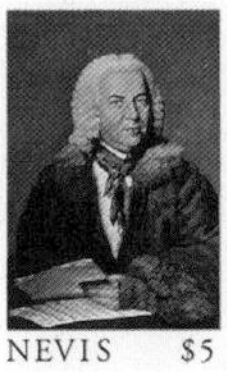

150d Johann Sebastian Bach

2000. 250th Death Anniv of Johann Sebastian Bach (German composer). Sheet 76×88 mm, containing vert design.

MS1512	$5 multicoloured	3·50	3·75

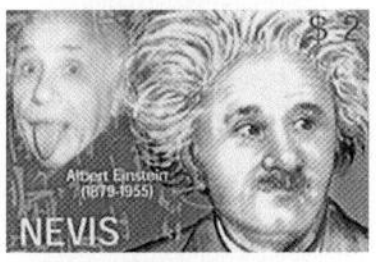

151 Albert Einstein

2000. Election of Albert Einstein (mathematical physicist) as Time Magazine "Man of the Century". Showing portraits with photographs in background. Multicoloured.

1513	$2 Type **151**	1·60	1·60
1514	$2 Riding bicycle	1·60	1·60
1515	$2 Standing on beach	1·60	1·60

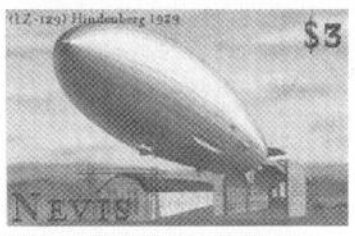

151a LZ-129 *Hindenburg*, 1929

2000. Centenary of First Zeppelin Flight.

1516	**151a**	$3 green, purple and black	2·00	2·25
1517	-	$3 green, purple and black	2·00	2·25
1518	-	$3 green, purple and black	2·00	2·25
MS1519		116×76 mm. $5 green, mauve and black	3·50	3·75

DESIGNS: (38×24 mm)—No. 1517, LZ-1, 1900; 1518, LZ-11 *Viktoria Luise*. (50×37 mm)—No. **MS**1519, LZ-127 *Graf Zeppelin*, 1928.

No. 1516 is inscribed "Hindenberg" in error.

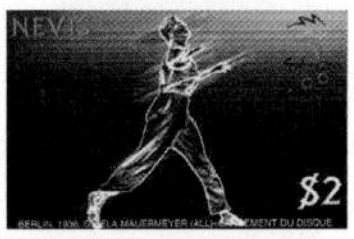

151b Gisela Mauermeyer (discus), Berlin (1936)

2000. Olympic Games, Sydney. Multicoloured.

1520	$2 Type **151b**	1·40	1·40
1521	$2 Gymnast on uneven bars	1·40	1·40
1522	$2 Wembley Stadium, London (1948) and Union Jack	1·40	1·40
1523	$2 Ancient Greek horseman	1·40	1·40

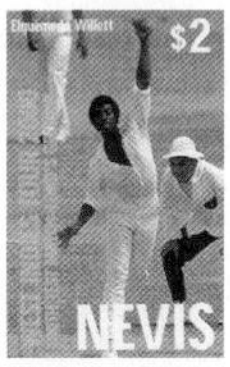

151c Elquemeda Willett

2000. West Indies Cricket Tour and 100th Test Match at Lord's. Multicoloured.

1524	$2 Type **151c**	1·50	1·25
1525	$3 Keith Arthurton	2·00	2·25
MS1526	121×104 mm. $5 Lord's Cricket Ground (horiz)	3·25	3·50

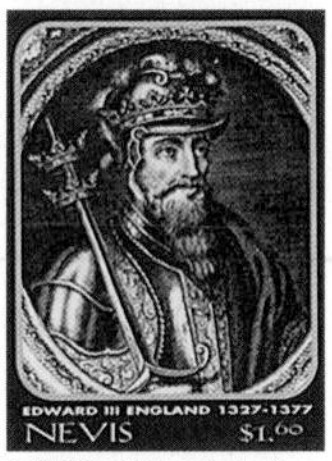

152 King Edward III of England

2000. Monarchs of the Millennium.

1527	**152**	$1.60 black, stone and brown	1·25	1·25
1528	-	$1.60 multicoloured	1·25	1·25
1529	-	$1.60 multicoloured	1·25	1·25
1530	-	$1.60 black, stone and brown	1·25	1·25
1531	-	$1.60 black, stone and brown	1·25	1·25
1532	-	$1.60 purple, stone and brown	1·25	1·25
MS1533		115×135 mm. $5 multicoloured	3·50	3·75

DESIGNS: No. 1528, Emperor Charles V (of Spain); 1529, King Joseph II of Hungary; 1530, Emperor Henry II of Germany; 1531, King Louis IV of France; 1532, King Ludwig II of Bavaria; **MS**1533, King Louis IX of France.

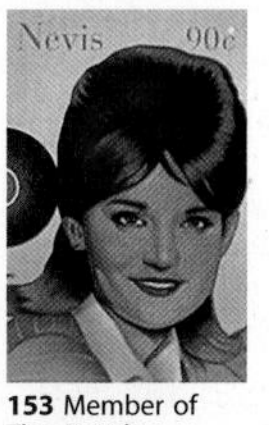

153 Member of The Angels

2000. Famous Girl Pop Groups. Multicoloured.

1534	90c. Type **153**	60	60
1535	90c. Member of The Angels with long hair	60	60
1536	90c. Member of The Angels with chin on hand	60	60
1537	90c. Member of The Dixie Cups (record at left)	60	60
1538	90c. Member of The Dixie Cups with shoulder-length hair	60	60
1539	90c. Member of The Dixie Cups with short hair and slide	60	60
1540	90c. Member of The Vandellas (record at left)	60	60
1541	90c. Member of The Vandellas ("Nevis" clear of hair)	60	60
1542	90c. Member of The Vandellas ("is" of "Nevis" on hair)	60	60

Each horizontal row depicts a different group with Nos. 1534/6 having green backgrounds, Nos. 1537/9 yellow and Nos. 1540/2 mauve.

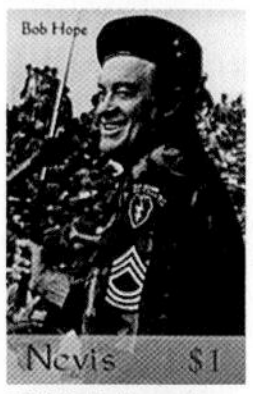

154 Bob Hope in Ranger Uniform, Vietnam

2000. Bob Hope (American entertainer).

1543	**154**	$1 black, grey and mauve	75	75
1544	-	$1 Indian red, grey and mauve	75	75
1545	-	$1 black, grey and mauve	75	75
1546	-	$1 multicoloured	75	75
1547	-	$1 black, grey and mauve	75	75
1548	-	$1 multicoloured	75	75

DESIGNS: No. 1544, On stage with Sammy Davis Jnr.; 1545, With wife Dolores; 1546, Playing golf; 1547, Making radio broadcast; 1548, Visiting Great Wall of China.

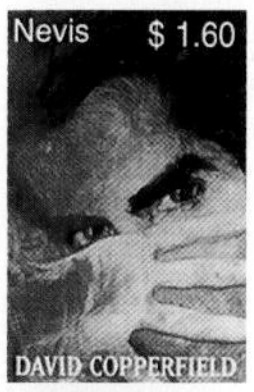

155 David Copperfield

2000. David Copperfield (conjurer).

1549	**155**	$1.60 multicoloured	1·25	1·25

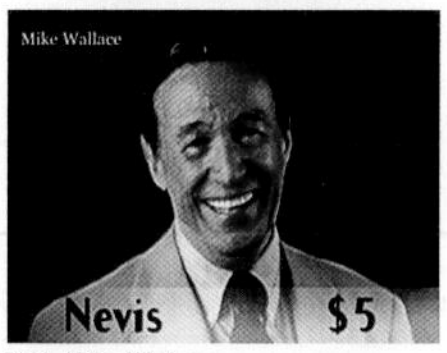

156 Mike Wallace

2000. Mike Wallace (television journalist). Sheet 120×112 mm.

MS1550	**156** $5 multicoloured	3·25	3·50

2000. 2nd Caribbean Beekeeping Congress. No. MS801 optd 2nd Caribbean Beekeeping Congress August 14–18, 2000 on top margin.

MS1551	100×70 mm. $6 Queen and workers in hive and mechanical honey extractor	3·75	4·00

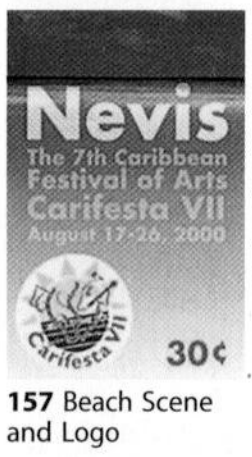

157 Beach Scene and Logo

2000. "Carifesta VII" Arts Festival. Multicoloured.

1552	30c. Type **157**	30	15
1553	90c. Carnival scenes	65	45
1554	$1.20 Stylized dancer with streamers	90	1·10

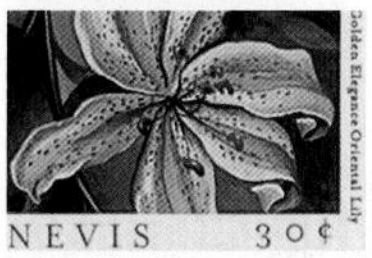

158 Golden Elegance Oriental Lily

2000. Caribbean Flowers. Multicoloured.

1555	30c. Type **158**	30	20
1556	80c. Frangipani	60	35
1557	90c. Star of the March	70	75
1558	90c. Tiger lily	70	75
1559	90c. Mont Blanc lily	70	75
1560	90c. Torch ginger	70	75
1561	90c. Cattleya orchid	70	75
1562	90c. St. John's wort	70	75
1563	$1 Culebra	70	75
1564	$1 Rubellum lily	70	75
1565	$1 Silver elegance oriental lily	70	75
1566	$1 Chinese hibiscus	70	75
1567	$1 Tiger lily (different)	70	75
1568	$1 Royal poincia	70	75
1569	$1.60 Epiphyte	1·00	1·10
1570	$1.60 Enchantment lily	1·00	1·10
1571	$1.60 Glory lily	1·00	1·10
1572	$1.60 Purple granadilla	1·00	1·10
1573	$1.60 Jacaranda	1·00	1·10
1574	$1.60 Shrimp plant	1·00	1·10
1575	$1.60 Garden zinnia	1·00	1·10
1576	$5 Rose elegance lily	3·25	3·50
MS1577	Two sheets. (a) 75×90 mm. $5 Bird of paradise (plant). (b) 90×75 mm. $5 Dahlia Set of 2 sheets	7·00	7·50

Nos. 1557/62, 1563/8 and 1569/74 were each printed together, se-tenant, with the backgrounds forming composite designs.

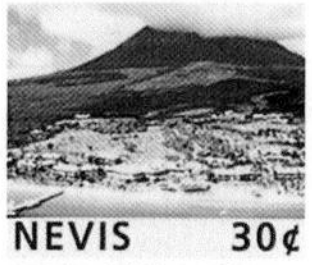

159 Aerial View of Resort

2000. Re-opening of Four Seasons Resort. Mult.

1578	30c. Type **159**	50	50
1579	30c. Palm trees on beach	50	50
1580	30c. Golf course	50	50
1581	30c. Couple at water's edge	50	50

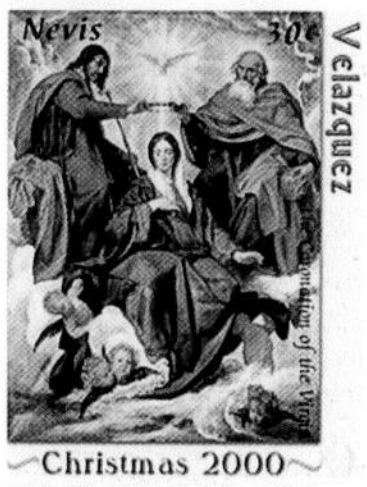

160 "The Coronation of the Virgin" (Velazquez)

2000. Christmas. Religious Paintings. Multicoloured.

1582	30c. Type **160**	25	15
1583	80c. "The Immaculate Conception" (Velazquez)	55	35
1584	90c. "Madonna and Child" (Titian) (horiz)	60	40
1585	$1.20 "Madonna and Child with St. John the Baptist and St. Catherine" (Titian) (horiz)	90	1·10
MS1586	108×108 mm. $6 "Madonna and Child with St. Catherine" (Titian) (horiz)	3·75	4·00

Nos. 1584/5 are both inscribed "Titien" in error.

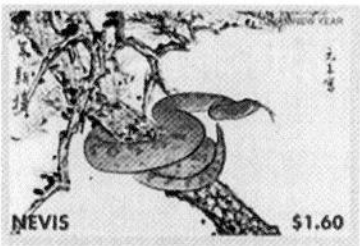

161 Snake coiled around Branch

2001. Chinese New Year. "Year of the Snake". Multicoloured.

1587	$1.60 Type **161**	1·10	1·10
1588	$1.60 Snake in tree	1·10	1·10
1589	$1.60 Snake on path	1·10	1·10
1590	$1.60 Snake by rocks	1·10	1·10
MS1591	70×100 mm. $5 Cobra at foot of cliff	3·25	3·50

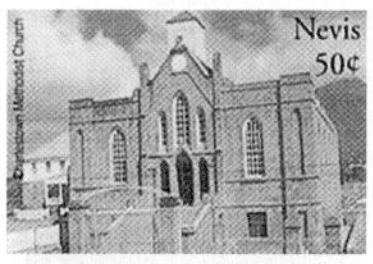

162 Charlestown Methodist Church

2001. Leeward Islands District Methodist Church Conference. Multicoloured.

1592	50c. Type **162**	35	40
1593	50c. Jessups Methodist Church	35	40
1594	50c. Clifton Methodist Church	35	40
1595	50c. Trinity Methodist Church	35	40
1596	50c. Combermere Methodist Church	35	40

1597	50c. New River Methodist Church	35	40
1598	50c. Gingerland Methodist Church	35	40

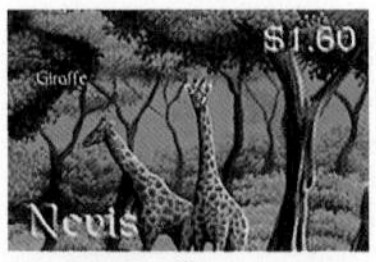

163 Two Giraffes

2001. Wildlife from "The Garden of Eden". Multicoloured.

1599	$1.60 Type **163**	1·10	1·10
1600	$1.60 Rainbow boa constrictor	1·10	1·10
1601	$1.60 Suffolk sheep and mountain cottontail hare	1·10	1·10
1602	$1.60 Bluebuck antelope	1·10	1·10
1603	$1.60 Fox	1·10	1·10
1604	$1.60 Box turtle	1·10	1·10
1605	$1.60 Pileated woodpecker ("Red-crested Woodpecker") and unicorn	1·10	1·10
1606	$1.60 African elephant	1·10	1·10
1607	$1.60 Siberian tiger	1·10	1·10
1608	$1.60 Greater flamingo and Adam and Eve	1·10	1·10
1609	$1.60 Hippopotamus	1·10	1·10
1610	$1.60 Harlequin frog	1·10	1·10
MS1611	Four sheets, each 84×69 mm. (a) $5 Keel-billed toucan ("Toucan") (vert). (b) $5 American bald eagle. (c) $5 Koala bear (vert). (d) $5 Blue and yellow macaw (vert) Set of 4 sheets	13·00	14·00

Nos. 1599/1604 and 1605/10 were each printed together, se-tenant, with the backgrounds forming composite designs.

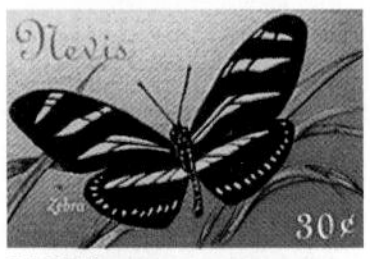

164 Zebra

2001. Butterflies of Nevis. Multicoloured.

1612	30c. Type **164**	35	20
1613	80c. Julia	65	40
1614	$1 Ruddy dagger	75	80
1615	$1 Common morpho	75	80
1616	$1 Banded king shoemaker	75	80
1617	$1 Figure of eight	75	80
1618	$1 Grecian shoemaker	75	80
1619	$1 Mosaic	75	80
1620	$1 White peacock	75	80
1621	$1 Hewitson's blue hairstreak	75	80
1622	$1 Tiger pierid	75	80
1623	$1 Gold drop helicopsis	75	80
1624	$1 Cramer's mesene	75	80
1625	$1 Red-banded pereute	75	80
1626	$1.60 Small flambeau	1·10	1·10
1627	$5 Purple mort bleu	3·25	3·50
MS1628	Two sheets, each 72×100 mm. (a) $5 Common mechanitis. (b) $5 Hewitson's pierella Set of 2 sheets	7·00	7·50

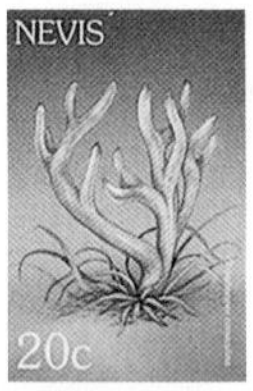

165 *Clavulinopsis corniculata*

2001. Caribbean Fungi. Multicoloured.

1629	20c. Type **165**	25	20
1630	25c. *Cantharellus cibarius*	25	20
1631	50c. *Chlorociboria aeruginascens*	40	30
1632	80c. *Auricularia auricula-judae*	65	40
1633	$1 *Entoloma incanum*	75	80
1634	$1 *Entoloma nitidum*	75	80
1635	$1 *Stropharia cyanea*	75	80
1636	$1 *Otidea onotica*	75	80
1637	$1 *Aleuria aurantia*	75	80
1638	$1 *Mitrula paludosa*	75	80
1639	$1 *Gyromitra esculenta*	75	80
1640	$1 *Helvella crispa*	75	80
1641	$1 *Morcella semilibera*	75	80
1642	$2 *Peziza vesiculosa*	1·40	1·50
1643	$3 *Mycena acicula*	1·90	2·25
MS1644	Two sheets, each 110×85 mm. (a) $5 *Russula sardonia*. (b) $5 *Omphalotus olearius* Set of 2 sheets	7·00	7·50

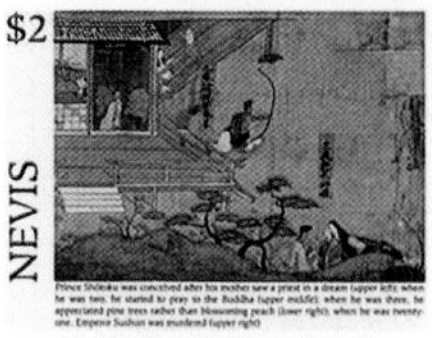

166 Early Life of Prince Shotoku

2001. "Philanippon 01" International Stamp Exhibition, Tokyo. Prince Shotoku Pictorial Scroll. Multicoloured.

1645	$2 Type **166**	1·40	1·40
1646	$2 With priests and nuns, and preaching	1·40	1·40
1647	$2 Subduing the Ezo	1·40	1·40
1648	$2 Playing with children	1·40	1·40
1649	$2 Passing through gate	1·40	1·40
1650	$2 Battle against Mononobe-no-Moriya	1·40	1·40
1651	$2 Yumedono Hall	1·40	1·40
1652	$2 Watching dog and deer	1·40	1·40

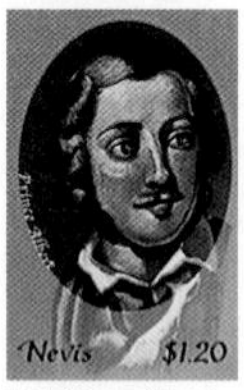

167 Prince Albert

2001. Death Centenary of Queen Victoria. Multicoloured.

1653	$1.20 Type **167**	90	90
1654	$1.20 Queen Victoria at accession	90	90
1655	$1.20 Queen Victoria as a young girl	90	90
1656	$1.20 Victoria Mary Louisa, Duchess of Kent (Queen Victoria's mother)	90	90
1657	$1.20 Queen Victoria in old age	90	90
1658	$1.20 Albert Edward, Prince of Wales as a boy	90	90
MS1659	97×70 mm. $5 Queen Victoria at accession	3·25	3·50

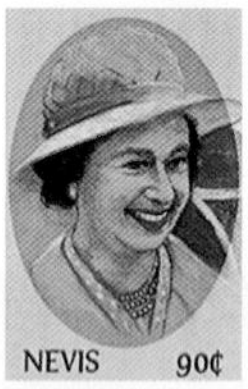

168 Queen Elizabeth II wearing Blue Hat

2001. Queen Elizabeth II's 75th Birthday. Multicoloured.

1660	90c. Type **168**	80	80
1661	90c. Wearing tiara	80	80
1662	90c. Wearing yellow hat	80	80
1663	90c. Wearing grey hat	80	80
1664	90c. Wearing red hat	80	80
1665	90c. Bare-headed and wearing pearl necklace	80	80
MS1666	95×107 mm. $5 Wearing blue hat	4·00	4·25

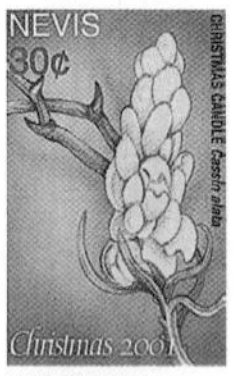

169 Christmas Candle (flower)

2001. Christmas. Flowers. Multicoloured.

1667	30c. Type **169**	25	15
1668	90c. Poinsettia (horiz)	60	40
1669	$1.20 Snowbush (horiz)	85	65
1670	$3 Tiger claw	1·90	2·25

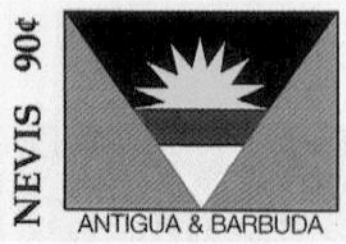

170 Flag of Antigua & Barbuda

2001. Flags of the Caribbean Community. Multicoloured.

1671	90c. Type **170**	1·00	1·00
1672	90c. Bahamas	1·00	1·00
1673	90c. Barbados	1·00	1·00
1674	90c. Belize	1·00	1·00
1675	90c. Dominica	1·00	1·00
1676	90c. Grenada	1·00	1·00
1677	90c. Guyana	1·00	1·00
1678	90c. Jamaica	1·00	1·00
1679	90c. Montserrat	1·00	1·00
1680	90c. St. Kitts & Nevis	1·00	1·00
1681	90c. St. Lucia	1·00	1·00
1682	90c. Surinam	1·00	1·00
1683	90c. St. Vincent and the Grenadines	1·00	1·00
1684	90c. Trinidad & Tobago	1·00	1·00

No. 1675 shows the former flag of Dominica, superseded in 1990.

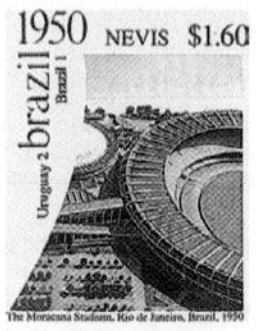

171 Maracana Football Stadium, Brazil 1950

2001. World Cup Football Championship, Japan and Korea (2002). Multicoloured.

1685	$1.60 Type **171**	1·10	1·10
1686	$1.60 Ferenc Puskas (Hungary), Switzerland 1954	1·10	1·10
1687	$1.60 Luiz Bellini (Brazil), Sweden 1958	1·10	1·10
1688	$1.60 Mauro (Brazil), Chile 1962	1·10	1·10
1689	$1.60 West German cap, England 1966	1·10	1·10
1690	$1.60 Pennant, Mexico 1970	1·10	1·10
1691	$1.60 Passarella (Argentina), Argentina 1978	1·10	1·10
1692	$1.60 Dino Zoff (Italy), Spain 1982	1·10	1·10
1693	$1.60 Azteca Stadium, Mexico 1986	1·10	1·10
1694	$1.60 San Siro Stadium, Italy 1990	1·10	1·10
1695	$1.60 Dennis Bergkamp (Holland), U.S.A. 1994	1·10	1·10
1696	$1.60 Stade de France, France 1998	1·10	1·10
MS1697	Two sheets, each 88×75 mm. (a) $5 Detail of Jules Rimet Trophy, Uruguay 1930. (b) $5 Detail of World Cup Trophy, Japan/Korea 2002 Set of 2 sheets	7·00	7·50

Nos. 1685 and 1687 are inscribed "Morocana" and "Luis" respectively, both in error.

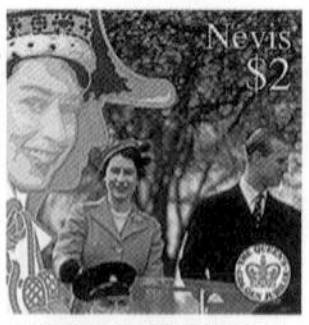

172 Queen Elizabeth and Duke of Edinburgh in reviewing Car

2002. Golden Jubilee. Multicoloured.

1698	$2 Type **172**	1·75	1·75
1699	$2 Prince Philip	1·75	1·75
1700	$2 Queen Elizabeth wearing yellow coat and hat	1·75	1·75
1701	$2 Queen Elizabeth and horse at polo match	1·75	1·75
MS1702	76×108 mm. $5 Queen Elizabeth with Prince Philip in naval uniform	3·50	3·75

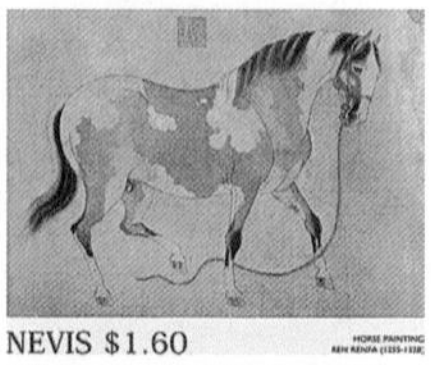

173 Chestnut and White Horse

2002. Chinese New Year ("Year of the Horse"). Paintings by Ren Renfa. Multicoloured.

1703	$1.60 Type **173**	1·10	1·10
1704	$1.60 Bay horse	1·10	1·10
1705	$1.60 Brown horse	1·10	1·10
1706	$1.60 Dappled grey horse	1·10	1·10

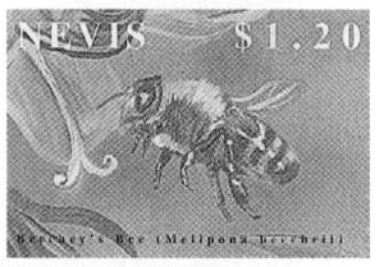

174 Beechey's Bee

2002. Fauna. Multicoloured.

1707	$1.20 Type **174**	90	90
1708	$1.20 Banded king shoemaker butterfly	90	90
1709	$1.20 Streaked sphinx caterpillar	90	90
1710	$1.20 Hercules beetle	90	90
1711	$1.20 South American palm weevil	90	90
1712	$1.20 Giant katydid	90	90
1713	$1.60 Roseate spoonbill	1·10	1·10
1714	$1.60 White-tailed tropicbird	1·10	1·10
1715	$1.60 Ruby-throated tropicbird	1·10	1·10
1716	$1.60 Black skimmer	1·10	1·10
1717	$1.60 Black-necked stilt	1·10	1·10
1718	$1.60 Mourning dove	1·10	1·10
1719	$1.60 Sperm whale and calf	1·10	1·10
1720	$1.60 Killer whale	1·10	1·10
1721	$1.60 Minke whales	1·10	1·10
1722	$1.60 Fin whale	1·10	1·10
1723	$1.60 Blaineville's beaked whale	1·10	1·10
1724	$1.60 Pygmy sperm whale	1·10	1·10
MS1725	Three sheets, each 105×78 mm. (a) $5 Click beetle. (b) $5 Royal tern. (c) $5 Humpback whale (vert)	9·50	10·50

Nos. 1707/12 (insects), 1713/18 (birds) and 1719/24 (whales) were each printed together, se-tenant, with the backgrounds forming composite designs.

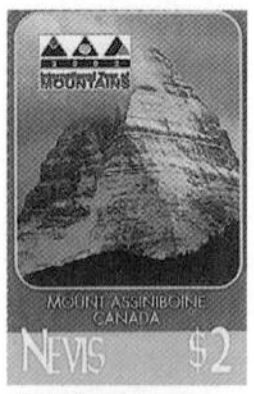

175 Mount Assiniboine, Canada

2002. International Year of Mountains. Multicoloured.

1726	$2 Type **175**	1·40	1·40
1727	$2 Mount Atitlan, Guatemala	1·40	1·40
1728	$2 Mount Adams, U.S.A.	1·40	1·40
1729	$2 The Matterhorn, Switzerland	1·40	1·40
1730	$2 Mount Dhaulagiri, Nepal	1·40	1·40
1731	$2 Mount Chamlang, Nepal	1·40	1·40
MS1732	106×125 mm. $5 Mount Kvaenangen, Norway	3·25	3·50

Nos. 1727 and 1729 are inscribed "ATAILAN" and "MATTHERORN", both in error.

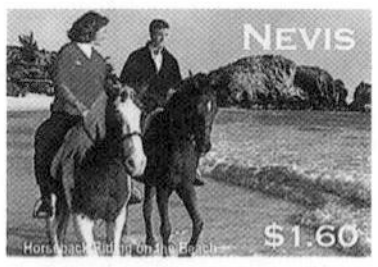

176 Horse-riders on Beach

2002. Year of Eco Tourism. Multicoloured.

1733	$1.60 Type **176**	1·40	1·40
1734	$1.60 Windsurfing	1·40	1·40
1735	$1.60 Pinney's Beach	1·40	1·40
1736	$1.60 Hikers by beach	1·40	1·40
1737	$1.60 Robert T. Jones Golf Course	1·40	1·40
1738	$1.60 Scuba diver and fish	1·40	1·40
MS1739	115×90 mm. $5 Snorkel diver on reef	3·25	3·50

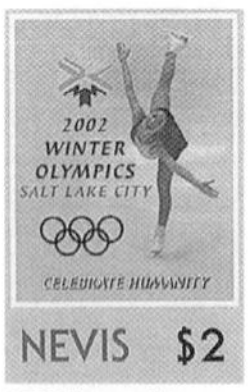

177 Women's Figure Skating

2002. Winter Olympic Games, Salt Lake City. Multicoloured.

1740	$2 Type **177**	1·40	1·50
1741	$2 Aerial skiing	1·40	1·50
MS1742	88×119 mm. Nos. 1740/1	2·75	3·00

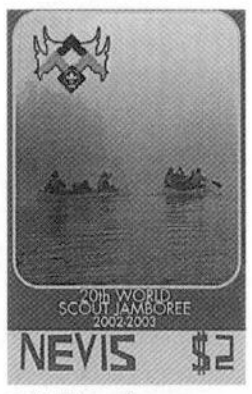

178 Two Scout Canoes in Mist

2002. 20th World Scout Jamboree, Thailand. Multicoloured.

1743	$2 Type **178**	1·40	1·40
1744	$2 Canoe in jungle	1·40	1·40
1745	$2 Scout on rope-ladder	1·40	1·40
1746	$2 Scouts with inflatable boats	1·40	1·40

MS1747 105×125 mm. $5 Scout
painting 3·25 3·50

179 U.S. Flag as
Statue of Liberty
with Nevis Flag

2002. "United We Stand". Support for Victims of 11
September 2001 Terrorist Attacks.
1748 **179** $2 multicoloured 1·40 1·40

180 "Nevis Peak with
Windmill" (Eva Wilkin)

2002. Art. M**m**ulticoloured (except Nos. 1750/1).
1749 $1.20 Type **180** 90 90
1750 $1.20 "Nevis Peak with ruined
Windmill" (Eva Wilkin) (brown
and black) 90 90
1751 $1.20 "Fig Tree Church" (Eva
Wilkin) (brown and black) 90 90
1752 $1.20 "Nevis Peak with Blossom"
(Eva Wilkin) 90 90
1753 $2 "Golden Pheasants and
Loquat" (Kano Shoei) (30×80
mm) 1·40 1·40
1754 $2 "Flowers and Birds of the
Four Seasons" (Winter) (Ikeda
Koson) (30×80 mm) 1·40 1·40
1755 $2 "Pheasants and Azaleas"
(Kano Shoei) (30×80 mm) 1·40 1·40
1756 $2 "Flowers and Birds of the
Four Seasons" (Spring) (Ikeda
Koson) (different) (30×80
mm) 1·40 1·40
1757 $3 "White Blossom" (Shikibu
Terutada) (38×62 mm) 1·75 1·90
1758 $3 "Bird and Flowers" (Shikibu
Terutada) (38×62 mm) 1·75 1·90
1759 $3 "Bird and Leaves" (Shikibu
Terutada) (38×62 mm) 1·75 1·90
1760 $3 "Red and White Flowers"
(Shikibu Terutada) (38×62
mm) 1·75 1·90
1761 $3 "Bird on Willow Tree" (Yosa
Buson) (62×38 mm) 1·75 1·90
1762 $3 "Bird on Peach Tree" (Yosa
Buson) (62×38 mm) 1·75 1·90
MS1763 Two sheets, each 105×105
mm. (a) $5 "Golden Pheasants
among Rhododendrons" (Yamamoto
Baiitsu) (38×62 mm). (b) $5 "Musk
Cat and Camellias" (Uto Gyoshi)
(62×38 mm) 7·00 7·50
Nos. 1757/62 were printed together, se-tenant, with
the backgrounds forming a composite design.

181 "Madonna
and Child
Enthroned with
Saints" (Pietro
Perugino)

2002. Christmas. Religious Art. Multicoloured.
1764 30c. Type **181** 25 15
1765 80c. "Adoration of the Magi"
(Domenico Ghirlandaio) 50 35
1766 90c. "San Zaccaria Altarpiece"
(Giovanni Bellini) 60 40
1767 $1.20 "Presentation at the
Temple" (Bellini) 90 75
1768 $5 "Madonna and Child"
(Simone Martini) 3·25 3·50
MS1769 102×76 mm. $6 "Maesa"
(Martini) 3·50 4·00

182 Claudio
Reyna (U.S.A.)
and Torsten
Frings
(Germany)

2002. World Cup Football Championship, Japan and
Korea. Multicoloured.
1770 $1.20 Type **182** 90 90
1771 $1.20 Michael Ballack
(Germany) and Eddie Pope
(U.S.A.) 90 90
1772 $1.20 Sebastian Kehl (Germany)
and Brian McBride (U.S.A.) 90 90
1773 $1.20 Carlos Puyol (Spain) and
Eul Yong Lee (South Korea) 90 90
1774 $1.20 Jin Cheul Choi (South
Korea) and Gaizka Mendieta
(Spain) 90 90
1775 $1.20 Juan Valeron (Spain) and
Jin Cheul Choi (South Korea) 90 90
1776 $1.60 Emile Heskey (England)
and Edmilson (Brazil) 1·10 1·10
1777 $1.60 Rivaldo (Brazil) and Sol
Campbell (England) 1·10 1·10
1778 $1.60 Ronaldinho (Brazil) and
Nicky Butt (England) 1·10 1·10
1779 $1.60 Ilhan Mansiz (Turkey) and
Omar Daf (Senegal) 1·10 1·10
1780 $1.60 Hasan Sas (Turkey) and
Pape Bouba Diop (Senegal) 1·10 1·10
1781 $1.60 Lamine Diata (Senegal)
and Hakan Sukur (Turkey) 1·10 1·10
MS1782 Four sheets, each 82×82 mm.
(a) $3 Sebastian Kehl (Germany); $3
Frankie Hejduk (U.S.A.). (b) $3 Hong
Myung Bo (South Korea); $3 Gaizka
Mendieta (Spain). (c) $3 David Beck-
ham (England) and Roque Junior
(Brazil); $3 Paul Scholes (England)
and Rivaldo (Brazil). (d) $3 Alpay
Ozalan (Turkey); $3 Khalilou Fadiga
(Senegal) 13·00 15·00
No. 1780 is inscribed "Papa" in error.

183 Ram and Two
Ewes

2003. Chinese New Year ("Year of the Ram").
1783 **183** $2 multicoloured 1·40 1·40

184 Marlene
Dietrich

2003. Famous People of the 20th Century. (a) 10th Death
Anniv of Marlene Dietrich. Multicoloured.
MS1784 127×165 mm. $1.60×2 Type
184; $1.60×2 Wearing white coat
and black hat; $1.60×2 Holding
cigarette 5·50 6·00
MS1785 76×51 mm. $5 Marlene
Dietrich 3·25 3·50

(b) 25th Death Anniv of Elvis Presley. Sheet 154×151 mm.
Multicoloured.
MS1786 $1.60×6 Elvis Presley 6·00 6·50

(c) Life and Times of President John F. Kennedy. Two
sheets, each 126×141 mm.
MS1787 $2 Taking Oath of Office, 1961
(black, brown and rose); $2 Watch-
ing swearing in of Cabinet Officers
(black, brown and rose); $2 With
Andrei Gromyko (Soviet Foreign
Minister), 1963 (multicoloured); $2
Making speech during Cuban Missile
Crisis, 1962 (black, violet and rose) 5·00 5·50

MS1788 $2 Robert and Ted Kennedy
(brothers) (slate, violet and rose); $2
John F. Kennedy (slate, violet and
rose); $2 John as boy with brother
Joe Jnr (maroon, black and rose); $2
With Robert Kennedy in Rose Gar-
den of White House (multicoloured) 5·00 5·50

(d) 75th Anniv of First Solo Transatlantic Flight. Two
sheets, each 142×126 mm. Multicoloured.
MS1789 $2 Ryan Airlines crew at-
taching wing to fuselage of NYP
Special *Spirit of St. Louis*; $2 Charles
Lindbergh with Donald Hall and
Mr. Mahoney (president of Ryan
Airlines); $2 Lindbergh planning
flight; $2 Donald Hall (chief engineer
of Ryan Airlines) working on plans
of aircraft 5·00 5·50
MS1790 $2 Donald Hall and drawing
of *Spirit of St. Louis*; $2 Charles
Lindbergh; $2 *Spirit of St. Louis* being
towed from factory; $2 *Spirit of St.
Louis* at Curtis Field before flight 5·00 5·50

185 Princess Diana

2003. 5th Death Anniv of Diana, Princess of Wales.
Multicoloured.
MS1791 203×150 mm. $2 Type **185**;
$2 Wearing white dress and four
strings of pearls; $2 Wearing black
sleeveless dress; $2 Wearing black
and white hat 5·00 5·50
MS1792 95×116 mm. $5 Wearing pearl
and sapphire choker 3·25 3·50

186 Abraham Lincoln
Bear

2003. Centenary of the Teddy Bear. Multicoloured.
MS1793 137×152 mm. $2 Type **186**; $2
Napolean bear; $2 Henry VIII bear;
$2 Charlie Chaplin bear 3·75 4·00
MS1794 100×70 mm. $5 Baseball bear 3·25 3·50

186a Gustave
Garrigou
(1911)

2003. Centenary of Tour de France Cycle Race. Showing
past winners. Multicoloured.
MS1795 160×100 mm. $2 Type **186a**;
$2 Odile Defraye (1912); $2 Philippe
Thys (1913); $2 Philippe Thys (1914) 6·00 6·00
MS1796 100×70 mm. $5 Francois Faber 5·50 5·50

187 Cadillac 355-C V8 Sedan (1933)

2003. Centenary of General Motors Cadillac.
Multicoloured.
MS1797 120×170 mm. $2 Type **187**; $2
Eldorado (1953); $2 Coupe Deville
(1977); $2 Seville Elegante (1980) 5·00 5·50
MS1798 84×120 mm. $5 Cadillac
(1954) 3·25 3·50

188 Corvette (1970)

2003. 50th Anniv of General Motors Chevrolet Corvette.
Multicoloured.
MS1799 120×140 mm. $2 Type **188**; $2
Corvette (1974); $2 Corvette (1971);
$2 Corvette (1973) 5·00 5·50
MS1800 120×85 mm. $5 C5 Corvette
(1997) 3·25 3·50

189 Queen
Elizabeth II on
Coronation Day

2003. 50th Anniv of Coronation. Multicoloured.
MS1801 156×93 mm. $3 Type **189**; $3
Queen wearing Imperial State Crown
(red background); $3 Wearing Impe-
rial State Crown (in recent years) 7·50 7·50
MS1802 106×76 mm. $5 Wearing tiara
and blue sash 4·50 4·50

190 Prince William

2003. 21st Birthday of Prince William of Wales.
Multicoloured.
MS1803 147×86 mm. $3 Type **190**; $3
Wearing jacket and blue and gold
patterned tie; $3 Wearing fawn
jumper 7·50 7·50
MS1804 98×68 mm. $5 Prince William 4·50 4·50

190a A. V. Roe's Triplane I, 1909

2003. Centenary of Powered Flight. A. V. Roe (aircraft
designer) Commemoration. Multicoloured.
MS1805 177×96 mm. $1.80 Type
190a; $1.80 Avro Type D biplane,
1911; $1.80 Avro Type F, 1912; $1.80
Avro 504 4·75 5·00
MS1806 106×76 mm. $5 Avro No.
561, 1924 3·25 3·50

191 Phalaenopsis
joline

2003. Orchids, Marine Life and Butterflies. Multicoloured.
1807 20c. Type **191** 30 20
1808 30c. Nassau grouper (fish) 35 30
1809 30c. *Perisama bonplandii* (butterfly) (horiz) 35 30
1810 80c. Acropora (coral) 55 35
1811 90c. Doubletooth soldierfish
(horiz) 65 55
1812 90c. *Danaus Formosa* (butterfly)
(horiz) 65 55
1813 $1 *Amauris vasati* (butterfly)
(horiz) 75 60
1814 $1.20 Vanda thonglor (orchid)
(horiz) 90 70
1815 $2 Potinara (orchid) 1·40 1·40
1816 $3 *Lycaste aquila* (orchid) (horiz) 2·00 2·25
1817 $3 *Lycorea ceres* (butterfly)
(horiz) 2·00 2·25
1818 $5 American manatee (horiz) 3·25 3·50

MS1819 136×116 mm. $2 *Brassolaelia cattleya*; $2 *Cymbidium claricon*; $2 *Calanthe restita*; $2 *Odontoglossum crispum* (orchids) (all horiz)   5·50   6·00

MS1820 116×136 mm. $2 Lionfish; $2 Copper-banded butterflyfish; $2 Honeycomb grouper; $2 Blue tang (all horiz)   5·50   6·00

MS1821 136×116 mm. $2 *Kallima rumia*; $2 *Nessaea anceaus*; $2 *Callicore cajetani*; $2 *Hamadryas guatemalena* (butterflies) (all horiz)   5·50   6·00

MS1822 Three sheets, each 96×66 mm. (a) $5 *Odontioda brocade* (orchid). (b) $5 Blue-striped grunt (fish). (c) $5 *Euphaedra medon* (butterfly) (all horiz)   9·75   10·50

192 "Madonna of the Magnificat" (Botticelli)

2003. Christmas. Multicoloured.
1823	30c. Type **192**	25	15
1824	90c. "Madonna with the Long Neck" (detail) (Parmigianino)	60	40
1825	$1.20 "Virgin and Child with St. Anne" (detail) (Da Vinci)	90	60
1826	$5 "Madonna and Child and Scenes from the Life of St. Anne" (detail) (Filippo Lippi)	3·25	3·50

MS1827 96×113 mm. $6 "The Conestabile Madonna" (Raphael)   3·50   4·00

193 Two Stylised Men and AIDS Ribbon

2003. World AIDS Awareness Day. Multicoloured.
1828	90c. Type **193**	90	50
1829	$1.20 Nevis flag and map and ribbon	1·75	1·75

194 Monkey King

2004. Chinese New Year ("Year of the Monkey"). Grey, black and brown (MS1830) or multicoloured (MS1831).

MS1830 Sheet 102×130 mm. $1.60 Type **194**×4   3·75   4·00

MS1831 Sheet 70×100 mm. $3 Monkey King (29×39 mm)   1·90   2·25

195 Guide Badges

2004. 50th Anniv of Nevis Girl Guides. Multicoloured.
1832	30c. Type **195**	25	15
1833	90c. Mrs Gwendolyn Douglas-Jones and Miss Bridget Hunkins (past and present Commissioners) (horiz)	60	40
1834	$1.20 Lady Olave Baden Powell	85	60
1835	$5 Photographs of Girl Guides	3·25	3·50

196 "The Morning After" (1945)

2004. 25th Death Anniv of Norman Rockwell (artist) (2003). Multicoloured.

MS1836 150×180 mm. $2 Type **196**; $2 "Solitaire" (1950); $2 "Easter Morning" (1959); $2 "Walking to Church" (1953)   5·50   6·00

MS1837 90×98 mm. $5 "The Graduate" (1959) (horiz)   3·50   3·75

197 "Woman with a Hat" (1935)

2004. 30th Death Anniv of Pablo Picasso (2003) (artist). Multicoloured.

MS1838 Two sheets each 133×168 mm. (a) $2 Type **197**; $2 "Seated Woman" (1937); $2 "Portrait of Nusch Eluard" (1937); $2 "Woman in a Straw Hat" (1936). (b) $2 "L'Arlesienne" (1937); $2 "The Mirror" (1932); $2 "Repose" (1932); $2 "Portrait of Paul Eluard" (1937). Set of 2 sheets   9·50   10·50

MS1839 Two sheets. (a) 75×100 mm. $5 "Portrait of Nusch Eluard" (with green ribbon in hair) (1937). (b) 100×75 mm. $5 "Reclining Woman with a Book" (1939). Imperf. Set of 2 sheets   7·00   7·50

198 "Still Life with a Drapery" (1899)

2004. 300th Anniv of St. Petersburg. "Treasures of the Hermitage". Multicoloured.
1840	30c. Type **198**	25	15
1841	90c. "The Smoker" (1895) (vert)	60	40
1842	$2 "Girl with a Fan" (1881) (vert)	1·40	1·25
1843	$5 "Grove" (1912) (vert)	3·25	3·50

MS1844 94×74 mm. $5 "Lady in the Garden" (1867). Imperf   3·25   3·50

199 John Denver

2004. John Denver (musician) Commemoration. Sheet 127×107 mm containing T 199 and similar vert designs. Multicoloured.

MS1845 $1.20 Type **199**; $1.20 Wearing patterned shirt; $1.20 Wearing dark shirt; $1.20 Wearing white shirt   3·25   3·50

200 Marilyn Monroe

2004. Marilyn Monroe Commemoration. Multicoloured.
1846	60c. Type **200**	70	60

MS1847 175×125 mm. $2 Pouting; $2 Laughing and looking left; $2 Laughing with head tilted back; $2 Smiling wearing drop earrings (37×50 mm)   5·00   5·50

201 Brain

2004. Arthur the Aardvark and Friends. Multicoloured.

MS1848 Three sheets, each 152×185. (a) $1×6, Type **201**; Sue Ellen; Buster; Francine; Muffy; Binky. (b) $2×4, Binky inside heart; Sue Ellen inside heart; Brain inside heart; Francine inside heart wearing red top. (c) $2×4, Arthur inside heart; D.W. inside heart; Francine inside heart wearing pink top; Buster inside heart   12·00   13·00

202 HMCS *Penetang*

2004. 60th Anniv of D-Day Landings. Multicoloured.

MS1849 Two sheets. (a) 136×122 mm. $1.20×6 Type **202**; Infantry disembarking from landing craft; Landing craft tank from above; Two landing craft tanks; Landing barge kitchen; Battleship *Texas*. (b) 96×76 mm. $6 HMS *Scorpion*   10·00   10·50

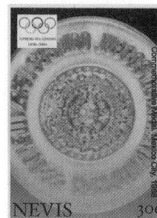

203 Medal (Mexico City, 1968)

2004. Olympic Games, Athens. Multicoloured.
1850	30c. Type **203**	30	20
1851	90c. Pentathlon (Greek art)	65	50
1852	$1.80 Avery Brundage (International Olympic Committee, 1952–1972)	1·30	1·30
1853	$3 Tennis (Antwerp, 1920) (horiz)	1·75	1·90

204 Deng Xiaoping

2004. Birth Centenary of Deng Xiaoping (leader of China, 1978–89). Sheet 96×66 mm.

MS1854 **204** $5 multicoloured   3·25   3·00

205 Peace Dove carrying Olive Branch

2004. United Nations International Year of Peace. Sheet 142×82 mm containing horiz designs as T 205. Multicoloured.

MS1855 $3×3, Type **205**; Dove from front; Dove angled left   5·25   5·50

206 Elvis Presley

2004. Elvis Presley (entertainer) Commemoration. Multicoloured.

MS1856 Two sheets, each 146×103 mm. (a) $1.20×6, Type **206**×3; magenta background×3. (b) $1.20×6, scarlet jumper; yellow jumper; blue jumper; turquoise jumper; purple jumper; green jumper   11·00   10·00

207 Nery Pumpido (Argentina)

2004. Centenary of FIFA (Federation Internationale de Football Association) (MS1857) and World Cup Football Championship (MS1858). Multicoloured.

MS1857 192×96 mm. $2×4, Type **207**; Gary Lineker (England); Thomas Hassler (Germany); Sol Campbell (England). (b) 107×86 mm. $5 Michael Owen (England)   3·25   3·50

MS1858 90×115 mm. $5 Jason Berkley Joseph (Nevis) (38×50 mm)   3·25   3·50

208 "Santa's Good Boys"

2004. Christmas. Paintings by Norman Rockwell. Multicoloured.
1859	25c. Type **208**	25	15
1860	30c. "Ride 'em Cowboy"	30	20
1861	90c. "Christmas Sing Merrillie"	65	50
1862	$5 "The Christmas Newsstand"	3·25	3·50

MS1863 63×72 mm. $5 "Is He Coming". Imperf   3·25   3·50

209 Steam Idyll, Indonesia

2004. Bicentenary of Steam Trains. Multicoloured.
1864	$3 Type **209**	2·00	2·00
1865	$3 2-8-2, Syria	2·00	2·00
1866	$3 Narrow Gauge Mallet 0-4-4-0, Portugal	2·00	2·00
1867	$3 Western Pacific Bo Bo Road Switcher, USA	2·00	2·00

MS1868 100×70 mm. $5 LMS 5305, Great Britain   3·75   3·75

210 Gekko Gecko

2005. Reptiles and Amphibians. Multicoloured.
1869	$1.20 Type **210**	90	90
1870	$1.20 Eyelash viper	90	90
1871	$1.20 Green iguana	90	90
1872	$1.20 Whistling frog	90	90

MS1873 96×67 mm. $5 Hawksbill turtle   3·25   3·50

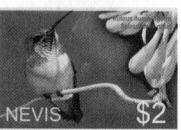

211 Rufous Hummingbird

2005. Hummingbirds. Multicoloured.
1874	$2 Type **211**	1·90	1·90
1875	$2 Green-crowned brilliant	1·90	1·90
1876	$2 Ruby-throated hummingbird	1·90	1·90
1877	$2 Purple-throated carib	1·90	1·90

MS1878 79×108 mm. $5 Rivoli's ("Magnificent") Hummingbird   4·50   4·50

212 *Xeromphalina campanella*

2005. Mushrooms. Multicoloured.
MS1879 137×127 mm. $2×4, Type **212**;
Calvatia sculpta; Mitrula elegans;
Aleuria aurantia — 6·00 6·50
MS1880 97×68 mm. $5 *iSarcoscypha*
coccinea — 4·00 4·25

213 Hawksbill Turtle (Leon
Silcott)

2005. Hawksbill Turtle. Children's Drawings.
Multicoloured.
1881	30c. Type **213**	25	15
1882	90c. Hawksbill turtle on sand (Kris Liburd)	60	35
1883	$1.20 Spotted hawksbill turtle (Alice Webber)	95	75
1884	$5 Hawksbill turtle in water (Jeuaunito Huggins)	3·25	3·50

214 Zebra Shark

2005. Sharks. Multicoloured.
MS1885 99×137 mm. $2×4, Type **214**;
Caribbean reef shark; Blue shark;
Bronze whaler — 5·00 5·50
MS1886 96×67 mm. $5 Blacktip reef
shark — 3·25 3·50

215 Rooster

2005. Chinese New Year ("Year of the Rooster").
Multicoloured.
1887	75c. Type **215**	50	55
1888	75c. Pink silhouette of rooster	50	55
1889	75c. Grey silhouette of rooster	50	55
1890	75c. Rooster on rose-lilac background	50	55

216 Enola Gay and Flight
Crew

2005. 60th Anniv of Victory in Japan. Multicoloured.
1891	$2 Type **216**	1·75	1·75
1892	$2 Bomb exploding over Hiroshima	1·75	1·75
1893	$2 Souvenir of Japanese Surrender Ceremony	1·75	1·75
1894	$2 Japanese Delegation aboard USS *Missouri*	1·75	1·75
1895	$2 General Macarthur speaking	1·75	1·75

217 Brazil Team, 1958

2005. 75th Anniv of First World Cup Football
Championship. Multicoloured.
1896	$2 Type **217**	1·40	1·40
1897	$2 Brazil and Sweden	1·40	1·40
1898	$2 Rasunda Stadium, Stockholm	1·40	1·40
1899	$2 Edson Arantes do Nascimento (Pele)	1·40	1·40
MS1900 115×89 mm. $5 Brazil celebrating with Swedish flag — 3·25 3·50

218 Friedrich von
Schiller

2005. Death Bicentenary of Friedrich von Schiller (poet
and dramatist). Multicoloured.
1901	$3 Type **218**	1·75	1·90
1902	$3 Friedrich von Schiller (black and white portrait)	1·75	1·90
1903	$3 Birthplace of Friedrich von Schiller	1·75	1·90
MS1904 100×70 mm. $5 Friedrich von
Schiller statue, Chicago — 3·25 3·50

219 Young Boy

2005. Centenary of Rotary International (humanitarian
organisation). Multicoloured.
1905	$3 Type **219**	1·75	1·90
1906	$3 Immunising child	1·75	1·90
1907	$3 Boy with leg braces and crutches	1·75	1·90
MS1908 103×70 mm. $5 Two children
and adult (horiz) — 3·25 3·50

220 Admiral Sir William Cornwallis

2005. Bicentenary of the Battle of Trafalgar.
Multicoloured.
1909	30c. Type **220**	50	25
1910	90c. Captain Maurice Suckling (Comptroller of the Navy)	1·00	60
1911	$1.20 Richard Earl Howe (First Lord of the Admiralty)	1·40	1·10
1912	$3 Sir John Jervis (First Earl of St Vincent)	3·00	3·50
MS1913 83×119 mm. $5 Richard Earl
Howe on quarterdeck of *Queen*
Charlotte — 4·75 5·00

221 General
Charles de Gaulle

2005. 60th Anniv of Victory in Europe.
1914	**221**	$2 multicoloured	1·75	1·75
1915	**221**	$2 sepia and pink	1·75	1·75
1916	**221**	$2 black and yellow	1·75	1·75
1917	**221**	$2 brown, stone and blue	1·75	1·75
1918	**221**	$2 multicoloured	1·75	1·75
DESIGNS: No. 1914, Type **221**; 1915, General George S.
Patton; 1916, Field Marshall Bernhard Montgomery; 1917,
Prisoners of War; 1918, "Germany Defeated!".

222 "The Little
Mermaid"
(sculpture)

2005. Birth Bicentenary of Hans Christian Andersen
(writer). Multicoloured.
1919	$2 Type **222**	1·40	1·40
1920	$2 *Thumbelina*	1·40	1·40
1921	$2 *The Snow Queen*	1·40	1·40
1922	$2 *The Emperor's New Clothes*	1·40	1·40
MS1923 100×75 mm. $6 Hans Christian
Andersen — 3·50 3·75

223 Tyrannosaurus Rex

2005. Prehistoric Animals. Multicoloured.
| 1924 | 30c. Type **223** | 60 | 30 |
| 1925 | $5 Hadrosaur | 2·75 | 3·00 |
MS1926 Three sheets. (a) 104×128 mm.
$1.20×6, Apatosaurus; Camarasaurus;
Iguanodon; Edmontosaurus; Centrosaurus; Euoplocephalus. (b) 128×104
mm. $1.20×6 (vert), Deinotherium;
Platybelodon; Palaeoloxodon;
Arsinoitherium; Procoptodon; Macrauchenia; (c) 104×128 mm. $1.20×6,
Ouranosaurus; Parasaurolophus;
Psittacosaurus; Stegasaurus; Scelidosaurus; Hypsilophodon — 12·00 13·00
MS1927 Three sheets. (a) 97×77 mm.
$5 Brontotherium. (b) 98×87 mm.
$5 Daspletosaurus; (c) 98×92 mm.
$5 Pliosaur — 9·75 10·50
The backgrounds of Nos. **MS**1926a/c form a composite
design which bleeds onto the sheet margins.

224 Captain Nemo
("20,000 Leagues
under the Sea")

2005. Death Centenary of Jules Verne (writer).
Multicoloured.
1928	$2 Type **224**	1·90	1·90
1929	$2 Michael Strogoff	1·90	1·90
1930	$2 Phileas Fogg ("Around the World in 80 Days")	1·90	1·90
1931	$2 Captain Cyrus Smith ("Mysterious Island")	1·90	1·90
MS1932 78×100 mm. $5 Pat Boone
("Journey to the Centre of the
Earth") — 4·25 4·50
No. 1930 is inscribed "Phinias Fogg".

225 No. SG69 of Vatican
City optd with Type **69**

2005. Pope John Paul II Commemoration. Multicoloured.
| 1933 | 90c. Type **225** | 1·00 | 70 |
| 1934 | $4 Pope John Paul II (28×42 mm) | 4·00 | 4·25 |

226 Shareef
Abdur-Rahim
(Portland Trail
Blazers)

2005. National Basketball Association. Multicoloured.
1935	$1 Type **226**	90	70
1936	$1 Vince Carter (New Jersey Nets)	90	70
1937	$1 Shaun Livingston (Los Angeles Clippers)	90	70
1938	$1 Theo Ratliff (Portland Trail Blazers)	90	70
1938b	$1 Portland Trail Blazers emblem	90	70
1939	$1 Rasheed Wallace (Detroit Pistons)	90	70

227 Dr Sun Yat-Sen

2005. TAIPEI 2005 International Stamp Exhibition.
80th Death Anniv of Dr Sun Yat-Sen (Chinese
revolutionary leader). Multicoloured.
1940	$2 Type **227**	1·40	1·40
1941	$2 Wearing jacket and tie	1·40	1·40
1942	$2 In front of statue	1·40	1·40
1943	$2 In front of building	1·40	1·40

228 "Madonna
and the Angels"
(detail) (Fra
Angelico)

2005. Christmas. Multicoloured.
1944	25c. Type **228**	25	15
1945	30c. "Madonna and the Child" (detail) (Filippo Lippi)	30	20
1946	90c. "Madonna and Child" (detail) (Giotto)	65	50
1947	$4 "Madonna of the Chair" (detail) (Raphael)	2·75	3·00
MS1948 67×97 mm. $5 "Adoration of
the Magi" (Giovanni Batista Tiepolo)
(horiz) — 3·25 3·00

229 "A Dog" (Ren Xun)

2006. Chinese New Year ("Year of the Dog").
| 1949 | **229** | 75c. multicoloured | 70 | 60 |

230 Eldorado National
Forest, California

2006. Centenary of United States Forest Service (2005).
Multicoloured.
1950	$1.60 Type **230**	1·20	1·20
1951	$1.60 Pisgah National Forest, North Carolina	1·20	1·20
1952	$1.60 Chattahoochee-Oconee National Forests, Georgia	1·20	1·20
1953	$1.60 Nantahala National Forest, North Carolina	1·20	1·20
1954	$1.60 Bridger-Teton National Forest, Wyoming	1·20	1·20
1955	$1.60 Mount Hood National Forest, Oregon	1·20	1·20
MS1956 Two sheets, each 104×70
mm. (a) $6 Klamath National Forest,
California (horiz). (b) $6 The Source
Rain Forest Walk, Nevis — 7·00 7·25

231 Queen Elizabeth II
wearing Garter Robes

2006. 80th Birthday of Queen Elizabeth II. Multicoloured.
1957	$2 Type **231**	1·40	1·40
1958	$2 Wearing white dress	1·40	1·40
1959	$2 Wearing tiara and evening dress	1·40	1·40
1960	$2 Waving, wearing white hat and gloves	1·40	1·40
MS1961 120×120 mm. $5 Queen
Elizabeth II, c. 1955 — 3·25 3·50

232 Italy 1956 Winter Olympics 10l.
Ski-jump Stamp

2006. Winter Olympic Games, Turin. Multicoloured.

1962	25c. USA 1980 Winter Olympics 15c.downhill skiing stamp	25	15
1963	30c. Type **232**	25	15
1964	90c. Italy 1956 Winter Olympics 25l. ice stadium stamp	60	40
1965	$1.20 Emblem of Winter Olympic Games, Lake Placid, USA, 1980 (vert)	1·40	1·10
1966	$4 Italy 1956 Winter Olympics 60l. skating arena stamp	2·50	2·75
1967	$5 Emblem of Winter Olympic Games, Cortina d'Ampezzo, 1956 (vert)	3·00	3·25

233 Mahatma Gandhi

2006. Washington 2006 International Stamp Exhibition. Sheet 140×152 mm.

1968	**233**	$3 multicoloured	1·75	1·90

234 "The Anatomy Lesson of Dr. Tulp" (detail)

2006. 400th Birth Anniv of Rembrandt Harmenszoon van Rijn (artist). Multicoloured.

1969	$2 Type **234**	1·25	1·40
1970	$2 "The Anatomy Lesson of Dr. Tulp" (detail of man leaning forward)	1·25	1·40
1971	$2 "The Anatomy Lesson of Dr. Tulp" (detail of man seen in profile)	1·25	1·40
1972	$2 "The Anatomy Lesson of Dr. Tulp" (detail)	1·25	1·40
MS1973 70×100 mm. $6 "Bald-headed Old Man". Imperf		3·50	3·75

235 "Saturn 1B" Launch KSC's from Launch Complex 39B

2006. Space Anniversaries. Multicoloured. (a) 30th Anniv (2005) of "Apollo" "Soyuz" Test Project.

1974	$2 Type **235**	1·40	1·40
1975	$2 Astronaut Donald Slayton and cosmonaut Aleksey Leonov	1·40	1·40
1976	$2 Liftoff of "Soyuz 19" from Baikonur Cosmodrome	1·40	1·40
1977	$2 "Soyuz" spacecraft seen from Apollo CM	1·40	1·40
1978	$2 American and Soviet crewmen	1·40	1·40
1979	$2 "Apollo CSM" with docking adapter seen from "Soyuz"	1·40	1·40

(b) 30th Anniv of "Viking 1" Landing on Mars.

1980	$3 "Titan"/"Centaur" rocket lifting off from Cape Canaveral	1·75	1·90
1981	$3 "Viking 1"	1·75	1·90
1982	$3 "Viking Lander"	1·75	1·90
1983	$3 Global view of Mars taken from "Viking 1"	1·75	1·90

236 Christmas Tree, Charlestown, Nevis

2006. Christmas. Multicoloured.

1984	25c. Type **236**	25	15
1985	30c. Snowman and other decorations, Bath, Nevis	25	15
1986	90c. Three white reindeer and other decorations, Bath, Nevis	60	40
1987	$4 Decorated Christmas tree (vert)	1·50	2·75
MS1988 100×70 mm. $6 Children meeting Santa		3·50	3·75

237 Map of United Kingdom and Centenary Flag

2007. Centenary of World Scout Movement and 21st World Scout Jamboree, Chelmsford, England. Multicoloured.

1989	$3 Type **237**	1·75	1·90
MS1990 80×111 mm. $5 Centenary flag and streamer of national flags (horiz)		3·25	3·50

238 Marilyn Monroe

2007. 80th Birth Anniv (2006) of Marilyn Monroe (actress). Multicoloured.

1991	$2 Type **238**	1·25	1·40
1992	$2 Wearing necklace	1·25	1·40
1993	$2 Wearing pearl earrings	1·25	1·40
1994	$2 Wearing white dress	1·25	1·40

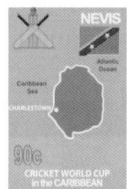

239 Outline Map of Nevis and Flag of St. Kitts and Nevis

2007. World Cup Cricket, West Indies. Multicoloured.

1995	90c. Type **239**	55	60
1996	$2 Runako Morton	1·25	1·40
MS1997 120×93 mm. $6 World Cup Cricket emblem		3·50	3·75

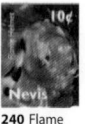

240 Flame Helmet

2007. Shells. Multicoloured.

1998	10c. Type **240**	10	15
1999	25c. Rooster tail conch	15	20
2000	30c. Three beaded periwinkles	15	20
2001	60c. Emperor helmet	35	40
2002	80c. Scotch bonnet	45	50
2003	90c. Milk conch	55	60
2004	$1 Beaded periwinkle	60	65
2005	$1.20 Alphabet cone	70	75
2006	$1.80 Measled cowrie	1·10	1·20
2007	$3 King helmet	1·75	1·90
2008	$5 Atlantic hairy triton	2·75	3·00
2009	$10 White lined mitre	5·00	5·50
2010	$20 Reticulated cowrie shell	11·25	11·50

241 *Pimenta racemosa* (wild cilliment)

2007. Flowers of Nevis. Multicoloured.
MS2011 108×131 mm. $2×4 Type **241**; *Abrus precatorius* (jumbie beads); *Lantanacamara* (wild sage); *Asclepias curassasavica* (blood flower/milky-milky) 4·75 5·00
MS2012 70×100 mm. $6 *Tabebuia heterophylla* (pink trumpet) 3·50 3·75

The stamps and margins of No. **MS**2011 form a composite background design.

242 *Battus zetides* (Zetides swallowtail)

2007. Butterflies of Nevis. Multicoloured.
MS2013 131×108 mm. $2×4 Type **242**; *Parides hahnell* (Hahnel's amazon swallowtail); *Dismorphia spio* (Haitian mimic); *Hesperocharis graphites* (marbled white) 4·75 5·00
MS2014 100×70 mm. $6 *Papilio multicaudata* (three-tailed tiger swallowtail) 3·50 3·75

The stamps and margins of No. **MS**2013 form a composite background design.

243 Rainbow Parrotfish

2007. Endangered Species. Rainbow Parrotfish (Scarus guacamaia). Multicoloured.

2015	$1.20 Type **243**	70	75
2016	$1.20 Pair	70	75
2017	$1.20 In close-up, facing to left	70	75
2018	$1.20 Facing to right	70	75
MS2019 115×168 mm. Nos. 2015/18, each ×2		5·50	6·00

244 Elvis Presley

2007. 30th Death Anniv of Elvis Presley. Multicoloured.

2020	$1.20 Type **244**	70	75
2021	$1.20 Wearing white jumpsuit, playing guitar	70	75
2022	$1.20 As No. 2021, but seen three-quarter length, spotlight at top right	70	75
2023	$1.20 Wearing black leather jacket	70	75
2024	$1.20 As No. 2023, seen three-quarter length	70	75
2025	$1.20 As Type **244**, seen in close-up	70	75

245 Concorde 02 on Ground

2007. Concorde. Multicoloured.

2026	$1.20 Type **245**	70	75
2027	$1.20 Concorde 02 flying over snowy mountains (blue inscriptions)	70	75
2028	$1.20 As Type **245** (lemon inscriptions)	70	75
2029	$1.20 As No. 2027 (lemon inscriptions)	70	75
2030	$1.20 As Type **245** (blue inscriptions)	70	75
2031	$1.20 As No. 2027 (white inscriptions)	70	75
MS2032 150×100 mm. $1.20×6 Concorde F-BTSD: Flying to right, dark blue background (over upper left part of globe); Flying to left, azure background (over map 'MERICA'); Flying right, dark blue background (over upper right part of globe); Flying left, azure background (over equator line); Flying right, dark blue background (over map of islands); Flying left, azure background (equator line at lower right)		4·25	4·50

Nos. 2026/31 commemorate the Washington to Paris record flight of Concorde 02, the second pre-production aircraft, on September 26 1973.

The stamps and margins of No. **MS**2032 form a composite background design. **MS**2032 commemorates the eastbound round the world record of Concorde F-BTSD on August 15–16 1995.

246 Diana, Princess of Wales

2007. 10th Death Anniv of Diana, Princess of Wales. Multicoloured.

2033	$2 Type **246**	1·25	1·40
2034	$2 Wearing black evening dress and choker	1·25	1·40
2035	$2 Wearing pale jacket and pearl necklace	1·25	1·40
2036	$2 Wearing white dress with narrow shoulder straps	1·25	1·40
MS2037 70×100 mm. $6 Wearing blue and white jacket and hat		3·50	3·75

247 Pope Benedict XVI

2007. 80th Birthday of Pope Benedict XVI.

2038	**247**	$1 multicoloured	60	65

248 Queen Elizabeth II and Prince Philip

2007. Diamond Wedding of Queen Elizabeth II and Prince Philip. Multicoloured.

2039	$1.20 Type **248**	1·25	1·40
2040	$1.20 Queen Elizabeth and Prince Philip waving	1·25	1·40
2041	$1.20 In Garter robes	1·25	1·40
2042	$1.20 Waving from Coronation coach at Golden Jubilee	1·25	1·40
2043	$1.20 Waving from carriage at Ascot	1·25	1·40
2044	$1.20 Waving from balcony	1·25	1·40

249 Begonias and Rock

2007. 50th Death Anniv of Qi Baishi (artist). Designs showing paintings. Multicoloured.

2045	$3 Type **249**	1·75	1·90
2046	$3 *Mother and Child*	1·75	1·90
2047	$3 *Fish and Bait*	1·75	1·90
2048	$3 *Solitary Hero* (bird)	1·75	1·90
MS2049 100×70 mm. $6 *Chrysanthemums and Insects* (28×42 mm)		3·50	3·75

250 Westland Sea King Naval Helicopter

2007. Centenary of the First Helicopter Flight. Multicoloured.
MS2050 $3×4 Type **250**; Schweizer N330TT light utility helicopter; Sikorsky R-4/R-5 first production helicopter; PZL Swidnik W-3 Sokol 7·00 7·25
MS2051 100×70 mm. $6 MIL V-12 heavy transport helicopter 3·50 3·75

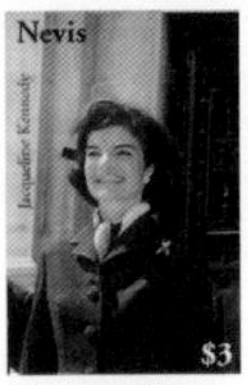

251 Jacqueline Kennedy

2007. 90th Birth Anniv of John F. Kennedy (US President 1960–3). Multicoloured.

2052	$3 Type **251**	1·75	1·90
2053	$3 John F. Kennedy (in library)	1·75	1·90
2054	$3 John F. Kennedy (clapping)	1·75	1·90
2055	$3 Vice President Lyndon B. Johnson	1·75	1·90

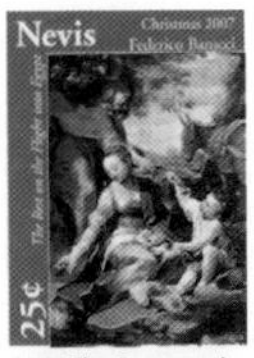

252 *The Rest on the Flight into Egypt* (Federico Barocci)

2007. Christmas. Paintings. Multicoloured.

2056	25c. Type **252**	15	20
2057	30c. *The Annunciation* (detail) (Federico Barocci)	15	20
2058	90c. *The Annunciation* (Cavalier d'Arpino)	55	60
2059	$4 *The Rest on the Flight into Egypt* (Francesco Mancini)	2·50	2·60
MS2060	100×70 mm. $5 *The Virgin and Child between Saints Peter and Paul and the Twelve Magistrates of the Rota* (Antoniazzo Romano)	2·75	3·00

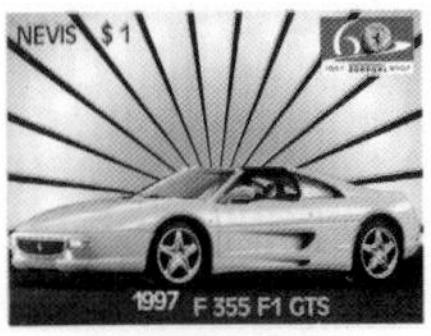

253 F 355 F1 GTS, 1997

2007. 60th Anniv of Ferrari. Multicoloured.

2061	$1 Type **253**	60	65
2062	$1 412, 1985	60	65
2063	$1 158 F1, 1964	60	65
2064	$1 375 MM, 1953	60	65
2065	$1 330 P4, 1967	60	65
2066	$1 512 BB LM, 1978	60	65
2067	$1 312 B3-74, 1974	60	55
2068	$1 308 GTB Quattrovalvole, 1982	60	65

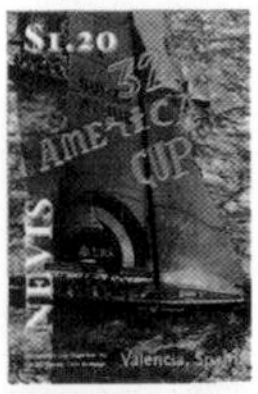

254 Yacht

2007. 32nd Americas Cup Yachting Championship, Valencia, Spain. Multicoloured.

2069	$1.20 Type **254**	60	65
2070	$1.80 White-hulled yacht	1·40	1·50
2071	$3 Yacht, 'T Systems' on sail	1·75	1·90
2072	$5 Yachts, sail with orange stripes in foreground	4·50	4·75

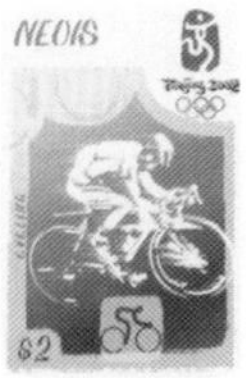

255 Cycling

2008. Olympic Games, Beijing. Multicoloured.

2073	$2 Type **255**	1·50	1·75
2074	$2 Kayaking	1·50	1·75
2075	$2 Yachting	1·50	1·75
2076	$2 Three-day eventing	1·50	1·75

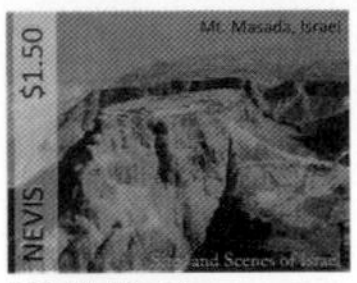

256 Mt. Masada

2008. Israel 2008 World Stamp Championship, Tel-Aviv. Natural Sites and Scenes of Israel. Multicoloured.

2077	$1.50 Type **256**	1·40	1·50
2078	$1.50 Red Sea and desert mountains	1·40	1·50
2079	$1.50 Dead Sea	1·40	1·50
2080	$1.50 Sea of Galilee	1·40	1·50
MS2081	100×70 mm. $5 Mt. Hermon	4·50	4·50

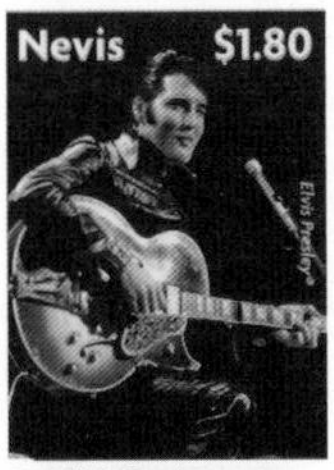

257 Elvis Presley

2008. 40th Anniv of Elvis Presley's '68 Special'. Multicoloured.

2082	$1.80 Type **257**	1·40	1·50
2083	$1.80 Wearing black leather, facing forward	1·40	1·50
2084	$1.80 Standing, seen three-quarter length (red background)	1·40	1·50
2085	$1.80 Wearing black leather, facing left	1·40	1·50
2086	$1.80 Wearing blue shirt	1·40	1·50
2087	$1.80 Wearing black leather, facing right	1·40	1·50

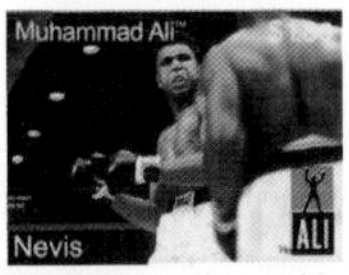

258 Muhammad Ali and Opponent

2008. Muhammad Ali (world heavyweight boxing champion, 1964, 1974–8). Multicoloured .

2088	$1.80 Type **258**	1·40	1·50
2089	$1.80 In ring with fists raised, opponent at right	1·40	1·50
2090	$1.80 Punched by opponent	1·40	1·50
2091	$1.80 Seated by ring ropes	1·40	1·50
2092	$1.80 With arms raised in victory	1·40	1·50
2093	$1.80 Muhammad Ali and trophy	1·40	1·50
2094	$2 In profile, speaking (37×50 mm)	1·50	1·75
2095	$2 Seen full face, speaking (37×50 mm)	1·50	1·75
2096	$2 Looking towards left (37×50 mm)	1·50	1·75
2097	$2 Eyes looking to right, speaking (37×50 mm)	1·50	1·75

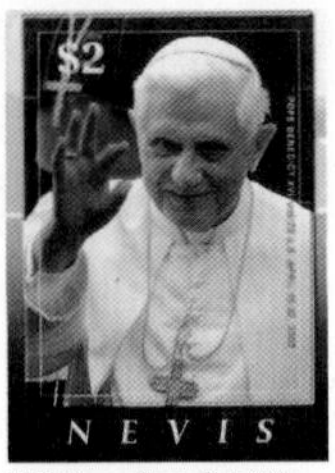

259 Pope Benedict XVI

2008. 1st Visit of Pope Benedict XVI to the United States. Sheet 178×127 mm containing T 259 and similar vert designs.

MS2098	multicoloured	6·00	6·00

The four stamps within **MS**2103 are as Type **259** but have slightly different backgrounds at the foot of the stamps, the middle two showing parts of the UN emblem.

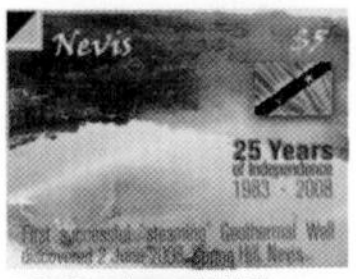

260 Geothermal Well, Spring Hill, discovered June 2008

2008. 25th Anniv of Independence.

2099	**260**	$5 multicoloured	4·50	4·50

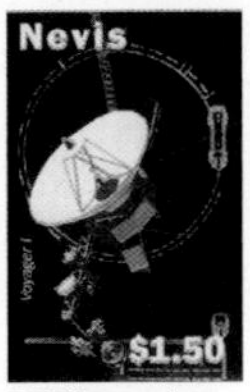

261 *Voyager I*

2008. 50 Years of Space Exploration and Satellites. Multicoloured.

2100	$1.50 Type **261**	1·40	1·50
2101	$1.50 *Voyager I*, Io, and part of Ganymede and Callisto	1·40	1·50
2102	$1.50 *Voyager I*, Europa and part of Ganymede and Callisto	1·40	1·50
2103	$1.50 *Voyager I*	1·40	1·50
2104	$1.50 *Voyager I*, Dione and part of Titan	1·40	1·50
2105	$1.50 *Voyager I*, Enceladus and part of Titan	1·40	1·50
2106	$1.50 *Galileo* spacecraft	1·40	1·50
2107	$1.50 *Galileo* (without sun shields)	1·40	1·50
2108	$1.50 *Galileo* Probe	1·40	1·50
2109	$1.50 Technical drawing of *Galileo* Probe	1·40	1·50
2110	$1.50 *Galileo* passing Io	1·40	1·50
2111	$1.50 Technical drawing of *Galileo*	1·40	1·50
2112	$2 Van Allen radiation belt	1·50	1·75
2113	$2 Technical drawing of *Explorer I*	1·50	1·75
2114	$2 James Van Allen	1·50	1·75
2115	$2 *Explorer I* above Earth	1·50	1·75
2116	$2 Technical drawing of *Apollo 11* Command Module	1·50	1·75
2117	$2 Saturn V Apollo Programme Launcher	1·50	1·75
2118	$2 Edwin 'Buzz' Aldrin Jr. walking on Moon, 1969	1·50	1·75
2119	$2 Technical drawing of *Apollo 11* Lunar Module	1·50	1·75

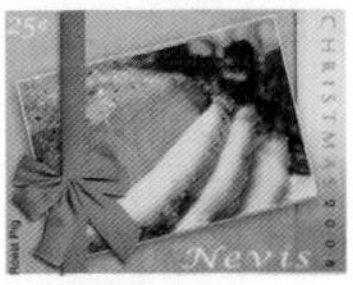

262 Roast Pork

2008. Christmas. Multicoloured.

2120	25c. Type **262**	10	15
2121	30c. Fruit-topped sponge cake	15	20
2122	80c. Pumpkin pie	55	60
2123	90c. Sorrel drink	55	60
2124	$2 Fruit cake	1·50	1·75
MS2125	100×70 mm. $6 Baked ham and turkey (vert)	4·50	4·50

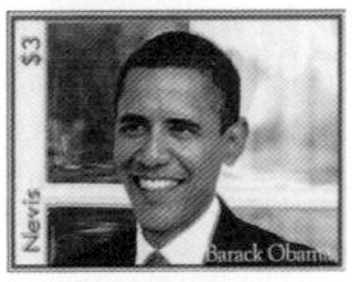

263 Pres. Barack Obama

2009. Inauguration of President Barack Obama. Sheet 180×100 mm containing T 263 and similar horiz designs showing Pres. Obama. Multicoloured.

MS2126	$3×4 Type **263**; US flag in background; White House garden in background; Black background	5·50	5·50

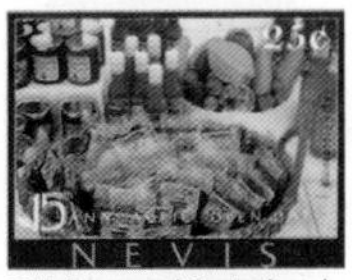

264 Processed Agricultural Products

2009. 15th Anniv of Agriculture Open Day. Multicoloured.

2127	25c. Type **264**	10	15
2128	30c. Fruits	15	20
2129	90c. Goats	55	60
2130	$5 Plant propagation	4·50	4·50
MS2131	100×70 mm. $6 Entertainment	4·50	4·50

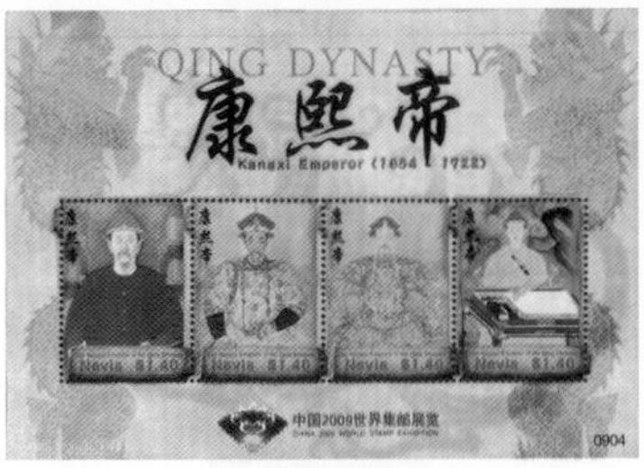

265 Kangxi, Second Emperor of the Qing Dynasty (image scaled to 33% of original size)

2009. China 2009 World Stamp Exhibition, Luoyang (1st issue). Kangxi, Second Emperor of the Qing Dynasty (1654–1722). Multicoloured. .

MS2132	146×100 mm. $1.40×4 Type **265**; Wearing gold with blue armlets; Wearing gold with gold armlets; At desk writing	5·25	5·25

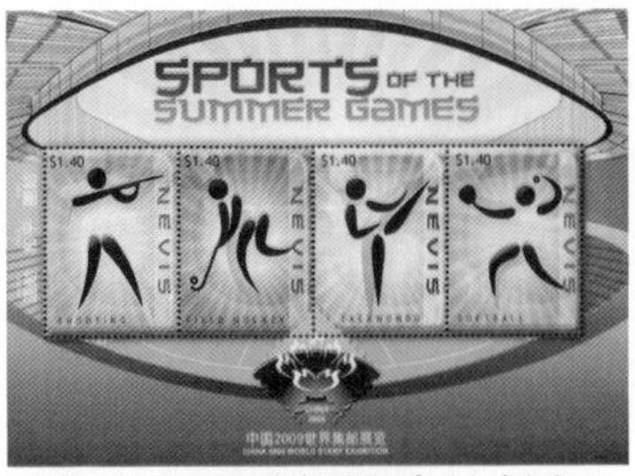

266 Shooting (image scaled to 35% of original size)

2009. China 2009 World Stamp Exhibition, Luoyang (2nd issue). Sports of the Summer Games.

MS2133	137×98 mm. $1.40×4 Type **266**; Field hockey; Taekwondo; Softball	5·25	5·25

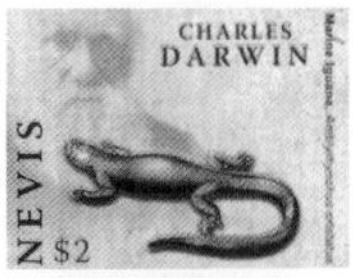

267 Marine Iguana (*Amblyrhynchus cristatus*)

2009. Birth Bicentenary of Charles Darwin (naturalist and evolutionary theorist). Multicoloured.

MS2134	Type **267**; Statue of Charles Darwin, Shrewsbury, England; Platypus (*Ornithorhynchus anatinus*); Vampire bat (*Desmodus rotundus* incorrectly inscr*Desmodus d'Orbignyi*); Portrait of Charles Darwin in late 1830s by George Richmond; Large ground-finch (*Geospiza magnirostris*)	9·00	9·00
MS2135	100×70 mm. $6 Charles Darwin (photograph), 1881 (37×50 mm)	4·50	4·50

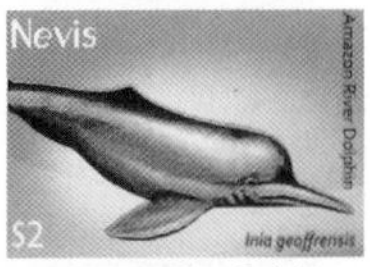

268 Amazon River Dolphin (*Inia geoffrensis*)

2009. Dolphins and Whales. Multicoloured.

MS2136	140×116 mm. $2×6 Type **268**; Indus river dolphin (*Platanista minor*); Atlantic white-sided dolphin (*Lagenorhynchus acutus*); La Plata dolphin; Peale's dolphin (*Lagenorhynchus australis*); White-beaked dolphin (*Lagenorhynchus albirostris*)	9·00	9·00
MS2137	100×70 mm. $3×3 Killer whale (*Orcinus orca*); Pygmy killer whale (*Feresa attenuata*)	4·25	4·25
MS2138	100×70 mm. $3×2 Long-finned pilot whale (*Globicephala melas*); Short-finned pilot whale (*Globicephalamacrorhynchus*)	4·50	4·50

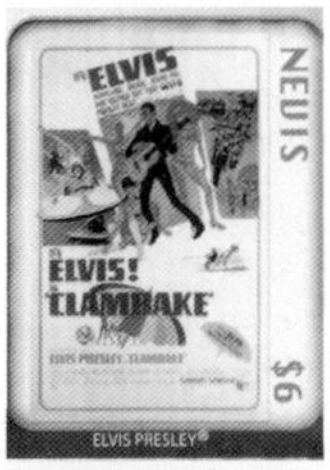

269 Film Poster for *Clambake*

2009. Elvis Presley in Film Clambake

MS2139	125×90 mm. $6 Type **269**	4·50	4·50
MS2140	90×125 mm. $6 Wearing black stetson and white jacket	4·50	4·50

MS2141 90×125 mm. $6 On motorcycle	4·50	4·50
MS2142 125×90 mm. $6 Wearing white jacket	4·50	4·50

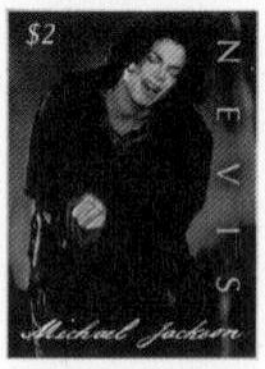

270 Michael Jackson

2009. Michael Jackson Commemoration. Two sheets, each 178×127 mm, containing T 270 and similar multicoloured designs. Litho.

MS2143 Wearing black: Type **270** (pale blue inscr); Three-quarter length (yellow inscr); Type **270** (lavender inscr); Three-quarter length (red inscr)	5·75	5·75
MS2144 Wearing white: With both hands raised to face; In profile; With microphone; With both arms raised	6·50	6·50

On No. **MS**2143 the colours givan are for the country inscription 'NEVIS'.

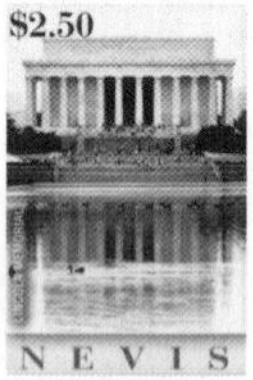

271 Lincoln Memorial

2009. Birth Bicentenary of Abraham Lincoln (US President 1861–5). Sheet 175×136 mm containing T 271 and similar vert designs. Multicoloured. Litho.

MS2145 Type **271**; Statue of Abraham Lincoln; Head and upper body of statue; Lincoln Memorial from air	6·25	6·25

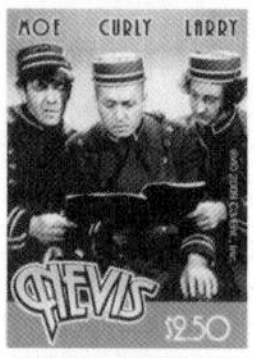

272 Moe, Curly and Larry

2009. The Three Stooges. Sheet 130×150 mm containing T 272 and similar vert designs. Multicoloured.

MS2146 Type **272**; Curly; Moe; Larry	6·25	6·25

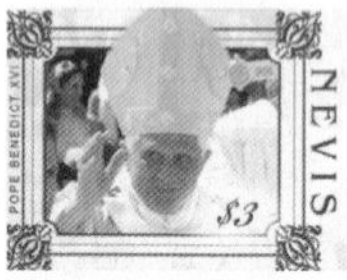

273 Pope Benedict XVI wearing Mitre

2009. Visit of Pope Benedict XVI to Israel. Sheet 100×150 mm containing T 273 and similar horiz designs. Multicoloured.

MS2147 Type **273**; As Type **273** (gold frame); Pope Benedict XVI wearing skull cap (brown frame); Pope wearing skull cap (gold frame)	6·25	6·25

274 *Genipa americana*

2009. Flowers of the Caribbean. Multicoloured.

2148	25c. Type **274**	15	15
2149	30c. *Clusia rosea*	25	25
2150	80c. *Browallia americana*	70	70
2151	90c. *Bidens alba*	75	75
2152	$1 *Begonia odorata*	80	80
2153	$5 *Jatropha gossypiifolia*	4·00	4·00
MS2154	150×100 mm. $2.50×4 *Crantzia cristata; Selaginella flabellata; Hibiscus tiliaceus; Heliconia psittacorum*	6·25	6·25

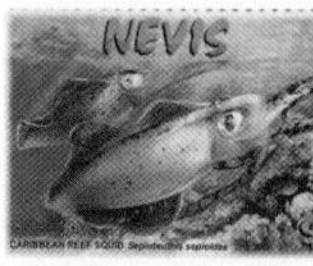

275 Caribbean Reef Squid

2009. Endangered Species. Caribbean Reef Squid (Sepioteuthis sepioidea). Multicoloured.

2155	$2 Type **275**	1·50	1·50
2156	$2 One squid	1·50	1·50
2157	$2 One squid (body bent showing head and tail)	1·50	1·50
2158	$2 Two squid (foreground squid swimming to left)	1·50	1·50
MS2159	112×165 mm. Nos. 2155/8, each ×2	12·00	12·00

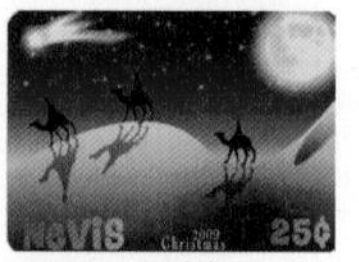

276 Journey of the Magi

2009. Christmas. Multicoloured.

2160	25c. Type **276**	15	15
2161	30c. Nativity with magi on star	25	25
2162	90c. Magi and camel in stars	80	80
2163	$5 Nativity with angels	3·25	3·25

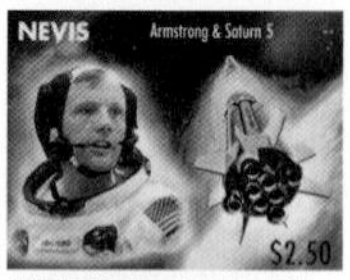

277 Neil Armstrong and Saturn 5 Rocket

2009. 40th Anniv of First Manned Moon Landing. International Year of Astronomy. T 277 and similar horiz designs. Multicoloured.

MS2164 150×100 mm. $2.50×4 Type **277**; Lunar Module, Buzz Aldrin and Michael Collins; Command Module in Moon orbit; Lunar Module leaving the Moon	6·50	6·50
MS2165 100×70 mm. $6 Neil Armstrong and Lunar Module taking off	4·00	4·00

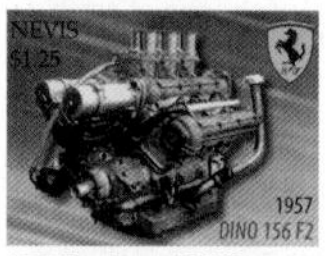

278 Engine of DINO 156 F2, 1957

2010. Ferrari Cars. Multicoloured.

2166	$1.25 Type **278**	1·25	1·25
2167	$1.25 DINO 156 F2, 1957 (car no. 122)	1·25	1·25
2168	$1.25 Diagram of engine and chassis of 125 S, 1947	1·25	1·25
2169	$1.25 125 S, 1947 (car no. 56)	1·25	1·25
2170	$1.25 Exhaust pipes of 553 F2, 1953	1·25	1·25
2171	$1.25 553 F2, 1953	1·25	1·25
2172	$1.25 Engine of 500 F2, 1951	1·25	1·25
2173	$1.25 500 F2, 1951 (car no. 15)	1·25	1·25

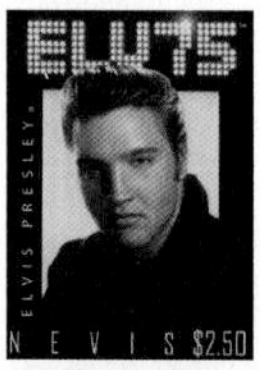

279 Elvis Presley

2010. 75th Birth Anniv of Elvis Presley. Multicoloured.

MS2174 $2.50×4 Type **279**; Wearing brown jacket and tie; Wearing cream jacket; Wearing pale grey shirt	6·50	6·50

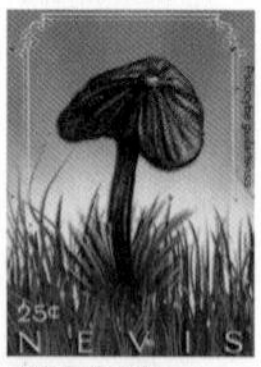

280 *Psilocybe guilartensis*

2010. Fungi. Multicoloured.

2175	25c. Type **280**	15	15
2176	80c. *Alboleptonia flavifolia*	70	70
2177	$1 *Agaricus* sp.	80	80
2178	$5 *Psilocybe caerulescens*	3·25	3·25
MS2179	125×158 mm. $1.50×6 *Psilocybe portoricensis; Boletus ruborculus; Psilocybe plutonia* (one mushroom); *Alboleptonia largentii; Psilocybe plutonia* (three mushrooms); *Collybia aurea*	4·25	4·25

The stamps and margins of **MS**2179 form a composite background design.

MS2179 is inscr 'MUSHROOMS' on the sheet margin.

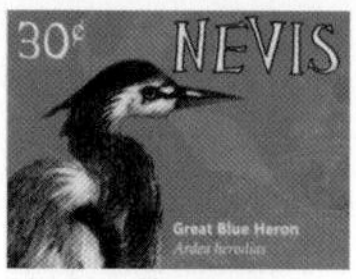

281 Great Blue Heron (*Ardea herodias*)

2010. Birds of Nevis

2180	30c. Type **281**	25	25
2181	90c. Magnificent frigatebird (*Fregata magnificens*)	75	75
2182	$1 Masked booby (*Sula dactylatra*)	80	80
2183	$5 Great egret (*Ardea alba*)	4·00	4·00
MS2184	150×110 mm. $2×4 White-tailed tropicbird (*Phaethon lepturus*); Audubon's shearwater (*Puffinus lherminieri*); Red-billed tropicbird (*Phaethon aethereus*); Leach's storm-petrel (*Oceanodroma leucorhoa*) (all vert)	6·00	6·00
MS2185	120×80 mm. $3 Brown pelican (*Pelecanus occidentalis*); $3 Brown booby (*Sula leucogaster*)	4·00	4·00

The stamps and margins of **MS**2184 form a composite background design of grassland.

The stamps and margins of **MS**2185 form a composite background design of trees at sunset.

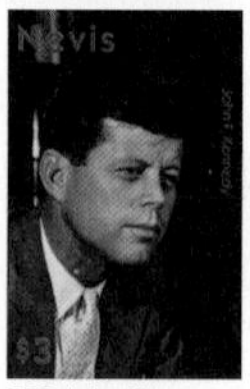

282 John F. Kennedy

2010. 50th Anniv of Election of Pres. John F. Kennedy (1st issue). Multicoloured.

MS2186 $3×4 Type **282**; Nikita Khrushchev; Nikita Khrushchev seated; Pres. Kennedy seated	5·50	5·50
MS2187 $3×4 Richard NIxon (Republican Candidate); John F. Kennedy (Democratic Candidate); John F. Kennedy (Democratic Candidate) (black/white photo); Richard Nixon (Republican Candidate) (black/white photo)	5·50	5·50

The two lower stamps within **MS**2187 form a composite design.

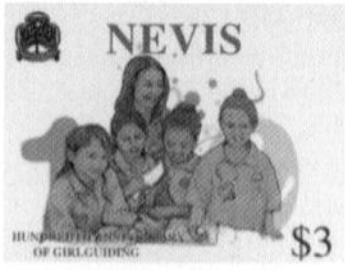

283 Four Brownies and Leader

2010. Centenary of Girlguiding

MS2188 150×100 mm. $3×4 Type **283**; Four guides; Guide abseiling; Three guides	5·50	5·50
MS2189 70×100 mm. $6 Four guides (vert)	6·00	6·00

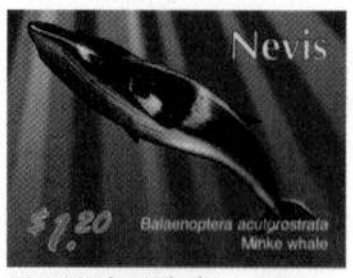

284 Minke Whale (*Balaenoptera acutorostrata*)

2010. Sea Mammals of the Caribbean. Multicoloured.

2190	$1.20 Type **284**	1·20	1·20
2191	$1.80 Northern right whale (*Eubalaena glacialis*)	1·70	1·70
2192	$3 Fin whale (*Balaenoptera physalus*)	2·50	2·50
2193	$5 Sei whale (*Balaenoptera borealis*)	3·50	3·50
MS2194	101×70 mm. $3 Caribbean monk seal (*Monachus tropicalis*); $3 West Indian manatee (*Trichechus manatus*)	2·20	2·20
MS2195	99×70 mm. $6 Blue whale (*Balaenoptera musculus*)	4·00	4·00

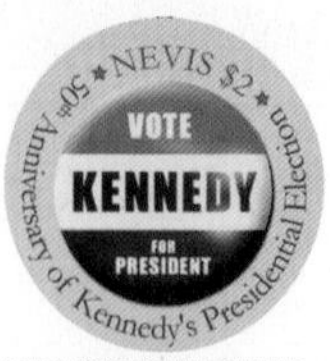

285 'VOTE KENNEDY FOR PRESIDENT' Badge

2010. 50th Anniv of Election of Pres. John F. Kennedy (2nd issue). Campaign Badges. Sheet 182×122 mm. Multicoloured.

MS2196 $2×4 Type **285**; Portrait and 'FOR PRESIDENT JOHN F. KENNEDY'; 'KENNEDY JOHNSON'; Portraits and 'AMERICA NEEDS KENNEDY JOHNSON'	6·00	7·00

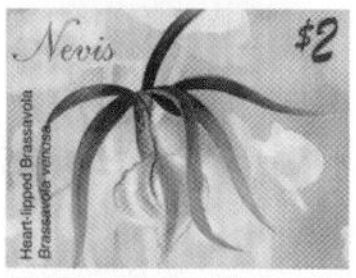

286 Heart-lipped Brassavola (*Brassavola venosa*)

2010. Orchids of the Caribbean

MS2197 150×100 mm. $2×6 Type **286**; Waunakee Sunset (*Phragmepidium* Jason Fisher); Moss-loving Cranichis (*Cranichis muscosa*); Longclaw orchid (*Eltroplectris calcarata*); Golden yellow cattleya (*Cattleya aurea*); Fat cat (*Zygoneria* Adelaide Meadows)	9·00	10·50
MS2198 100×70 mm. $6 Von Martin's Brassavola (*Brassavola martiana*) (vert)	4·75	5·25

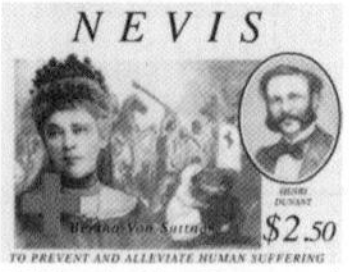

287 Bertha Von Suttner and Henri Dunant

2010. Death Centenary of Henri Dunant (founder of Red Cross). Multicoloured.

MS2199 151×100 mm. Type **287**; Victor Hugo; Charles Dickens; Harriet Beecher Stowe	6·25	6·25
MS2200 71×101 mm. $6 Abolition of slavery, Washington DC, 1862	4·50	4·50

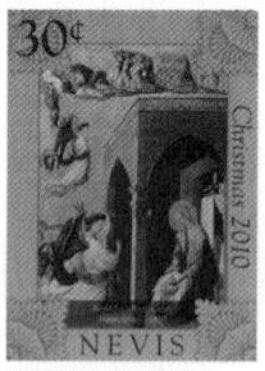

288 *Annunciation* (Paolo Uccello), c. 1420

2010. Christmas. Multicoloured.

2201	30c. Type **288**	15	20
2202	90c. The Altarpiece of the Rose Garlands (Albrecht Dürer)	55	60
2203	$1.80 As 30c.	1·40	1·50
2204	$2 Sistine Madonna (Raffaello Sanzlo da Urbino), c. 1513	1·50	1·75
2205	$2.30 As $2	1·90	2·00
2206	$3 The Adoration of the Magi (Giotto di Bondone), c. 1305	2·25	2·50

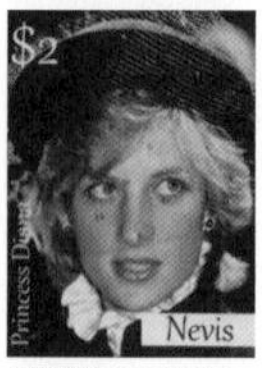

289 Princess Diana

2010. Princess Diana Commemoration. Multicoloured.

MS2207 130×150 mm. $2×6 Type **289**×2; Wearing white jacket and tiara; Wearing white hat and jacket×2	9·00	9·00
MS2208 140×100 mm. $3 Wearing white sleeveless dress×4	2·25	2·25

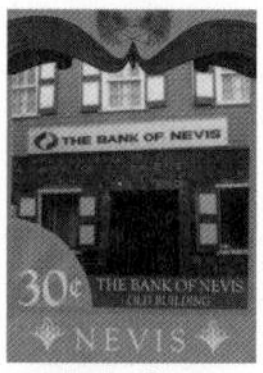

290 Bank of Nevis Building, Charlestown

2010. 25th Anniv of the Bank of Nevis. Multicoloured.

2209	30c. Type **290**	15	20
2210	$5 Projected new Bank of Nevis building	3·25	3·25

291 Marek Hamsik (Slovakia)

2010. World Cup Football Championship, South Africa. Multicoloured.
MS2211 131×155 mm. $1.50×6 Netherlands vs. Slovakia: Type **291**; Giovanni Van Bronckhorst (Netherlands); Robert Vittek (Slovakia); Eljero Elia (Netherlands); Miroslav Stoch (Slovakia); Dirk Kuyt (Netherlands)   7·50   8·50
MS2212 130×155 mm. $1.50×6 Brazil vs. Chile: Lucio (Brazil); Alexis Sanchez (Chile); Dani Alves (Brazil); Arturo Vidal (Chile); Gilberto Silva (Brazil); Rodrigo Tello (Chile)   7·50   7·50
MS2213 130×155 mm. $1.50×6 Paraguay vs. Japan: Paulo Da Silva (Paraguay); Yoshito Okubo (Japan); Edgar Barreto (Paraguay); Yuichi Komano (Japan); Cristian Riveros (Paraguay); Yasuhito Endo (Japan)   7·50   7·50
MS2214 130×155 mm. $1.50×6 Spain vs. Portugal: Liedson (Portugal); Xavi Hernandez (Spain); Simao (Portugal); Jasper Juinen (Spain); Cristiano Ronaldo (Portugal); David Villa (Spain)   7·50   7·50
MS2215 85×90 mm. $1.50 Bert van Marwijk (Netherlands); $1.50 Joris Mathijsen   2·50   2·50
MS2216 85×90 mm. $1.50 Dunga (coach, Brazil); Kaka (Brazil)   1·25   1·25
MS2217 85×90 mm. $1.50 Gerardo Martino (coach, Paraguay); $1.50 Roque Santa Cruz   2·50   2·50
MS2218 85×90 mm. $1.50 Vicente del Bosque (coach, Spain); Sergio Ramos (Spain)   1·25   1·25

292 Abraham Lincoln

2011. Birth Bicentenary (2009) of Abraham Lincoln (US President, 18615). Multicoloured.
MS2219 100×150 mm. $2 Type **292**×4   1·50   1·75
MS2220 110×150 mm. $2×4 Abraham Lincoln portraits: With sepia background; With grey background; Oval portrait with white background but facing forwards; Black background   6·00   7·00

293 Elvis Presley

2011. Elvis Presley Commemoration. Multicoloured.
MS2221 100×168 mm. $3 Type **293**×4   2·25   2·50
MS2222 167×100 mm. $3 Elvis Presley (wearing black jacket)×4   2·50   2·75

294 Buckingham Palace (image scaled to 57% of original size)

2010. Royal Engagement. Multicoloured.
MS2223 130×140 mm. $3×4 Type **294**; Miss Catherine Middleton (black/white photo); Coat of arms of Prince William of Wales (circular 38 mm diameter); Prince William (black/white photo)   2·50   2·50
MS2224 130×140 mm. $3×4 Prince William and Miss Catherine Middleton; Miss Catherine Middleton (wearing red jacket and black hat); Coat of arms of Prince William of Wales (circular 38 mm diameter); Prince William (colour photo)   2·50   2·50

MS2225 70×120 mm. $6 Prince William and Miss Catherine Middleton (40×30 mm)   5·00   5·00
Nos. **MS**2223/4 each contain a central circular stamp surrounded by three semi-circular stamps as T **294**.

295 Pres. Barack Obama and Mrs. Michelle Obama

2011. Visit of President Barack Obama to India. Multicoloured.
MS2226 157×100 mm. $3×4 Type **295**; Pres. Obama addressing Inidan students in Mumbai; Pres. Obama signing condolence book for Mumbai terror attack; Pres. Obama with Indian Prime Minister Singh   9·00   10·50
MS2227 70×100 mm. $6 Pres. Obama addressing Indian students in Mumbai (horiz)   4·75   5·00

296 Buckingham Palace

2011. Fifth Death Anniv of Pope John Paul II. Multicoloured.
MS2228 110×170 mm. $3 Type **296**×4   2·25   2·50
MS2229 110×170 mm. $4 Pope John Paul II wearing red brimmed hat×4   3·00   3·25

297 Mahatma Gandhi

2011. Indipex 2011 International Stamp Exhibition, Delhi. Mahatma Gandhi. Multicoloured.
MS2230 $3 Type **297**×4   2·50   2·50
MS2231 $3 Mahatma Gandhi (facing left)×4   2·50   2·50

298 Elvis Presley

2011. Elvis Presley Commemoration. Multicoloured.
MS2232 $3×4 Type **298**; Elvis Presley wearing cap; Head tilted to left; In profile   2·50   2·50
MS2233 $3×4 Elvis Presley smiling, wearing dark jacket; Singing, wearing white jacket and bow tie; Singing, wearing dark shirt; Smiling, wearing white (all vert)   2·50   2·50

299 Pope Benedict XVI

2011. Pope Benedict XVI. Multicoloured.
MS2234 109×173 mm. $3×4 As Type **299** but with different backgrounds showing interior of Basilica: Type **299** (windows in dome); Top of pillar at bottom left; Pillars; Statue with cross at foot   2·50   2·50
MS2235 180×140 mm. $3 Pope Benedict XVI (in profile) (vert)×4   2·50   2·50

300 Elvis Presley as Guy Lambert in *Double Trouble*, 1967

2011. Elvis Presley in *Double Trouble*. Multicoloured.
MS2236 90×125 mm. $6 Type **300**   5·00   5·00
MS2237 125×90 mm. $6 Poster for *Double Trouble*   5·00   5·00
MS2238 90×125 mm. $6 Elvis Presley (wearing grey jacket and bow tie) (horiz)   5·00   5·00
MS2239 125×90 mm. $6 Elvis Presley playing guitar   5·00   5·00

301 Queen Elizabeth II

2011. 85th Birthday of Queen Elizabeth II and 90th Birthday of Prince Philip. Multicoloured.
MS2240 $2 Type **301**×2 $2 Queen Elizabeth II (wearing mauve)×2   3·50   3·50
MS2241 $2 Prince Philip×4   3·50   3·50

302 Meadow Argus (*Junonia villida*)

2011. Butterflies of the World. Multicoloured.
MS2242 104×150 mm. $2×6 Type **302**; Gulf fritillary (*Agraulis vanillae*); Eastern tiger swallowtail (*Papilio glaucus*); Gabb's checkerspot (*Chlosyne gabbii*); Indian leafwing (*Kallima paralekta*); Blue diadem (*Hypolimnas salmacis*)   10·00   10·00
MS2243 70×100 mm. $6 Monarch (*Danaus plexippus*)   5·00   5·00

303 Maine Coon

2011. Cats of the World. Multicoloured.
MS2244 $2.50×4 Type **303**; Norwegian forest cat; Ragdoll; Turkish angora   8·50   8·50
MS2245 $2.50×4 Russian blue; Siamese; Abyssinian; Bombay   8·50   8·50

304 King George V

2011. Centenary of the Coronation of King George V. Sheet 150×101 mm. Multicoloured.
MS2246 $3 Type **304**×4   2·50   2·50

305 King George VI

2011. 75th Anniv of the Accession of King George VI. Sheet 150×100 mm. Multicoloured.
MS2247 $3 Type **305**×4   2·50   2·50

306 Shoaib Akhtar (Pakistan)

2011. Cricket World Cup, India, Sri Lanka and Bangladesh. Multicoloured.
MS2248 $3×4 Type **306**; Shoaib Akhtar (head and shoulders); Pakistan team; Emblem (all with yellow-olive background)   10·00   10·00
MS2249 $3×4 A. B. De Villiers batting; A. B. De Villiers ; South Africa team; Emblem (all with orange-yellow backgrounds)   10·00   10·00
MS2250 $3×4 Kumar Sangakkara on pitch; Kumar Sangakkara; Sri Lanka team; Emblem (all with reddish-orange background)   10·00   10·00
MS2251 $3×4 Chris Gayle on pitch; Chris Gayle; West Indies team; Emblem (all with brown-red background)   10·00   10·00
MS2252 $3×4 A. B. De Villiers batting; A. B. De Villiers ; South Africa team celebrating; Emblem (all with pale orange background)   10·00   10·00

307 Miss Catherine Middleton on Wedding Day

2011. Royal Wedding. Multicoloured.
MS2253 100×150 mm. $3 Type **307**×2; $3 Prince William (in profile)×2   7·50   7·50
MS2254 100×150 mm. $3 Duke and Duchess of Cambridge in carriage×2; $3 Duchess of Cambridge; $3 Prince William   7·50   7·50
MS2255 100×90 mm. $6 Duke and Duchess of Cambridge; $6 Duke and Duchess of Cambridge riding in carriage   7·50   7·50

308 Princess Diana

2011. 50th Birth Anniv of Princess Diana. Multicoloured.
MS2256 150×130 mm. $2×4 Type **308**; Wearing cap; Waving, in profile; Wearing dark purple and maroon hat   6·50   6·50
MS2257 160×125 mm. $2×4 Princess Diana wearing bright mauve jacket; Wearing black and white hat and jacket; Wearing navy blue jacket and white top; Wearing red dress   6·50   6·50

309 Pres. Abraham Lincoln and 'Government of the People by the People for the People shall not perish from the Earth'

2011. 150th Anniv of the American Civil War. Multicoloured.
MS2258 $2×4 all showing Pres. Abraham Lincoln and quotation: Type **309**; 'The best way to destroy an enemy is to make him a friend'; 'A house divided against itself cannot stand'; 'Avoid popularity if you would have peace'   6·50   6·50
MS2259 $2×4 Union Army soldier; Shield and Constitution ('The American Civil War'); Union Army soldiers in trenches; Pres. Abraham Lincoln   6·50   6·50

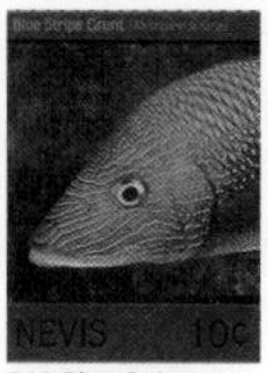

310 Blue Stripe Grunt (*Haemulon sciurus*)

2011. Tropical Fish of the Caribbean. Multicoloured.

2260	10c. Type **310**	10	10
2261	30c. Red hind (*Cephalopholis miniatus*)	30	20
2262	40c. Red snapper (*Lutjanus campechanus*)	35	25
2263	$5 Old wife (*Enoplosus armatus*)	4·50	5·00
MS2264	102×123 mm. $2×6 Spotfin butterflyfish (*C. ocellatus*); Caribbean reef squid (*S. sepioidea*); Chubs (*K. bigibbus*); Surgeonfish (*A. olivaceus*); Blue-headed wrasse (*T. bifasciatum*); Long-spine porcupinefish (*D. holocanthus*) (all horiz)	5·50	6·50
MS2265	100×71 mm. $6 Anemone fish (*Amphiprioninae*) (horiz)	5·00	5·00

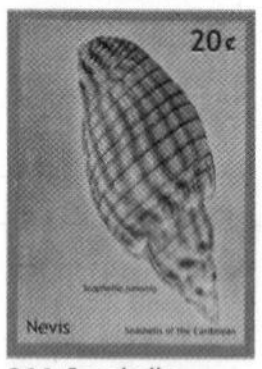

311 *Scaphella junonia*

2011. Seashells of the Caribbean. Multicoloured.

2266	20c. Type **311**	15	10
2267	30c. *Strombus gigas*	30	20
2268	$1.80 *Busycon contrarium*	1·50	1·50
2269	$5 *Arca zebra*	4·50	5·00
MS2270	150×101 mm. $2.50×4 *Charonia variegata*; *Cyphraea aurantium*; *Cyphoma gibbosa*; *Chicoreus articulatus*	8·50	8·50
MS2271	100×71 mm. $6 *Thais deltoidea*	5·00	5·00
MS2272	100×71 mm. $6 *Cittarium pica*	5·00	5·00

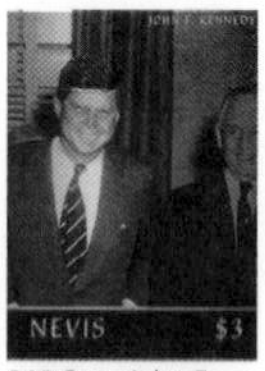

312 Pres. John F. Kennedy

2011. 50th Anniv of the Inauguration of Pres. John F. Kennedy. Multicoloured.

MS2273	120×180 mm. $3×4 Type **312**; Pres. Kennedy in front of microphones; Facing microphones, in profile; Shaking hands	10·00	10·00
MS2274	90×100 mm. $6 Pres. Kennedy	5·00	5·00

313 Memorial, Staten Island, New York

2011. Tenth Anniv of Attack on World Trade Center, New York. Black and turquoise-green.

MS2275	161×100 mm. $2.75×4 Type **313**; Memorial, Bayonne, New Jersey; Memorial, The Pentagon; Memorial, Jerusalem	8·50	8·50
MS2276	100×100 mm. $6 Ground Zero Reflecting Pools	5·00	5·00

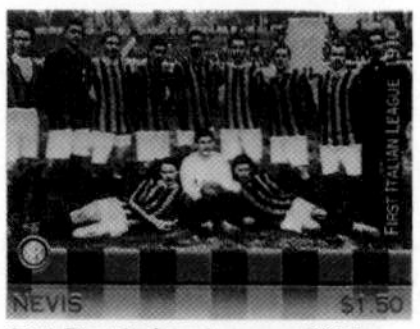

314 First Italian League, 1910

2011. Juventus Football Club, Turin, Italy. Multicoloured.

MS2277	$1.50×9 Type **314**; Giorgio Muggiani; Angelo Moratti; Helenio Herrera; Tim Cup, 2011; Giacinto Facchetti; Sandro Mazzola; Mario Corso; Luis Suarez	9·75	9·75

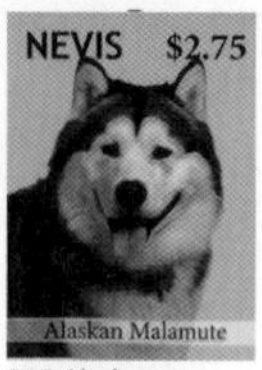

315 Alaskan Malamute

2011. Dogs of the World. Multicoloured.

MS2278	140×100 mm. $2.75×4 Type **315**; Yorkshire terrier; Black labrador; Dachshund	8·50	8·50
MS2279	100×70 mm. $6 Beagle	5·00	5·00

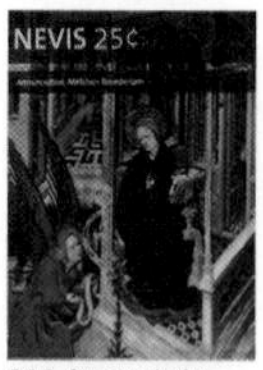

316 *Annunciation*

2011. Christmas. Paintings by Melchior Broederlam. Multicoloured.

2280	25c. Type **316**	20	15
2281	30c. *Visitation*	30	20
2282	90c. *Presentation in the Temple*	80	50
2283	$5 *Flight into Egypt*	2·75	3·25

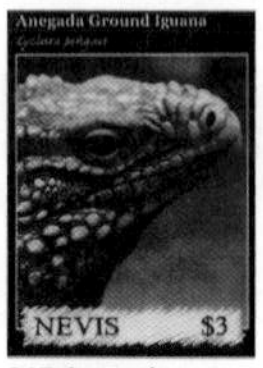

317 Anegada Ground Iguana (*Cyclura pinguis*)

2011. Reptiles of the Caribbean. Multicoloured.

MS2284	150×100 mm. $3×4 Type **317**; Antilles racer (snake) (*Alsophis antillensis*); Brown anole (*Anolis sagrei*); Lesser Antillean iguana (*Iguana delicatissima*)	2·50	2·50
MS2285	70×101 mm. $6 Anegada ground iguana (*Cyclura pinguis*) (51×38 mm)	5·00	5·00

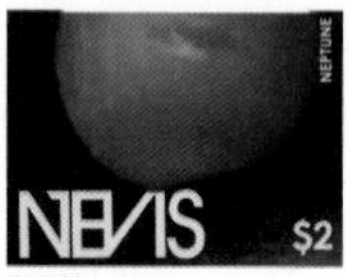

318 Neptune

2011. 50th Anniv of the First Man in Space. Multicoloured.

MS2286	210×140 mm. $2×6 Type **318**; Uranus; Earth and Mars; Venus and Mercury; Jupiter; Saturn	5·00	5·00
MS2287	220×80 mm. $3×4 Full moon; Waxing gibbous moon; First quarter; Waxing crescent moon (all circular 35 mm diameter)	2·50	2·50

OFFICIAL STAMPS

1980. Nos. 40/49 optd OFFICIAL.

O1	15c. Sugar cane being harvested	10	10
O2	25c. Crafthouse (craft centre)	10	10
O3	30c. "Europa" (liner)	10	10
O4	40c. Lobster and sea crab	15	15
O5	45c. Royal St. Kitts Hotel and golf course	20	20
O6	50c. Pinney's Beach, Nevis	15	20
O7	55c. New runway at Golden Rock	15	20
O8	$1 Picking cotton	15	25
O9	$5 Brewery	45	55
O10	$10 Pineapples and peanuts	70	90

1981. Nos. 60/71 optd OFFICIAL.

O11	15c. New River Mill	10	10
O12	20c. Nelson Museum	10	10
O13	25c. St. James' Parish Church	10	15
O14	30c. Nevis Lane	15	15
O15	40c. Zetland Plantation	15	20
O16	45c. Nisbet Plantation	20	25
O17	50c. Pinney's Beach	20	25
O18	55c. Eva Wilkin's Studio	25	30
O19	$1 Nevis at dawn	30	30
O20	$2.50 Ruins of Fort Charles	40	50
O21	$5 Old Bath House	50	65
O22	$10 Beach at Nisbet's	80	1·00

1983. Nos. 72/7 optd or surch OFFICIAL.

O23	45c. on $2 "Royal Sovereign"	10	15
O24	45c. on $2 Prince Charles and Lady Diana Spencer	20	25
O25	55c. "Royal Caroline"	10	15
O26	55c. Prince Charles and Lady Diana Spencer	25	25
O27	$1.10 on $5 "Britannia"	20	25
O28	$1.10 on $5 Prince Charles and Lady Diana Spencer	55	60

1985. Nos. 187/98 optd OFFICIAL.

O29	15c. Flamboyant	20	20
O30	20c. Eyelash orchid	30	30
O31	30c. Bougainvillea	30	40
O32	40c. Hibiscus sp	30	40
O33	50c. Night-blooming cereus	35	40
O34	55c. Yellow mahoe	35	45
O35	60c. Spider-lily	40	50
O36	75c. Scarlet cordia	45	55
O37	$1 Shell-ginger	60	60
O38	$3 Blue petrea	1·25	1·75
O39	$5 Coral hibiscus	2·00	2·25
O40	$10 Passion flower	3·00	2·50

1993. Nos. 578/91 optd OFFICIAL.

O41	5c. Type **63**	45	60
O42	10c. "Historis odius"	50	60
O43	15c. "Marpesia corinna"	60	50
O44	20c. "Anartia amathea"	60	40
O45	25c. "Junonia evarete"	60	40
O46	40c. "Heliconius charithonia"	75	45
O47	50c. "Marpesia petreus"	75	45
O48	75c. "Heliconius doris"	1·00	60
O49	80c. "Dione juno"	1·50	50
O50	$1 "Hypolimnas misippus"	1·00	80
O51	$3 "Danaus plexippus"	2·25	2·75
O52	$5 "Heliconius sara"	3·00	3·50
O53	$10 "Tithorea harmonia"	5·50	6·50
O54	$20 "Dryas julia"	11·00	12·00

1999. Nos. 1166/77 optd OFFICIAL.

O55	25c. Guava	15	20
O56	30c. Papaya	15	20
O57	50c. Mango	25	30
O58	60c. Golden apple	30	35
O59	80c. Pineapple	40	45
O60	90c. Watermelon	45	50
O61	$1 Bananas	50	55
O62	$1.80 Orange	90	95
O63	$3 Honeydew	1·50	1·60
O64	$5 Cantaloupe	2·50	2·75
O65	$10 Pomegranate	5·00	5·25
O66	$20 Cashew	10·00	10·50

Pt. 1

NEW BRUNSWICK

An eastern province of the Dominion of Canada, whose stamps are now used.

1851. 12 pence = 1 shilling; 20 shillings = 1 pound.
1860. 100 cents = 1 dollar.

1 Royal Crown and Heraldic Flowers of the United Kingdom

1851

2	**1**	3d. red	£2750	£325
4	**1**	6d. yellow	£4500	£700
5	**1**	1s. mauve	£18000	£4500

2 Locomotive

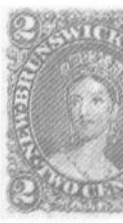

3 Queen Victoria

1860

8	**2**	1c. purple	65·00	50·00
10	**3**	2c. orange	30·00	28·00
13	-	5c. brown	£8000	
14	-	5c. green	27·00	18·00
17	-	10c. red	65·00	70·00
18	-	12½c. blue	70·00	42·00
19	-	17c. black	42·00	75·00

DESIGNS—VERT: 5c. brown, Charles Connell; 5c. green, 10c. Queen Victoria; 17c. King Edward VII when Prince of Wales. HORIZ: 12½c. Steamship.

Pt. 6

NEW CALEDONIA

A French Overseas Territory in the S. Pacific, E. of Australia, consisting of New Caledonia and a number of smaller islands.

100 centimes = 1 franc.

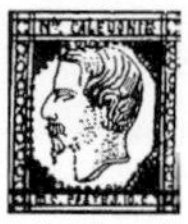

1 Napoleon III

1860. Imperf.

1	**1**	10c. black	£275	

1881. "Peace and Commerce" type surch N C E and new value. Imperf.

5	**H**	05 on 40c. red on yellow	23·00	18·00
8a	**H**	5 on 40c. red on yellow	14·00	14·00
9	**H**	5 on 75c. red	65·00	41·00
6	**H**	25 on 35c. black on orange	£275	£275
7	**H**	25 on 75c. red	£350	£350

Nos. 5/30 are stamps of French Colonies optd or surch.

1886. "Peace and Commerce" (imperf) and "Commerce" types surch N.C.E. 5c.

10	**J**	5c. on 1f. green	42·00	46·00
11	**H**	5c. on 1f. green	£11000	£12000

1891. "Peace and Commerce" (imperf) and "Commerce" types surch N.-C.E. 10 c. in ornamental frame.

13		10c. on 40c. red on yellow	40·00	55·00
14	**J**	10c. on 40c. red on yellow	28·00	14·50

1892. "Commerce" type surch N.-C.E. 10 centimes in ornamental frame.

15	10c. on 30c. brown on drab	23·00	13·00

1892. Optd NLLE CALEDONIE. (a) "Peace and Commerce" type. Imperf.

16	**H**	20c. red on green	£300	£325
17	**H**	35c. black on orange	90·00	80·00
19	**H**	1f. green	£250	£250

(b) "Commerce" type.

20	**J**	5c. green on green	48·00	18·00
21	**J**	10c. black on lilac	£130	90·00
22	**J**	15c. blue	£120	60·00
23	**J**	20c. red on green	£130	85·00
24	**J**	25c. brown on yellow	50·00	9·25
25	**J**	25c. black on pink	£130	18·00
26	**J**	30c. brown on drab	£120	95·00
27	**J**	35c. black on orange	£225	£160
29	**J**	75c. red on pink	£170	£140
30	**J**	1f. green	£140	£140

1892. "Tablet" key-type inscr "NLLE CALEDONIE ET DEPENDANCES".

31	**D**	1c. black and red on blue	90	55
32	**D**	2c. brown and blue on buff	45	45
33	**D**	4c. brown and blue on grey	1·80	4·50
55	**D**	5c. green and red	3·25	30
34	**D**	10c. black and blue on lilac	4·50	75
56	**D**	10c. red and blue	6·50	45
35	**D**	15c. blue and red	6·50	3·00
57	**D**	15c. grey and red	7·75	30
36	**D**	20c. red and blue on green	38·00	90
37	**D**	25c. black and red on pink	6·00	8·25
58	**D**	25c. blue and red	10·00	3·75
38	**D**	30c. brown and blue on drab	16·00	1·20
39	**D**	40c. red and blue on yellow	13·00	17·00
40	**D**	50c. red and blue on pink	16·00	7·75
59	**D**	50c. brown and red on blue	60·00	£110
60	**D**	50c. brown and blue on blue	55·00	37·00
41	**D**	75c. brown & red on orange	85·00	29·00
42	**D**	1f. green and red	19·00	23·00

1892. Surch N-C-E in ornamental scroll and new value. (a) "Peace and Commerce" type. Imperf.

44	**H**	10 on 1f. green	£5500	£4500

(b) "Commerce" type.

45	**J**	5 on 20c. red on green	55·00	9·25
46	**J**	5 on 75c. red on pink	24·00	25·00
48	**J**	10 on 1f. green	19·00	12·00

1899. Stamps of 1892 surch (a) N-C-E in ornamental scroll and 5.

50	**D**	5 on 2c. brown & bl on buff	11·00	17·00
51	**D**	5 on 4c. brown & bl on grey	2·30	3·75

(b) N.C.E. and 15 in circle.

52		15 on 30c. brown and blue on drab	3·75	7·00
53		15 on 75c. brown and red on orange	13·00	23·00
54		15 on 1f. green and red	60·00	44·00

1902. Surch N.-C.E. and value in figures.

61		5 on 30c. brown and blue on drab	3·25	9·25
62		15 on 40c. red and blue on yellow	4·50	8·50

1903. 50th Anniv of French Annexation. Optd CINQUANTENAIRE 24 SEPTEMBRE 1853 1903 and eagle.

63		1c. black and red on blue	75	1·20
64		2c. brown and blue on buff	2·30	2·75
65		4c. brown and blue on grey	7·00	5·75
66		5c. green and red	2·00	3·50
69		10c. black and blue on lilac	3·75	5·50
70		15c. grey and red	8·25	1·80
71		20c. red and blue on green	11·00	28·00
72		25c. black and red on pink	11·00	18·00
73		30c. brown and blue on drab	20·00	29·00
74		40c. red and blue on yellow	55·00	23·00
75		50c. red and blue on pink	55·00	60·00
76		75c. brown & blue on orange	70·00	£120
77		1f. green and red	£120	£130

1903. Nos. 64 etc further surch with value in figures within the jubilee opt.

78		1 on 2c. brown & bl on buff	90	90
79		2 on 4c. brown & bl on grey	3·50	5·25
80		4 on 5c. green and red	1·20	2·75
82		10 on 15c. grey and red	75	2·75
83		15 on 20c. red and blue on green	2·00	5·50
84		20 on 25c. black and red on pink	3·75	6·50

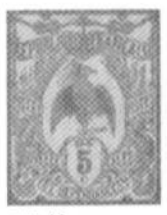
15 Kagu

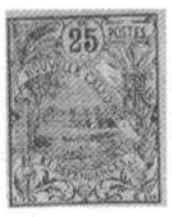
16

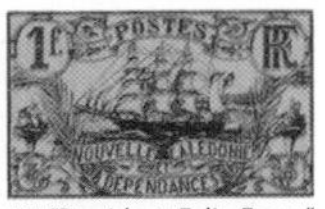
17 "President Felix Faure" (barque)

1905

85	15	1c. black on green	10	30
86	15	2c. brown	20	65
87	15	4c. blue on orange	35	65
88	15	5c. green	1·40	20
112	15	5c. blue	10	30
113	15	10c. green	1·50	65
114	15	10c. red	45	45
90	15	15c. lilac	50	70
91	16	20c. brown	45	10
92	16	25c. blue on green	1·40	35
115	16	25c. red on yellow	20	10
93	16	30c. brown on orange	65	2·30
116	16	30c. red	1·70	3·50
117	16	30c. orange	35	1·00
94	16	35c. black on yellow	1·50	1·10
95	16	40c. red on green	1·70	1·80
96	16	45c. red	1·50	2·50
97	16	50c. red on orange	5·50	4·00
118	16	50c. blue	1·20	85
119	16	50c. grey	1·10	75
120	16	65c. blue	1·80	3·25
98	16	75c. olive	2·75	3·75
121	16	75c. blue	30	1·80
122	16	75c. violet	90	5·50
99	17	1f. blue on green	1·80	2·50
123	17	1f. blue	2·75	3·25
100	17	2f. red on blue	4·50	5·00
101	17	5f. black on orange	16·00	19·00

1912. Stamps of 1892 surch.

102	D	05 on 15c. grey and red	85	1·20
103	D	05 on 20c. red and blue on green	30	1·40
104	D	05 on 30c. brown and blue on drab	55	2·75
105	D	10 on 40c. red and blue on yellow	90	1·80
106	D	10 on 50c. brown and blue on blue	1·20	2·50

1915. Surch NCE 5 and red cross.

107	15	10c.+5c. red	2·30	1·40

1915. Surch 5c and red cross.

109		10c.+5c. red	2·30	6·25
110		15c.+5c. lilac	35	5·00

1918. Surch 5 CENTIMES.

111		5c. on 15c. lilac	6·00	7·75

1922. Surch 0 05.

124		0.05 on 15c. lilac	30	2·00

1924. Types 15/17 (some colours changed) surch.

125		25c. on 15c. lilac	55	4·25
126	17	25c. on 2f. red on blue	1·10	4·75
127	17	25c. on 5f. black on orange	45	7·25
128	16	60 on 75c. green	20	1·80
129	16	65 on 45c. purple	1·00	3·50
130	16	85 on 45c. purple	1·40	4·00
131	16	90 on 75c. red	45	3·25
132	17	1f.25 on 1f. blue	75	7·25
133	17	1f.50 on 1f. blue on blue	1·50	3·25
134	17	3f. on 5f. mauve	2·00	7·50
135	17	10f. on 5f. green on mauve	2·30	25·00
136	17	20f. on 5f. red on yellow	13·00	50·00

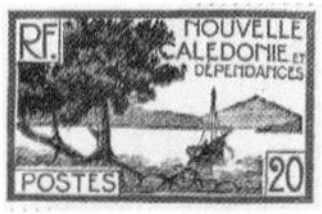
22 Pointe des Paletuviers

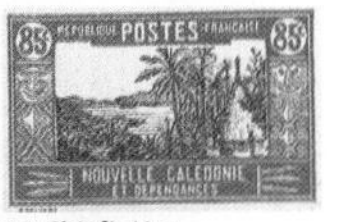
23 Chief's Hut

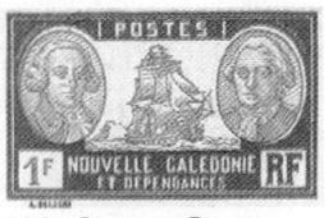
24 La Perouse, De Bougainville and "L'Astrolabe"

1928

137	22	1c. blue and purple	30	2·00
138	22	2c. green and brown	10	2·30
139	22	3c. blue and red	20	6·25
140	22	4c. blue and orange	20	2·50
141	22	5c. brown and blue	20	1·30
142	22	10c. brown and lilac	20	45
143	22	15c. blue and brown	20	45
144	22	20c. brown and red	55	1·40
145	22	25c. brown and green	45	10
146	23	30c. deep green and green	20	65
147	23	35c. mauve and black	55	10
148	23	40c. green and red	20	2·75
149	23	45c. red and blue	2·75	7·00
150	23	45c. green and deep green	3·00	3·75
151	23	50c. brown and mauve	20	10
152	23	55c. red and blue	4·75	1·50
153	23	60c. red and blue	30	7·25
154	23	65c. blue and brown	1·40	90
155	23	70c. brown and mauve	1·80	7·25
156	23	75c. drab and blue	2·30	1·80
157	23	80c. green and purple	1·50	6·50
158	23	85c. brown and green	3·50	3·75
159	23	90c. pink and red	2·75	2·30
160	23	90c. red and brown	2·00	4·50
161	24	1f. pink and drab	6·00	2·30
162	24	1f. carmine and red	3·00	1·60
163	24	1f. green and red	85	4·75
164	24	1f.10 brown and green	11·00	38·00
165	24	1f.25 green and brown	4·50	7·50
166	24	1f.25 carmine and red	1·80	7·75
167	24	1f.40 red and blue	2·00	7·25
168	24	1f.50 light blue and blue	45	1·80
169	24	1f.60 brown and green	2·75	8·25
170	24	1f.75 orange and blue	4·25	5·00
171	24	1f.75 blue and ultramarine	3·75	7·00
172	24	2f. brown and orange	65	35
173	24	2f.25 blue and ultramarine	2·50	6·75
174	24	2f.50 brown	1·70	5·50
175	24	3f. brown and mauve	75	2·75
176	24	5f. brown and blue	75	2·30
177	24	10f. brown & pur on pink	2·00	6·25
178	24	20f. brown & red on yellow	2·75	5·50

1931. "Colonial Exhibition" key-types.

179	E	40c. green and black	5·50	14·50
180	F	50c. mauve and black	5·50	6·00
181	G	90c. red and black	5·50	14·50
182	H	1f.50 blue and black	5·50	6·00

1932. Paris–Noumea Flight. Optd with Couzinet 33 airplane and PARIS-NOUMEA Verneilh-Deve-Munch 5 Avril 1932.

183	23	40c. olive and red	£400	£425
184	23	50c. brown and mauve	£400	£425

1933. 1st Anniv of Paris–Noumea Flight. Optd PARIS-NOUMEA Premiere liaison aerienne 5 Avril 1932 and Couzinet 33 airplane.

185	22	1c. blue and purple	6·50	29·00
186	22	2c. green and brown	7·25	26·00
187	22	4c. blue and orange	5·75	27·00
188	22	5c. brown and blue	7·00	24·00
189	22	10c. brown and lilac	9·00	28·00
190	22	15c. blue and brown	5·50	27·00
191	22	20c. brown and red	5·50	27·00
192	22	25c. brown and green	8·25	30·00
193	23	30c. deep green and green	6·75	28·00
194	23	35c. mauve and black	7·00	28·00
195	23	40c. green and red	6·75	19·00
196	23	45c. red and blue	9·25	28·00
197	23	50c. brown and mauve	5·00	29·00
198	23	70c. brown and mauve	6·75	32·00
199	23	75c. drab and blue	10·00	24·00
200	23	85c. brown and green	6·75	24·00
201	23	90c. pink and red	6·75	24·00
202	24	1f. pink and drab	10·00	34·00
203	24	1f.25 green and brown	9·25	32·00
204	24	1f.50 light blue and blue	11·00	34·00
205	24	1f.75 orange and blue	6·50	20·00
206	24	2f. brown and orange	9·25	38·00
207	24	3f. brown and mauve	9·75	38·00
208	24	5f. brown and blue	11·00	40·00
209	24	10f. brown & pur on pink	6·75	38·00
210	24	20f. brown & red on yellow	5·75	38·00

1937. International Exhibition, Paris. As T 4a of Niger.

211		20c. violet	1·10	5·00
212		30c. green	75	7·75
213		40c. red	35	3·50
214		50c. brown and blue	45	2·75
215		90c. red	75	5·25
216		1f.50 blue	55	2·50
MS216a		120×100 mm. 3f. sepia	14·00	46·00

DESIGNS—HORIZ: 30c. Sailing ships; 40c. Berber, Negress and Annamite; 90c. France extends torch of civilization; 1f.50, Diane de Poitiers. VERT: 50c. Agriculture.

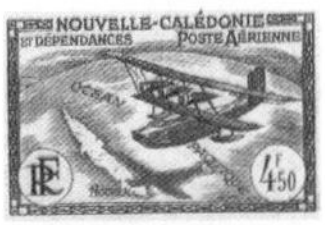
27 Breguet Saigon Flying Boat over Noumea

1938. Air.

217	27	65c. violet	1·50	7·00
218	27	4f.50 red	4·00	6·75
219	27	7f. green	75	6·00
220	27	9f. blue	5·50	6·25
221	27	20f. orange	3·25	5·00
222	27	50f. black	3·75	10·50

1938. Int Anti-cancer Fund. As T 17a of Oceanic Settlement.

223		1f.75+50c. blue	4·00	46·00

1939. New York World's Fair. As T 17b of Oceanic Settlement.

224		1f.25 red	55	8·50
225		2f.25 blue	75	4·25

1939. 150th Anniv of French Revolution. As T 17c of Oceanic Settlement.

226		45c.+25c. green and black (postage)	11·00	23·00
227		70c.+30c. brown and black	11·00	23·00
228		90c.+35c. orange and black	11·00	23·00
229		1f.25+1f. red and black	11·00	23·00
230		2f.25+2f. blue and black	11·00	23·00
231		4f.50+4f. black and orange (air)	23·00	46·00

1941. Adherence to General de Gaulle. Optd France Libre.

232	22	1c. blue and purple	3·75	30·00
233	22	2c. green and brown	4·50	32·00
234	22	3c. blue and red	4·00	55·00
235	22	4c. blue and orange	4·00	23·00
236	22	5c. brown and blue	3·25	23·00
237	22	10c. brown and lilac	3·50	60·00
238	22	15c. blue and brown	20·00	38·00
239	22	20c. brown and red	18·00	32·00
240	22	25c. brown and green	17·00	38·00
241	23	30c. deep green and green	14·50	30·00
242	23	35c. mauve and black	18·00	29·00
243	23	40c. green and red	20·00	30·00
244	23	45c. green and deep green	22·00	34·00
245	23	50c. brown and mauve	16·00	25·00
246	23	55c. red and blue	21·00	30·00
247	23	60c. red and blue	13·00	25·00
248	23	65c. blue and brown	25·00	38·00
249	23	70c. brown and mauve	12·00	42·00
250	23	75c. drab and blue	16·00	30·00
251	23	80c. green and purple	17·00	26·00
252	23	85c. brown and green	12·00	29·00
253	23	90c. pink and red	16·00	38·00
254	24	1f. carmine and red	11·00	55·00
255	24	1f.25 green and brown	10·00	36·00
256	24	1f.40 red and blue	15·00	29·00
257	24	1f.50 light blue and blue	11·50	29·00
258	24	1f.60 brown and green	13·00	28·00
259	24	1f.75 orange and blue	18·00	28·00
260	24	2f. brown and orange	17·00	28·00
261	24	2f.25 blue and ultramarine	14·50	28·00
262	24	2f.50 brown	18·00	32·00
263	24	3f. brown and mauve	11·50	30·00
264	24	5f. brown and blue	11·50	30·00
265	24	10f. brown & pur on pink	14·00	60·00
266	24	20f. brown & red on yellow	14·00	65·00

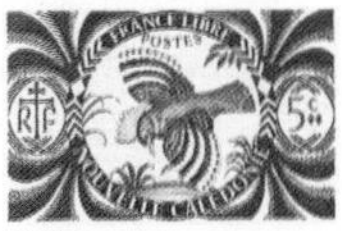
29 Kagu

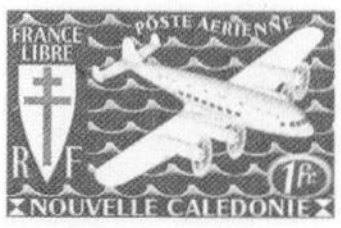
30 Fairey FC-1 Airliner

1942. Free French Issue. (a) Postage.

267	29	5c. brown	10	5·00
268	29	10c. blue	10	4·25
269	29	25c. green	20	3·00
270	29	30c. red	45	3·25
271	29	40c. green	45	3·00
272	29	80c. purple	65	2·30
273	29	1f. mauve	85	65
274	29	1f.50 red	75	35
275	29	2f. black	1·00	35
276	29	2f.50 blue	1·60	5·00
277	29	4f. violet	90	85
278	29	5f. yellow	75	60
279	29	10f. brown	1·10	45
280	29	20f. green	1·40	2·30

(b) Air.

281	30	1f. orange	45	3·50
282	30	1f.50 red	45	6·50
283	30	5f. purple	90	3·75
284	30	10f. black	55	5·00
285	30	25f. blue	55	2·50
286	30	50f. green	65	1·50
287	30	100f. red	1·00	1·70

1944. Mutual Aid and Red Cross Funds. As T 19b of Oceanic Settlements.

288		5f.+20f. red	75	8·25

1945. Eboue. As T 20a of Oceanic Settlements.

289		2f. black	35	6·00
290		25f. green	1·10	4·00

1945. Surch.

291	29	50c. on 5c. brown	65	35
292	29	60c. on 5c. brown	60	7·25
293	29	70c. on 5c. brown	55	7·50
294	29	1f.20 on 5c. brown	60	4·25
295	29	2f.40 on 25c. green	1·30	8·00
296	29	3f. on 25c. green	1·70	2·00
297	29	4f.50 on 25c. green	90	6·75
298	29	15f. on 2f.50 blue	1·40	75

1946. Air. Victory. As T 20b of Oceanic Settlements.

299		8f. blue	45	6·00

1946. Air. From Chad to the Rhine. As T 25a of Madagascar.

300	35	5f. black	90	4·75
301	-	10f. red	90	3·00
302	-	15f. blue	90	7·50
303	-	20f. brown	90	7·50
304	-	25f. green	90	7·50
305	-	50f. purple	1·20	8·25

DESIGNS: 5f. Legionaries by Lake Chad; 10f. Battle of Koufra; 15f. Tank Battle, Mareth; 20f. Normandy Landings; 25f. Liberation of Paris; 50f. Liberation of Strasbourg.

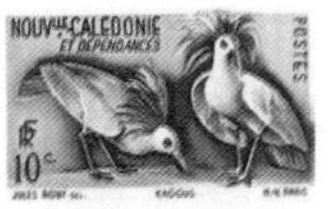
36 Two Kagus

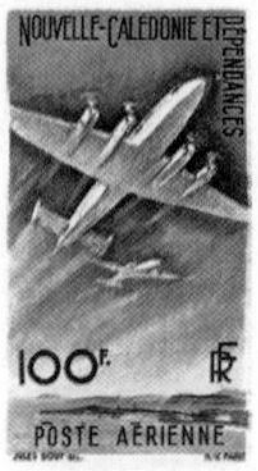
37 Sud Est Languedoc Airliners over Landscape

1948. (a) Postage.

306	36	10c. purple and yellow	10	3·75
307	36	30c. purple and green	10	7·00
308	36	40c. purple and brown	20	3·00
309	-	50c. purple and pink	55	35
310	-	60c. brown and yellow	65	3·25
311	-	80c. green and light green	55	4·00
312	-	1f. violet and orange	85	35
313	-	1f.20 brown and blue	1·30	5·00
314	-	1f.50 blue and yellow	55	85

315	-	2f. brown and green	1·20	10
316	-	2f.40 red and purple	1·30	7·00
317	-	3f. violet and orange	1·50	45
318	-	4f. indigo and blue	1·00	20
319	-	5f. violet and red	1·60	30
320	-	6f. brown and yellow	1·10	45
321	-	10f. blue and orange	1·60	30
322	-	15f. red and blue	1·10	45
323	-	20f. violet and yellow	1·00	45
324	-	25f. blue and orange	2·30	65

(b) Air.

325		50f. purple and orange	3·50	3·25
326	**37**	100f. blue and green	7·75	2·75
327	-	200f. brown and yellow	5·50	5·50

DESIGNS—As T **36**: HORIZ: 50c. to 80c. Ducos Sanatorium; 1f.50, Porcupine Is; 2f. to 4f. Nickel foundry; 5f. to 10f. "The Towers of Notre Dame" Rocks. VERT: 15f. to 25f. Chief's hut. As T **37**: HORIZ: Sud Est Languedoc airliner over- 50f. St. Vincent Bay; 200f. Noumea.

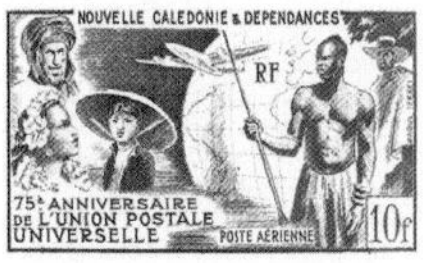
38 People of Five Races, Bomber and Globe

1949. Air. 75th Anniv of U.P.U.

328	**38**	10f. multicoloured	2·50	7·25

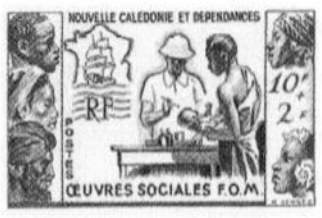
39 Doctor and Patient

1950. Colonial Welfare Fund.

329	**39**	10f.+2f. purple & brown	1·60	17·00

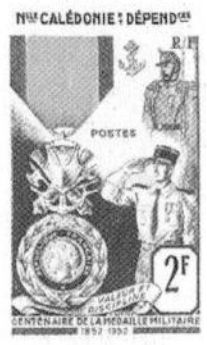
40

1952. Military Medal Centenary.

330	**40**	2f. red, yellow and green	2·20	5·50

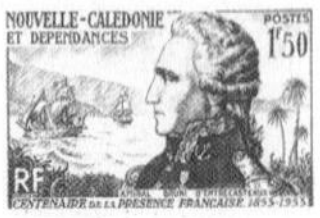
41 Admiral D'Entrecasteaux

1953. French Administration Centenary. Inscr "1853 1953".

331	**41**	1f.50 lake and brown	1·40	1·30
332	-	2f. blue and turquoise	75	45
333	-	6f. brown, blue and red	1·80	1·40
334	-	13f. blue and green	2·00	1·50

DESIGNS: 2f. Mgr. Douarre and church; 6f. Admiral D'Urville and map; 13f. Admiral Despointes and view.

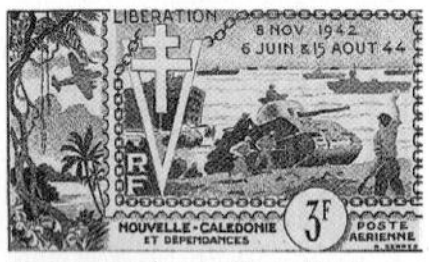
42 Normandy Landings, 1944

1954. Air. 10th Anniv of Liberation.

335	**42**	3f. blue and deep blue	8·75	12·50

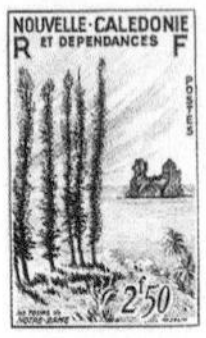
43 Towers of Notre-Dame (rocks)

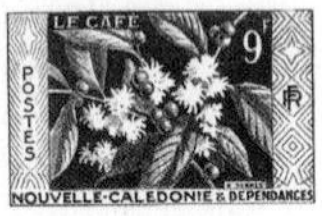
44 Coffee

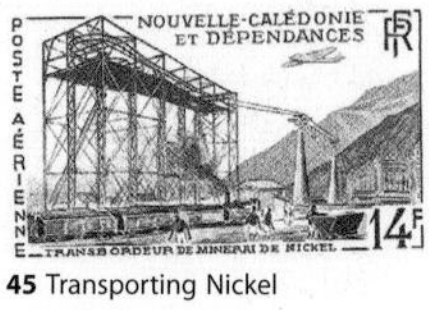
45 Transporting Nickel

1955

336	**43**	2f.50c. blue, green and sepia (postage)	45	1·30
337	**43**	3f. blue, brown and green	1·80	2·75
338	**44**	9f. deep blue and blue	60	30
339	**45**	14f. blue and brown (air)	1·30	90

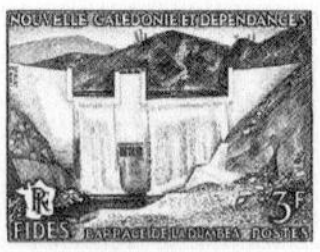
46 Dumbea Barrage

1956. Economic and Social Development Fund.

340	**46**	3f. green and blue	1·00	35

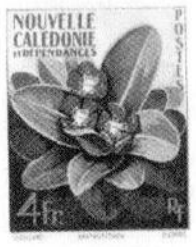
47 "Xanthostemon"

1958. Flowers.

341	**47**	4f. multicoloured	80	1·10
342	-	15f. red, yellow and green	1·30	90

DESIGN: 15f. Hibiscus.

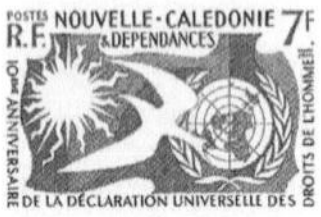
48 "Human Rights"

1958. 10th Anniv of Declaration of Human Rights.

343	**48**	7f. red and blue	45	90

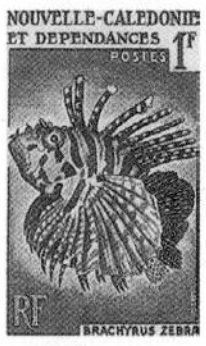
49 Zebra Lionfish

1959

344	**49**	1f. brown and grey	30	20
345	-	2f. blue, purple and green	2·00	1·30
346	-	3f. red, blue and green	35	55
347	-	4f. purple, red and green	2·00	2·75
348	-	5f. bistre, blue and green	3·25	2·30
349	-	10f. multicoloured	70	35
350	-	26f. multicoloured	1·10	5·25

DESIGNS—HORIZ: 2f. Outrigger canoes racing; 3f. Harlequin tuskfish; 5f. Sail Rock, Noumea; 26f. Fluorescent corals. VERT: 4f. Fisherman with spear. 10f. Blue sea lizard and "Spirographe" (coral).

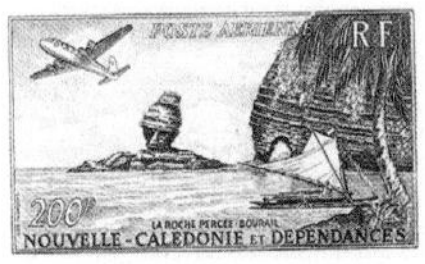
49a The Carved Rock, Bourail

1959. Air.

351		15f. green, brown and red	1·80	2·30
352		20f. brown and green	8·25	4·50
353		25f. black, blue and purple	8·00	3·25
354		50f. brown, green and blue	3·75	3·25
355		50f. brown, green and blue	7·00	3·25
356		100f. brown, green & blue	21·00	6·50
357	**49a**	200f. brown, green & blue	8·50	7·75

DESIGNS—HORIZ: 15f. Fisherman with net; 20f. New Caledonia nautilus; 25f. Underwater swimmer shooting bump-headed unicornfish; 50f. (No. 355), Isle of Pines; 100f. Corbeille de Yate. VERT: 50f. (No. 354), Yate barrage.

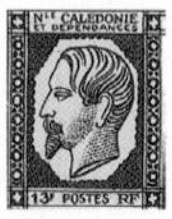
49b Napoleon III

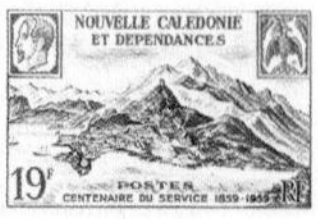
49c Port-de-France, 1859

1960. Postal Centenary.

358	**15**	4f. red	30	85
359	-	5f. brown and lake	35	1·30
360	-	9f. brown and turquoise	45	1·80
361	-	12f. black and blue	45	2·30
362	**49b**	13f. blue	90	3·00
363	**49c**	19f. red, green & turquoise	75	1·60
364	-	33f. red, green and blue	85	2·75
MS364a		150×80 mm. Nos. 358, 362 and 364	8·25	29·00

DESIGNS—As Type **49c**: HORIZ: 5f. Girl operating cheque-writing machine; 12f. Telephone receiver and exchange building; 33f. As Type **49c** but without stamps in upper corners. VERT: 9f. Letter-box on tree.

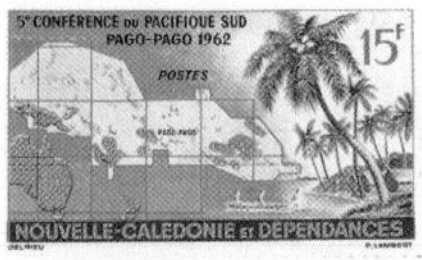
49d Map of Pacific and Palms

1962. 5th South Pacific Conference, Pago-Pago.

365	**49d**	15f. multicoloured	2·50	2·75

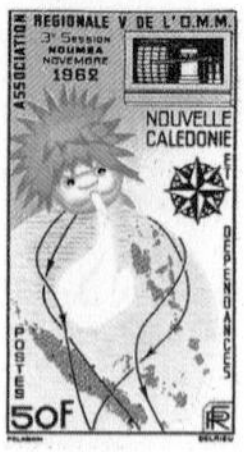
49e Map and Symbols of Meteorology

1962. 3rd Regional Assembly of World Meteorological Association, Noumea.

366	**49e**	50f. multicoloured	3·75	11·50

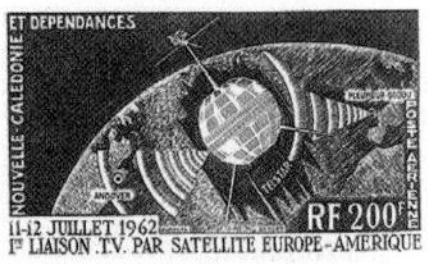
50 "Telstar" Satellite and part of Globe

1962. Air. 1st Transatlantic TV Satellite Link.

367	**50**	200f. turquoise, brown & bl	11·00	14·00

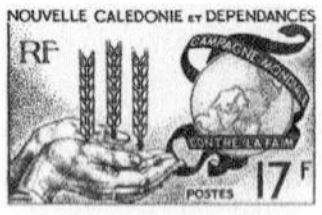
51 Emblem and Globe

1963. Freedom from Hunger.

368	**51**	17f. blue and purple	1·50	2·75

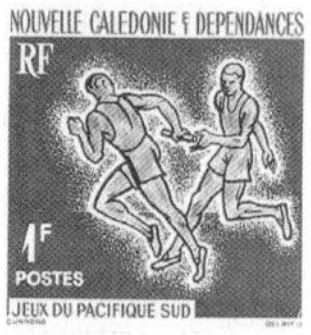
52 Relay-running

1963. 1st South Pacific Games, Suva, Fiji.

369	**52**	1f. red and green	45	2·30
370	-	7f. brown and blue	65	5·25
371	-	10f. brown and green	90	2·50
372	-	27f. blue and deep purple	2·10	4·75

DESIGNS: 7f. Tennis; 10f. Football; 27f. Throwing the javelin.

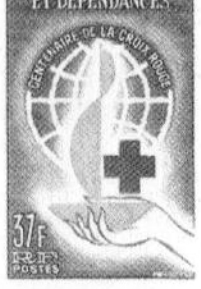
53 Centenary Emblem

1963. Red Cross Centenary.

373	**53**	37f. red, grey and blue	3·75	11·00

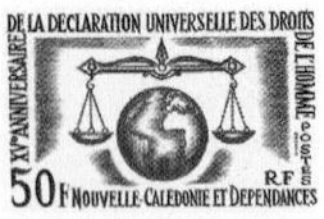
54 Globe and Scales of Justice

1963. 15th Anniv of Declaration of Human Rights.

374	**54**	50f. red and blue	5·25	14·00

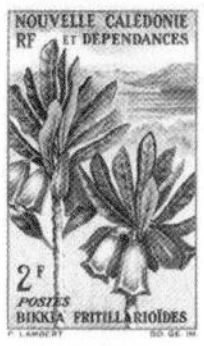
54a "Bikkia fritillarioides"

1964. Flowers. Multicoloured.

375	1f. "Freycinettia"	75	3·25
376	2f. Type **54a**	55	1·60
377	3f. "Xanthostemon francii"	90	2·20
378	4f. "Psidiomyrtus locellatus"	1·60	2·00
379	5f. "Callistemon suberosum"	2·10	2·50
380	7f. "Montrouziera sphaeroidea" (horiz)	2·30	2·75
381	10f. "Ixora collina" (horiz)	2·30	2·50
382	17f. "Deplanchea speciosa"	3·75	4·00

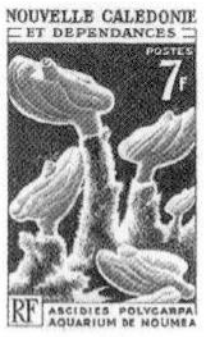
54b "Ascidies polycarpa"

1964. Corals and Marine Animals from Noumea Aquarium.

383	**54b**	7f. red, brown and blue (postage)	1·60	1·70
384	-	10f. red and blue	2·30	1·80
385	-	17f. red, green and blue	3·75	90
386	-	27f. multicoloured	3·25	4·50
387	-	37f. multicoloured	5·50	9·00
388	-	13f. bistre, black and orange (air)	4·25	4·75
389	-	15f. green, olive and blue	5·00	4·75
390	-	25f. blue and green	7·00	9·00

DESIGNS—As T **54b**: VERT: 10f. "Alcyonium catalai" (coral). 17f. "Hymenocera elegans" (crab). HORIZ: 48×28 mm: 27f. Palette surgeonfish; 37f. "Phyllobranchus" (sea slug). 48×27 mm: 13f. Twin-spotted wrasse (young); 15f. Twin-spotted wrasse (subadult); 25f. Twin-spotted wrasse (adult).

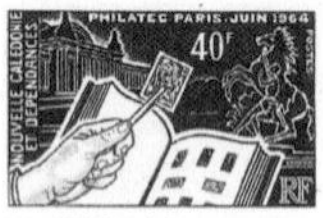
54c "Philately"

1964. "PHILATEC 1964" Int Stamp Exn, Paris.

391	**54c**	40f. brown, green & violet	3·75	7·25

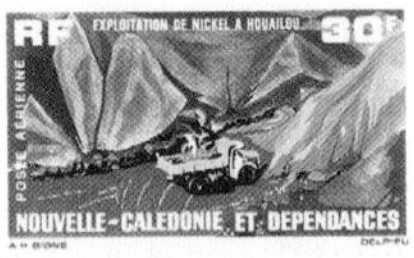
54d Houailou Mine

1964. Air. Nickel Production at Houailou.

392	**54d**	30f. multicoloured	2·30	10·00

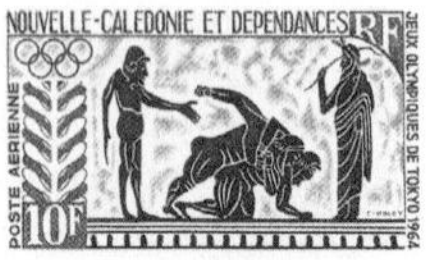
54e Ancient Greek Wrestling

1964. Air. Olympic Games, Tokyo.

393	**54e**	10f. sepia, mauve & green	9·25	13·00

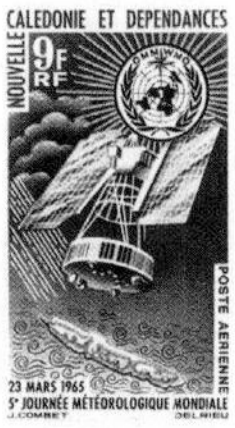
55 Weather Satellite

1965. Air. World Meteorological Day.

394	**55**	9f. multicoloured	4·25	4·50

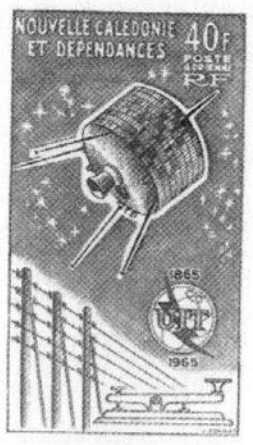

56 "Syncom" Communications Satellite, Telegraph Poles and Morse Key

1965. Air. Centenary of I.T.U.

395	**56**	40f. purple, brown and blue	6·75	12·50

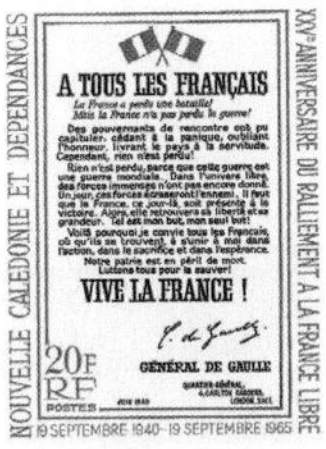

56a De Gaulle's Appeal of 18 June 1940

1965. 25th Anniv of New Caledonia's Adherence to the Free French.

396	**56a**	20f. black, red and blue	5·50	10·00

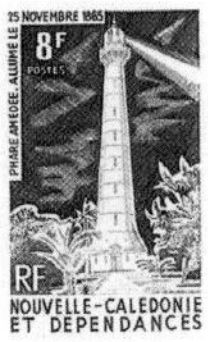

56b Amedee Lighthouse

1965. Inauguration of Amedee Lighthouse.

397	**56b**	8f. bistre, blue and green	2·30	2·30

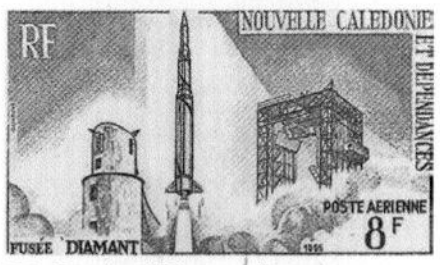

56c Rocket "Diamant"

1966. Air. Launching of 1st French Satellite.

398	**56c**	8f. lake, blue and turquoise	3·25	5·00
399	-	12f. lake, blue & turquoise	4·25	5·50

DESIGN: 12f. Satellite "A1".

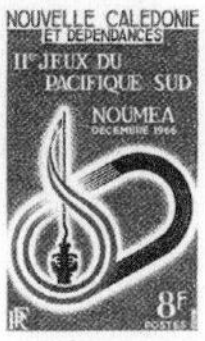

56d Games Emblem

1966. Publicity for 2nd South Pacific Games, Noumea.

400	**56d**	8f. black, red and blue	1·00	2·30

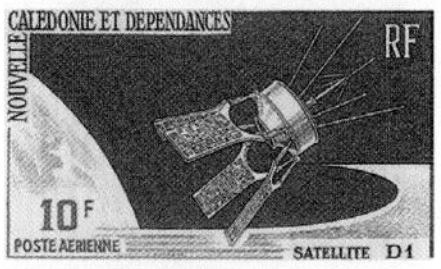

56e Satellite "D1"

1966. Air. Launching of Satellite "D1".

401	**56e**	10f. brown, blue and buff	1·70	3·00

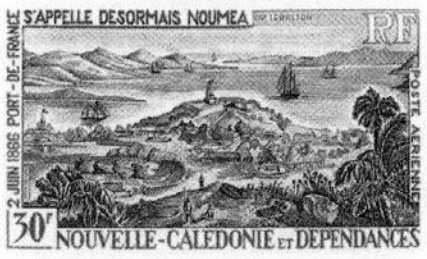

57 Noumea, 1866 (after Lebreton)

1966. Air. Centenary of Renaming of Port-de-France as Noumea.

402	**57**	30f. slate, red and blue	3·25	12·50

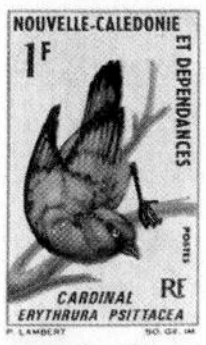

58 Red-throated Parrot Finch

1966. Birds. Multicoloured.

403	1f. Type **58** (postage)	2·30	3·50
404	1f. New Caledonian grass warbler	2·00	1·70
405	2f. New Caledonian whistler	2·50	1·50
406	3f. New Caledonian pigeon ("Notou")	3·25	2·10
407	3f. White-throated pigeon ("Collier blanc")	2·75	2·00
408	4f. Kagu	3·75	1·80
409	5f. Horned parakeet	6·25	2·75
410	10f. Red-faced honeyeater	11·00	4·50
411	15f. New Caledonian friarbird	8·25	3·75
412	30f. Sacred kingfisher	12·50	11·00
413	27f. Horned parakeet (diff) (air)	6·25	4·50
414	37f. Scarlet honeyeater	9·50	10·00
415	39f. Emerald dove	21·00	12·50
416	50f. Cloven-feathered dove	13·00	14·00
417	100f. Whistling kite	50·00	34·00

Nos. 413/14 are 26×45½ mm; Nos. 415/17 are 27½×48 mm.

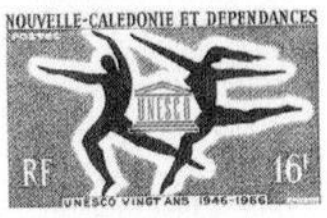

59 UNESCO Allegory

1966. 20th Anniv of UNESCO.

418	**59**	16f. purple, ochre and green	3·00	2·50

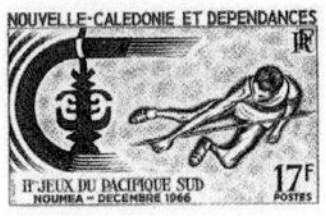

60 High Jumping

1966. South Pacific Games, Noumea.

419	**60**	17f. violet, green and lake	2·30	1·50
420	-	20f. green, purple and lake	3·00	2·75
421	-	40f. green, violet and lake	3·50	4·50
422	-	100f. purple, turq & lake	7·25	11·00
MS423		149×99 mm. Nos. 419/22	25·00	70·00

DESIGNS: 20f. Hurdling; 40f. Running; 100f. Swimming.

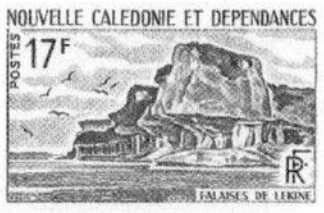

61 Lekine Cliffs

1967

424	**61**	17f. grey, green and blue	1·50	1·20

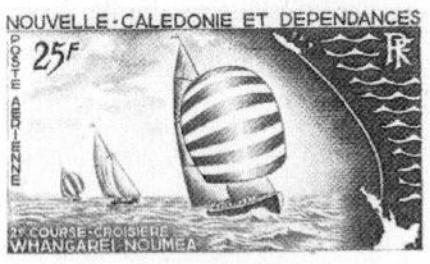

62 Ocean Racing Yachts

1967. Air. 2nd Whangarei–Noumea Yacht Race.

425	**62**	25f. red, blue and green	4·25	4·50

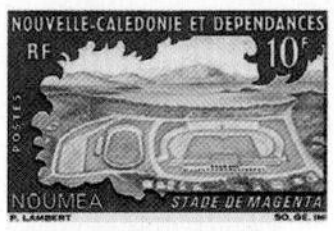

63 Magenta Stadium

1967. Sport Centres. Multicoloured.

426	10f. Type **63**	2·75	2·00
427	20f. Ouen-Toro swimming pool	4·00	1·40

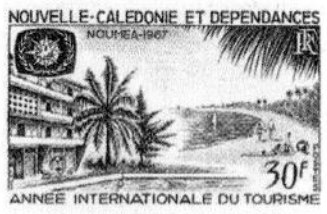

64 New Caledonian Scenery

1967. International Tourist Year.

428	**64**	30f. multicoloured	3·25	3·75

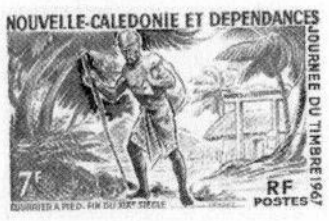

65 19th-century Postman

1967. Stamp Day.

429	**65**	7f. red, green and turquoise	2·50	2·30

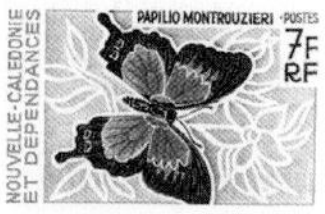

66 "Papilio montrouzieri"

1967. Butterflies and Moths.

430	**66**	7f. blue, black and green (postage)	3·25	1·80
431	-	9f. blue, brown and mauve	3·00	1·60
432	-	13f. violet, purple & brown	4·75	7·00
433	-	15f. yellow, purple and blue	7·25	4·00
434	-	19f. orange, brown and green (air)	7·00	2·75
435	-	29f. purple, red and blue	8·50	9·25
436	-	85f. brown, red and yellow	21·00	30·00

BUTTERFLIES—As T **66**: 9f. "Polyura clitarchus"; 13f. Common eggfly (male), and 15f. (female). 48×27 mm: 19f. Orange tiger; 29f. Silver-striped hawk moth; 85f. "Dellas elipsis".

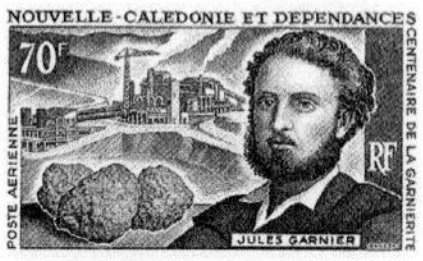

67 Garnierite (mineral), Factory and Jules Garnier

1967. Air. Centenary of Garnierite Industry.

437	**67**	70f. multicoloured	6·75	20·00

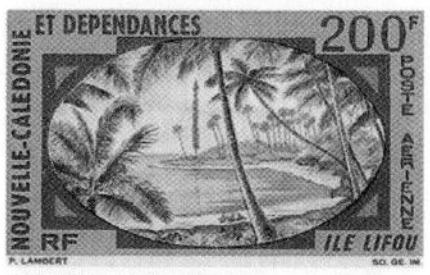

67a Lifou Island

1967. Air.

438	**67a**	200f. multicoloured	10·00	9·25

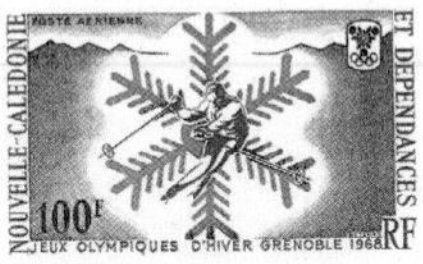

67b Skier and Snow-crystal

1967. Air. Winter Olympic Games, Grenoble.

439	**67b**	100f. brown, blue & green	9·25	18·00

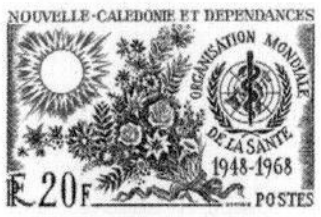

68 Bouquet, Sun and W.H.O. Emblem

1968. 20th Anniv of W.H.O.

440	**68**	20f. blue, red and violet	2·75	1·80

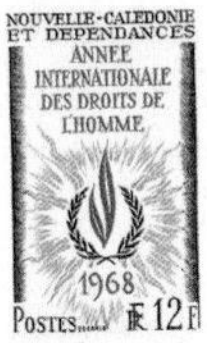

69 Human Rights Emblem

1968. Human Rights Year.

441	**69**	12f. red, green and yellow	1·50	2·50

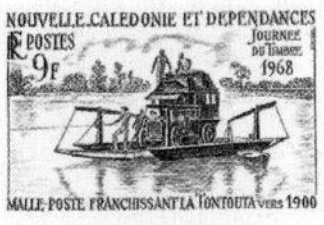

70 Ferrying Mail Van across Tontouta River

1968. Stamp Day.

442	**70**	9f. brown, blue and green	4·00	2·20

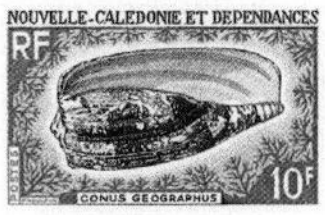

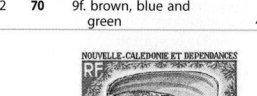

71 Geography Cone

1968. Sea Shells.

443	-	1f. brn, grey & grn (postage)	2·30	2·50
444	-	1f. purple and violet	2·00	2·00
445	-	2f. purple, red and blue	3·75	2·30
446	-	3f. brown and green	1·80	1·60
447	-	5f. red, brown and violet	2·75	1·00
448	**71**	10f. brown, grey and blue	2·50	2·00
449	-	10f. yellow, brown and red	3·25	2·75
450	-	10f. black, brown & orange	3·25	2·00
451	-	15f. red, grey and green	7·25	5·75
452	-	21f. brown, sepia and green	6·00	3·75
453	-	22f. red, brown & blue (air)	7·50	3·75
454	-	25f. brown and red	3·25	3·75
455	-	33f. brown and blue	7·50	7·25
456	-	34f. violet, brown & orange	9·25	3·75
457	-	39f. brown, grey and green	8·75	9·25
458	-	40f. black, brown and red	8·25	4·50
459	-	50f. red, purple and green	4·50	8·00
460	-	60f. brown and green	16·00	21·00
461	-	70f. brown, grey and violet	12·00	9·25
462	-	100f. brown, black and blue	18·00	26·00

DESIGNS—VERT: 1f. (No. 443) Swan conch ("Strombus epidromis"); 1f. (No. 444) Scorpion conch ("Lambis scorpius"); 3f. Common spider conch; 10f. (No. 450) Variable conch ("Strombus variabilis"). 27×48 mm: 22f. Laciniate cone; 25f. Orange spider conch; 34f. Vomer conch; 50f. Chiragra spider conch. HORIZ: 36×22 mm: 2f. Snipe's-bill murex; 5f. Troschel's murex; 10f. (No. 449) Sieve cowrie; 15f. "Murex sp."; 21f. Mole cowrie. 48×27 mm: 33f. Eyed cowrie; 39f. Lienardi's cone; 40f. Cabrit's cone; 60f. All-red map cowrie; 70f. Scarlet cone; 100f. Adusta murex.

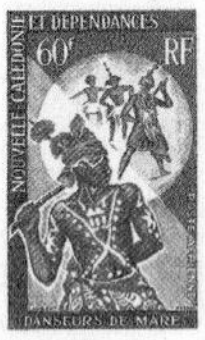

72 Dancers

1968. Air.

463	**72**	60f. red, blue and green	6·50	11·50

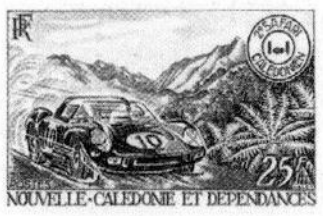

73 Rally Car

1968. 2nd New Caledonian Motor Safari.

464	**73**	25f. blue, red and green	3·75	4·25

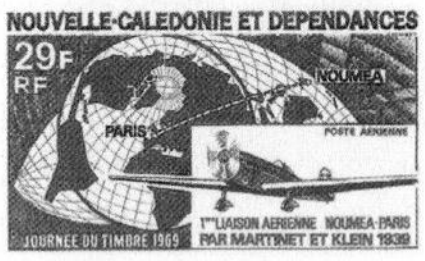

74 Caudron C-60 "Aiglon" and Route Map

1969. Air. Stamp Day. 30th Anniv of 1st Noumea–Paris Flight by Martinet and Klein.

465	**74**	29f. red, blue and violet	4·50	2·75

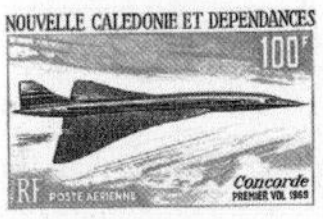

75 Concorde in Flight

1969. Air. 1st Flight of Concorde.

466	**75**	100f. green and light green	18·00	29·00

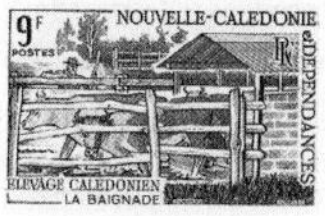

76 Cattle-dip

1969. Cattle-breeding in New Caledonia.

467	76	9f. brown, green and blue (postage)	2·50	2·00
468	-	25f. violet, brown and green	3·75	4·25
469	-	50f. purple, red & grn (air)	6·00	5·00

DESIGNS: 25f. Branding. LARGER 48×27 mm; 50f. Stockman with herd.

77 Judo

1969. 3rd South Pacific Games, Port Moresby, Papua New Guinea.

470	77	19f. purple, bl & red (post)	2·50	1·80
471	-	20f. black, red and green	3·00	2·75
472	-	30f. black and blue (air)	5·50	6·75
473	-	39f. brown, green and black	8·25	11·00

DESIGNS—HORIZ: 20f. Boxing; 30f. Diving (38×27 mm). VERT: 39f. Putting the shot (27×48 mm).

1969. Air. Birth Bicentenary of Napoleon Bonaparte. As T 114b of Mauritania. Multicoloured.

474		40f. "Napoleon in Coronation Robes" (Gerard) (vert)	17·00	18·00

78 Douglas DC-4 over Outrigger Canoe

1969. Air. 20th Anniv of Regular Noumea–Paris Air Service.

475	78	50f. green, brown and blue	20·00	9·25

79 I.L.O. Building Geneva

1969. 50th Anniv of I.L.O.

476	79	12f. brown, violet & salmon	2·75	4·25

80 "French Wings around the World"

1970. Air. 10th Anniv of French "Around the World" Air Service.

477	80	200f. brown, blue and violet	26·00	11·00

81 New U.P.U. Building, Berne

1970. Inauguration of New U.P.U. Headquarters Building, Berne.

478	81	12f. red, grey and brown	3·50	2·30

82 Packet Steamer "Natal", 1883

1970. Stamp Day.

479	82	9f. black, green and blue	8·00	2·30

83 Cyclists on Map

1970. Air. 4th "Tour de Nouvelle Caledonie" Cycle Race.

480	83	40f. brown, blue & lt blue	9·75	7·25

84 Mt. Fuji and Japanese "Hikari" Express Train

1970. Air. "EXPO 70" World Fair, Osaka, Japan. Multicoloured.

481		20f. Type **84**	5·50	5·75
482	-	45f. "EXPO" emblem, map and Buddha	7·25	3·25

85 Racing Yachts

1971. Air. One Ton Cup Yacht Race Auckland, New Zealand.

483	85	20f. green, red and black	5·50	2·50

86 Steam Mail Train, Dumbea

1971. Stamp Day.

484	86	10f. black, green and red	6·50	6·25

87 Ocean Racing Yachts

1971. 3rd Whangarei–Noumea Ocean Yacht Race.

485	87	16f. turquoise, green and blue	8·75	4·75

88 Lieut.-Col. Broche and Theatre Map

1971. 30th Anniv of French Pacific Battalion's Participation in Second World War Mediterranean Campaign.

486	88	60f. multicoloured	10·00	8·50

89 Early Tape Machine

1971. World Telecommunications Day.

487	89	19f. orange, purple and red	4·25	4·75

90 Weightlifting

1971. 4th South Pacific Games, Papeete, French Polynesia.

488	90	11f. brown & red (postage)	3·75	2·75
489	-	23f. violet, red and blue	4·50	90
490	-	25f. green and red (air)	4·50	4·00
491	-	100f. blue, green and red	5·75	6·50

DESIGNS—VERT: 23f. Basketball. HORIZ: 48×27 mm: 25f. Pole-vaulting; 100f. Archery.

91 Port de Plaisance, Noumea

1971. Air.

492	91	200f. multicoloured	17·00	16·00

92 De Gaulle as President of French Republic, 1970

1971. 1st Death Anniv of General De Gaulle.

493	92	34f. black and purple	6·50	4·50
494	-	100f. black and purple	11·00	10·00

DESIGN: 100f. De Gaulle in uniform, 1940.

93 Publicity Leaflet showing De Havilland Gipsy Moth "Golden Eagle"

1971. Air. 40th Anniv of 1st New Caledonia to Australia Flight.

495	93	90f. brown, blue and orange	13·00	17·00

94 Downhill Skiing

1972. Air. Winter Olympic Games, Sapporo, Japan.

496	94	50f. green, red and blue	9·75	7·00

95 St. Mark's Basilica, Venice

1972. Air. UNESCO "Save Venice" Campaign.

497	95	20f. brown, green and blue	5·50	5·25

96 Commission Headquarters, Noumea

1972. Air. 25th Anniv of South Pacific Commission.

498	96	18f. multicoloured	2·75	4·75

97 Couzinet 33 "Le Biarritz" and Noumea Monument

1972. Air. 40th Anniv of 1st Paris–Noumea Flight.

499	97	110f. black, purple & green	4·50	5·50

98 Pacific Island Dwelling

1972. Air. South Pacific Arts Festival, Fiji.

500	98	24f. brown, blue and orange	5·00	2·50

99 Goa Door-post

1972. Exhibits from Noumea Museum.

501	99	1f. red, green & grey (post)	1·60	1·50
502	-	2f. black, green & deep grn	1·80	1·50
503	-	5f. multicoloured	2·30	1·80
504	-	12f. multicoloured	4·50	2·30
505	-	16f. multicoloured (air)	3·75	2·75
506	-	40f. multicoloured	6·50	4·00

DESIGNS: 2f. Carved wooden pillow; 5f. Monstrance; 12f. Tchamba mask; 16f. Ornamental arrowheads; 40f. Portico, chief's house.

100 Hurdling over "H" of "MUNICH"

1972. Air. Olympic Games, Munich.

507	100	72f. violet, purple and blue	8·75	10·50

101 New Head Post Office Building, Noumea

1972. Air.

508	101	23f. brown, blue and green	4·25	2·50

102 J.C.I. Emblem

1972. 10th Anniv of New Caledonia Junior Chamber of Commerce.

509	102	12f. multicoloured	2·50	2·30

103 Forest Scene

1973. Air. Landscapes of the East Coast. Multicoloured.

510		11f. Type **103**	4·00	2·10
511	-	18f. Beach and palms (vert)	4·50	4·75
512	-	21f. Waterfall and inlet (vert)	6·50	7·50

See also Nos. 534/6.

104 Moliere and Characters

1973. Air. 300th Death Anniv of Moliere (playwright).

513	104	50f. multicoloured	4·50	4·50

105 Tchamba Mask

1973

514	105	12f. purple (postage)	11·00	6·00
515	-	23f. blue (air)	14·50	14·00

DESIGN: 23f. Concorde in flight.

106 Liner "El Kantara" in Panama Canal

1973. 50th Anniv of Marseilles–Noumea Shipping Service via Panama Canal.
516 **106** 60f. black, brown & green 19·00 12·00

107 Globe and Allegory of Weather

1973. Air. Centenary of World Meteorological Organization.
517 **107** 80f. multicoloured 8·25 7·50

108 DC-10 in Flight

1973. Air. Inauguration of Noumea–Paris DC-10 Air Service.
518 **108** 100f. green, brown & blue 24·00 10·50

109 Common Egg Cowrie

1973. Marine Fauna from Noumea Aquarium. Multicoloured.
519 8f. Black-wedged butterflyfish (daylight) 3·00 2·30
520 14f. Black-wedged butterflyfish (nocturnal) 3·75 4·25
521 3f. Type **109** (air) 2·00 2·00
522 32f. Orange-spotted surgeon-fish (adult and young) 6·50 5·25
523 32f. Green-lined paper bubble ("Hydatina") 3·75 5·50
524 37f. Pacific partridge tun ("Dolium perdix") 5·50 3·00

111 Office Emblem

1973. 10th Anniv of Central Schools Co-operation Office.
532 **111** 20f. blue, yellow and green 2·75 2·00

112 New Caledonia Mail Coach, 1880

1973. Air. Stamp Day.
533 **112** 15f. multicoloured 4·25 1·80

1974. Air. Landscapes of the West Coast. As T 103. Multicoloured.
534 8f. Beach and palms (vert) 2·75 5·75
535 22f. Trees and mountain 3·50 5·25
536 26f. Trees growing in sea 2·75 3·25

113 Centre Building

1974. Air. Opening of Scientific Studies Centre, Anse-Vata, Noumea.
537 **113** 50f. multicoloured 4·50 4·50

114 "Bird" embracing Flora

1974. Nature Conservation.
538 **114** 7f. multicoloured 1·70 1·90

115 18th-century French Sailor

1974. Air. Discovery and Reconnaissance of New Caledonia and Loyalty Islands.
539 - 20f. violet, red and blue 5·50 4·75
540 - 25f. green, brown and red 4·50 5·25
541 **115** 28f. brown, blue and green 4·50 3·75
542 - 30f. blue, brown and red 7·25 4·25
543 - 36f. red, brown and blue 7·00 9·50
DESIGNS—HORIZ: 20f. Captain Cook, H.M.S. "Endeavour" and map of Grand Terre island; 25f. La Perouse, "L'Astrolabe" and map of Grand Terre island (reconnaissance of west coast); 30f. Entrecasteaux, ship and map of Grand Terre island (reconnaissance of west coast); 36f. Dumont d'Urville, "L'Astrolabe" and map of Loyalty Islands.

116 "Telecommunications"

1974. Air. Centenary of U.P.U.
544 **116** 95f. orange, purple & grey 5·50 10·00

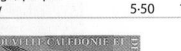
117 "Art"

1974. Air. "Arphila 75" International Stamp Exhibition, Paris (1975) (1st issue).
545 **117** 80f. multicoloured 6·50 5·75
See also No. 554.

118 Hotel Chateau-Royal

1974. Air. Inauguration of Hotel Chateau Royal, Noumea.
546 **118** 22f. multicoloured 2·75 2·50

118a Animal Skull, Burnt Tree and Flaming Landscape

1975. "Stop Bush Fires".
547 **118a** 20f. multicoloured 1·90 1·80

119 "Cricket"

1975. Air. Tourism. Multicoloured.
548 3f. Type **119** 2·75 2·10
549 25f. "Bougna" ceremony 3·00 4·25
550 31f. "Pilou" native dance 3·75 2·30

120 "Calanthe veratrifolia"

1975. New Caledonian Orchids. Multicoloured.
551 8f. Type **120** (postage) 3·00 2·00
552 11f. "Lyperanthus gigas" 2·75 1·80
553 42f. "Eriaxis rigida" (air) 8·25 3·75

121 Global "Flower"

1975. Air. "Arphila 75" International Stamp Exhibition, Paris (2nd issue).
554 **121** 105f. purple, green & blue 8·25 5·00

122 Throwing the Discus

1975. Air. 5th South Pacific Games, Guam.
555 24f. Type **122** 5·75 4·75
556 50f. Volleyball 6·75 3·25

123 Festival Emblem

1975. "Melanesia 2000" Festival, Noumea.
557 **123** 12f. multicoloured 2·30 2·00

124 Birds in Flight

1975. 10th Anniv of Noumea Ornithological Society.
558 **124** 5f. multicoloured 1·80 1·60

125 Pres. Pompidou

1975. Pompidou Commemoration.
559 **125** 26f. grey and green 3·00 3·00

126 Concordes

1976. Air. First Commercial Flight of Concorde.
560 **126** 147f. blue and red 17·00 19·00

127 Brown Booby

1976. Ocean Birds. Multicoloured.
561 1f. Type **127** 1·50 2·00
562 2f. Blue-faced booby 1·80 1·90
563 8f. Red-footed booby (vert) 3·75 2·50

128 Festival Emblem

1976. South Pacific Festival of Arts, Rotorua, New Zealand.
564 **128** 27f. multicoloured 3·25 4·50

129 Lion and Lions' Emblem

1976. 15th Anniv of Lions Club, Noumea.
565 **129** 49f. multicoloured 5·50 9·00

130 Early and Modern Telephones

1976. Air. Telephone Centenary.
566 **130** 36f. multicoloured 4·25 5·00

131 Capture of Penbosct

1976. Air. Bicent of American Revolution.
567 **131** 24f. purple and brown 4·00 2·75

132 Bandstand

1976. "Aspects of Old Noumea". Multicoloured.
568 25f. Type **132** 2·75 3·25
569 30f. Monumental fountain (vert) 3·25 2·50

133 Athletes

1976. Air. Olympic Games, Montreal.
570 **133** 33f. violet, red and purple 3·75 3·25

134 "Chick" with Magnifier

1976. Air. "Philately in Schools", Stamp Exhibition, Noumea.
571   **134**   42f. multicoloured   4·50   5·50

135 Dead Bird and Trees

1976. Nature Protection.
572   **135**   20f. multicoloured   2·75   2·30

136 South Pacific Heads

1976. 16th South Pacific Commission Conference.
573   **136**   20f. multicoloured   2·40   1·80

137 Old Town Hall, Noumea

1976. Air. Old and New Town Halls, Noumea. Mult.
574   75f. Type **137**   6·50   4·75
575   125f. New Town Hall   9·25   5·25

138 Water Carnival

1977. Air. Summer Festival, Noumea.
576   **138**   11f. multicoloured   2·75   1·80

139 "Pseudophyllanax imperialis" (cricket)

1977. Insects.
577   **139**   26f. emerald, green
                    & brn   4·50   7·00
578   -   31f. brown, sepia &
                    green   4·75   3·75
DESIGN: 31f. "Agrianome fairmairei" (long-horn beetle).

140 Miniature Roadway

1977. Air. Road Safety.
579   **140**   50f. multicoloured   4·25   4·00

141 Earth Station

1977. Earth Satellite Station, Noumea.
580   **141**   29f. multicoloured   3·00   4·00

142 "Phajus daenikeri"

1977. Orchids. Multicoloured.
581   22f. Type **142**   3·75   6·00
582   44f. "Dendrobium finetianum"   5·50   7·50

143 Mask and Palms

1977. La Perouse School Philatelic Exn.
583   **143**   35f. multicoloured   2·50   4·25

144 Trees

1977. Nature Protection.
584   **144**   20f. multicoloured   1·80   2·30

145 Palm Tree and Emblem

1977. French Junior Chambers of Commerce Congress.
585   **145**   200f. multicoloured   10·00   9·00

146 Young Bird

1977. Great Frigate Birds. Multicoloured.
586   16f. Type **146** (postage)   3·75   4·50
587   42f. Adult male bird (horiz) (air)   7·00   6·25

147 Magenta Airport and Map of Internal Air Network

1977. Air. Airports. Multicoloured.
588   24f. Type **147**   3·75   4·50
589   57f. La Tontout International
           Airport, Noumea   6·25   8·25

1977. Air. 1st Commercial Flight of Concorde, Paris–New York. Optd 22.11.77 PARIS NEW-YORK.
590   **126**   147f. blue and red   44·00 42·00

149 Horse and Foal

1977. 10th Anniv of S.E.C.C. (Horse-breeding Society).
591   **149**   5f. brown, green and
                    blue   2·75   5·00

150 "Moselle Bay" (H. Didonna)

1977. Air. Views of Old Noumea (1st series).
592   **150**   41f. multicoloured   8·00   8·25
593   -   42f. purple and brown   5·50   6·00
DESIGN—49×27 mm: 42f. "Settlers Valley" (J. Kreber).

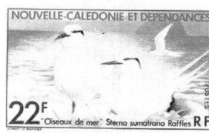

151 Black-naped Tern

1978. Ocean Birds. Multicoloured.
594   22f. Type **151**   2·75   6·00
595   40f. Sooty tern   4·50   3·25

152 "Araucaria montana"

1978. Flora. Multicoloured.
596   16f. Type **152** (postage)   2·00   4·00
597   42f. "Amyema scandens"
           (horiz) (air)   3·75   2·50

153 "Halityle regularis"

1978. Noumea Aquarium.
598   **153**   10f. multicoloured   2·30   1·80

154 Turtle

1978. Protection of the Turtle.
599   **154**   30f. multicoloured   2·30   6·00

155 New Caledonian Flying Fox

1978. Nature Protection.
600   **155**   20f. multicoloured   3·00   2·30

156 "Underwater Carnival"

1978. Air. Aubusson Tapestry.
601   **156**   105f. multicoloured   7·00   9·75

157 Pastor Maurice Leenhardt

1978. Birth Centenary of Pastor Maurice Leenhardt.
602   **157**   37f. sepia, green &
                    orange   3·75   5·25

158 Hare chasing "Stamp" Tortoise

1978. School Philately (1st series).
603   **158**   35f. multicoloured   4·50   4·25

159 Heads, Map, Magnifying Glass and Cone Shell

1978. Air. Thematic Philately at Bourail.
604   **159**   41f. multicoloured   4·00   6·50

160 Candles

1978. 3rd New Caledonian Old People's Day.
605   **160**   36f. multicoloured   2·50   5·00

161 Footballer and League Badge

1978. 50th Anniv of New Caledonian Football League.
606   **161**   26f. multicoloured   2·75   4·50

162 "Fauberg Blanchot" (after Lacouture)

1978. Air. Views of Old Noumea.
607   **162**   24f. multicoloured   3·25   5·75

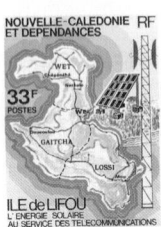

163 Map of Lifou, Solar Energy Panel and Transmitter Mast

1978. Telecommunications through Solar Energy.
608   **163**   33f. multicoloured   4·00   6·50

164 Petroglyph, Mere Region

1979. Archaeological Sites.
609   **164**   10f. red   2·30   1·00

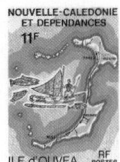

165 Ouvea Island and Outrigger Canoe

1979. Islands. Multicoloured.
610   11f. Type **165**   2·50   4·50
611   31f. Mare Island and ornaments
       (horiz)   2·10   1·10
       See also Nos. 629 and 649.

166 Satellite Orbit of Earth

1979. Air. 1st World Survey of Global Atmosphere.
612   **166**   53f. multicoloured   3·25   5·00

167 19th-century Barque and Modern Container Ship

1979. Air. Centenary of Chamber of Commerce and Industry.
613   **167**   49f. mauve, blue &
                  brown   4·50   5·75

168 Child's Drawing

1979. Air. International Year of the Child.
614   **168**   35f. multicoloured   3·50   6·25

169 House at Artillery Point

1979. Views of Old Noumea.
615   **169**   20f. multicoloured   2·30   3·50

170 Skipjack Tuna

1979. Air. Sea Fishes (1st series). Multicoloured.
616   29f. Type **170**   2·75   5·25
617   30f. Black marlin   2·75   3·75
       See also Nos. 632/3 and 647/8.

171 L. Tardy de Montravel (founder) and View of Port-de-France (Noumea)

1979. Air. 125th Anniv of Noumea.
618   **171**   75f. multicoloured   7·00   6·00

172 The Eel Queen (Kanaka legend)

1979. Air. Nature Protection.
619   **172**   42f. multicoloured   3·75   3·50

173 Auguste Escoffier

1979. Auguste Escoffier Hotel School.
620   **173**   24f. brown, green and
                  turquoise   2·30   6·00

174 Games Emblem and Catamarans

1979. 6th South Pacific Games, Fiji.
621   **174**   16f. multicoloured   2·30   2·75

175 Children of Different Races, Map and Postmark

1979. Air. Youth Philately.
622   **175**   27f. multicoloured   2·50   4·00

176 Aerial View of Centre

1979. Air. Overseas Scientific and Technical Research Office (O.R.S.T.O.M.) Centre, Noumea.
623   **176**   25f. multicoloured   3·25   4·75

177 "Agathis ovata"

1979. Trees. Multicoloured.
624   5f. Type **177**   2·00   1·90
625   34f. "Cyathea intermedia"   2·75   3·00

178 Rodeo Riding

1979. Pouembout Rodeo.
626   **178**   12f. multicoloured   2·75   2·30

179 Hill, 1860 10c. Stamp and Post Office

1979. Air. Death Centenary of Sir Rowland Hill.
627   **179**   150f. black, brown
                  & orge   8·25   8·00

180 "Bantamia merleti"

1980. Noumea Aquarium. Fluorescent Corals (1st issue).
628   **180**   23f. multicoloured   2·50   4·00
       See also No. 646.

1980. Islands. As T 165. Multicoloured.
629   23f. Map of Ile des Pins and
       ornaments (horiz)   2·00   2·50

181 Outrigger Canoe

1980. Air.
630   **181**   45f. blue, turq & indigo 2·75 2·75

182 Globe, Rotary Emblem, Map and Carving

1980. Air. 75th Anniv of Rotary International.
631   **182**   100f. multicoloured   5·50   4·00

1980. Air. Sea Fishes (2nd series). As T 170. Multicoloured.
632   34f. Angler holding dolphin
       (fish)   2·30   4·00
633   39f. Fishermen with sailfish
       (vert)   2·75   4·00

183 "Hibbertia virotii"

1980. Flowers. Multicoloured.
634   11f. Type **183**   1·50   1·50
635   12f. "Grevillea meisneri"   1·80   1·80

184 High Jumper, Magnifying Glass, Albums and Plimsoll

1980. School Philately.
636   **184**   30f. multicoloured   2·75   3·75

185 Scintex Super Emeraude Airplane and Map

1980. Air. Coral Sea Air Rally.
637   **185**   31f. blue, green and
                  brown   2·75   5·25

186 Sailing Canoe

1980. Air. South Pacific Arts Festival, Port Moresby.
638   **186**   27f. multicoloured   2·10   5·00

187 Road Signs as Road-users

1980. Road Safety.
639   **187**   15f. multicoloured   1·40   2·75

188 "Parribacus caledonicus"

1980. Noumea Aquarium. Marine Animals (1st series). Multicoloured.
640   5f. Type **188**   90   1·70
641   8f. "Panulirus versicolor"   1·00   1·70
       See also Nos. 668/9.

189 Kiwanis Emblem

1980. Air. 10th Anniv of Noumea Kiwanis Club.
642   **189**   50f. multicoloured   3·00   4·25

190 Sun, Tree and Solar Panel

1980. Nature Protection. Solar Energy.
643   **190**   23f. multicoloured   1·70   3·50

191 Old House, Poulou

1980. Air. Views of Old Noumea (4th series).
644   **191**   33f. multicoloured   2·00   3·00

192 Charles de Gaulle

1980. Air. 10th Death Anniv of Charles de Gaulle (French statesman).
645   **192**   120f. green, olive and
                  blue   5·50   5·50

1981. Air. Noumea Aquarium. Fluorescent Corals (2nd series). As T 180. Multicoloured.
646   60f. "Trachyphyllia geoffroyi"   2·75   2·75

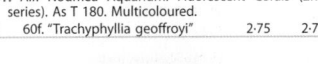

193 Manta Ray

1981. Sea Fishes (3rd series). Multicoloured.
647   23f. Type **193**   1·80   4·75
648   25f. Grey reef shark   1·80   4·75

1981. Islands. As T 165. Multicoloured.
649   26f. Map of Belep Archipelago
       and diver (horiz)   2·75   4·50

194 "Xeronema moorei"

1981. Air. Flowers. Multicoloured.
650   38f. Type **194**   2·00   3·00
651   51f. "Geissois pruinosa"   2·50   3·25

195 Yuri Gagarin and "Vostok 1"

1981. Air. 20th Anniv of First Men in Space. Multicoloured.

652	195	64f. Type **195**	2·75	3·75
653		155f. Alan Shepard and "Freedom 7"	5·50	5·00
MS654		149×119 mm. As Nos. 652/3 but colours changed (sold at 225f.)	21·00	36·00

196 Liberation Cross, "Zealandia" (troopship) and Badge

1981. Air. 40th Anniv of Departure of Pacific Battalion for Middle East.

655	196	29f. multicoloured	4·75	5·25

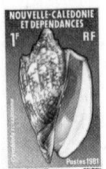

197 Rossini's Volute

1981. Shells. Multicoloured.

656	197	1f. Type **197**	85	1·60
657		2f. Clouded cone	90	1·70
658		13f. Stolid cowrie (horiz)	1·80	3·00

198 Sail Corvette "Constantine"

1981. Ships (1st series).

659	**198**	10f. blue, brown and red	1·80	2·75
660	-	25f. blue, brown and red	2·50	3·75

DESIGN: 25f. Paddle-gunboat "Le Phoque", 1853.
See also Nos. 680/1 and 725/6.

199 "Echinometra mathaei"

1981. Air. Water Plants. Multicoloured.

661	199	38f. Type **199**	1·50	4·75
662		51f. "Prionocidaris verticillata"	1·60	3·25

200 Broken-stemmed Rose and I.Y.D.P. Emblems

1981. International Year of Disabled Persons.

663	**200**	45f. multicoloured	2·30	3·25

201 25c. Surcharged Stamp of 1881

1981. Air. Stamp Day.

664	**201**	41f. multicoloured	2·30	5·00

202 Latin Quarter

1981. Air. Views of Old Noumea.

665	**202**	43f. multicoloured	2·50	5·00

203 Trees and Unicornfish

1981. Nature Protection.

666	**203**	28f. blue, green and brown	1·40	5·00

204 Victor Roffey and "Golden Eagle"

1981. Air. 50th Anniv of First New Caledonia–Australia Airmail Flight.

667	**204**	37f. black, violet and blue	3·25	4·75

1982. Noumea Aquarium. Marine Animals (2nd series). As T 188. Multicoloured.

668		13f. "Calappa calappa"	90	4·25
669		25f. "Etisus splendidus"	1·40	2·75

205 "La Rousette"

1982. Air. New Caledonian Aircraft (1st series).

670	**205**	38f. brown, red and green	3·50	4·25
671	-	51f. brown, orange & grn	3·75	4·25

DESIGN: 51f. "Le Cagou".
See also Nos. 712/13.

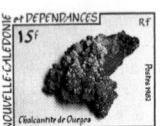

206 Chalcantite, Ouegoa

1982. Rocks and Minerals (1st series). Multicoloured.

672		15f. Type **206**	90	4·25
673		30f. Anorthosite, Blue River	1·30	5·00

See also Nos. 688/9.

207 De Verneilh, Deve and Munch (air crew), Couzinet 33 "Le Biarritz" and Route Map

1982. Air. 50th Anniv of First Flight from Paris to Noumea.

674	**207**	250f. mauve, blue and black	17·00	12·50

208 Scout and Guide Badges and Map

1982. Air. 50th Anniv of New Caledonian Scout Movement.

675	**208**	40f. multicoloured	1·80	3·75

209 "The Rat and the Octopus" (Canaque legend)

1982. "Philexfrance 82" International Stamp Exhibition, Paris.

676	**209**	150f. blue, mauve and deep blue	5·50	7·50

210 Footballer, Mascot and Badge

1982. Air. World Cup Football Championship, Spain.

677	**210**	74f. multicoloured	2·50	5·00

211 Savanna Trees at Niaoulis

1982. Flora. Multicoloured.

678		20f. Type **211**	1·50	4·50
679		29f. "Melaleuca quinquenervia" (horiz)	1·70	3·25

1982. Ships (2nd series). As T 198.

680		44f. blue, purple and brown	3·25	2·50
681		59f. blue, light brown and brown	3·75	3·50

DESIGNS: 44f. Naval transport barque "Le Cher"; 59f. Sloop "Kersaint", 1902.

212 Islanders, Map and Kagu

1982. Air. Overseas Week.

682	**212**	100f. brown, green & blue	4·50	3·00

213 Ateou Tribal House

1982. Traditional Houses.

683	**213**	52f. multicoloured	2·30	3·25

214 Grey's Fruit Dove

1982. Birds. Multicoloured.

684		32f. Type **214**	2·50	4·75
685		35f. Rainbow lory	2·50	5·25

215 Canoe

1982. Central Education Co-operation Office.

686	**215**	48f. multicoloured	2·30	5·00

216 Bernheim and Library

1982. Bernheim Library, Noumea.

687	**216**	36f. brown, purple & blk	1·60	3·75

1983. Air. Rocks and Minerals (2nd series). As T 206. Multicoloured.

688		44f. Paya gypsum (vert)	1·80	4·00
689		59f. Kone silica (vert)	2·75	4·00

217 "Dendrobium oppositifolium"

1983. Orchids. Multicoloured.

690		10f. Type **217**	1·10	3·00
691		15f. "Dendrobium munificum"	1·40	2·30
692		29f. "Dendrobium fractiflexum"	1·80	1·80

218 W.C.Y. Emblem, Map of New Caledonia and Globe

1983. Air. World Communications Year.

693	**218**	170f. multicoloured	5·50	7·75

219 "Crinum asiaticum"

1983. Flowers. Multicoloured.

694		1f. Type **219**	45	60
695		2f. "Xanthostemon aurantiacum"	45	1·20
696		4f. "Metrosideros demonstrans" (vert)	45	3·50

220 Wall Telephone and Noumea Post Office, 1890

1983. 25th Anniv of Post and Telecommunications Office. Multicoloured.

697		30f. Type **220**	1·90	3·75
698		40f. Telephone and Noumea Post Office, 1936	2·00	4·25
699		50f. Push-button telephone and Noumea Post Office, 1972	2·50	4·50
MS700		114×94 mm. As Nos. 697/9 but colours changed	11·00	30·00

221 "Laticaudata laticaudata"

1983. Noumea Aquarium. Sea Snakes. Multicoloured.

701		31f. Type **221**	2·00	1·20
702		33f. "Laticauda colubrina"	2·30	4·25

1983. Air. New Caledonian Aircraft (2nd series). As T 205. Each red, mauve & brown.

712		46f. Mignet HM14 "Pou du Ciel"	4·25	5·00
713		61f. Caudron C-600 "Aiglon"	5·00	4·50

223 Bangkok Temples

1983. Air. "Bangkok 1983" International Stamp Exhibition.

714	**223**	47f. multicoloured	2·00	5·50

224 Volleyball

1983. 7th South Pacific Games, Western Samoa.
715 **224** 16f. purple, blue and red 1·40 4·50

225 Oueholle

1983. Air.
716 **225** 76f. multicoloured 2·75 5·00

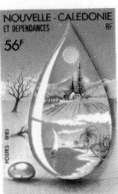

226 Desert and Water Drop showing Fertile Land

1983. Water Resources.
717 **226** 56f. multicoloured 2·30 4·75

227 Barn Owl

1983. Birds of Prey. Multicoloured.
718 34f. Type **227** 2·50 5·50
719 37f. Osprey 2·75 5·50

228 "Young Man on Beach" (R. Mascart)

1983. Air. Paintings. Multicoloured.
720 100f. Type **228** 3·75 5·00
721 350f. "Man with Guitar" (P. Nielly) 10·00 12·00

229 "Conus chenui"

1984. Sea Shells (1st series). Multicoloured.
722 5f. Type **229** 1·50 1·80
723 15f. Molucca cone 1·60 4·00
724 20f. "Conus optimus" 1·80 4·50
See also Nos. 761/2 and 810/11.

230 "St. Joseph" (freighter)

1984. Ships (3rd series). Each black, red and blue.
725 18f. Type **230** 2·30 4·50
726 31f. "Saint Antoine" (freighter) 2·50 3·25

231 Yellow-tailed Anemonefish

1984. Air. Noumea Aquarium. Fishes. Multicoloured.
727 46f. Type **231** 2·10 3·25
728 61f. Bicoloured angelfish 2·75 6·00

232 Arms of Noumea

1984
729 **232** 35f. multicoloured 2·30 2·50

233 "Araucaria columnaris"

1984. Air. Trees. Multicoloured.
730 51f. Type **233** 3·00 2·50
731 67f. "Pritchardiopsis jeanneneyi" 3·75 3·50

234 Tourist Centres

1984. Nature Protection.
732 **234** 65f. multicoloured 2·30 4·75

235 Swimming

1984. Air. Olympic Games, Los Angeles. Multicoloured.
733 50f. Type **235** 2·30 5·75
734 83f. Windsurfing 4·50 5·00
735 200f. Marathon 7·75 14·00

236 "Diplocaulobium ou-hinnae"

1984. Orchids. Multicoloured.
736 16f. Type **236** 1·40 4·50
737 38f. "Acianthus atepalus" 2·30 3·75

237 Royal Exhibition Hall, Melbourne

1984. Air. "Ausipex 84" International Stamp Exhibition, Melbourne.
738 **237** 150f. green, brown & mve 5·50 11·50

MS739 143×104 mm. **237** 150f. mauve and violet 10·00 19·00

238 School and Arrow Sign-post

1984. Centenary of Public Education.
740 **238** 59f. multicoloured 2·30 2·50

239 Anchor, Rope and Stars

1984. Air. Armed Forces Day.
741 **239** 51f. multicoloured 2·30 4·50

240 "Women looking for Crabs" (Mme. Bonnet de Larbogne)

1984. Air. Art. Multicoloured.
742 120f. Type **240** 3·75 4·00
743 300f. "Cook discovering New Caledonia" (tapestry by Pilioko) 9·25 19·00

241 Kagu

1985
744 **241** 1f. blue 75 2·75
745 **241** 2f. green 75 1·40
746 **241** 3f. orange 85 2·10
747 **241** 4f. green 85 3·50
748 **241** 5f. mauve 75 2·75
749 **241** 35f. red 1·60 3·00
750 **241** 38f. red 1·60 2·50
751 **241** 40f. red 2·00 4·25
For similar design but with "& DEPENDANCES" omitted, see Nos. 837/43.

1985. Sea Shells (2nd series). As T 229. Multicoloured.
761 55f. Bubble cone 2·50 2·75
762 72f. Lambert's cone 2·75 4·00

243 Weather Station transmitting Forecast to Boeing 737 and Trawler

1985. World Meteorology Day.
763 **243** 17f. multicoloured 2·30 3·50

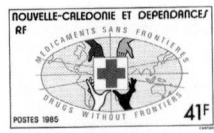

244 Map and Hands holding Red Cross

1985. International Medicines Campaign.
764 **244** 41f. multicoloured 2·50 4·50

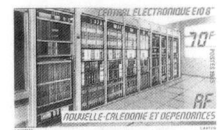

245 Electronic Telephone Exchange

1985. Inaug of Electronic Telephone Equipment.
765 **245** 70f. multicoloured 2·50 3·50

246 Marguerite la Foa Suspension Bridge

1985. Protection of Heritage.
766 **246** 44f. brown, red and blue 2·10 4·75

247 Kagu with Magnifying Glass and Stamp

1985. "Le Cagou" Stamp Club.
767 **247** 220f. multicoloured 7·25 11·50
MS768 120×100 mm. No. 767 (sold at 230f.) 13·00 21·00

248 Festival Emblem

1985. 4th Pacific Arts Festival, Papeete. Mult.
769 55f. Type **248** 1·80 5·25
770 75f. Girl blowing trumpet triton 2·30 6·00

249 Flowers, Barbed Wire and Starving Child

1985. International Youth Year.
771 **249** 59f. multicoloured 1·80 4·75

250 "Amedee Lighthouse" (M. Hosken)

1985. Electrification of Amedee Lighthouse.
772 **250** 89f. multicoloured 2·75 3·25

251 Tree and Seedling

1985. "Planting for the Future".
773 **251** 100f. multicoloured 2·75 4·50

252 De Havilland Dragon Rapide and Route Map

1985. Air. 30th Anniv of First Regular Internal Air Service.
774 **252** 80f. multicoloured 5·25 6·00

253 Hands and U.N. Emblem

1985. 40th Anniv of U.N.O.
775 **253** 250f. multicoloured 7·25 11·50

254 School, Map and "Nautilus"

1985. Air. Jules Garnier High School.
776   **254**   400f. multicoloured   14·50   15·00

255 Purple Swamphen

1985. Birds. Multicoloured.
777   50f. Type **255**   1·80   5·25
778   60f. Island thrush   2·30   4·75

256 Aircraft Tail Fins and Eiffel Tower

1986. Air. 30th Anniv of Scheduled Paris–Noumea Flights.
779   **256**   72f. multicoloured   3·25   5·75

257 Merlet Scorpionfish

1986. Noumea Aquarium. Multicoloured.
780   10f. Emperor angelfish   55   2·30
781   17f. Type **257**   70   4·25

258 Kanumera Bay, Isle of Pines

1986. Landscapes (1st series). Multicoloured.
782   50f. Type **258**   1·60   4·75
783   55f. Inland village   1·70   3·00
      See also Nos. 795/6 and 864/5.

259 "Bavayia sauvagii"

1986. Geckos. Multicoloured.
784   20f. Type **259**   1·20   3·00
785   45f. "Rhacodactylus leachianus"   1·80   5·00

260 Players and Azteca Stadium

1986. World Cup Football Championship, Mexico.
786   **260**   60f. multicoloured   1·80   5·75

261 Vivarium, Nou Island

1986. Air. Protection of Heritage.
787   **261**   230f. deep brown, blue
                 and brown   7·25   10·50

262 Pharmaceutical Equipment

1986. 120th Anniv of First Pharmacy.
788   **262**   80f. multicoloured   2·30   6·00

263 "Coelogynae licastioides"

1986. Orchids. Multicoloured.
789   44f. Type **263**   1·80   4·75
790   58f. "Calanthe langei"   2·30   3·00

264 Black-backed Magpie

1986. "Stampex 86" National Stamp Exhibition, Adelaide.
791   **264**   110f. multicoloured   4·00   9·50

265 Aerospatiale/Aeritalia ATR 42 over New Caledonia

1986. Air. Inaugural Flight of ATR 42.
792   **265**   18f. multicoloured   2·10   4·25

266 Emblem and 1860 Stamp

1986. Air. "Stockholmia 86" International Stamp Exhibition.
793   **266**   108f. black, red and lilac 3·75   6·75

267 Arms of Mont Dore

1986
794   **267**   94f. multicoloured   2·75   6·00

1986. Landscapes (2nd series). As T **258**. Multicoloured.
795   40f. West coast (vert)   90   2·00
796   76f. South   1·80   2·75

268 Wild Flowers

1986. Association for Nature Protection.
797   **268**   73f. multicoloured   3·50   5·75

269 Club Banner

1986. 25th Anniv of Noumea Lions Club.
798   **269**   350f. multicoloured   8·25   21·00

270 "Moret Bridge" (Alfred Sisley)

1986. Paintings. Multicoloured.
799   74f. Type **270**   2·75   4·00
800   140f. "Hunting Butterflies"
      (Berthe Morisot)   4·50   4·00

271 Emblem and Sound Waves

1987. Air. 25th Anniv of New Caledonia Amateur Radio Association.
801   **271**   64f. multicoloured   90   5·50

272 "Challenge France"

1987. America's Cup Yacht Race. Multicoloured.
802   30f. Type **272**   1·80   4·75
803   70f. "French Kiss"   2·50   6·00

273 "Anona squamosa" and "Graphium gelon"

1987. Plants and Butterflies. Multicoloured.
804   46f. Type **273**   2·75   5·00
805   54f. "Abizzia granulosa" and
      "Polyura gamma"   3·25   5·50

274 Peaceful Landscape, Earphones and Noisy Equipment

1987. Air. Nature Protection. Campaign against Noise.
806   **274**   150f. multicoloured   4·50   5·25

275 Isle of Pines Canoe

1987. Canoes. Each brown, green and blue.
807   72f. Type **275**   2·10   5·75
808   90f. Ouvea canoe   2·50   4·00

276 Town Hall

1987. New Town Hall, Mont Dore.
809   **276**   92f. multicoloured   2·75   6·00

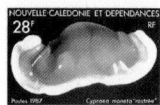

277 Money Cowrie

1987. Sea Shells (3rd series). Multicoloured.
810   28f. Type **277**   1·30   4·50
811   36f. Martin's cone   1·80   4·75

278 Games Emblem

1987. 8th South Pacific Games. Noumea (1st issue).
812   **278**   40f. multicoloured   1·40   3·00
      See also Nos. 819/21.

279 Emblem

1987. 13th Soroptimists International Convention, Melbourne.
813   **279**   270f. multicoloured   8·00   14·50

280 New Caledonia White-Eye

1987. Birds. Multicoloured.
814   18f. Type **280**   1·40   4·25
815   21f. Peregrine falcon (vert)   1·40   4·25

281 Flags on Globe

1987. 40th Anniv of South Pacific Commission.
816   **281**   200f. multicoloured   6·50   10·50

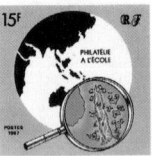

282 Globe and Magnifying Glass on Map of New Caledonia

1987. Schools Philately.
817   **282**   15f. multicoloured   90   4·00

283 Cricketers

1987. Air. French Cricket Federation.
818   **283**   94f. multicoloured   3·25   5·75

284 Golf

1987. 8th South Pacific Games, Noumea (2nd issue). Multicoloured.
819   20f. Type **284**   1·20   4·00
820   30f. Rugby football   2·20   4·25
821   100f. Long jumping   2·75   6·00

285 Arms of
Dumbea

1988. Air.
822 **285** 76f. multicoloured   3·00   2·75

286 Route Map, "L'Astrolabe", "La
Boussole" and La Perouse

1988. Bicentenary of Disappearance of La Perouse's
Expedition.
823 **286** 36f. blue, brown and red   4·75   3·50

287 University

1988. French University of South Pacific, Noumea and
Papeete.
824 **287** 400f. multicoloured   10·00 13·50

288 Semicircle Angelfish

1988. Noumea Aquarium. Fishes. Multicoloured.
825 Type **288** 30f.   2·50   4·00
826 46f. Sapphire sergeant major   2·75   4·75

289 Mwaringou
House, Canala

1988. Traditional Huts. Each brown, green and blue.
827 Type **289** 19f.   1·10   4·00
828 21f. Nathalo house, Lifou (horiz)   1·10   3·75

290 Anniversary Emblem

1988. 125th Anniv of International Red Cross.
829 **290** 300f. blue, green and red   10·00 7·75

291 "Ochrosia elliptica"

1988. Medicinal Plants. Multicoloured.
830 Type **291** 28f. (postage)   1·40   4·00
831 64f. "Rauvolfia sevenetii" (air)   2·00   4·75

292 "Gymnocrinus richeri"

1988
832 **292** 51f. multicoloured   1·80   4·50

293 Furnished Room and Building
Exterior

1988. Bourail Museum and Historical Association.
833 **293** 120f. multicoloured   3·75   7·50

294 La Perouse sighting Phillip's
Fleet in Botany Bay

1988. "Sydpex 88" Stamp Exhibition, Sydney.
Multicoloured.
834 42f. Type **294**   2·75   5·00
835 42f. Phillip sighting "La Bous-
     sole" and "L'Astrolabe"   2·75   5·00
MS836 175×120 mm. Nos. 834/5 (sold
     at 120f.)   5·50   11·50

295 Kagu

1988
837 **295** 1f. blue   1·80   2·75
838 **295** 2f. green   1·80   3·25
839 **295** 3f. orange   1·80   3·75
840 **295** 4f. green   1·80   2·75
841 **295** 5f. mauve   1·80   3·50
842 **295** 28f. orange   2·30   3·75
843 **295** 40f. red   3·50   4·00

296 Table Tennis

1988. Olympic Games, Seoul.
846 **296** 150f. multicoloured   4·50   6·50

297 Laboratory Assistant,
Noumea Institute and
Pasteur

1988. Centenary of Pasteur Institute, Paris.
847 **297** 100f. red, black and blue   3·75   5·50

298 Georges Baudoux

1988. Writers.
848 **298** 72f. brown, green and
             purple (postage)   2·30   4·00
849 -   73f. brown, bl & blk (air)   2·10   3·00
DESIGN: 73f. Jean Mariotti.

299 Map and Emblems

1988. Air. Rotary International Anti-Polio Campaign.
850 **299** 220f. multicoloured   5·00   6·50

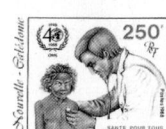

300 Doctor examining
Child

1988. 40th Anniv of W.H.O.
851 **300** 250f. multicoloured   6·50   9·75

301 "Terre des Hommes" (L.
Bunckley)

1988. Paintings. Multicoloured.
852 54f. Type **301**   3·25   4·75
853 92f. "Latin Quarter" (Marik)   2·75   6·00

302 Arms of
Koumac

1989
854 **302** 200f. multicoloured   7·75   10·50

303 "Parasitaxus
ustus"

1989. Flowers. Multicoloured.
855 80f. Type **303**   2·20   5·75
856 90f. "Tristaniopsis guillainii"
          (horiz)   2·30   6·00

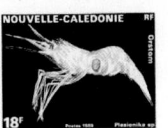

304 "Plesionika sp."

1989. Marine Life. Multicoloured.
857 18f. Type **304**   2·20   3·75
858 66f. Sail-backed scorpionfish   2·50   5·50
859 110f. Cristiate latiaxis   3·75   3·50

305 "Liberty"

1989. Bicentenary of French Revolution and "Philexfrance
89" International Stamp Exhibition, Paris.
Multicoloured.
860 40f. Type **305** (postage)   1·80   2·30
861 58f. "Equality" (air)   2·30   1·60
862 76f. "Fraternity"   3·50   3·00
MS863 155×110 mm. 180f. "Liberty"
     "Equality" and "Fraternity" (92×51
     mm)   8·75   13·00

1989. Landscapes (3rd series). As T 258. Mult.
864 180f. Ouaieme ferry (post)   5·50   5·00
865 64f. "The Broody Hen" (rocky
          islet), Hienghene (air)   2·00   5·00

306 Canoe and
Diamond Decoration

1989. Bamboo Decorations by C. Ohlen. Each black,
     bistre and orange.
866 70f. Type **306** (postage)   2·40   3·25
867 44f. Animal design (air)   1·40   4·25

307 "Hobie Cat 14"
Yachts

1989. 10th World "Hobie Cat" Class Catamaran
Championship, Noumea.
868 **307** 350f. multicoloured   9·25   17·00

308 Book Title Pages and Society
Members

1989. 20th Anniv of Historical Studies Society.
869 **308** 74f. black and brown   2·75   2·75

309 Fort Teremba

1989. Protection of Heritage.
870 **309** 100f. green, brown
             & blue   3·00   6·00

310 "Rochefort's Escape"
(Edouard Manet)

1989. Paintings. Multicoloured.
871 130f. Type **310**   4·50   3·75
872 270f. "Self-portrait" (Gustave
           Courbet)   8·25   14·00

311 Fr. Patrick
O'Reilly

1990. Writers.
873 **311** 170f. black and mauve   5·50   8·25

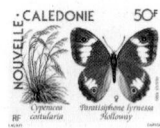

312 Grass and Female
Butterfly

1990. "Cyperacea costularia" (grass) and "Paratisiphone
lyrnessa" (butterfly). Multicoloured.
874 50f. Type **312** (postage)   2·75   4·75
875 18f. Grass and female butterfly
          (different) (air)   1·80   1·80
876 94f. Grass and male butterfly   3·75   6·00

313 "Maize" Stem
with Face

1990. Kanaka Money.

877	**313**	85f. olive, orange & green	2·75	2·30
878	-	140f. orange, black & grn	4·50	7·00

DESIGN: 140f. "Rope" stem with decorative end.

314 Exhibit

1990. Jade and Mother-of-pearl Exhibition.

879	**314**	230f. multicoloured	6·50	11·00

315 Ocellate Nudibranch

1990. Noumea Aquarium. Sea Slugs. Multicoloured.

880	10f. Type **315**	65	4·00
881	42f. "Chromodoris kuniei" (vert)	1·40	4·50

316 Head of "David"
(Michelangelo) and Footballers

1990. World Cup Football Championship, Italy.

882	**316**	240f. multicoloured	8·75	8·00

317 De Gaulle

1990. Air. 50th Anniv of De Gaulle's Call to Resist.

883	**317**	160f. multicoloured	4·50	9·00

318 Neounda Site

1990. Petroglyphs.

884	**318**	40f. brown, green and red (postage)	1·60	3·25
885	-	58f. black, brown and blue (air)	2·30	2·50

DESIGN—HORIZ: 58f. Kassducou site.

319 Map and Pacific International
Meeting Centre

1990

886	**319**	320f. multicoloured	7·25	8·00

320 New Zealand
Cemetery, Bourail

1990. Air. "New Zealand 1990" International Stamp
Exhibition, Auckland. Multicoloured.

887	80f. Type **320**	2·50	4·25

888	80f. Brigadier William Walter Dove	2·50	4·25

MS889 140×100 mm. 150f. Kagu, brown kiwi and maps of New Caledonia and New Zealand | 6·50 | 13·00

321 Kagu

1990

890	**321**	1f. blue	2·00	4·00
891	**321**	2f. green	2·00	3·00
892	**321**	3f. yellow	2·00	3·75
893	**321**	4f. green	2·00	4·00
894	**321**	5f. violet	2·00	2·75
895	**321**	9f. grey	2·00	4·00
896	**321**	12f. red	2·00	4·00
897	**321**	40f. mauve	90	4·25
898	**321**	50f. red	1·00	4·50
899	**321**	55f. red	2·75	4·50

The 5 and 55f. exist both perforated with ordinary gum and imperforate with self-adhesive gum.
For design with no value expressed see No. 994.

322 "Munidopsis
sp"

1990. Air. Deep Sea Animals. Multicoloured.

900	30f. Type **322**	90	3·00
901	60f. "Lyreidius tridentatus"	1·80	3·50

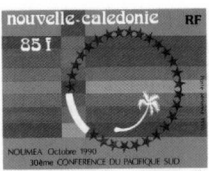

323 Emblem

1990. Air. 30th South Pacific Conference, Noumea.

902	**323**	85f. multicoloured	1·80	5·75

324 "Gardenia aubryi"

1990. Flowers. Multicoloured.

903	105f. Type **324**	3·00	6·00
904	130f. "Hibbertia baudouinii"	3·75	7·00

325 De Gaulle

1990. Air. Birth Centenary of Charles de Gaulle (French statesman).

905	**325**	410f. blue	11·00	13·00

326 "Mont Dore,
Mountain of Jade" (C. Degroiselle)

1990. Air. Pacific Painters. Multicoloured.

906	365f. Type **326** (postage)	10·00	11·00
907	110f. "The Celieres House" (M. Petron) (air)	3·00	5·00

327 Fayawa-Ouvea Bay

1991. Air. Regional Landscapes. Multicoloured.

908	36f. Type **327**	2·10	3·25
909	90f. Coastline of Mare	2·40	4·00

328 Louise Michel and Classroom

1991. Writers.

910	**328**	125f. mauve and blue	5·25	7·00
911	-	125f. blue and brown	5·25	7·00

DESIGN: No. 911, Charles B. Nething and photographer.

329 Houailou Hut

1991. Melanesian Huts. Multicoloured.

912	12f. Type **329**	1·80	2·75
913	35f. Hienghene hut	2·40	4·25

330 Northern Province

1991. Provinces. Multicoloured.

914	45f. Type **330**	1·30	3·75
915	45f. Islands Province	1·30	3·75
916	45f. Southern Province	1·30	3·75

331 "Dendrobium biflorum"

1991. Orchids. Multicoloured.

917	55f. Type **331**	2·75	4·75
918	70f. "Dendrobium closterium"	3·00	5·00

332 Japanese
Pineconefish

1991. Fishes. Multicoloured.

919	60f. Type **332**	3·25	4·75
920	100f. Japanese bigeye	4·00	5·00

333 Research Equipment and Sites

1991. French Scientific Research Institute for Development and Co-operation.

921	**333**	170f. multicoloured	7·25	7·00

334 Emblem

1991. 9th South Pacific Games, Papua New Guinea.

922	**334**	170f. multicoloured	7·25	7·00

335 Map and Dragon

1991. Centenary of Vietnamese Settlement in New Caledonia.

923	**335**	300f. multicoloured	10·00	13·00

336 Emblems

1991. 30th Anniv of Lions International in New Caledonia.

924	**336**	192f. multicoloured	7·25	7·75

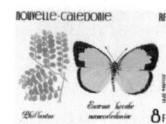

337 Map, "Camden" (missionary
brig), Capt. Robert Clark Morgan
and Trees

1991. 150th Anniv of Discovery of Sandalwood.

925	**337**	200f. blue, turquoise & grn	7·25	8·25

338 "Phillantus" and
Common Grass Yellow

1991. "Phila Nippon '91" International Stamp Exhibition, Tokyo. Plants and Butterflies. Mult.

926	8f. Type **338**	1·60	3·00
927	15f. "Pipturus incanus" and "Hypolimnas octocula"	1·60	3·00
928	20f. "Stachytarpheta urticaefolia" and meadow argos	1·80	3·25
929	26f. "Malaisia scandens" and "Cyrestis telamon"	1·80	3·25

MS930 100×122 mm. 75f. *Cyrestis telamon*; 75f. *Hypolimnas octocula*; 75f. *Eurema hecabe*; 75f. *Precis villida* (all vert) | 16·00 | 23·00

339 Nickel Processing Plant and
Dam

1991. 50th Anniv of Central Economic Co-operation Bank. Multicoloured.

931	76f. Type **339**	3·25	5·25
932	76f. Housing and hotels	3·25	5·25

340 "Caledonian Cricket" (Marcel
Moutouh)

1991. Air. Pacific Painters. Multicoloured.

933	130f. Type **340**	5·75	6·00
934	435f. "Saint Louis" (Janine Goetz)	14·00	19·00

341 Blue River

1992. Air. Blue River National Park.

935	**341**	400f. multicoloured	10·00	13·00

MS936 127×91 mm. No. 935 (sold at 450f.) 14·00 17·00

342 La Madeleine Falls

1992. Nature Protection.
937 **342** 15f. multicoloured 1·30 3·25
MS938 122×88 mm. No. 937 (sold at 150f.) 6·25 6·75

343 Lapita Pot

1992. Air. Noumea Museum.
939 **343** 25f. black and orange 1·30 3·25

344 Barqueta Bridge

1992. Air. "Expo '92" World's Fair, Seville.
940 **344** 10f. multicoloured 1·50 2·00

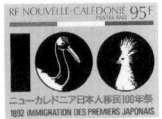

345 "Pinta"

1992. Air. "World Columbian Stamp Expo '92", Chicago. Multicoloured.
941 **345** 80f. Type **345** 2·75 4·00
942 **345** 80f. "Santa Maria" 2·75 4·00
943 **345** 80f. "Nina" 2·75 4·00
MS944 160×70 mm. 110f. Eric the Red and longship; 110f. Christopher Columbus and arms; 110f. Amerigo Vespucci (sold at 360f.) 10·00 13·00

346 Manchurian Crane and Kagu within "100"

1992. Centenary of Arrival of First Japanese Immigrants. Multicoloured, background colours given.
945 **346** 95f. yellow 3·75 4·00
946 **346** 95f. grey 3·75 4·00

347 Synchronised Swimming

1992. Olympic Games, Barcelona.
947 **347** 260f. multicoloured 4·50 6·50

348 Bell Airacobra, Grumman F4F Wildcat, Barrage Balloon, Harbour and Nissen Huts

1992. 50th Anniv of Arrival of American Forces in New Caledonia.
948 **348** 50f. multicoloured 3·25 3·50

349 "Wahpa" (Paul Mascart)

1992. Air. Pacific Painters.
949 **349** 205f. multicoloured 5·50 5·25

350 Australian Cattle Dog

1992. Air. Canine World Championships.
950 **350** 175f. multicoloured 3·75 5·00

351 Entrecasteaux and Fleet

1992. Air. Navigators. Bicentenary of Landing of Admiral Bruni d'Entrecasteaux on West Coast of New Caledonia.
951 **351** 110f. orange, blue & green 3·00 4·25

352 "Amalda fuscolingua"

1992. Air. Shells. Multicoloured.
952 **352** 30f. Type **352** 1·80 3·25
953 **352** 50f. "Cassis abbotti" 2·00 3·50

353 Deole

1992. Air. "La Brousse en Folie" (comic strip) by Bernard Berger. Multicoloured.
954 **353** 80f. Type **353** 2·75 2·75
955 **353** 80f. Tonton Marcel 2·75 2·75
956 **353** 80f. Tathan 2·75 2·75
957 **353** 80f. Joinville 2·75 2·75

354 Lagoon

1993. Lagoon Protection.
958 **354** 120f. multicoloured 3·00 4·25

355 Harbour (Gaston Roullet)

1993. Air. Pacific Painters.
959 **355** 150f. multicoloured 3·50 4·75

356 Symbols of New Caledonia

1993. School Philately. "Tourism my Friend".
960 **356** 25f. multicoloured 1·60 2·30

357 Still and Plantation

1993. Air. Centenary of Production of Essence of Niaouli.
966 **357** 85f. multicoloured 1·40 1·80

358 Planets and Copernicus

1993. Air. "Polska '93" International Stamp Exhibition, Poznan. 450th Death Anniv of Nicolas Copernicus (astronomer).
967 **358** 110f. blue, turquoise & grey 1·80 4·00

359 Noumea Temple

1993. Air. Centenary of First Protestant Church in Noumea.
968 **359** 400f. multicoloured 7·25 7·25

1993. No. 898 surch 55F.
969 **321** 55f. on 50f. red 1·80 3·50

361 Malabou

1993. Air. Regional Landscapes.
970 **361** 85f. multicoloured 2·30 2·75

362 Locomotive and Bridge

1993. Air. Centenary of Little Train of Thio.
971 **362** 115f. red, green and lilac 2·50 3·75

363 Rochefort

1993. Air. 80th Death Anniv of Henri Rochefort (journalist).
972 **363** 100f. multicoloured 1·80 4·00

364 "Megastylis paradoxa"

1993. Air. "Bangkok 1993" International Stamp Exhibition, Thailand. Multicoloured.
973 **364** 30f. Type **364** 1·40 3·00
974 **364** 30f. "Vanda coerulea" 1·40 3·00
MS975 120×90 mm. 140f. Exhibition centre (51×39 mm) 5·50 6·75

365 Route Map and Boeing 737-300/500

1993. Air. 10th Anniv of Air Cal (national airline).
976 **365** 85f. multicoloured 2·50 2·75

366 "Francois Arago" (cable ship)

1993. Air. Centenary of New Caledonia–Australia Telecommunications Cable.
977 **366** 200f. purple, blue & turq 4·50 5·00

367 "Oxypleurodon orbiculatus"

1993. Air. Deep-sea Life.
978 **367** 250f. multicoloured 5·50 6·25

368 Aircraft, Engine and Hangar

1993. Air. 25th Anniv of Chamber of Commerce and Industry's Management of La Tontouta Airport, Noumea.
979 **368** 90f. multicoloured 2·75 2·50

369 First Christmas Mass, 1843 (stained glass window, Balade church)

1993. Air. Christmas.
980 **369** 120f. multicoloured 3·00 4·00

370 Bourail

1993. Town Arms. Multicoloured.
981 **370** 70f. Type **370** 2·30 3·75
982 **370** 70f. Noumea 2·30 3·75
983 **370** 70f. Canala 2·30 3·75
984 **370** 70f. Kone 2·30 3·75
985 **370** 70f. Paita 2·30 3·75
986 **370** 70f. Dumbea 2·30 3·75
987 **370** 70f. Koumac 2·30 3·75
988 **370** 70f. Ponerihouen 2·30 3·75
989 **370** 70f. Kaamoo Hyehen 2·30 3·75
990 **370** 70f. Mont Dore 2·30 3·75
991 **370** 70f. Thio 2·30 3·75

992	70f. Kaala-Gomen	2·30	3·75
993	70f. Touho	2·30	3·75

1994. No value expressed.

994	**321**	(60f.) red	1·80	2·30

371 Dog, Exhibition Emblem and Chinese Horoscope Signs (New Year)

1994. Air. "Hong Kong '94" International Stamp Exhibition. Multicoloured.

995		60f. Type **371**	1·80	3·50
MS996		161×120 mm. 105f. Giant panda (51×39 *mm*); 105f. Kagu (51×39 *mm*)	5·50	10·00

372 Airbus Industrie A340

1994. Air 1st Paris–Noumea Airbus Flight. Self-adhesive.

997	**372**	90f. multicoloured	2·75	4·00

1994. "Philexjeunes '94" Youth Stamp Exhibition, Grenoble. No. 960 optd PHILEXJEUNES'94 GRENOBLE 22–24 AVRIL.

998	**356**	25f. multicoloured	90	3·00

374 Photograph of Canala Post Office and Post Van

1994. 50th Anniv of Noumea–Canala Postal Service.

999	**374**	15f. brown, green and blue	1·50	3·00

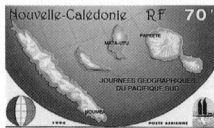

375 Pacific Islands on Globe

1994. Air. South Pacific Geographical Days.

1000	**375**	70f. multicoloured	2·30	3·00

376 Post Office, 1859

1994. Postal Administration Head Offices. Mult.

1001		30f. Type **376**	3·00	3·00
1002		60f. Posts and Telecommunications Office, 1936	4·00	3·25
1003		90f. Ministry of Posts and Telecommunications, 1967	4·75	4·00
1004		120f. Ministry of Posts and Telecommunications, 1993	5·75	4·50

377 "The Mask Wearer"

1994. Pacific Sculpture.

1005	**377**	60f. multicoloured	2·50	3·25

378 "Legend of the Devil Fish" (Micheline Neporon)

1994. Air. Pacific Painters.

1006	**378**	120f. multicoloured	3·00	4·00

379 "Chambeyronia macrocarpa"

1994

1007	**379**	90f. multicoloured	3·25	3·50

380 Podtanea Pot

1994. Air. Noumea Museum.

1008	**380**	95f. multicoloured	3·00	4·00

381 Trophy, U.S. Flag and Ball

1994. Air. World Cup Football Championship, U.S.A.

1009	**381**	105f. multicoloured	3·00	4·25

1994. No. D707 with "Timbre Taxe" obliterated by black bar.

1010	**D222**	5f. multicoloured	14·50	6·00

382 Timor Deer

1994. Bourail Fair.

1011	**382**	150f. multicoloured	3·75	4·50

383 Korean Family

1994. Air. "Philakorea 1994" International Stamp Exhibition, Seoul. Multicoloured.

1012		60f. Type **383**	2·75	3·25
MS1013		110×110 mm. 35f. Containers, peppers and emblem (36×37 mm); 35f. Carafe, celery, cannage and garlic (36×37 mm); 35f. Container and turnips (36×37 mm); 35f. Jug, seafood and lemon (36×37 mm)	7·75	7·75

384 "L'Atalante" (oceanographic research vessel)

1994. Air. ZoNeCo (evaluation programme of Economic Zone).

1014	**384**	120f. multicoloured	3·00	4·50

385 "Nivose"

1994. Attachment of the "Nivose" (French surveillance frigate) to New Caledonia. Multicoloured.

1015		30f. Type **385**	3·25	3·00
1016		30f. Aircraft over frigate	3·25	3·00
1017		30f. Frigate moored at quay	3·25	3·00
1018		60f. Frigate and map of New Caledonia on parchment	4·00	3·50
1019		60f. Ship's bell	4·00	3·50
1020		60f. Frigate and sailor	4·00	3·50

386 Driving Cattle

1994. Air. 1st European Stamp Salon, Flower Gardens, Paris. Multicoloured.

1021		90f. Aerial view of island	2·75	3·75
1022		90f. Type **386**	2·75	3·75

387 Paper Darts around Girl

1994. School Philately.

1023	**387**	30f. multicoloured	1·40	3·00

388 Jaques Nervat

1994. Writers.

1024	**388**	175f. multicoloured	4·50	4·75

389 Satellite transmitting to Globe and Computer Terminal

1994. Air. 50th Anniv of Overseas Scientific and Technical Research Office.

1025	**389**	95f. multicoloured	3·00	2·75

390 Emblem and Temple

1994. Air. 125th Anniv of Freemasonary in New Caledonia.

1026	**390**	350f. multicoloured	8·75	7·75

391 Thiebaghi Mine

1994. Air.

1027	**391**	90f. multicoloured	2·50	3·75

392 Place des Cocotiers, Noumea

1994. Christmas.

1028	**392**	30f. multicoloured	1·40	3·00

No. 1028 covers any one of five stamps which were issued together in horizontal se-tenant strips, the position of the bell, tree and monument differing on each stamp. The strip is stated to produce a three-dimensional image without use of a special viewer.

393 Globe and Newspapers

1994. 50th Anniv of "Le Monde" (newspaper).

1029	**393**	90f. multicoloured	3·00	3·75

394 1988 100f. Pasteur Institute Stamp

1995. Death Centenary of Louis Pasteur (chemist).

1030	**394**	120f. multicoloured	3·00	4·00

395 Pictorial Map

1995. Air. Tourism.

1031	**395**	90f. multicoloured	2·30	3·75

396 Profile of De Gaulle (Santucci) and Cross of Lorraine

1995. 25th Death Anniv of Charles de Gaulle (French President, 1959–69).

1032	**396**	1000f. deep blue, blue and gold	24·00	34·00

397 Emblem

1995. Pacific University Teachers' Training Institute.

1033	**397**	100f. multicoloured	2·50	4·00

398 "Sylviornis neocaledoniae"

1995

1034	**398**	60f. multicoloured	1·80	3·25

399 Swimming, Cycling and Running

1995. Triathlon.

1035	**399**	60f. multicoloured	1·80	3·50

400 Tent and Trees

1995. 50th Anniv of Pacific Franc.

1036	**400**	10f. multicoloured	1·10	2·75

No. 1036 covers any one of four stamps which were issued together in horizontal se-tenant strips, the position of the central motif rotating slightly in a clockwise direction from the left to the right-hand stamp. The strip is stated to produce a three-dimensional image without use of a special viewer.

401 Bourbon Palace (Paris), Map of New Caledonia and Chamber

1995. 50th Anniversaries. Multicoloured.
1037	60f. Type **401** (first representation of New Caledonia at French National Assembly)		1·80	3·25
1038	90f. National emblems, De Gaulle and Allied flags (end of Second World War)		2·50	3·75
1039	90f. U.N. Headquarters, New York (U.N.O.)		2·30	3·75

402 "Sebertia acuminata"

1995
1040	**402**	60f. multicoloured	2·10	3·25

403 Common Noddy

1995. "Singapore'95" International Stamp Exhibition. Sea Birds. Multicoloured.
1041	5f. Type **403**	1·00	1·80
1042	10f. Silver gull	1·10	2·00
1043	20f. Roseate tern	1·20	2·50
1044	35f. Osprey	1·60	3·00
1045	65f. Red-footed booby	1·80	3·75
1046	125f. Great frigate bird	2·75	4·50
MS1047	130×100 mm. Nos. 1041/6	8·25	9·25

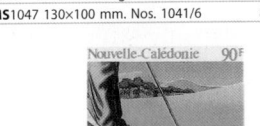

404 Golf

1995. 10th South Pacific Games.
1048	**404**	90f. multicoloured	2·50	4·00

405 "The Lizard Man" (Dick Bone)

1995. Pacific Sculpture.
1049	**405**	65f. multicoloured	2·00	3·50

406 Venue

1995. Air. 35th South Pacific Conference.
1050	**406**	500f. multicoloured	8·25	12·50

407 Silhouette of Francis Carco

1995. Writers.
1051	**407**	95f. multicoloured	1·80	4·00

408 Ouare

1995. Air. Kanak Dances. Multicoloured.
1052	95f. Type **408**	1·80	3·75
1053	100f. Pothe	1·80	3·75

409 Saw-headed Crocodilefish

1995. World of the Deep.
1054	**409**	100f. multicoloured	2·50	4·00

410 "Mekosuchus inexpectatus"

1996. Air.
1055	**410**	125f. multicoloured	3·00	4·25

411 Vessel with decorated Rim

1996. Noumea Museum.
1056	**411**	65f. multicoloured	1·70	3·50

412 "Captaincookia margaretae"

1996. Flowers. Multicoloured.
1057	65f. Type **412**	1·70	3·25
1058	95f. "Ixora cauliflora"	2·50	3·75

413 Pirogue on Beach

1996. World Pirogue Championships, Noumea. Multicoloured.
1059	30f. Type **413**	2·00	3·00
1060	65f. Pirogue leaving shore	2·75	3·25
1061	95f. Double-hulled pirogue	3·25	3·75
1062	125f. Sports pirogue	3·25	4·75

Nos. 1059/62 were issued together, se-tenant, forming a composite design.

414 Red Batfish

1996. "China'96" International Stamp Exhibition, Peking. Deep Sea Life. Multicoloured.
1063	25f. Type **414**	1·20	2·75
1064	40f. "Perotrochus deforgesi" (slit shell)	1·40	3·00
1065	65f. "Mursia musorstomia" (crab)	1·80	3·25
1066	125f. Sea lily	3·25	4·25

415 "Sarcolchilus koghiensis"

1996. "Capex'96" International Stamp Exhibition, Toronto, Canada. Orchids. Multicoloured.
1067	5f. Type **415**	30	2·30
1068	10f. "Phaius robertsii"	1·10	2·50
1069	25f. "Megastylis montana"	1·20	2·75
1070	65f. "Dendrobium macrophyllum"	1·60	3·25
1071	95f. "Dendrobium virotii"	2·20	3·75
1072	125f. "Ephemerantha comata"	2·75	4·00

416 Indonesian Couple beneath Tree

1996. Air. Centenary of Arrival of First Indonesian Immigrants.
1073	**416**	130f. multicoloured	3·50	4·50

417 Louis Brauquier

1996. Air. Writers.
1074	**417**	95f. multicoloured	2·40	3·75

1996. 50th Anniv of UNICEF. No. 1023 optd unicef and emblem.
1075	**387**	30f. multicoloured	1·40	3·00

419 Dish Aerial

1996. Air. Anniversaries. Multicoloured.
1076	95f. Type **419** (20th anniv of New Caledonia's first Earth Station)	2·50	3·75
1077	125f. Guglielmo Marconi (inventor) and telegraph masts (centenary of radio-telegraphy)	3·00	4·50

420 Tribal Dance

1996. Air. 7th South Pacific Arts Festival.
1078	**420**	100f. multicoloured	2·40	4·00

421 "The Woman" (Elija Trijikone)

1996. Sculptures of the Pacific.
1079	**421**	105f. multicoloured	2·50	2·30

422 Ordination, St. Joseph's Cathedral, Noumea

1996. 50th Anniv of Ordination of First Priests in New Caledonia.
1080	**422**	160f. multicoloured	3·75	4·75

423 "Man" (Paula Boi)

1996. Pacific Painters.
1081	**423**	200f. multicoloured	4·50	4·00

424 Gaica Dance

1996
1082	**424**	500f. multicoloured	11·00	8·75

425 Great Reef

1996. Air. 50th Autumn Stamp Show, Paris. Multicoloured.
1083	95f. Type **425**	3·00	3·75
1084	95f. Mount Koghi	3·00	3·75

426 Decorated Sandman

1996. Christmas.
1085	**426**	95f. multicoloured	2·20	3·50

427 Horned Tortoises

1997. Air.
1086	**427**	95f. multicoloured	2·20	4·00

428 Emblem

1997. Air. 50th Anniv of South Pacific Commission.
1087	**428**	100f. multicoloured	2·30	3·75

429 Junk, Hong Kong, Ox and Flag

1997. Air. Hong Kong '97 International Stamp Exhibiton. Year of the Ox. Multicoloured.

1088	**429**	95f. Type **429**	2·20	3·75
MS1089		121×91 mm. 75f. Farmer ploughing with ox (39×29 mm); 75f. Cattle grazing (39×29 mm)	5·00	7·75

430 Mitterrand

1997. 1st Death Anniv of Francois Mitterrand (French President, 1981–95).

1090	**430**	1000f. multicoloured	20·00	27·00

431 Windmill ("Letters from My Windmill")

1997. Death Centenary of Alphonse Daudet (writer). Multicoloured.

1091	**431**	65f. Type **431**	2·00	2·30
1092		65f. Boy sitting by wall ("The Little Thing")	2·00	2·30
1093		65f. Hunter in jungle ("Tartarinde Tarascon")	2·00	2·30
1094		65f. Daudet at work	2·00	2·30
MS1095		100×120 mm. Nos. 1091/4	7·25	11·00

432 Lapita Pot with Geometric Pattern

1997. Air. Melanesian Pottery in Noumea Museum. Multicoloured.

1096	**432**	95f. Type **432**	2·50	3·75
1097		95f. Lapita pot with "face" design	2·50	3·75

433 French Parliament Building and Lafleur

1997. Appointment of Henri Lafleur as First New Caledonian Senator in French Parliament.

1098	**433**	105f. multicoloured	2·50	4·00

434 Cotton Harlequin Bug

1997. Insects. Multicoloured.

1099	**434**	65f. Type **434**	3·00	3·75
1100		65f. "Kanakia gigas"	3·00	3·75
1101		65f. "Aenetus cohici" (moth)	3·00	3·75

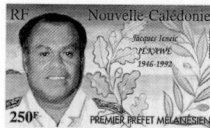

435 Iekawe

1997. 5th Death Anniv of Jacques Ieneic Iekawe (first Melanesian Prefect).

1102	**435**	250f. multicoloured	6·00	6·75

436 Consolidated Catalina Flying Boat and South Pacific Routes Map

1997. Air. 50th Anniv of Establishment by TRAPAS of First Commercial Air Routes in South Pacific. Multicoloured.

1103	**436**	95f. Type **436**	2·50	3·75
1104		95f. TRAPAS emblem, seaplane and New Caledonia domestic flight routes	2·50	3·75

437 Kagu

1997

1105	**437**	5f. violet	1·30	1·30
1107	**437**	30f. orange	1·20	3·00
1113	**437**	95f. blue	2·20	3·00
1114	**437**	100f. blue	3·00	3·50

No. 1114 also comes self-adhesive. See also No. 1128.

438 Cup and Harness Racing

1997. Equestrian Sports. Multicoloured.

1118	**438**	65f. Type **438**	2·10	3·25
1119		65f. Cup and horse racing	2·10	3·25

439 Port de France (engraving)

1997

1120	**439**	95f. multicoloured	2·30	3·50

440 "Marianne", Voter and Tiki

1997. 50th Anniv of First Elections of Melanesian Representatives to French Parliament.

1121	**440**	150f. multicoloured	3·50	4·50

441 Seahorses

1997. 5th Indo-Pacific Fishes Conference.

1122	**441**	100f. multicoloured	2·30	3·50

442 Hammerhead Shark Dance Mask (Ken Thaiday)

1997. Pacific Art and Culture. Multicoloured.

1123	**442**	100f. Type **442**	2·30	3·50
1124		100f. Painting of traditional Melanesian images by Yvette Bouquet	2·30	3·50
1125		100f. "Doka" (figurines by Frank Haikiu)	2·30	3·50

443 Father Christmas surfing to Earth

1997. Christmas. Multicoloured.

1126	**443**	95f. Type **443**	2·30	3·50
1127		100f. Dolphin with "Meilleurs Voeux" banner	2·40	3·50

1998. As Nos. 1107/13 but with no value expressed. Ordinary or self-adhesive gum.

1128	**437**	(70f.) red	1·80	3·00

444 "Lentinus tuber-regium"

1998. Edible Mushrooms. Multicoloured.

1130	**444**	70f. Type **444**	1·80	2·00
1131		70f. "Morchella anteridiformis"	1·80	2·00
1132		70f. "Volvaria bombycina"	1·80	2·00

445 Mask from Northern Region

1998. Territorial Museum. Multicoloured.

1133	**445**	105f. Type **445**	2·20	1·80
1134		110f. Section of door frame from Central Region	2·20	1·80

446 Painting by Gauguin

1998. 150th Birth Anniv of Paul Gauguin (painter).

1135	**446**	405f. multicoloured	8·00	7·25

447 Player

1998. World Cup Football Championship, France.

1136	**447**	100f. multicoloured	2·20	3·50

448 "Mitimitia"

1998. Tjibaou Cultural Centre. Multicoloured.

1137	**448**	30f. Type **448**	1·50	2·75
1138		70f. Jean-Marie Tjibaou (politician) and Centre	1·80	3·25
1139		70f. Detail of a Centre building (Renzo Piano) (vert)	1·80	3·25
1140		105f. "Man Bird" (Mathias Kauage) (vert)	2·30	3·50

449 Broken Chains and Slaves

1998. 150th Anniv of Abolition of Slavery.

1141	**449**	130f. brown, blue and purple	2·50	2·40

450 Dogs watching Postman delivering Letter

1998. Stamp Day.

1142	**450**	70f. multicoloured	2·00	3·00

451 Vincent Bouquet

1998. 50th Anniv of Election of First President of Commission of Chiefs.

1143	**451**	110f. multicoloured	2·10	2·00

452 Noumea Fantasia, 1903

1998. 100 Years of Arab Presence.

1144	**452**	80f. multicoloured	2·00	1·70

453 Departure

1998. "Portugal 98" International Stamp Exhibition, Lisbon. 500th Anniv of Vasco da Gama's Voyage to India via Cape of Good Hope. Multicoloured.

1145	**453**	100f. Type **453**	2·50	2·00
1146		100f. Fleet at Cape of Good Hope	2·50	2·00
1147		100f. Vasco da Gama meeting Indian king	2·50	2·00
1148		100f. Vasco da Gama in armorial shield flanked by plants	2·50	2·00
MS1149		160×130 mm. 70f. Route map (39×51 mm); 70f. Vasco da Gama (39×51 mm); 70f. Sao Gabriel (flagship) and fleet (39×51 mm)	6·50	7·75

454 Kagu

1998. Endangered Species. The Kagu. Multicoloured.

1150	**454**	5f. Type **454**	1·00	85
1151		10f. Kagu by branch	1·10	85
1152		15f. Two kagus	1·20	90
1153		70f. Two kagus, one with wings outspread	1·80	1·30

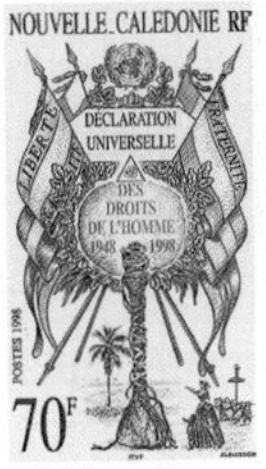

455 Liberty Trees

1998. 50th Anniv of Universal Declaration of Human Rights.
1154 **455** 70f. green, black and blue 2·00 1·30

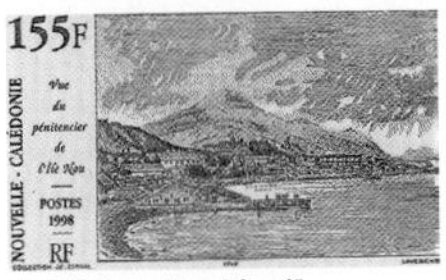

456 "Prison, Nou Island" (engraving)

1998
1155 **456** 155f. multicoloured 2·75 2·75

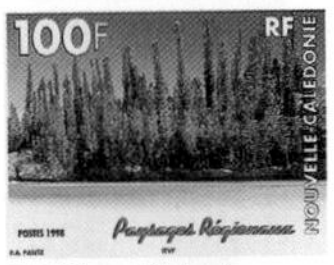

457 View of Island

1998. Regional Scenes. Multicoloured.
1156 100f. Type **457** 2·50 3·50
1157 100f. View of sea 2·50 3·50

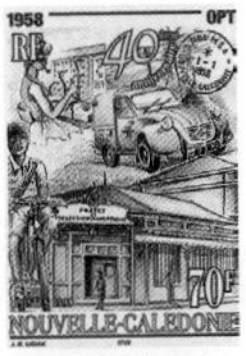

458 Switchboard, Post Van, Postman on Bicycle and Post Office (1958)

1998. 40th Anniv of Posts and Telecommunications Office. Multicoloured.
1158 70f. Type **458** 1·70 1·30
1159 70f. Automatic service machine, woman with mobile phone, dish aerial, motor cycle courier and post office (1998) 1·70 1·30

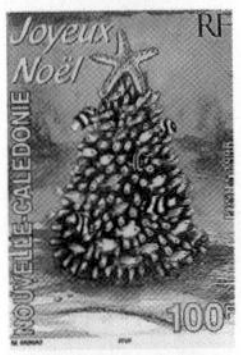

459 Marine Life forming Christmas Tree ("Merry Christmas")

1998. Greetings stamps. Multicoloured.
1160 100f. Type **459** 3·00 3·25
1161 100f. Treasure chest ("Best Wishes") 3·00 3·25
1162 100f. Fish ("Good Holiday") 3·00 3·25
1163 100f. Fishes and reefs ("Happy Birthday") 3·00 3·25

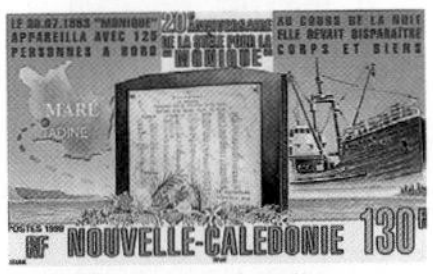

460 Map, Memorial and "Monique"

1998. 20th Anniv of Erection of Memorial to the Victims of the "Monique" (inter-island freighter) Disaster.
1164 **460** 130f. multicoloured 3·00 3·50

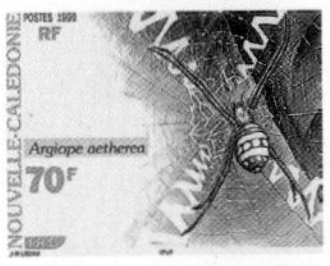

461 "Argiope aetherea"

1999. Spiders. Multicoloured.
1165 70f. Type **461** 2·30 1·20
1166 70f. "Latrodectus hasselti" 2·30 1·20
1167 70f. "Cyrtophora moluccensis" 2·30 1·20
1168 70f. "Barycheloides alluviophilus" 2·30 1·20

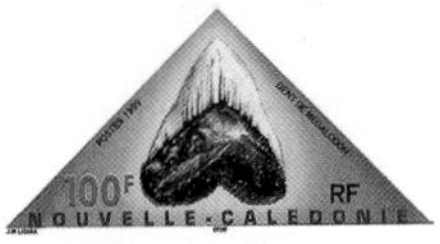

462 Tooth

1999. Giant-toothed Shark. (Carcharodon megalodon). Multicoloured.
1169 100f. Type **462** 2·50 1·80
MS1170 90×120 mm. 70f. Giant-toothed shark (29×39 mm); 70f. Diver, giant-toothed shark and great white shark (39×29 mm); 70f. Decaying tooth and section of jawbone (triangular, 55×28 mm) 4·50 5·00

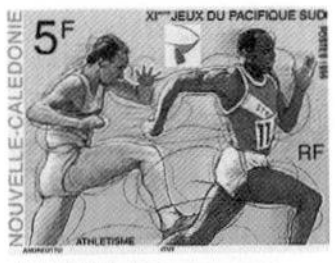

463 Athletics

1999. 11th South Pacific Games. Multicoloured.
1171 5f. Type **463** 1·60 70
1172 10f. Tennis 1·70 75
1173 30f. Karate 1·80 2·50
1174 70f. Baseball 2·30 2·75

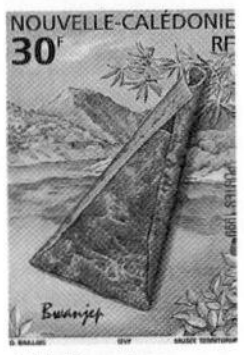

464 Bwanjep

1999. Traditional Musical Instruments. Mult.
1175 30f. Type **464** 1·70 85
1176 70f. Bells 2·30 1·30
1177 100f. Flutes 2·50 1·80

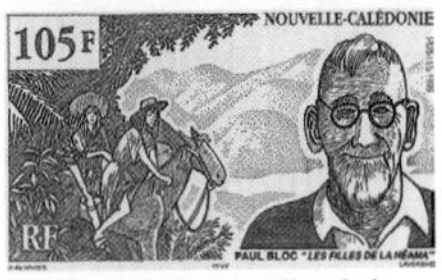

465 Scene from "Les Filles de la Neama" and Bloc

1999. 29th Death Anniv of Paul Bloc (writer).
1178 **465** 105f. blue, green & purple 3·00 1·80

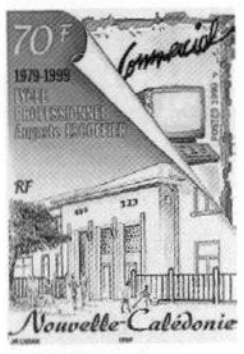

466 School Building and Computer

1999. 20th Anniv of Auguste Escoffier Commercial and Hotelier Professional School. Multicoloured.
1179 70f. Type **466** 1·50 1·30
1180 70f. School building and chef's hat 1·50 1·30

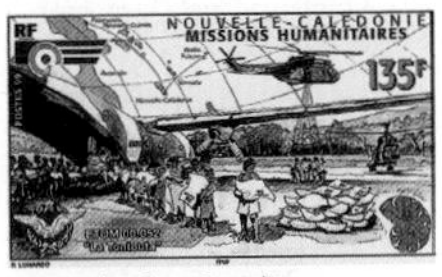

467 Unloading Supplies, Helicopters and Map

1999. Humanitarian Aid.
1181 **467** 135f. multicoloured 3·25 3·00

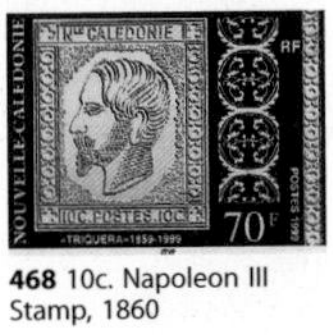

468 10c. Napoleon III Stamp, 1860

1999. 140th Anniv (2000) of First New Caledonian Stamp and "Philexfrance 99" International Stamp Exhibition, Paris.
1182 **468** 70f. multicoloured 1·20 1·40
MS1183 155×110 mm. 100f. black (two 1860 10c. stamps) (recess) (36×29 mm); 100f. multicoloured (1860 10c. stamp) (thermography) (36×29 mm); 100f. Close-up of Napoleon's head (litho) (36×29 mm); 100f. gold and black (1860 10c. stamp) (embossing); 700f. 1997 Kagu design and hologram of Napoleon's head (44×35 mm) 26·00 28·00

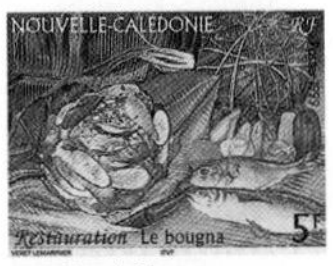

469 Food Platter

1999. Hotels and Restaurants. Multicoloured.
1184 5f. Type **469** 1·30 70
1185 30f. Seafood platter 1·50 80
1186 70f. Hotel cabins by lake 1·90 1·30
1187 100f. Modern hotel and swimming pool 2·30 3·25

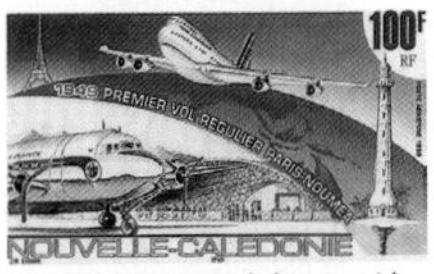

470 Eiffel Tower, Lighthouse with 1949 and 1999 Aircraft

1999. Air. 50th Anniv of First Paris–Noumea Scheduled Flight.
1188 **470** 100f. multicoloured 2·40 3·00

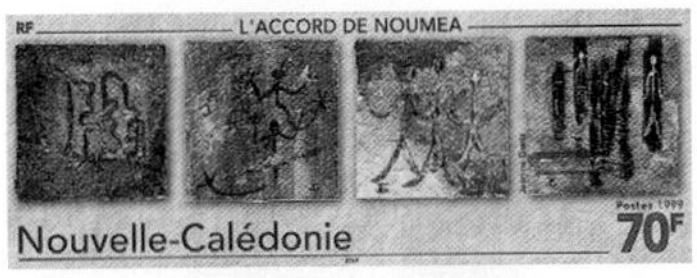

471 Paintings

1999
1189 **471** 70f. multicoloured 3·25 1·40

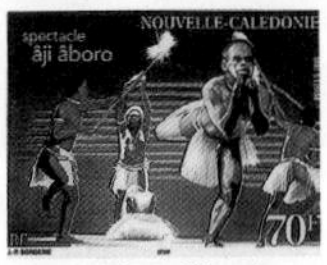

472 Aji Aboro (Kanak dance)

1999
1190 **472** 70f. multicoloured 3·25 1·40

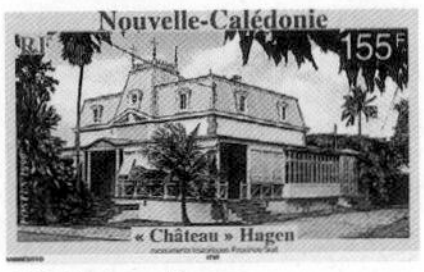

473 Chateau Hagen

1999. Historic Monuments of South Province.
1191 **473** 155f. multicoloured 4·25 2·75

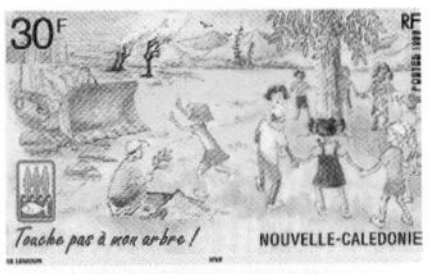

474 Children protecting Tree

1999. Nature Protection: "Don't touch my Tree".
1192 **474** 30f. multicoloured 2·75 75

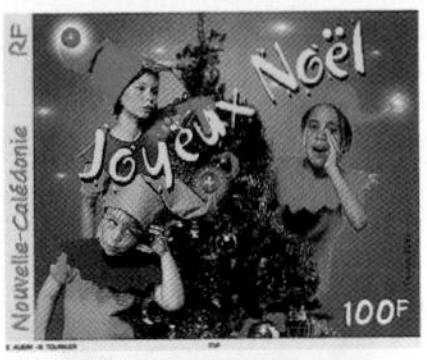

475 Children around Tree

1999. Greetings Stamps. Multicoloured.
1193 100f. Type **475** ("Merry Christmas") 3·50 1·80
1194 100f. Children with flowers and star ("Best Wishes 2000") 3·50 1·80
1195 100f. Children and Year 2000 cake ("Happy Birthday") 3·50 1·80
1196 100f. Children looking in pram ("Congratulations") 3·50 1·80

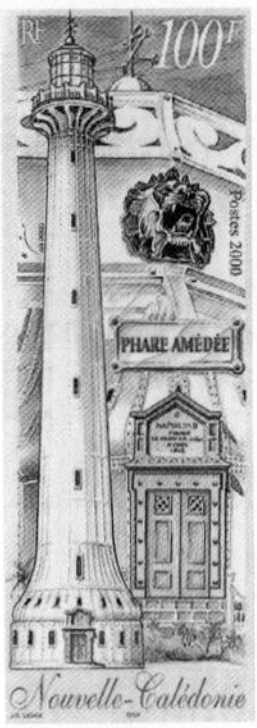

476 Amedee Lighthouse

2000
1197 **476** 100f. multicoloured 3·50 3·00

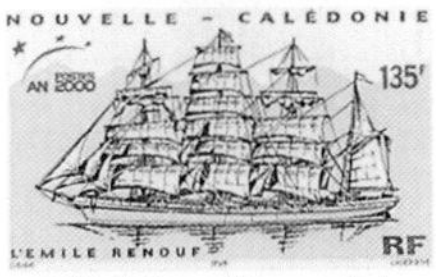

477 *L'Emile Renouf* (four-masted steel barque)

2000. Centenary of Loss of Emile Renouf on Durand Reef, Insel Mare.
1198 **477** 135f. multicoloured 4·00 3·25

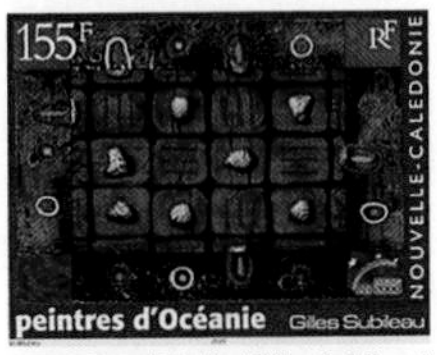

478 Painted Shells (Gilles Subileau)

2000. Pacific Painters.
1199 **478** 155f. multicoloured 4·25 3·50

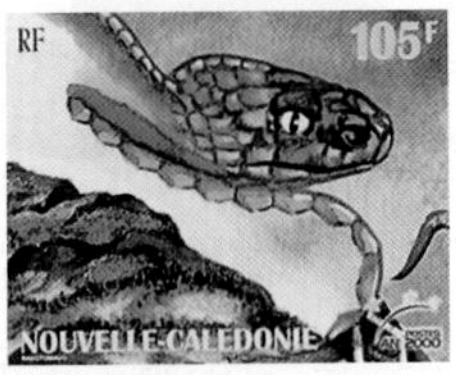

479 Snake

2000. Chinese New Year. Year of the Dragon. Sheet 121×90 mm containing T 479 and similar horiz design. Multicoloured.
MS1200 105f. Type **479**; 105f. Dragon 5·75 5·75

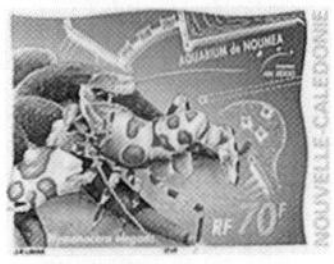

480 Prawn

2000. Noumia Aquarium. Multicoloured.
1201 70f. Type **480** 3·25 1·90
1202 70f. Fluorescent corals 3·25 1·90
1203 70f. Hump-headed wrasse (*Cheilinus undulatus*) 3·25 1·90

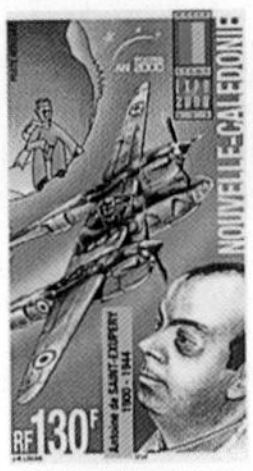

481 Lockheed P-38 Lightning Fighter

2000. Air. Birth Centenary of Antoine de Saint-Exupery (writer and pilot).
1204 **481** 130f. multicoloured 4·25 2·50

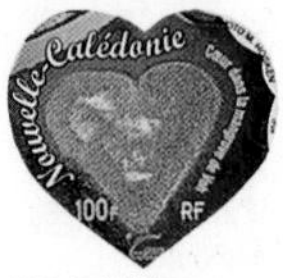

482 Aerial View

2000. Mangrove Swamp, Voh.
1205 **482** 100f. multicoloured 3·50 1·90

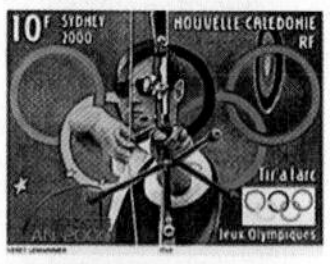
483 Archery

2000. Olympic Games, Sydney. Multicoloured.
1206 10f. Type **483** 2·50 1·80
1207 30f. Boxing 2·75 1·90
1208 80f. Cycling 3·25 2·20
1209 100f. Fencing 3·50 2·50

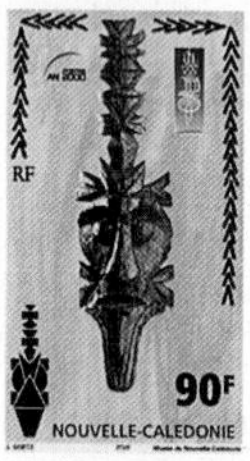
484 Museum Exhibit

2000. Museum of New Caledonia. Multicoloured.
1210 90f. Type **484** 3·50 2·30
1211 105f. Museum exhibit 3·75 2·75

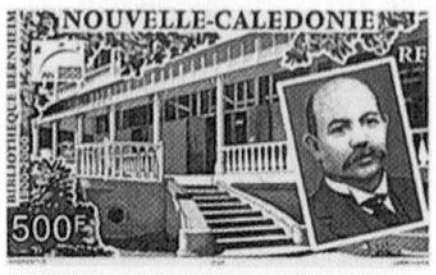
485 Library Building and Lucien Bernheim

2000. Bernheim Library, Noumea.
1212 **485** 500f. brown, blue and green 11·00 9·25

486 Painting

2000. Eighth Pacific Arts Festival, Kanaky, New Caledonia. Sheet 120×90 mm containing T 486 and similar horiz designs. Multicoloured.
MS1213 70f. Type **486**; 70f. Human figures; 70f. Stylized faces and fish; 70f. Stylized faces and fishes on coloured squares 7·00 7·00

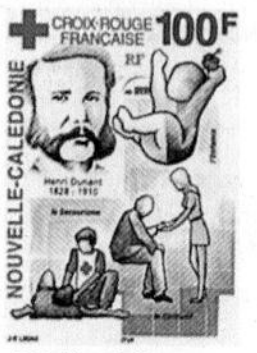
487 Henri Dunant (founder), Baby and Patients with Volunteers

2000. Red Cross.
1214 **487** 100f. multicoloured 3·50 2·50

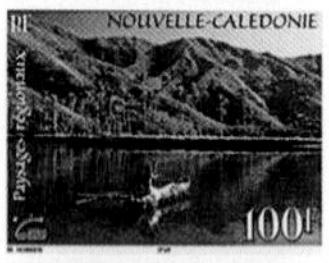
488 Canoeist

2000. Regional Landscapes. Multicoloured.
1215 100f. Type **488** 3·50 2·50
1216 100f. Speedboat near island 3·50 2·50
1217 100f. Sunset and man on raft 3·50 2·50

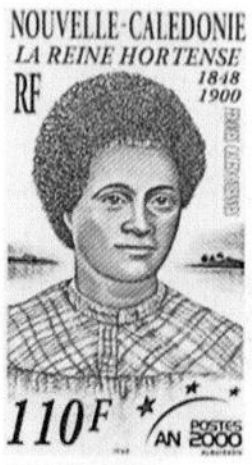
489 Queen Hortense

2000
1218 **489** 110f. red, green and blue 3·75 2·75

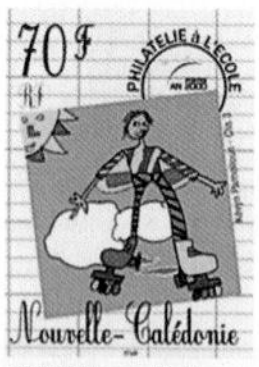
490 Boy on Roller Skates (Kevyn Pamoiloun)

2000. "Philately at School". Entries in Children's Painting Competition. Multicoloured.
1219 70f. Type **490** 2·20 1·80
1220 70f. People using airborne vehicles (Lise-Marie Samanich) 2·20 1·80
1221 70f. Aliens (Alexandre Mandin) 2·20 1·80

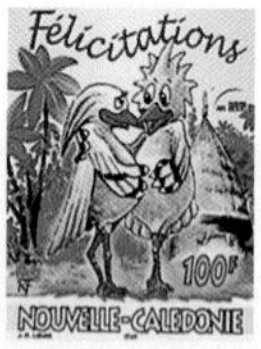
491 Kagu Parents ("Congratulations")

2000. Greetings Stamps. Multicoloured.
1222 100f. Type **491** 3·00 2·50
1223 100f. Kagu on deck chair ("Happy Holidays") 3·00 2·50
1224 100f. Kagu with bunch of flowers ("Best Wishes") 3·00 2·50

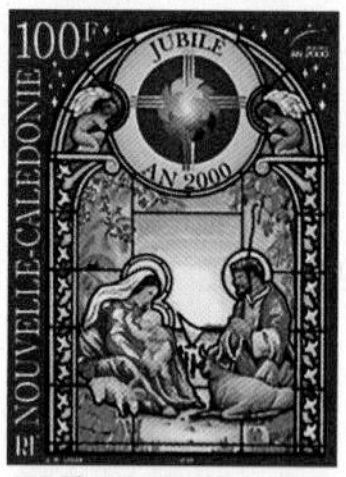
492 The Nativity

2000. Christmas.
1225 **492** 100f. multicoloured 3·25 2·75

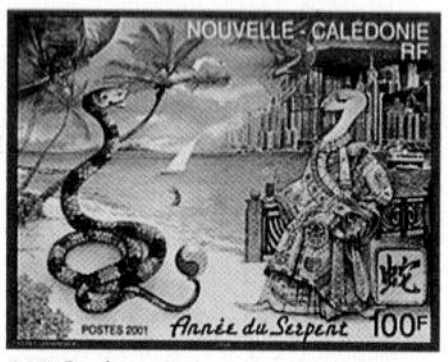
493 Snakes

2001. Chinese New Year. Year of the Snake. Multicoloured.
1226 100f. Type **493** 3·25 2·75
MS1227 130×91 mm. 70f. Snake and Pacific island; 70f. Snake and Chinese symbols 4·25 4·25

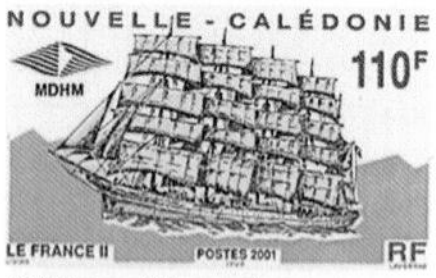
494 *France II* (barque)

2001. Reconstruction of France II.
1228 **494** 110f. multicoloured 3·25 2·75

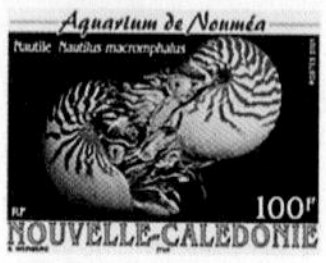
495 Two Nautili

2001. Noumea Aquarium. The New Calendonia Nautilus. Multicoloured.
1229 100f. Type **495** 3·00 2·30
1230 100f. Section through nautilus 3·00 2·30
1231 100f. Two nautili (different) 3·00 2·30

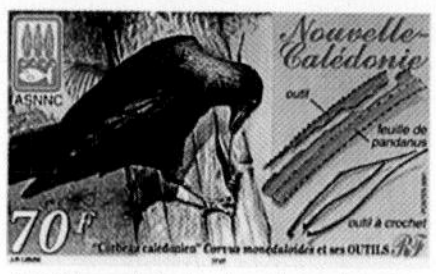
496 New Caledonian Crow, Tools and Emblem

2001. Association for the Protection of New Caledonian Nature (ASNNC).
1232 **496** 70f. multicoloured 2·10 1·70

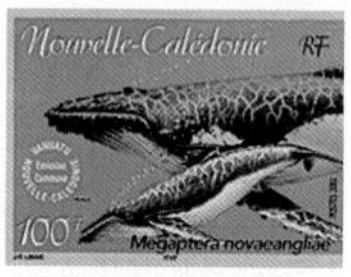
497 Humpback Whale and Calf

2001. Operation Cetaces (marine mammal South Pacific study programme). Multicoloured.
1233 100f. Type **497** 2·75 2·30
1234 100f. Whales leaping 2·75 2·30

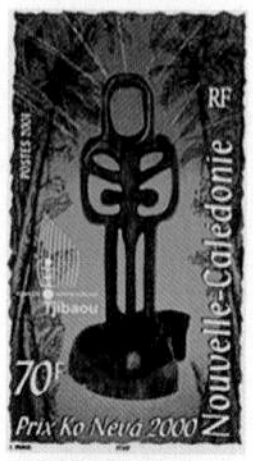
498 "Guards of Gaia" (statue) (I. Waia)

2001. Ko Neva 2000 Prize Winner.
1235 **498** 70f. multicoloured 2·10 1·70

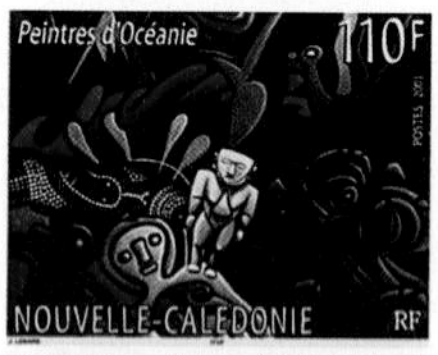
499 "Vision of Oceania" (J. Lebars)

2001
1236 **499** 110f. multicoloured 3·25 2·75

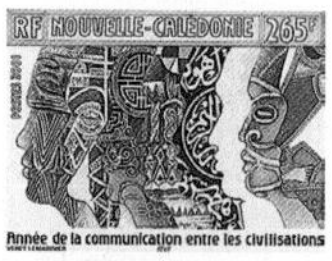
500 Profiles

2001. Year of Communication.
1237 **500** 265f. multicoloured 7·75 6·25

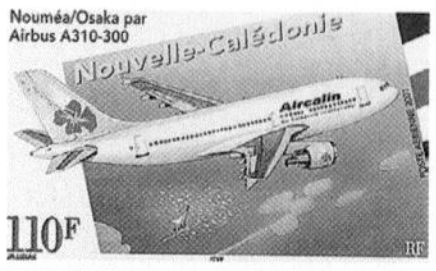
501 Air International Caledonie Airbus A310-300

2001. Air. First Anniv of Noumea–Osaka Passenger Service.
1238 **501** 110f. multicoloured 3·25 2·75

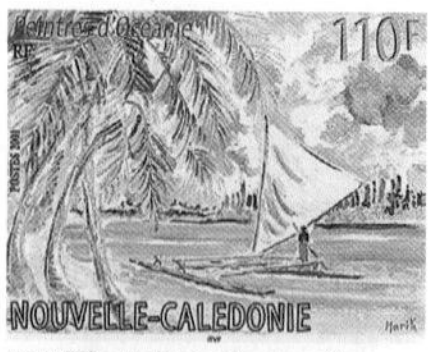
502 "The Solitary Boatman" (Marik)

2001. Pacific Painters.
1239 **502** 110f. multicoloured 3·25 2·75

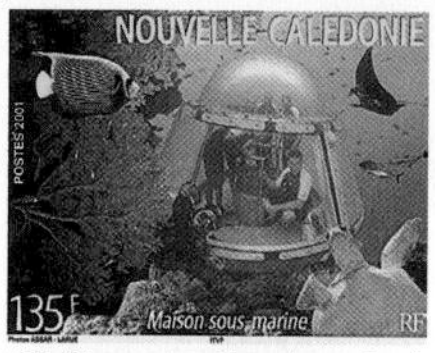
503 Observation Capsule on Coral Reef

2001
1240 **503** 135f. multicoloured 3·50 3·00

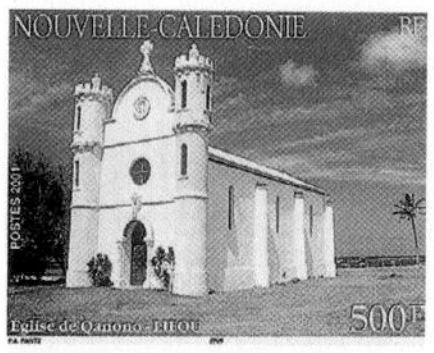
504 Qanono Church, Lifou

2001
1241 **504** 500f. multicoloured 13·00 10·50

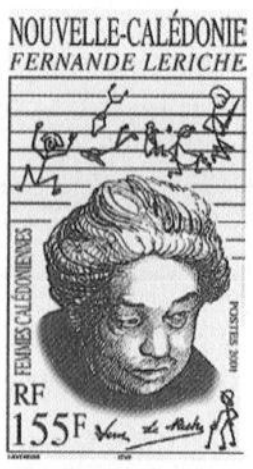
505 Fernande Leriche (educator and author)

2001
1242 **505** 155f. brown, red and blue 4·50 3·75

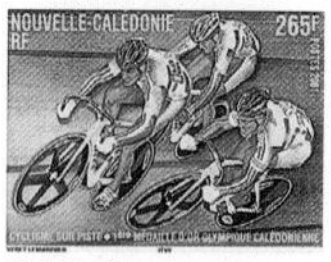
506 Cyclists

2001. 1st Olympic Gold Medal for New Caledonian Sportsman.
1243 **506** 265f. multicoloured 7·75 6·25

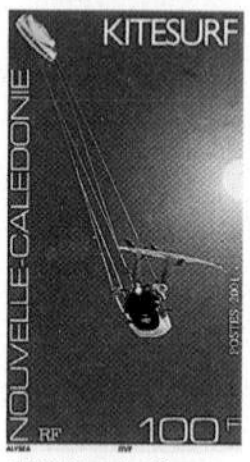
507 Kite Surfer

2001
1244 **507** 100f. multicoloured 3·00 2·50

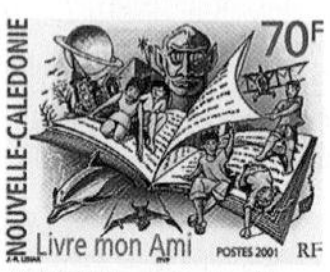
508 Children on Book

2001. School Philately.
1245 **508** 70f. multicoloured 2·10 1·70

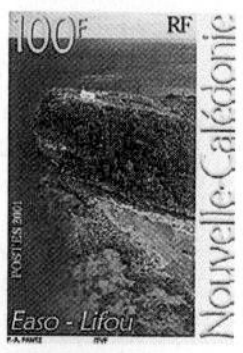
509 Easo

2001. Lifou Island. Multicoloured.
1246 100f. Type **509** 3·00 2·50
1247 100f. Jokin 3·00 2·50

510 Father Christmas

2001. Christmas. Multicoloured.
1248 100f. Type **510**   3·00   2·50
1249 100f. Bat with spotted wings
      and "Meilleurs Voeux"   3·00   2·50
1250 100f. Bat with party hat and
      red nose and "Vive la Fete"   3·00   2·50

511 Horse and Sea Horse

2002. Chinese New Year. Year of the Horse. Multicoloured.
1251 100f. Type **511**   3·00   2·50
MS1252 190×30 mm. 70f. Horse's head;
      70f. Sea horse   4·00   4·00

512 Two Flying Foxes

2002. St. Valentine's Day.
1253 **512** 100f. multicoloured   3·00   2·50

513 Cricketer in Traditional Dress

2002. Cricket.
1254 **513** 100f. multicoloured   3·00   2·50

514 Ancient Axe

2002.
1255 **514** 505f. multicoloured   10·50   9·50

515 Hobie 16 Catamaran

2002. Hobie 16 Catamaran World Championship.
1256 **515** 70f. multicoloured   2·10   1·70

516 Loggerhead Turtle
(*Caretta caretta*)

2002. Noumea Aquarium. Sheet 185×120 mm in shape
of turtle containing T 516 and similar horiz designs.
Multicoloured.
MS1257 30f. Type **516**; 30f. Green sea
turtle (*Chelonia mydas*); 70f. Hawksbill turtle (*Eretmochelys imbricata*)
(inscr "imbricat"); 70f. Leatherback
sea turtle (*Dermochelys coriacea*)   5·75   5·75

517 Player

2002. World Cup Football Championship 2002, Japan and
South Korea.
1258 **517** 100f. multicoloured   3·00   2·50

518 Coffee Bean Plant

2002. Coffee Production. Multicoloured.
1259 70f. Type **518**   2·10   1·70
1260 70f. Coffee production process   2·10   1·70
1261 70f. Cafe and cup of coffee   2·10   1·70

519 *Alcmene* (French corvette)

2002. Exploration of Coast of New Caledonia by Alcmene.
1262 **519** 210f. multicoloured   6·00   5·00

520 Emma Piffault
(statue)

2002. Emma Piffault Commemoration.
1263 **520** 10f. multicoloured   65   55

521 Circus School

2002.
1264 **521** 70f. multicoloured   2·10   1·70

522 Telescope and Caillard

2002. 90th Birth Anniv of Edmond Caillard (astronomer).
1265 **522** 70f. multicoloured   2·10   1·70

523 Face in Landscape, Couple,
Ship and Birds

2002. Jean Mariotti (writer).
1266 **523** 70f. multicoloured   2·10   1·70

524 Adult Sperm Whale
and Calf

2002. New Caledonia–Norfolk Island Joint Issue.
Operation Cetaces (marine mammal study).
Multicoloured.
1267 100f. Type **524**   3·00   2·50

1268 100f. Sperm whale attacked by
      giant squid   3·00   2·50
Stamps of similar designs were issued by Norfolk Islands.

525 Coral Snake Musicians

2002. Christmas.
1269 **525** 100f. multicoloured   3·00   2·50

526 Central Mountain Chain

2002. International Year of Mountains. Litho.
1270 **526** 100f. multicoloured   3·00   2·50

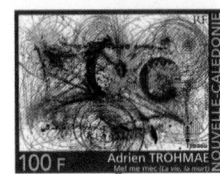

527 Powder Store, Bourail Military Post

2002.
1271 **527** 1000f. multicoloured   28·00 23·00

528 "Life and Death" (Adrien
Trohmae)

2002. Pacific Painters.
1272 **528** 100f. multicoloured   3·00   2·50

529 Couple enclosed in
Heart

2003. St. Valentine's Day.
1273 **529** 100f. multicoloured   3·00   2·50

530 Goat's Head

2003. Chinese New Year. Year of the Goat.
1274 **530** 100f. multicoloured   3·00   2·50

644 Kagu

2003. Kagu.
1274a 1f. light yellowish green (8.05)   45   40
1274b 3f. light greenish blue (8.05)   55   50
1274c 5f. violet (1.07)   75   70
1275   10f. myrtle-green   1·50   1·45
1276   15f. agate   1·80   1·60
1277   30f. bright orange   2·00   1·90
1277a 100f. ultramarine (2.04)   4·50   4·25
1277b 110f. blue-black (1.06)   4·50   4·25

       (ii) Self-adhesive gum.
1277c 110f. blue-black (1.06)   4·50   4·25

       (b) No value espressed. Ordinary gum.
1278   (70c.) bright scarlet   3·25   3·00

       (ii) Self-adhesive gum.
1279   (70c.) scarlet (5.03)   3·25   3·00

1279a (70c.) bright scarlet (7.09)   3·25   3·00

532 1903 Stamp

2003. Centenary of First Kagu Stamp.
1290 **532** 70f. multicoloured   2·10   1·70

533 High-finned Grouper
(*Epinephelus maculates*)

2003. Noumea Aquarium. Groupers. Multicoloured.
1291 70f. Type **533**   2·10   1·70
1292 70f. Purple-spotted grouper
      (*Plectropomus leopardus*)   2·10   1·70
1293 70f. Hump-back grouper
      (*Cromileptes altivelis*)   2·10   1·70

534 School Building

2003. Grand Noumea High School.
1294 **534** 70f. multicoloured   2·10   1·70

535 Shooting

2003. 12th South Pacific Games, Suva. Multicoloured.
1295 5f. Type **535**   25   20
1296 30f. Rugby   90   75
1297 70f. Tennis   2·10   1·70

536 Adult Sea Cow and Calf

2003. Sea Cow (Dugong dugon). Operation Cetaces
(marine mammal study). Multicoloured.
1298 100f. Type **536**   3·00   2·50
1299 100f. Adult and calf grazing
      (40×30 mm)   3·00   2·50
Nos. 1298/9 were printed together, se-tenant, forming
a composite design.

537 "The Harvest"

2003. Death Centenary of Paul Gauguin (artist) (1st
issue).
1300 **537** 100f. multicoloured   3·00   2·50
See also No. **MS**1303.

538 Governor
Feillet

2003. Death Centenary of Governor Feillet (first governor).
1301   **538**   100f. black and green   3·00   2·50

539 Aircalin Airbus A330–200

2003. 20th Anniv of Aircalin.
1302   **539**   100f. multicoloured   3·00   2·50

540 Tahitian Heads (sketch)

2003. Death Centenary of Paul Gauguin (artist) (2nd issue). Sheet 130×90 mm containing T 540 and similar vert design. Multicoloured.
MS1303 100f. Type **540**; 100f. Still-life with Maori statue   6·25   6·25
Stamps of a similar design were issued by Wallis et Futuna.

541 *Bavayia cyclura*

2003. Geckos. Sheet 140×110 mm containing T 541 and similar horiz designs. Multicoloured.
MS1304 30f.×2, Type **541**; *Rhacodactylus chahoua*; 70f.×2, *Rhacodactylus ciliatus*; *Eurydactylodes vieillardi*   6·25   6·25

542 German Shepherd Dog

2003
1305   **542**   105f. multicoloured   3·25   2·75

543 Rade de Balade (1853)

2003
1306   **543**   110f. brown, green and blue   3·50   2·75

544 Men and Women surrounding Port (painting) (Robert Tatin)

2003. Pacific Painters.
1307   **544**   135f. multicoloured   4·00   3·50

2003. World Cup Football Championships, Japan and South Korea. As No. 1257 but with inscription added to sheet margin.
MS1308 185×120 mm 30f. Type **516**; 30f. Green sea turtle (*Chelonia mydas*); 70f. Hawksbill turtle (*Eretmochelys imbricate* (inscr "imbricat"); 70f. Leatherback sea turtle (*Dermochelys coriacea*)   6·25   6·25

545 Ouen Island

2003
1309   **545**   100f. multicoloured   3·00   25·00

546 Characters from "Brousse en Folie"

2003. Christmas. "Brousse en Folie" (Bush in Madness) (comic strip created by Bernard Berger).
1310   **546**   100f. multicoloured   3·00   2·50

547 Tiger King

2003. Year of the Monkey (1st issue). Sheet 130×100 mm containing T 547 and similar vert design. Multicoloured.
MS1311 100f.×2 Type **547**; Monkey King on horseback   6·25   6·25

548 Three Monkeys

2004. Year of the Monkey (2nd issue).
1312   **548**   70f. multicoloured   2·20   1·80

549 Cupid enclosed in Heart

2004. St. Valentine's Day.
1313   **549**   100f. multicoloured   3·00   2·50

550 Whale

2004. Blainville's Beaked Whales (*Mesoplodon densirostris*). Operation Cetaces (marine mammal study). Sheet 196×96 mm containing T 550 and similar horiz design. Multicoloured.
MS1314 100f.×2 Type **550**; Head of whale (40×30 mm)   6·25   6·25
The stamps and margin of **MS**1314 form a composite design.

551 Blue-spotted Stingray (*Dasyatis kuhlii*)

2004. Noumea Aquarium. Rays. Multicoloured.
1315   100f. Type **551**   3·00   2·50
1316   100f. Spotted eagle ray (*Aetobatus narinari*)   3·00   2·50
1317   100f. Marbled stingray (*Taeniura meyrni*)   3·00   2·50

552 Postman on Horseback

2004. Postal Service.
1318   **552**   105f. multicoloured   3·25   2·75

553 Decauville C/N 637 Locomotive (1905)

2004. Railways.
1319   **553**   155f. multicoloured   4·75   4·00

554 *Oxera sulfurea*

2004. Endangered Species. Forest Flowers. Multicoloured.
1320   100f. Type **554**   3·00   2·50
1321   100f. *Turbina inopinata*   3·00   2·50
1322   100f. *Gardenia urvillei*   3·00   2·50

555 Carving, House and Tree

2004. Sandalwood. Multicoloured.
1323   200f. Type **555**   6·25   5·00

(b) Size 40×30 mm.
MS1324 141×110 mm. 100f.×3, Fruit; Distillery; Sandalwood products   9·00   9·00

556 Early and Modern Noumea

2004. 150th Anniv of Noumea.
1325   **556**   70f. multicoloured   2·20   1·80

557 Cat

2004. Cats. Multicoloured.
1326   100f. Type **557**   3·00   2·50
1327   100f. Oriental   3·00   2·50
1328   100f. White Persian   3·00   2·50
1329   100f. Birman   3·00   2·50
1330   100f. European shorthair   3·00   2·50
1331   100f. Abyssinian   3·00   2·50

558 Gymnasts

2004. Olympic Games, Athens. Multicoloured.
1332   70f. Type **558**   2·20   1·80
1333   70f. Women's relay   2·20   1·80
1334   70f. Men's volleyball   2·20   1·80

559 Face, Butterfly, Hut and Trees

2004. French Research in the Pacific. Multicoloured.
1335   100f. Type **559**   3·00   2·50
1336   100f. Palms, dolphin and woman   3·00   2·50

560 Walla Bay, Belep

2004. Tourism.
1337   **560**   100f. multicoloured   3·00   2·50

561 "Tradimodernition" (Nat D.)

2004. Pacific Painters.
1338   **561**   505f. multicoloured   15·00   13·50

562 Nativity

2004. Christmas.
1339   **562**   100f. multicoloured   3·00   2·50

563 Rooster

2005. New Year. "Year of the Rooster".
1340   **563**   100f. multicoloured   3·00   2·50

564 Anniversary Emblem

2005. Centenary of Rotary International.
1341   **564**   110f. multicoloured   3·25   2·75

565 People from Many Nations

2005. French-speaking Culture.
1342   **565**   135f. multicoloured   4·25   3·50
A stamp of similar design was issued by Wallis et Futuna.

566 Swimming, Cycling and Running

2005. International Triathlon Competition, Noumea.
1343   **566**   80f. multicoloured   2·75   2·30

567 Passenger Ship

2005. Coastal Tour.
1344   **567**   75f. multicoloured   2·50   2·10

568 Pan-tropical Spotted Dolphins (*Stenella attenuate*)

2005. Operation Cetaces (marine mammal study). Multicoloured.

1345	100f. Type **568**	3·00	2·50
1346	100f. Bottle-nose dolphin (*Tursiop truncates*) (inscr "Tiurciop")	3·00	2·50
1347	100f. Spinner dolphin (*Stenella longirostris*)	3·00	2·50

569 Corpet et Louvet 0-6-OTs Locomotive

2005. Railways.

1348	**569**	745f. multicoloured	23·00	23·00

570 Black-tip Reef Shark (*Carcharhinus melanopterus*)

2005. Noumea Aquarium. Sheet 140×90 mm containing T 570 and similar horiz design. Multicoloured.

MS1349 110f.×2, Type **551**; Tawny nurse shark (*Nebrius ferrugineus*)   7·00   7·00

The stamps and margin of **MS**1349 form a composite design.

571 *Eunymphicus uvaeensis*

2005. Endangered Species. Birds. Multicoloured.

1350	75f. Type **571**	2·30	1·90
1351	75f. *Eunymphicus cornutus*	2·30	1·90
1352	75f. *Cyanoramphus saisseti*	2·30	1·90

572 Luengoni Beach, Lifou

2005. Tourism.

1353	**572**	85f. multicoloured	2·75	2·30

573 Emblem and People of Many Nations

2005. East Pacific Region IOMS Conference, Noumea.

1354	**573**	150f. multicoloured	4·75	4·00

574 "My Dream of Peace" (Mendoza)

2005. International Day of Peace.

1355	**574**	85f. multicoloured	2·75	2·30

2005. Nos. 1114 and 1277a surch.

1356	110f. on 100f. blue (No. 1114)	3·00	2·50
1357	110f. on 100f. ultramarine (No. 1277a)	3·00	2·50

2005. Nos. 1345/7 surch.

1358	110f. on 100f. multicoloured	3·00	2·50

1359	110f. on 100f. multicoloured	3·00	2·50
1360	110f. on 100f. multicoloured	3·00	2·50

577 Ouare

2005. Petroglyphs (rock paintings).

1361	**577**	120f. violet and vermilion	4·00	3·50
1362	-	120f. chocolate and blue	4·00	3·50
1363	-	120f. green and scarlet vermilion	4·00	3·50

DESIGNS: 1361, Type **577**; 1362, Balade; 1363, Croix enveloppees (wrapped crosses).

578 Marquis du Bouzet

2005. Birth Bicentenary of Marquis du Bouzet (governor).

1364	**578**	500f. black, blue and violet	15·00	14·00

579 Santa sailing Yacht

2005. Christmas.

1365	**579**	110f. multicoloured	3·50	3·25

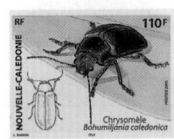

580 *Bohumiljania caledonica*

2005. Insects. Multicoloured.

1366	110f. Type **580**	3·50	3·25
1367	110f. *Bohumiljania humboldti*	3·50	3·25
1368	110f. *Cazeresia Montana*	3·50	3·25

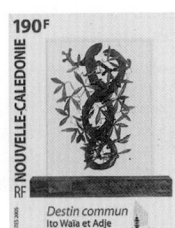

581 Snakes and Twigs

2005. Kanak and Oceanic Art Fund.

1369	**581**	190f. multicoloured	6·00	5·50

582 Nokanhoui Island

2006. Tourism.

1370	**582**	110f. multicoloured	3·50	3·25

583 Georges Richard (1903)

2006. Vintage Cars. Multicoloured.

1371	110f. Type **583**	3·50	3·25
1372	110f. Renault NN 6cv (1925)	3·50	3·25
1373	110f. Citroen Trefle (1926)	3·50	3·25

584 Emblem

2006. 50th Anniv of National Red Cross.

1374	**584**	75f. vermilion and black	2·50	2·30

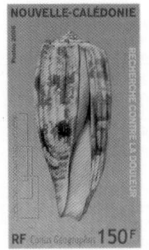

585 *Conus geographus*

2006. Pain Relief Research. Discovery of Anaesthetic in Cone Shellfish.

1375	**585**	150f. multicoloured	5·00	4·50

586 Colonists and Tractor

2006. 80th Anniv of Arrival of Northern Colonists.

1376	**586**	180f. multicoloured	5·75	5·25

587 *Gallirallus lafresnayanus*

2006. Endangered Species. Birds. Multicoloured.

1377	75f. Type **587**	2·50	2·30
1378	75f. *Charmosyna diadema*	2·50	2·30
1379	75f. *Aegotheles savesi*	2·50	2·30

MS1380 100×130 mm. 110f.×3, *Charmosyna diadema* (52×31 mm); *Aegotheles savesi* (31×52 mm); *Gallirallus lafresnayanus* (52×31 mm)   10·50   10·50

The stamps and margins of **MS**1380 form a composite design of the forest.

588 Players

2006. World Cup Football Championship, Germany.

1381	**588**	110f. multicoloured	3·50	3·25

589 *Artia balansae*

2006. Ornamental Vines. Multicoloured.

1382	110f. Type **589**	3·50	3·25
1383	110f. *Oxera brevicalyx*	3·50	3·25
1384	110f. *Canavalia favieri*	3·50	3·25

590 Aircraft and Route

2006. 25th Anniv of Voluntary Aid to Caledonian Evacuees.

1385	**590**	85f. multicoloured	2·75	2·50

591 Mobile Post Office

2006. Stamp Day.

1386	**591**	75f. chocolate, black and ultramarine	2·50	2·30

592 Turtle, Starfish and Palm Trees

2006. Regional Ocean and Environmental Programme (PROE) Conference.

1387	**592**	190f. multicoloured	6·00	5·50

593 SACM 030T Mining Locomotive Nakale

2006. Railways.

1388	**593**	320f. multicoloured	9·75	9·00

594 Cell Phone and Tower

2006. 10th Anniv of MobiLis (mobile telephone network).

1389	**594**	75f. multicoloured	2·50	2·30

595 Musicians

2006. 20th Anniv of Kaneka (music style).

1390	**595**	75f. multicoloured	2·50	2·30

596 Animals

2006. Les Comediens de Bois.

1391	**596**	280f. multicoloured	8·75	8·00

597 Madonna and Child

2006. Christmas.

1392	**597**	110f. multicoloured	3·50	3·25

598 "L'homme lezard"

2006
| 1393 | **598** | 110f. multicoloured | 3·50 | 3·25 |

599 Emblem

2007. 60th Anniv of CPS (Secretariat of the Pacific Community).
| 1394 | **599** | 120f. multicoloured | 3·75 | 3·50 |

600 Boar

2007. New Year. Year of the Pig.
| 1395 | **600** | 110f. multicoloured | 3·75 | 3·50 |

601 Building Facade

2007. Bicentenary of Court of Auditors.
| 1396 | **601** | 110f. blue and vermilion | 3·75 | 3·50 |

602 EU Stars and Children

2007. 50th Anniv of Treaty of Rome.
| 1397 | **602** | 110f. multicoloured | 3·75 | 3·50 |

603 *Siganus lineatus*

2007. Fish. Multicoloured.
1398		35f. Type **603**	1·20	1·10
1399		75f. *Lutjanus adetii*	2·50	2·30
1400		110f. *Naso unicornis*	3·75	3·50

604 Swimmer

2007. South Pacific Games.
| 1401 | **604** | 75f. multicoloured | 2·50 | 2·30 |

605 Cable and Ship

2007. Sub-marine Cable Between Sydney and Noumea.
| 1402 | **605** | 280f. multicoloured | 9·25 | 8·50 |

606 Rescue

2007. National Society for Sea Rescue.
| 1403 | **606** | 75f. multicoloured | 2·75 | 2·50 |

607 Post Box

2007. Stamp Day. Letter Boxes. Multicoloured.
1404		75f. Type **607**	2·40	2·20
1405		75f. Thatched roof and open sides	2·40	2·20
1406		75f. Rectangular with square opening, coloured roof and shells	2·40	2·20
1407		75f. Corrugated roof (vert)	2·40	2·20
1408		75f. Red rectangular with white edges (vert)	2·40	2·20
1409		75f. Metal with circular opening	2·40	2·20
1410		75f. Circular with triangular opening	2·40	2·20
1411		75f. House shaped	2·40	2·20
1412		75f. Motor cycle helmet used as post box (vert)	2·40	2·20
1413		75f. Wooden with steep roof (vert)	2·40	2·20

608 *Gymnomyzaaubryana*

2007. Endemic Birds. Multicoloured.
1414		35f. Type **608**	1·30	1·20
1415		75f. *Coracina analis*	2·75	2·50
1416		110f. *Rhynochetos jubatus*	4·00	3·75

609 Magnifier and 1942 4f. Stamp (No. 277)

2007. 60th Anniv of Cagou Philatelic Club. Sheet 90×120 mm containing T 609 and similar horiz design. Multicoloured.
| **MS**1417 | | 110f.×2, Type **609**; Cagou | 7·25 | 7·25 |

The stamps and margins of **MS**1417 form a composite design.

610 New Caledonian and New Zealand Traditional Dress and Body Decoration

2007. New Caledonia in New Zealand.
| 1418 | **610** | 190f. multicoloured | 6·25 | 5·75 |

611 *Gymnothoraxpolyranodon*

2007. Inauguration of New Aquarium, Noumea. Multicoloured.
1419		110f. Type **611**	4·00	3·75
1420		110f. Aquarium building (80 ×30 mm)	4·00	3·75
1421		110f. *Monodactylus argenteus*	4·00	3·75
1422		110f. *Negaprion brevirostris*	4·00	3·75
1423		110f. *Pseudanthias bicolour*	4·00	3·75

612 Player

2007. Rugby World Cup Championship, France.
| 1424 | **612** | 110f. multicoloured | 4·00 | 3·75 |

613 Jules Repiquet

2007. Jules Repiquet (governor 1914–23) Commemoration.
| 1425 | **613** | 320f. multicoloured | 11·00 | 10·00 |

614 Bananas and Pomegranate

2007. Fruit. Multicoloured.
1426		35f. Type **614**	1·40	1·30
1427		75f. Vanilla (vert)	3·25	3·00
1428		110f. Pineapple and lychees	4·25	4·00

615 Globe and Couple

2007. Happy New Year.
| 1429 | **615** | 110f. multicoloured | 4·00 | 3·75 |

No. 1430 and Type **616** have been left for 'Arrows (Fleches)', issued on 9 November 2007, not yet received.

617 Cascade de Tao

2007. Waterfalls.
| 1431 | **617** | 110f. multicoloured | 4·00 | 3·75 |

618 Baby in Seashell

2007
| 1432 | **618** | 110f. multicoloured | 4·00 | 3·75 |

619 *Les damnes* (dance by Najib Guerfi Company)

2007. Tjibaou Cultural Centre.
| 1433 | **619** | 110f. multicoloured | 4·00 | 3·75 |

620 *La Montagnarde* Locomotive

2007. Caledonian Railways.
| 1434 | **620** | 400f. multicoloured | 13·00 | 12·00 |

621 Rat

2008. New Year. Year of the Rat.
| 1435 | **621** | 110f. multicoloured | 4·50 | 4·25 |

622 Laurel Wreath

2008. Bicentenary of Palmes Academiques.
| 1436 | **622** | 110f. multicoloured | 4·50 | 4·25 |

623 *Pseudobulweria rostrata* (Tahiti petrel)

2008. Endangered Species. Sea Birds. Multicoloured.
1437		110f. Type **623**	4·50	4·25
1438		110f. *Pterodroma leucoptera* (Gould's petrel)	4·50	4·25
1439		110f. *Nesofregetta fuliginosa* (white-throated storm-petrel)	4·50	4·25

624 Mango

2008. Fruit. Multicoloured.
1440		110f. Type **624**	4·50	4·25
1441		110f. Papaya	4·50	4·25
1442		110f. Mandarin	4·50	4·25

625 Stylized Great House (part of centre complex) (designed by Renzo Piano)

2008. 10th Anniv of Tjibaou Cultural Centre, Tina Peninsula, Noumea.
| 1443 | **625** | 120f. multicoloured | 5·00 | 4·50 |

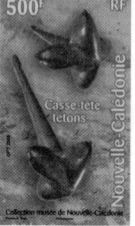

626 Symbols of Accord

2008. 20th Anniv of Matignon Accords.
| 1444 | **626** | 430f. multicoloured | 17·00 | 16·00 |

627 Casse-tete Tetons (ceremonial objects)

2008. Museum Exhibits.
| 1445 | **627** | 500f. multicoloured | 19·00 | 17·00 |

628 1960 5f. Stamp (No. 359), Debit Card and Online Banking ('Le financier')

2008. 50th Anniv of OPT (Office des Postes et Telecommunications). Multicoloured.

1446	75f. Type **628**	3·50	3·25
1447	75f. Sorting, 1973 15f. stamp (Type **112**) and mail box ('Le courier')	3·50	3·25
1448	75f. Fibre optic cable, 1960 12f. stamp (No. 359) and satellite dish ('Les Telecommunications')	3·50	3·25

629 Table Tennis

2008. Olympic Games, Beijing. Multicoloured.

1449	75f. Type **629**	3·50	3·25
1450	75f. Taekwondo	3·50	3·25
1451	75f. Weightlifting	3·50	3·25

630 Telegraph

2008. Stamp Day. History of Telecommunications on New Caledonia. Sheet 100×130 mm containing T 630 and similar vert designs. Multicoloured.

MS1452	75f.×4, Type **630**; Radio telephone; Satellite; Fibre optic cable	12·00	12·00

631 Fort de Kone Ancient and Modern

2008. 130th Anniv of Fort de Kone (military installation).

1453	**631**	220f. multicoloured	8·75	8·00

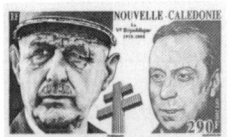

632 General de Gaulle and Michel Debre (first Prime Minister of Fifth Republic)

2008. 50th Anniv of Fifth Republic.

1454	**632**	290f. ultramarine and vermilion	11·00	10·00

633 Symbols of New Caledonia

2008. Christmas.

1455	**633**	110f. multicoloured	5·50	5·00

634 Fields, River and Bridge

2008. River Diahot (Le Fleuve Diahot). Multicoloured.

1456	110f. Type **634**	5·00	4·50
1457	110f. Delta	5·00	4·50

635 Clasped Hands

2008. HANDICAP—Charter for Disabilities.

1458	**635**	120f. multicoloured	5·75	5·25

636 Masked Boobies

2008. World Heritage Site. Caledonia Lagoons. Sheet 184×102 mm containing T 636 and similar multicoloured designs.

MS1459	75f.×6, Type **636**; Sea snake (Tricot raye) (horiz); Marine turtles (horiz); Humphead wrasse; Dugong; Humpback whale (horiz)	21·00	21·00

637 Emblem

2008. Pacific Games.

1460	**637**	110f. multicoloured	5·00	4·50

638 Lethrinus atkinsoni

2009. Fish. Multicoloured.

1461	75f. Type **638**	3·25	3·00
1462	75f. Chlorurus microrhinuos	3·25	3·00
1463	75f. Letherinus nebulosus	3·25	3·00

Nos. 1461/3 were printed, se-tenant, forming a composite design.

639 Ox on Lantern

2009. Chinese New Year. Year of the Ox. Multicoloured.

1464	75f. Type **639**	3·25	3·00

MS1465	120×90 mm.110f.×2, Ox amongst flowers; Ox as constellation	9·25	9·00

The stamps and margins of **MS**1469 form a composite design.

640 Turtle Carrier (Tein Thavouvace)

2009. Ngan Jila Cultural Centre.

1466	**640**	180f. multicoloured	8·00	7·25

641 Sterna nereis (fairy tern)

2009. Terns. Multicoloured.

1467	75f. Type **641**	3·25	3·00
1468	75f. Sterna sumatrana (black-naped tern)	3·25	3·00
1469	75f. Sterna dougallii (roseate tern) (inscr 'Sterna dougalli')	3·25	3·00

642 Entrance

2009. Tenth Anniv of Cinema de la Foa.

1470	**642**	75f. multicoloured	3·25	3·00

643 Flower containing Globe

2009. Third France–Oceania Summit. Multicoloured.

1471	110f. Type **643**	4·50	4·25
1472	110f. Hands holding globe	4·50	4·25

644 Kagu

2009. Kagu

(a) Ordinary gum

1473	**644**	5f. violet		
1474		10f. pale green		
1475		(75f.) scarlet-vermillion		
1476		110f. blue		

(b) Self-adhesive

1480	(75f.) scarlet-vermilion	3·50	3·25

645 Mail Coach

2009. 150th Anniv of Postal Services. Sheet 130×100 mm containing T 645 and similar multicoloured designs.

MS1491	110f.×4, Type **645**; Pony express messenger (vert); Modern mail van; Indigenous messenger (vert)	19·00	19·00

The stamps and margins of **MS**1491 form a composite design.

646 Symbols of Astronomy and Astronaut

2009. International Year of Astronomy.

1492	**646**	110f. multicoloured	4·50	4·25

647 Kagu

2009. Kagu on Stamps. Self-adhesive.

1493	**647**	500f. multicoloured	22·00	22·00

No. 1493 shows five designs of Kagu, and the names of the stamp designers, when tilted.

648 Armand Weneguei, Father Joseph-Marie Dubois and Henry Daly

2009. 40th Anniv of Society for Historical Studies.

1494	**648**	75f. sepia, red-brown and black	3·50	3·25

649 Joemy (games mascot)

2009. Pacific Games 2009, Rarotonga.

1495	**649**	75f. multicoloured	3·25	3·00

650 Museum Buiding and Ships

2009. Tenth Anniv of Maritime Museum. Multicoloured.

1496	75f. Type **650**	3·25	3·00
1497	75f. Symbols of La Perouse's wreck on Vanikoro	3·25	3·00

651 Santa and Reindeer

2009. Christmas.

1498	**651**	110f. multicoloured	4·50	4·25

652 Valley

2009. Tontouta River. Multicoloured.

1499	110f. Type **652**	5·00	4·50
1500	110f. Delta	10·50	9·50

653 Block House

2009. 150th Anniv of Blockhouse, Canala.

1501	**653**	120f. multicoloured	5·50	4·75

654 Dugong Cow and Calf

2009. Coastal Lagoon West–UNESCO World Heritage Site.

1502	**654**	75f. multicoloured	3·25	3·00

655 Women and Children (Micheline Neporon)

2010. Art

1502a	**655**	110f. multicoloured	5·00	4·75

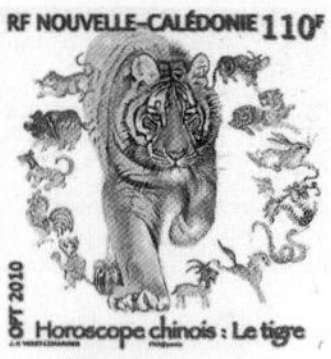

656 Tiger

2010. Chinese New Year

1503	**656**	110f. multicoloured	5·00	4·75

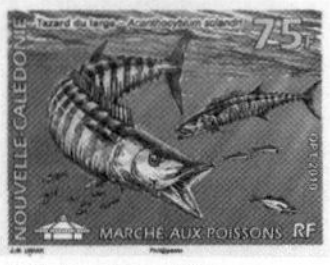

657 *Acanthocybium solandri*

2010. Fish. Multicoloured.

1504	75c. Type **657**	3·50	3·00
1505	75c. *Thunnus albacares*	3·50	3·00
1506	75c. *Coryphaena hippurus*	3·50	3·00

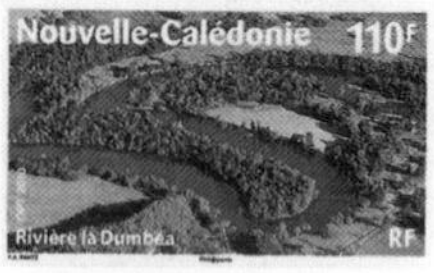

658 Dumbea River

2010. Tourism. Multicoloured.

1507	110f. Type **658**		
1508	110f. Conoeists and bridge		

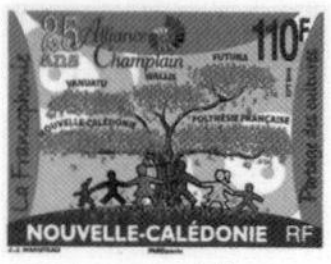

659 Figures encircling Tree

2010. 25th Anniv of Alliance Champlain (Francophones in the Pacific)

1509	**659**	110f. multicoloured	5·00	4·75

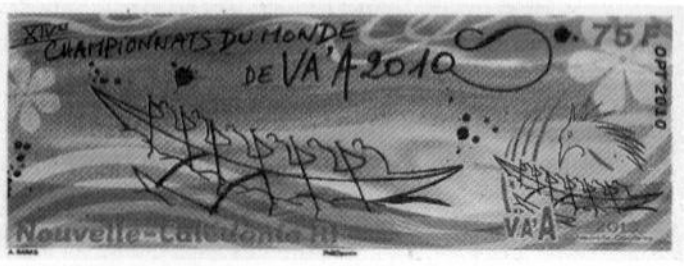

660 Stylized Canoe

2010. Va'a (canoe) World Championships–2010, New Caledonia

1510	**660**	75f. multicoloured	3·25	3·00

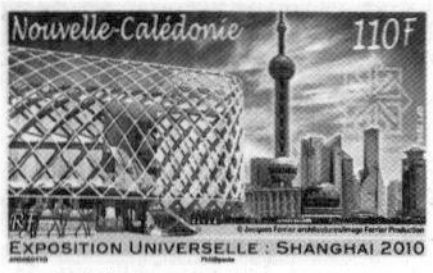

661 Exhibition Site

2010. Expo 2010, Shanghai

1511	**661**	110f. multicoloured	4·25	4·00

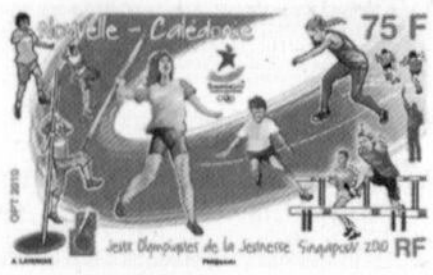

662 Young Athletes

2010. Olympic Youth Games, Singapore

1512	**662**	75f. multicoloured	3·25	3·00

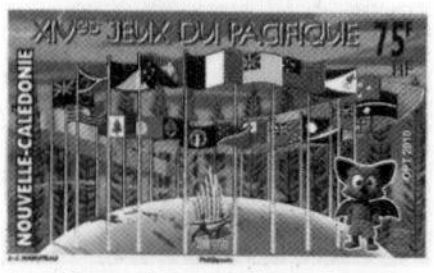

663 Flags of Competitors, Games Emblem and Joemy (games mascot)

2010. NC2011–Pacific Games, New Caledonia

1513	**663**	75f. multicoloured	3·25	3·00

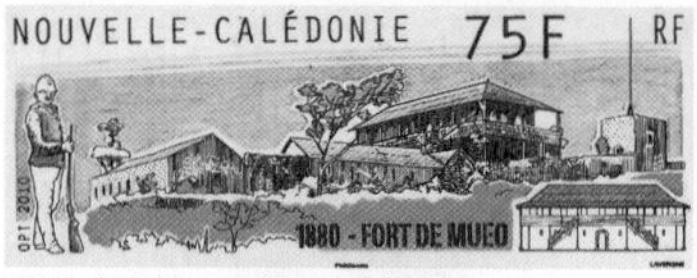

664 Early Soldier and Fort Buildings

2010. Fort Mueo

1514	**664**	75f. multicoloured	3·50	3·25

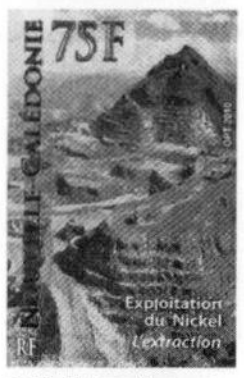

665 Extraction

2010. Nickel Production. Multicoloured.

1515	75f. Type **665**	3·25	3·00
1516	75f. Smelting	3·25	3·00
1517	75f. Ship transportation	3·25	3·00

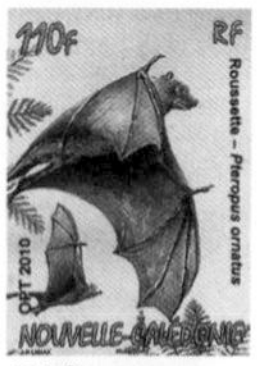

666 *Pteropus ornatus* (ornate flying fox)

2010. Grandes Fougeres Park. Multicoloured.

MS1518 110f.×4, Type **666**; *Ducula goliath* (Goliath Imperial pigeon); *Cyathea* (fern); *Calanthe langel* (flowering plant) 19·00 19·00

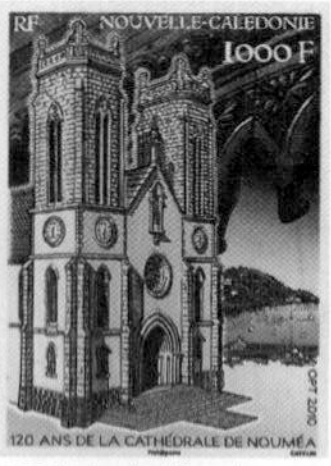

667 Cathedral Facade

2010. 120th Anniv of St. Joseph Cathedral, Noumea

1519	**667**	1000f. multicoloured	40·00	35·00

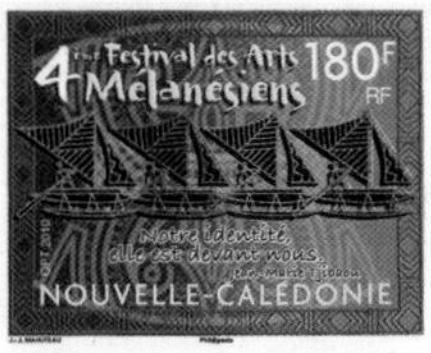

668 Pirogues

2010. Melanesian Arts Festival–2010, New Caledonia

1520	**668**	180f. multicoloured	8·00	7·75

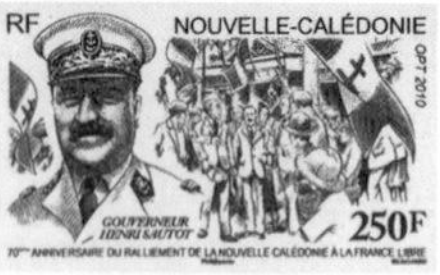

669 Henri Sautot and Soldiers

2010. 70th Anniv of New Caledonia joining Free French Forces

1521	**669**	250f. multicoloured	11·00	10·00

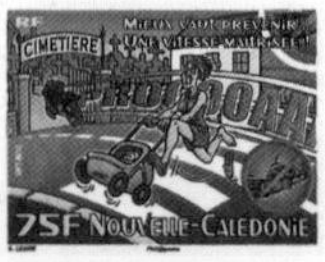

670 Woman with Pushchair avoiding Speeding Motor Cyclist

2010. Road Safety Awareness Campaign. Multicoloured.

1522	75f. Type **670**	3·50	3·25
1523	75f. Drunken driver	3·50	3·25

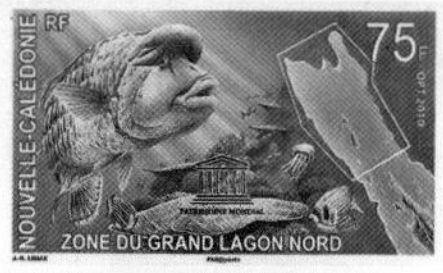

671 Wrasse and UNESCO Emblem

2010. World Heritage Site

1524	**671**	75f. multicoloured	3·50	3·25

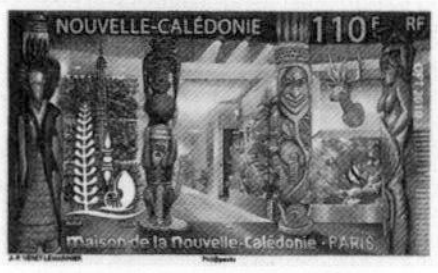

672 Symbols of New Caledonia on Display

2010. Culture

1525	**672**	110f. multicoloured	5·00	4·75

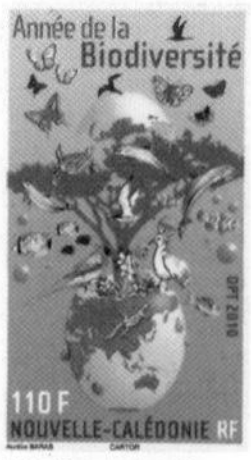

673 Symbols of Biodiversity erupting from Globe

2010. International Year of Biodiversity

1526	**573**	110f. multicoloured	5·00	4·75

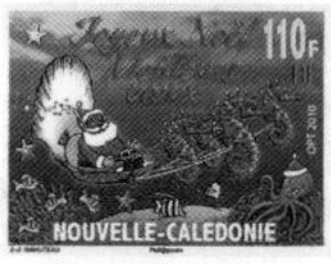

674 Santa's Sleigh drawn by Seahorses

2010. Christmas

1527	**674**	110f. multicoloured	5·00	4·75

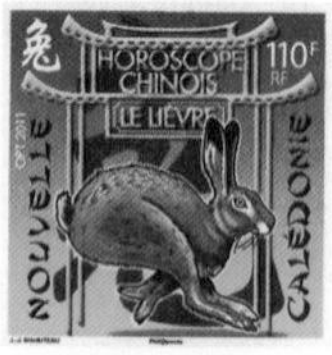

676 Hare and Chinese Symbols

2011. Chinese New Year. Year of the Rabbit

1529	**676**	110f. multicoloured	5·00	4·75

OFFICIAL STAMPS

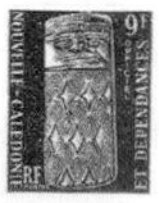

O49 Ancestor Pole

1958. Inscr "OFFICIEL".

O344	**O49**	1f. yellow	40	75
O345	**O49**	3f. green	55	75
O346	**O49**	4f. purple	65	45
O347	**O49**	5f. blue	55	90
O348	**O49**	9f. black	85	1·10
O349	**A**	10f. violet	2·20	55
O350	**A**	13f. green	1·20	2·30
O351	**A**	15f. blue	2·00	1·30
O352	**A**	24f. mauve	2·75	1·70
O353	**A**	26f. orange	1·60	3·25
O354	**B**	50f. green	1·90	5·00
O355	**B**	100f. brown	5·50	14·00
O356	**B**	200f. red	5·00	29·00

DESIGNS: A, B, Different idols.

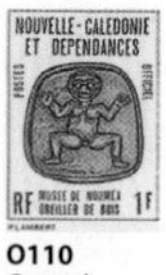

O110 Carved Wooden Pillow (Noumea Museum)

1973

O525	**O110**	1f. green, blk & yell	2·30	2·50
O526	**O110**	2f. red, black & grn	2·30	5·25
O527	**O110**	3f. green, blk & brn	2·30	2·75
O528	**O110**	4f. green, black & bl	2·30	3·00
O529	**O110**	5f. green, blk & mve	2·50	2·10
O530	**O110**	9f. green, black & bl	2·50	3·75
O531	**O110**	10f. green, blk & orge	2·75	2·10
O532	**O110**	11f. grn, blk & mve	3·25	5·25
O533	**O110**	12f. green, blk & turq	2·50	4·00
O534	**O110**	15f. green, blk & lt grn	2·00	3·50
O535	**O110**	20f. green, blk & red	3·25	3·50
O536	**O110**	23f. green, blk & red	3·00	5·75
O537	**O110**	24f. green, blk & bl	2·00	5·50
O538	**O110**	25f. green, blk & grey	2·30	4·00
O539	**O110**	26f. green, blk & yell	2·30	5·25
O540	**O110**	29f. red, black & grn	2·20	4·00
O541	**O110**	31f. red, black & yell	2·30	4·75
O542	**O110**	35f. red, black & yell	2·00	2·75
O543	**O110**	36f. green, blk & mve	3·00	5·50
O544	**O110**	38f. red, black & brn	2·30	5·75
O545	**O110**	40f. red, black & bl	2·30	5·75
O546	**O110**	42f. green, blk & brn	3·00	5·25
O547	**O110**	50f. green, blk & bl	2·50	4·50
O548	**O110**	58f. blue, blk & grn	2·75	6·25
O549	**O110**	65f. red, black & mve	2·50	6·25
O550	**O110**	76f. red, black & yell	3·25	6·50
O551	**O110**	100f. green, blk & red	3·50	5·00
O552	**O110**	200f. green, blk & yell	6·50	10·50

PARCEL POST STAMPS

1926. Optd Colis Postaux or surch also.

P137	**17**	50c. on 5f. green on mauve	65	8·00
P138	**17**	1f. blue	75	9·00
P139	**17**	2f. red on blue	1·20	10·00

1930. Optd Colis Postaux.

P179	**23**	50c. brown and mauve	45	3·00
P180	**24**	1f. pink and drab	75	7·50
P181	**24**	2f. brown and orange	90	8·25

POSTAGE DUE STAMPS

1903. Postage Due stamps of French Colonies optd CINQUANTENAIRE 24 SEPTEMBRE 1853 1903 and eagle. Imperf.

D78	**U**	5c. blue	2·30	1·40
D79	**U**	10c. brown	11·50	6·00
D80	**U**	15c. green	30·00	2·50
D81	**U**	30c. red	14·50	28·00
D82	**U**	50c. purple	95·00	9·25
D83	**U**	60c. brown on buff	£225	55·00
D84	**U**	1f. pink	28·00	16·00
D85	**U**	2f. brown	£800	£850

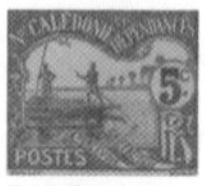

D18 Outrigger Canoe

1906

D102	**D18**	5c. blue on blue	30	35
D103	**D18**	10c. brown on buff	30	2·75
D104	**D18**	15c. green	35	3·00
D105	**D18**	20c. black on yellow	55	1·60
D106	**D18**	30c. red	1·30	3·25
D107	**D18**	50c. blue on cream	1·60	8·50
D108	**D18**	60c. green on blue	1·20	7·25
D109	**D18**	1f. green on cream	1·70	8·50

1926. Surch.

D137	2f. on 1f. mauve	65	9·25
D138	3f. on 1f. brown	2·50	12·50

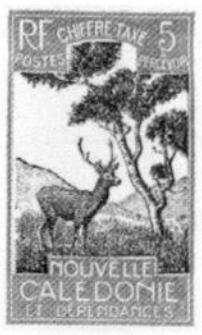

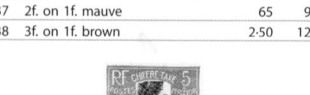

D25 Sambar Stag

1928

D179	**D25**	2c. brown and blue	10	2·75
D180	**D25**	4c. green and red	10	3·00
D181	**D25**	5c. grey and orange	30	3·75
D182	**D25**	10c. blue and mauve	10	1·20
D183	**D25**	15c. red and olive	20	2·75
D184	**D25**	20c. olive and red	1·40	6·75
D185	**D25**	25c. blue and brown	10	4·50
D186	**D25**	30c. olive and green	30	5·75
D187	**D25**	50c. red and brown	1·70	4·00
D188	**D25**	60c. red and mauve	2·50	6·25
D189	**D25**	1f. green and blue	2·30	3·00
D190	**D25**	2f. olive and red	3·25	6·25
D191	**D25**	3f. brown and violet	2·50	4·75

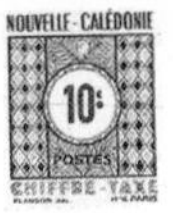

D38

1948

D328	D38	10c. mauve	10	5·25
D329	D38	30c. brown	10	7·50
D330	D38	50c. green	20	7·50
D331	D38	1f. brown	30	7·50
D332	D38	2f. red	45	6·75
D333	D38	3f. brown	35	6·75
D334	D38	4f. blue	55	7·75
D335	D38	5f. red	60	8·25
D336	D38	10f. green	1·20	8·75
D337	D38	20f. blue	1·20	7·25

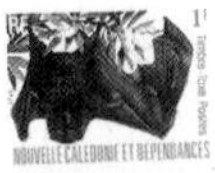

D222 New Caledonian Flying Fox

1983

D703	D223	1f. multicoloured	85	4·00
D704	D223	2f. multicoloured	85	4·00
D705	D223	3f. multicoloured	85	4·00
D706	D223	4f. multicoloured	90	4·00
D707	D223	5f. multicoloured	90	4·00
D708	D223	10f. multicoloured	90	4·00
D709	D223	20f. multicoloured	1·30	4·50
D710	D223	40f. multicoloured	1·90	5·50
D711	D223	50f. multicoloured	2·00	5·75

Pt. 1

NEWFOUNDLAND

An island off the east coast of Canada. A British Dominion merged since 1949 with Canada, whose stamps it now uses.

1857. 12 pence = 1 shilling; 20 shillings = 1 pound.
1866. 100 cents = 1 dollar.

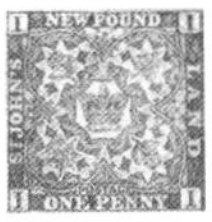

1

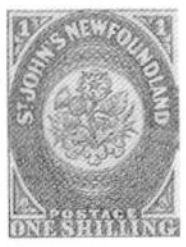

2

3 Royal Crown and Heraldic Flowers of the United Kingdom

1857. Imperf.

1	1	1d. purple	£160	£250
10	2	2d. red	£500	£600
11	3	3d. green	£100	£180
12	2	4d. red	£3750	£950
13	1	5d. brown	£140	£400
14	2	6d. red	£4500	£700
7	2	6½d. red	£4000	£4000
8	2	8d. red	£375	£700
9	2	1s. red	£23000	£8500

The frame design of Type **2** differs for each value.

1861. Imperf.

16	1	1d. brown	£325	£425
17	2	2d. lake	£275	£500
18	2	4d. lake	50·00	£110
19a	1	5d. brown	90·00	£200
20	2	6d. lake	32·00	£100
21	2	6½d. lake	£100	£450
22	2	8d. lake	£120	£650
23	2	1s. lake	50·00	£300

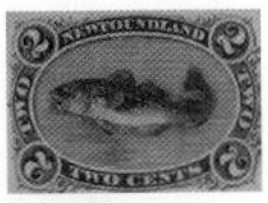

6 Codfish

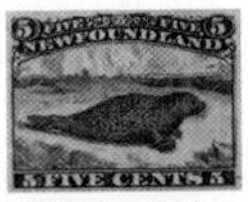

7 Common Seal on Ice-floe

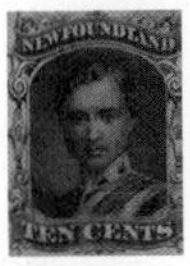

8 Prince Consort

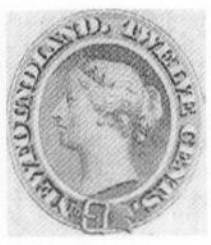

9 Queen Victoria

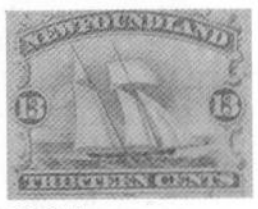

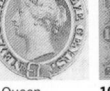

10 Schooner

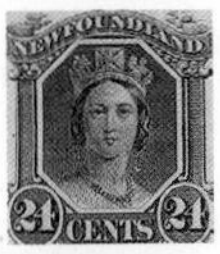

11 Queen Victoria

1866. Perf (2c. also roul).

31	6	2c. green	£100	50·00
26	7	5c. brown	£550	£180
32	8	10c. black	£275	48·00
33	9	12c. brown	60·00	48·00
29	10	13c. orange	£120	£120
30	11	24c. blue	48·00	38·00

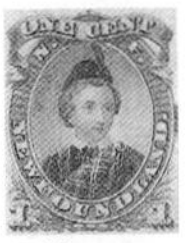

12 King Edward VII when Prince of Wales

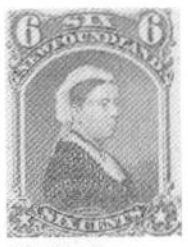

14 Queen Victoria

1868. Perf or roul.

34	12	1c. purple	75·00	60·00
36	14	3c. orange	£300	£100
37	14	3c. blue	£275	27·00
38	7	5c. black	£300	£110
43	7	5c. blue	£180	3·50
39	14	6c. red	13·00	28·00

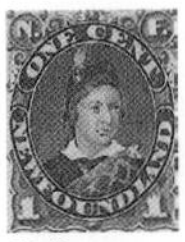

15 King Edward VII when Prince of Wales

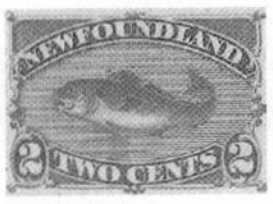

16 Codfish

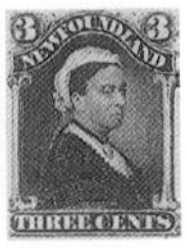

17

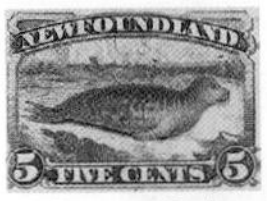

18 Common Seal on Ice-floe

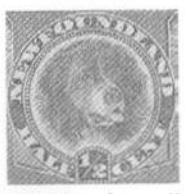

19 Newfoundland Dog

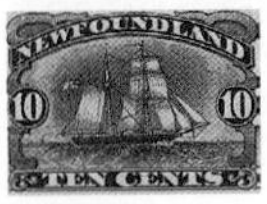

20 Atlantic Brigantine

1880

49	19	½c. red	15·00	10·00
59	19	½c. black	10·00	7·50
44	15	1c. brown	42·00	16·00
50a	15	1c. green	6·00	4·00
46	16	2c. green	55·00	32·00
51	16	2c. orange	24·00	7·50
47a	17	3c. blue	80·00	6·50
52	17	3c. brown	70·00	2·75
59a	18	5c. blue	70·00	4·75
54	20	10c. black	70·00	65·00

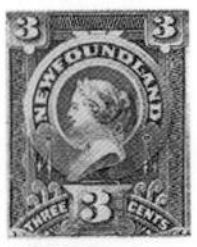

21 Queen Victoria

1890

55	21	3c. grey	48·00	3·25

This stamp on pink paper was stained by sea-water.

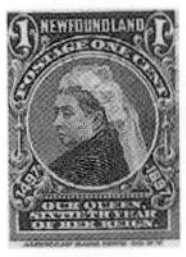

22 Queen Victoria

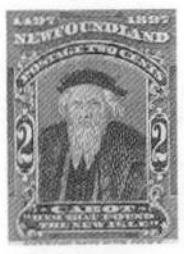

23 John Cabot

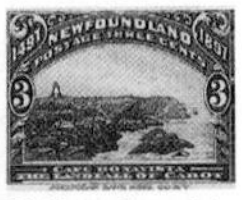

24 Cape Bonavista

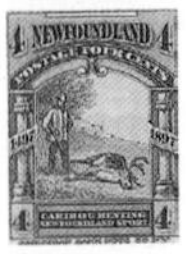

25 Caribou-hunting

1897. 400th Anniv of Discovery of Newfoundland and 60th Year of Queen Victoria's Reign. Dated "1497 1897".

66	22	1c. green	6·50	9·50
67	23	2c. red	2·75	2·75
68	24	3c. blue	3·50	1·00
69	25	4c. olive	11·00	7·00
70	-	5c. violet	14·00	3·50
71	-	6c. brown	9·50	3·25
72	-	8c. orange	21·00	9·00
73	-	10c. brown	42·00	12·00
74	-	12c. blue	40·00	10·00
75	-	15c. red	24·00	19·00
76	-	24c. violet	28·00	29·00
77	-	30c. blue	50·00	95·00
78	-	35c. red	65·00	85·00
79	-	60c. black	25·00	19·00

DESIGNS—As Type **24**: 5c. Mining; 6c. Logging; 8c. Fishing; 10c. Cabot's ship, the "Matthew"; 15c. Seals; 24c. Salmon-fishing; 35c. Iceberg. As Type **23**: 12c. Willow/red grouse; 30c. Seal of the Colony; 60c. Henry VII.

1897. Surch ONE CENT and bar.

80	21	1c. on 3c. grey	70·00	32·00

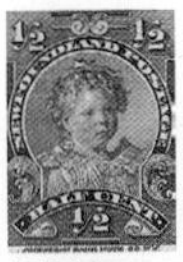

39 Prince Edward, later Duke of Windsor

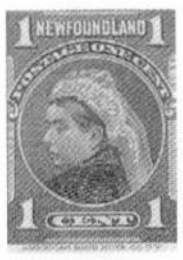

40 Queen Victoria

1897. Royal portraits.

83	39	½c. olive	2·25	1·50
84	40	1c. red	5·50	5·50
85	-	1c. green	16·00	20
86	-	2c. orange	8·50	7·00
87	-	2c. red	21·00	40
88	-	3c. orange	27·00	30
89	-	4c. violet	32·00	8·00
90	-	5c. blue	48·00	3·00

DESIGNS: 2c. King Edward VII when Prince of Wales; 3c. Queen Alexandra when Princess of Wales; 4c. Queen Mary when Duchess of York; 5c. King George V when Duke of York.

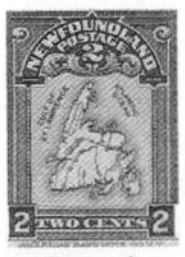

45 Map of Newfoundland

1908

94	45	2c. lake	27·00	1·00

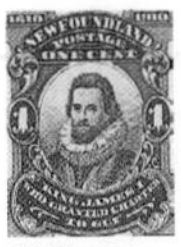

46 King James I

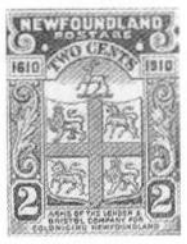

47 Arms of Colonisation Co.

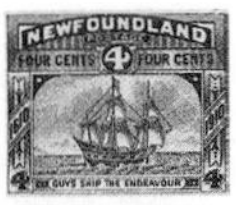

49 "Endeavour" (immigrant ship), 1610

1910. Dated "1610 1910".

109	46	1c. green	3·25	30
107	47	2c. red	8·00	40
97	-	3c. olive	14·00	22·00
98	49	4c. violet	24·00	21·00
108	-	5c. blue	9·00	3·00
111	-	6c. purple	18·00	50·00
112	-	8c. bistre	50·00	75·00
102	-	9c. green	65·00	£100
103	-	10c. grey	65·00	£130
115	-	12c. brown	70·00	70·00
105	-	15c. black	65·00	£130

DESIGNS—HORIZ: 5c. Cupids; 8c. Mosquito; 9c. Logging camp, Red Indian Lake; 10c. Paper mills, Grand Falls. VERT: 3c. John Guy; 6c. Sir Francis Bacon; 12c. King Edward VII; 15c. King George V. (Cupids and Mosquito are places).

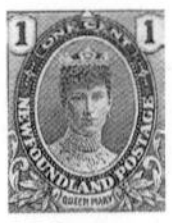

57 Queen Mary

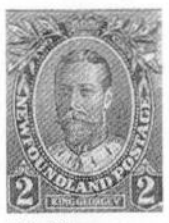

58 King George V

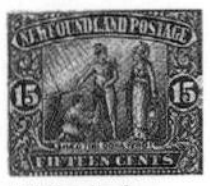

67 Seal of Newfoundland

1911. Coronation.

117	57	1c. green	10·00	30
118	58	2c. red	10·00	20
119	-	3c. brown	23·00	48·00
120	-	4c. purple	22·00	38·00
121	-	5c. blue	8·00	1·50
122	-	6c. grey	13·00	25·00
123	-	8c. blue	60·00	85·00
124	-	9c. blue	29·00	55·00
125	-	10c. green	42·00	50·00
126	-	12c. plum	30·00	50·00
127	67	15c. lake	27·00	50·00

PORTRAITS—VERT (As Type **57/8**): 3c. Duke of Windsor when Prince of Wales; 4c. King George VI when Prince Albert; 5c. Princess Mary, the Princess Royal; 6c. Duke of Gloucester when Prince Henry; 8c. Duke of Kent when Prince George; 9c. Prince John; 10c. Queen Alexandra; 12c. Duke of Connaught.

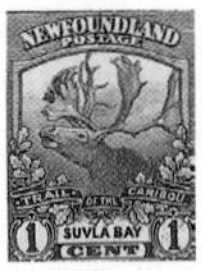

68 Caribou

1919. Newfoundland Contingent, 1914–18.

130	68	1c. green	3·75	20
131	68	2c. red	3·75	85
132	68	3c. brown	8·00	20
133	68	4c. mauve	13·00	80
134	68	5c. blue	15·00	1·25
135	68	6c. grey	17·00	65·00
136	68	8c. purple	17·00	65·00
137	68	10c. green	8·00	6·00
138	68	12c. orange	20·00	75·00
139	68	15c. blue	16·00	85·00
140	68	24c. brown	32·00	42·00
141	68	36c. olive	21·00	48·00

DESIGNS—Each inscr with the name of a different action: 1c. Suvla Bay; 3c. Gueudecourt; 4c. Beaumont Hamel; 6c. Monchy; 10c. Steenbeck; 15c. Langemarck; 24c. Cambrai; 36c. Combles. The 2, 5, 8 and 12c. are inscribed "Royal Naval Reserve-Ubique".

1919. Air. Hawker Flight. No. 132a optd FIRST TRANS-ATLANTIC AIR POST April, 1919.

142	3c. brown	£21000	£11000

1919. Air. Alcock and Brown Flight. Surch Trans-Atlantic AIR POST, 1919. ONE DOLLAR.

143	$1 on 15c. red (No. 75)	£120	£130

1920. Surch in words between bars.

144	2c. on 30c. blue (No. 77)	5·00	27·00
146	3c. on 15c. red (No. 75)	32·00	30·00
147	3c. on 35c. red (No. 78)	16·00	24·00

1921. Air. Optd AIR MAIL to Halifax, N.S. 1921.

148a	35c. red (No. 78)	£120	85·00

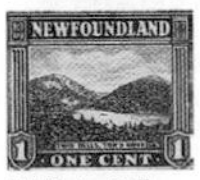

73 Twin Hills, Tor's Cove

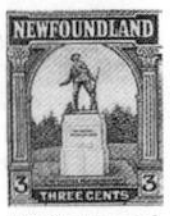

75 Statue of Fighting Newfoundlander, St. John's

1923

149	73	1c. green	2·25	20
150	-	2c. red	1·00	10
151	75	3c. brown	3·25	10
152	-	4c. purple	1·00	30
153	-	5c. blue	4·25	1·75
154	-	6c. grey	9·50	15·00
155	-	8c. purple	13·00	3·50
156	-	9c. green	18·00	35·00
157	-	10c. violet	12·00	7·00
158	-	11c. olive	4·75	28·00
159	-	12c. lake	6·00	16·00
160	-	15c. blue	6·00	32·00
161	-	20c. brown	23·00	18·00
162	-	24c. brown	60·00	90·00

DESIGNS—HORIZ: 2c. South-west Arm, Trinity; 6c. Upper Steadies, Humber River; 8c. Quidi Vidi, near St. John's; 9c. Caribou crossing lake; 11c. Shell Bird Island; 12c. Mount Moriah, Bay of Islands; 20c. Placentia. VERT: 4c. Humber River; 5c. Coast at Trinity; 10c. Humber River Canon; 15c. Humber River, near Little Rapids; 24c. Topsail Falls.

1927. Air. Optd Air Mail DE PINEDO 1927.

163	60c. black (No. 79)	£38000	£12000

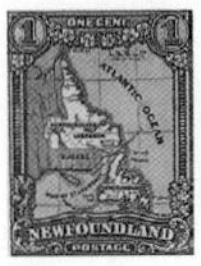

88 Newfoundland and Labrador

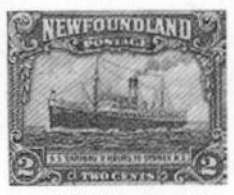

89 S.S. "Caribou"

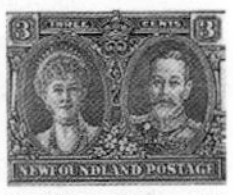

90 King George V and Queen Mary

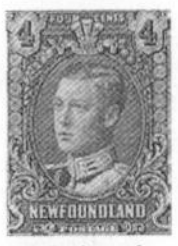

91 Duke of Windsor when Prince of Wales

1928. Publicity issue.

164	88	1c. green	3·75	1·25

180	**89**	2c. red	1·75	40
181	**90**	3c. brown	1·00	20
201	**91**	4c. mauve	3·50	1·25
183	-	5c. grey	7·00	5·00
184a	-	6c. blue	3·00	27·00
170	-	8c. brown	8·00	48·00
171	-	9c. green	2·50	24·00
185	-	10c. violet	6·50	5·50
173	-	12c. lake	2·50	27·00
174a	-	14c. purple	17·00	9·00
175	-	15c. blue	9·50	45·00
176a	-	20c. black	6·50	9·50
177	-	28c. green	28·00	65·00
178	-	30c. brown	6·00	22·00

DESIGNS—HORIZ: 5c. Express train; 6c. Newfoundland Hotel, St. John's; 8c. Heart's Content; 10c. War Memorial, St. John's; 15c. Vickers Vimy aircraft; 20c. Parliament House, St. John's. VERT: 9, 14c. Cabot Tower, St. John's; 12, 28c. G.P.O., St. John's; 30c. Grand Falls, Labrador.

1929. Surch THREE CENTS.

188		3c. on 6c. (No. 154)	2·50	9·00

1930. Air. No. 141 surch Trans-Atlantic AIR MAIL By B. M. "Columbia" September 1930 Fifty Cents.

191	**68**	50c. on 36c. olive	£6500	£5500

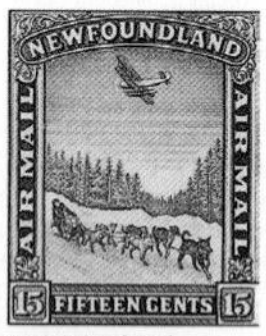
103 Westland Limousine III and Dog-team

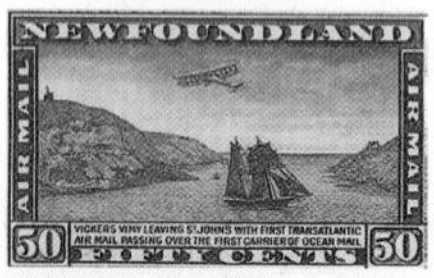
104 Vickers Vimy Biplane and early Sailing Packet

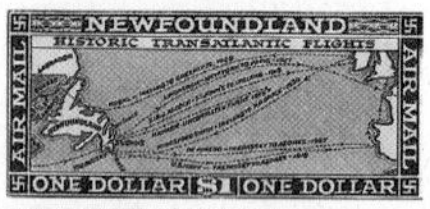
105 Routes of historic Trans-Atlantic Flights

1931. Air.

192	**103**	15c. brown	9·00	18·00
193	**104**	50c. green	38·00	55·00
194	**105**	$1 blue	50·00	95·00

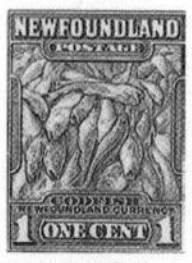
107 Codfish

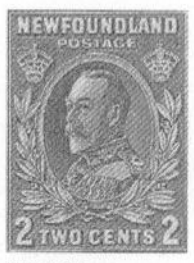
108 King George V

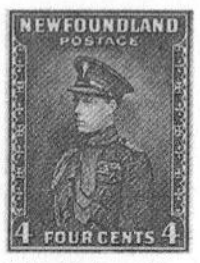
110 Duke of Windsor when Prince of Wales

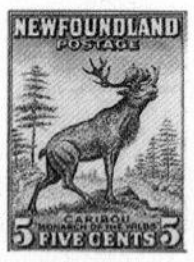
111 Reindeer

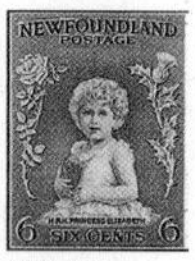
112 Queen Elizabeth II when Princess

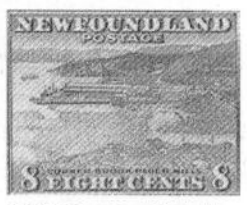
121 Corner Brook Paper Mills

1932

209	**107**	1c. green	3·50	30
276	**107**	1c. grey	20	2·75
210	**108**	2c. red	1·50	20
223	**108**	2c. green	2·50	10
211	-	3c. brown	1·50	20
212	**110**	4c. lilac	9·00	2·25
224	**110**	4c. red	5·50	40
213	**111**	5c. purple	8·50	5·50
225c	**111**	5c. violet	1·00	30
214	**112**	6c. blue	4·00	14·00
226	-	7c. lake	3·00	3·75
227	**121**	8c. red	3·75	2·00
215	-	10c. brown	85	65
216	-	14c. black	4·50	5·50
217	-	15c. purple	1·25	2·00
218	-	20c. green	1·00	1·00
228	-	24c. blue	1·00	3·25
219	-	25c. grey	2·00	2·25
220	-	30c. blue	42·00	38·00
289	-	48c. brown	5·00	9·50

DESIGNS—VERT: 3c. Queen Mary; 7c. Queen Mother when Duchess of York. HORIZ: 10c. Salmon; 14c. Newfoundland dog; 15c. Harp seal; 20c. Cape Race; 24c. Loading iron ore, Bell Island; 25c. Sealing fleet; 30, 48c. Fishing fleet.

1932. Air. Surch TRANS-ATLANTIC WEST TO EAST Per Dornier DO-X May, 1932. One Dollar and Fifty Cents.

221	**105**	$1.50 on $1 blue	£250	£225

1933. Optd L. & S. Post. ("Land and Sea") between bars.

229	**103**	15c. brown	4·75	18·00

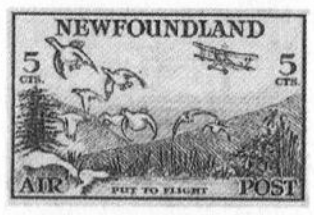
124 Put to Flight

1933. Air.

230	**124**	5c. brown	22·00	22·00
231	-	10c. yellow	18·00	35·00
232	-	30c. blue	32·00	48·00
233	-	60c. green	50·00	£120
234	-	75c. brown	50·00	£120

DESIGNS: 10c. Land of Heart's Delight; 30c. Spotting the herd; 60c. News from home; 75c. Labrador.

1933. Air. Balbo Trans-Atlantic Mass Formation Flight. No. 234 surch 1933 GEN. BALBO FLIGHT. $4.50.

235		$4.50 on 75c. brown	£275	£325

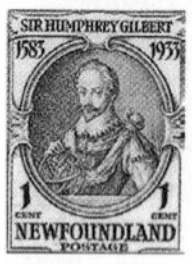
130 Sir Humphrey Gilbert

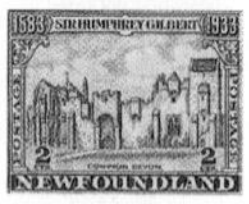
131 Compton Castle, Devon

1933. 350th Anniv of Annexation. Dated "1583 1933".

236	**130**	1c. black	1·25	1·50
237	**131**	2c. green	2·00	70
238	-	3c. brown	2·50	1·25
239	-	4c. red	1·00	50
240	-	5c. violet	2·00	1·00
241	-	7c. blue	15·00	17·00
242	-	8c. orange	9·50	21·00
243	-	9c. blue	7·00	22·00
244	-	10c. brown	7·00	16·00
245	-	14c. black	22·00	42·00
246w	-	15c. red	7·50	30·00
247	-	20c. green	19·00	21·00
248	-	24c. purple	21·00	29·00
249	-	32c. black	13·00	65·00

DESIGNS—VERT: 3c. Gilbert coat of arms; 5c. Anchor token; 14c. Royal Arms; 15c. Gilbert in the "Squirrel"; 24c. Queen Elizabeth I; 32c. Gilbert's statue at Truro. HORIZ: 4c. Eton College; 7c. Gilbert commissioned by Elizabeth; 8c. Fleet leaving Plymouth, 1583; 9c. Arrival at St. John's; 10c. Annexation, 5 August, 1583; 20c. Map of Newfoundland.

1935. Silver Jubilee.

250	**143a**	4c. red	1·00	1·75
251	**143a**	5c. violet	1·25	4·25
252	**143a**	7c. blue	3·75	7·00
253	**143a**	24c. olive	5·00	26·00

1937. Coronation.

254	**143b**	2c. green	1·00	3·00
255	**143b**	4c. red	1·60	4·00
256	**143b**	5c. purple	3·00	4·00

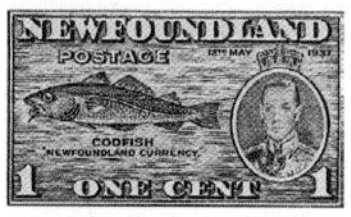
144 Atlantic Cod

1937. Coronation.

257	**144**	1c. grey	3·50	30
258ed	-	3c. brown	9·50	4·75
259	-	7c. blue	4·00	1·25
260	-	8c. red	4·25	4·00
261	-	10c. black	7·00	9·00
262	-	14c. black	2·25	4·00
263	-	15c. red	20·00	9·00
264f	-	20c. green	5·00	9·50
265	-	24c. blue	2·75	3·00
266	-	25c. black	5·00	4·50
267	-	48c. purple	11·00	6·50

DESIGNS: 3c. Map of Newfoundland; 7c. Rein-deer; 8c. Corner Brook Paper Mills; 10c. Atlantic salmon; 14c. Newfoundland dog; 15c. Harp seal; 20c. Cape Race; 24c. Bell Island; 25c. Sealing fleet; 48c. The Banks fishing fleet.

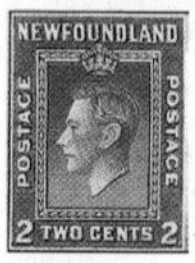
155 King George VI

1938

277	**155**	2c. green	40	75
278	-	3c. red	40	30
279	-	4c. blue	2·75	40
271		7c. blue	1·00	12·00

DESIGNS: 3c. Queen Mother; 4c. Queen Elizabeth II, aged 12; 7c. Queen Mary.

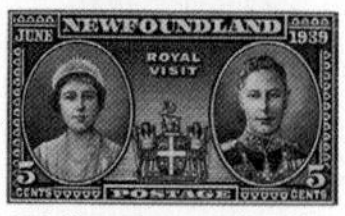
159 King George VI and Queen Elizabeth

1938. Royal Visit.

272	**159**	5c. blue	3·25	1·00

1939. Surch in figures and triangles.

273		2c. on 5c. blue	2·50	50
274		4c. on 5c. blue	2·00	1·00

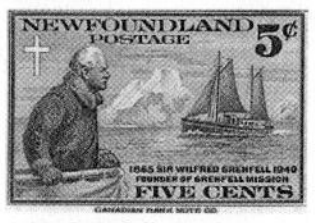
161 Grenfell on the "Strathcona" (after painting by Gribble)

1941. 50th Anniv of Sir Wilfred Grenfell's Labrador Mission.

275	**161**	5c. blue	30	1·00

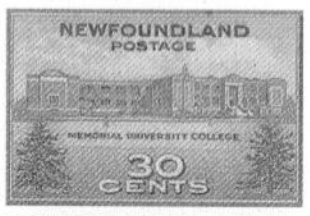
162 Memorial University College

1942

290	**162**	30c. red	1·75	5·00

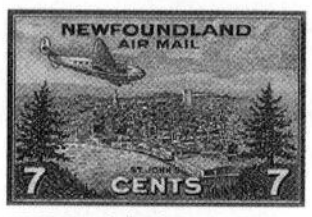
163 St. John's

1943. Air.

291	**163**	7c. blue	50	1·25

1946. Surch TWO CENTS.

292	**162**	2c. on 30c. red	30	2·25

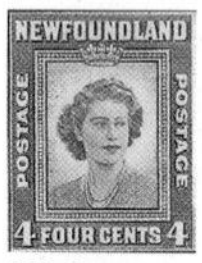
165 Queen Elizabeth II when Princess

1947. 21st Birthday of Princess Elizabeth.

293	**165**	4c. blue	40	1·00

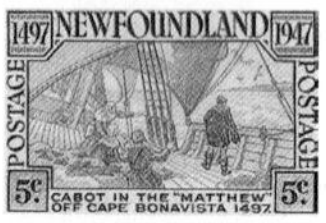
166 Cabot off Cape Bonavista

1947. 450th Anniv of Cabot's Discovery of Newfoundland.

294	**166**	5c. violet	50	1·00

POSTAGE DUE STAMPS

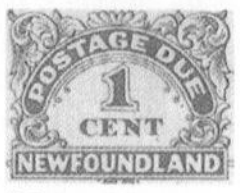
D1

1939

D1	**D 1**	1c. green	2·25	20·00
D2	**D 1**	2c. red	15·00	8·50
D3	**D 1**	3c. blue	5·00	35·00
D4	**D 1**	4c. orange	9·00	28·00
D5	**D 1**	5c. brown	7·50	40·00
D6	**D 1**	10c. purple	11·00	27·00

Pt. 1

NEW GUINEA

Formerly a German Colony, part of the island of New Guinea. Occupied by Australian forces during the 1914–18 war and subsequently joined with Papua and administered by the Australian Commonwealth under trusteeship. After the Japanese defeat in 1945 Australian stamps were used until 1952 when the combined issue appeared for Papua and New Guinea (q.v.). The stamps overprinted "N.W. PACIFIC ISLANDS" were also used in Nauru and other ex-German islands.

12 pence = 1 shilling; 20 shillings = 1 pound.

1914. "Yacht" key-types of German New Guinea surch G.R.I. and value in English currency.

16	**N**	1d. on 3pf. brown	65·00	80·00
17	**N**	1d. on 5pf. green	27·00	45·00
18	**N**	2d. on 10pf. red	40·00	60·00
19	**N**	2d. on 20pf. blue	42·00	70·00
5	**N**	2½d. on 10pf. red	95·00	£200
6	**N**	2½d. on 20pf. blue	£110	£225
22	**N**	3d. on 25pf. blk & red on yell	£170	£250
23	**N**	3d. on 30pf. blk & orge on buff	£150	£200
24	**N**	4d. on 40pf. black and red	£160	£275
25	**N**	5d. on 50pf. black & pur on buff	£275	£350
26	**N**	8d. on 80pf. blk & red on rose	£425	£600
12	**O**	1s on 1m. red	£3000	£4000
13	**O**	2s. on 2m. blue	£2750	£3750
14	**O**	3s. on 3m. black	£4750	£6500
15	**O**	5s. on 5m. red and black	£12000	£14000

Nos. 3/4 surch 1.

31		"1" on 2d. on 10pf. red	£27000	£27000
32		"1" on 2d. on 20pf. blue	£27000	£16000

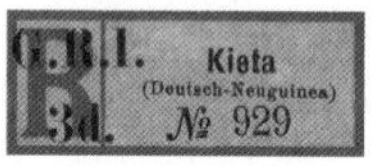

4

1914. Registration labels with names of various towns surch G.R.I. 3d.

33	**4**	3d. black and red	£275	£325

1914. "Yacht" key-types of German Marshall Islands surch G.R.I. and value in English currency.

50	**N**	1d. on 3pf. brown	80·00	£130
51	**N**	1d. on 5pf. green	80·00	85·00
52	**N**	2d. on 10pf. red	24·00	38·00
53	**N**	2d. on 20pf. blue	26·00	42·00
64g	**N**	2½d. on 10pf. red	£25000	
64h	**N**	2½d. on 20pf. blue	£38000	
54	**N**	3d. on 25pf. black and red on yellow	£425	£550
55	**N**	3d. on 30pf. black and orange on buff	£425	£550
56	**N**	4d. on 40pf. black and red	£160	£225
57	**N**	5d. on 50pf. black and purple on buff	£225	£325
58	**N**	8d. on 80pf. black and red on rose	£475	£700
59	**O**	1s. on 1m. red	£3500	£4750
60	**O**	2s. on 2m. blue	£1700	£4000
61	**O**	3s. on 3m. black	£5500	£8500
62	**O**	5s. on 5m. red and black	£12000	£13000

1915. Nos. 52 and 53 surch 1.

63		"1" on 2d. on 10pf. red	£180	£275
64		"1" on 2d. on 20pf. blue	£3750	£2500

1915. Stamps of Australia optd N. W. PACIFIC ISLANDS.

102	**3**	½d. green	1·75	3·50
103	**3**	1d. red	3·75	1·60
120	**3**	1d. violet	2·50	6·50
94	**1**	2d. grey	6·50	25·00
121	**3**	2d. orange	8·00	2·75
122	**3**	2d. red	9·50	2·50
74	**1**	2½d. blue	2·75	16·00
96	**1**	3d. olive	5·50	11·00
70	**3**	4d. orange	4·00	15·00
123	**3**	4d. violet	20·00	40·00
124	**3**	4d. blue	11·00	60·00
105	**3**	5d. brown	3·75	12·00
110	**1**	6d. blue	4·50	14·00
89	**1**	9d. violet	16·00	21·00
90	**1**	1s. green	11·00	24·00
115	**1**	2s. brown	21·00	38·00
116	**1**	5s. grey and yellow	65·00	70·00
84	**1**	10s. grey and pink	£140	£170
99	**1**	£1 brown and blue	£325	£450

1918. Nos. 105 and 90 surch One Penny.

100		1d. on 5d. brown	90·00	80·00
101	**1**	1d. on 1s. green	£100	80·00

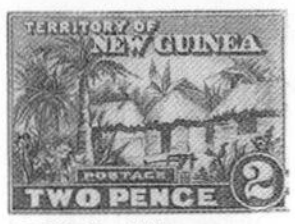

12 Native Village

1925

125	12	½d. orange	2·50	7·00
126	12	1d. green	2·50	5·50
126a	12	1½d. red	3·25	2·75
127	12	2d. red	5·00	4·50
128	12	3d. blue	5·50	4·00
129	12	4d. olive	13·00	21·00
130a	12	6d. brown	6·00	50·00
131	12	9d. purple	13·00	45·00
132	12	1s. green	15·00	27·00
133	12	2s. lake	30·00	48·00
134	12	5s. brown	50·00	65·00
135	12	10s. pink	£120	£180
136	12	£1 grey	£190	£300

1931. Air. Optd with biplane and AIR MAIL.

137	½d. orange	1·50	8·50
138	1d. green	1·60	5·00
139	1½d. red	1·25	7·00
140	2d. red	1·25	7·00
141	3d. blue	1·75	13·00
142	4d. olive	1·25	9·00
143	6d. brown	1·75	14·00
144	9d. purple	3·00	17·00
145	1s. green	3·00	17·00
146	2s. lake	7·00	45·00
147	5s. brown	20·00	65·00
148	10s. pink	85·00	£110
149	£1 grey	£160	£250

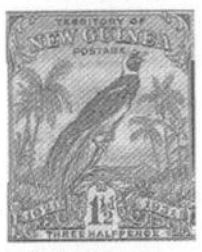

14 Raggiana Bird of Paradise (Dates either side of value)

1931. 10th Anniv of Australian Administration. Dated "1921–1931".

150	14	1d. green	4·00	4·50
151	14	1½d. red	5·00	10·00
152	14	2d. red	5·00	2·25
153	14	3d. blue	5·00	4·75
154	14	4d. olive	6·50	27·00
155	14	5d. green	6·50	21·00
156	14	6d. brown	5·00	19·00
157	14	9d. violet	8·50	19·00
158	14	1s. grey	6·00	15·00
159	14	2s. lake	10·00	45·00
160	14	5s. brown	42·00	55·00
161	14	10s. pink	£120	£140
162	14	£1 grey	£250	£275

1931. Air. Optd with biplane and AIR MAIL.

163	½d. orange	3·25	3·25
164	1d. green	4·00	6·50
165	1½d. red	3·75	10·00
166	2d. red	3·75	3·00
167	3d. blue	6·00	6·50
168	4d. olive	6·00	6·00
169	5d. green	6·00	11·00
170	6d. brown	7·00	26·00
171	9d. violet	8·00	15·00
172	1s. grey	7·50	15·00
173	2s. lake	16·00	48·00
174	5s. brown	42·00	70·00
175	10s. pink	80·00	£120
176	£1 grey	£150	£250

1932. As T 14, but without dates.

177	1d. green	5·00	20
178	1½d. red	5·00	15·00
179	2d. red	5·00	20
179a	2½d. green	6·50	25·00
180	3d. blue	5·50	1·00
180a	3½d. red	13·00	17·00
181	4d. olive	5·50	6·00
182	5d. green	6·50	70
183	6d. brown	6·50	3·25
184	9d. violet	9·50	22·00
185	1s. grey	5·50	10·00
186	2s. lake	5·00	17·00
187	5s. brown	27·00	45·00
188	10s. pink	55·00	70·00
189	£1 grey	£120	£100

1932. Air. T 14, but without dates, optd with biplane and AIR MAIL.

190	½d. orange	60	1·50
191	1d. green	1·25	2·50
192	1½d. mauve	1·75	9·50
193	2d. red	1·75	30
193a	2½d. green	8·50	2·50
194	3d. blue	3·25	3·00
194a	3½d. red	4·75	3·25
195	4d. olive	4·50	10·00
196	5d. green	7·00	7·50
197	6d. brown	4·50	15·00
198	9d. violet	6·00	9·00
199	1s. grey	6·00	9·00
200	2s. lake	10·00	48·00
201	5s. brown	48·00	60·00
202	10s. pink	95·00	85·00
203	£1 grey	85·00	55·00

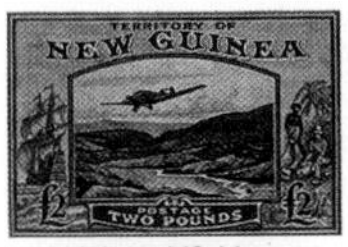

16 Bulolo Goldfields

1935. Air.

204	16	£2 violet	£350	£140
205	16	£5 green	£750	£450

1935. Silver Jubilee. Nos. 177 and 179 optd HIS MAJESTY'S JUBILEE. 1910–1935.

206	1d. green	1·00	65
207	2d. red	3·00	65

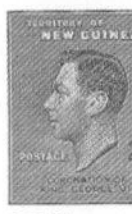

18 King George VI

1937. Coronation.

208	18	2d. red	50	1·50
209	18	3d. blue	50	1·75
210	18	5d. green	50	1·75
211	18	1s. purple	50	2·25

1939. Air. As T 16 but inscr "AIR MAIL POSTAGE".

212	½d. orange	3·75	7·00
213	1d. green	3·25	4·50
214	1½d. purple	4·00	15·00
215	2d. red	8·00	3·50
216	3d. blue	16·00	18·00
217	4d. olive	14·00	8·50
218	5d. green	13·00	4·00
219	6d. brown	38·00	26·00
220	9d. violet	38·00	35·00
221	1s. green	38·00	27·00
222	2s. red	80·00	70·00
223	5s. brown	£170	£140
224	10s. pink	£500	£375
225	£1 olive	£120	£130

OFFICIAL STAMPS

1915. Nos. 16 and 17 optd O. S.

O1	N	1d on 3pf. brown	29·00	75·00
O2	N	1d. on 3pf. green	90·00	£140

1925. Optd O S.

O22	12	1d. green	2·75	4·50
O23	12	1½d. red	5·50	17·00
O24	12	2d. red	2·50	3·75
O25	12	3d. blue	6·00	10·00
O26	12	4d. olive	4·50	8·50
O27a	12	6d. brown	7·00	35·00
O28	12	9d. purple	4·00	35·00
O29	12	1s. green	5·50	35·00
O30	12	2s. lake	32·00	65·00

1931. Optd O S.

O31	14	1d. green	11·00	13·00
O32	14	1½d. red	11·00	12·00
O33	14	2d. red	11·00	7·00
O34	14	3d. blue	7·00	6·00
O35	14	4d. olive	7·50	8·50
O36	14	5d. green	10·00	12·00
O37	14	6d. brown	14·00	17·00
O38	14	9d. violet	16·00	28·00
O39	14	1s. grey	16·00	28·00
O40	14	2s. lake	40·00	70·00
O41	14	5s. brown	£110	£180

1932. T 14, but without dates, optd O S.

O42	1d. green	15·00	16·00
O43	1½d. red	16·00	16·00
O44	2d. red	16·00	3·25
O45	2½d. green	7·00	8·50
O46	3d. blue	11·00	38·00
O47	3½d. red	7·00	9·00
O48	4d. olive	16·00	27·00
O49	5d. green	9·00	27·00
O50	6d. brown	21·00	55·00
O51	9d. violet	15·00	42·00
O52	1s. grey	15·00	29·00
O53	2s. lake	30·00	75·00
O54	5s. brown	£120	£180

For later issues see **PAPUA NEW GUINEA**.

Pt. 1

NEW HEBRIDES

A group of islands in the Pacific Ocean, E. of Australia, under joint administration of Gt. Britain and France. The Condominium ended in 1980, when the New Hebrides became independent as the Republic of Vanuatu.

1908. 12 pence = 1 shilling; 20 shillings = 1 pound.
1938. 100 gold centimes = 1 gold franc.
1977. 100 centimes = 1 New Hebrides franc.

BRITISH ADMINISTRATION

1908. Stamps of Fiji optd. (a) NEW HEBRIDES. CONDOMINIUM. (with full points).

1a	23	½d. green	40	7·00
2	23	1d. red	50	40
5	23	2d. purple and orange	60	70
6	23	2½d. purple and blue on blue	60	70
7	23	5d. purple and green	80	2·00
8	23	6d. purple and red	70	1·25
3	23	1s. green and red	24·00	3·75

(b) NEW HEBRIDES CONDOMINIUM (without full points).

10	23	½d. green	3·50	28·00
11	23	1d. red	11·00	8·50
12	23	2d. grey	70	3·00
13	23	2½d. blue	75	4·75
14	23	5d. purple and green	2·25	5·50
15	23	6d. purple and deep purple	1·50	6·00
16	23	1s. black and green	1·50	7·50

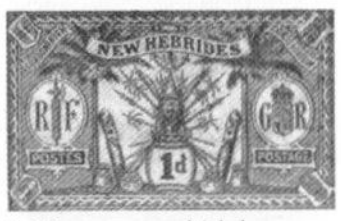

3 Weapons and Idols

1911

18	3	½d. green	85	1·75
19	3	1d. red	5·00	2·00
20	3	2d. grey	9·00	3·00
21	3	2½d. blue	4·25	5·50
24	3	5d. green	4·50	7·00
25	3	6d. purple	3·00	5·00
26	3	1s. black on green	2·75	13·00
27	3	2s. purple on blue	38·00	22·00
28	3	5s. green on yellow	45·00	55·00

1920. Surch. (a) On T 3.

40	3	1d. on ½d. green	4·00	24·00
30	3	1d. on 5d. green	8·50	60·00
31	3	1d. on 1s. black on green	3·25	13·00
32	3	1d. on 2s. purple on blue	1·00	10·00
33	3	1d. on 5s. green on yellow	1·00	10·00
41	3	3d. on 1d. red	4·00	11·00
42	3	5d. on 2½d. blue	7·50	26·00

(b) On No. F16 of French New Hebrides.

34	34	2d. on 40c. red on yellow	1·00	22·00

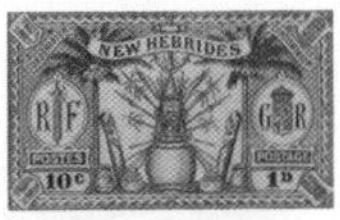

5

1925

43	5	½d. (5c.) black	1·25	19·00
44	5	1d. (10c.) green	1·00	17·00
45	5	2d. (20c.) grey	1·75	2·50
46	5	2½d. (25c.) brown	1·00	13·00
47	5	5d. (50c.) blue	3·00	2·75
48	5	6d. (60c.) purple	3·50	16·00
49	5	1s. (1f.25) black on green	3·25	19·00
50	5	2s. (2f.50) purple on blue	6·00	22·00
51	5	5s. (6f.25) green on yellow	6·00	25·00

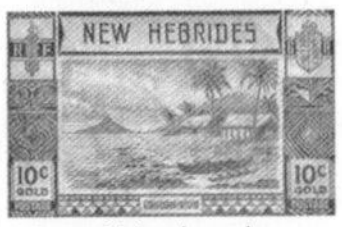

6 Lopevi Islands and Outrigger Canoe

1938

52	6	5c. green	2·50	4·50
53	6	10c. orange	2·00	2·25
54	6	15c. violet	3·50	4·50
55	6	20c. red	2·50	4·25
56	6	25c. brown	1·60	3·00
57	6	30c. blue	4·00	2·75
58	6	40c. olive	4·50	6·50
59	6	50c. purple	1·60	2·75
60	6	1f. red on green	6·00	9·00
61	6	2f. blue on green	30·00	23·00
62	6	5f. red on yellow	75·00	55·00
63	6	10f. violet on blue	£225	80·00

1949. U.P.U. As T 4d/g of Pitcairn Islands.

64	10c. orange	30	1·00
65	15c. violet	30	1·00
66	30c. blue	30	1·00
67	50c. purple	40	1·00

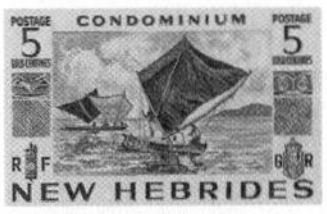

7 Outrigger Sailing Canoes

1953

68	7	5c. green	1·00	1·00
69	7	10c. red	1·00	35
70	7	15c. yellow	1·00	20
71	7	20c. blue	1·00	20
72	-	25c. olive	60	20
73	-	30c. brown	60	20
74	-	40c. sepia	60	20
75	-	50c. violet	1·00	20
76	-	1f. orange	6·00	2·00
77	-	2f. purple	6·00	8·50
78	-	5f. red	8·00	22·00

DESIGNS: 25c. to 50c. Native carving; 1f. to 5f. Two natives outside hut.

1953. Coronation. As T 8a of Pitcairn Islands.

79	10c. black and red	75	50

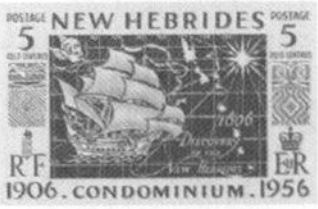

10 "San Pedro y San Paulo" (Quiros) and Map

1956. 50th Anniv of Condominium. Inscr "1906 1956".

80	10	5c. green	15	10
81	10	10c. red	15	10
82	-	20c. blue	10	10
83	-	50c. lilac	15	15

DESIGN: 20, 50c. "Marianne", "Talking Drum" and "Britannia".

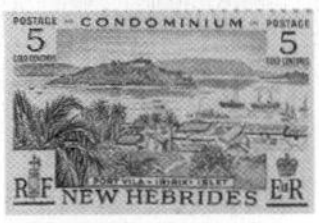

12 Port Villa; Iririki Islet

1957

84	12	5c. green	40	1·50
85	12	10c. red	30	10
86	12	15c. yellow	50	1·50
87	12	20c. blue	40	10
88	-	25c. olive	45	10
89	-	30c. brown	45	10
90	-	40c. sepia	45	10
91	-	50c. violet	45	10
92	-	1f. orange	1·00	1·00
93	-	2f. mauve	4·00	3·00
94	-	5f. black	9·00	4·75

DESIGNS: 25c. to 50c. River scene and spear fisherman; 1f. to 5f. Woman drinking from coconut.

1963. Freedom from Hunger. As T 20a of Pitcairn Islands.

95	60c. green	50	15

1963. Centenary of Red Cross. As T 20b of Pitcairn Islands, but with British and French cyphers in place of the Queen's portrait.

96	15c. red and black	30	10
97	45c. red and blue	45	20

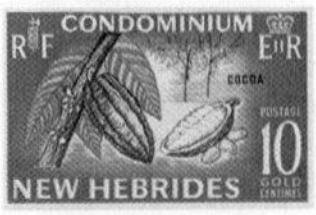

17 Cocoa Beans

1963

98	-	5c. red, brown and blue	2·00	50
99	17	10c. brown, buff and green	15	10
100	-	15c. bistre, brown and violet	15	10
101	-	20c. black, green and blue	55	10
102	-	25c. violet, brown and red	50	70
103	-	30c. brown, bistre and violet	75	10
104	-	40c. red and blue	80	1·40
105	-	50c. green, yellow and blue	60	10
129	-	60c. red and blue	40	15
106	-	1f. red, black and green	2·00	3·25

107	- 2f. black, purple and green	2·00	1·75
108	- 3f. multicoloured	6·00	4·50
109	- 5f. blue, deep blue and black	6·00	19·00

DESIGNS: 5 c Exporting manganese, Forari; 15c. Copra; 20c. Fishing from Palikulo Point; 25c. Picasso triggerfish; 30c. New Caledonian nautilus shell; 40, 60c. Lionfish; 50c. Clown surgeonfish; 1f. Cardinal honeyeater (bird); 2f. Buff-bellied flycatcher; 3f. Thicket warbler; 5f. White-collared kingfisher.

1965. Centenary of I.T.U. As T 24a of Pitcairn Islands, but with British and French cyphers in place of the Queen's portrait.

110	15c. red and drab	20	10
111	60c. blue and red	35	20

1965. I.C.Y. As T 24b of Pitcairn Islands, but with British and French cyphers in place of the Queen's portrait.

112	5c. purple and turquoise	15	10
113	55c. green and lavender	20	20

1966. Churchill Commemoration. As T 24c of Pitcairn Islands, but with British and French cyphers in place of the Queen's portrait.

114	5c. blue	20	15
115	15c. green	70	10
116	25c. brown	80	10
117	30c. violet	80	15

1966. World Cup Football Championship. As T 25 of Pitcairn Islands, but with British and French cyphers in place of the Queen's portrait.

118	20c. multicoloured	30	15
119	40c. multicoloured	70	15

1966. Inauguration of W.H.O. Headquarters, Geneva. As T 25a of Pitcairn Islands, but with British and French cyphers in place of the Queen's portrait.

120	25c. black, green and blue	15	10
121	60c. black, purple and ochre	40	20

1966. 20th Anniv of UNESCO. As T 25b/d of Pitcairn Islands, but with British and French cyphers in place of the Queen's portrait.

122	15c. multicoloured	25	10
123	30c. yellow, violet and olive	65	10
124	45c. black, purple and orange	75	15

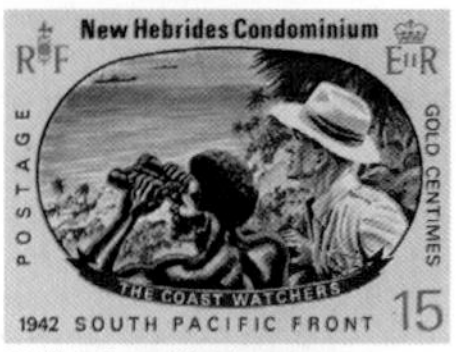

36 The Coast Watchers

1967. 25th Anniv of Pacific War. Multicoloured.

125	15c. Type **36**	30	10
126	25c. Map of war zone, U.S. marine and Australian soldier	60	20
127	60c. H.M.A.S. "Canberra" (cruiser)	65	30
128	1f. Boeing B-17 "Flying Fortress"	65	80

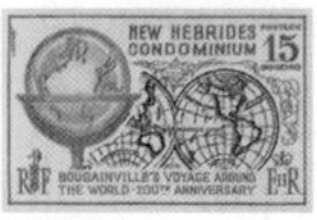

40 Globe and Hemispheres

1968. Bicent of Bougainville's World Voyage.

130	**40** 15c. green, violet and red	15	10
131	- 25c. olive, purple and blue	30	10
132	- 60c. brown, purple & green	35	10

DESIGNS: 25c. Ships "La Boudeuse" and "L'Etoile", and map; 60c. Bougainville, ship's figure-head and bougainvillea flowers.

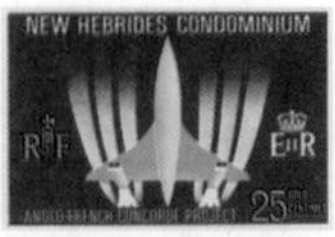

43 Concorde and Vapour Trails

1968. Anglo-French Concorde Project.

133	**43** 25c. blue, red and blue	35	30
134	- 60c. red, black and blue	40	45

DESIGN: 60c. Concorde in flight.

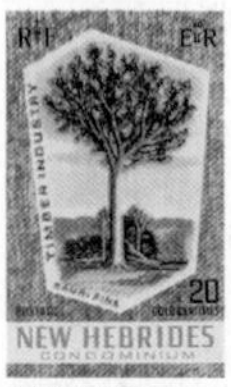

45 Kauri Pine

1969. Timber Industry.

135	**45** 20c. multicoloured	10	10

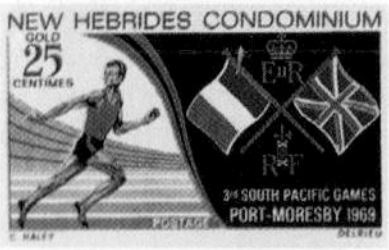

46 Cyphers, Flags and Relay Runner receiving Baton

1969. 3rd South Pacific Games, Port Moresby. Multicoloured.

136	25c. Type **46**	10	10
137	1f. Runner passing baton	20	20

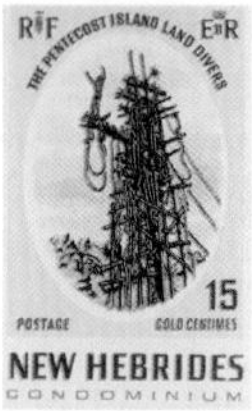

48 Diver on Platform

1969. Pentecost Island Land Divers. Mult.

138	15c. Type **48**	10	10
139	25c. Diver jumping	10	10
140	1f. Diver at end of fall	20	20

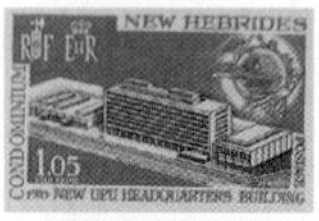

51 U.P.U. Emblem and Headquarters Building

1970. New U.P.U. Headquarters Building.

141	**51** 1f.05 slate, orange & purple	20	20

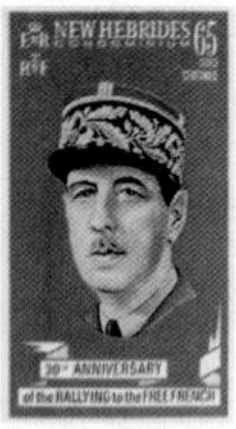

52 General Charles de Gaulle

1970. 30th Anniv of New Hebrides' Declaration for the Free French Government.

142	**52** 65c. multicoloured	35	70
143	**52** 1f.10 multicoloured	45	70

1970. No. 101 surch 35.

144	35c. on 20c. black, green and blue	30	30

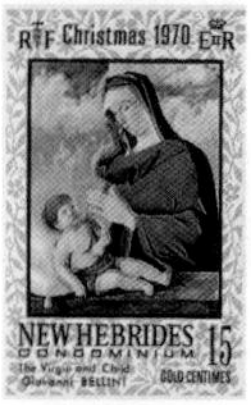

54 "The Virgin and Child" (Bellini)

1970. Christmas. Multicoloured.

145	15c. Type **54**	10	10
146	50c. "The Virgin and Child" (Cima)	20	20

1971. Death of General Charles de Gaulle. Nos. 142/3 optd 1890-1970 IN MEMORIAM 9-11-70.

147	65c. multicoloured	15	10
148	1f.10 multicoloured	15	20

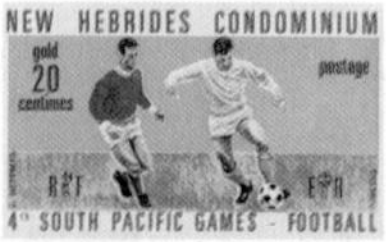

56 Football

1971. 4th South Pacific Games, Papeete, French Polynesia.

149	20c. Type **56**	10	10
150	65c. Basketball (vert)	30	20

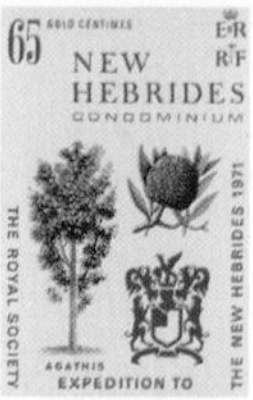

57 Kauri Pine, Cone and Arms of Royal Society

1971. Royal Society's Expedition to New Hebrides.

151	**57** 65c. multicoloured	20	15

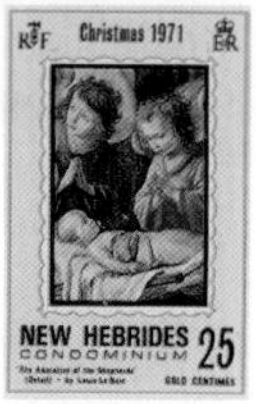

58 "The Adoration of the Shepherds" (detail, Louis le Nain)

1971. Christmas. Multicoloured.

152	25c. Type **58**	10	10
153	50c. "The Adoration of the Shepherds" (detail, Tintoretto)	30	90

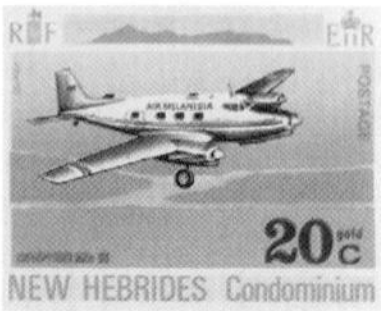

59 De Havilland Drover 3

1972. Aircraft. Multicoloured.

154	20c. Type **59**	30	15
155	25c. Short S25 Sandringham 4 flying boat	30	15
156	30c. De Havilland Dragon Rapide	30	15
157	65c. Sud Aviation SE 210 Caravelle	75	1·25

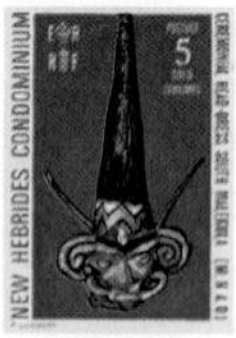

60 Ceremonial Headdress, South Malekula

1972. Multicoloured.

158	5c. Type **60**	10	20
159	10c. Baker's pigeon	30	20
160	15c. Gong and carving, North Ambrym	15	20
161	20c. Red-headed parrot finch	50	25
162	25c. Graskoin's cowrie (shell)	40	25
163	30c. Red-lip olive (shell)	50	30
164	35c. Chestnut-bellied kingfisher	80	40
165	65c. Pretty conch (shell)	75	60
166	1f. Gong (North Malekula) and carving (North Ambrym)	50	1·00
167	2f. Palm lorikeet	3·50	4·50
168	3f. Ceremonial headdress, South Malekula (different)	1·50	6·00
169	5f. Great green turban (shell)	4·00	13·00

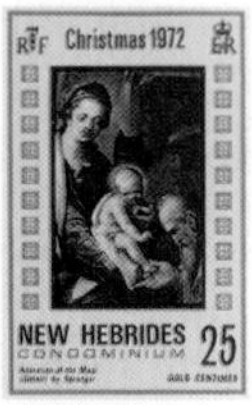

61 "Adoration of the Kings" (Spranger)

1972. Christmas. Multicoloured.

170	25c. Type **61**	10	10
171	70c. "The Virgin and Child in a Landscape" (Provoost)	20	20

1972. Royal Silver Wedding. As T 73 of Pitcairn Islands, but with Royal and French cyphers in background.

172	35c. violet	15	10
173	65c. green	20	10

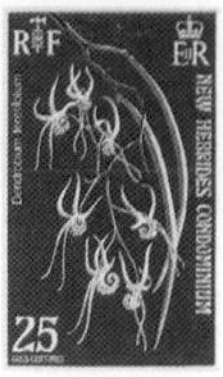

63 "Dendrobium teretifolium"

1973. Orchids. Multicoloured.

174	25c. Type **63**	25	10
175	30c. "Ephemerantha comata"	25	10
176	35c. "Spathoglottis petri"	30	10
177	65c. "Dendrobium mohlianum"	60	55

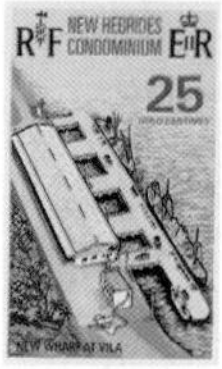

64 New Wharf at Vila

1973. Opening of New Wharf at Villa. Mult.

178	25c. Type **64**	20	10
179	70c. As Type **64** but horiz	40	30

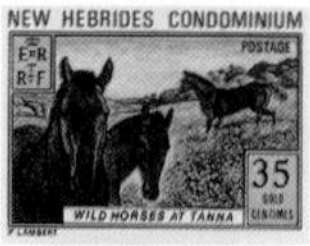

65 Wild Horses

1973. Tanna Island. Multicoloured.

180	35c. Type **65**	45	15
181	70c. Yasur Volcano	55	20

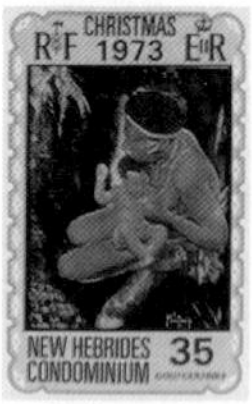

66 Mother and Child

1973. Christmas. Multicoloured.

182	35c. Type **66**	10	10
183	70c. Lagoon scene	20	20

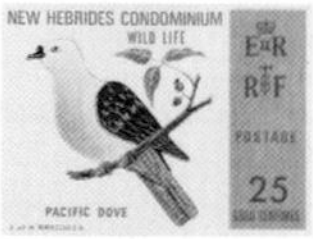

67 Pacific Pigeon

1974. Wild Life. Multicoloured.

184	25c. Type **67**	60	25
185	35c. "Lyssa curvata" (moth)	60	60
186	70c. Green sea turtle	60	70
187	1f.15 Grey-headed flying fox	80	1·50

1974. Royal Visit. Nos. 164 and 167 optd ROYAL VISIT 1974.

188	35c. multicoloured	40	10
189	2f. multicoloured	60	40

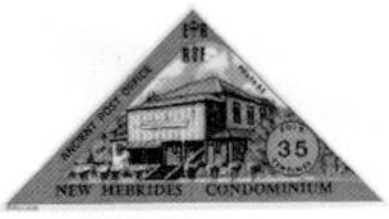

69 Old Post Office

1974. Inaug of New Post Office, Vila. Mult.

190	35c. Type **69**	15	50
191	70c. New Post Office	15	60

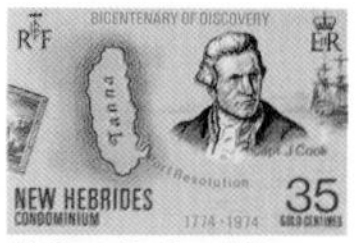

70 Capt. Cook and Map

1974. Bicent of Discovery. Multicoloured.

192	35c. Type **70**	1·25	2·00
193	35c. William Wales and beach landing	1·25	2·00
194	35c. William Hodges and island scene	1·25	2·00

195	1f.15 Capt. Cook, map and H.M.S. "Resolution" (59×34 mm)	2·50	3·50

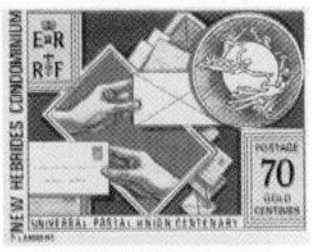

71 U.P.U. Emblem and Letters

1974. Centenary of U.P.U.

196	**71**	70c. multicoloured	30	70

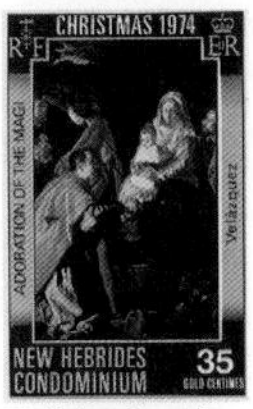

72 "Adoration of the Magi" (Velazquez)

1974. Christmas. Multicoloured.

197	35c. Type **72**	10	10
198	70c. "The Nativity" (Gerard van Honthorst)	20	20

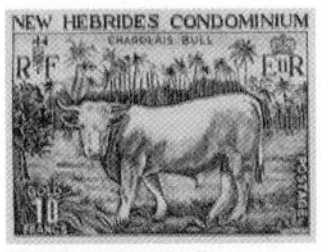

73 Charolais Bull

1975

199	**73**	10f. brown, green and blue	7·00	18·00

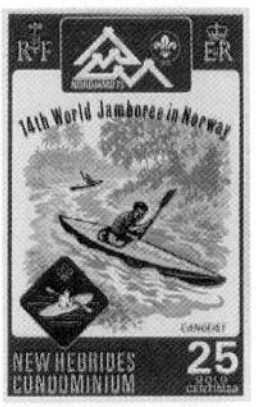

74 Canoeing

1975. World Scout Jamboree, Norway. Mult.

200	25c. Type **74**	15	10
201	35c. Preparing meal	15	10
202	1f. Map-reading	35	15
203	5f. Fishing	1·25	2·50

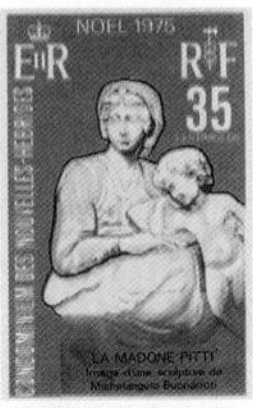

75 "Pitti Madonna" (Michelangelo)

1975. Christmas. Michelangelo's Sculptures. Mult.

204	35c. Type **75**	10	10
205	70c. "Bruges Madonna"	15	10
206	2f.50 "Taddei Madonna"	70	50

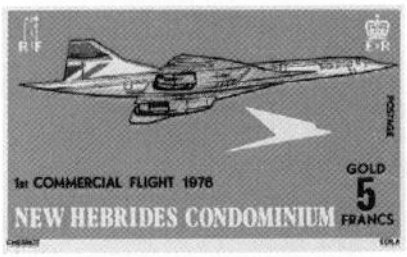

76 Concorde in British Airways Livery

1976. 1st Commercial Flight of Concorde.

207	**76**	5f. multicoloured	4·00	5·00

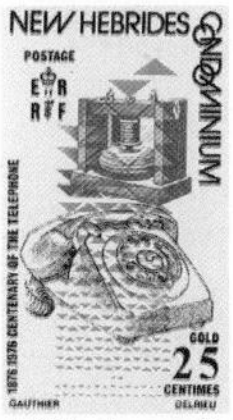

77 Telephones of 1876 and 1976

1976. Centenary of Telephone. Multicoloured.

208	25c. Type **77**	15	10
209	70c. Alexander Graham Bell	30	10
210	1f.15 Satellite and Noumea Earth Station	50	50

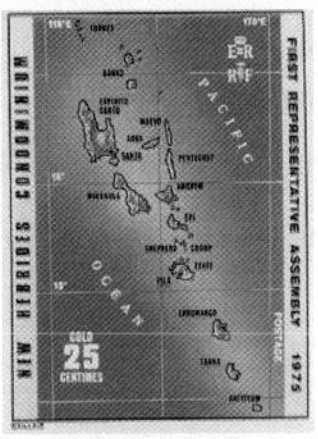

78 Map of the Islands

1976. Constitutional Changes. Multicoloured.

211	25c. Type **78**	40	15
212	1f. View of Santo (horiz)	75	60
213	2f. View of Vila (horiz)	1·10	2·25

Nos. 212/13 are smaller, 36×26 mm.

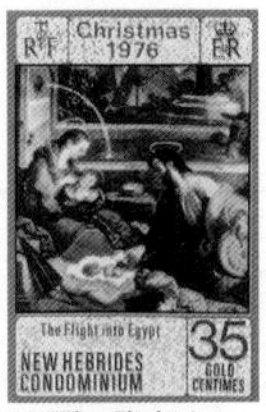

79 "The Flight into Egypt" (Lusitano)

1976. Christmas. Multicoloured.

214	35c. Type **79**	10	10
215	70c. "Adoration of the Shepherds"	15	10
216	2f.50 "Adoration of the Magi"	45	50

Nos. 215/16 show retables by the Master of Santos-o-Novo.

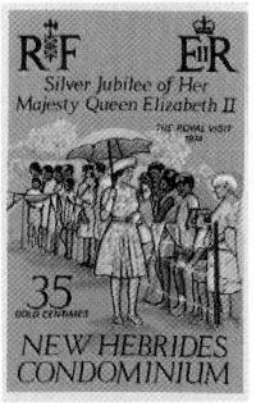

80 Royal Visit, 1974

1977. Silver Jubilee. Multicoloured.

217	35c. Type **80**	10	10
218	70c. Imperial State Crown	15	10
219	2f. The Blessing	30	65

1977. Currency change. Nos. 158/69 and 199 surch.

233	5f. on 5c. Type **60**	50	15
234	10f. on 10c. Baker's pigeon	70	15
222	15f. on 15c. Gong and carving	60	1·50
223	20f. on 20c. Red-headed parrot finch	1·25	55
224	25f. on 25c. Gaskoin's cowrie (shell)	1·75	2·00
225	30f. on 30c. Red-lip olive (shell)	1·75	1·10
226	35f. on 35c. Chestnut-bellied kingfisher	1·75	1·25
239	40f. on 65c. Pretty conch (shell)	1·50	55
228	50f. on 1f. Gong and carving	1·00	1·75
229	70f. on 2f. Palm lorikeet	6·50	75
230	100f. on 3f. Ceremonial head-dress	1·00	3·75
231	200f. on 5f. Great green turban (shell)	5·00	14·00
241	500f. on 10f. Type **73**	19·00	14·00

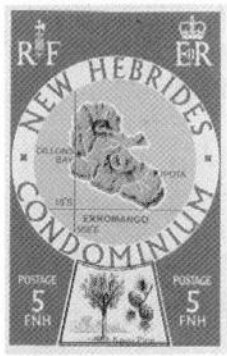

89 Island of Erromango and Kauri Pine

1977. Islands. Multicoloured.

242	5f. Type **89**	30	10
243	10f. Territory map and copra-making	40	30
244	15f. Espiritu Santo and cattle	30	30
245	20f. Efate and Vila P.O.	30	25
246	25f. Malekula and headdresses	40	40
247	30f. Aobe, Maewo and pigs' tusks	45	50
248	35f. Pentecost and land diver	50	65
249	40f. Tanna and John Frum Cross	70	60
250	50f. Shepherd Is. and canoe	1·50	40
251	70f. Banks Is. and dancers	1·75	3·50
252	100f. Ambrym and idols	1·75	90
253	200f. Aneityum and baskets	1·75	2·50
254	500f. Torres Is. and archer fisherman	3·50	7·50

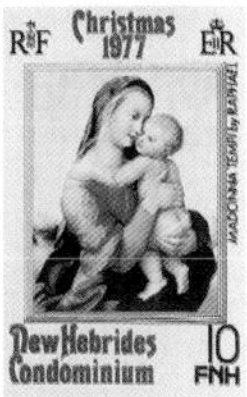

90 "Tempi Madonna" (Raphael)

1977. Christmas. Multicoloured.

255	10f. Type **90**	20	45
256	15f. "The Flight into Egypt" (Gerard David)	30	60
257	30f. "Virgin and Child" (Batoni)	40	90

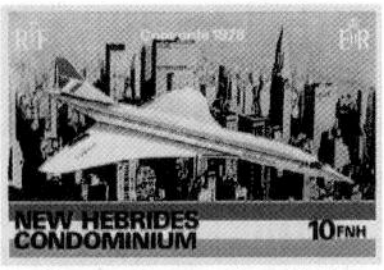

91 Concorde over New York

1978. Concorde Commemoration.

258	10f. Type **91**	1·00	75
259	20f. Concorde over London	1·00	1·00
260	30f. Concorde over Washington	1·25	1·40
261	40f. Concorde over Paris	1·50	1·60

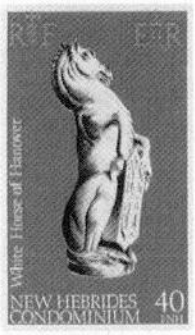

92 White Horse of Hanover

1978. 25th Anniv of Coronation.

262	**92**	40f. brown, blue and silver	15	30
263	-	40f. multicoloured	15	30
264	-	40f. brown, blue and silver	15	30

DESIGNS: No. 263, Queen Elizabeth II; 264, Gallic Cock.

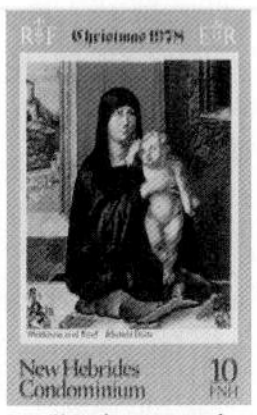

93 "Madonna and Child"

1978. Christmas. Paintings by Durer. Mult.

265	10f. Type **93**	10	10
266	15f. "The Virgin and Child with St. Anne"	10	10
267	30f. "Madonna of the Siskin"	15	10
268	40f. "Madonna of the Pear"	20	15

1979. 1st Anniv of Internal Self-Government. Surch 166°E 11.1.79 FIRST ANNIVERSARY INTERNAL SELF-GOVERNMENT and new value.

269	**78**	10f. on 25f. multi-coloured (blue background)	10	10
270	**78**	40f. on 25f. multi-coloured (green background)	20	20

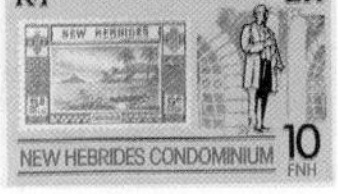

95 1938 5c. Stamp and Sir Rowland Hill

1979. Death Centenary of Sir Rowland Hill. Mult.

271	10f. Type **95**	10	10
272	20f. 1969 25c. Pentecost Island Land Divers commemorative	20	10
273	40f. 1925 2d. (20c.)	25	20
MS274	143×94 mm. Nos. 272 and F286	75	90

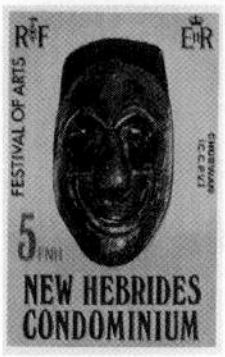

96 Chubwan Mask

1979. Arts Festival. Multicoloured.

275	5f. Type **96**	10	10
276	10f. Nal-Nal clubs and spears	10	10
277	20f. Ritual puppet	15	10
278	40f. Neqatmalow headdress	25	15

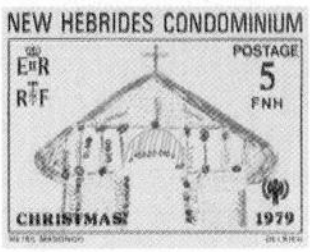

97 "Native Church" (Metas Masongo)

1979. Christmas and International Year of the Child. Children's Drawings. Multicoloured.

279	5f. Type **97**	10	10
280	10f. "Priest and Candles" (Herve Rutu)	10	10
281	20f. "Cross and Bible" (Mark Deards) (vert)	10	10
282	40f. "Green Candle and Santa Claus" (Dev Raj) (vert)	15	15

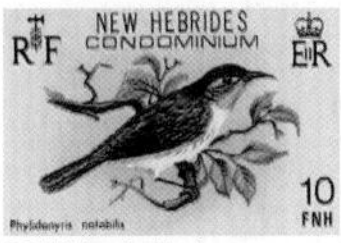

98 White-bellied Honeyeater

1980. Birds. Multicoloured.

283	10f. Type **98**	50	10
284	20f. Scarlet robin	70	10
285	30f. Yellow-fronted white-eye	90	45
286	40f. Fan-tailed cuckoo	1·00	70

POSTAGE DUE STAMPS

1925. Optd POSTAGE DUE.

D1	**5**	1d. (10c.) green	30·00	1·00
D2	**5**	2d. (20c.) grey	32·00	1·25
D3	**5**	3d. (30c.) red	32·00	2·75
D4	**5**	5d. (50c.) blue	35·00	4·75
D5	**5**	10d. (1c.) red on blue	40·00	6·00

1938. Optd POSTAGE DUE.

D6	**6**	5c. green	28·00	50·00
D7	**6**	10c. orange	28·00	50·00
D8	**6**	20c. red	35·00	75·00
D9	**6**	40c. olive	42·00	85·00
D10	**6**	1f. red on green	45·00	90·00

1953. Nos. 68/9, 71, 74 and 76 optd POSTAGE DUE.

D11	**7**	5c. green	5·00	19·00
D12	**7**	10c. red	1·75	16·00
D13	**7**	20c. blue	5·00	25·00
D14	-	40c. sepia (No. 74)	15·00	45·00
D15	-	1f. orange (No. 76)	4·50	45·00

1957. Optd POSTAGE DUE.

D16	**12**	5c. green	30	1·50
D17	**12**	10c. red	30	1·50
D18	**12**	20c. blue	75	1·75
D19	-	40c. sepia (No. 90)	1·00	2·50
D20	-	1f. orange (No. 92)	1·25	3·25

FRENCH ADMINISTRATION

1908. Stamps of New Caledonia optd NOUVELLES HEBRIDES.

F1	**15**	5c. green	8·50	4·75
F2	**15**	10c. red	9·00	3·50
F3	**16**	25c. blue on green	9·00	2·25
F4	**16**	50c. red on green	8·50	4·75
F5	**17**	1f. blue on green	21·00	20·00

1910. Nos. F1/5 further optd CONDOMINIUM.

F6	**15**	5c. green	5·50	3·00
F7	**15**	10c. red	5·50	1·25
F8	**16**	25c. blue on green	2·50	3·75
F9	**16**	50c. red on orange	8·00	16·00
F10	**17**	1f. blue on green	23·00	22·00

The following issues are as stamps of British Administration but are inscr "NOUVELLES HEBRIDES" except where otherwise stated.

1911

F11	**3**	5c. green	1·00	2·75
F12	**3**	10c. red	50	1·00
F13	**3**	20c. grey	1·00	2·25
F25	**3**	25c. blue	1·25	7·00
F15	**3**	30c. brown on yellow	6·50	5·25

F16	3	40c. red on yellow	1·40	5·50
F17	3	50c. olive	2·00	6·00
F18	3	75c. orange	7·00	27·00
F19	3	1f. red on blue	4·00	4·25
F20	3	2f. violet	11·00	22·00
F21	3	5f. red on green	12·00	42·00

1920. Surch in figures.

F34	5c. on 40c. red on yellow (No. F16)	27·00	£100
F32a	5c. on 50c. red on orange (No. F4)	£550	£600
F33	5c. on 50c. red on orange (No. F9)	2·40	18·00
F38	10c. on 5c. green (No. F11)	1·00	9·00
F33a	10c. on 25c. blue on green (No. F8)	50	1·50
F35	20c. on 30c. brown on yellow (No. F26)	15·00	70·00
F39	30c. on 10c. red (No. F12)	1·00	2·50
F41	50c. on 25c. blue (No. F25)	2·50	28·00

1921. Stamp of New Hebrides (British) surch 10c.

F37	10c. on 5d. green (No. 24)	14·00	60·00

1925

F42	5	5c. (½d.) black	75	11·00
F43	5	10c. (1d.) green	1·00	9·00
F44	5	20c. (2d.) grey	2·50	2·75
F45	5	25c. (2½d.) brown	1·50	9·00
F46	5	30c. (3d.) red	1·50	15·00
F47	5	40c. (4d.) red on yellow	1·75	15·00
F48	5	50c. (5d.) blue	1·50	1·75
F49	5	75c. (7½d.) brown	1·50	19·00
F50	5	1f. (10d.) red on blue	1·50	2·50
F51	5	2f. (1s.8d.) violet	2·50	32·00
F52	5	5f. (4d.) red on green	3·50	32·00

1938

F53	6	5c. green	4·00	9·50
F54	6	10c. orange	4·00	3·25
F55	6	15c. violet	4·00	7·00
F56	6	20c. red	4·00	5·50
F57	6	25c. brown	8·50	7·50
F58	6	30c. blue	8·50	7·50
F59	6	40c. olive	4·00	14·00
F60	6	50c. purple	4·00	4·75
F61	6	1f. red on green	4·50	8·50
F62	6	2f. blue on green	42·00	45·00
F63	6	5f. red on yellow	60·00	70·00
F64	6	10f. violet and blue	£140	£150

1941. Free French Issue. As last, optd France Libre.

F65	6	5c. green	2·00	25·00
F66	6	10c. orange	5·00	24·00
F67	6	15c. violet	9·00	40·00
F68	6	20c. red	23·00	32·00
F69	6	25c. brown	26·00	42·00
F70	6	30c. blue	26·00	38·00
F71	6	40c. olive	26·00	40·00
F72	6	50c. purple	23·00	38·00
F73	6	1f. red on green	24·00	38·00
F74	6	2f. blue on green	23·00	38·00
F75	6	5f. red on yellow	19·00	38·00
F76	6	10f. violet on blue	18·00	38·00

1949. 75th Anniv of U.P.U.

F77	10c. orange	3·50	7·50
F78	15c. violet	4·75	12·00
F79	30c. blue	7·50	16·00
F80	50c. purple	8·50	19·00

1953

F81	7	5c. green	3·25	5·50
F82	7	10c. red	5·00	5·50
F83	7	15c. yellow	5·00	5·50
F84	7	20c. blue	5·00	4·50
F85	-	25c. olive	2·00	4·50
F86	-	30c. brown	1·50	4·75
F87	-	40c. sepia	1·75	4·75
F88	-	50c. violet	1·75	4·25
F89	-	1f. orange	12·00	11·00
F90	-	2f. purple	18·00	50·00
F91	-	5f. red	18·00	85·00

1956. 50th Anniv of Condominium.

F92	10	5c. green	1·50	2·25
F93	10	10c. red	1·50	2·25
F94	-	20c. blue	1·50	2·75
F95	-	50c. violet	1·50	2·75

1957

F96	12	5c. green	1·75	2·75
F97	12	10c. red	2·25	2·75
F98	12	15c. yellow	2·50	3·50
F99	12	20c. blue	2·25	2·75
F100	-	25c. olive	2·00	2·50
F101	-	30c. brown	2·00	1·75
F102	-	40c. sepia	2·25	1·25
F103	-	50c. violet	2·50	1·60
F104	-	1f. orange	8·00	4·00
F105	-	2f. mauve	12·00	21·00
F106	-	5f. black	30·00	48·00

1963. Freedom from Hunger. As T 51 of New Caledonia.

F107	60c. green and brown	18·00	18·00

1963. Centenary of Red Cross. As T 53 of New Caledonia.

F108	15c. red, grey and orange	11·00	11·00
F109	45c. red, grey and bistre	14·00	29·00

1963

F110	-	5c. lake, brown and blue	55	1·75
F111	-	10c. brown, buff and green*	2·00	3·50
F112	-	10c. brown, buff and green	1·00	2·00
F113	18	15c. bistre, brown and violet	6·00	1·25
F114	-	20c. black, green and blue*	2·25	5·00
F115	-	20c. black, green and blue	1·50	2·25
F116	-	25c. violet, brown and red	70	1·75
F117	-	30c. brown, bistre and violet	7·50	1·25
F118	-	40c. red and blue	3·25	8·50
F119	-	50c. green, yellow and turquoise	8·50	2·25
F120	-	60c. red and blue	1·75	2·25
F121	-	1f. red, black and green	2·00	5·00
F122	-	2f. black, brown and olive	17·00	9·00
F123	-	3f. multicoloured*	8·50	26·00
F124	-	3f. multicoloured	8·50	15·00
F125	-	5f. blue, indigo and black	28·00	29·00

The stamps indicated by an asterisk have "RF" wrongly placed on the left.

1965. Centenary of I.T.U. As T 56 of New Caledonia.

F126	15c. blue, green and brown	10·00	9·00
F127	60c. red, grey and green	28·00	35·00

1965. I.C.Y. As Nos. 112/13.

F128	5c. purple and turquoise	3·00	6·00
F129	55c. green and lavender	10·00	12·00

1966. Churchill Commem. As Nos. 114/17.

F130	5c. multicoloured	2·10	8·00
F131	15c. multicoloured	3·00	3·00
F132	25c. multicoloured	3·50	9·00
F133	30c. multicoloured	4·25	10·00

1966. World Cup Football Championship. As Nos. 118/19.

F134	20c. multicoloured	2·75	5·50
F135	40c. multicoloured	4·75	5·50

1966. Inauguration of W.H.O. Headquarters, Geneva. As Nos. 120/1.

F136	25c. black, green and blue	3·75	4·25
F137	60c. black, mauve and ochre	5·50	8·50

1966. 20th Anniv of UNESCO. As Nos. 122/4.

F138	15c. multicoloured	2·50	3·25
F139	30c. yellow, violet and olive	3·50	4·75
F140	45c. black, purple and orange	4·00	6·50

1967. 25th Anniv of Pacific War. As Nos. 125/8.

F141	15c. multicoloured	1·40	1·50
F142	25c. multicoloured	2·00	3·00
F143	60c. multicoloured	2·00	2·50
F144	1f. multicoloured	2·25	2·75

1968. Bicentenary of Bougainville's World Voyage. As Nos. 130/2.

F145	15c. green, violet and red	55	1·10
F146	25c. olive, purple and blue	65	1·25
F147	60c. brown, purple and green	1·10	1·50

1968. Anglo-French Concorde Project. As Nos. 133/4.

F148	25c. blue, red and violet	1·90	2·40
F149	60c. red, black and blue	2·25	4·25

1969. Timber Industry. As No. 135.

F150	20c. multicoloured	45	1·00

1969. 3rd South Pacific Games, Port Moresby, Papua New Guinea. As Nos. 136/7.

F151	25c. multicoloured	50	1·40
F152	1f. multicoloured	1·50	2·00

1969. Land Divers of Pentecost Island. As Nos. 138/40.

F153	15c. multicoloured	55	1·25
F154	25c. multicoloured	45	1·25
F155	1f. multicoloured	1·10	2·00

1970. Inauguration of New U.P.U. Headquarters Building, Berne. As No. 141.

F156	1f.05 slate, orange & purple	1·00	2·75

1970. New Hebrides' Declaration for the Free French Government. As Nos. 142/3.

F157	65c. multicoloured	2·75	2·00
F158	1f.10 multicoloured	3·00	2·25

1970. No. F115 surch 35.

F159	35c. on 20c. black, green and blue	65	1·75

1970. Christmas. As Nos. 145/6.

F160	15c. multicoloured	25	1·00
F161	50c. multicoloured	45	1·25

1971. Death of General Charles de Gaulle. Nos. F157/8 optd 1890-1970 IN MEMORIAM 9-11-70.

F162	65c. multicoloured	1·00	1·50
F163	1f.10 multicoloured	1·50	2·00

1971. 4th South Pacific Games, Papeete, French Polynesia. As Nos. 149/50.

F164	20c. multicoloured	75	1·00
F165	65c. multicoloured	1·00	1·50

1971. Royal Society Expedition to New Hebrides. As No. 151.

F166	65c. multicoloured	1·00	1·50

1971. Christmas. As Nos. 152/3.

F167	25c. multicoloured	50	75
F168	50c. multicoloured	60	1·25

1972. Aircraft. As Nos. 154/7.

F169	20c. multicoloured	1·00	1·60
F170	25c. multicoloured	1·00	1·60
F171	30c. multicoloured	1·10	1·60
F172	65c. multicoloured	2·75	5·00

1972. As Nos. 158/69.

F173	5c. multicoloured	85	1·40
F174	10c. multicoloured	1·90	1·75
F175	15c. multicoloured	90	1·25
F176	20c. multicoloured	2·50	1·50
F177	25c. multicoloured	1·90	1·60
F178	30c. multicoloured	1·90	1·50
F179	35c. multicoloured	3·00	1·50
F180	65c. multicoloured	2·40	2·00
F181	1f. multicoloured	1·75	2·75
F182	2f. multicoloured	15·00	14·00
F183	3f. multicoloured	5·50	16·00
F184	5f. multicoloured	8·50	25·00

1972. Christmas. As Nos. 170/1.

F185	25c. multicoloured	45	1·00
F186	70c. multicoloured	65	1·50

1972. Royal Silver Wedding. As Nos. 172/3.

F187	35c. multicoloured	50	50
F188	65c. multicoloured	60	1·25

1973. Orchids. As Nos. 174/7.

F189	25c. multicoloured	2·75	1·40
F190	30c. multicoloured	2·75	1·60
F191	35c. multicoloured	2·75	1·60
F192	65c. multicoloured	4·75	5·00

1973. Opening of New Wharf at Vila. As Nos. 178/9.

F193	25c. multicoloured	80	1·10
F194	70c. multicoloured	1·10	2·25

1973. Tanna Island. As Nos. 180/1.

F195	35c. multicoloured	2·25	2·25
F196	70c. multicoloured	3·25	3·25

1973. Christmas. As Nos. 182/3.

F197	35c. multicoloured	50	1·00
F198	70c. multicoloured	75	2·75

1974. Wild Life. As Nos. 184/7.

F199	25c. multicoloured	4·50	3·25
F200	35c. multicoloured	5·75	2·40
F201	70c. multicoloured	6·00	4·75
F202	1f.15 multicoloured	7·50	11·00

1974. Royal Visit of Queen Elizabeth II. Nos. F179 and F182 optd VISITE ROYALE 1974.

F203	35c. Chestnut-bellied kingfisher	3·00	90
F204	2f. Green palm lorikeet	6·50	8·25

1974. Inauguration of New Post Office, Vila. As Nos. 190/1.

F205	35c. multicoloured	1·00	2·00
F206	70c. multicoloured	1·00	2·00

1974. Bicent of Discovery. As Nos. 192/5.

F207	35c. multicoloured	4·50	5·75
F208	35c. multicoloured	4·50	5·75
F209	35c. multicoloured	4·50	5·75
F210	1f.15 multicoloured	9·00	12·00

1974. Centenary of U.P.U. As No. 196.

F210a	70c. blue, red and black	1·75	3·00

1974. Christmas. As Nos. 197/8.

F211	35c. multicoloured	40	75
F212	70f. multicoloured	60	1·25

1975. Charolais Bull. As No. 199.

F213	10f. brown, green and blue	20·00	40·00

1975. World Scout Jamboree, Norway. As Nos. 200/3.

F214	25c. multicoloured	70	50
F215	35c. multicoloured	75	60
F216	1f. multicoloured	1·25	1·25
F217	5f. multicoloured	5·00	10·00

1975. Christmas. As Nos. 204/6.

F218	35c. multicoloured	35	50
F219	70c. multicoloured	55	90
F220	2f.50 multicoloured	1·90	3·00

1976. 1st Commercial Flight of Concorde. As No. 207, but Concorde in Air France livery.

F221	5f. multicoloured	9·00	9·00

1976. Centenary of Telephone. As Nos. 208/10.

F222	25c. multicoloured	60	50
F223	70c. multicoloured	1·50	1·50
F224	1f.15 multicoloured	1·75	2·75

1976. Constitutional Changes. As Nos. 211/13.

F225	25c. multicoloured	60	50
F226	1f. multicoloured	1·50	1·25
F227	2f. multicoloured	2·50	2·75

1976. Christmas. Paintings. As Nos. 214/16.

F228	35c. multicoloured	30	30
F229	70c. multicoloured	50	50
F230	2f.50 multicoloured	1·75	3·00

1977. Silver Jubilee. As Nos. F217/9.

F231	35c. multicoloured	30	20
F232	70c. multicoloured	55	35
F233	2f. multicoloured	55	65

1977. Currency change. Nos. F173/84 and F213, surch.

F234	5f. on 5c. multicoloured	1·50	1·50
F235	10f. on 10c. multicoloured	2·50	1·25
F236	15f. on 15c. multicoloured	1·25	1·25
F237	20f. on 20c. multicoloured	3·00	1·50
F238	25f. on 25c. multicoloured	2·50	1·75
F239	30f. on 30c. multicoloured	2·50	2·25
F240	35f. on 35c. multicoloured	4·25	2·25
F241	40f. on 65c. multicoloured	3·25	3·00
F242	50f. on 1f. multicoloured	2·00	3·00
F243	70f. on 2f. multicoloured	7·50	4·00
F244	100f. on 3f. multicoloured	2·75	6·00
F245	200f. on 5f. multicoloured	9·00	25·00
F246	500f. on 10f. multicoloured	16·00	45·00

1977. Islands. As Nos. 242/54.

F256	5f. multicoloured	1·50	1·75
F257	10f. multicoloured	1·50	1·75
F258	15f. multicoloured	2·00	1·75
F259	20f. multicoloured	2·00	1·75
F260	25f. multicoloured	2·00	1·75
F261	30f. multicoloured	2·00	1·75
F262	35f. multicoloured	2·75	1·75
F263	40f. multicoloured	1·50	2·25
F264	50f. multicoloured	2·75	2·25
F265	70f. multicoloured	5·00	4·50
F266	100f. multicoloured	2·75	3·25
F267	200f. multicoloured	3·75	9·00
F268	500f. multicoloured	6·50	17·00

1977. Christmas. As Nos. 255/7.

F269	10f. multicoloured	30	30
F270	15f. multicoloured	50	50
F271	30f. multicoloured	80	1·40

1978. Concorde. As Nos. 258/61.

F272	10f. multicoloured	2·50	1·50
F273	20f. multicoloured	2·75	1·75
F274	30f. multicoloured	3·25	2·25
F275	40f. multicoloured	3·75	3·50

1978. Coronation. As Nos. 262/4.

F276	40f. brown, blue and silver	25	70
F277	40f. multicoloured	25	70
F278	40f. brown, blue and silver	25	70

1978. Christmas. As Nos. 265/8.

F279	10f. multicoloured	20	30
F280	15f. multicoloured	25	35
F281	30f. multicoloured	30	70
F282	40f. multicoloured	35	85

1979. Internal Self-Government. As T 37 surch 166°E PREMIER GOUVERNEMENT AUTONOME 11.1.78. 11.1.79 and new value.

F283	10f. on 25f. multicoloured (blue background)	90	1·00
F284	40f. on 25f. multicoloured (green background)	1·60	1·75

1979. Death Centenary of Sir Rowland Hill. As Nos. 271/3.

F285	10f. multicoloured	35	50
F286	20f. multicoloured	35	60
F287	40f. multicoloured	40	1·00

1979. Arts Festival. As Nos. 275/8.

F288	5f. multicoloured	30	60
F289	10f. multicoloured	30	60
F290	20f. multicoloured	40	80
F291	40f. multicoloured	60	1·25

1979. Christmas and International Year of the Child. As Nos. 279/82.

F292	5f. multicoloured	85	60
F293	10f. multicoloured	1·00	60
F294	20f. multicoloured	1·10	80
F295	40f. multicoloured	1·90	2·00

1980. Birds. As Nos. 283/6.

F296	10f. multicoloured	1·10	1·75
F297	20f. multicoloured	1·40	2·00
F298	30f. multicoloured	1·75	2·75
F299	40f. multicoloured	1·90	3·25

POSTAGE DUE STAMPS

1925. Nos. F32 etc, optd CHIFFRE TAXE.

FD53	**5**	10c. (1d.) green	55·00	3·75
FD54	**5**	20c. (2d.) grey	55·00	3·75
FD55	**5**	30c. (3d.) red	55·00	3·75
FD56	**5**	50c. (5d.) blue	55·00	3·75
FD57	**5**	1f. (10d.) red on blue	55·00	3·75

1938. Optd CHIFFRE TAXE.

FD65	**6**	5c. green	18·00	75·00
FD66	**6**	10c. orange	21·00	75·00
FD67	**6**	20c. red	27·00	80·00
FD68	**6**	40c. olive	60·00	£160
FD69	**6**	1f. red on green	60·00	£160

1941. Free French Issue. As last optd France Libre.

FD77	5c. green	19·00	45·00
FD78	10c. orange	19·00	45·00
FD79	20c. red	19·00	45·00
FD80	40c. olive	24·00	45·00
FD81	1f. red on green	22·00	45·00

1953. Optd TIMBRE-TAXE.

FD92	**7**	5c. green	10·00	25·00
FD93	**7**	10c. red	9·00	24·00
FD94	**7**	20c. blue	24·00	40·00
FD95	-	40c. sepia (No. F87)	17·00	38·00
FD96	-	1f. orange (No. F89)	19·00	60·00

1957. Optd TIMBRE-TAXE.

FD107	**12**	5c. green	1·50	9·50
FD108	**12**	10c. red	2·00	9·50
FD109	**12**	20c. blue	3·50	14·00
FD110	-	40c. sepia (No. F102)	8·00	27·00
FD111	-	1f. orange (No. F104)	7·00	35·00

For later issues see **VANUATU**.

`Pt. 1`

NEW REPUBLIC

A Boer republic originally part of Zululand. It was incorporated with the South African Republic in 1888 and annexed to Natal in 1903.

12 pence = 1 shilling;
20 shillings = 1 pound.

1

1886. On yellow or blue paper.

1	**1**	1d. black		£3000
2	**1**	1d. violet	16·00	18·00
73	**1**	2d. violet	14·00	14·00
79	**1**	3d. violet	22·00	23·00
75	**1**	4d. violet	23·00	23·00
81	**1**	6d. violet	13·00	14·00
82	**1**	9d. violet	13·00	16·00
83	**1**	1s. violet	15·00	15·00
84	**1**	1s.6d. violet	40·00	32·00
85	**1**	2s. violet	35·00	38·00
86	**1**	2s.6d. violet	32·00	32·00
87	**1**	3s. violet	55·00	55·00
88b	**1**	4s. violet	55·00	55·00
16	**1**	5s. violet	48·00	55·00
90	**1**	5s.6d. violet	25·00	27·00
91	**1**	7s.6d. violet	28·00	30·00
92	**1**	10s. violet	25·00	28·00
93	**1**	10s.6d. violet	21·00	26·00
44	**1**	12s. violet		£375
23	**1**	13s. violet		£550
94	**1**	£1 violet	65·00	70·00
25	**1**	30s. violet		£120

Some stamps are found with Arms embossed in the paper, and others with the Arms and without a date above "ZUID-AFRIKA".

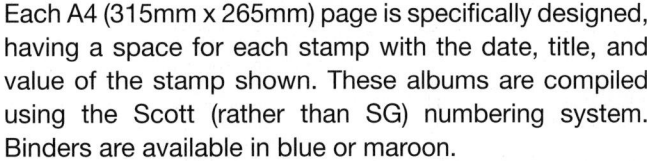

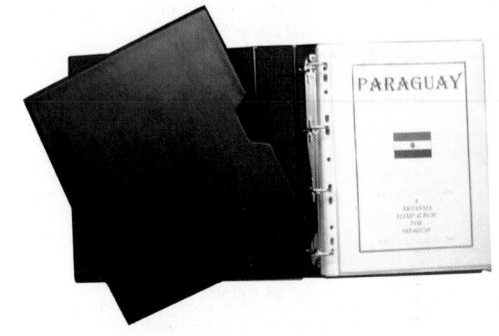

Index